PENGUIN HANDBOOKS

THE PENGUIN GUIDE TO COMPACT DISCS
NEW EDITION

EDWARD GREENFIELD, until his retirement in 1993, was for forty years on the staff of the *Guardian*, succeeding Neville Cardus as Music Critic in 1975. He still contributes regularly to the record column which he founded in 1954. At the end of 1960 he joined the reviewing panel of *Gramophone*, specializing in operatic and orchestral issues. He is a regular broadcaster on music and records for the BBC, not just on Radios 3 and 4 but also on BBC World Service, latterly with his weekly programme, 'The Greenfield Collection'. In 1958 he published a monograph on the operas of Puccini. More recently he has written studies on the recorded work of Joan Sutherland and André Previn. He has been a regular juror on International Record awards and has appeared with such artists as Dame Elisabeth Schwarzkopf, Dame Joan Sutherland and Sir Georg Solti in public interviews. In October 1993 he was given a *Gramophone* Award for Special Achievement and in June 1994 received the OBE for services to music and journalism.

ROBERT LAYTON studied at Oxford with Edmund Rubbra for composition and with Egon Wellesz for the history of music. He spent two years in Sweden at the universities of Uppsala and Stockholm. He joined the BBC Music Division in 1959 and has been responsible for such programmes as *Interpretations on Record*. He has contributed a 'Quarterly Retrospect' to *Gramophone* for a number of years, and he has written books on Berwald and Sibelius and has specialized in Scandinavian music. He has written a monograph on the Dvořák symphonies and concertos for the BBC Music Guides, of which he was General Editor for many years. His translation of the first two volumes of Erik Tawastsjerna's definitive study of Sibelius was awarded the 1984 Finnish State Literary Prize. In 1987 he was awarded the Sibelius Medal and in the following year was made a Knight of the Order of the White Rose of Finland for his services to Finnish music.

IVAN MARCH is a former professional musician. He studied at Trinity College of Music, London, and at the Royal Manchester College. After service in the Central Band of the RAF, he played the horn professionally for the BBC and travelled with the Carl Rosa and D'Oyly Carte opera companies. Now director of the Long Playing Record Library, the largest commercial lending library for classical music on compact discs in the British Isles, he is a well-known lecturer, journalist and personality in the world of recorded music. As a journalist, he contributes to a number of record-reviewing magazines, including *Gramophone*, where his regular monthly 'Collector's Corner' deals particularly with important reissues.

The present volume is dedicated with admiration, warmth and respect (but, alas, without permission) to

CHRISTOPHER HEADINGTON
(1930–1996)

composer, musician, fine pianist and highly regarded colleague. He loved life and people; he made friends readily but discerningly and those who knew him found him a stimulating and spirited companion with the widest interests, which he enthusiastically shared – for he was always seeking to expand his horizons, both musical and human.

All this was reflected in his music, which was unashamedly tonal and blossomed readily with appealingly communicative melodic invention. Yet underneath its surface lyricism there was at times an underlying vein of nostalgia or meditative feeling, suggesting that although he was essentially an outward-looking musician who enjoyed life, he took nothing for granted.

Christopher also loved to drive fast and he was an expert skier. He was killed on a ski-ing holiday in France, just after supervising two days of recording sessions of his own music at London's Henry Wood Hall. He was so proud that there was going to be an 'all Headington' disc. We shall look forward to hearing that CD, which will include concertante works for both piano and cello, plus a song-cycle. Meanwhile we already have Xue Wei's splendid recording of his *Violin concerto*, and Christopher could have no better memorial than that.

The Penguin Guide to Compact Discs and Cassettes
New Edition

Ivan March, Edward Greenfield and Robert Layton
Edited by Ivan March

Penguin Books

PENGUIN BOOKS

Published by the Penguin Group
Penguin Books Ltd, 27 Wrights Lane, London W8 5TZ, England
Penguin Books USA Inc., 375 Hudson Street, New York, New York 10014, USA
Penguin Books Australia Ltd, Ringwood, Victoria, Australia
Penguin Books Canada Ltd, 10 Alcorn Avenue, Toronto, Ontario, Canada M4V 3B2
Penguin Books (NZ) Ltd, 182–190 Wairau Road, Auckland 10, New Zealand
Penguin Books Ltd, Registered Offices: Harmondsworth, Middlesex, England

This edition first published 1996
10 9 8 7 6 5 4 3 2

Set in 8/9.5 pt Monotype Times New Roman
Typeset from data supplied by Datix International Ltd, Bungay, Suffolk
Made and printed in Great Britain by Clays Ltd, St Ives plc

Contents

Preface

The arrival of a seven-CD box from EMI entitled 'Great Conductors of the Past', not long before we went to press, seemed to us to underscore what our present and continuing survey is all about. It followed after a deservedly successful Teldec video tape, which won a special award from *Gramophone* magazine in 1995, compiling rare film footage to show almost all the key conductors from the first half of the twentieth century actually making music. It even included Arthur Nikisch – captured on silent film, with no indication as to what he was directing!

But the others can all be seen and heard, often creating electrifying intensity. And listening to the growing range of CDs of increasingly successful transfers of highly distinguished interpretations by these great musicians from that earlier generation gives cause for reflection. Do performers of our own era measure up to what has gone before?

In the years between the two world wars, and stretching forward into the post-war era, such musical giants were working in almost every major city of the world. Berlin had Furtwängler and Fricsay, later to be followed by Karajan; Koussevitzky conducted the Boston Symphony; Chicago became the home of Fritz Reiner, and Szell left Europe to turn the Cleveland Orchestra into one of the world's greatest virtuoso ensembles. In London there was the inimitable Beecham, the modestly unassuming Boult and that great musical innovator and father of the Proms, Sir Henry Wood (still underrated as an interpreter), and his colleague, Sir Malcolm Sargent; later came the magisterial Klemperer. Manchester was rightly proud of Barbirolli, while in New York Toscanini and Mitropoulos were to be followed by Leonard Bernstein.

Stokowski, the orchestral magician (with the help of Disney and Hollywood), put Philadelphia on the world's musical map and made music with a special kind of charisma which Eugene Ormandy, who followed, sometimes found difficult to match. Monteux, most versatile of interpreters, first made his mark in San Francisco. Vienna had Richard Strauss, Felix Weingartner and Bruno Walter, the latter forced to emigrate in the late 1930s and who capped his career with a glorious post-war Indian summer in the USA.

Then there were the extraordinary, larger-than-life instrumental soloists: the incomparable Casals, Heifetz, Horowitz, Kempff, Kreisler, Menuhin, Schnabel, Solomon, Stern, Szigeti; these are all names that immediately spring to mind, alongside those of the legendary Busch and Pro Arte Quartets.

As the century progressed, more and more composers recorded their own music: Elgar and Stravinsky and, later, Britten, Copland and Walton. Gershwin used pianola rolls; and today it is taken for granted that contemporary figures will want – at the very least – to supervise authoritative interpretations of their own music. Indeed Sir Malcolm Arnold is currently overseeing a cycle of his symphonies on the Naxos super-bargain label.

If today there are fewer obvious star personalities around, Brendel, Kovacevich, Perlman, Richter and Rostropovitch are with us, and Kissin, Perahia and Pletnev have come to join them. In the world of violin playing, Korea and Japan are providing an astonishing new source of great talent from Chung to Chang, while we have an impressive new pantheon of conductors, including Colin Davis and Dutoit, Handley and Hickox, Järvi and Muti, Masur, Rattle and Solti, Tennstedt and Wand; their combined coverage of the repertoire is astonishingly wide-ranging and, like Marriner before them, they have the gift of being able to bring music (orchestral, choral and operatic) spontaneously to life in the recording studio. Hopefully in America a new generation is in chrysalis, following on after Levine, Slatkin and Schwarz.

Most remarkable of all for our own time are the leading purveyors of 'authenticity', using period instruments. We do not know what music *sounded* like in the baroque era, and attempted simulations over the years from various scholar-musicians have brought astonishingly varying results. Earlier groups led by the distinguished recorder players, Frans Brüggen and David Munrow, or resonantly presented by Maier's Collegium Aureum, provided stimulating but comparatively smooth listening, whereas from the very beginning Harnoncourt's manner with the Vienna Concentus Musicus was determinedly abrasive, and rhythmically eruptive.

Contrast the Concerto Köln – a dedicated but sober German ensemble – with the exuberant Roy Goodman, and one again discovers two entirely different sound-worlds. There are similar differences in the Hogwood and Pinnock approaches to the performance of the Mozart symphonies, but it is Pinnock who has shown in his most recent recordings that it is possible to combine vitality and transparency of texture with fine intonation and at the same time achieve lyrical warmth in slow movements.

In the symphonies of Haydn, Tafelmusik, directed by Bruno Weil (with H. C. Robbins Landon as musical consultant), are creating a stimulating new niche for themselves, although in this area Roy Goodman and Kuijken are still making their mark. But it is good to see that Dorati's pioneering set of all the Haydn symphonies, the very first complete recording, has returned to the catalogue at budget price. Modern instruments were used for this project by the Philharmonia Hungarica, but there was nothing dated about their spirited style of performance.

The agreeable aspect of all this enterprise is that performances on period instruments are becoming more pleasing to the ear: they are better tuned, and phrasing (surely at the very heart of music-making) is moving away from the linear eccentricity that once seemed to be inevitable whenever there was sparing use of vibrato, or none at all.

Undoubtedly the reigning monarch of period performance is John Eliot Gardiner. Very perceptively, he changed over from using modern instruments at exactly the right moment, and his Monteverdi Choir and English Baroque Soloists are to the 1990s what Marriner's comparably successful Academy of St Martin-in-the-Fields was to the 1970s. Gardiner's versatility is typical of the finest of today's recorded performers, and he is usually admirably supported by his recording engineers.

Chamber music is alive and well, and the CD is its ideal medium. Instrumentalists like Arthur Grumiaux and the Beaux Arts Trio are synonymous with musical excellence, while the Kodály, Lindsay, Talich and Végh Quartets, and – using period instruments – the Mosaïques and Festetics groups have given us much musical refreshment. Equally a new generation of organists is bringing new life to the repertoire of Bach, Buxtehude, Franck and others, led by Peter Hurford's unsurpassed complete Bach survey, another of Decca's 'budget boxes' which are as economical of space as they are in cost.

For the general public it is the operatic tenors who are today's star 'classical' artists, and who would suggest that Pavarotti does not deserve his huge popular acclaim when he can produce a ringing 'Nessun dorma' ten times out of ten! Callas and Sutherland, Janet Baker and Schwarzkopf have all retired, but the gramophone keeps their singing fresh and alive, and there are plenty of fine newcomers, from the vivacious Sumi Jo and the superb Welsh bass-baritone, Bryn Terfel, to the glorious mezzo, Cecilia Bartoli, and the current star duo of Angela Gheorghiu (fresh from her triumphant Decca *La Traviata*) and Roberto Alagna, who are already planning a future *La Bohème* together.

So clearly we do have an answer to the question posed above. The present-day recording scene includes much to tempt, fascinate and stimulate listeners, and the future undoubtedly contains much promise.

Edward Greenfield, Robert Layton and Ivan March

Introduction

As in previous editions, the object of the current *Penguin Guide to Compact Discs and Cassettes* is to give the serious collector a comprehensive survey of the finest recordings of permanent music on CD. As most records are issued almost simultaneously on both sides of the Atlantic and use identical international catalogue numbers, this *Guide* should be found to be equally useful in Great Britain and the USA. The internationalization of repertoire and numbers now applies to almost all CDs issued by the major international companies and by many smaller ones too, while most of the smaller European labels are imported in their original formats into both Britain and the USA.

The sheer number of records of artistic merit now available causes considerable problems in any assessment of overall and individual excellence. While in the case of a single popular repertoire work it might be ideal for the discussion to be conducted by a single reviewer, it has not always been possible for one person to have access to every version, and division of reviewing responsibility becomes inevitable. Also there are certain works and certain recorded performances for which one or another of our team has a special affinity. Such a personal identification can often carry with it a special perception too. We feel that it is a strength of our basic style to let such conveyed pleasure or admiration for the merits of an individual recording come over directly to the reader, even if this produces a certain ambivalence in the matter of choice between competing recordings. Where disagreement is more positive (and this has rarely happened), readers will find an indication of this difference in the text.

We have considered (and rejected) the use of initials against individual reviews, since this is essentially a team project. The occasions for disagreement generally concern matters of aesthetics, for instance in the manner of recording-balance, where a contrived effect may trouble some ears more than others, or in the matter of style, where the difference between robustness and refinement of approach appeals differently to listening sensibilities, rather than involving a question of artistic integrity. But over the years our views seem to grow closer together rather than to diverge; perhaps we are getting mellower, but we are seldom ready to offer strong disagreement following the enthusiastic reception by one of the team of a controversial recording, if the results are creatively stimulating. Our perceptions of the advantages and disadvantages of performances of early music on original (as against modern) instruments seem fairly evenly balanced; again, any strong feelings are indicated in the text.

EVALUATION

Most recordings issued today by the major companies are of a high technical standard and offer performances of a quality at least as high as is experienced in the concert hall. In adopting a starring system for the evaluation of records, we have decided to make use of from one to three stars. Brackets round one or more of the stars indicate some reservations about its inclusion, and readers are advised to refer to the text. Brackets round all the stars usually indicate a basic qualification: for instance, a mono recording of a performance of artistic interest, where considerable allowances have to be made for the sound-quality, even though the recording may have been digitally remastered.

Our evaluation system may be summarized as follows:

*** An outstanding performance and recording in every way.

** A good performance and recording of today's normal high standard.

* A fair performance, reasonably well or well recorded.

Our evaluation is normally applied to the record as a whole, unless there are two main works or groups of works, and by different composers. In this case, each is dealt with separately in its appropriate place. In the case of a collection of shorter works we feel that there is little point in giving a separate starring to each item, even if their merits are uneven, since the record has to be purchased as a complete programme.

ROSETTES

To a very few records we have awarded a Rosette: ✹.

Unlike our general evaluations, in which we have tried to be consistent, a Rosette is a quite arbitrary compliment by a member of the reviewing team to a recorded performance which, he finds, shows special illumination, magic, or a spiritual quality, or even outstanding production values, that places it in a very special class. Occasionally a Rosette has been awarded for an issue that seems to us to offer extraordinary value for money, but that presupposes that the performance or performances are outstanding too. The choice is essentially a personal one (although often it represents a shared view) and in some cases it is applied to an issue where certain reservations must also be mentioned in the text of the review. The Rosette symbol is placed before the usual evaluation and the record number. It is quite small – we do not mean to imply an 'Academy Award' but a personal token of appreciation for something uniquely valuable. We hope that, once the reader has discovered and perhaps acquired a 'rosetted' CD, its special qualities will soon become apparent.

DIGITAL RECORDINGS

Nearly all new compact discs are recorded digitally, but an increasingly large number of digitally remastered, reissued analogue recordings are now appearing, and we think it important to include a clear indication of the difference:

Dig. This indicates that the master recording was digitally encoded.

BARGAIN AND SUPER-BARGAIN ISSUES

Since the publication of our last main volume we have seen a further huge expansion of the mid- and bargain-price labels from all the major companies. These are usually standard-repertoire works in excellent analogue recordings, digitally remastered. Often these reissue CDs are generous in playing time, increasing their value to the collector. There are also even cheaper classical CDs at super-bargain price, usually featuring performances by artists whose names are not internationally familiar, notably on the now rightly famous Naxos label. While many of these recordings derive from Eastern Europe, where recording costs have in the past been much lower than in the West, now this enterprising company is spreading its wings to embrace major orchestras and ensembles from Great Britain and Ireland.

The major companies have responded vigorously to this competition, not only by issuing super-bargain issues of their own (as on the DG Classikon, Decca Eclipse and Polygram Belart logos) but also by the introduction of Duos and Doubles: two CDs packaged back-to-back in a single jewel-case, generously filled with top-line repertoire and offered for the cost of a single premium-price CD. More recently EMI have introduced their even less expensive Seraphim duos, which offer two discs for the cost of a single *mid-priced* CD. Thus the collector has plenty of scope in deciding how much to pay for a recorded performance, with a CD range from just under £5 up to three times that amount.

Our listing of each recording first indicates if it is not in fact in the premium-price category, as follows:

(M) Medium-priced label
(B) Bargain-priced label
(BB) Super-bargain label

See below for price structures for CDs and cassettes in the UK and the USA.

LAYOUT OF TEXT

We have aimed to make our style as simple as possible, even though the catalogue numbers of recordings are no longer as straightforward as they once were. So, immediately after the evaluation and before the catalogue number, the record make is given, often in abbreviated form. In the case of a set of two or more CDs, the number of units involved is given in brackets after the catalogue number. Cassette numbers are still denoted by being given in italic type.

AMERICAN CATALOGUE NUMBERS

The numbers which follow in square brackets are US catalogue numbers, while the abbreviation [id.] indicates that the American number is identical to the European, which is increasingly becoming the case. Even RCA has recently moved over to completely identical numbers, although earlier issues have an alphabetical prefix in the UK which is not used by the *Schwann* catalogue in the USA.

There are certain other small differences to be remembered by American readers. For instance, a CBS/Sony number could have a completely different catalogue number on either side of the Atlantic, or it could use the same digits with different alphabetical prefixes, although this now seldom occurs. Both will be clearly indicated. EMI/Angel use extra digits for their British compact discs; thus the US number CDC 47001 becomes CDC7 47001-2 in Britain (the -2 is the European indication that this is a compact disc). We have taken care to check catalogue information as far as is possible, but as all the editorial work has been done in England there is always the possibility of error; American readers are therefore invited, when ordering records locally, to take the precaution of giving their dealer the fullest information about the music and recordings they want.

The indications (M), (B) and (BB) immediately before the starring of a disc refer only to the British record, as pricing systems are not always identical on both sides of the Atlantic.

Where no American catalogue number is given, this does not necessarily mean that a record is not available in the USA; the transatlantic issue may not have been made at the time of the publication of this *Guide*. Readers are advised to check the current *Schwann* catalogue and to consult their local record store.

ABBREVIATIONS

To save space we have adopted a number of standard abbreviations in listing orchestras and performing groups (a list is provided below), and the titles of works are often shortened, especially where they are listed several times. Artists' forenames are sometimes omitted if they are not absolutely necessary for identification purposes. Also we have not usually listed the contents of operatic highlights and collections; these can sometimes be found in *The Classical Catalogue*, published by *Gramophone* magazine (135 Greenford Road, Sudbury Hill, Harrow, Middx. HA1 3YD).

We have followed common practice in the use of the original language for titles where it seems sensible. In most cases, English is used for orchestral and instrumental music and the original language for vocal music and opera. There are exceptions, however; for instance, the Johann Strauss discography uses the German language in the interests of consistency.

ORDER OF MUSIC

The order of music under each composer's name broadly follows that adopted by *The Classical Catalogue*: orchestral music, including concertos and symphonies; chamber music;

solo instrumental music (in some cases with keyboard and organ music separated); vocal and choral music; opera; vocal collections; miscellaneous collections.

The Classical Catalogue now usually includes stage works alongside opera; in the main we have not followed this practice, preferring to list, say, ballet music and incidental music (where no vocal items are involved) in the general orchestral group. Within each group our listing follows an alphabetical sequence, and couplings within a single composer's output are *usually* discussed together instead of separately with cross-references. Occasionally and inevitably because of this alphabetical approach, different recordings of a given work can become separated when a record is listed and discussed under the first work of its alphabetical sequence. The Editor feels that alphabetical consistency is essential if the reader is to learn to find his or her way about.

CATALOGUE NUMBERS

Enormous care has gone into the checking of CD catalogue numbers and contents to ensure that all details are correct, but the editor and publishers cannot be held responsible for any mistakes that may have crept in despite all our zealous checking. When ordering CDs, readers are urged to provide their record-dealer with full details of the music and performers, as well as the catalogue number.

DELETIONS

Compact discs, especially earlier, full-priced issues not too generous in musical content, are now steadily succumbing to the deletions axe, and more are likely to disappear during the lifetime of this book. Sometimes copies may still be found in specialist shops, and there remains the compensatory fact that most really important and desirable recordings are eventually reissued, usually costing less!

Readers will have noted that EMI's new Special Import Service, which began in August 1995, means that the whole EMI international catalogue will be available to UK customers. EMI suggest that dealers should be able to get these special import discs quite quickly, and such records will probably cost about £1 more than those in the UK catalogue.

Polygram have now followed suit with their own import service, and we hope that this will provide a more stable supply situation for British collectors.

COVERAGE

As the output of major and minor labels continues to expand, it will obviously be impossible for us to mention *every* CD that is available, within the covers of a single book; this is recognized as a practical limitation if we are to update our survey regularly. We have to be carefully selective in choosing the discs to be included (although on rare occasions a recording has been omitted simply because a review copy was not available); anything which eludes us can always be included next time. However, we do welcome suggestions from readers about such omissions if they seem to be of special interest, and particularly if they are inexpensive. But borderline music on specialist labels that are not readily and reliably obtainable on both sides of the Atlantic cannot be given any kind of priority.

ACKNOWLEDGEMENTS

Our thanks, as ever, are due to Roger Wells, our copy editor, who has worked closely alongside us throughout the preparation of this book and, as a keen CD collector himself, also frequently made valuable creative suggestions.

Kathleen March once again zealously checked the proofs for errors and reminded us when the text proved ambiguous, clumsily repetitive in its descriptive terminology, or just plain contradictory, occasionally removing reviews that had somehow appeared twice!

Barbara Menard and Roy Randle contributed to the titling – never an easy task, and especially complicated in the many boxed anthologies involving a bouquet of different performers. Alan Livesey also cast an eagle eye over the proofs, especially looking for mistakes in the musical listings; he also helped with both titling and retrieval of earlier material (connected with reissues) in the hectic period immediately before we sent off our final copy. Our team of Penguin proofreaders are also indispensable.

Grateful thanks also go to all those readers who write to us to point out factual errors and remind us of important recordings which have escaped our notice.

Finally, we again welcome back to our cover the whimsical portrait of Nipper, the most famous dog in the world. He is associated with a deservedly world-famous trademark and reminds us that fine records have been available from this source for almost exactly one hundred years!

To American Readers

From your many letters and from visiting record stores in the USA, we know that our *Penguin Guide* is read, enjoyed and used as a tool by collectors on both sides of the Atlantic. We also know that some of you feel that our reviews are too frequently orientated towards European and British recordings and performances.

In concentrating on records which have common parlance in both Europe and the USA, we obviously give preference to the output of international companies, and in assessing both performers and performances we are concerned with only one factor: musical excellence. In a 400-year-old musical culture centred in Europe, it is not surprising that a great number of the finest interpreters should have been Europeans, and many of them have enjoyed recording in London, where there are four first-class symphony orchestras and many smaller groups at their disposal, supported by recording producers and engineers of the highest calibre.

However, the continued reissue of earlier recordings by major American recording orchestras and artists is slowly redressing the balance, not least in the present volume by the inclusion of Isaac Stern's 'Life in Music' survey, a pair of Horowitz Editions, and a similar coverage of Pierre Monteux. Stokowski's discography has greatly expanded, while many of the recordings made by Bruno Walter in the last years of his life and featured in the Bruno Walter Edition were recorded in the USA with American musicians. Ironically, the latest Bernstein Edition from DG conversely features recordings made mostly in Israel, but also in London and Vienna!

Of course new names are always appearing, and we must mention again here Gerard Schwarz in Seattle, who has revealed another great orchestra in the making and is making distinguished recordings of music by the (until recently) almost forgotten generation of American composers of the inter-war years, including Creston, Diamond, Hanson and Piston.

Our performance coverage in the present volume – helped by the huge proportion of reissued older records – certainly reflects the American achievement, past and present; with the current phenomenal improvements in transferring technology we hope that more of the early recordings made by the great names from America's musical past mentioned in our Preface will enjoy the attention of the wider public.

An International Mail-order Source for Recordings in the UK

Readers are urged to support a local dealer if he is prepared and able to give a proper service, and to remember that obtaining many CDs involves expertise and perseverance. However, because of the recession many specialist sources have disappeared and, for that reason, if any difficulty is experienced in obtaining the CDs you want, we suggest the following mail-order alternative, which offers competitive discount, operates world-wide and is under the direction of the Editor of *The Penguin Guide to Compact Discs*, whose advice on choice of recordings is always readily available to mail-order customers:

Squires Gate Music Centre (PG Dept)
   Rear 13 St Andrew's Road South
   St Annes on Sea
   Lancashire FY8 1SX
   England
   Tel.: 01253 782588; Fax: 01253 782985

This organization patiently extends compact disc orders until they finally come to hand. A full guarantee of safe delivery is made on any order undertaken. Please write for further details, or make a trial credit card order, by fax or telephone.

✸ The Rosette Service

Squires Gate also offers a try-before-you-buy weekly loan service (within the UK only) so that customers can try out at home rosetted recordings, plus a hand-picked group of recommended key repertoire works, for a small charge, without any obligation to purchase. If a CD is subsequently purchased, it will be discounted and the trial charge waived. Full details sent on request.

Squires Gate Music Centre also offers a simple three-monthly mailing, listing a hand-picked selection of current new and reissued CDs, chosen by the Editor of the *Penguin Guide*, Ivan March. Regular customers of Squires Gate Music Centre, both domestic and overseas, receive the bulletin as available, and it is sent automatically with their purchases.

An International Mail-order Source for Recordings in the USA

American readers seeking a domestic mail-order source may write to the following address, where a comparably expert and caring supply service is in operation (for both American and imported European labels). Please write for further details (enclosing a stamped, self-addressed envelope if within the USA) or make a trial order by letter, fax or phone to:

Serenade Records (PG Dept)
   1800 M St, N.W.
   Washington DC 20036
   USA
   Tel.: (202) 638-5580; Fax: (202) 783-0372
   Tel.: (for US orders only) 1-800-237-2930

Regular customers of Serenade Records, both domestic and overseas, can also on request receive the mailing, with a hand-picked selection of current new and reissued CDs chosen by the Editor of the *Penguin Guide*, Ivan March.

Price Differences in the UK and USA

Compact discs and cassettes in all price ranges are more expensive in Britain and Europe than they are in the USA but, fortunately, in nearly all cases the various premium-price, mid-price, bargain and super-bargain categories are fairly consistent on both sides of the Atlantic. However, where records are imported in either direction, this can affect their domestic cost. For instance, (British) EMI's Classics for Pleasure and Eminence labels are both in the mid-price range in the USA, whereas CfP is a bargain series in the UK. Similarly Naxos, a super-bargain digital label in the UK, is a bargain label in the USA.

Of course retail prices are not fixed in either country, and various stores may offer even better deals at times, so our price structure must be taken as a guideline only. One major difference in the USA is that almost all companies make a dollar surcharge (per disc) for mid-priced opera sets (to cover the cost of librettos) and Angel apply this levy to all their boxed sets. The Carlton compact disc series appears to be available only as a special import in the USA. The Vanguard CD label (except for the 8000 Series, which retails at around $15) is upper-mid-price in the USA but lower-mid-price in the UK. In *listing* records we have not used the major record companies' additional label subdivisions (like Decca/London's Ovation, DG's Galleria, EMI's Studio and Références, Philips's Concert Classics, Sony's Essential Classics and so on) in order to avoid further confusion, although these designations are sometimes referred to in the text of reviews.

Comparable Prices in the UK and USA

Premium-priced CDs (although they cost less west of the Atlantic) are top-price repertoire the world over. Here are comparative details of the other price ranges:

(M) MID-PRICED SERIES (sets are multiples of these prices)
Includes: Chandos (Collect); Decca/London; DG; EMI/Angel (Studio and Références; Eminence); Erato/Warner (UK), Erato/WEA (USA); DHM; Mercury; Philips; RCA Gold Seal; Saga; Sony; Teldec/Warner (UK), Teldec/WEA (USA); Unicorn (UK only).
  UK
  CDs: under £10; more usually £8–£9
  Cassettes: around £5
  USA
  CDs: under $12
  Cassettes: $5–$6.50 – but very few are available

(B) DUOS – two CDs for the cost of one premium-priced CD, which results in an 'upper' bargain price per disc but compensates by offering exceptionally generous playing time.
Includes: Erato Bonsai Duos; Decca/London and DG Doubles; Philips Duos; EMI Rouge et Noir (CZS). (The EMI forte series is available only in Europe; Angel have decided to call their equivalent series double forte and it will feature a mixture of American and European recordings.)

BARGAIN-PRICED SERIES (sets are multiples of these prices)
Includes: CfP (UK only); Decca Eclipse/London; Discover; Harmonia Mundi Musique d'Abord; Philips; Sony. Also includes EMI Scraphim – two CDs for the cost of one mid-priced CD.
  UK
  CDs: £5–£7.50
  Cassettes: around £4

USA
CDs: under $7
Cassettes: around $4

SPECIAL SETS: Decca, DG, Nimbus and Philips (as indicated); EMI CZS multiple sets are also within the bargain range in the UK but may cost rather more in the USA.

(BB) SUPER-BARGAIN SERIES – CDs
Includes: ASV Quicksilva (UK only); DG Classikon; Naxos; Polygram Belart; RCA Navigator (UK only).
UK
CDs: under £5; some (including Navigator) cost even less
USA
CDs: under $5–$6
(In some cases, equivalent cassettes are available, usually costing slightly less than bargain cassettes.)

Abbreviations

AAM	Academy of Ancient Music	GO	Gewandhaus Orchestra
Ac.	Academy, Academic	HM	Harmonia Mundi France
Amb. S.	Ambrosian Singers	Hung.	Hungaroton
Ang.	Angel	[id.]	same record number for US
Ara.	Arabesque		and European versions
arr.	arranged, arrangement	L.	London
ASMF	Academy of St Martin-in-the-Fields	LAPO	Los Angeles Philharmonic Orchestra
(B)	bargain-price CD	LCO	London Chamber Orchestra
(BB)	super-bargain-price CD	LMP	London Mozart Players
Bar.	Baroque	LOP	Lamoureux Orchestra of
Bav.	Bavarian		Paris
BBC	British Broadcasting Corporation	LPO	London Philharmonic Orchestra
BPO	Berlin Philharmonic Orchestra	LSO	London Symphony Orchestra
Cal.	Calliope	(M)	mid-price CD
Cap.	Caprice	Mer.	Meridian
CBSO	City of Birmingham Symphony Orchestra	Met.	Metropolitan
		Mo C	Ministry of Culture
CfP	Classics for Pleasure	movt	movement
Ch.	Choir; Chorale; Chorus	(N)	a new or reissued recording
CO	Chamber Orchestra		which appears for the first
COE	Chamber Orchestra of Europe		time in this *Guide*
Col. Mus. Ant.	Musica Antiqua, Cologne	N.	North, Northern
Coll.	Collegium	nar.	narrated
Coll. Aur.	Collegium Aureum	Nat.	National
Coll. Mus.	Collegium Musicum	NY	New York
Concg. O	Royal Concertgebouw Orchestra of Amsterdam	O	Orchestra, Orchestre
		OAE	Orchestra of the Age of Enlightenment
cond.	conductor, conducted	O-L	Oiseau-Lyre
Cons.	Consort	Op.	Opera (in performance
d.	different coupling		listings); opus (in music
DG	Deutsche Grammophon		titles)
DHM	Deutsche Harmonia Mundi	ORR	Orchestre Révolutionnaire
Dig.	digital recording		et Romantique
E.	England, English	ORTF	L'Orchestre de la radio et
ECCO	European Community Chamber Orchestra		télévision française
		Ph.	Philips
ECO	English Chamber Orchestra	Phd.	Philadelphia
ENO	English National Opera Company	Philh.	Philharmonia
		PO	Philharmonic Orchestra
Ens.	Ensemble	Qt	Quartet
ESO	English Symphony Orchestra	R.	Radio
		RLPO	Royal Liverpool Philharmonic Orchestra
Fr.	French		

ROHCG	Royal Opera House, Covent Garden	trans.	transcription, transcribed
		V.	Vienna
RPO	Royal Philharmonic Orchestra	Van.	Vanguard
		VCM	Vienna Concentus Musicus
RSNO	Royal Scottish National Orchestra	VPO	Vienna Philharmonic Orchestra
RSO	Radio Symphony Orchestra	VSO	Vienna Symphony Orchestra
S.	South		
SCO	Scottish Chamber Orchestra	W.	West
Sinf.	Sinfonietta	WNO	Welsh National Opera Company
SO	Symphony Orchestra		
Soc.	Society	(Y/B)	a new or reissued recording which first appeared in the 1995 *Yearbook*
Sol. Ven.	I Solisti Veneti		
SRO	Suisse Romande Orchestra		
Sup.	Supraphon		

Editor's Note

This new edition of *The Penguin Guide to Compact Discs and Cassettes* offers a completely fresh look at the vast range of readily available recordings of permanent music at each price level. There is nothing new about that, but one of the great joys of the current marketplace is the profusion of excellence in the lower ranges, so that fine recorded music is on average considerably less expensive now than it ever was. However, the continuing expansion of recorded repertoire outside the 'standard classics' has brought an urgent new problem for us. Even if we include only the very finest available versions of major works, we now have barely enough room within the pages of a single volume to cover the periphery of the repertoire, where there are so many fascinating and musically rewarding discoveries to be made.

The size of the present *Guide* has been expanded to the maximum number of pages which it is feasible to bind securely in paperback format, but that is still not big enough for our needs! We have *just* managed to find room for all our composer entries, but the appearance of a number of special editions celebrating the achievement of a single performer puts additional pressure on the space reserved for Concert/Recital collections.

Most single-CD collections have necessarily been carried forward to our next *Yearbook*, in order to make room for those special editions featuring star artists which demand immediate attention, as some may have only a limited catalogue life. Readers must therefore regard the forthcoming *Yearbook* as a further extension of the present volume, to be used in conjunction with it. We plan to expand the compilation coverage considerably within its pages, while it will also update our assessment of the repertoire as a whole and provide a revised series of 'best buys'.

The special rewards of compact discs hardly need restating: ease of access, great presence and clarity of the sound-image, with background noise either (as in a digital master) obliterated or greatly minimized, and made unobtrusive by modern technology. It is sad that the tape cassette has now been all but superseded by the bargain-price CD. Few recordings are available on musicassettes, but honourable exceptions are provided by the analogue bargain Sony 'Essential Classics' series and the resuscitated Decca Eclipse bargain label – in which the repertoire is now exclusively digital. All issues in both series have cassette equivalents and we have included the tape catalogue number in each instance.

We have thought it useful to indicate recordings (or reissued recordings) which are new to the present survey by using the abbreviation (N) placed immediately before the evaluation, catalogue number and performance details, while (Y/B) indicates a similar new recording carried forward from our last *Yearbook*.

As we go to press, the Gimell catalogue has been taken over by Polygram, and their recordings will now be reissued on the Philips label with new catalogue numbers.

Ivan March (Editor)

Abel, Carl Friedrich (1723–87)

Overtures: In C, Op. 1/2; in C, Op. 5/4; in D, Op. 7/3; in G, Op. 14/5; Symphonies: in E flat, Op. 4/3; in B flat, Op. 12/2.
(N) (M) ** Van. Dig. 99703 [id.]. Il Fondamento, Paul Dombrecht.

It was Abel who (as impresario) joined forces with J. C. Bach in London between 1765 and 1781 to give a series of concerts which put the symphony, as developed from the Italian overture, firmly on the map. However, on the evidence here, his own music (especially in the three-part overtures) is pretty thin and full of routine gestures. Il Fondamento, directed by Paul Dombrecht, give faithful period-instrument performances but fail to make a very enticing case for this repertoire. They are acceptably recorded.

6 Symphonies, Op. 7.
**(*) Chandos Dig. CHAN 8648 [id.]. Cantilena, Shepherd.

The six *Symphonies* of Op. 7 speak much the same language as J. C. Bach or early Mozart. The performances are not the last word in elegance, but they are both lively and enjoyable as well as being well recorded.

Adam, Adolphe (1803–56)

Le Corsaire (ballet): complete.
*** Decca Dig. 430 286-2 (2) [id.]. ECO, Richard Bonynge.

Le Corsaire is agreeably colourful and amiably melodic, but has little of the distinction of *Giselle*. Bonynge conducts it with finesse, warmth and drama, and the recording is out of Decca's top drawer.

Le Diable à quatre (ballet): complete.
(Y/B) (M) *** Decca 444 111-2 [id.]. LSO, Richard Bonynge (with MASSENET: *La Navarraise: Nocturne. Don César de Bazan: Sévillana. Les Erinnyes: Invocation;* BIZET: *Don Procopio: Entr'acte to Act II;* GOUNOD: *Le Tribut de Zamora, Act III: Danse grecque* ***).

Adam's *Le Diable à quatre* was recorded in a vintage period (1964) and, as the opening Act immediately demonstrates, produces Decca's top ballet quality, with glowing horns and woodwind, and wonderfully vivid detail. This was the seventh of Adam's thirteen ballets, arriving in 1845, four years after *Giselle*, and when Richard Bonynge points the elegant writing for the strings so seductively, it makes a splendid entertainment. Moreover, for this reissue Decca have found five equally winning *entr'actes* from their vaults (bringing the playing time up to 75 minutes), and these pieces are even more melodically characterful than the main work. Bonynge clearly relishes all these items and presents them with characteristic polish and spontaneity. The 1971 Decca sound is every bit as warm, richly hued and immediate as the complete ballet.

Giselle (ballet): complete.
(B) *** Decca Double Dig. 452 185-2 (2) [id.]. ROHCG O, Richard Bonynge.
(Y/B) (PB) *** Naxos Dig. 8.550755/6 [id.]. Slovak RSO, Mogrelia.

Giselle (ballet): abridged version.
(Y/B) (M) *** Sony Dig. SMK 42450 [id.]. LSO, Michael Tilson Thomas.

Giselle (1841) is the first of the great classical ballets. Andrew Mogrelia's complete recording uses the normal performing edition, including interpolated scenes by Friedrich Burgmüller, and by Minkus, which means that it offers some 1 hour 54 minutes of music. The orchestral playing has grace and elegance and plenty of life: the brass are not ashamed of the melodrama. The recording is resonantly full and warm in ambience, yet well detailed. Bonynge's performance on Decca is just that bit more strongly characterized and the Decca sound has a slightly sharper profile. That remains first choice (at Double Decca price), but this Naxos set costs slightly less. However, Michael Tilson Thomas's generous (77-minute) single-CD selection with the LSO on Sony, which offers all the important music and was recorded, like Bonynge's set, in the Henry Wood Hall, could well be a first choice for many collectors now that it is offered at mid-price, for the LSO playing is beautifully polished.

Adams, John (born 1947)

Chamber symphony; Grand pianola music.
(Y/B) *** Elektra Nonesuch/Warner Dig. 7559 79219-2 [id.]. L. Sinf., composer.

This Elektra coupling combines the *Grand pianola music*, one of the most immediately accessible and inspired examples of minimalism, with a piece that is initially more intractable, the *Chamber symphony*, written for 15 instruments and inspired by Schoenberg's Opus 9 (the choice of instrumentation is both comparable and different). Unlike the Schoenberg, this piece is in three clearly defined movements, requiring great virtuosity from its performers. It is surely given a definitive performance here.

In the composer's hands *Grand pianola music* projects with overwhelmingly thrilling impact, and throughout the balancing of the composite elements, notably the three 'siren' soprano voices, is near ideal. With extensive and illuminating notes from John Adams himself, this is a key issue in the Adams discography.

(i) *Violin concerto;* (ii) *Shaker loops.*
*** Nonesuch/Warner Dig. 7559 79360-2 [id.]. (i) Kremer, LSO, Nagano; (ii) O of St Luke's, composer.

This concerto has had a good press, and undoubtedly Gidon Kremer's account of the fiendishly demanding solo part is dazzling. The violently rhythmic pulsations and brilliant ostinatos of the outer movements gnaw at the consciousness and, even though the dream-like *Chaconne* which forms the central slow movement offers aural and spiritual balm, the mood is swept away by the manic energy of the closing *Toccata*. The performance is superb but, with the soloist closely balanced, not all listeners will find it easy to last out the bravura battering provided by the 15-minute opening movement. *Shaker loops* is hypnotically involving, and the atmospherically recorded performance by the composer tends to trump previous versions.

Grand pianola music; Short ride in a fast machine (arr. for wind band by Lawrence T. Odom).
(Y/B) **(*) Chandos Dig. CHAN 9393 [id.]. Netherlands Wind Ens., Stephen Moscow – LANG: *Are you experienced?* etc. (***)

John Adams' *Short ride in a fast machine* brings great exhilaration and, as presented here, does not go on for a moment too long. It sounds splendid in the clever arrangement for wind ensemble by Lawrence T. Odom. *Grand pianola music* also suits the Netherlands group as it is scored for two obbligato pianos, three sopranos and an ensemble of woodwind, brass and percussion. It is very seductively played, even if detail is less well defined than in the composer's own recording, notably the female voices, and Stephen Moscow's account of the last movement also misses some of the sheer physical exhilaration of the climax. The couplings, too, are a highly debatable proposition.

Harmonielehre; The Chairman dances; (i) *2 Fanfares: Tromba Lontana; Short ride in a fast machine.*
*** EMI Dig. CDC5 55051-2 [id.]. CBSO, Simon Rattle; (i) with Jonathan Holland, Wesley Warren.

Harmonielehre is an extraordinary, large-scale (39-minute) work in three parts. Its minimalist progress is powerfully sustained by Rattle. *The Chairman dances* his foxtrot for a full 13 minutes, if with unabated energy. The *Two Fanfares* mystically and hauntingly pay their respects to Ives as well as Copland while the *Short* (exhilarating) *ride in a fast machine*, propelled by what sounds like bursts of rocket power, is just as described in the title and has an agreeably unstoppable momentum. The performances bring the most persuasive advocacy and the excellent recording, clear, vivid and spacious, speaks well for the acoustics of Birmingham's Symphony Hall.

Harmonium (for large orchestra and chorus).
**(*) ECM 821 465-2 [id.]. San Francisco SO & Ch., Edo de Waart.

Harmonium is a setting of three poems. John Donne's curiously oblique 'Negative love' opens the piece, with the orchestra lapping gently round the chorus. The other two poems are by Emily Dickinson. The magnificent, resonantly expansive 1984 analogue recording is certainly worthy of the performance; one might complain that this CD plays for only just over 32 minutes, yet for some ears it may seem longer.

Shaker loops.
❀ (M) *** Virgin/EMI CUV5 61121-2 [id.]. LCO, Warren-Green – GLASS: *Company* etc.; REICH: *8 Lines;* HEATH: *Frontier.* ***

The inspired performance by Christopher Warren-Green and his London Concert Orchestra is full of imaginative intensity, and understandably it received the composer's imprimatur. Outstandingly vivid recording.

OPERA

The Death of Klinghoffer (complete).
*** Elektra-Nonesuch/Warner Dig. 7559 79281-2 (?) [id.]. Sylvan, Maddalena, Friedman, Hammons, E.
  Op. Ch., Op. de Lyon, Nagano.

As in his first opera, the headline-catching *Nixon in China*, so too in *The Death of Klinghoffer* Adams has moved away from subjective expression, traditional in opera, to a stylized setting of a modern myth. He even dares to relate his opera to the Bach *Passions*, and the gravity and intensity of what he is saying is never in doubt. That brings *The Death of Klinghoffer* far closer to a dramatic oratorio than to an opera, with its lack of incident and its sequence of meditative solos and choruses of comment.

A recording loses very little, and that is particularly true in as strong a performance as this one in which Kent Nagano conducts Lyon Opéra forces with the original singers who directly inspired the composer. The treatment of the story, based on the age-old conflict between Palestinians and Jews, is conscientiously dispassionate. The closing scene brings the one solo of fully operatic intensity, the bitter concluding lament of Klinghoffer's wife, Marilyn. It is as though, after all the detachment, Adams is bringing us back finally to emotional reality, and the result is the more moving. The mezzo, Sheila Nadler, rises to the challenge superbly, and the baritone Sanford Sylvan is comparably sensitive as Klinghoffer himself, well matched by James Maddalena as the Captain, an Evangelist-like commentator, and by Thomas Hammons and Janice Felty in multiple roles. The recorded sound is excellent, but the booklet reproduces an unrevised version of the libretto.

Addinsell, Richard (1904–77)

Film and theatre music: *Fire over England: suite. Goodbye Mr Chips: theme* (arr. Alwyn). *Journey to Romance* (radio feature): *Invocation. The Prince and the Showgirl:* selection (arr. Felton Rapley). *Ring round the Moon: Invitation waltz* (orch. Alwyn). (i) *A Tale of Two Cities: Theme* (arr. Gamley). *Tom Brown's Schooldays: Overture* (arr. Alwyn). (ii) *Trespass: Festival* (beguine). *The Isle of apples;* (ii) *Smokey Mountain concerto;* (i) *Tune in G.*
(Y/B) **(*) Marco Polo Dig. 8.223732 [id.]. BBC Concert O, Kenneth Alwyn, with (i) Roderick Elms;
  (ii) Philip Martin.

Throughout his composing career Addinsell left the scoring and arrangements of his ideas to others, and the present recorded collection owes much to the skill of its conductor, Kenneth Alwyn, who has pieced a good deal of the material together where original scores are lost, notably in the 'Overture' from the film music for *Tom Brown's Schooldays* and the charming introductory sequence for *Goodbye Mr Chips*. Not all Addinsell's invention is distinguished, and, as with most film music, there is a good deal of hyperbole, but the *Invitation waltz* for Christopher Fry's translation, *Ring round the Moon*, of Jean Anouilh's *L'Invitation au château* is quite haunting, as is the gentle idyll, *The Isle of apples*, and the simple *Tune in G* with its piano embroidery. These pieces, like the *Smokey Mountain concerto*, were independent compositions. Alwyn and the BBC Concert Orchestra are thoroughly at home in this repertoire and they present it all freshly. The acoustic of the Golders Green Hippodrome gives a suitably bright but rather brash sonority to the orchestra.

Warsaw concerto.
(M) *** Decca Dig. 430 726-2 [id.]. Ortiz, RPO, Atzmon – GERSHWIN: *Rhapsody* **(*); GOTTSCHALK: *Grand fantasia* ***; LITOLFF: *Scherzo* ***; LISZT: *Hungarian fantasia.* ***

Richard Addinsell's pastiche miniature concerto, written for the film *Dangerous Moonlight* in 1942, is perfectly crafted and its atmosphere combines all the elements of the Romantic concerto to great effect; moreover it has a truly memorable main theme.

Addison, John (born 1920)

Carte blanche (ballet suite).
(M) (***) EMI mono CDM7 64718-2 [id.]. Pro Arte O, composer – ARNELL: *Great Detective;* ARNOLD: *A Grand Grand Overture;* BLISS: *Checkmate;* RAWSTHORNE: *Madame Chrysanthème* etc.
  (***)

John Addison is known mainly for his film music (including *A Taste of Honey, Reach for the Sky* and *The Charge of the Light Brigade*). The ballet, *Carte blanche*, written for Sadler's Wells, attracted the attention of Sir Thomas Beecham. It is wittily precocious writing (immediately introducing a xylophone solo in the *Prelude*), readily melodic and nicely scored. Unpretentious but entertaining, and well played and brightly recorded under the composer in 1960.

Aguado, Dionisio (1784–1849)

Adagio; Polonaise; Introduction and Rondo, Op. 2/1–3.
(M) **(*) RCA Dig.09026 61607-2. Julian Bream (guitar) – SOR: *Collection.* **(*)

The *Adagio* is the most striking piece here, serene and introspective; it might have been even more effective had Bream been slightly less deliberate and reflective and chosen to move the music on a little more. However, the other pieces have plenty of life, and all are played with Bream's characteristic feeling for colour. The New York recording is truthful and realistic.

Aho, Kalevi (born 1949)

(i) *Violin concerto; Hiljaisuus (Silence); Symphony No. 1.*
*** BIS Dig. CD 396 [id.]. (i) Manfred Gräsbeck; Lahti SO, Vänskä.

Aho's *First Symphony* betokens an impressive musical personality at work. *Silence* is an imaginative piece. It is related to (and was conceived as an introduction to) the post-expressionist and more 'radical' and trendy *Violin concerto*; it is a work of considerable resource and imaginative intensity. Good performances and recording.

(i) *Symphony No. 8;* (ii) *Pergamon.*
(Y/B) *** BIS Dig. CD 646 [id.]. (i) Hans-Ola Ericsson; (ii) Pauili Pietiläinen, Lilli Paasikivi, Eeva-Liisa Saarinen, Tom Nyman, Matti Lehtinen; Lahti SO, Osmo Vänskä.

The *Eighth Symphony* for organ and orchestra is an ambitious 50-minute piece of unusual design. It is often imaginative and at times imposing in its massive sonorities, and the integration of the organ into the orchestral texture is masterly. The filler is *Pergamon*, a pretentious multi-lingual setting (four narrators speak a text of Peter Weiss simultaneously in German, Finnish, Swedish and Ancient Greek, with elaborate instrumental support) to pretty negligible effect.

Albéniz, Isaac (1860–1909)

Iberia (suite; orch. Arbós).
*** Chandos Dig. CHAN 8904 [id.]. Philh. O, Yan Pascal Tortelier – FALLA: *Three-cornered hat.* ***

The transcriptions of five of the twelve piano pieces which make up *Iberia* were made by Albéniz's contemporary and friend, Enrique Arbós. The music itself glows and flickers with the nuances of Spanish dance-rhythms. The Philharmonia's response brings glowing woodwind colours and seductive string phrasing, well projected by the warmly resonant recording.

Iberia: Triana; Fête-dieu à Seville. Navarra (all orch. Arbós).
(N) (M) *** RCA 09026 62586-2 [id.]. Chicago SO, Reiner – FALLA: *El amor brujo* etc.; GRANADOS: *Goyescas: Intermezzo.* ***

This vintage Reiner collection of Spanish music is especially notable for the remarkably idiomatic account of these Albéniz pieces. The Latin passion of the climax of *Navarra* is matched by the climax of *Fête-dieu à Seville*, in which Reiner captures the boisterous vulgarity of a Spanish religious procession with superb aplomb. Vintage Chicago recording from 1958, still sounding amazingly ripe and vivid.

Rapsodia española (arr. Halfter).
(N) (B) *** Decca Eclipse Dig. 448 243-2; *448 243-4* [id.]. Alicia de Larrocha, LPO, Frühbeck de Burgos – RODRIGO: *Concierto de Aranjuez* etc.; TURINA: *Rapsodia sinfónica.* ***

Albéniz's *Rapsodia española*, originally written for solo piano but heard here in Cristobal Halfter's arrangement for piano and orchestra, is a chimerical piece constructed fairly loosely from a series of contrasting Spanish dances. Alicia de Larrocha's performance is both evocative and dazzling, and she is given splendid support by Frühbeck de Burgos and brilliant Decca sound.

Suite española (arr. Frühbeck de Burgos).
(M) *** Decca 448 601-2 [id.]. New Philh. O, Frühbeck de Burgos – FALLA: *El amor brujo* *** (with GRANADOS: *Goyescas: Intermezzo* ***).

Albéniz's early *Suite española* offers light music of the best kind, colourful, tuneful, exotically scored and providing orchestra and recording engineers alike with a chance to show their paces, the sound bright and glittering, and fully worthy of reissue in Decca's Classic Sound series.

GUITAR MUSIC

Cantos de España: Córdoba, Op. 232/4; Mallorca (Barcarola), Op. 202; Piezás características: Zambra Granadina; Torre Bermeja, Op. 92/7, 12; Suite española: Granada; Sevilla; Cádiz; Asturias, Op. 47/1, 3–5.
*** Sony Dig. SK 36679 [id.]. John Williams (guitar).

Some of Albéniz's more colourful miniatures are here, and John Williams plays them most evocatively.

Cantos de España: Córdoba, Op. 232/4; Mallorca (Barcarola), Op. 202. Suite española: Cataluña; Granada; Sevilla; Cádiz, Op.47/1–4.
(Y/B) ✿ (BB) *** RCA Navigator Dig. 74321 17903-2. Julian Bream (guitar) – GRANADOS: *Collection;* RODRIGO: *3 Piezas españolas.* *** ✿

Julian Bream is in superb form in this splendid recital (apparently his own favourite record), vividly recorded in the pleasingly warm acoustic of Wardour Chapel, near his home in Wiltshire. The CD is electrifying, giving an uncanny impression of the great guitarist sitting and making music just beyond the loudspeakers. The playing itself has wonderfully communicative rhythmic feeling, great subtlety of colour, and its spontaneity increases the impression that one is experiencing a 'live' recital. The performance of the haunting *Córdoba*, which ends the group, is unforgettable. The new super-bargain Navigator reissue includes additionally the *Tres piezas españolas* of Rodrigo. This is perhaps the finest single recital of Spanish guitar music in the catalogue and, at its new price, a bargain of bargains.

Cantos de España; Suite española.
(M) *** Decca Analogue/Dig. 433 923-2 (2). Alicia de Larrocha – GRANADOS: *12 Danzas españolas* etc.
***

This is most rewarding repertoire and de Larrocha's playing is imbued with many subtle changes of colour and has refreshing vitality.

Iberia; Navarra; Suite española.
✿ *** Decca Dig. 417 887-2 [id.]. Alicia de Larrocha.

On her digital Decca version, Alicia de Larrocha brings an altogether beguiling charm and character to these rewarding miniature tone-poems and makes light of their sometimes fiendish technical difficulties. The recording is among the most successful of piano sounds Decca has achieved.

Iberia (complete); España (6 Hojas de album), Op. 165: Malagueña; Tango. Pavana capricho, Op. 12. Recuerdos de viaje: Puerta de Tierra; Rumores de la caleta.
(M) *** Decca 433 926-2 (2) [id.]. Alicia de Larrocha – FALLA: *Fantasía bética* etc. ***

Iberia (complete); Navarra.
(N) (B) *** Decca Double 448 191-2 (2) [id.]. De Larrocha – GRANADOS: *Goyescas.* ***

Alicia de Larrocha's second analogue set of *Iberia* was made in 1972, a decade after her earliest stereo version for Hispavox. As in that version (recently available on EMI), she plays with full-blooded temperament and fire, and although there are occasional touches of wilful rubato her natural overriding spontaneity carries the day, both here and in *Navarra*. The piano recording is excellent in its realism, and the Double Decca reissue, coupled with Granados's *Goyescas*, makes a formidable bargain, for on both artistic and technical merits *Iberia* loses little ground to her later, digital set which has rather more subtlety.

The alternative mid-priced set (coupled with Falla) remains an attractive alternative, with its other colourful genre pieces played with comparable understanding.

Sonata in D.
(M) *** Decca 433 920-2 (2) [id.]. Alicia de Larrocha – GRANADOS: *Goyescas* etc. *** ✿; SOLER: *Sonatas.* ***

Albéniz's delectably cool *Sonata*, with its obvious homage to Domenico Scarlatti, has enormous character. It is beautifully played and recorded.

Suite española, Op. 47.
(BB) **(*) ASV CDQS 6079. Alma Petchersky – FALLA: *Fantasía bética* (with GRANADOS: *Allegro de concierto*). **(*)

Alma Petchersky plays engagingly and with a natural spontaneity that gives pleasure. The recording is generally faithful, without being in the top bracket. At super-bargain price this is worth considering.

d'Albert, Eugen (1864–1932)

Piano concertos Nos. 1 in B min., Op. 2; 2 in E, Op. 12.
(Y/B) *** Hyperion Dig. CDA 66747 [id.]. Piers Lane, BBC Scottish SO, Alun Francis.

The *Piano concerto No. 1 in B minor* (1884), the inspiration of a twenty-year-old, is the more ambitious of the two works, a 45–minute span, written in a style half-way between Liszt and Rachmaninov, a warmly lyrical mix, lacking only the sharp memorability of a masterwork. This, its first recording, is an unqualified success, and Piers Lane plays with delicacy and virtuosity and is well supported by the BBC Scottish Symphony Orchestra. Its musical substance may not be immediately memorable but is always pleasing, and almost (but not quite) sustains its length. There is a rather extraordinary fugal outburst towards the end of the work. The *Piano concerto No. 2 in E major* is a one-movement piece, though in four sections, following the style of Liszt's concertos. The recording is expertly balanced by Tony Kime. In Hyperion's outstanding 'Romantic Piano Concerto' series this is one of the most successful issues yet, very well recorded.

Albert, Stephen (1941–92)

Cello concerto.
(Y/B) *** Sony Dig. SK 57961 [id.]. Yo-Yo Ma, Baltimore SO, David Zinman – BARTOK: *Viola concerto;* BLOCH: *Schelomo.* ***

Stephen Albert's *Cello concerto* (1989–90) was written for Yo-Yo Ma. The idiom is both tonal and distinctive. Albert is very much his own man and his music is both inventive and imaginative. Yo-Yo Ma and the Baltimore orchestra give a passionately committed account of it and are superbly recorded.

Albinoni, Tommaso (1671–1751)

Adagio in G min. for organ and strings (arr. Giazotto).
(M) *** Virgin/EMI Dig. CUV5 61145-2 [id.]. LCO, Warren-Green – VIVALDI: *4 seasons;* PACHELBEL: *Canon.* ***
(Y/B) (M) *** Carlton Dig. PCD 2001. Scottish CO, Laredo (with String masterpieces ***).
(N) (M) *** DG 449 724-2 [id.]. BPO, Karajan – RESPIGHI: *Ancient airs* etc. ***

Christopher Warren-Green's version is as impressive as any in the catalogue, opening with an attractively volatile violin solo and leading to a richly upholstered climax.

No less telling is the mid-priced, digitally recorded Carlton account, strongly contoured and most responsively played by the Scottish Chamber Orchestra under Jaime Laredo.

Karajan's view is stately and measured, and the Berlin Philharmonic strings respond with dignity and sumptuous tone. The anachronism of Giazotto's arrangement is obviously relished, and this is certainly a reasonable way of approaching it. The remastered recording sounds very good.

12 Concerti a cinque, Op. 5.
(Y/B) (M) *** Ph. Dig. 442 658-2 [id.]. Pina Carmirelli, I Musici.

This fine body of concertos has variety and resource to commend it. I Musici, with Pina Carmirelli as the solo player, are every bit as fresh as the music, and they are accorded altogether first-rate sound. This is one of the best sets of its kind among recent reissues; those prepared to explore these concertos will be well rewarded.

12 Concerti, Op. 7; Sonatas for strings a 5: in D & G min., Op. 2/5–6.
*** Ph. Dig. 432 115-2 (2) [id.]. Heinz Holliger, Maurice Bourgue, I Musici.

Albinoni's Op. 7 consists of four each of solo oboe concertos, double oboe concertos and concertos for strings, with continuo. This recording by Heinz Holliger and Maurice Bourgue and I Musici is comparatively robust in using modern instruments but is eminently stylish, the effect sunny and lively by turns. The digital recording is fresh and naturally balanced. The two *String sonatas* from Op. 2 are particularly attractive works, and here the recording is slightly closer.

(i) *Concerti a cinque, Op. 7/2–3, 5–6, 8–9, 11–12;* (ii) *Adagio in G min.* (arr. Giazotto).

[B] *** DG 439 509-2 [id.]. (i) Holliger, Elhorst, Bern Camerata; (ii) Lucerne Festival Strings, Baumgartner.

The playing of Heinz Holliger, Hans Elhorst and the Bern Camerata is refined, persuasive and vital, and the CD could hardly be more truthful or better detailed. This excellent collection has now been relegated to DG's bargain Classikon label and the famous *Adagio* (in a perfectly acceptable performance under Baumgartner) has been added to tempt a wider public. Let us hope it does so.

Oboe concertos, Op. 7/3, 6, 9 & 12; Op. 9/2, 5, 8 & 11.
*** Unicorn Dig. DKPCD 9088; *DKPC 9088* [id.]. Sarah Francis, L. Harpsichord Ens.
(Y/B) *** Chandos Dig. CHAN 0579 [id.]. Anthony Robson, Coll. Mus. 90, Simon Standage.

Those looking for a selection of *Oboe concertos* from both Opp. 7 and 9 will find that Sarah Francis is an immensely stylish and gifted soloist. She is accompanied with warmth and grace, and the recording is first class, transparent yet full and naturally balanced.

Anthony Robson also plays all eight solo concertos from Op. 7 and Op. 9, but using a period oboe. His tone is most appealing and his phrasing and musicianship are second to none. Simon Standage provides alert accompaniments, also using original instruments, and creates bright, athletic string-timbres. The effect has slightly less flexibility in matters of dynamic than is possible using a modern instrument, but it is still both pleasing and stimulating. Authenticists need not hesitate.

Concerti a cinque, Op. 9/1, 4, 6–7, 10 & 12.
(M) *** Ph. 426 080-2. Ayo, Holliger, Bourgue, Garatti, I Musici.

Concerti a cinque, Op. 9/2, 3, 5, 8, 9 & 11.
(M) *** Ph. 434 157-2 [id.]. Holliger, Bourgue, I Musici.

This pair of excellent mid-priced CDs includes all the Opus 9 concertos with Heinz Holliger and Maurice Bourgue. They are played with much finesse and style and the 1966 recording is brightly remastered.

Concerti a cinque, Op. 9/1–3, 5, 6, 10 & 11.
(B) *** Erato/Warner 2292 45921-1 [id.]. Pierlot, Chambon, Toso, Sol. Ven., Scimone.

Albinoni's music continues to be underrated – his best concertos are as fine as the finest Vivaldi, as this collection readily demonstrates. Pierre Pierlot, with his elegant phrasing and lovely tone, Jacques Chambon (in the *Double Oboe concerto in F*, Op. 9/3) and Piero Toso (in the two concertos for violin) all make impressive contributions. Scimone and I Solisti Veneti are also on form, and the recording is full and naturally balanced.

Concerti a cinque, Op. 9/2, (i) *3; 5, 8,* (i) *9; 11.*
(BB) *** Naxos Dig. 8.550739; *4.550739* [id.]. Anthony Camden, (i) Julia Girdwood, L. Virtuosi, John Georgiadis.

The calibre of Anthony Camden's playing is shown in the *Adagio* of the *D minor Concerto*, Op. 9/5, which opens with a long, controlled crescendo on a sustained note, which is beautifully managed, but both the solo playing (with Julia Girdwood an excellent partner in the two double concertos) and the lively and sensitive accompaniments give great pleasure throughout this freshly recorded disc, another of Naxos's best bargains.

Concerti a cinque, Op. 9/2, 5, 8 & 11.
(Y/B) (M) *** Virgin/EMI Veritas Dig. VER5 61152–2 [id.]. Hans de Vries, Alma Musica Amsterdam, Bob van Asperen – TELEMANN: *Oboe concertos.* ***

Hans de Vries plays a baroque oboe, made by Gottlob Crone in Leipzig around 1735, and produces a most appealing timbre, while his technique is remarkably assured and true. There are several fine collections of Op. 9, but none more authentic than this. There is one cavil: the solo balance seems a shade too forward, even though the interaction with the strings (which are well in the picture) is effectively managed. The accompaniments are as alert and stylish as the solo playing and there is not a trace of vinegar in the string-timbre.

12 Concerti (Opera decima), Op. 10.
(N) (M) *** Erato/Warner 0630 11222-2 (2) [id.]. Toso, Carmignola, Sol. Ven., Claudio Scimone.

Although the existence of this set of concertos was long known and was listed by the Amsterdam publisher, Le Cène, their rediscovery is comparatively recent. They came to light as late as the 1960s, when Michael Talbot found them in a Swedish library at the castle of Leufsta. They were immediately recorded by I Musici but now appear in a more recent (1979) two-record set from I Solisti Veneti. Four of the set are violin concertos (Nos. 6, 8, 10 and 12) and three are concerti grossi with a small concertino group (2, 3 and 4), while the remainder are without soloists and have non-fugal last movements. They were composed in the mid-1730s, thirteen years after Op. 9 and after the composer had been absorbed by operatic ventures. They are of special interest, both in showing the development of the solo violin writing by the side of his earlier sets, and for their participation in the gestation of the string sinfonia (all the works are in the three-part format of the Italian overture – quick-slow-quick). But it is for their lyricism and warmth that these concertos will be cherished, readily demonstrated by the lovely slow movement of the *D major Violin concerto* (No. 6) or the serene *Adagio* of the *C major Concerto grosso* (No. 3) and the gracious, imitative Minuet finale of the same work. They radiate simple vitality and love of life and a youthful exuberance that belies the composer's age. The playing is warm and musical, and the recording is made in an ample acoustic. Some may prefer more sharply etched detail (particularly in the concerti grossi), but the resonant string-timbres are agreeably natural and immaculately transferred to CD.

6 Sonate da chiesa, Op. 4; 12 Trattenimenti armonici per camera, Op. 6.
(Y/B) *** Hyperion Dig. CDA 66831/2 [id.]. Locatelli Trio.

The set of '*Church*' *sonatas*, showing the composer at his most lyrically appealing, contrasts with Op. 6. *Trattenimento* indicates 'Entertainment', suggesting a more secular style; and certainly the allegros of Op. 6 are strikingly lively and infectiously dance-like in character. The slow movements are often more formal, although never dull. The excellent continuo player of the Locatelli Trio uses a discreet and often touchingly understated organ continuo to support the violin and cello in Op. 4 and a harpsichord in Op. 6. The performances, using original instruments, are of high quality, well paced, sensitive and fresh, and the recording is well balanced and vivid.

Il nascimento dell'Aurora (festa pastorale; complete).
(Y/B) (B) **(*) Erato/Warner Dig. 4509 96374-2 (2) [id.]. Anderson, Zimmermann, Klare, Browne, Yamaj, Sol. Ven., Scimone.

Written as a court celebration, probably on the birth of Princess Maria-Theresa, daughter of Charles VI of Austria, *Il nascimento dell'Aurora* makes a substantial and attractive two-hour stage entertainment or 'festa pastorale'. This well-balanced live recording, made in Vicenza, Italy, puts forward a persuasive case despite some roughness in the choral singing (which is particularly distracting in the first chorus) and some intrusive audience applause. Soloists are first rate and the orchestra generally stylish. The CD transfer is excellently managed. With full libretto and translation included, this is well worth exploring.

Alfvén, Hugo (1872–1960)

A Legend of the Skerries, Op. 20; Swedish rhapsodies Nos. 1 (Midsummer vigil), Op. 19; 2 (Uppsala rhapsody), Op. 24; 3 (Dala rhapsody), Op. 47; King Gustav II Adolf, Op. 49: Adagio.
(Y/B) *** Chandos Dig. CHAN 9313 [id.]. Iceland SO, Sakari.

Petri Sakari is a totally unaffected guide in this repertory and secures excellent playing from the Icelandic orchestra. *Midsummer vigil*, Alfvén's masterpiece, is quintessential Sweden and so, too, is the affecting *Elegy* from the incidental music to Ludwig Nordström's play about *Gustav II Adolf*. Sakari produces musically satisfying results, and this useful anthology can be warmly recommended. The Chandos sound is excellent.

Symphony No. 1 in F min., Op. 7; Andante religioso; Drapa (Ballad for large orchestra); Uppsala rhapsody, Op. 24.
*** BIS Dig. CD 395 [id.]. Stockholm PO, Neeme Järvi.

Järvi's version of the *First Symphony* supersedes the earlier Westerberg version; it is superior both artistically and technically and leaves the listener more persuaded as to its merits. The *Uppsala rhapsody* is based on student songs but it is pretty thin stuff, and the *Andante religioso* is rather let down by its sugary closing pages. *Drapa* opens with some fanfares, full of sequential clichés and with a certain naïve pomp and splendour that verges on bombast.

Symphony No. 2 in D, Op. 11; Swedish rhapsody No. 1 (Midsummer vigil).
*** BIS Dig. CD 385 [id.]. Stockholm PO, Neeme Järvi.

Like those of its predecessor, the ideas of the *Second Symphony* are pleasing though they do not possess a particularly individual stamp. On the whole, Järvi is very persuasive in the symphony and gives a delightful performance of the popular *Midsummer vigil*.

(i) *Symphony No. 4 (Havsbandet – From the outermost skerries), Op. 29; A Legend of the Skerries, Op. 20.*
*** BIS Dig. CD 505 [id.]. Stockholm PO, Järvi, (i) with Christina Högman, Claes-Håkan Ahnsjö.

Alfvén's *Fourth Symphony* is perhaps his most ambitious work. There is a romantic programme relating to the emotions of two young lovers, whose wordless melisma is heard to excellent effect in this very fine recording. However, the results are conventionally voluptuous rather than ethereal. Alfvén's scoring is eminently resourceful, and no one with an interest in this composer will be disappointed either by the performance, which is sensitive and persuasive, or by the superbly balanced recording with its natural perspective and admirable detail.

Symphony No. 5 in A min.; The Mountain King (Bergakungen): suite; Gustav II Adolf: Elegy.
*** BIS Dig. CD 585 [id.]. Royal Stockholm PO, Neeme Järvi.

The *Fifth Symphony* is a late work; it draws freely on ideas from the ballet, *The Mountain King*, whose suite completes this CD. The first movement is by far the best, despite its echoes of Wagner and Sibelius. The second movement has some beautiful ideas but the last two movements, which became 'problem children' in his old age, are really rather feeble. *The Mountain King* is an inventive and attractive score; and both works, as well as the touching *Elegy* from the music to *Gustav II Adolf*, could hardly be presented more persuasively. The engineering is absolutely first class.

Choral music: (i) *Aftonen; Anders, han var en hurtiger dräng; Berceuse;* (ii) *Glädjens blomster. Gryning vid havet; Gustaf Frödings jordafärd; Hör I Orphei Drängar; Kulldansen;* (ii) *Lindagull (Serenade). Min kära;* (ii) *Natt. Och jungfrun hon går i ringen; Oxbergsmarschen; Papillon;* (ii) *Prövningen. Roslagsvår; Stemning; Sveriges flagga; Trindskallarna; Uti vår hage; Vaggvisa;* (ii) *Vallgossens visa;* (ii) *Värmlandsvisan.* Songs (ii; iii) *Du är stilla ro; I stilla timmar; Jag längtar dig; Saa tag mit Hjerte; Skogen sofver; Sommardofter.* (i) SODERMAN, arr. ALFVEN: *I månans skimmer.*
*** BIS Dig. CD 633 [id.].(i) Orphei Drängar Ch., Robert Sund; (ii) with Claes-Håkan Ahnsjö; (iii) Folke Alin.

Some of the part-songs Alfvén composed for the Orphei Drängar (Sons of Orpheus) are collected here and are sung to the highest standards of tonal virtuosity. Their singing is quite remarkable: wide in dynamic range and cultured in tonal blend – in terms of male choir singing, the equivalent of the Berlin Philharmonic. It is superbly recorded too. Recommended with enthusiasm even to those who find the symphonies inflated and self-indulgent.

Aliabiev, Alexander (1787–1851)

(i; ii) *Introduction and theme with variations in D min.;* (iii; ii) *Souvenir de Moscou, Op. 6;* (iv) *Piano trio in A min.;* (v) *12 Romances.*
*** Olympia OCD 181 [id.]. (i) Venyavsky; (ii) USSR Ac. SO, Verbitsky; (iii) Grauch; (iv) Voskresensky, Ambarpumyan, Knyasev; (v) Pluzhnikov, Mishuk.

Aliabiev's (or Alyabiev's) *Trio in A minor* is a delightful piece with something of the fluency of Weber and Mendelssohn, and it is heard to good advantage here. The *Introduction and theme with variations in D minor* is sandwiched between two groups of songs, nearly all of which have great charm and appeal. The recording of the two insubstantial pieces for violin and orchestra comes off less well. This disc almost gives the lie to the impression that Russian music begins with Glinka.

Alkan, Charles (1813–88)

Barcarolle; Gigue, Op. 24; Marche, Op. 37/1; Nocturne No. 2, Op. 57/1; Saltarelle, Op. 23; Scherzo diabolico, Op. 39/3; Sonatine, Op. 61.
(B) *** HM HMA 190 927 [id.]. Bernard Ringeissen.

Bernard Ringeissen could be more flamboyant but he is fully equal to the cruel technical demands of this music. The recording, from the beginning of the 1970s, is first class.

12 Etudes in the minor keys, Op. 39/1–12. Etudes, Op. 3/5: Allegro barbaro. Chants: Assez vivement, Op. 38/1; Barcarolle, Op. 65/6. Esquisses: La staccatissimo; Les cloches; Les soupirs; En songe, Op. 63/2, 4, 11 & 48. Les Mois: Gros temps, Op. 74 (Suite 1: No. 2). Nocturne in B, Op. 22; Preludes: La chanson de la folle au bord de la mer; Le temps qui n'est plus; J'étais endormie, mais mon cœur veillait, Op. 31/8, 12 & 13.
(N) *** ASV Dig. CDDCS 227 (2) [id.]. Jack Gibbons.

Liszt himself spoke of Alkan as having the finest piano technique he had ever known, and Alkan's music (like Medtner's and Scarlatti's) is almost exclusively for the keyboard but, unlike theirs, rarely finds its way into the modern concert hall – not surprisingly, given its fiendish, hair-raising difficulties and (to be fair) uneven quality. Jack Gibbons is up to the formidable demands this music makes on technique and intelligence alike and he gives outstanding accounts, very well recorded too, of the *Symphony for piano* (the *Etudes Nos. 4–7*) and the *Concerto for piano* (*Nos. 8–10*). He is no less persuasive and convincing in the smaller pieces. He has obviously inherited the mantle of Ronald Smith, to whom his notes pay homage, and he rises to the challenge these pieces present with triumphant virtuosity. Good sound, too.

Grande sonate (Les quatre âges), Op. 33; Barcarolle; Le festin d'Esope; Sonatine, Op. 61.
(Y/B) *** Hyperion Dig. CDA 66794 [id.]. Marc-André Hamelin.

Under studio conditions, Marc-André Hamelin records works by Alkan with a virtuosity just as breathtaking as on his live Wigmore Hall disc, also for Hyperion (see our Recitals section, below). In his flair and brilliance he has rarely, if ever, been matched. Written six years before the Liszt *Sonata*, Alkan's *Grande sonate* over its four massive movements represents the hero at various ages, with the second, *quasi-Faust*, the key one. The *Sonatine*, the most approachable of Alkan's major works, is just as dazzlingly done, with the hauntingly poetic *Barcarolle* and the swaggering *Festin d'Esope* as valuable makeweights.

Grande sonate (Les quatre âges), Op. 33; Prelude: La chanson de la folle au bord de la mer, Op. 31/8. 12 Studies in all minor keys, Op. 39 (excerpts): *Comme le vent; En rythme molossique; Scherzo diabolique; Le festin d'Esope. 12 Studies in all major keys, Op. 35: Allegro barbaro* (only).
(M) *** EMI CDM7 64280-2 [id.]. Ronald Smith.

The *Grande sonate* is a quite extraordinary piece. Some of the other music here is also quite astonishing, and it goes without saying that Ronald Smith's virtuosity is remarkable and his understanding of this repertoire beyond question. The piano sound is realistic and clean. Inadequate back-up notes.

25 Preludes, Op. 31.
*** Decca Dig. 433 055-2 [id.]. Olli Mustonen – SHOSTAKOVICH: *24 Preludes*. ***

The *Preludes* are more poetic than barnstorming and date from 1847. They go through all the major and minor keys, returning to C major in No. 25. The young Finnish pianist Olli Mustonen plays them supremely well. The recording is absolutely first class, though the pedal-stamping in the *Tenth Prelude*, *Dans le style fugué*, should have been curbed. Strongly recommended.

ORGAN MUSIC

8 Petits Préludes sur les huit gammes du plainchant; 13 Prières, Op. 64; Impromptu on Luther's 'Un fort rampart est notre Dieu', Op. 69.
*** Nimbus Dig. NI 5089 [id.]. Kevin Bowyer (organ of Salisbury Cathedral).

One does not think of Alkan as a composer for the organ, and indeed only the eight *Little preludes on the eight modes of plainchant* were actually conceived for this instrument. Kevin Bowyer is clearly a master of this repertoire and conveys his enjoyment in music which has personality and is readily melodic. Perhaps the mellow Salisbury Cathedral organ was not an ideal choice (a French instrument would have had more reedy bite), but this remains an attractive and generous (74 minutes) recital.

Allaga, Géza (1841–1913)

Concerto hongrois for (solo) *cymbalum; Etudes de concert: in A; A min. (Tempest); C; D; D min.; B flat; F (Chorale); Pizzicato and glissando;* (i) *Hungarian rhapsody for cymbalom and string quintet.* arr. of Liszt: *Le Dieu des Hongrois; Arrangements for flute and cymbalom:* (ii) SCHUBERT: *Ave Maria.* FIELD: *Nocturne.*
(B) *** HM Dig. HMA 1903075 [id.]. Viktória Herrencsár; (i) Zsolnai, Tóth, Papp, Nagy, Tibay; (ii) Béla Drahos.

A fascinating collection. Géza Allaga founded a school for what has come to be regarded as Hungary's national instrument, the cymbalum (though it was in use in various forms for thousands of years and originated in Asia). He left a complete course of study for beginners and experts: many of these pieces obviously demand much bravura. Allaga's invention is always agreeable and his use of folk-tunes in the two extended works, the one solo and the other with an agreeably warm string backing, is also very pleasing. The soloist here is both a virtuoso and a sensitive musician. Here there is much subtlety, both of colour and of dynamic range, while Béla Drahos produces an elegant flute line in the Schubert and Field arrangements. The recording is excellent.

Allegri, Gregorio (1582–1652)

Miserere.
*** Gimell CDGIM 339; *1585-T-39* [id.]. Tallis Scholars, Phillips – MUNDY: *Vox patris caelestis;* PALESTRINA: *Missa Papae Marcelli.* ***
(M) *** Decca 421 147-2 [id.]. King's College Ch., Willcocks – PALESTRINA: *Collection.* ***

Mozart was so impressed with Allegri's *Miserere* when he heard it in the Sistine Chapel (which originally claimed exclusive rights to its performance) that he wrote the music out from memory so that it could be performed elsewhere. On the much-praised Gimell version, the soaring treble solo is taken by a girl, Alison Stamp, and her memorable contribution is enhanced by the recording itself.

The famous King's performance of Allegri's *Miserere*, with its equally arresting treble solo so beautifully and securely sung by Roy Goodman, is now coupled with Palestrina at mid-price.

Almeida, Francisco António de (c. 1702–55)

La Giuditta (oratorio).
(N) *** HM Dig. HMC 901411/12 [id.]. Lootens, Congiu, M. Hill, Köhler, Concerto Köln, Jacobs.

Here is a superb oratorio (based on the story from the Apocrypha of Judith's deception of Holofernes) by a virtually unknown Portuguese composer who studied Italian music in Rome between 1722 and 1726. Although his visit did not coincide with that of Handel, his music is every bit the equal of that master – indeed, without any hint of plagiarism it keeps reminding one of Handel at his finest. Almeida is surely lucky that René Jacobs has assembled such a fine cast, with Lena Lootens singing freshly and appealingly as Giuditta, Martyn Hill a generally fine Holofernes (though perhaps not an entirely convincing seducer) and Alex Köhler most impressive of all as Ozia, Commander of Bethulia, a male alto role which he makes totally convincing. The work is brimful of melody, its invention of such consistently high quality that one hardly misses the choruses that Handel would surely have provided. To discover the remarkable range of this music, try Ozia's lovely first aria, *Tortorella, se rimira*, or Giuditta's extraordinarily dramatic call for God's wrath to avenge the insults of the heathen, which opens Part 2. The orchestral writing, using flutes, oboes, horns – which come through spectacularly – and strings, shows a true feeling for the orchestral palette and the way it can be used to sharpen and colour the narrative. Jacobs directs a performance that springs vividly to life, and everything about this production, including the recording, is first class. With excellent documentation this is very highly recommended.

Alwyn, William (1905–85)

(i) *Autumn legend* (for cor anglais and string orchestra); (ii) *Lyra Angelica* (concerto for harp and string orchestra); (iii) *Pastoral fantasia* (for viola and string orchestra); *Tragic interlude.*
*** Chandos Dig. CHAN 9065 [id.]. (i) Nicholas Daniel; (ii) Rachel Masters; (iii) Stephen Tees; City of L. Sinfonia, Richard Hickox.

Autumn legend (1954) is a highly atmospheric tone-poem, very Sibelian in influence. It is beautifully played. The *Pastoral fantasia* also contains a curious Sibelius quotation – perhaps unconscious – near the beginning. Yet the piece has its own developing individuality. Again a fine performance, with Stephen Tees highly sympathetic to the music's fluid poetic line. The *Tragic interlude* is a powerful lament for the dead of wars past, written on the eve of the Second World War. But the highlight of the disc is the *Lyra Angelica*, a radiantly beautiful, extended piece (just over half an hour in length), inspired by the metaphysical poet, Giles Fletcher's '*Christ's victorie and triumph*'. The performance here is very moving, and the recording has great richness of string-tone and a delicately balanced harp texture. Rachel Masters's contribution is distinguished. This is the record to start with for those beginning to explore the music of this highly rewarding composer.

Concerti grossi Nos. 1 in B flat for chamber orchestra; 2 in G for string orchestra; 3 for woodwind, brass and strings; (i) Oboe concerto.
*** Chandos Dig. CHAN 8866 [id.]. (i) Daniel; City of L. Sinfonia, Hickox.

The improvisatory feeling and changing moods of the *Oboe concerto* are beautifully caught by Nicholas

Daniel, with Hickox and the Sinfonia players providing admirable support. They then turn to the more extrovert and strongly contrasted *Concerti grossi*, the first a miniature concerto for orchestra, the second in the ripest tradition of English string writing. The third is a fine *in memoriam* for Sir Henry Wood. Excellent Chandos sound, gaining from the warm ambience of St Jude's in north-west London, yet with textures unclouded.

(i) *Piano concerto No. 1. Symphony No. 1.*
*** Chandos Dig. CHAN 9155 [id.]. (i) Howard Shelley; LSO, Hickox.

Hickox's performance of the *First Symphony* is just as compelling as the composer's own version on Lyrita (coupled with No. 4 – SRCD 227). Its unashamed flamboyance and energy, helped by Chandos's spectacular recording, brings great vitality to the music. The *First Piano concerto* is also a flamboyant piece, in a single movement. Howard Shelley is a splendid soloist, fully up to the rhetoric and touching the listener when the passion subsides, creating a haunting stillness at the very end. Again splendid recording.

(i) *Piano concerto No. 2; Sinfonietta for strings; Symphony No. 5 (Hydriotaphia).*
*** Chandos Dig. CHAN 9196 [id.]. (i) Howard Shelley; LSO, Richard Hickox.

The *Piano concerto No. 2* opens boldly and expansively and is romantically rhetorical, with sweeping use of the strings. The imaginative *Andante* is its highlight, but the jazzy 'fuoco' finale with its calm central section is overlong (13 minutes). Howard Shelley plays with brilliance and much sensitivity, and Alwyn admirers will be glad to have the work available on record, even if it is flawed.

The cogent *Fifth Symphony* (1973), with its dense argument distilled into one movement with four sub-sections, has a strange subtitle. It is called '*Hydriotaphia*' and the work is dedicated to the memory of physician/philosopher Sir Thomas Browne (1605–82), whose writings were always on the composer's bedside table.

The *Sinfonietta for strings*, a much more expansive piece, is almost twice as long as the symphony. The string writing, very much in the English tradition, is vigorous in the first movement and hauntingly atmospheric, especially in the beautiful *Adagio*, desperate in its melancholy. The recordings were made in the resonant acoustic of All Saints', Tooting, which provides spectacular results although detail is not always sharply defined. But it suits the string work especially well. Hickox is consistently sympathetic, with the structure of the symphony held in a strong grip.

(i) *Violin concerto. Symphony No. 3.*
*** Chandos Dig. CHAN 9187 [id.]. (i) Lydia Mordkovitch; LSO, Hickox.

The *Violin concerto* – so sympathetically played here by Lydia Mordkovitch – is, like the *Piano concerto No. 2*, unknown. It is discursive but has moments of intense beauty, especially at the rapt closing section of the first movement, where Lydia Mordkovitch plays exquisitely. Indeed her performance is very sensitive and often touchingly beautiful. Hickox's reading of the *Third Symphony* is every bit as convincing as that of the composer on Lyrita, while the LSO again respond to a symphony that is strongly conceived, powerfully argued, consistently inventive and impressively laid out. The expansive Chandos recording suits both works admirably, and the *Violin concerto* is balanced most convincingly.

4 Elizabethan dances (from the set of 6); *Derby Day overture; Festival march; The Magic island* (symphonic prelude); *Sinfonietta for strings.*
*** Lyrita SRCS 229 [id.]. LPO, composer.

An exceptionally attractive compilation and one of the composer's most successful records. Alwyn's *Elizabethan dances* are extrovert and tuneful in the Malcolm Arnold tradition (if not quite so ebullient in orchestration). Alwyn is no less successful in *Derby Day* with its pithily rhythmic main theme, and he is both poetic and romantically expansive in the Shakespearean evocation of *The Magic island*. In the *Festival march*, while acknowledging his debt to Elgar and Walton, he brings an individual, restrained nobilmente to the main lyrical tune. But the most important work here is the *Sinfonietta for strings*. The Lyrita recordings were made between 1972 and 1979 and show the usual engineering flair which distinguishes all issues on this label.

Film scores: *The Fallen Idol; The History of Mr Polly; Odd Man Out; The Rake's Progress: Calypso* (all restored and arr. Christopher Palmer).
*** Chandos Dig. CHAN 9243 [id.]. LSO, Richard Hickox.

Alwyn made his name as a film composer in the days when the immediate post-war British films as often as not had a 'symphonic score'. Unfortunately the major scores were all inadvertently destroyed at Pinewood Studios, and Christopher Palmer has had to return to the composer's sketches for these recordings. The result is impressive. *Odd Man Out* (about the IRA) has the most compellingly poignant music, but the lightweight *History of Mr Polly* is charming and *The Fallen Idol* sophisticated in its delineation of action and character. The orchestral playing is both warmly committed and polished, and the recording is out of Chandos's top drawer.

Symphonies Nos. 1–4; 5 (Hydriotaphia); Sinfonietta for strings.
(N) *** Chandos Dig. CHAN 9429 (3) [id.]. LSO, Richard Hickox.

William Alwyn's five symphonies plus the expansive *Sinfonietta for strings* are given outstanding performances from the LSO under Hickox to match the composer's own in natural understanding. Here they are separated from their various couplings and fitted snugly on to three CDs. The Chandos recordings are consistently up to the high house standard, and this set can be commended without reservation to all collectors interested in the twentieth-century English symphony which, on the evidence of this box, is alive and well.

Symphonies Nos. 1; 4.
*** Lyrita SRCD 227 [id.]. LPO, composer.

The first of Alwyn's symphonies dates from 1950 and is a work of considerable power and maturity. Its gestures are occasionally overblown, particularly in the finale, and offer obvious echoes of the film-scores of which Alwyn is so consummate a master. The LPO responds splendidly to the composer's direction and the Lyrita analogue recording has fine presence, body and clarity.

Symphony No. 2; Derby Day overture; Fanfare for a joyful occasion; The Magic island; Overture to a masque.
*** Chandos Dig. CHAN 9093 [id.]. LSO, Richard Hickox.

Hickox's account of the Sibelian *Second Symphony* is every bit as fine as the composer's own performance on Lyrita, and the modern Chandos digital recording provides even fuller and more expansive sound for brass and strings and a natural concert-hall balance. *The Magic island* is a fine piece, inspired by *The Tempest*, and Hickox's account is beautifully played and full of atmosphere. The pithy *Derby Day overture* has plenty of energy here, but the *Overture to a masque* with its 'pipe and tabor' Elizabethan flavour is comparatively slight. The brilliant *Fanfare*, appropriately dedicated to the percussion player, James Blades, ends the concert spectacularly with the bright, sonorous recording impressively wide in range.

Symphony No. 4; Elizabethan dances; Festival march.
*** Chandos Dig. CHAN 8902 [id.]. LSO, Richard Hickox.

Richard Hickox's conception of the *Fourth* is marginally more spacious than the composer's own – as the timings of the outer movements demonstrate. Yet he has a masterly grip on the score. The Chandos digital recording, made in St Jude's, in London NW 11, is superbly rich and spacious. The *Elizabethan suite* doesn't bridge the opposing styles of the times of the queens, Elizabeth I and II, too convincingly, but there is a graceful waltz, an engaging mock-morris dance and a pleasing pavane. The *Festival march* is agreeable enough, but its grand tune lacks the memorability of those by Elgar and Walton.

CHAMBER MUSIC

Concerto for flute and 8 wind instruments; Music for three players; Naiades fantasy (Sonata for flute and harp); Suite for oboe and harp; Trio for flute, cello and piano.
*** Chandos Dig. CHAN 9152 [id.]. Haffner Wind Ens. of L., Daniel, with Jones, Drake.

Alwyn's part-writing, pleasing invention and skilful manipulation of colour and texture make this a particularly rewarding collection. The *Concerto for flute and eight wind instruments* is richly textured, yet the consistent inner movement fascinates the ear. The charmingly pastoral *Suite for oboe and harp* is most delectably played by Nicholas Daniel (oboe) and Ieuan Jones (harp), its closing *Jig* winningly articulated. The *Naiades fantasy for flute and harp* is a chimerical piece in six movements (alas, not cued individually). The final work is an equally attractive two-movement *Trio*. The Haffner Wind Ensemble are very impressive, both individually as solo personalities and as a team, expertly matching timbres in part-writing which always rewards their skill and musicianship. The recording is admirably balanced and very realistic. A concert that can be recommended with no reservations whatsoever.

Crépuscule for solo harp; Divertimento for solo flute; Clarinet sonata; Flute sonata; Oboe sonata; Sonata impromptu for violin and viola.
(Y/B) *** Chandos Dig. CHAN 9197 [id.]. L. Haffner Wind Ens. (members), Nicholas Daniel; Julius Drake (piano).

The *Oboe sonata* is an inspired work; it is beautifully played here by Nicholas Daniel and Julius Drake.

The *Clarinet sonata* is a fantasy piece in which Joy Farrall combines extrovert freedom with a more thoughtful reserve, yet with wild excursions into the upper tessitura. By contrast the solo *Divertimento* for flute (the responsive Kate Hill) is neo-classical. The *Crépuscule* for solo harp (Ieuan Jones) is a quiet evocation of a cold, clear and frosty Christmas Eve. The *Sonata for flute and piano* and the *Sonata impromptu for violin and viola* are no less striking. Alwyn demonstrates in all these works a natural skill in interweaving his part-writing and his usual ready flow of appealing melody. Overall this programme is consistently rewarding and the recording is very real and immediate.

(i) *Rhapsody for piano quartet. String quartet No. 3; String trio.*
*** Chandos Dig. CHAN 8440 [id.]. (i) David Willison; Qt of London.

The *Third Quartet* is the most important work on this record; like its two predecessors, it is a concentrated and thoughtful piece of very considerable substance, elegiac in feeling. The playing of the Quartet of London throughout (and of David Willison in the *Rhapsody*) is both committed and persuasive. The recording brings the musicians vividly into one's living-room.

String quartets Nos. 1 in D min.; 2 (Spring waters).
**(*) Chandos Dig. CHAN 9219 [id.]. Qt of London.

Both quartets are works of substance. The *First* has a probing, deeply felt first movement, a dancing, gossamer Scherzo and a profound, yearning *Andante*. Its companion comes 20 years later and derives its subtitle, *Spring waters*, from Turgenev. Both works are well played and the performances are obviously felt and thoroughly committed. The digital recording from the early 1980s has clarity and presence and sounds admirably natural in its CD format. However, the playing time is too short for a full-priced record (45 minutes).

Fantasy-waltzes; 12 Preludes.
**(*) Chandos Dig. CHAN 8399 [id.]. John Ogdon.

This record has been restored to the catalogue at full price (even though it dates from 1985) and a price reduction might have been feasible. The *Fantasy-waltzes* are highly attractive and are excellently played by John Ogdon, who is also responsible for a perceptive insert-note. The *Twelve Preludes* are equally fluent and inventive pieces that ought to be better known and well repay investigation.

VOCAL MUSIC

(i) *Invocations;* (ii) *A Leave-taking* (song-cycles).
*** Chandos Dig. CHAN 9220 [id.]. (i) Jill Gomez, John Constable; (ii) Anthony Rolfe Johnson, Graham Johnson.

In each of these two song-cycles, with a distinctive and unexpected choice of poems, Alwyn shows a keen ear for matching word-movement in music with a free arioso style. Notable in the tenor cycle, *A Leave-taking*, is *The ocean wood*, subtly evocative in its sea inspirations. The soprano cycle is almost equally distinguished, leading to a beautiful *Invocation to the Queen of Moonlight*, which suits Jill Gomez's sensuous high soprano perfectly. Excellent performances, not least from the accompanists, and first-rate recording.

Miss Julie (complete).
*** Lyrita SRCD 2218 (2) [id.]. Jill Gomez, Benjamin Luxon, Della Jones, John Mitchinson, Philh. O, Tausky.

Alwyn's operatic gestures are big and, though the melodies hardly match Puccini's, the score is rich and confident, passionately performed by the Philharmonia under Tausky's direction. Jill Gomez sings ravishingly as Miss Julie and Benjamin Luxon gives a most convincing characterization of the man-servant lover, with roughness a part of the mixture. Della Jones's mezzo is not contrasted enough with the heroine's soprano, but she sings warmly, and it is good to have as powerful a tenor as John Mitchinson in the incidental role of Ulrik. The 1983 Lyrita recording is well up to standard, beautifully clear as well as full, and it projects the narrative evocatively and involvingly.

Amirov, Fikret (1922–84)

(i) *The Arabian Nights* (complete ballet); (ii) *Shur (Symphonic Mugam);* (iii) *Symphony for strings.*
(N) *(*) Olympia Analogue/Dig. OCD 578 A/B (2) [id.]. (i) Bolshoi Theatre O, Nazim Rzaev; (ii) Moscow RSO, Abdullayev; (iii) Azerbaijan SO, Rozhdestvensky.

The Azeri composer, Fikret Amirov, will hardly be even a name to most collectors and, apart from half a dozen pieces for flute and piano, is unrepresented in the catalogue. He studied in Baku, where his full-length choral ballet, *The Arabian Nights*, was produced in 1979. This occupies about 90 minutes in all, and the second CD includes two earlier works, a *Symphony for strings* (1947) and *Shur* (1948). The ballet is heavily indebted to Khachaturian, though the latter seems the soul of subtlety by comparison. *The Arabian Nights* is very noisy indeed, but ideas are not in such abundant supply as are the decibels. The shallow, rather strident (1982) recording does not help matters. The early *Symphony for strings* offers evidence of distinct talent, though again Khachaturian is the dominant influence. The recording under Rozhdestvensky is from 1964. *Shur* is a 30-minute, symphonic 'mugam' (*mugam* is related to the Arab *maqam*), which suggests that this composer, perhaps, has been stronger on promise than fulfilment. Recorded in 1993, it is a digital recording and is considerably better balanced than its companions.

Anderson, Leroy (1908–75)

Arietta; Balladette; Belle of the ball; Blue tango; Bugler's holiday; Clarinet candy; Fiddle-faddle; The first day of spring; Forgotten dreams; Home stretch; Horse and buggy; Jazz legato; Jazz pizzicato; The penny whistle song; The phantom regiment; Plink, plank, plunk!; Promenade; Sandpaper ballet; Saraband; Serenata; Sleigh ride; The syncopated clock; Trumpeter's lullaby; The typewriter; The waltzing cat.
(N) *** RCA 09026 68131-2 [id.]. Saint Louis SO, Leonard Slatkin.

With over two dozen items included, Slatkin's is the most winning, generous and comprehensive single-disc Leroy Anderson collection now on offer. The orchestral playing combines an easy-going zest with warmth and finesse and, if the acoustic of Powell Symphony Hall is rather resonant, it adds to the *galant* elegance of the lyrical numbers, which are played with much affection. The various soloists (three trumpets in *Bugler's holiday* and four clarinets in *Clarinet candy*) obviously enjoy their own infectious bravura. Fennell's Eastman-Rochester performances are not entirely upstaged (some may prefer the brightly etched Mercury sound), but on most counts this new RCA CD is the one to have. Anderson produced a ready flow of indelible tunes over three decades after the first two, *Jazz pizzicato* and its complement, *Jazz Legato*, were a hit at Arthur Fiedler's Boston Pops Concerts in 1938. Slight though they may be, one cannot help but reflect on the formidable quantity of more 'serious' music composed during that period (and afterwards) without any tunes at all! The CD is presented in a specially designed jewel case which provides a vulgar optical illusion of a self-motivating typewriter – but don't let that put you off.

Belle of the ball; Blue tango; Chicken reel; China doll; Fiddle-faddle; The first day of spring; The girl in satin; Horse and buggy; Jazz legato; Jazz pizzicato; The phantom regiment; Plink, plank, plunk!; Promenade; Saraband; Scottish suite: The bluebells of Scotland. Serenata; Sleigh ride; Song of the bells; Summer skies; The syncopated clock; The typewriter; The waltzing cat. Arr. of HANDEL: *Song of Jupiter.*
(M) *** Mercury 432 013-2 [id.]. Eastman-Rochester Pops O, or O, Frederick Fennell.

The reissue of Fennell's Mercury performances is most welcome; although certain key numbers such as *Bugler's holiday*, *Forgotten dreams* and *A Trumpeter's lullaby* are missing; they will no doubt, arrive on a later issue. His performances have a witty precision which is most attractive. The sound throughout is truthful, if not opulent.

Andriessen, Hendrik (1892–1981)

(i) *Chromatic variations; Variations and fugue on a theme by Kuhnau;* (ii) *Variations on a theme by Couperin;* (iii) *Fiat Domine; Magna res est amor; Miroir de Peine* (song-cycle).
*** NM Classics Dig. 92023 [id.]. Netherlands R. CO, Porcelijn; with (i) Reinders, Vincken, Bosman, Ferschtman; (ii) Verhey, Stoop; (iii) Alexander.

Andriessen's melodic gift is very appealing and his scoring for strings shows a remarkable grasp of sonority and textural colour: there is much imaginative and haunting writing in his three sets of variations. The Couperin set (1944) also includes some delightfully delicate scoring for flute and harp, while the *Chromatic variations* (1970), among his last works, is virtually a miniature sinfonia concertante, with felicitous interweaving of the soloists: flute, oboe, violin and cello. *Magna res est amor* is very operatic in its rapturous line. Roberta Alexander soars aloft with glorious tone and she is hardly less ravishing in the song-cycle, setting poems by Henri Ghéon which illustrate Christ's passion as seen through Mary's eyes. This very rewarding music is performed with persuasive depth of feeling and considerable subtlety too, and the glowingly warm recording increases the listener's pleasure.

Antill, John (1904–86)

Corroboree (ballet suite).
(Y/B) **(*) Everest EVC 9007 [id.]. LSO, Sir Eugene Goossens – GINASTERA: *Estancia; Panambi* ***;
  VILLA-LOBOS: *Little train of the Caipira*. **(*)

The ballet-score *Corroboree*, the best-known work by the Australian composer, John Antill, is based on
an aboriginal dance ceremony. Its primitivism generates imaginatively exotic invention, very colourfully
scored, to include an enticing *Dance to the Evening Star*, a strongly rhythmic *Rain dance* and a boisterously frantic *Closing fire ceremony*. The performance here generates plenty of energy, and if the recording is over-resonant it is immensely vivid. It is a pity that this Everest series is not in the mid-priced
range, although it costs slightly less than the highest premium-priced CDs.

Arensky, Anton (1861–1906)

Piano concerto in F min., Op. 2; Fantasia on Russian folksongs, Op. 48.
(Y/B) **** Hyperion Dig. CDA 66624 [id.]. Coombs, BBC Scottsh SO, Maksymiuk – BORTKIEWICZ:
  Piano concerto. ***

Arensky's *Piano concerto in F minor* is an endearing piece, highly Chopinesque in feeling and with some
very appealing ideas. Coombs is an artist of great sensitivity and effortless virtuosity, and he makes out
the best possible case for both the *Concerto* and the much shorter *Fantasia on Russian folksongs*. Good
orchestral support and recording.

Silhouettes (Suite No. 2), Op. 23.
*** Chandos Dig. CHAN 8898 [id.]. Danish Nat. RSO, Järvi – SCRIABIN: *Symphony No. 3*. ***

Arensky's *Silhouettes* have a lot of period charm – particularly *Le rêveur*, which is almost the Russian
equivalent of Elgar's *Dream children*. The Danish Radio Orchestra play for Neeme Järvi with great
freshness and elegance, as if they are enjoying making the acquaintance of this rarely heard music – as
we did!

Symphonies Nos. 1 in B min., Op. 4; 2 in A, Op. 22; Dream on the Volga overture.
** Olympia OCD 167 [Mobile Fidelity MFCD 878 (without Overture)]. USSR Ac. SO, Svetlanov.

Arensky's *First Symphony* is beautifully put together and has considerable melodic freshness. The
Second is the more individual of the two and is full of highly attractive ideas. The *Overture* opens
bombastically but also has its attractive moments, though its inspiration is less consistent than either of
the symphonies. The performances are spirited, though the brass are at times raw in climaxes.

Piano trio No. 1 in D min., Op. 32.
*** CRD CRD 3409; *CRDC 3409* [id.]. Ian Brown, Nash Ens. – RIMSKY-KORSAKOV: *Quintet*. ***
*** Chandos Dig. CHAN 8477 [id.]. Borodin Trio – GLINKA: *Trio*. ***
(Y/B) **(*) Sony Dig. SK 53269 [id.]. Yefim Bronfman, Cho-Liang Lin, Gary Hoffman – TCHAIKOV-
  SKY: *Piano trio*. **(*)

Arensky's delightful *D minor Piano trio* was composed a year after Tchaikovsky's death and a decade
after Tchaikovsky's own contribution to the genre. The account by members of the Nash Ensemble is
first class in every way. These fine players capture the Slav melancholy of the *Elegia*, and in the delightful
Scherzo Ian Brown is both delicate and nimble-fingered. The warm, resonant 1982 analogue recording
has transferred naturally to CD.

  The Borodins, too, give a lively and full-blooded account of the *Trio*. The *Scherzo* comes off well, and
the whole does justice to the Borodins' genial playing.

  Yefim Bronfman, Cho-Liang Lin and Gary Hoffman give a strongly characterized performance of the
First Trio which would be a credible first choice, were it not for the recording. Bronfman is allowed to
swamp his string partners. Both Cho-Liang Lin and Gary Hoffman are players of such refinement and
insight that their contribution cannot fail to afford great pleasure. So does Yefim Bronfman, but he
would have afforded more had he been more discreetly balanced.

Piano trios Nos. 1 in D min., Op. 32; 2 in F min., Op. 73.
(Y/B) *** Ph. Dig. 442 127-2 [id.]. Beaux Arts Trio.

The Beaux Arts offer the more logical coupling. While the *D minor Trio* is well represented in the
catalogue, its later companion is neglected, and the Beaux Arts is a first recommendation now: lively
playing, full of engagement and sparkle, and very well recorded.

String quartet No. 2 in A min., Op. 35.
*** Mer. Dig. CDE 84211; *KE 77211* [id.]. Arienski Ens. – BORODIN: *Sextet movements;* TCHAIKOV-SKY: *Souvenir de Florence.* **

A charming three-movement work whose middle movement, the variations on a theme of Tchaikovsky, is best known in its transcription for full strings, it has, like so much of this composer's music, real quality. The playing is very committed indeed.

Suites for 2 pianos Nos. 1, Op. 15; 2 (Silhouettes), Op. 23; 3 (Variations), Op. 33; 4, Op. 62.
(Y/B) *** Hyperion Dig. CDA 66755 [id.]. Stephen Coombs, Ian Munro.

Arensky was enormously fluent and his invention proceeds with apparently effortless ease. Only the *Valse* from the *Suite No. 1* of 1888 is at all known, yet all the music here is endearingly fresh. The *Polonaise*, which ends this suite, would not disgrace a ballet by Tchaikovsky. *Suite No. 2*, written four years later, is subtitled *Silhouettes*, and each of its five movements represents a different character, *Le Savant* ('The Scholar'), *La Coquette*, and so on. *Suite No. 3* is a set of nine variations and is the most brilliant and pianistically resourceful of all four. *Suite No. 4* was written five years before the composer's death and is hardly less beguiling than its companions: its third movement, *La rêve*, would also grace a Tchaikovsky or Glazunov ballet. Two pianos are difficult to record and the recording, though too resonant, reproduces them very truthfully. Altogether delightful music and captivating playing. Were it not so resonant, it would have a Rosette.

Arne, Thomas (1710–78)

Keyboard concertos (played as listed): *Harpsichord concertos: in C; in G min.; Organ concertos: in B flat; in G; Piano concertos: in A; in B flat.*
(N) *** Hyperion Dig. CDA 66509 [id.]. Paul Nicholson, Parley of Instruments, Holman.

These are exhilarating performances of delightful works, beautifully recorded. The six keyboard concertos of Arne date from different periods in his career and have a wide variety of movement-structures. It is a wonder that they survive at all, when they were not published until 15 years after his death. Arne followed in the tradition set by Handel, with the organ the regular solo instrument; but that was varied more and more as the idea took hold of the harpsichord and, later, the piano as the solo instrument. Holman varies the solo instrument according to the character of each work, with the earliest, *No. 2 in G major*, given on the organ, but the next oldest, *No. 5 in G minor*, played on the harpsichord, when the Scarlattian cross-hands writing is better suited to that instrument. As a sampler, try the delectable *No. 3 in A*, given here on a gentle-toned fortepiano. The instrumental balances are perfectly managed, achieving clarity without exaggeration.

Harpsichord concerto No. 5 in G min.; Overture No. 1 in E min.
(M) *** Decca 440 033-2 [id.]. George Malcolm, ASMF, Marriner – C. P. E. BACH: *Harpsichord concerto in C min.;* J. C. BACH: *Harpsichord concerto in A min.;* HAYDN: *Harpsichord concerto in D* etc. ***

This is the pick of the six concertos above and a most winning example of post-Handelian concertante writing. It is part of a most attractive anthology, recorded in 1967 with the Academy under Marriner at its early peak. George Malcolm not only plays a fine solo role in the concerto but provides the continuo for the attractive *Overture*, in effect a four-part sinfonia (slow-fast-slow-fast). The harpsichord is recorded realistically and life-size, too, not overblown.

Organ concertos Nos. 1 in C; 2 in G; 3 in A; 4 in B flat; 5 in G min.; 6 in B flat.
**(*) Chandos Dig. CHAN 8604/5; *DBTD 2013* (2) [id.]. Roger Bevan Williams, Cantilena, Shepherd.

Though Arne's concertos are simpler in style and construction than those of Handel, their invention is consistently fresh. The performances here have admirable style and spirit, and the recording is ideally balanced – the organ seems perfectly chosen for this consistently engaging music. A recommendable set in every respect, except for the playing time (only 86 minutes).

Cymon and Iphigenia; Frolic and free (cantatas); Jenny; The Lover's recantation; The Morning (cantata); Sigh no more, ladies; Thou soft flowing Avon; What tho' his guilt.
*** Hyperion Dig. CDA 66237 (id.]. Emma Kirkby, Richard Morton, Parley of Instruments, Goodman.

The present collection admirably shows the ingenuous simplicity of Arne's vocal writing, very much in the mid-eighteenth-century English pastoral school with its 'Hey down derrys'. Excellent, warm recording, with the voices naturally projected. A most entertaining concert.

Artaxerxes (complete).
(N) *** Hyperion Dig. CDA 67051/2 [id.]. Robson, Bott, Partridge, Spence, Edgar-Wilson, Hyde, Parley of Instruments, Roy Goodman.

Artaxerxes was the first *opera seria* with words in English and, though the language often seems oddly matched with the formality of the structure, this sparkling, lively performance impressively explains why Arne's opera was such a success when it was first produced at Covent Garden in February 1762, three years after Handel died. One reason for its success was that it provides a splendid challenge to the singers, most of all to the soprano who takes the role of Mandane, sister of Artaxerxes, whose love for Arbaces, her brother's friend, provides a central theme of the libretto, translated from Metastasio. The one number that has latterly become popular – largely thanks to Joan Sutherland's brilliant recording – is *The soldier tir'd*, but that dazzling climactic number is only one of Mandane's formidable solos, whether expressive or vehement. Catherine Bott gives a masterly performance, with the counter-tenor, Christopher Robson, also impressive in the castrato title-role, and with Ian Partridge pure-toned and incisive in the role of the villain, Artabanes, even if his sweet tenor hardly conveys evil. With the mezzo-soprano, Patricia Spence, taking the castrato role of Arbaces, the others are first rate too. On two very well-filled CDs the set owes much of its success to the inspired direction of Roy Goodman, who from the overture onwards electrifies the players and singers, pointing rhythms and aerating textures to bring out the point and charm as well as the vigour of the writing. The reconstruction of the score – involving the recitatives which were separated from the original – has been most capably achieved by Peter Holman, who contributes an excellent note.

Arnell, Richard (born 1917)

The Great Detective (ballet suite).
(M) (***) EMI mono CDM7 64718-2 [id.]. Pro Arte O, composer – ADDISON: *Carte blanche;* ARNOLD: *A Grand Grand Overture;* BLISS: *Checkmate;* RAWSTHORNE: *Madame Chrysanthème* etc. (***)

The Great Detective is of course Sherlock Holmes and Richard Arnell's ballet was written for Sadler's Wells in 1953. Arnell described the music as 'a mixture of wit, self-importance, low cunning and, where it depicts the fiend, animal ferocity'. The writing is engagingly lightweight and tuneful, with a *Pas de deux for Distressed lady and a suspect* and a *Pas de trois for Doctor and Ladies*. In the *Dance of deduction* Sherlock briefly plays his fiddle. The lively performance under the composer makes for a highlight in this collection of unpretentious, well-written British music, vividly recorded.

Arnold, Malcolm (born 1921)

Overture: *Beckus the Dandipratt, Op. 5; Commonwealth Christmas, Op. 64; The Fair field, Op. 110; The Smoke, Op. 21; A Sussex overture.*
(N) *** Reference Dig. R R 48CD [id.]. LPO, composer.

This collection of overtures valuably fills in gaps in the Arnold discography, notably *Beckus the Dandipratt*, his very first orchestral work. If its scherzando rhythms owe much to Walton's *Scapino*, the fizzing energy and brilliant orchestration are very much Arnold's own. The early Decca 78 record of this piece, with the composer still principal trumpet in the LPO under Eduard van Beinum, had a biting zest not quite matched here, but the skipping rhythms are still sprung infectiously. Arnold at seventy is perhaps a less exhilarating conductor than in his earlier recordings, but only *The Fair field* (celebrating the Croydon Fairfield Halls) lacks something in effervescence. *The Smoke* brings a contrasting sultry atmosphere in its central section and the Prokofievian *Sussex overture* is jauntily full of good spirits, as is the exuberant *Commonwealth Christmas overture*; with its injection of West Indian popular music, complete with steel band evocations. The LPO playing is strikingly alert throughout and the recording suitably brilliant. Christopher Palmer, the recording producer, provides excellent documentation.

Carnival of the animals, Op. 72; (i) *Concerto for 2 pianos, 3 hands (Concerto for Phyllis and Cyril), Op. 104; A Grand grand overture, Op. 57; Symphony No. 2, Op. 40.*
(Y/B) *** Conifer Dig. 75605 51240-2 [id.]. (i) David Nettle and Richard Markham; RPO, Vernon Handley.

Malcolm Arnold's *Double piano concerto* was originally the '*Concerto for Phyllis and Cyril*', written in 1969 for Phyllis Sellick and Cyril Smith when Cyril lost the use of his left hand and he and his wife continued as a highly successful piano duo. The piano duo here, Nettle and Markham, are obviously captivated by the piece, which they play with much flair and understanding. The *Second Symphony* is fresh and colourful, far more complex in structure than it may initially seem. The tension is released in the finale, which has all the assertive self-confidence of the composer's earlier writing. Vernon Handley is a persuasive advocate, and the spectacular recording is especially effective in the moments of brassy flamboyance in the outer movements. The *Grand, grand overture* was written for the famous Hoffnung Festivals and comes up remarkably effectively in this spectacular modern recording. It has a character- istically high-spirited, Arnoldian tune but is mainly notable for its outrageous scoring, including three vacuum-cleaners and a floor-polisher! Arnold's supplement to Saint-Saëns's *Carnival of the animals*, written for a Hoffnung memorial concert, fails to match the French whimsy it simulates, but individual numbers have a certain charm. However the *Jumbo* joke, to music of Delibes, is unashamedly vulgar.

Concerto for 28 players, Op. 105; (i) *Viola concerto, Op. 108. Larch trees, Op. 3; Serenade for small orchestra, Op. 105.*
(N) *** Conifer Dig. 75605 51211-2 [id.]. (i) Rivka Golani; L. Musici, Stephenson.

Following up his other excellent Conifer disc of Arnold concertos, Mark Stephenson here fills in more important gaps in the CD catalogue of Arnold's music. *Larch trees* dates from as early as 1943, written when he was only 21. It is his first orchestral work, a tone-poem that instantly reveals his natural feeling for effective, evocative instrumentation. There are one or two obvious echoes of Debussy and Delius, and Arnold never again took nature so overtly as his inspiration, but it is good to have so likeable a piece recorded. The *Viola concerto* and the *Concerto for 28 players* both date from the period 1970–71. The *Viola concerto* is the more immediately approachable, with Arnold exploiting the lower register of the solo instrument more consistently than Walton did in his concerto, notably in the richly lyrical, central slow movement, much the longest of the three, between lively and tuneful allegros. The most enigmatic work here is the *Concerto for 28 players*, chamber-music writ large, often abrasive in an almost Stravinskian way. Here again the emotional weight is borne by the central slow movement, where even the hesitant, ostensibly serial opening theme is warmly expressive. Stephenson and his talented team are just as convincingly idiomatic in the charming *Serenade*.

Clarinet concertos Nos. 1, Op. 20; 2, Op. 115; Scherzetto.
*** Hyperion Dig. CDA 66634 [id.]. Thea King, ECO, Wordsworth – BRITTEN: *Clarinet concerto movement;* MACONCHY: *Concertinos.* ***

Designed in part as a tribute to the great clarinettist, Frederick Thurston, Thea King's collection of short concertante works for clarinet makes an exceptionally attractive disc, beautifully recorded and superbly performed. The *Scherzetto* is a delightfully jaunty piece adapted by Christopher Palmer from Arnold's music for the film, *You Know What Sailors Are.* Not only Thea King but the ECO (the orchestra in which she has been a distinguished principal for many years) under Barry Wordsworth bring out the warmth as well as the rhythmic drive.

Clarinet concertos Nos. 1, Op. 20; 2, Op. 115; Divertimento for flute, oboe and clarinet, Op. 37; Fantasy for B flat clarinet, Op. 87; Clarinet sonatina, Op. 29; 3 Shanties for wind quintet.
(Y/B) *** ASV Dig. CDDCA 922 [id.]. Emma Johnson, Jaime Martin, Jonathan Kelly, Claire Briggs, Susanna Cohen, Malcolm Martineau; ECO, Ivor Bolton.

With the characterful Emma Johnson as the central figure in all five works, this makes a delightful collection of what is labelled as Arnold's 'Complete Works for Clarinet'. Above all, these performances bring out the fun in Arnold's music, his bluff sense of humour set alongside a vein of warm lyricism matched by few of his contemporaries. Though Emma Johnson is the leader in this ensemble, she is matched in both expressive warmth and wit by her young colleagues, notably the flautist, Jaime Martin, and the horn player, Claire Briggs. Compared with Thea King on Hyperion, Emma Johnson has a rather reedier tone, less smooth, and her speeds tend to be a little more relaxed. Choice can safely be left to preference over coupling, though the recording of the orchestra is rather less transparent than in the rival versions. Otherwise first-rate sound.

(i) *Clarinet concerto No. 2, Op. 115;* (ii) *Flute concerto No. 2, Op. 111;* (iii) *Horn concerto No. 1, Op. 11;* (iv) *Concerto for piano duet and strings, Op. 32.*
*** Conifer Dig. 75605 51228-2 [id.]. (i) Michael Collins; (ii) Karen Jones; (iii) Richard Watkins; (iv) David Nettle & Richard Markham; L. Musici, Mark Stephenson.

In the *Second Clarinet concerto,* written for Benny Goodman in 1974, Michael Collins (who played it at the 1993 Last Night of the Proms) is even more persuasive, more volatile than Thea King in her fine Hyperion version. Karen Jones, principal flute of the Bournemouth orchestra and Shell–LSO prize-winner in 1985, is equally sympathetic in the *Flute Concerto No. 2.* The *Concerto for piano duet* of 1950 should not be confused with the three-handed *Concerto for two pianos* that Arnold wrote for Cyril Smith and Phyllis Sellick. In its use of block chords for the four hands at one keyboard, it is a chunkier work but is full of characteristic Arnold touches. Nettle and Markham play as one at their single keyboard; and under Mark Stephenson the young musicians of London Musici perform throughout with the understanding and precision that have marked all their Conifer recordings.

(i) *Flute concerto No. 1, Op. 45;* (ii) *Oboe concerto, Op. 39; Sinfoniettas Nos. 1–3, Opp. 48, 65 & 81.*
*** Hyperion Dig. CDA 66332 [id.]. (i) Beckett, (ii) Messiter; L. Festival O, Ross Pople.

It makes a delightful programme having Arnold's three *Sinfoniettas* framing two wind concertos that come from the same early period, the 1950s. The performances here are all excellent, with warm, well-balanced sound.

Guitar concerto, Op. 67.
(M) *** RCA 09026 61598-2. Julian Bream, Melos Ens., composer – Richard Rodney BENNETT: *Concerto;* RODRIGO: *Concierto de Aranjuez.* ***
*** EMI Dig. CDC7 54661-2 [id.]. Julian Bream, CBSO (members), Rattle – RODRIGO: *Concierto de Aranjuez.* TAKEMITSU: *To the Edge of Dream.* ***

There are few guitar concertos to match the effectiveness of this jazz-inflected piece, written in 1957 for Julian Bream, whose first recording, made two years later with the composer directing the Melos Ensemble, is surely definitive. It was recorded by Decca engineers, so the balance is exemplary and the sound has plenty of atmosphere and the most vivid colouring.

Bream's second recording, with Rattle, is also very successful indeed and gains from the modern digital sound, which is vividly focused. As with the earlier version, the work is recorded in its original chamber scoring, which is especially effective in the infectious finale.

(i) *Double violin concerto. Serenade for small orchestra, Op. 26; Sinfoniettas Nos. 1–2.*
**(*) Koch Dig. 37134-2 [id.]. (i) Igor and Vesna Gruppman; San Diego CO, Barra.

These are warm-hearted performances, very well recorded, of four of Malcolm Arnold's most attractive earlier works, each in his favourite form of three compact movements. The *Serenade for small orchestra,* the first of the four, with the most ambitious orchestration, is particularly valuable, when otherwise it is unavailable on CD. The San Diego Chamber Orchestra gives a winning account, full of high spirits, but they are less successful in evoking the Bachian overtones of the *Double Violin concerto,* with the central *Andantino* too romantic in style, and the soloists consistently adopting too heavy a vibrato, with the occasional portamento.

(i) *4 Cornish dances; 8 English dances, Sets 1, Op. 27; 2, Op. 33; 4 Scottish dances, Op. 59* (all arr. Farr); *Fantasy for brass band, Op. 114; Little suites for brass band Nos. 1, Op. 80; 2, Op. 92;* (ii) *The Padstow Lifeboat* (march), *Op. 94.*
*** Conifer Dig. 74321 16848-2 [id.]. Grimethorpe Colliery Band, (i) Elgar Howarth; (ii) composer.

Sir Malcolm Arnold, who was present at the recording sessions, gave high praise to Elgar Howarth's carefully prepared yet winningly spontaneous performances, unerringly paced. The composer himself directs the final march, *The Padstow Lifeboat,* with its warning off-key foghorn (based on the pitch of the foghorn at Trevose in Cornwall). The astonishing virtuosity and the wide palette of colour achieved by the Grimethorpe Colliery Band is consistently stimulating throughout this highly enjoyable programme. The performances are superb and the recording, made – appropriately – in Dewsbury Town Hall, Yorkshire, is completely natural and very realistically balanced. This is very much in the demonstration bracket and is also a most entertaining 66 minutes of good tunes and brilliant invention, very cleverly scored.

4 Cornish dances, Op. 91; 8 English dances, Set 1, Op. 27; Set 2, Op. 33; 4 Irish dances, Op. 126; 4 Scottish dances, Op. 59; Solitaire (ballet): *Sarabande; Polka.*
*** Chandos Dig. CHAN 8867 [id.]. Philh. O, Bryden Thomson.

Arnold's four sets of British national dances make a wonderfully varied and colourful musical entertainment. The two numbers specially written for *Solitaire* in 1956 augmented the eight *English dances*, to form the ballet of this name. The *Sarabande* has a wistful charm and the *Polka* brings characteristically witty orchestral colouring. Bryden Thomson has the advantage of the extra definition superb digital sound brings, with no loss of ambient feeling, and this set of performances is admirable.

Film music: *The Bridge on the River Kwai* (suite for large orchestra); *Hobson's Choice* (orchestral suite); *The Inn of the Sixth Happiness* (suite); *The Sound Barrier* (rhapsody), *Op. 38; Whistle Down the Wind* (small suite for small orchestra).
*** Chandos Dig. CHAN 9100 [id.]. LSO, Richard Hickox.

Malcolm Arnold wrote over 100 film scores, and it was the music for *The Bridge on the River Kwai* which – as the composer has acknowledged – put his name before the wider public. He justly won an Oscar for what in essence was the provision of an exuberant counter-melody to sail over the top of Kenneth Alford's march, *Colonel Bogey*. What is so exasperating is that the Alford estate refused permission for this inimitable musical amalgam to be recorded, so what we are given here is separate performances of the Alford march and Arnold's breezy counter-theme. What is so striking here and throughout this 78-minute collection is the sheer fecundity of Arnold's invention. In *Kwai* Christopher Palmer, Arnold's amanuensis for this project, took various fragments and sections and reassembled them with the composer's blessing: the result is very strong. Much the same applies to the lighter score for *Hobson's Choice*. But how charmingly melodic it is. *Whistle Down the Wind*, also set in Lancashire, brings in its *Prelude* one of Arnold's most indelible ideas originally including a human whistle, which the producer, Richard Attenborough, provided in the soundtrack but which here is a piccolo. *The Inn of the Sixth Happiness* is more Hollywoodian in its flamboyance, but it has a charming central romantic interlude. All this music is superbly played by Hickox and the LSO (who obviously relish the often virtuoso instrumental scoring), and the recording is as lavish as anyone could wish – very much in the Chandos demonstration bracket.

A Grand Grand Overture.
(M) (***) EMI mono CDM7 64718-2 [id.]. Pro Arte O, composer – ADDISON: *Carte blanche;* ARNELL: *Great Detective;* BLISS: *Checkmate;* RAWSTHORNE: *Madame Chrysanthème* etc. (***)

Malcolm Arnold's *Grand Grand Overture*, with its rifle-shots and parts in the score for three vacuum-cleaners and a floor-polisher, was written for the first Hoffnung Festival in 1956. It has quite a good main theme but its flagrant audacity wears a bit thin, away from the visual occasion. It is perhaps the least repeatable offering on this otherwise attractive collection of British lightweight composer-conducted music. The mono sound is vivid enough, and the rest of the compilation is recorded in stereo.

(i) *Symphony No. 1;* (ii) *Concerto for 2 pianos (3 hands), Op. 104;* (iii) *English dances Nos. 3 & 5;* (i) *Solitaire: Sarabande; Polka;* (iii) *Tam O'Shanter: overture, Op. 51.*
(M) *** EMI CDM7 64044-2. (i) Bournemouth SO; (ii) Phyllis Sellick and Cyril Smith, CBSO; (iii) Philh. O; composer.

This is a strong performance of the *First Symphony* under the composer, while the concerto is a delightful, undemanding work, superbly played by the dedicatees, which makes a good foil alongside the rumbustious overture, *Tam O'Shanter*. Finally come the two pieces Arnold added to his *English dances* for the ballet *Solitaire*, and two of the most attractive of the *Dances*.

Symphonies Nos. 1, Op. 22; 2, Op. 40.
(Y/B) *** Chandos Dig. CHAN 9335 [id.]. LSO, Richard Hickox.
(N) (BB) **(*) Naxos Dig. 8.553406 [id.]. Nat. SO of Ireland, Andrew Penny.

Richard Hickox takes naturally to the Malcolm Arnold idiom and moves easily from geniality to angry intensity, as in the first movement of No. 1; and he is particularly impressive in the two slow movements, which are full of atmosphere, vividly coloured and strongly felt. The rumbustious finale of No. 2 brings a splendid release of tension, and throughout the LSO response is powerful and thoroughly committed. The recording is well up to the high standard we expect from this label and the spontaneity of the playing communicates the feeling of live music-making. A first-rate coupling.

Comparison between Hickox's account and the composer's own recording of the *First Symphony* is instructive. With Hickox, the first movement is much more tautly paced. Andrew Penny in his Naxos version matches Hickox closely, but the National Orchestra of Ireland cannot command the richness of sonority of the LSO, nor are their (otherwise excellent) wind soloists quite so strong in personality. However, there is an agreeable lightness of touch in Dublin, and the presentation of the delectable melody of the *Andantino* (shared by flute and violins) brings a whimsical charm. Indeed the Dublin performances of both symphonies are fresh and spontaneous, but in the poignant *Lento* of the *Second*, with its plangent funeral march, Hickox's much more spacious tempo is profoundly moving when the

LSO playing sustains such a high degree of concentration. The finale, too, is joyously exuberant, whereas the genial skittishness of the Dublin orchestra has less abandon. However, it must be said that the composer was present at these sessions and undoubtedly Penny consulted him over questions of tempo and especially that for the slow movement of the *Second Symphony*, which certainly communicates strongly in the Dublin performance. The Naxos recording is excellent, full and spacious, but the Chandos is very much in the demonstration bracket.

(i) *Symphony No. 2, Op. 40;* (ii) *Symphony No. 5, Op. 74;* (i) *Peterloo: overture.*
(M) *** EMI CDM7 63368-2 [id.]. (i) Bournemouth SO, Groves; (ii) CBSO, composer.

The recoupling of two of Arnold's most impressive symphonies can be warmly welcomed. Both recordings date from the 1970s. The composer secures an excellent response from the Birmingham orchestra, and Groves, in Bournemouth, is equally dedicated. The CD transfer is outstandingly successful, and the overture makes a highly effective encore. Splendid value at mid-price.

Symphony No. 3, Op. 63.
(Y/B) **(*) Everest EVC 9001 [id.]. LPO, composer – VAUGHAN WILLIAMS: *Symphony No. 9.* **(*)

Arnold made his first recording of the *Third Symphony* at Walthamstow in the late 1950s. In the outer movements the performance has a certain chimerical, spontaneous quality that balances out the deeper feelings which are beneath the music's surface. The result is uncommonly fresh, even if Hickox's later recording has more gravitas. The early stereo is remarkably spacious and the brass writing is given fine sonority, though the violins are less full-bodied than we would expect today.

Symphonies Nos. 3, Op. 63; 4, Op. 71.
*** Chandos Dig. CHAN 9290 [id.]. LSO, Hickox.

Arnold's symphonies mirror his experience of life in its broader context, with disappointment, frustration and even tragedy all included within the package that humanity has to accept. As it happens, the immediately communicative *Third Symphony* does have a good-natured finale; even if there is a sting at the end with a fierce, Holst-like rhythmic warning in the coda, the despair is met head on in the final few bars. The work, commissioned by the Royal Liverpool Philharmonic Society and first performed in 1957, is more notable for the long, expressively austere string-melody in the opening movement and the desolation of its *Lento* slow movement, both played with great expressive intensity under Hickox.

The first movement of the *Fourth Symphony* is dominated by one of those entirely winning, Arnoldian lyrical tunes, even though there is jagged dissonance in the central episode. The slow movement brings another long-breathed, almost Mahlerian, melodic flow, although with more overt sensuousness, and the finale, complete with fugue, has its bizarre, indeed raucous moments, including a curious march sequence. Richard Hickox has the work's full measure, and the Chandos recording is superb, full of colour and atmosphere.

Symphonies Nos. 5, Op. 74; 6, Op. 95.
(N) *** Chandos Dig. CHAN 9385 [id.]. LSO, Richard Hickox.

Arnold has developed the habit of hiding his deeper emotions behind a bright, extrovert manner, and his *Fifth Symphony* brings out this dichotomy very clearly. It is a consciously elegiac work, written in memory of friends who died young; it contains some of his most intense and emotional music but remains easily approachable. The *tempestuoso* first movement, starting with a solitary oboe, is punctuated with bursts of anger and with percussion adding brilliance; it is both tenderly valedictory and nostalgic. So too the gracefully lyrical slow movement before the dazzling Scherzo and the drum-and-fife finale. While the first movement brings moments of valedictory evocation in Hickox's hands, it is also dramatically vibrant, and the *Andante* has a certain restrained warmth of feeling to balance its dejection. Whereas the jocularly brash Scherzo and finale are bursting with rhythmic life and colour, the work's ambivalent close is caught perceptively. The disconsolate *Sixth Symphony* is a good deal less comfortable than the *Fifth*, but Hickox handles the powerfully menacing climax of the *Lento* quite superbly, gripping the listener in the music's bleak despair, which then suddenly evaporates with the arrival of the joyous, syncopated brass fanfares of the rondo finale. In both symphonies the committed response of the LSO, together with the richly expansive Chandos recording, increases the weight and power of the readings, and this coupling stands out as a highly suitable point of entry for those collectors wanting to explore Arnold's symphonic canon.

Symphony No. 6, Op. 95; (i) *Fantasy on a theme of John Field for piano and orchestra, Op. 116. Sweeny Todd* (ballet): *concert suite, Op. 68a; Tam O'Shanter overture, Op. 51.*
*** Conifer Dig. 74321 16847-2 [id.]. RPO, Vernon Handley, (i) with John Lill.

Written in 1967 during his unhappy Cornish period, the powerfully bleak *Sixth Symphony* brings a striking example of the darker, more troubled side of Arnold's genius. The work finally resolves its enigmatic despondency in the up-beat *Con fuoco* finale, a rondo based on a characteristically ebullient Arnoldian trumpet-tune, a movement somewhat Shostakovich-like in its quirkiness. The *Fantasy on a theme of John Field*, written for John Lill during the composer's Irish period, is a splendid example of the more extrovert Arnold in the bravura of the piano writing. It uses one of Field's most innocently charming nocturnes, in which John Lill revels with much delicate poetry. The *Sweeney Todd* music, drawn from a ballet score with the help of David Ellis, brings a contradiction between the grimness of the subject and the open jollity of the treatment, with cakewalks, polkas and other dance-rhythms freely used. The *Tam O'Shanter overture*, the best-known item, is an idiosyncratic, rumbustious showpiece characteristic of the early Arnold. Handley draws colourful and committed playing from the orchestra, with John Lill a masterful, flamboyant soloist in the music written for him. First-class recording.

Symphonies Nos. 7, Op. 113; 8, Op. 124.
*** Conifer 74321 15005-2 [id.]. RPO, Vernon Handley.

The bitterness in the *Seventh* is inescapable. Dedicated to the composer's three children, the writing is most strongly influenced by his son Edward, tragically autistic. The *Eighth* is emotionally hardly less pungent. Handley's performances of both symphonies generate great power and depth of feeling, with the most eloquent response from the RPO players, and the recording is outstandingly real and vivid. However, neither work offers an easy listening experience.

Symphony No. 9, Op. 128.
(N) (BB) *** Naxos Dig. 8.553540 [id.]. Nat. SO of Ireland, Andrew Penny.

Just ten years after Sir Malcolm Arnold wrote his *Ninth Symphony* this superb first recording arrived to confirm the work as a fitting culmination to his symphonic series. The baldness of the arguments, with two-part writing the general rule, and with structure built on repetition and juxtaposition rather than thematic development, might initially be thought disconcerting. What matters are the actual results, and they consistently speak in a true Arnoldian accent. With occasional echoes of Shostakovich, the ear is regularly tweaked by the terracing of sounds, at extremes of register as well as of dynamic, culminating in the long slow finale, almost as long as the other three movements together, registering a mood of tragedy and disillusion. The parallel with the final *Adagio* of Mahler's *Ninth Symphony* is clear, though without neurosis or self-pity. As Arnold explains in his interview included on the disc, the whole piece reflects 'the five years of hell' he suffered before writing this work. The symphony ends quietly on a major triad, a firm D major chord, a mere sop towards granting release. The other three movements are just as direct, bald in their arguments but pointful, not facile, built on instantly memorable material. So the first movement, *Vivace*, quickly establishes Arnold's mode of duetting, with occasional jazzy slur-rings. The second movement, *Allegretto*, brings hypnotic, chaconne-like repetitions on a theme with modal overtones. The third movement starts like a typical Arnold Scherzo, weightier than the rest of the work, but then grows ever angrier. As to the performance, this is not just concentrated and consistently committed but warmly resonant, with the strings sounding glorious and the woodwind and brass consistently brilliant. The recording is rich and firmly focused.

CHAMBER MUSIC

Divertimento for flute, oboe and clarinet, Op. 37; Duo for flute and viola, Op. 10; Flute sonata, Op. 121; Oboe quartet, Op. 61; Quintet for flute, violin, viola, horn and piano, Op. 7; 3 Shanties for wind quintet, Op. 4.
*** Hyperion Dig. CDA 66173 [id.]. Nash Ens.

Duo for 2 cellos, Op. 85; Piano trio, Op. 54; Viola sonata No. 1, Op. 17; Violin sonatas Nos. 1, Op. 15; 2, Op. 43; Pieces for violin and piano, Op. 54.
*** Hyperion Dig. CDA 66171 [id.]. Nash Ens.

Clarinet sonatina, Op. 29; Fantasies for wind, Opp. 86–90; Flute sonatina, Op. 19; Oboe sonatina, Op. 28; Recorder sonatina, Op. 41; Trio for flute, bassoon and piano, Op. 6.
*** Hyperion Dig. CDA 66172 [id.]. Nash Ens.

There is much here that belies Malcolm Arnold's image as just an entertaining and genial tunesmith. All the pieces on the first disc show conspicuous resource in the handling of the instruments. The second disc includes two *Violin sonatas* which are cool, civilized and intelligent. The *Piano trio* of 1956 has a powerful sense of direction. The third listing concentrates on the wind music. This is perhaps more for admirers of Arnold's music than for the generality of collectors. The playing is brilliant and sympathetic throughout all three discs and the recording first rate.

PIANO MUSIC

Allegro in E min.; 2 Bagatelles, Op. 18; 8 Children's pieces, Op. 36; Children's suite, Op. 16; 3 Fantasies; 3 Pieces (1937); *2 Pieces* (1941); *3 Pieces* (1943); *Prelude; Serenade in G; Sonata; Variations on a Ukrainian folksong, Op. 9.*
(Y/B) *** Koch Dig. 3-7162-2 [id.]. Benjamin Frith.

This splendid disc spans Malcolm Arnold's almost unknown piano output, from his earliest pieces (including the *Allegro in E minor*) from 1937, dedicated to his mother and firmly neo-classical in the manner of Bach, to the *Three Fantasies* of 1986, terse in structure and much more ambivalent in expressive mood to match the composer's last symphonies. In between are some highly atmospheric pieces with a strong popular influence. The *Sonata* (1942), succinct and strongly argued, brings motoric pungency and in the finale a reminder of Prokofiev; the slow movement, however, still has a popular ambience in its harmony and melodic style. The formidable quarter-of-an-hour-long *Variations on a Ukrainian theme* (1948) makes a bold contrast, its complexities demonstrating the composer imaginatively stretched. The two groups of short pieces for children are very much in the spirit of Elgar's nursery music. The comparatively enigmatic, more sombrely coloured *Ballades* provide further contrast. Benjamin Frith is clearly at home in all this music, presenting it discerningly and spontaneously in order of composition, to make a thoroughly rewarding 72-minute recital. Arnold communicates in every bar, and the piano recording is very fine indeed.

Arriaga, Juan (1806–26)

Symphony in D; Overture: Los esclavos felices.
(N) *** Hyperion Dig. CDA 66800 [id.]. SCO, Sir Charles Mackerras – VORISEK: *Symphony in D*. ***

The *Overture*, which comes before the *Symphony*, is a real charmer, opening with a gracious melody that is almost Schubertian, and then carrying on very much in the style of Rossini, complete with crescendo. The *Symphony* (1824) is contemporary with the better-known string quartets – and indeed the Vorišek coupling as well. Arriaga opens with an *Adagio* and the main allegro quickly establishes a *Sturm und Drang* ambivalence, though the secondary theme has a certain elegance. The *Andante* is charming, and Schubert again comes to mind both here and in the hardly less winning Minuet with its innocent flute-led Trio. The agitated closing allegro confirms this to be an original and individual work of great appeal which ought to be in the repertoire. It could scarcely be played with more character, and the somewhat resonant but very well-balanced recording does not cloud detail. Highly recommended.

String quartets Nos. 1 in D min.; 2 in A; 3 in E flat.
*** CRD CRD 33123 (2) [id.]. Chilingirian Qt – WIKMANSON: *String quartet No. 2*. ***
*** Ph. Dig. 446 092-2 [id.]. Guarneri Qt.
(Y/B) **(*) Claves Dig. CD 50-9501 [id.]. Sine Nomine Qt.

These three *Quartets* are marvellous works of great warmth and spontaneity that can hold their own in the most exalted company. It is barely credible that a boy still in his teens could have produced them. The Chilingirians play with both conviction and feeling. But they involve a pair of CDs (admittedly with an interesting coupling) and many collectors will now be looking for a single disc containing the triptych. In many ways the Claves set, by the excellent Sine Nomine Quartet, fills the bill. One has only to listen to the raptly sustained opening of the *Pastorale Andantino* slow movement of the *E flat Quartet* to find playing which is sensitive to the music's atmosphere and which has appealing lyrical feeling. But as soon as the impetus becomes more impassioned, a degree of aggressiveness is imparted to the string timbre, and one realizes that the microphones are uncomfortably close. Yet the playing has warmth and subtlety, clean ensemble and plenty of verve, and those who do not object to the up-front sound-image and the degree of edge on the leader's attack will count this worth having, for there is no lack of ambience.

Fortunately the newest set by the Guarneri Quartet, although still too up-front as a recording, offers smoother quality, coupled with a truthful balance and a vivid presence. They play the *Adagio* of the *D minor Quartet* very beautifully, and the *Theme and variations* of the *A major* work is hardly less appealing. Their playing throughout is immaculate in ensemble yet has both warmth and ardour. But if the Chilingirians were to be reissued on a single disc, they would still take pride of place.

Atterberg, Kurt (1887–1974)

Symphonies Nos. (i) *1 in B min., Op. 3;* (ii) *4 in G min. (Sinfonia piccola), Op. 14.*
**(*) Complete Record Co. Sterling CDS 1010-2 [id.].* (i) Swedish RSO, Westerberg; (ii) Norrköping
SO, Frykberg.

Although Atterberg composed nine symphonies, only the *Sixth* has made any headway abroad.
However, he had a well-stocked imagination and a good feeling for the orchestra and he deserves wider
dissemination. The *First Symphony* (1909, revised 1913) is derivative but well fashioned, and well played
too. The *Sinfonia piccola* (1922) is slight, almost sinfonietta-like; it makes extensive use of folk material.
A useful coupling, though the performance of the folksy *Sinfonia piccola* is not quite top-drawer.

Symphony No. 6 in C, Op. 31; Ballad without words, Op. 56; A Värmland rhapsody, Op. 36.
** BIS Dig. CD 553 [id.]. Norrköping SO, Jun'ichi Hirokami.

Atterberg's *Sixth Symphony* is a colourful and inventive score which deserves wide popularity. *A
Värmland rhapsody* is, appropriately enough, strongly folkloric. The *Ballad without words* has many
imaginative touches. The Norrköping orchestra includes many sensitive players, but the string-tone
lacks weight and opulence. The recording is very clean.

*Autumn ballads, Op. 15; Rondo rétrospectif, Op. 26; Trio concertante in G min./C, Op. 57; Valse monotone
in C; Violin sonata in B min., Op. 27.*
** Marco Polo Dig. 8.223404 [id.]. Eszter Pérényi, András Kiss, Ilona Prunyi, Sándor Falvay, György
    Kertész, Deborah Sipkay.

The *Violin sonata* is a well-wrought piece. The *Autumn ballads*, however, are rather banal. The *Valse
monotone* is a piano transcription of the last movement of the *Suite for violin, viola and strings*, one of
the composer's very best works. The *Rondeau rétrospectif* is an entertaining piece from the 1920s for
piano (four hands), much in the irreverent spirit of the finale of the *Sixth Symphony*, and which quotes
freely from various classics including the *Pathétique Symphony* and the *Emperor concerto*. The *Trio
concertante* is an arrangement for violin, cello and harp of his *Double concerto* for violin, cello and
orchestra (1960). None of this is great music but it is well played and more than adequately recorded.

Auber, Daniel (1782–1871)

Overtures: The Bronze horse; Fra Diavolo; Masaniello.
❀ (M) *** Mercury 434 309-2 [id.]. Detroit SO, Paray – SUPPE: *Overtures.* ***

Dazzling performances, full of verve and style, which will surely never be surpassed. The present
recordings, made in the suitably resonant acoustic of Detroit's Old Orchestra Hall, shows Mercury
engineering (1959 vintage) at its very finest.

(i) *Le domino noir* (complete); *Gustave III ou Le Bal masqué* (Overture & ballet music)
(N) ❀ *** Decca Dig. 440 646-2 (2) (i) Sumi Jo, Vernet, Ford, Power, Bastin, Olmeda, Cachemaille, L.
    Voices; ECO, Bonynge.

Richard Bonynge here fulfils a long-held ambition to record this enchanting opéra-comique about two
novices in a convent illicitly attending a masked ball. The hero, Horace, falls in love with one of them,
Angèle, only to have her running off, Cinderella-like, as midnight strikes – a scene that recalls (as well as
'Cinderella') the end of the ball in *Fledermaus*. Act II, set in the apartment of Juliano, the hero's friend,
also involves Angèle in a different disguise, this time as a servant, while in Act III, about to take her final
vows before becoming abbess in the convent on the orders of the queen, she is absolved at the last
minute, so allowing the hero and heroine finally to fall into each other's arms.To a libretto by Scribe –
one of dozens he provided for Auber's many operas – Auber was inspired to write a sparkling score, full
of delightful invention. So the opening number, after the Spanish-flavoured overture, has a passage in
thirds for the heroine and her confidante, Brigitte, that directly anticipates the celebrated duet in
Delibes's *Lakmé*, and other numbers bring clear anticipations of Gounod's *Faust* and of Verdi's *Il
trovatore*, not to mention Gilbert and Sullivan. Bonynge's advocacy stems from his finding a first edition
score of the opera, as well as a set of orchestral parts. His researches led him to find accompanied
recitatives, written by Tchaikovsky for a planned performance in St Petersburg, three of which he uses
very effectively in Act II. Otherwise dialogue is crisply tailored and is very well delivered. Bonynge
makes the ideal advocate, moulding melodies, springing rhythms and aerating textures to make the
music sparkle from first to last. The playing of the ECO is outstanding, not least from the wind soloists,
and the casting is near-perfect. Sumi Jo takes on a role that is lower in tessitura than usual, but with

elaborations devised by Bonynge leading her into dazzling coloratura. Bruce Ford as the hero and Patrick Power as his friend, Juliano, sing stylishly in well-contrasted tenor tones, while Isabelle Vernet is excellent as Brigitte. Martine Olmeda and Jules Bastin are both characterful in servant roles. The recording is among Decca's most vivid. On the second disc, after Act III, the fill-up aptly comes from another colourful but more serious opera of Auber, also inolving a masked ball and a libretto by Scribe, the one which, translated into Italian, prompted Verdi's *Ballo in maschera*.

Fra Diavolo (complete).
*** EMI Dig. CDS7 54810-2 (2) [id.]. Gedda, Mesplé, Corazza, Berbié, Dran, Bastin, Jean Laforge Ch.
   Ens., Monte Carlo PO, Soustrot.

With a comic English milord and two comic bandits (played by Laurel and Hardy in the Hollywood film version of 1933), *Fra Diavolo* is a delightful piece, given a sparkling performance under Marc Soustrot. Some of the patter ensembles suggest that Sullivan and maybe Gilbert too knew this comic opera. The numbers are separated by spoken French dialogue but, with a cast very much in tune with the style of the piece, it adds to the dramatic point. Though Nicolai Gedda's voice has lost its youthful sweetness and often sounds strained, he is very characterful in the title, and similarly Mady Mesplé with her typically French, tinkly soprano is very idiomatic as Zerline. The others are all excellent, and the 1984 digital sound is well balanced.

Aubert, Jacques (1689–1753)

Concerts de simphonies for violins, flutes & oboes: Suites: Nos. 2 in D; 5 in F; Concertos for 4 violins, cello & bass continuo: in D & G min., Op. 17/1 & 6; in E min. (Le Carillon), Op. 26/4.
(N) *** Chandos Dig. 0577 [id.]. Coll. Mus. 90, Simon Standage.

Here is another unfamiliar name from the world of French baroque whose music proves to be of more than merely historical and academic interest. Jacques Aubert was a contemporary of Rameau and Leclair; he possessed much of the former's melodic flair and feeling for orchestral colour and shared the latter's interest in extending violin technique. His concertos for four violins also bring a whiff of Vivaldi, even if none of them has the inspirational ingenuity of the *Quadruple concerto* from *L'Estro armonico*. The leader (here the inestimable Simon Standage, sounding much sweeter than he did in the earliest days of period performances on record) has most of the bravura; the other violin soloists are subservient, and sometimes the cello joins the solo team. The invention is always agreeable and the gracioso *Gavotte* which forms the centrepiece of Op. 17/6 anticipates Boccherini in its courtly charm. The *E minor* work, Op. 26/4, closes with a robust carillon effect. The orchestral concertos are neatly scored and full of attractive ideas. They are each in eight sprightly movements with a brief overture or introduction and a closing chaconne. The performances here are polished, refreshingly alive and invigorating, and the recording is first class. Well worth investigating.

Aubert, Louis (1887–1968)

Cinéma (six tableaux symphoniques); Dryade; Feuilles d'images; Offrande; Tombeau de Chateau-briand.
(Y/B) ** Marco Polo 8.223531 [id.]. Rheinland-Pfalz PO, Leif Segerstam.

The pieces recorded here span the period from 1924, the year in which Aubert composed his tableau symphonique, *Dryade*, through to 1956, the year of the ballet, *Cinéma. Offrande* (1952) is a short tone-poem dedicated to the victims of war, strongly reminiscent of Florent Schmitt, and much of the music here recalls others: the first of the *Feuilles d'images* evokes *Le jardin féerique* from Ravel's *Ma Mère l'oye*. Accomplished though it is, the music as a whole is too derivative to maintain a hold on the repertory. It is well played and recorded.

Auric, Georges (1899–1983)

L'éventail de Jeanne (complete ballet, including music by Delannoy, Ferroud, Ibert, Milhaud, Poulenc, Ravel, Roland-Manuel, Roussel, Florent Schmitt). *Les Mariés de la Tour Eiffel* (complete ballet, including music by Honegger, Milhaud, Poulenc, Tailleferre).
(✹) *** Chandos Dig. CHAN 8356 [id.]. Philh. O, Simon.

A carefree spirit and captivating wit run through both these composite works. In fact these pieces are full of imagination and fun. Geoffrey Simon and the Philharmonia Orchestra give a very good account of themselves and the Chandos recording is little short of spectacular.

Overture.
(M) *** Mercury 434 335-2 [id.]. LSO, Dorati – FETLER: *Contrasts;* FRANCAIX: *Piano concertino;* MILHAUD: *Le bœuf sur le toit;* SATIE: *Parade.* ***

Georges Auric's breezy *Overture* is irrepressibly high-spirited and its melodic freshness and Dorati's vivacious performance help to dispel the impression that it is a shade too long for its content. Vividly clear and transparent sound from near the end of the Mercury vintage era: 1965.

Violin sonata in G.
(Y/B) *** EMI Dig. CDC7 54541-2 [id.]. Frank Peter Zimmermann, Alexander Lonquich – FRANCAIX: *Sonatine;* MILHAUD: *Sonata No. 2;* POULENC: *Sonata;* SATIE: *Choses vues.* ***

The *Violin sonata in G major* is quite attractive but completely inconsequential, and it leaves no strong impression on the listener. Frank Peter Zimmermann and Alexander Lonquich play it with great spirit and elegance and are well recorded, though the balance rather favours the piano.

Avison, Charles (1709–70)

12 Concerti grossi after Scarlatti.
(B) *** Ph. Duo 438 806-2 (2) [id.]. ASMF, Marriner.
(Y/B) *** Hyperion CDA 66891/2 [id.]. Brandenburg Consort, Roy Goodman.

Marriner and the ASMF pioneered a complete recording of these works by the Newcastle-upon-Tyne composer, Charles Avison, which he ingeniously based on the keyboard sonatas of Domenico Scarlatti, and Marriner's fine set, with Iona Brown leading the solo group, has much grace and style. It makes a fine bargain on a Philips Duo two-discs-for-the-price-of-one.

Those seeking a period-instrument performance will find Roy Goodman's version has plenty of vitality. Fast movements fizz spiritedly, but the linear style of the slower movements, though not lacking expressive feeling, is altogether less smooth, and these performances are essentially for those totally converted to the authentic style. The recording is excellent.

The Bach family, including Johann Sebastian

Johann Christoph (1642–1703) Johann Michael (1648–94)

Johann Bernhard (1676–1749) Johann Sebastian (1685–1750)

Johann Lorenz (1695–1773) Johann Ernst (1722–77)

'The Bach family: Organ works': J. S. BACH: *Toccata and Fugue in D min., BWV 565; Fantasia and fugue in A min., BWV 904; Prelude and fugue in C, BWV 547; Prelude (Fantasia) and fugue in G min., BWV 542; Chorale with 6 variations on 'Wenn wir in höchsten Nöten sein', BWV Anh. 78; Capriccio in E, BWV 993.* J. L. BACH: *Prelude and fugue in D min.* J. M. BACH: *Chorales: Allein Gott in der Höh sei Ehr; Wenn wir in höchsten Nöten sein.* J. C. BACH: *Prelude and fugue in E flat;* Chorales: *Warum betrübst du dich, mein Herz; Wach auf, mein Herz, und singe; Aus meines Herzens Grunde.* J. B. BACH: *Passacaglia (Chaconne) in B flat; Partita on 'Du Friedefürst, Herr Jesu Christ'.* J. E. BACH: *Fantasia and fugue in F.*
(M) *** Teldec/Warner 4505 92176 (2) [id.]. Wilhelm Krumbach (Herbst organ of the Schlosskirche, Lahm/Itzgrund, Germany).

Seven generations of Bach's family were professional or semi-professional musicians, most employed as church Kantors, which inevitably involved composing. Johann Christoph and Johann Michael Bach were distant uncles of Johann Sebastian; Johann Bernhard Bach was his first cousin once removed; Johann Lorenz was his first nephew once removed (and also his pupil); Johann Ernst was the son of Johann Bernhard. So much for the family tree, but what of the music? The whole family were – naturally enough – good at chorales, and both Johann Lorenz and Johann Christoph could write a respectable prelude and fugue. But the star here is Johann Bernhard, whose *Passacaglia in B flat* is a splendid piece, while the *Chorale partita on Du Friedefürst Herr Jesu Christ* is also very inventive. The programme ends with Johann Ernst's remarkably flamboyant *Fantasia and fugue in F*, but that is much later than the other works. Performances are first class and so is the organ. It was good to have the *Chorale variations* and *Capriccio* of Johann Sebastian as an illuminating yardstick but, had the other of his works been omitted, this programme could have fitted economically on to a single CD. Nevertheless this is a fascinating set.

Bach, Carl Philipp Emanuel (1714–88)

Cello concertos: in A min., Wq.170; in B flat, Wq.171; in A, Wq.172.
*** Virgin/EMI Dig. VC7 59541-2 [id.]. Anner Bylsma, OAE, Leonhardt.

These concertos also have alternative versions for both keyboard and flute, but they suit the cello admirably. Bylsma's expressive intensity communicates strongly, without ever taking the music outside its boundaries of sensibility, and these artists convey their commitment to this music persuasively.

Flute concertos: in D min., Wq.22; in A min., Wq.166; in B flat, Wq.167; in A, Wq.168; in G, Wq.169.
*** Capriccio Dig. 10 104 (Wq.22, 166, 168); 10 105 (Wq.167, 169) [id.]. Eckart Haupf, C. P. E. Bach CO, Haenchen.

Eckart Haupf gives lively, cleanly articulated performances of these concertos, written for the court of Frederick the Great, well supported by the strong, full-bodied and vigorous accompaniments of the C. P. E. Bach Chamber Orchestra under Hartmut Haenchen. Full, atmospheric recording from East German VEB engineers.

Flute concerto in D min., Wq.22.
(BB) **(*) ASV CDQS 6012. Dingfelder, ECO, Mackerras – HOFFMEISTER: *Concertos Nos. 6 & 9.*
**(*)

Those who are interested in the Hoffmeister coupling will find Ingrid Dingfelder's playing both spirited and stylish.

(i) *Flute concertos: in A min., Wq.166; in B flat, Wq.167; in A, Wq.168; in G, Wq.169;* (ii; iii) *Oboe concertos: in B flat, Wq.164; in E flat, Wq.165;* (ii; iv; v) *Solo in G min., for oboe and continuo;* (v) *Solo in G for harp, Wq.139.*
(Y/B) (B) **(*) Ph. Duo 442 592-2 (2) [id.]. (i) Aurèle Nicolet, Netherlands CO, David Zinman; (ii) Heinz Holliger; (iii) ECO, Leppard; (iv) Rama Jucker; (v) Ursula Holliger.

Nicolet uses a modern instrument and plays very well, but the effect with a rather heavy string accompaniment (partly the result of the acoustic) makes less of the music than the rival versions on Capriccio. But those are at full price, and the Philips Duo set offers a great deal more music. Holliger's accounts of the *Oboe concertos* are masterly. In addition to the excellence of the support from the ECO under Leppard, the Philips engineering is distinguished. The bonuses for oboe and continuo (in this instance harp and cello) and Ursula Holliger's harp *Solo* also add to the attractions of this very generous set.

Flute concertos: in A, Wq.168; in G, Wq.169; in D min. (from *Harpsichord concerto*).
*** RCA Dig. RD 60244 [60244-2-RC]. James Galway, Württemberg CO, Joerg Faerber.

James Galways plays these three works with his customary musicianship, virtuosity and polish. Faerber and his Württemberg orchestra accompany persuasively, with no attempt made to create 'authentic' textures. Excellent recording. Recommended, except to authenticists.

Harpsichord concerto in G min., Wq.6.
*** Capriccio Dig. 10 283 [id.]. Gerald Hambitzer, Concerto Köln – J. C. BACH: *Sinfonia;* J. C. F. BACH: *Sinfonias;* W. F. BACH: *Sinfonia* etc. ***

The *G minor Concerto*, Wq.6 (1740), is one of the most remarkable of C. P. E. Bach's early works. Gerald Hambitzer is an expert and persuasive soloist, and the performance has abundant vitality and imagination. The recording is very naturally balanced.

Harpsichord concerto in C min., Wq.43/4.
(M) *** Decca 440 033-2 [id.]. George Malcolm, ASMF, Marriner – ARNE: *Harpsichord concerto No. 5* etc; J. C. BACH: *Harpsichord concerto in A min.;* HAYDN: *Harpsichord concerto in D* etc. ***

The *C minor Concerto* comes from Bach's Hamburg period and is highly inventive and brilliant; the musical material is as interesting as its formal layout. The performance has splendid life and vitality, and the 1968 recording is as fresh as you could wish, with the harpsichord most naturally caught. A first-rate collection.

Double concerto for harpsichord and fortepiano in E flat.
(N) (M) *** Teldec/Warner 0630 12326-2 [id.]. Uittenbosch, Antonietti, Leonhardt Cons. – J. C. BACH: *Sinfonia concertante in F;* W. F. BACH: *Double concerto for 2 harpsichords.* **(*)

(i) *Double concerto in E flat for harpsichord & fortepiano, Wq.47;* (ii) *Double concerto in F, for 2 harpsichords, Wq.46;* (i) *Sonatina for 2 harpsichords & orchestra in D, Wq.109.*

(N) (B) *** DHM 05472 77410-2 [id.]. (i) Eric Lynn Kelley, Jos van Immersel (fortepiano or harpsichord); (ii) Alan Curtis, Gustav Leonhardt; Coll. Aur., Maier.

The spirited and delightful *E flat Concerto for harpsichord and fortepiano* comes from Bach's last year and ought to be far better known than it is. It has a chirpily inviting opening theme and is given a wholly persuasive account here, with the solo instruments naturally balanced and a warm acoustic assisting a lively (but painless) authentic accompaniment, although the orchestral flutes seem rather forward. The *Sonatina for two harpsichords and orchestra* is one of fifteen; it was written in 1762 and is ambitiously scored – as the lively opening tutti demonstrates – for three trumpets, two each of flutes, oboes and horns, bassoon and strings. The first movement (of two), which opens with an exuberantly brief *Presto* (to return later) and then mellows, is a free fantasia, characteristically quirky and diverse. There are surprises, too, towards the end of the second, which is a Minuet with variations. The *F major Concerto*, scored for strings with the addition of two horns, comes from a different world: it was composed much earlier (probably in 1740) for Frederick II's court, yet is still thoroughly representative of this composer, with a memorable *Largo* slow movement. It is also very well played and, at its very economical price, this is a reissue not to be missed. It completely upstages the competing Erato disc from Koopman and Mathot with the Amsterdam Baroque Orchestra (2292 45306-2) which offers only two of the three works here.

A hardly less attractive account of the *Concerto for harpsichord and fortepiano* also comes on Teldec in a higher price-range. The orchestral balance is somewhat better here and the fortepiano has a slightly bolder, more tangible image. The interplay between the two soloists is felicitous, and choice between the two performances must depend on couplings.

Oboe concertos: in B flat, Wq.164; in E flat, Wq.165; Sonata for oboe and continuo in G min., Wq.135.
(M) *** Erato/Warner Dig. 2292 45430-2 [id.]. Ku Ebbinge, Amsterdam Bar. O, Koopman.

C. P. E. Bach's pair of *Oboe concertos* is very appealing in their wide range of mood, and the *Largo e mesto* of Wq.164 is plaintively haunting in Ku Ebbinge's hands. Koopman provides gracefully alert accompaniments and the recording balance is fresh and realistic, with textures transparent.

Oboe concertos: in B flat, Wq.164; in E flat, Wq.165; (Unaccompanied) *Oboe sonata in A min., Wq.132.*
(BB) **(*) Naxos Dig. 8.550556 [id.]. József Kiss, Ferenc Erkel CO – MARCELLO: *Concerto.* **(*)

József Kiss's account of Bach's pair of *Oboe concertos* is sensitive and musical, if without quite the individuality of Ebbinge's versions on Erato, but they are very well accompanied and beautifully recorded. The solo *Sonata* is also worth having on disc, although one might have liked more dynamic light and shade here. But with an enjoyable Marcello coupling, this is well worth its modest cost.

Organ concerto in G, Wq. 34.
(B) **(*) Erato/Warner 4509 94581 [id.]. Marie-Claire Alain, Jean-François Paillard CO, Paillard – HAYDN: *Organ concertos.* ***

The *G major Organ concerto*, which also exists in a version for the flute, dates from the mid-1730s and is representative of C. P. E. Bach at something like his best. Marie-Claire Alain plays with excellent style, and the orchestra accompanies with spirit, even if ensemble is not always impeccable. The sound is not quite as rich as the original LP but is bright and generally well focused.

Organ concertos: in G; in E flat, Wq.34–5; Fantasia and fugue in C min., Wq.119/7; Prelude in D, Wq.70/7.
*** Capriccio Dig. 10 135 [id.]. Roland Munch, C. P. E. Bach CO, Haenchen.

Hartmut Haenchen and his admirable C. P. E. Bach Chamber Orchestra reinforce the lively expressiveness of the music, alongside the soloist, Roland Munch, on a Berlin baroque organ of the 1750s.

Berlin sinfonias: in C; in F, Wq.174/5; in E min.; in E flat, Wq.178/9; in F, Wq.181.
*** Capriccio Dig. 10 103 [id.]. C. P. E. Bach CO, Haenchen.

The playing of Haenchen's excellent C. P. E. Bach group is alert and vigorous, with airy textures and attractively sprung rhythms. Modern instruments are used in the best possible way. Excellent sound.

6 Hamburg sinfonias, Wq.182/1–6.
*** DG 415 300-2 [id.]. E. Concert, Pinnock.
(M) *** O-L 443 192-2 [id.]. AAM, Hogwood.

The six *Hamburg string sinfonias* are magnificent examples of Bach's later style when, after the years at the Berlin court, he had greater freedom in Hamburg. The English Concert under Pinnock offers an authentic performing style which retains great concern for eighteenth-century poise and elegance. The 1960 analogue recording sounds splendidly fresh and clear.

On the other hand, the abrasiveness of the writing comes out more sharply in the kind of authenticity favoured by Hogwood's Academy of Ancient Music in 1979. They have mellowed somewhat since then, but the music-making here is typical of their earlier style and some listeners may find that their angularity, though undoubtedly stimulating, does not make for relaxed listening. No complaints about the recording, and the Oiseau-Lyre disc has a distinct price advantage.

4 Hamburg sinfonias, Wq.183/1–4.
(N) (BB) **(*) Naxos Dig. 8.553289 [id.]. Salzburg CO, Yoon K. Lee – W. F. BACH: *Sinfonia in F.* **(*)

4 Hamburg sinfonias, Wq.183/1–4; String sinfonia in B min., Wq.182/5 (H661).
(Y/B) (M) *** Virgin Veritas/EMI Dig. VER5 61182-2 [id.]. OAE, Gustav Leonhardt.

Unlike the six *Hamburg sinfonias* which C. P. E. Bach wrote earlier for Baron von Swieten, these four later works involve wind as well as strings. The writing is just as refreshing in its unexpectedness and originality. Gustav Leonhardt's account of this second set, Wq.183, is the one to have if you want them on period instruments. They are lively and alert, and distinguished by fine musical intelligence. This set is to be preferred, albeit by a small margin, to that by Koopman (Erato 2292 45430-2) and in any case includes an extra work.

The Naxos Salzburg versions are also freshly played, the results spick and span, with polished playing from strings and woodwind alike. Obviously Yoon K. Lee knows about period-performance styles and, though modern instruments are used here, textures are clear and clean. While there is plenty of dramatic contrast, by the side of Leonhardt the expressive music seems just a shade cool. But the results are certainly stimulating, and this disc is worth its modest cost.

CHAMBER AND INSTRUMENTAL MUSIC

Fantasia (Fantasy-sonata) in F sharp min. (Empfindungen), Wq.80; Sonatas for piano and violin in B min., Wq.76; C min., Wq.78.
*** Denon Dig. CO 72434 [id.]. Huguette Dreyfus, Eduard Melkus.

The subtitle of the *Fantasy-sonata*, *Empfindungen* ('The Sentiments'), gives some idea of its introspective character, which emerges immediately in the first of its twelve sections; it finds Bach at his most individual. Its two companions are less striking – though in their different way they are rewarding. They are excellently played.

Flute sonatas: in D, Wq.83; in E, Wq.84; in G, Wq.85; in G, Wq.86; in C, Wq.87.
(BB) **(*) Naxos Dig. 8.550513 [id.]. Béla Drahos, Zsuzsa Pertis (harpsichord).

These sonatas sound less exploratory in idiom and less unpredictable than is often the case with this composer in these simply stated and highly musical performances by Drahos and Pertis. They are recorded in an ecclesiastical acoustic and, although the acoustic could with advantage have been drier, the effect is natural.

Flute sonatas: in E min., Wq.124; in G; in A min.; in D, Wq.127–9; in G, Wq.133; in G, Wq.134.
*** Capriccio Dig. 10 101 [id.]. Eckart Haupf, Siegfried Pank, Armin Thalheim.

Six of the composer's eleven flute sonatas in fresh, lively performances, well recorded, ending with one written in Bach's Hamburg period, two years before he died, altogether lighter and more conventionally classical, presenting an interesting perspective on the rest.

Trio sonatas: in B min., Wq.76 (H.512); in A, Wq.146 (H.570); in D, H.585.
*** HM/BMG Dig. RD 77250 [77050-2-RC]. Les Adieux – J. C. BACH: *Quintets;* J. C. F. BACH: *Quartet.* ***

These three sonatas span three decades: between them, they give a good idea of the composer's artistic development. They are played with admirable style and no mean virtuosity by Les Adieux. Excellent recording.

Trio sonata in E, W.162.
(N) (M) *** Erato/Warner 0630 12977 [id.]. Nicolet, Finke, Picht-Axenfeld – J. C. BACH: *6 Quintets, Op. 11.* ***

A pleasing little work, stylishly presented, with a neat, jocular finale, to act as bonus for the Op. 11 *Quintets* of Johann Christian.

Quartets (Trios) for flute, viola, fortepiano: in A min., D & G, Wq.93/5.
(M) *** HM/BMG GD 77052 [77052-2-RG]. Les Adieux.

Although these works were designated by Bach as *Quartets*, no bass part survives. Piano, flute and viola are musically handled so equally, and everything is so minutely written out, that an added cello would always remain 'the fifth wheel on the wagon'. The playing of Les Adieux matches the music in its finish, lightness of touch and spontaneity.

Sinfonia a tre voci in D; 12 Variations on La Folia, Wq.118/9; Trio sonatas: in B flat, Wq.158; in C min. (Sanguineus & Melancholicus), Wq.161/1; Viola da gamba sonata in D, Wq.137.
*** Hyperion Dig. CDA 66239 [id.]. Purcell Qt.

The *Variations on La Folia* are fresh and inventive, particularly in Robert Woolley's hands, but the remaining pieces are hardly less rewarding. The Purcell Quartet play with sensitivity and seem well attuned to the particularly individual sensibility of this composer. The Hyperion recording is well balanced, faithful and present.

KEYBOARD MUSIC

Concerto for harpsichord solo in C, Wq.112/1; 6 Prussian sonatas, Wq.48; 6 Württemberg sonatas, Wq.49.
(M) *** Teldec/Warner 9031 77623-2 (3). Bob van Asperen (harpsichord).

Bach's six *Prussian sonatas* were written between 1740 and 1742; they immediately demonstrate the formal and expressive adventurousness which characterizes so much of this composer's music. The *Württemberg sonatas* date from 1744 and are at once even more daring and powerfully expressive than their immediate predecessors. They are arguably more suited to the clavichord than to the harpsichord (they are too early for the fortepiano) and one small criticism of Bob van Asperen's performances concerns the range of dynamic contrast he achieves: this could ideally be wider. The solo *Concerto* is a much later work, more elaborately Italianate and florid – perhaps suitable for the fortepiano, but here sounding well on the plucked instrument. Van Asperen uses a fine reproduction of a Dulcken harpsichord, and his approach throughout has a welcome rhythmic freedom, a fine sense of line and an appropriate intensity of feeling when required. He is very well recorded and, if the volume level is judiciously set, the effect brings both realism and a natural presence.

Essay on the True Art of Playing Keyboard Instruments: 6 Sonatas, Wq.63/1–6; 6 Sonatinas, Wq.63/7–12.
(Y/B) (M) *** O-L 444 162-2 [id.]. Christopher Hogwood.

This record contains the twelve keyboard sonatas that were to wield enormous influence for the remainder of the century on composers such as Haydn, Mozart and Beethoven. Despite their didactic intention, they are pieces of expressive power and are played by Christopher Hogwood not only with virtuosity but with a rare vein of poetic feeling. He is recorded excellently, though the disc should be played at a low level: remember that the clavichord has a very limited upper range of dynamic.

ORGAN MUSIC

Organ sonatas: in F; A min.; D; G min., Wq.70/3–6; Fantasia and fugue in C min., Wq.119/7; Fugue in D min.; Prelude in D, Wq.70/7; 6 Variations.
(N) **(*) Meridian Dig. CDE 84313 [id.]. Gerald Gifford (Organ of the Chapel of Hull University).

Carl Philipp Emanuel's organ music is a far cry from the magisterial polyphony of his father's output. The *Prelude in D major* opens grandly, but its imitative passage-work is simplicity itself and rather jolly. The *Fantasia and fugue* is a little more aspiring, but not that ambitious, and neither is the *D minor Fugue*. However, while the four lightweight *Sonatas* make no great technical demands on the performer, they are engaging enough when freshly presented, as here, with a lively, 'orchestral' palette. They were written for Princess Amalie, sister of Fredrick the Great, and are Italianate in feeling, not least in their construction (fast–slow–fast), while the *Variations* are in much the same style. The chapel organ at Hull University has bright, glowing reeds and Gerald Gifford's registration reflects the Italian sunshine in the music. The recording is excellent, but this music is not among the composer's most stimulating output.

VOCAL MUSIC

Anbetung dem Erbarmer (Easter cantata) Wq.243; Auf schicke dich recht feierlich (Christmas cantata), Wq.249; Heilig, Wq.217; Klopstocks Morgengesang am Schöpfungsfeste, Wq.239.
*** Capriccio Dig. 10 208 [id.]. Schlick, Lins, Prégardien, Elliott, Varcoe, Schwarz, Rheinische Kantorei, Kleine Konzert, Hermann Max.

Klopstocks Morgengesang am Schöpfungsfeste ('Klopstock's morning song on the celebration of creation') is a work of many beauties and is well performed by these artists. *Anbetung dem Erbarmer* ('Worship of the merciful') is another late work, full of modulatory surprises. *Auf schicke dich recht feierlich* ('Up, be reconciled') and *Heilig* ('Holy') (1779) are Christmas works. A record of unusual interest, very well performed and naturally recorded.

(i) *Die Auferstehung und Himmelfahrt Jesu (The Resurrection and Ascension of Jesus), Wq.240;* (ii) *Gott hat den Herrn auferweckt (Easter cantata), Wq.244.*
*** Capriccio Dig. 10 206/7 (2) [id.]. (i) Schlick, Lins, Prégardien; (ii) Elliott, Varcoe, Schwarz; Rheinische Kantorei, Kleine Konzert, Hermann Max.

Carl Philipp Emanuel numbered *Die Auferstehung und Himmelfahrt Jesu* among his finest works. This two-CD set offers good solo singing and generally very good playing; the choral singing for the most part is respectable without being distinguished. Impressive music which no one with an interest in this composer should pass over.

Die letzten Leiden des Erlösers (The Last Sufferings of the Saviour), Wq.233.
(M) *** HM/BMG GD 77042 [77042-2-RG]. Schlick, Reyghere, Patriasz, Prégardien, Egmond, Ghent Coll. Vocale, La Petite Bande, Kuijken.

Die letzten Leiden has good claims to be considered one of Carl Philipp Emanuel's masterpieces, and it is given a first-class performance by the excellent team of soloists assembled here. Fine, well-balanced recording.

Magnificat, Wq.215.
(M) *** Decca 421 148-2. Palmer, Watts, Tear, Roberts, King's College Ch., ASMF, Ledger – J. S. BACH: *Magnificat.* ***

With vividly atmospheric recording, the performance under Philip Ledger comes electrically to life, with choir, soloists and orchestra all in splendid form. Aptly coupled with Johann Sebastian's earlier setting, this CD can be strongly recommended. It sounds extremely vivid.

Bach, Johann Christian (1735–82)

Harpsichord concertos, Op. 1/1–6.
(N) *** CPO Dig. 999 299-2 [id.]. Anthony Halstead, Hanover Band.

Those wanting a set of Op. 1 on period instruments could hardly better this CPO disc. These are all simple two-movement works, except for No. 4 with its wistful central *Andante* and No. 6 which closes with variations on *God save the King*. The performances are sprightly and perfectly in scale and the balance quite excelllent.

Clavier concertos, Op. 1/1–6; Op. 7/1–6.
(B) *** Ph. Duo 438 712-2 (2) [id.]. Ingrid Haebler, V. Capella Academica, Eduard Melkus.

J. C. Bach composed three sets of *Clavier concertos*, each comprising six works. All the concertos here are in major keys and are attractive, well-wrought compositions. It would be difficult to find a more suitable or persuasive advocate than Ingrid Haebler, who is excellently accompanied and most truthfully recorded. There is some delightful invention here and it is difficult to imagine it being better presented.

Harpsichord concerto in A min., T 297/1.
(M) *** Decca 440 033-2 [id.]. George Malcolm, ASMF, Marriner – ARNE: *Harpsichord concerto No. 5* etc. C. P. E. BACH: *Harpsichord concerto in C min.;* HAYDN: *Harpsichord concerto in D.* ***

This is a delightful concerto, though its authenticity is doubtful. The playing is extremely crisp and vital, with a sensitively shaped *Andante* which uses moments of pizzicato charmingly. The recording is a model of its kind: the harpsichord is not too forwardly balanced and sounds completely lifelike. This collection is strongly recommended.

Sinfonia concertante in C for flute, oboe, violin, cello and orchestra; Sinfonia in G min., Op. 6/6; Sinfonia for double orchestra in E flat, Op. 18/1; Sinfonia in D, Op. 18/4; Overture: Adriano in Siria.
**(*) Chandos Dig. CHAN 0540 [id.]. AAM, Standage.

An enterprising and enjoyable programme. The *Sinfonia concertante* is perhaps the most conventional piece but it has a memorable finale. The *G minor Sinfonia* shows J. C. Bach's imagination at full stretch, lively and intense. The little overture is given three separate bands to show how its fast–slow–fast format was the basis of the symphony. Excellent, well-played 'authentic' performances, but the characteristic Chandos resonance prevents the crispest focus.

Sinfonia concertante in F for oboe, cello and orchestra, T.VIII/6.
(N) (M) **(*) Teldec/Warner 0630 12326-2 [id.]. Schaeftlein, Bylsma, Leonhardt Cons. – C. P. E. BACH: *Double concerto for harpsichord and fortepiano* ***; W. F. BACH: *Double concerto for 2 harpsichords.* **(*)

The *Sinfonia concertante in F* is a pleasing but not distinctive work in two movements, given a good rather than distinctive performance.

Sinfonia concertante in A for violin, cello and orchestra; Grand Overture in E flat.
(*) Sony MK 39964 [id.]. Yo-Yo Ma, Zukerman, St Paul CO – BOCCHERINI: *Cello concerto* (arr. Grützmacher). ***

Generally this is an enjoyable pairing and the playing of the soloists in the *Sinfonia concertante* establishes a fine musical interplay, although the cadenza is over-elaborated. Good sound, with excellent stereo effects.

Sinfonias concertantes in A for violin, cello and orchestra, SC 3; E flat for 2 violins, 2 violas, cello and orchestra (MSC E flat 1); E flat for 2 clarinets, bassoon and orchestra (MSC E flat 4); G for 2 violins, cello and orchestra, SC 1.
(BB) *** ASV CDQS 6138 [id.]. London Festival O, Ross Pople.

The performances here are eminently vital and enthusiastic, and the recording is very bright and present. This is an invigorating disc which can be recommended strongly, especially at super-bargain price.

Sinfonias, Op. 3/1–6.
(N) *** CPO Dig. 999268-2 [id.]. Hanover Band, Anthony Halstead.
(Y/B) (BB) ** Naxos Dig. 8.553083 [id.]. Camerata Budapest, Gmür.

This excellent CPO disc offers a lively group of six symphonies (or overtures), each in three brief movements, which were dedicated to the then Duke of York, the younger brother of George III, given at a concert series organized by Bach in 1765. These are all excellent examples of a fast-developing genre, offering arguments both pithy and imaginative, with the vigorous finales particularly enjoyable. Though the strings of the Hanover Band under Anthony Halstead are on the abrasive side, performances are fresh and alert. Enjoyment is much enhanced by the authoritative notes of Ernest Warburton.

    Bach's Op. 3 symphonies are essentially three-part Italian overtures and are full of lyrical melody, often of considerable charm. These works break no barriers but they clearly influenced the young Mozart, and the writing is easy-going and fluent. The *cantabile* quality of the writing is well captured by these elegant and polished performances by the Camerata Budapest, and Hanspeter Gmür's pacing of allegros is well judged and lively. The recording, however, made at the Festetich Castle, is very resonant. Yet horns and oboes are nicely integrated in a slightly recessed balance which is wholly natural.

Sinfonias, Op. 6/1–6.
(Y/B) (BB) **(*) Naxos 8.553084 [id.]. Camerata Budapest, Hanspeter Gmür.

The music of Op. 6 shows a distinct advance on Op. 3, with allegros more dramatic and often very spirited, and slow movements touchingly expressive. Affinities with Mozart are the more striking, and a link with Haydn is also suggested, particularly in the remarkable *G minor Symphony*, the last of the set, with its stormy outer movements suggesting *Sturm und Drang* and a darkly dramatic *Andante*. This is very strongly played here, as is the striking *E flat Symphony*, Op. 6/3; the weightiness of the recordings, which is very well balanced, suits the added gravitas of the performances, which retain also the music's 'singing' qualities.

6 Sinfonias, Op. 6; 6 Sinfonias, Op. 9; 6 Sinfonias, Op. 18; Overture, La calamità de cuori.
(B) *** Ph. Duo 442 275-2 (2) [id.]. Netherlands CO, David Zinman.

David Zinman secures good, lively playing from the Netherlanders and few (except dedicated authenticists) will quarrel with the results. A case could be made for giving some of the outer movements less elegance and greater weight. But if there are times when one feels that Zinman is too brisk, any newer versions using original instruments are likely to be brisker! Certainly Zinman gives stimulation and pleasure with the vigour of his presentation of the outer movements and the charm of the slower ones.

Sinfonias, Op. 9/1–4; Sinfonia concertante in A for violin and cello; Sinfonia concertante in E flat, for 2 violins, oboe and orchestra.
(Y/B) (BB) **(*) Naxos 8.553085 [id.]. Camerata Budapest, Hanspeter Gmür.

This disc is of interest not so much for the symphonies as for the two *Sinfonias concertantes* which are beautifully played, with stylish and appealing contributions from the soloists, all drawn from the orchestra. The solo writing in the *A major Sinfonia concertante* is quite elaborate, and in the *Andante* of the E flat work there is a surprise when the two solo violins introduce Gluck's *Che farò senza Euridice*, which is then taken up by the oboe. The Op. 9 symphonies are not perhaps as interesting overall as Op. 6, but the second of the set of four has a real lollipop *Andante con sordini*, presented over a pizzicato accompaniment. The balance is excellent.

Sinfonia in G min. Op. 6/6.

*** Capriccio Dig. 10 283 [id.]. Concerto Köln – C. P. E. BACH: *Harpsichord concerto;* J. C. F. BACH: *Sinfonias;* W. F. BACH: *Sinfonia* etc. ***

This remarkable symphony, written in 1770 when Johann Christian was at the height of his fame, is altogether darker than is usual with this most gracious and genial of composers, and the Concerto Köln discover greater dramatic intensity in it than do most ensembles. It is recorded as excellently as it is played.

6 Sinfonias (Grand overtures), Op. 18.

(N) (BB) **(*) Naxos Dig. 8.553367 [id.]. Failoni O, Hanspeter Gmür.

Continuing their Naxos series, Gmür and the Failoni Orchestra give warm and graceful accounts of Op. 18. The spirited allegros are slightly cushioned by the resonance, but slow movements are phrased very musically (particularly the lovely, almosty Handelian melody of Op. 18/2, which also has a fine oboe solo from Laszló Párkányi).

Oboe quartet in B flat, Op. 8/6.

*** Denon Dig. C37 7119 [id.]. Holliger, Salvatore Qt – M. HAYDN: *Divertimenti;* MOZART: *Adagio.* ***

The unpretentious elegance of J. C. Bach's *Oboe quartet* is beautifully caught by the incomparable Holliger and his stylish partners. An excellent coupling for even more compelling works, all vividly recorded.

6 Quintets, Op. 11.

(N) (M) *** Erato/Warner 0630 12977 [id.]. Rampal, Pierlot, Fr. String Trio – C. P. E. BACH: *Trio sonata in E.* ***

The six Op. 11 *Quintets* were published in London in 1776. They are written for flute, oboe, violin, viola and cello, and the delectable scoring varies the colour felicitously. The invention is fresh and, with Rampal and Pierlot as the leading wind soloists, the listener is assured that the performances will be expert and spirited.

Quintets (for flute, oboe, violin, viola & continuo) in G & F, Op. 11/2–3.

*** HM/BMG Dig. RD 77250 [77050-2-RC]. Les Adieux – C. P. E. BACH: *Trio sonatas;* J. C. F. BACH: *Quartet.* ***

The *Quintets* find Johann Christian at his most delightful; there are moments of considerable expressive poignancy, which these imaginative and elegant players make the most of. This is one of the best records devoted to the sons of Bach and the sound-quality is first class.

Bach, Johann Christoph Friedrich (1732–95)

Sinfonias: in D min.; E flat, Wfv 1/3 & 10.

*** Capriccio Dig. 10 283 [id.]. Concerto Köln – C. P. E. BACH: *Harpsichord concerto;* J. C. BACH: *Sinfonia;* W. F. BACH: *Sinfonia* etc. ***

Both works recorded here are elegantly written and are well worth investigating, even if Johann Christoph Friedrich does not have the strong musical personality of his brothers. The playing of the Concerto Köln is enthusiastic, sprightly and sensitive, and they are excellently recorded.

Flute quartet No. 3 in C.

*** HM/BMG Dig. RD 77250 [77050-2-RC]. Les Adieux – C. P. E. BACH: *Trio sonatas;* J. C. BACH: *Quintets.* ***

Johann Christoph Friedrich's music is untroubled by any depths but has a genuine charm that is beautifully communicated by these accomplished players. Excellent recording.

Musikalisches Vielerley: Cello sonata in A.

*** Sony Dig. SK 45945 [id.]. Anner Bylsma, Bob van Asperen – J. S. BACH: *Viola da gamba sonatas Nos. 1–3.*

This *Sonata* is a work of slight but not negligible musical interest, and it is here played imaginatively by Anner Bylsma, using a piccolo cello, and by Bob van Asperen on a 'trunk' or chamber organ. Excellently recorded.

The Resurrection of Lazarus (Die Auferweckung Lazarus).
(N) (M) *** Erato/Warner 0630 11224-2 [id.]. Borst, Finnilä, Ramirez, Huttenlocher, de Kermel, Valence
   Vocal Ens., Paillard CO, Paillard.

This is the finest work we have yet encountered by Johann Christoph Friedrich, the least-known of
Johann Sebastian's sons, and it reveals him to be a composer who can match a sense of the dramatic
with vocal writing of considerable expressive power. A modern edition of this fine oratorio has existed
since the time of the First World War, yet it has remained unknown and virtually unperformed; this is its
first recording. It opens without preamble with Maria's touching lament for Lazarus, leading to a
moving duet with Martha, who tries to comfort her – superbly sung here by Birgit Finnilä and Danièle
Borst. The work then proceeds with a sequence of arias and recitatives (including a dialogue between
Martha, Jesus and two witnesses), interspersed with brief choruses and chorales leading to a remarkable
Terzetto between the two women and Jesus. Later Maria and Lazarus share a further extended duet and,
after a series of further comments from the chorus, the work ends unusually with an eloquent tenor solo.
All the soloists are on top form and, although the chorus lacks bite (partly the resonant acoustic), the
expansive sound gives the performance proper weight. Well worth exploring; any minor inadequacies
here are unimportant when the music itself is so fine and so strongly projected. A full text and translation are provided.

Bach, Johann Sebastian (1685–1750)

The Art of fugue, BWV 1080.
(N) (M) ** DG Dig. 447 293-2 [id.]. Col. Mus. Ant., Goebel.

The Cologne performance has the advantage of being fitted on to a single, mid-priced disc. The movements are divided between strings and solo harpsichord, and the two harpsichord players are often
imaginative and expressive. The rhythmic vigour of the playing of Musica Antiqua confounds the
scholarly idea that this is music *not* intended for public performance. But there are snags to the authentic
style, notably the bite on the string-tone and also the expressive bulges which are at times exaggerated.
The recording is remarkably clean and present.

The Art of fugue, BWV 1080; A Musical offering, BWV 1079.
(Y/B) (B) *** Ph. Duo 442 556-2 (2) [id.]. ASMF, Marriner.

How to perform *The Art of fugue* has always presented problems, since Bach's own indications are so
sparse. Sir Neville Marriner in the edition he prepared with Andrew Davis has varied the textures most
intelligently, giving a fair proportion of the fugues and canons to keyboard instruments, organ as well as
harpsichord. In each instance the instrumentation has been chosen as specially suitable to that particular movement. Marriner's style of performance is profoundly satisfying, with finely judged tempi,
unmannered phrasing and resilient rhythms, and the 1974 recording is admirably refined. Similarly, in
The Musical offering Marriner uses his own edition and instrumentation: strings with three solo violins,
solo viola and a solo cello; flute, organ and harpsichord. The performance here is of high quality,
though some of the playing is a trifle bland. It is, however, excellently recorded and overall must be
numbered among the most successful accounts of the work.

Brandenburg concertos Nos 1–6, BWV 1046–51.
*** DG Dig. 410 500/1-2 [id.]. E. Concert, Trevor Pinnock.
(Y/B) *** Sony Dig. S2K 66289 (2) [id.]. Tafelmusik, Jeanne Lamon.
(N) *** Telarc Dig. CD 80368 (*Nos. 1–3*), CD 80354 (*Nos. 4–6*) (2) [id.]. Boston Bar., Pearlman.
(M) *** EMI Dig. CD-EMX 2200 (*Nos. 1, 3 & 4*); CD-EMX 2201 (*Nos. 2, 5 & 6*). Hanover Band,
   Anthony Halstead.
*** Ph. 400 076/7-2 (2) [id.]. ASMF, Marriner.
(Y/B) (B) *** Carlton Dig. PCD 2006 (*Nos. 1–3*); PCD 2009 (*Nos. 4–6*) [id.]. ECO, Ledger.
(Y/B) (M) *** Virgin/EMI Dig. CUV5 61114-2 (2) [id.]. Scottish Ens., Jonathan Rees.
(Y/B) (BB) **(*) EMI Seraphim CES5 68516-2 (2) [CDEB 68516]. Bath Festival CO, Sir Yehudi
   Menuhin.
(Y/B) **(*) HM/BMG Dig. 05472 77308-2 (2) [id.]. La Petite Bande, Sigiswald Kuijken.

Brandenburg concertos Nos. 1–6; A musical offering, BWV 1079.
(Y/B) (M) *** Virgin Veritas/EMI Dig./Analogue VED5 61154–2 (2) [id.]. Linde Consort, Hans-
   Martin Linde.

Undoubtedly Pinnock's DG set of *Brandenburgs*, played on original instruments, represents the peak of his achievement as an advocate of authentic performance with sounds that are clear and refreshing but not too abrasive. After a period when a limited edition of this set was available at mid-price, this now reverts to DG's full-price Archiv label and the set now seems expensive. The recordings are, however, alternatively available on three mid-priced CDs (423 492-2) coupled with the *Orchestral Suites*, but the latter are somewhat controversial, bringing a distinct loss of breadth and grandeur.

With sprung rhythms and generally well-chosen tempi, the Linde Consort deserve to rank alongside Pinnock's set. Quite apart from the considerable bonus of the *Musical offering*, many will prefer their version of the *Brandenburgs*, for the 1981 EMI recording is rather fuller than the DG Archiv sound, with the strings very slightly less immediate. Linde is as stylish and accomplished as any of his rivals, and he and his six colleagues offer another preferred version of this work using original instruments. They are again warmly as well as clearly recorded. *Concertos* Nos. 1–4 and 6 are on the first CD, and No. 5 with the *Musical offering* on the second.

Tafelmusik seldom disappoint, and their set of *Brandenburgs* is enjoyably robust and spontaneous, if inevitably not always as polished as the best versions on modern instruments. Many will find this more infectious than Pinnock, with the horn soloists in No.1, Ab Koster and Derek Conrod, playing mid-eighteenth-century hand horns with lustily extrovert vigour and bravura, so that one does not mind that intonation is not always exact. Crispian Steele-Perkins, the trumpet soloist in No. 2, plays a modern copy of a 1667 instrument with remarkable sophistication. Tempi are brisk (the finale of No. 3 is most invigorating) but never hurried, and slow movements relax warmly as they should, with bulges in phrasing fairly minimal. The recording is excellent.

Another most enjoyable set on period instruments comes from the Boston Baroque under Martin Pearlman. He sets attractively lively and spirited tempi in outer movements, yet for once slow movements are not pressed on but are allowed space to expand. Solo playing is excellent, although Friedemann Immer's trumpet does have a few moments of ungainliness in No. 2. But there is no vinegar here in the string timbre, even in the *Sixth Concerto*, which is played with one instrument to a part and uses violas da gamba. Not quite a first choice but, with first-class Telarc sound and a feeling that the players are enjoying themselves, this is well worth considering.

In addition a recommendable new recording from Anthony Halstead and the Hanover Band has arrived on EMI Eminence which will surely meet the needs of collectors looking for a recommendable authentic mid-priced set. The playing is consistently fresh and tempi are admirably chosen to give a feeling of liveliness and a joyful alertness without pressing on too hard while, throughout, lyrical lines flow pleasingly and textures are clean and transparent. The recording was made in the Henry Wood Hall and its warm acoustic provides an admirable background ambience for the music-making.

Marriner's analogue Philips set has been remastered since it was first issued and the sound is both natural and lively. Above all, these performances communicate warmth and enjoyment; and they are strong in personality. However, this set has to face strong competition in the mid-priced range. Those wanting a first-class set using modern instruments can still rest content with Marriner – if paying a premium price is acceptable. With star soloists and beautifully sprung performances, this is very enjoyable indeed, with sound that is natural and lively.

On Carlton, Ledger has the advantage of fresh and detailed digital recording. He directs resilient, well-paced readings of all six concertos on modern instruments, lively yet never over-forced. The slow movements in particular are most beautifully done, persuasively and without mannerism. Flutes rather than recorders are used in No. 4.

From Virgin an excellent new Scottish set of *Brandenburgs*, directed with much spirit by Jonathan Rees, freshly played and with a warm yet clear recording, with excellent internal balance. The tempi seem very apt when the players so convey their enjoyment and the sound has such a pleasing bloom. A fine new mid-priced recommendation using modern instruments to put alongside the 'authentic' Halstead/Hanover Band set on EMI Eminence which is comparably joyful.

Menuhin's stylish 1959 set of *Brandenburgs* has stood the test of time. It is played by the chamber-sized Bath Festival Orchestra, which includes gambas – Dennis Nesbitt and Ambrose Gauntlett – and recorders. Rhythms are sprung lightly and joyfully, and tempi are uncontroversially apt. The excellent soloists (unnamed in the current – inadequate – documentation) include Barry Tuckwell, Janet Craxton and Michael Dobson, while Dennis Clift is the first-rate trumpeter. Throughout there is a spontaneity that is consistently refreshing. With the pair of CDs offered for the price of one mid-priced disc, this is the least expensive among the more distinguished recordings of these much-recorded works.

La Petite Bande under Kuijken are stylish and musical and they are well recorded. The performance of No. 5 shows the group at its finest, with some particularly fine playing in the slow movement. But elsewhere, although the performances bring both vigour and polish, they have a less strong profile than Tafelmusik, whose performance of the first two concertos is much more compulsively alive. An enjoyable set, but not a distinctive one.

(i) *Brandenburg concertos Nos. 1–6;* (ii) *Flute concerto in G min.* (from *BWV 1056*); *Double concerto for violin, oboe and strings in D min.* (from *BWV 1060*).
(Y/B) (B) *** Decca Double 443 847-2 (2) [id.]. (i) ECO, Britten; (ii) ASMF, Marriner.

Britten made his recordings in the Maltings concert-hall in 1968. The result is a fairly ample sound that in its way goes well with Britten's interpretations. There is some lack of textural delicacy in the slow movements of Nos. 1, 2, 4 and 6; but the bubbling high spirits of the outer movements are hard to resist, and the harpsichordist, Philip Ledger, follows the pattern he had set in live Britten performances, with Britten-inspired extra elaborations a continual delight. As a makeweight for the Double Decca reissue, two more of Marriner's stylish performances of reconstructions of Bach's harpsichord concertos for alternative instruments have been added. First-class (originally Argo) recording, too.

Brandenburg concertos Nos. 1–6; (i) *Oboe concertos: in A* (from *BWV 1055*); *in D min.* (from *BWV 1059*); *in F* (from *BWV 1053*).
(N) (M) **(*) DG 445 578-2 (2) [id.]. COE, (i) with Douglas Boyd.

A spirit of fun infects the COE version of the *Brandenburg concertos*. Using modern instruments, these are among the happiest performances ever, marked by easily bouncing rhythms and warmly affectionate – but never sentimental – slow movements. Some may want more severity, but the joyful exuberance of Bach's inspiration is inescapable. Unfortunately, the first movement of No. 1 – the movement which many will sample first – takes relaxation too far, becoming almost ragged; conversely, the first movement of No. 6 is uncharacteristically rigid. Otherwise these performances, well recorded, give pure joy. However, to make this mid-priced reissue more inviting, DG have added the three *Oboe concertos*, reconstructed from keyboard concertos and cantata movements. The soloist, Douglas Boyd, principal oboe of the COE from its foundation, directs his colleagues in delectable performances. His resilient and imaginative playing goes with well-sprung rhythms, matching the infectious sense of fun found in the *Brandenburgs*. First-rate sound.

Brandenburg concertos Nos. 1–6; (i) *Organ concerto in D min., BWV 1059;* (ii) *Triple concerto for flute, violin and harpsichord in A min., BWV 1044.*
(N) (M) *** Erato/ Warner Dig. 0630 13733-2 (2). Amsterdam Bar. O, Koopman, with (i) Koopman (organ); (ii) Hazelzet, Manze, Koopman (harpsichord).

Relaxed and intimate, Koopman's account of the *Brandenburgs* makes a recommendable alternative to Pinnock, for those who prefer expressive contrasts to be less sharply marked. As with Pinnock, players are one to a part, with excellent British soloists included in the band. In the *Third Concerto*, Koopman effectively interpolates the *Toccata in G*, BWV 916, as a harpsichord link between the two movements. The sound on CD is immediate, but not aggressively so. The two additional concertos make an attractive bonus, well played and recorded. In each case the slow movement is a highlight, particularly that of the reconstructed organ concerto, heard in a revision by Koopman himself.

Brandenburg concertos Nos. 1–3; (i) *Violin concertos Nos. 1 in A min.; 2 in E, BWV l041–2.*
(Y/B) (M) *** Ph. 442 386-2 [id.]. ECO, Leppard; (i) with Arthur Grumiaux.

Brandenburg concertos Nos. 4–6; (i) *Triple concerto in A min. for violin, flute and harpsichord, BWV 1044.*
(Y/B) (M) *** Ph. 442 387-2 [id.]. ECO, Leppard; (i) with Grumiaux, Garcia & Adeney.

Brandenburg concertos Nos. 1–6, BWV 1046–51; Violin concertos Nos. (i) *1 in A min.;* (ii) *2 in E;* (i; ii) *Double violin concerto in D min., BWV 1041–3.*
(N) (BB) **(*) CfP Silver Double CDCFPSD 4769 (2). (i) Kenneth Sillito; (ii) Hugh Bean; Virtuosi of England, Davison.

Leppard's mid-1970s Philips set with the ECO is higher-powered than the Rees Scottish performances, whose relaxed manner will for many be easier to live with. But the exhilaration of the Leppard set is undeniable: there is much to enjoy here and the soloists include John Wilbraham's trumpet in No. 2 and a piquant recorder contribution from David Munrow in No.4. The remastered sound is fresh and full. Grumiaux's accounts of the two solo concertos come from 1964, but the playing from one of the most musical soloists of our time is extremely satisfying. It has a purity of line and an expressive response that communicate very positively, and Leppard's stylish accompaniments have striking buoyancy. The *Triple concerto* (recorded two decades later) has plenty of vitality, too; although the balance is a little contrived, the effect is certainly vivid.

Arthur Davison's set of *Brandenburgs* was vividly recorded (in 1972), although the microphones are close, somewhat limiting the dynamic range. The playing is polished, robust and lively; slow movements are sensitive, and the brisk, unfussy approach of the conductor is impressive; however, in the last resort these performances lack the individuality of the Menuhin set offered at the same price on Seraphim (see above). What rights the balance on this CfP Silver Double is the set of *Violin concertos* which have been added to the second disc. Kenneth Sillito and Hugh Bean, both of them distinguished orchestral leaders as well as fine virtuosi, are outstandingly successful as soloists in the *Double concerto*. This is one of the most beautiful accounts of the lovely slow movement on record, deeply felt but pure and restrained. Though the accompaniments are not always ideally resilient, all three performances can be recommended warmly. The solo concertos are shared, Kenneth Sillito playing the *A minor Concerto* and Hugh Bean the *E major*. The spacious (1975) recording was made in the Fairfield Halls, Croydon. Excellent value.

Brandenburg concertos Nos. 1–3; Orchestral Suite No. 1 in C, BWV 1066.
(N) (M) (*) DG Dig. 447 287-2. Col. Mus. Ant., Goebel.

Brandenburg concertos Nos. 4–6; Orchestral Suite No. 4 in D, BWV 1069.
(N) (M) (*) DG Dig. 447 288-2. Col. Mus. Ant., Goebel.

Reinhard Goebel's set with Cologne Musica Antiqua is one to have you disbelieving your ears. Even in an age of period performance that favours fast speeds, his allegros are hectic to the point of recklessness, in several instances comically impossible. It is hard not to laugh out loud at the speeds for both movements of No. 3 (the second more than the first) and even more at the sketchy strumming which purports to be the first movement of No. 6, 'without tempo indication', as the booklet reminds us. At Goebel's headlong speed the semiquaver arpeggios are hardly audible and even the repeated quavers sound rushed. It is a tribute to the virtuosity of the Cologne ensemble that otherwise they cope so well, usually playing with a good rhythmic spring. Abrasive, choppy of phrasing and employing squeeze techniques on sustained notes, they use a normal baroque orchestra with four first and four second violins, and again allegros are pushed forward to the point of frenzy. Vivid recording, but these reissues (available separately) cannot be recommended with any confidence, even to the most dedicated proponents of authenticity.

Harpsichord concertos Nos. 1 in D min.; 2 in E; 3 in D; 4 in A; 5 in F min.; 6 in F; 7 in G min., BWV 1052–8; (i) Double harpsichord concertos: Nos. 1 in C min.; 2 in C; 3 in C min., BWV 1060–62; (i; ii) Triple harpsichord concertos Nos. 1 in D min.; 2 in C, BWV 1063–4; (i–iii) Quadruple harpsichord concerto in A min., BWV 1065.
(N) (B) *** DG Analogue/Dig. 447 709-2 (3) [id.]. Pinnock with (i) Gilbert; (ii) Mortensen; (iii) Kraemer; E. Concert.

Pinnock's performances of the Bach *Harpsichord concertos* first appeared in 1981, and they have dominated the catalogue ever since. In the solo concertos he plays with real panache, his scholarship tempered with excellent musicianship. Pacing is brisk, but to today's ears, used to period performances, the effect is convincing when the playing is so spontaneous and the analogue sound bright and clean. The *Double*, *Triple* and *Quadruple concertos* are digital, and the combination of period instruments and playing of determined vigour certainly makes a bold effect. There is a bit more edge on the strings and everything is clearly laid out and forwardly projected. Outer movements emphasize the bravura of Bach's conceptions and, if slow movements could at times be more relaxed, those ears prepared to accept a hint of aggressiveness in the energetic musical flow will find this set as stimulating now as when it first appeared.

Harpsichord concertos Nos. 1–7, BWV 1052–8; No. 8 in D min. (reconstructed Kipnis), BWV 1059.
(B) *** Sony SB2K 53243 (2). Kipnis, L. Strings, Marriner.

Between 1967 and 1970 Igor Kipnis undertook a series of sessions with the London Strings (the St Martin's Academy under a pseudonym), recording not merely the well-known keyboard concertos but also an eighth work reconstructed by Kipnis himself from a fragment of nine bars identical with the *Sinfonia* of *Cantata No. 35*. Kipnis scored that movement for concertante forces and added two other movements from the same cantata; that is typical of his eager approach to Bach. The recording was made either in EMI's No. 1 Studio at Abbey Road or at the London Olympic studios, which produce a very similar balance of sound. This is more realistic than many made by CBS records at that time and the effect on CD is full and vivid. The music-making is infectious, the accompaniments are characteristic of the vintage ASMF recordings. At budget price this can certainly be recommended.

Clavier concertos Nos. 1–5; 7, BWV 1052–6, 1058.
(M) (**) Sony mono (*No. 1*)/stereo SM2K 52591 (2) [id.]. Glenn Gould (piano), Columbia SO, Bernstein (*No. 1*) or Golschmann.

The quality is variable; the *D minor Concerto* was recorded in 1957 with Bernstein conducting and the remainder date from various times: the *F minor*, BWV 1056, from 1958; the *D major*, BWV 1054, and *G minor*, BWV 1058, from 1967 and the remaining two from 1969, all with Vladimir Golschmann conducting. The performances are strongly personal and, whether or not you like them, strangely compelling. The finale of the *A major* is very, very fast and there is some odd but not excessively intrusive vocalise.

Clavier concertos Nos. 1 in D min.; 2 in E; 3 in D, 4 in A; 5 in F; 6 in F; 7 in G min., BWV 1052–8.
*** Decca Dig. 425 676-2 (2) [id.]. András Schiff (piano), COE.

Clavier concertos Nos. 1 in D min., BWV 1052; 2 in E, BWV 1053; 3 in D, BWV 1054.
(BB) *** Naxos Dig. 8.550422; *4.550422* [id.]. Hae-won Chang (piano), Camerata Cassovia, Stankovsky.

Clavier concertos Nos. 4 in A, BWV 1055; 5 in F min., BWV 1056; 6 in F, BWV 1057; 7 in G min., BWV 1058.
(BB) *** Naxos Dig. 8.550423; *4.550423* [id.]. Hae-won Chang (piano), Camerata Cassovia, Stankovsky.

As in his solo Bach records, Schiff's control of colour and articulation never seeks to present merely a harpsichord imitation, and his shaping of Bach's lovely slow movements brings fine sustained lines and a subtle variety of touch. He directs the Chamber Orchestra of Europe from the keyboard and chooses spirited, uncontroversial tempi for allegros, at the same time providing decoration that always adds to the joy and sparkle of the music-making. This makes a clear first choice for those who, like us, enjoy Bach on the piano.

Miss Chang is a highly sympathetic Bach exponent, playing flexibly yet with strong rhythmic feeling, decorating nimbly and not fussily. Robert Stankovsky directs freshly resilient accompaniments; and both artists understand the need for a subtle gradation of light and shade. The digital recording, made in the House of Arts, Košice, is first class, with the piano balanced not too far forward. A fine super-bargain alternative.

Clavier concertos Nos. 1 in D min., BWV 1052; 2 in E, BWV 1053; 3 in D, BWV 1054; 4 in A, BWV 1055; 5 in F min., BWV 1056; 6 in F, BWV 1057; 7 in G min., BWV 1058; French suite No. 5.
(M) **(*) EMI Dig. CDM5 65173/4-2 [id.]. Andrei Gavrilov (piano), ASMF, Marriner.

In terms of dexterity and clarity of articulation, Andrei Gavrilov cannot be faulted and he produces some beautiful sound when his playing is lyrical and relaxed. If at times one feels he pushes on relentlessly, and his incisive touch can be a bit unremitting in some movements, there are also a lot of memorable things. Indeed in the slow movement of the *D minor* and *F minor concertos* there is playing of real poetry and delicacy – and, for that matter, in the finale of the *A major*. The recordings are excellently balanced, with the piano well integrated into the overall picture.

Clavier concertos Nos. 1 in D min., BWV 1052; 3 in D, BWV 1054; 5 in F min., BWV 1056; 6 in F, BWV 1057.
(M) *** Teldec/Warner Dig. 9031 74779-2 [id.]. Cyprien Katsaris (piano), Liszt CO, Rolla.

Cyprien Katsaris possesses the most remarkable technique and feeling for colour, which are to be heard to excellent advantage in this vividly recorded and well-filled disc. Exhilarating and imaginative performances all round.

Clavier concertos Nos. 1 in D min., BWV 1052; 4 in A, BWV 1055; 5 in F min., BWV 1056.
(N) (M) *** Erato/Warner 4509 96949-2 [id.]. Maria-João Pires (piano), Gulbenkian Foundation CO (Lisbon), Corboz.

Maria-João Pires provides admirable mid-priced versions of these concertos on the piano. Her crisp and nimble fingerwork is a joy in the allegros and the orchestral strings are not too heavy, with Corboz providing plenty of lift in the allegros. The famous *Largo* of the *F minor Concerto* is beautifully serene. The sound-balance is fresh and believable. Most enjoyable.

Double harpsichord concertos Nos. 1 in C min.; 2 in C; 3 in C min., BWV 1060–62.
(N) *(*) Virgin/EMI Dig. VC5 45054-2. Bob van Asperen, Gustav Leonhardt, Melante Amsterdam, cond. Van Asperen.

More slimline, one-to-a-part Bach, which no doubt underlines a chamber-music-like quality. It goes without saying that the two distinguished soloists offer many insights, but these performances do not convey much sense of spontaneity or joy. The recorded sound is very good, but readers are best advised to look elsewhere.

Oboe concerto in F (from BWV 1053); Oboe d'amore concerto in A (from BWV 1055); Triple concerto in D min. for violin, oboe, flute and strings (from BWV 1063); Triple violin concerto in D (from BWV 1064).
(M) *** Decca 440 037-2 [id.]. Soloists, ASMF, Marriner.

The idea behind this reissued (Argo) disc is to present Bach harpsichord concertos in reconstructions for alternative instruments that either did exist or might have existed. Purists may throw up their hands in horror, but the sparkle, charm and sensitivity of all these performances under Marriner, with soloists from among early Academy members, should silence all but the severest Bachian, and it will certainly please those for whom three harpsichords is too much of a good thing. Indeed the *Triple harpsichord concerto in D minor* sounds wonderfully fresh, arranged for violin, oboe and flute, while its companion appears with three violins taking over the solo roles. Most beautiful is the *Oboe d'amore concerto*, arranged from the solo *Harpsichord concerto*, BWV 1055. Splendidly lively and naturally balanced recording, made in the Henry Wood Hall in 1973–4, admirably transferred to CD.

(i) *Piano concerto in D, BWV 1054;* (ii) *Piano concerto in G min., BWV 1058;* (iii) *Concerto for piano, violin, flute & orchestra, BWV 1044;* (iv) *Concerto for piano, 2 flutes & orchestra, BWV 1057.*
(N) ** EMI Dig. CDC5 55059-2. Ensemble O de Paris, Jean-Pierre Wallez, with (i) Gabriel Tacchini; (ii) Michel Béroff; (iii) Jean-Philippe Collard, Jean-Jacques Kantorow, Philippe Bernold; (iv) Bruno Rigutti, Philippe Bernold, Emmanuelle Reville.

The distinguished line-up of soloists ensures playing of quality, and readers need not feel anxiety on this score. All the concertos have one thing in common: they are transcriptions of other works – the *F major Concerto* is a transposition downwards of the *Fourth Brandenburg* and the *D major*, BWV 1054, the *E major Violin concerto*. But this issue is rather let down by the recording, which lacks transparency and bloom.

Violin concertos Nos. (i) *1–2;* (ii) *Double violin concerto, BWV 1041–3;* (iii) *Double concerto for violin & oboe in C min., BWV 1060.*
✸ (M) *** Ph. 420 700-2. Grumiaux; (ii) Krebbers, (iii) Holliger; (i–ii) Les Solistes Romandes, Arpad Gerecz; (iii) New Philh. O, Edo de Waart.
(N) (M) **(*) Sony Stern Edition I Analogue/Dig. SMK 66471 [id.]. Isaac Stern, with (i) ECO/ Schneider; (ii) Perlman, NYPO, Mehta; (iii) Gomberg, NYPO, Bernstein.

Arthur Grumiaux is joined in the *Double concerto* by Hermann Krebbers. The result is an outstanding success. The way Grumiaux responds to the challenge of working with another great artist comes over equally clearly in the concerto with oboe, reconstructed from the *Double harpsichord concerto in C minor*. Grumiaux's performances of the two solo concertos are equally satisfying.

At a time when the pursuit of authenticity has accustomed us to pinched sound in Bach and Vivaldi, it is good to have such rich performances as these by Stern, although one has to accept that orchestral accompaniments are heavier and tempos of allegros are slower under Schneider and Bernstein than we would expect today. Stern's glorious tone and richness of line is compensation enough. The solo concertos were recorded in London in 1976, the *Concerto for violin and oboe* in the Avery Fisher Hall a decade earlier; but the *Double concerto*, most inspirational of all, came from Stern's sixtieth birthday concert in the autumn of 1980. Stern nobly concedes first place to Perlman in this work. Mehta is perhaps not the ideal conductor in this music, but the feeling of a live occasion comes over strikingly and the slow movement is glorious. The applause at the close is well deserved. Bernstein takes over for the *Concerto for oboe and violin* and, with tempi relaxed, he clearly relishes the beauty of the *Adagio* in which Gomberg and Stern exchange the melody in a gentle conversation. In this work the recording is very resonant, and at times in the finale the balance between the soloists has the violin dominating at the expense of the oboe.

(i) *Violin concertos Nos. 1 in A min.; 2 in E;* (i; ii) *Double violin concerto in D min., BWV 1041–3;* (i; iii) *Double concerto for violin and oboe in C min., BWV 1060. Orchestral Suites Nos. 1 in C;* (iv) *2 in B min.* (for flute and strings); *3 in D, BWV 1066–8.*
(Y/B) (BB) *** EMI Seraphim CES5 68517-2 (2) [CDEB 68517]. (i) Y. Menuhin; (ii) Christian Ferras; (iii) Leon Goossens; (iv) Elaine Schaffer; Bath Festival CO, Sir Yehudi Menuhin.

This is one of the very best bargains in the EMI/Seraphim catalogue, offering a pair of discs for the cost of one premium-priced CD. The documentation – or lack of it – is no credit to the famous old EMI trademark, but the music-making is of the highest order. The *Violin concertos* date from 1960 and, played as they are here by Menuhin (in very good form), both the solo concertos take flight, for their balance of warmth, humanity and classical sympathy is very appealing. In the *Double violin concerto* Ferras matches his timbre beautifully to that of Menuhin and the duet is a real partnership, with the slow movement especially fine. Leon Goossens makes a ravishing contribution to the *Adagio* of the *Concerto for violin and oboe*, the only slight snag being that the oboe is too backwardly balanced in the outer movements. To complete this attractive Menuhin/Bach package, we are offered three of the four *Orchestral Suites*, where Menuhin finds an admirable balance between freshness and warmth, conveying the music's spirit and breadth without inflation. The *Suites* date from 1961 and the *Concerto for violin and oboe* from 1962; and the current remastering brings sound which is quite full, yet clear.

(i) *Violin concertos Nos. 1 in A min.; 2 in E;* (ii) *Double concerto, BWV 1041–3;* (iii) *Orchestral Suite No. 4 in D, BWV 1068.*

(N) (B) **(*) DG Classikon 449 844-2 [id.]. (i–ii) D. Oistrakh, RPO, Goossens; (ii) with I. Oistrakh; (iii) Munich Bach O, Karl Richter.

It is good to have David Oistrakh's justly renowned performances back in the catalogue on DG's bargain Classikon label, since the playing is peerless and can be ranked alongside the Grumiaux versions. In the *Double concerto* father and son are suitably contrasted in timbre and the performance of the great slow movement is Elysian. The 1961 recording hardly sounds dated. Richter's account of the *Fourth Orchestral Suite* is rhythmically unstylish in the matter of double-dotting, but is otherwise alert – less heavy than we had remembered.

Violin concertos Nos. 1 in A min.; 2 in E; (i) *Double concerto, BWV 1041–3.*
(M) *** HM/BMG GD 77006 [77006-2-RG]. Sigiswald Kuijken; (i) Lucy van Dael; La Petite Bande.

Violin concertos Nos. 1 in A min.; 2 in E; (i) *Double concerto, BWV 1041–3;* (ii) *Triple violin concerto in D, BWV 1064 (arr. of Triple harpsichord concerto).*
(M) *** Virgin Veritas/EMI Dig. VC7 59319-2 [id.]. Elisabeth Wallfisch; (i) Alison Bury; (ii) Pavlo Beznosiuk; Catherine Mackintosh, OAE.
(N) **(*) Sony Dig. SK 66265 [id.]. Jean Lamon, with (i) Linda Melstead; (ii) David Greenberg; Tafelmusik.

This Virgin Veritas 'authentic' collection of the Bach *Violin concertos* is vigorously stimulating and does not shirk tasteful expressiveness. All the soloists are expert and their playing has plenty of character, with felicitous, unfussy decoration; the arrangement of the *Triple harpsichord concerto* is particularly convincing. Excellent balance and believable sound make this highly recommendable, alongside Kuijken, with the advantage of first-class modern digital recording.

The Tafelmusik collection is most appealing in the two solo concertos, where Jean Lamon is warmly stylish, and in outer movements the accompaniment is rhythmically buoyant. But the account of the *Double concerto* is let down by the slow movement, which moves forward very positively, with the solo interchanges neatly integrated yet comparatively cool and just that bit too precise. The recording is agreeably warm and natural, but the *Triple concerto* is also less appealing than its Virgin Veritas competitor.

Kuijken is a fine Bach player, and these performances of the *Violin concertos* are also worth considering by those who want period performances on original instruments. The slight edge on the solo timbre is painless and La Petite Bande provide lively, resilient allegros, the playing both polished and alert. Excellent, well-balanced, 1981 digital recording.

(i) *Violin concertos Nos. 1 in A min.; 2 in E;* (i–ii) *Double violin concerto in D min., BWV 1041–3. Orchestral suites Nos. 1–4, BWV 1066–9.*
(N) (B) ** Ph. Duo 446 533-2 (2) [id.]. ASMF, Marriner; with (i) Henryk Szeryng; (ii) Maurice Hasson.

Henryk Szeryng first recorded the Bach *Violin concertos* for Philips with the Winterthur Collegium Musicum in the 1960s, and those performances were imbued with both dignity and classical feeling; the slow movements were particularly fine. Alas, his later (1976) recordings with Marriner cannot match the earlier versions in spontaneity, depth of feeling or understanding; moreover they do not displace the finest of rival accounts. The *Double concerto* (with Maurice Hasson) is particularly disappointing. Similarly, Marriner's second analogue recording of the four *Orchestral Suites*, made in 1978, is no match for his first (1970) set for Argo/Decca (see below). The movements in which he has has changed his mind – for example the famous *Air* from the *Suite No. 3*, which here is dangerously slow – are almost always less convincing, and that reflects the very qualities of urgency and spontaneity which made the earlier, Argo version so enjoyable. It must be said, however, that the Philips sound is full and naturally balanced, though ears used to period instruments may find textures too ample (not the case in the remastered Decca record).

(i) *Double violin concerto in D min., BWV 1043. Suite in D, BWV 1068: Air* (arr. Wilhelmj). (Unaccompanied) *Violin sonata No. 1 in G min., BWV 1001: Adagio.*
(M) (***) Biddulph mono LAB 056-7[id.]. Arnold Rosé, (i) with Alma Rosé, O – BEETHOVEN: *String quartets Nos. 4, 10 & 14.* (***)

The issue is valuable in that it affords an insight into a style of playing that has long passed into history. Arnold Rosé's sonata-partner was Bruno Walter and his brother-in-law was Mahler. His daughter,

Alma, with whom he is heard in a 1931 recording of the Bach *D minor Double concerto*, perished in Auschwitz. Interesting though these recordings are, the principal musical rewards in the set come from the three Beethoven quartets with which they are coupled.

Orchestral suites Nos. 1–4, BWV 1066–9.
(N) (M) *** Erato/Warner Dig. 4509 99615-2 (2) [id.]. E. Bar. Soloists, Gardiner.
(M) *** Decca 430 378-2; *430 378-4* [id.]. ASMF, Marriner.
(Y/B) (M) *** EMI Dig. CDM5 68331-2 [id.]. Linde Consort, Hans-Martin Linde.
(N) (B) * Decca Dig. 448 231-2 [id.]. Stuttgart CO, Karl Münchinger.

Orchestral suites Nos. 1–4, BWV 1066–9; Triple concerto for flute, violin & harpsichord, BWV 1044.
(N) *** EMI Dig. CDS7 54653-2 (2) [id.]. Boston Early Music Festival O, Andrew Parrott.

Gardiner's four *Orchestral Suites* at last return to the catalogue at mid-price, making a clear first recommendation for those wanting these works played on period instruments. In his characteristic manner, allegros tend to be fast and lightly sprung, with slower movements elegantly pointed. Though the edginess of baroque violins using a squeeze technique on sustained notes makes for some abrasiveness, Gardiner avoids the extremes which mark even Pinnock's English Concert version on CD. Thanks to full and immediate recording, textures are fresh and clear, with trumpet and timpani biting through but not excessively.

Deserting his own Taverner Players for one of the most talented American period-performance groups, Andrew Parrott directs the *Orchestral suites* in exceptionally transparent and well-sprung readings. With one instrument to a part and with balance perfectly judged (also a question of recording), one registers many details normally obscured, with dance rhythms made the more infectious. Christopher Krueger, the flautist in *Suite No. 2*, is also an outstanding soloist in the *Triple concerto*, joined by Daniel Stepner on the violin and John Gibbons on harpsichord. There too textures are lightened in a small-scale reading, one instrument to a part. A thoroughly stimulating new look at much-recorded repertoire, even if Gardiner's set still remains a more obvious primary recommendation. However, the Linde version is also very competitive.

Marriner's 1970 recording of the Bach *Suites* with the ASMF comes on a single CD (77 minutes 48 seconds) and the remastering of the fine (originally Argo) recording is fresh and vivid. The playing throughout is expressive without being romantic, and always buoyant and vigorous. A fine bargain for those not insisting on original instruments; there is nothing remotely unstylish here.

The previous issue of the Linde performances was also on a single (full-priced) CD, but it omitted the *Second suite*. Now this is added and the price reduced, making this reissue very competitive and recommendable alongside Marriner. As with the companion set of *Brandenburgs*, for those wanting period instruments and digital sound Linde should make an excellent choice. The string style is less abrasive than that of the English Concert (currently on two full-priced CDs) and the rhythmic spring in allegros generally lighter. Nor is the grandeur of the music missed, and the famous *Air* is pointed and elegant. The acoustic is warm, the recording cleanly focused.

Münchinger's 1985 digital set of the four *Orchestral Suites* has, alas, been bypassed by musical history. In the days of LP he pioneered the performance of Bach on an apt scale, but the present performances, although well played and brilliantly recorded, sound unattractively heavy, with rhythms unlifted.

Orchestral suites Nos. 1–4; Concerto movement in D, BWV 1045; Sinfonias from Cantatas Nos. 29; 42; 209.
(Y/B) *** Hyperion Dig. CDA 66701/2 [id.]. Brandenburg Consort, Roy Goodman.

Orchestral suites Nos. 1 in C, 2 in B min., BWV 1066–7; Cantatas Nos. 42, 209: sinfonias.
(Y/B) *** Hyperion Dig. CDA 66501 [id.]. Brandenburg Consort, Roy Goodman.

(Y/B) *Orchestral suites Nos. 3 in D, 4 in D, BWV 1068–9; Concerto movement in D, BWV 1045; Cantata No. 29: sinfonia.*
(Y/B) *** Hyperion Dig. CDA 66502 [id.]. Brandenburg Consort, Roy Goodman.

Roy Goodman directs brisk and stylish readings of the four Bach *Orchestral Suites*, which are aptly supplemented by four *Sinfonias*, each following a suite in the same key. Though in the *Suites* Goodman in eagerness occasionally chooses too breathless a tempo for fast movements, the lightness of rhythm and the crispness of ensemble are consistently persuasive, with textures cleanly caught in excellent, full-bodied sound. These are among the finest versions on a long list, with Rachel Brown an exceptionally warm-toned flautist in No. 2. Goodman observes all repeats, making the opening overtures longer than usual. As indicated above, the discs are available either separately or in a box.

Orchestral suites Nos. 1–4, BWV 1066–9. Sinfonias from Cantatas Nos. 42; 174 & Easter Oratorio, BWV 249; (i) *Cantata No. 118: Chorus: Ich liebe den Höchsten von ganzem Gemüte.*
(N) *** DG Dig. 439 780-2 (2) [Id.]. E. Concert, Pinnock; (i) with Ch.

With sound rather warmer and string-tone sweeter, Trevor Pinnock and the English Concert manage to improve on their benchmark readings of 16 years earlier. In the dance movements of the *Suite No. 2* Lisa Beznosiuk takes her flute solos faster and more brilliantly than her predecessor, Stephen Preston, but otherwise speeds are generally a fraction broader in all four suites, with allegros more jauntily sprung and phrasing a degree more espressivo. Above all, the great *Air* of the *Suite No. 3* sounds far warmer, persuasively phrased on multiple violins instead of on a single, acid-toned instrument. This time Pinnock also opts to observe the marked repeats not only in the slow introductions to the opening overtures but in the main allegros as well, making them substantially longer. The fill-ups are brief but make a fascinating bonus, winningly performed. The chorus from *Cantata No. 118* is a brilliant choral setting of the opening *Overture* of *Suite No. 4*, while the *Sinfonias* from *Cantatas Nos. 42* and *174* are re-orchestrations of the opening movements of the *First* and *Third Brandenburg Concertos* respectively, the latter with oboes and horns delightfully elaborating the original string textures. While Gardiner, who tends to press ahead more than Pinnock, remains a more obvious first choice for the *Orchestral Suites*, this DG collection will prove a stimulating alternative for Pinnock's admirers.

Orchestral suites Nos. 1–2, BWV 1066–7; (i) *Double harpsichord concerto No. 1 in C min., BWV 1060.*
(M) *** O-L Dig. 443 181-2 [id.]. (i) Rousset, Hogwood; AAM, Hogwood.

Orchestral suites Nos. 3–4, BWV 1068–9; (i) *Double harpsichord concerto No. 3 in C min., BWV 1062.*
(M) *** O-L Dig. 433 182-2 [id.]. (i) Rousset, Hogwood; AAM, Hogwood.

Hogwood's set of the Bach orchestral *Suites* illustrates how the Academy of Ancient Music has developed in refinement and purity of sound, modifying earlier abrasiveness without losing period-instrument freshness. That comes out in the famous *Air* from *Suite No. 3* where, with multiple violins and an avoidance of the old squeezed style, the tone is sweet even with little or no vibrato – a movement which in the Pinnock version on DG Archiv, for example, sounds very sour. *Allegros* tend to be on the fast side but are well sprung, not breathless. The *Concertos for two harpsichords* added for the mid-priced reissue are imaginatively played by Christopher Hogwood and Christophe Rousset. Hogwood aficionados need not hesitate.

Orchestral suites Nos. 1–3, BWV 1066–8.
(N) (BB) ** RCA Navigator 74321 24196-2. Lucerne Festival Strings, Baumgartner.

Rudolf Baumgartner offers quite stylish performances, beautifully recorded in the late 1970s. This is the way we used to hear these works played before the advent of period instruments. He has excellent wind players, notably the flautist Aurèle Nicolet, the soloist in No. 2. Only three of the four *Suites* are included, but this Navigator CD is in the very lowest price-range and is certainly enjoyable.

CHAMBER MUSIC

The Art of fugue, BWV 1080.
*** Sony Dig. S2K 45937 (2) [id.]. Juilliard Qt.

The Juilliard Quartet's new version has the field virtually to itself, and hearing it again in this medium gives undoubted pleasure. They play with far less vibrato than usual (at times one is tempted to feel that they are aspiring to the condition of a consort of viols) and they convey a feeling of intimacy and a clarity of the part-writing that is very satisfying. This is a very worthwhile alternative to the relatively abundant keyboard versions, and musically very satisfying.

(Unaccompanied) *Cello suites Nos. 1–6, BWV 1007–12.*
(Y/B) ✸ *** EMI Dig. CDS5 55363-2 (2) [id.]. Mstislav Rostropovich.
*** Virgin/EMI Dig. VCD5 45086-2 (2) [id.]. Ralph Kirshbaum.
*** EMI Dig. CDS7 47471-8 (2). Heinrich Schiff.
*** RCA Dig. RD 70950 (2). Anner Bylsma.
(N) (M) *** DG 449 711-2 (2) [id.]. Pierre Fournier.
(Y/B) *** DG Dig. 445 373-2 (2) [id.]. Mischa Maisky.
(B) *** Ph. Duo 442 293-2 (2) [id.]. Maurice Gendron.
(M) (***) EMI mono CHS7 61027-2 (2) [Ang. CDH 61028/9]. Pablo Casals.

Rostropovich, the most intrepid of cellists, ever eager to tackle concertos by the score, has nevertheless approached these supreme masterpieces of the solo cello repertory with caution. He played them all in his teens but, until the 1990s, refrained from recording them as a complete cycle. The result is revelatory, in many ways the most powerful recording of all, positive and personal, full of individual perceptions. Rostropovich verbally characterizes each one of the series: 'No. 1, lightness; No. 2, sorrow and intensity; No. 3, brilliance; No. 4, majesty and opacity; No. 5, darkness; and No. 6, sunlight'. True to his word, more than usual he draws distinctions between each, also reflecting the point that the structure of each suite grows in complexity. He pays tribute to the example of Casals and, like Casals, Rostropovich takes a broadly romantic view but, far more than that master, he keeps the basic rhythm of each movement clearly defined, whatever his expressive freedom. The results are both moving and strong with the sound of the cello, as recorded in a warm acoustic, full and powerful. He is just as positive in his choice of speeds, often fast and volatile, vigorously sprung, but with the slow sarabande in each suite made to represent the inner heart. His dynamics are romantically free but always compelling, making one hear the music afresh, with pianissimo repeats magically achieved. Anyone who has ever been daunted by solo cello music will find its range of expression astonishingly expanded by Rostropovich.

Ralph Kirshbaum's 'authentic' set of the Bach *Cello suites* is also very fine. He also has the advantage of an absolutely natural recording which displays his full timbre to great advantage. He plays a Domenico Montagnana Venetian cello of 1729 and gives it a warmly vivid personality. Articulation in the dance movements is clear; expressive playing is without bulges and does not shirk a degree of vibrato. The performances have intensity, dedication, spontaneity and an intimate thoughtfulness which is genuinely moving.

Strong and positive, producing a consistent flow of beautiful tone at whatever dynamic level, Schiff here establishes his individual artistry very clearly, his rhythmic pointing a delight. He is treated to an excellent recording, with the cello given fine bloom against a warm but intimate acoustic.

Using a baroque cello, Bylsma brings a vivid musical imagination and an ardent intensity to each movement. He is rhythmically flexible and always thoughtful, and he brings the music alive in an unforced, seemingly natural way. This is worth acquiring as it offers new insights.

Fournier's richly phrased and warm-toned performances carry an impressive musical conviction. Fournier can be profound and he can lift rhythms infectiously in dance movements, but above all he conveys the feeling that this is music to be enjoyed. This recording has been remastered splendidly for reissue in DG's 'Legendary Recordings' series and now has even greater presence and realism.

Mischa Maisky's 1985 set, originally on three CDs, now reappears, remastered on to two, but still at full price. Maisky's performances are beautifully cultured and at a high emotional temperature. He is rather less inclined to let the music speak for itself than some of his rivals and is at times even self-indulgent. The *Sarabande* of the *D minor Suite* is a little narcissistic and the impatient may find it interminable; nor is that of *No. 5 in C minor* free from affectation. There are times in the quicker dance movements when one longs for him to move on. However, there is no doubt that he makes an absolutely glorious sound and commands an unusually wide range of colour and tone.

No one artist holds all the secrets in this repertoire, but few succeed in producing such consistent beauty of tone as Maurice Gendron, with the digital remastering firming up the focus of what was originally an excellent and truthful analogue recording. His phrasing is unfailingly musical, and although these readings have a certain sobriety (save, perhaps, for No. 6 which has distinct flair) their restraint and fine judgement command admiration. At Philips's Duo price, they can be given a warm welcome back to the catalogue.

It was Casals who restored these pieces to the repertory after long decades of neglect. Some of the playing is far from flawless; passage-work is rushed or articulation uneven, and he is often wayward. But he brought to the *Cello suites* insights that remain unrivalled. Casals brings one closer to this music than do most of his rivals. The sound is inevitably dated but still comes over well in this transfer.

Flute sonatas Nos. 1–6, BWV 1030–35; in G min., BWV 1020; Partita in A min. (for solo flute), *BWV 1013.*
*** CRD CRD 3314/5 (2) [id.]. Stephen Preston, Trevor Pinnock, Dordi Savall.

Two of these *Sonatas*, BWV 1031 and 1033, are unauthenticated, but still contain attractive music. Using an authentic one-key instrument, Stephen Preston plays all six with a rare delicacy. Throughout, the continuo playing, led by Trevor Pinnock, is of the highest standard; for those willing to stretch to the expense of two premium-priced records, this is a clear first choice for this repertoire.

Flute sonatas Nos. 1 in B min.; 2 in E flat; 3 in A; 4 in C; 5 in E min.; 6 in E, BWV 1030–35.
(BB) *** ASV CDQS 6108 [id.]. William Bennett, George Malcolm, Michael Evans.

William Bennett uses a modern flute, and in the first three sonatas he and George Malcolm manage without the nicety of including a viola da gamba in the continuo. In *Sonatas Nos. 4–6* the two players are joined by Michael Evans and the bass is subtly but tangibly reinforced and filled out, though the balance remains just as impressive. The playing, as might be expected of these artists, has superb character: it is strong in personality yet does not lack finesse. Moreover it is strikingly alive and spontaneous and, since the CD transfer brings the most vivid presence without the sound being in the least overblown, this can be enthusiastically recommended at super-bargain price to all but those who demand the finer points of authenticity above all else. Bennett himself has made the reconstruction of the first movement of BWV 1032.

Lute music transcribed for guitar

Lute suites (arr. for guitar): *Nos. 1–4, BWV 995–7 and 1006a.*
*** Sony MK 42204 [id.]. John Williams (guitar).

With all four *Suites* conveniently fitted on to a single compact disc, this CBS issue offers a clear first choice in this repertoire.

(i) *Lute suites Nos. 1 in E min., BWV 996; 2 in C min., BWV 997;* (ii) *Trio sonatas Nos. 1 in E flat, BWV 525; 5 in C, BWV 529* (ed. Bream).
(M) *** RCA 09026 61603-2. Julian Bream (i) (guitar); (ii) (lute), George Malcolm.

This compilation comes from records made between 1965 and 1969. The two *Lute suites* are played with great subtlety and mastery on the guitar; the *Trio sonatas* were originally written for organ; here they are heard on lute and harpsichord and are elegantly played and cleanly recorded within a convincing ambience. Perhaps the harpsichord is a little less well defined in the bass register than is ideal, but the effect is pleasingly transparent and intimate.

A Musical offering, BWV 1079.
(N) (M) *** Virgin Veritas/EMI Dig. VC5 45139-2 [id.]. Ens. Sonnerie.

It is good to have a scholarly and thoroughly fresh account of the *Musical offering* on period instruments. Monica Huggett, who leads the Ensemble Sonnerie, favours a colourful instrumentation drawing on solo violin, a dark-timbred oboe da caccia, viola da gamba, viola, flute and bassoon, although the harpsichord (Gary Cooper) is used to open the work thoughtfully with the *Ricercar a 3* and close it with the *Ricercar a 6*, where perhaps a little more panache might have been effective. The *Sonata sopr'il Soggetto Reale* is most sensitively presented as a trio sonata by flute, violin, viola da gamba and harpsichord. Certainly the sounds of these baroque instruments prevent a feeling of blandness, and the polyphony is very clear within a warm ambience.

Trio sonatas Nos. 1 in D min., 2 in C, 3 & 4 in G, BWV 1036–9.
*** HM Dig. HMC 901173[id.]. L. Bar.

This disc contains two sonatas of established authenticity, the *G major*, BWV 1039, and (perhaps less certain) its companion in the same key, BWV 1038, which exists in a set of parts in Bach's own hand. The other two are of less certain authorship. The playing of the London Baroque has great freshness and spirit, and readers wanting this repertoire need not hesitate. The recording is eminently satisfactory, too.

6 (organ) *Trio sonatas: Nos. 1 in E flat* (arr. for 2 violins & continuo); *2 in C min.* (for violin, viola & continuo); *3 in D min.* (for oboe, violin & continuo); *4 in E min.* (for oboe d'amore, viola & continuo); *5 in C* (for oboe, viola & continuo); *6 in G* (for 2 violins & continuo), *BWV 525–30.*
(N) *** Hyperion Dig. CDA 666843 [id.]. King's Consort, Robert King.

Trio sonatas Nos. 1 in G, BWV 525; 3 in G min., BWV 527; 5 in F, BWV 529; 6 in C, BWV 530; Duettos in E min.; in F; in G; in A min., BWV 802–5; 14 Goldberg Canons, BWV 1087 (arr. for recorder or voice, flute, violin, viola da gamba, archlute or theorbo).
(N) **(*) Linn Dig. CDK 036 [id.]. Palladian Ens.

Bach's organ *Trio sonatas* not only have a layout similar to Italian instrumental chamber sonatas, but at least two of the movements have instrumental associations. They readily invite transcription, and Robert King makes a good case for presenting them in such arrangements as are offered here, all retaining the original keys. Not only are the 'solo' parts imaginatively varied but the continuo variously combines theorbo, harpsichord and organ with cello. The baroque oboe and oboe d'amore suit Bach's invention especially well and the resulting ranges of colour are very appealing, giving this music a completely new dimension. The dark opening *Adagio* of the *E minor Sonata*, for instance, shared by cor anglais and organ, is very striking and the *Andante* of the same work is haunting. The allegros, too, are vivaciously coloured: the outer movements of BWV 529 even recall the *Brandenburg concertos*. The playing is joyous and light-hearted and always warm in spirit. First-class recording, too.

The arrangements used by the Palladian Ensemble necessitate transpositions to place the upper voices in a suitable range for the recorder, partnered by the violin, with the viola da gamba given the upper bass lines and the archlute or theorbo completing the continuo. This works well enough and the sound is fresh and transparent. Allegros are lively, but slow movements here are rather cool, although the playing is expert and impeccably stylish. The four *Duetti*, which come from Part III of the *Clavierübung*, are shared by viola da gamba and violin, and again the polyphony is laid out in front of the listener rather literally. What makes this collection enticing is the inclusion of the 14 *Canons*, discovered as recently as 1975 on the back of Bach's own personal manuscript of the *Goldberg variations*. Their presentation in a masterly connected sequence could hardly be bettered, and here the players are clearly enjoying themselves, and so do we.

Viola da gamba sonatas Nos. 1–3, BWV 1027–9.
*** Sony Dig. MK 37794 [id.]. Yo-Yo Ma (cello), Kenneth Cooper.
*** DG Dig. 415 471-2 [id.]. Mischa Maisky (cello), Martha Argerich (piano).
(M) *** HM/BMG GD 77044 [77044-2-RG]. Wieland Kuijken, Gustav Leonhardt.

Yo-Yo Ma plays with great eloquence and natural feeling. His tone is warm and refined and his technical command remains, as ever, irreproachable. Kenneth Cooper is a splendid partner.

Mischa Maisky is also a highly expressive cellist and he opts for the piano – successfully, for Martha Argerich is a Bach player of the first order. In fact the sonority of the cello and the modern piano seems a happier marriage than the compromise Ma and Cooper adopt. A most enjoyable account for collectors who do not care for period instruments.

Kuijken and Leonhardt are both sensitive and scholarly musicians. This is the most authentic account to have appeared on the market in recent years and is among the most rewarding.

(i) *Viola da gamba sonatas Nos. 1–3, BWV 1027–9;* (ii) *Violin sonatas* (for violin and harpsichord) *Nos. 1–6, BWV 1014–19.*
(Y/B) (M) ** Sony SM2K 52615 (2) [id.]. (i) Leonard Rose or (ii) Jaime Laredo; Glenn Gould (piano).

Leonard Rose does not project a larger-than-life instrumental personality like Rostropovich, but his tone is subtly coloured and beautifully focused, his playing shows a fine sensibility, and his slightly introvert style is admirably suited to the *Viola da gamba sonatas* of Bach. Moreover, he and Glenn Gould achieve a very close partnership indeed, although some of Gould's ornamentation is questionable. At times Glenn Gould's clean, staccato articulation in outlining the rhythm of slow movements (usually taken very slowly) seems a shade eccentric, but when both artists do it together, as in the *Andante* of BWV 1027, the effect is both individual and pleasing. In the *Violin sonatas* there is some lovely quiet lyrical playing from Laredo. Again Gould's unforced staccato style is very apparent in slow movements but the violin line floats serenely above, and again faster movements are enjoyably spirited. There is undoubtedly pleasure to be had from this pair of discs, for all the unconventionality of Gould's contribution.

(Unaccompanied) *Violin sonatas Nos. 1–3, BWV 1001, 1003 & 1005; Violin partitas Nos. 1–3, BWV 1002, 1004 & 1006.*
✪ *** EMI Dig. CDS7 49483-2 (2) [id.]. Itzhak Perlman.
(M) *** DG 423 294-2 (2) [id.]. Milstein.
(B) *** Ph. Duo 438 736-2 (2) [id.]. Arthur Grumiaux.
(M) *** HM/BMG GD 77043 (2) [77043-2-RG]. Sigiswald Kuijken.

The range of tone in Perlman's playing adds to the power of these performances, infectiously rhythmic in dance movements but conveying the intensity of live performance in the great slow movements in hushed playing of great refinement. Some may still seek a greater sense of struggle conveyed in order to bring out the full depth of the writing, but the sense of spontaneity, of the player's own enjoyment in the music, makes this set a unique, revelatory experience.

Milstein's set from the mid-1970s remains among the most satisfying of all versions. Every phrase is beautifully shaped and there is a highly developed feeling for line, and these performances have an aristocratic poise and a classical finesse which is very satisfying.

Arthur Grumiaux's fine performances were recorded in Berlin in 1960–61. The venue offers a pleasingly warm background ambience against which the violin is forward, recorded in strong profile with complete realism and with no microphonic exaggeration of the upper partials. He strikes just the right balance between expressive feeling and purity of style. Some may prefer a rhythmically freer, more charismatic approach, as with Perlman and Milstein for instance; but Grumiaux's simplicity of manner, without exaggerated temperament, lets the music unfold naturally, and his readings of all six works are the product of superlative technique and a refined musical intellect. At bargain price this set is very tempting.

Kuijken's accounts are as little painful or scratchy as you are ever likely to get in the authentic field.

(Unaccompanied) *Violin partitas Nos. 2, BWV 1004* (complete); *3 (Minuets I & II* only), *BWV 1006; Violin sonatas Nos. 1, BWV 1001; 3, BWV 1005* (complete); (i) *English suite No. 3 in E, BWV 808: Sarabande; Gavottes Nos. I & II.*

(M) (***) EMI mono CDH7 64492-2 [id.]. Heifetz, (i) with Arpad Sándor.

Heifetz's Bach was by no means romantic, indeed this is thoughtfully inspirational playing, but his chimerical bowing produces more variety of timbre and subtlety of dynamic shading in the *Allemanda* and *Giga* of the *D minor Partita* than would have been likely or possible in Bach's time, while the great *Chaconne* has wonderful detail, without losing strength. Such is the spontaneity of effect that the result gives enormous pleasure, with the *Giga* running like quicksilver. The transfer is bright but truthful: the violin image is real if the volume level is not set too high.

Violin sonatas (for violin and harpsichord) Nos. 1–6, BWV 1014–19.

(M) *** HM/BMG GD 77170 (2) [77170-2-RG]. Sigiswald Kuijken, Gustav Leonhardt.

Violin sonatas Nos. 1–6, BWV 1014–19; Cantabile, ma un poco adagio; Adagio; BWV 1019a/1–2.

(N) (M) **(*) Complete Record Co. Maya Dig. MCD 9503 (2). Maya Homburger, Malcolm Proud.

Violin sonatas Nos. 1–6, BWV 1014–19; 1019a; Sonatas for violin and continuo, BWV 1020–24.

(N) ✪ [B] *** Ph. Duo 454 011-2 (2) [id.]. Arthur Grumiaux, Christiane Jaccottet, Philippe Mermoud (in *BWV 1021 & 1023*).

Violin sonatas (for violin and harpsichord) Nos. 1–6, BWV 1014–19; Sonatas for violin and continuo, BWV 1021 & 1023.

(N) (M) **(*) Virgin Veritas/EMI Dig. VED5 61237-2 (2). John Holloway, Davitt Moroney, Susan Sheppard.

The Bach *Sonatas for violin and harpsichord* and for *violin and continuo* are marvellously played, with all the beauty of tone and line for which Grumiaux is renowned; they have great vitality too. His admirable partner is Christiane Jaccottet, and in BWV 1021 and 1023 Philippe Mermoud (cello) joins the continuo. There is endless treasure to be discovered here, particularly when the music-making is so serenely communicative.

Sigiswald Kuijken uses a baroque violin, and both he and Gustav Leonhardt give us playing of rare eloquence. This reissue is an admirable example of the claims of authenticity and musical feeling pulling together rather than apart. This is a wholly delightful set and the transparency of the sound is especially appealing.

In addition to the six *Sonatas for violin and harpsichord*, the Virgin set presents the two surviving *Sonatas for violin and continuo* (in the latter, Davitt Moroney uses a chamber organ) known to be authentic. (Grumiaux also includes them, plus two more sonatas now thought not to be by Bach.) John Holloway has long experience in the early-music field, but violin tone is as much a matter of personal taste as is the human voice. Some will find the actual sound he makes unpleasing: it is vinegary and at times downright ugly. Yet those who take a different view will find him not wanting in artistry. Both Davitt Moroney and Susan Sheppard give excellent support, and the recording cannot be faulted in its clarity and presence; for those who must have original-instrument performances, first choice remains with Kuijken who, although he omits BWV 1021 and 1023, is no less authentic.

An enjoyably fresh set of these attractive works comes from Maya Homburger (who plays regularly in period-instrument ensembles under both John Eliot Gardiner and Trevor Pinnock), using a baroque violin by Antonio dalla Costa of 1740. She certainly makes it sing, and Malcolm Proud (playing a two-manual copy of an appropriate period harpsichord) is her excellent partner. They are recorded in a church and, while the sound is pleasingly open (and the keyboard instrument is well balanced), the resonance does affect the crispness of focus of the violin very slightly, although this seems rather more noticeable on the second disc than on the first. As a bonus, they offer Bach's alternative versions of two movements of the final sonata. Most refreshing.

KEYBOARD MUSIC

'Bach and Tureck at home' (A birthday offering): (i) *Adagio in G, BWV 968; Aria and 10 variations in the Italian style, BWV 989; Capriccio on the departure of a beloved brother, BWV 992; Chromatic fantasia and fugue, BWV 903; Fantasia, adagio and fugue in D, BWV 912; The Well-tempered clavier, Book 1: Prelude & fugue in B flat, BWV 866.* (ii) *English suite No. 3 in G min., BWV 808; Italian concerto, BWV*

971; Sonata in D min., BWV 964 (trans. from Unaccompanied *Violin sonata No. 2 in A min., BWV 1003*); *Well-tempered clavier, Book 1: Preludes & fugues: in C min; in C, BWV 847–8; Book 2: Preludes & fugues in C sharp, BWV 872; in G, BWV 884.* (iii) *Goldberg variations, BWV 988;* (iv) *Partitas Nos. 1 in B flat, BWV 825; 2 in C min., BWV 826; 6 in E min., BWV 830.*

❀ *** (i) VAIA 1041; (ii) VAIA 1051; (iii) VAIA 1029; (iv) VAIA 1040 (available separately). Rosalyn Tureck (piano).

These recordings originated in the home of William F. Buckley at Wallach's Point, Stamford, Connecticut. They were planned as an inspired birthday present by his wife, but the initial event expanded to five evenings, the first on 24 November 1979 and the last in May 1984. The result is a series of Bach programmes that have all the advantages of live music-making – notably a wonderfully spontaneous feeling of music taking wing as one listens – and none of the disadvantages.

Rosalyn Tureck's Bach playing is legendary, and the performances here show that her keyboard command and fluent sense of Bach style are as remarkable as ever. Miss Tureck uses a wide dynamic and expressive range with consummate artistry, her decoration always adds to the musical effect, and she makes us feel that Bach's keyboard music could be played in no other way than this – the hallmark of a great artist.

These recordings, originally issued on the Troy label, are now on the American VAI Audio label (158 Linwood Plaza, Suite 301, Fort Lee, New Jersey 07024, USA) and are distributed in the UK by Parsifal Distribution (Bridge Studios, Suite 7, 318–326 Wandsworth Bridge Road, London SW6 2TZ).

Aria variata in A min., BWV 989; Capriccio on the departure of a beloved brother, BWV 992; Prelude and fugue in A min., BWV 894; Toccatas: in F sharp min., BWV 910; C min., BWV 911.
(N) (M) *** DG Dig. 447 297-2 [id.]. Kenneth Gilbert.

These are all brilliant and colourful works, and Kenneth Gilbert plays them with panache. The recording of the Jan Couchet harpsichord in a fairly resonant acoustic makes it sound a little larger than life-size, but at mid-price such a reservation need not inhibit a fairly strong recommendation.

The Art of fugue, BWV 1080 (see also string quartet and orchestral versions).
*** HM HMC 901169/70 [id.]. Davitt Moroney (harpsichord).

Davitt Moroney's account commands not only the intellectual side of the work but also the aesthetic, and his musicianship is second to none.

The Art of fugue, BWV 1080; Italian concerto, BWV 971; Partita in B min., BWV 831; Prelude, fugue and allegro in E flat, BWV 998.
(M) *** HM/BMG GD 77013 (2) [77013-2-RG]. Gustav Leonhardt (harpsichord).

Under the fingers of Leonhardt every strand in the texture emerges with clarity and every phrase is allowed to speak for itself. This is a very impressive and rewarding set, well recorded and produced.

Capriccio in B flat (on the departure of a beloved brother), BWV 992; Chorale preludes: Befiehl du deine Wege, BWV 727; Es ist gewisslich an der Zeit, BWV 307 & 734; Ich ruf zu dir, Herr Jesu Christ, BWV 639; In dulci jubilo, BWV 751; Jesu, joy of man's desiring, from BWV 147; Nun komm' der Heiden Heiland, BWV 659; Wachet auf, from BWV 140; Wir danken dir, Gott, BWV 29; Harpsichord concerto in F min., BWV 1056: Largo. Flute sonata in E flat, BWV 1031: Siciliano. English suite No. 3 in G, BWV 808; French suite No. 5 in G, BWV 816; Toccata in D, BWV 912; The Well-tempered Clavier, Book I, excerpts: Preludes and fugues Nos. 4, BWV 849; 9–14, BWV 854–9; Book II, excerpts: Preludes Nos. 3, BWV 872; 6–7, BWV 875–6; 15, BWV 884; 24, BWV 893.
(B) *** DG Double 439 672-2 (2) [id.]. Wilhelm Kempff (with GLUCK: *Orfeo ed Euridice: Ballet music* ***).

Played like this, Bach is a joyful and compelling master, far removed from the relentless plod favoured by some harpsichordists. Though Kempff was well into his eighties when these recordings were made, his intellectual vigour, technical command and musical feeling seem ever fresh. The sound is truthful, warm and clear, and everyone who cares about Bach and piano playing should investigate this issue. One can only lament that, although this new Double DG series (two CDs for the price of one) is generous value, the documentation is inadequate.

Chaconne in D min. (arr. Busoni from (unaccompanied) *Violin partita No. 2 in D min., BWV 1004*).
(Y/B) (M) *** RCA 09026 62590-2 [id.]. Artur Rubinstein – FRANCK: *Prelude, chorale and fugue* ***; LISZT: *Piano sonata in B min.* **(*)

Rubinstein recorded this performance in Rome in 1970, when he was already in his eighties, but the freshness and spirit are a delight. The transfer of the 1970 recording is just a little clangy, but not unpleasantly so.

Chromatic fantasia and fugue in D min., BWV 903; Chorale Preludes: Ich ruf zu dir, BWV 639; Nun komm' der Heiden Heiland, BWV 659 (both arr. Busoni); *Fantasia in A min., BWV 922; Fantasia and fugue in A min., BWV 904; Italian concerto in F, BWV 971.*
(Y/B) (M) *** Ph. 442 400-2 [id.]. Alfred Brendel.

Brendel's fine Bach recital originally appeared in 1978. The performances are of the old school, with no attempt made to strive after harpsichord effects and with every piece creating a sound-world of its own. The *Italian concerto* is particularly imposing, with a finely sustained sense of line and beautifully articulated rhythms. The recording is in every way truthful and present. Masterly.

Chromatic fantasia and fugue in D min., BWV 903; 4 Duets, BWV 802–5; Italian concerto in F, BWV 971; Partita in B min., BWV 831.
🏵 *** O-L Dig. 433 054-2 [id.]. Christophe Rousset (harpsichord).

Christophe Rousset's playing combines the selfless authority and scholarly dedication of such artists as Leonhardt and Gilbert with the flair and imagination of younger players, and all the performances here have a taste and musical vitality that reward the listener.

Chromatic fantasia & fugue in D min., BWV 903; Fantasias: in C min., BWV 906; G min., BWV 917; C min., BWV 919; Fantasia & fugue in A min., BWV 904; Preludes: in C min., BWV 921; A min., BWV 922; Preludes & fugues: in A min., BWV 894; F, BWV 901; G, BWV 902.
*** HM/BMG RD 77039 [RCA 77039-2-RC]. Andreas Staier (harpsichord).

What is good about Staier's playing is its air of freedom, for although he keeps a firm grip on rhythm he is never rigid or inflexible, and his approach and registration are varied enough for his programme to be heard at one sitting. The recording has impressive clarity and presence and is made in a pleasingly warm acoustic. Strongly recommended.

English suites Nos. 1–6, BWV 806–11.
*** Decca Dig. 421 640-2 (2) [id.]. András Schiff (piano).
(Y/B) (M) *** Virgin Veritas/EMI Dig. VER5 61157-2 (2) [id.]. Gustav Leonhardt (harpsichord).
(Y/B) (M) ** Sony SM2K 52606 (2) [id.]. Glenn Gould (piano).

Schiff is straightforward, finely articulated, rhythmically supple and vital. Ornamentation is stylishly and sensibly observed. Everything is very alive, without being in the least over-projected or exaggerated in any way. The Decca recording is altogether natural and present.

Leonhardt's playing here has a flair and vitality that one does not always associate with him, and there is no doubt that he makes the most of the introspective *Sarabande* of the *G minor Suite*. He is better served by the EMI engineers than when he last recorded these for Philips; his performances, too, are more flexible and relaxed. The harpsichord is present without being right on top of the listener.

Glenn Gould often inspires the adjective 'wilful', and certainly these performances have much that is eccentric. At the same time there is undoubtedly a strong musical personality to which the listener cannot remain indifferent. The vocalizations are tiresome and, although phrasing is often imaginative, there is some bizarre ornamentation and accentuation and the piano sound tends to be dry and unappealing, although it represents the effect intended by Gould himself.

English suites Nos. 2 in A min.; 3 in G min., BWV 807–8.
(N) (M) *** DG Dig. 445 573-2 [id.]. Ivo Pogorelich (piano) (with Domenico SCARLATTI: *Keyboard sonatas Kk. 87, 135, 380 & 450 ***).

The young Yugoslav pianist plays both *Suites* with a welcome absence of affectation. It is all beautifully articulate and fresh. Moreover, to make this reissue even more attractive, DG have added four well-chosen keyboard sonatas of Domenico Scarlatti, which also show this artist at his most perceptive. The recording is one of DG's best, with natural piano-sound and an excellent sense of presence.

English suite No. 2 in A min., BWV 807; Partita No. 2 in C min., BWV 826; Toccata in C min., BWV 911.
(M) *** DG 423 880-2 [id.]. Martha Argerich (piano).

Martha Argerich's playing is alive and keenly rhythmic but also wonderfully flexible and rich in colour. She is very well recorded.

French suites Nos. 1–6, BWV 812–17.
*** Erato/Warner Dig. 4509 94805-2 [id.]. Ton Koopman (harpsichord).
(Y/B) *** DG Dig. 445 840-2 [id.]. Andrei Gavrilov (piano).
**(*) Collins Dig. 1371-2 [id.]. Joanna MacGregor (piano).

French suites Nos. 1–6, BWV 812–17 (including 3 additional movements); *18 Little Preludes, BWV 924–8; 930; 933–43; 999; Prelude and fugue in A min., BWV 894; Sonata in D min., BWV 964.*
(N) *** Hyperion Dig. CDA 67121/2 [id.]. Angela Hewitt (piano).

Readers who enjoy Bach on the piano but who do not welcome a nineteenth-century approach will warm to Angela Hewitt's set of the *French suites*. We have had good accounts of them in recent years, most notably Gavrilov's excellent DG set. However, Angela Hewitt, who made her CD début on DG, need not fear any comparison. Her playing is informed by an intelligence and musicianship that are refreshing. Whether in the *Preludes*, written for Wilhelm Friedemann, or the suites themselves she displays an imaginative vitality of a high order. The recorded sound is very natural.

Ton Koopman fits all six *French suites* on to a single, 70–minute CD. He uses a copy of a Ruckers to admirable effect and these performances are stimulatingly rhythmic, exciting and thoughtful by turns. The best-known *Fifth suite* is especially spontaneous. The effect of the recording – not too closely balanced – is vivid and realistic. Ornaments are nicely handled and there is not a trace of pedantry here. A first choice for those not wanting the extra suites offered by Hogwood.

Andrei Gavrilov conveys the enormous inner vitality of these suites and makes this music vibrant. Such is the conviction he conveys that while he is playing one feels there is no other way to play this music and no other instrument to play it on. Very good sound.

Joanna MacGregor's style is relatively soft-grained to which the warm acoustics of The Maltings, Snape, contribute not a little. So the effect is mellow rather than incisive, quite unlike a clavichord or harpsichord. Indeed the characterization in both the *Fourth* and *Fifth suites* gives special pleasure. In spite of the hall resonance, MacGregor conveys intimacy of feeling alongside spontaneous joy in the music, and and many will enjoy this playing a lot.

French suites Nos. 1–6; Suites: in A min., BWV 818a; in E flat, BWV 819; Allemande, BWV 819a.
*** O-L Dig. 411 811-2 (2) [id.]. Christopher Hogwood (harpsichord).

Christopher Hogwood's performances have both style and character and can be recommended with some enthusiasm. To the *French suites* themselves he adds the two others that Bach had obviously intended to include as Nos. 5 and 6.

French suites Nos. 1–6; Italian concerto in F, BWV 971; Partita in B min., BWV 831.
*** Decca Dig. 433 313-2 (2). András Schiff (piano).

András Schiff has few peers in playing Bach on the piano. He continues his distinguished series with highly rewarding performances of the *French suites*, his expressive style entirely without personal indulgence, his freedom in slow movements seemingly improvisatory and spontaneous, and his faster dance movements an unqualified delight. The *Partita in B minor* is slightly more severe in style than the rest of the programme. As with the rest of his series, the Decca recording is appealingly realistic and an ideal acoustic has been chosen.

French suites Nos. 1–6; Partita No. 7 in B min., BWV 831.
(Y/B) (M) ** Sony SM2K 52609 (2) [id.]. Glenn Gould (piano).

Brilliant though Glenn Gould's playing is, it is far too idiosyncratic to justify an unqualified recommendation. Needless to say, there are revealing touches, marvellously clear part-writing and some impressive finger dexterity. There are some odd tempi and a lot of very detached playing that inspires more admiration than conviction. The sound is clear and clean and is acceptably transferred.

Goldberg variations, BWV 988.
(N) *** O-L Dig. 444 866-2 [id.]. Christophe Rousset (harpsichord).
*** DG 415 130-2 [id.]. Trevor Pinnock (harpsichord).
⚛ *** VAI Audio VAIA 1029 [id.]. Rosalyn Tureck (piano).
(Y/B) (M) *** Virgin Veritas/EMI Dig. VER5 61153-2 [id.]. Maggie Cole (harpsichord).
(Y/B) (M) *** DG 439 978-2 [id.]. Wilhelm Kempff (piano).
(M) *(**) Sony Dig. SMK 52619 [id.] (1981 recording). Glenn Gould (piano).
(N) (M) ** Teldec/Warner 4509 97994-2 [id.]. Gustav Leonhardt (harpsichord).
(N) ** Ongaku Dig. 024 107 [id.]. Sergey Schepkin (piano).

Goldberg variations; Fughetta in C min., BWV 961; Preludes and fugues: in A min., BWV 895; D min., BWV 899; E min., BWV 900; F, BWV 901; G, BWV 902.
(N) **(*) Mer. CDA 84291 [id.]. Julia Cload (piano).

Goldberg variations; Well-tempered Clavier: Fugues in E, BWV 878; F sharp min., BWV 883.
(M) (**(*)) Sony mono SMK 52594 [id.] (1955 recording). Glenn Gould (piano).

Christophe Rousset takes his place fairly easily at the top of the list. He plays a 1751 Hemsch, which is superbly recorded within a generous but not too resonant acoustic, so that the harpsichord is very real and believable. His performance opens with an appealingly thoughtful account of the *Aria*, and the variations which follow are strong in character and consistently imaginative in presentation. A playing time of 77 minutes ensures that repeats can be fully observed, and the playing has great freshness and spontaneity.

Trevor Pinnock retains repeats in more than half the variations – which seems a good compromise, in that variety is maintained yet there is no necessity for an additional disc. The playing is eminently vital and intelligent, with alert, finely articulated rhythm. The recording is very truthful and vivid.

While this work should properly be heard on the harpsichord and Christophe Rousset and Trevor Pinnock will fully satisfy in this respect, Rosalyn Tureck's recording is very special indeed – there is no other record of Bach played on the piano quite as compelling as this, and for I. M. it would be a desert island disc. (The circumstances of this recording are discussed above under '*Bach and Tureck at home*'.)

Maggie Cole's playing is completely straightforward and she holds the listener's interest throughout. At mid-price this make a very strong recommendation for those wanting a digital harpsichord version of this work.

Kempff's version is not for purists, but it has a special magic of its own. Ornaments are ignored altogether in the outlining of the theme and the instances of anachronisms of style are too numerous to mention. Yet, for all that, the sheer musicianship exhibited by this great artist fascinates and his playing is consistently refreshing. The 1969 recording is very natural. Rosalyn Tureck's version, however, remains very special indeed.

Julia Cload observes the repeats in the opening *Aria* but not elsewhere; she therefore finds room for the '*Little*' *Preludes and fugues*, which she plays appealingly and fluently. Her account of the *Goldberg variations* is strong and thoughtful; not as inspirational as Tureck's, but some may like its directness of manner. The piano is well recorded but the ear needs to adjust to the 'empty studio' acoustic.

Glenn Gould's famous (1955) mono recording enjoyed cult status in its day, and its return will occasion rejoicing among his admirers. He observes no repeats and in terms of sheer keyboard wizardry commands admiration, even if you do not respond to the results. There is too much that is wilful and eccentric for this to be a straightforward recommendation, but it is a remarkable performance nevertheless.

Gould's later, stereo version was one of the last records he made. In his earlier record he made no repeats; now he repeats a section of almost half of them and also joins some pairs together (6 with 7 and 9 with 10, for example). Yet, even apart from his vocalise, he does a number of weird things – fierce staccatos, brutal accents, and so on – that inhibit one from suggesting this as a first recommendation even among piano versions. The recording is, as usual with this artist, inclined to be dry and forward, which aids clarity.

Leonhardt's Das Alte Werk set of the *Goldberg variations* is now more than thirty years old, but the sound remains undimmed. Indeed the transfer to CD freshens it and the focus is beautifully clear and immediate. It is eminently scholarly but without the vitality of Pinnock. Leonhardt's later recording for Deutsche Harmonia Mundi is preferable, and that will no doubt reappear before too long.

Sergey Schepkin opens impressively, and much of his playing is poised and thoughtful, his bravura effortless, his articulation clear. But in the faster variations he is almost inclined to let the music run away with him and at times his forceful pacing becomes relentless. The spirit of Bach's music does not elude him and a willingness to hold back a bit more would have made this a considerable achievement, for with such urgency he has no trouble fitting in repeats. The recording has fine presence.

Goldberg variations, BWV 988; Fantasia in C min., BWV 906; Fantasia and fugue in F min., BWV 904; Italian concerto in F, BWV 971.
(Y/B) (M) **(*) DG 439 465-2 [id.]. Ralph Kirkpatrick (harpsichord).

Ralph Kirkpatrick is at his best in this work, providing light and subtle registration, and the music benefits both in clarity and in colour. The playing is lively when it should be, controlled and steady in the slow, stately, contrapuntal variations. He is a scholarly rather than an intuitive player and his thoughts are rarely without interest. Though not a first choice, this version includes three extra items where he uses his modern Neupert harpsichord to good effect, while sounding more pedantic, particularly in the *Italian concerto*.

15 2-Part Inventions, BWV 772–86; 15 3-Part Inventions, BWV 787–801.
*** Capriccio Dig. 10 210 [id.] (with *6 Little preludes, BWV 933–8*). Ton Koopman (harpsichord).
**(*) Decca Dig. 411 974-2 [id.]. András Schiff (piano).

15 2-Part Inventions; 15 3-Part Inventions; Fragments of Anna Magdelena's Notebook: March in D; 3 Minuets in G; Minuet in D min.; Musette in D; 2 Polonaises in G min.
(BB) ** Naxos Dig. 8.550679 [id.]. János Sebestyén (piano).

Ton Koopman scores over rivals in offering the *Six Little preludes* in addition to the two sets of *Inventions*, and Koopman plays with spontaneity and sparkle.

András Schiff's playing is (for this repertoire) rather generous with rubato and other expressive touches, but elegant in the articulation of part-writing. Such is his musicianship and pianistic sensitivity, however, that the overall results are likely to persuade most listeners. The recording is excellent.

János Sebestyén is by no means inflexible, but his performances are straighter than those of Schiff. They have less individuality, but this is sensitive, well-structured Bach playing, truthfully recorded, and there is the welcome bonus of eight small-scale keyboard pieces which Bach provided for his second wife.

Partitas Nos. 1–6, BWV 825–30.
*** O-L Dig. 440 217-2 (2) [id.]. Christophe Rousset (harpsichord).
*** Decca Dig. 411 732-2 (2) [id.]. András Schiff (piano).

Partitas Nos. 1–6, BWV 825–30; Partita in B min. (Overture in the French style), BWV 831.
(Y/B) (B) *** Ph. Duo 442 559-2 (2) [id.]. Blandine Verlet (harpsichord).

Bach playing doesn't come much better than it does in Christophe Rousset's two-CD set on Oiseau-Lyre. Here is an artist who wears his elegance and erudition lightly; there are none of the scholarly hang-ups that so often afflict performers of this repertoire. The playing has complete naturalness and is obviously the product of a vital musical imagination. This must now be the first recommendation in this repertoire.

Blandine Verlet's Philips Duo set is not only inexpensive, it is the only set of the *Partitas* to include the later *Overture in the French style*, BWV 831, which is played with much character. Indeed the performances throughout are direct and spontaneous, thoughtful and strongly characterized. Not an out-and-out first choice, which lies with Christophe Rousset on Oiseau-Lyre. But he does not give us the *B minor Partita* and, in its price range, Verlet can certainly be strongly recommended.

Schiff is a most persuasive advocate of Bach on the piano. Though few will cavil at his treatment of fast movements, some may find him a degree wayward in slow movements, though the freshness of his rubato and the sparkle of his ornamentation are always winning. The sound is outstandingly fine.

8 Preludes for W. F. Bach, BWV 924–31; 6 Little Preludes, BWV 933–8; 5 Preludes, BWV 939–43; Prelude, BWV 999; Prelude, fugue and allegro in E flat, BWV 998; Preludes and fughettas: in F & G, BWV 901–2; Fantasia in C min., BWV 906; Fantasia and fugue in A min., BWV 904.
(Y/B) (M) **(*) DG Dig. 447 278-2 (id.]. Kenneth Gilbert (harpsichord).

Splendid artistry from this scholar-player; he is predictably stylish and authoritative. He uses a harpsichord by a Flemish maker, Jan Couchet, enlarged by Blanchet in 1759 and by Taskin in 1778, overhauled by Hubert Bédard. Even played at the lowest setting, the sound seems a bit unrelieved and overbright. This really has 'presence' with a vengeance. The excellence of the playing however is not in question.

Toccatas: in F sharp min.; C min.; D; D min.; E min.; G min.; G; BWV 910–16.
(M) ** Sony SM2K 52612 (2). Glenn Gould (piano).

The seven *Toccatas* offer some of Glenn Gould's finest Bach playing. They are often quite complex in structure, but Gould has their full measure. The recording balance is close and rather dry but truthful and with rather more bloom than in previous incarnations. The one overriding snag is the vocalise.

The Well-tempered Clavier (48 Preludes & fugues), BWV 846–93.
*** DG Dig. 413 439-2 (4) [id.]. Kenneth Gilbert (harpsichord).
(N) (B) **(*) Ph. Duo 446 548-2 (2) [id.]. Friedrich Gulda (piano).

The Well-tempered Clavier, Book I, Preludes and fugues Nos. 1–24, BWV 846–69.
⊛ *** Decca Dig. 414 388-2 (2) [id.]. András Schiff (piano).

The Well-tempered Clavier, Book II, Preludes and fugues Nos. 25–48, BWV 870–93.
⊛ *** Decca Dig. 417 236-2 (2) [id.]. András Schiff (piano).

Gilbert has made some superb harpsichord records, but his set of the 'Forty-eight' crowns them all. By a substantial margin it now supplants all existing harpsichord versions, with readings that are resilient and individual, yet totally unmannered, although some might feel that the acoustic is just a shade too resonant.

Schiff often takes a very individual view of particular preludes and fugues, but his unexpected readings regularly win one over long before the end. Consistently he translates this music into pianistic terms, rarely if ever imitating the harpsichord, and though his very choice of the piano will rule him out with those seeking authenticity, his voyage of discovery through this supreme keyboard collection is the more riveting, when the piano is an easier instrument to listen to over long periods. First-rate sound.

Gulda's recording of the '48' was originally made in 1973. The bold CD transfer brings out the more sharply not only the relative dryness of acoustic (although it is by no means confined) but also the pianist's commendable reluctance to use the sustaining pedal. His approach is strong and direct, sometimes severe, yet has undoubted dedication. In Book I the listener is occasionally aware of strong accenting, yet Gulda can also play lightly and thoughtfully (as in the *Preludes in C sharp minor* and *G sharp minor*) and provide keen but unexaggerated virtuosity (as in the *moto perpetuo* of the *D major*). He uses a fairly wide dynamic range with fine judgement and can build a fugue impressively to an unexaggerated climax (as in the *A flat*). In Book II the playing often seems more serene, and again the use of light and shade is always apt. Pacing is generally convincing and if at times his musical personality brings a degree of eccentricity in this respect (the organ-like *C minor fugue* is very slow and deliberate and the *E major* of the same book is very strong and loud) at others his playing can be pleasingly light and unassertive, as in the flowing *G minor Prelude* and its neat, yet precise, following fugue. If not matching Schiff, these readings are sound and certainly not dull.

The Well-tempered Clavier, Book II, Preludes and fugues Nos. 25–48, BWV 870–93.
*** ECM Dig. 847936-2 [id.]. Keith Jarrett (harpsichord).
(Y/B) (BB) *** Naxos Dig. 8. 550970/1 (2) [id.]. Jenö Jandó (piano).

Keith Jarrett is a highly intelligent and musical player whose readings can hold their own against the current opposition.

Like András Schiff on Decca, Jandó sees the *Well-tempered Clavier* in pianistic terms; he varies his touch from boldly assertive to a light staccato or a more mellow, expressive style. He can also be thoughtful, almost improvisatory, and then commanding. He uses light and shade judiciously. His approach brings great variety to the music and, like his choice of tempi, seems apt, although some listeners may not always agree with his choices. The piano timbre is firm, clear and realistic, and this makes a thoroughly recommendable super-bargain alternative to Schiff, who remains rather special.

ORGAN MUSIC
Complete organ music

Peter Hurford Complete Decca series
Disc 1: *Preludes & fugues, BWV 531–2, 548–50; Toccatas & fugues, BWV 540, 565* (444 411-2).
Disc 2: *Fantasias & fugues, BWV 542, 561; Kleines harmonisches Labyrinth, BWV 591; Preludes & fugues, BWV 533, 551; Toccata, adagio & fugue, BWV 564; Toccata & fugue, BWV 538; Trio, BWV 585* (444 412-2).
Disc 3: *Fantasias, BWV 562, 572; Fantasia & fugue, BWV 537; Fugues, BWV 575–7, 579, 581; Passacaglia & fugue, BWV 582; Pedal-Exercitium, BWV 598; Prelude & fugue, BWV 535; Trio, BWV 583* (444 413-2).
Disc 4: *Clavier-Übung, Part 3* (beginning): *German organ Mass (Prelude & fugue in E flat, BWV 552, & Chorale preludes, BWV 669–71, 676, 678, 680, 682, 684, 686, 688)* (444 414-2).
Disc 5: *Clavier-Übung, Part 3* (conclusion): *Chorale preludes, BWV 672–5, 677, 679, 681, 683, 685, 687, 689; 24 Kirnberger Chorale preludes, BWV 690–713* (444 415-2).
Disc 6: *6 Trio sonatas, BWV 525–30* (444 416-2).
Disc 7: *Canonic variations: Vom Himmel hoch, BWV 769; Chorale partitas: Christ, du bist der helle Tag; O Gott, du frommer Gott; Sei gegrüsset, Jesu gütig, BWV 766–8; Chorale variations: Ach, was soll ich Sünder machen, BWV 770* (444 417-2).
Disc 8: *Chorale preludes, BWV 730–40; Schübler chorale preludes, BWV 645–50; Chorale variations: Allein Gott in der Höh' sei Ehr, BWV 771* (444 418-2).
Disc 9: *Chorale preludes, BWV 726–9; Concertos Nos. 1–6, BWV 592–7* (444 419-2).
Disc 10: *Arnstadt chorale preludes, BWV 714, 719, 742 & 1090–1117* (from Yale manuscript, copied Neumeister) (444 420-2).
Disc 11: *Arnstadt chorale preludes, BWV 957, 1118–20* (from Yale manuscript, copied Neumeister); *Leipzig chorale preludes, BWV 651–62* (444 421-2).
Disc 12: *Leipzig chorale preludes, BWV 663–8. Chorale preludes, BWV 714–25* (444 422-2).
Disc 13: *Allabreve in D, BWV 589; Fugue, BWV 580; Prelude, BWV 568; Preludes & fugues, BWV 534, 536, 539, 541; 8 Short Preludes & fugues, BWV 553–60; Trios, BWV 584 & 586* (444 423-2).

Disc 14: *Aria in F, BWV 587; Canzona in D min., BWV 588; Fantasia, BWV 571; Fugues, BWV 574 & 578; Pastorale, BWV 590; Preludes, BWV 567 & 569; Preludes & fugues, BWV 546–7 (444 424–2).*

Disc 15: *Fantasia, BWV 563; Musical offering: Ricercar, BWV 1079/5. Preludes & fugues, BWV 535a* (incomplete), *543–5; Prelude, trio & fugue, BWV 545b; Toccata & fugue in E, BWV 566; Trio, BWV 1027a* (444 425-2).

Disc 16: *Chorale preludes Nos. 1–41 (Orgelbüchlein), BWV 599–639* (444 426-2).

Disc 17: *Chorale preludes Nos. 42–6 (Orgelbüchlein), BWV 640–44. Chorale preludes, BWV 620a, BWV 741–8, BWV 751–2, BWV 754–5, BWV 757–63, BWV 765, BWV Anh. 55; Fugue in G min., BWV 131a* (444 427-2).

(N) ✹ (B) *** Decca Analogue/Dig. 444 410-2 (17) [id.]. Peter Hurford (organs of Ratzeburg Cathedral, Germany; Church of Our Lady of Sorrows, Toronto, Canada; New College Chapel, Oxford; Knox Grammar School Chapel, Sydney, Australia; Eton College, Windsor; Stiftskirche, Melk, Austria; Augustinerkirche, Vienna, Austria; All Souls Unitarian Church, Washington, DC, USA; Domkirche, St Pölten, Austria; St Catharine's College Chapel, Cambridge).

With the exception of the 35 *Arnstadt chorale preludes*, as copied by Neumeister – discovered quite recently in the Music Library of Yale University – which were added in 1986, Peter Hurford recorded his unique survey of Bach's organ music for Decca's Argo label over a period of eight years, 1974–82. One of the activities for which Bach was renowned was trying out organs, especially new ones (and he was hard to please), so it is highly appropriate that Hurford uses ten different organs, moving from Ratzeburg in Germany to Toronto in Canada, back home to New College, Oxford, then to Sydney, Australia, and so on. Each organ is caught superbly by the recording engineers, and the registration features a range of baroque colour that is almost orchestral in its diversity. The digital recording of the Vienna Bach organ chosen for the *Neumeister chorales* is particularly beautiful. Hurford here omits the three pieces which are already familiar (BWV 601 and 639 from the *Orgelbüchlein*, and BWV 637), all of which can be found within their proper sequences in the order in which they were published by the Bach Gesellschaft edition which was followed in Schmieder's catalogue. However, Hurford does include BWV 714 (which in the Neumeister manuscript is 27 bars longer than previously known versions), BWV 719 and 742 (hitherto not thought to be authentic Bach) and BWV 957 (until now not regarded as an organ work).

It was Peter Hurford's achievement to influence a complete change in approach to this repertoire, moving away from an enduring and essentially pedagogic, German tradition (shown at its best by organists like Helmut Walcha on DG Archiv). Wolfgang Rübsam on Philips (see below) had already pioneered a new look at Bach's organ music on record, and Hurford carried it forward to fruition, choosing organs which could produce a fine palette of colour, yet carefully registering textures which do not cloud the polyphonic argument, notably in the chorale preludes which can so easily become overladen. Vigour and energy are the keynotes of his approach to the large-scale works and, without losing their majesty, he never lets the fugal momentum get bogged down by the the music's weight and scale. We hear Bach's organ writing with new ears, its human vitality revealed alongside its extraordinary architecture. It can readily be seen that the new layout has been well thought out. Moreover it is supported with extensive notes by Clifford Bartlett which are both scholarly and readable; full specifications of all the organs used are included. The recordings are splendidly transferred to CD and remain among the finest ever and, with its greatly improved documentation, this set of 17 bargain-price CDs must be counted a supreme investment in this repertoire.

Wolfgang Rübsam Philips series

Volume 1: *Allabreve, BWV 589; Canzona, BWV 588; Fantasias, BWV 562 & 572; in C min.; Fugues, BWV 575, 577–9; 581; Passacaglia, BWV 582; Pedal-Exercitium, BWV 598; Prelude, adagio-trio, fantasia & fugue; Prelude, BWV 568; Preludes & fugues, 531–6; 538–9; 541; 543–550; Toccata, BWV 564; Toccatas & fugues, BWV 540, 564–566; Trios, BWV 583, 586, 1027a.* (4 discs)

Volume 2: *Canonic variations on the Christmas chorale, Vom Himmel hoch, BWV 769; Chorale partitas: Christ, der du bist der helle Tag, BWV 766; O Gott, du frommer Gott, BWV 767; Sei gegrüsset, Jesu gütig, BWV 768; Ach, was soll ich Sünder machen?, BWV 770; Chorales & Chorale preludes: BWV 691a, 717, 725, 739, 745, 747; Chorale variations: Allein Gott in der Höh' sei Ehr', BWV 717; Fantasia, BWV 571; Fugue on a theme of Legrenzi, BWV 574; Orgelbüchlein, BWV 599–644; Pastorale in F, BWV 590; Trio sonatas Nos. 1–6, BWV 525–30.* (4 discs)

Volume 3: *Chorales & Chorale preludes: BWV 653b, 748–750, 754, 756, 759; Chorale: O Lamm Gottes unschuldig; 6 Schübler chorales, BWV 645–650; Clavierübung, Part III: German organ mass: (Prelude in E flat,BWV 552/1; Catechism chorales, Kyrie and Gloria BWV 669–689; Duets Nos. 1–4, BWV 802–5; Fugue in E flat, BWV 552/2). 18 Leipzig chorales, BWV 651–668; 6 Concertos after other composers, BWV 592–7; Fugue on the Magnificat, BWV 733.* (4 discs)

Volume 4: *Aria in F after Couperin, BWV 587; The Art of Fugue, BWV 1080; Chorales & Chorale preludes: BWV 668a; 690–695, 700, 705–707, 708–711, 712–715, 716, 718–720, 722–724, 726–727, 728–732, 734–736, 737, 740, 738, 741–744, 746, 751–752, 755, 757–758, 760–763, 765, 795–796; Fughettas on: Christum wir sollen loben schon, BWV 696; Gelobet seist du, Jesu Christ BWV 697; Herr Christ, der ein'ge Gottes Sohn, BWV 698; Nun komm' der Heiden Heiland, BWV 699; Vom Himmel hoch, BWV 701; Das Jesulein soll doch mein Trost, BWV 702; Gottes Sohn ist kommen, BWV 703; Lob sei dem allmächt'gen Gott, BWV 704; Allein Gott in der Höh' sei Ehr', BWV 716; Fantasia in C, BWV 570; Fantasia and fugue in A min., BWV 561; Fantasia con imitazione in B min., BWV 563; Fugues: in G, BWV 576; in D, BWV 580; Kleine harmonisches Labyrinth, BWV 591; Preludes in C, BWV 567; in A min., BWV 569; Prelude and fugue in A min., BWV 551; Trio from Cantata BWV 166, BWV 584; Trio after Fasch, BWV 585.* (4 discs)

(B) *** Ph. 438 170-2 (16) [id.]. Wolfgang Rübsam (organs of Frauenfeld & Freiburg).

Wolfgang Rübsam made his highly recommendable complete survey at the beginning of the 1970s, using two organs. He recorded the bulk of the music on the fine instrument at St Nikolaus in Frauenfeld, Switzerland. For the chorale preludes and fughettas and a few miscellaneous works on CDs 14 and 15 he turned to the Belgian Hockhois organ at Freiburg Münster. Sonically the results are highly stimulating and in works calling for a wide range of colour, including the *Leipzig chorales, Orgelbüchlein,* and the chorale variants of all kinds, one could not ask for more suitable reeds or more innocent piping in flute stops, while there is plenty of supporting weight in the pedals. The *Trio sonatas* are especially attractive and compare well with Simon Preston's set (see below) in both their luminous palette and their liveliness. The six solo *Concertos* based on music of others, principally Ernst and Vivaldi, are comparably successful, although here Rübsam adopts extreme tempi, with adagios very measured against sprightly allegros. The so-called *German Organ Mass* is by no means heavy-going, while in *The Art of Fugue* Rübsam generally chooses a bright, somewhat swift (but by no means hurried) presentation of the *Contrapuncti.*

But the key to the success of any Bach survey must lie with the way the performer approaches the large-scale concert pieces, notably the *Preludes and fugues* and *Toccatas and fugues,* and these are nearly all in the first volume. Certainly in these works Rübsam is consistently vital, and his registration often tickles the ear. The famous *Toccata, adagio and fugue,* BWV 564, is very well judged, a work that can easily become ponderous, while the *Passacaglia in C minor,* BWV 582, has a convincing forward momentum and plenty of imaginative detail. The set comes on 16 bargain-priced CDs, laid out in four boxes of four CDs within a slipcase. The documentation is excellent.

Kevin Bowyer Nimbus series
Aria in F (after Couperin), *BWV 587; Concerto in A min.* (after Vivaldi), *BWV 593; Fugue in G, BWV 576; Prelude and fugue in D min., BWV 539; Toccata and fugue in F, BWV 540.*
*** Nimbus Dig. NI 5400 [id.]. Kevin Bowyer (Marcussen organ of Sct. Hans Kirke, Odense, Denmark).

Chorale partita: Sei gegrüsset, Jesu gütig, BWV 768; Concerto in D min. after Vivaldi, BWV 596; Preludes and fugues: in F min., BWV 534; in F min., BWV 543.
**(*) Nimbus Dig. NI 5290 [id.]. Kevin Bowyer (Marcussen organ of Sct. Hans Kirke, Odense, Denmark).

Chorale preludes: Aus tiefster Not schrei ich zu dir, BWV 1099; Erbarm' dich mein, O Herre Gott, BWV 721; Concerto in G (after Prince Johann Ernst), *BWV 592; Fantasia and fugue in G min., BWV 542; Trio sonata No. 1 in E flat, BWV 525.*
*** Nimbus Dig. NI 5280 [id.]. Kevin Bowyer (Marcussen organ of Sct. Hans Kirke, Odense, Denmark).

Kevin Bowyer is another of the younger generation of organists who is embarking on a complete Bach survey, but he has chosen to produce a series of carefully planned recitals rather than grouping works together in their respective genres. For the collector this may bring the problem of duplication unless the intention is to acquire the whole series, but the advantage is that each CD can be enjoyed as an individual recital. Characteristically, the Nimbus engineeers produce a sound-image with plenty of ambience, with glowing, colourful pipings and throaty reeds, the effect often expansively grand.

The first volume in the series (NI 5280) sets the pattern by framing a collection of lighter pieces and chorale preludes with two ambitious major works. Bowyer's opening *Toccata and fugue in D minor* is second to none, the Toccata strong yet improvisational in feeling; then, after a solemn cadence, the fugue is vividly brilliant with a powerful apotheosis. The sound is magnificently rich in colour.

Volume 3 (NI 5290) seems slightly less successful overall than some of Bowyer's collections, with a rather easy-going approach to the *Sei gegrüsset variations* and the Vivaldi concerto, too, not as sprightly as it might be. The framing *Preludes and fugues* are powerful and vigorous, especially the closing *A minor*, but the recording seems fractionally brighter than usual and the reeds just a trifle grainy.

Volume 5 in the series (NI 5400) begins with Bach's arrangement of Vivaldi, the *Concerto in A minor*, opening jauntily, and almost immediately brings some engaging fluting in the glowing registration, as does the brightly extrovert *Fugue in G*. The colouring of the chorale preludes is nicely varied. The *Prelude and fugue in D minor* again has an improvisational thoughtfulness, while the closing Weimar *Toccata and fugue in F* is vigorously articulated and suitably resplendent and weighty. The expansive recording provides a broad canvas but with the lighter detail bright and clear.

Chorale preludes: Ein feste Burg ist unser Gott, BWV 720; Gelobet seist du, Jesu Christ, BWV 697 & BWV 722; In dulci jubilo, BWV 751 & BWV 729; Vom Himmel hoch, BWV 738; Fugue (Gigue) in G, BWV 577; Prelude and fugues: in D, BWV 532; in G, BWV 541; Trio sonata No. 5 in C, BWV 529.
*** Nimbus Dig. NI 5289 [id.]. Kevin Bowyer (Marcussen organ of Sct. Hans Kirke, Odense, Denmark).

Fantasia & imitatio in B min., BWV 563; Fugue in C min., BWV 575; 2 Fugues on themes of Albinoni: in A & B min., BWV 950–1; 8 Short Preludes and fugues, BWV 553–60; Toccatas: in G min., BWV 915; in G, BWV 915.
🏵 *** Nimbus Dig. NI 5377 [id.]. Kevin Bowyer (Marcussen organ of Sct. Hans Kirke, Odense, Denmark).

Volume 2 of Kevin Bowyer's survey (NI 5289), a predominantly cheerful programme, brings more examples of his lively rhythmic style and the appealing colours and husky reeds of this fine Danish organ.

Volume 4 is even more stimulating, opening with the brilliantly flamboyant *Toccata in G minor* which, after its thoughtful centrepiece, encapsulates a bouncing, minor-key version of the '*Gigue' fugue*. This is marvellously played; yet the highlight of the recital is surely the set of *Short Preludes and fugues*, BWV 553–60, conceived by Bach in pedagogical style and planned in an ascending scale of major and minor keys from C major to B flat. Finally the three-part Weimar *G minor Toccata* again opens with cascading brilliance, leading to a quietly reflective arioso, then closes the programme with sprightly, dancing 6/8 exuberance. The bright, clear recording seems ideally judged, cleaner in focus than the earlier Nimbus CDs in this fine series. There are few more invigorating Bach organ recitals than this.

Volume 6: *Chorale partita 'Wenn wir in höchsten Nöten sein', BWV Anh. 78; Fantasias super 'Valet will ich dir geben', BWV 735–6; Prelude and fugues in E min., BWV 533; G min., BWV 535; Toccata in E, BWV 566; Toccata, adagio and fugue in C, BWV 564; Trio in G min., BWV 584; Trio sonata No. 6 in G, BWV 630.*
(N) *** Nimbus Dig. NI 5423 [id.]. Kevin Bowyer (Marcussen organ of Sct. Hans Kirke, Odense, Denmark).

Another well-planned and highly successful collection, that works well as an ongoing recital, on this superb Danish organ which is recorded most spectacularly. The powerful *Toccata, adagio and fugue in C* makes an arresting opener and Bowyer's bravura in the two contrasted Fantasias on '*Valet will ich dir geben*' is remarkable: both works are highly stimulating. His playing is no less stimulating in the two often flamboyant *Preludes and fugues* which are among Bach's most interesting (and exciting). Then the flowing variants on the very attractive chorale, '*Wenn wir in höchsten Nöten sein*' (with an engagingly wide palette), make a perfect contrast before the powerful *Toccata in E*, which demands more and more bravura as it proceeds to its majestic denouement.

Christopher Herrick Hyperion series
Canonic variations: Vom Himmel hoch, BWV 769; Chorale partitas: Christ, der du bist der helle Tag, BWV 766; O Gott, du frommer Gott, BWV 767; Sei gegrüsset, Jesu gütig, BWV 767–8; Ach, was soll ich Sünder machen, BWV 770.
*** Hyperion Dig. CDA 66455 [id.]. Christopher Herrick (organ of St Nicholas Church, Bremgarten, Switzerland).

Christopher Herrick is very much of the new generation of organists, giving equal precedence to momentum and vitality and colourful registration, alongside a feeling for the musical architecture. There is certainly no lack of momentum here, and in his hands the splendid Metzler organ at Bremgarten illuminates Bach's intricate divisions with a wide colouristic range. Herrick always keeps the music moving and in the *Chorale partitas* this is to advantage. Certainly the recording does the organ justice in vivid palette and truthful balance, and the music-making is consistently alive.

Fantasias: in C min., BWV 562; in G, BWV 572; in C min., BWV 537; in G min., BWV 542; Preludes and fugues: in A, BWV 536; in A min., BWV 543; in B min., BWV 544; in C, BWV 545; in C min., BWV 546; in C, BWV 547; in D, BWV 532; in E min. (Wedge), BWV 548; in E flat (St Anne), BWV 552; in F min., BWV 534; in G, BWV 541.
*** Hyperion Dig. CDA 66791/2 [id.]. Christopher Herrick (organ of Jesuits' Church, Lucerne).

Among all the complete sets and individual mixed recitals, this very imposing two-disc set centres on some of the most powerfully structured and intellectually cogent of all Bach's major organ works. Christopher Herrick offers a presentation which is obviously built on a background of careful preparation, with a spontaneously vivid presentation that never gives an impression of the music simply 'trundling on' and is as emotionally compelling as it is authoritative, with each fugue moving on to a gripping apotheosis. The chosen Swiss instrument seems ideal for the repertoire and it is superbly recorded, giving weight, amplitude and clarity in equal measure.

'The Italian connection': Concertos (for solo organ) Nos. 1 in G, BWV 592 (after ERNST); *2 in A min. (after* VIVALDI: *Concerto in A min., Op. 3/8, RV 522), BWV 593; 3 in C (after* VIVALDI: *Concerto in D, Op. 7/11, RV 208), BWV 594; 4 in C (after* ERNST), *BWV 595; 5 in D min. (after* VIVALDI: *Concerto in D min., Op. 3/11, RV 565), BWV 596; Fugue on a theme of Corelli, BWV 579; Fugue on a theme of Legrenzi in C min., BWV 574.*
(N) **(*) Hyperion Dig. CDA 66813 [id.]. Christopher Herrick (organ of St Peter and St Paul, Villmergen, Switzerland).

This is somewhat disappointing. The Metzler organ Christopher Herrick uses for these concerto transcriptions has a splendid range of colour – witness the *Adagio* of *No. 2 in A minor* (after Vivaldi), which is most imaginatively registered, or the delightful palette of the *Largo e spiccato* of Vivaldi's *D minor concerto* (which nevertheless could have been moved on just a fraction faster). But in the allegros Christopher Herrick is not helped by the lack of bite in the reeds, although the spirited finale of that same *D minor Concerto* still sounds splendid. The Corelli *Fugue* on the other hand tends to jog along and the *Concerto movement in C major* for Johann Ernst is quite heavy going.

Orgelbüchlein: Chorale preludes Nos. 1–46, BWV 599–644.
(N) *** Hyperion Dig. CDA 66756 [id.]. Christopher Herrick (Metzler organ of Stadkirche, Rheinfelden, Switzerland).

Herrick's *Orgelbüchlein* is in every way recommendable and these performances can stand among the finest in the catalogue. The Swiss Metzler organ seem just right for these relatively simple yet sometimes florid pieces: it has a wide palette and an equal range of sonorities. The effect is never plangent, yet Herrick readily keeps the cantus firmus in front of the listener without exaggeration. His tempi invariably seem apt and his approach is obviously aware of the word-meaning of each chorale and its expressive implications. The recording is beautiful, smooth yet clear.

Passacaglia in C min., BWV 582; Toccatas and fugues: in D min. (Dorian), BWV 538; in D min., BWV 565; in F, BWV 540; Toccata, adagio and fugue in C, BWV 564.
*** Hyperion Dig. CDA 66434 [id.]. Christopher Herrick (Metzler organ of Stadkirche, Zofingen, Switzerland).

These are all powerfully structured yet attractively lively performances. Christopher Herrick yet again is obviously determined not to get bogged down with the pedagogues, and his forward thrust is consistently impressive: the famous *D minor* work certainly sparkles yet does not lack power, while the *Fugue in C major* which follows on after the *Toccata and adagio*, BWV 564, is not too heavy. Similarly the *Passacaglia in C minor* has gravitas without seeming too sombre and is glowingly decorated. The recording has fine spectacle and realism.

Trio sonatas Nos. 1–6, BWV 525–30.
*** Hyperion Dig. CDA 66390 [id.]. Christopher Herrick (Metzler organ of St Nicholas Church, Bremgarten, Switzerland).

Herrick's performances are comparatively relaxed, but the playing has plenty of lift and he produces colours in slow movements to charm the ear, with the lyrical lines flowing. He has an instrument well suited to this repertoire and he is in full command of its palette, with registration suited to the character of each movement and articulation that is precise without pedantry. The Hyperion recording, too, cannot be faulted, and even the order of works is chosen to make the most of their variety of style.

Marie-Claire Alain Erato series
(Y/B) (M) **(*) Erato/Warner Dig. 4509 96358-2 (14) [id.]. Marie-Claire Alain.

Marie-Claire Alain's series has much to offer the lover of Bach's organ music, and she plays to excellent effect on some splendid instruments. The complete set of fourteen records is available in a slipcase at a small saving in cost, and admirers of this artist should not be disappointed with such an investment. But competition is strong, and for most collectors a choice from among the separate issues, all at mid-price, would seem more sensible.

Volume 1: *Leipzig chorale preludes: An Wasserflüssen Babylon, BWV 653; Schmücke dich, o liebe Seele, BWV 654; Von Gott will ich nicht lassen, BWV 658; Triple chorale (with Trio): Allein Gott in der Höh' sei Ehr', BWV 662–4; Preludes and fugues: in B min., BWV 544; in E min., BWV 548.*
(Y/B) (M) **(*) Erato/Warner Dig. 4509 96718-2 [id.]. Marie-Claire Alain (organ of Martinikerk, Groningen).

Volume 1 is recorded on the Martinikerk organ in Groningen and the results are not entirely satisfactory, for the engineers obtain a rich, weighty sound as in the opening *E minor Prelude and fugue*, but the resonance makes the result rather opaque, which does not enable Alain to clarify detail. The fugue, however, is measured and powerful. This whole programme bears out her comments about tempi, which are essentially relaxed.

Volume 2: *Orgelbüchlein: Chorale preludes, BWV 618–32; Prelude and fugue in G min., BWV 535; Toccatas and fugues: in D min. (Dorian), BWV 538; in C, BWV 566.*
(Y/B) (M) **(*) Erato/Warner Dig. 4509 96719-2 [id.]. Marie-Claire Alain (organ of Freiburg Cathedral).

Volume 2 was recorded in 1991 on the early eighteenth-century Silbermann organ at Freiburg, and the sound is immediately more vivid and clear. The opening *Dorian Toccata in D minor* is brightly registered and lively and, if the fugue is unhurried, the tension is well sustained. The *C major Toccata*, however, is one of the finest performances in the cycle. Alain presents the earlier chorales from the *Orgelbüchlein* gently and persuasively. Generally these simple pieces come off very well, although she does not always make the cantus firmus stand out. The second group of chorales, BWV 625–30, are richly textured until *Erschienen ist der herrliche Tag*, BWV 629, which makes an engaging lighter contrast.

Volume 3: *Allabreve in D, BWV 589; Canzona in D min., BWV 588; Fugues: in C min., BWV 575; in G, BWV 577; Fugue sopra 'Meine Seele erhebet den Herren'; Kirnberger chorale preludes: Wo soll ich fliehen hin, BWV 694; Wir Christenleut hab'n jetzund Freud, BWV 710; Kleines harmonisches Labyrinth, BWV 591; Partita sopra 'O Gott, du frommer Gott', BWV 767; Preludes and fugues: in D min., BWV 539; in C, BWV 545; in A min., BWV 551.*
(Y/B) (M) **(*) Erato/Warner Dig. 4509 96720-2 [id.]. Marie-Claire Alain (organ of Freiburg Cathedral).

The Freiburg organ is again used in Volume 3 (also recorded in 1991) and Alain uses its fullest sonority for her weighty presentation of the opening *Prelude and fugue in C*. However, the following *G major fugue* (better known as the *Fugue à la gigue* and of questionable authenticity) is impossibly slow and heavy. Alain is much more impressive in the *D minor fugue*, BWV 539, which is cleanly pointed and rhythmically positive. The splendid virtuoso *Fugue in C minor* (which reminds one of the more famous *D minor*, BWV 565) is fluent and quite dramatic at the end, while in the fugue, based on the *Magnificat*, Alain uses the pedals impressively to build a most powerful climax. The *Kleines harmonisches Labyrinth* has sounded more original in other hands, but here the registration is certainly interesting.

Volume 4: *Chorale preludes: BWV 711, 714–18, 722, 724–32, 734, 737–9, 765; Fantasia in B min., BWV 563; Preludes and fugues: in C, BWV 531; in E min., BWV 533.*
(Y/B) (M) **(*) Erato/Warner Dig. 4509 96721-2 [id.]. Marie-Claire Alain (organ of Georgenkirche, Rötha).

The Silbermann organ at Rötha (still 1991) proves ideal for this repertoire, and it stimulates Alain to some of her most spontaneous performances so far in this variable series. After a robust *Prelude and fugue in E minor*, Marie-Claire Alain is at her most chimerical in the Christmas chorale, *Nun freut euch, lieben Christen g'mein*, with the registration like tinkling bells. The two settings of *Liebster Jesu* then seem rather staid and solemn, and *In dulci jubilo* is very grand indeed. Alain clearly revels in the elaborate passage on the pedals which opens the *Prelude in C*, BWV 531, and even conveys exuberance (not a quality for which her Bach playing is notable), while the fugue is equally alive and vivid. The contrapuntally grand *Herr Gott, dich loben wir* ends the recital massively, and here one feels Alain could have moved the music on a bit. But there is no doubt that Alain is really enjoying this organ, which sounds as if it answers readily to her touch.

Volume 5: *Chorale preludes: BWV 690–91, 695, 700, 706, 709, 712, 721; Fantasia ('Jesu, meine Freude'), BWV 713; Fugue (on a theme of Corelli) in B min., BWV 579; Kirnberger chorale preludes for Christmas, BWV 696–704; Partita sopra 'Christ, der du bist der helle Tag', BWV 766; Preludes and fugues: in C min., BWV 537, in C min., BWV 549.*

(Y/B) (M) **(*) Erato/Warner Dig. 4509 96722-2 [id.]. Marie-Claire Alain (organ of Georgenkirche, Rötha).

Alain opens Volume 5 with the early *Prelude and fugue in C minor* (1703/4) using the Rötha organ's pedals to bravura effect, following with a fairly spontaneous account of the jolly fugue. The first chorale, *Herr Jesus Christ, dich zu uns wend*, BWV 709, is full of gleaming sunshine, while *Erbarm' dich mein O Herre Gott* brings that dedicated feeling of repose which Alain manages so well. The *Partita sopra 'Christ, der du bist der helle Tag'* brings six variations and Alain finds an orchestral range of colour for them, with a gigue movement finally leading to a majestic close.

Volume 6: *Canonic variations: Vom Himmel hoch, BWV 769; Chorale preludes: BWV 669–79; Clavier-Ubung, Part 3: German organ Mass: Prelude in E flat, BWV 552; Prelude and fugue in C, BWV 547.*

(Y/B) (M) **(*) Erato/Warner Dig. 4509 96723-2 [id.]. Marie-Claire Alain (organ of Martinikerk, Groningen).

Volume 6 was one of the earlier sets of recordings, made in 1985 in Groningen, but the organ is beautifully focused and detail hardly ever clouds. If the *C major fugue*, BWV 547, proceeds on its way somewhat remorselessly, the *Canonic variations* (as with other similar, expansive sets of divisions) bring out the very best in Marie-Claire Alain, and the opening presentation, in which the Christmas chorale cantus firmus subtly creeps through the flowing decorative lines, is very cunningly managed, while the intricate contrapuntal writing remains clear throughout, and the chorales which follow have plenty of variety in presentation and mood.

Volume 7: *Chorale preludes: 'Herr Jesu Christ, dich zu uns wend', BWV 655; 'Vor Deinen Thron tret' ich', BWV 668; Clavier-Ubung, Part 3: German organ Mass: Chorale preludes, BWV 680–89; 4 Duets, BWV 802–5; Fugue in E flat, BWV 552.*

(Y/B) (M) *** Erato/Warner Dig. 4509 96724-2 [id.]. Marie-Claire Alain (organ of Martinikerk, Groningen).

Marie-Claire Alain returned to the Groningen organ in 1990, having decided that its range of colours was especially suitable for this collection of chorales, plus the four *Duets* and *Fugue in E flat* which make up the so-called 'German organ Mass'. (Its opening *Prelude in E flat* had already been included in the previous volume.) This is repertoire which finds Alain at her very finest, for her performances of the chorales clearly identify with their spiritual implications. Splendid recording: this can be strongly recommended.

Volume 8: *Chorale preludes: Orgelbüchlein Nos. 35–46, BWV 633–44; Fantasia in C, BWV 570; Partita sopra 'Sei gegrüsset, Jesu gütig', BWV 768; Preludes and fugues: in F min., BWV 534; in C min., BWV 546.*

(Y/B) (M) **(*) Erato/Warner Dig. 4509 96725-2 [id.]. Marie-Claire Alain (organ of St Laurentskerk, Alkmaar).

The famous Schnitger organ at Alkmaar has stimulated many Bach performers on record, but one has to say that Alain's opening *Prelude and fugue in C minor* is rather stoic, though it is certainly a powerful utterance. The dozen chorale preludes from the *Orgelbüchlein* bring the usual simplicity and variety, but it is the Partita on *'Sei gegrüsset, Jesu gütig'* which really excites Alain's imagination – not surprisingly, as it is one of Bach's very finest sets of keyboard variations; again one laments that there is no separate cueing for this expansive work (19 minutes 50 seconds) which reaches such a stunning apotheosis here. The recording dates from 1990.

Volume 9: *Chorale preludes: Orgelbüchlein Nos. 1–19, BWV 599–617; 'Valet will ich dir geben', BWV 735; Fantasias: in C min., BWV 562; in G, BWV 572; Fugue on a theme of Legrenzi in C min., BWV 574.*

(Y/B) (M) **(*) Erato/Warner Dig. 4509 96742-2 [id.]. Marie-Claire Alain (organ of St Laurentskerk, Alkmaar).

The *Très vitement* opening of the *G major Fantasia* is always appealing, and Alain plays it perkily enough, then returning to her full-bodied style for the *Gravement–Lentement*, which she takes very literally. The first of the Orgelbüchlein chorales included here, *Nunn komm' der Heiden Heiland*, BWV 599, is also very fully orchestrated, but in *Gottes Sohn ist kommen*, BWV 600, the balance between decoration and chorale is felicitous (something Alain does not always manage ideally). The host of ascending and descending angels in BWV 606 is evocatively pictured, but it is in a quietly reflective piece like *Das alte Jahr vergangen ist*, BWV 614, that Alain is at her finest.

Volume 10: *Leipzig chorale preludes: BWV 651–2, 656–7, 659–61, 665–7; Prelude and fugue in D, BWV 532; Trio in D min., BWV 583.*

(Y/B) (M) **(*) Erato/Warner Dig. 4509 96743-2 [id.]. Marie-Claire Alain (organ of St Laurentskerk, Alkmaar).

There is no denying the grandeur of Alain's opening *D major Prelude*, BWV 532, and the fugue is ebullient. The *Trio in D minor* provides a comparatively lightweight transition to a further extended grouping of Bach's splendid Leipzig chorales, including three different settings of *Nun komm der Heiden Heiland*, and two each of *Komm, heiliger Geist* and *Jesus Christus, unser Heiland*. They definitely suit the panoply of colour possible with the Alkmaar organ, and Alain is generally very persuasive. Recording date: again 1990.

Volume 11: *Concertos* (for solo organ): *Nos. 1 in G* (after ERNST); *2 in A min.* (after VIVALDI: *Concerto, Op. 3/8*); *3 in C* (after VIVALDI: *Concerto, Op. 7/11*); *4 in C* (after ERNST); *5 in D min.* (after VIVALDI: *Concerto, Op. 3/11*), *BWV 592/6; Aria in F, BWV 587; Chorale prelude 'An Wasserflüssen Babylon', BWV 653b; Preludes and fugues: in A, BWV 536; in G, BWV 550; Trio in G min., BWV 584.*

(Y/B) (M) *** Erato/Warner Dig. 4509 96744-2 [id.]. Marie-Claire Alain (organ of St Martin, Masevaux).

For Volume 11 (recorded in 1992) Marie-Claire Alain went to France, and this splendid Müller organ with its bright, sunny reeds sounds just right for Bach's vivacious Vivaldi transcriptions. Moreover the manuals and pedals have a compass sufficiently wide for these arrangements to be played as Bach conceived them, which is not possible on certain of the other organs in use for this series. The works by Johann Ernst are also most rewarding. Alain's tempi are apt; allegros are not raced, but they are certainly infectious. The *Aria in F* is a Couperin transcription (from *Les Nations*). The two *Preludes and fugues* are also comparatively lightweight, although still first-class Bach, from the early Weimar period. They are given attractively lively performances. A splendid disc and an ideal sampler to show this artist at her most perceptive.

Volume 12: *Pastorale, BWV 590; Prelude (Fantasia) and fugue in G min., BWV 542; Prelude and fugue in A min., BWV 543; Toccatas: in C, BWV 564; in D min., BWV 565; Toccata and fugue in F, BWV 540.*

(Y/B) ✪ (M) *** Erato/Warner Dig. 4509 96745-2 [id.]. Marie-Claire Alain (organs of St Bavokerk, Haarlem; Jakobijnkerk, Leeuwarden).

Using a pair of magnificent Dutch organs, Marie-Claire Alain here (in 1992) surveys an ideally chosen group of Bach's organ works on the largest scale, and she is not found wanting. The pedal solo in the *Toccata in F* is spectacular indeed, while the *Fantasia and Fugue in G minor*, BWV 542, is particularly imposing, with the fugue given a thrilling impetus. The famous *Toccata and fugue in D minor* is a shade resonant – there have been clearer-focused versions – but the performance certainly does not lack panache. The *Prelude and fugue in A minor*, too, has unquestioned flair, while in the *Toccata, Adagio and fugue in C* the clarity of articulation (again with the pedals used spectacularly) is very commanding indeed, and the lyrical feeling in the *Adagio* provides fine contrast. This performance climaxes a recital of the very highest calibre, superbly recorded.

Volume 13: *6 Trio sonatas, BWV 525–30.*

(Y/B) (M) **(*)Erato/Warner Dig. 4509 96746-2 [id.]. Marie-Claire Alain (organ of Aa Kerk, Groningen).

Marie-Claire Alain decided to use the 'other' (Schnitger) organ in Groningen for the *Trio sonatas* and to our ears the organ sounds very good indeed and, if there is a criticism of the sound, it is its relative lack of intimacy as recorded. Alain plays these Italianate works with considerable flair, and she is particularly appealing in slow movements. Just occasionally the running passages of the outer movements seem almost too mellifluous but for the most part these are fresh and highly enjoyable performances that do justice to this splendid old instrument.

Volume 14: *Adagio (& Allegro), BWV 1027; Chorale prelude, 'Ein feste Burg ist unser Gott', BWV 720; Fugue in G min., BWV 578; Passacaglia and fugue in C min., BWV 582; Preludes: in G, BWV 568; in A min., BWV 569; Prelude and fugue in G, BWV 541; Ricercare a 6, BWV 1079; 6 Schübler chorale preludes, BWV 645–50.*

(Y/B) (M) **(*) Erato/Warner Dig. 4509 96747-2 [id.]. Marie-Claire Alain (organ of Stiftskirche, Goslar).

The famous *Schübler chorales* are the highlight of Marie-Claire Alain's final volume. They are particularly imaginative and pleasing. The action of the Goslar organ is more audible than in some of this series, but that is hardly a problem. Alain takes the famous *Passacaglia in C minor* very spaciously, and here she miscalculates slightly, for she does not quite generate a high enough degree of tension to carry it at such a slow speed. The *Fugue in G minor* is a little didactic, too – although again very effectively registered. On the other hand, the *Prelude and fugue in G major* is a considerable success, and the *Prelude in G major* is also a fine performance.

Other organ music

33 Arnstadt chorale preludes (from Yale manuscript).
(B) *** HM Dig. HMA 1905158 [id.]. Joseph Payne (organ of St Paul's, Brookline, Mass.).

Joseph Payne collects the complete set together on a single CD and is very economically priced. Now reissued on Harmonia Mundi's budget Musique d'Abord label, this is even more attractive.

The Art of fugue, BWV 1080.
*** Erato/Warner Dig. 4509 91946-2 [id.]. Marie-Claire Alain (organ of Saint-Martin à Masevaux, Haut-Rhin).

Marie-Claire Alain has at Saint-Martin à Masevaux an almost ideal instrument for presenting *The Art of fugue*, with a clear focus and a wide range of effective colouring. The digital recording provides an excellent focus and her performance is admirable.

Chorale preludes Nos. 1–45 (Orgelbüchlein), BWV 599–644 (complete).
*** DG Dig. 431 816-2 [id.]. Simon Preston (organ of Sorø Abbey, Denmark).

Simon Preston conveniently gathers all 45 chorales of the *Orgelbüchlein* on to a single (74-minute) CD and plays them with persuasive musicianship on a fine Danish organ.

Concertos (for solo organ) *Nos. 1 in G* (after ERNST: *Concerto*); *2 in A min.* (after VIVALDI: *Concerto, Op. 3/8*); *3 in C* (after VIVALDI: *Concerto, Op. 7/11*); *4 in C* (after ERNST: *Concerto*); *5 in D min.* (after VIVALDI: *Concerto, Op. 3/11*), *BWV 592–6.*
*** DG Dig. 423 087-2 [id.]. Simon Preston (organ of Lübeck Cathedral).

It was Prince Johann Ernst who introduced Bach to the Italian string concertos; these are Bach's arrangements, with the music for the most part left with little alteration or embellishment. The two Ernst works show a lively and inventive if not original musicianship. The performances are first class and the recording admirably lucid and clear, yet with an attractively resonant ambience.

6 Trio sonatas, BWV 525–30 (see also arrangements under Chamber Music – above).
(N) (M) **(*) DG Dig. 447 277-2 [id.]. Ton Koopman (organ of Waalse Kerk, Amsterdam).

Ton Koopman's set comes from 1982 and is very well recorded on a highly suitable Dutch organ. The opening of the very first sonata promises well, with a buoyant rhythmic lift; the central *Adagio* is nicely coloured and the finale spirited. The *Adagio e dolce* of *No. 3 in D minor* again shows an apt choice of colouring, but the finale (marked *Vivace*) tends to jog along and the similarly indicated opening movement of *No. 6* is also relaxed. Other versions of these works are that bit more spirited but not more glowing, and this is certainly enjoyable.

Organ recitals

Allabreve in D, BWV 589; Canzona in D min., BWV 588; Fantasie in G, BWV 572; Passacaglia and fugue in C min., BWV 582; Pastorale in F, BWV 590; Prelude in A min., BWV 569; Toccata and fugue in D min., BWV 565; Toccata and fugue in D min. (Dorian), BWV 538.
(N) (M) **(*) DG Dig. 447 292-2 [id.]. Ton Koopman (organ of Maassluis Grote Kerk).

This recital comes into competition with an earlier bargain recital (see below) which duplicates four items here. Choice between the two programmes will be a matter of taste; this one has the advantage of placing the two *D minor Toccatas and fugues* side by side, although the layout is less than ideally planned, with the *Allabreve* coming immediately after the sombre *Canzona.*

Allabreve in D, BWV 589; Chorale prelude: Ach Gott und Herr, BWV 714; Preludes and fugues, BWV 532 and BWV 553–60; Toccata and fugue in D min., BWV 565.
*** Mer. ECD 84081 [id.]. David Sanger (organ of St Catharine's College, Cambridge).

The organ at St Catharine's College, Cambridge, was completely rebuilt in 1978–9. The result is a great success, and its reedy clarity and brightness of timbre are especially suitable for Bach. David Sanger's playing throughout is thoughtful and well structured; registration shows an excellent sense of colour without being flamboyant.

Canzona in D min., BWV 588; Fantasie in G, BWV 572; Passacaglia and fugue in C min., BWV 582; 6 Schübler chorales, BWV 645–50; Toccatas and fugues in F, BWV 540; in D min., BWV 565.
(Y/B) (B) **(*) DG Dig. 439 477-2 [id.]. Ton Koopman (various organs).

Ton Koopman uses two different organs here, principally that of the Grote Kerk, Maassluis, but the *Schübler chorales* are recorded on the Waalse Kerk, Amsterdam, whose reeds are brightly and colourfully projected. The recital opens with the famous *Toccata and fugue in D minor*, BWV 565, and this performance has an engaging eccentricity in that Koopman introduces decoration into the opening flourishes. The performance has an excitingly paced fugue and is superbly recorded. Contrast is provided by the *Canzona in D minor*, a slow and rather solemn contrapuntal exercise. Overall the performances are well structured and alive, if sometimes rather considered in feeling. The recital ends with the mighty *Passacaglia and fugue in C minor*, BWV 582.

Chorale partita on Sei gegrüsset, Jesu gütig, BWV 768; Prelude and fugue in D, BWV 532; Prelude in G, BWV 568; Sonata No. 4 in E min., BWV 528.
*** Denon Dig. C37 7376 [id.]. Jacques Van Oortmerssen (organ of Waalse Kerk, Amsterdam).

The organ of the Waalse Kerk is a magnificent instrument. The playing here, always alive, is traditional in the best sense, and the CD recording is superbly realistic. A most rewarding recital.

Chorale preludes: Erbarm' dich mein, O Herre Gott, BWV 721; Herzlich tut mich verlangen, BWV 727; O Mensch, bewein' dein' Sünde gross, BWV 622; Wir gläuben all an einen Gott, BWV 680; Fugue in B min. on a theme of Corelli, BWV 579; Passacaglia and fugue in C min., BWV 582; Pastorale in F, BWV 590; Toccata and fugue in D min., BWV 565.
(N) (M) *** EMI Dig. CD-EMX 2218; *TC-EMX 2218*. Peter Hurford (organ of Martinikerk, Groningen, Holland).

Having left his complete Decca Bach series long behind him, Peter Hurford here sets off on his travels again to record a familiar programme on a remarkably fine Groningen organ. This new recital whets the appetite for more. Perhaps the most famous *Toccata and fugue* is a fraction less flamboyant than before, and several of the chorale preludes are very relaxed and thoughtful. The *Pastorale*, too, is fairly static. But in the closing *Passacaglia and fugue* he demonstrates how he can hold and build tension when setting off at a very measured pace. What a masterpiece this is! The EMI engineers do him proud.

Chorale preludes: Herzlich tut mich verlangen, BWV 727; In dulci jubilo, BWV 729; Liebster Jesu, wir sind hier, BWV 730; Nun freut euch, lieben Christen g'mein, BWV 734; Nun komm, der Heiden Heiland, BWV 659; Wachet auf, ruft uns die Stimme, BWV 645; Wo soll ich fliehen hin, BWV 694; Fantasias: in C min., BWV 562; in G, BWV 572; Fantasia and fugues: in C min., BWV 537; in G min., BWV 542; Passacaglia and fugue in C min., BWV 582; Preludes and fugues: in A min., BWV 543; in D, BWV 532; in E flat (St Anne), BWV 552; Toccata, Adagio and fugue in C, BWV 564; Toccatas and fugues in D min. (Dorian), BWV 538; BWV 565.
(Y/B) (B) *** Decca Duo 443 485-2 (2) [id.]. Peter Hurford (organs of Ratzeburg Cathedral; Knox Grammar School, Sydney, Chapel; Church of Our Lady of Sorrows, Toronto; New College, Oxford, Chapel; All Souls' Unitarian Church, Washington, DC).

A generous 146-minute collection of major Bach organ works, taken from Peter Hurford's complete survey (see above), brings two separate recitals, each framed by major concert pieces, with the beautifully played chorales used in between the large-scale pieces to add contrast. The current bright transfers seem to have added an extra sharpness of outline to the sound of some of the big set pieces, but this is something which will be more noticeable on some reproducers than on others, and the various organs are caught with fine realism and plenty of depth.

Chorale preludes: Herzlich tut mich verlangen, BWV 727; In dulci jubilo, BWV 729; Liebster Jesu, wir sind hier, BWV 730; Wachet auf, BWV 645; Fantasia and fugue in G min., BWV 542; Passacaglia and fugue in C min., BWV 582; Prelude and fugue in E flat (St Anne), BWV 552; Toccata, Adagio and fugue in C, BWV 564; Toccata and fugue in D min., BWV 565.
(N) (M) *** Decca 444 569-2 [id.]. Peter Hurford (organs of Knox Grammar School, Sydney; Church of Our Lady of Sorrows, Toronto; New College, Oxford; Ratzeburg Cathedral).

Bach organ recitals do not come any better than this – Volume III in Decca's 'Organ Masterpieces series' – and none is better planned or more effective in its choice of instruments. The recital opens with the justly famous *D minor Toccata and fugue*, BWV 565 (Ratzeburg), and ends with the massive '*St Anne' Prelude and fugue* (New College, Oxford). These are used as an outer frame for three *Chorale preludes*, including a splendid version of the famous Schübler *Wachet auf* (Knox Grammar School), which in turn are separated by the other three major pieces, all among Bach's very finest organ works and sounding marvellous on the Toronto organ. Hurford's pacing and control of tension are masterly, his registration is unerringly apt, and he is superbly recorded. The programme timing is 78 minutes 30 seconds.

Fantasia in C min., B W V 562; Fantasia in G, B W V 572; Preludes and fugues: in A min., B W V 543; in D, B W V 532; Toccata, adagio and fugue in C, B W V 564. Toccatas and fugues: in D min. (Dorian), B W V 538; in D min., B W V 565.
(M) *** Decca 436 225-2 [id.]. Peter Hurford (organs of Church of Our Lady of Sorrows, Toronto; Chapel of New College, Oxford; Ratzeburg Cathedral, Germany).

Another splendid recital culled from Peter Hurford's integral Bach recordings, made in the late 1970s, and, even though it duplicates the ubiquitous B W V 565, the 75-minute programme is highly recommendable for its colour, power and rhythmic felicity, which so often brings a sense almost of fantasy. The vividly projected sound is always excellent and usually on a demonstration level; there is just a hint of harshness at the opening of the *D major Prelude*.

Fantasia and fugue in G min., B W V 542; Passacaglia and fugue in C min., B W V 582; 6 Schübler chorales, B W V 645–50; Toccata, adagio and fugue in C, B W V 564; Toccata and fugue in F, B W V 540.
⊛ *** DG Dig. 435 381-2 [id.]. Simon Preston (Sauer organ in St Peter's, Waltrop, near Dortmund).

Simon Preston's recital at St Peter's, Waltrop, is a magnificent demonstration of the splendour and power of Bach's more ambitious organ statements, admirably contrasted with music which is inherently less weighty, if not less inspired. The engaging *Schübler chorales* are used to provide contrast at the centre of the 71-minute recital, and Preston chooses a lighter, more pointed style than usual. The Sauer organ in Waltrop is a modern instrument (1984) of splendid range, with a diversity of colour that is ideal for baroque repertoire and Bach in particular. There is an enormous reserve of power in the pedals, and the richer sonorities elsewhere bring no attendant clouding. This is one of the very finest Bach collections of the digital C D era.

Organ and vocal chorales combined

18 Leipzig chorale preludes, with chorales, B W V 651–68; 6 Schübler chorale preludes with chorales, B W V 645–50.
(N) *** Teldec/Warner Dig. 4509 94459-2 (2) [id.]. Ton Koopman (Müller organ of Grote Kerk, Leeuwarden).

Ton Koopman is beginning a new, complete survey of Bach's organ music for Teldec which we hope to cover in full in our next volume. As an auspicious start (like Peter Hurford before him), he has had the happy and useful idea of presenting two major sets of organ chorale preludes together with the vocal chorales on which they are based. These chorales are sung simply and very beautifully by the Amsterdam Baroque Choir, and the appropriate organ work follows. In the case of the famous *Schübler* set, with which he begins, there are (in all but *Kommst du nun, Jesu, vom Himmel herunter,* B W V 650) two different vocal chorales for each of the organ pieces, which here are played as concert pieces. The *Leipzig chorales* are played and registered very simply, so that the organ variants still carry the (usually) serene character of each hymn-like vocal setting. Both organ and choir are recorded most naturally.

Kevin Bowyer Nimbus recordings
Volume 7: *Orgelbüchlein: Chorales and chorale preludes Nos. 1–46, B W V 599–644.*
(N) **(*) Nimbus Dig. NI 5457/8 [id.]. Kevin Bowyer (organ of Sct Hans Kirke, Odense, Denmark); Fynske Chamber Ch., Alice Joensen.

This Nimbus set presents each organ chorale prelude immediately preceded by the sung chorale, and while that is an admirable plan its drawback is that there are no separate cues on the pair of CDs for each organ entry, and this is not even indicated by the overall times for each piece in the back-up documentation. The Danish choir sing admirably, but the choral focus is not as uniformly smooth as with the Amsterdam group on Koopman's set of the *Leipzig* and *Schübler chorales*.

Comparing Kevin Bowyer's performances of the *Orgelbüchlein* directly with Christopher Herrick's versions (which in general we find more satisfying) reveals an astonishing difference of sound and characterization. The Danish organ has much more plangent reeds and Bowyer's performances are less warmly mellifluous, more dramatic. This usually works very well, and often (as with *In dulci jubilo*) the effect is piquant, but at times the characterization seems almost too bold. Of course the Odense organ is a splendid instrument, and those who like a lively presentation will find this set very much to their taste, for Bowyer's tempi are usually brisker than Herrick's. He is recorded very vividly. The set runs to a pair of discs, with the second playing for only 47 minutes.

VOCAL MUSIC

Cantatas Nos. 1–14; 16–52; 54–69; 69a; 70–117; 119–140; 143–159; 161–188; 192; 194–199 (complete). (Y/B) (B) *** Teldec/Warner Analogue/Dig. 4509 91765-2 (60) [id.]. Treble Soloists from V. Boys' & Regensburg Choirs, Esswood, Equiluz, Van Altena, Van Egmond, Hampson, Nimsgern, Van der Meer, Jacobs, Iconomou, Holl, Immler, King's College, Cambridge, Ch., V. Boys' Ch., Tölz Boys' Ch., Ch. Viennensis, Ghent Coll. Vocale, VCM, Harnoncourt; Leonhardt Cons., Leonhardt.

Cantatas Nos. (i) *1: Wie schön leuchtet uns der Morgenstern; 2: Ach Gott, vom Himmel; 3: Ach Gott, wie manches Herzeleid; 4: Christ lag in Todesbanden; 5: Wo soll ich fliehen hin; 6: Bleib bei uns;* (ii) *7: Christ unser Herr zum Jordan kam; 8: Liebster Gott; 9: Es ist das Heil; 10: Meine Seele erhebt den Herrn;* (i) *11: Lobet Gott in seinen Reichen;* (ii) *12: Weinen, klagen, sorgen, zagen; 13: Meine Seufzer, meine Tränen; 14: Wär Gott nicht mit uns diese Zeit; 16: Herr Gott, dich loben wir;* (i) *17: Wer Dank opfert, der preiset mich; 18: Gleichwie der Regen und Schnee vom Himmel; 19: Es erhub sich ein Streit.*
(M) *** Teldec/Warner 4509 91755-2 (6) [id.]. Esswood, Equiluz, Van Altena, Van Egmond, treble soloists; (i) V. Boys' Ch., Ch. Viennensis, VCM, Harnoncourt; (ii) Tölz Boys' Ch., King's College Ch., Leonhardt Cons., Leonhardt.

Cantatas Nos. (i) *20: O Ewigkeit, du Donnerwort; 21: Ich hatte viel Bekümmernis;* (ii) *22: Jesus nahm zu sich die Zwölfe; 23: Du wahrer Gott und Davids Sohn;* (i) *24: Ein ungefärbt Gemüte; 25: Es ist nicht Gesundes an meinem Leibe; 26: Ach wie flüchtig, ach wie nichtig; 27: Wer weiss, wie nahe mir mein Ende!; 28: Gottlob! nun geht das Jahr zu Ende; 29: Wir danken dir, Gott; 30: Freue dich, erlöste Schar; 31: Der Himmel lacht! die Erde jubilieret;* (ii) *32: Liebster Jesu, mein Verlangen; 33: Allein zu dir, Herr Jesu Christ;* (i) *34: O ewiges Feuer, O Ursprung der Liebe; 35: Geist und Seele wird verwirret; 36: Schwingt freudig euch empor.*
(M) *** Teldec/Warner 4509 91756-2 (6) [id.].
Esswood, Jacobs, Van Altena, Equiluz, Van Egmond, Van der Meer, Nimsgern, Wyatt, (i) V. Boys' Ch., Ch. Viennensis, VCM, Harnoncourt; (ii) Hanover Boys' Ch., King's College Ch., Leonhardt Cons., Leonhardt.

Cantatas Nos. (i) *37: Wer da gläubet und getauft wird; 38: Aus tiefer Not schrei ich zu dir; 39: Brich dem Hungrigen dein Brot; 40: Dazu ist erschienen der Sohn Gottes;* (i) *41: Jesu, nun sei gepreiset; 42: Am Abend aber desselbigen Sabbats; 43: Gott fähret auf mit Jauchzen; 44: Sie werden euch in die Bann tun;* (ii) *45: Es ist dir gesagt, Mensch, was gut ist; 46: Schauet doch und sehet;* (i) *47: Wer sich selbst erhöhet; 48: Ich elender Mensch, wer wird mich erlösen; 49: Ich geh' und suche mit Verlangen; 50: Nun ist das Heil und die Kraft;* (ii) *51: Jauchzet Gott in allen Landen; 52: Falsche Welt, dir trau ihr nicht; 54: Widerstehe doch der Sünde; 55: Ich armer Mensch, ich Sündenknecht; 56: Ich will den Kreuzstab gerne tragen;* (i) *57: Selig ist der Mann; 58: Ach Gott, wie manches Herzeleid; 59: Wer mich liebet, der wird mein Wort halten; 60: O Ewigkeit, du Donnerwort.*
(M) *** Teldec/Warner 4509 91757-2 (6) [id.]. Kweksilber, Jelosits, Esswood, Jacobs, Van Altena, Equiluz, Van Egmond, Van der Meer, Kunz, Schopper, (i) V. Boys' Ch., Tölz Boys' Ch., Ch. Viennensis, VCM, Harnoncourt; (ii) Hanover Boys' Ch., Leonhardt Cons., Leonhardt.

Cantatas Nos. (i) *61: Nun komm, der Heiden Heiland; 62: Nun komm, der Heiden Heiland; 63: Christen, ätzet diesen Tag; 64: Sehet, welch eine Liebe; 65: Sie werden aus Saba alle kommen;* (ii) *66: Erfreut euch, ihr Herzen; 67: Halt im Gedächtnis Jesum Christ;* (i) *68: Also hat Gott die Welt geliebt; 69 & 69a: Lobe den Herrn, meine Seeele; 70: Wachet! betet! betet! wachet!; 71: Gott ist mein König; 72: Alles nur nach Gottes Willen* (ii) *73: Herr, wie du willt, so schicks mit mir; 74: Wer mich liebet, der wird mein Wort halten; 75: Die Elenden sollen essen;* (i) *76: Die Himmel erzählen die Ehre Gottes;* (ii) *77: Du sollt Gott, deinen Herren, lieben; 78: Jesu, der du meine Seele.*
(M) **(*) Teldec/Warner 4509 91758-2 (6) [id.]. Esswood, Equiluz, Kraus, Van Egmond, Van der Meer, Visser, (i) Tölz Boys' Ch., VCM, Harnoncourt; (ii) Hanover Boys' Ch., Ghent Coll. Vocale, Leonhardt Cons., Leonhardt.

Cantatas Nos. (ii) *79: Gott der Herr ist Sonn' und Schild;* (i) *80: Ein feste Burg; 81: Jesus schläft, was soll ich hoffen?; 82: Ich habe genug; 83: Erfreute Zeit im neuen Bunde; 84: Ich bin vergnügt mit meinem Glücke; 85: Ich bin ein guter Hirt; 86: Wahrlich, wahrlich, ich sage euch; 87: Bisher habt ihr nichts gebeten;* (ii) *88: Siehe, ich will viel Fischer aussenden; 89: Was soll ich aus dir machen, Ephraim?; 90: Es reisset euch ein schrecklich Ende; 91: Gelobet seist du, Jesus Christ; 92: Ich habe in Gottes Herz und Sinn;* (i) *93: Wer nur den lieben Gott lässt walten; 94: Was frag' ich nach der Welt; 95: Christus, der ist mein Leben; 96:*

Herr Christ, der ein'ge Gottes-Sohn; 97: In allen meinen Taten; (ii) *98: Was Gott tut, das ist wohlgetan; 99: Was Gott tut, das ist wohlgetan.*

(M) **(*) Teldec/Warner 4509 91759-2 (6) [id.].

Esswood, Equiluz, Van Egmond, Huttenlocher, Van der Meer, (i) Tölz Boys' Ch., V. Boys' Ch., Ch. Viennensis, VCM, Harnoncourt; (ii) Hanover Boys' Ch., Ghent Coll. Vocale, Leonhardt Cons., Leonhardt.

Cantatas Nos. (ii) *100: Was Gott tut, das ist wohlgetan;* (i) *101: Nimm von uns, Herr, du treuer Gott; 102: Herr, deine Augen sehen nach dem Glauben;* (ii) *103: Ihr werdet weinen und heulen;* (i) *104: Du Hirte Israel, höre; 105: Herr, gehe nicht ins Gericht;* (ii) *106: Gottes Zeit ist die allerbeste Zeit (Actus tragicus); 107: Wass willst du dich betrüben;* (i) *108: Es ist euch gut, dass ich hingehe; 109: Ich glaube, lieber Herr, hilf meinem Unglauben!; 110: Unser Mund sei voll Lachens; 111: Was mein Gott will, das g'scheh allzeit; 112: Der Herr ist mein getreuer Hirt;* (ii) *113: Herr Jesu Christ, du höchstes Gut; 114: Ach, lieben Christen, seid getrost;* (i) *115: Mache dich, mein Geist, bereit; 116: Du Friedefürst, Herr Jesu Christ;* (ii) *117: Sei Lob und Ehr dem höchsten Gut.*

(M) *** Teldec/Warner 4509 91760-2 (6) [id.]. Esswood, Jacobs, Van Altena, Equiluz, Van Egmond, Huttenlocher, Lorenz, Van der Meer, (i) Tölz Boys' Ch., VCM, Harnoncourt; (ii) Hanover Boys' Ch., Ghent Coll. Vocale, Leonhardt Cons., Leonhardt.

Cantatas Nos. (i) *119: Preise, Jerusalem, den Herrn; 120: Gott, mann lobet dich in der Stille; 121: Christum wir sollen loben; 122: Das neugebor'ne Kindelein; 123: Liebster Immanuel, Herzog der Frommen; 124: Meinen Jesum lass ich nicht; 125: Mit Fried und Freud ich fahr dahin; 126: Erhalt uns, Herr, bei deinem Wort;* (ii) *127: Herr Jesu Christ wahr' Mensch und Gott; 128: Auf Christi Himmelfahrt allein; 129: Gelobet sei der Herr, mein Gott;* (i) *130: Herr Gott, dich loben alle wir; 131: Aus der Tiefen rufe ich, Herr, zu dir;* (ii) *132: Bereitet die Wege, bereitet die Bahn; 133: Ich freue mich in dir; 134: Ein Herz, das seinen Jesum lebend weiss; 135: Ach Herr, mich armen Sünder;* (i) *136: Erforsche mich, Gott, und erfahre mein Herz; 137: Lobe den Herren, den mächtigen König der Ehren.*

(M) **(*) Teldec/Warner 4509 91761-2 (6) [id.]. Esswood, Jacobs, Van Altena, Equiluz, Van Egmond, Hartinger, Heldwein, Holl, Huttenlocher, Thomaschke, (i) Tölz Boys' Ch., VCM, Harnoncourt; (ii) Hanover Boys' Ch., Ghent Coll. Vocale, Leonhardt Cons., Leonhardt.

Cantatas Nos. (i) *138: Warum betrübst du dich, mein Herz?; 139: Wohl dem, der sich auf seinen Gott; 140: Wachet auf, ruft uns die Stimme;* (ii) *143: Lobe den Herrn, meine Seele; 144: Nimm, was dein ist, und gehe hin;* (i) *145: Ich lebe, mein Herze, zu deinem Ergötzen; 146: Wir müssen durch viel Trübsal; 147: Herz und Mund und Tat und Leben; 148: Bringet dem Herrn Ehre seines Namens;* (ii) *149: Man singet mit Freuden vom Sieg; 150: Nach dir, Herr, verlanget mich; 151: Süsser Trost, mein Jesus kömmt;* (i) *152: Tritt auf die Glaubensahn; 153: Schau, lieber Gott, wie meine Feind; 154: Mein liebster Jesus ist verloren; 155: Mein Gott, wie lang, ach lange; 156: Ich steh' mit einem Fuss im Grabe* (ii) *157: Ich lasse dich nicht, du segnest mich denn; 158: Der Friede sei mit dir; 159: Sehet, wir gehn hinauf gen Jerusalem;* (i) *161: Komm, du süsse Todesstunde; 162: Ach! ich sehe, jetzt, da ich zur Hochzeit gehe.*

(M) **(*) Teldec/Warner Analogue/Dig. 4509 91762-2 (6) [id.]. Esswood, Equiluz, Van Egmond, Hampson, Holl, (i) Tölz Boys' Ch., VCM, Harnoncourt; (ii) Hanover Boys' Ch., Ghent Coll. Vocale, Leonhardt Cons., Leonhardt.

Cantatas Nos. (i) *163: Nur jedem das Seine;* (ii) *164: Ihr, die ihr euch von Christo nennet; 165: O heil'ges Geist und Wasserbad; 166: Wo gehest du hin?;* (i) *167: Ihr Menschen, rühmet Gottes Liebe; 168: Tue, Rechnung! Donnerwort; 169: Gott soll allein mein Herze haben;* (ii) *170: Vergnügte Ruh', beliebte Seelenlust;* (i) *171: Gott, wie dein Name, so ist auch dein Ruhm;* (ii) *172: Erschallet, ihr Lieder;* (i) *173: Erhöhtes Fleisch und Blut; 174: Ich liebe den Höchsten von ganzem Gemüte;* (ii) *175: Er rufet seinen Schafen mit Namen; 176: Es ist ein trotzig und verzagt Ding;* (i) *177: Ich ruf zu dir, Herr Jesu Christ; 178: Wo Gott der Herr nicht bei uns hält; 179: Siehe zu, dass deine Gottesfurcht.* (ii) *180: Schmücke dich, O liebe Seele; 181: Leichtgesinnte Flattergeister;* (i) *182: Himmelskönig, sei willkommen.*

(M) **(*) Teldec/Warner Dig. 4509 91763-2 (6) [id.]. Esswood, Equiluz, Van Altena, Van Egmond, Holl, (i) Tölz Boys' Ch., VCM, Harnoncourt; (ii) Hanover Boys' Ch., Ghent Coll. Vocale, Leonhardt Cons., Leonhardt.

Cantatas Nos. (i) *183: Sie werden euch in den Bann tun;* (ii) *184: Erwünschtes Freudenlicht;* (i) *185: Barmherziges Herze der ewigen Liebe; 186: Argre dich, O Seele, nicht;* (ii) *187: Es wartet alles auf dich;* (i) *188: Ich habe meine Zuversicht; 192: Nun danket alle Gott; 194: Höchsterwünschtes Freudenfest;* (ii) *195: Dem Gerechten muss das Licht immer wieder aufgehen;* (i) *196: Der Herr denket an uns;* (ii) *197: Gott ist unsrer Zuversicht; 198: Lass, Fürstin, lass noch einen Strahl;* (i) *199: Mein Herze schwimmt im Blut.*

(M) **(*) Teldec/Warner Dig. 4509 91764-2 (6) [id.]. Bonney, Esswood, Jacobs, Elwes, Equiluz, Van

Egmond, Hampson, Holl, Van der Kamp, (i) Tölz Boys' Ch., VCM, Harnoncourt; (ii) Hanover
Boys' Ch., Ghent Coll. Vocale, Leonhardt Cons., Leonhardt.

The remarkable Teldec project, a recording of all Bach's church cantatas begun in the 1970s, has
reached completion. These were originally offered in 45 volumes, each usually combining two CDs at
upper-mid-price. Now the whole series has been repackaged and is offered in two alternative choices: as
a 60-CD box (with more music on each disc) at bargain price or as a series of ten separate collections,
each of six CDs, at mid-price.

The recordings got off to a very good start but, later in the project, various flaws of intonation, and
sometimes a feeling that the ensemble would have benefited from more rehearsal, plus occasionally
sluggish direction, slightly undermined the overall excellence. However, the authentic character of the
performances is in no doubt. Boys replace women not only in the choruses but also as soloists (which
brings occasional minor lapses of security), and the size of the forces is confined to what we know Bach
himself would have expected. The simplicity of the approach brings its own merits, for the imperfect yet
otherworldly quality of some of the treble soloists refreshingly focuses the listener's attention on the
music itself. Less appealing is the quality of the violins, which eschew vibrato and, it would sometimes
seem, any kind of timbre! Generally speaking, there is a certain want of rhythmic freedom and some
expressive caution. Rhythmic accents are underlined with some regularity and the grandeur of Bach's
inspiration is at times lost to view. Nevertheless, overall this is an astonishing achievement, and there is
much glorious music here which, to do justice to Harnoncourt and Leonhardt, usually emerges freshly
to give the listener much musical nourishment. The CD transfers of the earlier analogue recordings are
first class. There is no background noise to speak of and the sound is clarified and refined to bring
striking presence to voices and accompaniment. The acoustic is usually not too dry – and not too
ecclesiastical, either – and the projection is realistic. The later digital recordings are altogether excellent,
and this is an infinitely rewarding series.

Cantatas (for Easter): Nos. 1: Wie schön leuchtet der Morgenstern; 4: Christ lag in Todesbanden; 6: Bleib
bei uns, denn es will Abend werden; 12: Weinen, Klagen, Sorgen, Zagen; 23: Du wahrer Gott und Davids
Sohn; 67: Halt im Gedächtnis Jesum Christ; 87: Bisher habt ihr nichts gebeten in meinem Namen; 92: Ich
habe in Gottes Herz und Sinn; 104: Du Hirte Israel, höre; 108: Es ist euch gut, dass ich hingehe; 126:
Erhalt uns, Herr, bei deinem Wort; 158: Der Friede sei mit dir; 182: Himmelskönig, wei willkommen.
(B) ** DG 439 374-2 (5) [id.]. Edith Mathis, Anna Reynolds, Hertha Töpper, Peter Schreier, Ernst
Haefliger, Dietrich Fischer-Dieskau, Theo Adam, Munich Bach Ch. & O, Karl Richter.

DG's Archiv label have offered a major reissue from Karl Richter's series of Bach's cantata recordings,
made over the years. Thanks to Richter, we had the most comprehensive survey of Bach cantatas ever to
be put on record before the ambitious Harnoncourt/Leonhardt venture got into its stride. The present
reissues are grouped into five bargain boxes, the first three centring on the three key celebrations of the
Church year and Volumes 4 and 5 covering the middle and later Sundays after Trinity. The set of
thirteen cantatas in Volume 2 are all linked by the theme of Easter and the Passion. The performances
are variable, some being impressive and spacious, others less sensitive. There is not space here to detail
every performance; suffice to say that readers wanting a more vigorous and full-blooded approach to
this repertoire than Harnoncourt's and Leonhardt's will find this a welcome offering, particularly as
solos are reliable, as indeed is the fine obbligato playing. The digitally remastered transfers sound very
good indeed, and collectors need have no worries on that score. Richter, of course, was heavy-handed at
times, but he often brought a weight and dignity to this music that are sometimes missing in the more
authentic versions.

Complete cantatas, Volume I: Cantatas Nos. 4: Christ lag in Todes Banden; 21: Ich hatte viel
Bekümmernis (with Appendix: Chorus: Sie nun wieder zufrieden); 31: Der Himmel lacht! die Erde jubi-
lieret; 71: Gott ist mein König; 106: Gottes Zeit ist die allerbeste Zeit (Actus tragicus); 131: Aus der
Tiefen rufe ich, Herr, zu dir; 150: Nach dir, Herr, verlanget mich; 185: Barmherziges Herze der ewigen
Liebe; 196: Der Herr denket an uns (Wedding cantata).
(N) *** Erato/Warner Dig. 4509 98536-2 (3) [id.]. Barbara Schlick, Kai Wessel, Guy de Mey, Klaus
Mertens, Amsterdam Bar. Ch. & O, Ton Koopman.

Volume II: Cantatas Nos. 12: Weinen, Klagen, Sorgen, Zagen; 18: Gleichwie der Regen und Schnee vom
Himmel fällt (with Appendix); 61: Nun komm, der Heiden Heiland; 132: Bereitet die Wege, bereitet die
Bahn; 152: Tritt auf die Glaubensbahn; 172: Erschallet, ihr Lieder; 182: Himmelskönig, sei willkommen
(with Appendix); 199: Mein Herze schwimmt im Blut; 203: Amore traditore. Quodlibet, BWV 524.
(N) *** Erato/Warner Dig. 0630 12598-2 (3) [id.]. Schlick, Wessel; Christoph Prégardien, Mertens,
Amsterdam Bar. Ch. & O, Koopman.

Ton Koopman has now embarked on a complete cycle which looks set to challenge the famous Leonhardt–Harnoncourt survey on Teldec. They differ in some important respects and readers will have to decide for themselves how these various factors weigh in their own balance-sheet. First, Koopman favours the Rifkin approach to choruses – namely one voice to a part – which may not worry some collectors as much as it will depress others! It seems to the present writer to rob this repertory of some of the sheer majesty and breadth. Second, unlike Leonhardt–Harnoncourt, Koopman opts for female soloists rather than boys, as would have been the case in Bach's day, and he favours mixed rather than solely male choirs. For many this will be a plus point – and it is good news for fans of Barbara Schlick who is pretty well everywhere. Thirdly, and again unlike Leonhardt–Harnoncourt, he goes for a higher than normal pitch – a semitone above present-day pitch which, as Christoph Wolff's notes point out, is what Bach used in Mühlhausen and Weimar, brightening the sonority quite a lot. (Readers with absolute pitch will have to stick to modern performances.) The singing in virtually all the cantatas is pretty impressive and the instrumental playing is of a high order of accomplishment, more finished than is often the case in the Teldec set. Those who set store by security of intonation and excellence of ensemble will probably prefer this new survey to the earlier set. Moreover Koopman offers the collector variants and alternative versions, which will again be an undoubted plus.

Cantatas Nos. 4: Christ lag in Todesbanden; 131: Aus der Tiefen rufe ich, Herr, zu dir.
(N) (M) **(*) Erato/Warner 4509 99614-2 [id.]. Kendall, Varcoe, Monteverdi Ch., E. Bar. Soloists, Gardiner.

These recordings, using original instruments and the style of squeezed phrasing associated with 'authenticity' in that period, first appeared in LP form in the early 1980s, linked with other cantatas and the *Motets*, which are all now included in the second volume of the Gardiner Collection at bargain price, together with his outstanding set of the four *Orchestral Suites* (see below under Collections: Vocal Recitals). However, the present disc is also available separately at mid-price. This account of one of the best-loved of all the cantatas, *Christ lag in Todesbanden*, is expressively rich, yet Gardiner's lively tempi ensure plenty of life in the music-making. Smooth, natural transfers, though the disc's timing (44 minutes) is not generous.

Cantatas Nos. 4: Christ lag in Todes Banden; 150: Nach dir, Herr, verlanget mich; 196: Der Herr denket an uns.
(N) *** BIS Dig. CD 751 [id.]. Kuriso, Tachikawa, Katano, Kooy, Japan Bach Coll., Masaaki Suzuki.

Although by now we are used to first-class Japanese orchestras and soloists, who could have possibly suspected that we should be embarking on a Bach cantata complete series on period instruments from Japanese singers and players – and recorded by a Swedish record company! The organist and harpsichordist, Masaaki Suzuki, comes from Kobe; after his studies in Tokyo, he went to the Sweelinck Conservatoire in Amsterdam, where he became a pupil of Ton Koopman. Since 1990 he has directed the Bach Collegium Japan and teaches at the Tokyo National University and Fine Arts and Music, from which many of the soloists are drawn. The only European soloist is Peter Kooy, also from the Sweelinck Conservatory. Like Koopman, Suzuki uses a higher pitch (A = 465) with its concomitant brighter sound, and he also favours female voices. This naturally places an additional hurdle before the soprano, Yumiko Kuriso, which she surmounts with conspicuous distinction. In some ways one wonders whether the results of the pupil do not outstrip those of the master, for these performances radiate more joy in music-making and give more consistent pleasure than many European ones. The strings are clean, and the sense of inhibition, of excessive awareness of the constraints of period performance that occasionally mar the Harnoncourt–Leonhardt set, is refreshingly absent here. Knowing the problems European languages pose for the Japanese, their German diction is more than acceptable. If the remainder of the series is as enjoyable as this first instalment – and as well recorded – this is going to be an important contribution to the Bach discography. Recommended with enthusiasm.

Cantatas (for the latter part of the Church year) *Nos. 5: Wo soll ich fliehen hin; 26: Ach wie flüchtig, ach wie nichtig; 38: Aus tiefer Not schrei ich zu dir; 55: Ich armer Mensch, ich Sündenknecht; 56: Ich will den Kreuzstab gerne tragen; 60: O Ewigkeit, du Donnerwort; 70: Wachet! betet! betet! wachet!; 80: Ein feste Burg ist unser Gott; 96: Herr Christ, der ein'ge Gottessohn; 106: Gottes Zeit ist die allerbeste Zeit (Actus tragicus); 115: Mache dich, mein Geist, bereit; 116: Du Friedefürst, Herr Jesu Christ; 130: Herr Gott, dich loben alle wir; 139: Wohl dem, der sich auf seinen Gott; 140: Wachet auf, ruft uns die Stimme; 180: Schmücke dich, O liebe Seele.*
(BB) **(*) DG 439 394-2 (5) [id.]. Mathis, Buckel, Schmidt, Töpper, Schreier, Haefliger, Fischer-Dieskau, Adam, Engen, Munich Bach Ch. & O, Karl Richter.

This fifth Richter box collects cantatas that Bach composed for the last ten Sundays of Trinity, plus three others, a Reformation Festival piece (No. 80), a cantata for St Michael's Day (No. 130) and Bach's funeral cantata, *Gottes Zeit* – the so-called *Actus tragicus* (No. 106); it is given a first-rate performance, with fine solo singing and committed direction. Most of these cantatas are chorale-based and nearly all emerge with the dignity and majesty one expects from these forces. They were all recorded in the Munich Herkulessaal, for the most part in 1978, and the sound is warm and spacious. Karl Richter's heavy tread seems over the years to have moderated into a more flexible and human gait, though a certain inflexibility and lack of imagination still surface occasionally.

Cantatas Nos. 6: Bleib bei uns, denn es will Abend werden; 31: Der Himmel lacht! die Erde jubilieret; 67, Halt im Gedächtnis Jesum Christ; 76: Die Himmel erzählen die Ehre Gottes; 80: Ein feste Burg ist unser Gott; 87: Bisher habt ihr nichts gebeten.
(N) (M) *** Erato/Warner 4509 98525-2 (2) [id.]. Reichelt, Giebel, Hellman, Töpper, Hoffgen, Krebs, Kelch, Wenk, Heilbronn Schütz Ch. & Instrumental Ens.; Pforzheim Chamber O, Fritz Werner.

Cantatas Nos. 8: Liebster Gott, wann werd' ich sterben?; 26: Ach wie flüchtig, ach wie nichtig; 43, Gott fähret auf mit Jauchzen; 61: Nun komm, der Heiden Heiland; 85, Ich bin ein guter Hirt; 130: Herr Gott, dich loben alle wir; 182: Himmelskönig, sei willkommen.
(N) (M) *** Erato/Warner 4509 97407-2 (2) [id.]. Sailer, Reichelt, Hellman, Töpper, Krebs, Wenk, Stämpfli, Kelch, Heilbronn Schütz Ch. & Instrumental Ens.; Pforzheim Chamber O, Fritz Werner.

Erato's sets collect various performances, conducted by Fritz Werner, made in the 1960s and early 1970s, before the period-performance bandwagon began to sweep all before it. When they first appeared on LP, they were rather overshadowed by Karl Richter's mammoth Archiv series, which has the advantage of more internationally celebrated soloists. However, in terms of natural musicianship Werner's versions are not only every bit as fine as the Richter but they have a warmth and sense of space that are very appealing. To start with, Werner rarely goes into overdrive as Richter was wont to do, and he certainly phrases with imagination. Richter possessed an undoubted feeling for Bach but he could be unyielding and Teutonic in his approach. At his best, Werner has greater humanity and vision, and in the above volumes Erato have collected most of his finest performances. Comparison of the inspired opening of *Liebster Gott, wann werd' ich sterben?*, BWV 8, is not to Richter's advantage. Collectors unseduced or unconvinced by the various authentic performances now on offer and looking for good modern instrument performances of the cantatas in decent recordings could do worse than go for these. Most of the singing is very fine and Werner has the gift of drawing the best from his choral and instrumental forces. As far as the recorded quality is concerned, it is far more than decent; in many instances it holds up well against 1990s' sound. While on the subject of 1960s' recordings of Bach cantatas, a plea for the reissue of Jürgen Jürgens's enchanting account of *Gottes Zeit ist die allerbeste Zeit*, BWV 106.

Cantatas (for the middle Sundays after Trinity) Nos. 8: Liebster Gott, wann werd'ich sterben?; 9: Es ist das Heil uns kommen her; 17: Wer Dank opfert, der preiset mich; 27: Wer weiss, wie nahe mir mein Ende!; 33: Allein zu dir, Herr Jesu Christ; 45: Es ist dir gesagt, Mensch, was gut ist; 51: Jauchzet Gott in allen Landen; 78: Jesu, der du meine Seele; 100: Was Gott tut, das ist wohlgetan; 102: Herr deine Augen sehen nach dem Glauben; 105: Herr, gehe nicht ins Gericht; 137: Lobe den Herren, den mächtigen König der Ehren; 148: Bringet dem Herrn Ehre seines Namens; 178: Wo Gott der Herr nicht bei uns hält; 179: Siehe zu, dass deine Gottesfurcht nicht Heuchelei sei; 187: Es wartet alles auf dich; 199: Mein Herz schwimmt im Blut.
(B) **(*) DG 439 387-2 (6) [id.]. Buckel, Mathis, Stader, Hamari, Töpper, Schreier, Haefliger, Van Kesteren, Fischer-Dieskau, Engen, Munich Bach Ch. & O, Karl Richter.

The fourth box in Richter's series runs to six CDs and offers the cantatas composed for the sixth Sunday after Trinity through to the seventeenth. Like the others, it continues the 'unauthentic' approach of Karl Richter and forms a welcome alternative to the Harnoncourt/Leonhardt venture. Again the spacious venue is the Munich Herkulessaal. The chorus is probably larger than it should be, but the results are invariably musical, and Richter shows greater flexibility and imagination than often has been the case. Just occasionally his heavy touch is felt, but so much of this set is first rate that reservations can be all but overruled. The soloists are thoroughly dependable.

Cantatas Nos. 8: Liebster Gott, wenn werd ich sterben; 99: Was Gott tut, das ist wohlgetan, BWV 99; 106: Gottes Zeit ist die allerbeste Zeit (Actus tragicus); 131: Aus der Tiefen rufe ich, Herr zu dir.
(Y/B) (M) *** O-L Dig. 444 166-2 [id.]. Monoyios, Baird, Rickards, Fast, Brownless, Kelley, Opalach, Bach Ens., Joshua Rifkin.

Rifkin's performances opt for the one-to-a-part principle not only in his instrumental ensemble but also as far as the choruses are concerned. He opts for female sopranos rather than boy trebles but uses adult male altos. Not all will find his solutions congenial and the use of one voice to a part in the chorales is not always convincing. But there is some good singing in this series, and the playing is lively enough. Even those for whom the avoidance of vocal vibrato seems an unnatural constraint may find themselves persuaded. One feels the need for greater weight and a more full-blooded approach at times, but this is outweighed by the sensitivity and intelligence that inform these excellently balanced recordings.

Cantatas (for Ascension Day; Whitsun; Trinity): *Nos. 10: Meine Seele erhebt den Herrn; 11: Lobet Gott in seinen Reichen; 21: Ich hatte viel Bekümmernis; 24: Ein ungefärbt Gemüte; 30: Freue dich, erlöste Schar; 34: O ewiges Feuer, O Ursprung der Liebe; 39: Brich dem Hungrigen dein Brot; 44: Sie werden euch in den Bann tun; 68: Also hat Gott die Welt geliebt; 76: Die Himmel erzählen die Ehre Gottes; 93: Wer nur den lieben Gott lässt walten; 129: Gelobet sei der Herr, mein Gott; 135: Ach, Herr, mich armen Sünder; 147: Herz und Mund und Tat und Leben; 175: Er rufet seinen Schafen mit Namen.*
(B)**(*) DG 439 380-2 (6) [id.]. Edith Mathis, Ursula Buckel, Anna Reynolds, Hertha Töpper, Peter Schreier, Ernst Haefliger, John van Kesteren, Dietrich Fischer-Dieskau, Kurt Moll, Kieth Engen, Munich Bach Ch. & O, Karl Richter.

The first performance offered here (Volume 3 of the Richter series) is the glorious Ascension cantata, *Lobet Gott in seinen Reichen* (No. 11), which opens and closes joyfully with resplendent trumpets. All four soloists are first rate, and Anna Reynolds is especially memorable in her famous aria, *Ach, bleib doch, mein liebstes Leben,* warmly supported by the strings of the Munich ensemble. Richter's other performances have a breadth and sense of space that are really quite impressive. He makes heavy weather of *Ein ungefärbt Gemüte* (No. 24), but on the whole the dignity of these performances outweighs the occasional pedestrian moments. No. 147, *Herz und Mund und Tat und Leben* (which includes *Jesu, joy of man's desiring*), is among the best of Richter's series. Ursula Buckel sings beautifully, as does the tenor, John van Kesteren, and the choral singing is also very good. On the whole a successful box.

Cantatas (for Advent and Christmas): *Nos. 13: Meine Seufzer, meine Tränen; 28: Gottlob! nun geht das Jahr zu Ende; 58: Ach Gott, wie manches Herzeleid; 61: Nun komm, der Heiden Heiland; 63: Christen ätzet diesen Tag; 64: Sehet, welch eine Liebe hat uns der Vater erzwiget; 65: Sie werden aus Saba alle kommen; 81: Jesus schläft, was soll ich hoffen?; 82: Ich habe genug; 111: Was mein Gott will, das g'scheh allzeit; 121: Christum wir sollen loben schon; 124: Meinen Jesum lass ich nicht; 132: Bereitet die Wege, bereitet die Bahn; 171: Gott, wie dein Name, so ist auch dein Ruhm.*
(B) **(*) DG 439 369-2 (4) [id.]. Edith Mathis, Sheila Armstrong, Lotte Schädle, Anna Reynolds, Hertha Töpper, Peter Schreier, Ernst Haefliger, Dietrich Fischer-Dieskau, Theo Adam, Munich Bach Ch. & O, Karl Richter.

It is useful to have this anthology (Volume 1 in this Richter series), which collects the cantatas appropriate to the Christmas festival; though there are some reservations to be made, there need be nothing but admiration for the purpose of the enterprise. The instrumental playing is extremely fine throughout and much of the solo singing is of genuine distinction. There is a greater boldness about Richter's approach than, say, Harnoncourt's, but he is at times a little earthbound and not free from pedantry. However, it is good to hear full-bodied choral singing and warm orchestral textures. The acoustic is a pleasing one; it has warmth and clarity at the same time, considering the forces used. There is much noble music-making and much noble music in this set.

Cantatas Nos. 27: *Wer weiss, wie nahe mir mein Ende!; 158: Der Friede sei mit dir; 198: Lass, Fürstin, lass noch einen Strahl (Trauer-Ode).*
(M) *** Teldec/Warner 4509 93687-2 [id.]. Rotraud Hansmann, Helen Watts, Kurt Equiluz, Max van Egmond, Hamburg Monteverdi Ch., Concerto Amsterdam, Jürgen Jürgens.

This is one of the most outstanding Bach cantata records on the market. Not only are the performances extremely sensitive yet vital, with excellent solo and choral singing as well as enthusiastic but disciplined instrumental support, but the cantatas themselves are among Bach's most inspired. The recording, from the mid-1960s, is also first rate.

Cantatas Nos. 50: *Nun ist das Heil und die Kraft; 118: O Jesu Christ, meine Lebens Licht.*
(N) (M) *** Erato/Warner 4509 99613-2 (2) [id.]. Monteverdi Ch., E. Bach. Soloists, Gardiner – *Motets.* ***

These cantatas are combined with the *Motets* (see below) in a superb two-disc set. The magnificent cantata movement, BWV 50, for double choir, is used as an epilogue to the glorious *Singet dem Herrn.* Alongside this, the high point is *O Jesu Christ, meine Lebens Licht,* given in its second version and with genuine majesty. Gardiner's tempi are often characteristically brisk and there is no question about the vitality of the music-making, both here and in the coupled *Motets.* The CD transfers are vivid and immediate and make the very most of the fine analogue recording, made in All Saints', Tooting, in 1980. The *Motets* are equally fine.

Cantata No. 51: Jauchzet Gott in allen Landen.
*** Ph. Dig. 411 458-2 [id.]. Emma Kirkby, E. Bar. Soloists, Gardiner – *Magnificat.* ***

Jauchzet Gott is one of Bach's most joyful cantatas; Emma Kirkby follows the example of the opening trumpeting (Crispian Steele-Perkins – in excellent form) when she begins. It is a brilliantly responsive performance, admirably accompanied and very well recorded.

Cantatas Nos. 51: Jauchzet Gott in allen Landen; 78: Jesu, der du meine Seele; 140: Wachet auf, ruft uns die Stimme.
(Y/B) (M) *** O-L Dig. 443 188-2 [id.]. Baird, Minter, Fast, Thomas, Kelley, Opalach, Bach Ens., Rifkin.

As in his other Bach records, Joshua Rifkin goes for the one-to-a-part principle in his instrumental ensemble (save for the violins), resting his case on the number of copies of the parts surviving at Leipzig. Rifkin uses a later Leipzig text for *Jauchzet Gott*. Julianne Baird is an excellent singer who possesses a pleasing voice and has commendable technique. The recording is excellent. For the reissue *Jesu, der du meine Seele* has been added, another very fine work which shows all the four soloists (here Julianne Baird, Allan Fast, Frank Kelley and Jan Opalach) to good advantage.

Cantatas Nos. (i) 51: Jauchzet Gott in allen Landen; (ii; iii; iv; v; vi) 80: Ein feste Burg is unser Gott; (vii; viii) 82: Ich habe genug; (ix; iv; vi) 106: Gottes Zeit ist die allerbeste Zeit (Actus tragicus); (ii; iii; iv; v; vi) 140: Wachet auf, ruft uns die Stimme; (x; viii) 147: Herz und Mund und Tat und Leben.
(Y/B) (B) **(*) EMI Analogue/Dig. (No. 51) CZS5 68544-2 (2) [CDZB 68544]. (i) Donath, ASMF, Marriner; (ii) Ameling; (iii) J. Baker, (iv) Altmeyer; (v) Sotin; (vi) S. German Madrigal Ch. & Consortium Musicum, Gönnenwein; (vii) Souzay; (viii) Geraint Jones O, Jones; (ix) Mathis, Michelow, Crass; (x) Sutherland, Watts, Wilfred Brown, Hemsley, Geraint Jones Singers.

Although by today's authentic standards these now sound to be rather old-fashioned Bach performances, they are certainly not unstylish. Gönnenwein is thoroughly reliable and *Eine feste Burg* achieves generally high standards. *Wachet auf* is equally attractive and Janet Baker's contribution, though small, is distinguished. The singing throughout is admirable, as it is in *Gottes Zeit*, Bach's funeral cantata, which has different soloists. Gönnenwein secures highly musical results on the whole but misses the last ounce of inspiration. For the solo cantata, *Jauchzet Gott*, Helen Donath's performance, though fresh, is slightly marred by her close vibrato. When one turns to *Ich habe genug*, it is to encounter artistry of a very high order indeed. Gérard Souzay, recorded at his peak in 1958, gives an intimate, wonderfully dedicated performance which is surely one of the finest recorded accounts of any of Bach's solo cantatas.

Joan Sutherland is not usually associated with Bach, but in the famous *Herz und Mund und Tat und Leben*, dating from the very beginning of her recording career, she displays an unfamiliar facet of her vocal facility, making of Bach's tricky lines a memorably beautiful impression, rich in ornament and variety of timbre. Helen Watts is impressive too, and the other soloists also sing with heart as well as the voice. The Geraint Jones Singers and Orchestra give firm and buoyant support and the famous chorale, *Jesu joy of man's desiring*, is beautifully sung. Good, vivid recording.

Cantatas Nos. (i) 51: Jauchzet Gott in allen Landen; (ii) 202: Weichet nur (Wedding cantata); (i) 209: Non sa che sia dolore.
(M) *** Van. 08.2028.71. (i) Teresa Stich-Randall, V. State Op. O, Anton Heiller; (ii) Anny Felbermeyer, Bach Guild O, Felix Prohaska.

Teresa Stich-Randall, in one of her finest records, gives a glorious account of the two solo cantatas. In *Jauchzet Gott* she is supported by an estimably brilliant trumpet soloist and in the Italian cantata by a sensitive, if not quite so striking, flute obbligato (neither player is named in the documentation) and Heiller provides fresh accompaniments. Anny Felbermeyer is pleasingly fresh in the *Wedding cantata*, if perhaps not quite so distinctive, and here the 1953 recording is from a mono source, disguised by the pleasing resonance. Overall a very good disc, cleanly remastered.

Cantatas Nos. 51: Jauchzet Gott in allen Landen; 208: Was mir behagt, ist nur die muntre Jagd (Hunt cantata).
(BB) **(*) Naxos Dig. 8.550643 [id.]. Kertesi, Pászthy, Nemeth, Mukk, Gáti, Hungarian R. Ch., Failoni CO, Budapest, Antál.

The Naxos accounts offer excellent value artistically for those who do not insist on period instrument ensembles. The soloists are all of a high standard and, although the recorded balance is not always ideal, the sound has warmth and immediacy, and Matyás Antál gets good results from his orchestra.

Cantatas Nos. 54: Widerstehe doch der Sünde; 169: Gott soll allein; 170: Vergnügte Ruh'.
*** Hyperion Dig. CDA 66326 [id.]. James Bowman, King's Consort, King.

James Bowman is on impressive form and his admirers need not hesitate here. The present disc is very desirable and the King's Consort under Robert King give excellent support. Good recorded sound.

(i) *Cantatas Nos. 80: Ein feste Burg ist unser Gott; 140: Wachet auf, ruft uns die Stimme;* (ii) *Organ concerto No. 3 in D min.* (reconstructed Schureck from *BWV 35* & *BVW 1059*).
(N) (B) **(*) Decca Eclipse Dig. 448 706-2; *448 706-4* [id.]. (i) Fontana, Hamari, Winbergh, Krause, Stuttgart Hymnus Ch., Stuttgart CO, Münchinger; (ii) Peter Hurford, N. Sinf., Hickox.

This digital coupling of two of Bach's most popular cantatas is most welcome at bargain price. Münchinger has the advantage of excellently transparent and well-detailed Decca digital recording and a fine team of soloists and there is little of the pedantry that has at times afflicted his performances. On CD, extra pleasure is afforded by the attractive ambience and by the tangibility of the chorus, whose vigorous contribution is given striking body and presence. For the Eclipse reissue a reconstructed organ concerto has been added, with movements taken partly from the *D minor Harpsichord concerto*, BWV 1059, and partly from a sinfonia in Cantata No. 35, *Geist und Seele sind verwirret*, featuring a solo organ. Peter Hurford is the admirable soloist, and this makes an enjoyable interlude between the two cantatas.

Cantatas Nos. (i) *80: Ein feste Burg ist unser Gott; 140: Wachet auf, ruft uns die Stimme;* (ii; iii) *147: Herz und Mund und Tat und Leben;* Motet: (iii) *Jesu, meine Freude, BWV 227.*
(N) (B) (*) EMI forte CZS5 68670-2 (2) [id.]. (i) Ameling, Baker, Altmeyer, Sotin, S. German Madrigal Ch. & Instrumentalists, Consortium Musicum, Gönnenwein; (ii) Sutherland, Watts, Brown, Hemsley; (iii) Geraint Jones Singers & O, Jones.

This is obviously a British replacement for the collection above from EMI France which is much more generous and far preferable. Here three cantantas are omitted (Nos. 51, 82 and 106) and Bach's most famous motet is added. But as this is sung comparatively indifferently, that is no advantage. Moreover the new transfers of the Gönnenwein performances on the second disc leave much to be desired, with the opening chorus of each poorly focused – and particularly *Ein feste Burg*, with its distorting trumpets bringing unpleasant roughness and congestion.

Cantatas Nos. 80: Ein feste Burg ist unser Gott; 147: Herz und Mund und Tat und Leben.
(BB) **(*) Naxos Dig. 8.550642 [id.]. Kertesi, Nemeth, Mukk, Gáti, Hungarian R. Ch., Failoni CO, Budapest, Antál.

Like its companion above, this Naxos disc is eminently good value. Neither performance disappoints in any significant respect; both are reasonably spirited in direction and offer satisfactory singing. Those who do not insist on period-instrument ensembles will find a great deal to enjoy here, particularly the singing of Ingrid Kertesi. The sound has real warmth and immediacy.

Cantata No. 82: Ich habe genug.
✪ (M) (***) EMI CDH7 63198-2 [id.]. Hans Hotter, Philh. O, Bernard – BRAHMS: *Lieder*. (***) ✪
(N) (BB) *(*) Naxos Dig. 8.550763 [id.]. Nicholas Gedge, Oxford Schola Cantorum, N. CO, Ward – *Magnificat*. **(*)

One of the greatest cantata performances ever. Glorious singing from Hans Hotter and wonderfully stylish accompanying from Anthony Bernard and the Philharmonia. This 1950 mono recording was never reissued on LP, and it sounds eminently present in this fine transfer.

Nicholas Gedge's account of this famous cantata is basically fresh, but his curiously quavery tone-production and style of phrasing will not appeal to all tastes.

Cantatas Nos. (i; ii) *82: Ich habe genug;* (i; iii; iv) *159: Sehet, wir gehn hinauf gen Jerusalem;* (iii) *170: Vergnügte Ruh', beliebte Seelenlust.*
✪ (M) *** Decca 430 260-2. (i) Shirley-Quirk; (ii) Lord; (iii) J. Baker; (iv) Tear, St Anthony Singers; ASMF, Marriner.

John Shirley-Quirk's performance of *Ich habe genug* is much to be admired, not only for the sensitive solo singing but also for the lovely oboe obbligato of Roger Lord. But this reissue is to be prized even more for the other two cantatas. Both Dame Janet Baker and Shirley-Quirk are in marvellous voice, and *Vergnügte Ruh'* makes a worthy companion. This is among the half-dozen or so cantata records that ought to be in every collection.

Cantatas Nos. 106: Gottes Zeit ist die allerbeste Zeit; 118: O Jesu Christ, mein Lebens Licht (2nd version); *198: Lass, Fürstin, lass noch einen Strahl.*

*** DG Dig. 429 782-2 [id.]. Argenta, Chance, Rolfe Johnson, Varcoe, Monteverdi Ch., E. Bar. Soloists, Gardiner.

Gardiner directs dedicated, intense performances of three of Bach's finest cantatas, all valedictory works. The new account of No. 118 is more intimate than the 1980 version, less grandly dramatic, more devotional; the whole record suggests a scale of performance apt for a small chapel.

Cantatas Nos. 140: Wachet auf, ruft uns die Stimme; 147: Herz und Mund und Tat und Leben.
*** DG Dig. 431 809-2; *431 809-4* [id.]. Holton, Chance, Rolfe Johnson, Varcoe, Monteverdi Ch., E. Bar. Soloists, Gardiner.
(Y/B) (M) **(*) Teldec/Warner Dig./Analogue 4509 95987-2 [id.]. Bergius, Rampf, Esswood, Equiluz, Hampson, Tölz Boys' Ch., VCM, Harnoncourt.

Two popular Bach cantatas are coupled in highly accomplished performances under John Eliot Gardiner. The level of instrumental playing is generally more polished than in the celebrated Teldec series, and Ruth Holton, Anthony Rolfe Johnson, Michael Chance and Stephen Varcoe make equally satisfying contributions. The recordings are immediate and well balanced. A strong recommendation.

This separate reissue accompanies the complete Teldec cantata series, offering a coupling of two familiar cantatas, both made famous by their chorales. In No. 147, some may be a little disconcerted by the minor swelling effect in the phrasing of *Jesu, joy of man's desiring*, but otherwise the authentic approach brings much to enjoy. The production and recording are well up to the usual Telefunken standard. However, John Eliot Gardiner's highly accomplished performances on DG Archiv are well worth the extra money.

(i) *Cantatas Nos. 197: Gott ist unsre Zuversicht (Wedding cantata);* (ii) *205: Der Zufriedengestellte Aolus.*
(N) (M) *** Teldec/Warner Dig. 0630 12321 [id.]. (i) Treble and alto soloists from V. Boys' Ch., Max von Egmond, Ch. Viennensis; (ii) Kenny, Lipovšek, Equiluz, Holl, Arnold Schönberg Ch.; VCM, Harnoncourt.

The performance of *Gott ist unsre Zuversicht* does not come from the complete Teldec set, above, but was recorded independently in 1969. It is a wedding cantata and an imposing work in two parts, the second of which was sung after the ceremony. It is on a large scale and the performance is fine, though the aria '*Schläfert aller Sorgen*' is a little sluggish. The use of boy treble and alto soloists may not be to all tastes but they put up a good showing and the recording is excellent. No. 205 is a much later recording (from 1983) and is digital. Bach describes this cantata as '*Dramma per musica*'. The performance is very good indeed, and the recording has a decently spacious acoustic and no lack of detail.

Cantata No. 208: Was mir behagt, ist nur die muntre Jagd! (Hunt cantata).
*** Hyperion Dig. CDA 66169 [id.]. Jennifer Smith, Emma Kirkby, Simon Davis, Michael George, Parley of Instruments, Goodman.

This is a cantata rich in melodic invention of the highest quality. The performance has the benefit of excellent soloists and first-class instrumental playing.

Cantatas Nos. (i) 208: Was mir behagt, ist nur die muntre Jagd! (Hunt). 212: Mer hahn en neue Oberkeet (Peasant).
(Y/B) (M) *** Teldec/Warner Dig. 4509 97501-2 [id.]. Angela Maria Blasi, Robert Holl; (i) with Yvonne Kenny, Kurt Equiluz; Arnold Schönberg Ch., VCM, Harnoncourt.

Harnoncourt tops off the complete Teldec set of Bach's church cantatas with admirably ebullient accounts of a pair of Bach's secular cantatas, celebrating the name-days of two local dignitaries. The delightful *Hunt cantata* is rich in melodic invention of the highest quality, including the famous aria, *Schafe können sicher weiden*, with its obbligato for a pair of flutes, better known as 'Sheep may safely graze', sung here quite gloriously by Angela Maria Blasi. Indeed the solo contributions in both works are splendid, and Blasi and the robust Robert Holl both enjoy themselves hugely in the boisterous *Peasant cantata* in their alternating bursts of extravagant praise, lyrical and exuberant, for Carl Heinrich von Dieskau, Chamberlain at the Court of the Elector of Saxony and Lord of the Manor. A later lyrical eulogy from the soprano is introduced by a quotation of the famous *La Folia*, and the musical interest of this remarkably inspired cantata (considering its ragbag of a text) is Bach's use of various old melodies familiar to his audience; and indeed the Overture is a patchwork, almost a musical swatch of such tunes. The exuberance of the performance carries over to Harnoncourt's accompaniments – no scholarly rectitude here – and the recording is first rate.

Cantatas Nos. 211: Schweigt stille, plaudert nicht (Coffee cantata); 212: Mer hahn en neue Oberkeet (Peasant cantata).

*** O-L Dig. 417 621-2 [id.]. Kirkby, Rogers, Covey-Crump, Thomas, AAM, Hogwood.

(BB) **(*) Naxos Dig. 8.550642 [id.]. Kertesi, Mukk, Gáti, Failoni CO, Budapest, Mátyás Antál.

Emma Kirkby is particularly appealing in the *Coffee cantata* and her father is admirably portrayed by David Thomas. Hogwood opts for single strings, and some may find they sound thin. However, there is a corresponding gain in lightness and intimacy. The recording is altogether first class.

Very serviceable accounts on Naxos of the *Coffee* and *Peasant cantatas*, and those who appreciated Ingrid Kertesi's *Jauchzet Gott* will find her singing gives as much pleasure here. Mátyás Antál's direction is lively and this is as enjoyable an issue as the other cantatas from this source, save only for the tenor, who falls short of distinction. The recording is warm and spacious.

Christmas oratorio, BWV 248.

*** DG Dig. 423 232-2 (2) [id.]. Rolfe Johnson, Argenta, Von Otter, Blochwitz, Bär, Monteverdi Ch., E. Bar. Soloists, Gardiner.

(M) **(*) Teldec/Warner 9031 77610-2 (2) [id.]. Treble soloists from V. Boys' Ch., Esswood, Equiluz, Nimsgern, V. Boys' Ch., Ch. Viennensis. VCM, Harnoncourt.

**(*) Collins Dig. 7028-2 (2). Russell, Padmore, Wyn-Rogers, George, The Sixteen, Christophers.

The freshness of the singing and playing in the DG set is a constant pleasure, with Gardiner's often brisk speeds sounding bright and eager, not breathless. Far more than usual, one registers the joyfulness of the work, from the trumpets and timpani at the start onwards. Anthony Rolfe Johnson makes a pointful and expressive Evangelist, and also outstanding is Anne Sofie von Otter with her natural gravity and exceptionally beautiful mezzo. Beauty of tone consistently marks the singing of Nancy Argenta, Hans-Peter Blochwitz and Olaf Bär. The whole oratorio is neatly contained on only two discs, with three cantatas on each instead of two. The sound is full and atmospheric.

Harnoncourt has rarely been more successful than here. It will not be to everyone's taste to have a boy treble and male counter-tenor instead of women soloists, but the purity of sound of these singers is most affecting. Above all, Harnoncourt in this instance never allows his pursuit of authentic sound to weigh the performance down: it has a lightness of touch which should please everyone. The sound, from 1971/2, as usual from this source is excellent.

Harry Christophers conducts a crisp, sympathetic reading, very well played and sung, which at speeds generally a little slower than John Eliot Gardiner's just fails to match that rival in exhilaration and intensity. He has a first-rate quartet of soloists – where Gardiner has different soloists for the arias from those for the Christmas narrative – with the tenor, Mark Padmore, particularly impressive not just in the arias but as the Evangelist. Good, atmospheric recording, with trumpets and drums dramatically prominent.

Christmas oratorio: Arias and choruses.

(M) *** Teldec/Warner 9031 74893-2 [id.]. Treble soloists from V. Boys' Ch., Esswood, Equiluz, Nimsgern, V. Boys' Ch., Ch. Viennensis, VCM, Harnoncourt.

The highlights from Harnoncourt's outstandingly spontaneous performance of the *Christmas oratorio* are attractive, particularly as the CD plays for nearly 78 minutes.

Magnificat in E flat, BWV 243a (original version).

(Y/B) (M) *** O-L 443 199-2 [id.]. Nelson, Kirkby, C. Watkinson, Elliot, D. Watkinson, Christ Church Ch., AAM, Preston – KUHNAU: *Der Gerechte kommt um;* VIVALDI: *Nisi dominus; Nulla in mundo pax sincera.* ***

The original version of the *Magnificat* is textually different in detail (quite apart from being a semitone higher) and has four interpolations for the celebration of Christmas. Preston and the Academy of Ancient Music present a characteristically alert and fresh performance, and the Christ Church Choir is in excellent form. One might quibble at the use of women soloists instead of boys, but these three specialist singers have just the right incisive timbre and provide the insight of experience. The reissue is now joined with two Vivaldi motets and an interesting piece by Kuhnau, which is much more generous than the old full-priced coupling.

Magnificat in D, BWV 243.

*** Ph. Dig. 411 458-2 [id.]. Argenta, Kwella, Kirkby, Brett, Rolfe Johnson, David Thomas, E. Bar. Soloists, Gardiner – *Cantata No. 51.* ***

*** Chandos Dig. CHAN 0518 [id.]. Kirkby, Bonner, Chance, Ainsley, Varcoe, Coll. Mus. 90, Hickox – VIVALDI: *Gloria.* ***

*** EMI Dig. CDC7 54283-2 [id.]. Hendricks, Murray, Rigby, Heilmann, Hynninen, ASMF Ch. & O,

Marriner – VIVALDI: *Gloria*. ***
(M) *** Decca 421 148-2. Palmer, Watts, Tear, Roberts, King's College Ch., ASMF, Ledger – C. P. E.
BACH: *Magnificat*. ***
(N) (BB) **(*) Naxos Dig. 8.550763 [id.]. Crookes, Whitaker, Trevor, Robinson, Gedge, Oxford Schola
Cantorum, N. CO, Nicholas Ward – *Cantata No. 82*. *(*)

The better-known, D major version of the *Magnificat* receives an exhilarating performance from
Gardiner. Tempi are consistently brisk but the vigour and precision of the chorus are such that one
never has the feeling that the pacing is hurried. A splendid team of soloists, and the accompaniment and
recording are no less impressive.

Both Richard Hickox and Neville Marriner couple the *Magnificat* with the popular D major *Gloria*, RV
589, of Vivaldi, and for collectors seeking this coupling the clear choice is between period and modern
instruments. Those who like the former will gravitate towards Hickox, who directs a most musical
account and has the benefit of such fine singers as Emma Kirkby, Michael Chance and Stephen Varcoe,
and good Chandos recording. Marriner's performance with the Academy is well paced and executed
with precision and fine musical intelligence. No quarrel with the soloists either or the splendidly warm
and present recording. Both can be recommended with confidence.

Philip Ledger's account, recorded by Argo in the late 1970s, is also most attractive, highly recommendable if boys' voices are preferred in the chorus, and is excellent value.

The Naxos performance is strikingly fresh, with generally good soloists drawn from the excellent Oxford
Schola Cantorum who sing brightly and incisively. Nicholas Ward directs with style and spirit, but this
CD is let down by its coupling, a famous solo cantata in which the soloist's vocal production and
phrasing are individual to the point of eccentricity.

*Magnificat in D, BWV 243; Masses (Missae breves): in F, BWV 233; in A, BWV 234; in G min., BWV
235; in G, BWV 236*.
(N) *** Ph. Dig. 438 873-2 (2) [id.]. Bonney, Remmert, Trost, Bär, Berlin RIAS Chamber Ch., C. P. E.
Bach CO, Peter Schreier.

*Masses (Missae breves): in F, BWV 233; in A, BWV 234; in G min., BWV 235; in G, BWV 236. 5
Sanctuses: in C; D; D min.; G; D, BWV 237–41; Christe eleison in G min., BWV 242*.
(N) (M) ** Erato/Warner 4509 97236-2 (2) [id.]. Staempfli, Capt, Rossier-Maradan, Perret, Schaer,
Elwes, Dufour, Huttenlocher, Brodard, Lausanne Vocal Ens., Michel Corboz.

Masses (Missae breves): in F, BWV 233; in G, BWV 236.
(N) **(*) Virgin/EMI Veritas Dig. VC7 59634-2 [id.]. Mellon, Lesne, Prégardien, Kooy, Coll. Voc.,
Herreweghe.

Masses (Missae breves): in A, BWV 234; in G min., BWV 235. Sanctus in D, BWV 238.
(N) **(*) Virgin/EMI Veritas Dig. VC7 59587-2 [id.]. Mellon, Lesne, Prégardien, Kooy, Coll. Voc.,
Herreweghe.

Bach's *Short Masses* (sometimes described as 'Lutheran' – although they are sung in Latin) are comparatively little known. Taking their material from cantatas, they have considerable musical interest,
with the *A major*, BWV 234 (which draws on *Cantata No. 67* for its *Gloria*), perhaps the most inspired.
Yet all four offer many beauties and it is difficult to understand their neglect. We hope Hickox's old
Argo performances may resurface soon on a Double Decca set; meanwhile the Schreier version can be
warmly recommended, for he also includes a fine, fresh account of the *Magnificat*. He has excellent
soloists, notably Barbara Bonney and Olaf Bär, and the Philips digital sound is first class. Schreier uses a
chamber chorus and their lightly rhythmic singing in the *Kyries* is most refreshing, while the *Glorias* are
exuberant. Stylistically these modern-instrument performances show that Schreier has absorbed much
that is attractive from period-instrument practice, with his lively tempi and fresh orchestral textures.
Moreover the ambience is particularly pleasing, bringing atmosphere without clouding detail.

Those who seek authenticity as a first priority should be fairly well satisfied with the quite spirited and
certainly stylish Herreweghe versions on a pair of Virgin Veritas discs, which however are apparently
now available only via EMI's Special Import Service, which takes them out of the mid-price range. The
snag here is the very resonant ecclesiastical acoustic which, while it provides a smooth freedom from
period-instrument abrasiveness, also takes some of the edge off the choruses and detracts from the
presence of the soloists. Even so, these performances are still warmly enjoyable.

The Corboz versions date from 1974 and their style now seems rather old-fashioned, with weighty
sounds from both chorus and orchestra. The spacious tempi in the *Kyries* seem almost lethargic alongside Schreier; in both BWV 234 and 235 Corboz takes two minutes longer than his colleague. Yet the
Glorias are ebullient and the solo singing from a very good team is of high quality: indeed Wally

Staempfli's *Qui tollis* in the *A major Mass* is even more lyrically beautiful than Barbara Bonney's account. In their more leisured way these performances are still enjoyable, for the recording is full-bodied and mostly pleasing, not as clear as with Schreier but better defined than with Herreweghe, although the horns are not cleanly caught in BWV 233. What makes the Corboz set the more interesting is his inclusion of a brief *Christe eleison* (a duet, nicely sung here by Staempfli and Nicole Rössler-Maradan) and five settings of the *Sanctus*, of varying length from less than two minutes (BWV 237, 239 and 241) to the ambitious BWV 238, scored for trumpets, which Herreweghe also includes. These scores exist in Bach's own hand, so, while doubt has been cast on the authenticity of the four shorter pieces, Bach obviously admired them.

Mass in B min., BWV 232.
*** DG Dig. 415 514-2 [id.]. Argenta, Dawson, Fairfield, Knibbs, Kwella, Hall, Nichols, Chance, Collin, Stafford, Evans, Milner, Murgatroyd, Lloyd-Morgan, Varcoe, Monteverdi Ch., E. Bar. Soloists, Gardiner.
*** EMI Dig. CDS7 47293-8 [Ang. CDCB 47292] (2). Kirkby, Van Evera, Iconomou, Immler, Kilian, Covey-Crump, David Thomas, Taverner Cons. and Players, Parrott.
(N) (B) *** EMI forte Dig. CZS5 68640-2 (2). Donath, Fassbaender, Ahnsjö, Hermann, Holl, Bav. R. Ch. & O, Jochum.
(N) **(*) Chandos Dig. CHAN 0533/4. Argenta, Denley, Tucker, Varcoe, Coll. Mus. 90 Ch. & O, Hickox.
(Y/B) **(*) Erato/Warner Dig. 4509 98478-2 (2) [id.]. Schlick, Wessel, De Mey, Mertens, Amsterdam Bar. Ch. & O, Ton Koopman.
(Y/B) (M) **(*) Teldec/Warner 4509 95517-2 (2) [id.]. Hansmann, Iiyama, Watts, Equiluz, Van Egmond, V. Boys' Ch., Ch. Viennensis, VCM, Harnoncourt.
(Y/B) (B) **(*) Decca Duo 440 609-2 (2) [id.]. Ameling, Minton, Watts, Krenn, Krause, V. Singakademiechor, Stuttgart O, Münchinger.
(Y/B) (B) ** DG Double 439 696-2 (2) [id.]. Janowitz, Ludwig, Schreier, Kerns, Ridderbusch, V. Singverein, Karajan.
(Y/B) ** Collins Dig. 7032-2 (2) [id.]. Dubosc, Denley, Bowman, Ainsley, George, The Sixteen & O, Christophers.
(Y/B) (BB) ** Naxos Dig. 8.550585/6 [id.]. Wagner, Schäfer-Subrata, Koppelstetter, Schäfer, Elbert, Slovak Philharmonic Ch., Capella Istropolitana, Christian Brembreck.
(N) ** Sony Dig. S2K 66354 (2) [id.]. Ruth Ziesak, Roberta Alexander, Jard Van Nes, Keith Lewis, David Wilson-Johnson, Bav. R. Ch. & SO, Giulini.

John Eliot Gardiner gives a magnificent account of the *B minor Mass*, one which attempts to keep within an authentic scale but which also triumphantly encompasses the work's grandeur. Gardiner masterfully conveys the majesty (with bells and censer-swinging evoked) simultaneously with a crisply resilient rhythmic pulse. The choral tone is luminous and powerfully projected. The regular solo numbers are taken by choir members making a cohesive whole. The recording is warmly atmospheric but not cloudy.

Parrott, hoping to re-create even more closely the conditions Bach would have expected in Leipzig, adds to the soloists a ripieno group of five singers from the Taverner Consort for the choruses. The instrumental group is similarly augmented with the keenest discretion. Speeds are generally fast, with rhythms sprung to reflect the inspiration of dance; however, the inner darkness of the *Crucifixus*, for example, is conveyed intensely in its hushed tones, while the *Et resurrexit* promptly erupts with a power to compensate for any lack of traditional weight. Soloists are excellent, with reduction of vibrato still allowing sweetness as well as purity. If you want a performance on a reduced scale, the recording, made in St John's, Smith Square, is both realistic and atmospheric.

Jochum's memorable, dedicated (1980) performance, marked by resilient rhythms, remains among the most completely satisfying versions even today. It makes a superb bargain on EMI's forte label, with two discs offered for the cost of a single premium-priced CD. The choral singing – by far the most important element in this work – is superb and, though the soloists are variably balanced, they make a fine, clear-voiced team. Brigitte Fassbaender's *Agnus Dei* is very beautiful; coming as it does before the final choral *Donna nobis pacem*, it helps to leave Bach's inspired music resonating in the listener's memory. The digital recording is admirably spacious and clear. Presentation is attractive; documentation is just about adequate, but with no text.

With an excellent chorus and a first-rate quartet of soloists, Richard Hickox conducts a period performance that emerges on a larger scale than many. This is thanks to a reverberant recording rather than to large-scale forces. His speeds are on the fast side, though never breathless-sounding, and his springing of rhythms is always infectious. With a relatively close recording-balance for the orchestra, the panoply of trumpets and drums in the more extrovert numbers comes over dramatically, and the soloists too are presented in close-up. That makes the recording of the chorus – more vital than any other element in this work – seem too distant and less involving than in such a version as Gardiner's.

Ton Koopman directs a purposeful, consistently persuasive account of the *B minor Mass* with four excellent, stylish soloists. With keenly responsive choral singing – as recorded, rather soft-grained – it is warmer than most period performances but lacks some of the brightness and bite that mark the very finest versions. So in Koopman's reading the opening fugue of the *Credo* starts softly and gently, building up its affirmation of faith only later. The great censer-swinging motif in the *Sanctus* is easy and persuasive, but neither the alto solo of the *Agnus Dei* (Kai Wessel the assured counter-tenor) nor the final *Dona nobis pacem* has quite the devotional quality one finds, for example, in Gardiner's outstanding version, an even clearer recommendation.

Harnoncourt's version marked a breakthrough in the development of the authentic movement. It confirms that, in parallel with his account of the *Christmas oratorio*, this is one of his most effective Bach performances on a chamber scale, with the choir, including boys' voices, projecting keenly. Rhythmically he is not as imaginative as his finest authentic rivals, and the brisk *Sanctus* is disappointing, but he rises warmly to the final *Dona nobis pacem*, given a real sense of occasion. First-rate solo singing, notably from Helen Watts, aptly firm and even. Nicely balanced recording, good for its late-1960s vintage.

Münchinger's is a strong, enjoyable performance with an exceptionally fine quintet of soloists and very good recording. On balance it makes a fair recommendation; however, with fastish tempi and a generally extrovert manner it is efficient rather than inspiring. The chorus sings well but is placed rather backwardly. The recording dates from 1971 and has been successfully remastered. The chorus sounds vibrant and clear and the trumpets offer no transfer problems. Good value in Decca's Duo series, but not a first choice.

Karajan conveys intensity, even religious fervour, and the very opening brings an impressive first entry of the choir on *Kyrie*. But then, after the instrumental fugue, the contrapuntal entries are sung in a self-consciously softened tone. There is a strong sense of the work's architecture, and the highly polished surfaces do not obscure the depths of the music, but (despite a fine solo team) this is hardly a first choice, although in its two-for-the-price-of-one format it is certainly reasonably priced.

Harry Christophers, with the Sixteen expanded to 26 singers, gives a fresh, direct period performance, marked by well-chosen speeds and bright choral singing. It wears its period manners easily, which many will welcome. The stylistic plainness, less detailed in such matters as appoggiaturas, is certainly refreshing but rarely allows the sharply distinctive characterization which marks such outstanding versions as Gardiner's on DG Archiv. The great *Sanctus* lacks a little in gravity, and the slightly distanced recording takes some of the impact from bright, vigorous movements, where trumpets are less forward than usual. Though Catherine Dubosc's vibrato is obtrusive at times, the soloists make an excellent team.

There is certainly room for a bargain digital version of the *B minor Mass*, and the Naxos set offers a chamber-scale performance on modern instruments. With generally well-chosen speeds it offers a good middle-of-the-road approach, and the orchestral playing is first rate, very well recorded, with string-playing finely detailed and with trumpets braying out superbly to bring out the joy of such numbers as the *Gloria*. The soloists are a reliable team, with the contralto, Martina Koppelstetter, outstanding in her two big solos, *Qui tollis* and *Agnus Dei*, the latter taken broadly with fine concentration. In this of all Bach's choral works the chorus is central to any performance, and sadly the backward placing of the chorus takes away bite from the singing except in the big, extrovert moments like the very opening of the *Kyrie* and the *Sanctus*, where the singers suddenly seem more confident.

The expression of Giulini as portrayed on the cover of his Sony set resembles that of the suffering Christ and, deeply religious himself, he conducts a devotional performance, recorded live, with a weighty chorus and some first-rate soloists. Yet the smoothness, the absence of dramatic bite overall, is debilitating, with the mood of meditation hampering forward movement and rhythmic spring. There are finer traditional readings than this, notably Jochum on EMI forte.

Motets: *Singet dem Herrn ein neues Lied, BWV 225; Der Geist hilft unser Schwachheit auf, BWV 226; Jesu, meine Freude, BWV 227; Fürchte dich nicht, BWV 228; Komm, Jesu, komm!, BWV 229; Lobet den Herrn alle Heiden, BWV 230; Sei Lob und Preis mit Ehren, BWV 231.*

(N) (M) *** Erato/Warner 4509 99613-2 (2) [id.]. Priday, Fisher, Stafford, McKenzie, Savage (soloists in BWV 227), Monteverdi Ch., E. Bar. Soloists, Gardiner – *Cantatas Nos. 50 & 118*. ***

*** Conifer Dig. 74321 15350-2 [id.] (without *BWV 231*). Trinity College, Cambridge, Ch., Marlow, G. Jackson and R. Pearce.

(N) **(*) Hyperion Dig. CDA 66369 [id.] (without *BWV 231*). The Sixteen, Harry Christophers.

John Eliot Gardiner's set of Bach's great *Motets*, recorded for Erato in 1980, was one of his first major

Bach recordings with the Monteverdi Choir. As well as bringing exceptionally strong and stylish performances, spaciously conceived and with crisp, clean, resilient rhythms, the set has the attendant
advantage of including not just the six *Motets* normally recognized in the Bach Gesellschaft Edition but
also two motet-like works that have been counted as cantatas. The set also includes a rarity in *Sei Lob
und Preis mit Ehren*. It all makes a superb collection in such performances, beautifully recorded in the
helpful acoustic of All Saints', Tooting, and vividly transferred to CD. This is a clear first choice among
the recordings of the Bach *Motets*, irrespective of the bonuses.

The Conifer issue of Bach's great motets by Richard Marlow and the Trinity College Choir brings
delightfully crisp and resilient performances of the six regular motets, marked by refined ensemble and
transparent textures. With discreet organ accompaniment this is a fine single-disc or -tape version,
consistently stylish and set against a helpful acoustic, with plenty of presence.

Christophers and The Sixteen give elegant readings, beautifully tuned and balanced, of the six principal
motets, not as strongly characterized as some but consistently refreshing and satisfying. Gardiner's
Erato readings are even more vital but, with the seventh motet and related cantatas as additional items,
that set spreads to two discs.

St John Passion, BWV 245.
*** DG Dig. 419 324-2 (2) [id.]. Rolfe Johnson, Varcoe, Hauptmann, Argenta & soloists, Monteverdi
Ch., E. Bar. Sol., Gardiner.
(Y/B) *** Teldec/Warner Dig. 9031 74862-2 (2) [id.]. Blasi, Lipovšek, Rolfe Johnson, Holl, Scharinger,
Arnold Schoenberg Ch., VCM, Harnoncourt.
(Y/B) *** Virgin/EMI Dig. VCD5 45096-2 (2) [id.]. Covey-Crump, Thomas, Bonner, Van Evera,
Trevor, Taverner Consort & Players, Parrott.
(M) **(*) RCA GD 77041 (2) [77041-2-RG]. Prégardien, Van der Kamp, Schlick, Jacobs, Van der Meel,
Van Egmond, La Petite Bande Ch. & O, Sigiswald Kuijken.
(N) (BB) ** Naxos Dig. 8.550664/5 [id.]. Soloists, Scholars Baroque Ens.
(N) *(*) HM Dig. HMC 901264/65 [id.]. Crook, Lika, Kooy, Schlick, Patriasz, Kendell, Ghent Coll.
Vocale, Paris Chapelle Royale O, Philippe Herreweghe.

Gardiner conducts an exhilarating performance, so dramatic in its approach and so wide-ranging in the
emotions conveyed it might be a religious opera. Speeds are regularly on the fast side but, characteristically, Gardiner consistently keeps a spring in the rhythm. Chorales are treated in contrasted ways, which
may not please the more severe authenticists but, as with so much of Gardiner's work, here is a
performance using authentic scale and period instruments which speaks in the most vivid way to anyone
prepared to listen, not just to the specialist. Soloists – regular contributors to Gardiner's team – are all
first rate. Warm and atmospheric, yet clear and detailed recording. A selection of arias and choruses is
available on DG 427 319-2.

Harnoncourt's 1993 recording brings an astonishing contrast with his pioneering set of 22 years earlier.
Where the earlier one used all-male forces, with boy trebles in the choir as well as singing soprano and
alto arias, here Harnoncourt opts for an outstanding professional mixed chorus, the Arnold Schoenberg
Choir, singing with biting incisiveness, helped by close balance and – like the Parrott version – a
relatively dry acoustic. The soloists too include characterful, finely focused women singers, Angela
Maria Blasi and Maria Lipovšek, with Anthony Rolfe Johnson a searchingly expressive Evangelist, as
he is also for Gardiner on DG Archiv. Consistently Harnoncourt's speeds are faster than before,
markedly so in the chorales, and though the performing style is lighter and more detached the thrust is
keener. Gardiner is more resilient in his rhythms, leading the ear on; but, for a period performance using
modest forces, this is another outstanding recommendation.

Andrew Parrott's version offers an intimate view that yet has sharp focus and plenty of power. Though
speeds are generally fast and rhythms resilient, he allows himself a broader tempo for the great final
chorus and the concluding *Chorale*, giving them an aptly expressive weight. The Taverner Consort here
has only two choristers per part, with soloists included among the singers, while Rogers Covey-Crump
as the Evangelist, light and alert, also sings the tenor arias, and David Thomas as Jesus sings the bass
arias. The soprano soloists, Tessa Bonner and Emily van Evera, are both bright-toned and boyish, while
the alto, Caroline Trevor, has a counter-tenor-like timbre. In compensation for any lack of weight from
the scale of forces, the recording balance keeps the voices well forward, both in solo and in choral work.
An outstanding recommendation for those who fancy an intimate but powerfully dramatic view.

At mid-price on BMG/Deutsche Harmonia Mundi, directed by Sigiswald Kuijken, Prégardien as the
Evangelist provides a beautiful and intense performance. Harry van der Kamp as Jesus also stands out
with his fresh, firm and resonant bass, while Barbara Schlick is the radiant soprano. With excellent
sound, the chorus sings the brief, elaborate 'turba' choruses of comment with exemplary point, and only
the big choruses fall short.

With a choir of only eight singers providing the soloists too, the Scholars Ensemble takes an attractively intimate view of this masterpiece, both dramatic and meditative. With no director, the ensemble relies on understanding and team-work, which generally works well. The 'turba' choruses of crowd-comment are most effective, but eagerness does not always go with precision. One registers the soloists, not as vocal stars, but as intelligent young singers with fresh rather than beautiful voices. As the Evangelist, Roger Doveton uses his clean, light tenor with imagination, even if he is not quite flexible enough to make the longer recitatives as compelling as they should be.

Herreweghe has directed some impressive Bach recordings, but in the *St John Passion* he is let down by the variable 15-voice choir, generally lacking in the bite needed for this most dramatic of Bach choral works. The instrumental ensemble is also flawed and, though Howard Crook is an excellent Evangelist and Barbara Schlick a radiant soprano soloist, others fall seriously short.

St John Passion, BWV 245 (sung in English).
(Y/B) ✹ (B) *** Decca Double 443 859-2 (2) [id.]. Peter Pears, Heather Harper, Alfreda Hodgson, Robert Tear, Gwynne Howell, John Shirley-Quirk, Wandsworth School Boys' Ch., ECO, Britten.

Benjamin Britten directed live performances of this, the more dramatic of Bach's *Passions*, at the Aldeburgh Festival and elsewhere, which culminated in this wonderfully vivid recording, made at The Maltings in April 1971. Britten characteristically refuses to follow any set tradition, whether baroque, Victorian or whatever; and, with greater extremes of tempo than is common (often strikingly fast), the result makes one listen afresh. The soloists are all excellent, Heather Harper radiant, and though the Wandsworth School Boys' Choir has its rough edges, it reinforces the freshness of the interpretation. The excellent accompaniments from the English Chamber Orchestra resonate grandly, and the ear relishes the richly resilient textures of modern string instruments giving splendidly full support to the singers, while there is also outstanding continuo playing from Philip Ledger. A superb bargain.

St Matthew Passion, BWV 244.
*** DG Dig. 427 648-2 (3) [id.]. Rolfe Johnson, Schmidt, Bonney, Monoyios, Von Otter, Chance, Crook, Bär, Hauptmann, Monteverdi Ch., E. Bar. Soloists, Gardiner.
(M) *** EMI CMS7 63058-2 (3). Pears, Fischer-Dieskau, Schwarzkopf, Ludwig, Gedda, Berry, Hampstead Parish Church Ch., Philh. Ch. & O, Klemperer.
(BB) *** Naxos Dig. 8.550832/34 [id.]. József Mukk, István Gáti, Judit Németh, Ibolya Verebits, Péter Köves, Péter Cser, Ferenc Korpás, Rózsa Kiss, Agnes Csenki, Hungarian R. Children's Ch., Hungarian Festival Ch. & State SO, Géza Oberfrank.

Gardiner's version of the *St Matthew Passion*, the culminating issue in his Bach choral series for DG Archiv, brings an intense, dramatic reading which now makes a clear first choice, not just for period-performance devotees but for anyone not firmly set against the new authenticity. The result is an invigorating, intense telling of the story, with Gardiner favouring high dynamic contrasts and generally fast speeds which are still geared to the weighty purpose of the whole work. He and his performers were recorded in what proved an ideal venue, The Maltings at Snape, where the warm acoustic gives body and allows clarity to period textures.

While it certainly will not appeal to the authentic lobby, Klemperer's 1962 Philharmonia recording of the *St Matthew Passion* represents one of his greatest achievements on record, an act of devotion of such intensity that points of style and interpretation seem insignificant. The whole cast clearly shared Klemperer's own intense feelings, and one can only sit back and share them too, whatever one's preconceptions.

At bargain price the new version from Naxos uses modern, not period, instruments but, following authentic trends, has brisk speeds and well-sprung rhythms. Though the performance takes no less than 35 minutes less than, say, Richter's, in its alertness it never seems rushed, with the Hungarian State Symphony Orchestra and Festival Choir on excellent form, conducted by Géza Oberfrank. A refreshingly lithe and young-sounding Evangelist, József Mukk, leads a team of Hungarian soloists with fresh, clear voices. The obbligato wind-playing is also attractive (if closely balanced) and the recording is spacious and full, and kind to voices.

St Matthew Passion, BWV 244 (abridged).
(N) (**) EMI mono CMS5 65509-2 (2). Grümmer, Höffgen, Dermota, Fischer-Dieskau, Edelmann, V. Singakademie, V. Boys' Ch., VPO, Furtwängler.

Furtwängler conducted the *St Matthew Passion* at Easter 1954, barely six months before he died, and the recording, arriving belatedly, gives a vivid reminder of a great, dedicated occasion. The sound is limited and the choral sound lacks definition; despite that, however, the power of the massive double chorus at the start comes over strongly with the chorale descant for trebles shining brightly above.

Speeds are consistently slow, never more disconcertingly to the modern ear than in the chorales, made heavy and funereal, and slowness regularly begets monstrous rallentandos. In addition, 14 numbers were omitted at the performance, and two more have been cut because of technical problems with the recording. However damaging that may be, the result is neatly contained on two well-filled discs in place of the usual three. The four soloists, well caught by the recording, sing the arias as well as contributing to the narrative, with Anton Dermota light and sweet as the Evangelist and the young Fischer-Dieskau thrilling as Jesus.

St Matthew Passion: Arias and choruses.
(Y/B) (B) **(*) DG 439 447-2 [id.] (from complete recording with Schreier, Fischer-Dieskau, Mathis, J. Baker, Salminen, Regensburger Domspatzen, Munich Bach Ch. & O, Karl Richter).

Many collectors who have another complete set will be glad to have this 73-minute Classikon bargain selection from Richter's dedicated second (1979) stereo recording, particularly as Dame Janet Baker's *Erbarme dich* is included.

St Matthew Passion (complete; in English).
(BB) ** ASV CDQSS 324 (3) [id.]. Robert Tear, John Shirley-Quirk, Felicity Lott, Alfreda Hodgson, Neil Jenkins, Stephen Roberts, Bach Ch., St Paul's Cathedral Ch. Boys, Thames CO, Willcocks.

For anyone wanting the *St Matthew Passion* in English, ASV on its super-bargain Quicksilva label offers Sir David Willcocks's traditional account, recorded in 1978 with the Bach Choir, a splendid memento for anyone who has enjoyed his annual performances at the Festival Hall in London. The outstanding soloists include Robert Tear's Evangelist and John Shirley-Quirk's Christus, with Felicity Lott as the soprano soloist and the late Alfreda Hodgson as the contralto; but Peter's denial – usually a supremely moving moment – is here less powerful than usual. The pity is that this version fails to lift quite as it ought. Willcocks, most experienced of choirmasters, draws light and rhythmic singing from the chorus, and the chorales avoid heaviness. The (originally) Argo recording is clear and well balanced.

Vocal collections

Arias: *Bist du bei mir; Cantata 202: Weichet nur, Betrübte Schatten. Cantata 209: Ricetti gramezza. St Matthew Passion: Blute nur; Ich will dir mein Herze schenken.*
**(*) Delos Dig. D/CD 3026 [id.]. Arleen Augér, Mostly Mozart O, Schwarz – HANDEL: *Arias.* **(*)

Arleen Augér's pure, sweet soprano, effortlessly controlled, makes for bright performances of these Bach arias and songs, very recommendable for admirers of this delightful singer, well coupled with Handel arias.

Arias: *Mass in B min.: Agnus dei; Qui sedes. St John Passion: All is fulfilled. St Matthew Passion: Grief for sin.*
(M) (***) Decca mono 433 474-2. Kathleen Ferrier, LPO, Boult – HANDEL: *Arias.* (***) ⊛

On 7th and 8th October 1952, Kathleen Ferrier made her last and perhaps greatest record in London's Kingsway Hall, coupling four arias each by Bach and Handel. The combined skill of John Culshaw and Kenneth Wilkinson ensured a recording of the utmost fidelity by the standards of that time. Now it re-emerges with extraordinary naturalness and presence.

Transcriptions

Transcriptions: arr. BUSONI: *Chaconne* (from *Violin Partita No. 2*); *Chorales: Ich ruf zu dir; Nun freut euch, lieben Christen; Nun komm der Heiden Heiland; Wachet auf; Toccata & fugue in D min.* arr. LISZT: *Prelude & fugue in A min.* arr. LORD BERNERS: *In dolci jubilo.* arr. MYRA HESS: *Jesu, joy of man's desiring.* arr. KEMPFF: *Siciliano.* arr. LE FLEMING: *Sheep may safely graze.* arr. RACHMANINOV: *Suite from Partita No. 3 in E.*
*** ASV Dig. CDDCA 759 [id.]. Gordon Fergus-Thompson (piano).

A highly entertaining collection, played with much flair and, in the case of the lyrical pieces at the centre of the recital (notably Wilhelm Kempff's delightful *Siciliano* and Dame Myra Hess's famous arrangement of *Jesu, joy of man's desiring*), stylish charm.

Arrangements: Bach–Stokowski

Adagio in C, BWV 564; Chorales: Jesus Christus Gottes Sohn (from *Easter cantata*); *Komm süsser Tod; Mein Jesu; Sheep may safely graze; Wir glauben all' an Einen Gott (Giant fugue), BWV 680. Fugue in G min. (Little), BWV 578; Passacaglia and fugue in C min., BWV 582; Suite No. 3 in D, BWV 1068: Air.*

Toccata and fugue in D min., BWV 565; Violin & harpsichord sonata No. 4, BWV 1017: Siciliano; Well-tempered Clavier, Book 1, Prelude No. 24.
*** Chandos Dig. CHAN 9259 [id.]. BBC PO, Matthias Bamert.

This sumptuously recorded Chandos CD brings together the dozen published Stokowski Bach transcriptions. Bamert's warmly sympathetic readings obviously follow his mentor's way with this music, if without quite managing the naturally spontaneous rubato which was one of Stokowski's special gifts. Nor is the playing as vital and electrifying as the great conductor's own record. But the result is very enjoyable, and the Chandos stereo here is very much in the demonstration bracket.

Chorales: Jesu, joy of man's desiring; Sheep may safely graze; We all believe in one God (Fugue on *Wir glauben all' an einen Gott*), *BWV 680; English suite No. 2, BWV 807: Bourrée. Komm süsser Tod, BWV 478; Chaconne* (from *Partita No. 2 in B min.* for unaccompanied violin), *BWV 1004; Well-tempered Clavier*, Book 1: *Prelude in B min., BWV 869. Easter oratorio: Chorale. Toccata and fugue in D minor, BWV 565.*
❀ (M) *** RCA mono GD 60922 [id.]. SO, Leopold Stokowski.

The *Toccata and fugue in D minor* is a mono recording made in 1947, and absolutely no technical apologies need be made for it. The sound is clear and full and has an impressively resonant bass. The violins sound more real than many stereo recordings made in America over the next two decades. The rest of the programme dates from three years later. The sobriquet, 'Symphony Orchestra', in this case describes a pick-up group of musicians drawn from the New York Philharmonic and NBC Symphony. They play marvellously. The collector's item here is the incredibly wayward account of Bach's famous *Chaconne*, with its funereal opening tempo. Milstein's account takes 14 minutes; Stokowski stretches it out to 17 minutes 22 seconds and his indulgent *espressivo* alters its character entirely.

Bach, Wilhelm Friedemann (1710–84)

Harpsichord concertos: in D, F41; in F, F44; in A min., F45.
(N) *** HM Dig. HMC 901558 [id.]. Richard Egar, L. Bar., Charles Medlam.

These three concertos have plenty of interest. The often intricate solo writing always holds the listener's attention in these lively performances from Richard Egar, more particularly as the harpsichord is very truthfully caught and is not made to seem larger than life-size. The earliest work here, in A minor, dates from 1733 and has a sunny *Cantabile* slow movement which brings an engaging interplay between soloist and orchestra. The first movement is often dramatic and by no means predictable. The *Molto adagio* of the F major work is more poignant in feeling and shows the composer at his most darkly expressive, while the *Presto* finale is quirky in its rhythmic high spirits. The London Baroque provide alert, polished accompaniments, but the sharp-edged timbre of leader Ingrid Seifert and her period style, with its swelling out on individual notes, may not appeal to all, although the ear does adjust to it.

Double concerto for 2 harpsichords in D, F46.
(N) (M) **(*) Teldec/Warner 0630 12326-2 [id.]. Uittenbosch, Curtis, VCM, Harnoncourt – C. P. E. BACH: *Double concerto for harpsichord and fortepiano* ***; J. C. BACH: *Sinfonia concertante in F.* **(*)

Wilhelm Friedemann's *Double concerto* is a much less remarkable piece than Carl Philipp Emanuel's concerto for harpsichord and fortepiano. It is well enough played here, though tuttis are a bit gruff and rather heavily accented.

Sinfonia in F.
(N) (BB) **(*) Naxos Dig. 8.553289 [id.]. Salzburg CO, Yoon K. Lee – C. P. E. BACH: *Sinfonias.* **(*)

Wilhelm Friedemann Bach's *F major Sinfonia* is not really a match for those by his brother, Carl Philipp Emanuel, with which it is coupled. But it is agreeable enough and certainly not entirely conventional. It is given a lively account in Salzburg; modern instruments are used but textures are clean and fresh and the recording is faithful and well balanced.

Sinfonia in D, F64; Adagio & fugue in D min., F65.
*** Capriccio Dig. 10 283 [id.]. Concerto Köln – J. C. F. BACH: *Sinfonia;* C. P. E. BACH: *Harpsichord concerto;* J. C. BACH: *Sinfonia.* ***

Wilhelm Friedemann's three-movement *Sinfonia in D major* was intended for use as an introduction to the Whitsun cantata, *Dies ist der Tag*. The better-known *Adagio and fugue in D minor* is possibly the last two movements of a symphony. It is a very extraordinary and expressive piece and makes one wonder whether Wilhelm Friedemann did not possess the most powerful imagination of all the sons. It is played by this period group with great expressive vitality and is well recorded.

Fantasia in C min., F2; 8 Fugues, F31; March, F30; Prelude, F29; Sonatas: in G, F7; F min., F8; Suite in G min., F24.
(B) *** HM Dig. HMA 1901305 [id.]. Christophe Rousset (harpsichord).

Here is another recital to confirm Wilhelm Friedemann's strong musical personality. The extraordinary *Fantasia in C minor* has a darkly dramatic opening, then immediately evokes memories of Johann Sebastian's *Chromatic fantasia* in its florid brilliance. The two sonatas are also impressive works. Christophe Rousset was nineteen when he recorded this recital and he plays with remarkable maturity and discernment throughout. He certainly brings out the diversity of the eight succinct miniature *Fugues* which readily demonstrate Wilhelm's contrapuntal mastery.

Keyboard fantasias: Nos. 1–8 & 10, F14–21 & F23.
*** Denon Dig. CO 72588 [id.]. Huguette Dreyfus (harpsichord).

These works are engagingly unpredictable, all bringing quite bold and daring harmonic sleights of hand. So, too, is the excellent playing of Huguette Dreyfus, who has the advantage of an outstanding recording.

Baermann, Heinrich (1784–1847)

Adagio for clarinet and orchestra.
*** ASV Dig. CDDCA 559 [id.]. Emma Johnson, ECO, Groves – CRUSELL: *Concerto No. 2* *** ⊛;
  ROSSINI: *Introduction, theme and variations*** ; WEBER: *Concertino.* ***

Heinrich Baermann's rather beautiful *Adagio*, once attributed to Wagner, is offered by a young clarinettist who plays the work warmly and sympathetically.

Baird, Tadeusz (1928–81)

Colas Breugnon: suite.
(Y/B) (M) *** EMI CDMS5 65418-2 [id.]. Polish CO, Jerzy Maksymiuk – SZYMANOWSKI: *Violin concertos Nos. 1–2.* **(*)

Baird's delightful neo-classical suite (for flute and strings) has much in common with Warlock's *Capriol suite.* It is beautifully played and recorded.

Bairstow, Edward (1874–1946)

Organ sonata in E flat.
*** Priory Dig. PRCD 401 [id.]. John Scott (St Paul's Cathedral organ) (with William HARRIS: *Sonata* ***) – ELGAR: *Sonata No. 1.* ***

Bairstow's *Organ sonata* was written in 1937 and is Elgarian in feeling and the central Scherzo produces a blaze of orchestral sound unsurpassed by Elgar in either of his works for the instrument. The performance here is admirable and the St Paul's Cathedral organ is just right for it. The third work on the disc, a much more conventional sonata by William Harris (1883–1973), at least has a rather pleasing central *Adagio.*

Anthems and choral settings: *Blessed city, heavenly Salem; Blessed Virgin's cradle song; Evening Canticles in D; If the Lord had not helped me; Jesu, grant me this I pray; Jesu, the very thought; Lamentation* (from *Jeremiah*); *Let all mortal flesh keep silence; Lord I call upon Thee; Lord thou has been our refuge; Save us O Lord.*
*** Priory Dig. PRDC 365 [id.]. York Minster Ch., Philip Moore; John Scott Whiteley.

Bairstow is (rightly) best known for his moving and comparatively short anthem, *Let all mortal flesh keep silence*; but, as this collection shows, he wrote much else that gives full rein to his subtle understanding of choral blending and instinctive response to liturgical texts, especially those drawn from the Psalms which were one of his favourite scriptural sources. The gloriously expansive *Blessed city, heavenly Salem*, which opens the concert, makes the firmest of Christian statements and the depth of the composer's religious feeling is expressed touchingly in the poignant *Jesu, the very thought of you.* The performances here are very well prepared and excitingly committed and spontaneous. The chorus is set back in the ample and resonant Minster acoustic, which provides plenty of space for climaxes to expand gloriously, while the balance with the excellent organ accompaniments could hardly be bettered.

Balakirev, Mily (1837–1910)

Piano concertos Nos. 1 in F sharp min., Op. 1; 2 in E flat, Op. posth.
*** Hyperion Dig. CDA 66640 [id.]. Malcolm Binns, E. N. Philh. O, Lloyd-Jones – RIMSKY-KORSAKOV: *Concerto.* ***

The one-movement *First Piano concerto* (*Youth*) was composed when Balakirev was eighteen and is modelled on his adored Chopin. All the same, there are some touches of individuality, and it is well served by Malcolm Binns' intelligent and sensitive performance, which also has the advantage of fine orchestral support and up-to-date recording. It also has the only available account of the more characteristic *Second Concerto*, which Balakirev started in 1861 but (like the *First Symphony*) put on one side. It was left incomplete and finished after his death by Lyapunov.

Symphony No. 1 in C; Islamey (orch. Lyapunov); *Tamara.*
(BB) *** Naxos Dig. 8.550792 [id.]. Russian State SO, Igor Golovschin.

Symphony No. 1; Russia (symphonic poem).
**(*) Hyperion Dig. CDA 66493 [id.]. Philh. O, Svetlanov.

Symphony No. 1 in C; Tamara (symphonic poem).
(M) **(*) EMI CDM7 63375-2 [id.]. RPO, Beecham.

Balakirev's sumptuously lyrical *First Symphony* has had a chequered gramophone career. Beecham's 1955 has always been the yardstick by which other versions were judged. It has many felicities and is coupled at mid-price with *Tamara*, with the early stereo responding quite well to the CD face-lift, although the lack of amplitude in the string-tone is disadvantageous.

Golovschin may not quite have the uncanny grip on the rather loose-structured first movement that Beecham found, but his reading is exciting, convincing in its pacing and control of tension. Moreover it is very well played by a Russian ensemble who have this music in their bones. The two supporting works are hardly less successful. *Islamey* starts off with tremendous Slavonic bustle and again produces a subtly alluring oriental flavour in its central section, while *Tamara* is warmly atmospheric and held together very well, again with glowing woodwind contributions and the Eastern melodic influences deliciously caught. The 1993 recording was made at the Mosfilm Studio and is vivid and full; although the acoustic is inevitably drier and less open than the Hyperion, it is not confining and the stereo ambience brings plenty of bloom.

Svetlanov's performance brings some beautiful playing from the Philharmonia Orchestra in both works. The soaring clarinet solo at the beginning of the slow movement is ravishingly done (presumably by Michael Collins). However, there is some disagreement among us concerning Svetlanov's grip on the first three movements, although in the finale the emotional thrust of this music is powerfully caught, and the Hyperion recording, warm and full, deserves the highest grading. The coupling is both apt and successful in all respects.

Symphony No. 2 in D min.; Russia.
(BB) *** Naxos Dig. 8.550793 [id.]. Russian State SO, Igor Golovschin.

Symphony No. 2 in D min.; Overture on 3 Russian themes; Tamara.
**(*) Hyperion Dig. CDA 66586 [id.]. Philh. O, Svetlanov.

The *Second Symphony* is a late work. The first movement is tautly constructed; Golovschin controls its layout impressively and at the same time provides plenty of impetus. The Scherzo has Slavonic gusto but, as with the *First Symphony*, it is the *Andante* where this very Russian performance is so telling – spacious and refined, the strings swelling out spontaneously from a romantic onward flow that is beautifully shaped. The opening of *Russia* is warmly atmospheric and its integrated folk material again brings seductive woodwind playing and highly responsive strings; after the brass livens things up in a folk dance, Golovschin sustains a raptly beautiful close.

In the *Second Symphony* the playing of the Philharmonia is cultured and the sound pleasingly natural and well balanced. It comes with the attractive *Overture on three Russian themes* and *Tamara*, arguably Balakirev's masterpiece. Yet once again there is lack of consensus over Svetlanov's reading. R.L. enjoys its spacious breadth; however, while agreeing that it is tauter than that of the *First*, E.G. suggests that it does little to promote a symphony which inevitably runs the risk of seeming a repetition of the earlier work. *Tamara* too – almost as extended as a one-movement symphony – needs to be stronger and more purposeful, as Beecham's version demonstrates.

Islamey (oriental fantasy).
(N) ⊛ *** Teldec/Warner Dig. 4509 96516-2 [id.]. Boris Berezovsky (with LIADOV: *Preludes, Opp. 39/4; 40/2; 57/1;* MEDTNER: *Fairy tales, Opp. 20/1; 34/2–3; 51/1;* RACHMANINOV: *Etudes-tableaux, Op. 39/3–4, 7 & 9* ***) – MUSSORGSKY: *Night on a bare mountain.* *** ⊛
(M) *** EMI CDM7 64329-2. Andrei Gavrilov – PROKOFIEV: *Concerto No. 1;* TCHAIKOVSKY: *Piano concerto No. 1* etc. ***

An amazing account of *Islamey* from Boris Berezovsky, the 1991 Tchaikovsky Competition prize-winner. One is tempted to hail it as the best *Islamey* ever – certainly the finest since the legendary Parlophone 78-r.p.m. disc by Simon Barere, and possibly even finer. Stunning, effortless virtuosity. Berezovsky makes an ideal Rachmaninov interpreter too, and it would be difficult to flaw these fine accounts of four of the Op. 39 set of *Etudes-tableaux*. Berezovsky is also a champion of Medtner and has an obvious affinity with his music. He has all the subtlety, poetic feeling and keyboard mastery that this music calls for. The Liadov *Preludes* too are played impeccably. This is in every respect an outstanding recital.

Gavrilov's dazzling account of Balakirev's fantasy is outstandingly charismatic; it is well recorded, too. It comes in harness with an equally dazzling version of Prokofiev's *First Piano concerto* and a performance of the Tchaikovsky *B flat minor Concerto* which is rather less convincing.

Piano sonata in B flat min.
**(*) Olympia OCD 354 [id.]; Archduke *MARC 2*. Donna Amato – DUTILLEUX: *Sonata.* **(*)
**(*) Kingdom Dig. KCLCD 2001 [id.]. Gordon Fergus-Thompson – SCRIABIN: *Sonata No. 3* etc. **(*)

The Balakirev is arguably the greatest Russian piano sonata of the pre-1914 era. Donna Amato gives a musicianly account of it, well paced and authoritative. The recording is very lifelike, and this is a most desirable issue, even if the playing time at 47 minutes is not particularly generous.

Gordon Fergus-Thompson, too, is fully equal to the considerable demands of the Balakirev *Sonata* and offers excellent playing, though the recording is reverberant and the piano not always dead in tune. Fergus-Thompson also includes Balakirev's arrangement of Glinka's *The Lark* as an encore.

Bantock, Granville (1868–1946)

Celtic Symphony; Hebridean Symphony; The Sea reivers; The Witch of Atlas.
*** Hyperion Dig. CDA 66450 [id.]. RPO, Handley.

Vernon Handley conducts warmly atmospheric performances of four of Bantock's Hebridean inspirations. Most ambitious is the *Hebridean Symphony* of 1913, with nature music echoing Wagner and Delius as well as Sibelius, whose music Bantock introduced into Britain. The two tone-poems are attractive too, but best of all is the *Celtic Symphony*, a late work written in 1940, which uses strings and six harps. This is in the grand string tradition of Vaughan Williams's *Tallis fantasia* and Elgar's *Introduction and allegro*, a beautiful, colourful work that deserves to be far better known. With warm, atmospheric recording to match, Handley draws committed performances from the RPO.

Pagan Symphony; Fifine at the fair; 2 Heroic ballads.
*** Hyperion Dig. CDA 66630 [id.]. RPO, Handley.

A fine successor to Handley's earlier pairing of the *Celtic* and *Hebridean Symphonies*. The *Pagan Symphony* dates from 1928, so it comes mid-way between the others, and the writing brings touches of Elgar as well as German influences. It is tuneful and well crafted. Perhaps it isn't as individual a work as *Fifine at the fair*, with which Beecham understandably identified; but Handley is equally at home in this colourful tone-poem, and it is good to have it presented in stereo as vivid as this. The two *Ballads* are rather more conventional but still make a considerable impression.

The Pierrot of the minute: overture.
(M) *** Chandos CHAN 6566 [id.]. Bournemouth Sinf., Norman Del Mar – BRIDGE: *Summer* etc.; BUTTERWORTH: *Banks of Green Willow.* ***

Bantock's overture is concerned with Pierrot's dream, in which he falls in love with a Moon Maiden who tells him their love must die at dawn, but he will not listen. He wakes to realize that his dream of love lasted a mere minute. The writing is often delicate and at times Elgarian, and the piece is well worth investigating. The 1978 recording sounds remarkably fresh.

Symphony No. 3 (The Cyprian Goddess); Dante and Beatrice (poem for orchestra); *Helena (variations on the theme HFB).*
(N) *** Hyperion Dig. CDA 66810 [id.]. RPO, Vernon Handley.

As in his two previous Hyperion issues of Bantock, Vernon Handley draws from the RPO ripely persuasive performances of high romantic works that have been too long neglected. It emerges that Bantock wrote some of his finest music in his last years when neglect had already overtaken him. *The Cyprian Goddess*, completed in 1939 when the composer was seventy, echoes Strauss in its sumptuous orchestration and melodic writing, and in its refinement it has something of the elegiac tone of late Strauss. The *Helena variations*, written in tribute to his wife, echo the freshness and variety of Elgar's newly completed *Enigma*, while *Dante and Beatrice* is a free-ranging programme work which in its warmth and dramatic contrasts echoes Tchaikovsky's *Romeo and Juliet*. Whatever the echoes, in each piece Bantock establishes his own distinctive voice, here more tautly controlled than in his expansive, middle-period works. First-rate sound.

Barber, Samuel (1910–81)

Adagio for strings, Op. 11.
*** Argo 417 818-2 [id.]. ASMF, Marriner – COPLAND: *Quiet city;* COWELL: *Hymn;* CRESTON: *Rumor;* IVES: *Symphony No. 3.* ***
(M) *** DG Dig. 427 806-2; *427 806-4.* LAPO, Bernstein – BERNSTEIN: *Overture Candide; West Side Story; On the Town* ***; GERSHWIN: *Rhapsody in blue.* **(*)
(M) *** DG Dig. 439 528-2 [id.]. LAPO, Bernstein – COPLAND: *Appalachian spring* ***; GERSHWIN: *Rhapsody in blue.* **(*)
*** Koch Schwann Dig. 3-7243-2 [id.]. New Zealand SO, James Sedares – DELLO JOIO: *The Triumph of St Joan* etc. ***

Marriner's 1976 performance of Barber's justly famous *Adagio* is arguably the most satisfying version we have had since the war, although Bernstein's alternative has the advantage of digital recording. The quality of sound on the remastered Argo CD retains most of the richness and body of the analogue LP, but at the climax the brighter lighting brings a slightly sparer violin texture than on the original LP.

Bernstein's 1971 Sony account is slow and intense, the brightly lit sound revealing all the linear detail. The later DG recording (variously coupled), with more modern digital sound, is preferable, but the earlier version is just as deeply felt.

The principal interest of this Koch CD is the coupled music by Norman Dello Joio, but the programme ends with a deeply felt account of Barber's *Adagio*, given in memory of Andrew Schenck who conducted many of the New Zealand orchestra's earlier records on this label.

(i) *Adagio for strings;* (i; ii) *Cello concerto, Op. 22;* (ii; iii) *Cello sonata, Op. 6.*
*** Virgin/EMI Dig. VC7 59565-2 [id.]. (i) SCO; Saraste; (ii) Ralph Kirshbaum; (iii) Roger Vignoles.

Kirshbaum's view of the Barber *Cello concerto*, with splendid support from Saraste and the Scottish Chamber Orchestra, is darker and spikier than those of his direct rivals, and rather more urgent in the outer movements, yet it is just as beautifully played. He is equally convincing in Barber's other, much rarer cello work, the *Cello sonata* of 1932. Roger Vignoles copes well with piano-writing unhelpful to a degree surprising from a pianist-composer. The celebrated *Adagio*, coolly done, makes a worthwhile fill-up. Spacious, well-focused recording.

Adagio for strings; (i) *Piano concerto, Op. 38; Medea's meditation and Dance of vengeance, Op. 23a.*
*** ASV Dig. CDDCA 534 [id.]. (i) Joselson; LSO, Schenck.

In Barber's *Concerto* Tedd Joselson is marvellously and dazzlingly brilliant, as well as being highly sensitive and poetic with an unforced and responsive orchestral contribution from the LSO under Andrew Schenck. The LSO also give a singularly fine account of the *Medea* excerpt (not to be confused with the Suite) and a restrained and noble one of the celebrated *Adagio*.

Adagio for strings, Op. 11; Essays Nos. 1, Op. 12; 2, Op. 17; Music for a scene from Shelley, Op. 7; Overture, The School for Scandal, Op. 5; Symphony No. 1, Op. 9.
*** Argo Dig. 436 288 [id.]. Baltimore SO, Zinman.

These performances are very alert and vital, particularly that of the *First Symphony,* which is as good as any now available; the recording has superb presence and detail. Apart from the first two *Essays* for orchestra, Zinman's disc includes the more rarely heard *Music for a scene from Shelley*, a sumptuously scored and gloriously atmospheric work inspired by lines from *Prometheus Unbound*. This is the best account of it since Golschmann's from the late 1960s, and adds greatly to the attractions of an already desirable issue. Zinman and his excellent orchestra play the *Overture* to Sheridan's *The School for Scandal*, Barber's celebrated graduation exercise on leaving the Curtis Institute, with equal commitment. Strongly recommended.

(i) *Adagio for strings;* (ii) *Essay No. 2 for orchestra; Music for a scene from Shelley; Serenade for strings, Op. 1;* (ii; iii) *A Stopwatch and an ordnance map, Op. 15;* (iv) Chorus: *Let down the bars, O Death!* (ii; v) *A Hand of bridge* (chamber opera), *Op. 35.*
(M) *** Van. 08.4016.71 [OVC 4016]. (i) I Solisti di Zagreb, Antonio Janigro; (ii) Symphony of the Air, Golschmann; (iii) with Robert De Cormier Chorale; (v) with Neway, Alberts, Lewis, Maero; (iv) Washington Cathedral Ch., Callaway.

An admirable and highly rewarding anthology of works by a composer whose *Adagio for strings* has wrongly overshadowed his achievement elsewhere. Excellent singing and playing throughout.

Adagio for strings, Op. 11; Knoxville, Summer of 1915; Songs, Op. 13: Nocturne; Sure on the shining night.
(Y/B) *** EMI Dig. CDC5 55358-2 [id.]. Barbara Hendricks, LSO, Tilson Thomas – COPLAND: *Quiet city* etc. ***

Between them, Tilson Thomas and Barbara Hendricks have devised a programme of Copland as well as Barber with both composers at their most radiantly inspired. *Knoxville*, to a poem by James Agee, is one of the most magically evocative pieces of its kind, and is the more magical here for the authentically American inflexions that Hendricks gives it, together with glowing string-tone. The two songs which Barber orchestrated from his Opus 13 are most beautifully done too, while the celebrated *Adagio* is taken at a flowing tempo with no self-indulgence or sentimentality at all. A radiant disc.

Adagio for strings, Op. 11. Medea: Medea's Meditation and Dance of vengeance, Op. 23a.
(M) *** RCA 09026 61424-2 [id.]. Boston SO, Munch – ELGAR: *Introduction and allegro* **; TCHAIKOVSKY: *Serenade.* **(*)

Munch's performance of the *Adagio* has a spacious nobility and generates great passion and ardour at the climax. It is marvellously played, and the playing in the excerpts from *Medea* is equally electrifying. The 1957 recording now sounds fuller and much more realistic than on LP: indeed the CD remastering is remarkably convincing.

(i) *Canzonetta;* (ii) *Souvenirs.*
(N) ** ASV Dig. CDDCA 737. (i) Julia Girdwood, SCO; (ii) LSO; Serebrier – BRITTEN: *Les Illuminations* etc. ***

With Julia Girdwood a deeply moving oboe soloist, the *Canzonetta*, shortest item on this Barber/Britten disc, is the most valuable of all. It is a piece left incomplete at the composer's death, the slow movement of a projected oboe concerto, with the strings of the Scottish Chamber Orchestra sweetly expressive too. This is a 'three-star' performance; but in *Souvenirs*, by turns nostalgic and witty, the LSO playing boldly under Serebrier sound too heavy, missing the wit of the parodies. Full-blooded recording.

Cave of the heart (original version of *Medea*).
*** Koch Dig. 3-7019-2 [id.]. Atlantic Sinf., Schenck – COPLAND: *Appalachian spring.* ***

The original version of *Medea* was entitled *Cave of the heart*; in this original form it sounds much darker in feeling and harder-edged, and it has stronger Stravinskian overtones. The effect in this full-blooded, vividly present recording is, if anything, brawnier than the more sumptuous revision. A most interesting and stimulating score.

Cello concerto, Op. 22.
*** Chandos Dig. CHAN 8322 [id.]. Wallfisch, ECO, Simon – SHOSTAKOVICH: *Cello concerto No. 1.* ***

Wallfisch gives an impressive and eloquent reading, and the elegiac slow movement is especially fine. Wallfisch is forwardly balanced, but otherwise the recording is truthful; the orchestra is vividly detailed.

(i; ii) *Piano concerto, Op. 38;* (ii) *Symphony No. 1, Op. 9;* (i; iii) *Souvenirs, Op. 28* (arr. piano, 4 hands); *Canzone.*
*** RCA Dig. RD 60732 [60732-2-RC]. (i) John Browning; (ii) St Louis SO, Leonard Slatkin; (iii) Slatkin (piano).

In his version of Samuel Barber's *Symphony No. 1*, Slatkin has an obvious advantage. At the very start, the tautness of attack by the St Louis players immediately commands attention, while Järvi (see below) builds tension more gradually. Though Järvi's sense of spontaneity gives extra warmth at times, Slatkin secures ensemble a degree crisper. The coupling will be the decisive point for many, and on RCA it is good to have a new recording of the *Piano concerto* by John Browning, the pianist for whom Barber originally wrote this formidable half-hour work. As an exceptionally generous makeweight Slatkin joins Browning in a piano duo playing Barber's two-piano piece, *Souvenirs*, as Browning points out a work of 'pure nostalgia', played here with winning lightness.

Violin concerto, Op. 14.
(N) ✪ (M) *** Sony Stern Edition II SMK 64506 [id.]. Stern, NYPO, Bernstein – MAXWELL DAVIES: *Violin concerto.* ***
(Y/B) ✪ *** DG Dig. 439 886-2 [id.]. Gil Shaham, LSO, Previn – KORNGOLD: *Violin concerto* etc. *** ✪
(Y/B) *** EMI Dig. CDC5 55360-2 [id.]. Perlman, Boston SO, Ozawa – BERNSTEIN: *Serenade;* FOSS: *Three American pieces.* ***

Isaac Stern gave the Barber *Violin concerto* its stereo première in 1964 and his performance, which is consistently inspired, is of superlative quality. It has warmth, freshness and humanity, and the slow movement is glorious. The CBS forward balance for the orchestra is less than ideal, but the recording is otherwise very good and has been impressively remastered. This is one of Stern's most important and most distinguished recordings: one feels that he realized that the work was a masterpiece from the very beautiful opening phrase. And yet it has taken three decades for the work to begin to find a permanent place in the concert repertoire.

Gil Shaham's performance of the Barber has great virtuosity and is a reading of strong profile, with every moment of dramatic intensity properly characterized. The effect is warm and ripe, with the sound close and immediate, bringing out above all the work's bolder side. There have been subtler readings of Barber's lovely *Concerto*, with the soloist not always helped by the close balance, but it is good to have a sharp distinction drawn between the purposeful lyricism of the first movement, marked *Allegro*, and the withdrawn, tender lyricism of the heavenly *Andante*. In the *moto perpetuo* finale Shaham brings out the fun behind the movement's manic energy, with Previn pointing the Waltonian wit. This really *is* good – and worthy to rank alongside the Stern/Bernstein (Sony). Indeed it is to be preferred to the richly extrovert Perlman account.

For Perlman the kernel of the Barber *Concerto* lies in the central slow movement. When the soloist enters after the extended orchestral introduction, he plays with a warmth and intensity that even he has rarely matched, making the return of the main theme on the G-string a wonderful resolution, with vibrato so perfectly controlled that there is no hint of soupiness. Weight, power and virtuoso brilliance then come together in Perlman's dazzling account of the finale. Though orchestral textures could be more open, the rich tapestry of the Boston sound is moulded beautifully to the fullness of Perlman's violin.

Essays Nos. 1, Op. 12; 2, Op. 17; 3, Op. 47.
*** Chandos Dig. CHAN 9053 [id.]. Detroit SO, Järvi – IVES: *Symphony No. 1.* ***

Both in terms of sonority and approach, Neeme Järvi's account of these appealing works differs from their American predecessors. The strings have a lightness and subtlety and are highly responsive. The recording is very natural and present, and beautifully balanced.

Essay for orchestra No. 3, Op. 47; Fadograph of a Yestern Scene, Op. 44; Medea: suite, Op. 23.
*** Koch Dig. 3-7010-2 [id.]. New Zealand SO, Andrew Schenck.

A welcome recording of two Barber rarities from the 1970s in sympathetic performances by the New Zealand orchestra under Andrew Schenck. The recording has outstanding clarity and definition, but the acoustic has the very slightly dry quality of a studio rather than the expansiveness of a concert hall.

Medea (ballet): suite.
(M) *** Mercury 432 016-2 [id.]. Eastman-Rochester O, Howard Hanson – GOULD: *Fall River legend* etc. ***

Hanson's performance is both polished and dramatic, and the brilliant 1959 Mercury recording has astonishing clarity and vivid presence.

Medea's meditation and dance of vengeance, Op. 23a; Music for a scene from Shelley, Op. 7; Vanesssa: 2 excerpts.
*** Chandos Dig. CHAN 9253 [id.]. Detroit SO, Järvi – CHADWICK: *Symphony No. 3.* ***

Music for a scene from Shelley is a powerfully atmospheric, rich and haunting score, already available on the Argo disc from Zinman and the Baltimore orchestra (as well as Golschmann's version from the

1970s), but this proves to be as appealing an alternative. The two excerpts (the vocal line being taken by solo instruments) from *Vanessa* are captivating; the celebrated dance from *Medea* comes off splendidly under Neeme Järvi and the recording is absolutely state-of-the-art.

Souvenirs.
*** Koch Dig. 3-7005-2 [id.]. New Zealand SO, Schenck – MENOTTI: *Amahl* etc. ***

Souvenirs is an absolutely enchanting score which has bags of charm and, unlike the delightful Menotti with which it is coupled, every idea is so memorable that it instantly replaces the one that came before. It is very well played here by the New Zealand Symphony Orchestra under Andrew Schenck and is eminently well recorded too. Strongly recommended.

Symphony No. 1, Op. 9.
(Y/B) (M) (**) Bruno Walter Edition: Sony mono SMK 64466 [id.]. NYPO, Bruno Walter (with DVORAK: *Slavonic dance, Op. 46/1*) – R. STRAUSS: *Death and transfiguration* etc. (**(*))

Symphony No. 1 (in one movement), Op. 9; Essays for Orchestra Nos. 1, Op. 12; 2, Op. 17; Night flight, Op. 19a.
(M) *** Unicorn UKCD 2046 [id.]. LSO, David Measham.

Symphony No. 1; The School for scandal: Overture, Op. 5.
*** Chandos Dig. CHAN 8958 [id.]. Detroit SO, Järvi – BEACH: *Symphony in E min.* ***

Neeme Järvi's account of Barber's *First Symphony* is broader than usual and gains enormously in symphonic coherence. Barber's youthful *Overture* to *The School for scandal* with its marvellously fresh and lyrical second theme is equally well served. Good playing from the Detroit orchestra and very good recorded sound.

David Measham also proves a splendid advocate of Barber's *First Symphony*, securing a passionately committed performance and bringing out its (at times) somewhat Waltonian manner. Those looking for a mid-priced version should be well pleased, for the first two *Essays for orchestra* are very well played, as is the hauntingly evocative movement, *Night flight*, all that the composer wanted to survive from his *Symphony No. 2*.

Walter is an unexpected conductor in the music of Samuel Barber, but he recorded the *First Symphony* in 1945, two years after the composer had revised his score. It is a fresh, powerfully intense reading, let down by harsh, two-dimensional, mono sound.

Symphony No. 2, Op. 19; Adagio for strings, Op. 11.
*** Chandos Dig. CHAN 9169 [id.]. Detroit SO, Järvi – BRISTOW: *Symphony No. 2.* ***

The *Second Symphony* is a powerful work with a strong first movement. There is a particularly beguiling second group which has some of the innocence and warmth of the second theme from the *School for Scandal* Overture. Of the performances available, Neeme Järvi on Chandos is the one to have: the Detroit orchestra turn in polished playing and the Chandos recording is rich and vivid.

CHAMBER MUSIC
(i; ii) *Canzone for flute and piano, Op. 38;* (iii; ii) *Cello sonata, Op. 6;* (iv) *Summer music* (for wind quintet)*, Op. 31;* (ii) (Piano) *Excursions, Op. 20; Nocturne (Homage to John Field), Op. 33; Souvenirs, Op. 28: Pas de deux; Two-step.*

(Y/B) *** EMI Dig. CDC5 55400-2 [id.]. (i) Jeanne Baxtresser; (ii) Israela Margalit; (iii) Alan Stepansky; (iv) Baxtresser, Robinson, Drucker, Le Clair, Myers.

The performances here are warmly spontaneous in feeling, readily demonstrating that these players have lived with this music before recording it. The *Canzone for flute and piano* has an Elysian, soaring melody (slightly French in atmosphere). Jeanne Baxtresser plays it very beautifully. The splendid *Cello sonata* has a powerful impulse and is given the most eloquent advocacy here, although Alan Stepansky and Israela Margalit are not helped by a rather too resonant acoustic. But better this than a dry studio, and the finely played piano works are beautifully full in timbre. The four *Excursions* have wit and elegance, and the *Nocturne* for John Field is quite charming. The concert closes with the gently sombre *Pas de deux* (which has something of Ravel in its poise and colouring) and the audacious and witty *Two-step*, both from the ballet *Souvenirs*. They originated as piano pieces (in 1951), but were written for four hands. Israela Margalit manages admirably with only two. Overall, this hour-long concert is very rewarding indeed and it cannot be too highly recommended.

(i) *Serenade for string quartet, Op.1; String quartet, Op. 11;* (i; ii) *Dover Beach, Op. 3;* (ii; iii) *3 Songs (The daisies; With rue my heart is laden; Bessie Bobtail), Op. 2; 3 Songs (Rain has fallen; Sleep now; I hear an army), Op. 10; Sure on this shining night; Nocturne, Op. 13/3–4; Solitary hotel; Despite and still, Op. 41/ 4–5; 3 Songs (Now I have fed and eaten up; A green lowland of pianos; O boundless, boundless evening), Op. 45.*

(Y/B) *** Virgin/EMI Dig. VC5 45033-2 [id.].(i) Endellion Qt; (ii) Thomas Allen; (iii) Roger Vignoles.

Where the DG set of his complete songs centred round John Browning at the piano, this single disc is geared to the Endellion Quartet, both as accompanist in *Dover Beach* and in the two early string quartet works. The *Serenade*, Op. 1, was written when Barber was only nineteen, with the first two of its three brief movements belying any idea of a lightweight work, even bringing echoes of late Beethoven. The Endellion Quartet play with the hushed gravity and clear intensity that it deserves, and their reading of the Opus 11 *Quartet* – best known as the original source of Barber's celebrated *Adagio for strings* – has points of advantage over even the finest rivals, with more mystery and variety of expression, and with the *Adagio* kept flowing. With Thomas Allen a superb soloist, this account of *Dover Beach* not only conveys more mystery and a keener feeling for atmosphere than current rivals, it builds to a thrilling climax on the poet's expression of love. In the solo songs Allen and Vignoles opt consistently for speeds on the fast side, so that the slow tango of the Joyce setting, *Solitary hotel*, is more clearly established.

String quartet, Op. 11.
*** ASV Dig. CDDCA 825 [id.]. Lindsay Qt – A. TCHAIKOVSKY: *String quartet No. 2;* WIREN: *String quartet No. 3;* WOOD: *String quartet No. 3.* ***
*** RCA Dig. 09026 61387-2 [id.]. Tokyo Qt – BRITTEN: *Quartet No. 2;* TAKEMITSU: *A Way A Lone.* ***
**(*) DG Dig. 435 864-2 [id.]. Emerson Qt – IVES: *Quartets 1–2.*

The Lindsays give the more humane and deeply felt account of Samuel Barber's early *String quartet*, and no one wanting to add the piece to their collection is likely to be disappointed. Their performance comes from a broadcast given in 1987 and so has the feel of live music-making. Their coupling blends enterprise and interest, offering quartets by André Tchaikovsky, better known during his lifetime as an accomplished pianist, Hugh Wood and Dag Wirén.

The Tokyo Quartet's account of the Barber is also hard to beat. They produce a sumptuous and beautifully blended sonority and they play with feeling. Choice will no doubt be affected by the coupling, but there is no doubt that theirs is very remarkable playing, and no one wanting the coupling should hesitate.

The Emerson Quartet play with all the brilliance and technical expertise with which one associates them, but there is something rather soulless about them. The tone is rich, their tonal blend immaculate and their ensemble impeccable – indeed nothing can be faulted; but their expressive eloquence sounds over-rehearsed as if the feeling is painted on afterwards. All the same it is in its way stunningly played, and those who admire their brilliance and tonal sheen will find it eminently well captured by the DG engineers. Given this level of accomplishment, it would be curmudgeonly to deny them a strong recommendation.

Summer music.
*** Crystal CD 750 [id.]. Westwood Wind Quintet – CARLSSON: *Nightwings;* LIGETI: *Bagatelles;* MATHIAS: *Quintet.* ***

Samuel Barber's *Summer music* is an evocative mood-picture of summer, a gloriously warm and lyrical piece whose neglect on record is difficult to understand. The Crystal CD offers superbly committed and sensitive playing and vivid, warm recording.

PIANO MUSIC

Ballade, Op. 46; 4 Excursions, Op. 20; Nocturne (Homage to John Field), Op. 33; Sonata, Op. 26.
**(*) Hyperion CDH 88016 [id.]. Angela Brownridge.

This CD accommodates Barber's entire output for the piano. Angela Brownridge gives a good account of herself in the dazzling *Sonata*. The recording is not first class; the resonant acoustic makes the piano sound slightly unfocused, though the ear soon adjusts.

Piano sonata, Op. 26.
(M) (***) RCA mono GD 60377. Vladimir Horowitz (with FAURE: *Nocturne No. 13;* POULENC: *Presto* ***) – KABALEVSKY; PROKOFIEV: *Sonatas* etc. (***)
(M) **(*) RCA GD 60415 [60415-2-RG]. Van Cliburn (with DEBUSSY: *Estampes: Soirée dans Grenade;*

Jardins sous la pluie; Etude No. 5; Images, Book I: Reflets dans l'eau; Préludes, Book 2: La terrasse des audiences du clair de lune; Feux d'artifice **; MOZART: *Piano sonata No. 10* **).

Horowitz gave the première of Barber's *Sonata* and his performance has never been surpassed. It is a remarkable work and, in Horowitz's hands, completely riveting: sample his playing in the quicksilver Scherzo or the articulation of the spirited closing *Fuga*. The 1950 sound is confined but fully acceptable. Of the encores, the scintillating Poulenc *Presto* shows the great pianist at his most dazzling, with a good (if not outstanding) supporting programme.

Van Cliburn's recording is pretty masterly and, although the sound could be more ingratiating and have a warmer ambience, it is still acceptable.

VOCAL MUSIC

Agnus Dei.
*** Hyperion Dig. CDA 66219 [id.]. Corydon Singers, Matthew Best – BERNSTEIN: *Chichester Psalms;* COPLAND: *In the beginning* etc. ***

Barber's *Agnus Dei* is none other than our old friend the *Adagio*, arranged for voices by the composer in 1967. Matthew Best's fine performance moves spaciously and expansively to an impressive climax.

(i) *Andromache's farewell;* (ii) *Dover Beach;* (iii) *Hermit songs;* (iv) *Knoxville: summer of 1915.*
(M) (***) Sony mono/stereo MPK 46727 [id.]. (i) Arroyo, NYPO, Schippers; (ii) Fischer-Dieskau, Juilliard Qt; (iii) Leontyne Price, composer; (iv) Eleanor Steber, Dumbarton Oaks O, William Strickland.

This collection of vintage recordings makes a splendid mid-priced Barber compendium, representing four of his finest vocal works, all in superb performances. Excellent CD transfers. No texts are provided but words are exceptionally clear.

Despite and still (song-cycle), *Op. 41; 10 Hermit songs* (to poems translated from anonymous Irish texts of 8th to 13th centuries), *Op. 29; Mélodies passagères (Puisque tout passe; Un cygne; Tombeau dans un parc; Le clocher chante), Op. 27; 3 Songs (The daisies; With rue my heart is laden; Bessie Bobtail), Op. 2; 3 Songs (Rain has fallen; Sleep now; I hear an army), Op. 10; 4 Songs (A nun takes the veil; The secrets of the old; Sure on this shining night; Nocturne), Op. 13; 2 Songs (The Queen's face on a summery coin; Monks and raisins), Op. 18; 3 Songs (Now I have fed and eaten up the rose; A green lowland of pianos; O boundless, boundless evening), Op. 45; Beggar's song; Dover Beach; In the dark pinewood; Love at the door; Love's caution; Night wanderers; Nuvoletta; Of that so sweet imprisonment; Serenades; A slumber song of the Madonna; Strings in the earth and air; There's nae lark.*
*** DG Dig. 435 867-2 (2) [id.]. Cheryl Studer, Thomas Hampson, John Browning; Emerson Qt.

Samuel Barber wrote songs throughout his composing career. Barber's style, easily lyrical, sensitively responding to the cadences of English verse, remained remarkably consistent. Barber had no special wish to write American songs, and very few of the poems he set are by his compatriots. Rather he chose to set British – and particularly Irish – poets, with whom he felt a special affinity, notably James Joyce. Cheryl Studer sings beautifully in the *Hermit songs*, but it is Thomas Hampson who establishes the full flavour of the collection, which includes a sprinkling of vigorous, extrovert songs. He is particularly fine in Barber's best-known song, the extended *Dover Beach*, a setting of Matthew Arnold, written early in Barber's career. In that Hampson is accompanied immaculately by the Emerson Quartet. Otherwise it is John Browning – a pianist specially associated with Barber's music and the prime mover behind this recording project – who sharpens the focus and heightens the fantasy in deeply sympathetic accompaniments. Excellent, natural recording, first-class documentation and full texts.

(i) *Hermit songs, Op. 29;* (ii) *Knoxville: Summer of 1915* (cantata); (i) *Songs: The Daisies; Nocturne; Nuvoletta; Sleep now.* (ii) *Antony and Cleopatra* (opera): scenes: *Give me some music; Give me my robe.*
(M) (***) RCA mono/stereo 09026 61983-2 [id.]. Leontyne Price, with (i) composer (piano); (ii) New Philh. O, Schippers.

The evocative cantata to words by James Agee, *Knoxville: Summer of 1915*, has never been done more hauntingly and is well coupled with the heroine's arias from the opera, *Antony and Cleopatra*. Far rarer is the private recording of the *Hermit songs*, also specially written for her. Accompanied by the composer, she is more rugged than Studer in the collected song edition, but just as intense. The mono sound is very limited but conveys the atmosphere of a historic occasion. Otherwise good stereo sound.

The Lovers, Op. 43. Prayers of Kierkegaard, Op. 30.
*** Koch Dig. 3-7125-2. Dale Duesing, Sarah Reese, Chicago Ch. & SO, Andrew Schenck.

The Lovers, written in 1971, was Barber's last major work, a substantial choral cantata setting nine erotic poems by the Chilean, Pablo Neruda. It makes a moving sequence, with the soloist, Dale Duesing, matching the responsiveness of the outstanding Chicago Symphony Chorus. *The Prayers of Kierkegaard*, written in 1952, is a tougher, more uncompromising work, but approachable too, again with magnificent writing for chorus.

Vanessa (opera): complete.
(M) *** RCA GD 87899 (2) [7899-2-RG]. Steber, Elias, Resnik, Gedda, Tozzi, Met. Op. Ch. & O, Mitropoulos.

Vanessa inhabits much the same civilized world as Strauss or Henry James. Although it has not held the stage, its melodic freshness and warmth will ensure a reversal of its fortunes some day. This, its only recording so far, was made at the time of its first performance in 1958, but no apologies are needed for its quality; it stands the test of time as well as does the opera itself.

Bargiel, Woldemar (1828–97)

Octet in C min. for strings, Op. 15a.
*** Hyperion Dig. CDA 66356 [id.]. Divertimenti – MENDELSSOHN: *Octet.* ***

What strikes one about this music is its independence of outlook and dignity. Indeed it is something of a discovery; the delightful scherzo-like section embedded in the slow movement is particularly felicitous. Divertimenti play it with real feeling and conviction and are excellently recorded.

Barrios, Agustin (1885–1944)

Las abejas; Aconquija; Aire de zamba; La catedral; Choro de saudade; Cueca; Julia Florida; Una limosna por el amor de Dios; Medallon antiguo; Maxixa; Mazurka appassionata; Preludios: in C min.; in G min. Un sueño en la floresta; Valses Nos. 3–4; Villancico de navidad.
(N) *** Sony Dig. SK 64396 [id.]. John Williams.

This duplicates almost all the music on John Williams's first (bargain-priced) recital of music by this fine Paraguayan composer and has the advantage of the complete background silence of digital recording. The playing is of the highest calibre and has both concentration and charisma. However, the earlier disc (see below) offers about 10 minutes' more music by including the Ponce *Variations* and it remains very attractive in its own right.

Aconquija; Aire de Zamba; Le catedral; Cueca; Estudio; Una limosna por el amor de Dios; Madrigal (Gavota); Maxixa; Mazurka appassionata; Minuet; Preludio; Un sueño en la floresta; Valse No. 3; Vallancico de Navidad.
(M) *** Sony SBK 47669; SBT 47669 [id.]. John Williams – PONCE: *Folia de España.* ***

In the expert hands of John Williams this collection provides a very entertaining recital, ideal for late-evening listening. The recording is excellent. The remarkable extended set of Ponce *Variations* added for the CD reissue brings the total playing time up to 77 minutes.

Bartók, Béla (1881–1945)

Concerto for orchestra.
(M) *** Decca 417 754-2 [id.]. Chicago SO, Solti – MUSSORGSKY: *Pictures.* ***
(N) **(*) Chandos Dig. CHAN 8947 [id.]. RSNO, Järvi – ENESCU: *Romanian rhapsodies Nos. 1–2.* ***
(M) **(*) Telarc Dig. CD 82010 [id.]. Los Angeles PO, André Previn – JANACEK: *Sinfonietta.* **(*)

Solti gave Bartók's *Concerto for orchestra* its compact disc début. The upper range is very brightly lit indeed, which brings an aggressive feeling to the upper strings. This undoubtedly suits the reading, fierce and biting on the one hand, exuberant on the other. Superlative playing from Solti's own Chicago orchestra, and given vivid sound.

Recorded in opulent sound with the Royal Scottish Orchestra, Järvi directs an amiable reading, not as brilliant or precise in ensemble as the finest but warm and convincing, with some fine solo playing. Anyone who also wants the Enescu *Rhapsodies*, the rare No. 2 as well as the popular No. 1, could well consider this.

Previn and the Los Angeles Philharmonic give a comfortable, relaxed reading of Bartók's *Concerto*. Previn is at his best in the fun of the couple-play in the second movement or the Shostakovich parody of the fourth movement. For him, it is above all a work of fun, although there is no lack of excitement in the finale. The Telarc recording captures the full bloom of the orchestra as few recordings from Los Angeles have. The coupling is unique.

(i) *Concerto for orchestra;* (ii) *Piano concertos Nos. 1–3;* (i; iii) *Violin concerto No. 2 in B min.*
(B) *** Ph. Duo 438 812-2 (2) [id.]. (i) Concg. O, Haitink; (ii) Kovacevich, LSO or BBC SO (in *No. 2*), Sir Colin Davis; (iii) Szeryng.

This is as enticing a bargain Bartók collection as you could find. Not unexpectedly in Haitink's 1960 *Concerto for orchestra*, the orchestral playing is of the highest quality and the recording is both atmospheric and clear. The performance is more subtle, less tense than Solti's mid-priced version, although the element of dramatic contrast is not missing. Szeryng joins Haitink for the *B minor Violin concerto* with equally satisfying artistic results. Haitink keeps a firm grip on proceedings and there is a genuine sense of momentum and impetus about the performance that is really exciting. The 1969 recording is vivid, and firmly and realistically focused. Kovacevich's direct, concentrated readings of the three *Piano concertos* are hardly less persuasive. Sir Colin Davis accompanies sensitively and vigorously. No complaints about the bright, full recording.

(i) *Concerto for orchestra;* (ii) *Dance suite; 2 Portraits, Op. 5; Mikrokosmos* (orch. Serly): *Bourrée; From the diary of a fly.*
(M) *** Mercury 432 017-2 [id.]. (i) LSO; (ii) Philharmonia Hungarica, Dorati.

Dorati secures outstandingly brilliant and committed playing from the LSO. The recording, made in Wembley Town Hall, shows characteristic expertise of balance. The rest of the programme was recorded in 1958 in the Grosse Saal of the Vienna Konzerthaus, which affords Dorati's fine orchestra of Hungarian émigrés plenty of body without blurring outlines.

Concerto for orchestra; Kossuth.
(Y/B) *** Decca Dig. 443 773-2 [id.]. San Francisco SO, Blomstedt.

Written in 1903, after the young Bartók had heard and admired Strauss's *Ein Heldenleben*, the symphonic poem *Kossuth* was inspired by the Hungarian revolutionary hero in the 1848 uprising. Except in the Hungarian rhythms it may give little indication of the mature Bartók, but in its opulence it makes a most satisfying piece. A modern recording has been badly needed that would do justice to its refinement as well as to its vigour. Blomstedt fills the gap very well indeed. In the *Concerto for orchestra* Blomstedt takes an equally refined view, missing some of the fire but genially bringing out not just the exotic colours but the warm lyricism of this late masterpiece.

Concerto for orchestra; (i) *The Miraculous Mandarin* (complete ballet).
(Y/B) (M) **(*) Virgin/EMI Dig. CUV5 61192-2 [id.]. (i) Dumont Singers; Melbourne SO, Iwaki.
(N) ** RCA Dig. 09028 61702-2 [id.]. (i) St Louis Ch.; St Louis SO, Leonard Slatkin.
(N) ** Ph. Dig. 442 783-2 [id.]. (i) Tanglewood Festival Ch.; Boston SO, Ozawa.

Iwaki and the Melbourne orchestra have an obvious advantage over their direct mid-priced and bargain rivals in presenting the complete *Miraculous Mandarin* ballet, not just the suite, as coupling for the *Concerto for orchestra*. The recording is excellent, spacious and full, though transferred at a rather low level. The playing is finely pointed but is often too well-mannered for Bartók, lacking something in fierceness and excitement. The ballet is generously indexed with tracks.

Slatkin draws refined playing from the St Louis orchestra in both works, but the bite of Bartók and his earthier qualities are largely missing. In the *Concerto for orchestra* there is a case for transparency, and this version has a tiny bonus in providing the alternative ending (which sounds disconcertingly truncated, next to the usual one) but, for all the purposefulness of the playing, the ballet sounds underpowered and lacking in beef, with its violence muted.

Like Sir Simon Rattle in his EMI issue, Ozawa offers a live recording of the *Concerto for orchestra* in coupling with the *Miraculous Mandarin* recorded in the studio; however, Ozawa offers the complete ballet, rather than the suite. The virtuoso brilliance of the Boston players is impressive, and Ozawa is masterly in drawing out the sensuous elements in the ballet, but the bite and energy are less in both works and his account is not as fresh or as atmospheric as, say, Reiner or Lehel; despite the distinction of the orchestral playing, it is not quite the equal of the best in terms of personality. It is, however, a highly professional account and with a *Miraculous Mandarin* that has plenty of savagery, but not a first choice in either score. Ozawa also opts for the original, truncated ending to the *Concerto*, which is disconcerting for anyone who knows the usual, revised one.

Concerto for orchestra; The Miraculous Mandarin (ballet suite).
(N) *** EMI Dig. CDC5 55094-2 [id.]. CBSO, Sir Simon Rattle.

Even Sir Simon Rattle has rarely matched his achievement in his superb Bartók coupling, a brilliant studio recording of the violent *Miraculous Mandarin* ballet suite married to a live recording of the *Concerto for orchestra* which draws on an exceptionally wide emotional and expressive range. With Rattle taking a warmer view than most rivals, Bartók's wit is delicately pointed to give extra sparkle, and the poetry of much of the writing is sharply counterpointed against scintillating playing in the many virtuoso passages. Equally, the ballet score is here as remarkable for the sensuousness of much of the playing as for the biting energy of the violent music. Rich, full and well-balanced recording, to match the brilliance of the performances. There are no finer readings of either work.

Concerto for orchestra; The Miraculous Mandarin: suite; 2 Pictures, Op. 10.
(B) *(**) Sony SBK 48263; *SBT 48263* [id.]. Phd. O, Ormandy.

The Philadelphia *Concerto for orchestra* is superbly played and there is plenty of panache in Ormandy's reading. The snag is that, even with careful digital remastering, the upper strings are inclined to be a bit shrill. Predictably, Ormandy also draws a brilliant, polished performance from his orchestra in *The Miraculous Mandarin*. Opus 10 combines an uninhibitedly romantic piece, fittingly labelled *In full bloom* (cue for the full Philadelphia sound), with a *Village dance*, fairly easy-going by Bartókian standards. A generous triptych (74 minutes) and it is a pity there have to be reservations about the recording, which certainly does not lack vividness.

(i) *Concerto for orchestra;* (ii) *Music for strings, percussion and celesta.*
*** EMI Dig. CDC7 54070-2 [id.]. Oslo PO, Jansons.
(N) *** DG Dig. 429 747-2 [id.]. Chicago SO, Levine.
(Y/B) **(*) Chant du Monde Praga PR 254047 [id.].(i) Czech PO, Lehel; (ii) Leningrad PO, Mravinsky.

James Levine gives larger-than-life performances of both these favourite Bartók works. The results are thrillingly magnetic, whatever the more sensitive devotees of the composer may feel. Only Sir Georg Solti can match Levine here in the thrust and drama of the performances, and the recording, far finer than most from this source, adds to the impact, immediate and resonant and with the widest colour range.

Jansons and the Oslo Philharmonic also give outstanding performances of both works, making this a fine alternative recommendation in this now-favourite coupling of two Bartók masterpieces. The Oslo orchestra plays with unfailingly crisp ensemble, and the sound is excellent too, full and open.

The Mravinsky version of the *Music for strings, percussion and celesta* was recorded at a concert during the Prague Spring in 1967. In this performance the slow movement has tremendous mystery and intensity, and it makes one regret the rather less than opulent sound. The *Concerto for orchestra*, conducted by György Lehel, is highly atmospheric and has both a magisterial sweep and a sensitive ear for detail. Even in a catalogue rich in versions of this work, this deserves a special place. While it is not superior to such classic accounts as Reiner nor as well recorded as Jansons, it is completely gripping in its atmosphere, though the recording is not quite comparable in quality with the very best. Nevertheless it is warm and spacious and truthfully balanced – and infinitely superior to that accorded Mravinsky.

Concerto for orchestra; Music for strings, percussion and celesta; Hungarian sketches.
(M) *** RCA 09026 61504-2 [id.]. Chicago SO, Fritz Reiner.

Reiner's version of the *Concerto for orchestra* was recorded in 1955 but in its latest CD format the sound approaches demonstration standard in its spacious warmth, clarity and impact. The performance is most satisfying, surprisingly straightforward from one brought up in central Europe, but with plenty of cutting edge. The *Music for strings, percussion and celesta*, recorded three years later, suffers from a forward balance which prevents a true pianissimo, yet the concentration of the playing all but overcomes this defect, and the folk-based set of five *Hungarian sketches*, which completes the programme, is utterly seductive when played and recorded with such vividness of colour and a natural understanding of the music's rhythmic impetus.

Concerto for orchestra; 4 Orchestral pieces, Op. 12.
**(*) DG Dig. 437 826-2 [id.]. Chicago SO, Boulez.

Boulez's is a strong and perceptively detailed account of the *Concerto for orchestra*. He secures brilliant playing from the Chicago orchestra, but they are able to relax in the central movements – which is just as well, for the finale is very powerfully driven indeed. The *Four Orchestral Pieces* was the nearest Bartók came to writing a symphony, complete with Scherzo and melancholy slow movement.

Piano concertos Nos. 1–3.
(N) *** Ph. Dig. 446 366-2 [id.]. Zoltán Kocsis, Budapest Festival O, Ivan Fischer.
*** EMI Dig. CDC7 54871-2 [id.]. Peter Donohoe, CBSO, Rattle.
(Y/B) (M) *** DG 447 399-2 [id.]. Géza Anda, Berlin RSO, Ferenc Fricsay.
(Y/B) (BB) **(*) Naxos Dig. 8.550771 [id.]. Jenö Jandó, Budapest SO, András Ligeti.

The Kocsis performances, extracted from the Philips box listed below, are probably a marginal first choice for the three piano concertos, although one could be equally happy with the Donohoe/Rattle EMI disc.

Peter Donohoe and Sir Simon Rattle give first-class accounts of all three Bartók concertos and they have the advantage of equally impressive sound. Apart from Kocsis, the keenest competition comes from Stephen Kovacevich and Sir Colin Davis (Philips), also accommodated on one CD and now available in one of Philips's Duo couplings, along with Szeryng's account of the 1938 *Violin concerto* and the *Concerto for orchestra*, all at the same price (see above). At the same time, taken in isolation and purely on its own merits, this EMI CD is a highly recommendable issue which offers thoroughly idiomatic playing.

The Géza Anda recordings with Fricsay from the beginning of the 1960s are rather special. Both artists show a feeling for the music's inner world and its colouring, which is magnetic in the slow movements. The performances are refined yet urgent, incisive but red-blooded too. They make a worthy addition to DG's series of 'Originals'. The recording, from the beginning of the 1960s, is vivid and remarkably atmospheric, yet still tangible in detail.

With an all-Hungarian cast, Naxos offers invigorating accounts of the three Bartók *Piano concertos* with Jandó on top form, playing with exciting bravura throughout. The energy of the motoric *First Concerto* is not brutalized; and in the slow movement with its important percussion parts and the haunting 'Night music' of the *Second* the resonance of the recording ensures that there is plenty of atmosphere, even if in outer movements the violent brass interjections could be more cleanly focused. Apart from the excess of resonance, the recording is vivid and well balanced.

(i) *Piano concertos Nos. 1–3. Allegro barbaro; 14 Bagatelles, Op. 6; 4 Dirges, Op. 9a; 2 Elegies, Op. 8b; First term at the piano; For Children, Books I–IV; 3 Hungarian folksongs from Csík; 3 Hungarian folk tunes; Rumanian Christmas carols; 6 Rumanian folk tunes; 2 Rumanian dances, Op. 8a; 3 Rondos on folk tunes; Sonatina; 3 Studies, Op. 18; Suite, Op. 14.*
(Y/B) *** Ph. Dig. 446 368-2 (4) [id.]. Zoltán Kocsis; (i) Budapest Festival O, Iván Fischer.

The calibre of this Philips set cannot be denied, but it is relatively expensive: four full-price CDs for the price of three. Kocsis's recordings of the three concertos are as idiomatic as they are vibrant, and the *Third* is superbly done, among the finest on record. The Philips recording is admirably bold and full-bodied. But there are other fine versions which cost less (notably Anda), and many may prefer to approach the solo piano music separately.

Piano concerto No. 2 in G.
(N) (B) *(*) EMI forte CZS5 68637-2 (2). Sviatoslav Richter, O de Paris, Maazel – PROKOFIEV: *Piano concerto No. 5* *(*); TCHAIKOVSKY: *Piano concertos 1–3.* **

Richter seldom disappoints in the recording studio, but his 1969 partnership with Maazel did not seem to strike any sparks and, although his bravura cannot be gainsaid, the musical effect has far less than his usual incisiveness and strength of projection. The recording is not special either.

Piano concerto No. 3.
(N) (M) *** DG 447 666-2 [id.]. Géza Anda, Dresden State O, Karajan – SCHUMANN: *Symphony No. 4.* ***

A most lyrical account of the concerto from the 1972 Salzburg Festival by Géza Anda, more spacious and ruminative than his earlier version with Fricsay, and accompanied with enormous sensitivity and imagination by Karajan and the Staatskapelle, Dresden. A very special performance, and very well recorded too.

Viola concerto (ed. Tibor Serly).
*** EMI Dig. CDC7 54101-2 [id.]. Tabea Zimmermann, Bav. RSO, David Shallon – HINDEMITH: *Der Schwanendreher.* ***
(Y/B) *** Sony Dig. SK 57961 [id.]. Yo-Yo Ma, Baltimore SO, David Zinman – ALBERT: *Cello concerto;* BLOCH: *Schelomo.* ***

Tabea Zimmermann and the Orchestra of Bayerischen Rundfunk are strongly recommendable. This is playing of great eloquence and taste, and the balance is much finer than that offered by the DG engineers on their newest version – see below. The soloist is helped, but she is not so forward as to mask orchestral detail, which is wonderfully present and beautifully placed.

Yo-Yo Ma had originally intended to record the cello version of the Bartók concerto which Tibor Serly made at the instigation of the Bartók Estate; but eventually he discovered he could play it at the correct pitch on the alto violin or vertical viola, in which the instrument is fitted with a long end-pin and played upright like a cello. His performance has characteristic finesse and eloquence, and it gains from the transparent sound which Zinman draws from the Baltimore orchestra.

Viola concerto; Violin concerto No. 1; (i) *Rhapsodies Nos. 1–2.*
(M) *** EMI CDM7 63985-2 [id.]. Sir Yehudi Menuhin, New Philh. O, Dorati; (i) BBC SO, Boulez.

Menuhin with his strongly creative imagination plays these concertos with characteristic nobility of feeling, and he and Dorati make much of the Hungarian dance rhythms. There is a comparably earthy, peasant manner in Menuhin's playing of the two *Rhapsodies*, and it is matched by Boulez's approach, warm and passionate rather than clinical. The soloist is rather close. However, the balance responds to the controls, and this remains one of Menuhin's most worthwhile reissues.

Viola concerto; Violin concerto No. 2.
*** RCA Dig. RD 60749 [60749-2-RC]. Zukerman, St Louis SO, Slatkin.

Pinchas Zukerman gives an attractively lively account of the Bartók *Violin concerto No. 2*, aptly coupled with the *Viola concerto*, with Zukerman once again demonstrating his supreme mastery on the bigger string instrument. Fine orchestral playing and excellent sound.

(i) *Viola concerto* (ed. Tibor Serly); *Music for strings, percussion and celesta.*
**(*) DG Dig. 437 993-2 [id.]. (i) Wolfram Christ, BPO, Ozawa.

In the 1989 DG account of the *Viola concerto* the soloist is very forward; the recording is multi-mike rather than a natural concert-hall balance and there is often a two-dimensional effect with little back-to-front perspective. All the same, Wolfram Christ plays marvellously and in view of its artistic excellence it would be curmudgeonly to deny a third star. Ozawa's dramatic and highly charged account of the *Music for strings, percussion and celesta* is first rate and there is more air round the sound. Recorded at a concert in 1993, the audience is impressively silent.

Violin concertos Nos. (i) *1;* (ii) *2.*
(N) (M) *** Sony Stern Edition II SMK 64502 [id.]. Stern; (i) Phd. O, Ormandy; (ii) NYPO, Bernstein.
(M) *** Decca Dig./Analogue 425 015-2 [id.]. Kyung Wha Chung, Chicago SO or LPO, Solti.
*** Nimbus Dig. NI 5333 [id.]. Gerhart Hetzel, Hungarian State SO, Adám Fischer.

Stern recorded what was known then as the Bartók *Violin concerto* in 1958, and it was among the 'Late arrivals' in our very first hardback *Stereo Record Guide*. Stern brings to this mature masterpiece an enviable combination of tautness and lyricism, steely strength and melting beauty of tone. The accompaniment is sensitive and subtle; Bernstein is evidently in complete sympathy with both the music and the soloist, and the overall impression is of understanding between these two inspirational artists. The earlier concerto was written in 1907–8 for the violinist Stefi Geyer as the composer's love-token, and Stern's passionate playing suits it to perfection, his ardour readily surmounting the clash of styles in the second and final movement, with Debussy and Strauss – particularly the latter – alternating with the genuine Hungarian Bartók. The 1961 recording brings a balance which favours the soloist in a manner typical of CBS, but otherwise it sounds well in its successfully remastered format.

Though on Decca the soloist is rather forwardly balanced, the hushed intensity of the writing, as well as bitingly Hungarian flavours, is caught superbly, thanks to the conductor as well as to the soloist. The expressive warmth behind Bartók's writing is fully brought out, and there is no sentimental lingering. Among modern recordings, this leads the field in both works.

Gerhart Hetzel plays both concertos with great feeling and understanding. There is no want of virtuosity, but nor is there virtuosity for its own sake (or, rather, that of the soloist's ego). Ideas are fashioned with great sensitivity and, although dynamic nuances are scrupulously observed, there is none of the exaggeration which draws attention to the soloist rather than to Bartók. These are performances of strong but unintrusive personality. Both concertos are very well recorded, with a natural, excellent balance which helps the soloist to just the right extent, and it must rank among the very best now available.

Violin concerto No. 2.
(M) (**(*)) RCA mono 09026 61395-2 [id.]. Menuhin, Dallas SO, Dorati (with ELGAR: *Salut d'amour;* DEBUSSY: *Prélude: La fille aux cheveux de lin;* LALO: *Symphonie espagnole* (**(*))).

Menuhin's première recording of the Bartók *Violin concerto* has an immediacy and freshness that neither of his later records surpassed. There is a strong sense of atmosphere and colour here (the texture is generally lighter and more transparent than it is in the Furtwängler/Philharmonia issue, though that was superb in other ways). The transfers are adequate rather than outstanding; however, one can imagine another team making a more expert job of it. Artistically this still remains a very strong account. The Lalo coupling is an admirable 1945 performance, with the San Francisco Symphony under Monteux, which has never been released before.

Violin concerto No. 2; 2 Rhapsodies for violin and orchestra.
*** EMI Dig. CDC7 54211-2 [id.]. Kyung Wha Chung, CBSO, Rattle.

Kyung Wha Chung in her EMI version gives a commanding, inspired performance, full of fire and imagination, helped by the inspirational accompaniment of Rattle and the Birmingham orchestra. The same qualities come out just as vividly in the two flamboyant *Rhapsodies*, each in two nicely contrasted movements.

(i) *Violin concerto No. 2; Second Suite for orchestra* (revised, 1943 version).
(N) (M) **(*) Mercury 434 350-2 [id.]. (i) Sir Yehudi Menuhin; Minneapolis SO, Dorati.

Menuhin's third version of the *Second Violin concerto* dates from 1957. It is much better recorded than either of his earlier records, and (even taking into account the comments above) remains thoroughly worthwhile, with the solo playing demonstrating those special qualities of lyrical feeling and warmth for which Menuhin was justly famous. His performance is especially appealing in the haunting theme and variations of the central *Andante tranquillo* but, with Dorati accompanying animatedly, the finale has plenty of impetus and fire. The rare coupling makes this Mercury reissue doubly attractive. Anyone who enjoys the *Concerto for orchestra* will respond to the early *Second Orchestral Suite*, which was revised in the year (1943) when the former was written. It is a colourful, half-hour-long piece in four movements; the second introduces a vibrant fugue and the *Andante* opens with an unusual extended recitative from the bass clarinet. The energetic, folksy finale ends serenely (*molto quieto*). Dorati is a persuasive advocate, and the characteristically graphic Mercury recording has no lack of primary colours.

Dance suite; Divertimento; Hungarian sketches; 2 Pictures.
(N) **(*) DG Dig. 445 825-2 [id.]. Chicago SO, Boulez.

As in their other Bartók recordings together, the partnership of Pierre Boulez and the Chicago orchestra makes for brilliant results, if here rather smoother and less sharply focused than usual. So the *Dance suite* has its Hungarian flavours muted and in the *Divertimento* the contrasts between solos and tutti are underplayed, though the hushed intensity of the slow movement is magical. The slower movements among the *Two Pictures* and the five *Hungarian sketches* are also done most poetically.

(i) *Dance suite;* (ii) *Music for strings, percussion and celesta;* (i) *The Wooden Prince* (complete), *Op. 13.*
(Y/B) (M) **(*) Sony SM2K 64100 (2) [id.]. (i) NYPO; (ii) BBC SO; Boulez – SCRIABIN: *Poème de l'exstase.* ***

In *The Wooden Prince* Boulez is the most compelling of advocates, maintaining his concentration throughout; the *Dance suite* brings a performance just as warm, but a degree less precise. The 1975 analogue recording, originally among CBS's best, emerges vividly on CD with plenty of atmosphere, although the upper strings could be more expansive. The *Music for strings, percussion and celesta* was made in Walthamstow two years later and was one of Boulez's finest records of that period. Unfortunately the recording suffers from the artificial balance sometimes favoured by CBS. However, for those who can overlook this there are genuine rewards in this magnetic music-making, and the Scriabin coupling is quite superb.

Divertimento for strings.
(M) *** EMI CDM5 65079-2 [id.]. ECO, Daniel Barenboim – HINDEMITH: *Trauermusik;* SCHOEN-
BERG: *Verklaerte Nacht.* ***

Barenboim's passionate earthiness makes this a very strong account of the *Divertimento* and the result is red-bloodedly involving, with a vigorous communication of high spirits in the finale. The work is, of course, in concerto grosso style and here the solo quartet is a distinguished one (José-Luis Garcia, John Tunnel, Cecil Aronowitz and Adrian Beers). The 1969 Abbey Road recording brings admirably full string textures. With excellent couplings this makes a first-rate triptych.

Divertimento for strings; Music for strings, percussion and celesta.
(N) (M) *** Decca 448 577-2 [id.]. ASMF, Marriner – SHOSTAKOVICH: *Piano concerto No. 1.* ***
(N) (B) *** HM HMA Dig. 190 3052 [id.]. Liszt CO, Rolla.

Divertimento for strings; Music for strings, percussion and celesta; (i) *2 Portraits.*
(M) (***) DG mono 437 675-2 [id.]. (i) Rudolf Schulz; Berlin RIAS SO, Fricsay.

A superlative coupling from Marriner, fully worthy of Decca's Classic Sound series, even though the recording originally appeared (in 1970) on the Argo label. Marriner follows the composer's intentions, like Sacher using a chamber-sized group, and his reading (helped by the superb Argo engineering) also reveals extra detail, extra expressiveness, extra care for tonal and dynamic nuances. In the slow opening fugue Marriner meticulously observes Bartók's instructions to keep the music down to a pianissimo as far as bar 26, yet there is no sense of cold, withdrawn playing; quite the opposite. In the second movement the terracing of subtly different tempi is managed much more adeptly than usual, and all the playing reflects the working together beforehand in democratic conference which was the general procedure in preparing a St Martin's performance at that time. The *Divertimento* is given a similarly vivid performance and the recording is again outstandingly good. With a generous and attractive Shostakovich bonus, this is a reissue not to be missed.

The *Music for strings, percussion and celesta* (1936) and the *Divertimento for strings* (1939) were both written for Paul Sacher's Basle Chamber Orchestra. The Liszt Chamber Orchestra comprises seventeen players, including Janos Rolla who directs from the first desk, though they are augmented for the *Music for strings, percussion and celesta*. These are both expert performances and distil a powerful atmosphere in the slow movements of both pieces. They command beautifully rapt *pianissimo* tone and keen intensity. The sound is less reverberant than for some rivals, but there is no lack of ambience. Readers who want accounts of these works that would not have greatly differed from Sacher's at the first performance will not be disappointed: indeed, this is the best available.

There is also something special about Ferenc Fricsay's Bartók: a total identification with the idiom and an authentic sense of pace and atmosphere. Both the *Music for strings, percussion and celesta* and the *Divertimento* were recorded in 1953, and the *Two Portraits* in the previous year; few allowances need be made for the quality (except perhaps for the string timbre above the stave in louder passages). Rudolf Schulz plays with great eloquence in the *Portraits*.

(i) *Divertimento for strings;* (ii) *Music for strings, percussion and celesta;* (iii) *Sonata for 2 pianos & percussion.*
(N) **(*) Oxford OOCD-CD2 (1/2) (2). (i–ii) Oxford O da Camera, Paul Sacher; (ii–iii) Tristan Fry, James Holland; (iii) Boris Berman, Stephane Lemin.

In September 1995, to commemorate the fiftieth anniversary of Bartók's death and within months of his own ninetieth birthday, Paul Sacher recorded these live performances with the Oxford Orchestra da Camera. It was Sacher who commissioned all three works in the 1930s, and he here introduces each with his own unique commentary in English. At speeds generally broader than usual, these unique performances may lack the vitality and bite of the finest rivals, but they have a compelling warmth and concentration, along with fine playing from the professional band, and they are atmospherically recorded. The two discs may be obtained from the orchestra direct (2 Axtell Close, Kidlington, Oxford).

Divertimento for strings; Rumanian folk dances.
(Y/B) (M) **(*) DG Dig. 445 541 [id.]. Orpheus CO – STRAVINSKY: *Dumbarton Oaks Concerto* etc.

The American Orpheus Chamber Orchestra give an eminently well-prepared account of the *Divertimento*. A good performance with a sense of mystery and intensity of feeling, if not entirely idiomatic. The recording is very clean and well balanced. The *Rumanian folk dances* are also attractively done, and the recording is fresh and immediate.

(i) *Hungarian pictures;* (ii) *The Miraculous Mandarin* (complete ballet); *Music for strings, percussion and celesta;* (iii) *Rhapsody for piano and orchestra;* (ii) *Suite No. 1, Op. 3; 2 Pictures, Op. 10.*
(N) (B) **(*) Decca Double 448 276-2 (2) [id.]. (i) Israel PO, Mehta; (ii) Detroit SO, Dorati; (iii) Pascal Rogé, LSO, Weller.

Mehta gives a fine performance of the five *Hungarian pictures* which Bartók scored for orchestra in 1931, some 20 years after their original composition as piano pieces. They have great charm, and the glowing orchestral colours are well realized here. The Israel Philharmonic, recorded in Kingsway Hall, sounds far finer than when it faces the microphones on home ground. Pascal Rogé shows genuine feeling for the keyboard colour of Bartók's *Rhapsody*: in his hands the music is far from abrasive, with an atmospheric recording to match. The rest of the programme is in the hands of Antal Dorati.The *Suite No. 1*, regarded as revolutionary at its first Viennese performance in 1905, now strikes the ear as conservative, but it is a warm and colourful work, impressive in structural control, with the five movements in arch form. Dorati's approach is strong and vigorous to match, as it is in the much more advanced *Pictures* of 1910. The two major works here, the complete *Miraculous Mandarin* ballet and the

Music for strings and percussion, are recorded digitally, and the range and brilliance of the sound are spectacular. This makes up for any lessening of tension in the actual performances compared with Dorati's previous recordings of both works for Mercury. Though the playing in the early ballet is polished enough, it finally lacks the flamboyance needed, the bold display of controlled barbarism. The *Music for strings, percussion and celesta* also lacks the final degree of intensity, although both make a considerable impact when the recording is so vividly projected.

Hungarian sketches; Romanian folk dances.
(M) *** Mercury 432 005-2 [id.]. Minneapolis SO, Dorati – KODALY: *Dances; Háry János*. ***

Dorati, himself a Hungarian, provided the pioneer stereo recording of these works, yet the 1956 sound is vivid and full and wears its years very lightly indeed. The Minneapolis orchestra, on top form, provides plenty of ethnic feeling and colour.

The Miraculous Mandarin (complete ballet), *Op. 19.*
(N) **(*) Chandos Dig. CHAN 9029 [id.]. L. Voices, Philh. O, Järvi – WEINER: *Hungarian folk-dance suite*. ***
(*) Delos Dig. DE 3083 [id.]. Seattle SO, Gerard Schwarz – KODALY: *Háry János; Galánta dances*. *

The Miraculous Mandarin (complete); *Dance suite.*
(N) ** EMI Dig. CDC7 54858-2 [id.]. LPO, Welser-Möst – KODALY: *Peacock variations*. ***

The Miraculous Mandarin; Divertimento for strings; (i) *2 Portraits, Op. 5.*
(N) *** Decca Dig. 436 210-2 [id.]. (i) Chantal Juillet; Montreal SO, Dutoit.

The Miraculous Mandarin (complete); *Music for strings, percussion and celesta.*
(N) ** DG Dig. 447 747-2 [id.]. Chicago SO, Boulez.

(i) *The Miraculous Mandarin* (complete); (ii) *2 Portraits, Op. 5.*
(Y/B) (M) *** DG Dig. 445 501-2 [id.]. LSO, Abbado; (i) with Amb. S.; (ii) Shlomo Minz – JANACEK: *Sinfonietta*. ***

(i) *The Miraculous Mandarin* (complete). *4 Orchestral pieces, Op. 12;* (ii) *3 Village scenes.*
(M) *** Sony SMK 45837 [id.]. (i) Schola Cantorum; (ii) Camerata Singers; NYPO, Pierre Boulez.

Abbado directs a fiercely powerful performance of Bartók's barbarically furious ballet – including the wordless chorus in the finale – but one which, thanks to the refinement of the recording, makes the aggressiveness of the writing more acceptable while losing nothing in power. The Janáček coupling is highly appropriate and equally successful; before that, however, the ear is sweetened by Minz's warmth in the *Portraits*.

Dutoit conducts the Montreal orchestra in a ripe and resonant account of Bartók's most violent orchestral score. Superbly recorded, and played with bite and energy, the performance combines precision with the manic wildness that this score needs. In the *Divertimento* Dutoit gives a delightful bounce to the dance rhythms in a winning and warm performance, and Chantal Juillet is a sensitive violin soloist in the first of the *Two Portraits* – in effect the first movement of the *Violin concerto No. 1*.

Boulez also proves a strong and sympathetic advocate in all this music, and his approach is surprisingly warm. This is even more striking in *The Miraculous Mandarin*. The New York orchestra responds with deeply expressive playing and, with spacious recording, many will prefer it on that account.

Neeme Järvi conducts a strong, rugged reading of *The Miraculous Mandarin*, opulently recorded. There are more sharply focused versions than this, but the energy of this performance convincingly brings out the barbaric quality of the score, getting one vividly to visualize the gruesome plot as it develops. The amiable and colourful Weiner *Folk dances* make an unusual and attractive coupling.

Gerard Schwarz directs the Seattle orchestra in a powerfully atmospheric account of Bartók's malignant ballet score, not as idiomatically aggressive as some, but with plenty of grip and excitement at the climax. Aptly and generously coupled with Kodály, this can be strongly recommended.

Franz Welser-Möst draws refined playing from the LPO in Bartók's violent ballet score, making it sound too civilized. The brutality of the writing is missing so that the impact is much reduced, and the *Dance suite* is also not biting or violent enough for this rugged but sophisticated, peasant-based inspiration. By contrast, the Kodály fill-up shows conductor and orchestra totally in sympathy with the music. Warm but slightly distanced sound.

Boulez takes a characteristically objective view of both works. The playing is brilliant and the recording full and detailed, but in the ballet the clinical approach means that there is a total absence of sensuousness, not to mention the other dramatic qualities which can make this violent piece so involving. With Boulez it is a musical tapestry and not much more. His objectivity works better in the *Music for strings, percussion and celesta*, which begins with the most refined pianissimo. Boulez's speeds are not extreme, which encourages clean textures, but ultimately tension is too low to convey the inner urgency of this masterpiece.

The Miraculous Mandarin (suite); *Music for strings, percussion and celesta.*
(M) **(*) EMI CDC5 65175-2 [id.]. Phd. O, Ormandy – HINDEMITH: *Symphonic metamorphoses.* **(*)

This (1978) EMI version of *The Miraculous Mandarin*, recorded in the Old Met., does greater justice to the body of the Philadelphia strings and the sonorities of their cellos and basses than the earlier, Sony/CBS recording. The playing here is dazzling; the only reservations concern the *Music for strings, percussion and celesta*, where greater mystery is neeeded (at least in the first and third movements). There is no want of eloquence and passion, but the dynamic range at the bottom end of the spectrum leaves something to be desired. That said, there is much to enjoy here: the orchestral playing is of the very first order.

The Miraculous Mandarin: suite; The Wooden Prince (suite, arr. Järvi).
(N) **(*) Chandos Dig. CHAN 9133 [id.]. Philh. O, Järvi.

These suites from Bartók's two ballets are taken from Järvi's separate recordings of the complete ballet scores of each. It makes a useful and illuminating coupling of two works which could hardly be more sharply contrasted, though the suite versions simply involve the omission of some 15 minutes of music from each score – from the end of *The Miraculous Mandarin* and from the middle of *The Wooden Prince*.

2 Pictures, Op. 10.
(N) *** Sony Dig. SK 58949 [id.] La Scala, Milan, PO, Muti – STRAVINSKY: *Le baiser de la fée.* ***

A puzzling coupling, as an all-Bartók or all-Stravinsky record would have made better sense. However, there is nothing wrong with either the playing or the recording here. Muti gets an orchestral response that stands up well to the competition from native Hungarians.

Rhapsodies for violin and orchestra Nos. 1 in G min., 2 in D min.
(N) (M) ** Sony Stern Edition II SMK 64503 [id.]. Stern, NYPO, Bernstein – PROKOFIEV: *Violin concertos.* **(*)

Stern and Bernstein seem less happy with the *Rhapsodies* than with the mature *Concerto*. The first, a colourful and immediately attractive piece, is played well enough; however, the second, taut and pithily rhythmic, surely needs a drier acoustic. Neither Stern nor Bernstein seems comfortable, and the constant rhythmic thrusting becomes monotonous.

Rhapsody for piano and orchestra; Scherzo for piano and orchestra.
(N) **(*) Ph. Dig. 446 472-2 [id.]. Zoltán Kocsis, Budapest Festival O, Iván Fischer – DOHNANYI: *Variations on a nursery tune.* **

The *Rhapsody* is familiar, and it is very well played; but the *Scherzo* is especially welcome. Its style is fascinatingly eclectic, yet the writing is extremely spontaneous and the work springs to life when the performers are so obviously enjoying themselves. The recording is full and well balanced, but there seems no reason why these recordings from 1985–6 should have been reissued at full price, and the coupling is less distinctive.

The Wooden prince (complete ballet), *Op. 13* (complete); *Hungarian pictures.*
*** Chandos Dig. CHAN 8895 [id.]. Philh. O, Järvi.

The Wooden prince (complete); *Music for strings, percussion and celesta.*
(N) (M) **(*) Mercury 434 357-2 [id.]. LSO, Dorati.

The Wooden prince (complete); (i) *Cantata profana.*
(N) *** DG Dig. 435 863-2 [id.]. Chicago SO Ch. & SO, Boulez; (i) with Aler, Tomlinson.

With the Chicago Symphony Orchestra Pierre Boulez gives a bitingly powerful reading of Bartók's often uncharacteristically mild ballet-score of 1914. Since he recorded it earlier with the New York Philharmonic (for CBS/Sony), Boulez's view has grown noticeably more expansive and a degree warmer, though at times the DG recording puts an edge on the sound to the point of abrasiveness. The enigmatic *Cantata profana* of 1930 is superbly done with the Chicago Symphony Chorus responding in total confidence to the challenge of the thorny choral writing, and with John Aler incisive in the taxing tenor role.

Järvi's red-blooded performance relates the work to romantic sources, even to Wagner's *Rheingold* at the very start. The drama of the fairy story is told in glowing colours and, unlike most rivals, Järvi ignores the many little cuts that the composer sanctioned, reluctantly or not, over the years. The opulent playing of the Philharmonia is greatly enhanced by the full, vivid Chandos recording. The suite, *Hungarian pictures*, drawn from various folk-based piano pieces, provides a colourful if trivial makeweight.

Dorati's performances of both works are brilliantly authentic. *The Wooden Prince* is given a fresh, dynamic reading, vivid in its detail, with the reminders of Stravinsky and the Debussian textures brilliantly caught. The *Music for strings, percussion and celesta* is comparably atmospheric, the playing full of tension, and Dorati brings out the Hungarian dance inflexions in the finale. The recordings, from 1964 and 1960 respectively, hardly sound their age except for a degree of rawness in the upper range of the strings in the more strident moments of the ballet.

CHAMBER AND INSTRUMENTAL MUSIC

(i) *Andante* (for violin and piano); (ii) *Piano quintet;* (iii) *Rhapsodies Nos. 1 & 2.*
(N) (BB) *** Naxos Dig. 8.550886-2. (i; iii) Pauk; (i; ii) Jandó; (ii) Kodály Qt.

The *Piano quintet* dates from 1903–4 (there were two earlier attempts at the medium) and is closer to the world of Strauss and Dohnányi than to the Bartók with which we are familiar. A substantial work in the received idiom over 40 minutes in length, it is wholly uncharacteristic. The *Andante* for violin and piano is also early (1902) and is otherwise not recorded. It is slight but charming. The two *Rhapsodies* come from 1928, written respectively for Joseph Szigeti and Zoltán Székely, and are more popular in style than the *Fourth Quartet*, written the same year. Very good playing from György Pauk and alert playing from Jenö Jandó, whose humming is at times faintly audible. No quarrels with either recording or performances. Excellent value.

Contrasts for clarinet, violin and piano.
*** Delos Dig. D/CD 3043 [id.]. Shifrin, Bae, Lash – MESSIAEN: *Quatuor*. ***

David Shifrin and his colleagues from Chamber Music Northwest admirably capture the diverse moods of Bartók's triptych, including the mordant wit and vitality of the outer sections and the dark colouring of the centrepiece. They are very well recorded in an agreeable acoustic.

(i) *Contrasts. Mikrokosmos:* excerpts.
(M) (***) Sony mono MPK 47676 [id.]. Composer; (i) with Joseph Szigeti, Benny Goodman.

Contrasts was commissioned by Benny Goodman. In 1940 Bartók added a further movement, and it was in this form that the three artists made their recording. That same year Bartók recorded 31 pieces from *Mikrokosmos* and these performances are indicative of the wide range and delicacy of keyboard colour that Bartók commanded. The sound is surprisingly good, given that it is over half a century old! An indispensable issue.

(i; ii) *Contrasts;* (ii) *2 Rhapsodies; Rumanian folk dances.* (Solo) *Violin sonata.*
(Y/B) *** Hyperion Dig. CDA 66415 [id.]. Krysia Osostowicz; with (i) Michael Collins; (ii) Susan Tomes.

Hyperion's coupling of the Bartók *Contrasts*, *Rhapsodies* and the *Sonata for solo violin* is a distinguished and well-recorded issue which finds all these artists on excellent form. Krysia Osostowicz is as good as any of her rivals in the *Sonata for solo violin*, and the remainder of the programme is hardly less impressive.

(i) *Contrasts. Violin sonatas Nos. 1–2.*
(Y/B) (BB) *** Naxos Dig. 8.550749 [id.]. György Pauk, Jenö Jandó; (i) with Kálmán Berkes.

The appearance of both the *Violin sonatas*, together with *Contrasts* for clarinet, violin and piano, making 75 minutes of music for less than £5 (or its equivalent), will cause a stir, particularly when they are played by such an experienced artist as György Pauk and his fellow Hungarian, Jenö Jandó. Given the refinement and subtlety of Pauk's playing here, it would be churlish not to give it a three-star recommendation, the only very small qualification being the balance, which favours the piano too much in both sonatas. In the superb account of *Contrasts*, in which Kálmán Berkes joins them, the balance is better. Outstanding value.

44 Duos for 2 violins.
*** Astrée E7720 [id.]. Sandor Végh, Albert Lysy.
(Y/B) ** Hyperion Dig. CDA 66453 [id.]. Ferenc Balogh, András Kiss.

The *44 Duos* are very much to violinists what *Mikrokosmos* is to pianists, but although they were educational in origin and purpose they were also intended (as was *Mikrokosmos*) for concert performance. Ferenc Balogh and András Kiss are the violinists of the New Budapest Quartet and give a very good account of themselves, though they are heard in a somewhat resonant acoustic environment. Their disc can be recommended, albeit not in preference to Sandor Végh and Albert Lysy (on the Astrée label), who bring greater expressive meaning to these pieces.

(i) *7 Hungarian folk tunes; 6 Romanian folk dances* (both arr. Szigeti). *Allegro barbaro; Bagatelle No. 2; Burlesque No. 2; Easy pieces Nos. 5 & 10; Mikrokosmos: Staccato, Ostinato. Romanian dance No. 1; Suite, Op. 14.* (ii) *5 Hungarian folksongs;* (iii) *8 Hungarian folksongs* (without No. 4).
(M) (***) EMI mono CDC5 55031-2 [id.]. Composer (piano), with (i) Joseph Szigeti; (ii) Vilma Medgyaszay; (iii) Mária Basildes (*Nos. 1, 2, 3 & 5*), Ferenc Székelyhidy (*Nos. 6–8*) – DOHNANYI: *Variations.* (***)

The majority of these performances were recorded in Budapest in 1929 and the remainder at various times between 1928 and 1937. They sound remarkably good for their period and the special character of Bartók's playing comes over with great clarity. There is in all 50 minutes of him, either as a brilliant and subtle soloist or accompanying the three singers listed above and, of course, Szigeti who, incidentally, plays wonderfully but not quite with the same rapture as the young Menuhin. The 'Composers in Person' series enjoys extensive and perceptive documentation, nowhere more so than in Zoltán Kocsis's notes to this disc.

Sonata for 2 pianos and percussion.
(Y/B) *** DG Dig. 439 867-2 [id.]. Argerich, Freire, Sadlo, Guggeis – RAVEL: *Ma Mère l'oye* etc. ***
*** Sony Dig. MK 42625 [id.]. Perahia, Solti, Corkhill, Glennie – BRAHMS: *Variations on a theme by Haydn.* ***
(N) *** Chandos Dig. CHAN 9398 [id.]. Safri Duo & Slovak Piano Duo – LUTOSLAWSKI: *Paganini variations* ***; HELWEG: *American fantasy.* **

Martha Argerich recorded the Bartók *Sonata* with Stephen Bishop-Kovacevich in the late 1970s, and this performance with Nelson Freire and the percussionists, Peter Sadlo and Edgar Guggeis, is a worthy successor artistically. It has tremendous fire and intensity. The aural image is not quite as fresh or open as the sound Philips produced for the earlier recording, though it is still very good and discreetly balanced. It comes with two Ravel transcriptions made by Peter Sadlo which, though of interest, are ultimately less satisfying than the originals.

On Sony an unexpected and highly creative partnership produces a vivid and strongly characterized performance. The recording is vivid to match, giving the players great presence.

The Slovak Piano Duo was formed in 1986 while they were still students, and the Safri Duo, two Danish percussion players, came together two years later. They are all dazzlingly alive and vital. All the same, their CD labours under a handicap: it is not good value at full price, lasting about 50 minutes; competition is not exactly thin on the ground and offers more substantial couplings. The Lutoslawski is a five-minute piece and the Helweg *American fantasy* will be an unknown quantity to most people and it is not great music. Nevertheless, given the brilliance of the playing and the vividness of the sound, it would be curmudgeonly to withhold three stars even if this is not a first choice.

String quartets Nos. 1–6.
(N) *** RCA Dig. 09026 68286-2 (3) [id.]. Tokyo Qt – JANACEK: *Quartets Nos. 1–2.* ***
(M) *** DG 445 241-2 (3). Tokyo Qt.
*** DG Dig. 423 657-2 (2) [id.]. Emerson Qt.
(N) (B) *** Teldec/Warner 0630 12334-2 (2) [id.]. Eder Qt.
**(*) EMI Dig. CDS7 47720-8 (3) [Ang. CDCC 47720]. Alban Berg Qt.
(**(*)) ASV Dig. CDDCS 301 (3) [id.]. Lindsay Qt.
(B) **(*) Ph. Duo 442 284-2 (2) [id.]. Novák Qt.

The Tokyo Quartet's DG version of the Bartók cycle, made in the 1970s, has long been our preferred version. Like that set (which is at mid-price), this RCA newcomer also encompasses a third disc, but it includes the two Janáček *Quartets* as well. These are on the first disc along with the *First Quartet*. Nos. 2, 3 and 4 occupy the second, and 5 and 6 the third. The same beauty of tone and finesse that mark the earlier set are everywhere in evidence, and the playing has intensity and authority. If you have the earlier set there is no need to make a change, but newcomers to this repertoire who are also attracted by the idea of the Janáček coupling need not hesitate.

The DG performances by the Tokyo Quartet bring an almost ideal combination of fire and energy with detailed point and refinement. The readings are consistently satisfying, outshining even the Emersons. Though the polish is high, the sense of commitment and seeming spontaneity are greater too. So the range of expression includes in the fullest measure not only the necessary Bartókian passion but the sparkle and wit, each interpretative problem closely considered and solved with finesse and assurance. Unlike the other DG set, the layout of the Tokyo performance is on three discs, but they are offered at mid-price and the splendid recording is admirably transferred to CD.

The Emerson Quartet's set comes on only two CDs. They project very powerfully and, in terms of virtuosity, finesse and accuracy, outstrip most of their rivals. If at times their projection and expressive vehemence are a bit too much of a good thing, these are concentrated and brilliant performances that are very well recorded.

Considerable competition comes from the Eder Quartet, a much-respected Hungarian ensemble whose complete digital set now returns to the catalogue on a pair of budget-priced CDs. Their playing has great intensity and is full of insights. There is a sense of onward movement without any feeling that the music is over-projected or held on a tight rein; on the contrary, one is hardly aware of the bar-line. And what a wonderful quality of sound they produce in No. 1 at the Debussy-like episode (fig. 9) and such rapt tone and concentration of atmosphere at the *pianopianissimo* passage into which it leads. The same must be said about nearly all the playing here. The recording too approaches the demonstration bracket.

The Alban Berg Quartet's are very impressive performances indeed, technically almost in a class of their own. They are very well recorded too, but at times they appear to treat this music as a vehicle for their own supreme virtuosity.

The Lindsay performances, searching, powerful and expressive, are now reissued together. The digital recording, though first class, occupies three discs which, like the Alban Berg set, places it at a distinct disadvantage to the DG Emerson version.

The Novák Quartet, a fine Czech group, bring plenty of grip to their performances and there is certainly no lack of fire and expressive intensity. If not as polished as the Tokyo versions, they have the advantage of being complete on a pair of Duo CDs, which Philips offer for the cost of one premium-price disc. So there is no question of their bargain status, as the recording is firm and well balanced.

String quartets Nos. 1, Op. 7; 5.
*** Collins Dig. 1279-2 [id.]. Talich Qt.

String quartets Nos. 2; 6.
*** Collins Dig. 1188-2 [id.]. Talich Qt.

No need for reservations about the Talich Quartet, who are completely inside this music, and the Talich pianissimo tone has a rapt quality that seems just right. These are finely argued, marvellously played and splendidly and truthfully recorded versions that can be recommended without any serious qualification.

Violin sonata No. 1.
*** DG Dig. 427 351-2 [id.]. Gidon Kremer, Martha Argerich – JANACEK: *Sonata* **(*); MESSIAEN: *Theme and variations.* ***

The *First Violin sonata* is played with great expressive intensity, enormous range of colour and effortless virtuosity by Gidon Kremer and Martha Argerich; but the ASV alternative is more sensibly coupled.

Violin sonata No. 1; Sonatina (trans. André Gertler); *Rhapsody No. 2 for violin and piano; Hungarian folksongs* (trans. Tivadar Országh); *Hungarian folk-tunes* (trans. Jozsef Szigeti).
(Y/B) *** ASV Dig. CDDCA 883 [id.]. Susanne Stanzeleit, Gusztáv Fenyö.

Susanne Stanzeleit has a distinguished pedigree, having studied with Kogan, Parachkevov, Milstein, Sándor Végh and practically every great violinist or violin teacher you care to think of. She and her partner, Gusztáv Fenyö, are completely inside the idiom – as you might expect, since the latter is related to Jelly d'Arányi, for whom Bartók composed the sonatas. The *Violin sonata No. 1* and the *Rhapsody No. 2* are every bit as well played and recorded as on the companion disc (see below), and this makes a worthy successor. Strongly recommended.

(Solo) *Violin sonata; Violin sonata No. 2; Rhapsody No. 1; Rumanian folk dances.*
*** ASV Dig. CDDCA 852 [id.]. Susanne Stanzeleit, Gusztáv Fenyö.

The young German-born violinist Susanne Stanzeleit plays the *Solo sonata* and the *Second Sonata* for violin and piano (1922) with uncommon authority. This is totally committed playing – and the performances are as good as any you can find in the current catalogue. The recording, too, is altogether first rate.

PIANO MUSIC

Allegro barbaro; 6 Dances in Bulgarian rhythm; 3 Hungarian folksongs; 15 Hungarian peasant songs; Mikrokosmos: Vol. 2/37, 40 & 50; Vol. 3/73, 82 & 87; Vol. 4/100, 113, 115–16 & 120; Vol. 5/122, 126, 128–31, 133, 135 & 138; Vol. 6/140, 144, 146–7; 3 Rondos on Slovak folk tunes; Sonatina.
(N) (BB) *** Naxos Dig. 8.550451-2. Balázs Szokolay.

Balázs Szokolay is a highly musical player, as befits the son of a distinguished composer (his father is the composer of the opera, *Blood Wedding*, after the Lorca play). His playing is always vitally intelligent and perceptive, and he is acceptably recorded. This is a thoroughly recommendable recital and excellent value, though Szokolay is by no means as well recorded as Kocsis on Philips, nor does he quite have the latter's subtlety or distinction.

Allegro barbaro; 4 Dirges, Op. 9a; First term at the piano; 3 Hungarian folksongs from Csík; Romanian Christmas carols; 2 Romanian dances, Op. 8a; 3 Rondos on folk tunes; 3 Studies, Op. 18; Suite, Op. 14.
(Y/B) *** Ph. Dig. 442 016-2 [id.]. Zoltán Kocsis.

Zoltán Kocsis recorded some of these pieces (the *Allegro barbaro*, the *Quatre Nénies* ('Dirges') and the *3 Hungarian folksongs from the Csík district*) for Philips way back in the last days of LP, and these performances are no less immaculate. This is every bit as impressive as the first CD (see below) in what is to be a complete survey of the piano music from him. Like Perahia in his CBS recital and Bishop-Kovacevich on Philips (now deleted), Kocsis penetrates to the very centre or soul of this music more deeply than almost any other rival – certainly such pioneering artists as György Sándor or Andor Foldes. This is likely to be the classic set for a long time to come, and the recorded sound is altogether natural and realistic. The disc is also included with the concertos in the four-CD box listed above.

14 Bagatelles, Op. 6; 2 Elegies, Op. 8b; 3 Hungarian folk tunes; 6 Rumanian folk tunes; Sonatina.
✪ *** Ph. Dig. 434 104-2 [id.]. Zoltán Kocsis.

Earlier surveys by Andor Foldes in the 1950s and by György Sándor have carried the authenticity of close association with the composer, but this has the advantage not only of state-of-the-art recording quality but of playing that is far more subtle and imaginative than Foldes'. Kocsis can produce power and drama when required, but he also commands a wide-ranging palette and a marvellously controlled vitality. The sound is never beautified but is also never aggressive; indeed his playing calls to mind Bartók's own injunction that performances must be 'beautiful but true'.

Dance suite; Hungarian peasant songs; 3 Rondos on folk tunes; Rumanian dances.
*** Denon Dig. C37 7092 [id.]. András Schiff (piano).

András Schiff's range of mood, tone and expression brings vivid colouring and these *Rumanian dances* have rarely been played with such infectious rhythms. The piano sound is first rate, with plenty of bite, and losing inner clarity only with the heaviest textures of the *Dance suite*.

For Children, Books 1–4.
(Y/B) *** Ph. Dig. 442 146-2 [id.]. Zoltán Kocsis.

As in the earlier volumes, Zoltán Kocsis has been scrupulously attentive to Bartók's own wishes as expressed not only in autographs and revised editions of the published scores but as expressed on record. Kocsis's playing is both more subtle and refined (and better recorded) than his earlier, Hungaroton set. Bartók playing doesn't come much better than this.

For Children (Books 1–4) complete; Mikrokosmos (Books 1–6) complete.
(M) *** Teldec/Warner 9031 76139-2 (3). Dezsö Ránki.

Dezsö Ránki here shows his musicianship and plays all 85 pieces with the utmost persuasion and with the art that conceals art, for the simplicity of some of these pieces is deceptive; darker currents lurk beneath their surface. He gives us the composer's original edition of 1908–9. Ránki also plays the *Mikrokosmos* with an effortless eloquence and a welcome straightforwardness. He is very clearly if forwardly recorded, and he is given a realistic presence.

For Children, Books I & II (revised version); *15 Hungarian peasant songs; Mikrokosmos: 6 Bulgarian dances. 10 easy pieces; 6 Rumanian popular dances; A simple air; Sonata; Sonatine.*
(B) *** EMI CZS5 68101-2 (2) [id.]. Michel Béroff.

Bartók's pieces for children are a collection of Hungarian (Book I) and Slovak (Book II) folksongs which possess a beguiling simplicity and (when taken in small doses) unfailing musical interest. Choice between Michel Béroff and Dezsö Ránki is simplified by the fact that Béroff records the revised score and Ránki gives us the original edition of 1908/9. Moreover Ránki's set is coupled with *Mikrokosmos*, whereas Béroff offers a number of Bartók's other major piano works. Béroff's playing has an unaffected eloquence that is touching, and the recording is very good.

Mikrokosmos (complete).
(B) **(*) HM HMA 190968/9 [id.]. Claude Helffer (with Haakon Austbö).

Bartók originally intended the piano pieces he began composing in 1926 as a pedagogic exercise with his young son Péter in mind, and it is naturally of great value to hear so intelligent a voice in this repertoire, though to record the complete set may be taking comprehensiveness a bit too far; music-lovers will be concentrating on the second of these CDs. Claude Helffer gives an intelligent account of all six Books, though at times he tends to invest detail with rather more expressive emphasis than this most simple of music can bear. The piano recording is realistic and naturally remastered. Even though the cueing is ungenerous (there are only twelve bands to cover 153 pieces), this is good value in the bargain range.

OPERA

Bluebeard's Castle (sung in Hungarian).
*** Sony Dig. MK 44523 [id.]. Marton, Ramey, Hungarian State O, Adám Fischer.
(M) *** Decca 433 082-2 [id.]. Kovats, Sass, Sztankay (speaker), LPO, Solti.
(Y/B) (M) *** Sony SMK 64110 [id.]. Nimsgern, Troyanos, BBC SO, Boulez.
(Y/B) (M) *** Decca 443 571-2 [id.]. Berry, Ludwig, LSO, Kertész.
(M) **(*) Mercury Dig. 434 325-2 [id.]. Mihály Székely, Olga Szönyi, LSO, Dorati – BERG: *Wozzeck* (excerpts). **(*)

Bartók's idea of portraying marital conflict as an opera was as unpromising as could be, but in the event *Bluebeard's Castle* is an enthralling work with its concentration on mood, atmosphere and slow development, as Bluebeard's wife finds the key to each new door. Its comparative absence of action makes it ideal for the gramophone. The glory of the Sony version is the magnificent singing of Samuel Ramey in the title-role. Eva Marton, also Hungarian-born, may lack the vulnerability as well as the darker tone-colours of the ideal Judith but, with more than a touch of abrasiveness in the voice, she still gives a powerful reading. The recording brings full and brilliant sound, well balanced and clear. The single CD comes with libretto in a separate box.

Solti directs a richly atmospheric reading, not as searingly dramatic as one might have expected but with analogue recording of spectacular range. The Hungarian soloists are tangily authentic, though their voices are not always perfectly steady, but Sylvia Sass with her exquisite pianissimo singing is more appealing than Eva Marton on Sony. The resulting effect is more romantic than usual, even revealing an affinity with Richard Strauss. With full libretto included, this makes a fine mid-priced alternative to the CBS/Sony version, dominated by Samuel Ramey.

Boulez reveals himself as an impressively warm Bartókian, the soloists are vibrantly committed and the recording is outstandingly vivid, presenting the singers in a slightly contrasted acoustic as though on a separate stage. Boulez has rarely if ever made a finer Bartók record. A full libretto is provided.

In 1965 Kertész set new standards in his version of *Bluebeard's Castle* with Christa Ludwig and Walter Berry, not only in the playing of the LSO at its peak, in the firm sensitivity of the soloists and the brilliance of the recording, but also in the natural Hungarian inflexions inspired by the conductor. There is still a strong case for preferring the reading conducted by a Hungarian, especially as the Decca sound approaches demonstration standard, but on performance the later, Sony CD has the balance of advantage.

Antal Dorati, drawing brilliant playing from the LSO, recorded in vivid, immediate Mercury sound, finds power rather than mystery in Bartók's unique one-Acter. Székely as Bluebeard is taut and intense, using his characterful bass imaginatively. Olga Szönyi is more uneven, strong and incisive but with squally moments. Though rival versions are more atmospheric than this, Dorati relates the work more clearly to later Bartók. The CD transfer is very vivid, though tape-hiss is quite high. As a practical advantage, the disc uniquely offers an equally positive account of the three concert-excerpts from Berg's *Wozzeck*. There are adequate notes, but no libretto.

Bax, Arnold (1883–1953)

(i) *Christmas eve; Dance of Wild Irravel; Festival overture; Nympholept; Paean;* (ii) *Tintagel.*
**(*) Chandos Dig. CHAN 9168 [id.]. (i) LPO; (ii) Ulster O, Bryden Thomson.

These shorter works were originally used as fillers for the separate issues of the symphonies, and it might have been more generous of Chandos to reissue them at mid-price. Apart from *Tintagel*, *Nympholept* is probably the most interesting piece. The *Paean* and the *Dance of Wild Irravel* may strain the allegiance of some. Performances and recordings give absolutely no cause for complaint.

(i) *Cello concerto; Cortège; Mediterranean; Northern Ballad No. 3; Overture to a picaresque comedy.*
*** Chandos Dig. CHAN 8494 [id.]. (i) Wallfisch; LPO, Bryden Thomson.

The *Cello concerto* is rhapsodic in feeling and Raphael Wallfisch plays it with marvellous sensitivity and finesse, given splendid support by the LPO under Bryden Thomson. The other pieces are of mixed quality: in the *Overture to a picaresque comedy* Bryden Thomson sets rather too measured a pace for it to sparkle as it should. The recording maintains the high standards of the Bax Chandos series.

(i) *Violin concerto. Golden Eagle* (incidental music): *suite; A Legend; Romantic overture.*
*** Chandos Dig. CHAN 9003 [id.]. (i) Lydia Mordkovitch; LPO, Bryden Thomson.

The *Violin concerto* is full of good, easily remembered tunes, yet there is a plangent, bitter-sweet quality about many of its ideas and an easygoing Mediterranean-like warmth that is very appealing. Lydia Mordkovitch plays it with commitment and conviction. The *Romantic overture* is for chamber orchestra and has a prominent role for the piano. All this music is new to the catalogue and the concerto deserves to be popular.

The Garden of Fand; The happy forest; November woods; Summer music.
*** Chandos Dig. CHAN 8307 [id.]. Ulster O, Bryden Thomson.

The Celtic twilight in Bax's music is ripely and sympathetically caught in the first three items, while *Summer music*, dedicated to Sir Thomas Beecham and here given its first ever recording, brings an intriguing kinship with the music of Delius. The Chandos recording is superb.

The Garden of Fand (symphonic poem); *Mediterranean; Northern ballad No. 1; November Woods; Tintagel* (symphonic poems).
*** Lyrita SRCD 231 [id.]. LPO, Boult.

Sir Adrian Boult's recording of *The Garden of Fand* is full of poetry and almost erases memories of Beecham's magical account. *Tintagel* is no less involving and beguiling and, though not as uninhibited as Barbirolli's, is equally valid. The *Northern ballad No. 1*, though less memorable than either *Fand* or *Tintagel*, is well worth having, as is *November Woods*, a lush, romantic score. *Mediterranean*, a Spanish picture postcard and almost a waltz, has an endearing touch of vulgarity uncharacteristic of its composer. Excellent sound.

In the faery hills; Into the twilight; Rosc-Catha; The tale the pine-trees knew.
*** Chandos Dig. CHAN 8367 [id.]. Ulster O, Bryden Thomson.

The tale the pine-trees knew is here done with total sympathy. The other three tone-poems form an Irish trilogy. The performances and recording are well up to the high standard of this series.

Malta G.C. (complete); *Oliver Twist: suite* (film-scores).
(M) *** ASV Dig. CDWHL 2058. RPO, Kenneth Alwyn – ARNOLD: *The Sound Barrier.* ***

Both these film-scores are in the form of a series of miniatures; on the whole, *Oliver Twist* stands up more effectively without the visual imagery. Kenneth Alwyn conducts the RPO with fine flair and commitment.

On the sea-shore.
*** Chandos Dig. CHAN 8473 [id.]. Ulster O, Handley – BRIDGE: *The Sea;* BRITTEN: *Sea interludes.*
***

Bax's Prelude, *On the sea-shore*, makes a colourful and atmospheric companion to the masterly Bridge and Britten pieces on the disc, played and recorded with similar warmth and brilliance.

Spring fire; Northern ballad No. 2; Symphonic scherzo.
*** Chandos Dig. CHAN 8464 [id.]. RPO, Vernon Handley.

Highly idiomatic playing from Vernon Handley and the RPO, and a thoroughly lifelike and characteristically well-detailed recording from Chandos.

Symphonic variations for piano and orchestra; Morning Song (Maytime in Sussex).
*** Chandos Dig. CHAN 8516 [id.]. Margaret Fingerhut, LPO, Bryden Thomson.

Margaret Fingerhut reveals the *Symphonic variations* as a work of considerable substance with some sinewy, powerful writing in the more combative variations, thoughtful and purposeful elsewhere. This CD is in the demonstration class.

Symphonies 1–7.
(M) *** Chandos Dig. CHAN 8906/10 [id.]. LPO or Ulster O, Bryden Thomson.

Chandos have repackaged the cycle of seven symphonies and it makes better sense for those primarily interested in these richly imaginative symphonies to pay for five rather than seven CDs. The recordings continue to make a strong impression. For those who prefer to have the symphonies separately and with their original couplings, we list below full details.

Symphony No. 1 in E flat; Christmas Eve.
*** Chandos Dig. CHAN 8480 [id.]. LPO, Bryden Thomson.

Symphonies Nos. 1 in E flat; 7 in A flat.
*** Lyrita SRCD 232 [id.]. LPO, (i) Fredman; (ii) Leppard.

Symphony No. 2; Nympholept.
*** Chandos Dig. CHAN 8493 [id.]. LPO, Bryden Thomson.

Symphony No. 3; Paean; The Dance of Wild Irravel.
*** Chandos Dig. CHAN 8454 [id.]. LPO, Bryden Thomson.

Symphony No. 4; Tintagel.
*** Chandos Dig. CHAN 8312 [id.]. Ulster O, Bryden Thomson.

Symphony No. 5; Russian suite.
*** Chandos Dig. CHAN 8669 [id.]. LPO, Bryden Thomson.

Symphony No. 6; Festival overture.
*** Chandos Dig. CHAN 8586 [id.]. LPO, Bryden Thomson.

Symphony No. 7 in A flat; (i) 4 Songs: Eternity; Glamour; Lyke-wake; Slumber song.
*** Chandos Dig. CHAN 8628 [id.]. (i) Martyn Hill; LPO, Bryden Thomson.

Bax's symphonies remain controversial and some listeners find their quality of invention and argument less intensely sustained than the composer's shorter orchestral tone-poems. Nevertheless they have a breadth of imagination which the smaller structures do not always carry. The Lyrita coupling is particularly generous (78 minutes) and the performances by Myer Fredman and Raymond Leppard respectively are powerful and finely shaped and can well hold their own with the later, Chandos digital versions. The Lyrita 1970s analogue sound, too, is vivid and clear.

The Chandos couplings have their own interest. *Christmas Eve* is an early work, coming from the Edwardian era, and it displays a less developed idiom than the symphonies. The four songs offer great contrasts of manner and style, and Martyn Hill presents them very sensitively.

The Truth about the Russian dancers (incidental music); *From dusk till dawn* (ballet).
*** Chandos Dig. CHAN 8863 [id.]. LPO, Bryden Thomson.

The Truth about the Russian dancers is vintage Bax, full of characteristic writing decked out in attractive orchestral colours. *From dusk till dawn* has many evocative ideas with some impressionistic orchestral touches. Not top-drawer Bax but often delightful, and very well played by the London Philharmonic under Bryden Thomson, and splendidly recorded.

Winter Legends; Saga fragment.
*** Chandos Dig. CHAN 8484 [id.]. Margaret Fingerhut, LPO, Bryden Thomson.

The *Winter Legends*, for piano and orchestra, comes from much the same time as the *Third Symphony*, to which at times its world seems spiritually related. The soloist proves an impressive and totally convincing advocate for the score and it would be difficult to imagine the balance between soloist and orchestra being more realistically judged. The companion piece is a transcription of his one-movement *Piano quartet* of 1922. A quite outstanding disc.

CHAMBER AND INSTRUMENTAL MUSIC

Cello sonata in E flat; Cello sonatina in D; Legend sonata in F sharp min.; Folk tale.
** ASV Dig. CDDCA 896 [id.]. Bernard Gregor-Smith, Yolande Wrigley.

The *Cello sonata* is a big piece, lasting over half an hour; it has many characteristic touches and an imaginative slow movement. Bernard Gregor-Smith and Yolande Wrigley are both highly sensitive and responsive players who command a wide dynamic range and variety of colour. In the *Sonata* the recording does not give quite enough back-to-front depth and there is a touch of glassiness about the sound. Things are a bit better in the *Folk Tale* (1920), but the recording is sufficiently wanting in bloom to inhibit a three-star recommendation.

Clarinet sonata.
**(*) Chandos CHAN 8683 [id.]. Janet Hilton, Keith Swallow – BLISS: *Clarinet quintet;* VAUGHAN
    WILLIAMS: *6 Studies.* ***

Bax's *Clarinet sonata* opens most beguilingly, and Janet Hilton's phrasing is quite melting. Moreover the Bliss coupling is indispensable.

(i) *Clarinet sonata;* (ii) *Elegiac trio* (for flute, viola & harp); (iii) *Harp quintet;* (iv) *Nonet;* (v) *Oboe quintet.*

(N) *** Hyperion Dig. CDA 66807 [id.]. (i; iv) Michael Collins; (i) Ian Brown (piano); (ii; iv) Philippa Davies; (ii–v) Roger Chase; (ii–iv) Skaila Kanga; (iii–v) Marcia Crayford, Christopher van Kampen; (iii; v) Iris Juda; (iv) Elizabeth Wexler, Duncan McTier, Ian Brown (cond.); (iv–v) Gareth Hulse.

These are performances of exemplary quality, ranging from the *Elegiac trio* of 1916 through to the *Clarinet sonata* of 1934. In the chamber-music field Bax wrote with a fantasy and sensibility that are no less captivating than in *The Garden of Fand* or *Tintagel*. This music is characterized by seductive and alluring sonorities and a haunting atmosphere which lends it strong appeal. The members of the Nash Ensemble, including Michael Collins in the *Clarinet sonata* and Gareth Hulse in the *Oboe quintet*, seem totally attuned to the idiom, and they play with their usual artistry and dedication. Excellent recording.

(i) *Harp quintet;* (ii) *Piano quartet; String quartet No. 1.*
*** Chandos Dig. CHAN 8391 [id.]. (i) Skaila Kanga, (ii) John McCabe; English Qt.

The *First String quartet* is music with a strong and immediate appeal. The *Harp quintet* is more fully characteristic and has some evocative writing to commend it, alongside the *Piano quartet*, with its winning lyricism. These may not be Bax's most important scores, but they are rewarding; and the performances are thoroughly idiomatic and eminently well recorded.

Nonet.
(N) (M) (***) Dutton Lab. mono CDAX 8014 [id.]. Goossens, Thurston, Slater, Watson, Korchinska, Griller Qt – MOERAN: *String trio;* FERGUSON: *Octet;* DELIUS: *Violin sonata No. 3.* (***)

The *Nonet* for flute, oboe, clarinet, string quartet, double-bass and harp is one of Bax's most magical and inventive works, and its neglect on record is quite unaccountable. (There are in it touches reminiscent of the *Third Symphony*, which was finished at about the same time.) After these 78s were made in 1937 with the same artists (save only for the clarinettist, Frederick Thurston) who had given its première in 1930, the piece remained unrecorded throughout both the mono and stereo LP eras. Now a modern version has arrived from the Nash Ensemble – see above. But this remains a beautiful and totally committed performance well worth having in its own rights, as indeed are the various couplings.

Oboe quintet.
*** Chandos Dig. CHAN 8392 [id.]. Sarah Francis, English Qt – HOLST: *Air & variations*, etc.; MOERAN: *Fantasy quartet;* JACOB: *Quartet.* ***

Bax's *Oboe quintet* is a confident, inventive piece. Sarah Francis proves a most responsive soloist – though she is balanced too close; in all other respects the recording is up to Chandos's usual high standards, and the playing of the English Quartet is admirable.

(i) *Piano quintet in G min.; String quartet No. 2.*
**(*) Chandos Dig. CHAN 8795 [id.]. Mistry Qt; (i) with David Owen Norris.

The *Piano quintet* is symphonic in scale. The playing of the Mistry Quartet is dedicated and David Owen Norris is the excellent and sensitive pianist. The *Second Quartet* is tauter and more powerful. The performance has plenty of feeling and the recording is excellent.

Rhapsodic Ballad (for solo cello).
*** Chandos Dig. CHAN 8499 [id.]. Raphael Wallfisch – BRIDGE: *Cello sonata;* DELIUS: *Cello sonata;* WALTON: *Passacaglia.* ***

The *Rhapsodic Ballad* for cello alone is a freely expressive piece, played with authority and dedication by Raphael Wallfisch. The recording has plenty of warmth and range.

Violin sonatas Nos. 1 in E; 2 in D.
*** Chandos Dig. CHAN 8845 [id.]. Erich Gruenberg, John McCabe.

The *Second* is the finer of the two sonatas and is thematically linked with *November woods*. Rhapsodic and impassioned, this is music full of temperament. Erich Gruenberg is a selfless and musicianly advocate and John McCabe makes an expert partner.

PIANO MUSIC

Apple-blossom time; Burlesque; The maiden with the daffodil; Nereid; O dame get up and bake your pies (Variations on a north country Christmas carol); On a May evening; The princess's rose-garden (Nocturne); Romance; 2 Russian tone pictures: Nocturne (May night in the Ukraine; Gopak); Sleepy-head.
**(*) Chandos Dig. CHAN 8732 [id.]. Eric Parkin.

The smaller pieces are not among Bax's most important works, but in Eric Parkin's hands they certainly sound pleasingly spontaneous.

Piano sonatas Nos. 1 in E flat; 2 in G; Legend.
*** Continuum Dig. CCD 1045 [id.]. John McCabe.

Both Bax's *Piano sonatas* are convincing in John McCabe's hands – in fact, more convincing than the *Legend*, written for an Australian pianist, John Simons, in the mid-1930s but not performed by its dedicatee until 1969. A thoroughly enterprising issue, excellently recorded.

Piano sonatas Nos. 1 & 2; Country Tune; Lullaby (Berceuse); Winter waters.
**(*) Chandos Dig. CHAN 8496 [id.]. Eric Parkin (piano).

Piano sonatas Nos. 3 in G sharp min.; 4 in G; A Hill tune; In a vodka shop; Water music.
**(*) Chandos Dig. CHAN 8497 [id.]. Eric Parkin.

These *Sonatas* are grievously neglected in the concert hall. Eric Parkin proves a sympathetic guide in this repertoire. The recording is on the resonant side, but the playing is outstandingly responsive.

Beach, Amy (1867–1944)

Symphony in E min. (Gaelic).
*** Chandos Dig. CHAN 8958 [id.]. Detroit SO, Järvi – BARBER: *Symphony No. 1* etc. ***

Amy Beach is a rather more remarkable figure than she is given credit for. She was largely self-taught. Her *Symphony in E minor* operates at a high level of accomplishment and has a winning charm, particularly its delightful and inventive second movement. Once heard, this haunting movement is difficult to exorcize from one's memory. A very persuasive performance by the Detroit orchestra under Neeme Järvi, and good recorded sound.

Piano quintet in F sharp, Op. 67.
(N) *** ASV Dig. CDDCA 932-2 [id.]. Martin Roscoe, Endellion Qt – CLARKE: *Piano trio; Viola sonata.* ***

The Boston composer, Amy Beach, composed this *Piano quintet* in 1908 during the period when, as the dutiful wife of a businessman, she gave up her career as a pianist, and composed instead. She uses a post-Brahmsian idiom in an individual and lyrical way, with the slow movement centred on a ravishing main theme, almost Elgarian. With Roscoe's characterful playing well matched by the masterly Endellion Quartet, the performance is magnetic and very well recorded.

Beethoven, Ludwig van (1770–1827)

Piano concertos Nos. 1–5.
*** Sony S3K 44575 (3) [id.]. Perahia, Concg. O, Haitink.
*** DG Dig. 435 467-2 (3) [id.]. Krystian Zimerman, VPO (*Nos. 3–5* cond. Bernstein).

(i) *Piano concertos Nos. 1–5;* (ii) *Triple concerto for violin, cello and piano, Op. 56.*
(M) *** Sony SB3K 48397 (3) [id.]. (i) Fleisher, Cleveland O, Szell; (ii) Stern, Rose, Istomin, Phd. O, Ormandy.

Piano concertos Nos. 1–5; Rondos, Op. 51/1–2.
(M) (***) DG mono 435 744-2 (3) [id.]. Wilhelm Kempff, BPO, Van Kempen.

(i) *Piano concertos Nos. 1–5. 6 Bagatelles, Op. 126; Für Elise.*
(N) (B) **(*) Decca 443 723-2 (3) [id.]. Ashkenazy, (i) Chicago SO, Solti.

(i) *Piano concertos Nos. 1–5. Piano sonata No. 32 in C min., Op. 111.*
(B) *** DG 427 237-2 (3) [id.]. Kempff; (i) BPO, Leitner.

(i) *Piano concertos Nos. 1–5. Diabelli variations, Op. 120.*
(M) **(*) Decca 433 891-2 (3) [id.]. Wilhelm Backhaus; (i) VPO, Schmidt-Isserstedt.

Piano concertos Nos. 1–5; (i) *Choral Fantasia, Op. 80.*
(M) *** EMI CMS7 63360-2 (3) [Ang. CDMC 63360]. Daniel Barenboim, New Philh. O, Klemperer, (i) with John Alldis Ch.

Perahia brings us as close to the heart of this music as any. These are masterly performances, and it is good that their more competitive price will bring them within the reach of an even wider audience. The sound is full and well balanced. This set has now reverted to full price, but it has to be said that it is still worth it.

Kempff's stereo accounts all come from the early 1960s and still sound remarkably good for their age, and the wisdom Kempff dispensed is as fresh as ever. A set to invest in, even if you have other recordings.

Krystian Zimerman, a thinker and poet among pianists, recorded the last three Beethoven concertos with Leonard Bernstein, less than a year before the conductor died. Zimerman then completed the cycle, after Bernstein died, directing from the keyboard in light, crisp performances. The recording of the piano is on the bright side, not always allowing a full pianissimo. Not a first choice, then, but a stimulating alternative view.

Fleisher made his series with Szell during 1961. Throughout their musical partnership was at its peak, and these performances are uncommonly rewarding. The remastering has greatly improved the recording, flattering the piano more than it did on LP, while the orchestra gains from the Severance Hall ambience. However, the balance in the *Triple concerto* has the soloists placed unnaturally forward.

The combination of Barenboim and Klemperer, recording together in 1967/8, is nothing if not stimulating and, for every wilfulness of a measured Klemperer, there is a youthful spark from the spontaneously combusting Barenboim. The concentration is formidable and especially compelling in the slow movements. The *Choral Fantasia* too is given an inspired performance. The remastered sound is vivid and clear and quite full.

There is a mood of carefree delight running through the earlier of Kempff's two cycles of the Beethoven *Piano concertos*. Even more than his stereo cycle, this one, recorded in mono in 1953, finds Kempff at his most individual, turning phrases and pointing ornamentation with a sparkle and sense of fun to have you smiling in response. Kempff is often idiosyncratic, as in his decision in the first four concertos to play his own cadenzas, making them sound like spontaneous improvisations. This is a classic recording guaranteed to give delight, which has been transferred to CD in full, immediate, well-detailed sound.

The partnership of Ashkenazy and Solti is fascinating. Where Solti is fiery and intense, Ashkenazy provides an introspective balance. Ashkenazy brings a hushed, poetic quality to every slow movement, while Solti's urgency maintains a vivid forward impulse in outer movements. Sometimes, as in the *C minor Concerto*, one feels that the music-making is too intense. Here a more relaxed and lyrical approach in the first movement can find a warmth that Solti misses. But for the most part the listener is given an overriding impression of freshness, and the *Emperor* performance, while on the grandest scale, has a marvellous individual moment in the first movement when Ashkenazy lingers over the presentation of the second subject. The Chicago orchestral playing is characteristically brilliant, and the one real snag is the very bright recording, which on CD is made to sound uncomfortably fierce at times, while the piano timbre is not as full in sonority as Decca usually provides.

Backhaus recorded the Beethoven concertos with the highly supportive Schmidt-Isserdtedt in 1958–9 when he was in his mid-seventies (the *Diabelli variations* date from 1955). His bold style, sometimes lacking in grace and wit, yet had remarkable authority, and now these early stereo recordings emerge with remarkable freshness. For every moment of wilfulness there is a balancing sense of spontaneity; if charm and subtlety of touch are not his strong points, the composer's spirit is ever present. Not surprisingly, it is the *Emperor* which shows the pianist at his most commanding. The recordings, made in the Sofiensaal, are amazingly good. In the *Diabelli variations* the moments of brusqueness are much more apparent and the close balance prevents a real pianissimo.

(i) *Piano concerto No. 1 in C, Op. 15. Piano sonatas Nos. 23 in F min. (Appassionata), Op. 57; 24 in F sharp, Op. 78.*
(N) (BB) **(*) Belart 461 050-2. Friedrich Gulda, (i) VPO, Horst Stein.

Piano concertos Nos. 2 in B flat, Op. 19; 3 in C min., Op. 37.
(N) (BB) **(*) Belart 450 102-2. Friedrich Gulda, VPO, Horst Stein.

Piano concertos Nos. 4 in G, Op 58; 5 in E flat (Emperor).
(N) (BB) *** Belart 450 022-2. Friedrich Gulda, VPO, Horst Stein.

Excellently recorded by Decca at the beginning of the 1970s, Gulda's fine set is in every way recommendable. He chose to use a Bösendorfer piano – which at the time seemed idiosyncratic but which, to present-day ears, offers a sound with something of the clean profile and tang of a fortepiano, while bringing a wider range of colour to slow movements. The strings are bright and fresh, yet there is a satisfying weight, noticeable immediately in the bold opening *tutti* of No. 1, which makes a bright start to the series. All the performances are most enjoyable, strong and direct and with a consistent spontaneity. No. 2 is perhaps marginally less impressive than the rest, yet it has a memorable finale; No. 3 is rhythmically fresh and sparkling; No. 4, with its eloquent opening, is particularly fine, with a memorable central *Andante*. But then all the slow movements are wisely paced and eloquent. The *Emperor* is another marked success, with tempi maintained consistently through each movement and strength rather than inflexibility emerging through the compulsive quality of the playing from soloist and orchestra alike. The two sonatas which are used to fill up the first disc are direct and purposeful, the *Appassionata* lacking something in fantasy but satisfying on its own terms. At super-bargain price, the set can be given the warmest welcome.

Piano concertos Nos. 1 in C, Op. 15; 3 in C min., Op. 37.
(N) (BB) ** RCA Navigator 74321 29240-2. Emanuel Ax, RPO, Previn.

(i) *Piano concerto No. 2 in B flat, Op. 19*; (ii) *Violin concerto in D, Op. 61.*
(N) (BB) ** RCA Navigator 74321 24200-2. (i) Ax, RPO, Previn; (ii) Ughi, LSO, Sawallisch.

These are thoughtful, unassertive performances, which in the first two concertos clearly relate the music to Mozart. Previn gives his very musical soloist good support, particularly in the slow movements, which are gentle and touching. Finales are enjoyably brisk and sparkling. The *Third Concerto* is given rather more weight, without ever being forceful: here the finale is more relaxed and measured – pleasingly lyrical in feeling. Excellent, natural, 1985–6 digital recording, warmly resonant but clear. Ughi's 1981 account of the *Violin concerto* also has realistic and well-balanced sound. His performance is in every way recommendable, fresh and unaffected, marked by consistent purity of tone in every register. If the last degree of imagination of the kind which creates special magic is missing in all these performances, their freshness makes them well worth considering for those with limited budgets.

(i) *Piano concertos Nos. 1–4;* (ii) *Romances for violin and orchestra Nos. 1–2, Opp. 40 & 50.*
(Y/B) (B) *** Ph. Duo 442 577-2 (2) [id.]. (i) Steven Kovacevich, BBC SO, Sir Colin Davis; (ii) Arthur Grumiaux, Concg. O, Haitink.

The first four concertos bring characteristically crisp and refreshing readings from Kovacevich and Davis which convey their conviction with no intrusive idiosyncrasy, while Nos. 3 and 4 would be top recommendations even if they cost far more. These are model performances and, throughout, the playing of Kovacevich has a depth and thoughtful intensity that have rarely been matched. The recording, from the early 1970s, is refined and well balanced and has been admirably transferred to CD. Grumiaux's *Romances* date from a decade earlier, but the Concertgebouw acoustic brings a characteristic fullness, and the solo playing is peerless.

Piano concertos Nos. 1 in C, Op. 15; 2 in B flat, Op. 19.
*** Sony Dig. SK 42177 [id.]. Perahia, Concg. O, Haitink.
(Y/B) (M) *** DG Dig. 445 504-2 [id.]. Martha Argerich, Philh. O, Sinopoli.
(N) (M) *** Virgin Veritas/EMI Dig. VER5 61296-2 [id.]. Tan (fortepiano), L. Classical Players, Norrington.
*** DG Dig. 437 545-2 [id.]. Krystian Zimerman, VPO.
(N) (M) *(**) Beethoven Edition DG Dig. 447 908-2 [id.]. Pollini, VPO, Jochum.

Murray Perahia's coupling of Nos. 1 and 2 brings strong and thoughtful performances very characteristic of this pianist, which yet draw a sharp distinction between the two works. No. 2, the earlier, brings a near-Mozartian manner in the first movement, but then rightly a deep and measured account of the slow movement takes Beethoven into another world, hushed and intense. The *First Concerto* finds Perahia taking a fully Beethovenian view from the start. Bernard Haitink proves a lively and sympathetic partner, with the Concertgebouw playing superbly. The recording sets the orchestra in a pleasingly warm acoustic.

The conjunction of Martha Argerich and Giuseppe Sinopoli in Beethoven produces performances which give off electric sparks, daring and volatile. Argerich's contribution in phrase after phrase brings highly individual pointing. She is jaunty in allegros rather than lightweight – one might even ask for more pianissimo – and slow movements are songful, not solemn. Very distinctive and stimulating performances, given full, vivid – albeit not ideally balanced – sound in a rather reverberant acoustic.

Melvyn Tan's coupling of the first two concertos, using a fortepiano, brings performances of natural, unselfconscious expressiveness which will delight those looking for versions on period instruments. Even when Tan's speeds for slow movements are very fast indeed, his ease of expression makes them very persuasive, avoiding breathlessness while simultaneously conveying more gravity than you might expect.

Zimerman, completing the cycle he began with Bernstein, directs the Vienna Philharmonic in bright, elegant, often witty performances that bring home the point that these are early works. Bright recording.

Pollini's second (digital) Beethoven cycle with Abbado (DG 439 770-2) – recorded live in December

1992 and January 1993 – proved something of a disappointment. One problem is that the piano-sound in the latter is often shallower than that of the first set; Pollini admirers will therefore be glad to see this earlier series reappearing as part of DG's Beethoven Edition. Pollini is sometimes wilful in his earlier account of the *First Concerto* but, with refreshing clarity of articulation, his is a performance, brisk rather than poetic, which vividly reflects the challenge of an unexpected partnership between pianist and conductor, and it has a keener sense of spontaneity than his later, digital version with Abbado. The recording was taken from live performances but betrays little sign of that. The *Second Concerto* (also live) is one of the more attractive of his Beethoven concerto series, but it cannot match its finest rivals. This CD was an early (1983) digital issue and it provides excellent presence for the piano, but the strings are curiously lacking in fullness of focus; the earlier, analogue recordings with Boehm were rather warmer and more natural-sounding.

Piano concertos Nos. 1 in C, Op. 15; 3 in C min., Op. 37.
(N) *(*) RCA Dig. 09026 68226-2 [id.]. Gerhard Oppitz, Leipzig GO, Janowski.

Gerhard Oppitz has many admirers in Germany and they will surely welcome the prospect of Beethoven concertos from him.. He has many sterling qualities and is not an idiosyncratic or self-regarding artist. However, his performances are not touched with sufficient distinction or poetic feeling to warrant an enthusiastic recommendation.

Piano concertos Nos. 2; 4.
(M) *** Sony SBK 48165 [id.]. Fleisher, Cleveland O, Szell.

This coupling by Leon Fleisher and George Szell brings masterly examples of their inspired artistry. No. 2 receives a powerful, intense, spontaneous-sounding performance, giving weight to early Beethoven. In No. 4 Fleisher and Szell are even more searching, with the soloist's refreshingly imaginative playing matched by glorious sounds from the Cleveland Orchestra. The bright, forward recordings, both made in Severance Hall, have been transferred with satisfying fullness and body.

Piano concertos Nos. 2 in B flat, Op. 19; 4 in G, Op. 58 (with the composer's final revisions).
(Y/B) *** Conifer Dig. 75605 51237-2 [id.]. Mikhail Kazakevich, ECO, Mackerras.

Dr Barry Cooper, whose earlier researches into Beethoven's sketchbooks gave us an illuminating reconstruction of the fragmentary *Tenth Symphony*, has here investigated Beethoven's amendments on a score the composer himself used for a public performance of the *Fourth Piano concerto*. Though the differences are relatively minor, it is fascinating to find Beethoven regularly adding virtuoso figuration to the solo part, making the result sparkle even more brightly. The poetry of Kazakevich's crisply articulated playing is then heightened, not least in the dialogue of the slow movement, by the sharply dramatic conducting of Sir Charles Mackerras with the ECO. In the *Second Piano concerto* the amendments come only in the first movement – inked into the autograph too late to be included in the published score. They involve the orchestra as well as the solo part, and include cuts of ten complete bars, tautening and clarifying the result. This is not just a curiosity but a viable coupling to recommend generally, for the performances, particularly of the *G major Concerto*, are memorable in their own right.

Piano concerto No. 3 in C min., Op. 37.
(N) (M) (**) DG 447 976-2 [id.]. Kempff, Dresden PO, Paul van Kampen – MOZART: *Piano concerto No. 20 etc.* (**)
Issued in the Dokumente series to celebrate Kempff's centenary, the CD transfer of his 78 recording of the *Third* Beethoven *Concerto*, dating from 1941, brings a performance fascinating interpretatively but very limited and scratchy in orchestral sound. If the first movement is less alert than in his later recordings, the slow movement is markedly broader and more warmly expressive.

Piano concertos Nos. 3 in C min., Op. 37; 4 in G, Op. 58.
*** Sony Dig. SK 39814 [id.]. Murray Perahia, Concg. O, Haitink.
(N) *** Ph. Dig. 446 082-2 [id.]. Mitsuko Uchida, Concg. O, Sanderling.
*** DG Dig. 429 749-2 [id.]. Krystian Zimerman, VPO, Bernstein.
(N) (M) **(*) Beethoven Edition DG 447 909-2 [id.]. Pollini, VPO, Boehm.
(N) (B) ** Decca Dig. 448 230-2 [id.]. Alicia de Larrocha, Berlin RSO, Chailly.

Perahia gives readings that are at once intensely poetic and individual, but also strong, with pointing and shading of passage-work that consistently convey the magic of the moment caught on the wing, helped by fine, spacious and open recorded sound.

Uchida proves a much stronger soloist in Beethoven's *C minor Concerto* than in her Mozart concerto records. She is admirably supported by Sanderling, whose accompaniments have much character: the dotted rhythmic figure which dominates the first movement bounces resiliently. The beautiful *Largo*, very spaciously presented, has real depth and serenity; the lyricism of the finale is uppermost, at an unforced pace, yet with a spurt of high spirits in the coda. Uchida's gently persuasive opening of the *G major Concerto* makes it immediately apparent that her performance is going to bring a freely improvisational quality and that its poetic feeling is in no doubt. Sanderling holds the first movement together splendidly and their interchange in the *Andante* is potent. The finale, again essentially lyrical, is also consistently imaginative and in both outer movements the cadenzas have impressive power. With superb Concertgebouw recording this is a highly enjoyable coupling, with much that is refreshingly individual and a feeling of live music-making holding the concentration span from the first note to the last.

Zimerman finds the vein of poetry not only in No. 4, but in the much earlier No. 3, very sympathetically accompanied by Bernstein, who exactly matches his soloist in the thoughtful dialogue of the central *Andante* of No. 4. Bright sound that yet does not allow a full pianissimo. But this is refreshing music-making that consistently rewards the listener.

The concentration of the playing and the single-minded clarity of Pollini's reading of the *Third Concerto* are matched by Boehm's strong, clear-minded accompaniment. The result is strikingly fresh, and Pollini brings undoubted personal insights to bear on his reading, with the slow movement serenely dedicated. Yet overall the performance is on the sober side for a youthful concerto that should perhaps sparkle more than it does here, although the result is by no means lacking in spontaneity. There is an aristocratic feeling about Pollini's account of the *Fourth,* and the clarity of his vision achieves a delicate balance between classical poise and poetic sensitivity. Boehm is a faithful accompanist who prevents the end result from being too chilly, although the 'question-and-answer' approach to the *Andante* is coolly individual. The closeness of the piano's balance is apparent in the transfer to CD, but the recordings, from the latter part of the 1970s, are of fine DG analogue quality.

Alicia de Larrocha's set of the Beethoven concertos with the Berlin Radio Symphony Orchestra, made in the mid-1980s, proved to be very uneven, with Nos. 3 and 4 the least attractive. Here de Larrocha sounds self-conscious in her somewhat weighty manner. She receives good support from Chailly and the Decca sound is full and vivid.

Piano concertos Nos. 3 in C min., Op. 37; 4 in G, Op. 58; 5 in E flat (Emperor), Op. 73; (i) *Choral Fantasia in C min., Op. 80.*
(Y/B) (B) **(*) Decca Double 440 839-2 (2) [id.]. Julius Katchen, LSO, Piero Gamba; (i) with London Symphony Ch.

Julius Katchen's account of the *C minor Concerto* dates from 1958, the *G major* from five years later. Both were well recorded and there is a good balance and plenty of ambient warmth. Katchen's *Emperor* is an excellent performance, full of characteristic animal energy and superbly recorded (and remastered). The first and last movements are taken at a sparkling pace, but not so fast that Katchen sounds at all rushed. With this pianist, who has sometimes seemed too rigid in his recorded playing, it is good to find that here he seems to be coaxing his orchestra to match his own delicacy. Overall, this is an enjoyable set of recordings and is undoubtedly good value. The performance of the *Choral Fantasia* is highly compelling. Katchen is very commanding in the opening cadenza, and later in the work there are some delightfully light touches from the orchestra. Very well recorded in 1965, it remains among the freshest versions in the catalogue.

(i) *Piano concerto No. 3 in C min., Op. 37;* (ii) *Piano trio No. 7 (Archduke), Op. 97.*
(Y/B) (M) (***) Dutton Lab. mono CDLX 7015 [id.]. Solomon; (i) BBC SO, Boult; (ii) Henry Holst, Anthony Pini.

Solomon's 1944 performance is one of the great interpretations of this concerto. He holds the listener in the palm of his hand from his entry throughout the whole; every phrase is alive and sharply and compellingly characterized, yet at no time is it for the glory of Solomon. Another point of interest is that he plays the Clara Schumann cadenza in the first movement. Sir Adrian gets a very good response from the orchestra. The Dutton CD brings another wartime performance, from 1943, of the *Archduke Trio* with Henry Holst and Anthony Pini – not really in the same class, but Solomon himself is in very good form. Superb transfers.

Piano concertos Nos. (i) *4 in G, Op. 58;* (ii) *5 in E flat (Emperor).*
(Y/B) (M) *** DG 447 402-2 [id.]. Wilhelm Kempff, BPO, Leitner.
(N) (B) *** DG Classikon 439 483-2 [id.]. Pollini, VPO, Boehm.
(N) (M) ** BBC Recordings Dig. BBCRD 9110-2. (i) Anthony Goldstone, RPO; (ii) Peter Donohoe, BBC SO; both cond. Norman Del Mar.
(N) (M) *(*) Ph. Dig. 446 193-2 [id.]. Brendel, Chicago SO, Levine.

The Kempff/Leitner performances, now reissued in DG's 'Originals' series, bring an outstanding mid-priced recommendation for this particular coupling. The digital remastering has perceptibly enhanced the sound, with the most natural balance in the *Fourth Concerto*. Here Kempff's delicacy of fingerwork and his shading of tone-colour are as effervescent as ever, and the fine control of the conductor ensures the unity of the reading. Although Kempff's version of the *Emperor* is not on an epic scale, it has power in plenty, and excitement, too. As ever, Kempff's range of tone-colour is extraordinarily wide, from the merest half-tone, as though the fingers were barely brushing the keys, to the crisp impact of a dry fortissimo. Leitner's orchestral contribution is of high quality and the Berlin orchestral playing has vigour and warmth. Here some reservations need to be made about the quality of the remastered CD. The bass is somewhat over-resonant and the orchestral tuttis are very slightly woolly; the piano timbre is natural but the slight lack of firmness in the orchestral focus is a drawback, though it does not seriously detract from the music-making.

Those wanting to sample Pollini's earlier set of the Beethoven concertos could hardly do better than invest in this bargain Classikon coupling of two of the most strikingly individual performances, of Nos. 4 and 5, excellently transferred, with believable piano-timbre and a full orchestral tapestry well focused within the warm ambience of the Grosser Saal of the Vienna Musikverein. After the poised account of the *Fourth Concerto*, the distinction of Pollini's interpretation of the *Emperor* is never in doubt and, though recorded in the studio, the performance sounds more spontaneously expressive, with a vein of poetry that is largely missing in the later, live recording. If at times the solo playing sounds a little withdrawn, the strong and wise accompaniment of Boehm and the Vienna Philharmonic again provides a nice balance. The slow movement is elegant and the finale is urgent and energetic; those not seeking a grand romantic manner in this concerto will find this satisfying in a quite different way.

The BBC performances emanate from Proms broadcasts in 1981–2 and, although they may not represent a serious challenge to the greatest studio recordings, they still give pleasure of a kind that one expects to find on such occasions. Donohoe gives a vital and often sensitive account of the *Emperor*, though his instrument does not sound as fresh in timbre. Anthony Goldstone, whose talents have never been accorded the recognition they deserve, gives a more than acceptable account of the *G major concerto*.

Brendel's digital coupling of Nos. 4 and 5 – like the live complete set from which it is taken – is a disappointment. Though Brendel's mastery and highly individual imagination are never in doubt, the performances are far less spontaneous-sounding than those he recorded earlier with Haitink in the studio. The audience noises, odd balances and intrusive applause are other disadvantages, while in the *Emperor* the relative constriction of the sound is distracting.

(i) *Piano concertos Nos. 4 in G, Op. 58; 5 in E flat (Emperor), Op. 73. Andante in F (Andante favori), WoO 57; Bagatelle in A min. (Für Elise), WoO 59; 6 Bagatelles, Op. 126; 6 Ecossaises, WoO 83; Piano sonatas Nos. 3 in C, Op. 2/3; 11 in B flat, Op. 22; 18 in E flat, Op. 31/3; 23 in F min. (Appassionata), Op. 57; 24 in F sharp, Op. 78; 29 in B flat (Hammerklavier), Op. 106; 30 in E, Op. 109; 5 Variations on 'Rule Britannia', WoO 79; 6 Variations in F, Op. 34; 15 Variations and fugue on a theme of Prometheus (Eroica), Op. 35; 33 Variations on a waltz by Diabelli, Op. 120.*

(N) (M) **(*) Ph. Brendel Edition Analogue/Dig. 446 922-2 (5) [id.]. Brendel, (i) with Chicago SO, Levine.

Brendel's coupling of the *Fourth* and *Fifth Concertos* is also available separately (see above) and its disappointments are indicated there. Brendel's command and individuality come over more powerfully in the *Emperor concerto*, but the poorly balanced sound and audience noises remain a problem. The *Sonatas* are altogether more successful, with Op. 2/3 fresh and sparkling and *No. 11 in B flat* among the very best of his analogue cycle, with first-class sound. No. 18 is marvellously responsive to the changing character of the invention: Brendel is aware of the interpretative pitfalls and how to solve them! The *Appassionata* is undeniably an impressive performance and excellent recording. Again, very truthful piano-sound. The digital *Hammerklavier* and Opus 78 both come, not from Brendel's complete sonata cycle, but from live recordings, made at the Queen Elizabeth Hall in London a decade later. Though there is greater urgency and dramatic tension in the allegro movements, the great *Adagio* of the *Hammerklavier*, intense as it is, lacks the spacious sublimity of his earlier version, taken even more slowly. The audience make their presence felt only between movements, and the recording is very believable. Brendel's *Diabelli variations* were also recorded live. The playing has energy and urgency; understandably it is not flawless, but the tensions are conveyed superbly. The sound is again excellent, though not as delicate in dynamic range as in a studio recording. The *Eroica variations*, not as flamboyant as with some, plainly point to the magnificence of their culminating development in the *Eroica* finale. Again very realistic recording. The other variations (recorded digitally) show Brendel's consistent thoughtfulness and imagination which bring out the truly Beethovenian qualities in even the most trivial pieces. It is a pity that Philips did not choose the analogue recordings of the two concertos, but for the most part this is an impressive box.

Piano concerto No. 5 in E flat (Emperor), Op. 73.
*** Ph. Dig. 416 215-2 [id.]. Arrau, Dresden State O, Sir Colin Davis.
*** DG Dig. 429 748-2 [id.]. Krystian Zimerman, VPO, Bernstein.
*** Sony Dig. SK 42330 [id.]. Perahia, Concg. O, Haitink.
(M) *** RCA 09026 61961-2 [id.]. Van Cliburn, Chicago SO, Reiner – TCHAIKOVSKY: *Piano concerto No. 1.* ***

Piano concerto No. 5 (Emperor); Grosse Fuge in B flat, Op. 133.
✪ (M) *** EMI Dig. CD-EMX 2184. Stephen Kovacevich, Australian CO.

(i) *Piano concerto No. 5 (Emperor); Piano sonata No. 21 in C (Waldstein), Op. 53.*
(N) (M) ** Carlton IMP Dig. PCD 2038 [id.]. Cristina Ortiz, City of L. Sinfonia, Hickox.

Kovacevich is unsurpassed today as an interpreter of this most magnificent of concertos. His superb account for Philips, now on Concert Classics, has set a model for everyone and, with its sonata coupling, remains highly recommendable. This Eminence version, with the soloist directing from the keyboard, is recognizably from the same inspired artist, though speeds are consistently faster and the manner is sharper and tauter. The piano sound on the digital recording is aptly brighter and more faithful than on the Philips, making this a first choice for this much-recorded work, even with no allowance for price. For fill-up, Kovacevich conducts a comparably electrifying account of the *Grosse Fuge*.

The wonder is that Arrau, for so long an inhibited artist in the studio, should in his *Emperor* recording, made when he was over eighty, sound so carefree. There are technical flaws, and the digital recording is rather resonant in bass, but with Sir Colin Davis and the Dresden State Orchestra as electrifying partners, the voltage is even higher than in his earlier versions of the mid-1960s. This is a thrillingly expansive *Emperor* which will give much satisfaction.

Zimerman reserves for the *Emperor* his most powerful playing, and Bernstein sensitively encourages him into spontaneous-sounding expressiveness, turning phrases with consistent imagination.

Perahia's account of the *Emperor*, strong and thoughtful yet with characteristic touches of poetry, rounds off an outstanding cycle of the Beethoven concertos. The approach is spacious, and with Bernard Haitink and the Concertgebouw Orchestra firm, responsive partners, each movement immediately takes wing, though a touch of bass-heaviness in the recording needs correcting.

Van Cliburn creates much excitement and intensity in the outer movements, with powerful support from Reiner. It is an individual but satisfying reading, with the slow movement a little restrained in the phrasing but poised in its beauty, and this effectively offsets the virtuosity of the outer movements. The finale is by no means driven too hard; if anything it is slower than usual but has a fine lilt and genuine bravura. The remastered recording sounds very well indeed.

A generally sound reading of the *Emperor* from Cristina Ortiz and Hickox, with a strong feeling of forward momentum in the first movement but without sufficient relaxation for the work's lyrical contrasts. The beautiful slow movement, however, is not lacking in poise, and the finale is brightly vivacious. With excellent, modern, digital recording, this has its attractions for a newcomer to the music. Ortiz is undoubtedly articulate and strong in the first movement of the *Waldstein*. After preparing with considerable skill for the entry of the great lyrical theme of the finale, however, she then sets off buoyantly and entirely without subtlety – whereas Kempff, for instance, gives the listener the impression that the famous melody is growing spontaneously out of the music which has gone before.

(i) *Piano concerto No. 5 (Emperor); (ii) Piano concerto in E flat, WoO 4 (arr. & orch. Willy Hess); (iii) Violin concerto in D, Op. 61; (iv) Triple concerto for violin, cello and piano in C, Op. 56.*
(Y/B) (B) **(*) Ph. Duo 442 580-2 (2) [id.]. (i) Kovacevich, LSO, Sir Colin Davis; (ii) Lidia Grychtolowna, Folkwang CO, Heinz Dressel; (iii) Herman Krebbers, Concg. O, Haitink; (iv) Szeryng, Starker, Arrau, New Philh. O, Inbal.

Kovacevich's superb 1969 account of the *Emperor* is here part of an attractive Duo compilation which includes also the early *E flat Piano concerto* (WoO 4) which the composer wrote when he was only fourteen. The present performance uses a reconstruction by Willy Hess in which the dominating flute colouring of the orchestration is hardly characteristic and not helped by less than distinguished playing from the wind section of the Folkwang Chamber Orchestra. The performance is spirited, especially the finale; but the piece sounds more like a concerto in the style of the sons of Bach rather than showing much evidence of the pen of even an immature Beethoven. Krebbers' 1974 recording of the *Violin concerto* is distinguished and will disappoint no one. In his hands the slow movement has a tender simplicity which is irresistible, and it is followed by a delightfully relaxed and playful reading of the finale. In the first movement Haitink and his soloist form a partnership which brings out the symphonic strength more than almost any other reading. If the balance of the soloist is a shade too close, the recording is otherwise excellent, and it has transferred with vivid fullness to CD. The companion account of the *Triple Concerto* with Arrau, Szeryng and Starker again brings full and spacious Concertgebouw recording, but Arrau and his colleagues are less strongly projected and, by adopting very unhurried tempi, they run the risk of losing concentration. The outer movements, with the solo playing almost on a chamber scale, lack the bite and bravura of the finest rivals. However, at 'two CDs for the price of one', this set remains well worth consideration for both the *Emperor* and the *Violin concerto*.

(i) *Piano concerto No. 5 (Emperor);* (ii) *Violin concerto in D; Romances Nos. 1–2, Opp. 40 & 50.*
(Y/B) (BB) **(*) EMI Seraphim Dig./Analogue CES5 68520-2 (2) [CDEB 68520]. (i) Youri Egorov, Philh. O, Sawallisch; (ii) Josef Suk, New Philh. O, Boult, or ASMF, Marriner – MOZART: *Piano concerto No. 20.* **(*)

Youri Egorov in his first concerto recording, made in the early 1980s, gives a refreshingly direct but still individual account of the *Emperor*, helped by authoritative conducting from Sawallisch. The slow movement is the controversial point, taken at a very measured *Adagio* which might have flowed better had Egorov adopted a more affectionate style of phrasing. Suk also chooses a very measured tempo for the first movement of the *Violin concerto*, and some may feel that there is not enough urgency and concentration to sustain the interpretation, especially as Suk's tone, as recorded, is on the small side. But otherwise the analogue recording, from the beginning of the 1970s, is excellent, and Suk's playing is both noble and spacious. The *Romances* are very successful, too. Good value at EMI's bargain-basement price for the two discs.

(i) *Piano concerto No. 5 in E flat (Emperor);* (ii) *Triple concerto for violin, cello and piano in C, Op. 56.*
(M) *** Sony SBK 46549 [id.]. (i) Leon Fleisher, Cleveland O, Szell; (ii) Stern, Rose, Istomin, Phd. O, Ormandy.

Leon Fleisher is a pianist who worked with special understanding in the Szell regime at Cleveland, and by any count his reading of the *Emperor* is impressive for its youthful dramatic vigour. For the coupling, Stern, Rose and Istomin – three friends who invariably reveal their personal joy in making music together – make a wonderful trio of soloists. Unfortunately the CBS balance, as usual, favours the soloists so that the contrast of their soft playing is endangered; but the performance as a whole is so compelling that it would take a much more serious recording fault to undermine the concentration.

Piano concerto No. 5 (Emperor); (i) *Choral Fantasia, Op. 80.*
✦ *** EMI Dig. CDC7 49965-2. Melvyn Tan, (i) Schütz Ch.; L. Classical Players, Roger Norrington.
(N) (M) **(*) Beethoven Edition DG Analogue/Dig. 447 910-2 [id.]. Pollini, VPO; (i) Boehm; (ii) Soloists, V. State Op. Ch., VPO, Abbado.

Melvyn Tan plays with real flair and musical imagination. He has a poetic fire and brilliance all his own. The disc conveys the feeling of a live performance rather than an academic exercise, and the artists follow Czerny's brisk (and authoritative) tempo markings. The inspiriting account of the *Choral Fantasia* possesses a mercurial quality and a panache that show this sometimes underrated work in a most positive light. Norrington and the chorus and orchestra are no less persuasive. A splendidly natural recording completes the attractiveness of this fine disc.

Although perhaps not the most joyful of *Emperors*, the command and individuality of Pollini's performance are compelling, helped by Boehm's warmth. The coupled *Choral Fantasia* is comparatively lightweight, with a very poised introductory cadenza, but proves enjoyably fresh. Rarely, each of its nine sections is separately cued.

Violin concerto in D, Op. 61.
(N) (M) *** Teldec/Warner Dig. 0630 10015-2 [id.]. Gidon Kremer, COE, Harnoncourt – SCHUMANN: *Violin concerto.* *(*)
(Y/B) ✦ (M) *** DG 447 403-2 [id.]. Schneiderhan, BPO, Jochum – MOZART: *Violin concerto No. 5.* ***
*** EMI Dig. CDC7 54072-2 [id.]. Kyung Wha Chung, Concg. O, Tennstedt – BRUCH: *Violin concerto No. 1.* ***
**(*) EMI Dig. CDC7 54574-2; *EL 754574-4* [id.]. Kennedy, N. German RSO, Tennstedt (with BACH: (Unaccompanied) *Violin Sonatas* and *Partitas*).
(**) Pearl mono GEMMCDS 9996 (2) [id.]. Fritz Kreisler, Berlin State Op. O, Leo Blech – BACH: *Double violin concerto;* BRAHMS; MENDELSSOHN; MOZART: *Violin concertos.* (**)

(i) *Violin concerto in D, Op. 61. Overtures: The Consecration of the house, Op. 124; Coriolan, Op. 62; Zur Namensfeier, Op. 115.*

(N) (M) ** Beethoven Edition DG 447 906-2 [id.]. (i) Ferras; BPO, Karajan.

(i) *Violin concerto in D;* (ii) *Romances Nos. 1 in G, Op. 40; 2 in F, Op. 50.*
✪ *** Teldec/Warner Dig. 9031 74881-2 [id.]. Kremer, COE, Harnoncourt.
*** EMI Dig. CDC7 49567-2 [id.]. Perlman, BPO, Barenboim.
(BB) *** Naxos Dig. 8.550149; *4550149* [id.]. Takako Nishizaki, Slovak PO (Bratislava), Kenneth Jean.
(N) (M) **(*) Carlton Dig. 30367 00242 [id.]. Jaime Laredo, SCO.

(i) *Violin concerto in D;* (ii) *Violin sonata No. 10 in G, Op. 96.*
**(*) RCA 09026 61219-2 [id.]. Zukerman, (i) LAPO, Mehta; (ii) Marc Neikrug.

Gidon Kremer's Teldec account of Beethoven's *Violin concerto* was taken from performances with Nikolaus Harnoncourt and the COE in Graz in July 1992, and offers one of his most commanding recordings, both polished and full of flair, magnetically spontaneous from first to last, with tone ravishingly pure. Harnoncourt's contribution as conductor is vital too, for, as in his records of the Beethoven symphonies, also with the COE, he applies lessons he learnt over his years as a pioneer of period performance. The controversial point for some will be the cadenza in the first movement. It is described as by 'Beethoven/Kremer', for (like Wolfgang Schneiderhan in his classic DG recording) he uses a transcription of the big cadenza which Beethoven wrote for his piano arrangement of the work. But where Schneiderhan had the solo violin backed up by only the timpani (just as Beethoven does), Kremer introduces a piano as well. It makes a very long cadenza indeed – 5 minutes exactly – but he can quote Beethoven in his support. He also plays violin versions of the other cadenzas and flourishes that punctuate Beethoven's piano version – many more than in normal performances. Altogether one of the most refreshing versions of the concerto ever put on disc, backed up by crisp, unsentimental readings of the two *Romances*, with the first of the two flowing faster and more freshly than we are used to.

Kremer's performance of the *Violin concerto*, without the *Romances*, comes additionally in an alternative, mid-priced coupling with the Schumann *Violin concerto*, which he recorded earlier with much less success.

Perlman's Berlin recording was made at a live performance in the Philharmonie in Berlin in 1986. The live occasion prompts the soloist to play with extra flair and individuality, spontaneous in imagination, with depth of insight married to total technical command. Though (as always with Perlman) the solo violin is balanced well forward, the sound is not overbearing. Anyone wanting an uncontroversial, modern, digital version cannot do better than opt for this. The two *Romances*, recorded by the same performers in the studio, are just as persuasive.

Wolfgang Schneiderhan's stereo version of the *Violin concerto* is among the greatest recordings of this work: the serene spiritual beauty of the slow movement, and the playing of the second subject in particular, have never been surpassed on record; the orchestra under Jochum provides a background tapestry of breadth and dignity. As an added point of interest, Schneiderhan uses cadenzas that were provided for the transcription of the work for piano and orchestra. This makes an entirely justified reissue in DG's 'Legendary recordings' series, and the current transfer of the well-balanced (1962) analogue recording is fresh and realistic. Moreover the new Mozart coupling is both more appropriate and more generous.

Kyung Wha Chung's EMI performance, recorded live in the Concertgebouw, is searching and intense. Next to Perlman on another live recording from EMI, Chung is lighter and more mercurial. The element of vulnerability in Chung's reading adds to the emotional weight, above all in the slow movement, which in its wistful tenderness is among the most beautiful on record, while the outer movements are full of flair. The recording, with the soloist not balanced too close, is remarkably full and atmospheric for one made live.

Those looking for a super-bargain, digital version will find that Nishizaki's highly spontaneous performance can measure up to many accounts by more famous names. Helped by a strongly sympathetic backing from the excellent Slovak Philharmonic under Kenneth Jean, her playing is individual yet unselfconscious and has a fresh simplicity of approach which is consistently appealing. The *Larghetto* is poised and serene, and the finale is nicely buoyant. The two *Romances* are also very well played. The digital recording, made in the Reduta Concert Hall in Bratislava, is first class, the violin well forward but with the resonantly full orchestral tapestry spaciously caught.

Compared with Zukerman's spacious reading from the late 1970s with Daniel Barenboim and the Chicago Symphony Orchestra, his new RCA version has an extra depth. If in the earlier version the characteristic warmth of Zukerman's tone marked the whole performance, this one brings greater emphasis on purity and refinement. The result may be more disciplined, but never too rigid, with even the opening of the finale on the main rondo theme given a sense of gentle communing, not as outward-going as before. The recording helps, with the solo violin less forwardly balanced. It makes an apt and surprisingly unusual coupling to have the concerto presented alongside the last and most elusive of the Beethoven *Violin sonatas*, taken from Zukerman's complete cycle with the pianist Marc Neikrug, who sadly fails to match the violinist in imagination.

Nigel Kennedy's performance was recorded live, not by editing various performances together (the general practice) but taken from a single performance in Lübeck, presented complete with encores (movements from the solo Bach *Sonatas* and *Partitas*). The snag is that many minutes of tuning up and applause have also been included. Like his interpretation of the Brahms, issued a year earlier, Kennedy's reading of the Beethoven is in principle wilfully slow but, far more than in that studio recording of the Brahms, the sense of spontaneity carries persuasion even when, after the big Kreisler cadenza in the first movement, he and Tennstedt threaten to come to a dead halt. The cadenza in the finale brings the most controversial point: Kennedy's own protracted improvisation which, towards the end, lapses into quarter-tones and hints of the twentieth century. Whatever the hype surrounding him these days, Kennedy here still produces much magical playing, but this well-recorded performance will not be to all tastes.

Laredo, directing the outstanding players of the Scottish Chamber Orchestra, gives a clean-cut, satisfy-ing reading of the *Concerto*, presented on a convincing chamber scale. Speeds are a degree faster than usual in all three movements and some of the dramatic contrasts are reduced, with the closeness of sound in the slow movement not allowing a really gentle pianissimo, but that is apt for the scale. There are more inspired readings but, with the *Romances* as coupling, well recorded in full digital sound, this is certainly worth considering.

In spite of the strong impact from the orchestra, Ferras's reading is not memorable. His tone is small, like Schneiderhan's, and he attempts a classical reading, but there the comparison ends. The first movement is cool, although gracious, and even though the second subject of the slow movement is played with very considerable tension it does not convey the quality of magic that Schneiderhan finds. The overtures come from Karajan's outstanding survey of the mid-1960s, but they are also available separately as a set.

When Kreisler recorded the Beethoven concerto with Barbirolli he was in his sixties, and this 1926 account with Leo Blech, which sonically was quite good for its period, shows his wonderful tone and consummate artistry to better advantage. However, those who have the earlier LP transfer (EMI HLM 7016), with which we compared this, will probably be better satisfied with the smoother, warmer sound on the HMV LP. The Pearl transfer has greater presence and detail, but there is some roughness and a lot more hiss.

(i) *Violin concerto in D, Op. 61;* (ii) *Triple concerto in C, Op. 56.*
(N) (M) **(*) Sony Stern Edition I SM2K 66941 (2) [id.]. Isaac Stern, with (i) NYPO, Barenboim; (ii) Leonard Rose, Eugene Istomin, Phd. O, Ormandy – BRAHMS: *Concertos.* ***

It was a pity that Sony chose Stern's later recording of the *Violin concerto* with Barenboim, instead of his earlier version which showed so readily the intensely creative bond that had been established between Stern and Bernstein in those early years. The account with Barenboim dates from 1975. Stern gives here a characteristically romantic reading but one that is less spontaneous-sounding than his earlier version and, although the sound is fuller, the CBS highlighting gets in the way of an ideal balance. The *Triple concerto*, recorded a decade earlier in 1964, brings a recording from three friends who reveal their personal joy in making music together. Though Stern is undoubtedly the leader of the trio, the domin-ance over his colleagues is benevolent. Rose's cello solos are so superbly expressive in the slow move-ment that it acquires a depth beyond its spare proportions, and the finale brings some wonderful springy polacca rhythms that take Beethoven very close to Eastern Europe. Unfortunately the close CBS balance is unflattering to the soloists so that their soft playing is endangered, but the performance as a whole is so compelling that it would take a much more serious recording fault to undermine the listener's attention.

Konzertsatz (Concerto movement) in C, WoO 5; Romance No. 1 in G, Op. 40.
(M) *** DG 431 168-2 [id.]. Kremer, LSO, Tchakarov – SCHUBERT: *Konzertstück* etc. ***

The early *Concerto movement in C* is performed in a completion by Wilfried Fischer that is effective enough; and the mixed bag of Schubert which acts as coupling is certainly apt. All the music is beauti-fully played by Kremer; the 1978 recording, made in the London Sir Henry Wood Hall, has transferred splendidly to CD.

Triple concerto for violin, cello and piano in C, Op. 56.

(M) *** EMI CDM7 64744-2 [id.]. D. Oistrakh, Rostropovich, S. Richter, BPO, Karajan – BRAHMS: *Double concerto.* ***

(N) (B) *** EMI forte CZS5 69331-2 (2) [id.]. David Oistrakh, Lev Oborin, Sviatoslav Knushevitzky, Philh. O, Sargent – BRAHMS: *Double concerto;* MOZART: *Violin concerto No. 3;* PROKOFIEV: *Violin concerto No. 2.* ***

(N) (BB) *** CfP Silver Double Dig. CDCFPSD 4775 (2). Zimmermann, Cohen, Manz, ECO, Saraste – DVORAK: *Cello concerto;* ELGAR: *Cello concerto;* TCHAIKOVSKY: *Variations on a rococo theme.* ***

(B) *** Carlton IMP Classics Dig. 30367 0091-2 [id.]. Trio Zingara, ECO, Heath – BOCCHERINI: *Concerto No. 7.* ***

(i) *Triple concerto, Op. 56. Overtures: King Stephen, Op. 117; Leonora No. 3, Op. 72b; The Ruins of Athens, Op. 113.*

(N) (M) **(*) Beethoven Edition DG 447 907-2 [id.]. (i) Mutter, Ma, Zeltser; BPO, Karajan.

(i) *Triple concerto, Op. 56;* (ii) *Symphony No. 10: First movement* (realized & completed Cooper).

(M) *** Chandos Dig. CHAN 6501 [id.]. (i) Kalichstein–Laredo–Robinson Trio, ECO, Gibson; (ii) CBSO, Weller.

The star-studded cast on the EMI recording makes a breathtaking line-up. This is warm, expansive music-making that confirms even more clearly than before the strength of the piece. The resonant recording suffers from loss of focus in some climaxes, but this is not too serious. The new transfer is remarkably vivid and has firmed up the orchestral tuttis most satisfactorily. Now recoupled with a similarly commanding account of the Brahms *Double concerto*, this is an irresistible mid-priced bargain.

The earlier EMI recording, also featuring distinguished Russian soloists, dates from the early days of stereo, yet the sound is excellent for its period and the balance (with Walter Legge producing) perhaps the most successful this concerto has received in the recording studio. Sargent does not direct the proceedings with Karajan's flair, but he is authoritative and musical, and his soloists make a good team as well as displaying plenty of individual personality. The slow movement is strikingly eloquent. On EMI's two-for-the-price of one forte label, this concertante collection is highly recommendable.

On Classics for Pleasure, with first-rate modern digital recording and with Robert Cohen leading an excellent team of prize-winning young soloists (his solo in the slow movement is superb), this makes an outstanding bargain version, keenly competitive with almost any full-priced issue, if not always as elegantly pointed as some. Jukka-Pekka Saraste and the ECO provide a lively, understanding accompaniment and the performance has splendid spontaneity throughout, with the finale sparkling in its sense of occasion. The recording is exceptionally well balanced, with most of the problems solved: the soloists forward, but not exaggeratedly so, and the orchestral backing given fine impact within the convincing acoustics of London's Henry Wood Hall. Coupled with three outstanding performances by Cohen, this is among the finest of these very economically priced Silver Doubles.

The 1984 Chandos version of the *Triple concerto* with three young American soloists is exceptionally well recorded. Sharon Robinson, the cellist, takes the lead with pure tone and fine intonation, though both her partners are by nature more forceful artists. A clean-cut, often refreshing view of the work, it is now reissued coupled with Weller's strong version of Barry Cooper's completion of the first movement of Beethoven's projected *Tenth Symphony*, also very well recorded.

On Carlton, Felix Schmidt, who is also the cello soloist in the Boccherini, plays with consistently beautiful, firm and clean tone, well matched by his two partners, creating the illusion of live performance, full of bounce and vigour. At bargain price, in full and vivid digital sound, it makes an excellent recommendation.

After the formidable crescendo within Karajan's very positive opening tutti, the soloists seem rather small-scale. But there are benefits from the unity brought by the conductor when each of the young players has a positive contribution to make, no less effectively when the recording balance for once in this work does not favour the solo instruments unduly. Yo-Yo Ma's playing is not immaculate, and he does not dominate each thematic statement, but the urgency, spontaneity and – in the slow movement – the depth of expressiveness make for an enjoyable version, well recorded. Throughout the overtures one cannot but marvel at the superlative playing of the Berlin Philharmonic Orchestra, without a suggestion of routine in pieces that must be almost over-familiar, and this applies especially to *Leonora No. 3* with its electrifying coda.

(i) *Triple concerto, Op. 56;* (ii) *Choral Fantasia* (for piano, chorus & orchestra), *Op. 80.*

(N) *** EMI Dig. CDC5 55516-2 [id.]. Barenboim; (i) Perlman; Ma; (ii) German Op. Ch.; BPO, Barenboim.

*** Ph. Dig. 438 005-2 [id.]. (i) Beaux Arts Trio; (ii) Menahem Pressler, Mid-German R. Ch.; Leipzig GO, Masur.

With such starry soloists, it is not surprising that these are strongly characterized, spontaneous-sounding performances which compel attention. Here are great musicians who in the *Triple concerto* challenge and respond to one another, phrase by phrase, just as Oistrakh, Rostropovich and Richter did (with Karajan conducting) on an earlier EMI recording. Barenboim as conductor here keeps tension overall taut, and in the opening solo of the *Choral Fantasia* he instantly conveys the impression of a Beethovenian improvisation, while the Berlin wind soloists are encouraged to play with wit in the engaging variations. The Beaux Arts Trio on Philips offer the same coupling (with Menahem Pressler as pianist in the *Fantasia*), but theirs are brisker, less warmly relaxed readings, though with recording marginally more transparent. The Berlin sound tends to grow a little opaque in tuttis, even if it conveys fine presence. Choice between this and the Philips disc is hard to assess and might well be left to a preference between crisp co-ordination and the inspiration of the moment.

Not only does Menahem Pressler's playing sparkle even more brightly in the concerto than before, he is an inspired protagonist in the *Choral Fantasia*, setting the pattern of joyfulness in this performance from his opening improvisation-like solo onwards. The other prime mover is Kurt Masur, who has rarely conducted more electrifying Beethoven performances on disc. What marks this performance out, distinguishing it not just from the previous Beaux Arts one but from most others, is its exhilarating urgency, quicker in its speeds than most rivals. The soloists are well focused in the front, with the orchestra warm and full behind – though, in a way typical of Leipzig sound, the bass is at times boomy and thick. The performance of the *Choral Fantasia* is most persuasive too, largely because it takes the work less seriously than most, with witty pointing of the variations.

12 Contredanses, WoO 14; 12 German dances, WoO 8; 12 Minuets, WoO 7; 11 Mödlinger dances, WoO 17.
(BB) *** Naxos 8.550433 [id.]. Capella Istropolitana, Oliver Dohnányi.

It is always a delight to catch Beethoven relaxing and showing how warmly he felt towards the Viennese background in which he lived. The excellent Capella Istropolitana group used for the recording seems to be of exactly the right size, and they play the music with light rhythmic feeling, yet with plenty of spirit. Dipped into, this will give pleasure.

The Creatures of Prometheus: Overture and ballet music, Op. 43 (complete).
(Y/B) *** Hyperion Dig CDA 66748 [id.]. SCO, Sir Charles Mackerras.
(N) (M) *** Beethoven Edition DG Dig. 447 911-2 [id.]. Orpheus CO.
(Y/B) **(*) Teldec/Warner Dig. 4509 90876-2 [id.]. COE, Harnoncourt.

The 18 numbers of Beethoven's early ballet about Prometheus, the bringer of fire, are recorded all too rarely. Here in fresh, vigorous performances Sir Charles Mackerras and the Scottish Chamber Orchestra bring out not only the drama of the piece but those colourful qualities which made Beethoven a great composer of light music. Exceptionally for him, he included an important part for the harp, and the ballet ends with the number that gave him one of his most fruitful themes, ultimately used for the finale of the *Eroica Symphony*. Recommended.

The very talented conductorless Orpheus Chamber Orchestra also plays most stylishly, helped by bright, clean recording, and this makes an equally recommendable alternative version.

Harnoncourt's comparative gruffness in the *Overture*, with its bold opening chords, prepares the listener for robust accents and strongly rhythmic allegros, and his performance reminds the listener more than usual of Beethoven the symphonist, most appropriately so in the finale. The solo playing from the COE is peerless. Excellent, resonant recording and a performance which is full of individuality and character.

OVERTURES

Overtures: The Consecration of the house, Op. 124; Coriolan, Op. 62; The Creatures of Prometheus, Op. 43; Egmont, Op. 84; Fidelio, Op. 72c; King Stephen, Op. 117; Leonora Nos. 1–3, Opp. 138; 72a; 72b; The Ruins of Athens, Op. 113; Zur Namensfeier, Op. 115.
(M) *** DG 427 256-2 (2) [id.]. BPO, Karajan.

Karajan's set of overtures was recorded in the middle and late 1960s. They are impressive performances that have stood the test of time. They show an imposing command of structure and detail as well as the customary virtuosity one expects from this conductor and the Berlin Philharmonic. The sound is fresh and bright.

(i) Overtures: *The Consecration of the house, Op. 124; Coriolan, Op. 62; The Creatures of Prometheus, Op. 43; Egmont, Op. 84; Fidelio, Op. 72c; King Stephen, Op. 117; Leonora Nos. 1–3, Opp. 138, 72 a–b; The Ruins of Athens, Op. 113; Zur Namensfeier, Op. 115;* (ii) *12 Contredanses, WoO 14; 12 German dances, WoO 8; 12 Minuets, WoO 7.*

(B) *** Ph. Duo 438 706-2 (2) [id.]. (i) Leipzig GO, Masur; (ii) ASMF, Marriner.

Masur's performances of the *Overtures* are more direct than those of Karajan and they are wholly satisfying in their strong motivation and lack of mannerism. The Philips recording from the early 1970s is of high quality, and the remastering has enhanced its vividness and impact, although the characteristic Leipzig resonance remains. To complete the second CD, Marriner and the Academy offer a splendid foil with the dance music. Even as a composer of light music Beethoven was a master, and this collection, beautifully played and recorded (in 1978), can be equally warmly recommended though, again, the acoustic is perhaps slightly over-resonant.

Overtures: The Consecration of the house, Op. 124; Coriolan, Op. 62; The Creatures of Prometheus, Op. 43; Egmont, Op. 84; Fidelio, Op. 72c; King Stephen, Op. 117; Leonora No. 2, Op. 72a; The Ruins of Athens, Op. 113.

**(*) Nimbus NI 5205 [id.]. Hanover Band, Roy Goodman or Monica Huggett.

Recorded at various periods in conjunction with the Hanover Band's other Beethoven recordings for Nimbus, this compilation makes a generous and attractive collection. Anyone who wants the principal Beethoven overtures played on period instruments will be well pleased.

Overtures: *Coriolan; Creatures of Prometheus; Egmont; Fidelio; Leonora No. 1; Leonora No. 3; The Ruins of Athens.*

(Y/B) (BB) *** RCA Navigator 74321 21281-2. Bamberg SO, Eugen Jochum.

Not surprisingly, Jochum provides a superb collection of overtures, naturally spontaneous and full of warmth and drama. The finest performance of all is *Leonora No. 3*, which makes a thrilling end to the programme. The Bamberg Symphony Orchestra are in excellent form and the recording has a full, spacious acoustic with a natural brilliance. A real bargain.

Overtures: *Coriolan, Op. 62; Leonore No. 2, Op. 72.*

(Y/B) (M) (***) EMI mono CHS5 65513-2 (3) [id.]. BPO or VPO, Furtwängler – BRAHMS: *Symphonies Nos. 1–4* etc. (**(*))

These studio recordings of Beethoven overtures, the one from Vienna in 1947, the other from Berlin in 1954, make a good supplement to Furtwängler's Brahms cycle, with Vienna mellower-sounding than Berlin, but both less harshly recorded than on the Brahms broadcasts.

SYMPHONIES

Symphonies Nos. 1–9; 10 (realized Dr Barry Cooper): *1st movt.*

(N) (M) *** Chandos CHAN 7042 (5) [id.]. CBSO, Weller (with Barstow, Finnie, Rendall, Tomlinson, CBSO Ch. in *No. 9*).

Symphonies Nos. 1–9.

(Y/B) (B) *** RCA Dig. 74321 20277-2 (5). N. German RSO, Günter Wand (with Wiens, Hartwig, Lewis, Hermann, combined Ch. from Hamburg State Op. and N. German R. in *No. 9*).

*** DG Dig. 439 900-2 (5) [id.]. ORR, Gardiner (with Orgonasova, Von Otter, Rolfe Johnson, Cachemaille, Monteverdi Ch. in *No. 9*).

*** Teldec/Warner Dig. 2292 46452-2 (5) [id.]. COE, Harnoncourt (with Margiono, Remmert, Schasching, Holl, Arnold Schoenberg Ch. in *No. 9*).

(B) *** DG 429 036-2 (5) [id.]. BPO, Karajan (with Janowitz, Rössel-Majdan, Kmentt, Berry, V. Singverein in *No. 9*).

(N) **(*) Ph. Dig. 446 067-2 (6) [id.]. Dresden State O, Sir Colin Davis (with Sharon Sweet, Jadwiga Rappé, Paul Frey, Franz Grundheber & Dresden State Op. Ch. in *No. 9*).

(Y/B) **(*) Everest EVC 901014 (5) [id.]. LSO, Krips (with Vyvyan, Verrett, Petrak, Bell, BBC Ch. in *No. 9*).

Symphonies Nos. 1–9; Coriolan overture.

(N) (M) *** Carlton IMG Dig. 30368 00025 [id.]. Sinfonia Varsovia, Sir Yehudi Menuhin (with Jean Glennon, Dalia Schaechter, Algirdas Janutas, Benno Schollum & Lithuanian Kaunas State Ch. in *No. 9*).

Symphonies Nos. 1–9; Overtures: Coriolan; Creatures of Prometheus; Egmont.
(M) ** EMI CMS5 65184-2 (6) [id.]. L. Classical Players, Norrington (with Kenny, Walker, Power, Salomaa, L. Schütz Ch. in *No. 9*).

Symphonies Nos. 1–9; Overtures: Coriolan; Egmont; Fidelio; Leonora No. 3.
**DG Dig. Gold 439 200-2 (6) [id.]. BPO, Karajan (with Perry, Baltsa, Cole, Van Dam, V. Singverein in *No. 9*).

Symphonies Nos. 1–9; Overtures: Egmont; Fidelio; King Stephen.
(M) **(*) Sony SB5K 48396 (5). Cleveland O, George Szell (with Addison, Hobson, Lewis, Bell, Cleveland Ch. in *No. 9*).
(N) (M) ** Sony SX5K 64201 (5) [id.]. NYPO, Bernstein (with Arroyo, Sarfaty, de Virgilio, Scott & Juilliard Ch. in *No. 9*).

Symphonies Nos. 1–9; Overture Leonora No. 3.
(M) (***) RCA mono GD 60324 (5) [60324-2-RG]. NBC SO, Toscanini (with Farrell, Merriman, Peerce, Scott, Shaw Chorale in *No. 9*).

Wand's digital set with the North German Radio Orchestra, recorded between 1985 and 1988, makes a first-class bargain choice, and indeed is thoroughly recommendable irrespective of cost, offering performances without idiosyncrasy yet full of character that are consistently satisfying to live with. There is a directness about Wand's approach to Beethoven, both early and mature, which is the opposite of dull or stuffy. Throughout the orchestral playing is of the highest quality and the recording is superb, both clean and atmospheric, and admirably transparent (witness the very opening of the first movement of No. 9). The *First Symphony* is strikingly fresh, with briskly vivacious allegros matched by those in the *Fourth*, which is particularly attractive and has splendid rhythmic bounce. No. 2 and the vigorous No. 8 have hardly less vitality, while slow movements have a simple eloquence and warmth that are most satisfying. Wand is generous with exposition repeats. In the *Seventh* – with the horns beautifully balanced in textures both clear and full-bodied – every single repeat is observed; yet, although tempi are relatively steady, the propulsion remains unflagging from first to last. The *Eroica* is admirably paced, a strong reading with plenty of underlying lyrical feeling, and again the horns are impressive in the Trio of the Scherzo and in the joyous finale. The *Pastoral*, taken rather steadily, does not have a very resonant bass, but the cello line is full and warm and the finale radiant. It is far preferable to the Karajan account in his 1961–2 analogue set and, while at times those performances may have a more dramatic edge, there is no lack of urgency and adrenalin flow with Wand; and the added fullness and naturalness of the RCA recording are especially telling in the even-numbered symphonies. The *Fifth* makes a powerful statement and, with its fine slow movement (bringing a neat coda to lead to the Scherzo) and compulsive finale, can be mentioned alongside Giulini's Los Angeles version – see below. The whole series is capped by a powerful account of the *Ninth* with weight and rhythmic bite in equal measure and here, like the *Eroica*, the *Adagio* is movingly intense. The finale is led by a fine team of soloists with the tenor, Keith Lewis, appealingly ardent and the soprano, Edith Wiens, notably secure in her big moment. The combined choruses of North German Radio and Hamburg State Opera, very effectively balanced, sing with fervour, and after Wand's spacious broadening at the centre of the movement the closing pages bring a thrilling culmination. You can't better this if you want a complete set of the Beethoven symphonies played on modern instruments. RCA have now made Wand's discs available separately at mid-price: *Symphonies Nos. 1* and *6* (74321 20278-2); *Symphonies Nos. 2* and *7* (74321 20279-2); *Symphonies Nos. 3* and *8* (74321 20280-2); *Symphonies Nos. 4–5* (74321 20281-2); *Symphony No. 9* (74321 20282-2).

Gardiner's cycle makes a clear first choice for those wanting period performances. With sound that is warmer and weightier than in the first generation of such versions, yet still transparent, it can also be recommended strongly to those who would normally opt for modern instruments. These are exhilarating performances which have bite and imagination and a sense of spontaneity, reflecting the shrewd programme of recording, linked to live performances. Like Norrington, Gardiner observes Beethoven's own fast metronome markings, but less rigidly, so that he allows himself a degree more expansion in the slow movements of the *Eroica* and the *Ninth*. By contrast, his speeds for the opening *Allegros* of both these key symphonies are even faster than Norrington's, yet more resilient. Significant among Gardiner's many corrections of traditional scores – with Jonathan Del Mar a scholarly helper – is his amendment of the marking for the Turkish March in the finale of the *Ninth*, twice as brisk as Norrington and leading logically into the fugue. This inspired account of the *Ninth* – recorded immediately after live performances in Britain and Japan – crowns the whole cycle, as it should. The set, given full, luminous sound, is complete on only five discs, with a sixth containing an illustrated talk by Gardiner in three languages.

Reflecting his work as a period-performance pioneer, Harnoncourt makes rhythms light and textures clean and with sparing vibrato. Periodically, as in the opening movement of the *Eroica*, he adopts a hectically fast tempo, but that is the exception. More usually, his choice of speeds is regularly geared to bringing out the rhythmic and expressive finesse characteristic of this brilliant young orchestra. That the performances so consistently display the joy in Beethoven, his natural exuberance, reflects the way they were made, done live over an intensive period in Graz in the summer of 1990. The *Ninth* was recorded almost a year after the rest and equally refreshingly reflects the lessons of period performance, though the dry manner in the great *Adagio*, taken at a flowing speed, underplays the emotional depth. Excellent sound. Admirers of Harnoncourt need not hesitate.

Of Karajan's four recorded cycles, the 1961-2 set is the most consistent and in many ways the most compelling, combining high polish with a biting sense of urgency and spontaneity. There is one major disappointment, in the over-taut reading of the *Pastoral*, which in addition omits the vital repeat in the scherzo. Otherwise these are incandescent performances, superbly played. On CD the sound is still excellent, the best-balanced in any of his Beethoven series and on five CDs at bargain price, this makes outstanding value for money.

Walter Weller's Beethoven cycle for Chandos is by far his finest achievement on record. Although this is the City of Birmingham Symphony Orchestra, there is a warm, refined, Viennese quality in the playing and interpretation, to remind you that this conductor started his career as concertmaster of the Vienna Philharmonic. The Chandos sound is full and glowing to match, the best to date given to any conductor in a collected Beethoven cycle. Now reissued at medium price and still including Barry Cooper's realization of the *Tenth Symphony*, though now without the rehearsals and the overtures, this set represents even better value for money.

Yehudi Menuhin's cycle, issued to celebrate his eightieth birthday, represents the refreshing response to Beethoven of a great interpretative musician who remains perennially young. Earlier he recorded late Mozart symphonies with outstanding success using this same Polish chamber orchestra, and much of the same freshness and fire inhabit these Beethoven performances. It helps that five of the nine symphonies (Nos. 1, 2, 4, 5 and 9) were recorded live in the Palais de Musique in Strasbourg, a helpful hall. Though the applause which greets the opening of each is irritating, the tensions of live performance regularly bring magical results, as in the dedicated, ecstatic performance of the great *Adagio* of the *Ninth*. Though the first movement is less biting than the rest, that last symphony, often a disappointment in complete cycles, here brings a fitting culmination, thanks also to the fresh, clear singing of the Lithuanian choir and a young, rather lightweight quartet of soloists. Following the Gardiner thesis, the drum-and-fife sequence in the finale of No. 9 is taken very fast like a French military march. In the studio performances, as well as in those recorded live, Menuhin uses the chamber scale positively, not only clarifying textures but achieving hushed pianissimos of ravishing beauty, as in the *Allegretto* of the *Seventh* or in the broken close of the *Eroica* funeral march. Hairpin dynamics are most subtly shaded throughout, and regularly in slow movements Menuhin's cunning in moulding string melodies, born of his violin mastery, is reflected in the imaginative beauty of line. Only in the *Allegretto* of the *Eighth* does he choose a tempo too slow for rhythms to lift. Allegros generally tend to be on the brisk side, with lightly sprung rhythms adding to the freshness; some of the very fast speeds, as in the finales of Nos. 5 and 7, seem to reflect not so much latterday period practice as the early influence of Toscanini. Menuhin adds an interpretative note about the very opening of the *Fifth*, vigorously rejecting the idea of 'artificial pompousness' in fate knocking on the door. The result in his live performance is deliberately understated, for once not very cleanly executed. Such flaws are minimal next to the shining merits of the set. Exposition repeats are observed, and not everyone will object that, like Günter Wand among others, Menuhin omits second-half repeats in the Scherzos of Nos. 7 and 9. With recording that puts a fine bloom on the sound without obscuring detail, this is an excellent set for those wanting dedicated performances on a chamber scale, which yet never underplay the strength and power of these masterpieces.

As a Beethoven interpreter Krips is in the central tradition, with speeds well chosen if rather broader than has latterly become the rule. In such a symphony as the *Pastoral* or the *Eighth*, one regularly registers that here is a great Schubertian, for Krips makes the music sing, giving it a glow of warmth. That is not to say that the performances lack dramatic bite. No. 4, for example, is given with great flair and panache, with the syncopations in the first movement sharply driven home and the great violin melody of the slow movement flowing sweetly. In the great opening movements of the *Eroica* and No. 9, weight and incisiveness go together, helped by the sharp focus of the 1960 sound, transferred from the original masters to give a fine sense of presence, though often with an acid edge on high violins in tuttis. Otherwise one would hardly register that these are vintage recordings. The *Funeral march* in the *Eroica*, against the general rule, is taken fast at a speed one nowadays associates with period performances, making its march-like qualities clearer without sounding perfunctory. After the sunny and lyrical performance of No. 8, the cycle is crowned by the *Ninth*, particularly the choral finale which, with excellent soloists and chorus, builds to a thrilling climax, giving the illusion of live performance. Only No. 5 is a degree disappointing, well shaped and pointed but too relaxed, lacking some of the tensions needed. In the manner of the time, exposition repeats are not observed in Nos. 3, 6 and 7, and neither repeat is observed in the finale of No. 5. This remains a highly stimulating set, but it is much more expensive than the superb Wand set – indeed, with the discs costing only a little below premium price, and bearing in mind the edge on the violin timbre, it cannot be regarded as a primary recommendation until the cost is reduced.

In opulent sound Sir Colin Davis takes a spacious view of the Beethoven symphonies, drawing consistently beautiful playing from the Dresden State Orchestra. He sustains broad speeds in total concentration to give each symphony a rugged strength. This could almost be regarded as a latterday equivalent of the Klemperer cycle, except that Davis is far warmer in the tone-colours he draws on. So it is that even the first two symphonies represent the mature Beethoven rather than a youthful revolutionary, and even the grinding dissonances at the heart of the development section in the first movement of the *Eroica* are warm rather than violent. Reflecting the mature responses of a conductor in his late sixties, Davis's approach may lack the bite which marked his very first Beethoven recording – of the *Seventh* for EMI in the early 1960s – but this is comfortable Beethoven, consistently alert and compelling. The slow movement of the *Ninth* may not scale the full heights of sublimity, and at times the reverberance of the Lukaskirche in Dresden, where the recordings were made, obscures detail; but anyone wanting a mellow view of Beethoven will be very well pleased.

Norrington's determination to observe Beethoven's metronome markings regularly leads to refreshing results, though some of the more extreme speeds come to sound wilful, especially in the *Choral Symphony* where the slow movement becomes a sweet interlude rather than a meditation, far shorter than the other movements. The male soloists, too, leave much to be desired. Hogwood is to be preferred here, as he is in the *Pastoral*, although Norrington scores in the *Eroica*, a very convincing and powerful performance. The recording, made in Abbey Road, is faithful and well balanced, though not always as full and immediate as it might be.

Szell's compellingly strong, direct view of Beethoven brings much to stimulate. The marvellously polished and always responsive Cleveland playing never brings a suspicion of routine, but reservations must be made about the close CBS sound-balance which prevents a real pianissimo from registering, even though the ear readily senses when the orchestra is playing gently.

In Karajan's last, digital set, the recording seems to have been affected by the need to make a version on video at the same sessions. The gain is that these performances have keener spontaneity, the loss that they often lack the brilliant, knife-edged precision of ensemble one has come to regard as normal with Karajan. The six discs are now remastered to Digital Gold standards – for comments see the individual issues below – and are offered at a slightly reduced price for the set: six CDs for the price of five.

The *Eroica* in Bernstein's earlier, New York cycle of the Beethoven symphonies was a mould-breaking interpretation, with a fast speed for the first movement made to sound fresh and exhilarating. The other symphonies too are given high-voltage performances, strong and purposeful, if occasionally self-indulgent; but the recordings are relatively coarse and lacking in contrast. The finer performances include No. 2 (where the orchestra play as if their very lives depended upon it) and No. 8, an interpretation with considerable sweep and genuine stature. No. 4 is also impressive; though tempi are on the brisk side, the playing pulsates with highly disciplined energy. Yet there is a loss of mystery at the opening. The *Pastoral* is admirably free of undue expressive vehemence; at the same time there is not the subtlety or richness of detail that one finds in the finest readings. The *Seventh* is characteristically vital, but only in the *Eroica* does the New York version outshine Bernstein's later readings for DG. However, the *Fifth* is also one of the finest of the earlier cycle. It is a strong, dramatic reading, not quite as distinguished as the *Eroica*, but as concentrated and vital as the *Eighth*. The *Ninth* is by no means to be dismissed, with a finely shaped first movement which has genuine breadth and eloquence. However, many will find the Scherzo too frenetic: it must be one of the fastest on record. The slow movement has considerable warmth, but not quite enough inwardness and repose; but the finale is dramatic and intense, with some fine contributions from the soloists and chorus, the latter quite well caught by the CBS engineers. The CD transfers make the most of the original masters, but the quality cannot match the later, DG recordings. These have been reissued individually as part of DG's Beethoven Edition, and each is discussed below.

The NBC Toscanini versions are faster and more tense than the earlier Beethoven readings that he committed to records, but they are far from rigid or unloving, and they are crowned by performances of breathtaking power in the *Eroica* and the *Ninth*. Listening to this Beethoven is never a relaxing experience, but it is a uniquely involving one.

Symphonies Nos. 1–4.
(N) (B) *** Ph. Duo 454 032-2 (2) [id.]. Leipzig GO, Kurt Masur.

Symphonies Nos. 5–8.
(N) (B) ** Ph. Duo 454 035-2 (2) [id.]. Leipzig GO, Masur.

(i) *Symphony No. 9 (Choral);* (ii) *Overtures: Consecration of the house; Fidelio; Leonora Nos. 1–3;* (iii) *Choral Fantasia, Op. 80.*
(N) (B) *(*) Ph. Duo 454 038-2 (2) [id.]. (i) Tomowa-Sintow, Burmeister, Schreier, Adam and Ch.; (i–ii) Leipzig GO, Masur; (iii) Brendel, LPO, Haitink.

Kurt Masur's earlier, analogue Beethoven cycle has a very great deal to recommend it. In sheer natural-ness of utterance, unforced expressiveness and the superlatively disciplined response of the orchestral playing, the Gewandhaus set has a good deal to offer. The first two symphonies are attractively fresh, with the slow movement of the *Second* memorable. The *Eroica* is uncommonly fine, particularly its nobly paced slow movement which is totally free of excessive emphasis in expression. In the *Fourth Symphony* Masur is particularly successful, and the Gewandhaus Orchestra respond with marvellously alert playing. In the slow movement Masur brings great imagination and poetry to his reading; the homogeneous, cultured orchestral sound of the Gewandhaus Orchestra and its rhythmic resilience and vitality are in themselves a source of pleasure. So the first of these three Duos is certainly recommend-able. However, neither the *Fifth* nor the *Pastoral* matches the finest in the catalogue: the former does not have the blazing intensity of Carlos Kleiber and the latter does not eclipse Boehm, Ashkenazy or, indeed, Klemperer. Nor can one say that the *Choral Symphony* has the stature of Karajan. It is a spacious, well-proportioned and noble account, well worth hearing; but competition is stiff and other versions are more strongly characterized. Thus the last of the Duo sets is the least recommendable, despite the inclusion of Haitink's fine account with Brendel of the *Choral Fantasia.*

Symphonies Nos. 1 in C, Op. 21; 3 in E flat (Eroica); 6 in F (Pastoral); 8 in F, Op. 93.
(Y/B) (B) **(*) Decca Double 440 627-2 (2) [id.]. VPO, Pierre Monteux.

Symphonies Nos. 2 in D, Op. 36; 4 in B flat, Op. 60; 5 in C min., Op. 67; 7 in A, Op. 92; Overtures: Egmont; King Stephen.
(Y/B) (B) *** Decca Double 443 479-2 (2) [id.]. LSO, Pierre Monteux.

Pierre Monteux, recording for Decca in his last years, did not include the *Choral Symphony* (the com-pany turned to Ansermet and Stokowski instead). But he recorded all the rest, and with distinction. Listening to these performances together as a sequence, the listener discovers the continuing thread of enhancing energy that brings all Monteux's music-making to life, together with consistent imagination in his phrasing and glowing treatment of the detail of slow movements. The Double Decca reissues have been sensibly divided into the performances with the VPO and those with the LSO and thus provide an obvious first choice for those not wanting both sets.

For some reason, the 1960 VPO coupling of Nos. 1 and 8 brings a hint of discoloration in the woodwind. But the ear soon adjusts when in both works Monteux steers an ideal course, neither underestimating the weight nor making the music too heavy. The *Eroica* was the first to be recorded (in 1957) and again it is as masterly as it is individual. The first movement (without exposition repeat) is superbly dramatic – the climax of the development wonderfully built up – and only in the *Funeral march* are there any real reservations. A slower speed would have allowed a greater sense of tragedy; and his oboe soloist is on the flat side, though never beyond tolerance. The early stereo is relatively coarse and does not allow a real pianissimo. The *Pastoral* dates from only a year later, yet the recording is strikingly better, full, warm and vivid. The performance emerges as finer than we had remembered it, even if the VPO were not on the form they were for the *Eroica.*

At the beginning of the 1960s Monteux achieved a special understanding with the players of the LSO, and his 1960 coupling of Nos. 2 and 4 shows this genial rapport to rewarding effect. The performance of No. 2 is essentially light in style, and the alertness of the LSO playing makes it strong and enjoyable. No. 4 is hardly less successful. You have only to listen to the way Monteux leads into the second subject or the way he floats the high violin melody in the slow movement to realize that a master is at work. The finale is exhilaratingly hectic in the fast, flying manner that he tends to adopt in Beethoven finales: it is very exciting when played with such precision. In a hardly less memorable performance of the *Fifth*, the volatile Frenchman plays his part. Where hitherto these Beethoven performances have tended to be straight and direct, here there is not only strength and drive but an element of waywardness. It is a personal reading, but a compelling one in all four movements, with fine articulation from the LSO, unashamedly strong, even aggressive in the finale.

The series is capped by an unforgettable account of the *Seventh Symphony.* Monteux opens with a powerful slow introduction, followed by a hard-driven 6/8 *Allegro* but with the rhythms nicely pointed, and a fast *Allegretto* to recall the famous early mono LP by Erich Kleiber. Then comes a wide speed-change for the trio after the Scherzo and an absolute headlong finale, out-Toscanini-ing Toscanini in its incandescent excitement, with the horns singing out flamboyantly at the close. Throughout, the full, atmospheric recording adds just the right degree of weight, and this Monteux/LSO box offers Beethoven performances as stimulating as any available. This Double Decca is well worth having in its own right.

Symphonies Nos. 1 in C, Op. 21; 2 in D, Op. 36.
(N) *** DG Dig. 447 049-2 [id.]. ORR, Gardiner.
**(*) DG Dig. Gold 439 001-2 [id.]. BPO, Karajan.
(N) (B) **(*) Carlton IMP Dig. 30369 0001-2 [id.]. LSO, Wyn Morris.

Symphonies Nos. 1 in C; 2 in D; Overture Coriolan.
(Y/B) (M) *** Bruno Walter Edition: Sony SMK 64460 [id.]. Columbia SO, Bruno Walter.

(i) *Symphonies Nos. 1 in C; 2 in D;* (ii) *Overture: Leonora No. 1.*
(N) (M) *** Sony Dig. SMK 66927 [id.]. (i) ECO, Michael Tilson Thomas, (ii) Bav. RSO, Sir Colin Davis.

Rather than treating the two early symphonies as Mozartian in the way most period performers do, John Eliot Gardiner uses his sonorous but clean-textured forces to bring out the power and revolutionary bite of the young Beethoven, as ever opting for speeds on the fast side. Vivid, immediate sound in both the live recording of No. 1 and the studio one of No. 2.

Bruno Walter's CBS recordings of the Beethoven symphonies now reappear on a series of mid-priced discs as part of the Bruno Walter Edition. They were recorded in 1958/9 in the American Legion Hall in Hollywood, which provided an attractive ambient warmth, while the upper-string timbre remained fresh and lively. The Columbia Symphony was a pick-up orchestra of outstanding musicians whom Walter moulded into a cohesive body of players of some distinction. The most controversial point about his interpretation of the *Second Symphony* is the slow movement, which is taken very slowly indeed, with plenty of rubato. But the rich warmth of the recording makes the effect very involving. For the rest, the speeds are well chosen, with a fairly gentle allegro in the finale which allows the tick-tock accompaniment to the second subject to have a delightful lift to it. On technical grounds this reissue can stand alongside most of the more recent competition, and the remaining hiss is not disturbing.

Michael Tilson Thomas offers excellent accounts of the first two symphonies with the ECO, both apt in scale but with no loss of weight because of the reduced number of players. Pacing is admirable, with vigour and urgency never leading to aggressiveness in outer movements. Slow movements are graciously phrased and fresh; and alert, clean articulation brings a buoyant Scherzo in No. 2 and delicately traced string-detail in the Trio of the Minuet of No. 1. The 1982 recording is well balanced internally, although the forward projection does mean that the difference between *piano* and *pianissimo* is reduced. Nevertheless these are spirited and involving performances which give much pleasure. Both first-movement exposition repeats are made to seem an essential part of the structure. Davis's fine account of *Leonora No. 1*, warmly recorded in Munich's famous Herkulessaal three years later, follows on after the symphonies.

Karajan's digital Beethoven series brings some surprisingly slack ensemble in the recording of the first two symphonies. The performances are relaxed in good ways too, with Karajan's flair and control of rhythm never leading to breathless speeds. Not unexpectedly, there are moments when detail is perceptively revealed, but the heavy reverberation of the recording makes the result arguably too weighty for these works and pianissimos are rarely gentle enough.

Wyn Morris draws a clear distinction between the two earliest symphonies: the *First*, brightly paced, resilient and strongly classical in feeling; the *Second* clearly looking forward, with a particularly eloquent account of the slow movement, not overlooking its anticipations of the *Pastoral Symphony*. Both first-movement exposition repeats are included. The recording is full-bodied, but the resonance prevents absolute sharpness of detail, and the violins could be sweeter on top. Nevertheless this is a most rewarding coupling.

Symphonies Nos. 1 and 2 (trans. Liszt).
(N) (M) *** Teldec/Warner Dig. 4509 97952-2 [id.]. Cyprien Katsaris (piano).

Transcendental technique and a fine musical intelligence are the distinguishing features of these performances, which remain without peer in the Beethoven–Liszt discography. Well worth having at mid-price.

Symphonies Nos. 1–2; 4–5.
(B) **(*) DG Double 439 681-2 (2) [id.]. VPO, Karl Boehm.

Boehm's performances come from his Vienna cycle of the early 1970s, centrally satisfying readings (especially Nos. 2 and 4), smoothly yet vividly recorded, with a good deal of resonance in the lower range to add weight without clouding the upper range. The performances are mature and completely reliable and surely represent an admirable first way to come to terms with these four masterpieces. What the readings lack is the sort of sharp idiosyncrasy which makes for dramatic individuality. If Boehm misses some of the tensions, there is no lack of weight or strength. The transfers to CD retain the full character of the original sound.

Symphonies Nos. 1 in C; 3 in E flat (Eroica), Op. 55.
(Y/B) *** EMI Dig. CDC7 54501-2 [id.]. Concg. O, Sawallisch.
*** Teldec/Warner Dig. 9031 75708-2 [id.]. COE, Harnoncourt.
(Y/B) **(*) Decca Dig. 430 515-2 [id.]. San Francisco SO, Blomstedt.
(M) (***) RCA mono GD 60252 [60252-2-RG]. NBC O, Toscanini.

The *First Symphony* sounds fresh and vibrant in Sawallisch's hands and the textures are clean and transparent in this splendidly engineered EMI recording. However, it is the *Eroica* for which collectors will buy this disc. It is a performance of some stature and has breadth and dignity; the orchestral playing is a joy in itself. The recording, too, is very good.

Harnoncourt's *Eroica* brings an extremely fast tempo in the first movement, and his austere view of the great *Funeral march* is chillingly intense. The result is as individual as it is powerful. No. 1, too, is splendidly alive.

Blomstedt's coupling provides satisfyingly weighty and strong performances, superbly played with outstanding wind solos (notably from the oboe in the *Funeral march*). These are most satisfying, sharply focused readings, notably of the *Eroica*, lacking only a little in Beethovenian dynamism. Speeds are relatively broad, but brisk enough for the exposition repeat to be observed in the *Eroica* first movement and for repeats to be included in the da capo of the Scherzo of the *First Symphony*. Fine recording.

Toscanini's are performances which convey breathtaking power, notably the magnificent account of the *Eroica*, never comfortable but far from rigid or unloving.

(i) *Symphonies Nos. 1 in C, Op. 21; 3 in E flat, Op. 55; 5 in C min., Op. 67;* (ii) *Overtures: Creatures of Prometheus; Egmont; Fidelio.*
(Y/B) (BB) **(*) EMI Seraphim CES5 68518-2 (2) [CEDB 68518]. (i) Munich PO; (ii) BPO; Rudolf Kempe.

Kempe's performances were recorded over a relatively brief period, and this shows in their merits as well as their limitations. Plainly the Munich orchestra responded to this challenge, producing fresh, spontaneous-sounding playing, not always perfectly disciplined but natural and communicative. Kempe as a Beethovenian believes in letting the music speak for itself at sensitive and unexaggerated tempi, so that even the introduction of No. 1 is weighty. Otherwise the crisp articulation of the Munich woodwind makes for refreshing results in the allegros, with the Munich strings producing sweet tone in the slow movement. Not all the symphonies sound as intense as they might – No. 5, for example. But even here the performance is warmly enjoyable, if not electrifying. Exposition repeats are normally observed, though not in the *Eroica*. Here Kempe takes a spacious view of the first movement. Initially it may sound unexciting, but then (as with Klemperer) the structure builds up strongly and compellingly. The *Funeral march* is subdued and inward, spontaneous-sounding in its concentration up to the hushed distintegration of the main theme. The oboe solos (Kempe himself was an oboist before he became a conductor) are beautiful. Fast speeds and fine articulation in the last two movements, although here the violins lose just a little of their bloom. The overtures feature the Berlin Philharmonic and are very well played indeed. Good value.

Symphonies Nos. 1 in C; 4 in B flat, Op. 60; Egmont overture.
(M) *** DG 419 048-2; *419 048-4* [id.]. BPO, Karajan.

Symphonies Nos. 1 in C; 4 in B flat; Overture Leonora No. 1.
(N) (B) (***) Dutton Lab. mono CDEA 5004 [id.]. BBC SO, Toscanini.

Karajan's 1977 version of No. 1 is exciting, polished and elegant; in No. 4 the balance is closer, exposing every flicker of tremolando. Yet the body and ambience of the recording combine to give a realistic presence, and overall this is very impressive.

The Toscanini recordings were made in London's Queen's Hall in 1937 and 1939, and they remain among the most treasurable Beethoven performances in the Toscanini legacy. All the electricity and concentration are here, yet there is a degree of warmth not often present in his NBC records. The sound too is remarkably good, and the Dutton transfers betray the 78 shellac source only with the slight hint of wow on the woodwind, caused by the pressings not being centred absolutely perfectly; one immediately adjusts to this when the playing has such magnetism. On our copy the cueing for the individual movements of the *Fourth Symphony* was faulty.

Symphonies Nos. 1 in C; 6 in F (Pastoral), Op. 68.
(N) (M) **(*) Beethoven Edition DG 447 901-2 [id.]. VPO, Bernstein.

Symphonies Nos. 1 in C; 6 in F (Pastoral), Op. 68; Overture Egmont, Op. 84.
(B) **(*) Sony SBK 46532; *SBT 46532* [id.]. Cleveland O, Szell.

Bernstein's second stereo cycle of the Beethoven symphonies was made with the Vienna Philharmonic Orchestra and first released as a set in 1980. Highly dramatic, perceptive, rich in emotion but never sentimental, these performances have a spontaneous quality that stemmed in part from his technique of recording. As in his other records for DG, Bernstein opted to have live performances recorded and then – with some tidying of detail – edited together. Balances are not always perfect, with microphones placed in order to eliminate audience noise, but the results are generally undistracting and the projection is very immediate. In No. 1 the allegros are fast but not hectic, the slow introductions and slow movements carefully moulded but not mannered. In this work the live recording is not ideally clear but is very acceptable. The reading of the *Pastoral* has plenty of character and, with its combination of joy and serenity, is persuasive, even if the performance fails to bite in the *Storm* sequence. There are some inevitable inconsistencies in the sound-balance, which is vivid rather than refined and mellow.

Szell's dynamic performance of the *First Symphony* makes up for any absence of charm. In the *Pastoral* Szell is subtle in his control of phrasing, for all the firmness of his style. However, it is a pity that the close-up sound robs the slow movement of much of its gentleness and delicacy of atmosphere. The finale, by contrast, is attractively relaxed.

Symphonies Nos. 1; 7 in A, Op. 92.
*** Sony Dig. SK 48236 [id.]. La Scala PO, Giulini.
(BB) **(*) ASV CDQS 6066. N. Sinfonia of England, Richard Hickox.
(M) **(*) EMI CDM7 63354-2 [id.]. Philh. O, Klemperer.
(N) (BB) **(*) RCA Navigator 74321 29239-2. Boston SO, Erich Leinsdorf.

Giulini in his late seventies takes a more expansive view of both symphonies than almost any predecessor. This was the first disc in his projected cycle of the symphonies with the La Scala Philharmonic, an orchestra drawn not just from the opera-house but from other leading Italian orchestras too. With sympathetic players he finds a rare lyricism, moulding phrases persuasively, but without making them seem mannered. And his gift of springing rhythms prevents the result from stagnating. Warm, if not ideally clear, sound.

Hickox's view of both works is unaffected and direct and so gets the best of both worlds: finely detailed yet substantial; and the very lack of idiosyncrasy makes for easy listening. The CD transfer is full and agreeable but provides a rather resonant bass.

With Klemperer the slow speeds and heavyweight manner in both works will for many get in the way of enjoyment. That said, the compulsion of Klemperer in Beethoven remains strong, with rhythmic pointing consistently preventing stagnation.

Leinsdorf's Beethoven is a bit gruff but is very compelling when the Boston orchestral playing has such polish and character. The *First Symphony* hardly ever smiles, but its vigour and strength clearly look forward to the *Eroica Symphony*. The *Seventh* brings relatively measured but rhythmically strong outer movements which, like the *Allegretto*, generate considerable tension: its conclusion is powerfully positive and really lifts off at the exciting close. The Boston acoustic adds a weighty resonance to the sound, without blurring; indeed these late-1960s recordings are very successful in their clear, full CD transfers. Excellent value.

Symphonies Nos. 2 in D; 4 in B flat, Op. 60.
(M) *** EMI CDM7 63355-2 [id.]. Philh. O, Klemperer.

The coupling for CD emphasizes the consistency of Klemperer's approach to Beethoven, with both the *Second* and *Fourth* symphonies sounding the more powerful through weighty treatment. The *Fourth* brings one of the most compelling performances of all. The sound is fresh yet full.

Symphonies Nos. 2 in D; 5 in C min., Op. 67.
*** Teldec/Warner Dig. 9031 75712-2 [id.]. COE, Harnoncourt.
(N) (M) **(*) Beethoven Edition DG 447 902-2 [id.]. VPO, Bernstein.
(B) **(*) Sony SBK 47651; *SBT 47651* [id.]. Cleveland O, George Szell.

Harnoncourt's exuberance does not mean a lack of weight in the *Fifth*, while the slow movement is particularly fine and the finale grows seamlessly out of the Scherzo. This Teldec record makes a clear first choice in this coupling. The orchestral playing has splendid bite and lift.

Bernstein's performance of No. 2 has touches that obviously stemmed from the inspiration of the moment, and the tension rises superbly at the end of the finale. He seems intent on emphasizing how much bigger a symphony this is than No. 1 and, though the ensemble is not always flawless and the recording has a rather boomy bass, the liveness is captivating. For his Vienna version, Bernstein rethought his reading of the *Fifth*, giving it resonance and spaciousness as well as drama. Some of the Toscanini-like tension of his earlier, New York account has evaporated from the first movement, but the warmth and conviction of the whole performance are most persuasive, ending with a blazing account of the finale. Again the recording balance is good, if not ideal.

There is some marvellously clean articulation from the strings in the first movement of Szell's No. 2 and the adrenalin runs free; yet here, as in the similarly brilliant account of No. 5, Szell understands the need to give full scope to the lyrical elements.

Symphonies Nos. 2 in D; 7 in A, Op. 92.
(M) *** DG 419 050-2; *419 050-4* [id.]. BPO, Karajan.

In Karajan's *Second*, the firm lines give the necessary strength. The *Seventh* is tense and exciting, with the conductor emphasizing the work's dramatic rather than its dance-like qualities.

Symphonies Nos. 2; 8 in F, Op. 93.
(Y/B) *** EMI Dig. CDC7 54502-2 [id.]. Concg. O, Sawallisch.
*** EMI Dig. CDC7 47698-2 [id.]. L. Classical Players, Norrington.
(BB) **(*) ASV CDQS 5067. N. Sinfonia, Hickox.
**(*) Sony Dig. SK 48238 [id.]. La Scala PO, Giulini.
(N) (BB) **(*) Tring TRP 039 [id.]. RPO, James Lockhart.

A lovely, alert account of both symphonies from Sawallisch that gives much pleasure. The *Second Symphony* in particular sounds beautifully fresh; the orchestral playing is of the high standard one expects from this great orchestra and Sawallisch has a fine sense of proportion. The recording is first class.

The coupling of Nos. 2 and 8 was the first of Norrington's Beethoven series and showed the London Classical Players as an authentic group with a distinctive sound, sweeter and truer in the string section than most, generally easier on non-specialist ears. In following Beethoven's own metronome markings for both symphonies the results are exhilarating, never merely breathless, bringing far more than proof of an academic theory.

Richard Hickox directs his chamber-scale orchestra in fresh, warm and relaxed readings of these two even-numbered symphonies. Playing is refined and rhythms resilient. The scale is well established by the slightly backward balance of the modest string section, with the focus rather sharper in No. 8 than in No. 2.

Predictably spacious readings from Giulini of both symphonies, the expansiveness working better in the glowing account of No. 2 than in No. 8 which lacks mercurial feeling; yet the purposeful strength of this reading remains impressive. Playing is excellent; the sound is good, better in No. 2 than in No. 8, which is not quite as full or as vivid.

Well-played, sensibly paced and very well-recorded accounts from the RPO under James Lockhart. The electricity of Monteux is missing, but there is an agreeable weight, and the easygoing account of No. 8 is particularly warm and enjoyable. Exposition repeats are observed. Excellent value.

Symphony No. 3 in E flat (Eroica), Op. 55.
(Y/B) *** DG Dig. 439 862-2 [id.]. Met. Op. O, Levine – SCHUBERT: *Symphony No. 8.* ***
(M) (***) RCA mono GD 60271 [60271-2-RG]. NBC SO, Toscanini – MOZART: *Symphony No. 40.*
     (**)
(N) (M) **(*) DG 447 444-2 [id.]. LAPO, Giulini (with SCHUMANN: *Manfred overture* ***).

Symphony No. 3 (Eroica); Grosse Fuge, Op. 133.
(M) *** EMI CDM7 63356-2 [id.]. Philh. O, Klemperer.

Symphony No. 3 (Eroica); Overture, Coriolan.
(M) *** Carlton Dig. PCD 900 [id.]. LSO, Wyn Morris.

Symphony No. 3 (Eroica); Overtures: Coriolan; Fidelio.
(M) **(*) RCA 09026 60962-2 [id.]. Chicago SO, Reiner.

Symphony No. 3 (Eroica); Creatures of Prometheus: Overture.
*** EMI Dig. CDC7 49101-2. L. Classical Players, Norrington.

Symphony No. 3 (Eroica); Overture Egmont, Op. 84.
*** Ph. Dig. 434 120-2 [id.]. Dresden State O, Sir Colin Davis.
**(*) DG Dig. Gold 439 002-2 [id.]. BPO, Karajan.

Symphony No. 3 (Eroica); Overture Fidelio.
(N) (BB) *** Tring TRP 026 [id.]. RPO, Guenther Herbig.

Symphony No. 3 (Eroica); Overtures: Leonora Nos. 2 & 3.
(M) (***) EMI mono CDM7 63855-2 [id.]. Philh. O, Klemperer.

With the Dresden Staatskapelle, Sir Colin Davis conducts a splendid account of the *Eroica* that master-fully sustains spaciousness and expansive speeds. Davis is electrifying in the great build-up of the development, leading to grinding dissonances. Equally, the hushed intensity of Davis's slow, concen-trated reading of the *Funeral march* has rarely been matched on disc, helped by superb sound. It is good to have a fresh *Eroica* to take its place comfortably at the top of the list.

As he shows in his dedicated reading of the *Missa solemnis*, James Levine can on occasion expand his usual image and interpret Beethoven with a rare depth and intensity. This account of the *Eroica*, recorded with his own opera orchestra, provides a clear instance, a reading that in its high drama and extremes of dynamic and tempo seems to reflect the influence of Toscanini. The first movement at a brisk speed is bright and bold, leading up powerfully to the great dissonances of the central develop-ment section. The *Funeral march* is taken spaciously, with concentration never slipping and with the measured tread of the central fugato as tense as in a Toscanini performance. There is plenty of fire in the last two movements, to confirm this as a first-rate recommendation for anyone wanting this unusual and generous coupling. Full-bodied sound, with more reverberation than you normally have in the Manhattan Center.

The digital remastering of Klemperer's spacious 1961 version of the *Eroica* reinforces its magnificence, keenly concentrated to sustain speeds slower than in his earlier, mono account. That alternative, mono version by Klemperer was among the very first records he made with the Philharmonia for EMI, but the success of these first Beethoven works revealed his full strength. This *Eroica* is one of his supreme achievements.

Although he does not include the first-movement exposition repeat, Guenther Herbig's 1994 recording of the *Eroica* with the RPO is most compelling, strong and aptly paced, and with the concentration of the playing at a high level throughout. The climax of the *Funeral march* has real emotional intensity and, after an exhilarating Scherzo with superb horn-playing, the genial finale caps the performance with the horns again impressive in a thrilling coda. The RPO are clearly on their toes and begin the CD with a fresh and vital account of the *Fidelio overture*. With full, brilliant, digital sound, naturally balanced in a concert-hall acoustic, this is very highly recommendable in the lowest price-range.

Norrington's account of the *Eroica* is consistently even faster than his closest period-performance rivals, yet one quickly forgets any feeling of haste when rhythms are so crisp and supple in their spring, and the great *Funeral march* has natural gravity.

Wyn Morris on the Carlton label conducts a taut reading of the *Eroica*, dark and intense, with allegros consistently urgent, and the LSO responds with both bite and refinement. An excellent bargain.

Toscanini's version has a far keener emotional intensity than the studio recording which appeared earlier as part of his Beethoven cycle in the BMG Toscanini series. Toscanini had a special insight into this of all Beethoven's symphonies, making this disc a valuable addition to his discography.

The gain in Karajan's digital version of the *Eroica* over his previous recordings lies most of all in the *Funeral march*, very spacious and intense, with dynamic contrasts intensified. Here, and even more noticeably in the allegros, the playing is marginally less polished than before, lacking something of the knife-edged bite associated with Karajan. The recording, remastered for the Karajan Gold series, now sounds cleaner and firmer, but there is still a degree of congestion in big tuttis. Nevertheless, the power and concentration make it an epic reading.

Reiner's is undoubtedly a compulsive *Eroica*, big-boned and spectacular in its epic qualities, but the first movement does not maintain an unerring single sweep forward, and the *Funeral march* is majestic and not greatly touched by tragedy. Characteristically full, late-1950s Chicago sound.

Giulini's refined and individual reading, with its almost eccentrically measured view of the first move-ment, was an early product of his love affair with the Los Angeles orchestra. Even though it is by no means a general recommendation among recordings of the *Eroica*, there is some justification for its reissue in DG's series of 'Legendary' Originals, for it remains an extraordinary example of a conductor transforming an orchestra's usual character, and it can also be valued for its new revelations. The coupling, an excellent performance of Schumann's *Manfred overture*, was originally offered as a make-weight for the *Rhenish Symphony*, which is now much more generously re-coupled.

Symphony No. 3 (Eroica) (trans. Liszt); *Eroica variations, Op. 35*.
(N) (M) ** Teldec/Warner Dig. 4509 97953-2 [id.]. Cyprien Katsaris (piano).

This is one of the less impressive of the Katsaris series of Liszt's remarkable transcriptions. The first movement of the *Eroica* is heavily rhetorical and the *Marcia funèbre* sounds comparatively uninvolved. The rest of the work is more impressive, as are the appropriately coupled *Variations*.

Symphonies Nos. 3 in E flat (Eroica), Op. 55; 4 in B flat, Op. 60.
(N) *** DG Dig. 447 050-2 [id.]. ORR, Gardiner.

Gardiner's fast speeds mean that, exceptionally, he can fit Nos. 3 and 4 on the same disc. The *Eroica* first movement may for some be too fast for comfort, but the argument is presented purposefully with full weight and biting intensity, helped by vivid recording. The Funeral march then has natural gravity even at a flowing speed, with high dynamic contrasts, and Gardiner's ability to spring rhythms has one quickly accepting fast tempi, not just in the *Eroica* but also in No. 4, where the sublime melody of the slow movement is sweeter than usual with period violins.

Symphonies Nos. 3 (Eroica); 7–8; Overture: Consecration of the house.
❀ (M) (***) Ph. mono 438 533-2 (2) [id.]. BPO, Paul van Kempen.

Astonishingly few allowances need be made for these mono recordings by Paul van Kempen and the Berlin Philharmonic. The *Eroica* dates from 1954, a year before the conductor's death (not 1959, as stated on the sleeve and labels), and the *Seventh* and *Eighth* from 1953. These are performances of classic profile: they have grandeur, integrity and power. Both the *Eroica* and the *Eighth* are worth a Rosette, so strong is their fallout! Had van Kempen lived, no doubt he would have assumed the mantle of Furtwängler that fell instead to Klemperer. Very impressive indeed.

Symphonies Nos. 3 (Eroica); 8 in F, Op. 93.
(Y/B) (M) **(*) Bruno Walter Edition: Sony SMK 64461 [id.]. Columbia SO, Bruno Walter.
(M) (***) RCA mono GD 60269 [60269-2-RG]. NBC SO, Toscanini.
(B) **(*) Sony SBK 46328; *SBT 46328* [id.]. Cleveland O, Szell.
(N) (M) **(*) Beethoven Edition DG 447 903-2 [id.]. VPO, Bernstein.

It is a pleasure to turn from other accounts of the *Eroica* and hear as beautiful and sympathetic a performance as Walter's. He is not monumental in the different ways of Klemperer and, before him, Toscanini; but this interpretation has all the ripeness of the best of Walter's work with the Vienna Philharmonic Orchestra between the wars. The digitally remastered recording has all the amplitude one needs for such a reading: its expansive qualities bring rich horns as well as full-bodied strings. The coupled *Eighth* has comparatively slow speeds, especially in the inner movements. The first goes well enough, but after that the pacing hampers the sustaining of any high degree of intensity, although the reading is of course interesting and sympathetic.

Toscanini's 1939 recording of the *Eroica*, made live, brings one of the most compelling recordings he ever made. Not only does he conduct at white heat, he is far more flexible in his musical manners than he became later, both moulding melodic lines with Italianate warmth and allowing himself far freer rubato. The *Eighth* is hard-driven and on the biggest scale (Toscanini, exceptionally for the days of 78s, observes the exposition repeat in the first movement). Yet this is a performance which sustains a satisfying power, far more persuasive in rhythm and phrasing than Toscanini's later NBC version.

Szell's is a fine performance in the Toscanini tradition, hard-driven and dramatic. The digital remastering is very successful: the sound is firm, full and brilliant. The performance of the *Eighth* is also a compelling one. The first-movement repeat is taken and the performance is not over-driven.

Bernstein's 1980 Vienna Philharmonic recording of the *Eroica* brings a degree of disappointment compared with his earlier (1964) Sony record (SMK 47514), which is electrically intense. There is less incandescence in the first movement, after a very powerful emphasis for the opening chords. The first-movement exposition repeat is still observed and this is undoubtedly a strong and dramatic reading, with a dedicated account of the *Funeral march*. This emerges as more clearly a march than before, yet is very measured indeed; but its intensity is enhanced by the presence of an audience. The *Eighth* is both strong (first-movement exposition repeat again included) and genial, coming out not so much a 'little' symphony as a jovial yet commanding one, with a bouncing, neatly pointed *Allegretto*, a mellow Minuet and a vigorous though not overdriven finale with a crisp, positive coda.

Symphonies Nos. 4 in B flat; 5 in C min., Op. 67.
*** EMI Dig. CDC7 49656-2 [id.]. L. Classical Players, Norrington.
(Y/B) (M) *** O-L Dig. 444 164-2 [id.]. AAM, Hogwood.
(M) *** Carlton Dig. PCD 869 [id.]. LSO, Wyn Morris.

Symphonies Nos. 4 in B flat; 5 in C min.; Egmont: Overture.
(B) **(*) Decca 433 600-2. VPO, Schmidt-Isserstedt.

This coupling of Nos. 4 and 5 – the same as Oiseau-Lyre offers in the rival Hogwood series – shows Norrington at his most refreshing and inspired, relishing his fast speeds; and the finale of No. 5 has infectious swagger. The sound is up to the high standard of the series.

Hogwood's generous coupling of Nos. 4 and 5 presents excellent versions for anyone wanting perform-ances on period instruments. Dramatic contrasts are strongly marked, with no feeling of miniaturiza-tion, and the clarity of textures is admirable, with natural horns in particular braying out superbly. This is now the more tempting at mid-price.

Wyn Morris generally adopts speeds close to those of Karajan and, though he cannot match that master in sharpness of focus or pointed intensity, his urgency goes with fine, biting strength, helped by some first-rate playing from the LSO. A bargain.

Schmidt-Isserstedt's late-1960s account of the first movement of the *Fourth* has more relaxation in it than is common these days. This does not mean that the reading is too small-scale or wayward, but that he finds a different range of Beethoven qualities. The *Fifth* is strong and direct, only the Scherzo offers controversy in its slow tempo. Both recordings are vivid and full; the *Fifth* has a slightly less clean transfer than the *Fourth*, which sounds excellent.

Symphonies Nos. 4 in B flat; 6 in F (Pastoral), Op. 68.
(Y/B) ✣ (M) *** Bruno Walter Edition: Sony SMK 64462 [id.]. Columbia SO, Walter.
(M) (***) RCA mono GD 60254 [60254-2-RG]. NBC SO, Toscanini.

For those collectors wanting a sampler of Bruno Walter's Beethoven series of the late 1950s, the coupling of the *Fourth* and *Sixth Symphonies* is the one to go for. Walter's reading of the *Fourth* is splendid, the finest achievement of his whole cycle. There is intensity and a feeling of natural vigour which makes itself felt in every bar. All aspects of this symphony – so much more varied than we have realized – are welded together here and show what depths it really contains. The recording is full, yet clear, sweet-toned with a firm bass. The pairing with the *Pastoral* is apt. The present version dates from the beginning of the 1960s and, like his recording of the *Fourth Symphony*, it represents the peak of his Indian summer in the American recording studios. It is an affectionate and completely integrated performance from a master who thought and lived the work all his life. The sound is beautifully balanced, with sweet strings and clear, glowing woodwind, and the bass response is firm and full.

The *Pastoral* was one of Toscanini's favourite Beethoven symphonies and the performance has a nat-ural, unforced freshness which allows the most delicate shading and persuasive moulding between sections. No. 4 is more characteristic of the later Toscanini, though the fast, fierce manner in the first movement conveys joyful exuberance, and the slow movement brings fine moulding.

Symphonies Nos. 4 in B flat; 7 in A, Op. 92.
*** Teldec/Warner Dig. 9031 75714-2 [id.]. COE, Harnoncourt.
(N) (M) *** Beethoven Edition DG 447 904-2 [id.]. VPO, Bernstein.
**(*) DG Dig. Gold 439 003-2 [id.]. BPO, Karajan.

Symphonies Nos. 4 in B flat; 7 in A; King Stephen overture, Op. 117.
(B) *** Sony SBK 48158; *SBT 48158* [id.]. Cleveland O, Szell.

Brilliant, vital readings from Harnoncourt, with high contrasts in the slow movement of No. 4, bringing soaring lyricism over nagging rhythmic figures below. In the outer movements of No. 7 – wonderfully spirited – the horns shine out, adding to the joyous release after an *Allegretto* full of under-the-surface tension.

Szell is at his finest in both symphonies. Along with powerful outer movements, tense and spontaneous-sounding, go exceptional accounts of the slow movements in both symphonies and in No. 7 Szell makes the second movement a genuine *Allegretto*, taking it almost as fast as a period specialist like Roger Norrington, and with magnetic concentration.

In No. 4, Bernstein's taut manner brings out the compactness of argument. The development is espe-cially fine: in context one registers it as the message of No. 1 retold in the language of the *Fifth*. If the Beethovenian tensions in Bernstein's Vienna performance of the *Seventh* are less marked than in his earlier, New York recording, here that makes for extra spring and exhilaration in the lilting rhythms of the first movement, while the *Allegretto* is reposeful without falling into an ordinary *Andante*, and the last two movements have the adrenalin flowing with a greater sense of occasion than in most of this Bernstein series. One almost regrets the lack of applause. The recordings are among the best and brightest in the series, with No. 7 especially vivid and full-blooded. An outstanding coupling.

Weller and the CBSO are at their best in both works, warm and companionable, giving the impression of live communication. Warm, full recording.

Karajan's digital coupling of the *Fourth* and *Seventh Symphonies* brings an impression of more spontaneous, less meticulous performances than in his previous versions of these works, presumably recorded this time with longer takes. The bravura is most compelling, but too much is lost. The slow movement of the *Fourth* is never hushed; and the *Allegretto* of No. 7, taken characteristically fast, is so smooth that the dactylic rhythm at the start is almost unidentifiable. The recording – remastered for reissue in the Karajan Gold series – is resonantly full.

Symphonies Nos. 4; 5 in C min. (trans. Liszt).
(N) (M) *** Teldec/Warner Dig. 4509 98954-2 [id.]. Cyprien Katsaris (piano).

Simply astonishing! Apart from his dazzling technique, Katsaris has enormous musicianship, a great range of colour and a real sense of scale. It is as if one is encountering this music for the first time. Readers will note that this mid-priced reissue is a recoupling.

Symphony No. 5 in C min., Op. 67.
(Y/B) (M) *** DG Dig. 445 502-2 [id.]. LAPO, Giulini – SCHUMANN: *Symphony No. 3 (Rhenish).* ***

Giulini's 1982 Los Angeles recording of Beethoven's *Fifth* is among the finest performances this symphony has ever received on record. The performance possesses majesty in abundance and conveys the power and vision of this inexhaustible work. The slow movement is glorious; the horn entry in the Scherzo is stunning and the finale almost overwhelming in its force and grandeur. Giulini also has the advantage of outstanding digital sound, clear, full and splendidly balanced, and the Schumann coupling is hardly less distinguished.

Symphonies Nos. 5 in C min.; 6 (Pastoral).
(N) **(*) DG Dig. 447 062-2 [id.]. ORR, Gardiner.
(B) **(*) DG 439 403-2 [id.]. BPO, Karajan.
**(*) DG Dig. Gold 439 004-2 [id.]. BPO, Karajan.

Gardiner's fast speeds in No. 5, like No. 1 recorded live, mean that the allegros have a manic energy and thrust, pushing the music to the limit in a way that Beethoven himself might well have approved, however unusual it sounds to our ears. The *Pastoral*, at comparably fast speeds, is crisp and light, with fine shading of phrase and dynamic, not least in the slow movement, though the exposed violin melody in the finale inevitably lacks the full sweetness of modern strings, making this one of the more controversial performances. Vivid, forward sound, full of presence.

Karajan's 1962 *Fifth* is thoroughly recommendable, if anything more intense than his later (1977) version, more spacious in the *Andante* and with blazing horns in the finale. The *Pastoral* is a brisk, lightweight performance, very well played, and marred only by the absence of the repeat in the Scherzo. The sound has freshness and body, and this is undoubtedly good value.

Karajan's digital versions of the *Fifth* and *Sixth* present characteristically strong and incisive readings, recorded in longer takes than previously. The sound may not be as cleanly focused as in his earlier Berlin versions, but the feeling of spontaneous performance is most compelling, so that the typically fast speed for the first movement of the *Pastoral* no longer sounds too tense.

Symphonies Nos. 5; 7 in A, Op. 92.
(Y/B) ✸ (M) *** DG 447 400-2 [id.]. VPO, Carlos Kleiber.
(M) *** EMI Dig. CD-EMX 2212; *TC-EMX 2212*. RLPO, Sir Charles Mackerras.
(N) (M) *** Decca Eclipse Dig. 448 222-2; *448 222-4* [id.]. Philh. O, Ashkenzy.
(Y/B) (M) **(*) Bruno Walter Edition: Sony SMK 64463 [id.]. Columbia SO, Bruno Walter.
(M) (***) EMI mono CDM7 63868-2 [id.]. Philh. O, Klemperer.

Symphonies Nos. 5; 8 in F, Op. 93.
(M) **(*) EMI CDM7 63357-2 [id.]. Philh. O, Klemperer.

Symphonies Nos. 5; 8; Fidelio: overture.
(M) *** DG 419 051-2; *419 051-4* [id.]. BPO, Karajan.

If ever there was a legendary recording, it is Carlos Kleiber's version of the *Fifth* from the mid-1970s. In Kleiber's hands the first movement is electrifying but still has a hushed intensity. The slow movement is tender and delicate, with dynamic contrasts underlined but not exaggerated. In the Scherzo the horns, like the rest of the VPO, are in superb form, and the central section has enormous energy; the finale, even more than usual, releases the music into pure daylight. The latest remastering has certainly enhanced the sound. Textures are drier than with Giulini's somewhat more expansive account with the Berlin Philharmonic (see above), but the upper range of the strings has more body than before, and there is little to complain of when this is undoubtedly one of the greatest performances of the work ever put on record. Kleiber's *Seventh* is a performance in which symphonic argument never yields to the charm of the dance. Kleiber's incisively dramatic approach is marked instead with sharp dynamic contrasts and thrustful rhythms. Another controversial point is that Kleiber, like his father, maintains the pizzicato for the strings on the final phrase of the *Allegretto*, a curious effect. The current digital remastering has again greatly improved the sound, with more resonance and weight in the middle strings – and how gloriously the horns come through in the tuttis of the outer movements.

Sir Charles Mackerras and the Royal Liverpool Philharmonic also give revelatory performances of both the *Fifth* and *Seventh*. The speed for the first movement of the *Fifth* initially takes one's breath away, so fast is it. Sir Charles has learnt from period practice. Here he demonstrates that fast speeds in Beethoven can go with clarity and rhythmic spring. Tempi are on the fast side in all four movements but, thanks to the rhythmic control, they never sound hectic. The dramatic contrasts in this exhilarating performance are underlined by the superb recording, both weighty and atmospheric. The coupling is an equally refreshing account of the *Seventh Symphony*. Those two favourite symphonies are normally too long to fit on a single disc, if (as here) exposition repeats are observed: the brisker speeds make all the difference.

Karajan's 1977 version of the *Fifth* is magnificent in every way, tough and urgently incisive, with fast tempi bringing weight as well as excitement. The coupling is an electrically intense performance of the *Eighth* plus the *Fidelio overture*.

Ashkenazy's reading of the *Fifth* is urgent and vivid and is notable for its rich, Kingsway Hall recording. Well-adjusted speeds here, with joyful exuberance a fair substitute for grandeur. The reading of the *Seventh* is equally spontaneous. This CD ranks high among records of these two symphonies, especially for those for whom outstanding recording quality is a priority.

In Bruno Walter's reading of the *Fifth*, the sound-balance is richer and more satisfying than in many more modern recordings. The first movement is taken very fast, yet it lacks the kind of nervous tension that distinguishes Carlos Kleiber's famous version. The middle two movements are contrastingly slow. In the *Andante* (more like an *adagio*) there is a glowing, natural warmth, but the Scherzo at this speed is too gentle. The finale, taken at a spacious, natural pace, is joyous and sympathetic, but again fails to convey the ultimate in tension. Walter's *Seventh* has a comparatively slow first-movement allegro. The *Allegretto* also seems heavier than usual (partly because of the rich, weighty recording). It is rather mannered, with *marcato* emphases on most of the down beats, but the important point is that genuine tension is created with the illusion of an actual performance. The Scherzo is also rather wayward, but in contrast the finale goes with a splendid lift to the playing and very brilliant horns and trumpets in the exciting coda.

Klemperer never surpassed these first EMI interpretations of either symphony. Though the recording is in mono only, both works have a clarity, immediacy and fidelity of balance that enhance electrifying readings, revealing Klemperer at his peak.

Klemperer's stereo renditions of Nos. 5 and 8 bring a clean and natural sound on top, notably in violin tone. The *Fifth* is plainly less electric than his earlier, mono version but, with exposition repeats observed in both outer movements, this retains its epic quality.

Symphony No. 6 in F (Pastoral), Op. 68.
(N) (M) *** DG 447 433-2 [id.]. VPO, Boehm – SCHUBERT: *Symphony No. 5.* ***

Symphonies No. 6 (Pastoral); Overtures: Coriolan; Creatures of Prometheus.
(BB) *** ASV CDQS 6053. N. Sinfonia, Richard Hickox.

Symphony No. 6 (Pastoral); Overtures: Coriolan; Egmont.
*** Sony Dig. SK 53974 [id.]. La Scala PO, Giulini.

Symphony No. 6 (Pastoral); Overtures: The Creatures of Prometheus; Egmont; (i) *Romance for violin and orchestra in No. 2 in F.*
(N) (B) *(*) BBC Radio Classics BBCRD 9114 [id.]. BBC SO, Sir Adrian Boult; (i) with Hugh Bean.

Symphony No. 6 (Pastoral); Overture: The Creatures of Prometheus; (i) *Egmont: Overture; Die Trommel geruhet; Freudvoll und leidvoll; Klärchens Tod, Op. 84.*
(M) *** EMI CDM7 63358-2 [id.]. Philh. O, Klemperer; (i) with Birgit Nilsson.

Symphony No. 6 (Pastoral); Overtures: Egmont; Leonora No. 3.
(M) *** Decca Dig. 430 721-2 [id.]. Philh. O, Vladimir Ashkenazy.

Boehm's 1971 version of the *Pastoral* is as fine as any offered at full price. It is a beautiful, unforced reading, one of the best played, and in its day one of the best recorded. It still sounds fresh in its current reissue in DG's 'Originals' series with a Schubert coupling. In the first movement Boehm observes the exposition repeat (not all versions do); and though the dynamic contrasts are never underplayed and the phrasing is affectionate, there is a feeling of inevitable rightness about Boehm's approach, no sense of an interpreter forcing his will. Only the slow movement with its even stressing raises any reservation, and that very slight.

Giulini's newest version of the *Pastoral*, measured, essentially warm and relaxed, speaks very much of the sunny Italian scene where it was recorded. Even the peasants sound Mediterranean in their robust vigour. The La Scala players are on their finest form throughout and play with great radiance in the glorious finale. The symphony is framed by the two overtures, *Coriolan* ruggedly powerful at the open- ing and *Egmont* highly histrionic at the somewhat manipulated climax. But the coda is strong. Excellently full recording.

Ashkenazy's performance has a beguiling warmth and it communicates readily. With generally spacious tempi, the feeling of lyrical ease and repose is most captivating, thanks to the response of the Philharmonia players and the richness of the recording, made in the Kingsway Hall. The two overtures make a thoroughly satisfactory makeweight.

Klemperer's account of the *Pastoral* is one of the very finest of all his records. The scherzo may be eccentrically slow but, with superbly dancing rhythms, it could not be more bucolic, and it falls naturally into place within the reading as a whole. The exquisitely phrased slow movement and the final *Shep- herds' hymn* bring peaks of beauty, made the more intense by the fine digital transfer, reinforcing the clarity and balance of the original sound. The *Egmont* music follows the *Symphony*, an unusual but valuable coupling with Nilsson in her prime, unexpectedly but effectively cast in the two simple songs, the first made to sound almost Mahlerian.

Hickox directs a persuasively paced reading, with a small orchestra used to give a performance of high contrasts, intimate in the lighter textures but expanding dramatically in the tuttis, while the finale, fresh and pure, brings a glowing climax. With warm, analogue recording giving a fine sense of presence, this is one of the best of the Hickox Beethoven series. The two *Overtures* come in vigorously dramatic readings.

On BBC Radio Classics is an enjoyable concert, with Hugh Bean playing most beautifully in the *F major Romance* and Boult's warmly persuasive view of the *Pastoral Symphony* matched by vivid per- formances of the two overtures. The snag is the audience's too frequent bronchial afflictions: the worst coughs usually come near the beginning of each work and the rustling of the audience between move- ments of the *Pastoral* also intrudes; it is also difficult to ignore the applause at the end. The sound itself is pleasing.

Symphonies Nos. 6 (Pastoral), Op. 68; 8 in F, Op. 93.
*** Teldec/Warner Dig. 9031 75709-2 [id.]. COE, Harnoncourt.

There is nothing over-tense about Harnoncourt's *Pastoral*, with the brook flowing and perhaps bubbling a little, over the stream bed; No. 8 has drama and bite and resilience too.

Symphonies Nos. 6 (Pastoral); 8 in F (trans. Liszt).
(N) (M) **(*) Teldec/Warner Dig. 4509 97955-2 [id.]. Cyprien Katsaris (piano).

Katsaris, using an instrument with the ideal combination of weight and clarity, makes an excellent exponent of Liszt's transcription of the *Pastoral Symphony*, direct and fresh, if not especially illuminat- ing interpretatively. The *Eighth* is much more perceptive. Good if rather resonant recording.

Symphonies Nos. (i) 6 in F (Pastoral); 8 in F, Op. 93; (ii) 9 in D min. (Choral), Op. 125.
(Y/B) (BB) **(*) EMI Seraphim CES5 68519-2 (2) [CDEB 68519]. (i) Munich PO, Rudolf Kempe; (ii) Armstrong, Reynolds, Tear, Shirley-Quirk, London Symphony Ch., LSO, Giulini.

Kempe's performance of the *Pastoral* is one of the most genially satisfying in the set. With warm, reverberant sound, few will be disappointed with either this or the comparable No. 8 (first-movement exposition repeat included). For the *Choral Symphony* EMI turned to Giulini's LSO account, also from the early 1970s. This is affected positively by the recording acoustic: close, immediate and full. Giulini's tempo in the first movement is unusually slow. He insists on precise sextuplets for the opening trem- olando, with no mistiness – and he builds the architecture relentlessly, finding the resolution only in the concluding coda. The Scherzo is lithe and powerful, with shattering timpani. The slow movement is warm and Elysian rather than hushed, while the finale, not always quite perfect in ensemble, is dedi- catedly intense, with excellent contributions from chorus and the solo team.

Symphony No. 7 in A, Op. 92.
(N) ✪ (B) *** EMI forte CZS5 69364-2 (2) [id.]. RPO, Sir Colin Davis – SCHUBERT: *Symphony No. 9* ***; ROSSINI: *Overtures.* **(*)
**(*) DG Dig. 431 768-2. Boston SO, Bernstein – BRITTEN: *Peter Grimes: Sea interludes.* **(*)

Symphony No. 7; Overtures: Coriolan; Creatures of Prometheus; Egmont.
(B) *** DG 429 509-2 [id.]. VPO, Boehm.

Symphony No. 7; Overture: The Creatures of Prometheus.
(M) *** EMI CDM7 69183-2 [id.]. Philh. O, Klemperer.

Sir Colin Davis's early (1961) *Seventh* is a great performance than can be spoken of in the same breath as Carlos Kleiber's *Fifth*. Originally issued as a bargain LP on the HMV Concert Classics label, it soon established itself as a firm recommendation and dominated the catalogue in the early stereo era. It sounds marvellous in its current remastering, the horns coming through thrillingly in the codas of both outer movements. As for the performance overall: here is an ideal illustration of the difference between a studio run-through and an interpretation that genuinely takes one forward compellingly from bar to bar. Admittedly the opening of the slow introduction is a shade lacking in weight, but from then on there is scarcely a blemish. The first movement, with delicious pointing of the dotted rhythms, has both stylishness and strength. The slow movement, taken at a measured speed, is beautifully controlled, not only in the detailed phrasing but over the architectural span of the whole movement. The scherzo, with all repeats taken, is wonderfully rumbustious, with some superb woodwind playing. The finale, taken very fast indeed, barely allows one to breathe for excitement. Unforgettable!

Klemperer's 1955 recording of the *Seventh* is among his very finest Beethoven interpretations on disc. Speeds are consistently faster, the tension more electric, with phrasing moulded more subtly, than in the later Philharmonia version.

Boehm's 1972 recording with the VPO is excellent, full and fresh, and the whole performance has lift and spontaneity. Boehm's direct style is most satisfying: full of impetus, yet with plenty of weight. The overtures go well too, especially *Egmont*.

Leonard Bernstein, recorded live with the Boston Symphony Orchestra, at the very last concert he ever conducted in Tanglewood on 19 August 1990, takes an extraordinarily expansive view, quite different from his previous recordings. Yet, for all the slowness of the basic speeds, he consistently conveys the joy of Beethoven's inspiration while springing rhythms with characteristic infectiousness. First-rate sound, considering the problems of live recording at Tanglewood, and an unusual coupling.

Symphony No. 7 (trans. Liszt).
(N) (M) *** Teldec/Warner Dig. 4509 97957-2 [id.]. Cyprien Katsaris (with SCHUMANN: *Exercises on Beethoven's Seventh Symphony* **).

Cyprien Katsaris does wonders in translating Liszt's transcription into orchestral terms, providing an unexpectedly illuminating listening experience. The sound is excellent. Well worth having at mid-price.

Symphonies Nos. 7; 8 in F, Op. 93.
*** DG Dig. 423 364-2 [id.]. VPO, Abbado.
(N) *** DG Dig. 447 063-2 [id.]. ORR, Gardiner.
(N) (B) **(*) Carlton IMP Dig. 30369 00022 [id.]. LSO, Wyn Morris.

The *Seventh* has always been a favourite symphony with Abbado, and the main allegro of the first movement is beautifully judged, as also is the *Eighth*, which is instantly established as more than a little symphony. As in the *Seventh*, speeds are beautifully judged, and the tensions of a live occasion are vividly conveyed. A splendid coupling.

As in No. 5, with Gardiner the first movements of both Nos. 7 and 8 are very highly charged, but textures and rhythms are lightened. Though there is comparable thrust in the finale of No. 7, the speed is not extreme, marginally slower in fact than Menuhin's. The *Allegretto* and Scherzo are fast and light too, as are the comparable movements of No. 8, as well as the hectic finale. Firm, forward sound.

Wyn Morris directs strong, spontaneous-sounding readings of both symphonies, not always as refined in execution as the finest, but superbly recorded. In a generous coupling on the bargain Carlton IMP label, they make an excellent recommendation. Though there are some distracting fluctuations of speed, Morris draws consistently resilient playing from the LSO, a vital quality in these two works written in parallel, with No. 8 becoming, like No. 7, an apotheosis of the dance.

Symphony No. 8 in F, Op. 93; Overtures: Coriolan; Fidelio; Leonora No. 3.
**(*) DG Dig. Gold 439 005-2 [id.]. BPO, Karajan.

Karajan's more relaxed view of the *Eighth* (compared with his 1977 Berlin version) is almost always pure gain. Nevertheless, Karajan's is a massive view of what has often been dubbed Beethoven's 'little symphony', taking it well into the powerful world of the nineteenth century, with fierceness part of the mixture in the outer movements. The three overtures are made massively Olympian too, with *Coriolan* especially impressive.

Symphony No. 9 in D min. (Choral), Op. 125.

(M) *** EMI Dig. CD-EMX 2186; *TC-EMX 2186*. Joan Rodgers, Della Jones, Peter Bronder, Bryn Terfel, R LPO Ch. & O, Sir Charles Mackerras.

(M) *** DG 415 832-2 [id.]. Tomowa-Sintow, Baltsa, Schreier, Van Dam, V. Singverein, BPO, Karajan.

*** DG 429 861-2 [id.]. Anderson, Walker, König, Rootering, various Chs., Bav. R SO, Dresden State O, etc., Bernstein.

(N) *** DG Dig. 447 074-2; *447 074-4* [id.]. Orgonasova, Von Otter, Rolfe Johnson, Cachemaille, Monteverdi Ch., O R R, Gardiner.

(Y/B) (M) *** DG Dig. 445 503-2 [id.]. Norman, Fassbaender, Domingo, Berry, V. State Op. Ch. Soc., VPO, Karl Boehm.

*** Teldec/Warner Dig. 9031 75713-2 [id.]. Margiono, Remmert, Schasching, Holl, Schoenberg Ch., C O E, Harnoncourt.

(BB) *** ASV CDQS 6069 [id.]. Harper, Hodgson, Tear, Howell, Sinfonia Ch., London Symphony Ch. (members), N. Sinfonia, Hickox.

(N) (BB) *** Tring TR P 051. Gillian Webster, Catherine Wyn-Rogers, Martyn Hill, Robert Hayward, Amb. S., RPO, Leppard.

(N) (B) *** DG 439 495-2 [id.]. G. Jones, Schwarz, Kollo, Moll, V. State Op. Ch., VPO, Bernstein.

(N) (M) *** Beethoven Edition DG 447 905-2 [id.]. Gwyneth Jones, Schwarz, Kollo, Moll, V. State Op. Ch., VPO, Bernstein.

*** O-L Dig. 425 517-2 [id.]. Augér, Robbin, Rolfe Johnson, Reinhart, London Symphony Ch., A A M, Hogwood.

(M) **(*) RCA 09026 61795-2 [id.]. Curtin, Kopleff, McCollum, Gramm, Chicago SO & Ch., Fritz Reiner.

(BB) **(*) Discover Dig. DICD 920151 [id.]. Gauci, Van Deyck, George, Rosca, Cantores Oratorio Ch., Belgian Nat. R. & TV PO, Rahbari.

**(*) DG Dig. Gold 439 006-2 [id.]. Perry, Baltsa, Cole, Van Dam, V. Singverein, BPO, Karajan.

(M) (**(*)) RCA mono G D 60256; [60256-2-RG]. Farrell, Merriman, Peerce, Scott, Shaw Ch., NBC O, Toscanini.

(N) ** EMI Dig. CDC7 54505-2 [id.]. Margaret Price, Marjana Lipovšek, Peter Seiffert, Jan-Hendrik Rootering, Concg. Ch. & O, Sawallisch.

(Y/B) (M) *(*) Bruno Walter Edition: Sony S M K 64464 [id.]. Cundari, Rankin, Da Costa, Wilderman, Westminster Ch., Columbia SO, Bruno Walter.

(N) (M) *(*) Carlton I M P Dig. 30369 00032 [id.]. Hargen, Della Jones, Rendall, Howell, London Symphony Ch., LSO, Wyn Morris.

(i) *Symphony No. 9 (Choral), Op. 125. Overture Fidelio.*

(B) **(*) Sony S B K 46533; *S B T 46533* [id.]. (i) Addison, Hobson, Lewis, Bell, Cleveland O Ch.; Cleveland O, Szell.

Symphony No. 9 (Choral); Overture: Coriolan.

(Y/B) (M) *** DG 447 401-2 [id.]. Janowitz, Rössl-Majdan, Kmentt, Berry, V. Singverein, BPO, Karajan.

Sir Charles Mackerras conducts the Royal Liverpool Philharmonic in an exceptional, inspired account of the *Ninth*, one which – more than any other with a traditional symphony orchestra – has learnt from the lessons of period performance. Articulation is light and clean, vibrato is used sparingly, making textures unusually clear; and, like Roger Norrington, Sir Charles has taken careful note of Beethoven's controversial metronome markings. The recording is among the very finest ever given to this symphony, warm yet transparent and with plenty of body; and the singing in the finale is splendid, even if the tenor, Peter Bronder, is on the strenuous side. Anyone wanting a refreshingly different version of the *Ninth*, which yet brings all the dramatic power and intensity of a more conventional reading, need not hesitate.

Of the three stereo recordings Karajan has made of the *Ninth*, his 1977 account (415 832-2) is the most inspired in its insight, above all in the *Adagio*, where he conveys spiritual intensity at a slower tempo than in his earlier, 1962 version. In the finale, the concluding eruption has an animal excitement rarely heard from this highly controlled conductor. The soloists make an excellent team, with contralto, tenor and bass all finer than their predecessors. The sound has tingling projection and drama.

Recorded live on the morning of Christmas Day 1989, Bernstein's Berlin version brings a performance that has something special to say, even after all the many recordings of this work, and not only because Bernstein substitutes the word '*Freiheit*', 'Freedom', for '*Freude*', 'Joy', in the choral finale, something Beethoven himself might well have approved of. The orchestra, drawn mainly from Germany, both East and West, the Bavarian RSO and Dresden Staatskapelle, also included members of the Kirov Theatre Orchestra in Leningrad, the New York Philharmonic, the Orchestre de Paris and the LSO. The choirs similarly came from East and West Germany, while the soloists represented four countries: America (June Anderson), Britain (Sarah Walker), Germany (Klaus König) and Holland (Jan-Hendrik Rootering). For many, the uniqueness of this version and the emotions it conveys will make it a first choice, despite obvious flaws.

With Gardiner and his period forces, recorded close, there is no mystery in the tremolos at the start of the *Ninth*, but the movement at its brisk speed builds up inexorably, and the Scherzo is well sprung at a relatively modest tempo. The slow movement is far faster than usual but still conveys repose, and the climax of the movement in compound time brings a most satisfying resolution. The finale, urgent and dramatic, gains from Gardiner's cunning as a choral conductor, drawing incandescent sounds from his own professional choir, and the quartet of fresh-voiced soloists is exceptionally strong. An exuberant conclusion confirms this as a clear first choice among period versions.

Karl Boehm's reading is spacious and powerful, and in its broad concept it has much in common with Klemperer's version. Yet overall there is a transcendent sense of a great occasion; the concentration is unfailing, reaching its peak in the glorious finale, where ruggedness and strength well over into inspiration. With a fine, characterful team of soloists and a freshly incisive chorus formed from singers of the Vienna State Opera, this is strongly recommendable.

Karajan's 1962 version is less hushed and serene in the slow movement than either of his two later versions, but the finale blazes even more intensely, with Janowitz's contribution radiant in its purity. This reflected the electricity of the Berlin sessions, when it rounded off a cycle recorded over two weeks. Even so, it is strange that DG chose this recording rather than the 1977 account for reissue in their 'Originals' series of legendary recordings, as the latter version is even finer. The *Coriolan* coupling is an added bonus.

For some listeners the fast pace of the slow movement of Harnoncourt's *Ninth* will seem a drawback, but otherwise the performance caps the cycle splendidly, with a very compelling account of the finale.

Hickox's performance, using an orchestra of the size Beethoven originally had, brings some of the advantages of period performance: clarity of articulation and texture; otherwise one might not realize that the string band is any smaller than one on a regular recording of the *Ninth*. In his pacing throughout the work, Hickox is unerring and conveys from first to last the tension of a genuine performance, in a way that some of his rivals among international stars do not manage. This is the most successful issue in his Beethoven series for ASV. The performance culminates in a glowing account of the choral finale with four excellent soloists. At super-bargain price this is very competitive indeed.

Raymond Leppard and the RPO offer a bright, incisive performance, enhanced by sharply focused, forward and well-detailed recording. The precise triplets in the opening tremolos may lack mystery but they lead to a well-terraced reading in which the entry of the recapitulation makes a shattering impact. Speeds, on the broad side in all the fast movements, never sound too slow, thanks to rhythmic lift and crisp ensemble, while the slow movement flows smoothly and songfully rather than meditating deeply. The fresh, forward balance of voices, both chorus and soloists, adds to the impact of the finale, making this an excellent recommendation at super-bargain price.

Bernstein's characterful VPO account of the *Ninth* crowns his Beethoven series superbly. The very start conveys immediate electricity, reflecting the presence of an audience, and the first movement is presented at white heat from first to last, with only a slight rallentando detracting from the thrust. The Scherzo is resilient, the *Adagio* deeply convincing in its distinctive contrasting of inner meditation in a very slow first theme with lighter, more carefree interludes in a fast-flowing *Andante*. In the finale Gwyneth Jones's soprano is as well controlled as it ever has been on record, and otherwise this is a superb account, sung and played with dedication, if a fraction less intense than the earlier movements. The recording needs no apology: it is bright, full and immediate. This seems to be available both on DG's Classikon bargain label (with very limited documentation) and, at mid-price, as part of the Beethoven Edition.

As bitingly dramatic as Toscanini in the first movement and electrically intense all through, Szell directs a magnetic, seemingly inevitable account of the *Ninth* which demonstrates the glories of the Cleveland Orchestra. The chorus sings with similarly knife-edged ensemble, set behind the orchestra but not too distantly. The performance of the *Fidelio overture* is electrifying.

Sawallisch's version was recorded live in the Concertgebouw, taken from three separate performances, but a sense of occasion is surprisingly muted, with little to indicate a live event until the applause at the end. Interpretatively it is a middle-of-the-road reading, with admirably chosen speeds but with playing too relaxed, lacking dramatic tension. Even the finale, with an impressive quartet of soloists, is disappointing when the chorus is placed backwardly and the singing lacks sharpness of focus.

Hogwood with his period forces is very well recorded. The ensemble is clear and well balanced both in the instrumental movements and in the choral finale, where an apt scale is achieved, neither too large nor too small. Hogwood has taken close note of Beethoven's controversial metronome markings. But Hogwood's manner is not too rigorous and he scores significantly over his direct rivals, not just in the sound-quality but in the quality of solo and choral singing. Though rhythms are not always ideally resilient, this is among the most recommendable period performances of the *Ninth* currently available.

Reiner's 1961 reading conveys power rather than mystery. Ensembles have knife-edged precision, rhythms are beautifully sprung and speeds are relatively broad, not least in the slow movement which, like the first, is presented in the full light of day. In the drum-and-fife episode of the finale too, Reiner's speed is surprisingly slow, but there and throughout he sustains tension magnetically, helped by the warm Chicago ambience. This is a fine example of Reiner's mastery and well worth hearing, even if there are greater accounts of the *Ninth* on CD.

Among versions at super-bargain price, Rahbari's Brussels version, digitally recorded, makes an excellent recommendation, consistently conveying vigour and spontaneity, as in a live, rather than a studio performance. The first movement is strong and purposeful, the Scherzo excitingly fast, with the slow movement sustaining measured speeds well, and the finale is helped by confident choral and solo singing. The recording is reverberant, but not so as to muddle an involving performance.

The high point of Karajan's digital version of the *Ninth* is the sublime slow movement, here exceptionally sweet and true, with the lyricism all the more persuasive in a performance recorded in a complete take. The power and dynamism of the first two movements are also striking, but the choral finale is flawed above all by the singing of the soprano, Janet Perry, far too thin of tone and unreliable. The sound of the choir has plenty of body, and definition has been improved in this remastered version.

Toscanini's electrifying account of the *Ninth* is marred somewhat by the excessive treble emphasis, more noticeable than on the earlier, full-priced reissue.

Walter's *Ninth* has many fine moments but suffers from slow tempi and a comparatively low level of tension. The first three movements were recorded in California in January 1959 and the finale in New York City four months later. Somehow the interpretation went off the boil and the choral finale fails to rise to the sense of occasion that a really great *Ninth* should have. Those interested in discovering Walter's methods of preparation for the final performances will be glad to know that there is a separate disc including recorded excerpts from the rehearsals of *Symphonies Nos. 4, 5, 7* and *9* (SMK 64465).

Wyn Morris's Beethoven cycle for Carlton came to a disappointing conclusion with this account of the *Ninth*, which displayed too many signs of haste in the recording; where most of the earlier issues in the series found the LSO in excellent form, the ensemble here is often slack. Even at bargain price there are many versions finer than this; though it has the benefit of modern, digital recording, the sound here is little more faithful than that on some of the vintage versions.

Symphony No. 9 (trans. Liszt).
(N) (M) *** Teldec/Warner Dig. 4509 97956-2 [id.]. Cyprien Katsaris (piano).

Cyprien Katsaris's performance is nothing short of a *tour de force*: his virtuosity is altogether remarkable and there is a demonic Beethovenian vehemence and drive. The piano is closely observed in a reverberant acoustic ambience and listeners may at times be disturbed by its somewhat jangly quality. But at mid-price this should not be missed.

Symphony No. 10 in E flat: 1st movement (realized and completed by Dr Barry Cooper – includes lecture by Dr Cooper).
(M) *** Carlton Dig. PCD 911 [id.]. LSO, Wyn Morris.

As re-created from Beethoven's sketches by Dr Barry Cooper, this movement from what was planned as the *Tenth Symphony* is, as Dr Cooper says, no more than an 'artist's impression'. The master would have moulded this into something far greater, but it is well worth hearing music that so dwells in the mind. Wyn Morris in this first recording directs a broad, strong reading, very well played and recorded. Dr Cooper's half-hour lecture fascinatingly amplifies and illustrates his detailed notes, making clear his scholarly credentials as well as his devotion to Beethoven's plan.

Wellington's victory (Battle symphony), Op. 91.
(N) ✸ (M) *** Mercury 434 360-2 [id.]. Cannon & musket fire directed Gerard C. Stowe, LSO, Dorati (with separate descriptive commentary by Deems Taylor) – TCHAIKOVSKY: *1812; Capriccio italien.* *** ✸

(N) (M) ** Beethoven Edition DG 447 912-2 [id.]. BPO, Karajan – *Ecossaise* etc. **; *Egmont.* **(*)
** Telarc Dig. CD 80079 [id.]. Cincinnati SO, Kunzel – LISZT: *Hunnenschlacht.* **

This most famous of all Mercury records was one of the most successful classical LPs of all time, selling some two million copies in the analogue era. Remastered for CD, it sounds far more convincing than it ever did in its vinyl format – indeed its sense of spectacle is quite extraordinary. Until 1804 Beethoven had been a Bonapartist and dedicated the *Eroica Symphony* to Napoleon; later, much disillusioned by events, he withdrew the dedication and instead became an anti-Bonapartist. No one was more pleased than he when in 1813 the Emperor's army was defeated by the British near the Basque city of Vitoria; encouraged by an entrepreneurial inventor, Johann Nepomuk Maelzel, Beethoven wrote a very commercial piece to celebrate the occasion. It was conceived to be performed on Maelzel's panharmonicon, a huge orchestral machine incorporating flutes, trumpets and percussion; but Beethoven also made an orchestral version, indicating in the score the exact spots at which the cannon and musketry were to be fired. It was in its orchestral form that the piece was eventually performed, and it is good to know that the venture was financially successful for both parties!

As the opposing armies march in, one on each side of the stereo spectrum, Beethoven represents the French army with a popular war-ditty, '*Malbrouck s'en va t'en guerre*' which, at the moment of defeat, reappears dejectedly in the minor key. The British are allotted *Rule Britannia* and, at the moment of victory, *God save the King*. In between comes an astonishing fusillade of fire, in which no one could complain at the use of period cannon and muskets or the engaging way the firing peters out as the battle comes to an end. Gerard C. Stowe deserves his share of the Rosette for these authentic special effects, as does Wilma Cozart Fine for her expert and painstaking re-editing and, not least, Dorati and the LSO for the excellent performance of Beethoven's music. This is surely an account which is unlikely to be bettered or realistically simulated in a live performance, and it is good to hear the endearing voice of Deems Taylor (famous for his commentary in Walt Disney's *Fantasia*) explaining how it was all done. Moreover the presentation, with handsome colour reproductions of appropriate paintings (and excellent documentation), is a model of its kind.

Karajan's version of *Wellington's Victory* is elegant rather than spectacular. It is beautifully played and the digital remastering adds presence to the opening assembly to left and right; but there is no sense of occasion and the battle-sounds are not entirely convincing, with the resonant acoustics of the Berlin Jesus-Christus Kirche bringing atmosphere but not helping to focus the spectacle. This cannot compare with its Mercury competitor, although the refined bravura of the Berlin Philharmonic in the closing section is impressive.

With a characteristically natural overall sound-balance, Kunzel's Telarc recording is also technically sophisticated, though the real musketry and cannon featured in the recording sound curiously like a fireworks display.

CHAMBER MUSIC

(i) *Cello sonatas Nos. 1–5;* (ii) *7 Variations on 'Bei Männern, welche Liebe fühlen'* (from Mozart's *Die Zauberflöte*), *WoO 46; 12 Variations on 'Ein Mädchen oder Weibchen'* (from Mozart's *Die Zauberflöte*), *Op. 66; 12 Variations on 'See the conqu'ring hero comes'* (from Handel's *Judas Maccabaeus*), *WoO 45*.
(Y/B) (B) *** Ph. Duo 442 565-2 (2) [id.]. (i) Mstislav Rostropovich, Sviatoslav Richter; (ii) Maurice Gendron, Jean Françaix.
(M) *** EMI CMS7 63015-2 (2). Jacqueline Du Pré, Daniel Barenboim.
(M) *** DG 437 352-2 (2) [id.]. Pierre Fournier, Friedrich Gulda.
(M) *** DG 423 297-2 (2) [id.]. Pierre Fournier, Wilhelm Kempff.
(Y/B) (B) *** EMI CZS5 68348-2 (2). Paul Tortelier, Eric Heidsieck.

Cello sonatas Nos. 1 in F, Op. 5/1; 2 in G min., Op. 5/2; 7 Variations on 'Bei Männern', WoO 46; 12 Variations on 'Ein Mädchen', Op. 66.
*** DG Dig. 431 801-2 [id.]. Mischa Maisky, Martha Argerich.

Cello sonatas Nos. 3 in A, Op. 69; 4 in C, Op. 102/1; 5 in D, Op. 102/2; 12 Variations on 'See the conqu'ring hero comes' (from Handel's *Judas Maccabaeus*), *WoO 45.*
*** DG Dig. 437 514-2 [id.]. Mischa Maisky, Martha Argerich.

Made in the early 1960s, the classic Philips performances by Mstislav Rostropovich and Sviatoslav Richter, two of the instrumental giants of the day, have withstood the test of time astonishingly well and sound remarkably fresh in this transfer. The performances of the *Variations* by Maurice Gendron and Jean Françaix have an engagingly light touch and are beautifully recorded. Indeed by their side the Rostropovich/Richter recording is noticeably drier and less vivid. But at its new price this reissue is very tempting.

The set of performances by Jacqueline Du Pré with Daniel Barenboim was recorded live for the BBC during the Edinburgh Festival of 1970. The playing may not have the final polish that studio performances would no doubt have achieved, but the concentration and intensity of the playing are wonderfully caught.

Fournier was to re-record Beethoven's complete music for cello and piano again for DG with Wilhelm Kempff, but those were 'live' performances, spontaneously fresh, yet some of the weight was missing. Even so, this was intensely expressive playing, marked by light, clear textures and rippling scale-work, even in the slow introductions, which are taken relatively fast.

The earlier accounts, made in the Brahms-Saal of the Vienna Musikverein in 1959, though not less spontaneous have more gravitas. Gulda's contribution is strong: he is more than a passive partner. The *Variations* are slight pieces, intended to divert, but once again in Fournier's hands they assume a greater significance than one might expect. The recording of both instruments is close but full and natural, beautifully balanced against an ideal acoustic.

Mischa Maisky and Martha Argerich make a strong partnership and there is enormous character about their playing here. Indeed it would be possible to feel that their readings are overcharacterized, so attentive are they to every dynamic nuance and hairpin that is marked (and plenty that aren't). All the same the performances are exhilarating and will be relished by many collectors, particularly in such vivid recordings.

The Tortelier set with Eric Heidsieck dates from the early 1970s and has the advantage of more modern and perhaps slightly better sound than the Philips set. The performances are distinguished and make a useful alternative, as the style is bolder than the way of Fournier and Kempff on DG, and less chimerical, too; indeed Tortelier and Heidsieck are nearer to Rostropovich and Richter, although they have their own insights. The variations have been added and make a bonus for the reissue, which comes at two CDs for the price of one. The CD transfer is admirably natural and clean, with the variations sounding particularly fresh.

Cello sonatas Nos. 1 in F; 2 in G min., Op. 5/1–2; 7 Variations on Mozart's 'Bei Männern', WoO 45; 12 Variations on Handel's 'See the conqu'ring hero comes', WoO 46; 12 Variations on Mozart's 'Ein Mädchen', Op. 66.
(BB) ** Naxos Dig. 8.550479 [id.]. Csaba Onczay, Jenö Jandó.

Although they do not have the personality of, say, Maisky and Argerich – let alone Rostropovich and Richter – Csaba Onczay and Jenö Jandó turn in serviceable accounts of both *Sonatas*. The cellist is a little colourless and does not have quite as much fervour or character as the pianist. Decent recording.

Cello sonatas Nos. 3 in A, Op. 69; 5 in D, Op. 102/2.
(M) *** EMI CDM7 69179-2. Jacqueline du Pré, Kovacevich.

The Du Pré/Bishop-Kovacevich recordings of Nos. 3 and 5 come from 1966, the year after Jacqueline had made her definitive record of the Elgar *Concerto*. Du Pré's tone ranges from full-blooded fortissimo to the mere whisper of a half-tone, and these artists allow the most free range of expressive rubato. With excellent recording, these performances are most welcome on CD, sounding crisp and present in their new format.

Duo for viola and cello in E flat, WoO 32; Sextet for 2 horns, 2 violins, viola & cello, Op. 81b; String quintet in A (arr. of Violin sonata in A, Op. 47 (Kreutzer)).
** Sony Dig. SK 48076 [id.]. L'Archibudelli.

L'Archibudelli play on period instruments and are an accomplished group. The arrangement of the *Kreutzer sonata* is not Beethoven's but is possibly by Ferdinand Ries. There is some striking horn playing here in the *Sextet*, Op. 81b, and elsewhere some occasional moments of vulnerable intonation. Very good 20–bit recording.

Ecossaise, WoO 22; March for wind sextet, WoO 29; Military marches, WoO 18–20; 24; Polonaise, WoO 21.
(N) (M) ** Beethoven Edition DG 447 912-2 [id.]. BPO Wind Ens., Hans Priem-Bergrath – *Egmont* **(*); *Wellington's victory.* **

The performances of Priem-Bergrath and the BPO Wind Ensemble are routine ones but vigorous and well played. The mellow piece for wind sextet (WoO 29) without percussion, the *Ecossaise* and *Polonaise* bring variety, although one or two of the military pieces are quite attractive, notably the '*Yorkshire*' *March in F*, WoO 19. The 1969 recording, made in the Jesus-Christus Kirche, Berlin (a curious venue), is brightly resonant and, considering the acoustic, the CD definition is surprisingly good.

(i) *Flute trio in G* (for flute, bassoon & piano), *WoO 37; (ii–iii) Horn sonata in F, Op. 17; (iii; v) Piano and wind quintet, Op. 16; (iv) Serenade in D for flute, violin & viola, Op. 25; (v) Septet, Op. 20; Sextet in E flat, Op. 81b; Wind octet in E flat, Op. 103; Wind sextet in E flat, Op. 71.*

(M) *** DG 439 852-2 (3) [id.]. (i) Zöller, Thunemann, Kontarsky; (ii) Seifert; (iii) Demus; (iv) Zöller, Brandis, Ueberschaer; (v) BPO (members).

These are all beautifully alert, civilized performances and they are recorded with clarity and definition and an appealing bloom. There are some minor reservations. There are perhaps more starry accounts of the *Piano and wind quintet* (although Demus and his colleagues play freshly and spontaneously). In the *Septet*, Op. 20, the Berlin players are richly mellifluous in style, especially noticeable in the Minuet. There is no rival compilation of this scope on the market at present and, even if there were, it is difficult to imagine it surpassing the present set (originally issued on five LPs).

Notturno, Op. 42.
(Y/B) *** EMI Dig. CDC5 55166-2 [id.]. Caussé, Duchable – REINECKE: *Fantasiestücke* ***; SCHU-
BERT: *Arpeggione sonata.* **(*)

Beethoven's *Notturno* is an 1803 arrangement by Franz Xaver Kleinheinz of the *Serenade*, Op. 8, for string trio. It is a slight work, but Gérard Caussé and François-René Duchable give a nicely turned and musicianly account of it. Exemplary recording.

Octet in E flat, Op. 103.
(Y/B) *** Decca Dig. 436 654-2 [id.]. Vienna Wind Soloists – MOZART: *Serenades.* ***

Nothing much to say about the new recording by the Vienna Wind Soloists on Decca. This is delightful playing, fresh and natural – as is the recorded sound. If the two Mozart *Serenades* the disc offers are what you want for your collection, there is no need to hesitate.

Piano quartets Nos. 1 in E flat; 2 in D; 3 in C, WoO 36.
(N) (B) **(*) Discover Dig. DICD 920254 [id.]. Scheuerer Qt.

The enterprising Discover label does it again by giving Beethoven's three early *Piano quartets* their CD début. Written in Bonn when the composer was fifteen, they are obviously Mozart-influenced, as the charming *Rondo* finales of Nos. 1 and 3 readily demonstrate. Indeed that for the *D major* (otherwise perhaps the least interesting) is little short of a lollipop. The *Theme and variations finale* of No. 1 is attractive too, but it is the central *Adagio* of No. 3 which hints at the mature Beethoven, and the opening *Adagio assai* of No. 1 even more so – beginning like the slow movement for a piano concerto. The bold *Allegro con spirito* second movement of the *E flat Quartet* is also obviously post-Mozartian and the four sibling performers here make the very most of it. Indeed they play throughout with pleasing freshness and plenty of vitality. The excellent pianist leads strongly, but (as we have commented before) the principal violinist could have a more generous tone. Fortunately the microphones are not near enough to exaggerate this, and the overall balance is good within a fairly resonant acoustic. This well worth its modest cost.

Piano trios Nos 1–9; 10 (Variations on an original theme in E flat), Op. 44; 11 (Variations on 'Ich bin der Schneider Kakadu'), Op. 121a; Allegretto in E flat, Hess 48.
*** EMI Dig. CDS7 47455-8 (4) [Ang. CDCD 47455]. Ashkenazy, Perlman, Harrell.

Piano trios Nos. 1–3, Op. 1; 4 in B flat, Op. 11; 5 in D (Ghost), Op. 70/1; 6 in E flat, Op. 70/2; 7 in B flat (Archduke), Op. 97; 14 Variations on an original theme in E flat, Op. 44; 10 Variations on 'Ich bin der Schneider Kakadu', Op. 121a.
(M) **(*) Teldec/Warner Dig. 9031 73281-2 (3) [id.]. Trio Fontenay.

Piano trios Nos. 1–11.
(M) *** Ph. 438 948-2 (3) [id.]. Beaux Arts Trio.

Piano trios Nos. 1–3, Op. 1; 8 in E flat, WoO 38; 10 (Variations on an original theme in E flat), Op. 44.
(N) (M) *** Sony Stern Edition III SM2K 64510 (2) [id.]. Stern, Rose, Istomin.

Piano trios Nos. 4 in B flat, Op. 11; 5 in D (Ghost), Op. 70/1; 6 in E flat, Op. 70/2; 7 in B flat (Archduke), Op. 97; 9 in B flat, WoO 39; 11 (Variations on 'Ich bin der Schneider Kakadu'), Op. 121a.
(N) (M) *** Sony Stern Edition III SM2K 64513 (2) [id.]. Stern, Rose, Istomin.

Piano trios Nos. 1–11; Trio in E flat (from Septet), Op. 38; Trio in D (from Symphony No. 2); Trio movement in E flat.
(M) **(*) Ph. Analogue/Dig. 432 381-2 (5) [id.]. Beaux Arts Trio.

Piano trios Nos. 1–3; 5–7; 9–10 (Variations on an original theme in E flat); 11 (Variations on 'Ich bin der Schneider Kakadu'); Allegretto in E flat, Hess 48.
(M) **(*) EMI CMS7 63124-2 (3) [Ang. CDMC 63124]. Daniel Barenboim, Pinchas Zukerman, Jacqueline du Pré.

Piano trios Nos. 7 (Archduke); 9 in B flat, WoO 39.
*** EMI Dig. CDC7 47010-2 [id.]. Ashkenazy, Perlman, Harrell.

Ashkenazy, Perlman and Harrell lead the field in this repertoire. The recordings have been made over a period of five years and at various locations, but the sound is consistently fresher, warmer, more richly detailed and more present than with most other rivals. The playing is unfailingly perceptive and full of those musical insights that make one want to return to the set. The *Archduke*, coupled with *No. 9 in B flat*, is available separately.

The Stern/Rose/Istomin recordings were made between 1968 and 1970, though the *Archduke* is earlier and was recorded in Switzerland in 1965. The results are outstanding: the music-making is strong, polished and alive, and Istomin is always thoughtful and imaginative in slow movements, while Rose, although a less extrovert artist than Stern, holds his own by the warmth and finesse of his lyrical phrasing. One of the highlights of the set is the *Archduke*, commandingly bold and immediate, with a glorious slow movement; the *Ghost trio* also shows these artists at their most communicative, while they do not miss the charm of the early, Op. 1 works. The recording is characteristically forward, in the CBS manner of the late 1960s, but the remastering for CD has improved the sonority at the lower end of the spectrum immeasurably. The shallowness of the piano has all but disappeared: indeed it is now a very convincing image and, while Stern is obviously close to the microphones, the fierceness noticeable on the LPs has been tamed. In every sense these recordings rank highly in the discography of the Beethoven *Piano trios* and may be recommended with enthusiasm alongside the Perlman/Ashkenazy/Harrell set, with which they have much in common.

In their analogue set, dating from 1965, the Beaux Arts are let down a little by the ungenerous tone of their leader, Daniel Guilet; set against the refreshing spontaneity of the playing as a whole, however, this is of little moment. Tempi are admirably chosen (save for the *Ghost Trio*, which is very brisk; the work's drama and intensity, however, are projected to brilliant effect) and phrasing is marvellously alive. Ultimately the Beaux Arts score here on account of the chamber-music quality of their playing. They convey a sense of music-making in the home rather than in the concert hall, and the naturally balanced recording also has an attractive combination of warmth and intimacy.

The Fontenay versions were recorded between 1990 and 1992 in the Teldec studios in Berlin. Alert and intelligent playing throughout, attentive phrasing and bright, well-lit recorded sound. The *Ghost* is rather closely balanced; the Op. 1 *Trios* are much better in this respect. Very good playing, without perhaps the last touch of humanity and depth, such as we find in the Beaux Arts – particularly in their earlier set from the 1960s.

The Barenboim/Zukerman/du Pré set (by omitting Nos. 4 and 8) is fitted economically on to three mid-priced CDs. Even more than usual, the individual takes involved long spans of music, often complete movements, sometimes even a complete work. The result is music-making of rare concentration, spontaneity and warmth. The excellent recording has been freshened on CD.

Unlike their earlier set, the later Beaux Arts box offers absolutely everything Beethoven composed (or arranged) for this grouping. However, five (well-filled) CDs are involved; four of the recordings are digital. The transfers are well up to the usual high Philips standard and the performances are as accomplished and musical as one would expect from this celebrated team. However, it has to be said that the earlier, analogue set had a freshness and sparkle that these new accounts do not wholly match.

Piano trios Nos. 1 in E flat; 2 in G, Op. 1/1–2.
(N) (B) *** HM HMA Dig. 1901361 [id.]. Patrick Cohen, Erich Höbarth, Christophe Coin.
*** Hyperion Dig. CDA 66197 [id.]. L. Fortepiano Trio.
(BB) ** Naxos Dig. 8.550946 [id.]. Stuttgart Piano Trio.

Even more than in the recordings by the London Fortepiano Trio, Patrick Cohen's group shows how fresh, alive and clear-textured these engaging works can be made to sound on period instruments, and how effective is the fortepiano, not only in the vivacious allegros but also in the slow movement of the *E flat major* and the *Largo con espressione* of the *G major*. The recording is first class, and this is a real bargain in its new Musique d'Abord format.

The London Fortepiano Trio play with considerable virtuosity, particularly in the finales, which are taken at high speed and to considerable effect. The use of a fortepiano serves to enhance clarity of texture in this particular repertoire, and readers should make an effort to sample what one assumes will be a complete cycle.

The Stuttgart Piano Trio play these early works of Beethoven with pleasing simplicity. They have not quite the individuality of the Beaux Arts, yet both slow movements are eloquently sustained and finales have sparkle, especially that to the G major which is infectious. The recording is naturally balanced in a warm acoustic which provides a clean realistic focus.

Piano trios Nos. 3 in C min., Op,. 1/3; 8 in E flat, WoO 38; 10 (Variations in E flat), Op. 44; Allegretto in E flat, Hess 48.

(BB) **(*) Naxos Dig. 8.550947 [id.]. Stuttgart Piano Trio.

Although the first movement of Op. 1/3 is on the brisk side, it springs to life spontaneously and the variations which follow are appealingly fresh. The other early *Trio in E flat* is very persuasively done and the *Variations*, Op. 44, are hardly less successful. With excellent recording, performances on this CD have obviously more sparkle than those on its earlier companion. Again the sound is fresh and naturally balanced.

Piano trios Nos. 5 in D (Ghost); 6 in E flat, Op. 70/1–2.

(N) (BB) * Naxos Dig. 8.550948 [id.]. Stuttgart Trio.

The Stuttgart Trio take Beethoven's marking for the first movement of the *Ghost trio* ('*Allegro vivace e con brio*') very literally indeed and they dash into the opening like an express train. Their nervous intensity permeates the performance, though the arrival of the 'Ghost' is eerily effective. The *E flat Quartet* is only marginally more relaxed and the finale totally lacks geniality. The players are not helped by the dry recording, with microphones unflatteringly close in the Clara Wieck Auditorium, and this gives the impression of brisk efficiency rather than musical enjoyment.

Piano trios Nos. 5 in D (Ghost); 6 in E flat, Op. 70/1–2; 7 (Archduke); ll (Variations on 'Ich bin der Schneider Kakadu'); 12 (Allegretto in E flat).

(N) [B] *** Carlton Double Dig. 30366 00107 (2). Solomon Trio.

Three of Beethoven's greatest trios played with fine dedication and intelligence by Yonty Solomon, Rodney Friend and Timothy Hugh in lively but not over-bright acoustics that do justice to their music-making. These artists have an excellent rapport; there is no playing to the gallery and one is left in no doubt that it is Beethoven's muse they are trying to serve rather than any corporate ego. The only real snag is the dominance in the aural picture of the pianist – up to a point understandable, since the keyboard part is so important, although in the *Archduke* Timothy Hugh's rich cello is very much in the picture, suitably so for what is a comparatively mellow performance. The *Kakadu variations* are also done splendidly and the brief *Allegretto in E flat* makes a fresh bonus.

Piano trios Nos. 5 in D (Ghost), Op. 70/1; 7 in B flat (Archduke).

(B) **(*) Sony SBK 53514; *SBT 53514* [id.]. Eugene Istomin, Isaac Stern, Leonard Rose.

The playing from the Istomin/Stern/Rose trio is strong, polished and alive, with good teamwork and the individual personality of each player coming over forcefully. The *Archduke* is a very impressive perform-ance indeed (preferable to the Beaux Arts), bold and traditional in approach and full of energy. One of the slight drawbacks of the transatlantic recording is the comparative shallowness of the piano tone and the touch of thinness on the violin timbre, but the ambience is convincing, the basic sound is warm and the balance not too close to rob the music-making of its dynamic range. An impressive coupling.

(i) *Piano trio No. 5 in D (Ghost), Op. 70/1;* (ii) *Violin sonata No. 9 in A (Kreutzer), Op. 47.*

(N) (M) **(*) Beethoven Edition DG 447 917-2 [id.]. (i) Szeryng, Fournier; (ii) Y. Menuhin; (i; ii) Kempff.

This account of the *Ghost trio*, like the *Archduke*, below, comes from the complete cycle which these artists made for DG and which first appeared in 1970. The performance opens dramatically but is for the most part comparatively restrained, sweet and lyrical rather than dramatic, with Kempff very much the dominating influence. The recording has good presence and separation, but the blend of the three instruments is not altogether homogeneous. If the Menuhin/Kempff performance of the *Kreutzer son-ata* is not as immaculate as other accounts, the spontaneous imagination of the playing, the challenge between great artists on the same wavelength, is consistently present.

(i) *Piano trio No. 7 in B flat (Archduke), Op. 97;* (ii) *Violin sonata No. 5 in F (Spring), Op. 24.*

(N) (M) **(*) Beethoven Edition DG 447 916-2 [id.]. (i) Szeryng, Fournier; (ii) Menuhin; (i; ii) Kempff.

Kempff and his colleagues give a crystalline reading of the *Archduke*. It is the clarity and imagination of Kempff's playing which sets the tone of the whole performance. He it is who grips the listener's attention with his individual touches of genius, so that by comparison Szeryng and Fournier sound less than inspired. An interesting but not a definitive version. The reading of the *Spring sonata* has the magic which characterizes the whole Menuhin/Kempff cycle, and it was a pity that DG chose not to couple the violin sonatas together instead of mixing them up with the piano trios.

Piano and wind quintet in E flat, Op. 16.
(Y/B) (M) *** Sony Dig. SMK 42099 [id.]. Perahia, members of ECO – MOZART: *Quintet.* ***
(N) *** Decca Dig. 443 892-2 [id.]. Pascal Rogé, London Winds – SPOHR: *Septet.* ***
(M) *** Decca 421 151-2. Ashkenazy, L. Wind Soloists – MOZART: *Quintet.* ***

First choice for Beethoven's *Piano and wind quintet* lies with Perahia's CBS version, recorded at The Maltings. The first movement is given more weight than usual, with a satisfying culmination. In the *Andante*, Perahia's playing is wonderfully poetic and serene, and the wind soloists are admirably responsive. With the recording most realistically balanced, this issue can be recommended with all enthusiasm.

Pascal Rogé and the London Winds also give an altogether delightful account of Beethoven's early *E flat Quintet* which can stand alongside Perahia and members of the ECO – which, however, now has a price advantage. Rogé and his colleagues have sensitivity, vitality and charm, and would still make a viable first choice if the coupling is desirable. The Decca recording is in the best traditions of the house.

Ashkenazy's recording from 1966 is also in every way recommendable. The sound is first class, the balance rather forward but very vivid and real.

Septet in E flat, Op. 20.
(N) (B) *** Decca Eclipse Dig. 448 232-2; *448 232-4* [id.]. Vienna Octet (members) – MOZART: *Clarinet quintet.* ***
(Y/B) (M) *** Teldec/Warner Dig. 4509 97451-2 [id.]. Berlin Soloists – MOZART: *Horn quintet.* **(*)
(*) O-L Dig. 433 044-2 [id.]. AAM Chamber Ens. – WEBER: *Clarinet quintet.* *
(N) **(*) Nimbus Dig. NI 5461 [id.]. BPO Octet – HINDEMITH: *Octet.* **(*)

Over the years the Vienna Octet have been justly famous for their recordings of Beethoven's *Septet* for Decca, and this newest version is no disappointment. Brio and good humour mark the performance, with a warmly elegant account of the slow movement to offset the high spirits of the Minuet and the Scherzo with its galumphing horn-playing. The finale is no less infectious. The recording is wonderfully warm and real; it was made as recently as 1991. The coupled Mozart *Clarinet quintet* is somewhat cooler but no less beautifully played (using a basset clarinet) and recorded.

The Teldec Berlin recording is rich and expansive in its bass resonance, but that does not inhibit the vivacity of the playing. The opening movement (exposition repeat included) sets off with a sparkling tempo, and such verve is irresistible. The *Adagio* has a gloriously rich melodic flow, offset by the elegantly measured minuet. The *Theme and variations* has the most delightfully perky rhythmic lightness from the very opening, and the fun of the Scherzo is appreciated by one and all, not least the solo horn. The finale has spendid impetus and a glowing warmth of timbre. This is all very enticing indeed, and the recording is appealingly atmospheric. Perhaps the Vienna account occasionally has a touch more rustic charm, but this Teldec version (dating from 1990) is equally enjoyable in its slightly more sumptuous way.

The Academy of Ancient Music give a light-textured and lively account of this genial work. Solo playing of the early instruments is impeccable, but somehow the lack of opulence of timbre is accompanied by lack of a sense of sheer infectious joy in the music. There is no absence of vivacity but other versions are more endearingly seductive. No complaints about the recording.

The Berlin Philharmonic Octet give a thoroughly delightful and characterful account of the *Septet*. Their polish and finesse excite admiration and their artistry pretty well silences criticism. The only snag is that the recording, made in the Teldec Studios, Berlin, is a bit too closely balanced and upfront. Recommended nonetheless.

(i) *Septet in E flat, Op. 20;* (ii) *Wind sextet in E flat.*
*** Hyperion Dig. CDA 66513 [id.]. Gaudier Ens.

The young members of the Gaudier Ensemble give an exuberant performance of the *Septet*, bringing it home as one of the young Beethoven's most joyfully carefree inspirations. The rarer *Sextet* for two horns and string quartet makes a generous coupling. Excellent sound, with the wind well forward.

Septet in E flat, Op. 20; Clarinet trio, Op. 11.
(Y/B) (M) *** Virgin/EMI Dig. CUV5 61233-2 [id.]. Nash Ens.

There is sheer magic in these performances on the Virgin Ultraviolet label, with the members of the Nash Ensemble conveying their own enjoyment in the young Beethoven's exuberant inspiration. So the *Clarinet trio* finds each player, not just the fine clarinettist Michael Collins but also the pianist Ian Brown and the cellist Christopher van Kampen, pointing rhythms and phrases as a friendly challenge to be answered and capped by colleagues, the spontaneous interplay of the moment. It is a happy phenomenon, too rarely evident on record but delectably present here. An apt sense of fun also infects the *Septet*, though the allegros in the outer movements, exhilaratingly fast, would have been even more winning at speeds a shade more relaxed. But here too the performance brims with joy. Good, atmospheric sound. This is an obvious first choice at mid-price for this coupling.

Serenade in D for flute, violin and viola, Op. 25.
✵ (M) *** Carlton/CDI Dig. PWK 1139. Israel Flute Trio (with Recital: '*Flute Serenade*' ***).

The light and charming combination of flute, violin and viola inspired the youthful Beethoven to write in an unexpectedly carefree and undemanding way. The sequence of tuneful, unpretentious movements reminds one of Mozart's occasional music, and this delectable Israel performance brings out all its charm. Er'ella Talmi is a superb flautist and she receives admirable support from her colleagues. The recording is wonderfully natural in sound and balance: it is as if the players were making music in one's own room.

Serenade in D, Op. 8 (arr. Matiegka).
*** Mer. Dig. CDE 84199 [id.]. Clive Conway, Paul Silverthorne, Gerald Garcia – KREUTZER; MOLINO: *Trios.* ***

Beethoven's early *Serenade* for string trio was arranged for violin, viola and guitar as early as 1807 by the Bohemian composer and guitarist, Wenceslaus Matiegka. Gerald Garcia has here rearranged it for the present unusual and delightful combination, offering the violin part to the flute, and giving the guitar a more taxing contribution. As a companion-piece for the rare Kreutzer and Molino items, it makes a charming oddity in its seven brief movements, very well played and warmly recorded.

String quartets

String quartets Nos. 1–16; Grosse Fuge, Op. 133.
(M) *** Valois V 4400 (8) [id.]. Végh Qt.
*** Valois V 4401 (*Nos. 1 & 5*); V 4402 (*Nos. 2–4*); V 4403 (*Nos. 6–7*); V 4404 (*Nos. 8–9*); V 4405 (*Nos. 10 & 12*); V 4406 (*Nos. 11 & 15*); V 4407 (*Nos. 13 & Grosse Fugue*); V 4408 (*Nos. 14 & 16*) [id.]. Végh Qt.
(M) (***) EMI mono CZS7 67236-2 (7). Hungarian Qt.

String quartets Nos. 1, 3 & 4, Op. 18/1, 3 & 4; 7 (Rasumovsky No. 1), Op. 59/1; 10 (Harp), Op. 74; 12, Op. 127; 13, Op. 130; 14, Op. 131.
(Y/B) *** EMI Dig. CDS7 54587-2 (4) [Ang. ZDCD 54587]. Alban Berg Qt.

String quartets Nos. 2, 5 & 6, Op. 18/2, 5 & 6; 8–9 (Rasumovsky Nos. 2–3), Op. 59/2–3; 11, Op. 95; 15, Op. 132; 16, Op. 135; Grosse Fuge, Op. 133; Cavatina from Op. 130.
(Y/B) *** EMI Dig. CDS7 54592-2 (4) [Ang. ZDCD 54592]. Alban Berg Qt.

The Végh performances were recorded in the mid-1970s; they have been rightly hailed for their simplicity and depth. Intonation may not always be absolutely immaculate, but flaws are few and trivial when one considers the wisdom and experience the Végh communicate. In short they are in a different league from most of their rivals: there is no cultivation of surface polish though there is both elegance and finesse. The CD transfers are successful in producing an altogether cleaner image and a slightly firmer focus than the original analogue LPs, although the imbalance towards the cello remains. The eight discs are now available together at mid-price.

The Hungarian Quartet's first recorded cycle of the Beethoven *Quartets*, with the mono sound firm and full, is superb, with tonal beauty never an end in itself. Polished ensemble goes with a sense of spontaneity in readings fresher and more direct than those of 1966. The spacious, unhurried playing of the great slow movements here has rarely been matched. Those primarily concerned with the music as opposed to sound-quality will find little difficulty in adjusting to the recording.

The Alban Berg's new set originates at public concerts and is, perhaps, an attempt to ensure that the greater intensity and spontaneity generated in the presence of an audience finds its way on to records. Generally speaking it does; on balance, these performances, when listened to alongside the earlier set, are freer and more vital, but the differences are small. It may seem perverse to say so, but even now there is perfection of ensemble and sheer beauty of sound that will not strike all listeners as altogether appropriate in this repertoire. However, these are not by any means superficial or slick – and admirers of this ensemble need have no hesitation in acquiring them.

String quartets Nos. 1–2, Op. 18/1–2.
(Y/B) ** Hyperion Dig. CDA 66401 [id.]. New Budapest Qt.

String quartets Nos. 3, 4 & 6, Op. 18/3, 4 & 6.
(Y/B) *** Hyperion Dig. CDA 66402 [id.]. New Budapest Qt.

String quartets Nos. 8–9 (Rasumovsky Nos. 2–3), Op. 59/2–3.
(Y/B) *** Hyperion Dig. CDA 66404 [id.]. New Budapest Qt.

String quartets Nos. 10 in E flat (Harp), Op. 74; 14 in C sharp min., Op. 131.
(Y/B) *** Hyperion Dig. CDA 66405 [id.]. New Budapest Qt.

String quartets Nos. 11 in F min., Op. 95; 15 in A min., Op. 132.
(Y/B) *** Hyperion Dig. CDA 66406 [id.]. New Budapest Qt.

String quartets Nos. 12 in E flat, Op. 127; 16 in F, Op. 135.
(Y/B) *** Hyperion Dig. CDA 66408 [id.]. New Budapest Qt.

String quartet No. 13 in B flat, Op. 130; Grosse Fuge, Op. 133.
(Y/B) *** Hyperion Dig. CDA 66407 [id.]. New Budapest Qt.

Generally speaking, the New Budapest Quartet produces fine results, not only in the Op. 127, which we much liked, but also in the companions in the series. Throughout the cycle their playing is distinguished by consistent (but not excessive) refinement of sonority, spot-on intonation, excellent ensemble and tonal blend. Their performances are never less than intelligent and are often touched by considerable insight. Given their first-class technical credentials and musicianship, as well as the excellence of the Hyperion recording, there is no justification for withholding a third star, except in the case of Op. 18/1–2 which are somewhat lacking in vitality. Yet the fact remains that the temptation to return to them for pleasure is not strong. Is it because they are somehow too clean and occasionally a shade characterless? They are certainly less searching than the Talich, the Lindsays, the Tokyo (in Opp. 18 and 59) – and, above all, the Végh. Recommendable, then, but not with the same enthusiasm as rival sets.

String quartets Nos. 1–6, Op. 18/1–6.
*** EMI Dig. CDS7 47127-8 [Ang. CDC 47126] (3). Alban Berg Qt.
(M) (***) Sony mono M2K 52531 (2) [id.]. Budapest Qt.
(M) **(*) Ph. 426 046-2 (3) [id.]. Italian Qt.

The Alban Berg's earlier set undoubtedly offers polish and tonal finesse. The playing is immaculate and the sound has all the usual advantages of the medium: excellent definition, presence and body. The CDs are also available separately (CDC7 47127/8/9-2).

The celebrated set by the Budapest Quartet first appeared in the UK on the Philips label in 1956. Unlike their 1960s re-make, which was pretty rough-and-ready, the sonority is perfectly focused and the readings have weight, animation and dedication. They have command of the music's architecture and of expressive detail that is captured in sound of outstanding fidelity, given the period. The Sony engineers have effected transfers of excellent quality which can hold their own against many later versions. These finely balanced and warmly musical readings are something special and not to be missed.

The Italian performances are in superb style. The only reservations concern Nos. 2 and 4: the latter is perhaps a little wanting in forward movement, while the conventional exchanges at the opening of No. 2 seem a shade too deliberate. The balance is truthful but the digital remastering does draw the ear to a certain thinness in the treble, slightly more noticeable in the earliest recordings.

String quartets Nos. 1–6, Op. 18/1–6; F (arr. of Piano sonata in E, Op. 14/1); (i) String quintet in C, Op. 29.
*** RCA Dig. 09026 61284-2 (3) [id.]. Tokyo Qt; (i) Zukerman.

There may be some quartet groups in the world that are as fine as the Tokyo, but one is hard pushed to think of one that is finer. They produce a sumptuous, beautifully blended sonority and play with impeccable ensemble; nor are they in any way wanting in musical insight. Their account of the Op. 18 *Quartets* is surely the best to have appeared for many years; it is more imaginative than the Talich, has greater finesse than the Lindsay and can match, though not surpass, the Végh in depth. First-movement exposition repeats are all observed. The three CDs offer an additional *bonne bouche* in the form of Beethoven's own transcription of the *E major Piano sonata* and the more substantial bonus of the *C major String quintet*, Op. 29, which at times almost seems to anticipate Schubert. There is plenty of space round the sound and a good back-to-front perspective. Among modern recordings this must now be a first recommendation.

String quartets Nos. 1–6, Op. 18/1–6; 10 in E flat (Harp), Op. 74; 11 in F min., Op. 95.
(Y/B) (M) *** ASV CDDDCS 305 (3) [id.]. Lindsay Qt.

It is good to have the Lindsay recordings now reissued at mid-price (retaining their old catalogue numbers). Their great merit in Beethoven lies in the natural expressiveness of their playing, most strikingly of all in slow movements, which brings a hushed inner quality too rarely caught on record.

The sense of spontaneity necessarily brings the obverse quality: these performances are not as precise as those in the finest rival sets; but there are few Beethoven quartet recordings that so convincingly bring out the humanity of the writing, its power to communicate. The recording of Op. 18, set against a fairly reverberant acoustic, is warm and realistic; the transfers reflect the fact that the recordings are more modern and rather fuller than the remastered Philips quality for the Italian group (see above).

String quartets Nos. 1–3, Op. 18/1–3.
*** Nimbus Dig. NI 5173 [id.]. Medici Qt.

The Medici are not a jet-set ensemble; their playing is refreshingly unglamorous and yet thoroughly polished; nor do they fail to penetrate the depths. They are given a very natural and well-balanced recording, and these performances will give considerable satisfaction.

String quartets Nos. 1 in F; 2 in G, Op. 18/1–2.
(BB) ** Naxos Dig. 8.550558 [id.]. Kodály Qt.

At super-bargain price, the Kodály Quartet deserve favourable consideration. They do not attempt to dress things up in the manner of jet-setting quartets and their readings of both *Quartets* are decent and straightforward, and free from idiosyncrasy. Tempi are well judged and the Naxos recordings are first rate.

String quartets Nos. 1 in F, Op. 18/1; 4 in C min., Op. 18/4; 6 in B flat, Op. 18/6.
(N) (M) **(*) Beethoven Edition DG Dig. 447 918-2 [id.]. Melos Qt.

The performances by the Melos Quartet offer a refined blend, impeccable intonation and superb ensemble. However, admiration rather than unalloyed pleasure is one's final reaction. Speeds are on the fast side, and too often this group does not convey a sufficient sense of pleasure in the courtly exchanges that take place among the four instruments, while at times their playing has an aggressive edge. There is, however, no question as to the finesse and mastery of the playing, nor the vividness of the recording.

(i) *String quartets Nos. 1 in F, Op. 18/1; 9 in C, Op. 59/3; 11 in F min., Op. 95; 12 in E flat, Op. 127; 14 in C sharp min., Op. 131; 15 in A min., Op. 132; 16 in F, Op. 135;* (ii) *Violin sonata No. 3 in E flat, Op. 12/3.*
(Y/B) ✲ (M) *** EMI mono CHS5 65308-2 (4) [id.]. (i) Busch Qt; (ii) Adolf Busch, Rudolf Serkin –
    SCHUBERT: *String quartet No. 8.* ***

Beethoven's greatest music, it is often rightly said, is better than any performance of it can ever be. Listening to the Busch Quartet's pre-war HMV accounts of the quartets, however, one is almost tempted to doubt this received wisdom. Certainly no group since has ever penetrated deeper into the heart of these scores. And one is also tempted to say that the (very occasional) technical imperfections (or frailties of intonation in Op. 132) are of greater musical interest than the meticulous perfection of most modern ensembles. In addition to the Beethoven quartets there is a bonus in the form of the *Violin sonata in E flat,* Op. 12, No. 3, from Busch and Serkin, playing of warmth and humanity, and a sparkling account of the early *B flat Quartet,* D.112, of Schubert. These are classics of the gramophone and not to be missed, and they are excellently remastered and transferred.

String quartets Nos. 1 in F, Op. 18/1; 14 in C sharp min., Op. 131.
(Y/B) *** Capriccio Dig. 10510 [id.]. Petersen Qt.

Quite easily the best account of the Op. 131 *Quartet* to have appeared in recent years. Both here and in the less successful *F major Quartet,* Op. 18, No. 1, the Petersen Quartet prove dedicated and character-ful. (The first movement is a bit rushed and the *Adagio* does not have the depth of the Végh, but it is still a very good performance.) For those who are unduly worried by the odd blemish in the Végh (or the leader's intakes of breath) or who do not care for the slightly dryish, bottom-heavy sound in the Talich, this could well be a satisfying alternative recommendation.

String quartets Nos. 3 in D; 4 in C min., Op. 18/3–4.
(N) (BB) ** Naxos Dig. 8.550559 [id.]. Kodály Qt.

These are acceptable performances which are perfectly good value for money. Taken in isolation, they are satisfactory without being in any way exceptional. They are to be preferred to many glossier alterna-tives at full price, and the recording quality is very good indeed. The *C minor Quartet* needs greater dramatic fire and urgency of pulse, but the *D major* has much to recommend it. Decent but undistinguished must be the verdict here.

String quartets Nos. 3 in D, Op. 18/3; 7 in F (Rasumovsky), Op. 59/1.
(Y/B) *** Channel Classics Dig. CCS 6094 [id.]. Orpheus Qt.

The Orpheus Quartet are first class in every way. Their account of the *First Rasumovsky quartet* is among the best to have appeared in recent years. This is real music-making: the finale of the *D major Quartet*, for example, is not rushed off its feet, as is so often the case nowadays; in short, this group are attuned to the sensibility of the period. This is very natural playing; much felt without being over-intense. The recording has clarity and presence.

String quartets Nos. 3 in D, Op. 18/3; 13 in B flat, Op. 130; Grosse Fuge, Op. 133.
(N) *(**) DG Dig. 449 404-2 [id.]. Emerson Qt.

In one sense the playing of the Emerson Quartet is in a class of its own. Few – if any – quartets on this planet can match their sheer perfection of ensemble, polish, power of attack and refinement of tonal shading. Their technical finish is incredible, amazing – indeed, awesome. The *Quartet in D major*, Op. 18, No. 3, offers many beauties – particularly the second movement. The allegro section of the *B flat*, Op. 130, is immaculate in its precision and dazzling in its unanimity. But the sheer thrust of this playing is less appropriate in music composed before the discovery of electricity, let alone jet propulsion. The second movement, which normally runs to about 2 minutes 8 seconds (Quartetto Italiano) or 2 minutes 12 seconds (Brandis) 'lifts off' at 1 minute 49 seconds. They do not give us the finale Beethoven substituted for the *Grosse Fuge*. Those who want high-powered, gleaming Beethoven will find much to please them, but others will find that the Emersons make only intermittent contact with this great music. The DG recording is marvellous; but we are well served for Beethoven *Quartet* cycles, and readers would do better to look elsewhere.

String quartets Nos. 4 in C min.; 5 in A, Op. 18/4–5.
(N) *(*) Telarc Dig. CD 80414 [id.]. Cleveland Qt.

The Cleveland Quartet possess impeccable technical address and it is difficult to flaw their playing or the quality of the Telarc recording. Their account of the *C minor Quartet* is much tauter than that of the Kodály and, as quartet playing, at an altogether higher level of finish and proficiency. Tempi are better judged, save for the *Minuet* of the *C minor*, which is absurdly rushed: the Clevelands get through it in 3 minutes 26 seconds, as opposed to the 4 minutes 28 seconds of the Végh or 4 minutes 41 seconds of the Kodály. The *A major* is the more enjoyable of the two performances, but again there is not a great deal of freshness or spontaneity. Only rarely does one feel any sense of deeper engagement.

String quartets Nos. 4 in C min., Op. 18/4; 10 in E flat (Harp), Op. 74; 14 in C sharp min., Op. 131.
(M) (***) Biddulph mono LAB 056-7 [id.]. Rosé Qt – BACH: *Double concerto* etc.

Music-making from another age and totally selfless. These performances bring us as close as we can possibly get to the kind of playing Brahms and Mahler would have heard. Indeed it is the sheer musical personality of the playing that is so refreshing after the relative anonymity we encounter so often today. The recordings were made in 1930 and 1932, while the *C sharp minor Quartet* dates from 1927, so allowance has to be made for pretty primitive sound.

String quartets Nos. 4 in C min., Op. 18/4; 15 in A min., Op. 132.
(N) *** Capriccio Dig. 10722 [id.]. Petersen Qt.

The Petersen Quartet here confirm the positive impression made by their first Beethoven recording (Opp. 18/1 and 131). The *Heiliger Dankgesang* inspires playing of real depth and, though they press ahead very slightly at one or two points (at the reprise of the main section of Op. 132/II and at the return of the theme in the finale), these are minor points. These are very fine peformances which can be recommended with confidence.

String quartets Nos. 5 in A; 6 in B flat, Op. 18/5 & 6.
(N) (BB) ** Naxos 8.550560 [id.]. Kodály Qt.

As with the earlier recordings in their series, this Naxos coupling is well played but not well enough to displace such distinguished accounts as the Quartetto Italiano or the Tokyo. The recording is eminently acceptable, but for Beethoven only the best is good enough.

String quartets Nos. 7 in F; 8 in E min.; 9 in C (Rasumovsky), Op. 59/1–3.
(Y/B) (M) *** ASV Dig. CDDCS 207 (2) [id.]. Lindsay Qt.

The Lindsay set contains performances of real stature; and though they are not unrivalled in some of their insights, among modern recordings they are not often surpassed. As a recording, this set is comparable with most of its competitors and superior to many; artistically, it can hold its own with the best. They are now reissued in a box, retaining the old catalogue number, but with further reduction to mid-price.

String quartets Nos. 7–9 (Rasumovsky Nos. 1–3), Op. 59/1–3; 10 in E flat (Harp), Op. 74; 11 in F min., Op. 95.
*** RCA Dig. R D 60462 (3) [60462-2-RC]. Tokyo Qt.
(M) *** Ph. 420 797-2 (3) [id.]. Italian Qt.

The Tokyo Quartet's account of *No. 7 in F major* is one of the very finest in the catalogue. The tempi throughout are splendidly judged and the performance as a whole is beautifully proportioned. There is, however, some minor cause for reservation in Op. 59, No. 3. The fugal finale is rather too headlong in pace and there are some traces of slickness elsewhere. But for the most part this is a powerful set and its strengths far outweigh its weaknesses. The account of the *F minor*, Op. 95, is appropriately taut and concentrated. The recording is excellent, rich in sonority yet completely truthful and unglamorized.

The remastered Italian set still sounds well: there is now only a slight thinness on top to betray their age, with no lack of body and warmth in the middle range. Their superiority in terms of sheer quartet playing is still striking: purity of intonation, perfectly blended tone and superb ensemble and attack. Their tempi are perfectly judged and every phrase is sensitively shaped, and these performances remain very recommendable at mid-price.

String quartets Nos. 7 in F, Op. 59/1; 9 in C, Op. 59/3 (Rasumovsky Nos. 1 & 3).
**(*) Nimbus Dig. NI 5382 [id.]. Brandis Qt.

There is much to admire in the Brandis Quartet's account of the *F major* and *C major Rasumovsky Quartets*; they are distinguished by musical phrasing, good ensemble and tonal blend, well-judged tempi and a feeling for the architecture of each piece. They are very well played indeed and are refreshingly unconcerned with outward show; yet their virtuosity in, say, the fugal finale of Op. 59/3 is not in question. The recording is acceptable but not worthy of a three-star grading; the sound is a bit hard.

String quartets Nos. 7 in F (Rasumovsky), Op. 59/1; 10 in E flat (Harp), Op. 74.
(N) (M) *** Beethoven Edition DG 447 919-2 [id.]. Amadeus Qt.

The recording of Op. 59/1 is taken from the first *Rasumovsky* set to be issued in stereo, in 1960. The four instruments of the quartet are perfectly balanced and the stereo is warm yet remarkably clear. The *F major Quartet*, a tough nut to crack both technically and from the interpretative angle, comes off very successfully, not least because of the players' attention to Beethoven's dynamic and other markings. The *Adagio* brings considerable concentration and characteristically fine tonal matching. The *Harp quartet* benefits from similarly lively, sensitive and deeply musical playing, which makes it really come out of its shell; again the sound is remarkably present and well integrated. Although not all will take to Norbert Brainin's vibrato in the slow movement, the closing *Allegretto* with variations shows this ensemble playing with extraordinary unanimity and much vigour. This is one of the very finest of the Amadeus's early stereo records and can be recommended to all their admirers.

String quartet No. 7 in F (Rasumovsky), Op. 59/1; (ii) Violin sonata No. 9 in A (Kreutzer), Op. 47.
(Y/B) (B) **(*) DG 439 453-2 [id.]. (i) Amadeus Qt; (ii) Sir Yehudi Menuhin, Wilhelm Kempff.

An unusual coupling that might well appeal to impecunious collectors. There is some splendid playing from the Amadeus in the *First Rasumovsky Quartet*. Perhaps they do not uncover all its secrets, but the self-assurance and polish of the playing does not mean that the *Adagio* is unfeeling. The 1959 recording sounds well (with a touch of thinness on top), and the same comment might apply to the 1970 *Kreutzer Sonata*, although the sound is obviously more modern. Here the Kempff/Menuhin partnership is unique. In many ways it is not as immaculate as earlier accounts, but the spontaneous imagination of the playing, the challenging between great artists on the same wavelength, is consistently present.

String quartet No. 10 in E flat (Harp), Op. 74.
(B) **(*) Discover Dig. D I C D 920171 [id.]. Sharon Qt – MOZART: *Quartet No. 1; ****; RAVEL: *Quartet.* **(*)

The Sharon Quartet give a remarkably enjoyable account of the the *Harp Quartet*, expressive and sensitive in the *Adagio* and perceptive in the closing *Allegretto con variazioni*. They are recorded in a Cologne church, which means that the sound is a shade reverberant (the Scherzo is affected most), but the blend is attractively full and it would be carping to complain when the playing is so well matched and responsive and gives the impression of a real performance.

String quartets Nos. 12 in E flat, Op. 127; 13 in B flat, Op. 130; 14 in C sharp min., Op. 131; 15 in A min., Op. 132; 16 in F, Op. 135.
**(*) RCA Dig. R D 60975 (3) [09026 60975-2]. Tokyo Qt.

String quartets Nos. 12–16; Grosse Fuge in B flat, Op. 133.
(Y/B) (M) *** ASV Dig. CDDCS 403 (4) [id.]. Lindsay Qt.
(M) **(*) Ph. 426 050-2 (4) [id.]. Italian Qt.

The Lindsays get far closer to the essence of this great music than most of their rivals. They have the benefit of very well-balanced recording; the sound of the ASV set is admirably present. They seem to find tempi that somehow strike the listener as completely right and which enable them to convey so much of both the letter and the spirit of the music. They bring much rich musical characterization and musical strength. Taken overall, these are among the very finest versions to have been made in recent years. They now reappear, their catalogue number unchanged, but at mid-price – excellent value.

The merits of the Italian Quartet's performances are considerable. The sonority that they produce is beautifully blended and splendidly focused. They do not sound as sumptuous as some modern quartet recordings and their reissue on four instead of three medium-price CDs is less competitive than it might be. However, for many the Italians' searching and thoughtful interpretations will ultimately prove most satisfying.

The Tokyo Quartet play marvellously and on that score are a joy to listen to. Even if they do not displace earlier recommendations (Lindsay, Végh, Quartetto Italiano, etc.), they are well worth considering as an alternative. They are superbly recorded and, although they are just too beautiful at times to be ideal in this great music, they have obviously thought long and hard about it.

String quartets Nos. 13 in B flat, Op. 130; 16 in F, Op. 135; Grosse Fuge in B flat, Op. 133.
(N) (M) ** Beethoven Edition DG 447 920-2 [id.]. Amadeus Qt.

The Amadeus provide refined performances, and there is much subtle playing here of a very high technical standard. The refinement does not prevent vigour when needed, and the performance of the *Grosse Fuge* may surprise some with the strength of the Amadeus attack. But in the last analysis the performances suffer from a lack of the 'inner' quality which should make both slow movements into experiences beyond anything else in music. Not one of the *Adagios* is taken quite slowly enough, and the great *Cavatina* of Op. 130 sounds almost casual at a swinging *Andante*. The recording sounds very fresh and vivid.

String quartet No. 13 in B flat, Op. 130; Grosse Fuge in B flat, Op. 133.
*** ASV CDDCA 602 [id.]. Lindsay Qt.
(N) **(*) Nimbus Dig. NI 5465 [id.]. Brandis Qt.

The Lindsay's account of Op. 130 includes both the *Grosse Fuge* as an ending and also the finale Beethoven substituted, so that listeners can choose for themselves.

The Brandis also offer both finales to this great quartet. Theirs is a decent performance, free from the razzle-dazzle of the Emersons and infinitely more humane in its musical approach. Tempi are well judged and the performances are completely musical, refreshingly selfless and thoroughly recommendable. The Nimbus recording is eminently satisfactory.

String quartet No. 14 in C sharp min., Op. 131.
*** ASV CDDCA 603 [id.]. Lindsay Qt.

The Lindsay's account of Op. 131 is as fine as any in the catalogue.

String quartets No. 14 in C sharp min., Op. 131; 16 in F, Op. 135 (versions for string orchestra).
*** DG Dig.435 779-2 [id.]. VPO, Bernstein.

Not long before he died, Bernstein nominated his string-orchestra version of Op. 131 as his personal favourite among his own recordings. Basing the adaptation on one prepared by his mentor, Dmitri Mitropoulos, he draws dedicated playing from the Vienna Philharmonic, finding a concentration and an inner quality too often missing in recordings by four players alone. The CD version adds a similar string version of Op. 135, a work which Toscanini presented in this form a generation earlier.

String trios Nos. 1 in E flat, Op. 3; 2 in G; 3 in D; 4 in C min., Op. 9/1–3; Serenade in D (for string trio), Op. 8.
** EMI Dig. CDS7 54198-2 (2) [id.]. Perlman, Zukerman, Harrell.

String trio No. 1 in E flat, Op. 3; Serenade in D, Op. 8.
(N) (M) *** Unicorn Dig. UKCD 2081 [id.]. Cummings Trio.

String trios Nos. 2 in G; 3 in D; 4 in C min., Op. 9/1–3.
(N) (M) *** Unicorn Dig. UKCD 2082 [id.]. Cummings Trio.

The playing of the Cummings Trio is cultured but not over-civilized; there is an unforced naturalness about it all. These players let Beethoven speak for himself, and in quieter moments there is a winning sense of repose; in short, this is real chamber-music-making, with excellent recording – in the demonstration class. Now at mid-price, it will be difficult to surpass this set.

The Perlman–Zukerman–Harrell performances were recorded at public performances in New York in 1989 and 1990. No one could complain that this distinguished trio do not bring zest in plenty to their music-making, though subtlety is not always in strong supply. Dynamic markings tend to be strongly contrasted, yet the performances are in other respects surprisingly routine and they are undoubtedly handicapped by the very close balance chosen by their engineers (doubtless to minimize extraneous audience-noise), which does not flatter the tone of any of the artists and which lends them an edge which would not be apparent were the listener more discreetly placed. To be frank, these performances fail to yield compellingly positive musical results.

VIOLIN SONATAS
Clara Haskil: The Legacy, Volume 1: Chamber music

Violin sonatas Nos. 1–10.
(Y/B) (M) (***) Ph. mono 442 625-2 (5) [id.]. Arthur Grumiaux, Clara Haskil – MOZART: *Violin sonatas.* (***)

Violin sonatas Nos. 1 in D; 2 in A; 3 in E flat, Op. 12/1–3; 4 in A min., Op. 23.
(Y/B) (M) (***) Ph. mono 442 626-2. Arthur Grumiaux, Clara Haskil.

Violin sonatas Nos. 5 in F (Spring), Op. 24; 6 in A; 7 in C min., Op. 30/1–2.
(Y/B) (M) (***) Ph. mono 442 627-2. Arthur Grumiaux, Clara Haskil.

Violin sonatas Nos. 8 in G, Op. 30/3; 9 in A (Kreutzer), Op. 47; 10 in G, Op. 96.
(Y/B) (M) (***) Ph. mono 442 628-2. Arthur Grumiaux, Clara Haskil.

Arthur Grumiaux and Clara Haskil made their celebrated recordings in 1956–7 and these versions sound remarkably well for their age. The performances are wonderfully civilized and aristocratic, and no one investing in them will regret it. They accommodate all ten *Sonatas* on three CDs at mid-price, as opposed to the four of Perlman and Ashkenazy, but they come in harness with two further CDs (equally desirable) of Mozart's mature *Violin sonatas*, as part of the 'Clara Haskil Legacy'. The discs are not at present available separately.

Violin sonatas Nos. 1–10.
(N) *** DG Dig. 447 058-2 (3) [id.]. Gidon Kremer, Martha Argerich.

Violin sonatas Nos. 1 in D; 2 in A; 3 in E flat, Op. 12/1–3.
*** DG Dig. 415 138-2 [id.]. Kremer, Argerich.

Violin sonatas No. 9 (Kreutzer); 10 in G, Op. 96.
(N) *** DG Dig. 447 054-2; *447 054-4* (from above). Kremer, Argerich.
(M) *** Decca 421 453-2 (4); 436 892-2 (*Nos. 1–3*), 436 893-2 (*Nos. 4–5*), 436 894-2 (*Nos. 6–8*), 436 895-2 (*Nos. 9–10*). Itzhak Perlman, Vladimir Ashkenazy.

(i) *Violin sonatas Nos. 1 in D; 2 in A; 3 in E flat, Op. 12/1–3; 4 in A min., Op. 23; 5 in F (Spring), Op. 24;* (ii) *Romances for violin and orchestra Nos. 1–2, Opp. 40 & 50.*
(N) (B) *** Ph. Duo 446 521-2 (2) [id.]. Henryk Szeryng; (i) Ingrid Haebler; (ii) Concg. O, Haitink.

Violin sonatas Nos. 6 in A; 7 in C min.; 8 in G, Op. 30/1–3; 9 in A (Kreutzer); 10 in G, Op. 96.
(N) (B) *** Ph. Duo 446 524-2 (2) [id.]. Henryk Szeryng, Ingrid Haebler.

Having two such volatile artists as Kremer and Argerich in partnership for the Beethoven *Violin sonatas* makes for exciting, heart-warming results. Perlman and Ashkenazy may be more centrally recommendable for being just as communicative and less idiosyncratic, but Kremer and Argerich have one magnetized from first to last by their individuality in performances that consistently sound spontaneous and fresh. So the three early sonatas of Opus 12, taken at high speed with wonderfully clean piano articulation, have rare sparkle and wit, and the openings of both the *Spring Sonata* and the *Kreutzer*, less plain than usual, convey a thoughtfulness that looks forward to the last, most enigmatic of the sonatas, *No. 10 in G*. Later in the *Kreutzer* too, there is an improvisatory feeling, with each artist challenging the other in bravura and flair. The performance is crowned by a dashing and light account of the tarantella finale which, so far from sounding rushed, is exhilaratingly joyful. As to the *G major Sonata*, the contrasts of mood are vividly caught, with rapt mystery at the very start giving way to lightness and point in the dotted rhythms of the second theme. That is typical, and the recorded sound, well balanced, adds to one's impression of overhearing two artists simply enjoying themselves in revealing Beethoven. Note that all ten sonatas are squeezed on to only three discs.

Perlman and Ashkenazy's set of the *Violin sonatas*, now reissued on four mid-priced CDs, will be difficult to surpass. These performances offer a blend of classical purity and spontaneous vitality that it is hard to resist; moreover the realism and presence of the recording in its CD format are very striking. They are also now available on four separate mid-priced CDs.

Szeryng and Haebler made their recordings between January 1978 and December 1979, with the *Kreutzer* saved until the end of the cycle. Philips used a favourite venue, La Chaux-de-Fonds in Switzerland; with clear CD transfers, the effect is very realistic and the balance impressive. Szeryng's timbre is small and thin, much less ample than Perlman's, yet firmly focused, with the recording slightly more flattering in the later sonatas. There is always a poised line and a natural warmth in his phrasing of slow movements, and allegros often gain from this relative lack of opulence. For example, the delightfully whimsical playing in the first movement of the *Second Sonata* of the Opus 12 set is captivating, as is the finale, which dances with chimerical grace. Haebler's lilt again adds to one's pleasure in the delightful *Andante scherzoso* of Op. 23, while her natural pacing and nobility of line draw the listener right into the *Adagio* of the *Spring Sonata*, a performance which is every bit as fresh as its title suggests. Throughout, her superbly eloquent playing makes an artistic bedrock over which Szering weaves his spell, and in the earlier sonatas Beethoven's designation that they are for piano and violin is the more apparent. Yet the violin is not dwarfed and in the later works assumes increasing dominance. The *Allegretto con variazioni* finale of Op. 30/1 is another highlight, as is the glorious slow movement of the *C minor*, Op. 30/2. Perhaps the first movement of the *Kreutzer* ideally requires a richer timbre from the violin, but the central variations are most satisfying, and the dancing finale is as light as quicksilver. The final *G major Sonata*, with its gently persuasive opening, does not disappoint either; again the finesse of Szeryng's light bowing draws a magical response from the pianist; the lovely *Adagio espressivo* is truly memorable and the *Poco allegro* finale full of graceful charm. Haebler surely has never played with more obvious distinction or greater spontaneity on record, and the recording is fully worthy of her range of pianistic colour. With the two *Romances for violin and orchestra* thrown in for good measure, this pair of Duos, taken together, make a very good bargain and, while the Perlman/Ashkenazy Decca set remains a primary recommendation for these sonatas, the inspiration of the Szeryng/Haebler partnership is very cherishable.

Violin sonatas Nos. 1 in D; 2 in A; 3 in E flat, Op. 12/1–3.
(BB) *** Naxos Dig. 8.550284 [id.]. Takako Nishizaki, Jenö Jandó.

Violin sonatas No. 4 in A min., Op. 23; 10 in G, Op. 96; 12 variations on Mozart's 'Se vuol ballare' from 'Le nozze di Figaro', WoO 40.
(BB) *** Naxos Dig. 8.550285 [id.]. Takako Nishizaki, Jenö Jandó.

Naxos are on to a winning combination here. These performances are wonderfully fresh and alive. Takako Nishizaki isn't a 'big' player but her timbre is admirably suited to Beethoven and she is clearly in complete rapport with Jandó, who is in excellent form. The *Mozart variations*, too, are winningly done. The recording is most naturally balanced, the acoustic is spacious without in any way clouding the focus.

Violin sonatas Nos. 5 in F (Spring), Op. 24; 7 in C min., Op. 30/2.
(M) (***) EMI CDH7 63494-2. Adolf Busch, Rudolf Serkin (with BACH: *Violin partita No. 2* (***)).

Music-making from another age, unhurried, humane and of supreme integrity. Playing of such naturalness and artistry transcends the inevitable sonic limitations.

Violin sonatas Nos. 5 in F (Spring); 8 in G, Op. 30/3; 9 in A (Kreutzer).
(M) *** EMI CDM7 64631-2 [id.]. Pinchas Zukerman, Daniel Barenboim.
(M) ** RCA 09026 61861-2 [id.]. Henryk Szeryng, Artur Rubinstein.

The Zukerman/Barenboim 1973 coupling of the *Spring* and *Kreutzer sonatas*, long a favourite recommendation, is made even more attractive by the inclusion of the *G major Sonata*, Op. 30/3, an equally memorable work, when the playing is just as disarmingly spontaneous. The CD transfer scarcely betrays its age.

The Szeryng/Rubinstein account of *No. 8 in G* is a particularly fine one and the 1961 recording, although dry, is quite full. The *Spring* and *Kreutzer sonatas* date from 1958, and the microphones are less flattering to Szeryng's timbre, which sounds slightly wiry. The *Spring sonata* is effective enough, but the *Kreutzer* is the least penetrating of the three performances.

Violin sonatas Nos. 5 in F (Spring), Op. 24; 9 in A (Kreutzer), Op. 47.
(BB) *** Naxos Dig. 8.550283; 4550283 [id.]. Takako Nishizaki, Jenö Jandó.
**(*) RCA Dig. 09026 61561-2 [id.]. Pinchas Zukerman, Marc Neikrug.

Takako Nishizaki does not produce a large sound but the balance with Jandó is expertly managed, and the result is very natural and real. The performances are delightful in their fresh spontaneity. This is a bargain.

The partnership of Zukerman and Neikrug produces enjoyable but not distinctive performances. Mostly the playing is fresh and committed, but there are other even more spontaneous versions of these two favourite works. The artists have good presence, but at times the balance is not wholly natural.

Violin sonatas Nos. 6 in A; 7 in C min.; 8 in G, Op. 30/1–3.
(BB) *** Naxos Dig. 8.550286; *4.550286* [id.]. Takako Nishizaki, Jenö Jandó.

All three of the Op. 30 *Sonatas* on one CD represents very good value for money, particularly as the playing is of considerable quality.

Wind music

(Wind) *Octet in E flat, Op. 103; Quintet in E flat for oboe, 3 horns & bassoon; Rondino in E flat for wind octet, WoO 25; Sextet in E flat, Op. 71.*
*** ASV Dig. CDCOE 807 [id.]. Wind Soloists of COE.

The wind soloists of the Chamber Orchestra of Europe give strong and stylish performances of this collection of Beethoven's wind music, marked by some outstanding solo work, notably from the first oboe, Douglas Boyd. They are recorded in warm but clear sound, with good presence.

SOLO PIANO MUSIC

Piano sonatas Nos. 1–32 (complete).
(Y/B) *** Elektra Nonesuch/Warner Dig. 7559 79328-2 (10). Richard Goode.
(N) ✿ (B) (***) DG mono 447 966-2 (8) [id.]. Wilhelm Kempff.
(B) *** DG 429 306-2 (9) [id.]. Wilhelm Kempff.
(B) *** EMI CZS7 62863-2 (10). Daniel Barenboim.
(Y/B) (B) *** Decca 443 706-2 (10) [id.] (with *Andanti favori*). Vladimir Ashkenazy.
✿ (M) (***) EMI mono CHS7 63765-2 (8) [Ang. CDHH 3765]. Artur Schnabel.
(M) **(*) Decca 433 882-2 (8). Wilhelm Backhaus.

Piano sonatas Nos. 1–32; 6 Variations in F, Op. 43; Variations and fugue in E flat on a theme from Prometheus (Eroica), Op. 35; 32 Variations in C min., WoO 80.
(M) *** Ph. 432 301-2 (11) [id.]. Claudio Arrau.

In America, Goode has often been likened to Schnabel or Serkin, rugged Beethovenians, but that is misleading. It is not just the power of Goode's playing that singles him out, but the beauty, when he has such subtle control over a formidably wide tonal and dynamic range. Even at its weightiest, the sound is never clangorous. Particularly in the early sonatas Goode brings out the wit and parody, while slow movements regularly draw sensuously velvety legato. Helped by an unusually full and clear recording, with no haze of reverberation, the clarity of his articulation is breathtaking, as in the running semi-quavers of the finale of the *Appassionata sonata*. Above all, Goode has a natural gravity which compels attention. One has to go back to the pre-digital era to find a Beethoven cycle of comparable command and intensity – to the earlier of Barenboim's two cycles on EMI, daringly spacious in its speeds, or to the jewelled clarity of Wilhelm Kempff. We feel this is now a clear first choice for those wanting a modern digital cycle.

In celebration of the centenary in November 1995 of the birth of Wilhelm Kempff, most inspirational of Beethoven pianists, DG have issued this welcome bargain box of the earlier of his two Beethoven sonata cycles. Those who have cherished the later, stereo cycle for its magical spontaneity will find Kempff's qualities even more intensely conveyed in this mono set, recorded between 1951 and 1956. The interpretations are the more personal, the more individual, at times the more wilful; but for any listener who responds to Kempff's visionary concentration, it is a magical series of interpretations. No other set of the sonatas so clearly gives the impression of new discovery, of fresh inspiration in the composer as a pianist. Amazingly, the sound has more body and warmth than the stereo set, with Kempff's unmatched transparency and clarity of articulation even more vividly caught, both in sparkling allegros and in deeply dedicated slow movements. A ninth disc comes free, celebrating Kempff's achievement in words and music, on the organ in Bach, on the piano in Brahms, Chopin and Beethoven (a masterly pre-war recording of the *Pathétique sonata*) and accompanying Fischer-Dieskau in four of his own songs. The discs are engagingly packaged with a portrait of Kempff on each CD jacket, although the documentation is not as lavish as when these recordings last appeared on LP in 1980 to celebrate Kempff's eighty-fifth birthday. It is worth recalling what the great pianist wrote for the booklet offered with those LPs: 'No finer 85th-birthday present could have been given to me. Not only I, but thus also listeners, have the opportunity to delve into my musical biography. For undoubtedly between the mono recordings and the stereo records which I made much later there lay changes in my own artistic viewpoint. It will be fascinating to pinpoint the differences. I should however like to emphasize that to me interpretation has always centred upon a creative or, more correctly, a post-creative element. It was so then as in later years – and it is still so today.'

Kempff's stereo recordings, all dating from 1964/5, are to the 1960s what Schnabel's were to the pre-war years – performances that represent a yardstick by which all others are judged. Kempff's shading of pianistic colour is so imaginative that the ear readily accommodates any slight dryness in the upper range. The interpretations have a commanding stature, yet Kempff brings his own individuality to every bar and a clarity and sparkle that make you want to go on listening.

Barenboim's earlier set of the Beethoven *Sonatas*, recorded for EMI when he was in his late twenties, remains one of his very finest achievements on record. The readings are sometimes idiosyncratic, with unexpected tempi both fast and slow, but the spontaneous style is unfailingly compelling. At times Barenboim's way is mercurial, with an element of fantasy. But overall this is a keenly thoughtful musician living through Beethoven's great piano cycle with an individuality that puts him in the line of master pianists.

Decca have now reissued Ashkenazy's set which occupied him over a decade from 1971 until 1980, with the *Andante favori* added on as an encore in 1981. He brings to the early sonatas the concentrated, unaffected qualities which make his recordings of the *Violin sonatas* with Perlman so eminently compelling. Interpretatively the manner is strong and direct, rightly treating the young Beethoven as a fully mature composer, no imitator of Haydn and Mozart; but the important point is that, whether in fast music or slow, he conveys the feeling of new discovery and ready communication. He is also especially persuasive in the two Op. 14 sonatas (Nos. 9 and 10). Among the famous named sonatas, there is much to admire in the *Moonlight* and, if his *Pathétique* is perhaps understated for so youthfully ebullient a work, the finale, unusually gentle, conveys the underlying power. He gives a deeply satisfying reading of the *Waldstein sonata*, where the degree of restraint, the occasional hesitations, intensify his thoughtful approach, never interrupting the broader span of the argument. The Op. 31 *D minor Sonata*, nicknamed *Tempest*, and its companion in E flat, Op. 31/3, are among the best of his cycle. He brings concentration of mind, together with a spontaneity of feeling, that illumines both works. The command of keyboard colour is as always impressive and, in terms of both dramatic tension and the sense of architecture, these are thoroughly satisfying performances. His readings of the middle-period sonatas are as masterly and penetrating as anything he has given us, and he is pretty impressive in the late sonatas. There is a rapt sense of repose in the slow movement of Op. 109 (*No. 30 in E major*) and the last two sonatas are played with a depth and spontaneity which put these readings among the finest available. However, the *Hammerklavier*, one of the last to be recorded, is not quite on this level. Curiously, it is coupled with the more *Andante favori* (which comes first on the CD). The performance of the sonata is fresher and more spontaneous-sounding than in his earlier Decca version, not quite so immaculate in the playing, but still strong and direct, with power and speed in the outer movements; but the total experience is less than monumental. Overall the sound is excellent, vivid and present, if not always quite as full and natural as Barenboim's alternative and highly recommendable bargain-priced EMI set.

Arrau's Beethoven cycle, recorded during the 1960s, is a survey of extreme distinction. The great Chilean pianist possessed a quite distinctive keyboard sonority, rich and aristocratic in its finesse. The late sonatas show his artistry at its most consummate: one of the very finest of these performances (and one of the very finest records he ever made) is his *Hammerklavier*, which represents his art at its most fully realized. No apologies need be made for the recordings, which belie their age.

For many music-lovers and record collectors of an older generation, Schnabel was the voice of Beethoven; returning to this pioneering set again, one realizes that his insights were deeper than those of almost anyone who followed him, though his pianism has been surpassed. This is one of the towering classics of the gramophone and, whatever other individual Beethoven sonatas you may have, this is an indispensable reference point.

Backhaus recorded his survey over a decade, from 1958 to 1969 (with the exception of the *Hammerklavier*, which came much earlier, in 1953, and is mono). As it happens, the latter represents the peak of the cycle, offering playing of great power and concentration. Backhaus's direct, sometimes brusque manner does not derive from any lack of feeling, rather from a determination to present Beethoven's thoughts adorned with no idiosyncratic excrescences. At his best, as in the *Waldstein* and *Appassionata sonatas*, the performances present a characteristic mixture of rugged spontaneity and wilfulness which can be remarkably compelling. But there are many other examples of his positive, alert and imaginative response which balance the apparently uncompromising wilfulness of manner. He was less suited to the more lightweight works, yet even here he plainly enjoyed himself in his own way, so that his own responses are conveyed to the listener. Generally – as with the *Hammerklavier* – the bigger the challenge for him, the more impressive the performance. His massive, rather gruff style naturally suits the later rather than the earlier sonatas, but even in Op. 101, where the challenge is greatest, the uningratiating manner will not suit all tastes, and the very powerful accounts of Op. 109 and Op. 111 do not always leave the music quite enough space to breathe. But overall the set is a formidable achievement and a reminder of a keyboard giant. The recording is remarkably faithful; the only real drawback is that the close balance brings a comparative lack of dynamic range.

Piano sonatas Nos. 1 in F min.; 2 in A; 3 in C, Op. 2/1–3.
(N) *** Sony Dig. SK 64397 [id.]. Murray Perahia.
*** Chandos Dig. CHAN 9212 [id.]. Louis Lortie.
(BB) **(*) Naxos Dig. 8.550150; *4550150* [id.]. Jenö Jandó.

As his accounts of the concertos have shown, Murray Perahia is as authoritative and sensitive an interpreter of Beethoven as he is of Mozart. These are commanding accounts of the greatest elegance and freshness. The *C major Sonata* recalls the classic Solomon account and, along with the Gilels on DG, is arguably the best we have had since the days of Kempff.

Louis Lortie has the benefit of an immediate and truthful recording, made at The Maltings, Snape, which greatly enhances the satisfaction his playing gives. He brings his usual refined musical intelligence to all three of the Op. 2 *Sonatas* and gives ample evidence of his instinctive musicianship and artistry. Lortie sustains momentum throughout and characterizes each phrase with a real sense of the music's meaning.

Jenö Jandó's complete recording of the Beethoven *Piano sonatas* is also available in two flimsy slip-cases, each comprising five CDs (8.505002 and 8.505003). This first CD (actually Volume 3) establishes Jandó's credentials as a strong, unidiosyncratic Beethovenian. If there is not the individuality of a Kempff or a Barenboim, the playing is always direct and satisfying. The piano sound is real, full and bold.

Piano sonatas Nos. 1 in F min.; 2 in A, Op. 2/1–2; 19 in G min.; 20 in G, Op. 49/1–2.
(BB) **(*) ASV CDQS 6055. John Lill.

This first record of John Lill's cycle offers some of the most characteristic performances in the series. There is a directness of utterance about Lill's Beethoven which is undoubtedly compulsive, particularly as the recording has great presence and the tone is admirably secure and realistic. Lill brings a formidable technique to all these sonatas and his deliberation at the opening of the *F minor Sonata* (No. 1) gives the first movement great character. The slow movement too is eloquently played, and the *Largo appassionato* of No. 2 also makes a strong impression, though some will feel that the fortissimo outbursts are over-characterized.The closing Rondo (*Grazioso*), however, lilts appealingly. As he shows in the two Opus 49 *Sonatas*, Lill is not strong on charm, yet there is an appealing simplicity and a strong profile. Moreover, there is an integrity about this playing that the listener cannot fail to notice.

Piano sonatas Nos. 4 in E flat, Op. 7; 13 in E flat, Op. 27/1; 19 in G min., 20 in G, Op. 49/1–2; 22 in F, Op. 54.
(BB) **(*) Naxos Dig. 8.550167; *4550167* [id.]. Jenö Jandó.

The performances of both the *E flat Sonata*, Op. 7, and the *Sonata quasi una fantasia*, Op. 27/1, in which Jandó is totally responsive to Beethoven's wide expressive range, show the continuing excellence of this series, and the three shorter works are also freshly presented.

Piano sonatas Nos. 5 in C min.; 6 in F; 7 in D, Op. 10/1–3.
(BB) *(*) ASV CDQS 6057 [id.]. John Lill.

These are among the more disappointing of Lill's sonata readings, rather square and charmless. The great D major slow movement of Op. 10/3 is taken challengingly slowly, but there is little feeling of flow. Bright, realistic, well-focused recording.

Piano sonatas Nos. 5 in C min.; 6 in F; 7 in D, Op. 10/1–3; 25 in G, Op. 79.
(BB) *** Naxos Dig. 8.550161; *4.550161* [id.]. Jenö Jandó.

The three splendid Op. 10 *Sonatas* show Jandó at his most perceptive and unselfconscious.

Piano sonatas Nos. 5 in C min.; 10 in G, Op. 14/2; 19 in G min.; 20 in G, Op. 49/1–2.
**(*) DG Dig. 419 172-2 [id.]. Emil Gilels.

Gilels manages to make one believe that his is exactly the *tempo giusto* even when one feels tempted to question the very deliberate speed he adopts in the slow movement of the *C minor*, Op. 10, No. 1. Such is his magic that, while under his spell, doubts are silenced. He is well recorded, too.

Piano sonatas Nos. 7 in D, Op. 10/3; 9 in E, Op. 14/1; 30 in E, Op. 109; 31 in A flat, Op. 110.
(N) *** EMI Dig. CDC5 55290-2 [id.]. Awadagin Pratt.

Born in Pittsburgh, Awadagin Pratt looks set to become the first black American pianist to establish an international reputation in classical music, rather than in the fields of jazz or the popular repertoire. These early sonatas have the flow and spontaneity of a natural Beethovenian: Op. 10/3 is a particularly appealing performance. He is hardly less impressive in the two late sonatas, with the *Theme and variations* which ends Op. 109 both moving and penetrating and the finale of Op. 110 conveying a similar concentration, with an impulsively individual close. Pratt is beautifully recorded, and this recital is both rewarding and stimulating.

Piano sonatas Nos. 7 in D, Op. 10/3; 18 in E flat, Op. 31/3; 15 Variations and fugue on a theme from Prometheus (Eroica variations), Op. 35.
*** DG 423 136-2 [id.]. Emil Gilels.

Gilels's account of the *Eroica variations* is masterly. In the *D major Sonata* he is hardly less impressive, though there are odd mannerisms. Op. 31, No. 3 is distinguished, too, though the recording acoustic is somewhat drier than that of its companions.

Piano sonatas Nos. 7 in D; 23 in F min. (Appassionata), Op. 57.
(Y/B) (M) *** Sony Dig. SMK 39344 [id.]. Murray Perahia.

Intense, vibrant playing from Perahia in the *D major Sonata*, with great range of colour and depth of thought, and the *Appassionata* is a performance of comparable stature. These are among the few interpretations to have appeared in recent years that can be recommended alongside Gilels. The recorded sound is truthful, and this issue is made even more attractive by being offered at mid-price.

Piano sonatas Nos. 8 (Pathétique), Op. 13; 13; 14 (Moonlight), Op. 27/1–2.
**(*) DG Dig. 400 036-2 [id.]. Emil Gilels.

Gilels's opening movement of the *E flat Sonata* is strangely reserved, as if he feared the charge of self-indulgence or out-of-period sentiment. However, such are the strengths of this playing that few will quarrel with the magnificence of his conceptions of all three pieces. The digital recording is lifelike, although the balance is very close.

Piano sonatas Nos. 8 (Pathétique), Op. 13; 14 (Moonlight), Op. 27/2; 15 (Pastoral), Op. 28; 17 (Tempest), Op. 31/2; 21 (Waldstein), Op. 53; 23 (Appassionata), Op. 57; 26 (Les Adieux), Op. 81a.
(B) *** Ph. Duo 438 730-2 [id.]. Alfred Brendel.

In offering seven of Beethoven's most popular named sonatas, this Duo set – two discs for the price of one – is in every way an outstanding bargain, well worth having even if duplication is involved. All the performances are undeniably impressive and the recording consistently excellent. The *Tempest*, Op. 31/2, is finely conceived and thoroughly compelling, and the central movements of the *Pastoral* resonate in the memory, the performance radiant and beautifully shaped, with every detail fitting in harmoniously with the artist's conception of the whole. While Brendel's earlier *Waldstein* (on Vox/Turnabout) has claims to be considered among the very finest on record, this is only marginally less impressive and is certainly much better recorded.

Piano sonatas Nos. 8 in C min. (Pathétique), Op. 13; 14 in C sharp min. (Moonlight), Op. 27/2; 17 in C sharp min. (Tempest), Op. 31/2.
(N) (BB) **(*) Tring Dig. TRP 027 [id.]. Cristina Ortiz.

Cristina Ortiz is at her finest on this inexpensive Tring triptych. These are considerable performances, and they are beautifully recorded. The *Pathétique* is strong and fluent; the *Tempest*, with its impulsive fluctuations of tempo handled very individually but always poetically and spontaneously, is most refreshing, especially the delightfully articulated *Allegretto* finale. However, Ortiz chooses to play the opening of the *Moonlight* very quietly indeed, and in a manner that seems deliberate as well as thoughtful. The second movement is lilting and the finale swift and strong, so the necessary contrasts are present; but not all will find the opening completely convincing.

Piano sonatas Nos. 8 in C min. (Pathétique), Op. 13; 14 in C sharp min. (Moonlight), Op. 27/2; 21 in C (Waldstein), Op. 53; 23 in F min. (Appassionata).
(Y/B) (M) *** DG 447 404-2 [id.]. Wilhelm Kempff.

Kempff's masterly recordings are truly legendary and make a fitting contribution to DG's series of 'Originals'. Each performance here shows so well his ability to rethink Beethoven's music within the recording studio. Everything he does has his individual stamp; above all, he never fails to convey the deep intensity of a master in communication with Beethoven. In the *Waldstein*, although the opening movement is dramatic, Kempff's preparation for the great theme of the finale is gentle, and when it appears the effect is to give the melody a less joyous quality than we are used to. But the result is magical, for there is a compensating spiritual quality and, with the suggestion of a more restrained forward momentum, the finale gains in breadth and boldness what it loses in sheer vivacity. The *Appassionata* is characteristically clear and classically straight. Although less weightily dramatic than in other readings, the concentration is irresistible. The recording has undoubtedly gained in firmness with the clean sound of the digital remastering, and there is plenty of warmth and colour at lower dynamic levels.

Piano sonatas Nos. 8 in C min. (Pathétique), Op. 13; 14 in C sharp min. (Moonlight), Op. 27/2; 23 in F min. (Appassionata), Op. 57.
(BB) **(*) Naxos Dig. 8.550045; 4550045 [id.]. Jenö Jandó.

Jandó's clean, direct style and natural spontaneity are particularly admirable in the slow movements of the *Pathétique* and *Appassionata*, warmly lyrical in feeling, yet not a whit sentimental. Only in the coda of the finale of the *Appassionata* does one feel a loss of poise, when the closing *presto* becomes *prestissimo* and the exuberance of the music-making nearly gets out of control.

Piano sonatas Nos. 8 (Pathétique); 14 (Moonlight); 23 (Appassionata); 26 (Les Adieux).
⊛ (M) *** RCA 09026 61443-2 [id.]. Artur Rubinstein.

Artur Rubinstein almost always conveys a sense of spontaneity in his recorded performances, and the sense of a live interpretation is specially vivid here. He was not a Beethoven specialist, but it is perhaps surprising that he had never recorded the *Moonlight* before this version (dating from 1962), nor even played it in public. But there is a combination of freshness and maturity in his reading which makes it stand out even among many fine recorded versions. The improvisatory feeling in the opening movement is remarkable. The *Pathétique* has a youthful urgency in the outer movements, yet the *Adagio cantabile* has a wonderful simplicity. The impulsive surge of feeling in the *Appassionata* is equally compelling, with the finale reminding one of Richter's famous record. The exhilaration and power of Rubinstein's playing, both here and in *Les Adieux*, are beyond praise. If he has forged a special link with any Beethoven work, it is with Op. 81a. The recordings, made in the Manhattan Center, New York City, sound firmer and fuller than they did on LP and reflect great credit on John Pfeiffer's remastering for CD.

Piano sonatas Nos. 8 in C min. (Pathétique); 21 in C (Waldstein); 23 in F min. (Appassionata).
(N) ⊛ [M] *** Beethoven Edition DG Analogue/Dig. 447 914-2 [id.]. Emil Gilels.

Piano sonatas Nos. 8 in C min. (Pathétique); 23 in F min. (Appassionata), Op. 57; 31 in A flat, Op. 110.
(B) *** DG Dig./Analogue 439 426-2 [id.]. Gilels.

Gilels's account of the *Appassionata* has previously been hailed by us as among the finest ever made, and much the same must be said of the *Waldstein*. It has a technical perfection denied even to Schnabel and, though in the slow movement Schnabel found special depths, Gilels is hardly less searching and profound. If the *Pathétique* does not quite rank among his very best, such are the strengths of his playing that the reading still leaves a profound impression. In this sonata the 1980 digital recording, though real and present, is nevertheless balanced too close (which brings a touch of hardness on fortissimos). In the analogue recordings of the other two sonatas, the piano is much less closely observed, to great advantage.

The *Pathétique* and *Appassionata sonatas* are also available on Classikon, in a coupling with Op. 110, and this makes a formidable bargain alternative, for the *A flat Sonata*, too, is given a performance of real stature. Even when Gilels storms the greatest heights in the closing fugue, no fortissimo ever sounds percussive or strained. This was (digitally) recorded five years later than the *Pathétique* and the balance is better judged.

Piano sonatas Nos. 9 in E; 10 in G, Op. 14/1–2; 24 in F sharp, Op. 78; 27 in E min., Op. 90; 28 in A, Op. 101.
(BB) *** Naxos Dig. 8.550162; 4550162 [id.]. Jenö Jandó.

Opp. 90 and 101 show this artist at full stretch. These are demanding works and Jandó does not fall short, particularly in the slow movements, which are very eloquent indeed. The piano sound is most believable.

Piano sonatas Nos. 11 in B flat, Op. 22; 13 in E flat (Sonata quasi una fantasia); 14 (Moonlight), Op. 27/ 1–2; 19 in G min.; 20 in G, Op. 49/1–2.
(N) (M) *** Virgin Veritas/EMI Dig. VER5 61238-2 [id.]. Melvyn Tan (fortepiano).

Melvyn Tan, now transferred to the Virgin Veritas label, here continues his stimulating Beethoven series, opening with the two Op. 49 *Sonatas* which, unsurprisingly, are a great success, as is (less predictably) the *Sonata quasi una fantasia*. Only in the first movement of the *B flat Sonata*, Op. 22, does the ear perceive the need for somewhat more weight and poise; but the first movement of the *Moonlight* has no lack of warmth or colour, and this highly spontaneous performance is a splendid demonstration of the sonority which Tan can achieve on his fortepiano (on this occasion a Nanette Streicher).

Piano sonatas Nos. 11 in B flat, Op. 22; 29 in B flat (Hammerklavier), Op. 106.
(BB) **(*) Naxos Dig. 8.550234; *4550234* [id.]. Jenö Jandó.

From its very opening bars, the *Hammerklavier* is commanding; there is rapt concentration in the slow movement, and the closing fugue runs its course with a powerful inevitability. Again, most realistic recording.

Piano sonatas Nos. 12 in A flat, Op. 26; 16 in G; 18 in E flat, Op. 31/1 & 3.
(BB) **(*) Naxos Dig. 8.550166 [id.]. Jenö Jandó.

Volume 7 with its trio of middle-period sonatas can be recommended with few reservations. No. 18 is a considerable success, and there is much to stimulate the listener's interest here. Excellent sound.

Piano sonatas Nos. 14 in C sharp min. (Moonlight), Op. 27/2; 17 in D min. (Tempest), Op. 31/2; 26 in E flat (Les adieux), Op. 81a.
(N) (M) **(*) Beethoven Edition DG Dig. 447 913-2 [id.]. Daniel Barenboim.

Spontaneity and electricity, extremes of expression in dynamic, tempo and phrasing, as well as mood, marked Barenboim's complete DG cycle. The plainness in the first movement of the *Moonlight* is disappointing, with little veiled tone; but the light, flowing finale of the *Tempest* is magically Mendelssohnian. The *Andante espressivo* of *Les Adieux* is also played touchingly. The 1984 digital recording is firm and the acoustic spacious.

Piano sonatas Nos. 14 in C sharp min. (Moonlight), Op. 27/2; 21 in C (Waldstein), Op. 53; 23 in F min. (Appassionata), Op. 57.
*** Virgin/EMI Dig. VC5 45131-2 [id.]. Mikhail Pletnev.
(M) *** Decca 417 732-2. Vladimir Ashkenazy.
(M) **(*) RCA GD 60375 [60375-2-RG]. Vladimir Horowitz.

Some will find the Pletnev *Moonlight* a bit mannered, but he has the capacity to make you listen intently – as every great pianist does, and he also finds the right depths in the slow movement and finale of the *Waldstein*. The account of the *Appassionata* is masterly. The engineering is immaculate and does justice to Pletnev's individual sound-world.

An excellent mid-priced grouping of three popular sonatas from Ashkenazy. The *Waldstein* (1975) is splendidly structured and the *Appassionata* (1973) superb, although those who feel strongly about matters of tempo may well find Ashkenazy a little too free in the first movement.

Horowitz was not thought of primarily as a Beethoven pianist, but these recordings, made in 1956 (the *Moonlight* and *Waldstein*) and 1959, show how powerful he could be in the music of this composer. His delicacy, too, is equally impressive. The sound has been improved in the remastering process; there is some hardness on top but little shallowness, and the bass sonority is telling.

Piano sonatas: No. 15 in D (Pastoral), Op. 28; (Kurfürstensonaten) in E flat, F min., D, WoO 47/1–3; in C (incomplete), WoO 51; Sonatinas: in G, F, Anh. 5/1–2.
(BB) ** Naxos Dig. 8.550255 [id.]. Jenö Jandó.

Jandó's playing is fresh, clean and intelligent and, if the two *Sonatinas* are not authentic, they make agreeable listening here. The *Pastoral sonata* is admirably done.

Piano sonatas Nos. 16 in G; 17 in D min. (Tempest); 18 in E flat, Op. 31/1–3.
(N) *** EMI Dig. CDC5 55226-2 [id.]. Stephen Kovacevich.
(BB) **(*) ASV CDQS 6060 [id.]. John Lill.

Even in this highly competitive field Stephen Kovacevich brings some extra distinction which makes this set special. This is playing of insight and of unfailing artistry that illumines and delights the listener. It is in the same class as his Opp. 110 and 111. If this cycle continues as it has begun, the Kovacevich could well be to the 1990s what Schnabel was to the 1930s and '40s.

On ASV this is one of the most impressive discs in John Lill's series and it is very well recorded. Obviously the Op. 31 *Sonatas* strike a spark in his consciousness and the first movement of No. 16 is keenly alive, while the slow movement is characteristically direct and there are some sensitive touches. There is no want of fire in *The Tempest*, and there is much to admire in the *E flat Sonata*, although Lill's tendency to aggressiveness brings some exaggerated sforzandos in the Scherzo. But the playing through-out is strong and keenly intelligent.

Piano sonatas Nos. 17 in D min., Op. 31/2; 18 in E flat, Op. 31/3; 26 in E flat (Les Adieux), Op. 81a.
*** Sony Dig. MK 42319 [id.]. Murray Perahia.

Wonderfully concentrated performances. All these readings have the blend of authority, finesse and poetry that distinguishes this great artist at his best.

Piano sonatas Nos. 17 in D min. (Tempest), Op. 31/2; 21 in C (Waldstein), Op. 53; 26 in E flat (Les Adieux), Op. 81a.
(BB) **(*) Naxos Dig. 8.550054 [id.]. Jenö Jandó.

Jandó offers here the other three famous named sonatas, and very enjoyable they are in their direct manner.

Piano sonatas Nos. 17 in D min. (Tempest), Op. 31/2; 29 in B flat (Hammerklavier), Op. 106.
(M) *** DG 419 857-2 [id.]. Wilhelm Kempff.

Kempff's preference for measured allegros and fastish andantes gives a different weighting to move-ments from the usual, but there is a profound thoughtfulness of utterance.

Piano sonatas Nos. 21 in C (Waldstein), Op. 53; 23 in F min. (Appassionata), Op. 57; 26 in E flat (Les Adieux), Op. 81a.
(Y/B) (M) *** Virgin Veritas/EMI Dig. VER5 61160-2 [id.]. Melvyn Tan (fortepiano).

Melvyn Tan's playing is for those yet unconverted to the fortepiano and who find its exponents tame. In all three sonatas he exhibits consummate artistry and real temperament and fire. Nor is there any want of poetic feeling. The EMI recording is excellent; in short, an outstanding issue.

Piano sonatas Nos. 21 (Waldstein); 24 in F sharp, Op. 78; 31 in A flat, Op. 110.
*** EMI Dig. CDC7 54896-2 [id.]. Stephen Kovacevich.

This second disc in Stephen Kovacevich's projected Beethoven cycle for EMI brings revelatory per-formances from one of the deepest thinkers among Beethoven pianists. Compared with Richard Goode – whose cycle has now appeared complete – Kovacevich allows himself a degree more expressive free-dom, giving foretastes of romantic music to come. The *Waldstein* as well as Op. 110 has a visionary quality. As with the first disc, the piano is set at a distance in a reverberant acoustic, blurring the edges.

Piano sonatas Nos. 24 in F sharp, Op. 78; 29 in B flat (Hammerklavier), Op. 106.
*** Sony SMK 52645 [id.]. Glenn Gould.

Whether or not you are a Gould devotee, no one could miss his unique magnetism in this long-buried recording. The first movement of the *Hammerklavier* must be the slowest version ever. It is not just that his basic tempo is very measured indeed, but that he takes every opportunity to linger over linking passages, coming virtually to a halt at the start of the development section. By personal magnetism the result is compelling, aptly rugged and muscular. The other movements too have their Gouldian eccen-tricities – quite apart from his incurable habit of singing and humming, particularly at the start of a new theme – but there the approach is rather less extreme, with the great *Adagio* no more spacious than, say, with Solomon. Gould's shading of phrase and tone is often persuasive, despite the unhelpfully dry, if full and immediate, recorded CBC sound of 1970. In the little Op. 78 *Sonata*, recorded by CBS in their New York studios almost three years earlier, Gould again consciously avoids lightness and charm, but his weighty, muscular approach to the first movement and his bright, sparky and ultimately hectoring view of the *Allegro vivace* are again magnetic.

Piano sonatas Nos. 27 in E min., Op. 90; 28 in A, Op. 101; 29 in B flat (Hammerklavier), Op. 106; 30 in E, Op. 109; 31 in A flat, Op. 110; 32 in C min., Op. 111.
(B) *** Sony SB2K 53531 (2) [id.]. Charles Rosen.
(B) *** Ph. Duo 438 374-2 (2) [id.]. Alfred Brendel.

Charles Rosen is one of the most commanding interpreters of Beethoven's longest and most taxing sonatas. The first movement of the *Hammerklavier* is magnificently strong and the fast tempo – as near Beethoven's impossible metronome marking as is reasonable – makes for an absolute concentration and no sense of hastiness. The great *Adagio* (taken slower than in his first, American recording) is played with an inner depth that allows no sentimentality, and the finale has rarely if ever been played on record with such dynamic power and clarity. A performance even for those who otherwise follow Barenboim or Brendel in their Beethoven cycles. The little *E minor Sonata* begins a little gruffly, but later Rosen shows that he can encompass the softer mood of this very different work. In the visionary last two sonatas, less searingly intense than those preceding them, some may resist the uningratiating manner, but Rosen's commanding toughness compels attention, and repeated hearings are the more rewarding. The recordings, made at the EMI studios between November 1968 and July 1970, are firm and realistic, and allow a wide range of dynamic.

Reissued in Philips's Duo bargain series, this Brendel set of the late sonatas is certainly value for money. In the glorious *E minor Sonata*, Op. 90, there are some expressive rubati that may worry some listeners, but Brendel provides a thoughtful, sensitive reading of the *E major Sonata*, Op. 109. The *A major*, Op. 101, is one of the finest of his cycle, and the sheer beauty of tone in the *A flat major*, Op. 110, is most persuasive: the playing of a thoughtful dreamer. There is a tendency in the *Adagio* of Op. 111, beautifully played as it is, for the forward impulse to lose its spontaneity, and the carefully considered account of the *Hammerklavier* has not quite the fire and sense of spontaneity that marked Brendel's earlier account on Turnabout. Yet with the help of the Philips engineers the great *Adagio* has a genuinely hushed tone (which the forward balance on Turnabout prevented from registering) and this is undoubtedly a fine performance, very well recorded. Generally speaking, this is among the most distinguished Beethoven playing of the analogue era. The recordings were made in the 1970s and are most realistic and satisfying in the latest CD transfers. The documentation, too, can be commended.

Piano sonatas Nos. 27 in E min., Op. 90; 28 in A, Op. 101; 32 in C min., Op. 111.
*** EMI Dig. CDC7 54599-2 [id.]. Stephen Kovacevich.

Stephen Kovacevich's Op. 90 is among the finest in the catalogue and the *A major*, Op. 101, is among the most serene since the eloquent account by Gilels on a beautifully recorded DG LP. Its first movement has a subtlety of colour and tone that long resonates with the listener, and its short slow movement seems to commune with another world. The *C minor*, Op. 111, is a performance of stature, free from any attempt to beautify. The recording is excellent, and the only reservation to make is that some may be distracted by the pianist's breathing which is audible at moments of strain.

Piano sonata No. 29 (Hammerklavier), Op. 106.
*** DG Dig. 410 527-2 [id.]. Emil Gilels.

Gilels's *Hammerklavier* is a performance of supreme integrity, Olympian, titanic, subtle, imperious, one of the finest accounts ever recorded. However, the recording is close and bright and harder than ideal.

Piano sonatas Nos. 30 in E, Op. 109; 31 in A flat, Op. 110.
*** DG Dig. 419 174-2 [id.]. Emil Gilels.

On DG, both sonatas are given performances of stature that seek out their profoundest truths. Even when Gilels storms the greatest heights in the closing fugue of Op. 110, no fortissimo ever sounds percussive or strained.

Piano sonatas Nos. 30 in E, Op. 109; 31 in A flat, Op. 110; 32 in C min., Op. 111.
(N) (M) *** Beethoven Edition DG 447 915-2 [id.]. Wilhelm Kempff.
*** MusicMasters Dig. 67098-2 [id.]. Vladimir Feltsman.
(N) (M) *** Cal. Dig./Analogue CAL 6648 [id.]. Inger Södergren.
(BB) *** Naxos Dig. 8.550151 [id.]. Jenö Jandó.

The reading of Op. 109 sets the style for Kempff's performances of the late sonatas, intense in its control of structure, but with a feeling of rhapsodic freedom too, of new visions emerging. The second movement of Op. 110 is not as fast as it might be, but the result is the cleaner for that and, in typical Kempff style, the great *Arietta* of Op. 111 is taken at a flowing tempo, not nearly as slowly as with many a recorded rival. These are all great performances, and the recordings are clean and firm.

Vladimir Feltsman, born in Moscow in 1952 and since 1987 established in the United States, demonstrates in the last three sonatas that age is not an essential even with the most searching Beethoven works. Interestingly, Feltsman's recordings were supervised by the same recording producer as Goode's, Max Wilcox, and the clean, bright, well-focused sound reflects that. The sound underlines unexpected differences in Feltsman's approach to each of the sonatas. In the first movement of Op. 109 he is freely rhapsodic to the point of wildness, with the piano made to clatter, as it does in the central Scherzo too. The simple dedication of Feltsman's playing in the sublime last movement then takes one by surprise. Similarly, in Op. 110 too Feltsman's fresh, simple account of the measured paragraphs of the final fugue happily tends to cancel out any disappointment over the bright forcefulness earlier. Opus 111 then comes as a culmination, for here his many qualities focus splendidly, not just in the drama of the compressed first movement but in the spaciousness of the final *Arietta*.

Inger Södergren, little known in her native country, is a Swedish pianist who lives in France, where she enjoys a considerable reputation; indeed her performances and recordings are regarded there with as much respect as those of Brendel. Her analogue accounts of Opp. 110 and 111 come from 1979, when they earned golden opinions. They are musically most impressive; she is obviously a pianist of keen musical insights. Her recording of Op. 109 is new: it is brighter and more forward. Op. 110 reminds one a little of Myra Hess's old mono LP, but this reading is even stronger. These performances are fit to keep exalted company and the earlier, analogue recordings are most naturally balanced. A first-class mid-priced recommendation.

The last three sonatas of Beethoven, offered in Naxos's Volume 4, are very imposing indeed in Jandó's hands. There is serenity and gravitas in these readings and a powerful control of structure.

Miscellaneous piano music

Allegretto in C min., WoO 53; Andanti favori, WoO 57; 'Für Elise', WoO 59; 6 Variations on an original theme in F, Op. 34.
(Y/B) (M) *** Virgin Veritas/EMI Dig. VER5 61161-2 [id.]. Melvyn Tan (fortepiano) – SCHUBERT: Moments musicaux etc. ***

Melvyn Tan is a spirited artist and an enormously persuasive exponent of the fortepiano. The *F major Variations* come off splendidly; this is a thoroughly enjoyable recital and is recorded with great realism and presence in the Long Gallery, Doddington Hall, Lincolnshire.

7 Bagatelles, Op. 33; 11 Bagatelles, Op. 119; 6 Bagatelles, Op. 126.
(B) *** Ph. 426 976-2. Stephen Kovacevich.
(BB) **(*) Naxos Dig. 8.550474 [id.]. Jenö Jandó.

Bagatelles, Op. 33; 119; 126; WoO 52 & 56.
*** Chandos Dig. CHAN 9201 [id.]. John Lill.

Beethoven's *Bagatelles*, particularly those from Opp. 119 and 126, have often been described as chips from the master's workbench; but rarely if ever has that description seemed so apt as in these searchingly simple and completely spontaneous readings by Kovacevich.

John Lill's collection of Beethoven's *Bagatelles*, the fill-up for his fine *Concerto* cycle for Chandos, is here brought together. Characteristically he takes a serious view of these chips from the master's workbench, bringing out their relationship to some of the full masterpieces.

Jandó plays the early set of *Bagatelles*, which date from 1802, with a crisply rhythmic style, almost at times as if he was thinking of a fortepiano. Then in the later works he finds more depth of tone and is thoughtful as well as flamboyant. He has an excellent, modern, digital recording.

Bagatelles, Opp. 33 & 119; Fantasia in G min.; Variations on 'God save the King' & 'Rule Britannia'.
*** EMI Dig. CDC7 54526-2. Melvyn Tan.

Melvyn Tan plays these pieces with all the spontaneity and flair which he exhibits consistently and in the *G minor Fantasy* conveys an improvisatory quality far removed from the judicious, scholarly rectitude of so many period-instrument specialists. He could allow himself more time in some of the *Bagatelles*, but there are no real quibbles here in what is a record of enormous interest, offering refreshing insights into the sound-world with which Beethoven himself would have been familiar. The recording has great realism and presence.

7 Bagatelles, Op. 33; 6 Bagatelles, Op. 126; 6 Variations in F, Op. 34; 15 Variations with fugue in E flat (Eroica), Op. 35; 32 Variations on an original theme in C min., WoO 80.
(M) *(**) Sony SM2K 52646 (2) [id.]. Glenn Gould (piano).

Glenn Gould's *Bagatelles* and *Variations* are a good deal better and less quirky than his Beethoven *Piano sonatas*, which are not competitive, given the number of great cycles in the catalogue. Gould fanatics can invest in them; others who are not converted can be assured that any eccentricity is positive and thought-provoking. Not a first choice (or anywhere near it) but deserving of a place in the catalogue.

6 Bagatelles, Op. 126; 6 Ecossaises, WoO 83; 'Für Elise', WoO 59; 15 Variations and fugue on a theme from Prometheus (Eroica variations), Op. 35.
*** Ph. 412 227-2 [id.]. Alfred Brendel.

Brendel may lack some of the sheer bravura of his own early playing in this collection of shorter pieces, but his consistent thoughtfulness and imagination bring out the truly Beethovenian qualities of even the most trivial pieces.

6 Bagatelles, Op. 126; Polonaise in C, Op. 89; Variations and fugue on a theme from Prometheus (Eroica variations), Op. 35.
*** Nimbus Dig. NIM 5017 [id.]. Bernard Roberts.

Bernard Roberts gives a characteristically fresh and forthright reading of the *Eroica variations*, recorded in exceptionally vivid sound. He may not have quite the dash of Brendel, but the crispness and clarity of his playing are most refreshing. The shorter pieces bring performances even more intense, with the *Bagatelles* for all their brevity given last-period intensity.

6 Variations in F, Op. 34; 6 Variations on 'Nel cor più non mi sento', WoO 70; 15 Variations and fugue on a theme from Prometheus in E flat (Eroica variations), Op. 35; 32 Variations in C min., WoO 80.
(BB) **(*) Naxos Dig. 8.550676 [id.]. Jenö Jandó.

Jandó essays the same strong, direct style in his performances of the two major sets of variations that he does in the sonatas. Occasionally his forceful manner in Op. 35 and the *C minor Variations* reaches the point of brusqueness in its forceful accenting but no one could deny the strength of this playing. His approach is appropriately lighter in Op. 34 and the very agreeable short set based on the duet by Paisiello. Excellent recording, clear and vivid, to match the other records in his Naxos series.

6 Variations in F, Op. 34; 15 Variations and fugue on a theme from Prometheus in E flat (Eroica variations), Op. 35; 2 Rondos, Op. 51; Bagatelle: 'Für Elise', WoO 59.
*** Chandos Dig. CHAN 8616 [id.]. Louis Lortie.

The Canadian pianist Louis Lortie is an artist of distinction; his readings have both grandeur and authority. This account of the *Eroica variations* belongs in exalted company and can be recommended alongside such magisterial accounts as that of Gilels.

6 Variations in F, Op. 34; 6 Variations in G on 'Nel cor più non mi sento', WoO 70; 5 Variations in D on 'Rule Britannia', WoO 79.
*** Ph. Dig. 432 093-2 [id.]. Alfred Brendel – SCHUMANN: *Symphonic études.* ***

This is among the best records Brendel has given us in recent years, full of intelligence and, in the *Rule Britannia* variations, wit. Exemplary recordings made in The Maltings, Snape.

33 Variations on a waltz by Diabelli, Op. 120.
(Y/B) *** Hyperion Dig. CDA 66763 [id.]. William Kinderman.
*** Ph. Dig. 426 232-2 [id.]. Alfred Brendel.
(N) (M) ** Carlton IMP 30367 00112 [id.]. Charles Rosen.

33 Variations on a waltz by Diabelli, Op. 120; Piano sonata No. 28 in A, Op. 101.
(Y/B) *** EMI Dig. CDC7 54792-2 [id.]. Peter Donohoe.

33 Variations on a waltz by Diabelli, Op. 120; 32 Variations in C min., WoO 80.
(N) (B) *** ASV Dig. CDQS 6155 [id.]. Benjamin Frith.

The *Diabelli* is the greatest set of variations ever written. William Kinderman's version on Hyperion is really in a class of its own, remarkably fresh and well thought out, and it is almost worth buying the present disc for the sake of his illuminating liner-notes. Although a reputable scholar, however, his is playing of real temperament and psychological insight. He is not excessively judicious in his interpretative judgements, carefully weighing one view against another, but is sparkling with life and character. He is very well recorded, too. The most outstanding *Diabelli variations* to have appeared for ages.

Now reissued in the lowest price range and with an equally fine account of the *32 Variations on an original theme in C minor* thrown in for good measure, the ASV reissue tends to sweep the board. Benjamin Frith gives a fresh and clear reading; tense and dedicated, this conveys Beethoven's mastery without exaggeration or self-indulgence. Clear, realistic recording to match.

On Philips, Brendel, here working in the studio, captures the music's dynamism, the sense of an irresistible force building up this immense structure, section by section. It would be hard to imagine a more dramatic reading, sparked off by the cheeky wit of Brendel's treatment of the Diabelli theme itself. The whirlwind power of the whole performance is irresistible, and the piano sound is full and immediate.

Peter Donohoe's EMI recording offers an additional work, the *A major Sonata*, Op. 101. Donohoe also has the advantage of excellent recorded sound, realistic and fresh in equal measure. His performance of both pieces is intelligent and vigorous, eminently recommendable, if not quite the equal of Kinderman (Hyperion) or Brendel (Philips). But there is no want of characterization and he has a good feeling for Beethoven's humour. No reason to withhold a third star, but this is not a first recommendation.

Admirers of Charles Rosen will be glad to have his recording available again. His view of this Everest of piano literature is purposeful and tough, hard to the point of being unrelenting. With clear, somewhat twangy recording to match, one misses the gentler half-tones (as for example in the great *Adagio* variation, No. 29, where Rosen ignores the *mezza-voce* marking at a trivially fast tempo); yet there is still much to satisfy in such a formidably intense reading.

VOCAL MUSIC

(i) *An die ferne Geliebte, Op. 98*. Lieder: *Abendlied unterm gestirnten Himmel;* (ii) *Adelaide;* (i) *Andenken; An die Hoffnung; Die Ehre Gottes aus der Natur; Es war einmal ein König; In questa tomba oscura; Der Jüngling in der Fremde;* (ii) *Der Kuss;* (i) *Der Liebende; Lied aus der Ferne; Maigesang; Marmotte; Mit einem gemalten Band;* (ii) *Resignation;* (i) *Sehnsucht; Seufzer eines Ungeliebten und Gegenliebe; Der Wachtelschlag; Wonne der Wehmut;* (ii) *Zärtliche Liebe.*

(N) (M) **(*) Beethoven Edition DG 447 921-2 [id.]. (i) Fischer-Dieskau, Demus; (ii) Wunderlich, Giesen.

Recorded in 1966, Fischer-Dieskau's Beethoven selection finds him at his vocal peak, especially in the song-cycle which he has made very much his own; though Demus's accompaniments are not as imaginative as the singer has received in other versions of these songs, Fischer-Dieskau's individuality is as positive as ever, with detail touched in as with no one else. Even so, the four items (*Adelaide, Zärtliche Liebe, Resignation* and *Der Kuss*) from Fritz Wunderlich, which are placed together immediately after the song-cycle, resonate in the memory. He was thirty-five when he recorded them and the unique bloom of the lovely tenor voice is beautifully caught to make an effective contrast. Though the accompanist is too metrical at times, the freshness of Wunderlich's singing makes one grieve again at his untimely death.

An die ferne Geliebte (song-cycle), *Op. 98; Goethe Lieder: Aus Goethes Faust; In questa tomba oscura; Mailied; Neue Liebe, neues Leben; Wonne der Wehmut.*

(N) (M) *** Ph. 442 741-2 (2) [id.]. Gérard Souzay, Dalton Baldwin – BRAHMS: *Lieder;* SCHUMANN: *Dichterliebe; Liederkreis* etc. ***

Souzay's lightness of touch and chimerical approach, with bursts of spontaneous ardour, suit Beethoven especially well, and any criticisms of this composer's vocal style are banished. The last song, *Nimm sie hin denn, diese Lieder*, is particularly touching. Among the miscellaneous songs Souzay finds humour in the *Flea song* from *Faust* and then brings a breath of spring to *Mailied*. Almost best of all is the delightfully gay *Neue Liebe, neues Lieben*, which sounds for all the world like Schubert. The recording projects the voices vividly; although Souzay was very close to the microphone, Dalton Baldwin's support comes over strongly. It is a pity that in an important set like this no translations are provided, just the German texts.

Bundeslied, Op. 122; Elegischer Gesang, Op. 118; King Stephen (incidental music), *Op. 117; Meeresstille und glückliche Fahrt (Calm sea and a prosperous voyage), Op. 112; Opferlied, Op. 121b.*

*** Sony Dig. MK 76404 [MK 33509]. Amb. S., LSO, Tilson Thomas.

Tilson Thomas's collection of Beethoven choral rarities plus the *King Stephen* incidental music makes an attractive out-of-the-way disc for Beethovenians. With excellent singing and playing, they are all enjoyable.

Che fa il mio bene? (2 versions); *Dimmi, ben mio; Ecco quel fiero istante!; In questa tomba oscura; T'intendo, si, mio cor.*

(N) *** Decca Dig. 440 297-2 [id.]. Cecilia Bartoli, András Schiff – HAYDN: *Arianna a Naxos;* MOZART: *Ridente la calma;* SCHUBERT: *Da quel sembiante appresi* etc. ***

These rare Italian songs come as part of a recital which has an outstanding account of Haydn's *Arianna a Naxos* as its highlight. *La Partenza* has a winningly ingenuous simplicity and the *Ariettas* (including two completely contrasting settings of *Che fa il mio bene?*) are also full of charm.

(i) *Choral Fantasia* (for piano, chorus & orchestra), *Op. 80;* (ii) *Missa solemnis in D, Op. 123.*

(M) *** Sony SM2K 47522 (2) [id.]. (i) Rudolf Serkin, (i; ii) Westminster Ch.; (ii) Farrell, Carol Smith, Lewis, Borg; NYPO, Bernstein – HAYDN: *Mass No. 12.* ***

Bernstein is at his most intense in this fine, dedicated account of Beethoven's supreme choral masterpiece. It is an inspirational performance, though it is a drawback that, like the Jochum set, it overlaps on to a second disc when, with an overall playing time of about 77 minutes, it could easily have been accommodated on a single CD. However, the couplings are recommendable and worth having, especially the Haydn (digital) *Theresia Mass*. Serkin's *Choral Fantasia* opens with a solo cadenza almost to rival Brendel's.

Christus am Olberge, Op. 85.

(M) **(*) Sony MPK 45878 [id.]. Raskin, Lewis, Herbert Beattie, Temple University Choirs, Phd. O, Ormandy.

**(*) HM HMC 905181 [id.]. Pick-Hieronimi, Anderson, Von Halem, Ch. & O Nat. de Lyon, Baudo.

Ormandy is at his most purposeful and warmly understanding, and the soloists are outstandingly fine, with the pure-toned Judith Raskin very aptly cast as the Seraph and with Richard Lewis at his freshest and most expressive as Jesus.

Monica Pick-Hieronimi, a singer of some power, brings Leonore-like qualities to her role as Seraph. Baudo directs an energetic and lively account of it which, if lacking the utmost refinement of detail, generates urgency and breadth in the fine closing section.

Egmont: Overture and incidental music (abridged), *Op. 84.*
(N) (M) **(*) Beethoven Edition DG 447 912-2 [id.]. Janowitz, Schellow, BPO, Karajan – *Ecossaise* etc.; *Wellington's victory*. **

(i) *Egmont: Overture and incidental music* (complete), *Op. 84;* (ii) *Leonora overture No. 3.*
(B) *** Discover Dig. DICD 920114. (i) Miriam Gauci, Dirk Schortemeier, Belgian R. & TV O; (ii) LPO; Rahbari.

On the bargain Discover label, Alexander Rahbari offers all ten movements of Beethoven's *Egmont* music, not just the selection made by Szell, whose 1969 version has just been reissued in Decca's Classic Sound series (448 593-2). Such rarities as the third and fourth entr'actes and the melodrama, *Süsse Schlaf,* with Schortemeier as the speaker, are chips from the master's workbench rather than significant pieces, but together with the well-known items they present an attractive whole. Both in *Egmont* and in the *Leonora No. 3 overture* (with the LPO) Rahbari conducts crisp, well-sprung, often exciting performances, with Miriam Gauci the warm-toned soprano. Atmospheric recording, pleasantly reverberant.

Karajan's abridged recording of *Egmont* dates from 1969 and was originally part of DG's Beethoven Edition, then as now. There is no lack of drama, and Gundula Janowitz sings the two Lieder beautifully; Erich Schellow's narration is reduced to a single melodrama before the finale. The sound is clear and vivid, and the CD transfer has brought more depth and warmth of atmosphere than one remembers on the original LP. The couplings, however, are uninspiring.

Mass in C, Op. 86.
(BB) *** Belart 461 317-2 [id.]. Palmer, Watts, Tear, Keyte, St John's College, Cambridge, Ch., ASMF, Guest – BRUCKNER: *Motets.* ***

(i) *Mass in C, Op. 86; Meeresstille und glückliche Fahrt (Calm sea and a prosperous voyage), Op. 112.*
*** DG Dig. 435 391-2 [id.]. Margiono, Robbin, Kendall, Miles, Monteverdi Ch., ORR, Gardiner.

(i) *Mass in C, Op. 86. The Ruins of Athens (Overture and incidental music), Op. 113.*
(M) *** EMI CDM7 64385-2 [id.]. (i) Vyvyan, Sinclair, Lewis, Nowakowski, Beecham Ch. Soc.; RPO, Beecham.

It is only in relation to the vast vision of the *Missa solemnis* that the *Mass in C* unfairly tends to be regarded as less than a masterpiece. With clean textures and sprung rhythms married to an expressive warmth not regularly associated with period manners, Gardiner's is just as refreshing a performance as his earlier, prize-winning account of the *Missa solemnis*. Aptly clear-toned soloists match the freshness of the Monteverdi Choir: Charlotte Margiono, Catherine Robbin, William Kendall and Alastair Miles. As an imaginatively chosen coupling Gardiner offers the dramatic soprano scena, *Ah! perfido*, with Charlotte Margiono as soloist, and the brief choral cantata, *Meeresstille und glückliche Fahrt*.

With a first-rate team of soloists and excellent choral singing, Beecham is fully competitive. The fill-up of incidental music is equally vibrant, and the transfer is vivid and lively with clear choral sound.

George Guest's reading is designedly intimate. Naturally, with boys' voices in the choir and a smaller band of singers, the results are less dramatic; but, with splendid recording, the scale works admirably and the result is refreshing. Excellent value at super-bargain price.

(i) *Mass in C, Op. 86;* (ii) *Missa solemnis, Op. 123.*
(B) **(*) Ph. Duo 438 362-2 (2) [id.]. (i) Eda-Pierre, Moll; (ii) Tomowa-Simtow, Lloyd; (i; ii) Payne, Tear, L. Symphony Ch., LSO, C. Davis.

The freshness of the choral singing and the clarity of the sound make Sir Colin Davis's an outstandingly dramatic version of the *Mass in C*. The cry, *'Passus'* ('suffered'), in the *Credo* has rarely been so tellingly presented on record, and the quartet of soloists is first rate. As it is in the *Missa solemnis*, and this too is a fine performance, if not consistently generating quite the same degree of intensity: this is especially noticeable when one moves to the second disc, which opens with the *Agnus Dei* of the *Missa solemnis*, where there is a fall-off in concentration. The 1977 recording, well focused, spacious and atmospheric, is given a natural, concert-hall balance and the CD transfer is first class. Good documentation.

Missa solemnis in D, Op. 123.

*** DG Dig. 435 770-2 (2) [id.]. Studer, Norman, Domingo, Moll, Leipzig R. Ch., Swedish R. Ch., VPO, Levine.

*** DG Dig. 429 779-2; *429 779-4* [id.]. Margiono, Robbin, Kendall, Miles, Monteverdi Ch., E. Bar. Soloists, Eliot Gardiner.

(N) *** HM Dig. HMC 901557 [id.]. Mannion, Remmert, Taylor, Hauptmann, La Chapelle Royale, Collegium Vocale, O des Champs Elysées, Herreweghe.

*** EMI Dig. CDC7 49950-2 [id.]. Vaness, Meier, Blochwitz, Tschammer, Tallis Chamber Ch., ECO, Tate.

(N) (M) *** Beethoven Edition DG 447 922-2 (2) [id.]. Moser, Schwarz, Kollo, Moll, Hilversum R. Ch., Concg. O, Bernstein.

(Y/B) (B) *** Sony SBK 53517; *SBT 53517* [id.]. Arroyo, Forrester, Lewis, Siepi, Singing City Choirs, Phd. O, Eugene Ormandy.

(Y/B) (M) **(*) DG Dig. 445 543-2 (2) [id.]. Cuberli, Schmidt, Cole, Van Dam, V. Singverein, BPO, Karajan – MOZART: *Mass No. 16.* **(*)

(M) **(*) Teldec/Warner Dig. 9031 74884-2 (2). Mei, Lipovšek, Rolfe Johnson, Holl, Schoenberg Ch., COE, Harnoncourt.

(M) (**(*)) RCA mono GD 60272 (2) [60272-RG-2]. Marshall, Merriman, Conley, Hines, Robert Shaw Ch., NBC SO, Toscanini – CHERUBINI: *Requiem.* (**(*))

(i) *Missa solemnis in D;* (ii) *Choral Fantasia in C, Op. 80.*

(M) **(*) EMI CMS7 69538-2 (2) [Ang. CDMB 69538-2]. (i) Söderström, Höffgen, Kmentt, Talvela, New Philh. Ch.; (ii) Barenboim, Alldis Ch.; New Philh. O, Klemperer.

Just two years after Herbert von Karajan died, the 1991 Salzburg Festival honoured its late music director in a performance of Beethoven's *Missa solemnis* conducted by James Levine. As the discs consistently demonstrate, the results have an incandescence that conveys the atmosphere of a great occasion, as this work should. This version has no rival, and the DG engineers have obtained the richest, weightiest sound yet on any recording made in the tricky Salzburg venue, not least from the massed choruses. The two-disc format may be extravagant, but for such an intense visionary experience, defying the conventional view of Levine, this is a version not to be missed.

Gardiner's inspired reading matches even the greatest of traditional performances on record in dramatic weight and spiritual depth, while bringing out the white heat of Beethoven's inspiration with new intensity. Though the performers are fewer in number than in traditional accounts, the Monteverdi Choir sings with bright, luminous tone, and the four soloists are excellent. The recording is vivid too. Even those who normally resist period performance will find this very compelling.

Philippe Herreweghe's live recording of the *Missa solemnis* (edited together from two performances) makes a good alternative to Gardiner's prize-winning version on DG Archiv for a period-scale reading. The relative distancing of the voices, both of soloists and of chorus, prevents it from having the dramatic impact of Gardiner's bitingly urgent account; but, with more conventionally relaxed speeds in the outer movements, the *Kyrie* and the *Agnus Dei*, this will please those who want a less radical view. Even at the start, with its odd balance, there is no mistaking that we are on a visionary journey, with an inner quality intensely conveyed. Despite the balance too, the sharpness of attack is refreshing, amply justifying a performance on a relatively intimate, period scale. The four young soloists make an excellent team, headed by the sweet, firm, Canadian soprano, Rosa Mannion, previously heard as Dorabella in the Gardiner *Così.*

Tate, with chorus and orchestra on a modest chamber scale, gains in incisiveness and loses hardly at all in weight, with bright, fresh singing from the Tallis Chamber Choir. The soloists make an outstanding quartet, with Hans Tschammer adding to Tate's deeply devotional treatment of the *Agnus Dei.* The well-balanced recording is at rather a low level, but sounds well at full volume.

Bernstein's DG recording was edited together from tapes of two live performances, and the result has a spiritual intensity matched by few rivals. Edda Moser is not an ideal soprano soloist, but the others are outstanding, and the *Benedictus* is made angelically beautiful by the radiant playing of the Concertgebouw concertmaster, Hermann Krebbers. The recording is a little light in bass but is outstandingly clear, as well as atmospheric.

The glory of Klemperer's set is the superb choral singing of the New Philharmonia Chorus. The soloists are less happily chosen: Waldemar Kmentt seems unpleasantly hard and Elisabeth Söderström does not sound as firm as she can be. It was, however, a happy idea to include the *Choral Fantasia* as a bonus.

On a single disc in Sony's Essential Classics series at budget price, Ormandy's 1967 Philadelphia recording makes an excellent bargain. Ormandy takes a bold and firm view of this masterpiece. It may not plumb all the spiritual depths of the work but, with four outstanding soloists and an excellent, well-focused choir, this is an account which takes you magnetically through the drama of Beethoven's personal view of the liturgy. The vintage recording gives plenty of body to the sound, both of voices and of orchestra, not least the bright-toned trumpets.

Karajan conducts a powerful reading marked by vivid and forward recording for orchestra and soloists, less satisfactory in rather cloudy choral sound. This was one of Karajan's recordings made in conjunction with a video film, and that brings both gains and losses. The sense of spontaneity, of a massive structure built dramatically with contrasts underlined, makes for extra magnetism, but there are flaws of ensemble and at least one serious flaw of intonation in the singing of Lella Cuberli, otherwise a full, sweet-toned soprano.

Like Levine's performance a year earlier, Harnoncourt's was recorded live at the Salzburg Festival but it represents the new, post-Karajan era at that grandest of music festivals. Like Harnoncourt's Beethoven symphony cycle, this performance conveys the dramatic tensions of a live occasion, with finely matched forces performing with freshness and clarity. As with Levine, the devotional element is clear, though the rather distanced sound makes the results marginally less involving than either the Levine version or John Eliot Gardiner's period-performance.

Toscanini's tensely dramatic account of the *Missa solemnis* leaves you in no doubt as to the work's magisterial power, even if the absence of a true pianissimo makes it less meditative than usual. Fine singing from choir and soloists alike, though the typical harshness of the recording is unappealing.

OPERA

Fidelio (complete).
(Y/B) ⊛*** EMI CDS5 55170-2 (2). Ludwig, Vickers, Frick, Berry, Crass, Philh. Ch. & O, Klemperer.
*** Ph. Dig. 426 308-2 (2) [id.]. Jessye Norman, Goldberg, Moll, Wlaschiha, Coburn, Blochwitz, Dresden State Op. Ch. & O, Haitink.
(N) *** Teldec/Warner Dig. 4509 94560-2 (2) [id.]. Margiono, Seiffert, Bonney, Skovhus, Leiferkus, Polgár, Van der Walt, Arnold Schönberg Ch., COE, Harnoncourt.
(Y/B) (M) *** EMI CMS7 69290-2 (2) [CDMB 769290]. Dernesch, Vickers, Kélémen, Ridderbusch, German Op. Ch., BPO, Karajan.
(M) (***) EMI mono CHS7 64901-2 (2) [id.]. Kirsten Flagstad, Julius Patzak, Paul Schoeffler, Josef Greindl, Elisabeth Schwarzkopf, Anton Dermota, V. State Op. Ch., VPO, Furtwängler.
(M) (**) RCA mono GD 60273 (2) [62073-RG]. Bampton, Peerce, Laderoute, Steber, Belarsky, Janssen, Moscona, Ch., NBC SO, Toscanini.
(N) (B) *(*) Decca Double 446 104-2 (2). Nilsson, McCracken, Böhme, Krause, Sciutti, Grobe, Prey, V. State Op. Konzertvereinigung, VPO, Maazel.
(N) (B) * DG Double 445 448-2 (2). Gwyneth Jones, King, Crass, Adam, Mathis, Schreier, Talvela, Leipzig R. Ch., Dresden Op. Ch. & State O, Boehm.
(N) (M) * Beethoven Edition DG 447 925-2 (2) [id.]. Jones, King, Crass, Adam, Mathis, Schreier, Talvela, Leipzig R. Ch., Dresden Op. Ch. & State O, Boehm.

Klemperer's great set of *Fidelio* is now reissued, but at full price. However, it has been superbly remastered. The sound has a depth, beauty and realism far beyond any previous incarnation of this splendid 1962 Kingsway Hall recording. The result is a technical triumph to match the unique incandescence and spiritual strength of the performance, with wonderful contributions from all concerned and a final scene in which, more than in any other recording, the parallel with the finale of the *Choral Symphony* is underlined. It remains first choice; but the price rise is a move in the wrong direction, even though the reissue has been repackaged with an admirably clear libretto. We have to say, however, that it is well worth its cost.

The unsurpassed nobility of Jessye Norman's voice is perfectly matched to this noblest of operas. In detail of characterization she may not outshine Christa Ludwig, Klemperer's firm and incisive Leonore, but her reading is consistently rich and beautiful, like those rivals bringing a new revelation. With excellent digital sound and with strong, forthright conducting from Haitink, this is the finest of modern versions, even if it does not replace Klemperer or Karajan.

As you would expect, Nikolaus Harnoncourt, tackling *Fidelio*, reflects the climate of period performance, even though – with the Chamber Orchestra of Europe as immaculate as ever – modern instruments are used. At chamber scale, textures are consistently clean, with crisply sprung rhythms at surprisingly relaxed speeds. The casting matches this approach, with the central role of Leonore given not to a dramatic soprano but to a singer best known till now for singing Mozart and Bach, Charlotte Margiono. The voice here is warmer than we have known it, with marked but unobtrusive vibrato, so that the *Abscheulicher* has a bite and clarity which make up for not pinning you back in your seat. The casting of the rest is similar, though the radiant Barbara Bonney would be a winner in any production on whatever scale, alternately spunky and wistful, very well contrasted with Margiono. Peter Seiffert sings with unforced clarity as Florestan, and Deon van der Walt is a fresh Jaquino. Contrasts of character are well established among the lower voices too, with Sergei Leiferkus an aptly sinister Pizarro, László Polgár a darkly resonant Rocco and Boje Skovhus a noble Don Pedro, even if his vibrato is exaggerated by the microphones. With his relaxed speeds, Harnoncourt encourages his singers to articulate cleanly. The two striking exceptions of very fast speeds – in the march before Pizarro's entry and at the start of the finale – both reflect French-style military marches such as Beethoven knew, something which John Eliot Gardiner also brought out in his recording of the finale of the *Ninth Symphony*. Highlights are available (70 minutes) on Teldec 0630 13800-9.

Comparison between Karajan's strong and heroic reading and Klemperer's version is fascinating. Both have very similar merits, underlining the symphonic character of the work with their weight of utterance. Both may miss some of the sparkle of the opening scene, but it is better that seriousness should enter too early than too late. Since seriousness is the keynote, it is rather surprising to find Karajan using bass and baritone soloists lighter than usual. Both the Rocco (Ridderbusch) and the Don Fernando (Van Dam) lack something in resonance in their lower range. Yet they sing dramatically and intelligently, and there is the advantage that the Pizarro of Zoltan Kélémen sounds the more biting and powerful as a result – a fine performance. Jon Vickers as Florestan is, if anything, even finer than he was for Klemperer; and although Helga Dernesch as Leonore does not have quite the clear-focused mastery of Christa Ludwig in the Klemperer set, this is still a glorious, thrilling performance, outshining lesser rivals than Ludwig. The orchestral playing is superb.

Taken from performances at the Salzburg Festival in 1950, with Wilhelm Furtwängler conducting an incomparably starry cast, this should not be confused with the studio recording he made with some of the same cast two years later. This is an Austrian Radio recording, previously available in pirated versions, but here treated to sound which captures the voices on stage with astonishing vividness. The epic scale of Kirsten Flagstad's voice as Leonore sometimes blasts the microphone, but it is a joy to hear such forthright power and security in a role nowadays too often given to squally singers. Elisabeth Schwarzkopf is a delight as Marzelline, vivacious in the dialogue and masterfully sustaining Furtwängler's expansive speed for the Act I quartet. With dialogue included, this is even more compelling than Furtwängler's studio recording, also with Julius Patzak as a superb Florestan, but with Paul Schoeffler a powerful Pizarro and Josef Greindl as Rocco.

Recorded in December 1944, when victory was in sight in the Second World War, this was the first of the concert performances of complete operas that Toscanini conducted in New York. There is no attempt at a dramatic presentation. This is just Beethoven's score with no dialogue whatever, not even in the great confrontation of the Act II quartet; but that makes one concentrate the more on the music, which is plainly what Toscanini wants. Typically his choice of soloists favours voices that are clean-cut and accurate rather than conventionally beautiful, and it is good to have Rose Bampton as a powerful Leonore, an American singer too little appreciated in Europe and too little recorded. Eleanor Steber is a weightier Marzelline than usual, but the clarity and precision are impressive, well matched by the Jaquino of Joseph Laderoute. Sidor Belarsky as Rocco is similarly clean of attack and, though Herbert Janssen is not as fresh-toned as he was earlier, this is a strong and characterful performance. As Florestan, Jan Peerce, Toscanini's favourite American tenor of the time, sings cleanly too if not with great imagination. The transfer follows the honest if unflattering pattern favoured in RCA's Toscanini Edition.

Maazel's Double Decca was recorded in the Sofiensaal in 1964 and the recording is characteristically clear and vivid. Although there is no libretto, the documentation is excellent, far preferable to Boehm's DG competitor in the same price-range. But Birgit Nilsson as Leonora is below her best, and none of the other principals is particularly characterful. Moreover Maazel's direction is erratic and sounds mannered or over-forced.

Boehm, returning to the orchestra he directed in the 1930s, brings a mature warmth to the score; but there are too many flaws in the singing for the set to compete seriously. Gwyneth Jones produces too many squally notes to be a satisfying Leonore, and James King is an uninspired Florestan. Theo Adam as Pizarro is no more appealing to the ear and, in spite of good recording, the DG Double set is put out of court by a complete absence of documentation, except for a list of the 20 cues and a brief background note which devotes just one paragraph to the plot.

However, the recording has also been reissued (at mid-price) as part of DG's Beethoven Edition, and this does include a proper synopsis linked to the generous cueing throughout,

Fidelio: highlights.
(M) *** EMI CDM7 63077-2. Dernesch, Vickers, Ridderbusch, Van Dam, Kélémen, German Op. Ch., BPO, Karajan.

(Y/B) (M) *** DG 445 461-2 [id.] (from complete set, with Janowitz, Kollo, Sotin, Jungirth, Fischer-Dieskau, Popp; cond. Bernstein).

Those who acquire Klemperer's classic set will welcome just under an hour of well-chosen highlights from the fine alternative Karajan recording, made in 1970.

It is also good to have a set of highlights from the Bernstein set, recorded in conjunction with live performances at the Vienna State Opera and full of dramatic flair, yet which presents the drama on a human scale, less monumental than with Klemperer. Janowitz sings most beautifully as Leonore and, although Hans Sotin is not an especially villainous Pizarro, his vocal projection is impressive, Kollo is an intelligent and musicianly Florestan and Lucia Popp is at her delightful best as Marzelline. The selection is generous (71 minutes), including the *Overture* and the final scene, and contains a cued synopsis of the narrative.

Bellini, Vincenzo (1801–35)

Beatrice di Tenda (complete).
(N) (M) ** Sony Dig. SM3K 64539 (3) [id.]. Nicolesco, Cappuccilli, Toczyska, La Scola, Prague Philharmonic Ch., Monte Carlo O, Alberto Zedda.

Beatrice di Tenda (complete); Arias: *Norma: Casta diva. I Puritani: Son vergin vezzosa; Oh rendetemi la speme. La sonnambula: Ah, non credea mirarti.*
(M) *** Decca 433 706-2 (3) [id.]. Sutherland, Pavarotti, Opthof, Veasey, Ward, Amb. Op. Ch., LSO, Bonynge.

Beatrice di Tenda was Bellini's last opera but one, coming after *La sonnambula* and *Norma* and before *I Puritani*. It had an unfortunate birth, for the composer had to go to the law courts to wring the libretto out of his collaborator, Romani; the result is not exactly compelling dramatically. The story involves a whole string of unrequited loves. Bellini always intended to revise the score but failed to do so before his death. As it is, the piece remains essentially a vehicle for an exceptional prima donna with a big enough voice and brilliant enough coloratura. Dame Joan Sutherland has made it her own in recent years – this recording was made in 1966 – and although here she indulges in some of the 'mooning' one hoped she had left behind, there are many dazzling examples of her art. The other star of the set is Richard Bonynge, whose powers as a Bellini conductor are most impressive. The supporting cast could hardly be better, with Pavarotti highly responsive. The recording, made in Walthamstow Assembly Hall, is of Decca's best vintage and it has transferred splendidly to CD, with vivid atmosphere and colour. Four famous arias are provided as a filler: one from Sutherland's 1964 *Norma*, two from her 1963 *I Puritani* and one from the 1962 *La sonnambula*.

Originally issued on the Ricordi label, the Sony set offers a live recording made in Monte Carlo in 1986. The scholar, Alberto Zedda, conducts most sympathetically, and Mariana Nicolesco in the title-role sings with strength and character, often using exciting and distinctive tone-colours, but spoiling Bellinian legato lines with squeezing and gusting and sudden moments of edginess. Others in the cast sing stylishly; but the Sutherland/Bonynge set is far preferable, both for the fresher, more beautiful performance and for the bright Decca sound of good (1966) vintage.

I Capuleti ed i Montecchi (complete).
(Y/B) (M) **(*) EMI Dig. CMS7 64846-2 (2) [CDMB 64846]. Baltsa, Gruberová, Raffanti, Gwynne Howell, Tomlinson, ROHCG Ch. & O, Muti.

Muti's set was recorded live at a series of performances at Covent Garden when the production was new, in March 1984. With the Royal Opera House a difficult venue for recording, the sound is hard and close, far less agreeable and well balanced than in the previous EMI version of this opera, recorded in the studio with Beverley Sills and Dame Janet Baker and now deleted. On the later version, Agnes Baltsa makes a passionately expressive Romeo and Edita Gruberová a Juliet who is not just brilliant in coloratura but also sweet and tender. It is an unlikely but successful matching of a Carmen with a Zerbinetta; but it is the masterful conducting of Muti that, more than anything, makes one tolerant of the indifferent sound. That mastery is especially striking at the end of Act I, when the five principals sing a hushed quintet in which Romeo and Juliet musically reveal their understanding, singing sweetly in thirds. With excellent contributions from the refined tenor Dano Raffanti (as Tebaldo), Gwynne Howell and John Tomlinson, it is a performance to blow the cobwebs off an opera that – even in the earlier recording – seemed one of Bellini's less compelling pieces.

Norma (complete).

(M) *** Decca 425 488-2 (3) [id.]. Sutherland, Horne, Alexander, Cross, Minton, Ward, London Symphony Ch., LSO, Bonynge.

**(*) Decca Dig. 414 476-2 (3) [id.]. Sutherland, Pavarotti, Caballé, Ramey, Welsh Nat. Op. Ch. & O, Bonynge.

(M) **(*) EMI CMS7 63000-2 (3) [Ang. CDMC 63000]. Callas, Corelli, Ludwig, Zaccharia, Ch. & O of La Scala, Milan, Serafin.

(N) (M) ** Sony SM2K 35902 (2) [id.]. Scotto, Troyanos, Giacomini, Plishka, Amb. Op. Ch., Nat. PO, Levine.

(N) (M) ** EMI Dig. CMS5 55471-2 (3) [CDCC 55471]. Eaglen, La Scola, Mei, Kavrakos, Remigio, Gavazzi, Maggio Musicale Fiorentino Ch. & O, Muti.

Norma: highlights.

(M) *** Decca 421 886-2 [id.] (from above complete recording with Sutherland, Horne; cond. Bonynge).

(M) **(*) EMI CDM7 63091-2 (from above complete recording with Callas, Corelli; cond. Serafin).

In her first, mid-1960s recording of *Norma*, Sutherland was joined by an Adalgisa in Marilyn Horne whose control of florid singing is just as remarkable as Sutherland's own, and who sometimes even outshines the heroine in musical imagination. The other soloists are very good indeed. Overall this is a most compelling performance, helped by the conducting of Richard Bonynge, and the Walthamstow recording is vivid but also atmospheric in its CD format.

Dame Joan Sutherland was fifty-eight when her second *Norma* recording was made. The conjunction of Sutherland with Pavarotti and Caballé does not always work easily. Though Pavarotti is in some ways the set's greatest strength, easily expressive yet powerful as Pollione, Caballé as Adalgisa seems determined to outdo Sutherland in mooning manner, cooing self-indulgently. Full, brilliant, well-balanced recording of the complete score.

By the time Callas came to record her 1960 stereo version, the tendency to hardness and unsteadiness in the voice above the stave, always apparent, had grown more serious, but the interpretation was as sharply illuminating as ever, a unique assumption, helped by Christa Ludwig as Adalgisa, while Corelli sings heroically. Serafin as ever is the most persuasive of Bellini conductors.

Renata Scotto as Norma has many beautiful moments but, above pianissimo in the upper register, the voice too regularly acquires a heavy beat and the sound becomes ugly. The close (1979) recording, made in the Henry Wood Hall, does not help, any more than it does with Tatiana Troyanos as Adelgisa, whose vibrato is exaggerated, Giuseppe Giacomini sings with fair style but little imagination, and Levine's conducting is far too brutal for such a piece, favouring aggressively fast tempi.

Recorded live at the Ravenna Festival in July 1994, Muti's performance is powerfully dramatic. Muti remains characteristically forceful but is also more considerate of the singers than he once was, allowing a degree more rubato. In the title-role Eaglen is a fire-eater, formidably expressing vehemence more readily than love, and the recitative before *Casta diva* is superb. For the start of that great aria she shades down her big, bright, resonant tone, but when the voice rises above the stave, particularly in coloratura, too often it acquires an unpleasant edge. The recording does not help, with voices balanced close and with little bloom allowed. This means that the first-rate Handel tenor, Vincenzo La Scola, sounds more heroic of tone than he perhaps is, but it is a clean-cut, incisive performance; and Dimitri Kavrakos is a forthright Oroveso with a distinctive flutter vibrato. Eva Mei makes an interesting choice as Norma's sister, Adalgisa, another soprano who is much lighter and purer than the protagonist and thus easily and convincingly distinguished, even if the matching in duet is not easy. Stage and audience noises tend to be intrusive, which in so poised a work is a marked drawback.

Il Pirata (complete).

(M) ** EMI CMS7 64169-2 (2). Cappuccilli, Caballé, Martí, Raimondi, Rome R. & TV Ch. & O, Gavazzeni.

(N) (M) (**) EMI mono CMS7 64938-2 (2) [CDMB 64938]. Callas, Ego, Miranda Ferraro, Peterson, Watson, Sarfaty, American Op. Soc. Ch. & O, Rescigno.

Gavazzeni's is the first complete recording of *Il Pirata*, the composer's third opera, written for La Scala and first produced in 1827. In the best traditions of Italian opera, in the finale the pirate-hero is killed, his rival is condemned to death, and the heroine loses her mind. With a not very promising scenario the opera is too long for its material. Caballé is well suited to the role of the heroine, though by her finest standards there is some carelessness in her singing – clumsy changes of register and less than the expected beauty of tonal contrast. Nor is the conducting and presentation sparkling enough to mask the comparative poverty of Bellini's invention at this early stage of his career. Bernabé Martí makes a fair stab at the difficult part of the pirate. The 1970 recording flatters the voices and has plenty of atmosphere but it is not as vividly projected as the best Decca offerings from this period.

Recorded live at a concert performance in New York in January 1959, the Callas version is inevitably flawed, with harsh sound and intrusive audience noises. Though Callas herself shows signs of the vocal deterioration which afflicted her all too early in her career, with top notes often raw and uneven, hers is a fire-eating performance, totally distinctive, instantly magnetic from the moment she utters her first word, 'Sorgete', in Act I. The rest of the cast is indifferent, with Constantine Ego strenuous in the tenor role of Ernesto. The second disc offers an alternative recording of the final scene, made in Amsterdam six months later, with Rescigno conducting the Concertgebouw Orchestra and with Callas in smoother vocal form, helped by less raw recording.

I Puritani (complete).
*** Decca 417 588-2 (3). Sutherland, Pavarotti, Ghiaurov, Luccardi, Caminada, Cappuccilli, ROHCG Ch. & O, Bonynge.
(Y/B) (M) **(*) EMI CMS7 69663-2 (2) [Ang. CDMC 69663]. Caballé, Kraus, Manuguerra, Hamari, Ferrin, Amb. Op. Ch., Philh. O, Muti.

Whereas her earlier set was recorded when Sutherland had adopted a soft-grained style, with consonants largely eliminated and a tendency to lag behind the beat, this time her singing is fresher and brighter. Pavarotti shows himself a remarkable Bellini stylist, Ghiaurov and Cappuccilli make up an impressive cast, and the only disappointing contributor is Anita Caminada in the small role of Enrichetta. Vivid, atmospheric recording.

In the EMI version of *I Puritani*, Riccardo Muti's contribution is most distinguished. As the very opening demonstrates, his attention to detail and pointing of rhythm make for refreshing results, and the warm but luminous recording is excellent. But both the principal soloists – Bellini stylists on their day, but here below form – indulge in distracting mannerisms, hardly allowing even a single bar to be presented straight in the big numbers, pulling and tugging in each direction, rarely sounding spontaneous. The big ensemble, *A te, o cara*, in its fussiness at slow speed loses the surge of exhilaration which Sutherland and Pavarotti show so strongly.

La Sonnambula (complete).
*** Decca Dig. 417 424-2 (2) [id.]. Sutherland, Pavarotti, Della Jones, Ghiaurov, L. Op. Ch., Nat. PO, Bonynge.
(***) EMI mono CDS7 47378-8 (2) [CDCB 47377]. Callas, Monti, Cossotto, Zaccaria, Ratti, La Scala, Milan, Ch. and O, Votto.

Sutherland's singing here is even more affecting and more stylish than her earlier version, generally purer and more forthright, if with diction still clouded at times. The challenge of singing opposite Pavarotti adds to the bite of the performance, crisply and resiliently controlled by Bonynge.

Substantially cut, the Callas version was recorded in mono in 1957, yet it gives a vivid picture of the diva at the peak of her powers. Nicola Monti makes a strong rather than a subtle contribution but blends well with Callas in the duets; and Fiorenza Cossotto is a good Teresa.

Ben-Haim, Paul (1897–1984)

Violin concerto.
*** EMI Dig. CDC7 54296-2 [id.]. Perlman, Israel PO, Mehta – CASTELNUOVO-TEDESCO: *Concerto No. 2.* ***

Perlman's coupling of concertos by Castelnuovo-Tedesco and Ben-Haim brings a heartfelt tribute to his Jewish background. These are live recordings, made in the Mann Auditorium in Tel Aviv, happily with the orchestral sound less brutally dry than usual, here given an acceptable bloom. The Hindemithian vigour of the outer movements of Ben-Haim's compact work readily gives way to Bloch-like melodic writing, with augmented intervals reflecting the music of the synagogue. The central *Andante affettuoso* too is a simple Jewish song, with the main melody returning at the end stratospherically high. As in the Castelnuovo-Tedesco work, Perlman is inspired to some of his most masterly playing, not just breathtakingly brilliant but deeply felt.

Sweet Psalmist of Israel.
(M) **(*) Sony SM2K 47533 (2). Marlowe, Stavrache, NYPO, Bernstein – BLOCH: *Sacred service;* FOSS: *Song of songs.* ***

As the biblical King David was a versatile musician, Ben-Haim represents him here by the use of both concertante harp and (more dubiously) harpsichord in his vividly scored triptych. The recording is balanced very forwardly, with the microphones too close, especially to the solo instruments. However, the early movements have a certain textural charm.

Benjamin, George (born 1960)

(i) *Ringed by the flat horizon.* (ii) *At first light. A Mind of winter.*
*** Nimbus Dig. NI 5075 [id.]. (i) BBC SO, Elder; (ii) Penelope Walmsley-Clark, L. Sinf., composer.

Ringed by the flat horizon is a 20-minute orchestral piece, with the big climax masterfully built. *A Mind of winter* is a 9-minute setting of *The Snowman* by Wallace Stevens, beautifully sung by the soprano Penelope Walmsley-Clark. Sound of great warmth and refinement to match the music make this a collection well worth exploring.

Piano sonata.
** Nimbus Single NI 1415 [id.]. Composer.

George Benjamin is one of the most imaginative composers of the younger generation. His *Piano sonata* dates from 1978 when he was still a student at the Paris Conservatoire. The influences are predominantly Gallic, and in particular the music of Messiaen (hardly surprising, considering that he studied with both that master and Yvonne Loriod). Benjamin is also a very good pianist, but the recording, made in 1980, is not quite three-star and sounds a bit synthetic. A 'single', this runs to 22 minutes 26 seconds.

Bennett, Richard Rodney (born 1936)

Guitar concerto (for guitar and chamber ensemble).
(M) *** RCA 09026 61598-2. Julian Bream, Melos Ens., Atherton – ARNOLD: *Concerto;* RODRIGO: *Concierto de Aranjuez.* ***

Bennett's concerto, written in 1970, is dedicated to Bream. It is imaginatively conceived, and its variety of texture, glittering and transparent, consistently intrigues the ear. If the work's idiom and language start out from the twelve-tone system, there is nothing difficult for the listener to assimilate. The performance, like its Arnold coupling, is definitive and the 1972 recording is first class in every way.

Bennett, Robert Russell (1894–1981)

Symphonic songs for band.
(M) *** Mercury 432 009-2 [id.]. Eastman Wind Ens., Fennell – HOLST: *Hammersmith* ***; JACOB: *William Byrd suite* ***; WALTON: *Crown Imperial.* *** ✪

Bennett's triptych, not surprisingly, relies more on colouristic manipulation and sonority than on content. Marvellous playing and Mercury's best recording. The disc also includes a *Fanfare and allegro* by Clifton Williams.

Benoit, Peter (1834–1901)

Hoogmis (High Mass).
(B) *(**) Discover Dig. DICD 920178 [id.]. Donald George, Belgian R. & TV Philharmonic Ch., Koninklijk Vlaams Antwerp Music Conservatoire Ch. & Caecilia Chorale, Gemengd Ars Musica Merksem Ch., Zingende Wandelkring Saint Norbertus Ch., Belgian R. & TV PO, Rahbari.

The bargain Discover label offers a fascinating rarity, the *Hoogmis* (*High Mass*), by the Belgian composer, Peter Benoit, a contemporary of Brahms. Alexander Rahbari's account with the BRTN Philharmonic Orchestra of Brussels and massed choirs, with the tenor, Donald George, taking the solos in the *Benedictus* and *Dona nobis pacem*, has all the thrust you need for an ambitious work lasting 55 minutes. With themes square-cut rather than individual and with crisply effective choral writing, the piece echoes Beethoven's *Missa solemnis* rather than any French model. The trouble is that the live recording, though atmospheric and full of presence, brings washy sound, and starts without warning.

Bentzon, Niels Viggo (born 1919)

Feature on René Descartes, Op. 357.
(*) BIS CD 79 [id.]. Danish Nat. R. O, Schmidt – JORGENSON: *To love music;* NORBY: *The Rainbow snake.* *

Krönik om René Descartes ('Feature on René Descartes') comes from 1975, and this recording was made at its première that year. The first movement gives a 'musical version of the Cartesian vortex which refers to a medieval notion of rotating heavenly bodies moving at enormous speed'; in other movements we are at the centre of the Aristotelean storm, and the final movement addresses Descartes' celebrated proposition, *Cogito ergo sum.* There are occasional flashes during its 27-minute duration that remind one of his best and most visionary music and, although there are enough good things to make it worth investigating, it is not a recommended or even characteristic entry-point into his world. An eminently well-prepared performance and good recording.

Symphonies Nos. 3, Op. 46 (1947); 4 (Metamorphoses), Op. 55 (1949).
*** Marco Polo DaCapo DCCD 9102 [id.]. Aarhus SO, Ole Schmidt.

Bentzon's music fuses something of the lean, rhythmic neo-classicism of Stravinsky, the contrapuntal vitality of Hindemith and the open-air diatonicism of Nielsen. Both the symphonies recorded here are teeming with invention: the pastoral opening of the *Third* unleashes a rich flow of ideas, all of memorable quality. The *Fourth* (*Metamorphoses*) is a most imaginative work, music of real vision and individuality, powerful, concentrated and inventive. Along with the *Sixth* and *Seventh Symphonies* of Holmboe, this is arguably the finest Nordic symphony after Nielsen and Ole Schmidt, and the Aarhus orchestra play it with all the conviction and passion they can muster. Although, ideally, the acoustic of the Aarhus hall is not quite ample enough for big climaxes, the recording is very good indeed, with plenty of detail and a good balance. Two remarkable works.

Berg, Alban (1885–1935)

Chamber concerto for piano, violin & 13 wind instruments, Op. 6.
(Y/B) (M) *** DG 447 405-2 [id.]. Barenboim, Zukerman, Ens. Intercontemporain, Boulez – STRAVINSKY: *Concerto in E flat* etc. ***

(i) *Chamber concerto;* (ii) *3 Pieces for orchestra;* (iii) *Violin concerto.*
(N) (M) ** Sony SMK 68331 [id.]. (i) Barenboim, Gavrilov; (i–ii) BBC SO; (iii) Zukerman, LSO; (i–iii) Boulez.

(i) *Chamber concerto;* (ii) *Violin concerto.*
(N) (M) ** Sony Stern Edition II SMK 64504 [id.]. Isaac Stern, with (i) Peter Serkin, LSO members, Abbado; (ii) NYPO, Bernstein.

On DG, Boulez sets brisk tempi in the *Chamber concerto*, seeking to give the work classical incisiveness; but the strong and expressive personalities of the pianist and violinist tend towards a more romantic view. The result is characterful and convincing, though unaccountably Boulez omits the extended repeat in the finale. The recording is attractively atmospheric, and those who regard this as a difficult work will find the music-making here not in the least intimidating.

This Sony issue conveniently couples Berg's two concertante works with violin, featuring Isaac Stern in both. The yoking, however, is uneven, when these are recordings made 26 years apart. The 1959 recording of the *Violin concerto* underlines the coarser side of the performance in which Stern takes a redblooded, romantic view of the work, as does Bernstein, with finer points skated over. There is coarseness in the *Chamber concerto* too, when the recording balance is aggressively close, though in other respects the sound is truthful. This is undoubtedly a virtuoso performance, but the interplay of instrumentalists is much less subtle than it might be, with Stern's violin for once placed rather backwardly in relation to the wind players. The digital sound is very immediate indeed.

Boulez's personality strongly dominates the Sony performances, the *Chamber concerto* and Op. 6 *Orchestral pieces*, sharply focused in 1967, with the solo passages very forward, and the *Violin concerto* with the soloist very close indeed, recorded two decades later in 1984. Zukerman's strong, urgent reading matches Boulez's toughness; his virtuoso flair makes for a robust rather than a subtle or poetic reading. The elegiac quality is missing.

Violin concerto.

(N) (M) *** DG 447 445-2 [id.]. Itzhak Perlman, Boston SO, Ozawa – RAVEL: *Tzigane;* STRAVINSKY: *Concerto.* ***

(Y/B) *** Teldec/Warner Dig. 4509 97449-2 [id.]. Zehetmair, Philh. O, Holliger – HARTMANN: *Concerto funèbre;* JANACEK: *Violin concerto.* ***

*** DG Dig. 437 093-2 [id.]. Mutter, Chicago SO, Levine – RIHM: *Gesungene Zeit; Time chant.* ***

(N) (BB) *** RCA Navigator 74321 29243-2. Hoelscher, Cologne RSO, Wakasugi – SCHOENBERG: *Verklerte Nacht;* WEBERN: *Passacaglia for orchestra.* ***

(N) (M) *** Sup. SU 1939-2 011 [id.]. Josef Suk, Czech PO, Karel Ančerl – BRUCH: *Concerto* **; MENDELSSOHN: *Concerto.* **(*)

(M) *** EMI CDM7 63989-2 [id.]. Sir Yehudi Menuhin, BBC SO, Boulez – BLOCH: *Violin concerto.* ***

The Berg *Concerto* currently must outstrip most other modern concertos, if the CD catalogues are an accurate barometer of taste. There are more than twice as many versions than of the Bartók or the Walton; only the Prokofiev *D major concerto* has comparable representation. Perlman's performance is totally commanding. The Boston orchestra accompanies superbly and, though the balance favours the soloist, the recording is excellent. This is an obvious candidate for DG's series of 'Originals' and is the more welcome at mid-price with the added bonus of the Ravel *Tzigane*. The current transfer shows the Boston acoustic at its most seductive: Berg's *Concerto* has never sounded richer or texturally more opulent on disc.

The Teldec recording by Thomas Zehetmair and the Philharmonia Orchestra under Heinz Holliger is one of the best to appear for a long time. Zehetmair plays with great sensitivity and a natural eloquence that many will prefer to the much (and rightly) admired account by Mutter on DG. That has tremendous brilliance and panache, but the glitzy elegance and slight coolness are less affecting than Zehetmair's reading. His version is less sensational and brings you closer to the heart of this poignant music. It offers more interesting couplings in the form of the Hartmann *Concerto funèbre* and the fragmentary Janáček *Concerto* of 1927–8. The recording, made at The Maltings in Snape, is of exemplary clarity and has great presence.

Anne-Sophie Mutter begins the *Concerto* with a pianissimo of such delicacy that it has one's ears pricking. She proceeds to give an intensely passionate reading, both freely expressive and intensely purposeful, with James Levine and the Chicago orchestra matching her in subtle shading. As an imaginative coupling, Mutter offers a concerto written for her by the 40-year-old German composer, Wolfgang Rihm.

Ulf Hoelscher is particularly well balanced in this fine (1977) Cologne recording, and he gives a passionately dedicated account of Berg's concerto, splendidly supported by Wakasugi and the excellent Cologne Radio Orchestra. The recording, though not as smooth and rich as Perlman's on DG, has plenty of warmth and the closing *Adagio* is very moving in its haunting intensity. This comes at the lowest possible price with two other key twentieth-century works, both very well played and recorded, although the documentation is totally inadequate.

Suk's sweet, unforced style brings out the work's lyrical side without ever exaggerating the romanticism, and the result is most moving. The arrival of the chorale theme (which Berg took from a Bach cantata) is achieved most delicately and the final coda has rarely sounded more tender and hushed on record. A most beautiful performance, with the excellent (1965) recording very firmly and naturally transferred to CD.

Menuhin's is a warm and vibrant performance and, though technically this is not as dashing or immaculate a performance as several others on record, it is one that compels admiration on its own terms of greatness.

(i) *Violin concerto;* (ii) *Lyric suite: 3 Pieces; 3 Pieces for orchestra, Op. 6.*

(Y/B) (B) *** DG 439 435-2 [id.].(i) Szeryng, Bav. RSO, Kubelik; (ii) BPO, Karajan.

(***) Testament mono SBT1004 [id.]. (i) Louis Krasner, BBC SO, Anton Webern; (ii) Galimir Qt.

Another outstanding version of Berg's *Violin concerto* comes from Henryk Szeryng, who gives a persuasive, perceptive and sympathetic account of this fine work and is well accompanied by the Bavarian orchestra under Kubelik. Superb playing, and a recording that has transferred well to CD. It is perhaps remarkable that, for their bargain Classikon reissue, DG have chosen to add to this two of Karajan's key recordings of Berg's orchestral music. Karajan's purification process gives wonderful clarity to these often complex pieces, with expressive confidence bringing out the romantic overtones. A beautiful, refined recording, admirably transferred to CD.

The Testament CD is of enormous interest as it brings back to life a broadcast of the *Violin concerto* by Louis Krasner who commissioned it and gave its first performance (and who subsequently made the first commercial recording on 78-r.p.m. discs). This is the second performance of the work ever, given only five months after Berg's death, and it is laden with an intensity and feeling that it would be impossible for anyone else to recapture. The quality is poor (it comes from the soloist's own acetates) but the spirit is extraordinarily powerful and vibrant, and the BBC orchestra play superbly. It comes with another 1936 recording, the Galimir Quartet's pioneering Polydor 78s of the *Lyric suite* – impeccably played but recorded in a horribly dry acoustic. Never mind, the concerto is a document of quite extraordinary interest.

Lyric suite: 3 Pieces; 3 Pieces for orchestra, Op. 6.
(M) *** DG 427 424-2 (3) [id.]. BPO, Karajan – SCHOENBERG; WEBERN: *Orchestral pieces.* ***

Karajan's justly famous collection of music by the Second Viennese School is here available as a set of three mid-priced CDs. Beautiful, refined recording, admirably transferred to CD.

3 Pieces for orchestra, Op. 6.
*** DG Dig. 419 781-2 [id.]. BPO, Levine – SCHOENBERG; WEBERN: *Pieces.* ***

Levine gives a powerful, warmly emotional reading of Berg's Opus 6, though odd emphasis of individual lines is intrusive in an otherwise full and vivid recording.

3 Pieces for orchestra, Op. 6; (i) Lulu: symphonic suite.
(M) *** Mercury 432 006-2 [id.]. (i) Helga Pilarczyk; LSO, Dorati – SCHOENBERG; WEBERN: *Orchestral pieces.* ***

In his pioneering 1962 Mercury coupling Dorati set the pattern for later recordings of this twentieth-century orchestral triptych, none recorded more clearly or vividly. The LSO plays fluently and warmly. For the *Lulu suite*, recorded a year earlier, Helga Pilarczyk is most impressive: the murder produces the most blood-curdling scream.

3 Pieces for orchestra, Op. 6; 5 Orchestral songs, Op. 4; (i) Lulu: symphonic suite.
(M) *** DG 449 714-2 [id.]. (i) M. Price; LSO, Abbado.

Abbado makes it clear above all how beautiful Berg's writing is, not just in the *Lulu* excerpts but in the early Opus 4 *Songs* and the Opus 6 *Orchestral pieces*. Now remastered and reissued as part of DG's 'Legendary Recordings', this mid-priced 'Original' offers even better value.

Lyric suite; String quartet, Op. 3.
(Y/B) *** EMI Dig. CDC5 55190-2 [id.]. Alban Berg Qt.

The eponymous Alban Berg Quartet give masterly and authoritative accounts of the early *String quartet* of 1910 and of the *Lyric suite*. It is difficult to imagine these works being better played or recorded. There is room for another work – say, the Webern 1905 *Quartet* – the playing time is no more than 47 minutes; but if it is short on quantity, it is emphatically not on quality. Of the ten or so versions now on the market, this *Lyric suite* is a good first choice, and that of the Op. 3 *Quartet* is arguably the best ever. The recording has a comparable finesse and is realistic and truthful.

Piano sonata, Op. 1.
** DG Dig. 423 678-2 [id.]. Maurizio Pollini – DEBUSSY: *Etudes.* **

An impressive enough account of Berg's one-movement *Sonata*, as powerful as any on disc. But it is not helped by a clinical, rather closely balanced recording, and the Debussy *Etudes* with which it is coupled are conspicuously wanting in atmosphere and poetry.

7 Early songs (1905–8 versions).
*** DG Dig. 437 515-2. Anne Sofie von Otter, Bengt Forsberg – KORNGOLD: *Lieder;* STRAUSS: *Lieder.* ***

In the seven early songs of Berg, Anne Sofie von Otter and Bengt Forsberg follow up the success of their prize-winning disc of Grieg songs with inspired playing and singing, drawing out the intensity of emotion to the full without exaggeration or sentimentality. Along with Strauss and Korngold songs, a fascinating programme, magnetically performed.

Lulu (with orchestration of Act III completed by Friedrich Cerha).
*** DG 415 489-2 (3) [id.]. Stratas, Minton, Schwarz, Mazura, Blankenheim, Riegel, Tear, Paris Op. O, Boulez.
*** EMI Dig. CDS7 54622-2 (3) [Ang. CDCC 54622]. Wise, Fassbaender, Straka, Clark, Schone, Clarey, O Nat. de France, Tate.

The full three-Act structure of Berg's *Lulu*, with Yvonne Minton singing the Countess Geschwitz's lament, is most moving, though Lulu remains to the last a repulsive heroine. Teresa Stratas's bright, clear soprano is well recorded. Altogether this is an intensely involving performance of a work which in some ways is more lyrically approachable than *Wozzeck*.

Jeffrey Tate's live recording of the full three-Act version provides a welcome alternative to the pioneer DG recording from Pierre Boulez with the original Paris Opéra cast. Tate's reading is more flexible, more volatile, more emotional than Boulez's. There are stage noises and some minor flaws of ensemble, and the recording is at a relatively low level, not as satisfying as the firmer, clearer, better-balanced DG sound for Boulez, who as a Berg interpreter is forceful, direct and rugged rather than affectionate. On casting, Tate's set is marginally preferable, with Patricia Wise in the title-role more sensuous than Teresa Stratas for Boulez, and with Brigitte Fassbaender incomparable as the predatory Countess Geschwitz, spontaneously expressive for Tate. Otherwise Graham Clark is a fine match for Robert Tear in various tenor roles, and Peter Straka is a more idiomatic Alwa than the clear-toned Kenneth Riegel for Boulez.

Lulu: symphonic suite.
*** EMI Dig. CDC7 49857-2 [id.]. Arleen Augér, CBSO, Rattle – SCHOENBERG: *5 Pieces;* WEBERN: *6 Pieces.* ***

Augér's pure, true soprano in the vocal passages of the *Lulu suite* is presented as an adjunct to the orchestra, rather than as a salient solo. The sound is of demonstration quality, adding enormously to the attractiveness of the disc.

Wozzeck (complete).
*** Decca Dig. 417 348-2 (2) [id.]. Waechter, Silja, Winkler, Laubenthal, Jahn, Malta, Sramek, VPO, Dohnányi – SCHOENBERG: *Erwartung.* ***
**(*) DG 423 587-2 (2) [id.]. Grundheber, Behrens, Haugland, Langridge, Zednik, V. State Op. Ch., VPO, Abbado.

Dohnányi, with refined textures and superb playing from the Vienna Philharmonic, presents an account of *Wozzeck* that not only is more accurate than any other on record but also is more beautiful.

The Abbado version, recorded live in the opera house, is very compelling in its presentation of the drama, given extra thrust through the tensions of live performance. However, there are drawbacks, too. Not only do you get the stage noises; the voices are also set behind the orchestra, with the instrumental sound putting a gauze between listener and singers.

Wozzeck (excerpts).
(M) **(*) Mercury Dig. 434 325-2 [id.]. Pilarczyk, LSO, Dorati – BARTOK: *Bluebeard's castle* (complete). **(*)

These three concert-excerpts from *Wozzeck* come as a very generous fill-up to Dorati's 1962 recording of Bartók's *Bluebeard's Castle*. The LSO play brilliantly, with the highly analytical Mercury recording bringing out both the power and the delicate poetry, even though pianissimos tend to be overamplified. The snag is the abrasive, at times under-the-note singing of Helga Pilarczyk in the brief vocal passages.

Berio, Luciano (born 1925)

Différences; 2 Pieces; (i) *Sequenza III;* (ii) *Sequenza VII;* (i) *Chamber music.*
(M) *** Ph. 426 662-2. (i) Cathy Berberian; (ii) Heinz Holliger; Juilliard Ens. (members), composer.

The biggest work here is *Différences* for five instruments and tape; but the two virtuoso solos – *Sequenza III* for voice and *Sequenza VII* for oboe – are if anything even more striking in their extensions of technique and expressive range. First-rate sound, well transferred.

Eindrücke; Sinfonia.
*** Erato/Warner Dig. 2292 45228-2 [id.]. Pasquier, New Swingle Singers, O Nat. de France, Boulez.

It was in 1969 that Berio's *Sinfonia*, written for the New York Philharmonic, made a far wider impact on the music world than is common with an avant-garde composer. Boulez records the complete work for the first time in this fine Erato version. *Eindrücke* is another powerful work, much more compressed, bare and uncompromising in its layering of strings and wind.

Coro (revised version).
(M) *** DG 423 902-2 [id.]. Cologne R. Ch. and SO, composer.

Coro is one of the most ambitious of Berio's works, with each of forty singers paired with an instrumentalist and with folk verse on basic themes contrasted with poems of Pablo Neruda. The composer directs a committed performance here, helped by the impact of the forward sound.

(i) *Recital I (for Cathy);* (ii) *Folk-song suite;* (iii) *3 Songs by Kurt Weill* (arr. Berio).

(Y/B) (M) *** RCA 09026 62540-2 [id.]. Cathy Berberian, with (i) L. Sinf.; (ii, iii) Juilliard Ens.; all cond. composer.

Recital I is the most elaborate, colourful work that Berio ever wrote for Cathy Berberian. Against fragmentary accompaniment from the instrumental band, the soloist in this semi-dramatic piece (presented in live performances as music theatre) thinks back through her repertoire as a concert-singer from Monteverdi to the present day. The end-product is a collage of musical ideas of a kind that Berio has always handled most skilfully and, with Berberian at her most intense, the result is very compelling. Excellent recording. Also included is a first-rate recording of an enchanting collection of folksongs arranged with twinkling ingenuity by Berio, again with Berberian very much in mind. The record concludes with three Kurt Weill songs, arranged by Berio, including the *Song of sexual slavery* intended for *The Threepenny Opera.* Cathy Berberian relishes every word, and she sings *Surabaya Johnny* with comparable enjoyment to Berio's effective scoring.

Requiem of Reconciliation (written in conjunction with 13 other composers): BERIO: *Prolog.* CERHA: *Introitus and Kyrie.* DITTRICH: *Dies irae.* KOPELENT: *Judex ergo.* HARBISON: *Juste Judex.* NORDHEIM: *Confutatis.* RANDS: *Interludium.* DALBAVIE: *Domine Jesu Christe.* WEIR: *Sanctus.* PENDERECKI: *Agnus Dei.* RIHM: *Communio I.* SCHNITTKE/ROZHDESTVENSKY: *Communio II.* YUASA: *Responsorium.* KURTAG: *Epilog.*

(N) *** Hänssler Dig. CD 98.931 (2) [id.]. Janzik, Donna Brown, Moffat, Danz, Randle, Schmidt, Stuttgart Gachinger Kantorei; Cracow Chamber Ch., Israel PO, Rilling.

First given in Stuttgart on 16 August 1995, this collaboration of 14 composers has produced an amazingly consistent result. It was the idea of the conductor, Helmuth Rilling – who earlier won fame for the Hänssler Classics label, reconstructing and recording another collaborative effort, the *Messa per Rossini* (as originally organized by Verdi) – to celebrate in this way the fiftieth anniversary of the ending of the Second World War. He asked composers from the combatant nations – the Dutch sadly missing – to collaborate in a work which would reflect the suffering of war and to symbolize the reconciliation which has followed. Rilling has long had a special relationship with the Israel Philharmonic, and it was felt apt that the Jewish contribution should be the attendant one of interpretation. On this live recording the sound is spectacular. The vast forces, superbly balanced, are caught with a bite and immediacy which allow one to appreciate every detail. Luciano Berio's dramatic *Prologue* re-creates the raw sound of the Jewish Shofar on heavy brass, leading to a dark and taxing first half. Only towards the end of that sequence does John Harbison's fine setting of *Juste Judex* lighten the mood and textures, with Nordheim then the first identifiably to use the secondary idea presented to all the composers of linking the *Requiem* with Gregorian chant. Nordheim uses the notes of the chant vertically as well as horizontally, while in the second half the Frenchman, Marc-André Dalbavie, in his *Domine Jesu Christe* goes much further in direct Gregorian echoes. After Bernard Rands' thoughtful introduction, the second half brings a brassily incandescent setting of the *Sanctus* from Judith Weir. There was a question-mark concerning Schnittke's contribution to the *Commmunio* when he suffered a stroke, but Gennadi Rozhdestvensky came to the rescue, orchestrating the completed sketch. Following that, the Japanese, Joji Yuasa, offers an atmospheric *Libera me* as a culmination, with Gyorgy Kurtag's *Epilogue* striking but rather perfunctory. Only one of the 14 contributions is a total disappointment, but that a serious one: the noisy *Dies irae* of the German, Paul-Heinz Dittrich, using extravagant extra percussion within a general flight from precise pitching. From a fine team of soloists the Canadian soprano, Donna Brown, stands out, while chorus and orchestra perform with thrilling attack.

Berkeley, Lennox (1903–89)

Guitar concerto.

(M) *** RCA 09026 61605-2 [id.]. Julian Bream, Monteverdi O, Gardiner – BROUWER; RODRIGO: *Concertos.* ***

This is a really splendid concerto with memorable invention and elegant architecture which presents a serious as well as attractive argument and a stylish brand of guitar writing that never leans barrenly on Spanish models. The *Lento* is particularly atmospheric. Bream's performance is superb and the recording vivid. This, with the equally stimulating Brouwer, makes an attractive if out-of-the-way coupling for the most popular of all guitar concertos.

Divertimento in B flat, Op. 18; Partita for chamber orchestra, Op. 66; Serenade for strings, Op. 12; (i)
Sinfonia concertante for oboe and chamber orchestra, Op. 84: Canzonetta (only). *Symphony No. 3 in one
movement, Op. 74; Mont Juic* (with Britten), *Op. 9.*
*** Lyrita SRCD 226 [id.]. LPO, composer; (i) with Roger Winfield.

This beautifully planned Lyrita collection introduces some of the most elegant and enjoyable music that
Berkeley wrote. The *Divertimento* is enchanting, with its four stylish and highly inventive movements,
while the *String serenade*, similarly in four sections, is hardly less attractive and brings a beautiful *Lento*
closing movement. In its rather weightier tone of voice the *Partita* belies that it was written originally
with a youth orchestra in mind, while the fourth movement from the *Sinfonia concertante* makes a
splendid interlude before the closing *Symphony No. 3*. This is a concise, one-movement work, slightly
more austere in its lyricism, but with a popular element entering the finale. Here at times one has the
feeling that the composer would have created an even stronger effect had he held the performance more
tautly. The recording, too, from the early 1970s, is first class, and the CD transfers only improve the
sense of presence and realism. The programme opens with the charmingly spontaneous *Mont Juic* suite
which Berkeley wrote in collaboration with Benjamin Britten, two movements each (Berkeley contributing the opening pair), and the work was later published jointly as Berkeley's Op. 9 and Britten's Op. 12.

*Improvisation on a theme of Falla, Op. 55l2; Mazurka, Op. 101l2; 3 Mazurkas (Hommage à Chopin), Op.
32; Paysage; 3 Pieces; Polka, Op. 5a; 6 Preludes, Op. 23; 5 Short pieces, Op. 4; Sonata, Op. 20.*
**(*) Kingdom KCLCD 2012; *CKCL 2012* [id.]. Christopher Headington (piano).

With the exception of the *Sonata*, all these pieces are miniatures, some of considerable elegance.
Christopher Headington is a sympathetic exponent and he is completely attuned to the idiom. The
recording is eminently serviceable and truthful.

Berkeley, Michael (born 1948)

(i; ii) *Clarinet concerto;* (i) *Flighting;* (iii; ii) *Père du doux repos (Father of sweet sleep from Speaking
silence).*
*** ASV Dig. Single CDDCB 1101 [id.]. (i) Emma Johnson; (ii) N. Sinfonia, Sian Edwards; (iii) Henry
    Herford.

The *Clarinet concerto*, written for Emma Johnson in 1991, represents a new generation in Michael
Berkeley's work, less lyrical, more abrasive and, above all, concentrated. The soloist's concentration
leads one magnetically through a thicket of virtuoso writing, often marked by stratospheric shrieks,
which she consistently makes compelling, thanks also to the dedicated accompaniment under Sian
Edwards. A central, meditative *Adagio* leads to a climactic screech of pain, which is then released into a
brief elegiac epilogue. That closing section leads logically on to the two much briefer works on the disc,
what the composer describes as 'fitting pendants'. The vocal work is a setting of a sonnet by the
sixteenth-century French poet, Pontus de Tyard, while the solo clarinet piece grows out of the song,
bringing out the soloist's warmly lyrical side further.

Berlin, Irving (1888–1989)

Annie get your gun (musical).
✷ *** EMI Dig. CDC7 54206-2 [id.]. Criswell, Hampson, Graee, Luker, Amb. Ch., L. Sinf., John
    McGlinn.

This is one of the most delectable of all show records. John McGlinn follows up the pattern of his best-
selling set of Jerome Kern's *Show Boat* with another performance that is at once scholarly and pulsing
with life. Not only is the singing strong, characterful and idiomatic, the whole performance – not least
from the players of the London Sinfonietta – is full of fun. Kim Criswell as Annie with her electric
personality and bitingly bright voice here confirms herself as the natural successor to Ethel Merman,
the original Annie Oakley, characterizing strongly while pitching precisely. Equally remarkably, Thomas
Hampson makes an ideal hero, an opera-singer with an exceptionally rich and firm baritone who
naturally gets inside the idiom. First-rate, full-bodied sound.

Berlioz, Hector (1803–69)

(i) *Harold in Italy, Op. 16;* (ii) *La damnation de Faust, Op. 24: Hungarian march; Ballet des sylphes; Menuet des follets;* (iii) *Les Troyens: Trojan march;* (iv) *Royal Hunt & Storm.*
(B) **(*) Sony SBK 53255; *SBT 53255* [id.]. (i) Joseph de Pasquale; (i; iii) Phd. O, Ormandy; (ii) Phd. O, Munch; (iv) O de Paris, Barenboim.

(i) *Harold in Italy, Op. 16;* (ii) *Overtures: Benvenuto Cellini, Op. 23; Les Francs-juges, Op. 3.*
(M) *** EMI CDM7 64745-2 [id.]. (i) Donald McInnes, O Nat. de France, Bernstein; (ii) LSO, Previn.

(i) *Harold in Italy;* (ii) *Tristia (Méditation religieuse; La mort d'Ophélie; March funèbre pour la dernière scène de Hamlet), Op. 18.*
(N) *** Ph. Dig. 446 676-2 [id.]. (i) Gérard Caussé; (ii) Monteverdi Ch.; ORR, Gardiner.

(i) *Harold in Italy;* (ii) *Tristia (Méditation religieuse; La mort d'Ophélie; Marche funèbre pour la dernière scène de Hamlet), Op. 18; Les Troyens à Carthage: Prelude to Act II.*
*** Ph. 416 431-2 [id.]. (i) Imai; (ii) Alldis Ch.; LSO, C. Davis.

With the understanding players of the Orchestre National, Bernstein gives a performance that is both exciting and introspective. His earlier account with his own New York Philharmonic for CBS was sharper-focused than this. But with French players Bernstein's slightly more relaxed manner is in some ways more authentic, so that the galloping rhythms of the first and third movements are more lilting, if fractionally less precise. Donald McInnes is a violist with a superbly rich and even tone. His first entry, with the phrase echoed, is a ravishing moment and he responds at all times to the conductor, yet has plenty of individuality. The 1976 recording, made in the Salle Wagram, has an opulent spread and plenty of warmth; on CD it is brighter and more firmly focused. This goes to the top of the list of available recordings of this somewhat elusive work and is certainly first choice at mid-price. It is made the more attractive by the addition of the two overtures. Under Previn, the swing-along melody of *Les Francs-juges* swaggers boldly. Again excellent transfers, with rich, deep brass.

Gardiner's pioneering account of *Harold in Italy* on period instruments is searingly dramatic, the more biting in its impact with textures transparent yet with plenty of weight and high dynamoic contrasts. Gérard Caussé, earlier the soloist in the Plasson version, here produces far sparer sounds than before, making the result more eerie, though he allows himself warm vibrato in the lyrical Harold theme. The three separate movements of *Tristia* are equally refreshing and dramatic, with sharp dynamic contrasts. Excellent sound.

Davis's Philips account offers even better value. In addition to a noble account of *Harold* in which Nobuko Imai is on top form, this CD offers the *Tristia*, which includes the haunting *Funeral march for the last scene of Hamlet* given with chorus; this CD also offers the *Prelude* to the second Act of *Les Troyens*. The sound is completely natural and realistic, and has impressive transparency and detail.

Ormandy's 1965 recording of *Harold in Italy* with the Philadelphia Orchestra has a lot going for it. Joseph de Pasquale is a thoughtful and cultured soloist and he is truthfully and expertly balanced in relation to the orchestra. The performance is beautifully shaped, though the finale could perhaps do with a shade more abandon. Although the recording perspective is excellent, the sound is not as transparent as some rivals, thanks to the reverberant acoustic. For all that, this is an impressive *Harold*, superbly played. The three excerpts from *La damnation de Faust* were recorded in 1963, when Munch was guest conductor in Philadelphia, and they have a Beecham-like elegance. Daniel Barenboim's recording of the *Royal Hunt and Storm* from *Les Troyens* with the Orchestre de Paris comes from the mid-1970s and has the benefit of better sound; it is well enough played though it is not really in the same street as the Munch or Ormandy performances. Nevertheless this CD is eminently recommendable and very good value.

(i) *Harold in Italy. Roméo et Juliette* (excerpts).
(M) (***) RCA mono GD 60275 [60275-2-RG]. (i) Carlton Cooley; NBC SO, Toscanini.

Toscanini's famous 1953 recording of *Harold in Italy* is of very high voltage, with Carlton Cooley an excellent soloist. The demonic fires glow with great intensity in the *Orgy of the Brigands*; perhaps the *Pilgrims' march* is just a shade hard driven. In spite of the sonic limitations, the excitement of the performance still comes across the decades.

Overtures: Béatrice et Bénédict; Benvenuto Cellini; Le Carnaval romain; Le Corsaire. Roméo et Juliette: Queen Mab scherzo. Les Troyens: Royal hunt and storm.
✪ (M) *** RCA 9026 61400-2 [id.]. Boston SO, Munch (with SAINT-SAENS: *Le rouet d'Omphale* ***).

Dazzlingly brilliant performances of four favourite overtures – the virtuosity of the Boston players, especially the violins in *Béatrice et Bénédict* and *Le Corsaire* – is breathtaking. But it is for the wonderfully poetic and thrilling account of the *Royal hunt and storm* from *Les Troyens* that this CD earns its Rosette. The horn solo is ravishing and the brass produce a riveting climax as the storm reaches its peak. Then the scene of a rain-drenched countryside is magically evoked as the horn steals back in the closing bars. The early stereo (1957/9) is remarkable: one really feels the hall ambience, and John Pfeiffer's remastering is expert. *Romeo and Juliet* was recorded in 1961, and again one marvels at the articulation of the Boston violins and horns. The Saint-Saëns bonus is the earliest recording of all (1957). It is beautifully played and, after a robust climax, has the most delicate, pianissimo ending.

Overtures: *Béatrice et Bénédict; Le Carnaval romain, Op. 9; Le Corsaire, Op. 21; Rob Roy; Le Roi Lear, Op. 4.*
**(*) Chandos Dig. CHAN 8316 [id.]. SNO, Gibson.

Rob Roy finds Gibson and the SNO at their most dashingly committed. *King Lear*, another rarity, also comes out most dramatically, and though *Béatrice et Bénédict* is not quite so polished, the playing is generally excellent. With first-rate digital recording, this can be generally recommended.

Overtures: *Le Carnaval romain; Le Corsaire; Damnation de Faust: Hungarian march.*
(N) (M) **(*) Decca 448 571-2 [id.]. Paris Conservatoire O, Martinon – BIZET: *Jeux d'enfants;* IBERT: *Divertissement;* SAINT-SAENS: *Danse macabre* etc. ***

Martinon's Berlioz recordings have been added as a bonus for this reissue (in Decca's Classic Sound series) of his highly praised 1960 collection of French music. They were recorded two years earlier and, although the playing is both brilliant and exciting, it is not on the level of the later performances. There are moments of faulty intonation in both woodwind and brass, not very serious, of course, but marring the effect for the critical ear.

Overtures: *Le Carnaval romain, Op. 9; Le Corsaire, Op. 21; Les Francs-juges, Op. 3; Le Roi Lear, Op. 4; Waverley, Op. 1.*
**(*) Ph. 416 430-2. LSO, C. Davis.

This is music which ideally calls for modern digital sound; in spite of this, Sir Colin's collection can hold its own, even though it should now be in the mid-price bracket. The playing undoubtedly has fire and brilliance.

Rêverie et caprice, Op. 8.
(Y/B) (M) *** DG Dig. 445 549-2 [id.]. Perlman, O de Paris, Barenboim – LALO: *Symphonie espagnole;* SAINT-SAENS: *Concerto No. 3.* ***

Berlioz's short concertante work for violin and orchestra uses material originally intended for *Benvenuto Cellini*. Perlman's ripely romantic approach to the *Rêverie* brings out the individuality of the melody and, with a sympathetic accompaniment from Barenboim, the work as a whole is given considerable substance. First-rate digital recording.

Roméo et Juliette: Queen Mab scherzo.
(M) (**) RCA mono GD 60314 [60314-2-RG]. Phd. O, Toscanini – MENDELSSOHN: *Midsummer Night's Dream.* (***)

Toscanini's quicksilver reading of this fairy scherzo has much in common with his fine Philadelphia recording of Mendelssohn's fairy music. The 1941 recording is clear.

Symphonie fantastique, Op. 14.
(N) *** DG Dig. 445 878-2 [id.]. Paris Opéra-Bastille O, Myung-Whun Chung (with DUTILLEUX: *Métaboles ***).
*** Ph. Dig. 434 402-2 [id.]. ORR, Gardiner.
**(*) EMI Dig. CDC7 49541-2 [id.]. L. Classical Players, Norrington.
(Y/B) (M) **(*) Telarc Dig. CD 82014 [id.]. Cleveland O, Lorin Maazel.
(N) (**) VAI mono VAIA 1081-2. Paris Conservatoire O, Walter – HAYDN: *Symphony No. 92 (Oxford).* (**)

Symphonie fantastique; Overtures: Béatrice et Bénédict; Le Carnaval romain.
(N) ** Teldec/Warner Dig. 4509 90855-2 [id.]. LPO, Mehta.

(i) *Symphonie fantastique;* (ii) *Overtures: Béatrice et Bénédict; Le Carnaval romain; Le Corsaire.*
(M) **(*) EMI CDM7 64630-2 [id.]. (i) O Nat. de France, Bernstein; (ii) LSO, Previn.
(Y/B) (BB) **(*) RCA Navigator 74321 21283-2. Boston SO, (i) Prêtre; (ii) Munch.

Symphonie fantastique; Overture: Le Carnaval romain, Op. 9.
(Y/B) **(*) Ph. Dig. 438 939-2 [id.]. O. de Paris, Bychkov.

Symphonie fantastique; Overtures: Le Carnaval romain; Le Corsaire.
(BB) **(*) ASV CDQS 6090. RPO, Bátiz.

Symphonie fantastique; Overtures: Le Carnaval romain; Le Corsaire; La damnation de Faust: Marche hongroise. Les Troyens: Trojan march.
(M) **(*) Mercury 434 328-2 [id.]. Detroit SO, Paul Paray.

Symphonie fantastique; Overture: Le Corsaire, Op. 21.
(M) *** Carlton/RPO Dig. 3036 60022-2 [id.]. RPO, Previn.

(i) *Symphonie fantastique;* (ii) *Roméo et Juliette: Love scene; Queen Mab scherzo.*
(N) (M) *** Ph. 446 202-2 [id.]. (i) Concg. O; (ii) LSO; Sir Colin Davis.

With Myung-Whun Chung and the Bastille Orchestra the *Symphonie fantastique* has rarely seemed so fantastic, for he conveys to a rare degree the nervously impulsive inspiration of a young composer. With the hints of hysteria and overtones of nightmare in Berlioz's programme freshly brought out, the result is volatile rather than symphonically foursquare, and the originality of the inspiration seems all the greater. Such an approach might easily have sounded self-indulgent, but with such rapport between the conductor and the orchestra the subtleties of expression seem natural and spontaneous in a very French, idiomatic-sounding way. Speeds tend to be extreme in both directions, but tension is superbly sustained. An outstanding, strongly characterized reading, very well recorded. Chung's unusual coupling adds to the disc's attractions – the set of five brief and brilliant pieces which Dutilleux wrote for Szell and the Cleveland Orchestra in 1964. Chung's view is both poetic and atmospheric, bringing out the subtly contrasting timbres in each piece, leading to the culminating *Presto*, where Chung relishes the marking 'Flamboyant', underlining jazzy syncopations.

Sir Colin Davis's 1974 Concertgebouw recording – his first with that orchestra – has dominated the catalogue for two decades. Now reissued at mid-price, with two excerpts from Davis's *Roméo et Juliette* as a fine bonus, it still remains a primary recommendation. The performance has superb life and colour, the slow movement memorably atmospheric and the final two movements very exciting. If the sound does not quite match recent rivals in brilliance and definition, the overall balance is very satisfying and believable. However, Martinon's fine account (coupled with *Lélio* – see below) should not be forgotten.

John Eliot Gardiner, with his Orchestre Révolutionnaire et Romantique, has followed Roger Norrington in recording the *Symphonie fantastique* on period instruments, and the comparisons are fascinating. Instead of working in the studio, Gardiner opted to go to the old hall of the Conservatoire in Paris, where the symphony was first heard in 1830. Gardiner uses the extra sharpness of focus to add to the dramatic bite, without undermining the intensely atmospheric moments in this colourful programme work. Thus the opening of the second-movement waltz, the *Scene at the ball*, is more sinister than with Norrington, with the interpretation faster and more impulsive. The evocation of thunder at the end of the slow movement, the *Scene in the country*, is even more dramatic and, though the brass in the last two movements lacks the bloom given to Norrington in his EMI recording, Gardiner conducts the *March to the scaffold* and the *Witches' Sabbath* with more excitement and panache and, despite the unhelpful acoustic, the violins have more body than those of Norrington's London Classical Players. Gardiner's performance also gains from his more openly expressive style of phrasing, while in Berlioz's wild syncopations he is second to none in conveying the astonishing modernity of music written within three years of Beethoven's death. Some will still prefer the Norrington version for its warmer sound; but Gardiner is more electrifying, building imaginatively on similar ingredients.

Norrington does his utmost to observe the composer's metronome markings; but where his Beethoven is consistently fast, some of these speeds are more relaxed than we are used to – as in the *March to the scaffold* and the *Ronde du sabbat*. As usual, his lifting of rhythms prevents the music from dragging, at the same time giving new transparency; and his revelations here certainly give his version a key place.

With full-ranging digital sound, well balanced with fine presence and atmosphere, André Previn conducts the RPO in a keenly dramatic reading marked by characteristically well-lifted rhythms, with dynamic contrasts powerfully underlined, which heightens the sinister side of the composer's nightmare vision. This is one of Previn's RPO recordings which matches his achievements in his vintage days with the LSO, and it makes an excellent, mid-priced, alternative recommendation.

Bernstein directs a brilliant and understanding performance which captures more than most the wild, volatile quality of Berlioz's inspiration. Sir Colin Davis may give a clearer idea of the logic of the piece, but Bernstein (unlike Davis, omitting the exposition repeat) has even more urgency, and his reading culminates in superb accounts of the *March to the scaffold* and the *Witches' sabbath*, full of rhythmic swagger and natural flair. However, the remastering of the late-1970s analogue recording gives slight over-emphasis to the brilliance with its tendency to shrillness in the upper strings. Some weight has also been lost at the bass end, but the warm resonance of the recording retains the body of the orchestral sound. The three overtures make a fine bonus.

Paray's excitingly hard-pressed reading is full of passionate, mercurial neurosis. The first movement immediately spurts away, and it is only the conductor's firm grip that prevents the movement from getting out of hand. The *Waltz*, too, is fast, though not inelegant, and the *Adagio*, even though it has moments of pastoral repose, never drags its feet. The final two movements have great verve, and there are few performances that combine such a high level of tension with a true understanding of the music's inner pulse. Fine playing, of course, and brilliant recording, with a tendency to thinness in the violins. The encores are similarly exciting and vivid, and again one marvels that a stereo recording from as early as 1958/9 should sound so impressive today.

Philips provide superb recording quality for the Orchestre de Paris and Semyon Bychkov in the *Symphonie fantastique* and it must be said that the quality of the orchestral response is very high. As an interpretation it is rather less impressive. Bychkov freely indulges in some wilful agogic touches, only some of which strike an idiomatic note. While it is far from being a front runner, Bychkov's is not a negligible account either – and the fine recording may well sway some collectors.

Bátiz's ASV CD is fully competitive in the super-bargain range. It has the advantage of an excellent digital recording, which is brilliant and well balanced. As always in the recording studio, he brings the score vividly to life, and his consistent warmth and intensity are highly persuasive. Points of detail may be less subtle than with Davis, for instance, but one has the feeling here of live music-making, and the two overtures are equally strong and spontaneous. The sound balance is more convincing than in Bernstein's remastered EMI version.

Prêtre's excitingly chimerical Boston account was recorded in 1969, and the upper range is far from full. However, the Boston ambience brings weight and the sound is otherwise resonantly spacious, with exciting projection for the brass. It is a highly volatile performance but Prêtre's sense of neurosis is convincing, and the finale combines an element of the grotesque with high adrenalin flow. An individual and involving account. Munch's famous accounts of the three *Overtures* make a thrilling bonus, but here the sound tends to shrillness.

Maazel's Telarc version dates from 1982, and the spectacular Severance Hall recording brings some superbly tangible brass sounds in the last two movements, not only in the clipped rhythms of the *March to the scaffold* but, notably, at the powerful entry of the *Dies irae* in the finale. Apart from this emphasis, the refined recording has a warm concert-hall perspective and the performance is naturally expressive in a spontaneous-sounding way without losing anything in precision of ensemble. Even so, this rather plain reading competes with the finest rivals only in its demonstration-worthy sonics and, with no fill-up, the disc has a playing time of only 49 minutes.

Mehta's view of the *Symphonie fantastique*, direct and solid, is strong and well sustained, with the LPO playing superbly; but it is not remarkable for poetry. The weighty recording-quality reinforces that impression. As fill-up, Mehta offers comparably direct and well-played readings of the two overtures, with the weight of the recording helping rather than hindering the mercurial qualities of *Béatrice et Bénédict*, thanks to crisp ensemble. But the performance of the *Symphonie* is not a front runner.

Immediately after the Anschluss Bruno Walter, who had made his historic recording of Mahler's *Ninth Symphony* only a few days before the Nazis marched in, was offered refuge in Paris, where he made his memorable recordings of Haydn symphonies and, in May 1939, the present account of the *Symphonie fantastique*. It immediately superseded the earlier, dimly recorded, predominantly classical account from Weingartner on Columbia. It balances the romantic fires and the classical poise of Berlioz to splendid effect. It appeared in France in the 1980s on an excellent EMI Références LP, but this has not yet appeared in the UK on CD. The present transfer from Canada is not quite as clean in focus or as richly detailed as one would like, but it is perfectly satisfactory. One is more aware of the 78-r.p.m. surfaces but, in the absence of any alternative, it must be welcomed as a reminder of a great performance.

Symphonie fantastique, Op. 14; La damnation de Faust, Op. 24: Dance of the sylphs; Minuet of the Will o'the wisps; Hungarian march. Overtures: *Béatrice et Bénédict; Benvenuto Cellini; Le Carnaval romain, Op. 9; Le Corsaire, Op. 21; Le Roi Lear, Op. 4;* (i) *L'enfance du Christ, Op. 25: Shepherds' farewell.*
(N) (BB) *(*) CfP Silver Double CDCFPSD 4751 (2). Hallé O, James Loughran, (i) with Hallé Ch., cond. Handford.

Loughran's Berlioz collection opens strongly with a vibrant account of the *Le Corsaire overture*. The *Symphonie fantastique*, however, is disappointing, heavy in places and rarely exciting, although there are touches which reveal this conductor's characteristic freshness of approach, shown at its best in the three orchestral excepts, all strongly characterized, from the *Damnation of Faust*. The other overtures are played well but lack a really powerful adrenalin flow. *King Lear* is easily the most impressive with fine brass playing and some nice points of orchestral detail. Maurice Handford's account of the delightful *Shepherds' chorus* from *L'enfance du Christ* with the Hallé Choir is quite sensitively done (if rather leisurely) and beautifully recorded, and the sound throughout (from the late 1970s) is very good.

Symphonie fantastique, Op. 14; (i) *Lélio (Le retour à la vie), Op. 14b.*
(B) *** EMI CZS7 62739-2 (2). (i) Gedda, Burles, Van Gorp, Sendrez, Topart, Ch. of R. France; ORTF Nat. O, Martinon.

Berlioz intended *Lélio* as a sequel to the *Symphonie fantastique*, and Martinon conveniently offers the works paired at bargain price. His account of the *Symphonie* shows a unique seductiveness. Martinon gives the first-movement exposition repeat and provides the often omitted extra brass parts; though the result is brilliant, he never presses on too frenetically. But most of all this reading is outstanding for its warm shaping of phrase, even if the finale, with its tolling bells of doom, has a flamboyance and power to match any available. The 1973 sound remains remarkably vivid. *Lélio* quotes the *idée fixe* from the *Symphonie*, which helps the listener to feel at home. It is difficult to imagine this performance being bettered, and the 1974 sound is suitably atmospheric.

(i) *Symphonie fantastique;* (ii) *Lélio, ou Le Retour à la vie, Op. 14b;* (iii; iv) *La Mort de Cléopâtre;* (iii–v) *Les Nuits d'été, Op. 7;* (vi) *Béatrice et Bénédict: Overture & Entr'acte;* Overtures: *Benvenuto Cellini; Le carnaval romain, Op. 9; Les Troyens: Royal hunt and storm.*
(Y/B) (M) *** Sony SM3K 64103 (3) (i) LSO; (ii) with Jean-Louis Barrault (narrator), John Mitchinson, John Shirley-Quirk, L. Symphony Ch.; (iii) Yvonne Minton; (iv) BBC SO; (v) Stuart Burrows; (vi) NYPO; all cond. Boulez.

A thoroughly worthwhile Berlioz anthology, spanning a decade of Boulez recordings for CBS from 1967 (the *Symphonie* and *Lélio*) to 1976 (the two song-cycles). Though the spoken dialogue remains obtrusively long (even when spoken most beautifully by M. Barrault), the individual cueing on CD allows one access to the music itself and the six numbers make a fascinating suite. Coupled with a unique reading of the *Fantastique* (clear-headed and intense rather than atmospheric), it shows Boulez at his most searchingly convincing. Very good recording, except for the difference of levels in *Lélio* between speech (loud and forward) and music. The dramatic scena, *La Mort de Cléopâtre*, an early work which yet gives many hints of the mature Berlioz, makes a particularly suitable companion, as it offers specific quotations of material later used in the *Symphonie fantastique* (the *idée fixe*) and the *Roman carnival overture* (the melody of the introduction). Yvonne Minton's account is dramatically incisive, less varied of expression than Dame Janet Baker's famous recording, but strongly committed. When Berlioz orchestrated *Les nuits d'été* he specified the use of more than one voice in the score, and here the cycle is shared by Minton and Stuart Burrows, with Minton's passionate response showing her at her most movingly eloquent and Burrows also at his finest. The 1972 New York collection of *Overtures* is warmer, less concerned with sharpness of detail than the earlier recordings, yet they still show toughness taking priority over flexible brilliance and the sound-balance matches the readings in its brightness, although it also has weight and atmosphere. Overall this is strongly recommended to Boulez admirers, and others will find it highly stimulating.

VOCAL MUSIC

La damnation de Faust, Op. 24.
*** Ph. 416 395-2 (2) [id.]. Veasey, Gedda, Bastin, Amb. S., Wandsworth School Boys' Ch., London Symphony Ch., LSO, C. Davis.
*** Decca Dig. 414 680-2 (2) [id.]. Riegel, Von Stade, Van Dam, King, Chicago Ch. & SO, Solti.
(Y/B) (B) *** DG Double 437 931-2 (2) [id.]. Rubio, Verreau, Roux, Mollet, Elisabeth Brasseur Ch., RTF Children's Ch., LOP, Markevitch.

Both Gedda as Faust and Bastin as Mephistopheles are impressive in the 1974 Philips set. The response of the chorus and orchestra is never less than intelligent and, in the quieter passages, highly sensitive and the recording perspective is outstandingly natural and realistic.

Solti's performance, searingly dramatic, is given stunning digital sound to make the *Ride to Hell* supremely exciting. But with Von Stade singing tenderly, this is a warmly expressive performance too; and the *Hungarian march* has rarely had such sparkle and swagger. The extra brightness matches the extrovert quality of the performance, less subtle than Davis's.

Reissued as a bargain DG Double, Markevitch's performance is also extremely dramatic and vivid, and the recording, which dates from the very end of the 1950s, sounds remarkably fresh, with an attractive bloom on the sound and no lack of atmosphere. The orchestral contribution emerges with fine colour and Markevitch draws the full effect from Berlioz's quirky touches of scoring. Richard Verreau, a distinctly Gallic tenor, as Faust, is especially impressive among the soloists, but Consuelo Rubio is also very good, as is Pierre Mollet, and Michel Roux makes an effective Mephistopheles. The choral contribution is very French, not always too sophisticated but committed and vibrant, with plenty of character. In short, this is very stimulating and enjoyable, and one notices especially some lovely sounds from the orchestral strings in the score's more expressive moments. The vivid CD transfer gives the performance all the immediacy of a live performance.

L'enfance du Christ, Op. 25.
(N) *** Hyperion Dig. CDA 66991/2 [id.]. Rigby, Miles, Finley, Aler, Howell, Corydon Singers & O, Best.
**(*) Ph. 416 949-2 (2) [id.]. Baker, Tappy, Langridge, Allen, Herincx, Rouleau, Bastin, Alldis Ch., LSO, C. Davis.
**(*) Erato/Warner Dig. 4509 99767-2 (2) [id.]. Von Otter, Rolfe Johnson, Van Dam, Cachemaille, Bastin, Monteverdi Ch., Lyon Op. O, Gardiner.
(M) **(*) RCA 09026 61234-2 (2) [id.]. Valletti, Kopleff, Souzay, Tozzi, New England Conservatory Ch., Boston SO, Munch – *Nuits d'été.* *

Vividly recorded in beautifully balanced digital sound, immediate yet warm, Matthew Best's version offers a keenly dramatic view, with the story of the Flight into Egypt made vital and involving. So Alastair Miles conveys pure evil in Herod's monologue at the start and, with words exceptionally clear, Joseph's pleas for shelter are movingly urgent. Though Best takes such passages faster than usual, his timings are unusually spacious in the more meditative passages, giving extra repose to the duet of Mary and Joseph. As an exception, the *Farewell of the Shepherds* flows easily and sweetly, beautifully sung by the Corydon Singers. Jean Rigby is a fresh, young-sounding Mary, with Gerald Finley warm and expressive as Joseph. John Aler is a powerful Reciter, and Gwynne Howell a strong, benevolent-sounding Father of the family. Though Sir Colin Davis's vintage Philips version has a starrier team of soloists, this one is no less consistent vocally and makes an ideal choice for those who want a more intimate view than Davis's and a superb modern recording with vivid presence.

In Sir Colin Davis's second version for Philips the beautifully balanced recording intensifies the colour and atmosphere of the writing, so that for example the *Nocturnal march* in the first part is wonderfully mysterious. There is a fine complement of soloists, and though Eric Tappy's tone as narrator is not always sweet, his sense of style is immaculate. Others are not always quite so idiomatic, but Dame Janet Baker and Thomas Allen, as ever, both sing beautifully. Even so, Davis's earlier set remains very competitive – see below.

John Eliot Gardiner has the advantage of fine modern recording, made in the Church of Sainte-Madeleine, Pérouges, very well balanced but with the resonance bringing warm atmosphere rather than great clarity. He has some fine soloists, too. Anne Sofie von Otter's Mary is outstanding, by far the best currently on record, sung with rapt simplicity. Gardiner often – though not always – adopts brisker tempi than Davis, and his vibrancy brings a new dimension to some of the music. This is a very vivid reading, marred only by two questionable speeds. Generally, however, Davis's choice of pacing is even more apt.

Charles Munch's account of *L'enfance du Christ* comes from 1956 and makes a welcome return to circulation in the economically packaged two-CD sets that look like one. Needless to say, the performance is thoroughly idiomatic and the playing of the Boston Symphony has a splendour and sonority that the (obviously dated) recording still conveys. The line-up as far as the soloists are concerned is impressive: Florence Kopleff as Mary and Gérard Souzay, then at the height of his powers, as Joseph. The chorus is a weakness; they do not have the tenderness and flexibility to be found in either of Colin Davis's accounts, and even Munch himself must yield in that Berliozian fervour to the English conductor. Leontyne Price is gloriously full-toned in her 1963 recording of *Nuits d'été*, though in terms of characterization she is no match for Danco or Crespin. She produces much the same colour in each of the songs, but the performance is well worth having for the sake of the magical playing of the Chicago orchestra under Reiner. The transfers are excellently effected.

(i; ii) *L'enfance du Christ*; (ii; iii) *Méditation religieuse; La mort d'Ophélie; Sara la baigneuse*; (iii; iv) *La mort de Cléopâtre.*
(Y/B) (B) *** Double Decca 443 461-2 (2) [id.]. (i) Pears, Morison, Cameron, Rouleau, Frost, Fleet, Goldsbrough O; (ii) St Anthony Singers, (iii) ECO; (iv) Anne Pashley; Sir Colin Davis.

Davis's 1961 recording of *L'enfance du Christ* (originally made for L'Oiseau-Lyre) is by no means inferior to his later, Philips set. At times the earlier performance was fresher and more urgent, and Peter Pears was a sweeter-toned, more characterful narrator. Elsie Morison and John Cameron are perfectly cast as Mary and Joseph, and Joseph Rouleau makes an impressive contribution as the Ishmaelite Father. Such moments as the famous *Shepherds' chorus* and the angelic hosannas which end Part 2 are ravishingly beautiful, particularly when the recording has transferred so freshly and atmospherically to its new format. Moreover this Decca reissue offers (on a Double Decca set with two CDs for the price of one) the entire contents of a third LP, issued in 1968 and also sounding freshly minted. This is an invaluable collection of off-beat vocal works, with fine choral singing and a splendid contribution from Anne Pashley. In a wonderfully intense account of the early scena, *La mort de Cléopâtre*, she even manages to rival Dame Janet Baker's version; in this most substantial of pieces Miss Pashley is if anything the more dramatic: the closing section, where Cleopatra in her death throes can merely mutter disconnected phrases, is most affectingly done. The other three pieces are for chorus: the gentle *Méditation religieuse* is a setting of Thomas Moore in translation; *La mort d'Ophélie*, for women's chorus, brings overtones of the choruses in *Roméo et Juliette*; and *Sara la baigneuse* is a strong, flowing setting of a Victor Hugo poem.

(i) *L'enfance du Christ, Op. 25;* (ii) *Roméo et Juliette, Op. 17* (orchestral music only).
(N) (B) *** EMI forte CZS5 88586-2 (2). (i) De los Angeles, Gedda, Soyer, Blanc, Depraz, Cottret, René Duclos Ch., Paris Conservatoire O, Cluytens; (ii) Chicago SO, Giulini.

This Cluytens performance of *L'enfance du Christ* from the mid-1960s emerges on CD with remarkable freshness and, although the earlier Colin Davis set tends to trump it on a Double Decca, it remains very competitive on EMI's forte label with its generous new coupling. Gedda may not be as sensitive as Pears on that Davis version, but de los Angeles is superlative and so, of course, is Ernest Blanc as Herod. The orchestra gives sensitive support and the choral singing is agreeably fresh – the *Shepherds' farewell*, taken at a flowing pace, is particularly beautiful. The remastered recording sounds very good indeed (much smoother than the original LPs) and shows the Salle Wagram acoustic at its most spacious. This is undoubtedly a version that will give much pleasure to Berlioz lovers; moreover it is coupled with one of Giulini's best records from the same period (1969). The Chicago orchestra responds with predictably fine discipline and beauty of tone, and also with great conviction. The brass in the opening *Combats et tumulte* sequence are characteristically impressive and, whether in the gossamer-like delicacy of the *Queen Mab scherzo* or the brilliance of the Capulets' festivities, Giulini shapes each phrase with the right degree of poetic feeling. This is an incandescent performance, and *Roméo seul* and the *Scène d'amour* are beautifully done, with the most refined response from the strings. Good recording quality, though the focus is not always absolutely clean on the otherwise well-balanced CD transfer.

Irlande, Op. 2: excerpts; Mélodies: *La belle voyageuse; Adieu, Bessy!; Le coucher du soleil; Elégie; L'origine de la harpe.*
✷ *** EMI Dig. CDC5 55047-2 [id.]. Thomas Hampson, Geoffrey Parsons – LISZT; WAGNER: *Lieder.* *** ✷

Thomas Hampson gives glowing performances of five of the nine songs, using translations from English texts by the poet Thomas Moore, which Berlioz wrote very early in his career. In their expressive warmth they make a perfect match for the fascinating selections of songs by Wagner and Liszt, with Geoffrey Parsons adding to the impact. Warm, helpful sound.

Mélodies: *Adieu Bessy; Amitié, reprends ton empire; La belle Isabeau; La belle voyageuse; Boléro; Canon libre à la quinte; La captive; Les champs; Chanson à boire; Chansonette de M. Léon de Wailly; Le chant des bretons; Chant guerrier; Le chasseur danois; Je crois en vous; Elégie en prose; Hélène; Le jeune pâtre breton; Le matin; Le Maure jaloux; Le Montagnard exilé; La mort d'Ophélie; Nocturnes à deux voix; L'Origine de la harpe; Pleure, pauvre Colette; Prière du matin; Le roi de Thulé; Sara la baigneuse; Sérénade de Méphistophélès; Le Trébuchet; Zaïde.*
(Y/B) *** DG Dig. 435 860-2 (2) [id.]. Françoise Pollet, Anne Sofie von Otter, John Aler, Thomas Allen, Cord Garben (with Bernd Schenk, Christine Mühlbach, Göran Söllscher, Torleif Thedéen, Thomas Lutz, Royal Op. Ch., Stockholm (members)).

Starting magically with a little duet for soprano and mezzo to guitar accompaniment, this collection of 29 of Berlioz's songs and ensembles includes many rarities previously unrecorded. With four outstanding soloists, it makes a unique and attractive collection which no Berlioz enthusiast should ignore, despite piano accompaniment from Cord Garben that is often rhythmically too square . No one will fail to spot the Berlioz flavour in the first drafts, included here, of two numbers later celebrated in *La damnation de Faust*, *Le roi de Thulé* and *Mephistopheles' serenade* – for tenor here, not bass. The second disc includes many fine songs that are familiar, notably *La captive* (here with Berlioz's cello obbligato), *La mort d'Ophélie* and *Sara la baigneuse*. Such a witty little duet for tenor and baritone as *Le trébuchet* ('The snare') proves a charmer with its bird-like accompaniment, and so does the *Boléro*, with castanets as well as piano. *Le matin*, Berlioz's last song, was written as early as 1850, and it makes one regret that from then on he ignored the genre. Though the recordings were made in different venues over several years, they present a consistent series, and one specially values the rare opportunity of having such fine singers as these in duets and ensembles as well as solo songs.

Mélodies: *Aubade; La belle voyageuse; La captive; Le chasseur danois; Le jeune pâtre breton; La mort d'Ophélie; Les nuits d'été; Zaïde.*
*** Erato/Warner Dig. 4509 99768-2 [id.]. Montague, Robbin, Fournier, Crook, Cachemaille, Lyon Op. O, Gardiner.

John Eliot Gardiner here divides the six keenly atmospheric songs of *Les nuits d'été* between four singers, in some ways an ideal solution when each song demands such different timbre and different tessitura. His choice of singers is inspired and the presiding genius of the conductor makes this a memorable Berlioz disc.

Mélodies: (i) *La belle Isabeau; La belle voyageuse; La captive; Le matin; La mort d'Ophélie.* (ii) *Nuits d'été* (song-cycle); (ii; iii) *Roméo et Juliette:* Prologue: *Premiers transports* (*Strophes*).
(Y/B) *** DG Dig. 445 823-2 [id.]. Anne Sophie von Otter, with (i) Royal Stockholm Op. Ch.; Cord Garben; (ii) BPO, Levine; (iii) Berlin RIAS Chamber Ch.

This is an excellent, most attractive compilation, bringing together von Otter's outstanding contributions both to DG's Berlioz song collection and to the Levine set of *Roméo et Juliette*, which had *Nuits d'été* as a fill-up. It allows those who do not want those bigger sets to savour von Otter's masterly singing. Hers is the most strikingly warm and characterful contribution to the song series, and the five solo songs here are among the most moving and individual of all, notably *La mort d'Ophélie*, the most extended of the songs. In *Les nuits d'été* von Otter is fresh and radiant, bringing out the dramatic contrasts between the songs, and the poise and weight of *Strophes* from *Roméo* is magical.

Mélodies: *La belle voyageuse; La captive; Les nuits d'été, Op. 7; Zaïde.*
(M) *** Virgin/EMI Dig. CUV5 61118-2 [id.]. Dame Janet Baker, City of L. Sinfonia, Hickox –
RESPIGHI: *La sensitiva.* ***

Dame Janet Baker's new recording of *Les nuits d'été* also includes extra orchestral songs. Helped by full, rich recording and a warmly sympathetic accompaniment from Hickox, the interpretation, if anything, glows even more warmly than in Dame Janet's classic EMI reading with Barbirolli, and the voice shows next to no sign of the passing years.

Messe solennelle; Resurrexit (revised version).
*** Ph. Dig. 442 137-2 [id.]. Donna Brown, Jean-Luc Viala, Gilles Cachemaille, Monteverdi Ch., ORR, Gardiner.

This massive work, completed in 1824, was among the first that the young Berlioz wrote. He was twenty and largely untrained, but both the scale of the inspiration and its actual execution are remarkable considering that background. It is an uneven work, but the glow of inspiration shines out over any shortcomings. Especially illuminating are the passages where Berlioz draws on themes we know from other contexts – a *Roman carnival* theme in the vigorous *Gloria*, a *Fantastic Symphony* theme in the *Gratias*, used totally differently. In 1849, 25 years after writing the Mass, Berlioz re-used the *Agnus* with its tenor solo in his *Te Deum*. Gardiner conducts with characteristic flair and sense of drama, bringing brilliant singing from the Monteverdi Choir, though the choral sound is backwardly balanced. A second, modified and slightly expanded version of the violent *Resurrexit* is included as a supplement, a revised version that Berlioz himself acknowledged.

Les nuits d'été (song-cycle), *Op. 7.*
*** Decca 417 813-2 [id.]. Régine Crespin, SRO, Ansermet (with *Recital of French songs* ***).
**(*) RCA GD 60681 (2) [09026 60681-2]. De los Angeles, Boston SO, Munch – *Roméo et Juliette.* (***)
*(M) RCA 09026 61234-2 (2) [id.]. Leontyne Price, Chicago SO, Reiner – *L'enfance du Christ.* **(*)

(i) *Les nuits d'été* (song-cycle), *Op. 7;* (ii) *La mort de Cléopâtre* (lyric scena); (ii; iii) *Les Troyens, Act V, Scenes ii & iii.*
❀ (M) *** EMI CDM7 69544-2. Dame Janet Baker, (i) New Philh. O, Barbirolli; (ii) LSO, Gibson; (iii) with Greevy, Erwen, Howell & Amb. Op. Ch.

The collaboration of Dame Janet Baker at the peak of her powers and Sir John Barbirolli in what is probably the most beautiful of all orchestral song-cycles produces ravishing results.

Crespin's richness of tone and a style which has an operatic basis do not prevent her from bringing out the subtlety of detail and, with Ansermet accompanying brilliantly, this glowing performance is a tour de force.

Victoria de los Angeles's celebrated recording comes from 1955 and still possesses a luminous freshness and purity that come over very well in this new transfer, where they are coupled with Munch's *Roméo et Juliette*. This is far more beautifully characterized than Leontyne Price's account, which suffers from rather generalized responses and little variety of colour or dynamics, though her voice is striking enough and she is well supported by Reiner and the Chicago orchestra in its heyday.

(i) *Requiem Mass (Grande messe des morts). Overtures: Benvenuto Cellini; Le Carnaval romain; Le Corsaire.*
**(*) DG Dig. 429 724-2 (2) [id.]. (i) Pavarotti, Ernst-Senff Ch.; BPO, Levine.

(i) *Requiem Mass;* (ii) *Symphonie funèbre et triomphale, Op. 15.*
**(*) Ph. 416 283-2 (2) [id.]. (i) Dowd, Wandsworth School Boys' Ch., London Symphony Ch.; (ii) John Alldis Ch.; LSO, Sir Colin Davis.

For Sir Colin Davis's recording of the *Requiem* Philips went to Westminster Cathedral and, thanks to the closeness of the microphones, in many passages one can hear individual voices in the choir. However, the large-scale brass sound is formidably caught and the choral fortissimos are glorious, helped by the fresh cutting edge of the Wandsworth School Boys' Choir. The LSO provides finely incisive accompaniment, and there is no doubt that the CD remastering has added to the overall impact and tangibility. However, the *Symphonie funèbre et triomphale* needs more persuasive handling than Sir Colin's if it is not to outstay its welcome.

Levine's account of the *Requiem*, one of his Berlioz series with the Berlin Philharmonic, is the most recommendable of the modern, digitally recorded versions, though in dramatic bite it cannot quite match the vintage Colin Davis and the Ernst-Senff Choir falls short of its usual high standards in the raggedness of some of the choral entries. Having Pavarotti as a characterful, imaginatively expressive soloist in the *Sanctus* is an advantage. Levine's coupling of three of Berlioz's most popular overtures is not as unusual as Davis's *Symphonie funèbre* but works very well in these excellent performances.

Roméo et Juliette, Op. 17.
(M) **(*) DG 437 244-2 (2) [id.]. Minton, Araiza, Bastin, Ch. & O de Paris, Barenboim – FRANCK: *Chasseur maudit* etc. **(*)
(M) (***) RCA mono GD 60681 (2) [09026 60681-2]. Roggero, Chabay, Yi-Kwei-Sze, Harvard Glee Club, Radcliffe Ch. Soc., Boston SO, Munch – *Nuits d'été.* **(*)
(M) (**) RCA mono GD 60274 (2) [60274-2-RG]. Gladys Swarthout, John Garris, Nicola Moscona, NBC Ch. & SO, Toscanini (with BIZET: *L'Arlésienne & Carmen suites* **).

(i) *Roméo et Juliette. Symphonie funèbre et triomphale, Op. 15.*
*** Decca 417 302-2 (2) [id.]. (i) Quivar, Cupido, Krause, Tudor Singers, Montreal Ch. & SO, Dutoit.

Dutoit's is a masterly, heart-warming reading of Berlioz's curious mixture of symphony, cantata and opera, superbly recorded in richly atmospheric sound, with a triumphantly successful account of the *Symphonie funèbre et triomphale* as a generous coupling. Dutoit is here at his most uninhibited, brilliantly skirting the very edge of vulgarity in this outgoing ceremonial piece.

Barenboim's Paris recording, reissued at mid-price with an unusual Franck coupling, offers the only current version with a French orchestra. It is a warmly idiomatic reading, not as brilliant as some and not always as well-played, but with a satisfying weight that relates such a sequence as the love music to Wagner's *Tristan*. The soloists are first rate and the recording is atmospheric. The Franck coupling is also successful.

Charles Munch's version dates from 1953. The RCA remastering has done wonders for the sound and in the three orchestral movements the playing of the Boston orchestra is superb, but it also occasionally sounds in its sheer brilliance (in the *Queen Mab Scherzo*, for example) as if Munch was carried away by the sheer feats of virtuosity this great orchestra could perform. This was the first recording of the whole work and the soloists, Margaret Roggero, Leslie Chabay and Yi-Kwei-Sze, are impressive. While it would be an exaggeration to call the recording boxy, the mono sound does not convey much sense of space; this nevertheless remains a valuable historical document and a welcome supplement. Moreover, it comes with a lovely account of *Nuits d'été* from Victoria de los Angeles at her prime.

Toscanini's concert performance of February 1947 brings many electrifying moments, with the melodic lines often drawn out lovingly in a Verdian way and with the virtuoso passages delivered with panache. But the sound, recorded in the notorious Studio 8H, is dry and fizzy, far less full than the RCA recording for Charles Munch in Boston, made only two years later. The Bizet coupling offers brilliant playing, but Munch is a more idiomatic Berliozian and offers a more interesting coupling in *Les nuits d'été* with Victoria de los Angeles.

Te Deum, Op. 22.
*** DG Dig. 410 696-2 [id.]. Araiza, London Symphony Ch., LPO Ch., Woburn Singers, Boys' Ch., European Community Youth O, Abbado.

The DG recording from Abbado is very impressive. The sound is wide-ranging, with striking dynamic contrasts: Abbado brings great tonal refinement and dignity to this performance, and the spacious sound helps. Francisco Araiza is altogether first class.

OPERA

Béatrice et Bénédict (complete).
*** Ph. 416 952-2 (2) [id.]. Baker, Tear, Eda-Pierre, Allen, Lloyd, Van Allan, Watts, Alldis Ch., LSO, C. Davis.
*** Erato/Warner Dig. 2292 45773-2 (2) [id.]. Graham, Viala, McNair, Robbin, Bacquier, Cachemaille, Le Texier, Lyon Opera Ch. & O, John Nelson.

(i) *Béatrice et Bénédict* (complete); (ii) *Chant de la Fête de Pâcques; Irlande (9 Mélodies), Op. 2; La Mort d'Ophélie, Op. 18/2; Le Trébuchet, Op. 13.*
(N) (B) *** Decca Double 448 113-2 (2) [id.]. (i) Veasey, Mitchinson, Cantelo, Cameron, Watts, Shirley-Quirk, Shilling, St Anthony Singers, LSO, Sir Colin Davis; (ii) Cantelo, Watts, Tear, Salter, Monteverdi Ch., Gardiner; Tunnard (piano).

Béatrice et Bénédict presents not just witty and brilliant music for the heroine and hero (Dame Janet Baker and Robert Tear at their most pointed) but sensuously beautiful passages too. First-rate solo and choral singing, brilliant playing and sound refined and clear in texture, bright and fresh, even if minimal hiss betrays an analogue source.

The Lyon Opera version conducted by John Nelson makes an excellent alternative to the vintage Colin Davis recording. In spacious, modern, digital sound it offers substantially more of the French dialogue, well spoken by actors but more dryly recorded than the musical numbers. Susan Graham is a characterful Béatrice, lighter in the big aria than Janet Baker for Davis but aptly younger-sounding. Jean-Luc Viala is a comparably light Bénédict, pointing the fun in his big aria, and Sylvia McNair and Catherine Robbin are superb as Hero and Ursule.

It is good to have back the early (1962) Oiseau-Lyre set sounding so fresh and vivid. Above all it is a triumph for Sir Colin Davis, who readily responds to Berlioz's quirkiness, bringing out the delicacy as well as both the humour and power. The singing is equally fresh and vigorous with April Cantelo in really top form, coping splendidly with Héro's fearsome opening aria, even if she does not always avoid some ungainliness on exposed entries. Josephine Veasey as Béatrice presents an appropriately formidable figure, singing with masterly precision and confidence. John Mitchinson as Bénédict does not attempt a conventional tenor-hero approach and his distinctive voice matches an offbeat part. The other soloists and the chorus are excellent and the recording is beautifully balanced and vividly clear in detail. The result scintillates. To make the Double Decca reissue even more tempting, Decca have added the contents of a third LP of little-known vocal Berlioz. The nine songs grouped together under the title *Irlande* were inspired by the words of Thomas Moore (set here in translation) and reflect early romantic ardour for the newly discovered ballad tradition. *Le Trébuchet* is a charming Scherzo, and it is valuable to have *La Mort d'Ophélie* in the alternative solo version. The performances are all of a high standard.

Les Troyens, Parts 1 & 2 (complete).
*** Ph. 416 432-2 (4) [id.]. Veasey, Vickers, Lindholm, Glossop, Soyer, Partridge, Wandsworth School Boys' Ch., ROHCG Ch. & O, C. Davis.
(Y/B) *** Decca Dig. 443 693-2 (4) [id.]. Lakes, Pollet, Voigt, Montreal Schubert Ch. & SO, Dutoit.

Throughout this long and apparently disjointed score Davis compels the listener to concentrate, to appreciate its epic logic. Only in the great love scene of *O nuit d'ivresse* would one have welcomed the more expansive hand of a Beecham. Veasey on any count, even next to Dame Janet Baker, makes a splendid Dido, singing always with fine heroic strength, with Vickers a ringing Aeneas. The Covent Garden Chorus and Orchestra excel themselves in virtuoso singing and playing, while CD brings out the superb quality of sound all the more vividly.

The alternative Decca recording was linked to two concert performances of each of the parts of the opera, *La prise de Troie* and *Les Troyens à Carthage*. The church of St Eustache, the orchestra's regular recording venue, was not big enough to accommodate all the separate ensembles and choirs in the *Trojan march* at the end of Act I, and to synchronize everything they needed 64 tracks. Interpretatively, the contrasts between Dutoit and Davis are quickly established at the very start of *La prise de Troie*. Dutoit launches in at high voltage, more volatile than Davis, conveying exuberance, consistently preferring faster speeds. Davis may be marginally less exciting, but he often compensates in the extra crispness and clarity of the playing of the Covent Garden Orchestra. The advantage of Dutoit's faster speeds – reflecting the metronome markings – comes not just in thrilling allegros but also in flowing andantes. So Cassandra's first solo is more persuasively moulded at a flowing speed, with Deborah Voigt far warmer than Berit Lindholm for Davis, both in her beauty of tone and in her espressivo phrasing. Lindholm is accurate, but her tone too readily becomes raw and throaty under pressure, where Voigt's portrait is far more feminine and movingly vulnerable. She crowns her performance at the end of Act II, triumphantly leading the final ensemble of defiant Trojan women, more impetuous than her rival. For completeness, Dutoit includes the brief prelude that Berlioz wrote for the garbled 1863 performances of the second part of the opera, but not intended to be given in the full five-Act version. The other textual addition comes in Act I. After the Andromache scene – with a clarinet solo of breathtaking gentleness from the Montreal player – there is an extra scene, lasting six minutes, which the Berlioz scholar, Hugh MacDonald, editor of the Bärenreiter score, has orchestrated from the surviving piano score.

The role of Chorebus, Cassandra's lover, in the first part of the opera is very well taken in both sets, by Peter Glossop for Davis, by Gino Quilico for Dutoit, both in rich, firm voice. As Aeneas, Gary Lakes may not have as richly heroic a voice as Jon Vickers for Davis, being rather more easily stressed at the top; among today's tenors, however, he is the most experienced of all in this role, having sung it close on two dozen times on both sides of the Atlantic. His big advantage over Vickers, most of all in the great love scene with Dido in Act IV, is that he shades his voice far more subtly. Though the role of Dido very often goes to a mezzo – Josephine Veasey in the Davis set, Dame Janet Baker in EMI's set of excerpts, with Sir Alexander Gibson conducting – here Decca firmly opts for a soprano, Françoise Pollet. Very much attuned to the idiom, she sings consistently with full, even tone, so that, matching Dutoit's expressiveness and the richness of the Montreal sound, she brings out the feminine sensuousness of the role more than a mezzo normally would. Where there is a disadvantage in having a soprano as Dido is in the darker passages. Pollet has a formidable chest register, but at the start of Dido's final monologue, *Je vais mourir*, she does not convey the heart-aching desolation that the finest mezzos achieve. She sounds purposeful instead of resigned, and the lyrical section that follows, '*Adieu, fière cité*', brings a tender contrast, with the reference back to the love duet most poignant. Then, in the final solo, Pollet portrays the distraught Dido, all purpose gone in the disjointed recitative. She may not have the dark colourings of a Baker or a Veasey, but her dramatic power is just as intense.

Though on balance the Covent Garden Chorus in the Davis set sing with even crisper ensemble, the passionate commitment of the performance matches the fire of Dutoit's whole reading. This is a thrilling set, to have one marvelling afresh at the electric vitality of Berlioz's inspiration – and marvelling too that the formidable problems of recording so massive a work have been accomplished so confidently. But above all this score depends on the spell that the conductor can cast over orchestra and thus on audience and, while Dutoit brings many moments of splendour and magic, allegiance to Sir Colin's set remains unchanged.

Les Troyens (abridged).
(**) VAIA mono VAIA 1006-3 (3) [id.]. Regina Resnik, Steber, Cassilly, Singher, Sarfaty, Ch. & O, Robert Lawrence.

The sound on this 1960 live recording is very variable and always limited so that at its worst it is dim and distant. The playing of the orchestra (or orchestras, when the recordings spanned performances in both New York and Washington) is generally rough, but there is an excitement conveyed, and some of the singing is thrilling, notably from Eleanor Steber as a magnificent Cassandra, perhaps finer than any on disc yet, and Regina Resnik as Dido. Both Richard Cassilly, a clear, strong Aeneas, and Resnik sound fresher and firmer than they often have on commercial discs. Yet ensembles hardly make the impact they should in this work, and with 3¼ hours of music recorded, as against four in the complete Davis version, these concert performances involved more cuts than we should allow nowadays.

Bernstein, Leonard (1918–90)

Bernstein Edition

(i) *Candide overture;* (ii) *On the Waterfront* (symphonic suite); (iii) *Prelude, fugue and riffs;* (i) *West Side Story:* symphonic dances.
(N) (M) *** DG Dig. 447 952-2 [id.]. (i) LAPO; (ii) Israel PO; (iii) Peter Schmidl, VPO; composer.

In his later, DG account of the *Overture* to *Candide* the composer still directs with tremendous flair, his speed a fraction slower than in his New York studio recording for CBS. The score for *On the Waterfront* is film music pure and simple and, expertly though it may underline the film's action, it does not bear too much repetition on its own. Bernstein's Israeli recording sounds fuller than his earlier version on Sony, and the same comment applies to the *West Side Story symphonic dances*. Bernstein, recorded live, is here at his most persuasive, conducting a highly idiomatic account of the orchestral confection devised from his most successful musical. It may not be quite as crisp of ensemble as his earlier, New York version, but it has even more spirit, with the players contributing the necessary shouts in the Mambo representing a street fight. The *Prelude, fugue and riffs* was also recorded live and its vibrant, rhythmic feeling does not sound in the least Viennese, although Peter Schmidl is a comparatively reticent soloist.

(i) *Concerto for orchestra (Jubilee Games);* (ii) *Dybbuk* (ballet): *suites Nos. 1–2.*
(N) (M) *** DG Dig. 447 956-2 [id.]. (i) Chama, Israel PO; (ii) Sperry, Fifer, NYPO; composer.

The *Concerto for orchestra* shows Bernstein in audacious yet searching mood. Originally planned as a two-movement work to celebrate the Jubilee of the Israel Philharmonic, it opens with the aleatory raucousness of *Free-style events*, featuring vociferous orchestral shouts; then comes the sparely scored and haunting *Mixed doubles*, a theme with seven variations given to pairs of orchestral soloists, which was added in 1989. The third-movement *Diaspora dances* is the high-spirited rhythmic composer we know from the musicals, while the final touching *Benediction* (which was added for the re-opening of a refurbished Carnegie Hall in 1986) is eloquently sung here by José Eduardo Chama. The live recording brings music-making of striking intensity, even if the Israeli playing is shown not always to be technically immaculate, especially in the demanding second movement.

The two suites taken from *Dybbuk* are no shorter than the original ballet (one of Bernstein's toughest works on a sinister subject – see below), dividing the score broadly between passages involving vocal elements and those purely instrumental. The first suite is the longer and more dramatic, the second the more contemplative. Even the jazzy dance-sequences so typical of Bernstein (often in seven-in-a-bar rhythms) acquire a bitter quality. Bernstein directs strong, colourful performances, cleanly and atmospherically recorded, with excellent vocal contributions from Paul Sperry and Bruce Fifer. The transfer to CD of the 1975 analogue studio recording is first class.

Facsimile (choreographic essay); (i) *Fancy free* (ballet); *On the Town* (3 dance episodes).
(N) (M) *** DG Dig./Analogue 447 951-2 [id.]. (i) Ruth Mense; Bernstein (vocals); Israel PO, composer.

Facsimile, written in 1946 for Jerome Robbins, tells of two boys and a girl and their balletic flirtations; its beach scenario recalls Poulenc's *Les biches*. It is an attractively inventive and resourceful, even charming score, but with no want of atmosphere and imagination, and this live performance from 1981 shows the Israel Philharmonic at their finest. The companion ballet, *Fancy free*, one of Bernstein's early successes from 1944, is another attractive example of his freely eclectic style, here raiding Stravinsky, Copland or Gershwin and putting the result effectively together, thanks to his exuberant sense of colour and rhythm. The Israel Philharmonic does not match the New York Philharmonic Orchestra (see below) in virtuosity or in command of jazz rhythms, but it still plays with tremendous spirit and also enjoys the merit (both here and in *Facsimile*) of outstanding recorded quality. What makes this version of *Fancy free* special is Bernstein's own performance of the blues number, *Big stuff*, as the ballet's epilogue; he also proves just a snippet of this number to set the scene at the opening. The colourful and vigorous dances from *On the Town* are given vivid if close-up digital sound, obviously more modern than in the CBS/Sony versions.

Divertimento for orchestra; (i) *Halil* (Nocturne for solo flute, strings and percussion); (ii) *3 Meditations* (from *Mass*) for cello and orchestra; *A Musical toast.*
(N) (M) *** DG Dig./Analogue 447 955-2 [id.]. Israel PO, Bernstein; with (i) Rampal; (ii) Rostropovich.

The *Divertimento* (written for the Boston Symphony Orchestra), easily and cheekily moving from one idiom to another, is often jokey (it even quotes the brief oboe cadenza from Beethoven's *Fifth Symphony* as a coda for the third-movement *Mazurka*) but agreeably so. *Halil*, for flute and strings, and the *Meditation* also beautifully reflect the individual poetry of the two artists for whom they were written and who perform in masterful fashion here. The other two party-pieces were recorded live in fizzing performances, *A Musical toast* for André Kostelanetz, and *Slava* (a 'political overture, fast and flamboyant') to celebrate Rostropovich in Washington. Excellent recording throughout.

Symphonies Nos. (i) *1 (Jeremiah);* (ii) *2 (The Age of anxiety)* for piano and orchestra.
(N) (M) *** DG 447 953-2 (2) [id.]. Israel PO, composer; with (i) Christa Ludwig; (ii) Lukas Foss.

(i) *Symphony No. 3 (Kaddish);* (ii) *Chichester Psalms.*
(N) (M) *** DG 447 954-2 [id.]. (i) Caballé, Wager, V. Boys' Ch.; (ii) Soloist from V. Boys' Ch.; (i;ii) Wiener Jeunnesse Ch., Israel PO, composer.

Bernstein's three symphonies have been undervalued because of his theatre music and his willingness to draw on popular influences, but their surface facility is deceptive. The *Jeremiah Symphony* dates from the composer's early twenties and ends with a moving passage from Lamentations for the mezzo soloist – here with Christa Ludwig responding sensitively. As the title suggests, the *Second Symphony* was inspired by the poem of W. H. Auden, and the work includes a concertante piano part, admirably played by Lukas Foss. The *Third Symphony,* written in memory of John F. Kennedy, is recorded here in its revised version (with a male speaker), which concentrates the original concept of a dialogue between man and God, a challenge from earth to heaven. The performances here are not always quite as polished or as forceful as those Bernstein recorded earlier for CBS in New York, but they never fail to reflect the warmth of Bernstein's writing. and the playing of the Israel Philharmonic is extremely vivid throughout. The *Chichester Psalms* were recorded live in 1977. One might have slight reservations over the treble soloist from the Vienna Boys' Choir, but otherwise the performance is first class, with the music's warmth and vigour compellingly projected. So are the CD transfers throughout both discs of (1977/8) recordings.

(i) *Serenade after Plato's Symposium* (for solo violin, string orchestra, harp and percussion); (ii) *Songfest* (cycle of American poems).
(N) (M) *** DG 447 957-2 [id.]. (i) Gidon Kremer, Israel PO; (ii) Dale, Elias, Nancy Williams, Rosenheim, Reardon, Gramm Nat. SO of Washington; composer.

The *Serenade* must rank among Bernstein's most resourceful and inspired creations, full of ideas, often thrilling and exciting, and equally often moving. Gidon Kremer has all the nervous intensity and vibrant energy to do justice to this powerful and inventive score. *Songfest,* too, is one of the composer's most richly varied works – a sequence of poems which ingeniously uses all six singers solo and in various combinations. Characteristically, Bernstein often chooses controversial words to set, and by his personal fervour welds a very disparate group of pieces together into a warmly satisfying whole. Both recordings (from the late 1970s) are of excellent quality, atmospheric and clear.

(i) *Candide* (final, revised version); (ii) *West Side story:* complete recording.
(N) ✾ *** DG Dig. 447 958-2 (3) [id.]. (i) Hadley, Anderson, Green, Ludwig, Gedda, Della Jones, Ollmann, London Symphony Ch., LSO; (ii) Te Kanawa, Carreras, Troyanos, Horne, Ollmann, Ch. and O; composer.

The composer's complete recordings of *Candide* and *West Side story* have been coupled together on three mid-priced discs for the Bernstein Edition to make an irresistible bargain for those who have not already aquired one or the other of these inspired scores. The humour of *Candide,* satirically reflecting Voltaire's rubbishing of enforced establishment values, at one point draws a ready parallel between the Spanish Inquisition and Bernstein's own experience during America's darkest political era. The result is a triumph, both in the studio recording (which Bernstein made immediately after the concert performances) and in the video recording of the actual concert at the Barbican. It confirms *Candide* as a classic, bringing out not just the vigour, the wit and the tunefulness of the piece more than ever before, but also an extra emotional intensity, something beyond the cynical Voltaire original. There is no weak link in the cast. Jerry Hadley is touchingly characterful as Candide, producing heady tone, and June Anderson as Cunegonde is not only brilliant in coloratura but also warmly dramatic. The character roles are also brilliantly cast. It was an inspired choice to have Christa Ludwig as the Old Woman, and equally original to choose Adolph Green, lyric writer for Broadway musicals as well as cabaret performer, for the dual role of Dr Pangloss and Martin. Nicolai Gedda also proves a winner in his series of cameo roles, and the full, incisive singing of the London Symphony Chorus adds to the weight of the performance without inflation.

What is missing in the CD set is the witty narration, prepared by John Wells and spoken by Adolph Green and Kurt Ollmann in the Barbican performance. As included on the video of the live concert (Laser disc DG 072 423-1; VHS DG 072 423-3), those links leaven the entertainment delightfully. Even those with the CDs should investigate the video version, which also includes Bernstein's own moving speeches of introduction before each Act.

Bernstein's recording of the complete score of *West Side Story* takes a frankly operatic approach in its casting, but the result is highly successful, for the great vocal melodies are worthy of voices of the highest calibre. Tatiana Troyanos, herself brought up on the West Side, spans the stylistic dichotomy to perfection in a superb portrayal of Anita. The clever production makes the best of both musical worlds, with Bernstein's son and daughter speaking the dialogue most affectingly. Bernstein conducts a superb instrumental group of musicians 'from on and off Broadway', and they are recorded with a bite and immediacy that is captivating. The power of the music is greatly enhanced by the spectacularly wide dynamic range of the recording, with a relatively dry acoustic keeping the sound-picture within an apt scale but without losing bloom.

A Quiet place (complete).
(N) (M) *** DG Dig. 447 962-2 (2) [id.]. Wendy White, Chester Ludgin, Beverly Morgan, John Brandstetter, Peter Kazaras, Vocal Ens., Austrian R SO, composer.

In flashbacks in Act II of *A Quiet place*, Bernstein incorporates his 1951 score, *Trouble in Tahiti*, with its popular style set in relief against the more serious idiom adopted for the main body of the opera. Bernstein's score is full of thoughtful and warmly expressive music, but nothing quite matches the sharp, tongue-in-cheek jazz-influenced invention of *Trouble in Tahiti*. The recording was made in Vienna, with an excellent cast of American singers and with the Austrian Radio orchestra responding splendidly on its first visit to the Vienna State Opera.

Bernstein Edition (complete; as listed above).
(N) (B) *** DG 447 950-2 (12) [id.]. Various artists and orchestras, cond. composer.

DG's complete Bernstein Edition is offered at bargain price and it would be difficult to think of a dozen CDs of twentieth-century music more varied, more approachable or more stimulating.

(i) *Candide: overture; Facsimile* (choreographic essay); *Fancy Free* (ballet); *On the Town* (3 dance episodes); (ii) *On the Town* (musical); (i) *On the Waterfront* (symphonic suite); (iii) *Trouble in Tahiti (opera in 7 scenes);* (i) *West Side story: Symphonic dances* (orch. Sid Ramin & Irwin Kostal).
(M) *** Sony SM154 (3) [id.]. (i) NYPO; (ii) Betty Comden, Adolph Green, Nancy Walker, John Reardon, Cris Alexander, George Gaynes, Ch. & O; (iii) Nancy Williams, Julian Patrick & Vocal Trio, Columbia Wind Ens.; all cond. composer.

Candide overture – placed at the beginning of Disc 2 – provides the perfect curtain-raiser for this indispensable box of Bernstein's vibrant early recordings of his theatrical and film music. The New York Philharmonic, in cracking form, display virtuosity and tremendous spirit in the ballet music and comparable gusto in the noisily pungent film score, plus a natural command of the jazz rhythms, while the tender moments in the *West Side Story* dances have great poignancy. The recordings are remarkably vivid and have been impressively remastered.

Candide: overture; West Side Story: symphonic dances.
(M) *** Sony SMK 47529 [id.]. NYPO, composer – GERSHWIN: *American in Paris* etc. ***

Fancy free (ballet); *On the Town* (3 dance episodes); *On the Waterfront* (symphonic suite).
(M) **(*) Sony SMK 47530 [id.]. NYPO, composer.

Bernstein's exhilarating early New York performances of his theatre music are now reissued separately as part of the Sony 'Royal Edition'.

Candide: overture; Facsimile (choreographic essay); *Fancy free* (ballet); *On the Town: 3 Dance episodes.*
(Y/B) (M) **(*) EMI Eminence CD-EMX 2242; *TC-EMX 2242* [id.]. St Louis SO, Slatkin.

Though Slatkin cannot quite match Bernstein himself in the flair he brings to his jazzier inspirations, this is an attractive and generous collection. Next to Bernstein, Slatkin sounds a little metrical at times, but it is a marginal shortcoming, and he directs a beautiful, refined reading of the extended choreographic essay, *Facsimile*. As a gimmick, the song 'Big Stuff' before *Fancy Free* is recorded in simulation of a juke-box, complete with 78-r.p.m. surface-hiss and a blues singer (Jean Kittrell) with very heavy vibrato. The sound otherwise is full rather than brilliant, set in a helpful, believable acoustic.

(i) *Candide: overture;* (ii) *On the Town: 3 Dance episodes;* (i) *West Side Story: Symphonic dances;* (iii) *America.*
(M) *** DG Dig. 427 806-2. (i) LAPO; (ii) Israel PO; (iii) Troyanos with O; composer – BARBER: *Adagio* ***; GERSHWIN: *Rhapsody in blue.* **(*)

This alternative collection offers the same performances as those included in the Bernstein Edition, and has the added attraction of including a characteristically intense account of Barber's *Adagio*. The other coupling of *Rhapsody in Blue* is, however, less successful than Bernstein's earlier, CBS/Sony account.

3 Meditations for cello and orchestra (from *Mass*).
(B) *** DG Double 437 952-2 (2) [id.]. Rostropovich, Israel PO, composer – BOCCHERINI: *Cello concerto No. 2;* GLAZUNOV: *Chant du Ménestrel;* SHOSTAKOVICH: *Cello concerto No. 2;* TARTINI: *Cello concerto;* TCHAIKOVSKY: *Andante cantabile* etc.; VIVALDI: *Cello concertos.* ***

Bernstein's concertante piece, *Meditations for cello and orchestra*, is fully worthy of the subtlety of Rostropovich's art, and he plays it masterfully. This is part of a remarkably generous Double DG bargain anthology.

(i) *On the Town: suite;* (ii) *7 Anniversaries.*
(M) (***) RCA mono GD 60915 [60915-2]. (i) On the Town O, Bernstein; (ii) Bernstein (piano) – COPLAND: *Billy the Kid* etc. (***)

There is always something special about first recordings. There is great vitality and swagger here, and no apologies need be made for the mono recording which, though slightly shrill, has great vividness. The stage music is followed by *Seven anniversaries*, a set of vignettes composed in 1943, dedicated to family and musical friends, opening with Aaron Copland and closing with William Schuman.

Prelude, fugue and riffs.
(***) Sony MK 42227 [id.]. Goodman, Columbia Jazz Combo, composer – COPLAND: *Clarinet concerto;* STRAVINSKY: *Ebony concerto;* BARTOK: *Contrasts;* GOULD: *Derivations.* (***)
*** RCA Dig. 09026 61350-2 [id.]. Stolzman, LSO, Leighton Smith – COPLAND: *Concerto;* CORIGLIANO: *Concerto;* STRAVINSKY: *Ebony concerto.*

Bernstein's exuberant, sometimes wild, yet structured *Prelude, fugue and riffs* fits well within this CBS collection of jazz-inspired pieces in a vintage performance, directed by the composer. It sounds exceptionally vivid on CD.

Like Benny Goodman before him, Richard Stolzman couples Bernstein's *Prelude, fugue and riffs* with Copland's masterly concerto and Stravinsky's *Ebony concerto*, and he makes the most of its unbuttoned jazziness. He is better recorded than Goodman, and his record can be recommended strongly on all counts.

Serenade after Plato's Symposium (for solo violin, string orchestra, harp & percussion).
(Y/B) *** EMI Dig. CDC5 55360-2 [id.]. Perlman, Boston SO, Ozawa – BARBER: *Violin concerto;* FOSS: *Three American pieces.* ***
(N) (M) *(**) Sony Stern Edition II SMK 64508 [id.]. Stern, Symphony of the Air, composer – DUTILLEUX: *Violin concerto.* ***

The *Serenade* is based on Plato's account of an Ancient Greek banquet in which those present take turns to soliloquize on the nature of love. Perlman may initially seem almost too confident, missing an element of fantasy in Bernstein's personalized meditation on Plato's *Symposium*, where the more reticent view of Gidon Kremer with the composer conducting (see above) seems to delve deeper. Yet increasingly through the five contrasted movements the purposefulness as well as the masterful power of Perlman's playing adds to the work's impact, eliminating any thought that the piece might be too episodic. He brings home the more tellingly how each movement leads thematically out of the preceding one, until the final movement, much the longest, completes the circle in its references back to the opening. He makes it seem a warmer piece too, thanks to his range of incomparably rich tone-colours. The richness of the Boston string-sound is beautifully set against the fullness of Perlman's violin.

Stern's temperament makes him an ideal soloist and he plays very beautifully and with intense feeling. The snag is the balance of the early 1956 stereo, with the violin right out in front and climaxes unpleasantly coarse. There is no mistaking the adrenalin flow, but the lack of any kind of refinement in the orchestral tuttis is a severe drawback.

Symphonies Nos. (i) *1 (Jeremiah);* (ii) *2 (The Age of anxiety)* for piano and orchestra; (i; iii) *3 (Kaddish): To the beloved memory of President Kennedy* (original version); (vi) *Prelude, fugue and riffs;* (iv) *Serenade after Plato's Symposium* (for solo violin, string orchestra, harp & percussion); (v) *Chichester Psalms.*
(M) **(*) Sony SM3K 47162 (3) [id.]. (i) Tourel; (ii) Entremont; (iii) F. Montealegre (speaker), Camerata Singers; Columbus Boychoir; (iv) Francescatti; (v) J. Bogart, Camerata Singers; (i–iv) NYPO; (vi) Benny Goodman, Columbia Jazz Combo; all cond. composer.

All three New York recordings were made in the Manhattan Center in the early 1960s; the acoustic is agreeably spacious, the bass resonantly full and the strings have plenty of body, so that no apologies need be made for the sound-quality. The *Chichester Psalms*, also impressively transferred to CD, was written in response to a commission from the Dean of Chichester. It must rank among Bernstein's most resourceful and inspired creations. Francescatti responds naturally to the Hebrew flavour of the lyrical writing of the *Serenade* but he is very closely balanced, as is the orchestra, and Bernstein's passionate climaxes are given an aggressive fierceness.

(i–iii) *Symphony No. 1 (Jeremiah);* (iv) *Anniversaries: In memoriam Nathalie Koussevitzky;* (ii; v) *Songfest.*

(M) (***) RCA stereo/mono 09026 61581-2 [id.]. (i) Nan Merriman; (ii) St Louis SO; (iii) composer; (iv) Leonard Slatkin (piano); (v) Hohenfeld, White, Spence, Planté, Hartman, Cheek, cond. Slatkin.

Songfest, a cycle for six soloists and orchestra celebrating all things American, finds Bernstein's inspiration focused sharply within a limited frame, and the result is one of his finest works. Specially moving, and beautifully sung by John Cheek, is the setting of a long-buried Whitman poem, celebrating male love; but each poem has been perceptively chosen to illustrate the variegated strands of American society. Leonard Slatkin's new recording hardly replaces Bernstein's own (currently withdrawn) on DG, but it offers another fine performance, recorded in a more mellow acoustic and with a warmer ensemble. In place of the *Seernade* on the DG issue comes Bernstein's own historic first recording of the *Jeremiah Symphony,* made for RCA in 1945, with Nan Merriman the clear-toned soloist. The mono sound is limited but conveys the high voltage of the performance. Between the two main works Slatkin plays the brief piano piece commemorating the first wife of Serge Koussevitzky, taken from the *Anniversaries* suite.

(i) *Symphony No. 2 (Age of anxiety); Overture: Candide; Fancy Free* (ballet).

(M) *** Virgin/EMI Dig. CUV5 61119-2 [id.]. (i) Kahane; Bournemouth SO, Andrew Litton.

Bernstein holds nothing back, but Litton in his less thrusting way is just as compelling and often more subtly expressive, helped by a more poetic, less muscular pianist, Jeffrey Kahane. Anyone fancying Litton's popular coupling need not hesitate.

VOCAL MUSIC

Arias and Barcarolles. On the Town: Some other time; Lonely town; Carried away; I can cook. Peter Pan: Dream with me. Songfest: Storyette, H. M.; To what you said. Wonderful Town: A little bit in love.

*** Koch International Classics Dig. 37000-2 [id.]. Judy Kaye, William Sharp; Michael Barrett, Steven Blier.

Arias and Barcarolles for two soloists and piano duet is a family charade of a work. It is a charming piece, here given – with the composer himself approving the performance – in the original version with piano and excellent, characterful soloists. The bizarre title relates to a comment made by President Eisenhower, after he had heard Bernstein play a Mozart concerto: 'I like music with a theme, not all them arias and barcarolles.' It became a Bernstein family joke. That half-hour work, very well recorded, is coupled with an equivalent collection of eight of Bernstein's most haunting songs and duets.

Chichester Psalms.

(M) *** Carlton Dig. 30366 0009-2 [id.]. Aled Jones, London Symphony Ch., RPO, Hickox – FAURE: *Requiem.* ***

Chichester Psalms (reduced score).

*** Hyperion Dig. CDA 66219 [id.]. Martelli, Corydon Singers, Masters, Kettel, Trotter; Best – BARBER: *Agnus Dei;* COPLAND: *In the beginning* etc. ***

Bernstein's *Chichester Psalms* make an instant communication and respond to familiarity too, especially in Richard Hickox's fresh and colourful reading, with Aled Jones bringing an ethereal contribution to the setting of the 23rd Psalm. The recorded sound is firm and well focused.

Martin Best uses the composer's alternative reduced orchestration. The treble soloist, Dominic Martelli, cannot match Aled Jones, but his chaste contribution is persuasive and the choir scales down its pianissimos to accommodate him, to elegiac effect. Excellent sound, with the acoustic of St Jude-on-the-Hill, Hampstead, creating the right atmosphere.

(i) *Dybbuk* (ballet): complete; (ii) *Mass (for the death of President Kennedy).*

(M) *** Sony SM3K 47158 (3) [id.]. (i) David Johnson, John Ostendorf, NY City Ballet O; (ii) Alan Titus (celebrant), Scribner Ch., Berkshire Boys' Ch., Rock Band & O; composer.

Outrageously eclectic in its borrowings from pop and the avant garde, Bernstein's *Mass* presents an extraordinary example of the composer's irresistible creative energy. Bernstein's ghoulish ballet on lost spirits presents much the same happy and colourful amalgam of influences as you find in other Bernstein ballets, a touch of the *Rite of spring* here and a whiff of *West Side Story* there. The vocal parts, although fairly substantial (and very well done here), are merely incidental.

Songs: *La bonne cuisine* (French and English versions); *I hate music* (cycle); *2 Love songs; Piccola serenata; Silhouette; So pretty; Mass: A simple song; I go on. Candide: It must be so; Candide's lament. 1600 Pennsylvania Ave: Take care of this house. Peter Pan: My house; Peter Pan; Who am I; Never-Never Land.*
*** Etcetera Dig. KTC 1037 [id.]. Roberta Alexander, Tan Crone.

A delightful collection, consistently bearing witness to Bernstein's flair for a snappy idea as well as his tunefulness. Roberta Alexander's rich, warm voice and winning personality are well supported by Tan Crone at the piano. The recording is lifelike and undistracting.

STAGE WORKS

Candide (musical: original Broadway production): *Overture and excerpts.*
(M) *** Sony SK 48017 [id.]. Adrian, Cook, Rounseville and original New York cast, Krachmalnick.

This exhilarating CBS record encapsulates the original 1956 Broadway production and has all the freshness of discovery inherent in a first recording, plus all the zing of the American musical theatre. The lyrics, by Richard Wilbur, give pleasure in themselves. Brilliantly lively sound.

Candide (final, revised version).
⊛ *** DG Dig. 429 734-2 (2) [id.]. Hadley, Anderson, Green, Ludwig, Gedda, Della Jones, Ollmann, London Symphony Ch., LSO, composer.

Candide: highlights.
*** DG Dig. 435 487-2 [id.] (from above set, cond. composer).

John Mauceri, dissatisfied with the results of his 1982 score of *Candide*, undertook a further revision in the mid-1980s, this time with Bernstein's collaboration, and the result was a triumphant success. The composer's splendid DG recording is now available at mid-price as part of the Bernstein Edition – see above – but the set also remains available separately, costing approximately the same price. For those who already have *West Side Story*, the highlights disc would seem a better buy.

'Bernstein on Broadway': Highlights from (i) *Candide;* (ii) *On the Town;* (iii) *West Side Story.*
(N) *** DG Dig. 447 898-2 [id.]. (i) Hadley, Anderson, Green, Ludwig, Gedda, Della Jones, L. Symphony Ch.; LSO, composer; (ii) Von Stade, Daly, Hampson, Garrison, Ramey, Laine, L. Voices, Tilson Thomas; (iii) Te Kanawa, Carreras, Troyanos; (i–iii) Ollmann; (iii) Ch. & O, composer.

A self-recommending selection of the principal numbers from Bernstein's three key musicals to tempt those who have not invested in the complete sets. The 77 minutes is divided reasonably fairly among the three, with *West Side Story* understandably given the lion's share. The *Candide* excerpts include the touchingly optimistic finale, which runs completely counter to Voltaire's intentions – but who will resist, when the music itself is so heart-warming? From *West Side Story* the very touching Balcony scene and Tatiana Troyanos's unforgettably exuberant *America* are both included and, of course, the finest tune of all, *Maria.*

On the Town (complete; with narration by Comden and Green).
*** DG Dig. 437 516-2 [id.]. Frederica von Stade, Tyne Daly, Marie McLaughlin, Thomas Hampson, David Garrison, Kurt Ollmann, Samuel Ramey, Evelyn Lear, Adolph Green, Cleo Laine, Meriel Dickinson, LSO, Tilson Thomas.

In this 1992 concert performance with the LSO at the Barbican of Bernstein's earliest musical, *On the Town*, with the librettists, Betty Comden and Adolph Green, as narrators, it is as though Bernstein himself was performing as well as providing the music, another triumph. If anything, the full score in the exuberance of youth is even richer in catchy tunes than *West Side Story* or *Candide.* A concert performance, bringing in some of the extra numbers that were originally cut from the Broadway show for lack of time, provides the perfect formula.

As in *Candide* (if not *West Side Story*), the mixing of opera stars with the Broadway tradition works like a charm. Thomas Hampson, rich and resonant, sings Gabey, the lead-sailor in search of Miss Turnstiles, with another fine American baritone, Kurt Ollmann, as Chip and David Garrison giving authentic point to the third sailor, Ozzie. Then in opulent casting Samuel Ramey sings a series of incidental roles, including the ever-understanding Pitkin, constantly pushed aside by his man-mad girlfriend, Claire. In that role Frederica von Stade firmly establishes herself as the central star, and anyone hesitating should hear the way she leads the ensemble in the climactic nostalgia of *Some other time.* Marie McLaughlin as Ivy, Miss Turnstiles, is slightly less at home, but Tyne Daly – the Cagney of TV's 'Cagney and Lacey' – as the predatory taxi-driver, Hildy, is winningly larger than life.

In contrast to *Candide*, the live recording has been used for both the CD and the video (072 197-3

[VHS], 072 197-1 [Laserdisc]), yet the results are startlingly different. With the CD, the numbers are presented dry, as though recorded in the studio, with no linking narration and no applause. Not only that, but two of the extra numbers and several encores are omitted to keep the result on a single, well-filled CD. In recompense, an extra number, omitted from the video, *The intermission's great*, is included on the CD. As with *Candide*, the video version, over half an hour longer, proves even more enjoyable, including narration as well as extra numbers. As narrators, Comden and Green are the most winning of guides, ending up by leading a final encore of the big weepy tune, *Some other time*, helping to convey the magic and electricity of a great occasion. The video not only shows Patricia Birch's clever staging of the story (uncostumed), but punctuates it with black-and-white newsreel clips of wartime New York. So it must be the video which earns our Rosette.

West Side Story: complete recording; *On the Waterfront (Symphonic suite)*.
✹ *** DG Dig. 415 253-2 (2) [id.]. Te Kanawa, Carreras, Troyanos, Horne, Ollmann, Ch. and O, composer.

The composer's complete recording of *West Side Story* is more attractively coupled at mid-price with *Candide* in the Bernstein Edition (see above) but, for those collectors seeking a separate issue of the composer's most popular musical, the original issue remains available at premium price, and this two-disc set also includes the vivid symphonic suite from *On the Waterfront*.

West Side story: highlights.
(M) *** DG Dig. 431 027-2 (from complete recording, with Te Kanawa, Carreras, Troyanos, Horne, Ollmann; cond. composer).

The highlights disc, including virtually all the key numbers, could be a preferable choice to the complete set for those not wanting it in harness with *Candide*.

West Side Story (film soundtrack recording).
(M) **(*) Sony SK 48211 [id.]. Nixon, Bryant, Tamblyn, Wand, Chakaris, Ch. & O, Johnny Green.

Few musicals have been transferred to the screen with more success than *West Side Story*, and there are some who feel that, even though the principals' voices are ghosted, the soundtrack recording is preferable to Bernstein's own version using opera stars. The film was splendidly cast and the 'ghosts' were admirably chosen. In the romantic scenes, *Tonight* and *One hand, one heart*, the changes from sung to spoken words are completely convincing and the tragic (mostly spoken) final scene – here included on record for the first time – is very moving. Russ Tamblyn, who sings his own songs, is first class and Marni Nixon and Jim Bryant as the pair of lovers sing touchingly and with youthful freshness. The performance is vibrantly conducted by Johnny Green, and it is a pity that the CD transfer is so 'toppy', bringing a degree of edge both to voices and to the brilliant orchestral playing.

West Side Story: Symphonic dances.
(N) (BB) ** RCA/Navigator 74321 24218-2. RCA Victor O, Bennett – GERSHWIN: *Porgy and Bess*: highlights. **

The music included in Robert Russell Bennett's early (1959) RCA recording is basically the same as that included by Bernstein himself, but with a few minor additions. The playing is extremely brilliant and the dance sequences are rhythmically idiomatic in a uniquely American manner. The sound is very resonant, noisy at times but also attractively atmospheric.

Bertrand, Anthoine de (1540–81)

Amours de Ronsard, Book 1; *Amours de Cassandre:* excerpts.
(B) *** HM Dig. HMA 1431147 [id.]. Clément Janequin Ens.

Anthoine de Bertrand's chansons as recorded here by the Clément Janequin Ensemble show him to be, if not a great master, at least a composer of feeling and considerable resource. The performances are excellent throughout, and admirably recorded. At bargain price this is well worth trying.

Berwald, Franz (1796–1868)

(i) *Piano concerto in D*; (ii) *Violin concerto in C sharp min., Op. 2; Festival of the Bayadères; Overture: The Queen of Golconda; Serious and joyful fancies*.
(M) *** EMI CDM5 65073-2 [id.]. (i) Marian Migdal; (ii) Arve Tellefsen; RPO, Björlin.

All these performances were recorded in 1976. The *Violin concerto* (1820) is an early work, written in the shadow of Spohr and Weber, but it has great charm and a keen melodic facility. A beautiful and elegant performance from Arve Tellefsen and the RPO under the late Ulf Björlin. The *Piano concerto* (1855) is a strange piece. There are some beautiful ideas, including the Chopinesque second group, and they are heard to splendid advantage in Marian Migdal's poetic and imaginative reading. The three shorter pieces are also delightful: the two tone-poems are vintage Berwald and come from the same period (1841–2) as the *Sinfonie sérieuse*, and it is possible that the *Queen of Golconda overture* (1862) also incorporates (either in part or in whole) a lost *Humoristisches Capriccio* written in the 1840s. Very acceptable performances of the orchestral pieces, excellent ones of the *Concertos*, and very good transfers make this a highly desirable issue, particularly at its competitive price.

Symphony in A (1820; fragment); Symphonies Nos. 1–4; Overtures: Estrella di Soria; The Queen of Golconda.
(N) *** Hyperion Dig. CDA 67081/2 [id.] Swedish RSO, Roy Goodman.

Congratulations are owed to Hyperion for their championship of Berwald. As we go to press, we hear that they also plan to record all the chamber music. Roy Goodman's set with the Swedish Radio Symphony Orchestra has the advantage of including the early fragment of the *Symphony in A major* which Berwald completed (it was performed in the same concert as the *Violin concerto* in 1821) but which survives only in fragmentary form. It has been completed – and very well, too – by Duncan Druce, and makes its début on records. It is distinctively Berwaldian, though there are touches of Weber in the opening introduction and of Schubert in the second group (even a foretaste of Mendelssohn). Goodman is always alert and intelligent, though he tends to favour brisk tempi. He starts the *Sinfonie singulière* far too quickly and is forced to pull back when the brass enter. He does not allow the movement to unfold naturally but tends to push ahead at times, and in the slow movement he underlines dynamic contrasts. There is a certain loss of breadth here, and again in the *Sinfonie sérieuse*. The *Overture* to *The Queen of Golconda* comes off very well. Berwald's orchestration tends to be top-heavy and the cool acoustic of the Berwald Hall in Stockholm slightly accentuates that.

Symphonies Nos. 1 in G min. (Sérieuse); 2 in D (Capricieuse); 3 in C (Singulière); 4 in E flat.
(N) (B) *** DG Dig. 445 581-2 (2) [id.]. Gothenburg SO, Järvi.

Neeme Järvi's set of the Berwald *Symphonies* appeared in the mid-1980s and is still eminently recommendable; this is music that is wholly in the life-stream of the Gothenburg orchestra. The only reservation one might make concerns the brisk opening movement to the *Sinfonie singulière*, but Järvi's most recent rival (Roy Goodman on Hyperion) is, if anything, faster. Järvi's account of the *E flat Symphony* has marginally greater sparkle and lightness of touch. The DG recording, balanced by Michael Bergek (more familiar on the BIS label), is excellent in every way, and the warmer acoustic of the Gothenburg Concert Hall may sway some readers in favour of this version, particularly in view of the much more modest outlay involved.

Symphonies Nos. 1–4; (i) *Piano concerto in D.*
(N) (BB) ** Naxos Dig. 8.553051/2 [id.]. (i) Niklas Sivelöv; Helsingborg SO, Okko Kamu.

All four Berwald *Symphonies*, with the *Piano concerto* thrown in for good measure – and all at super-bargain price! The recordings are very good and the performances decent. The Helsingborg orchestra is impressive, though their strings are not as fine as those of the Gothenburg orchestra. Okko Kamu's performance of the *Sinfonie singulière* is impressive and is to be preferred to Goodman or Järvi, but the *E flat Symphony* needs a more mercurial touch and greater lightness. The standard is that of a very acceptable broadcast by one of the old regional BBC orchestras. Niklas Sivelöv in the 1855 *Piano concerto in D major* gives a good account of himself, though Marian Migdal on EMI is the more poetic player. Very good recorded sound.

Symphonies Nos. 1 in G min. (Sérieuse); 3 in C (Singulière); Play of the elves (Elfenspiel).
(Y/B) (M) **(*) EMI CDM5 65303-2 [id.]. RPO, Björlin.

Symphonies Nos. 2 (Capricieuse); 4 in E flat; Overture: Estrella de Soria; Racing; Reminiscences from the Norwegian mountains.
(N) (M) **(*) EMI CDM5 65866-2 [id.]. RPO, Björlin.

These CDs continue EMI's reissues from a 1976 boxed set containing all Berwald's orchestral music. The performances here are thoroughly sympathetic and certainly worth considering at mid-price. They sound warm and fresh, though the orchestral playing under the late Ulf Björlin is a little deficient in vitality; the recordings were made during a heat-wave. Both Järvi and Ehrling with the LSO are more vital and alert in the *Singulière*, and the former's account of the *Sérieuse* is comparably rewarding, while Erling's account of No. 4 is also more vital and alert. By their side, Björlin does not succeed in creating the same degree of tension in shaping melodic lines. The tone-poems are wholly neglected, but their invention is often captivating. The *Reminiscences from the Norwegian mountains* is attractively atmospheric, while *Play of the elves* is a delightful piece under whose deceptively Mendelssohnian surface resides an inventive and original mind. The *Overture Estrella de Soria* is full of resourceful and finely drawn ideas. There are no current alternatives at present, so this pair of CDs is by no means to be written off, as the EMI engineers have provided excellent recording, well transferred to CD.

Symphonies Nos. 1 (Sinfonie sérieuse); 4 in E flat (Sinfonie naïve).
**(*) Decca Dig. 436 597-2 [id.]. San Francisco SO, Blomstedt.

Blomstedt gets very good playing from the San Francisco orchestra and his accounts of the *Sérieuse* and the *E flat Symphonies* are eminently civilized. *No. 4 in E flat* is the sunniest of the symphonies, though in Blomstedt's realization the sun has a rather cool pallor. Tempi are somewhat measured and there is little of the infectious sparkle that Neeme Järvi gets in his communicative and enthusiastic performances on DG, which have the advantage of the livelier, warmer acoustic of the Gothenburg hall. The Decca recording has a truthful perspective to commend it and clean, well-detailed sound, but the strings are a bit top-heavy and have a chilly timbre, doubtless induced by the acoustic. Yet these are well-shaped, highly intelligent readings that deserve a three-star recommendation, though by the side of Järvi and Ehrling they sound a bit laid back.

Symphonies Nos. 3 in C (Sinfonie singulière); No. 4 in E flat.
*** Bluebell ABD 037 [id.]. LSO, Sixten Ehrling.

Sixten Ehrling's records of Berwald's masterpiece, the *Sinfonie singulière*, and its sunny and high-spirited companion, the *Symphony No. 4 in E flat*, were made in 1967 for Decca and still sound as fresh and satisfying as ever. Although the sound is not digital, there is no reason to withhold a third star.

Grand septet in B flat.
*** CRD CRD 3344 [id.]. Nash Ens. – HUMMEL: *Septet.* ***

Berwald's only *Septet* is a work of genuine quality and deserves a secure place in the repertory instead of on its periphery. It is eminently well played by the Nash Ensemble, and finely recorded.

Grand Septet in B flat; Piano and wind quartet in E flat; Piano trio in F min.
(N) *** Hyperion Dig. CDA 66834 [id.]. Gaudier Ens.

The first in a series to mark the bicentenary of Berwald's birth. The *Quartet in E flat for piano and wind* of 1819 is the earliest piece here and is good but not vintage Berwald, though it could not sound more persuasive in this performance. However, the *Grand Septet* (1828) is a captivating piece, and so is the inventive *F minor Piano trio* of 1851. Delightful performances on which it would be difficult to improve, and excellent recording too. This augurs well for this enterprise.

(i) *Piano quintet No. 1 in C min.;* (ii) *Piano trios Nos. 1 in E flat; 3 in D min.*
**(*) MS Dig. MSCD 521 [id.]. (i) Stefan Lindgren, Berwald Qt; (ii) Bernt Lysell, Ola Karlsson, Lucia Negro.

The performances of the *Trios* are very good indeed, though not necessarily superior to those of the Prunyi–Kiss–Onczay team on Marco Polo. One minor quibble: a little more space round and distance from the instruments would have shown these fine players to even greater advantage.

Piano trios Nos. 1 in E flat; 2 in F min.; 3 in D min.
*** Marco Polo Dig. 8.223170 [id.]. Prunyi, Kiss, Onczay.

These Hungarian players give spirited accounts of all three trios recorded here and make out a persuasive case for this music. The string players (András Kiss and Czaba Onczay) are both highly accomplished; perhaps the most demanding writing is for the piano and it is a pity that Ilona Prunyi proves at times to be a little less imaginative than her companions. The recording, made at the Italian Institute in Budapest, is very good indeed, fresh and present.

Piano trios: in C (1845); No. 4 in C (1853); in C (fragment); in E flat (fragment).
**(*) Marco Polo Dig. 8.223430 [id.]. Kalman Drafi, Jozsef Mondrian, György Kertész.

The *C major Trio*, like its companions and the fragments recorded here, is fresh and inventive. These performances by Kalman Drafi, Jozsef Mondrian and György Kertész are faithful and committed and are very well recorded at the Festetic Castle in Budapest.

String quartet in G min.
*** CRD CRD 3361; CRDC 4061 [id.]. Chilingirian Qt – WIKMANSON: *Quartet.* ***

The *G minor Quartet* is, as one would expect from an accomplished violinist, a remarkably assured piece, and the first movement is full of modulatory audacities. The thematic substance is both characterful and appealing. The trio of the Scherzo has a touching charm that is almost Schubertian, though it is impossible that Berwald could have been aware of his great contemporary. This is a highly interesting and often bold *Quartet*, and the Chilingirian players give a well-shaped and sensitive account of it. They are truthfully recorded, and the coupling – another Swedish quartet – enhances the attractions of this issue. The CD transfer is fresh and clear, and there is an excellent cassette equivalent. Strongly recommended.

Biber, Heinrich (1644–1704)

Arien à 4; Balletti lamentabili à 4; Mensa sonora.
(N) ** Lyrichord Dig. LEMS 8017 [id.]. La Follia Strasburg.

The major work here is the *Mensa sonora*, a set of six suites from 1680, Biber's equivalent of Telemann's *Tafelmusik*. They are usually in six or seven movements, including an *Intrada* and various dances: *Balletto, Allemande, Gagliarda, Courante, Gigue*, and so on. But the invention here is less winning than with Telemann. However, Biber's writing is not helped by the (at times) heavy-handed approach of this period German group, who only occasionally lighten the pervading tutti string texture, which tends to be somewhat thick-textured and gruff. When they do, as in the *Gigues* of Parts I and IV, and almost the whole of Part V, which is treated like a ballet suite, the effect is very diverting. The *Arien à 4* (from 1673–4) which opens the concert is a more dramatically diverse, six-movement suite, while in the early *Balletti lamentabili*, the final item, the six movements are similar in form to those of *Mensa sonora* but all are of a melancholy disposition.

Balletae à 4 violettae Nos. 1–7; Battalia in D; Peasants' churchgoing sonata in B flat à 6; Sonatas Nos. 1–2 à 8 for 2 clarini, 6 violae; 3–4 à 5 violae; Sonata à 7 for 6 trumpets, tramburin and organ (168).
(N) (M) *** Teldec/Warner 4509 97914-2 [id.]. VCM, Harnoncourt.

This is as good and varied an introduction to Biber's music as any. His *Battle* evocation is as spectacular as any of the baroque era and Harnoncourt is just the man for it. The battle sequence itself has some hair-raising instrumental effects, including barbaric pizzicati representing the cannon. The picture of '*the dissolute company*' brings a half-minute of well-organized instrumental cacophony to suggest that Biber could even anticipate Charles Ives. In the *March* there is a bizarre fife-and-drum imitation by violin and double bass. The piece closes with a *Lament of the wounded musketeers*. The *Sonatas* for strings and clarini (and notably the *Peasants' churchgoing*) show this Bohemian-born Viennese Court Kapellmeister as a resourceful and inventive musician who knew how to manage lyrical pictorial effects as well as dramatic ones. His musical ideas are certainly attractive. The performances have great character – Nikolaus Harnoncourt was always good at explosive accents – and are very well recorded.

Harmonia artificiosa-ariosa (7 Partitas), Nos. 1–3 & 5 for 2 scordatura violins & continuo; 4 for scordatura violin, viola di braccio & continuo; 6 for 2 violins & continuo; 7 for 2 violas d'amore & continuo (complete).
(Y/B) *** Sony Dig. SK 58920 [id.]. Tafelmusik, Jeanne Lamon.
(Y/B) (M) *** Chandos Dig. 0575/6 [id.]. Purcell Quartet with Elizabeth Wallfisch.

Two complete recordings of Biber's masterly *Harmonia artificosa-ariosa*, equally distinguished, show us the amazing range of these seven partitas (or suites), which were published posthumously in 1712. (The term *scordata*, incidentally, indicated a different system of tuning.) Each work consists of a very free opening *Prelude* or a more structured *Sonata* (slow–fast–slow), usually improvisational in feeling, and includes the usual dance forms of *Allemande* and *Sarabande*, plus an *Aria* with divisions, and often closes with a lighthearted *Gigue*, although the *Third* ends with a remarkable *Canon in uniso*, liberally decorated with violin cascades, which readily relates to the more famous piece by Biber's contemporary, Pachelbel. The *Fifth Sonata in G* ends with a splendid *Passacaglia*. The *Aria* in the *Sixth* has thirteen variations plus finale, and, including all repeats, the Purcell performance extends this remarkable movement to over 13 minutes, with playing of the highest order to hold the listener's attention readily throughout; the Tafelmusik account is half as long. But in many ways the two sets of performances are alike, and they certainly share the spontaneity and scholarship of the very best period-instrument performances. Tempi are usually similar, although the Purcell Consort tend to bring a slightly more spacious espressivo to slower movements. Their extra weight (with use of organ continuo) is especially telling in the passacaglias. On the other hand, the airy sprightliness of Tafelmusik, especially in the *Gigues*, often more dashing, is very attractive. In short, you cannot go wrong with either of these recordings, which are both splendidly balanced and truthful. We have listed Tafelmusik first as (for some of the reasons stated above) Sony squeeze all seven partitas on to a single CD. Chandos have been forced to use a pair, playing for 43 minutes and 47 minutes respectively. But the cost has been reduced accordingly, and this set retails at upper-mid-price, probably costing slightly under £20 for the two CDs.

Harmonia artificiosa-ariosa (for 2 violins scordatura and continuo): *Partitas III & V. Rosenkranz sonata No. 10* (for violin scordatura and continuo); *Passacaglia No. 16 for solo violin; Sonata No. VI; Sonata representativa* (both for violin and continuo).
*** BIS Dig. CD 608 [id.]. Maria Lindal, Ens. Saga.

Heinrich Biber is fast emerging as a major personality, and the melancholy *Passacaglia* for solo violin is totally memorable. But the hit of the programme is the *Sonata representativa* with its bird evocations – they are more than just imitations – including the nightingale, thrush, cuckoo (a most striking approach) and cockerel. Maria Lindal is a splendid soloist, and the style of the playing here is vibrantly authentic: the ear quickly adjusts to the plangent (but in no way anaemic) timbres which suit this repertoire admirably.

Rosenkranz sonatas Nos. 1–16.
(M) **(*) HM/BMG Dig. GD 77102 (2) [77102-RG]. Franzjosef Maier, Franz Lehrndorfer, Max Engel, Konrad Junghänel.

Biber's *Sonatas* for violin and basso continuo, based on the Mysteries of the rosary, include music of great poetic feeling and sensibility. The playing here is of high quality, and although the recording could provide better internal definition it is full and pleasing.

12 Sonatae tam aris, quam aulis servientes.
(N) *** Chandos Dig. CHAN 0591 [id.]. Bennett, Laird, McGillivray, Cronin, Purcell Qt.

Sonatae tam aris, quam aulis servientes: Nos. 2 in D; 3 in G min.; 5 in E min.; 11 in A.
**(*) HM/BMG 05472 77303-2 [id.]. Freiburg Bar. Cons. – MUFFAT: *Sonatas.* **(*)

Biber's *Sonatae tam aris, quam aulis servientes* were written in 1670, intended, as the title suggests, for use in church (at the altar) or court. Each is short (4–7 minutes) and structured in a single movement, yet each combines both expressive elements and a rhythmic vitality deriving from the dance. They are splendidly chimerical miniatures and confirm yet again the fecundity of the composer's imagination, with sleight-of-hand changes of tempo and apt use of contrapuntal devices. The result is wittily entertaining, yet retains its propriety, with the dance elements thoroughly absorbed so as not to offend the clergy with any vulgar associations. The new Chandos complete set from the augmented Purcell Quartet is excellent in every way, full of life and imaginative detail, with the expressive music not at all intimidated by the use of period instruments. The sound is first class.

Those wanting a selection only will find the Freiburg Baroque Consort equally persuasive. Their performances too are winningly vital (try No. 2 as a sampler as it is briefest of all) and the only drawback for some ears is the tendency in sustained, chordal writing for the well-blended 'authentic' string group to sound a bit like a harmonium. Also the playing time is not generous (59 minutes) and there would certainly have been room for a couple more of these sonatas.

8 Violin sonatas (for violin and continuo) (1681); *Sonata pastorella; Sonata representativa in A* (for solo violin); *Passacaglia for solo violin; Passacaglia for lute.*
(Y/B) *** HM Dig. HMU 907134/5 (2) [id.]. Romanesca (Andrew Manze, Nigel North, John Toll).

As a performer, Biber was obviously a virtuoso of the highest order, for these phenomenally difficult *Sonatas*, with their chimerical upper tessitura and sometimes bizarre effects, could be played only by a violinist of remarkable technical gifts. Such is Andrew Manze, whose baroque violin encompasses all the demands made on it with consummate mastery. He conveys to the full the tension which always springs from strong performances of technically demanding music, yet at the same time retains an essentially expressive style. For with all the extraordinary decorative divisions inherent in Biber's writing, it is essentially melodic, and the tunes come out fast and furious. He is an unashamed borrower, using *La Folia* readily enough and drawing on other composers' ideas without shame (Schmelzer among them). What is remarkable in these superbly played performances is the conveyed improvisatory feeling in the writing, to say nothing of its sublimely volatile unpredictability. Although the solo lute *Passacaglia*, which is a simplified piece, does not give him much of a chance to shine, Nigel North's often plangent continuo on lute and theorbo makes a major contribution to the imaginative vitality of the music-making, and John Toll is a good keyboard partner (for instance, the organ underpinning of the *Passacaglia* which opens the *Sixth Sonata*). But it is Andrew Manze who makes these performances so exciting and stimulating: surely the composer himself must have played them like this. The recording has a fine, spacious acoustic, and only those who find the abrasiveness of authentic fiddling aurally difficult should stay away from this highly stimulating pair of discs.

Requiem à 15 in A.
(N) *** DHM Dig. 05472 77344-2 [id.]. Almajano, Van der Sluis, Elwes, Padmore, Huijts, Van der Kamp, Netherlands Bach Festival Ch. & O, Leonhardt – STEFFANI: *Stabat Mater*. ***

Requiem a 15 in A; Vesperae a 32.
*** Erato/Warner Dig.4509 91725-2 [id.]. Bongers, Grimm, Wessel, De Groot, Reyans, S. Davies, Steur, De Koning, Amsterdam Bar. Ch. & O, Koopman.

As might be expected from the major key (hardly a usual one for a post-Renaissance requiem) Biber's A major setting is more robust than its companion in F minor. It is a gloriously exultant piece. Here death has very little sting, with the promises of forgiveness and heaven to come, and Biber immediately in the opening *Introitus* uses rich brass sonorities and his combined forces of singers in the grandest manner. In the Salzburg Court Cathedral of his day it was possible to place soloists, brass and choral groups in five different places. Here the polyphonic and polychoral writing is spread across a wide proscenium with brass and voices echoing each other ambitiously in overlapping phrases. There is plenty of vitality in the writing. Although the *Vespers* is hardly less complex and its writing equally inventive, this work depends more on continual contrast to makes its effect, with the soloists consistently used in alternation with the more massive choral and brass outbursts. It has some splendid moments. The *Magnificat* brings a fine flowing fugato and, after much interplay between the solo group and the others, ends with a very positive closing *Amen*. The performances here are inspired with the most glorious sounds coming from all concerned, and the solo team matching voices and singing splendidly together. The performances under Koopman are inspired.

Leonhardt's account is also very fine indeed. There is no lack of spectacle, but the acoustic of Pieterskerk, Utrecht, is ideally free from excess resonance so that the results are particularly fresh with remarkably clear detail, yet there is the right warmth of ambience and a bloom on the excellent soloists, choir and orchestra alike. The performance has plenty of vitality and, for those interested in having a beautiful setting of *Stabat Mater* by Biber's contemporary, Agostino Steffani, this is an excellent alternative recommendation.

(i) *Requiem in F min.;* (ii) *Serenada 'Der Nachtwächter'; Balletae à 4; Battalia à 10; Sonata à 6 in B (Die Bauern Kirchfarht genandt).*
*** O-L Dig. 436 460-2. (i) Catherine Bott, Tessa Bonner, Christopher Robson, John Mark Ainsley, Michael George; (ii) Simon Grant; New L. Cons., Pickett.

Philip Pickett calls the *Serenada* (in which Simon Grant participates characterfully, and the sonata, *Die Bauern Kirchfarht genandt*, 'a programmatic *tour de force*', and they are both quite astonishingly vivid pieces. In the *Requiem in F minor* Pickett lays out his forces as they would have been positioned in Salzburg Cathedral in the 1690s, 'recreating the spatial polychoral effects which the surviving performance parts suggest'. The piece is powerful and makes a stronger effect than in the 1968 Harnoncourt performance, coupled with the *St Polycarpi sonata* and the *Cantata, Laetatus sum*, which we much admired in its day. Fine singing, remarkable music and excellent recording.

Binge, Ronald (1910–79)

Las Castañuelas; (i) *Concerto for E flat saxophone. Dance of the snowflakes; Elizabethan serenade; Faire Frou-Frou; High stepper, Madrugado; Miss Melanie; The red sombrero; Sailing by; Scherzo; Scottish rhapsody; String song; Trade winds; Venetian carnival; The watermill;* (ii) *The whispering valley: Prelude.*
(Y/B) ** Marco Polo Dig. 8.223515 [id.]. Slovak RSO (Bratislava), Ernest Tomlinson; (i) with Kenneth Edge; (ii) Silvia Cápová.

Ronald Binge created the Mantovani 'sound', a cascading string effect cleverly achieved not by studio reverberation alone but by overlapping the part-writing for the violins. (Glazunov had already hinted at how it could be done in his *Seasons* ballet.) Binge's ingenious arrangement helped to make *Charmaine* one of the great post-war instrumental hits. Later he went on to use this effect, slightly modified, in one of his own pieces – pointing the string phrasing with the harp, in *The dance of the snowflakes*. Then came his own great personal success, *Elizabethan serenade* (first called simply 'Andante cantabile'), which Mantovani premièred in 1951. It immediately caught the public fancy and became a signature-tune *par excellence*. Binge's other striking lyrical success was *Sailing by*, but his most delectable miniature is undoubtedly *The watermill*. The *Saxophone concerto* is lively enough, with the finale the most striking movement. It is given a first-rate performance by Kenneth Edge but is not as memorable as the Eric

Coates *Rhapsody*. The whole programme is freshly played by this excellent Slovak orchestra under the sympathetic Ernest Tomlinson, although he phrases the *Elizabethan serenade* rather angularly. The one snag is that the microphones have been placed too close to the violins, which produces an unflattering, grainy patina of string-tone. The conductor provides nine pages of biography and excellent descriptive notes.

Birtwistle, Harrison (born 1934)

Carmen Arcadiae mechanicae perpetuum; Secret theatre; Silbury air.
*** Etcetera Dig. KTC 1052 [id.]. L. Sinf., Elgar Howarth.

Silbury air is one of Birtwistle's 'musical landscapes', bringing ever-changing views and perspectives on the musical material and an increasing drawing-out of melody. With melody discarded, *Carmen Arcadiae mechanicae perpetuum* (*The perpetual song of Mechanical Arcady*) superimposes different musical mechanisms to bring a rhythmic kaleidoscope of textures and patterns. The title of *Secret theatre* is taken from a poem by Robert Graves which refers to 'an unforeseen and fiery entertainment', and there is no doubting the distinctive originality of the writing, utterly typical of the composer. Howarth and the Sinfonietta could hardly be more convincing advocates, recorded in vivid, immediate sound.

Earth dances.
*** Collins Dig. Single 2001-2. BBC SO, Eötvös.

This is a characteristically rugged and characterful piece by Birtwistle, recorded live at the Proms in 1991 in spectacular sound. It is a generally slow-moving ritual, brilliantly written for the orchestra. Unfortunately, there are no separate tracks for the individual sections.

(i; iii) *Melencolia I;* (ii; iii) *Meridian;* (iii) *Ritual Fragment*.
*** NMC Dig. NMCD 009 [id.]. (i) Antony Pay; (ii) Mary King, Michael Thompson, Christopher van Kampen; L. Sinf. Voices; (iii) L. Sinf. (members); Oliver Knussen.

The NMC Birtwistle disc has the London Sinfonietta under Oliver Knussen in three works revealing the composer at his most uncompromising. *Ritual Fragment* was inspired by the death of Michael Vyner, the dynamic and influential artistic director of London Sinfonietta. It was perhaps the most moving of the pieces specially written for the Vyner memorial concert at Covent Garden. Just as dark and even more obsessive are the two longer works on the disc, *Melencolia I* and *Meridian*, that last the grimmest of love-songs.

Secret theatre; Tragoedia; Five distances for five instruments; (i) *3 settings of Celan* (for soprano and 5 instruments).
(N) *** DG Dig. 439 910-2 [id.]. Ens. InterContemporain, Pierre Boulez; (i) with Christine Whittlesey.

Pierre Boulez has been a champion of Birtwistle's music for many years – one of the few British composers he recognizes – and here he delivers performances sharply focused and powerfully intense. The earliest work here is *Tragoedia*, not a tragedy in the conventional sense but a ritual in eight compact, tensely argued sections. It was this work – involving material used later in the opera, *Punch and Judy* – which in 1965 alerted us to a formidable new voice in British music, conveying deep, dark emotions behind a brutal façade. *Secret theatre* over a span of nearly half an hour presents another ritual, contrasting timbres and moods, dance and song, with the brutality tempered by overt lyricism. The close of the piece is hauntingly poetic, one of Birtwistle's most telling moments. The other two works are shorter but hardly less intense, with the five players in the *Five distances* widely separated (an instruction not well conveyed in this otherwise excellent recording) and with the Celan settings a poignant tribute to a Romanian-Jewish poet who suffered severely in the Second World War. The recording lets one hear every detail of the rugged textures, but with fine bloom on the instruments.

Secret theatre; Ritual fragment; (i) *Nenia: The Death of Orpheus*.
(N) *** CPO Dig. CPO 9993602 [id.]. (i) Rosemary Hardy; Musikfabrik NRW, Johannes Kalitzke.

It is fascinating to compare this German reading of Birtwistle's impressive *Secret theatre* with Boulez's on DG. The playing of Musikfabrik may not seem so powerful, partly because of a less forward recording, but the concentration builds up with comparable intensity, and the final climax is if anything even more maniacally uninhibited, leading to a more warmly poetic conclusion. *Nenia: The Death of Orpheus*, the earliest work here, is an elegiac piece in which the soloist's vocalizing is punctuated by percussive sing-speech, an early example of the composer's obsession with the Orpheus legend which culminated in the large-scale opera, *The Mask of Orpheus*. *Ritual fragment*, dating from 1990, is a moving lament on the death of Michael Vyner, artistic director of London Sinfonietta, not just dark and intense but at times angry, demonstrating that, for all the brutality of expression, Birtwistle's emotions are fundamental.

Punch and Judy (opera) complete.
*** Etcetera KTC 2014 (2) [id.]. Roberts, DeGaetani, Bryn-Julson, Langridge, Wilson-Johnson, Tomlinson, L. Sinf., David Atherton.

Punch and Judy is a brutal, ritualistic piece, 'the first modern English opera', as it was called when it first appeared at the Aldeburgh Festival in 1968. It may not make easy listening, but nor is it easy to forget for, behind the aggressiveness, Birtwistle's writing has a way of touching an emotional chord, just as Stravinsky's so often does. Stephen Roberts is outstanding as Punch, and among others there is not a single weak link. David Atherton, conductor from the first performances, excels himself with the Sinfonietta. The clear, vivid recording, originally made by Decca for their enterprising LP Headline series, has been licensed by Etcetera.

The Triumph of Time; Gawain (opera): *Gawain's journey.*
*** Collins Dig. 1387-2 [id.]. Philh. O, Elgar Howarth.

In their unmistakable power and authority, the two major works on this Collins disc are typical of the mature Birtwistle. *The Triumph of Time*, inspired by the Breughel engraving, was the piece which – with Pierre Boulez responsible for its first recording – was influential in making Birtwistle an international figure. Its power is undiminished: a grim, relentless processional. Even more welcome is *Gawain's journey*, one of Birtwistle's richest and most approachable scores, which in its 25-minute span reworks salient passages from his unforgettable Covent Garden opera, *Gawain*, first heard in 1991. Under Elgar Howarth, both works are brilliantly played by the Philharmonia and stunningly recorded.

Bizet, Georges (1838–75)

L'Arlésienne (complete incidental music; ed. Riffauld).
*** EMI Dig. CDC7 47460-2 [id.]. Orféon Donstiarra, Toulouse Capitole O, Plasson.

The EMI recording of the complete incidental music appears to have returned to the catalogue, although it may take perseverance to obtain. The score that Michel Plasson and his excellent French forces have recorded is based on the 1872 autograph, and the singing of the Orféon Donstiarra is as excellent as the orchestral playing. The less familiar music is every bit as captivating as the suites so that the performance has great charm, and the EMI recording is very good indeed. Strongly recommended.

L'Arlésienne: suites Nos. 1–2; Symphony in C.
*** EMI CDC7 47794-2 [id.]. RPO, Beecham.
**(*) EMI Dig. CDC5 55118-2 [id.]. ASMF, Marriner.
(N) (M) ** Erato/Warner Dig. 4509 99769-2 [id.]. Lyon Op. O, Gardiner.

L'Arlésienne: suites Nos. 1–2: excerpts; *Carmen: suites Nos. 1–2:* excerpts; *Symphony in C.*
(Y/B) (BB) *** RCA Navigator 74321 17901-2. Bamberg SO, Georges Prêtre.

Beecham's magical set of the incidental music for *L'Arlésienne*, dating from 1957, still sounds remarkably well. Besides the beauty and unique character of the wind solos, Beecham's deliciously sprightly *Minuet* and his affectingly gentle sense of nostalgia in the *Adagietto* (both from the first suite) are as irresistibly persuasive as the swaggering brilliance of the closing *Farandole* of the second. Beecham's version of the *Symphony* above all brings out its spring-like qualities. The playing of the French orchestra is not quite as polished as that of Marriner's group, but Beecham's panache more than compensates. The remastered sound is bright on top, without glare.

From Prêtre a most enjoyable and generous super-bargain disc, originating from the Eurodisc catalogue, very warmly and naturally recorded, most elegantly played and offering 77 minutes of music. The most important numbers are included in the two orchestral suites and, if the playing in *L'Arlésienne* is a little low-key, the *Carmen* vignettes alternate vividness with pleasing instrumental delicacy. The performance of the *Symphony*, complete with exposition repeat, is alert, yet has much refinement as well as warmth, the oboe solo in the slow movement played most engagingly. There is plenty of vigour in the outer movements and, although the ambience is resonant, it does not cloud detail.

Marriner's latest EMI account of Bizet's *Symphony*, which is generous with repeats in the outer movements, does not quite re-create the sparkling lightness of touch of his early Argo (now Decca) version, currently withdrawn. In the first movement there is plenty of energy, but not the same sense of complete spontaneity. The two *L'Arlésienne suites* are beautifully played, the *Adagietto* given a gossamer delicacy, and the Abbey Road recording is first class.

John Eliot Gardiner's Bizet coupling is a disappointment. Although he secures polished playing in Lyon, his conception of the Bizet *Symphony* is a fully romanticized one. The choice of the Eglise Sainte-Madeleine de Pérouges (Ain) as a recording venue was unfortunate, for the reverberation inflates Bizet's textures. Both here and in *L'Arlésienne* they are made to lose much of their transparent subtlety of colouring. Although in its way the account of the *Symphony* makes a strong impression, especially in the *Adagio*, the outer movements lose their light-hearted feeling, and the finale sounds far more sprightly elsewhere. The sound itself is not very refined.

L'Arlésienne: suites Nos. 1–2; Carmen: suite No. 1.
(M) *** DG 423 472-2 [id.]. LSO, Abbado.

L'Arlésienne: suites Nos. 1–2; Carmen: suites Nos. 1–2.
*** Decca Dig. 417 839-2 [id.]. Montreal SO, Dutoit.

(i) *L'Arlésienne: suites Nos. 1–2; Carmen: suites Nos. 1–2;* (ii) *Jeux d'enfants.*
(N) (M) **(*) Ph. 446 198-2 [id.]. (i) ASMF, Marriner; (ii) Concg. O, Haitink.

L'Arlésienne: suites Nos. 1–2; Carmen: suite No. 1; suite No. 2: excerpts; *Patrie overture.*
(M) **(*) Mercury 343 321-2 [id.]. Detroit SO, Paray – THOMAS: *Overtures: Raymond; Mignon.* ***

With playing that is both elegant and vivid, and with superb, demonstration-worthy sound, Dutoit's polished yet affectionate coupling of the *L'Arlésienne* and *Carmen* suites makes a clear first choice.

Among analogue couplings of *L'Arlésienne* and *Carmen* suites, Abbado's 1981 DG recording stands out, available at medium price on CD. The orchestral playing is characteristically refined, the wind solos cultured and eloquent, especially in *L'Arlésienne*, where the pacing of the music is nicely judged.

The Mercury *L'Arlésienne* and *Carmen* suites were recorded as early as 1956 and, apart from some background hiss, it would be impossible to guess, so full is the sound. Paray's performances are neat and polished, certainly Gallic if without quite the panache of Beecham's version, made for EMI a year later. Paray adopts a phlegmatic tempo for the famous dotted tune in *L'Arlésienne*; by the same token, his *Minuetto* in the second suite is very brisk indeed. But this music-making is attractively alive, and in the flamboyant (if slightly empty) *Patrie overture*, recorded two years later in Old Orchestral Hall, the Detroit brass enjoy themselves hugely. What makes this disc especially attractive is the inclusion of the two overtures of Thomas, which are superbly done.

Marriner's collection is generous, offering 11 items from *Carmen* and both *L'Arlésienne suites*, while Haitink's *Jeux d'enfants* is delectably played and superbly recorded in the Concertgebouw. The London recording, too, is attractively rich and naturally balanced. But the musical characterization – despite fine LSO playing, notably from the flautist, Peter Lloyd – is sometimes lacking in flair and the last degree of *brio*. There are minor touches of eccentricity: Marriner's tempo suddenly quickens for the middle section of the *Menuet* from the second *L'Arlésienne suite* and, although there is much to ravish the ear, the orchestrations of the vocal numbers from *Carmen* are sometimes less than convincing.

L'Arlésienne: suite No. 1 (with *Andante molto*); *Jeux d'enfants* (*suite*; including *Les quatre coins*); *Overture in A; Marche funèbre in B min.*
*** EMI Dig. CDC7 54765-2 [id.]. Toulouse Capitole O, Michel Plasson.

L'Arlésienne: suite No. 1; Jeux d'enfants (petite suite); La jolie Fille de Perth (suite).
(M) *** EMI CDM7 64869-2 [id.]. O de Paris, Barenboim.

Neither Barenboim nor Plasson offers the second *L'Arlésienne* suite, although Plasson includes the delicate *Andante molto* with its refined saxophone solo. He also offers an attractively busy extra movement (*Les quatre coins*) from *Jeux d'enfants* which the composer unaccountably discarded, even though he had reworked and extended the piano duet original. The other important novelty here is the delightful *Overture in A* which is contemporary with the *Symphony* and is equally felicitously scored. The *Marche funèbre* is in fact the relatively flamboyant *Prélude* to the discarded opera, *La Coupe du roi de Thulé*. Plasson's performances are alive and persuasive throughout. The recording, made in the Hall-aux-Grains, Toulouse, is of best EMI quality.

But then so is the analogue sound (from 1972 and 1975) of Barenboim's earlier programme, and those who want this particular grouping of works will find the mid-priced CD thoroughly recommendable. The performances are vivid and affectionate and Barenboim's winning combination of delicacy and sparkle in *La jolie fille de Perth* suggests that he has been influenced by the Beecham recordings of this music. The CD transfer is one of EMI's best in its combination of fullness and brilliance. The *Patrie overture*, which can sound over-melodramatic, is here presented most convincingly.

Jeux d'enfants (Children's games), Op. 22.

(N) (M) *** Decca 448 571-2 [id.]. Paris Conservatoire O, Martinon – BERLIOZ: *Overtures* **(*); IBERT: *Divertissement* ***; SAINT-SAENS: *Danse macabre* etc. ***

(B) *** CfP CD-CFP 4086; *TC-CFP 40086.* SNO, Gibson – RAVEL: *Ma Mère l'Oye;* SAINT-SAENS; *Carnival.* ***

(N) (BB) ** Tring Dig. TRP 046 [id.]. RPO, Andrea Licata – PROKOFIEV: *Peter;* SAINT-SAENS: *Carnival.* **(*)

Martinon's memorable account of *Jeux d'enfants* was part of a famous 1960 Decca anthology of French orchestral music, now reissued in the 'Classic Sound' series. The crisp trumpet fanfares in the opening piece set the seal on a performance notable for its vivid colour and delicacy of feeling. The sound is remarkably good.

From Classics for Pleasure a fresh approach, lively orchestral playing and excellent mid-1970s sound; with excellent couplings, this is highly recommendable.

The RPO under the Italian conductor, Andrea Licata, play sympathetically and are well recorded, and this makes a fully acceptable coupling for Gielgud's *Peter and the wolf.*

Roma suite; Patrie overture, Op. 19; Symphony in C.

(Y/B) **(*) EMI Dig. CDC5 55057-2 [id.]. Capitole Toulouse O, Michel Plasson.

(Y/B) (BB) **(*) ASV Dig. CDQS 6135 [id.] (without *Patrie*). RPO, Enrique Bátiz.

Roma was written over a period, some years after the *Symphony in C.* It has not the overall spontaneity of the *Symphony* and is uneven in quality, but it remains a piece easy to indulge if you are a lover of Bizet's feeling for the orchestral palette. The warmth of the opening horn chorale and the gaiety of the finale, with its pleasing secondary tune, are brought out enjoyably in Toulouse and the orchestral playing is excellent. The recording, too, is very good, vividly coloured, if not of demonstration standard. *Patrie,* too, comes over with plenty of gusto, and again its lyrical theme is warmly presented. The *Symphony* is lively and well played (with an imaginative oboe soloist) and is certainly enjoyable if not distinctive. Martinon's version (see below) has more sheer *joie de vivre* and Prêtre's slightly more character. But the disc is worth considering for *Roma.*

Bátiz's performances are also attractive, with very good playing from the RPO. As with the Plasson account of *Roma,* it is the first and last movements which come off the most effectively. Although he omits *Patrie,* Bátiz has a considerable price advantage and he receives excellent (1990) digital recording, engineered by Brian Culverhouse. In the *Symphony* the sound is noticeably full and weighty, and this adds to the impression that the performance is less lighthearted than usual in the first movement (repeat included), though there is no lack of vitality and, with its more serious manner, it is still both effective and enjoyable.

Symphony in C.

*** DG Dig. 423 624-2 [id.]. Orpheus CO – BRITTEN: *Simple symphony;* PROKOFIEV: *Symphony No. 1.* ***

(M) *** Sony SBK 48264; *SBT 48264* [id.]. Nat. PO, Stokowski – MENDELSSOHN: *A Midsummer Night's Dream* ***; SMETANA: *Vltava.* ***

Symphony in C; Jeux d'enfants; La jolie fille de Perth: suite.

(Y/B) (B) **(*) DG Double 437 371-2 (2) [id.]. Fr. R. & TV O, Jean Martinon – LALO: *Cello concerto; Namouna* etc. **(*)

The freshness of the seventeen-year-old Bizet's *Symphony* is well caught by the Orpheus group who present it with all the flair and polished ensemble for which they are famous. First-rate sound, most realistic in effect.

Stokowski's exhilaratingly polished account of the Bizet *Symphony* was recorded at Abbey Road in May/June 1977, only three months before he died; it is a superb example of his last vintage recording period, as vital and alive as anything he recorded in his youth. David Theodore's oboe solo in the *Adagio* is very elegantly done and the *moto perpetuo* finale is wonderfully light and sparkling. A fine bargain coupling, ranking alongside the top recommendations of Beecham and Marriner. The couplings, too, show Szell at his finest.

Martinon's performance of the *Symphony* is very good indeed, with both charm and sparkle, and the couplings make this Double DG set worth considering, even though the early-1960s string timbre is somewhat lacking in allure.

PIANO MUSIC

2 Caprices; Les chants du Rhin (suite); La chasse fantastique; 3 Esquisses musicales; Magasin des

familles (suite); Marine; Nocturnes Nos. 1 in F; 2 in D; 4 Préludes; Romance sans paroles; Thème;
Variations chromatiques; Waltz in C; Grande valse de concert.
(N) (B) *(*) HM Dig. HMA 1905223/4 [id.]. Par Setrak.

Bizet was a formidable pianist, but his output for the instrument is not extensive. Much of it is eclectic
and derivative: the early pieces (and this two-disc set includes three recently discovered juvenilia) inherit
the pyrotechnics of Liszt and Thalburg, while the *Nocturne in F major* and the *Romance sans paroles* (the
second comes as the opening movement of the *Magasin des familles*) obviously use both Chopin and
Liszt as models. By far the most interesting pieces are the *Variations chromatiques*, which Glenn Gould
has recorded, and the *Trois Esquisses musicales*, which show some of the composer's charm and individuality. Par Setrak makes rather heavy going of the opening of the *Variations* and the piece takes some
time to get under way. However, he is quite persuasive in the *Esquisses*. Elsewhere the playing, though
unidiosyncratic and often sympathetic, lacks the extra degree of subtlety that can make second-rate
music seem better than it is. The recording is a bit hard, but otherwise is quite truthful, the acoustic
rather dry but not unacceptably so.

Jeux d'enfants, Op. 22.
*** Ph. Dig. 420 159-2 [id.]. Katia and Marielle Labèque – FAURE: *Dolly;* RAVEL: *Ma Mère l'Oye.* ***

The Labèque sisters characterize Bizet's wonderfully inventive cycle of twelve pieces with vitality, great
wit and delicacy of feeling and touch. Superb recording in the best Philips tradition.

OPERA

Carmen (opera; complete).
*** DG Dig. 410 088-2 (3) [id.]. Baltsa, Carreras, Van Dam, Ricciarelli, Barbaux, Paris Op. Ch.,
    Schoenberg Boys' Ch., BPO, Karajan.
(B) *** DG 427 440-2 (3) [id.]. Horne, McCracken, Krause, Maliponte, Manhattan Op. Ch., Met. Op.
    O, Bernstein.
(M) *** RCA GD 86199 (3) [6199-2-RG]. Leontyne Price, Corelli, Merrill, Freni, Linval, V. State Op.
    Ch., VPO, Karajan.
**(*) Decca 414 489-2 (2) [id.]. Troyanos, Domingo, Van Dam, Te Kanawa, John Alldis Ch., LPO,
    Solti.
(Y/B) (B) **(*) DG 427 885-2; *427 885-4* (3/2) [id.]. Berganza, Domingo, Cotrubas, Milnes, Amb. S.,
    LSO, Abbado.
(Y/B) (B) **(*) CfP CD-CFPD 4454 (2). Grace Bumbry, Jon Vickers, Mirella Freni, Les Petites
    Chanteurs à la Croix de Bois, Paris Op. Ch. & O, Frühbeck de Burgos.
(N) (M) (**) EMI mono CMS5 65318-2 (2). Michel, Angelici, Jobin, Dens, Chellet, Notti, Vieuille,
    Leprin, Thirace, Smati, Arschodt, Théâtre Nat. de l'Opéra-Comique Ch. & O, Cluytens.

Karajan's DG set of *Carmen* makes a clear first choice among currently available versions. In Carreras
he has a Don José, lyrical and generally sweet-toned. José van Dam is incisive and virile, the public hero-
figure; which leaves Agnes Baltsa as a vividly compelling Carmen, tough and vibrant, yet with tenderness under the surface.

Bernstein's 1973 *Carmen* was recorded at the New York Metropolitan Opera. Some of his slow tempi
will be questioned, but what really matters is the authentic tingle of dramatic tension which permeates
the whole entertainment. Marilyn Horne – occasionally coarse in expression – gives a most fully satisfying reading of the heroine's role, a great vivid characterization. The rest of the cast similarly works to
Bernstein's consistent overall plan. It is very well transferred and comes on three bargain CDs.

With Karajan's RCA version, made in Vienna in 1964, much depends on the listener's reaction to the
conductor's tempi and to Leontyne Price's smoky-toned Carmen. Corelli has moments of coarseness,
but his is still a heroic performance. Robert Merrill sings with gloriously firm tone, while Mirella Freni
is, as ever, enchanting as Micaëla. With often spectacular recording, this three-disc set, now offered at
mid-price, remains a keen competitor.

Solti's Decca performance is remarkable for its new illumination of characters whom everyone thinks
they know inside out. Tatiana Troyanos is quite simply the subtlest Carmen on record. Escamillo too is
more readily sympathetic, not just the flashy matador who steals the hero's girl, whereas Don José is
revealed as weak rather than just a victim. Troyanos's singing is delicately seductive too, with no hint of
vulgarity, while the others make up a most consistent singing cast. Solti, like Karajan, uses spoken
dialogue and a modification of the Oeser edition, deciding in each individual instance whether to accept
amendments to Bizet's first thoughts. Though the CD transfer brings out the generally excellent balances of the original analogue recording, it exaggerates the bass to make the orchestra sound boomy,
although the voices retain their fine realism and bloom.

Superbly disciplined, Abbado's performance nails its colours to the mast at the very start with a breathtakingly fast account of the opening prelude. Conductor and orchestra can take a large share of credit for the performance's success for, though the singing is never less than enjoyable, it is on the whole less characterful than on some rival sets. Teresa Berganza is a seductive if somewhat unsmiling Carmen – not without sensuality, and producing consistently beautiful tone, but lacking some of the flair which makes for a three-dimensional portrait. Ileana Cotrubas as Micaëla is not always as sweetly steady as she can be; Milnes makes a heroic matador. The spoken dialogue is excellently produced, and the sound is vivid and immediate. This makes a possible bargain alternative to the Bernstein set with Marilyn Horne and James McCracken, and readers will note that it is now again available on cassette as well as CD.

Frühbeck's version of 1970, made before the Oeser edition appeared, was the first to use the original (1875) version of Bizet's score without the cuts that were made after experience in the theatre, and with spoken dialogue instead of the recitatives which Guiraud composed after Bizet's early death. Well recorded on two bargain-priced discs, it makes a fair recommendation, though Grace Bumbry gives a generalized portrait of the heroine, singing with firm tone but too rarely with musical or dramatic individuality. Vickers makes a strong, heroic Don José; and though, surprisingly, Frühbeck's conducting lacks sparkle, it is very well paced. Paskalis makes a gloriously rich-toned Escamillo and Freni an exquisite Micaëla.

Recorded in 1950 in close, immediate mono sound, the Cluytens set from the Opéra-Comique may seriously lack atmosphere and poetry, but it is worth hearing for its all-French cast, representatives of a well-trained, stylish generation soon to disappear. Solange Michel's mezzo in the title-role is firm and rich if hardly voluptuous in a Carmen-like way. One admires the singing, not least for its flawless diction, but not the characterization. It is much the same with the Escamillo of Michel Dens, and equally Raoul Jobin as Don José who, with Martha Angelici, seems more concerned for beauty of production than for portrayal of character. Cluytens as ever times the score beautifully.

Carmen: highlights.
(M) *** Decca 436 310-2; *436 310-4* (from above recording with Troyanos; cond. Solti).
(Y/B) (B) **(*) DG 439 496-2 [id.] (from above set with Berganza, Domingo; cond. Abbado).

The reissued compilation of 'scenes and arias' from Solti's sharply characterful set is generous and is offered at medium price; the remastered recording sounds better than on the complete set.

The bargain highlights selection on DG Classikon offers a fairly generous sampler of the Berganza/ Domingo/Abbado set with some 69 minutes of well-chosen excerpts, including all the hits. The documentation relates the music to the narrative in a brief but succinct synopsis.

Carmen: highlights (sung in English).
(B) **(*) CfP CD-CFP 4596; *TC-CFP 4596*. Johnson, Smith, Herincx, Robson, Hunter, Greene, Stoddart, Moyle, Sadler's Wells Ch. & O, Sir Colin Davis.

Those who enjoy opera in English will find this a highly successful example, thanks both to the strongly animated conducting of Sir Colin Davis and to the rich-voiced, reliable singing of Patricia Johnson as Carmen.

Les pêcheurs de perles (complete).
(N) (M) (***) EMI mono CMS5 652662 (2). Angelici, Legay, Dens, Noguera, Théâtre Nat. de l'Opéra-Comique Ch. & O, Cluytens.

(i) *Les pêcheurs de perles* (complete). (ii) *Ivan IV:* highlights.
** EMI Dig. CDS7 49837-2 (2) [Ang. CDCB 49837]. Hendricks, Aler, Quilico, Capitole, Toulouse, Ch. & O, Plasson.

Unavailable since the early days of LP, this superb EMI Cluytens set of 1954 offers the finest, most warmly expressive performance on disc of this delectable opera. Ironically, its nearest rival is the Philips set of the previous year under Jean Fournet, also in mono, both of them outshining later stereo sets. Cluytens is an even more sensitive conductor than his Philips rival, less foursquare, getting the music to flow flexibly; and his cast, idiomatically French, has no weak link. Martha Angelici as the heroine, Leila, is both sweet and bright, with no Gallic shrillness, and Henry Legay has a degree of heroic timbre in the rounded, lyric quality of his tenor, while Michel Dens, as in other French opera recordings of the period, proves a firm, characterful baritone. With excellent choral and orchestral work, one gets the impression of a stage experience translated to the studio. The mono transfer is a little dull on orchestral sound, but it captures voices vividly.

Michel Plasson with the choir and orchestra of the Capitole, though sympathetic, fails to draw out as warmly committed a performance as he usually does in his French opera recordings. John Aler and Gino Quilico as the two fishermen sing cleanly and with lyrical freshness, but often their phrasing could be more affectionate. Barbara Hendricks is aptly alluring as Leila, beloved of both of them, but too often she attacks notes from below.

Blake, Howard (born 1938)

Clarinet concerto.
*** Hyperion Dig. CDA 66215 [id.]. Thea King, ECO, composer – LUTOSLAWSKI: *Dance preludes;* SEIBER: *Concertino.* ***

Howard Blake provides a comparatively slight but endearing *Clarinet concerto,* which is played here with great sympathy by Thea King, who commissioned the work.

(i) *Violin concerto (Leeds); A Month in the Country* (film incidental music): *suite; Sinfonietta for brass.*
(Y/B) *** ASV Dig. CDDCA 905 [id.]. (i) Christiane Edlinger; E. N. Philh., Paul Daniel.

It was the success of his music for *The Snowman* that gave Howard Blake the encouragement and the artistic breathing-space to write his beautiful and stimulating *Violin concerto.* Christiane Edlinger, who gave its première, is the soloist in what proves to be an inspired performance, caught 'on the wing' to join a select group of very special first recordings made over the years. The work, written in the received tradition of Elgar, Vaughan Williams, Walton and, more recently, Christopher Headington, has a ready and appealing melodic impulse, and the playing here is as intense and communicative as it is spontaneous. The only snag is the very wide dynamic range of the recording; this means that the spectacular bursts of percussion interrupting the reverie, which opens the first movement and which reappears at the climax of the *Adagio,* are almost overwhelming when one has set the volume level to accommodate the music's quieter moments. Blake's suite of string music written for the film, *A Month in the Country,* brings moments of comparable bitter-sweet elegiac feeling. It is most sensitively played, as is the brass *Sinfonietta,* sonorous and jolly by turns. In terms of overall concert-hall realism the recording is impressive and this record is strongly recommended.

Bliss, Arthur (1891–1975)

(i; ii) *Adam Zero* (ballet): *suite; Mêlée fantasque; Hymn to Apollo;* (i; ii; iii) *Rout for soprano and orchestra;* (i; iv; v) *Serenade for orchestra and baritone;* (i; vi; vii) *The World is charged with the grandeur of God.*
*** Lyrita SRCS 225 [id.]. (i) LSO; (ii) cond. composer; (iii) with Rae Woodland; (iv) John Shirley-Quirk; (v) cond. Brian Priestman; (vi) with Amb. S.; (vii) cond. Philip Ledger.

The ballet *Adam Zero* may not show Bliss at his finest but the four excerpts here contain some attractive moments. The *Mêlée fantasque* (well named) is even more striking with strong Stravinskian influences but with a characteristic elegiac section at its centre. After the *Hymn to Apollo,* although the rest of the programme is primarily vocal, it is in fact the orchestral writing that one remembers most vividly, for the *Serenade* has two purely orchestral movements out of three. The second, *Idyll,* shows Bliss's lyrical impulse at its most eloquent. The orchestra is almost more important than the voice in *Rout.* The solo vocal performances throughout this CD are of high quality, and John Shirley-Quirk's swashbuckling account of the gay finale of the *Serenade* must have pleased the composer greatly. In *The World is charged with the grandeur of God,* the invention is less memorable, and it is again the orchestration that shows the composer's imagination at work, notably the atmospheric scoring for the flutes in the second section. The recordings date from the early 1970s and are of high quality.

Checkmate (ballet): *5 dances.*
(M) *** Chandos CHAN 6576 [id.]. West Australian SO, Schönzeler – RUBBRA: *Symphony No. 5* ***; TIPPETT: *Little music.* **(*)

Checkmate (ballet suite).
(M) (***) EMI mono CDM7 64718-2 [id.]. Pro Arte O, composer – ADDISON: *Carte blanche;* ARNELL: *The Great Detective;* ARNOLD: *A Grand Grand Overture;* RAWSTHORNE: *Madame Chrysanthème* etc. (***)

The idea of a ballet based on chess with all its opportunities for symbolism and heraldic splendour appealed to Bliss, and the score he produced remains one of his most inventive creations. The five dances on the Chandos issue are well played under Hans-Hubert Schönzeler and, with its valuable Rubbra coupling, this is welcome back in the catalogue at mid-price.

It is good to have the composer's own performance of the *Checkmate ballet suite*, admirably recorded in the Kingsway Hall in 1960. He conducts his score with obvious authority and plenty of vitality.

(i) *Cello concerto; Introduction and allegro; Meditations on a theme of John Blow*.
**(*) Argo 443 170-2 [id.]. (i) Robert Cohen; RPO, Wordsworth.

Bliss wrote his *Cello concerto* for Rostropovich. Its great advantage is that it gets better as it goes along. The *Larghetto* is much more attractive than the weak first movement and the finale gathers together the best of the composer's ideas, including the main theme of the opening movement. Robert Cohen gives a committed performance and he is well accompanied. The *Introduction and allegro* (1923) is flamboyantly scored (with the Philadelphia Orchestra in mind) and has a striking lyrical idea; the *Meditations on a theme of John Blow* was written for the CBSO in 1955. The composer thought highly of it, but it is an amiable and rather rambling piece. It is certainly well played here and the Walthamstow recording is spectacular.

(i) *Piano concerto; March of homage*.
(M) **(*) Unicorn Dig. UKCD 2029. (i) Philip Fowke; RLPO, David Atherton.

Bliss's concerto is a work which needs a passionately committed soloist, and that is what it finds in Philip Fowke, urgent and expressive, well matched by David Atherton and the Liverpool orchestra. The occasional piece is also given a lively performance. The digital recording is full and vivid.

A Colour Symphony; Checkmate (ballet): *suite*.
*** Chandos Dig. CHAN 8503 [id.]. Ulster O, Handley.

Each of the movements of Bliss's *Colour Symphony* evokes the heraldic symbolism of four colours – purple, red, blue and green – and the quality of his invention and imagination is fresh. Vernon Handley directs with complete authority and evident enthusiasm; the *Checkmate* ballet is given with equal success. Excellent sound.

(i) *A Colour Symphony; Introduction and allegro;* (ii) *Men of Two Worlds: Baraza;* (i) *Things to come* (film music): *suite* and excerpts: *Ballet for children; Pestilence; Attack; The world in ruins*.
(Y/B) (M) (***) Dutton Lab. CDLXT 2501 [id.]. (i) LSO, composer; (ii) Eileen Joyce, Ch. & Nat. SO, Muir Mathieson.

A Colour Symphony was the work that brought Bliss fame as an *enfant terrible*, but nowadays its flavour seems more Elgarian than modern, with the merest hint that Bliss knew his early Stravinsky. The sounds are attractive and the recording (1956 vintage) captures them well (courtesy of Mike Dutton's admirably faithful CD transfer of Decca's excellent Kingsway Hall recording). But, as with so much of this composer's output, in all honesty the thematic material is never very memorable. The *Introduction and allegro*, written for Stokowski (also in the early 1920s), is another well-constructed, completely professional but unmemorable work. For the film *Men of Two Worlds: Baraza* Eileen Joyce was recruited to the piano part of a score of which only a snippet survives, including a chorus and some touches of syncopation. It is quite vigorous, if at times somewhat coarse, but nevertheless rather endearing. Again, the 1946 recording in Dutton's vivid transfer sounds astonishingly good, like a broadcast transcription rather than an old record, only with more ambience. But Bliss's masterpiece was his incidental music for Korda's H. G. Wells film, *Things to come*. Bliss rescued his material and recorded an early set of four excerpts for Decca on 78-r.p.m. discs in 1936. This included a section called *The world in ruins*, missing from the final orchestral suite, which the composer published and recorded later in stereo in 1957. In terms of memorability of ideas, Bliss never surpassed this music, and the *March* is unforgettable in its gutsy, flamboyantly tuneful vitality.

A Colour Symphony; Metamorphic variations.
*** Nimbus Dig. NI 5294 [id.]. BBC Welsh SO, Wordsworth.

The title, *Metamorphic variations*, may be unattractive, but this is one of the most cogent of Bliss's mature works. In *A Colour Symphony* Wordsworth is a degree broader in his approach than Vernon Handley on the rival Chandos version, yet his control of rhythm and line makes his reading just as warm and sympathetic. As recorded, the Welsh string-tone is not quite so full and warm as that of Handley's Ulster Orchestra, but anyone who wants this apt coupling is unlikely to be disappointed.

Things to come: suite; Welcome the Queen.
(Y/B) (BB) ** Belart 450 143-2 [id.]. LSO, composer – ELGAR: *Pomp and circumstance marches 1–5*. **

The composer's own excellent (1957) recording of his *Things to come suite* is additionally available on a super-bargain Belart reissue, offering its original couplings of *Welcome the Queen* and Elgar's five *Pomp and circumstance marches*. The former was an occasional piece, written by Bliss in the Elgar tradition of pageantry; the piece is of no particular distinction except for a very gracious middle tune. The perform- ance could hardly be more authentic but the (originally very good) recording is not flattered by the current transfer, which is excessively bright and thin on top.

Conversations; Madam Noy; (i; ii) *Rhapsody;* (ii) *Rout; The Women of Yueh; Oboe quintet.*
*** Hyperion CDA 66137 [id.]. Nash Ens., (i) Anthony Rolfe Johnson; (ii) Elizabeth Gale.

The predominant influence in *Rout*, for soprano and chamber orchestra, and in the *Rhapsody*, with its two wordless vocal parts, is Ravel. The *Oboe quintet* is a work of considerable quality. The music assembled here represents Bliss at his very best. A lovely disc, which can be warmly recommended, and eminently well engineered, too.

Clarinet quintet.
(N) *** Redcliffe Dig. R R 010 [id.]. Nicholas Cox, Redcliffe Ens. – RAWSTHORNE: *Clarinet quartet;*
    ROUTH: *Clarinet quintet.* ***
*** Chandos Dig. CHAN 8683 [id.]. Hilton, Lindsay Qt – BAX: *Sonata;* VAUGHAN WILLIAMS: *Studies.*
    ***

The *Clarinet quintet* is Bliss's masterpiece. The flowing lyricism of the opening movement is matched by the intense valedictory feeling of the *Adagietto*, in which the composer remembers his younger brother, Kennard, killed at the Somme in 1916. The work could not be better played than in this very beautiful performance by Nicholas Cox and members of the Redcliffe Ensemble. The recording, too, in the glowing acoustic of St George's, Brandon Hill, Bristol, is quite ideal to capture the music's radiance of texture, yet detail in the lively Scherzo and *energico* finale is well captured.
    Janet Hilton and the Lindsays also have the measure of its autumnal melancholy; the recording is natural and well focused, and the music-making is of the highest quality.

String quartets Nos. 1 in B flat; 2 in F min.
*** Hyperion CDA 66178 [id.]. Delmé Qt.

These performances by the Delmé Quartet are not only thoroughly committed but enormously per- suasive and can be recommended even to readers not normally sympathetic to this composer. Strongly recommended.

Piano sonata; Pieces: *Bliss (One-step); Miniature scherzo; Rout trot; Study. Suite; Triptych.* Arr. of BACH: *Das alte Jahr vergangen ist (The old year has ended).*
*** Chandos Dig. CHAN 8979 [id.]. Philip Fowke.

The biggest work on the disc is the *Sonata*. Its neo-romantic rhetoric is less convincing than some of the earlier pieces he composed, in particular the *Suite* (1925). There are some other lighter pieces like the *The Rout trot* and *Bliss (One-step)*, written in the 1920s when his inspiration was at its freshest. Good performances and excellent recording, made in The Maltings, Snape.

VOCAL MUSIC

Lie strewn the white flocks.
*** Hyperion CDA 66175 [id.]. Shirley Minty, Judith Pierce (flute), Holst Singers & O, Hilary Davan
    Wetton – BRITTEN: *Gloriana: Choral dances;* HOLST: *Choral hymns from Rig Veda.* ***

Bliss's *Pastoral* is given a winning performance by the Holst Singers and Orchestra, with the choral sections (the greater part of the work) aptly modest in scale but powerful in impact. With glowing sound and very attractive works for coupling, this is an outstanding issue.

Morning heroes.
(M) **(*) EMI CDM7 63906-2. Westbrook (nar.), RLPO Ch. & O, Groves.

Morning heroes is an elegiac work, written as a tribute to the composer's brother and to all who fell in the First World War. This is a strong performance, even if the music itself has a curious element of complacency. Fine recording and an excellent transfer.

Bloch, Ernest (1880–1959)

Concerti grossi Nos. 1 & 2; (i) *Schelomo.*
(M) *** Mercury 432 718-2 [id.]. Eastman-Rochester O, Hanson, (i) with Miquelle.

In Bloch's two *Concerti grossi* the neo-classical style brings a piano continuo in the Baroque manner in No. 1; the second, for strings alone, is more intense in feeling. The performances here are admirable, although the violin-timbre is distinctly astringent. *Schelomo*, with Georges Miquelle its soloist, makes a useful bonus for this mid-priced reissue.

Violin concerto.
(M) *** EMI CDM7 63989-2 [id.]. Y. Menuhin, Philh. O, Kletzki – BERG: *Violin concerto.* ***

(i) *Violin concerto. Baal Shem.*
*** ASV Dig. CDDCA 785. (i) Michael Guttman; RPO, Serebrier (with SEREBRIER: *Momento; Poema **).

Menuhin's deeply felt and finely recorded 1963 account is passionate and committed from the very first note, and any weaknesses in the score are quite lost when the playing is so compelling. Paul Kletzki accompanies with equal distinction. The 1964 Kingsway Hall recording sounds very well indeed.

The newcomer from Michael Guttman has plenty going for it: it has both fire and colour, and no attempt is made to rein in the freely rhapsodic flow of the piece. It also has well-balanced modern digital recording.

From Jewish life (orch. Palmer).
*** RCA Single 09026 61966-2 [id.]. Steven Isserliss, Moscow Virtuosi, Spivakov – TAVENER: *Eternal memory.* ***

Bloch's soliloquy, if more extrovert and tangible than the drifting mysticism of Tavener's *Eternal memory*, nevertheless makes an apt coupling, especially when played with poignant warmth of feeling in this judicious expansion by Christopher Palmer of the composer's original version (for cello and piano) to feature instead orchestral strings. Excellent recording.

(i) *Israel Symphony;* (ii) *Schelomo.*
(M) **(*) Van. 08 4047.71 [OVC 4047]. (i) Christensen, Basinger, Fraenkel, Politis, Heder, Watts; (ii) Nelsova; Utah SO, Abravanel.

Bloch's *Israel Symphony* is a large-scale work, but its way of anticipating the style of Hollywood film composers means that the music has something in common with the soundtracks of Hollywood's biblical epics. The performance here has the vigour and spontaneity that are characteristic of Abravanel's Utah performances, and the only snag is that the soloists, who are introduced at the end of the work, are wobbly and not especially distinguished. *Schelomo* is an appropriate coupling. The recordings were made in 1967 and are transferred to CD with great success.

Schelomo (Hebraic rhapsody) for cello and orchestra.
(Y/B) (M) *** Virgin/EMI Dig. CUV5 61125-2 [id.]. Steven Isserlis, LSO, Hickox – ELGAR: *Cello concerto.* **(*)
*** RCA Dig. RD 60757 [60757-2-RC]. Ofra Harnoy, LPO, Mackerras – BRUCH: *Adagio on Celtic themes* etc. ***
(Y/B) *** Sony Dig. SK 57961 [id.]. Yo-Yo Ma, Baltimore SO, David Zinman – ALBERT: *Cello concerto;* BARTOK: *Viola concerto.* ***
(M) *** Sony SBK 48278; *SBT 48278* [id.]. Leonard Rose, Phd. O, Ormandy – FAURE: *Elégie ***; LALO: *Concerto **(*);* TCHAIKOVSKY: *Rococo variations.* ***

The dark intensity of Isserlis's solo playing and the sharp, dramatic focus of Hickox in the big climactic orchestral tuttis are magnetic, preventing Bloch's youthful outpouring on Solomon and the Song of Songs from sounding self-indulgent. Warm, refined recording.

Harnoy also catches the passionate, Hebraic feeling of the melodic line and in this is matched by Mackerras, whose central climax is riveting. Fine, well-balanced and expansive sound.

Yo-Yo Ma is more cultured and refined than many of his current rivals, but there are moments when Solomon drops his voice, as it were, and dispenses his wisdom in a whisper rather than in full-throated fervour. It comes with an interesting first recording of a rewarding *Cello concerto* by the New York composer, Stephen Albert.

A darkly passionate, rhapsodical account from Leonard Rose, with an equally strong accompaniment from Ormandy. The recording balance is close, which reduces the possible dynamic range, but the compelling power of the music-making triumphs – this very good 71-minute compilation is worthy of a fine (perhaps underrated) cellist.

Sacred service (Avodath Hakodesh).
(M) *** Sony SM2K 47533 (2) [id.]. Robert Merrill, Rabbi Juhah Cahn, Choirs of Metropolitan Synagogue & NY Community Church, NYPO, Bernstein – FOSS: *Song of songs* ***; BEN-HAIM: *Psalmist of Israel.* **(*)

Bernstein pioneered this work on record as early as 1958, but the age of the recording, made in the St George Hotel, Brooklyn, is disguised by the remastering which preserves the spaciousness and enhances the vividness of this persuasively committed performance, which has far more ardour and intensity than the more recent version on Chandos. Robert Merrill is the excellent soloist and the only possible drawback for repeated listening by the non-Jewish listener is the inclusion in the Epilogue of the spoken Kaddish Prayer and, of course, the Benediction. The documentation helpfully includes the picturesque original Hebrew, and a line-by-line translation of romanized Hebrew text. The irritating thing about this reissue is that the Bloch and the stimulating Foss coupling could both have been fitted on to a single CD, as their total playing time is just over 78 minutes.

Blomdahl, Karl-Birger (1916–68)

Symphonies Nos. 1–2; 3 (Facetter).
*** BIS Dig. CD 611 [id.]. Swedish RSO, Segerstam.

Karl-Birger Blomdahl's *First Symphony*, written in his mid-twenties during the war, is not particularly individual and, though more than student work, is less than a mature one. There is a certain debt to his master, Hilding Rosenberg, and, in the slow movement, Honegger. At the same time a strong symphonic impulse runs through it. Blomdahl is an eclectic figure: there are echoes of Bartók, Hindemith and serial composers in the *Second* and *Third Symphonies*. The *Third* is a dark and powerful piece and though it is, as one critic put it, 'deficient in thematic vitality', there is a powerful atmosphere. Good performances by the Swedish Radio Orchestra under Segerstam and excellent BIS recording.

Blow, John (1649–1708)

Anthems: *Blessed is the man; God spake sometimes in visions.*
(M) **(*) Decca 436 259-2 [id.]. King's College, Cambridge, Ch., Willcocks – HANDEL: *Ode for St Cecilia's Day.* **

Anthems: *Cry aloud, and spare not; I was glad; O sing unto the Lord.*
(M) **(*) Decca 436 256-2 [id.]. King's College, Cambridge, Ch., ASMF, Willcocks – HANDEL: *Coronation anthems.* ***

These anthems impress, both by their grandeur and by the confidence of the part-writing for individual solo voices, sung here by members of the choir. *O sing unto the Lord* is a particularly eloquent and expressive piece; *God spake sometimes in visions* was written for the coronation of James II in 1685, while *I was glad*, with its trumpet obbligato, was composed for the opening of the chancel of St Paul's Cathedral (all that was completed in 1697). The performances, if lacking something in robust flair, are agreeably secure, and the recording is spacious and full, even if the focus of the King's acoustic lacks something in sharpness.

(i) *Ode on the death of Mr Henry Purcell;* (ii) *Amphion Angelicus* (song collection): *Ah, heaven! What is't I hear?; Cloe found Amintas lying all in tears; Loving above himself; Shepherds deck your crooks; Why weeps Asteria? ; Epilogue: Sing, sing, ye muses.*
(M) **(*) HM/BMG GD 71962. (i) René Jacobs, James Bowman; (ii) Yamamoto, Van der Speek, Jacobs, Van Altena, Van Egmond, Ens., Leonhardt.

John Blow's *Ode on the death of Purcell*, a highly eloquent setting of an allegorical poem by John Dryden, makes a worthy memorial to the great English composer. The other items in the programme are admirably presented, especially the closing *Epilogue* for vocal quartet. Gustav Leonhardt and his chamber ensemble accompany authentically, and the 1973 recording has a good ambience and no lack of presence.

Ode on the death of Mr Henry Purcell: Mark how the lark and linnet sing. Ah, heav'n! What is't I hear?.
*** Hyperion Dig. CDA 66253 [id.]. James Bowman, Michael Chance, King's Consort, King – PURCELL: *Collection.* ***

Where Leonhardt on RCA is spacious in his concept and more detailed in his concern for word-meanings, the result also more polished, Robert King's spontaneous style is infectious with the orchestral comments engagingly animated. Both performances are highly rewarding, and in the last resort couplings will dictate choice. The Hyperion disc is more expensive but includes a quarter of an hour more music.

Venus and Adonis.
(M) *** HM/BMG GD 77117 (2). Kirkby, Tubb, King, Wistreich, Bonner, Holden, Cass, Nichols, Cornwell, Müller, Consort of Musicke, Rooley – GIBBONS: *Cupid and Death*. ***
(B) *** HM Dig. HMA 190 1276 [id.]. Argenta, Dawson, Varcoe, Covey-Crump, L. Bar. & Ch., Medlam.

Venus and Adonis is like a Lully opera in miniature. Rooley directs an elegant, lightly sprung performance, very well sung, recorded in good analogue sound (1984) in a warm acoustic.

Charles Medlam with London Baroque gives a period performance and takes care that the early instruments are well blended rather than edgy and the choral sound is full, bright and clean. The soloists too are all remarkable for sweetness and freshness of tone. This record is now offered at bargain price in the Musique d'Abord series.

Boccherini, Luigi (1743–1805)

Cello concertos Nos. 1 in E flat, G.474; 7 in G, G.480; 9 in B flat, G.482.
(N) (M) **(*) Virgin Veritas/EMI Dig. VER5 61239-2 [id.]. Wouter Möller, Linde Consort, Linde.

The Linde Consort, renowned for their baroque repertoire, now venture equally authentically into the *galant* world of Boccherini. Here we have the original version of the *B flat Concerto* played freshly, if without strong individuality, by the excellent Wouter Möller. The orchestral group (4.2.2.1, with 2 oboes, 2 hand horns and harpsichord) plainly seeks a chamber style, but the resonant acoustic amplifies the effect of both the forwardly placed soloist and the accompanying group. Möller plays the fine slow movement of G.482 with restrained *espressivo*, and his articulation in allegros is neatly rhythmic throughout. Linde provides polished accompaniments, and intonation (so important when there is only the merest hint of vibrato) is excellent: the finale of the *B flat Concerto* has an attractively easy pacing. The other works are hardly less successful, and the *G major* (No. 7) brings out the very best in the performers, with articulate, resilient strings in the outer movements and Möller comparatively intense in the *Adagio*.

Cello concerto No. 2 in D, G.479.
(B) *** DG Double 437 952-2 (2) [id.]. Rostropovich, Zurich Coll. Mus., Sacher – BERNSTEIN: *3 Meditations;* GLAZUNOV: *Chant du Ménestrel;* SHOSTAKOVICH: *Cello concerto No. 2;* TARTINI: *Cello concerto;* TCHAIKOVSKY: *Andante cantabile* etc; VIVALDI: *Cello concertos*. ***

Although essentially a performance in the grand manner, Rostropovich is so compelling that reservations are swept aside. He is given an alert accompaniment by Sacher, and the recording has fine body and presence. This is now part of a self-recommending Double DG bargain anthology.

Cello concertos Nos. 3 in D, G.476; 7 in G, G.480; 9 in B flat, G.482. (i) *Aria accademica in B flat, G.557*.
(N) **(*) Astrée Audivis Dig. E 8517 [id.]. Christophe Coin, Limoges Bar. Ens., Coin; (i) with Marta Almajano.

Christophe Coin directs this excellent Limoges period-instrument group from the bow, and they accompany most stylishly. But his baroque cello image is small, his playing is subtle and fastidiously elegant, its expressive feeling never worn on the sleeve. He is the exact opposite of Rostropovich, and those who enjoy intimacy in these works may find this much to their taste. One of the highlights is the *Largo* of the *D major Concerto*, which is introduced exquisitely by the orchestra and its gentle atmosphere is then continued by the soloist; but even here the effect is just a little wan. The *Aria accademica* is included for its cello obbligato, and indeed it opens as if it is going to be another concerto, but then makes even greater bravura demands on its soprano soloist. It is sung expertly though brightly rather than seductively.

Cello concertos Nos. 4 in C, G.477; 6 in D, G.479; 7 in G, G.480; 8 in C, G.481.
(Y/B) (M) *** Teldec/Warner Dig. 9031 77624-2 [id.]. Anner Bylsma, Concerto Amsterdam, Schröder.

These concertos were originally published as Nos. 1–4 but are numbered as above in the Gérard catalogue. They are scored for strings with the addition of simple horn parts in Nos. 4 and 8 and are agreeable works which sit easily between the galant and classical styles. There are few moments of routine in the writing, and it is always elegant and pleasing. *No. 6 in D major* is a particularly fine work, while the finale of No. 8 is very jolly. Anner Bylsma is a fine player and seems eminently suited to this repertoire, while Schröder's accompaniments are most stylish and full of vitality. Charm, too, is an important element and it is not missing here, while the sombre *Adagio* of No. 7 has undoubted eloquence and is ideally paced to contrast with the sprightly and tuneful finale. The 1965 recording is first class and, like so many of Teldec's *Das Alte Werk* series, the immaculate CD transfer makes the very most of the sound.

(i) *Cello concertos Nos. 6 in D, G.479; 7 in G, G.480;* (ii) *9 in B flat, G.482; 10 in D, G.483.*

(Y/B) (M) *** Erato/Warner 4509 97408-2 (2) [id.]. Frédéric Lodéon, (i) Lausanne CO, Jordan; (ii) Bournemouth Sinf., Guschlbauer.

This set combines two sets of performances, recorded four years apart. Lodéon was in his thirties at the time and plays splendidly throughout. His playing has genuine style and real eloquence and in the *G major concerto*, G.480, originally unearthed by Maurice Gendron, he is wonderfully fresh and fervent; in his hands the better-known *D major Concerto*, G.479 (also recorded by Bylsma and Rostropovich), has genuine tenderness and depth. He is well accompanied by both groups, but the two Lausanne performances (1981) have slightly superior sound and the balance of the soloist is less obviously spotlighted. The snag to this pair of records is the playing time of only 85 minutes, whereas the competing Bylsma collection manages to get four concertos (including G.479 and 480) on a single CD.

Cello concerto No. 7 in G, G.480.

(M) *** Carlton IMP Classics Dig. 30367 00912. Felix Schmidt, ECO, Heath – BEETHOVEN: *Triple concerto.* ***

This is the concerto from which Grützmacher extracted the slow movement in his phoney, cobbled-together 'Boccherini Concerto', the movement everyone remembers. It makes an unusual but apt and attractive coupling for the Trio Zingara's excellent version of the Beethoven *Triple concerto*.

(i) *Cello concerto No. 9 in B flat* (original version, revised Gendron); (ii; iii) *Flute concerto in D, Op. 27* (attrib.; now thought to be by Franz Pokorny); (iv) *Symphonies Nos. 3 in C; 5 in B flat, Op. 12/3 & 5;* (v) *Guitar quintets Nos. 4 in D (Fandango); 9 in C (La Ritirata di Madrid);* (vi) *String quartet in D, Op. 6/1;* (iii) *String quintet in E, Op. 13/5: Minuet* (only).

(B) *** Ph. Duo 438 377-2 (2) [id.]. (i) Gendron, LOP, Casals; (ii) Gazzelloni; (iii) I Musici; (iv) New Philh. O, Leppard; (v) Pepe Romero, ASMF Chamber Ens.; (vi) Italian Qt.

Entitled 'The best of Boccherini including the *Minuet*', this most attractive anthology was assembled especially for the Philips Duo series. It is well documented and the famous *Minuet* could hardly be presented more winningly. It is the one digital recording here. It is good, too, that Gendron's version of the *Cello concerto* is included, for he pioneered the return of the original version (without Grützmacher's reworking), and he plays it admirably. The *Flute concerto* is a galant piece, elegantly played by Gazzelloni, and one can see why it was mistakenly attributed; Boccherini is all too readily dismissed as *la femme de Haydn*, but underneath the surface charm and elegance that one associates with him there are deeper currents and an altogether special pathos to disturb the attentive listener. Both *Symphonies* are full of vitality in these excellent performances under Raymond Leppard and are very well recorded. The Italian Quartet's performance of the *D major Quartet* is notable for its freshness and refinement. The *Guitar quintets* were arranged by Boccherini for his Spanish patron, the Marquis Benavente. The guitar part was obviously intended for the Marquis to perform, so its contribution is sometimes limited to an accompanying role; but the music has considerable charm, though it is somewhat uneven. The performances are unfailingly warm and sensitive and they are well recorded too, although there is a touch of thinness on top. The set is supported with good documentation.

Cello concerto in B flat (arr. Grützmacher).

*** Sony MK 39964 [id.]. Yo-Yo Ma, St Paul CO, Zukerman – J. C. BACH: *Sinfonia concertante* etc. **(*)

(BB) *** Naxos Dig. 8.550059; *4550059* [id.]. Ludovít Kanta, Capella Istropolitana, Peter Breiner – HAYDN: *Cello concertos Nos. 1 & 2.* ***

(*) EMI CDC7 47840-2 [id.]. Jacqueline du Pré, ECO, Barenboim – HAYDN: *Concerto in D.* *

Like Jacqueline du Pré before him, Yo-Yo Ma chooses the Grützmacher version. He plays it with taste and finesse, not wearing his heart on his sleeve as obviously as du Pré, but with his warm, if refined, timbre and style not missing the romanticism. The recording is first class.

Ludovít Kanta's playing is distinguished by imaginative and musicianly phrasing and a warm tone. The Slovak players under Peter Breiner give a good account of themselves, and this can hold its own against versions costing twice or three times as much.

Working for the first time in the recording studio with Daniel Barenboim, du Pré was inspired to some really heart-warming playing, broadly romantic in style – but then that is what Grützmacher plainly asks for.

Symphonies, Op. 12, Nos. 1 in D; 2 in E flat; 3 in C; 4 in D min.; 5 in B flat; 6 in A.
(M) *** Ph. 438 314-2 (2) [id.]. New Philh. O, Leppard.

Boccherini's Op. 12 was published in 1776. The scoring is for the normal classical orchestra, including two flutes or oboes and horns, but the composer's individuality emerges in his writing for the strings – with divided cellos – which are always predominant in the main argument. Even so, there are many pleasing touches of woodwind colour. The *E flat Symphony* (No. 2) is a remarkably fine work, virtually a sinfonia concertante with important bravura duets, first for two violins, then for a pair of cellos (the composer's own instrument); there is even a cadenza. The other symphonies are all of comparable interest, with Boccherini's silken melancholy strongly featured in the lyrical writing. The composer's craftsmanship is as ever deft, although perhaps his attempt at cyclic construction brings a too easy solution in *No. 6 in A major* when, after the *Grave* introduction to the finale, he simply repeats the latter part of the first movement, starting at the central double bar! In short, this set of six attractive symphonies is well worth exploring, particularly as Leppard consistently secures playing from the highly alert New Philharmonia Orchestra that is polished, elegant and never superficial. The Philips 1971 recording is excellent and so is the CD transfer, losing nothing of the bloom but firming up the overall focus admirably.

Symphonies: in D; in C, Op. 12/3; in D min., Op. 12/4; in B flat, Op. 35/6; in D min., Op. 37/3; in A, Op. 37/4.
**(*) Chandos Dig. CHAN 8414/5 (3) [id.]. Cantilena, Adrian Shepherd.

These are sympathetic rather than high-powered performances and will give considerable pleasure, though lacking the last ounce of finish. But there is no want of feeling for this unjustly neglected repertoire, and the symphonies are well recorded.

Symphonies: in D min. (La casa del diavolo), Op. 12/4; in A, Op. 12/6; in A, Op. 21/6.
*** Hyperion Dig. CDA 66236 [id.]. L. Festival O, Ross Pople.

Ross Pople's record duplicates only one work included in the more ambitious Chandos collection, *La casa del diavolo*, Op. 12/4; in his account the demons are certainly let loose in the finale, with the most frantically energetic playing from the strings. Elsewhere the performances are the soul of elegance; altogether this well-played and well-recorded collection can be given the warmest welcome.

Symphonies: in D min. (La casa del diavolo), Op. 12/4; in F, Op. 35/4; in C min., Op. 41.
(N) **(*) O-L Dig. 436 993-2 [id.]. AAM, Hogwood.

Christopher Hogwood's period-instrument performances have great character and his slightly more severe manner adds to the music's strength and gravitas. Although there is rather less charm, the *Pastoral Lentarello* which forms the slow movement of Op. 41 has a nice rustic flavour. Excellent recording, but this is less winning than Pople's series.

Symphonies: in D; in E flat; in A; in F; in E flat; in B flat, Op. 35/1–6.
(N) *** Hyperion Dig. CDA 66903 [id.]. L. Festival O, Ross Pople.

The Op. 35 symphonies date from 1782. They are each in the three-movement, Italian overture style and are scored for oboes and horns (often used tellingly, especially in the finales of the *A major* and *B flat* works). The standard of invention is high and the music has plenty of vitality. Indeed the opening *D major Symphony* with its dancing theme for the violins and strong tuttis might almost be middle-period Mozart, although the spirit of the *Andantino* is closer to Haydn. In the *E flat* work the orchestral colouring is felicitous, and its C minor slow movement has a nice touch of pathos. The elegant *Andante* of the *A major* has much wistful charm – but then all the slow movements here are very attractive, not least the *soave* central movement of the *E flat Symphony* and the gentle march of the *B flat*, which then ends the set with a jolly finale. The performances here could hardly be bettered: crisp and neat, warm yet vital, and the recording is excellent. Boccherini set out to entertain his listeners and he surely succeeds here.

CHAMBER MUSIC

Guitar quintets Nos. 1–7, G.445/51; 9 (La Ritirata di Madrid), G.453.
(B) *** Ph. Duo 438 769-2 (2) [id.]. Pepe Romero, ASMF Chamber Ens.

Boccherini wrote or arranged twelve *Guitar quintets*, but only the present eight have survived, plus another version of *No. 4 in D (Fandango)*, G.448. Although some of the music is bland, it is nearly all agreeably tuneful in an unostentatious way, and there are some highly imaginative touches, with attractive hints of melancholy and underlying passion. These performances by Pepe Romero (often willing to take a relatively minor role) and members of the ASMF Chamber Ensemble are wholly admirable, and Philips are especially good at balancing textures of this kind in the most natural way, the guitar able to be assertive when required without overbalancing the ensemble. The recording is slightly less smooth than the original LPs, but the CD transfer has brought greater presence and a bolder outline. This is an engagingly undemanding set to dip into in the late evening.

Guitar quintets Nos. 1 in D min.; 2 in E, G.445/6; 7 in E min., G.451; 9 in C (La Ritirata di Madrid), G.543.
(N) (B) ** Teldec/Warner 4509 97975-2 (2). Daniel Benkö, Eder Qt.

Daniel Benkö and the Eder Quartet play well enough, even if the effect, though musical, is just a trifle faceless. They have the seeming advantage of digital recording, but the close balance means that the result is less natural than the Philips analogue sound for Pepe Romero. Moreover he offers four more concertos in the same price-range.

Guitar quintets Nos. (i) 4 in D (Fandango); 7 in E min., G.451; 9 in C (La ritirata di Madrid).
(B) *** DG 429 512-2 [id.]. Yepes, Melos Qt; (i) with Lucero Tena.

In the DG bargain compilation from 1971 the sound is very good, full yet lively and well projected. The playing is expert and, in the boisterous *Fandango* finale of No. 4, Lucero Tena makes a glittering contribution with his castanets.

Piano quintets: in E min., G.407; in F, G.408; in D, G.411, Op. 56/1.
*** Audivis Dig. E 8518 [id.]. Patrick Cohen, Mosaïques Qt.

Piano quintets: in B flat, G.414; in E min., G.415; in C, G.418, Op. 57/2, 3 & 6.
*** Audivis Dig. E 8721 [id.]. Patrick Cohen, Mosaïques Qt.

The scope of Boccherini's achievement in the field of chamber music is becoming more and more apparent. There are twelve piano quintets and Patrick Cohen and the Mosaïques Quartet are obviously embarking – so far with great success – on a complete set. There is drama and grace and warmth of feeling, balanced by elegance, in this music; and the playing here also emphasizes its vitality. Slow movements are particularly eloquent and the use of period instruments in no way inhibits the expressive range of the music.

Piano quintets: in A min., Op. 56/2, G.412; in E flat, Op. 56/3, G.410; in E min., Op. 57/3, G.415; in C, Op. 57/6, G.418.
(M) *** RCA Dig. GD 77053 [77053-2-RG]. Les Adieux.

The lovely *E minor* (Op. 57/3) which starts the disc and the *A minor* (Op. 56/2) both have those hints of beguiling, almost sultry melancholy that makes this composer's musical language so distinctive. This accomplished period-instrument group turn in performances of great finesse and charm, though the recording balance places the listener very much in the front row of the salon.

String quartets, Op. 32/1–6.
(Y/B) (M) *** Teldec/Warner 4509 95988-2 (2) [id.]. Esterházy Qt.

This set dates from 1780, about the same period as Haydn's Op. 33. They may ultimately lack the depth and vision of Haydn and Mozart, but to listen to this pioneering recording is to be amazed that music of this quality has been so long neglected. Its originality and the quality of the inspiration, its freshness and grace can scarcely be exaggerated, and these performances on original-period instruments are both committed and authoritative, with no want of charm to boot. The Esterházy Quartet are led by Jaap Schröder and theirs is thoroughly rewarding music-making. The Quartet was beautifully recorded in Haarlem, Holland, in 1976 and the CD transfer and excellent documentation of this Das Alte Werke reissue are both commendable. The only snag is the short overall playing time of the pair of CDs – 89 minutes, but every one of them is enjoyable.

String quartet in E flat, Op. 58/2.
(N) (M) *** Cal. CAL 6698 [id.]. Talich Qt – HAYDN: *Quartet No. 74;* MENDELSSOHN: *Quartet No. 2;*
    MICA: *Quartet No. 6.* ***

Boccherini's tuneful *E flat major Quartet*, Op. 58/2, opens with a friendly *Allegro lento*, yet characteristically its *Larghetto* brings a touch of gentle melancholy. The finale is a spirited *Allegro vivo*, played here with much geniality. Indeed the Talich are on top form and are very naturally recorded, so that this well-planned collection amounts to more than the sum of its parts.

String quintets: in E, Op. 11/5, G.275; in D min., Op. 13/4, G.280; in D, Op. 39/3, G.339; in C min., Op. 51/ 2, G.377.
**(*) Denon Dig. CO 2199 [id.]. Berlin Philh. Ens.

The Denon disc offers music-making of great elegance and charm. There is depth and pathos in some of these *Quintets* (the *Andante* of the *D minor* or the *Andantino con innocenza* of the *C minor*, for example). These fine musicians play with dedication, though at times there is a degree of caution as if they are a little inhibited by courtly manners. Good if rather forward recording.

String sextets Nos. 1 in E flat, G.454; 2 in B flat, G.455; 5 in D, G.458, Op. 23/1–2 & 5.
**(*) HM Dig. HMC 90 1478 [id.]. Ens. 415.

Boccherini's special vein of melancholy, which yet never suggests gloom and indeed refreshes the spirit, is heard at its most appealing in these works, which are played with refined polish and feeling by this sensitive ensemble who use original instruments with much finesse. However, it must be said that the overall texture produced here is somewhat meagre, and at times one feels the need for the fuller, more robust sound of modern instruments.

Boeck, August de (1865–1937)

Symphony in G.
(Y/B) (B) *** Discover Dig. DICD 920126 [id.]. Brussels BRT PO, Karl Anton Rickenbacher – GILSON: *De Zee.* ***

The *Symphony in G* of August de Boeck, like Paul Gilson's suite, *De Zee*, with which it is coupled, is a ripely exotic work, full of Russian echoes. You might describe it as the Borodin symphony that Borodin didn't write, sharply rhythmic in the fast movements and sensuous in the slow movement, brilliantly orchestrated and full of tunes that are only marginally less memorable than those of the Russian master. Well played and recorded and, at Discover International's bargain price, an ideal disc for experimenting with.

Böhm, Georg (1661–1733)

Capriccio in D; Chorale partitas on 'Ach wie nichtig, ach wie flüchtig'; on 'Wer nur den lieben Gott lässt walten'; Overture in D; Praeludium in G min.; Suites in C min.; E flat; F min.
*** Sony Dig. SK 53114 [id.]. Gustav Leonhardt (harpsichord/clavichord).

Böhm was one of the most interesting and influential North German precursors of Bach, and this excellent recital by Gustav Leonhardt makes a useful introduction to his art. His chorale partitas exercised a strong influence on Bach himself and his suites are both resourceful and inventive. Leonhardt intersperses the suites with the other pieces and ensures variety of texture and colour by using both clavichord and harpsichord, the latter a copy of an early-eighteenth-century instrument from Berlin and the clavichord a modern instrument by Skowroneck of Bremen. Excellent recording.

Boieldieu, François (1775–1834)

Harp concerto in 3 tempi in C.
✹ (M) *** Decca 425 723-2; 425 723-4. Marisa Robles, ASMF, Iona Brown – DITTERSDORF; HANDEL: *Harp concertos* etc. *** ✹

Boieldieu's *Harp concerto* has been recorded elsewhere but never more attractively. The (originally Argo) recording is still in the demonstration class and very sweet on the ear. To make the reissue even more attractive, three beguiling sets of *Variations* have been added, including music by Handel and Beethoven and a *Theme, variations and Rondo pastorale* attributed to Mozart.

Boismortier, Bodin de (1689–1755)

Première suite de clavecin.
(N) (M) ** Cal. CAL 6838 [id.]. Mireille Lagacé – RAMEAU: *6 Concerts en sextuor.* **

Bodin de Boismortier was a contemporary of Rameau, and his musical career was divided between Spain and France. His harpsichord pieces (each of which have sobriquets, like those of Rameau) have a reasonable degree of individuality, particularly the gentle melancholy of the sarabande (*La Valtudinière*) and the rhythmically winning closing *Pièce en rondeau* (*La Décharnée*). They are expertly played by Mireille Lagacé, who uses a restored 1754 Hemsch, and the recording is realistic, provided you turn down the volume.

Boito, Arrigo (1842–1918)

Mefistofele (complete).
**(*) Decca Dig. 410 175-2 [id.]. Ghiaurov, Pavarotti, Freni, Caballé, L. Op. Ch., Trinity Boys' Ch., Nat. PO, Fabritiis.
(N) (M) (**(*)) EMI mono CMS5 65655-2 (2) [CDMB 65655] with Act IV omitted. Christoff, Prandelli, Moscucci, Rome Op. Ch. & O, Gui.
(M) **(*) Decca 440 054-2 [id.]. Siepi, Del Monaco, Tebaldi, Cavalli, Santa Cecilia Academy, Rome, Ch. & O, Serafin.

The modern digital recording given to the Fabritiis set brings obvious benefits in the extra weight of brass and percussion – most importantly in the heavenly prologue. With the principal soloists all at their best – Pavarotti most seductive, Freni finely imaginative on detail, Caballé consistently sweet and mellifluous as Elena – this is a highly recommendable set.

Though it omits Act IV, the episodic scene with Helen of Troy in the Underworld, there is much to enjoy in Vittorio Gui's 1955 mono recording with Boris Christoff in the title-role. Gui is a master at building tension and, though the chorus has a backward balance, the choral close to the Prologue is hardly less incandescent than in Toscanini's classic concert performance. Giacinto Prandelli, who made several important recordings in the early days of LP, is here a lyrical Faust, stylish if lacking full heroic power, while Orietta Moscucci is a soprano not afraid to sing softly, as at the opening of her big aria, *L'altra notte*. Hers is a sweet voice, if with edge at the top under pressure. But the glory of the set is the towering impersonation of Christoff as Mefistofele, thrillingly dark-toned and intense from first to last, the more vivid for being balanced close. Orchestral sound is dim, but Gui's conducting compensates.

On the earlier (1958) Decca Rome set, Serafin, the most persuasive Italian conductor of his day, draws glorious sounds from his performers, even from Mario del Monaco, who is here almost sensitive. Tebaldi is a rich-toned Margherita – almost too rich-toned for so frail a heroine – and Siepi makes an excellent Mefistofele. The Decca engineers came up trumps: the stereo remains remarkably spacious, particularly in the Prologue, making a good mid-priced alternative to the later Decca version.

Mefistofele: Prologue.
(M) (***) RCA mono GD 60276 [60276-2-RG]. Moscona, Robert Shaw Ch., Columbus Boychoir, NBC SO, Arturo Toscanini – VERDI: *I Lombardi; Rigoletto*: excerpts. (**)

The hair-raising intensity of Toscanini's performance gives Boito's multi-layered *Prologue* a cogency never matched since on record. The dryness of sound even seems to help, when offstage choruses are accurately focused, and the singing of the Robert Shaw Chorale has thrillingly dramatic bite.

Bononcini, Antonio (1677–1726)

Stabat Mater.
(Y/B) (B) *** Decca Double 443 868-2 (2) [id.]. Palmer, Langridge, Esswood, Keyte, St John's College, Cambridge, Ch., Philomusica, Guest – PERGOLESI: *Magnificat in C; Stabat Mater **(*)*; D. SCARLATTI: *Stabat Mater;* A. SCARLATTI: *Domine, refugium factus es nobis; O magnum mysterium;* CALDARA: *Crucifixus;* LOTTI: *Crucifixus.* ***

This fascinating Double Decca collection centres on three different settings of the *Stabat Mater dolorosa*, a medieval poem describing the anguish of Mary during her son's crucifixion, an experience with which women, especially, have readily identified down through the ages. Although its origins date from the end of the thirteenth century, it was not until 1727 that it became part of the Roman liturgy.

Antonio Bononcini is not to be confused with Handel's rival, Giovanni, his older brother. Antonio's *Stabat Mater* is a work of genuine melodic distinction and affecting tenderness; there are some striking harmonies, even moments of drama, and in general a nobility and simple expressiveness that leave a strong impression. The St John's performance is wholly admirable and is very well recorded.

Bononcini, Giovanni (1670–1747)

Cello sonata in A min.; Trio sonata for 2 violins and continuo in D min. (i) Cantatas: *Già la stagion d'amore; Lasciami un sol momento; Misero pastorello; Siedi, Amarilli mia.*
*** Virgin/EMI Dig. VC5 45000-2 [id.]. Gérard Lesne, Il Seminario Musicale.

Giovanni Bononcini's cantatas were popular and were published in London in 1721. They reveal their composer to be far more than a historical figure. *Lasciami un sol momento* stands out as a particularly moving work with its melancholy opening aria ('Leave me but for one moment, O bitter memory of my betrayed love') leading to a bravura finale, *Soffro in pace* ('I bear these chains in peace'). The instrumental works are also highly inventive and characterful: the *Lento* of the lively *Trio sonata* is gently touching and its finale wonderfully spirited. All this music is worth knowing, and the advocacy of these fine artists brings it fully to life. If you believe you may not respond to four cantatas sung by a male alto, your doubts will be swept away by the vocal skill and expressive eloquence of Gérard Lesne's singing, here using the most felicitous ornamentation. The recording too is first class.

Borodin, Alexander (1833–87)

'The World of Borodin': (i) *In the Steppes of Central Asia; Prince Igor:* (ii) *Overture;* (ii–iii) *Polovtsian dances;* (iv) *Symphony No. 2 in B min.;* (v) *String quartet No. 2: Nocturne;* (vi) *Scherzo in A flat;* (vii, viii) *Far from the shores of your native land;* (vii, ix) *Prince Igor: Galitzky's aria.*
(Y/B) (M) *** Decca Analogue/Dig. 444 389-2; *444 389-4.* (i) SRO, Ansermet; (ii) LSO, Solti; (iii) with London Symphony Ch.; (iv) LSO, Martinon; (v) Borodin Qt; (vi) Ashkenazy; (vii) Nicolai Ghiaurov; (viii) Zlatina Ghiaurov; (ix) London Symphony Ch. and LSO, Downes.

An extraordinarily successful disc that will provide for many collectors an inexpensive summation of the art of Borodin. The compilation, which was originally offered on LP, has been updated and extended, with the changes of performers all to advantage. There can be few if any other collections of this kind that sum up a composer's achievement so succinctly or that make such a rewarding and enjoyable 76-minute concert. Solti's *Prince Igor overture* is unexpectedly romantic, and very exciting too; there is no finer account in the current catalogue, and the same can be said for the *Polovtsian dances*, with splendid choral singing – even if the chorus takes a little longer to warm up than in the famous Beecham version. Both recordings date from 1966 and have vintage Decca sound. The *Nocturne* follows the *Overture* so effectively that one might have thought it the composer's own plan. Then comes *Galitzky's aria* (complete with chorus), where the sound is over-bright, but no matter, and the *Scherzo in A flat* follows – with Ashkenazy in fine form – before the choral *Polovtsian dances*. Ansermet's *In the Steppes of Central Asia* is warmer and more atmospheric than we had remembered it and, if the Suisse Romande violins fail to do its voluptuous main theme full justice, Ansermet's interpretation is spacious and vivid. After Nicolai Ghiaurov has reminded us of the melancholy side of the Russian spirit, we come finally to Martinon's unsurpassed 1960 LSO performance of the *B minor Symphony*, notable for its fast tempo for the famous opening theme. The strong rhythmic thrust suits the music admirably, the Scherzo has vibrant colouring and the slow movement, with a beautifully played horn solo, is most satisfying. The sound has remarkable presence and sparkle, and only in the massed violin tone (which is good) is there a suggestion that the recording is not modern.

In the Steppes of Central Asia; (i) *Nocturne* (from *String quartet No. 2*) arr. for violin & orchestra by Rimsky-Korsakov; *Petite suite* (orch. Glazunov); (ii; iii) *Requiem* (orch. Stokowski, arr. Simon). *Prince Igor: Overture;* (iii) *Chorus of Polovtsian maidens. Dance of Polovtsian maidens; Polovtsian march; Polovtsian dances.*
**(*) Cala Dig. CACD 1011; CAMC 1011 [id.]. Philh. O, Geoffrey Simon, with (i) Stephanie Chase; (ii) Ian Boughton; (iii) BBC SO Ch.

An interesting and valuable anthology that is recommendable, but for one curious and serious drawback. Borodin's 5-minute piano piece called *Requiem* is played in Stokowski's flamboyantly expansive orchestration, to which Geoffrey Simon has added solo tenor and male chorus to great effect. The piece is ingeniously based on 'Chopsticks'. It is in the form of a long crescendo and diminuendo, and the great double climax has been recorded with an exaggerated dynamic range which is ridiculously too wide. The other works are all given full-bodied sound, a shade lacking in sparkle, and a normal dynamic range. *In the Steppes of Central Asia*, rather forwardly recorded, would have been more effective with a bit more dynamic contrast. It is a warmly languorous but not distinctive performance. The excerpts from *Prince Igor* include the sinuously seductive *Chorus of Polovtsian maidens* which opens Act II of the opera and also a version of the *Polovtsian march* which includes both chorus and off-stage band. In the march and the famous *Polovtsian dances*, the singing of the BBC Chorus is of a high standard, though Geoffrey Simon's direction is lively rather than electrifying, both here and in the Overture. Rimsky-Korsakov's concertante arrangement of the famous *Nocturne* for violin and orchestra – in spite of Stephanie Chase's pleasing advocacy – gives the piece the character of a salon encore, charming but insouciant. The *Petite suite*, a set of six piano miniatures orchestrated by Glazunov, comes off very engagingly.

Prince Igor: Overture and Polovtsian dances.
(Y/B) (M) *** Virgin/EMI Dig. CUV5 61135-2 [id.]. Royal Liverpool PO. Ch. & O, Mackerras –
     MUSSORGSKY: *Night* etc. **

A splendid account of the *Prince Igor overture*, with the brilliant, jaggedly thrusting imitation in the allegro given plenty of bite and the lyrical secondary melody glowingly phrased by principal horn and strings alike. The *Polovtsian dances* proceed with comparable brilliance and fervour, with the Royal Liverpool Philharmonic Choir producing expansive lyrical tone and joining in the frenzy of the closing section with infectious zest. Excellent recording too, vivid and full; if only the Mussorgsky coupling had produced comparable electricity, this record would have been a world-beater.

Symphonies Nos. 1 in E flat; 2 in B min.; 3 in A min. (completed Glazunov); *In the Steppes of Central Asia; Nocturne* (orchestrated Nicolai Tcherepnin); *Petite suite* (arr. Glazunov); *Prince Igor: Overture;* (i) *Polovtsian dances.*
*** DG Dig. 435 757-2 (2) [id.]. Gothenburg SO, Neeme Järvi; (i) with Gothenburg Ch.

For those wanting all three symphonies, the Järvi DG set remains recommendable. The alternative versions by Serebrier (ASV CDDCA 706) and Gunzenhauser (Naxos 8.550238) each have the advantage of being offered on a single CD, but Serebrier's performances – recorded in Rome – lack Russian feeling, and one needs a more sumptuous body of tone for this music than the Bratislava Radio Symphony Orchestra on Naxos can provide. While Gunzenhauser's accounts are fresh and pleasing and undoubtedly good value, this is not a distinctive triptych.

Järvi's *First* has plenty of individuality and colour; the slow movement is radiant, the Scherzo beautifully sprung and the finale made to anticipate the *Prince Igor overture* in its bright, rhythmic pointing. The *Second* is a strong, spacious reading; however, alongside Martinon and Ashkenazy, the first movement is somewhat lacking in bite and thrust. The *Third Symphony* (completed by Glazunov), comes off vividly, although it is not as strong a work as the other two. The other pieces are equally well played by the excellent Gothenburg orchestra, notably the *Petite suite*, although there are some reservations about Tcherepnin's very exotic orchestration of the famous *Nocturne* from the *D major String quartet*, and perhaps Järvi doesn't pull out all the stops in his undoubtedly vivid account of the *Polovtsian dances*. Yet the choral Swedish singing, if not uninhibited, is vital enough and even includes a brief solo interpolation representing the Khan. The digital recording throughout is from DG's top drawer.

Symphonies Nos. 1 in E flat; 2 in B min.; In the Steppes of Central Asia.
*** Decca Dig. 436 651-2 [id.]. RPO, Ashkenazy.

With the opening in octaves brisk and dramatic and with speeds throughout that never drag, Ashkenazy's Decca reading of Borodin's *Second Symphony* is exceptionally warm and brilliant, helped by full-bodied Decca recording. The RPO wind soloists are outstanding, and the horn solo in the slow movement is satisfyingly opulent. The prestissimo Scherzo of the second movement is a special delight, not just brilliant but witty, and the dashing speed for the finale is thrilling. The coupling is both apt and generous. *In the Steppes of Central Asia* is a fine example of Borodin's genius, and it is given a warmly atmospheric performance here. If in the *Symphony No. 1* Ashkenazy's performance is less high-powered than in the *Second*, its many delights come over richly, thanks not only to the quality of the RPO's playing but also to the warm recording. For these two works alone this makes a clear first choice.

Symphony No. 2 in B min.
(N) (***) Testament mono SBT 1048 [id.]. Philh. O, Paul Kletzki – TCHAIKOVSKY: *Manfred Symphony.* (***)

Kletzki draws superb playing from the Philharmonia at a vintage period in the mid-1950s. The ravishing account of the slow movement has Dennis Brain at his peak in the big horn solo, backed by Bernard Walton on the clarinet and Sidney Sutcliffe on the oboe producing whispered pianissimos that caress the ear. The first movement is brisk and dramatic, while in the Scherzo the tonguing of the woodwind makes for phenomenal precision. As for the transfer, after a dull opening the bite and immediacy of the brass and woodwind are so vivid they give an illusion of stereo.

Symphony No. 2 in B min.; Nocturne (orch. Tcherepnin).
(N) (M) *** DG Dig. 445 568-2 [id.]. Gothenburg SO Järvi – RIMSKY-KORSAKOV: *Symphony No. 2 (Antar).* ***

In a surprisingly rare coupling, Järvi's expansive approach to both these Russian symphonies works well when the DG recording is so warm and full-bodied. His account of the Borodin *Second* is at its finest in the *Andante* in which the key melody, so beautifully introduced by the solo horn, returns on the full strings in a flood of romanticism; but even in the first movement, which lacks the exhilaration of Martinon's much faster basic tempo, the return of the dominating idea on the brass in the coda is very powerful. Tcherepnin's added orchestral colour in the *Nocturne* remains controversial, but this too is very well played and recorded.

Piano quintet in C min.
(Y/B) ** Auvidis Valois Dig. V 4702 [id.]. Monte Carlo Pro Arte Quintet – SHOSTAKOVICH: *Piano quintet.* **

Borodin's *Piano quintet in C minor* is an early and uncharacteristic piece, without the technical finesse that distinguished his mature work. Ideally it needs a rather more mercurial touch than this team bring to it. The recording is perhaps a bit two-dimensional with little back-to-front depth, but there is currently no alternative. It is coupled to a very good account of the Shostakovich *Piano quintet.*

Sextet (2 movements).
** Mer. Dig. CDE 84211 [id.]. Arienski Ens. – ARENSKY: *Quartet* ***; TCHAIKOVSKY: *Souvenir de Florence.* **

Borodin composed his *Sextet* on a visit to Heidelberg in 1860 but, unfortunately, only two of its movements survive. The Arienski Ensemble play with enthusiasm and conviction and are decently recorded.

String quartets Nos. 1 in A; 2 in D.
** Olympia OCD 538 [id.]. Shostakovich Qt.
(Y/B) (BB) ** Naxos Dig. 8.550850 [id.]. Haydn Qt of Budapest.

The Olympia performances were recorded at the studios of Moscow Radio in 1977–8 and are thoroughly enjoyable, though they offer no real challenge to the version of No. 2 with the Hollywood Quartet.

The Haydn Quartet of Budapest play both works with a passionate display of Slavonic temperament. Their playing does not lack light and shade but the Unitarian Church acoustic makes their agreeably sumptuous textures seem forwardly orchestral, and the close microphones restrict the dynamic range. Perhaps that will not be a drawback for some listeners, and such opulence of tone suits the music, even if it robs the performances of subtlety.

String quartet No. 2 in D.
(N) *** Decca Dig 425 239-2 [id.]. Takács Qt – SMETANA: *String quartet No. 1.* ***
(Y/B) (***) Testament mono SBT 1061 [id.]. Hollywood Qt – GLAZUNOV: *5 Novelettes;* TCHAIKOVSKY: *String quartet No. 1.* (***)
(N) (BB) *** CfP Silver Double CDCFPSD 4772 (2). Gabrieli String Qt – BRAHMS: *Clarinet quintet* **(*); DVORAK: *String quartet No. 12* ***; SCHUBERT: *String quartet No. 14.* ***
(N) (M) **(*) Cal. CAL 6202 [id.]. Talich Qt – TCHAIKOVSKY: *Quartet No. 1.* ***
(M) **(*) Decca 425 541-2; *425 541-4* [id.]. Borodin Qt – SHOSTAKOVICH; TCHAIKOVSKY: *Quartets.* **(*)

An outstanding new version of Borodin's *D major Quartet* comes from the Takács group, who play with fine ensemble and plenty of feeling, yet bring subtlety of colour and delicacy of texture, as well as warmth, to the famous *Notturno.* The recording has striking presence, and the Smetana coupling is hardly less impressive.

At the time when the Hollywood Quartet's version of the Borodin *Second Quartet* first appeared in 1953, there were complaints that the sound was steely and hard. At the same time, the work itself was in the doldrums – 'the Hollywood Quartet do all that is possible to revive the faded colours of this melodious but weak composition,' was one verdict. Although, for once, it is possible to speak of later recordings (most notably by the eponymous Borodin Quartet) as matching – and even surpassing – the Hollywood group, this is still a performance that has a freshness and an ardour which are very persuasive. The sound has been improved, and the addition of the Glazunov, which is new to the catalogue, enhances the disc's value. The playing-time runs to one second short of 80 minutes.

As part of an outstanding Classics for Pleasure Silver Double compilation of Romantic string quartets, the Gabrielis offer a finely wrought, sensitive and thoroughly polished performance of the Borodin, warm in feeling. At less than half the price of its main competitor, this is excellent value, for the recording is first class and beautifully transferred to CD.

The Talich performance is characteristically refined and beautifully played; although there is no lack of warmth and the leader shapes the famous theme of the *Notturno* with ravishing purity of timbre and line, the performance lacks something in Slavonic voluptuousness compared with the Borodin Quartet. The digital recording is, however, first class, full and naturally balanced, and this is easily preferable to the Borodins' Decca alternative. Moreover the Tchaikovsky coupling is outstanding in every way.

The Borodins' version of the *Second Quartet* on Decca is very fine. However, the forward recording, though rich-textured, approaches fierceness in the CD transfer, and most will prefer a softer-grained effect.

Songs: *Arabian melody; Arrogance; The beauty no longer loves me; The false note; The fisher-maiden; From my tears; From the shores of thy far native land; Listen to my song little friend; The magic garden; The queen of the sea; The sea; The sleeping princess; Song of the dark forest; There is poison in my songs; Those people; Why art thou so early, dawn?*
(M) *** EMI CMS7 63386-2 (3) [Ang. CDMC 63386]. Christoff, Tcherepnin, Reiss, Lamoureux O, Tzipine – *Prince Igor*. **(*)

Accompanied at the piano in all but three of the songs by the composer Alexander Tcherepnin, Christoff gives glorious performances of these rare items, sung, of course, in Russian.

Prince Igor (opera) complete.
(Y/B) *** Ph. Dig. 442 537-2 (3) [id.]. Kit, Gorchakova, Ognovienko, Minjelkiev, Borodina, Grigorian, Kirov Ch. & O, St Petersburg, Gergiev.
*** Sony Dig. S3K 44878 (3) [id.]. Martinovich, Evstatieva, Kaludov, Ghiuselev, Ghiaurov, Miltcheva, Sofia Nat. Op. Ch. & Festival O, Tchakarov.
(M) **(*) EMI CMS7 63386-2 (3) [Ang. CDMC 63386]. Chekerliiski, Christoff, Todorov, Sofia Nat. Theatre Op. Ch. & O, Jerzy Semkow – *Songs*. ***

Gergiev has been an inspired musical director of the Kirov company in St Petersburg, and this electrifying account of Borodin's epic opera reflects not only his own magnetic qualities as a conductor but also the way he has welded his principal singers as well as the chorus and orchestra into a powerful team. Textually the oddity of this version is that Acts I and II are given in reverse order from the usual, with the substantial Prologue here followed by the first Polovtsian scene and its spectacular dances. Only then do you get the scene at Prince Galitzky's court, normally Act I, leading up to Yaroslavna's great lament, here superbly sung by Galina Gorchakova. The reordering works well, with contrasting elements better separated. Otherwise Gergiev generally follows that well-established edition, but he has included material omitted from Borodin's copious sketches, notably an extended monologue of lament for Igor himself as a prisoner of Khan Konchak in Act III, '*Why did I not fall on the field of battle*'. It may not be as fine as the aria Igor sings in the first Polovtsian scene, using the great melody introduced in the overture, but that and other supplementary passages are very welcome. That alone puts this ahead of the fine rival Sony recording from Tchakarov with Bulgarian forces, and Gergiev is even more sharply dramatic, generally adopting faster speeds. The Philips recording too is weightier than the Sony, with the chorus in particular sounding satisfyingly large as well as incisive. On the solo casting, honours are much more even. The two principal women here, not just Gorchakova but Olga Borodina too as Konchak's daughter, Konchakovna, are both magnificent, even finer than their Bulgarian rivals, but neither principal bass, Vladimir Ognovienko as Galitsky and Bulat Minjelkiev as Konchak, can match the vocal richness or character of the Bulgarians, Ghiuselev and Ghiaurov, both older-sounding but still compelling. Gegam Grigorian in the tenor role of Igor's son gives a lusty performance, while Mikhail Kit as Igor himself, though often gritty and even fluttery of tone, sings thoughtfully and intelligently, making him a fair match for his Bulgarian rival. Yet in the end the overall control of this massive score is what matters, and there Gergiev, with a finer and more polished orchestra, clearly takes the palm.

On Sony, Nicola Ghiuselev as Galitzky is powerful but rather unsteady and Nicolai Ghiaurov makes a splendid Konchak. Boris Martinovich makes a firm, very virile Igor, and both the principal women have vibrantly Slavonic voices which still never distract in wobbling. The dramatic tension in this long work is held very well and its richness of invention over its very episodic span comes across vividly, notably in all its memorable melody and high colour.

In the colourful EMI recording, Act III is completely omitted, on the grounds that it was almost entirely the work of Rimsky-Korsakov and Glazunov. Boris Christoff as both Galitzky and Konchak easily outshines all rivals. Jerzy Semkow with his Sofia Opera forces is most sympathetic, but the other soloists are almost all disappointing, with the women sour-toned and the men often strained and unsteady. The sound is limited but agreeably atmospheric.

Prince Igor: Overture and Polovtsian dances.
*** EMI CDC7 47717-2 [id.]. Beecham Choral Soc., RPO, Beecham – RIMSKY-KORSAKOV: *Scheherazade.****

Prince Igor: Polovtsian dances.
(M) *** DG 419 063-2 [id.]. BPO, Karajan – RIMSKY-KORSAKOV: *Scheherazade.* ***
(N) (M) *** Decca Phase 4 443 896-2 [id.]. Welsh Nat. Op. Ch., RPO Ch., RPO, Stokowski – MUSSORGSKY: *Night on the bare mountain* etc. **; TCHAIKOVSKY: *1812 overture* etc. **(*)
(M) **(*) Mercury 434 308-2 [id.]. London Symphony Ch., LSO, Dorati – RIMSKY-KORSAKOV: *Capriccio espagnol* etc. ***

Beecham's 1957 recording of the *Polovtsian dances* sweeps the board, even though it omits the percussion-led opening *Dance of the Polovtsian maidens*. Beecham draws an almost Russian fervour from his choristers. The recorded sound is little short of astonishing in its fullness, vividness and clarity.

Karajan's Berlin Philharmonic version has great flair and excitement, though it lacks a chorus.

Stokowski misses out the percussion-led opening dance, but there is no question about the excitement he creates at the climax, with the chorus singing their hearts out. The recording is sumptuous and spectacular.

Dorati's Mercury recording is not among the most refined from this source, but no one could say that effect lacks vividness or boisterous vitality, and the climax is exhilarating.

Bortkiewicz, Serge (1877–1952)

Piano concerto No. 1 in B flat min., Op. 16.
(Y/B) *** Hyperion Dig. CDA 66624 [id.]. Coombs, BBC Scottish SO, Maksymiuk – ARENSKY: *Piano concerto.* ***

Serge Bortkiewicz's concerto is conservative in idiom, a conventional, romantic, virtuoso offering without much individual flavour. Stephen Coombs takes its considerable difficulties in his stride and plays the work as if it is great music, and at times he almost persuades one that it is; and he receives excellent support from the BBC Scottish Orchestra under Jerzy Maksymiuk, and good recording quality.

Bottesini, Giovanni (1821–89)

(i) *Double-bass concertino in C min.; (i; ii) Duo concertante on themes from Bellini's 'I Puritani' for cello, double-bass and orchestra; (i) Elégie in D; (i; iii) Passioni amorose (for 2 double-basses); Ali Baba overture; Il Diavolo delle notte; Ero e Leandro: Prelude.*
(Y/B) *** ASV Dig. CDDCA 907 [id.]. (i) Thomas Martin; (ii) Moray Welsh; (iii) Francesco Petracchi; LSO, Petracchi, or (iii) Matthew Gibson.

Bottesini must have been a double-bass player *extraordinaire*! A contemporary said of his playing: 'Under his bow the double-bass sighed, cooed, sang, quivered,' and it does all those things here on the flamboyant bow of Thomas Martin, himself a musician of the strongest personality. He 'coos' mellifluously in the *Elégie*, a conventional piece but agreeably melodic; then he sings the yearning cantilena which forms the slow movement of the *Concertino* with a grace unexpected from his comparatively unwieldy instrument. In this work the composer resourcefully commands the soloist to tune his instrument a minor third above the orchestra, which increases the instrument's projection. For the *Passioni amorose* the conductor, Francesco Petracchi (professor of the double-bass at the Geneva Conservatoire), exchanges his baton for another bow to join his colleague, establishing a close, decisive partnership. Further contrast is provided when Moray Welsh successfully interweaves with his larger instrumental cousin in the *Duo concertante* on melodies of Bellini. To prevent the ear from being over-lubricated with sounds from the orchestral basement, the programme is interspersed with colourful orchestral miniatures. The *Prelude to Ero e Leandro* has a distinctly Neapolitan flavour (and a nice oboe solo); the *Sinfonia, Il Diavolo della notte*, turns naturally from warm lyricism to galloping liveliness, and the brief *Ali Baba overture* brings a spirited whiff of Rossini. The recording engineers have done marvels to balance everything so convincingly; thus the persuasive Thomas Martin can play with delicacy and easy virtuosity within his instrument's little-heard upper tessitura and be sure he is clearly audible. His intonation is remarkably true, and this programme is surprisingly rewarding and entertaining, far more than a specialist collection for the musically curious.

Gran duo concertante for violin, double-bass and orchestra; Gran concerto in F sharp min. for double-bass;
Andante sostenuto for strings; Duetto for clarinet and double-bass.
**(*) ASV Dig. CDDCA 563 [id.]. Garcia, Martin, Emma Johnson, ECO, Andrew Litton.

The ASV recording combines the *Gran duo concertante* with another *Duetto for clarinet and double-bass* which Emma Johnson ensures has plenty of personality. To be frank, none of this amiable music is very distinctive. The recording is excellent, well balanced and truthful.

Capriccio di bravura; Elegia in Re; Fantasia on Beatrice di Tenda; Fantasia on Lucia di Lammermoor;
Grand allegro di concerto; Introduzione e Bolero; Romanza drammatica; (i) *Romanza: Une bouche aimée.*
**(*) ASV Dig. CDDCA 626 [id.]. Thomas Martin, Anthony Halstead; (i) with J. Fugelle.

Thomas Martin is a superb virtuoso of the double-bass, and he obviously relishes these display pieces, but some of the high tessitura is inevitably uncomfortable. The recording is most realistic.

Boughton, Rutland (1878–1960)

(i) *Oboe concerto; Symphony No. 3 in B min.*
*** Hyperion Dig. CDA 66343 [id.]. (i) Sarah Francis; RPO, Vernon Handley.

Rutland Boughton's *Third Symphony* is old-fashioned in idiom, expertly fashioned and often imaginative, and it hardly puts a foot wrong. The *Oboe concerto* is hardly less rewarding. The recording is in the demonstration class and the performances are totally committed, even if the strings of the RPO are not quite on top form.

Bethlehem (choral drama, adapted from the Coventry Nativity Play).
(N) *** Hyperion Dig. CDA 66690 [id.]. Field, Bryan, Bryson, R. Evans, Bowen, Peacock, Opie,
    MacDougall, Van Allan, Seaton, Campbell, I. Boughton, Matheson-Bruce, Holst Singers, New L.
    Children's Ch., City of L. Sinf., Alan Melville.

Rutland Boughton wrote this choral drama in 1915 for the festival he had founded the previous year at Glastonbury. Boughton's score, lyrical and undemanding, with carols punctuating the scenes as chorales punctuate the Bach Passions, is an aptly fresh and innocent setting of an edited version of the Coventry Nativity Play. The scenes start with the annunciation and carry on the nativity story in a direct, uncomplicated way which, within its limits, is most moving. The villainous role of Herod is unexpectedly consigned to a tenor (perhaps for a composer representing unreliability) but otherwise there are no more surprises than you would find in a church pageant. Alan G. Melville conducts a warm, fluent performance generally well sung, though for the central role of the Virgin Mary it would have been better to have a voice caught more sweetly by the microphone than Helen Field's. Alan Opie and the two other wise men are outstanding, and the three shepherds characterize well in their pastoral cavortings without overdoing the Mummerset accents. The score has been discreetly cut to fit the two Acts on a single CD – mainly involving the removal of an incidental ballet for Herod – with little loss. First-rate, well-balanced sound.

The Immortal hour (opera): complete.
*** Hyperion Dig. CDA 66101/2 [id.]. Kennedy, Dawson, Wilson-Johnson, Davies, Geoffrey Mitchell
    Ch., ECO, Melville.

Analysed closely, much of *The Immortal hour* may seem like Vaughan Williams and water; but this fine performance, conducted by a lifelong Boughton devotee, brings out the hypnotic quality which had 1920s music-lovers attending performances many times over, entranced by its lyrical evocation of Celtic twilight. The simple tunefulness goes with a fine feeling for atmosphere. The excellent cast of young singers includes Anne Dawson as the heroine, Princess Etain, and Maldwyn Davies headily beautiful in the main tenor rendering of the *Faery song*. Warm, reverberant recording, undoubtedly enhanced in its CD format.

Boulanger, Lili (1893–1918)

(i) *Cortège; D'un matin de printemps; Nocturne* (3 pieces for violin & piano); (ii) *Du fond de l'abîme;* (iii)
Pié Jesu; (iv) *Psaume 24;* (v) *Psaume 129;* (vi) *Vieille prière bouddhique.*
(M) *(**) EMI mono/stereo CDM7 64281-2 [id.]. (i) Menuhin, Curzon; (ii) Dominguez, Amade; (iii)
    Fauqueur; (iii; iv) Grunenwald; (iv) Sénéchal; (v) Mollet; (ii; iv–vi) Chorale Elizabeth Brasseur; (ii–
    vi) LOP, Markevitch.

Du fond de l'abîme is a haunting piece that quite transcends its very dated, dryish 1958 mono recording by Oralia Dominguez and the Lamoureux Orchestra of Paris under Igor Markevitch. The opening of the *Psaume 24* almost looks forward to the Honegger of *Le roi David*, and the *Vieille prière bouddhique* to Holst. The three pieces for violin and piano, *Cortège, D'un matin de printemps* and *Nocturne*, are more Ravel-like, and are beautifully played by Yehudi Menuhin and Clifford Curzon. An altogether fascinating disc: the music deserves three stars, the recordings only one.

Boulez, Pierre (born 1926)

Eclat-Multiples; Rituel: In memoriam Bruno Maderna.
(M) *** Sony SK 45839 [id.]. BBC SO, Ens. InterContemporain, composer.

Eclat-Multiples started (in 1964) simply as *Eclat*, a brilliant showpiece, an exuberant mosaic of sounds; but then, in 1970, it started developing from there in the pendant work, *Multiples*. *Rituel* is the most moving music that Boulez has ever written, inspired by the premature death of his friend and colleague, Bruno Maderna. This record, very well played and recorded, provides both a challenge and a reward.

(i) *Livre pour cordes;* (ii) *Pli selon pli.*
(N) (M) *** Sony SMK 68335 [id.]. (i) New Philh. O. Strings; (ii) Halina Lukomska, Maria Bergman (piano), Paul Stingle (guitar), Hugo d'Alton (mandolin), BBC SO; composer.

Pli selon pli is a grandly conceived work to refute the idea that serialists and their progeny are necessarily cramped in their inspiration. The title (literally 'fold upon fold') comes from the poet Mallarmé, and Boulez's layers of invention are used to illuminate as centrepieces three Mallarmé sonnets. Neither these craggy vocalizations nor the purely instrumental passages are at all easy to understand in a conventional sense, but the luminous texture of Boulez's writing is endlessly fascinating and, for the listener with an open mind, this is rewarding way of widening experience of the avant-garde. *Livre pour cordes*, adapted from an early string quartet, is a less demanding piece, but one equally worth studying. Definitive performances and excellent (late-1960s) recording under the composer's sharp-eared and electrifying direction.

Le soleil des eaux.
(M) *** EMI CDM7 63948-2 [id.]. Nendick, McDaniel, Devos, BBC Ch. & SO, composer – KOECK- LIN: *Les Bandar-Log;* MESSIAEN: *Chronochromie* etc. ***

Boulez's cantata is best thought of initially in its atmospheric context. Josephine Nendick, the principal soloist, is breathtakingly precise and the result is far more enjoyable as a result. Both performance and recording are of a high standard and the CD transfer gives striking presence.

Bouzignac, Guillaume (*c.* 1590–*c.* 1640)

Te Deum. Motets: *Alleluia, venite amici; Ave Maria; Clamant clavi; Dum silentium; Ecce Aurora; Ecce festivitas; Ecce homo; Flos in flores; Ha! Plange; In pace, in idipsum; Jubilate Deo; Salve Jesu Piissime; Tota pulchra es; Unus ex vobis; Vulnerasti cor meum.*
(Y/B) ✸ *** HM Dig. HMC 901471 [id.]. Les Pages de la Chapelle, Les Arts Florissants, William Christie.

You might call Bouzignac the Charles Ives of the sixteenth century. His music was almost totally forgotten for 250 years until rediscovered by a scholar at the beginning of this century. On record he has continued to be neglected, and this pioneering disc brings a revelation. The great refreshing quality of Bouzignac for the modern ear is that consistently he responds vividly and unpredictably to the texts of each of these motets. Often his response is so wildly individual that you would be unlikely to deduce which century the music came from, let alone which country. Vigour is the essence, as in the exuberantly light-hearted setting of *Jubilate Deo*, yet such a motet as *In pace, in idipsum* in its sustained lines has a rare meditative beauty, and the dialogue of *Unus ex vobis* even brings echoes of Russian Orthodox music. The response of William Christie, always a vivid interpreter of early music, brings out the colour in all its variety, for once with boy trebles (Les Pages de la Chapelle) added to the finely disciplined forces, vocal and instrumental, of Les Arts Florissants. This will be a thrilling discovery for many, helped by vividly immediate sound.

Boyce, William (1710–79)

Overtures Nos. 1–9.
(M) *** Chandos CHAN 6531 [id.]. Cantilena, Adrian Shepherd.

Overtures Nos. 10–12; Concerti grossi: in B flat; in B min.; in E min.
(M) *** Chandos CHAN 6541 [id.]. Cantilena, Adrian Shepherd.

This reissue offers Cantilena's complete set of the Boyce *Overtures* and includes the three *Concerti grossi*. Though these works do not quite have the consistent originality which makes the Boyce *Symphonies* so refreshing, the energy of the writing – splendidly conveyed in these performances – is recognizably the same, with fugal passages that turn in unexpected directions. Cantilena's performances readily convey the freshness of Boyce's inspiration. The recording is oddly balanced but is both atmospheric and vivid and provides a refreshing musical experience.

Symphonies Nos. 1–8, Op. 2.
(Y/B) (M) *** Decca 444 523-2 [id.]. ASMF, Marriner.
*** O-L Dig. 436 761-2 [id.]. AAM, Hogwood.
*** DG Dig. 419 631-2 [id.]. E. Concert, Pinnock.
*** CRD CRD 3356 [id.]. Bournemouth Sinf., Ronald Thomas.

Marriner treats these superb examples of English baroque to exhilarating performances, with the rhythmic subtleties in both fast music and slow guaranteed to enchant. The recording was made in 1978 at St John's, Smith Square, and it has plenty of ambience, while the digital remastering ensures brighter lighting to the upper strings in a beneficial way. The listener now experiences more of the bite one would expect from an authentic version, yet the expressive style of modern instruments and the absence of bulges in the phrasing bring an approach that should satisfy most ears. Those requiring a period performance should turn to Hogwood.

Christopher Hogwood and the Academy of Ancient Music turn in performances that are every bit as lively and well played as Trevor Pinnock's set with the English Concert, and perhaps more sensitively shaped. By comparison, Pinnock now sounds just a bit bright and business-like. The Academy version is now a safe first choice among period-instrument versions.

However, Pinnock's disc of the Boyce *Symphonies* wears its scholarship very easily and in so doing brings not only lively, resilient playing but fresh revelation in the treatment of the *vivace* movements. Nicely scaled recording, bright but atmospheric.

Thomas's tempi are often brisk, and certainly swifter-paced than Pinnock's 'new look'. But even against such strong competition as this, the buoyant playing of the Bournemouth Sinfonietta still gives much pleasure by its sheer vitality. Bright, clear sound.

(i) *Anthems: By the waters of Babylon; I have surely built Thee a house; O where shall wisdom be found; Turn unto me, O Lord. Organ voluntaries Nos. 1, 2, 4 & 10.*
(M) *** Saga EC 3379-2. Arthur Wills, (i) Ely Cathedral Ch., Gerald Clifford.

The music of Boyce is most compelling, especially when sung with such warmth. The organ voluntaries have plenty of character. This makes a most stimulating introduction to valuable and rare repertoire, and the CD transfer catches the cathedral ambience to perfection.

Solomon (serenata).
*** Hyperion Dig. CDA 66378 [id.]. Bronwen Mills, Howard Crook, Parley of Instruments, Goodman.

William Boyce's *Solomon* is a totally secular piece, a dialogue between She and He, with the verses freely based on the *Song of Solomon*. As this stylish and alert period performance using young, fresh-voiced soloists makes clear, it has some delightful inspirations, less influenced by Italian models than by popular English song. First-rate sound.

Brade, William (1560–1630)

Hamburger Ratsmusik: Allemandes, Canzonas, Courantes, Galliards, Intradas (1609, 1614 & 1617 collections).
(M) *** HM/BMG Dig. GD 77168 (2) [77168-2-RG]. Hespèrion XX, Jordi Savall.

This collection of dances is absolutely delightful, varied in both content and instrumental colour, and excellently played by Hespèrion XX under Jordi Savall, while the recording, from 1981, is very good indeed.

Bræin, Edvard Fliflet (1924–76)

Anne Pedersdotter (opera; complete).
(Y/B) *** Simax Dig. PSC3121 (2) [id.]. Ekeberg, Handssen, Carlsen, Sandve, Thorsen, Norwegian Nat. Op. Ch. & O, Per Ake Andersson.

Edvard Fliflet Bræin was a highly talented Norwegian composer who died in his early fifties. His opera, *Anne Pedersdotter* (1971), is based on the most famous of witchcraft trials in Norway, the burning of Anne Pedersdotter in Bergen in 1590. Fliflet Bræin called it 'a symphonic opera' and, like Schoeck's *Venus*, its invention unfolds in an effortlessly organic fashion; in other words, his is the art that conceals art. It is effective music-theatre, and many of its ideas, as is so often the case with this composer, are memorable. It gets an eminently serviceable performance, with good singing from Kjersti Ekeberg as the eponymous heroine, Svein Carlsen as her husband, Absolon Pedersøn-Beyer, and Kjell Magnus Sandve as his son by his first marriage. The Norwegian Opera forces under the baton of Per Ake Andersson are excellent, and the recording, produced by Michael Woodcock, is very good indeed. Strongly recommended.

Brahms, Johannes (1833–97)

(i) *Piano concertos Nos. 1–2. Academic festival overture; Tragic overture; Variations on a theme of Haydn.*
(B) **(*) Ph. Duo 438 320-2 (2) [id.]. (i) Claudio Arrau; Concg. O, Haitink.

(i) *Piano concertos Nos. 1 in D min., Op. 15; 2 in B flat, Op. 83;* (ii) *Academic festival overture, Op. 80; Variations on a theme of Haydn, Op. 56a.*
(N) (BB) *** CfP Silver Double CDCFPSD 4766 (2). (i) Tirimo, LPO, Sanderling or Yoel Levi; (ii) Hallé O, Loughran.

Piano concertos Nos. (i) *1 in D min., Op. 15;* (ii) *2 in B flat, Op. 83. Variations and fugue on a theme of Handel, Op. 24; Variations on a theme of Paganini, Op. 35.*
(Y/B) (B) **(*) Decca Double 440 612-2 (2) [id.]. Julius Katchen; (i–ii) LSO; (i) Pierre Monteux; (ii) János Ferencsik.

(i) *Piano concertos Nos. 1–2. 4 Ballades, Op. 10; 8 Pieces, Op. 76; Scherzo in E flat, Op. 4.*
(B) *** Ph. Duo 442 109-2 (2) [id.]. Steven Kovacevich; (i) LSO, Sir Colin Davis.

(i) *Piano concertos Nos. 1–2. 4 Ballades, Op. 10; Theme and variations in D min.* (from *String sextet, Op. 18*).
(N) (M) *** Ph. Brendel Edition Dig. 446 925-2 (5) [id.]. Alfred Brendel, (i) BPO, Abbado – SCHU-MANN: *Collection.* ***

(i) *Piano concertos Nos. 1–2. Capriccio in B min., Op. 76/2; Intermezzi: in E, Op. 116/6; in E flat, Op. 117/ 1; in E min.; in C, Op. 119/2–3; Rhapsody in B min., Op. 79/1; 6 Pieces, Op. 118.*
(M) **(*) Decca 433 895-2 (2) [id.]. Wilhelm Backhaus; (i) VPO, Boehm.

Piano concerto No. 2 in B flat, Op. 83.
(M) *** Decca 448 600-2 (2) [id.]. Backhaus, VPO, Boehm – MOZART: *Piano concerto No. 27.* **(*)

(i) *Piano concertos Nos. 1–2. Fantasias, Op. 116.*
(N) (M) *** DG 447 446-2 (2) [id.]. Gilels; (i) BPO, Jochum.

The Gilels performances were an obvious candidate for DG's 'Originals' series and can still hold their own against virtually all the competition, but the two concertos are also available separately – see below. However, the present set is offered at a reduced price and the remastered recording is quite outstanding: for these 'Legendary Recordings' DG have improved the sound well beyond previous incarnations of these works.

The *Second concerto* was Tirimo's début recording, made in 1974. He gives a commanding if measured account of the first movement, not always quite tidy in its occasional impulsiveness (but then neither is Richter). The second and fourth movements too have slow basic tempi, but the clarity of articulation gives a sharpness of focus to conceal that, and both are made exuberant and joyful. Similarly in the *First concerto*, made six years later, Sanderling and Tirimo amply justify their straight and measured manner in the thoughtful concentration of the whole reading. One has no feeling of the performance dragging, for the crisp, lifted rhythms prevent that in the outer movements, and the slow movement has a rapt quality, holding one's attention as a live performance would. With such excellent sound, this is one of the very best of Classics for Pleasure's Silver Doubles, and the set is made the more competitive by the addition of Loughran's accounts of the *Variations* and the *Academic festival overture*, fine performances both, although the latter has a rather subdued start.

In the *D minor concerto* Kovacevich plays with great tenderness and lyrical feeling. Similarly, No. 2 combines poetic feeling and intellectual strength and reflects an unforced naturalness that compels admiration. Sir Colin Davis provides wholly sympathetic support throughout, and this set can be spoken of alongside Gilels; the recording is less well balanced, but still full and quite satisfying. The piano music originally took up a whole LP by itself. The accounts of the *Ballades* and the Op. 76 *Klavierstücke* have both fire and tenderness and are truthfully recorded.

Brendel's digital recordings of the two Brahms *Concertos* with Claudio Abbado and the Berlin Philharmonic as understanding partners show him at his finest. In the *D minor Concerto* the result is both strong and spontaneous. His control of Brahmsian rubato is masterly, easily flexible but totally unexaggerated, and the basic tempi are set well and steadily. The balance is not too forward and the effect is warmly satisfying. The account of the *B flat Concerto* is hardly less striking. It has the advantage of impressive and weighty recorded sound, and the Berlin Philharmonic under Abbado produce an equally splendid warmth. The account of the Op. 10 *Ballades* is also a performance of distinction. There is some highlighting of subsidiary part-writing that may strike some as just a little self-conscious, but much else will delight the listener. The digital recording is first class.

In the *First Concerto* Katchen was not particularly well served by the balance provided by the Decca engineers, but he plays superbly, particularly in the first movement, and is sonorously matched by some fine playing by the LSO under Monteux. Again in No. 2 he gives an impassioned and exciting account of the solo piano part, combining great drive with the kind of ruminating delicacy Brahms so often calls for in his piano writing. The balance places the piano well within the orchestral framework and the sound is not too dated. The sets of solo variations, brilliant though they are, are not among the most compelling of Katchen's solo Brahms recordings for Decca. Oddly enough, for all their sheer pyro-technical display, they sound comparatively unspontaneous.

Arrau's readings undoubtedly have vision and power, and the *D minor Concerto* is majestic and elo-quent. There is some characteristic agogic distortion that will not convince all listeners, and, by the side of Gilels, Arrau seems idiosyncratic. In the *Second Concerto* his playing has a splendid combination of aristocratic finesse and warmth of feeling, and in both concertos Haitink and the Royal Concertgebouw Orchestra give excellent support. Excellent value, and the set is well documented.

Backhaus recorded the *First Concerto* in 1953 and no apologies need be made for the mono recording. The acoustics of the Musikverein ensure a fine spread of sound and the performance has great impetus and authority. The *Second Concerto* was made in the Sofiensaal in 1967 when Backhaus was in his eighties, and the rugged strength of his conception is matched by playing of remarkable power. His is a broad, magisterial account. The recording wears its years remarkably lightly: it sounds fresh, full-bodied and is finely detailed. (As can be seen above, this is also available separately in Decca's Classic Sound series, coupled with Mozart's *Piano concerto No. 27*.) The solo pieces date from 1956. Backhaus is again in excellent form, though the *Intermezzi*, which are played sensitively, come in for rather more subtle treatment than the *Capriccio* and *Rhapsody*.

Piano concerto No. 1 in D min., Op. 15.
*** Ph. Dig. 420 071-2 [id.]. Brendel, BPO, Abbado.
(Y/B) (M) *** Decca 425 082-2 [id.]. Clifford Curzon, LSO, Szell – FRANCK: *Symphonic variations;* LITOLFF: *Scherzo.* ***
(B) **(*) Sony SBK 48166; *SBT 48166* [id.]. Rudolf Serkin, Cleveland O, Szell – MENDELSSOHN: *Capriccio brilliant* **; SCHUMANN: *Intro. and allegro appassionata.* **(*)
**(*) Decca Dig. 410 009-2 [id.]. Ashkenazy, Concg. O, Haitink.
(BB) **(*) ASV CDQS 6083. John Lill, Hallé O, Loughran.

(i) *Piano concerto No. 1. Variations and fugue on a theme of Handel, Op. 24.*
(***) Testament mono SBT1041 [id.]. Solomon, (i) Philh. O, Kubelik.
(N) (M) (**) DG mono 447 977 [id.]. Kempff, (i) Dresden State O, Konwitschny.

(i) *Piano concerto No. 1;* (ii) *Variations on a theme of Haydn, Op. 56a.*
(M) *** EMI CDM7 63536-2 [id.]. (i) Barenboim, Philh. O; (ii) VPO; Barbirolli.

(i) *Piano concerto No. 1. 4 Ballades, Op. 10.*
(Y/B) (M) *** DG 439 979-2 [id.]. Gilels; (i) BPO, Jochum.

(i) *Piano concerto No. 1. Capriccio in B min., Op. 76/2; Intermezzo in E flat min., Op. 118/6; Rhapsody in B min., Op. 79/1.*
(M) **(*) RCA 09026 61263-2 [id.]. Artur Rubinstein; (i) Chicago SO, Reiner.

(i) *Piano concerto No. 1;* (ii) *2 Songs, Op. 91.*
🏵 *** EMI Dig. CDC7 54578-2. (i) Stephen Kovacevich, LPO, Sawallisch; (ii) Anne Murray, Nobuko Imai.

Noble and dedicated, Stephen Kovacevich's account of the Brahms *D minor Concerto* is a performance of stature which belongs in the most exalted company. It can be recommended alongside such classic accounts as the Gilels/Jochum (DG); indeed, it must now take precedence. Moreover it is accorded fine digital sound which has all the warmth and spaciousness one could ask for, together with splendid presence and detail. There is a welcome fill-up in the form of the two Op. 91 *Songs* with viola, admirably presented by Anne Murray and Nobuko Imai.

Gilels's reading of the *D minor Concerto* has a magisterial strength blended with a warmth, humanity and depth that are altogether inspiring. Jochum is a superb accompanist and the remastered 1972 recording has a better focus on CD. The *Ballades* have never been played so marvellously on record, and the recording is very believable.

Brendel produces a consistently beautiful sound and balances the combative and lyrical elements of the work with well-nigh perfect judgement.

Barenboim's performance of the *First Concerto* with Barbirolli is also among the most inspired ever committed to disc. The playing is heroic and marvellously spacious, and the performance is sustained by the intensity of concentration, especially in the pianissimo passages of the slow movement; the joyous finale uplifts the spirit and communicates a life-enhancing confidence. The *Variations* again show the conductor at his finest; the late-1960s recordings have transferred splendidly to CD.

Clifford Curzon's 1962 recording, produced by John Culshaw in Kingsway Hall, returns to the catalogue, carefully remastered by the Decca engineers. The fierceness of attack in the upper strings, especially in the powerful opening tutti, sounds naturally focused on CD, adding a leonine power to Szell's orchestral contribution, and the piano tone is admirably natural. Curzon has the full measure of Brahms's keyboard style and penetrates both the reflective inner world of the slow movement and the abundantly vital and massive opening movement. The piano balance is most satisfying. For this generous reissue in Decca's Classic Sound series, the Franck *Symphonic variations* and Litolff *Scherzo* have been added.

Serkin's 1968 account with Szell, his third on LP, brought tremendous command and grandeur. This is undoubtedly a memorable performance and the support from Szell and the Cleveland Orchestra has great power. The Schumann coupling is very fine too. The CBS/Sony recording has been considerably improved in the current remastering and is fuller than before, but the balance still lacks a natural perspective and the sound ideally needs more opulence and depth. However, the hall's ambience prevents brashness, and admirers of Serkin will still want this CD.

Ashkenazy gives a commanding and magisterial account of the solo part that is full of poetic imagination. The performance is very impressive indeed and there is superlative playing from the Concertgebouw Orchestra. The recording is enormously vivid.

Rubinstein's Chicago recording was made in stereo as early as 1954 and the sound remains remarkably good, thanks to the sympathetic Chicago acoustics. This is a poetic and essentially lyrical reading, impulsive and intent on avoiding Brahmsian stodginess, for Reiner's control of the orchestra, volatile and imaginative, has a spacious strength. The three solo piano pieces, now added as a bonus, are characteristically chimerical. This is a fine memento of a great artist, not the most profound version but a consistently enjoyable one.

Solomon's magisterial account with Rafael Kubelik and the Philharmonia Orchestra belongs among the greatest ever made. It has a majestic grandeur and blends the dramatic power of youth with the wisdom of old age. Of course the 1952 recording does not possess the range or bloom of subsequent versions, but the transfer succeeds in making it sound astonishingly present. Of his celebrated 1942 set of the Brahms *Handel variations* one is tempted to say the same.

John Lill has the measure of the work's fire and drama, yet his playing is fundamentally classical; indeed, it is unfailingly impressive and scrupulous in its observance of every dynamic marking and expressive nuance. He is given warm and spirited support from Loughran and the Hallé – natural Brahmsians – even though woodwind intonation in one or two places is not wholly above reproach. Masterly and commanding playing, although at times there is a slightly reserved quality that inhibits unqualified recommendation. Nevertheless, with very good (1978) recording, this is well worth considering in the lowest price range.

Kempff's Brahms disc, issued to celebrate his centenary in 1995, offers 1957 recordings with harsh, even clangy sound in the concerto. Kempff, though as rapt and spontaneous-sounding as ever, playing with fine, individual imagination, seems however less concentrated than usual over the whole span. This reading is also available coupled (at bargain price on a DG Double) with stereo versions of the *F minor*

Sonata and other major solo works, played by Kempff with great warmth and sympathy – see below. The *Handel variations* are much more characteristic, again transparent, with the crispest possible ornamentation, purposefully conveying pure joy. This calls for a separate issue.

(i) *Piano concerto No. 1 in D min. 4 Ballades Op. 10; 2 Capricci, Op. 76/1–2; Intermezzo in B flat, Op. 76/ 4; 2 Rhapsodies, Op. 79; Piano sonata No. 3 in F min., Op. 5; Scherzo in E flat, Op. 4.*
(B) *** DG Double mono/stereo 437 374-2 (2) [id.]. Wilhelm Kempff; (i) Dresden State O, Konwitschny.

Kempff was born in 1895, two years before the death of Brahms, and the great pianist himself died in 1991. This set spans his major solo Brahms recordings, made between 1957 and 1963, and includes the mono account of the Brahms *D minor Concerto* from 1956; no complaints about the DG recording of this work. Kempff entering thoughtfully is able immediately to create rapt inner tension, yet providing the necessary bravura while investing the *Adagio* with characteristic poetry and bringing joyfully articulated vigour to the finale. This version of the concerto is also available at mid-price on a single CD, coupled with Kempff's mono reading of the *Handel variations*, less desirable than the present coupling. In the solo items, mostly recorded in the early 1960s, poetry is emphasized rather than brilliance, and the absence of extrovert virtuosity in Op. 79 does not mean that the music is without a strong impulse. The four *Ballades* emerge very much as a young man's music, full of ardour, as does the *F minor Sonata* which could hardly be warmer or more sympathetic. The *Scherzo in E flat minor* – still comparatively rarely heard – makes a fine encore. We noted at the time of the LP issue that the recording was splendidly full and clear and that the acoustic of the studio seemed just about right.

Piano concerto No. 2 in B flat, Op. 83.
*** Ph. Dig. 432 975-2 [id.]. Brendel, BPO, Abbado.
(BB) **(*) ASV CDQS 6088. John Lill, Hallé O, Loughran.
(B) **(*) Sony SBK 53262; *SBT 53262* [id.]. Rudolf Serkin, Cleveland SO, Szell – R. STRAUSS: *Burleske.* *(**)

(i) *Piano concerto No. 2;* (ii) *Academic festival overture; Tragic overture.*
(M) *** EMI CDM7 63537-2 [id.]. (i) Barenboim, Philh. O; (ii) VPO; Barbirolli.

(i) *Piano concerto No. 2; 4 Ballades, Op. 10.*
(Y/B) (M) *** DG 439 466-2 [id.]. Gilels; (i) BPO, Jochum.

(i) *Piano concerto No. 2. Intermezzi: in E min., Op. 116/5; in B flat min., Op. 117/2; Rhapsody in G min., Op. 79/2.*
(M) *** RCA 09026 61442-2 [id.]. Rubinstein, (i) RCA Victor SO, Krips.

(i) *Piano concerto No. 2. Intermezzo in B flat min., Op. 117/2; in C, Op. 119/3; Rhapsody in G min., Op. 79/ 2.*
(***) Testament mono SBT1042 [id.]. Solomon, (i) Philh. O, Dobrowen.

(i) *Piano concerto No. 2;* (ii) *5 Lieder, Op. 105.*
(Y/B) **(*) EMI Dig. CDC5 55218-2 [id.]. (i–ii) Stephen Kovacevich; (ii) Ann Murray; (i) LPO, Wolfgang Sawallisch.

The partnership of Gilels and Jochum produces music-making of rare magic and the digital remastering has improved definition: the sound is full in an appropriately Brahmsian way. Readers will note that this reissue is now recoupled with the *4 Ballades*, Op. 10 (instead of the *Fantasias*, Op. 116), which seems perverse when the Gilels version of the *First Concerto* has the same coupling.

Brendel's new account of the concerto is massive and concentrated, and has greater depth than his earlier account with Haitink. It is a worthy successor to their *D minor*, though in terms of humanity and wisdom it does not displace the celebrated Gilels–Jochum version.

With Barenboim's reading with Barbirolli, the first two movements remain grandly heroic and the slow movement has something of the awed intensity you find in the middle movement of the *First Concerto*, while the finale erupts gracefully into rib-tickling humour. This is a performance to love in its glowing spontaneity. Of the fill-ups, the *Tragic overture* is a performance of considerable distinction; but the measured account of the *Academic festival overture* could do with more sparkle.

Rubinstein was at his peak in 1958, and his technical mastery brings a charismatic response to the changing moods of the first movement, while the finale is a delight with its deftness of articulation and rippling lyricism. Rubinstein was lucky to have Josef Krips as his collaborator, for he brings a Viennese touch to the orchestra and matches Rubinstein's spontaneity. This is a reading which emphasizes the bright and luminous aspects of the work and is all the more refreshing for that, even if other accounts have more gravitas and weight. The three substantial encores are well chosen to make a miniature (15-minute) solo recital after the concerto; once again, the sound is realistic and the playing distinguished.

The commanding Solomon version of the *B flat Concerto* with Issay Dobrowen and the Philharmonia Orchestra comes from 1947. There is a leonine nobility about this performance and an immediacy, spontaneity and dramatic fire that sweep all before it. Like his *D minor Concerto*, this is a classic account, which no admirer of this artist (or of Brahms, for that matter) should pass over. The piano is not always perfect (the C above the stave is out of tune in one passage) but the pianist is! One soon forgets the sonic limitations and is swept along by the performance.

After his noble and dedicated account of the *First Piano concerto* with Wolfgang Sawallisch and the LPO, Stephen Kovacevich's version of its successor brings admiration tinged with disappointment. Not that his playing is anything other than magisterial; it does not match this partnership's *First*. This does not take wing or catch fire in quite the same way; memories of Gilels and Jochum, still our first recommendation for this concerto, are not displaced. Some have been disappointed with the sound, which will naturally give diverse results in different acoustic environments.

John Lill's 1982 version with the Hallé Orchestra under James Loughran is in many ways a strong account, well thought out, finely paced and without the slightest trace of self-indulgence, and it is the space and power of Brahms's conception that are given priority, rather than his poetry. Not that the performance is wanting in feeling or imagination. There is a stronger sense of the philosopher musing than of the poet dreaming. The recorded sound is eminently well balanced, and in the budget range this is competitive.

Serkin achieves an ideal balance between straightforwardness and expressiveness, while the slow movement has a genuine 'inner' intensity, with some wonderfully expressive playing by the Cleveland principal cellist. Serkin chooses a comparatively slow speed for the finale, but the flow and energy of the music are not impaired and the Hungarian motifs of the second subject sparkle with point and wit. Unfortunately the piano tone is not as full as one would ideally like, but the remastering produces a firm orchestral image and the hall ambience contributes to a Brahmsian sonority.

Violin concerto in D, Op. 77.

(N) *** Decca Dig. 444 811-2 [id.]. Joshua Bell, Cleveland O, Christoph von Dohnányi – SCHUMANN: *Violin concerto.* ***

(M) *** EMI Dig. CD-EMX 2203; *TC-EMX 2203* [id.]. Tasmin Little, RLPO, Handley – SIBELIUS: *Violin concerto.* ***

(Y/B) (M) *** DG Dig. 445 515-2 [id.]. Anne-Sophie Mutter, BPO, Karajan – MENDELSSOHN: *Violin concerto.* ***

*** EMI Dig. CDC7 54580-2 [id.]. Itzhak Perlman, BPO, Barenboim.

*** ASV CDDCA 748 [id.]. Xue-Wei, LPO, Ivor Bolton – MENDELSSOHN: *Violin concerto.* ***

(M) *** RCA 09026 61495-2. Heifetz, Chicago SO, Reiner – TCHAIKOVSKY: *Concerto.* ***

*** Chandos Dig. CHAN 8974 [id.]. Hideko Udagawa, LSO, Mackerras – BRUCH: *Concerto No. 1.* ***

(M) (***) EMI mono CDH7 61011-2. Ginette Neveu, Philh. O, Issay Dobrowen – SIBELIUS: *Concerto.* (***)

(***) Testament mono SBT 1037 [id.]. Johanna Martzy, Philh. O, Kletzki – MENDELSSOHN: *Concerto.* (***)

(***) Testament mono SBT 1038 [id.]. Ida Haendel, LSO, Celibidache – TCHAIKOVSKY: *Concerto.* (***)

**(*) EMI Dig. CDC7 54187-2; *EL 754187-4* [id.]. Nigel Kennedy, LPO, Klaus Tennstedt.

(M) **(*) EMI CDM7 64632-2 [id.]. David Oistrakh, Fr. Nat. RSO, Klemperer – MOZART: *Sinfonia concertante.* **

(N) **(*) EMI Dig. CDC5 55426-2 [id.]. Frank Peter Zimmermann, BPO, Sawallisch – MOZART: *Violin concerto No. 3.* ***

(N) (BB) **(*) RCA/Navigator Dig. 74321 29245-2 [60479-2-TV]. Ughi, Philh. O, Sawallisch – BRUCH: *Violin concerto.* **(*)

(N) ** RCA Dig. 09026 68046-2 [id.]. Pinchas Zukerman, LAPO, Mehta – BRUCH: *Violin concerto No. 1.* **

(**) Pearl mono GEMMCDS 9996 (2) [id.]. Kreisler, Berlin State Op. O, Leo Blech – BACH: *Double violin concerto;* BEETHOVEN; MENDELSSOHN; MOZART: *Violin concertos.* (**)

Joshua Bell is an outstanding young soloist who, though very highly regarded in America, has only just begun to establish himself on this side of the Atlantic. This commanding performance of the Brahms *Concerto* will surely confirm his reputation as a major recording artist. The playing is full of flair, demonstrating not only his love of bravura display, but also his ready gift for turning a phrase individually in a way that catches the ear, always sounding spontaneous. Regularly one registers moments of new magic, not least when, in the most delicate half-tones, pianissimos seem to convey an inner communion.

He rounds the first movement off with his own big cadenza and a magically hushed link into the coda, rapt and intense. The slow movement, sweet and songful, gains too from Bell's love of playing really softly, not least in stratospheric registers. Then in the finale the vein of fantasy is less apparent in a strong but plain reading at a fairly measured tempo. Full, atmospheric recording and a no less outstanding coupling put this among the very finest versions.

Tasmin Little gives a warmly satisfying account of the Brahms, at once brilliant and deeply felt. The rapt poetry she finds in the first two movements has rarely been matched, with powerful bravura set against yearning pianissimos. She also brings an element of fun to the Hungarian dance finale, rarely caught so winningly. Even more than in her earlier recordings, there is a dramatic thrust and intensity that mirrors live communication, strongly matched by the R LPO under Handley. At mid-price the disc is even more recommendable when it also contains an equally searching and exuberant account of the Sibelius *Violin concerto*.

In many ways the playing of Anne-Sophie Mutter combines the unforced lyrical feeling of Krebbers (currently withdrawn) with the flair and individuality of Perlman. There is a lightness of touch, a gentleness in the slow movement that is highly appealing, while in the finale the incisiveness of the solo playing is well displayed by the clear (yet not clinical) digital recording. Needless to say, Karajan's accompaniment is strong in personality and the Berlin Philharmonic play beautifully; the performance represents a genuine musical partnership between youthful inspiration and eager experience. The recording balance places the soloist rather close, but on this newly remastered CD the orchestral sound, while retaining its vivid presence, is smoother on top. The coupling is hardly less attractive.

Perlman's newest digital account of the Brahms finds him at his most commanding, powerful and full of nonchalant flair to a degree that no rival today can quite match. With Perlman the advantage of a live recording is that, as here, there is an extra warmth of commitment, with no sense that the performance has been too easily achieved. There is no fill-up, but few will complain with a reading that is so strong and compelling.

Xue-Wei's version of the Brahms is fresh and well-mannered. There is a degree of emotional reticence here compared with more flamboyant performers but, with Ivor Bolton drawing first-rate playing from the LPO, it is a performance to live with and can be warmly recommended. The sound is first rate too.

Heifetz's performance is both dazzling and enormously stimulating, and the new CD transfer has quite transformed the 1955 recording, making it vivid and fresh instead of harsh, while the excellent qualities of the balance in the warm acoustics of Orchestra Hall come out in full, giving a fine three-dimensional focus. The speeds for all three movements may be fast but Heifetz's ease and detailed imagination make them more than just dazzling, while the central *Andante* at a flowing speed is delectably songful. Recoupled with the Tchaikovsky *Concerto* – a work which Heifetz made his own in the 78-r.p.m. era – this is a reissue not to be missed.

Hideko Udagawa gives a powerful, persuasively spontaneous-sounding reading. Her biting attack on the most taxing passages is often thrilling, even if her violin-sound is not always the sweetest. The personality of the player and her magnetic temperament submerge reservations on detail, particularly when Mackerras draws comparably powerful playing from the LSO. Warm, full and well-balanced recording.

Ginette Neveu's is a magnificent performance, urgently electric, remarkable not just for sweetness of tone and her pinpoint intonation but also for the precision and clarity of even the most formidable passages of double stopping. The transfer from the original 78s brings satisfyingly full-bodied sound, surprisingly good on detail.

Johanna Martzy's warmth of temperament is also ideal. She always sounds spontaneous in her freely flexible rubato which never falls into wilfulness or sentimentality. Hers is an exceptionally warm and persuasive account of the Brahms, marked by a very wide range of dynamic and tone. Few versions of whatever period can match the hushed tenderness of Martzy in the coda of the first movement, and so it is too in the slow movement, while the finale is played with Hungarian point and flair. Kletzki proves an ideal accompanist. The Testament reissue, superbly transferred, ideally coupled with an equally inspired account of the Mendelssohn, at last does justice to a long-underappreciated artist.

With Sergiu Celibidache making a rare appearance as conductor on disc, Ida Haendel, too, gives a powerful, full-toned reading of the Brahms. Recorded in mono in 1953, it comes up very freshly and intensely in this superb CD transfer from Testament, and the clarity and bite of the playing, as well as its strength and nobility, are splendidly caught, confirming the mastery of a great violinist too little heard on disc.

Kennedy's version of the Brahms is by a fair margin the slowest ever put on disc, but Kennedy's musical personality and his devotion to the work give an intensity to sustain all the eccentricities. Tennstedt draws concentrated playing from the LPO, the whole richly recorded.

The conjunction of two such positive artists as Oistrakh and Klemperer makes for a reading characterful to the point of idiosyncrasy, monumental and strong rather than sweetly lyrical. Oistrakh sounds superbly poised and confident, and in the finale, if the tempo is a shade deliberate, the total effect is one of clear gain. The 1961 recording seems smoother than in its most recent incarnation.

Zimmermann's recording is taken from live performances given in the Philharmonie in Berlin, but only in the finale does this add to the lift and imagination of the performance. Until then his clean, direct approach seems a little too well-mannered for such a bravura work, beautiful as the playing is. Well recorded, and coupled with an inspired, quicksilver performance of the Mozart.

Uto Ughi's account has the advantage of a strong and passionate orchestral backing from Sawallisch and first-rate (1983) digital sound, with a good balance. As with the Bruch coupling, this is a fresh and direct reading, not as charismatic as some, but with moments of considerable lyrical intensity and by no means unimaginative in the control of light and shade. In the bargain basement it is well worth considering – and even at mid-price, as issued in the USA.

The big contrast between Pinchas Zukerman's latest readings of these two central masterpieces and those he recorded earlier (the Brahms for DG in Paris in 1979, the Bruch for CBS (Sony) in Los Angeles in 1977) lies in the more natural placing of the violin. Though the earlier recordings may initially seem to pack a weightier punch, the power of Zukerman's playing remains very clear, and the reflective quality in his later interpretations – one of the most striking developments – is all the more intensely conveyed in readings regularly marked by hushed poetry. What is less welcome in the RCA recording is the slight edginess in the solo violin sound, missing the roundness which always used to mark Zukerman's tone on disc. Though Zukerman is more reflective than before, he is also a degree less expansive, more tautly disciplined, with Mehta a rather stiff Brahmsian. A fair recommendation for this apt coupling, though hardly a match for Grumiaux's analogue version coupled on a Philips Duo with the Beethoven, Mendelssohn and Tchaikovsky concertos (see below).

Kreisler's Brahms *Concerto* was made in 1926, and its lyrical fervour and warmth give it a special place in the catalogue. As a performance it rates more stars and rosettes than most versions of the CD era put together, but the untamed surfaces and edgy treble will pose a problem to all but devoted enthusiasts, even though some ears do adjust and, of course, Kreisler's commanding entry silences any criticism. He is very closely balanced indeed and one is tempted to be grateful for that. But it ought to be possible to improve greatly on this transfer with the technical facilities currently available.

Violin concerto (with cadenzas by Busoni, Joachim, Singer, Hermann, Auer, Ysaÿe, Ondricek, Kneisel, Marteau, Kreisler, Tovey, Kubelik, Busch, Heifetz, Milstein, Ricci).
*** Biddulph Dig. LAW 002 [id.]. Ruggiero Ricci, Sinf. of London, Del Mar.

The veteran Ruggiero Ricci not only gives a strong, assured performance of the concerto, he adds no fewer than 16 cadenzas as well, any of which can be programmed into the main performance on CD. Though Ricci is no longer as fiery or incisive as he once was, his is an attractive performance of the concerto, well recorded.

(i) *Violin concerto in D, Op. 77;* (ii) *Double concerto for violin, cello and orchestra in A min., Op. 102.*
(B) **(*) Sony SBK 46335; *SBT 46335* [id.]. Stern, (ii) with Rose; Phd. O, Ormandy.
(N) (M) **(*) Sony Stern Edition I SM2K 66941 (2) [id.]. Isaac Stern, with (i) NYPO, Mehta; (ii) Rose, Phd. O, Ormandy – BEETHOVEN: *Concertos.* **(*)
(N) (M) ** Ph. 446 194-2 [id.]. Henryk Szeryng, (ii) with János Starker; Concg. O, Haitink.

Stern's glorious 1959 account of the *Violin concerto* with Ormandy is now given a coupling that is both generous and suitable, the mid-1960s' collaboration with Leonard Rose in the *Double concerto.* The two soloists unfailingly match each other's playing, with Ormandy always an understanding accompanist.

Once again a wrong choice has been made for the Sony Stern Edition: instead of the above 1959 account of the *Violin concerto* with Ormandy, the later (1978) version has been selected. Here Stern certainly has the measure of the *Violin concerto*'s lyricism and also its rhetoric. There are many thoughtful touches, but the orchestral playing under Mehta is not particularly distinguished; it is a little undercharacterized, and the recording is not in the first flight either. The mid-1960s recording of the *Double concerto* is another matter. Here, each soloist has a creative ear in pointing a comment so that the response is made to sound like an unfolding conversation. The forward balance brings glorious tone, even if this means that there are no pianissimos (although one can tell when they are playing quietly from the tone-colour). The CD transfer is well managed; the sound overall is full and clear.

Szeryng recorded the Brahms *Concerto* three times in stereo. The first (with Monteux on RCA) was the most mercurial. Here he has the advantage of much richer (early-1970s) recording and a superb accompaniment from Haitink, who holds the whole structure spaciously together so that the comparatively slow tempi for the outer movements remain convincing. Szeryng's playing is lyrically passionate and assured, and it communicates strongly: the reading has impressive breadth. However, when Starker joins

Szeryng for the *Double concerto*, the result remains obstinately unmemorable and ultimately disappointing. Although it is not easy to fault any individual detail, the overall impact is not strong. The recording
balances both soloists very closely, though the engineers produce truthful results in other respects.

(i) *Violin concerto in D;* (ii) *Hungarian dances Nos. 1 & 3* (orch. Brahms); *5–6* (orch. Schmedling); (iii; iv)
Symphony No. 4 in E min., Op. 98; (v; iv) *Variations on a theme of Haydn (St Anthony chorale), Op. 56a.*
(Y/B) (BB) *** EMI Seraphim CES5 68526-2 (2) [CDEB 68526]. (i) Sir Yehudi Menuhin, BPO,
    Kempe; (ii) RPO, Kubelik; (iii) New Philh. O; (iv) Giulini; (v) Philh. O.

Reissued in EMI's Seraphim series (two CDs for the cost of one mid-priced disc), Menuhin's recording
from the end of the 1950s can be given the strongest recommendation. He was in superb form, producing tone of great beauty, while the reading is memorable for its warmth and nobility. He was
splendidly accompanied by Kempe, and the sound remains satisfyingly well balanced, and now compares very favourably indeed with any of the top recommendations for this work. Giulini's account of
the *Fourth Symphony* shows him as a typically thoughtful and direct Brahmsian, using measured tempi:
the very opening of the work has a coaxing warmth which is persuasive. The slow movement is beautifully played too, the finale is strong, and the only snag is the relative absence of bloom on the violins,
although the recording itself is full and expansive. The *St Anthony variations* date from 1962 and show
Giulini and the Philharmonia on their very finest form. The recording still sounds well, and this pair of
discs is more than worth its modest cost.

Double concerto for violin, cello and orchestra in A min., Op. 102.
(N) (B) *** EMI forte CZS5 69331-2 (2) [id.]. David Oistrakh, Pierre Fournier, Philh. O, Galliera –
    BEETHOVEN: *Triple concerto;* MOZART: *Violin concerto No. 3;* PROKOFIEV: *Violin concerto No. 2.*
    ***
(M) *** EMI CDM7 64744-2 [id.]. D. Oistrakh, Rostropovich, Cleveland O, Szell – BEETHOVEN: *Triple*
    concerto. ***
*** Sony Dig. MK 42387 [id.]. Isaac Stern, Yo-Yo Ma, Chicago SO, Abbado – *Piano quartet No. 3.* **
(N) (BB) *** Naxos 8.550938 [id.]. Ilya Kaler, Maria Kliegel, Nat. SO of Ireland, Andrew Constantine –
    SCHUMANN: *Cello concerto.* ***
(M) (***) RCA mono 09026 61485-2 [id.]. Milstein, Piatigorsky, Robin Hood Dell O of Philadelphia,
    Reiner – R. STRAUSS: *Don Quixote.* (***)
(N) (M) **(*) Bruno Walter Edition Sony SMK 64479. Francescatti, Fournier, Columbia SO, Walter
    (with BEETHOVEN: (mono) *Triple concerto for piano, violin and cello in C, Op. 56* – Walter Hendl,
    John Corigliano, Leonard Rose, NYPO, Walter *(*)).

David Oistrakh's first stereo account with Fournier dates from 1959, but the recording was balanced by
Walter Legge and the sound is remarkably satisfying. The performance is distinguished, strong and
lyrical – the slow movement particularly fine – and, with Galliera and the Philharmonia providing
excellent support, this version, coupled with three other outstanding concerto recordings, makes an
ideal choice for bargain-hunters.

    This (1969) EMI recording of the *Double concerto* has claims to be regarded with equal esteem as one
of the finest of all versions. The remastered sound is full and vivid and has great presence. If it places the
soloists too far forward, few will grumble when the playing is so ripely, compellingly Brahmsian and the
solo timbres so richly projected. The *Andante* is glorious. Szell's powerful tutti and warmly sympathetic
backing keep the Cleveland Orchestra well in the picture. Coupled with an equally arresting version of
Beethoven's *Triple concerto*, this reissue is a superb bargain of the first order.

    The CBS version with Isaac Stern, Yo-Yo Ma and the Chicago Symphony Orchestra under Claudio
Abbado is one of the more successful of recent years. The balance is well judged and the playing of both
soloists and orchestra alike is glorious. The *Piano quartet* coupling, however, is rather less successful.

    The apt but rare coupling of the Brahms and Schumann concertos is the more attractive for coming on
the Naxos super-budget label in warmly expressive performances, very well recorded. The violinist, Ilya
Kaler (about whom the notes give no background information), is as clean in attack and intonation as is
Maria Kliegel, who firmly established her credentials with her excellent Naxos coupling of the Dvořák
and Elgar *Concertos*. The matching of the two players is first-rate too, not least in the difficult double-
stopped chords for them both together. In the slow movement warmth is conveyed without a hint of
self-indulgence, and the relaxed account of the finale brings plenty of wit.

    The Milstein–Piatigorsky–Reiner account also ranks with the great performances of the *Double con-
certo*. It has warmth, vitality, nobility and power; Reiner gets some fabulous playing from his
Philadelphia Orchestra. It comes with a no less remarkable *Don Quixote* from Piatigorsky which should
not be missed. A very good transfer.

    Bruno Walter's recording with Francescatti and Fournier is welcome back to the catalogue. Fournier is magnificent, and if one adjusts to Francescatti's rather intense vibrato there is much to relish here, not least the playing of the Columbia Symphony Orchestra. The remastering is clear and immediate, and the real snag for most listeners will be the mono sound of the coupling. Walter's soloists make a fine team, but John Corigliano's violin is very near the microphones and is wiry in timbre; although the performance has plenty of vitality, its warmth is minimized by the top-heavy sound-balance.

(i) *Double concerto in A min. for violin, cello and orchestra;* (ii) *Symphony No. 4 in E min.*
(N) (B) (**(*)) Dutton Lab. mono CDEA 5006 [id.]. (i) Jacques Thibaud, Pablo Casals, Pau Casals O, Barcelona, Alfred Cortot; (ii) Dresden State O, Karl Boehm.

The Thibaud/Casals/Cortot recording of the *Double concerto* is a gramophone classic, with superb contributions from all concerned; and Mike Dutton's transfer (from 78 shellac pressings) is worthy of it. Sadly the sound-balance in Boehm's superb 1939 account of the *Fourth Symphony* with the Dresden Staatskapelle sounds less convincing. The focus is admirably clear, but the strings lack body and there is not enough middle and bass (so essential in a Brahms symphony) to balance the clean, bright upper range. Both IM and RL grew up on this performance and still hold it in great esteem, but the results here are comparatively disappointing.

Hungarian dances Nos. 1–21 (complete).
❀ (BB) *** Naxos Dig. 8.550110; *4550110 (Nos. 1–2; 4–21).* Budapest SO, István Bogár.
(N) (B) *** Decca Dig. 448 240-2 [id.]. RPO, Walter Weller (with DVORAK: *Slavonic dances, Op. 46/1–3 & 6–8;* cond. Dorati **(*)).

The Budapest recording of the Brahms *Hungarian dances* is sheer delight from beginning to end. The playing has warmth and sparkle, and the natural way the music unfolds brings a refreshing feeling of rhythmic freedom. Bogár's rubato is wholly spontaneous. The recording is warm and full, yet transparent, with just the right brilliance on top. This is an outright winner among the available versions.

The RPO also play with wonderful spirit, as if they were enjoying every moment, and Walter Weller secures excellent playing from every department of the orchestra. The Kingsway Hall recording is lively and bright, eminently truthful in timbre and with good natural perspective. Moreover the Decca Eclipse reissue offers six *Slavonic dances* from Dvořák's Op. 46 as a considerable bonus. Dorati's performances have comparable *brio*, and the recording (in the same venue) is just as vivid, if not quite so sweet on top.

Hungarian dances Nos. 1–2, 4 & 7.
*** EMI Dig. CDC7 54753-2 [id.]. Sarah Chang, Jonathan Feldman – TCHAIKOVSKY: *Violin concerto.*
***

It may be an ungenerous coupling for the Tchaikovsky *Concerto*, but Chang's performances of four of the Brahms *Hungarian dances* – recorded with Jonathan Feldman in New York – are delectable.

Hungarian dances Nos. 1, 3, 5–6, 17–20.
(N) (M) *** DG 447 434-2 [id.]. BPO, Karajan – DVORAK: *Scherzo capriccioso; 5 Slavonic dances.* **(*)

Karajan's performances have great panache and brilliance. But the brightly lit (1959) recording, reissued in DG's 'Originals' series, is given added fullness in the current remastering, and the superlative orchestral playing is by turns warmly affectionate and dazzling. The coupling offers comparably virtuoso performances of Dvořák's *Slavonic dances* and the *Scherzo capriccioso.*

Hungarian dances Nos. 1, 5–7, 12–13, 19, 21.
(N) (M) **(*) Decca 448 568-2 [id.]. VPO, Fritz Reiner – DVORAK: *Slavonic dances;* R. STRAUSS: *Till Eulenspiegel.* **(*)

Reiner's coupling of Brahms and Dvořák dances was a favourite record of the late John Culshaw, and the 1960 Sofiensaal recording wears its years fairly lightly, although it hasn't the allure of Reiner's Chicago records for RCA. Reiner indulges himself in rubato and effects of his own (witness No. 12), but the affection of the music-making is obvious. For the reissue, a vintage Richard Strauss performance has been added, but this disc would have been more tempting at Eclipse price than in the more expensive 'Classic Sound' series.

Piano quartet in G min. (orch. Schoenberg); *Variations and fugue on a theme by Handel, Op. 24* (orch. Rubbra).
*** Chandos Dig. CHAN 8825 [id.]. LSO, Järvi.

The current craze for Schoenberg's transcription of the Brahms *Piano quartet in G minor* is puzzling. Neeme Järvi's new version with the LSO is as good as any. It is performed with some enthusiasm and well recorded.

Serenades Nos. 1 in D, Op. 11; 2 in A, Op. 16.
(N) (B) **(*) Carlton IMP Dig. PCD 2046 [id.]. West German Sinfonia, Dirk Joeres.

An excellent, digital, bargain CD, coupling two of Brahms's most endearing works. The boisterous first movement of No. 1 with its exuberant horns is very jolly, and the beguilingly warm lyricism of the opening of the *A major* work is equally well conveyed. The orchestral playing is responsive and polished throughout. The resonant acoustic makes textures sound rather ample, but this is a genuine Brahmsian sound; the recording, made by West German Radio in Cologne, is naturally balanced, its richness never congealing. The charming *Rondo* finale of No. 2 brings some neat woodwind articulation, and again the genial horns add to the listener's pleasure.

(i) *Serenades Nos. 1 in D, Op. 11; 2 in A, Op. 16; Academic festival overture;* (ii) *Tragic overture, Op. 81;* (i) *Variations on a theme of Haydn, Op. 56a;* (i, iii) *Alto rhapsody, Op. 53.*
(N) (B) **(*) EMI forte CZS5 68655-2 (2). (i) LPO; (ii) LSO; (iii) with J. Baker, John Alldis Ch.; all cond. Boult.

Sir Adrian Boult's warmly lyrical approach to the two *Serenades* is less ebullient and sparkling than that of Kertész (see below, under *Symphonies*), yet he gives pleasure in a different way. The mellow opening of No. 2 is particularly appealing and with excellent orchestral playing he produces ripe performances, glowing and fresh. His spacious tempi are not always conventional, but Boult's way with these delightful scores is engaging enough to blunt any criticism, when the late-1970s Abbey Road recording is suitably full. What makes this inexpensive forte reissue even more attractive is the inclusion of Dame Janet Baker's devoted account of the *Alto rhapsody*, the performance essentially meditative, even though Boult's style is unlingering and the manner totally unindulgent, supported by warm, Abbey Road sound. The *Academic festival overture* opens the programme in a rather more extrovert fashion, and the *Variations* are also vividly presented and strongly characterized, the sound here rather more lively. The eloquent *Tragic overture* also shows Boult as a true Brahmsian. In playing time (just under two hours), however, this is rather less generous than some forte doubles.

Serenade No. 1 in D, Op. 11.
(Y/B) *** Sony Dig. SK 57973 [id.]. La Scala O, Muti – ELGAR: *In the South.* ***

Muti's reading of the Brahms brings out the fun and beefy good humour over the six movements, but the recording is very good and is well focused, if with a weighty bass and less body given to the high violins. Even so, the rustic quality of many of Brahms's ideas is well caught, with some outstanding wind solo playing, and with Muti giving the central *Adagio*, much the longest movement, a tender expressiveness. A most winning account of this endearing and high-spirited music.

SYMPHONIES

Symphonies Nos. 1–4.
(M) **(*) DG 429 644-2 (3) [id.]. BPO, Karajan.
(Y/B) (B) **(*) RCA Dig. 74321 20283-2 (2). N. German RSO, Günter Wand.

Symphonies Nos 1–4, Hungarian dances Nos. 1, 3 & 10; Variations on a theme of Haydn.
(Y/B) (M) (**(*)) EMI CHS5 65513-2 (3). BPO or VPO, Furtwängler – BEETHOVEN: *Overtures.* (***)

Symphonies Nos. 1–4; Academic festival overture; Tragic overture; Variations on a theme of Haydn, Op. 56a.
**(*) Erato/Warner Dig. 4509 94817-2 (4). Chicago SO, Barenboim.

Symphonies Nos. 1–4; Academic festival overture; Tragic overture; Variations on a theme of Haydn; (i) *Hungarian dances Nos. 17–21.*
(M) **(*) Sony SB3K 48398 (3). Cleveland O, George Szell; (i) Phd. O, Ormandy.

Symphonies Nos. 1–4; Academic festival overture; Tragic overture; Variations on a theme of Haydn, Op. 56a; (i) *Alto rhapsody, Op. 53; Fragment from Goethe's Harz Journey in Winter;* (ii) *Gesang der Parzen (Song of the Fates), Op. 89; Nänie, Op. 82; Schicksalslied, Op. 54.*
*** DG Dig. 435 683-2 (4) [id.]. BPO, Abbado; (i) with Marjana Lipovšek, Ernest Senf Ch.; (ii) Berlin R. Ch.

Symphonies Nos. 1–4; Tragic overture; Variations on a theme of Haydn.
(Y/B) (***) Testament mono/stereo SBT 3054 (3) [id.]. BPO, Rudolf Kempe.
**(*) DG Dig. 427 602-2 (3) [id.]. BPO, Karajan.

(i) *Symphonies Nos. 1–2;* (ii) *Serenade No. 2 in A, Op. 16;* (i) *Variations on a theme by Haydn, Op. 56a.*
(N) (B) **(*) Decca Double 448 197-2 (2) [id.]. (i) VPO; (ii) LSO; Kertész.

(i) *Symphonies Nos. 3–4;* (ii) *Serenade No. 1 in D, Op. 11.*
(N) (B) **(*) Decca Double 448 200-2 (2) [id.]. (i) VPO; (ii) LSO; Kertész.

Abbado's is the most successful of the modern, digital cycles and makes a clear first choice, with playing at once polished and intense, glowingly recorded. Perhaps surprisingly, Abbado proves a more passionate, more romantic Brahmsian than either of his Italian rivals, Muti and Chailly, presenting the warmth of Brahms in full strength, never sentimentally. The set gains from having a generous collection of imaginatively chosen couplings: the rare, brief, choral works, as well as the usual supplements in the overtures and variations.

Kempe's magnetism in Brahms lies very much in his compelling ability to draw out the lyrical warmth of the writing. Like Furtwängler, Kempe is freely expressive, but his freedom is very different, with far less extreme tempo changes. Speeds and timings are often very similar, but results are strikingly different, with Kempe's Brahms above all glowing with warmth and beauty. This conductor also brought great fire to the quicker movements and a tremendous sense of breadth. First and foremost, Kempe has his finger on the natural flow and pulse of these symphonies in a way which calls to mind only the most exalted comparisons. The *First* and *Third* were recorded in 1959 and 1960 in stereo, and are accommodated on the first disc; the *Second* and the *Fourth* (from 1955 and 1956 respectively) are both mono, and the sound is less transparent and fresh – but, ironically, they are at least as vivid and are rather better focused. The *Tragic Overture* is one of the best ever committed to disc. The noble performance of the *St Anthony chorale variations* was never issued in the UK and comes from 1957. The recording venue is the same throughout, the Grünewaldkirche in Berlin. Excellent transfers.

Broadly, Karajan's 1978 cycle shows that his readings of the Brahms *Symphonies*, with lyrical and dramatic elements finely balanced, changed little over the years. The playing of the Berlin Philharmonic remains uniquely cultivated: the ensemble is finely polished, yet can produce tremendous bravura at times. The remastering has freshened the sound: textures are clear and clean. There is less emphasis in the middle frequencies so that the Brahmsian richness is conveyed less readily.

Kertész's Decca cycle was recorded in the Sofiensaal in 1973, except for No. 2, which came nearly a decade earlier (1965). They are straightforward performances, full of affectionate but not fussy detail, with first-class playing from the Vienna Philharmonic and fine recording, lucid yet full-bodied. The CD transfers add digital brightness to the violins, most noticeably in Nos. 2 and 3, both of which include exposition repeats. No. 2 has striking freshness and youthful vigour, and No. 3 also has a fine, direct impetus. All four symphonies are capped with exciting finales, which at a concert would send one home properly exhilarated, and overall the cycle can be be widely recommended, even though in the last analysis the performances are less strongly characterized than Karajan's, though the sound is fuller. No. 4 is perhaps the finest of the cycle, a strong but comparatively serious reading with dignity and grandeur balanced by delicacy and lyricism, the slow movement emerging as a passionate elegy – aptly enough, as this was one of the last recordings the conductor made before his tragic early death. With their natural flow and lack of idiosyncrasy these highly sympathetic readings are easy to live with, and this pair of Double Deccas is made the more attractive by the inclusion of the two still underrated early *Serenades*, which show the conductor at his finest: the first both fresh and warm-hearted; the second, with its autumnal colourings, alert yet at the same time amiably relaxed. The 1977 recording is both excellently balanced and vivid.

As with his companion box of Beethoven symphonies, Günter Wand's Brahms set, now reissued on a pair of CDs, is highly recommendable for providing spontaneously compelling readings of all four works, very well played. The snag is that the early digital recording (1982/3) brings a degree of fierceness on violin tone in all but No. 2 and verges on shrillness in No. 3. Wand's is a consistently direct view of Brahms, yet the reading of each symphony has its own individuality. In the *First* the extra unity is clear and the performance is made convincing by its spontaneity. Even though he does not observe the exposition repeat, Wand's reading of the *Second* is the pick of his Brahms series, a characteristically glowing but steady reading, recorded with a fullness and bloom that are missing in the companion issues. His unsensational approach exactly matches this sunniest of symphonies. In the *Third Symphony* Wand does observe the exposition repeat and his wise way with Brahms, strong and easy and steadily paced, works beautifully here, bringing out the autumnal moods, ending with a sober view of the finale. By contrast, the reading of No. 4 initially seems understated. At a fastish speed, the first movement is melancholy rather than tragic, while the slow movement, similarly steady and flowing, makes no great expansion for the big melody of the counter-subject. It is quite a strong reading and, though the recording is less than ideally clear, it provides a generally satisfying culmination to an inexpensive modern set of the four symphonies and is well worth considering. As we go to press, Wand's recordings have been made available separately at mid-price: *Symphonies Nos. 1 and 3* (74321 20284-2); *Symphonies Nos. 2 and 4* (74321 20285-2).

Szell's powerful view of Brahms is consistently revealed in this masterful series of performances, recorded in the 1960s when he had made the Cleveland Orchestra America's finest. His approach is generally plain and direct, crisp and detached rather than smooth and moulded. Speeds are broad, and in the manner of the time no exposition repeats are observed, not even in No. 3. Though the sound, as transferred, is not as full as on the original LPs, it is clear and bright, with superb detail.

With variably focused sound, Karajan's last cycle of the Brahms *Symphonies* is not his finest; but he remained a natural Brahmsian to the last, and this compilation, with Nos. 2 and 3 on the second disc, and No. 4 coupled with the *Variations*, makes a better investment than the original issues, for those who must have digital sound. However, this set is at full price.

Barenboim dons his Furtwänglerian mantle for his Erato accounts of the first two symphonies which, though very well played, suffer from his wilful flexibility and eccentric structural control: at one point in the finale of the *First Symphony*, the great Chicago orchestra is very nearly brought to a dead stop but subsequently recovers to end the work very positively. Barenboim's inspirational volatility works well in the *Third Symphony*, which does not lose its ongoing purpose and brings beautiful orchestral playing in the central movements. No. 4 is finest of all, a highly concentrated interpretation that moves forward powerfully; even though the tempo for the *Andante* is slow, it is ardently presented and capped by a gripping performance of the closing *Passacaglia*.

Furtwängler's EMI compilation brings together the studio recording of the *First Symphony* that he made with the Vienna Philharmonic in 1949 and live recordings of the remaining three symphonies made with the Berlin Philharmonic in 1948 and 1952, presumably taken from radio sources. The sound is disappointingly thin, lacking in body and with some harshness in the live recordings; but the electricity of Furtwängler in Brahms is vividly captured. His freedom of expression, with speeds varied far more extremely than by any latterday conductor, is essentially a spontaneous style, however carefully planned. Far from making the symphonies seem rhapsodic, with structure undermined, the results are totally cohesive, thanks also to Furtwängler's magnetic concentration. Though his moulding of phrase is affectionate, with rubato freely used (rather more than tenuto), these are not performances that set Brahmsian lyricism above drama. Despite the limitations of the sound, lacking in body but with plenty of detail, and despite the bronchial audiences in Nos. 2, 3 and 4, this is an inspirational set, with the makeweights an added attraction.

Symphonies Nos. 1–4; Academic festival overture; (i) *Double concerto in A min., Op. 102. Hungarian dances Nos. 1, 17, 20 & 21; Tragic overture; Variations on a theme of Haydn;* (ii) *Liebeslieder-Walzer, Op. 52;* (iii) *Song of the Fates (Gesang der Parzen). Op. 89.*
(M) (*(**)) RCA mono GD 60325; *GK 60325* (4) [60325-2-RG; *60325-4-RG*]. NBC SO, Toscanini, with (i) Mischakoff, Miller; (ii) Ch., Artur Balsam, Joseph Kahn; (iii) (without O) Robert Shaw Ch.

The *First Symphony* starts very fast and intensely; but often speeds are surprisingly broad, and the *Fourth Symphony*, Toscanini's favourite, brings a magnificent performance. The soloists in the *Double concerto* were principals in the NBC orchestra, even though Toscanini allowed them less expressive freedom than they really needed. The CD transfers do everything possible for the dry and limited original sound.

Symphony No. 1 in C min., Op. 68.
(Y/B) (M) *** DG 447 408-2 [id.]. BPO, Karajan – SCHUMANN: *Symphony No. 1.* ***
(B) *** DG 431 161-2 [id.]. BPO, Karajan – SCHUMANN: *Overture, Scherzo and Finale.* ***
(BB) **(*) ASV Dig. CDQS 6101. RLPO, Marek Janowski.
(Y/B) **(*) Decca Dig. 436 289-2 [id.]. Cleveland O, Ashkenazy (with DVORAK: *Othello* **(*)).

Symphony No. 1; Academic festival overture, Op. 80.
(Y/B) (M) *** Carlton Dig. PCD 2014 [id.]. Hallé O, Skrowaczewski.

Symphony No. 1; Academic festival overture; Tragic overture.
(M) *** EMI CDM7 69651-2 [id.]. Philh. O, Klemperer.

Symphony No. 1; Academic festival overture; Variations on a theme of Haydn, Op. 56a.
(N) (M) **(*) Bruno Walter Edition Sony SMK 64470 [id.]. Columbia SO, Walter.

Symphony No. 1; Serenade No. 2 in A, Op. 16.
(M) (**) RCA mono GD 60277 [60277-2-RG]. NBC SO, Toscanini.

Symphony No. 1 in C min.; Variations on a theme of Haydn, Op. 56a.
*** EMI Dig. CDC7 54286-2 [id.]. L.Classical Players, Norrington.

(i) *Symphony No. 1; Variations on a theme of Haydn;* (ii) *Hungarian dances Nos. 17–21.*
(B) **(*) Sony SBK 46534; *SBT 46534* [id.]. (i) Cleveland O, Szell; (ii) Phd. O, Ormandy.

Symphony No. 1; (i) *Gesang der Parzen (Song of the Fates), Op. 89.*
*** DG Dig. 431 790-2 [id.]. BPO, Abbado, (i) with Berlin R. Ch.

After a spacious introduction, Abbado launches into a warm, dramatic reading, rhythmically well sprung and finely shaded, with the full power of the great dramatic climaxes brought out in the finale, from the rapt pianissimo of the opening onwards. The *Gesang der Parzen* makes an unusual and warmly attractive coupling, very well sung. A clear first choice.

Karajan's 1964 recording of Brahms's *First Symphony* (the conductor's third version of five – DG 447 408-2) seems by general consensus to be regarded as his finest. The control of tension in the first movement is masterly, the orchestral playing is of superlative quality and the result is very powerful, with the finale a fitting culmination. The remastering has restored the original full, well-balanced, analogue sound, with plenty of weight in the bass (as is obvious at the timpani-dominated opening), yet detail is firmer. The coupling with Schumann's *First Symphony* makes this a very desirable record indeed – an obvious candidate for inclusion in DG's set of legendary 'Originals'.

Klemperer's spacious opening with its thundering, relentless timpani strokes is as compelling as ever and the close of the work has a comparable majesty; and the reading remains unique for its feeling of authority and power, supported by consistently fine Philharmonia playing. The remastered sound has gained in clarity while retaining its fullness.

Karajan's 1978 analogue recording – his fourth (DG 431 161–2) – is also highly recommendable, especially at bargain price and now with its present Schumann coupling, and the sound is still remarkably good.

Walter's set of the Brahms symphonies now returns to the catalogue in the second box of Sony's 'Bruno Walter Edition' (see below), but each disc is available separately. The recordings have been carefully remastered to emerge clearer than before but with very slight loss of bloom on the high violins; otherwise the sound is full and well balanced. Walter's first two movements of the *First Symphony* have a white-hot intensity that shows this conductor at his very finest: he conveys the architecture of the first movement strongly; the second movement too is most impressive, warm and with natural, unforced phrasing. The third movement begins with a less than ravishing clarinet solo and, though the 6/8 section is lively enough, the playing is not as crisp as in the first two movements. In the finale the performance reasserts itself, although some might find the big string tune too slow. The performance of the *Variations* is relaxed and smiling, and the genial account of the *Academic festival overture* gains from the extra brightness on top.

Skrowaczewski conducts the Hallé in a powerful performance of No. 1, both warmly sympathetic and refined, with sound which is fresh, bright and clear and with a good, open atmosphere. The first movement is ideally paced, but without the exposition repeat. His view of the finale is big and bold, but with a rather old-fashioned slowing for the final appearance of the chorale theme in the coda. Nevertheless it makes an excellent bargain-price digital choice.

Norrington takes the opening introduction surprisingly fast – rather as Toscanini used to – but then adopts a relaxed tempo for the main *Allegro*, making it easy and bouncy rather than dramatic. More characteristically, he then adopts a flowing speed for the *Andante*, and in the finale the natural horn and dry timpani add to the dramatic impact. A very good recommendation, well coupled, if a period performance is wanted.

Szell's account of No. 1 is one of the most impressive of his set. His bold, direct thrust gives the outer movements plenty of power and impetus, and the inner movements bring relaxation and a fair degree of warmth.

Janowski's plain yet sympathetic reading is greatly enhanced on a CD which is full-bodied, clearly detailed and well balanced. The added fullness is much more flattering to the orchestral timbres and makes a very satisfying sound overall. Janowski, unlike most, does observe the exposition repeat in the first movement. At super-bargain price, this is excellent value.

Ashkenazy, with full, weighty recording of an exceptionally rich and resonant orchestra, gives a strong, warmly expressive reading, with no self-indulgence. If the slow movement lacks a little in hushed intensity, the freshness of the rest compensates, and the disc could be considered by anyone fancying the unusual Dvořák coupling, equally well played and recorded.

The *First Symphony* is the performance Toscanini recorded in Carnegie Hall during 1941. It differs from the version he made ten years later with the same orchestra in the greater breadth of the first movement allegro, and in the tenderness he shows in the *Andante*, which at the same time remains completely unsentimental. The sound is not at all bad for the period. There is however little one can do with the 1942 broadcast – made in Studio 8-H – of the *Serenade*. The performance, too, is held together on a tight rein and sounds unrelaxed.

Symphony No. 2 in D, Op. 73.
(M) *** DG 435 067-2 [id.]. BPO, Karajan – SCHUMANN: *Symphony No. 2.* ***
(***) Testament mono SBT 1015 [id.]. BBC SO, Toscanini (with MENDELSSOHN: *Midsummer Night's Dream:* excerpt; ROSSINI: *Semiramide: Overture* ***).
**(*) DG Dig. 435 348-2 [id.]. VPO, Giulini.

Symphony No. 2; Tragic overture.
**(*) EMI Dig. CDC7 54875-2 [id.]. L. Classical Players, Norrington.
**(*) Ph. Dig. 432 094-2 [id.]. Boston SO, Haitink.
(BB) **(*) ASV Dig. CDQS 6102. RLPO, Marek Janowski.

Symphony No. 2; Variations on a theme of Haydn, Op. 56a.
*** DG Dig. 423 142-2 [id.]. BPO, Karajan.

Symphony No. 2; (i) Alto rhapsody, Op. 53.
*** DG Dig. 427 643-2 [id.]. (i) Lipovšek, Senff Ch.; BPO, Abbado.
(M) *** EMI CDM7 69650-2 [id.]. (i) Ludwig, Philh. Ch.; Philh. O, Klemperer.

Among modern versions Abbado's now stands as an easy first choice, particularly when, with Marjana Lipovšek a radiant soloist, it also contains a gravely beautiful account of the *Alto rhapsody*. Abbado's approach to Brahms is generally direct, but his control of rhythm and phrase makes the performance instantly compelling. He observes the exposition repeat in the first movement, while in the finale, through his rhythmic control, Abbado makes a relatively measured speed sound much more exciting than it does with any of the speed-merchants. This is an outstanding version in every way.

Karajan's 1978 reading (DG 435 067-2) is more direct, less mellow than the 1964 account – see below – and this is most striking in the third movement. The finale has even more impetus than before, its brilliant pacing challenging the Berliners to exciting virtuosity. Some will prefer the earlier version, but the coupling with Schumann is very generous.

Karajan's digital reading of the *Second Symphony* suffers less than the *First* from the thick, undifferentiated recording. It is a magnificent reading, even warmer and more glowing than his previous versions, with consistently fine playing from the Berlin Philharmonic, who approach with striking freshness a symphony which they must have played countless times. As in the *First Symphony*, Karajan omits the first-movement exposition repeat, but compensates with an appealing performance of the *Haydn variations*.

Klemperer's is also a great performance, the product of a strong and vital intelligence. He may seem a trifle severe and uncompromising, but he was at his peak in his Brahms cycle and he underlines the power of the *Symphony* without diminishing its eloquence in any way. The *Alto rhapsody*, with Klemperer at his most masterful and Ludwig on fine form, is a beautifully expressive performance. Ludwig sings gloriously in the opening section, and later her voice blends naturally with the male chorus.

Toscanini's account with the BBC Symphony Orchestra on Testament, recorded in 1938, will come as a revelation to those who view the legendary Italian as a hard-driving, demonic maestro. Tempi are relaxed, the first movement is unhurried and the mood is sunny and smiling. There is none of the hard-driven momentum and over-drilled intensity that marked his final, NBC version. Gratitude is in order that this performance has been rescued for posterity: the sound calls for tolerance but the playing is worth it.

Norrington, with his London Classical Players presenting leaner textures than usual, takes a clean, direct view, adopting speeds on the fast side in all four movements. He misses some of the work's charm but consistently makes it sound fresh and bright. A fair recommendation if you need a period performance.

Haitink directs a strong, steady reading, in which the rapt pianissimos convey tension quite as much as the dramatic outbursts. That is partly the result of the Boston sound, generally warm and full, which yet does not expand in richness for climaxes.

Janowski's plain style is least convincing in this most lyrical of symphonies, with rhythms tending to sound too rigid, whether in his metrical view of the slow movement or the rather charmless account of the third. The overture is much more successful, and the digital recording is excellently balanced: this is certainly worth considering at its super-bargain price.

Giulini takes an exceptionally spacious view of the *Second*, understandably preferring not to observe the exposition repeat in the first movement, which in his hands becomes very long, even without it. The weight and warmth of Giulini's approach go with ripe and resonant playing from the Vienna Philharmonic, richly recorded. Yet such an approach misses some of the charm of this fundamentally lyrical work.

Symphonies Nos. 2–3.
(N) (M) *** Bruno Walter Edition Sony SMK 64471 [id.]. Columbia SO, Walter.
(B) *** DG 429 153-2 [id.]. BPO, Karajan.
(N) (B) *** Sony SBK 47652; *SBT 47652* [id.]. Cleveland O, George Szell.
(M) **(*) Ph. 426 632-2. Concg. O, Haitink.

The new Bruno Walter coupling of the *Second and Third Symphonies* is very recommendable indeed. Walter's performance of the *Second* is wonderfully sympathetic, with an inevitability, a rightness which makes it hard to concentrate on the interpretation as such, so cogent is the musical argument. As though to balance the romanticism of his approach on detail, Walter keeps his basic speeds surprisingly constant, yet little of the passion is lost in consequence. It is a masterly conception overall and one very easy to live with. Walter's pacing of the *Third* is admirable and the vigour and sense of joy which imbues the opening of the first movement (exposition repeat included) dominates throughout, with the second subject eased in with wonderful naturalness. The central movements provide contrast, though with an intense middle section in II. There is beautifully phrased string and horn playing in the *Poco Allegretto*. The finale goes splendidly, the secondary theme given characteristic breadth and dignity, and the softening of mood for the coda sounding structurally inevitable. The upper strings are brighter than before, and at times (most noticeably in the opening movement of the *Third*) they sound thinner on top than in previous incarnations; on the other hand there is an added bite, and the ambient warmth and glowing woodwind remain, while there is plenty of supporting weight.

Karajan's 1964 reading of the *Second* is among the sunniest and most lyrical accounts, and its sound is competitive even now. The companion performance of the *Third* is marginally less compelling, but still very fine. He takes the opening expansively and omits the exposition repeat. But clearly he sees the work as a whole: the third movement is also slow and perhaps slightly indulgent, but the closing pages of the finale have a memorable autumnal serenity. A bargain.

With the Cleveland Orchestra at its peak and on its toes throughout, this is an inexpensive reissue that should be in every comprehensive Brahms collection. The Severance recordings have been improved immeasurably in the remastering for CD and, although the *Second* (1967) is smoother than the *Third* (1964), that works well, for the latter is well served by the brighter lighting. When the *Second* first appeared we were unimpressed by 'the characteristic Cleveland recording quality' and found that its unexpansiveness helped to give the feeling 'that Brahms's heart is being encased in a precision-made casket'. That impression all but disappears now. The orchestral virtuosity remains and at times Szell's care for detail does become predominant, but the underlying ardour and warmth are in no doubt, especially in the *Adagio*, while the *Allegretto grazioso* has an appealing simplicity. The *Third* is a magnificent performance. Szell had recorded it in mono previously for Decca with the Concertgebouw Orchestra, and the extra polish of the Cleveland players in no way detracted from a sense of committedness in the new interpretation. Szell is dashing and heroic at the opening, then slows very unselfconsciously for the lyrical second subject, neatly dovetailing speed-changes so that the casual listener will hardly notice them. The slow movement is very much on the slow side, warmly lyrical and full of expressive emotion. So is the lovely third movement – no reserve here, rather heartbreaking romantic nostalgia. The finale brings the expected return to the dashing, dramatic approach, and overall this is a reading to set alongside that of Bruno Walter, even if (as in the *Second Symphony*), the exposition repeat is omitted.

Haitink's account of No. 2 opens soberly. The sunshine quickly breaks through, however, so that the gentle high entry of the violins is magically sweet. This is a thoughtful reading, marked by beautifully refined string playing, but in a way it is too controlled. The *Third* is much more impressive, and Haitink's firmness of grip and lyrical eloquence make this a very satisfying account. The sound is fresh yet full in the Philips manner.

Symphony No. 3 in F, Op. 90.
(Y/B) (M) *** RCA 09026 61793-2 [id.]. Chicago SO, Fritz Reiner – SCHUBERT: *Symphony No. 5.* ***

Symphony No. 3; Tragic overture; (i) Song of Destiny (Schicksalslied), Op. 54.
*** DG Dig. 429 765-2 [id.]. BPO, Abbado; (i) with Ernest Senff Ch.

Symphony No. 3; Variations on a theme of Haydn, Op. 56a.
*** DG Dig. 431 681-2 [id.]. VPO, Carlo Maria Giulini.
*** Erato/Warner Dig. 4509 95193-2 [id.]. Chicago SO, Daniel Barenboim.
(N) (M) *** Carlton IMP Dig. PCD 2039 [id.]. Hallé O, Scrowaczewski.
(BB) *** ASV Dig. CDQS 6103. RLPO, Marek Janowski.
(Y/B) **(*) Decca Dig. 433 548-2 [id.]. Cleveland O, Ashkenazy (with DVORAK: *Carnival overture* ***).

Symphony No. 3; (i) *Alto rhapsody, Op. 53.*
(Y/B) **(*) Ph. Dig. 442 120-2 [id.]. (i) Jard van Nes, Tanglewood Festival Ch.; Boston SO, Haitink.

Abbado directs a glowing, affectionate performance of No. 3, adopting generally spacious speeds and finely moulded phrasing but never sounding self-conscious, thanks to the natural tension which gives the illusion of live, spontaneous music-making. The rich, well-balanced, clean-textured recording underlines the big dramatic contrasts. This now heads the list of modern digital recordings of this symphony.

Reiner's magnificent performance dates from 1956. It is a glowing, marvellously proportioned account, exposition repeat included, and prepared in masterly fashion, and with the close of the work given a touchingly gentle, valedictory feeling. Yet there is no want of momentum in the outer movements and the lyrical intensity and warmth in the slow movement are equally memorable. Here the Chicago ambience adds to the atmosphere and it is a pity that in tuttis there is some loss of refinement in the upper strings. This has been improved in the CD transfer and this is a reading of stature. Besides the estimable Schubert coupling there is an exciting account of Mendelssohn's *Fingal's Cave overture.*

In the *Third Symphony* Giulini is recorded live. The speeds, though on the expansive side, are not so extreme, with the finale no slower than in many other versions. The result is a big-scaled, powerful reading, marked by ripe, resonant playing, given full and satisfying sound. The second-movement *Andante* is particularly beautiful. The *Variations* are similarly expansive and compelling, a welcome coupling.

Barenboim's volatile approach works well in the *Third Symphony* and, although there must be some minor reservations about his freely spacious treatment of both central movements, they are beautifully played and warmly lyrical. The first movement (exposition repeat very much part of the interpretation) has plenty of power and glowing lyrical feeling, ensuring that Barenboim's flexible style is convincing. The finale has exciting thrust and the valedictory ending is managed most sensitively. The *Variations*, too, are full of imaginative touches. Fine, committed orchestral playing and richly expansive sound suit the nature of the interpretation.

Skrowaczewski chooses consistently slow tempi for the central movements, yet with refined playing there is no hint of dragging. In the third movement he underlines the tender wistfulness, with a gorgeous horn solo in the reprise, full and spacious. The hush at the start of the finale then leads to a powerfully rhythmic performance, ending with a most refined account of the gentle coda. An excellent digital lower mid-price version, well coupled with a fresh reading of the *Haydn variations.*

The *Third* is the finest of Janowski's Brahms cycle, with surging outer movements (exposition repeat included) and the central *Andante* and *Poco allegretto* given an appealing, unforced Brahmsian lyricism. An exciting and satisfying performance, given bright, full, digital sound, not absolutely refined on top. The *Variations* also have plenty of impetus and are strongly characterized. In its price-range this is very recommendable.

The weight and resonance of the Cleveland Orchestra as recorded by the Decca engineers helps to make Ashkenazy's version a competitive one for anyone who fancies the coupling, not just the *Haydn Variations* but with the Dvořák overture as an extra. In the *Symphony* Ashkenazy takes a direct view, characteristically fresh and lacking in mannerism but with plenty of dramatic tension, helped by clean, incisive playing.

Beautifully moulded and refined, Haitink's recording of the *Third Symphony* is impressive in its directness and want of any kind of artifice. Here is Brahms pure and simple, the music left to speak for itself. Haitink draws playing of exemplary culture from the Boston orchestra, and the Philips recording is judiciously balanced and truthful. Some may feel that the first movement in particular could be more urgent in feeling; although there have been more highly charged accounts from Kempe and Walter, this is an eminently sane and civilized performance. However, the *Alto rhapsody* is an exceptionally broad account which is better played than it is sung; Jard van Nes has too wide a vibrato.

Symphonies Nos. (i) *3 in F, Op. 90;* (ii) *4 in E min., Op. 98.*
(M) *** EMI CDM7 69649-2 [id.]. Philh. O, Klemperer.
(M) *** DG 437 645-2 [id.]. BPO, Karajan.
(M) **(*) Teldec/Warner Dig. 4509 92144-2 [id.]. Cleveland O, Dohnányi.

In No. 3, there is a severity about Klemperer's approach which may at first seem unappealing but which comes to underline the strength of the architecture. Similarly in No. 4, Klemperer's granite strength and his feeling for Brahmsian lyricism make his version one of the most satisfying ever recorded. The finale may lack something in sheer excitement, but the gravity of Klemperer's tone of voice, natural and unforced in this movement as in the others, makes for a compelling result.

In his 1978 recording Karajan gives superb grandeur to the opening of the *Third Symphony* but then characteristically refuses to observe the exposition repeat. Comparing this reading with Karajan's earlier, 1964 version (coupled with No. 2), one finds him more direct and strikingly more dynamic and compelling. In the *Fourth Symphony* Karajan refuses to overstate the first movement, starting with deceptive reticence. His easy, lyrical style, less moulded in this 1978 reading than in his 1964 account, is fresh and unaffected and highly persuasive. The scherzo, fierce and strong, leads to a clean, weighty account of the finale.

Those for whom quality of sound is of the highest consideration will certainly find Dohnányi's mid-priced Cleveland coupling tempting. The performances are clean and direct and superbly played. The fine tonal blend and balance in the *Third* means that the often thick orchestration is made clear as well as naturally weighty in a version which (exposition repeat included) emphasizes classical values. In the second-movement *Andante*, taken on the slow side, Dohnányi does not entirely avoid squareness and, although the third-movement *Allegretto* flows warmly, the horn reprise of the main theme is forthright rather than affectionate. The opening of the finale lacks mystery and the hemiola rhythms of the second subject, for all the power of the performance, fail to leap aloft. These detailed criticisms are given merely to suggest why, with such superlative playing and an irreproachably direct manner, the result finally lacks something in Brahmsian magic. The *Fourth* opens simply and seductively, a strong and finely controlled reading, lacking only occasionally in a flow of adrenalin. The slow movement is hushed and thoughtful, the third clear and fresh in its crisp articulation, while the weight of the finale is well caught – even if it is not thrust home at the close as sharply as it might be.

Symphony No. 4 in E min., Op. 98.
**(*) DG Dig. 400 037-2 [id.]. VPO, Carlos Kleiber.
(*) Decca Dig. 433 151-2 [id.]. Concg. O, Chailly – SCHOENBERG: *5 Orchestral pieces.* *
(Y/B) (BB) **(*) BBC Radio Classics BBCRD 9107 [id.]. New Philh. O, Stokowski (with Concert) –
   VAUGHAN WILLIAMS: *Tallis Fantasy;* RAVEL: *Rapsodie espagnole.* **(*)

Symphony No. 4; Hungarian dances Nos. 1, 3 & 10.
(N) (M) *** Carlton Dig. 30367 00272 [id.]. Hallé O, Skrowaczewski.

Symphony No. 4; Academic festival overture.
*** Erato/Warner 4509 95194-2 [id.]. Chicago SO, Barenboim.
(M) *** Telarc Dig. CD 82006 [id.]. RPO, Previn.
(BB) **(*) ASV Dig. CDQS 6104. RLPO, Marek Janowski.

Symphony No 4; Tragic overture, Op. 81.
*** DG Dig. 429 403-2 [id.]. VPO, Giulini.
(Y/B) (M) *** DG Dig. 445 508-2 [id.]. VPO, Bernstein.

Symphony No. 4; Tragic overture; (i) *Song of Destiny (Schicksalslied), Op. 54.*
(N) (M) *** Bruno Walter Edition Sony SMK 64472 [id.]. Columbia SO, Walter, (i) with Occidental
   College Concert Ch.

Symphony No. 4; Variations on a theme by Haydn, Op. 56a.
(N) (BB) **(*) RCA/Navigator 74321 24206-2. Dresden State O, Kurt Sanderling.

Symphony No. 4; Variations on a theme of Haydn; (i) *Nänie, Op. 82.*
*** DG Dig. 435 349-2 [id.]. BPO, Abbado, (i) with Berlin R. Ch.

Abbado rounds off his outstanding series with an incandescent performance of the *Fourth*, marked by strong, dramatic contrasts and finely moulded phrasing. The coupling is exceptionally generous, not just the *Haydn variations* but the rare choral piece to words by Schiller, *Nänie*.

Barenboim's Chicago reading is grippingly compulsive. He opens the first movement gently and affectionately, but the performance soon develops a compulsive lyrical power. Barenboim takes the *Andante* more slowly than marked but, with a richly ardent response from the Chicago strings, the result is eloquently convincing, with much refined orchestral detail. After an excitingly ebullient Scherzo, the finale sets off with a powerful thrust that carries through to the final bar, though Barenboim's flexible style prevents any feeling of rigidity. There is a tremendous burst of energy in the coda to make the *Passacaglia*'s final apotheosis very gripping indeed. The *Academic festival overture* is unusually expansive, bringing superb playing from the Chicago brass. Throughout the sound is suitably full-bodied within the aptly resonant acoustics of Chicago's Orchestra Hall.

As the delicate opening demonstrates, Giulini's affectionate control of line completely disguises any slowness, and in the development the big, dramatic fortissimo contrasts bring a rugged manner, equally compelling. The great melody of the slow movement is rapt and refined as well as warm, and the last two movements bring satisfyingly extreme contrasts of tension and dynamic, helped by the rich and refined recording. The *Tragic overture* is given a similarly spacious and affectionate reading.

Walter's opening is simple, even gentle, and the pervading lyricism is immediately apparent; yet power and authority are underlying. The conductor's refusal to linger by a wayside always painted in gently glowing colours adds strength and impetus, building up to an exciting coda, the unanimity and cutting edge of the strings bringing a cumulative effect. A beautifully moulded slow movement, intense at its central climax, is balanced by a vivacious, exhilarating Scherzo. The finale has an underlying impetus so that Walter is able to relax for the slow middle section. The new transfer is very successful: the recording has never sounded fresher or warmer and there is plenty of necessary weight in the bass. The *Tragic overture* has characteristic breadth and vigour, while the *Song of destiny*, both warm and dramatic, displays the capability of the chorus to good effect. The recording is excellent.

Bernstein's 1981 Vienna version of Brahms's *Fourth*, recorded live, is exhilaratingly dramatic in fast music, while the slow movement brings richly resonant playing from the Vienna strings, not least in the great cello melody at bar 41, which with its moulded rubato comes to sound surprisingly like Elgar. This is easily the finest of Bernstein's Vienna cycle and, with generally good sound, is well worth considering.

There is a Boultian directness about the opening of Previn's account, fresh and alert, which immediately commands attention, helped by naturally balanced Telarc sound, just a little distanced. The finale is similarly strong and energetic, well drawn together; only in the bold third movement does the distancing detract from the impact of the performance, while allowing some clouding of inner detail. With a good – if hardly generous – coupling and now reissued on Telarc's Bravo! mid-priced label, it is one of the best of the modern digital versions.

The refinement of the very opening in Skrowaczewski's Carlton version leads to an exceptionally satisfying reading, outstanding in the lower mid-price range and finer than many full-price versions. The phrasing is affectionate without ever sounding self-conscious, and the alertness as well as the refinement of the Hallé playing confirms the excellence; if the coupling of only three *Hungarian dances* is hardly generous, they are certainly attractively presented.

Any record from Carlos Kleiber is an event, and his is a performance of real stature. Everything is shaped with the attention to detail one would expect from this great conductor. A gripping and compelling performance. However, the limitations of the early digital recording are exposed here. The strings above the stave sound a little shrill and glassy, while there is a want of opulence in the bass.

Part of a live concert, recorded at the Royal Albert Hall in May 1974, Stokowski's is a masterly reading of pretty high voltage, with notably fast tempi in outer movements but never sounding hurried; he pulls back, as he always did, just before the end of the exposition of the first movement but, generally speaking, this is pretty free from exaggeration. The playing has you sitting on the edge of your seat. Even if at times ensemble could be more precise, the performance is thrilling with the New Philharmonia playing with great eloquence. There is intrusive applause at the end of the first movement (over the last chord); the recording is inclined to be opaque and it is a pity that the reverberant acoustic has necessitated close microphones, which are not entirely flattering to the violins. All the same, this is a disc well worth investigating in this new series from the BBC's archives.

Sanderling's super-bargain Dresden version has genuine fire and eloquence. It is finely recorded (in 1971), beautifully played and splendidly shaped, with some of the classical strength that distinguished this orchestra's account of the work under Karl Boehm in the days of 78s. However, it has a warmth and sense of enjoyment that make it a very rewarding performance indeed, and the *Variations* are also very successful. The warmth of the Dresden acoustic means that the quality remains pleasingly full, although the violins sound a little thin on top.

Following the success of the *Third*, Janowski gives a refreshingly direct reading of the *Fourth*. Speeds are unexceptionable, with the second-movement *Andante*, introduced very gently, slower than usual, but certainly expressive. The recording sounds vivid and full on CD and the weight of the final *Passacaglia* is well established. The coda of the symphony, like the overture which follows, brings real excitement.

Variations on a theme of Haydn, Op. 56a.
(N) **(*) Decca Dig. 444 458-2 [id.]. Carnegie Hall Project O, Solti – SHOSTAKOVICH: *Symphony No. 9* **(*); R. STRAUSS: *Don Juan* *** (with Concert **(*)).
** Teldec/Warner Dig. 9031 74007-2 [id.]. NYPO, Masur – IVES: *Variations on America;* REGER: *Variations and fugue on a theme of Mozart.* **

This Decca recording was made at the end of a special workshop in which gifted instrumentalists were assembled in Carnegie Hall and given the opportunity to work with Sir Georg Solti. Generally speaking the playing is very good and the result is undoubtedly tingling fresh, but Sir Georg keeps things on a fairly taut rein and some will prefer a more relaxed approach.

The *St Antoni Chorale variations* find Kurt Masur in a leisurely mood. Some collectors may want them to move on just a little more. This is a cultured, measured and judicious reading, and it is pleasing to find the New York Philharmonic playing with greater refinement and subtlety than they have for many years. A valid reading, but not a front-runner perhaps.

CHAMBER MUSIC

Cello sonatas Nos. 1 in E min., Op. 38; 2 in F, Op. 99.
*** DG Dig. 410 510-2 [id.]. Mstislav Rostropovich, Rudolf Serkin.
*** Hyperion Dig. CDA 66159 [id.]. Steven Isserlis, Peter Evans.
*** Channel Classics Dig. CCS 5483 [id.]. Pieter Wispelwey, Paul Komen.
(M) **(*) RCA Dig. 09026 61355-2. Yo-Yo Ma, Emanuel Ax.

Cello sonatas Nos. 1 in E min., Op. 38; 2 in F, Op. 99; in D min., Op. 108 (arr. of *Violin sonata in D min.*).
*** Sony Dig. SK 48191 [id.]. Yo-Yo Ma, Emanuel Ax.

The partnership of the wild, inspirational Russian cellist and the veteran Brahmsian pianist on DG is a challenging one. It proves an outstanding success, with inspiration mutually enhanced, whether in the lyricism of Op. 38 or the heroic energy of Op. 99. Good if close recording.

Although with the Rostropovich/Serkin account available, Yo-Yo Ma and Emanuel Ax may not be a first choice in the Brahms *Cello sonatas*, their performances on Sony are certainly among the finest in the current lists. Both are highly responsive artists and are of one mind concerning matters of phrasing. As always, Ma produces tone of great beauty and refinement and Ax plays with great sensitivity, though there are times when he is in danger of overpowering his partner. In addition to the two sonatas, they add their own transcription of the *D minor Violin sonata*. Distinguished playing and very good recording, even if the piano is slightly favoured.

Using gut strings, Isserlis produces an exceptionally warm tone, here nicely balanced in the recording against the strong and sensitive playing of his regular piano partner. In every way these perceptive and well-detailed readings stand in competition with the finest.

The Dutch partnership, Pieter Wispelwey and Paul Komen, offer something rather different. The cellist plays a nineteenth-century Bohemian cello and the pianist a Viennese period instrument: thus theirs is the only version of the sonatas to approximate to the sound Brahms himself might have heard. There is nothing anaemic or academic about their playing and no sense of scholarly inhibition. These are full-blooded performances, vivid in feeling and passionate, at no time wanting in eloquence.

In the alternative performances from Yo-Yo Ma and Emanuel Ax on RCA the balance favours the piano, for Ax sometimes produces too thick a sound in climaxes and Ma is, as always, sensitive and smaller in tone. Theirs is an essentially romantic view, and they are certainly more measured in their tempi than almost any of their rivals. Yo-Yo Ma's pianissimos occasionally draw attention to themselves, though the grace and tenderness of his playing is not in question. The claims of these readings reside in their refined lyricism rather than in their muscularity, and these artists have splendid rapport. The RCA recording is very truthful.

Clarinet quintet in B min., Op. 115.
(M) *** EMI CDM7 63116-2 [id.]. Gervase de Peyer, Melos Ens. – MOZART: *Quintet.* ***
(M) *** Carlton Dig. 3036 70097-2 [id.]. Keith Puddy, Delmé Qt – DVORAK: *Quartet No. 12.* ***
(N) (BB) **(*) CfP Silver Double CDCFPSD 4772 (2). Keith Puddy, Gabrieli String Qt – BORODIN:
    String quartet No. 2; DVORAK: *String quartet No. 12;* SCHUBERT: *String quartet No. 14.* ***

(i) *Clarinet quintet;* (ii) *Clarinet sonata No. 2 in E flat, Op. 120/2.*
(M) *** Chandos CHAN 6522 [id.]. Janet Hilton, (i) Lindsay Qt; (ii) Peter Frankl.

(i) *Clarinet quintet;* (ii) *Clarinet trio in A min., Op. 114.*
*** Hyperion CDA 66107 [id.]. King, (i) Gabrieli Qt; (ii) Georgian, Benson (piano).
(BB) **(*) Naxos Dig. 8.550391. József Balogh, with (i) Danubius Qt; (ii) Jenö Jandó, Csaba Onczay.

Gervase de Peyer's vintage performance of the *Clarinet quintet* with the Melos Ensemble is a warmly lyrical reading, dominated by the clarinettist, who brings out wistfully autumnal overtones. The sound is full and immediate, set in a relatively dry acoustic.

Keith Puddy's warm tone is well suited to Brahms and, with spacious speeds in all four movements, this is a consistently sympathetic reading; the Carlton digital recording is equally fine, vivid and full. Excellent value.

Janet Hilton's essentially mellow performance of the *Clarinet quintet*, with the Lindsay Quartet playing with pleasing warmth and refinement, has a distinct individuality. Her lilting syncopations in the third movement are delightful. Hilton's partnership with Peter Frankl in the *E flat Clarinet sonata* is rather less idiosyncratic and individual; nevertheless this performance offers considerable artistic rewards, even if the resonance means that the aural focus is a little diffuse.

Thea King and the Gabrieli Quartet give a radiantly beautiful performance of the *Clarinet quintet*, as fine as any put on record, expressive and spontaneous-sounding, with natural ebb and flow of tension as in a live performance. The recording of the strings is on the bright side, very vivid and real.

Although the CD transfer of the 1970 recording brings a certain thinness in the violin timbre, Keith Puddy's earlier, CfP account with the Gabrielis of this elusive work rises to fine, intense poetry in the slow movement and in the visionary closing pages of the finale. There is a spontaneity in the playing here which is a vital quality in this work, far more important than mechanical precision. Moreover all three couplings on this Silver Double are highly recommendable.

József Balogh, principal clarinet with both the Hungarian State Opera and Radio Orchestras, is a highly sensitive player with a lovely tone. He is well supported by the Danubius Quartet and their account of the *Clarinet quintet* is a rewarding one, with warmth and atmosphere, and rising to considerable heights of intensity in the *Adagio*. The *Clarinet trio* is an enjoyably fresh account, though not quite so memorable, except in the *Andantino grazioso* which is delightfully done. Nevertheless Balogh, Jandó and Onczay are thoroughly sympathetic and, with excellent recording, this is still a worthwhile disc and inexpensive to boot.

(i) *Clarinet quintet in B min., Op. 115;* (ii) *Piano quintet in F min., Op. 34; String quintets Nos. 1 in F, Op. 88; 2 in G, Op. 111.*
(Y/B) (B) *** Ph. Duo 446 172-2 (2) [id.]. (i) Herbert Stähr; (ii) Werner Haas; Berlin Philharmonic Octet (members).

The Berlin performance of the *Clarinet quintet* is both beautiful and faithful to Brahms's instructions, an outstanding version in every way. The delicacy with which the 'Hungarian' middle section of the great *Adagio* is interpreted gives some idea of the insight of these players. It is an autumnal reading, never overforced, and is recorded with comparable refinement. The two *String quintets* are also admirably served by these same players (with Dietrich Gerhard, viola, replacing the clarinettist, Herbert Stähr). The performances are searching and artistically satisfying, combining freshness and polish, warmth with well-integrated detail. For the *Piano quintet* Werner Haas joins the group, and they give a strongly motivated, spontaneous account of this splendid work that is in every way satisfying. The piano is most convincingly balanced. The recordings come from the early 1970s and the sound is remarkably full and warm, the richness of texture suiting the *String quintets* especially well. This is among the finest bargains in the Philips Duo list.

(i) *Clarinet quintet in B min., Op. 115; String quartet No. 1 in C min., Op. 51/1.*
(M) (**(*)) EMI mono CDH7 64932-2 [id.]. (i) Reginald Kell; Busch Qt.

Reginald Kell's beauty of tone was legendary and his 1937 account of the *Clarinet quintet* with the Busch Quartet is among the greatest recordings of the piece. Kell's vibrato was not to all tastes, but his playing here is heard at its most refined and the Busch produce a splendidly autumnal feeling in the slow movement. The *C minor Quartet*, recorded in 1932, may not be as polished as in some more recent accounts (and certainly sounds its age), but the playing is full of imagination and vitality.

(i) *Clarinet quintet in B min., Op. 115. String quintet No. 2 in G, Op. 111.*
**(*) Delos Dig. DE 3066 [id.]. (i) David Shifrin; Chamber Music NorthWest.

David Shifrin plays most beautifully in the *Clarinet quintet* and fully catches its serenity and autumnal nostalgia. He receives highly sympathetic support from Chamber Music NorthWest who find a parallel in the atmosphere of the *Adagio* of the *String quintet*, which is also played with a natural Brahmsian feeling.

Clarinet sonatas Nos. 1 in F min.; 2 in E flat, Op. 120/1–2.
*** Chandos Dig. CHAN 8563 [id.]. Gervase de Peyer, Gwenneth Prior.
(Y/B) *** Decca Dig. 430 149-2 [id.]. Cohen, Ashkenazy – SCHUMANN: *Fantasiestücke.* ***

Superb performances from Gervase de Peyer and Gwenneth Prior, commanding, aristocratic, warm and full of subtleties of colour and detail. The recording too is outstandingly realistic.

Franklin Cohen and Vladimir Ashkenazy give an eloquent account of both sonatas. What glorious pieces they are, and how well they sound here. The Decca recording has an exemplary balance and the overall sound-picture is rich.

(i) *Clarinet trio in A min.* (for clarinet, cello and piano), *Op. 114; Clarinet sonatas Nos. 1–2, Op., 120/1–2.*
*** Gutman Records Dig. CD 931 [id.]. Hein Wiedijk, Frank van de Laar; (i) with Pieter Wispelwey.

It has taken a small label to provide this ideal coupling of the three major Brahms works featuring the clarinet. Hein Wiedijk is a most sensitive player, with a warm timbre and clear articulation. He can be persuasively gentle as well as ardent, and he has the full measure of Brahms's lyricism. This is playing of subtlety as well as warmth, and Frank van de Laar is an excellent partner. They are then joined by Pieter Wispelwey for an equally persuasive account of the *Clarinet trio*, full of autumnal feeling. The recording is real and vivid and well balanced in a slightly dry but not unsympathetic acoustic. However, this is available only as a special import from Europe and may take some perseverance to obtain.

(i; ii) *Clarinet trio in A min., Op. 114;* (iii) *Horn trio in E flat, Op. 40;* (ii) *Piano trios Nos. 1 in B, Op. 8; 2 in C, Op. 87; 3 in C min., Op. 101; 4 in A, Op. posth.*
(B) *** Ph. Duo 438 365-2 (2) [id.]. (i) George Pieterson; (ii) Beaux Arts Trio; (iii) Francis Orval, Arthur Grumiaux, Gyorgy Sebok.

The splendid Beaux Arts set of the *Piano trios* come on a pair of joined CDs at bargain price, with two other outstanding performances thrown in for good measure. George Pieterson is a first-rate artist and his account of the *Clarinet trio* with members of the Beaux Arts group offers masterly playing from all three participants and a very well-integrated recording. The balance in the *Horn trio* is even more adroitly managed, perhaps the most successful on record. The fine horn player, Francis Orval, seeks not to dominate but to be one of the group, and he achieves this without any loss of personality in his playing (note the richness of his contribution to the Trio of the Scherzo). The performance is warmly lyrical and completely spontaneous, with a racy finale to round off a particularly satisfying reading, never forced but deeply felt. Arthur Grumiaux's playing is a constant pleasure, and the pianist, Gyorgy Sebok, is hardly less admirable.

As for the *Piano trios*, the performances are splendid, with strongly paced, dramatic allegros, consistently alert and thoughtful, and with sensitive playing in slow movements. The sound is first class and the resonance of Bernard Greenhouse's cello is warmly caught without any clouding of focus. The CD transfer has brightened the top a little, but not excessively. Excellent notes, too.

Horn trio in E flat, Op. 40 (see also above).
(M) *** Decca 433 695-2 [id.]. Tuckwell, Perlman, Ashkenazy – FRANCK: *Violin sonata;* SAINT-SAENS: *Romance;* SCHUMANN: *Adagio & allegro.* ***
(BB) **(*) Naxos Dig. 8.550441 [id.]. Jenö Keveházi, Jenö Handó, Ildikó Hegyi (with Heinrich HERZOGENBERG: *Trio for horn, oboe & piano, Op. 61* (with Józef Kiss); Frédéric DUVERNOY: *Horn trio* **(*)).

A superb performance of Brahms's marvellous *Horn trio* from Tuckwell, Perlman and Ashkenazy. They realize to the full the music's passionate impulse, and the performance moves forward from the gentle opening, through the sparkling scherzo and the more introspective but still outgiving *Adagio*, to the gay and spirited finale. The recording is worthy of the playing, although the new ADD transfer of the 1968 recording seeks to provide a more sharply defined sound-picture than before, and the attempt to clarify its imagery brings moments when the refinement of texture slips at climaxes.

The Naxos version has plenty of vitality and romantic ardour, but rather less in the way of refinement. The excellent horn player, Jenö Keveházi, has a touch of vibrato but the ear soon adjusts, and he makes a strong, full-blooded contribution. The players are somewhat backwardly placed in the fairly resonant Unitarian Church, Budapest, but the result is convincing with a good relationship between the three instruments. The other two *Horn trios* are enjoyable but not distinctive. The oboe makes an effective substitute for the violin in the Herzogenberg piece, which cribs from the Brahms finale in its second-movement *Presto*. The Duvernoy *Trio* has two movements only, slow–fast, with the second rather jolly. They are both well played and recorded.

(i) *Horn trio in E flat;* (ii) *Piano quintet in F min., Op. 34.*
**(*) CRD Dig. CRD 3489 [id.]. Nash Ens.: (i) Frank Lloyd; (i; ii) Marcia Crayford, Ian Brown; (ii) Elizabeth Layton, Roger Chase, Christopher van Kampen.

The Nash Ensemble have extra expressive warmth at spacious speeds, firmly underpinned by the incisive playing of the pianist, Ian Brown, and this is heard at its best in the *Piano quintet*. The romanticism of the Nash approach also comes out in the *Horn trio*, but the horn soloist, Frank Lloyd, is rather too reticent here. He produces an exceptionally rich tone to remind one of Dennis Brain and helps the group to give a raptly beautiful account of the *Adagio*. Following these relaxed accounts of the first three movements, the galloping finale is then given with joyful panache, with the horn braying splendidly. Thanks partly to the CRD recording, the Nash performances are made to sound satisfyingly beefy, almost orchestral. Yet, with both performances undoubtedly characterful and enjoyable, the disc can be recommended, particularly when this is the only issue coupling these two works.

(i) *Horn trio in E flat;* (ii) *String sextet No. 2 in G, Op. 36.*
❀ (M) **(*) Sony SMK 46249 [id.]. (i) Myron Bloom, Michael Tree, Rudolph Serkin; (ii) Pina Carmirelli, Toth, Naegele, Caroline Levine, Arico, Reichenberger.

The performance of the *Horn trio*, recorded at the Marlboro Festival in 1960, is quite splendid. Myron Bloom's horn playing is superb, and Michael Tree matches his lyrical feeling, while Serkin holds the performance together so that, when the fervour of the music-making brings a few slips in rhythmic precision, the listener is carried along by the exhilaration of the moment. The *Trio* comes paired with another Marlboro performance, of the *G major String sextet*, by a string group led by Pina Carmirelli. Recorded in 1967, this is at an altogether lower voltage.

Piano quartets Nos. 1 in G min., Op. 25; 2 in A, Op. 26; 3 in C min., Op. 60.
*** Sony Dig.S2K 45846 (2) [id.]. Jaime Laredo, Isaac Stern, Yo Yo Ma, Emanuel Ax.

(i) *Piano quartets Nos. 1–3;* (ii) *Piano trios Nos. 1 in B, Op. 8; 2 in C, Op. 87; 3 in C min., Op. 101.*
(N) (M) *** Sony Stern Edition III Dig./Analogue SM3K 64520 (3) [id.]. Isaac Stern, with (i) Laredo, Yo-Yo Ma, Ax; (ii) Rose, Istomin.

The Stern–Laredo–Ma–Ax partnership produces some pretty high-voltage playing and a real sense of give-and-take. There is little sense of four stars just coming together for a recording session but more of a genuine musical rapport. The listener is placed rather closer to the artists than some readers might like. All the same, no one investing in the Sony set is likely to be in the least disappointed.

This set is still available separately on two premium-priced CDs, but the three-disc set (taken from Volume III of Sony's celebration of Stern's 'Life in Music') is the one to go for. This includes equally fine versions of the *Piano trios*, recorded in New York two decades earlier, in 1964 and 1966. Here Stern joins with Rose and Istomin to give committed, romantic performances of comparable magnetism. Allegros are relaxed but alive and there are many individual touches in the phrasing to give pleasure. The *Adagio* of the *B major*, taken very slowly, has rapt concentration; that for Op. 101 is by comparison a nicely flowing *Andante grazioso*. As with the Beethoven *Piano trios* from the same source, the remastering has improved the original recording almost out of recognition, especially in relation to the piano sonority. The balance is close, but one relishes the presence of these fine artists.

(i) *Piano quartets Nos. 1–3; Piano quintet in F min., Op. 34. String quartet in A min., Op. 51/2.*
(N) (***) Testament mono SBT 3063 (3) [id.]. (i) Victor Aller; Hollywood Qt – SCHUMANN: *Piano quintet* (***).

For a brief period in the 1950s the Hollywood Quartet dominated the chamber-music scene. Their records were as eagerly awaited as were their rare visits to the concert hall. Their discography was not extensive and nearly all of it is self-recommending. Certainly the Brahms *Piano quartets* have hardly been surpassed since, and the *A minor Quartet* has tremendous grip and an ardent lyricism. At the time they seemed to be more or less ideal performances, and so they do now. Due to the microphone placement there is a strident quality in the upper register in the *A minor Quartet*, but it can easily be tamed. There was nothing in the least strident about their tone in the flesh. Desmond Shawe-Taylor and Edward Sackville-West's *The Record Guide* (1955) spoke of the *A minor Quartet* having 'a sensibility that reveals the romantic soul beneath the classical surface'. Performances of this integrity do not come often.

(i) *Piano quartets Nos. 1 in G min., Op. 25; 2 in A, Op. 26; 3 in C min., Op. 60. Piano trio in A, Op. posth.*
(N) (B) *** Ph. Duo 454 017-2 (2) [id.]. Beaux Arts Trio, (i) with Walter Trampler.

The Beaux Arts set of *Piano quartets* is self-recommending at Duo price, with the *A major Piano trio* thrown in as a bonus. The recording is bold and full-bloodedly Brahmsian in outer movements, which have splendid impetus. Thoughtful, sensitive playing in slow movements, lively tempi in allegros, characteristic musicianship plus spontaneity combine to make these recordings highly recommendable throughout, alongside the Stern Sony set (see above), which is in a higher price bracket.

Piano quartet No. 1 in G min.
*** Sony Dig. MK 42361 [id.]. Murray Perahia, Amadeus Qt (members).

Piano quartets Nos. 1 in G min.; 3 in C min.
*** Virgin/EMI Dig. VC7 59248-2 [id.]. Domus.

Perahia's version of the *G minor Piano quartet* has an expressive power and eloquence that silence criticism. The sound has both warmth and presence in its CD format and this is arguably the finest account of the work since Gilels recorded it with the same string group (see below).

However, Domus offer not only the *G minor Quartet* but also the *C minor*, and they give marvellously spontaneous accounts of both works, urgent and full of warmth, yet with no lack of subtlety. The full, vivid recording can be recommended strongly.

(i) *Piano quartet No. 1 in G min., Op. 25. 4 Ballades, Op. 10.*
(Y/B) (M) **(*) DG 447 407-2 [id.]. Gilels, (i) with Amadeus Qt.

As might be expected, Gilels' account of the *G minor Quartet* with members of the Amadeus has much to recommend it. The great Russian pianist is in impressive form, and most listeners will respond to the withdrawn delicacy of the Scherzo and the gypsy fire of the finale. The slow movement is perhaps somewhat wanting in ardour and the Amadeus do not sound as committed or as fresh as their keyboard partner. At medium price, however, this version enjoys an advantage, and the 1971 DG recording is well balanced and sounds very natural in its new transfer. Moreover in the *Ballades* Gilels offers artistry of an order that silences criticism. In terms of imaginative vitality and musical insight it would be difficult to surpass these readings, and the 1976 recording is also first class. This certainly is a recording worthy of inclusion in DG's Legendary series of 'Originals'.

Piano quartet No. 3 in C min., Op. 60.
** Sony Dig. MK 42387 [id.]. Stern, Ma, Laredo, Ax – *Double concerto.* ***

Excellent playing from all concerned on the Sony/CBS disc, even if Emanuel Ax delivers too thick a fortissimo tone at times – though he can produce beautiful pianissimo tone as well. There are pianists more sensitive in this respect on rival recordings.

Piano quintet in F min., Op. 34.
(BB) *** Naxos Dig. 8.550406; 4550406 [id.]. Jenö Jandó, Kodály Qt – SCHUMANN: *Piano quintet.* ***

This fine Naxos account has a great deal going for it, even though it does not include the first-movement exposition repeat. The playing is boldly spontaneous and has plenty of fire and expressive feeling. The opening of the finale has mystery too, and overall, with full-bodied recording and plenty of presence, this makes a strong impression. It is certainly a bargain.

(i) *Piano quintet in F min., Op. 34; String sextet No 1 in B flat, Op. 18.*
(N) (B) **(*) DG 439 490-2 [id.]. (i) Eschenbach, Amadeus Qt (augmented).

Christoph Eschenbach gives a powerful – sometimes overprojected – account of his part in the *Quintet*, yet this is undoubtedly a moving performance with plenty of vitality. Good piano quality and, although the piano dominates, the Amadeus players remain well in the picture. The performance of the *Sextet* lacks something in purity of style, but the obvious tonal warmth and the undoubted merits of the ensemble, coupled with very good late-1960s recording, make this a pretty good recommendation for those with limited budgets.

Piano trios Nos. 1 in B, Op. 8; 2 in C, Op. 87; 3 in C min., Op. 101; 4 in A, Op. posth.
*** Teldec/Warner Dig. 9031 76036-2 (2) [id.]. Trio Fontenay.
*** Ph. Dig. 416 838-2 (2) [id.]. Beaux Arts Trio.
(BB) ** Naxos Dig. 8.550746 (*Nos. 1 & 2*); 8.550747 (*Nos. 3 & 4*). Vienna Piano Trio.

Powerful, spontaneous playing with a real Brahmsian spirit, given excellent, modern recording, puts these admirable performances by the Trio Fontenay at the top of the list.

The new digital recordings by the Beaux Arts Trio were made in La Chaux-de-Fonds, Switzerland, and they bring one close to the artists. The playing is always highly vital and sensitive. There is a splendid, finely projected sense of line and the delicate, sensitive playing of Menahem Pressler is always a delight.

The accounts by the Vienna Piano Trio on Naxos are warm and unidiosyncratic and have no lack of vitality. Slow movements are shaped and phrased very musically, and the stronger allegros are well paced. These are not distinctive performances but they are fresh and worth their modest cost. The recording in a resonant acoustic (a hall in a castle in Budapest) has brought fairly close microphones, but the presence given to the group does not sound too noticeably artificial.

Piano trios Nos. 1 in B, Op. 8; 2 in C, Op. 87.
(M) *** Decca 421 152-2. Julius Katchen, Josef Suk, János Starker.
(N) *** DG Dig. 447 055-2 [id.]. Pires, Dumay, Wang.
(N) **(*) Virgin/EMI Dig. VC5 45184-2 [id.]. Grieg Trio.

The Katchen/Suk/Starker performances are warm, strong and characterful. The richness of the acoustics at The Maltings adds to the Brahmsian glow; and if the sound of the remastered disc is a little limited in the upper range, it provides a real Brahmsian amplitude which is very satisfying.

Following their fine accounts of the violin sonatas, Augustin Dumay and Maria João Pires are joined by the young Chinese cellist, Jian Wang. (RL recalls hearing him as an eleven-year-old in Shanghai, playing the *Sarabande* of a Bach suite.) His contribution is certainly eloquent here and the performances overall have authority and finesse. Though the recording is not absolutely ideal in balance (the listener is placed far too forwardly) and the instruments are not always cleanly focused, it has a pleasing warmth and amplitude. The performance has greater personality and earns three stars. It is to be preferred artistically though not as a recording to the recent Grieg Trio account.

The Grieg Trio made a strong impression in 1988 at Esterháza at the last Interforum mounted in Hungary, and they subsequently went on to collect prizes elsewhere. These young Norwegian players give exemplary and highly professional accounts of the two Brahms *Trios*. Perhaps they miss some of the insights that the Beaux Arts bring to this repertoire, and they are not to be preferred to them or to the old Katchen–Suk–Starker set. Their pianist is certainly not the equal of Menahem Pressler. All the same, no one wanting a good set of the two *Trios* should feel short-changed if they get this well-recorded disc.

Piano trios No. 3 in C min., Op. 101; in E flat, Op. 40; in A, Op. 114.
(N) * Chandos Dig. CHAN 9400 [id.]. Bekova Sisters.

Here the *C minor Trio*, Op. 101, is the only one to be recorded in unaltered form. The wonderful *Clarinet trio* can of course be played by viola, cello and piano, and the viola can replace the horn in the *Horn trio*, but they are heard here in arrangements for piano trio. There is nothing special about the playing and the record is a complete non-starter.

String quartets Nos. 1 in C min.; 2 in A min., Op. 51/1–2; 3 in B flat, Op. 67.
*** EMI Dig. CDS7 54829-2 (2) [id.]. Alban Berg Qt.
**(*) Claves Dig. 50-9404/5 (2) [id.]. Quartet Sine Nomine.

On EMI, the outer quartets, the *C minor*, Op. 51/1, and the *B flat*, Op. 67, were recorded in Switzerland (in a church) and are accommodated on the first CD; the *A minor*, Op. 51/2, is from a live performance given at the Palais Yusopov in St Petersburg and is on the second CD – rather short measure these days for a full-price CD. All the same there is nothing short-measured about the performances, which have all the finesse and attack one expects from the Alban Berg Quartet along with impeccable technical address. The *A minor* has just the right kind of dramatic intensity, and the range of colour and dynamics they produce in all three works is impressive. The EMI engineers produced well-detailed, truthful sound in the Swiss venue; the slightly greater freshness and spontaneity of the St Petersburg performance is offset by a slight loss in tonal radiance. All the same, these are all performances of quality and can be recommended even to those who find this ensemble at times a little too glossy.

The Sine Nomine Quartet are splendidly recorded in a helpful acoustic, and the effect here is just like a series of live performances. The playing, though well integrated and responsive with plenty of Brahmsian spirit, has not the degree of sophistication and finesse the Alban Berg Quartet displays, but it does have consistent vitality and spontaneity; the *Third, B flat major Quartet* is particularly alive: it leaps out of the speakers towards the listener, and again the closing variations are a highlight of the performance.

String quartets Nos. 1 in C min.; 2 in A min., Op. 51/1–2; 3 in B flat, Op. 67; (i) Piano quintet in F min., Op. 34.
*** Hyperion Dig. CDA 66651/52 [id.]. (i) Lane; New Budapest Qt.

The New Budapest Quartet bring warmth and spontaneity to all three scores, responding to their dramatic fervour and lyrical flow in equal measure. Their intonation is altogether impeccable and they are scrupulously attentive to Brahms's dynamic markings, with pleasing results in terms of clarity and transparency. Both the *C minor* and *A minor Quartets* can so often sound opaque, and in this respect the New Budapest produce as clean and open a sonority as any. They also have plenty of character and rhythmic vitality. They enjoy two further advantages over some earlier rivals in that, first, they also offer an excellently shaped and musicianly account of the *F minor Piano quintet* with responsive playing from Piers Lane and, secondly, they are among the best and most naturally recorded to have appeared in recent years. Moreover the two CDs come separately and not as a package. But most collectors will surely want both.

String quartets Nos. 1 in C min.; 2 in A min., Op. 51/1–2.
*** Denon Dig. CD75756 [id.]. Carmina Qt.
*** Chandos Dig. CHAN 8562 [id.]. Gabrieli Qt.
*** Decca Dig. 425 526-2 [id.]. Takács Qt.

The Denon coupling of the Op. 51 *Quartets* is one of the best recent issues – and perhaps the finest since the Quartetto Italiano's account in the days of vinyl. The *A minor Quartet* is placed first, and some may find its opening a little too sweet-toned; but they have a firm grasp on the architecture of the music and convey pleasure in music-making. They are recorded with presence and body.

Richly recorded in an agreeably expansive ambience, the Gabrielis give warm, eloquent performances of both the Op. 51 *Quartets*, deeply felt and full-textured without being heavy; the *Romanze* of Op. 51, No. 1, is delightfully songful. There are both tenderness and subtlety here, and the sound is first class.

The Takács Quartet's coupling of the *C minor* and *A minor Quartets* has vitality and sensitivity, and their accounts of both works are eminently well shaped. They may be recommended alongside the Gabrielis on Chandos.

String quartets Nos. 1 in C min., Op. 51/1; 3 in B flat, Op. 67.
**(*) Teldec/Warner Dig. 4509 90889-2 [id.]. Borodin Qt.

Marvellously sophisticated playing from the Borodins, with wonderful tonal blending, absolute security of intonation and immaculate ensemble. The first movement of No. 1 sets off with considerable impetus, but the thoughtfulness of the performance establishes itself within a few bars, and the inner movements of this *Quartet* have much grace and delicacy of feeling, while in Op. 67 the subtle treatment of the variations which make up the last movement is a high point of the record. The digital recording is firm and truthful, if a shade close and bright; but the main reservation here is that these performances, although they offer much to admire and enjoy, lack the kind of spontaneity that really grips the listener; moreover many listeners might like their Brahms to sound rather more robust.

String quartet No. 2 in A min., Op. 51/2.
(Y/B) *** RCA Dig. 09026 61866-2 [id.]. Vogler Qt – SCHUMANN: *String quartet No. 3.* ***

String quartet No. 3 in B flat, Op. 67.
(Y/B) *** RCA Dig. 09026 61438-2 [id.]. Vogler Qt – SCHUMANN: *String quartet No. 1.* ***

The Vogler is an extremely fine ensemble who have been engaged on recording the Brahms and Schumann quartets, as the Quartetto Italiano did on LP in the 1970s. Tough luck if you already have one and want the other (though there is no lack of alternatives) but, if you do want both in modern, digital recordings, it would be difficult to improve on them. They have the advantage of a rich and beautifully blended sonority and refined musicianship. Moreover the RCA recording is very good indeed. Recommended with enthusiasm. If the remaining disc (which will couple the Brahms *C minor*, Op. 51, No. 1, with the Schumann *F major*, Op. 41, No. 2) is their equal, this is likely to be a first recommendation for this repertoire.

String quintets Nos. 1 in F, Op. 88; 2 in G, Op. 111.
(N) *** Hyperion Dig. CDA 66804 [id.]. Raphael Ens.
(M) **(*) Ph. 426 094-2. BPO Octet (members).

With the *First Quintet* opening seductively, these are fine, vital performances of both works from the Raphael Ensemble, who show themselves particularly sensitive to the grave melancholy of the slow movement of the *F major* and the wistfully gentle mood of the *Intermezzo* in the *G major*. Indeed these performances are on the same level of distinction as their accounts of the *String sextets* and, like that companion Hyperion disc, the recording is very present indeed, which to some ears may seem a minor drawback.

Although the remastering has brought a thinner, more astringent treble response than the original LP, the performances by the Berlin Philharmonic group are searching and artistically satisfying, combining freshness with polish, warmth with well-integrated detail.

String quintet No. 2 in G, Op. 111.
(N) *** Naim Dig. CD 010 [id.]. Augmented Allegri Qt – BRUCH: *String quintet.* ***

The second of the two string quintets that Brahms wrote late in his career makes the ideal coupling for the long-buried Bruch *Quintet*, which was also the product of old age. Very well played and recorded.

String sextets Nos. 1 in B flat, Op. 18; 2 in G, Op. 36.
*** Hyperion Dig. CDA 66276 [id.]. Raphael Ens.
*** Sony Dig. S2K 45820 (2) [id.]. Stern, Lin, Ma, Robinson, Laredo, Tree.
*** Chandos Dig. CHAN 9151 [id.]. ASMF Chamber Ens.

The *Sextets* are among Brahms's most immediately appealing chamber works. The Raphael Ensemble are fully responsive to all their subtleties as well as to their vitality and warmth. In short, these are superb performances; the recording is very vivid and immediate, although some ears might find it a shade too present.

The Sony award-winning version of the *String sextets* deserves its laurels. Names alone are not in themselves enough to ensure success, even if they are as resplendent as those of Isaac Stern, Cho-Liang Lin, Yo-Yo Ma, Jaime Laredo and so on; but the rapport and interplay so vital in chamber-music playing is in ample evidence. There is a keen feeling for the warmth and generosity of feeling, as well as for the strength and architecture of these masterpieces, and the Sony engineering is impressive. In spite of awards and razzmatazz, this can be recommended alongside the Raphael Ensemble (Hyperion), which have the advantage of being accommodated on one CD. The Sony issue involves two premium-priced CDs, so many may feel that the Hyperion remains 'best buy'.

The Chandos alternative is also highly recommendable, with both *Sextets* again accommodated on one CD without sacrificing the exposition repeats, so that at almost 78 minutes the Academy of St Martin-in-the-Fields offer excellent value for money. Moreover these well-prepared and musical performances are perceptive and intelligent. Free from interpretative point-making, these performances are musically satisfying and are given finely detailed and present recording.

String sextet No. 1 in B flat, Op. 18.
(Y/B) (***) Biddulph mono LAB 093 [id.]. Pro Arte Qt, with Hobday, Pini – SCHUBERT: *String quintet in C.* (***)

Although they enjoyed much renown in the concert hall, the Pro Arte Quartet were rather over-shadowed in the recording studios of the 1930s by the Busch and Budapest Quartets. True, they were allocated the task of recording what was to have been a complete cycle for the Haydn Quartet Society, but this was a subscription set. They made a handful of other discs, including some Mozart (K.428 and, with Alfred Hobday, the *G minor Quintet*, K.516), which were classics of their day. They also recorded Bartók's *First Quartet* and championed the new music of the time (Honegger, Roussel, Tansman and Milhaud). Their impeccable technical address shows here, and their warmth and finesse make their Brahms as satisfying as any account recorded since. Needless to say, some allowance has to be made for the 1935 recording, eminently well transferred though it is.

Viola sonatas Nos. 1 in F min.; 2 in E flat, Op. 120/1–2.
❀ *** Virgin/EMI Dig. VC7 59309-2 [id.]. Lars Anders Tomter, Leif Ove Andsnes – SCHUMANN: *Märchenbilder.* ***

Viola sonatas Nos. 1 in F min.; 2 in E flat, Op. 120/1–2; F.A.E. Sonata: Scherzo.
**(*) Chandos Dig. CHAN 8550 [id.]. Nobuko Imai, Roger Vignoles – SCHUMANN: *Märchenbilder.* **(*)
(M) **(*) DG 437 248-2 [id.]. Pinchas Zukerman, Daniel Barenboim.

This young Norwegian partnership gives us the best account of these sonatas in their viola form now on CD. Theirs is playing of great sensitivity and imagination. Lars Anders Tomter and Leif Ove Andsnes bring a wide range of colour to this music and phrase with an unforced naturalness that is very persuasive. Very well balanced, though there is a slight bias in favour of the piano. Altogether rather special.

Nobuko Imai is an almost peerless violist and it is difficult to find a flaw in her accounts of the two Op. 120 *Sonatas* with Roger Vignoles. The reverberant acoustic does not show the piano to good advantage but, apart from that, this is an impressive issue.

Zukerman's 1975 recording with Barenboim, which we liked enough at the time to award it three stars, is back in circulation on the DG Galleria label. Although it will be too sweet for some tastes, these are spontaneous-sounding performances, and the expressiveness never sounds contrived, always buoyant. After the sonatas, Zukerman shows his versatility by changing over to the violin for the lively *Scherzo in C minor* from the *F.A.E. Sonata*, a work composed jointly with Schumann and Albert Dietrich. The recording has good presence.

Violin sonatas Nos. 1 in G, Op. 78; 2 in A, Op. 100; 3 in D min., Op. 108.
*** Hyperion Dig. CDA 66465 [id.]. Krysia Osostowicz, Susan Tomes.
*** Sony Dig. SK 45819 [id.]. Itzhak Perlman, Daniel Barenboim.
*** EMI Dig. CDC7 47403-2 [id.]. Itzhak Perlman, Vladimir Ashkenazy.
*** DG Dig. 435 800-2 [id.]. Augustin Dumay, Maria João Pires.
(***) Testament mono SBT 1024 [id.]. Gioconda De Vito, Edwin Fischer; Tito Aprea (in *No. 2*).
(N) (M) **(*) Ph. 446 570-2 [id.]. Arthur Grumiaux, György Sebök.

Krysia Osostowicz and Susan Tomes give performances of such natural musicality that criticism is almost disarmed. They phrase with great spontaneity yet with apparently effortless care and artistry, and the interplay between the two partners is instinctive. The Hyperion engineers manage the sound and balance with their customary skill, and theirs is certainly to be preferred to some of the more glamorous rivals now on the market.

The Sony recording, made at a live recital in Chicago, finds Perlman in far more volatile form, more urgently persuasive with naturally flowing speeds and more spontaneous rubato than he adopts in his spacious readings with Ashkenazy on EMI. Barenboim too is less aggressive and more fanciful than he was with Zukerman on DG (now deleted).

Perlman and Ashkenazy bring out the trouble-free happiness of these lyrical inspirations, fully involved yet avoiding underlying tensions. In their sureness and flawless confidence at generally spacious speeds, they are performances which carry you along, cocooned in rich sound.

Augustin Dumay and Maria João Pires on DG are certainly among the most interesting of the other CD couplings. They bring temperament and finesse to all three sonatas and, though there are one or two interpretative touches that may not enjoy universal appeal, these are too trifling to detail and are unlikely to inhibit pleasure. These are artists of strong personality: certainly those with a special admiration for this partnership need not hesitate, for they are very well recorded.

Gioconda De Vito made all too few records. Her accounts of the *G major* and *D minor Sonatas* with Edwin Fischer come from 1954 and show her to excellent advantage. She possessed warmth and finesse in equal measure, and her playing conveys a sense of expressive freedom which makes one regret that her recording career was so short. Fischer's playing is characteristically magisterial and the *A major Sonata*, which she recorded with her normal partner, Tito Aprea, is hardly less beautiful. This is all rather special playing, and few allowances need be made for the excellent mono recording.

When they were issued on LP, we found these Grumiaux performances from the mid-1970s slightly disappointing, mellifluous rather than vital, with even an element of blandness. Returning to them in this superb CD transfer, we must revise our response, however. The very opening of the *G major Sonata* is gently appealing in a typically unassertive, Grumiaux way, and the first movement soon generates a full head of steam. The opening of the *Adagio* is restrained but tender, and the finale has an appealing lyrical flow. Moreover these artists exactly capture the nostalgic mood of the first movement of the *A major* (marked 'Allegro amabile') to perfection. If the opening of the *D minor* is reticent, again the *Adagio* is very lovely and the *Un poco presto e con sentimento* brings the lightest touch. In short, while other versions of these works may be more volatile and passionate, Grumiaux, expertly partnered by Sebök, is very persuasive, and never short of Brahmsian warmth. The recording too is beautifully balanced and natural.

Piano music, four hands

Piano music, 4 hands: *Hungarian dances Nos. 1–21; Waltzes, Op. 39.*
**(*) Sony Dig. SK 53285 [id.]. Yaara Tal and Andreas Groethuysen.

The playing here has enormous verve and energy and is seemingly spontaneous in the way the two artists play as one, with considerable rubato flowing quite naturally. Their style, however, brings the very widest dynamic range and is very percussive at fortissimo level. (This is even more striking at a live recital.) So this is not intimate playing, although the *Waltzes* provide plenty of examples when the brilliance scintillates, and there is also some beguilingly gentle pianism at times, especially in the delightful closing *D minor Waltz*, better known as Brahms's *Lullaby*.

Solo piano music

4 Ballades, Op. 10; 7 Fantasias, Op. 116; Hungarian dances Nos. 1–10; (i) Nos. 11–21. 3 Intermezzi, Op. 117; 8 Piano pieces, Op. 76; 6 Piano pieces, Op. 118; 4 Piano pieces, Op. 119; Piano sonatas Nos. 1 in C, Op. 1; 2 in F sharp min., Op. 2; 3 in F min., Op. 5; 2 Rhapsodies, Op. 79; Variations on a Hungarian song, Op. 21/2; Variations on a theme by Paganini, Op. 35; Variations and fugue on a theme by Handel, Op. 24; Variations on a theme by Schumann, Op. 9; Variations on an original theme, Op. 21/1; Waltzes, Op. 39.
(M) **(*) Decca mono/stereo 430 053-2 (6). Julius Katchen, (i) with J.-P. Marty.

Brahms often brought out the best in Katchen, and he is particularly good in the impulsive early music. If at times one could make small criticisms, the spontaneity and understanding are always there, and of course the excitement that comes when bravura is controlled by a sensitive and musical mind. Katchen's style in Brahms is distinctive: there is a boldness about it that suits some works more than others. The playing is extremely brilliant and assured. The lesser-known *Variations on a Hungarian song* and *On an original theme*, plus those *On a theme by Schumann*, are particularly successful. They are played with the utmost persuasiveness and artistry. Katchen plays Book One of the *Hungarian dances* in Brahms's later arrangement for piano solo; the remaining dances are offered in the more traditional form with Jean-

Pierre Marty as Katchen's partner. On CD the recordings, made between 1962 and 1966, are remarkably realistic. The four *Ballades* are mono.

4 Ballades, Op. 10.
*** DG Dig. 400 043-2 [id.]. Michelangeli – SCHUBERT: *Sonata No. 4.* **
*** Ph. Dig. 426 439-2 [id.]. Alfred Brendel – WEBER: *Piano sonata No. 2.* ***

Michelangeli gives the *Ballades* a performance of the greatest distinction and without the slightly aloof quality that at times disturbs his readings. He is superbly recorded.

A thoughtful (and at times self-aware) account of the Op. 10 *Ballades* by Brendel in a wonderfully clear, digital recording. This is playing of stature that should be heard by all the great pianist's admirers.

4 Ballades, Op. 10; Piano sonata No. 3 in F min., Op. 5.
(Y/B) (BB) **(*) Naxos Dig. 8.550352 [id.]. Idil Biret.

As a pupil of Kempff, Idel Biret has a fine understanding of this repertoire, although her approach is more muscular than Kempff's. Thus the first of the *Four Ballades* opens with enticing lyrical feeling but has the most powerfully dramatic climax, to match the feeling of the Scottish ballad, *Edward*, on which it is based. The *Fourth Ballade* is gravely beautiful and shows her at her finest. The *Sonata* opens commandingly and its lyrical side is well balanced. These performances are full of character. Good recording, made in the Heidelberg studio.

4 Ballades, Op. 10; Variations and fugue on a theme by Handel, Op. 24; Variations and fugue on a theme by Schumann, Op. 9.
(N) (BB) *** ASV Dig. CDQS 6161 [id.]. Jorge Federico Osorio.

The young Mexican pianist, Jorge Federico Osorio, has been winning golden opinions in recent years and his account of the *Variations and fugue on a theme by Handel* is tremendously impressive. There is no want of clarity, but the texture has plenty of warmth and colour and he balances the sonorities in a most musical way. He possesses an unfailing sense of the Brahms style, giving us playing that is selfless and with no hint of the idiosyncratic. This is undoubtedly his best record to date, for the Schumann set is hardly less impressive and the four *Ballades* are also played with fine sensitivity and character. On top of all this, ASV provide excellent, well-focused sound, with plenty of depth, and this now comes in the super-bargain category.

Fantasias, Op. 116.
*** Ottavio Dig. OTRC 39027 [id.]. Imogen Cooper – SCHUMANN: *Abegg variations* etc. ***

The impulsively spontaneous flow of Imogen Cooper's stirring account of the *Capriccio* which opens the set captures the listener immediately and the variety of colour and mood gives enormous pleasure throughout. The gentle *Intermezzi* are most beautiful, for the recording does this memorable playing full justice. The listening experience here is as if one was present at a live recital.

Fantasias, Op. 116; 3 Intermezzi, Op. 117; 6 Pieces, Op. 118; 4 Pieces, Op. 119.
(M) **(*) DG 437 249-2 [id.]. Wilhelm Kempff.

Kempff's style in Brahms is characteristically individual: poetry emphasized rather than brilliance, subtle timbres rather than virtuosity. It follows that Kempff shines in the gentle fancies of Brahms's last period, with his magic utterly beguiling in the *Intermezzi in A minor*, *E major* and *E minor* from Op. 116 and especially in the lovely *E flat major Andante* of Op. 117. Don't be put off by the opening *Capriccio in D minor* of Op. 116 which sounds rather hard, the piano timbre lacking sonority; at lower dynamic levels the piano colouring is exquisite.

(i) *Fantasias, Op. 116; Intermezzi, Op. 117;* (ii) *Pieces, Op. 76;* (i) *Pieces, Opp. 118/119;* (ii) *Rhapsodies Nos. 1 in B min.; 2 in G min., Op. 79/1–2;* (i) *Variations and fugue on a theme by Handel, Op. 24;* (iii) *Variations on a theme by Paganini, Op. 35.*
(Y/B) (B) *(**) Ph. Duo Analogue/Dig. 442 589-2 (2) [id.]. (i) Stephen Kovacevich; (ii) Dinorah Varsi; (iii) Adam Harasiewicz.

The performances by Stephen Kovacevich can receive the strongest recommendation. He finds the fullest range of emotional contrast in the Op. 116 *Fantasias*, but is at his finest in the Op. 117 *Intermezzi* and the four *Klavierstücke*, Op. 119, which contain some of Brahms's most beautiful lyrical inspirations for the keyboard, while the *Allegro risoluto* of the final *Rhapsodie* of Op. 119 has splendid flair and presence. On the second CD the *Handel variations* are also impressive and it seems perverse that Philips then turned to recordings by Dinorah Varsi of the two *Rhapsodies* and eight *Klavierstücke*, Op. 76, when Kovacevich has also recorded them. However, these are already available, coupled with the two piano concertos, on another Duo. Varsi's playing is at times very impulsive (as in the Op. 79 *Rhapsody*) and her performances of the *Klavierstücke* also lack the necessary degree of poise. Adam Harasiewicz, however, plays the *Paganini variations* with some flair and towards the end produces some exciting bravura. Generally the recordings are very good; Kovacevich's Op. 116 and Op. 118 are digital.

7 Fantasias, Op. 116; 8 Pieces, Op. 76; 2 Rhapsodies, Op. 79.
(Y/B) (BB) **(*) Naxos Dig. 8.550353 [id.]. Idil Biret.

Biret opens her programme strongly with the agitato *Capriccio in F sharp minor* (the first of the Op. 76 group), and then articulates the second lightly and engagingly. She readily captures the graceful intimacy of the *A flat* and *B flat Intermezzi*. Of the two *Rhapsodies*, the first is very impulsive indeed, but the second is particularly fine, boldly spontaneous, its dark colouring caught well. The *Fantasias*, Op. 116, bring some beautifully reflective playing, notably in the three *Intermezzi* grouped together (in E major and E minor), while the framing *G minor* and *D minor Capriccios* are passionately felt, the latter ending the recital strongly. This is all impressively characterized Brahms playing, and the recording does not lack sonority.

3 Intermezzi, Op. 117; 6 Pieces, Op. 118; 4 Pieces, Op. 119; 2 Rhapsodies, Op. 79.
*** Decca 417 599-2 [id.]. Radu Lupu.

Radu Lupu's late Brahms is quite outstanding in every way. There is great intensity and inwardness when these qualities are required and a keyboard mastery that is second to none. This is undoubtedly one of the most rewarding Brahms recitals currently before the public.

Intermezzi, Op. 117; 6 Pieces, Op. 118; Variations on a theme by Paganini, Op. 35.
*** DG Dig. 431 123-2 [id.]. Lilya Zilberstein.

Lilya Zilberstein has flawless technique and keen musical instincts. The recording is marvellously present and clear.

Piano sonatas Nos. 1 in C, Op. 1; 2 in F sharp min., Op. 2.
*** Decca Dig. 436 457-2 [id.]. Sviatoslav Richter.

Recorded in Mantova in February 1987, these performances show Richter at his most commanding. He makes the most heavily chordal piano writing sound totally pianistic and there is exquisite shading of tone and flawless legato. Both slow movements are most subtly coloured and the opening of the finale of the *F sharp minor Sonata* has a wonderful improvisational feeling. The playing throughout has the spontaneity of live music-making and the Decca engineers have secured most realistic sound.

Piano sonata No. 3; 4 Ballades; Intermezzo in E, Op. 116/6; Romance in F, Op. 118/5.
(M) ** RCA 09026 61862-2 [id.]. Artur Rubinstein.

Piano sonata No. 3; Intermezzi: in E flat, Op. 117/1; in C, Op. 119/3.
(N) (M) *** Decca 448 578-2 [id.]. Clifford Curzon – SCHUBERT: *Piano sonata No. 21.* ***

Curzon's account of the *F minor Sonata* is special. His approach is both perceptive and humane, and his playing has great intensity and freshness. Curzon was at his peak, powerful and sensitive and, above all, spontaneous-sounding, both in the *Sonata* and in the two *Intermezzi* which act as encores. The 1962 recording was among the finest of its day and is worthy to be reissued in Decca's 'Classic Sound' series. The generous coupling with Schubert (an equally fine performance) makes this CD very desirable indeed.

  Rubinstein's impulsive way with Brahms, though arresting at the opening of the *Sonata*, is not always convincing. His comparatively fast pacing of the second and fourth movements means that he does not entirely catch the feeling of reverie in the *Andante*. The rather hard, unexpansive (1959) recording does not help the *Sonata*; but the two shorter pieces seem to have slightly more bloom, and the *Ballades*, too, recorded in Rome in 1970, are fuller although the balance remains close and the acoustic cool. They are given a totally unsentimental approach and there are times when one feels the playing is somewhat shorn of mystery: one misses the extremes of both tension and repose.

Theme and variations in D min. (1860); *Variations and fugue on a theme by Handel, Op. 24; Variations on a Hungarian song, Op. 21; Variations on a theme by Schumann, Op. 9.*
(Y/B) *** EMI Dig. CDC5 55167-2 [id.]. Mikhail Rudy.

The Russian pianist Mikhail Rudy proves to be a Brahms interpreter of considerable insight. He keeps a firm grasp on the musical structure of each of these sets of variations, not least the 1860 D minor transcription of the slow movement of the *Sextet in B flat*, Op. 18; and he produces a sonority of consistent beauty. The *Handel variations* are the best to appear more recently. Very good sound.

Variations on a theme of Haydn, Op. 56a (arr. for piano duet).
*** Sony Dig. MK 42625 [id.]. Murray Perahia, Sir Georg Solti – BARTOK: *Sonata for 2 pianos and percussion.* ***

Murray Perahia and Solti bring out the fullest possible colouring in their performance, so that one hardly misses the orchestra.

Variations on a theme of Paganini, Op. 35.
(N) **(*) Decca Dig. 444 338-2 [id.]. Jean-Yves Thibaudet – SCHUMANN: *Arabesque* etc. **(*)

Although Jean-Yves Thibaudet is a cultured player and has an impressive technical address, his set of the *Paganini variations* lacks the very last ounce of fire. The Decca sound is good, and it goes without saying that there is much to admire in Thibaudet's playing.

ORGAN MUSIC

11 Chorale preludes, Op. 122. Chorale prelude and fugue on 'O Traurigkeit, O Herzeleid'; Fugue in A flat min. (original and published versions); *Preludes and fugues: in A min.; G min.*
*** Nimbus Dig. NI 5262 [id.]. Kevin Bowyer (organ of Odense Cathedral).

11 Chorale preludes, Op. 122; Chorale prelude and fugue on 'O Traurigkeit, O Herzeleid'; Fugue in A flat min.; Preludes and fugues: in A min.; G min.
*** CRD Dig. CRD 3404; *CRDC 4104* [id.]. Nicholas Danby (organ).

Kevin Bowyer, already successful in the music of Bach, now provides an admirable Brahms survey. He has the advantage of the splendid Danish organ in Odense Cathedral which combines a full tone and a warmly coloured palette with a clear profile. Like Nicholas Danby, Bowyer is obviously at home both in the early *Preludes and fugues* in which he produces considerable bravura (helped by the fresh, bright sound of the organ) and in the very late set of *Chorale preludes*, from the period of the *Four Serious Songs*, and which are comparably mellow. He then closes the recital with Brahms's original manuscript forms of the two earliest pieces (which we have already heard in their published formats), the *Chorale prelude and fugue on 'O Traurigkeit'* and the unpolished *A flat minor fugue*. The disc is very well documented.

    Nicholas Danby playing the organ of the Church of the Immaculate Conception in London, which also seems ideally suited to this repertoire, gives restrained, clean-cut readings (which yet have a strong profile). The sound of the Farm Street organ is beautifully caught by the recording. Choice between these two discs might well depend on preference for the type of organ used. The effect on CRD is rather more incisive, yet has firmness and weight of tone and certainly does not lack amplitude.

Chorale preludes: Es ist ein Ros entsprungen; Herzlich tut mich verlangen; O Welt, ich muss dich lassen; O wie selig seid ihr doch; Schmücke dich, o liebe Seele, Op. 122.
(N) (M) *** Decca Dig. 444 570-2 [id.]. Peter Hurford (organ of Ratzeburg Cathedral) – MENDELSSOHN: *Organ sonatas* etc. *** ❀

Brahms's *Chorale preludes* were written in the last year of his life as a serene tribute to Bach, often recalling the mood of the *Orgelbüchlein*. Five of the eleven are played here with engaging simplicity by Peter Hurford as a postlude to his Mendelssohn recital, and they are admirably recorded.

VOCAL MUSIC

Lieder: Ach, wende diesen Blick; Die Mainacht; Heimweh; Mädchenlied; Meine Liebe ist grün; O kühler Wald; Ständchen; Unbewegte laue Luft; Von ewiger Liebe; Wie rafft' ich mich auf; Wiegenlied. (i) *2 Songs with viola (Gestilte Sehnsucht & Geistliches Wiegenlied), Op. 91. 3 Volkslieder: Dort in den Weiden; Sonntag; Vergebliches Ständchen. 8 Zigeunerlieder Op. 103/1–7 & 11.*
*** DG Dig. 429 727-2 [id.]. Anne Sofie von Otter, Bengt Forsberg, (i) with Nils-Erik Sparf.

Anne Sofie von Otter gives these Brahms Lieder the natural freshness of folksong, which so often they resemble, or even quote, as in the radiant melody of *Sonntag*. She phrases unerringly, holding and changing tension and mood as in a live recital. Compared with some, there is still a degree of expressive restraint, but there are few Brahms song-recital discs to match this one, and her accompanist is strongly supportive. In the Op. 91 settings they are joined by Nils-Erik Sparf, who plays with admirable taste.

Vier ernste Gesänge, Op. 121; Lieder: Auf dem Kirchhofe; Botschaft; Feldeinsamkeit; Im Waldeseinsamkeit; Minnelied III; Mondenschein; O wüsst ich doch den Weg zurück; Sapphische Ode; Sommerabend; Ständchen.
❀ (M) (***) EMI CDH7 63198-2 [id.]. Hotter, Moore – BACH: *Cantata No. 82: Ich habe genug.* (***) ❀
Glorious singing from Hans Hotter, wonderfully accompanied by Gerald Moore. An excellent transfer.

Lieder: *Abendregen; Alte Liebe; Feldeinsamkeit; Immer leiser wird mein Schlummer; Der Jäger; Liebestreu; Mädchenfluch; Mädchenlied; Das Mädchen spricht; Meine Liebe ist grün; Regenlied; Salome; Der Schmied; Sommerabend; Therese; Der Tod, das ist die kühle Nacht; Von ewiger Liebe; Vor dem Fenster; Wir wandelten.*
*** Orfeo C 058831A [id.]. Margaret Price, James Lockhart.

Margaret Price sings radiantly, with the voice ideally suited to the soaring lines of many of these songs, finely coloured over the changes of mood in a song such as *Alte Liebe*. Clean, bright recording.

Lieder: *Alte Liebe; Auf dem Kirchhofe; Auf dem See; Es liebt sich so lieblich; Geheimnis; Die Mainacht; O liebliche Wangen; Sapphische Ode; Sonntag; Verzagen.*
(N) (M) *** Ph. 442 741-2 (2) [id.]. Gérard Souzay, Dalton Baldwin – BEETHOVEN: *An die ferne Geliebte* etc.; SCHUMANN: *Dichterliebe; Liederkreis* etc. ***

Not even Souzay's lightness (at its finest in *Geheimnis* and the flowingly passionate *O liebliche Wangen*) can prevent some of these songs sounding heavy in texture. Yet his gently grave account of *Die Mainacht* is very touching, and all this singing is persuasive. Comparison with the coupled Beethoven – who comes off better as a song writer than his successor on this showing – is fascinating. Recording is close but otherwise excellent. Alas, no translations are provided.

(i) *Alto rhapsody, Op. 53; Deutsche Volkslieder:* (ii) *Ach, englische Schäferin; All mein' Gedanken; Da unten im Tale; Dort in den Weiden;* (iii) *Es war einmal ein Zimmergesell;* (ii) *Es wohnet ein Fiedler; In stiller Nacht; Maria ging aus wandern; Mein Mädel hat einen Rosenmund; Schwesterlein; Die Sonne scheint nicht mehr;* (iii) *Verstohlen geht der Mond auf.* (ii) *Wach auf, mein' Herzensschöne.* (iv) Lieder: *Am Sonntagmorgen; Botschaft; Heimweh II; Junge Lieder I; Die Mainacht; Minnelied; O liebche Wangen; Regenlied; Sonntag; Uber die Heide; Von ewiger Liebe.*
(N) (B) *** DG 439 441-2 [id.]. (i) Christa Ludwig, V. Singverein, VPO, Boehm; (ii) Edith Mathis or Peter Schreier, Karl Engel; (iii) N. German R. Ch., Jena; Kahl; (iv) Fischer-Dieskau, Barenboim.

Although the initial attraction of this highly recommendable bargain collection may be Christa Ludwig's strong and eloquent account of the *Alto rhapsody* (recorded in 1977) or the Lieder recital from Fischer-Dieskau and Barenboim (both in superb form), taken from a comprehensive survey recorded in the early 1980s, the highlight is the well-chosen selection from Brahms's folksong arrangements. These are simple, glowing settings, published only three years before the composer's death, but the product of a lifetime's love-affair with the music. Edith Mathis and Peter Schreier capture their innocent spirit delightfully, never overplaying their hands (sample Schreier's charming *Mein Mädel hat einen Rosenmund* or Mathis's lovely *Maria ging aus wandern*). Karl Engel accompanies sympathetically and the Chorus of the North German Radio (digitally recorded) provides two of the attractive choral settings.

(i) *Alto rhapsody, Op. 53;* (ii) *German Requiem; Song of destiny (Schicksalslied), Op. 54. Academic festival overture; Tragic overture; Variations on a theme by Haydn.*
(B) **(*) Ph. Duo 438 760-2 (2) [id.]. (i) Aafjé Heynis; (ii) Wilma Lipp, Franz Crass; (i; ii) V. Singverein; VSO, Sawallisch.

In the *German Requiem* Sawallisch may not penetrate the spiritual depths as deeply as a conductor like Haitink but, with a simple, dedicated manner that lets the music flow naturally and with the help of very fine choral singing and recording to point the climaxes, it is still a deeply satisfying version, with an account of the final movements both dramatic and ethereal. Franz Crass's dark bass colouring make his solos tonally distinctive, but the singing of Wilma Lipp in *Ihr habt nun Traurigkeit* is a blot, wobbly and plaintive-sounding. However, what makes this inexpensive set worth considering, even against the competition, is Aafjé Heynis's lovely singing in the *Alto rhapsody*. It is even more dedicated and 'inner' than Kathleen Ferrier's, and the tonal shading is most beautiful. The emotionally more turbulent *Song of destiny* is also a considerable success. Not all collectors will need the overtures, but they are well enough played and recorded, although the early date (1959) of the *Variations* shows in the violin timbre. Sawallisch's performance is brisk and alive, with the slower variations not quite as convincing as the quick ones.

49 Deutsche Volkslieder; 14 Folksongs for children.
(N) (M) *** DG 449 087-2 (2) [id.]. Edith Mathis, Peter Schreier, Karl Engel; N. German R. Ch., Günter Jena.

The writing here represents Brahms at his most engagingly domestic in these lovely folksong settings and the *Volks-Kinderlieder*, originally designed for the family of Robert and Clara Schumann. There is much to treasure here and the performances are fresh and brightly affectionate. The sound is first class and the documentation includes full translations. Recommended.

German Requiem, Op. 45.
⊛ *** Ph. Dig. 432 140-2 [id.]. Margiono, Gilfry, Monteverdi Ch., ORR, Eliot Gardiner.
(M) *** Teldec/Warner Dig. 9031 75862-2 [id.]. M. Price, Ramey, Amb. S., RPO, Previn.
(N) (M) (***) EMI mono CDH7 64705-2 [id.]. Grümmer, Fischer-Dieskau, St Hedwig's Cathedral Ch., BPO, Kempe.
(M) **(*) RCA Dig. 09026 61349-2. Battle, Hagegård, Chicago Ch. & SO, Levine.
(B) **(*) EMI Dig. CZS7 67819-2 (2) [id.]. Jessye Norman, Jorma Hynninen, LPO Ch., LPO, Tennstedt – SCHUMANN: *Requiems.* ***
(N) ** DG Dig. 437 517-2 [id.]. Studer, Schmidt, Swedish R. Ch., Eric-Ericson Chamber Ch., BPO, Abbado.
(N) *(*) RCA Dig. 09026 60868-2 [id.]. Blasi, Terfel, Bav. R. Ch. & RSO, Sir Colin Davis.
(N) * Erato/Warner Dig. 4509 92856-2 [id.]. Williams, Hampson, Chicago SO, Barenboim.
(N) (BB) * Naxos Dig. 8.550213 [id.]. Gauci, Tumagian, Slovak Philharmonic Ch., Slovak RSO, Alexander Rahbari.

(i) *German requiem. Burial song, Op. 13.*
(N) *** EMI Dig. CDC7 54658-2 [id.]. L. Dawson, Bär, L. Schütz Ch., LCP, Norrington.

Gardiner's 'revolutionary' account of the *German Requiem* brings a range of choral sound even more thrilling than in the concert hall. With period instruments and following Viennese practice of the time, speeds tend to be faster than usual, though the speed for the big fugue is surprisingly relaxed. Charlotte Margiono makes an ethereal soprano soloist, while Rodney Gilfry, despite a rapid vibrato, is aptly fresh and young-sounding. One could not ask for a more complete renovation of a masterpiece often made to sound stodgy and square.

It is the seeming simplicity of Previn's dedicated approach, with radiant singing from the chorus and measured speeds held steadily, that so movingly conveys an innocence in the often square writing, both in the powerful opening choruses and in the simple, songful *Wie lieblich.* The great fugatos are then powerfully presented. Both soloists are outstanding, Margaret Price golden-toned, Samuel Ramey incisively dark. The recording is warmly set against a helpful church acoustic with the chorus slightly distanced.

Roger Norrington, using period forces, comes into direct rivalry with John Eliot Gardiner in his Philips version recorded 18 months earlier. At speeds even faster and taking a plainer view but drawing equally fine singing from his choir, Norrington lacks some of Gardiner's dramatic flair, but Lynne Dawson sings with ravishing sweetness in her central solo, and Olaf Bär brings a lieder-like intensity to the baritone solos, even if he lacks a degree of darkness. Unlike Gardiner and most other rivals, Norrington offers a brief coupling, the dark *Burial song* with wind accompaniment.

Rudolf Kempe's mono recording of 1955 is incandescent, glowing with warmth, a characteristic example of his dedicated intensity in such a work. His view is flexibly expressive rather than rugged and, though the mono recording is limited on orchestral sound, the voices are caught vividly and atmospherically, with the choir the more involving for being forwardly balanced, something which modern digital recordings should heed more often. There is vintage singing too from both soloists, with the young Fischer-Dieskau darkly intense and with Elisabeth Grümmer sweetly radiant, superbly sustaining Kempe's exceptionally slow speed for *Ihr habt nun Traurigkeit.*

Levine's version features the Chicago Symphony Chorus, which is probably the finest in America, while his two soloists both prove excellent, Kathleen Battle pure and sweetly vulnerable-sounding, Hagegård clear-cut and firm. Levine is not the most illuminating conductor in this work and his pacing is not always convincing; yet the performance is alive, with power as well as impetus, and it undoubtedly gives pleasure. The recording is not ideal, with inner textures growing cloudy in tuttis.

Tennstedt's is an unusually spacious view of the *Requiem*, with speeds slower than on any rival version. His dedication generally sustains them well, with a reverential manner always alert, never becoming merely monumental, though the choir's ensemble is not always perfect. Jorma Hynninen proves an excellent soloist. What does sound monumental rather than moving is Jessye Norman's solo, *Ihr habt nun Traurigkeit,* though the golden tone is glorious. On CD, generally fine, spacious recording which matches the spaciousness of the interpretation.

Claudio Abbado conducts a strong and fresh if not especially distinctive reading, marked by excellent singing from the Swedish chorus as well as from the two soloists, Cheryl Studer and Andreas Schmidt. For all the warmth of expressiveness and the dynamic strength, the emotions of the piece are a degree underplayed, making this a safe reading rather than an inspired one.

Sir Colin Davis conducts his Munich forces in a weighty, at times four-square account, with unusually broad speeds in the outer movements punctuated in the middle by an exceptionally brisk and light one of the most celebrated movement, the chorus, *Wie lieblich* ('How lovely are thy dwellings'). The soprano solo, warmly sung by Angela Maria Blasi, also flows easily but rather lacks poetry. The most compelling moments involve the singing of Bryn Terfel in the third and sixth movements, more electrifyingly intense than anyone. Warm, atmospheric sound with choral detail not ideally clear.

Barenboim's Erato version from Chicago cannot match his earlier recording for DG in intensity. Exceptionally slow speeds for the first two movements sound dull and lacking in bite and tension, not helped by rather distant balance for the excellent chorus. Thomas Hampson is a splendid baritone soloist, but the warm-toned soprano, Janice Williams, does not sound quite secure.

On Naxos, Rahbari's reading at brisk speeds tends to be too matter-of-fact and lacking in detail, with the choral singing rather dull and inexpressive. By contrast the baritone, Eduard Tumagian, is warm and resonant, and Miriam Gauci takes a big-scale, operatic view of the soprano solo.

Liebeslieder waltzes, Op. 52; New Liebeslieder waltzes, Op. 65/15.
(M) (***) Decca mono 425 995-2 [id.]. Irmgaard Seefried, Kathleen Ferrier, Julius Patzak, Günter, Curzon, Gá – MAHLER: *Kindertotenlieder*. (**)
(N) ** EMI CDC5 55430-2 [id.]. Bonney, Von Otter, Streit, Bär, Deutsch, Forsberg – SCHUMANN: *Spanische Liebeslieder*. ***

Liebeslieder waltzes, Op. 52; New Liebeslieder waltzes, Op. 65; 3 Quartets, Op. 64.
*** DG Dig. 423 133-2 [id.]. Mathis, Fassbaender, Schreier, Fischer-Dieskau; Engel and Sawallisch (pianos).

On DG one of the most successful recordings yet of the two seductive but surprisingly difficult sets of *Liebeslieder waltzes*. The CD has fine realism and presence.

Recorded at the Edinburgh Festival in September 1952, the Decca historic performance brings a dazzling team together. Though it is not the most relaxed account, there are countless touches of imagination, not least from the very distinctive tenor, Julius Patzak, and the ever-responsive Clifford Curzon taking the upper piano part. Limited but clear sound.

With a most gifted quartet of young soloists recorded live at the 1994 Edinburgh Festival, the EMI version should be even more of a winner than it is: a crisp and clear reading, well sprung, that yet misses much of the magic caught by the earlier, equally distinguished quartet on the DG disc. Recommended only to those who want the very rare Schumann coupling.

Motets: *Ave Maria, Op. 12; 3 Fest-und Gedenksprüche, Op. 109; Geistliche Chöre, Op. 37; Geistliches Lied, Op. 30; 2 Motets, Op. 29; 2 Motets, Op. 74; 3 Motets, Op. 110; Psalm 13, Op. 27.*
*** Conifer Dig. 74321 15352-2 [id.]. Trinity College, Cambridge, Ch., Richard Marlow.

Richard Marlow and his excellent Cambridge choir add to their distinguished list of records with this invaluable collection, bringing together all sixteen of the motets which Brahms wrote over the course of his long career. With superb singing recorded vividly, this is an outstanding issue.

Die schöne Magelone (15 Romances), Op. 33.
(N) *** Teldec/Warner Dig. 4509 90854-2 [id.]. Brigitte Fassbaender, Elisabeth Leonskaya.

Brigitte Fassbaender's highly spontaneous account of Brahms's cycle is given a novel presentation here by the use of the original narrative, Ludwig Tieck's *The Love story of the Fair Magelone and Count Peter of Provence*. Fassbaender prefaces each song with a brief spoken narrative, placing it within the context of the story. Of course, like the songs, the commentary is in German (it would have been a happy idea if she had recorded an English alternative of the spoken text), but the translation booklet is complete. Miss Fassbaender characterizes strongly and is obviously highly involved herself in the progress of the tale, and therefore so are we. Fischer-Dieskau's recording of the songs had rather more subtlety of colour and mood, but not more life; Elisabeth Leonskaya's accompaniments participate strongly. The recording balance is excellent. The spoken introductions can be programmed out if the listener wishes.

Brian, Havergal (1876–1972)

(i) *Violin concerto; The Jolly Miller (comedy overture); Symphony No. 18.*
(**) Marco Polo Dig. 8.223479 [id.]. (i) Marat Bisengaliev, BBC Scottish SO, Lionel Friend.

Havergal Brian's *Violin concerto* has attractive and readily identifiable folksong-like ideas, notably the second subject of the first movement and the lyrical theme on which the slow movement's fifteen chimerical variations are based. The finale, like the Elgar *Concerto*, has an important cadenza in which the orchestra finally joins and it is the orchestra which, unusually, finishes the concerto without the soloist. It is an impressive work and is played with much feeling by Marat Bisengaliev, who is given powerful support by the BBC Scottish Orchestra under Lionel Friend. The snag is the close-miked recording, which at times brings an edge to the solo violin timbre and makes the many passionate orchestral tuttis sound fierce and aggressive instead of opulent in an Elgarian way. The concerto is prefaced by a jolly little overture introducing the folksong, *The Miller of Dee*, and is followed by a rather good small-scale symphony, with its three movements all based on march-like themes, ranging over a whole gamut of emotions and ending forcefully.

Symphony No. 1 (Gothic).
*** Marco Polo Dig. 8.223280/1; *4.223280/1* [id.]. Jenisová, Pecková, Dolezal, Mikulás, Slovak Philharmonic Ch., Slovak Nat. Theatre Op. Ch., Slovak Folk Ens. Ch., Lucnica Ch., Bratislava Chamber Ch. & Children's Ch., Youth Echo Ch., Czech RSO (Bratislava), Slovak PO, Ondrej Lenárd.

This first of the symphonies here receives a passionately committed performance from Slovak forces. Despite a few incidental flaws, it conveys surging excitement from first to last, helped by a rich recording which gives a thrilling impression of massed forces. The final *Te Deum*, alone lasting 72 minutes, brings fervent choral writing of formidable complexity, with the challenge superbly taken up by the Czech musicians.

Symphony No. 3 in C sharp min.
**(*) Hyperion Dig. CDA 66334. Ball, Jacobson, BBC SO, Friend.

The *Third Symphony* began life as a concerto for piano; this perhaps explains the prominent role given to two pianos in the score. The work is full of extraordinarily imaginative and original touches, but the overall lack of rhythmic variety is a handicap. The playing of the BBC Symphony Orchestra under Lionel Friend is well prepared and dedicated, but the recording does not open out sufficiently in climaxes.

Symphonies Nos. 7 in C; 31; The Tinker's wedding: comedy overture.
(M) *** EMI CDM7 64717-2 [id.]. RLPO, Mackerras.

Mackerras and the Royal Liverpool Philharmonic bring together the last of the expansive works, No. 7, completed in 1948, allying Brian's earlier style with the often elliptical manners of his later, more concentrated work, and the penultimate symphony of the whole series, written just 20 years later, after an amazing eruption of creative activity. The brilliant comedy overture, *The Tinker's wedding*, more conventional in its material and manner if still at times unpredictable, provides an attractive make-weight. The unconverted may still have doubts whether Brian's music has quite the cohesion and musical strength it obviously aims at, but this collection presents him and his achievement more effectively than any other disc. Beautifully played and vividly recorded, it can be recommended to anyone fascinated by an extraordinary, offbeat composer.

Bridge, Frank (1879–1941)

Cherry ripe; Sir Roger de Coverley; Suite for strings; There is a willow grows aslant a brook.
**(*) Koch Dig. 3-7139-2 [id.]. New Zealand CO, Nicholas Braithwaite – DELIUS: *Sonata for strings.* **(*)

A nicely played, pastel-shaded performance of Bridge's *Suite for string orchestra*, with the delicacy of feeling in the lovely, ethereal *Nocturne* making amends for any lack of robustness elsewhere. The folk-song arrangements are also attractively done and, if Britten's old ECO recording of *Sir Roger de Coverley* was even wittier, the poignant 'impression' (the composer's own term), *There is a willow grows aslant a brook* is beautifully played. The modern digital recording is both fresh and transparent.

Oration (Concerto elegiaco) for cello and orchestra.
(M) *** EMI Dig. CDM7 63909-2. Isserlis, City of L. Sinfonia, Hickox – BRITTEN: *Symphony for cello and orchestra.* **(*)

Oration is in effect a massive cello concerto in nine linked sections. Though Isserlis is not always as passionate as Baillie, his focus is sharper, and with Hickox he brings out the originality of the writing all the more cleanly. It is fascinating to find some passages anticipating the more abrasive side of Britten, and specifically the *Cello symphony* with which this is coupled.

Phantasm for piano and orchestra.
*** Conifer Dig. 74321 15007-2 [id.]. Kathryn Stott, RPO, Handley – IRELAND: *Piano concerto;*
WALTON: *Sinfonia concertante.* ***

Bridge's curiously titled *Phantasm* is a large-scale piano concerto, some 26 minutes long, in a single, massive movement. Kathryn Stott, most sympathetically accompanied by Vernon Handley and the RPO, proves a persuasive, committed interpreter, matching her achievement in the other two works on the disc. Warm, generally well-balanced recording.

The Sea (suite).
*** Chandos Dig. CHAN 8473 [id.]. Ulster O, Handley – BAX: *On the sea-shore;* BRITTEN: *Sea interludes.* ***

The Sea receives a brilliant and deeply sympathetic performance from Handley and the Ulster Orchestra, recorded with a fullness and vividness to make this a demonstration disc.

Suite for strings.
*** Chandos Dig. CHAN 8390 [id.]. ECO, Garforth – IRELAND: *Downland suite; Holy Boy; Elegiac meditations.* ***
*** Nimbus Dig. NI 5068 [id.]. E. String O, Boughton – BUTTERWORTH: *Banks of green willow; Idylls; Shropshire lad;* PARRY: *Lady Radnor's suite.* ***

Suite for string orchestra; Summer; There is a willow grows aslant a brook.
(M) *** Chandos CHAN 6566 [id.]. Bournemouth Sinf., Norman Del Mar – BANTOCK: *Pierrot of the minute;* BUTTERWORTH: *Banks of green willow.* ***

Summer is beautifully played by the Bournemouth Sinfonietta under Norman Del Mar. The same images of nature permeate the miniature tone-poem, *There is a willow grows aslant a brook*, an inspired piece, very sensitively managed. The *Suite for strings* is equally individual. Its third movement, a *Nocturne*, is lovely. The CD transfer is excellent and one can relish its fine definition and presence.

The ECO also play well for David Garforth in the *Suite for strings*. This performance is extremely committed; it is certainly excellently recorded, with great clarity and presence.

The Nimbus collection is more generous and is certainly well chosen. Here Bridge's *Suite* again receives a lively and responsive performance, from William Boughton and his excellent Birmingham-based orchestra, treated to ample, sumptuously atmospheric recording, more resonant than its competitors.

CHAMBER MUSIC

Cello sonata.
(Y/B) (M) *** Decca 443 575-2 [id.]. Rostropovich, Britten – SCHUBERT: *Arpeggione sonata.* **(*)
*** Chandos Dig. CHAN 8499 [id.]. Raphael and Peter Wallfisch – BAX: *Rhapsodic ballad;* DELIUS: *Sonata;* WALTON: *Passacaglia.* ***

Cello sonata; 2 Pieces: Meditation; Spring song.
**(*) ASV Dig. CDDCA 796 [id.]. Bernard Gregor-Smith, Yolande Wrigley – DEBUSSY; DOHNANYI: *Sonatas.* **(*)

Bridge wrote his *Cello sonata* during the First World War. The craftsmanship is distinguished and the lines delicately traced, and the modulations are often personal. The playing on Decca is of an altogether rare order, even by the exalted standards of Rostropovich and Britten, and the recording, made at The Maltings in 1968, has immediacy, warmth and great response. The reissue features its original coupling in Decca's Classic Sound series.

It is a distinctive world that Bridge evokes in the *Cello sonata* and one to which Raphael Wallfisch and his father, Peter, are completely attuned, and they are beautifully recorded.

The ASV account by Bernard Gregor-Smith and Yolande Wrigley can hold its head high. It is played with intensity and sensitivity. The recording is a bit close, but those wanting the coupling (and the Dohnányi is an excellent piece) need not hesitate.

3 Idylls for string quartet.
(Y/B) *** Hyperion Dig. CDA 66718 [id.]. Coull Qt – ELGAR: *Quartet* **(*); WALTON: *Quartet.* ***
*** Conifer Dig. 74321 15006-2. Brindisi Qt – BRITTEN: *String quartet No. 2;* Imogen HOLST: *String quartet No. 1.* ***

The *Three Idylls* date from 1906, soon after Bridge's first regular quartet. As this superb, purposeful performance by the Coull Quartet shows, the separate pieces, each marked by sharp changes of mood as a phantasie-form, make up a satisfying whole, a quartet in all but name. They provide a superb bonus to a fine performance of the Elgar and an outstanding performance of the Walton *Quartet*. Excellent sound.

They are also well served by the Brindisi Quartet.

(i) *Phantasy (quartet) in F sharp min. Phantasy trio in C min.; Piano trio No. 2.*
*** Hyperion Dig. CDA 66279 [id.]. Dartington Trio; (i) with P. Ireland.

The playing of the *Phantasy trio* by the Dartington Trio is of exceptional eloquence and sensitivity. They are no less persuasive in the *F sharp minor Phantasy*. Their account of the visionary post-war *Piano trio No. 2* of 1929 is completely inside this score. The Hyperion recording is altogether superb, in the demonstration bracket, perfectly natural and beautifully proportioned.

PIANO MUSIC

Arabesque; Capriccios Nos. 1–2; Dedication; Fairy tale suite; Gargoyle; Hidden fires; In autumn; 3 Miniatures; Pastorals, Sets 1–2; Sea idyll; 3 Improvisations for the left hand; Winter pastoral.
*** Continuum Dig. CCD 1016 [id.]. Peter Jacobs.

Berceuse; Canzonetta; 4 Characteristic pieces; Dramatic fantasia; Etude rhapsodic; Lament; Pensées fugitives; 3 Pieces; 4 Pieces; 3 Poems; Scherzettino.
*** Continuum Dig. CCD 1018 [id.]. Peter Jacobs.

Piano sonata; Graziella; The Hour-glass; 3 Lyrics; Miniature pastorals, Set 3; Miniature suite (ed. Hindmarsh); *3 Sketches.* arr. of BACH: *Chorale: Komm, süsser Tod, BWV 478.*
*** Continuum Dig. CCD 1019 [id.]. Peter Jacobs.

Peter Jacobs provides a complete survey of the piano music of Frank Bridge, and it proves an invaluable enterprise. The recorded sound is very good indeed: clean, well defined and present, and the acoustic lively. Calum MacDonald's excellent notes tracking his development over these years are worth a mention too.

Piano sonata; Capriccios Nos. 1 & 2; Ecstasy; The Hour-glass; Sea Idyll; Vignettes de Marseille.
*** Conifer Dig. 75605 51186-2 [id.]. Kathryn Stott.

Kathryn Stott provides a formidable and illuminating single-disc selection from the piano music of Frank Bridge, for those who are unable or unwilling to stretch to Peter Jacobs's indispensable complete survey. Kathryn Stott's recital culminates in the masterly large-scale *Sonata* that Bridge wrote in disillusion in the years after the First World War, and she gives it a powerfully concentrated account. It is arguably the greatest piano sonata ever written by a British composer. The short early pieces, brilliantly and imaginatively written, give little inkling of such a development. Kathryn Stott is responsive to every changing mood, and these are outstanding performances, very well recorded.

Bristow, George Frederick (1825–98)

Symphony in F sharp min., Op. 26.
*** Chandos Dig. CHAN 9169 [id.]. Detroit SO, Järvi – BARBER: *Symphony No. 2.* ***

Although George Frederick Bristow was a vigorous campaigner for American music, there is little distinctively American in his *Symphony in F sharp minor* (1858). Its speech is rather Mendelssohnian and, although it serves to fill in our picture of American music of the period, its claims to mastery are slim.

Britten, Benjamin (1913–76)

An American overture; Ballad of heroes; The building of the house; Canadian carnival; (i) *Diversions for piano (left hand) and orchestra. Occasional overture; Praise we great men; Scottish ballad; Sinfonia da Requiem; Suite on English folk tunes; A time there was . . .; Young Apollo;* (ii) *4 Chansons françaises.*
(Y/B) *** EMI Dig. CDS7 54270-2 (2) [CDCB 54270]. (i) Peter Donohoe; (ii) Jill Gomez; CBSO, Rattle.

A valuable compilation from the various recordings of Britten's music, most of it rare, which Rattle has made over the years. It is good to have the *Diversions for piano (left-hand) and orchestra* with Peter Donohoe as soloist – amazingly this was the first version in stereo – and the most cherishable item of all is the radiant performance given by Jill Gomez of the *Four Chansons françaises*, the remarkable and tenderly affecting settings of Hugo and Verlaine composed by the fifteen-year-old Britten. This collection of reissues is offered at full rather than medium price, but it is worth it.

An American overture; Sinfonia da Requiem, Op. 20; Peter Grimes: 4 Sea interludes and Passacaglia, Op. 33.
(N) (BB) **(*) Naxos Dig. 8.553107 [id.]. New Zealand SO, Fredman.

Myer Fredman conducts warm and purposeful performances of this group of orchestral works from early in Britten's career. Though the New Zealand strings are not as rich or as resonant as most, the purity of sound makes up for power in spontaneous-sounding performances. Dramatic and atmospheric points are well made with the help of a warm hall acoustic and full-ranging recording. Recommendable at super-budget price.

Clarinet concerto movement (orch. Colin Matthews).
*** Hyperion Dig. CDA 66634 [id.]. Thea King, ECO, Wordsworth – ARNOLD: *Clarinet concertos* etc.; MACONCHY: *Concertinos.* ***

Benny Goodman, having commissioned Bartók to write *Contrasts*, turned in 1942 to the young Benjamin Britten, then in the United States, to write a concerto for him. Sadly, just before Britten returned to England, Goodman suggested a delay, and the composer never even sorted out the sketches. Colin Matthews, who worked closely with Britten during his last three years, has here fathomed what Britten intended and has orchestrated the result to make a highly attractive short piece, alternately energetic and poetic, with material adroitly interchanged and with percussion used most imaginatively. Thea King, as in the rest of the disc, plays the piece most persuasively, making one regret deeply that it was never completed.

Piano concerto in D, Op. 13.
(M) **(*) Chandos CHAN 6580 [id.]. Gillian Lin, Melbourne SO, John Hopkins – COPLAND: *Concerto.* **(*)
(Y/B) (M) **(*) Hyperion Dig. CDA 66293 [id.]. Annette Servadei, LPO, Giunta – KHACHATURIAN: *Piano concerto.* **(*)

(i) *Piano concerto, Op. 13;* (ii) *Violin concerto, Op. 15.*
(M) *** Decca 417 308-2. (i) Sviatoslav Richter; (ii) Lubotsky; ECO, composer.

(i) *Piano concerto, Op. 13. Paul Bunyan overture.*
*** Collins Dig. 1102-2 [id.]. (i) Joanna MacGregor; ECO, Bedford – SAXTON: *Music to celebrate the resurrection of Christ.* ***

Britten wrote his formidable *Piano concerto* for a Prom in 1938. He later rejected the slow movement and replaced it in 1945 with an *Impromptu*, simpler and more obviously apt. The characterful young Joanna MacGregor gets the best of both worlds by recording both slow movements, so that you can take your pick. With Steuart Bedford a deeply understanding conductor, this is a ripe and refreshing performance, well recorded. The brassy *Paul Bunyan overture*, never used with the operetta, has been orchestrated by Colin Matthews.

Richter is incomparable in interpreting the *Piano concerto*, not only the thoughtful, introspective moments but the Liszt-like bravura passages. With its highly original sonorities the *Violin concerto* makes a splendid vehicle for another Soviet artist, Mark Lubotsky. Recorded in The Maltings, the playing of the ECO under the composer's direction matches the inspiration of the soloists.

Gillian Lin provides a useful alternative to Richter's classic recording. Miss Lin cannot match the Soviet master in detailed imagination but, from her sharp attack on the opening motif onwards, she gives a strong and satisfying reading, well accompanied by Hopkins and the Melbourne orchestra. The 1978 recorded sound is wide-ranging and well balanced on this lively CD, which makes a useful mid-priced alternative, with its rarer Copland coupling.

With good, well-balanced digital recording, Annette Servadei gives a strong, dedicated, muscular performance. South-African born but trained mainly in Italy, Servadei is nevertheless a devotee of British music. She is particularly impressive in the hushed and sustained passacaglia, entitled *Impromptu*, which takes the place of the slow movement and provided Walton with the theme of his *Variations on an Impromptu of Britten.*

Violin concerto, Op. 15.
(M) *** EMI CDM7 64202-2 [id.]. Ida Haendel, Bournemouth SO, Berglund – WALTON: *Violin concerto.* ***

(i) *Violin concerto, Op. 15. Canadian carnival overture, Op. 19; Mont Juic* (written with Lennox Berkeley). ✱ *** Collins Dig. 1123-2 [id.]. (i) Lorraine McAslan, ECO, Steuart Bedford.

(i) *Violin concerto in D min., Op. 15;* (ii) *Serenade for tenor, horn and strings, Op. 31.*
(N) (BB) *** CfP Silver Double CDCFPSD 4754 (2). (i) Rodney Friend; (ii) Ian Partridge, Busch; LPO, Pritchard – TIPPETT: *Concerto for double string orchestra ***;* VAUGHAN WILLIAMS: *Tallis fantasia* etc. ***; WALTON: *Belshazzar's feast.* **(*)

Lorraine McAslan's virtuosity is effortless and always subservient to musical ends; her artistic insights are unusually keen and she brings to the *Concerto* a subtle imagination and great emotional intensity. Steuart Bedford gets first-class playing from the English Chamber Orchestra and emphasizes the pain and poignancy underlying much of this music. The recording is remarkably well balanced, truthful and exceptionally wide-ranging and vivid. *Mont Juic* and the *Canadian carnival overture* are eminently well served by these splendid musicians and the engineers.

It was a happy idea to combine the most colourful of Britten's song-cycles with the *Violin concerto*. It was an equally good idea to exploit the artistry of two outstanding performers. Rodney Friend, at the time (1974) leader of the LPO, later concertmaster of the New York Philharmonic, proves a masterful soloist, magnificently incisive and expansive. As for Ian Partridge – one of the most consistently stylish of recording tenors – he gives a reading often strikingly new in its illumination, more tenderly beautiful and purer than Peter Pears's classic reading, culminating in a heavenly performance of the final Keats sonnet setting. With vivid recording, this is part of a highly desirable Silver Double aptly entitled '*The Best of England*', with only James Loughran's account of Walton's *Belshazzar's feast* below the overall high standard of all the rest.

Ida Haendel's ravishing playing places the work firmly in the European tradition. She brings great panache and brilliance to the music, as well as great expressive warmth. This is a reading very much in the grand manner and it finds Paavo Berglund in excellent form. His support is sensitive in matters of detail and full of atmosphere. The recording is full and realistic, with a beautifully spacious perspective that creates a positively Mediterranean feeling. The soloist is balanced a little close, but the security of her technique can stand up to such a spotlight and the performance has great conviction.

Diversions for piano (left hand) and orchestra.
*** Sony Dig. SK 47188 [id.]. Fleisher, Boston SO, Ozawa – PROKOFIEV: *Piano concerto No. 4;* RAVEL: *Left-hand concerto.* ***

Leon Fleisher lost the use of his right hand at the height of his career and is currently engaged on an ambitious project with Sony to record repertoire for the left hand. The present issue assembles three of the most brilliant and rewarding pieces for the medium, all commissioned by Paul Wittgenstein, brother of the philosopher, who lost his right hand during the First World War. The *Diversions* is a wartime work, highly inventive and resourceful, whose neglect over the years is puzzling. Fleisher gives a sensitive and intelligent account with great sympathy and skill. His playing has strong character and he receives more than decent support from Ozawa and the Boston orchestra and eminently truthful recording.

(i) *Diversions for piano (left hand) and orchestra, Op. 21;* (ii) *Sinfonia da Requiem, Op. 20;* (iii) *Young person's guide to the orchestra, Op. 34.*
(M) **(*) Sony Dig./Analogue SMK 58930 [id.]. (i) Leon Fleisher, Boston SO, Ozawa; (ii) St Louis SO, Previn; (iii) LSO, Andrew Davis.

Fleisher's recording is also available differently coupled – see above. The St Louis orchestra plays with great spirit in the *Sinfonia da Requiem* and Previn's performance is obviously deeply felt. If it is not quite a match for the composer's own, it has a well-detailed (1963) recording. To complete the disc, Andrew Davis directs an account of the *Young person's guide* that is bright and workmanlike, rather than one with any special flair or brilliance. But it is enjoyable enough, and the (1975) Abbey Road recording sounds well on CD.

(i; ii) *Lachrymae (Reflections on a song by Dowland);* (i) *Prelude and fugue, Op. 29; Simple Symphony, Op. 4; Variations on a theme of Frank Bridge, Op. 10;* (ii) *Elegy for solo viola.*
(Y/B) ✱ *** Virgin/EMI Dig. VC5 45121-2 [id.]. (i) Norwegian CO, Iona Brown; (ii) Lars Anders Tomter.

Iona Brown gives performances of the *Simple Symphony* and the *Frank Bridge variations* to match and almost surpass the composer's own. The *Simple Symphony* fizzes with youthful energy, yet Iona Brown brings an unusually wide dynamic and expressive range to the first movement and the poignant *Sentimental sarabande*, which elevates Britten's writing far beyond any suggestion of juvenilia. The *Playful pizzicato* has a splendid bounce. The *Frank Bridge variations* have never sounded more emotionally powerful on record and, after the opening flourish, the raptly quiet playing of the solo strings draws

a parallel with the Vaughan Williams *Tallis fantasia*. The starkness of the *Funeral march* compares with
the famous Karajan/Philharmonia version in its intensity, and in the following *Chant* the Norwegian
players show they understand all about icy landscapes. The finale brings a release of the utmost virtuosity, crisp ensemble, and then great tenderness, leading to a hushed pianissimo from the violins to surpass
even the opening solo passages. In the *Lachrymae* Lars Anders Tomter is an outstanding soloist, not
least in the touching full presentation of Dowland's tune, *If my complaints could passions move*, in the
haunting coda. He follows the *Lachrymae* with an ardent account of the solo *Elegy*. The recording is in
the demonstration bracket, and this fine concert throughout conveys the natural spontaneity of seemingly live music-making.

(i) *Lachrymae. Simple Symphony, Op. 4; Variations on a theme of Frank Bridge, Op. 10; Young Apollo,
Op. 16.*
(N) *** Chandos Dig. CHAN 8817 [id.]. (i) Rivka Golani; Montreal I Musici, Turovsky.

Under Yuli Turovsky the Montreal players give passionate performances of another attractively chosen
group of Britten works, two popular, two rare. *Young Apollo*, resurrected after Britten's death, is particularly successful, with vivid recording capturing the unusual textures with piano and string quartet as
well as strings. Rivka Golani is a resonant soloist in *Lachrymae*, and the *Variations* and *Simple
Symphony* have similar heft, helped by the rich, upfront recording.

Matinées musicales; Soirées musicales.
(Y/B) (M) *** Decca Dig. 444 109-2 [id.]. Nat. PO, Bonynge – ROSSINI: *La Boutique fantasque.* ***

Matinées musicales; Soirées musicales; Variations on a theme of Frank Bridge.
(B) *** CfP Dig. CD-CFP 4598. ECO, Gibson.

Britten wrote his *Soirées musicales* for a GPO film-score in the 1930s; the *Matinées* followed in 1941 and
were intended as straight ballet music. Both are wittily if rather sparsely scored, deriving their musical
content directly from Rossini. Bonynge's versions are brightly played and extremely vividly recorded in
the best Decca manner, and are now reissued at mid-price in this company's Ballet Gala series.

The ECO play very well indeed for Sir Alexander Gibson, and readers requiring this particular coupling
need not hesitate on either artistic or technical grounds. The *Frank Bridge variations* display strong
characterization and virtuosity in equal measure. The recording is full and resonant; only the bright
lighting of the violin-timbre above the stave betrays the early date of the digital recording (1982).

(i) *Matinées musicales; Soirées musicales;* (ii; iv) *Young person's guide to the orchestra;* (iii; iv) *Peter
Grimes: 4 Sea interludes and Passacaglia.*
(M) *** Decca 425 659-2 [id.]. (i) Nat. PO, Bonynge; (ii) LSO; (iii) ROHCG O; (iv) composer.

Bonynge's versions of the *Matinées* and *Soirées musicales* are here reissued, coupled with Britten's
accounts of the *Young person's guide to the orchestra* and the *Sea interludes and Passacaglia*.

*Prelude and fugue for 18 solo strings, Op. 29; Simple Symphony, Op. 4; Variations on a theme of Frank
Bridge, Op. 10.*
*** ASV Dig. CDDCA 591 [id.]. N. Sinfonia, Hickox.

The ASV issue is notable for an outstandingly fine account of the *Frank Bridge variations*, which stands
up well alongside the composer's own version. Throughout, the string playing is committedly responsive, combining polish with eloquence, the rich sonorities resonating powerfully in the glowing ambience
of All Saints' Quayside Church, Newcastle.

The Prince of the Pagodas (complete).
⚜ *** Virgin/EMI Dig. VCD7 59578-2 (2) [id.]. L. Sinf., Knussen.

The multicoloured instrumentation – much influenced by Britten's visit to Bali – is caught with glorious
richness in Oliver Knussen's really complete version. Most importantly he opens out more than 40 cuts,
most of them small, which Britten sanctioned to fit his own recording on to four LP sides. The
performance is outstanding and so is the recording.

Prince of the Pagodas: Pas de six. Gloriana: symphonic suite; Peter Grimes: 4 Sea interludes.
(N) (M) *** EMI Dig. CD-EMX 2231; *TC-EMX 2231*. RLPO, Takuo Yuasa.

Takuo Yuasa conducts these orchestral pieces, drawn from Britten's stage works, with great colour and
flair, matching and even outshining any rival versions. The Liverpool orchestra is in virtuoso form, and
the recording is full and rich. If the programme appeals, this is good value.

Simple Symphony (for strings), Op. 4.
*** DG Dig. 423 624-2 [id.]. Orpheus CO – BIZET: *Symphony;* PROKOFIEV: *Symphony No. 1.* ***

Simple Symphony, Op. 4; Prelude and fugue for 18-part string orchestra, Op. 29.
(N) (M) *** Decca 448 569-2 [id.]. ECO, composer – Concert of *English string music.* *** ⊛

(i) *Simple Symphony, Op. 4; Variations on a theme of Frank Bridge, Op. 10;* (ii) *The Young person's guide to the orchestra (Variations and fugue on a theme of Purcell), Op. 34.*
(M) *** Decca 440 321-2 [id.]. (i) ECO; (ii) LSO, composer (with DELIUS: (i) *2 Aquarelles;* BRIDGE: *Sir Roger de Coverley for string orchestra* ***).

(i) *Simple Symphony, Op. 4; Variations on a theme of Frank Bridge;* (ii) *Young person's guide to the orchestra; Peter Grimes: 4 Sea interludes.*
(Y/B) (M) **(*) Nimbus NI 7017 [id.]. (i) E. String O; (ii) E. SO, Boughton.

The composer's own recording of the *Simple Symphony* was originally contained in an outstanding anthology called 'Britten conducts English music' – see the Concerts section – but is also here available in a slightly different permutation. Britten's three most famous orchestral works are generously supplemented with warmly atmospheric accounts of the two Delius *Aquarelles* and a refreshingly lively performance of Bridge's *Sir Roger de Coverley*, which wittily interpolates *Auld lang syne*. The three Britten works are very brightly transferred with very tangible strings and great clarity and presence overall; some ears, however, might decide that the violins are too brightly lit. Britten takes a very brisk view of his *Young person's guide*, so brisk that even the LSO players cannot always quite match him. But every bar has a vigour which makes the music sound more youthful than usual, and the headlong, uninhibited account of the final fugue (trombones as vulgar as you like) is an absolute joy. In the *Frank Bridge variations* Britten goes more for half-tones and he achieves an almost circumspect coolness in the waltz-parody of the *Romance*; in the *Viennese waltz* section later, he is again subtly atmospheric; and in the *Funeral march* he is relatively solemn. The *Simple Symphony* makes a splendid foil, with its charm and high spirits, aided by the glowing resonance of The Maltings where the recording was made.

The *Simple Symphony* goes nicely alongside the Bizet and Prokofiev works, especially when played as freshly and characterfully as here by the Orpheus group. Britten himself found more fun in the *Playful pizzicato*, but the reading is all-of-a-piece and enjoyably spontaneous. Excellent, realistic sound.

William Boughton offers an attractive and generous 75-minute Britten anthology, very well played and showing the sumptuous Nimbus recording style at its most effective. The *Simple Symphony* and *Frank Bridge variations* were recorded in the Great Hall of Birmingham University in 1985 and are most sympathetically played (the *Playful pizzicato* has a resonance to match the composer's own version). The *Young person's guide* and *Sea interludes* were recorded in Birmingham's new Symphony Hall in 1991 and, while equally rich in texture, have even better definition. The famous *Variations* are amiably colourful, but Boughton is fired with a strongly emotional response to the *Sea Interludes*, bringing out the inner tensions in *Moonlight* most involvingly, while the powerful *Storm* sequence is highly spectacular.

Sinfonia da Requiem, Op. 20.
(M) *** EMI Dig. CDM7 64870-2 [id.]. CBSO, Simon Rattle – SHOSTAKOVICH: *Symphony No. 10.* **

Rattle's passionate view of the *Sinfonia da Requiem* is unashamedly extrovert, yet it finds subtle detail too. The EMI recording is admirably vivid and clear, but the Shostakovich coupling is less convincing.

(i) *Sinfonia da Requiem, Op. 20;* (ii) *Symphony for cello and orchestra, Op. 68;* (iii) *Cantata misericordium, Op. 69.*
(M) *** Decca 425 100-2 [id.]. (i) New Philh. O; (ii) Rostropovich, ECO; (iii) Pears, Fischer-Dieskau, London Symphony Ch., LSO; composer.

All the performances here are definitive, and Rostropovich's account of the *Cello symphony* in particular is everything one could ask for. The CD transfers are admirably managed.

Sinfonia da Requiem, Op. 20; The Young person's guide to the orchestra, Op. 34; Peter Grimes: 4 Sea interludes & Passacaglia, Op. 33.
(Y/B) (M) **(*) Virgin/EMI Dig. CUV5 61195-2 [id.]. RLPO, Libor Pešek.

Sinfonia da Requiem; Young person's guide to the orchestra, Op. 34; Peter Grimes: 4 Sea interludes and Passacaglia. arr. of PURCELL: *Chacony for strings in G min.*
(N) ** RCA Dig. 09026 61226-2 [id.]. LPO, Leonard Slatkin.

Though Pešek fails to convey the full ominous weight of the first movement of the *Sinfonia da Requiem*, he then directs a dazzling account of the central *Dies Irae Scherzo*, taken breathtakingly fast, and finds an intense repose in the calm of the final *Requiem aeternam*. The *Sea interludes* sound very literal, not ideally atmospheric. The *Young person's guide* lacks a degree of tension, with the fugue not dashing enough. The recording is comfortably reverberant.

Helped by vivid recording, Leonard Slatkin draws brilliant playing from the LPO in this group of popular Britten works. The approach is objective rather than expressive, so the very precision detracts a degree from warmth and purposefulness: these are pieces that gain from not sounding too easy.

Sinfonia da Requiem; Gloriana: symphonic suite; Peter Grimes: 4 Sea interludes and Passacaglia.
(N) *** Collins Dig. 1019-2 [id.]. LSO, Bedford.

In his Britten series for Collins, Steuart Bedford conducts strong, idiomatic performances of these works, helped by exceptionally vivid recording. The atmosphere of the *Peter Grimes Interludes* is caught superbly, and the *Sinfonia da Requiem*, treated expansively, culminates in a radiant account of the final *Requiem aeternam*, much more telling than the Slatkin account. Recommended.

Sinfonietta, Op. 1.
(N) *** BIS Dig. CD 540 [id.]. Tapiola Sinf., Vänskä – *Nocturne; Serenade* etc. ***

The *Sinfonietta* (also available in a chamber performance – see below) is busier in its textures than mature Britten; it is here presented with rare strength and warmth to make it totally convincing. It is very well recorded and comes with an attractive collection of vocal music.

Suite on English folksongs (A time there was); Young person's guide to the orchestra, Op. 34; Peter Grimes: 4 Sea interludes and Passacaglia.
(M) **(*) Sony SMK 47541. NYPO, Leonard Bernstein.

Bernstein's charismatic account of the *Young person's guide to the orchestra* brings much exhilarating bravura from the New York soloists, notably the flutes, clarinets and trumpets. The 1961 recording, made in the New York Manhattan Center, is fuller than usual from this source. The performance of *A time there was* (its title quoting Hardy) reveals a darkness and weight of expression behind the seemingly trivial plan. For violins alone, *Hunt the squirrel* is brief, brilliant and witty. Bernstein misses a little of the wit but is warmly sympathetic, and the dramatic account of the *Grimes interludes*, with a powerful *Passacaglia*, makes a good coupling.

Symphony for cello and orchestra, Op. 68.
(M) *** Sony Dig. SMK 58928 [id.]. Yo-Yo Ma, Baltimore SO, David Zinman – MAXWELL DAVIES: *Violin concerto*. ***
(M) **(*) EMI Dig. CDM7 63909-2. Stephen Isserlis, City of L. Sinfonia, Hickox – BRIDGE: *Oration*. ***
(*) Russian Disc RDCD 11108 [id.]. Rostropovich, Moscow PO, composer – SAUGUET: *Mélodie concertante*. *

(i) *Symphony for cello and orchestra, Op. 68. Death in Venice: suite, Op. 88* (arr. Bedford).
*** Chandos Dig. CHAN 8363 [id.]. (i) Wallfisch; ECO, Bedford.

Sounding less improvisatory than Rostropovich (see above), Wallfisch and Bedford give a more consistent sense of purpose, and the weight and range of the brilliant and full Chandos recording quality add to the impact, with Bedford's direction even more spacious than the composer's. Steuart Bedford's encapsulation of Britten's last opera into this rich and colourful suite makes a splendid coupling.

What predominates in Yo-Yo Ma's partnership with David Zinman is the wayward mystery in the first movement, rather than its more aggressive qualities, and in the Scherzo Ma is masterly in bringing out the lightness and fantasy. The third-movement *Adagio* is softer-grained than usual, with the soloist placed naturally, leading on to an account of the finale, a shade faster than usual, compellingly purposeful, which brings out the Copland-like swagger of the main passacaglia theme. The orchestra plays with brilliance and commitment in a full and well-balanced recording.

Stephen Isserlis provides a valuable mid-priced alternative to Wallfisch and Ma. With speeds generally a little slower, Isserlis is not quite as taut and electric as his rival, partly because the recording does not present the solo instrument so cleanly.

The special interest of the Russian Disc issue resides in the fact that it includes a recording of the very first performance of the *Cello Symphony* on 12 March 1964, given by its dedicatee and 'onlie begetter' with Britten himself conducting. It is not as well recorded as the version Rostropovich and Britten made for Decca not long afterwards, but there is terrific intensity and concentration here.

A time there was (suite on English folk tunes), *Op. 90; Johnson over Jordan* (suite, arr. P. Hindmarsh); *Young person's guide to the orchestra, Op. 34; Peter Grimes: 4 Sea interludes.*
(N) *** Chandos Dig. CHAN 9221 [id.]. Bournemouth SO, Hickox.

Richard Hickox and the Bournemouth orchestra offer an attractive coupling, opulently recorded, of two of Britten's most popular works, both done with flair, set against two rarities. *A time there was* is the suite which Britten wrote at the very end of his life, characteristically original and with a new, elusive vein. The *Johnson over Jordan suite* is drawn from the incidental music which Britten wrote in 1939 for an experimental play of J. B. Priestley in which music and mime played an integral part. If the style is uncharacteristic of the later Britten, the colour and vitality are most winning, played here with verve.

Variations on a theme of Frank Bridge, Op. 10; Simple Symphony, Op. 4.
(M) (***) Dutton mono CDAX 8007 [id.]. Boyd Neel O, Neel – VAUGHAN WILLIAMS: *Concerto accademico* etc. (***)

In 1937 the Boyd Neel String Orchestra commissioned the 23–year-old Benjamin Britten to write a new work for them to take to that year's Salzburg Festival; the *Variations on a theme of Frank Bridge* was the result. They recorded it on three gold-label Decca 78s the following year and, although Britten's own Decca performance remains indispensable, there is something very special about this pioneering recording. The playing is full of imaginative touches and there is a poetic intensity that brings this music vividly to life. Michael Dutton has done a splendid job in restoring these discs, and those who are acquainted with or possess the originals will be astonished at his results. The same applies to the *Simple Symphony*, which the same artists recorded some months later.

Variations and fugue on a theme by Frank Bridge; Young person's guide to the orchestra; Peter Grimes: 4 Sea interludes & Passacaglia.
(N) *** Teldec/Warner Dig. 9031 73126 [id.]. BBC SO, Andrew Davis.

In his admirable British music series for Teldec, Andrew Davis gives full weight as well as brilliance to these masterpieces from early in Britten's career, making a particularly attractive triptych. The *Frank Bridge variations*, set here against the more popular Purcell set, gain particularly from large-scale treatment, with each variation strongly characterized. Excellent recording.

Young Apollo, Op. 16; (i) Les Illuminations, Op. 18.
(N) ** ASV Dig. CDDCA 737 [id.]. (i) Carole Farley, SCO, Serebrier – BARBER: *Canzonetta; Souvenirs.* **

Carole Farley is a forceful soloist in *Les illuminations*, incisive in attack but missing the subtlety and beauty of the piece, with the voice raw under pressure. *Young Apollo* too needs a subtler, less square reading than this for its full originality to be appreciated.

Young person's guide to the orchestra (with narration).
(N) ** Cala Dig. CACD 1022 [id.]. Ben Kingsley, LSO, Mackerras – DUKAS: *L'apprenti sorcier;* PROKOFIEV: *Peter and the wolf.* **

Not surprisingly, the LSO play very well for Mackerras, bringing out Britten's imaginative instrumental colour luminously (the harp variation a good example). But Ben Kinsley's narration is low-key and needs to offer a brighter, more enthusiastic advocacy. However, after he has finished, the final fugue is very spirited indeed.

The Young person's guide to the orchestra (Variations and fugue on a theme of Purcell), Op. 34.
(M) *** EMI Dig. CD-EMX 2165; *TC-EMX 2165* (without narration). LPO, Sian Edwards – PROKOFIEV: *Peter and the wolf* **(*); RAVEL: *Ma Mère l'Oye.* **

Sian Edwards does not press the earlier variations too hard, revelling in the colour of her wind soloists, yet the violins enter zestfully and the violas make a touching contrast. The brass bring fine bite and sonority. The fugue has plenty of vitality and the climax is spectacularly expansive in the resonant acoustics of Watford Town Hall.

CHAMBER MUSIC

Alla marcia; 3 Divertimenti for string quartet; 2 Insect pieces; Phantasy oboe quartet, Op. 2; Phantasy in F min. for string quintet; Temporal variations for oboe and piano.
(M) *** Unicorn Dig. UKCD 2060 [id.]. Derek Wickens, John Constable, Augmented Gabrieli Qt.

Derek Wickens is heard at his finest in his contributions to the *Phantasy oboe quartet* (with its passages of seeming improvisation) as well as to the two rediscovered works, the *Temporal variations* and the evocatively etched *Insect pieces*, which are incisive and poised, with a most effectively restrained, lyrical feeling. The Gabrieli Quartet too play with a degree of restraint which works especially well in the two works for strings. The *Phantasy in F minor* is a finely wrought piece but not as striking as the *Phantasy oboe quartet* in its material. This ends the recital quite memorably, but there is striking material in plenty in the *Alla marcia* of 1933 and the three string *Divertimenti* of 1936, with ideas in both pointing forward to the song cycle, *Les Illuminations*. A rewarding reissue on all counts.

Cello sonata, Op. 65.
**(*) Sony Dig. MK 44980 [id.]. Yo-Yo Ma, Emanuel Ax – R. STRAUSS: *Sonata*. **(*)

(i) *Cello sonata in C, Op. 65;* (Unaccompanied) *Cello suites Nos. 1, Op. 72; 2, Op. 80.*
(M) *** Decca 421 859-2 [id.]. Rostropovich; (i) with composer.

This strange five-movement *Cello sonata* is coupled with two of the *Suites for unaccompanied cello*. This is rough, gritty music in Britten's latterday manner, but Rostropovich gives such inspired accounts that the music reveals more and more with repetition.

Yo-Yo Ma and Emanuel Ax give an account of the *Cello sonata* which is very carefully thought out, with exaggerated pianissimi and self-conscious phrasing. The recording is very truthful.

(i) *Cello sonata in C, Op. 65;* (ii) *Elegy for solo viola;* (iii) *6 Metamorphoses after Ovid, for solo oboe, Op. 49;* (iv) *Suite for violin and piano, Op. 6.*
(Y/B) *** EMI Dig. CDC5 55398-2 [id.]. (i) Moray Welsh, John Lenehan; (ii) Paul Silverthorne; (iii) Roy Carter; (iv) Alexander Barantschick, John Alley.

In the Britten *Cello sonata*, Moray Welsh and John Lenehan make no attempt to ape the famous Rostropovich account, but instead choose their own approach, thoughtful, ardent (especially in the central *Elegia*) and strong (as in the *Marcia* – very *echt*–Shostakovich) and highly spontaneous. The *moto perpetuo* finale has great energy and develops a vibrant intensity at the close, and the whole performance is very immediate. Paul Silverthorne gives a touchingly valedictory account of the *Elegy* and Roy Carter is rhapsodically free in the six piquant oboe miniatures, capturing their wistful innocence to perfection. But perhaps most memorable of all is the compellingly alive account of the early *Suite for violin and piano*. Throughout, the recordings, made in the Conway Hall, have a pleasing degree of resonance: the effect is real and present in the most natural way.

Cello suites (Suites for unaccompanied cello) Nos. 1, Op. 72; 2, Op. 80; 3, Op. 87.
*** BIS Dig. CD 446 [id.]. Torleif Thedéen.

Torleif Thedéen has magnificent tonal warmth and eloquence, and he proves a masterly advocate of these *Suites*, which sound thoroughly convincing in his hands.

Cello suite No. 3.
*** Virgin/EMI Dig. VC7 59052-2 [id.]. Steven Isserlis – TAVENER: *The Protecting veil.* ***

Steven Isserlis brings out the spiritual element in a work which draws on traditional Russian themes, including Orthodox church music, and such a performance relates well to the Tavener work with which it is coupled.

Lachrymae, Op. 48.
*** EMI Dig. CDC7 54394-2 [id.]. Tabea Zimmermann, Hartmut Höll – SHOSTAKOVICH: *Viola sonata;* STRAVINSKY: *Elégie.* ***

Tabea Zimmermann gives the moving *Lachrymae* ('Reflections on a song of John Dowland') with an altogether exemplary eloquence and is recorded with great naturalness and presence.

(i) *6 Metamorphosen after Ovid;* (i; ii) *Phantasy quartet* (for oboe, violin, viola & cello), *Op. 2;* (i; iii) *2 Insect pieces; Temporal variations;* (iii) *Holiday diary, Op. 5; Night piece; 5 Waltzes.*
(N) *** Hyperion Dig. CDA 66776 [id.]. (i) Sarah Francis; (ii) Delmé Qt (members); (iii) Michael Dussek.

Sarah Francis has long had a special association with Britten's oboe music, studying the *Ovid* pieces with the composer himself. She gives strong and distinctive characterizations not only to those six unaccompanied pieces but also to the early *Phantasy quartet* and to the pieces for oboe and piano as well. Michael Dussek proves a magnetic interpreter of the solo piano music, bringing out the sparkle of the boyhood waltzes (or 'Walztes' as Britten originally called them) and the *Holiday diary*. He then finds intense poetry and magic in the *Night piece*, written for the first Leeds Piano Competition with deliberately awkward keyboard layout.

(i) *Sinfonietta, Op. 1;* (ii) *String quartets Nos. 2, Op. 36; 3, Op. 94.*
(M) *** Decca 425 715-2. (i) Vienna Octet; (ii) Amadeus Qt.

Britten's Opus 1 was written when he was in his teens. Its mixture of seriousness and assurance is not unappealing and its astringency is brought out well in this appropriately Viennese chamber performance. The *Third Quartet*, a late work, was written for the Amadeus, who play it convincingly. The *Second* ends with a forceful *Chaconne*. The contrasts of style and mood are developed well here, in performances that could be regarded as definitive.

(i) *String quartets Nos. 1 in D, Op. 25; 2 in C, Op. 36; 3, Op. 94; String quartet in D; Quartettino; Alla marcia; 3 Divertimenti; Rhapsody* (all for string quartet); (ii) *Elegy for solo viola;* (i; iii) *Phantasy for oboe and string trio, Op. 2;* (i; iv) *Phantasy in F min. for string quintet.*
(Y/B) (M) *** EMI Dig. CMS5 65115-2. (i) Endellion Qt; (ii) Garfield Jackson; (iii) Douglas Boyd; (iv) Nicholas Logie.

In addition to the three mature *Quartets* which are familiar to collectors, this set brings a number of early works, many of which are completely new (although some have appeared in alternative versions since this EMI compilation first appeared in 1987). The early *Rhapsody* (1929) is followed on the first disc by the remarkable three-movement *Quartettino* (1930) which is at times almost Berg-like and shows how exploratory were Britten's musical instincts and how keenly he responded to the stimulus of Frank Bridge. Also offered is the *Quartet in D* (1931) which the composer later reworked when he was convalescing from open-heart surgery. The *Phantasy quintet* for strings comes from 1932, the same year as the eloquent *Oboe Phantasy quartet*; one is taken aback by the sheer fertility of its invention and the abundance of his imagination. The *Alla marcia* followed a year afterwards, and the three *Divertimenti* derive from a suite of contrasting character movements entitled *Alla quartetto serioso*, written three years earlier. The playing throughout is as responsive and intelligent as one could wish for. In the three published *Quartets* both performances and recordings are exemplary.

String quartet No. 1 in D, Op. 25a.
*** CRD CRD 3351 [id.]. Alberni Qt – SHOSTAKOVICH: *Piano quintet.* **(*)

String quartets Nos. 2 in C, Op. 36; 3, Op. 94.
*** CRD CRD 3395 [id.]. Alberni Qt.

The Alberni Quartet have good ensemble and intonation, and they play with considerable feeling; moreover the CDs are available separately. The recording is vivid and clear.

String quartet No. 1 in D, Op. 25; String quartet in D (1931); Simple Symphony.
(N) **(*) Collins Dig. 1115-2 [id.]. Britten Qt.

The Britten Quartet's warm and spacious treatment of Britten's quartet writing brings out to the full the distinctive imagination of the fully mature *Quartet No. 1* of 1940, made more expressive. Their similarly strong qualities in the early work of 1930 are very convincing, but lighter treatment would have brought out the Britten flavour more. Full-blooded, wide-ranging sound.

String quartet No. 2 in C.
*** RCA Dig. 09026 61387-2 [id.]. Tokyo Qt – BARBER: *Quartet;* TAKEMITSU: *A Way A Lone.* ***
*** Conifer Dig. 74321 15006-2. Brindisi Qt – BRIDGE: *3 Idylls;* Imogen HOLST: *String quartet No. 1.* ***

In the Britten *Second Quartet*, the Tokyo Quartet are little short of superb. Their sound has consistent beauty and refinement. However, the problem with hybrid records is that those wanting the Britten will probably be tempted to the more logical coupling offered by the Alberni Quartet. However, there is no doubt that the Tokyo give a remarkable performance, arguably the best now available; and no one wanting the coupling should hesitate. The recording is as superb as the playing.

The Brindisi on Conifer give an excellent account of the *Second Quartet* which can hold its own with the best and comes with interesting and more sensibly chosen couplings.

String quartets Nos. 2 in C, Op. 36; 3, Op. 94.
(N) *** Collins Dig. 1025-2 [id.]. Britten Qt.

The Britten Quartet gives exceptionally powerful readings of Britten's two best-known quartets, the magnificent No. 2 completed in 1945, with its rare example of Britten using sonata-form, and the very late No. 3 with its rarefied, elliptical thoughts. The brilliant young players treat both works with red-blooded intensity, sustaining very broad speeds in slow movements. In their inner concentration they never let you forget the emotion behind the writing.

String quartet No. 3, Op. 94.
*** ASV Dig. CDDCA 608 [id.]. Lindsay Qt – TIPPETT: *Quartet No. 4.* ***

The Lindsay performance brings the most expansive and deeply expressive reading on record. The ASV recording is vivid, with fine presence; but extraneous sounds are intrusive at times: heavy breathing, snapping of strings on finger-board, etc.

(i) *Suite for harp, Op. 83;* (ii) *2 Insect pieces, for oboe & piano; 6 Metamorphoses after Ovid (for oboe solo), Op. 49.*
*** Mer. CDE 84119 [id.]. (i) Osian Ellis; (ii) Sarah Watkins; Ledger – *Tit for Tat* etc. ***.

It was for Osian Ellis that Britten wrote the *Harp suite*, and Ellis remains the ideal performer. Sarah Watkins gives biting and intense performances of the unaccompanied *Metamorphoses*, as well as the two early *Insect pieces*, with Philip Ledger. The sound is full and immediate, set convincingly in a small but helpful hall.

VOCAL MUSIC

Advance democracy; Antiphon; The ballad of Little Musgrave and Lady Barnard; Rejoice in the Lamb; Sacred and profane; The Sycamore tree; Te Deum; A Wedding anthem.
*** Collins Dig. 1343-2 [id.]. The Sixteen, Harry Christophers.

The two main works of this third of Christophers' Britten series represent two very different periods: the delightful cantata to words by Christopher Smart, *Rejoice in the Lamb*, dating from 1943, and *Sacred and profane*, setting medieval lyrics, his last work for unaccompanied voices. Among the rest are celebratory works like the *Te Deum* and the *Wedding anthem* for Lord Harewood and Marion Stein. Even the anthem, *Advance democracy*, written during Britten's actively left-wing phase before the war, transcends Randall Swingler's propagandist words in its musical imagination. Bright, clear singing from The Sixteen with their boyish-sounding sopranos.

Cabaret songs (to words of W. H. Auden): *As it is, plenty; Calypso; Funeral blues; O tell me the truth about love; Johnny; When you're feeling like expressing your affection.* Blues: *Blues; Boogie-Woogie; The Clock on the wall; The Spider and the fly.*
*** Unicorn Dig. DKPCD 9138 [id.]. Jill Gomez, Martin Jones, Instrumental Ens. – PORTER: *Songs.* **(*)

Jill Gomez finds a winning compromise between art-song and cabaret proper. These are all fun-pieces, and as a bonus Gomez includes the jazzy song, *As it is, plenty*, from the cycle, *On this Island*. The accompanist, Martin Jones, is far less helpful and more deadpan in five classic Cole Porter songs which Jill Gomez also sings. To fill the disc, an instrumental ensemble plays Daryl Runswick's inventive arrangements of four blues numbers by Britten, drawn from the operetta *Paul Bunyan* as well as his early incidental music for plays.

A Boy was born; A Ceremony of carols; Rejoice in the lamb.
(N) **(*) Argo Dig. 433 215-2 [id.]. Masters, Barley, King's College, Cambridge, Ch., Stephen Cleobury.

Stephen Cleobury conducts refined, beautifully controlled readings of three works from early in Britten's career, all with the sound of boy-trebles as a source of inspiration. These performances, set against a reverberant acoustic, may lack the bite and earthiness of the readings Britten is known to have preferred (including those he himself conducted), but they still have plenty of energy and can be recommended to those who fancy this very apt coupling.

A Boy was born; Christ's nativity; Hymn to the Virgin; Jubilate in C; Shepherd's carol; Te Deum in C.
(N) *** Hyperion CDA 66285 [id.]. Gritton, Wyn-Rogers, Holst Singers, St Paul's Cathedral Choristers, Steven Layton; David Goode (organ).

Here is a disc to illustrate Britten's special fascination with the Christmas story, including the first ever recording of the Christmas suite for chorus, *Christ's nativity*. It was written early in 1931 when Britten was a first-year student at the Royal College of Music; but it was not performed complete until 60 years later, well after his death. The writing has many bold and original touches typical of the mature composer, not least in the opening cries of *Awake!*. Steven Layton conducts a finely controlled performance, full of sharp dynamic and rhythmic contrasts. Despite speeds slower than usual, the performance of the cantata, *A Boy was born*, of 1934 has similar merits, with the *Jubilate* and *Te Deum* made the more vigorous by the organ accompaniment of David Goode. Atmospheric, spacious choral sound.

A Boy was born; 5 Flower songs; Hymn to St Cecilia; Gloriana: Choral dances.
*** Collins Dig. 1286-2 [id.]. The Sixteen, Harry Christophers.

This first of Harry Christophers' Britten series for Collins sets the fine pattern for the following issues, starting with the early cantata, *A Boy was born*, and including the brilliant Auden setting, *Hymn to St Cecilia*, and the choral dances taken from the opera, *Gloriana*. Bright, fresh soprano tone, atmospherically recorded, puts these among the finest versions of these works; if this particular grouping is wanted, this is very recommendable.

A Boy was born, Op. 3; Festival Te Deum, Op. 32; Rejoice in the Lamb, Op. 30; A Wedding anthem, Op. 46.
*** Hyperion CDA 66126 [id.]. Corydon Singers, Westminster Cathedral Ch., Best; Trotter (organ).

All the works included here are sharply inspired. The refinement and tonal range of the choirs could hardly be more impressive, and the recording is refined and atmospheric to match.

The Burning fiery furnace (2nd Parable), Op. 77.
(M) *** Decca 414 663-2. Pears, Tear, Drake, Shirley-Quirk, Ch. & O of E. Op. Group, composer and Viola Tunnard.

The story of *Burning fiery furnace* is obviously dramatic in the operatic sense, with vivid scenes like the *Entrance of Nebuchadnezzar*, the *Raising of the Idol*, and the putting of the three Israelites into the furnace. The performers, both singers and players, are the same hand-picked cast that participated in the first performance at Orford Parish Church, where this record was made.

5 Canticles.
(N) **(*) Hyperion Dig. CDA 66498 [id.]. Rolfe Johnson, Chance, Opie, Vignoles, Williams, Thompson (with PURCELL, arr. Britten: *An evening hymn; In the black dismal dungeon of despair; Let the dreadful engines* ***).

Canticles Nos. 1, My beloved is mine, Op. 40; 2, Abraham and Isaac, Op. 51; 3, Still falls the rain, Op. 55; 4, Journey of the Magi, Op. 86; 5, Death of St Narcissus, Op. 89. A birthday hansel. Arr. of PURCELL: *Sweeter than roses.*
(M) *** Decca 425 716-2. Peter Pears, Hahessy, Bowman, Shirley-Quirk, Tuckwell, Ellis, composer.

This CD brings together on a single record all five of the miniature cantatas to which Britten gave the title 'Canticle', plus the *Birthday hansel*, written in honour of the seventy-fifth birthday of Queen Elizabeth the Queen Mother, and a Purcell song-arrangement. A beautiful collection as well as a historical document, with recording that still sounds well.

Though even Vignoles cannot always match the magic of Britten himself as accompanist, and the original Decca recordings are even more characterful and intense than these, yet the newer Hyperion versions make an excellent alternative. Rolfe Johnson's tenor is sweeter even than Pears', most of all in the fifth of the *Canticles*, *The Death of St Narcissus*, written with harp accompaniment at the very end of Britten's life. Like the fourth, *The journey of the Magi*, it sets a T. S. Eliot poem. The three Purcell realizations are shared among the soloists, one apiece, all representing Purcell at his most beautiful and intense.

(i; ii; iii) *Canticle II: Abraham and Isaac;* (ii; iv) *6 Songs from the Chinese.* Folksongs: (i; iii) *The Ash grove;* (ii; iv) *Bonny at morn;* (ii; iii) *The Bonny Earl O'Moray;* (ii; iv) *I will give my love an apple;* (ii; iii) *Little Sir William;* (ii; iv) *Master Kilby;* (i; iii) *O Waly, Waly;* (ii; iii) *Oliver Cromwell; The Plough boy;* (ii; iv) *Sailor-boy;* (i; iii) *The Salley Gardens;* (ii; iv) *The Shooting of his dear; The Soldier and the sailor;* (i; iii) *There's none to soothe.*
(N) ** Carlton IMP Masters Dig. MCD 57 [id.]. (i) Paul Esswood; (ii) James Griffett; (iii) Judith Ridgway (piano); (iv) Timothy Walker (guitar).

This varied collection of Britten's folksong settings leads logically up to the final piece, by far the longest, the *Canticle II*, *Abraham and Isaac*, which involves both the counter-tenor, Paul Esswood, and the tenor, James Griffett. The most successful items are those with guitar, not only five folksongs but the *Songs from the Chinese* of 1957, setting translations by Arthur Waley, a rare item. Though Griffett brings out word-meaning well, the voice has too little tonal variety and, for all the artistry of Paul Esswood, it sounds odd having a counter-tenor in such folksongs as the *Foggy dew*.

A Ceremony of carols; Deus in adjutorium meum; Hymn of St Columba; Hymn to the Virgin; Jubilate Deo in E flat; Missa brevis, Op. 63.
*** Hyperion Dig. CDA 66220 [id.]. Westminster Cathedral Ch., David Hill; (i) with S. Williams; J. O'Donnell (organ).

Particularly impressive here is the boys' singing in the *Ceremony of carols*, where the ensemble is superb, the solo work amazingly mature, and the range of tonal colouring a delight. Along with the other, rarer pieces, this is an outstanding collection, beautifully and atmospherically recorded.

A Ceremony of carols, Op. 28; Festival Te Deum; Hymn of St Columba; Hymn to St Peter; Hymn to the Virgin; Jubilate Deo; Missa brevis; Rejoice in the Lamb, Op. 30.
(M) *** Decca 430 097-2. Tear, Forbes Robinson, St John's College Ch., Guest; Robles; Runnett.

Guest's account of the delightful *Ceremony of carols* has tingling vitality, spacious sound and a superb contribution from Marisa Robles. The performance of *Rejoice in the Lamb* is very similar to Britten's own, but much better recorded, and the *Missa brevis* has the same striking excellence of style. All the shorter pieces show the choir in superb form and the Argo analogue engineering at its most impressive.

A Ceremony of carols; Festival Te Deum; Jubilate Deo!; A Hymn of Saint Columba; Hymn to Saint Peter; Hymn to the Virgin; Missa brevis in D; A New Year carol; A Shepherd's carol; Sweet was the sound.
*** Collins Dig. 1370-2 [id.]. The Sixteen, Harry Christophers.

With bright-toned sopranos taking the place of boy trebles, Harry Christophers in his Britten series for Collins directs superbly incisive, refreshingly dramatic performances of all these works, giving extra bite even to so well-known a piece as the *Ceremony of carols*. The delightful *Missa brevis*, written for the boys of Westminster Cathedral, has never been more telling, and the shorter pieces all confirm Britten's mastery in choral writing, with Christophers terracing the dynamic contrasts with fine precision. Excellent sound, both warm and well detailed. Highly recommended.

(i; ii) *Ceremony of carols, Op. 28;* (i; iii) *Friday afternoons, Op. 7; Francie; King Herod and the cock; The oxen;* (i) *Sweet was the song;* (iv) Song: *The Birds;* (iv; v; iii) *3 2–part settings of Walter de la Mare: The Ride-by-nights; The Rainbow; The Ship of Rio. A Wealden trio.*
(N) (B) *** Naxos Dig. 8.553183 [id.]. (i) New L. Children's Ch., Ronald Corp; (ii) Skaila Kanga; (iii) Alexander Wells; (iv) Catherine Hopper; (v) Emily Attree; Anna Kenyon.

Ronald Corp directs bright, refreshing performances of a delightful collection of Britten choral pieces written with children's voices in mind. The New London Children's Choir is relatively large and is recorded against a lively hall acoustic, but there is no lack of impact, and the tenderness of expression as well as the liveliness is consistently refreshing. Though the *Processional* is recorded statically, losing in atmosphere, the *Ceremony of carols* brings ensemble remarkably crisp for a biggish choir, and these performances justify the decision to have full ensemble treatment for all of the *Friday afternoons* sequence. A splendid bargain.

(i) *A Ceremony of carols, Op. 28; Hymn to St Cecilia, Op. 27;* (ii) *Jubilate Deo;* (i) *Missa brevis in D, Op. 63;* (ii) *Rejoice in the Lamb* (Festival cantata), *Op. 30; Te Deum in C.*
(M) *** EMI CDM7 64653-2 [id.]. King's College, Cambridge, Ch.; (i) Osian Ellis, Willcocks; (ii) James Bowman, Ledger.

The King's trebles may still have less edge in the *Ceremony of carols* than their Cambridge rivals at St John's College, and the *Missa brevis* can certainly benefit from a throatier sound, but the results here are dramatic as well as beautiful. To make a generous reissue EMI have added Philip Ledger's 1974 version of the cantata, *Rejoice in the Lamb*, with timpani and percussion added to the original organ part. Here the biting climaxes are sung with passionate incisiveness, while James Bowman is in his element in the delightful passage which tells you that 'the mouse is a creature of great personal valour'. The *Te Deum* setting and *Jubilate* make an additional bonus and are no less well sung and recorded.

Orchestral song-cycles: (i) *4 Chansons françaises (1928);* (ii) *Our Hunting Fathers, Op. 8;* (i) *Les illuminations, Op. 18;* (iii) *Nocturne, Op. 60;* (iv) *Phaedra, Op. 93;* (iii;v) *Serenade for tenor, horn and strings, Op. 31.*
(Y/B) *** Collins Dig. 7037-2 (2) [id.]. (i) Felicity Lott; (ii) Phyllis Bryn-Julson; (iii) Philip Langridge; (iv) Ann Murray; (v) Frank Lloyd; ECO or (in *Nocturne*) N. Sinf., Steuart Bedford.

Steuart Bedford, successor to Britten himself as conductor, here offers fresh, clear readings of the five orchestral song-cycles, plus the scena, *Phaedra*, written in 1975 long after the rest. In that Ann Murray may not match the dedicatee, Janet Baker, but the dramatic bite is intense. Similarly in the anti-blood-sports cantata, *Our Hunting Fathers*, Phyllis Bryn-Julson is refreshingly fluent and agile. In the even earlier cycle, *Quatre chansons françaises*, Felicity Lott could be warmer, but she is masterly in the Baudelaire cycle, *Les illuminations*. Best of all, with Philip Langridge the characterful, heady-toned tenor, are the two most popular cycles, the *Serenade* (horn soloist Frank Lloyd) and the *Nocturne*. Bright, forward sound.

4 Chansons françaises; Les illuminations; Serenade for tenor, horn and strings.
**(*) Chandos Dig. CHAN 8657 [id.]. Felicity Lott, Anthony Rolfe Johnson, Michael Thompson, SNO, Bryden Thomson.

The *Four French songs* were written when Britten was only fourteen. Felicity Lott gives a strong and sensitive performance, as she does of the other early French cycle on the disc, *Les illuminations*, bringing out the tough and biting element rather than the sensuousness. Anthony Rolfe Johnson, soloist in the *Serenade*, gives a finely controlled performance, but Michael Thompson is not as evocative in the horn solo as his most distinguished predecessors have been. Bryden Thomson draws crisp, responsive playing from the SNO.

(i) *Children's crusade;* (ii) *The Little Sweep (Let's make an opera);* (iii) *Gemini variations.*
(M) (***) Decca stereo/mono 436 393-2 [id.]. (i) Hartnett, Purcell Singers, English Op. Group Boys' Ch.;
  Choristers of All Saints', Margaret St, composer; (ii) Soloists, Wandsworth School Boys' Ch.,
  Burgess; composer (piano); (iii) G. & Z. Jeney.

Britten's own mono recording of *The Little Sweep* sounds amazingly vivid, with voices in particular full
and immediate. As a performance it has never been surpassed in its vigour and freshness, with David
Hemmings here impressive in the title-role for treble. Others in the cast, like Jennifer Vyvyan and April
Cantelo, represent the accomplished group of singers that Britten gathered for his Aldeburgh Festival
performances. The choruses, usually sung by the audience, are here done by the school choir. The
Children's crusade, written for the Save the Children Fund, is darker but equally vivid. The *Gemini
variations* (interchanging flute, violin and piano) was written for the Jeney twins, who play it here.

The Company of Heaven; Paul Bunyan: Overture; Inkslinger's aria; Lullaby of dream shadows.
(Y/B) *** Virgin/EMI Dig. VC5 45093-2 [id.]. Allen, Barkworth (narrators), Pope, Dressen, LPO Ch.,
  ECO, Brunelle.

The Company of Heaven links extensive readings from texts on the theme of angels, and there is much
that echoes such works of the time as the *Frank Bridge variations* and *Les illuminations*, with Britten's
use of a congregational hymn in the last item anticipating both *Noye's Fludde* and *St Nicholas*. Also very
striking is the movement, *War in heaven*, with the men in the chorus delivering the words in sing-speech.
Philip Brunelle made this recording soon after the first concert performance at The Maltings in 1989,
using the same excellent forces, with the spoken contributions more effective on record than in concert.
The brief excerpts from *Paul Bunyan* include an infectious 'Overture' (completed, from sketches, by
Colin Matthews) and a rather engaging *Lullaby*, here performed most persuasively. The recording
throughout is excellent, spacious and with fine balance and presence.

Curlew River (1st parable for church performance).
(N) *** Koch-Schwann 3-1397-2 [id.]. Milhofer, Hargreaves, Hughes-Jones, M. Evans, Guildhall
  Chamber Ens., David Angus.
(M) *** Decca 421 858-2 [id.]. Pears, Shirley-Quirk, Blackburn, soloists, Instrumental Ens., composer
  and Viola Tunnard.

Recorded at a single performance in St Giles', Cripplegate, in February 1993, directed by David Angus
with students of the Guildhall School of Music, this superb Koch version of *Curlew River* is in many
ways even more involving than the original recording of almost 30 years earlier. Britten's daringly
original concept of transferring the story of a Japanese Noh play to a mystery play in a medieval
monastery can seem cold and detached, but having fresh, firm voices makes the drama much more
compelling, with a live performance, often at broader speeds, conveying dramatic tension more hypnotically. In particular the predicament of the madwoman searching for her child becomes more touching
when the voice is as young and clear as Mark Milhofer's. The on-stage voices are set at a slight distance
but words are commendably clear, and the bite of the chorus and of the instrumental ensemble (notably
horn and percussion) makes this a moving experience, with stage and audience noises at a minimum.

  In Britten's own version, which has its own special character, Harold Blackburn plays the Abbot of the
monastery who introduces the drama, while John Shirley-Quirk plays the ferryman who takes people
over the Curlew River and Peter Pears sings the part of the madwoman who, distracted, searches
fruitlessly for her abducted child. The recording is outstanding even by Decca standards.

Folksong arrangements (complete): Volume 1: *British Isles; Unpublished folksongs;* Volume 2: *France;*
Volume 3: *British Isles; Unpublished folksongs;* Volume 4: *Moore's Irish melodies;* Volume 5: *British
Isles;* Volume 6: *England; Unpublished folksongs; 8 Folksong arrangements for high voice and harp;
Miscellaneous published and unpublished folksongs; Orchestral arrangements.*
(N) *** Collins Dig. 7039-2 (3) [id.]. Felicity Lott, Philip Langridge, Thomas Allen, Carlos Bonell,
  Osian Ellis, Graham Johnson, Wenhaston Boys' Ch., BBC Singers, N. Sinf., Steuart Bedford.

This three-disc collection follows closely on Hyperion's two-disc set, including as important extras ten
unpublished settings as well as 14 orchestral arrangements. With Philip Langridge, Felicity Lott and
Thomas Allen more positively characterful than their opposite numbers, and with Graham Johnson
grippingly imaginative at the piano, one appreciates far more here that Britten's folksongs were not
simple settings but original art-songs. Among the extra ten *I wonder as I wander* (unaccompanied except
for interstanza commentary on the piano) is specially moving, a song that Pears often performed with
Britten but which was never included in the regular collections. Tantalizingly, no one has yet identified
the words for one tenderly beautiful setting, superbly performed here on the cello by Christopher van
Kampen.

Folksong arrangements: *The ash grove; Avenging and bright; La belle est au jardin d'amour; The bonny Earl o' Moray; The brisk young widow; Ca' the yowes; Come you not from Newcastle?; Early one morning; The foggy, foggy dew; How sweet the answer; The last rose of summer; The Lincolnshire poacher; The miller of Dee; The minstrel boy; Oft in the stilly night; O Waly, Waly; The plough boy; Le roi s'en va-t'en chasse; Sally in our alley; Sweet Polly Oliver; Tom Bowling.*
(M) *** Decca 430 063-2 [id.]. Peter Pears, Benjamin Britten.

It is good to have the definitive Pears/Britten collaboration in the folksong arrangements. Excellent, faithful recording, well transferred to CD.

The Golden Vanity; Ballad of Little Musgrave and Lady Barnard; Friday afternoons; Holiday diary; Night; Sailing.
(N) **(*) DG Dig. 439 778-2 [id.]. V. Boys' Ch., Ch. Viennensis, Andrei Gavrilov.

(i) *The Golden Vanity;* (ii) *Noye's Fludde.*
(M) *** Decca 436 397-2. (i) Wandsworth School Boys' Ch., Burgess, composer (piano); (ii) Brannigan, Rex, Anthony, East Suffolk Children's Ch. & O, E. Op. Group O, Del Mar.

Britten originally wrote his 'vaudeville', *The Golden Vanity*, for the Vienna Boys, who wanted a piece in which they would not have to take the roles of girls, and they give a performance at once superbly controlled and lusty. The Wandsworth boys are completely at home in the music and sing with pleasing freshness. The coupling was recorded during the 1961 Aldeburgh Festival, and not only the professional choristers but the children too have the time of their lives to the greater glory of God. All the effects have been captured miraculously here, most strikingly the entry into the Ark, while a bugle band blares out fanfares, with the stereo readily catching the sense of occasion and particularly the sound of *Eternal Father* rising above the storm at the climax of *Noye's Fludde.*

The sheer fun you find in Britten's own recording is lacking in DG's alternative, Vienna account, but this is an attractive and unusual coupling, recorded in upfront sound. In the school songs, *Friday afternoons*, seven out of the twelve are done with solo voices, and some of them, like the *New-year carol*, lose in magic; but with Andrei Gavrilov both a positive accompanist and a sympathetic soloist in the two early piano pieces this is a fresh and lively disc, even if the *Ballad of Little Musgrave* for men's voices, well sung by members of the Chorus Viennensis, is taken a little too slowly to bring the narrative to life.

The Holy Sonnets of John Donne, Op. 35; Harmonia Sacra (realizations of Pelham HUMFREY): *Hymn to God the Father; Lord I have sinned* (realization of William CROFT): *A Hymn on Divine Musick. The Way to the Tomb* (incidental music for Ronald Duncan's masque): *Evening; Morning; Night.* W. H. Auden settings: *Fish in the unruffled lakes; Night covers up the rigid land; To lie flat on the back with the knees flexed.* Songs: *Birthday song for Erwin; Cradle song for Eleanor; If thou wilt ease thine heart; Not even summer yet; The Red cockatoo; Um Mitternacht. When you're feeling like expressing your affection; Wild with passion.*
(N) ✿ *** Hyperion Dig. CDA 66823 [id.]. Ian Bostridge, Graham Johnson.

In his first solo recital disc, Ian Bostridge to an astonishing extent makes one forget the example of Peter Pears in songs inspired and performed by him. Few other tenors have even attempted to record the Donne *Sonnet* cycle, written when the composer returned in deep shock after playing at the death camp of Belsen at the end of the war. Here one concentrates afresh on Britten's powerful response to Donne's grittily uncompromising poems. Bostridge's voice may be lighter than that of Pears on either of his two recordings (1949 and 1967), but in its lyrical beauty it can encompass a wider range of tone and dynamic. So in the opening sonnet one registers the anger of the words even more bitingly than with Pears, thanks also to the inspired accompaniment of Graham Johnson. Bostridge's reading of the honeyed setting of *Since she whom I loved* is not just more seductive, it expands thrillingly at the climax. Here is a tenor who not only possesses an exceptionally sweet and beautiful voice, but who is a fine musician and a thinker too.

The Donne cycle is only one item in a disc that also offers inspired performances of 18 of the Britten songs which earlier fell by the wayside. It is astonishing that Britten could allow such jewels to be forgotten: the four Auden settings here, which include a provocatively sexual one, a dreamily atmospheric setting of *Fish in the unruffled lakes*, and a jolly cabaret song. The evocative title given to this CD collection '*The Red Cockatoo*' refers to the shortest song of all, a striking setting of Arthur Waley.

Holy sonnets of John Donne, Op. 35; 7 Sonnets of Michelangelo, Op. 22.
(***) EMI mono CDC7 54605-2 [id.]. Peter Pears, composer – POULENC: *Songs.* (***)

Peter Pears's early EMI recordings of Britten's two sonnet-cycles, both made soon after the works had been composed, have a freshness and vigour that he did not quite recapture in his later versions for

Decca. Even among the many recordings that Britten made with Pears of the works which his voice inspired, these have a special place, well transferred in the 'Composers in Person' series, and imaginatively coupled with the Bernac/Poulenc collection.

(i) *Les Illuminations* (song-cycle), *Op. 18;* (ii) *Nocturne;* (iii) *Serenade for tenor, horn and strings, Op. 31.*
(M) *** Decca 436 395-2 [id.]. (i–iii) Peter Pears; (i) ECO; (ii) wind soloists; (ii; iii) LSO strings, composer; (iii) with Barry Tuckwell.

With dedicated accompaniments under the composer's direction, these Pears versions of *Les Illuminations* and the *Serenade* (with its horn obbligato superbly played by Barry Tuckwell) make a perfect coupling. For the CD release Decca have added the recording of the *Nocturne* from 1960. It is a work full – as is so much of Britten's output – of memorable moments. Each song has a different obbligato instrument (with the ensemble unified for the final Shakespeare song) and each instrument gives the song it is associated with its own individual character. Pears, as always, is the ideal interpreter, the composer a most efficient conductor, and the fiendishly difficult obbligato parts are played superbly. The recording is brilliant and clear, with just the right degree of atmosphere although, for some reason, the transfer of *Les Illuminations* is brighter than the other two works.

Nocturne, Op. 60; Now sleeps the crimson petal; Serenade, Op. 31 (both for tenor, horn & strings).
(N) *** BIS Dig. CD 540 [id.]. Prégardien, Lanzky-Otto, Tapiola Sinf., Vänskä – *Sinfonietta.* ***

Drawing brilliant, expressive and purposeful playing from the Tapiola Sinfonietta, the players totally at home in this music, Osmo Vänskä brings together not only the two best-loved orchestral song-cycles but also the supplementary Tennyson setting intended for the *Serenade* and the elusive work, the *Sinfonietta*, which Britten honoured as his Opus 1. Christoph Prégardien has an ideally light and sweet tenor which, even in the high tessitura of the *Lyke-Wake dirge* from the *Serenade*, shows no strain whatever. Though one detects that he is not English, that is a tribute to his articulation, and he is totally in tune with the idiom. Excellent, spacious sound, if with the tenor soloist slightly backward.

(i) *Noye's Fludde;* (ii) *Serenade for tenor, horn & strings, Op. 31.*
(M) **(*) Virgin/EMI Dig. CUV5 61122-2 [id.]. (i) Maxwell, Ormiston, Pasco, Salisbury & Chester Schools Ch. & O, Coull Qt, Alley, Watson, Harwood, Endymion Ens. (members); (ii) Martyn Hill, Frank Lloyd, City of L. Sinfonia, Hickox.

On the Virgin disc the instrumental forces, including a schools' orchestra as well as professional soloists, are relatively recessed. Compare the storm sequence here with the Decca account, and the distancing undermines any feeling of threat so that the entry of the hymn, *Eternal Father*, instantly submerges the orchestral sound, instead of battling against it. Not even Donald Maxwell as Noah, strong and virile, can efface memories of the incomparable Owen Brannigan.

(i) *Our Hunting Fathers, Op. 8; Folksong arrangements: The bonny Earl o'Moray; Come you not from Newcastle?; Little Sir William; Oliver Cromwell; O Waly, Waly; The plough boy;* (ii) *Serenade for tenor, horn and strings.*
(M) **(*) EMI Dig./Analogue CDM7 69522-2 [id.]. (i) Elisabeth Söderström, Welsh Nat. Op. O, Richard Armstrong; (ii) Robert Tear, Alan Civil, N. Sinfonia, Marriner.

W. H. Auden put together the sequence of poems on an anti-bloodsport theme, *Our Hunting Fathers*, designing it to shock the Norwich audience (which it did) and providing two of the poems himself. The piece, with its obvious acerbities – like the shrieks in *Rats away* – still has the power to shock, and this performance finds Söderström a committed soloist, even if a tenor voice suits this work even more. The folksongs make an attractive bonus, and the new coupling with Robert Tear's 1970 version of the *Serenade* adds to the interest of this reissue. Tear is very much in the Aldeburgh tradition set by Pears, yet he gives a new and positive slant to each of Britten's lovely songs, with the Johnson *Hymn to Diana* given extra jollity, thanks partly to the brilliant galumphing of Alan Civil on the horn. The recording's resonance provides atmosphere without clouding.

The Prodigal Son (3rd parable), Op. 81.
(M) *** Decca 425 713-2. Pears, Tear, Shirley-Quirk, Drake, E. Op. Group Ch. & O, composer and Viola Tunnard.

The last of the parables is the sunniest and most heart-warming: Britten cleverly avoids the charge of oversweetness by introducing the Abbot, even before the play starts, in the role of Tempter, confessing he represents evil and aims to destroy contentment in the family he describes: 'See how I break it up' – a marvellous line for Peter Pears. An ideal performance is given here with a characteristically real and atmospheric Decca recording.

Purcell realizations: *Orpheus Britannicus: The Knotting song; 7 Songs* (1947); *6 Songs* (1948); *O Solitude; 5 Songs* (1960); *Celemene; 6 Duets* (1961). *Harmonia Sacra: The Blessed Virgin's expostulation; The Queen's Epicedium; Saul and the Witch of Endor; 3 Divine hymns* (1947); *2 Divine hymns & Alleluia* (1960). Miscellaneous songs (1971): *Dulcibella; When Myra sings*.
(N) *** Hyperion Dig. CDA 67061/2 [id.]. Lott, Gritton, S. Walker, Bowman, Ainsley, Bostridge, Rolfe Johnson, Jackson, Keenlyside; Johnson.

As a result of giving recitals with Peter Pears during and after the war, Britten was encouraged to make a whole series of realizations using the figured basses Purcell provided in his big collections, *Orpheus Britannicus* and *Harmonia Sacra*. Though most of the arrangements date from the immediate post-war period, Britten made more in about 1960 and again towards the very end of his life in 1971. The accompaniments for piano may defy latterday ideas of authenticity but, as Purcell intended, Britten follows the harmonic indications given, to produce entirely distinctive results, regularly displaying an individual lyricism rare in keyboard continuo. With an outstanding team of soloists and with Graham Johnson as the inspired pianist, this collection stands as a monument to the devotion of one English master to another. The first disc, drawn from the *Orpheus Britannicus* collection, includes songs like *Fairest isle*, better known in the context of *King Arthur* or other entertainments. The second, from *Harmonia Sacra*, has darker, weightier and more extended items, notably the magnificent scena, *Saul and the Witch of Endor*, involving three singers and with side-slipping chromatics as daring as any Purcell ever imagined. Among the newcomers, the tenor Ian Bostridge confirms the high mastery he also displays in the *Red Cockatoo* collection of Britten songs, and Simon Keenlyside sings magnificently in the dark, bass items like *Job's curse* and the late *Let the dreadful engines*. Excellent, well-balanced sound.

(i) *The Rescue of Penelope;* (ii) *Phaedra*.
(N) *** Erato/Warner Dig. 0630 12713-2 [id.]. (i) Alison Hagley, Catherine Wyn-Rogers, John Mark Ainsley, William Dazeley, Dame Janet Baker (narrator); (ii) Lorraine Hunt; Hallé O, Kent Nagano.

Soon after his return from America at the height of the war, Britten wrote the incidental music for a radio play by Edward Sackville-West on the Homeric subject of Odysseus's return to Penelope. Drawn from the complete score with barely any amendment of the original and compressed into a 36-minute cantata with the help of Colin Matthews, Britten's last amanuensis, the result is extraordinarily powerful, with emotions intensified. The most important role is that of the narrator, here masterfully taken by Janet Baker to bring the story vividly to life despite the stylized classical language (e.g. 'Odysseus, Lord of sea-girt Ithaca' or 'His fair wife, white-armed Penelope'). The commentaries, beautifully sung, regularly add to the atmospheric beauty of the piece. In its richness of idiom this may not be distinctively Britten-ish, with unexpected echoes of Walton film-music and even of Wagner, but it is endlessly inventive in a very Britten-like way, not just illustrative but strong and purposeful, a valuable addition to the Britten *œuvre*. Lorraine Hunt's performance of *Phaedra*, Britten's last vocal work, characteristically spare, may not quite match that of the dedicatee, Dame Janet, in conveying the heroine's agony, but the portrait of a deranged woman is chillingly powerful, with singing comparably beautiful and intense.

St Nicholas; Hymn to St Cecilia.
*** Hyperion Dig. CDA 66333 [id.]. Rolfe Johnson, Corydon Singers, St George's Chapel, Windsor, Ch., Girls of Warwick University Chamber Ch., Ch. of Christ Church, Southgate, Sevenoaks School, Tonbridge School, Penshurst Ch. Soc., Occasional Ch., Edwards, Alley, Scott, ECO, Best.

For the first time in a recording, the congregational hymns are included in Matthew Best's fresh and atmospheric account of *St Nicholas*. That adds enormously to the emotional impact of the whole cantata. Though the chorus is distanced slightly, the contrasts of timbre are caught well, with the waltz-setting of *The birth of Nicholas* and its bath-tub sequence delightfully sung by boy-trebles alone. The *Hymn to St Cecilia* is also beautifully sung, with gentle pointing of the jazzy syncopations in crisp, agile ensemble and with sweet matching among the voices.

(i) *St Nicholas, Op. 42;* (ii) *Rejoice in the Lamb, Op. 30*.
(M) (***) Decca mono 425 714-2. (i) Hemmings, Pears, St John Leman School, Beccles, Girls' Ch., Ipswich School Boys' Ch., Aldeburgh Festival Ch. & O; R. Downes; (ii) Hartnett, Steele, Todd, Francke, Purcell Singers, G. Malcolm; composer.

With rare exceptions, Britten's first recordings of his own works have a freshness and vigour unsurpassed since. Britten's performances capture the element of vulnerability, not least in the touching setting of words by the deranged poet, Christopher Smart, *Rejoice in the Lamb*.

Serenade for tenor, horn and strings.
(Y/B) (B) *** DG 439 464-2 [id.]. Robert Tear, Dale Clevenger, Chicago SO, Giulini – DELIUS: *On hearing the first cuckoo; Summer night on the river*; VAUGHAN WILLIAMS: *Greensleeves; Lark ascending*. ***

Robert Tear's 1977 interpretation of the *Serenade* is very much in the Aldeburgh tradition set by Pears, and Giulini has long been a persuasive advocate of Britten's music. He presents the cycle as a full-scale orchestral work and Tear is at his finest, more open than in his earlier, EMI recording. Dale Clevenger is a superb horn player, and though in places some may find him unidiomatic it is good to have a fresh view of the music, especially when inexpensively coupled with fine performances of music by Delius and Vaughan Williams.

(i) *Serenade for tenor, horn and strings, Op. 31;* (ii) *7 Sonnets of Michelangelo, Op. 22; Winter words, Op. 52.*

(M) (***) Decca mono 425 996-2 [id.]. Peter Pears, (i) Dennis Brain, Boyd Neel String O, composer; (ii) composer (piano).

This compilation brings together some of Britten's historic early recordings for Decca. This first record-ing of the *Serenade*, though not helped by unatmospheric sound, is wonderfully intense, with Dennis Brain uniquely magnetic on the horn. The first recording of the Hardy song-cycle, *Winter words*, has never been matched by more recent recordings, an intensely evocative performance with Britten drawing magical sounds from the piano in support of Pears. This version of the *Michelangelo sonnets* is not quite as fresh-toned as the even earlier EMI one, but it still offers a searchingly intense performance. Limited but clear mono sound.

Songs and proverbs of William Blake, Op. 74; Tit for Tat; 3 Early songs: Beware that I'd ne'er been married; Epitaph; The clerk. Folksong arrangements: Bonny at morn; I was lonely; Lemady; Lord! I married me a wife!; O Waly, Waly; The Salley Gardens; She's like the swallow; Sweet Polly Oliver.
**(*) Chandos Dig. CHAN 8514 [id.]. Benjamin Luxon, David Williamson.

Benjamin Luxon's lusty baritone gives an abrasive edge whether to early songs, folksong settings or the Blake cycle. Only rarely does he become too emphatic. Excellent, sensitive accompaniment and first-rate recording.

(i) *Songs from the Chinese, Op. 58;* Folksong arrangements: *I will give my love an apple; Master Kilby; Sailor boy; The shooting of his dear; The soldier and the sailor. Gloriana: Second lute song of the Earl of Essex. Nocturnal* (for solo guitar), *Op. 70.*
(M) *** RCA 09026 61601-2 [id.]. Julian Bream (guitar); (i) Peter Pears (with FRICKER: *O Mistress mine*) – SEIBER: *French folksongs;* WALTON: *Anon in love.* ***

Nearly all the music on this record was written with Julian Bream in mind, and the *Nocturnal*, based on a tune by Dowland, was dedicated to him. Characteristically Britten exploits every nuance of expression that Bream's virtuosity makes possible. The haunting lute song from *Gloriana* by contrast brings a remarkable Elizabethan feeling. The *Songs from the Chinese* are based on Arthur Waley's translations of Chinese poetry. Of the folksong arrangements, it is *I will give my love an apple* where Pears's tender vocal-line is particularly memorable, while the closing *Soldier and the sailor* has all the pay-off wit for which Britten's arrangements are famous. Peter Racine Fricker's soaring setting of *O Mistress mine* seems tailor-made for Pears, his voice at its freshest throughout. With Seiber and Walton couplings equally rewarding, this (Volume 18) is outstanding among the reissues in the Julian Bream Edition where he is joined by other artists.

(i) *Spring symphony, Op. 44;* (ii) *Cantata academica;* (iii) *Hymn to St Cecilia.*
(M) *** Decca 436 396-2 [id.]. (i; ii) Vyvyan, Pears; (i) Procter, Emanuel School, Wandsworth, Boys' Ch., ROHCG O, composer; (ii) Watts, Brannigan; (ii; iii) L. Symphony Ch.; (ii) LSO; (ii; iii) Malcolm.

(i) *Spring symphony, Op. 44; Peter Grimes: 4 Sea interludes.*
(M) *** EMI CDM7 64736-2 [id.]. (i) Armstrong, J. Baker, Tear, St Clement Dane's School Boys' Ch., L. Symphony Ch.; LSO, Previn.

(i) *Spring Symphony, Op. 44;* (ii) *Welcome ode, Op. 95;* (iii) *Psalm 150, Op. 67.*
**(*) Chandos Dig. CHAN 8855 [id.]. (i) Gale, Hodgson, Hill, Southend Boys' Ch., LSO; (ii) City of London Schools' Ch., LSO; (iii) City of London Schools' Ch. and O; Hickox.

It is the freshness of Britten's imagination in dozens of moments that makes this work as memorable as it is joyous. Thanks to the Decca engineers, one hears more than is usually possible in a live perform-ance. Jennifer Vyvyan and Peter Pears are both outstanding, and Britten shows that no conductor is more vital in his music than he himself. The Decca reissue couples the work to the *Cantata academica*, with its deft use of a 12-note row, written for Basel, and the *Hymn to St Cecilia*, an ambitious piece written just before the war, when Britten's technique was already prodigious. The setting exactly matches the imaginative, capricious words of Auden. Performances are first class and so is the CD transfer.

Like Britten, Previn makes this above all a work of exultation, a genuine celebration of spring; but here, more than in Britten's recording, the kernel of what the work has to say comes out in the longest of the solo settings, using Auden's poem *Out on the lawn I lie in bed*. With Dame Janet Baker as soloist it rises above the lazily atmospheric mood of the opening to evoke the threat of war and darkness. The *Four Sea interludes*, which make a generous bonus, are presented in their concert form, with tailored endings. Previn springs the bouncing rhythms of the second interlude – the picture of Sunday morning in the Borough – even more infectiously than the composer himself in his complete recording of the opera.

With more variable soloists – the tenor Martyn Hill outstandingly fine, the soprano Elizabeth Gale often too edgy – Hickox's version of the *Spring Symphony* does not quite match the composer's own in gutsy urgency. But this CD brings the advantage of a first recording of Britten's last completed work, the *Welcome ode*. The third work, equally apt, is the boisterous setting of *Psalm 150*.

(i) *Tit for Tat;* (ii) Folksong arrangements: *Bird scarer's song; Bonny at morn; David of the White Rock; Lemady; Lord! I married me a wife!; She's like the swallow.*
*** Mer. CDE 84119 [id.]. Shirley-Quirk; (i) Ledger; (ii) Ellis – *Suite for harp* etc. ***

John Shirley-Quirk was the baritone who first sang the cycle, *Tit for Tat*, with the composer at the piano, and he is still unrivalled in the sharp yet subtle way he brings out the irony in these boyhood settings of De la Mare poems. It is also good to have him singing the six late folk-settings with harp accompaniment, here played by Osian Ellis for whom (with Peter Pears) they were originally written.

War Requiem, Op. 66.
*** Decca 414 383-2 [id.]. Vishnevskaya, Pears, Fischer-Dieskau, Bach Ch., London Symphony Ch., Highgate School Ch., Melos Ens., LSO, composer.
*** EMI Dig. CDS7 47034-8 [id.]. Söderström, Tear, Allen, Trebles of Christ Church Cathedral Ch., Oxford, CBSO Ch., CBSO, Rattle.
**(*) DG Dig. 437 801-2 (2) [id.]. Orgonasova, Rolfe Johnson, Skovhus, Monteverdi Ch., Tölz Boys' Ch., N. German R. Ch. & SO, Gardiner.

(i) *War Requiem;* (ii) *Ballad of heroes, Op. 14; Sinfonia da requiem, Op. 20.*
*** Chandos Dig. CHAN 8983/4 [id.]. (i) Harper, Langridge, Shirley-Quirk, (ii) Hill; St Paul's Cathedral Choristers, London Symphony Ch., LSO & CO, Richard Hickox.

Richard Hickox's Chandos version rivals even the composer's own definitive account in its passion and perception, and must be now regarded as a first choice. Hickox thrusts home the big dramatic moments with unrivalled force, helped by the weight of the Chandos sound. The boys' chorus from St Paul's Cathedral is exceptionally fresh. Heather Harper is as golden-toned as she was at the very first Coventry performance, fearless in attack. Philip Langridge has never sung more sensitively on disc, and both he and John Shirley-Quirk bring many subtleties to their interpretations. Adding to the attractions of the set come two substantial choral works, also in outstanding performances.

Britten's own 1963 recording of the *War Requiem* comes near to the ideal, but it is a pity that Britten insisted on Vishnevskaya for the soprano solos. Having a Russian singer was emotionally right, but musically Heather Harper would have been better still. The digital remastering, as with *Peter Grimes*, brings added textural refinement and makes the recording sound newly minted; it also reveals a degree of background hiss.

With Elisabeth Söderström a far more warmly expressive soloist than the oracular Vishnevskaya, the human emotions behind the Latin text come out strongly with less distancing than from the composer. If Tear does not always match the subtlety of Pears on the original recording, Allen sounds more idiomatic than Fischer-Dieskau. Rattle's approach is warm, dedicated and dramatic, with fine choral singing (not least from the Christ Church Cathedral trebles). The various layers of perspective are impressively managed by the digital recording. Yet in its combination of imaginative flair with technical expertise, the Culshaw recording of two decades earlier is by no means surpassed.

Recorded live in Lübeck by the North German Radio Orchestra and Choir under their chief conductor, John Eliot Gardiner, this is a thoughtful rather than a dramatic reading. It is intense and compelling, as one would expect from Gardiner, but it is seriously undermined by dim, inconsistent recording, with soloists and chorus often ill-focused. In every way Richard Hickox's Chandos version is warmer and more powerful as an interpretation, as well as far better recorded. For the same price the two Chandos discs also contain the *Sinfonia da Requiem* and the early *Ballad of heroes*.

What works far better than Gardiner's CD is the video version of the same performance (LaserDisc 072 198-1; VHS 072 198-3), set in the beautiful Marienkirche. With the singers in close-up, the ear obligingly ignores bad balances to have one appreciating the firm Slavonic tang of Luba Orgonasova, the intimate intensity of Anthony Rolfe Johnson and the youthful ardour of the baritone, Boje Skovhus. Another advantage is that on a single VHS cassette there is no break in the middle.

Winter words (song-cycle), *Op. 52*.
(N) (BB) *** ASV CDQS 6172 [id.]. Ian Partridge, Jennifer Partridge – PURCELL: '*Sweeter than Roses*' (songs). ***

Ian Partridge's soaringly fresh timbre brings surprising reminders of Peter Pears in these highly sensitive performances of atmospheric Hardy settings dating from 1953. Ian is admirably supported by sister Jennifer Partridge, and she makes the very most of the imaginative piano-writing, whether in simulating railway noises in *Midnight on the Great Western*, the creaks of *The little old table*, or setting the melancholy mood for *The choirmaster's burial* and creating the joyful chorus of the *Proud songsters*. Excellent late-1970s recording. A worthy coupling for a warmly sympathetic collection of favourite Purcell songs.

OPERA

Albert Herring (complete).
**(*) Decca 421 849-2 (2) [id.]. Pears, Fisher, Noble, Brannigan, Cantelo, ECO, Ward, composer.

Britten's own 1964 recording of the comic opera, *Albert Herring*, is a delight. Peter Pears's portrait of the innocent Albert was caught only just before he grew too old for the role, but it is full of unique touches. Sylvia Fisher is a magnificent Lady Billows, and it is good to have so wide a range of British singers of the 1960s so characterfully presented. The recording, made in Jubilee Hall, remains astonishingly vivid.

Billy Budd (complete).
*** Decca 417 428-2 (3) [id.]. Glossop, Pears, Langdon, Shirley-Quirk, Wandsworth School Boys' Ch., Amb. Op. Ch., LSO, composer (with *Holy Sonnets of John Donne; Songs and Proverbs of William Blake* ***).
(**) VAIA mono 1034-3 (3) [id.]. Pears, Uppman, Dalberg, Alan, G. Evans, Langdon, ROHCG Ch. & O, Britten.

An ideal cast, with Glossop a bluff, heroic Billy, and Langdon a sharply dark-toned Claggart, making these symbol-figures believable. Magnificent sound, and the many richly imaginative strokes – atmospheric as well as dramatic – are superbly managed. The layout on three CDs begins with the *John Donne Holy Sonnets* (sung by Pears) and the *Songs and Proverbs of William Blake* (sung by Fischer-Dieskau), with the Prologue and Act I of the opera beginning thereafter. They are equally ideal performances.

Though the sound is very scrubby, disconcertingly so at the very start, this historic recording of the very first performance of the opera in December 1951 is doubly valuable: not only does it let us hear the fresh, youthful-sounding performance of Theodor Uppman in the title-role, as well as Peter Pears as Captain Vere, clearer and more flexible than in his studio recording of 16 years later; it also presents the original, four-Act text, with its substantial muster scene at the end of the original Act I, later cut. Other passages were also elided. Philip Reed provides a brief but informative comment on the text and the recording, but there is no libretto. It is interesting that, though the orchestra sounds dim and limp at the start, Britten as conductor whips up searing tension through the opera.

Death in Venice (complete).
*** Decca 425 669-2 (2) [id.]. Pears, Shirley-Quirk, Bowman, Bowen, Leeming, E. Op. Group Ch., ECO, Bedford.

Thomas Mann's novella, which made an expansively atmospheric film, far removed from the world of Mann, here makes a surprisingly successful opera. Pears's searching performance in the central role of Aschenbach is set against the darkly sardonic singing of John Shirley-Quirk in a sequence of roles as the Dionysiac figure who draws Aschenbach to his destruction and, though Steuart Bedford's assured conducting lacks some of the punch that Britten would have brought, the whole presentation makes this a set to establish the work outside the opera house.

Gloriana (complete).
*** Decca Dig. 440 213-2 (2) [id.]. Josephine Barstow, Philip Langridge, Della Jones, Jonathan Summers, WNO Ch. & O, Mackerras.

Gloriana is a portrait of a lonely monarch forced to do her duty and condemn to the scaffold a man, the Earl of Essex, whom she loved more than anyone, but who had rebelled against her. Without effacing memories of earlier interpreters, Josephine Barstow gives a splendid performance as the Virgin Queen, tough and incisive, with the slight unevenness in the voice adding to the abrasiveness. No easy option, this one. Only in the final scene when, after the execution of Essex, the queen muses to herself in fragments of spoken monologue does the reading lack weight. A chestier speaking voice would have helped but, just before that, the final confrontation between Elizabeth and Essex brings a thrilling climax in what amounts to an 'out-of-love' duet. Elizabeth attacks her lover not for infidelity but for treason.

Philip Langridge's portrait of Essex is, if anything, even more striking. More than the original interpreter, Peter Pears, he consistently brings out the character's arrogant bravado, the quality which first attracted the queen but which then finally destroyed the man. Though Langridge's voice is mellifluous and flexible in the lute songs, its bright, cutting quality helps to enhance that characterization. The rest of the cast is equally starry, with Alan Opie as the queen's principal adviser, Sir Robert Cecil, balefully dark rather than sinister, while the warm-toned Della Jones as Essex's wife and the abrasive Yvonne Kenny as his sister, Lady Penelope Rich, both well cast, sharply draw out the opposing sides of the queen's character, when in turn they make their final pleas for Essex's life, the latter with disastrous results. Sir Charles Mackerras directs his Welsh National Opera forces in a performance that brings out the full splendour of this rich score. The Decca recording, made in Brangwyn Hall, Swansea, is comparably splendid, a crowning achievement in the complete cycle of Britten operas begun by the composer himself.

Gloriana: Choral dances.
*** Hyperion CDA 66175 [id.]. Martyn Hill, Thelma Owen, Holst Singers & O, Hilary Davan Wetton –
    BLISS: *Lie strewn the white flocks;* HOLST: *Choral hymns from the Rig Veda.* ***

The composer's own choral suite, made up of unaccompanied choral dances linked by passages for solo tenor and harp, makes an excellent coupling for the equally attractive Bliss and Holst items. Excellent, atmospheric recording.

A Midsummer Night's Dream (complete).
*** Decca 425 663-2 (2) [id.]. Deller, Harwood, Harper, Veasey, Watts, Shirley-Quirk, Brannigan,
    Downside and Emmanuel School Ch., LSO, composer.

The beauty of the instrumental writing comes out in this recording even more than in the opera house, for John Culshaw, the recording manager, put an extra halo round the fairy music to act as a substitute for visual atmosphere. Britten again proves himself an ideal interpreter of his own music and draws virtuoso playing from the LSO. Peter Pears has shifted to the straight role of Lysander. The mechanicals are admirably led by Owen Brannigan as Bottom; and among the lovers Josephine Veasey (Hermia) is outstanding. Deller, with his magical male alto singing, is the eerily effective Oberon.

(i) *Owen Wingrave* (complete); (ii) *6 Hölderlin fragments, Op. 61;* (iii) *The Poet's echo, Op. 76.*
*** Decca 433 200-2 (2) [id.]. (i) Pears, Fisher, Harper, Vyvyan, J. Baker, Luxon, Shirley-Quirk, ECO,
    composer; (ii) Pears, composer; (iii) Vishnevskaya, Rostropovich.

Britten's television opera marked a return after the *Church parables* to the mainstream pattern of his operatic style, with a central character isolated from society. Each of the seven characters is strongly conceived, with the composer writing specially for the individual singers in the cast. The performance is definitive and the recording very atmospheric. The set is filled out with the *Six Hölderlin fragments* and *The Poet's echo*, Russian settings of Pushkin, written for Vishnevskaya who performs them with her husband at the piano.

Paul Bunyan (complete).
✪ *** Virgin/EMI Dig. VCD7 59249-2 (2) [id.]. James Lawless, Dan Dressen, Elisabeth Comeaux
    Nelson, soloists, Ch. & O of Plymouth Music Series, Minnesota, Philip Brunelle.

Aptly, this first recording of Britten's choral operetta comes from the state, Minnesota, where the story is set. When the principal character is a giant who can appear only as a disembodied voice, the piece works rather better on record or radio than on stage. Musically, Britten's conscious assumption of popular American mannerisms does not prevent his invention from showing characteristic originality. Recorded in clean, vivid sound, with Philip Brunelle a vigorous conductor, this excellent first recording richly deserves the prizes it won for the Virgin Classics label.

Peter Grimes (complete).
(N) *** Chandos Dig. CHAN 9447/8 (2) [id.]. Langridge, Watson, Opie, Connell, Harrison, Opera
    London, L. Symphony Ch., City of L. Sinf., Hickox.
✪ *** Decca 414 577-2 (3) [id.]. Pears, Claire Watson, Pease, Jean Watson, Nilsson, Brannigan, Evans,
    Ch. and O of ROHCG, composer.

*** EMI Dig. CDC7 54832-2 (2) [id.]. Anthony Rolfe Johnson, Felicity Lott, Thomas Allen, Ch. & O of ROHCG, Bernard Haitink.

(M) *** Ph. 432 578-2 (2) [id.]. Vickers, Harper, Summers, Bainbridge, Cahill, Robinson, Allen, ROHCG Ch. & O, C. Davis.

On Chandos, Richard Hickox follows up the success of his award-winning sets of the *War requiem* and of Walton's *Troilus and Cressida* with a comparably warm and involving performance, more atmospheric than any since the composer's own original version. The rhythmic spring which Hickox gives this colourful score harks back to that classic set, and Chandos backs him up with an exceptionally rich recording, with bloom on the voices and full, immediate orchestral sound. The casting of Philip Langridge in the title-role is central to the set's success. As on stage, he is unrivalled at conveying the element of hysteria in Grimes's character, of manic obsession gathering ground, leading to madness in the final mad scene. The result is chilling, making most rivals seem too secure. With his and other voices less closely focused than in other versions, one may not register vocal power so clearly, but the spread of the stereophonic stage is just as vivid as in the composer's original recording. Janice Watson makes a most touching Ellen Orford, younger and less maternal than her rivals, but all the more tender, with the golden tones of the voice well caught. The others make a superb team, with Alan Opie an outstanding Bulstrode and John Connell commanding as lawyer Swallow at the start. This is a warmer, more atmospheric performance than the only digital rival, from Haitink on EMI, and is just as powerful, with choral singing even more sharply disciplined.

The Decca recording of *Peter Grimes* was one of the first great achievements of the stereo era. Few opera recordings can claim to be so definitive, with Peter Pears, for whom it was written, in the name-part, Owen Brannigan (another member of the original team) and a first-rate cast. Britten conducts superbly and secures splendidly incisive playing, with the whole orchestra on its toes throughout. The recording, superbly atmospheric, has so many felicities that it would be hard to enumerate them, and the Decca engineers have done wonders in making up aurally for the lack of visual effects.

Bernard Haitink's reading of *Grimes*, helped by one of EMI's most spectacular recordings yet, finds more light and shade in this extraordinarily atmospheric score. Anthony Rolfe Johnson too comes far closer to Peter Pears in the Britten recording than Jon Vickers does for Davis, with his rugged, bull-like portrait. Rolfe Johnson is the most inward of the three, singing the most beautifully, less troubled than Pears by the high tessitura. He presents Grimes as suffering from hysteria rather than outright madness, and the result is at least as touching. Felicity Lott makes a tenderly sympathetic Ellen Orford, less mature than Heather Harper for Davis, more characterful than Claire Watson for Britten. Sarah Walker is unforgettable as Mrs Sedley, the laudanum-taking gossip, and Thomas Allen is a wise and powerful Balstrode, making the Act III duel with Ellen an emotional resolution, preparing for the final tragedy. The Covent Garden Chorus and Orchestra are used in all three recordings, outstanding in all three but with the extra range and vividness of EMI's latest digital recording adding to the impact, not least of the chorus, whether singing on stage or in evocative off-stage effects. The set has the advantage over Britten's own of coming (like the Davis) on two instead of three discs.

Sir Colin Davis takes a fundamentally darker, tougher view of *Peter Grimes* than the composer himself. Jon Vickers' heroic interpretation sheds keen new illumination on what arguably remains the greatest of Britten's operas, even if it cannot be said to supplant the composer's own version. Heather Harper as Ellen Orford is very moving, and there are fine contributions from Jonathan Summers as Captain Balstrode and Thomas Allen as Ned Keene. The recording is full and vivid, with fine balancing.

(i, ii) *Peter Grimes* (scenes); (i, iii) *The Rape of Lucretia* (abridged); (iv) French folksong arrangements: *La belle est au jardin d'amour; La fileuse; Quand j'étais chez mon père; Le roi s'en va-t'en chasse; Voici le printemps;* (v) English folksongs: *The Ash grove; The Bonny Earl o' Moray; Come you not from Newcastle?; The Foggy, foggy dew; Heigh ho, heigh hi!; The King is gone a-hunting; Little Sir William; O, Waly, Waly; Oliver Cromwell; The Plough boy; The Salley Gardens; Sweet Polly Oliver; There's none to soothe.*

(M) (***) EMI mono CMS7 64727-2 (2) [id.]. (i) Joan Cross, Peter Pears; (ii) Nancy Evans, E. Op. Group Chamber O; (iii) BBC Theatre Ch., ROHCG O, Reginald Goodall; (iv) Sophie Wyss, composer; (v) Peter Pears, composer.

Both of these abridged recordings of Britten's earliest operas, made in the 1940s, have a freshness and energy that reflect the excitement they aroused at their first appearance, transforming the British musical scene. More specifically, they illustrate both the resilient energy of Peter Pears at this early stage, lighter and fresher of voice than later, and the urgent intensity of Reginald Goodall, conducting Britten in a way very different from his later, solidly weighty manner in Wagner. Though the recordings, transferred from 78s, are boxy in sound, the closeness adds to the bite and impact. They are particularly valuable for demonstrating the character and point of Joan Cross as Ellen Orford. It was a role written for her, as indeed was the Female Chorus part in *Lucretia*. In the latter opera it is good to have Nancy Evans in the title-role, tenderly affecting, with the contrasts between the heroine's tragic grief and the beauty of the serving maids' Flower duet superbly brought out.

The recordings of folksong settings are delightful, made not just by Peter Pears for both Decca and EMI, but by Sophie Wyss (for whom *Les illuminations* was written). The wit and point of such songs as *The foggy, foggy dew* and *Little Sir William* come out even more delightfully than in later recordings, with Britten as accompanist at his most inspired.

Peter Grimes: 4 Sea interludes and Passacaglia.
*** Chandos Dig. CHAN 8473 [id.]. Ulster O, Handley – BAX: *On the Sea-shore;* BRIDGE: *The Sea.* ***

Handley draws brilliant and responsive playing from the Ulster Orchestra in readings that fully capture the atmospheric beauty of the writing, helped by vivid recording of demonstration quality.

The Rape of Lucretia (complete).
*** Chandos Dig. CHAN 9254/5 [id.]. Rigby, Robson, Pierard, Maxwell, Miles, Rozario, Gunson, City of L. Sinf., Hickox.

(i) *The Rape of Lucretia* (complete); (ii) *Phaedra, Op. 93*.
*** Decca 425 666-2 (2) [id.]. (i) Pears, Harper, Shirley-Quirk, J. Baker, Luxon, ECO, composer; (ii) J. Baker, ECO, Bedford.

In combining on CD *The Rape of Lucretia* with *Phaedra*, Decca celebrates two outstanding perform-ances by Dame Janet Baker, recorded at the peak of her career. Among other distinguished vocal contributions to the opera, Peter Pears and Heather Harper stand out, while Benjamin Luxon makes the selfish Tarquinius into a living character. The seductive beauty of the writing – Britten then at his early peak – is splendidly caught, the melodies and tone-colours as ravishing as any that he ever conceived.

Richard Hickox follows up his outstanding version of Britten's *War Requiem* for Chandos, as well as his version of *A Midsummer Night's Dream* for Virgin, with this colourful and atmospheric account of *The Rape of Lucretia*. The cast is a strong one, with no weak link. Though the soloists in the Britten recording – notably Janet Baker in the title-role – are more sharply characterful and well-contrasted, the alternative views presented here are comparably convincing. Jean Rigby as Lucretia may lack the warmth and weight of Baker, but she gains from having a younger-sounding voice. Equally the timbre of Nigel Robson as the Male Chorus, rather darker than Peter Pears's, adds to the dramatic bite of his characterization, virile in attack. Catherine Pierard as the Female Chorus has a more sensuous voice than most sopranos taking this role, making it a more involved commentary. The digital sound is warm and glowing, fully revealing the sensuous beauty of Britten's chamber orchestration. Quite apart from its unique authority, Britten's Decca set (also at full price) comes with a valuable fill-up in *Phaedra*, the work he wrote for Janet Baker; but the Chandos rival gives an equally strong, in some ways more dramatic view of a masterly opera.

The Turn of the screw.
*** Collins Dig. 7030-2 (2) [id.]. Langridge, Lott, Pay, Hulse, Cannan, Secunde, Aldeburgh Festival Ens., Bedford.
(M) (***) Decca mono 425 672-2 (2) [id.]. Pears, Vyvyan, Hemmings, Dyer, Cross, Mandikian, E. Op. Group O, composer.
(N) **(*) Ph. 446 325-2 (2) [id.]. Helen Donath, Robert Tear, Heather Harper, Ava June, Lillian Watson, Michael Ginn, ROHCG O (members), Sir Colin Davis.

Steuart Bedford here presents a highly idiomatic performance of *The Turn of the screw* with a compar-able sharpness and magnetism which, thanks to the spacious recording, brings out the eerie atmosphere of the piece. The singers too have been chosen to follow the pattern set by the original performers. Langridge here, like Pears before him, takes the double role of narrator and Peter Quint, echoing Pears's inflexions but putting his own stamp on the characterization. Felicity Lott is both powerful and vulner-able as the Governess, rising superbly to the big climaxes which, thanks to the recording quality, have a chilling impact, not least at the very end. Sam Pay is a fresh-voiced Miles, less knowing than David Hemmings in the Britten set, with Eileen Hulse bright and girlish as Flora. Nadine Secunde is a strong Miss Jessel, and Phyllis Cannan even matches up to the strength of her predecessor, Joan Cross. An outstanding set.

Though the recording is in mono only, the very dryness and the sharpness of focus give an extra intensity to the composer's own incomparable reading of his most compressed opera. Peter Pears as Peter Quint is superbly matched by Jennifer Vyvyan as the governess and by Joan Cross as the housekeeper, Mrs Grose. It is also fascinating to hear David Hemmings as a boy treble, already a confident actor. Excellent CD transfer.

Sir Colin Davis's 1981 Covent Garden recording has the benfit of spacious and atmospheric sound, but the composer's mono recording is in some ways better-balanced and clearer of detail. Britten's own reading is a degree tougher and at times more intense, but Davis's extra ability to relax, to vary the expression, brings many dividends. As before, there is no weak link in the singing cast, with Tear underlining the devilish side of Peter Quint's character, more forcefully sinister than was Peter Pears, but at times too melodramatic. Helen Donath sings feelingly as the Governess, making her a neurotic character; but she hardly erases memories of Jennifer Vyvyan. The treble, Michael Ginn, as Miles, is excellent, and Heather Harper as Miss Jessel is a warmly persuasive ghost. The playing of the Covent Garden orchestra is superb, to bring out the formidable compassion of the piece, and the transfer to CD is first class in every way. A full libretto is included, but the words are for the most part very clear.

Collection

'The world of Britten': (i; ii) Simple Symphony; (iii; ii) Young person's guide to the orchestra. (iv; v) Folksong arrangements: Early one morning; The plough boy. (vi) Hymn to the Virgin. (iv; vii; iii; ii) Serenade for tenor, horn & strings: Nocturne. Excerpts from: Ceremony of carols; Noye's Fludde; Spring Symphony; Billy Budd; Peter Grimes.
(M) *** Decca 436 990-2; 436 990-4. (i) ECO; (ii) cond. composer; (iii) LSO; (iv) Pears; (v) composer (piano); (vi) St John's College Ch., Guest; (vii) Tuckwell; & var. artists.

The Britten sampler is well worth having for the composer's own vibrant account of the Variations on a theme of Purcell and the Simple Symphony, where the Playful pizzicato emerges with wonderful rhythmic spring and resonance (in the warm Maltings acoustics). The Pears contributions are very enjoyable too, notably the haunting Nocturne from the Serenade, with Barry Tuckwell in splendid form. Excellent sound throughout, although the tuttis in the Young person's guide to the orchestra could with advantage have had a more expansive sonority.

Brouwer, Leo (born 1939)

Concerto elegiaco (Guitar concerto No. 3).
(M) *** RCA 09026 61605-2 [id.]. Julian Bream, RCA Victor CO, composer – LENNOX BERKELEY; RODRIGO: Concertos. ***

Leo Brouwer has blended earlier Afro-Cuban and Javanese influences with romantic feeling, even adopting a cyclic structure as 'a homage to César Franck or the leitmotif of the nineteenth century'. The result is a piece with a short but haunting central Lento and a brilliant Toccata-like finale which sums up the earlier lyrical ideas. Bream's performance draws the music's threads together and yet displays much bravura. He is very well recorded.

Bruch, Max (1838–1920)

Adagio on Celtic themes, Op. 56; Ave Maria, Op. 61; Canzone, Op. 55; Kol Nidrei, Op. 55.
*** RCA Dig. RD 60757 [60757-2-RC]. Ofra Harnoy, LPO, Mackerras – BLOCH: Schelomo etc. ***

Ofra Harnoy undoubtedly has the full measure of Bruch's sombre, Hebraic lyricism in the best-known piece here, Kol Nidrei, and she receives warm support from Mackerras. The rest of the programme creates a lighter mood, with the engaging Adagio on Celtic themes recalling the Scottish fantasia. An excellent recording, made in Watford Town Hall.

Double piano concerto in A flat min., Op. 88a.
**(*) Ph. Dig. 432 095-2 [id.]. Katia and Marielle Labèque, Philh. O, Bychkov – MENDELSSOHN: Double concerto. **(*)

Bruch's Double piano concerto was given its concert première by the Cann Duo (who, one hopes, may be persuaded to record it). Bychkov makes a meal of the opening, but the contrapuntal writing for the pianos that follows is rather agreeable; one thinks of Reger. After a second movement which moves from Andante to Allegro molto, there is a romantic Adagio more typical of the composer. The Labèques play with bravura and panache and are given good solid support. The recording is full and resonant but lacks transparency, and the effect is surely heavier than need be.

Violin concertos Nos. 1 in G min.; 2 in D min., Op. 44; 3 in D min., Op. 58; Adagio appassionato, Op. 57; In Memoriam, Op. 65; Konzertstück, Op. 84; Romanze, Op. 42; Serenade, Op. 75.
(M) *** Ph. 432 282-2 (3) [id.]. Salvatore Accardo, Leipzig GO, Kurt Masur.

This valuable set gathers together all Bruch's major works for violin and orchestra. Although no other piece quite matches the famous *G minor Concerto* in inventive concentration, the delightful *Scottish fantasia*, with its profusion of good tunes, comes near to doing so, and the first movement of the *Second Concerto* has two themes of soaring lyrical ardour. The *Third Concerto* brings another striking lyrical idea in the first movement and has an endearing *Adagio* and a jolly finale. The engagingly insubstantial *Serenade* was originally intended to be a fourth violin concerto. The two-movement *Konzertstück* dates from 1911 and is one of Bruch's last works. *In Memoriam* is finer still and the *Adagio appassionato* and *Romanze* are strongly characterized pieces. Throughout the set Accardo's playing is so persuasive in its restrained passion that even the less inspired moments bring pleasure. Because of the resonant Leipzig acoustics, the Philips engineers put their microphones rather too close to the soloist and there is at times a degree of shrillness on his upper range. This is most noticeable on the first disc, containing the *G minor Concerto*, but the ear adjusts; throughout the rest of the collection one's pleasure is hardly diminished, for the orchestral recording is full and spacious.

Violin concerto No. 1 in G min., Op. 26.
(Y/B) (M) *** Sony Dig. SMK 64250 [id.]. Cho-Liang Lin, Chicago SO, Slatkin – MENDELSSOHN: *Concerto;* VIEUXTEMPS: *Concerto No. 5.* ***
*** EMI Dig. CDC7 54072-2 [id.]. Kyung Wha Chung, LPO, Tennstedt – BEETHOVEN: *Concerto.* ***
*** ASV Dig. CDDCA 680. Xue Wei, Philh. O, Bakels – SAINT-SAENS: *Concerto No. 3.* ***
(B) *** CfP Dig. CD-CFP 4566; *TC-CFP 4566* [Ang. CDB 62920]. Tasmin Little, RLPO, Handley – DVORAK: *Concerto.* ***
(Y/B) (M) *** Carlton Dig. PCD 2005 [id.]. Jaime Laredo, SCO – MENDELSSOHN: *Concerto.* ***
(N) (M) *** DG 449 091-2 [id.]. Shlomo Mintz, Chicago SO, Abbado – DVORAK: *Concerto.* ***
*** Chandos Dig. CHAN 8974 [id.]. Hideko Udagawa, LSO, Mackerras – BRAHMS: *Concerto.* ***
(Y/B) (BB) *** EMI Seraphim CES5 68524-2 (2) [CEDB 68524]. Sir Yehudi Menuhin, LSO, Boult – MENDELSSOHN: *Violin concerto* etc. ***
*** EMI Dig. CDC7 49663-2; *EL 749663-4* [id.]. Nigel Kennedy, ECO, Tate – MENDELSSOHN: *Concerto;* SCHUBERT: *Rondo.* ***
(N) (BB) **(*) RCA/Navigator Dig. 74321 29245-2 [60479-2-TV]. Uto Ughi, LSO, Prêtre – BRAHMS: *Violin concerto.* **(*)
(N) (M) **(*) Sony Stern Edition I SMK 66830 [id.]. Stern, Phd. O, Ormandy – TCHAIKOVSKY: *Méditation; Sérénade mélancolique* ***; WIENIAWSKI: *Violin concerto No. 2.* **(*)
(M) **(*) Sony SBK 48274; *SBT 48274* [id.]. Zukerman, LAPO, Mehta – LALO: *Symphonie espagnole;* VIEUXTEMPS: *Concerto No. 5.* **(*)
(N) (M) ** Sup. SU 1939-2 011 [id.]. Josef Suk, Czech PO, Karel Ančerl – BERG: *Concerto* ***; MENDELSSOHN: *Concerto.* **(*)
(N) ** RCA Dig. 09026 68046-2 [id.]. Pinchas Zukerman, LPO, Mehta – BRAHMS: *Violin concerto.* **

There have been few accounts on record of Bruch's slow movement that begin to match the raptness of Lin. He is accompanied most sensitively by Slatkin and the Chicago orchestra, and this reading is totally compelling in its combination of passion and purity, strength and dark, hushed intensity. The addition of the attractive *Fifth Concerto* of Henri Vieuxtemps makes this CD more attractive than ever. The recording is excellent.

Compared with her earlier Decca recording, Chung's expressive rubato is more marked, so that in the first movement the opening theme is more impulsive, and her freedom in the second subject vividly conveys the sort of magic you find in her live performances. The slow movement brings extreme contrasts of dynamic and expression from orchestra as well as soloist, and the finale is again impulsive in its bravura. That makes this an exceptionally attractive issue and an essential one for this much-loved violinist's admirers.

Xue Wei's approach to the concerto is at once passionately committed and refined in its delicacy of detail. Fortunately he is accompanied superbly by Kees Bakels, while Wei can equally seduce the listener with a most magical pianissimo. The slow movement is ravishing in its poetic flair, and the finale is full of fire. An outstanding début.

The movement in the Bruch where Tasmin Little's individuality comes out most clearly is the central *Adagio*, raptly done with a deceptive simplicity of phrasing, totally unselfconscious, that matches the purity of her sound. Her speeds in the outer movements are broader than those of such rivals as Lin. At full price this would be a first-rate recommendation: on CfP it is an outstanding bargain.

Jaime Laredo with consistently fresh and sweet tone gives a delightfully direct reading, warmly expressive but never for a moment self-indulgent. The orchestral ensemble is particularly impressive, when no conductor is involved. With first-rate modern digital recording, this is a highlight of the Carlton (formerly Pickwick) mid-price catalogue.

Shlomo Mintz certainly makes the listener hang on to every phrase, and his playing is undoubtedly compelling. The vibrato is wide, but his approach is so distinctive and interesting that few listeners will not be fired. The Chicago Symphony Orchestra plays with great brilliance and enthusiasm, and Abbado's direction is most sympathetic. The vivid recording has transferred splendidly to CD.

Full of temperament, Hideko Udagawa gives a persuasively passionate performance of the Bruch, very well recorded, and with strong, colourful playing from the orchestra the hushed opening of the slow movement is caught beautifully.

Menuhin's second stereo recording of the Bruch *Concerto* was made in the early 1970s. While he is obviously on familiar ground, there is no sign of over-familiarity and the lovely slow movement is given a performance of great warmth and humanity. Boult accompanies admirably, and the recording is obviously fuller and more modern than the earlier version with Susskind, even if the solo playing is technically less immaculate and the solo timbre a little spare. On EMI's bargain-basement Seraphim label, this coupling with Mendelssohn remains very attractive.

Nigel Kennedy's masculine strength goes with a totally unsentimental view of Bruch's lyricism, as in the central slow movement. This may not have quite the individual poetry of the very finest versions; but, coupled with an outstanding account of the Mendelssohn and the rare Schubert *Rondo*, it makes an excellent recommendation. The recording is full, warm and well balanced.

Those looking for a bargain-basement coupling with the Brahms *Concerto* (though this CD is at mid-price in the USA), and very good (1982) digital recording, might well choose Ughi on RCA Navigator. His is a fresh, direct reading. It may not have the individuality of Lin, but it is still a fine performance and excellent value.

Stern's vintage account from 1966 with Ormandy is one of the great classic recordings of the work, gloriously warm-hearted and passionate, with a very involving account of the slow movement, which sustains the greatest possible intensity. The finale, too, has wonderful fire and spirit. Ormandy's accompaniment is first class and triumphs over the hopelessly unrealistic balance, with the violin way out front.

Zukerman's reissued Sony triptych shows him at his finest, and it is a pity that the close-up balance brings inevitable reservations. His Bruch is a passionately extrovert performance, tempered by genuine tenderness in the slow movement. The brilliantly lit recording increases the sense of fiery energy in the outer sections and, with the excitement of the solo playing and the strongly committed accompaniment, the larger-than-life effect is almost overwhelming.

Josef Suk's recording from the early 1960s has been remastered effectively to sound fresh and clear. He is less suited to the Bruch than to the other concertos here; although his natural warmth and simplicity of line are appealing, his account is not as imaginative as some. The finale, taken slowly, draws on the affinity with the Brahms *Concerto*.

As in the Brahms, with which Zukerman's RCA version is coupled, the violin is placed more naturally than in his earlier, Sony version, also with Mehta conducting. As before, he takes an exceptionally expansive view in all three movements. The big gain in the new recording is the hushed, inner intensity of the reading, helped by the recording balance, and though the finale may be less beefy the clarity of Zukerman's articulation means that he is no less biting. However, for those who insist on a digital recording, Ughi on superbargain-priced RCA Navigator offers readings of both the Bruch and the Brahms that are both fresh and ardent.

Violin concerto No. 1 in G min., Op. 26; Scottish fantasy, Op. 46.
(N) (M) *** Decca 448 597-2 [id.]. Kyung-Wha Chung, RPO, Kempe.

The magic of Kyung-Wha Chung, a spontaneously inspired violinist if ever there was one, comes over beguilingly in this very desirable Bruch coupling from 1972, reissued in Decca's Classic Sound series. Chung goes straight to the heart of the famous *G minor Concerto*, finding mystery and fantasy as well as more extrovert qualities. Just as strikingly in the *Scottish fantasia* she transcends the episodic nature of the writing to give the music a genuine depth and concentration, above all in the lovely slow movement. Kempe and the RPO accompany sympathetically, well caught in a glowing recording.

Violin concerto No. 2 in D min., Op. 44.
(N) ⊛ *** Delos Dig. DE 3156 [id.]. Nai-Yan Hu, Seattle SO, Schwarz – GOLDMARK: *Violin concerto.*
*** ⊛

As with the Goldmark coupling, Nai-Yan Hu is ideally balanced and Schwarz and the Seattle orchestra provide a highly supportive accompaniment. The composer could not understand why this very tuneful concerto was so dwarfed by the earlier, G minor work, and Hu's soaring lyrical lines underline its warmth and consistent melodic inspiration. Though Perlman strikes a high profile in his EMI version, the sympathetic warmth of this Hu/Schwarz partnership and the concert-hall fullness of the Delos recording is altogether preferable.

Violin concerto No. 2 in D min., Op. 44; Scottish fantasy, Op. 46.
**(*) EMI Dig. CDC7 49071-2 [id.]. Perlman, Israel PO, Mehta.

Perlman may be less intimately reflective in both works than he was when he recorded this coupling before with the New Philharmonia, but in the fast movements there are ample compensations in the sharp concentration from first to last.

Kol Nidrei, Op. 47.
*** DG Dig. 427 323-2 [id.]. Matt Haimovitz, Chicago SO, Levine – LALO: *Concerto;* SAINT-SAENS: *Concerto No. 1.* ***

Matt Haimovitz, born in Israel, has a natural feeling for the piece and his performance, balancing restraint with expressive intensity, is serenely moving.

Scottish fantasia for violin and orchestra, Op. 46.
*** RCA Dig. RD 60942. Anne Akiko Meyers, RPO, López-Cobos – LALO: *Symphonie espagnole.* **(*)

Anne Meyers is admirably partnered by López-Cobos and the RPO. The very opening, with its melancholy, sonorous brass, is unforgettable, and the hushed violin entry is to be matched later by most tender playing in the *Andante*, where the response of the RPO is equally warm. First-class Abbey Road recording, expansive and very well balanced.

Symphonies Nos. 1 in E flat, Op. 28; 2 in F min., Op. 36; 3 in E, Op. 51.
**(*) EMI CDS5 550 046-2 (3) [id.]. Gürzenich O; Cologne PO, James Conlon.

When the first of Bruch's three symphonies is the one that is most striking in its invention and each has its weaknesses, one has to deduce that he was more a symphonist by default than by nature. On the whole, James Conlon's performances are convincing, if not ideal. Both orchestras (it is not clear which plays which work, or indeed if these are two different names for the same group) emphasize the music's Brahmsian and Schumannesque derivations, and indeed a rather good case is made for the *Third Symphony* here. The romantic opening is richly done, the slow-movement variations are warmly effective and the Scherzo (which the composer regarded as the finest movement in all three works) is made to sound quite original in its scoring. Only the finale rather lets the piece down. The orchestral playing is committed throughout, but at times one feels that greater drive is needed from the conductor. There is no fill-up, and the second CD plays for only 36 minutes.

String quintet in A min., Op. posth.
(N) *** Naim Dig. CD 010 [id.]. Augmented Allegri Qt – BRAHMS: *String quintet No. 2.* ***

Written in 1918, two years before he died, Bruch's *A minor Quintet* was one of two he wrote for sheer joy at the age of eighty. The scores were lost by the publisher at the end of the First World War, and we owe the rediscovery of this one to the fact that Bruch's daughter-in-law made a copy of her own. Though it was in the BBC Music Library and two broadcasts were given over the years, this is its first recording. It is an unashamed throwback in idiom to Beethoven and Brahms, but the freshness of ideas and argument is most winning. Starting with what sounds like late Beethoven updated, the strongly constructed outer movements frame a jolly Scherzo full of cross-rhythms and a sweetly lyrical interlude. Like the Brahms *G major Quintet*, with which it is ideally coupled, it is very well performed and vividly recorded.

Bruckner, Anton (1824–96)

Symphonies Nos. '0'; 1–9; (i) Helgoland; (i; ii) Psalm 150; (i; iii) Te Deum.
(B) **(*) DG Dig./Analogue 429 025-2 (10) [id.]. Chicago SO, Barenboim, (i) with Chicago SO Ch.; (ii) Ruth Welting; (iii) Jessye Norman, Yvonne Minton, David Rendall, Samuel Ramey.

Barenboim's inexpensive cycle has many excellent things, not least the account of No. 8, volatile and passionate, with flexible phrasing and urgent stringendi. The *Ninth*, too, is very well done, if not a first choice. Barenboim gives us the underrated *Nullte*, a performance comparable to Chailly's, though less successful than with Haitink. Barenboim brings keener and deeper responses to No. 3, and his *Seventh* has a strongly flowing current; although these performances are not to be recommended in preference to Karajan or Jochum at their best – as in the *Eighth* – they deserve to rank alongside them, which is no mean achievement. In Nos. 1–3 and 8 (and also the *Te Deum*) Barenboim has the advantage of excellent digital sound, and the analogue recordings are spaciously transferred, though with just a hint of fierceness on Bruckner's massive fortissimos, noticeable immediately in No. 4. But no one investing in this set is likely to be greatly disappointed, and the magnificent *Te Deum* and *Psalm 150* are majestically done, though Ruth Welting is too shallow in the *Psalm* and David Rendall too tight of tone in the *Te Deum*. *Helgoland* is the valuable rarity.

Symphonies Nos. '0'; 1–9.
(b) **(*) Ph. 442 040-2 (9) [id.]. Concg. O, Haitink.

Haitink's set of Bruckner symphonies (reissued as part of the Haitink Edition) has all the classic virtues: they are well shaped and free from affectation or any kind of agogic distortion. Haitink's grasp of the architecture is strong and his feeling for beauty of detail refined. He has a less developed sense of mystery and atmosphere than Jochum, whose readings have a spiritual dimension at which Haitink only hints; however, Jochum recorded the Nowak edition. Haitink's judgements on matters of text are as sound as his approach is dedicated, and he secures consistently fine playing from the Concertgebouw Orchestra. Only the *Eighth* with its generally brisk tempi is at all controversial. The CD transfers bring much more vivid sound than on LP, yet the overall balance is always convincing. The set also has the additional advantage of economy, with only No. 1 split between CDs; the other symphonies each occupy a single CD.

Symphonies Nos. 1–9.
(m) *** DG 429 648-2 (9) [id.]. BPO, Karajan.
(b) *** DG 429 079-2 (9) [id.]. BPO or Bav. RSO, Jochum.

The reappearance of Karajan's magnificent cycle, long a yardstick by which others were measured – and at mid-price, too – must be warmly welcomed. We have sung the praises of these recordings loud and long, and in their new format they are outstanding value.

Jochum's DG cycle was recorded between 1958 and 1967 and costs even less. It enjoys the advantage of accommodating one symphony per disc. No apology need be made for the quality of the recorded sound. Jochum still has special claims as a guide in this terrain. He communicates a lofty inspiration to his players, and many of these readings can more than hold their own with later rivals.

Symphony No. 0 in D min.; Overture in G min.
**(*) Decca Dig. 421 593-2 [id.]. Berlin RSO, Chailly.

Riccardo Chailly's account of the unnumbered *D minor* (the so-called *Die Nullte*) is eminently acceptable. The Berlin Radio Orchestra respond well to Chailly's direction and, both as a recording and as a performance, this deserves recommendation.

Symphony No. 0 in D min.; (i) *Helgoland* (for male chorus & orchestra); (i; ii) *Psalm 150* (for soprano, chorus & orchestra).
(m) **(*) DG 437 250-2 [id.]. Chicago SO, Barenboim, with (i) Chicago Symphony Ch., (ii) Ruth Welting.

Bruckner's early *D minor Symphony* contains some inspired music. Barenboim shows evident affection for it but, once again donning his Furtwänglerian mantle, he is not always content to let the music speak for itself. However, he gets a generally positive response from the Chicago Symphony, and the 1979 recording is full and spacious. In *Helgoland* the islanders pray to be spared from the marauding Romans; a storm saves them in this brief but graphic piece. The Chicago forces sing and play with heartwarming resonance in both this and the Psalm setting and, although Ruth Welting is too shallow a soloist in the *Psalm*, this disc is well worth considering.

Symphony No. 1 in C min.
*** Orfeo Dig. C 145851A [id.]. Bav. State O, Sawallisch.

Symphony No. 1 in C min.; (i) *Te Deum.*
(m) **(*) DG Dig. 435 068-2 [id.]. Chicago SO, Barenboim; (i) with Jessye Norman, Minton, Rendall, Ramey, Chicago Symphony Ch.

Sawallisch's interpretation of the *First* is impressive in its honesty and dignity. There is warmth and some beautiful playing from the fine Bavarian orchestra, which is recorded in a spacious, yet not over-reverberant acoustic.

Barenboim's version of the *Symphony No. 1* comes with the *Te Deum* with its starry quartet of soloists and the magnificent Chicago Symphony Chorus. In both works he directs beautifully played, spontaneous-sounding performances that mould Brucknerian lines persuasively, but in the *Symphony* the dramatic tension is less keen, lacking something in concentration. The early digital recording is good but not ideally clear, with a brightness that needs a little taming.

Symphony No. 2 in C min.
*** Decca Dig. 436 154-2 [id.]. Concg. O, Chailly.
*** Decca Dig. 436 844-2 [id.]. Chicago SO, Solti.
*** DG Dig. 415 988-2 [id.]. BPO, Karajan.

Bruckner's *Second Symphony* is very long. Chailly uses the complete, Haas edition and his laid-back performance does not shirk that problem. It is a beautifully simple reading, with the slow-movement climax nobly graduated, a strong Scherzo without repeats (the Trio has a tuneful charm) and a finale that is not pressed forward ruthlessly but generates a positive and exciting closing section. The Decca recording is appropriately spacious and luminous, and for many this will be a first choice for the most elusive work in the Bruckner canon.

Solti, too, follows Haas. His overall momentum is characteristically more urgent than Chailly but there is no real sense of too much emotional pressure; indeed some will feel Chailly is too relaxed with his spaciously moulded paragraphs. The effect of the Chicago recording, too, is more robust and full-blooded. It is a satisfying alternative view. Solti aficionados need not hesitate.

Karajan modifies the Nowak edition by opening out some of the cuts, but by no means all. He starts reticently, only later expanding in grandeur. The scherzo at a fast speed is surprisingly lightweight, the finale relatively slow and spacious. It is a noble reading, not always helped by rather bright digital recording.

Symphony No. 3 in D min. (original, 1873 version).
(N) (B) *** Teldec/Warner Dig. 0630 14197-2 [id.]. Frankfurt RSO, Eliahu Inbal.

There are in all three versions of the *Third Symphony*: the first completed on the last day of 1873, a second which Bruckner undertook immediately after the completion of the *Fifth Symphony* in 1877, and then, after that proved unsuccessful, a third which he made in 1889. The 1873 is by far the longest version, running to nearly 66 minutes (the first movement alone lasts 24 minutes), and for those who have either of the others it will make far more than a fascinating appendix. The playing of the Frankfurt Radio Orchestra under Eliahu Inbal is very respectable indeed, with a sensitive feeling for atmosphere and refined dynamic contrasts; the recording is most acceptable without being top-drawer. Reissued at bargain price, this disc is even more tempting.

Symphony No. 3 in D min. (1877 version).
*** Ph. Dig. 422 411-2 [id.]. VPO, Bernard Haitink.

Haitink gives us the 1877 version, favoured by many Bruckner scholars. Questions of edition apart, this is a performance of enormous breadth and majesty, and Philips give it a recording to match. The playing of the Vienna Philharmonic is glorious throughout, and even collectors who have alternative versions should acquire this magnificent issue.

Symphony No. 3 in D min. (Nowak edition).
**(*) RCA Dig. 09026 61374-2. N. German RSO, Hamburg, Wand.

As in his earlier version from 1981, made with the Cologne orchestra, Günter Wand also opts for the 1889 version. This recording was compiled from public performances given at the Hamburg Musikhalle in January 1992, and the feeling of a live occasion comes across. The new version is better played and more sumptuously recorded, even though the sound is not in the demonstration bracket. Generally speaking, Wand's overall conception of the work is largely unchanged. The only flaw in what remains an altogether compelling account is the slow movement, which some Brucknerians may find a shade brisk.

Symphonies Nos. 3 in D min.; 4 in E flat (Romantic) (Nowak editions).
(N) (B) *** Decca Double 448 098-2 (2) [id.]. VPO, Karl Boehm.

There are many who admire Boehm's Bruckner, and he certainly controls the lyrical flow of these two symphonies convincingly, helped by first-rate playing from the VPO. Both recordings offer vintage Decca sound from 1970 and 1973 respectively; each has the advantage of the spacious acoustics of the Sofiensaal, and the balance provides splendid detail and a firm sonority. The effect is certainly compelling, and Boehm's sobriety was also his strength. In every bar he gives the impression that he knows exactly where he is going and, choosing the Nowak edition, he shapes each structure compellingly. If neither of these accounts is as individually imaginative as with Jochum nor as keenly dramatic as in the hands of Karajan, both have genuine stature.

Symphonies Nos. 3 in D min.; 7 in E.
(N) (B) *** EMI forte CZS5 68652-2 (2). Dresden State O, Jochum.

As a Brucknerian, Eugen Jochum has a special magnetism. Whatever the reservations that may be made on detailed points of style – Jochum believes in a free variation of tempo within a movement – his natural affinity of temperament with the saintly, innocent Austrian gives these massive structures an easy, warm, unforced concentration which brings out their lyricism as well as their architectural grandeur. So it is in these fine performances with the Dresden orchestra, made at the beginning of the 1980s. As in his earlier cycle with the Berlin Philharmonic and Bavarian Radio orchestras, he uses the Nowak edition. Thus No. 3 is based on Bruckner's 1888–9 revision, rather than the earlier and more extended score edited by Oeser. Readers wanting this alternative version will need to turn to the noble account given by Haitink. However, Jochum's Dresden readings of both the *Third* and *Seventh Symphonies* are exceptionally fine. With somewhat fuller, 1976–7 recording (made in the Lukaskirche), the *Seventh* opens magnetically; though it may miss a little of the hushed intensity that marked Jochum's earlier Berlin recording for DG, it is very compulsive. With his understanding of Bruckner developing towards a more direct and monumental approach, the authority is never in doubt, and this is matched by splendid playing from the Dresden orchestra.

Symphonies Nos. 3 in D min.; 8 in C min.
(B) **(*) Sony SB2K 53519 (2) [id.]. Cleveland O, Szell.
(N) ** Decca Dig. 443 753-2 [id.]. Cleveland O, Dohnányi.

In No. 3 Szell does not indulge the listener in a gentle, moulded style and the close-up Cleveland recording adds to the tangibility of his reading. But this outstanding American orchestra – here at its peak in 1966 – under the most incisive of conductors is hard to resist. Szell also uses the 1889 Nowak Edition and this reissue presents a marvellously strong interpretation which is well worth having in its own right even if, for some reason, the second part of the Scherzo is omitted when the outer section is repeated. In No. 8 Szell again uses a revised text, but here the differences between this and the Nowak edition favoured by Jochum are relatively minor. Szell's interpretation as a whole is masterly, and the Cleveland Orchestra produces glorious playing, recorded, like No. 3, in the spacious acoustics of Severance Hall (in 1969). Szell's manner is direct and tempi are generally uncontroversial, the exception being the Scherzo where, like Klemperer, Szell favours a massively measured tempo to bring out the bell-like tolling of the ostinato figures. The last two movements are held together superbly. The CD transfers are expertly done: the sound remains brightly lit but the dynamic range in No. 8 is wide, partly because Szell insists on real pianissimo playing.

There is also much magnificent playing from the Clevelanders in Dohnányi's similar coupling, particularly in slow movements. But Dohnányi (who uses the Oeser Edition in No. 3 and Haas in No. 8) fails to exert the same grip on the proceedings that makes the Szell performances so compelling: while there are moments of high drama, the tension ebbs and flows very unevenly and tuttis are emphatically stoic. Even the Decca sound, spectacular as it is, does not match Chailly's *Seventh* in naturalness of perspective and fullness of sonority.

Symphony No. 4 in E flat (Romantic) (original, 1874 version).
(N) (B) **(*) Teldec/Warner 0630 14198-2 [id.]. Frankfurt RSO, Inbal.

Like the *Third*, there are three versions of the *Romantic Symphony*, and no one has recorded the original before. The differences are most obvious in the Scherzo, a completely different and more fiery movement, but the opening of the finale is also totally different. Inbal's performance is more than adequate – indeed he has a genuine feeling for the Bruckner idiom and pays scrupulous attention to dynamic refinements. The recording is well detailed, though the climaxes almost (but not quite) reach congestion. An indispensable and fascinating issue, especially attractive at bargain price.

Symphony No. 4 in E flat (Romantic).
(N) *** EMI Dig. CDC5 55119-2 [id.]. Phd. O, Sawallisch.
(N) (M) *** DG 449 718-2 [id.]. BPO, Jochum (with SIBELIUS: *Night ride and sunrise, Op. 55* with Bav. RSO (***)).
(M) *** DG 439 522-2 [id.]. BPO, Karajan.
*** Denon Dig. C37 7126 [id.]. Dresden State O, Blomstedt.
(Y/B) *** Decca Dig. 443 327-2 [id.]. San Francisco SO, Herbert Blomstedt.
(N) (M) **(*) Sony Bruno Walter Edition SMK 64481 [id.]. Columbia SO, Bruno Walter.
(M) **(*) EMI CDM7 69006-2 [id.]. BPO, Karajan.
(Y/B) (BB) **(*) RCA Navigator 74321 17895-2. Leipzig GO, Kurt Masur.
(N) (M) **(*) Carlton IMP Dig. 30367 00282 [id.]. Hallé O, Skrowaczewski.

Symphony No. 4 in E flat; Overture in G min.
(Y/B) (***) Testament mono/stereo SBT 1050 [id.]. Philh. O, Lovro von Matačić.

Jochum is very special in this work, and Karajan also has a unique feeling for it – to say nothing of
Bruno Walter, now happily restored to the catalogue. But there is room for a first-class new recording,
and this EMI version from Sawallisch and the Philadelphia Orchestra (in superb form) is very compelling indeed. His grip on the first two movements is unerring; the Scherzo is suitably boisterous, with the
horns clearly enjoying themselves, and the finale is superbly expansive and exciting: a real apotheosis.
The recording really does justice to the Philadelphia sound.

   Jochum's way with Bruckner is unique. So gentle is his hand that the opening of each movement or even
the beginning of each theme emerges into the consciousness rather than starting normally. The purist
may object that, in order to do this, Jochum reduces the speed far below what is marked, but Jochum is
for the listener who wants above all to love Bruckner. The recording has undoubtedly been further
enhanced in this reissue in DG's 'Originals' series, and a fascinating mono recording of Sibelius's *Night
ride and sunrise* has been added. Jochum was not thought of as a Sibelian, but this performance is
undoubtedly impressive and well worth having.

   Karajan's opening (on his DG version) also has more beauty and a greater feeling of mystery than
almost anyone else on CD. As in his earlier, EMI record, Karajan brings a keen sense of forward
movement to this music as well as showing a firm grip on its architecture. His slow movement is
magnificent. The current remastering of the 1975 analogue recording, made in the Philharmonie, is very
impressive. The sound may lack the transparency and detail of the very finest of his records, but it is full
and firmly focused and there is no doubt that this is a performance of considerable stature.

   On Denon, Blomstedt opts for the Nowak edition, and the spacious and resonant acoustic in which his
version is recorded lends it a pleasing sense of atmosphere. The performance has a certain ardour and
conviction that impress. The slow movement has more feeling and poetry than one normally associates
with this conductor, and the sumptuous tone produced by the Dresden orchestra is a joy in itself. This is
not bright and analytical, but it is a beautiful sound and it suits Bruckner.

   The new Blomstedt account with the San Francisco orchestra is, as always with this conductor, a
performance of the old school. He uses the Haas edition with a few minor adjustments that Bruckner
made for the New York première of 1886. The acoustic of the Davies Symphony Hall does not have the
opulence or warmth of the Lukaskirche in Dresden where Blomstedt made his 1981 recording with the
Staatskapelle (on Denon); nor are the strings as rich and luxuriant. But this is an admirably direct and at
times moving performance and is cleanly recorded.

   Although not quite as impressive as his Bruckner *Ninth*, Bruno Walter's 1960 recording is transformed
by its CD remastering, with textures clearer, strings full and brass sonorous. It is not quite as rich as the
Blomstedt Dresden recording on Denon but is still pretty impressive, and the superbly played 'hunting
horn' Scherzo is wonderfully vivid. Walter makes his recording orchestra sound remarkably European
in style and timbre. The reading is characteristically spacious. Walter's special feeling for Bruckner
means that he can relax over long musical paragraphs and retain his control of the structure, while the
playing has fine atmosphere and no want of mystery.

   Karajan's earlier recording for EMI had undoubted electricity and combines simplicity and strength.
The playing of the Berlin Philharmonic is very fine. The resonance means that there is a touch of
harshness on the considerable fortissimos, while pianissimos are relatively diffuse. However, at mid-price
this remains well worth considering.

   Lovro von Matačić's Philharmonia account of the *Fourth Symphony* dates from 1954 and used the
Franz Schalk–Karl Loewe edition of 1889. Apart from retouching the orchestration, it involved a cut of
some 70 bars in the repeat of the Scherzo and half that number from the finale. Its Testament transfer is
tribute to the fine ears of the Walter Legge/Douglas Larter recording team; every detail in the orchestral
texture is transparent and finely delineated and the sound beautifully blended. When it was issued in the
USA, the *Overture in G minor* was added two years later, and this was also recorded in stereo. It is state-
of-the-art recording for its period, and impressive even now. The performance has both lucidity and
majesty, and Dennis Brain's horn-playing is a source of great pleasure.

   In RCA's super-bargain Navigator series, Masur with the Leipzig orchestra is obviously a sound guide
in Bruckner (no pun intended) and after opening poetically he shapes individual movements spaciously
and convincingly and his conception of the overall span is impressive. The horns roister appropriately in
the hunting Scherzo and the *Andante* has a gentle concentration and genuine atmosphere. The resonant
Leipzig recording has brought some problems with the digital remastering: there is at times an element
of minor coarseness in fortissimos, but at super-bargain price one can make allowances when the
interpretation is so instinctively sympathetic.

   Stanislav Skrowaczewski's reading with the Hallé Orchestra is eminently straightforward and well shaped. As one would expect from this conductor, the tempi are well judged and the concept spacious and majestic, with scrupulous attention to detail in matters of both phrasing and dynamics. The playing from the Hallé is responsive and sensitive, and there is no idiosyncrasy or self-indulgence. Overall this is a fine performance, full of perceptive touches. The recording has plenty of back-to-front perspective and no lack of atmosphere, though the acoustic does not have great warmth. There is a certain digital chill in big climaxes.

Symphonies Nos. 4 in E flat; 9 in D min.
(Y/B) (BB) *** EMI Seraphim CES5 68527-2 (2) [CDEB 68627]. Dresden State O, Jochum.

In Jochum's Dresden account of No. 4 the playing of the orchestra cannot always quite match that of the West German rival of a decade and more earlier, and that earlier Berlin Philharmonic record (see above) has a special claim on the collector for its subtlety and persuasiveness. But the newer version is very fine too, and both this and No. 9 have the advantage of a more modern and somewhat more opulent yet wide-ranging recording, although the remastering has brought extra brightness on top which is not entirely natural. The Dresden account of the last, uncompleted symphony shows the newer combination at its most persuasive, giving an impression of spontaneity such as you would expect in the concert hall; it is a splendid example of Jochum's art, with the Dresden strings sounding full and sonorous. On Seraphim, the two discs are offered together for the cost of a single medium-priced CD.

Symphony No. 5 in B flat.
*** Decca Dig. 433 819-2 [id.]. Concg. O, Chailly.
(Y/B) *** EMI Dig. CDC5 551255 [id.]. LPO, Franz Welser-Möst.
(N) (M) *(*) Decca 448 581-2 [id.]. VPO, Hans Knappertsbusch (with WAGNER: *Götterdämmerung: Dawn and Siegfried's Rhine journey* **).

Chailly gave us an outstanding Bruckner *Seventh* with the Berlin Radio Symphony Orchestra in the early days of CD which still ranks high among all the competition (see below). This new version of the *Fifth* is, if anything, even finer. The Royal Concertgebouw Orchestra play with sumptuous magnificence, and Chailly's overall control of a work that is notable for its diversive episodes is unerring, moving towards an overwhelming final apotheosis. The *Adagio* is very beautiful and never sounds hurried. The Decca recording is superb, very much in the demonstration bracket, with the brass attacking brilliantly, yet producing the fullest sonority, and the strings equally expansive. An easy first choice.

However stormy their relations may or may not have been, the London Philharmonic play well for Franz Welser-Möst on this occasion. They were recorded at the Konzerthaus, Vienna, in late May–early June 1993 before an attentive and silent audience whose presence emerges only at the very end. The applause is deserved. There are some potentially disruptive agogic touches, but he succeeds in persuading you that they have some logical motivation. There is nothing bland or 'general purpose' about this reading, and the LPO play with an impressive eloquence and radiance. The wide-ranging dynamics are well captured by the engineers.

Recorded in the earliest days of stereo (1956) Knappertsbusch's VPO version of the *Fifth* uses the Schalk edition with its truncated finale. Knappertsbusch can be a persuasive Bruckner conductor, but here the reading, though spaciously conceived, does not achieve a high level of tension, and it is not helped by the sound, which has a restricted dynamic range.

Symphony No. 6 in A.
*** Decca Dig. 436 129-2 [id.]. San Francisco SO, Blomstedt (with WAGNER: *Siegfried Idyll* ***).
*** Orfeo Dig. C 024821 [id.]. Bav. State O, Sawallisch.
(M) *** EMI CDM7 63351-2 [id.]. New Philh. O, Klemperer.
(N) (M) **(*) DG 477 525-2 [id.]. BPO, Karajan.

Blomstedt uses the Nowak edition, and in warmth and intensity the San Francisco strings readily match those of any rival, even Karajan's Berlin Philharmonic. The performance is splendidly shaped and the broad-spanned slow movement is particularly fine. Quite apart from providing a generous and beautifully played coupling (which no rival does), Decca's recording is also outstanding, at once full-bodied and warm but cleanly defined.

Sawallisch's account of the *Sixth Symphony* is beautifully shaped, spacious yet never portentous or inflated. Tempi – never too slow but never hurried – are beautifully judged, and the Bavarian State Orchestra respond splendidly to his direction. The acoustic has plenty of warmth but is not too reverberant, and the recording sounds excellent.

Klemperer directs a characteristically strong and direct reading. It is disarmingly simple rather than expressive in the slow movement (faster than usual) but is always concentrated and strong, and the finale is particularly well held together. Splendid playing from the orchestra and clear, bright recording.

Karajan is not as commanding here as in his other Bruckner recordings, yet this is still a compelling performance, tonally very beautiful and with a glowing account of the slow movement that keeps it in proportion. The 1979 analogue recording might ideally have been more expansive.

Symphony No. 7 in E (original edition).
(N) (B) *(*) Teldec/Warner Dig. 0630 14201-2 [id.]. Frankfurt RSO, Inbal.

Inbal uses the original score, published by Nowak, which omits the famous cymbal strokes which cap the climax of the slow movement. Alas, the tension level here is not high enough to manage without them, and overall this is a sound, well-played reading, given excellent mid-1980s digital recording, which fails to rise to the occasion.

Symphony No. 7 in E.
(N) (B) *** Decca Eclipse Dig. 448 710-2; *448 710-4* [id.]. Berlin RSO, Chailly (with MAHLER: *Des Knaben Wunderhorn: Des Antonius von Padua Fischpredigt; Das irdische Leben* – with Brigitte Fassbaender ***).
(N) (M) *** Ph. 446 580-2 [id.]. Concg. O, Haitink.
(M) *** EMI CDM7 69923-2. BPO, Karajan.
(N) *** DG Gold Dig. 437 037-2 [id.]. VPO, Karajan.
*** Denon Dig. C37 7286 [id.]. Dresden State O, Blomstedt.
*** DG Dig. 435 786-2 [id.]. Dresden State O, Sinopoli.
(Y/B) *** DG Dig. 437 518-2 [id.]. VPO, Abbado.
*** EMI Dig. CDC7 54434-2 [id.]. LPO, Welser-Möst.
(N) (M) **(*) DG Dig. 445 553-2 [id.]. VPO, Carlo Maria Giulini.
(N) (M) ** Sony Bruno Walter Edition SMK 64481 [id.]. Columbia SO, Bruno Walter.
(N) ** ASV Dig. CDQS 6154 [id.]. Philh. O, D'Avalos.
(N) (BB) *(*) RCA Navigator 74321 24207-2. Leipzig GO, Masur.

Chailly's account, with its superb Decca digital recording, ranks among the best available and makes an obvious first choice. He obtains some excellent playing from the Berlin Radio Symphony Orchestra and, though he may not attain the spirituality of Karajan and Jochum, his is a committed and very moving performance, and the apparent lack of weight soon proves deceptive. He has a considerable command of the work's architecture and controls its sonorities expertly. The recording, made in the Jesus-Christus Kirche, Berlin, is outstanding in every way. Warm, full tone throughout all the departments of the orchestra, yet a clean and refined sound, which is especially impressive on CD. Reissued on Eclipse with the bonus of two delightful songs from Mahler's *Des Knaben Wunderhorn* sung by Brigitte Fassbaender, this is an unbeatable bargain.

Haitink's 1978 version offers a fine alternative at mid-price. The recording is wide in range and refined in detail, yet retains the ambient warmth of the Concertgebouw. Haitink's reading is more searching than his earlier version, made in the 1960s. The Concertgebouw Orchestra play with their accustomed breadth of tone and marvellously blended ensemble.

Karajan's reading of No. 7 for EMI shows a superb feeling for the work's architecture, and the playing of the Berlin Philharmonic is gorgeous. The recording has striking resonance and amplitude, making a further good alternative medium-price choice for this favourite Bruckner symphony, generally preferable to his later, digital recording for DG. The EMI reading has a sense of mystery that is really rather special.

Karajan's digital account of the *Seventh* was his last recording, and he secures a marvellous response from the Vienna Philharmonic. This features in the lists without displacing his earlier accounts: in fact the 1977 version has slightly more grip and the 1971 EMI account has a sense of mystery that is also rather special. Those who have either need not make the change. The 'original image' reprocessing of the 1989 digital recording offers marginally cleaner sound, but there is a slightly artificial brightness on fortissimos.

A well-shaped account of the *Seventh* comes from Herbert Blomstedt and the Staatskapelle, Dresden; the beautiful playing of the orchestra and the expansive acoustic of the Lukaskirche are strong points in its favour. The reading is totally dedicated and Blomstedt has both strength and imagination to commend him.

It is not uncommon to hear Sinopoli spoken of as a 'stop-go' conductor, and it is true that he sometimes tends to cosset this or that detail and is reluctant to allow the musical argument to speak for itself. His account of the *Seventh Symphony* with the Staatskapelle, Dresden, is, however, unaffected, very well held together and beautifully played. Indeed it must be numbered among the best of Sinopoli's recordings, both artistically and technically, although Blomstedt's set with the same orchestra has greater nobility.

It is difficult to fault Claudio Abbado's DG account, which brings playing of great eloquence from the Vienna Philharmonic. The sound has splendid lustre and the architecture is impressively realized. No one listening to it is likely to feel short-changed – but at the same time one comes away from it with the sense that, despite its tonal finesse and opulent recording, there are depths undiscovered and terrain unexplored. Nevertheless, given its many splendours, the fine playing and recording, it would be curmudgeonly to withhold a third star.

EMI's version with the LPO conducted by Franz Welser-Möst comes from a 1991 Prom and so enjoys a warmer ambience than most studio performances. The LPO are responsive and produce a real Bruckner sound, save perhaps at the bottom end of the aural spectrum. As one would expect from a native Austrian, Welser-Möst has a natural feel for Bruckner's spacious lyricism and there is little here to quarrel with. Audience noise is minimal, save at the very end, when it is anything but!

Giulini secures playing of the utmost refinement from the Vienna Philharmonic and shapes each paragraph lovingly – indeed, at times some might think too lovingly: the Vienna strings are occasionally prone to a little too much sweetness. All the same, here are some wonderful things and music-making of a real and affecting eloquence. The only major reservation to be made concerns a want of a consistent forward movement. The DG recording has splendid warmth and does justice to the sumptuous sounds that the Vienna orchestra produce. The balance and perspective are natural.

Walter's reading suffers from the basic fault of concentrating on detail at the expense of structure. The outer movements bring many illuminating touches and the final climax of the first is imposingly built, but overall the tension is loosely held. In the *Adagio*, which is kept moving fairly convincingly, the climax is disappointing, and made the more so by the absence of the famous cymbal clash, as Walter uses the original text. The 1963 recording has been opened up in its remastering for CD and sounds fuller and more spacious than the original LPs. The present reissue places the work on a single CD for the first time, but this is not one of Walter's finest Bruckner records.

There is some respectable orchestral playing from the Philharmonia Orchestra under Francesco D'Avalos on ASV and the quality of the recorded sound gives no ground for complaint. But the performance is not strong on personality and it would be impossible to recommend it while such excellent accounts as those by Haitink, Karajan and Blomstedt remain in currency.

Masur secures fine playing from the Leipzig Gewandhaus Orchestra and the recording is spacious. But the very expansive reading lacks the grip of real concentration and (whichever edition is used) the absence of cymbals at the climax of the slow movement is a great drawback.

Symphony No. 8 in C min.
⊛ *** DG Dig. 427 611-2 (2) [id.]. VPO, Karajan.
(Y/B) (M) *** DG 439 969-2 (2) [id.]. BPO, Karajan – WAGNER: *Siegfried idyll*.***
(N) (BB) *** EMI Seraphim CES5 69092 [CDEB 69092] (2). BPO, Karajan – WAGNER: *Lohengrin; Parsifal Preludes*. ***
(B) **(*) DG 431 163-2. BPO, Jochum.
(M) *** EMI Dig. CDM7 64849-2 [id.]. LPO, Tennstedt.
(Y/B) (B) *** RCA Dig. 09026 68047-2 (2) [id.]. N. German RSO, Wand.

Karajan's last version of the *Eighth Symphony* is with the Vienna Philharmonic Orchestra and is the most impressive of them all. The sheer beauty of sound and opulence of texture is awe-inspiring but never draws attention to itself: this is a performance in which beauty and truth go hand in hand. The recording is superior to either of its predecessors in terms of naturalness of detail and depth of perspective. This is quite an experience!

Karajan's earlier (1975) Berlin Philharmonic recording sounds very impressive in the current CD transfer. Moreover it has the advantage, not only of a lower price, but also of a first-class coupling in Wagner's *Siegfried idyll*. The analogue recording of the symphony has fine body and refinement of texture. Sonically it does not perhaps quite match the later, Vienna Philharmonic account but there is very little in it, and no one investing in this noble account is likely to be disappointed. The reading is majestic, massive in scale, yet immaculate in detail. Excellent value.

The Seraphim transfer of Karajan's 1958 Berlin Philharmonic recording is remarkably successful. The EMI sound is spacious and, if the sonorities are not quite as sumptuous as we would expect today, the strings do not lack body and the brass makes a thrilling impact. The performance has much in common with Karajan's later (mid-price version) for DG and has compelling power. The slow movement is very fine indeed, conveying dark and tragic feelings, and the finale makes a fine apotheosis. While Karajan's last VPO version remains special, this is very worth while. As well as the advantage of great economy, it offers outstanding performances of the *Preludes* to Acts I and III of both *Lohengrin* and *Parsifal*.

Jochum uses the Nowak Edition, which involves cuts in the slow movement and finale, and in addition he often presses the music on impulsively in both the outer movements and especially in his account of the *Adagio*, where the climax has great passion and thrust. The symphony fits on to a single bargain-priced CD – which is worth any Brucknerian's money.

The plainness and honesty of Tennstedt in Bruckner is heard at its finest in this impressive account of the *Eighth*. It may not have the degree of exaltation which marked the performance which he conducted with this same orchestra at the Proms just after he made this record, but the inwardness and hushed beauty of the great *Adagio* in particular are superbly projected in unforced concentration. Though Karajan conveys more of the work's visionary power, Tennstedt in his comparative reticence carries similar conviction. Where generally in the other symphonies he prefers the Haas editions to those of Nowak, here he is firmly in favour of Nowak without the additional material in the recapitulation. Fine, well-balanced recording, with the CD clarity filled out by the fullness of ambience. EMI's No. 1 Studio is made to sound like a concert hall.

Günter Wand is as far removed from the jet-set maestro as it is possible to get, and his new recording of the *Eighth Symphony* has a patrician eloquence that is impressive. It is the product of three live concerts from December 1993, and is a straightforward, selfless reading of integrity and vision. All the same, it does not significantly add to his view of the work as exemplified in his earlier cycle. The Hamburg orchestra is a fine body, though it does not quite possess the tonal lustre of the Berlin Philharmonic or Concertgebouw. This comes on two CDs, packaged as one and costing as much. Given its artistic claims and the very truthful sound, it is certainly worth considering.

Symphony No. 8 in C min. (Scherzo; Adagio; Finale only).
(Y/B) (***) Koch Schwann mono/stereo 314482 [id.]. Prussian State O, Karajan.

Who would ever have thought that a Bruckner symphony *without its first movement* would ever score so resounding a success? Karajan's 1944 recording, made at a time when the war was at so crucial a stage, was among those which were spirited off to the then Soviet Union after the Nazi collapse. Technically the sound is quite astonishing – and in the finale, an early example of stereo, is little short of incredible. ('It beggars belief' was one verdict.) Not only is it extraordinary in terms of sound, it is also of exceptional artistic interest. The finale has a breadth and spaciousness, a grandeur and, above all, a sense of repose, that Karajan does not surpass in his later recordings with the Berlin Philharmonic (1958 and 1975) or the Vienna Philharmonic (1987). The slow movement is also intense, yet natural in feeling. It is amazing that such artistic and technical results could have been achieved under wartime conditions.

Symphonies Nos. 8 in C min.; 9 in D min.
(N) (M) (***) Ph. mono 442 730-2; 430 731-2 (available separately) [id.]. Concg. O, van Beinum.

Although van Beinum's *Ninth* has been reissued on LP, the *Eighth* makes its first appearance since the 1950s. It is a performance of considerable stature and sounds astonishingly good. One critic, Richard Osborne, writing in *Gramophone* magazine, went so far as to say that the recording has 'a splendour, and a sense of rightness that make me wonder why anyone ever bothered to convert to stereo'! In the *Eighth Symphony* tempi are on the brisk side and the musical argument proceeds with an impressive and compelling logic. And what a glorious sound the Concertgebouw Orchestra makes! These are perform-ances of commanding integrity, well worth adding to any collection, and they are to be preferred to many full-price versions of the 1990s.

Symphony No. 9 in D min. (1896 original version).
(N) (B) **(*) Teldec/Warner Dig. 0630 14203-2 [id.]. Frankfurt RSO, Eliahu Inbal.

Eliahu Inbal's reading of the *Ninth* with the Frankfurt Radio Orchestra is far from negligible, even though it may not be a performance of the highest stature. The playing is often very fine, and Inbal is scrupulously attentive to detail; however, there is not the sense of scale that is to be found in the finest of his rivals.

Symphony No. 9 in D min.
(N) ⊛ (M) *** Sony Bruno Walter Edition SMK 64483 [id.]. Columbia SO, Bruno Walter.
(M) *** DG 429 904-2 [id.]. BPO, Karajan.
*** Teldec/Warner Dig. 9031 72140-2 [id.]. BPO, Barenboim.
*** DG Dig. 427 345-2 [id.]. VPO, Giulini.
(B) **(*) DG 429 514-2 [id.]. BPO, Jochum.
(N) (BB) ** RCA Navigator 74321 29247-2. Leipzig GO, Masur.

Bruno Walter's 1959 account of Bruckner's *Ninth Symphony* represents the peak of his achievement during his Indian summer in the CBS recording studios just before he died. Walter's mellow, persuasive reading leads one on through the leisurely paragraphs so that the logic and coherence seem obvious where other performances can sound aimless. Perhaps the Scherzo is not vigorous enough to provide the fullest contrast – though the sound here has ample bite – yet it exactly fits the overall conception. The final slow movement has a nobility which makes one glad that Bruckner never completed the intended finale. After this, anything would have been an anticlimax.

The DG Galleria reissue offers a glorious performance of Bruckner's last and uncompleted symphony, moulded in a way that is characteristic of Karajan and displaying a simple, direct nobility that is sometimes missing in this work. Even in a competitive field, this 1966 disc stands out at mid-price, to rank alongside Bruno Walter's noble 1959 version.

Daniel Barenboim's new account has depth and strength and, of course, the advantage of superb orchestral playing. Moreover the recorded sound has splendid body and transparency and, although it does not displace the Karajan account or the old Bruno Walter, must be numbered among the strongest newer recommendations.

Giulini's *Ninth* is a performance of great stature, the product of deep thought. As always, there is the keenest feeling for texture and beauty of contour, and he distils a powerful sense of mystery from the first and third movements. The DG recording has a welcome sense of space and transparency of texture.

Jochum's reading has greater mystery than any other and the orchestral playing reaches a degree of eloquence that disarms criticism. If at times Jochum tends to phrase too affectionately so that consequently the architecture does not emerge unscathed, he is still magnetic in everything he does. The 1966 recording sounds remarkably good. A fine bargain version.

As in his Leipzig recording of the *Seventh Symphony*, Masur's reading is leisured and expansive, but there is rather more tension in the *Ninth*. The Leipzig orchestra certainly understands Bruckner's expansive paragraphs, and the recording is warm and spacious. A fair recommendation in the bargain basement.

CHAMBER MUSIC

String quintet in F; Intermezzo in D min.; Rondo in C min.; String quartet in C min.
(Y/B) *** Sony Dig. SK 66251 [id.]. L'Archibudelli.

String quintet in F; Intermezzo for string quintet.
(Y/B) **(*) Hyperion Dig. CDA 66704 [id.]. Raphael Ens. – R. STRAUSS: *Capriccio: Sextet.* ***
(Y/B) **(*) CRD Dig. CRD 3456 [id.]. Alberni Qt.

Sony's newest version of the beautiful Bruckner *String quintet* as played by L'Archibudelli has much going for it. Moreover it includes three more Bruckner works. However, its appeal rests not so much in terms of the interest of the early and uncharacteristic *String quartet in C minor*, a student work lasting over twenty minutes to which few are likely to return, but in the care these players exercise over matters of phrasing and dynamics. As usual (as is the case with the symphonies) there is no escape from editions here: L'Archibudelli give us the later, longer version which Novak edited, whereas rivals give us the shorter coda. They use gut strings, which initially give the impression of being under-projected – or would do, were it not for the careful dynamic perspective.

The Raphael Ensemble, coupling their performance with the *Intermezzo in D minor* and the opening *Sextet* from Strauss's *Capriccio*, are more full-blooded, more obviously ardent and they have the benefit of rich recorded sound. Theirs is an eloquent account which, coming after the Sony, could seem over-stated.

The Alberni version comes from the early 1980s without any additional fill-up. It is nicely played without affectation and, taken in isolation, provides considerable musical satisfaction. However, where the above rivals are to be found, they should probably take precedence.

VOCAL MUSIC

Helgoland (cantata).
(M) *** Carlton PCD 1042. Ambrosian Male Voice Ch., L. Symphonica, Wyn Morris – WAGNER: *Liebesmahl der Apostel.* **(*)

Helgoland was written during the long-delayed composition of Bruckner's *Ninth Symphony*, and it might be regarded as a secular counterpart to the *Te Deum*. Though latterly the work was underprized, early responses were more enthusiastic than was common with Bruckner, and this recording, ardently conducted by Wyn Morris, helps to explain why. The Ambrosians sing with fervour and – despite the relatively small chorus being just a little dwarfed by the orchestra – the final climax has splendid bite and breadth. The sound is atmospheric and the CD transfer highly successful.

Masses Nos. (i) *1 in D min.* (for soloists, chorus and orchestra); *2 in E min.* (for 8-part chorus and wind ensemble); (ii) *3 in F min.* (for soloists, chorus and orchestra).
(Y/B) ✹ (M) *** DG 447 409-2 (2) [id.]. (i) Mathis, Schiml, Ochman, Ridderbusch; (ii) Stader, Hellman, Haefliger, Borg; Bav. R. Ch. & O, Jochum.

Bruckner composed his three *Masses* between 1864 and 1868, although all three works were revised two decades later. Each contains magnificent music; Eugen Jochum is surely an ideal interpreter, finding their mystery as well as their eloquence, breadth and humanity. The *Kyrie* of the *E minor* swelling out gloriously from its gentle opening is quite breathtaking, while the fervour of the passionate *F minor* work is extraordinarily compelling, with all the intensity and drive of an inspirational live performance. But throughout all three works the scale and drama of Bruckner's inspiration are fully conveyed. In these outstanding new transfers, the analogue recordings from the early 1970s are given remarkable vividness and presence, while the warm atmosphere is fully retained. A remarkable achievement and a splendid choice for DG's 'Original' series of Legendary Recordings.

Motets: *Afferentur regi virgines; Ave Maria; Christus factus est; Ecce sacerdos magnus; Inveni David; Locus iste; Os justi; Pange lingua; Tota pulchra es, Maria; Vexilla regis; Virga Jesse.*
**(*) Hyperion CDA 66062 [id.]. Salmon, Corydon Singers, Best; Trotter (organ).

Motets: *Afferentur regi virgines; Ecce sacerdos magnus; Inveni David; Os justi; Pange lingua gloriosa.*
(N) (BB) Belart 461 317-2 [id.]. St John's College, Cambridge, Ch., ASMF, Guest – BEETHOVEN: *Mass in C.* ***

The Corydon Singers under Matthew Best are not quite as well blended or as homogeneous in tone as the Bavarian Radio Chorus, but Best's direction is often imaginative and he achieves a wide tonal range.
   The St John's performances are also of the highest quality and the recording is marvellously spacious. They come in the lowest price range, coupled with a fine account of Beethoven's *C major Mass.*

Requiem in D min.; Psalms 112 and 114.
**(*) Hyperion CDA 66245 [id.]. Rodgers, Denley, Maldwyn Davies, George, Corydon Singers, ECO, Best; T. Trotter (organ).

Matthew Best here tackles the very early setting of the *Requiem* which Bruckner wrote at the age of twenty-five. The quality of the writing in the Psalm settings also varies; but with fine, strong performances from singers and players alike, including an excellent team of soloists, this is well worth investigating by Brucknerians. First-rate recording.

Bruhns, Nicolaus (1665–97)

2 Preludes in E min.; Preludes: in G; G min.; (i) Fantasia on *'Nun komm der Heiden Heiland'.*
*** Chandos Dig. CHAN 0539 [id.]. Piet Klee (organ of Roskilde Cathedral, Denmark), (i) with Elisabeth Rehling – BUXTEHUDE: *Chorale preludes.* ***

Just five Bruhns organ works survive (all included in this recital). Though he uses the term '*Praeludium*', each consists of an introduction and one or two fugues, written with an eager flair that recalls the early organ works of the young Johann Sebastian, who certainly knew of this music. The spirited opening *Prelude in E minor* is striking enough, but most remarkable of all is the flamboyant G major work with its bravura writing for the pedals. It also has a jolly fugue subject. The *Fantasia on 'Nun komm der Heiden Heiland'* has its *cantus firmus* introduced by a soprano voice, and she returns to repeat the chorale (undecorated) at a central point, after three variants. Piet Klee presents all this music with splendid life and colour, and his Danish organ, recently restored, brings vivid registration which is a pleasure to the ear. The recording is in the demonstration bracket. If you enjoy Bach's Arnstadt and Weimar preludes and fugues, you should certainly try this.

Brumel, Antoine (c. 1460–c. 1520)

Missa: Et ecce terrae motus; Sequentia: Dies irae, dies illa.
✹ *** Sony/Vivarte Dig. SK 46348 [id.]. Huelgas Ens., Paul van Nevel.

Missa: Et ecce terrae motus; Lamentations. Magnificat secundi toni.
*** Gimell Dig. CDGIM 026 [id.]. Tallis Scholars, Peter Phillips.

Brumel succeeded Josquin as *maestro di cappella* at Ferrara. Lassus himself prepared and took part in a performance of the twelve-part Mass, *Et ecce terrae motus*, in Munich in the 1570s, and this is the only copy of the work that survives. But it is not just the contrapuntal ingenuity of Brumel's music that impresses but the sheer beauty of sound with which we are presented. Brumel was not only one of the first to write a polyphonic *Requiem* but the very first to make a polyphonic setting of the sequence, *Dies irae, dies illa*. This is a more severe work than the glorious 12-part Mass which occupies the bulk of this CD, and it is written in a more medieval tonal language. The performances by the Huelgas Ensemble under its founder-director, Paul van Nevel, are fervent and eloquent and vividly bring this music back to life. This was its first recording, made in the ample acoustic of the Irish Chapel in Liège, and is resplendent.

The Tallis Scholars follow hot on the heels of the Sony issue and are hardly less impressive. In some respects their disc is complementary in that they opt for a different solution to the *Agnus Dei*, which is incomplete in the Munich manuscript. Nevel favours a Danish source that Phillips and his editor reject on the grounds that it uses six voices and voices of different range. The texture in their performance has greater transparency and clarity than the richer, darker sonority of the Nevel. Both can be recommended; neither should be ignored, and either or both should be acquired.

Bull, John (1562/3?–1628)

Keyboard music: *Canon in subdiapente, two parts in one with a running basse ad placitum; Dr Bull's myselfe; Dutch dance; Fantasias X & XII; Fantastic pavan and galiarda; Germain's alman; In nomine IX & XII; The King's hunt; The Queen Elizabeth's chromatic pavan and galliard.*
(Y/B) (M) **(*) Teldec/Warner Dig. 4509 95532-2. Bob van Asperen (harpsichord).

Apart from the justly famous, rhythmically vigorous *King's hunt*, most of Bull's music is unfamiliar compared to that of his contemporaries, yet he wrote for the keyboard expressively and with intellectual command (witness the *In Nomine IX* and the impressive *Canon*) and many of his pieces demand great bravura from their exponents. (Thomas Tomkins described his keyboard writing as 'for the hand' as distinct from Byrd's which was 'for substance'.) Yet Bull could write with simple charm, as in the two vignettes in the treble clef, *Germain's alman* and the engaging *Dutch dance*. The performances here are distinguished in every way, as we expect from Bob van Asperen; but his 1624 Ruckers harpsichord is too closely observed and made to sound metallic. Nevertheless, at a low volume setting, fully acceptable results can be achieved.

Burgon, Geoffrey (born 1941)

At the round earth's imagined corners; But have been found again; Laudate Dominum; Magnificat; Nunc dimittis; A prayer to the Trinity; Short mass; This world; Two hymns to Mary.
**(*) Hyperion Dig. CDA 66123 [id.]. Chichester Cathedral Ch., Alan Thurlow.

Burgon's famous *Nunc dimittis* is well matched here with the *Magnificat* that he later wrote to complement it and a series of his shorter choral pieces, all of them revealing his flair for immediate, direct communication, and well performed. First-rate recording.

Bush, Geoffrey (born 1920)

Symphonies Nos. (i) *1;* (ii) *2 (Guildford);* (iii) *Music for orchestra;* (iv) *Overture Yorick.*
(N) *** Lyrita Analogue/Dig. SRCD 252 [id.]. (i) LSO, Nicholas Braithwaite; (ii) RPO, Barry Wordsworth; (iii) LPO, or (iv) Philh. O, Vernon Handley.

Full of colourful and striking thematic material, with occasional echoes of Walton and Lambert, Geoffrey Bush's music is consistently warm and appealing. This very well-filled disc brings together fine Lyrita recordings made between 1972 and 1982, and adds a superb, completely new recording of the *Symphony No. 2*. The vigorous *Yorick overture* (1949), written in memory of the comedian, Tommy Handley, opens this concert most invitingly. It has all the exuberance of a Walton overture and is an immensely jolly piece, with wit and warm lyricism nicely balanced; in one brief, syncopated idea it offers a rhythmic reminder of Lambert's *Horoscope*. Geoffrey Bush was a pupil of John Ireland and he belongs to the lost generation of fine English composers whose music was upstaged for more than three decades by the barbed-wire school. The first of his two symphonies dates from 1954 and is a positive, three-movement structure centring on an elegiac slow movement with blues overtones, written in memory of Constant Lambert. The slow movement, *Elegiac Blues*, actually quotes from *The Rio Grande*. The work exhibits the traditional values of fine craftsmanship and directness of utterance by which

Bush sets great store. He does not shrink from the notion that music should entertain, and the main body of the first movement, as well as the finale, is much lighter in character than those of many contemporary British symphonists.

The *Second Symphony* is outgoing, too. It was commissioned to celebrate the 700th anniversary of the granting of a Royal Charter to the City of Guildford and was first heard there in 1957; it then had to wait 30 years for its first broadcast performance. This was no formal exercise but a warm statement of personal feeling, built on a strong and complex structure in four linked sections. Its four clearly defined sections are played without a break, the first and last suitably genial and festive. Both the central slow movement and the witty Scherzo, with two catchy trios, draw on earlier material, which is then recapitulated in reverse for the finale.

Music for orchestra (1967) is also designed to be played continuously. It was commissioned by the Shropshire Schools Symphony Orchestra and is, in the composer's words, 'a miniature symphony', with the string parts carefully written so that they are not beyond the reach of inexperienced players, yet with plenty of opportunities for bravura offered to the wind and brass. Ample percussion and a piano add to the vividness. It is a formidable and by no means lightweight piece with a bleakly poignant *Lento* at its centre, with the threads of the structure drawn together in the finale, called an *Epilogue* but which becomes energetic towards the close. All the performances and recordings are outstandingly good, notably that of the *Symphony No. 2*, conducted by Barry Wordsworth.

Farewell, earth's bliss; 4 Hesperides songs; A Menagerie; (i) *A Summer serenade.*
*** Chandos Dig. CHAN 8864 [id.]. Varcoe, Thompson, Westminster Singers, City of London Sinfonia, Hickox, (i) with Eric Parkin.

The delightful *Summer serenade* of seven song-settings, written in 1948, five years after Britten's very comparable *Serenade*, has long been Bush's most frequently performed work – a favourite with small choral groups – and this first recording glowingly brings out the sharp contrasts of mood within and between the songs. The instrumentation is just as felicitous as the choral writing, with a spiky concertante part for piano played by Eric Parkin. It is well coupled with a solo song-cycle of comparable length, *Farewell, earth's bliss*, with Stephen Varcoe the baritone soloist; four songs from Herrick's *Hesperides*, also for baritone and strings; and three for unaccompanied voices, including an insistently menacing setting of Blake's *Tyger*. The tenor, Adrian Thompson, not ideally pure-toned, contributes to only two of the *Serenade* songs; otherwise these are near-ideal performances in warm, open sound.

Busoni, Ferruccio (1866–1924)

Berceuse élégiaque.
(N) (M) *** EMI CDM7 65869-2 [id.]. New Philh. O, Prausnitz – SCHOENBERG: *Chamber Symphony No. 2* **(*); WEILL: *Symphonies Nos. 1–2.* **

Busoni's *Berceuse élégiaque* is a moving and original piece, and it is very well played and recorded here. This is the highlight of an interesting group of works which are rather less successful as performances.

Comedy overture, Op. 38.
(N) (M) ** BBC Radio Classics 15656 91372 [id.]. LSO, Mackerras – CHERUBINI: *Symphony;* RESPIGHI: *The Birds* etc. **

What a delight this overture is! It was once an ingredient of the more exploratory Third Programme concerts, but it has the lightness of touch, the bustle, sparkle and grace of Wolf-Ferrari's *Jewels of the Madonna*. Why have composers stopped composing this kind of music, and why is this astonishing little masterpiece so seldom performed? The BBC label has performed a valuable service in giving it to us, for it is not otherwise available on CD. It is a good performance too, though it is possible to imagine one with greater finish, had Sir Charles and his musicians had more time.

Clarinet concertino.
*** Denon Dig. CO 75289 [id.]. Paul Meyer, ECO, Zinman – COPLAND; MOZART: *Concertos.* ***

Busoni's *Concertino* (1918) lasts about ten minutes and encompasses two quite striking ideas, the first soon heard in fugato style; but this is a not-too-serious but very well-crafted rhapsodical piece that is a worthwhile addition to the repertoire. It is played with elegance and improvisational spirit by the excellent Paul Meyer, and David Zinman and the ECO provide an equally well-judged accompaniment. They are given first-rate recording within a pleasantly resonant acoustic.

Piano concerto, Op. 39.
(M) *** Telarc Dig. CD 82012 [id.]. Garrick Ohlsson, Cleveland Men's Ch., Cleveland O, Dohnányi.

Busoni's marathon *Piano concerto* is unique, running to 70 minutes, roughly the same time as Beethoven's *Choral Symphony*, with which it has another parallel in its choral finale. Garrick Ohlsson's bravura display is very exciting, and the pianist's own enjoyment in virtuosity enhances his electricity and flair, even if the first-rate modern digital sound brings fewer advantages than expected, other than highlighting the solo piano.

(i) *Violin concerto, Op. 35a;* (ii) *Violin sonata No. 2 in E min., Op. 36a.*
(M) (***) Sony mono MPK 52537 [id.]. Szigeti, with (i) Little O Soc., Scherman; (ii) Horszowski.

In recent years Busoni's *Piano concerto* has come in from the cold; it is puzzling that the somewhat earlier *Violin concerto* has still to be recorded in stereo. Szigeti's pioneering LP was made in 1954, when he was well past his prime. The *Concerto* has a warmth and lyricism that reflect something of Busoni's admiration for Brahms and Strauss, and yet the afterglow of romanticism is still tinged with the forward-looking Busoni to come. The opening theme is particularly memorable. It is good to have Szigeti's 1956 mono recording of the *Second Violin sonata*, since he knew the composer. Despite the wide vibrato and slightly dry timbre Szigeti had developed by this time, the performance is well worth having – not least for the sake of Horszowski's artistry. Some allowance must be made for the sound, but the disc deserves a three-star recommendation purely on interest grounds and as the only version of a beautiful concerto.

Turandot suite, Op. 41.
*** Sony Dig. SK 53280 [id.]. La Scala PO, Muti – CASELLA: *Paganiniana;* MARTUCCI: *Giga* etc. ***

Busoni's *Turandot suite* has all the ingredients of popularity: colour, a captivating lightness of spirit and vivid musical ideas presented with wonderful imagination. It is good that its CD première is so successful in every respect; with excellent playing from the La Scala Orchestra under Muti, its wit and character are splendidly conveyed. Muti conducts the 1905 version of the suite. Good, well-detailed recording in a slightly dryish acoustic.

Violin sonatas Nos. 1 in E min., Op. 29; 2 in E min., Op. 36a.
*** Chandos Dig. CHAN 8868 [id.]. Lydia Mordkovitch, Victoria Postnikova.

Busoni's two *Violin sonatas* are rarities in the concert hall. There is no current alternative to the *First*, and Lydia Mordkovitch and Victoria Postnikova are impressive advocates of this somewhat uneven piece. The *Second* is a one-movement piece, dating from 1898, with a *langsam* opening, a Presto and a most beautiful *Andante* section leading to a set of variations. Mordkovitch and her partner give a sympathetic reading and, with excellent recording, this disc should be sought out by admirers of this composer.

Fantasia contrappuntistica; Fantasia after J. S. Bach; Toccata.
**(*) Altarus AIR-2-9074. John Ogdon.

Ronald Stevenson calls Busoni's remarkable *Fantasia contrappuntistica* a masterpiece and, listening to John Ogdon's performance, one is tempted to agree. The *Fantasia after J. S. Bach* was written a year earlier and is among Busoni's most concentrated and powerful piano works. The balance places Ogdon rather far back and, as the acoustic is somewhat reverberant, the piano sounds a little clangy.

OPERA

(i) *Arlecchino* (complete); (ii) *Turandot* (complete).
*** Virgin/EMI Dig. VCD7 59313-2 (2) [id.]. (i) Ernst Theo Richter, Mohr, Holzmair, Huttenlocher, Dahlberg, Mentzer; (ii) Gessendorf, Selig, Dahlberg, Schäfer, Kraus, Holzmair, Struckmann, Sima, Rodde; Lyon Op. Ch. & O, Nagano.

Kent Nagano follows up the success of his previous Lyon Opéra recordings with a set which vividly illustrates the elusive genius of Busoni. *Arlecchino* ('Harlequin') is a sparkling comedy that builds on *commedia dell'arte* conventions with a point rarely matched in opera, though for the non-German-speaking listener a snag of the piece is that the title-role is a speaking part. On disc, prolonged passages of spoken German give anything but an impression of frothiness, providing a deterrent to frequent repetition. Even so, it would be hard to imagine a finer performance than this, with the conductor's finesse, not least in controlling tension, matched by a brilliant German cast with no weak link.

Busoni's *Turandot* evokes a fantasy fairy-tale atmosphere in a piece that is light in texture, with motivation aptly quirky rather than realistic. In place of Puccini's Liù you have Adelma, Turandot's maid-servant, and the *commedia dell'arte* element is more central than with Puccini's Ping, Pang and Pong.

The surreal atmosphere is enhanced when the improbable theme for the evocative interlude before Act II is not Chinese but English – *Greensleeves*. Again Nagano's conducting gives a thrusting intensity to a piece that might seem wayward, and the casting is comparably brilliant, with Mechthild Gessendorf masterly as Turandot and Stefan Dahlberg heady-toned as Kalaf. The recording is vividly atmospheric, with plenty of presence.

Doktor Faust (opera) complete.
(M) *** DG 427 413-2 (3) [id.]. Fischer-Dieskau, Kohn, Cochran, Hillebrecht, Bav. Op. Ch. & R. O, Leitner.

Busoni's epic *Doktor Faust* was left incomplete at the composer's death. Unfortunately, this recording is full of small cuts; however, with superb, fierily intense conducting from Leitner, it fully conveys the work's wayward mastery, the magnetic quality which establishes it as Busoni's supreme masterpiece, even though it was finished by another hand. The cast is dominated by Fischer-Dieskau, here in 1969 at his very finest; and the only weak link among the others is Hildegard Hillebrecht as the Duchess of Parma. Though this is a mid-price set, the documentation is generous.

Butterworth, George (1885–1916)

The banks of green willow.
(M) *** Chandos CHAN 6566 [id.]. Bournemouth Sinf., Norman Del Mar – BANTOCK: *The Pierrot of the minute: overture;* BRIDGE: *Summer* etc. ***

The banks of green willow; 2 English idylls; A Shropshire lad (rhapsody).
(M) *** Decca 440 325-2 [id.]. ASMF, Marriner – VAUGHAN WILLIAMS: *Lark ascending* etc.; WAR-LOCK: *Capriol suite* etc. ***
*** Nimbus Dig. NI 5068 [id.]. E. String O, Boughton – BRIDGE: *Suite;* PARRY: *Lady Radnor's suite*. ***

Reissued in Decca's 'British Classics' series, this collection of music by Butterworth, Vaughan Williams and Warlock makes an exceptionally generous anthology (74 minutes). Butterworth's *Shropshire lad* represents the English folksong school at its most captivatingly atmospheric, and the other works are in a similarly appealing pastoral vein. Marriner's performances with the Academy are stylishly beautiful, without the last degree of finesse but very fine indeed, with vivid, wide-ranging recording quality.

Boughton secures from his Birmingham-based orchestra warm and refined playing in well-paced readings. In an ample acoustic, woodwind is placed rather behind the strings.

On Chandos, Del Mar gives a glowingly persuasive performance of *The banks of green willow*, which comes as part of another highly interesting programme of English music, devoted also to Butterworth's somewhat older contemporaries, Bantock and Frank Bridge. The digital transfer of a 1979 analogue recording has the benefit of even greater clarity without loss of atmosphere.

Love blows as the wind (3 songs).
(M) *** EMI CDM7 64731-2 [id.]. Robert Tear, CBSO, Vernon Handley – ELGAR; VAUGHAN WIL-LIAMS: *Songs.* ***

These three charming songs (*In the year that's come and gone, Life in her creaking shoes, Coming up from Richmond*), to words by W. E. Henley, provide an excellent makeweight for a mixed bag of orchestral songs based on the first recording of Vaughan Williams's *On Wenlock Edge* in its orchestral form. The sound is clear yet enjoyably warm and atmospheric.

A Shropshire lad (song-cycle).
(M) *** Decca 430 368-2 [id.]. Benjamin Luxon, David Willison – VAUGHAN WILLIAMS: *Blake songs* etc. ***

Benjamin Luxon gives powerful, dramatic performances of songs which can take such treatment, not quite the miniatures they may sometimes seem. Well-balanced recording and an admirable coupling.

Buxtehude, Diderik (c. 1637–1707)

Trio sonatas: in G; B flat and D min., Op. 1/2, 4 & 6 (BuxWV 253, 255 & 257); in D and G min., Op. 2/2–3, (BuxWV 260–1).
*** ASV/Gaudeamus CDGAU 110. Trio Sonnerie.

Make no mistake, this is music of real quality: its invention is fertile and distinguished by a lightness of touch and colour that is quite individual; the melodic lines are vivacious and engaging, and their virtuosity inspiriting. The Trio Sonnerie show real enthusiasm and expertise, and their virtuosity is agreeably effortless and unostentatious.

Trio sonatas for violin, viola da gamba and harpsichord: in A min., Op. 1/3; in B flat, Op. 1/4; in G min., Op. 2/3; in E, Op. 2/6 (BuxWV 254–5, 261; 264).

(B) *** HM HMA 901089 [id.]. Boston Museum Trio.

The Boston Museum Trio are a highly accomplished group and display an exemplary feeling for style. The music is unfailingly inventive and, despite the obvious Italianate elements, distinctive. Not only are the playing, recording and presentation of high quality, but the cost is modest.

Canzona in E min., BuxWV 169; Canzonetta in G, BuxWV 171; Ciacona in E min., BuxWV 160; Chorales: *Ach Herr, mich armen Sünder, BuxWV 178; In dulci jubilo, BuxWV 197; Komm, Heiliger Geist, Herre Gott, BuxWV 199; Vater unser im Himmelreich, BuxWV 219; Magnificat primi toni, BuxWV 203; Preludes: in C, BuxWV 137; in D, BuxWV 139.*

(*) Chandos Dig. CHAN 0514 [id.]. Piet Kee (organ of St Laurent Church, Alkmaar) – SWEELINCK: *Collection.* *

Kee's performance of the opening *Magnificat primi toni* is little short of magnificent. The closing *Ciacona in E minor* is pretty impressive too, while the *Canzonetta in G* is deliciously registered, with piping flute colouring. One's reservations, however, concern the presentation of the chorales, which, Kee suggests, 'require poetic expression'. Perhaps they do, but they also need to be moved on rather faster. The Chandos recording is superb.

Canzonetta in G, BuxWV 171; Ciaconas: in C min., BuxWV 159; in E min., BuxWV 160. Chorales: *Ach, Herr, mich armen Sünder, BuxWV 178; Der Tag der ist so freudenreich, BuxWV 182; Durch Adams Fall ist ganz verderbt, BuxWV 183; In dulci jubilo, BuxWV 197; Komm, heiliger Geist, Herr Gott, BuxWV 199; Nimm von uns, BuxWV 207; Nun komm der Heiden Heiland, BuxWV 211; Wie schön leuchtet der Morgenstern, BuxWV 223. Fugue in C, BuxWV 174; Magnificat primi toni, BuxWV 203; Passacaglia in D min., BuxWV 161; Preludes: in A min., BuxWv 153; in C, BuxWV 137; in D, BuxWV 139; in D min., BuxWV 140; E min., BuxWV 142; F, BuxWV 145; F sharp min., BuxWV 146; G min., BuxWV 149. Te Deum laudamus, BuxWV 218; Toccatas: in D min., BuxWV 155; in F, BuxWV 156.*

(N) (M) *** Erato/Warner Dig. 0630 12979-2 (2). Marie-Claire Alain (Schnitger-Ahrend organ, Groningen).

Marie-Claire Alain's admirable mid-priced, two-disc set on Erato currently seems just about the best buy for those wanting a comprehensive survey of Buxtehude's splendid organ music. The magnificent opening *Prelude in C* shows not only how ideally the Groningen organ suits this repertoire, with its bright reeds and weighty yet never clouding sonorities, but also the full calibre of Buxtehude's music. Beginning floridly and thrillingly over massive pedals, it then produces a flowing fugue, with a following lively dance section and a final toccata. Marie-Claire Alain presents it powerfully and spontaneously, and she is equally impressive in registering the chorales, using a wide palette of colour: they are gently paced but never drag. The second disc opens with the ebullient *Fugue in C* which is so like the *Fugue à la gigue* attributed to Bach (BWV 577). Then, after the impressive chaconnes, the *Canzonetta in G* is piped quite deliciously. The complex *Magnificat primi toni* and the large-scale chorale fantasia on the *Te Deum* (in which Buxtehude and Alain always ensure that the cantus firmus emerges clearly) make one understand why Bach so admired this music. The arresting *Toccata in D minor*, with its dramatic pauses, undoubtedly influenced Bach's most famous organ work in the same key. Superb playing throughout, and demonstration-standard recording.

Chorales: *Auf meinen lieben Gott, BuxWV 179; Gott der Vater wohn uns bei, BuxWV 190; Nimm von uns, Herr du treuer Gott, BuxVW 207; Nun komm der Heiden Heiland, BuxWV 211; Puer natus in Bethlehem, BuxWV 217; Von Gott will ich nicht lassen (2 settings), BuxWV 220/221.*

*** Chandos Dig. CHAN 0539 [id.]. Piet Klee (organ of Roskilde Cathedral, Denmark) – BRUHNS: *Preludes.* ***

The restored baroque organ at Roskilde Cathedral has a palette to tempt the most jaded listener and, although Piet Klee still persists in playing these chorales and their variants rather slowly, his piquant registration is very effective, so that they serve as attractively serene interludes between the remarkably flamboyant *Preludes* by Buxtehude's precociously inspired pupil, Nicolaus Bruhns, whose genius was sadly cut short when he died before his mentor, at the early age of thirty-two. The recording is very much in the demonstration class throughout this disc.

Chorales: *Christ unser Herr zum Jordan kam; Durch Adams Fall ist ganz verderbt; Ein feste Burg ist unser Gott; Erhalt uns, Herr, bei deinem Wort; Es ist das Heil uns kommen her; Es spricht der unweisen Mund wohl; Gelobet seist du, Jesu Christ; Gott der Vater, wohn uns bei; Magnificat primi toni; 2 Preludes and fugues in A min.; Preludes and fugues: in C; F sharp min.*
(B) *** HM HMA 190942 [id.]. René Saorgin (Schnitger organ of the Church of St Michel de Zwolle, Holland).

The Schnitger organ is sensitively and colourfully registered by Saorgin: he is particularly impressive in the serene, reflective chorales, *Durch Adams Fall* and *Es spricht der unweisen Mund wohl*, while the elaborations of the *Magnificat* are finely made. Excellent recording, vividly transferred.

Ciaconas: *in C min.; E min., BuxWV 159–60; Passacaglia in D min., BuxWV 161; Preludes and fugues: in D; D min.; E; E min., BuxWV 139–42; in F; F sharp min., BuxWV 145–6; in G min., BuxWV 149.*
(M) *** DG 427 133-2. Helmut Walcha (organ of Church of SS Peter and Paul, Cappel, West Germany).

Helmut Walcha has the full measure of this repertoire and these performances on the highly suitable Arp Schnitger organ in Cappel, Lower Saxony, are authoritative and spontaneous. The 1978 recording is excellent and the disc comprises generous measure: 73 minutes.

(i) Preludes and fugues: *in G min.; F.* Chorales: *Herr Christ, der einig Gottes Sohn; In dulci jubilo; Lobt Gott, ihr Christen allzugleich; Chorale fantasy: Gelobet seist du, Jesu Christ.* Cantatas: (ii) *In dulci jubilo; Jubilate Domino.*
(B) *** HM HMA 190700 [id.]. (i) René Saorgin (organ of St Laurent Church, Alkmaar); (ii) Alfred Deller, Deller Cons., Perulli, Chapuis.

A good, inexpensive sampler of Buxtehude, dating from 1971. The opening *Prelude and fugue in G minor* is fully worthy of the young J. S. Bach and, like its companion, is splendidly played by René Saorgin. The chorales are more static and less interesting than Bach's treatment of the same ideas. Of the cantatas, *In dulci jubilo* is a florid piece for four voices with instrumental accompaniment, while *Jubilate Domino* is a solo cantata accompanied by viola da gamba and organ continuo. Deller is in good form throughout.

Cantatas: *An Filius non est Dei, BuxWV 6; Cantata Domino, BuxWV 12; Frohlocket mit Händen, BuxWV 29; Gott fähret auf mit Jauchzen, BuxWV 33; Herr, wenn ich nur Dich habe, BuxWV 39; Heut triumphieret Gottes Sohn, BuxWV 43; Ich bin die Auferstehung, BuxWV 44; Ich habe Lust abzuscheiden, BuxWV 46; Ihr lieben Christen, BuxWV 51; In dulci jubilo, BuxWV 52; Jesus dulcis memoria, BuxWV 56; Jesu meines Lebens Leben, BuxWV 62; Jubilate Deo, BuxWV 64; Mein Gemüt erfreuet sich, BuxWV 72; Nichts soll uns scheiden, BuxWV 77; Nun danket alle Gott, BuxWV 79; Wie wird erneuet, wie wird er freuet, BuxWV 110.*
*** Erato/Warner Dig. 2292 45294-2 (3) [id.]. Schlick, Frimmer, Chance, Jacobs, Prégardien, Kooy, Hannover Knabenchor, Amsterdam Bar. O, Koopman.

All the works here are of a pietist religious character, although the music readily expands into joyously extrovert expressions of praise. Some attractively combine the form of a concerto grosso, with alternating solos and tuttis, and a few are more ambitious, including chorus, trumpets and cornetts, and even trombones, and drums too. The brass writing is inevitably primitive, but highly effective in its stylized way. The solo singing is excellent, and the soloists match pleasingly when they sing in duet or trio. There is plenty to discover here for any collector who enjoys the pre-Bach era. Accompaniments are alive, textures transparent, and the recording balance is altogether excellent.

Membra Jesu nostri, *BuxWV 75.*
(N) (M) *** DG Dig. 447 298-2 [id.]. Monteverdi Ch., E. Bar. Soloists, Gardiner – SCHUTZ: *O bone Jesu.* ***

Membra Jesu nostri, *BuxWV 75; Heut triumphieret Gottes Sohn, BuxWV 43.*
**(*) HM Dig. HMC 901333 [id.]. Concerto Vocale & Instrumental Ens., Jacobs.

The *Membra Jesu nostri* is a cycle of seven cantatas, each addressed to different parts of the body of the crucified Christ, all of a simple, dignified, expressive power that, as always with this composer, make a strong impression. Of the two performances John Eliot Gardiner's is the more searching and devotional; the Concerto Vocale, though beautifully sung, is less atmospheric both as a performance and as a recording. The Harmonia Mundi is more forwardly balanced; the Gardiner has more space and the sense of one of Buxtehude's own Abendmusik. Compare the sixth of the cantatas, *Ad cor*, and the more reverential approach and feeling of the Gardiner tells. There are only a few seconds between the two, but the latter feels wonderfully spacious and unhurried. But both issues can be recommended; the impressive *Heut triumphieret Gottes Sohn* comes with the Harmonia Mundi disc and a Schütz *Geistliches Konzert, O bone Jesu,* related in spirit, comes on the Archiv recording, which is now offered at mid-price.

Byrd, William (1543–1623)

Complete consort music: *Christe qui lux a 4, Nos. 1–3; Christe redemptor a 4; Fantasia a 3, Nos. 1–3; Fantasia a 4, No. 1; Fantasia a 5 (Two in one); Fantasia a 6, Nos. 2–3; In nomine a 4, Nos. 1–2; In nomine a 4, Nos. 1–5; Miserere a 4; Pavan & Galliard a 5; Pavan & Galliard a 6; Prelude & Ground a 5; Sermon blande blando a 3; Sermon blando a 4, No. 1; Te lucis a 4, No. 2, verse 2.*
*** Virgin/EMI Dig. VC5 45031-2 [id.]. Fretwork, with Christopher Wilson (lute).

Fretwork have now completed their survey of Byrd's consort music – part of which was originally issued coupled with Dowland's *Lachrimae* – and the complete consort music (76 minutes) is now fitted on to a single CD. The grave feeling of much of this music is apparent in the opening *Prelude and Ground a 5;* then the mood quickly lightens as the texture is woven in more swiftly moving configurations to make a typically satisfying whole. *Browning* has the alternative title of *The leaves be green* and consists of divisions on a popular song, while the *Fantasia a 6* which closes the concert is a masterly compression of ideas into a fluid structure as powerful as Purcell's famous *Chaconne*. Performances have consistent authority and freshness and, although the recording seems rather close, it is vivid and realistic.

My Ladye Nevells Booke, 1591 (42 keyboard pieces).
✸ *** O-L 430 484-2 (3). Christopher Hogwood (virginal, harpsichord, chamber organ).

This collection of Byrd's music was compiled by John Baldwin of Windsor, 'a gentleman of the Chapel Royal', and must be reckoned the finest collection in Europe of keyboard writing of the sixteenth century. Christopher Hogwood rings the changes by using a variety of instruments: a virginal, two harpsichords (one Flemish and the other Italian) and a fine chamber organ, all of which he plays with sympathy and vitality. Hogwood's scholarly gifts are shown in the fine notes that accompany the set, but, more importantly, his masterly keyboard technique and artistic sensitivity are sustained throughout the three discs. The recording is exemplary, very real and in excellent perspective. A landmark in records of early keyboard music.

VOCAL MUSIC

Motets in paired settings: *Ave verum corpus* (with PHILIPS: *Ave verum corpus*); *Haec dies* (with PALESTRINA: *Haec Dies*); *Iustorum animae* (with LASSUS: *Iustorum animae*); *Miserere mei* (with G. GABRIELI: *Miserere mei*); *O quam gloriosum* (with VICTORIA: *O quam gloriosum*); *Tu es Petrus* (with PALESTRINA: *Tu es Petrus*).
(B) *** CfP CD-CFP 4481; *TC-CFP 4481*. King's College, Cambridge, Ch., Sir David Willcocks.

This is an imaginatively devised programme of motets in which settings of Latin texts by Byrd are directly contrasted with settings of the same words by some of his greatest contemporaries. As was the intention, quite apart from adding variety to the programme, the juxtaposition makes one listen to the individual qualities of these polyphonic masters the more keenly, and register their individuality. The recording emerges with remarkable freshness on CD, and the beauty of the singing is never in doubt.

Cantiones sacrae, Book 1: Aspice Domine; Domine secundum multitudinem; Domine tu iurasti; In resurrectione tua; Ne irascaris Domine; O quam gloriosum; Tristitia et anxiestas; Vide Domine afflictionem; Virgilate.
**(*) CRD Dig. CRD 3420; *CRDC 4120* [id.]. New College, Oxford, Ch., Higginbottom.

Cantiones sacrae, Book 2: Circumdederunt me; Cunctis diebus; Domine, non sum dignus; Domine, salva nos; Fac sum servo tuo; Exsurge, Domine; Haec dicit Dominus; Haec dies; Laudibus in sanctis Dominum; Miserere mei, Deus; Tribulatio proxima est.
**(*) CRD Dig. CRD 3439; *CRDC 4139* [id.]. New College, Oxford, Ch., Higginbottom.

Though the New College Choir under its choirmaster Edward Higginbottom does not sing with the variety of expression or dynamic which marks its finest Oxbridge rivals, it is impossible not to respond to the freshness of its music-making. The robust, throaty style suggests a Latin feeling in its forthright vigour, and the directness of approach in these magnificent *cantiones sacrae* is most attractive, helped by recording which is vividly projected, yet at once richly atmospheric.

The Great Service (with anthems).
*** Gimell Dig. CDGIM 011; *1585T-11* [id.]. Tallis Scholars, Phillips.
*** EMI Dig. CDC7 47771-2. King's College, Cambridge, Ch., Cleobury; Richard Farnes (organ).
Peter Phillips and the Tallis Scholars give a lucid and sensitively shaped account of Byrd's *Great Service*. Theirs is a more intimate performance than one might expect to encounter in one of the great English

cathedrals; they are fewer in number and thus achieve greater clarity of texture. The recording is quite excellent: it is made in a church acoustic (the Church of St John, Hackney) and captures detail perfectly. It includes three other anthems, two of which (*O Lord make thy servant Elizabeth* and *Sing joyfully unto God our strength*) are included on the rival EMI disc. This CD will give great musical satisfaction.

Collectors wanting *The Great Service* in a cathedral acoustic will turn to the King's version, which is beautifully recorded on EMI. They have the advantages of boy trebles, a larger complement of singers who can offer more contrast between solo and full verses, and a well-played organ accompaniment, which it probably had in the 1580s. Stephen Cleobury also sets the music in a more authentic liturgical background: he offers the *Kyrie* and puts the two canticles for Evensong into their context with anthems and responses.

Mass for 3 voices; Mass for 4 voices; Mass for 5 voices.
❀ (M) *** Decca 433 675-2 [id.]. King's College, Cambridge, Ch., Willcocks.
(B) **(*) HM HMA 90211[id.]. Deller Cons.

Masses for 3, 4 and 5 voices; Ave verum corpus.
*** Gimell Dig. CDGIM 345 [id.]. Tallis Scholars, Phillips.

Although later versions of the *Mass for 5 voices* have produced singing that is more dramatic and more ardent, the serenity of the King's account with its long, flowing paragraphs remains very appealing. The performances of the *Masses for 3 and 4 voices*, dating from 1963, remain classics of the gramophone. Under Willcocks there is an inevitability of phrasing and effortless control of sonority and dynamic that completely capture the music's spiritual and emotional feeling. The Argo recording – a great tribute to the late Harley Usill – is extraordinarily real.

Peter Phillips is a master of this repertoire; undoubtedly these performances have more variety and great eloquence so that, when the drama is varied with a gentler mood, the contrast is the more striking; and certainly the sound made by the Scholars in Merton College Chapel is beautiful, both warm and fresh.

Whether or not it is historically correct for Byrd's Masses to be sung by solo voices, the great merit of these French Harmonia Mundi performances is their clarity, exposing the miracle of Byrd's polyphony, even though the tonal matching is not always flawless. The 1968 recording is clean and truthful, although it lacks something in ecclesiastical atmosphere.

Mass for 3 voices; Mass for 4 voices; Mass for 5 voices; Ave verum corpus; Infelix ego; The Great Service. Anthems: O God, the Proud are risen against me; O Lord, make thy servant; Sing joyfully unto God.
*** Gimell Dig. CDGIM 343/4 [id.]. Tallis Scholars, Peter Phillips.

In honour of the 450th anniversary of Byrd's birth, Gimell have reissued their key performances coupled into a two-disc set, which seems no great advantage when there is no perceptible saving in cost.

Mass for 4 voices; Mass for 5 voices; Infelix ego.
(BB) *** Naxos Dig. 8.550574; 4.550574 [id.]. Oxford Camerata, Jeremy Summerly.

This new coupling from the Oxford Camerata represents one of Naxos's most enticing bargains. The full-throated singing has spontaneous ardour but no lack of repose in the music's more serene moments. Summerly offers the motet, *Infelix ego*, as a bonus. These readings are distinctive in a different way from those by the Tallis Scholars. They are recorded outstandingly vividly, and this super-bargain coupling gives every satisfaction.

Mass for five voices.
(N) (M) *** EMI CDM5 65211-2 [id.]. King's College, Cambridge, Ch., Ledger – TALLIS: *Mass: Puer natus est nobis;* TYE: *Mass: Euge Bone.* ***

Ledger in his last two years (1980–81) as choirmaster at King's made a series of superb recordings with what must still be counted the premier collegiate/cathedral choir. The richest and most complex of Byrd's settings of the Mass here receives a superbly poised yet deeply expressive reading, atmospherically set against a warm, reverberant acoustic. Ledger combines the contemplative intensity that his predecessor, Sir David Willcocks, instilled in this choir, with an extra rhythmic urgency, and the apt couplings with music of Tallis and Tye make this a particularly desirable and generous reissue, with first-class analogue sound impressively transferred to CD.

Anthems: *Praise our Lord, all ye Gentiles; Sing joyfully; Turn our captivity.* Motets: *Attolite portas; Ave verum corpus; Christus resurgens; Emendemus in melius; Gaudeamus omnes; Justorum animae; Laudibus in sanctis Dominum; Non vos relinquam; O magnum mysterium; O quam suavis; Plorans plorabit; Siderum rector; Solve iubente Deo; Veni, Sancte Spiritus; Visita quaesumus Domine.*

*** Coll. Dig. COLCD 110; *COLC 110* [id.]. Cambridge Singers, John Rutter.

John Rutter brings a composer's understanding to these readings, which have a simple, direct eloquence, the music's serene spirituality movingly caught; and the atmospheric recording is very faithful, even if detail could be sharper. The programme is divided into four groups: Anthems; then Motets: of penitence and prayer; of praise and rejoicing; and for the Church year.

Caldara, Antonio (*c.* 1670–1736)

Crucifixus.
(Y/B) (B) *** Decca Double 443 868-2 (2) [id.]. Palmer, Langridge, Esswood, Keyte, St John's College, Cambridge, Ch., Philomusica, Guest – BONONCINI: *Stabat Mater* ***; PERGOLESI: *Magnificat in C; Stabat Mater* **(*); D. SCARLATTI: *Stabat Mater;* A. SCARLATTI: *Domine, refugium factus es nobis; O magnum mysterium;* LOTTI: *Crucifixus.* ***

Antonio Caldara settled in Vienna and established an enviable reputation as a master of opera – he composed nearly a hundred! The *Crucifixus* is an elaborate sixteen-part setting of great eloquence, texturally rich and concentrated into a few seconds short of five minutes. It follows on naturally after Bononcini's beautiful *Stabat Mater*. The treble lines have some moments of insecurity but otherwise the performance is impressive and the (originally Argo) recording first class.

Camilleri, Charles (born 1931)

Piano concertos Nos. 1 (Mediterranean); 2 (Maqam); 3 (Leningrad).
**(*) Unicorn Dig. DKPCD 9150 [id.]. André de Grotte, Bournemouth SO, Michael Laus.

Charles Camirelli was born in Malta and there is an Italianate, sunny good nature about the *First Piano concerto* (1948), unashamedly popular and agreeably slight when presented with such sparkle. The *Second Concerto* (1967/8) came from what is described as the composer's 'Afro-Arabic-Hindu period'. The even thornier *Leningrad Concerto* dates from a Russian visit in 1985 and has a political inspiration and a philosophical basis. Much of what goes on here is not very coherent but the work ends with a ruthless toccata that finds no solution and ends abruptly. Performances of all three works are full of vitality and the recording sharply observes and vividly details yet has plenty of atmosphere. But neither of the two later concertos is easily fathomed and the back-up notes offer the listener few guidelines.

Campra, André (1660–1744)

Cantatas: Arion; La dispute de l'Amour et de l'Hymen; Enée et Didon; Les femmes.
(B) *** HM Dig. HMA 1901238 [id.]. Jill Feldman, Dominique Visse, Jean-François Gardeil, Les Arts Florissants, William Christie.

Jill Feldman is at her most spirited and eloquent in the dramatic narrative of *Arion* (which has an effective flute obbligato) and Dominique Visse's tangy alto is equally telling in the altercation of the conflicting interests of Marriage and Love which need to be resolved harmoniously. In *Les Femmes* there is disillusion from a male lover who, first dolorously and then with considerable animation, laments the vagaries of the fair sex; his final conclusions are far from optimistic. This is sung with both feeling and sparkle by Jean-François Gardeil. The most ambitious of the four works is a brilliant duet celebrating the nuptials of Aeneas and Dido, which conveniently leaves out the unhappy ending to come later in the story. With sensitive and strongly paced accompaniments from Christie and Les Arts Florissants, it is difficult to imagine that these works could be re-created more tellingly, helped by the presence and atmosphere of the excellent recording.

Requiem Mass.
(N) (M) *** Gardiner Collection: Erato/Warner 4509 99714-2 [id.]. Nelson, Harris, Orliac, Evans, Roberts, Monteverdi Ch., E. Bar. Soloists, Gardiner.
**(*) HM HMC 901251 [id.]. Baudry, Zanetti, Benet, Elwes, Varcoe, Chapelle Royale Ch. & O, Herreweghe.

This *Requiem* is a lovely work, with luminous textures and often beguiling harmonies, and its neglect is difficult to understand. John Eliot Gardiner and his team of fine singers and players have clearly lavished much affection on this performance and they bring to it intelligence and sensitivity. The radiance of the singing of the Monteverdi Choir is caught all the more vividly on CD, as well as the bloom on the voices of the excellent team of soloists, with the contrasted tenor timbres of the Frenchman, Jean-Claude Orliac, and of the Welsh singer, Wynford Evans, brought out the more sharply. The intimacy of the accompaniment in such a number as the *Agnus Dei*, with its delicate flute solo, is set nicely in scale, though in slow sections the strings of the English Baroque Soloists are edgier and more squeezy than they became after 1981, when this recording was made.

Herreweghe's performance, with refined solo and choral singing, makes a good alternative to John Eliot Gardiner's version, for those who prefer a cooler approach to church music of 1700. The recording is refined, to match the performance.

L'Europe galante (opera-ballet): suite.
(M) *** HM/BMG GD 77059 (2) [77059-2-RG]. Yakar, Kweksilber, René Jacobs, La Petite Bande, Leonhardt – LULLY: *Bourgeois gentilhomme*. ***

Like Couperin's *Les Nations*, though in a very different fashion, this enchanting divertissement attempts to portray various national characteristics: French, Spanish, Italian and Turkish. The three soloists all shine and the instrumentalists, directed by Leonhardt, are both expert and spirited. The recording too is well balanced and sounds very fresh on CD.

Idomenée (tragédie lyrique).
**(*) HM HMC 901396/8 [id.]. Delétré, Piau, Zanetti, Fouchécourt, Boyer, Les Arts Florissants, Christie.

In the manner of the time, Campra's *Idomenée* relies on free cantilena rather than formal numbers, with set-pieces kept short and with the chorus often contributing to such brief arias as there are. Christie with his talented Les Arts Florissants team presents the whole work with a taut feeling for its dramatic qualities, though there is nothing here to compare with the big moments in Mozart's opera. The matching of voices to character is closer here than we would conventionally expect in Mozart, and in the breadth of its span and its frequent hints as to what Purcell might have achieved, had he tackled a full-length opera, this is a fascinating work, vividly recorded.

Idoménée (opera): highlights.
(Y/B) *** HM Dig. HMC 901506 [id.] (from complete set with Delétré, Piau, Zanetti, Fouchécourt, Boyer, Les Arts Florissants, Christie).

Here are some 70 minutes, with items well balanced to include the Overture, a brief reminder of the Prologue and excerpts from all five Acts. The complete work runs to three CDs, and this makes a very useful sampler. A full translation is provided.

Canning, Thomas (born 1911)

Fantasy on a hymn tune by Justin Morgan (for double string quartet and string orchestra).
(Y/B) *** Everest EVC 9004 [id.]. Houston SO, Stokowski – R. STRAUSS: *Don Juan* etc. ***

The Pennsylvanian composer, Thomas Canning, has clearly modelled his *Fantasy* on the Vaughan Williams *Tallis fantasia*. Although the contrast with the secondary string group is less ethereal, in Stokowski's hands the work reaches a thrilling climax, and this fine if derivative piece is well worth having on disc when the recording is so rich and well focused. This CD is offered at slightly under premium price.

Canteloube, Marie-Joseph (1879–1957)

Songs of the Auvergne: Series 1–5 (complete).
(N) (B) *** Decca Double Dig. 444 995-2 (2) [id.]; *444 995-4*. Kiri Te Kanawa, ECO, Jeffrey Tate – VILLA-LOBOS: *Bachianas brasileiras No. 5*. ***

(i) *Chants d'Auvergne: Series 1–5* (complete); (ii) Appendix: *Chants d'Auvergne et Quercy: La Mère Antoine; Lorsque le meunier; Oh! Madelon, je dois partir; Reveillez-vous, belle endormie. Chants paysans Béarn: Rossignolet qui chants. Chants du Languedoc: La fille d'un paysan; Moi j'ai un homme; Mon père m'a plasée; O up!; Quand Marion va au moulin. Chants des Pays Basques: Allons, beau rossignol; Comment donc Savoir; Dans le tombeau; J'ai une douce amie; Le premier de tous les oiseaux.*
✹ (M) *** Van. 08.8002.72 [OVC 8001/2]. Netania Davrath, O, (i) Pierre de la Roche; (ii) Gershon Kingsley.

It was Netania Davrath who in 1963 and 1966 – a decade before the De los Angeles selection – pioneered a complete recording of Canteloube's delightful song-settings from the Auvergne region of France. While her voice has a lovely, sweet purity and freedom in the upper range, she also brings a special kind of colour and life to these infinitely varied settings. All 30 songs from the five series are included, plus an important appendix of 15 more, collected by Canteloube and admirably scored by Gershon Kingsley, very much in the seductive manner of the others. They are quite as delightful as any of the more familiar chants, and some of them are unforgettable, providing a programme of two hours of enchanting music which, when dipped into, will give endless pleasure. The accompaniments are freshly idiomatic, warm but not over-upholstered, and the CD transfers retain all the sparkle and atmosphere of the original recordings.

In Dame Kiri Te Kanawa's recital the warmly atmospheric Decca recording brings an often languorous opulence to the music-making. In such an atmosphere the quick songs lose a little in bite, and *Baïlèro*, the most famous, is taken extremely slowly. With the sound so sumptuous, this hardly registers and the result remains compelling, thanks in large measure to sympathetic accompaniment from the ECO under Jeffrey Tate. At Double Decca price, this now makes a formidable bargain, for Dame Kiri's voice was at its freshest and most beautiful when she made these recordings in 1983/4. This set is now also available on cassette.

Chants d'Auvergne: L'Aio dè rotso; L'Antouèno; Baïlèro; Brezairola; Malurous qu'o uno fenno; Passo pel prat; Pastourelle.
(M) *** RCA GD 87831 [7831-2-RG]. Anna Moffo, American SO, Stokowski – RACHMANINOV: *Vocalise;* VILLA-LOBOS: *Bachianas brasileiras No. 5.* ***

Moffo gives radiant performances, helped by the sumptuous accompaniment which Stokowski provides. The result is sweet, seductively so. The recording, from the early 1960s, is opulent to match.

Chants d'Auvergne: L'Antouèno; Baïlèro; 3 Bourrées; Lou Boussu; Brezairola; Lou coucut; Chut, chut; La Délaïssádo; Lo Fïolairé; Jou l'pount d'o Mirabel; Malurous qu'o uno fenno; Passo pel prat; Pastourelle; Postouro, sé tu m'aymo; Tè, l'co, tè.
❀ (M) *** EMI Dig. CD-EMX 9500; *TC-EMX 2075* [Ang. CDM 62010]. Jill Gomez, RLPO, Handley.

Jill Gomez's selection of these increasingly popular songs, attractively presented on a mid-price label, makes for a memorably characterful record which, as well as bringing out the sensuous beauty of Canteloube's arrangements, keeps reminding us, in the echoes of rustic band music, of the genuine folk base. An ideal purchase for the collector who wants just a selection.

Chants d'Auvergne: Baïlèro; 3 Bourrées; Brezairola; Lou Boussu; Lou coucut; Chut, chut; La Délaïssádo; Lo Fïolairé; Jou l'pount d'o Mirabel; Malurous qu'o uno fenno; Oï ayaï; Pastourelle; La pastrouletta; Postouro, sé tu m'aymo; Tè, l'co, tè; Uno jionto postouro.
(M) *** Virgin/EMI Dig. CUV5 61120-2 [id.]. Arleen Augér, ECO, Yan Pascal Tortelier.

Arleen Augér's lovely soprano is ravishing in the haunting, lyrical songs like the ever-popular *Baïlèro*. In the playful items she conveys plenty of fun, and in the more boisterous numbers the recording has vivid presence.

Caplet, André (1878–1925)

La Masque de la mort rouge (Conte fantastique for harp and orchestra).
(M) **(*) EMI Dig. CDM7 64687-2 [id.]. Cambreling, Monte Carlo PO, Prêtre – DEBUSSY: *Chute de la Maison Usher;* SCHMIDT: *Palais hanté.* ***

La Masque de la mort rouge (Conte fantastique); Divertissements; Les Prières; Septet; 2 Sonnets.
*** HM Dig. HMC 901417 [id.]. Soloists of Ens. Musique Oblique.

André Caplet's best-known work is the *Conte fantastique* for harp and strings, based on Edgar Allan Poe's *Masque of the Red Death*, a work strong on evocative menace. This new Harmonia Mundi offers the more intimate, chamber version of the score and makes a strong challenge to the EMI alternative. This new programme is admirably chosen and serves to flesh out a portrait of Caplet himself. Moreover it is better balanced than the EMI reissue, which presents the work (dating from 1908) in its original form: the composer later transcribed it for chamber forces. Here it is eminently well played by Frédérique Cambreling and the Monte Carlo orchestra under Georges Prêtre, but the placing of the harp so forwardly diminishes the sense of mystery and atmosphere. However, the EMI Debussy and Schmidt couplings are rare – the Debussy uniquely so and very desirable – and the EMI CD also has a price advantage.

5 Ballades françaises; Chanson d'automne; 3 Fables de Jean de la Fontaine; Green; Nuit d'automne; Oraison dominicale; La Part à Dieu; Pie Jesu; 3 Poèmes de Jean-Aubry; Prière normande; Quand reverrai-je, hélas; Salutation angélique; Viens! Une flûte invisible soupire.
*Unicorn Dig. DKPCD 9142 [id.]. Claudette Leblanc, Boaz Sharon.

This CD presents 21 of Caplet's songs, many of which are of great beauty. The Canadian singer, Claudette Leblanc, sings them with undoubted intelligence, but the voice has little tonal beauty or bloom and has an unpleasing vibrato. Her partner, Boaz Sharon, accompanies sensitively and they are well recorded. A disappointment.

Cardoso, Frei Manuel (c. 1566–1650)

Lamentatio; Magnificat secundi toni.
(N) (BB) *** Naxos Dig. 8.553310 [id.]. Ars Nova, Bo Holten – LOBO: *Motets;* MAGALHAES: *Missa O Soberana luz* etc. *** (with Concert of Portuguese polyphony ***).

Cardoso's serene, flowing polyphony with its forward-looking use of augmented chords is heard at its most striking in the *Magnificat*, while his *Lamentatio* for six voices is touchingly beautiful. Remarkably eloquent singing from this fine Danish choir and good recording in a suitably ecclesiastical acoustic. The rest of the programme is hardly less stimulating.

Missa pro defunctis.
(Y/B) (BB) *** Naxos Dig. 8.550682 [id.]. Oxford Schola Cantorum, Jeremy Summerly – LOBO: *Missa pro defunctis.* ***

Cardoso's *Missa pro defunctis* is not as dramatic in its contrasts as the coupled setting of Duarte Lôbo, but its polyphony is characteristically long-breathed and expressively powerful. As with the Lôbo performance, a solo treble makes a brief but effective introduction for each movement, a device which works very touchingly. Here it is the *Sanctus* that one especially remembers as being gloriously rich in expressive feeling, although the *Communio* closes the work with rapt intensity. The performance by Jeremy Summerly and his Oxford Schola Cantorun is beautifully paced and the calibre of the singing itself is very impressive indeed, as is the Naxos recording.

Requiem: Magnificat; Motets, Mulier quae erat; Non mortui; Nos autem gloriari; Sitivit anima mea.
⊛ *** Gimell CDGIM 021; *1585T-21* [id.]. Tallis Scholars, Phillips.

Cardoso's *Requiem* opens in striking and original fashion. The polyphony unfolds in long-breathed phrases of unusual length and eloquence, and both the motets, *Mulier quae erat* ('A woman, a sinner in that city') and the short *Nos autem gloriari* ('Yet should we glory'), are rich in texture and have great expressive resplendence. Cardoso's use of the augmented chord at the opening of the *Requiem* gives his music some of its distinctive stamp. The Tallis Scholars sing with characteristic purity of tone and intonation, and they are splendidly recorded. A glorious issue.

Carissimi, Giacomo (1605–74)

Duos & cantatas: A piè d'un verde alloro; Bel tempo per me; Così volete, così sarà; Deh, memoria è che più chiedi; Hor che si Sirio; Il mio cor è un mar; Lungi homai deh spiega; Peregrin d'ignote sponde; Rimati in pace homai; Scrivete, occhi dolente (Lettera amorosa); Tu m'hai preso à consumare; Vaghi rai, pupille ardenti.
(B) *** HM Dig. HMA 1901262 [id.]. Concerto Vocale, René Jacobs.

Carissimi's achievement as a sacred composer has long overshadowed his secular music, whose riches are generously displayed here and whose inspiration and mastery are immediately evident. These are performances of great style and are beautifully recorded. A bargain.

(i) *Jepthe;* (ii) *Jonas;* (iii) *Judicium Salomonis (The Judgement of Solomon)* (oratorios).
(N) (M) *** Gardiner Collection: Erato/Warner Dig. 4509 99715–2 [id.]. Holton, (i) Robson, Stafford; (ii) Tucker, Varcoe; (iii) Varcoe, Charlesworth, Hemmington; His Majesties Sagbutts & Cornetts; (i–iii) soloists, Monteverdi Ch., E. Bar. Soloists, Gardiner.
*** Mer. Dig. CDE 84132 [id.]. Coxwell, Hemington Jones, Harvey, Ainsley, Gabrieli Cons. 8 Players, Paul McCreesh.

The reissue of Gardiner's 1988 triptych (as part of the 'Gardiner Collection') tends rather to upstage the earlier Meridian CD in offering strikingly vivid performances of three of the best known of Carissimi's chamber oratorios. Indeed the addition of His Majesties Sagbutts & Cornetts brings an added sense of scale to *Judicium extremum*, where the Monteverdi Choir sings the final chorus, *Quam magna, quam amara*, most movingly. Throughout the soloists, notably Ruth Holton and Mark Tucker (as Jonah) are very fine, and the supporting continuo (including harp, three different lutes, virginals and chamber organ) matches the stylishness of the accompanying string-group. But most of all it is the vigorous and strongly characterized choral contribution that carries the day, helped by excellent recording – cleanly focused yet atmospheric. The documentation is admirably extensive, with full translations included.

The Meridian CD is also worth considering. No opening sinfonia survives for *Jepthe*, and Paul McCreech chooses to preface this oratorio with a Frescobaldi *Toccata*, which works well (whereas Gardiner goes straight into the opening vocal ensemble). *Jepthe* is affectingly presented, and the McCreech performance at times has more overt expressive feeling than with Gardiner, despite some vocal insecurities at the very top. Overall these are well-prepared and intelligent performances. The continuo part is imaginatively realized with some pleasing sonorities (organ, double harp, chitarrone, etc.) and, despite some undoubted minor shortcomings, these are most convincing accounts of all three works, if on a more intimate scale than Gardiner's. However, the back-up documentation is inadequate.

Carlsson, Mark (born 1952)

Nightwings.
*** Crystal Dig. CD 750 [id.]. Westwood Wind Quintet – BARBER: *Summer music;* LIGETI: *Bagatelles;* MATHIAS: *Quintet.* ***

In *Nightwings* the flute assumes the persona of a dreamer, the taped music may be perceived as a dream-world, and the other four instruments appear as characters in a dream. On this evidence, however, the conception is in some respects more interesting than the piece itself. Excellent playing and recording.

Carmina Burana (c. 1300)

Carmina Burana – songs from the original manuscript.
*** O-L Dig. 417 373-2 [id.]. New L. Cons., Pickett.
**(*) HM HMC 90335 [id.]. Clemencic Cons., René Clemencic.

Carmina Burana – songs from the original manuscript, Vol. 2.
*** O-L Dig. 421 062-2 [id.]. New L. Cons., Pickett.

This was the collection on which Carl Orff drew for his popular cantata. The original manuscript comprises more than 200 pieces from many countries, dating from the late eleventh to the thirteenth century, organized according to subject-matter: love songs, moralizing and satirical songs, eating, drinking, gambling and religious texts. The performances on these well-filled Oiseau-Lyre discs have the merit of excellent singing from Catherine Bott and Michael George, and sensitive playing from the instrumentalists under Pickett.

René Clemencic's performances, recorded in 1977, have immense spirit and liveliness, and there is much character. The presentation suffers slightly in comparison with its rival from slightly over-reverberant sound, though this at times brings a gain in atmosphere.

Carter, Elliott (born 1908)

(i) *Piano concerto. Variations for orchestra.*
*** New World NW 347 [id.]. (i) Ursula Oppens; Cincinnati SO, Gielen.

The *Concerto* is a densely argued piece, complex in its structure, with a concertino of seven instruments, surrounding the piano, who act as 'a well-meaning but impotent intermediary'. The *Variations* is an inventive and fascinating work, splendidly played by these Cincinnati forces. The recording was made at concert performances and is excellent.

Carulli, Ferdinando (1770–1841)

Guitar concerto in A.

(Y/B) (M) **(*) DG 439 984-2 [id.]. Siegfried Behrend, I Musici – GIULIANI: *Concerto in A* ***;
   VIVALDI: *Guitar concertos* **(*).

The Italian virtuoso Ferdinando Carulli made his reputation in Paris, where this innocent post-
Mozartian one-movement piece was written. It is elegantly played by Behrend and I Musici and
immaculately recorded. A touch more vitality would have been welcome, but this is enjoyable enough.

Carver, Robert (c. 1484–c. 1568)

Mass: Cantate Domino for 6 voices.

*** Gaudeamus/ASV Dig. CDGAU 136 [id.]. (i) Graham Lovett; David Hamilton, Cappella Nova,
   Alan Tavener (with: ANGUS: *All my belief;* (i) *The Song of Simeon.* ANON.: *Descendi in hortum
   meum.* BLACK: *Ane lesson upone the feiftie psalme; Lytill Blak.* PEEBLES: *Psalms 107; 124; Si quis
   diligit me* ***).

This anthology celebrates the music heard in the 1560s after the return from France of Mary, Queen of
Scots. Most of the pieces, by David Peebles (who flourished 1530–76), John Black (*c.* 1520–87) and John
Angus (fl. 1562–90), come from *Musica Britannica* Vol. XV ('Music of Scotland, 1500–1700') and
appear on record for the first time. Though the authorship of the *Mass: Cantate Domino* is not definitely
established, it is related to the five-part *Fera pessima* by Robert Carver and is almost certainly a reworking, possibly by Carver himself, of the earlier, five-part piece for six voices. In any event, this is a
record of much interest, well sung and recorded.

Missa: L'Homme armé for 4 voices; Mass for 6 voices.

*** Gaudeamus/ASV Dig. CDGAU 126 [id.]. Cappella Nova, Alan Tavener.

Masses: Fera pessima for 5 voices; Pater creator omnium for 4 voices.

*** Gaudeamus/ASV Dig. CDGAU 127 [id.]. Cappella Nova, Alan Tavener.

These two CDs, together with his ten-part *Missa Dum sacrum mysterium* (and probably the *Cantata
Domino* listed above) which is thought to have accompanied the coronation of the young King James V
in Stirling in 1513, represent the complete sacred music of the early-sixteenth-century Scottish composer, Robert Carver. In the *L'Homme armé Mass* of 1520, Carver is the only British composer to make
use of the French popular song which inspired so many Mass settings by continental composers, from
Josquin onwards. The six-part *Mass* of 1515 is cyclic (each Mass section opens with similar music), and
the presence of other common material suggests that it is a parody Mass, possibly based, it is thought,
on an earlier Carver motet.

   Like the *L'Homme armé,* the *Fera pessima* is another *cantus firmus* Mass (i.e. based on a recurring
melody, mostly in longer notes and usually placed in the tenor) and dates from 1525; its companion, the
four-part *Pater creator omnium,* comes from 1546 and reflects the changing style of the period. Much of
the music Carver composed in the intervening years has been lost and the *Pater creator* survives only in
incomplete form; the two missing parts in the *Kyrie* and *Gloria* have been added by Kenneth Elliott.
Committed singing from the Cappella Nova and Alan Tavener, and very well recorded too. A rewarding
series.

Mass in 10 parts, 'Dum sacrum mysterium'; Motets: Gaude flore Virginali; O bone Jesu.

*** Gaudeamus Dig. CDGAU 124 [id.]. Cappella Nova, Alan Tavener.

The opening piece here, the motet *O bone Jesu,* is in 19 parts and is of exceptional luminosity and
richness. The 10-part *Mass, Dum sacrum mysterium,* was written at the beginning of the sixteenth
century, and it is thought that in its final form it was performed at the coronation of the infant James V
at Stirling. As the note puts it, among Carver's *Masses* this is 'undoubtedly the grandest in scope, the
most extended in development and the richest in detail'. The motet, *Gaude flore Virginali* for five voices,
though less sumptuous, has some adventurous modulations. The Cappella Nova under Alan Tavener
give a thoroughly dedicated account of all three pieces, though the pitch drops very slightly in the *Gaude
flore Virginali.* The recording is very good indeed.

Casella, Alfredo (1883–1947)

Paganiniana, Op. 65.
*** Sony Dig. SK 53280 [id.]. La Scala PO, Muti – BUSONI: *Turandot suite;* MARTUCCI: *Giga* etc. ***
(***) Testament mono SBT 1017 [id.]. St Cecilia, Rome, O, Cantelli – DUKAS: *L'apprenti sorcier;*
   FALLA: *Three-cornered hat;* RAVEL: *Daphnis et Chloé: suite No. 2.* (***)

Paganiniana was commissioned by the Vienna Philharmonic to mark its centenary in 1942. It is a
delightful, effervescent score whose sparkling yet dry wit and exuberance fare well in Muti's hands (as
they did in Ormandy's celebrated recording with the Philadelphia Orchestra). It also has the advantage
of an enterprising and imaginative coupling.

   Cantelli's pioneering record dates from 1949 and comes up sounding very well in a marvellously transferred Testament issue which also offers his 1955–6 Philharmonia recording of the *Daphnis* suite and his
1954 *Three-cornered hat.* Elegant playing.

Casken, John (born 1949)

Cello concerto.
*** Collins Dig. CD single 2006-2 [id.]. N. Sinfonia, Heinrich Schiff.

John Casken wrote this 20-minute *Cello concerto* for Schiff and the Northern Sinfonia in a shrewdly
practical way so that it does not need a separate conductor. On the Collins recording, as in his live
performances, Schiff directs the orchestra from the cello, and the result is one of the richest, most
powerful accounts of a new work on any recent disc. Collins has issued it in its twentieth-century-plus
series as a CD 'single', costing about £6, the sort of price to encourage anyone to experiment.

Castelnuovo-Tedesco, Mario (1895–1968)

Guitar concertos Nos. 1 in D, Op. 99; 2 in C, Op. 160; (i) Double guitar concerto, Op. 201.
** RCA Dig. RD 60355 [60355-2-RC]. Kazuhito Yamashita; (i) with Naoko Yamashita; LPO, Slatkin.

It is sensible to put all three of the Castelnuovo-Tedesco concertos together, even if the first is by far the
best. The second opens invitingly but does not sustain its length, although the central *Sarabanda con
variazione* has some nice touches of colour. The quality of invention of the *Double concerto* is unimpressive to say the least, although some might find the Mexican *mariachi* influences in the finale suitably
exotic. The Yamashitas are excellent guitarists but the performances here are too cosy by half, with the
mellow, over-resonant sound contributing to the enervating atmosphere. The Naxos version of the *First
concerto* is infinitely fresher and more enjoyable.

Guitar concerto No. 1 in D, Op. 99.
(BB) *** Naxos Dig. 8.550729 [id.]. Norbert Kraft, Northern CO, Nicholas Ward – RODRIGO; VILLA-
   LOBOS: *Concertos.* ***
(N) (M) **(*) DG 449 098-2 [id.]. Narciso Yepes, LSO, Navarro – HALFFTER: *Concerto;* RODRIGO:
   Fantasía. **

On Naxos a first-class version of this slight but attractive concerto, which is well suited by the relatively
intimate scale of the performance. The recording is well balanced and vivid, and this is happily coupled
with enjoyable versions of two other favourite concertos. The soloist, Norbert Kraft, has plenty of
personality and the accompaniment is fresh and polished. Typically excellent Naxos value.

   Narciso Yepes's playing is distinguished, but he has not always been lucky in choosing his accompanists.
He plays this concerto admirably, receiving attentive support from Navarro and the LSO and fresh,
vivid recording from DG; for the two coupled works, however, his partner was Odón Alonso and the
results are less impressive, with a dry studio acoustic not flattering the music-making. The Naxos CD is
a far more attractive proposition.

Violin concerto No. 2 (I Profeti), Op. 66.
*** EMI Dig. CDC7 54296-2 [id.]. Perlman, Israel PO, Mehta – BEN-HAIM: *Concerto.* ***

Castelnuovo-Tedesco's *Violin concerto No. 2* is the best-known of the three he wrote, a favourite of
Jascha Heifetz, who commissioned it and recorded it in 1954. Perlman is just as commanding as Heifetz
himself, relishing not just the bravura of the piece but the warm lyricism. The subtitle of this work is *I
Profeti* ('The Prophets'), with the three movements devoted respectively to Isaiah, Jeremiah and Elijah.
As in the Ben-Haim work, Perlman is inspired to dazzling fiddle-playing, helping to conceal any weak-
nesses in the episodic structure. Recorded live in the Mann Auditorium, Tel-Aviv, the sound is warmer

and less aggressive than usual in this venue, with Mehta drawing committed if not always ideally polished playing from the Israel orchestra.

Catalani, Alfredo (1854–93)

La Wally (opera): complete.
(M) *** Decca 425 417-2 (2) [id.]. Tebaldi, Del Monaco, Diaz, Cappuccilli, Marimpietri, Turin Lyric Ch., Monte Carlo Op. O, Fausto Cleva.

The title-role of *La Wally* prompts Renata Tebaldi to give one of her most tenderly affecting performances on record, a glorious example of her singing late in her career. Mario del Monaco begins coarsely, but the heroic power and intensity of his singing are formidable, and it is good to have the young Cappuccilli in the baritone role of Gellner. The sound in this late-1960s recording is superbly focused and vividly real.

Cavalli, Francesco (1602–76)

La Calisto (complete).
(Y/B) **(*) HM Dig. HMC 1901515/17 (3) [id.]. Bayo, Lippi, Keenlyside, Pushee, Mantovani, Concerto Vocale, René Jacobs.

La Calisto (complete version – freely arranged by Raymond Leppard).
(M) *** Decca 436 216-2 (2) [id.]. Cotrubas, Trama, J. Baker, Bowman, Gottlieb, Cuénod, Hughes, Glyndebourne Festival Op. Ch., LPO, Leppard.

No more perfect Glyndebourne entertainment has been devised than Leppard's freely adapted version of an opera written for Venice in the 1650s but never heard since. It exactly relates that permissive society of the seventeenth century to our own. It is the more delectable because of the brilliant part given to the goddess, Diana, taken by Dame Janet Baker. In this version she has the dual task of portraying first the chaste goddess herself, then in the same costume switching immediately to the randy Jupiter disguised as Diana, quite a different character. The opera is splendidly cast. Parts for such singers as James Bowman draw out their finest qualities, and the result is magic. No one should miss Dame Janet's heartbreakingly intense singing of her tender aria *Amara servitù*, while a subsidiary character, Linfea, a bad-tempered, lecherous, ageing nymph, is portrayed hilariously by Hugues Cuénod. The opera has transferred admirably to a pair of CDs, with each of the two Acts offered without a break; the recording, made at Glyndebourne, is gloriously rich and atmospheric, with the Prologue in a different, more ethereal acoustic than the rest of the opera. A full libretto is provided.

Jacobs directs a lively account, recorded in vivid, immediate sound, readily sustaining the extra length of the original score (2 hours 45 minutes), helped by some characterful, generally well-sung solo performances. In the title-role Maria Bayo has a sweet and fresh, very girlish-sounding soprano, and Alessandra Mantovani as Diana sings warmly, though with some unsteadiness. The disappointment is that when Jove is disguised as Diana, the part is sung by the weighty baritone, Marcello Lippi, taking the role of Jove, in a piping falsetto. Graham Pushee, a reliable but hooty counter-tenor, takes the role of Endimione and, as at Glyndebourne, the comic role of the nymph, Linfea, is taken by a male singer, Gilles Ragon, capable but nowhere near as characterful as Hugues Cuénod at Glyndebourne. However inauthentic the Leppard version is, it conveys more intense enjoyment than this and, though the vigour and variety of Cavalli's inspiration are brought out well by Jacobs and his team, the Decca mid-priced reissue is the one to go for.

Ecole amante (complete).
(N) (M) *** Erato/Warner 0630 12980-2 (3) [id.]. Cold, Miller, Tomlinson, Minton, Alliot-Lugaz, Hill-Smith, Palmer, Hardy, Crouzat, Lewis, Cassinelli, E. Bach Festival Ch. & Bar. O, Corboz.

Originally commissioned for the wedding celebrations of Louis XIV but finally performed (with little success) some two years late, *Ecole amante* is one of Cavalli's later and greatest operas. Its profundity, with moving laments and monumental choral passages, brings it closer to the operas of Monteverdi than the other Cavalli works so far recorded. The snag is the libretto, but on record that drawback is minimized. This fine performance under Michel Corboz was a direct result of the enterprise of Lina Lalandi and her English Bach Festival at the beginning of the 1980s. Ulrik Cold with his clean-cut bass makes a fine Hercules, and the rest of the cast is excellent, with outstanding contributions from John Tomlinson in three roles and Patricia Miller as Dejanira. The recording is first class, but in the remastering for CD the choral sound is not absolutely sharp in focus.

Giasone (complete).
*** HM Dig. HMC 1901282/4 [id.]. Chance, Schopper, Dubosc, Deletré, Mellon, Banditelli, Visse, De Mey, Concerto Vocale, Jacobs.

With the brilliant and sensitive counter-tenor, Michael Chance, in the title-role, René Jacobs's recording of Cavalli's opera is a remarkable achievement. The admixture of comedy that can be embarrassing in operas of this period is here handled splendidly. The vividly characterful Dominique Visse in particular scores a huge success in the drag-role of the nurse, Delfa, very much in the tradition of Hugues Cuénod's performances for Raymond Leppard in Cavalli at Glyndebourne. It is a pity that none of the others characterize like Visse, beautifully as they sing. Clean, well-balanced sound.

L'Ormindo (complete) (ed. Raymond Leppard).
(Y/B) (M) *** Decca 444 529-2 (2) [id.]. Wakefield, Howells, Runge, Garcisanz, Berbié, Cuénod, Van Bork, F. Davis, Alister, Van Allan, LPO, Leppard.

We owe it above all to Raymond Leppard that the name of Francesco Cavalli has become famous again. As with *La Calisto*, he subjected *L'Ormindo* to his own magical Leppardization process, to produce another enchanting Glyndebourne entertainment. The gaiety of Glyndebourne is superbly caught, for wisely Decca (or, rather, Argo) opted to record the work on the editor's home ground in Sussex, using the Organ Room for studio instead of the excessively dry acoustic of the old opera house. With modern instruments in the orchestra, the sounds are nothing short of luscious, often almost Straussian in their opulence, and Leppard's array of continuo instruments constantly charms the ear. Anne Howells makes a fine Erisbe, so pure-sounding one scarcely credits the blatant immorality of the story. Indeed the whole point is that one should not question it but accept it as a product of the permissive society of 1650. Excellent contributions from the whole team, with special mention required for the veteran Hugues Cuénod in the 'drag' part of the maid, Erice. The gloriously full recorded quality has not been lost in the CD transfer.

Xerse (complete).
*** HM HMC 1901175/8 [id.]. René Jacobs, Nelson, Gall, Poulenard, Mellon, Feldman, Elwes, De Mey, Visse, Instrumental Ens., Jacobs.

'Ombra mai fù,' sings King Xerxes in the opening scene, addressing a plane tree, and most listeners will have a double-take, remembering Handel's *Largo*, which comes from a later setting of the same libretto. As well as directing his talented team, Jacobs sings the title-role, only one of the four counter-tenors, nicely contrasted, who take the castrato roles. The fruity alto of Dominique Visse in a comic servant role is particularly striking, and among the women – some of them shrill at times – the outstanding singer, Agnès Mellon, takes the other servant role, singing delightfully in a tiny laughing song.

Certon, Pierre (died 1572)

Chansons: *Amour a tort; Ce n'est a vous; C'est grand pityé; De tout le mal; En espérant; Entre vous gentilz hommes; Heilas ne fringuerons nous; Je l'ay aymé; Je neveulx poinct; Martin s'en alla; Plus nu suys; Que n'est auprès de moy; Si ta beaulté; Ung jour que Madame dormait.* Mass: *Sur le pont d'Avignon.*
(B) *** HM HMA 190 1034 [id.]. Boston Camerata, Joel Cohen.

The Mass, *Sur le pont d'Avignon*, has genuine appeal, and the chansons also exercise a real charm over the listener. The Mass is performed *a cappella*, and the chansons enjoy instrumental support. In both sacred and secular works the Boston Camerata bring freshness, musical accomplishment and stylistic understanding to bear; the recording, made in a spacious acoustic, creates the most beautiful sounds.

Cesti, Antonio (1623–69)

Cantatas: *Amanti, io vi disfido; Pria ch'adori.*
(B) **(*) HM HMA 1901011 [id.]. Concerto Vocale – D'INDIA: *Duets, Laments & Madrigals.* **(*)

Cesti's 17-minute cantata, *Pria ch'adori*, is a serenata for two voices, after the Monteverdi style, including even a *Lamento d'Arianna* in duet form. *Amanti, io vi disfido* is a much shorter, bravura piece. The performances by Judith Nelson and René Jacobs are certainly pleasingly fresh, and the distinguished instrumental group includes William Christie providing the continuo.

Chabrier, Emmanuel (1841–94)

Bourrée fantasque; España (rhapsody); *Joyeuse marche; Menuet pompeux; Prélude pastorale; Suite pastorale; Le Roi malgré lui: Danse slave; Fête polonaise.*
*** EMI Dig. CDC7 49652-2. Capitole Toulouse O, Plasson.

Bourrée fantasque; España (rhapsody); *Joyeuse marche; Suite pastorale; Gwendoline: Overture; Le Roi malgré lui: Danse slave.*
(Y/B) (M) *** Erato/Warner Dig. 4509 96730-2 [id.]. Fr. Nat. PO, Armin Jordan.

Bourrée fantasque; España (rhapsody); *Joyeuse marche; Suite pastorale; Gwendoline: Overture. Le Roi malgré lui: Danse slave; Fête polonaise.*
(M) *** Mercury 434 303-2 [id.]. Detroit SO, Paray – ROUSSEL: *Suite.* **(*)

Chabrier is Beecham territory and he calls for playing of elegance and charm. Michel Plasson and his excellent Toulouse forces bring just the right note of exuberance and *joie de vivre* to this delightful music. The recording is eminently satisfactory, though it is a shade resonant and, as a result, lacks the last ounce of transparency. Even so, the effect suits the music, and the elegant performance of the delightful *Suite pastorale* ensures a strong recommendation for this CD, recently restored to the EMI catalogue, still at full price.

On Erato a sparkling collection which (originally) provided Chabrier's CD début. The playing is admirably spirited, even boisterous in the *Marche joyeuse*, and the melodramatic *Gwendoline overture* is relished with proper gusto. Perhaps Paray's account of the engaging *Suite pastorale* is that bit more distinctive, but here the tempo of the third movement, *Sous bois*, is less controversial. *España* has infectious élan, yet rhythms are nicely relaxed so that the gaiety is never forced. The recording is generally first class, with the body and range especially telling.

The return of the finely played and idiomatically conducted Mercury collection of Chabrier's best orchestral pieces does not disappoint. Paray's whimsically relaxed and sparkling account of *España* gives great pleasure and his rubato in the *Fête polonaise* is equally winning. The *Suite pastorale* is a wholly delightful account, given playing that is at once warm and polished, neat and perfectly in scale, with the orchestra beautifully balanced. The *Marche joyeuse* was recorded in Detroit's Old Orchestral Hall a year before the rest of the programme.

España (rhapsody).
(N) (M) **(*) Decca 448 576-2 [id.]. SRO, Ansermet – DUKAS: *L'apprenti sorcier* ***; DEBUSSY: *La Mer* **(*); HONEGGER: *Pacific 231* ***; RAVEL: *Boléro; La Valse.* ***

España (rhapsody); *Suite pastorale.*
*** Chandos Dig. CHAN 8852 [id.]. Ulster O, Yan Pascal Tortelier – DUKAS: *L'apprenti sorcier; La Péri.* **(*)

Yan Pascal Tortelier and the excellent Ulster Orchestra give an altogether first-rate account of Chabrier's delightful *Suite pastorale*, distinguished by an appealing charm and lightness of touch. There is a spirited account of *España*, too.

Ansermet's performance lacks something in uninhibited exuberance but is lively enough and is excellently recorded (in 1964).

PIANO MUSIC

(i) Piano music, four hands: *Cortège burlesque; Joyeuse marche; Souvenirs de Munich (Quadrille* on themes from Wagner's *Tristan und Isolde); 3 Valses romantiques.* (Piano): *Air de ballet; Bourrée fantasque; Capriccio* (finished by Maurice le Boucher); *Habañera; Impromptu; Marche des Cipayes; Petite valse; 5 Pièces (Ballabile; Feuillet d'album; Aubade; Caprice; Ronde champêtre); 10 Pièces pittoresques; Souvenirs de Brunehaut (Grande valse); Suite de valses.*
(Y/B) (M) **(*) Erato/Warner 4509 95309-2 (2) [id.]. Pierre Barbizet; (i) with Jean Hubeau.

It is good to see Chabrier's piano music receiving the attention of the record companies. In its day it exerted quite an influence over Ravel, Debussy, Poulenc and others. The most striking solo work is the set of ten *Pièces pittoresques*: these are the source of Chabrier's charming orchestral *Suite pastorale*. Like much twentieth-century French piano music, the medium seems interchangeable without too much loss either way. Some of the other music is trivial, if engaging (the *Air de ballet*, for instance), but the music for piano, four hands, is particularly enticing. The delectable Gallic joke of doing quadrilles on themes from Wagner's *Tristan* could be what first attracts the new listener to this repertoire, and Barbizet recorded for the first time another Wagner joke, an elaborate waltz called *Souvenirs de Brunehaut* (Brünnhilde). Vigorous, jolly music makes up a high proportion of this collection and

Barbizet in his tough, brightly rhythmic style is excellently suited, recorded in clear, vivid sound with the piano close and real.

Music for piano duet: *Air de ballet; Cortège burlesque; Prélude et marche française; Souvenirs de Munich; Suite des valses.* Music for 2 pianos: *España; 3 Valses romantiques.*
(Y/B) (BB) ** Naxos Dig. 8.550380 [id.]. Georges Rabol, Sylvie Dugas.

The works for two pianos come off with some flair on the Naxos disc, and the acoustic is more open: indeed the recording is more than satisfactory. The programme opens with *España*, which has plenty of gusto (and distinct touches of orchestral colouring) while the *Marche française* (better known as the *Joyeuse marche*) is also ebullient. The second of the *Trois valses romantiques* displays real charm, while the *Cortège burlesque* and *Souvenirs de Munich* are lively and spirited. The exaggerated parody rubato in the *Air de ballet* is a minus point, and *Suite des valses* is also rhythmically self-conscious, but not irredeemably so.

Aubade; Ballabile; Caprice; Feuillet d'album; Impromptu; Pièces pittoresques; Ronde champêtre; (i) *3 Valses romantiques.*
(Y/B) *** Unicorn-Kanchana DKPCD 9158 [id.]. Kathryn Stott, (i) with Elizabeth Burley.

While some readers will be drawn to the complete survey listed above, for those wanting a representative single-CD selection, Kathryn Stott provides the ideal answer. She plays this long-neglected but rewarding repertoire with intelligence, wit and elegance. Perhaps the very last ounce of charm is missing, but there is enough of it to provide delight. She is moreover recorded with great presence and fidelity; the piano-sound is very alive, natural and fresh.

Bourrée fantasque; 5 Pièces posthumes; 10 Pièces pittoresques; Suite de valses.
(N) (BB) **(*) ASV Dig. CDQS 6166 [id.]. Alan Schiller.

For those wanting an inexpensive entry into the world of Chabrier's piano music, this ASV Quicksilva disc should serve well enough. Alan Schiller, if not quite as sympathetic as Kathleen Stott on Unicorn-Kanchana, can play tenderly (as in the *Feuillet d'album* from the *Pièces posthumes*) as well as brilliantly, and he is only occasionally percussive. He lifts rhythms nicely in the *Bourrée fantasque* and characterizes strongly, although perhaps the *Idylle* (made famous in the orchestral *Suite pastorale*) could be a shade more relaxed. On the whole tempi are well chosen and his rubato is-convincing. Good, clear piano recording.

OPERA

Briseis (complete).
(Y/B) ✿ *** Hyperion Dig. CDA 66803 [id.]. Rodgers, Padmore, Keenlyside, Harries, George, BBC
  Scottish SO, Jean-Yves Ossonce.

Starting with a ripely seductive sailors' chorus, few operas are as sensuous as *Briseis*, subtitled 'The Lovers of Corinth'. Chabrier, with his flair for colour in vocal and instrumental sound, completed the long first Act of this tale of conflict between early Christianity and pagan indulgence, then hit a block. The piece remained unfinished when he died, but Richard Strauss, no less, conducted the first staging, and it plainly influenced him when later he was writing *Salome*, built on a similar conflict. This passionate performance was recorded live at the 1994 Edinburgh Festival, the first-ever hearing in Britain. On disc it matters little that this is a torso. The writing is not just sensuous but urgent, a warm bath of sound that is also exhilarating. Casting is near ideal, with Joan Rodgers in the title-role rich and distinctive, and with Mark Padmore as the sailor, Hylas, equally warm, producing heady, clear tenor tone. Symbolizing the forces of Christian good, Simon Keenlyside as the Catechist and Kathryn Harries as the mother of Briseis, cured through faith, both sing with character and apt resonance. Full, atmospheric sound.

L'Etoile (complete).
✿ *** EMI Dig. CDS7 47889-8 (2) [Pathé id.]. Alliot-Lugaz, Gautier, Bacquier, Raphanel, Damonte,
  Le Roux, David, Lyon Opéra Ch. and O, Gardiner.

This fizzing operetta is a winner: the subtlety and refinement of Chabrier's score go well beyond the usual realm of operetta, and Gardiner directs a performance that from first to last makes the piece sparkle bewitchingly. Colette Alliot-Lugaz and Gabriel Bacquier are first rate and numbers such as the drunken duet between King and Astrologer are hilarious. Outstandingly good recording, with excellent access.

Le roi malgré lui (complete).
(M) **(*) Erato/Warner 2292 45792-2 (2) [id.]. Hendricks, Garcisanz, Quilico, Jeffes, Lafont, French R.
    Ch. & New PO, Dutoit.

This long-neglected opera is another Chabrier masterpiece, a modified Cinderella story, ending happily,
which prompts a series of superb numbers, some *España*-like in brilliance (the well-known Waltz of Act
II transformed in its choral form) and some hauntingly romantic, with even one sextet suggesting a
translation of Wagner's Rhinemaiden music into waltz-time. The pity is that the linking recitatives have
been completely omitted from this recording, and in addition the score has been seriously cut. But
Charles Dutoit is a most persuasive advocate. Star among the singers is Barbara Hendricks as the slave-
girl Cinderella figure, Minka. The recording is naturally balanced and has plenty of atmosphere.

Chadwick, George (1854–1931)

Symphony No. 2 in B flat; Symphonic sketches.
(Y/B) *** Chandos Dig. CHAN 9334 [id.]. Detroit SO, Neeme Järvi.

Chadwick's *Second Symphony* is fresh and appealing. It dates from the early 1880s, though its delightful
Scherzo was premièred two years ahead of the rest of the work. When this was first heard, it had to be
encored, which is hardly surprising. It has an engaging, cheeky quality (one contemporary review in the
Boston Transcript wrote that 'it positively winks at you'). The *Symphonic sketches* are later, occupying
the composer over the best part of a decade (1895–1904). Neither work is a masterpiece but both are
pleasing, and the Detroit orchestra under Neeme Järvi make out a very persuasive case for it.

Symphony No. 3 in F.
*** Chandos Dig. CHAN 9253 [id.]. Detroit SO, Järvi – BARBER: *Medea's meditation* etc. ***

Chadwick's *Third Symphony* is an attractive piece in the received idiom of the day. In 1894 it won first
prize in a competition whose jury was chaired by Dvořák, and it breathes much the same air as Brahms,
Dvořák and Svendsen; although its musical language is not strongly individual, it is fresh and compelling, particularly in so persuasive a performance. The *Largo* is beautifully shaped and the Scherzo
delightfully light and piquant. Absolutely first-class recording too.

Serenade for strings.
*** Albany Dig. TROY 033-2 [id.]. V. American Music Ens., Hobart Earle – GILBERT: *Suite*. ***

Chadwick's *Serenade*, written in 1890, is here given its European première. This very well-crafted piece
by the so-called 'Boston classicist' gives much pleasure. It is quite beautifully played by this excellent
Viennese group, drawn from younger members of the Vienna Symphony Orchestra. The sound too is
first rate, a successful example of a 'live recording' bringing no loss in realism and a gain in spontaneity.

Chambonnières, Jacques Champion de (c. 1602–72)

Pièces de clavecin, Livres I & II: Suites in A, C, D & G.
*** HM/BMG Dig. 05472 77210-2. Skip Sempé (harpsichord).

Chambonnières is spoken of as the father of the French harpsichord school, but Sempé speaks of his
music as 'a keyboard synthesis of the *Air de cour* and Italian recitative, the declamation and rhetoric of
Italian monody'. While retaining a feeling of dance, Sempé is able to convey an improvisatory touch
that brings every piece alive. He plays a Flemish instrument of about 1680, and in four of them he is
joined by Brian Feehan as theorbo continuo. Very good recording.

Chaminade, Cécile (1857–1944)

*Air à danser, Op. 164; Air de ballet, Op. 30; Automne; Autrefois; Contes bleus No. 2, Op. 122; Danse
créole, Op. 94; Guitare, Op. 32; La Lisonjera, Op. 50; Lolita, Op. 54; Minuetto, Op. 23; Pas des écharpes,
Op. 37; Pas des sylphes: Intermezzo; Pierette, Op. 41; 3 Romances sans paroles, Op. 76/1, 3 & 6; Sérénade,
Op. 29; Sous la masque, Op. 116; Toccata, Op. 39; Valse arabesque.*
*** Chandos Dig. CHAN 8888 [id.]. Eric Parkin.

*Autrefois; Callirhoë; Elévation in E; Etude mélodique in G flat; Etude pathétique in B min.; Etude scholas-
tique; La Lisonjera; L'Ondine; Pêcheurs de nuit; Romance; Scherzo in C; Sérénade in D; Solitude;
Souvenance; Thème varié in A; Valse romantique; Waltz No. 2.*

*** Hyperion Dig. CDA 66584 [id.]. Peter Jacobs.

These days Chaminade occupies a more peripheral position than she did in Victorian drawing-rooms, when her piano miniatures gained wide currency, and it is for her piano music that she is best remembered. Both Eric Parkin and Peter Jacobs offer excellent and well-filled selections. Only a handful overlap, so both discs can be acquired without risk of much duplication. Artistically these pieces are rather stronger than one had suspected and, although they are by no means the equal of Grieg or early Fauré, they can hold their own with Saint-Saëns and are more inventive than the *Brises d'orient* of Félicien David. There is a quality of gentility that has lent a certain pallor to Chaminade's charms, but both pianists here make out a stronger case for her than most people would imagine possible. Both are well recorded and in this respect there is little to choose between the two. Nor is there much to choose as far as the performances are concerned; both are persuasive, though Parkin has a slight edge over his colleague in terms of elegance and finesse.

Charpentier, Gustave (1860–1956)

Louise (gramophone version conceived and realized by the composer).
(M) (***) Nimbus mono NI 7829 [id.]. Vallin, Thill, Pernet, Lecouvreur, Gaudel, Ch. Raugel & O, Eugène Bigot.

These substantial excerpts from *Louise* were recorded in 1935 under the 75-year-old composer's supervision; they feature two ideally cast French singers as the two principals, Ninon Vallin enchanting in the title-role and the tenor, Georges Thill, heady-toned as the hero, Julien. France has produced few singers to rival them since. The original eight 78-r.p.m. records are fitted neatly on to a single CD, and – in the selection of items, made by the composer himself – just the delights and none of the *longueurs* of this nostalgically atmospheric opera are included. The voices are caught superbly in the Nimbus transfers, but their system of playing the original 78s on an acoustic horn gramophone works far less well for the orchestral sound: with an early electrical recording like this it becomes muddled. Yet even Nimbus has rarely presented voices as vividly as here.

Louise (opera): complete.
(M) *** Sony S3K 46429 (3) [id.]. Cotrubas, Berbié, Domingo, Sénéchal, Bacquier, Amb. Op. Ch., New Philh. O, Prêtre.
(M) **(*) Ph. 442 082-2. Monmart, Larose, Michel, Musy, Opéra-Comique Ch. & O, Jean Fournet.

This fine, atmospheric Sony recording, the first in stereo, explains why *Louise* has long been a favourite opera in Paris. The love-duets are enchanting and Ileana Cotrubas makes a delightful heroine, not always flawless technically but charmingly girlish. Plácido Domingo is a relatively heavyweight Julien, and Jane Berbié and Gabriel Bacquier are excellent as the parents. Under Georges Prêtre, far warmer than usual on record, the ensemble is rich and clear, with refined recording every bit as atmospheric as one could want. A set which splendidly fills an obvious gap in the catalogue.

Dating from 1956, the Philips version also offers a keenly idiomatic performance, beautifully paced thanks to the warmly understanding direction of Fournet, a conductor too little known on disc. The Opéra-Comique cast contains no stars but relies on singers with experience of their roles in the theatre. It is hardly a direct rival to the Sony version with Cotrubas and Domingo, but with Monmart a bright-toned, very French and girlish Louise and Larose a ringing tenor, equally French in tone, the set conveys the authentic atmosphere, despite close and limited recording.

Charpentier, Marc-Antoine (1634–1704)

Concert à 4 (for viols), H.545; Musique de théâtre pour Circé et Andromède; Sonata à 8 (for 2 flutes & strings), H.548.
**(*) HM Dig. HMC 1901244 [id.]. London Baroque, Medlam.

These pieces are most expertly played here by the members of London Baroque (though the string sound still does not entirely escape the faint suspicion that it has been marinaded in vinegar) and will reward investigation. The sound is excellent.

Le malade imaginaire (incidental music).
*** Erato/Warner Dig. 2292 45002-2 [id.]. Poulenard, Feldman, Ragon, Les Musiciens du Louvre, Marc Minkowski.

*** HM Dig. HMC 90-1336 [id.]. Zanetti, Rime, Brua, Visse, Crook, Gardeil, Les Arts Florissants, Christie.

This sequence of extended prologue and three *intermèdes* tingles with energy, and is superbly realized on this first recording of the complete incidental music, much of which was lost for three centuries. Eight first-rate soloists and a lively period orchestra are spurred by the consistently animated direction of Marc Minkowski, and the vivid recording adds to the illusion of live performance.

With rather less forward and more refined sound, Christie – though he uses percussion just as dramatically as his rival – is lighter in his textures and rhythms, often opting for faster speeds. The format is cumbersome, with a single disc contained in a double jewel-case, but the libretto is far more readable.

Motets: *Alma redemptoris; Amicus meus; Ave regina; Dialogus inter Magdalenam et Jesum; Egredimini filiae Sion; Elevations; O pretiosum; O vere, o bone; Magdalena lugens; Motet du saint sacrement; O vos omnes; Pour le Passion de notre Seigneur* (2 settings); *Salve regina; Solva vivebat in antris Magdalena lugens.*
*** HM HMC 1901149 [id.]. Concerto Vocale.

Half of the motets on this record are for solo voice and the others are duets. Among the best and most moving things here are *O vos omnes* and *Amicus meus*, which are beautifully done. Another motet to note is *Magdalena lugens*, in which Mary Magdalene laments Christ's death at the foot of the Cross. Expressive singing from Judith Nelson and René Jacobs, and excellent continuo support. Worth a strong recommendation.

Caecilia, virgo et martyr; Filius prodigus (oratorios); *Magnificat.*
*** HM Dig. HMC 90066 [id.]. Grenat, Benet, Laplenie, Reinhard, Studer, Les Arts Florissants, Christie.

The music's stature and nobility are fully conveyed here. The *Magnificat* is a short piece for three voices and has an almost Purcellian flavour. One thing that will immediately strike the listener is the delicacy and finesse of the scoring. All this music is beautifully recorded; the present issues can be recommended with enthusiasm.

Elévation; In obitum augustissimae nec non piissimae gallorum Reginae lamentum; Luctus de morte augustissimae Mariae Theresiae Reginae Galliae.
(M) *** Erato/Warner Dig. 2292 45339-2 [id.]. Degelin, Verdoodt, Smolders, Crook, Vandersteene, Widmer, Namur Chamber Ch., Musica Polyphonica, Devos.

All three works here lament the death in 1683 of Queen Maria Teresa, wife of Louis XIV of France since 1660. Clearly the event moved Charpentier deeply, and each reflects the paradox of the Christian faith in contrasting grief with joy and hope in the life hereafter. The performances could hardly be bettered, bringing out all the music's drama, joy and depth of feeling. The recording, made in a spacious acoustic, is also first class in every way. Very highly recommended.

In navitatem Domini nostri Jésus Christi (canticum), H.414; Pastorale sur la naissance de notre Seigneur Jésus Christ, H.483.
*** HM HMC 901082. Les Arts Florissants Vocal & Instrumental Ens., Christie.

This *Canticum* has much of the character of an oratorio. The invention has great appeal and variety. The *Pastorale* is a most rewarding piece, and the grace and charm of the writing continue to win one over to this eminently resourceful composer. This collection by William Christie is self-recommending, so high are the standards of performance and recording, and so fertile is Charpentier's imagination.

In navitatem Domini nostri Jésus Christi, H.416; Pastorale sur la naissance de notre Seigneur Jésus Christ.
*** HM HMC 905130 [id.]. Les Arts Florissants Vocal & Instrumental Ens., Christie.

The cantata is one of Charpentier's grandest, a finely balanced edifice in two complementary halves, separated by an instrumental section, an eloquent evocation of the night. The little pastorale was written in the tradition of the ballet de cour or divertissement. This is enchanting music, elegantly played and excellently recorded.

Leçons de ténèbres.
*** HM HMC 901005 [id.]. Jacobs, Nelson, Verkinderen, Kuijken, Christie, Junghänel.

These *Leçons de ténèbres* are eloquent and moving pieces, worthy of comparison with Purcell. René Jacobs's performance, like that of his colleagues, is so authentic in every respect that it is difficult to imagine it being surpassed. The recording is as distinguished as the performances.

9 Leçons de ténèbres, H.120–125; H.135–137.
(Y/B) (M) **(*) Erato/Warner Dig. 4509 96376-2 (2) [id.]. Widmer, Verschaeve, Crook, Caals, De Meulenaere, Ruyl, Musica Polyphonica, Louis Devos.

The first six *Leçons de ténèbres* for solo voices included here (H.120–125) come from Volume XXIII and were probably written in 1680 for the Abbaye-aux-Bois; the remainder are for three voices and, though not unrelated to the earlier ones, are later still. Neither set duplicates the repertoire already covered by the Harmonia Mundi and Virgin issues; but the performances here, although sensitive and lyrically eloquent, lack something in vitality. In that respect the solo works are rather more positive than those for three voices. The stylish instrumental accompaniments using original instruments are suitably pastel-shaded and the recording is excellent; but one feels that a rather stronger characterization would have made these performances even more appealing.

Leçons de ténèbres for Wednesday in Holy Week.
(Y/B) (M) *** Virgin/EMI VC5 45107-2 [id.]. Catherine Greuillet, Caroline Pelon, Gérard Lesne, Christopher Purves, Il Seminario Musicale.

Leçons de ténèbres for Maundy Thursday.
(Y/B) (M) *** Virgin/EMI VC5 45075-2 [id.]. Sandrine Piau, Gérard Lesne, Ian Honeyman, Peter Harvey, Il Seminario Musicale.

Leçons de ténèbres for Good Friday.
*** Virgin/EMI Dig. VC7 59295-2 [id.]. Gérard Lesne, Agnès Mellon, Ian Honeyman, Jacques Bona, Il Seminario Musicale.

This series of Charpentier's *Leçons de Ténèbres* from Il Seminario Musicale offers music of great variety and beauty, featuring soloists who are naturally attuned to this repertoire. The accompaniment is provided by a varied instrumental group, including recorders, treble and bass viols, with a continuo of theorbo, bass viol and organ, and their use is consistently imaginative and refreshing to the ear. The Psalms are sung by a small choral group. The effect is warm yet refined and the lyrical melancholy of much of this music is quite haunting. It is difficult to imagine these inspired and highly expressive settings being presented more persuasively or better balanced, and the acoustic of L'Abbaye Royale de Fontevraud is ideal for the music. The documentation is first class. Charpentier's settings were enormously admired in his own time, and rightly so. No collection is complete without at least one of these CDs.

The attempt on the third disc to reconstruct a Tenebrae Office for Good Friday poses many problems: although the three on this recording were all composed for Good Friday, they were not necessarily intended for the same Good Friday. Be that as it may, as the music unfolds, its effect is both powerful and elevating. In the context of this service, Charpentier's music has a quiet and affecting directness as well as spirituality.

Méditations pour le Carême; Le reniement de St Pierre.
*** HM Dig. HMC 1905151 [id.]. Les Arts Florissants, William Christie.

Le reniement de Saint Pierre is one of Charpentier's most inspired and expressive works and its text draws on the account in all four Gospels of St Peter's denial of Christ. The *Méditations pour le Carême* are a sequence of three-voice motets for Lent with continuo accompaniment (organ, theorbo and bass viol) that may not have quite the same imaginative or expressive resource but which are full of nobility and interest. The performances maintain the high standards of this ensemble, and the same compliment can be paid to the recording.

(i) *Messe de minuit pour Noël (Midnight Mass for Christmas Eve); (ii) Te Deum.*
(M) **(*) EMI CDM7 63135-2. (i) Cantelo, Gelmar, Partridge, Bowman, Keyte, King's College Ch., ECO, Willcocks; (ii) Lott, Harrhy, Brett, Partridge, Roberts, King's College Ch., ASMF, Ledger.

There is a kinship between Charpentier's lovely *Christmas Mass* and Czech settings of the Mass that incorporate folk material, even the *Kyrie* having a jolly quality about it. The King's performance is warm and musical, but there isn't much Gallic flavour. The recording comes from the late 1960s and certainly now has more bite than it did; but reservations remain about the basic style of the singing. The coupling is the best known of the *Te Deum* settings, and this time the King's performance has a vitality and boldness to match the music and catches also its douceur and freshness.

Messe pour les Trépassés, H.2; Dies irae, H.12; Motet pour les Trépassés, H.311.
(Y/B) (M) **(*) Erato/Warner 4509 92738-2 [id.]. Rosat, Jennifer Smith, Schaer, Elwes, Serafim, Huttenlochwer, Brodard, Gulbenkian Foundation Ch. & O, Lisbon, Corboz.

The *Messe pour les Trépassés* (Mass for All Souls' Day) is scored for large forces: soloists, double-chorus and orchestra. In this account a *Dies irae* and a motet are inserted into its course. They were all recorded in 1972. Readers who welcome the opportunity to hear this music on modern instruments, however, will find much to reward them. Corboz draws some lively singing from both soloists and choir, and the generous acoustic in which the recording was made serves to give a pleasing effect. The music itself dates from the 1670s, not long after Charpentier's return from Italy, and is both powerful and eloquent. The recorded sound, if not up to the best modern standards, is eminently acceptable.

Miserere, H.219; Motets: *pour la seconde fois que le Saint Sacrament vien au même reposoir, H.372; pour le Saint Sacrement au reposoir, H.346. Motet pour une longue offrande, H.434.*
*** HM Dig. HMC 901185 [id.]. Mellon, Poulenard, Ledroit, Kendall, Kooy, Chapelle Royale, Herreweghe.

Charpentier's *Motet pour une longue offrande* is one of his most splendid and eloquent works. The *Miserere* was written for the Jesuit Church on Rue Saint-Antoine, whose ceremonies were particularly sumptuous. All four works on the disc are powerfully expressive and beautifully performed. The recording, made in collaboration with Radio France, is most expertly balanced.

OPERA

Actéon (complete).
(B) *** HM HMA 1901095 [id.]. Visse, Mellon, Laurens, Feldman, Paut, Les Arts Florissants Vocal & Instrumental Ens., Christie.

Actéon is particularly well portrayed by Dominique Visse; his transformation in the fourth tableau and his feelings of horror are almost as effective as anything in nineteenth-century opera! The other singers are first rate, in particular the Diane of Agnès Mellon. Alert playing and an altogether natural recording, as well as excellent presentation, make this a most desirable issue and a real bargain.

Les Arts Florissants (opéra et idyle en musique).
(B) *** HM HMA 1901083 [id.]. Les Arts Florissants Vocal & Instrumental Ens., William Christie.

Les Arts Florissants is a short entertainment in five scenes; the libretto tells of a conflict between the Arts, who flourish under the rule of Peace, and the forces of War, personified by Discord and the Furies. This and the little Interlude that completes the music include some invigorating and fresh invention, performed very pleasingly indeed by this eponymous group under the expert direction of William Christie. Period instruments are used, but intonation is always good and the sounds often charm the ear. The recording is excellent. A bargain.

David et Jonathas (complete).
(M) *** Erato/Warner 2292 45162-2 [id.]. Esswood, Alliot-Lugaz, Huttenlocher, Soyer, David, Jacobs, Lyon Opera Ch., E. Bar. Festival O, Corboz.
**(*) HM Dig. HMC 90 1289/90 [id.]. Lesne, Zanetti, Gardeil, Visse, Les Arts Florissants, Christie.

David et Jonathas confirms the impression, made by many other Charpentier records during the last few years, that in him France has one of her most inspired Baroque masters. The Erato performance is marked by some good singing, though there are passages which would, one feels, benefit from greater finish. But Michel Corboz gets generally excellent results from his artists and is well recorded.
  Christie's version on Harmonia Mundi may not always be especially dramatic, but it has a notably sure sense of authentic Baroque style and scale, as well as fine choral singing. However, only one of Christie's soloists is really outstanding, the characterfully distinctive counter-tenor, Dominique Visse, who gives a vivid, highly theatrical performance; but those who relish authenticity above all else will clearly take to this version, very well recorded.

La descente d'Orphée aux Enfers (chamber opera; complete).
(N) *** Erato/Warner Dig. 0630 11913-2 [id.]. Agnew, Daneman, Zanetti, Petibon, Károlyi, Gardeil, Les Arts Florissants, William Christie.

William Christie on this charming disc unearths a dramatic entertainment on an intimate scale, lasting just under an hour, which Charpentier wrote for a private function in a noblewoman's mansion around 1686. It is sad that through lack of opportunity Charpentier was then given little chance to develop as a composer for the theatre as opposed to the church. The piece starts with lightweight, sparkling movements in dance rhythms, but then dramatically changes tone with the death of Euridice, a moment superbly interpreted by Sophie Daneman. The following lament of Orphée is just the first of his moving and expressive solos, each of them brief but intense and beautifully sung by Paul Agnew. They culminate in a sequence when he seeks to charm Pluton in the Underworld, finally succeeding. Their impact is the greater by being regularly set against light, rhythmic numbers. The piece ends with the lamenting of Pluton's subjects at losing Orphée and his musical magic. The pattern is far more compact than in the great settings of this favourite classical subject by Monteverdi and Gluck on either side but, with Christie drawing superb playing and singing from his well-chosen team, it is good to have such a delightful rarity revived, probably given once at the time and no more.

Médée (complete).
(Y/B) ✹ *** Erato/Warner Dig. 4509 96558-2 (3) [id.]. Hunt, Padmore, Delétré, Zanetti, Salzmann, Les Arts Florissants, William Christie.

Barely ten years after making his prize-winning recording of this rare opera for Harmonia Mundi (HMC 901139/41), Christie, again with his group, Les Arts Florissants, has re-recorded it. He explained in a note that ten years of experience actually staging this and other operas had modified his view. The earlier set was 'a brave beginning' but, with experience, the orchestra had learnt above all to respond in a livelier way. He was also glad to be able to open out the small cuts that were made before so as to fit the LP format. Christie's claims are readily borne out in the finished performance, which easily surpasses the previous one in its extra brightness and vigour, with consistently crisper and more alert ensembles, often at brisker speeds, with the drama more clearly established. With a libretto by Thomas Corneille, younger brother of the celebrated dramatist, Pierre, this is a powerful and moving piece, readily matching the finest of the exploratory operas of Charpentier's predecessor, Lully.

The casting is first rate, with Lorraine Hunt outstanding in the tragic title-role. Her soprano has satisfying weight and richness, as well as the purity and precision needed in such classical opera; and Mark Padmore's clear, high tenor copes superbly with the role of Jason, with no strain and with cleanly enunciated diction and sharp concern for word-meaning. The others follow Christie's pattern of choosing cleanly focused voices, even if the tone is occasionally gritty.

Chausson, Ernest (1855–99)

Poème for violin and orchestra.
*** EMI Dig. CDC7 47725-2 [id.]. Perlman, O de Paris, Martinon – RAVEL: *Tzigane;* SAINT-SAENS: *Havanaise* etc. ***
(N) (M) *** Sony Stern Edition II SM2K 64501 (2) [id.]. Stern, O de Paris, Barenboim (with Concert ***).
(N) (M) **(*) RCA Heifetz Collection 09026 61753-2 [id.]. Heifetz, RCA Victor SO, Izler Solomon – LALO: *Symphonie espagnole* (**(*)); SAINT-SAENS: *Havanaise* etc.; SARASATE: *Zigeunerweisen.* (***)

Chausson's beautiful *Poème* has been generously represented on records; Perlman's 1975 recording with the Orchestre de Paris under Jean Martinon is a classic account by which newcomers are measured. What a glorious and inspired piece it is when played with such feeling! The digital transfer exchanges some of the opulence of the original for a gain in presence (not that Perlman isn't near enough already) but still sounds full. Perlman's glorious tone is undiminished, even if now the ear perceives a slightly sharper outline to the timbre.

In Stern's admirable reading, the *Poème* has strength and no sentimentality. He is well recorded and is better balanced than usual.

Heifetz is recorded very closely, as if in the glare of a spotlight, and the performance is robbed of much of its subtlety. Even so, the playing itself is quite remarkable.

(i) *Poème for violin & orchestra;* (ii) *Poème de l'amour et de la mer.*
*** Chandos Dig. CHAN 8952. (i) Yan Pascal Tortelier; (ii) Linda Finnie; Ulster O, Tortelier – FAURE: *Pavane* etc. ***

No quarrels with Yan Pascal Tortelier's playing in the *Poème*, which he directs from the bow. There is consistent beauty of tone and, what is more important, refinement of feeling. In the *Poème de l'amour et de la mer* Linda Finnie can hold her own with the very best; her feeling for the idiom is completely natural and her voice is beautifully coloured. Ferrier and de los Angeles are, of course, special cases; but among newer recordings this has very strong claims. Indeed in rapport between singer and orchestra none is better.

(i) *Poème, Op. 25. Symphony in B flat, Op. 20.*
(M) **(*) RCA GD 60683 [0926 60683-2]. (i) David Oistrakh; Boston SO, Munch (with SAINT-SAENS: *Introduction & Rondo capriccioso* ***).

Munch's 1962 account of the *Symphony in B flat* is high-powered and splendidly played. The CD transfer has, of course, improved matters, but the orchestral texture, which is fairly thick at times, is not perhaps as transparent as it might be. Some may also find the performance just a shade overdriven. David Oistrakh's 1955 account of the *Poème* is masterly – were there nothing else on this disc, it would still be worth buying, and the Saint-Saëns encore tops it off nicely.

Symphony in B flat, Op. 20.
*** Denon Dig. CO 73675 [id.]. Netherlands R. PO, Jean Fournet – FAURE: *Pelléas et Mélisande.* ***

Symphony in B flat; Soir de fête, Op. 32; The Tempest, Op. 18: 2 Scenes.
**(*) Chandos Dig. CHAN 8369 [id.]. Radio-Télévision Belge SO, Serebrier.

Symphony in B flat; Soir de fête; Viviane, Op. 5.
(M) ** EMI CDM7 64686-2 [id.]. Toulouse Capitole O, Michel Plasson.

Jean Fournet's new account of the *Symphony in B flat* is arguably the finest now on the market. Not only is it very well shaped, but the texture in the voluptuous slow movement is heard in excellent focus. Fournet paces all three movements well and gets sensitive results from his players. It is to be preferred to Serebrier's account, though that is more logically coupled with other Chausson pieces, *Soir de fête* plus two scenes from the incidental music for *The Tempest*. Serebrier's account of the *Symphony* has real conviction and receives good recording, but on balance Fournet is first choice.

   Michel Plasson gives a sensitive account of the Chausson *Symphony* and, particularly in the powerful introduction and the somewhat Tristanesque slow movement, secures playing of real feeling from the Toulouse orchestra. This is an eloquent performance and, were the recording more refined, it would be a high recommendation, particularly as the couplings are such rarities – *Soir de fête*, with its the poetic middle section, and the early tone-poem, *Viviane*. The recordings were made in the somewhat reverberant acoustic of the Halle-aux-Graines, Toulouse. Detail could be better focused, and the digital remastering of the two analogue masters has emphasized an unpleasing edge on the strings, though fairly acceptable results can be secured by the manipulation of the controls.

CHAMBER MUSIC

Concert in D for violin, piano and string quartet, Op. 21.
(N) *** Decca Dig. 444 172-2 [id.]. Pierre Amoyal, Pascal Rogé, Ysaÿe Qt – FRANCK: *Violin sonata.* ***
(*) Essex CDS 6044. Accardo, Canino, Levin, Batjer, Hoffman, Wiley – SAINT-SAENS: *Violin sonata No. 1.* *

(i) *Concert for violin, piano and string quartet;* (ii) *Pièce in C for cello and piano, Op. 39.*
(B) ** HM HMP 3901135 [id.]. (i) R. Pasquier, Daugareil, Simonot, B. Pasquier; (ii) Ridoux; (i; ii) Pennetier.

The natural idiomatic response to this high romantic work of a superb all-French team results in a warmly spontaneous-sounding performance at speeds rather broader than usual, made the more involving by the full and immediate recording. Contrasts of dynamic and texture, of light and shade, warmly and strongly brought out, give concentration to a work which can seem too rhapsodic. It helps too that the string quartet is given full weight, with the Ysaÿe Quartet matching Amoyal and Rogé in their virtuosity. With an equally persuasive account of the Franck *Sonata* for coupling, this makes an outstanding disc.

   Salvatore Accardo and Bruno Canino and their four colleagues convey a sense of effortless music-making and of pleasure in making music in domestic surroundings. Accardo is particularly songful in the third movement, light and delicate elsewhere. It is a thoroughly enjoyable account, recorded in a warm acoustic.

   The Harmonia Mundi alternative is inexpensive and it includes also the Op. 39 *Pièce for cello and piano*. This is good value. The French team here are by no means wanting in imagination, but the effect is less poetic than the Essex CD.

Piano quartet in A, Op. 30; Piano trio in G min., Op. 3.
(B) **(*) HM HMA 1901115 [id.]. Les Musiciens.

The Op. 30 *Piano quartet* of 1896 is one of Chausson's finest works. Les Musiciens comprise the Pasquier Trio and Jean-Claude Pennetier, but they are recorded rather closely, and their performance is lacking some of the subtlety and colour one knows this ensemble can command. The effect both here and in the early *G minor Trio*, Op. 3, is somewhat monochrome. However, the playing is both warm and spontaneous, and the ambience of the acoustic is pleasing.

Piano trio in G min., Op. 3.
*** Ph. Dig. 411 141-2 [id.]. Beaux Arts Trio – RAVEL: *Trio in A min.* ***

The early *G minor Trio* will come as a pleasant surprise to most collectors, for its beauties far outweigh any weaknesses. The playing of the Beaux Arts Trio is superbly eloquent and the recording is very impressive on CD.

VOCAL MUSIC

(i) *Chanson perpétuelle;* (ii) *Poème de l'amour et de la mer, Op. 19;* (iii) *5 mélodies, Op. 2/2–5 & 7 (Le charme; Le colibri; La dernière feuille; Sérénade italienne; Les papillons).*
*** Erato/Warner 2292 45368-2 [id.]. Jessye Norman, (i) Monte Carlo Qt, Dalberto; (ii) Monte Carlo PO, Jordan; (iii) Michel Dalberto.

Although Jessye Norman's account of the glorious *Poème de l'amour et de la mer* does not wholly eclipse memories of Dame Janet Baker's version, it is still very competitive in its own right. The orchestral texture is splendidly opulent and atmospheric, and Jessye Norman makes an impressive sound throughout.

(i) *La Légende de Sainte Cécile, Op. 22;* (ii) *La Tempête, Op. 18.*
(N) (M) *** EMI Dig. CDM5 55323-2 (2) [id.]. (i) Isabelle Verner, Chœur de Femmes de Radio France; (ii) Laurence Dale, Raphaëlle Farman, Marie-Ange Todorovitch, François le Roux, Jean-Philippe Lafont, Ens. O de Paris, Jean-Jacques Kantorow.

Two Chausson rarities, beautiful pieces both, expertly performed by these distinguished artists. *La Tempête* comprises a dozen or so settings and is scored for unusual forces: three strings, flute, harp and celeste (the latter instrument, which Tchaikovsky presented in *Nutcracker*, making its bow, as it predates the Tchaikovsky by four years). *La Légende de Sainte Cécile*, as its opus number indicates, comes from the same period as the *Symphony in B flat* and was first put on in 1892. The shades of Wagner and Franck are never far away but, as always with this composer, the invention is fluent, the music often imaginative and always rewarding. The performances are expert and persuasive and the recording very natural. This is something of a find.

Poème de l'amour et de la mer.
(M) **(*) Carlton 3036 70100-2 [id.]. Caballé, L. Symphonica, Wyn Morris – DEBUSSY: *La damoiselle elue.* **(*)

Montserrat Caballé, singing a role often taken by a mezzo-soprano, gives a warm and expressive reading – though, compared with Dame Janet Baker's version, it centres less on word-meanings and seeks instead to create an impressionistic melisma. Caballé's tone is lovely and the voice floats within the acoustic of All Saints' Church, Tooting, in the most beguilingly sensuous way, with the warm, slightly vague recording given a clearer focus on CD without loss of ambience.

Le roi Arthus (opera): complete.
(M) *** Erato/Warner Dig. 2292 45407 (3) [id.]. Zylis-Gara, Quilico, Winbergh, Massis, Fr. R. Ch. & New PO, Jordan.

This first ever recording of *Le roi Arthus* reveals it to be a powerful piece, full of overt Wagnerian echoes. Armin Jordan directs a warmly committed performance which brings out the full stature of the work. Gino Quilico in the name-part sings magnificently, and the freshness and freedom of Gösta Winbergh's tone are very apt for Lancelot's music. Teresa Zylis-Gara, though not always ideally sweet-toned, is an appealing Guinevere; the recorded sound is generally full and well balanced.

Cherubini, Luigi (1760–1842)

Symphony in D.
(N) (M) ** BBC Radio Classics 15656 91372 [id.]. LSO, Mackerras – BUSONI: *Comedy overture;* RESPIGHI: *The Birds* etc. **

Symphony in D; Overtures: Ali-Baba; Anacréon; Médée.
(M) (***) RCA mono GD 60278 [60278-2-RG]. NBC SO, Toscanini (with CIMAROSA: *Overtures: Il matrimonio per raggiro; Il matrimonio segreto* (**)).

The Cherubini *Symphony* is rightly one of Toscanini's most famous records. It was made in the Carnegie Hall, so even the sound is good. The playing has great finesse and the performance sparkles, though some ears may find its high level of underlying intensity out of place in such repertoire. The overtures are just as characterful, *Anacréon* taken from a broadcast concert, again using Carnegie Hall. The other performances, including the brilliant – some might say hard-driven – Cimarosa items, were done in the famously dry Studio 8-H. The sheer incandescent energy of *Il matrimonio per raggiro* is remarkable and *Ali-Baba*, too, is very brisk indeed. With its 'Turkish' percussion, it sounds very piquant and the end is very like the 'chase' music in a silent movie. The transfers are first class.

A well-paced and more than decently played version of Cherubini's *Symphony in D major* from Mackerras, recorded in Walthamstow Town Hall by the BBC Transcription Service in 1969. Well worth the money, and it brings some pleasing Respighi and Busoni's captivating *Comedy overture* as a makeweight.

String quartets Nos 1–6.
(M) *** DG 429 185-2 (3). Melos Qt.

Cherubini's melodic inspiration is often both distinguished and distinctive, although there are times when it falls short of true memorability; but a fine musical intelligence and polished craftsmanship are always in evidence. The Melos Quartet play these works with real commitment and authority, while the remastered recorded sound is well balanced and clear.

String quartet No. 1 in E flat.
*** Collins Dig. 1267-2 [id.]. Britten Qt – VERDI: *Quartet;* TURINA: *La Oración del Torero.* ***

Cherubini's early *First Quartet* (1814) apparently uses ideas borrowed from the symphonies of Méhul, but they are thoroughly absorbed, so that all four movements spring from the same basic material. This is a highly rewarding work and one cannot imagine it being better played or recorded. The sound and balance are very realistic indeed and the acoustic perfectly judged.

(i) *Coronation Mass for King Charles X; Marche religieuse.* (ii) *Requiem in C min.;* (iii) *Requiem in D min. for male voices;* (iv) *Solemn Mass in G for the Coronation of Louis XVIII.*
(M) *** EMI Dig./Analogue CMS7 63161-2 (4). (i) Philh. Ch. & O; (ii) Amb. S., Philh. O; (iii) Amb. S., New Philh. O; (iv) LPO Ch., LPO; Muti.

Three of these records are digital, the *D minor Requiem* (recorded in 1975) is analogue. They come in a handsome slip-case and, at mid-price, should bring this fine repertoire to a wider audience. Muti is well served both by his orchestra and by the relatively small professional choir; and the full, clear recording is most satisfying.

Requiem in C min.
(N) (B) *** EMI forte Dig. CZS5 68613-2 (2). Ambrosian Ch., Philh. O, Muti – VERDI: *Requiem.* ***
(M) (**(*)) RCA mono GD 60272 (2) [60272-RG-2]. Marshall, Merriman, Conley, Hines, Robert Shaw Ch., NBC SO, Toscanini – BEETHOVEN: *Missa solemnis.* (**(*))

The *C minor Requiem*, the best known, was called by Berlioz 'the greatest of the greatest of his [Cherubini's] work', and he went on to claim that 'no other production of this great master can bear any comparison with it for abundance of ideas, fullness of form and sustained sublimity of style'. Muti directs a tough, incisive reading, underlining the drama, to remind one that this was a work also recorded by Toscanini some three decades earlier. The digital recording is excellent.

Toscanini was an admirer of Cherubini's choral music, and though the start of this live performance of 1950 lacks the full Toscanini electricity, the Shaw Chorale, superbly disciplined, quickly responds to the maestro, to produce searingly incisive singing in such movements as the *Dies irae*. Characteristically dry recording.

OPERA

Lodoïska (complete).
**(*) Sony Dig. S2K 47290 (2) [id.]. Devia, Lombardo, Moser, Corbelli, Shimell, Luperi, La Scala, Milan, Ch. & O, Muti.

Muti's conviction in this live recording brings much to enjoy, suggesting that the piece is more effective on disc when the staging is left to one's imagination. The British baritone, William Shimell, is a splendid Dourlinski. As Lodoïska herself, the soprano Mariella Devia sounds sweeter and purer than when heard live, and so does Thomas Moser in the heavyweight tenor role of the Tartar chief, Titzikan. In the high tenor role of the hero, Floreski, Bernard Lombardo copes well with the high tessitura, but the voice bleats disagreeably. In the dry acoustic of La Scala the voices have been recorded close, so that there is a lack of atmosphere, and stage noises keep intruding, though the Sony engineers have done well to get such body in the sound.

Medea (complete).
(M) ** EMI CMS7 63625-2 (2) [Ang. CDMB 63625]. Callas, Scotto, Pirazzini, Picchi, La Scala Ch. &
O, Serafin (with BEETHOVEN: *Ah! perfido* **).

Callas's 1957 studio recording of *Medea* is a magnificent example of the fire-eating Callas. She completely outshines any rival. A cut text is used and Italian instead of the original French, with Serafin less
imaginative than he usually was; but, with a cast more than competent – including the young Renata
Scotto – it is an enjoyable set. Callas's recording of the Beethoven scena, *Ah! perfido*, makes a powerful
fill-up, even though in this late recording (1963/4) vocal flaws emerge the more.

Chopin, Frédéric (1810–49)

Idil Biret Complete Chopin Edition

*Piano concerto No. 1, Op. 11; Andante spianato et Grande Polonaise brillante, Op. 22; Fantasia on Polish
airs, Op. 13.*
(BB) **(*) Naxos Dig. 8.550368; *4.550368* [id.] (with Slovak State PO, Stankovsky).

Piano concerto No. 2, Op. 21; Krakowiak, Op. 14; Variations on Mozart's 'Là ci darem la mano', Op. 2.
(BB) ** Naxos Dig. 8.550369; *4.550369* [id.] (with Slovak State PO, Stankovsky).

*Ballades Nos. 1–4; Berceuse, Op. 57; Cantabile; Fantaisie, Op. 49; Gallop marquis; Largo; Marche fun-
èbre; 3 Nouvelles Etudes.*
(BB)** Naxos Dig. 8.550508; *4.550084* [id.].

*Mazurkas, Op. posth: in D; A flat; B flat; G; C; B flat; Rondos, Op. 1, Op. 16 & Op. 73; Rondo à la
Mazurka, Op. 5; Souvenir de Paganini; Variations brillantes; (i) Variations for four hands; Variations on a
German theme; Variations on themes from 'I Puritani' of Bellini.*
(BB) *** Naxos Dig. 8.550367 [id.] ((i) with Martin Sauer).

Nocturnes Nos. 1–21.
(BB) *** Naxos Dig. 8.550356/7 [id.] (available separately).

Polonaises Nos. 1–6; 7 (Polonaise fantaisie).
(BB) **(*) Naxos Dig. 8.550360 [id.].

*Polonaises Nos. 8–10, Op. 71; in G min.; B flat; A flat; G sharp min.; B flat min. (Adieu); G flat, all Op.
posth.; Andante spianato et Grande Polonaise in E flat, Op. 22 (solo piano version).*
(BB) **(*) Naxos Dig. 8.550361 [id.].

Piano sonatas Nos. 1, Op. 4; 2 (Funeral march); 3, Op. 58.
(BB) *** Naxos Dig. 8.550363; *4.550363* [id.].

Waltzes Nos. 1–19; Contredanse in G flat; 3 Ecossaises, Op. 72; Tarantelle, Op. 43.
(BB) ** Naxos Dig. 8.550365; *4.550365* [id.].

The Turkish pianist, Idil Biret, has recorded a Complete Chopin Edition for Naxos which has been
made available as a boxed set in France but in England is being issued a disc at a time. She has all the
credentials for the undertaking. Among others, she studied with both Cortot and Wilhelm Kempff. She
has a prodigious technique and the recordings we have heard so far suggest that overall her Chopin
survey is an impressive achievement.

Her impetuous style and chimerical handling of phrasing and rubato are immediately obvious in the
First Concerto, especially in the freely poetic account of the *Larghetto* and her very flexible rhythmic
approach to the *Polacca* finale. Following Stankovsky's bold tutti, Biret makes a commanding entry in
the *F minor Concerto*; in the *Larghetto*, too, the solo playing brings a gently improvisational manner,
and the finale really gathers pace only at the entry of the orchestra (which is recorded rather resonantly
throughout). Later there is more dash from the soloist. Of the other short concertante pieces, the
opening of the *Andante spianato* is very delicate and there is some scintillating playing in the following
Grande Polonaise and *Fantasia on Polish airs* – and a touch of heaviness, too, in the former, but here
Stankovsky and the Slovak State Philharmonic Orchestra, who are generally sympathetic in the concertos and quite strong in No. 1, rather take a back seat. The introductory *Largo* of the *Mozart
variations* is a bit too dreamy and diffuse but, once the famous tune arrives, the performance springs to
life. Similarly, the introduction to the charming *Krakowiak Rondo* hangs fire, but again the *Rondo*
sparkles, with the rhythmic rubato nicely handled, though the orchestral tuttis could ideally be firmer.

The first of the solo recordings were made in the Clara Wieck Auditorium, Heidelberg; the sound is a little studio-ish but truthful and often expands impressively in fortissimo. The *Ballades* brings impetuously romantic interpretations where the rubato at times seems mannered; the *Berceuse* is tender and tractable, the *Fantaisie in F minor* begins rather deliberately but opens up excitingly later; though the playing is rather Schumannesque, it is also imaginative; the three *Nouvelles Etudes*, too, are attractively individual.

The disc called '*Rondos and variations*' (8.550367) is worth anyone's money. Much of the music here is little known and none of it second rate. The *Rondos* are more ambitious than one would expect, and the sets of *Variations* show Biret's technique at its most prodigious and glittering. Perhaps not surprisingly, the *Nocturnes* are a great success, the rubato simple, the playing free and often thoughtful, sometimes dark in timbre, but always spontaneous. The recording venue has now changed to the Tonstudio van Geest in Heidelberg and throughout is pleasingly full in timbre. The *Polonaises* demonstrate Biret's sinewy strength: the famous *A major* is a little measured, but the *A flat* is fresh and exciting and the whole set commanding, while the *Polonaise fantaisie* shows imaginative preparation yet comes off spontaneously like the others. Nos. 8–10, published as Op. 71, are early works, written between 1825 and 1828, and Biret at her most appealing makes all three sound mature. The recital ends with a fine account of the solo piano version of the *Andante spianato* (quite lovely) and *Grande Polonaise*, which is more appealing than the concertante version.

The three *Sonatas* are fitted comfortably on to one CD (75 minutes) and, irrespective of cost, this represents one of the finest achievements in Biret's series so far. The *Waltzes* brought another change of venue, to the Tonstudio in Sandhausen. The recording is bright, somewhat more resonant. Idil Biret starts impetuously and immediately favours a fast tempo in the *Grande valse brillante*, Op. 18/1. This is charismatic playing, giving opportunities for exciting bravura, but too many of these pieces are pressed on without respite. The *Ecossaises* and *Tarantelle* are also thrown off at almost breakneck speed.

(i) *Piano concertos Nos. 1–2. Andante spianato et Grande polonaise brillante; Ballades Nos. 1–4; Barcarolle* (1946 & 1962 recordings); *Berceuse* (1946 & 1962 recordings); *Boléro; Fantaisie in F min.; Impromptus Nos. 1–4; 51 Mazurkas; 19 Nocturnes; 3 Nouvelles-études; 6 Polonaises; Polonaise-Fantaisie; 24 Préludes; Scherzi Nos. 1–4; Sonata No. 2* (1946 & 1961 recordings); *Sonata No. 3; Tarantelle; 14 Waltzes.*

(M) *** RCA GD 60822 [60822-2-RG] (11). Artur Rubinstein, (i) with London New SO, Scrowaczewski; or Symphony of the Air, Wallenstein.

Rubinstein's principal Chopin œuvre is offered here on eleven CDs at mid-price. His achievement was unique in this repertoire, and for the most part the remastered recordings are almost worthy of the playing. Alternative versions are offered of several pieces, but most of the recordings listed are discussed below as individual issues, many still at full price.

(i) *Piano concertos Nos. 1 in E min., Op. 11; 2 in F min., Op. 21. Andante spianato et Grande Polonaise brillante, Op. 22; Barcarolle, Op. 60; Berceuse, Op. 57; Mazurkas Nos. 1–51; Nocturnes Nos. 1–19; Polonaises Nos. 1–7; Scherzi Nos. 1–4 Waltz in C sharp min., Op. 64/1.*

(M) (***) EMI mono CHS7 64933-2 (5) [id.]. Rubinstein, (i) with LSO, Barbirolli.

Andante spianato et Grande Polonaise brillante, Op. 22; Barcarolle, Op. 60; Berceuse, Op. 57; Mazurkas Nos. 1–51; Polonaises Nos. 1–7; Scherzi Nos. 1–4; Waltz in C sharp min., Op. 64/1.

(M) (***) EMI mono CHS7 64697-2 (3) [id.]. Arthur Rubinstein.

The five-CD set listed above falls into two parts, the first consisting of the two piano concertos, recorded with Barbirolli and the LSO in 1937 (*E minor*) and 1931 (*F minor*), the *C sharp minor Waltz*, recorded in 1930, and the celebrated set of the *Nocturnes* from 1936–7. The second set of three CDs comprises the *Mazurkas* (recorded in 1938), some of the most totally idiomatic Chopin playing ever committed to record, the 1932 *Scherzi* and the *Polonaises* (1934) and various other pieces. They can be bought in two separate packages or together. Quite simply, the best advice is to get both; each of the discs is packed to capacity and the transfers are excellent. Rubinstein was at the height of his powers when he made these recordings and he rarely equalled and never surpassed them in the post-war, LP era. The *Mazurkas* and *Nocturnes* have a poetic spontaneity and aristocratic finesse that are totally convincing.

Piano concertos Nos. (i) 1 in E min., Op. 11; (ii) 2 in F min., Op. 21.
*** DG 415 970-2 [id.]. Zimerman, LAPO, Giulini.
*** Sony Dig. SK44922 [id.]. Perahia, Israel PO, Mehta.
(Y/B) *** Conifer Dig. 76505 51247-2 [id.]. Martino Tirimo, Philh. O, Fedor Glushchenko.
(Y/B) (BB) *** RCA Navigator 74321 17892-2. Emanuel Ax, Phd. O, Ormandy.
(BB) *** Naxos Dig. 8.550123; *4550123* [id.]. István Székely, Budapest SO, Gyula Németh.

(Y/B) (M) **(*) Sony Analogue/Dig. SMK 64241 [id.]. (i) Hiroko Nakamura, LSO, Fistoulari; (ii) Cécile Licad, LPO, Previn.

(B) *** DG 429 515-2 [id.]. Tamás Vásáry, BPO, (i) Semkow; (ii) Kulka.

**(*) Hyperion Dig. CDA 66647 [id.]. Nikolai Demidenko, Philh. O, Heinrich Schiff.

The CD coupling of Zimerman's performances of the two Chopin concertos with Giulini is hard to beat. Elegant, aristocratic, sparkling, it has youthful spontaneity and at the same time a magisterial authority, combining sensibility with effortless pianism. Both recordings are cleanly detailed.

Perahia's effortless brilliance and refinement of touch recall artists like Hofmann and Lipatti. Mehta provides a highly sensitive accompaniment once the soloist enters but is curiously offhand and matter-of-fact (indeed almost brutal) in the orchestral ritornelli. The sound is dryish and far from ideal. The three stars are for Perahia's playing, not the sound!

Martino Tirimo's performances are worthy to rank alongside those of Perahia and Zimerman. Poetic feeling is paramount: Tirimo's readings often bring exquisite delicacy and they are totally without barnstorming, yet there is spontaneity in every bar, and both slow movements bring playing where one has an impression of musing reverie. In outer movements passage-work is scintillatingly alive, and finales have a beguiling rhythmic lift. There is strong orchestral support and sparkling dance rhythms.

Emanuel Ax offers fine performances of both concertos at super-bargain price. His account of the *F minor* has admirable taste and finesse, though not quite the sense of character of his finest full-priced rivals – Rubinstein for instance. Nevertheless this is genuinely poetic playing and the finale with its light, chimerical touch is particularly pleasing. This is a digital recording and not quite top-drawer in the matter of transparency. Yet it provides a fuller and more flattering sound for the Philadelphia Orchestra than on many of their recent records. Ormandy is a highly sensitive accompanist in both works and this Navigator reissue, with its frontispiece map to show the source of the music, is well worth its modest price.

István Székely is particularly impressive in the *E minor Concerto*, but in both works he finds atmosphere and poetry in slow movements and an engaging dance spirit for the finales, with rhythms given plenty of character. Németh accompanies sympathetically; the orchestral contribution here is quite refined. The recording is resonantly full in the Hungarian manner, not absolutely clear on detail; but the piano image is bold and realistic. A splendid bargain in every sense of the word.

The Sony coupling is also an attractive proposition. Fistoulari never lets one down and, though he provides a comparatively gentle tutti in the first movement of No. 1, he sets the scene for a pleasingly delicate and poetic contribution from his young Japanese soloist, while there is plenty of rhythmic life in the finale. Cécile Licad gives a very impressive account of the *F minor Concerto*: she has the appropriate fire and delicacy. Comparisons with the most distinguished versions are not to her disadvantage; more-over her sense of style earned her the imprimatur of the International Chopin Competition in Warsaw, who chose this for their concerto record prize in 1985. She has excellent support from the LPO under Previn and the benefit of very natural recording.

Vásáry's approach is much more self-effacing: his gentle poetry is in clear contrast with the opulent orchestral sound (especially in No. 1, where the recording is more resonantly expansive than in No. 2). Yet soloist and orchestra match their styles perfectly in both slow movements, which are played most beautifully, and the finales have no lack of character and sparkle. In their way, these performances will give considerable pleasure and, with recording that retains its depth and bloom, this makes a fine bargain coupling.

Nikolai Demidenko's recording of the two concertos can be strongly recommended to his admirers, but those who are not always persuaded by him should approach it with some caution. He produces consistent beauty of sound but his rubati can be disruptive: his slowing down for the second group of the *E minor Concerto* will not be to all tastes – certainly not ours! As in his earlier CDs, finesse and elegance are much in evidence but, if his pianistic control is not in question, it is considerably offset by moments of disturbing self-consciousness. Probably the best things are in the middle movements, though even these are not always allowed to speak for themselves. Heinrich Schiff gets an excellent response from the Philharmonia Orchestra throughout and the recording, though not top-drawer, is perfectly acceptable. For the dedicated admirer of the pianist rather than of the composer.

(i) *Piano concertos Nos. 1–2;* (ii) *Impromptus Nos. 1–3; Waltzes Nos. 1–19.*

(N) (BB) ** EMI Seraphim CES5 68528-2 [CDEB 68528] (2). (i) Garrick Ohlsson, Polish Nat. RSO, Maksymiuk; (ii) Agustin Anievas.

Garrick Ohlsson won the Warsaw International Chopin prize in 1970, and his set of the two concertos is to be reckoned with. He is an impressive player with no lack of technical aplomb and finesse to commend him. But he is not as subtle and aristocratic as Zimmerman or Perahia – nor for that matter is his conductor, who is prone to making bold gestures and is distinctly earthbound in the opening tutti of the *F major Concerto*. The recording is brilliant, not exactly shallow but not ideally expansive. On the second disc of this inexpensive Seraphim set, Anievas gives us the three *Impromptus* (but not the *Fantaisie-impromptu*) and all the *Waltzes*, including the five published posthumously. The opening *Grande valse brillante* is somewhat lacking in flair by the side of Ohlsson, and generally Anievas is better in the reflective music than in providing glitter. His technique is absolutely secure and there is much to enjoy, but there is a great deal of competition in this repertoire.

(i) *Piano concertos Nos. 1 in E min., Op. 11; 2 in F min., Op. 21. 2 Mazurkas in F min., Opp. 63/2 & 68/4; Waltz in E min., Op. posth.*
(N) *** RCA 09026 68378-2 [id.]. Evgeny Kissin, Moscow PO, Dmitri Kitaenko.

This reissue is remarkable testimony to the precociousness of Evgeny Kissin's astonishing musicianship. This programme was recorded at the Moscow Conservatory in 1984 when he was a boy of twelve (and here pictured winningly on the CD backing slip), though he sounds like a seasoned master. His later recitals have shown greater depth and poetic feeling, though there is no lack of either here and this still remains a pretty extraordinary feat. Kissin follows the concertos with three encores, again proclaiming his mastery of this repertoire, with the closing waltz thrown away with captivating insouciance. The applause is well justified. The recording is excellent, and this is a useful supplement to the later recitals he gave in Tokyo and in the Carnegie Hall, not to mention his recent RCA Chopin discs.

Piano concerto No. 1.
(N) (M) *** DG 449 719-2 Martha Argerich, LSO, Abbado – LISZT: *Piano concerto No. 1.* ***
(*) Chesky CD 93 [id.]. Earl Wild, RPO, Sargent – FAURE: *Ballade;* LISZT: *Concerto No. 1.* *
(N) * Decca Dig. 444 518-2 [id.]. Olli Mustonen, San Francisco SO, Herbert Blomstedt – GRIEG: *Piano concerto.* *

(i) *Piano concerto No. 1. Ballade No. 1, Op. 23; Nocturnes Nos. 4 & 5, Op. 15/1–2; 7, Op. 27/1; Polonaise No. 6, Op. 53.*
(M) *** EMI CDM7 64354-2 [id.]. Pollini, (i) Philh. O, Kletzki.

(i) *Piano concerto No. 1. Barcarolle in F sharp, Op. 60; Preludes, Op. 28/1, 3, 6, 10, 15–17, 20–21 & 24; Scherzo No. 3, Op. 39.*
(Y/B) (B) **(*) DG 439 459-2 [id.]. Argerich; (i) LSO, Abbado.

Pollini's classic recording still remains among the best available of the *E minor Concerto*. This is playing of such total spontaneity, poetic feeling and refined judgement that criticism is silenced. The digital remastering has been generally successful. The additional items come from Pollini's first EMI solo recital, and the playing is equally distinguished, the recording truthful.

Martha Argerich's recording dates from 1968 and helped to establish her international reputation. The distinction of this partnership is immediately apparent in the opening orchestral ritornello with Abbado's flexible approach. Argerich follows his lead and her affectionate phrasing provides some lovely playing, especially in the slow movement. Perhaps in the passage-work she is rather too intense, but this is far preferable to the rambling style we are sometimes offered. This version is now reissued in two different formats. The first comes as one of DG's 'Originals' in a coupling with an equally individual and charismatic account of Liszt's *First Concerto*, and great trouble has been taken by the DG engineers to add lustre to a recording which was originally of very high quality and which now sounds even fresher. For the bargain Classikon alternative a miscellaneous programme of encores has been added, showing well the impulsive qualities of her solo playing; however, the offering of just a (well-chosen) selection of the *Préludes* may not suit collectors who would prefer to invest in a complete set.

Earl Wild offers a flamboyantly romantic account of Chopin's *E minor Concerto*, well supported by Sargent and the RPO. This was one of the RCA recordings produced for *Reader's Digest* in the mid-1960s and engineered by Decca. The vintage recording hardly sounds dated at all. A pity this has to be at full-price.

Olli Mustonen is a gifted and intelligent artist, and one wonders how he could come up with something so grotesquely mannered and affected. He pulls this lovely work about quite intolerably. The recording is good and so are Blomstedt and the orchestra – hence the star. As a performance no stars, and not recommended.

Cziffra Edition, Volume 2: (i) *Piano concerto No. 1. Ballade No. 4, Op. 52; Etudes Nos. 3 & 10, Op. 10/3 & 10; 13–14, Op. 25/1–2; Impromptu No. 1, Op. 29; Nocturne No. 2, Op. 9/2; Polonaise in A (Military), Op. 40/1.*
(Y/B) (M) ** EMI CDM5 65251-2 [id.]. György Cziffra; (i) O de Paris, György Cziffra, Jr.

Cziffra's account of the Chopin *E minor Concerto* has plenty of life, helped by a robust orchestral contribution from his son, who yet opens the central *Romance* with some delicacy. There are moments of genuine poetry, and the first movement's secondary theme is coaxed seductively. The finale has plenty of lift and rhythmic impetus, passage-work never drags and one cannot but admire the soloist's glittering dexterity. But the solo performances are less attractive and, despite much deft articulation, too often sound calculated. Fair recording, using the Paris Salle Wagram. The concerto dates from 1968 and the rest from over the next decade.

Piano concerto No. 2 in F min., Op. 21.
(M) *** Decca 417 750-2 [id.]. Ashkenazy, LSO, Zinman – TCHAIKOVSKY: *Piano concerto No. 1.* ***

Ashkenazy's 1965 recording is a distinguished performance: his sophisticated use of light and shade in the opening movement, and the subtlety of phrasing and rubato, are a constant source of pleasure. David Zinman and the LSO are obviously in full rapport with their soloist, and the vintage recording has been remastered most satisfactorily.

(i) *Piano concerto No. 2. Ballades Nos. 1–4; Barcarolle, Op. 60; Berceuse, Op. 57* (2 versions); *Chants polonais, Op. 74* (trans. Liszt); *Etudes, Op. 10/1–12* (2 versions); *Op. 25/1–12* (2 versions); *Nouvelles Etudes; Impromptus, Opp. 29, 36; Nocturnes Opp. 9/2; 15/1–2; 27/1; 55/1–2; 24 Preludes, Op. 28; Prelude in C sharp min., Op. 45; Piano sonatas Nos. 2, Op. 35; 3, Op. 58; Waltzes Nos. 1–14.*
(M) (***) EMI CZS7 67359-2 (6). Alfred Cortot, (i) with O, Barbirolli.

This Cortot compilation encompasses most (but not all) of the recordings he made between 1920 and 1949, arranged in roughly chronological order. His 1933 set of the *Preludes* is omitted (perhaps logically, as they appeared separately, together with the *Fantaisie-impromptu*, also omitted, some time ago). The quality of the performances is such that they would need several pages to do them justice; Cortot's spontaneity, poetic feeling and keyboard refinement are heard to prodigal effect on these six CDs. Several alternative versions (for example, both sets of the Opp. 10 and 25 *Etudes* from 1934 and 1942 are included) offer food for thought. But in any event this is playing of a quite special quality: aristocratic yet full of fire and spontaneity. The transfers are strikingly good and bring Cortot very much before one's eyes.

(i) *Piano concerto No. 2. Mazurkas Nos. 5 & 7, Op. 7/1 & 3; 15 & 17, Op. 24/2 & 4; 20–21, Op. 30/3–4; 22–23 & 25, Op. 33/1–2 & 4; 27, Op. 41/2; 32, Op. 50/3; 41, Op. 63/3; 45, Op. 67/4; 47 & 49, Op. 68/2 & 4; Piano sonata No. 3, Op. 58; Waltzes Nos. 1–14.*
(Y/B) (B) **(*) EMI CZS5 68226-2 (2). Witold Malcuzynski; (i) with LSO, Walter Susskind.

Malcuzynski's recordings were made between 1959 and 1961. They project his musical personality with great intensity. This is especially apparent in his brilliant and highly individual collection of the fourteen *Waltzes* (a favourite of IM's), which glitter and sparkle whenever they should – and sometimes when they should not. Yet the crisp, assured playing is undeniably attractive, especially in the more extrovert numbers, thrown off with splendid panache. But his finest EMI LP was his collection of *Mazurkas*, brilliantly successful in every way. The playing is again immensely polished, yet finds an infinite range of mood and expression in a very well-chosen programme. The performance of the *B minor Sonata* is undoubtedly commanding, mannered perhaps, sometimes glittering, and certainly not insensitive. But there is a dimension missing compared with Rubinstein. The concerto is a disappointment. Again Malcuzynski offers confident, extrovert playing which inevitably provides much excitement, but this is altogether too glittering to be an ideal account of Chopin's delicate inspiration. However, it would be wrong to suggest that Malcuzynski's *Larghetto* lacks poetic feeling, and the finale has much dash and fire. The LSO under Susskind provide good support and the recording is bold, rather loud and rather over-projected. For all one's reservations, there is nothing pallid or routine about this Chopin playing, and this inexpensive 'Profile' is a thoroughly worthwhile reissue and worth seeking out before it disappears back into the EMI vaults.

Les Sylphides (ballet; orch. Douglas).
⊛ (B) *** DG Double 437 404-2 (2) [id.]. BPO, Karajan – DELIBES: *Coppélia suite* ***; GOUNOD: *Faust* etc. **(*); OFFENBACH: *Gaîté parisienne;* RAVEL: *Boléro* ***; TCHAIKOVSKY: *Sleeping Beauty* (suite). **(*)
(N) (B) *** Sony SBK 46550; *SBT 46550* [id.]. Phd. O, Ormandy – DELIBES: *Coppélia; Sylvia: suites* ***; TCHAIKOVSKY: *Nutcracker suite.* **(*)
(B) **(*) Ph. Duo 438 763-2 (2) [id.]. Rotterdam PO, David Zinman – DELIBES: *Coppélia;* GOUNOD: *Faust: ballet music.* **(*)

Karajan conjures consistently beautiful playing with the Berlin Philharmonic Orchestra, and he evokes a delicacy of texture which consistently delights the ear. The woodwind solos are played gently and lovingly, and one can feel the conductor's touch on the phrasing. The upper register of the strings is bright, fresh and clearly focused, the recording is full and atmospheric. Within a two-disc Double DG set it is now coupled not only with the *Coppélia suite* (no longer truncated) but also with ballet music by Offenbach, Gounod and Tchaikovsky. However, the inclusion of Ravel's *Boléro*, very well played though it is, was a curious choice.

The Philadelphia strings are perfectly cast in this score and, although the CBS sound is less svelte than the DG quality for Karajan, it is still very good. Ormandy begins gently and persuasively. Later the lively sections are played with irrepressible brilliance.

David Zinman's approach is less suavely characterful than Karajan's, but he secures smoothly beautiful playing from his Rotterdam orchestra and there is no lack of vitality. Most enjoyable, when the 1980 recording is so natural and resonantly full (obviously more modern than the DG).

CHAMBER MUSIC

Cello sonata in G min., Op. 65.
(M) **(*) EMI CMS7 63184-2. Du Pré, Barenboim – FRANCK: *Cello sonata.* **(*)

The easy romanticism of the *Cello sonata* is beautifully caught by Jacqueline du Pré and Daniel Barenboim. Though the cellist phrases with all her usual spontaneous-sounding imagination, this is one of her more reticent records, while still bringing an autumnal quality to the writing which is very appealing. The recording is excellently balanced.

SOLO PIANO MUSIC

Vladimir Ashkenazy Chopin Edition
Albumblatt in E; Allegro de concert in A, Op. 46; Barcarolle in F sharp, Op. 60; Berceuse in D flat, Op. 57; Boléro in A min., Op. 19; 2 Bourrées; Cantabile in B flat; Fugue in A min.; Galop marquis; Hexameron: Variation in E min.; Largo in E flat; 3 Nouvelles études; Rondo in E flat, Op. 16; Souvenir de Paganini (Variations in A); Tarantelle in A flat, Op. 43; Variations brillantes in B flat, Op. 12; Wiosna (Spring) from Op. 74/2 (443 751-2).
Ballades Nos. 1–4; Scherzi Nos. 1–4 (443 740-2).
12 Etudes, Op. 10; 12 Etudes, Op. 25 (443 743-2).
Impromptus Nos. 1–3; 4 (Fantaisie-impromptu); 24 Preludes, Op. 28; Preludes: in C sharp min., Op. 45; in A flat (443 739-2).
Mazurkas Nos. 1–29 (443 747-2); *Nos. 30–68 (including 2 versions of Op. 68/4)* (443 748-2).
Nocturnes Nos. 1–12 (443 741-2); *Nos. 13–21* (443 742-2).
Polonaises Nos. 1–6; No. 7, Polonaise-fantaisie (443 744-2); *Nos. 8–16* (443 745-2).
Sonata No. 1; Contredanse in G flat; 3 Ecossaises; Marche funèbre in C min., Op. 72/2; Rondo in C min., Op. 1; Rondo à la Mazur in F, Op. 5; Rondo in C, Op. 73; Variations on a German national air; (i) Variations in D (for piano duet – with Vovka Ashkenazy) (443 750-2).
Sonatas Nos. 2–3; Fantaisie in F min., Op. 49 (443 749-2).
Waltzes Nos. 1–19 (443 746-2).
(N) (B) *** Decca Analogue/ Dig. 443 738-2 (13) [id.].

Ashkenazy made his Chopin recordings for Decca over a decade from 1974 to 1984, using seven different locations, yet the recorded sound is remarkably consistent, always natural in colour and balance and with a good presence, whether from an analogue or a digital source. His playing is appealingly fresh, never idiosyncratic to the point of trying to superimpose his own personality over that of the composer. Consistently persuasive, these readings combine poetry with flair and (as in the *Ballades*) often bring a highly communicated warmth. The bravura brings genuine panache, whether in the large-scale, virtuoso pieces like the *Scherzi* or in the chimerical approach to a miniature like the *Souvenir de Paganini*. At bargain price this set makes an unbeatable investment. It seems likely that many of these records will become available separately during the lifetime of this book, and the *Mazurkas* – see below – make an admirable first instalment. The *Polonaises* are due to appear at about the time we are published (see below), while the *Etudes* (414 127-2), *Preludes* (417 476-2) and *Waltzes* (414 600-2) remain available at full price.

Andante spianato et Grande polonaise brillante, Op. 22; Barcarolle in F sharp min., Op. 60; Berceuse in D flat, Op. 57; Boléro in C, Op. 19; Impromptus Nos. 1–4; Fantaisie-impromptu, Op. 66; 3 Nouvelles études, Op. posth.; Tarantelle in A flat, Op. 43.
*** RCA RD 89911 [RCA 5617-2-RC]. Artur Rubinstein.

In Chopin piano music generally, Rubinstein has no superior. The *Andante spianato and Grande polon-aise* obviously inspires him, and his clear and relaxed accounts of the *Impromptus* make most other interpretations sound forced by comparison. The magnificent *Barcarolle* and *Berceuse* contain some of Chopin's finest inspirations – and if the *Tarantelle* may appear musically less interesting and not very characteristic, in Rubinstein's hands it is a glorious piece, full of bravura.

Ballades Nos. 1–4; Allegro de concert, Op. 45; Introduction and variations on 'Je vends des scapulaires', Op. 12.
*** CRD CRD 3360; *CRDC 4060*. Hamish Milne.

Hamish Milne gives thoughtful and individual performances of the *Ballades*. They may initially sound understated, but in their freshness and concentration they prove poetic and compelling. Similarly he plays the two rarities with total conviction, suggesting that the *Allegro de concert* at least (originally a sketch for a third piano concerto) is most unjustly neglected. The recorded sound is first rate.

Ballades Nos. 1–4; Barcarolle, Op. 60; Fantaisie in F min., Op. 49.
*** DG Dig. 423 090-2 [id.]. Krystian Zimerman.

Ballades Nos. 1–4; Etudes: in E; C sharp min., Op. 10/3–4; Mazurkas: in F min., Op. 7/4; in A min., Op. 17/4; in D, Op. 33/2; Nocturne in F, Op. 15/1; Waltzes: in E flat (Grande valse brillante), Op. 18; in A flat, Op. 42.
(Y/B) ✿ *** Sony Dig. SK 64399 [id.]. Murray Perahia.

Ballades Nos. 1–4; Scherzi Nos. 1–4.
*** RCA RD 89651 [RCD1 7156]. Artur Rubinstein.

Ballades Nos. 1–4; Piano sonata No. 2 in B flat min. (Funeral march), Op. 35.
*** DG Dig. 435 622-2 [id.]. Andrei Gavrilov.
(N) (BB) **(*) RCA Navigator Dig. 74321 24204-2. Ax.

Murray Perahia was absent from the concert platform for much of 1992/3, and this was his first record for some time. Chopin playing does not come better than this, and this set of the *Ballades* is unlikely to be surpassed. One has to go back to Hofmann, recorded in 1937, to find a more searching or poetic account of the *G minor Ballade*, and the *Waltzes* not only prompt thoughts to turn to the classic post-war Lipatti set, but comparison does not find Perahia less poetic. Moreover the Sony engineers do him justice. In every respect a masterly recital that is in a class of its own and which readers should not miss.

Krystian Zimerman's impressive set of the *Ballades* and the other two works on this disc are touched by distinction throughout and have spontaneity as well as tremendous concentration to commend them, and the modern digital recording is of fine DG quality.

Rubinstein's readings are unique and the digital remastering has been highly successful. The performances of the *Ballades* are a miracle of creative imagination, with Rubinstein at his most inspired. The *Scherzi*, which gain most of all from the improved sound (they were originally very dry), are both powerful and charismatic.

Gavrilov's set of the *Ballades*, coupled with the *B flat minor Sonata*, finds him in excellent form. Here we find finesse and control as well as real poetic feeling. It is good to be able to recommend this without any serious reservation, and to note that the DG engineers produce very good and realistic sound.

Emanuel Ax, recorded in 1985, is a good deal more extrovert in Chopin than in the Beethoven concertos. Indeed the *Ballades* bring volatile, boldly romantic readings, with the *A flat major* and *F minor* particularly successful. Just occasionally – as at the opening of the *G minor* – the rubato seems a little studied, but spontaneity soon reasserts itself. The *Sonata* is also a commanding performance, but with striking contrast provided in the central section of the *Funeral march*, which is played very gently. Clear recording, with just a touch of hardness. But this is very reasonably priced and good value.

Barcarolle, Op. 60; Berceuse, Op. 57; Cantabile in B flat; Contredanse in G flat; Fantaisie in F min., Op. 49; Feuille d'album in E; Fugue in A min.; Funeral march in C min., Op. 72/2; Largo in E flat; 3 Nouvelles-Etudes, Op. posth; Polonaise-Fantaisie, Op. 61; Souvenir de Paganini in A (Variations).
(B) *** Sony Analogue/Dig. SBK 53515 [id.]. Fou Ts'ong.

Fou Ts'ong is a pianist of intelligence and sensibility and his admirers need not hesitate here. The programme is enterprising – how many readers, we wonder, have heard Chopin's succinct little *Fugue in A minor*? The smaller pieces are played with a distinction and dedication that completely win one over, and the closing *Paganini variations* are disarmingly attractive. The recording, partly analogue, partly digital, is good but not quite top-drawer: in general the analogue items sound best. But this 66-minute bargain recital is well worth exploring.

Barcarolle, Op. 60; Berceuse, Op. 57; Fantaisie in F min., Op. 49; Impromptu No. 1 in A flat, Op. 29; Impromptu No. 2 in F sharp, Op. 36; Impromptu No. 3 in G flat, Op. 51.
*** Sony Dig. MK 39708 [id.]. Murray Perahia.

Perahia is a Chopin interpreter of the highest order. There is an impressive range of colour and an imposing sense of order. This is highly poetic playing and an indispensable acquisition for any Chopin collection. The CBS recording does him justice.

Barcarolle, Op. 60; Berceuse, Op. 57; Fantaisie, Op. 49; Nocturne No. 4 in F, Op. 15/1; Polonaise No. 4 in C min., Op. 40/2; Sonata No. 3 in B min., Op. 58.
(Y/B) (M) **(*) Carlton Dig. PCD 2008 [id.]. John Ogdon.

John Ogdon's collection presents fresh and thoughtful performances, not as electrifying as some he recorded earlier in his career but often bold and full of individual insights. His speeds for the slower pieces are at times daringly extreme, but he sustains them well and the delicacy of much that he does is a delight, set in contrast to his natural strength in bravura. Bright, clear, realistic recording, giving the piano a powerful presence.

Barcarolle, Op. 60; Berceuse, Op. 57; Scherzi Nos. 1–4.
**(*) DG Dig. 431 623-2 [id.]. Maurizio Pollini.

Berceuse, Op. 57; Fantaisie in F min., Op. 49; Scherzi Nos. 1–4.
*** Chandos Dig. CHAN 9018 [id.]. Howard Shelley.

Howard Shelley offers much the same programme as Maurizio Pollini on DG. He emerges unscathed from any comparison; he has the advantage of a more sympathetic recording. But there is a greater freshness and tenderness about his approach and though he is obviously totally inside this music, he manages to convey the feeling that he is discovering it for the first time. These are performances of no mean quality.

There is no want of intellectual power or command of keyboard colour in Maurizio Pollini's accounts of the Chopin *Scherzi*. This is eminently magisterial playing with powerfully etched contours and hard surfaces that inspires more admiration than pleasure.

Etudes, Op. 10/1–12; Op. 25/1–12; 3 Nouvelles études.
*** Chandos Dig. CHAN 8482 [id.]. Louis Lortie.

Etudes, Op. 10/1–12; Op. 25/1–12.
*** DG 413 794-2 [id.]. Maurizio Pollini.
(N) (BB) ** CfP Silver Double CDCFPSD 4748 (2). Ian Hobson – RACHMANINOV: *Piano transcriptions.* **

Louis Lortie's set of the 24 *Etudes* can hold its own with the best. His playing has a strong poetic feeling and an effortless virtuosity. He is beautifully recorded at The Maltings, Snape (whose acoustic occasionally clouds the texture).

Pollini's record also comes from 1975 and sounds splendidly fresh in its digitally remastered form. These are vividly characterized accounts, masterly and with the sound eminently present, although not as full in sonority as the more recent versions.

Ian Hobson was the winner of the 1981 Leeds Piano Competition and he recorded the Chopin *Etudes* the following year, proving a formidable virtuoso. The incisiveness and dexterity of his playing in these ever demanding studies are never in doubt, yet Chopin really requires more affection than Hobson allows here, more lyrical warmth. The famous *E major* is just a little stiff and the *G flat Study* is a hard-edged butterfly. The recording is truthful and the Rachmaninov couplings suit him better.

Mazurkas Nos. 1–51.
*** RCA RD 85171 (2) [RCA 5614-2-RC]. Artur Rubinstein.

Mazurkas Nos. 1–57.
(B) **(*) Sony Dig. S2BK 53246 (2) [id.]. Fou Ts'ong.

Mazurkas Nos. 1–59, Op. 6/1–4; Op. 7/1–5; Op. 17/1–4; Op. 24/1–4; Op. 30/1–4; Op. 33/1–4; Op. 41/1–4; Op. 50/1–3; Op.56/1–3; Op. 59/1–3; Op. 63/1–3; Op. 67/1–4; Op. 68/1–4; & Op. 68/4 (revised version); Nos. 60–68, Op. posth.
(N) (B) *** Decca Double Dig./Analogue 448 086-2 (2) [id.]. Vladimir Ashkenazy.

As can be seen, Ashkenazy's survey of Chopin's *Mazurkas* is the most comprehensive available and as such must take pride of place over Rubinstein's set (irrespective of its extremely modest cost). Ashkenazy's recordings were made over a decade in various venues between 1976 and 1985; about two-thirds of them are digital. His are finely articulated, aristocratic accounts and the sound is amazingly fresh and consistent, considering the time-span involved. He includes the posthumously published *Mazurkas* and the recording quality is more modern and more natural than that afforded to Rubinstein, with a believable presence.

Rubinstein could never play in a dull way to save his life, and in his hands these fifty-one pieces are endlessly fascinating, though on occasion in such unpretentious music one would welcome a completely straight approach. As with the *Ballades* and *Scherzi*, the digital remastering has brought a much more pleasing piano timbre.

After recording the *Nocturnes*, Fou Ts'ong went on to record all the *Mazurkas*, including two early works from 1826 in G and B flat major, another two in D and B flat (the latter dedicated to Alexandrine Wolowaska in 1832), the *Mazurkas in C* (1833) and *A flat* (1834) and the two A minor works of 1840 (*Notre temps* and *à Emile Gaillard*). Fou Ts'ong's style is distinctive and rhythmically strong but not lacking poetry. Sometimes the rubato seems a shade too impulsive, but for the most part the playing is compelling. The digital recording from 1984 is bold and clear.

Nocturnes Nos. 1–19.
*** RCA RD 89563 (2) [RCA 5613-2-RC]. Artur Rubinstein.

Nocturnes Nos. 1–21.
(Y/B) (B) *** DG Double Dig. 437 464-2 (2). Daniel Barenboim.
**(*) Hyperion Dig. CDA 66341/2 [id.]. Lívia Rév.
**(*) Ph. 416 440-2 (2) [id.]. Claudio Arrau.
(B) **(*) Sony SB2K 53249 (2) [id.]. Fou Ts'ong.

Nocturnes Nos. 1–21; Barcarolle; Fantaisie-impromptu.
**(*) Unicorn Dig. DKPCD 9147/8 [id.]. Kathryn Stott.

Nocturnes Nos. 1–4; 7–10; 12–13; 15; 18–19.
(Y/B) (B) *** DG Dig. 439 497-2 [id.]. Daniel Barenboim.

Rubinstein in Chopin is a magician in matters of colour; his unerring sense of nuance and the seeming inevitability of his rubato demonstrate a very special musical imagination in this repertoire. The recordings were the best he received in his Chopin series for RCA.

Re-listening to Barenboim's performances, which are beautifully recorded, gave much pleasure. His phrasing is beautifully moulded, the nuancing of tempi thoughtful and poetic, yet seemingly spontaneous. While the mercurial dimension of Rubinstein's performances gives them a special claim on the listener, Barenboim's set will give genuine satisfaction, his style essentially relaxed, becoming really impetuous only in the music's more passionate moments. There is an excellent, well-chosen single-disc selection on DG's bargain label which offers 72 minutes of music and scores thirteen out of the total of twenty-one. The recording remains first class.

As is immediately apparent in the *Fantaisie-impromptu* which acts an introduction to her survey, Kathryn Stott's Chopin is very romantic, seldom understated and with a wide dynamic range. Op. 48/1 (on disc 2) shows how she can change from a raptly gentle manner to passionate ardour, yet with her quiet playing of the chorale theme in Op. 37/1 she touches the listener by her very calmness. Rubato is convincingly managed and overall her playing has a stronger profile than that of Lívia Rév. She is most realistically recorded.

Lívia Rév is an artist of refined musicianship and impeccable taste, selfless and unconcerned with display or self-projection. Indeed there are times when she comes too close to understatement. But still these are lovely performances and the recording has great warmth.

Arrau's approach clearly reflects his boyhood training in Germany, creating tonal warmth coupled with inner tensions of the kind one expects in Beethoven. With the *Nocturnes* it can be apt to have an element of seriousness, and this is a very compelling cycle, full of poetry, the rubato showing an individual but very communicable sensibility.

Fou Ts'ong sometimes reminds one of Solomon – and there can surely be no higher tribute. He is at his very best in the gentle, poetic pieces; in the more robust *Nocturnes* his rubato is less subtle, the style not so relaxed. But this is undoubtedly distinguished and, with good transfers of well-balanced recording from the late 1970s, this is competitive at budget price.

Nocturnes Nos. 2 in E flat, Op. 9/2; 5 in F sharp min., Op. 15; 7 in C sharp min.; 8 in D flat, Op. 27/1–2; 9 in B; 10 in A flat, Op. 32/1–2; 12 in G, Op. 37/2; Waltzes Nos. 1 in E flat (Grande Valse brillante), Op. 18; 3 in A min.; 4 in F, Op. 34/2–3; 5 in A flat, Op. 42; 9 in A flat; 10 in E min., Op. 69/1–2; 11 in G flat; 12 in F min.; 13 in D flat Op. 70/1–3.
(M) *** Decca Dig. 430 751-2 [id.]. Vladimir Ashkenazy.

Ashkenazy's selection of waltzes and nocturnes is aptly chosen and felicitously arranged to make a most satisfying programme of two groups in each genre. The *Nocturnes* are mostly reflective and poetically create a magical atmosphere in Ashkenazy's hands. The famous *E flat*, the very beautiful *D flat* and *B major* and the *Sylphides Nocturne in A flat*, Op. 32/2, are highlights. First-class digital sound ensures a welcome for this reissue.

Polonaises Nos. 1–6; 7 (Polonaise-fantaisie); 8–9, 10 (2 versions), *Op. 71; in G min.; B flat; A flat; G sharp min.; B flat min. (Adieu); G flat, all Op. posth.; Andante spianato et Grande Polonaise in E flat, Op. 22; Marche funèbre in C min., Op. 72/2* (3 versions).
*** Sony Dig. S2K 53967 [id.]. Cyprien Katsaris.

Cyprien Katsaris provides a fine new survey of the Chopin *Polonaises*, excellently recorded. We know he can sometimes rush his fences and here in the central section of the famous *Polonaise in A flat major* he does almost let the music run away with him in his spontaneous fervour. But the performance is undoubtedly thrilling and we can forgive him this when for the most part there is a strong sense of structure in these readings, a wide range of colour and plenty of flexibility. The *Andante spianato* is gentle and poetic and the posthumously published early works are presented with flair, more extrovert than Idil Biret's performances; the difference of approach of these two artists makes a fascinatuing comparison as surely both approaches are valid. Katsaris's virtuosity, one need hardly say, is never in doubt; indeed it is often breathtaking. A stimulating set. To tidy up properly, he includes both the autograph and an edited version by Julian Fontana of Op. 71/3 and three different versions of the *Marche funèbre* which the composer never finalized and which exists in a number of differing editions.

Polonaises Nos. 1–16.
(N) (B) *** Decca Double 452 167-2 (2). Vladimir Ashkenazy.

Ashkenazy's performances of the *Polonaises* have been out of the catalogue for some time. At Double Decca price they are self-recommending.

Polonaises Nos. 1–7.
*** RCA RD 89814 [RCA 5615-2]. Artur Rubinstein.
*** DG 413 795-2 [id.]. Maurizio Pollini.

Master pianist that he was, Rubinstein seems actually to be rethinking and re-creating each piece, even the hackneyed '*Military*' and *A flat* works, at the very moment of performance in this recording, made in Carnegie Hall. His easy majesty and natural sense of spontaneous phrasing give this collection a special place in the catalogue.

   Pollini offers playing of outstanding mastery as well as subtle poetry, and the DG engineers have made a decent job of the transfer. This is magisterial playing, in some ways more commanding than Rubinstein (and rather better recorded) though not more memorable.

(i) *Polonaises Nos. 1–6;* (ii) *Piano sonata No. 3 in B min., Op. 58.*
(N) (M) **(*) DG 449 090-2 [id.]. (i) Lazar Berman; (ii) Emil Gilels.

Gilels' account of the *B minor Sonata* is thoughtful and ruminative, seen through a powerful mind and wholly individual fingers; there are some highly personal touches, for example the gentle undulating accompaniment,like a quietly tolling bell, caressing the second subject of the first movement. There is a pensive and delicately coloured slow movement; the first movement is expansive and warmly lyrical, and there is not a bar that does not set one thinking anew about this music. An altogether haunting reading. Lazar Berman's *Polonaises* are not of this calibre. He gives bold character and colour to these works and these readings possess a certain magisterial command, while the recording is good; but Berman does not invest each phrase with the intensity of Pollini or the sheer poetry of Gilels.

24 Preludes, Op. 28; Prelude in C sharp min., Op. 45; Prelude in A flat, Op. posth.; Allegretto & Mazur; Allegretto in F sharp; Boléro in C, Op. 19; 2 Bourrées; Cantabile in B flat; Contredanse in G flat; 3 Ecossaises, Op. 72/3; Ecossaises, WN 27; Feuille d'album in E; Fugue in A min.; Galop Marquis in A flat; Largo in E flat; Wiosna in G min., Op. 74/2.
**(*) Sony Dig. SK 53355 [id.]. Cyprien Katsaris.

One of the attractions of the Sony recital disc by Cyprien Katsaris is the inclusion of a dozen or so miniatures, some trifles of less than a minute. His account of the *Préludes* has no want of panache or virtuosity, though he does not perhaps match the very finest versions in terms of poetic feeling or Lívia Rév in naturalness. There are some idiosyncratic touches (he pulls back a few bars into the very first prelude), but to be fair his rubati are not unduly obtrusive. But if the playing is brilliant and command-ing, it is rarely touching. These matters are highly personal and readers should perhaps investigate the set for themselves, but the overall impression of the set is a shade charmless. It is, of course, good to have the rarities: the manuscript version of the *Ecossaises*, WN 27, and the two *Allegrettos* are new to the gramophone. In some but not all of the preludes the sound is wanting in transparency; the instrument is closely observed and the balance seems to favour the middle and bass end of the instrument at the expense of the treble.

24 Preludes, Op. 28; Preludes Nos. 25–26; Barcarolle, Op. 60; Polonaise No. 6 in A flat, Op. 53; Scherzo No. 2 in B flat min., Op. 31.
(M) **(*) DG 415 836-2; *415 836-4* [id.]. Martha Argerich.

Preludes, Op. 28; Preludes Nos. 25–26; Berceuse, Op. 57; Fantasy in F min., Op. 4.
*** Hyperion Dig. CDA 66324 [id.]. Lívia Rév.

Lívia Rév's playing has an unforced naturalness that is most persuasive. She is an artist to her fingertips and, though she may not have the outsize musical personality of some great pianists, she does not have the outsize ego either. She includes not only the extra *Preludes*, but two other substantial pieces as well.

   The *Preludes* show Martha Argerich at her finest, spontaneous and inspirational, though her moments of impetuosity may not appeal to all tastes. But her instinct is sure, with many poetic, individual touches. The other pieces are splendidly played.

24 Preludes, Op. 28; Etudes, Op. 10/4–6; Op. 25/1–2; 6 & 12.
(N) **(*) Erato/Warner Dig. 0630 11726-2 [id.]. Moura Lympany.

Dame Moura Lympany seldom disappoints on record. Hers may not be the most dazzling version of the Op. 28 *Preludes*, but she is often technically impressive and her feeling for keyboard colour is matched by the natural spontaneity of her rubato. She plays the whole set as an ongoing sequence and then adds a baker's half-dozen hand-selected *Etudes* for good measure in which her pedalling covers the not always quite precise articulation (in Op. 25/12, for instance). The piano recording is truthful, warm rather than brilliant.

Scherzos Nos. 1–4; Introduction and variations on a German air; Variations on 'La ci darem la mano', Op. 2.
**(*) Hyperion Dig. CDA 66514 [id.]. Nikolai Demidenko.

Scherzos Nos. 1–4; Polonaise-fantaisie, Op. 61.
(Y/B) (M) *** Ph. Dig. 442 407-2 [id.]. Claudio Arrau.

Arrau's last recording of the four *Scherzi* was made in Munich, just after the artist's eightieth birthday. There is little sign of age, even if he would have produced a greater weight of sonority at the height of his powers. However, these accounts are full of wise and thoughtful perceptions and remarkable pianism, recorded with great presence and clarity. The middle section of the *First Scherzo* may strike some collectors as unusually slow and a trifle mannered, but there are magical things elsewhere, notably in the *Fourth*. Arrau's fire may have lost some of its youthful charisma, but the gains in wisdom and delicacy of feeling are adequate compensation. The Philips engineers seem to produce piano quality of exceptional realism. However, this is short measure (55 minutes).

   Nikolai Demidenko plays with magisterial keyboard authority and command of colour. There are narcissistic and idiosyncratic touches to which not all listeners will respond; all the same, there is still much that will (and does) give pleasure, but this artist does not offer the 100 per cent Chopin we get, for instance, from Kissin's recital (see below).

Piano sonatas Nos. 1 in C min., Op. 4; 2 in B flat min. (Funeral march), Op. 35; 3 in B min., Op. 58.
*** Sony Dig. SK 48483 [id.]. Cyprien Katsaris.

Piano sonatas Nos. 1–3; Etudes, Op. 10/6; Op. 25/3, 4, 10 & 11; Mazurkas, Op. 17/1–4.
(N) (B) *** Virgin/EMI Dig. VCD5 45187-2 (2) [id.]. Leif Ove Andsnes.

The young Norwegian pianist has the advantage of state-of-the-art piano-sound and his recital comes in a slim, two-for-the-price-of-one CD pack. As such it is splendid value. Andsnes proves as idiomatic an interpreter of Chopin as he has done of Grieg. He also makes out a very good case for the early *C minor Sonata*, Op. 4, which is less well represented on disc and which he plays with real conviction and flair. The other pieces generally come off well and collectors can invest in this set with complete confidence.

   Cyprien Katsaris gives highly characterized and well-thought-out readings of all three *Sonatas* and he is often challenging and thought-provoking. Ultimately, however, though less outwardly virtuosic, Leif Ove Andsnes is the more musically satisfying, and his is the preferred version.

Piano sonatas Nos. 2 in B flat min. (Funeral march), Op. 35; 3 in B min., Op. 58.
*** DG Dig. 415 346-2 [id.]. Maurizio Pollini.
*** Sony MK 76242 [MK 37280]. Murray Perahia.
**(*) Ph. Dig. 420 949-2 [id.]. Mitsuko Uchida.

Piano sonatas Nos. 2 (Funeral march); 3 in B min., Op. 58; Fantaisie in F min., Op. 49.
*** RCA RD 89812 [RCA 5616-2-RC]. Artur Rubinstein.

Rubinstein's readings of the *Sonatas* are unsurpassed, with a poetic impulse that springs directly from the music and a control of rubato to bring many moments of magic. The sound is improved, too, though Pollini gains in this respect.

Pollini's performances are enormously commanding; his mastery of mood and structure gives these much-played *Sonatas* added stature. The slow movement of Op. 35 has tremendous drama and atmosphere, so that the contrast of the magical central section is all the more telling. Both works are played with great distinction, but the balance is just a shade close.

Murray Perahia's technique is remarkable, but it is so natural to the player that he never uses it for mere display; always there is an underlying sense of structural purpose. The dry, unrushed account of the finale of the *B flat Sonata* is typical of Perahia's freshness, and the only pity is that the recording of the piano is rather clattery and close.

Mitsuko Uchida's Chopin is not quite as successful as her extraordinary set of the Debussy *Etudes*, though she always produces a beautiful sound and there is some particularly refined tone in the slow movements of both sonatas. A very present and realistic piano image, and plenty of sensitive touches, even if she lacks the sweep and power of many rivals.

Piano sonatas Nos. 2 in B flat min., Op. 35; 3 in B min, Op. 58; Waltzes Nos. 1–19.
(N) (BB) **(*) CfP Silver Double CDCFPSD 4790 (2). Philip Fowke.

Philip Fowke, recorded in 1983, gives polished, elegant, meticulously accurate accounts of the *Waltzes*, nicely nuanced and not without sparkle but curiously cool. Yet if here he displays his inhibitions in the recording studio, four years later in 1987, he gives highly impressive readings of both *Sonatas*, wide-ranging in their expression, dramatic and poetic, as when he is playing live. He is perhaps at his finest in the *B minor Sonata*, the first movement freely rhapsodic in feeling, the *Largo* both thoughtful and intense. His formidable articulation in the Scherzo is not quite matched in the finale of the *B flat minor Sonata*, but this too is a fine performance, the *Funeral march* gently solemn and the middle section touchingly nostalgic. The recording, in the *Waltzes* analogue in the *Sonatas* digital, is excellent, full in timbre and presence and with an agreeable ambience.

Piano sonata No. 3 in B min., Op. 58; Barcarolle, Op. 60; Fantaisie-impromptu, Op. 66; Impromptus Nos. 1–3, Opp. 29, 36 & 51.
*** Chandos Dig. CHAN 9175 [id.]. Howard Shelley.

An outstanding Chopin recital from Howard Shelley whose interpretative powers continue to grow in stature. His playing has poetic feeling and ardent but well-controlled temperament. Very good sound.

Piano sonata No. 3 in B min., Op. 58; Mazurkas, in A min., Op. 17/4; in B flat min., Op. 24/4; in D flat, Op. 30/3; in D, Op. 33/2; in G; in C sharp min., Op. 50/ 1 & 3; in C, Op. 56/2; in F sharp min., Op. 59/3; in B; in F min.; in C sharp min., Op. 63/1–3; in F min., Op. 68/4.
(Y/B) *** RCA Dig. 09026 62542-2 [id.]. Evgeny Kissin.

Evgeny Kissin plays not only with an effortless mastery but with a naturalness and freshness that silence criticism. His sense of poetry and his idiomatic rubato are combined with impressive technical address and impeccable taste. Along with Perahia's recent set of the *Ballades*, this is one of the best Chopin recitals to have appeared recently.

Waltzes Nos. 1–14.
*** RCA RD 89564 [RCD1-5492]. Artur Rubinstein.

Waltzes Nos. 1–14; Barcarolle, Op. 60; Mazurka in C sharp min., Op. 50/3; Nocturne in D flat, Op. 27/2.
⊛ (M) (***) EMI CDH7 69802-2. Dinu Lipatti.

Lipatti's classic performances were recorded by Walter Legge in the rather dry acoustic of a Swiss Radio studio at Geneva in the last year of Lipatti's short life, and with each LP reincarnation they seem to have grown in wisdom and subtlety. The reputation of these meticulous performances is fully deserved.

Rubinstein's performances have a chiselled perfection, suggesting the metaphor of finely cut and polished diamonds, emphasized by the crystal-clear quality of the RCA recording. The digital remastering has softened the edges of the sound-image, and there is an illusion of added warmth.

RECITAL COLLECTIONS

Andante spianato et Grande polonaise brillante, Op. 22; Ballades Nos. 1, Op. 23; 4, Op. 52; Barcarolle, Op. 60;
Etudes: in G flat, Op. 10/5; in C sharp min., Op. 25/7; Polonaise-fantaisie, Op. 61; Waltz in A flat, Op. 69/1.
(M) *** RCA GD 87752 [7752-2-RG]. Vladimir Horowitz.

All these performances derive from live recitals. The performances are fabulous; to the end of his career
Horowitz's technique was transcendental and his insights remarkable. There is much excitement – but
even more that is unforgettably poetic, and not a bar is predictable. With the sound so realistic, his
presence is very tangible.

'Favourite piano works': Ballades Nos. 1 in G min., Op. 23; 3 in A flat, Op. 47; Barcarolle, Op. 60; Etudes: in
E; in G flat (Black keys); in C min. (Revolutionary), Op. 10/3, 5 & 12; in A min. (Winter wind), Op. 25/11;
Fantaisie-impromptu, Op. 66; Mazurkas: in B flat, Op. 7/1; in D, Op. 33/1; Nocturnes: in E flat, Op. 9/2; in
F sharp min., Op. 15/2; in B, Op. 32/1; in F min., Op. 55/1; Polonaises: in A (Military), Op. 40/1; in A flat,
Op. 53; Preludes: in D flat (Raindrop), Op. 28/15; in C sharp min., Op. 45; Scherzos Nos. 1 in B flat min.,
Op. 31; 3 in C sharp min., Op. 39; Waltzes: in E flat (Grande valse brillante), Op. 18; in A min., Op. 34/2; in
D flat (Minute); in C sharp min., Op. 64/1-2,; in A flat, Op. 69/1; in B min., Op. 69/2; in G flat, Op. 70/1.
(N) (B) *** Decca Double 444 830-2 (2) [id.]. Vladimir Ashkenazy.

Most music-lovers would count themselves lucky to attend a recital offering the above programme, as
effectively laid out as it is on these two discs and with a total playing time of 130 minutes. The first CD,
which is an all-digital programme, opens commandingly with the *Grande valse brillante* and closes with
the *Polonaise in A flat*; the second (an analogue collection, but of excellent technical quality) begins with
the *A flat Ballade* and ends with the *Scherzo in C sharp minor*. Overall the recordings date from between
1972 and 1984. The two discs are offered for the price of one within a standard-width jewel case,
centrally hinged.

Ballades Nos. 1 in G min., Op. 23; 3 in A flat, Op. 47; Barcarolle, Op.60; Etudes: in A flat; in F min.; in A
min., Op. 25/1, 2 & 11; Nocturnes: in E flat, Op. 9/2; in F sharp, Op. 15/2; in D flat, Op. 27/2; Preludes: in
A; in D flat (Raindrop), Op. 28/7 & 15; Waltzes: in D flat (Minute), Op. 64/1; in E min., Op. posth.
(N) (B) **(*) Decca Dig. 448 244-2 [id.]. Jorge Bolet.

There is some really lovely playing from Jorge Bolet in this recital, assembled from recordings made
between 1985 and 1987, though there is also a certain want of youthful fire. Bolet is happiest when he is
at his most reflective and contemplative, less so when in the *Ballades* the music calls for more abandon.
He brings keen musical insights to this music, but he is at his best in the *Barcarolle* and the quieter
Nocturnes and the more inward-looking *Preludes*. The recording is in every way first class, and this is
surely an ideal recital to relax to in the late evening.

Ballade No. 1 in G min., Op. 23; Barcarolle, Op. 60; Fantaisie-impromptu, Op. 66; Mazurkas: in B flat, Op.
7/1; in D, Op. 33/2; Nocturnes: in E flat, Op. 9/2; in F sharp, Op. 15/2; in D flat, Op. 27/2; in G min., Op.
37/1; Polonaises: in A (Military), Op. 40/1; in A flat, Op. 53; Waltzes: in A flat, Op. 34/1; in D flat
(Minute); in C sharp min., Op. 64/1–2.
(M) *** RCA GD 87725 [7725-2-RG]. Artur Rubinstein.

An outstanding mid-priced recital – there is no more distinguished miscellaneous Chopin collection in
the catalogue – with fourteen contrasted pieces, well programmed.

Ballade No. 1 in G min.; Berceuse in D flat; Etudes, Op. 10/1, 5, 6, & 12 (Revolutionary); Impromptu No. 1
in A flat, Op. 29; Mazurkas: in B flat, Op. 7/1; in C, Op. 67/3; in A min., Op. 68/2; in A flat, Op. posth.;
Polonaise No. 6 in A flat, Op. 53; Scherzos No. 3 in C sharp min.; 4 in E, Op. 54; Waltzes Nos. 3 in A min.,
Op. 34/2; 14 in E min., Op. posth.
(B) **(*) DG 439 406-2 [id.]. Tamás Vásáry.

An excellent bargain recital, compiled for DG's Classikon label from Vásáry's mid-1960s recordings.
The layout is attractive, opening poetically with the *G minor Ballade* and *Berceuse*, ranging through the
Waltzes, Etudes, Scherzos (very well done) and *Mazurkas*, and ending with the *A flat Polonaise*. But why
no *Nocturnes*? The sound is a fraction dry but firm and believable. The documentation – which begins
on the front of the liner-leaflet – is impressive.

'Favourites': Ballade No. 1 in G min., Op. 23; Fantaisie-impromptu, Op. 66; Mazurkas: in B flat, Op. 7/1;
in D, Op. 33/2; Nocturnes: in E flat, Op. 9/2; in F sharp, Op. 15/2; in B, Op. 32/1; Polonaise in A flat, Op.
53; Scherzo in B flat min., Op. 31; Waltzes: in E flat (Grande valse brillante), Op. 18; in A min., Op. 34/2;
in A flat; B min., Op. 69/1–2; in G flat, Op. 70/1.
(M) *** Decca Dig. 417 798-2; 417 798-4. Vladimir Ashkenazy.

An exceptionally attractive recital, with many favourites, played with Ashkenazy's customary poetic flair and easy brilliance. The digital recordings were made at various times during the early 1980s but match surprisingly well: the sound has striking realism and presence.

Ballade No. 1 in G min., Op. 23; Mazurkas Nos. 19 in B min., 20 in D flat, Op. 30/2–3; 22 in G sharp min., 25 in B min., Op. 33/1 and 4; 34 in C, Op. 56/2; 43 in G min., 45 in A min., Op. 67/2 and 4; 46 in C; 47 in A min., 49 in F min., Op. 68/1–2 and 4; Prelude No. 25 in C sharp min., Op. 45; Scherzo No. 2 in B flat min., Op. 31.
**(*) DG 413 449-2 [id.]. Arturo Benedetti Michelangeli.

Although this recital somehow does not quite add up as a whole, the performances are highly distinguished. Michelangeli's individuality comes out especially in the *Ballade* and is again felt in the *Mazurkas*, which show a wide range of mood and dynamic. The *Scherzo* is extremely brilliant, yet without any suggestion of superficiality. The piano tone is real and lifelike.

Ballade No. 3 in A flat, Op. 47; Barcarolle in F sharp, Op. 60; Fantaisie in F min., Op. 49; Fantaisie-impromptu, Op. 66; Nocturnes Nos. 2 in E flat, Op. 9/2; 5 in F sharp, Op. 15/2; Prelude in D flat, Op. 28/15; Waltzes Nos. 7 in C sharp min., Op. 64/2; 9 in A flat, Op. 69/1.
(M) *** Ph. 420 655-2 [id.]. Claudio Arrau.

A fine recital, showing both poetry and the thoughtful seriousness which distinguishes Arrau's Chopin, which is West rather than East European in spirit. The CD is admirably transferred.

Ballade No. 4 in F min., Op. 52; Berceuse, Op. 57; Etudes, Opp. 10/3, 8 & 9; 25/1–3; Fantaisie in F min., Op. 49; Mazurka in A min., Op. 68/2; Nocturnes in E flat, Op. 9/2; D flat, Op. 27/2; Polonaise in A, Op. 40/1; A flat, Op. 53; Waltzes in A flat, Op. 42; E min., Op. posth.
(**(*)) Testament mono S BT 1030 [id.]. Solomon.

Although he was thought of primarily as a master of the central Viennese repertoire (and particularly Beethoven) rather than a Chopin interpreter, this anthology affords ample proof of Solomon's power to distil magic in pretty well whatever composer he touched. Most of these 78 recordings were made between 1942 and 1946; the F minor *Fantaisie* is pre-war (1932), a wonderfully searching account, and the sheer delicacy and poetry of the playing shine through the often frail recorded sound. Good transfers.

'Chopin masterpieces': (i) *Etudes: Op. 10, Nos. 3 in E; 5 in G flat; 12 in C min. (Revolutionary);* (ii) *Op. 25, No. 9 in G flat;* (iii) *Fantaisie-impromptu, Op. 66; Nocturnes: Nos. 2 in E flat, Op. 9/2;* (ii) *10 in A flat, Op. 32/2;* (iv) *Polonaises: Nos. 3 in A, Op. 40/1;* (v) *6 in A flat (Heroic), Op. 53;* (vi) *Preludes, Op. 28, Nos. 7 in A; 20 in C min.;* (vii) *Waltzes Nos. 1 in E flat (Grande valse brillante), Op. 18; 6 in D flat (Minute); 7 in C sharp min., Op. 64/1–2.*
(B) *** CfP CD-CFP 4501; *TC-CFP 4501* (i) Anievas; (ii) Adni; (iii) Ogdon; (iv) Ohlsson; (v) Pollini; (vi) Orozco; (vii) Malcuzynski.

EMI first made this compilation available in 1974 and it is as successful today as it was then. The programme includes many favourites and the selection has been made with skill. The recital opens and closes with a polonaise (Pollini is in splendid form in the final item). But this excellent roster of pianists never disappoints and the quality is consistently good. Malcuzynski's contribution is among the highlights: his *Grande valse brillante* has a characteristic glitter, while other attractive performances include the *Sylphides Nocturne in A flat* and Daniel Adni's *'Butterfly' Study*, which takes wing with charming grace. The transfers are all well managed.

Fantaisie in F min., Op. 49; Nocturnes in C sharp min., Op. 27/1; in D flat, Op. 27/2; in A flat, Op. 32/2 ; Polonaise in F sharp min., Op. 44; Scherzo No. 2 in B flat min., Op. 31; Waltzes: in A flat, Op. 34/1; in A min., Op. 34/2; in A flat, Op. 42.
(✸) *** RCA Dig. 09026 60445-2 [id.]. Evgeny Kissin.

Evgeny Kissin's Chopin anthology comes from a Carnegie Hall recital given early in 1993 when he was still only twenty-one. His playing remains remarkably unaffected and, in the *F minor Fantasy* for example, touchingly direct. His virtuosity and brilliance are always harnessed to musical ends and there is total dedication to Chopin and no indulgence in the narcissistic idiosyncrasies that at times have afflicted such young talents as Demidenko and Pogorelich. Chopin playing of real quality and well recorded, though the sound is a bit thick in the bass.

Arrangements

Arrangements by Leopold Godowsky: *Etudes, Op. 10/1, 3, 5 (2 versions), 6, 7; Op. 25/1. 3 Nouvelles études No. 1, Op. posth.; Waltzes, Op. 64/1 & 3; Op. 69/1; Op. 70/2–3; Op. 18* (concert paraphrase).
(M) ** Decca 425 059-2 [id.]. Jorge Bolet.

It seems remarkable today that anyone should want to try to 'improve' Chopin, yet Leopold Godowsky (1870–1938) made transcriptions of a great deal of his music, elaborating the textures in such a way as to place the new versions beyond the reach of all but the bravest virtuosi. It must be said that these performances by Jorge Bolet show the most remarkable technical command of Godowsky's complexities, but what Bolet fails to do is convince the listener that the prodigious effort is really worth while. A degree more audacity of manner might have helped, but, brilliant though the playing is, one is not persuaded to enjoy oneself despite all preconceptions. The recording is admirably realistic.

Cilea, Francesco (1866–1950)

Adriana Lecouvreur (complete).
*** Decca Dig. 425 815-2 (2) [id.]. Sutherland, Bergonzi, Nucci, d'Artegna, Ciurca, Welsh Nat. Op. Ch. & O, Bonynge.
(M) **(*) Decca 430 256-2 (2) [id.]. Tebaldi, Simionato, Del Monaco, Fioravanti, St Cecilia, Rome, Ac. Ch. & O, Capuana.

Sutherland's performance in the role of a great tragic actress could not be warmer-hearted. She impresses with her richness and opulence in the biggest test, the aria *Io son l'umile ancella*, an actress's credo, and her formidable performance is warmly backed up by the other principals, and equally by Richard Bonynge's conducting, not just warmly expressive amid the wealth of rich tunes, but light and sparkling where needed, easily idiomatic.

Tebaldi's consistently rich singing misses some of the flamboyance of Adriana's personality but in her characterization both *Io son l'umile ancella* and *Poveri fiori* are lyrically very beautiful. One wishes that Del Monaco had been as reliable as Tebaldi but, alas, there are some coarse moments among the fine, plangent top notes. Simionato is a little more variable than usual but a tower of strength nevertheless. The recording is outstanding for its time (early 1960s), brilliant and atmospheric.

Cimarosa, Domenico (1749–1801)

(i) *Requiem* (revised Vittorio Negri); *Concertante in G for flute, oboe and orchestra* (arr. Holliger).
(Y/B) (M) *** Ph. Analogue/Dig. 442 657-2 [id.]. (i) Ameling, Finnilä, Van Vrooman, Widmer, Montreux Festival Ch., Lausanne CO, Negri; (ii) Nicolet, Holliger, ASMF, Sillito.

Cimarosa's *Requiem* is an impressive, even formidable work. The singing here by the Montreux Festival Choir conveys a feeling of spacious eloquence and it is a pity that the recording is rather too reverberant to produce an incisive edge to the choral sound; its warm atmosphere, however, adds to the feeling of weight and serenity. The soloists are very good, though some might find the tenor, Richard van Vrooman, a trifle histrionic in the *Preces meae*. Elly Ameling's lovely singing more than compensates, and the bass, Kurt Widmer, is impressive in the *Inter oves*. Vittorio Negri secures excellent playing from the Lausanne orchestra, and the CD transfer, as usual with Philips, greatly enhances a 1969 recording which does not sound dated. What makes this reissue especially attractive is the inclusion of Cimarosa's best-known concertante work. This engaging *Concertante* is aptly operatic in feeling. The music is not without substance, but the singing lyrical secondary theme in the first movement and the interplay of flute and oboe in the *Largo* show a distinct vocal style. With such superb playing from Nicolet and Holliger, nicely turned accompaniments and first-rate digital recording, this CD, with its attractive coupling, is most entertaining.

Il maestro di cappella (complete).
(M) *** Decca 433 036-2 (2) [id.]. Fernando Corena, ROHCG O, Argeo Quadri – DONIZETTI: *Don Pasquale*. ***

Corena's classic assumption of the role of incompetent Kapellmeister has been out of the catalogue for too long. Corena shows complete mastery of the buffo bass style, and he is so little troubled by the florid passages that he can relax in the good humour. The vintage 1960 recording is clear and atmospheric, with the directional effects naturally conveyed.

Il pittor parigino (complete).
**(*) Hung. Dig. HCD 12972/3-2 [id.]. Szucs, Kincses, Garino, Gregor, Klietmann, Salieri CO, Pál.

Tamás Pál is an efficient conductor, himself playing harpsichord recitatives, and he draws a lively performance – using modern instruments – from the Salieri Chamber Orchestra. The cast is a strong one, using a number of soloists from the Budapest Opera who are becoming increasingly well known on record. The outstanding performance comes from the veteran buffo bass, József Gregor, brilliant as the Baron.

Clarke, Rebecca (1886–1979)

(i) *Piano trio*; (ii) *Viola sonata*.
(N) ✹ *** ASV Dig. CDDCA 932 [id.]. Martin Roscoe, with (i) Andrew Watkinson, David Waterman; (ii) Garfield Jackson – BEACH: *Piano quintet*. ***

Not many chamber works from the early years of the century match these two masterpieces of Rebecca Clarke for power or passion. Born and educated in Britain, she was a frequent visitor to the United States and lived there permanently from the Second World War onwards. As well as composing, she played the viola, and the bitingly romantic *Viola sonata*, superbly written for the instrument, is here given a warm and purposeful performance. The *Piano trio* of two years later (1921) is, if anything, even more striking, with clean-cut, thrusting themes bringing echoes of Bartók and Bloch which never submerge Clarke's individual voice. Sadly, she stopped writing in 1930. The performances by Roscoe with members of the Endellion Quartet are masterly, with full-bodied, well-balanced recording.

Clemens non Papa, Jacob (c. 1510/15–c. 1555/6)

Missa Pastores quidnam vidistis; Motets: *Pastores quidnam vidistis; Ego flos campi; Pater peccavi; Tribulationes civitatum.*
✹ *** Gimell Dig. CDGIM 013; *1585T-13* [id.]. Tallis Scholars, Peter Phillips.

This admirable disc serves as an introduction to the music of Jacob Clement or Clemens non Papa (who was jokingly known as Clemens-not-the-Pope, so as to distinguish him from either Pope Clement VII or the Flemish poet, Jacobus Papa). The beauty of line and richness of texture in the masterly *Missa Pastores quidnam vidistis* are unforgettable in this superb performance by the Tallis Scholars. The programme opens with the parody motet associated with the Mass, which has a glorious eloquence. Of the other motets, *Pater peccavi*, solemnly rich-textured, is especially memorable; but the whole programme is designed to reveal to twentieth-century ears another name hitherto known only to scholars. The recording is uncannily real and superbly balanced. It was made in the ideal acoustics of the Church of St Peter and St Paul, Salle, Norfolk.

Clementi, Muzio (1752–1832)

(i) *Piano concerto in C. Symphonies: in B flat & D, Op. 18; Nos. 1–4; Minuetto pastorale; Overtures in C & D.*
(M) ** ASV Dig. CDDCS 322 (3) [id.]. (i) Pietro Spada; Philh. O, Francesco D'Avalos.

(i) *Piano concerto in C; Symphonies in B flat & D, Op. 18; Minuetto pastorale.*
(M) **(*) ASV Dig. CDDCA 802 [id.]. (i) Pietro Spada; Philh. O, D'Avalos.

Symphonies Nos. 1 in C; 2 in D; 3 (Great National) in G; 4 in D.
(M) *** Erato/Warner 4509 92191-2 (2) Philh. O, Claudio Scimone.

Symphonies Nos. 1 in C; 3 in G (Great National); Overture in C.
** ASV Dig. CDDCA 803 [id.]. Philh. O, D'Avalos.

Symphonies Nos. 2 in D; 4 in D; Overture in D.
** ASV Dig. CDDCA 804 [id.]. Philh. O, D'Avalos.

Clementi, publisher as well as composer, tragically failed to put most of his symphonic output into print. Six of his 20 symphonies survive, and these are here made available thanks to the researches of Pietro Spada. The four numbered works come from the first decade of the nineteenth century. They are all scored for much larger forces than the Op. 18 set and even include trombones. Their musical content explains Clementi's high reputation in his lifetime as a composer for the orchestra, not just the piano.

If the *Great National Symphony* is the most immediately striking, with *God save the King* ingeniously worked into the third movement so that its presence does not emerge until the very end, the other works are all boldly individual. The *Fourth* is a remarkably powerful symphonic statement which brings some striking modulations, and there is some unexpected chromatic writing (unexpected, that is, to those who are not familiar with the famous set of the piano sonatas that Horowitz recorded). Moreover Clementi's use of the orchestra is often very imaginative, though his indebtedness to the Haydn of the *London Symphonies* is very striking. Scimone's performances with the Philharmonia are strong and sympathetic, and the recording, made in London's Henry Wood Hall in 1978, is full, resonant and natural, bringing weight as well as freshness.

The three-disc ASV set includes also the two Op. 18 symphonies on the first disc. These were published in London in 1787 and are much indebted to Haydn, even if they want his melodic distinction and imagination; the *Piano Concerto in C*, an arrangement of a piano sonata, is a later piece with a good deal of Mozart and some Beethoven, though without their inventive fertility. Pietro Spada, who has edited all the pieces on these records, himself appears as the secure and accomplished soloist. Francesco D'Avalos gets spirited playing from the Philharmonia, though he is not strong on subtleties of phrasing; Scimone with the Philharmonia finds rather more finesse, and no less energy or commitment. The ASV digital sound is bright and a bit forward, but the texture is insufficiently transparent and clean to warrant a three-star grading. The sound is certainly not preferable to the analogue quality of the Erato discs. There is some arresting music in the course of the four mature symphonies to make them worth investigating, and the reissued Erato set takes precedence for this purpose, although the first ASV disc – though it makes the least urgent claims on the collector – could be chosen as a supplement.

Symphonies: No. 1 in C; in B flat and D, Op. 18/1–2 (1787).
*** Chandos Dig. CHAN 9234 [id.]. LMP, Matthias Bamert.

Bamert's performances are on a chamber scale and are refreshingly alive and polished. They are given top-class Chandos sound. If you want just one CD of Clementi symphonies, this is the one to have, and indeed the music here is rather engaging.

Piano sonatas in G min., Op. 7/3; in F min., Op. 13/6; in B flat, Op. 24/2; in F sharp min.; in D; Op. 25/5–6.
**(*) D & J Athene Dig. ATH CD 4 [id.]. Peter Katin.

Peter Katin plays a square piano, built by Clementi and Company in 1832 (the year of the composer's death), which has subsequently been restored. So the sounds he creates are as authentic as one could find. The work which comes off best in his recital is the *G minor Sonata*, Op. 7/3, which sounds so effective on the fortepiano. So does the finale of the *D major*, Op. 25/5, very nicely articulated, and the *F minor Sonata*, Op. 13/6, also seems exactly suited to the instrument. The slow movement of the *F sharp minor*, Op. 25/5, sounds utterly different here from Maria Tipo's version, the playing altogether more direct, seeking no romantic overtones; generally, Peter Katin's approach is plainspun to suit the somewhat dry sonority of his instrument. He is very realistically recorded.

Piano sonatas: in G min., Op. 8/1; in F, Op. 13/6; in F sharp min., Op. 25/5; in D, Op. 40/3; Introduction, Andante grazioso, Allegretto and coda on *'Batti batti'* from Mozart's *Don Giovanni.*
**(*) EMI Dig. CDC7 54766-2 [id.]. Maria Tipo (piano).

Maria Tipo plays sensitively and musically and produces an attractive range of colour; moreover she is very realistically recorded – this is EMI's best piano-quality. She finds Clementi essentially a romantic composer (the *Lento e patetico* of Op. 25/5, which is beautifully played, is made to sound like Schubert). Elsewhere her personal touches of rubato bring a style more appropriate for Chopin. Even so, she brings all this music to life, and she is particularly impressive in the splendid *D major Sonata*, Op. 40/3: in her hands the first movement is particularly engaging.

Piano sonatas: in F min., Op. 13/6; in B flat, Op. 24/2; in F sharp min., Op. 25/5; in G, Op. 37/1.
*** Accent ACC 67911D [id.]. Jos van Immerseel.

Very fleet and brilliant performances from Jos van Immerseel. The slow movements of these sonatas have some considerable expressive depth, and the outer ones are full of a brilliance that is well served by this eminently skilful and excellent artist.

Piano sonatas: in F min., Op. 14/3; in F sharp min., Op. 26/2; in C (quasi concerto), Op. 33/3; in G min., Op. 34/2; Rondo (from Sonata, Op. 47/2).
(M) *** RCA GD 87753 [7753-2-RC]. Vladimir Horowitz (piano).

These electrifying performances from the 1950s show a Clementi of greater substance and sterner mettle than the composer we thought we knew and, though the piano sound is shallow by the side of most up-to-date recordings, the quality is a great improvement upon either of the vinyl transfers with which we have compared it.

Coates, Eric (1886–1958)

Ballad; By the sleepy lagoon; London suite; The Three Bears (phantasy); *The Three Elizabeths* (suite).
(M) *** ASV Dig. CDWHL 2053. East of England O, Malcolm Nabarro.

Nabarro has the full measure of Coates's leaping allegros and he plays the famous marches with crisp buoyancy. *The Three Bears* sparkles humorously, as it should; only in *By the sleepy lagoon* does one really miss a richer, more languorous string-texture. Excellent, bright recording, and the price is right.

(i) *By the sleepy lagoon;* (ii) *Calling all workers* (march); (iii) *Cinderella* (phantasy); *From meadow to Mayfair: suite; London suite; London again suite;* (i) *The Merrymakers overture;* (iii) *Music everywhere* (march); (iv) *Saxo-rhapsody;* (i) *The Three Bears* (phantasy); (ii) *The Three Elizabeths* (suite); (i) *The three men* (suite): *Man from the sea.* (iii) *Wood nymphs* (valsette).
(B) *** CfP CD-CFPD 4456 (2) [id.]. (i) LSO, Mackerras; (ii) CBSO, Kilbey; (iii) R LPO, Groves; (iv) with Jack Brymer.

This collection of the music of Eric Coates includes, besides some very lively performances from Sir Charles Mackerras, several outstanding ones from the CBSO under Reginald Kilbey, who proves the ideal Coates conductor. Although the CDs bring out the brittleness in the upper range, notably in the Groves recordings, the ambient effect helps to prevent too great an imbalance towards the treble.

Calling all workers march; Dambusters march; The Jester at the wedding; London suite; The Merrymakers overture; The Three Elizabeths; (i) *The Green hills; Stonecracker John.*
(Y/B) (B) ** BBC Radio Classics BBCRD 9106 [id.]. BBC Concert O, Sir Adrian Boult; (i) with Ian Wallace.

An exceptionally generous collection (76 minutes) of Eric Coates favourites, including the three best-known marches, *Dambusters*, *Knightsbridge* (once used as the introduction to the BBC's vintage radio show, 'In Town Tonight') and *Calling all workers*, specifically written as the signature-tune for later wartime broadcasts of 'Music while you work'. Most importantly, the programme includes Coates's finest orchestral work, *The Three Elizabeths* (1944), in which the Queen Mother (*Elizabeth of Glamis*) got the best tune – scored for the oboe, and with a delightful, Scottish snap (although as played here it does not beguile the ear as much as it can). Queen Elizabeth II (then a princess) was celebrated with yet another swinging march. The charming and little-known ballet suite, *The Jester at the wedding*, is played quite delightfully and Boult sees that the marches have plenty of rhythmic swing. The fine bass-baritone, Ian Wallace, is also on hand to give resonant accounts of two of Coates's most successful ballads. The orchestral playing is lively enough, if not immaculate; but the recording, although quite satisfactorily balanced in the Hippodrome Studio, Golders Green, does not flatter the violins and suggests that there were not too many of them. Good value, nevertheless.

The 4 Centuries: suite; The Jester at the wedding: ballet suite; The 7 Dwarfs.
(M) **(*) ASV Dig. CDWHL 2075 [id.]. East of England O, Malcolm Nabarro.

For their second anthology of music by Eric Coates, the orchestra based in Nottinghamshire (where the composer was born) offer a particularly delectable account of *The Jester at the wedding ballet suite*. *The Four Centuries* is a masterly and engaging pastiche of styles from four different periods, and again it receives a performance of some subtlety, although at times one wishes for a more opulent sound from the violins, and the closing jazzy evocation of the 1930s and 1940s could be more uninhibitedly rumbustious. *The Seven Dwarfs* is an early work (1930), a ballet written for a short-lived London revue. It is nicely coaxed back into life and the recording is very good.

The Three Elizabeths (suite).
(M) **(*) Mercury 434 330-2 [id.]. London Pops O, Fennell – GRAINGER: *Country gardens* etc. **

Fennell's performance is notable for its spirit and polish: the closing march, *The Youth of Britain*, sounds particularly fresh and alert, while the slow movement is nicely expressive. But the 1965 Mercury recording, made in Watford Town Hall, though fuller and with a more attractive ambience than the coupled Grainger items, still lacks something in expansiveness, though not clarity of detail.

VOCAL MUSIC

Songs: *Always as I close my eyes; At sunset; Bird songs at eventide; Brown eyes I love; Dinder courtship; Doubt; Dreams of London; Green hills o'Somerset; Homeward to you; I heard you singing; I'm lonely; I pitch my lonely caravan; Little lady of the moon; Reuben Ranzo; Song of summer, A song remembered; Stonecracker John; Through all the ages; Today is ours.*
(M) *** ASV Dig. CDWHL 2081. Brian Rayner Cook, Raphael Terroni.

Eric Coates, as well as writing skilful orchestral music, also produced fine Edwardian ballads which in many instances transcended the limitations of the genre, with melodies of genuine refinement and imagination. Most date from earlier in his career, prior to the Second World War. Brian Rayner Cook, with his rich baritone beautifully controlled, is a superb advocate and makes a persuasive case for every one of the 19 songs included in this recital. His immaculate diction is infectiously demonstrated in the opening *Reuben Ranzo* (a would-be sailor/tailor), in which he breezily recalls the spirited projection of another famous singer of this kind of repertoire in the early days of the gramophone, Peter Dawson. The recording is admirably clear.

Colding-Jørgenson, Henrik (born 1944)

To love music.
** BIS CD 79 [id.]. Danish Nat. RO, Schmidt – BENTZON: *Feature on René Descartes* **; NORBY: *The Rainbow snake.* ***

At elske musikken ('To love music') falls into two parts: 'To love music with the head' and, secondly, '. . . with the heart'. Its musical language is eclectic and far from inaccessible; indeed, during the course of its 26 minutes there are many moments of beauty. But while it is undeniably imaginative, it is difficult to discern any strong sense of musical purpose and organic growth. One feels that the music could stop or start anywhere and, given the thinness of some of the musical substance, it outstays its welcome. Dedicated playing from the Danish orchestra under Ole Schmidt, and a good analogue recording.

Constantinescu, Paul (1909–63)

The Nativity (Byzantine Christmas oratorio).
**(*) Olympia OCD 402 (2) [id.]. Emelia Petrescu, Martha Kessler, Valentin Teodorian, Helge Bömches, Bucharest Georges Enescu Ch. & PO, Mircea Basarab.

Paul Constantinescu's *The Nativity*, which he subtitles *Byzantine Christmas oratorio*, is an extended work of some quality in three parts: *Annunciation, Nativity* and *The Three Magi*. This impressive performance comes from the late 1970s. Apart from the exoticism of the Byzantine material and liturgical references, there are reminders of expressionism (Constantinescu studied in Vienna) and of such contemporary models as Honegger and Bartók. Constantinescu writes effectively both for the chorus and for solo voices, and his orchestration too is expert. The soloists are excellent (and in different circumstances might well have made names for themselves outside their native country) and the analogue recording is very good indeed. Readers with an interest in the exotic and a touch of enterprise are recommended to investigate this set.

Cooke, Arnold (born 1906)

Clarinet concerto.
*** Hyperion CDA 66031 [id.]. Thea King, NW CO of Seattle, Alun Francis – JACOB: *Mini-concerto;* RAWSTHORNE: *Concerto.* ***

Arnold Cooke's music contains an element of Hindemithian formalism, carefully crafted, but the slow movement of this concerto soars well beyond. Thea King makes a passionate advocate, brilliantly accompanied by the Seattle Orchestra in excellent 1982 analogue sound, faithfully transferred.

Copland, Aaron (1900–90)

Appalachian spring (ballet; complete original version)
*** Koch Dig. 3-7019-2; 2-7019-4 [id.]. Atlantic Sinf., Schenck – BARBER: *Cave of the heart.* ***

This Koch International issue offers a welcome chance to hear a modern digital recording of

Appalachian spring in its original form for thirteen instruments and the bright, upfront recording presents the chamber version in the best possible light. This is a most interesting and stimulating issue.

(i) *Appalachian spring* (ballet) *suite; Billy the Kid: ballet suite;* (ii) *Clarinet concerto;* (i) *Danzón Cubano; Fanfare for the common man; John Henry; Letter from home;* (i; iv) *Lincoln portrait;* (iii) *Music for movies;* (i) *Our Town; An Outdoor overture; Quiet city; Rodeo (4 Dance episodes);* (iii) *El Salón México;* (i) *Symphony No. 3;* (v) *Las agachadas.*
(M) *** Sony SM3K 46559 (3) [id.]. (i) LSO; (ii) Benny Goodman, Columbia Symphony Strings; (iii) New Philh. O; (iv) with Henry Fonda; (v) New England Conservatory Ch.; composer.

Sony here offer a comprehensive anthology of the major orchestral works, ballet suites and film scores dating from Copland's vintage period, 1936–48. The composer directs with unrivalled insight throughout. The remastering for CD is done most skilfully, retaining the ambience of the originals, while achieving more refined detail.

Appalachian spring (ballet) *suite.*
(Y/B) *** Everest EVC 9003 [id.]. LSO, Walter Susskind – GOULD: *Spirituals* ***; GERSHWIN: *American in Paris.* **(*)
(M) *** DG Dig. 439 528-2 [id.]. LAPO, Bernstein – BARBER: *Adagio for strings* ***; GERSHWIN: *Rhapsody in blue.* **(*)

Susskind's dramatic and sympathetic reading of what is perhaps Copland's finest orchestral score is most spaciously and vividly recorded. Although it is an English performance, it compares very favourably indeed with the composer's own – see below – and the American-style engineering with wide dynamics adds plenty of drama, but not at the expense of amplitude. Susskind conducts the piece in a completely spontaneous way: the string ostinatos have the proper rhythmic bite, the quieter, more reflective pages bring serenity, and the unfolding of the Shaker variations is managed with a simplicity of great charm. With its apt Gould coupling – no less well done – this is an outstanding reissue. It is a pity that it is offered at only slightly less than full price, but it is worth its cost.

Bernstein's DG version of *Appalachian spring* was recorded at a live performance, and the conductor communicates his love for the score in a strong yet richly lyrical reading, and the compulsion of the music-making is obvious. The recording is close but not lacking in atmosphere, and it sounds extremely vivid. It is here recoupled with his rather less recommendable second recording of Gershwin's *Rhapsody in blue.*

Appalachian spring (concert version); *Billy the Kid: suite; El Salón Mexico; Fanfare for the common man; Rodeo: Hoe-down.*
(N) (BB) *(*) Tring Dig. TRPO 40 [id.]. RPO, Philip Ellis.

The RPO play well, if without that special transatlantic syncopated bite in the popular dance rhythms, and they are richly and atmospherically recorded. *Appalachian spring* is suitably evocative, with good detail and a touching closing section, and (apart from a tiny slip of ensemble near the opening) the *Fanfare* is arresting and spectacularly resonant. The characterization of the other music is vivid; but while Bernstein's NYPO collection is available the main attraction of this disc is its remarkably low cost.

(i) *Appalachian spring;* (ii) *Billy the Kid* (suite); *Rodeo* (suite).
(Y/B) (BB) *** RCA Navigator 74321 21297-2. (i) Boston SO, composer; (ii) Morton Gould and his Orchestra.

Copland's first recording of *Appalachian spring* was recorded in Boston in 1959 and is alone worth the modest price of this disc. The performance has an appealing breadth and warmth of humanity, helped by the Symphony Hall resonance: the Shaker climax is wonderfully expansive. Morton Gould conducts the other two ballets with enormous zest and vitality, and 'his' orchestra play as if their very lives depended on it. The early (1957) stereo is a little dated but remains arrestingly spectacular and the quieter, evocative writing is haunting, distilling a special combination of tender warmth and underlying tension. The *Corral Nocturne* and wistful *Saturday night waltz* in *Rodeo* are especially fine, and here Gould also includes the *Honky-tonky interlude* on an appropriate piano. The closing *Hoe-down* is refreshingly folksy and has great rhythmic energy.

(i) *Appalachian spring* (ballet) *suite; Billy the Kid* (ballet) complete; (ii) *Danzón cubano; El salón México.*
(M) *** Mercury 434 301-2 [id.]. (i) LSO; (ii) Minneapolis SO, Antal Dorati.

Dorati pioneered the first stereo recording of the complete *Billy the Kid* ballet, and the 1961 Mercury LP caused a sensation on its first appearance for its precision of detail and brilliance of colour, while the generous acoustics of Watford Town Hall added ambient warmth. The gunshots (track 13) were and remain electrifying, with their clean percussive transients, while the LSO playing combines tremendous vitality and rhythmic power with genuine atmospheric tension. For the CD, earlier (1957) Minneapolis versions of the *Danzón cubano* and *El salón México* have been added. The recording is crisp and clean to suit his approach.

Appalachian spring: ballet suite; Billy the Kid: ballet suite; Rodeo: 4 dance episodes; Symphony No. 3: Fanfare for the common man.
⚛ (M) *** Sony SMK 47543 [id.]. NYPO, Leonard Bernstein.

Bernstein recorded these ballet scores in the early 1960s when he was at the peak of his creative tenure with the NYPO, and we are fortunate that the recordings are so good, vivid, spacious and atmospheric. No one – not even the composer   has approached these performances for racy rhythmic exuberance or for the tenderness and depth of nostalgia in the lyrical music, especially in the opening sequence of *Appalachian spring* and the *Corral nocturne* from *Rodeo*. The opening *Buckaroo holiday* and the final *Hoe-down* from the latter ballet, taken at a tremendous pace, have an unforgettable rhythmic bite and zest, with amazing precision of ensemble from the New York players, whose adrenalin is obviously running at unprecedented levels. The evocation of *The open prairie* in *Billy the Kid* is magical and the picture of a *Street in a frontier town* has a piquant charm, while the projection of the score's more strident moments brings a characteristic pungency. The *Fanfare for the common man* is not the original, commissioned in 1942 by Eugene Goossens for the Cincinnati Orchestra, but the composer's reworking, when he introduced it as a springboard for the finale of his *Third Symphony*. *Appalachian spring* (1961) and *Rodeo* (1960) were made at the Manhattan Center (once again put to use by DG for their recordings by the Orpheus Chamber Orchestra) and *Billy the Kid* in Symphony Hall, Boston, in 1959.

(i) *Appalachian spring* (ballet) *suite;* (ii) *Ceremonial fanfare;* (iii) *Dance symphony; El salón México;* (i) *Fanfare for the common man;* (i; iv) *Lincoln portrait;* (v) *Music for movies;* (vi) *Quiet city;* (iii) *Rodeo: 4 Dance episodes;* (vii) *Old American songs* (excerpts): *Simple gifts; Ching-a-ring-chaw; Long time ago; I bought me a cat; At the river.*
(N) (B) *** Decca Double Analogue/Dig. 448 261-2 (2) [id.]. (i) LAPO, Mehta; (ii) Philip Jones Brass Ens.; (iii) Detroit SO, Dorati; (iv) Gregory Peck; (v) L. Sinf., Elgar Howarth; (vi) ASMF, Marriner; (vii) Marilyn Horne, ECO, Carl Davis.

Mehta's performance of *Appalachian spring*, made for Decca in the late 1970s, is one of the most distinguished of several fine recordings, which also included the spectacular *Fanfare for the common man* and the *Lincoln portrait*, with Gregory Peck a comparatively laid-back narrator who speaks Lincoln's prose with dignity and restraint. Dorati's performances of the *Dance symphony*, *El salón México* and *Rodeo* were digitally recorded in 1981. They are notable for their bright, extrovert brilliance, having evidently been chosen for their immediate, cheerful qualities. The playing demonstrates very clearly the degree of orchestral virtuosity available in Detroit, and the only reservation is that, somewhat surprisingly, Dorati's treatment of jazzy syncopations is rather literal, though it has undoubted idiomatic feeling. But as sound this is very impressive, and the performances have much vitality. The *Music for movies* was drawn together by the composer from his film scores for *The City*, *Of Mice and Men* (both 1939) and *Our Town* (1940). The evocative opening picture of the *New England Countryside* occupies the same musical world as *Appalachian spring*, and the jaunty third piece, *Sunday traffic*, has a marked choreographic feeling. Again fine playing from the London Sinfonietta under Elgar Howarth (though not perhaps as brightly idiomatic as with Dorati) and vivid recording. Marriner's account of *Quiet city* is second to none, but the highlight of the second CD is Marilyn Horne's delightful performances of five *Old American songs*: the rhythmic sparkle of *Ching-a-ring-raw* and the charm of *I bought me a cat* contrasting with the moving simplicity of the closing *At the river*. Excellent value.

Appalachian spring (ballet; chamber version) *suite; 3 Latin-American sketches; Quiet city; Short symphony.*
*** DG 427 335-2 [id.]. Orpheus CO.

With exceptionally vivid sound, bright and immediate, giving a realistic sense of presence, the Orpheus Chamber Orchestra's collection makes for a very distinctive Copland record of four works in which the composer is at his most approachable. The version of *Appalachian spring* here is the shortened text of the suite allied to the original 13-instrument ballet scoring. The performances, immaculately drilled, have a consistent sense of corporate purposefulness, of live communication made the more intense by the realism of the recording.

Appalachian spring (ballet) *suite; Short symphony.*
*** Pro Arte Dig. CDD 140 [id.]. St Paul CO, Russell Davies – IVES: *Symphony No. 3.* ***

On Pro Arte, using a smaller ensemble than is usual, Russell Davies conducts fresh and immediate performances of both the *Short symphony* and the well-known suite from *Appalachian spring*, which was

originally conceived for chamber orchestra. The recording is bright and forward to match the performances. An excellent and recommendable anthology.

Appalachian spring (ballet) *suite; The Tender Land* (opera): *suite*.
(M) *** RCA 09026 61505-2 [id.]. Boston SO, composer – GOULD: *Fall River legend* etc. ***

The composer's first (1959) Boston recording of the *Appalachian spring suite* (also available less expen-
sively, differently coupled – see above) has moments of special resonance, its atmospheric feeling at
times quite profound, helped by splendid orchestral playing and the warm Boston acoustic. The suite
from *The Tender Land* is also well worth having. We are given the *Love duet* virtually complete, the Party
music from Act II and the quintet, *The promise of living* (all, of course, without voices). The 'Living
Stereo' remastering by John Pfeiffer and his team creates the most vivid and full-bodied sound-picture.

(i) *Billy the Kid* (ballet suite); (ii) *Piano sonata*.
(M) (***) RCA mono GD 60915 [60915-2]. (i) RCA Victor SO, Bernstein; (ii) Bernstein (piano) –
BERNSTEIN: *On the Town: suite* etc. (***)

Bernstein got to know the music of *Billy the Kid* by sitting with the composer and playing the full score
on the piano. He also learned the formidable *Sonata* as it was being written in 1941. Both performances
are full of nervous energy and must be regarded as definitive.

Ceremonial fanfare; John Henry (A railroad ballad); Jubilee variations; (i) *Lincoln portrait;* (ii) *Old
American songs, set 1; An Outdoor overture; The Tender Land: The promise of living.*
*** Telarc Dig. CD 80117 [id.]. Cincinnati Pops O, Kunzel; (i) with Katharine Hepburn (nar.); (ii)
    Sherrill Milnes.

Katharine Hepburn's remarkable delivery of Abraham Lincoln's words quite transcends any limitations
in Copland's *Lincoln portrait* and makes it an undeniably moving experience, and Kunzel, clearly
inspired by the authority of her reading, punctuates the text with orchestral comments of singular
power. The shorter pieces are also given splendid life. Sherrill Milnes's highly infectious performance of
the first set of *Old American songs* shows a spirited boisterousness that recalls Howard Keel in *Seven
Brides for Seven Brothers*. Altogether a collection that is more than the sum of its parts, given superlative
Telarc recording, highly spectacular and realistic, yet with natural balance.

Clarinet concerto.
*** RCA Dig. 09026 61350-2. Stoltzman, LSO, Leighton Smith – BERNSTEIN: *Prelude, fugue and riffs.*
    CORIGLIANO: *Concerto;* STRAVINSKY: *Ebony concerto.* ***
*** Sony MK 42227 [id.]. Benny Goodman, Columbia SO, composer – BERNSTEIN: *Prelude, fugue and
    riffs;* GOULD: *Derivations;* STRAVINSKY: *Ebony concerto* ***; BARTOK: *Contrasts.* (***)
*** Chandos Dig. CHAN 8618 [id.]. Janet Hilton, SNO, Bamert – NIELSEN: *Concerto;* LUTOSLAWSKI:
    Dance preludes. ***
*** ASV Dig. CDDCA 568 [id.]. MacDonald, N. Sinfonia, Bedford – FINZI: *Concerto;* MOURANT:
    Pied Piper. ***
**(*) Denon Dig. CO 75289 [id.]. Paul Meyer, ECO, Zinman – BUSONI: *Adagio;* MOZART: *Concerto.*
    ***

Copland's splendid *Clarinet concerto* is at last coming into its own, on record at least. Stoltzman is
effectively cool in the serene opening and catches the work's later quirky jazz elements to perfection; in
this he is well matched by Lawrence Leighton Smith and the LSO players, who let their hair down
without losing rhythmic sharpness or crispness of ensemble. The finale's flair is exhilarating and, with
first-rate RCA recording, this bids to upstage even Benny Goodman in its combination of idiomatic
understanding, natural virtuosity and superior sound. Now reissued with Stravinsky's *Ebony concerto*
added to the original programme, this CD is even more attractive.

  Benny Goodman gives a splendid account of the concerto he commissioned in 1947, and the recording
from the early 1960s sounds admirably fresh in remastered form.

  Janet Hilton's performance is softer-grained and has a lighter touch than Stolzman's, yet she finds
plenty of sparkle for the finale and her rhythmic felicity is infectious. She is at her very finest, however, in
the gloriously serene opening, where her tender poetic line is ravishing.

  George MacDonald gives a virtuoso performance, not quite as dramatic and full of flair as that of the
dedicatee, Benny Goodman, but in many ways subtler in expression and particularly impressive in the
long lyrical paragraphs of the first of the two movements.

  The gifted French clarinettist Paul Meyer plays with characteristic Gallic finesse and offers a winningly
sprightly cadenza; he and Zinman wring remarkably felt intensity from the expressive opening section.
Surprisingly, the popular rhythmic elements which come in the Rondo finale are presented straight,
without jazzy inflexions. Fine, spacious recording.

(i; ii) *Piano concerto;* (iii) *Dance symphony;* (ii) *Music for the theatre;* (iii) *2 Pieces for string orchestra; Short symphony (Symphony No. 2); Statements; Symphonic ode;* (iv; ii) *Symphony for organ and orchestra.*

(M) *** Sony SM2K 47232 (2) [id.]. (i) Composer (piano); (ii) NYPO, Bernstein; (iii) LSO, composer; (iv) with E. Power Biggs.

This second Sony Copland collection covers early orchestral and concertante music written between 1922 and 1935 and is, if anything, more valuable than the first box. The 1923 *Rondino,* the second of his *Two Pieces for string orchestra,* is the earliest work here. The *Lento* is a totally memorable piece. The *Symphony for organ and orchestra* is a powerful and strikingly innovative work, dating from 1924. It is given an extremely idiomatic and responsive performance by Power Biggs, who is fully sensitive to its atmosphere, and Bernstein balances the overall sounds with great skill and a marvellous feeling for colour. The *Piano concerto* (1927) is both abrasive and strongly jazz-influenced. The pungently flamboyant *Symphonic ode,* commissioned by the Boston Symphony, helped the orchestra to celebrate its fiftieth anniversary: it was written between 1927 and 1929. The *Dance symphony* was completed that same year. The *Short symphony* dates from 1931–3; both works are full of originality and energy and are tautly constructed. *Statements* (1934–5), as the bald title suggests, is one of Copland's less expansive works, but its six vignettes, *Militant, Cryptic, Dogmatic, Subjective, Jingo* and *Prophetic,* reveal a compression of thought and sharpness of idea that are most refreshing. All these performances have a definitive authority combined with total spontaneity of response from the participants which makes them compelling listening, and the recordings – dating from between 1964 and 1967 – are very well engineered, extremely vivid in the excellent CD transfers.

Piano concerto.
(M) *** Van. 08.4029.71 [OVC 4029]. Earl Wild, Symphony of the Air, composer – MENOTTI: *Piano concerto.* **(*)
(M) **(*) Chandos CHAN 6580 [id.]. Gillian Lin, Melbourne SO, John Hopkins – BRITTEN: *Piano concerto.* **(*)

This Vanguard record, with a supreme piano virtuoso providing a glittering account of the piano part, is very recommendable. The 1961 recording is first rate.

Gillian Lin is undoubtedly successful in the Copland *Concerto,* bringing out the jazz element in this syncopated music. The 1978 stereo recording is well balanced and realistically transferred to CD. A thoroughly worthwhile mid-priced coupling.

(i) *Connotations;* (ii) *Dance panels; Down a country lane;* (i) *Inscape;* (ii) *3 Latin-American sketches; Music for a great city; Orchestral variations; Preamble for a solemn occasion; The Red Pony* (film score).
(M) *(**) Sony SM2K 47236 (2) [id.]. (i) NYPO, Bernstein; (ii) LSO or New Philh. O, composer.

This third Copland box from Sony is something of a disappointment – not the music, which is even rarer than before and of great interest. *The Red Pony* is vintage Copland, and the *Orchestral variations,* though strictly an orchestral version of the *Piano variations* of 1930, make a unique and impressive contribution to Copland's oeuvre. *Connotations* and to a lesser extent *Inscape,* the major work of the composer's final period, are serially orientated. *Dance panels* is an abstract ballet without a narrative line, and *Music for a great city,* with its jazz influences and nocturnal scene, derives from another filmscore (*Something Wild*). The performances are all extremely successful, but the CD transfers are overbright and, for all their vividness of detail, tiring to the ear, particularly the thin violins and the more pungent climaxes of the later works.

(i) *Grogh* (complete ballet); (ii) *Hear ye! Hear ye!* (ballet; complete version for small orchestra); *Prelude for chamber orchestra.*
(Y/B) *** Argo Dig. 443 203-2 [id.]. (i) Cleveland O; (ii) L. Sinf., Oliver Knussen.

Copland's full score for *Grogh* was apparently lost; then Oliver Knussen found it, hidden away in the Library of Congress. Inspired by the images of the German horror film, *Nosferatu,* it is a strange early score (1922–5, revised 1932), given a superbly played, atmospheric performance here. *Hear ye! Hear ye!* is a curious burlesque, about a nightclub murder, set in a courtroom, with all kinds of influences, including jazz and even a parody of Mendelssohn's *Wedding march* on four violins. The *Prelude for chamber orchestra* uses material from the *Symphony for organ and orchestra* in a very succinct form. Excellent performances of not always entirely convincing music, given first-class recording.

Quiet city.
*** Argo 417 818-2 [id.]. ASMF, Marriner – BARBER: *Adagio;* COWELL: *Hymn;* CRESTON: *Rumor;* IVES: *Symphony No. 3.* ***

Marriner's 1976 version is both poetic and evocative, and the playing of the trumpet and cor anglais soloists is of the highest order. The digital remastering has brought added clarity without loss of atmosphere.

Quiet city; (i) *8 Poems of Emily Dickinson.*
(Y/B) *** EMI Dig. CDC5 55358-2 [id.]. (i) Barbara Hendricks; LSO, Tilson Thomas – BARBER: *Adagio for strings* etc. ***

Tilson Thomas and Barbara Hendricks have between them devised a programme of Copland as well as Barber, with both composers at their most radiantly inspired. This is an intensely beautiful disc that in its deep thoughtfulness belies the conventional idea of American culture being brash. Tilson Thomas describes *Quiet city,* adapted from film music, as 'Mahler in Manhattan', but that hardly gives a fair idea of its rapt individuality, with solo trumpet and cor anglais (superbly played by Maurice Murphy and Christine Pendrill) adding atmospheric intensity. Copland himself orchestrated eight of his twelve settings of Emily Dickinson poems for chamber orchestra for his seventieth birthday concert, and Tilson Thomas as a young conductor was in charge. The freshness and sharp imagination of the accompaniments are enhanced in support of vocal lines lovingly matched to Dickinson's distinctive poetic style. Radiant singing from Hendricks, and equally sensuous sounds from the orchestra.

Symphony No. 3; Quiet city.
*** DG Dig. 419 170-2 [id.]. NYPO, Bernstein.

With Bernstein conducting Copland's *Third Symphony,* you appreciate more than with rival interpreters that this is one of the great symphonic statements of American music. The electricity of the performance is irresistible. The recording is full-bodied and bright, but its brashness is apt for the performance. The hushed tranquillity of *Quiet city,* another of Copland's finest scores, is superbly caught by Bernstein in the valuable fill-up.

PIANO MUSIC

Down a country lane; In the evening air; Midday thoughts; Midsummer nocturne; 3 Moods; Night thoughts (Homage to Ives); Passacaglia; Petite portrait; 4 Piano blues; Piano fantasy; Proclamation; Piano variations; Scherzo humoristique: The cat and the mouse; Sentimental melody (Slow dance); Sonata; Sunday afternoon music; The Young Pioneers.
(Y/B) (M) *** Sony Analogue/Dig. SM2K 66345 (2) [id.]. Leo Smit.

The sound-quality here may not be ideal – the piano is recorded in a rather small acoustic – but this is nevertheless an important and valuable set, containing a collection of all Copland's important piano music from the very earliest pre-Boulanger days – the abrasively impressionistic *Scherzo, The cat and the mouse* (1920) – right down to his most recent works, *Midday thoughts* and *Proclamation* completed in November 1982. The hauntingly atmospheric yet audaciously conceived *Night thoughts* was composed in 1972 as an apt tribute to Ives. The three most important works, the *Variations* (1930), the *Sonata* (1941) and the *Fantasy* (1957), were not otherwise available at the time Smit's recordings were made. Copland's own response when questioned about the three works was: 'I think that has a lot to do with the quality of the piano itself and with the kind of sound – lean, percussive and rather harmonically severe – that I like to make at the keyboard.' But of course not all this writing is uncompromising. Apart from the bluesy and jazzy pieces, the wistful *In the evening air* and *Midday thoughts* have something of the evocation of the atmospheric writing in the three great ballets, and *Down a country lane* brings a comparable brand of pastoralism. Both are played very sympathetically. Leo Smit has been closely associated with Copland's music over the years (the first of the *Four Piano blues* and the *Midsummer nocturne* of 1947 were here receiving their first recording and both are dedicated to Smit), and he recorded the *Sonata* in the days of 78s. It would be difficult to find anyone who is more inside the idiom and whose command of nervous energy so well matches the needs of this vital music. Authoritative, stimulating and vivid performances.

VOCAL MUSIC

(i) *In the Beginning. Help us, O Lord; Have mercy on us, O my Lord; Sing ye praises to our King.*
*** Hyperion Dig. CDA 66219 [id.]. (i) Catherine Denley; Corydon Singers, Best – BARBER: *Agnus Dei;* BERNSTEIN: *Chichester Psalms.* ***

In the Beginning is a large-scale, fifteen-minute motet for unaccompanied chorus and soprano solo, written in 1947, and the long span of the work is well structured with the help of the soprano soloist, here the fresh-toned Catherine Denley. The chorus is just as clear and alert in its singing, not only in the big motet but also in the three delightful little pieces which come as an appendix. Vivid recording, full of presence.

Old American songs: Sets 1 and 2 (original versions).
*** Chandos Dig. CHAN 8960 [id:]. Willard White, Graeme McNaught (with collection: *'American spirituals; Folk-songs from Barbados and Jamaica'* ***).

Characteristically White's opulent bass comes with a pronounced vibrato which on disc tends to get exaggerated. Yet with its helpful acoustic the Chandos recording captures the richness of his voice most attractively, very characterfully black in its evocations.

Corelli, Arcangelo (1653–1713)

Concerti grossi, Op. 6/1–12.
*** RCA Dig. RD 60071 (2) [09026 60071-2]. Guildhall Ens., Robert Salter.
(Y/B) *** HM Dig. HMC90 1406/7 [id.]. Ensemble 415, Banchini.
(Y/B) *** Hyperion Dig. CDA 66741/2 [id.]. Brandenburg Consort, Goodman.
*** DG Dig. 423 626-2 (2) [id.]. E. Concert, Pinnock.
(BB) *** Naxos Dig. 8.550402/3 [id.]. Capella Istropolitana, Jaroslav Kr(e)chek.
(M) *** HM/BMG GD 77007 (2) [77077-2-RG]. La Petite Bande, Kuijken.
(Y/B) (B) **(*) Decca Double 443 862-2 [id.]. ASMF, Marriner.
(N) (BB) ** EMI/Seraphim CES5 69143-2 (2) [CES 69143]. SW German R. CO, Günter Wich.

For a long time relatively (though not entirely) neglected in the days of LP and the early days of CD, Corelli's glorious set of *Concerti grossi*, Op. 6, is at long last gaining a strong hold on the catalogue. In fact one really can't go far wrong with any of the three-star listings here. The Guildhall Ensemble and Robert Salter, for example, are very fine indeed and are probably a first choice for those who prefer modern instruments. They have the benefit of really excellent recording: immediate and present without being too forward, full-bodied and transparent in detail. The playing is really vital and imaginative and has plenty of warmth and imagination.

For those who want period instruments, there are now two more alternatives to list alongside (and in some ways in preference to) Pinnock. Annoying though it may be for readers who want a definite preference declared for one or the other (or for us, who like to give clear-cut recommendations), the two newcomers are both almost equally recommendable in different ways. One can invest in either with confidence. Roy Goodman and the Brandenburg Consort use the smaller forces (17 string players) plus harpsichord continuo, archlute and organ; Harmonia Mundi's Ensemble 415, with Chiara Banchini and Jesper Christensen, number 32 strings and a comparably larger continuo section with several archlutes, chitarrone, harpsichords and organ. The richer bass and altogether fuller sonority may cause some readers to prefer it (if pressed, we would incline towards it for its greater splendour and the imaginative use of continuo instruments). However, there is a sense of style and a freshness of approach in the Goodman that is very persuasive. In both instances the recorded sound is first class. Choice will largely rest on whether you want a more chamber-like approach, as on Hyperion, or the richer sonority the Harmonia Mundi set offers.

The DG performances bring not only an enthusiasm for this music but a sense of its spacious grandeur. The English Concert are entirely inside its sensibility, and the playing of the concertino group (Simon Standage, Micaela Comberti and Jaap Ter Linden) is wonderfully fresh-eyed and alert, yet full of colour.

At super-bargain price, the Naxos set by the Capella Istropolitana under Jaroslav Kr(e)chek represents very good value indeed. The players are drawn from the Slovak Philharmonic and have great vitality and, when necessary, virtuosity to commend them. The digital recording is clean and well lit, but not over-bright, and makes their version strongly competitive.

La Petite Bande offers a further (mid-price) alternative to the Pinnock set. Authentic instruments are used to excellent effect, and the playing is always expressive and musical. The 1977 recordings were made in a highly sympathetic acoustic, that of the Cedernsaal at Schloss Kirchheim; besides being splendidly lifelike, they are also impressive in conveying the nobility and grandeur of Corelli.

The reissued ASMF version uses a performing edition by Christopher Hogwood and has been prepared with evident thought and care; if one cavils it is only at two small points: some fussy continuo playing here and there, and a certain want of breadth and nobility of feeling in some of the slow movements. These are perhaps small points when weighed alongside the liveliness and intelligence of these perform-ances, so expertly played. Yet compared to the issues mentioned above, there is at times a hint of blandness, and those wanting a bargain version should turn to the Naxos recording by the excellent

Capella Istropolitana under Jaroslav Kr(e)chek, which is even more vital and has first-rate, modern, digital sound.

The performances from the excellent South West German Radio Chamber Orchestra are lively, well played, warmly expressive and not too heavily textured. The concertino group is impressive and the balance between this solo group and the ripieno is well managed. This set is inexpensive and collectors with limited budgets buying it on impulse should not be disappointed, for the breadth of Corelli's inspiration is well conveyed. But the Naxos set, which costs about the same, is even fresher and has the advantage of digital recording.

Concerti grossi, Op. 6/1–6.
(N) (BB) *** DHM Baroque Esprit 05472 77432-2 [id.]. La Petite Band, Sigiswald Kuijken.

La Petite Band have recorded the complete Op. 6, and the present CD offers the first half-dozen concertos at a very economical price; no doubt the rest will follow. In many respects this is superior to the ASMF/Marriner set. Authentic instruments are used to excellent effect: textures are more transparent as a result and the playing is always expressive and musical. The 1977 recordings were made in a warm and highly sympathetic acoustic: besides being splendidly lifelike, they are also impressive in conveying the nobility and grandeur of Corelli.

Concerti grossi, Op. 6/1, 3, 7, 8 (Christmas), 11 & 12.
(N) (M) *** DG Dig. 447 289-2 [id.]. E. Concert, Pinnock.

At mid-price, with the *Christmas Concerto* included, this will admirably suit those collectors who want an original-instrument version and who are content with a single-disc selection.

Trio sonatas, Op. 1/1, 3, 7, 9, 11–12; Op. 2/4, 6, 9, 12.
*** DG Dig. 419 614-2 [id.]. E. Concert (members), Pinnock.

Trio sonatas, Op. 1/9, 10 & 12 (Ciacona); Op. 2/4; Op. 3/5; Op. 4/1; Violin sonata, Op. 5/3; Concerto grosso in B flat, Op. 6/5.
(N) (M) *** Virgin Veritas/EMI Dig. VER5 61210-2 [id.]. L. Baroque, Medlam.

Trio sonatas, Op. 1/9; Op. 2/4 & 12 (Ciacona); Op. 3/12; Op. 4/3; Op. 5/3, 11 & 12 (La Folia).
*** Hyperion Dig. CDA 66226 [id.]. Purcell Qt.

The quality of invention in these pieces underlines the injustice of their neglect. The players from the English Concert dispatch them with a virtuosity and panache that are inspiriting, and their evident enthusiasm for this music is infectious. This is a most impressive and rewarding issue – and excellently recorded into the bargain.

Though not lacking vitality, the London Baroque performances here are graceful and comparatively restrained, lighter in feeling and texture than Pinnock and his English Concert, thus providing a genuine alternative approach. Reissued on Virgin Veritas, they also now have a price advantage.

The Hyperion disc is one of six designed to illustrate the widespread use in the eighteenth century of the famous *La Folia* theme. It includes a varied collection of sonate da chiesa and sonate da camera. Excellent performances from all concerned, and recording to match.

Violin sonatas, Op. 5/1, 3, 6, 11 and 12 (La Follia).
*** Accent Dig. ACC 48433D [id.]. Sigiswald & Wieland Kuijken, Robert Kohnen.

When authenticity of spirit goes hand in hand with fine musical feeling and accomplishment, the results can be impressive, as they undoubtedly are here, drawing one into the sensibility of the period. This is a thoroughly recommendable issue which deserves to reach a wider audience than early-music specialists; the recording is natural and the musicianship refined and totally at the service of Corelli.

Corigliano, John (born 1938)

Clarinet concerto.
*** RCA Dig. 09026 61350-2. Stoltzman, LSO, Leighton Smith – BERNSTEIN: *Prelude, fugue and riffs;* COPLAND: *Concerto;* STRAVINSKY: *Ebony concerto.* ***

Stoltzman gives an outstanding performance of John Corigliano's attractive *Concerto*, his richly expressive treatment of the slow movement balanced by superb flair and virtuosity in the finale. Moreover his reissued CD sweeps the board in including three equally outstanding couplings.

Flute concerto (Pied Piper fantasy); Voyage.
**(*) RCA Dig. R D 86602 [6602-2-RC]. James Galway, Eastman Philh. O, David Effron.

Galway is at his inimitable best in Corigliano's *Flute concerto*. The picaresque qualities of its invention in detailing the Pied Piper narrative are spread thinly in memorability of material, although the closing section when the children are led away into the distance is right up Galway's street. The serene *Voyage* is shorter and more memorable.

(i) *Oboe concerto;* (ii; iii) *3 Irish folksong settings: The Sally Gardens; The foggy dew; She moved thro' the fair;* (ii; iv) *Poem in October.*
(M) *** BMG Analogue/Dig. GD 60395 [60395-2-RG]. (i) Humbert Lucarelli, American SO, Kazuyoshi Akiyama; (ii) Robert White; (iii) Ransom Wilson; (iv) Nyfenger, Lucarelli, Rabbai, American Qt, Peress (cond. from harpsichord).

John Corigliano's highly imaginative *Oboe concerto* opens ingeniously with the orchestra tuning up, and the music springs fairly naturally from this familiar aleatory pattern of sound. The performance here is outstanding, expert and spontaneous and very well recorded. The three *Folksong settings* are for tenor and flute; Robert White's headily distinctive light tenor gives much pleasure, as he does in the Dylan Thomas setting, *Poem in October.*

Piano concerto.
(Y/B) *** Koch 3-7250-2 [id.]. Alain Lefevre, Pacific SO, Carl St Clair -TICHELI: *Postcard* etc. ***

Dating from 1968, long before Corigliano's Aids-inspired *Symphony No. 1* and the brilliantly successful Met. opera, *The Ghosts of Versailles*, this *Piano concerto* communicates with similar immediacy. Starting with an expansive Allegro, it is in four sharply contrasted movements. Here, as later, Corigliano unashamedly uses a freely eclectic style, positive and energetic, with Gershwin and jazz among the influences, and with the lyrical slow movement bringing repose. It is well coupled with two similarly unproblematic works by Frank Ticheli, composer-in-residence to this orchestra of musicians from the film studios. First-rate performances and sound.

Symphony No. 1.
*** Erato/Warner Dig. 2292 45601-2 [id.]. Stephen Hough, John Sharp, Chicago SO, Barenboim.

This fine, deeply felt work is an elegy for friends of the composer, three in particular who have died of Aids. The symphony opens with an expression of rage while the brief finale is an epilogue quoting all three movements. Barenboim and the Chicago orchestra bring out the full passionate intensity of the inspiration in this live recording. The sound is immediate and full-bodied, giving full scope to the colourful and often spectacular orchestral writing. This is well worth exploring and very rewarding.

Troubadours (variations for guitar and orchestra).
(N) **(*) Virgin/EMI Dig. CDC5 55083-2 [id.]. Sharon Isbin, St Paul CO, Hugo Wolff – SCHWANT-NER: *From afar* **; FOSS: *American landscapes.* ***

Corigliano's very free set of variations is an elliptical work, beginning and ending in the mists of time. Two-thirds of the basic theme is Corigliano's own, but the final cadence comes from an actual twelfth-century song. When the troubadours enter, they do so boisterously to dance rhythms from a raucously exuberant 'shawm band', and it has to be said that the climax becomes rather ugly. However, the work's reflective passages, notably the melancholy final section, communicate readily. Like the companion *Fantasy* by Joseph Schwantner, this is a piece that undoubtedly makes a strong impression in live performance, although the playing and recording by its dedicatee do it full justice.

Cornysh, William (c. 1468–1523)

Adieu, adieu my heartes lust; Adieu, courage; Ah Robin; Ave Maria, mater Dei; Gaude, virgo, mater Christi; Magnificat; Salve regina; Stabat Mater; Woefully arrayed.
⊛ *** Gimell Dig. CDGIM 014; *1585T-14* [id.]. Tallis Scholars, Phillips.

Cornysh's music is quite unlike much other polyphony of the time and is florid, wild, complex and, at times, grave. The Tallis Scholars give a magnificent, totally committed account of these glorious pieces – as usual their attack, ensemble and true intonation and blend are remarkable. Excellent recording.

Corrette, Michel (1709–95)

6 Organ concertos, Op. 26.
(b) *** HM HMA 190 5148 [id.]. René Saorgin (organ of L'Eglise de l'Escarène, Nice), Bar. Ens., Gilbert Bezzina.

These lively and amiable concertos are here given admirably spirited and buoyant performances, splendidly recorded using period instruments. The orchestral detail is well observed and René Saorgin plays vividly on an attractive organ. Michel Corrette's invention has genuine spontaneity and this makes an enjoyable collection to dip into, though not to play all at one go.

Sonatas: for bassoon and continuo: in F & G (Les Délices de la Solitude), Op. 20/1 & 5; for flute and continuo: in E min.; D min., Op. 13/2 & 4; for harpsichord and flute in E min., Op. 15/4; for oboe and continuo in D min. (L'école d'Orphée). Suite for recorder and continuo in C min. (from Les Pièces, Op. 5). (Harpsichord): Les Amusements du Parnasse: La Furstemberg and variations; Le Sabotier Hollandois and variations; Première Livre de Pièces de Clavecin: Suite in D (complete); Suite No. 3 (Les Etoiles): Rondeau, Op. 12 (both from Op. 12).
(n) *** Mer. Dig. CDE 84325 [id.]. Paul Carroll, David Rowland, Sally Civil.

These attractive instrumental works from a minor French composer, born in Rouen in 1709, were written with an eye to maximum sales, so his designated instrumentation was interchangeable. The rather agreeable *Oboe sonata*, for instance, comes from *L'école d'Orphée*, a violin tutor, and the Op. 5 *Pièces*, from which the *Suite for recorder and continuo* is taken, were primarily designated for the musette (an aristocratic set of bagpipes). However, the composer suggested a whole range of alternatives (including vielle, oboe and viola d'amore) as well as the recorder, which they suit rather well. The versatile and expert Paul Carroll has mastered all the baroque instruments featured in these works and plays each of them with spirit and character (his oboe and bassoon timbres are particularly striking). But it is perhaps his harpsichord music for which Corrette is best remembered – and justly so. The *D major Suite* is strikingly inventive and the final two movements, the *Faste milannoise* and the hurdy-gurdy-like *Bal*, are real lollipops. David Rowland plays them on excellent modern copies of two different period instruments, and he is beautifully recorded. The instrumental works, too, are naturally balanced. An entertaining 73 minutes – but not necessarily to be taken all at once.

Couperin, François (1668–1733)

L'apothéose de Corelli; L'apothéose de Lully; Concert 'dans le goût théâtral'.
*** Erato/Warner Dig. 4509 99761-2 [id.]. Bury, Wilcock, Campbell, E. Bar. Soloists, Gardiner.

Gardiner here presents an ideal Couperin coupling in superb performances, bringing together the two great instrumental works, both called apothéoses, celebrating first Corelli and then, even more grandly, Lully. The disc is completed with a fine *Concerto 'in the theatrical style'*, in which the instrumentation has been realized by Peter Holman. First-rate sound.

Concerts Royaux Nos. 1 in G; 2 in D; 3 in A; 4 in E min.
*** ASV Gaudeamus CDGAU 101 [id.]. Trio Sonnerie.
(b) ** HM HMA 190 1151 [id.]. Robert Claire, Davitt Moroney, Jaap ter Linden, Janet See.

The *Concerts Royaux* can be performed in a variety of forms. The Trio Sonnerie give them in the most economical fashion (violin, viola da gamba and harpsichord) and the contribution of all three musicians is unfailingly imaginative. Excellent recording.

Davitt Moroney and his colleagues opt for two flutes, bass viol and harpsichord in the *Concerts Royaux*. This was music intended for Louis XIV's diversion of a Sunday evening, and here the effect is just a shade wan. There is a certain uniformity of colour, and in addition their playing is just a little wanting in panache and vitality.

Les Goûts-réunis: Nouveaux concerts Nos. 8; 9 (Ritratto dell'amore).
(m) **(*) HM/BMG GD 71968. Kuijken Ens.

The Kuijken Ensemble use original instruments, and one only has to sample the *Overture* of the *Eighth Concert* to find how attractive is their sound-world. The *Ninth Concert* has a linking programme and its eight dance movements contrast the many facets of love.

Les Nations (complete).
(m) *** Teldec/Warner 4509 93689-2 (2) Quadro Amsterdam (Frans Brüggen, Jaap Schröder, Anner Bysma, Gustav Leonhardt).

Couperin's *Les Nations*, published in 1726, divides into four sections: *La Françoise*, *L'Espagnole* (where there is a touch of flamenco influence in the *Sonata*), *L'Impériale* and *La Piémontoise*, but the music itself is not really programmatic, though the invention is full of diversity and colour. The performance by the starry Quadro Amsterdam, using period instruments without any of those excesses of phrasing which sometimes affect much so-called 'authentic' music-making, is another of the treasures of the mid-1960s Telefunken Das Alte Werk catalogue. They are alive, elegant, polished and thoroughly idiomatic. Moreover they are beautifully recorded. Highly recommended.

L'apothéose de Lulli; La Parnasse ou l'apothéose de Corelli; Pièces de clavecin: 9e Ordre: Allemande à deux. 14e Ordre: La Juilliet. 15e Ordre: Muséte de Choisi; Muséte de Taverni. 16e Ordre: La Létiville.
*** HM Dig. HMC 901269 [id.]. William Christie, Christophe Rousset (harpsichords).

Couperin's preface explains that he himself played these works on two harpsichords with members of his family and pupils; and William Christie has chosen to follow his example. Surprisingly, they sound rather more exciting in this form than in the more familiar instrumental versions, largely perhaps because of the sheer sparkle and vitality of these performers.

L'Art de toucher le clavecin: Preludes in A, C, B flat, D min., E flat, F, & G min. L'Arlequine; Les Baricades mistérieuses; Suites in C min., Ordre 3; B min., Ordre 8; Suite in A.
⚅ *** HM/BMG Dig. RD77219 [77219-2-RC]. Skip Sempé (harpsichord).

This is playing of real insight and flair, by far the best Couperin recital to have appeared in recent years and one of the most imaginative. There is expressive freedom about this playing and a poetic vitality that will persuade those who have hitherto found it difficult to come to terms with eighteenth-century French keyboard music. Sempé plays a modern copy by Bruce Kennedy of a Ruckers-Taskin and is very well recorded.

Harpsichord suites, Book 1, Ordres 1–5.
(Y/B) *** HM Dig. HMC 901450/2 [id.]. Christophe Rousset (harpsichord).

(i) *Harpsichord suites, Book 2, Ordres 6–12. L'Art de toucher le clavecin.*
(Y/B) *** HM Dig. HMC 901447/9 [id.]. Christophe Rousset (harpsichord), (i) with William Christie.

Harpsichord suites, Book 3, Ordres 13–19; Concerts royaux Nos. 1–4.
*** HM Dig. HMC 901442/4 [id.]. Christophe Rousset (with Blandine Rannou).

Harpsichord suites, Book 4, Ordres 20–27.
*** HM Dig. HMC 901445/6 [id.]. Christophe Rousset (with Kaori Uemura).

Rousset's distinguished series of the *Pièces de clavecin* includes *L'Art de toucher le clavecin*, using appropriate instruments. Apart from his inherent sense of style and feeling for decoration, Rousset well understands terms like *gracieusement, gayement, très tendrement* and *agréable, sans lenteur*, which he realizes to perfection. The *Concerts royaux* were of course written for a small chamber group, but the composer also encouraged their performance on the keyboard alone. In Book 2, Rousset is joined in certain pieces (the *Allemande* which opens Ordre No. 9 is for two harpsichords) by the estimable William Christie. In Book 3, he is joined in a very few items by Blandine Rannou on a second harpsichord; and in *La Croûilli ou la Couperinète*, from Book 4, Ordre 20, Kaori Uemura provides a vigorous basso continuo for the closing section. One could carp here and there about choice of tempi and so on, but Couperin wanted his music to be played creatively and flexibly, and that is what Christophe Rousset does – and with total spontaneity, too. He is beautifully recorded within an open but not too resonant acoustic, and this series can be welcomed very cordially indeed. Bargain hunters will note that Kenneth Gilbert's earlier, analogue set is still available and can be recommended as a much less expensive alternative.

Harpsichord suites, Book 1, Ordres 1–5.
(B) *** HM HMA 190351/3 [id.]. Kenneth Gilbert.

Harpsichord suites, Book 2, Ordres 6–12.
(B) *** HM HMA 190354/6 [id.]. Kenneth Gilbert.

Harpsichord suites, Book 3, Ordres 13–19.
(B) *** HM HMA 190357/8 [id.]. Kenneth Gilbert.

Harpsichord suites, Book 4, Ordres 20–27.
(B) *** HM HMA 190359/60 [id.]. Kenneth Gilbert.

Professor Gilbert's performances are scrupulous in matters of registration, following what is known of eighteenth-century practice in France. There is no want of expressive range throughout the series and

Gilbert plays with authority and taste – and, more to the point, artistry. He is also well served by the engineers.

Harpsichord suites, Book 2, Ordres 8 & 9.
*** Denon Dig. CO 1719 [id.]. Huguette Dreyfus (harpsichord).

Huguette Dreyfus plays with her customary authority and restraint. The *Huitième ordre* includes the famous *Passacaille* that Landowska played with such panache and flair. Excellent balance and recording.

Harpsichord suites, Book 2, Ordre 11; Book 3, Ordre 13.
*** Denon Dig. C37 7070 [id.]. Huguette Dreyfus (harpsichord).

For Ordres 11 and 13, Huguette Dreyfus plays a Dowd and shows herself yet again to have great understanding of this style. She is impeccably recorded.

3 Leçons de ténèbres.
(Y/B) (M) *** O-L 444 169-2 [id.]. Nelson, Kirkby, Ryan, Hogwood – MONTECLAIR: *Cantatas.* ***.
(B) *** HM HMA 190210 [id.]. Deller, Todd, Perulli, Chapuis.

The *Trois leçons de ténèbres* were written for performance on Good Friday. Couperin's settings had female voices in mind, and he could scarcely have hoped for more ethereal timbres than those of Judith Nelson and Emma Kirkby. Purity and restraint rather than warmth and humanity are the keynote of these performances, but few are likely to complain of the results. The recordings are admirably vivid, and the *Easter motet* is another attraction. But what makes this reissue especially appealing is the additional coupling of two delightful cantatas by Michel Pignolet de Montéclair, a bass viol player at the Opéra who was also employed to teach Couperin's daughters. His setting of the story of *Pan et Syrinx* is particularly graphic, both lyrically and dramatically.

   Deller's account of the *Trois Leçons* is inevitably less authentic, since this music, written for a convent, did not envisage performances by male voices. In every other respect, however, it has a wonderful authenticity of feeling and a blend of scholarship and artistry that gives it a special claim on the attention of collectors.

Motets: *Domine salvum fac regem; Jacunda vox ecclesiae; Laetentur coeli; Lauda Sion salvatorem; Magnificat; O misterium ineffabile; Regina coeli; Tantum ergo sacramentum; Venite exultemus Domine; Victoria! Christo resurgenti.*
(B) *** HM HMA 1901150 [id.]. Feldman, Poulenard, Reinhart, Linden, Moroney.

The motets on this record cover a wider spectrum of feeling and range of expressive devices than might at first be imagined. The performances are eminently acceptable, with some particularly good singing from Jill Feldman; the recording is made in a spacious and warm acoustic.

Couperin, Louis (c. 1626–61)

Suites de pièces and complete harpsichord music.
(B) *** HM 901124/27 (4) [id.]. Davitt Moroney (harpsichord).

Louis Couperin was a pupil of Chambonnières, and his keyboard output comprises enough individual dance pieces to make sixteen suites, as well as other pieces. This comprehensive survey makes out a strong case for this repertoire; readers expecting it to be greatly inferior in quality to the clavecin music of François-le-Grand will be pleasantly surprised – though, of course, there is less of the poetic fantasy of his nephew at his best. The recording is eminently truthful and the CD transfer wholly natural.

Harpsichord suites: in A min.; in C; in F; Pavane in F sharp min.
(M) *** HM/BMG GD 77058 [77058-2-RG]. Gustav Leonhardt (harpsichord).

Leonhardt has such subtlety and panache that he makes the most of the grandeur and refinement of this music to whose sensibility he seems wholly attuned. This is the best introduction to Louis Couperin's keyboard suites now before the public.

Harpsichord suites: in A min.; C; D; F (including Le Tombeau de M. de Blancrocher).
(Y/B) (BB) *** Naxos Dig. 8.550922 [id.]. Laurence Cummings.

Harpsichord suites: in C min.; D min.; F.
(Y/B) (M) **(*) O-L Dig. 443 189-2 [id.]. Christopher Hogwood (harpsichord).

Laurence Cummings was an organ scholar at Christ Church, Oxford, and he seems quite as much at home in this repertoire as Hogwood. He plays a modern copy of a Ruckers, which is very well recorded by Naxos. His selection is more generous than Hogwood's and he arranges his own groupings. His decoration is convincing and he plays with more spontaneity and flair than his illustrious colleague. The CD offers some 75 minutes of music and is one of Naxos's best bargains.

Christopher Hogwood plays a Couchet harpsichord of 1646. Louis Couperin's teacher, Chambonnières, used such an instrument and, observed not too closely in a pleasing acoustic, it sounds beautiful. Hogwood plays expertly and these performances give pleasure. The *Tombeau de Monsieur de Blancrocher* which ends the *F major Suite* and the *Chaconne la bergeronette* which closes the *C minor* are characteristic of his style, thoughtful and with unexaggerated rubato, but here, as in the more lively movements, a little more panache would have been welcome.

Coward, Noël (1899–1973)

After the ball: I knew that you would be my love. Bitter Sweet: I'll see you again; Zigeuner. Conversation piece: I'll follow my secret heart; Never more; Melanie's aria (sung in French); *Charming. Operette: Dearest love; Where are the songs we sung? Countess Mitzi. Pacific 1860: Bright was the day; This is a changing world.*
(Y/B) (BB) *** Belart 450 014-2. Dame Joan Sutherland, Noël Coward, soloists, Ch. & O, Richard Bonynge.

It is fairly easy to criticize this disc on the grounds that a full operatic style does not always suit Noël Coward and that Joan Sutherland does not always get right inside the characters Coward created (she tries very hard with Countess Mitzi). But all this is swept aside in the sheer pleasure of hearing such a wonderful voice sing such delightful music. Dame Joan Sutherland's tonal lustre and sense of line in *I'll see you again* are incomparable, as is her display of fireworks in *Zigeuner*, and her gentle delicacy in *I knew that you would be my love*, with its ravishing final cadence. Noël Coward's own vocal contributions are quite small but they magically create atmosphere, and Richard Bonynge's affectionate and stylish conducting is a model.

Cowell, Henry (1897–1965)

Hymn and fuguing tune No. 10 for oboe and strings.
*** Argo 417 818-2 [id.]. Nicklin, ASMF, Marriner – BARBER: *Adagio;* COPLAND: *Quiet city;* CRESTON: *Rumor;* IVES: *Symphony No. 3.* ***

This likeable *Hymn and fuguing tune*, by a composer otherwise little known, is well worth having and is expertly played and recorded here. The digital remastering has slightly clarified an already excellent recording.

Cowen, Frederick (1852–1935)

Symphony No. 3 in C min. (Scandinavian); The Butterfly's ball: concert overture; Indian rhapsody.
** Marco Polo Dig. 8.220308 [id.]. Czechoslovak State PO (Košice), Adrian Leaper.

The *Symphony No. 3* (1880) shows (to borrow Hanslick's judgement) 'good schooling, a lively sense of tone painting and much skill in orchestration, if not striking originality'. But what Cowen lacks in individuality he makes up for in natural musicianship and charm. His best-known work is the *Concert overture, The Butterfly's ball* (1901), which is scored with Mendelssohnian delicacy and skill. The *Indian rhapsody* (1903) with its naïve orientalisms carries a good deal less conviction. The performances are eminently lively. The recording is pleasingly reverberant but somewhat lacking in body.

Creston, Paul (born 1906)

A Rumor.
*** Argo 417 818-2 [id.]. ASMF, Marriner – BARBER: *Adagio;* COPLAND: *Quiet city;* COWELL: *Hymn;* IVES: *Symphony No. 3.* ***

A Rumor is a witty and engaging piece and is played here with plenty of character by the Academy under Sir Neville Marriner. It completes a thoroughly rewarding and approachable disc of twentieth-century American music that deserves the widest currency. The sound is first class.

Symphony No. 2, Op. 35.
(N) *** Chandos Dig. CHAN 9390. Detroit SO, Järvi – IVES: *Symphony No. 2.* ***

Symphony No. 2, Op. 35; Corinthians XIII, Op. 82; Walt Whitman, Op. 53.
*** Koch Dig. 37036-2 or KI 7036 [id.]. Krakow PO, David Amos.

Paul Creston's *Second* is one of the most inventive of American symphonies and it is good to see it getting the attention it deserves. It has lush orchestral textures and a refreshing, exhilarating vitality. This well-recorded and excellently performed version makes a viable first choice and can be recommended to all with an interest in the American symphony.

Creston's musical language is strongly influenced by French music. His orchestration is both opulent and expert, though some climaxes are overblown. The *Second Symphony* (1944) opens rather like a Roy Harris symphony but subsequently becomes highly exotic in the manner of a Roussel or a Villa-Lobos, with infectiously vital rhythms and lush textures. It is played with real enthusiasm and affection by these Polish forces and is very well recorded, even though the sound could do with greater transparency in the upper range. This should enjoy wide appeal.

Symphony No. 3 (Three Mysteries), Op. 48; Invocation and Dance; Out of the cradle; Partita for flute, violin and strings.
*** Delos Dig. DEL 3114 [id.]. Seattle SO, Schwarz.

At last it would seem that Paul Creston is coming in from the cold. A generation force-fed on Elliott Carter and Milton Babbitt is now beginning to rediscover the American symphonic tradition of the 1940s and '50s. True, Creston's work is uneven, but the idiom is approachable, nowhere more so than in the *Third Symphony*, a work of strong invention and lyrical impulse. Incidentally, the *Three Mysteries* of the subtitle allude to the Nativity, Crucifixion and Resurrection. Gerard Schwarz gives a fervent and committed account, drawing excellent playing from his Seattle orchestra, and completely supersedes the earlier account. The exhilarating *Invocation and Dance*, the *Partita*, which is somewhat more austere, and the less successful *Out of the cradle*, benefit not only from Schwarz's committed advocacy but also from superb engineering. The sound is in the demonstration class.

String quartet, Op. 8.
(Y/B) (***) Testament mono SBT 1053 [id.]. Hollywood Qt – DEBUSSY: *Danse sacrée* etc. RAVEL: *Intro & allegro;* TURINA: *La Oración del torero;* VILLA-LOBOS: *Quartet No. 6.* (***)

The *String quartet*, Op. 8, is a pleasing, well-fashioned piece, slightly Gallic in feeling but not possessed of strong individuality. The *Adagio* is perhaps the most memorable of the four movements, and its argument unfolds with eloquence. It could not be better served than it is by the Hollywood Quartet, recorded in 1953: the playing is stunning, and the recording, too, is very good for its period, even if the acoustic is on the dry side.

Crusell, Bernhard (1775–1838)

Clarinet concertos Nos. 1 in E flat, Op. 1; 2 in F min., Op. 5; 3 in E flat, Op. 11.
⊛ *** ASV Dig. CDDCA 784 [id.]. Emma Johnson, RPO/ECO, Herbig; Groves; or Schwarz.
*** Virgin/EMI Dig. VC7 59287-2 [id.]. Antony Pay, O of Age of Enlightenment.
*** Hyperion CDA 66708 [id.]. Thea King, LSO, Alun Francis.

Crusell, born in Finland but working in Stockholm most of his career, was himself a clarinettist and these delightful concertos demonstrate his complete understanding of the instrument. There are echoes of Mozart, Weber and Rossini in the music, with a hint of Beethoven.

No one brings out the fun in the writing quite as infectiously as Emma Johnson, and this generous recoupling (74 minutes) bringing all three concertos together is a delight. With well-structured first movements, sensuous slow movements and exuberant finales, Johnson establishes her disc as a first choice above all others.

Pay's is the first period performance of these works. As well as directing the Orchestra of the Age of Enlightenment himself, he uses a reproduction of a nine-key clarinet as made around 1810 by Heinrich Grenser; Crusell himself is known to have used a ten-key Grenser clarinet. The slight edginess of the sound goes well with Pay's preference for fastish – often very fast – speeds which yet never get in the way of his imaginative rhythmic pointing. The results in outer movements are exhilarating, with phenomenal articulation of rapid passage-work, while slow movements have a flowing songfulness that is comparably persuasive. The Virgin recording, made at Abbey Road studio, is clear, well balanced and atmospheric.

Thea King with her beautiful, liquid tone also makes an outstanding soloist. Her approach is often more serious, especially in the *Second Concerto*, where she brings out the Beethovenian character of the first movement, while the *Andante pastorale* slow movement is played with the widest range of tone-colour. Throughout, she is well accompanied by Alun Francis; and the resonant Hyperion recording, with the soloist balanced forward, emphasizes the feeling of added gravitas.

Clarinet concerto No. 1 in E flat, Op. 1.
*** ASV Dig. CDDCA 763 [id.]. Emma Johnson, RPO, Herbig – KOZELUCH; KROMMER: *Concertos.* ***

Even though many collectors may prefer the CD containing all three of the Crusell concertos, Emma Johnson's version of the *First Clarinet concerto* makes a highly attractive compilation with lesser-known but enticing works by Kozeluch and Krommer, especially when her warm-toned playing is magnetically individual, and the ASV recording brings out the great range of sensuously beautiful tone-colours she produces.

Clarinet concerto No. 2 in F min., Op. 5.
❀ *** ASV Dig. CDDCA 559 [id.]. Emma Johnson, ECO, Groves – BAERMANN: *Adagio;* ROSSINI: *Introduction, theme and variations;* WEBER: *Concertino.* ***

Crusell's *Second Clarinet concerto* made Emma Johnson a star, and in return she put Crusell's engagingly lightweight piece firmly on the map. Her delectably spontaneous performance is now caught on the wing and this recording sounds very like a live occasion.

Concertino for bassoon and orchestra in B flat; Introduction et air suédois for clarinet and orchestra, Op. 12; Sinfonia concertante for clarinet, horn, bassoon and orchestra, Op. 3.
*** BIS Dig. BIS CD 495 [id.]. Hara, Korsimaa-Hursti, Lanski-Otto, Tapiola Sinf., Vänskä.

The most substantial piece here is the *Sinfonia concertante for clarinet, horn, bassoon and orchestra*. The finale is a set of variations on a chorus from Cherubini's opera, *Les deux journées*. The much later *Concertino for bassoon and orchestra* is an altogether delightful piece, which quotes at one point from Boïeldieu. It is played with appropriate freshness and virtuosity by László Hara. The *Introduction et air suédois for clarinet and orchestra* is nicely done by Anna-Maija Korsimaa-Hursti. The Tapiola Sinfonietta, the orchestra of Esspoo, play with enthusiasm and spirit for Osmo Vänskä, and the BIS recording has lightness, presence and body.

Clarinet quartets Nos. 1 in E flat, Op. 2; 2 in C min., Op. 4; 3 in D, Op. 7.
*** Hyperion CDA 66077 [id.]. Thea King, Allegri Qt (members).

These are captivatingly sunny works, given superb performances, vivacious and warmly sympathetic. Thea King's tone is positively luscious, as recorded, and the sound is generally excellent. The CD transfer is highly successful.

Divertimento in C, Op. 9.
*** Hyperion CDA 66143 [id.]. Francis, Allegri Qt – KREUTZER: *Grand quintet;* REICHA: *Quintet.* ***

No one wanting this slight but charming piece and its companions need look further than this nicely played and well-recorded account.

Cui, César (1835–1918)

(i) *Suite concertante* (for violin & orchestra), *Op. 25. Suite miniature No. 1, Op. 20; Suite No. 3 (In modo populari), Op. 43.*
**(*) Marco Polo Dig. 8.220308 [id.]. (i) Nishizaki; Hong Kong PO, Schermerhorn.

These pieces have a faded period charm that is very appealing (try the *Petite Marche* and the equally likeable *Impromptu à la Schumann* from the *Suite miniature*) and are very well played by the Hong Kong Philharmonic. Takako Nishizaki is the expert soloist in the *Suite concertante*. An interesting issue that fills a gap in the repertoire, and very decently recorded too.

Curzon, Frederick (1899–1973)

The Boulevardier; Bravada (Paso doble); Capricante (Spanish caprice); Cascade (Waltz); Galavant; In Malaga (Spanish suite); Punchinello: Miniature overture; Pasquinade; La Peineta; Robin Hood suite; (i) *Saltarello for piano and orchestra; Simionetta (Serenade).*

*** Marco Polo Dig. 8.223425 [id.]. (i) Silvia Cápová; Slovak RSO (Bratislava), Leaper.

The best-known piece here is *Dance of an ostracised imp*, a droll little scherzando, much played on the radio during the Second World War. But the *Galavant* is hardly less piquant and charming, the delicious *Punchinello* sparkles with miniature vitality, and the *Simionetta* serenade is sleekly beguiling. Curzon liked to write mock Spanishry, and several pieces here have such a Mediterranean influence. Yet their slight elegance and economical scoring come from cooler climes farther north. Both *In Malaga* and the jolly *Robin Hood suite* are more frequently heard on the (military) bandstand, but their delicate central movements gain much from the more subtle orchestral scoring. The performances throughout are played with the finesse and light touch we expect from this fine Slovak series, so ably and sympathetically conducted by Adrian Leaper. The recording is admirable.

Czerny, Karl (1791–1857)

Andante e polacca in E for horn and piano, Op. posth.; 3 Fantasias brillantes on themes of Schubert for horn and piano, Op. 339.
*** Etcetera Dig. KTC 1121 [id.]. Barry Tuckwell, David Blumenthal.

The *Andante and polacca* is a characteristically ripe piece which is enjoyable enough when played with such aplomb, but the real interest of this recital lies with the three Schubertian *Fantasias*. In effect they are pot-pourris of favourite Schubert songs, with the horn given the vocal melody against a background of glittering piano cascades. The performances could hardly be bettered; if you want Schubert Lieder without the words, then the present recording is most pleasing, the resonance flattering to both artists but the focus realistically firm.

Damase, Jean-Michel (born 1928)

Quintet for flute, harp, violin, viola & cello (1948); Sonata for flute & harp (1964); Trio for flute, harp & cello (1946); Variations 'Early Music' for flute & harp (1980).
*** ASV Dig. CDDCA 898 [id.]. Noakes, Tingay, Friedman, Atkins, Szucs.

Jean-Michel Damase was a pupil of Alfred Cortot and Henri Büsser, and his chamber music (and in particular the *Trio for flute, harp and cello* and the *Quintet*) has a fluent, cool charm which will delight many listeners; there is little substance but it is beautifully fashioned and makes some very pleasing sounds. Those coming to it for the first time will find it very attractive. Very Gallic, with touches of Poulenc without his harmonic subtlety. It is nicely played and very well recorded.

Danzi, Franz (1763–1826)

Flute concertos Nos. 1 in G, Op. 30; 2 in D min., Op. 31; 3 in D min., Op. 42; 4 in D, Op. 43.
*** Orfeo Dig. C 00381-2H [id.]. András Adorján, Munich CO, Stadlmair.

Danzi wrote four flute concertos, all included here, which suggest a style midway between eighteenth-century classicism and the more romantic manner of Weber. All four performances by András Adorján and Stadlmair with his Munich Chamber Orchestra are impeccably stylish and have plenty of vitality, and the recording is both full and transparent and is well balanced.

(i) *Piano quintet in F, Op. 53. Wind quintets, Op. 67/1–3.*
*** BIS Dig. CD 539 [id.]. (i) Love Derwinger; BPO Wind Qt.

Danzi was one of the first composers to cultivate the wind quintet. These are light, diverting pieces of no great musical substance but when played with such distinction and recorded with such great clarity and presence they offer unexpected pleasure. The *Piano quintet*, in which the Berlin quintet are joined by the young Swedish pianist, Love Derwinger, is also pretty empty-headed but rather delightful all the same.

Da Ponte, Lorenzo (1749–1838)

L'ape musicale.
**(*) Nuova Era Dig. 6845/6 (2). Scarabelli, Matteuzzi, Dara, Comencini, Teatro la Fenice Ch. & O, Vittorio Parisi.

This greatest of librettists was no composer, but he was musical enough to devise a pasticcio like *L'ape musicale* ('The musical bee') from the works of others, notably Rossini and Mozart. It makes a delightful if offbeat entertainment, generally well sung in a lively performance. The first Act – full of Rossinian passages one keeps recognizing – leads up to a complete performance of Tamino's aria, *Dies Bildnis*, sung in German at the end of the Act. Similarly, Act II culminates in an adapted version of the final cabaletta from Rossini's *Cenerentola*. The sound is dry, with the voices slightly distanced. The stage and audience noises hardly detract from the fun of the performance.

Dawson, William (1899–1990)

Negro Folk Symphony.
*** Chandos Dig. CHAN 9226 [id.]. Detroit SO, Neeme Järvi – STILL: *Symphony No. 2;* ELLINGTON: *Harlem.* ***

William Dawson began life the son of a poor Alabama labourer, yet he worked his way up to become Director of Music at the Tuskegee Institute. His *Negro Folk Symphony* is designed to combine European influences and Negro folk themes. All three movements are chimerical. The first is rhapsodic with a scherzando character, interrupted by lyrical interludes. It has plenty of energy and ideas, but they are inclined to run away with their composer. The central movement is basically lyrical and passionate, opening and closing with a marching theme. The finale becomes energetic at the very close. Järvi has the advantage of excellent orchestral playing and first-class Chandos sound.

Debussy, Claude (1862–1918)

Complete orchestral music (as below).
(N) (M) *** Chandos Dig. CHAN 7019 (4) [id.]. Soloists, Ulster O, Yan Pascal Tortelier.

La boîte à joujoux; Children's corner (orch. Caplet); *Danse (Tarantelle styrienne,* orch. Ravel); *Marche écossaise sur un thème populaire; Petite suite* (orch. Büsser).
(N) (M) *** Chandos Dig. CHAN 7017 [id.]. Ulster O, Y. P. Tortelier.

(i) *Fantaisie for piano and orchestra;* (ii) *Danse sacrée et danse profane for harp and strings; L'Isle joyeuse* (orch. Molinari); (iii) *La plus que lente;* (iv) *Première rapsodie for clarinet and orchestra;* (v) *Rapsodie for alto saxophone and orchestra* (orch. Roger-Ducasse); *Sarabande* (orch.Ravel); *Suite bergamasque: Clair de lune* (orch. Caplet).
(N) (M) *** Chandos Dig. CHAN 7018 [id.]. Ulster O, Y. P. Tortelier, with (i) Anne Queffélec; (ii) Rachel Masters; (iii) Derek Bell (cimbalom); (iv) Christopher King; (v) Gerard McChrystal.

Images; Jeux; Khamma.
(N) (M) **(*) Chandos Dig. CHAN 7016 [id.]. Ulster O, Y. P. Tortelier.

La Mer; Nocturnes; Printemps; Prélude à l'après-midi d'un faune.
(N) ** Chandos Dig. CHAN 7015 [id.]. Ulster O, Y. P. Tortelier.

As can be seen, Chandos have now assembled Debussy's orchestral music (previously coupled with Ravel) in an upper-mid-priced box in recordings which generally represent the state of the art. There are excellent soloists in the concertante works. The subtlety and atmosphere of *La boîte à joujoux* are captured splendidly, and the concertante works are equally sensitive. Not all the performances are a first choice; *Jeux, La Mer* and *Printemps* spring to mind: Tortelier's *La Mer* is taut and well held together, though his generally brisk tempi do not enhance the atmosphere; and *Printemps,* though intelligently shaped, is not as evocative and relaxed as the finest versions on disc. The shorter works come off particularly well. Debussy himself orchestrated *La plus que lente* and he explained to his publisher, tongue in cheek, that the opening cimbalom solo was added because 'It's impossible to begin the same way in a brasserie as in a salon: you absolutely need a few bars' preparation!' It is a charmingly inconsequential performance with the cimbalom lacing the texture like a continuo. At present these four CDs are available only in a box at a special price; when they become available separately, CHAN 7017 and 7018 will prove very desirable indeed.

2 Arabesques (orch. Mouton); (i) *La cathédrale engloutie* (orch. Stokowski); *La mer; Petite suite* (orch. Henri Büsser); *Pagodes* (orch. Grainger). *Première rapsodie for clarinet and orchestra; Suite bergamasque: Clair de lune* (orch. Caplet).
(Y/B) *** Cala Dig. CACD 1001 [id.]. (i) James Campbell; Philh. O, Geoffrey Simon.

Geoffrey Simon's warm, urgent reading of *La Mer,* very well recorded, comes in coupling with six items originally involving piano. Debussy did his own arrangement of the *Clarinet rhapsody* and approved André Caplet's arrangement of *Clair de lune* as well as Henri Büsser's of the *Petite suite.* Stokowski's freely imagined orchestral version of *La cathédrale engloutie* is effectively opulent, and the most fascinating instrumentation of all comes in Percy Grainger's transcription of *Pagodes*, with an elaborate percussion section simulating a Balinese gamelan.

(i) *Berceuse héroïque;* (ii; iii) *Danses sacrée et profane* (for harp and strings); (ii) *Images; Jeux; Marche écossaise; La Mer;* (ii; iv) *Nocturnes;* (ii) *Prélude à l'après-midi d'un faune;* (ii; v) *Première rapsodie for clarinet and orchestra.*

✿ (B) *** Ph. Duo 438 742-2 (2) [id.]. Concg. O, (i) Eduard van Beinum; (ii) Bernard Haitink; with (iii) Vera Badings; (iv) women's Ch. of Coll. Mus.; (v) George Pieterson.

This must now rank as the finest Debussy collection in the CD catalogue and one of the greatest bargains that the gramophone has to offer at present – all for the cost of a single premium-priced CD. Although the programme as a whole is directed by Haitink, it is good that his distinguished predecessor, Eduard van Beinum, is remembered by the opening *Berceuse héroïque*, played with great delicacy and a real sense of mystery, with the early stereo (1957) highly effective. For the *Danses sacrée et profane* Haitink takes over, with elegant playing from the harpist, Vera Badings, who is excellently balanced. Haitink's reading of *Images* is second to none and is beautifully played by the wonderful Dutch orchestra; the sonorities are delicate and the dynamic shadings sensitively observed. The superlative quality of the playing is matched by analogue recording of the very highest order. This applies equally to *Jeux*, where Haitink's reading is wonderfully expansive and sensitive to atmosphere and easily matches any recent rivals. Competition is even stiffer in the *Nocturnes*, but this great orchestra and conductor hold their own. The cruel vocal writing in *Sirènes* taxes the women of the Collegium Musicum Amstelodamense, but the choral balance is perfectly judged and few versions are quite as beguiling and seductive as Haitink's. His pacing of *La Mer* is comparable with Karajan's tempo in his 1964 recording. Both conductors pay close attention to dynamic gradations and both secure playing of great sensitivity and virtuosity from their respective orchestras; the *Dialogue du vent et de la mer* is both fast and exciting. An interesting point is that the brief fanfares that Debussy removed, eight bars before fig. 60, are here restored (as they were by Ansermet), but Haitink gives them to horns. The hazily sensuous *Prélude à l'après-midi d'un faune* and the undervalued *Clarinet rhapsody* are also played atmospherically, although the former is more overtly languorous in Karajan's hands. Again the Philips recording is truthful and natural, with beautiful perspectives and realistic colour, a marvellously refined sound.

La boîte à joujoux (orch. Caplet): complete.
(M) **(*) Erato/Warner 2292 45819-2 [id.]. Basle SO, Armin Jordan – DUKAS: *L'apprenti sorcier* etc. **(*)

Debussy's enchanting ballet score depicts adventures in a children's box of toys, and is full of delights. Armin Jordan's account is enjoyably atmospheric, helped by very good (1981) analogue recording. Although not distinguished by playing of the very first order, the performance is thoroughly idiomatic and sympathetic, and this is fair value at mid-price.

La boîte à joujoux; Jeux; Prélude à l'après-midi d'un faune.
*** Sony Dig. SK 48231 [id.]. LSO, Tilson Thomas.

La boîte à joujoux is ideally suited to Michael Tilson Thomas's talents. His account is second to none and has the right lightness of touch and wistful charm. Nor will collectors be disappointed with his account of *Jeux*, which is admirably unhurried and atmospheric, or his dreamy, languorous *Prélude à l'après-midi d'un faune*. The Sony recording is first class – very natural and spacious. *Jeux* does not displace the Haitink Duo version on Philips but can be recommended alongside it.

Children's corner; Danse (Tarantelle styrienne) (arr. Ravel); *Estampes: La soirée dans Grenade* (arr. Stokowski). *L'isle joyeuse; Nocturnes; Préludes: Bruyères; La fille aux cheveux de lin.*
*** Cala CACD 1002; *CAMC 1002* [id.]. Philh. O, Geoffrey Simon.

Geoffrey Simon's version of the three *Nocturnes* is colourful and atmospheric, with nothing vague in *Fêtes*. The orchestrations of piano music include Stokowski's vivid realization of *La soirée dans Grenade*, as well as Ravel's magical re-interpretation of *Danse* and André Caplet's sensitive orchestration of *Children's corner*. Full, vivid recorded sound.

Danse (Tarantelle styrienne); Sarabande (orch. Ravel).
(Y/B) (M) *** Virgin/EMI Dig. CUV5 61206-2 [id.]. Lausanne CO, Zedda – MILHAUD: *Création du monde;* PROKOFIEV: *Sinfonietta.* ***

Zedda's performances with the Lausanne Chamber Orchestra are neat and polished, full of character and well recorded. But it is the couplings that make this disc especially attractive.

Danse sacrée et danse profane (for harp and string orchestra).
(Y/B) (***) Testament mono SBT 1053 [id.]. Anne Mason Stockton, Concert Arts Strings, Slatkin – CRESTON: *Quartet;* RAVEL: *Intro & allegro;* TURINA: *La Oración del torero;* VILLA-LOBOS: *Quartet No. 6.* (***)

Felix Slatkin and his Hollywood colleagues give as atmospheric an account of the *Danse sacrée et danse profane* as any on record, and Anne Mason Stockton is the excellent harpist. The mono recording dates from 1951 but is uncommonly good. This comes as part of a remarkably fine anthology of Hollywood Quartet recordings.

(i) *Danses sacrée et profane; Images. Jeux; La Mer;* (ii) *Nocturnes; Printemps;* (iii) *Première rapsodie for clarinet and orchestra.*
(N) (M) **(*) Sony SM2K 68327 (2) [id.]. New Philh. O or (i) Cleveland O; Boulez; with (i) Alice Chalifoux; (ii) John Alldis Ch.; (iii) Gervase de Peyer.

These (originally CBS) Boulez recordings come from between 1966 and 1968 and won considerable critical acclaim when they first appeared. He secures consistently first-class playing from the New Philharmonia Orchestra, but in terms of atmosphere and poetry the results are uneven. *Jeux*, a work of seminal importance in Boulez's development, is given persuasively, and the *Images* are carefully shaped and balanced. This work, like the coolly distinctive *Danses sacrée et profane*, was recorded in Cleveland and gain from the ambience of Severance Hall, even if the balance is close (the harp assumes an importance equal to the strings). *La Mer* and the *Prélude à l'après-midi d'un faune* (which certainly does not lack passionate feeling) are a good deal better than some accounts, but *La Mer* cannot compare with the Karajan version from the same era in subtly conveying the briny marine atmosphere. Needless to say, Gervase de Peyer gives a distinguished account of the lovely *Clarinet rhapsody*, and the contribution of the John Alldis Choir to *Sirènes*, the third of the *Nocturnes*, is poised, even if the effect overall is cool rather than ethereal. But those who respond to Boulez's clarity of vision in this repertoire will find that the Sony engineers have made a marvellous job of these transfers to CD, maximizing the ambient effect and retaining the sharply defined detail – at Barking and Abbey Road as well as at Cleveland.

(i) *Fantaisie for piano and orchestra. 2 Arabesques; Ballade; Berceuse héroïque; Children's corner; Danse; Danse bohémienne; D'un cahier d'esquisses; Estampes; 12 Etudes; Hommage à Haydn; Images 1–2; L'isle joyeuse; Masques; Mazurka; Nocturne; Le petit nègre; La plus que lente; Pour le piano; Préludes, Books 1–2; Rêverie; Suite bergamasque; Valse romantique.*
(N) (M) (***) EMI mono CHS5 65855-2 (4) [CDHD 65855]. Walter Gieseking; (i) with Hessischen R. O, Schröder.

Gieseking's Debussy enjoyed legendary status in the 1930s and '40s, and EMI are to be congratulated for not only restoring to circulation the famous recordings he then made but also, in the case of the *Fantaisie*, even adding to them. The two sets of *Préludes* date from 1953 and 1954, as indeed do most of the recordings collected here. The earliest is *Children's corner* from 1951 when Walter Legge was pro- ducer. He and Geraint Jones between them were responsible for most of these records. The 1951 Frankfurt recording of the *Fantaisie* calls for some (albeit not great) tolerance, but the remaining performances sound better than ever. Some critics maintain that his pre-war Debussy was even finer, and some of these are to be found on Pearl and other specialist labels. Gieseking's artistry is too well known to need further exegesis or advocacy. As Bryce Morrison puts it in the accompanying notes, 'Deeply sensitive and personal, virtuosic in the truest sense, Gieseking's performances are quite without preen- ing mannerisms or idiosyncrasy and are, from this point of view alone, instantly recognizable.' A marvellous set which all pianists should investigate.

Images.
(Y/B) **(*) Sony Dig. SK 53284 [id.]. BPO, Levine – ELGAR: *Enigma variations.* **(*)
(N) (M) **(*) BBC Radio Classics 15656 91362 [id.]. BBC N. SO, Leppard – FAURE: *Ballade;* ROUS- SEL: *Symphony No. 3.* **(*)

Images; Jeux; Le Roi Lear (incidental music).
*** EMI Dig. CDC7 49947-2 [id.]. CBSO, Rattle.

Images; (i) Nocturnes.
*** Decca Dig. 425 502-2 [id.]. Montreal SO, Dutoit; (i) with chorus.

In *Images* Rattle is memorably atmospheric, while in *Jeux* he is just a touch more expansive than most rivals, and also more evocative, though he does not depart from the basic metronome markings. Haitink probably remains a first choice in this score, for he has atmosphere and a tauter grip on the music's flow, but Baudo's mid-priced EMI version (see below) should not be forgotten either. The *King Lear* excerpts sound splendid. First-rate recording, very vivid but beautifully balanced.

Dutoit is freer in his use of rubato, as well as in his warm, espressivo moulding of phrase. His sharp pointing of rhythm, as in the Spanish dances of *Ibéria* or the processional march in *Fêtes*, is also highly characteristic of his approach to French music. For those who like these impressionistic masterpieces to be presented in full colour, with a vivid feeling for atmosphere, this is an ideal choice.

This is hardly central repertory for the Berlin Philharmonic and it brings a degree of controversy among us. For EG, Levine draws thrilling, intense performances from the players, clear-cut rather than atmospheric, making an unexpected but exciting coupling. Unlike *Enigma*, this was recorded under studio conditions, offering sound as full and immediate as has ever been achieved in the Philharmonie. RL feels that the sonority produced by the Berlin Philharmonic is much changed since Karajan's days and, although these fine players are incapable of falling below a certain standard, the orchestra's corporate personality of the previous era is here replaced by a general-purpose sound such as any orchestra of the first rank might produce. The recording is very good indeed, with good definition and dynamic range.

Although Raymond Leppard is identified in the public mind with baroque music, his wide-ranging sympathies and his sheer musicianship can never be overlooked. The disc places *Rondes de printemps* between *Gigues* and *Ibéria*. He gets an evocative atmosphere in the former without relaxing a firm grip on the music's flow. The first movement of *Ibéria*, *Par les rues et par les chemins*, is splendidly crisp. A vital and imaginative performance, though one has to make allowances for a dryish acoustic (a presumably well-filled Free Trade Hall in Manchester). Allowances are well worth making, given the quality of the performance. Not a first choice in a strongly competitive field, but recommended and well worth the asking price, given the excellence of the couplings.

Images; (i) Nocturnes; Le Martye de Saint-Sébastien: 2 Fanfares and symphonic fragments; Printemps; Prélude à l'après-midi d'un faune; (ii) 3 Ballades de François Villon; (iii) La Damoiselle élue.
(B) **(*) DG Double Dig./Analogue 437 934-2 (2) [id.]. O de Paris, Daniel Barenboim; with (i) Ch. de l'O de Paris; (ii) Dietrich Fischer-Dieskau; (iii) Barbara Hendricks.

This DG Double set includes a 72-minute single-disc collection to which we awarded a Rosette in a previous volume; it included not only the early *Printemps* and the fragments from *Le Martyre de Saint-Sébastien* but also Barenboim's splendid set of *Nocturnes*. This performance, although highly individual in its control of tempo, has great fervour. Comparably in *Le Martyre* Barenboim succeeds in distilling an intense, rapt quality and brings to life its evocative atmosphere. He is no less persuasive in *Printemps*. This receives a performance as good as any in the catalogue. The 1977/8 recordings are spacious, rich in texture and well balanced, with good definition and range.

The second of the two CDs offers rather a mixed bag. The *3 Ballades de François Villon* are well sung by Dietrich Fischer-Dieskau and are valuable, as they are seldom heard in their orchestral form. Also welcome is *La Damoiselle élue*, which Barbara Hendricks sings with great sensitivity and beauty, and Barenboim draws playing of genuine atmosphere from the Orchestre de Paris. However, the other additions rather tend to dilute the appeal of this reissue. The *Prélude* brings languorous feeling which is undoubtedly telling, but there is nothing very special about the *Images*. Indeed the performances of both these works remain serviceable rather than distinguished. It is a pity these discs were paired!

Images; Printemps; Prélude à l'après-midi d'un faune.
**DG Dig. 435 766-2 [id.]. Cleveland O, Boulez.

Pierre Boulez has recorded all this repertoire before, though not with the success his DG engineers have achieved here. There is more atmosphere this time round in the *Gigues* and much to admire in the sheer beauty and finesse of the orchestral playing. *Printemps* is far more successful than before. For all that, one remains outside this music looking in admiringly; one is not drawn into its world in the same way as is the case with the greatest Debussy interpreters. Atmosphere, yes; but magic, no.

Images; (i) Première rapsodie for clarinet and orchestra.
(M) **(*) Sony SMK 47545 [id.]. (i) Stanley Drucker; NYPO, Bernstein – RAVEL: *Ma Mère l'Oye* etc.
***

Bernstein recorded Debussy's *Images* in 1958, and that early date shows in the upper strings, notably in the sparkling *Rondes de printemps*. But the playing has both unforced virtuosity and atmosphere, and *Gigues* has great character. In *Ibéria* the 'Perfumes of the night' are gently yet headily sensuous. This is the highlight of the performance, and at times the balmy fragrance of the nocturnal breeze is almost overwhelming, with the lead into *Le matin d'un jour de fête* exquisitely managed, bringing an explosion of colour and rhythmic energy. The *Clarinet rhapsody* is extremely well played here, and it is a pity that the recording – otherwise excellent – is still somewhat unflattering to the upper strings. Nevertheless these performances have great magnetism.

Images: Ibéria.
(❀) (M) *** RCA GD 60179 [60179-2-RG]. Chicago SO, Fritz Reiner – RAVEL: *Alborada* etc. *** (❀)

Fritz Reiner and the Chicago orchestra give a reading that is immaculate in execution and magical in atmosphere. This marvellously evocative performance, and the Ravel with which it is coupled, should not be overlooked, for the recorded sound with its natural concert-hall balance is greatly improved in terms of body and definition. It is amazingly realistic even without considering its vintage.

Images: Ibéria. La Mer; Nocturnes: Nuages; Fêtes. Prélude à l'après-midi d'un faune.
(M) (**(*)) RCA mono GD 60265 [60265-2-RG]. NBC SO, Toscanini.

By emphasizing clarity, Toscanini with his electric intensity and sense of purpose consistently compels attention. One thinks of these supreme examples of musical impressionism, not as colour pieces but as masterly structures of great originality in purely musical terms. Clean, bright transfers.

Images: Ibéria. La Mer; Prélude à l'après-midi d'un faune.
(Y/B) (M) *** Mercury 434 343-2 [id.]. Detroit SO, Paray – RAVEL: *Ma Mère l'oye.* ***

Paray's collection, dating (unbelievably) from as early as 1955, gave us the first stereo recording of *La Mer* which is very exciting, balancing powerful evocation and firm overall control. The balance is slightly recessed, which provides plenty of atmosphere and a hazy warm sentience to the sound, adding luminosity to Paray's glowingly voluptuous account of *L'après-midi* with its ardently beautiful string climax. The recording was made in Detroit's Old Orchestra Hall, where the resonance adds great warmth but prevents sharply delineated detail. Yet for body, natural concert-hall balance and richness of orchestral colour there are few stereo recordings made in the mid-to late-1950s to match this.

Images: Ibéria. Prélude à l'après-midi d'un faune; (i) *La damoiselle élue.*
*** DG Dig. 423 103-2 [id.]. (i) Maria Ewing, Brigitte Balleys, London Symphony Ch.; LSO, Abbado.

Maria Ewing has never sounded sweeter on record, and Brigitte Balleys, a touch raw-toned on some notes, sings with attractive freshness. The purely orchestral works bring more urgent, even impulsive performances, marked by a warmly persuasive rubato style. Though balances are not always quite natural, the ambient warmth of All Saints', Tooting, seems ideal for the music, orchestral as well as vocal, and the effect is very vivid and glowing, without loss of detail.

Jeux; Le Martyre de Saint-Sébastien: symphonic fragments; La Mer; Prélude à l'après-midi d'un faune.
(N) **(*) Decca Dig. 430 240-2 [id.]. Montreal SO, Dutoit.

With vivid and immediate sound, Dutoit conducts taut and powerful readings of this generous selection from orchestral works. They are strong on purposeful strength rather than evocative magic, though few versions of *L'après-midi* match this one in the seductive beauty of Timothy Hutchins' flute.

Jeux; La Mer; (i) *Nocturnes;* (ii) *Première rapsodie for clarinet and orchestra.*
(Y/B) **(*) DG Dig. 439 896-2 [id.].(i) Cleveland O Ch.; (ii) Franklin Cohen; Cleveland O, Boulez.

Readers who normally respond to Boulez will probably like all these performances for the clarity of his readings, the meticulous balance and lucidity of his textures. At the same time there is a cool, neutral quality about these readings. The orchestra play well for him and the sound is admirably balanced; there is even some atmosphere at times, but little sense of mystery or discovery. The *Jeux* is no match for such rivals as Bernard Haitink or Simon Rattle; and in *La Mer* Karajan, Giulini, Reiner, Baudo and Ormandy are greatly to be preferred.

Jeux; La Mer; Nocturnes: Nuages; Fêtes (only); *Prélude à l'après-midi d'un faune.*
(M) **(*) Sony SMK 47546 [id.]. NYPO, Bernstein.

These recordings were made in the Manhattan Center in 1960/61 and show Bernstein at his most charismatic.There is plenty to admire in the orchestral playing and Bernstein has an undoubted feeling for atmosphere which he sustains even when, as in *La Mer*, the adrenalin is running very freely. Both *Jeux* and the *Prélude à l'après-midi d'un faune* have more than a whiff of voluptuousness and the phrasing in the *Prélude* is self-conscious in places. But the feeling throughout is of live music-making, and such performances would receive a standing ovation at a concert. The remastered sound is remarkably convincing. The diffuse recording – though woodwind are picked out by the microphones – adds to the evocative feeling, and the remastered sound is remarkably convincing, although the balance is contrived.

Jeux; La Mer; Prélude à l'après-midi d'un faune.
⊛ (M) *** EMI Dig. CD-EMX 9502; *TC-EMX 2090* [Ang. CDM 62012]. LPO, Baudo.

Serge Baudo's version of *La Mer* is first class. The recording is beautifully natural and expertly balanced. The same may be said for his lovely account of *Prélude à l'après-midi d'un faune*, as atmospheric as any in the catalogue and more beautifully shaped than many. In the faster sections, *Jeux* is at times brisker than we are used to and well conveys the sense of the playfulness of the tennis match. Its competitive price makes it even more enticing.

Khamma (Légende dansée).
(N) *** Decca Dig. 443 934-2 [id.]. Conc. O, Chailly – RAVEL: *Daphnis et Chloé* (complete). ***

Debussy's *Khamma* was composed in response to a commission from Maud Allan, whom he refers to in his letters as '*la girl anglaise*'. There are good things in it and the orchestration was entrusted to Koechlin, who put the work into a performable state. In any event it makes a good fill-up to *Daphnis* and is well played and recorded.

La Mer.
(Y/B) (M) *** DG 447 426-2 [id.]. BPO, Karajan – MUSSORGSKY: *Pictures;* RAVEL: *Boléro.* ***
(Y/B) (M) *** RCA 0926 68079-2 [id.]. Chicago SO, Fritz Reiner – RESPIGHI: *Fountains & Pines of Rome.* *** ⊛
(M) *** RCA GD 60875 [60875-2-RG]. Chicago SO, Reiner – RIMSKY-KORSAKOV: *Scheherazade.* ***
(M) **(*) RCA 09026 61500-2 [id.]. Boston SO, Munch – IBERT: *Escales* ***; SAINT-SAENS: *Symphony No. 3.* *** ⊛
(N) (M) **(*) Decca 448 576-2 [id.]. SRO, Ansermet – CHABRIER: *España* **(*); DUKAS: *L'apprenti sorcier* ***; HONEGGER: *Pacific 231* ***; RAVEL: *Boléro; La Valse.* ***

La Mer; Danse (Tarantelle styrienne); (i) Nocturnes. Prélude à l'après-midi d'un faune.
(B) *** Sony SBK 53266; *SBT 53266* [id.]. Phd. O, Ormandy, (i) with Temple University Womens' Ch.

La Mer; (i) Nocturnes.
(N) (BB) *** EMI Seraphim Dig. CES5 68539-2 (2) [CDEB 68539]. (i) Amb. S.; LSO, Previn – MUSSORGSKY: *Pictures;* RAVEL: *Alborada* etc. **(*)

La Mer; (i) Nocturnes. Prélude à l'après-midi d'un faune.
(B) *** DG 439 407-2 [id.]. O de Paris, Barenboim, (i) with Ch.
(M) *** Carlton Dig. PCD 915. LSO, Frühbeck de Burgos, (i) with Ch.
(N) (B) * Decca Dig. 448 229-2 [id.]. Cleveland O, Ashkenazy; (i) with women's chorus (with RAVEL: *Rapsodie espagnole* **).

La Mer; Nocturnes: Nuages; Fêtes (only). Prélude à l'après-midi d'un faune. Printemps (symphonic suite).
(Y/B) (BB) *** RCA Navigator 74321 21293-2. Boston SO, Munch.

La Mer; Prélude à l'après-midi d'un faune.
(M) *** DG 427 250-2. BPO, Karajan – RAVEL: *Boléro; Daphnis et Chloé.* ***
(M) *** EMI CDM7 64357-2 [id.]. BPO, Karajan – RAVEL: *Alborada* etc. ***
** DG Gold Dig. 439 008-2 [id.]. BPO, Karajan – RAVEL: *Pavane; Daphnis.* **

After three decades, Karajan's 1964 account of *La Mer*, now reissued in DG's Legendary Recordings series of 'Originals', is still very much in a class of its own. So strong is its evocative power that one feels one can almost see and smell the ocean. It enshrines the spirit of the work as effectively as it observes the letter, and the superb playing of the Berlin orchestra, for all its virtuosity and sound, is totally self-effacing. For CD reissue, the performance is coupled with Karajan's outstanding (1966) record of Mussorgsky's *Pictures at an exhibition* and a gripping account of Ravel's *Boléro*, but it is still also available with an equally unforgettable coupling of the *Prélude à l'après-midi d'un faune* and Ravel's *Daphnis et Chloé*.

Reiner's 1960 recording is available coupled with either Rimsky-Korsakov's *Scheherazade* or Respighi's *Fountains* and *Pines of Rome*. It has all the warmth and atmosphere that make his version of *Ibéria*, recorded at about the same time (see above), so unforgettable. The pianissimo opening has enormous evocative feeling and the *Jeux des vagues* has the same haunting sense of colour. Of course the marvellous acoustics of the Chicago Hall contribute to the appeal of this superbly played account: the effect is richer and fuller than in Karajan's remastered DG version, and Reiner's record gives no less pleasure. With Karajan, one could picture the bracing air of the northern Atlantic, whereas with Reiner, although the dialogue of the wind and waves is no less powerful, one senses a more southerly latitude. The new coupling with Respighi is surely ideal, for Reiner's magical Roman evocations are among the most unforgettably evocative recorded performances the gramophone has to offer.

The new CD transfers on the inexpensive RCA Navigator reissue have completely transformed the Munch recordings, the Boston acoustic now casting a wonderfully warm aura over the orchestra; and the sound, hitherto rather fierce in its original LP format, is gloriously expansive and translucent. The result is that the opening of *Printemps* is ravishingly sensuous and the 1956 *La Mer* (also available alternatively coupled) has plenty of atmosphere to match its undoubted excitement. There is marvellous Boston playing here, especially from the violins, and the climax of the former is driven very hard indeed (*Fêtes* is similarly pressed on with comparable emotional force). Munch's inclination to go over the top may not appeal to all listeners, but the results are very compelling when the orchestral bravura is so thrilling. The *Prélude* makes a ravishing interlude, expanding to a rapturous climax.

Ormandy is a master of French repertoire, and in his 1964 set of *Nocturnes* the orchestral playing has the superb subtlety of timbre we expect from a Philadelphia performance of a great score and it is only in the last piece, *Sirènes*, where, as so often happens, the female chorus refuses to sound quite ethereal enough. The recording is quite full and atmospheric. *La Mer* dates from the early days of stereo (1959). It is relatively closely balanced and the dynamic range is somewhat more restricted, though not impossibly so. The orchestral playing in *Jeux de vagues* has thrilling virtuosity, and subtlety too, and the sustained gentle playing at the halfway point of the *Dialogue du vent et de la mer* means that the climax in the strings which follows seems the more ecstatic. The *Prélude à l'après-midi d'un faune* (with a fine flute solo from William Kincaid) is sensuous but refined, although the early recording date is conveyed by the timbre of the violins above the stave; the *Danse* is stunningly played, yet the conductor's touch is as light as anyone could wish. Indeed, all the technical reservations notwithstanding, this is one of Ormandy's most impressive Sony reissues.

Barenboim's 1978 coupling of *La Mer* and *Nocturnes*, reissued on DG's Classikon bargain label, offers not only first-class analogue recording but performances which, although highly individual in their control of tempo, have great electricity. For some ears the effect (with the wind balanced rather forward) may lack the subtlety that distinguishes Karajan's analogue version, but there is an ardour that more than compensates. The *Prélude à l'après-midi d'un faune* has comparable languor to *Sirènes*, the last of the *Nocturnes*, if not quite the same refinement of feeling. This too is very well recorded.

Previn's ocean, like Reiner's, is clearly in the southern hemisphere, with Debussy's orchestral colours made to sound more vividly sunlit. The playing of the LSO is extremely impressive, particularly the ardour of the strings. The recording has glittering detail and expands brilliantly at climaxes (though, even on CD, there is a slight loss of refinement at the very loudest peaks). The *Nocturnes* have even greater spontaneity. Some might feel that the *Sirènes* are too voluptuous, but this matches Previn's extrovert approach. The new couplings which make up this inexpensive, Seraphim, two-CD package comprise quite an attractive collection.

Although also strong in Mediterranean atmosphere, Frühbeck de Burgos's account of *La Mer* has an underlying grip, helped by the wide dynamic range of the Walthamstow recording. There is much subtlety of detail, both here and in the *Nocturnes*, where textures again have the sensuousness of southern climes. The *Prélude à l'après-midi d'un faune* brings lovely delicate flute-playing from Paul Edmund-Davies and a richly moulded string climax. If these are not conventional readings, they are full of impulse and superbly recorded.

Karajan's 1978 analogue re-recording of *La Mer* for EMI may not have quite the supreme refinement of his earlier DG version – partly a question of the warmer, vaguer recording – but it has a comparable concentration, with the structure persuasively and inevitably built. The *Prélude* has an appropriate languor, and there is a persuasive warmth about this performance, beautifully moulded; but again the earlier version distilled greater atmosphere and magic.

Ansermet's 1964 *La Mer*, although vibrant and vividly detailed, did not match his earlier recordings in the quality of the orchestral playing, with moments of suspect intonation. The rest of this concert, however, shows the Swiss conductor on top form.

The digital reprocessing of Karajan's 1985 recordings is impressively clear and vivid, with the Philharmonie acoustic very well managed. But the improved sound serves only to emphasize the lack of magic in the playing compared with his earlier (1964) account. The *Prélude à l'après-midi d'un faune* is beautifully played, although the flautist has a very pronounced vibrato; and, again, the earlier version distils a more subtle fragrance.

Ashkenazy's Cleveland versions, although having the advantage of superb (1987) digital sound, seem unable to get inside the music; tempi are often unconvincing, and the beautiful *Prélude à l'après-midi d'un faune* lacks shape without a really strong central climax.

La Mer; Nocturnes: Nuages; Fêtes (only); *Le Martyre de Saint-Sébastien* (symphonic fragments);
Prélude à l'après-midi d'un faune.
(***) Testament mono SBT 1011. Philh. O, Guido Cantelli.

Cantelli's classic accounts have been beautifully restored and come up sounding both natural and fresh.
Cantelli's account of the four symphonic fragments from *Le Martyre de Saint-Sébastien* is one of the
most beautiful performances he ever committed to vinyl; the textures are impeccably balanced and
phrases flawlessly shaped. Its atmosphere is as concentrated as that of the legendary first recording
under Coppola. *La Mer* and the *Prélude à l'après-midi d'un faune* are hardly less perfect.

Symphony in B min.
** Koch Dig. 3-7067-2 [id.]. Sinfonia O of Chicago, Barry Faldner – GOUNOD: *Petite symphonie for
winds;* MILHAUD: *Symphonies for chamber orchestra.* **

Debussy composed his *Symphony in B minor* when he was eighteen and staying in Russia with
Tchaikovsky's patron, Madame von Meck. He sketched out this ten-minute piece for piano, four hands,
in which form it has been recorded. To be truthful, there are few signs of the Debussy to come and much
that is derivative. Barry Faldner's orchestration includes a piano so that it sounds rather like a concertante work. It is very well played but of limited musical interest. The time would have been better spent
on recording all six rather than only four of the Milhaud *Petites symphonies.*

CHAMBER MUSIC

*Cello sonata; Petite pièce for clarinet and piano; Première rapsodie for clarinet and piano; Sonata for flute,
viola and harp; Violin sonata; Syrinx for solo flute.*
*** Chandos CHAN 8385 [id.]. Athena Ens.

The most ethereal of these pieces is the *Sonata for flute, viola and harp,* whose other-worldly quality is
beautifully conveyed here. In the case of the other sonatas, there are strong competitors but, as a
collection, this is certainly recommendable.

Cello sonata in D min.
*** Decca 417 833-2 [id.]. Rostropovich, Britten – SCHUBERT: *Arpeggione sonata* **(*); SCHUMANN: *5
Stücke.* ***
**(*) ASV Dig. CDDCA 796 [id.]. Bernard Gregor-Smith, Yolande Wrigley – BRIDGE; DOHNANYI:
Sonatas. **(*)

(i) *Cello sonata;* (ii) *Violin sonata.*
**(*) Chandos Dig. CHAN 8458 [id.]. (i) Yuli Turovsky; (ii) Rostislav Dubinsky; Luba Edlina – RAVEL:
Piano trio. ***

Like Debussy's other late chamber works, the *Cello sonata* is a concentrated piece, quirkily original. The
classic version by Rostropovich and Britten has a clarity and point which suit the music perfectly. The
recording is first class, and if the couplings are suitable, this holds its place as first choice.
    Bernard Gregor-Smith and Yolande Wrigley play with great refinement and authority, as well as much
sensitivity. They are perhaps too closely balanced but this does not prevent their record being a highly
desirable one.
    Turovsky gives a well-delineated, powerful account with Luba Edlina. In the *Violin sonata,* Rostislav
Dubinsky and Luba Edlina (his wife) are in excellent form, though this is red-blooded Slavonic Debussy
rather than the more ethereal, subtle playing of a Grumiaux.

(i) *Cello sonata in D min.;* (ii) *Violin sonata in G min.*
(N) *(*) Decca Dig. 444 318-2 [id.]. (i) Harrell; (ii) Perlman; Ashkenazy – RAVEL: *Piano trio.* *(*)

'Star' performances, completely wanting in intimacy of feeling. The closely balanced recording does not
help. There are many more idiomatic accounts in circulation, and at less than 50 minutes this is not
highly competitive.

*Le petit nègre; Petite pièce; Première rapsodie; Rapsodie for cor anglais; Rapsodie for saxophone; Sonata
for flute, viola and harp;* (i) *Syrinx.*
(Y/B) (B) *** Cala Dig. CACD 1017 (2) [id.]. William Bennett, Nicholas Daniel, James Campbell,
Rachael Gough, (i) Simon Haram & Ens. – SAINT-SAENS: *Chamber music.* ***

Another two-CD set for the price (and shape) of one, the first volume of French chamber music for
woodwind. The *Rapsodie for cor anglais* with which it opens is more familiar in its form for alto
saxophone, which was originally to have been called *Rapsodie Mauresque.* Daniel plays it with great

sensitivity. It is also heard in its alternative form, splendidly played by Simon Haram. The performance of the *Sonata for flute, viola and harp* is highly sensitive.

Sonata for flute, viola and harp.
*** Koch Dig. 3-7016-2 [id.]. Atlantic Sinf. – JOLIVET: *Chant de Linos;* JONGEN: *Concert.* ***

The three members of the Atlantic Sinfonietta are well balanced and achieve a feeling of repose and mystery. This is the best of the recent recordings of this enormously civilized and ethereal music.

Piano trio in G (1880).
*** Carlton Dig. MCD 41 [id.]. Solomon Trio – FAURE; RAVEL: *Piano trios.* ***
(Y/B) **(*) Ara. Dig. Z 6643 [id.]. Golub Kaplan Carr Trio – FAURE: *Piano trio* ***; SAINT-SAENS: *Piano trio.* **(*)

The *G major Trio* undoubtedly shows more promise than fulfilment and is almost entirely uncharacter-istic. On Carlton, Rodney Friend, Yonty Solomon and Timothy Hugh give as fine an account as any, and they are very well recorded indeed. They play with considerable finesse and sensitivity, and persuade the listener that this piece is stronger than in fact it is.

The Golub–Kaplan–Carr Trio also give a good account of this slender piece, and they are decently recorded.

String quartet in G min.
*** DG Dig. 437 836-2 (id.]. Hagen Qt – RAVEL; WEBERN: *Quartets.* ***
*** Denon Dig. CO 75164 [id.]. Carmina Qt – RAVEL: *Quartet.* ***
*** RCA Dig. 09026 61816-2 [id.]. Vogler Qt – JANACEK; SHOSTAKOVICH: *Quartets.* ***
*** Sony Dig. SK 52554 [id.]. Juilliard Qt – DUTILLEUX; RAVEL: *Quartets.* ***
(M) *** Ph. 420 894-2 [id.]. Italian Qt – RAVEL: *Quartet.* ***
(M) *** DG 435 589-2 [id.]. LaSalle Qt – RAVEL: *Quartet.* ***
(B) *** CfP Dig. CD-CFP 4652; *TC-CFP 4652* [id.]. Chilingirian Qt – RAVEL: *Quartet.* ***
(BB) **(*) Naxos Dig. 8.550249 [id.]. Kodály Qt – RAVEL: *Quartet* etc. ***
(N) **(*) ASV Dig. CDDCA 930 [id.]. Lindsay Qt – RAVEL: *String quartet* **(*); STRAVINSKY: *3 Pieces.* **(*)
(Y/B) **(*) RCA Dig. 09026 62552-2 [id.]. Tokyo Qt – RAVEL: *Introduction and allegro; Quartet.* **(*)
(N) (M) **(*) Carlton Dig. 3036 70105-2 [id.]. New World Qt – RAVEL: *Quartet* **(*); DUTILLEUX: *Ainsi la nuit.* ***

The Debussy and Ravel quartets are an almost mandatory coupling these days and even Dover Scores reprint the two together! The Hagen Quartet on DG produce the greatest refinement of sound without beautifying the score; they also enjoy the benefit of superb engineering. Indeed, if pressed, this might well be a first choice, at least among recent issues.

The Carmina Denon disc can certainly be given the strongest recommendation for those willing to accept short measure, as they do not offer a third work as coupling. However, the recordings are fresh and wide-ranging (perhaps a trace fierce right at the very top) and the playing is of the highest quality.

The Vogler on RCA offer a more unusual combination, likely to fit the needs of any collector who just happens to want the eleventh of the Shostakovich quartets and the Janáček No. 1. This is an exception-ally fine account of the Debussy, fiery when required, highly sensitive to dynamic nuance and keenly atmospheric; it is as good as any now before the public. Put the Vogler slow movement, say, alongside the Juilliard, and comparison is very much to their advantage.

The Juilliard performance is impressive all the same, in spite of the wider vibrato these players employ, which one barely notices except when making a direct comparison. Their first movement is not as fresh and ardent as the Vogler, but overall this is very satisfying. They are well recorded (though the balance in the fine Dutilleux bonus is much closer than in the Debussy or Ravel).

Turning now to the mid-and bargain-priced versions, it need hardly be said that the playing of the Quartetto Italiano is outstanding. Perfectly judged ensemble, weight and tone still make this a most satisfying choice and, even if it is rather short measure, the Philips recording engineers have produced a vivid and truthful sound-picture.

The LaSalle Quartet are also on top form and their reading takes a place of honour alongside – but not in preference to – the Quartetto Italiano. The 1971 recording was of high quality and the CD transfer in no way degrades its natural balance.

At bargain price the Chilingirian coupling is in every way competitive. They give a thoroughly commit-ted account with well-judged tempi and very musical phrasing. The Scherzo is vital and spirited, and there is no want of poetry in the slow movement. The recording has plenty of body and presence and has the benefit of a warm acoustic: the sound is fuller than on the competing version by the Italian Quartet.

As we know from their Haydn recordings, the Kodály Quartet are an excellent ensemble and they give a thoroughly enjoyable account that can be recommended to those who do not want to spend that bit extra on the mid-priced Quartetto Italiano version. There are moments here (in the slow movement, for example) when the Kodály, too, are touched by distinction. This music-making has the feel of a live performance and is to be preferred to some of the glossier, mechanized accounts at full price: these players also have the benefit of a generous fill-up and very good recorded sound. Excellent value.

The Lindsays play with their usual aplomb and panache. There are splendid things here, notably the youthful fire of the opening movement and the finely etched finale. They do not always match the *douceur* and *tendresse* which the Quartetto Italiano, the Hagen and the Tokyo find, but they are always stimulating. Fine recording.

The Tokyo Quartet play with great beauty and sweetness of tone. Their tonal refinement and perfect ensemble are a joy in themselves and are heard to great advantage in the inner movements. Unfortunately the first movement is pulled around rather more than is acceptable on a disc designed for repeated hearing, and some listeners will find this problematic.

The New World Quartet is Harvard-based and their playing gives undoubted pleasure. The Debussy is very well played but a bit overprojected. The expressive rubato of the leader may pose problems for those with austere tastes. However, these artists add an interesting Dutilleux piece. They are very well recorded. This CD comes at slightly more than mid-price.

Violin sonata in G min.
(N) *** DG Dig. 445 880-2 [id.]. Dumay, Pires – FRANCK: *Violin sonata in A;* RAVEL: *Berceuse* etc. ***
(N) *** Virgin/EMI Dig. VC5 45122-2. Tetzlaff, Andsnes – JANACEK: *Sonata;* RAVEL: *Sonata;* NIELSEN: *Sonata No. 2.* ***

(i) *Violin sonata in G min.;* (ii) *Sonata for flute, viola and harp.*
(M) *** Decca 421 154-2. (i) Kyung Wha Chung, Radu Lupu; (ii) Melos Ens. (members) – FRANCK: *Violin sonata;* RAVEL: *Introduction and allegro.* *** ✪

Kyung Wha Chung plays with marvellous character and penetration, and her partnership with Radu Lupu could hardly be more fruitful. Nothing is pushed to extremes, and everything is in perfect perspective. The *Sonata for flute, viola and harp* and the Ravel *Introduction and allegro* are wonderfully sensitive and the music's ethereal atmosphere well caught. The recording sounds admirably real.

Augustin Dumay and Maria João Pires give as idiomatic and sensitive an account of the Debussy *Sonata* as one could wish for, and those wanting their particular coupling with Franck and Ravel need not really hesitate.

However, Christian Tetzlaff and Leif Ove Andsnes provide as expert and imaginative a partnership as any of their rivals. The sheer interest of their couplings, not least the Nielsen *G minor Sonata*, and the quality of the performances make this also one of the strongest contenders in the current catalogue. Both the DG and Virgin performances are very well recorded.

PIANO MUSIC
Music for two pianos

Danses sacrée et profane; En blanc et noir; Lindaraja; Nocturnes (trans. Ravel); *Prélude à l'après-midi d'un faune.*
*** Hyperion Dig. CDA 66468 [id.]. Stephen Coombs and Christopher Scott.

Stephen Coombs and Christopher Scott made an outstanding début with this fine recording, which leads the field in this repertoire.

Solo piano music

2 Arabesques; Children's corner; Estampes; Images, Books 1–2; L'isle joyeuse; Mazurka; Pour le piano; Préludes, Books 1–2.
(B) **(*) Ph. Duo 438 718-2 (2) [id.]. Werner Haas.

(i) *En blanc et noir; 6 Epigraphes antiques; Lindaraja; Marche écossaise; Petite suite.* (Solo piano): *Ballade slave; Berceuse héroïque; Danse (Tarantelle styrienne); Danse bohémienne; D'un cahier d'esquisses; 12 Etudes; Hommage à Haydn; Masques; Nocturne; Le petit nègre; La plus que lente; Rêverie; Suite bergamasque; Valse romantique.*
(B) *** Ph. Duo 438 721-2 (2) [id.]. Werner Haas, (i) with Noël Lee.

2 Arabesques; Children's corner; Estampes; Images, Books 1–2; L'Isle joyeuse; Pour le piano; Préludes, Book 1; Rêverie; Suite bergamasque.
(Y/B) (B) *** Decca Double 443 021-2 (2) [id.]. Pascal Rogé.

Pascal Rogé's playing is distinguished by a keen musical intelligence and sympathy, as well as by a subtle command of keyboard colour, and this Double Decca set must receive the warmest welcome. *Children's corner* is played with neat elegance and the characterization has both charm and perception, while the *Suite bergamasque* brings crisp, well-articulated playing in the *Passepied* and genuine poetry in the famous *Clair de lune*. *Pour le piano* is no less distinguished, and the *Images* are full of evocative imagery. In *Estampes* there are occasional moments when the listener senses the need for more dramatic projection, but Rogé brings genuine poetic feeling to the first book of the *Préludes*. Here he communicates atmosphere and character in no small measure and has greater warmth than Michelangeli and Zimerman, perhaps partly the effect of the 1978 recording, which has a slightly fuller recording in the bass than the rest of the programme. The other recordings were made in 1977 and 1979 and the CD transfers are clear and firm.

   The playing of Werner Haas is rarely routine. Book II of the *Préludes* (sample *Feux d'artifice*) and many of the pieces from Book 1 are very well worth having; the *Images* are pretty good too (*Reflets dans l'eau* sparkles iridescently), and many of the shorter pieces in the first listed volume are neatly and sensitively characterized. What makes this particular pair of CDs indispensable is the splendid collection of Debussy's music for piano duet (four hands or two pianos), recorded a decade later, in which Haas is joined by Noël Lee. The *Petite suite* is delightfully fresh, and *En blanc et noir* and the *Six épigraphes antiques* are very distinguished indeed. The (early 1960s) piano recording throughout is well up to Philips's high standard, and the CD transfers are first class. As usual with this bargain series, the documentation is very good.

2 Arabesques; Berceuse héroïque; Etudes Nos. 7–8, 10–12; Images (1905; 1907); L'Isle joyeuse; Masques; La plus que lente; Préludes, Books 1–2; Rêverie.
(N) (B) ** EMI CZS5 68562-2 (2) [id.]. Samson François.

There is some spirited playing from Samson François and the piano is well enough recorded (between 1968 and 1970), but François is not consistently sensitive nor does he always observe the dynamic nuances so important in this repertoire. Robust rather than refined, and no match for Rogé.

2 Arabesques; Children's corner; Etudes: Pour les cinq doigts d'après M. Czerny; Pour les arpèges composés. Images: Poissons d'or. L'Isle joyeuse; Le petit nègre; La plus que lente; Préludes, Book 1: Des pas sur la neige; Book 2: Ondine; La terrasse des audiences du clair de lune; Feux d'artifice. Suite bergamasque: Prélude.
(B) *** CfP Dig. CD-CFP 4653; *TC-CF 4653* . Moura Lympany.

Dame Moura Lympany's choice cannot be faulted and this is among the finest recitals of its kind in the catalogue. The subtle colouring of *La plus que lente* is as impressive as the power and glowing ardour of the closing *L'Isle joyeuse*. The *Arabesques* are played rhapsodically with distinct individuality and there are few finer or more imaginative performances of *Children's corner*, here presented as children's imagery seen through adult eyes. Among the *Préludes* the remarkably compelling *La terrasse des audiences du clair de lune* comes over as truly impressionistic in feeling rather than in any way pictorial. *Feux d'artifice* flashes with brilliance. The whole recital emerges as a spontaneous experience, and it is worth noting that the pianist was 76 years young when she went into EMI's Abbey Road Studio to make this record, which is very realistically recorded indeed. The notes by Peter Avis are a model of what documentation for a miscellaneous recital should be.

2 Arabesques; Images oubliées; Préludes, Book 1.
*** ASV Dig. CDDCA 720 [id.]. Gordon Fergus-Thompson.

Ballade; Berceuse héroïque; Danse; Danse bohémienne; D'un cahier d'esquisses; Elégie; Hommage à Haydn; L'isle joyeuse; Masques; Mazurka; Morceau de concours; Nocturne; Page d'album; Le petit nègre; La plus que lente; Valse romantique.
*** ASV Dig. CDDCA 711 [id.]. Gordon Fergus-Thompson.

Children's corner; Estampes; Images, Books 1–2.
*** ASV Dig. CDDCA 695 [id.]. Gordon Fergus-Thompson.

Etudes, Books 1–2; Pour le piano.
*** ASV Dig. CDDCA 703 [id.]. Gordon Fergus-Thompson.

Préludes. Book 2; Suite bergamasque.
*** ASV Dig. CDDCA 723 [id.]. Gordon Fergus-Thompson.

Gordon Fergus-Thompson's survey maintains a consistently high standard of artistry. If one places his sets of *Préludes* alongside recordings by Arrau or Gieseking, then they are clearly less individually distinctive, but overall this playing shows a genuine feeling for the Debussy palette and, with fine, modern, digital sound, these records will give considerable satisfaction. The collection of shorter pieces is particularly successful.

2 Arabesques; Ballade; Danse bohémienne; Images, Books 1–2; Images (1894); Mazurka; Nocturne.
(M) *** Saga EC 3376-2 [id.]. Lívia Rév.

For a long time Lívia Rév was underrated as a pianist; it was these Debussy recordings which established her reputation, receiving just acclaim when they first appeared on CD. This compilation (77 minutes 38 seconds) can hold its own with any in the catalogue. Lívia Rév has sensibility, a finely developed sense of colour, a keen awareness of atmosphere and fleet fingers. She is moreover decently recorded in a spacious acoustic, and the CD transfers are extremely successful.

2 Arabesques; Ballade; Images, Book 1: Reflets dans l'eau; Mouvement. Book 2: Poissons d'or. L'isle joyeuse; Préludes, Book 2: Feux d'artifice. Suite bergamasque.
(M) *** EMI CD-EMX 2055-2; *TC-EMX 2055.* Daniel Adni.

This collection dates from 1972 and is outstanding in every way: this young Israeli pianist proves himself a Debussian of no mean order. His recital is well planned and offers playing that is as poetic in feeling as it is accomplished in technique.

2 Arabesques; Berceuse héroïque; D'un cahier d'esquisses; Hommage à Haydn; Images, Books 1–2; L'isle joyeuse; Page d'album; Rêverie.
⊛ *** Ph. Dig. 422 404-2 Zoltán Kocsis.

Artistically, this new recital is if anything even more distinguished in terms of pianistic finesse, sensitivity and tonal refinement than Kocsis's earlier (1983) Debussy collection – see below.

2 Arabesques; Danse bohémienne; D'un cahier d'esquisses; Estampes; Images oubliées; L'isle joyeuse; Morceau de concours; Nocturne; Pour le piano; Préludes, Books 1–2 (complete); *Masques; Rêverie.*
(N) *** Decca Dig. 452 022-2 (2) [id.]. Jean-Yves Thibaudet.

Beautifully recorded, Thibaudet's new survey of Debussy's piano music (this is Volume I of an ongoing series) looks set to take first place in a competitive field. Thibaudet's wide range of tone and dynamic is used with great imagination, and his playing often suggests an improvisatory quality. The music's subtlety of colour, with half-lights as well as sudden blazes of light (as in the stunning *Feux d'artifice*), is fully understood by this fine artist, and there is no question as to the spontaneity of his playing. The *Préludes* are among the finest on record.

2 Arabesques; L'isle joyeuse; Masques; La plus que lente; Pour le piano; Suite bergamasque; Danse (Tarantelle styrienne).
(B) *** DG 429 517-2 [id.]. Tamás Vásáry.

Vásáry is at his very best in the *Suite bergamasque*, and *Clair de lune* is beautifully played, as are the *Arabesques*. *La plus que lente* receives the least convincing performance. But overall this is a satisfying recital, particularly as the piano is so realistic.

Berceuse héroïque; Children's corner suite; Danse; D'un cahier d'esquisses; Mazurka; Morceau de concours; Nocturne; Le petit nègre; La plus que lente; Rêverie.
*** Denon Dig. C37 7372 [id.]. Jacques Rouvier.

An enjoyable and interesting Debussy recital from Jacques Rouvier, which has the advantage of very truthful recording. This serves as a very useful addition to the catalogue and can be thoroughly recommended.

Berceuse héroïque; D'un cahier d'esquisses; Etudes, Books 1–2; Morceau de concours; Suite bergamasque.
(M) *** Saga EC 3383-2 [id.]. Lívia Rév.

Lívia Rév is consistently imaginative and her playing has considerable poetic feeling, as well as great technical accomplishment. The *Suite bergamasque* is also highly sensitive. The 1980 recording is excellent and the disc offers 75 minutes of music.

Children's corner; Elégie; Hommage à Haydn; Page d'album; Préludes, Book 1; La plus que lente; Danse (Tarantelle styrienne).
(M) *** Saga EC 3377-2 [id.]. Lívia Rév.

Lívia Rév plays *Children's corner* very well, and her performance of the *Préludes* holds its own in terms of sensitivity and atmosphere. Her keyboard mastery is beyond question (just sample *La cathédrale engloutie*) and she is a fine colourist. The recording, too, is first class.

Children's corner; Images, Books 1–2; Préludes, Books 1–2.
(N) **(*) DG 449 438-2 (2) [id.]. Michelangeli.

'Immaculate' is one of the words that spring to mind when one hears Michelangeli's Debussy. There is no doubt that his performances of *Children's corner* and the two sets of *Images* are very distinguished. The recording, good as it is, dates from 1971 – which might have indicated a price reduction for this new collection. The *Préludes* undoubtedly bring piano playing which is pretty flawless. At the same time, it is very cool and detached and, although Book II excited enormous enthusiasm in some quarters, both Books here will strike many as somewhat glacial and curiously unatmospheric.

Children's corner suite; La plus que lente; Préludes, Book 1: La fille aux cheveux de lin. Suite berga-masque: Clair de lune.
(N) (BB) (*) RCA Navigator 74321 24214-2. Weissenberg – SATIE: *Piano music.* ***

Alas, Alexis Weissenberg is an insensitive Debussian. He begins *Children's corner* much too fast and adds unnecessary rubato to *Clair de lune*, while similarly *La fille aux cheveux de lin* lacks the simplicity which conveys innocence.

Estampes; Images, Books 1–2; Images oubliées (1894); Pour le piano.
*** Denon Dig. CD 1411 [id.]. Jacques Rouvier.

Jacques Rouvier is very well recorded; there is plenty of atmosphere and space round the sound. His account of the *Cloche à travers les feuilles* has great poise and *Et la lune descend sur le temple qui fut* has wonderful atmosphere and repose.

Estampes; Images, Books 1–2; Préludes, Books 1–2.
(M) *** Ph. 432 304-2 (2) [id.]. Claudio Arrau.

Claudio Arrau's versions of these solo piano works by Debussy are very distinguished. The piano timbre in these 1978/9 analogue recordings has a consistent body and realism typical of this company's finest work.

Estampes; Préludes, Books 1–2 (complete); Images: Reflets dans l'eau.
(N) (BB) *** CfP Dig. Silver Double CDCFPSD 4805 (2). Youri Egorov.

The Classics for Pleasure Silver Double has the advantage of considerable economy since it brings us the *Estampes* and the first of the *Images*, *Reflets dans l'eau*, as well as the two Books of *Préludes*, at the cost of a single medium-priced CD. Youri Egorov is a very fine player indeed; he gives performances of commanding keyboard technique, exquisite refinement and atmosphere. The recording is very good, a shade too reverberant perhaps and not quite as clear as Arrau (Philips) or Rogé (Decca). However, the hazy atmosphere in evocations like *Voiles*, *La cathédrale engloutie* and indeed in *Reflets dans l'eau* is very telling, and this must rank high in current CD sets of the complete *Préludes*.

Etudes, Books 1–2.
❀ *** Ph. Dig. 422 412-2 [id.]. Mitsuko Uchida.

12 Etudes; Estampes; L'isle joyeuse.
(N) (M) **(*) Carlton Dig. 30367 0018-2 [id.]. Martino Tirimo.

Mitsuko Uchida's remarkable account of the *Etudes* on Philips is not only one of the best Debussy piano records in the catalogue and arguably her finest recording, but also one of the best ever recordings of the instrument.

Martino Tirimo offers not only the *Etudes*, played with imagination and much subtlety of colour, but also a set of *Estampes* and *L'isle joyeuse*, neither quite as impressive but still worth having. He is very well recorded. But first choice for the *Etudes* remains with Uchida.

Préludes, Books 1–2 (complete).
❀ (M) *** EMI mono CDH7 61004-2 [id.]. Walter Gieseking.
(M) *** Carlton IMP Classics Dig. 30367 0079-2. Martino Tirimo.
*** DG Dig. 435 773-2 (2) [id.]. Krystian Zimerman.

Gieseking penetrates the atmosphere of the *Préludes* more deeply than almost any other artist. This is playing of rare distinction and great evocative quality. However, the documentation is concerned solely with the artist and gives no information about the music save the titles and the cues.

No grumbles about value for money or about quality from Martino Tirimo on Carlton; he accommodates both Books on the same disc. His playing is very fine indeed and can withstand comparison with most of his rivals – and, apart from the sensitivity of the playing, the recording is most realistic and natural. This is probably a first choice for those wanting a modern digital record offering the complete set, although Egorov's CfP Silver Double (see above) offers more music.

There is no want of atmosphere or poetic feeling in Krystian Zimerman's account of the *Préludes*. This is a very distinguished performance indeed, though some may find the level of intensity too much to live with. Every note, whether the quietest of pianissimi or the strongest fortissimo, is highly charged. But if Zimerman makes a meal of every small detail, his playing is imaginative and concentrated. The DG recording is analytical and sensitively balanced, but even so there is more than a hint of hardness in climaxes.

Préludes, Book 1; Images oubliées (1894).
(M) **(*) Channel Classics Dig. CCS 4892 [id.]. Jos van Immerseel.

The special interest of Jos van Immerseel's recording of the first book of *Préludes* lies in his instrument, an Erard of 1897, of the kind which Debussy would have known and played. The sonority is gentle and veiled and curiously seductive except in *forte* passages; the timbre, particularly in the upper register of the instrument, is monochrome and dry, and this tells in a piece such as *La sérénade interrompue*. There is a real turn-of-the-century feel to the shadowy sound-world of *Des pas sur la neige* and the first of the *Images oubliées*. An interesting appendix for a Debussy discography, but essentially this is an issue for specialist collections.

Préludes, Book 2.
(Y/B) (M) **(*) Saga EC 3347-2 [id.]. Lívia Rév.

Lívia Rév's Saga recording of the second book of *Préludes* comes from the 1970s. We thought quite highly of it at the time, giving it a full three-star grading. The playing has great polish and finesse, and it gives pleasure. However, at 39 minutes it is no bargain. Book 2 is less well represented in the catalogue than its companion, but there is no shortage of excellent packages that offer both books in distinguished performances which are worth the extra outlay (Gieseking etc).

VOCAL MUSIC

3 Chansons de Charles d'Orléans.
(Y/B) *** Ph. Dig. 438 149-2 [id.]. Monteverdi Ch., O Révolutionnaire et Romantique, Gardiner –
    FAURE: *Requiem;* RAVEL; SAINT-SAENS: *Choral works.* ***

With Gardiner and his period forces bringing out the medieval flavour of these charming choral settings, this adds to a generous and unusual coupling for Gardiner's expressive reading of the Fauré *Requiem*.

La damoiselle élue.
(M) **(*) Carlton 3036 70100-2 [id.]. Caballé, Coster, Ambrosian Ladies Ch., L. Symphonica, Wyn
    Morris – CHAUSSON: *Poème de l'amour et de la mer.* **(*)

Debussy's early cantata, *La damoiselle élue*, has been seriously neglected on record. It is a highly evocative setting of Rossetti in translation, using women's chorus and mezzo-soprano solo for the central role of the Blessed Damozel. This richly expressive performance is focused on Caballé's radiant account of the principal solo, with her timbre sometimes suggesting her compatriot, Victoria de los Angeles. She produces ecstatic high pianissimos and, even if at times she allows sensuous scooping up to notes and her French enunciation is idiosyncratic, this is a beautiful and involving performance. The warmly atmospheric recording, bringing out some unexpected *Parsifal* echoes, is very well transferred to CD, and altogether this Carlton reissue is excellent value.

Le Martyre de Saint-Sébastien (incidental music): complete.
*** Sony Dig. SK 48240 [id.]. Leslie Caron; McNair, Murray, L. Symphony Ch., LSO, Tilson Thomas.

(i) *Le Martyre de Saint-Sébastien* (incidental music, complete); *Images: Ibéria.*
(M) **(*) RCA GD 60684 [id.]. (i) Kopleff, Akos, Curtin; Boston SO, Munch.

Debussy produced music that is far less concentrated than in his major masterpieces, but its sweetness and simplicity often point forward to his late works. Michael Tilson Thomas here records the complete incidental music in a form that the composer approved, using a narrator, Leslie Caron, to provide the spoken links between sections. What it shows is how much richer and more varied the complete score is than the usual symphonic fragments. This is as near an ideal performance as could be imagined, with Sylvia McNair singing radiantly in the principal soprano roles, with brilliant playing from the LSO, and glorious recording which brings out the full atmospheric beauty of the choral singing, often off-stage.

Charles Munch's recording of the complete *Le Martyre de Saint-Sebastien* comes from 1957 and offers sumptuous orchestral sound, though the recording does not have front-to-back depth and transparency. It is still very good – and what magnificent playing the Boston orchestra give us! However, Munch's New England Chorus is a bit too well drilled. He gives us the narration, which he speaks very expressively himself (with a slight Alsatian accent). Though he is a bit too closely recorded, anyone needing a mid-price *Martyre* need look no further. However, Munch's version does not compete with Michael Tilson Thomas's new, sumptuously recorded, full-price version on Sony. The *Ibéria* comes from the set of *Images* Munch recorded in 1956.

OPERA

La chute de la Maison Usher (unfinished opera, arr. Blin).
(M) *** EMI CDM7 64687-2 [id.]. Barbaux, Lafont, Le Roux, Le Maigat, Monte Carlo PO, Prêtre –
  CAPLET: *Masque* **(*); SCHMIDT: *Palais hanté*. ***

In the 1970s the Chilean scholar and composer, Juan Allende Blin, put together the rediscovered fragments of *The Fall of the House of Usher*, and managed to reconstitute 400 bars of music. Debussy left the most scanty indications concerning the orchestration and the scoring is the work of Allende Blin himself. The music has extraordinary novelty, great harmonic freedom and a liberty of prosodic treatment far surpassing *Pelléas*. The score has a great sense of mystery in the manner of *Jeux* and, perhaps, *Le martyre*, and is a real discovery. It makes, if not a full dramatic entertainment, at least a fascinating cantata, very original indeed, and very well performed here in this first commercial recording in which Jean-Philippe Lafont is outstanding in the baritone role of Roderick, the doomed central character. The direction of Georges Prêtre is dedicated and the 1983 recording, although an example of early digital techniques, is reasonably atmospheric. Alas, the documentation is almost non-existent, with the libretto included with the original issue now omitted.

Pelléas et Mélisande (complete).
*** DG Dig. 435 344-2 (2) [id.]. Ewing, Le Roux, Van Dam, Courtis, Ludwig, Pace, Mazzola, Vienna
  Konzertvereingung, VPO, Abbado.
*** Decca Dig. 430 502-2 (2) [id.]. Alliot-Lugaz, Henry, Cachemaille, Thau, Carlson, Golfier, Montreal
  Ch. & SO, Dutoit.
(M) **(*) Sony SM3K 47265 (3) [id.]. Shirley, Söderström, McIntyre, Ward, Minton, ROHCG Ch. &
  O, Boulez.
(N) *** EMI Dig. CDS7 49350-2 (3) [id.]. Stilwell, Von Stade, Van Dam, Raimondi, Ch. of German
  Op., Berlin, BPO, Karajan.
(***) EMI mono CHS7 61038-2 (3). Joachim, Jansen, Etcheverry, Paris CO, Désormière (with
  Mélodies).
(Y/B) (***) Testament mono SBT 3051 (3) [id.]. Jansen, De los Angeles, Souzay, Froumenty, Collard,
  French Nat. R. O, Cluytens.

Abbado's outstanding version broadly resolves the problem of a first recommendation in this opera, which has always been lucky on record. If among modern versions the choice has been hard to make between Karajan's sumptuously romantic account, almost Wagnerian, and Dutoit's clean-cut, direct one, Abbado satisfyingly presents a performance more sharply focused than the one and more freely flexible than the other, altogether more urgently dramatic. The casting is excellent, with no weak link.

Charles Dutoit brings out the magic of Debussy's score with an involving richness typical of that venue which has played so important a part in the emergence of the Montreal orchestra into the world of international recording. This is not the dreamy reading which some Debussians might prefer, but one which sets the characters very specifically before us as creatures of flesh and blood, not mistily at one remove.

Boulez's sharply dramatic view of Debussy's atmospheric score is a performance which will probably not please the dedicated Francophile – for one thing there is not a single French-born singer in the cast – but it rescues Debussy from the languid half-tone approach which for too long has been accepted as authentic. He is supported by a strong cast; the singing is not always very idiomatic but it has the musical and dramatic momentum which stems from sustained experience on the stage. In almost every way this has the tension of a live performance.

EMI have restored the rich and passionate Karajan set to the catalogue, still at full price. It is a performance that sets Debussy's masterpiece as a natural successor to Wagner's *Tristan*, with the orchestral tapestry at the centre and the singers providing a verbal obbligato, but Karajan's concentration carries one in total involvement through a story that can seem inconsequential. Frederica von Stade is a tenderly affecting heroine and Richard Stilwell a youthful and upstanding hero, set against the dark, incisive Golaud of Van Dam. The playing of the Berlin Philharmonic is both polished and deeply committed.

Roger Désormière's wartime recording still has a special claim on the collector's attention in spite of its sonic limitations. Etcheverry is arguably the most strongly characterized Golaud committed to disc, and neither Joachim's Mélisande nor Jansen's Pelléas has been readily surpassed. A *Pelléas* without atmosphere is no *Pelléas*, and this classic reading puts you under its spell immediately. Like so many pre-war performances, it is distinguished not only by wonderful singing but also by marvellous articulation and there is a sense that every detail is in the right perspective and every nuance perfectly inflected. A further inducement for collectors is a generous selection of Debussy songs from Maggie Teyte and the celebrated recording of *Mes longs cheveux* by the original Mélisande, Mary Garden, accompanied on the piano by Debussy himself in 1904. A very special – indeed indispensable – set.

It is good to see the Cluytens (1956) recording return to currency. Victoria de los Angeles as Mélisande is often affecting and always sings the role exquisitely, and readers will obviously want the set for her. Souzay's Golaud is also magnificent vocally. André Cluytens gets superior playing from the Orchestre National de la Radiodiffusion Française and casts a strong spell even if he does not always distil as powerful an atmosphere. The transfer is altogether exemplary, a model of its kind, and the well-focused mono sound gives unalloyed pleasure.

Rodrigue et Chimène (opera; completed Langham Smith; orch. Denisov).
(N) *** Erato/Warner Dig. 4509 98508-2 (2) [id.]. Donna Brown, Dale, Jossoud, Van Dam, Bastin, Le Texier, Lyon Op. Ch. & O, Nagano.

In the years immediately before he started work on his masterpiece, *Pelléas et Mélisande*, Debussy all but completed this opera to a much more conventional libretto, telling the story of El Cid. The project was prompted by the over-insistent librettist, Catulle Mendès, and during its composition Debussy came to appreciate very clearly how far the piece departed from his concept of an opera in short, visionary scenes. He later claimed to have destroyed the score, but in fact the manuscript was virtually complete, mainly in well-detailed short-score. Richard Langham Smith reconstructed the rest, and Edison Denisov did the inspired orchestration, adding music from other sections to fill in a few gaps. The best comes first. The duet between Rodrigue et Chimène at the start of Act I is vintage Debussy, already distinctive, sweet and fluent, with radiant singing from Laurence Dale, ideal as Rodrigue, and the fresh and expressive soprano, Donna Brown, as Chimène. Atmospheric off-stage choruses are distinctive too, but little of Act III gives much clue as to the identity of the composer, enjoyable though it is. Kent Nagano chose this as the opera to open the new opera house in Lyon, and this superb recording was then made in studio sessions with vividly atmospheric sound. José van Dam sings strongly and clearly as the heroine's father, Don Diègue, with the veteran, Jules Bastin, in splendid voice as Don Gomez.

Delalande, Michel-Richard (1657–1726)

Symphonies pour les soupers du roy (complete).
*** HM Dig. HMC 901337/40 (4) [id.]. Ensemble La Simphonie du Marais, Reyne.

In the last years of his life, Louis XIV could choose from among a dozen suites to accompany his meal. This is the first time all have been committed to disc. Each of these four CDs contains between 36 and 45 individual movements, much of it as charming and inventive as the familiar excerpts. The young members of the Ensemble La Simphonie du Marais, led by Hugo Reyne, give thoroughly fresh and stylish accounts of them.

Cantate Domino; De profundis; Regina coeli.
(Y/B) *** ASV/Gaudeamus Dig. CDGAU 141 [id.]. Ex Cathedra Chamber Ch. & Bar. O, Skidmore.

Jeffrey Skidmore with his fine, Birmingham-based choir and orchestra presents vividly characterized performances of three of Delalande's '*grands motets*', written to be performed simultaneously with the daily celebration of Mass at Louis XIV's court. *De profundis* is a magnificent piece, as are the two lighter, joyful motets. As the title indicates, *Regina coeli* has a Marian text, while *Cantate Domino* represents the peak of Delalande's long career. With their sequences of brief, sharply contrasted movements, these motets, in performances as lively and sensitive as these, can be warmly recommended to many more than baroque specialists. Warm, full sound.

Confitebor tibi Domine; Super flumina Babilonis; Te Deum.
*** HM Dig. HMC 901351 [id.]. Gens, Piau, Steyer, Fouchécourt, Piolino, Corréas, Les Arts
   Florissants, Christie.

Confitebor tibi Domine (1699) and *Super flumina Babilonis* (1687) have much expressive writing, and the
performances under William Christie are light and airy but not wanting in expressive feeling. The more
familiar *Te Deum* is given as good a performance as any that has appeared in recent years. The sound is
airy and spacious and the performances combine lightness and breadth.

3 Leçons de ténèbres.
(Y/B) (M) *** Erato/Warner 4509 98528-2 [id.]. Etcheverry, Charbonnier, Boulay.

These *Leçons de ténèbres* are for the relatively austere combination of voice and continuo favoured in
France at this time and perhaps best known from their use by Couperin and Charpentier. Delalande
brings a distinctive personal stamp to these settings and is no less a master of the ariosa style than his
contemporaries; indeed, in melodic richness some of this is even finer than the Couperin version. And
the continuo realization (viola da gamba; harpsichord; chamber organ) was spontaneous and not
prepared in every detail beforehand; it sounds fresh and immediate without having the fussiness that
often marks continuo realizations. Micaëla Etcheverry is an excellent soloist; she sings with considerable
lyrical beauty, and the artists are eminently well balanced and recorded. A welcome reissue.

Delden, Lex van (1919–88)

(i) *Concerto for double string orchestra, Op. 71; Piccolo concerto, Op. 67;* (ii) *Musica sinfonica, Op. 93;* (iii)
Symphony No. 3 (Facets), Op. 45.
(Y/B) *(**) Etcetera stereo/mono KTC 1156 [id.]. Concg. O; (i) Eugen Jochum; (ii) Bernard Haitink;
   (iii) George Szell.

The idiom of the Dutch composer, Lex van Delden, is predominantly tonal and his style offers occasional reminders of Roussel, Honegger and Stravinsky. The strongest of the works here are the *Third
Symphony* and the brilliant *Piccolo concerto* for twelve wind instruments, timpani, percussion and
piano. Van Delden is inventive and intelligent, and these four pieces leave you wanting to hear more. The
recordings were made at various times and are of varying quality, all in the Concertgebouw Hall and
taken from various broadcast tapes, the two concertos conducted by Jochum in 1968 and 1964 respectively (the latter is mono), the *Musica sinfonica* with Haitink in 1969, and the *Third Symphony* with Szell,
again mono, in 1957.

Delibes, Léo (1836–91)

Coppélia (ballet): complete.
*** Erato/Warner Dig. 4509 91730-2 (2) [id.]. Lyon Opéra O, Kent Nagano.
*** Decca Dig. 414 502-2 (2) [id.]. Nat. PO, Richard Bonynge.
(N) (B) *** Decca Double 444 836-2 [id.]. SRO, Bonynge – MASSENET: *Le Carillon.* ***
(B) **(*) Ph. Duo 438 763-2 [id.]. Rotterdam PO, David Zinman – CHOPIN: *Les Sylphides;* GOUNOD:
   Faust: ballet music. **(*)

Delibes's delightful score for *Coppélia*, which Tchaikovsky admired so much, is available in a number of
different formats, but Kent Nagano's new complete set rises fairly easily to the top of the current list of
recommendations. The performance has many felicities and the Orchestre de L'Opéra de Lyon bring a
sure sense of style to this elegantly crafted and engagingly tuneful music. Their playing is polished, yet
warm and graceful and, under the lively yet nicely detailed direction of Kent Nagano, the spontaneity
of the music-making seems to grow as the ballet proceeds. The recording has a nicely judged acoustic,
warm yet clear.

   The only slight drawback to Bonynge's digital recording is the relatively modest number of violins
which the clarity of the digital recording makes apparent. In all other respects the recording is praiseworthy, not only for its vividness of colour but for the balance within a concert-hall acoustic (Walthamstow Assembly Hall).

   On the Double Decca reissue of his earlier (1969) analogue set, Bonynge secures a high degree of polish
from the Suisse Romande Orchestra, with sparkling string and wind textures, and with sonority and bite
from the brass. The Decca recording sounds freshly minted and, with its generous Massenet bonus,
little-known music of great charm, this set remains very competitive.

   David Zinman's performance of *Coppélia* is beautifully played and most naturally recorded. The warm acoustic of the Rotterdam concert hall certainly suits Delibes's colourful scoring and the gracefully delicate string-playing is nicely flattered. The performance has no want of vigour or refinement and, if it is without the sheer character of Kent Nagano's performance, it is still very enjoyable in its own right. The Chopin and Gounod couplings are similarly smooth and elegant, and all are offered at the cost of one premium-priced CD.

Coppélia (ballet; complete); *La Source: suites Nos. 2 & 3; Intermezzo: Pas de fleurs.*
(N) (BB) *** Naxos Dig. 8.553356/7 [id.]. Slovak RSO (Bratislava), Mogrelia.

Mogrelia's complete Naxos set of *Coppélia* is very attractive indeed. The Bratislava orchestra plays with characteristic finesse and grace and with glowing lyrical feeling. There is both drama and vitality. The recording is warm and spacious, with the orchestra set slightly back. Other versions may have more surface brilliance (the *Musique des automates* in Act II could glitter more brightly), but most lovers of ballet music will enjoy the naturalness of perspective and the attractively smooth string-quality. *La Source* somes off equally well. The *Pas de fleurs Grande valse* is a real lollipop and in the two suites the music (selected rather arbitrarily) has plenty of colour and rhythmic life.

(i) *Coppélia* (ballet): complete; *Sylvia* (ballet): complete.
(M) *** Mercury 434 313-2 (3) [id.]. (i) Minneapolis SO, Dorati; (ii) LSO, Fistoulari.

Both Mercury recordings are very early stereo (*Coppélia* 1957, *Sylvia* 1958), but neither sounds its age and *Sylvia*, using the expansive acoustics of Watford Town Hall, approaches the demonstration bracket. Fistoulari was among the very greatest of ballet interpreters and this shows him at his most inspired. The conductor displays his deep affection for the ballet in every bar; his sense of delicacy and grace and his feeling for the specially French elegance of the woodwind writing are demonstrated throughout. The LSO play superbly for him, the woodwind ensemble is outstanding and the solo playing most beautiful.

Dorati's recording of *Coppélia* makes a lively contrast. This Minneapolis recording has never sounded better than it does here. The acoustic is rather more confined at the bottom end, but the conductor's vivid combination of energy and grace is appealing in a score that teems with bright melodies and piquant orchestral effects.

Coppélia (ballet) extended excerpts: Act I, Nos. 1–2, 6–8, 10; Act II, Nos. 12, 14, 15–20, 22; Act III, Nos. 23–8, 30, 32, 34–6.
(Y/B) *** Erato/Warner 4509 96368-2 [id.]. Lyon Opéra O, Kent Nagano.

A very comprehensive selection from our top recommendation for Delibes's delightful score for *Coppélia*, which Tchaikovsky admired so much. The whole set on two CDs (see above) plays for only 99 minutes and here are 74 minutes 35 seconds of them. Every bar of the music-making is of the highest quality, and the recording, with its nicely judged acoustic, is as attractive as the playing. Self-recommending.

Coppélia: extended excerpts; *Sylvia:* extended excerpts.
(B) *** EMI CZS7 67208-2 (2). Paris Op. O, Mari.

Jean-Baptiste Mari's pair of CDs are offered for the price of one in the French Rouge et Noir series. The sound is fresh and the extra brightness of focus brings no attendant edginess. Mari uses ballet tempi throughout, yet there is never any loss of momentum, and the long-breathed string phrasing and the felicitous wind solos are a continual source of delight. Mari's natural sympathy and warmth make the very most of the less memorable parts of the score for *Sylvia* (and they are only slightly less memorable). Seventy-five minutes is offered from each ballet.

Coppélia (ballet): suite.
(B) *** DG Double 437 404-2 (2) [id.]. BPO, Karajan – CHOPIN: *Les Sylphides* *** ⊛; GOUNOD: *Faust* etc. **(*); OFFENBACH: *Gaîté parisienne;* RAVEL: *Boléro* ***; TCHAIKOVSKY: *Sleeping Beauty* (suite). **(*)

(i) *Coppélia* (ballet) suite; (ii) *Sylvia* (ballet) suite.
(N) (B) *** Sony SBK 46550; *SBT 46550* [id.]. Phd. O, Ormandy – CHOPIN: *Les Sylphides* ***; TCHAIKOVSKY: *Nutcracker suite.* **(*)

Ormandy and the Philadelphia Orchestra are on top form here. The playing sparkles and has a fine sense of style. Both suites are done in a continuous presentation but are, unfortunately, not banded. The recording is notably full and brilliant in the CBS manner.

Karajan secures some wonderfully elegant playing from the Berlin Philharmonic Orchestra, and generally his lightness of touch is sure; the *Csárdás*, however, is played very slowly and heavily. The recording is impressive and DG have now returned the suite to its original format so that the three movements omitted on its last appearance have been restored. Other ballet music has now been added, plus Ravel's ubiquitous *Boléro*, all played with considerable panache.

Coppélia: suite; *Kassya: Trepak; Le roi s'amuse:* suite; *La Source:* suite; *Sylvia:* suite.
(BB) **(*) Naxos Dig. 8.550080; *4550080* [id.]. Slovak RSO (Bratislava), Ondrej Lenárd.

An attractive hour of Delibes, with five key items from *Coppélia*, including the *Music for the Automatons* and *Waltz*, four from *Sylvia*, not forgetting the *Pizzicato*, and four from *La Source*. Perhaps most enjoyable of all are the six pastiche ancient airs de danse, provided for a ballroom scene in Victor Hugo's play, *Le roi s'amuse*. They are played most gracefully here, and the excerpts from the major ballets are spirited and nicely turned. The brightly lit digital sound has body too, and the acoustics of the Bratislava Concert Hall are not unflattering to Delibes's vivid palette.

Sylvia (ballet): complete.
(N) (B) *** Decca Double 448 095-2 (2) [id.]. New Philh. O, Richard Bonynge – MASSENET: *Le Cid.*
    ***

(N) (BB) *** Naxos Dig. 8.553338/9 [id.]. Razumovsky Sinfonia, Mogrelia – SAINT-SAENS: *Henry VIII ballet music.* ***

Sylvia is played by Richard Bonynge with wonderful polish and affection, and the recording is full, brilliant and sparkling in Decca's best manner. The CDs offer a splendid Massenet bonus, another recording out of Decca's top drawer, and this is even more attractive as a Double Decca.

Mogrelia's performance of *Sylvia* is above all spacious, bringing out the music's pastel-shaded lyricism yet finding plenty of weight for the more vigorous music depicting the hunters. The relaxed tempo for the famous *Valse lente* is quite well sustained and the Razumovsky Sinfonia carries this slighter of Delibes's two most famous ballet scores very pleasingly, with the gentle wind solos matching the caressing warmth of the strings. The *Divertissement* of Act III (which includes some of the best numbers, including the famous '*Pizzicato*') is vividly done. However, in the performance as a whole, glowing sentience takes precedence over vitality, and some might find the atmosphere at times a little sleepy. Excellent, naturally balanced recording.

OPERA

Lakmé (complete).
(M) *** Decca 425 485-2 (2). Sutherland, Berbié, Vanzo, Bacquier, Monte Carlo Op. Ch. and O, Bonynge.

Lakmé is a strange work, not at all the piece one would expect knowing simply the famous *Bell song*. This performance seizes its opportunities with both hands. Sutherland swallows her consonants, but the beauty of her singing, with its ravishing ease and purity up to the highest register, is what matters; and she has opposite her one of the most pleasing and intelligent of French tenors, Alain Vanzo. Excellent contributions from the others too, spirited conducting and brilliant, atmospheric recording.

Delius, Frederick (1862–1934)

The Delius Collection

With many of the performances directed by the composer's devoted amanuensis and dedicated interpreter, Eric Fenby, the Unicorn Delius Collection can be given the strongest recommendation. Quite apart from the consistent quality of the music-making, the warm and spacious digital sound seems ideally suited to music which depends on atmosphere and evocation to make its fullest effect.

Volume 1: (i–ii) *Dance rhapsody No. 1* (ed. Beecham); (i; iii) *Dance rhapsody No. 2; Fantastic dance;* (iv) (Piano) *Preludes Nos. 1–3; Zum carnival* (polka); (v; i; iii) *Song of the high hills.*
(Y/B) ❀ (M) *** Unicorn Dig. UKCD 2071 [id.]. (i) RPO; (ii) Del Mar; (iii) Fenby; (iv) Parkin; (v) Amb. S.

Norman Del Mar, a natural Delian, gives a spontaneously volatile performance of the *Dance rhapsody No. 1*, and the spacious recording with its wide dynamic range captures well the music's sudden mood-changes. The *Dance rhapsody No. 2* is not much more than half as long but, even more than the first, it gives the lie to the idea of Delius as an unrhythmic composer. Fenby's performance is both fluid and crisply sprung. The *Fantastic dance* is an agreeable late miniature. Eric Parkin also breathes Delian air naturally. The *Preludes* for piano are typical miniatures, the *Polka* an oddity. The piano is naturally caught. But the highlight of this well-planned programme is the *Song of the high hills*, written in 1911. Fenby, the composer's life-long advocate, draws a richly atmospheric performance from Beecham's old orchestra in what proves to be one of the most ravishingly beautiful of Delius's choral works, here finely balanced within an evocative sound-picture, ideally warm yet with the most delicate pianissimo detail.

Volume 2: (i–ii) *Piano concerto;* (iii–iv) *Violin concerto;* (v) *Irmelin: Prelude; A Late lark; A Song of summer.*
(Y/B) (M) *** Unicorn Dig. UKCD 2072 [id.]. RPO; (i) Fowke; (ii) Del Mar; (iii) Holmes; (iv) Handley; (v) Fenby.

Philip Fowke rides confidently over the orchestra in this impassioned account of the one-movement *Piano concerto*, a work admired by Busoni. As ever, Del Mar is the responsive accompanist. Ralph Holmes and Vernon Handley form a comparable symbiosis in their strong and beautiful account of the *Violin concerto*, one of Delius's supreme masterpieces, recorded shortly before the premature death of the soloist. Holmes and Handley together bring out the Delian warmth in their shaping of phrase and pointing of rhythm while keeping firm overall control. Holmes's beautifully focused playing is nicely balanced against the wide span of the orchestra behind him. *A Late lark* was the last composition which Delius was able to finish, except for a few bars, before the arrival of Eric Fenby; while *A Song of summer* is the finest of the works which Fenby subsequently took down from the dictation of the blind, paralysed and irascible composer; the performance is loving and dedicated. The programme opens with a ravishingly atmospheric account of the *Irmelin Prelude*, arranged by Fenby with the composer's approval.

Volume 3: (i) *Koanga: La Calinda;* (i–iii) *Idyll;* (i–iv) *Songs of sunset;* (v) *A Village Romeo and Juliet: Walk to the Paradise Garden.*
(Y/B) (M) *** Unicorn Dig. UKCD 2073 [id.]. RPO; (i) Fenby; with (ii) Felicity Lott, (iii) Thomas Allen; (iv) Sarah Walker, Amb. S.; (v) Del Mar.

In this continuing series, conducted for the most part by Eric Fenby, Volume 3 is particularly valuable. The love scene entitled *Idyll* was rescued from an abortive opera project (*Margot la rouge*) and the composer reworked the music to words of Walt Whitman, arranged by Robert Nichols. It becomes a beautiful, extended duet in this impressive performance by Felicity Lott and Thomas Allen. Allen is no less persuasive in the *Songs of sunset*, where he is joined by Sarah Walker, and this fine recording brings ravishing sounds from the Ambrosians, with both soloists deeply expressive. The concert opens with Norman Del Mar's languorously brooding yet passionate account of the *Walk to the Paradise Garden* and ends with Fenby's expansive performance of *La Calinda*, which begins with deceptive delicacy. First-class digital sound throughout.

Volume 4: (i) *Cello sonata;* (ii) *Violin sonatas Nos. 1–3.*
(Y/B) (M) *** Unicorn Dig./Analogue UKCD 2074 [id.]. (i) Julian Lloyd Webber; (ii) Ralph Holmes; Eric Fenby.

The *Cello sonata* dates from the fruitful period of the First World War, when Delius wrote a sequence of richly lyrical and imaginative works – concertos as well as sonatas – which he moulded to his very own personal expression. Lloyd Webber is a warmly persuasive advocate and Fenby partners him admirably. The three *Violin sonatas*, particularly the last, are also among the finest of Delius's chamber works. Though Fenby as pianist may not be a virtuoso, the natural affinity of his playing and that of Ralph Holmes with the composer's muse makes this one of the most treasurable and moving of Delius recordings. The *Cello sonata* was recorded digitally in 1981 and is set in a natural and pleasing acoustic. The *Violin sonatas*, dating from a decade earlier, are also atmospheric in ambience, but the violin timbre has just a hint of thinness on top.

Volume 5: Orchestral songs: (i) *The bird's story;* (ii) *I-Brasil;* (i) *Le ciel est par-dessus le toit;* (ii) *La lune blanche;* (i) *Let springtime come;* (ii) *Il pleure dans mon cœur;* (iii) *To daffodils; Twilight fancies; Wine roses.* Songs with piano: (iii) *Autumn;* (i) *Avant que tu ne t'en ailles;* (iii) *Chanson d'automne;* (i) *Le ciel est par-dessus le toit;* (ii) *I-Brasil;* (i) *In the garden of the Seraglio; Irmelin Rose;* (iii) *Let springtime come;* (ii) *La lune blanche; Il pleure dans mon cœur; Silken shoes; So white, so soft, so sweet is she;* (i) *Sweet Venevil;* (iii) *To daffodils; Twilight fancies;* (i) *The violet.*
(N) (M) *** Unicorn Dig. UKCD 2075 [id.]. (i) Felicity Lott; (ii) Anthony Rolfe Johnson; (iii) Sarah Walker; RPO, Eric Fenby; or Fenby (piano).

The very generous (73 minutes) collection of Delius songs is particularly valuable in including the beautiful and virtually unknown orchestral arrangements. All the orchestral songs are sung in the original language, whereas in the larger collection of English, French and Scandinavian songs – in which Eric Fenby accompanies on Delius's own piano – except for three in German, the Scandinavian settings are sung in English. Apart from the early *Twilight fancies* they are little known, but they consistently reflect the composer's feeling for words. Almost all of them are slow and dreamy, to provide a charming sidelight on Delius's art. The duplications in both versions are particularly welcome. All three soloists sing most understandingly and characterfully. Excellent recording.

Volume 6: (i) *Fennimore and Gerda: intermezzo;* (ii) *Paris* (*the song of a great city*; ed. Beecham); (iii; iv) *Suite for violin and orchestra;* (i; v) *An Arabesque.*

(N) (M) *** Unicorn Dig. UKCD 2076 [id.]. RPO, cond. (i) Eric Fenby; (ii) Norman Del Mar; (iii) Vernon Handley; with (iv) Ralph Holmes; (v) Thomas Allen, Amb. S.

Paris is more spaciously conceived by Norman Del Mar than by Mackerras (or, indeed, by Collins) but the splendidly atmospheric Unicorn sound-picture suits this evocatively leisurely, less vibrant reading. In Fenby's hands, *An Arabesque* emerges as a masterpiece. The emotional thrust of the opening sequence, superbly sung by Thomas Allen and with passionate singing from the chorus too, subsides into characteristic Delius reflectiveness. The early *Suite for violin and orchestra* is played with much understanding, with Holmes and Handley naturally attuned to its rhapsodical feeling; and Fenby closes the programme with a warmly evocative account of the best-known piece here, the lovely *Intermezzo* from *Fennimore and Gerda*.

Volume 7: (i) *2 Aquarelles;* (i; iv) *Caprice and elegy;* (ii; v) *Légende;* (iii) *Life's dance;* (i; vi) *Cynara;* (i; vii) *Songs of farewell.*

(N) (M) *** Unicorn Dig. UKCD 2077 [id.]. RPO, cond. (i) Eric Fenby; (ii) Vernon Handley; (iii) Norman Del Mar; with (iv) Julian Lloyd Webber; (v) Ralph Holmes; (vi) Thomas Allen; (vii) Amb. S.

Once again Eric Fenby draws loving and dedicated performances from the RPO and the Ambrosian Singers: the *Songs of farewell* are most beautiful; and Thomas Allen is very impressive in *Cynara*. *Life's dance*, conceived at the same time as *Paris* (1889), certainly does not lack ebullience in Norman Del Mar's hands, and Ralph Holmes and Handley again find an admirable partnership in the *Légende*. The two gentle *Aquarelles* for strings are Fenby's transcriptions of two choruses for unaccompanied mixed voices 'to be sung of a summer night on the water', and these, together with the *Caprice and elegy* (dedicated to Fenby) for cello and small orchestra, make an attractive central interlude in the programme. Julian Lloyd Webber is very persuasive as soloist in the latter piece. As throughout this series, the recording is warmly atmospheric and beautifully balanced.

Air and dance for string orchestra; Fennimore and Gerda: Intermezzo. Hassan: Intermezzo and Serenade (arr. Beecham). *Irmelin: Prelude. Koanga: La Calinda. On hearing the first cuckoo in spring; Sleigh ride; A song before sunrise; Summer evening* (ed. Beecham); *Summer night on the river.*

(M) *** EMI Dig. CDM5 65067-2 [id.]. N. Sinfonia, Richard Hickox.

Richard Hickox's 1985 Delius collection neatly brings together most of the shorter pieces in finely shaped, well-played readings, recorded in aptly atmospheric sound. Hickox's warm moulding of phrase goes with fine playing from the Northern Sinfonia. This is currently the best-recorded of the post-Beecham digital collections. However, Marriner's comparable analogue CD also offers lovely sound-quality and is much more generous in including also *Sea drift*.

Air and dance; Fennimore and Gerda: Intermezzo. Hassan: Intermezzo and Serenade; Koanga: La Calinda. On hearing the first cuckoo in spring; A Song before sunrise; Summer night on the river; A Village Romeo and Juliet: The Walk to the Paradise Garden. (i) *Sea drift.*

(M) *** Decca 440 323-2 [id.]. ASMF, Marriner; (i) John Shirley-Quirk, L. Symphony Ch., RPO, Hickox.

This orchestral collection was admirably recorded in 1977, but the quality is not in the least dated. These are lovely performances, warm, tender and eloquent. They are played superbly and recorded in a flattering acoustic. The recording is beautifully balanced – the distant cuckoo is highly evocative – though, with a relatively small band of strings, the sound inevitably has less body than with a full orchestral group. *Sea drift* was recorded (also by Argo engineers) three years later in 1980 and is a total success. Rather than lingering, Richard Hickox is urgent in his expressiveness, but there is plenty of evocative atmosphere. John Shirley-Quirk sings with characteristic sensitivity and the chorus – trained by Hickox – is outstanding. The effect of the CD transfer is most real and tangible, the chorus set back within a warm ambience.

American rhapsody (Appalachia); Norwegian suite (Folkeraadet: The Council of the people); Paa Vidderne (On the heights); Spring morning.

**Marco Polo 8.220452 [id.]. Slovak PO, Bratislava, John Hopkins.

A fascinating collection of early Delius, mostly uncharacteristic, but with pre-echoes of his later work. *Paa Vidderne*, the most substantial piece, is rather melodramatic but has a distinct melodic interest. *Spring morning* is shorter and similarly picaresque, but the *Folkeraadet suite* displays a sure orchestral touch and is most attractive in its diversity of invention. The *American rhapsody* is a concise version of *Appalachia* without the chorus, given here in its original 1896 format. John Hopkins brings a strong sympathy and understanding to this repertoire and secures a committed and flexible response from his Czech players in music which must have been wholly unknown to them.

2 Aquarelles (arr. Fenby); *Fennimore and Gerda: Intermezzo. Hassan: Intermezzo and serenade* (all arr. Beecham); *Irmelin: Prelude. Late swallows* (arr. Fenby); *On hearing the first cuckoo in spring; A Song before sunrise; Summer night on the river*.
(M) *** Chandos CHAN 6502 [id.]. Bournemouth Sinf., Norman Del Mar.

There are few finer interpreters of Delius than the late Norman Del Mar. The 49-minute concert creates a mood of serene, atmospheric evocation – into which Eric Fenby's arrangement of *Late swallows* from the *String quartet* fits admirably – and the beauty of the 1977 analogue recording has been transferred very well to CD, with all its warmth and bloom retained.

2 Aquarelles; Fennimore and Gerda: Intermezzo. On hearing the first cuckoo in spring; Summer night on the river.
(M) *** DG 439 529-2 [id.]. ECO, Barenboim – VAUGHAN WILLIAMS: *Lark ascending* etc.; WALTON: *Henry V*. ***

Barenboim's luxuriant performances have a gorgeous sensuousness and their warm, sleepy atmosphere should seduce many normally resistant to Delius's pastoralism. The couplings are no less enticing; indeed, some might feel that this music-making has a touch of decadence in its unalloyed appeal to the senses.

Brigg Fair; Dance rhapsody No. 2; Fennimore and Gerda: Intermezzo. Florida suite; Irmelin: Prelude. Marche-caprice; On hearing the first cuckoo in spring; Over the hills and far away; Sleigh ride; Song before sunrise; Summer evening; Summer night on the river; (i) *Songs of sunset*.
⊛ *** EMI CDS7 47509-8 (2) [id.]. RPO, Beecham; (i) with Forrester, Cameron, Beecham Ch. Soc.

The remastering of the complete stereo orchestral recordings of Delius's music, plus the choral *Songs of sunset*, is something of a technological miracle. Beecham's fine-spun magic, his ability to lift a phrase, is apparent throughout. In the *Songs of sunset* the choral focus is soft-grained, but the words are surprisingly audible, and the backward balance of the soloists is made to sound natural against the rich orchestral textures. The gramophone here offers music-making which is every bit as rewarding as the finest live performances.

Brigg Fair; Eventyr; In a summer garden; A Song of summer.
(B) *** CfP CD-CFP 4568; *TC-CFP 4568*. Hallé O, Vernon Handley.

Although the tempi are sometimes controversial, Handley is an understanding and exciting Delian, and these pieces are beautifully played. The digital recording is of EMI's best quality, matching clarity of definition with ambient lustre and rich colouring. A bargain.

(i) *Brigg Fair; La Calinda* (arr. Fenby); *In a summer garden; Fennimore and Gerda: Intermezzo. Hassan: Intermezzo* and (iii) *Serenade* (arr. Beecham); (ii) *Irmelin prelude;* (i) *Late swallows* (arr. Fenby); *On hearing the first cuckoo in spring; A song before sunrise;* (ii) *A song of summer;* (i) *Summer night on the river;* (ii) *A Village Romeo and Juliet: Walk to the Paradise Garden* (arr. Beecham); (i; iv) *Appalachia* (with brief rehearsal sequence).
(Y/B) (M) *** EMI CMS5 65119-2 [Ang. ZDMB 65119]. (i) Hallé O; (ii) LSO; Sir John Barbirolli; (iii) with Robert Tear; (iv) Balun Jenkins, Amb. S.

Sir John shows an admirable feeling for the sense of light Delius conjures up and for the luxuriance of texture his music possesses. The languor of the string and horn tune in *Brigg Fair* is matched by the almost Mediterranean feeling of the works evoking summer, whilst the gentle evocation of *La Calinda* contrasts with the surge of passionate Italianate romanticism at the arching string-phrases of the climax of *The walk to the Paradise Garden*. Barbirolli's style is evanescent in repose and more romantic than the Beecham versions but, with lovely playing from both the Hallé and the LSO, the first-rate analogue sound from the mid-to late 1960s adds to the listener's pleasure. In *Appalachia*, perhaps Barbirolli dwells a little too lovingly on detail to suit all tastes, but for the most part he gives an admirably atmospheric reading that conveys the work's exotic and vivid colouring.

Brigg Fair; In a summer garden; Paris (The song of a great city); On hearing the first cuckoo in spring; A song of summer; Summer night on the river.
(Y/B) (M) (***) Dutton Lab. mono CDLXT 2503 [id.]. LSO, Anthony Collins.

Mike Dutton works another of his miracles here, achieving colour, body and translucence for these 1953

Decca recordings and revealing why they were so much admired in their day. Made in the Kingsway Hall, the ambient warmth of that famous venue means that the usual flatness of mono perspective all but disappears except in the complex fortissimos, and the glow of the sound, so essential in Delius, makes listening to this CD a real pleasure, with no apologies necessary for the body of string-tone. Collins's performance of *Paris* is spontaneously full of passionate evocation, confirms Collins as an inspired and individual Delian in his own right, able to create a subtle control of mood and texture reminiscent of Debussy in its atmospheric impressionism. *First cuckoo* is luminous in its woodwind detail. The recording shows how far Decca's engineers were ahead of the competition with their *ffrr* (full frequency range recording) technique, even in the earliest days of LP.

(i) *Caprice & elegy;* (ii; iii) *Piano concerto;* (iv; v) *Violin concerto;* (vi; iii) *Hassan: Intermezzo and serenade; Koanga: La Calinda;* (v) *On hearing the first cuckoo in spring;* (vii) *Legend for violin and piano.*
(***) Testament mono SBT 1014 [id.]. (i) Beatrice Harrison, CO, Eric Fenby; (ii) Moiseiwitsch, Philh. O; (iii) Constant Lambert; (iv) Albert Sammons; (v) Liverpool PO, Sargent; (vi) Hallé O; (vii) Henry Holst, Gerald Moore.

The greatest treasure here is the first ever recording of the *Violin concerto*, made in 1944 and featuring the original soloist, Albert Sammons, arguably the most eloquent and moving account of the work ever committed to disc. The thrusting passion of the performance comes not just from Sammons but from Sargent and the Liverpool orchestra, confirming this as one of Delius's supreme masterpieces. Moiseiwitsch's recording of the *Piano concerto*, also the first ever, is hardly less powerful, making a very good case for this warm but less cogent piece. The other items range from the 1930 recording of the *Caprice and elegy* by Beatrice Harrison, the dedicatee, with suspect intonation and plentiful portamento, to Sargent's 1947 recording of the *First cuckoo*, very warm and free in its rubato. Constant Lambert is also a first-rate interpreter of Delius, as the *Hassan* and *Koanga* excerpts show. This transfer has higher surface-hiss than later issues on this label, but the disc must be as strongly recommended as the Beecham transfers from Dutton – even if these are perhaps more sophisticated.

Cello concerto.
*** RCA RD 70800. Lloyd Webber, Philh. O, Handley – HOLST: *Invocation;* VAUGHAN WILLIAMS: *Fantasia.* ***
(N) *** EMI Dig. CDC5 55529-2 [id.]. Jacqueline du Pré, RPO, Sir Malcolm Sargent – Recital. ***

Lloyd Webber is inside the idiom and plays the *Cello concerto* with total conviction. Its lyricism is beguiling enough, but the work proceeds in wayward fashion, and the soloist must play every note as if he believes in it ardently – and this Lloyd Webber and his partners do. The RCA recording conveys an almost chamber-like quality at times, with great warmth and clarity.

The newly revamped version of the Delius (du Pré's first concerto recording) offers more body and warmth in the cello sound. The recital is a transfer of the material, mainly from her very first EMI sessions in 1962 which gave such clear promise of glories to come. Most recommendable, although readers will note that it remains at full price.

(i) *Cello concerto;* (ii) *Double concerto for violin and cello. Paris (the song of a great city).*
(M) *** EMI Dig. CD-EMX 2185; *TC-EMX 2185.* (i; ii) Rafael Wallfisch; (ii) Tasmin Little; RLPO, Mackerras.

This superb new recording of the *Double concerto*, with soloists who easily outshine their predecessors on record (however distinguished), confirms the strength of a piece which establishes its own logic, with each theme developing naturally out of the preceding one. Wallfisch is just as persuasive in the *Cello concerto*, and Mackerras proves an understanding interpreter of the composer in the big tone-poem, *Paris, the song of a great city.* The recording is comparably full and atmospheric.

Piano concerto in C min.
(N) (M) *** EMI Dig. CD-EMX 2239 [id.]. Piers Lane, RLPO, Handley – VAUGHAN WILLIAMS: *Piano concerto;* FINZI: *Eclogue.* ***
(B) *** Decca 433 633-2. Kars, LSO, Gibson – ELGAR: *Cello concerto* etc. ***

Piers Lane gives a masterly performance of the Delius *Piano concerto*, weighty without pomposity, which effectively counters ideas of this merely being 'sub-Grieg', early as it is. Lane's measured, concentrated reading of the slow movement is particularly compelling. An apt and unusual coupling.

Jean-Rodolphe Kars also proves a superb and eloquent advocate of what has previously been thought of as one of Delius's weaker pieces. The LSO under Sir Alexander Gibson provides admirable support, and the 1969 recording preserves an excellent balance between the two. Excellent value.

Violin concerto.
(M) **(*) EMI CDM7 64725-2 [id.]. Sir Yehudi Menuhin, RPO, Meredith Davies – ELGAR: *Violin concerto.* ***

(i) *Violin concerto. 2 Aquarelles* (arr. Fenby); *Dance rhapsodies 1 and 2; Fennimore and Gerda: Intermezzo. Irmelin prelude; On hearing the first cuckoo in spring; Summer night on the river.*
**(*) Decca Dig. 433 704-2 [id.]. (i) Tasmin Little; Welsh Nat. Op. O, Mackerras.

Tasmin Little's shading down to hushed pianissimos is ravishing, with the close of the work bringing a moment of total repose, while Mackerras draws strong, sympathetic playing from the orchestra of WNO. The *Dance rhapsodies*, works which similarly are far from rhapsodic, here receive fresh, taut performances, but the forwardness and clarity of the recording tend to make the results less evocative than they might be.

Menuhin's performance, recorded in 1976, does not show the polish of his playing in earlier years, and the timbre is not always ideally sweet; but he gives a heartfelt performance, and the semi-improvisational freedom and radiant beauty of the writing above the stave are superbly caught. Meredith Davies provides an accompaniment that is full of delicately sensitive detail, if not as richly expressive as Boult's partnership in the coupled Elgar *Concerto*. The Abbey Road recording is truthful, warmly atmospheric and well balanced, to make this an indispensable coupling for lovers of English music.

Dance rhapsodies Nos. 1–2; In a summer garden; North Country sketches; A Village Romeo and Juliet: Walk to the Paradise Garden.
(Y/B) **(*) Chandos Dig. CHAN 9355 [id.]. Bournemouth SO, Richard Hickox.

Hickox is a sensitive and flexible Delian and the Bournemouth orchestra play passionately for him, especially in the *Walk to the Paradise Garden*. The *Dance rhapsodies* are impulsively volatile and attractively so, but they are not held together quite so persuasively as by Eric Fenby, who also has the advantage of smoother and more natural string recording. *In a summer garden* is both ardent and luxuriant in its shimmering summer heat-haze, while the wintry landscape of the *North Country sketches* brings almost crystalline iciness from the violins. The *March of spring* with its 'light, lively and throbbing movement' is chimerically spontaneous in unfolding its kaleidoscopic detail. But the recording, made in the Winter Gardens, Bournemouth, although basically full and spacious, brings a somewhat two-dimensional effect in catching the fervent sweep of violin-tone, as if the microphones were a little too close.

Eventyr; Fennimore and Gerda: Intermezzo. Irmelin: prelude. Over the hills and far away; Paris (the song of a great city).
(***) Beecham Trust mono BEECHAM 2. LPO, Sir Thomas Beecham.

These recordings date from between 1935 and 1939. The transfers from the original 78 r.p.m. discs were made by the highly skilled Anthony Griffiths, and the further remastering for CD seems to have been entirely beneficial.

Fennimore and Gerda: Intermezzo. Irmelin: Prelude. Koanga: La Calinda (arr. Fenby). *On hearing the first cuckoo in spring; Sleigh ride; A Song before sunrise; Summer night on the river; A Village Romeo and Juliet: The Walk to the Paradise Garden.*
(B) *** CfP CD-CFP 4304; *TC-CFP 40304*. LPO, Vernon Handley.

Those looking for a bargain collection of Delius should find this very good value; Handley's approach to *The Walk to the Paradise Garden* is strongly emotional, closer to Barbirolli than to Beecham.

Florida suite; North Country sketches.
*** Chandos Dig. CHAN 8413 [id.]. Ulster O, Handley.

Handley's choice of tempi is always apt and it is fascinating that in the *North Country sketches* which evoke the seasons on the Yorkshire moors a Debussian influence is revealed. Handley's refined approach clearly links the *Florida suite* with later masterpieces. The recording is superbly balanced within the very suitable acoustics of the Ulster Hall.

On hearing the first cuckoo in spring; Summer night on the river.
(Y/B) (B) *** DG 439 464-2 [id.]. ECO, Barenboim – BRITTEN: *Serenade*; VAUGHAN WILLIAMS: *Greensleeves; Lark ascending.* ***

Hazily sensuous in the summer sunshine, Barenboim's performances are warmly and enticingly recorded, and here offered as part of a fine bargain collection of English music.

(i) *On hearing the first cuckoo in spring; Summer night on the river;* (ii) *Appalachia;* (iii) *Hassan: Intermezzo and Serenade; Closing Scene;* (iv) *Koanga: Closing Scene;* (v) *3 Songs: Cradle song; The Nightingale; Twilight fancies.*

(M) (***) Dutton mono CDLX7011 [id.]. (i) Royal Philharmonic Soc. O; (ii) BBC Ch., LPO; (iii) Royal Op. Ch., LPO; (iv) Jan van der Gucht, London Select Ch., LPO; (v) Dora Labette; Sir Thomas Beecham (i–iv) cond.; (v) (piano).

Appalachia, subtitled *Variations on an old slave song*, is the product of Delius's years in the Deep South and this, its première recording, dating from 1938, is generally speaking the more atmospheric of the two that Beecham made. In fact all these performances (particularly the excerpts from *Hassan, On hearing the first cuckoo in spring* and *Summer night on the river*) reinforce Beecham's legendary reputation as Delius's greatest interpreter. The recordings, all pre-war, are as beautifully presented as is possible and, although their frequency-range is inevitably limited (*On hearing the first cuckoo* and *Summer night* date from 1928), they wear their years gracefully. One is unlikely ever to hear this music better played than it is here.

Sonata for strings (arr. from *String quartet* by Eric Fenby).
(*) Koch Dig. 3-7139 [id.]. New Zealand CO, Nicholas Braithwaite – BRIDGE: *Suite* etc. *

It was Sir John Barbirolli who in 1963 commissioned Delius's amanuensis, Eric Fenby, to score the 'Late swallows' slow movement of the *String quartet* for full orchestral strings, and in 1977 he completed the arrangement of the whole work. It is arguable whether the other movements transcribe as effectively as the third (marked by the composer 'Slow and wistfully') but the performance here is persuasive, and the warm yet transparently natural sound seems right for the music.

CHAMBER MUSIC

Cello sonata.
*** Chandos Dig. CHAN 8499 [id.]. Raphael and Peter Wallfisch – BAX: *Rhapsodic ballad;* BRIDGE: *Cello sonata;* WALTON: *Passacaglia.* ***

In this alternative version of the *Cello sonata* these Chandos performers give as strong and sympathetic an account as is to be found. They are also excellently recorded.

(i) *Cello sonata; Violin sonatas Nos.* (ii) *1–2;* (iii) *3.*
(Y/B) *** EMI Dig. CDC5 55399-2 [id.]. (i) Moray Welsh; (ii) Janice Graham; (iii) Alexander Barantschik; (i–iii) Israela Margalit.

Those looking for modern digital recordings of these four works will find that the performances by members of the LSO, in EMI's Anglo-American Chamber Music series, are in every way satisfying. Moray Welsh provides warm tone and much depth of feeling in the *Cello sonata* and Janice Graham's passionate advocacy in the earlier *Violin sonatas* matches that of Alexander Barantschik in the *Third*, which opens the record. Israela Margalit's pianism in all four works is full of personality. The recording is both resonant and forwardly balanced, and satisfyingly full.

Violin sonata No. 3.
(N) (M) (***) Dutton Lab. mono CDAX 8014 [id.]. Sammons, Long – BAX: *Nonet;* MOERAN: *String trio;* FERGUSON: *Octet.* (***)

The *Violin sonata No. 3* was one of the pieces which Delius dictated to Eric Fenby during his last years at Grez-sur-Loing. It was written in 1930, the same year as the Bax *Nonet* (Bax, incidentally, was the pianist at its first performance the same year with May Harrison, its dedicatee). The present recording was made 14 years later, during the war, by Albert Sammons, who had championed Delius's concerto and subsequently recorded it. Both he and Kathleen Long play it *con amore* but without excess of feeling. There are modern alternatives, but this performance has something special.

String quartet.
*** ASV Dig. CDDCA 526 [id.]. Brodsky Qt – ELGAR: *Quartet.* ***

In this music, the ebb and flow of tension and a natural feeling for persuasive but unexaggerated rubato is vital; with fine ensemble but seeming spontaneity, the Brodsky players consistently produce that. First-rate recording.

VOCAL MUSIC

Hassan (incidental music).
(M) *** EMI CD-EMX 2207. Hill, Rayner Cook, Bournemouth Sinf. Ch. & O, Handley.

A most valuable reissue, beautifully transferred to CD. The 1979 recording, made in the Guildhall, Southampton, is fairly immediate (some might prefer a mistier atmosphere) but the focus of chorus and the balance of soloists is realistic and Handley is a naturally sympathetic advocate of the score, bringing vitality and evocation in equal measure to his reading; even if memories of Beecham's briefer selection from the incidental music are not effaced, both playing and singing are first rate and the music springs vividly to life, including a choral version of the famous *Serenade*.

(i) *Koanga: La Calinda;* (ii) *Late swallows;* (iii; iv) *Margot La Rouge: Prelude.* (iii; v) *A Song before sunrise;* (iii; iv) *A Village Romeo and Juliet: Walk to the Paradise Garden.* (vi) *Cynara;* (vii; iii; v) *Songs of farewell;* (viii) *To be sung of a summer night on the water;* (ix) *Wanderer's song.*
(M) *** EMI CD-EMX 2198; *TC-EMX 2198.* (i) Philh. O, Weldon; (ii) Hallé O, Barbirolli; (iii) RPO; (iv) Meredith Davies; (v) Sargent; (vi) Shirley-Quirk, RPO, Groves; (vii) Royal Choral Soc.; (viii) Tear, King's College Ch., Ledger; (ix) Baccholian Singers of L.

A highly successful anthology, worth any Delian's money. Only George Weldon's *La Calinda* is a little stiff, and that comes at the very end. The programme opens with a ravishing account of the *Songs of farewell* under Sargent, who proves highly sympathetic in both the items he directs. This was the most ambitious work the composer attempted to write after he had become blind and paralysed. Sir Malcolm conducted the first performance in March 1932 with the Royal Choral Society, and his presentation is committed and warm-hearted in the best tradition of Delius recording, while the Abbey Road sound is full and sensuous. Barbirolli's *Late swallows* (another piece in which Eric Fenby had a hand) is hardly less evocative, and John Shirley-Quirk is equally at home in *Cynara*, a Dowson setting, while the wordless songs *To be sung of a summer night on the water* sound particularly well in their original *a cappella* vocal form. The transfers of recordings, all made in the 1960s – except the *Wanderer's song*, which is later – are managed most pleasingly.

(i) *A Mass of Life;* (ii) *An Arabesque;* (iii) *Songs of sunset.*
(M) *** EMI CMS7 64218-2 (2) [id.]. (i) Harper, Watts, Tear, Luxon, LPO Ch., LPO; (ii) J. Baker, Shirley-Quirk; (ii; iii) RLPO Ch. & O; Groves.

Groves inspires his performers to a magnificent account of the *Mass of Life*, fully worthy of the work. It is good to have this music on CD in such fine, clearly focused sound – though, curiously, the very mistiness of some passages in Beecham's old mono set made the results more evocative still. The other two works are also very successful here: the *Songs of sunset* and *An Arabesque*. John Shirley-Quirk does the solo part impressively and the results fall not far short of Beecham's standard, though they lack his sense of magic. He is joined by Dame Janet Baker singing most affectingly in the *Songs of sunset*. Again very good transfers of recordings made in the Philharmonic Hall, Liverpool, in 1968.

4 Old English lyrics. Songs: *I-Brasil; Indian love song; Love's philosophy; The nightingale; The nightingale has a lyre of gold; Secret love; Sweet Venevil; Twilight fancies.*
**(*) Chandos Dig. CHAN 8539 [id.]. Benjamin Luxon, David Willison – ELGAR: *Songs.* **(*)

This group of Delius songs draws most persuasive performances from Luxon and Willison, sadly marred by the rough tone which has latterly afflicted this fine baritone. Excellent, well-balanced recording.

Sea drift.
(N) (B) *** Decca Double 443 170-2 (2) [id.]. Shirley-Quirk, L. Symphony Ch., RPO, Hickox – ELGAR: *Dream of Gerontius* **(*); HOLST: *Hymn of Jesus.* ***

This dedicated performance under Richard Hickox, urgent in its expressiveness rather than lingering, brings John Shirley-Quirk as a characteristically sensitive soloist, and the chorus – trained by Hickox – is outstanding. The 1980 Kingsway Hall recording is both fresh and warmly atmospheric. Even though this is an inexpensive reissue, a full text is provided.

(i) *Sea drift; Songs of farewell;* (i; ii) *Songs of sunset.*
(N) *** Chandos Dig. CHAN 9214 [id.]. (i) Bryn Terfel; (ii) Sally Burgess; Bournemouth Symphony Ch., Waynflete Singers, Southern Voices, Bournemouth SO, Hickox.

Having earlier recorded *Sea drift* for Decca (now reissued as a tempting Double – see above), Hickox in this second recording of Delius's masterpiece finds even more magic, again taking a spacious view – which keeps the flow of the music going magnetically. Bryn Terfel adds to the glory of the performance, the finest since Beecham, as he does in the *Songs of sunset*, with Sally Burgess the other characterful soloist. The *Songs of farewell*, helped by incandescent choral singing, complete an ideal triptych, presented in full and rich Chandos sound.

OPERA

A Village Romeo and Juliet (complete).
*** Argo Dig. 430 275-2 [id.]. Field, Davies, Hampson, Mora, Dean, Schoenberg Ch., Austrian RSO, Mackerras.

(i) *A Village Romeo and Juliet* (opera; complete); (ii) *Sea drift*.
(M) (***) EMI mono CMS7 64386-2 (2) [id.]. (i) Ritchie, Soames, Dowling, Sharp, Bond, Dye; (i; ii) Clinton; Ch. & RPO, Beecham.

This is one of Delius's most beautiful and heart-warming scores, and Sir Charles Mackerras – even more than Sir Charles Groves on his earlier recording – brings that out lovingly. His approach is rather broader and more affectionate, with each scene timed to convey its emotional thrust, however flimsy the story-line. The Argo cast is even finer than the EMI one, with Helen Field and Arthur Davies very sympathetic as the lovers. The spacious, atmospheric recording has the voices cleanly focused, with offstage effects beautifully caught.

Beecham made this complete recording of Delius's evocative opera in the days of 78s in 1948, and though the mono sound is limited in range, it is well focused, and Beecham's ability to mould Delius's melodic lines gives it an extra warmth and magic, even compared with later stereo recordings. It is worth any Delian getting this set for the magnificent performance of *Sea drift*, even warmer than the two other Beecham recordings, early and late, of this most moving setting of Walt Whitman, expansive but tautly held together.

Dello Joio, Norman (born 1913)

The Triumph of St Joan (Symphony); Variations, chaconne and finale.
*** Koch Schwann Dig. 3-7243-2 [id.]. New Zealand SO, James Sedares – BARBER: *Adagio for strings.*
***

Norman Dello Joio is little played outside America, and his *Triumph of St Joan Symphony* makes a welcome CD début here and has worn well. For those who do not know it, the idiom relates loosely to early Bernstein and more closely to Hindemith, Piston and Honegger; the music is spacious, dignified and imaginative. The *Variations, chaconne and finale* is a little earlier and a good deal less convincing. However, the disc is well worth investigating for the sake of the symphony (and there are good things in the companion work).

Denisov, Edison (born 1929)

Variations on Haydn's Canon, 'Tod ist ein langer Schlaf' (Death is a long sleep).
(Y/B) *** RCA Dig. 09026 68061-2 [id.]. Moscow Virtuosi, Vladimir Spivakov – SHOSTAKOVICH: *Chamber symphony No. 2;* PART: *Collage on B-A-C-H* etc.; SHCHEDRIN: *Stalin cocktail.* ***

The Soviet composer Edison Denisov kept a low enough profile to survive the Zhdanov witch-hunt and, like his contemporary, Alfred Schnittke, was later able to write experimental music. His *Variations* celebrated the 250th anniversary of Haydn's birth in 1982, and one wonders what Haydn would have made of this 13–minute concertante cello piece. The soloist's eloquent soliloquy reaches a climax against weird slithers and oscillations from the strings and woodwind, then finally vanquishes their intrusions and breaks free into a touching unaccompanied elegy. The piece closes with three gentle bell-strokes, thus preparing the way for the Arvo Pärt *Cantus*, which follows in this well-planned, very well-played and admirably recorded concert.

Dett, R. Nathaniel (1882–1943)

8 Bible vignettes; In the bottoms; Magnolia suite.
**(*) New World Dig. NW 367 [id.]. Denver Oldham.

Robert Nathaniel Dett graduated from Oberlin Conservatory in 1908, the first African American to gain a Bachelor of Music degree. His writing is at times colourful and, though limited in its range of expressive devices, is attractive, particularly so in the suite *In the bottoms*, which evokes the moods and atmosphere of life in the 'river bottoms' of the Deep South. However, this is not a disc to be taken all at once. Denver Oldham is a persuasive enough player and he is decently recorded.

Devreese, Frédéric (born 1929)

Belle; Benvenuta (suite); *L'œuvre au noir* (suite); *Un soir, un train.*
(Y/B) ** Marco Polo Dig. 8.223681 [id.]. Belgian R. & TV PO (Brussels), composer.

Effective and at times appealing film scores by an accomplished composer, the son of Godfried Devreese. They do not amount to anything more than their objective, which is to provide atmospheric background to events on the screen. Taken out of context, they provide some pleasure but little substance. They are well played by the Belgian Radio and Television Philharmonic under the composer's own direction, and are very well recorded, too.

Piano concertos Nos. 2–4.
(Y/B) ** Marco Polo Dig. 8.223505 [id.]. Daniel Blumenthal, Belgian R. & TV PO (Brussels), composer.

There is a lot of Prokofiev in the *Piano concerto No. 2*, and there are also similarities with, say, Malcolm Arnold. There are occasional reminders of the Honegger of the middle movement of the *Concerto* as well as Prokofiev in the *Piano concerto No. 3*. Nearly three decades separate it from the shorter and rather Bartókian *Piano concerto No. 4*, which is in two movements – *Introduction and variations* and *Finalé*. Daniel Blumenthal plays this and the earlier concertos brilliantly and is well supported by the excellent Belgian Radio and Television Orchestra under the composer's direction. Well-crafted, literate music and, if it is of no great individuality, it is still worth hearing.

Devreese, Godfried (1893–1972)

(i) *Cello concertino;* (ii) *Violin concerto No. 1. Tombelène* (choreographic suite).
(Y/B) *** Marco Polo Dig. 8.223680 [id.]. (i) Viviane Spanoghe, (ii) Guido de Neve. Belgian R. & TV PO (Brussels), Frédéric Devreese.

Godfried Devreese is a Belgian composer whose work is little known outside his native country. The ballet, *Tombelène*, dates from 1925–6 and was premièred under Gabriel Pierné. It is rather derivative – but none the worse for that – close in atmosphere and idiom to early Stravinsky and Florent Schmitt's *Tragédie de Salomé*. But Devreese is imaginative as well as a gifted and colourful orchestrator, and this suite gives pleasure. His *Violin concerto No. 1* sounds balletic in inspiration, and if you respond to the Bloch and Delius concertos, you would find much here to engage your sympathies. The *Cello concertino* (1930) originally appeared scored for 15 wind instruments, celesta, harp, six double-basses and variously tuned side-drums. The present version is rescored by his son for more practical forces; it, too, is imaginative without possessing a strong individual voice. Very good performances and vivid, well-detailed recording.

Diabelli, Anton (1781–1858)

Guitar sonata in A (ed. Bream).
(M) **(*) RCA 09026 61593-2. Julian Bream (guitar) – GIULIANI: *Grand overture* etc.; SOR: *Grand solo Sonata in C.* **(*)

Bream combined the first two movements of Diabelli's (guitar) *Sonata in F* with the two final movements of his *Sonata in A* into a single composite work with appropriate transpositions. The result makes a quite strong (if conventional) piece, which Bream brings fully to life, even if it is perhaps a shade long for its material at 18 minutes.

Diamond, David (born 1915)

(i) *Concerto for small orchestra;* (ii) *Symphonies Nos 2; 4.*
*** Delos Dig. D/CD 3093 [id.]. (i) NY CO; (ii) Seattle SO, Gerard Schwarz.

The *Second Symphony* is a large-scale work lasting nearly three-quarters of an hour, written in 1942–3 at the height of the war, and it has great sweep and power. There is a lot of Roy Harris in the opening measures and the music unfolds with a similar sense of inevitability and purpose. The *Concerto for small orchestra* is original in form; there are two parts which open and conclude with a Fanfare with two preludes and fugues in between. The Mediterranean-like *Fourth Symphony* with its glowing, luminous textures sounds even more relaxed and lyrical in this performance than in Bernstein's account from the

1960s. Dedicated and expert performances from the Seattle Orchestra under Gerard Schwarz. The acoustic is spacious and the balance is very well judged.

(i) *Violin concerto No. 2. The Enormous room; Symphony No. 1.*
*** Delos Dig. DE 3119 [id.]. (i) Ilkka Talvi; Seattle SO, Gerard Schwarz.

A further addition to Diamond's growing representation in the catalogue brings the *First Symphony*, an urbane and intelligently wrought piece which has a strong sense of both purpose and direction. The *Second Violin concerto* is a bit Stravinskian with a dash of Walton and keeps the excellent soloist fully stretched. Not perhaps top-drawer Diamond, though *The Enormous room* shows the composer at his most imaginative. It derives its title from e. e. cummings's 'high and clear adventure'. It is rhapsodic in feeling, with orchestral textures of great luxuriance. Excellent performances from Gerard Schwarz and the Seattle orchestra, and outstanding recording.

(i) *Kaddish for cello and orchestra. Psalm; Romeo and Juliet; Symphony No. 3.*
*** Delos Dig. DE 3103 [id.]. (i) Starker; Seattle SO, Gerard Schwarz.

The *Third Symphony* is a four-movement work of no mean power. The *Romeo and Juliet* music is an inventive score, full of character and atmosphere, which shows Diamond as a real man of the orchestra; and the Seattle orchestra proves an eloquent advocate. *Kaddish* is a more recent piece and is played here by its dedicatee, János Starker.

Symphony No. 8; Suite No. 1 from the ballet, Tom; (i) *This sacred ground.*
(Y/B) *** Delos Dig. DE 3141 [id.]. (i) Erich Parce, Seattle Ch., Seattle Girls' Ch., NorthWest Boys' Ch.; Seattle SO, Gerard Schwarz.

The *First Suite from the ballet, Tom* is often powerful and inventive, and inhabits much the same musical world as Aaron Copland, Diamond's mentor and friend, for whose sixtieth birthday the *Eighth Symphony* was composed. Although it makes use of serial technique, it will still present few problems to those familiar with Diamond's earlier music, for it remains lyrical and thought-provoking. It culminates in a double fugue of considerable ingenuity. *This sacred ground* is a short setting for soloist, choirs and orchestra of the Gettysburg Address, which may not travel so well. Well worth investigating for the ballet and the symphony. Committed performances and excellent, natural, recorded sound.

Dibdin, Charles (1745–1814)

(i) *The Brickdust man* (musical dialogue); (ii) *The Ephesian Matron* (comic serenata); (iii) *The Grenadier* (musical dialogue).
*** Hyperion Dig. CDA 66608 [id.]. (i) Barclay, West; (ii) Mills, Streeton, Padmore, Knight; (iii) Bisatt, West, Mayor; Opera Restor'd, Parley of Instruments, Holman.

Dibdin, best known as the composer of *Tom Bowling*, the song heard every year at the Last Night of the Proms, here provides three delightful pocket operas, the shorter ones officially described as musical dialogues and *The Ephesian Matron* as a comic serenata. *The Grenadier* – dating from 1773 – lasts well under a quarter of an hour, using a text that is possibly by David Garrick. The brief numbers – duets and solos – are linked by equally brief recitatives, then rounded off with a final trio. The other two pieces are just as delightful in these performances by a group that specializes in presenting just such dramatic works of this period in public. Excellent Hyperion sound.

Diepenbrock, Alphons (1862–1921)

Elektra suite; (i) *Hymn for violin & orchestra. Marsyas suite; Overture: The Birds.*
*** Chandos Dig. CHAN 8821 [id.]. (i) Emmy Verhey; Hague Residentie O, Vonk.

The *Birds Overture*, written for a student production of Aristophanes, is rather delightful if very Straussian, with some vaguely Impressionist touches. The *Marsyas music* (1910) is expertly and delicately scored with touches of Strauss, Reger and Debussy. Good performances from the Residentie Orchestra under Hans Vonk and eminently truthful recording quality. Recommended.

(i) *Hymne an die Nacht;* (ii) *Hymne;* (i) *Die Nacht;* (iii) *Im grossen Schweigen.*
*** Chandos Dig. CHAN 8878 [id.]. (i) Linda Finnie; (ii) Christoph Homberger; (iii) Robert Holl; Hague Residentie O, Hans Vonk.

This second volume brings four symphonic songs, all of great beauty and with an almost Straussian melancholy. There are touches of Reger and Debussy as well as Strauss, and all four pieces are expertly and delicately scored. Good performances from all three soloists and the Residentie Orchestra under Hans Vonk, and very good recording indeed.

Dieupart, Charles (after 1667–1740)

Suites in G min. and A.
(Y/B) (M) *** Teldec/Warner Frans Brüggen Edition 4509 97468-2 [id.]. Frans Brüggen, Kees Boeke, Nikolaus Harnoncourt, Anner Bylsma, Gustav Leonhardt – HOTTETERRE: *Suite No. 1.* ***

These two suites by Dieupart are very much cast in the style favoured by Telemann. Both are contrived so that each movement is derived from the opening phrase of the music first heard in the *Overture*: the result is like an ingenious set of divisions, although each dance has its own completeness. Brüggen uses a different instrument for each suite. For the *G major* he chooses a bright, early eighteenth-century English Bressan recorder, but the 'voice flute' used in the *A major Suite* is another Bressan with a paler personality. Brüggen's usual team provide thoroughly stylish accompaniments and the early-1970s recording is excellent.

Dittersdorf, Carl Ditters von (1739–99)

(i) *Double-bass concerto in E;* (ii) *Flute concerto in E min.;* (iii) *Symphonies in C & D.*
** Olympia OCD 405 [id.]. (i) Stefan Thomas, Arad PO, Boboc; (ii) Gavril Costea, Cluj-Napoca PO, Cristescu; (iii) Oradea Philharmonic CO, Ratiu.

The *C major* is an agreeably conventional three-movement symphony, but the *D major* is more elaborate, with an infectious opening movement, an engaging *Chanson populaire d'Elsass* for its *Andante*, a minuet with two trios and a set of variations for its modestly paced finale. Both the concertos are attractive and require considerable bravura from their soloists. The recorded sound varies somewhat but is always fully acceptable and quite well balanced.

Harp concerto in A (arr. Pilley).
❀ (M) *** Decca 425 723-2; *425 723-4* [id.]. Marisa Robles, ASMF, Iona Brown – BOIELDIEU; HANDEL: *Harp concertos* etc. *** ❀

Dittersdorf's *Harp concerto* is a transcription of an unfinished keyboard concerto with additional wind parts. It is an elegant piece, thematically not quite as memorable as the Boieldieu coupling, but captivating when played with such style.

6 Symphonies after Ovid's Metamorphoses.
**(*) Chandos Dig. CHAN 8564/5 (2). Cantilena, Shepherd.

All the *Ovid symphonies* have a programmatic inspiration and relate episodes from the *Metamorphoses* of Ovid, such as *The fall of Phaeton*, which are vividly portrayed. *The rescue of Andromeda by Perseus* is a particularly effective work (it has an inspired *Adagio*) and the slow movement of the *D major*, *The petrification of Phineus and his friends*, is a delight. One well appreciates the contemporary verdict that Dittersdorf 'spoke to the heart'. *The transformation of the Lycian peasants into frogs* could hardly be more graphic and is full of wit. This is inventive and charming music that will give much pleasure, and it is generally well served by Cantilena under Adrian Shepherd.

Dodgson, Stephen (born 1924)

(i) *Flute concerto* (for flute and strings); (ii) *Duo concertant for violin, guitar and strings;* (iii) *Last of the leaves* (cantata for bass, clarinet and strings)
*** Biddulph Dig. LAW 015 [id.]. (i) Robert Stallman; (ii) Jean-Jacques Kantorow, Anthea Gifford; (iii) Michael George, John Bradbury, N. Sinfonia, Zollman.

As Dodgson himself says in his illuminating note, 'I have developed a particular fondness for music which outwardly has the manner of a divertimento, but inwardly is quite otherwise.' All three of these works illustrate that equivocal quality in the writing, not least the *Flute concerto* which Dodgson wrote for the American flautist, Robert Stallman, who is also the fine soloist on this disc. Dodgson wanted to draw not only on Stallman's agility and rhythmic flair, but on his tonal bloom and subtlety, and the performance bears that out. The *Duo concertant* also receives a persuasive performance. With its hints of an English Stravinsky, this is another work that is at once thoughtful and charming. *Last of the leaves* is a cantata for bass soloist accompanied by clarinet and strings, more consistently autumnal and elegiac. The image of leaves being burnt is used as a metaphor for the tragic loss of life in the First World War, and the result is the more moving for its relative reticence. Framing the work are settings of poems by poets now neglected, Austin Dobson and Harold Monro, with the necessary contrast provided by the best-known poem, G. K. Chesterton's *The Donkey*, light-hearted, leading up to its surprise reference at the end to Christ's entry into Jerusalem. Though Michael George's noble bass voice is not as sweetly caught as it might be, it is a tenderly moving performance, with John Bradbury equally expressive and with the Belgian conductor, Ronald Zollman, as in the other works, a sympathetic accompanist.

Dohnányi, Ernst von (1877–1960)

Piano concertos Nos. 1 in E min., Op. 5; 2 in B min., Op. 42.
*** Hyperion Dig. CDA 66684 [id.]. Martin Roscoe, BBC Scottish SO, Fedor Glushchenko.

The note provided with this coupling places Dohnányi's writing style as lying somewhere between that of Brahms and Saint-Saëns, but these concertos suggest that he is hardly a musical individualist in his own right. They are well wrought, with a melodic warmth that fails to be indelible; they provide bravura for the soloist and contrast for the orchestra. The present performances are surely unlikely to be surpassed for their commitment, and the playing is finished as well as ardent; the recording, too, is excellent. But both works, ambitious as they are, are agreeable rather than distinctive.

Konzertstück for cello and orchestra, Op. 12.
*** Chandos Dig. CHAN 8662 [id.]. Wallfisch, LSO, Mackerras – DVORAK: *Cello concerto.* ***

Dohnányi's *Konzertstück* has many rich, warm ideas, not least a theme in the slow movement all too close to *Pale hands I loved beside the Shalimar*, and none the worse for that. Wallfisch's performance, as in the Dvořák, is strong, warm and committed, and the Chandos sound is first rate.

Variations on a nursery tune (for piano and orchestra), *Op. 25.*
(N) (M) (***) Dutton mono CDLXT 2504 [id.]. Julius Katchen, LPO, Boult – RACHMANINOV: *Piano concerto No. 2* etc. (***)
(M) (***) EMI mono CDC5 55031-2 [id.]. Composer, LSO, Lawrance Collingwood – BARTOK: *Collection.* (***)
(N) ** Ph. Dig. 446 472-2 [id.]. Zoltán Kocsis, Budapest Festival O, Iván Fischer – BARTOK: *Rhapsody* etc. **(*)

It is surprising that the *Nursery variations*, once a regular repertory work, have fallen into relative neglect both on disc and in the concert hall. Katchen's 1954 mono recording with Boult has never been surpassed: there is a sense of new discovery, and the humour is all the more delightful for not being overplayed. So Boult conducts the grand orchestral introduction with a biting intensity worthy of Wagner, leaving Katchen to enunciate the nursery theme ('*Ah vous dirai-je maman*', or 'Twinkle twinkle little star'), not labouring the humour with any hint of archness at all. The waltz variation is given the most delectable Viennese lilt, and the final pay-off after the fugue is charmingly pointed. This vivid Dutton transfer offers full and firm piano-sound with fine presence, though there is a degree of edge on the thin, exposed high violins.

Dohnányi made two recordings of his celebrated *Variations on a nursery tune*, the first in 1931 with the LSO and Lawrance Collingwood and the second in 1956 with the RPO and Sir Adrian Boult (with Collingwood producing), when the composer-pianist was approaching eighty. Remarkable though the latter is, the earlier account has much greater character and more effortless virtuosity. This was its première recording and has great freshness and naturalness. The sound was always a little dry and the strings wanting in richness, but the engineers have given it a completely new lease of life.

Zoltán Kocsis plays with dazzling brilliance, though the orchestral playing could be more subtle. By the side of past recordings of this masterpiece the Kocsis/Fischer account is rather plain and, though not wanting in humour, rarely commands real wit.

(i) *Variations on a nursery tune, Op. 25. Capriccio in F min., Op. 28.*
*** Chesky CD-13 [id.]. Earl Wild, (i) New Philh. O, Christoph von Dohnányi – TCHAIKOVSKY: *Piano concerto No. 1.* ***

A scintillating account of the piano part from Earl Wild is matched by a witty accompaniment directed by the composer's grandson, who doesn't miss a thing. Splendid vintage analogue recording from the early 1960s. The *Capriccio*, brilliantly played, acts as an encore (before the Tchaikovsky coupling), but the recording is rather recessed.

Cello sonata in B flat min., Op. 8.
**(*) ASV Dig. CDDCA 796[id.]. Bernard Gregor-Smith, Yolande Wrigley – BRIDGE; DEBUSSY: *Sonatas.* **(*)

Like so much of Dohnányi's early music, the *Cello sonata* (1899) is very Brahmsian in feeling. There is a marvellously inventive scherzo, which leaves no doubt that it is the work of a great pianist-composer. The finale is a theme and variations and what a superb theme it is too. It is played with great expertise and fine musicianship by this excellent duo partnership. The recording is just a bit too bright and forward to be ideal but, with that proviso, the disc can be cordially recommended.

(i) *Piano quintet No. 1 in C min., Op. 1. String quartet No. 2 in D flat, Op. 15.*
**(*) Chandos Dig. CHAN 8718 [id.]. (i) Wolfgang Manz; Gabrieli Qt.

(i; ii) *Piano quintets Nos. 1 in C min., Op. 1; 2 in E flat min., Op. 28;* (i) *Suite in the old style, Op. 24.*
(Y/B) *** ASV Dig. CDDCA 915 [id.]. (i) Martin Roscoe; (ii) Vanbrugh Qt.

It is good to have three works that winningly bring out Dohnányi's lyrical warmth and his keen instrumental mastery. He wrote the first of his two *Piano quintets* when still in his teens, ripely Brahmsian, built strongly on memorable themes. The *Second quintet*, dating from twenty years later, just after the *Nursery variations*, is sharper and more compact, with Hungarian flavours more pronounced, if never Bartókian. The *Suite in the old style*, for piano alone, is an amiable example of pre-Stravinsky neo-classicism, again beautifully written for the instrument. The prize-winning Vanbrugh Quartet is well matched by Martin Roscoe in keen, alert performances, warmly recorded.

Manz's performance of Dohnányi's *First Piano quintet* lacks something in fantasy and lightness of touch. But the bigger-boned, somewhat Brahmsian effect of this performance is certainly compelling, if less strong on charm. The scherzo of the *Second String quartet* is reminiscent of the opening of *Die Walküre* and there are reminders of Dvořák and Reger as well as Brahms. It is a strong piece, splendidly played by the Gabrielis and beautifully recorded.

Donizetti, Gaetano (1797–1848)

Ballet music from: *L'assedio di Calais; Dom Sébastien; La favorita; Les martyres.*
(Y/B) (B) *** Ph. Duo 442 553-2 (2) [id.]. Philh. O, Antonio de Almeida – ROSSINI: *Ballet music.* **(*)

Music from the baroque period has given us dozens of records which are validly used for aural wall-paper. The ballet music from four of Donizetti's operas which were presented in Paris provides a nineteenth-century equivalent, sparkling, refreshing dances of no great originality, delivered here with great zest and resilience and fine solo playing, and excellently recorded. The Rossini coupling offers even more characterful music, and if the playing of the Monte Carlo Orchestra cannot match that of the Philharmonia, this is still very enjoyable.

Sinfonias (String quartets): in A; D min. (both arr. Benedek); *D* (arr. Angerer).
**(*) Marco Polo Dig. 8.223577 [id.]. Failoni CO, Géza Oberfrank.

We have had the *D major Sinfonia* (arranged here by Paul Angerer) from the ASMF under Marriner (see below). It is a delightfully spontaneous piece with a graciously beautiful *Larghetto*. The D minor work opens darkly, but the sun soon comes out and at times we are reminded of Rossini. The *Larghetto* is pensive. The *A major* has a fine, siciliano-like *Larghetto cantabile*. All this is warmly appealing music, well played and flatteringly recorded; a touch more wit and sparkle would not have come amiss, but the music is well worth having. A pity that this was not issued on the Naxos label.

String quartet in D (arr. for string orchestra).
(Y/B) (B) *** Decca Double 443 838-2 (2) [id.]. ASMF, Marriner – ROSSINI: *String sonatas Nos. 1–6* (with CHERUBINI: *Etude No. 2 for French horn and strings* (with Barry Tuckwell); BELLINI: *Oboe concerto in E flat* (with Roger Lord) ***).

This delightful 'prentice work has a sunny lyricism and a melodic freshness that speak of youthful genius. The composer's craftsmanship is obvious and the writing is such that (unlike Verdi's *String quartet*) it lends itself readily to performance by a string orchestra, especially when the playing is so warm-hearted and polished and the recording transferred so immaculately to CD. A fine bonus for the irresistible Rossini *String sonatas*.

Il Barcaiolo; Cor anglais concerto in G; Oboe sonata in F; (Piano) Waltz in C.
*** Mer. CDE 84147 [id.]. Jeremy Polmear, Diana Ambache (with PASCULLI: *Concerto on themes from La Favorita; Fantasia on Poliuto;* LISZT: *Réminscences de Lucia di Lammermoor*).

The *Sonata in F* is an agreeable piece with a fluent *Andante* and a catchy finale; and the vignette, *Il Barcaiolo*, is even more engaging. The *Cor Anglais concerto* centres on a set of variations which are not unlike the fantasias on themes from his operas by Pasculli. However, these demand the utmost bravura from the soloist. Diana Ambache proves a sympathetic partner and gives a suitably flamboyant account of Liszt's famous *Lucia* paraphrase.

String quartets Nos. 7 in F min.; 8 in B flat; 9 in D min.
(Y/B) * CPO Dig. CPO 999170-2 [id.]. Revolutionary Drawing Room.

If would be useful to have a recommendable CD of the Donizetti *String quartets*, but this will not do. The players here may be revolutionary in their approach to authenticity, but the Gillette-edged timbre of the leader would not be welcome in an elegant nineteenth-century drawing-room. Its thin penetration dominates the texture to such an extent that any convincing overall blend of sonority between the four instruments seems possible only very occasionally.

String quartet No. 13 in A.
*** CRD CRD 3366; *CRDC 4066* [id.]. Alberni Qt – PUCCINI: *Crisantemi;* VERDI: *Quartet.* ***

This is an endearing work, with a scherzo echoing that in Beethoven's *Eroica*, and with many twists of argument that are attractively unpredictable. It is given a strong, committed performance and is well recorded.

Requiem.
(M) ** Decca 425043-2 [id.]. Cortez, Pavarotti, Bruson, Washington, Arena di Verona Lyric Ch. & O, Fackler.

There are many passages in Donizetti's *Requiem* which may well have influenced Verdi when he came to write his masterpiece. Donizetti's setting lasts for 65 minutes, but its inspiration is short-winded and it is not helped here by limited performance and recording, deriving from the Cime label. The singing and playing are generally indifferent. Pavarotti, recorded in 1979, is the obvious star, singing flamboyantly in his big solo, *Ingemisco*. Of curiosity value only.

OPERA

Anna Bolena (complete).
*** Decca Dig. 421 096-2 (3) [id.]. Sutherland, Ramey, Hadley, Mentzer, Welsh Nat. Op. Ch. & O, Bonynge.
(N) (M) (**(*)) EMI mono CMS7 64941-2 (2) [CDMB 64941]. Callas, Simionato, Rossi-Lemeni, G. Raimondi, Carturan, La Scala, Milan, Ch. & O, Gavazzeni.

In this 1987 recording of *Anna Bolena*, Sutherland crowns her long recording career with a commanding performance. Dazzling as ever in coloratura, above all exuberant in the defiant final cabaletta, she poignantly conveys the tragedy of the wronged queen's fate with rare weight and gravity. Ramey as the king is outstanding in a fine, consistent cast. Excellent recording.

The Callas recording was made live at La Scala in 1957, with the great diva at her most searingly magnetic. This is a performance which, despite the occasional sour note, has one marvelling at the imaginative phrasing and subtlety of dynamic shading, with top notes firm and clear if characteristically edgy. Gavazzeni proves a most sympathetic conductor and, though the rest of the cast is no match for Callas, there is characterful if rather inflexible singing from Simionato as Giovanna and a fresh, clear contribution from Gianni Raimondi in the relatively small tenor role of Percy, here made the smaller by cuts. Nicola Rossi-Lemeni as Henry VIII is positive but gritty of tone in a less than convincing characterization. The radio sound is dry and limited with occasional interference, but for Callas fans this is well worth hearing.

L'assedio di Calais (complete).
*** Opera Rara OR 9 (2) [id.]. Du Plessis, Della Jones, Focile, Serbo, Nilon, Platt, Glanville, Smythe, Treleaven, Harrhy, Bailey, Geoffrey Mitchell Ch., Philh. O, David Parry.

Donizetti's invention was at its peak in *L'assedio di Calais*. What above all must strike us today is the weight and intensity he gave to the big ensembles, bringing them very close not just to early but to mature Verdi. The Opera Rara set is one of the most invigorating of all the complete opera recordings made over the years by that enterprising organization. With Della Jones and Christian du Plessis in the cast, as well as a newcomer, Nuccia Focile, as Queen Eleanor, David Parry conducts the Philharmonia in a fresh, well-sprung performance which gives a satisfying thrust to the big ensembles. The one which ends Act II, including a magnificent sextet and a patriotic prayer for the chorus, brings the opera's emotional high-point. When, in Act III, Edward III's big aria turns into a sort of jolly waltz song, the music seems less apt.

Il Campanello (complete).
*** Sony Dig. MK 38450 [id.]. Baltsa, Dara, Casoni, Romero, Gaifa, V. State Op. Ch., VSO, Bertini.

This sparkling one-Act piece is based on something like the same story which Donizetti developed later in *Don Pasquale*. Enzo Dara as the apothecary, Don Annibale, and Angelo Romero as the wag, Enrico, are delightful in their patter duet, and Agnes Baltsa is a formidable but sparkling Serafina. Gary Bertini is a sympathetic conductor who paces things well, and the *secco* recitatives – taking up rather a large proportion of the disc – are well accompanied on the fortepiano. Generally well-balanced recording.

Don Pasquale (complete).
(Y/B) *** RCA Dig. 09026 61924-2 (2) [id.]. Bruson, Mei, Allen, Lopardo, Bav. R. Ch., Munich R. O, Roberto Abbado.
*** EMI Dig. CDS7 47068-2 (2) [Ang. CDCB 47068]. Bruscantini, Freni, Nucci, Winbergh, Amb. Op. Ch., Philh. O, Muti.
(M) *** Decca 433 036-2 (2) [id.]. Corena, Sciutti, Oncina, Krause, V. State Op. Ch. & O, Kertész – CIMAROSA: *Il maestro di cappella.* ***
*** Erato/Warner Dig. 2292 45487-2 (2) [id.]. Bacquier, Hendricks, Canonici, Quilico, Schirrer, Lyon Opera Ch. & O, Ferro.

In vivid, immediate sound and with voices balanced well forward, Roberto Abbado's Munich set for RCA is on balance the finest modern version of Donizetti's sparkling comedy. Not only does Abbado spring rhythms cleanly and lightly, they are made the more infectious by the clarity of focus. The cast has no weak link. Renato Bruson may accentuate Pasquale's comic lines with little explosions of underlining, but that helps to distinguish him sharply as a *buffo* character from his opposite number, Malatesta, here sung with rare style and beauty by Thomas Allen, as well as with a nicely timed feeling for the comedy. Frank Lopardo as Ernesto shades his clear tenor most sensitively, singing his *Serenade* with far more refinement than most latterday rivals. Eva Mei sings the role of Norina with an apt brightness and precision (including an excellent trill), even if others have presented a more characterful heroine.

Muti's is a delectably idiomatic-sounding reading, one which consistently captures the fun of the piece. Freni is a natural in the role of Norina, both sweet and bright-eyed in characterization, excellent in coloratura. The *buffo* baritones, the veteran Bruscantini as Pasquale and the darker-toned Leo Nucci as Dr Malatesta, steer a nice course between vocal comedy and purely musical values. Muti is helped by the beautifully poised and shaded singing of Gösta Winbergh, honey-toned and stylish as Ernesto. Responsive and polished playing from the Philharmonia and excellent studio sound.

Under Kertész, Corena is an attractive *buffo*, even if his voice is not always focused well enough to sing semiquavers accurately. Juan Oncina, as often on record, sounds rather strained, but the tenor part is very small; and Krause makes an incisive Malatesta. Graziella Sciutti is charming from beginning to end, bright-toned and vivacious, and remarkably agile in the most difficult passages. The 1964 Decca recording is excellent, with plenty of atmosphere as well as sparkle.

The Erato version gains enormously from the rhythmic subtlety and affectionate phrasing encouraged by the conductor, Gabriele Ferro. This is a reading with more light and shade than Muti's or Kertész's, not so high-powered but more relaxed, genially capturing the spirit of comedy in this delightful score. Barbara Hendricks is a charming Norina with her sweet timbre, and Luca Canonici an engaging Ernesto, even if his production is not always perfectly even. The recording has fine atmosphere, though some of the vocal balances are inconsistent.

L'elisir d'amore (complete).
*** Decca 414 461-2 (2) [id.]. Sutherland, Pavarotti, Cossa, Malas, Amb. S., ECO, Bonynge.
(M) *** Sony CD 79210 (2) [M2K 34585]. Cotrubas, Domingo, Evans, Wixell, ROHCG Ch. & O, Pritchard.
(Y/B) (B) **(*) Decca Double 443 542-2 (2) [id.]. Gueden, Di Stefano, Corena, Capecchi, Mandelli, Maggio Musicale Fiorentino Ch. & O, Molinari-Pradelli.
(Y/B) (M) **(*) RCA Dig. 74321 25280-2 (2) [id.]. Popp, Dvorský, Weikl, Nesterenko, Munich R. Ch. & O, Wallberg.
(N) [M] **(*) EMI CMS5 65658-2 [CDMB 65658] (2). Carteri, Alva, Panerai, Taddei, La Scala, Milan, Ch. & O, Serafin.

Joan Sutherland makes Adina a more substantial figure than usual, full-throatedly serious at times, at others jolly like the rumbustious Marie; and in the key role of Nemorino Luciano Pavarotti proves ideal, vividly portraying the wounded innocent. Spiro Malas is a superb Dulcamara, while Dominic Cossa is a younger-sounding Belcore, more of a genuine lover than usual. Bonynge points the skipping rhythms delectably, and the recording is sparkling to match, with striking presence.

On the Sony reissue delight centres very much on the delectable Adina of Ileana Cotrubas. Plácido Domingo by contrast is a more conventional hero and less the world's fool that Nemorino should be. Sir Geraint Evans gives a vivid characterization of Dr Dulcamara, though the microphone sometimes brings out roughness of tone, and Ingvar Wixell is an upstanding Belcore. The stereo staging is effective and the remastered recording bright and immediate. This set remains at full price in the USA.

With Hilde Gueden at her most seductive – an enchanting, provocative Adina, characterfully using her golden tone to bring out the minx-like qualities of the heroine – the very early (1955) Decca stereo recording offers a delightful, spontaneous-sounding performance. Not just Gueden but also the other soloists are strikingly characterful, with Giuseppe di Stefano at his most headily sweet-toned, singing with youthful ardour, Fernando Corena a strong and vehement Dulcamara and Renato Capecchi well contrasted as Sergeant Belcore, though not quite so firm of tone, but both splendidly comic. Even without a libretto it makes a good bargain, with two CDs offered for the price of one.

Wallberg conducts a lightly sprung performance of Donizetti's sparkling comic opera, well recorded and marked by a charming performance of the role of Adina from Lucia Popp, bright-eyed and with delicious detail both verbal and musical. Nesterenko makes a splendidly resonant Dr Dulcamara with more comic sparkle than you would expect from a great Russian bass. Dvorský and Weikl, both sensitive artists, sound much less idiomatic, with Dvorský's tight tenor growing harsh under pressure, not at all Italianate, and Weikl failing similarly to give necessary roundness to the role of Belcore. Like other sets recorded in association with Bavarian Radio, the 1982 sound is excellent.

Although reissued at mid-rather than bargain price (it last appeared on Classics for Pleasure), the La Scala set of *L'elisir d'amore* now comes with a full translation instead of a synopsis. It is still worth considering: it was a fine cast in its day (1959). Alva is a pleasantly light-voiced and engaging Nemorino. Carteri's Adina ideally should be more of a minx than this, but the part is nicely sung all the same. Panerai as Belcore once again shows what a fine and musical artist he is, and Taddei is magnificent, stealing the show as any Dulcamara can and should. The drawback is Serafin's direction. The La Scala Chorus is lively enough, and it is not that the orchestral playing is slipshod, but they provide less sparkle than they should.

Emelia di Liverpool (complete). *L'eremitaggio di Liwerpool* (complete).
*** Opera Rara OR 8 (3) [id.]. Kenny, Bruscantini, Merritt, Dolton, George Mitchell Ch., Philh. O, David Parry.

The very name, *Emelia di Liverpool*, makes it hard to take this early opera of Donizetti seriously. In this set, sponsored by the Peter Moores Foundation, we have not only the original version of 1824 but also the complete reworking of four years later, which was given the revised title noted above. Such a veteran as Sesto Bruscantini makes an enormous difference in the *buffo* role of Don Romualdo in *Emelia*, a character who speaks in Neapolitan dialect. His fizzing duet with Federico (the principal tenor role, superbly sung by Chris Merritt) sets the pattern for much vigorous invention. With fresh, direct conducting from David Parry this is a highly enjoyable set for all who respond to this composer.

La Favorita (complete).
(M) **(*) Decca 430 038-2 (3). Cossotto, Pavarotti, Bacquier, Ghiaurov, Cotrubas, Teatro Comunale Bologna Ch. & O, Bonynge.

La Favorita may not have as many memorable tunes as the finest Donizetti operas, but red-blooded drama provides ample compensation. Fernando is strongly and imaginatively sung here by Pavarotti. The mezzo role of the heroine is taken by Fiorenza Cossotto, formidably powerful if not quite at her finest, while Ileana Cotrubas is comparably imaginative as her confidante Ines, but not quite at her peak. Bacquier and Ghiaurov make up a team which should have been even better but which will still give much satisfaction. Bright recording.

La Fille du régiment (complete).
*** Decca 414 520-2 (2) [id.]. Sutherland, Pavarotti, Sinclair, Malas, Coates, ROHCG Ch. & O, Bonynge.

It was with this cast that *La Fille du régiment* was revived at Covent Garden, and Sutherland immediately showed how naturally she takes to the role of Marie, a vivandière in the army of Napoleon. Sutherland is in turn brilliantly comic and pathetically affecting, and Pavarotti makes an engaging hero. Monica Sinclair is a formidable Countess in a fizzing performance of a delightful Donizetti romp that can be confidently recommended both for comedy and for fine singing. Recorded in Kingsway Hall, the CD sound has wonderful presence and clarity of focus.

(i) *Gabriella di Vergy* (1838 version); (ii) Scenes from 1826 version.
(N) **(*) Opera Rara Dig. ORC 3 (2) [id.]. (i) Andrew, Du Plessis, Arthur, Tomlinson, J. Davies, Winfield; (ii) Harrhy, Della Jones, RPO, Alun Francis.

Dating from 1979 and transferred well to CD, this Opera Rara set of *Gabriella di Vergy* (not to be confused with *Gemma di Vergy*) presents the rediscovered score, written in the composer's hand, of a piece which Donizetti himself never heard. It was unearthed by Don White and Patric Schmid, and makes one wonder how this inventive score with its many sparkling cabalettas and superb Act II finale could have been neglected for so long. The cast is a capable one with Alun Francis, as ever, a sympathetic conductor; it is interesting to hear John Tomlinson early in his career, slightly miscast. It is fascinating to have as appendix three excerpts from the original, 1836 score, with Della Jones taking the role of the hero, Raoul, later rewritten for tenor.

Linda di Chamounix (complete).
(N) (M) *(*) Ph. 442 093-2 (2). Stella, Valletti, Barbieri, Capecchi, Di Palma, Teatro di San Carlo, Naples, Ch. & O, Serafin.

Despite the conducting of Serafin and fine contributions from Barbieri and Valletti, this Philips recording of 1956 is too seriously flawed to recommend except out of interest in an attractive rarity. The aria *O luce in quest'anima* has been a showpiece of the coloratura repertory, and nothing else matches it. But this opera is far from boring, and it is a pity that Antonietta Stella with her shallow, ill-controlled voice is inadequate in the title-role. The San Carlo chorus is also far too rough, and the recording is limited.

Lucia di Lammermoor (complete).
*** Decca 410 193-2 (2) [id.]. Sutherland, Pavarotti, Milnes, Ghiaurov, Ryland Davies, Tourangeau, ROHCG Ch. & O, Bonynge.
(M) *** Decca 411 622-2 (2) [id.]. Sutherland, Cioni, Merrill, Siepi, St Cecilia Ac., Rome, Ch. & O, Pritchard.
(M) (***) EMI mono CMS7 63631-2 (2) [Ang. CDMB 63631]. Callas, Di Stefano, Panerai, Zaccaria, La Scala Ch. & O, Karajan.
*** DG Dig. 435 309-2 (2) [id.]. Studer, Domingo, Pons, Ramey, Amb. Op. Ch., LSO, Marin.
(M) (***) EMI mono CMS7 69980-2 (2) [Ang. CDMB 69980]. Callas, Di Stefano, Gobbi, Arie, Ch. & O of Maggio Musicale Fiorentino, Serafin.
(N) (B) **(*) Ph. Duo 446 551-2 (2) [id.]. Caballé, Carreras, Sardinero, Ramey, Murray, Ahnsjö, Amb. S., New Philh. O, López-Cobos.

Though some of the girlish freshness of voice which marked the 1961 recording disappeared in the 1971 set, Sutherland's detailed understanding was intensified. Power is there as well as delicacy, and the rest of the cast is first rate. Pavarotti, through much of the opera not as sensitive as he can be, proves magnificent in his final scene. The sound-quality is superb on CD. In this set, unlike the earlier one, the text is absolutely complete.

The 1961 Sutherland version of *Lucia* remains an attractive proposition in the mid-price range. Though consonants were being smoothed over, the voice is obviously that of a young singer and dramatically the performance was close to Sutherland's famous stage appearances of that time, full of fresh innocence. Sutherland's coloratura virtuosity remains breathtaking, and the cast is a strong one, with Pritchard a most understanding conductor.

Recorded live in 1955, when Karajan took the company of La Scala to Berlin, for years this finest of Callas's recordings of *Lucia* was available only on pirate issues. Despite the limited sound, Callas's voice is caught with fine immediacy. Her singing is less steely than in the 1953 studio recording, and far firmer than in the 1959 one (now withdrawn).

On DG, Cheryl Studer makes an affecting heroine, singing both brilliantly and richly, and Plácido Domingo rebuts any idea that his tenor is too cumbersome for Donizetti. This is the finest version yet in digital sound, with the young Romanian, Ion Marin, drawing fresh, urgent playing from the LSO. The rest of the cast is outstandingly strong too, with Juan Pons as Lucia's brother, Enrico, and Samuel Ramey as the teacher and confidant, Raimondo, Bide-the-Bent.

Callas's earlier mono set dates from 1953. The diva is vocally better controlled than in her later stereo set (indeed some of the coloratura is excitingly brilliant in its own right), and there are memorable if not always perfectly stylish contributions from Di Stefano and Gobbi. As in the later set, the text has the usual stage cuts.

The idea behind the set with Caballé is fascinating: a return to what the conductor, Jésus López-Cobos, believes is Donizetti's original concept, an opera for a dramatic soprano, not a light coloratura. Compared with the text we know, transpositions paradoxically are for the most part upwards (made possible when no stratospheric coloratura additions are needed); but López-Cobos's direction hardly compensates for the lack of brilliance and, José Carreras apart, the singing, even that of Caballé, is not very persuasive. The recording is warm, refined in detail and atmospheric, with the choral contribution well projected; those who seek emotional histrionics in the Mad scene will find that Caballé manages much of the high coloratura remarkably effectively. Certainly this is good value as a Philips Duo reissue and, although only a synopsis of the plot is included, it is generously cued.

Lucia di Lammermoor: highlights.
(M) *** Decca 421 885-2 [id.] (from above complete recording, with Sutherland, Pavarotti; cond. Bonynge).
(M) **(*) EMI CDM7 63934-2 [id.]. Callas, Tagliavini, Cappuccilli, Ladysz, Philh. Ch. & O, Serafin.

For those who have chosen Callas or Sutherland's earlier, complete set, this 63-minute selection from her later (1971) version should be ideal.

A satisfactory hour-long selection from Callas's 1959 Kingsway Hall stereo recording, with Callas not as completely in vocal control as she was in her earlier, mono sets.

Lucrezia Borgia (complete).
(M) *** Decca 421 497-2 (2) [id.]. Sutherland, Aragall, Horne, Wixell, London Op. Voices, Nat. PO, Bonynge.

Sutherland is in her element here. Aragall sings stylishly too, and though Wixell's timbre is hardly Italianate he is a commanding Alfonso. Marilyn Horne in the breeches role of Orsini is impressive in the brilliant *Brindisi* of the last Act, but earlier she has moments of unsteadiness. The recording is characteristically full and brilliant.

Maria Padilla (complete).
**(*) Opera Rara ORC 6 (3) [id.]. McDonall, Della Jones, Clark, Du Plessis, Earle, Caley, Kennedy, Joan Davies, Geoffrey Mitchell Ch., LSO, Francis.

Maria Padilla marks a return to Donizetti's Italian manner, a piece based on strong situations. It even matches *Lucia di Lammermoor* in places, with the heroine ill-used by the prince she loves, Pedro the Cruel. When the obligatory mad scene is given not to the heroine but to her father, even a tenor such as Graham Clark – future star in Bayreuth – can hardly compensate, however red-blooded the writing and strong the singing. In the title-role Lois McDonall is brightly agile, if at times a little raw. Alun Francis directs the LSO in a fresh, well-disciplined performance and, as ever with Opera Rara sets, the notes and commentary contained in the libretto are both readable and scholarly.

Maria Stuarda (complete).
(M) *** Decca 425 410-2 (2) [id.]. Sutherland, Tourangeau, Pavarotti, Ch. & O of Teatro Comunale, Bologna, Bonynge.

In Donizetti's tellingly dramatic opera on the conflict of Elizabeth I and Mary Queen of Scots, the contrast between the full soprano Maria and the dark mezzo Elisabetta is underlined by some transpositions, with Tourangeau emerging as a powerful villainess in this slanted version of the story. Pavarotti turns Leicester into a passionate Italian lover, not at all an Elizabethan gentleman. As for Sutherland, she is at her most fully dramatic too, and the great moment when she flings the insult *Vil bastarda!* at her cousin brings a superb snarl; Richard Bonynge directs an urgent account of an unfailingly enjoyable opera. Unusually for Decca, the score is slightly cut. The recording is characteristically bright and full.

Poliuto (complete).
*** Sony Dig. M2K 44821 (2) [id.]. Carreras, Ricciarelli, Pons, Polgar, V. Singakademie Ch., VSO, Oleg Caetani.

Set in Rome in the early Christian period, *Poliuto* is based on Corneille's tragedy, *Polyeucte*, a story of martyrdom. Carreras's voice is in splendid form. Ricciarelli as Paolina lacks something in dramatic bite, but she gives the heroine an inward warmth and tenderness. Pons and Polgar are also excellent and the piece is well worth investigating for one of Donizetti's most inspired ensembles in the Act II finale. The recording is clear and vivid, hardly betraying the fact that it was made live at a concert performance.

Ugo, conte di Parigi (complete).
*** Opera Rara ORC1 (3) [id.]. Della Jones, Harrhy, J. Price, Kenny, Arthur, Du Plessis, Geoffrey Mitchell Ch., New Philh. O, Francis.

The 1977 recording of *Ugo, conte di Parigi* was the result of formidable detective work, revealing in this early opera of 1832 a strong plot and some fine numbers, including excellent duets. Matching such singers as Janet Price and Yvonne Kenny, Maurice Arthur sings stylishly in the title-role, with a clear-cut tenor that records well. Della Jones and Christian du Plessis, regular stalwarts of Opera Rara sets, complete a stylish cast. Reissued on CD, thanks to the Peter Moores Foundation, it offers a fresh and intelligent performance under Alun Francis, and the scholarly, readable notes and commentary, as well as libretto and translation, are models of their kind.

Dowland, John (1563–1626)

Consort music: *Captain Digorie Piper, his pavan and galliard; Fortune my foe; Lachrimae; Lady Hunsdon's almain; Lord Souche's galliard; Mistress Winter's jump; The shoemaker's wife (a toy); Sir George Whitehead's almain; Sir Henry Guildford's almain; Sir Henry Umpton's funeral; Sir John Smith's almain; Sir Thomas Collier's galliard; Suzanna.*
*** Hyperion Dig. CDA 66010 [id.]. Extempore String Ens.

The Extempore Ensemble's technique of improvising and elaborating in Elizabethan consort music is aptly exploited here in an attractively varied selection of pieces by Dowland, and on record, as in concert, the result sounds the more spontaneous. Excellent recording.

Lachrimae, or Seaven Teares.
*** BIS Dig. CD 315 [id.]. Dowland Consort, Jakob Lindberg.

Jakob Lindberg and his consort of viols give a highly persuasive account of Dowland's masterpiece. The texture is always clean and the lute clearly present.

Lachrimae: Seven passionate pavans. Consort settings: *Captain Piper his galiard; The Earl of Essex galiard; The King of Denmarks galiard; M. Bucton his galiard; M. George Whitehead his almand. M. Giles Hoby his galiard; M. Henry Noell his galiard; M. John Langtons pavane; M. Nicholas Gryffith his galiard; M. Thomas Collier his galliard with two trebles; Mrs Nichols Almand; Semper Dowland, semper dolens; Sir Henry Umptons funerall; Sir John Souch his galiard.*
*** Virgin/EMI Dig. VC5 45005-2 [id.]. Fretwork, with Christopher Wilson.

This is a reissue of Fretwork's 1989 recording of excerpts from the *Lachrimae*, for which the 'passionate' pavans serve as introduction. Structurally they form a variation sequence, linked by a falling fourth at the opening of the first *Lachrimae antiquae* and by other common motifs of melodic line and harmony, an innovative procedure at the time. They are distinguished also by their pervading melancholy but are followed by a newly recorded collection of Dowland's own galliards, so one can choose to move over to more cheerful music at any time during the separately banded *Lachrimae*. All the performances are of undoubted merit and are well recorded.

Lute music: *Almaine; Captain Digorie Piper's galliard; Dowland's first galliard; The Earl of Derby, his galliard; The Earl of Essex galliard; Frog galliard; Galliard to lachrimae; Lachrimae antiquae; Lachrimae verae; Lady Rich, her galliard; Lord De L'Isle's galliard; Melancholy galliard; Mr Langton's galliard; Mrs Vaux's gigge; My Lady Hunsdon's puffe; My Lord Chamberlain, his galliard; Piper's pavan; Resolution; Semper Dowland, semper dolens; The shoemaker's wife; Sir Henry Gifford's almaine; Sir John Smith's almaine; Sir John Souche's galliard.*
(M) *** RCA 09026 61586-2. Julian Bream (lute).

Julian Bream captures the melancholy (the piece entitled *Semper Dowland, semper dolens* is certainly autobiographical) and the eloquence of these endlessly imaginative miniatures. He produces an astonishing range of colour from the lute: each phrase shows distinction, nothing is in the least routine. The recordings were made over a decade between 1967 and 1976.

Lute solos: *In darkness let me dwell; Lachrimae antiquae pavan; Semper Dowland, semper dolens.* Songs: *Can she excuse my wrongs?; Come again! Sweet love doth now invite; Far from triumphing court; Flow my tears; Flow not so fast, ye fountains; I saw my Lady weep; Lady, you so spite me; Shall I sue; Thou mighty God; Weep you no more, sad fountains.*
(N) *** Lyrichord LEMS 8011 [id.]. Russell Oberlin, Joseph Iadone.

The unique counter-tenor voice of Russell Oberlin is heard here to maximum advantage in the songs of William Byrd. Originally issued on LP on the Experiences Anonymes label in 1958, this CD is immaculately remastered. It is of comparatively short measure (48 minutes) but in every other respect this is a superb disc. Oberlin's voice is like a very fine wine: once tried, nothing else seems quite the same. The accompaniments by Joseph Iadone are admirably stylish, and he has two lute solos to provide central interludes for each group of six songs and a third to act as a postlude.

First Booke of Songes (1597): 1, Unquiet thoughts; 2, Whoever thinks or hopes; 3, My thoughts are wing'd with hopes; 4, If my complaints; 5, Can she excuse my wrongs; 6, Now, O now I needs must part; 7, Dear, if you change; 8, Burst forth my tears; 9, Go crystal tears; 10, Think'st thou then; 11, Come away, come sweet love; 12, Rest awhile; 13, Sleep wayward thoughts; 14, All ye who love or fortune; 15, Wilt thou unkind; 16, Would my conceit; 17, Come again; 18, His golden locks; 19, Awake, sweet love; 20, Come, heavy sleep; 21, Away with these self-loving lads.
*** O-L 421 653-2 [id.]. Cons. of Musicke, Rooley.

Rooley and the Consort of Musicke he directs have recorded all the contents of the *First Booke of Songes* of 1597 in the order in which they are published, varying the accompaniment between viols, lute with bass viol, voices and viols, and even voices alone. There is hardly any need to stress the beauties of the music itself, which is eminently well served by this stylish ensemble, and beautifully recorded.

Second Booke of Songes (1600): I saw my lady weep; Flow my tears; Sorrow, stay; Die not before thy day; Mourn day is with darkness fled; Time's eldest son; Then sit thee down; When others say Venite; Praise blindness eyes; O sweet words; If floods of tears; Fine knacks for ladies; Now cease my wond'ring eyes; Come, ye heavy states of night; White as lilies was her face; Woeful heart; A shepherd in a shade; Faction that ever dwells; Shall I sue; Toss not my soul; Clear or cloudy; Humour say what mak'st thou here.
*** O-L 425 889-2 [id.]. Kirkby, York Skinner, Hill, D. Thomas, Cons. of Musicke, Rooley.

The *Second Booke* contains many of Dowland's best-known songs. The solo songs are given with great restraint (sometimes perhaps rather too great) and good musical judgement, while the consort pieces receive expressive treatment. Refined intelligence is shown by all taking part. The recording is of the highest quality.

Third Booke of Songes (1603): 1, Farewell too fair; 2, Time stands still; 3, Behold a wonder here; 4, Daphne was not so chaste; 5, Me, me and none but me; 6, When Phoebus first did Daphne love; 7, Say, Love, if ever thou didst find; 8, Flow not so fast, ye fountains; 9, What if I never speed; 10, Love stood amazed; 11, Lend you ears to my sorrow; 12, By a fountain where I lay; 13, O, what hath overwrought; 14, Farewell unkind; 15, Weep you no more sad fountains; 16, Fie on this feigning; 17, I must complain; 18, It was a time when silly bees; 19, The lowest trees; 20, What poor astronomers; 21, Come when I call.
**(*) O-L 430 284-2 [id.]. Kirkby, Skinner, Hill, Thomas, Mackintosh, Cons. of Musicke, Rooley.

Although there are certain details with which to quarrel – a general air of sobriety and an excessive restraint in colouring words – the whole set is well worth investigation and an impressive achievement; the instrumental support is of high quality, as is the presentation. The CD transfer is absolutely refined and clear: this might almost be a digital recording.

Ayres and Lute-lessons: *Prelude and Galliard; All ye whom love; Away with these self-loving lads; Come again sweet love; Come heavy sleep; Go Christal teares; If my complaints; My thoughts are winged; Rest awhile;* (Lute): *Semper Dowland, semper dolens. A shepherd in a shade; Stay sweet awhile; Tell me, true love; What if I never speede; When Phoebus first did Daphne love; Wilt thou unkind.*
(B) **(*) H M H M A 901076 [id.]. Deller Consort, Mark Deller; Robert Spencer.

Dowland's 'ayres' were designed for a consort of singers as well as for solo singer and lute, and it is good to hear them in this form. Two of the Lute Lessons are excellently played by Robert Spencer. The performances for the most part give consistent pleasure. The sound is excellent.

Lute songs: *Awake sweet love, thou art returned; Can she excuse my wrongs?; Come again! sweet love doth now invite; Fine knacks for ladies; Flow not so fast, ye fountains; Go, crystal tears; Lady, if you so spite me; Me, me and none but me; Shall I strive with words to move?; Shall I sue?; Sorrow stay; Tell me true love; What if I never speed?; When Phoebus first did Daphne love;* Lute lessons: *Captain Candish's galliard; Lady Laiton's almain; Preludium and Lachrimae pavan; Semper Dowland, semper dolens.*
(M) *** Saga SCD 9004. James Bowman, Robert Spencer.

This record makes a fine single-disc introduction to Dowland's art. James Bowman brings sensitivity and intelligence to each song and characterizes them tellingly. The lute solos provide two central interludes. The recording is very good too, real and present.

Ayres: *Can she excuse my wrongs?; Come again, sweet love; Come heavy sleep; Flow not so fast, ye fountains; From silent night; Go nightly cares; In darkness let me dwell; I saw my lady weep; Shall I sue?.* Consort pieces: *Captain Digory Piper's pavane and galliard; The First galliard.* Lute lessons: *Melancholy galliard; Mistess White's nothing; Mistress Winter's jump; My Lady Hunsdon's puff.* Lute duets: *My Lord Chamberlain's galliard; My Lord Willoughby's welcome home.* Lute lessons: *Orlando sleepeth; Sir John Smith's almain; Tarlton's resurrection.*
*** H M H M C 90245 [id.]. Alfred Deller, Consort of Six, Robert Spencer.

Ayres: *Come away, come away sweet love; Flow my tears; If my complaints could passions move; If that a sinner's sighs be angel's food; Lasso, vita mia; Me, me and none but me; O gentle Death; Say, love, if ever thou didst find; Sorrow stay; Weep you no more sad fountain; What if I never speed?; Wilt thou unkind, thus reave me.* Consort pieces: *Can she excuse galliard; Fortune my foe; The Frog galliard; Katherine Darcy's galliard; Lachrimae pavane; The Round battle galliard.* Lute lessons: *Can she excuse galliard; Galliard; The Lady Laiton's almain; Midnight; Mistress White's thing; The shoemaker's wife (a toy).*
*** HM HMC 90244. Alfred Deller, Consort of Six, Robert Spencer.

Deller's two collections are admirably planned and beautifully recorded. He is in excellent voice, while variety is provided by interweaving his solos with lute pieces and music for Elizabethan consort of six instruments (two viols, flute, lute, cittern and bandora). The recording is naturally balanced and neither of these recitals outstays its welcome.

Dufay, Guillaume (c. 1400–1474)

Missa L'homme armé; Motet: *Supremum est mortalibus bonum.*
(Y/B) (BB) *** Naxos Dig. 8.553087 [id.]. Oxford Camerata, Jeremy Summerly.

Jeremy Summerly and his Oxford Camerata give a powerfully expressive and wholly convincing account of Dufay's masterly cyclic Mass using a Burgundian chanson as its basis. We hear this sung first in its original format as an introduction, and its message, 'The armed man should be feared', makes a dramatically appropriate contrast with the motet, *Supremum est mortalibus*, which is a peace song. The latter was written some 30 years earlier, yet shows just as readily the remarkable inventiveness and eloquence of this fifteenth-century French composer. The Mass movements are interspersed with plain-chant in the same Dorian mode. With vivid yet atmospheric recording, this can be given the strongest recommendation.

Dukas, Paul (1865–1935)

L'apprenti sorcier (The sorcerer's apprentice).
*** DG Dig. 419 617-2 [id.]. BPO, Levine – SAINT-SAENS: *Symphony No. 3.* ***
(N) (M) *** Decca 448 576-2 [id.]. SRO, Ansermet – CHABRIER: *España* **(*); DEBUSSY: *La Mer* **(*); HONEGGER: *Pacific 231* ***; RAVEL: *Boléro; La Valse.* ***
(*) Decca Dig. 421 527-2 [id.]. Montreal SO, Dutoit (with Concert: 'Fête à la française' *).
(M) **(*) Chandos CHAN 6503 [id.]. SNO, Gibson – ROSSINI/RESPIGHI: *La boutique fantasque;* SAINT-SAENS: *Danse macabre.* **(*)
(***) Testament mono SBT1017 [id.]. Philh O, Cantelli – CASELLA: *Paganiniana;* FALLA: *Three-cornered hat;* RAVEL: *Daphnis et Chloé: suite No. 2.* (***)
(N) ** Cala Dig. CACD 1022 [id.]. LSO, Mackerras – BRITTEN: *Young person's guide;* PROKOFIEV: *Peter and the wolf.* **

L'apprenti sorcier; Polyeucte overture.
(M) **(*) Erato/Warner Dig. 2292 45819-2 [id.]. Basle SO, Armin Jordan – DEBUSSY: *La boîte à joujoux.* ***

Levine chooses a fast basic tempo, though not as fast as Toscanini (who managed with only two 78 sides), but achieves a deft, light and rhythmic touch to make this a real orchestral scherzo. Yet the climax is thrilling, helped by superb playing from the Berlin Philharmonic. The CD has an amplitude and sparkle which are especially telling.

Ansermet's performance is more relaxed, yet it has a cumulative effect. There is plenty of atmosphere here and the detail of the recording shows the Swiss conductor at his finest. This was originally part of a very successful 1963 collection (with music by Honegger and Ravel) to which the Chabrier and Debussy works have been added for this reissue in Decca's 'Classic Sound' series.

Dutoit does not quite match Levine's zest (nor indeed achieves the sense of calamity at the climax that the latter does), but he is genially enjoyable and is featured within a desirable collection, given demonstration-worthy recording – see our Concerts section.

Gibson secures excellent playing from the SNO, if without the sheer panache of some of his competitors. The recording (made in City Hall, Glasgow, in 1972) is less overtly brilliant than Ormandy's but has plenty of atmosphere. The Chandos disc, however, is ungenerous in playing time (37 minutes).

Armin Jordan's account of *L'apprenti sorcier* is not without impetus but is rhythmically rather heavy. It is very well recorded, as is the *Polyeucte overture*, really a 16-minute symphonic poem after Corneille's allegorical Christian play. Although the work's melodrama shows influences of Wagner and its scoring has much in common with Lalo, the closing pages are beautiful, and are touchingly played here.

Cantelli's 1954 mono account still remains one of the very best performances ever recorded, and it is splendidly transferred.

A brilliant account from Mackerras, not lacking atmosphere at the opening but otherwise going for excitement rather than subtlety of detail. Good, atmospheric recording.

L'apprenti sorcier; La péri.
(*) Chandos Dig. CHAN 8852 [id.]. Ulster O, Yan Pascal Tortelier – CHABRIER: *España* etc. *

Yan Pascal Tortelier gives a very good performance indeed of *La péri*, with plenty of atmosphere and feeling, and *L'apprenti sorcier* is equally successful as a performance.

La péri: poème dansé (including *Fanfare*).
(N) (M) *** Sony SMK 68333 [id.]. NYPO, Boulez – FALLA: *Harpsichord concerto* etc. **(*)

A most sensitive and atmospheric account comes from Boulez. It is both imaginative and poetic, and the orchestral playing is of the highest quality. Even those who do not normally respond to this conductor will find their reservations swept aside. The recording, made in the Manhattan Center in 1975, is a little over-resonant (but that is not too serious a reservation, for the brass in the opening fanfare is suitably expansive); there is also a touch of stridency in the upper strings. Even so, this can be given a strong recommendation.

Symphony in C; L'apprenti sorcier; La péri: poème dansé (including *Fanfare*).
*** Denon Dig. CO 75284 [id.]. Netherlands R. PO, Fournet.

Along with d'Indy, Chausson and Magnard, Dukas carried the torch for the post-Franckian symphony in France with his well-argued and imaginatively scored contribution to the genre. *La péri* is very much to the French *art nouveau* movement in music what Balakirev's *Tamara* was to Russian music. With its voluptuous ideas and sumptuous scoring, full of colour, it ought to be as much a repertoire piece as Rimsky-Korsakov's *Antar* or *Scheherazade*. The Fournet recording is among the best ever and is second to none. *L'apprenti sorcier* has greater competition than either of its two companions – but, even so, this is among the best. Given the marvellously expansive yet well-focused recording, this deserves a strong recommendation.

Ariane et Barbe-bleue (opera): complete.
(M) *** Erato/Warner Dig. 2292 45663-2 (2) [id.]. Ciesinski, Bacquier, Paunova, Schauer, Blanzat, Chamonin, Command, Fr. R. Ch. & O, Jordan.

Ariane et Barbe-bleue is, like Debussy's *Pelléas*, set to a Maeterlinck text, but there is none of the half-lights and the dream-like atmosphere of the latter. The performance derives from a French Radio production and is, with one exception, well cast; its direction under the baton of Armin Jordan is sensitive and often powerful; the recording is eminently acceptable. The complete libretto is included, and this most enterprising and valuable reissue is strongly recommended.

Duparc, Henri (1848–1933)

Mélodies (complete): *Au pays où se fait la guerre; Chanson triste; Elégie; Extase; La fuite (duet); Le galop; L'invitation au voyage; Lamento; Le Manoir de Rosamonde; Phidylé; Romance de Mignon; Sérénade; Sérénade florentine; Soupir; Testament; La vague et la cloche; La vie antérieure.*
*** Hyperion Dig. CDA 66323 [id.]. Sarah Walker, Thomas Allen, Roger Vignoles.

The Hyperion issue is as near an ideal Duparc record as could be. Here are not only the thirteen recognized songs but also four early works – three songs and a duet – which have been rescued from the composer's own unwarranted suppression. Roger Vignoles is the ever-sensitive accompanist; and the recording captures voices and piano beautifully, bringing out the tang and occasional rasp of Walker's mezzo and the glorious tonal range of Allen's baritone.

Duphly, Jacques (1715–89)

Pièces pour clavecin: La Bouchon; Courante; La Félix; La Forqueray; Les Graces; La d'Héricourt; Légèrement; Menuets; Rondo in D; Rondeau in D min.; La Vanlo; La Victoire; La de Villeneuve.
*** Gaudeamus/ASV Dig. CDGAU 108 [id.]. Mitzi Meyerson (harpsichord).

Mitzi Meyerson's anthology is among the best records devoted to Duphly. These performances come from the mid-1980s (still analogue, and none the worse for that) and are very spirited and characterful. Duphly published four collections of harpsichord works between 1744 and 1768 and, though none of his music can lay a claim to greatness, it has undoubted charm and grace. Mitzi Meyerson plays a Goble harpsichord and uses no fewer than four tunings during the course of the recital. There are excellent notes by Nicholas Anderson. Recommended.

Dupré, Marcel (1886–1971)

Symphony in G minor for organ and orchestra, Op. 25.
*** Telarc Dig. CD 80136 [id.]. Michael Murray, RPO, Ling – RHEINBERGER: *Organ concerto No. 1.* ***

If you enjoy Saint-Saëns's *Organ Symphony* you'll probably enjoy this. The organ's contribution is greater, though it is not a concerto. It is a genial, extrovert piece, consistently inventive if not as memorably tuneful as its predecessor. The performance has warmth, spontaneity and plenty of flair, and the recording has all the spectacle one associates with Telarc in this kind of repertoire.

Chorale and fugue, Op. 57; 3 Esquisses, Op. 41; Preludes and fugues: in B; G min., Op. 7/1 & 3; Le tombeau de Titelouse: Te lucis ante terminum; Placare Christe servulis, Op. 38/6 & 16; Variations sur un vieux Noël, Op. 20.
*** Hyperion Dig. CDA 66205 [id.]. John Scott (St Paul's Cathedral organ).

An outstandingly successful recital, more spontaneous and convincing than many of the composer's own recordings in the past. Dupré's music is revealed as reliably inventive and with an atmosphere and palette all its own. John Scott is a splendid advocate and the St Paul's Cathedral organ is unexpectedly successful in this repertoire.

Duruflé, Maurice (born 1902)

Fugue sur la thème du Carillon des heures de la Cathédrale de Soissons; Prélude, adagio et choral varié sur la thème du Veni Creator; Prélude sur l'Introit de l'Epiphanie; Prélude et fugue sur le nom d'Alain, Op. 7; Scherzo, Op. 2; Suite, Op. 5.
**(*) Delos Dig. D/CD 3047 [id.]. Todd Wilson (Schudi organ of St Thomas Aquinas, Dallas, Texas).

The producer of this record, which contains all Duruflé's organ music, consulted the composer before choosing the present organ, and the performances of Duruflé's often powerful and always engagingly inventive music are of the highest quality. The account of the closing *Toccata* of the *Suite*, Op. 5, has breathtaking bravura and if here, as elsewhere, detail is not sharply registered, the spontaneity and power of the playing are compulsive.

Messe Cum jubilo, Op. 11; 4 Motets, Op. 10.
(N) *** Conifer Dig. 74321 15351-2 [id.]. Griffiths, Trinity College, Cambridge, Ch., Marlow – FAURE: *Requiem.* ***

Duruflé's *Requiem*, echoing Fauré's, is deservedly well known, but these four *a cappella* motets and the *Messe Cum jubilo* of 1966 equally reveal his feeling for evocative choral sound. The *Mass* here comes in its version for organ alone, with the highly distinctive organ-writing adding to the beauty and drama of the piece. An apt and attractive coupling, strongly performed, for a fine version of Fauré's *Requiem*.

Requiem, Op. 9.
*** Teldec/Warner Dig. 4509 90879-2 [id.]. Jennifer Larmore, Thomas Hampson, Amb. S., Philh. O, Legrand – FAURE: *Requiem.* ***
(N) (B) *** Decca Eclipse Dig. 448 711-2; *448 711-4* [id.]. Palmer, Shirley-Quirk, Boys of Westminster Cathedral Ch., L. Symphony Ch., LSO, Hickox – FAURE: *Pavane;* POULENC: *Gloria.* ***

(i; ii; iii) *Requiem. Op. 9;* (ii) *4 Motets (Ubi Caritas et Amor; Tota pulchra es; Tu es Petrus; Tantum ergo), Op. 10;* (iii) (Organ) *Prélude et fugue sur le nom d'Alain.*
(B) *** Decca Double 436 486-2 [id.]. (i) Robert King, Christopher Keyte; (ii) St John's College, Cambridge, Ch.; (iii) Stephen Cleobury (organ); George Guest – FAURE: *Requiem* etc.; POULENC: *Messe* etc. ***

Those who have sometimes regretted that the lovely Fauré *Requiem* remains unique in the output of that master of delicate inspiration should investigate this comparably evocative *Requiem* of Duruflé. The composer wrote it in 1947, overtly basing its layout and even the cut of its themes on the Fauré masterpiece. The result is far more than an imitation for (as it seems in innocence) Duruflé's inspiration is passionately committed.

On Teldec comes a splendidly vibrant new digital version. Michel Legrand uses the full orchestral version and makes the most of the passionate orchestral eruptions in the *Sanctus* and *Libera me*. He strikes a perfect balance between these sudden outbursts of agitation and the work's mysticism and warmth. The Ambrosian Choir sing ardently yet find a treble-like purity for the *Agnus Dei* and *In Paradisum*, while Jennifer Larmore gives the *Pié Jesu* more plangent feeling than its counterpart in the Fauré *Requiem*. The recording, made in Watford Town Hall, is spacious and most realistically balanced. A clear first choice.

Hickox tempers the richness of the orchestral version by using boys' voices in the choir. He relishes the extra drama of orchestral accompaniment with biting brass at the few moments of high climax. Felicity Palmer and John Shirley-Quirk sing with deep feeling and fine imagination, if not always with ideally pure tone. The recording has a pleasantly ecclesiastical ambience, which adds to the ethereal purity of the trebles, and the stereo spread is wide.

The (originally Argo) St John's version also uses boy trebles instead of women singers, even in the solo of the *Pié Jesu* – exactly parallel to Fauré's setting of those words, which was indeed first sung by a treble. The alternative organ version is used here, not so warmly colourful as the orchestral version, but very beautiful nevertheless. The 1974 recording is vividly atmospheric. To this have been added the *Four Motets* on plainsong themes, each quite short but greatly varied in character, with the final *Tantum ergo* perhaps the most ambitious. They are beautifully sung here. The organ piece, another sensitive example of Duruflé's withdrawn genius, makes a further substantial bonus, especially when one realizes that this remarkably generous pair of CDs includes also the *Mass* and *Salve Regina* of Poulenc, to make an unbeatable bargain.

Requiem, Op. 9 (3rd version); *4 Motets, Op. 10*.
*** Hyperion Dig. CDA 66191 [id.]. Ann Murray, Thomas Allen, Corydon Singers, ECO, Best; Trotter (organ).

Using the chamber-accompanied version, with strings, harp and trumpet – a halfway house between the full orchestral score and plain organ accompaniment – Best conducts a deeply expressive and sensitive performance of Duruflé's lovely setting of the *Requiem*. With two superb soloists and an outstandingly refined chorus, it makes an excellent recommendation, well coupled with motets, done with similar freshness, clarity and feeling for tonal contrast. The recording is attractively atmospheric yet quite clearly focused.

Dussek (Dusik), Jan Ladislav (1760–1812)

Keyboard sonatas: in D, Op. 31/2; in B flat; in G; in C min., Op. 35/1–3.
(Y/B) *** HM/BMG Dig. 05472 77286-2 [id.]. Andreas Staier (fortepiano).

The four sonatas in Andreas Staier's recital come from Dussek's London years in the 1790s, when he was befriended by Haydn and John Broadwood, the piano-maker, for whose five-and-a-half-octave grand the three sonatas of Op. 35 (1797) were written. Staier's exhilarating recital is recorded on a Broadwood of 1806, restored by Christopher Clarke, who describes it as 'loud, sonorous, dramatic, a little vulgar'. It has all the weight to cope with the dramatic flair which Staier brings to these highly interesting and occasionally prophetic sonatas. At one point the *B flat Sonata*, Op. 35/1, anticipates Schubert, and the *C minor*, Op. 35/3, has often been compared with the Beethoven *Pathétique*.

Elégie harmonique, Op. 61; Fantasia and fugue (composed and inscribed to J. B. Cramer by his friend, J. S. Dussek), Op. 55; Sonata (Le retour à Paris), Op. 64.
(N) *** HM/BMG 05472 77334-2 [id.]. Andreas Staier (fortepiano).

After his recital of works from Dussek's London years Andreas Staier follows him to France, celebrating appropriately with the remarkably romantic *Sonata, Le retour à Paris* (1806), with its touchingly expressive *Molto adagio*, quirky Minuet/Scherzo and boisterously rhythmic finale. But before that, in 1804 Dussek was engaged by Louis Ferdinand, Prince of Prussia, and wrote his striking, elegiac memorial, the first notes of which quote the *Consumatum est* from Haydn's *Seven Last Words*. The piece is in two movements, with the closing *Tempo vivace e con fuoco* providing a strong contrast, suggesting that the prince was a man of vigour and feeling. The recital opens by looking back towards London with the flamboyantly improvisational *Fantasia* and simpler *fugue*, dedicated to the composer's friend, J. B. Cramer, publisher and piano manufacturer. Once again the playing throughout has great impetus and all the panache needed to bring these remarkable works back to life on the same Broadwood fortepiano that was used for the earlier disc. First-class recording.

Dutilleux, Henri (born 1916)

Cello concerto (Tout un monde lointain).
*** EMI CDC7 49304-2 [id.]. Rostropovich, O de Paris, Baudo – LUTOSLAWSKI: *Cello concerto.* ***

Dutilleux's *Cello concerto* (whose subtitle translates as 'A whole distant world') is a most imaginative and colourful score which exerts an immediate appeal and sustains it over many hearings. Rostropovich plays it with enormous virtuosity and feeling, and the Orchestre de Paris under Serge Baudo gives splendid support. This record won the composer the 1976 Koussevitzky Award, and the 1975 recording is immensely vivid, with Rostropovich looming larger than life but given great presence. This is a straightforward full-priced reissue, retaining the original catalogue number.

(i) *Cello concerto (Tout un monde lointain);* (ii) *Violin concerto (L'Arbre des songes).*
(N) *** Decca Dig. 444 398-2 [id.]. (i) Harrell; (ii) Amoyal; Fr. Nat. O, Dutoit.

Both concertos have been recorded before and are listed here, but they have not been coupled together, so this remains in many respects an obvious choice for the serious collector. Both Pierre Amoyal and Lynn Harrell are first class and withstand the exalted comparisons they confront. The Decca recording is finer than that of rivals, clean, well detailed and with great presence and refinement. What imaginative music this is.

Violin concerto (L'Arbre des songes).
(N) (M) *** Sony Stern Edition II SMK 64508 [id.]. Stern, O Nat. de France, Maazel – BERNSTEIN: *Serenade.* *(**))

Dutilleux's *Violin concerto*, written for Isaac Stern, is a beautiful work. Always the perfect craftsman and consistently writing with refinement, Dutilleux shows how taut self-discipline can go with natural expressive warmth. There are passages in this tightly knit structure of seven linked sections which sound very like Walton updated; and the underlying romantic fervour finds Stern playing with warm commitment, strongly accompanied by Maazel and the Orchestre National. First-rate recording.

Métaboles.
(M) *** Erato/Warner 2292 45689-2 [id.]. French Nat. RO, Munch – HONEGGER: *Symphony No. 4.* ***

Métaboles is a marvellously atmospheric piece, with the fastidious orchestral palette this composer commands: it has something of the rhythmic energy of Stravinsky, the evocative atmosphere of Messiaen, but is wholly individual. It is played in splendid and exhilarating fashion by the French Radio Orchestra, and the recording could have been made yesterday. Strongly recommended.

(i) *Symphonies Nos. 1–2 (Le Double);* (ii) *Métaboles;* (iii) *Mystère de l'instant* (for 24 strings, cymbalum and percussion); (ii) *Timbres, espace, mouvement (La nuit étoilée);* (iv) *Ainsi la nuit (String quartet);* (v) *Les citations* (Diptych for oboe, harpsichord, double-bass & percussion); (vi) *3 Strophes sure le nom de Sacher* (for unaccompanied cello); (vii; viii) *Figures de résonances* (for 2 pianos); (vii) *Piano sonata; 3 Préludes Nos. 1–3;* (ix; viii) *2 Sonnets de Jean Cassou.*
(N) (M) *** Erato/Warner Dig./Analogue 0630 14068-2 (3) [id.]. (i) O de Paris, Barenboim; (ii) O Nat. de France, Rostropovich; (iii) Zurich Coll. Mus., Paul Sacher; (iv) Sine Nomine Qt; (v) Bourgue, Dreyfus, Cazauran, Balet; (vi) David Geringas; (vii) Geneviève Joy; (viii) composer; (ix) Gilles Chachemaille.

These three Erato CDs, issued to celebrate the composer's eightieth birthday, afford an excellent survey of Dutilleux's orchestral, chamber and instrumental music. If the exhilarating and aurally fascinating *First Symphony* is not as well served by Barenboim and the Orchestre de Paris as it is on Harmonia Mundi by their less celebrated colleagues in Lyons under Serge Baudo, it is still an involving performance, even if the Scherzo is scrambled. The *Second Symphony* is well played, and the recording of both is eminently serviceable, if neither music-making nor sound are a match for Tortelier on Chandos. *Métaboles* is otherwise the best-known orchestral work here and is now well represented in the catalogue. *Timbres, Espace, Mouvement*, inspired by Van Gogh's painting, *La nuit étoilée*, is highly imaginative, and it is good to have it under the baton of Rostropovich, who commissioned it. *Mystère de l'instant* is a set of ten miniatures, snapshots of both subtlety and ingenuity, splendid played by the Collegium Musicum under Sacher and digitally recorded. The chamber and instrumental performances date from 1982 and are analogue. They include the *Sonata* of 1947, played by the pianist most closely associated with it over the years, Geneviève Joy -and played with great zest and panache, too! Joy is no less excellent in the *Préludes*. Dutilleux is a composer of keen imaginative awareness and consistent inventive quality, who always holds the listener – *Les Citations* is a case in point. *Ainsi la nuit* is already represented on CD, but it is very well played here. Those coming to this music fresh need not hesitate. The performances and recordings are very fine and the music stimulating and rewarding. Unlike the four separate CDs which this compilation replaces, this is quite good value in terms of playing time, with the first two CDs each timed at just under an hour, and the third playing for 75 minutes. The documentation is excellent and is illustrated with photographs of the composer and major participants.

Symphony No. 1; Timbres, espace, mouvement.
*** HM Dig. HMC 905159 [id.]. O Nat. de Lyon, Serge Baudo.

In Dutilleux's *First Symphony* there is a mercurial intelligence and a vivid imagination at work, and the orchestral textures are luminous and iridescent. What is particularly impressive is its sense of forward movement: you feel that the music is taking you somewhere. *Timbres, espace, mouvement* is a more recent work, dating from 1978. Serge Baudo is an authoritative interpreter of this composer and the Lyon orchestra also serve him well. The engineering is superb: there is plenty of space round the various instruments, and the balance is thoroughly realistic.

Symphonies Nos. 1–2.
✸ *** Chandos Dig. CHAN 9194 [id.]. BBC PO, Tortelier.

Marvellously resourceful and inventive scores which are given vivid and persuasive performances by Tortelier and the BBC Philharmonic Orchestra. The engineers give us a splendidly detailed and refined portrayal of these complex textures – the sound is really state-of-the-art. This issue supersedes Serge Baudo's version with the Orchestre National de Lyon of the *First Symphony*, coupled with *Timbres, espace, mouvement*.

Symphony No. 2; Timbres, espace, mouvement (La nuit étoilée); Métaboles.
*** Ph. 438 008-2 [id.]. O de Paris, Bychkov.

Magnificent orchestral playing from the Orchestre de Paris and splendidly present and clear recording, made in the Salle Pleyel; the sound has exceptional body and range. The performance has all the virtuosity and brilliance you could want, and has real fire. All the same, Tortelier and the BBC Philharmonic on Chandos have greater atmosphere and their disc of the two symphonies remains the preferred recommendation. The *Timbres, espaces, mouvement* (*La nuit étoilée*) is very successful and those who do not have that or Munch's disc of the *Métaboles* might do well to consider this vividly recorded account.

Ainsi la nuit (String quartet).
*** Sony Dig. SK 52554 [id.]. Juilliard Qt – DEBUSSY; RAVEL: *Quartets.* ***
(N) *** Carlton Dig. 3036 70105-2 [id.]. New World Qt – DEBUSSY; RAVEL: *Quartets.* **(*)

There are other versions of Dutilleux's fascinating quartet, *Ainsi la nuit*, but this impressive account from the Juilliard Quartet is a clear first choice, offering superb playing and recording. The music conjures up the moods and impressions surrounding the idea of 'night' – not night itself so much as its aura. As so often with this composer, the writing is highly imaginative.

On Carlton, the New World Quartet offers a useful, slightly less expensive alternative, conveying the music's sense of mystery and scurrying whispers most effectively. Excellent recording too.

Piano sonata.
**(*) Olympia Dig. OCD 354 [id.]; Archduke MARC 2. Donna Amato – BALAKIREV: *Sonata.* **(*)

The Dutilleux *Sonata* has an almost symphonic breadth and sense of scale; it is tonal – the first movement is in F sharp minor and its centrepiece, a Lied, is finely wrought and original, and skilfully linked to the final chorale and variations. Donna Amato gives a totally committed and persuasive account of it, and the recording is very truthful.

Dvořák, Antonín (1841–1904)

Cello concerto in B min., Op. 104.
(Y/B) ✸ (M) *** DG 447 413-2 [id.]. Rostropovich, BPO, Karajan – TCHAIKOVSKY: *Variations on a rococo theme.* *** ✸
(N) *** Sony Dig. SK 67173 [id.]. Ma, NYPO, Masur – HERBERT: *Cello concerto No. 2.* ***

*** Chandos Dig. CHAN 8662 [id.]. Wallfisch, LSO, Mackerras – DOHNANYI: *Konzertstück*. ***

(N) (BB) *** CfP Silver Double CDCFPSD 4775 (2). Robert Cohen, LPO, Macal – BEETHOVEN: *Triple concerto;* ELGAR: *Cello concerto;* TCHAIKOVSKY: *Variations on a rococo theme*. ***

(M) (***) EMI CDH7 63498-2 [id.]. Casals, Czech PO, Szell – ELGAR: *Concerto* (**(*)) (with BRUCH: *Kol Nidrei* (***)).

(N) **(*) EMI CDC5 55527-2 [id.]. Jacqueline du Pré, Chicago SO, Barenboim – ELGAR: *Concerto*. ***

(N) **(*) Finlandia Dig. 4509 98886-2 [id.]. Arto Noras, Finnish RSO, Sakari Oramo – SCHUMANN: *Cello concerto*. **

(M) **(*) RCA 09026 61498-2 [id.]. Piatigorsky, Boston SO, Munch – WALTON: *Concerto*. ***

(N) (M) DG Dig. 445 574-2 [id.]. Maisky, Israel PO, Bernstein – SCHUMANN: *Concerto*. *

There have been a number of distinguished recordings of both the Dvořák *Concerto* and its equally seductive Tchaikovsky coupling over the two and a half decades since this DG record was made, but none to match it for intensity of lyrical feeling and the spontaneity of the partnership between Karajan and Rostropovich. The orchestral playing is glorious. Moreover the analogue recording, made in the Jesus-Christus Kirche in September 1969, is as near perfect as any made in that vintage analogue era. The CD transfer has freshened the original, and the metaphor of 'cleaning an Old Master' readily applies to this splendid reissue.

Ten years after his first recording of the Dvořák with Maazel and the Berlin Philharmonic, Yo-Yo Ma returned to this greatest of cello concertos to demonstrate his extra weight of expression, his firmer control, making for a performance that is both more commanding and more spontaneous-sounding. His expressiveness is simpler and nobler in such great lyrical passages as the second-subject melody, and Masur's vivid accompaniment adds to the drama, very well recorded with wide dynamic range in Avery Fisher Hall, New York, now much improved for sound. The result is one of the finest versions available, ideal if one wants for coupling the Victor Herbert concerto which sparked off Dvořák's inspiration.

Rafael Wallfisch's is also an outstanding version, strong and warmly sympathetic, masterfully played. This is a performance which, in its taut co-ordination between soloist, conductor and orchestra, far more than usual establishes the unity of the work. The excitement as well as the warmth of the piece comes over as in a live performance, and Wallfisch's tone remains rich and firm in even the most taxing passages. The orchestral playing, the quality of sound and the delightful, generous and unusual coupling all make it a recommendation which must be given the strongest advocacy.

Robert Cohen was only twenty when he recorded the Dvořák *Cello concerto*, but his is anything but an immature reading; it is strong and forthright, very secure technically, with poetry never impaired by his preference for keeping steady speeds. The result is most satisfying, helped by a comparably incisive and understanding accompaniment from the Czech conductor, Zdenek Macal. With first-class recording, orchestrally full-bodied and with a truthful balance, this is part of an outstanding quartet of works featuring this fine cellist, which makes a very recommendable Silver Double compilation.

Casals plays with astonishing fire and the performance seems to spring to life in a way that eludes many modern artists; the rather dry acoustic of the Deutsches Haus, Prague, and the limitations of the 1937 recording are of little consequence. This disc is one of the classics of the gramophone.

Jacqueline du Pré's version is newly transferred for a so-called 'dream coupling' with her unique Elgar performance. The original harshness of the Chicago Dvořák recording has been tamed and, though the exaggeratedly forward balance of the cello is still very noticeable, the sound has filled out nicely and is clearly detailed; the inspirational result is very rewarding.

The excellent Finnish cellist, Arto Noras – well remembered for making the first recording of the Bliss *Cello concerto* – gives a sensitive reading of the Dvořák, not helped by the backward balance of the soloist. Most impressive are the tender moments, not least the epilogue, raptly done.

Piatigorsky's recording has been improved remarkably for this CD and, although the balance is still too close and not always flattering to the soloist, with tuttis still inclined to be somewhat two-dimensional, the quality is now fully acceptable. There is no lack of orchestral colour and the acoustic of Symphony Hall is conveyed behind the music-making. The performance is the very opposite of routine, with Piatigorsky and Munch in complete rapport, producing a consistently spontaneous melodic flow; although there are also moments when intonation is less than immaculate, the inspiration of the performance carries the day.

Maisky and Bernstein in their live recording spread the *Concerto* to an extraordinary 43½ minutes. Even that might have been acceptable, had Maisky's playing been less perverse. His fluctuations of tempo and rhythm are so wilful that he sounds jerky, not persuasive. With the soloist too closely balanced and with dry orchestral sound in tuttis, this is not recommended.

(i) *Cello concerto; Symphony No. 8 in G, Op.35.*

(Y/B) (BB) **(*) RCA Navigator 74321 21289-2. (i) Piatigorsky; Boston SO, Munch.

Piatigorsky's 1960 recording (see above) is here also available coupled with Munch's account of the *G major Symphony*, recorded a year later. As in the *Concerto*, the improvement in the recorded sound is remarkable and the work is made to sound extremely vivid against the spacious Boston acoustic. Munch's reading is strongly characterized and, though he occasionally presses hard, the thrust comes from a natural ardour. Some might feel the finale a bit overdriven, but there is plenty of feeling in the slow movement and few would fail to respond to the passionate blossoming in the strings of the inspired lyrical theme that forms the centrepiece of the third-movement *Allegretto.*

(i) *Cello concerto;* (ii) *Symphony No.9 (New World).*

(Y/B) (M) *** Ph. 442 401-2 [id.]. (i) Heinrich Schiff; Concg. O; (i) Sir Colin Davis; (ii) Antal Dorati.

(N) (B) (***) Dutton Lab. mono CDEA 5002 [id.]. (i) Casals; Czech PO, Szell.

(i) *Cello concerto;* (ii) *Symphony No. 9 (New World); Carnival overture, Op. 92; Scherzo capriccioso, Op. 66.*

(Y/B) (BB) *** EMI Seraphim CES5 68521-2 (2) [CEDB 68521]. (i) Paul Tortelier, LSO, Previn; (ii) Philh. O, Giulini – TCHAIKOVSKY: *Variations on a Rococo theme.* ***

The two Philips performances are fascinatingly different in character. Schiff's earlier reading of the *Concerto* (from the beginning of the 1980s) brings an unexaggerated vein of poetry akin to the approach of Yo-Yo Ma – its range of emotion is on a relatively small scale, though satisfying in its intimacy. This performance sounds extremely well in its CD transfer. Dorati's *New World* is characteristically vibrant and extrovert, less subtle but compelling in its direct way; indeed the level of tension is high in the outer movements and the finale ends with a thrilling surge of adrenalin. Because of the rich Concertgebouw acoustic, the forwardly balanced recording from the late 1950s does not sound too dated; indeed the woodwind glow attractively in the *Largo.*

Tortelier's 1978 recording with Previn has a satisfying centrality, not as passionately romantic as Rostropovich's recording on DG, but with the tenderness as well as the power of the work held in perfect equilibrium. What is rather less perfect is the balance of the recording, with the microphones obviously rather too near the soloist. Giulini's recording of the *New World Symphony* was made when the Philharmonia was at its peak in 1962. The result has a refinement, coupled to an attractive directness, which for some will make it an ideal reading. The remastering gives the sound plenty of warmth and projection and, if the performance is not as physically exciting as some versions, like Reiner's Chicago account, the playing, with its beautiful moulding of phrase, is very refreshing. With two attractive bonuses (the lyrical side of the *Scherzo capriccioso* appealingly affectionate), this is a bargain on EMI's Seraphim series, offering two discs for the cost of one medium-priced CD.

When there has been such an explosion in the field of historic recordings on CD, it is specially welcome that Dutton Laboratories, responsible for some of the most vivid and truthful transfers yet, have established an attendant bargain label, the Essential Archive, with this Dvořák disc one of the first issues. In Casals' pioneering recording of the Dvořák concerto, there is little to choose between the Dutton transfer and EMI's most recent one, also using the CEDAR process, with the Dutton marginally brighter and more forward. What makes this disc fascinating is having, instead of more Casals, the recording of the *New World Symphony* made in London by Szell and the Czech Philharmonic six months after the concerto. It is a bitingly powerful performance, crisp and intense and with pinpoint articulation, all the more valuable when Szell seems not to have returned to it in later commercial recordings. And as Compton Mackenzie said at the time, it is 'trance-like' in the slow movement, to have one forgetting the limited 78 dynamic range.

(i) *Cello concerto; Rondo in G min., Op. 94; Silent woods, Op. 68/5;* (ii) *Polonaise, Op. posth; Slavonic dances, Op. 46/3 & 8.*

(N) ** RCA Dig. 09026 68186-2 [id.]. Ofra Harnoy; (i) Prague SO, Mackerras; (ii) Michael Dussek.

(i) *Cello concerto;* (ii) *Rondo in G min., Op. 94; Silent woods, Op. 68/5; Slavonic dance in G min., Op. 46/8.*

*** Ph. Dig. 434 914-2 [id.]. Heinrich Schiff, (i) VPO, Previn; (ii) Previn (piano).

Heinrich Schiff's newest recording of Dvořák's *Cello concerto*, at once fresh, direct and warm, shines out for the fidelity with which he observes the composer's detailed markings and is commanding and spontaneous-sounding, as well as urgent. The great second-subject melody is moving for its tender restraint. Unlike almost any rival, Schiff dares to play it pianissimo and at a flowing tempo, which is what the score asks for. The finale has more fun in it than before, bringing a more dramatic contrast with the meditation of the epilogue. Previn, drawing ravishing sounds from the Vienna Philharmonic, particularly the brass, gives an extra lift to the Slavonic rhythms. Then at the piano Previn similarly adds sparkle to the shorter Dvořák pieces that come as encore, all of them better-known in orchestral form, but here more winning still. An ungenerous coupling, but an attractive one.

The Ofra Harnoy version of this concerto is obviously aimed less at the general collector than at the cellist's many admirers. On the front of the liner booklet she is glamorously shown in a soft-focus portrait through twigs, hidden behind the title, 'Silent Woods'. As one would expect with a Czech orchestra under such a Czech specialist as Sir Charles Mackerras, the opening tutti is given a powerful performance, sharp in focus, though it is not helped by some constriction in the sound and a lack of bloom on high violins. Ofra Harnoy immediately establishes the warmth of her approach both in tone and in expressive freedom, though quickly one registers that her tendency to draw out linking passages grows wearisome when carried to such excess. More seriously, her vibrato grows obtrusive, so that it sounds almost like a sustained trill in many of the big sustained melodies. In the all-Dvořák coupling, Silent woods brings more flutter-vibrato and, next to a direct rival like Heinrich Schiff, Harnoy is heavy-handed in the other pieces too, though Michael Dussek proves a fresh and alert accompanist in all three of his items.

Piano concerto in G min., Op. 33.
*** RCA Dig. RD 60781 [60781-2]. Rudolf Firkušný, Czech PO, Václav Neumann – JANACEK: *Concertino; Capriccio.* ***

(i) *Piano concerto in G min., Op. 33; The Water Goblin (symphonic poem), Op. 107.*
(Y/B) (BB) *** Naxos Dig. 8.550896 [id.]. (i) Jenö Jandó; Polish Nat. RSO, Antoni Wit.

Firkušný has played the Dvořák *Piano concerto* in both the original version and that by Vilém Kurz, as well as this, a *mélange* of the two. The present recording conveys its sunny geniality to good effect, and although the great pianist was seventy-nine when this record was made, the playing still sounds both youthful and aristocratic. Firkušný now makes an admirable first choice, and his claims are enhanced by the value of the coupling, (and the 73 minutes' playing time of the CD).

An infectiously fresh and warmly lyrical account from Jandó and the highly supportive Polish National Radio Orchestra under Antoni Wit, which makes it difficult to understand why the piece is not a popular favourite. Jandó plays with engaging freshness and conveys his own pleasure, and Wit's accompaniment glows with colour; he then offers a splendidly vibrant and colourful portrayal of *The Water Goblin*, one of the composer's most vividly melodramatic symphonic poems. The recording is spacious and realistically balanced. The violins are a shade overbright, but otherwise the sound is first class. Very enjoyable and well worth its modest cost.

Violin concerto in A min., Op. 53.
(B) *** CfP Dig. CD-CFP 4566; *TC-CFP 4566* [Ang. CDB 62920]. Tasmin Little, RLPO, Handley – BRUCH: *Concerto No. 1.* ***
(Y/B) *** EMI Dig. CDC7 54872-2 [id.]. Zimmermann, LPO, Welser-Möst – GLAZUNOV: *Concerto.* ***
(M) *** Ph. 420 895-2. Accardo, Concg. O, C. Davis – SIBELIUS: *Violin concerto.* ***
(N) (M) *** DG Dig. 449 091-2 [id.]. Shlomo Mintz, BPO, Levine – BRUCH: *Concerto No. 1.* ***

Violin concerto in A min., Op. 53; Romance in F min., Op. 11.
*** EMI Dig. CDC7 49858-2 [id.]. Kyung Wha Chung, Phd. O, Muti.
*** EMI CDC7 47168-2 [id.]. Perlman, LPO, Barenboim.
(Y/B) (BB) *** Naxos Dig. 8.550758 [id.]. Ilya Kaler, Polish Nat. RSO (Katowice), Camilla Kolchinsky – GLAZUNOV: *Concerto.* ***
(N) (M) *** Sup. SU 1928-2 011 [id.]. Josef Suk, Czech PO, Karel Ančerl – SUK: *Fantasy.* ***
(M) **(*) Teldec/Warner Dig. 4509 91444-2 [id.]. Zehetmair, Philh. O, Inbal – SCHUMANN: *Violin concerto.* ***
(N) (M) ** Sony Stern Edition I SMK 66827 [id.]. Stern, Phd. O, Ormandy – MENDELSSOHN: *Violin concerto.* **(*)

Tasmin Little brings to this concerto an open freshness and sweetness, very apt for this composer, that are extremely winning. The firm richness of her sound, totally secure on intonation up to the topmost register, goes with an unflustered ease of manner, and the recording brings little or no spotlighting of the soloist; she establishes her place firmly with full-ranging, well-balanced sound that co-ordinates the soloist along with the orchestra.

Frank Peter Zimmermann's account of the Dvořák concerto is fresh and full of spirit. His rhythms are lightly sprung and he conveys great delight in this genial yet underrated score. There are some twenty or so accounts in the catalogue, and this belongs among the best. Certainly the LPO under Franz Welser-Möst are supportive, and the EMI recording is first class.

Kyung Wha Chung gives a heartfelt reading of a work that can sound wayward. The partnership with Muti and the Philadelphia Orchestra is a happy one, with the sound warmer and more open than it has usually been in the orchestra's recording venue. She finds similar concentration in the *Romance*, which is also the ungenerous coupling on Perlman's version.

In his Philips recording, Accardo is beautifully natural and unforced, with eloquent playing from both soloist and orchestra. The engineering is altogether excellent, and in a competitive field this must rank high, especially at mid-price.

Perlman and Barenboim still sound pretty marvellous and show all the warmth and virtuosity one could desire. This CD also has the eloquent and touching *F minor Romance*. Perlman is absolutely superb in both pieces: the digital remastering undoubtedly clarifies and cleans the texture, though there is a less glowing aura about the sound above the stave. However, this EMI record offers no other music.

The performance of the Russian violinist, Ilya Kaler, has great romantic warmth and natural Slavonic feeling, and he is given excellent support by Kolchinsky and the Polish orchestra. In short this is first class in every way. The very resonant acoustics of the recording, made in the Concert Hall of Polish Radio, give the soloist a somewhat larger-than-life image against a widely resonant orchestral back-cloth. But the effect is easy to enjoy when the playing is so ardent; moreover these artists tend to trump the opposition by offering (besides the Glazunov) the *Romance in F minor* as a considerable (13-minute) bonus, and that is also beautifully played.

Suk's earlier performance is back in the catalogue at mid-price, effectively remastered, recoupled with the Suk *Fantasy*. Its lyrical eloquence is endearing, the work is played in the simplest possible way and Ančerl accompanies glowingly. Readers will note that, since its last appearance, the *Romance* has been restored, an equally delightful performance. This is one of Suk's very finest records.

There is dazzling playing from Shlomo Mintz, whose virtuosity is effortless and his intonation astonishingly true. There is good rapport between soloist and conductor, and the performance has the sense of joy and relaxation that this radiant score needs. The digital sound is warm and natural in its upper range.

Thomas Zehetmair plays the concerto with brilliance and precision. He is satisfyingly clean in attack and is very sympathetic in the lovely *Romance*. He is well accompanied by Inbal, and the Teldec recording is natural and well balanced. Even so, this is a performance in the central Viennese tradition, with Czech flavours played down and little feeling for the Czech idiom, even in the Slavonic dance of the finale. But the Schumann coupling is first class, and this generous coupling of two less familiar concertos is welcome.

Stern's recording is a disappointment. It is not lacking in power or eloquence, but this fine soloist seems not entirely at home in the music: his playing is less natural in feeling and not as penetrating as the finest accounts. The recording, too, has the boosted quality and false balance that mar so many records from this source made in the 1960s.

Czech suite, Op. 39; A Hero's song, Op. 111; Festival march, Op. 54; Hussite overture, Op. 67.
(Y/B) (BB) **(*) Naxos Dig. 8.553005 [id.]. Polish Nat. RSO (Katowice), Antoni Wit.

Antoni Wit, who has already given us a memorable performance of Smetana's *Má Vlast*, is almost equally impressive in *A Hero's song*. It opens atmospherically and produces a characteristically Slavonic melodic flow, with some lovely writing for strings and horns. There is an outburst of patriotic hyperbole towards the close (with thundering trombones), which is considerably inflated by the resonant acoustics of the Concert Hall of Polish Radio, which have a similar effect on the *Hussite overture* and *Festival march*; however, no one could grumble that the result lacks spectacle, and Antoni Wit generates excitement without letting things get out of hand. The performance of the *Czech suite* is warm and relaxed, nicely rustic in feeling, but again is affected by the resonance.

Czech suite, Op. 39; Nocturne for strings, Op. 40; Prague waltzes.
(N) (B) *** Decca Double Dig. 443 015-2 (2) [id.]. Detroit SO, Dorati – SMETANA: *Má Vlast* etc. **

The *Czech suite* can sometimes outstay its welcome, but not here; and the charming set of waltzes, written for balls in Prague – Viennese music with a Czech accent – is complemented by the lovely *Nocturne* with its subtle drone bass. The recording has an attractive warmth and bloom to balance its brightness. However, the principal Smetana coupling is less readily recommendable. Readers will note that the *Czech suite* and *Prague waltzes* are also available on Eclipse, coupled with the *New World Symphony* – see below.

Czech suite, Op. 39; Serenade for strings, Op. 22.
(B) *** Erato/Warner Dig. 2292 45928-2 [id.]. Lausanne CO, Jordan (with SMETANA: *Vltava:* Strasbourg PO, Lombard *).

Jordan's bargain coupling of the *Czech suite* and *String serenade* is eminently recommendable. The performances are comparatively mellow but both works respond to this relaxed treatment, and the *Czech suite* in its undemanding, gently pastoral way becomes a charmer. First-rate playing and excellent recording. The Smetana coupling, however, is not an asset, a lifeless performance which begins too slowly and never gushes into life as a great river should.

Legends Nos. 1–10, Op. 59 (see also under *Stabat Mater*); *Nocturne for strings;* (i) *Romance in F min., Op. 11.*
(Y/B) (M) *** EMI Dig. CD-EMX 2232; *TC-EMX 2232* [id.]. (i) Stephanie Gonley; ECO, Mackerras.

Dvořák in lighter mood inspires a charmer of a record, perfect for relaxed listening. The ten *Legends*, like the *Slavonic dances*, were originally written for piano duet and were orchestrated later, easy-going pieces given winningly pointed performances by Mackerras and the ECO, helped by glowing recorded sound. The critic Eduard Hanslick, so far from acting like Beckmesser (as Wagner portrayed him in *Meistersinger*), was delighted to receive the dedication. The ECO strings play with similar refinement in the early *Nocturne*, and Stephanie Gonley, the ECO's leader, is the characterful soloist in the longest of the pieces, the haunting *Romance* for violin and orchestra.

Overtures: *Carnival, Op. 92; Hussite, Op. 67; In nature's realm, Op. 91; My home, Op. 62; Othello, Op. 93.* Symphonic poems: *The Golden spinning wheel, Op. 109; The Noonday witch, Op. 108; The Water goblin, Op. 107; The Wood dove, Op. 110. Symphonic variations, Op. 78.*
(M) *** DG 435 074-2 (2) [id.]. Bav. RSO, Rafael Kubelik.

Kubelik's performances are among his finest on record and they are superbly played. He is splendidly dashing in *Carnival*; in the two pieces there is magic and lustre in the orchestra, and the atmospheric tension is striking. The *Symphonic variations* opens warmly and graciously, yet Kubelik is obviously determined to minimize the Brahmsian associations; his light touch and apt pacing lead on to the lively finale. The recordings, made in the Munich Hercules-Saal between 1973 and 1977, are freshly transferred to CD and generally sound excellent.

Overtures: *Carnival, Op. 92; In Nature's realm, Op. 91; Othello, Op. 93. Scherzo capriccioso, Op. 66.*
*** Chandos Dig. CHAN 8453 [id.]. Ulster O, Handley.

Dvořák wrote this triptych immediately before his first visit to America in 1892. Handley's excellent performances put the three works in perspective. A splendid issue, superbly recorded.

Overtures: *Carnival, Op. 92; In Nature's realm, Op. 91; Othello, Op. 93. Scherzo capriccioso, Op. 66; Symphonic variations, Op. 78.*
*** ASV Dig. CDDCA 794 [id.]. RPO, Farrer.

John Farrer scores over Handley by including also the *Symphonic variations*, here given a performance of airy freshness which confounds any Brahmsian associations. The three linked overtures have comparable warmth and delicacy of colouring. There is plenty of drama too, and the only slight disappointment is that *Carnival*, while vigorous enough and with a richly hued central section, could have been even more exuberant. The *Scherzo capriccioso* is brightly vivacious. The recording, made at St Barnabas Church, Mitcham, is wide-ranging and naturally balanced.

The Cunning Peasant, Overture.
(N) (**) Sup. mono SU 1914 011 [id.]. Czech PO, Karel Sejna – SKROUP: *The Tinker overture;* SMETANA: *Festive Symphony* etc. (***)

The Cunning Peasant is not one of Dvořák's greatest overtures though Karel Sejna makes the most positive case for it in his mono recording. Acceptable sound, and a useful fill-up to Smetana's exhilarating *Festive Symphony*.

Symphonic poems: *The Golden spinning-wheel, Op. 109; The Noonday Witch, Op. 108; The Wood dove, Op. 110.*
(BB) *** Naxos Dig. 8.550598 [id.]. Polish Nat. RSO (Katowice), Stephen Gunzenhauser.

The Polish orchestra seem thoroughly at home in Dvořák's sound-world and Gunzenhauser gives warm, vivid performances and is especially evocative in the masterly *Golden spinning wheel* – a favourite of Sir Thomas Beecham – with its evocative horn-calls setting the opening hunting scene and immediately creating a romantic atmosphere. There is shapely string phrasing and a fine, sonorous contribution from the brass. The concert hall of Polish Radio in Katowice has expansive acoustics – just right for the composer's colourful effects.

Overture: *Othello, Op. 93*. Symphonic poems: *The Golden spinning-wheel, Op. 109; The Water goblin, Op. 107. Scherzo capriccioso, Op. 66*.
(M) **(*) Decca 425 060-2 [id.]. LSO, István Kertész.

These recordings come from a vintage Dvořák series which Kertész made for Decca in the 1960s and early 1970s. This group, coupling *The Golden spinning-wheel* and the tale of the malignant *Water goblin*, with an outstanding version of the *Scherzo capriccioso* and *Othello*, makes a most attractive anthology. Some of the richness of the original sound has been lost in the CD remastering: the violins are drier in timbre than they were on LP; but the ambient effect ensures plenty of colour.

Scherzo capriccioso, Op. 66; Slavonic dances, Opp. 46/1, 3 & 7; 72/2 & 8.
(N) (M) **(*) DG 447 434-2 [id.]. BPO, Karajan – BRAHMS: *8 Hungarian dances*. ***

These are essentially virtuoso performances from Karajan which remain stylish because of the superbly polished ensemble. The 1959 recording, originally very brightly lit, sounds better balanced in this carefully remastered reissue in DG's 'Legendary Recordings' series of 'Originals'. The *Scherzo capriccioso* is exhilarating, but, while it seems carping to criticize orchestral playing of such superlative quality, the lilt of the lyrical secondary tune does seem a trifle calculated. However, coupled with eight of the Brahms *Hungarian dances*, this reissue certainly shows the Karajan/BPO combination in dazzling form.

Scherzo capriccioso, Op. 66; Slavonic rhapsody No. 3, Op. 45/3.
(N) (B) *** EMI forte CZS5 68649-2 (2). Dresden State O, Berglund – GRIEG: *Old Norwegian romance* etc.; SMETANA: *Má vlast*. ***

Berglund's *Scherzo capriccioso* is warmly engaging, not the most brilliantly exciting version on record, but with plenty of impetus and a seductively lilting second subject. The *Slavonic rhapsody* (which, with its opening harp solo, has something in common with *Vyšehrad*, the opening tone-poem in the coupled *Má vlast*) is superbly done, and the recording is pleasingly warm and full.

Serenade for strings in E, Op. 22.
(M) **(*) Virgin/EMI Dig. CUV5 61144-2. LCO, Warren-Green – SUK: *Serenade* ***; TCHAIKOVSKY: *Serenade*. **(*)
(BB) **(*) Naxos Dig. 8.550419 [id.]. Capella Istropolitana, Kr(e)chek – SUK: *Serenade*. ***

Serenade for strings; Romance, Op. 11.
(N) (M) *** Carlton IMP Classics Dig. 30367 0029-2. Laredo, SCO, Laredo – WAGNER: *Siegfried idyll*. ***

Serenade for strings; Serenade for wind in D min., Op. 44.
*** ASV Dig. CDCOE 801 [id.]. COE, Alexander Schneider.
*** Ph. 400 020-2 [id.]. ASMF, Marriner.

Serenade for strings; Serenade for wind; Miniatures, Op. 74a.
(B) *** Discover Dig. DICD 920135 [id.]. Virtuosi di Praga, Oldrich Vlček.

The young players of the Chamber Orchestra of Europe give winningly warm and fresh performances of Dvořák's *Serenades*, vividly caught in the ASV recording.

Marriner's later, Philips performances are direct without loss of warmth, with speeds ideally chosen, refined yet spontaneous-sounding; in the *Wind serenade* the Academy produce beautifully sprung rhythms, and the recording has a fine sense of immediacy.

Laredo's performance of Dvořák's lovely *Serenade* is volatile, full of spontaneous lyrical feeling. The recording, made in City Hall, Glasgow, is admirably balanced to give a true concert-hall effect and add ambient lustre to the string timbre. As an encore Laredo takes the solo role in the *F minor Romance*, which he plays with appealing simplicity.

The wind players of the Virtuosi di Praga give a bright, idiomatic performance of Opus 44, using characteristically reedy tones. The *String serenade* is done with equal understanding, though the recording catches an edge on high violins. The rare *Miniatures* for string trio provide an attractive makeweight. An excellent bargain in full, bright sound.

Warren-Green and his excellent London Chamber Orchestra bring their characteristically fresh, spontaneous approach to the Dvořák *Serenade*. If without the winning individuality of the outstanding COE version under Schneider, this is still very enjoyable, and the Suk coupling is outstanding. Excellent sound.

Fine playing from the Capella Istropolitana on Naxos, and flexible direction from Jaroslav Kr(e)chek. His pacing is not quite as sure as in the delightful Suk coupling, and the *Adagio* could flow with a stronger current, but this is still an enjoyable and well-recorded performance.

Serenade for wind, Op. 44.
*** CRD CRD 3410; *CRD C 4110* [id.]. Nash Ens. – KROMMER: *Octet-Partita.* ***

The Nash Ensemble can hold their own with the competition in the *D minor Serenade*, and their special claim tends to be the coupling, a Krommer rarity that is well worth hearing. The CRD version of the Dvořák is very well recorded and the playing is very fine indeed, robust yet sensitive to colour, and admirably spirited.

Serenade for wind in D min., Op. 44; Hussite overture (Husitská), Op. 67; The Noonday witch, Op. 108; Symphonic variations, Op. 78.
(M) *** Decca 425 061-2 [id.]. LSO, István Kertész.

Kertész gives a delightfully fresh performance of the enchanting *Wind serenade*, with excellent (1967) Decca recording clearly defining detail and providing both warmth and bloom. The *Symphonic variations* is another splendid work, still played comparatively rarely. Under Kertész its Brahmsian derivations are all but submerged by the Czech composer's freshness of spirit. Kertész is even more remarkably successful in the *Hussite overture*. *The Noonday witch* (the traditional ogress threatened to erring children by distraught mothers) also has striking colour and warmth, and the transfers – the additional works were recorded in 1971 – are all well managed.

Slavonic dances Nos. 1–8, Op. 46; 9–16, Op. 72.
*** Decca Dig. 430 171-2 [id.]. Cleveland O, Christoph von Dohnányi.
❀ (M) *** Sony SBK 48161; *SBT 48161* [id.]. Cleveland O, George Szell.
(Y/B) *** Ph. Dig. 442 125-2 [id.]. VPO, André Previn.
(N) **(*) DG Dig. 447 056-2 [id.]. Russian Nat. O, Pletnev.

Dohnányi's rhythmic flexibility and the ebb and flow of his rubato are a constant delight. The recording is superb, very much in the demonstration bracket, with the warm acoustics of the Cleveland Hall ideal in providing rich textures and brilliance without edge. A delightful disc.

In Szell's exuberant, elegant and marvellously played set of the *Slavonic dances* the balance is close (which means pianissimos fail to register) but the charisma of the playing is unforgettable and, for all the racy exuberance, one senses a predominant feeling of affection and elegance. The warm acoustics of Severance Hall ensure the consistency of the orchestral sound.

Previn with his rhythmic flair brings out the playfulness of the *Slavonic dances* as few others do. One is regularly reminded of the closeness of Dvořák's Bohemia to Vienna, when in the warm Musikverein acoustic these dances become first-cousins to the waltzes and polkas of the Strauss family. Helped by the Vienna ambience, however, Previn has more light and shade than Szell. Whatever the contrasts, all three are outstanding versions, with Previn's the most genial.

Refinement and crispness of ensemble are the keynotes of Mikhail Pletnev's distinctive reading of the *Slavonic dances* with the Russian National Orchestra. The approach is at times almost Mozartian in its elegance, with little of the earthier Slavonic qualities and with even the wildest furiants kept under control. The crispness of ensemble and clarity of texture give a sharpness of focus to prevent any idea that these are performances lacking in bite, though one might well feel that they are on the cool side, with the extrovert joy of the music rather underplayed. Yet consistently Pletnev and his Russian players make one marvel at the beauty of the instrumentation, and this is a disc to give a fresh view of well-loved music. However, the acoustic of the Concert Hall of Moscow Conservatory is not particularly flattering, and competition is strong. In short, Pletnev's Russian set of the *Slavonic dances* does not match its two main competitors for infectious brilliance or panache.

Slavonic dances Nos. 1, 3, 8–10.
(N) (M) **(*) Decca 448 568-2 [id.]. VPO, Fritz Reiner – BRAHMS: *Hungarian dances;* R. STRAUSS: *Till Eulenspiegel.* **(*)

Reiner's way with Dvořák is indulgent but has plenty of sparkle, and the VPO are clearly enjoying themselves; any reservations about the conductor's idiosyncrasies are minor when the playing is so vivacious. The Sofiensaal recording is very good, though perhaps not quite worthy of Decca's 'Classic Sound' series.

SYMPHONIES

Symphonies Nos. 1–9.
(M) *** Chandos Dig. CHAN 9008/13 [id.]. SNO, Neeme Järvi.

Symphonies Nos. 1–9; Overtures: Carnival; In nature's realm; My home. Scherzo capriccioso.
🏵 (B) *** Decca 430 046-2 (6). LSO, István Kertész.

Järvi has the advantage of outstanding, modern, digital recording, full and naturally balanced. The set is offered at upper mid-price, six CDs for the price of four. Only the *Fourth Symphony* is split centrally between discs; all the others can be heard uninterrupted. But there are no fillers, as with Kertész on Decca.

For those not wanting to go to the expense of the digital Chandos Järvi set, Kertész's bargain box is an easy first choice among the remaining collections of Dvořák symphonies. The CD transfers are of Decca's best quality, full-bodied and vivid with a fine ambient effect. It was Kertész who first revealed the full potential of the early symphonies, and his readings gave us fresh insights into these often inspired works. To fit the symphonies and orchestral works on to six CDs some mid-work breaks have proved unavoidable; but the set remains a magnificent memorial to a conductor who died sadly young.

Symphonies Nos. 1 (Bells of Zlonice); 2 in B flat, Op. 2; 3 in E flat, Op. 10.
(N) (B) ** Ph. Duo 446 527-2 (2) [id.]. LSO, Witold Rowicki.

Symphonies Nos. 4 in D min., Op. 13; 5 in F, Op. 76; 6 in D, Op. 60; Overtures: Hussite, Op. 67; My home, Op. 62.
(N) (B) ** Ph. Duo 446 530-2 (2) [id.]. LSO, Witold Rowicki.

These Philips Duo reissues come into direct competition with the Decca set conducted by Kertész. Both conductors approach the music sympathetically and comparatively straightforwardly, although their tempi are not always alike, and indeed on the whole Rowicki's interpretative approach is to keep the music moving along fairly briskly. This has the advantage of freshness but in the first movement of No. 1 there is nearly three minutes' difference, and Rowicki sounds too fast. Similarly in No. 5, after Kertész's fine reading, Rowicki's initially sounds rushed and even perfunctory. He takes the outer movements very much faster, which makes for some added excitement but a less coherent argument and phrasing that inevitably sounds hurried. No. 4 is similar, although it certainly is not dull, and the Scherzo is undeniably lively. But even if there is a case for presenting the music in this way, in the middle movements, too, Rowicki's approach is a little stiffer than Kertész's. In the *Sixth* it is the *Adagio* slow movement which suffers from an over-fast tempo; it is taken as an andante, and the misjudgement is the more striking when one remembers the echo of the opening of the slow movement of Beethoven's *Ninth*. Rowicki does his best to draw flexible phrasing, despite the speed, but it would clearly have been better if he had relaxed more. The performances of the other three movements have much to be said for them, for Rowicki manages to point the phrasing engagingly – for example, in the way he leads to the oboe theme of the second subject group in the first movement, where (like Kertész) he observes the exposition repeat – very important when the fourteen bars of lead back would not otherwise be heard. In the last resort the Kertész readings of all these symphonies are more imaginative; the Philips sound (from the early 1970s) is smooth, bright and full, but the Decca is more dramatic in its incisiveness, with the orchestral colours showing rather more glow and sparkle. There is little difference in cost, and clearly the Decca complete set is the one to go for.

Symphony No. 1 in C min. (The Bells of Zlonice), Op. 3; A Hero's song, Op. 111.
*** Chandos Dig. CHAN 8597 [id.]. SNO, Järvi.

The first of Dvořák's nine symphonies is on the long-winded side. Yet whatever its structural weaknesses, it is full of colourful and memorable ideas, often characteristic of the mature composer. Järvi directs a warm, often impetuous performance, with rhythms invigoratingly sprung in the fast movements and with the slow movement more persuasive than in previous recordings. The recording is warmly atmospheric in typical Chandos style.

Symphony No. 1 in C min. (The Bells of Zlonice), Op. 3; Legends, Op. 59/1–5.
(BB) *** Naxos Dig. 8.550266 [id.]. Slovak PO, Czecho-Slovak RSO, Gunzenhauser.

Though on a super-bargain label, this Bratislava version rivals any in the catalogue both as a performance and in sound. The ensemble of the Slovak Philharmonic is rather crisper than that on the other modern rival, Järvi's Chandos disc, and the recording, full and atmospheric, has detail less obscured by reverberation. The first five of Dvořák's ten *Legends* make a generous coupling: colourful miniatures, colourfully played.

Symphony No. 2 in B flat, Op. 4; Legends, Op. 59/6–10.
(BB) *** Naxos Dig. 8.550267 [id.]. Slovak PO, Czecho-Slovak RSO, Gunzenhauser.

With speeds more expansive than those of his Chandos rival, Neeme Järvi (CHAN 8589), Gunzenhauser gives a taut, beautifully textured account, very well played and recorded, clearly preferable in every way, even making no allowance for price. The completion of the set of *Legends* makes a very generous coupling (73 minutes).

Symphony No. 3 in E flat, Op. 10; Carnival overture; Scherzo capriccioso.
*** Virgin/EMI Dig. VC7 59257-2 [id.]. RLPO, Pešek.

Symphony No. 3 in E flat, Op. 10; Carnival overture, Op. 92; Symphonic variations, Op. 78.
*** Chandos Dig. CHAN 8575 [id.]. SNO, Järvi.

Pešek's strong, direct manner in Dvořák here works to bring out the rhythmic freshness of the writing in a most persuasive reading. He has high concentration in sustaining a very slow speed for the central *Adagio*. The clarity of the recording, beautifully set against a believable acoustic, adds to the rhythmic freshness, not least in Pešek's account of the *Scherzo capriccioso*, in which he observes the central repeat.

Järvi's is also a highly persuasive reading, not ideally sharp of rhythm in the first movement but totally sympathetic. The recording is well up to the standards of the house and the fill-ups are particularly generous.

Symphonies Nos. 3 in E flat, Op. 10; 6 in D, Op. 60.
(BB) *** Naxos Dig. 8.550268; 4.550268 [id.]. Slovak PO, Stephen Gunzenhauser.

These exhilarating performances of the *Third* and *Sixth Symphonies* are well up to the standard of earlier records in this splendid Naxos series. Gunzenhauser's pacing is admirably judged through both works, and rhythms are always lifted. Excellent, vivid recording in the warm acoustics of the Bratislava Concert Hall.

Symphony No. 4 in D min., Op. 13; (i) Biblical songs, Op. 99.
*** Chandos Dig. CHAN 8608 [id.]. SNO, Järvi, (i) with Brian Rayner Cook.

Järvi's affectionate reading of this early work brings out the Czech flavours in Dvořák's inspiration and makes light of the continuing Wagner influences, notably the echoes of *Tannhäuser* in the slow movement. This is a performance to win converts to an often underrated work. The recording is well up to the Chandos standard.

Symphonies Nos. 4 in D min., Op. 13; 8 in G, Op. 33.
(BB) **(*) Naxos Dig. 8.550269; 4550269 [id.]. Slovak PO, Stephen Gunzenhauser.

Gunzenhauser's *Fourth* is very convincing. In his hands the fine lyrical theme of the first movement certainly blossoms and the relative lack of weight in the orchestral textures brings distinct benefit in the Scherzo. The slow movement, too, is lyrical without too much Wagnerian emphasis. The naturally sympathetic orchestral playing helps to make the *Eighth* a refreshing experience, even though the first two movements are rather relaxed and without the impetus of the finest versions. The digital sound is excellent, vivid and full, with a natural concert-hall ambience.

Symphony No. 5 in F, Op. 76; Othello overture, Op. 93; Scherzo capriccioso, Op. 66.
Ⓦ *** EMI Dig. CDC7 49995-2 [id.]. Oslo PO, Jansons.

Symphony No. 5 in F, Op. 75; The Water goblin, Op. 107.
*** Chandos Dig. CHAN 8552 [id.]. SNO, Järvi.

Jansons directs a radiant account of this delectable symphony and the EMI engineers put a fine bloom on the Oslo sound. With its splendid encores, equally exuberant in performance, this is one of the finest Dvořák records in the catalogue.

Järvi is also most effective in moulding the structure, subtly varying tempo between sections to smooth over the often abrupt links. His persuasiveness in the slow movement, relaxed but never sentimental, brings radiant playing from the SNO, and Czech dance-rhythms are sprung most infectiously, leading to an exhilarating close to the whole work, simulating the excitement of a live performance.

Symphonies Nos. 5 in F, Op. 76; 7 in D min., Op. 70.
(BB) *** Naxos Dig. 8.550270; 4550270 [id.]. Slovak PO, Stephen Gunzenhauser.

Gunzenhauser's coupling is recommendable even without the price advantage. The beguiling opening of the *Fifth*, with its engaging Slovak wind solos, has plenty of atmosphere, and the reading generates a natural lyrical impulse. The *Seventh*, spontaneous throughout, brings an eloquent *Poco adagio*, a lilting Scherzo, and a finale that combines an expansive secondary theme with plenty of excitement and impetus.

Symphony No. 6 in D, Op. 60; The Wood dove, Op. 110.
(N) *** Chandos Dig. CHAN 9170 [id.]. Czech PO, Jiří Bělohlávek.

Bělohlávek conducts a glowing performance of No. 6, rich in Brahmsian and Czech pastoral overtones, helped by satisfyingly full and immediate Chandos sound. This easily takes precedence over the Järvi version (CHAN 8350). His reading of the late symphonic poem is comparably warm and idiomatic in a relaxed way.

Symphonies Nos. 6 in D, Op. 60; 7 in D min., Op. 70; 8 in G, Op. 88; 9 (New World); Scherzo capriccioso, Op. 66.
(N) (M) **(*) EMI CMS5 65705-2 (3) [CDMC 65705]. LPO, Rostropovich.

Now reissued as part of EMI's Rostropovich Edition, these performances date from 1979–80. The *Sixth Symphony* opens freshly, the first movement quite relaxed until the coda which draws everything strongly together; the performance is notable for some lovely LPO wind-playing. The slow movement is leisurely and romantic but has an imposing climax and coda. The Scherzo brings an accent on forceful vigour and is in no way lightweight, although there is more lovely pastoral woodwind playing in the Trio. The finale certainly does not lack impetus and power and its forceful close is characteristic of Rostropovich's weighty approach throughout the set. The *Seventh* is a big, thrustful reading which underplays the genial Dvořák, who now becomes biting and unrelenting. The spaciousness of the speeds is designed not for lyrical self-indugence but to underline the symphonic breadth. Even the slow movement is big and powerful, highly charged rather than warm and refined; the Scherzo, the rhythmic nudgings a trifle calculated, is emphatic rather than urgent, the most controversial point of an unconventional interpretation. The *Eighth* produces slow tempi throughout and a consciously *espressivo* manner. The slow movement sounds too studied and unspontaneous, and the performance overall disappointingly refuses to catch fire. Rostropovich's very opening chords for the *New World* suggest an epic view, and from then on, with generally expansive tempi, the reading clearly follows this weighty conception. The exposition repeat brings a slight modification of treatment the second time, and some will resist such inconsistencies as that. The conscious weight of even the *Largo* is also controversial, though in all four movements Rostropovich contrasts the big tuttis with light pointing in woodwind solos. The *Scherzo capriccioso* is incisive and energetic, lilting yet essentially symphonic in feeling; with all reservations taken into account, these readings are all full of character and only the *Eighth* lacks the fullest concentration. The Kingsway Hall recording has been very effectively remastered so that the sound is bright and fresh on top, yet remains full and expansive.

Symphony No. 7 in D min., Op. 70; Nocturne for strings, Op. 40; The Water goblin, Op. 107.
(N) *** Chandos Dig. CHAN 9391 [id.]. Czech PO, Bělohlávek.

As he showed when he conducted Dvořák symphonies in London, Bělohlávek knows better than his direct rivals how to draw out idiomatic warmth from the Czech Philharmonic, and he is helped by satisfyingly full and glowing Chandos sound. Fresh, well paced and intelligently shaped, this is a thoroughly recommendable reading. Everything is perfectly straight without being undercharacterized in any way. Others offer the *G major Symphony* as coupling, but readers who have the latter will be rewarded by an excellent account of one of Dvořák's most inventive late tone-poems, *The Water goblin*, and the eloquent, poignant *Nocturne for strings*. In this spacious reading of the *Nocturne* the Czech strings produce ravishing sounds, and *The Water goblin* is similarly relaxed and warm rather than sharply dramatic.

Symphonies Nos. 7 in D min., Op. 70; 8 in G, Op. 88.
(N) *** EMI Dig. CDC7 54663-2 [id.]. Oslo PO, Jansons.
(M) *** Mercury 434 312-2 [id.]. LSO, Antal Dorati.
(M) *** Decca Dig. 430 728-2 [id.]. Cleveland O, Christoph von Dohnányi.
*** Virgin/EMI Dig. VC7 59516-2 [id.]. RLPO, Pešek.
(Y/B) (M) **(*) Telarc Dig. CD 82018 [id.]. LAPO, André Previn.
(N) (B) **(*) Sony SBK 67174; SBT 67174 [id.]. Philh. O, Andrew Davis.

Mariss Jansons's readings of both works are outstandingly fine, with the dramatic tensions of the *D minor* work bitingly conveyed, yet with detail affectionately treated, and with rhythms exhilaratingly sprung. No. 8 is given a performance of high contrasts too, with the slow movement warmly expansive and the whole crowned by a winningly spontaneous-sounding account of the finale, rarely matched in its exuberance. Excellent sound. This makes a new first choice for this coupling, although at mid-price there are strongly recommendable alternatives, notably Dorati on Mercury.

Dorati's coupling brings an extraordinary successful account of No. 7, with the spontaneous feel of a live performance enhanced by the vividly realistic concert hall balance of the (1963) Mercury recording

– one of their very finest. The interpretation is free, the *Poco Adagio* is impulsive and the Scherzo lifts off with a sparkle. The finale has enormous energy and bite, and an exuberant thrust, leading on to a thrilling coda. The *Eighth Symphony* was recorded four years earlier, with the acoustic of Watford Town Hall again providing a highly convincing ambience. Dorati's reading proves comparably vibrant.

Dohnányi's coupling of Dvořák's *Seventh* and *Eighth Symphonies* with the Cleveland Orchestra is also very attractive indeed. Tempi are all aptly judged. The playing of the Cleveland Orchestra is so responsive that the overall impression is one of freshness, and the recording is in the demonstration class, using the acoustics of the Masonic Auditorium to give a convincingly natural balance, the internal definition achieved without any kind of digital edge.

In Pešek's *D minor*, the fresh, direct manner relates it readily to other Dvořák. The slow movement is warm and relaxed, and the scherzo becomes a happy folk-like dance, despite the minor key, while Pešek's speed in the finale also allows him to give a lift to the stamping dance-rhythms. No. 8 receives a similarly refreshing performance, persuasive in a light, relaxed way, with the folk element again brought out, above all in the middle movements. The Scherzo is liltingly light; and again the performance benefits from the full, clear sound.

Andrew Davis's coupling with the Philharmonia is reissued in Sony's 'Essential Classics' bargain series but was recorded at EMI's Abbey Road studios with Neville Boyling the balance engineer. Yet, with the violins given a bright sheen, with good detail but lacking something in warmth, and with the brass given plenty of presence and bite, the sound is more like a CBS recording than a mellower, EMI offering. Davis's comparatively lightweight account of the *Seventh* has an attractive lyrical freshness, the *Poco Adagio* simple and songful though with an eloquent climax, the Scherzo vivaciously energetic, rhythms nicely lifted. But the finale hangs fire just a little until the very end. The *Eighth* is much more compulsive and dramatically spontaneous, making the most of the music's dynamic contrasts, with high drama in the climaxes of the *Adagio*, which also has plenty of expressive feeling, and a sense of vibrant energy throughout the outer movements. The Scherzo responds least well to this approach, but the finale is thrilling (although there is some raucous tone from the brass) and there is no doubt about the individuality of the reading as a whole.

Previn directs a tautly rhythmic account of the *Seventh Symphony*. Rather than developing Slavonic atmosphere, he tends to bring out the symphonic cohesion. The slow movement is warmly done, with fine horn solos; but some of the lightness of the last two movements is lost – notably in the lilting Scherzo – with such rhythmic emphasis. The *Eighth*, too, is sharply rhythmic but rather more idiomatic in feeling. Warmth and freshness here go with the finest orchestral sound yet achieved by this orchestra in Royce Hall, full and with a vivid sense of presence that allows fine inner quality. In the *Seventh Symphony* the upper range has marginally less bloom.

Symphonies Nos. (i) *7 in D min., Op. 70;* (ii) *8 in G, Op. 88; 9 (New World); Overture: Carnival, Op. 92; Scherzo capriccioso, Op. 66.*
(N) (B) **(*) EMI forte CZS5 68628-2 (2). (i) LPO; (ii) Philh. O; Giulini.

Giulini is at his finest in both the *Seventh* and the *New World*. In the *D minor Symphony* he and the LPO players really make the music sing, and the Dvořákian sunshine keeps breaking out. The glowing (1976) recording encourages rounded textures and rounded phrases, but it is not in any way a self-indulgent performance, and the concentration from first to last makes for buoyancy instead of the usual more biting qualities. No. 8 (like the *New World*), recorded with the Philharmonia 14 years earlier, brings a similar mellow approach, but the result is comparatively disappointing. Giulini's speeds are on the slow side, especially in the *Adagio* (though there is a spurt at the climax) and rather bland *Allegretto*, while the finale opens in a somewhat subdued fashion. Frankly this does not altogether come off. The *New World* is a different matter, refreshingly direct. It is discussed above in its alternative, Seraphim coupling with the *Cello concerto*.

(i) *Symphonies Nos. 7 in D min., Op. 70; 8 in G, Op. 88;* (ii) *9 (New World);* (i) *Symphonic variations, Op. 78.*
(B) *** Ph. Duo 438 347-2 (2) [id.]. (i) LSO; (ii) Concg. O, Sir Colin Davis.

Sir Colin Davis's performances of Nos. 7 and 8, with their bracing rhythmic flow and natural feeling for Dvořákian lyricism, are appealingly direct yet have plenty of life and urgency. In the *New World*, however, the very directness has its drawbacks. The cor anglais solo in the slow movement brings an appealing simplicity. The reading is completely free from egotistical eccentricity and, with beautiful orchestral playing throughout, this is enjoyable in its way. The set is made the more attractive by the inclusion of the *Symphonic variations* – one of Dvořák's finest works, much underrated by the public – and here Davis's performance has striking freshness. The remastering of all the recordings is very successful.

Symphonies Nos. 7 in D min., Op. 70; 9 in E min. (New World), Op. 95.
(N) (M) *** EMI Eminence Dig. CD-EMX 2202; *TC-EMX 2202* [id.]. LPO, Mackerras.
(N) (M) **(*) Sony Dig. SX2K 58946-2 (2) [id.]. Concg. O, Giulini.

At mid-price, Mackerras's coupling offers performances of both works which are among the finest ever. With Mackerras, tragedy is not uppermost in the *D minor Symphony* but rather Dvořákian openness. After a hushed, mysterious opening it is the lilting joy of the inspiration which makes the performance so winning. In the *New World* he takes a warmly expansive view, remarkable for a hushed and intense account of the slow movement and superb playing from the LPO, treated to warm, atmospheric recording.

Where others (notably Mackerras) manage to couple Nos. 7 and 9 together on a single disc, Giulini's speeds in his latest Sony recordings are so expansive that two discs are required, happily offered at mid-price. With Giulini, the open joy and rhythmic exuberance of Dvořák are underplayed in favour of rapt dedication, making the slow movement of the *New World* a deeply moving experience. One admires and is magnetized, but the vision is too personal to recommend as a first choice. Readers are referred to EMI's reissue of Giulini's earlier recordings of the late symphonies, including the Philharmonia account of the *New World* which shows the conductor at his finest, the interpretation quite free from personal indulgence.

Symphony No. 8 in G; The Golden spinning-wheel, Op. 109.
(N) **(*) Chandos Dig. CHAN 9048 [id.]. Czech PO, Bělohlávek.

Symphony No. 8 in G; Legends Nos. 4, 6 & 7, Op. 59; Scherzo capriccioso.
⊛ (M) *** EMI CDM7 64193-2 [id.]. Hallé O, Sir John Barbirolli.

Symphony No. 8 in G; Symphonic variations, Op. 78.
(N) (M) *** EMI Dig. CD-EMX 2216; *TC-EMX 2216* [id.]. LPO, Mackerras.

Symphony No. 8 in G; The wood dove, Op. 110.
*** Chandos Dig. CHAN 8666 [id.]. SNO, Järvi.

Barbirolli's account of this symphony was one of his best Pye records: the reading has immense vitality and forward impetus, the kind of spontaneous excitement that is rare in the recording studio, and yet the whole performance is imbued with a delightful, unforced lyricism. The *Scherzo capriccioso* is warm and very exciting too, and the *Legends* make a colourful bonus. This was always the finest of Barbirolli's late Dvořák symphonies technically, and the EMI documentation reveals why: it was made in 1957/8 in Manchester's recently rebuilt Free Trade Hall by the Mercury recording team, led by Wilma Cozart Fine. In remastered form it is tremendously real and vivid.

Mackerras's version of No. 8 matches in its effervescence his outstanding accounts of Nos. 7 and 9, also on Eminence. The colour and atmosphere of the piece are brought out vividly and with a lightness of touch that makes most rivals seem heavy-handed. In the *Symphonic variations* too, his relaxed treatment is consistently winning, helped by fine playing and recording. While Barbirolli's interpretation of the symphony remains very special, Mackerras has the advantage of first-rate digital recording.

Järvi's highly sympathetic account of the *Eighth* underlines the expressive lyricism of the piece, the rhapsodic freedom of invention rather than any symphonic tautness, with the SNO players reacting to his free rubato and affectionate moulding of phrase with collective spontaneity. The warm Chandos sound has plenty of bloom, with detail kept clear, and is very well balanced.

Bělohlávek directs the Czech Philharmonic in a warmly idiomatic reading of No. 8. He is helped by a satisfyingly beefy recording with plenty of bloom that yet focuses the players more sharply than most recordings with this orchestra. Though basic speeds are on the fast side, Bělohlávek is never reticent over giving full expansiveness to linking passages, so adding to the warmth. The longest and richest of Dvořák's late symphonic poems is given similarly idiomatic treatment but in a version with cuts, a considerable drawback.

Symphonies Nos. 8 in G; 9 in E min. (New World).
(N) (M) *** Sony Bruno Walter Edition SMK 64484 [id.]. Columbia SO, Bruno Walter.

Walter's account of Dvořák's *Eighth* was one of the last recordings he made (in 1962); the sound has been successfully freshened in the current remastering, but with the violas, cellos and basses remaining expansively resonant. It is a strong yet superbly lyrical reading, but the overall lyricism never takes the place of virility and Walter's mellowness is most effective in the *Adagio*. His pacing is uncontroversial until the finale, which is steadier than usual, more symphonic, though never heavy. The *New World* was recorded two years earlier and again has been effectively remastered. Once more, this is not a conventional reading, but it is one to fall in love with. Its recognizably Viennese roots lead to a more relaxed view of the outer movements than usual. Nevertheless, as so often with Walter, there is an underlying tension to knit the structure together; the *Largo* is radiant and the Scherzo lilting. The spacious finale finds dignity without pompousness and the result is more involving and satisfying than some other rivals which have greater surface excitement.

Symphony No. 9 in E min. (From the New World), Op. 95.
(M) *** Mercury 434 317-2 [id.]. Detroit SO, Paray – SIBELIUS: *Symphony No. 2.* **
(M) (***) RCA mono GD 60279 [60279-2-RG]. NBC SO, Toscanini – KODALY: *Háry János*: suite (***); SMETANA: *Má Vlast: Vltava.* (**)
**(*) DG Dig. 439 009-2 [id.]. VPO, Karajan – SMETANA: *Vltava.* **(*)
(M) **(*) Teldec/Warner CD 82007 [id.]. St Louis SO, Leonard Slatkin.

Symphony No. 9 (New World); Carnival overture, Op. 92.
(Y/B) (M) *** RCA 09026 62587-2 [id.]. Chicago SO, Fritz Reiner – SMETANA: *Bartered Bride overture;*
      WEINBERGER: *Schwanda polka and fugue.* ***

Symphony No. 9 (New World); Overtures: Carnival; Othello.
(N) (M) *** Decca 448 583-2 [id.]. LSO, Istvan Kertész.

Symphony No. 9 (New World); Carnival overture; Slavonic dances Nos. 1 & 3, Op. 46/1 & 3.
(M) ** Sony SMK 47547 [id.]. NYPO, Bernstein (with SMETANA: *Vltava* *(*)).

Symphony No. 9 (New World); (ii) Czech suite; Prague waltzes.
(N) (B) *** Decca Eclipse Dig. 448 245-2; *448 245-4* [id.]. (i) VPO, Kondrashin; (ii) Detoit SO, Dorati.

Symphony No. 9 (New World); My home overture, Op. 62.
*** Chandos Dig. CHAN 8510 [id.]. SNO, Järvi.

(i) *Symphony No. 9 (New World);* (ii) *Serenade for strings.*
(M) **(*) Sony SBK 46331 [id.]. (i) LSO, Ormandy; (ii) Munich PO, Kempe.

(i) *Symphony No.9 in E min. (New World);* (ii) *Slavonic dances Nos. 1, 2, 7 & 8, Op. 46/1, 2, 7 & 8; 16, Op. 72/8.*
(B) *** DG 439 436-2 [id.]. (i) BPO; (ii) Bav. RSO; Rafael Kubelik.

Symphony No. 9 (New World); Slavonic dances Nos. 1, 3 and 7, Op. 46/1, 3 & 7; 10 and 15, Op. 72/2 & 7.
(M) *** DG 435 590-2 [id.]. BPO, Karajan.

Symphony No. 9 (New World); Symphonic variations, Op. 78.
(B) *** CfP Dig. CD-CFP 9006; *TC-CFP 4382.* LPO, Macal.

Kondrashin's Vienna performance of the *New World Symphony* was one of Decca's first demonstration CDs and its impact remains quite remarkable. Recorded in the Sofiensaal, the ambience of the hall prevents a clinical effect, yet every detail of Dvořák's orchestration is revealed within a highly convincing perspective. Other performances may exhibit a higher level of tension but there is a natural spontaneity here, with the first-movement exposition repeat fitting naturally into the scheme of things. The cor anglais solo in the *Largo* is easy and songful, and the finale is especially satisfying, with the wide dynamic range adding drama and the refinement and transparency of the texture noticeably effective as the composer recalls ideas from earlier movements. Previously available in a mid-priced coupling with Dorati's RPO version of the engaging *American suite*, the new budget-priced Eclipse CD is enhanced by Dorati's bright, fresh Detroit versions of the *Czech suite* and the even rarer *Prague waltzes* (Viennese music with a Czech accent).

Among earlier analogue accounts, Kertész's LSO version stands out. It remains one of the finest performances ever committed to record, with a most exciting first movement (exposition repeat included) in which the introduction of the second subject group is eased in with considerable subtlety; the *Largo* brings playing of hushed intensity to make one hear the music with new ears. Tempi in the last two movements are perfectly judged. Reissued, very successfully remastered, as part of Decca's 'Classic Sound' series, with equally fine accounts of *Othello* and the *Carnival overture*, this remains very competitive, but for most collectors the Kondrashin version is even more attractive.

Reiner's 1957 *New World* is an essentially lyrical performance without idiosyncratic disturbances. There is no first-movement exposition repeat, but how naturally the second subject is ushered in and how well the music flows, both here and in the *Largo*, with consistently lovely playing, especially in the rapt closing section. The Scherzo sparkles and its lilting rustic interlude is especially beguiling, while there is no lack of excitement in the finale. Typically warm Chicago sound. What makes this disc the more attractive are the fill-ups, not just the brilliant *Carnival overture*, which bursts with energetic orchestral bravura and yet has ravishing Slavonic feeling in the middle section.

Macal as a Czech takes a fresh and unsentimental view of the *New World Symphony*. His inclusion of the repeat balances the structure convincingly. With idiomatic insights there is no feeling of rigidity, with the beauty of the slow movement purified, the Scherzo crisp and energetic, set against pastoral freshness in the episodes, and the finale again strong and direct, bringing a ravishing clarinet solo. The *Symphonic variations*, which acts as coupling, is less distinctive but is well characterized. A fine bargain recommendation.

Karajan's 1964 DG analogue recording is preferable to his digital version. It has a powerful lyrical feeling and an exciting build-up of power in the outer movements. The *Largo* is played most beautifully, and Karajan lets the orchestra speak for itself, which it does, gloriously. The rustic qualities of the Scherzo are affectionately brought out, and altogether this is very rewarding. The recording is full, bright and open. This is now reissued, sounding as good as ever, coupled with five favourite *Slavonic dances*, given virtuoso performances.

Kubelik's *New World* (see above) remains among the top recommendations. It is brightly transferred in this Classikon reissue, where it is recoupled with five sparkling *Slavonic dances*.

Järvi's opening introduction establishes the spaciousness of his view, with lyrical, persuasive phrasing and a very slow speed, leading into an allegro which starts relaxedly, but then develops in big dramatic contrasts. The expansiveness is underlined, when the exposition repeat is observed. The *Largo* too is exceptionally spacious, with the cor anglais player taxed to the limit but effectively supported over ravishingly beautiful string playing. The Scherzo is lilting rather than fierce, and the finale is bold and swaggering.

Paray's 1960 *New World* is uncommonly fresh. In the first-movement allegro he is airy and graceful; the exposition repeat is not observed. The *Largo*, with its poised cor anglais melody, makes a gentle contrast, and the Scherzo is admirably vivacious. The finale goes furiously and its spontaneity leaves the listener with that rare feeling that the music really has been made while he or she was listening. The recording, made in Detroit's Cass Technical High School auditorium, is well balanced in a typically natural Mercury way and adds to the freshness of effect. The Sibelius coupling is generous but the interpretation, though exciting, is rather less successful.

With speeds consistently fast and the manner clipped, Toscanini's reading of the *New World* is anything but idiomatic, but it still tells us something unique about Dvořák and his perennial masterpiece, presenting a fiery, thrilling experience. The sound is fuller than most from this source and the transfer brings that out, despite the usual dryness.

Under Ormandy the playing of the LSO has life and spontaneity, and the rhythmic freshness of the Scherzo (achieved by unforced precision) is matched by the lyrical beauty of the *Largo* and the breadth and vigour of the finale. Perhaps the reading has not the individuality of the finest versions; but the sound is full and firm in the bass to support the upper range's brilliance. For coupling, we are offered an essentially mellow account of the *String serenade*, directed by Kempe with affectionate warmth.

Karajan's digital recording of the *New World Symphony* is enjoyably alive and does not lack spontaneity, although the VPO playing is less refined than on either of Karajan's analogue versions with the BPO, especially in the *Largo*. However, those wanting a Karajan performance in modern digital sound could be well satisfied with this.

The St Louis Symphony plays for Slatkin with polish and refinement; the cor anglais solo of the slow movement is so velvety it hardly sounds like a reed instrument, and the brass which introduces the *Largo* is characteristically rich in sonority. One or two mannerisms apart, the reading is both enjoyably direct and vital, and the recording, full-bodied and naturally balanced, brings out the sweetness of the strings, even in the gentlest pianissimos. This is most enjoyable but even at mid-price (with a playing-time of only 44 minutes) remains uncompetitive without a coupling.

Bernstein's *New World* begins well with a fresh, brilliant account of the first movement (exposition repeat included) and a beautifully played *Largo*. The third movement, however, is very fast and does not relax enough or beguile as it should. The finale is done not very imaginatively: it is just played through, with no magic when the earlier themes are recalled. The recording, made in New York's Manhattan Center in 1962, is good; Bernstein is back on form in the two *Slavonic dances*, while the *Carnival overture* is brilliant enough. *Vltava* makes a colourful encore, but here the recording of the violins in their famous lyrical melody is not very flattering.

CHAMBER AND INSTRUMENTAL MUSIC

Flute sonatina in G min. (trans. Galway).
*** RCA Dig. 07863 57802-2 [7802-2-RC]. James Galway, Phillip Moll – FELD; MARTINU: *Sonatas*. ***

What the flute version of Dvořák's *Sonatina* underlines more than the violin original is how close this tuneful, unpretentious piece is to the *New World Symphony* of the same year, 1893. Well recorded, with characterful performances and an unusual and attractive coupling of two modern Czech flute works, it makes an excellent recommendation for anyone wanting a Galway record out of the ordinary.

Piano quartets Nos. 1 in D, Op. 23; 2 in E flat, Op. 87.
⊛ *** Hyperion Dig. CDA 66287 [id.]. Domus.

The Dvořák *Piano quartets* are glorious pieces, and the playing of Domus is little short of inspired. This is real chamber-music-playing: intimate, unforced and distinguished by both vitality and sensitivity. Domus are recorded in an ideal acoustic and in perfect perspective; they sound wonderfully alive and warm.

Piano quintet in A, Op. 81.
*** ASV Dig. CDDCA 889 [id.]. Peter Frankl, Lindsay Qt – MARTINU: *Piano quintet No. 2.* ***
(M) *** Decca 421 153-2 [id.]. Clifford Curzon, VPO Qt – FRANCK: *Quintet.* ***
(M) *** Decca 448 602-2 [id.]. Clifford Curzon, VPO Qt – SCHUBERT: *Trout quintet.* ***

This ASV account of Dvořák's glorious *Piano quintet* by the Lindsays with Peter Frankl is the finest of modern versions and can readily stand comparison with the famous early Decca account with Clifford Curzon. Apart from Peter Frankl's fine contribution, one especially responds to Bernard Gregor-Smith's rich cello-line. Because of the resonance, the recording is full and warm and, if there is just a hint of thinness on the violin timbre, the balance with the piano is particularly well managed.

This wonderfully warm and lyrical (1962) performance of Dvořák's *Piano quintet* by Clifford Curzon is a classic record, one by which all later versions have come to be judged, and the CD transfer retains the richness and ambient glow of the original analogue master, yet has improved definition and presence. The piano timbre remains full and real. This performance is available coupled either with the César Franck *Quartet* or, even more attractively, with Schubert's *Trout quintet* in Decca's Classic Sound series.

Piano quintet in A, Op. 81; Piano quartet No. 2 in E flat, Op 87.
**(*) DG Dig. 439 868-2 [id.]. Menahem Pressler, Emerson Quartet (augmented).

Menahem Pressler joins the Emerson Quartet in powerful, intense accounts of these two magnificent works, and they demonstrate how the *Second Piano quartet*, sketched immediately after the other work and completed two years later in 1889, is just as rich in invention, in some ways even more distinctive in its thematic material. If there is one movement that above all proves a revelation, it is the *Lento* of the *Quartet*, given with a rapt, hushed concentration to put it among the very finest of Dvořák inspirations. The performance of the *Quintet* is comparably positive in its characterization, even if many will prefer easier, even warmer readings such as that from Domus on Hyperion in the *Piano quartet*. The DG New York recording gives an unpleasant edge to high violins, making the full ensemble abrasive.

(i) *Piano quintet in A, Op. 81; String quartet No. 12 in F (American), Op. 96.*
(N) *** Testament SBT 1074 [id.]. (i) Pavel Stepán; Smetana Qt – JANACEK: *String quartet No. 1.* ***
*** RCA RD 86263 [6263-2-RC]. (i) Rubinstein; Guarneri Qt.

What a magnificent quartet the Smetanas were when they made these records in the mid-1960s! In terms of tonal finesse and bloom they had few peers, and their ensemble is perfect. Nor do any apologies need to be made for the quality of the recorded sound, which is as good as many being produced today. The *Piano quintet*, in which they are joined by Pavel Stepán, is glorious and can well withstand comparison with the celebrated version by Clifford Curzon and the Vienna Philharmonic Quartet (Decca) which appeared a few years earlier; the acoustic is perhaps slightly drier than the Decca. No quarrels with the *F major Quartet* either. The sound is analogue and has great warmth. Moreover this CD is generously full, and the Janáček coupling is very special.

Both the RCA performances are memorably warm and spontaneous; tempi tend to be brisk, but the lyrical element always underlies the music and the playing has both great vitality and warmth. Needless to say, Rubinstein's contribution to the *Quintet* is highly distinguished. The recordings, made in April 1971 and 1972 respectively, are well balanced, detailed and fairly full, helped by the attractive studio ambience.

(i) *Piano quintet in A, Op. 81. String quintet in G, Op. 77.*
(N) *** Hyperion Dig. CDA 66796 [id.]. Gaudier Ensemble, (i) with Susan Tomes.

With Susan Tomes (also of Domus) the inspired pianist, the Gaudier Ensemble gives a sparkling performance of the *Piano quintet*, full of mercurial contrasts that seem entirely apt and with rhythms superbly sprung. The *G major String quintet*, the earlier of the two which Dvořák wrote, the one with extra double-bass, is lighter than most rival versions, with speeds on the brisk side and with Marieke Blankestun's violin pure rather than rich in tone. Very well recorded, this makes an excellent recommendation if you fancy the coupling. In neither work are the exposition repeats observed, but Dvořák himself, as we know from the symphonies, was very doubtful about the need for them.

Piano trios Nos. 1 in B flat, Op. 21; 2 in G min., Op. 26; 3 in F min., Op. 65; 4 in E min. (Dumky), Op. 90.
(M) *** Teldec/Warner Dig. 9031 76458-2 (2) [id.]. Trio Fontenay.

First-class playing and expertly balanced modern recording combine to make this very attractive indeed. Wolf Harden, the pianist, dominates – but only marginally so: his colleagues match him in lyrical ardour, and they are as sympathetic to Dvořák's warm lyricism as to the Czech dance characteristics of the livelier allegros.

Piano trios Nos. 1 in B flat min., Op. 21; 2 in G min., Op. 26.
*** Chandos Dig. CHAN 9172 [id.]. Borodin Trio.

We liked the Borodins' earlier recording of the *F minor Piano trio* (see below) and find much to admire in the present disc: these are spontaneous yet finely shaped performances, very well recorded.

Piano trio No. 3 in F min., Op. 65.
**(*) Chandos Dig. CHAN 8320 [id.]. Borodin Trio.

Piano trios No. 3 in F min., Op. 65; 4 in E min. (Dumky), Op. 90.
*** Sony Dig. MK 44527 [id.]. Emanuel Ax, Young-Uck Kim, Yo-Yo Ma.
(M) **(*) Ph. 426 095-2. Beaux Arts Trio.

Piano trio No. 4 in E min. (Dumky), Op. 90.
*** Chandos Dig. CHAN 8445 [id.]. Borodin Trio – SMETANA: *Piano trio.* ***

The *F minor Trio* is given a powerful yet sensitive performance by the Ax/Kim/Ma trio and, like the *Dumky*, it has warmth and freshness. The recording is faithful and natural.

The Beaux Arts' 1969 performances of Op. 65 and the *Dumky* still sound fresh and sparkling, though the recording on CD is a little dry in violin timbre; the *F minor*, arguably the finer and certainly the more concentrated of the two, is played with great eloquence and vitality.

The playing of the Borodin Trio in the *F minor Trio* has great warmth and fire; such imperfections as there are arise from the natural spontaneity of a live performance; however, this now seems short measure. But in the *Dumky trio* it is the spontaneous flexibility of approach to the constant mood-changes that makes the splendid Borodin performance so involving, as well as the glorious playing from each of the three soloists. The recording here is naturally balanced and the illusion of a live occasion is striking.

String quartets Nos. 1–14; Cypresses, B.152; Fragment in F, B.120; 2 Waltzes, Op. 54, B.105.
(M) *** DG 429 193-2 (9). Prague Qt.

Dvořák's *Quartets* span the whole of his creative life. The glories of the mature *Quartets* are well known, though it is only the so-called *American* which has achieved real popularity. The beauty of the present set, made in 1973–7, is that it offers more *Quartets* (not otherwise available) plus two *Quartet movements*, in *A minor* (1873) and *F major* (1881), plus two *Waltzes* and *Cypresses* for good measure, all in eminently respectable performances and decent recordings.

String quartet No. 7 in A min., Op. 16; Cypresses.
**(*) Chandos Dig. CHAN 8826 [id.]. Chilingirian Qt.

String quartets Nos. 8 in E, Op. 80; 9 in D min., Op. 34.
**(*) Chandos Dig. CHAN 8755 [id.]. Chilingirian Qt.

String quartets Nos. 10 in E flat, Op. 51; 11 in C, Op. 61.
**(*) Chandos Dig. CHAN 8837 [id.]. Chilingirian Qt.

Chandos provide very fine recorded sound for the Chilingirians, who play with sensitivity in all five *Quartets*. These are straightforward, well-paced readings that are eminently serviceable. Some collectors may feel, perhaps, that they fall short of the very highest distinction, but they are unfailingly musicianly and vital.

String quartet No. 12 in F (American), Op. 96.
(N) (M) *** Carlton IMP Dig. 3036 70097-2 [id.]. Delmé Qt – BRAHMS: *Clarinet quintet.* ***
(N) (BB) *** CfP Silver Double CDCFPSD 4772 (2). Gabrieli String Qt – BORODIN: *String quartet No. 2* ***; BRAHMS: *Clarinet quintet* **(*); SCHUBERT: *String quartet No. 14.* ***
*** EMI Dig. CDC7 54215-2 [id.]. Alban Berg Qt – SMETANA: *Quartet.* ***
(N) (***) Testament mono SBT 1072 [id.]. Hollywood Qt – KODALY; SMETANA: *Quartets.* (***)

(M) **(*) DG 437 251-2 [id.]. Amadeus Qt. – SMETANA: *String quartet No. 1.* **(*)
**(*) Collins Dig. 1386-2 [id.]. Duke Qt – BARBER: *Quartet;* GLASS: *Quartet No. 1.* **

String quartet No. 12 (American); Cypresses.
*** DG Dig. 419 601-2 [id.]. Hagen Qt – KODALY: *Quartet No. 2.* ***

The Delmé Quartet on a superbly recorded Carlton IMP disc at bargain price give a winningly spontaneous-sounding performance, marked by unusually sweet matching of timbre between the players, which brings out the total joyfulness of Dvořák's American inspiration.

The Hagen Quartet make an uncommonly beautiful sound and their account of this masterly score is very persuasive indeed. Their playing is superbly polished, musical and satisfying, and they play the enchanting *Cypresses*, which Dvořák transcribed from the eponymous song-cycle, with great tenderness. The recording is altogether superb, very present and full-bodied.

A thoroughly satisfying account of the *American quartet* from the Gabrielis, notable for its warmth, vitality and polish, and a touching account of the slow movement. As part of a Classics for Pleasure Silver Double it makes an outstanding reissue, given first-class 1973 sound, smoothly yet vividly transferred to CD.

The Alban Berg also give a very fine account of the *F major*, Op. 96. They have their finger on the vital current that carries its musical argument forward. Phrasing is dextrously shaped and the polish and elegance of their playing are never in danger of diminishing the spontaneous-seeming character of this music. In this respect they are perhaps less successful in the Smetana coupling. Very good recording, and thoroughly recommendable to admirers of this ensemble.

The Hollywood Quartet is pretty well self-recommending, and their account of the *F major Quartet*, Op. 96, is everything one would expect: impeccable in terms of execution, ensemble and taste. This was a quartet which brought real artistry to everything they played.

Although we have some reservations about Norbert Brainin's vibrato, which at times sounds self-conscious (especially in the slow movement), admirers of the Amadeus will certainly want their 1977 coupling of Dvořák and Smetana, recorded in Finland. This is a strongly conceived performance, full of ardour. The Scherzo and exhilarating finale show their brilliance of ensemble at its most appealing and infectious. The sound is vivid, full and immediate.

The Duke Quartet is handicapped by a curiously hybrid coupling: two American works, though it would have been better to have had a Schuman or Piston quartet along with Barber's celebrated piece rather than the empty Glass. They play the *F major Quartet* well, but not better than many rivals in the catalogue: they are very well recorded, though the balance is a bit forward.

String quartet No. 12 in F (American), Op. 96; (i) String quintet in E flat, Op. 97.
(N) *** Erato/Warner Dig. 4509 96968-2 [id.]. Keller Qt; (i) with Anna Deeva.
(N) ** HM Dig. HMC 901509 [id.]. Melos Quartet; (i) with Gérard Causse.

Dvořák wrote the second of his string quintets, the one with extra viola, at the same period as the popular Opus 96 *Quartet*, similarly using thematic material with American inflexions, so that the two works make an apt and attractive coupling. The Keller Quartet give outstanding readings of both works, crisp and fanciful, with light, clear textures and with speeds generally on the fast side. The tenderness of the lyricism is beautifully caught in consistently imaginative phrasing, and the Erato recording is beautifully balanced.

After a withdrawn, reticent start, the Melos Quartet with Gérard Causse give a refined, finely tuned performance of the *Quintet* that lacks a little in colour, plain in approach rather than well characterized. In the *Quartet* they are more convincing but relatively heavy-handed. In this coupling, the Keller version is clearly preferable.

String quartets Nos. 12 in F (American), Op. 96; 13 in G, Op. 106.
*** ASV Dig. CDDCA 797. Lindsay Qt.

In the *F major Quartet* (*American*) the Lindsays' account is certainly among the very best in terms of both performance and recording. The *G major*, Op. 106, is also very well played, with much the same dedication and sensitivity. An outstanding coupling.

String quartets Nos. 12 in F (American), Op. 96; 14 in A flat, Op. 105.
**(*) Chandos Dig. CHAN 8919 [id.]. Chilingirian Qt.

These Chilingirian performances are well up the standard of their fine series, even if their version of the *American Quartet* would not be a first choice. The recording is first class and those needing this coupling will not be disappointed.

String quartet No. 13 in G, Op. 106; Quartet movement in F, B.120; 2 Waltzes, Op. 54.
**(*) Chandos Dig. CHAN 8874 [id.]. Chilingirian Qt.

In the last and perhaps most remarkable of Dvořák's string quartets the Chilingirians maintain the generally high quality of their cycle for Chandos. The playing has momentum and vitality and, though there are moments when they could make more of dynamic nuance, these are sympathetic and well-recorded performances. They include the *Quartet movement in F major* that Dvořák had originally intended for the piece, as well as two of the *Waltzes* he arranged from the Op. 54 piano pieces.

String quartet No. 14 in A flat, Op. 105.
*** Sony Dig. SK 53282 [id.]. Artis Qt – SMETANA: *String quartet.* ***

The Artis Quartet give one of the best accounts of the *A flat Quartet*, Op. 105, to have reached the catalogue since the Smetana Quartet recorded it in the early 1970s. It is ardent and expressive without being in the least overstated, and is compelling throughout. The Sony recording is in every way first class.

String quartet No. 14 in A flat, Op. 105; Terzetto in C, Op. 74.
(N) *** Testament SBT 1075 [id.]. Smetana Qt – JANACEK: *String quartet No. 2.* ***

The *Terzetto in C* for two violins and viola is a rarity in the concert hall and, although there are good recent alternatives, none of them surpasses this fresh yet elegant playing. Despite its earlier opus number, the *A flat Quartet*, Op. 105, is later than the Op. 106; in it the Smetanas observe the traditional cut in the finale, from 11 bars before fig. 11 until 4 bars after fig. 12. (Even Alec Robertson in his *Master Musician* volume complained that this movement was too long.) When this first appeared we thought this was a wonderful performance – and it still is! Moreover it comes with their outstanding account of Janáček's *Intimate letters* which is new to the British catalogues.

String quintets: (i) in G, Op. 77; (ii) in E flat, Op. 97.
*** Bayer Dig. BR 100 184CD [id.]. Stamitz Qt, with (i) Jiří Hudec; (ii) Jan Talich.

String quintets in G, Op. 77; in E flat, Op. 97; Intermezzo in B, Op. 40.
*** Chandos Dig. CHAN 9046 [id.]. Chilingirian Qt with D. McTier.

Artistically, honours are pretty evenly divided between the Stamitz Quartet and the Chilingirians in the quintets. The *E flat String quintet*, Op. 97, which dates from his American years, is one of Dvořák's very greatest works! The Stamitz Quartet is perhaps balanced more forwardly but is pleasantly recorded, and the Chilingirian set on Chandos has more air round the sound but without any loss of focus. Both performances have the warmth and humanity that Dvořák exudes, but the Chilingirians undoubtedly score in including the beautiful *B major Intermezzo* that the composer had originally intended for the *G major Quintet* and which he subsequently expanded into an independent work for full strings, the *Nocturne*, Op. 40. This tips the balance in its favour.

String quintet in E flat, Op. 97; String sextet in A, Op. 48.
*** Hyperion Dig. CDA 66308 [id.]. Raphael Ens.

The *E flat major Quintet*, Op. 97, is one of the masterpieces of Dvořák's American years, and it is most persuasively given by the Raphael Ensemble. It is also very well recorded, though we are placed fairly forward in the aural picture.

Slavonic dances Nos. 1–16, Op. 46/1–8; Op. 71/1–8.
**(*) Ph. Dig. 426 264-2 [id.]. Katia & Marielle Labèque.
**(*) Ara. Dig. Z 6559 [id.]. Artur Balsam, Gena Raps (piano, four hands).

The Labèque sisters obviously revel in their own cultured virtuosity and they know what they are about, so their brilliance is balanced with lyrical sensibility and a feeling for colour. However, the recording venue, an abbey, was a less than ideal choice. The engineers have put their microphones up close and, while the sound is basically natural, the resonance brings a slight preponderance of middle and bass.

Generally fine performances from Artur Balsam and Gena Raps, who respond to the music in a spirit of relaxed enjoyment, yet do not miss its brio. The recording too is well balanced in a pleasing acoustic.

VOCAL AND CHORAL MUSIC

(i) *Requiem, Op. 89;* (ii) *6 Biblical songs from Op. 99.*
(Y/B) ✪ (B) *** DG Double 437 377-2 (2) [id.]. (i) Maria Stader, Sieglinde Wagner, Ernst Haefliger, Kim Borg, Czech PO & Ch., Karel Ančerl; (ii) Dietrich Fischer-Dieskau, Joerg Demus.

This superb DG set from 1959 brings an inspired performance of a work that can sound relatively conventional but which here emerges with fiery intensity, helped by a recording made in an appropriately spacious acoustic that gives an illusion of an electrifying live performance, without flaw. The passionate singing of the chorus (in the *Hostias* and *Sanctus*, for instance) is unforgettable, and the soloists not only make fine individual contributions but blend together superbly in ensembles. Ančerl controls his forces with expert precision and the Czech chorus responds to the manner born. It was a good idea to choose good German soloists rather than Czech ones, who might have sounded unrefined in comparison with chorus and orchestra. Haefliger and Borg are particularly fine. The first entry of the chorus moaning away to a gentle '*Requiem aeternam*' suggests that the balance is going to favour the orchestra, but this is all part of the deliberate control of acoustic in which the balance between soloists, chorus and orchestra is particularly well handled in DG's best analogue manner. As if that were not enough, DG have added Fischer-Dieskau's 1960 recordings of six excerpts from Op. 99. He is at his superb best in these lovely songs. Brimming over with melody and never in the least sanctimonious, they deserve to be more generally known. (The numbers included are: *Rings an den Herrn*; *Gott, erhöre meine inniges Flahen*; *Gott ist mein Hirte*; *An den Wassern zu Babylon*; *Wende dich zu mir*; and *Singet ein neues Lied*.) Joerg Demus accompanies sensitively, and the recording balance is most convincing.

(i) *Requiem, Op. 89;* (ii) *Mass in D, Op. 86.*

(N) (B) *** Decca Double 448 089-2 (2) [id.]. (i) Lorengar, Komlóssy, Isofalvy, Krause, Amb. S., LSO, Kertész; (ii) Ritchie, Giles, Byers, Morton, Christ Church Cathedral Ch., Oxford, Cleobury (organ), Preston.

Kertész's fine (1968) account of Dvořák's *Requiem* acted as a distinguished pendant to his pioneering set of the symphonies, and it has comparable freshness. Kertész conducts with a total commitment to the score and secures from singers and orchestra an alert and sensitive response. The recording, which has the advantage of the Kingsway Hall ambience, has a lifelike balance and the CD remastering has been entirely beneficial. For this Double Decca reissue the work has been sensibly recoupled with Simon Preston's beautifully shaped Christ Church account of the *Mass in D*, recorded six years later. Again the CD remastering shows how good was the original (Argo) recording, and it is also impeccably balanced.

(i) *Stabat Mater, Op. 58;* (ii) *Legends Nos. 1–10, Op. 59.*

(M) *** DG 423 919-2 [id.]. (i) Mathis, Reynolds, Ochman, Shirley-Quirk, Bav. R. Ch. & O; (ii) ECO; Kubelik.

Dvořák's devout Catholicism led him to treat this tragic religious theme with an open innocence that avoids sentimentality. Kubelik is consistently responsive and this is a work which benefits from his imaginative approach. The recording, made in the Munich Herkules-Saal, is of very good quality. This set is well worth considering at this reasonable price, especially as the ten *Legends* are played so beautifully by the ECO. This music ought to be better known, with its colourful scoring and folksy inspiration of a high order. One is often reminded of the *Slavonic dances*; although the prevailing mood is more amiable, there is no lack of sparkle. Again very good recording.

OPERA

Dimitrij (complete).

(Y/B) **(*) Sup. Dig. 11 1259-2 (3) [id.]. Vodička, Drobková, Hajossyová, Aghová, Mikulas, Prague R. Ch., Czech PO Ch. and O, Albrecht.

Dimitrij, Dvořák's attempt to write a really grand opera, might be regarded as a sequel to *Boris Godunov*, following the career of the character who in Mussorgsky's opera is the Pretender who usurps Boris's throne. As in Mussorgsky but in a less rugged way, Dvořák contrasts large-scale ensemble scenes with intimate ones full of lyrical ideas as ripely inspired as he ever conceived for an opera. The title-role is taken by the tenor, Leon Marian Vodička, whose Slavonic timbre is very apt for the music, even if he is strained at times. Drahomira Drobková as Marfa and Magdalena Hajossyová as Marina sing strongly, but it is Livia Aghová as Xenia who with sweet, pure tone brings out the beauty of Dvořák's melodies more than anyone. Gerd Albrecht draws brilliant playing from the Czech Philharmonic, though the choral singing is less well disciplined. With the four Acts contained on three CDs, this recording follows a reconstruction of Dvořák's original score of 1882. So it is that this set contains sections of the score never previously heard this century.

The Jacobin.

(Y/B) *** Sup. 11 2190-2 (2) [id.]. Zítek, Sounová, Přibyl, Machotková, Blachut, Prusa, Tuček, Berman, Katilena Children's Ch., Kuhn Ch., Brno State PO, Pinkas.

The Jacobin dates from the most contented period of Dvořák's life and, though the background to the piece is one of revolt and political turmoil, he was more interested in individuals, so this is more a village comedy than a tract for the times. Though the drama is minimal, the sequence of exuberant, tuneful numbers, dances and choruses as well as arias, is more than enough to make the piece a delight on disc. Jiři Pinkas draws lively and idiomatic performances from a first-rate cast, including such stalwarts as Vilem Přibyl as the hero (a little old-sounding but stylish) and the veteran tenor Beno Blachut giving a charming portrait of the heroine's father. Václav Zítek sings the heroic part of the Jacobin himself with incisive strength and Daniela Sounová is bright and clear as the heroine. The analogue sound is clear and firmly focused. On CD, the three Acts are squeezed on to two extremely well-filled discs and a full libretto/translation is included.

The Jacobin: highlights.
(Y/B) (M) **(*) Sup. 11 2250-2 [id.] (from above complete recording, cond. Pinkas).

The highlights disc is at medium price and, with 62 minutes' playing time, makes a good sampler. However, there is no libretto included, not even a synopsis, which is unhelpful in an unfamiliar work of this kind.

Kate and the Devil (complete).
(Y/B) **(*) Sup. 11 1800-2 (2) [id.]. Barová, Ježil, Novák, Sulcová, Suryová, Horáček, Brno Janáček Op. Ch. & O, Pinkas.

Attracted by the combination of folk element and fairy-tale, Dvořák began composing this opera in 1898, a charming comic fantasy about the girl who literally makes life hell for the devil who abducts her. It inspired a score that might almost be counted an operatic equivalent of his *Slavonic dances*, full of sharply rhythmic ideas, colourfully orchestrated.

Kate, finding herself consigned to be a wallflower in her village, declares she would dance with the devil himself. A minor devil, Marbuel, appears and, spinning fantastic tales, persuades her to come away with him. She is whisked off to Hell, with the shepherd Jirka gallantly going off to save her. Not that she needs much help, for she defies Marbuel so successfully that he, Lucifer and the other devils are only too glad to be rid of her. The role of Kate is very well taken by Anna Barová, firm and full-toned, with Jirka sung attractively by Miloš Ježil, though his Slavonic tones are strained on top. The snag is the ill-focused singing of Richard Novák as the Devil, characterful enough but wobbly. Jiři Pinkas persuasively brings out the fun and colour of the score, drawing excellent singing from the chorus; and the 1979 recording has plenty of space, agreeably warm and atmospheric. The libretto is well produced and clear, but assumes that the set is on three CDs instead of two with Acts II and III together on the second.

Rusalka (complete).
*** Sup. Dig. 10 3641-2 (3) [id.]. Beňačková-Cápová, Novák, Soukupová, Ochman, Drobková, Prague Ch. & Czech PO, Neumann.

Dvořák's fairy-tale opera is given a magical performance by Neumann and his Czech forces, helped by full, brilliant and atmospheric recording which, while giving prominence to the voices, brings out the beauty and refinement of Dvořák's orchestration. The title-role is superbly taken by Gabriela Beňačková-Cápová, and the famous *Invocation to the Moon* is enchanting. Vera Soukupová as the Witch is just as characterfully Slavonic in a lower register, though not so even; while Wieslaw Ochman sings with fine, clean, heroic tone as the Prince, with timbre made distinctive by tight vibrato. Richard Novák brings out some of the Alberich-like overtones as the Watersprite, though the voice is not always steady. The banding could be more generous, but a full translation is included.

Rusalka: highlights.
(Y/B) (M) **(*) Sup. Dig. 11 2252-2 [id.] (from above complete recording; cond. Neumann).

This is a first-class selection, including, of course, the famous *Invocation to the moon* and offering an hour of music. But the current mid-priced reissue has neither libretto nor synopsis, merely a list of the excerpts.

Dyson, George (1883–1964)

(i)*Violin concerto. Children's suite* (after Walter De La Mare).
(Y/B) ✵ *** Chandos Dig. CHAN 9369 [id.]. (i) Mordkovitch; City of L. Sinfonia, Hickox.

Completed in 1941, Dyson's *Violin concerto* is a richly inspired, warmly lyrical work that readily sustains its 43-minute span. Not that the extended first movement, *Molto moderato*, lacks dark undercurrents. The idiom in all four movements is warm and distinctive, with the second-movement Scherzo and the finale both exhilarating, regularly veering towards waltz-rhythms. The third-movement *Andante* for violin and muted strings, divided into variations, brings a rare hushed beauty, superbly achieved in this dedicated performance. Lydia Mordkovitch makes light of the formidable technical difficulties to give a reading both passionate and deeply expressive. The *Children's suite* of 1924 has four sharply character-ized movements, inspired by De La Mare poems. In its lighter way it reflects similar qualities to those in the concerto, not least a tendency to switch into waltz-time and a masterly ability to create rich and transparent orchestral textures, beautifully caught in the opulent Chandos recording. Two rarities to treasure.

(i) *Concierto leggiero* (for piano & strings); *Concerto da camera; Concerto da chiesa* (both for string orchestra).
⊛ *** Chandos Dig. CHAN 9076 [id.]. (i) Eric Parkin; City of L. Sinfonia, Hickox.

Until now we have been inclined to think of Dyson as essentially a composer of vocal music, but this splendid Chandos CD rights the balance and brings not only an engagingly light-textured concertante item for piano but also two powerful and eloquent works in the great tradition of English string music. All these pieces belong to the composer's last composing years and date from 1949/51. The writing shows both a strongly burning creative flame as well as new influences from outside. The performances here are wonderfully fresh and committed and the string recording has plenty of bite and full sonority, while the balance with the piano is quite admirable. Highly recommended.

Symphony in D.
*** Chandos Dig. CHAN 9200 [id.]. City of L. Sinfonia, Richard Hickox.

Dyson's *Symphony*, composed in 1937, was played in the 1940s (Felix Aprahamian took Ansermet to hear it at a performance in Southwark Cathedral) and then forgotten. Its best movement by far is the third, an attractive and diverse theme and variations (in which Ansermet justly found an affinity with ballet music). The finale is confident in its use of ideas from *The Canterbury Pilgrims* with majestic scoring for the brass, but the charming second-movement *Andante* is rather slight and the first move-ment, marked *Energico*, flags and fails to sustain its initial Richard Straussian momentum. An enjoyable piece, very well played and resonantly and realistically recorded, in the way of Chandos, but not an essential acquisition, except for those especially attracted to this composer.

(Organ) *Fantasia and Ground bass. 3 Choral hymns; Hierusalem; Psalm 150; 3 Songs of praise.*
*** Hyperion CDA 66150 [id.]. Valery Hill, St Michael's Singers, Thomas Trotter, RPO, Jonathan Rennert.

Where the organ piece unashamedly builds on an academic model, *Hierusalem* reveals the inner man more surprisingly, a richly sensuous setting of a medieval poem inspired by the thought of the Holy City, building to a jubilant climax. It is a splendid work, and is backed here by the six hymns and the Psalm setting, all of them heartwarming products of the Anglican tradition. Performances are out-standing, with Rennert drawing radiant singing and playing from his team, richly and atmospherically recorded.

Egk, Werner (1901–83)

The Temptation of St Anthony (cantata).
(N) (M) *** DG 449 097-2 [id.]. Dame Janet Baker, Koeckert Qt, Bav. RSO (strings), composer – ORFF: *Catulli Carmina.* ***

Egk has never made much headway in this country. His music is not unattractive, in the sense that it falls easily on the ear, though its thematic substance is often unmemorable and the composer does not have a great deal of personality. His *Temptation of St Anthony*, however, shows him at his best: it is in effect a song-cycle and Dame Janet Baker was in particularly good voice at this period of her career (the mid-1960s) and sings with great beauty. The recording, too, is good, and this can be recommended as a good sampler for those who want to investigate Egk's music for themselves.

Elgar, Edward (1857–1934)

(i) *Adieu; Beau Brummel: Minuet;* (ii) *3 Bavarian dances, Op. 27; Caractacus, Op. 35: Woodland interlude. Chanson de matin; Chanson de nuit, Op. 15/1–2; Contrasts, Op. 10/3; Dream children, Op. 43; Falstaff, Op. 68: 2 Interludes. Salut d'amour; Sérénade lyrique;* (ii; iii) *Soliloquy for oboe* (orch. Gordon Jacob); (i) *Sospiri, Op. 70; The Spanish Lady: Burlesco. The Starlight Express: Waltz. Sursum corda, Op. 11.*
(M) *** Chandos CHAN 6544 [id.]. Bournemouth Sinf., (i) George Hurst; (ii) Norman Del Mar; (iii) with Goossens.

The real treasure in this splendid collection of Elgar miniatures is the *Soliloquy* which Elgar wrote right at the end of his life for Leon Goossens. Here the dedicatee plays it with his long-recognizable tone-colour and feeling for phrase in an orchestration by Gordon Jacob. Most of the other pieces in Norman Del Mar's programme are well known but they come up with new warmth and commitment here, and the 1976 recording, made in the Guildhall, Southampton, has an appealing ambient warmth and naturalness. For the CD reissue Chandos have generously added some delightful Elgar rarities recorded by George Hurst a year earlier in Christchurch Priory. Again the recording has plenty of fullness, but the CD transfer brings more thinness to the violins than in the Del Mar recording. The disc has an overall playing time of nearly 76 minutes.

Acoustic recordings (1914–25): Abridged or excerpts: *Bavarian dances; Carillon; Carissima; Chanson de nuit; Cockaigne overture;* (i) *Cello concerto;* (ii) *Violin concerto. Enigma variations; In the South; King Olaf; Light of life; Polonia; Pomp and circumstance marches Nos. 1 & 4; Salut d'amour; The Sanguine fan; Symphony No. 2* (complete). (iii) *Fringes of the fleet;* (iv) *Sea pictures;* (iii; v) *Starlight express; Fantasia and Fugue* (Bach, arr. Elgar); *Overture* (Handel, arr. Elgar).
(M) (**(*)) Pearl GEMM mono CDS 9951/5 (5). (i) Beatrice Harrison; (ii) Marie Hall; (iii) Charles
    Mott; (iv) Leila Megane; (v) Agnes Nicholls; O or Royal Albert Hall O, cond. composer.

This box of five Pearl CDs gathers together all of Elgar's recordings made in the days of the acoustic gramophone. With players in limited numbers gathered round an acoustic horn, the sounds are limited but have been transferred here with astonishing fidelity. Orchestrations had to be modified to bring out the bass line, and all but the *Symphony No. 2*, among the major works, had to be cut for the medium, often drastically, as when the *Violin concerto* is reduced from 50 to 15 minutes. Speeds here are generally brisker than in his later, electrical recordings, and performances are often flawed. Marie Hall adopts an exaggeratedly portamento style in the *Violin concerto*, and Beatrice Harrison is less assured here than in her electrical recording of the full *Cello concerto*, but Leila Megane proves a formidable contralto soloist in *Sea pictures*. The sense of witnessing historic events is irresistible, with Elgar consistently hypnotic as a conductor.

3 Bavarian dances, Op. 27; 3 Characteristic pieces, Op. 10; Chanson de nuit; Chanson de matin, Op. 15/1–2; (i) *Violin concerto in B min., Op. 61. Crown of India (suite), Op. 66; Enigma variations, Op. 36; Nursery suite; Severn suite; Wand of youth suites 1–2, Op. 1a/b; The Light of Life: Meditation.* arr. of Bach: *Fantasia & fugue in C min., Op. 86;* (ii) (Choral) *The Banner of St George: It comes from the misty ages. Land of hope and glory.* Arrangements of Croft: *O God, our help in ages past. National anthem.*
(***) EMI mono CDS7 54564-2 (3) [id.]. LSO, Royal Albert Hall O, New SO or LPO, composer, with
    (i) Y. Menuhin; (ii) Philharmonic Ch.

Volume 2 of the Elgar Edition centres on the two masterpieces which make up the first of the three discs: the *Enigma variations* in the 1926 recording with the Royal Albert Hall Orchestra, volatile and passionate, and the sixteen-year-old Menuhin's classic reading of the *Violin concerto*, as fresh and intense as ever. The *Wand of Youth, Nursery* and *Severn suites* make up the second disc, with Elgar sparkling as a conductor. The third disc of shorter works includes a number of rarities, all of them revealing. Excellent transfers and background notes.

Beau Brummel: minuet (2 versions); (i) *Caractacus: Woodland interlude and Triumphal march, Op. 35; Carissima;* (ii) *Cello concerto in E min, Op. 85; Cockaigne: concert overture, Op. 40* (2 versions); (iii) *Coronation march, Op. 65; Elegy, Op. 58; Falstaff: interludes, Op. 68; Froissart: concert overture, Op. 19; In the South: concert overture, Op. 50; Land of hope and glory; The Kingdom: prelude, Op. 51; May song;* (iv) *Mina* (2 versions); *Minuet, Op. 21; Pomp and circumstance marches Nos. 1–5, Op. 39* (2 versions); *Rosemary; Salut d'amour, Op. 12; Sérénade in E min., Op. 20; Sérénade lyrique;* (v) *5 Piano Improvisations.*
(***) EMI mono CDS7 54568-2 (3) [id.]. LPO, Royal Albert Hall O, LSO or New SO, composer, with
    (i) Collingwood; (ii) Beatrice Harrison; (iii) Ronald; (iv) Murray, Wood; (v) composer (piano).

This third and last issue of EMI's Elgar Edition centres on the *Cello concerto* (with Beatrice Harrison as soloist in another urgent performance) and the overtures, *Froissart* and *In the South* as well as *Cockaigne*, and, like the previous volumes, demonstrates from first to last how as a conductor Elgar could electrify players, drawing from them bitingly dramatic performances that have a natural flexibility and flow unsurpassed by anyone since. The most fascinating contrast is between the two versions of the overture, *Cockaigne*, both contained in this third volume. His remake in 1933 with the recently founded BBC Symphony Orchestra is far more polished, with portamento far less marked in the string-playing; but the earlier performance, recorded with the Royal Albert Hall Orchestra in 1926, marginally faster and at times ragged in ensemble, yet has a more intense emotional thrust. The incidental items are fascinating too, including multiple versions of the *Pomp and circumstance marches* and two *Caractacus* excerpts conducted by Lawrance Collingwood, which Elgar supervised by telephone from his sick-bed only a month before he died. Yet the items which give the most intimate portrait of Elgar are the five improvisations that he recorded at the piano in 1929. It is also good to have the soundtrack recording from the Pathé newsreel covering the opening of the Abbey Road studio. Preparing to conduct *Land of hope and glory*, Elgar asks the LSO to 'play this tune as though you've never heard it before'. Transfers are astonishingly clear and full, though at times the background hiss is higher than in previous volumes.

Caractacus: Triumphal march; Cockaigne overture, Op. 40; Coronation march (1911); *Empire march* (1924); *Imperial march, Op. 32; Pomp and circumstance marches Nos. 1–5.*
(Y/B) (M) **(*) Virgin/EMI Dig. CUV5 61199-2 [id.]. RPO, Sir Yehudi Menuhin.

Menuhin brings out the *nobilmente* in this patriotic programme, but there is certainly no lack of spirit. Tempi are at times extreme; thus the *First* and *Second Pomp and circumstance marches* are pressed on with such gusto that the orchestral ensemble is less crisp than it might be, while the *Coronation march* is very slow and grandiloquent, sustained by its rich sonority and expansive organ pedals. *Cockaigne* (which comes last in a generous programme) has plenty of life and colour, but Menuhin's lyrical broadening at the end may strike some ears as being not wholly spontaneous. The recording, made at EMI's Abbey Road Studio, has a convincing concert-hall effect without too much resonance, and the brass are resplendent, especially in the *Triumphal march* from *Caractacus*.

Carissima; Chanson de matin; Chanson de nuit, Op. 15/1–2; Contrasts (Gavotte), Op. 10/3; Dream children, Op. 43; May song; Mazurka, Op. 10/1; Nursery suite; Rosemary (That's for remembrance); Salut d'amour, Op. 12; Sérénade lyrique.
(N) (M) *** Nimbus Dig. NI 7029 [id.]. ESO, William Boughton.

The *Nursery suite* usually comes with the *Wand of Youth suites* (see below), but those favouring the delicate *Dream children* plus a group of Elgar's orchestral miniatures will find that William Boughton's performances are graceful and sympathetic and have plenty of character. The recording too (made in Birmingham's Symphony Hall) is pleasingly full and spacious without being over-resonant, as are some offerings from this label.

Cockaigne overture, Op.40.
(N) (BB) ** ASV Dig. CDQS 6162 [id.]. Philh. O, Arwel Hughes – VAUGHAN WILLIAMS: *London Symphony.* **

The playing in Arwel Hughes's version of *Cockaigne* is crisper and more alert than in the coupled *London Symphony* of Vaughan Williams; but here, too, speeds are very broad indeed, at times impairing the flow, though building to a fine, ripe climax. The recording is warm and atmospheric, but the timpani is imprecisely focused.

Cockaigne overture, Op. 40; (i) *Cello concerto in E min., Op. 85. Wand of youth suites 1–2; Elegy.*
(N) (**) Beulah mono 2PD 15 [id.]. (i) Anthony Pini; LPO, Eduard van Beinum.

Anthony Pini gives a most beautiful and moving account of the *Cello concerto* in which the gentle, lyrical style of the soloist is matched by sensitive orchestral playing under a devoted Elgarian. Indeed the Dutch conductor was highly attuned to Elgar's music, as his sparkling account of *Cockaigne* readily demonstrates, while the charming *Wand of Youth suites* (alas, without cues for individual movements) have an affecting sense of innocence to show how well he understood this more delicate side of the composer's orchestral palette. The *Cello concerto* was an early (1950) LP original, but the rest of the music comes from 78s (recorded in the previous year). The orchestral colours are characteristically luminous in the *Wand of Youth* (the recording venue was the Kingsway Hall), but both this and the *Elegy* (a performance which is full of the right kind of tension) bring noticeable surface noise and, occasionally, swish which could have been much reduced by the CEDAR process. In louder movements and in the fortissimos of *Cockaigne* the upper range is tight and fierce. One wishes that Mike Dutton could have made these transfers which (as usual in the Beulah series) were made from the Decca masters by Tony Hawkins.

Cockaigne overture, Op. 40; Elegy for strings, Op. 58; Enigma variations, Op. 36; Introduction and allegro for strings, Op. 47; Pomp and circumstance march No. 1; Sospiri, Op. 70.
(M) **(*) Nimbus Dig. NI 7075 [id.]. ESO, William Boughton.

Warmly affectionate performances, beautifully played and given characteristically spacious Nimbus sound, recorded in the Great Hall of Birmingham University. The resonance prevents absolute sharpness of detail, but the effect is natural. The *Introduction and allegro* has a ripely overwhelming climax, yet the fugal argument is not lost. The *Enigma variations* have many pleasingly delicate touches of colour (*Dorabella* is delightfully fey) and *Nimrod* expands spaciously from its genuine pianissimo open-ing to achieve a climax of dignity rather than great ardour (surely an authentic portrayal of its dedi-catee, A. E. Jaeger). There are more strongly characterized versions of the work, but this performance has undoubted spontaneity and is easy to enjoy. The brass and organ make a fine effect in the finale, which brings a noble summing up. With 75 minutes of music, this is certainly excellent value.

(i) *Cockaigne overture, Op. 40;* (ii) *Elegy for strings, Op. 58;* (i) *Overture, In the South; Pomp and circumstance marches Nos. 1–5; National anthem* (arrangement).
(M) *** Decca 440 317-2 [id.]. (i) LPO, Solti; (ii) ASMF, Marriner.

Solti's *Cockaigne* is sharply dramatic and exciting; his view of the marches is both vigorous and refined, with sharp pointing in the outer sections, spaciousness in the great melodies. The result is both striking and satisfying. Marriner's *Elegy*, beautifully played, follows the marches as an agreeable interlude before the erupting energy of *In the South*, which is excitingly volatile rather than ripely expansive. The vivid Decca sound and bright, clean transfers match the Solti charisma.

Cockaigne overture, Op. 40; Enigma variations, Op. 36; Introduction and allegro for strings; Serenade for strings, Op. 20.
🏵 *** Teldec/Warner Dig. 9031 73279-2 [id.]. BBC SO, Andrew Davis.

Andrew Davis's collection of favourite Elgar works is electrifying. The very opening of *Cockaigne* has rarely been so light and sprightly, and it leads on to the most powerful characterization of each con-trasted section. The two string works are richly and sensitively done. Similarly the big tonal contrasts in *Enigma* are dramatically brought out, notably in Davis's rapt and spacious reading of *Nimrod*, helped by the spectacular Teldec recording. This is surely a worthy successor to Barbirolli in this repertoire and is an outstanding disc in every way.

Cockaigne overture, Op. 40; Falstaff (symphonic study), Op. 68; Introduction and allegro for strings, Op. 47.
(B) *** CfP CD-CFP 4617. LPO, Vernon Handley.

Vernon Handley directs a superb performance of *Falstaff*, and the achievement is all the more remark-able because his tempi are unusually spacious (generally following the composer's marking). The play-ing of the LPO is warmly expressive and strongly rhythmic. *Cockaigne* is also given a performance that is expansive yet never hangs fire. The *Introduction and allegro* is digital and dates from 1983. It was made in Watford Town Hall, but the balance is closer, its string outline more brightly lit. The performance is direct and passionate, yet with the lyrical contrasts tenderly made. This reissue is a real bargain.

(i) *Cockaigne overture, Op. 40;* (ii) *Froissart overture, Op. 19; Pomp and circumstance marches, Op. 39, Nos* (i) *1 in D;* (ii) *2 in A min.; 3 in C min.;* (i) *4 in G;* (ii) *5 in C.*
(M) *** EMI CDM7 69563-2. (i) Philh. O; (ii) New Philh. O; Barbirolli.

It is good to have Barbirolli's ripe yet wonderfully vital portrait of Edwardian London on CD where the recording retains its atmosphere as well as its vividness. *Froissart* is very compelling too, and Barbirolli makes a fine suite of the five *Pomp and circumstance marches*, with plenty of contrast in Nos. 2 and 3 to offset the Edwardian flag-waving of Nos. 1 and 4.

Cello concerto in E min., Op. 85.
🏵 *** EMI CDC7 47329-2 [id.]; *TC-ASD 655.* Du Pré, LSO, Barbirolli – *Sea Pictures.* *** 🏵
(N) *** EMI CDC5 55527-2 [id.]. Jacqueline du Pré, LSO, Barbirolli – DVORAK: *Cello concerto.* **(*)
(M) *** Sony Dig. SMK 53333 [id.]. Yo-Yo Ma, LSO, Previn – WALTON: *Cello concerto.* ***
(B) *** Carlton IMP Dig. PCD 930 [id.]. (i) Felix Schmidt; LSO, Frühbeck de Burgos – VAUGHAN
   WILLIAMS: *Tallis fantasia; Greensleeves.* **(*)
(N) (BB) *** CfP Silver Double CDCFPSD 4775 (2). Robert Cohen, LPO, Del Mar – BEETHOVEN:
   Triple concerto; DVORAK: *Cello concerto;* TCHAIKOVSKY: *Variations on a rococo theme.* ***
(Y/B) *** BIS Dig. CD 486 [id.]. Torleif Thedéen, Malmö SO, Markiz – SCHUMANN: *Concerto.* ***
(Y/B) *** Finlandia Dig. 4509 95768-2 [id.]. Arto Noras, Finnish RSO, Saraste – LALO: *Cello concerto.*
   ***
(Y/B) (M) **(*) Virgin Dig. CUV5 61125-2 [id.]. Steven Isserlis, LSO, Hickox – BLOCH: *Schelomo.* ***
(M) (**(*)) EMI mono CDH7 63498-2 [id.]. Casals, BBC SO, Boult – DVORAK: *Concerto* (***) (with
   BRUCH: *Kol Nidrei* (***)).

(i) *Cello concerto;* (ii) *Cockaigne overture, Op. 40; Enigma variations, Op. 36.*
*** Sony SK 76529. (i) Du Pré, Phd. O; (ii) LPO; Barenboim.

(i) *Cello concerto. Enigma variations, Op. 36.*
*** Ph. Dig. 416 354-2 [id.]. (i) Julian Lloyd Webber; RPO, Menuhin.

(i) *Cello concerto. Enigma variations; Froissart: concert overture, Op. 19.*
(N) **(*) Argo Dig. 436 545-2 [id.]. (i) Robert Cohen; RPO, Mackerras.

Jacqueline du Pré was essentially a spontaneous artist. Her style is freely rhapsodic, but the result produced a very special kind of meditative feeling; in the very beautiful slow movement, brief and concentrated, her inner intensity conveys a depth of espressivo rarely achieved by any cellist on record. Brilliant virtuoso playing too in the Scherzo and finale. CD brings a subtle extra definition to heighten the excellent qualities of the 1965 recording, with the solo instrument firmly placed.

Alongside the original pairing with Dame Janet Baker's *Sea pictures*, EMI have now given an alternative so-called 'dream coupling' with the Dvořák *Concerto*, and this much-loved recording is given extra warmth and clarity in the new transfer. However, we retain our allegiance to the original coupling, which was earlier revamped when it won a platinum disc award.

In its rapt concentration Yo-Yo Ma's recording with Previn is second to none. The first movement is lighter, a shade more urgent than the Du Pré/Barbirolli version, and in the Scherzo he finds more fun, just as he finds extra sparkle in the main theme of the finale. The key movement with Ma, as it is with du Pré, is the *Adagio*, echoed later in the raptness of the slow epilogue; there, his range of dynamic is just as daringly wide, with a thread of pianissimo at the innermost moment, poised in its intensity. Warm, fully detailed recording, finely balanced, with understanding conducting from Previn. At mid-price a splendid bargain.

The Philips coupling of the *Cello concerto* and the *Enigma variations*, the two most popular of Elgar's big orchestral works, featuring two artists inseparably associated with Elgar's music, made the disc an immediate bestseller, and rightly so. These are both warmly expressive and unusually faithful readings, the more satisfying for fidelity to the score, and Julian Lloyd Webber in his playing has never sounded warmer or more relaxed on record, well focused in the stereo spectrum.

Jacqueline du Pré's second recording of the Elgar *Cello concerto* was taken from live performances in Philadelphia in November 1970, and this is a superb picture of an artist in full flight, setting her sights on the moment in the Epilogue where the slow-movement theme returns, the work's innermost sanctuary of repose. Barenboim's most distinctive point in *Enigma* is in giving the delicate variations sparkle and emotional point, while the big variations have full weight, and the finale brings extra fierceness at a fast tempo. *Cockaigne* is comparably lively and colourful. The sound of the CBS transfer lacks something in body and amplitude.

Felix Schmidt, a young cellist with the widest expressive range, gives a bold, emotionally intense reading which finds a most satisfying middle ground between the romantic freedom typified by the unique Jacqueline du Pré and the steadier way of a Paul Tortelier. With his rich, full tone opulently recorded, his account can be recommended beside the very finest versions.

Robert Cohen's performance is strong and intense, with steady tempi, the colouring more positive and less autumnal than usual, relating the work to the *Second Symphony*. Yet there is no lack of inner feeling. The ethereal half-tones at the close of the first movement are matched by the gently elegiac poignancy of the *Adagio*. Del Mar's accompaniment is wholly sympathetic, underlining the soloist's approach and his songful line. The 1978 Walthamstow recording is wide-ranging and brilliant but shows Cohen's tone as bright and well focused rather than especially resonant in the bass. Those for whom the Silver Double couplings are attractive will find this both individual and satisfying.

Two Nordic views of the Elgar *Cello concerto* come from BIS and Finlandia. The former offer the young Swedish virtuoso, Torleif Thedéen, splendidly recorded with the Malmö orchestra, and the latter brings his Finnish colleague, Arto Noras, with Finnish Radio forces; both artists seem completely attuned to the Elgar sensibility. Thedéen has a nobility and reticence that are strongly appealing and Noras is hardly less impressive. Neither will disappoint; both enrich and do justice to the Elgar discography.

The most distinctive point about Steven Isserlis's version of Elgar's *Cello concerto* on Virgin is his treatment of the slow movement, not so much elegiac as songful. Using a mere thread of tone, with vibrato unstressed, the simplicity of line and the unforced beauty are brought out. The very placing of the solo instrument goes with that, rather more distant than is usual, with the refinement of Elgar's orchestration beautifully caught by both conductor and engineers.

Robert Cohen's earlier recording, made when he was in his teens, remains an outstanding bargain version on CfP, but in his later (1992) recording he plays with extra weight and gravity, masterfully sustaining slower speeds in the first and third movements, though the latter is marginally marred by some excessive coloration on the flat side. The finale, faster than before and more volatile, crowns the whole performance. The bright, up-front Decca recording brings out the brasher rather than the mellow qualities in the *Froissart overture*. *Enigma* is rather sluggish at the start and in *Nimrod*, but erupts in a superb, impulsive finale, bold and brassy.

Casals recorded the Elgar *Cello concerto* in London in 1946, and the fervour of his playing caused some raised eyebrows. A powerful account, not least for Sir Adrian's contribution, even though its eloquence would have been even more telling were the emotion recollected in greater tranquillity. A landmark of the gramophone all the same, and the strongly characterized Max Bruch *Kol Nidrei* makes a fine encore.

(i) *Cello concerto in E min., Op. 85;* (ii) *Violin concerto in B min., Op. 61.*

(M) *** Decca 440 319-2 [id.]. (i) Lynn Harrell, Cleveland O, Maazel; (ii) Kyung Wha Chung, LPO, Solti.

(Y/B) (**(*)) EMI mono CDC5 55221-2 [id.]. (i) Beatrice Harrison. New SO; (ii) Sir Yehudi Menuhin, LSO; composer.

This Decca reissue coupling Chung's heartfelt performance of the *Violin concerto* with Lynn Harrell's outstanding account of the *Cello concerto* on Decca offers a strong challenge. With eloquent support from Maazel and his fine orchestra (the woodwind play with appealing delicacy), this reading, deeply felt, balances a gentle nostalgia with extrovert brilliance. In the *Violin concerto* Chung's dreamily responsive playing in the central movement is ravishing in its beauty, not least in the ethereal writing above the stave, and so too are the lyrical pages of the outer movements. Solti responds with warmth to the expressive breadth of his soloist, and no other recording brings a wider range of dynamic or tone in the soloist's playing. Both recordings are from the late 1970s and are transferred to CD with impressive body and clarity.

The 1932 Menuhin/Elgar recording of the *Violin concerto* emerges on CD with a superb sense of atmosphere and presence. As for the performance, its classic status is amply confirmed: in many ways no one has ever matched – let alone surpassed – the sixteen-year-old Menuhin in this work, even if the first part of the finale lacks something in fire. The performance of the *Cello concerto* has nothing like the same inspiration when Beatrice Harrison's playing is at times fallible, and there are moments which seem almost perfunctory; but there is still much Elgarian feeling. Readers will note that this reissue in EMI's Composer in Person series puts this coupling into the premium-price range.

(i) *Cello concerto in E min., Op. 85. Elegy, Op. 58. Enigma variations, Op. 36; Introduction and allegro, Op. 47.*

🏵 (M) *** EMI stereo/mono CDM7 63955-2 [id.]. (i) Navarra, Hallé O, Barbirolli.

This Hallé version of the *Enigma variations* was recorded in the Manchester Free Trade Hall in 1956 by the Mercury team, Wilma Cozart and Harold Lawrence. In its new CD transfer the sound is extraordinarily good, and the performance is revealed as Barbirolli's finest account ever on record. Barbirolli generates powerful fervour and an irresistible momentum: at the very end, the organ entry brings an unforgettable, tummy-wobbling effect which engulfs the listener thrillingly. The *Introduction and allegro* is mono and, though not quite so impressively recorded, has comparable passion – the recapitulation of the big striding tune in the middle strings has superb thrust and warmth. The concert closes with a moving account of the *Elegy*, simple and affectionate. In between comes Navarra's strong and firm view of the *Cello concerto*. With his control of phrasing and wide range of tone-colour this 1957 performance culminates in a most moving account of the Epilogue.

(i) *Cello concerto in E min., Op. 85; Enigma variations, Op. 36; Serenade for strings, Op. 20.*

(Y/B) (M) *** DG Dig. 445 511-2 [id.]. (i) Mischa Maisky; Philh. O, Sinopoli.

Maisky is highly persuasive in the *Cello concerto* and, with Sinopoli a willing partner, gives a warmly nostalgic performance, essentially valedictory in feeling. The slow movement is deeply felt, but not in an extrovert way, and the soloist's dedication is mirrored in the finale. The mood of the *Concerto* is carried over into the other works here. The lyrical variations of *Enigma* are expressively relaxed and *Nimrod* has a simple, direct nobility. Though Sinopoli avoids the usual speeding-up at the end of the finale, the thrust of that and the other vigorous climaxes is pressed home passionately. The *Serenade* is similarly expansive, and some may feel that the *Larghetto*, for all its sympathetic feeling, is too measured. The rich recording adds to the character of the readings, with the Philharmonia strings in particular playing superbly.

Violin concerto in B min., Op. 61.

🏵 (M) *** EMI Dig. EMX 2058; *TC-EMX 2058*. Nigel Kennedy, LPO, Handley.

(M) *** EMI CDM7 64725-2 [id.]. Sir Yehudi Menuhin, New Philh. O, Boult – DELIUS: *Violin concerto*. **(*)

(Y/B) (***) Beulah mono 1PD 10 [id.]. Campoli, LPO, Boult – MENDELSSOHN: *Violin concerto*. (***)

(N) (M) ** DG Dig. 445 564-2 [id.]. Itzhak Perlman, Chicago SO, Barenboim – CHAUSSON: *Poème*. ***

(i) *Violin concerto in B min.; Cockaigne overture*, Op. 40.
(BB) *** Naxos Dig. 8.550489; *4.550489* [id.]. Dong-Suk Kang, Polish Nat. RSO (Katowice), Adrian Leaper.

(i) *Violin concerto; In the South (Alassio)* (concert overture).
(M) *** Sony SMK 58927 [id.]. (i) Pinchas Zukerman; LPO, Barenboim.

(i) *Violin concerto in B min.;* (ii) *Violin sonata in E min., Op. 82.*
(B) *** CfP CD-CFP 4632; *TC-CFP 4632*. Hugh Bean; (i) RLPO, Groves; (ii) David Parkhouse.

This remains Nigel Kennedy's finest achievement on record, arguably even finer than the long line of versions with star international soloists from either outside or within Britain. With Vernon Handley as guide it is a truly inspired and inspiring performance and the recording is outstandingly faithful and atmospheric. At mid-price it is a supreme Elgarian bargain.

Menuhin's second stereo recording, in partnership with Sir Adrian Boult, is hardly less moving and inspirational than his first. Boult directs the performance with a passionate thrust in the outer movements and the warmest Elgarian understanding in the beautiful slow movement. There is an added maturity in Menuhin's contribution to compensate for any slight loss of poise or sweetness of tone, and the finale – the most difficult movement to keep together – is stronger and more confident than it was. The (1966) Kingsway Hall recording is characteristically warm and atmospheric, yet vividly focused by the CD transfer. A record indispensable for its documentary value as well as for its musical insights.

Hugh Bean has not the outsize personality of his most eloquent rivals, but his reading of the Elgar *Concerto* has a nobility and reticence well attuned to this composer, while his selfless artistry is wholly dedicated to the music rather than to ego projection. The introspective playing during the cadenza of the finale is particularly telling, with the secondary theme of the first movement movingly recalled. The 1973 record is extremely realistic, with the balance just as in the concert hall, and its perspective seems just right for the performance. Groves is at his very finest and his understanding support is excellent in every way. The performance of the *Sonata* is dramatically alive, but ripely autumnal too, and again the (Abbey Road) recording is of high quality.

Zukerman, coming fresh to the Elgar *Violin concerto* in 1976, was inspired to give a reading which gloriously combined the virtuoso swagger of a Heifetz with the tender, heartfelt warmth of the young Menuhin, plus much individual responsiveness. Barenboim is a splendid partner, brilliant but never breathless in the main allegro and culminating in a deeply felt rendering of the long accompanied cadenza, freely expansive yet concentrated. With full but clearly defined recording, naturally balanced, at EMI's Abbey Road studios, this is a version which all Elgarians should seek out. The coupling is an exciting and virile account of *In the South*, not quite as remarkable as the *Concerto* but a worthwhile bonus, even if the sound is marginally less full.

Dong-Suk Kang, immaculate in his intonation, plays the Elgar with fire and urgency. This is very different from most latterday performances, with markedly faster speeds; yet those speeds relate more closely than usual to the metronome markings in the score, and they never get in the way of Kang's ability to feel Elgarian rubato naturally, guided by the warmly understanding conducting of Adrian Leaper. Irrespective of price, this is a keenly competitive version, with excellent, wide-ranging digital sound, if with rather too forward a balance for the soloist.

Campoli gives a deeply felt but highly individual account of Elgar's great concerto. One can judge one's reaction to this performance by the control of vibrato on the opening phrase of his first entry. This is an essentially romantic approach, full of warmth, but there is no indulgence. Campoli's reading is based on an impeccable technique and he applies himself here with dedication to a work he obviously loves, and the result – with Boult securely and compellingly at the helm – is most rewarding. The 1954 Kingsway Hall recording has been impeccably transferred 'from the *ffrr* master tape' by Tony Hawkins at the Decca studios. With its outstanding Mendelssohn coupling this is a fully worthy memento of a strikingly fine soloist.

Perlman's ease in tackling one of the most challenging violin concertos ever written brings an enjoyable performance, though he misses some of the darker, more intense elements in Elgar's inspiration. The solo instrument is forwardly balanced and the recording is bright and vivid rather than rich, lacking some of the amplitude one expects in the Elgar orchestral sound. The CD emphasizes the presence of the soloist but confirms the lack of expansiveness in the orchestra. The Chausson coupling seems a strange choice, although it is beautifully played.

Coronation march, Op. 65; Froissart: concert overture, Op. 19; In the South (Alassio) (concert overture), *Op. 50; The Light of life: Meditation, Op. 29.*
*** ASV Dig. CDDCA 619 [id.]. RPO, Yondani Butt.

Yondani Butt draws warm and opulent performances from the RPO. Both overtures have splendid panache. Rich, atmospheric recording, yet with plenty of brilliance – an excellent Elgar sound, in fact.

Crown of India: suite, Op. 66; Enigma variations, Op. 36; Pomp and circumstance marches Nos. 1–5.
(M) **(*) Sony SBK 48265 [id.]. LPO, Barenboim.

Barenboim's view of *Enigma* is full of fantasy. Its most distinctive point is its concern for the miniature element, while the big variations have full weight, and the finale brings the fierceness of added adrenalin at a fast tempo. Tempi are surprisingly fast in the *Pomp and circumstance marches* (though Elgar's tended to be fast too) and not all Elgarians will approve of the updating of Elgarian majesty. The rumbustious approach to the *Crown of India suite* brings this patriotic celebration of the Raj vividly to life, though here the lack of opulence in the recording is a drawback. The marches, too, could do with a more expansive middle range, though *Enigma* is fully acceptable.

Enigma variations (Variations on an original theme), Op. 36.
(BB) *** DG 439 446-2 [id.]. LSO, Jochum – HOLST: *Planets.* ***
(M) *** EMI CDM7 64648-2 [id.]. LSO, Boult – HOLST: *Planets.* ***
(Y/B) *** Sony Dig. SK 53284 [id.]. BPO, Levine – DEBUSSY: *Images.* ***
(Y/B) (***) EMI mono CDC7 54837-2 [id.]. Royal Albert Hall O, composer – HOLST: *Planets.* (***)
(Y/B) (B) **(*) BBC Radio Classics BBCRD 9104 [id.]. BBCSO, Sir Malcolm Sargent – HOLST: *Planets* **(*)
(M) (***) RCA mono GD 60287 [60287-2-RG]. NBC SO, Toscanini – MUSSORGSKY: *Pictures.* (**)

The DG Classikon super-bargain CD couples Steinberg's exciting and brilliantly recorded complete set of the Holst *Planets* with Eugen Jochum's inspirational reading of *Enigma*. Like others – including Elgar himself – Jochum sets a very slow *Adagio* at the start of *Nimrod*, slower than the metronome marking in the score; unlike others, he maintains that measured tempo and, with the subtlest gradations, builds an even bigger, nobler climax than you find in *accelerando* readings. It is like a Bruckner slow movement in microcosm around which the other variations revolve, all of them delicately detailed, with a natural feeling for Elgarian rubato. The playing of the LSO matches the strength and refinement of the performance. The remastered recording, however, sounds brighter and more vivid than before but has lost none of its richness.

Boult's *Enigma* comes from the beginning of the 1970s, but the recording has lost some of its amplitude in its transfer to CD: the effect is fresh, but the violins sound thinner. The reading shows this conductor's long experience of the work, with each variation growing naturally and seamlessly out of the music that has gone before. Yet the livelier variations bring exciting orchestral bravura and there is an underlying intensity of feeling that carries the performance forward.

Levine and the Berlin Philharmonic may not be idiomatic but their live recording has a thrust and passion that are hard to resist, least convincing at the start, but spacious and unhurried in *Nimrod* and thrillingly powerful in the final variation, which draws cheers from the Berlin audience. However, this is not a first choice.

Elgar's own 1928 recording is too well known to require further comment. Now it represents Elgar in the 'Composers in Person' series and comes in harness with Holst's own version of *The Planets*. Both are remarkable in their different ways and are self-recommending. Although allowances have to be made for the sound, they are remarkably few.

With the BBC engineers capturing the atmospheric thrill of a Prom performance in the Royal Albert Hall, Sir Malcolm Sargent's account of Elgar's *Enigma variations* gives a better idea of why he was such a Proms favourite, with the result more spontaneous than almost any of his studio recordings. The live performance may be a degree less polished, but its thrust and urgency are irresistible, building up superbly to the final variation, in which the BBC brass and the obbligato organ convey an extra frisson, even if the sound is pretty opaque and there are too many extraneous noises. But this is an inexpensive disc and, with an equally warm and expressive account of *The Planets* as the generous coupling, in some ways this makes a more persuasive case for the conductor than the mid-price EMI pairing of Sargent's studio recordings of the same works.

It is a pity that Toscanini's sharply focused but warmly expressive NBC reading of *Enigma* should come in a coupling with his severe account of the Mussorgsky. The Elgar, often expansive as well as affectionately phrased, as in the statement of the theme, gives a much more sympathetic view of the taskmaster conductor than most of his late recordings. Though traditionalist Elgarians may not always approve, it makes for an electrifying experience. The transfer is clean but not too aggressive.

Enigma variations, Op. 36; Falstaff, Op. 68; Grania and Diarmid: Funeral march.
(Y/B) *** EMI CDC5 55001-2 [id.]. CBSO, Simon Rattle.

(i) *Enigma variations;* (ii) *Falstaff;* (iii) *Serenade for strings.*
(M) **(*) Decca 440 326-2 [id.]. (i) Chicago SO; (ii) LPO, Solti; (iii) ASMF, Marriner.

In *Enigma*, Rattle and the CBSO are both powerful and refined, overwhelming at the close, and they offer a generous and ideal coupling. *Falstaff* is given new transparency in a spacious reading, deeply moving in the hush of the final death scene, with the *Grania and Diarmid* excerpts as a valuable makeweight.

With Solti, the *Enigma variations* becomes a dazzling showpiece. Though the charm of the work is given short measure, the structure emerges the more sharply, with the fast variations taken at breakneck speed and with the Chicago orchestra challenged to supreme virtuosity. *Falstaff* is hardly a traditional view either, with the tensions too tautly held, and the effect just does not relax enough. Yet it is easy to be exhilarated by Solti's sense of momentum, and the recording, given more weight and body on CD, is impressive. By the side of these high-powered Solti readings, Marriner's simple approach to the *Serenade* is refreshing. This performance, warm and resilient, shows this conductor at his finest.

(i) *Enigma variations;* (ii) *Pomp and circumstance marches Nos. 1–5, Op. 39.*
(M) *** Chandos CHAN 6504 [id.]. SNO, Sir Alexander Gibson.
(M) *** DG 429 713-2 [id.]. RPO, Norman Del Mar.
(M) *** EMI CDM7 64015-2 [id.]. (i) LSO; (ii) LPO, Sir Adrian Boult.

Sir Alexander Gibson's reading of *Enigma* has stood the test of time and remains very satisfying, warm and spontaneous in feeling, with a memorable climax in *Nimrod*. The 1978 recording, made in Glasgow's City Hall, remains outstanding, with the organ sonorously filling out the bass in the finale, which has real splendour. The *Pomp and circumstance marches*, too, have fine *nobilmente* and swagger.

In the *Enigma variations* Del Mar comes closer than any other conductor to the responsive rubato style of Elgar himself, using fluctuations to point the emotional message of the work with wonderful power and spontaneity. The RPO plays superbly, both here and in the *Pomp and circumstance marches*, given Proms-style flair and urgency – although some might feel that the fast speeds miss some of the *nobilmente*. The reverberant sound here adds something of an aggressive edge to the music-making.

Boult's *Enigma* (also available coupled with Holst's *Planets* – see above) is self-recommending; it shows this conductor's long experience of the work, with each variation growing naturally and seamlessly out of the music that has gone before. Boult's approach to the *Pomp and circumstance marches* is brisk and direct, with an almost no-nonsense manner in places. There is not a hint of vulgarity and the freshness is most attractive, though it is a pity he omits the repeats in the Dvořák-like No. 2. The brightened sound brings a degree of abrasiveness to the brass.

(i) *Enigma variations;* (ii) *Pomp and circumstance marches Nos. 1–5;* (iii) *Serenade for strings.*
(B) *** Decca 433 629-2. (i) LAPO, Mehta; (ii), LSO, Bliss; (iii) ASMF, Marriner.

Mehta proves a strong and sensitive Elgarian, and this is a highly enjoyable performance. If there are no special revelations, the transition from the nobly conceived and spacious climax of *Nimrod* to a delightfully graceful *Dorabella* is particularly felicitous. The vintage Decca recording, with the organ entering spectacularly in the finale, is outstanding in its CD transfer, and this is one of Mehta's very finest records. Marriner's elegantly played yet highly sensitive account of the *String serenade* makes a fine bonus, and Sir Arthur Bliss's rumbustiously vigorous accounts of the *Pomp and circumstance marches* are worth anyone's money.

Falstaff, Op. 68; Froissart: concert overture, Op. 19; In the South (Alassio), Op. 50.
(N) *** EMI CDC7 54415-2 [id.]. LSO, Tate.

Helped by full, opulent recording, weighty in brass and timpani, Tate offers a strong and purposeful reading of *Falstaff*, well coupled with the two concert overtures. The swagger of *Froissart* and the atmospheric colourings of *In the South* are superbly caught, with the viola nocturne in the latter ravishingly played by Edward Vanderspar. If you want this particular programme, this CD is very recommendable.

(i) *Falstaff, Op. 68.* (ii) *Introduction and allegro for strings, Op. 47; Serenade for strings in E min., Op. 20.*
(N) (**) Beulah mono 1PD 15 [id.]. (i) LSO; (ii) Strings of New SO; Anthony Collins.

Dating from February 1954, this was the first recording of Elgar's *Falstaff* after the composer's own of 22 years earlier. Few versions since match Collins's in the way his timing helps you visualize the story. The reading is strong and purposeful, yet not at all rushed, with each section sharply characterized and beautifully timed. The crisp ensemble, not just in the woodwind and brass sections but also in the strings, defies the idea that the LSO was then at a low ebb. Collins also offers a taut and exciting performance of the *Introduction and allegro* (with a touching introduction for the lovely secondary theme) and, in suitable contrast, a mellow, poised reading of the softer and delightful *Serenade*. However, as with the Eduard van Beinum collection above, these transfers from the Decca masters by Tony Hawkins for Beulah cannot compare with the results obtained by Mike Dutton from other Decca records of the same period. They fail to capture the full vividness of the *ffrr* recording, although there is a fair body in the sound and the bite of the brass is splendid. Moreover it is irritating that there is only a single track for the 34-minute work, with no sections separately indexed, and there are no separate tracks even for the different movements of the *Serenade*. The string recordings were also made in the Kingsway Hall, but in 1952. It is assumed in both instances that Hawkins used the same tapes from which the later Decca Ace of Clubs LPs were transferred, in which the sound had already seemingly become degraded, compared with first pressings of the original full-priced discs. The violins sound distinctly thin and fizzy, even acidulated in climaxes, and although the playing is not nearly as polished as in *Falstaff* this is not entirely the fault of the relatively small number of players in what was called the New Symphony Orchestra. All three recordings were engineered by Kenneth Wilkinson, and this CD almost certainly does not do full justice to the balance of the sound he originally achieved.

Falstaff, Op. 68; Introduction and allegro for strings, Op. 47; arr. of BACH: *Fantasia and fugue in C min., Op. 86.*
(N) (M) *** Carlton IMP Dig. 3036 70030-2 [id.]. National Youth O of Great Britain, Christopher Seaman.

These works have rarely been given such heartfelt performances as those by Christopher Seaman and the National Youth Orchestra. The weight of string sound, combined with the fervour behind the playing, makes this an exceptionally satisfying reading of the *Introduction and allegro*, while *Falstaff* demonstrates even more strikingly how, working together intensively, these youngsters have learnt to keep a precise ensemble through the most complex variations of expressive rubato. Warm, full, digital recording adds to an outstanding bargain.

Falstaff; Symphonies Nos. 1–2; (i) *Dream of Gerontius: Prelude* and excerpts. *The Music makers*: excerpts. *Civic fanfare and National anthem.*
*** EMI mono CDS7 54560-2 (3). (i) Margaret Balfour, Steuart Wilston, Herbert Heyner, Tudor Davies, Horace Stevens, Royal Ch. Soc., Three Choirs Festival Ch., LSO or Royal Albert Hall O, composer.

It is thrilling in this first volume of EMI's Elgar Edition to find that the recordings, made between 1927 and 1932, have a body and immediacy that give the most astonishing sense of presence. Elgar is with us here and now, providing in these inspired performances an insight beyond that of any other conductor of his music. Consistently these are tough performances, with rhythms pressed sharply home and with speeds generally faster than has become normal today. In addition, Elgar's sense of line, his ability to mould rhythms with natural flexibility, regularly brings an extra emotional thrust and an extra intensity. What is special is the poignancy, the vulnerability conveyed in this music even at its grandest. Most thrilling of all is the *First Symphony*, where Elgar modifies some of the markings in the score on speed-changes; and this reading of *Falstaff*, too, has never been surpassed. *Symphony No. 2* comes with fascinating supplements, including a rehearsal of the Scherzo and an alternative take of the first part of the movement. Most atmospheric of all are the live recordings of *Gerontius* and *The Music makers* on the third disc, all recorded live at a time when recording on wax discs in short spans of under five minutes presented almost insoluble problems. The brief *Civic fanfare* is a curiosity, the only Elgar first performance preserved on record.

In the South (Alassio), Op. 50.
(Y/B) *** Sony Dig. SK 57973 [id.]. La Scala PO, Milan, Muti – BRAHMS: *Serenade No. 1.* ***

Muti's account of Elgar's *Alassio* or *In the South* is an almost unqualified success. The Straussian ebullience and Elgarian sentiment are nicely balanced and the music glows with the confidence of Edwardian Elgar, tinged with hints of melancholy forebodings. Like his compatriot, Sinopoli, Muti has a natural feeling for Elgarian rubato in this overture, and he too takes an expansive view. The recording is natural and well focused, and the Milan acoustic treats the Elgar kindly, though the violins are somewhat lacking in opulence.

Introduction and allegro for strings.
(M) ** RCA 09026 61424-2 [id.]. Boston SO, Munch – BARBER: *Adagio; Medea* excerpts ***; TCHAI-KOVSKY: *Serenade.* **(*)

A striking performance from Munch, individual in that his tempo for the big *Sul G* unison tune must be the slowest on record. In this he shows a lack of idiomatic understanding, but otherwise the perform-ance has plenty of vitality and the 1957 recording has filled out in the excellent remastering for CD.

Introduction and allegro for strings, Op. 47; Serenade for strings in E min., Op. 20.
(M) *** Virgin/EMI Dig. CUV5 61126-2 [id.]. LCO, Christopher Warren-Green – VAUGHAN
  WILLIAMS: *Tallis fantasia* etc. ***

(i; ii) *Introduction and allegro for strings, Op. 47;* (i) *Serenade for strings in E min., Op. 20;* (iii) *Elegy, Op.
58; Sospiri, Op. 70.*
(N) ⊛ *** EMI CDC7 47537-2 [id.]. (i) Sinfonia of L.; (ii) Allegri Qt; (iii) New Philh. O; Barbirolli –
  VAUGHAN WILLIAMS: *Greensleeves & Tallis fantasias.* *** ⊛
(N) (M) *(*) DG Dig. 445 561-2 [id.]. Orpheus CO (with BRITTEN: *Simple symphony* ***) – VAUGHAN
  WILLIAMS: *Greensleeves & Tallis fantasias.* *

As can be seen, EMI have remastered Barbirolli's inspirational coupling of the string music of Elgar
and Vaughan Williams. It was made in 1963, but no one could guess this from the present disc which,
both musically and technically, is in every way outstanding. Barbirolli brings an Italianate ardour and
warmth to this music without in any way robbing it of its Englishness, and the response of the string
players, full-throated or subtle as the music demands, was matched by superb analogue recording,
notable for its combination of clarity and ambient richness. For CD, the *Elegy* (like the *Serenade*,
showing Barbirolli in more gentle and beguiling mood) and the passionate *Sospiri* have been added for
good measure. The new CD transfer has retained the fullness, amplitude and analogue ambience and
has refocused the upper range most believably. A triumph!

  Christopher Warren-Green, directing and leading his London Chamber Orchestra, directs the *Introduction and allegro* with tremendous ardour: the great striding theme on the middle strings is unforgettable,
while the fugue has enormous bite and bravura. The whole work moves forward in a single sweep and
the sense of a live performance, tingling with electricity and immediacy, is thrillingly tangible. It is very
difficult to believe that the group contains only seventeen players (6-5-2-3-1), with the resonant but never
clouding acoustics of All Saints' Church, Petersham, helping to create an engulfingly rich body of tone.
Appropriately, the *Serenade* is a more relaxed reading yet has plenty of affectionate warmth, with the
beauty of the *Larghetto* expressively rich but not overstated.

  The recordings by the Orpheus Chamber Orchestra are disappointing. Though their keen articulation
tells in the *Allegro* of Op. 47, the playing overall suggests a lack of experience in this repertoire; the
sharply focused, vividly realistic recording of a string group that is plainly too few in number to be fully
effective in this music also emphasizes the lack of ripeness in the readings. The Britten *Simple symphony*
is by far the most attractive performance on this CD, fresh, sensitive and vital, missing only a degree of
geniality in the *Playful pizzicato.*

King Arthur: suite; (i) *The Starlight Express* (suite), *Op. 78.*
(M) **(*) Chandos CHAN 6582 [id.]. (i) Cynthia Glover, John Lawrenson; Bournemouth Sinf., George
  Hurst.

The *King Arthur suite* is full of surging, enjoyable ideas and makes an interesting novelty on record. *The
Starlight Express suite* is taken from music Elgar wrote for a children's play, with a song or two included.
Though the singers here are not ideal interpreters, the enthusiasm of Hurst and the Sinfonietta is
conveyed well, particularly in the *King Arthur suite.* The recording is atmospheric if rather over-
reverberant, but the added firmness of the CD and its refinement of detail almost make this an extra
asset in providing a most agreeable ambience for Elgar's music.

Nursery suite; Wand of Youth suites Nos. 1 and 2, Op. 1a and 1b.
*** Chandos Dig. CHAN 8318 [id.]. Ulster O, Bryden Thomson.

The playing in Ulster is attractively spirited; in the gentle pieces (the *Sun dance, Fairy pipers* and *Slumber
dance*) which show the composer at his most magically evocative, the music-making engagingly combines refinement and warmth. The *Nursery suite* is strikingly well characterized, and with first-class
digital sound this is highly recommendable.

Pomp and circumstance marches Nos. 1–5.
(Y/B) (BB) ** Belart 450 143-2 [id.]. LSO, Bliss – BLISS: *Things to come* etc. **

Sir Arthur Bliss was an admirable conductor for this music. He plays the marches with a rumbustious
vigour, yet preserves a sense of style so that the *nobilmente* is never cheapened. The recording is bright
but has less sonority than when it first appeared in 1959, and the upper range is thin.

Romance for cello and orchestra, Op. 62.
(M) *** EMI Dig. CDM7 64726-2 [id.]. Julian Lloyd Webber, LSO, Mackerras – SULLIVAN: *Cello
  concerto* etc. ***

Julian Lloyd Webber has rescued the composer's own version of the *Romance* for cello (originally for bassoon) and it provides a delightful makeweight for the Sullivan reissue, beautifully played and warmly recorded.

Serenade for strings in E min., Op. 20.
(B) *** Carlton IMP Dig. PCD 861 [id.]. Serenata of London – GRIEG: *Holberg suite;* MOZART: *Eine kleine Nachtmusik* etc. ***

A particularly appealing account of Elgar's *Serenade*, with unforced tempi in the outer movements admirably catching its mood and atmosphere. The Serenata of London is led rather than conducted by Barry Wilde, and it is recorded with remarkable realism and naturalness.

Symphonies Nos. 1–2; Overtures: Cockaigne; In the South.
(Y/B) (B) *** Decca Double 443 856-2 (2) [id.]. LPO, Solti.

Solti's recordings of the two Elgar symphonies are now offered very economically together as a Double Decca. In the *First Symphony* Solti's thrusting manner will give the traditional Elgarian the occasional jolt, but his clearing away of the cobwebs stems from the composer's own 78-r.p.m. recording. The modifications of detailed markings implicit in that performance are reproduced here, not with a sense of calculation but with very much the same rich, committed qualities that mark out the Elgar performance. Again modelled closely on the composer's own surprisingly clipped and urgent reading, the *Second Symphony* benefits from virtuoso playing from the LPO and full, well-balanced sound. Fast tempi bring searing concentration, yet the *nobilmente* element is not missed and the account of the finale presents a true climax. The effect is magnificent. The CD transfers bring out the fullness satisfyingly as well as the brilliance of the excellent 1970s sound, and this applies also to the sharply dramatic account of *Cockaigne. In the South*, recorded in 1979, is less successful, if still exciting. But the result is nervy and tense, although the playing is excellent. Here Solti is not helped by Decca recording in which the brilliance is not quite matched by weight or body (an essential in Elgar).

Symphony No. 1 in A flat, Op. 55.
(Y/B) ✸ (B) *** Carlton IMP Dig. PCD 2019 [id.]. Hallé O, James Judd.
(B) *** CfP CD-CFP 9018. LPO, Vernon Handley.

(i) *Symphony No. 1 in A flat;* (ii) *Cockaigne overture.*
(M) **(*) EMI CDM7 64511-2. Philh. O, Barbirolli.
(BB) **(*) ASV CDQS 6082 [id.]. Hallé O, James Loughran; (ii) Philh. O, Owain Hughes.
(N) **(*) EMI Dig. CDC7 54414-2 [id.]. LSO, Tate.

(i) *Symphony No. 1 in A flat; Cockaigne overture;* (ii) *Romance for bassoon and orchestra, Op. 62.*
(N) (B) ** Sony SBK 53510 [id.]. (i) LPO; (ii) Martin Gatt & ECO; both cond. Barenboim.

Symphony No. 1 in A flat; Chanson de matin; Chanson de nuit; Serenade for strings, Op. 20.
(M) *** EMI CDM7 64013-2 [id.]. LPO, Sir Adrian Boult.

Symphony No. 1 in A flat; Imperial march, Op. 32.
(BB) *** Naxos Dig. 8.550634 [id.]. BBC PO, George Hurst.

(i) *Symphony No. 1 in A flat;* (ii) *Introduction and allegro, Op. 47;* (iii) *Pomp and circumstance march No. 1.*
(N) (BB) *** RCA Navigator Dig./Analogue 74321 24217-2. (i) BBC SO, Sir Colin Davis; (ii) Boston SO, Charles Munch; (iii) Boston Pops O, Arthur Fiedler.

James Judd, more than any rival on disc, has learnt directly from Elgar's own recording of this magnificent symphony. So the reading has extra authenticity in the many complex speed-changes (sometimes indicated confusingly in the score), in the precise placing of climaxes and in the textural balances. Above all, Judd outshines others in the pacing and phrasing of the lovely slow movement which in its natural flowing rubato has melting tenderness behind the passion, a throat-catching poignancy not fully conveyed elsewhere but very much a quality of Elgar's own reading. The refinement of the strings down to the most hushed pianissimo confirms this as the Hallé's most beautiful disc in recent years, recorded with warmth and opulence.

Vernon Handley directs a beautifully paced reading which can also be counted in every way outstanding. The LPO has performed this symphony many times before but never with more poise and refinement than here. It is in the slow movement above all that Handley scores, spacious and movingly expressive. With very good sound, well transferred to CD, this is a highly recommendable alternative version.

On the bargain Naxos label comes Elgar's *First Symphony* in a warmly sympathetic version from the BBC Philharmonic under George Hurst, a conductor too long neglected on record. Masterly with

Elgarian rubato, he refreshingly chooses speeds faster than have become the norm, closer to those of Elgar himself. James Judd's even warmer, more tender, more ripely recorded version on Pickwick is still preferable, but no one will be disappointed with Hurst's powerful reading, well coupled with the *Imperial march*.

Boult clearly presents the *First Symphony* as a counterpart to the *Second*, with hints of reflective nostalgia amid the triumph. His EMI disc contains a radiantly beautiful performance, with no extreme tempi, richly spaced in the first movement, invigorating in the syncopated march rhythms of the Scherzo, and similarly bouncing in the Brahmsian rhythms of the finale.

The lyrical spontaneity of Sir Colin Davis's version of the *First Symphony* with the BBC Symphony Orchestra is very winning, an evocatively atmospheric live recording, made at the Royal Albert Hall during a Concertaid event in May 1985. Live recording conditions evidently relaxed Davis to give a beautifully paced performance which is warmer in its expressiveness than his usual studio performances. Though in the finale ensemble is not as crisp as earlier in the performance, and audience noises intrude in all four movements, this is persuasive in a way hard to achieve without an audience. The recording, though a little recessed, brings out the distinctive acoustic of the hall, with a real Elgarian rasp on trombones. Munch's vibrant if unidiomatic account of the *Introduction and allegro* makes a good bonus, and Fiedler is ebullient in *Pomp and circumstance*, which is also very well recorded. A fine bargain in the lowest price-range.

In Barbirolli's later (1962) Philharmonia acccount on EMI there is a hint of heaviness where, after the march introduction, the music should surge along. The slow movement, too, is very slow: it is done more affectionately in the earlier, Pye version, which we hope will reappear in due course. The present transfer of a Kingsway Hall recording has lost some of the fullness in the violins; otherwise, it sounds very well. The *Cockaigne overture* is one of Barbirolli's most notable Elgar recordings.

Loughran's performance, offered in the lowest price-range, is direct and understanding, reflecting the Hallé Orchestra's long familiarity with this symphony. There is an element of reserve here, but the performance makes a strong impression, with a memorably beautiful slow movement. The 1983 analogue recording is first class, naturally balanced but vivid. Owain Arwel Hughes's version of *Cockaigne* is crisp and alert, but speeds are very broad, at times impairing the flow, though building to a fine, ripe climax.

As in the *Symphony No. 2*, Tate takes an expansive view, generally sustaining slow speeds with keen concentration, but letting one or two passages sag. A warm-hearted reading nevertheless, helped by brilliant playing from the LSO and rich and full recording in both the symphony and the overture, but not a first choice.

Barenboim, like Solti, studied Elgar's own recording before interpreting the *First Symphony*, and the results are certainly idiomatic, though in the long first movement Barenboim overdoes the fluctuations, so losing momentum. The other three movements are beautifully performed, with the *Adagio* almost as tender as in Solti's reading with the same players. The snag is the recording, which is not as opulent or well balanced as Elgar's orchestration really demands; and the same comment applies to Barenboim's colourful account of *Cockaigne*. The well-played bassoon *Romance* is placed after the symphony and before the overture.

Symphony No. 2 in E flat, Op. 63.
(B) *** CfP CD-CFP 4544. LPO, Vernon Handley.
(BB) *** Naxos Dig. 8.550635 [id.]. BBC PO, Downes.

Symphony No. 2; Cockaigne overture, Op. 40.
(M) *** EMI CDM7 64014-2 [id.]. LPO, Sir Adrian Boult.

Symphony No. 2; The Crown of India (suite), Op. 66.
(M) *** Chandos CHAN 6523 [id.]. SNO, Gibson.

(i) *Symphony No. 2 in E flat;* (ii) *Elegy for strings, Op. 58; Serenade for strings, Op. 20.*
(N) (B) ** Sony SBK 67176 [id.]. (i) LPO; (ii) ECO, Daniel Barenboim.

(i) *Symphony No. 2;* (ii) *Elegy, Op. 58; Sospiri, Op. 70.*
(M) **(*) EMI CDM7 64724-2 [id.]. (i) Hallé O; New Philh. O, Barbirolli.

Symphony No. 2; In the South (Alassio), Op. 50.
(N) *** Teldec/Warner Dig. 9031 74888-2 [id.]. BBC SO, A. Davis.

(i) *Symphony No. 2;* (ii) *Serenade for strings, Op. 20.*
*** RCA Dig. 09026 60072 [60072-2-RC]. LPO, Slatkin.
(BB) **(*) ASV Analogue/Dig. CDQS 6087. (i) Hallé O, James Loughran; (ii) ASMF, Marriner.

Symphony No. 2; Dream of Gerontius: Prelude. Sospiri.
(N) (**) Beulah mono 3PD15 [id.]. BBC SO, Sir Adrian Boult.

Symphony No. 2; (i) *Sea pictures* (song-cycle), *Op. 37.*
(Y/B) **(*) Argo Dig. 443 321-2 [id.]. RPO, Sir Charles Mackerras; (i) with Della Jones.

Handley's remains the most satisfying modern version of a work which has latterly been much recorded. What Handley conveys superbly is the sense of Elgarian ebb and flow, building climaxes like a master and drawing excellent, spontaneous-sounding playing from an orchestra which, more than any other, has specialized in performing this symphony. The sound is warmly atmospheric and vividly conveys the added organ part in the bass, just at the climax of the finale, which Elgar himself suggested 'if available': a tummy-wobbling effect. This would be a first choice at full price, but as a bargain CD there are few records to match it.

Andrew Davis provides a strong and passionate account of Elgar's *Second*. It is an impetuous perform-ance, but convincingly so, with delicacy of texture telling equally, alongside the bold swagger of cli-maxes. The slow movement has great eloquence, and that strangely ominous warning passage in the Scherzo is conveyed powerfully. The finale has splendid impetus, and one can only lament that Davis did not insist on the organ reinforcement at the climax, which makes the Handley version unforgettable and contrasts with the valedictory feeling at the work's close. Handley remains first choice (and is much less expensive). But Davis offers an exuberant *In the South* as a bonus, catching the music's Straussian surge, yet tenderly depicting the melancholy moonlight of the central section. The recording is first class, with fine range and amplitude.

Downes uses an expansive speed in the first movement to give the writing its full emotional thrust, and the hushed tension of the slow movements leads up to towering climaxes, well controlled. The Scherzo is brilliant, delicate and witty, and the finale with its sequential writing is perfectly paced. Although it has not quite the bite and thrust of Handley's version (partly the effect of the recording-balance), its valedictory feeling at the close is very moving. Indeed the only reservation is that the sound, though warm and refined, is a degree too distanced, so that the noble opening of the work does not have its full impact. This does not displace Vernon Handley, except for those needing digital recording, but it can be recommended alongside it.

For his fifth recording of the *Second Symphony* Sir Adrian Boult, incomparable Elgarian, drew from the LPO the most richly satisfying performance of all. Over the years Sir Adrian's view of the glorious nobility of the first movement had mellowed a degree, but the pointing of climaxes is unrivalled. With Boult more than anyone else the architecture is clearly and strongly established, with tempo changes less exaggerated than usual. This is a version to convert new listeners to a love of Elgar, although, even more than in the *First Symphony*, the ear notices a loss of opulence compared with the original LP. This is also very striking in *Cockaigne*, which opens the disc.

Slatkin's account of the *Second Symphony* is splendid, timed beautifully to deliver authentic frissons, and it too has extra power in the finale from the addition of pedal notes on the organ, just before the epilogue – as Elgar once suggested to Sir Adrian Boult. Previously, only Vernon Handley had included them on his equally outstanding version for CfP. Though the new Slatkin is much more expensive than that, it also includes a strong account of the *Serenade for strings*. Those looking for a first-class modern digital recording of the symphony should be well satisfied.

Gibson's recording shows his partnership with the SNO at its peak, and this performance captures all the opulent nostalgia of Elgar's masterly score. The reading of the first movement is more relaxed in its grip than Handley's, but its spaciousness is appealing and, both here and in the beautifully sustained *Larghetto*, the richly resonant acoustics of Glasgow City Hall bring out the full panoply of Elgarian sound. The finale has splendid *nobilmente*. In the *Crown of India* suite Gibson is consistently imaginative in his attention to detail, and the playing of the Scottish orchestra is again warmly responsive.

In the outer movements Mackerras's speeds are markedly faster than on most modern versions, yet there is no feeling of rush. It may not be the most brilliantly played version of Elgar's *Second Symphony*, but the energetic thrust goes with an idiomatic feeling for Elgarian rubato. And though the recording is finely detailed, it still has plenty of body. As in most of her later recordings, Della Jones gives a commanding performance of the *Sea pictures*. As recorded, hers may not be a velvety voice, but its firm projection and tonal variety give a welcome toughness to a work which, thanks to the poems chosen, can fall into sentimentality. Excellent, well-detailed sound.

Even more than in his recording of No. 1, Loughran's *Second* has an element of emotional reticence. He chooses a steady pacing for the last two movements, and the finale has less exuberance than with Handley. This is still a performance of considerable character. The 1979 sound is fresh, well balanced and spacious, though the CD transfer is a little light at the bass end. Marriner's (1983) digital recording of the *Serenade* offers well-defined and cleanly focused sound; perhaps it is just a little too 'present', but the effect is truthful and never edgy. The performance adds nothing to his earlier recording, made for Argo/Decca in the late 1960s, which generates slightly greater atmosphere. All in all, however, this bargain disc is good value.

Barbirolli's 1964 Kingsway Hall recording shows its age a little in the massed violins (especially by comparison with the richer tapestry for the two short string-pieces, beautifully played, which were recorded two years later). Barbirolli's ardour is never in doubt – witness the exuberant horn-playing in the first movement and the passion of the finale – but his interpretation is a very personal one, deeply felt but with the pace of the music often excessively varied, sometimes coarsening effects which Elgar's score specifies very precisely and weakening the structure.

Having conducted this symphony all over the world, in 1972 Barenboim made it his first exercise in Elgar recording. Following very much in the path set by Barbirolli, Barenboim underlines and exaggerates the contrasts of tempi, pulling the music out to the expansive limit. Yet this is still a red-blooded, passionate performance, capable of convincing for the moment at least, and the only snag is that the Abbey Road recording is seriously lacking in body and warmth. The string pieces sound fuller, and in the *Serenade* the *Larghetto* is touching. But in the *Elegy* Barenboim tends to dwell too affectionately on detail and the result is almost schmaltzy.

Sir Adrian Boult made the first – and arguably the finest – of his five recordings of Elgar's *Second* in 1944, with sound which, on 78, at the time was regarded as spectacular. EMI reissued this in the 'Great Recordings of the Century' series, but that CD has disappeared; sadly, Beulah's transfer is even less faithful, dimmer, lacking in contrast and with hiss so high it is sometimes louder than the music. A pity, when the reading is revelatory, as are those of the *Gerontius Prelude* and *Sospiri*, recorded in the 1930s.

CHAMBER AND INSTRUMENTAL MUSIC

Piano quintet in A min., Op. 84; String quartet in E min., Op. 83.
(M) *** EMI Dig. CDM5 65099-2 [id.]. (i) Bernard Roberts; Chilingirian Qt.
(Y/B) **(*) Medici Qt MQCD 7002 [id.]. Medici String Qt, (i) with John Bingham.

(i–ii) *Piano quintet in A min.;* (i) *String quartet in E min.;* (ii–iii) *In moonlight (Canto popolare for viola and piano).*
(Y/B) (M) *** EMI Dig. CD-EMX 2229 [id.]. (i) Vellinger Qt; (ii) Piers Lane; (iii) James Boyd.

The Vellinger Quartet, winner of the London International Quartet Competition in 1994, is an unusually characterful group for whom contrasts of ensemble are as important as blending. In this first recording, the Vellinger approach to Elgar is impulsive, with allegros taken faster than in rival versions, to make the finale of the *Quintet* bold and thrusting and the finale of the *Quartet* light and volatile. The middle movement of the *Quartet* is light and flowing too, like an interlude rather than a meditation; but the central *Adagio* of the *Quintet* is by contrast very slow and weighty, not as thoughtful as in other versions. What crowns the disc is the little fill-up, a ravishing performance of the magical interlude which Elgar arranged for viola and piano from the central *Nocturne* passage from his *Overture In the South*. James Boyd, the Vellinger viola, plays with a richness and firmness of intonation that make one long to hear him in more solo work.

Bernard Roberts and the Chilingirian Quartet are well attuned to the Elgarian sensibility: they have dignity and restraint and they capture the all-pervading melancholy of the *Quintet*'s slow movement. In the *String quartet*, the Chilingirians are excellent too, though they do not quite match the ardour of the Medicis; indeed some people have found them too low-voltage. However, they are excellently recorded in a warm acoustic and there is plenty of space around the aural image. An impressive and rewarding issue.

John Bingham and the Medici Quartet play with a passionate dedication and bring an almost symphonic perspective to the *Piano quintet*, and there is no denying their ardour and commitment, particularly in the slow movement. They also give a fine and thoroughly considered account of the *Quartet*, and overall their reading is full of perceptive and thought-provoking touches. Unfortunately they are far too close in the *Quartet* (though less so in the *Quintet*) and it still remains difficult for a real *pp* to register, while tone tends to harden somewhat on climaxes. This is a straight reissue of a coupling previously available on Meridian, and it omits the extra item which makes the newer Eminence issue so enticing.

Piano quintet in A min., Op. 84; Violin sonata in E min., Op. 82.
(Y/B) *** Hyperion Dig. CDA 66645 [id.]. Nash Ens. (members).

With the violinist, Marcia Crayford, and the pianist, Ian Brown, as both the duo in the *Sonata* and the key players in the *Quintet*, these are performances, more volatile than usual, that bring out the fantasy behind these late chamber works of Elgar. The dedication behind the playing, the understanding of Elgarian rubato born of long study and affection, comes out in each movement, but the slow movements above all are what mark these performances as exceptional. The central *Adagio* of the *Quintet*, far slower than usual, then brings the most dedicated playing of all, making this not just a lyrical outpouring but an inner meditation. Warm, immediate recording.

String quartet in E min., Op. 83.
*** Collins Dig. 1280-2 [id.]. Britten Qt – WALTON: *Quartet.* ***
*** ASV Dig. CDDCA 526 [id.]. Brodsky Qt – DELIUS: *Quartet.* ***
(Y/B) **(*) Hyperion Dig. CDA 66718 [id.]. Coull Qt – BRIDGE: *3 Idylls;* WALTON: *Quartet.* ***

There is a poignancy in this late work which the beautifully matched members of the Britten Quartet capture to perfection. Not only do they bring out the emotional intensity, they play with a refinement and sharpness of focus that give superb point to the outer movements. With more portamento than one would normally expect today, the result is totally in style. Warmly expressive as the Gabrieli Quartet are in the Chandos coupling of these same works (CHAN 8474), the Brittens are even more searching.

The young players of the Brodsky Quartet take a weightier view than usual of the central, interlude-like slow movement but amply justify it. The power of the outer movements, too, gives the lie to the idea of this as a lesser piece than Elgar's other chamber works. First-rate recording.

The Elgar and Walton *Quartets,* both with elegiac qualities, make an apt and attractive coupling; here, generously, they come with a splendid bonus in the Bridge *Idylls.* Though in the Elgar the Coulls sound almost too comfortable, less successful at conveying the volatile mood-changes than the Vellinger Quartet on EMI Eminence (see above), their relaxed warmth is still very persuasive; and the Walton performance, with the melancholy of the slow movement intensified, compares very favourably even with that of the Brittens. Excellent sound.

Violin sonata in E min., Op. 82; Canto popolare; Chanson de matin, Op. 15/2; Chanson de nuit, Op. 15/1; Mot d'amour, Op. 13/1; Salut d'amour, Op. 12; Sospiri, Op. 70; 6 Easy pieces in the first position.
*** Chandos Dig. CHAN 8380 [id.]. Nigel Kennedy, Peter Pettinger.

At the start of the *Sonata,* Kennedy establishes a concerto-like scale, which he then reinforces in a fiery, volatile reading of the first movement, rich and biting in its bravura. The elusive slow movement, *Romance,* is sharply rhythmic in its weird Spanishry, while in the finale Kennedy colours the tone seductively. As a coupling, Kennedy has a delightful collection of shorter pieces, not just *Salut d'amour* and *Chanson de matin* but other rare chips off the master's bench. Kennedy is matched beautifully throughout the recital by his understanding piano partner, Peter Pettinger, and the recording is excellent.

Music for wind

Adagio cantabile (Mrs Winslow's soothing syrup); Andante con variazione (Evesham Andante); 5 Intermezzos; Harmony music No. 1.
(M) *** Chandos CHAN 6553 [id.]. Athena Ens.

4 Dances; Harmony music Nos. 2–4; 6 Promenades.
(M) *** Chandos CHAN 6554 [id.]. Athena Ens.

As a budding musician, playing not only the violin but also the bassoon, Elgar wrote a quantity of brief, lightweight pieces in a traditional style for himself and four other wind-players to perform. He called it 'Shed Music'; though there are few real signs of the Elgar style to come, the energy and inventiveness are very winning, particularly when (as here) the pieces – often with comic names – are treated to bright and lively performances. Excellent recording, with the CD transfers sounding as fresh as new paint.

PIANO MUSIC

Adieu; Carissima; Chantant; Concert allegro; Dream children, Op. 43; Griffinesque; In Smyrna; May song; Minuet; Pastorale; Presto; Rosemary; Serenade; Skizze; Sonatina.
**(*) Chandos Dig. CHAN 8438 [id.]. Peter Pettinger.

This record includes all of Elgar's piano music. It has not established itself in the piano repertoire but, as Peter Pettinger shows, there are interesting things in this byway of English music (such as the *Skizze* and *In Smyrna*). We get both the 1889 version of the *Sonatina* and its much later revision. Committed playing from this accomplished artist, and a pleasing recording too, with fine presence on CD.

Organ sonata No. 1 in G, Op. 28.
*** Priory Dig. PRDC 401 [id.]. John Scott (organ of St Paul's Cathedral) (with HARRIS: *Sonata* ***) – BAIRSTOW: *Organ sonata.* ***
(N) (BB) **(*) ASV CDQS 6160 [id.]. Jennifer Bate (Royal Albert Hall organ) – with Recital: *British organ music.* **(*)

Elgar's *Organ sonata* is a ripely expansive piece dating from 1895, written in the period leading up to the *Enigma variations*, a richly inspired work, more of a symphony than a sonata. John Scott gives an excitingly spontaneous performance and the St Paul's Cathedral organ seems an ideal choice, although some of the pianissimo passages become rather recessed (a feature of organ playing that works better 'live' than on a record, heard domestically). The recording has plenty of spectacle and the widest dynamic range.

The Royal Albert Hall organ is just the instrument for Elgar's early *Sonata*, a richly enjoyable piece, full of characteristic ideas, not least the grand opening. Jennifer Bate plays with all the necessary flair, with her rubato only occasionally sounding unidiomatic, bringing out the dramatic contrasts of dynamic encouraged by this vast organ in its massive setting – emphasized by its facility for causing the sound-image to recede in quieter passages. The analogue recording brings good detail, even if the very wide dynamic range means that Bate's *piano* registers as *pianissimo* because of the distancing. This is now part of a 75-minute collection of British organ music, discussed below under Recitals.

VOCAL AND CHORAL MUSIC

Songs: *After; Arabian serenade; Is she not passing fair; Like to the damask rose; Oh, soft was the song; Pleading; Poet's life; Queen Mary's song; Rondel; Shepherd's song; Song of autumn; Song of flight; Through the long days; Twilight; Was it some golden star?*
**(*) Chandos Dig. CHAN 8539 [id.]. Benjamin Luxon, David Willison – DELIUS: *Songs.* **(*)

Benjamin Luxon seemingly cannot avoid the roughness of production which has marred some of his later recordings, but gives charming freshness to this delightful selection. Brilliant and sensitive accompaniment, and a very fine recording balance.

Angelus, Op. 56/1; Ave Maria; Ave maris stella; Ave verum corpus, Op. 2; Ecce sacerdos magnus; Fear not, O land; Give unto the Lord, Op. 74; Great is the Lord, Op. 67; I sing the birth; Lo! Christ the Lord is born; O hearken thou, Op. 64; O salutaris hostia Nos. 1–3.
*** Hyperion Dig. CDA 66313 [id.]. Worcester Cathedral Ch., Donald Hunt; Adrian Partington.

Though one misses the impact of a big choir in the *Coronation anthem, O hearken thou*, and in the grand setting of Psalm 48, *Great is the Lord*, the refinement of Dr Hunt's singers, their freshness and bloom as recorded against a helpful acoustic, are ample compensation, particularly when the feeling for Elgarian phrasing and rubato is unerring. Vividly atmospheric recording, which still allows full detail to emerge.

The Apostles, Op. 49.
*** Chandos Dig. CHAN 8875/6 [id.]. Hargan, Hodgson, Rendall, Roberts, Terfel, Lloyd, London Symphony Ch., LSO, Hickox.
(M) *** EMI CMS7 64206-2 (2). Armstrong, Watts, Tear, Luxon, Grant, Carol Case, Downe House School Ch., LPO Ch., LPO, Boult.

Where Boult's reading has four-square nobility, Hickox is far more flexible in his expressiveness, drawing singing from his chorus which far outshines that on the earlier reading. Most of his soloists are preferable too, for example Stephen Roberts as a light-toned Jesus and Robert Lloyd characterful as Judas. Only the tenor, David Rendall, falls short, with vibrato exaggerated by the microphone. The recording, made in St Jude's, Hampstead, is among Chandos's finest, both warm and incandescent, with plenty of detail.

Boult's performance gives the closing scene great power and a wonderful sense of apotheosis, with the spacious sound-balance rising to the occasion. Generally fine singing – notably from Sheila Armstrong and Helen Watts – and a 1973/4 Kingsway Hall recording as rich and faithful as anyone could wish for. The powerfully lyrical *Meditation* from *The Light of Life* makes a suitable postlude without producing an anticlimax, again showing Boult at his most inspirational.

The Banner of St George, Op. 33; (i) Great is the Lord (Psalm 48), Op. 67; Te Deum and Benedictus, Op. 34.
(M) *** EMI Dig. CDM5 65108-2 [id.]. L. Symphony Ch., N. Sinfonia, Hickox; (i) with Stephen Roberts.

In telling the story of St George slaying the dragon and saving the Lady Sylene, Elgar is at his most colourful, with the battle sequence leading to beautifully tender farewell music (bringing one of Elgar's most yearningly memorable melodies) and a final rousing chorus. The three motets, written at the same period, bring 'Pomp and circumstance' into church and, like the cantata, stir the blood in Hickox's strong, unapologetic performances, richly recorded.

(i) *The Black Knight* (symphony for chorus and orchestra); Part-songs: *Fly singing bird; The snow; Spanish serenade;* (ii) *Scenes from the Saga of King Olaf, Op. 30.*

(M) *** EMI Dig. CMS5 65104-2 (2) [id.]. (i) R LPO Ch. & O, Groves; (ii) Cahill, Langridge, Rayner Cook, LPO Ch., LPO, Handley.

Charles Groves conducts a strong, fresh performance of *The Black Knight*, not always perfectly polished in its ensemble but with bright, enthusiastic singing from the chorus. Neurotic tensions here are far more distant, and the happiness and confidence of the writing are what come over with winning freshness, even though Elgarians must inevitably miss the deeper, darker and more melancholy overtones. Nevertheless, the rare couplings still make this a highly desirable set.

King Olaf was the last of Elgar's works to be put on disc, and Vernon Handley, outstanding among today's Elgarians, makes it an appropriate landmark. The emotional thrust in Handley's reading confirms this as the very finest of the big works Elgar wrote before the *Enigma variations* in 1899. In its proportions it almost exactly anticipates *The Dream of Gerontius*, 90 minutes long with the first half shorter than the second, while in its big choruses its style keeps anticipating the later masterpieces, equally reflecting the influence of Wagner's *Parsifal*. The wonder is that Elgar's inspiration rises high above the doggerel of the text (Longfellow, adapted by Harry Acworth) and, though the episodic dramatic plan eventually tails off, the opposite is the case with Elgar's music, which grows even richer. Towards the end the charming 'gossip' chorus leads to the radiant pastoral duet between Olaf and Thyri, the third of his brides, followed by the exciting, dramatic chorus, *The Death of Olaf* (very Wagnerian), and finally an epilogue which transcends everything, building to a heart-tugging climax on the return of the 'Heroic Beauty' theme. Though strained at times by the high writing, Philip Langridge makes a fine, intelligent Olaf, Teresa Cahill sings with ravishing silver purity and Brian Rayner Cook brings out words with fine clarity; but it is the incandescent singing of the London Philharmonic Chorus that sets the seal on this superb set, ripely recorded, one of the finest in EMI's long Elgar history.

The Black Knight, Op. 3; Scenes from the Bavarian Highlands, Op. 27.
(N) ✿ *** Chandos Dig. CHAN 9436 [id.]. L. Symphony Ch., LSO, Richard Hickox.

These two choral works, strongly contrasted, both date from the decade before Elgar achieved international fame with the *Enigma variations*, and they here receive incandescent performances, easily outshining previous recordings. The cantata, *The Black Knight*, is based on a similar story to that of Mahler's early cantata, *Das klagende Lied*, but Elgar's inspiration is more open and less tortured, with the orchestration already showing the mastery which was to bloom in *Enigma*. Hickox, helped by exceptionally rich and full recording, with vivid presence, consistently brings out the dramatic tensions of the piece as well as the refinement and beauty of the poetic sequences, to make the previous recording under Sir Charles Groves sound too easy-going, enjoyable as it is. The part-songs inspired by the composer's visit to Bavaria then add even more exhilaration, with the vigour and joy of the outer movements – better-known in Elgar's orchestral versions – winningly brought out, and with the London Symphony Chorus at its freshest and most incisive. A disc to win new admirers for two seriously neglected works.

(i) *Caractacus, Op. 35. Severn suite* (full orchestral version).
*** Chandos Dig. CHAN 9156/7 [id.]. (i) Howarth, Wilson-Johnson, Davies, Roberts, Miles, London Symphony Ch.; LSO, Hickox.

Elgar's *Caractacus* – the nearest the composer ever got to writing an opera – draws from Hickox and his splendid LSO forces a fresh, sympathetic reading of a disconcertingly episodic piece. The oratorio is generally very well sung, with David Wilson-Johnson in the title-role, recorded in opulent Chandos sound. This is Elgar at his happiest, inspired by the countryside, and one of the high spots is a glowing duet for Eigen, Caractacus's daughter, and her lover, Orbin, sung by Judith Howarth and Arthur Davies. Much the most memorable item is the well-known *Imperial march*, introducing the final scene in Rome, made the more exciting with chorus. One even forgives the embarrassment of the concluding chorus which predicts that 'The nations all shall stand, and hymn the praise of Britain hand in hand.' The only reservation is that the earlier, EMI recording conducted by Sir Charles Groves, a sure candidate for CD, was crisper in ensemble and even better sung, with even more seductive pointing of rhythm. For coupling, Hickox has the full orchestral arrangement of Elgar's very last work, originally for brass band, the *Severn suite*.

(i) *Coronation ode, Op. 44; The Spirit of England, Op. 80.*
(M) *** Chandos CHAN 6574 [id.]. Cahill, SNO Ch. and O, Gibson; (i) with Anne Collins, Rolfe Johnson, Howell.

Gibson's performances combine fire and panache, and the recorded sound has an ideal Elgarian expansiveness, the choral tone rich and well focused, the orchestral brass given plenty of weight, and the overall perspective highly convincing. He is helped by excellent soloists, with Anne Collins movingly eloquent in her dignified restraint when she introduces the famous words of *Land of hope and glory* in the finale; and the choral entry which follows is truly glorious in its power and amplitude. *The Spirit of England*, a wartime cantata to words of Laurence Binyon, is in some ways even finer, with the final setting of *For the fallen* rising well above the level of his occasional music.

The Dream of Gerontius, Op. 38.
*** Chandos Dig. CHAN 8641/2 [id.]. Palmer, Davies, Howell, London Symphony Ch. & LSO, Hickox
  – PARRY: *Anthems.* ***
(N) (B) **(*) Decca Double 443 170-2 (2) [id.]. Pears, Minton, Shirley-Quirk, L. Symphony Ch., King's
  College, Cambridge Ch., LSO, Britten – DELIUS: *Sea drift;* HOLST: *Hymn of Jesus.* ***

(i) *The Dream of Gerontius;* (ii) *Cello concerto.*
(***) Testament mono SBT 2025 (2) [id.]. (i) Heddle Nash, Gladys Ripley, Dennis Noble, Norman
  Walker, Huddersfield Ch. Soc., Liverpool PO; (ii) Tortelier, BBC SO; Sargent.

(i) *The Dream of Gerontius. Organ sonata in G, Op. 28.*
(M) ** EMI Dig. CD-EMXD 2500; *TC-EMXD 2500* (2). (i) Anthony Rolfe Johnson, Catherine Wyn-
  Rogers, Michael George, RLPO Ch., Huddersfield Ch. Soc.; RLPO, Handley.

(i) *The Dream of Gerontius. Sea pictures.*
(M) **(*) EMI CMS7 63185-2 (2). Dame Janet Baker, Hallé O, Barbirolli; (i) with Richard Lewis, Kim
  Borg, Hallé & Sheffield Philharmonic Ch., Amb. S.

It was not until 1945 that the *Dream of Gerontius* was recorded complete for the very first time. Sir Malcolm Sargent was never finer on disc, pacing the score perfectly and drawing incandescent singing from the Huddersfield Choral Society. The soloists too, led superbly by Heddle Nash as Gerontius, have a freshness and clarity rarely matched, with Nash's ringing tenor consistently clean in attack. Though Gladys Ripley's fine contralto is caught with a hint of rapid flutter, she matches the others in forthright clarity, with Dennis Noble as the Priest and Norman Walker as the Angel of the Agony, both strong and direct. The mono recording captures detail excellently, even if inevitably the dynamic range is limited. Having the soloists balanced relatively close allows every word to be heard; in the present transfer, though the chorus lacks something in body, such a climax as *Praise to the Holiest* has thrilling bite. The first and finest of Tortelier's three recordings of the Elgar *Cello concerto* makes an ideal coupling, emotionally intense within a disciplined frame. The third-movement *Adagio*, taken slowly at a very steady tempo, is given a rapt yet restrained performance, and the finale is strong, with the volatile element underplayed. The 1953 recording is transferred very clearly and vividly. Like all the Testament transfers of EMI material, it comes with excellent background notes.

Barbirolli's red-blooded reading of *Gerontius* is the most heart-warmingly dramatic ever recorded; here it is offered, in a first-rate CD transfer, in coupling with one of the greatest Elgar recordings ever made: Dame Janet Baker's rapt and heartfelt account of *Sea pictures.* No one on record can match Dame Janet in this version of *Gerontius* for the fervent intensity and glorious tonal range of her singing as the Angel, one of her supreme recorded performances; and the clarity of CD intensifies the experience. In pure dedication the emotional thrust of Barbirolli's reading conveys the deepest spiritual intensity, making most other versions seem cool by comparison. The recording may have its hints of distortion, but the sound is overwhelming. Richard Lewis gives one of his finest recorded performances, searching and intense, and, though Kim Borg is unidiomatic in the bass role, his bass tones are rich in timbre, even if his projection lacks the dramatic edge of Robert Lloyd on the full-price Boult set.

Hickox's version outshines all rivals in the range and quality of its sound. Quite apart from the fullness and fidelity of the recording, Hickox's performance is deeply understanding, not always ideally powerful in the big climaxes but most sympathetically paced, with natural understanding of Elgarian rubato. The soloists make a characterful team. Arthur Davies is a strong and fresh-toned Gerontius; Gwynne Howell in the bass roles is powerful if not always ideally steady; and Felicity Palmer, though untradi-tionally bright of tone with her characterful vibrato, is strong and illuminating. Though on balance Boult's soloists are even finer, Hickox's reading in its expressive warmth conveys much love for this score, and the last pages with their finely sustained closing *Amen* are genuinely moving.

The Britten version brings searching and inspired conducting from a fellow-composer not generally associated with Elgar. Britten's approach is red-blooded, passionate and urgent, and with speeds never languishing – as in this oratorio they can. The London Symphony Chorus – supplemented by the King's Choir – is balanced backwardly in the warmly atmospheric recording made at The Maltings, but the extra projection and precision of CD brings out how bitingly dramatic the singing is, even if the actual choral sound is poorly focused. The soloists are a fine, responsive team, with Pears an involving if sometimes over-stressed Gerontius, and Yvonne Minton and John Shirley-Quirk both excellent. On CD the layout, with Delius's *Sea drift* placed first, allows the break between discs to come in the ideal place, between the oratorio's two parts. The Holst work then follows on afterwards. Full texts are provided, and there is no doubt that in Double Decca format this set is a real bargain.

On EMI Eminence at mid-price Vernon Handley's version offers a modern, digital recording which captures the sound of the chorus vividly with plenty of church atmosphere. The impact of the performance is then weakened by a relatively backward placing of soloists and orchestra. One's involvement is reduced, even with Anthony Rolfe Johnson's thoughtful portrayal of Gerontius, and Catherine Wyn-Rogers as the Angel too often sounds matter-of-fact rather than dedicated. With Handley also less intense than usual, this is disappointing next to his earlier Elgar recordings, though it is welcome to have as fill-up his 1989 account of Elgar's magnificent *Organ sonata in G*, vividly orchestrated by Gordon Jacob to create what might almost be counted Elgar's 'Symphony No. 0'.

(i) *The Kingdom* (with BACH, arr. ELGAR: *Fantasia and fugue in C min. (BWV 537), Op. 86;* HANDEL, arr. ELGAR: *Overture in D min.* from *Chandos anthem No. 2*).
**(*) RCA Dig. 07863 57862-2 (2) [7862-2-RC]. (i) Kenny, Hodgson, Gillett, Luxon, LPO Ch.; LPO, Slatkin.

The Kingdom; Sursum corda; Sospiri.
*** Chandos Dig. CHAN 8788/9 [id.]. Marshall, Palmer, Davies, Wilson-Johnson, London Symphony Ch., LSO, Hickox.

On his RCA version Slatkin, like Hickox, proves a warmly understanding Elgarian, but Hickox's manner is more ripely idiomatic. With a more consistent team of soloists and richer recording, the Chandos is to be preferred. Hickox's soloists make a characterful quartet. Margaret Marshall is the sweet, tender soprano, rising superbly to a passionate climax in her big solo, *The sun goeth down*, and Felicity Palmer is a strong and positive – if not ideally warm-toned – Mary Magdalene. David Wilson-Johnson points the words of St Peter most dramatically, and Arthur Davies is the radiant tenor. The fill-ups are not generous: the intense little string adagio, *Sospiri*, and the early *Sursum corda*.

Slatkin sometimes jumps the gun in unleashing his forces, but he makes nonsense of any suggestion that this is an undramatic, merely meditative piece. Urgent as his view of Elgar is, Slatkin has a natural feeling for Elgarian rubato and is never rigid or breathless. When it comes to the gentler moments, he conveys a hushed dedication. The choral singing is incandescent; but sadly the set falls short in the choice of soloists. All four in varying degrees (Alfreda Hodgson less than the others) sing with uneven production and with noticeable flutter or vibrato amounting to wobble. The sound is full, rich and atmospheric, as it also is in the two ripely characteristic transcriptions of Bach and Handel that come as fill-ups.

The Light of Life (Lux Christi), Op. 29.
*** Chandos Dig. CHAN 9208 [id.]. Judith Howarth, Linda Finnie, Arthur Davies, John Shirley-Quirk, LSO Ch., LSO, Hickox.
(M) *** EMI CDM7 64732-2. Marshall, Watts, Leggate, Shirley-Quirk, RLPO Ch. & O, Groves.

The Light of Life was one of the works immediately preceding the great leap forward which Elgar made with *Enigma* in 1899, and this hour-long oratorio is full of Elgarian fingerprints, not least in the choral writing and the ripe orchestration. Notably more than Sir Charles Groves in the earlier, EMI recording, Hickox conveys the warmth of inspiration in glowing sound, with the chorus incandescent. The solo singing is richly characterful, even if the microphone catches an unevenness in the singing of the mezzo, Linda Finnie, and of John Shirley-Quirk; nevertheless he sings nobly as Jesus in the climactic Good Shepherd solo. Arthur Davies as the blind man and the soprano, Judith Howarth, are both excellent, singing with clear, fresh tone. Warm, full, atmospheric Chandos recording adds to the impact.

Sir Charles Groves's understanding performance features four first-rate soloists and strongly involving, if not always flawless, playing and singing from the Liverpool orchestra and choir. The recording is vivid and full in EMI's recognizable Elgar manner and has been admirably transferred, with cleaner focus and no appreciable loss of amplitude.

(i) *The Music Makers, Op. 69. Chanson de matin; Chanson de nuit, Op. 15/1–2; Dream children, Op. 43; Elegy, Op. 58; Salut d'amour, Op. 12; Sospiri, Op. 70; Sursum corda, Op. 11.*
(Y/B) **(*) Teldec/Warner Dig. 4509 92374-2 [id.]. (i) Jean Rigby, BBC Symphony Ch.; BBC SO, Andrew Davis.

The Music Makers, Op. 69; Sea pictures, Op. 37.
(Y/B) *** Chandos Dig. CHAN 9022 [id.]. Linda Finnie, LPO Ch., LPO, Bryden Thomson.
(N) (M) **(*) EMI Dig. CDM5 65126-2 [id.]. Felicity Palmer, L. Symphony Ch., LSO, Hickox.

Andrew Davis conducts a dedicated, refined reading of *The Music Makers*, giving a rare intensity to the quotations from such earlier works as the symphonies and the *Enigma variations*, making one catch the breath. The crisp ensemble, both in the singing and the playing, goes with freely flexible speeds and warm understanding of Elgarian rubato. Jean Rigby sings with clear, firm focus. The rather backward balance of the chorus prevents the performance from having the full impact it deserves; but the sound, both refined and atmospheric, consistently brings out the beauty of Elgar's orchestration, both in the cantata and in the very generous and imaginative selection of shorter pieces which come as coupling. Among the encores, the early *Sursum corda*, Op. 11, for brass, organ and strings, stands well between the two masterly elegiac pieces of his high maturity, *Elegy* and *Sospiri*.

On Chandos, the song-cycle and the neglected cantata make a good coupling, with a contralto soloist as the key figure in each work. Bryden Thomson directs warmly expressive, spontaneous-sounding performances of both works, easily flexible in an idiomatic way, and this now makes a first choice among modern recordings. The recording, full and atmospheric, with the chorus well balanced and with the organ obbligatos richly caught in both works, yet brings out an unevenness in Linda Finnie's strong, forthright voice, giving a hint of flutter.

Hickox's coupling of *Sea pictures* and the big cantata, *The Music makers*, brings strong, powerful performances, very individual in the song-cycle thanks to the urgent, tough and indeed characterful singing of Felicity Palmer. Hickox gives a convincing, red-blooded reading of the cantata, atmospherically recorded and with the voices well caught, but with reverberation masking some of the orchestral detail.

3 Partsongs, Op. 18; 4 Partsongs, Op. 53; 2 Partsongs, Op. 71; 2 Partsongs, Op. 73; 5 Partsongs from the Greek Anthology, Op. 45; Death on the hills; Evening scene; Go song of mine; How calmly the evening; The Prince of Sleep; Weary wind of the West.
*** Chandos Dig. CHAN 9269 [id.]. Finzi Singers, Paul Spicer.

Elgar's part-songs span virtually the whole of his creative career, and the 22 examples on the Finzi Singers' disc range from one of the most famous, *My love dwelt in a Northern land*, of 1889 to settings of Russian poems (in English translation) written during the First World War. *Death on the hills*, to words by Maikov, presents a chilling narrative about villagers on the hills being visited by the figure of Death. The basses in unison sing menacingly, representing Death, while the remaining voices sing a nagging ostinato to represent the villagers. Untypical as it is of the composer's usual style, he himself counted this motet 'one of the biggest things I have ever done'. The Finzi Singers under Paul Spicer give finely tuned, crisp and intense readings of all the pieces. The Hyperion two-disc collection also includes Elgar's ecclesiastical motets, but for the secular part-songs the Chandos performances are even finer.

4 Partsongs, Op. 53; 5 Partsongs from the Greek anthology, Op. 45. Choral songs: *Christmas greeting; Death on the hills; Evening scene; The fountain; Fly, singing bird; Goodmorrow; Go, song of mine; The herald; How calmly the evening; Love's tempest; My love dwelt; Prince of sleep; Rapid stream; Reveille; Serenade; The shower; Snow; Spanish serenade; They are at rest; The wanderer; Weary wind of the West; When swallows fly; Woodland stream; Zut! zut! zut!*
*** Hyperion Dig. CDA 66271/2 [id.]. Worcester Cathedral Ch.; Donald Hunt Singers, Hunt; K. Swallow, J. Ballard; R. Thurlby.

Though many of the partsongs, particularly the early ones, show Elgar at his most conventional, they bring many delights. The finest item is the last, in which both choirs join, the eight-part setting of *Cavalcanti* in translation by Rossetti, *Go, song of mine*. It is also fascinating to find Elgar in 1922, with all his major works completed, writing three charming songs for boys' voices to words by Charles Mackay, as refreshing as anything in the whole collection. Atmospherically recorded – the secular singers rather more cleanly than the cathedral choir – it is a delightful collection for anyone fascinated by Elgar outside the big works.

5 Partsongs from the Greek anthology, Op. 45: Yea, cast me from heights of the mountains; Whether I find thee; After many a dusty mile; It's oh! to be a wild wind; Feasting I watch. The Wanderer; The Reveille.
(N) (M) *** EMI CMS5 65123-2 (2) [id.]. Baccholian Singers; Jennifer Partridge (with HOWELLS: *A Dirge*; BAX: *The Boar's Head*; DELIUS: *Wanderer's song*; WARLOCK: *The Shrouding of the Duchess of Malfi; The Lady's birthday*; BRITTEN: *The ballad of Little Musgrave and Lady Barnard* ***) – HOLST: *Choral songs*; VAUGHAN WILLIAMS: *Folksong arrangements.* ***

This particularly desirable cornucopia of English songs is assembled from three different CDs, recorded at either Kingsway Hall or Abbey Road between 1969 and 1976. Elgar's *Part songs*, Op. 45, for male voices date from 1902 and are settings of Greek translations by English poets. They are all brief but vivid, and the miscellaneous group of choral songs by various other English composers brings great variety. Perhaps the most striking is Britten's extended *Ballad of Little Musgrave*, with piano accompaniment, a macabre piece presented with great drama. Here Jennifer Partridge provides a telling accompaniment, and she also contributes to the success of Peter Warlock's rollicking third 'Sociable song', *The Lady's birthday*. Excellent, truthful recording.

Songs: *Pleading; 3 Songs (Was it some golden star?; Oh, soft was the song; Twilight), Op. 59; 2 Songs (The torch; The river), Op. 60.*
*** (M) EMI CDM7 64731-2 [id.]. Robert Tear, CBSO, Vernon Handley – BUTTERWORTH: *Songs;* VAUGHAN WILLIAMS: *On Wenlock Edge* etc. ***

At his most creative period in the early years of the century, Elgar planned another song-cycle to follow *Sea pictures*, but he completed only three of the songs, his Op. 59. The other three songs here are even more individual, a fine coupling for Vaughan Williams and Butterworth. Incisive and characterful, yet expressively sympathetic performances from Tear. The recording, well focused, is appropriately warm and atmospheric.

Scenes from the Bavarian Highlands, Op. 27; Ecce sacerdos magnus; O salutaris Hostia (3 settings); *Tantum ergo. The Light of Life: Doubt not thy Father's care; Light of the World.*
(M) **(*) Chandos CHAN 6601 [id.]. Worcester Cathedral Ch., Christopher Robinson; Frank Wibaut; Harry Bramma.

It is good to have a fine mid-priced performance of the original piano-accompanied version of the charmingly tuneful *Bavarian scenes*. Even without the orchestra, the music lifts up with remarkable freshness when the singing in Worcester is appropriately committed and spontaneous. The three versions of *O salutaris Hostia* are also worth having, and the strong performances of *Tantum ergo* and *Ecce sacerdos magnus* add to the interest of this reissue.

Scenes from the Bavarian Highlands, Op. 27 (orchestral version).
(M) *** EMI CDM5 65129-2 [id.]. Bournemouth Ch. & SO, Del Mar – STANFORD: *Symphony No. 3.* ***

The EMI recording uses the orchestral version of the score; although the choral recording is agreeably full, balances are not always ideal, with the choral descant in the *Lullaby* outweighing the attractive orchestral detail. However, the performances are infectiously spirited, conveying warmth as well as vigour – Del Mar is a natural Elgarian. Moreover the EMI coupling of the Stanford *Third Symphony* was a happy and generous choice.

Sea pictures (song-cycle), *Op. 37.*
★ *** EMI CDC7 47329-2 [id.]; *TC-ASD 655*. Dame Janet Baker, LSO, Barbirolli – *Cello concerto.* *** ★

(i) *Sea pictures, Op. 37. Pomp and circumstance marches Nos. 1–5, Op. 39.*
(B) *** CfP CD-CFP 9004. (i) Bernadette Greevy; LPO, Handley.

Like du Pré, Baker is an artist who has the power to convey on record the vividness of a live performance. With the help of Barbirolli she makes the cycle far more convincing than it usually seems, with often trite words clothed in music that seems to transform them. On CD, the voice is caught with extra bloom, and the beauty of Elgar's orchestration is enhanced by the subtle added definition.

Bernadette Greevy – in glorious voice – gives the performance of her recording career in an inspired partnership with Vernon Handley, whose accompaniments are no less memorable, and with the LPO players finding a wonderful rapport with the voice. In the last song Handley uses a telling *ad lib*. organ part to underline the climaxes of each final stanza. The coupled *Marches* are exhilarating, and if Nos. 2 and (especially) 3 strike some ears as too vigorously paced, comparison with the composer's own tempi reveals an authentic precedent.

The Spirit of England, Op. 80; O give unto the Lord (Psalm 29); Land of hope and glory; O hearten Thou (Offertory); *The Snow.*
(N) (M) *** EMI Dig. CDM5 65586-2 [id.]. Felicity Lott, L. Symphony Ch., N. Sinfonia, Hickox.

In his series of lesser Elgar choral works for EMI, Hickox conducts a rousing performance of *The Spirit of England*, magnificently defying the dangers of wartime bombast. He adds three short choral pieces, including a setting of Psalm 29, and ends with *Land of hope and glory* in all its splendour. The London

Symphony Chorus is in radiant form and Felicity Lott is a strong soloist in the main work. First-rate EMI digital sound, made at Abbey Road in 1987.

The Starlight Express (incidental music), *Op. 78.*
(N) (M) *** EMI CD-EMX 2267 [id.]. Masterson, Hammond-Stroud, LPO, Handley.

The Starlight Express was a children's play of 1916, adapted from a novel by Algernon Blackwood, which its promoters hoped would prove a successor to J. M. Barrie's *Peter Pan.* Though the play failed to attract a comparable following, Elgar himself recorded a whole sequence of numbers from it at the time. Even that failed to keep the music alive, and it has been left to latterday Elgarians to revive a score which reveals the composer at his most charming. On CD in this dedicated reconstruction (without the spoken dialogue) one is conscious of the element of repetition, but the ear is constantly beguiled and the key sequences suggest that this procedure would have won the composer's approval. Some of the words reflect the coy manner of the original libretto, but much of the orchestral music has that nostalgically luminous quality which Elgarians will instantly recognize. Both soloists are excellent and the LPO plays with warmth and sympathy. The 1976 recording is excellent and it matters little that, in order to fit the piece complete on to a single CD, some minor cuts have had to be made.

Eller, Heino (1887–1970)

Dawn (tone poem); (i) *Elegia for harp & strings; 5 pieces for strings.*
*** Chandos Dig. CHAN 8525 [id.]. (i) Pierce; SNO, Järvi – RAID: *Symphony No. 1.* ***

Dawn is frankly romantic – with touches of Grieg and early Sibelius as well as the Russian nationalists. The *Five Pieces for strings* of 1953 are transcriptions of earlier piano miniatures and have a wistful, Grieg-like charm. The *Elegia for harp and strings* of 1931 strikes a deeper vein of feeling and has nobility and eloquence, tempered by quiet restraint; there is a beautiful dialogue involving solo viola and harp which is quite haunting. Excellent performances and recording, too. Strongly recommended.

Ellington, Edward Kennedy 'Duke' (1899–1974)

Harlem.
*** Chandos Dig. CHAN 9226 [id.]. Detroit SO, Neeme Järvi – DAWSON: *Negro Folk Symphony;*
    STILL: *Symphony No. 2.* ***

Duke Ellington wrote *Harlem* on board the *Ile de France* in 1950. It was intended for Toscanini but the old maestro never performed it, and it was left for the composer to record it instead – a wildly exuberant but essentially optimistic picture of Harlem as it used to be before the drug age. Ellington's own programme says, 'We are strolling from 110th Street up Seventh Avenue. Everybody is nicely dressed and in a friendly mood and on their way to or from church.' He pictures a parade and a funeral, and ends with riotous exuberance. This is true written-down orchestral jazz, more authentic than Gershwin and marvellously played by musicians who know all about the Afro-American musical tradition. The trumpets are terrific. Superb recording.

Emmanuel, Maurice (1862–1938)

Sonatine bourguignonne; Sonatine pastorale; Sonatines Nos. 3–4; Sonatine No. 5 (Alla francese); Sonatine No. 6.
⊛ *** Continuum CCD 1048 [id.]. Peter Jacobs.

Maurice Emmanuel was born in Burgundy and celebrated his native province in the *Sonatine bourguignonne* (1893), drawing on folk tunes as well as featuring the carillon and chimes of the cathedral at Beaune where he was a boy chorister. Later in his career he was to number Messiaen among his pupils and his *Sonatine pastorale* (1897) is inspired by the birdsong which fascinated his more famous contemporary, although Emmanuel is comparatively simplistic, more atune with Satie in wittily quoting the coda from the slow movement of Beethoven's *Pastoral Symphony* to conclude his portrayal of *Le Rossignol.* The later works are impressionistic, the *Third* (1920) very Debussian, then erupting into a Messiaen-like cascade of brilliance for the finale. The sinuous charms of the *Sonatine Hindous*, written in the same year, contrast with the elegant pastiche of the masterly *Sonatine alla francese* (1926), a 'French suite' in six dance movements of considerable appeal, not so far removed from Ravel's *Tombeau de Couperin.* All this music is superbly played by Peter Jacobs, whose clean articulation and vitality throughout the series afford as much pleasure as his feeling for the music's lyricism and atmosphere. Not to be missed.

Enescu, Georges (1881–1955)

Roumanian rhapsody No. 1.
(M) *** Mercury 432 015-2 [id.]. LSO, Dorati – LISZT: *Hungarian rhapsodies Nos. 1–6.* **(*)
(M) **(*) Sony SMK 47572 [id.]. NYPO, Bernstein – LISZT: *Hungarian rhapsodies; Les Préludes.* **(*)

Enescu's chimerical *First Roumanian rhapsody* combines a string of glowing folk-derived melodies with glittering scoring to make it the finest genre piece of its kind in laminating Eastern gypsy influences under a bourgeois orchestral veneer. Dorati finds both flair and exhilaration in the closing pages, and the Mercury sound, from the early 1960s, is of a vintage standard. The coupling with the Liszt *Hungarian rhapsodies* is entirely appropriate.

Not surprisingly, Bernstein's charisma comes well to the fore in Enescu's chimerical *First Rhapsody*, a vividly individual performance gathering excitement as it proceeds. The recording does not match Dorati's Mercury version in richness of colour, but it has been effectively remastered. The Liszt couplings are impressive too, and the CD also includes a pair of Brahms *Hungarian dances*.

Roumanian rhapsodies Nos. 1–2, Op. 11/1–2.
(N) *** Chandos Dig. CHAN 8947 [id.]. RSNO, Järvi – BARTOK: *Concerto for orchestra.* **(*)

Järvi has a warmly idiomatic feeling for these amiable, peasant-inspired rhapsodies, moulding phrases and linking sections with spontaneity, drawing committed playing from the Royal Scottish National Orchestra, ripely recorded. Though the first of the two rhapsodies is much the more popular, the second is also lively and colourful. Together they make an unusual coupling for Järvi's warmly sympathetic version of the much-recorded Bartók *Concerto for orchestra*.

Cello sonata, Op. 26/1.
**Marco Polo Dig. 8.223298 [id.]. Rebecca Rust, David Apter – VILLA-LOBOS: *Berceuse* etc. **

Despite its late opus number, the *First Cello sonata* is an early work. It reflects something of the climate of French music at the time (Franck and Fauré in particular) and, though it is well wrought and full of interesting ideas, at 37 minutes it rather outstays its welcome. However, it is admirably played by this duo, and well recorded too.

Octet in C, for strings, Op. 7.
*** Chandos Dig. CHAN 9131 [id.]. ASMF Chamber Ens. – SHOSTAKOVICH: *2 Pieces for string octet;* R. STRAUSS: *Capriccio: Sextet.* ***

(i) *Octet in C, Op. 7;* (ii) *Dixtuor for winds, Op. 14.*
(N) **(*) Olympia Dig. OCD 445 [id.] (i) Popescu, Morna, Morialanu, Winkler, Bala, Matel, Cazacu, Joitoiu; (ii) Frâncu, Maxim, Petrescu, Ionoaia, Barbuceany, Boanta; Orban, Feher, Jebeleanu, Cinca; Andreescu.
**(*) Marco Polo Dig. 8.223147 [id.]. (i) Voces and Euterpe Qts; (ii) Winds of Iasi Moldava PO, Ion Baciu.

Enescu's *C major Octet* for strings (1900) is an amazingly accomplished piece for a nineteen-year-old, and its contrapuntal mastery says much for his studies with André Gédalge, to whom the piece is dedicated. It is a masterly and inventive score whose inspiration flows with wonderful naturalness. From the Academy of St Martin-in-the-Fields Chamber Ensemble comes a very good performance and recording.

This Romanian account of the *Octet* does not displace the Academy of St Martin-in-the-Fields on Chandos, though it is a good performance and well recorded. So is the glorious *Dixtuor* for winds, though there are some minor blemishes of intonation hardly worth mentioning. Generally this is better than the rival coupling on Marco Polo.

One can have no quarrel with the playing of the Romanian strings on that latter CD, and the *Dixtuor* or *Decet* is very well played by the winds of the Iasi Moldova Philharmonic under Baicu. But the recording, though good, does not match that of either the Chandos or the Olympia CD.

Violin sonatas Nos. 2–3; Torso.
**(*) Hyperion Dig. CDA 66484 [id.]. Adelina Oprean, Justin Oprean.

Enescu's *Second Violin sonata* is an early work. The *Third* (1926) is masterly and shows an altogether different personality; the difference in stylistic development could hardly be more striking. Adelina Oprean is thoroughly inside the idiom and deals with its subtle rubati and quarter-tones to the manner born. She exhibits excellent musical taste but her partner (and brother) is somewhat less scrupulous in his observance of dynamic nuance. The additional *Torso* is a sonata movement from 1911, which was published only in the 1980s.

Oedipe (opera) complete.
*** EMI Dig. CDS7 54011-2 (2) [Ang. CDCB 54011]. Van Dam, Hendricks, Fassbaender, Lipovšek, Bacquier, Gedda, Hauptmann, Quilico, Aler, Vanaud, Albert, Taillon, Orfeon Donostiarra, Monte Carlo PO, Lawrence Foster.

This is an almost ideal recording of a rare, long-neglected masterpiece, with a breathtaking cast of stars backing up a supremely fine performance by José van Dam in the central role of Oedipus. The idiom is tough and adventurous, as well as warmly exotic, with vivid choral effects, a revelation to anyone who knows Enescu only from his *Roumanian rhapsody*. The only reservation is that the pace tends to be on the slow side, but the incandescence of the playing of the Monte Carlo Philharmonic under Lawrence Foster and the richness of the singing and recorded sound amply compensate for that, making this a musical feast.

Englund, Einar (born 1916)

Symphonies Nos. 1 (War) (1946); *2 ('Blackbird')* (1948).
**(*) Ondine Dig. ODE 751-2 [id.]. Estonian SO, Peeter Lilje.

Einar Englund's *First Symphony* is in his own words 'an expression of euphoric joy'. He has a spontaneous and natural gift, and his musical language is probably closer to Shostakovich than to anyone else. The *Second Symphony* presumably acquired its nickname from the apparent evocation of birdsong at the very opening. Englund may not be the equal of Tubin but his talents are far from negligible; he knows a thing or two about how to generate musical movement. Good performances and very acceptable (though not outstanding) recorded sound.

Symphonies Nos. 2 ('Blackbird'); (i) *4 for strings and percussion*; (ii) *Epinikia (Triumphal Hymn)*.
(M) ** Finlandia FACD 017 [id.]. Helsinki PO, Pertti Pekkanen; (ii) Berglund; (i) Espoo CO, Paavo Pohjola.

There is not a great deal to choose between the two versions of the *Second Symphony*; this analogue recording holds its own against its digital rival and, if anything, the Helsinki performance has the edge over the Estonian CD in terms of intensity. The *Fourth Symphony* was written in homage to Shostakovich, whose death in 1975 prompted its composition. There are some effective percussion effects, bells and ticking string pizzicati, designed – the composer says – to symbolize the brevity of existence; but for all its undoubted ingenuity, the debt to Shostakovich looms far too large. (There is also a brief allusion to *Tapiola*.)

Falla, Manuel de (1876–1946)

El amor brujo (Love the magician; ballet) (original version, complete with dialogue); (i) (Piano) *Serenata; Serenata andaluza; 7 Canciones populares Españolas*.
*** Nuova Era Dig. 6809 [id.]. Martha Senn, Carme Ens., Luis Izquierdo; (i) Maria Rosa Bodini.

(i) *El amor brujo* (original version); (ii) *El corregidor y la molinara*.
(M) *** Virgin/EMI Dig. CUV5 61138-2 [id.]. (i) Claire Powell; (ii) Jill Gomez; Aquarius, Cleobury.

By including the dialogue, spoken over music, the Nuova Era issue provides the complete original conception of *El amor brujo*, rather like a one-act zarzuela, with chamber scoring and a narrative line somewhat different from the ballet we know in its full orchestral dress. Martha Senn is perfectly cast in the role of the gypsy heroine. She sings flamboyantly and often ravishingly, both here and in the delectable *Canciones populares* and the other two songs offered as coupling, and she is accompanied very sympathetically. Luis Izquierdo directs the main work atmospherically and finds plenty of gusto for the piece we know as the *Ritual fire dance*; and the recording is suitably atmospheric and vivid.

The Virgin alternative, by omitting the dialogue, finds room for the original version of the *Three-cornered hat*, also conceived for chamber orchestra, which first appeared as a mime play with music. Much is missing from the ballet we know today. Claire Powell makes an admirable gypsy in *El amor brujo*, while Jill Gomez is equally vibrant in her contributions to the companion work. Nicholas

Cleobury concentrates on atmosphere rather than drama and, helped by the transluscent textures of the outstanding Virgin Classics recording, certainly seduces the ear.

(i; ii) *El amor brujo* (ballet; complete); (iii; iv) *Harpsichord concerto* (for harpsichord, flute, oboe, clarinet, violin & cello); (v) *Nights in the gardens of Spain;* (vi; ii) *The Three-cornered hat* (ballet; complete); (ii) *La vida breve: Interlude and dance;* (vii; iv) *Psyché;* (vii; viii; iv) *El retablo de Maese Pedro (Master Peter's puppet show)*.
(M) *** Decca 433 908-2 (2) [id.]. (i) Marina de Gabarain; (ii) SRO, Ansermet; (iii) John Constable; (iv) L. Sinfonia, Rattle; (v) De Larrocha, LPO, Frühbeck de Burgos; (vi) Teresa Berganza; (vii) Jennifer Smith; (viii) with Oliver, Knapp.

This is a wholly recommendable set offering 140 minutes of top-quality Falla; it is worth investigating even if some duplication is involved. Ansermet's vivaciously spirited complete *Three-cornered hat* is also available coupled with Alicia de Larrocha's distinguished earlier, analogue version of *Nights in the gardens of Spain* (see below); here we are offered her later, digital account which is finer still. The surprise is the Ansermet mid-1960s *El amor brujo*, glittering with flamenco colour and with a particularly appealing soloist in the vibrant Marina de Gabarain. John Constable proves an admirable interpreter of the *Concierto* and there is no doubting the truth and subtlety of the balance or the excellence of the performance. *Psyché* is a setting of words by Jean Aubry for voice and a small instrumental grouping of the size used in the *Harpsichord concerto*. Jennifer Smith is an excellent soloist and the orchestral response in both works is thoroughly alive and characterful. *Master Peter's Puppet show* is not really an opera but a play within a play, both audience and performers being puppets. A series of tableaux is presented with The Boy (Jennifer Smith) as MC. It would be difficult to imagine The Boy being better done than it is here, and the other singers are also excellent. Simon Rattle shows himself completely at home in the Spanish sunshine and the orchestral playing and recording are matchingly vivid.

El amor brujo: complete.
(M) *** Decca 448 601-2 [id.]. Nati Mistral, New Philh. O, Frühbeck de Burgos – ALBENIZ: *Suite española.* ***

(i) *El amor brujo* (complete); (ii) *Nights in the gardens of Spain.*
🏵 (M) *** Decca Dig. 430 703-2; *430 703-4* [id.]. (i) Tourangeau, Montreal SO, Dutoit; (ii) De Larrocha, LPO, Frühbeck de Burgos – RODRIGO: *Concierto.* *** 🏵
(Y/B) (B) **(*) DG 439 458-2 [id.]. (i) Teresa Berganza, LSO, Navarro; (ii) Margrit Weber, Bav. RSO, Kubelik – RODRIGO: *Concierto de Aranjuez.* **

Dutoit's brilliantly played *El amor brujo* has long been praised by us. With recording in the demonstration class, the performance has characteristic flexibility over phrasing and rhythm and is hauntingly atmospheric. The sound in the coupled *Nights in the gardens of Spain* is equally superb, rich and lustrous and with vivid detail. Miss de Larrocha's lambent feeling for the work's poetic evocation is matched by her brilliance in the nocturnal dance-rhythms.

Raphael Frühbeck de Burgos provides us with an excellent mid-priced version of *El amor brujo*, attractively coupled with Albéniz. The score's evocative atmosphere is hauntingly captured and, to make the most striking contrast, the famous *Ritual fire dance* blazes brilliantly. Nati Mistral has the vibrant open-throated projection of the real flamenco artist, and the whole performance is idiomatically authentic and compelling. Brilliant Decca sound to match. Well worthy of reissue in Decca's Classic Sound series.

Navarro conducts a vibrantly atmospheric account of *El amor brujo* and Terasa Berganza is a strong, dark-throated soloist. The LSO are on top form, especially in the *Ritual fire dance*, and the recording (made in the Henry Wood Hall) is both vivid and evocative. The performance of *Nights in the gardens of Spain* is similarly compelling. With Margrit Weber giving a brilliant account of the solo part, particularly in the latter movements, the effect is both sparkling and exhilarating. A little of the fragant nocturnal essence is lost, particularly in the opening section (where de Larrocha on Decca (430 703-2) is gentler), but the performance, with its strong sense of drama, is certainly not without its evocative qualities. A stimulating pairing; a pity the Rodrigo coupling is less recommendable.

(i; ii) *El amor brujo* (complete); (iii) *Nights in the gardens of Spain;* (ii) *The Three-cornered hat* (ballet): suite.
(M) **(*) EMI CDM7 64746-2 [id.]. (i) De los Angeles; (ii) Philh. O, Giulini; (iii) Soriano, Paris Conservatoire O, Frühbeck de Burgos.

Giulini's performances come from the early 1960s, and the disc also includes Soriano's excellent account of *Nights in the gardens of Spain*. The Philharmonia playing is polished and responsive and Giulini produces civilized, colourful performances. The recording, too, is brightly coloured and, although noticeably resonant in *The Three-cornered hat*, the present transfers offer vivid and full-bodied sound. *El amor brujo* is not as red-blooded here as it is in the hands of Dutoit, but Victoria de los Angeles's contribution is an undoubted point in its favour.

(i) *El amor brujo* (complete); (ii) *Nights in the gardens of Spain; The Three-cornered hat: Dance of the Neighbours; Dance of the Miller, Finale (Jota)*.
(Y/B) (BB) **(*) RCA Navigator 74321 24215-2. (i) Mistral; (ii) Achucarro; LSO, Mata.

The late Eduardo Mata made some fine recordings for RCA in Dallas during the early digital era, notably of the music of Ravel (see below), but his Falla sessions are analogue and date from the previous decade. His account of *El amor brujo* is much more exciting than Maazel's; although the famous *Ritual fire dance* is measured, it does not lack rhythmic force. Mata, too, has an uninhibited vocal soloist in Nancy Mistral and her singing is, if anything, even more earthy than Bumbry's. *Nights in the gardens of Spain* brings a highly sympathetic contribution from Joaquin Achucarro, and the performance is both evocative and exciting, if not as delicately refined as the Del Pueyo/Martinon account. The sound throughout is warmly atmospheric and vivid. The dances from the *Three-cornered hat* are more rhythmically subtle than Maazel's, although here the LSO violin timbre sounds thinner. A good super-bargain triptych, nevertheless.

(i) *El amor brujo* (complete); (ii) *Nights in the gardens of Spain; La vida breve: Interlude and dance*.
*** Chandos Dig. CHAN 8457 [id.]. (i) Sarah Walker; (ii) Fingerhut, LSO, Simon.

The brightly lit Chandos recording emphasizes the vigour of Geoffrey Simon's very vital account of *El amor brujo*, and Sarah Walker's powerful vocal contribution is another asset, her vibrantly earthy singing highly involving. The Simon/Fingerhut version of *Nights in the gardens of Spain* also makes a strongly contrasted alternative to Alicia de Larrocha's much-praised reading and the effect is more dramatic, with the soloist responding chimerically to the changes of mood, playing with brilliance and power, yet not missing the music's delicacy. The *Interlude and Dance* from *La vida breve* make a very attractive encore.

(i) *El amor brujo* (complete); *Three-cornered hat: Dance of the Miller's wife; Dance of the Neighbours; Dance of the Miller, Finale (Jota)*.
(Y/B) (M) ** DG 447 414-2 [id.]. (i) Bumbry; Berlin RSO, Maazel – STRAVINSKY: *Firebird suite*. ***

The most striking thing about Maazel's *El amor brujo* is the splendid contribution of Grace Bumbry. This black singer was an unexpected choice in music by Falla, but in fact she catches the flamenco style vibrantly and her dark timbre has an idiomatic 'throaty' clang. Unfortunately the rest of the performance, though warm and often vivid, is not really memorable and the four famous dances from the *Three-cornered hat* fail to take off.

(i) *El amor brujo* (complete); *Three-cornered hat* (ballet): *3 dances. La vida breve: Interlude and dance*.
(N) (M) *** RCA 09026 62586-2 [id.]. (i) Leontyne Price; Chicago SO, Reiner – ALBENIZ: *Iberia* etc.; GRANADOS: *Goyescas: Intermezzo*. ***

Reiner's complete *El amor brujo*, from a vintage period with the Chicago orchestra, is a fiery and colourful account, yet totally seductive in its nudging of rhythms in *The magic circle* and in the languorous *Pantomime*. Leontyne Price's contribution has all the dark, guttural fire you could ask for, flamenco singing to the manner born: the operatic voice is almost unrecognizable. The excerpts from *La vida breve* and three dances from *The Three-cornered hat* are both sultry and gripping; they have far more sparkle than many recordings made since: the final dance brings really exciting orchestral virtuosity. The recording (from 1958) still sounds amazingly good.

El amor brujo; The Three-cornered hat (ballet): complete.
✹ *** Decca Dig. 410 008-2 [id.]. Boky, Tourangeau, Montreal SO, Dutoit.

Dutoit provides the ideal and very generous coupling of Falla's two popular and colourful ballets, each complete with vocal parts. Few more atmospheric records have ever been made. Performances are not just colourful and brilliantly played, they have an idiomatic feeling in their degree of flexibility over phrasing and rhythm. The ideal instance comes in the tango-like seven-in-a-bar rhythms of the Pantomime section of *El amor brujo* which is lusciously seductive. The sound is among the most vivid ever; this remains in the demonstration class for its vividness and tangibility.

(i) *Harpsichord concerto* (for harpsichord, flute, oboe, clarinet, violin & cello); (ii) *The Three-cornered Hat* (complete ballet).
(N) (M) **(*) Sony SMK 68333 [id.]. NYPO, Boulez; with (i) Igor Kipnis; (ii) Jan de Gaetani – DUKAS: *La péri*. ***

The attraction of the Boulez CD resides both in its fine Dukas coupling and in the exhilarating Falla *Harpsichord concerto*, which Igor Kipnis plays with distinction and which is well recorded, if balanced slightly closely. *The Three-cornered Hat* ballet is vividly played, but here the recording (made in the Manhattan Center in 1975) is somewhat less flattering in terms of richness of sonority.

(i) *Harpsichord concerto;* (ii) *Soneto a Córdoba; 7 Spanish popular songs; El amor brujo: Canción del fuego fátuo.*

(M) (***) EMI mono CDC7 54836-2 [id.]. (i) Composer (harpsichord), Moyse, Bonneau, Godeau, Darrieux, Cruque; (ii) Maria Barrientos, composer (piano) – GRANADOS: *Danzas españolas* etc.; MOMPOU: *Piano pieces;* NIN: *Cantos populares españolas.* (***)

An invaluable addition to the 'Composers in Person' series which has enriched recent EMI lists. Maria Barrientos' account of the *Siete canciones populares españolas* was made in 1928 and 1930 in Paris, and it is marvellously intense from both singer and pianist; the *Asturiana* is particularly moving, as indeed are the *Canción del fuego fátuo* from *El amor brujo* ('Love, the magician') and the *Sonnet to Córdoba*. The *Harpsichord concerto* was recorded in Paris in 1930 with a group of distinguished soloists, including the incomparable Marcel Moyse; and again, though one would not mistake it for a modern recording, it sounds remarkably good.

Nights in the gardens of Spain.

(Y/B) ✿ (M) *** Ph. 442 751-2 (2) [id.]. Eduardo del Pueyo, LAP, Jean Martinon – GRANADOS: *Danzas españolas* etc. ***

(i) *Nights in the gardens of Spain. El amor brujo: Ritual fire dance.*

(M) **(*) RCA 09026 61863-2 [id.]. Rubinstein; (i) Phd. O, Ormandy – FRANCK: *Symphonic variations* ***; SAINT-SAENS: *Concerto No. 2.* **(*)

(i) *Nights in the gardens of Spain;* (ii) *The Three-cornered hat* (ballet): complete; *La vida breve: Interlude and dance.*

(M) *** Decca 417 771-2. (i) De Larrocha, SRO, Comissiona; (ii) SRO, Ansermet.

Dating from 1955, Del Pueyo's *Nights in the gardens of Spain* was one of the very first performances to be recorded in stereo, and it has never been surpassed. Martinon's magically evocative orchestral opening is matched by the delicacy of the solo entry, and the continuing dialogue between piano and the Paris orchestra brings incandescent subtlety of colour. The thrilling climax of *En la Generalife* has a glowing, spacious rapture and the following *Danza lejana* brings an almost dream-like quality. Somehow the vibrato of the (French) horn playing is not intrusive, and the slightly diffuse orchestral tapestry presented by the early stereo suits the music admirably. After the brilliance of *En los jardines de la Sierra de Córdoba* the music sinks gently back into the repose of its closing cadence. Unforgettable.

Alicia de Larrocha's earlier (1971) recording makes an excellent alternative mid-priced recommendation, coupled with Ansermet's lively and vividly recorded complete *Three-cornered hat*; she receives admirable support from Comissiona. The Decca analogue recording entirely belies its age. The *La vida breve* excerpts make an agreeable bonus.

Rubinstein's version dates from 1969. His is an aristocratic reading, treating the work as a brilliantly coloured and mercurial concert-piece rather than a misty evocation, with flamenco rhythms glittering in the finale. The two encores which follow are even more arresting.

The Three-cornered hat (ballet; complete).

*** Chandos Dig. CHAN 8904 [id.]. Jill Gomez, Philh. O, Yan Pascal Tortelier – ALBENIZ: *Iberia.* ***

The Three-cornered hat (complete); *Homenajes; La vida breve: Prelude and dance.*

(Y/B) (M) **(*) Telarc Dig. CD 82017 [id.]. Florence Quivar; Men of the May Festival Ch., Cincinnati SO, Jesús López-Cobos.

Yan Pascal Tortelier is hardly less seductive than Dutoit in handling Falla's beguiling dance-rhythms. The fine Chandos recording is full and vivid, if rather reverberant, and Jill Gomez's contribution floats within the resonance; but the acoustic warmth adds to the woodwind bloom and the strings are beguilingly rich. Tortelier brings out the score's humour as well as its colour and the closing *Jota* is joyfully vigorous.

Telarc's recording is cushioned by wider reverberation so that the opening of the ballet with its '*Olés!*' and castanets underlined by insistent timpani is much less sharply defined; elsewhere the warm ambience, with the orchestra set back in a concert-hall balance, is pleasingly atmospheric. But although the Cincinnati orchestra provides much felicitous detail (the violins in the *Grapes* sequence and the wit of the bassoon making fun of the Corregidor, for instance) this is overall a less distinctive and less dramatic reading than Tortelier's. The four *Homenajes* are impressively sombre, while the excerpts from *La vida breve* make an enjoyably contrasting end-piece. In the ballet, Florence Quivar's vocal contribution might with advantage have been earthier – it has more the feeling of the opera house than a gypsy encampment. However, with an hour of music, offered on Telarc's Bravo! mid-priced label, this is worth considering, for the sound is really very pleasing.

The Three-cornered hat (ballet): *3 Dances.*
(***) Testament mono SBT1017 [id.]. Philh O, Cantelli – CASELLA: *Paganiniana;* DUKAS: *L'apprenti sorcier;* RAVEL: *Daphnis et Chloé: suite No. 2.* (***)

It is good that Cantelli's excellent (1954) performances of these vivid dances are back in such fine transfers. Elegant, polished accounts, given very good mono sound.

PIANO MUSIC

Fantasía bética; 4 Piezas españolas.
(M) *** Decca 433 926-2 (2) [id.]. Alicia de Larrocha – ALBENIZ: *Iberia* etc. ***

These welcome and attractive couplings for Albéniz's *Iberia* are given exemplary performances and most realistic 1974 recording.

Fantasía bética.
(BB) ** ASV CDQS 6079. Alma Petchersky – ALBENIZ: *Suite española.* **(*)

Falla's masterly *Fantasía bética* calls for more dramatic fire and projection than Alma Petchersky commands. But she is a musical and neat player, the recording is very acceptable and this recital (which also includes Granados's *Allegro de concierto*) is competitively priced.

OPERA

La vida breve (complete).
**(*) DG 435 851-2 [id.]. Berganza, Nafé, Carreras, Iñigo, Ambrosian Op. Ch., LSO, Navarro.

La vida breve is a kind of Spanish *Cavalleria rusticana* without the melodrama. Teresa Berganza may not have the light-of-eye expressiveness of her compatriot, Victoria de los Angeles (whose version is currently withdrawn), but she gives a strong, earthy account; and it is good to have so fine a singer as José Carreras in the relatively small tenor role of Paco. With vivid performances from the Ambrosian Singers and LSO, idiomatically directed, the result here is convincing, even if the balance is not always ideal. However, while this 1978 recording comes in a box with libretto, is is ungenerously reissued at full price and so is rather uncompetitive.

Farnon, Robert (born 1917)

A la claire fontaine; Colditz march; Derby Day; Gateway to the West; How beautiful is night; 3 Impressions for orchestra: 2, In a calm; 3, Manhattan playboy. Jumping bean; Lake in the woods; Little Miss Molly; Melody fair; Peanut polka; Pictures in the fire; Portrait of a flirt; A Star is born; State occasion; Westminster waltz.
*** Marco Polo Dig. 8.223401 [id.]. Slovak RSO (Bratislava), Adrian Leaper.

Farnon's quirky rhythmic numbers, *Portrait of a flirt, Peanut polka* and *Jumping bean* have much in common with Leroy Anderson in their instant memorability; their counterpart is a series of gentler orchestral watercolours, usually featuring a wistful flute solo amid gentle washes of violins. *A la claire fontaine* is the most familiar. Then there is the film music, of which the *Colditz march* is rightly famous and the very British genre pieces, written in the 1950s. All this is played by this excellent Slovak orchestra with warmth, polish and a naturalness of idiomatic feeling that is quite astonishing. Adrian Leaper and the musicians obviously relish the atmospheric and delicately scored pastoral evocations. The recording is splendid, vivid with the orchestra set back convincingly in a concert hall acoustic.

Fauré, Gabriel (1845–1924)

Ballade for piano and orchestra, Op. 19.
*** Chandos Dig. CHAN 8773 [id.]. Louis Lortie, LSO, Frühbeck de Burgos – RAVEL: *Piano concertos.* **(*)
*** Chesky CD 93 [id.]. Earl Wild, Nat. PO, Gerhardt – CHOPIN: *Concerto No. 1* **(*); LISZT: *Concerto No. 1.* ***

(N) (B) **(*) BBC Radio Classics 15656 91362 [id.]. Malcolm Binns, BBC N. SO, Leppard – DEBUSSY: *Images;* ROUSSEL: *Symphony No. 3.* **(*)

(Y/B) (BB) **(*) Naxos 8.550754 [id.]. Thiollier, Nat. SO of Ireland, Antonio de Almeida – FRANCK: *Symphonic variations;* D'INDY: *Symphonie sur un air montagnard français.* **(*)

Louis Lortie is a thoughtful artist and his playing has both sensitivity and strength. This is as penetrating and well recorded an account of Fauré's lovely piece as any now available; however, the coupling is not one of the preferred versions of the Ravel concertos.

A comparatively extrovert account from Earl Wild, but spontaneous and not lacking in finesse or warmth. Gerhardt accompanies positively and is also responsible for the excellent (1967) recorded quality. Admirers of this fine pianist will find this triptych very successful.

Malcolm Binns captures the gentle, wistful character of the Fauré *Ballade* to perfection. He has every bit as much sensitivity and even greater charm than Kathryn Stott on Chandos (with the same orchestra under its old name). His performance comes from the same year (1976) but was recorded at a different venue from the Debussy and Roussel couplings. Raymond Leppard draws a sympathetic response from the Manchester orchestra and, although the sound is not absolutely top-class, at this price it deserves a strong recommendation on artistic grounds.

Naxos offer an intelligently planned coupling: none of these works is a concerto and all were written within a relatively brief time-span. François-Joël Thiollier shows some imagination and sensitivity in Fauré's lovely *Ballade*, which is not represented as generously on CD as it should be. The orchestral playing is perfectly acceptable, without being in any way out of the ordinary; likewise the recording. All the same, it is worth the money.

(i) *Ballade for piano and orchestra, Op. 19. Dolly suite;* (ii) *Elégie for cello and orchestra;* (iii) *Fantaisie for flute and orchestra* (orch. I. Aubert). *Masques et bergamasques, Pavane* (orch. H. Rabaud); *Pénélope: Prelude.*

(N) *** Chandos Dig. CHAN 9416. (i) Kathryn Stott; (ii) Peter Dixon; (iii) Richard Davis; BBC PO, Yan-Pascal Tortelier.

Beautifully played and richly recorded, with Yan-Pascal Tortelier a most understanding interpreter, this neatly brings together the most popular orchestral pieces of Fauré, miniatures which often convey surprising weight of feeling as well as charm, as for example the celebrated *Elégie*, here tenderly played by Peter Dixon. The most substantial work is the *Ballade for piano and orchestra*, which Fauré himself arranged from a solo piece. As a Fauré specialist, the soloist, Kathryn Stott, brings out not only the poetry in her freely expressive playing, but the scherzando sparkle of the virtuoso passages. Just as convincing are the *Fantaisie* for flute (soloist Richard Davis) and the ever-popular *Dolly suite*, both arranged by other hands. The four brief movements of *Masques et bergamasques* are charmingly done too. Tortelier's account of the *Overture* to *Masques et bergamasques* is the best since Anthony Bernard's marvellously stylish EMI account from the early 1950s. Indeed he has the measure of all the music on this disc, be it the poignancy of the *Pénélope Prelude* or the delicacy of the *Dolly* suite.

(i) *Ballade for piano and orchestra, Op. 19;* (ii) *Pavane, Op. 50;* (iii) *Pelléas et Mélisande* (incidental music); (iv) *Requiem, Op. 48.*

(N) (M) ** Ph. 446 201-2 [id.]. (i) Marie-Françoise Bucquet, Monte Carlo Op. O, Paul Capolongo; (ii–iv) Rotterdam PO; (iii) with Jill Gomez, cond. Zinman; (iv) with Ameling, Kruysen, Netherlands R. Ch., cond. Fournet.

A generous (74-minute) but somewhat mixed bag, recorded between 1970 and 1980. Unassuming, reticent and charming are adjectives that come to mind on hearing Bucquet's reading of the *Ballade*. The orchestra is somewhat recessed and the piano too forward, but the sound is very acceptable. Bucquet shows traces of impetuosity at times, but this remains a sympathetic and musical performance. Moreover Fauré's incidental music for *Pelléas et Mélisande* is beautifully played by the Rotterdam orchestra under David Zinman and, to make the selection complete, Jill Gomez gives a delightful account of the song, *The three blind daughters*, not previously recorded. David Zinman's refined approach suits Fauré admirably and there is a pervasive tenderness and delicacy (the *Sicilienne* is memorable). The recording too is naturally balanced and of good quality. So far so good, but unfortunately the Fournet performance of the *Requiem* is not very competitive. The singing of the Netherlands Radio Chorus is first class, but in most other respects this is a rather cool, almost routine account, and the balance makes both soloists and the organist, Daniel Chorzempa, seem too close.

Berceuse, Op. 16.

(N) (M) *** Sony Stern Edition II SM2K 64501 (2) [id.]. Stern, O de Paris, Barenboim (with Concert ***).

Fauré's lovely *Berceuse*, played unaffectedly, is part of a fine collection at the heart of Box II of Sony's 'Life in Music'.

(i) *Berceuse, Op. 16; Violin concerto;* (ii) *Elégie. Masques et bergamasques: Overture, Op. 112; Pelléas et Mélisande: suite, Op. 80; Shylock: Nocturne, Op. 57.*
** ASV Dig. CDDCA 686. (i) Bonucci; (ii) Ponomarev; Mexico City PO, Bátiz.

The allegro, which is all that survives of Fauré's projected *Violin concerto*, was first performed in 1880. Rodolfo Bonucci plays it with affection, as he does the charming *Berceuse* – though his tone above the stave can be a little wiry. Viocheslav Ponomarev produces a big, rich sonority in the celebrated *Elégie*, and Enrique Bátiz plays the orchestral pieces with evident feeling. Good rather than distinguished recorded sound.

Elégie in C min. (for cello and orchestra), *Op. 24.*
(M) *** Sony SBK 48278; *SBT 48278* [id.]. Leonard Rose, Phd. O, Ormandy – BLOCH: *Schelomo* ***; LALO: *Concerto* **(*); TCHAIKOVSKY: *Rococo variations.* ***
(B) *** DG 431 166-2. Heinrich Schiff, New Philh. O, Mackerras – LALO: *Cello concerto;* SAINT-SAENS: *Cello concerto No. 1.* ***
** Ph. Dig. 432 084-2 [id.]. Julian Lloyd Webber, ECO, Yan Pascal Tortelier – D'INDY: *Lied;* HONEGGER: *Concerto;* SAINT-SAENS: *Concerto* etc. **(*)

An ardent yet not over-pressed account from Leonard Rose of Fauré's lovely *Elégie* which admirably captures its idiom and its feeling of burgeoning yet restrained ecstasy. The recording is close, but the cello image is natural and firm. The rest of this collection is also highly recommendable.

Heinrich Schiff gives an eloquent account of the *Elégie*, and he is finely accompanied and superbly recorded.

Julian Lloyd Webber plays Fauré's *Elégie* sensitively enough. His account comes, however, on a disc of much interest in that it includes rarities by Honegger and Vincent d'Indy.

Pavane, Op. 60.
(N) (B) *** Decca Eclipse Dig. 448 711-2; *448 711-4* [id.]. ASMF, Marriner – DURUFLE: *Requiem;* POULENC: *Gloria.* ***

Marriner's warmly elegant account of the famous *Pavane* is used effectively on this Decca disc as an interlude between Duruflé's *Requiem* and Poulenc's *Gloria*, both fine performances.

Pelléas et Mélisande (suite), Op. 80.
*** Denon Dig. CO 73675 [id.]. Netherlands R. PO, Fournet – CHAUSSON: *Symphony.* ***

The *Prélude* to *Pelléas* must be one of the most beautiful things in all music. Jean Fournet's account has a charm that is essential in this repertoire, and the Netherlands Radio Orchestra plays most sensitively throughout. They are also very well recorded.

Pelléas et Mélisande (suite), Op. 80; (i) *Pavane, Op. 50.*
*** Chandos Dig. CHAN 8952 [id.]. (i) Renaissance Singers; Ulster O, Y. P. Tortelier – CHAUSSON: *Poème* etc. ***

These finely finished and atmospheric performances come in harness with a fine account from the soloist-conductor of Chausson's *Poème* and a perceptive and idiomatic performance of the *Poème de la mer et de l'amour*. Very good orchestral playing and exemplary recording.

CHAMBER MUSIC

(i) *Allegretto moderato for two cellos;* (ii) *Andante. Elégie, Op. 24; Papillon, Op. 77; Romance, Op. 69; Sérénade, Op. 98; Sicilienne, Op. 78; Sonatas Nos. 1 in D min. Op. 109; 2 in G min., Op. 117.*
(Y/B) **(*) RCA Dig. 09026 68049-2 [id.]. Steven Isserlis, Pascal Devoyon; with (i) David Waterman; (ii) Francis Greer.

The present issue presents Fauré's complete output for cello and piano and includes an *Allegretto moderato* for two cellos (which takes under a minute) and an *Andante* for cello and organ, which is the original version of the *Romance*. Steven Isserlis understands the essential reticence and refinement of Fauré's art and contributes perceptive notes on the music. Perhaps he is at times a shade too reticent in the music and could allow himself to produce a more ardent and songful tone. Maybe the balance, which slightly favours his partner, contributes to this impression. Pascal Devoyon is a no less perceptive and sensitive artist; were he less so, this imperfect balance would present greater problems. A welcome, then, for the artistry of these performances, but tinged with slight disappointment at the less than ideal balance.

Cello sonatas Nos. 1 in D min., Op. 109; 2 in G min., Op. 117; Elégie, Op. 24; Sicilienne, Op. 78.
**(*) CRD CRD 3316; *CRDC 4016* [id.]. Thomas Igloi, Clifford Benson.

Noble performances from the late Thomas Igloi and Clifford Benson that do full justice to these elusive and rewarding Fauré sonatas, and the recording is clear, if not one of CRD's finest in terms of ambient effect.

Piano quartets Nos. 1 in C min., Op. 15; 2 in G min., Op. 45.
❀ *** Hyperion CDA 66166 [id.]. Domus.
*** Sony Dig. SK 48066 [id.]. Ax, Stern, Laredo, Ma.
(Y/B) (B) ** Discover Dig. DIDC 920231 [id.]. Sheuerer Piano Qt.

Domus have the requisite lightness of touch and subtlety, and just the right sense of scale and grasp of tempi. Their nimble and sensitive pianist, Susan Tomes, can hold her own in the most exalted company. The recording is excellent, too, though the balance is a little close, but the sound is not airless.

Sony's starry version of the two *Piano quartets* with Emanuel Ax, Isaac Stern, Jaime Laredo and Yo-Yo Ma offers the first serious challenge to the Domus account on Hyperion. The performances are of high quality and anyone could rest happy with them. But Domus convey the more idiomatic feel; theirs is domestic music-making at the highest level of accomplishment and conveys an altogether special fresh-ness and spontaneity.

The Sheuerers (four siblings) display a real feeling for Fauré's elusive world, and the *C minor Quartet* is certainly successful in achieving an ardent, romantic flow in the outer movements, contrasted with a nimble Scherzo and a warm yet serene *Adagio*. Gertraud Scheuerer, the pianist, firmly recorded, plays with much character and holds the music-making together, and if her brother Franz leads the strings with a somewhat meagre timbre in the upper range, both viola and cello are more generous in tone, and the resonance of the Winterthur Studio provides plenty of fullness. While the recordings by Domus on Hyperion are in a class of their own, we hope this inexpensive Discover disc may tempt newcomers to sample these lovely works.

Piano quartets Nos. (i; ii) 1 in C min., Op. 15; (i; iii) 2 in G min., Op. 45; Piano quintets Nos. 1 in C min., Op. 89; 2 in D min., Op. 115; (iii) String quartet in E min., Op. 121.
(B) **(*) EMI CMS7 62548-2 (2). (i) Jean-Philippe Collard; (ii) Augustin Dumay, Bruno Pasquier, Frédéric Lodéon; (iii) Parrenin Qt.

The performances of the *Piano quartets* are masterly. In addition, there are authoritative and idiomatic readings of the two *Piano quintets* and other-worldly *Quartet*, Fauré's last utterance. This is enormously civilized music; however, one has to accept that, because the Paris Salle Wagram was employed for the recordings (made between 1975 and 1978), close microphones have been used to counteract the hall's resonance. The remastering has both increased the sense of presence and brought a certain dryness to the ambient effect, although the string timbres are fresh.

Piano quintets Nos. 1 in D min., Op. 89; 2 in C min., Op. 115.
(Y/B) ❀ *** Hyperion Dig. CDA 66766 [id.]. Domus, with Anthony Marwood.
*** Claves Dig. CD 50-8603 [id.]. Quintetto Fauré di Roma.

The playing of Domus in these two masterpieces is as light, delicate and full of insight as one would expect. They make one fall for this music all over again. The first and more elusive of the two took Fauré many years to write but, as Domus's rapt performance demonstrates, the slow movement shows the composer at his most deeply reflective. Broader and more outward-going, the second is among the masterpieces of Fauré's Indian summer as he approached his eighties. As this concentrated performance suggests, its autumnal lyricism brings likenesses to late Elgar, with the pianist, Susan Tomes, at her most sparkling in the mercurial Scherzo. Excellent sound.

The Quintetto Fauré di Roma also have the measure of Fauré's subtle phrasing and his wonderfully plastic melodic lines, and their performances are hard to fault. The recording, made in a Swiss church, is warm and splendidly realistic. This music, once you get inside it, has a hypnotic effect and puts you completely under its spell.

Piano trio in D min., Op. 120.
*** Carlton IMP Dig. MCD 41 [id.]. Solomon Trio – DEBUSSY; RAVEL: *Piano trios.* ***
(Y/B) *** Ara. Dig. Z 6643 [id.]. Golub Kaplan Carr Trio – DEBUSSY: *Piano trio* ***; SAINT-SAENS: *Piano trio.* **(*)

The Solomon Trio's account of this subtle and rewarding score, which eludes so many artists, has great finesse and has the advantage of an excellently balanced recording. No one wanting this particular coupling is likely to be disappointed, particularly in view of the price.

David Golub, Mark Kaplan and Colin Carr give as understanding and idiomatic a performance of the sublime Fauré *Trio* as is to be found. They convey its understatement and subtlety of nuance to perfection, and the interplay among them is a model of the finest chamber-music-making. The recording is very good indeed, with plenty of warmth.

Piano trio in D min., Op. 120; (i) *La bonne chanson, Op. 61.*
*** CRD CRD 3389; *CRDC 4089* [id.]. Nash Ens., (i) with Sarah Walker.

The characterful warmth and vibrancy of Sarah Walker's voice, not to mention her positive artistry, come out strongly in this beautiful reading of Fauré's early settings of Verlaine, music both tender and ardent. Members of the Nash Ensemble give dedicated performances both of that and of the late, rarefied *Piano trio*, capturing both the elegance and the restrained concentration. The atmospheric recording is well up to CRD's high standard in chamber music.

String quartet in E min., Op. 121.
*(*) Nimbus Dig. NI 5114 [id.]. Medici Qt – FRANCK: *Piano quintet.* **(*)

The Fauré *Quartet* is not generously represented on CD, but while the Parrenin version of this elusive work remains available in the EMI two-CD set of Fauré's chamber music there is no need to look further. The Medici seem only intermittently at ease in its other-worldly atmosphere. The players obviously like this music, but they have yet to come fully to terms with it. They are well recorded.

Violin sonatas Nos. 1 in A, Op. 13; 2 in E min., Op. 108.
(M) *** Ph. 426 384-2. Arthur Grumiaux, Paul Crossley – FRANCK: *Sonata.* **(*)
*** Hyperion Dig. CDA 66277 [id.]. Krysia Osostowicz, Susan Tomes.

Violin sonatas Nos. 1–2; Andante, Op. 75; Berceuse, Op. 16.
(N) (BB) **(*) ASV Dig. CDQS 6170 [id.]. Fujikawa, Osorio.

Violin sonatas Nos. 1 in A, Op. 13; 2 in E min., Op. 108; Andante in B flat, Op. 75; Berceuse, Op. 16; Romance in B flat, Op. 28.
(Y/B) ✿ *** Decca Dig. 436 866-2 [id.]. Pierre Amoyal, Pascal Rogé.
(N) (BB) *** Naxos Dig. 8.550906 [id.]. Dong-Suk Kang, Pascal Devoyon.

Readers wanting a modern recording of the two Fauré *Violin sonatas* need look no further. Pierre Amoyal and Pascal Rogé play them as to the manner born. As one would expect, they are totally inside the idiom and convey its subtlety and refinement with freshness and mastery. There are admirable alternatives from Grumiaux and Crossley at mid-price and from Krysia Osostowicz and Susan Tomes, but Amoyal and Rogé more than hold their own against them and throw new light on the three slight miniatures that they offer as a bonus. Impeccable recording, too. A lovely disc.

Now comes a version from no less accomplished a stylist, Dong-Suk Kang, splendidly partnered by another French pianist, Pascal Devoyon. They give us performances which are hardly less fine and which cost only a third as much as the Decca CD. Without disturbing our allegiance to other earlier issues (Grumiaux–Crossley among them, although they offer less music), this is a welcome newcomer – and very good value for money.

These *Sonatas* are beautifully played and recorded on the Philips reissue. Moreover the two artists sound as if they are in the living-room; the acoustic is warm, lively and well balanced. An excellent mid-priced recommendation.

Krysia Osostowicz and Susan Tomes bring an appealingly natural, unforced quality to their playing and they are completely persuasive, particularly in the elusive *Second Sonata*. The acoustic is a shade resonant but, such is the eloquence of these artists, the ear quickly adjusts.

Mayumi Fujikawa and Jorge Federico Osorio produce playing of the highest accomplishment and finesse. There is genuine passion here (particularly in the opening movement of the *E minor Sonata*) and real commitment. They are recorded in a resonant hall, and the fairly close microphones are not always flattering to the violin's upper range under stress, although not too much need be made of this: Fujikawa often makes a beautiful sound, and particularly so in the lovely *Berceuse*. For the sonatas, this would not be a first choice; but for those with limited budgets the collection is excellent value.

PIANO MUSIC

Ballade in F sharp, Op. 19; Barcarolles Nos. 1–13; (i) *Dolly, Op. 56. Impromptus Nos. 1–5; Impromptu, Op. 86; Mazurka in B flat, Op. 32; 13 Nocturnes; Pièces brèves Nos. 1–8, Op. 84; 9 Préludes, Op. 103; Romances sans paroles Nos. 1–3;* (i) *Souvenirs de Bayreuth. Theme & variations in C sharp min., Op. 73; Valses-caprices Nos. 1–4.*
(Y/B) ✿ *** Hyperion CDA 66911/4 (4) [id.]. Kathryn Stott, (i) with Martin Roscoe.

This four-disc set, issued to coincide with the 150th anniversary of the composer's death, is a revelation. Both the *13 Barcarolles*, written between 1880 and 1921, and the *13 Nocturnes*, from an even wider period between 1875 and 1921, give a most illuminating view of Fauré's career, gentle and unsensational like the music itself, but with the subtlest of developments towards a sparer, more rarefied style. That comes out all the more tellingly when, as here, they are given in succession and are played with such poetry and spontaneous-sounding freshness. Stott earlier recorded for Conifer a generous selection of Fauré piano music (see below) but, quite apart from the warmer, clearer and more immediate sound on the Hyperion issue, allowing for velvet tone-colours, the later performances are more winningly relaxed, ranging wider in expression. Each of the four discs contains well over 70 minutes of music, logically presented, with the second containing the *Barcarolles* and the early *Ballade* (more taxing than the later version with orchestra) and with the *Nocturnes* spread between the third and fourth discs, framing the lighter pieces, including such duets as the witty Wagner quadrille, *Souvenirs de Bayreuth*, and the ever-fresh *Dolly suite*, both with Stott ideally partnered by Martin Roscoe. Then, in preparation for the superb last six *Nocturnes* come the elusively poetic *9 Préludes* of 1910/11 and the solitary *Mazurka* of 1878 which, unlike the *Nocturnes* and *Barcarolles*, finds Fauré's gentle individuality rather submerged by the ever-present Chopin influence. A masterly set.

Ballade in F sharp, Op. 19; Mazurka in B flat, Op. 32; 3 Songs without words, Op. 17; Valses-caprices Nos. 1–4.
*** CRD Dig. CRD 3426; *CRDC 4126* [id.]. Paul Crossley.

Crossley's playing seems to have gone from strength to strength in his series, and he is especially good in the quirky *Valses-caprices*, fully equal to their many subtleties and chimerical changes of mood. He is extremely well recorded too.

Barcarolles Nos. 1–13 (complete).
*** CRD CRD 3422; *CRDC 4122* [id.]. Paul Crossley.

Barcarolles Nos. 1–13; (i) Dolly. Impromptus Nos. 1–5; Mazurka, Op. 32; Pièces brèves Nos. 1–8, Op. 84; Romances sans paroles Nos. 1–3; (i) Souvenir de Bayreuth. Valses-caprices Nos. 1–4.
(B) **(*) EMI CZS7 62687-2 (2) [id.]. Jean-Philippe Collard, (i) with Rigutto.

Paul Crossley has a highly sensitive response to the subtleties of this repertoire and is fully equal to its shifting moods. The CRD version was made in the somewhat reverberant acoustic of Rosslyn Hill Chapel, and is more vivid than the 1971 EMI recording of Jean-Philippe Collard.

Jean-Philippe Collard has the qualities of reticence yet ardour, subtlety and poetic feeling to penetrate Fauré's intimate world but, while Collard has exceptional beauty and refinement of tone at all dynamic levels, the only regret is that full justice is not done to it by the French engineers.

Barcarolles Nos. 1, 2, 4, Opp. 26, 41, 44; Impromptus Nos. 2 & 3, Opp. 31, 34; Nocturnes Nos. 4 & 5, Opp. 36–7; 3 Romances sans paroles, Op. 17; Valse-caprice, Op. 30.
*** Decca Dig. 425 606-2. Pascal Rogé.

This CD makes an ideal single-CD introduction to Fauré's piano music. Rogé brings warmth and charm as well as all his pianistic finesse to this anthology, and his artistry is well served by the Decca engineers.

Dolly, Op. 56.
*** Ph. Dig. 420 159-2 [id.]. Katia and Marielle Labèque – BIZET: *Jeux d'enfants;* RAVEL: *Ma Mère l'Oye.* ***

The Labèque sisters give a beautiful account of Fauré's touching suite, their playing distinguished by great sensitivity and delicacy. The recording is altogether first class.

Impromptus Nos. 1–5; 9 Préludes, Op. 103; Theme and variations in C sharp min., Op. 73.
*** CRD CRD 3423; *CRDC 4123* [id.]. Paul Crossley.

The *Theme and variations in C sharp minor* is one of Fauré's most immediately attractive works; Paul Crossley plays it with splendid sensitivity and panache, so this might be a good place to start for a collector wanting to explore Fauré's special pianistic world. The recorded sound, too, is extremely well judged.

Nocturnes (complete); *Pièces brèves, Op. 84.*
**(*) CRD CRD 3406/7; *CRDC 4106/7* [id.]. Paul Crossley.

Here the recording is rather closely balanced, albeit in an ample acoustic, but the result tends to emphasize a percussive element that one does not normally encounter in this artist's playing. There is much understanding and finesse, however, and the *Pièces brèves* are a valuable fill-up.

Nocturnes Nos. 1–6; Theme and variations in C sharp min., Op. 73.
(BB) ** Naxos Dig. 8.550794 [id.]. Jean Martin.

Nocturnes Nos. 7–13; Préludes, Op. 103/3 & 9; 3 Romances sans paroles, Op. 17.
(BB) ** Naxos Dig. 8.550795 [id.]. Jean Martin.

Immensely civilized yet never aloof, the *Nocturnes* take a greater hold of the listener at each hearing. The French pianist Jean Martin is obviously at home here, although he does not always catch the full delicacy of feeling, the quiet-spoken reticence which is so eloquent. He is at his best in the earlier *Nocturnes*. In the later works, notably the elusive *F sharp minor* (No. 12) and *E minor* (No. 13), his approach seems too direct and positive. The three *Songs without words* come off well, but the familiar *Theme and variations*, although strongly characterized, finds more subtlety in the hands of Collard and Stott. Like Collard and Crossley, Martin is fairly closely recorded in the Clara Wieck Auditorium, Heidelberg, a not unsympathetic acoustic, but greater distancing aids the effect of this music.

9 Préludes, Op. 103; Theme and variations, Op. 73; Adagietto, Op. 84/5; Capriccio, Op. 84/1; Improvisation, Op. 84/4.
(M) *** Saga EC 3397-2 [id.]. Albert Ferber.

This Saga disc is particularly valuable in making available, relatively inexpensively, the *Nine Préludes*, Op. 103, composed in 1909–10. These will repay the repeated attention the gramophone affords, for they are not immediately accessible yet are deeply rewarding. The *Theme and variations* is more extrovert and inventive in an instantly appealing way. It too is given a well-characterized and finely considered reading and there are some welcome smaller pieces. Albert Ferber is imaginative, poetic and content to let the music speak for itself. He is well recorded, too.

VOCAL MUSIC

Après un rêve; Au bord de l'eau; Aurore; Automne; Les Berceaux; Chanson du pecheur; Clair de lune; Lydia; Mai; 5 Mélodies de Venise, Op. 58; Nell; Nocturne; Notre amour; Le papillon et la fleur; Poème d'un jour, Op. 21; Prison; Rêve d'amour; Les Roses d'Ispahan; Le secret; Soir; Spleen; Tristesse.
**RCA Dig. 09026 61439-2 [id.]. Natalie Stutzmann, Catherine Collard.

Natalie Stutzmann has a striking voice of undoubted richness and beauty. The dark colour tends to produce a rather uniform effect, and there is not quite enough variety of character; her warm vibrato strikes too matronly a note at times. The disc is also a reminder of the artistry of Catherine Collard. Both artists are well served by good recording and, though this would not be a first recommendation in building a Fauré song library, admirers of this remarkable artist should investigate this issue.

La chanson d'Eve, Op. 95; Mélodies: Après un rêve; Aubade; Barcarolle; Les berceaux; Chanson du pêcheur; En prière; En sourdine; Green; Hymne; Des jardins de la nuit; Mandoline; Le papillon et la fleur; Les présents; Rêve d'amour; Les roses d'Ispahan; Le secret; Spleen; Toujours!.
⊛ *** Hyperion Dig. CDA 66320 [id.]. Dame Janet Baker, Geoffrey Parsons.

Dame Janet Baker gives magical performances of a generous collection of 28 songs, representing the composer throughout his long composing career, including many of his most winning songs. Geoffrey Parsons is at his most compellingly sympathetic, matching every mood. Many will be surprised at Fauré's variety of expression over this extended span of songs.

Requiem, Op. 48.
*** Teldec/Warner Dig. 4509 90879-2 [id.]. Barbara Bonnney, Thomas Hampson, Amb. S., Philh. O, Michel Legrand – DURUFLE: *Requiem.* ***

Requiem; Pavane, Op. 50.
(N) (M) *** Carlton/RPO Dig. 30366 0009-2 [id.]. Aled Jones, Stephen Roberts, London Symphony Ch., RPO, Hickox – BERNSTEIN: *Chichester Psalms.* ***
(N) *** Ph. Dig. 446 084-2 [id.]. (i) McNair, Allen; ASMF Ch. & O, Marriner (with KOECHLIN: *Choral sur le nom de Fauré;* SCHMITT: *In Memoriam No. 2: Scherzo sur le nom de Gabriel Fauré;* RAVEL: *Pavane pour une infante défunte* ***).
(M) **(*) EMI CDM7 64715-2 [id.]. Chilcott, Carol Case, King's College Ch., Cambridge, New Philh. O, Willcocks.

(i; ii) *Requiem, Op. 48;* (i) *Pavane; Pelléas et Mélisande: suite, Op. 80.*
*** Decca Dig. 421 440-2 [id.]. (i) Kiri Te Kanawa, Sherrill Milnes; (ii) Montreal Philharmonic Ch.; Montreal SO, Dutoit.

Requiem, Op. 48 (1893 version). *Ave Maria, Op. 67/2; Ave verum corpus, Op. 65/1; Cantique de Jean Racine, Op. 11; Maria, Mater gratiae, Op. 47/2; Messe basse; Tantum ergo, Op. 65/2.*
*** Collegium COLCD 109 [id.]. Ashton, Varcoe, Cambridge Singers, L. Sinfonia (members), Rutter.

Requiem, Op. 48 (1893 version); *Ave verum corpus, Op. 65/1; Cantique de Jean Racine, Op. 11; Messe basse; Tantum ergo, Op. 65/2.*
*** Hyperion Dig. CDA 66292 [id.]. Mary Seers, Isabelle Poulenard, Michael George, Corydon Singers, ECO, Matthew Best.

Requiem, Op. 48; Cantique de Jean Racine, Op. 11.
(N) *** Conifer Dig. 74321 15351-2 [id.]. Otaki, Griffiths, Trinity College, Cambridge, Ch., London Musici, Marlow (with MESSIAEN: *O sacrum convivium* ***) – DURUFLE: *Messe Cum jubilo* etc. ***

(i) *Requiem, Op. 48;* (ii) *Cantique de Jean Racine, Op. 11;* (ii; iii) *Messe basse.*
(Y/B) (BB) *** Naxos Dig. 8.550765 [id.]. Beckley, Gedge, Schola Cantorum of Oxford, Oxford Camerata, Summerly (with DE SEVERAC: *Tantum ergo;* VIERNE: *Andantino;* with Colm Carey, organ ***).

(B) *** Decca Double 436 486-2 (2) [id.]. (i) Jonathon Bond, Benjamin Luxon; (ii) Stephen Cleobury; (iii) Andrew Brunt; (i–iii) St John's College, Cambridge, Ch., Guest (i) with ASMF – FAURE: *Requiem;* POULENC: *Mass* etc. ***

(i; ii; iv) *Requiem, Op. 48;* (ii; iii) *Les Djinns, Op. 12;* (ii) *Madrigal, Op. 35.*
(Y/B) *** Ph. Dig. 438 149-2 [id.]. (i) Catherine Bott, Gilles Cachemaille; (ii) Monteverdi Ch., Salisbury Cathedral Boy Choristers; (iii) Sabine Vatin; (iv) ORR, Gardiner – DEBUSSY: *3 Chansons de Charles d'Orléans;* RAVEL: *3 Chansons;* SAINT-SAENS: *3 songs.* ***

Requiem, Op. 48 (1894 version); *Messe des pêcheurs de Villerville.*
*** HM Dig. HMC 90 1292 [id.]. Mellon, Kooy, Audoli, Petits Chanteurs de Saint-Louis, Paris Chapelle Royale Ch., Musique Oblique Ens., Herreweghe.

John Rutter's inspired reconstruction of Fauré's original 1893 score, using only lower strings and no woodwind, opened our ears to the extra freshness of the composer's first thoughts. Rutter's fine, bright recording includes the *Messe basse* and four motets, of which the *Ave Maria* setting and *Ave verum corpus* are particularly memorable. The recording is first rate but places the choir and instruments relatively close.

John Eliot Gardiner with period forces also chooses the version of the *Requiem* with the original instrumentation, using only the lower strings, plus a solo violin, and without woodwind. The darkness matches Gardiner's view of the work which, with expressive moulding and flexible rhythm and phrasing, he makes more dramatic than it often is. The mellow recording takes away some of the bite but, with excellent soloists – Catherine Bott radiantly beautiful in the *Pie Jesu*, Gilles Cachemaille vividly bringing out word-meaning – and a generous, unusual coupling, it makes an excellent choice. Fauré's atmospheric setting of Hugo's *Les Djinns* is specially welcome, with piano accompaniment on a gentle-toned Erard of 1874; and all the other pieces, including Fauré's enchanting *Madrigal*, are in various ways inspired by early French part-songs, with the medieval overtones brought out in the Debussy and with the humour of the Ravel nicely underlined.

Like Gardiner on Philips, Richard Marlow uses the Nectoux-Delage edition, but he gives the *Requiem* a more liturgical flavour, helped by a chapel acoustic, with an emphasis on fresh, young voices, soloists included. It is a strong, purposeful performance, warmly expressive. The disc can be strongly recommended to those who fancy the coupling of Messiaen's one motet and four of Duruflé, as well as the latter's superb *Messe Cum jubilo* of 1966 in its version with inspired organ accompaniment.

Matthew Best's performance with the Corydon Singers also uses the Rutter edition but presents a choral and orchestral sound that is more refined, set against a helpful church acoustic. *In paradisum* is ethereally beautiful. Best's soloists are even finer than Rutter's, and he too provides a generous fill-up in the *Messe basse* and other motets, though two fewer than Rutter.

The Naxos version makes an excellent bargain choice for the *Requiem* in its original orchestration. The fresh, forward choral tone goes with a direct, unmannered interpretation from Jeremy Summerly, with soloists comparably fresh-toned and English-sounding. The recording brings out the colourings of the orchestra in sharp detail, with the organ and brass vividly caught. The performance of the *Messe basse* is comparably direct, made to sound a little square at times, but *Le cantique de Jean Racine* is most winningly done. The little meditative organ piece by Vierne and the unaccompanied motet by de Severac are pleasing makeweights.

Philippe Herreweghe, unlike Rutter and Best, tends to adopt speeds that are a degree slower than those marked. His soloists are more sophisticated than their British rivals, tonally very beautiful but not quite so fresh in expression. The recording has chorus and orchestra relatively close, but there is a pleasant ambience round the sound.

Michel Legrand uses the full orchestral version of 1900 in the most dramatic way possible. In the *Sanctus* the cries of '*Hosanna in excelsis*' are immensely telling, yet the delicacy of the *In Paradisum* reflects an equally sympathetic response to the gentler, mystical side of the music. Barbara Bonney's *Pié Jesu* with its simplicity and innocence is very touching. Thomas Hampson makes an eloquent contribution to the *Libera me*, and after the climax the flowing choral line shows the subtle range of colour and dynamic commanded by the Ambrosian Singers (as well as the orchestra). With superb, spacious recording this performance is very compelling indeed, and it is aptly coupled with an equally fine account of the Duruflé work which was inspired by Fauré's masterpiece.

Richard Hickox also opts for the regular full-scale text of the *Requiem*, yet at speeds rather faster than usual – no faster than those marked – he presents a fresh, easily flowing view, rather akin to John Rutter's using the original chamber scoring on his Conifer issue. Aled Jones sings very sweetly in *Pié Jesu*. With its generous and equally successful coupling, this makes a strong alternative recommendation.

Not surprisingly, the acoustics of St Eustache, Montreal, are highly suitable for recording the regular full orchestral score of Fauré's *Requiem*, and the Decca sound is superb. Dutoit's is an essentially weighty reading, matched by the style of his fine soloists, yet the performance has both freshness and warmth and does not lack transparency. There are attractive bonuses.

The St John's account has a magic that works from the opening bars onwards. Jonathon Bond and Benjamin Luxon are highly sympathetic soloists and the 1975 (originally Argo) recording is every bit as impressive as its digital competitors, while the smaller scale of the conception is probably nearer to Fauré's original conception. The Double Decca reissue offers exceptionally generous couplings, not only the Duruflé *Requiem* but other fine music by both Duruflé and Poulenc.

Marriner in his 1993 recording for Philips returns to the fuller re-orchestration which has on disc been largely supplanted by Fauré's spare original. But where many larger forces encourage expansive speeds, Marriner's pacing is ideal, and the clean choral attack is matched by superb singing from Sylvia McNair and Thomas Allen. Though other versions convey even more magic, Marriner can be warmly recommended, particularly for those who fancy the instrumental pieces offered as coupling, including charming rarities by Koechlin and Schmitt.

The King's style is very much in the English cathedral tradition. On the earlier (1967) version, the solo soprano role is taken appealingly by a boy treble, Robert Chilcott. The recording, incidentally, was made in Trinity College Chapel and is very fine and splendidly remastered. The performance is eloquent and warmly moving, although some may feel its Anglican accents unidiomatic. The modest coupling is a melting version of the famous *Pavane*, with Gareth Morris playing the flute solo, given lovely, rich sound.

Ledger presents the *Requiem* on a small scale, with unusual restraint. Many will feel that this performance makes an excellent foil for the beautiful Duruflé coupling, as the digital recording allows many details of scoring to register that are normally hazed over. The singing is refreshingly direct, but anyone who warms to the touch of sensuousness in the work, its Gallic quality, may well find a degree of disappointment, though the *Sanctus* does not lack drama. This is less beautiful a performance than the earlier one, now also reissued, which was made with the same choir by Sir David Willcocks.

Fayrfax, Robert (1464–1521)

Antiphon: Tecum principium (plainsong); *Missa Tecum principium;* Motet: *Maria plena virtute;* Music for recorders: *Mese tenor; O lux beata trinitas; Parames tenor.*

(N) *** ASV Gaudeamus Dig. CDGAU 145 [id.]. Cardinall's Musick, Andrew Carwood; Frideswide Cons.

Andrew Carwood's first disc of Robert Fayrfax, issued last summer, promptly won the *Gramophone* Award for early vocal music, and this second in the series, flawlessly performed, brings comparably thrilling revelations of the most celebrated of early Tudor composers. Though the *Missa Tecum principium* is less complex than the brilliant Mass recorded before, the argument is not just more direct but even more extended, with the four big sections lasting almost 50 minutes. The final sublime *Agnus Dei* is followed by three tiny instrumental pieces played on recorders by the Frideswide Consort. An extended votive antiphon, *Maria plena virtute*, then rounds off the disc with the most moving music of all, a narrative on the Virgin Mary at the Cross, full of deeply personal responses immediately to involve the modern listener.

Ave Dei patris filia; Missa O quam glorifica; O quam glorifica (hymnus); Orbis factor (Kyrie). 3 secular songs: *Sumwat musyng; That was joy; To complayne me, alas.*
(Y/B) ✸ *** ASV/Gaudeamus Dig. CDGAU 142 [id.]. Cardinall's Musick, Andrew Carwood.

Cardinall's Musick, directed by Andrew Carwood, using editions specially prepared by David Skinner, here embark on another exciting voyage of discovery. As Skinner's notes explain, the Mass, *O quam glorifica,* is the most complex that Fayrfax ever wrote. Who would believe that a Mass written around 1500 would last, even with a chanted rather than a fully composed *Kyrie,* some 50 minutes, as here? The rhythmic complexities, too, are wonderfully fresh for the modern ear, with conflicting speeds often involving bold cross-rhythms, parading the composer's closely controlled freedom before bar-lines applied their tyranny. Above all, whatever the complexity, this is music immediately to involve one in its radiant beauty. The separate antiphon or motet, *Ave Dei patris filia,* is comparably adventurous and beautiful, and that church music is well supplemented by three secular part-songs for male voices. They even anticipate the Elizabethan madrigal, notably the third and most poignant, *To complayne me, alas.* As in Ludford, Carwood draws inspired performances from his singers, crisp and dramatic as well as beautifully blended, and most atmospherically recorded in the Fitzalan Chapel at Arundel Castle.

Feld, Jindřich (born 1925)

Flute sonata.
*** RCA Dig. 07863 57802 [7802-2-RC]. James Galway, Phillip Moll – DVORAK: *Sonatina;* MARTINU: *Sonata.* ***

Jindřich Feld writes in a relatively conservative idiom, only occasionally betraying a specifically Czech flavour. What matters is his understanding of the flute, when it prompts Galway to play with characteristic flair. The piece makes an unusual and attractive coupling to the Dvořák and Martinů works, all of them vividly recorded in a relatively dry acoustic.

Ferguson, Howard (born 1908)

(i) *Concerto for piano and string orchestra;* (ii) *Amore langueo, Op. 18.*
(M) *** EMI Dig. CDM7 64738-2 [id.]. (i) Howard Shelley; (ii) Martyn Hill, L. Symphony Ch.; City of L. Sinfonia, Hickox – FINZI: *Eclogue.* ***

Ferguson was a fine pianist in his younger days, and his concerto has something in common with the lyrical feeling of John Ireland's comparable work. As with Ireland, the finale is gay and melodically carefree. Howard Shelley's performance is admirable and Hickox secures highly sympathetic response from the City of London Sinfonia string section. *Amore langueo* is an extended cantata, lasting just over half an hour. To the medieval mind, spiritual and secular love were not always seen as separate experiences. The setting, for tenor solo and semi-chorus, with a strong contribution from Martyn Hill, brings a powerful response in the present performance, and Ferguson's music moves with remarkable ease from the depiction of Christ's suffering on the Cross to the sometimes even playful atmosphere of lovers in the bedchamber. An unusual and rewarding piece, recorded with great vividness on CD.

Overture for an occasion, Op. 16; Partita, Op. 5a; (i) *2 Ballads, Op. 1;* (ii) *The Dream of the Rood, Op. 19.*
(N) *** Chandos Dig. CHAN 9082 [id.]. (i) Rayner Cook; (ii) Dawson, London Symphony Ch.; LSO, Hickox.

It is sad that Ferguson gave up composing in 1959 at the age of fifty, after completing his superb choral work, *The Dream of the Rood.* His is one of the most rewarding voices among composers of his time, and this collection offers a splendid cross-section starting with his Opus 1 – which includes a striking setting of the *Lyke-Wake dirge,* written in 1928 long before Britten. The *Partita* of 1935–6 (also available in a two-piano version) is a compact, four-movement symphonic structure, surprisingly dark until the last movement, with a weirdly enigmatic second movement and a lamenting slow movement. The *Overture for an occasion,* written for the Queen's coronation, has the warmth and colour of comparable Walton works, and further echoes of Walton flavour the *Dream of the Rood,* a setting of an Anglo-Saxon poem with a radiant soprano solo introducing a sequence of richly atmospheric choruses. Hickox proves an ideal advocate, drawing incandescent singing and playing from his performers, with rich and clear Chandos sound to match.

Octet, Op. 4.

(N) (M) (***) Dutton Lab. CDAX 8014 [id.]. Juler, James, Dennis Brain, Merrett, Griller Qt – BAX: *Nonet;* MOERAN: *String trio;* DELIUS: *Violin sonata No. 3.* (***)

Now in his late eighties, Howard Ferguson has enjoyed something of a revival, thanks to smaller record producers such as Chandos and Hyperion. Dutton Laboratories are to be congratulated for restoring the 1943 Decca recording of his *Octet* by the Griller Quartet and the 22-year-old Dennis Brain in such fresh and present sound. This is civilized, finely crafted music in the received tradition, and none the worse for that.

(i) *Octet;* (ii; iii) *Violin sonata No. 2, Op. 10;* (iii) *5 Bagatelles.*
*** Hyperion Dig. CDA 66192 [id.]. (i) Nash Ens.; (ii) Levon Chilingirian; (iii) Clifford Benson – FINZI: *Elegy.* ***

Ferguson's *Octet* is written for the same instruments as Schubert's masterpiece, a delightful counterpart. The other works on the disc display the same gift of easy, warm communication, including the darker *Violin sonata* and Finzi's haunting *Elegy for violin and piano.*

(i) *Violin sonatas Nos. 1, Op. 2; 2, Op. 10;* (ii) *4 Short pieces;* (iii) *Three sketches, Op. 14;* (iv) *Discovery* (song-cycle), *Op. 13;* (v) *5 Irish folksongs, Op. 17;* (vi) *Love and reason;* (iv) *3 Mediaeval Carols, Op. 3.*
(N) *** Chandos Dig. CHAN 9316-2 [id.]. (i) Lydia Mordkovitch; (ii) Jane Hilton; (iii) David Butt; (iv) John Mark Ainsley; (v) Sally Burgess; (vi) Schneider-Waterberg; all with Clifford Benson.

This generous collection of Ferguson's chamber music, beautifully performed, provides a fine counterpart to Hickox's choral and orchestral disc. It is framed by the two *Violin sonatas* (1931 and 1946), both powerful works, with Lydia Mordkovitch a rich and persuasive interpreter. Clifford Benson is the lynchpin among the performers, contributing to all the works here. The *Four Short pieces* for clarinet and the *Three Sketches* for flute are delightful miniatures, as is the counter-tenor song, *Love and reason,* and the *Carols* and the *Discovery* cycle for tenor. Best of all is the colourful cycle of Irish folksongs for mezzo, vividly performed by Sally Burgess. Excellent, well-balanced sound.

(i) *Partita for 2 pianos, Op. 56. Piano sonata in F min., Op. 8.*
*** Hyperion CDA 66130 [id.]. Howard Shelley, (i) Hilary Macnamara.

Ferguson's *Sonata* is a dark, formidable piece in three substantial movements, here given a powerful and intense performance, a work which, for all its echoes of Rachmaninov, is quite individual. The *Partita* is a large-scale piece, full of good ideas, in which Howard Shelley is joined for this two-piano version by his wife, Hilary Macnamara. Excellent, committed performances and first-rate recording, vividly transferred to CD.

Ferranti, Marco Aurelio Zani de (1801–78)

Exercice, Op. 50/14; Fantaisie variée sur le romance d'Otello (Assisa à piè), Op. 7; 4 Mélodies nocturnes originales, Op. 41a/1–4; Nocturne sur la dernière pensée de Weber, Op. 40; Ronde des fées, Op. 2.
✹ *** Chandos Dig. CHAN 8512 [id.]. Simon Wynberg (guitar) – FERRER: *Collection.* ***

Simon Wynberg's playing fully enters the innocently compelling sound-world of this Bolognese composer; it is wholly spontaneous and has the most subtle control of light and shade. Ferranti's invention is most appealing, and this makes ideal music for late-evening reverie; moreover the guitar is most realistically recorded.

Ferrer, José (1835–1916)

Belle (Gavotte); La danse de naïades; L'étudiant de Salamanque (Tango); Vals.
*** Chandos Dig. CHAN 8512 [id.]. Simon Wynberg (guitar) – FERRANTI: *Collection.* *** ✹

José Ferrer is a less substantial figure than Ferranti, but these four vignettes are almost as winning as that composer's music. The recording has striking realism and presence.

Fesch, Willem de (1687–1761)

Concerti grossi, Op. 2/6; Op. 3/3–4; Op. 5/2; Op. 10/4–5; (i) *Violin concertos, Op. 2/2 & 5; Op. 3/6; Op. 5/5.*
(N) *** Olympia Dig. OCD 450 [id.]. (i) Gordon Nikolitch; O d'Auvergne, Arie van Beek.

This extremely rewarding first recorded collection will surely put the undeservedly neglected Dutch
baroque composer, Willem de Fesch, on the international musical map. His music is instantly appealing
and of high quality. De Fesch was born in Alkmaar, but his career took him to Amsterdam, Antwerp and
finally (in 1732) to London; his writing reflects influences absorbed from Italy and France, and also from
Handel, of whom he was an almost exact contemporary. His melodic inspiration in slow movements
often falls little short of that master, as in the wistfully lovely *Largo* of the *D major Violin concerto,* Op. 2/
6, or the *C minor,* Op. 5/5, a characteristic siciliano. He must have been a pretty impressive fiddler
himself, judging from the bravura demanded of the soloist in his violin concertos. The *Concerti grossi* are
first rate. Op.3/4 is very like a sinfonia concertante in the way de Fesch uses his solo group of two oboes
plus genial bassoon. The five-movement *G minor* work, Op. 5/2, features a pair of flutes with equal
felicity, its undoubted charm coming from delicate scoring and a melancholy atmosphere. In general,
allegros have simple yet refreshing contrapuntal vitality and, despite all the influences (including that of
Vivaldi in the solo concertos), De Fesch is very much his own man. The Orchestre d'Auvergne are an
excellent chamber group and Gordon Nikolitch an estimable soloist. Arie van Beek directs throughout
with spirit and nicely judged *espressivo.* Although modern instruments are used, the light textures and
resilient rhythms suggest a thorough knowledge of authentic practices, though melodic lines are merci-
fully unsqueezed. Excellent recording too. A strong recommendation for this pioneering CD.

Fetler, Paul (born 1920)

Contrasts for orchestra.
(M) *** Mercury 434 335-2 [id.]. Minneapolis SO, Dorati – AURIC: *Overture;* FRANCAIX: *Piano concertino;* MILHAUD: *Le bœuf sur le toit;* SATIE: *Parade.* ***

Paul Fetler's four-movement sinfonietta, *Contrasts,* is based on four notes (B flat, F, C, A flat) yet is as
impressive for its fine use of brass sonorities in the slow movement as for the neo-classical athleticism of
the opening *Allegro* and the pervading energy of the finale where everything comes together. It is an
eclectic work yet has distinct character. The performance is first rate, and so is the Mercury recording.

Fibich, Zdeněk (1850–1900)

Symphony No. 1 in F, Op. 17.
*** Chandos Dig. CHAN 9230 [id.]. Detroit SO, Neeme Järvi – SMETANA: *Má Vlast* (excerpts). ***

There is a strong Bohemian feel to this piece and though, like so much of Fibich's music, it is a little
square, such is the excellence of Neeme Järvi's performance that it doesn't feel so. This is its best
performance so far on record. The coupling, two Smetana tone-poems, is unlikely to influence a collector one way or the other. Hybrid programmes are not always satisfactory from the collector's viewpoint, but readers should not pass this by.

(i) *Symphonies Nos. 2 in E flat, Op. 38;* (ii) *3 in E min., Op. 53.*
**(*) Sup. 11 0657-2 [id.]. Brno State PO, (i) Waldhans; (ii) Bělohlávek.

Fibich's *Second Symphony* proceeds in a somewhat predictable way, yet the *Adagio* is undoubtedly
eloquent, and the Scherzo is stirring and colourful. The Brno orchestra under Jiří Waldhans give a
straightforward performance and the 1976 recording is clear, with plenty of body and a convincing
ambient effect. In the *Third Symphony* the invention is fresher than that of its predecessor, and the
Scherzo with its catchy syncopations has great charm. The performance, directed by Jiří Bělohlávek, is
sympathetic and alive.

Moods, impressions and reminiscences, Opp. 41, 44, 47 & 57; Studies of paintings, Op. 56.
**Unicorn-Kanchana Dig. DKPCD 9149 [id.]. Radoslav Kvapil.

These small vignettes are touching – they are a forerunner of Janáček's *Leaves from an overgrown path* –
and spring from a love affair he had towards the end of his life. They are played with great sensitivity
and subtlety by Radoslav Kvapil. The music deserves three stars and a Rosette – and so does the playing,
which has great sensitivity and artistry. But the recording is veiled and plummy and has no top – even
electrostatic speakers fail to reveal any transparency at the treble end of the spectrum. Even so, it is
worth while putting up with this for the sake of such haunting music and fine pianism.

Field, John (1782–1837)

Piano concertos Nos. 1 in E flat; 2 in A flat.
(Y/B) *** Chandos Dig. CHAN 9368 [id.]. Michëal O'Rourke, LMP, Bamert.

Michëal O'Rourke embarks on what appears to be a complete cycle of the Field concertos with hardly less success than with his first disc of solo piano music (see below). The music of the present pair of concertos is uneven, but the Scottish slow movement of No. 1 features the folk tune '*Within a mile of Edinburgh town*' rather winningly, while the characteristically ingenuous *Poco adagio* of No. 2 is followed by a *Moderato innocente* – another Field rondo with an engaging principal theme which becomes catchier as it is given more rhythmic treatment. Perhaps the movement is a shade over-extended, but the soloist is very persuasive, and he receives admirable support from Bamert and the London Mozart Players. First-class, naturally balanced recording. It is a pity that this fine record duplicates the *Second Concerto* (coupled with No. 3) on an equally recommendable Telarc CD by John O'Conor.

Piano concertos Nos. 2 in A flat; 3 in E flat.
⊛ *** Telarc Dig. CD 80370 [id.]. John O'Conor, SCO, Mackerras.

John O'Conor has recorded all the John Field concertos before with the New Irish Chamber Orchestra (Onyx CD 101/3) but these Telarc versions are distinctly superior. They are beautifully recorded and the warm, naturally balanced sound gives the music the elegance it needs. The first movement of No. 3 brings a nicely rhapsodical feeling and its *Andantino* (not a part of the original concerto) is one of the composer's daintiest *Nocturnes*, that in B flat, orchestrated to have a gentle string accompaniment. It is played with much grace and delicacy and is then followed by a Rondo, with a catchy, hopping main theme which is also one of Field's very best finales. O'Conor plays throughout with great distinction and always displays the lightest touch – his softly gleaming roulades are very fetching – and Mackerras accompanies with warmth and character. The recording has a somewhat resonant bass but the violins sing in an atmosphere of pleasing bloom.

Piano concertos Nos. 4 in E flat; 6 in C.
(N) *** Chandos Dig. CHAN 9442 [id.]. Michëal O'Rourke, LMP, Bamert.

O'Rourke continues his Chandos series with highly persuasive accounts of Nos. 4 and 6, with both works providing delightful slow movements. The *C major Concerto* is the more interesting of the two, giving the soloist some scintillating passage-work in the first movement and a lolloping Rondo finale. Excellent, sympathetic accompaniments and first-rate recording.

Air du bon roi Henri IV; 2 Album leaves in C min.; Andante inédit in E flat; Fantaisie sur un air russe, 'In the garden'; Fantaisie sur l'air de Martini; Irish dance: 'Go to the devil'; Marche triomphale; Nocturne in B flat; Nouvelle fantaisie in G; Polonaise en rondeau; Rondeau d'écossais; Rondo in A flat; Sehnsuchtswalzer; Variations in D min. on a Russian song, 'My dear bosom friend'; Variations in B flat on a Russian air: Kamarinskaya.
(Y/B) *** Chandos Dig. CHAN 9315 [id.]. Míceál O'Rourke.

Míceál O'Rourke is as sympathetic and sensitive an advocate of these rarities as one could wish for. He avoids any attempt to invest this music with more significance than it has, and presents this (nearly 80-minute) recital with intelligence and taste. Most of this repertory is not otherwise available, and much of it has the quiet charm one expects from this delightful composer. Whether it is in the *Andante inédit*, possibly Field's last composition, or the captivating *Sehnsuchtswalzer*, also published posthumously, Míceál O'Rourke proves a dedicated interpreter of real artistry. Recorded at The Maltings, Snape, he is admirably served by the Chandos team.

Nocturnes Nos. 1–16.
**(*) Athene ATH CD 1 [id.]. Joanna Leach (fortepiano).

Joanna Leach uses three 'square' fortepianos, by Stodart and Broadwood (both from the 1820s) and a D'Almain from a decade later. The latter instrument most closely approaches the quality of a modern piano, though the Broadwood is not far behind. Joanna Leach coaxes poetic sounds from these comparatively recalcitrant instruments and plays this repertoire very sensitively. However, it cannot be denied that for most ears this music (with its remarkable anticipations of Chopin) sounds even better on a modern concert grand.

Nocturnes 1, 2, 4–6, 8–16, 18.
*** Telarc Dig. CD-80199 [id.]. John O'Conor.

It would be difficult to better John O'Conor's sensitive and beautifully recorded accounts of his countryman's pioneering essays in the *Nocturnes*. He captures their character to perfection, and his tonal finesse is remarkable but never self-regarding. Strongly recommended.

Piano sonatas: Nos. 1 in E flat; 2 in A; 3 in C min., Op. 1/1–3; 4 in B.
**(*) Chandos Dig. CHAN 8787 [id.]. Míceál O'Rourke.

Míceál O'Rourke plays these two-movement *Sonatas* written by his countryman with some flair. He is particularly good in the famous *Rondo* finale of the *First Sonata*, which he plays with real Irish whimsy and sparkling touch. The *Allegretto scherzando* of No. 3 also has hit potential.

Finzi, Gerald (1901–56)

Cello concerto in A min., Op. 40.
*** Chandos Dig. CHAN 8471 [id.]. Wallfisch, R LPO, Handley – K. LEIGHTON: *Veris gratia.* ***

Finzi's *Cello concerto* is perhaps the most searching of all his works. Wallfisch finds all the dark eloquence of the central movement, and the performance overall has splendid impetus, with Handley providing the most sympathetic backing. The Chandos recording has an attractively natural balance.

Clarinet concerto, Op. 31.
*** Hyperion CDA 66001 [id.]. Thea King, Philh. O, Francis – STANFORD: *Concerto.* ***
*** ASV Dig. CDDCA 568 [id.]. MacDonald, N. Sinfonia, Bedford – COPLAND: *Concerto;* MOURANT: *Pied Piper.* ***

(i) *Clarinet concerto, Op. 31;* (ii) *5 Bagatelles for clarinet and piano.*
*** ASV CDDCA 787 [id.]. Emma Johnson; (i) RPO, Groves; (ii) Malcolm Martineau – STANFORD: *Clarinet concerto* etc. ***

There is no more delightful disc of British clarinet music than this, with Emma Johnson even more warmly expressive in the concertos than Thea King on her Hyperion disc, and with Sir Charles Groves and the RPO ideally sympathetic accompanists. Finzi's sinuous melodies for the solo instrument are made to sound as though the soloist is improvising them, and with extreme daring she uses the widest possible dynamic, ranging down to a whispered pianissimo that might be inaudible in a concert-hall.

On the Hyperion label, Thea King also gives a definitive performance, strong and clean-cut. Her characterful timbre, using little or no vibrato, is highly telling against a resonant orchestral backcloth. The accompaniment of the Philharmonia under Alun Francis is highly sympathetic. With Stanford's even rarer concerto, this makes a most attractive issue, and the sound is excellent.

The coupling of Finzi and Copland makes an unexpected but attractive mix, with the Canadian clarinettist, George MacDonald, giving a brilliant and thoughtful performance, particularly impressive in the spacious, melismatic writing of the slow movement. Refined recording, with the instruments set slightly at a distance.

(i) *Clarinet concerto;* (ii) *Introit for violin and orchestra.*
(Y/B) (B) ** BBC Radio Classics BBCRD 9119 [id.]. (i) Janet Hilton, BBC Northern SO, Bryden Thomson; (ii) Gerald Jarvis, LPO, Boult (with Concert). **(*)

The *Clarinet concerto* is well played, recorded in Milton Hall, Manchester, in 1978. Janet Hilton is the nimble soloist, with the performance of the lovely *Adagio* memorably intense. Though the quality is not as fresh or transparent as with such rivals as Thea King and Emma Johnson, and the transfer gives the solo instrument a flutter in the finale, the sound is otherwise acceptable. The virtually unknown *Introit for violin and orchestra* brings another memorable theme and is well worth having; it originally formed the middle movement of a larger work whose outer movements Finzi withdrew. It is a meditative, thoughtful work, very well played by Gerald Jarvis and the LPO under Sir Adrian Boult in 1969, even if the timbre of the solo violin as recorded could be sweeter. The recording does not have the transparency or dynamic range one would expect from a commercial recording of this period. However, this is part of a 77-minute concert of English music, including the *Harpsichord concertino* of Walter Leigh, which is well worth having at so modest a cost.

(i) *Clarinet concerto. Love's Labour's Lost: suite; Prelude for string orchestra; Romance for strings.*
*** Nimbus Dig. NI 5101 [id.]. (i) Alan Hacker; E. String O, Boughton.

Alan Hacker's reading of the *Concerto* is improvisatory in style and freely flexible in tempi, with the slow movement at once introspective and rhapsodic. The concert suite of incidental music for Shakespeare's *Love's Labour's Lost* is amiably atmospheric and pleasing in invention and in the colour of its scoring. The two string pieces are by no means slight and are played most expressively; the *Romance* is particularly eloquent in William Boughton's hands.

Eclogue for piano and string orchestra.
(M) *** EMI Dig. CDM7 64738-2 [id.]. Howard Shelley, City of L. Sinfonia, Hickox – FERGUSON: *Piano concerto No. 2* etc. ***
(N) (M) *** EMI Dig. CD-EMX 2239 [id.]. Piers Lane, RLPO, Handley – DELIUS: *Piano concerto;* VAUGHAN WILLIAMS: *Piano concerto.* ***

This is the central movement of an uncompleted piano concerto which the composer decided could stand on its own. It was Howard Ferguson who edited the final manuscript and set the title, and it is appropriate that this essentially valedictory piece should be coupled with his own concerto. The mood is tranquil yet haunting, and Shelley's performance brings out all its serene lyricism. The recording is admirably realistic.

Brief as it is, this concertante piece is a haunting work, a valuable makeweight for the Eminence coupling of the Delius and Vaughan Williams *Piano concertos.* Piers Lane gives it a tenderly sympathetic reading, even if this does not quite match in magic the Howard Shelley version on EMI.

Grand Fantasia and Toccata (for piano and orchestra), *Op. 38;* (ii) *Intimations of Immortality, Op. 29.*
(M) *** EMI Dig. CDM7 64720-2 [id.]. (i) Philip Fowke; (ii) Philip Langridge, RLPO Ch.; RLPO, Hickox.

Finzi's setting of Wordsworth, which is both eclectic and Elgarian in feeling, is delightfully spontaneous. His flamboyant presentation of *Now, while the birds thus sing a joyous song* – with its exuberant syncopations – even features a xylophone solo. The rich, lyrical cantilena of this music brings constant reminders of the Elgar of *Gerontius,* while the writing remains essentially within the pastoral tradition of English song-setting. The performance here is wholly committed, with the fervour of the chorus echoing the dedication of the soloist. The choral recording is both spacious and brilliant. The coupling is another fascinatingly eclectic piece, this time for piano and orchestra. The Bachian *Grand fantasia* is followed by a genial *Toccata,* fugal in style. The piece is played compellingly by Philip Fowke, and Hickox is a fine partner. Again vividly realistic sound. Highly recommended.

Elegy for violin and piano.
*** Hyperion Dig. CDA 66192 [id.]. Chilingirian, Benson – FERGUSON: *Octet* etc. ***

Finzi's moving little *Elegy for violin and piano* makes an apt fill-up for the record of chamber music by his friend, Howard Ferguson.

Dies natalis.
(N) (M) *** EMI CDM5 65588-2 [id.]. Wilfred Brown, ECO, Christopher Finzi – HOLST: *Choral fantasia; Psalm 86;* VAUGHAN WILLIAMS: *5 Mystical songs* etc. ***

Dies natalis is one of Finzi's most sensitive and deeply felt works, using meditative texts by the seventeenth-century writer, Thomas Traherne, on the theme of Christ's nativity. Finzi's profound response to the words inspires five intensely beautiful songs; only the central *Rapture,* subtitled *Danza,* provides vigorous contrast to the mood of contemplation. Finzi's setting is sung well here by Wilfred Brown. In a way, one may regard this as a preparation for Britten's later achievement in his orchestral song-cycles, and this record must be recommended to all interested in modern English song setting. The remastered recording sounds wonderfully fresh and is naturally balanced within a glowing acoustic. What a beautiful work this is!

Fiorillo, Federigo (1755–after 1823)

Violin concerto No. 1 in F.
*** Hyperion Dig. CDA 66210 [id.]. Oprean, European Community CO, Faerber – VIOTTI: *Violin concerto No. 13.* ***

Fiorillo's *Concerto* is charmingly romantic. Adelina Oprean's playing can only be described as quicksilver: her lightness of bow and firm, clean focus of timbre are most appealing. She is given a warm, polished accompaniment and the recording is eminently truthful and well balanced.

Flotow, Friedrich (1812–83)

Martha (complete).
(N) (M) *** RCA 74321 32231-2 (2) [id.]. Popp, Soffel, Jerusalem, Nimsgern, Ridderbusch, Bav. R. Ch. and O, Wallberg.

Martha is a charming opera, and the cast of this 1978 recording (originating with Eurodisc) is as near perfect as could be imagined. Lucia Popp is a splendid Lady Harriet, the voice rich and full yet riding the ensembles with jewelled accuracy. Doris Soffel is no less characterful as Nancy, and Siegfried Jerusalem is in his element as the hero, Lionel, singing ardently throughout. Siegmund Nimsgern is an excellent Lord Tristan, and Karl Ridderbusch matches his genial gusto. Wallberg's direction is marvellously spirited and the opera gathers pace as it proceeds. The Bavarian Radio Chorus sings with joyous precision and the orchestral playing sparkles. The first-class recording has been vividly tranferred, though there is a touch of edge on the voices of Lady Harriet and Nancy. The libretto promised on the back of the box is in German only, but the story of this opera is very easy to follow.

Floyd, Carlisle (born 1926)

Susannah (opera; complete).
(Y/B) *** Virgin/EMI Dig. VCD5 45039-2 (2) [id.]. Cheryl Studer, Samuel Ramey, Jerry Hadley, Lyon Op. Ch. & O, Kent Nagano.

This is an updating of the story of Susanna and the Elders in the Apocrypha, which readily adapts to the background of a traditional community in the Appalachian mountains. The hypocrisy of the Bible-thumping minister, Blitch, and of the elders of the church makes for an effective narrative-line, even if the dénouement goes over the top in melodrama. The idiom is tuneful and unashamedly tonal, influenced by American folk-music, just as atmospherically as in Copland (if far less distinctively). With echoes of Puccini on the one hand, of the American musical on the other, you might describe it as a cross between *Fanciulla del West* and *Carousel*. It is a pity that the musical invention is not more distinguished and that the words of the libretto are too often banal. The big dramatic climaxes quickly come to sound corny and a recording, even more than a live performance, makes one well aware of that. Most effective are the two big solos for the heroine, one in each of the compact Acts, both gloriously sung by Cheryl Studer, who as a native American sounds easily in character, taking to the idiom naturally. Samuel Ramey is similarly at home in this music, singing strongly with his richest tone, even if one can hardly believe in him as a vile hypocrite. With Jerry Hadley ideally cast as the tenor hero, Sam, Susannah's brother, who finally murders the predatory Blitch, the rest of the cast is first rate. The chorus and orchestra of the Lyon Opera are also inspired by their American conductor to give heartfelt, idiomatic performances. Excellent sound, as in previous Lyon Opera recordings with Nagano. It is surprising that an opera which has become such a favourite in America (even if it has so far failed to travel abroad) was not recorded earlier, but this set could not be more successful in filling the gap.

Foerster, Josef Bohuslav (1859–1951)

Symphony No. 4 in C min. (Easter), Op. 54; Springtime and desire, Op. 93.
(Y/B) *** Sup. Analogue/Dig. 111 822-2 [id.]. Prague SO, Smetáček.

Strange that this beautiful if overlong symphony has enjoyed such little exposure. Yet it is dignified and noble, and its Scherzo is infectiously memorable and could be as popular as any of the *Slavonic dances* if only it were known. Foerster was devout, and the symphony has a religious programme. The idiom is best described as being close to that of Josef Suk. Above all, Foerster has a feeling for architecture and there is a sweep to the first movement that is most impressive. The finale is the least successful of the four movements, and here attention flags. All the same, the symphony wears well and it is good to have it on CD, even if it would have been even better had we been given a new recording under, say, Bělohlávec. To this analogue recording Supraphon add a 1985 account, digitally recorded, of his *Springtime and desire*, a symphonic poem with a strong emphasis on the symphonic. Foerster has an inborn feeling for the natural growth of ideas and this, like the symphony, is a most welcome addition to the catalogue. Good performances, decent recording.

Forqueray, Antoine (1671–1745)

(i) *Pièces de viole;* (ii) *Pièces de clavecin.*
*** HM/BMG Dig. RD 77262 [77262-2]. (i) Jay Bernfeld; (ii) Skip Sempé.

Antoine Forqueray was a younger contemporary of Marin Marais and enjoyed a reputation as one of the greatest gamba players of his day. Skip Sempé's performances have all the expressive freedom and poetic feeling that the music calls for. The music has an intimacy and character that is beguiling, and Jay

Bernfeld's playing has a comparable instinctive artistry. Both players are well served by the engineers who do not attempt to make either instrument larger than life.

Foss, Lucas (born 1922)

American landscapes for guitar and orchestra.
(N) *** Virgin/EMI Dig. CDC5 55083-2 [id.]. Sharon Isbin, St Paul CO, Hugo Wolff – CORIGLIANO: *Troubadours* **(*); SCHWANTNER: *From afar.* **

Lucas Foss is a purveyor of real music, and so it is not surprising that this winning three-movement concertante evocation, written in 1989, has plenty of attractive invention and a vivid orchestral palette. Sharon Isbin had asked the composer for a work based on American folk and bluegrass music, and the haunting central variations on '*The wayfaring stranger*' are framed by a quirky *mélange* of folksy ideas. The whimsical finale dances along joyfully to tunes like '*Stay a little longer*' and '*Cotton-eyed Joe*'. The performance could hardly be more spontaneous and readily displays Sharon Isbin's virtuosity and range, although a great deal happens in the orchestra too (with violin and piano solos in the finale offering the guitar a little competition). The piece ends suddenly, immediately following the introduction of '*America the beautiful*'.

3 American pieces.
(Y/B) *** EMI Dig. CDC5 55360-2 [id.]. Perlman, Boston SO, Ozawa – BARBER: *Violin concerto;* BERNSTEIN: *Serenade.* ***

Foss's *Three American pieces* provide an attractive makeweight for Perlman's coupling of the two major works by Barber and Bernstein. As the title suggests, they have a strong element of Copland-like folksiness, married to sweet, easy lyricism and with some Stravinskian echoes. Skilfully orchestrated for a small orchestra with prominent piano, all three of the pieces, not just the final allegro, *Composer's holiday*, but the first two, *Early song* and *Dedication*, have a way of gravitating into hoe-down rhythms, often with a suddenness to remind one of the sharp contrasts in Bohemian *dumkas*.

Song of Songs.
(M) *** Sony SM2K 47533 [id.]. Jennie Tourel, NYPO, Bernstein – BLOCH: *Sacred service* ***; BEN-HAIM: *Sweet Psalmist of Israel.* **(*)

This highly imaginative cantata is an attractive mixture of Copland-flavoured sonorities and a wider folk influence, not unlike that found in Canteloube's *Songs of the Auvergne*. Jennie Tourel is a strong and compelling soloist, suitably histrionic, but her lyrical singing, especially in the final song which becomes more darkly intense as it unfolds, is memorable. Bernstein secures a bravura accompaniment from his New York players, strongly involved and at their peak in 1958. Like the coupled Bloch *Sacred service*, the remastered sound is surprisingly full and graphic.

Foulds, John (1880–1939)

Dynamic triptych for piano and orchestra.
*** Lyrita SRCD 211 [id.]. Howard Shelley, RPO, Handley – VAUGHAN WILLIAMS: *Piano concerto.* ***

John Foulds was working in Paris in the late 1920s when he wrote this ambitious concerto, and the profusion of memorable ideas, not always well disciplined, makes for an attractive piece, particularly so in the last of the three movements, *Dynamic rhythm*, with its extrovert references to Latin-American rhythms and the American musical. Played with dedication and beautifully recorded, it makes an interesting coupling for the masterly and underestimated Vaughan Williams *Piano concerto*. Howard Shelley and the RPO under Handley give a highly persuasive account of the *Triptych*, and the 1984 recording is well up to the usual high Lyrita standard.

String quartets Nos. 9 (Quartetto intimo), Op. 89; 10 (Quartetto geniale), Op. 97. Aquarelles, Op. 32.
⊛ *** Pearl SHECD 9564 [id.]. Endellion Qt.

The *Quartetto intimo*, written in 1931, is a powerful five-movement work in a distinctive idiom more advanced than that of Foulds' British contemporaries, with echoes of Scriabin and Bartók. Also on the disc is the one surviving movement of his tenth and last quartet, a dedicated hymn-like piece, as well as three slighter pieces which are earlier. Passionate performances and excellent recording, which is enhanced by the CD transfer. A uniquely valuable issue.

Françaix, Jean (born 1912)

Piano concertino.

(M) *** Mercury 434 335-2 [id.].Claude Françaix, LSO, Dorati – AURIC: *Overture;* FETLER: *Contrasts;*
MILHAUD: *Le bœuf sur le toit;* SATIE: *Parade.* ***

Claude Françaix, the composer's daughter and a pupil of Nadia Boulanger, partnered by Dorati made
the first recommendable stereo recording of this delectable, miniature, four-movement *Concertino* in
1965. The conductor's touch is deliciously light in the outer movements and the pianist's touch is neat
and accomplished. The Scherzo is also colourful but the gentle slow movement is the final test, and this
is taken a fraction too fast. However, the performance is undoubtedly successful overall, and the composer's delicate effects in the winsome finale are particularly successful when the Mercury sound-picture
is so lucid.

L'horloge de flore.

❀ (M) *** RCA GD 87989 [7989-2-RG]. John de Lancie, LSO, Previn (with SATIE: *Gymnopédies Nos.
1 & 3) –* IBERT: *Symphonie concertante;* R. STRAUSS: *Oboe concerto.* ***

*** Nimbus Dig. NI 5330 [id.]. John Anderson, Philh. O, Simon Wright – MARTINU; R. STRAUSS:
Concertos. ***

Inspired by the Linnaeus Flower Clock, *L'horloge de flore* is music of real memorability and much
charm. John de Lancie, the sponsor of the piece, plays delightfully, the accompaniment is a model of
felicity and good taste, and the recording is just about perfect. The Satie *Gymnopédies*, orchestrated by
Debussy, which follow as an encore, are played slowly and gravely and not ineffectively.

John Anderson's performance is hardly less enjoyable; the newer Nimbus recording is digital and has
each movement separately cued.

Violin sonatine.

(Y/B) *** EMI Dig. CDC7 54541-2 [id.]. Frank Peter Zimmermann, Alexander Lonquich – AURIC:
Sonate; MILHAUD: *Sonata No. 2;* POULENC: *Sonata;* SATIE: *Choses vues.* ***

Jean Françaix's engaging *Sonatine* for violin and piano of 1934 is a delight, and it is played with great
sparkle and Gallic charm by Zimmermann and Lonquich. Beautifully present and lively recording.

Wind quintets Nos. 1 & 2; (i) *L'heure du berger.*

(Y/B) *** Priory/MDG Dig. 603 0557-2 [id.]. Kammervereinigung Berlin; (i) Frank-Immo Zichner.

These Berliners put over Françaix's delightful *Wind quintets* with great charm and delicacy. These are
performances that radiate freshness and fun and, apart from the virtuosity of the performances, the
naturalness of the recording and the balance are a continuing source of delight. *L'heure du berger* is a
piano and wind sextet, but this is as good in its different way. Delicious playing and enchantingly light-
hearted music.

Franchomme, Auguste (1808–84)

(i) *Air auvergnat varié, Op. 26; Air russe varié No. 2; Grande valse: Morceau de concert* (all for cello and
strings); (ii) *Caprices, Op. 7/2, 4 & 7* (for 2 cellos); (iii) *Nocturne in A flat, Op. 15/2* (for cello and piano).
arr. of CHOPIN: *Nocturne in G, Op. 15/1 & Op. 37/1.* FRANCHOMME/CHOPIN: *Grand duo concertante on
themes from Robert le Diable* (for cello and piano).

*** Sony Dig. SK 53980 [id.]. Anner Bylsma, with (i) L'Archibudelli & Smithsonian Chamber Players;
(ii) Kenneth Slowik; (iii) Lamber Orkis (piano).

Auguste Franchomme was a Parisian cello virtuoso of great renown in his day, but he became even more
famous when, as a personal friend of Chopin, they collaborated in this rather jolly *Grand duo concertante.* His own variations are effective enough when using folk themes, though his melodic facility was
not really distinguished (as comparison of his own *Nocturne* with an arrangement of Chopin's readily
demonstrates). But Anner Bylsma is a superb advocate and the pieces for two cellos are made attractive
by his fine partnership with Kenneth Slowik. The back-up group for the amiable concertante pieces (of
which the *Air auvergnat* and – especially – the *Grande valse* are the most winning) enjoy themselves
playing splendid original instruments from the Smithsonian collection in Washington, DC. The result is
both authentic and entertaining, and the recording could hardly be bettered. It is very well balanced and
has vividness, warmth and transparency.

Franck, César (1822–90)

Le chasseur maudit; (i) *Les Djinns. Les Eolides; Rédemption.*
(N) (M) ** EMI CDM5 65153-2 [id.]. (i) Aldo Ciccolini; O Nat. de Belgique, André Cluytens.

When this collection was first issued on LP in 1963, we admired the performances but commented (in Volume IV of the *Stereo Record Guide*) that the reason why the programme overall is not a success is that 'the aesthetic which inspired the music is no longer acceptable and the music itself is not of sufficient interest to overcome its outdated philosophy'. We continued: 'Indeed *Rédemption*, which was originally the the orchestral centrepiece of an ambitious two-part choral work, was a failure at its first performance. *Les Eolides* has some imaginative orchestration and the closing pages of *Les Djinns* (for piano and orchestra) are effective simply because the rhetoric diminishes with the music's structural decrescendo. But the one inspiration here, our old friend *The accursed huntsman*, is worth all the rest put together.' While this dismissive statement may still be true in part (certainly there is no doubting the vitality of *Le chasseur maudit*), later recordings (by Barenboim, among others) have shown that *Rédemption* and certainly *Les Eolides* have been underrated, while Ashkenazy has made an excellent case for *Les Djinns.* Cluytens and the Belgian orchestra failed to find the *tendresse* of approach that can make much of this writing glow, and certainly here the opening of *Les Djinns* seems unnecessarily melodramatic, even though Ciccolini later finds an attractive affinity with the *Symphonic variations.* Moreover the rather dated, 1960s stereo, though not lacking fullness and atmosphere, is not kind to the Belgian violins, which sound a bit whiskery.

Le chasseur maudit (symphonic poem); *Rédemption (morceau symphonique);* (i) *Nocturne (O fraîche nuit).*
(M) *** DG 437 244-2 (2). (i) Christa Ludwig; O de Paris, Barenboim – BERLIOZ: *Roméo et Juliette.* ***

A most attractive coupling for a highly recommendable version of Berlioz's *Roméo et Juliette. Le chasseur maudit* is vividly exciting, with Franck's graphic portrayal of the accursed huntsman superbly energetic with its arresting horn calls. *Rédemption,* too, is highly convincing, again with the brass antiphonies most telling. In between comes an attractively simple but relatively brief nocturnal interlude from Christa Ludwig. Excellent mid-1970s recording, very well transferred to CD.

Symphonic variations for piano and orchestra.
⊛ (B) *** Decca 433 628-2 [id.]. Clifford Curzon, LPO, Sir Adrian Boult – GRIEG: *Concerto ***;* SCHUMANN: *Concerto.* **(*)
(Y/B) (M) *** Decca 425 082-2 [id.]. Curzon, LPO, Boult – BRAHMS: *Piano concerto No. 1;* LITOLFF: *Scherzo.* ***
(M) *** RCA 09026 61863-2 [id.]. Rubinstein; Symphony of the Air, Wallenstein (with PROKOFIEV: *Love for 3 oranges: March ***) –* FALLA: *Nights in the gardens of Spain* etc. SAINT-SAENS: *Concerto No. 2.* **(*)
(BB) **(*) ASV Dig. CDQS 6092. Osorio, RPO, Bátiz – RAVEL: *Left-hand concerto ***;* SAINT-SAENS: *Wedding-cake ***;* SCHUMANN: *Concerto.* **(*)
(Y/B) (BB) **(*) Naxos 8.550754 [id.]. Thiollier, Nat. SO of Ireland, Antonio de Almeida – FAURE: *Ballade;* D'INDY: *Symphonie sur un chant montagnard français.* **(*)

Clifford Curzon's 1959 recording of the Franck *Variations* has stood the test of time; even after three decades and more there is no finer version. It is an engagingly fresh reading, as notable for its impulse and rhythmic felicity as for its poetry. The vintage Decca recording is naturally balanced and has been transferred to CD without loss of bloom. The Grieg *Concerto* coupling is hardly less desirable, and there is also an alternative coupling with Brahms and Litolff.

Rubinstein's recording of the *Symphonic variations* was the first to appear in stereo, and it remains one of the finest available recorded performances of it. There is refinement and charm, yet his bravura tautens the structure while his warmth and freedom prevent it from seeming hard or in any way aggressive. The 1958 recording was made in the Manhattan Center, New York City, and a warm atmosphere in this work is far preferable to crystal clarity. The two solo encores are marvellously done, particularly the Prokofiev *March.*

The ASV super-bargain disc offers fine performances of four concertante works including a really outstanding version of the Ravel *Left-hand concerto* and it adds up to more than the sum of its parts. It can receive a strong recommendation, for reservations about the Franck performance are minor. It has both poetry and impulse and lacks only a little in sparkle at the very end. It is very well recorded.

Naxos's coupling is intelligent enough: none of these works is a concerto and all are written within a relatively brief time-span. But it would be idle to pretend that their anthology offers playing as distinguished as, say, Curzon. François-Joël Thiollier shows some imagination, and the orchestral playing is perfectly acceptable without being in any way distinguished. All the same, many will find it tempting at this price.

(i) *Symphonic variations for piano and orchestra;* (ii) *Symphony in D min.; Les Eolides;* (iii) *Violin sonata in A;* (iv) (Piano) *Prélude, choral et fugue;* (v) (Organ) *Cantabile in B; Choral No. 2; Pièce héroïque in B min.;* (vi) *Panis angelicus.*

(Y/B) (B) **(*) Ph. Duo 442 296-2 (2) [id.]. (i) Bucquet, Monte Carlo Op. O, Capolongo; (ii) Concg. O, Otterloo; (iii) Arthur Grumiaux, István Hajdu; (iv) Eduardo del Pueyo; (v) Pierre Cochereau (organ of Notre-Dame de Paris); (vi) José Carreras.

Although the performances are variable, this Philips Duo set is certainly worth its asking price. Its highlights are Otterloo's splendid (1964) account of the *Symphony* (plus *Les Eolides*) and the Grumiaux/Hajdu performance of the *Violin sonata.* Otterloo's reading of the *Symphony* has tremendous thrust and its romantic urgency is impossible to resist when the orchestral playing is so assured. *Les Eolides* is a welcome bonus. Grumiaux's account of the *Violin sonata* has both nobility and warmth, and if his partner is not quite his match this is still a memorable performance, most naturally recorded. Marie-Françoise Bucquet gives a perfectly satisfactory account of the *Symphonic variations,* and Carreras sings his heart out in *Panis angelicus.* But del Pueyo's piano contribution is a routine one and Cochereau's organ pieces are also unmemorable, not helped by wheezily unflattering sound.

Symphony in D min.

(N) (M) *** DG 449 720-2 [id.]. Berlin RSO, Maazel – MENDELSSOHN: *Symphony No. 5.* ***

*** Decca Dig. 430 278-2 [id.]. Montreal SO, Dutoit – D'INDY: *Symphonie sur un chant montagnard.* ***

(M) **(*) RCA GD 86805 [6805-2-RG]. Chicago SO, Monteux – D'INDY: *Symphonie sur un chant montagnard français* **(*) (with BERLIOZ: *Overture: Béatrice et Bénédict* ***).

(Y/B) (M) **(*) DG Dig. 445 512-2 [id.]. O Nat. de France, Bernstein – ROUSSEL: *Symphony No. 3.* **(*)

Symphony in D min.; Le chasseur maudit.

(Y/B) (M) **(*) EMI Eminence Dig. CD-EMX 2236; *TC-EMX 2236* [id.]. Phd. O, Riccardo Muti.

(i) *Symphony in D min.;* (iii) *Le chasseur maudit;* (iv) *Psyché: Psyché and Eros;* (ii; iii) *Symphonic variations for piano and orchestra.*

*** Chesky CD 87 [id.]. (i) London O, Boult; (ii) Earl Wild; (iii) RCA Victor SO, Freccia; (iv) RPO, Prêtre.

(i) *Symphony in D min.;* (ii) *Le chasseur maudit;* (iii) *Symphonic variations for piano and orchestra.*

(N) (BB) **(*) RCA Navigator 74321 29256-2. (i–ii) Boston SO, Munch; (iii) Leonard Pennario, Boston Pops O, Fiedler.

(M) **(*) EMI CDM7 64747-2 [id.].(i; iii) BPO, Karajan; (iii) with Alexis Weissenberg; (ii) Phd. O, Muti.

Symphony in D min.; Les Eolides.

**(*) Teldec/Warner Dig. 9031 74863-2 [id.]. NYPO, Masur.

(i) *Symphony in D min.;* (ii) *Pièce héroïque* (orch. Charles O'Connell).

✸ *** RCA 09026 61967-2 [id.]. (i) Chicago SO; (ii) San Francisco SO; Monteux (with (ii): D'INDY: *Istar* (***)).

(i) *Symphony in D min.;* (i; ii) *Symphonic variations for piano and orchestra;* (iii) *Prélude, choral et fugue.*

(B) *** Erato/Warner 4509 92871-2 [id.]. ORTF Nat. O, Martinon, (ii) with Philippe Entremont; (iii) Pascal Devoyon.

Monteux exerts a unique grip on this highly charged Romantic symphony, and his control of the continuous ebb and flow of tempo and tension is masterly, so that any weaknesses of structure in the outer movements are disguised. The splendid playing of the Chicago orchestra is ever responsive to the changes of mood, and the sound on GD 86805 is greatly improved.

However, the most recent remastering, by John Pfeifer for the Monteux Edition, brings a further improvement; indeed, now the quality reflects the acoustics of Chicago's Orchestra Hall in the same way as the Reiner recordings, with textures full-bodied and glowing without loss of detail. Vincent d'Indy's *Istar* (mono, from 1945) is a colourful and increasingly energetic piece. Although the mono sound is boxy, the strings have plenty of middle sonority, and the vivid performance is unlikely to be bettered. Those preferring a stereo version of d'Indy's *Symphonie cévenole* as coupling can rest assured that the earlier transfer of the Franck *Symphony* still sounds very well.

Maazel's account is beautifully shaped, both in its overall structure and in incidental details. However, though each phrase is sensitively moulded, there is no sense of self-conscious striving for beauty of effect. Maazel adopts a fairly brisk tempo in the slow movement, which, surprisingly enough, greatly enhances its poetry and dignity; his finale is also splendidly vital and succeeds in filtering out the excesses of grandiose sentiment and vulgarity which can disfigure this edifice. The work gains enormously from strong control and deliberate understatement, as well as from the refinement of tone and phrasing which mark this reading, for there is no lack of excitement. The recording, admirably well blended and balanced, is enhanced in this new CD transfer for DG's 'Legendary Recordings' series of 'Originals', and the coupling is aptly chosen, for Mendelssohn's *Reformation Symphony* was onother of this conductor's finest DG recordings.

Dutoit's account with the Montreal orchestra is very well proportioned, almost classical in its approach with the whole being the sum of its parts. It is magnificently played and recorded and though in terms of intensity and vision it would not dislodge Monteux, it provides a good choice for those who want a more up-to-date, near-state-of-the-art recording.

Martinon's 1969 reading of the *D minor Symphony* compares with Otterloo in the sheer gusto with which he presents the outer movements. The effect is gripping and exhilarating: there is no indulgence or hanging about, and the chromatic second subject of the first movement emerges with real fervour. The central *Allegretto*, too, is without idiosyncrasy but has genuine eloquence. Fine playing from the ORTF National Orchestra, with the brass not shirking their rumbustious moments. Philippe Entremont joins the orchestra for a fresh and exciting account of the *Symphonic variations*, also well recorded. For a bonus, Pascal Devoyon provides a fine version of the *Prélude, choral et fugue*, a work strangely poised between classic form and romantic expression, between the piano and the organ loft. Here it is heard on the piano and again is convincingly recorded.

Boult's manner after the rapt and dedicated account of the slow introduction is brisk, urgent and direct, with crisply pointed rhythms preventing any feeling of breathlessness and with all sentimentality and vulgarity completely removed. This is as compelling as Monteux's famous version, yet in Sir Adrian's hands much of this music might almost be by Elgar, with nobility one of the elements. The recording is bright, clean and well balanced. Fortunately Earl Wild's account of the *Symphonic variations* is memorable for its gentle lyricism and poetic feeling, while Freccia ensures a vigorously buoyant closing section. He also directs a thrilling account of *The accursed huntsman*. Prêtre's *Psyché and Eros* is idiomatic but nothing special as either a performance or recording. But no matter, this record is highly recommendable, even at full price.

Bernstein conducts a powerful, warmly expressive performance which, thanks in part to a live recording, carries conviction in its flexible spontaneity. It has its moments of vulgarity, but that is part of the work; the reservations are of less importance next to the glowing, positive qualities of the performance. The recording is vivid and opulent, but with the brass apt to sound strident.

Munch's 1957 performance of the *Symphony in D minor* was always among the finest ever recorded, but it suffered – as it still does – from the internal balance of the orchestra, which lets the trumpets (with a nasal edge to their tone) coarsen the texture of the loud moments. Otherwise the warm Boston acoustics are heard to good effect, although in the slow movement the harp is very forward. The finale begins with tremendous élan and the quotations from previous movements are not allowed to halt the onward flow of the music; it is this similar momentum in the first movement that allows the glorious second subject to emerge so swingingly. *Le chasseur maudit* (recorded five years later) also sounds spectacular: Franck's horn-calls come over arrestingly. The *Symphonic variations* are brilliantly played by Leonard Pennario, and if Fiedler's support is strong rather than subtle this is still enjoyable. Altogether this Navigator compilation is well worth its modest cost.

Karajan's tempi are all on the slow side, but his control of rhythm prevents any feeling of sluggishness or heaviness. There is always energy underlying the performance, and by facing the obvious problems squarely Karajan avoids the perils. The impact of the recording, now sounding more brightly lit but with textures still full and bold, is considerable; there is potent atmosphere and the finale has both amplitude and plenty of bite. Weissenberg's account of the *Symphonic variations* has less distinction, but the poetry of the lyrical sections is not missed and Karajan ensures that the orchestral contribution is a strong one. Muti's *Le chasseur maudit* is vividly dramatic and strongly presented, but there is a degree of glare on the otherwise brilliant digital recording.

Muti's is a strongly committed but unsentimental reading of the *Symphony*. The cor anglais solo in the *Allegretto* is most beautiful and the finale is particularly refreshing in its directness. The fill-up is welcome, a vividly dramatic symphonic poem, strongly presented, but this is not especially competitive, except for those seeking a digital master. The 1983 recording, robust and vivid, is certainly improved in its CD format, generally well integrated and among EMI's better Philadelphia records made in the 1980s.

Masur creates a sound-world with the New York Philharmonic which is totally different from that achieved by his predecessor, Zubin Mehta. The wind phrasing is sensitive, the brass blend more subtly and the strings produce a far more cultured sonority. Moreover the recording, too, is more sophisticated and without the brash, overlit quality we have noted in the past. The performances of both *Les Eolides* and the *Symphony* are very fine, sensitively shaped and with the architecture held together well. All the same, Masur's account of the *Symphony* does not generate quite the same excitement and blazing conviction that Monteux brought to it, and does not displace existing recommendations. Moreover at full price it offers rather less than good value with playing time of only 48 minutes.

CHAMBER MUSIC

Cello sonata in A (trans. of *Violin sonata*).
(M) **(*) EMI CDM7 63184-2. Du Pré, Barenboim – CHOPIN: *Sonata*. **(*)
**(*) CRD CRD 3391; *CRDC 4091* [id.]. Robert Cohen, Roger Vignoles (with DVORAK: *Rondo*) – GRIEG: *Cello sonata*. **(*)

Du Pré and Barenboim give a fine, mature, deeply expressive reading of a richly satisfying work. They are well balanced, but the effect of the music when transferred to the cello is inevitably mellower, less vibrant.

Cohen gives a firm and strong rendering of the Franck *Sonata* in its cello version, splendidly incisive and dashing in the second-movement *Allegro*, but the recording is more limited than one expects from CRD, a little shallow. The addition of the Dvořák *G minor Rondo*, Op. 94, makes a pleasing bonus.

Piano quintet in F min.
**(*) Nimbus Dig. NI 5114 [id.]. John Bingham, Medici Qt – FAURE: *String quartet*. *(*)
(M) **(*) Decca 421 153-2. Clifford Curzon, VPO Qt – DVORAK: *Quintet*. ***
(N) (***) Testament mono SBT 1077 [id.] Victor Aller, Hollywood Qt – SHOSTAKOVICH: *Piano quintet*. (***)

Ardent playing from the Medici and an especially imaginative contribution from their pianist, John Bingham. Artistically, this is very impressive, for the players seem more fully inside César Franck's world than they are in the Fauré coupling. In spite of somewhat excessive reverberance, there is much here that will give pleasure.

Not as seductive a performance on Decca as the glorious Dvořák coupling, partly because the sound, though basically full, has a touch of astringency on top; but Curzon and the VPO players are sensitive and firm at the same time. Curzon's playing is particularly fine.

Edward Sackville-West and Desmond Shawe-Taylor, the authors of *The Record Guide*, spoke of this four decades ago as a 'clean-limbed performance . . . the players' attack is extraordinarily vivid and the instrumental balance beautifully maintained'. It has lost none of its power (it dates from 1953) and even if there is no mistaking the mono sound as being of its time, the performance has such eloquence and power that the music leaps out of the speakers with a vibrant intensity. It comes coupled with a performance of the Shostakovich *Quintet* that is as commanding in its way as the Richter–Borodin account.

String quartet in D.
(Y/B) ** Koch Dig. 3-1053-2 [id.]. César Franck Ens.

With the Fitzwilliam account of the *String quartet* now withdrawn, the Koch version by the César Franck Ensemble becomes more attractive. The playing has no want of enthusiasm – nor, for that matter, does it lack finesse; but the quality of the recording may pose problems for some collectors. The quartet is placed fairly close to us, so that *pianissimo* markings do not register to full effect, and the acoustic has too much resonance. Still, there is more to admire in this issue than to cavil at, and it deserves its two stars.

Violin sonata in A.
⊛ (M) *** Decca 421 154-2. Kyung Wha Chung, Radu Lupu – DEBUSSY: *Sonatas;* RAVEL: *Introduction and allegro* etc. *** ⊛
(N) *** Decca Dig. 444 172-2 [id.]. Pierre Amoyal, Pascal Rogé – CHAUSSON: *Concert in D.* ***
(N) *** DG Dig. 445 880-2 [id.]. Dumay, Pires – DEBUSSY: *Violin sonata in G min.;* RAVEL: *Berceuse* etc. ***
(M) *** DG 431 469-2. Kaja Danczowska, Krystian Zimerman – SZYMANOWSKI: *Mythes* etc. *** ⊛
(M) *** Decca 433 695-2 [id.]. Itzhak Perlman, Vladimir Ashkenazy – BRAHMS: *Horn trio;* SAINT-SAENS: *Romance;* SCHUMANN: *Adagio and allegro*. ***
(M) **(*) Ph. 426 384-2. Arthur Grumiaux, György Sebok – FAURE: *Sonatas*. ***

Kyung Wha Chung and Radu Lupu give a glorious account, full of natural and not over-projected eloquence, and most beautifully recorded. The slow movement has marvellous repose and the other movements have a natural exuberance and sense of line that carry the listener with them. The 1977 recording is enhanced on CD and, with outstanding couplings, this record is in every sense a genuine bargain.

The Franck *Sonata* and the Chausson *Concert* make an attractive, generous and apt – if rare – coupling. Here it is made the more enticing by the warmly expressive, naturally idiomatic performances from French artists. It is remarkable what freedom over rhythm and tempo Amoyal and Rogé allow themselves without ever seeming undisciplined, so that the opening *Allegretto* even more than usual emerges as a dreamy meditation, a happy preparation for more serious argument later. With speeds in all four movements a degree broader than usual, this is a reading full of fantasy, giving the impression of music emerging spontaneously on the moment. The full and immediate recording helps.

The distinguished partnership of Augustin Dumay and Maria João Pires offers as assured and powerful an interpretation of Franck's indestructible *Sonata* as any now in the catalogue. They have a firm grip on line and combine both intellectual conviction and tenderness of feeling. The DG recording is more than acceptable, and readers wanting this particular coupling need not hold back. It is a pity that the opportunity was not taken to record the Ravel *Sonata*, for which there is room, which would have further enhanced the claims of this issue.

Kaja Danczowska's account of the Franck is distinguished by a fine sense of line and great sweetness of tone, and she is partnered superbly by Krystian Zimerman. Indeed, in terms of dramatic fire and strength of line, this version can hold its own alongside the finest, and it is perhaps marginally better-balanced than the Kyung Wha Chung and Radu Lupu recording.

With Perlman and Ashkenazy, the first movement catches the listener by the ears with the thrust of its forward impulse and the intensity of its lyrical flow. Yet there is no lack of flexibility and the sheer ardour of this interpretation makes it a genuine alternative to the Chung/Lupu account.

Grumiaux's account, if less fresh than Miss Chung's, has nobility and warmth to commend it. He is slightly let down by his partner, who is not as imaginative as Lupu in the more poetic moments, including the hushed opening bars.

ORGAN MUSIC

Andantino in E (arr. Vierne); *Cantabile; Chorales Nos. 2–3; Pièce héroïque; Prélude, fugue et variation, Op. 18.*
*** Chandos Dig. CHAN 8891 [id.]. Piet Kee (Cavaillé-Coll organ of Basilica de Santa Maria del Coro, San Sebastian).

The Dutch composer-organist Piet Kee omits the *Chorale No. 1*, for which room could surely have been found, as the playing-time is only 61 minutes 43 seconds, but, apart from this, there can be few grumbles about his record. His interpretations strike an excellent balance between expressive freedom and scholarly rectitude.

(i) *Chorales Nos. 1–3; Pastorale, Op. 19;* (ii) *Pièce héroïque;* (i) *Prélude, fugue et variation.*
(N) (M) *** Decca Dig. 444 568-2 [id.]. Peter Hurford (organs of (i) Basilica of Saint-Sernin, Toulouse; (ii) Royal Festival Hall).

Peter Hurford has a double advantage over Marcel Dupré on Mercury, in that he has exactly the right instrument, the Cavaillé-Coll organ at the Church of Saint-Sernin, Toulouse, and first-class 1983 Decca engineering. His are masterly performances of the three *Chorales* which Franck composed during the last years of his life: they are beautifully shaped and grandly paced. Moreover he also includes equally fine accounts of the *Pastorale* and the *Prélude, fugue et variation*, the third and fourth of the *Six Pièces*, written during the composer's early years at Sainte-Clotilde. The *Pièce héroïque* was recorded a year earlier on the organ at the Royal Festival Hall and sounds most spectacular. The organ's widely spread sound-sources add tellingly to the presentation and there is no doubt that, among modern digital recordings of this repertoire, this reissue (Volume II in Hurford's 'Organ masterpieces' series) leads the field.

Fantaisie in A; Pastorale.
*** Telarc Dig. CD 80096 [id.]. Michael Murray (organ of Symphony Hall, San Francisco) – JONGEN: *Symphonie concertante.* ***

Michael Murray plays these pieces very well, although the San Francisco organ is not tailor-made for them. The Telarc recording is well up to standard.

PIANO MUSIC

Prélude, choral et fugue.
*** Sony Dig. SK 47180 [id.]. Murray Perahia – LISZT: *Années de pèlerinage* etc. ***
(Y/B) (M) *** RCA 09026 62590-2 [id.]. Artur Rubinstein – BACH: *Chaconne* ***; LISZT: *Sonata.* **(*)

Murray Perahia's recording of the *Prélude, choral et fugue* is in a class of its own, carefully thought out yet apparently spontaneous and highly poetic.

In music like this, strangely poised between classical form and Romantic expression, between the piano and the organ-loft, Rubinstein is also very persuasive. This performance, recorded (like the Bach) in 1970, has fire and spontaneity. The piano-tone is firm and clear: its brightness suits the music.

Frankel, Benjamin (1916–71)

(i) *The Aftermath, Op. 17. Concertante lirico, Op. 27; 3 Sketches for strings, Op. 2; Solemn speech and discussion, Op. 11; Youth music, Op. 12.*
(Y/B) *** CPO Dig. 999 221-2 [id.]. (i) Robert Dan; Northwest CO, Seattle, Alun Francis.

All the works recorded here are for string orchestra and, with the exception of the *Concertante lirico*, all were composed before the *Violin concerto* of 1951, which was dedicated to the memory of the victims of the holocaust and which made so strong an impression at its première by Max Rostal. One of the strongest pieces here is *The Aftermath*, a song-cycle for tenor, strings and off-stage trumpet and timpani, to words of Robert Nichols. It is an evocative and imaginative piece. Frankel's craftsmanship is always of the highest order and his invention and imagination are more often impressive than not. This issue, like others in this series, is recommended to all with an interest in contemporary music that has real individuality and eschews trendiness like the plague. The notes are exceptionally helpful and informative.

Symphonies Nos. 1, Op. 33; 5, Op. 46; May Day overture, Op. 22.
*** CPO Dig. 999 240-2 [id.]. Queensland SO, Werner Andreas Albert.

Benjamin Frankel is one of the few composers of film music, like Rawsthorne or Walton, whose personality one can place before the credit titles reach his name. A master of the orchestra, as one knew from his earlier scores, the *First Symphony* (1959) leaves no doubt that he was also a master symphonist. It is a powerfully concentrated and finely argued piece which has a constant feeling of onward movement. The music develops organically; Frankel has something of the strength of Sibelius combined with a Mahlerian anguish, and his serialism, like that of Frank Martin, never undermines tonal principles. This symphony withstands much repetition and reveals more on each hearing. The *Fifth Symphony*, too, is a well-argued and impressive score. The Queensland orchestra play with dedication, and the performances of both symphonies and the inventive *May Day Overture* are very well recorded too. Frankel possessed a refined imagination and a completely natural musical facility and it is good news that all eight of his symphonies are to be recorded by this orchestra and their excellent conductor.

Symphonies Nos. 2, Op. 38 (1962); *3, Op. 40* (1964).
(Y/B) ✸ *** CPO Dig. 999 241-2 [id.]. Queensland SO, Werner Andreas Albert.

Like the *First*, his *Second Symphony* is a powerfully concentrated and finely argued piece which has a constant feeling of onward movement. While the *Second* springs from painful emotions, the *Third Symphony* with its almost Stravinskian opening is a compact one-movement work, predominantly positive in expression and compelling in its sense of purpose. Each symphony is prefaced by a paragraph or so of spoken introduction that the composer recorded at the time he conducted the first performance of these symphonies on the Third Programme. It is also supplemented by documentation and notes of exceptional quality. As was the case in the *First* and *Fifth Symphonies*, the playing of the Queensland Orchestra is excellent, and so, too, is the recording.

Frescobaldi, Girolamo (1583–1643)

Il Primo Libro di Toccate (1615–37): excerpts; *Il Secondo Libro di Toccate* (1637): excerpts.
*** O-L Dig. 436 197-2 (2) [id.]. Christopher Hogwood (harpsichord, virginal).

This pair of CDs covers about a third of the two books of *Toccatas* and *Partitas*, the first disc offering us two *Toccatas*, a set of variations on the *Follia* and various other pieces, while the second brings four *Toccatas* from the 1637 book and a number of other pieces, *Canzone, Gagliarde* and so on. Between them the two discs cover music suitable for the harpsichord or spinet from all periods of Frescobaldi's career, save only for the last years. Christopher Hogwood uses four instruments, all of which are reproduced pictorially in the accompanying booklet: three are from the last half of the seventeenth century, while there is an early Venetian spinet of 1540 for the *Aria detta balletto*. Frescobaldi's music is unfailingly interesting and its expressive freedom often takes the listener by surprise. Hogwood has both the artistic flair and the feeling for style to do it justice, and the clarity and presence of the recording are really beyond praise. But take care not to set the volume level too high.

Froberger, Johann (1616–67)

Canzon No. 2; Capriccio No. 10; Fantasia No. 4 sopra sollare; Lamentation faîte sur la mort très dou-loureuse de Sa Majesté Imperiale, Ferdinand le troisième; Ricercar No. 5; Suites Nos. 2 & 3; Suite No. 14: Lamentation sur ce que j'ay été volé. Toccatas Nos. 9, 10 & 114; Tombeau faict à Paris sur la mort de M. Blancrocher.
*** HM/BMG Dig. RD 77923 [7913-2-RC]. Gustav Leonhardt (harpsichord).

Froberger's music is highly exploratory in idiom and, in works such as the *Tombeau faict à Paris sur la mort de M. Blancrocher* and the *Plainte faite à Londres pour passer la Melancholie*, from the *Suite No. 3*, he reveals great expressive poignancy. There is space round the instrument and, heard at a low level-setting, this well-played recital produces very good results. Recommended with enthusiasm.

Fuchs, Robert (1847–1927)

Cello sonatas Nos. 1 in D min., Op. 29; 2 in E flat min., Op. 83; Phantasiestücke, Op. 78.
*** Marco Polo Dig. 8.223423 [id.]. Mark Drobinsky, Daniel Blumenthal.
*** Biddulph Dig. LAW005 [id.]. Nancy Green, Caroline Palmer.

The *First Sonata* was composed in 1881 for the celebrated Popper and, whatever the claims to the contrary, sounds very much like Brahms, who, incidentally, recommended it to the publisher, Simrock. The *Second* is much later (1908) and is, like the more Schumannesque *Phantasiestücke*, in the same conservative mould. It is well-fashioned, cultured and civilized music (no mean virtues) which may not have a strongly original profile but is well worth investigating for all that. After long neglect this music is available in two different versions. To be frank, there is not much to choose between them; both offer very good performances; both are very well recorded and deserve their three stars, so no agonies of choice are required: you can safely invest in one or the other.

Clarinet quintet, Op. 102.
*** Marco Polo Dig. 8.223282 [id.]. Rodenhäuser, Ens. Villa Musica – LACHNER: *Septet*. ***

This is beautifully crafted and speaks with the accents of Schubert and Brahms rather than with any strong individuality. It is nicely played by the Mainz-based Ensemble Villa Musica whose excellent clarinettist, Ulf Rodenhäuser, is worth a mention. A curiosity rather than a revelation then, but emi-nently well recorded.

Piano sonatas Nos. 1, Op. 19; 2, Op. 88.
*** Marco Polo Dig. 8.223377 [id.]. Daniel Blumenthal.

Robert Fuchs basked in the approval of Brahms, who called his music 'beautiful, skilful and attractive'. And so it is, particularly given such masterly and persuasive advocacy as it receives at the hands of Daniel Blumenthal. The early *F minor Sonata*, Op. 19, (1877) is indeed heavily indebted to Brahms, and the rondo finale with which it concludes seems heavily indebted to the latter's *Ballades*, Op. 10. All the same it has a certain breadth and lyrical fertility that impress. As its opus number indicates, the *Second Sonata*, Op. 88, is mature Fuchs, dating from 1910, which reflects the changed musical environment. Its invention is more chromatic and there are hints of Reger and even of Debussy and Fauré. Although Fuchs may lack a strong individual voice, he is a fine craftsman whose musical thinking has the merit of breadth and span.

Furtwängler, Wilhelm (1886–1954)

Symphony No. 2 in E min.
**(*) Marco Polo Dig. 8.2234436 [id.]. BBC SO, Alfred Walter.

Furtwängler regarded himself as primarily a composer and his conducting as a secondary pursuit. Although not quite as long as its predecessor in B minor, the *Second Symphony* (1944–5) still takes over

1¼ hours to perform. The invention itself does not possess strong individuality, and the shadow of Bruckner hangs heavily over the scene. However, there is a certain nobility and majesty that are at times rather imposing. Furtwängler himself spoke of it as his spiritual testament, and if you find it convincing it is worth noting that Alfred Walter has recorded the *First* with the Košice Orchestra (Marco Polo 8.223295) and *Third* with the Brussels Radio & Television Orchestra (Marco Polo 8.223105); the former takes 77 minutes 50 seconds! The BBC Symphony Orchestra respond to Alfred Walter's direction with warmth and, though the acoustic of the Maida Vale studios does not allow tutti to expand as they might, the recording is expertly balanced.

Fux, Johann (1660–1741)

Il Concentus musico instrumentalis (1701): Serenada a 8; Rondeau a 7; Sonata a 4.
(Y/B) (M) *** Teldec/Warner 4509 95989-2 (2) [id.]. VCM, Harnoncourt – SCHMELZER: *Sonatas*. **

Johann Fux was Kapellmeister to Emperor Charles VI at the Habsburg Court; until recently, the common view of him was as a dull academic. But the present collection suggests entirely the contrary. The *Serenada* consists of 17 (mostly brief) movements and is amazingly inventive. Scored for two clarinos (high trumpets), two oboes, bassoon, two violins, viola and basso continuo (but not horns), it is surely an early anticipation of Handel's *Water music* – a group of lively, contrasting dances: gigues, bourrées, rigadons, ciacona plus arias, which are very entertaining indeed. There is some highly original writing for the trumpets and a most beautiful Minuet. The other works are attractive too, and the performances show Harnoncourt at his finest, full of vitality, and his players convey their enjoyment. As usual with this Das Alte Werk series, the recording (1970) is first class. The drawback is that this 48-minute programme comes in harness with music by another Habsburg Kapellmeister, Johann Schmelzer, and his music is more uneven. It is a great pity that a shorter selection of Fux's music, including his string sonatas, was not used to fill out these discs, for the two CDs together play for only 96 minutes.

Il Concentus musico instrumentalis: Overtures (Suites) Nos. 2 in B flat; 4 in G min. Overtures (Suites) in B flat; D min.
(N) (M) *** Van. Dig. 99705 [id.]. Il Fondamento, Paul Dombrecht.

Fux wrote a great many overtures or suites which combine the French and Italian styles, of which the present four are lively and quite colourful examples. They have a good deal in common with similar works of Telemann, even if not nearly so skilfully scored. Il Fondamento, a period-instrument group under Paul Dombrecht, who have been less successful with the music of Abel, bring these works to life quite vividly. They are agreeably recorded; though the sound could ideally be more transparent. But the thickness of texture is partly caused by the doubling up in the scoring, with the wind playing in tutti with the strings. Perhaps this was an influence from Dresden, where tutti unisons were very fashionable.

Gabrieli, Andrea (1520–86)

Laudate Dominum.
(M) **(*) Decca 430 359-2. Magdalen College, Oxford, Ch., Wren O, Rose – G. GABRIELI: *Motets* **(*);
PERGOLESI: *Miserere II* *** (with BASSANO: *Ave Regina* **(*)).

This fine setting of *Laudate Dominum* for two five-part choirs is most stimulating. Also included is a splendid *Ave Regina* by Andrea's contemporary, Giovanni Bassano, which is laid out for three four-part choirs and brass in a similar polychoral style. Both are are well performed, if without strong individuality, and the recording is magnificently expansive.

Gabrieli, Giovanni (1557–1612)

Canzoni e Sonate: Canzon a 5; Canzon a 6; Canzon a 7; Canzon a 8; Sonata a 4; Sonata a 8; Sonata a 15. Sacrae symphoniae: 2 Canzoni septimi toni a 8; Canzon septimi e octavio toni a 12; Sonata octavi toni a 8; Sonata pian' e forte a 8.
(M) **(*) DG 437 073-2. London Cornett and Sackbutt Ens., Andrew Parrott.

Using authentic instruments, Andrew Parrott and the London Cornett and Sackbutt Ensemble present stylish performances of a well-chosen collection of Gabrieli's instrumental pieces, not as dramatic or incisive as some we have heard on modern brass instruments but beautifully recorded in spacious stereo and immaculately transferred to CD. Best known is the magnificent *Sonata pian' e forte*. However, this disc is not generous in content: 44 minutes.

Angelus ad pastores ait; Buccante in neomenia tuba; Canzon septimi toni à 8; Hodie Christus natus est; Hodie completi sunt; O Domine Jesu Christe; O magnum mysterium; Omnes gentes, plaudite manibus.

(N) (B) **(*) EMI forte CZS5 68631-2 (2). Cambridge University Musical Soc., Bach Ch., King's College Ch., Wilbraham Brass Soloists, Willcocks (with SCHEIDT: *In dulci jubilo* ***) – SCHUTZ: *Psalm 150* **(*); MONTEVERDI: *Vespers.* *(*)

Originally recorded in King's College Chapel, using quadraphonic sound, the CD transfer brings stereo which is notable for the opulent richness of brass and choral textures rather than inner clarity, yet is resonantly resplendent. There is an impressively wide dynamic range, as is shown by the serene motet, *O Domine Jesu Christe*. Added to the Gabrieli works is Scheidt's setting in eight parts of the famous *In dulci jubilo*, which is particularly successful. It is a pity that the principal Monteverdi coupling is not more recommendable.

Hodie Christus natus est; Plaudite; Virtute magna.

(M) **(*) Decca 430 359-2 [id.]. Magdalen College, Oxford, Ch., Gowman (organ), Wren O, Rose – A. GABRIELI: *Laudate Dominum* **(*); PERGOLESI: *Miserere II.* ***

The Christmas motet, *Hodie Christus natus est*, is justly the most celebrated; but the other pieces too are most beautiful, notably *Plaudite* for three separate choirs. The performances, though finely controlled, could be more positive and dramatic, but they are very well recorded.

Symphoniae sacrae II (1615): Buccinate in neomania (a 19); In ecclesiis (a 14); Jubilate Deo (a 10); Magnificat a 14; Magnificat a 17; Misericordia (a 12); Quem vidistis pastores (a 14); Suscipe a 12; Surrexit Christus (a 11).

*** O-L 436 860-2 [id.]. Taverner Ch., L. Cornett and Sackbutt Ens., Parrott.

As principal composer of ceremonial music at St Mark's, Venice, the younger Gabrieli had to write all kinds of appropriate church music, and this fine collection contains some of the pieces of his later years, when – relying on instrumentalists rather than choristers – he came to include elaborate accompaniments for cornetts and sackbutts. Here, for example, six sackbutts accompany the six-part setting of *Suscipe* with glowing results; after hearing modern brass instruments and without the benefits of the St Mark's acoustics, these more authentic instruments may seem on the gentle side, with Gabrielian panoply underplayed, but the singing and playing are most stylish, helped by first-rate 1977 recording, smoothly transferred to CD.

Gade, Niels (1817–90)

Symphony No. 1 in C min. (On Sjølund's fair plains), Op. 5; Overture, Echoes from Ossian, Op. 1; Hamlet Overture, Op. 37.

(N) *** Chandos Dig. CHAN 9422 [id.]. Danish Nat. RSO, Dmitri Kitaenko.

This performance of the *First Symphony* has an unaffected quality and an unforced eloquence that give much delight. The symphony is named after one of the folksongs which Gade's teacher, Andreas Peter Berggreen, had published two years earlier, though it includes references to several others as well. The two shorter works, *Hamlet* and the *Echoes from Ossian overture*, are also very well played. The latter (1992) recording has already appeared in harness with Gade's *Elverskud*. The recording, made in the fine concert hall of Danish Radio, is absolutely first rate, natural in perspective, with plenty of presence and detail. An excellent introduction to the composer and a first choice unless the coupling with the *Eighth* is preferred.

Symphonies Nos. 1 in C min. (On Sjøland's fair plains), Op. 5; 8 in B min., Op. 47.

*** BIS Dig. CD 339 [id.]. Stockholm Sinf., Järvi.

Gade's *First Symphony* is a charming piece. Thirty years separate it from his *Eighth* and last symphony, like the *First* much indebted to Mendelssohn. Despite this debt, there is still a sense of real mastery and a command of pace. The Stockholm Sinfonietta and Neeme Järvi give very fresh and lively performances, and the recording is natural and truthful.

Symphonies Nos. 2 in E, Op. 10; 7 in F, Op. 45.

**(*) BIS Dig. CD 355 [id.]. Stockholm Sinf., Järvi.

Schumann thought No. 2 'reminiscent of Denmark's beautiful beechwoods'. The debt to Mendelssohn is still enormous here, but it is very likeable, more spontaneous than the *Seventh*, though this work has a delightful Scherzo. Splendid playing from the Stockholm Sinfonietta under Järvi, and good recording too.

Symphonies Nos. 3 in A min., Op. 15; 4 in B flat, Op. 20.
*** BIS Dig. CD 338 [id.]. Stockholm Sinf., Järvi.

Gade's *Third* has great freshness and a seemingly effortless flow of ideas and pace, and a fine sense of musical proportion. No. 4 was more generally admired in Gade's lifetime, but its companion here is the more winning. It is beautifully played and recorded.

Symphonies Nos. 3 in A min., Op. 15; (i) *5 in D min., Op. 25.*
**(*) Dacapo Dig. DCCD 9004 [id.]. (i) Amalie Malling, Coll. Mus., Copenhagen, Schønwandt.

Michael Schønwandt's performances of these two Gade symphonies are most musical, and distinguished by sensitive phrasing and a fine feeling for line. In the *Fifth Symphony*, the piano is less closely observed than it is in the BIS recording. Amalie Malling is the more reticent player, too, and plays with taste and grace. However, the 1988 recording though perfectly acceptable is not as good or as fresh sounding as its BIS rival which is on balance to be preferred.

Symphonies Nos. (i) *5 in D min., Op. 25; 6 in G min., Op. 32.*
*** BIS Dig. CD 356 [id.]. Stockholm Sinf., Järvi; (i) with Roland Pöntinen.

The *Fifth Symphony* is a delightfully sunny piece which lifts one's spirits; its melodies are instantly memorable, and there is a lively concertante part for the piano, splendidly played by the young Roland Pöntinen. The *Sixth Symphony* is rather more thickly scored and more academic. The recording is very good and, given the charm of the *Fifth Symphony* and the persuasiveness of the performance, this coupling must be warmly recommended.

Allegro in A min., for string quartet; (i) *Andante and Allegro molto in F min., for string quintet. String quartet in F (Wilkommen und Abschied);* (ii) *Octet in F, Op. 17.*
(N) **(*) BIS Dig. CD545 [id.]. Kontra Qt, with (i–ii) Hans Nygaard; (ii) Anne Egendal, Per Lund Madsen, Sune Ranmo.

All this music is youthful. The *Allegro in A minor* for string quartet was written when Gade was nineteen and the *F minor quintet* (with two cellos) comes from the following year. The *'Wilkommen und Abschied' Quartet* was composed in 1840 and the *Octet in F*, Op. 17, in 1848 when Gade had succeeded Mendelssohn in Leipzig. The music has charm and freshness of invention. The influence of Mendelssohn had not become stultifying and, though Gade's work belongs to that tradition, it has a spontaneity – particularly the *F minor Quintet* — which is quite captivating. This is a useful supplement to the Kontra's recording of the three later *Quartets* discussed below, and in many ways it is to be preferred. The Kontra performance of the *Octet* is more persuasive than the Sony version discussed below. The excellent performances are well recorded, but there is a slightly strident edge in tutti passages which inhibits a full three-star recommendation.

Octet in F, Op. 17.
** Sony Dig. SK 48307 [id.]. L'Archibudelli, Smithsonian Chamber Players – MENDELSSOHN: *Octet.*
*(*)

Like so much of Gade's music, the *Octet*, composed in 1848, is heavily indebted to his mentor and champion, Mendelssohn. It is well played by the combined L'Archibudelli and Smithsonian ensembles and truthfully recorded, but it is hardly a compelling piece (it does not possess a fraction of the character or inspiration of Svendsen's essay in this genre).

String quartets Nos. 1 in F min., 2 in E min., 3 in D, Op. 63.
*** BIS Dig. CD 516 [id.]. Kontra Qt.

These are pleasing works of great facility and are worth hearing, particularly in such good performances and recordings as we are given here. However, the fact remains that they show too strong a gravitational pull of Mendelssohn. Nevertheless, in terms of invention and craftsmanship, they give a certain pleasure.

Comola, Op. 12.
(Y/B) ** Kontrapunkt Dig. 32180 [id.]. Dahl, Halling, Katagiri, Mannov, Canzone Ch., Sønderjylland SO, Frans Rasmussen.

Comola was Gade's first choral work. As always with Gade, the music is expertly crafted and the invention heavily indebted to Mendelssohn. There is a certain nobility and warmth about much of it, and one can understand why it enjoyed such popularity during his lifetime. All the same, inspiration flows less generously or naturally than in *Elverskud* or the *Fifth Symphony* for piano and orchestra. Like his Op. 1 *Overture*, the work draws on Ossian, and it receives a well-prepared and persuasive performance from both soloists and instrumentalists alike. The recording is decent rather than distinguished.

(i) *Efterklange af Ossian (Echoes from Ossian), Op. 1;* (ii) *Elverskud (The Elf-shot), Op. 30;* (iii) *5 Partsongs, Op. 13.*
*** Chandos Dig. CHAN 9075 [id.]. (ii) Johansson, Gjevang, Elming, Danish Nat. R. Ch.; (iii) Danish Nat. R. Chamber Ch., Parkman; (i; ii) Danish Nat. RSO, Kitaienko.

Elverskud, also translated as *The Elf-king's daughter* and *The Fairy spell*, was Gade's wedding present to his wife, Sophie; it is certainly a work of great charm and grace. It comes here with his very first opus, the *Ossian Overture*, which drew the composer to the attention of Mendelssohn, from whose pen the second group could easily have come. A further bonus is the delightful set of *Five Partsongs*, Op. 13, beautifully sung by the Danish Radio Chamber Choir; the fourth, *Autumn song*, is particularly memorable and haunting. Gade never escapes the embrace of Mendelssohn for long; if his world is urbane, well ordered and free from any hint of tragedy, *Elverskud*, like the *Fifth Symphony*, still gives unfailing pleasure, particularly in such a persuasive performance and excellent recording.

Korsfarerne (The Crusaders), Op. 50.
**(*) BIS Dig. CD 465 [id.]. Rorholm, Westi, Cold, Canzone Ch., Da Camera, Kor 72, Music Students' Chamber Ch., Aarhus SO, Frans Rasmussen.

Gade's *Korsfarerne* is in three sections, *In the desert*, *Armida* and *Towards Jerusalem*, and lasts the best part of an hour. The Danish forces assembled here do it proud, as do the BIS recording team, but the debt to Mendelssohn, say in the *Chorus of the Spirits of Darkness* which opens the second section, overwhelms any feeling of originality.

Galuppi, Baldassare (1706–85)

Motets: (i) *Arripe alpestri ad vallem;* (ii) *Confitebor tibi, Domine.*
⊛ *** Virgin/EMI Dig. VC5 45030-2 [id.]. (i) Gérard Lesne, (ii) with Véronique Gens, Peter Harvey; Il Seminario Musicale.

Galuppi was a very considerable figure in his time and undoubtedly had influence on C. P. E. Bach and Haydn. So it is not before time that we are made familiar with his music. The motet, *Confitebor tibi, Domine* (praising God for his munificence), is a masterly and very beautiful piece using three soloists with a skill in its overlapping part-writing worthy of Mozart. The flowing vocal lines of the duets and trios, with their touching melancholy and moving drama, are consistently involving. Gérard Lesne, the alto, comes into his own in the coupled solo cantata, *Arripe alpestri ad vallem* ('Stop, you people of the mountain tops, do not come down into the valley driving savage monsters towards me'), a metaphorical allusion to remorse for inescapable human sin. It is an extraordinary 18–minute declamation with two long arias framing a histrionic recitative ('Oh whither shall I flee') and ending with a highly individual setting of *Hallelujah*. The accompaniments from Il Seminario Musicale are refreshingly sensitive, alive and polished, and these players give splendid support to the singers while the recording has a natural presence and realism. Well worth seeking out.

Gardiner, Henry Balfour (1877–1950)

Humoresque; The joyful homecoming; Michaelchurch; Noel; 5 Pieces; Prelude; Salamanca; Shenandoah and other pieces (suite).
*** Continuum CCD 1049 [id.]. Peter Jacobs.

Balfour Gardiner was a musical contemporary of Cyril Scott, Roger Quilter and Percy Grainger. Like his musical friends he was at his finest in miniatures, and his writing has an attractive simplicity and innocence. Most of this music is slight, but its appeal is undeniable when it is presented with such authority and sympathy. It is very well recorded indeed. The source is analogue, but there is no background worth mentioning and the piano image is absolutely real, with a natural presence.

Gaubert, Philippe (1879–1941)

Music for flute and piano: *Sonatas Nos. 1–3; Sonatine. Ballade; Berceuse; 2 Esquisses; Fantaisie; Nocturne et allegro scherzando; Romance; Sicilienne; Suite; Sur l'eau.*
*** Chandos Dig. CHAN 8981/2 [id.]. Susan Milan, Ian Brown.

Gaubert had a genuine lyrical gift and his music has an elegance and allure that will captivate. He is eminently well served by Susan Milan and Ian Brown, and they are all well balanced by the Chandos engineers. Truthful sound; civilized and refreshing music, not to be taken all at one draught but full of delight. Edward Blakeman's notes are particularly informative and interesting and there are two charming illustrations.

Gay, John (1685–1732)

The Beggar's opera (arr. Pepusch and Austin).
(N) ✪ (BB) *** CfP Silver Double CDCFPSD 4778 (2). Morison, Cameron, M. Sinclair, Wallace, Brannigan, Pro Arte Ch. & O, Sargent.

The Beggar's Opera (arr. Bonynge and Gamley).
*** Decca Dig. 430 066-2 (2) [id.]. Te Kanawa, Sutherland, Morris, Dean, Mitchell, Hordern, Marks, Lansbury, Resnik, Rolfe Johnson, London Voices, Nat. PO, Bonynge.

The Beggar's Opera was the eighteenth-century equivalent of the modern American musical. It was first produced in 1728 and caused a sensation with audiences used to the stylized Italian opera favoured by Handel. Its impact produced a whole series of inferior ballad operas, culminating a century later in works like *Maritana* and *The Bohemian girl*, which are far removed from Gay's piece in spirit as well as in social content. This performance under Sargent is in every way first class, one of the finest things he did on record (comparable with his *Hiawatha's wedding feast* – alas, currently out of the catalogue – and the best of his Savoy operas). The soloists here could hardly be bettered, with Elsie Morison as Polly and Owen Brannigan a splendid Peachum; and the linking dialogue is spoken by actors to make the result most dramatic, with every word crystal clear. The chorus is no less effective, and the recording has a most appealing ambience. EMI chose *Let us take the road* for inclusion on their original stereo demonstration disc, and the sense of presence and atmosphere which it revealed is highly compelling throughout this highly successful 1995 remastering of a recording made at Abbey Road – astonishingly – as long ago as 1955.

The entertaining Decca digital version actually creates the atmosphere of a stage musical. The musical arrangements are free – including an unashamedly jazzy sequence in Act II, complete with saxophones – but the basic musical material is of vintage quality and responds readily to a modern treatment which is always sparkling and often imaginative. The casting is imaginative too. With Alfred Marks and Angela Lansbury as Mr and Mrs Peacham a touch of humour is assured; if James Morris is not an entirely convincing Macheath, he sings nicely, and Joan Sutherland makes a spirited Lucy. Kiri Te Kanawa as Polly undoubtedly steals the show, as well she should, for it is a peach of a part. She sings deliciously and her delivery of the dialogue is hardly less memorable. The whole show is done with gusto, and the digital recording is splendid, as spacious as it is clear.

Geminiani, Francesco (1687–1762)

Concerti grossi, Op. 2/1–6; Concerti grossi after Corelli, Op. 5/3 & 5.
*** Sony Dig. SK 48043 [id.]. Tafelmusik, Jeanne Lamon.

As with other recent recordings of the music of Geminiani, Tafelmusik's lively performances of the six concertos of Op. 2, using original instruments, show this composer as a more considerable and innovative figure than was once supposed. Although these works are essentially *concerti grossi*, the frequent dominance of the solo violin in the concertino points the way to the solo concertos of Vivaldi. Jeanne Lamon takes this solo role and directs the performances with plenty of vitality, and the recording produces clean, full, yet transparent textures. The recording is bright and immediately balanced within the warm acoustic of Notre Dame Convent in Waterdown, Ontario, Canada.

Concerti grossi, Op. 2/5–6; Op. 3/3; Op. 7/2; in G min. (after Corelli, *Op. 5/5*); *in D min.* (after Corelli, *Op. 5/12*); *Theme & variations (La Folia).*
(M) *** RCA Dig. GD 77010 [77010-2-RG]. La Petite Bande, Sigiswald Kuijken.

The quality of invention in the Geminiani concertos recorded here rises high above the routine. There is considerable expressive depth in some of the slow movements too. La Petite Bande is incomparably superior to many of the period-instrument ensembles. Those who are normally allergic to the vinegary offerings of some rivals will find this record a joy. It is beautifully recorded too, and makes an admirable and economical introduction to this underrated and genial composer.

6 Concerti grossi, Op. 3.
*** Novalis Dig. 150 083-2 [id.]. Bern Camerata, Thomas Füri.
**(*) Ph. Dig. 438 145-2 [id.]. I Musici.

This Novalis version of the Geminiani Op. 3 *Concertos* claims to be a first recording. Earlier recordings are of the 1733 edition, but between that time and the mid-1750s Geminiani made revisions, some quite extensive, to the six pieces; on this CD, Thomas Füri and the Bern Camerata make use of these later revisions. Their playing has the same merits of liveliness and sensitivity that have distinguished their earlier recordings of the late 1970s to early 1980s. They use modern instruments and play with a good, singing quality, consistent taste and expressive vitality. Moreover they receive eminently good recording from Novalis, well balanced and truthful.

I Musici offer a fine digital alternative, using the unrevised, 1733 edition and playing modern instruments convincingly enough, except that inevitably the harpsichord continuo is submerged under the fuller string textures. However, the playing has plenty of life and expressive warmth, and this music-making is easy to enjoy. Fairly short measure though for a 1994 issue (50 minutes).

12 Concerti grossi, Op. 5 (after Corelli).
(B) *** Ph. Duo 438 766-2 (2) [id.]. Michelucci, Gallozzi, Bennici, Centurione, I Musici.

The music on which Geminiani based his Op. 5 is drawn from the splendid *Sonatas for violin and continuo* of Corelli with the same opus number. Their skilful adaptation to *concerto grosso* form features a viola in the solo group as well as violins and cello. The basic musical material is unaltered in any harmonic or thematic sense, but textures are filled out and greater variety of colour is provided. The result is entirely successful. The music balances serenity and a noble expressive feeling in slow movements with vigorously spontaneous allegros. The performances by I Musici – at their very finest – are admirable in all respects, spirited and responsive, polished yet never bland. The recording is first class too, wide-ranging, full and clearly detailed. Highly recommended: if you enjoy Handel's Op. 6, this inexpensive reissue is not to be missed.

Concerti grossi: in D min. (*La Folia,* from CORELLI: *Sonata in D min., Op. 5/12*); *in G min., Op. 7/2; Trio sonatas Nos. 3 in F* (from *Op. 1/9*); *5 in A min.* (from *Op. 1/11*); *6 in D min.* (from *Op. 1/12*); *Violin sonatas: in E min., Op. 1/3; in A, Op. 4/12.*
*** Hyperion Dig. CDA 66264 [id.]. Purcell Band & Qt.

This record comes from Hyperion's '*La Folia*' series, though the only piece here using that celebrated theme is the arrangement Geminiani made of Corelli's *D minor Sonata.* Apart from the *G minor Concerto,* Op. 7, No. 2, the remainder of the disc is given over to chamber works. The Purcell Quartet play with dedication and spirit and convey their own enthusiasm for this admirably inventive music to the listener.

German, Edward (1862–1936)

The Conqueror: Berceuse. Gipsy suite. Henry VII: 3 Dances. Nell Gwyn: Overture & 3 Dances. Romeo and Juliet (incidental music): *Pavane; Nocturne; Pastorale. Merrie England: 4 Dances. Tom Jones: Waltz song.*
**(*) Marco Polo Dig. 8.223419 [id.]. Slovak RSO (Bratislava), Leaper.

The Edward German collection in Marco Polo's enterprising series of English light music is just a little disappointing. The Slovak Radio Orchestra play with their usual verve and Adrian Leaper is ever sympathetic. The opening *Overture* to *Nell Gwyn* introduces the folk tune, *Early one morning,* and ingeniously combines it later with German's own material. But in the series of numbers which follow, the 'Hey nonny nonny' English country-dance style becomes rhythmically rather repetitive. Moreover, it is a pity that the *Merrie England* excerpts could not have included vocalists – the *Minuet* delivers up the glorious 'With sword and buckler by my side' which cries out for a voice, as does *Sophia's waltz song* from *Tom Jones.* The most rewarding numbers are the *Berceuse* from *The Conquerer* and the three pieces written for the Forbes-Robertson production of *Romeo and Juliet* at the London Lyceum in 1895. All are charming and very nicely scored. Excellent recording.

Welsh rhapsody.
(B) *** CfP CD-CFP 4635; *TC-CFP 4635.* RSNO, Gibson – HARTY: *With the wild geese;* MACCUNN: *Land of mountain and flood;* SMYTH: *Wreckers overture.* ***

This collection, appropriately entitled 'Music of four countries', offers first-class sound from the late 1960s, extremely well transferred to CD and, with its interesting and rare couplings, makes a highly recommendable bargain. Edward German is content not to interfere with the traditional melodies he uses, relying on his orchestral skill to retain the listener's interest, and in this he is very successful. The closing pages, based on *Men of Harlech*, are prepared in a Tchaikovskian manner to provide a rousing conclusion. The CD transfer is very well managed, though the ear perceives a slight limitation in the upper range.

Merrie England (complete; without dialogue).
(N) (BB) (**) CfP Silver Double CDCFPSD 4796 (2). McAlpine, Bronhill, Glossop, M. Sinclair, Kern, Williams Singers, O, Michael Collins.

Although this recording dates from 1960, it cannot compare in stereo sophistication with EMI's *Beggar's Opera* of five years earlier. While all the present soloists came from Sadler's Wells, the production team was obviously drawn from EMI's popular department; the result, technically speaking, is a near disaster. All the solo voices are close-miked, usually in a most unflattering way, and too often they sound edgy, while the chorus is made artificially bright; the orchestra is lively enough, but the violins are thin. However, it must be said that Michael Collins directs the proceedings in an attractively spirited fashion. Taken as a whole, the score does not wear too well (much of it sounds like diluted Gilbert and Sullivan). But if the moments of coarseness in the libretto can be forgiven, there is much pleasing lyricism in German's music and one or two really outstanding tunes which will ensure that the score survives. Among the soloists Howell Glynne is splendid as King Neptune, and Monica Sinclair sings with her usual richness and makes *O peaceful England* more moving than usual. Patricia Kern's mezzo is firm and forward, while McAlpine as Sir Walter Raleigh sings with fine, ringing voice. The Rita Williams Singers are thoroughly professional even if just occasionally their style is suspect. However, another recording seems unlikely so this is acceptable, *faute de mieux*.

Gershwin, George (1898–1937)

An American in Paris.
(Y/B) **(*) Everest EVC 9003 [id.]. Pittsburgh SO, Steinberg – COPLAND: *Appalachian spring*; GOULD: *Spirituals*. ***

The recorded sound is rather dry and unexpansive, but otherwise vivid. Steinberg's performance is lively, idiomatic and convincing. The central blues tune is pleasingly sultry. Incidentally, the sleeve-note points out that the Parisian taxi horns that Gershwin took home with him to use in the orchestra and which Steinberg adopts now date the piece irretrievably, as horn-tooting is now forbidden in Paris by law.

An American in Paris; (i) Piano concerto in F; Rhapsody in blue.
(M) *** Carlton Dig. 30369 00072. (i) Gwenneth Pryor; LSO, Richard Williams.
(Y/B) (M) *** Ph. 442 395-2 [id.]. (i) Werner Haas; Monte Carlo Op. O, De Waart.

An American in Paris; (i) Piano concerto in F; Rhapsody in blue; Variations on 'I got rhythm'.
(Y/B) (BB) *** RCA Navigator 74321 17906-2. (i) Earl Wild; Boston Pops O, Arthur Fiedler.

From the opening glissando swirl on the clarinet, the performance of the *Rhapsody in blue* by Gwenneth Pryor and the LSO under Richard Williams tingles with adrenalin, and the other performances are comparable. In the *Concerto*, the combination of vitality and flair and an almost voluptuous response to the lyrical melodies is very involving. *An American in Paris*, briskly paced, moves forward in an exhilarating sweep, with the big blues tune vibrant and the closing section managed to perfection. The performances are helped by superb recording, made in the EMI No. 1 Studio; but it is the life and spontaneity of the music-making that enthral the listener throughout all three works.

The super-bargain CD on RCA's Navigator label is particularly generous (70 minutes) in including, besides the usual triptych, the *'I got rhythm' variations*, given plenty of rhythmic panache. Indeed these are essentially jazzy performances: Earl Wild's playing is full of energy and brio, and he inspires Arthur Fiedler to a similarly infectious response. In many ways these performances are as fine as any; if the *Rhapsody* has not the breadth of Bernstein's highly recommendable account (Sony SMK 47529), it is nearer the Paul Whiteman original and is rewarding in quite a different way. The outer movements of the *Concerto* are comparably volatile and the blues feeling of the slow movement is strong. At the end of *An American in Paris* Fiedler (like Steinberg) adds to the exuberance by bringing in a bevy of motor horns. The brightly remastered recording suits the music-making, though the resonant Boston acoustics at times prevent absolute sharpness of focus, but the current transfer gives a convincing overall sound-picture.

In Monte Carlo the *Concerto* is particularly successful; its lyrical moments have a quality of nostalgia which is very attractive. Werner Haas is a volatile and sympathetic soloist, and his rhythmic verve is refreshing. Edo de Waart's *An American in Paris* is not only buoyant but glamorous too – the big blues melody is highly seductive and, as with all the best accounts of this piece, the episodic nature of the writing is hidden. There is a cultured, European flavour to this music-making that does not detract from its vitality, and the jazz inflexions are not missed, with plenty of verve in the *Rhapsody*. Very good sound.

An American in Paris; (i) *Rhapsody in blue.*
(M) *** Sony SMK 47529 [id.]. NYPO, Bernstein; (i) Bernstein (piano) – BERNSTEIN: *Candide overture* etc. ***

Bernstein's 1958/9 CBS (now Sony) coupling was recorded when (at the beginning of his forties) he was at the peak of his creativity, with *West Side Story* only two years behind him. This record set the standard by which all subsequent pairings of *An American in Paris* and *Rhapsody in blue* came to be judged. It still sounds astonishingly well as a recording. Bernstein's approach is inspirational, exceptionally flexible but completely spontaneous. The performance of *An American in Paris* is vividly characterized, brash and episodic; an unashamedly American view, with the great blues tune marvellously timed and phrased as only a great American orchestra can do it.

An American in Paris (revised F. Cambell-Watson); (i) *Rhapsody in blue; Girl crazy*: excerpts (arr. Leroy Anderson); *Porgy and Bess* (suite, arr. R. R. Bennett & A. Courage).
*** Ph. Dig. 426 404-2 [id.]. (i) Misha Dichter; Boston Pops O, John Williams.

John Williams is just the man for a programme like this. His touch is light and *An American in Paris* is relaxed in a most appealing way – less 'symphonic' than usual. So is the *Rhapsody in blue*, yet Misha Dichter provides plenty of bravura. The selections from *Girl crazy* (with its two big hits, *Embraceable you*, and *I got rhythm*) is infectious, and each of the eight numbers from *Porgy and Bess* is given its full individual character, rather than being streamlined into an ongoing pot-pourri. The Boston sound is first class.

Broadway and film music: *A Damsel in distress:* suite, arr. McGlinn. *Stiff upper lip: Funhouse sequence.* Overtures: *Girl crazy; Of thee I sing; Oh, Kay!; Primrose; Tip-Toes.*
(N) (B) **(*) EMI forte Dig. CZS5 68589-2 (2). New Princess Theatre O, McGlinn – KERN: *Overtures* **; PORTER: *Overtures and film music.* ***

This inexpensive two-disc forte set makes a pretty good collection for those who enjoy authentic recreations of Broadway music composed by three of its greatest names. John McGlinn has recorded his selections using the original scores. The extended dance-sequence, *Stiff upper lip*, comes from a 1937 movie and has some good tunes. So has *Oh Kay!* (half a dozen) while *Girl crazy* offers the irresistible *I got rhythm*. Elsewhere the famous melodies are more thinly spread, but the marvellous playing of the New York pick-up orchestra (gorgeous saxes and brass) has splendid pep. The lively, close-miked sound gives an authentic theatre-pit brashness, with very bright violins, although the backgound ambience is warm enough.

Catfish Row (suite from *Porgy and Bess*).
*** Telarc Dig. CD 80086 [id.]. Tritt, Cincinnati Pops O, Kunzel – GROFE: *Grand Canyon suite.* ***

Catfish Row was arranged by the composer after the initial failure of his opera. It includes a brief piano solo, played with fine style by William Tritt in the highly sympathetic Telarc performance which is very well recorded.

(i) *Piano concerto in F; Rhapsody in blue. Cuban overture.*
(Y/B) (M) ** Mercury 434 341-2 [id.]. (i) Eugene List; Eastman-Rochester O, Howard Hanson (with SOUSA: *Stars and Stripes forever* **).

Quite highly regarded in its day, this is one Mercury reissue which sounds dated. The dry acoustics of the Eastman Theatre in Rochester are not flattering and the orchestral strings sound thin to today's ears. List and Hanson are both at home in this repertoire, but it is the scherzando element in the *Rhapsody* that one most remembers and, for the same reason, the finale of the *Concerto* is the most effective movement. The *Cuban overture* is probably the most successful piece here and *The Stars and Stripes forever* (credited to the Eastman Philharmonia) is robustly gutsy rather than particularly peppy.

Porgy and Bess: Symphonic picture (arr. Bennett).
(M) *** Decca 430 712-2 [id.]. Detroit SO, Dorati – GROFE: *Grand Canyon suite.* ***

Robert Russell Bennett's famous arrangement of Gershwin melodies has been recorded many times, but never more beautifully than on this Decca digital version from Detroit. The performance is totally memorable and the sound quite superb.

Rhapsody in blue (see also above, under *An American in Paris*).

(M) **(*) DG Dig. 439 528-2 [id.]. Bernstein with LAPO – BARBER: *Adagio for strings;* COPLAND: *Appalachian spring.* ***

In his last recording of this work for DG, Bernstein rather goes over the top with his jazzing of the solos in Gershwin. Such rhythmic freedom was clearly the result of a live rather than a studio performance. This does not match Bernstein's inspired 1959 analogue coupling for CBS.

Song arrangements for orchestra: *Bidin' my time; But not for me; Embraceable you; Fascinating rhythm; I got rhythm; Liza; Love is sweeping the country; Love walked in; The man I love; Oh, Lady be good; Someone to watch over me; 'S wonderful* (all arr. Ray Wright).

(M) **(*) Mercury 434 327-2 [id.]. O, Frederick Fennell – PORTER: *Song arrangements.* **(*)

This is reputed to be Fennell's favourite record, and he directs every one of these famous tunes with affectionate style and a sparkling rhythmic lift. Unusually for this label, the smooth (1961) Mercury sound is multi-miked, yet it has plenty of ambience as well as both a silky lustre and a natural clarity. The orchestral playing is fully worthy of the sophistication of the scoring, and Gershwin's songs with their ripe tunefulness respond more easily than Cole Porter's to presentation without the lyrics.

'The Piano rolls' Vol. 1: (i) *An American in Paris;* (ii) *Idle dreams; Kicking the clouds away; Novelette in fourths; On my mind the whole night long; Rhapsody in blue; Scandal walk; So am I; Swanee; Sweet and lowdown; That certain feeling; When you want 'em you can't get 'em, when you've got 'em you don't want 'em.*

(N) *** Nonesuch Dig. 7559 79287-2 [id.]. (i) Milne and Leith; (ii) composer.

This series, recorded by the composer between 1916 and 1926 using the Welte-Mignon and Duo-Art piano-roll systems, was reproduced through a 1911 pianola (operated by Artis Wodehouse) on a Yamaha Disklavier player-piano with computer links, and then recorded in digital stereo – with the umost realism. The result is as if Gershwin himself was playing in the studio. The four-handed arrangement of *An American in Paris*, attributed to Milne and Leith, dates from 1933. It seems, however, that Leith was one of Frank Milne's pseudonyms and that he was responsible for both parts. It is a marvellous 'orchestral' performance and matches the composer in its flamboyance and breadth of style. *Rhapsody in blue* is the composer's special arrangement which Michael Tilson Thomas used later for his recording with full orchestra by editing out Gershwin's transcription of the orchestral parts. But it sounds pretty good here, with the composer filling in. The sound is first class and admirably present.

'The Piano rolls' Vol. 2: FREY: *Havanola.* CONRAD/ROBINSON: *Singin' the blues.* GERSHWIN: *From now on.* AKST: *Jaz-o-mine.* SILVERS: *Just snap your fingers at care.* KERN: *Whip-poor-will.* GERSHWIN/ DONALDSON: *Rialto ripples.* PINKARD: *Waitin' for me.* WENDLING/WILLS: *Buzzin' the bee.* C. SCHON-BERG: *Darling.* BERLIN: *For your country and my country.* MORRIS: *Kangaroo hop.* MATTHEWS: *Pastime rag No. 3.* GARDNER: *Chinese blues.* SCHONBERGER: *Whispering.* GRANT: *Arrah go on I'm gonna go back to Oregon.*

(N) ** Nonesuch Dig. 7559 79370-2 [id.]. George Gershwin.

As can be seen, Volume II includes music by others, and few of these numbers even approach the quality of Gershwin's own output. But it is all played in good, lively style, although one senses that Gershwin was doing a professional job rather than acting as an enthusiastic advocate, and some pieces come off more appealingly than others. Frankly, much of this is cocktail bar music, although Chris Schonberg's *Darling* is a a rather effective exception. Again the recording cannot be faulted.

'The authentic George Gershwin' (Piano arrangements of songs)
Volume 1 (1918–25): *Come to the moon; Drifting along with the tide; Fascinatin' rhythm; The half of it, Dearie, blues; Hang on to me; I'd rather Charleston; I was so young; Kicking the clouds away; Limehouse nights; The man I love; Nobody but you; Oh Lady be good; So am I; Swanee; Tee-Oodle-Um-Bum-Bo. Piano concerto in F: slow movt. Rhapsody in blue.*

(N) (M) **(*) ASV Dig. CDWHL 2074 [id.]. Jack Gibbons.

Volume 2 (1925–30): *Clap yo' hands; Do, do, do; Embraceable you; He loves and she loves; I got rhythm* (2 versions); *Liza; Looking for a boy; Maybe; Meadow serenade; My one and only; Someone to watch over me; Sweet and low-down* (2 versions); *'S Wonderful; Funny face; That certain feeling; When do we dance? An American in Paris (overture); Strike up the band (overture); Irish waltz (Three-quarter blues); 3 Piano preludes.*

(N) (M) **(*) ASV Dig. CDWHL 2077 [id.]. Jack Gibbons.

Volume 3 (1931–37): *For you, for me, for evermore; Isn't it a pity; Jilted; Let's call the whole thing off; Our love is here to stay; They can't take that away from me. Cuban overture; Second rhapsody; Porgy and Bess: suite. Good morning, Brother: excerpts. Variations on 'I got rhythm'.*
(N) (M) **(*) ASV Dig. CDWHL 2082 [id.]. Jack Gibbons.

Volumes 1–3 (complete).
(N) (M) **(*) ASV Dig. CDWLS 328 (3) [id.].

Jack Gibbons has transcribed Gershwin's own piano transcriptions from the records and piano rolls made by the composer himself, and in certain cases from recorded radio programmes and film soundtracks. His playing is brightly idiomatic, fresh and spontaneous, and has received much praise for its closeness to the composer's own keyboard style. The modern digital recording adds to the appeal of this set. But the arrangements of the orchestral works (*An American in Paris*, for instance), the suite from *Porgy and Bess* and the solo piano versions of the *Rhapsody in blue*, the *Second Rhapsody* and the '*I got rhythm' variations* (drawn from the composer's four-handed versions) often sound rather prolix and are much less effective and enjoyable than the songs, although played with the same sense of style. There are also more impressive versions on disc of the three *Piano preludes*.

Gershwin Songbook (18 songs) complete; *Impromptu in two keys; Jazzbo Brown blues; Merry Andrew; 3 Preludes; Promenade; Rialto ripples; Three-quarter blues; 2 Waltzes in C* (arr. Chaplin). *Show tunes* (arr. Bennett): *Lady be good!: Little jazz bird. Oh Kay!: Someone to watch over me. Porgy and Bess: Oh Bess.*
(N) (M) **(*) Carlton IMP 30367 00372 [id.]. Richard Rodney Bennett

A generous and useful bargain anthology including all the key piano works and a *pot-pourri* of the hits in the *Gershwin Songbook* (the composer's transcriptions of 18 of his most popular numbers). Richard Rodney Bennett's own arrangements of key show tunes are effective and he plays the whole programme with lilting warmth and a genuine rhythmic understanding. Perhaps at times one thinks of the atmosphere of a piano bar, but that is no bad thing when the concert pieces are well understood, the *Three Preludes* standing out from the rest. Good, truthful recording. However, this inevetably is very much a second choice after Gershwin's own recordings on Elektra/Nonesuch.

Piano arrangements of songs: *Bidin' my time; But not for me; Clap yo' hands; Do, do, do; Embraceable you; Fascinating rhythm; A foggy day; Funny face; He loves and she loves; How long has this been going on; I got rhythm; I'll build a stairway to paradise; I've got a crush on you; Let's call the whole thing off; Liza; Love is here to stay; Love is sweeping the country; Love walked in; The man I love; Maybe; Mine; Of thee I sing; Oh, Lady be good; Somebody loves me; Someone to watch over me; Soon; Strike up the band; Swanee!; 'S Wonderful; That certain feeling; They can't take that away from me; Who cares;* Excerpts from: *An American in Paris;* Themes from *Concerto in F; Piano prelude No. 2; Rhapsody in blue*: excerpts.
(M) *** Van. 08.6002.71 [OVC 6002]. George Feyer (with Tommy Lucas, George Mell, Sy Salzberg, Edward Caccavate).

The American Hungarian émigré pianist, George Feyer, is unsurpassed in this repertory, playing all these tunes with a rhythmic lift and naturally lilting inflexions that make one almost forget that most of them also had lyrics! The rhythmic backing is first class and the 1974 recording very real. Offering some 64 minutes of marvellous melody, this CD is in a class of its own. An ideal disc to titillate the ear and senses on a late summer evening.

VOCAL MUSIC

'*Kiri sings Gershwin*': *Boy wanted; But not for me; By Strauss; Embraceable you; I got rhythm; Love is here to stay; Love walked in; Meadow serenade; The man I love; Nice work if you can get it; Somebody loves me; Someone to watch over me; Soon; Things are looking up. Porgy and Bess: Summertime.*
**(*) EMI Dig. CDC7 47454-2 [id.]; *EL 270574-4*. Kiri Te Kanawa, New Theatre O, McGlinn (with Chorus).

In Dame Kiri's gorgeously sung *Summertime* from *Porgy and Bess*, the distanced heavenly chorus creates the purest kitsch. But most of the numbers are done in an upbeat style. Dame Kiri is at her most relaxed and ideally there should be more variety of pacing: *The man I love* is thrown away at the chosen tempo. But for the most part the ear is seduced; however, the pop microphone techniques bring excessive sibilants on CD.

OPERA AND MUSICALS

Girl crazy (musical).

*** Elektra-Nonesuch/Warner Dig. 7559 79250-2. Judy Blazer, Lorna Luft, David Carroll, Eddie Korbich, O, John Mauceri.

Girl crazy with its hit numbers (*Embraceable you*, *I got rhythm* and *Bidin' my time*) is an escapist piece, typical of the early 1930s. The score has point and imagination from beginning to end. The casting is excellent. Judy Blazer takes the Ginger Rogers role of Kate, the post-girl, while Judy Garland's less well-known daughter, Lorna Luft, is delightful in the Ethel Merman part of the gambler's wife hired to sing in the saloon. David Carroll is the New Yorker hero, and Frank Gorshin takes the comic role of the cab-driver, Gieber Goldfarb. The whole score, 73 minutes long, is squeezed on to a single disc. The only serious reservation is that the recording is dry and brassy, aggressively so – but that could be counted typical of the period too.

Lady Be Good (musical).

*** Elektra Nonesuch/Warner Dig. 7559 79308-2; *7559 79308-4* [id.]. Teeter, Morrison, Alexander, Pizzarelli, Blier, Musto, Ch. & O, Stern.

This charming score, dating from 1924 (just after *Rhapsody in blue*), emerges as one of the composer's freshest. Such numbers as the title-song, as well as *Fascinatin' rhythm* and the witty *Half of it, dearie, blues*, are set against such duets as *Hang on to me* and *So am I*, directly reflecting the 1920s world that Sandy Wilson parodied so affectionately in *The Boy Friend*. *Lady Be Good* was the piece originally written for the brother-and-sister team of Fred and Adele Astaire, and the casting of the principals on the disc is first rate. These are not concert-singers but ones whose clearly projected voices are ideally suited to the repertory, including Lara Teeter and Ann Morrison in the Astaires' roles and Michael Maguire as the young millionaire whom the heroine finally marries. The score has been restored by Tommy Krasker, and an orchestra of first-rate sessions musicians is conducted by Eric Stern.

Let 'em Eat Cake; Of Thee I Sing (musicals).

*** Sony Dig. M2K 42522 (2) [id.]. Jack Gilford, Larry Kert, Maureen McGovern, Paige O'Hara, David Garrison, NY Choral Artists, St Luke's O, Tilson Thomas.

Of Thee I Sing and *Let 'em Eat Cake* are the two operettas that George Gershwin wrote in the early 1930s on a political theme, the one a sequel to the other. What the British listener will immediately register is the powerful underlying influence of Gilbert and Sullivan, not just in the plot – with Gilbertian situations exploited – but also in the music, with patter-songs and choral descants used in a very Sullivan-like manner. In every way these two very well-filled discs are a delight, offering warm and energetic performances by excellent artists under Michael Tilson Thomas. Both Larry Kert and Maureen McGovern as his wife make a strong partnership. With the recording on the dry side and well forward – very apt for a musical – the words are crystal clear.

Porgy and Bess (complete).

✿ *** EMI Dig. CDS7 49568-2 (3) [Ang. CDCC 49568]. Willard White, Cynthia Haymon, Harolyn Blackwell, Cynthia Clarey, Damon Evans, Glyndebourne Ch., LPO, Rattle.

Simon Rattle here conducts the same cast and orchestra as in the opera house, and the EMI engineers have done wonders in re-creating what was so powerful at Glyndebourne, establishing more clearly than ever the status of *Porgy* as grand opera, not a mere jumped-up musical or operetta. The impact of the performance is consistently heightened by the subtleties of timing that come from long experience of live performances. By comparison, Lorin Maazel's Decca version (414 559-2) sounds a degree too literal, and John DeMain's RCA set (RD 82109 [RCD3 2109]) is less subtle. More than their rivals, Rattle and the LPO capture Gershwin's rhythmic exuberance with the degree of freedom essential if jazz-based inspirations are to sound idiomatic. The chorus is the finest and most responsive of any on the three sets, and the bass line-up is the strongest. Willard White is superbly matched by the magnificent Jake of Bruce Hubbard and by the dark and resonant Crown of Gregg Baker. As Sportin' Life, Damon Evans gets nearer than any of his rivals to the original scat-song inspiration without ever short-changing on musical values. Cynthia Haymon as Bess is movingly convincing in conveying equivocal emotions, Harolyn Blackwell as Clara sensuously relishes Rattle's slow speed for *Summertime*, and Cynthia Clarey is an intense and characterful Serena. EMI's digital sound is exceptionally full and spacious.

Porgy and Bess: highlights.

*** EMI Dig. CDC7 54325-2 [id.]; *EL 754325-4* (from above recording, with White, Haymon; cond. Rattle).

(N) (BB) ** RCA Navigator 74321 24218-2 [5234-2RG]. Price, Warfield, Bubbles, Boatwright, Henson,

Webb, Burton, Alonzo Jones, Berneice Hall, Stewart, RCA Victor O, Skitch Henderson – BERN-
STEIN: *West Side Story: Symphonic dances*. **

Rattle's highlights disc is most generous (74 minutes) and most comprehensive. However, not all the
tailoring is clean: *Summertime* ends rather abruptly and there is at least one fade.

The RCA studio compilation was recorded in 1963. Both Price and Warfield sing magnificently, and the
supporting group is given lively direction by Skitch Henderson. The rest of the cast comes from the
opera house rather than the musical theatre, which underlined the claims of Gershwin's work to be
regarded as being in the mainstream of opera, some 25 years before this was confirmed by Rattle's
complete recording. (N.B.: In the USA this appears to be still available at mid-price without a
coupling.)

Strike up the Band (musical).
**(*) Nonesuch/Warner Dig. 7559 79273-2; *7559 79273-4* [id.]. Barrett, Luker, Chastain, Graae, Fowler,
    Goff, Lambert, Lyons, Sandish, Rocco, Ch. & O, Mauceri.

Strike up the Band was the nearest that George and Ira Gershwin ever came to imitating Gilbert and
Sullivan. The very subject is Gilbertian – a satirical story about the United States going to war with
Switzerland over the price of cheese. Quite apart from the two undoubted hits from the show, *The man I
love* and *Strike up the band*, there is a whole sequence of delightful numbers that it is good to have
revived in this first really complete recording. For all its vigour, the performance lacks something of the
exuberance which marks the recordings of musicals conducted by John McGlinn for EMI. It may be
correct to observe the dotted rhythms of *The man I love* as precisely as this performance does, but
something is lost in the flow of the music, and to latterday ears the result is less haunting than the
customary reading. The singers are first rate, but they would have been helped by having at least one of
their number with a more charismatic personality. The second disc includes an appendix containing
seven numbers used in the abortive 1930 revival.

Gesualdo, Carlo (*c.* 1561–1613)

Ave, dulcissima Maria; Ave, regina coelorum; Maria mater gratiae; Precibus et meritus beatae Mariae
(motets). *Tenebrae responsories for Holy Saturday*.
*** Gimell Dig. CDGIM 015; *1585-T-15* [id.]. Tallis Scholars, Peter Phillips.

The astonishing dissonances and chromaticisms may not be as extreme here as in some of Gesualdo's
secular music but, as elaborate as madrigals, they still have a sharp, refreshing impact on the modern ear
which recognizes music leaping the centuries. The Tallis Scholars give superb performances, finely
finished and beautifully blended, with women's voices made to sound boyish, singing with freshness and
bite to bring home the total originality of the writing with its awkward leaps and intervals. Beautifully
recorded, this is another of the Tallis Scholars' ear-catching discs, powerful as well as polished.

Leçons de Ténèbres: Responsories for Maundy Thursday.
(B) *** HM HMA 190220 [id.]. Deller Cons., Deller.

The Responses for Holy Week of 1611 are as remarkable and passionately expressive as any of
Gesualdo's madrigals, and in depth of feeling they should be compared only with the finest music of the
age. The invention is often unpredictable and nearly always highly original. The Deller Consort bring to
this music much the same approach that distinguishes their handling of the madrigal literature. The
colouring of the words is a high priority, yet it never oversteps the bounds of good taste to become
precious or over-expressive. The consort blends remarkably well and intonation is excellent. This is
temptingly inexpensive.

Motets for 5 voices (complete): *Ave dulcissima Maria; Ave Regina coelorum; Deus refugium et virtus;
Dignare me, laudare te; Domine ne despicias; Exaudit Deus deprecationem meam; Hei mihi, Domine;
Illumina faciem tuam; Laboravi in gemitu meo; Maria mater gratiae; O Crux benedicta; O vos omnes;
Peccanteum me quotidie; Precibus et meritus beatae Mariae; Reminiscere miserationum Tuarum; Sancti
Spiritus Domine; Tribularer si nescirem; Tribulationem meam; Venit lumen tuum Jerusalem.*
(BB) **(*) Naxos Dig. 8.550742 [id.]. Oxford Camerata, Jeremy Summerly.

The dozen singers of the Oxford Camerata sing these nineteen motets with beautifully blended tone and
thoughtfully moulded melodic lines. Tempi are spacious and, though not unvaried, at times perhaps
rather more movement would have been advantageous. Even so, *Ave dulcissima Maria* demonstrates
how well Jeremy Summerly understands Gesualdo's style, and the following, deeply felt *Domine ne
despicias* is another highlight of the programme. Similarly, the flowing *Sancti Spiritus Domine* and the

sustained *Hei mihi, Domine* heard together show well the expressive contrast of the writing. The recordings were made in the Chapel of Hertford College, Oxford, and the choral sound has great beauty, with a finely judged balance between atmosphere and clarity. Even without texts and translations this is a stimulating and rewarding disc, and excellent value.

Motets: *Ave, dulcissima Maria; Dolcissima mia vita; Ecco, morirò dunque; Hei mihi, Domine; Moro, lasso, al mio duolo; O vos omnes.*
(M) ** Decca 440 032-2 [id.]. Monteverdi Ch., John Eliot Gardiner – MONTEVERDI: *Madrigals.* **

John Eliot Gardiner, early in his recording career (1969), gives convincing and fluent performances of six Gesualdo pieces, music that is full of character even when it is not wholly convincing. The singers have excellent ensemble and intonation, though they tend to leave nothing to the listener's imagination. However, the (originally Argo) recording is particularly firm and realistic.

Getty, Gordon (20th century)

The White election (song-cycle).
*** Delos Dig. D/CD 3057 [id.]. Kaaren Erickson, Armen Guzelimian.

The simple, even primitive, yet deeply allusive poetry of Emily Dickinson is sensitively matched in the music of Gordon Getty. Here he tackles a sequence of 32 songs, building them into an extended cycle in four linked parts. Everything is aimed, in as simple a way as possible, at bringing out the meaning of the poems, which have been selected (as Getty puts it) 'to tell Emily's story in her own words'. He adds that 'The most salient features of Emily's life were taken to be the white election, with its theme of union in death, and her unsuspected poetic genius.' If at times the tinkly tunes seem to be an inadequate response to profound emotions, the total honesty of the writing disarms criticism, particularly in a performance as dedicated and sensitive as this, with Kaaren Erickson a highly expressive artist with a naturally beautiful voice. The pianist too is very responsive.

Gibbons, Christopher (1615–76)

Cupid and Death (with Matthew Locke).
(N) (B) *** DHM Baroque Esprit 0542 77428-2 [id.]. Kirkby, Tubb, Holden, Nichols, King, Cornwell, D. Thomas, Wistreich, Consort of Musicke, Rooley.

Cupid and Death, 'a masque in four entries', dates from 1653. Christopher Gibbons, the son of Orlando, seems to have been the lesser partner in the project, with Matthew Locke providing the bulk of the music for this rustic fantasy on an ancient fable. Each of the five 'entries' or Acts is formally laid out in a set sequence of items – a suite of dances, a dialogue, a song and a chorus – and Rooley's team consistently brings out the fresh charm of the music. The spoken sections have been edited out for this welcome reissue, and now the music fits neatly on to a single CD (71 minutes).

Gibbons, Orlando (1583–1625)

Fantasia in 2 Parts; 4 Fantasias in 3 parts; 3 Fantasias in 6 Parts; Go from my window in 6 parts. Galliard in 3 parts; 2 Fantasias in 3 parts; Fantasia in 4 parts (all 4 '*for the Great Dooble Bass*'); *In nomine in 4 parts; In nomine in 5 parts; Fantasia, Prelude and Ground* (for organ). (i) *The Cries of London:* Parts I & II.
(N) (M) **(*) Virgin/EMI Dig. VC5 45144-2 [id.]. Fretwork, with Paul Nicholson (organ); (i) with Red Byrd.

It is good to have comprehensive coverage of the instrumental music of Orlando Gibbons played by musicians who have a deep understanding of the period and idiom. This music is much less inspired than the comparable works of Purcell but is pleasingly inventive and often dolorous. Easily the most interesting items are the *Fantasias* (and *Galliard*) which feature – not too ostentatiously – 'the Great Dooble Bass' (in fact an oversized viol – pictured on the back of the excellent accompanying booklet). Its inclusion seemed to have inspired Gibbons to produce a sequence of his more attractive ideas. *Go from my window in 6 parts* is a set of divisions on a popular ballad which tends to outstay its welcome because of the lack of dynamic range in the music-making – a criticism which applies also to the simpler *Fantasias*. The viols are balanced closely and, with Paul Nicholson discreetly doubling the bass line on the organ, the homogeneity of tone emphasizes this limited range. Paul Nicholson provides variety with his organ solos, but the most memorably expressive pieces are the pair of *In nomine* settings, of which the piece in 5 parts is particularly appealing. In between come the two charming brief selections from the *Cries of London*, sung by the members of Red Byrd with a nice feeling for their popular declamatory style, yet with musical sophistication and good tuning.

Anthems & Verse anthems: *Almighty and everlasting God; Hosanna to the Son of David; Lift up your heads; O Thou the central orb; See, see the word is incarnate; This is the record of John. Canticles: Short service: Magnificat and Nunc dimittis. 2nd Service; Magnificat and Nunc dimittis. Hymnes & Songs of the church: Come kiss me with those lips of thine; Now shall the praises of the Lord be sung; A song of joy unto the Lord. Organ fantasia: Fantasia for double organ; Voluntary.*
*** ASV Gaudeamus CDGAU 123 [id.]. King's College Ch., L. Early Music Group, Ledger; John Butt.

This invaluable anthology was the first serious survey of Gibbons's music to appear on CD. It contains many of his greatest pieces. Not only are the performances touched with distinction, the recording too is in the highest flight and the analogue sound has been transferred to CD with complete naturalness. Strongly recommended.

(i) Anthems: *Almighty and everlasting God; Hosanna to the Son of David; O clap your hands together – God is gone up; O Lord, increase my faith; O Lord, in thy wrath rebuke me not;* (ii) *Introit: First Song of Moses; Second setting of Preces and Proper Psalm 145 for Whit Sunday; Second Service: Voluntary I & Te Deum; Voluntary II & Jubilate. Short Service: Voluntary I & Magnificat; Voluntary II & Nunc dimittis.* Verse anthems for voices and viols: *Glorious and powerful God; See, see, the word is incarnate; This is the record of John.*
(M) **(*) Decca mono/stereo 433 677-2. King's College, Cambridge, Ch., (i) with Boris Ord; Hugh McLean (organ); (ii) with Jacobean Consort of Viols, Willcocks; Simon Preston (organ).

Of the two groups of recordings, the first (mono) was made under Boris Ord in 1955; the second (stereo) came three years later directed by David Willcocks, but with Thurston Dart lending his influence and leading the consort of viols in the verse anthems (alongside Desmond Dupré). The mono recordings have plenty of ambience to disguise their lack of antiphony. But generally the effect is remarkably real, although the consort of viols is not always very well balanced. Juxtaposing the contents of two separate LPs means that there is plenty of variety and the later stereo collection is imaginatively chosen. Gibbons is a major musical personality and it was a happy idea in each case to preface the canticles from the two *Services* with an organ voluntary; it was customary in the early seventeenth century to have such a voluntary before the reading of the first Lesson.

Gilbert, Henry (1868–1928)

Suite for chamber orchestra.
*** Albany Dig. TROY 033-2 [id.]. V. American Music Ens., Hobart Earle – CHADWICK: *Serenade for strings.* ***

Henry Gilbert belonged to a time when almost all musical influences came from Europe and the American public did not value the output of its indigenous composers. This *Suite*, which harmonically is innocuous but which has an agreeable nostalgic languor, has something in common with Delius's *Florida suite*, although Gilbert's invention is less indelible. An excellent performance here from members of the Vienna Symphony Orchestra, who are completely at home in the music, as well they might be. The recording is excellent.

Gilles, Jean (1668–1705)

Messe des morts (Requiem Mass).
(M) *** DG 437 087-2. Rodde, Nirouët, Hill, U. Studer, Kooy, Ghent Coll. Voc., Col. Mus. Ant., Herreweghe (with CORRETTE: *Carillon des morts ***).

Like his English contemporary, Purcell, the Provençal Jean Gilles died sadly young. His *Requiem*, which for many years was a favourite work in France, was rejected by the two families who originally commissioned it, so Gilles decreed that it should be used for his own funeral. So great was regional pride in eighteenth-century Provence that the work was often heard alongside the *Requiem* of Campra with alternating movements from each! Gilles's rhythmic and harmonic vigour (with plentiful false relations to add tang) is well caught in this performance on original instruments, and the singers find the music's expressive style admirably. The *Carillon* was included by Michel Corrette in his own edition of the Gilles *Requiem*, printed in 1764, and is appropriately included here as a postlude.

Gilson, Paul (1865–1942)

De Zee (suite).
(Y/B) (B) *** Discover Dig. DICD 920126 [id.]. Brussels BRT PO, Karl Anton Rickenbacher – DE
    BOECK: *Symphony in G.* ***

Like August de Boeck, also represented on this disc, Paul Gilson was a Belgian composer, born in 1865.
His suite, *De Zee*, like de Boeck's *Symphony* is full of Russian echoes. It is a series of four seascapes half-
way between Wagner's *Flying Dutchman* and Debussy's *La Mer*, with Rimsky-Korsakov's *Scheherazade*
mixed in. Well played and recorded and, at Discover International's bargain price, an ideal disc for
experimenting with.

Ginastera, Alberto (1916–83)

Harp concerto, Op. 25.
*** Chandos Dig. CHAN 9094 [id.]. Rachel Masters, City of L. Sinfonia, Hickox – GLIERE: *Concertos*.
    ***

Ginastera's 1956 *Harp concerto*, written for Nicanor Zabaleta, who also recorded it, is one of his most
attractive and frequently heard works. It is full of vivid colours and snappy, incisive rhythms and has a
highly atmospheric slow movement. All its kaleidoscopic moods are keenly projected by Rachel Masters
in this refreshing and invigorating performance. Alert playing, too, from the City of London Sinfonia
under Richard Hickox. Strongly recommended, as are the two Glière concertos with which it is coupled.

(i) *Harp concerto, Op. 25;* (ii) *Piano concerto No. 1; Estancia* (ballet suite), *Op. 89.*
*** ASV Dig. CDDCA 654 [id.]. (i) Nancy Allen; (ii) Oscar Tarrago; Mexico City PO, Bátiz.

The *Harp concerto* is brought fully to life here by Nancy Allen and the Mexican orchestra. *Estancia* is a
comparably vivid piece of Coplandesque machismo, its character also very successfully realized. The
First Piano concerto is mildly serial but far from unattractive – and very brilliantly (and sensitively)
played by Oscar Tarrago. An excellent introduction to this composer.

Estancia (ballet suite); *Panambi* (choreographic legend).
(Y/B) *** Everest EVC 9007 [id.]. LSO, Sir Eugene Goossens – ANTILL: *Corroboree*; VILLA-LOBOS:
    Little train of the Caipira. **(*)

These vivid recordings of the music of Ginastera are a highlight of an anthology conducted with verve
and commitment by a conductor who championed much music at the edge of the repertoire. Both these
brightly hued scores bring a high standard of invention. *Panambi* is the earlier – written when the
composer was only twenty. It opens with a haunting picture of *Moonlight on the Panama* and the
Lament of the Maidens is gently touching, while the *Invocations of the Powerful Spirits* and *Dance of the
Warriors* are powerfully primitive. *Estancia* dates from a slightly later period. Again the scoring is exotic
and impressive, and the lively dances are full of primeval energy, notably the closing *Malambo*, while the
lovely *Wheat dance* brings another nostalgic interlude. The performances are in every way first class and
the atmospheric recording brilliantly captures the composer's imaginatively varied sound-world.

(i) *Cello sonata, Op. 49. Danzas argentinas, Op. 2; Estancia, Op. 8:* (i) *Pampeana No. 2, Op. 21* (rhapsody
for cello and piano). *Pequeña danza; Piano sonata No. 1, Op. 22; 5 Canciones populares argentinas:* (i)
Triste. (arr. Fournier)
*** ASV Dig. CDDCA 865 [id.]. Alberto Portugheis, (i) with Aurora Natola-Ginastera.

The four-movement *Cello sonata*, ardently rhapsodic, chimerical and full of atmosphere, is dedicated to
Ginastera's wife, who is the soloist here, while *Pampeana* is a rhapsody which has an Argentinian flavour
without using folk melodies. The *Piano sonata No. 1* (1952) is a powerful, integrated piece with a
desolate *Adagio* and a brilliant, rhythmically chimerical folk-dance finale. Alberto Portugheis is thoroughly at home in this repertoire and plays compellingly throughout. He is well recorded.

*Canciones, Op. 3: Milonga. Malambo, Op. 7; 3 Piezas, Op. 6; Piezas infantiles; Rondo sobre temas
infantiles argentinos, Op. 19; Sonatas Nos. 1, Op. 53; 3, Op. 58; Toccata.*
*** ASV Dig. CDDCA 880 [id.]. Alberto Portugheis.

This is the record to start with if you want to explore this Argentinian composer's characterful piano
music. The pieces for children are most welcoming and are delightfully varied and intimate: the *Milonga*
is seductive in a Latin-American way, as are the *Three Pieces*, Op. 6. The *Sonatas* are harder nuts to
crack: the first has a formidable opening movement and a ferocious closing toccata, and the *Toccata*,
written for the organ and played with great bravura here, is also a piece to make one sit up. Alberto

Portugheis is a first-rate artist and his natural sympathies for the music's idiom are apparent throughout. He is very well recorded.

Giordano, Umberto (1867–1948)

Andrea Chénier (complete).
(M) *** RCA GD 82046 (2) [RCD-2-2046]. Domingo, Scotto, Milnes, Alldis Ch., Nat. PO, Levine.
**(*) Decca Dig. 410 117-2 (2) [id.]. Pavarotti, Caballé, Nucci, Kuhlmann, Welsh Nat. Op. Ch., Nat. PO, Chailly.
(Y/B) (M) **(*) EMI CMS5 65287-2 (2) [Ang. CDMB 65287]. Corelli, Stella, Sereni, Rome Op. Ch. & O, Santini.

Andrea Chénier with its defiant poet hero provides a splendid role for Domingo at his most heroic and the former servant, later revolutionary leader, Gérard, is a character well appreciated by Milnes. Scotto gives one of her most eloquent and beautiful performances, and Levine has rarely displayed his powers as an urgent and dramatic opera conductor more potently on record, with the bright recording intensifying the dramatic thrust of playing and singing.

Pavarotti may motor through the role of the poet-hero, singing with his usual fine diction; nevertheless, the red-blooded melodrama of the piece comes over powerfully, thanks to Chailly's sympathetic conducting, incisive but never exaggerated. Caballé, like Pavarotti, is not strong on characterization but produces beautiful sounds, while Leo Nucci makes a superbly dark-toned Gérard. Though this cannot replace the Levine set, it is a colourful substitute with its demonstration sound.

The glory of the 1964 EMI version is the Chénier of Franco Corelli, one of his most satisfying performances on record with heroic tone gloriously exploited. The other singing is less distinguished. Though Antonietta Stella was never sweeter of voice than here, she hardly matches such rivals as Scotto or Caballé. The 1960s recording is vivid, with plenty of atmosphere, and has been transferred to CD most naturally, but the RCA set in the same price range, with Domingo and Scotto, remains a clear first choice.

Fedora (complete).
(M) **(*) Decca 433 033-2 (2) [id.]. Olivero, Del Monaco, Gobbi, Monte Carlo Nat. Op. Ch. & O, Gardelli – ZANDONAI: *Francesca da Rimini.* **(*)
(M) ** Sony Dig. M2K 42181 (2). Marton, Carreras, Hungarian R. & TV Ch. & O, Patanè.

Fedora will always be remembered for one brief aria, the hero's *Amor ti vieta*; but, as this highly enjoyable recording confirms, there is much that is memorable in the score, even if nothing else quite approaches it. Meaty stuff, which brings some splendid singing from Magda Olivero and (more intermittently) from Del Monaco, with Gobbi in a light comedy part. Fine, vintage (1969), atmospheric recording.

On Sony, Eva Marton as Fedora, the Romanov princess, is aptly cast, with José Carreras taking the role of hero. In a work that should sound sumptuous it is not a help that the voices are placed forwardly, with the orchestra distanced well behind. That balance exaggerates the vibrato in Marton's voice, but it is a strong, sympathetic performance; Carreras, too, responds warmly to the lyricism of the role of the hero, Loris, giving a satisfyingly forthright account of *Amor ti vieta*. The rest of the cast is unremarkable, and Patanè's direction lacks bite, again partly a question of orchestral balance.

Giuliani, Mauro (1781–1828)

Guitar concerto in A, Op. 30.
(Y/B) (M) *** DG 439 984-2 [id.]. Siegfried Behrend, I Musici – CARULLI: *Concerto in A* ***; VIVALDI: *Guitar concertos.* **(*)
(N) (B) *** Sony SBK 58168; *SBT 58168* [id.]. John Williams, ECO – RODRIGO: *Concierto de Aranjuez* etc; VIVALDI: *Concerto, RV 93.* ***

Giuliani's *A major Concerto* is presented by Behrend with much elegance and finesse and is immaculately recorded. Its catchy main theme is endearing; though the music overall is slight, it is nicely crafted.

John Williams's account, too, is elegantly turned and pleasingly recorded, and choice will no doubt rest with the coupling. This reissue is excellent value.

Duo concertante for violin & guitar, Op. 25; Gran duetto concertante for flute & guitar, Op. 52; Serenade for violin, cello & guitar in A, Op. 19.
**(*) RCA 09026 60237-2 [60237-2]. Swensen, Galway, Anderson, Yamashita.

Giuliani is an elegant purveyor of ingenuous, pleasing phrases, and these three works show him at his most gallantly generous. These four artists do the composer proud, playing with warmth and elegance – Joseph Swensen's timbre in the *Duo concertante* is sumptuous (almost too lush) and only in the *Serenade* is the penchant of American engineering – the recordings were made in New York City – for close balancing disturbing, when the violin catches the microphone in the galloping Scherzo. Even so, this concert is easy to enjoy.

Sonata for violin and guitar.
*** Sony MK 34508 [id.]. Itzhak Perlman, John Williams – PAGANINI: *Cantabile* etc.***

Giuliani's *Sonata* is amiable enough but hardly substantial fare; but it is played with such artistry here that it appears better music than it is. The recording is in need of more ambience, but sound is invariably a matter of taste, and there is no reason to withhold a strong recommendation. The CD transfer is admirably managed.

Grand overture, Op. 61; Rossiniana No. 3, Op. 121.
(M) **(*) RCA 09026 61593-2. Julian Bream (guitar) – SOR: *Grand solo sonata* etc.; DIABELLI: *Sonata in A.* **(*)

The *Grand Overture* is a rather imposing piece which Bream despatches with panache, whereas Giulini's six *Rossinianae* were, as the title suggests, based on the operas of Rossini, and one might expect the music of No. 3 to be witty and memorably tuneful, but that is not so. Bream makes cuts, but the music outstays its welcome. The playing is first class, of course, and the recording exemplary.

Glass, Louis (1864–1936)

Symphonies Nos. 5 in C (Svastika), Op. 57; 6 (Skoldungeaet), Op. 60.
(N) * Marco Polo Dig. 8.223486-2. S. African Broadcasting Corp. Nat. SO, Peter Marchbank.

Louis Glass is best known to collectors for his enchanting *Elverhøjsuite* ('The Hill of the Elves' suite), which the Odense orchestra recorded in 1986 on an LP called *Music inspired by Hans Christian Andersen* but which never appeared on CD. Those who know this piece will doubtless eagerly snap up this issue – but they will, alas, be disappointed. It has to be said that neither of these symphonies is of the same quality of inspiration, nor that the lacklustre, turgid performances are persuasive. The orchestral playing is very routine indeed, and the recording rather ordinary too.

Glass, Philip (born 1937)

Company; Façades.
(M) *** Virgin/EMI Dig. CUV5 61121-2. LCO, Warren-Green – ADAMS: *Shaker loops* *** ❀; REICH: *8 Lines* ***; HEATH: *Frontier.* ***

Company consists of four brief but sharply contrasted movements for strings; *Façades* offers a haunting cantilena for soprano saxophone, suspended over atmospherically undulating strings. The performances are full of intensity and are expertly played, and the recording is excellent.

Dance Pieces: Glasspieces; In the Upper Room: Dances Nos. 1, 2, 5, 8 & 9.
*** CBS Dig. MK 39539 [id.]. Ens., dir. Michael Riesman.

These two ballet scores bring typical and easily attractive examples of Glass's minimalist technique. Heard away from the stage, the music seems to have a subliminally hypnotic effect, even though rhythmic patterns often repeat themselves almost endlessly.

String quartets Nos. 2 (Company); 3 (Mishima); 4 (Buczak); 5.
(Y/B) *** Elektra-Nonesuch/Warner Dig. 7559 79356-2 [id.]. Kronos Quartet.

Happily, the quartets here are presented in reverse order, for the last of the four, No. 5, dating from 1991, presents Glass at his most warmly expressive and intense, the more moving for being conventionally beautiful in a way that for so long he tended to avoid. Textures are luminous, shimmering in their repetitions rather than thrusting them home relentlessly. The Kronos Quartet, for whom the work was written, give a heartfelt performance, as they do of the *Quartet No. 4* (1990), written in memory of Brian Buczak, who died of AIDS. The valedictory mood is intensified by a lyrical and poignantly beautiful middle movement, leading to a noble finale. The *Quartet No. 2* (1983) consists of four brief movements originally written to accompany the staged soliloquy of a dying man, entitled *Company*. Again it is valedictory in tone but is far less tender. The *Quartet No. 3* (1985) is repetitive in the characteristic Glass manner, this time with six brief movements. Though Nos. 4 and 5 most clearly reveal the hand of a master, the earlier works also represent Glass at his most approachable, the more so when they are treated to magnetic performances by the Kronos Quartet, superbly recorded.

OPERA

Akhnaten (complete).
*** CBS M2K 42457 (2) [id.]. Esswood, Vargas, Liebermann, Hannula, Holzapfel, Hauptmann, Stuttgart State Op. Ch. & O, Russell Davies.

Akhnaten, Glass's powerful third opera, is set in the time of Ancient Egypt. Paul Esswood in the title-role is reserved, strong and statuesque; this is an opera of historical ghosts, and its life-flow lies in the hypnotic background provided by the orchestra; indeed the work's haunting closing scene with its wordless melismas is like nothing else in music. It offers a theatrical experience appealing to a far wider public than usual in the opera house; and here the Stuttgart chorus and orchestra give the piece impressively committed advocacy.

La Belle et la Bête (opera based on the film of Jean Cocteau): complete.
(Y/B) *** Nonesuch-Elektra/Warner Dig 7559 794347 [id.]. Felty, Purnhagen, Kuether, Martinez, Neill, Zhou, Philip Glass Ens., Michael Riesman.

Philip Glass first saw Cocteau's films in Paris in 1954 at the age of seventeen, and he was so profoundly impressed that three of his works have been directly inspired by them: *Orpheé* and *Les enfants terribles*, as well as this most recent one. With *La Belle et la Bête* the composer tells us 'the story interests me less as a fairy tale than as a love story', and the tender emotions behind the score, as well as its evocative beauty, bear witness to that. What Glass has done is to provide a new musical accompaniment to a showing of the 90-minute film, dispensing with Auric's original film-music and synchronizing the singing-parts with the speech of the actors in the film. In the opening scenes the music is far lighter and more conventionally beautiful than most Glass, but then the poignancy of the story is more and more reflected in the score, both tender and mellifluous. Glass and Riesman had to use computers in the end in order to synchronize the vocal line and the actors' lips perfectly, but what matters on the disc is that the hypnotic quality of Glass's repetitions helps to enhance the magical atmosphere, while the use of the original French film-script prompts Glass to be more warmly melodic than usual. Glass himself recognizes that his score might be regarded as either presumptuous or gimmicky, but the justification lies in the intensity of the score overall, with Janice Felty and Gregory Purnhagen both clearly focused in the central roles, though Purnhagen's baritone suggests from the start a heroic, not a bestial, figure. Vividly atmospheric sound.

Einstein on the Beach (complete).
(Y/B) *** Teldec/Warner Dig. 7559 79323-2 (3) [id.]. Soloists, Philip Glass Ens., Riesman.

Glass himself explains the need for a new recording of this bizarre and relentless opera – as the surreal title implies, more dream than drama. 'To begin with, the new recording is almost 190 minutes long, as opposed to some 160 minutes in 1978 . . . and length is not a trivial matter in a performance of *Einstein* but part of the total experience.' Where the earlier recording of this opera had an abrasive edge, this new one is more refined, melding the different elements, electronic alongside acoustic, more subtly and persuasively than before. Even so, the first train episode, over 20 minutes long, remains mind-blowing in its relentlessness. The impact is heightened by the vividness of the recording, with spoken voices in particular given such presence that they startle you as if someone had burst into your room. The vision remains an odd one, and other examples of Glass's minimalist operatic style remain more immediately appealing, but, with a formidable group of vocalists and instrumentalists brilliantly directed, often from the keyboard, by Michael Riesman, the new recording certainly justifies itself.

Satyagraha (complete).
*** Sony Dig. M3K 39672 (3) [id.]. Perry, NY City Op. Ch. & O, Keene.

The subject here is the early life of Mahatma Gandhi, pinpointing various incidents; and the text is a selection of verses from the *Bhagavadgita*, sung in the original Sanskrit and used as another strand in the complex repetitive web of sound. The result is undeniably powerful. Where much minimalist music in its shimmering repetitiveness becomes static, a good deal of this conveys energy as well as power. The writing for chorus is often thrilling, and individual characters emerge in only a shadowy way. The recording, using the device of overdubbing, is spectacular.

Glazunov, Alexander (1865–1936)

Chant du ménestrel (for cello and orchestra), Op. 71.

(B) *** DG Double 437 952-2 (2) [id.]. Rostropovich, Boston SO, Ozawa – BERNSTEIN: *3 Meditations;* BOCCHERINI: *Cello concerto No. 2;* SHOSTAKOVICH: *Cello concerto No. 2;* TARTINI: *Cello concerto;* TCHAIKOVSKY: *Andante cantabile* etc.; VIVALDI: *Cello concertos.* ***

*** Chandos Dig. CHAN 8579 [id.]. Wallfisch, LPO, Bryden Thomson – KABALEVSKY; KHACHATURIAN: *Cello concertos.* ***

Glazunov's *Chant du ménestrel* shows the nostalgic appeal of 'things long ago and far away'. It is a short but appealing piece and is splendidly played by Rostropovich within a highly recommendable Double DG anthology. Alternatively, it becomes a welcome makeweight on the Chandos CD.

Violin concerto in A min., Op. 82.

(N) *** Teldec/Warner Dig. 4509-90881-2 [id.]. Vengerov, BPO, Abbado – TCHAIKOVSKY: *Violin concerto.* ***

(Y/B) *** EMI Dig. CDC7 54872-2 [id.]. Zimmermann, LPO, Welser-Möst – DVORAK: *Violin concerto.* ***

❀ (M) (***) EMI mono CDH7 64030-2 [id.]. Heifetz, LPO, Barbirolli – SIBELIUS: *Violin concerto* (**); TCHAIKOVSKY: *Violin concerto.* (***)

(M) *** RCA 09026 61744-2 [61744-2-RG]. Heifetz, RCA Victor SO, Hendl – PROKOFIEV: *Violin concerto No. 2;* SIBELIUS: *Concerto.* ***

*** EMI Dig. CDC7 49814-2 [id.]. Perlman, Israel PO, Mehta – SHOSTAKOVICH: *Violin concerto No. 1.* ***

(Y/B) (BB) *** Naxos Dig. 8.550758 [id.]. Ilya Kaler, Polish Nat. RSO (Katowice), Kolchinsky – DVORAK: *Concerto* etc. ***

(M) *** Carlton Dig. 30367 0031-2 [id.]. Udagawa, LPO, Klein – Concert ***.

Outstanding as Vengerov's Tchaikovsky performance is, his Glazunov is even more exceptional, for he gives a warhorse concerto extra dimensions, turning it from a display piece into a work of far wider-ranging emotions. Above all he makes one appreciate afresh what a wonderful sequence of melodies the composer here offers, when in each he contrasts and shades the tone-colours so magically, keeping his fattest tone in reserve for the third theme. Predictably, the dashing final section is breathtaking in its brilliance.

The Glazunov comes up sounding delightfully fresh in Frank Peter Zimmermann's hands. Among recent versions, however, this can hold its head high: Zimmermann plays with effortless virtuosity, great polish and great beauty of tone. Franz Welser-Möst provides excellent support, and the recording is outstandingly natural and realistic.

Heifetz's recording of the Glazunov *Violin concerto* with Barbirolli was made in 1934 when the composer was still alive. It has greater expressive breadth and spaciousness than his later record with Walter Hendl and the Chicago orchestra and there is great warmth. Intonation is incredibly sure and the tone sweet; generally speaking, this first Heifetz version of the concerto has never been surpassed. For those who want more modern, stereo sound, Heifetz is again incomparable; his account is the strongest and most passionate (as well as the most perfectly played) in the catalogue. The RCA orchestra under Hendl gives splendid support.

The command and panache of Perlman are irresistible in this showpiece concerto, and the whole performance, recorded live, erupts into a glorious account of the galloping final section, in playing to match that even of the supreme master in this work, Heifetz.

The Russian violinist Ilya Kaler gives a rapturously lyrical performance, and Camilla Kolchinsky's accompaniment is equally warm and supportive. The resonant acoustic of the Concert Hall of Polish Radio gives a big, spacious orchestral sound, but Ilya Kaler's tone is full to match, and the violin playing can certainly accommodate the scrutiny of the fairly close microphones. The Dvořák *Concerto* is hardly less successful, and the delightful *Romance* is thrown in for good measure.

The Glazunov also receives a heartfelt performance from Udagawa which is just as compelling as the virtuoso stereo accounts from such master violinists as Heifetz and Perlman. In the finale she may not offer quite such bravura fireworks as they do but, with more open sound, the result is very persuasive in its lilting way.

(i) *Violin concerto. The Seasons* (ballet), *Op. 67.*

*** Chandos Dig. CHAN 8596 [id.]. (i) Oscar Shumsky; SNO, Järvi.

Neeme Järvi obtains good results from the Scottish National Orchestra in *The Seasons*, though tempi tend to be brisk. The Chandos acoustic is reverberant and the balance recessed. In the *Violin concerto,*

Oscar Shumsky is perhaps wanting the purity and effortless virtuosity of Heifetz, but the disc as a whole still carries a three-star recommendation.

From the Middle Ages, Op. 79; Scènes de ballet, Op. 52.
*** Chandos Dig. CHAN 8804 [id.]. SNO, Järvi (with LIADOV: *A Musical snuffbox* ***).

Järvi makes out an excellent case for these charming Glazunov suites. Although this music is obviously inferior to Tchaikovsky, Järvi has the knack of making you think it is better than it is. The disc also includes a fine account of Liadov's delightful *A Musical snuffbox*.

Raymonda (ballet; complete), *Op. 57.*
(N) (M) *** Carlton Classics Dig. 30366 00067 [id.]. Kirov Op. O, Viktor Fedotov.

Although Glazunov lacks the incredible fund of invention or the musical substance that Tchaikovsky commanded, his three-Act *Raymonda* (1896–8) includes much music of great charm and grace. Not only is it expertly fashioned and orchestrated (as one might expect), it offers warmth and has the capacity to delight. If the outpouring of melody is not as rich and seemingly limitless as in the great Tchaikovsky ballets, its geniality and urbanity – and some endearing numbers – make it well worth having. This new performance from the Kirov orchestra finds them in good form, even if the upper strings could be richer; the recording, too, is more than serviceable. It is good without automatically reaching the distinction of some three-star recommendations. However, on balance it would be curmudgeonly to withhold the third star, for its merits are considerable and it is unlikely that a better version will come along in the immediate future. Not that it matters, but the disc deserves a special prize for having the ugliest label.

Raymonda (ballet), *Op. 57:* extended excerpts from Acts I & II.
*** Chandos Dig. CHAN 8447 [id.]. SNO, Järvi.

Järvi chooses some 56 minutes of music from the first two Acts, omitting entirely the Slavic/Hungarian Wedding *Divertissement* of the closing Act, and this contributes to the slight feeling of lassitude. But with rich Chandos recording this is a record for any balletomane to wallow in, even if a Russian performance would undoubtedly have more extrovert fire.

The Sea (fantasy), *Op. 28; Spring, Op. 34.*
*** Chandos Dig. CHAN 8611 [id.]. SNO, Järvi – KALINNIKOV: *Symphony No. 1.* ***

The tone-poem, *Spring*, was written two years after *The Sea* and is infinitely more imaginative; in fact, it is as fresh and delightful as its companion is cliché-ridden. At one point Glazunov even looks forward to *The Seasons*. Persuasive and well-recorded performances from the Scottish National Orchestra under Neeme Järvi. The spacious and vivid recording sounds well.

The Seasons (ballet; complete) *Op. 67.*
*** Decca Dig. 433 000-2 (2) [id.]. RPO, Ashkenazy – TCHAIKOVSKY: *Nutcracker.* ***
(BB) **(*) Naxos Dig. 8.550079; *4550079* [id.]. Czech RSO (Bratislava), Ondrej Lenárd – TCHAIKOV-SKY: *Sleeping Beauty suite.* **
(Y/B) (***) EMI mono CDC5 55223-2 [id.]. O, composer – PROKOFIEV: *Piano concerto No. 3* etc. (***)

The Seasons (ballet) complete; *Scènes de ballet, Op. 52.*
*** Telarc CD Dig. CD 80347 [id.]. Minnesota O, Edo de Waart.

The Seasons and Tchaikovsky's *Nutcracker* make a perfect coupling. Both scenarios occupy a fantasy world where frost and snowflakes are glitteringly magical rather than freezing. Ashkenazy's account of Glazunov's delightful ballet is the finest it has ever received. The RPO playing is dainty and elegant, refined and sumptuous, yet the strings respond vigorously to the thrusting vitality of the Autumnal *Bacchanale*. The Decca engineers, working in Watford Town Hall, provide digital sound of great allure and warmth, very much in the demonstration bracket.

If you want *The Seasons* separately on a single CD, you will be hard put to better the Minnesota performance, elegant, polished, warm and alive, and given Telarc's top-drawer sound. The famous thrusting tune of *Autumn* is only marginally less athletic than with Ashkenazy. The *Scènes de ballet* make an ideal coupling, not quite as melodically distinctive but still very enjoyable and cosily tuneful, although the second-movement *Marionnettes* matches Delibes at his most piquant.

Ondrej Lenárd gives a pleasing bargain account of Glazunov's delightful score, finding plenty of delicacy, while the entry of Glazunov's most famous tune at the opening of the *Autumn Bacchanale* is very virile indeed. The sound is atmospheric, yet with plenty of fullness.

Glazunov's 1929 recording is of remarkable quality. It was recorded at the Portman Rooms in London's

Baker Street. The playing is marvellously phrased and has great inner life and, above all, warmth and grace. Although, as one would expect from the period, the frequency range is limited, the actual orchestral texture is quite remarkably well detailed throughout the spectrum, and the present transfer does it justice. Strongly recommended, this comes with all of Prokofiev's commercial recordings as a pianist. An indispensable issue.

Stenka Razin (symphonic poem), *Op. 13.*
*** Chandos Dig. CHAN 8479 [id.]. SNO, Järvi – RIMSKY-KORSAKOV: *Scheherazade.* ***

Stenka Razin has its moments of vulgarity – how otherwise with the *Song of the Volga Boatmen* a recurrent theme? – but it makes a generous and colourful makeweight for Järvi's fine version of *Scheherazade*. The recording is splendid.

Symphonies Nos. 1 in E, Op. 5; 5 in B flat, Op. 55.
**(*) Orfeo Dig. C 093101A [id.]. Bav. RSO, Järvi.

Glazunov's prodigious *First Symphony* is not only remarkably accomplished but delightfully fresh. The playing of the Bavarian Radio Symphony Orchestra under Neeme Järvi is highly sympathetic and polished. The music is made to sound cogent and civilized, if perhaps a little bland at times. The Orfeo recording lacks something in glitter, although the Scherzos remain highly effective, and in their way Järvi's versions are certainly enjoyable.

Symphony No. 2 in F sharp min., Op. 16; Concert waltz No. 1, Op. 47.
**(*) Orfeo Dig. C 148101A [id.]. Bamberg SO, Järvi.

Järvi's Orfeo sound is comfortable, and the music-making is comfortable too. However, within its boundaries, which are comparatively inhibited, this is a very good performance. The recording is naturally balanced, but could do with just a bit more brilliance.

Symphony No. 3 in D, Op. 33; Concert waltz No. 2 in F, Op. 51.
*** Orfeo Dig. C 157101A [id.]. Bamberg SO, Järvi.

(i) *Symphony No. 3;* (ii) *Serenades Nos. 1 in A, Op. 7; 2 in F, Op. 11;* (i) *Stenka Razin, Op. 13.*
(Y/B) *** ASV Dig. CDDCA 903 [id.]. (i) LSO; (ii) RPO; Yondani Butt.

ASV have reissued Yondani Butt's performance (originally offered on its own) with substantial couplings. *Stenka Razin* (never quite the popular success Glazunov intended by incorporating the *Volga boat song*) comes off well enough; there is some impressive LSO brass playing and the sinuous secondary theme is well appreciated by the LSO strings. But it is the two charming early *Serenades* that catch the ear, seductively played by the RPO. The performance of the symphony is a good one. One would have liked a greater sense of soaring (over the throbbing wind chords) at the opening, but the response of the LSO catches the colour and melancholy of the slow movement, and the Scherzo (easily the best movement) has sparkle. However, Järvi is more successful in the finale, which seems rather too long here and could use a shade more adrenalin. But a cultivated approach overall is never amiss with this composer.

In Järvi's hands Glazunov's *Third Symphony* is rich and cultivated; the Scherzo is delectably played. The finale has plenty of energy and almost doesn't seem too long, when the momentum is so well sustained.

Symphonies Nos. 4 in E flat, Op. 48; 7 in F, Op. 77.
**(*) Orfeo C 148201A [id.]. Bamberg SO, Järvi.

Glazunov's *Fourth* is a charming and well-composed symphony, full of good things and distinctly Russian in outlook, and held together structurally by a theme which Glazunov uses in all three movements. The *Seventh* also has much to attract the listener. The *Andante* is undoubtedly eloquent in Järvi's performance and the Scherzo, marked 'giocoso', is well up to form. The finale has plenty of bustle, even if here it sounds rather long. The sound is full and naturally balanced, lacking something in spectacle.

Symphony No. 6 in C min., Op. 58; Poème lyrique, Op. 12.
*** Orfeo Dig. C 157201 [id.]. Bamberg SO, Neeme Järvi.

(i) *Symphony No. 6; Raymonda* (ballet), *Op. 57a: suite;* (ii) *Triumphal march, Op. 40.*
(Y/B) *** ASV Dig. CDDCA 904 [id.]. (i) LSO; (ii) RPO; Yondani Butt.

Taken overall, Yondani Butt's is the preferred choice for Glazunov's *Sixth*, although of course couplings do come into the matter. Yet Butt's performance is marginally fresher than Järvi's, helped by the more open sound of the ASV recording, and the fine wind and brass contributions from the LSO; the brass chorale at the end of the *Variations* is effectively sonorous. The selection from *Raymonda* concentrates on the first two Acts and offers only a brief *Entr'acte* from Act III; most of the music in fact comes from Act I, some 21 minutes out of a selection lasting just over half an hour. The playing is both graceful and lively, and the recording has plenty of amplitude and warmth.

Järvi makes more than usual of the first movement of the *Sixth*, building an impressive climax. The *Theme and variations* benefits greatly from the polished playing of the Bambergers. The finale produces energy and vigour without too much bombast, for the Bamberg brass is sonorous without being blatant. The *Poème lyrique* is full of romantic atmosphere; the full yet vivid recording seems just right for the music.

Symphony No. 8 in E flat, Op. 83; Overture solennelle, Op. 73; Wedding procession, Op. 21.
**(*) Orfeo C 093201A [id.]. Bav. RSO, Järvi.

As in the rest of his series, Järvi and the Bavarian players give the piece a cultivated, polished perform- ance of the *Eighth*, thoroughly musical and undoubtedly enjoyable, with spaciousness to some extent compensating for passion, when the sound is full and pleasing.

CHAMBER MUSIC

5 Novelettes, Op. 15.
(Y/B) (***) Testament mono SBT1061 [id.]. Hollywood Qt – BORODIN: *String quartet No. 2;* TCHAI-
    KOVSKY: *String quartet No. 1.* (***)

The Hollywood Quartet's recording dates from 1955 and has not appeared in the UK before. These players bring a freshness and ardour to these charming compositions that is most persuasive. The *Novelettes* last a little under half an hour, and as a result the disc is only one second short of eighty minutes long. The sleeve warns that some CD players may have difficulty in tracking it. We have not found this to be the case, but some caution may be necessary on the part of readers with older players.

String quartets Nos. 3 in G (Slavonic), Op. 26; 5 in D min., Op. 70; The Fridays, Book 2: Kuranta; Prelude and fugue in D min.
(Y/B) **(*) Olympia OCD 525 [id.]. Shostakovich Qt.

The appeal of the *Third Quartet* is immediate and the thematic inspiration folk-like and of the highest level. It comes over particularly well in the persuasive and enthusiastic hands of the Shostakovich Quartet. The *Fifth Quartet* (1898) opens with a noble and expressive fugue, and on hearing it one is tempted to agree with Calvocoressi that this is the finest of the seven (though his essay was published before the last, *Hommage au passé*, was written). Good performances, though they are not the last word in polish; but they are rather too closely balanced for complete comfort.

String quartets Nos. 6 in B flat, Op. 106; 7 in C, Op. 107.
(Y/B) ** Olympia OCD 526 [id.]. Shostakovich Qt.

The turbulence of the 1910s and '20s seems not to have cast any shadows here; the *Fifth* and *Sixth Quartets* have all the sad charm of old Russia. Glazunov – and who can blame him? – has retired into his own world and offers music that could have been composed at the beginning of his career. The Shostakovich Quartet generally play with conviction, though their performances are by no means as polished as those of Nos. 3 and 5. The recording is rather up-front and has some roughness on climaxes, but there is no alternative version of either work.

String quintet in A, Op. 39.
(N) *** Chandos Dig. CHAN 9878 [id.] ASMF Chamber Ens. – TCHAIKOVSKY: *Souvenir de Florence.*
    ***

Glazunov's *String quintet* (with second cello) dates from 1892 and so comes between the *Third* and *Fourth Symphonies*. It is a work of characteristic warmth and lyricism. (There is a long analysis of it by M. D. Calvocoressi in *Cobbett's Cyclopedic Survey of Chamber Music*.) The performance is thoroughly committed and persuasive, and very well recorded too. There is no alternative version in the catalogue – but, even if there were, this would be hard to beat.

Complete piano music

Grande valse de concert, Op. 41; 3 Miniatures, Op. 42; Petite valse, Op. 36; Sonata No. 1 in B flat min., Op. 74; Suite on the name 'Sacha'; Valse de salon, Op. 43; Waltzes on the theme 'Sabela', Op. 23.
(N) *** Hyperion Dig. CDA 66833 [id.]. Stephen Coombs.

Easy Sonata; 3 Etudes, Op. 31; Miniature in C; 3 Morceaux, Op. 49; Nocturne, Op. 37; 2 Pieces, Op. 22; 2 Poèmes-improvisations; Sonatina; Theme and variations, Op. 72.
(N) *** Hyperion Dig. CDA 66844 [id.]. Stephen Coombs.

When Glazunov himself was an indifferent pianist, it is astonishing how brilliant the piano writing is here. Even when he writes a simple melody at a spacious tempo, he regularly decorates it with cascades of notes. Marking the start of a new Russian series, each of these two discs, available separately, contains a major work, the *Piano sonata No. 1* on the first and the *Theme and variations*, Op. 72, on the second (both written in 1900). For the rest, you have a dazzling series of salon and genre pieces, full of the easy charm and winning tunefulness that mark Glazunov's ballet, *The Seasons*. Stephen Coombs proves a most persuasive advocate, consistently conveying sheer joy in keyboard virtuosity to a degree rare in British pianists. Making light of the most formidable technical difficulties and positively relishing the shoals of notes in every bar, Coombs plays with a natural warmth and a spontaneous feeling for line which give magic to pieces which otherwise might seem trivial. It makes a feast for any lover of piano music.

In the *First Piano sonata*, Op. 74, written in 1900, which Stephen Coombs in his excellent notes calls 'a colossal achievement for its day', the playing is always musical, often poetic and rarely falls short of distinction. Leading up to the sonata, the first disc starts with Glazunov's first published piece, the *Suite on the name 'Sacha'*, the work of a keenly confident eighteen-year-old. The three *Miniatures*, Op. 42, brilliantly exploit the piano's upper registers, ending with a waltz, and that leads to a sequence of waltzes ranging from the ambitious *Grande valse de concert* (almost anticipating Ravel's *La valse*) to the *Petite Valse*, Op. 36. As well as the *Variations*, Op. 72, simple in outline but elaborate and colourful in texture, the second disc offers what might be counted Glazunov's most assured piano work, the set of three *Etudes*, Op. 31, and more salon pieces, including several early miniatures written as exercises for Rimsky-Korsakov.

2 Impromptus, Op. 54; 3 Morceaux, Op. 49; 2 Poèmes-improvisations; Prelude and fugue, Op. 62; Theme and variations, Op. 72; Valse de salon, Op. 43.
(Y/B) *(**) Marco Polo Dig. 8.223152 [id.]. Tatjana Franová.

Glazunov is not at his most inventive or inspired in his keyboard music, though his writing for it is never less than cultivated and idiomatic. The best-known work is the *Theme and variations*, Op. 72, which Tatjana Franová plays with fluent sympathy. Generally speaking, the recital uncovers no masterpieces, though her playing could not be more persuasive. The recording, while not wholly unpleasing, does not really produce a realistic piano-sound: it is difficult to be sure where the instrument is in the aural picture. The bass is well defined but does not wholly relate to the rest of the instrument, and the overall effect is a shade synthetic.

Piano sonatas Nos. 1 in B flat min., Op. 74; 2 in E min., Op. 75; Grande valse de concert in E flat, Op. 41.
**(*) Pearl SHECD 9538 [id.]. Leslie Howard.

The Glazunov *Sonatas* are well worth investigating, particularly in performances as committed and as well recorded as these. Admirers of Glazunov's art should investigate this issue which sounds extremely impressive in its CD format.

Glière, Reinhold (1875–1956)

The Bronze Horseman: suite; (i) *Horn concerto, Op. 91.*
(N) ** Chandos Dig. CHAN 9379 [id.]. (i) Richard Watkins; BBC PO, Sir Edward Downes.

The Bronze Horseman is not great music – nor, for that matter, is the *Horn concerto*. Richard Watkins is a fine soloist in the latter; Downes gets good rather than really distinguished playing from the BBC Philharmonic, though the recording is excellent.

(i) *Concerto for coloratura soprano, Op. 82;* (ii) *Harp concerto, Op. 74.*
*** Chandos Dig. CHAN 9094 [id.]. (i) Eileen Hulse; (ii) Rachel Masters; City of L. Sinfonia, Hickox –
    GINASTERA: *Harp concerto*. ***

This digital recording of Glière's lush concertos is highly competitive in both works. The recording is suitably rich and opulent, yet every detail is audibly in place. Eileen Hulse is an impressive soloist with excellent control, well-focused tone and a good sense of line, and she is excellently supported by the City of London Sinfonia and Richard Hickox. Nor need Rachel Masters fear comparison with her predecessor, Osian Ellis; so, given such excellent sound, this is all highly self-indulgent and sybaritic.

Symphony No. 2 in C min, Op. 25; Zaporozhy Cossacks, Op. 64.
**(*) Chandos Dig. CHAN 9071 [id.]. BBC PO, Downes.

Not even the advocacy of Sir Edward Downes with his magnificent Manchester orchestra can conceal the banality of some of the writing in this early Glière symphony – it cannot compare with Glière's later and grander *Symphony No. 3. Zaporozhy Cossacks* is less ambitious but also contains banalities. Excellent performances and outstanding recording.

Symphony No. 3 in B min. (Ilya Murometz), Op. 42.
*** Chandos Dig. CHAN 9041 [id.]. BBC PO, Sir Edward Downes.
(BB) ** Naxos Dig. 8.550858 [id.]. Slovak RSO, Johanos.

Downes and the BBC Philharmonic in magnificent form give an urgently passionate performance of this colourful programme piece, more convincing than any rival in what can easily seem too cumbersome a work. Downes, taut and intense, relates the writing very much to the world of Glière's close contemporary, Rachmaninov. The recording, made in the concert hall of New Broadcasting House, Manchester, is one of Chandos's finest, combining clarity and sumptuousness.

Naxos have acted sensibly in reducing the price of the Johanos version (originally on Marco Polo). While the Chandos alternative is well worth the extra cost, the rougher Slovak Radio performance is perfectly acceptable and will suit those who want to explore this score at little cost.

Glinka, Mikhail (1805–57)

Ruslan and Ludmilla: Overture.
(M) *** RCA GD 60176 [60176-2-RG]. Chicago SO, Fritz Reiner – PROKOFIEV: *Alexander Nevsky* etc. ***

Reiner's performance is highly infectious and the (1959) Chicago sound brings plenty of colour and warmth.

Grand sextet in E flat.
*** Hyperion CDA 66163 [id.]. Capricorn – RIMSKY-KORSAKOV: *Quintet*. ***

Glinka's *Sextet* is rather engaging, particularly when played with such aplomb as it is here. The contribution of the pianist, Julian Jacobson, is brilliantly nimble and felicitous. The balance places the piano rather backwardly, but the CD provides good detail and presence.

Trio pathétique in D min.
*** Chandos Dig. CHAN 8477 [id.]. Borodin Trio – ARENSKY: *Piano trio*. ***

Glinka's *Trio* is prefaced by a superscription; '*Je n'ai connu l'amour que par les peines qu'il cause*' ('I have known love only through the misery it causes'). It is no masterpiece – but the Borodins almost persuade one that it is. The recording is vivid and has excellent presence.

A Life for the Tsar.
**(*) Sony Dig. S3K 46487 (3) [id.]. Martinovich, Pendachanska, Merritt, Toczyska, Sofia Nat. O Ch. & O, Tchakarov.

When this opera was first given in St Petersburg in November 1836 it marked a breakthrough in Russian music. Glinka introduced Russian themes far more than his predecessors, and the subject itself reflected the nationalist fervour behind his inspiration. There are many delightful sequences in the opera, not least the many choruses and dances, which regularly inspire the late Emil Tchakarov to spring rhythms infectiously, bringing out the peasant flavour. Against the background of a good ensemble performance the soloists are more than reliable, with Boris Martinovich singing characterfully, if not always steadily. Aleksandrina Pendachanska is bright and fresh as his daughter, only occasionally edgy in a Slavonic way, and Stefania Toczyaska sings beautifully as Vanya, singing this character's two arias delightfully. From outside the Slavonic area the American tenor Chris Merritt is well attuned, singing without strain. Though in its clear recording this gives little idea of a staged rather than a studio performance, it is more than a stop-gap for an essential work in the repertory.

Gluck, Christophe (1714–87)

Don Juan (ballet): complete.
(N) (M) *** Erato/Warner 4509 99608-2 [id.]. E. Bar. Soloists, Gardiner.

Reissued as part of the Gardiner Collection, this has much to recommend it. The 1981 recording is full and modern. The performance too has a clean and dramatic profile.

Alceste (complete).
** Orfeo Dig. C 02782 (3) [id.]. Jessye Norman, Gedda, Krause, Nimsgern, Weikl, Bav. R. Ch. and SO,
   Baudo.

The French version of *Alceste* in this very well-cast set has Jessye Norman commanding in the title-role,
producing gloriously varied tone in every register. What is rather lacking is a fire-eating quality such as
made Janet Baker's performance so memorable. That is mainly the fault of the conductor, who makes
Gluck's score sound comfortable rather than tense and, as a set, this does not quite rebut the idea that in
Gluck 'beautiful' means 'boring'. Good, well-focused sound.

Le Cinesi (The Chinese women).
(M) *** HM/BMG Dig. GD 77174 [77174-2-RG]. Poulenard, Von Otter, Banditelli, De Mey, Schola
   Cantorum Basiliensis O, Jacobs.

Gluck's hour-long opera-serenade provides a fascinating view of the composer's lighter side and, rather
like Mozart in *Entführung*, Gluck uses jangling and tinkling percussion instruments in the overture to
indicate an exotic setting. Otherwise the formal attitudes in Metastasio's libretto – written some twenty
years before Gluck set it – are pure eighteenth century.

(i) *La Corona* (complete). (ii) *La Danza* (dramatic pastoral).
**(*) Orfeo Dig. C 135872H (2) [id.]. (i) Slowakiewicz, Gorzynska, Nowicks, Bav. R. Ch; (ii) Ignatowicz,
   Myriak, Warsaw CO; Bugaj.

Hunting-calls set the scene evocatively in the three-movement sinfonia of *La Corona*, which is followed
by six arias, a delightful duet and a final quartet. This performance is fresh and direct, with first-rate
singing from the three sopranos. The much shorter fill-up, described as a dramatic pastoral, is less
interesting and is less reliably done.

Iphigénie en Aulide (complete).
(N) (M) *** Erato/Warner Dig. 4509 99609-2 (2) [id.]. Van Dam, Von Otter, Dawson, Aler, Monteverdi
   Ch., Lyon Op. O, Gardiner.

Iphigénie en Aulide was Gluck's first piece in French and it anticipated the *Tauride* opera in its speed and
directness of treatment, so different from the leisurely and expansive traditions of *opera seria*. Gardiner
here eliminates the distortions of the piece which the long-established Wagner edition created and
reconstructs the score as presented in the first revival of 1775; the recording conveys the tensions of a
live performance without the distractions of intrusive stage noise. The darkness of the piece is established at the very start, with men's voices eliminated, and a moving portrait built up of Agamemnon,
here sung superbly by José van Dam. In the title-role Lynne Dawson builds up a touching portrait of the
heroine. Her sweet, pure singing is well contrasted with the positive strength of Anne Sofie von Otter as
Clytemnestra, and John Aler brings clear, heroic attack to the tenor role of Achille. The performance is
crowned by the superb ensemble-singing of the Monteverdi Choir in the many choruses.

Iphigénie en Aulide (complete in German; arr. Wagner).
(N) (M) *** RCA 74321 32236-2 (2) [id.]. Moffo, Fischer-Dieskau, Schmidt, Spiess, Stewart, Augér, Bav.
   R Ch., Munich R. O, Eichhorn.

Look closely at the small print and you will find that this is hardly Gluck at all. Wagner's arrangement,
used here is, by the standards of modern purism, a total travesty and the use of German instead of
French only reinforces the stylistic conflict. But with an urgently dramatic performance, with a formidable list of soloists, excellent choral singing and fine playing, this is enjoyable entertainment in its own
right. Maybe, as the scholars tell us, we shall come to regard Raymond Leppard's arrangements of
Cavalli in the same light as this realization, with its enriched orchestration and harmony, its cuts
and additions and its amended plot. But, compact as it is, Gluck/Wagner is every bit as effective as
Cavalli/Leppard, and Wagnerians at least need not hesitate. Good stage atmosphere in the recording.
The German libretto comes without a translation.

Iphigénie en Tauride (complete).
⊛ *** Ph. Dig. 416 148-2 (2) [id.]. Montague, Aler, Thomas Allen, Argenta, Massis, Monteverdi Ch.,
   Lyon Op. O, Gardiner.
** Sony Dig. S2K 52492 (2) [id.]. Vaness, Surian, Allen, Winbergh, La Scala, Milan, Ch. & O, Muti.

Gardiner's electrifying reading of *Iphigénie en Tauride* is a revelation. Though his Lyon orchestra does
not use period instruments, its clarity and resilience and, where necessary, grace and delicacy are
admirable. Diana Montague in the name-part sings with admirable bite and freshness, Thomas Allen is
an outstanding Oreste, characterizing strongly but singing with classical precision. John Aler is a similarly strong and stylish singer, taking the tenor role of Pylade. The recording is bright and full.

Muti's set was recorded live at La Scala in March 1992, a big-scale version that provides a possible alternative to the superb Gardiner for those who insist on modern, not period, instruments. Muti's taut direction is comparably dramatic, but with its beefy orchestral sound and close-up recording it is an overweight performance that misses the essential elegance of Gluck in its lack of light and shade. Vaness's dramatic timbre is apt, but the microphone catches a flutter in the voice. Thomas Allen as Oreste is as telling as for Gardiner but, thanks to the recording, his subtler shading is missing, and Gösta Winbergh as Pylade sings with fine ringing tones yet lacks subtlety and variety.

Orfeo ed Euridice (complete).
*** Ph. Dig. 434 093-2 (2) [id.]. Ragin, McNair, Sieden, Monteverdi Ch., E. Bar. Soloists, Gardiner.
*** EMI Dig. CDS7 49834-2 (2). Hendricks, Von Otter, Fournier, Monteverdi Ch., Lyon Opera O, Gardiner.
(M) *** Erato/Warner Dig. 2292 45864-2 (2). J. Baker, Speiser, Gale, Glyndebourne Ch., LPO, Leppard.
(M) **(*) RCA GD 87896 (2) [7896-2-RG]. Verrett, Moffo, Raskin, Rome Polyphonic Ch., Virtuosi di Roma, Fasano.
(N) (M) **(*) RCA Dig. 74321 32238-2 (2). Lipovšek, Popp, Kaufmann, Bav. R. Ch., Munich R. O, Hager.

Gardiner's newest set for Philips could not be more sharply contrasted with the earlier recording he made for EMI in 1989. Then he was persuaded at the Lyon Opéra to record the Berlioz edition, in French. But all along Gardiner has much preferred the tautness of the original, Vienna version in Italian, which here on Philips he presents with a bite and sense of drama both totally in period and deeply expressive. The element of sensuousness, not least in the beautiful singing of the counter-tenor, Derek Lee Ragin, in the title-role, complements the Elysian beauty Gardiner finds in such passages as the introduction to *Che puro ciel*. Sylvia McNair as Euridice and Cyndia Sieden as Amor complete Gardiner's outstanding solo team. One's only regret is that the set does not provide as a supplement such numbers written for Paris as *The Dance of the Blessed Spirits*.

Many will be glad to have the Berlioz edition, sung in French, which aimed at combining the best of both the Vienna and Paris versions, although once again Gardiner omits the celebratory ballet at the end of the opera. Anne Sofie von Otter is a superb Orfeo, dramatically most convincing. The masculine forthrightness of her singing matches the extra urgency of Gardiner's direction; and both Barbara Hendricks as Eurydice and Brigitte Fournier as Amour are also excellent. The chorus is Gardiner's own Monteverdi Choir, superbly clean and stylish. The recording is full and well balanced.

The Erato version of *Orfeo ed Euridice*, directly based on the Glyndebourne production in which Dame Janet Baker made her very last stage appearance in opera, was recorded in 1982, immediately after the run of live performances. Often credited with being a romanticizer of the eighteenth century, Leppard in fact presents the score with freshness and power, indeed with toughness. Nowhere is that clearer than in the great scene leading up to the aria, *Che farò*, where Dame Janet commandingly conveys the genuine bitterness and anger of Orpheus at Eurydice's death. That most famous of Gluck's arias comes over fresh and clear with no sentimentality whatever, and conversely the display aria which brings Act I to a close has passion and expressiveness even in the most elaborate coloratura. Elisabeth Speiser as Eurydice and Elizabeth Gale as Amor are both disappointing but, as in the theatre, the result is a complete and moving experience centring round a great performance from Dame Janet. The complete ballet-postlude is included, delightful celebration music. The recording has been enhanced in the CD transfer, bright and vivid without edginess, with the modern orchestral strings sounding both fresh and warm. At mid-price this makes a clear first choice. Highlights (74 minutes) are available on Erato (0630 13805-9).

Clearly, if you have a mezzo as firm and sensitive as Shirley Verrett, then everything is in favour of your using the original Italian version. Fasano also uses the right-sized orchestra (of modern instruments) and adopts an appropriately classical style. Anna Moffo and Judith Raskin match Verrett in clean, strong singing, and the Rome Polyphonic Chorus is far more incisive than most Italian choirs. The recording is vivid and atmospheric but emphasizes the music's dramatic qualities rather than its tenderness. However, this makes a good alternative mid-priced recommendation.

Hager's Munich version, recorded in 1986 in full and atmospheric if slightly distanced sound, brings a good, enjoyable, middle-of-the-road performance. Marjana Lipovšek has a beautiful, rich mezzo inclined to fruitiness, which yet in this breeches role is well able to characterize Orfeo strongly and positively. So *Che farò* is warm and direct in its expressiveness, with Lipovšek avoiding distracting mannerism both here and in recitative. Lucia Popp makes a delightful Euridice and Julie Kaufman, though less distinctive, is fresh and bright as Amor. The chorus is on the heavyweight side for Gluck, but that adds to the power of the performance, which uses the 1762 Vienna version of the score, though with instrumental numbers added from the Paris version. The libretto has the full Italian text without translation.

La rencontre imprévue (or *Les Pèlerins de la Mecque*) (opéra-comique).
(N) (M) *** Erato/Warner Dig. 4509 99610-2 (2) [id.]. Dawson, Le Coz, Flechter, Dubosc, Marin-Degor, De Mey, Viala, Lafont, Cachemaille, Dudziak, Lyon Op. O, Gardiner.

John Eliot Gardiner demonstrates here that one of Gluck's comic operas can come up as freshly as the great reform operas. It is true that *Les Pèlerins de la Mecque* (as Gardiner prefers to call it, rather than using its duller, more common title, given above) has nothing like the comic timing of Mozart. Yet all through the brisk sequence of arias and ensembles Gardiner gives the lie to the idea of the score being banal. The sweet-toned Lynne Dawson is charming as the heroine, Rezia, and Guy de Mey as the hero, Ali, is one of the few tenors who could cope effortlessly with the high tessitura. Pierre Cachemaille sings powerfully in an incidental role. The Lyon acoustic, as usual, is on the dry side, as recorded, but that has many advantages in comic opera.

Goehr, Alexander (born 1932)

Metamorphosis/Dance, Op. 36; (i) *Romanza for cello and orchestra, Op. 24*.
(M) *** Unicorn Dig. UKCD 2039. (i) Moray Welsh; RLPO, Atherton.

Moray Welsh plays the *Romanza* warmly and stylishly. *Metamorphosis/Dance*, inspired by the Circe episode in the *Odyssey*, is a sequence of elaborate variations, full of strong rhythmic interest. The performance is excellent.

Goldmark, Karl (1830–1915)

Violin concerto No. 1 in A min., Op. 28.
(N) ✸ *** Delos Dig. DE 3156 [id.]. Nai-Yuan Hu, Seattle SO, Schwarz – BRUCH: *Violin concerto No. 2*. ***
*** EMI Dig. CDC7 47846-2 [id.]. Perlman, Pittsburgh SO, Previn – KORNGOLD: *Violin concerto*. ***

The Taiwanese soloist Nai-Yuan-Hu (pronounced Nigh-Yen Who) makes an outstanding début on CD with a coupling of two underrated concertos, both occupying a peripheral place in the catalogue, which on his responsively lyrical bow are made to sound like undiscovered masterpieces. The Goldmark is a tuneful and warm-hearted concerto that needs just this kind of songful, inspirational approach: Hu shapes the melodies so that they ravishingly take wing and soar. Moreover Schwarz and the Seattle orchestra share a real partnership with their soloist, helped by a perfectly balanced recording which does not place the violin too near the microphones and provides a full, detailed backcloth in a natural concert-hall framework.

Not surprisingly, the concerto is also beautifully played by Perlman, whose effortless virtuosity and strong profile in the bravura passage-work are combined with striking lyrical poise. In the first-movement cadenza he is unsurpassed. However, the EMI balance places the violin in a forward spot-light so that orchestral detail does not always register as it should: in this respect the Delos alternative is in almost every way preferable. Yet this is very charming and likeable music, and Perlman plays it most winningly.

Rustic Wedding Symphony, Op. 26; Overtures: In Italy, Op. 49; In the Spring, Op. 36.
(N) (BB) **(*) Naxos Dig. 8.550745 [id.]. Nat. SO of Ireland, Stephen Gunzenhauser.

Rustic Wedding Symphony, Op. 26; Sakuntala overture, Op. 13.
*** ASV Dig. CDDCA 791 [id.]. RPO, Yondani Butt.

Goldmark's *Rustic Wedding Symphony* opens with a distinctly rustic theme on the lower strings, which when taken up by the horns (with woodwind birdsong overhead) is as magical as any passage in the romantic symphonic repertory, not forgetting the beginning of Mahler's *First*. The hazily romantic evocation of a summer garden which forms the slow movement leads to a boisterous dance finale, with genial injections of fugato. Yondani Butt and the RPO clearly enjoy themselves. The recording has brightly lit violins, but plenty of bloom on the woodwind, and the only miscalculation of balance concerns the trombone entry in the first movement which is too blatant and too loud. Otherwise this is in every way enjoyable. The *Overture Sakuntala* opens impressively but does not quite sustain its 18 minutes. Butt presents it with persuasive vigour and lyrical feeling, and does not shirk the melodrama.

Gunzenhauser gives a fresh, bright-eyed account of the *Rustic Wedding Symphony*. He takes both the opening movement and the Andante (*In the garden*) appreciably faster than does Butt, and he loses something in poise and spacious eloquence in consequence. But the overall performance is spontaneous and enjoyable. It is well recorded and, although the violins sound thin (immediately noticeable at the opening of *In the Spring*), that is almost certainly not the fault of the engineers. Of the two jaunty overtures, *In Italy* is especially vivacious and sparkling.

Symphony No. 2 in E, Op. 35; In Italy overture, Op. 49; Prometheus bound, Op. 38.
(N) *** ASV Dig. CDDCA 934 [id.]. Philh. O, Yondani Butt

Goldmark's *First Symphony* (1860) came to nothing; only the Scherzo survives in published form. After the success of his *Rustic Wedding*, which is really a suite, the composer tried again, this time with more success. The *Second Symphony* is a highly confident piece with a strong opening movement possessing the symphonic impulse of Brahms and a flavour of Mendelssohn, an ambivalent but appealing Andante, and a vivaciously delicate Scherzo which is Mendelssohn undiluted. Yet it brings an individual touch in the Trio with its piquant trumpet chorale, and Goldmark concludes with a characteristically folksy, dance-like finale. Butt has the work's full measure: he does not reveal a forgotten masterpiece, but this is a piece worth having on disc. The Lisztian *Promtheus bound* on the other hand is overlong and melodramatic, and the main allegro is routine in its working out. Yet it has some winning lyrical ideas and Butt does his very best for it. The *Italian overture* is genuinely vivacious, though not especially Italianate: it has a rather beautiful nocturnal sequence as a central episode. The performance here has rather more substance than Gunzenhauser's on Naxos, which in turn is more chimerical. The ASV recording is in every way excellent.

Die Königin von Saba (opera).
** Hung. HCD 12179/82 [id.]. Sólyom-Nagy, Gregor, Kincses, Jerusalem, Miller, Takács, Hungarian State Op. Ch. & O, Fischer.

Klára Takács is dramatic and characterful as the Queen of Sheba while, in the tenor role of Asad, Siegfried Jerusalem gives a magnificent performance, not least in his aria, *Magische Töne*. Sándor Sólyom-Nagy is an impressive Solomon, and Adám Fischer draws lively performances from everyone. The recording is very acceptable, but there are many details which do not emerge as vividly as they might. The documentation, too, is poorly produced.

Goldschmidt, Berthold (born 1903)

(i) *String quartets Nos. 2–3;* (ii) *Letzte Kapitel; Belsatzar.*
*** Largo Dig. LC 5115 [id.]. (i) Mandelring Qt; (ii) Marks; Ars-Nova Ens., Berlin, Schwarz.

Berthold Goldschmidt was hounded from Nazi Germany in 1935 and settled in London. This disc collects his *Letzte Kapitel* for speaker and an instrumental ensemble, very much in the style of Kurt Weill, and the *Second Quartet*, which has something of the fluency of Hindemith. It is an excellently fashioned piece with a rather powerful slow movement, an elegy subtitled *Folia*. The CD is completed by *Belsatzar*, an *a cappella* setting of Heine, and the *Third Quartet*, a remarkable achievement for an 86-year-old, the product of a cultured and thoughtful musical mind. The performances are dedicated, the recordings satisfactory.

OPERA

(i) *Beatrice Cenci* (opera; complete). (ii) Songs: *Clouds; Nebelweben; Ein Rosenzweig.*
(N) *** Sony Dig. S2K 66836 (2) [id.]. Estes, Della Jones, Alexander, Kimm, Rose, Wottrich, Berlin R. Ch., German SO, Berlin, Zagrosek; (ii) Iris Vermillion, composer.

Commissioned to write an opera for the Festival of Britain in 1951, Berthold Goldschmidt responded with this richly imaginative rendering of a melodramatic play of Shelley, in which Beatrice is portrayed not as a murderess but as the victim of an evil father. The piece was never staged at the time; but it received a concert performance in 1988, before finally being presented in Germany. Much of the most moving music involves the relationship of Beatrice and her mother, Lucia, with Della Jones strongly cast against Roberta Alexander in the title-role, singing radiantly. Her big final aria brings the most moving moment of all. Simon Estes sings well, but is not evil-sounding enough to convey the full villainy of the father; but Goldschmidt's treatment of the story is vigorous and swift, inspiring him to more ripely lyrical writing than in his earlier opera, *Die gewaltige Hahnrei*. Vividly recorded and powerfully conducted by Lothar Zagrosek, the set makes generous amends for the work's long neglect. The songs, with Iris Vermillion accompanied by the nonagenarian composer, make a delightful bonus.

(i) *Der gewaltige Hahnrei* (complete); (ii) *Mediterranean songs.*
*** Decca Dig. 440 850-2 (2) [id.]. (i) Alexander, Wörle, M. Kraus, Otelli, Berlin R. Ch. & Deutsches
SO, Berlin; (ii) John Mark Ainsley, Leipzig GO, (i; ii) Zagrosek.

The opera, *Der gewaltige Hahnrei* ('The magnificent cuckold') with an excellent cast, powerfully conducted and played with thrust and polish, makes an invaluable addition to Decca's series of *Entartete
Musik*, so-called 'decadent music'. The Berlin Radio Symphony Orchestra under Lothar Zagrosek
brings out the point and wit of the writing from the very start. If in the ragtime rhythms of the opening
there are echoes of Kurt Weill, that likeness quickly evaporates. Goldschmidt even in his twenties was
less abrasive than Weill, more sweetly lyrical, less brutal in presenting a savagely ironic piece. Based on a
play by Fernand Cromelynck, it is a study of a man, Bruno, whose hysterical, unfounded jealousy of his
devoted wife, Stella, makes Othello look like a beginner. Bruno progressively destroys what he wants
most, the love of a devoted wife. Goldschmidt deftly compresses the original play to produce a colourful, fast-moving piece, with incidental figures well characterized and with complexities both of plot and
of texture skilfully clarified. One only regrets that he does not allow himself more repose, and with it a
more expansive lyricism. The tenor, Robert Wörle, as Bruno, and Roberta Alexander as Stella both give
rich and brilliant performances.

Dating from almost 30 years after the opera, the *Mediterranean songs* reveal Goldschmidt's lyrical gift
even more richly in colourful settings of such poets as Byron, Shelley and James Elroy Flecker, all
beautifully sung by John Mark Ainsley. Outstandingly vivid recording in both opera and song-cycle.

Gombert, Nicolas (*c.* 1495–*c.* 1557)

*Magnificat secundi toni; Missa Tempore paschali; Marian antiphon: Regina coeli. Motets: In te Domine
speravi; Media vita. Chansons: Je prens congie; Tous les regretz. Regina coeli.*
*** Sony Dig. SK48249 [id.]. Huelgas Ens., Paul van Nevel.

Gombert was born in southern Flanders and was probably a pupil of Josquin; his work is rich with full
harmonies and imitative counterpoint. Both his sacred and secular music is often dense in texture, and
both genres are represented in this beautifully sung collection, an ideal introduction to his music. There
is an unusually long, scholarly note by Paul van Nevel himself.

Górecki, Henryk (born 1933)

(i) *Harpsichord concerto;* (ii) *Little Requiem for a polka (Kleines Requiem für eine Polka);* (iii) *Good night
(In Memoriam Michael Vyner)* for soprano, alto flute, 3 tam-tams and piano.
(Y/B) *** Nonesuch/Warner Dig. 7559 79362-2 [id.]. L. Sinf.; (i) David Zinman; (ii) Ezbieta Chojnacka,
cond. Markus Stenz; (iii) Dawn Upshaw, Sebastian Bell, John Constable, David Hockings.

Those listeners who have encountered the *Third Symphony* and who are looking for further Górecki to
explore might well start here. The *Little Requiem* (1993) opens with a single quiet bell-stroke; a piano
(John Constable) then engages in a tranquil dialogue with the violins, to be rudely interrupted by a burst
of bell-ringing; the reverie returns momentarily before the energetic, marcato *Allegro impetutoso* which
follows. The piece ends with a raptly sustained elegiac *Adagio*, still dominated by the quietly assertive
tolling bells. The two-movement *Harpsichord concerto*, written a decade earlier, combines soloist and
strings in a vibrant, jangly ménage. *Good night* is nocturnally serene, the composer's repetitions used to
haunting effect. The soprano voice enters only in the third movement, with a cantilena to Shakespeare's
words from *Hamlet*: 'Good night . . . and flights of angels sing thee to thy rest!' The three tam-tams
poignantly add their own mystical requiem at the close. Both here and in the *Little Requiem* the very
atmospheric recording brings an added dimension to the communication from performers who are
obviously totally committed to the composer's cause.

Symphony No. 3 (Symphony of sorrowful songs), Op. 36.
*** Elektra Nonesuch Dig. 979282-2 [id.]. Dawn Upshaw, London Sinf., David Zinman.
(BB) *** Belart 450 148-2; *450 148-4.* Zofia Kilanowicz, Polish State PO (Katowice), Swoboda.

Symphony No. 3 (Symphony of sorrowful songs), Op. 36; 3 Pieces in the olden style.
(BB) *** Naxos Dig. 8.550822 [id.]. Zofia Kilanowicz, Polish Nat. RSO, Antoni Wit.
**(*) Koch Schwann 311041 [id.]. Stefania Woytowicz, Berlin RSO, Kamirski; or Warsaw CO, Karol
Teutsch;

(i) *Symphony No. 3 (Symphony of sorrowful songs)* for soprano and orchestra; (ii) *3 pieces in olden style for string orchestra;* (iii) *Amen for choir.*
**(*) Olympia OCD 313 [id.]. (i) Stefania Woytowicz, Polish R. Nat. SO (Katowice), Katlewicz; (ii) Warsaw Nat. Philharmonic CO, Teutsch (iii) Poznan Boys' Ch., Kurczewski.

Scored for strings and piano with soprano solo in each of the three movements, all predominantly slow, Górecki's *Symphony No. 3* sets three laments taking the theme of motherhood. The first movement, nearly half an hour long, resolves on the central setting of a fifteenth-century text from a monastic collection. The second movement incongruously brings a switch to a sensuously beautiful idiom, with the soprano solo soaring radiantly. The third movement is the setting of a folksong with a two-chord ostinato as accompaniment, concluding in a passage of total peace. The Sinfonietta's fine performance, beautifully recorded, is crowned by the radiant singing of Dawn Upshaw.

It is good to have two excellent super-bargain versions of this moving work. Katowice was where the symphony was written and the performance by the State Philharmonic is deeply felt, the hypnotic power of the undulating, arching climax of the first movement well caught. Zofia Kilanowicz's strong, richly timbred soprano contribution is well balanced with string textures that are satisfyingly full-bodied. There could perhaps be more variety of dynamic in the second and third movements, but the effect remains hypnotic.

The Naxos alternative has the advantage of digital recording, a wider dynamic range and, of course, background silence. The sound itself is full, but not quite as lavish as the Belart; on the other hand, detail is more refined and the focus more real. By the time she had come to re-record the work, Zofia Kilanowicz had obviously become even more immersed in the word-settings. In the work's closing section, with its hint of a gentle but remorseless tolling bell, Wit achieves a mood of simple serenity, even forgiveness. The *Three Pieces in olden style* make a fine postlude, the second with its dance figurations, the third with its fierce tremolando violins, like shafts of bright light, suddenly resolving to a very positive ending. All in all, this seems in many ways a 'best buy'.

The performance on Olympia shares the same soloist as the Koch alternative. Stefania Woytowicz sings this most rewarding solo part beautifully and the overall performance is very satisfying. The analogue sound is full and this disc includes not only the triptych of string pieces but also a brief but rather telling choral *Amen*. Excellent value.

The Koch performance is also most eloquent, with Woytowicz again completely at home in her solo role, but it is no more moving than either of the bargain versions and the analogue recording is not appreciably finer than that offered on Belart.

Genesis I (Elementi per tre archi); Sonata for 2 violins, Op. 10; String quartets Nos. 1 (Already it is dusk), Op. 62; 2 (Quasi una fantasia), Op. 64.
*** Olympia OCD 375 [id.]. Silesian Qt.

This record (74 minutes) contains all Górecki's chamber music written so far. As a listening experience it is certainly stimulating but hardly reassuring. Indeed one could be forgiven for thinking that the composer is very pessimistic about the human condition. The opening of the *Double violin sonata* is harsh and spiky and, although calm soon descends, it is an uneasy calm and the restlessness soon reasserts itself. Whether or not the opening of *Genesis* is meant to simulate an air-raid siren, it is an extraordinary effect. Indeed this work is full of extraordinary effects: some of the scrapings and fizzings here are remarkably imaginative. If this is the beginning of life, the bubblings and glissandi suggest a volatile primeval melting pot. The *First Quartet* opens with an emphatic chord which diminuendos; then mysticism takes over, with emphatic chordal interruptions; later there is a nagging ostinato which produces a climax of considerable power. The *Second Quartet* begins in an atmosphere of utter desolation; the effect is of a desperate plodding journey to nowhere: the music crescendos and then falls back. The *Arioso* slow movement begins in a mood of piercing despair – though, to be fair, there is a warmer, calmer interlude to follow. The finale moves on with a remorseless, toccata-like insistence, then the slow plodding of the work's opening reappears and, gradually becoming less insistent, returns the music to infinity. The playing throughout this collection combines power and intensity. The recording is of very high quality. The composer was present and there is something special about these performances.

VOCAL MUSIC

(i) *Miserere, Op. 44; Amen, Op. 35; Euntes ibant et flebant, Op. 32;* (ii) *Wuslo moja (My Vistula, grey Vistula), Op. 46; Szeroka woda (Broad waters): choral suite of folksongs, Op. 39 (Oh, our River Narew; Oh, when in Powistle; Oh, Johnny, Johnny; She picked wild roses; Broad waters).*
(Y/B) *** Nonesuch/Warner 7559 79348-2 [id.]. (i) Chicago Symphony Ch. & Lyric Op. Ch., Nelson; (ii) Lyra Chamber Ch., Lucy Ding.

Górecki's powerful *Miserere* was prompted by the political upheaval in Poland in 1981, when a demonstration by members of Solidarity was quelled by the militia and many workers were injured. Górecki set a text of only five words: *Domine Deus noster, Miserere nobis*; although the work's span is ambitious, it is sustained by profound intensity of feeling. The repetitions of the words '*Domine Deus*' call for all the composer's resourcefulness; the poignant final cry, '*Miserere nobis*', is kept for the last three minutes. The combined Chicago choirs maintain the sombrely atmospheric opening pianissimo with impressive concentration, and the dynamic climax of the piece, when the combined choirs sing in ten parts, is very compelling. The following *Amen* is powerfully concentrated, while *Euntes ibant et flebant* (the composer's first work for unaccompanied chorus) is simpler, more serene. The five folksong settings are also essentially expressive (even *Oh, Johnny, Johnny* is marked *Molto lento – dolce cantabile*) and all are harmonically rich. They are beautifully sung by the smaller group. The recording, made in the Church of St Mary of the Angels in Chicago, is admirable.

Gottschalk, Louis (1829–69)

(i; ii) *Grande tarantelle for piano and orchestra;* (ii) *Symphony No. 1 (A Night in the tropics);* (iii) Music for one piano, four hands: *L'étincelle; La gallina; La jota aragonesa; Marche de nuit; Orfa; Printemps d'amour; Radieuse; Réponds-moi; Ses yeux; Souvenirs d'Andalousie; Tremolo.* (2 pianos): *The Union* (concert paraphrase on national airs).
(M) *** Van. 08.4051 71. (i) Reid Nibley; (ii) Utah SO, Abravanel; (iii) Eugene List with Cary Lewis or Joseph Werner.

With nearly 77 minutes of music this well-recorded Vanguard reissue makes an ideal introduction to Gottschalk's music. The *Grande tarantelle* has a very catchy main theme which keeps returning and never wears out its welcome when the performance is so vivacious. As might be expected, the two-movement *Night in the tropics* uses its title of 'symphony' very loosely. It begins somewhat soupily, then in Abravanel's hands develops a full head of emotional steam; the second movement is a kind of samba, rhythmically very winning. The music for piano, four hands, is played with flair and scintillating upper tessitura. The opening arrangement of *La jota aragonesa* heads an ear-tickling programme, with a touch of wit in the piece called *Tremolo*. When the participants move to two pianos for *The Union* concert paraphrase, the acoustic expands and the effect is properly grand, yet the balance is not too close and the players are still able to produce delicate tonal contrasts. The orchestral recordings date from 1962, the piano pieces from 1976, and the sound is excellent throughout.

PIANO MUSIC
Piano music for four hands

Le Bananier (Chanson nègre), Op. 5; La Gallina (Danse cubaine), Op. 53; Grande Tarantelle, Op. 67; La jota aragonesa (Caprice espagnol), Op. 14; Marche de nuit, Op. 17; Ojos criollos (Danse cubaine – Caprice brillante), Op. 37; Orfa (Grande polka), Op. 71; Printemps d'amour (Mazurka-caprice de concert), Op. 40; Réponds moi (Danse cubaine), Op. 50; Radieuse (Grand valse de concert), Op. 72; La Scintilla (L'Etincelle – Mazurka sentimentale), Op. 21; Ses yeux (Célébre polka de concert), Op. 66.
**(*) Nimbus Dig. NI 5324 [id.]. Alan Marks & Nerine Barrett (piano, 4 hands).

Alan Marks and Nerine Barrett make an effervescent Gottschalk partnership, playing this repertoire to the manner born. *La jota aragonesa* shimmers with twinkling light, while the *Grande tarantelle* makes a splendid finale. The slight snag is that they are – very realistically – recorded in an empty, resonant hall.

Solo piano music

Bamboula; Le Bananier; Le Banjo; The Dying Poet; The Last hope; The Maiden's blush; Ojos criollos; Pasquinade; La Savane; Souvenir de Porto Rico; Suis-moi!; Tournament galop.
(M) *** Van. 08.4050.71 [OVC 4050]. Eugene List.

Eugene List made this repertoire very much his own in the USA in the late 1950s and early '60s, and his performances are second to none. The glittering roulades in *Le Bananier* and *Ojos criollos* are brought off with unaffected brilliance, and the plucking imitations at the close of *The Banjo* are equally successful. The pieces with sentimental titles are more appealing than their names might suggest. The *Souvenir de Porto Rico*, a set of variations, is given real substance, and the *Tournament galop* closes the recital at an infectious canter. The recording dates from 1956 but doesn't sound its age at all: it is very well balanced and realistic.

Le Banjo; Berceuse (cradle song); *The dying poet* (meditation); *Grand Scherzo; The last hope* (religious meditation); *Mazurka; Le Mancenillier* (West Indian serenade); *Pasquinade caprice; Scherzo romantique; Souvenirs d'Andalousie; Tournament galop; The Union: Concert paraphrase on national airs (The Star-spangled banner; Yankee Doodle; Hail Columbia).*
*** Nimbus Dig. NI 5014 [id.]. Alan Marks.

Alan Marks plays with unassuming panache: his *Souvenirs d'Andalousie* glitter with bravura, his felicity of touch and crisp articulation bring much sparkle to the *Grand scherzo* and *Scherzo romantique*, while he sounds like a full orchestra in the *Tournament galop*. Most importantly, he finds simplicity and charm in the delightful *Berceuse* and *Le Mancenillier*, while there is not a hint of sentimentality in *The last hope* or *The dying poet*. He is most realistically recorded in a fairly reverberant acoustic, which suits the flair of his playing.

Gould, Morton (1913–96)

Derivations for clarinet and band.
*** Sony MK 42227 [id.]. Benny Goodman, Columbia Jazz Combo, composer – BARTOK: *Contrasts;* BERNSTEIN: *Prelude, fugue and riffs;* COPLAND: *Concerto;* STRAVINSKY: *Ebony concerto.* (***)

Gould's *Derivations* is in Gershwinesque mould. Benny Goodman is in his element, and the accompaniment under the composer is suitably improvisatory in feeling.

Fall River legend (ballet; complete).
*** Albany Dig. TROY 035 [id.]. Brock Peters, National PO, Milton Rosenstock (with recorded conversation between Agnes de Mille and Morton Gould).

This complete recording of *Fall River legend* opens dramatically with the Speaker for the Jury reading out the Indictment at the trial, and then the ballet tells the story of Lizzie Borden in flashback. Gould's music has a good deal in common with the folksy writing in Copland's *Appalachian spring*, and it is given a splendidly atmospheric performance and recording by the New York orchestra under Rosenstock. There is also a 26-minute discussion on the creation of the ballet between Agnes de Mille and the composer.

Fall River legend (ballet): *suite. Latin-American symphonette: Tango and Guaracha.*
(M) *** RCA 09026 61505-2. O, composer – COPLAND: *Appalachian spring* etc. ***

Morton Gould's own recording of the suite from *Fall River legend* is so vivid and atmospheric that at times one almost thinks this could be Copland. The two movements from the engaging *Latin-American symphonette* are also splendidly done. With astonishingly full and vivid recording (made in the New York Manhattan Center in 1960), triumphantly remastered by John Pfeiffer, the irresistibly catchy *Guaracha* is demonstration-worthy.

Fall River legend: suite; Spirituals for string choir and orchestra.
(M) *** Mercury 432 016-2 [id.]. Eastman-Rochester SO, Howard Hanson – BARBER: *Medea: suite.* ***

The composer's orchestral suite from the ballet is brightly played by the Eastman-Rochester Orchestra under the highly sympathetic Howard Hanson, who also gives an outstandingly vibrant account of the *Spirituals*. The 1959/60 Mercury recording has astonishing clarity, range and presence.

Spirituals for string choir and orchestra.
(Y/B) *** Everest EVC 9003 [id.]. LSO, Walter Susskind – COPLAND: *Appalachian spring* ***; GERSHWIN: *American in Paris.* **(*)

It is unexpected to find an English performance of this essentially American piece, the more so as it has never been bettered, not even by the composer himself. The slow movement is really moving and *A little bit of sin* is wittily pungent, while the wide-ranging recording (brightly lit in a transatlantic way) looks after the dramatic needs of *Protest* and the ambivalent exuberance of *Jubilee*. The couplings are hardly less welcome.

Gounod, Charles (1818–93)

Faust: ballet music and Waltz.
(B) **(*) Ph. Duo 438 763-2 [id.]. Rotterdam PO, David Zinman – DELIBES: *Coppélia;* CHOPIN: *Les Sylphides.* **(*)
(B) **(*) DG Double 437 404-2 (2) [id.]. BPO, Karajan – CHOPIN: *Les Sylphides* *** ✿; DELIBES:

Coppélia (ballet) *suite;* OFFENBACH: *Gaîté parisienne;* RAVEL: *Boléro* ***; TCHAIKOVSKY: *Sleeping Beauty* (suite). **(*)

If without quite the panache of a Beecham, David Zinman's account of the *Faust ballet music* springs readily to life: it has polish and elegance. Very good (1980) recording in a warm acoustic ensures the listener's aural pleasure, making this collection a genuine bargain.

Brilliant orchestral playing from the Berlin Philharmonic and vivid recording, very brightly lit. But there is a degree of streamlining and the *Waltz*, though undoubtedly exuberant, lacks something in charm. Even so, the polish of the playing is impressive. This comes in an excellent Double DG anthology which as a whole is very good value.

Petite symphonie for winds.
** Koch Dig. 3-7067-2 [id.]. Sinfonia O of Chicago, Barry Faldner – DEBUSSY: *Symphony in B min,;* MILHAUD: *Symphonies for chamber orchestra.* **

A very polished and professional account of Gounod's delightful *Petite symphonie*, as one would expect from these first-desk players of the Chicago Symphony Orchestra. It is very well recorded too, and yields to rivals only in wanting just the last ounce of charm that is surely essential in this music.

Mélodies and songs: *L'absent; The arrow and the song; Au rossignol; Ave Maria; Boléro; Ma belle amie est morte; La Biondina* (song-cycle); *Ce que je suis sans toi; Chanson de printemps; Clos ta paupière; Envoi de fleurs; The fountain mingles with the river; If thou art sleeping, maiden; Ilala; A lay of the early spring; Loin du pays; Maid of Athens; Mignon; My true love hath my heart; Oh happy home! o blessed flower!; Où voulez-vous aller?; La Pâquerette; Prière; Rêverie; Sérénade; Le soir; Le temps des roses; Trust her not!; Venise; The worker.*
*** Hyperion Dig. CDA 66801/2 [id.]. Felicity Lott, Ann Murray, Anthony Rolfe Johnson, Graham Johnson.

As in his Schubert series, also for Hyperion, Graham Johnson here brings a revelation, thanks not only to his inspired playing but also to his devising of an enchanting programme of 41 songs. It presents the full span of Gounod's achievement not just in French mélodie (on the first of the two discs) but also in songs Gounod wrote during his extended stay in England. The lyrical innocence of the inspiration regularly conceals both the originality of the writing and the technical problems for the performers. The soloists here, all regular contributors to Johnson's Songmakers' Almanac, are at their very finest. So on the first disc, after charming performances of the opening items from Felicity Lott, Ann Murray enters magically, totally transforming the hackneyed lines of *Ave Maria*, before tackling the most joyous of Gounod songs, the barcarolle-like *Serenade*. Rolfe Johnson is comparably perceptive in *Biondina*, bringing out the Neapolitan-song overtones, as well as in six of the English settings. As in the Schubert series, Johnson's notes are a model of scholarship, both informed and fascinating.

Mélodies: *Crépuscule; Envoi de fleurs; Hymne à la nuit; Medjé; Si la mort est le but.*
**(*) EMI Dig. CDC7 54818-2 [id.]. José van Dam, Jean-Philippe Collard – MASSENET; SAINT-SAENS: *Mélodies.* **(*)

As in Massenet and Saint-Saëns, José van Dam's firm, dark tone brings out the beauty of these five Gounod songs, even though he tends to miss the subtler shades of meaning, not always helped by Collard, heavier-handed here than in his solo playing.

Messe solennelle de Saint Cécile.
*** EMI Dig. CDC7 47094-2 [id.]. Hendricks, Dale, Lafont, Ch. and Nouvel O Philharmonique of R. France, Prêtre.

Gounod's *Messe solennelle*, with its blatant march setting of the *Credo* and sugar-sweet choral writing, may not be for sensitive souls, but Prêtre here directs an almost ideal performance, vividly recorded, with glowing singing from the choir as well as the three soloists.

Faust (complete).
🏵 *** Teldec/Warner Dig. 4509 90872-2 (3) [id.]. Hadley, Gasdia, Ramey, Mentzer, Agache, Fassbaender, Welsh Nat. Op. Ch. & O, Rizzi.
*** EMI Dig. CDS7 54228-2 (3) [id.]. Leech, Studer, Van Dam, Hampson, Ch. & O of Capitole de Toulouse, Plasson.
(Y/B) (M) **(*) EMI CMS7 69983-2 (3) [Ang. CDMC 69983]. De los Angeles, Gedda, Blanc, Christoff, Paris Nat. Op. Ch. and O, Cluytens.
(N) (M) (***) EMI mono CMS5 65256-2 (3). De los Angeles, Gedda, Christoff, Borthayre, Angelici, Paris Opéra Ch. & O, Cluytens.

Rizzi, with an outstanding cast and vividly clear recording, makes the whole score with its astonishing sequence of memorable, tuneful numbers seem totally fresh and new. If the EMI version under Plasson offers a beefy, thrusting performance, together with a strong cast, Rizzi reminds one, generally with more spacious speeds, that such a strikingly eventful and expressive score is not totally unworthy of Goethe. Jerry Hadley as Faust has lyrical freshness rather than heroic power, brought out in his headily beautiful performance of *Salut! demeure*. Yet here is a positive figure and, like Rizzi's conducting, his singing has more light and shade in it than that of rivals. The tenderness as well as the bright agility of Cecilia Gasdia's singing as Marguerite brings comparable variety of expression, with the *Roi de Thulé* song deliberately drained of colour to contrast with the brilliance of the *Jewel song* which follows. Her performance culminates in an angelic contribution to the final duet, with Rizzi's slow speed encouraging refinement, leading up to a shattering moment of judgement and a fine apotheosis. Alexander Agache as Valentin may be less characterful than Hampson on the EMI set, but his voice is caught more richly; but it is the commandingly demonic performance of Samuel Ramey as Mephistopheles that sets the seal on the whole set, far more sinister than José van Dam on EMI. The clarity and precision of both performance and recording, so far from blunting the power of the piece, enhance it. Like the EMI set, the Teldec offers a valuable appendix, not just the full ballet music but numbers cut from the definitive score – a drinking song for Faust and a charming aria for Siebel. EMI's supplementary items, four, all different, are more generous, but musically less interesting.

With his excellent cast headed by three American singers, Plasson comes near to providing a completely recommendable *Faust*, even if José van Dam's gloriously dark, finely focused bass-baritone does not have the heft of a full-blooded bass voice such as is associated with the role of Mephistopheles. That said, it is a masterly performance, searching and sinister, with the singer consistently exploiting his idiomatic French. Cheryl Studer conveys the girlishness of Marguerite, using the widest range of dynamic and colour. If Richard Leech's voice might in principle seem too lightweight for the role of Faust, the lyrical flow and absence of strain make his singing consistently enjoyable. As Valentin, Thomas Hampson is strongly cast, with his firm, heroic baritone. The sound has a good sense of presence, set in a pleasantly reverberant acoustic which does not obscure necessary detail. In addition to supplementary numbers, the appendix offers the complete ballet music.

In the reissued Cluytens set, the seductiveness of De los Angeles's singing is a dream and it is a pity that the recording hardens the natural timbre slightly. Christoff is magnificently Mephistophelian. Gedda, though showing some signs of strain, sings intelligently, and among the other soloists Ernest Blanc has a pleasing, firm voice, which he uses to make Valentin into a sympathetic character. Cluytens's approach is competent but somewhat workaday. The set has been attractively repackaged and the libretto has strikingly clear print, to make a good mid-priced choice for this popular opera.

Not to be confused with the stereo remake of this opera with the same three principals (and conductor), this mono set of 1953 offers an advantage in the extra freshness of Victoria de los Angeles as Marguerite, sparkling and girlish, with Gedda also in fresher voice. Christoff is more uninhibited here, which makes his French even less idiomatic, but the result is thrilling; Jean Borthayre as Valentin and Martha Angelici as Siebel sing beautifully. The mono sound, less dry than others from this source, captures the voices well, and Cluytens proves a persuasive interpreter.

Faust (opera): highlights.
(N) (M) *** Teldec/Warner Dig. 0630 13806-9 [id.] (from above complete recording, with Hadley, Gasdia, Ramey; cond. Rizzi).
(M) *** EMI CD-EMX 2215 (from above complete set, with De los Angeles, Gedda; cond. Cluytens).

The Teldec CD makes an obvious first choice for highlights from this ever-tuneful opera. The 76-minute selection is well made to include both the finale and the ballet music. No translations are offered but there is a cued synopsis.

The one important snag in the EMI complete set was Cluytens's rather ungracious conducting. But in this generous 75–minute set of excerpts his crisp efficiency is more than acceptable. The singing gives much pleasure, particularly that of de los Angeles and Christoff, and the choral contribution is spirited. Excellent value and an ideal way of sampling a performance which has many virtues.

Faust (abridged version sung in English with ballet music; introduced by Sir Thomas Beecham).
(Y/B) (M) *** Dutton mono 2CDAX 2001 (2) [id.] Nash, Licette, Easton, Williams, Vane, Brunskill, Carr, BBC Ch. & SO, LPO, Sir Thomas Beecham.

Beecham's 1929 recording, superbly transferred on the Dutton label, with full-bodied sound for voices and orchestra alike, gives a vivid and refreshing idea of British opera performance in the 1920s. The old Chorley translation is used, stilted and creaking but memorable – 'What rubbishy wine!' says Mephistopheles – and the team of top British singers of the day is at one in enunciating words with crystal clarity. Voices are firm and cleanly projected, with the bright-toned Miriam Licette as Marguerite delivering a splendid trill at the start of the *Jewel song*. Heddle Nash sings with heady tone as Faust, Harold Williams is a youthfully fresh Valentine and the distinctive flicker in Robert Easton's bass never gets in the way of clean focus in the role of Mephistopheles. Beecham himself is inspired, pointing rhythms and phrases infectiously, though, curiously, four of the 32 sides of the original 78s were conducted by Clarence Raybould. A supplement on the second CD includes a brief spoken introduction by Beecham, as well as the *Nubian dance* and *Adagio* from the ballet music – otherwise omitted, like the *Walpurgisnacht* scene.

Mireille (complete).
(M) (**) EMI mono CMS7 64382-2 (2) [id.]. Vivalda, Gedda, Gayraud, Dens, Ignal, Aix-en-Provence Festival Ch., Paris Conservatoire O, Cluytens.

This EMI *Mireille* is disappointing, not only thanks to limited mono sound but also to the performance, far too rigidly conducted by Cluytens to bring out the Provençal charm of this rustic opera, with even the *Farandole chorus* sounding stiff. As Mireille, Janette Vivalda sings unimaginatively with shrill, bright tone, not helped by the recording. Happily, the other soloists are more sympathetic. The young Nicolai Gedda sings most beautifully as the hero, Vincent, and the mezzo Christiane Gayraud is comparably rich as the gypsy, Taven, with Michel Dens ringingly clear, if hardly sinister, as the villain, Ourrias.

Roméo et Juliette (complete).
(Y/B) (B) (**(*)) Decca Double mono 443 539-2 (2) [id.]. Jobin, Micheau, Mollet, Rialland, Rehfuss, Opéra Nat. Ch. & O, Erede.
(Y/B) (M) ** EMI CMS5 65290-2 (2) [CDMB 65290]. Corelli, Freni, Calès, Depraz, Paris Op. Ch. & O, Lombard.

This 1953 Decca mono set is well worth considering. With a first-rate cast singing idiomatically, the result is fresh and full of fire. It is an interesting comment that in 1953 Paris could offer a far finer team of singers than latterly, with the tenor Pierre Mollet, for example, light and airy as Mercutio, not least in the *Queen Mab aria*, and Charles Cambon a fine Capulet. The only non-French singer, Heinz Rehfuss, projects with the clearest focus as Frère Laurent, while the roles of the two lovers are taken by two vintage singers of the period, not always ideally caught on record but both warmly characterful. Janine Micheau is tenderly charming as a vulnerably girlish Juliette and, as Roméo, Raoul Jobin sings stylishly and with little of the pinched tone that too often has afflicted French tenors. The transfer is more than full-bodied enough to compensate for the slightly edgy top.

On EMI, the great pity is that the casting of this great and rich opera is basically inadequate. Neither Corelli as Romeo nor Freni as Juliet is remotely in style, even though their tones are often beautiful to the ear. Why was it not possible in a French-made recording to correct the often excruciating pronunciation of the two principals? Freni with her sweet tone and natural charm comes much closer to the mark than her partner and so much revolves around the lovers' four big duets. The conducting of Alain Lombard makes up some ground with its warm, idiomatic understanding; but it could all have been so much better without difficulty. The set is well presented and documented and brightly and vividly transferred, the chorus well focused yet with plenty of atmosphere overall. The break between the two CDs comes between the first and second scenes of Act III.

Sapho (complete).
** Koch Dig. 3-1311-2 (2) [id.]. Command, Coste, Papis, Faury, Sarrazin, St Etienne Lyric Ch., Nouvel O de St-Ètienne, Fournillier.

Sapho contains a sequence of delightful numbers, starting with a beautiful tenor aria, *Puis-je oublier*. There follows a splendid quartet, a baritone aria, *O liberté*, which provocatively hints at the *Marseillaise*, and some magnificent solos for the mezzo taking the title-role, culminating in a sombre and spacious suicide aria. Though the Saint-Etienne orchestra under Fournillier too often sounds limp, partly thanks to the washy live recording, the solo singing is strong enough to convey both the power and the beauty of much of the writing. The rich mezzo, Michèle Command, in the title-role is well contrasted with the sweet, bright soprano, Sharon Coste, as Glycère. Christian Papis as Phaon ably uses a head-voice to cope with stratospheric notes in the tenor role, and the young baritone, Eric Faury, is fresh and confident as the rival poet to Sappho, Alcée.

Gouvy, Louis Théodore (1819–98)

Aubade, Op. 77/2; Ghiribizzi, Op. 83; 6 Morceaux, Op. 59; Scherzo, P77/1; Sonatas: in D min., Op. 36; in C min., Op. 49; in F, Op. 51.
(✹) *** Sony Dig. SK 53110 [id.]. Yaara Tal, Andreas Groethuysen.

Louis Théodore Gouvy was born near Saarbrücken and was equally at home with French and German cultures. The artists say that on first hearing they noticed clear affinities with Bizet, Mendelssohn, Offenbach and Schumann before becoming conscious of 'the uniqueness of his musical language'. They also speak of falling in love with this music at first sight, and this is how the playing sounds: beautifully shaped without being in the slightest bit beautified, every shading of colour and dynamic scrupulously observed without the slightest exaggeration. As piano duet playing, it is absolutely outstanding; so, too, is the recording.

Grainger, Percy (1882–1961)

Blithe bells (Free ramble on a theme by Bach: Sheep may safely graze): Country gardens; Green bushes (Passacaglia); Handel in the Strand; Mock morris; Molly on the shore; My Robin is to the greenwood gone; Shepherd's hey; Spoon River; Walking tune; Youthful rapture.
(M) *** Chandos CHAN 6542 [id.]. Bournemouth Sinf., Montgomery.

For those wanting only a single Grainger orchestral collection, this could be first choice. Among the expressive pieces, the arrangement of *My Robin is to the greenwood gone* is highly attractive, but the cello solo in *Youthful rapture* is perhaps less effective. Favourites such as *Country gardens, Shepherd's hey, Molly on the shore* and *Handel in the Strand* all sound as fresh as new paint. The 1978 recording, made in Christchurch Priory, has retained all its ambient character in its CD transfer.

Children's march; Colonial song; Country gardens; Handel in the Strand; The immovable 'Do'; Irish tune from County Derry; Mock Morris; Molly on the shore; My Robin is to the greenwood gone; Shepherd's hey; Spoon River.
(M) ** Mercury 434 330-2 [id.]. Eastman-Rochester Pops O, Fennell – COATES: *Three Elizabeths suite.* **(*)

Lively and sympathetic performances from Fennell, and good playing. But the 1959 Mercury sound here is more dated than most CDs from this source: the acoustics of the Eastman Theatre in Rochester are too dry for Grainger's more expansive string writing in the *Colonial song* and the *Irish tune from County Derry*. The pithily rhythmic pieces like *Mock Morris* come off best as the sound is always clear and clean.

Children's march; Country gardens; Over the hills and far away; Irish tune from County Derry; The Lincolnshire posy; Molly on the shore.
(M) *** EMI Dig. CDM5 65122-2. Central Band of the RAF, Wing Commander Eric Banks – HOLST: *Suites;* VAUGHAN WILLIAMS: *English folksong suite.* ***

Marvellously spirited and colourful performances from the RAF Central Band under Wing Commander Banks. His sense of pacing is exhilarating, yet the band produces a fine, full sonority for the famous *Londonderry air*, thanks to the acoustics of Watford Town Hall and the excellent engineering of Brian Culverhouse. There are few military band records to match this.

Irish tune from County Derry; Lincolnshire Posy (suite); Molly on the shore; Shepherd's hey.
(M) *** ASV CDWHL 2067. L. Wind O, Wick – MILHAUD; POULENC: *Suite française.* ***

First-class playing and vivid recording, with the additional attraction of delightful couplings, make this very highly recommendable.

The Warriors (music for an imaginary ballet).
(Y/B) *** DG Dig. 445 860-2; 445 860-4 [id.]. Philh. O, Gardiner – HOLST: *The Planets.* ***

Colourful and vigorous, *The Warriors* is described as 'an imaginary ballet for orchestra and three pianos', a characteristically extrovert showpiece, Grainger's largest work. With richly scored echoes of *Rosenkavalier* and *Petrushka* brought improbably together at the start, the piece throbs with energy, at one point – in a gentler interlude – involving an offstage orchestra in Ivesian superimpositions. If much of the writing, with the piano prominent in the orchestra, sounds as though it is about to turn into Grainger's *Handel in the Strand*, plus an echo or two of Eric Coates, the result is hugely enjoyable in such a fine performance as Gardiner's. It makes an unexpected and valuable coupling for his brilliant account of the favourite Holst work. Dazzling sound.

PIANO MUSIC

'Dished up for piano', Volume 1: Andante con moto; Arrival platform humlet; Bridal lullaby; Children's march; Colonial song; English waltz; Gay but wistful; The Gum-suckers' march; Handel in the Strand; Harvest hymn; The immovable 'Do'; In a Nutshell (suite); In Dahomey; Mock morris; Pastoral; Peace; Sailor's song; Saxon twi-play; To a Nordic princess; Walking tune.
*** Nimbus Dig. NI 5220 [id.]. Martin Jones.

'Dished up for piano', Volume 2: Arrangements: BACH: Blithe bells. BRAHMS: Cradle song. Chinese TRAD.: Beautiful fresh flower. DOWLAND: Now, o now, I needs must part. ELGAR: Enigma variations: Nimrod. Stephen FOSTER: Lullaby; The rag-time girl. GERSHWIN: Love walked in; The man I love. RACHMANINOV: Piano concerto No. 2: Finale (abridged). R. STRAUSS: Der Rosenkavalier: Ramble on the last love-duet. TCHAIKOVSKY: Piano concerto No. 1 (opening); Paraphrase on the Flower waltz.
**(*) Nimbus Dig. NI 5232 [id.]. Martin Jones.

'Dished up for piano', Volume 3: Folksong arrangements: The brisk young sailor; Bristol Town; Country gardens; Died for love; Hard-hearted Barb'ra Helen; The hunter in his career; Irish tune from County Derry; Jutish medley; Knight and shepherd's daughter; Lisbon (Dublin Bay); The merry king; Mo Ninghean Dhu; Molly on the shore; My Robin is to Greenwood gone; One more day my John (2 versions, easy and complex); Near Woodstock Town; The nightingale and the two sisters; O gin I were where Gowrie rins; Rimmer and goldcastle; The rival brothers; Scotch Strathspey; Shepherd's hey; Spoon River; Stalt vesselil; Sussex mummer's Christmas carol; The widow's party; Will ye gang to the Hielands, Lizzie Lindsay.
*** Nimbus Dig. NI 5244 [id.]. Martin Jones.

Martin Jones's survey of Grainger's piano music is refreshingly lively and spontaneous. Volume 1 is particularly attractive, and that is the place to start, for there is not a dull item here. There is plenty of dash in the folksong arrangements, and charm too, and they display a much greater range than one might have expected. The transcriptions are the most fascinating of all. The opening of the Tchaikovsky Piano concerto – some would say the 'best bit' – is transcribed straightforwardly, with a flamboyant flourish to finish it off, and the purple patch at the end of the Rachmaninov No. 2 cannot fail to make an impact in a performance as brilliant as this. Martin Jones is equally good in the freely composed pastiche on Bach's Sheep may safely graze (Blithe bells). But he plays Nimrod and the Der Rosenkavalier excerpts too slowly; such a degree of languor might come off with the orchestra, but on the piano the effect is enervating. The piano is recorded reverberantly in the Nimbus manner – but it rather suits this repertoire, and the image is absolutely truthful.

VOCAL MUSIC

Folksong arrangements: The Bride's tragedy (for chorus & orchestra); Brigg Fair (for tenor & chorus); Danny Deever (for baritone, chorus & orchestra); Father and daughter (A Faeroe Island dancing ballad; for 5 solo narrators, double chorus, & 3 instrumental groups); I'm seventeen come Sunday (for chorus, brass & percussion); Irish tune from County Derry (Londonderry air; for wordless chorus); The Lost lady found; Love verses from The Song of Solomon (for tenor & chamber orchestra); The merry wedding (Bridal dances; for 9 soloists, chorus, brass, percussion, strings & organ); My dark-haired maiden (Mi nighean dhu; for mixed voices); Scotch strathspey and reel – inlaid with several Irish and Scotch tunes and a sea shanty (orchestral version); Shallow Brown (for solo voice or unison chorus, with an orchestra of 13 or more instruments); The Three ravens (for baritone solo, mixed chorus & 5 clarinets); Tribute to Foster (for vocal quintet, male chorus & instrumental ensemble).
(N) ❀ *** Ph. Dig. 446 657-2 [id.]. Soloists, Monteverdi Ch., English Country Gardiner O, Gardiner.

It would be hard to imagine a more exhilarating disc of Grainger's music than this collection of 'songs and dancing ballads'. John Eliot Gardiner met the eccentric composer as a child and has become devoted to his music. The variety is astonishing even among the folksong settings, which often use melodies transcribed from original sources by Grainger himself. Gardiner singles out the hypnotically measured sea-shanty, Shallow Brown, as the most 'searingly original' of Grainger's works and the most haunting. The performance here backs that up, with furious tremolandos from guitars and banjos, which Grainger called 'wogglings'. The richest, most exotic piece is the setting of Love verses from The Song of Solomon, while the longest and most elaborate items bring astonishingly original effects for both voices and orchestra, the richly evocative Tribute to Stephen Foster and the setting of a mock Scottish ballad by Swinburne, The Bride's tragedy, which Grainger described as a pained 'grumble-shout'. All 14 items, many of them first-ever recordings, bring typically quirky inspirations, superbly interpreted. Even if the choir's attempts at various dialects, from Mummerset onwards, may not be to everyone's taste, the virtuosity of the singing is breathtaking. The bitter element in some of the numbers provides a clue to the inspiration which fired Grainger, as in the grim setting of Kipling's *Danny Deever*, with its refrain, 'Oh they're hanging Danny Deever in the morning'. Echoing Mahler in its subject, it is far more angry. Superb sound, though (because of the complexity of textures) words are often inaudible. Full text and really outstanding notes – a model of what documentation should be with a full-priced CD.

Duke of Marlborough fanfare; Green bushes (Passacaglia); Irish tune from County Derry; Lisbon; Molly on the shore; My Robin is to Greenwood gone; Shepherd's hey; Piano duet: Let's dance gay in green meadow; Vocal & choral: *Bold William Taylor; Brigg Fair; I'm seventeen come Sunday; Lord Maxwell's goodnight; The lost lady found; The pretty maid milkin' her cow; Scotch strathspey and reel; Shallow Brown; Shenandoah; The sprig of thyme; There was a pig went out to dig; Willow willow.*
(M) *** Decca 425 159-2. Pears, Shirley-Quirk, Amb. S. or Linden Singers, Wandsworth Boys' Ch., ECO, Britten or Steuart Bedford; Britten and V. Tunnard (pianos).

This is an altogether delightful anthology, beautifully played and sung by these distinguished artists. Grainger's imagination in the art of arranging folksong was prodigious. Vocal and instrumental items are felicitously interwoven, and the recording is extremely vivid, though the digital remastering has put a hint of edge on the voices.

Granados, Enrique (1867–1916)

Goyescas: Intermezzo.
(N) (M) *** RCA 09026 62586-2 [id.]. Chicago SO, Reiner – ALBENIZ: *Iberia* etc.; FALLA: *El amor brujo* etc. ***

A totally memorable performance of the *Goyescas intermezzo* from Reiner, seductively sultry and vibrant by turns. The 1958 Chicago recording sounds amazingly rich and vivid.

Cuentos para la juventud, Op. 1: Dedicatoria. Danzas españolas Nos. 4 & 5, Op. 37/4–5; Tonadillas al estilo antiguo: La maja de Goya. Valses poéticos.
(Y/B) ✿ (BB) *** RCA Navigator Dig. 74321 17903-2. Julian Bream (guitar) – ALBENIZ: *Collection;* RODRIGO: *3 Piezas españolas.* *** ✿

Like the Albéniz items with which these Granados pieces are coupled, these performances show Julian Bream at his most inspirational. The illusion of the guitar being in the room is especially electrifying in the middle section of the famous *Spanish dance No. 5*, when Bream achieves the most subtle pianissimo. Heard against the background silence, the effect is quite magical. But all the playing here is wonderfully spontaneous. This is one of the most impressive guitar recitals ever recorded, and for this super-bargain reissue RCA have generously added the *Tres Piezas españolas* of Rodrigo, recorded a year later and no less distinguished.

12 Danzas españolas; Allegro de concierto; El pelele.
(M) *** Decca Analogue/Dig. 433 923-2 (2) [id.]. Alicia de Larrocha – ALBENIZ: *Suite española* etc. ***

Alicia de Larrocha has an aristocratic poise to which it is difficult not to respond, and she plays with great flair and temperament. *El pelele* is an appendix to the *Goyescas* collection and comes as one of two brilliant encores (the sparkling *Allegro de concierto* is digitally recorded). The transfer of the 1982 analogue master to CD has been very successful.

12 Danzas españolas; Goyescas.
(Y/B) (M) *** Ph. 442 751-2 (2) [id.]. Eduardo del Pueyo – FALLA: *Nights in the gardens of Spain.* *** ✿

This set is justly described as 'the quintessence of Spanish pianism', for playing of this repertoire does not come any better than this. Eduardo del Pueyo, born in Aragon, made these recordings in 1956 (although the ear would hardly guess, so natural is the piano recording). His playing of the colourful *Spanish dances* has much flair and poetic delicacy – sample *No. 2 in C minor*, so beautifully articulated – and the magical pianissimo at the centre of No. 5 makes one wonder if Julian Bream listened to Del Pueyo before making his equally memorable account of this famous piece. But it is in the *Goyescas* that Del Pueyo's evocation so immediately captures the Spanish atmosphere, as in *Los requiebros* and *Coloquios en la reja* and especially in the haunting *Quejas o la maja y el ruiseñor*, while the idiomatic brilliance of *El pele* shows restraint as well as spontaneous virtuosity. The Falla coupling is perhaps even more remarkable.

Danzas españolas: Valenciana; Danza triste. Goyescas; El pelele.
(M) (***) EMI mono CDC7 54836-2 [id.]. (i) Composer – FALLA: *Harpsichord concerto* etc.; MOMPOU:
    Piano pieces; NIN: *Cantos populares españolas.* (***)

Granados was a formidable pianist and it was a pity that he did not live long enough to make electric
recordings. The two *Danzas españolas* and *El pelele* from the *Goyescas* were recorded in Barcelona
around 1912 but the engineers have done a marvellous job in restoring them, though they have not been
able to remove all the surface noise in *El pelele* and the sound remains somewhat watery but gives a good
idea of what an impressive and sensitive player he must have been.

Goyescas (complete).
(N) ⊛ [B] *** Decca Double 448 191-2 (2) [id.]. Alicia de Larrocha – ALBENIZ: *Iberia* etc. ***

Goyescas (complete); *Escenas románticas; 6 Piezas sobre cantos populares españoles.*
(M) *** Decca Dig./Analogue 433 920-2 (2). Alicia de Larrocha – ALBENIZ: *Sonata;* SOLER: *8 Sonatas.*
***

Goyescas (complete); *Escenas románticas; 6 Piezas sobre cantos populares españoles; Valses poéticos.*
(M) *** EMI CMS7 64524-2 (2). Alicia de Larrocha.

Alicia de Larrocha brings special insights and sympathy to the *Goyescas* (given top-drawer Decca sound
in 1977); her playing has the crisp articulation and rhythmic vitality that these pieces call for, while she is
hauntingly evocative in *Quejas o la maja y el ruiseñor.* The overall impression could hardly be more
idiomatic in flavour nor more realistic as a recording. The subtle, expressively ambitious *Escenas románticas* again show the surprisingly wide range of Granados's piano music. They were recorded digitally in
1985, as were the *6 Piezas sobre cantos populares españoles.* However, many collectors will opt for the
alternative (and less expensive) Double Decca coupling with Albéniz's *Iberia* which is equally
distinguished.
    Alicia de Larrocha's EMI set of *Goyescas* derives from the Spanish Hispavox catalogue and was made
in 1963, a decade before her first Decca set. The performance is more impulsive, at times more intensely
expressive, if less subtle in feeling than the later version, and the recording, if not as fine as the Decca, is
eminently realistic. The closing *Zapateado* of the *Cantos populares españoles* has a fire and sparkle
characteristic of her playing at this stage of her career.

Grechaninov, Alexander (1864–1956)

Symphony No. 1 in B min., Op. 6; (i) Snowflakes, Op. 47; Missa Sancti Spiritus, Op. 169.
(N) *** Chandos Dig. CHAN 9397 [id.] (i) Russian State Symphony Cappella; Russian State SO,
    Valery Polyansky.

As its opus number indicates, the *First Symphony* is a student work, and it is not particularly individual.
Rimsky-Korsakov spoke of it dismissively ('if someone with a natural inclination to compose in the
style of Rubinstein suddenly takes a fancy to Borodin and begins to compose in his style, it won't
work'), and the debt to Borodin is striking. Even so, it is well-schooled music and, like so much Russian
music of the period, its craftsmanship is not in question. *Snowflakes* is a middle-period work, written
before Grechaninov moved to America after the revolution; and it has charm. The *Missa Sancti Spiritus*
comes from the other end of Grechaninov's long career, when he was living in America. Good performances and excellent recording.

String quartet No. 1 in G, Op. 2.
**(*) Olympia OCD 522 [id.]. Shostakovich Qt – TCHAIKOVSKY: *Adagio molto* etc. **(*)

Alexander Grechaninov was enormously prolific, though little of his music has gained much more than
a precarious foothold on the repertoire. (There are six operas, five symphonies and four quartets.) The
First Quartet in G major (1894) is very much in the mould of Tchaikovsky and Rubinstein, and shows
little individuality. It is unmemorable but is pleasing and well fashioned – and well played, too!

Greef, Arthur de (1862–1940)

Piano concerto No. 1 in C min.
(M) ** EMI CDM5 65075-2 [id.] Jean-Claude vanden Eynden, Liège PO, Pierre Bartholmée –
    JONGEN: *Symphonie concertante.* **

The *First Piano concerto* comes from 1914 and its ethos is clearly that of Liszt, César Franck and Saint-

Saëns, to whom the piece is dedicated. Some passages call Anton Rubinstein to mind, but de Greef has both facility and fantasy. Even if he does not have a strongly individual voice, he is a civilized composer and is well served by his countrymen, Jean-Claude vanden Eynden and the Liège Philharmonic under Pierre Bartholmée. The analogue recording dates from 1977 and is well balanced and spacious.

Gregorian chant

'*The Tradition of Gregorian Chant*': *Mass Propers and chants for Christmas* (Spain); *Easter and Epiphany* (Switzerland); *Good Friday with processionals* (Germany); *other Feast Days* (Italy); *and Vespers* (France).
(M) *** DG 435 032-2 (4) [id.]. Various monastic choirs.

Mass Propers for Good Friday and Easter.
(N) (M) *** DG 447 299-2 [id.]. Abteikirche Münsterschwarzach, Pater Godehard Joppich.
(BB) **(*) Naxos Dig. 8.550951. Nova Schola Gregoriana, Alberto Turco.

Mass Propers for the Church Year.
(BB) *** Naxos Dig. 8.550711. Nova Schola Gregoriana, Alberto Turco.

'*Gregorian chant according to the Aquitaine tradition*': *Mass for St John the Baptist; Mass for the Nativity of Jesus Christ*.
🏵 (B) *** HM HMA 190 3031 [id.]. Schola Hungarica, László Dobszay or Janka Szendrei.

Christmas Eve' (Gregorian chant and simple polyphony from the Middle Ages): *Noel settings; Alleluia and sequence; Antiphons; Chants; Graduals; Hymns; Responses and Tropes*.
(N) [B] *** HM Dig. HMA 190 3037 [id.]. Schola Hungarica, László Dobszay & Janka Szendrei.

The liturgy of the Catholic Church has the Mass as its central focus. The Ordinary of the Mass – those elements that are unchanging through the Church year – have been set by countless composers and include the *Kyrie* ('Lord have mercy'), the *Gloria*, *Credo* and *Sanctus* ('Holy, holy, holy') and the *Agnus Dei*, which is undoubtedly the most important of all for believers ('Lamb of God, who takes away the sins of the world, have mercy on us and grant us peace'). The Mass Propers are chants which change with the seasons of the year or the occasion of the celebration; they consist of Introit, Gradual, Alleluia, Tract, Offertory and Communion. These are amplified by Sequences (accretions to the liturgy) and Tropes (additions which amplify and heighten the meaning of the biblical text in prose or poetry). The changes brought about by the reforming Council of Trent in the sixteenth century removed many of these additions, but they are at the heart of medieval Church music.

To evaluate Gregorian Chant in a volume of this kind is hazardous and essentially subjective. Although this music does give much aesthetic pleasure in that these chants are of great antiquity and beauty, their purpose is devotional and the singers are not 'professional' in any normal sense of the word. The recent vogue for the two-CD EMI set by the monks of the Monasterio Benedictino de Santo Domingo de Silos (EMI CMS5 65217–2) is not directly related to its aesthetic merit, and it would be not entirely appropriate to compare their singing to that from other monasteries as if one were discussing various orchestras, instrumentalist or singers. Gregorian chant does induce a spirit of serenity and repose, but a study of its growth and interpretation is a highly specialized subject.

A useful starting-point for the lay listener might be the four-CD DG set which assembles some of the many fine recordings made by DG's Archiv label during the period 1968–77. This set, called *Die Tradition des gregorianischen Chorale*, collects chant from two Spanish monasteries, Montserrat (1973) and Silos, Burgos (1968), the Abbey of Notre-Dame de Fontgombault in France (1977), the Kloster Maria Einsiedeln in Switzerland (1972), the Cappella Musicale del Duomo di Milano from Italy (1974), and the Abteikirche Münsterschwarzach in Germany. These four CDs include examples of almost all varieties of chant, Gregorian, Ambrosian and Old Spanish. Archive also offer a number of seasonal discs, such as the Gregorian chant for Good Friday and Easter from the Abteikirche Münsterschwarzach, led by Pater Godehard Joppich and recorded in 1981–2, while an inexpensive Naxos disc (with full texts provided, though no translations) by the Nova Schola Gregoriana, directed by the Italian scholar, Alberto Turco, covers this same area very effectively, and this choir is recorded in the Parish Church of Quatrelle, Mantua, which provides a suitably atmospheric setting. However, this fine choral group are heard to even better effect in an excellently chosen 75-minute compilation of chants taken from different Sundays in the Church year.

The opening *Adorate Deum*, which gives the record its title, comes from the Introit of the Third Sunday after the Epiphany, and other chants derive from the Second, Fourth, Eighth and Ninth Sundays after Epiphany, while there are also Gradualia, Versus alleluiatici, Offertoria and Communions for the

Fourth, Ninth, Seventh, Eighteenth, Nineteenth and Twenty-third Sundays after Pentecost, the Fourth Sunday in Quadragesima (the last Friday before Passion Sunday), the Third and Fourth Sundays of Lent, and Sundays within the Octave of the Feast of the Sacred Heart, and the Sunday within the Octave of Corpus Christi. The singing has a firm profile and is well recorded, not seeking to create a purely atmospheric effect. It is a pity that texts and translations are not provided, but the back-up notes are very helpful.

The Chant of the Aquitaine tradition is quite different from anything else previously discussed, not least because it moves forward at a much faster pace, but also because the performances here use a choir which includes not only men but also both boy trebles and women's voices. While the men's voices remain dark-timbred and sonorous when singing alone, the soprano line is sweet, while the trebles are frequently plangent. For example, after they and the full choir have shared a radiant dialogue in the troped *Offertorium* of the *Mass for the Nativity*, the trebles re-enter in the *Ante communio cum tropis*, enthusiastically singing *Emitte Spiritum Sanctum tuum* and seeking the Holy Spirit with lusty fervour. The performances by the Schola Hungarica have remarkable feeling and rich, clean textures. The result is totally refreshing, and the choir is beautifully recorded within an ideal ambience: the Parish Church of Sainte Famille, Zugliget, Budapest.

Those who have enjoyed the Schola Hungarica's recording of chant according to the Aquitaine tradition will surely want to move on to their equally stimulating collection of chant and polyphony centring on Christmas, drawing on both English and Hungarian sources. Men's and women's voices are again used to create a rich tapestry, and the opening *Noel* polyphonic settings, first for two and then three voices, are memorable. There is, of course, soaring monody, and another fine example of an early *Alleluja* and sequence (*Dominus dixit/Grates nunc*). Tempi are kept moving onwards so that the music never drags, and the recording is full and expansive. This is much more enjoyable than many more famous recordings of such repertoire.

Canto live (Agnus Dei; Alleluias; Antiphon; Graduals; Hymns; Introits; Kyries; Responsories; Sequences; Tropes).
(N) **(*) EMI Dig. CDC5 55504-2 [id.]. Ch. of Monasterio Benedictino de Santo Domingo de Silos, Ismale Fernández de la Cuesta.

The latest collection of chant from the monks of the Benedictine monastery of Santo Domingo de Silos is apparently to be their last record, and it gives a good idea of their simple but robust monodic style. Appropriately, one of its highlights is the *Alleluia* framing a verse in honour of Saint Benedict.

'Liturgia defuntorum': Gregorian chant for the dead (from the Order of Burial and for All Souls' Day).
(N) (BB) **(*) Naxos Dig. 8.553192 [id.]. Aurora Surgit, Alessio Randon.

To use a group of female voices in this repertoire (but with a male cantor) may not be completely authentic but the soaring monody gains a special character from the use of female trebles, and the added element of contrast in the responsories is also attractive. By no means all this music is solemn or dark in feeling: the closing group of chants, the *Libera me*, and especially the soaring *In paradisum – Chorus angelorum*, followed by the *Ego sum Resurrectio*, are intended to give the Christian soul an eloquent send-off. Fine singing and atmospheric yet clear recording.

Grieg, Edvard (1843–1907)

Piano concerto in A min. (original 1868/72 version); *Larvikspolka* (1858); *23 Small pieces* (1859).
*** BIS Dig. CD 585 [id.]. Love Derwinger, Norrköping SO, Hirokami.

All his life Grieg tinkered with his orchestration of the *Piano concerto* and made no fewer than seven versions of the score, the last in 1907, only a few weeks before his death. In the first version many of the familiar orchestral landmarks are absent: the lyrical second theme of the first movement appears on solo trumpet rather than the cellos; the brief dialogue between horn and cello in the *Adagio*, which Gerald Abraham called 'one of the most memorable points in the whole score', is not there, the material being allocated to the first violins. This CD offers us a fascinating glimpse of how the concerto must have sounded to its contemporaries. Love Derwinger is the intelligent and accomplished soloist with the Norrköping orchestra, and he proves a sensitive guide in the collection of juvenilia that completes the disc. The *Larvikspolka*, written when Grieg was fifteen, is probably the very earliest of his piano pieces to survive, and the *Nine Children's Pieces* included in the set of *23 Small pieces* were written during his first months at the Leipzig conservatory. They are all very slight in substance, but they fill out the picture of the young composer and the world in which he grew up. The concerto is well balanced and Love Derwinger's solo pieces are well recorded too.

Historic recordings:
Disc 1: (i) *Piano concerto in A min., Op. 16. Album leaf, Op. 28/4; Ballade in G min., Op. 24; Lyric pieces: Op. 12/4, 5; Op. 38/1, 2, 5; Op. 43/1, 4; Op. 47/6; Op. 54/1, 3; Op. 68/5.*
(*(*)) RCA mono 09026 61883-2 [id.]. Rubinstein, (i) with Phd. O, Ormandy.

Disc 2: (i) *String quartet in G min., Op. 27;* (ii) *Violin sonata No. 3 in C min., Op. 45;* (iii) *Album leaf, Op. 28/2;* (iv) *The last spring.*
(***) RCA mono 09026 61826-2. (i) Budapest Qt; (ii) Kreisler, Rachmaninov; (iii) Elman; (iv) Boston SO, Koussevitzky.

Disc 3: Songs: *And I shall have a true love; At the brook; Bilberry slopes; A Dream* (3 versions); *Eros; Good morning; Greeting; I love thee* (5 versions); *In the boat; The mother sings; The Norse people; To Norway; A swan* (3 versions); *With a primrose; With a water lily* (2 versions); *Peer Gynt: Solveig's lullaby; Solveig's song.*
(**(*)) RCA mono 09026 61827-2. Björling; Crooks; Farrar; Flagstad; Frijsh; Galli-Curci; Kline; Krogh; Marsh; Melchior; Nilsson; Schumann-Heink; Traubel.
(**) (M) RCA mono 09026 61879-2 (3) [id.]: Discs 1–3 complete.

The three-CD RCA set has the great advantage of being available singly. The first disc couples Rubinstein's 1942 recording of the *Piano concerto* with the Philadelphia Orchestra under Ormandy with the 1953 recordings he made in Hollywood of the *G minor Ballade* and some of the *Lyric pieces*. This account of the *Concerto* has brilliance and sensitivity but is a little wanting in spontaneity. The 78 surface-noise, while not disturbing, is probably more discernible than some collectors would like, and the end of the second side of the 78-r.p.m. set used for this transfer is excessively busy. Nor are the solo pieces distinguished by the poetry and freshness one might expect. The *Lyric pieces* do not begin to compare with Gilels, and both they and the *Ballade*, arguably Grieg's most deeply felt piano work, are recorded in a shallow and claustrophobic acoustic environment.

The second CD brings the famous 1928 Kreisler–Rachmaninov set of the Op. 45 *C minor Sonata*, already available in RCA's ten-CD Rachmaninov retrospective. The superb (1937) Budapest version of the *G minor String quartet* is a masterly performance, with splendid grip but at the same time great lyrical warmth and freshness. The eloquence of the Boston Symphony Orchestra's strings in the days of Koussevitzky was legendary and their seamless phrasing and glorious tone shine vibrantly through the years.

With such celebrated singers as Björling, Farrar, Flagstad, Galli-Curci and Melchior represented on the generously filled last disc, RCA's song compilation is self-recommending. One might regret the absence of Flagstad's earliest *Haugtussa*, particularly when there are several duplications, but no doubt it will appear in subsequent reissues. Given the quality and interest of the singing, this CD will no doubt be eagerly sought by collectors. The transfers are acceptable, though not in any way superior to the specialist issues one encounters of this repertoire on the Danacord label.

Piano concerto in A min., Op. 16.
*** Sony Dig. SK 44899 [id.]. Perahia, Bav. RSO, Colin Davis – SCHUMANN: *Concerto.* ***
(B) *** Decca 433 628-2 [id.]. Curzon, LSO, Fjeldstad – FRANCK: *Symphonic variations* *** ✮; SCHUMANN: *Concerto.* **(*)
*** EMI Dig. CDC7 54746-2 [id.]. Lars Vogt, CBSO, Rattle – SCHUMANN: *Concerto.* ***
(B) *** CfP Dig. CD-CFP 4574 [id.]. Pascal Devoyon, LPO, Maksymiuk – SCHUMANN: *Piano concerto.* ***
(M) **(*) Decca 417 728-2 [id.]. Radu Lupu, LSO, Previn – SCHUMANN: *Concerto.* **(*)
(M) (***) EMI mono CDH7 63497-2. Lipatti, Philh. O, Galliera – with: CHOPIN: *Piano concerto No. 1.* (**)
(M) ** RCA 09026 61262-2. Artur Rubinstein, O, Wallenstein – TCHAIKOVSKY: *Piano concerto No. 1.* ***
(N) (B) * Decca Eclipse Dig. 448 235-2; *448 235-4* [id.]. Jorge Bolet, Berlin RSO, Chailly (with MENDELSSOHN: *Rondo capriccioso, Op. 14* **) – SCHUMANN: *Piano concerto.* *(*)
(N) * Decca Dig. 444 518-2 [id.]. Mustonen, San Francisco SO, Blomstedt – CHOPIN: *Piano concerto No. 1.* *

(i) *Piano concerto in A min. 6 Lyric pieces, Op. 65.*
*** Virgin/EMI Dig. VC7 59613-2 [id.]. Leif Ove Andsnes, (i) Bergen PO, Dmitri Kitaenko – LISZT: *Piano concerto No. 2.* ***

(i) *Piano concerto in A min. Lyric pieces: Arietta; Elves' dance; Folk melody, Op. 12/1, 4 & 5; Butterfly; Little bird; To spring, Op. 43/1, 4 & 6; Notturno, Op. 54/4; Gade, Op. 57/2; Sylph; French serenade, Op. 62/ 1 & 3; Salon, Op. 65/4; Summer evening, Op. 71/2.*

(Y/B) ❀ (BB) *** Tring Dig. TRPO 24 [id.]. Ronan O'Hora, (i) with RPO, James Judd.

(i) *Piano concerto in A min.;* (ii) *Piano sonata in E min., Op. 7.*

(N) (M) *** Ph. 446 192-2 [id.]. (i) Kovacevich, BBC SO, Sir Colin Davis; (ii) Zoltan Kocsis – SCHU-MANN: *Concerto*. ***

Whether in the clarity of virtuoso fingerwork or the shading of half-tone, Kovacevich is among the most illuminating of the many great pianists who have recorded the Grieg *Concerto*. He plays with bravura and refinement, the spontaneity of the music-making bringing a sparkle throughout, to balance the underlying poetry. The 1972 recording has been freshened most successfully and, for the mid-priced reissue, Philips have added a performance by Zoltán Kocsis of the *Piano sonata*, recorded digitally at the beginning of the 1980s. The brilliant young Hungarian pianist gives a strongly characterized reading. His style of pianism, impulsive and extrovert, is quite different from Kovacevich's (and, indeed, that of Andsnes – see below). But in his own way he is very persuasive in this early and not wholly convincing piece, in which the seams are clearly audible: the *Andante* shows him at his finest. The recording is bright and immediate and suits his style. With its new addition as a supplement to the Schumann coupling, this reissue has a playing time of 78 minutes.

Perahia revels in the bravura as well as bringing out the lyrical beauty in radiantly poetic playing. He is commanding and authoritative when required, with the blend of spontaneity, poetic feeling and virtu-oso display this music calls for. He is given sympathetic support by Sir Colin Davis and the fine Bavarian Radio Symphony Orchestra, and there is no finer version of the Grieg recorded in the digital age than this.

Curzon's approach to Grieg is wonderfully poetic and this is a performance with strength and power as well as lyrical tenderness. This ranks alongside Kovacevich and Perahia and the reading is second to none in distilling the music's special atmosphere. The sound is bright and open and the recording hardly shows its age in this crisply focused CD transfer.

The young Manchester pianist, Ronan O'Hora, with a totally sympathetic partner in James Judd, now provides us with a recorded performance which is for the mid-1990s what Solomon and Clifford Curzon were for the later 1950s, Steven Kovacevich for the 1970s, and Perahia for the end of the 1980s. Indeed in imagination and delicacy of feeling, combined with natural, authoritative brilliance, this new perform-ance is unsurpassed, especially the melting arrival of the lovely second group which brings a moment of the utmost magic, matched by the gentle reverie of the *Adagio* and the tranquil, flute-led central episode of the finale. Throughout the pacing seems just right, and the interchange between soloist and orchestra brings a natural, spontaneous flow. The piano is rather forwardly balanced and some listeners may find it a little bright, but in the music's gentler pages the piano's timbre is beautifully coloured. The pro-gramme is completed by a wholly delightful selection of a dozen of Grieg's most cherishable *Lyric pieces*, in which the pianist's simplicity of approach is consistently disarming. As if this were not enough, this record comes in the very lowest price-range and as such it is one of the great bargains of the catalogue.

Lars Vogt never allows his personality to obtrude; he colours the familiar phrases with great subtlety yet without the slightest trace of narcissism. He is very well supported by Rattle and the CBSO, and excellently recorded. An unusually sensitive player, his version, with the inevitable Schumann coupling, is eminently satisfying. Curzon, Kovacevich and O'Hora are top recommendations, but among new-comers this has strong claims to be put among them.

Pascal Devoyon's account of the Grieg *Concerto* is characteristic of him: aristocratic without being aloof, pensive without being self-conscious, and brilliant without being flashy. He is a poetic artist whose natural musicianship shines through, and this excellent account is very competitive. This is a very fine issue, with excellent playing from the LPO under Jerzy Maksymiuk.

Andsnes wears his brilliance lightly. There is no lack of display and bravura here, but no ostentation. Indeed he has great poetic feeling and delicacy of colour, and Grieg's familiar warhorse comes up with great freshness. His piano is in perfect condition (not always the case on records) and is excellently balanced in relation to the orchestra. This is one of the best modern accounts.

Radu Lupu's recording dates from 1974 and is now even more brightly lit than it was originally, not entirely to advantage. But the performance is a fine one; there is both warmth and poetry in the slow movement; the hushed opening is particularly telling. The orchestral contribution under Previn is a strong one.

The famous 1947 Lipatti performance remains eternally fresh, and its return to the catalogue is a cause for rejoicing, although the ear now notices a slightly drier quality and a marginal loss of bloom.

Rubinstein usually has something interesting to say about any major concerto; it is a great pity that his partner here, Alfred Wallenstein, shows little sensitivity or imagination in his handling of the light-textured but all-important orchestral contribution. Nevertheless Rubinstein produces some marvellously poetic and aristocratic playing towards the end of the slow movement, and the finale is both commanding and exciting, even if the orchestral response is aggressive.

Bolet shows little affinity with Grieg's delightful concerto. He seeks to give a spacious reading and the result is merely lethargic and heavy; even the first-movement cadenza drags. The recording is the best part of the affair – it is of Decca's finest quality. The Mendelssohn encore hardly affects the matter.

The gifted young Finnish pianist, Olli Mustonen, has succumbed to attention-seeking. He is very concerned to give us something different and the result is intolerably affected and mannered. It barely survives one hearing, let alone the repetition one anticipates from disc. The recording is good and so are Blomstedt and the orchestra – hence the star. Nevertheless it is impossible to recommend this version.

(i) *Piano concerto in A min.;* (ii; iii) *Holberg suite, Op. 40; Lyric suite, Op. 54;* (iv; iii) *4 Symphonic dances, Op. 64;* (ii; iii) *Peer Gynt (incidental music): suites Nos. 1, Op. 46; 2, Op. 55.* (v) (Piano) *Lyric pieces, Op. 12: Album leaf; Arietta; Fairy dance; National song; Norwegian melody; Popular melody; Waltz; Watchman's song; Op. 43: Butterfly; Erotik; In my native country; Little bird; Solitary traveller; To Spring.*
(M) **(*) Ph. Duo 438 380-2 (2) [id.]. (i) Kovacevich, BBC SO, C. Davis; (ii) ECO; (iii) Raymond Leppard; (iv) Philh. O; (v) Zoltán Kocsis.

Including as it does the highly praised Kovacevich/Davis account of the *Piano concerto,* so imaginatively illuminating, this bargain-priced anthology does indeed include much of 'The best of Grieg', if one leaves aside the vocal music. Leppard's accounts of the two *Peer Gynt suites* are fresh, and all his performances here have an air of thoughtfulness which will appeal to many, especially as the orchestral playing is so good. However, in the slow movements of the *Holberg suite* and also occasionally in *Peer Gynt* there is just a hint of a lack of vitality. *In the hall of the Mountain King,* for instance, opens slowly then does not build up quite the head of steam one expects. The *Lyric suite,* however, is beautifully done, and the four *Symphonic dances,* recorded digitally, are also very successful, with a refined response from the Philharmonia. What makes the collection especially attractive is the inclusion of 14 of the *Lyric pieces,* played by Zoltán Kocsis with much character. Perhaps he is a bit impetuous at times (as in the *Fairy dance*), but his approach certainly suits *To Spring,* his last item.

(i) *Piano concerto in A min.;* (ii) *Peer Gynt suites Nos. 1–2.*
(B) **(*) DG 439 427-2 [id.]. (i) Géza Anda, BPO, Kubelik; (ii) BPO, Karajan.

Anda's account of the *Piano concerto* is more wayward than some but is strong in personality and has plenty of life. Kubelik's accompaniment is good too, and the 1963 recording sounds well. However, Karajan's analogue *Peer Gynt suites* are in a class of their own. They were also recorded – a decade later – in the Berlin Jesus-Christus-Kirche but, for some reason, the CD transfer seems very brightly lit, although the fullness and analogue ambience are retained. They are played with much expressive feeling and demonstrate superlative orchestral skill and polish, yet at the same time sound admirably fresh: they have far more character than most of their bargain competitors.

2 Elegiac melodies, Op. 34; Erotik; 2 Melodies, Op. 53; 2 Norwegian airs, Op. 63.
(BB) **(*) Naxos Dig. 8.550330; *4550330* [id.]. Capella Istropolitana, Adrian Leaper – SIBELIUS: *Andante festivo* etc. **

Adrian Leaper secures responsive and sensitive playing from the Capella Istropolitana in this Grieg collection, and the recording is very good indeed and the balance natural.

2 Elegiac melodies; Holberg suite, Op. 40.
(BB) **(*) ASV CDQS 6094 Swiss CO – SUK; TCHAIKOVSKY: *String serenades.* ***

The Swiss Chamber Orchestra take the first movement of the *Holberg suite* very briskly, but it is an enjoyably spick-and-span account, with good lyrical contrast; although the *Elegiac melodies* lack opulence, these brightly recorded performances make a good bonus for outstanding versions of the Suk and Tchaikovsky *Serenades.*

2 Elegiac melodies (Heart's wounds; The last spring), Op. 34; Holberg suite, Op. 40; 2 Lyric pieces (Evening in the mountains; At the cradle); 2 Melodies (Norwegian; The first meeting), Op. 53; 2 Nordic melodies (In folk style; Cow-call), Op. 63.
*** DG Dig. 437 520-2 [id.]. Gothenburg SO, Neeme Järvi.

A most attractive and well-designed anthology. The *Holberg suite,* opening athletically, has not quite the ultimate polish and charm of Karajan's version but it is presented with much character, and the other folk melodies bring some beautiful playing from the Gothenburg strings. The two lovely *Elegiac melodies* sound freshly minted and the innocent appeal of the much less familiar *Nordic melodies* is fully captured. These are all works for string orchestra, save the first of the two *Lyric pieces, Evening in the mountains*, where the effect of oboe solo – backwardly placed as the composer intended – is piquantly and engagingly managed. The following *Cradle song* is very touching. Excellent, bright, modern recording with a good ambient effect.

(i) *2 Elegiac melodies, Op. 34; Lyric suite, Op. 54: Norwegian march and Nocturne. Norwegian dance, Op. 35/2;* (i) *Peer Gynt suites Nos. 1–2* (including *Solveig's lullaby*); (i) *Sigurd Jorsalfar: Homage march, Op. 56/3.*

(B) *** Sony SBK 53257; *SBT 53257* [id.]. (i) Phd. O, Ormandy; (ii) Elisabeth Söderström, New Philh. O, Andrew Davis.

Andrew Davis offers freshly thought performances of the two *Peer Gynt suites*, beautifully played and warmly recorded at Abbey Road in 1976. A special attraction is the singing of Elisabeth Söderström, not only in *Solveig's song* but also in *Solveig's lullaby*, which has been added to the second suite. The Ormandy recordings date from a decade earlier but they make up a most attractive anthology. The orchestral playing is very good indeed and Ormandy's warmth is obvious. The transfers are well managed.

Holberg suite, Op. 40.
(M) *** Carlton Dig. PCD 861 [id.]. Serenata of London – ELGAR: *Serenade;* MOZART: *Eine kleine Nachtmusik.* ***

The performance by the Serenata of London is first class in every way, spontaneous, naturally paced and played with considerable eloquence. The digital recording is most realistic and very naturally balanced.

Holberg suite, Op. 40; Peer Gynt suites Nos. 1 & 2.
*** DG Gold Dig. 439 010-2 [id.]. BPO, Karajan – SIBELIUS: *Finlandia; Valse triste; Swan of Tuonela.* ***

Karajan's performance of the *Holberg suite* is the finest currently available. The playing has wonderful lightness and delicacy, with cultured phrasing not robbing the music of its immediacy, while in Peer Gynt many subtleties of colour and texture are revealed by the vividly present recording, clear and full and with a firm bass-line, especially in the thrillingly gusty *In the hall of the Mountain King.* Grieg's perennially fresh score is marvellously played. *Anitra* dances with elegance, and the *Death of Aase* is movingly eloquent. The digital recording now proves to be one of the best to have emerged from the Philharmonie in the early 1980s.

In Autumn overture, Op. 11; Lyric piece: Erotik, Op. 43/5; Norwegian dances, Op. 35; Old Norwegian romance with variations, Op. 51.
*** Chandos Dig. CHAN 9028 [id.]. Iceland SO, Sakari (with SVENDSEN: *2 Icelandic melodies* for strings ***).

The Iceland orchestra play very responsively for their Finnish conductor, Petri Sakari, who gives very natural and straightforward accounts of this endearing music. There are no egocentric interpretative touches or unwelcome tonal sophistication; this is a kind of music-making one had thought belonged to a bygone age in these days of jet-setting virtuoso conductors. Highly musical performances, with no lack of personality, very truthfully recorded. Very recommendable.

Lyric suite, Op. 54; Sigurd Jorsalfar (suite), Op. 56; Symphonic dances, Op. 64.
**(*) ASV Dig. CDDCA 722 [id.]. RPO, Yondani Butt.

The *Symphonic dances* are particularly successful here. They are not easy to bring off, yet Butt and the RPO capture their charm and energy without succumbing to melodrama in No. 4. The *Lyric suite*, too, is fresh and the trolls in the finale have an earthy pungency. However, the outer movements of *Sigurd Jorsalfar* bring an element of ponderousness. Excellent, vivid recording.

Old Norwegian romance with variations, Op. 51; 4 Symphonic dances, Op. 64.
(N) (B) *** EMI forte Dig. CZS5 68649-2 (2). Bournemouth SO, Berglund – DVORAK: *Scherzo capriccioso* etc.; SMETANA: *Má vlast.* ***

Berglund has a special feeling for this composer and this was one of his finest Grieg records. The performances of the *Symphonic dances* are both fresh and volatile – as fine as any in the catalogue. They have a strong sense of drama, yet Berglund's beautifully moulded shaping of the lovely oboe solo (exquisitely delicate) in No. 2 gives a personal imprint to the music-making. The *Old Norwegian romance* is introduced persuasively, and the variations are sympathetically and imaginatively done. The digital recording, made in the Southampton Guildhall, is first class, warmly atmospheric yet with just the right degree of brilliance. On all counts this EMI forte double is highly recommendable.

Symphonic dances, Op. 64; Sigurd Jorsalfar (suite), *Op. 56;* (i) *Peer Gynt: Solveig's song: Solveig's lullaby.* Songs: *Fra Monte Pincio; En Swan; Våren; Henrik Wergeland.*
**(*) Chandos Dig. CHAN 9113 [id.]. (i) Solveig Kringelborn; Royal Stockholm Philh. O, Rozhdestvensky.

Rozhdestvensky and his fine Swedish orchestra offer the *Symphonic dances* and the popular *Sigurd Jorsalfar suite*, Op. 56, and, sandwiched in between, a group of songs with the young Norwegian soprano, Solveig Kringelborn. She has a light, pretty voice, though she is a little short on imagination; most of the songs tend to sound much the same. But the orchestral pieces are excellently done, and Chandos provide recording quality of the utmost naturalness and presence.

CHAMBER MUSIC

Cello sonata in A min., Op. 36.
(N) *** RCA Dig. 09026 68290-2 [id.]. Steven Isserlis, Stephen Hough – RUBINSTEIN: *Cello sonata No. 1; LISZT: Elégies* etc. ***
**(*) CRD CRD 3391; *CRDC 4091* [id.]. Robert Cohen, Roger Vignoles – FRANCK: *Cello sonata.* **(*)

Cello sonata in A min.; Intermezzo in A min.; Piano sonata, Op. 7.
(Y/B) (BB) *** Naxos Dig. 8.550878 [id.]. Oystein Birkeland, Håvard Gimse.

Written in 1882 when Grieg was thinking of composing a second piano concerto, the *Cello sonata* very much reflects the *A minor Concerto* in manner and material, with Grieg at his most richly distinctive. With Steven Isserlis and Stephen Hough an inspired duo, natural recording artists both, these are outstanding performances of high romantic works that deserve to be better known, defying the tacky title for the disc, '*Forgotten Romance*'. In an exhilarating performance Isserlis and Hough are consistently spontaneous-sounding and imaginative. Never running the risk of sounding sentimental, they give full emotional weight to each movement at speeds that flow easily and naturally. An outstanding cello disc in every way, very well recorded.

Oystein Birkeland and Håvard Gimse also give the sonata an alive and sensitive account, coupled with the early and unrepresentative *Intermezzo in A minor*. They are both imaginative players and are decently recorded. Given the modest outlay involved, this competes very strongly with its rivals, but even if it were at mid-or full-price it would be highly recommendable. Håvard Gimse's performance of the early *Piano sonata*, Op. 7, is also very good indeed. Altogether a first-rate bargain.

In the folk element Cohen might have adopted a more persuasive style, bringing out the charm of the music more, but certainly he sustains the sonata structures well. The recording presents the cello very convincingly. It has been most naturally transferred to CD.

String quartet No. 1 in G min., Op. 27.
(Y/B) (M) (***) Biddulph mono LAB 098 [id.]. Budapest Qt – SIBELIUS: *Quartet;* WOLF: *Italian serenade.* (***)

String quartets Nos. 1 in G min., Op. 27; 2 in F (unfinished).
(Y/B) (BB) *** Naxos Dig. 8.550879 [id.]. Oslo String Qt – JOHANSEN: *String quartet.* ***

String quartets Nos. 1–2; (i) *Andante con moto for piano trio. Fugue in F min.*
*** Olympia Dig. OCD 432 [id.]. Raphael Qt, (i) with Jet Röling.

The Naxos account of the quartets from the Oslo String Quartet, a relatively new group, proves the best of the lot – indeed it is the best version we have had since the Budapest. They would easily sweep the board even at full price, on account of their sensitivity, tonal finesse and blend, and the keenness of their artistic responses. They (rightly) play only the first two movements of the *F major Quartet*, leaving room for a fine quartet by Grieg's biographer, David Monrad Johansen. The recording balance, made in the Norwegian Radio studios, is excellent, neither too forward nor too recessed. Three stars – and indeed verging on a Rosette.

The Budapest Quartet's recording, dating from 1936, has already appeared on RCA, as part of a three-CD Historic Grieg anthology (see above). There is no difference in cost between this and the Biddulph transfer, both being at mid-price, but its attractions in terms of coupling here are even stronger. The Sibelius *Voces intimae* and the Hugo Wolf *Italian serenade* are both superb performances and still remain unsurpassed. The Biddulph transfer has a slight edge over the RCA.

The Raphael Quartet do not give quite as spirited an account of the *F major Quartet* as the Oslo

Quartet, but their CD enjoys two points of special interest: they give us Julius Röntgen's conjectural realization of the sketches to the remaining two movements Grieg had planned for the *F major Quartet*; and they also include another rarity in the shape of the *Andante con moto* for piano trio.

Violin sonatas Nos. 1 in F, Op. 8; 2 in G, Op. 13; 3 in C min., Op. 45.
(Y/B) *** DG Dig. 437 525-2 [id.]. Augustin Dumay, Maria João Pires.
(Y/B) *** Chandos Dig. CHAN 9184 [id.]. Lydia Mordkovitch, Elena Mordkovitch.
(Y/B) **(*) BIS Dig. CD 647 [id.]. Dong-Suk Kang, Roland Pöntinen.

After a long period of neglect, violin-and-piano partnerships are turning to the three Grieg *Sonatas*, and doing so with consistent success. Like the *Piano concerto*, these works possess extraordinary resilience and survive countless repetition. They have a perennial and indestructible freshness that is quite special. Indeed among the newcomers listed above it is not easy to establish any order of priority.

The French violinist, Augustin Dumay, and his distinguished partner, Maria João Pires, give poised, animated accounts of all three sonatas, and their CD is available both separately and as part of the six-CD Grieg Edition on DG. Their performances are exemplary in every way, and the recorded sound is also excellent in terms of both balance and realism.

Yet the same goes for Lydia and Elena Mordkovitch (*mère et fille*) on an admirably recorded Chandos CD. They, too, give splendidly fresh and well-shaped accounts of all three sonatas which give much pleasure in music-making. Affectionate yet virile performances – thoroughly recommendable.

Dong-Suk Kang produces a rich, finely focused tone, and his purity of style and intonation always inspire admiration. He is an artist of sensibility, and no one investing in the BIS recording is likely to be disappointed. Roland Pöntinen is a highly accomplished partner though a trifle too self-aware at times (the middle movement of the *C minor Sonata* is a case in point). Moreover the sound of the piano is less open and realistic than in rival versions.

PIANO MUSIC

Naxos Complete Edition
4 Album Leaves, Op. 28; Ballade, Op. 24; Melodies of Norway: Iceland. Pictures from everyday life (Humoresques), Op. 19; Poetic Tone-pictures, Op. 3; Sigurd Jorsalfar: Prayer, Op. 56/1.
(N) (BB) *** Naxos Dig. 8.550883 [id.]. Steen-Nøkleberg.

The first meeting, Op. 52/2; Improvisations on 2 Norwegian folksongs, Op. 29; Melodies of Norway: Ballad to St Olaf. 25 Norwegian folksongs and dances, Op. 17; 19 Norwegian folksongs, Op. 66.
(N) (BB) *** Naxos Dig. 8.550882 [id.]. Steen-Nøkleberg.

Funeral March in memory of Rikard Nordraak; Humoresques, Op. 6; I love you (Jeg elsker dig), Op. 41/3; Melodies of Norway: The Sirens' enticement. Moods (Stimmungen), Op. 73; 4 Piano pieces, Op. 1; Sonata in E min., Op. 7.
(N) (BB) *** Naxos Dig. 8.550881 [id.]. Steen-Nøkleberg.

Holberg suite, Op. 40; Melodies of Norway: I went to bed so late. 6 Norwegian mountain melodies; Peer Gynt suite No. 1, Op. 46/1: Morning. Norwegian peasant dances (Slåtter) Op. 72.
(N) (BB) *** Naxos Dig. 8.550884 [id.]. Steen-Nøkleberg.

Einar Steen-Nøkleberg is recording the complete Grieg piano music on 14 CDs, most of which will be in circulation by the time this volume is in print. The first eight augur well for the series. Steen-Nøkleberg won several prizes in Norway in his youth and was professor of the piano at the Hannover Musikhochschule for some years. He is also the author of a book on Grieg's piano music and its interpretation. Generally speaking, his survey looks set to displace such rivals as Einar Henning Braaten on the Victoria label and the RCA sets by Gerhard Oppitz. He is more responsive to mood and is more imaginative in his approach than they; apart from such outstanding discs as Leif Ove Andsnes's account of the Op. 7 *Sonata* and the Gilels anthology of *Lyric pieces* (as well as the 1986 selection by Pletnev, which RCA will presumably issue here as part of their Melodiya series), these are likely to be the first (as well as the most affordable) choice for most collectors.

Volume I (8.550881) couples early and late Grieg – the very earliest of his published pieces, written while he was still studying at Leipzig, the *Humoresques*, Op. 6, and the *E minor Piano sonata*, Op. 7, alongside the *Stimmungen* ('Moods'), Op. 73, composed in the early years of the present century (1901–5). Whether the music is early or late, Steen-Nøkleberg plays with total sympathy and dedication, and he is beautifully recorded throughout in the Lindeman Hall of the Norwegian State Academy of Music. Only in the *Sonata* is he a little mannered.

Volume II (8.550882) includes the remarkable *Nineteen Norwegian folksongs*, Op. 66, which are contemporaneous with what many would see as Grieg's masterpiece, the song-cycle *Haugtussa*, and which the composer himself spoke of as full of 'hair-raising' chromatic harmonies. (One of the folksongs appears in Delius's *On hearing the first cuckoo in spring*.) But the earlier set, Op. 17, written not long after the first version of the *Piano concerto*, is also full of delights.

Volume III (8.550883) brings the poignant *Ballade*, Op. 24, composed on the death of the composer's parents. Steen-Nøkleberg is highly imaginative and even if some may find his rubato a little extreme the keyboard colouring is subtle and rich. He conveys a splendidly rhapsodic spontaneity and there is much feeling. This and the companion disc, with the *Seventeen Norwegian peasant dances* ('*Slåtter*'), Op. 72, deserve a particularly strong recommendation. Steen-Nøkleberg recorded the *Slåtter*, interspersed with the hardangar-fiddle melodies on which they are based, for Simax on the late 1980s; he is perhaps the most characterful exponent of these extraordinary pieces with their quasi-Bartókian clashes now available. In any event, one could buy all four of these CDs for not much more than the cost of a single full-price disc, and they are full of surprises and will give much pleasure.

Norway's melodies Nos. 1–63.
(N) (BB) **(*) Naxos Dig. 8.550891 [id.]. Steen-Nøkleberg.

Norway's melodies Nos. 64–117.
(N) (BB) **(*) Naxos Dig. 8.550892 [id.]. Steen-Nøkleberg.

Norway's Melodies Nos. 118–52 (EG 108).
(N) (BB) **(*) Naxos Dig. 8.550893 [id.]. Steen-Nøkleberg.

The next three discs are devoted to *Norges Melodier* ('Norway's Melodies'), an anthology Grieg made in the mid-1870s for a Danish publisher who wanted 'easy-to-play arrangements for piano, while at the same time presenting a degree of challenge to the performer and adhering to a certain artistic standard'. In need of money, Grieg agreed to prepare this anthology of some 150-odd pieces, provided that his name was not mentioned on the title-page of the publication. The resulting anthology is of tunes – some of them charming, others less so – drawn from folk melodies collected by Lindemann in his *Old and New Mountain Melodies*, from such composers as Halfdan Kjerulf and Rikard Nordraak, as well as some of his own songs. Grieg regarded it as having little to do with art, and as being directed primarily at amateur pianists up and down the country. However, when Gerhard Schjelderup dismissed them many years later as 'scandalously common and completely lacking in sophistication', Grieg went to their defence. Einar Steen-Nøkleberg plays some on the house-organ or harmonium, some on the clavichord, some on a Graf piano (to match those sonorities which would have been familiar in Norwegian homes in the 1870s), and some on a Steinway. There is nothing wrong with the performances; on the contrary, Steen-Nøkleberg makes out the best case for them.

Lyric pieces: Book I, Op. 12; Book II, Op. 38; Book III, Op. 43; Book IV, Op. 47.
(N) (BB) *** Naxos Dig. 8.553394 [id.]. Steen-Nøkleberg.

Lyric pieces: Book V, Op. 54; Book VI, Op. 57; Book VII, Op. 62.
(N) (BB) *** Naxos Dig. 8.553395 [id.]. Steen-Nøkleberg.

Lyric pieces: Book VIII, Op. 65; Book IX, Op. 68; Book X, Op. 71.
(N) (BB) *** Naxos Dig. 8.553396 [id.]. Steen-Nøkleberg.

Volumes VIII–X survey the delightful *Lyric pieces*. They are admirably fresh and are presented with the utmost simplicity, yet are obviously felt. One has only to sample the opening piece of Book V (included in Volume 9), *Herd boy*, Op. 54/1, or the *Nocturne*, Op. 54/4 (both part of the well-known orchestral *Lyric suite*), to discover the poetic calibre of this playing. These performances come into direct competition with Daniel Adni's not quite complete but otherwise excellent set on an EMI forte double CD. Many will like to have the coverage absolutely complete, and the three Naxos discs cost about the same. The EMI piano-sound is perhaps very slightly warmer and fuller, but the Naxos recording is wholly natural and believable.

Agitato; Album Leaf; At the Halfdán Kjerulf Statute; 3 Pieces; 10 Norwegian melodies. Peer Gynt. arr. of HALVORSEN: *Entry of the Boyars.*
**(*) BIS Dig. CD 620 [id.]. Love Derwinger.

These are juvenilia which have never been recorded before and, although they are of interest to the Grieg specialist, they are not exactly essential listening: none of these pieces is in any sense a great discovery. The Swedish pianist, Love Derwinger, plays them sensitively and is decently recorded, and both performance and recording deserve a high rating; but it is difficult to imagine Grieg, who was fastidious in these matters, being overjoyed at seeing these slight pieces, which he chose not to publish, representing him in the catalogue.

Agitato; Album leaves, Op. 28/1 & 4; Lyric pieces, Opp. 43 & 54; Piano sonata in E min., Op. 7; Poetic tone pieces, Op. 3/4–6.

🏵 *** Virgin/EMI Dig. VC7 59300-2 [id.]. Leif Ove Andsnes.

A notable recital by Grieg's countryman, Leif Ove Andsnes, which has won golden opinions – and rightly so! He includes two sets of the *Lyric pieces*, the Op. 43 which begins with the famous *Butterfly*, and the Op. 54 which Grieg later scored; there are various other short pieces, as well as the *Sonata in E minor*, Op. 7, another piece which all young students had to learn in the 1940s and '50s. Andsnes's virtuosity is always at the service of the composer, and he has that ability to make familiar music sound fresh, as if you haven't heard it before. He plays with real imagination and lightness of touch.

(iii) *Album Leaf, Op. 28/3; Arietta, Op. 12/1;* (vi) *Ballade in G min., Op. 24;* (vii) *Cradle song, Op. 68/5; French serenade, Op. 62/3;* (i; ii; v) *Norwegian bridal procession, Op. 19/2;* (iv) *Piano concerto in A min., Op. 16:* (v) cadenza to 1st movt only; (i) *To spring, Op. 45/6;* (v) *Wedding day at Troldhaugen, Op. 65/6.*

(*) Pearl mono GEMMCD 9933 (i) Edvard Grieg; (ii) Joanne Stockmarr; (iii) Arthur de Greef; (iv) Severin Eisenberger, Cincinnati Conservatoire O, Alexander von Kreisler; (v) Percy Grainger; (vi) Leopold Godowsky; (vii) Walter Gieseking.

Primarily a historical document, but an interesting and valuable one for all who have a special interest in this composer. There are two of the recordings Grieg himself made in Paris in 1903, and they give some idea, albeit very faintly, of the delicacy and characterfulness of his playing. The actual sound might perhaps be said to fall short of the highest standards of 1903 and, though Pearl have done their best, use of modern technology should be able to make more of the original master. There are other performances of interest: Percy Grainger playing the cadenza of the *Piano concerto* the year after Grieg's death, not long after he had played the work to the composer; and a recently discovered (1937) recording by Severin Eisenberger, who had played the concerto in Germany under Grieg's baton. Artistically the most poetic performance is Godowsky's 1930 account of the *G minor Ballade* (which also sounds excellent), possibly the finest interpretation on record of this underrated piece. Gieseking's *French serenade*, made in 1937, is hardly less captivating and more strongly characterized than his post-war Grieg anthology on LP. The sound on some of the earlier discs varies from passable to grim; but the disc is perhaps worth the money for the Godowsky alone.

Ballade, Op. 24; 4 Lyric pieces: March of the dwarfs; Notturno, Op. 54/3–4; Wedding day at Troldhaugen, Op. 65/6; Peace of the woods, Op. 71/4. Sonata in E min., Op. 7; arr. of songs: *Cradle song; I love thee; The princess; You cannot grasp the wave's eternal course. Peer Gynt: Solveig's song.*

**(*) Olympia OCD 197 [id.]. Peter Katin.

The *Sonata* is not one of Grieg's finest works, but it has a touching *Andante* and is agreeably inventive, if perhaps conventionally so. Katin gives it a clean, direct performance, and he is impressive in the rather dolorous set of variations which forms the *Ballade*. The song arrangements, too, come off well, and the four *Lyric pieces* are presented very appealingly.

Holberg suite, Op. 40; Lyric pieces from *Opp. 12, 38, 43, 47, 54, 57, 68, 71; Norwegian dance No. 2; Peer Gynt: Morning.*

(M) *** Teldec/Warner Dig. 4509 92147-2 [id.]. Cyprien Katsaris.

Katsaris starts off with *Morning mood* from *Peer Gynt*; he then plays 18 of the *Lyric pieces* (often in groups of two or three), including favourites like *At the cradle, To spring, Butterfly, Little bird, Erotik* and the *Nocturne*, Op. 54/4 (some 39 minutes of music); the rest of the recital, apart from the opening ten minutes, is devoted to the suite, *From Holberg's time*, and one of the *Norwegian dances*, Op. 35. He is moreover accorded quite outstanding recording quality; the piano sound is particularly realistic and 'present', with plenty of range and colour. He plays with character, combining both temperament and sensitivity, and is generally scrupulous in observing dynamic nuances, and for the most part these are strong and idiomatic performances – perhaps too 'strong' in the *Holberg suite*, where he is masterful and exuberant and where more finesse could be in order. However, at mid-price this is a very attractive reissue.

Lyric pieces: Opp. 12; 38; 43; 47; 54; 57; 62; 65; 68 & 71 (complete).

(M) **(*) Unicorn Dig. UKCD 2033, *UKC 2033* (1–4); UKCD 2034, *UKC 2034* (5–7); UKCD 2035, *UKC 2035* (8–10) [id.]. Peter Katin.

Lyric pieces: Op. 12/3, 5, 7 & 8; Op. 38/1, 3 & 6; Opp. 43, 47 & 54; Op. 57; Opp. 62, 65, 68 & 71.

(N) (B) *** EMI forte CZS5 68634-2 (2). Daniel Adni.

Peter Katin is a persuasive and sensitive exponent of this repertoire, and he has the benefit of a recording of exceptional presence and clarity (though very occasionally it seems to harden in climaxes, when one notices that the microphone is perhaps a shade close). Katin has the measure of Grieg's sensibility and characterizes these pieces with real poetic feeling.

Daniel Adni has also made a complete recording but, in order to fit the majority of the works on to two CDs (with a total playing time of 155 minutes), some of the earlier pieces from Books I and II have been omitted. Adni plays with genuine feeling for their character and a strong sense of atmosphere, and the 1973 EMI recording is very good indeed: the piano is firmly in focus and well balanced; there is plenty of presence and the Abbey Road studio has agreeable ambience. This is excellent value. Those wanting the complete set can stay with Peter Katin; those satisfied with a single-disc selection (costing the same as this EMI forte double) will find Gilels finest of all.

Lyric pieces: Op. 12/1, 6; Op. 38/5; Op. 54/1, 4 & 5; Op. 57/4, 6; Op. 62/3, 4 & 6; Op. 65/1–4; Op. 68/2, 4 & 5; Op. 71/1.
**(*) Naxos Dig. 8.550650 [id.]. Balázs Szokolay.

Lyric pieces: Op. 12/3, 8; Op. 38/1; Op. 43/1, 3 & 6; Op. 47/3–7; Op. 54/3, 5–6; Op. 57/1–3; Op. 62/1–2, 5; Op. 65/6; Op. 71/7.
**(*) Naxos Dig. 8.550557 [id.]. Balázs Szokolay.

Naxos are not always lucky with their piano recordings, but the two CDs Balázs Szokolay has recorded are very good. Szokolay's playing is not as consistently subtle in colouring or as poetic in feeling as Leif Ove Andsnes, but it is pretty idiomatic. However, at super-bargain price it is really very good value indeed and the balance, though very slightly close, is not oppressively so. Both CDs give pleasure.

Lyric pieces: Op. 12/1; Op. 38/1; Op. 43/1–2; Op. 47/2–4; Op. 54/4–5; Op. 57/6; Op. 62/4 and 6; Op. 68/2, 3 and 5; Op. 71/1, 3 and 6–7.
(N) ⊛ (M) *** DG 449 721-2 [id.]. Emil Gilels.

With Gilels we are in the presence of a great keyboard master whose characterization and control of colour and articulation are wholly remarkable. An altogether outstanding record in every way. This recording has been admirably remastered for reissue in DG's 'Originals' series and now sounds better than ever.

Lyric pieces: Album leaf, Op. 47/2; Arietta, Op. 12/1; At the cradle, Op. 68/5; At your feet, Op. 68/3; Ballad, Op. 65/5; Brooklet, Op. 62/4; Butterfly, Op. 43/1; Homesickness, Op. 57/6; Cradle song, Op. 38/1; Ganger, Op. 54/2; Gone, Op. 71/6; Halling, Op. 47/4; Melody, Op. 47/3; Nocturne, Op. 54/4; Puck, Op. 71/ 3; Remembrances, Op. 71/7; Scherzo, Op. 54/5; Shepherd's boy, Op. 54/1; Solitary traveller, Op. 43/2; Summer's Eve, Op. 71/2.
**(*) DG Dig. 437 522-2 [id.]. Andrei Gavrilov.

Andrei Gavrilov's anthology of *Lyric pieces* is virtually identical to the celebrated Gilels record, which it does not challenge in any respect. All the same, it is very well played and recorded, and there is no reason to deny it a three-star recommendation. All credit, then, to Gavrilov – but buy the Gilels!

VOCAL MUSIC

Songs in historic performances (1888–1924): *Den første møte (First meeting); Dulgte kjaerlighed (Hidden love); En fuglevis (A Bird-Song); Eros; Fra Monte Pincio; Den gamle vise (The old song); God Morgen; Jag elsker Dig (I love thee); Jag reiste en deilig sommerkvaeld (I walked one balmy summer evening); Killingdans (Kids' dance); Kongekvadet (The King's Song); Margretas Vuggesang (Margreta's cradle song); Mens jeg venter (On the water); Moderen synger (The mother's lament); Norønnafolket (The Northland folk); Og jeg vil ha mig en Hjertenskaer (Midsummer Eve); Ragnhild; Solveig's Song; Solveigs vuggevise (Solveig's lullaby); Stambogsrim (Album Lines); En Svane (A swan); Takk for dit råd (Say what you will); Eine Traume (A dream); Trudom (Faith); Våren (Spring); Vaer hilset I Damer (Greetings, fair ladies).*
(*(**)) SIMAX mono PSC 1810 (3). Aino Ackté, Giuseppe Anselmi, Maria Barrientos, Borghild Bryhn-Landgaard, Otta Bronnum, Robert Burg, Eugenia Burzio, Erik Bye, Feodor Chaliapin, Edmund Clément, Peter Cornelius, Emmy Destinn, Kaia Eide, Gervase Elwes, Elisa Elizza, Geraldine Farrar, Kirsten Flagstad, John Forsell, Amelita Galli-Curci, Lucy Gates, Elena Gerhardt, Gunnar Graarud, Ellen Gulbranson, Nina Grieg, Hans Hedemark, Melitta Heim, Frida Hempel, Vilhelm Herold, Clara Hultgren, Hermann Jadlowker, Beatrice Kernic, Olive Kline, Salomea Kruszelnicka, Lilli Lehmann, Augusta Lütken, Magna Lykseth-Schjerven, Cally Monrad, Carl-Martin Ohman, Rosa Olitzka, Elisabeth Rethberg, Ernestine Schumann-Heink, Karl Scheidemantel, Leo Slezak, Greta Stückgold, Joseph Schwarz, Richard Tauber, Luisa Tetrazzini (various pianists).

As the cast-list shows, this is a veritable treasure-house of singing at the turn of the century, not only in northern Europe but elsewhere. Naturally in the early years of the gramophone singers tended to gravitate towards a handful of songs so that familiar numbers such as *Jag elsker Dig* and *En Svane* turn up in several versions, the former 11 times and the latter seven. There are no fewer than 16 different versions of *Solveig's song*, including a few bars sung without accompaniment by Nina Grieg in 1889 when she would have been forty-four. (She stopped singing in public in the 1890s.) Grieg himself declared her to be the finest interpreter of his songs and, although she is barely audible through the deluge of background noise, the voice is obviously of great purity. Listening to her across a divide of over a century is a curiously moving experience. The roll-call is pretty dazzling, ranging as it does from big names such as Aino Ackté (for whom Sibelius composed *Luonnotar*), to Chaliapin and Emmy Destinn (the copy of her *Mens jeg venter* is unfortunately pretty rough) and there are 47 singers in all, but the less familiar names also offer valuable insights into performance practice. There are nearly 80 performances altogether, and the quality of the recordings which have been subjected to the NoNoise system of reduction calls for more tolerance than many listeners will feel able to extend. This is a set for libraries, specialist collectors and students of song, and it is an invaluable resource into which to dip.

Songs: *Autumn storm (Efteråsstormen); I give my song to the spring (Jeg giver mit digt til våren); I would like a waistcoat of silk (Og jeg vil ha mig en silkevest); To you (Til én) I & II.*
(Y/B) (M) *** Decca 440 492-2 [id.]. Kirsten Flagstad, LSO, Oiven Fjeldstad – SIBELIUS: Songs (with: Arne EGGEN: *Praise to the eternal spring of life (Aere det evige forår i livet);* Eyvind ALNAES: *About love (Nu brister alle de kløfter); A February morning at the Gulf (Februarmorgen ved Golfen); A hundred violins (De hundrede fioliner); Yearnings of spring (Vårlængsler);* Harald LIE: *The key (Nykelen); The letter (Skinnvengbrev)* ***).

Flagstad is in fine voice in this carefully chosen recital of Norwegian songs, hardly any of which can be really well known to the average listener. Even Grieg's songs, with the possible exception of *Autumn storm*, are almost a closed book to all but the connoisseur. Perhaps *I would like a waistcoat of silk* might ideally have had a lighter touch but, for the most part, the nobility of Flagstad's line and her concern for the words are most illuminating, and it is all the more valuable to have this repertoire in such deeply felt performances, to which the London Symphony Orchestra and Oivin Fjeldstad contribute not a little. Excellent stereo sound too, using both Kingsway Hall and Walthamstow. The reissue is part of Decca's Kirsten Flagstad Edition and is well documented.

(i) *Bergliot, Op. 42;* (ii) *Den Bergtekne (The mountain thrall), Op. 32;* (iii & iv) *Foran sydens kloster (Before a southern convent);* (ii & iii) *7 Songs with orchestra: Den første møde; Solveigs sang; Solveigs vuggesang; Fra Monte Pincio; En svane; Våren; Henrik Wegeland.*
*** DG Dig. 437 519-2 [id.]. (i) Rut Tellefsen, (ii) Håkan Hagegård; (iii & iv) Barbara Bonney; (iii) Randi Stene; Gothenburg SO, Neeme Järvi.

Before a southern convent is based on a Bjørnson poem which tells how Ingigerd, the daughter of a chieftain, has seen her father murdered by the villainous brigand, Arnljot. He was on the verge of raping her but relented and let her go. Despite what she has suffered, she feels a certain attraction for Arnljot and now seeks expiation by entering a foreign convent. The piece is in dialogue form. When she is questioned, she speaks openly to the nuns about her feelings of guilt, and the piece ends with a chorus of nuns who admit her to their number. It's not great Grieg but it has a lot going for it. It's well worth investigating, very naturally balanced with plenty of air round the sound. The singers are well placed and not right on top of you. Generally speaking, the quality on all these DG recordings is excellent – which is not surprising, as they're made by the same Gothenburg team who have recorded for the BIS label.

(i) *Bergliot, Op. 42;* (ii) *Olav Trygvason, Op. 50; Funeral March for Rikard Nordraak.*
(Y/B) *** Virgin/EMI Dig. VC5 45051-2 [id.]. (i) Lise Fjeldstad; (ii) Solveig Kringelborn, Randi Stene, Per Vollestad, Trondheim Ch.; Trondheim SO, Ole Kristian Ruud.

Neither *Olav Trygvason* nor *Bergliot* is top-drawer Grieg, but this excellently balanced recording gives them a good run for their money. These Norwegian performances have great freshness and spirit, though the DG accounts have the greater polish and finesse. All the same, no one investing in this disc will have occasion to feel disappointed.

A Dream (3 versions); *Good morning; Greeting; The Mother sings; The Norse people; Solveig's lullaby; Solveig's song; With a water lily* (2 versions); *With a primrose; Eros; To Norway; I love thee* (5 versions); *A swan* (3 versions); *Bilbery slopes; At the brook; In the boat; And I shall have a true love.*
(Y/B) (M) (***) RCA mono/stereo 09026 61827-2 [id.]. Marsh, Melchior, Flagstad, Nilsson, Björling, Crooks, Traubel, Galli-Curci, Krogh, Schumann-Heink, Kline, Farrar, Frijsh.

The transfers here are acceptable and, with such celebrated singers as Björling, Farrar, Flagstad, Galli-Curci and Melchior represented, this compilation needs no further recommendation.

Haugtussa, Op. 67; 7 Children's songs, Op. 61; Melodies of the heart, Op. 5; 6 Songs, Op. 4; 6 Songs, Op. 25.
**(*) BIS Dig. CD 637 [id.]. Monica Groop, Love Derwinger.

Haugtussa (song-cycle), *Op. 67; 6 Songs, Op. 48. Songs: Beside the stream; Farmyard song; From Monte Pincio; Hope; I love but thee; Spring; Spring showers; A Swan; Two brown eyes; While I wait; With a waterlily* (sung in Norwegian).
⊛ *** DG Dig. 437 521-2 [id.]. Anne Sofie von Otter, Bengt Forsberg.

This recital of Grieg's songs by Anne Sofie von Otter and Bengt Forsberg is rather special. It begins with Grieg's most important song-cycle, *Haugtussa* ('The mountain maid'), and a generous helping of other songs includes the six songs of Op. 48, strongly characterized without being over-projected. Von Otter commands an exceptionally wide range of colour and quality and in Bengt Forsberg has a highly responsive partner. Altogether a captivating recital, and beautifully recorded too.

The Finnish soprano, Monica Groop, possesses a striking voice of considerable colour and does not disappoint in her excellently recorded recital. All the same, her *Haugtussa* is no match for von Otter's and her recital does not possess quite the strong interpretative personality of her Swedish colleague. This is the first of a complete survey on BIS and will provide a useful alternative to the current survey on RCA from Hagegård. It deserves warm support.

Haugtussa (The Mountain maid; song-cycle), Op. 67; Songs: Ambition (Der ærgjerrige); Among roses (Millom rosor); At Gjaetle Brook (Ved Gjætle-Bekken); Blueberry slope (Blåbær-Li); Children's dance (A hipp og hoppe); A dream (En drøm); The encounter (Møte); Enticement (Det syng); Eros; The first meeting (Det første møte); Fra Monte Pincio (from Monte Pincio); High up in the leafy hills (I liden højt der oppe); I give my song to the spring (Jeg giver mit digt til våren); I love you (Jeg elsker Dig); In the boat (Der gynger en Båd på Bølge); The little hut (Hytten); Little Kirsten (Liten Kirsten); The little maiden (Veslemøy); Love (Elsk); Sorrowful day (Vond Dag); The water-lily (Med en vanlilje); With a primrose (Med en primulaveris).
(Y/B) (M) (***) Decca mono 440 493-2 [id.]. Kirsten Flagstad, Edwin McArthur.

Flagstad is in splendid voice and this repertoire suits her admirably, for she had grown up with many of these songs. If the dark cycle about a peasant girl who falls in love and is deserted by her lover is conceived for a younger voice, Flagstad still makes it very much her own from the noble account of the very first song, 'Enticement' (*Det syng*). She is at her most compelling in the fifth (*Elsk*), about the passionate bondage of love itself, and she scales the big voice down delightfully for the light-hearted 'Children's dance'. Some of the other songs here are more familiar, none more so than *Jeg elsker dig* ('I love you') which is gloriously sung. As elsewhere in these recordings, her partner, Edwin McArthur, is wholly at one with her, much more than just an accompanist.

(i) *Landkjenning (Land-sighting), Op. 31;* (i & ii) *Olav Trygvason, Op. 50; Peer Gynt Suites Nos. 1 & 2.*
*** DG Dig. 437 523-2 [id.]. (i) Anne Gjevang; (ii) Randi Stene; (i; ii) Håkan Hagegård; Gothenburg SO, Neeme Järvi.

The great enthusiasm which greeted *Before a southern convent* prompted Bjørnson to plan an opera, *Olav Trygvason. Landkjenning* ('Land-sighting') and the three scenes that survive from the opera are on DG, coupled together with the two *Peer Gynt* suites. In the second tableau, the role of the priestess is sung by Anne Gjevang, the Erda in the Haitink *Ring* on EMI. Some may find her vibrato a bit excessive. The other soloists, Randi Stene and Håkan Hagegård, acquit themselves well, as does the Gothenburg Orchestra and Chorus under Neeme Järvi. The *Peer Gynt* suites are not new, though two of the numbers have been re-recorded. Recommended.

Melodies of the heart, Op. 5; 9 Songs, Op. 18; 6 Songs, Op. 25; The last spring, Op. 33/2; The Mountain thrall, Op. 32; Rocking, rocking on the gentles waves, Op. 49/2; Henrik Wergeland, Op. 58/3.
**(*) RCA Dig. 09026 61518-2. Håkan Hagegård, Warren Jones.

Songs and ballads, Op. 9; 4 Songs, Op. 21; 5 Songs, Op. 26; Romances & songs, Op. 39; Reminiscences from mountain and fjord, Op. 44.
**(*) RCA Dig. 09026 61629-2. Håkan Hagegård, Warren Jones.

Håkan Hagegård's two CDs with Warren Jones find the great Swedish baritone less than wholly persuasive. Here there is a certain uniformity of colour and approach in many of these songs, and an occasional hardness at the tenor end of the voice. However, these discs have been widely admired and Hagegård's artistry and musical intelligence are always in evidence.

Peer Gynt (incidental music), *Op. 23* (complete).
(M) *** Unicorn UKCD 2003/4 [id.]. Carlson, Hanssen, Bjørkøy, Hansli, Oslo PO Ch., LSO, Dreier.

Per Dreier achieves very spirited results from his soloists, the Oslo Philharmonic Chorus and our own LSO, with some especially beautiful playing from the woodwind; the recording is generally first class, with a natural perspective between soloists, chorus and orchestra. The Unicorn set includes 32 numbers in all, including Robert Henrique's scoring of the *Three Norwegian dances*, following the revised version of the score Grieg prepared for the 1886 production in Copenhagen. This music, whether familiar or unfamiliar, continues to astonish by its freshness and inexhaustibility.

Peer Gynt (incidental music), *Op. 23* (complete); *Sigurd Jorsalfar* (incidental music), *Op. 56* (complete).
*** DG Dig. 423 079-2 (2) [id.]. Bonney, Eklöf, Sandve, Malmberg, Holmgren; Foss, Maurstad, Stokke (speakers); Gösta Ohlin's Vocal Ens., Pro Musica Chamber Ch., Gothenburg SO, Järvi.

Neeme Järvi's recording differs from its predecessor by Per Dreier in offering the Grieg Gesamtausgabe *Peer Gynt*, which bases itself primarily on the 26 pieces he included in the 1875 production rather than the final published score, prepared after Grieg's death by Halvorsen. This well-documented set comes closer to the original by including spoken dialogue, as one would have expected in the theatre. The CDs also offer the complete *Sigurd Jorsalfar* score, which includes some splendid music. The performances by actors, singers (solo and choral) and orchestra alike are exceptionally vivid, with the warm Gothenburg ambience used to creative effect; the vibrant histrionics of the spoken words undoubtedly add to the drama.

Peer Gynt: extended excerpts.
*** DG Dig. 427 325-2 [id.]. Bonney, Eklöf, Malmberg, Maurstad, Foss, Gothenburg Ch. & SO, Järvi.
*** Decca Dig. 425 448-2 [id.]. Urban Malmberg, Mari-Ann Haeggander, San Francisco Ch. & SO, Blomstedt.
(N) (BB) *** Belart 450 018-2. VPO, Karajan – SIBELIUS: *En Saga* etc. ***

Neeme Järvi's disc offers more than two-thirds of the 1875 score, and the performance has special claims on the collector who wants one CD rather than two (half the second CD of the set is taken up by *Sigurd Jorsalfar*).

Decca's set of excerpts makes a useful alternative to the Järvi disc. All but about 15 minutes of the complete score is here and the spoken text is included too, all admirably performed. Perhaps the Gothenburg acoustic is to be preferred to the Davies Hall, San Francisco. However, the Decca recording approaches the demonstration class.

Karajan's shorter set of excerpts (from 1962) makes a first-class super-bargain alternative on Belart, with a particularly fresh response from the VPO. It includes a beautiful account of *Solveig's song*, and the sound is warm and atmospheric. The Sibelius couplings are equally recommendable.

(i) *Peer Gynt:* excerpts. *In Autumn* (overture), *Op. 11; An Old Norwegian song with variations, Op. 51; Symphonic dance No. 2.*
(M) *** EMI CDM7 64751-2 [id.]. (i) Ilse Hollweg, Beecham Ch. Soc.; RPO, Beecham.

Beecham showed a very special feeling for this score and to hear *Morning*, the gently textured *Anitra's dance* or the eloquent portrayal of the *Death of Aase* under his baton is a uniquely rewarding experience. Ilse Hollweg makes an excellent soloist. The recording dates from 1957 and, like most earlier Beecham reissues, has been enhanced by the remastering process. The most delectable of the *Symphonic dances*, very beautifully played, makes an ideal encore after *Solveig's lullaby*, affectingly sung by Hollweg. The *In Autumn* overture, not one of Grieg's finest works, is most enjoyable when Sir Thomas is so persuasive, not shirking the melodramatic moments. Finally for the present reissue, we are offered *An Old Norwegian folksong with variations* (not previously released in its stereo format). It is a piece of much colour and charm, which is fully realized here.

Peer Gynt (incidental music): *Overture; Suites 1–2. Lyric pieces: Evening in the mountain; Cradle song, Op. 68/5; Sigurd Jorsalfar: suite, Op. 56; Wedding day at Troldhaugen, Op. 65/6.*
(BB) **(*) Naxos Dig. 8.550140; *4550140* [id.]. CSSR State PO, Košice, Stephen Gunzenhauser.

A generous Grieg anthology on Naxos (70 minutes, all but 3 seconds) and the performances by the Slovak State Philharmonic Orchestra in Košice (in eastern Slovakia) are very fresh and lively and thoroughly enjoyable. There is wide dynamic range both in the playing and in the recording, and sensitivity in matters of phrasing.

Peer Gynt: suites Nos. 1, Op. 46; 2, Op. 55. Sigurd Jorsalfar: suite.
(N) (B) *** DG Double 447 358-2 (2) [id.]. BPO, Karajan – SIBELIUS: *The Bard* etc. ***

Karajan's earlier analogue performances from the early 1970s reappear here on a DG Double, coupled with a very generous and enticing Sibelius programme. The Grieg performances are highly expressive and superbly played. Anitra dances with allure and there is contrasting simplicity and repose in *Aase's death*. The current transfers are rather brightly lit, but there is no lack of body.

Peer Gynt: suites Nos. 1–2; Lyric pieces: Evening in the mountains; Cradle song, Op. 68/1–2; Wedding day at Troldhaugen, Op. 65/6; Sigurd Jorsalfar suite, Op. 56.
(BB) ** Naxos Dig. 8.550864 [id.]. BBC Scottish SO, Jerzy Maksymiuk.

The *Peer Gynt* music is presented with admirable simplicity by the excellent Scottish players. But although *Aase's death* brings a rapt closing pianissimo, *In the hall of the Mountain King* could use rather more impetus, and it is the second suite that has the greater character. What makes this disc worth considering is the very beautiful string-playing in the two *Lyric pieces* and the fine performance of the first two numbers from *Sigurd Jorsalfar*, *In the king's hall* engagingly presented and *Borghild's dream* full of atmosphere and drama. The famous *Homage march* is suitably regal but rather too slow and expansive. However, the jolly *Wedding dance* is very spirited.

(i) *Peer Gynt: suites Nos. 1–2. Lyric suite, Op. 54; Sigurd Jorsalfar: suite.*
(M) *** DG Dig. 427 807-2 [id.]. (i) Soloists, Ch.; Gothenburg SO, Järvi.

Järvi's excerpts from *Peer Gynt* and *Sigurd Jorsalfar* are extracted from his complete sets, so the editing inevitably produces a less tidy effect than normal recordings of the *Suites*. However, the performances are first class and so is the recording, and this comment applies also to the *Lyric suite*, taken from an earlier, digital orchestral collection.

4 Psalms, Op. 74.
**(*) Nimbus Dig. NI 5171 [id.]. Håkan Hagegård, Oslo Cathedral Ch., Terje Kvam – MENDELSSOHN: *3 Psalms.* **(*)

The *Four Psalms* are dignified, beautiful pieces, very well sung here by the choir and the Swedish baritone, Håkan Hagegård. The recording is eminently faithful, though the pauses between the Psalms are not long enough.

Griffes, Charles (1884–1920)

(i) *The Pleasure Dome of Kubla Khan, Op. 8;* (ii) *3 Tone pictures, Op. 5;* (ii; iii) *3 Poems of Fiona Macleod;* (iv) *4 German songs; 4 Impressions; Song of the Dagger.*
** New World NW 273/4 [id.]. (i) Boston SO; (ii) New World CO; Ozawa; (iii) with Bryn-Julson; (iv) Stapp, Milnes, Richardson, Spong.

The four *German songs* come from the early years of the century when Griffes was much influenced by Brahms; they are well sung here by Sherrill Milnes, but the four *Impressions* (1912–16) are less well served. Ozawa's performance of *The Pleasure Dome* conveys much of the work's strong atmosphere. By far the most persuasive performance comes from Phyllis Bryn-Julson in the Op. 11 settings of Fiona Macleod. The recordings date from the 1970s and are eminently acceptable.

Fantasy pieces; Legend; The Pleasure Dome of Kubla Khan; 3 Preludes; Rhapsody in B min.; Sonata; 3 Tone pictures.
** Kingdom Dig. KCLCD 2011 [id.]. James Tocco.

The *Sonata* is the most radical and expressionistic work here and *The Pleasure Dome of Kubla Khan* the best known. The three late *Preludes* have a keen sense of mystery and concentration. So, too, have the three *Tone pictures*. James Tocco plays with insight and sensitivity; he meets the virtuoso demands of the *Sonata* and is keenly responsive to the dynamic nuances of these scores. He is not well served by the acoustic, which has far too little space round the aural image. All the same, such is the interest of the music and the quality of the playing that this shortcoming should not be exaggerated.

Grigny, Nicolas de (1672–1703)

Organ Mass.
(N) (M) *** Cal. CAL 6911 [id.]. André Isoir (Cliquot organ at the Cathedral of Saint-Pierre de Poitiers).

Nicolas de Grigny was born in Reims and died there prematurely, just after his 31st birthday. He was principal organist both in Reims and at Notre-Dame Cathedral, where he succeeded his father in 1698. His fame as a composer rests upon one book, including 49 pieces of music, and the present Couperin-influenced *Organ Mass* which was very influential in its own right. We know Bach had a copy which survives in his own hand. Although the *Mass* (an extensive collection of 22 movements varying considerably in length, most lasting between two and four minutes) is presented here as a solo work, when it was performed in its own time the organ undoubtedly alternated with the sung sections of the Mass. The *Dialogues* and other sections (such as *Basse de Trompette* and the spectacular *Offertoire sur les grands Jeux*, with a span of over eight minutes) were intended as solo interludes. Movements such as the tranquil *Récit de Tierce pour le Bénédictus* and the coolly beautiful *Dialogue de Flûtes pour l'Elévation* created an atmosphere of mysticism so characteristic of French cathedral music. The variety of the writing is remarkable, and certainly André Isoir's performance on the Cliquot organ at Poitiers Cathedral (with its characteristically pungent reeds but full underlying sonority) readily demonstrates the music's imaginative range. As a double encore we are offered an *Elévation en sol* and a *Symphonie* by Nicolas LeBegue, both strong pieces. The analogue recording is of fine quality and, while this reissue has specialist rather than general appeal, it is a fine example of the contrapuntal church organ music being written in France before the later domination of this field by Bach.

Grofé, Ferde (1892–1972)

Grand Canyon suite.
(M) *** Decca 430 712-2 [id.]. Detroit SO, Dorati – GERSHWIN: *Porgy and Bess.* ***
*** Telarc Dig. CD 80086 [id.] (with additional cloudburst, including real thunder). Cincinnati Pops O, Kunzel – GERSHWIN: *Catfish Row.* ***

Antal Dorati has the advantage of superlative Decca recording, very much in the demonstration class, with stereoscopically vivid detail. Yet the performance combines subtlety with spectacle, and this version is very much in a class of its own.

The Cincinnati performance is played with great commitment and fine pictorial splendour, although Dorati scores at *Sunrise*, where his powerful timpani strokes add to the power of the climax. What gives the Telarc CD its special edge is the inclusion of a second performance of *Cloudburst* as an appendix with a genuine thunderstorm laminated on to the orchestral recording. The result is overwhelmingly thrilling, except that in the final thunderclap God quite upstages the orchestra, who are left trying frenziedly to match its amplitude in their closing peroration.

Grand Canyon suite; Mississipi suite.
(N) (M) **(*) Mercury 434 355-2 [id.]. Eastman-Rochester O, Hanson – HERBERT: *Cello concerto No. 2.* **

It is impossible not to respond to the pictorial vividness and gusto of Hanson's performances and, even if the studio-ish acoustic of the Eastman Theater is not ideally expansive, the 1958 Mercury stereo is brilliantly detailed in the *Grand Canyon suite*. The *Mississippi suite*, a much lesser piece, is also persuasively presented, especially the exuberant portrait of *Huckleberry Finn*. But the canyon storms rage much more spectacularly on the rival versions.

Guilmant, Félix Alexandre (1837–1911)

Symphony No. 1 for organ and orchestra, Op. 42.
*** Chandos Dig. CHAN 9271 [id.]. Ian Tracey (organ of Liverpool Cathedral), BBC PO, Yan Pascal Tortelier – WIDOR: *Symphony No. 5* ***; POULENC: *Organ concerto.* **(*)

This Guilmant *Symphony* (the composer's own arrangement of his *First Organ sonata*) is a real find, with all the genial vigour of the famous work of Saint-Saëns. The first movement has a galumphing main theme and an equally pleasing secondary idea. It is followed by a tunefully idyllic Pastorale (with some delicious registration from Ian Tracey) and a rumbustiously grandiloquent finale. All great fun, and well suited to the larger-than-life resonance of Liverpool Cathedral with its long reverberation period.

Haas, Pavel (1899–1944)

String quartets Nos. 2 (From the Monkey Mountains), Op. 7; 3, Op. 15.
(Y/B) *** Decca Dig. 440 853-2 [id.]. Hawthorne Qt – KRASA: *Quartet.* ***

Pavel Haas, like Hans Krása, was one of the many Jewish musicians who were murdered by the Nazis at the Terezín (Teresienstadt) camp. Haas's *String quartet No. 2* dates from 1925 and its sub-title, *From the*

Monkey Mountains, alludes to the Czech–Moravian highlands, which are so known in Brno. It is a highly imaginative and often beautiful score, with the strong, open-air feeling that one recognizes in Janáček. The *String quartet No. 3* (1938) comes after the lapse of a decade which had seen the rise of Nazism and the Munich treaty which led to the dismemberment and occupation of Czechoslovakia. It is a strong piece, more astringent in character than its predecessor, but it is well-argued and likeable music. The Hawthorne Quartet were members of the Boston Symphony Orchestra and have devoted them-selves to composers who suffered under Nazi persecution, and they give dedicated performances. Excellent recording.

Hadley, Patrick (1899–1973)

(i) *Lenten cantata. The cup of blessing; I sing of a maiden; My beloved spake; A Song for Easter*.
*** ASV Dig. CDDCA 881 [id.]. (i) John Mark Ainsley, Donald Sweeney; Ch. of Gonville & Caius College, Cambridge, Geoffrey Webber; Hill or Phillips (organ) – RUBBRA: *Choral music*. ***

The most substantial piece here is the *Lenten cantata* or *Lenten meditations* for two soloists, choir and orchestra (here given in an organ transcription), composed in 1963. Not a strongly individual voice, Hadley is nevertheless a refined craftsman whose feeling for line and texture is highly developed. The performances are of high quality, and so is the recording.

Hahn, Reynaldo (1875–1947)

Le bal de Béatrice d'Este (ballet suite).
*** Hyperion Dig. CDA 66347 [id.]. New London O, Ronald Corp – POULENC: *Aubade; Sinfonietta*.
***

Le bal de Béatrice d'Este is a rather charming pastiche, dating from the early years of the century and scored for the unusual combination of wind instruments, two harps, piano and timpani. Ronald Corp and the New London Orchestra play it with real panache and sensitivity.

Songs: *A Chloris; L'Air; L'Automne; 7 Chansons grises; La chère blessure; D'une prison; L'enamourée; Les étoiles; Fêtes galantes; Les fontaines; L'Incrédule; Infidélité; Offrande; Quand je fus pris au pavillon; Si mes vers avaient des ailes; Tyndaris*.
**(*) Hyperion CDA 66045 [id.]. Hill, Johnson.

If Hahn never quite matched the supreme inspiration of his most famous song, *Si mes vers avaient des ailes*, the delights here are many, the charm great. Martyn Hill, ideally accompanied by Graham Johnson, gives delicate and stylish performances, well recorded.

Halévy, Jacques Fromental (1799–1862)

La juive (opera): complete.
*** Ph. Dig. 420 190-2 (3). Varady, Anderson, Carreras, Gonzalez, Furlanetto, Amb. Op. Ch., Philh. O, Almeida.

La juive ('The Jewess') was the piece which, along with the vast works of Meyerbeer, set the pattern for the epic French opera, so popular last century. Eléazar was the last role that the great tenor, Enrico Caruso, tackled, and it was in this opera that he gave his very last performance. The greater part of the recording was completed in 1986, but that was just at the time when José Carreras was diagnosed as having leukaemia, and it was only in 1989 that he contributed his performance through 'overdubbing'. He sings astonishingly well, but the role of the old Jewish father really needs a weightier, darker voice, such as Caruso had in his last years. Julia Varady as Rachel makes that role both the emotional and the musical centre of the opera, responding both tenderly and positively. In the other soprano role, that of the Princess Eudoxia, June Anderson is not so full or sweet in tone, but she is particularly impressive in the dramatic coloratura passages, such as her Act III *Boléro*. Ferruccio Furlanetto makes a splendidly resonant Cardinal in his two big solos, and the Ambrosian Opera Chorus brings comparable bite to the powerful ensembles. Antonio de Almeida as conductor proves a dedicated advocate.

Halffter, Ernesto (1905–89)

Guitar concerto.

(N) (M) ** DG 449 098-2 [id.]. Narciso Yepes, Spanish R. & TV O, Alonso – CASTELNUOVO-
TEDESCO: *Concerto* **(*); RODRIGO: *Fantasía.* **

Halffter, the favourite pupil of Manuel de Falla, echoes some of his master's later music, developing on
the spareness of, for example, the Falla *Harpsichord concerto*. It is not what one thinks of as typical
Spanish music, but the Spanish flavour is still there behind a gritty façade. Superb playing from Yepes
and a competent accompaniment from Alonso, if not particularly glamorous recording.

Halvorsen, Johan (1864–1935)

Air norvégien, Op. 7; Danses norvégiennes.

(BB) *** Naxos Dig. 8.550329 [id.]. Dong-Suk Kang, Slovak (Bratislava) RSO, Adrian Leaper –
SIBELIUS: *Violin concerto;* SINDING: *Légende;* SVENDSEN: *Romance.* ***

Dong-Suk Kang plays the attractive *Danses norvégiennes* with great panache, character and effortless
virtuosity, and delivers an equally impeccable performance of the earlier *Air norvégien.*

Handel, George Frideric (1685–1759)

Gardiner Handel Edition
Handel Edition (complete in slipcase).

(N) (M) *** Erato/Warner 4509 99719-2 (7). Soloists, Monteverdi Ch., E. Bar. Soloists, Gardiner.

Gardiner's key Erato Handel recordings are brought together here in a new 'Handel Edition' (at a slight
price reduction) as a 7-disc, mid-priced set inside a slipcase. The only item about which there are some
reservations is the CD of the Op. 3 *Concerti grossi*, and these are relatively minor. The recordings are all
also available separately.

Ballet music: *Alcina: overture; Acts I & III: suites. Il pastor fido: suite. Terpsichore: suite.*
(N) (M) *** Erato/Warner 4509 99720-2 [id.]. E. Bar. Soloists, Gardiner.

John Eliot Gardiner is just the man for such a programme. He is not afraid to charm the ear, yet allegros
are vigorous and rhythmically infectious. The bright and clean recorded sound adds to the sparkle, and
the quality is first class. A delightful collection, and very tuneful too.

Concerti grossi, Op. 3/1–6.
(N) (M) **(*) Erato/Warner 4509 99721-2 [id.]. E. Bar. Soloists, Gardiner.

Gardiner's analogue set from 1980 has transferred well to CD. Recorded in the Henry Wood Hall,
textures are slightly more ample but still clear and admirably balanced. The starry cast-list includes
Simon Standage and Roy Goodman among the violins, and there is some very lively playing here and no
want of style. There is a slight lack of finish in one or two places and some poor intonation in *No. 2 in B
flat* – yet there are some very good things here too, as for instance the imaginative treatment of the *Largo
e staccato* of Op. 3/3 and its following *Adagio*, with Lisa Beznosiuk the engaging flute soloist.

L'allegro, il penseroso, il moderato.
(N) (M) *** Erato/Warner 4509 99723-2 (2) [id.]. Kwella, McLaughlin, Jennifer Smith, Ginn, Davies,
Hill, Varcoe, Monteverdi Ch., E. Bar. Soloists, Gardiner.

Taking Milton as his starting point, Handel illustrated in music the contrasts of mood and character
between the cheerful and the thoughtful. Then, prompted by his librettist, Charles Jennens, he added
compromise in *Il moderato*, the moderate man. The sequence of brief numbers is a delight, particularly
in a performance as exhilarating as this, with excellent soloists, choir and orchestra. The recording is first
rate.

Tamerlano (opera; complete).
(N) (M) *** Erato/Warner Dig. 4509 99722-2 (3) [id.]. Ragin, Robson, Argenta, Chance, Findlay,
Schirrer, E. Bar. Soloists, Gardiner.

John Eliot Gardiner's live concert performance of *Tamerlano* presents a strikingly dramatic and
immediate experience. The pacing of numbers and of the recitative is beautifully thought out and the
result is electrifying. Leading the cast are two outstanding counter-tenors whose encounters provide
some of the most exciting moments: Michael Chance as Andronicus, firm and clear, Derek Ragin in the

name-part equally agile and more distinctive of timbre, with a rich, warm tone that avoids womanliness. Nigel Robson in the tenor role of Bajazet conveys the necessary gravity, not least in the difficult, highly original G minor aria before the character's suicide; and Nancy Argenta sings with starry purity as Asteria. The only serious snag is the dryness of the sound, which makes voices and instruments sound more aggressive on CD than they usually do in Gardiner's recordings with the English Baroque Soloists.

Concerti grossi, Op. 3/1–6; Op. 6/1–12.
(Y/B) ❀ (M) *** Decca 444 532-2 (3) [id.]. ASMF, Marriner.

Concerti grossi, Op. 3/1–6 (including No. 4b); Concerti grossi, Op. 6/1–12.
(Y/B) (M) **(*) Teldec/Warner Analogue/Dig. 4509 95500-2 (4) [id.]. VCM, Harnoncourt.

This integral recording of the Handel *Concerti grossi* makes a permanent memorial of the partnership formed by the inspired scholarship of Thurston Dart and the interpretative skill and musicianship of (then plain Mr) Neville Marriner and his superb ensemble, at their peak in the late 1960s. Dart planned a double continuo of both organ and harpsichord, used judiciously to vary textural colour and weight. Flutes and oboes are employed (with delightful effect) where Handel suggested in Op. 3, and in Op. 6 the optional oboe parts are used in concertos 1, 2, 5 and 6. The final concerto of Op. 3 features the organ as a solo instrument, and Christopher Hogwood's more recent researches suggest that this was not what Handel originally intended (see below); but the result here very much conjures up the composer's spirit hovering in the background. Incidentally, Thurston Dart makes the point that the warm acoustic used for the recording is different from the relatively dry theatre ambience which the composer would have expected; thus the chamber organ has been balanced with discretion, for under such circumstances there is less need to add tonal body to the ripieno. The three records come at a special lower-mid-price. But, alas, the superb CD transfer brings no separate cues for individual movements, only one band for each work.

The Teldec set is easily the most endearing of Harnoncourt's earlier authentic performances of baroque music. In Op. 3, tempi tend to be relaxed, but the performances are very enjoyable in their easy-going way, the ripe, fresh colouring of the baroque oboes, played expressively, is most attractive to the ear, and the string-sound is unaggressive. Tuttis are curiously dry, suggesting that the microphones were close to the violins; otherwise the sound is very good and the whole effect quite distinctive. So it is in Op. 6, where the recording is much more ample: indeed the digital sound is among the best Harnoncourt has ever received, with the most naturally refined string timbre, excellent detail and an ideal depth of acoustic. Here, as always, Harnoncourt is rhythmically gruff, and his is a performance bringing extremes of light and shade, and with the gentle playing of the solo group often lingeringly expressive. Some may find the almost brutal accents of the ripieno overdone and the dynamic contrasts too exaggerated, but Harnoncourt obviously values the music and in his hands its greatness and diversity are always obvious. The famous melody of No. 12 (marked *Larghetto e piano*) is played *mezzo forte* and is fast and jaunty, utterly different from our experience of it in modern-instrument performances. But vitality is the keynote of Harnoncourt's approach and the sound of his original instruments is altogether more congenial than in Pinnock's Archiv set. Altogether a stimulating experience, to make one hear Handel's greatest orchestral work afresh. Unfortunately Op. 3 (with its extra concerto) plays for 71 minutes at Harnoncourt's chosen tempi and Teldec have spread Op. 6 uneconomically over three more CDs, playing for a total of 166 minutes, an expensive way of obtaining this music, even at mid-price.

Concerti grossi, Op. 3/1–6.
*** Sony Dig. SK 52553 [id.]. Tafelmusik, Jeanne Lamon.
*** DG 413 727-2 [id.]. E. Concert, Pinnock.
*** Ph. Dig. 411 482-2 [id.]. ASMF, Marriner.
(Y/B) (M) **(*) O-L Dig. 444 165-2 [id.]. Handel & Haydn Soc., Boston, Hogwood.

Those looking for a fine, modern, digital recording of Op. 3, with its woodwind complement added to the strings and a concertante organ in No. 6, will find the Tafelmusik disc eminently satisfactory. The playing is fresh and unfussy – plainer than with Gardiner, but none the worse for that. It is alert, elegant and with plenty of warmth, and tempi are admirably judged. Original instruments are used but not flaunted too abrasively and the sound is first class, clear as well as full. Indeed the resonance ensures that the music has plenty of breadth without being muddied.

The six Op. 3 concertos with their sequences of brief jewels of movements also find Pinnock and the English Concert at their freshest and liveliest, with plenty of sparkle and little of the abrasiveness associated with 'authentic' performance.

In Sir Neville Marriner's latest version with the Academy, tempi tend to be a little brisk, but the results are inspiring and enjoyable. Not unexpectedly, textures are fuller here than on Pinnock's competing Archiv recording, and the CD quality is admirably fresh.

Hogwood's set with his excellent Boston players has no lack of energy and life, and a fairly high degree of polish. Intonation, too, though not always quite immaculate, is by no means a problem; although the period wind instruments bring plenty of colour to Handel's scoring, the end result is a little deadpan and lacking in geniality. However, Hogwood has taken the opportunity of checking the sources of this music throughout and has come up with a more authentic revised score for the sixth concerto, with two new movements; the original organ concerto movement has been relegated as an appendix, and is played as a separate encore.

(i) *Concerti grossi, Op. 3/1–6;* (ii) *Organ concertos Nos. 1–6, Op. 4/1–6.*
(Y/B) (B) **(*) Ph. Duo 442 263-2 (2) (i) ECO, Leppard; (ii) Daniel Chorzempa, Concerto Amsterdam, Schröder.

Among versions of Handel's Op. 3, Leppard's set stands high. The playing is lively and fresh, and the remastered recording sounds very good. Leppard includes oboes and bassoons and secures excellent playing all round. At times one wonders whether he isn't just a shade too elegant, but in general this reissue offers one of the best versions of Op. 3 on modern instruments. In this Duo pairing we are also offered Daniel Chorzempa's set of Handel's Op. 4 *Organ concertos*, and here we move over to period instruments. The Concerto Amsterdam, however, create a robustly substantial sound so the difference is not all that striking. They bring plenty of rhythmic buoyancy and life to the accompaniments. Chorzempa uses an appropriate Dutch organ and the balance is admirable. Regarding ornamentation, Chorzempa's approach is fairly elaborate and he interpolates a sonata movement from Op. 1 after the *Adagio* of the *Third Concerto.* The recording is again excellent, and those for whom the coupling is suitable will find this is good value.

12 Concerti grossi, Op. 6/1–12.
⊛ *** Chandos Dig. CHAN 9004/6 [id.]. I Musici de Montréal, Yuli Turovsky.
*** O-L Dig. 436 845-2 (3). Handel & Haydn Soc., Christopher Hogwood.
**(*) DG Dig. 410 897-2 (1–4); 410 898-2 (5–8); 410 899-2 (9–12) [id.]. E. Concert, Pinnock.
(N) (BB) ** ASV Dig. CDQS 6163 (*Nos. 1–4*); **(*) CDQS 6164 (*Nos. 5–8*); ** CDQS 6165 (*Nos. 9–12*) [id.]. Northern Sinfonia, George Malcolm.

Concerti grossi, Op. 6/1–12; Concerto grosso in C (Alexander's Feast).
(M) **(*) HM/BMG 05472 77267-2 (3). Coll. Aur.

A refreshing and stimulating set of Handel's Opus 6 – the high-water mark of Baroque orchestral music – from Montreal. The group uses modern instruments and Yuli Turovsky's worthy aim is to seek a compromise between modern and authentic practice, by paring down vibrato in some of the expressive music, with just a hint of squeezing on the melodic line, as when the solo group make their restrained entry in the slow movement. The pointed, almost staccato treatment of the famous *Larghetto e piano* movement of No. 12 – one of the composer's most famous tunes – might be counted controversial, but many will like Turovsky's light touch and gentle grace. The concertino, Eleonora and Natalya Turovsky and Alain Aubut, play impressively, while the main group (6.3.1.1) produces full, well-balanced tone and Handel's joyous fugues are particularly fresh and buoyant. Turovsky paces convincingly, not missing Handel's breadth of sonority and moments of expressive grandeur. This is now our first choice for this wonderful music.

Admirers of Hogwood's characteristically astringent rhythmic style will be well satisfied with his Op. 6. The playing has enormous vitality, with bracingly brisk tempi and emphasis on refinement and transparency of texture rather than sonority. Two harpsichords and an arch-lute are used as continuo. The playing is heard at its finest in the masterly *Fifth Concerto in D major,* with the allegros sparkling with vivacity. The sound of the solo original instruments in the lyrical writing almost suggests viols rather than violins, although the forward balance gives the concertino soloists a strikingly firm presence. Listening to this exhilarating music-making is certainly a refreshing experience, and Hogwood is undoubtedly preferable to Pinnock, helped by the fuller, more naturally focused, Decca sound.

For all its 'authenticity', Pinnock's is never unresponsive music-making, with fine solo playing set against an attractively atmospheric acoustic. Ornamentation is often elaborate – but never at the expense of line. These are performances to admire and to sample, but not everyone will warm to them. If listened through, the sharp-edged sound eventually tends to tire the ear, and there is comparatively little sense of grandeur and few hints of tonally expansive beauty. The recording is first class.

In Handel's Op. 6 the Collegium Aureum, led by Franzjosef Maier, use original instruments, but the effect is tempererd by the warmth of the acoustic (the Cedernsaal in the Schloss Kirchheim). There is no acid-like astringency here and phrasing in slow movements is warmly expressive and unsqueezed.

Baroque oboes and bassoons are featured in Nos. 1, 2, 5 and 6 to add weight and colour within the string texture, rather than hinting at a solo role. They are fairly well submerged by the resonance. Throughout, tempi are uncontroversial and generally well judged, though the basic approach is mellow, with the famous melody in No. 12 sounding as gracious as anyone could wish. The effect is slightly old-fashioned compared to 'authentic' practices of today.

George Malcolm's set uses a full complement of modern string players; the playing is polished and alert but essentially expressive in style, heard at its best in the full-bodied opening of *Concerto No. 7*, with a genial fugato following. The best known, No. 5, is also strongly characterized and gives much pleasure, while throughout Malcolm conveys his own warmth for this endlessly inventive music. But although the playing is always spirited, in the faster movements rhythms are sometimes jogging rather than sprightly. The recording, made in All Saints' Church, Gosforth, is generally well balanced and agreeably realistic, although the harpsichord continuo might have been clearer. The transfer to CD creates a clean, bright focus with pleasingly natural string-timbres; moreover the set is inexpensive and has the advantage that the three discs are available separately. Those wanting a sampler could try the second (which includes Nos 5, 6 – which is hardly less successful – and 7), while the third CD includes No. 12 with its famous *Larghetto* melody which certainly sounds beautiful here, although Malcolm's tempo may seem too slow in the light of current period-instrument practice. Neverthess the breadth of Handel's inspiration is certainly not lost in Malcolm's spacious approach.

Concerti grossi, Op. 6/1, 2, 6, 7 & 10.
(Y/B) **(*) HM Dig. HMC 901507 [id.]. Les Arts Florissants O, William Christie.

Vital, athletic performances from Christie, and clean, transparent recording with no lack of body and with the concertino and ripieno clearly defined. The playing in slow movements is refined and there is no lack of expressive feeling, but the result is less touching than with Marriner and Turovsky and, although allegros are spirited, there is more to this music than these performers discover.

Harp concerto in B flat, Op. 4/5.
(B) *** DG 427 206-2. Zabaleta, Paul Kuentz CO – MOZART: *Flute and harp concerto;* WAGENSEIL: *Harp concerto.* ***

(i) *Harp concerto, Op. 4/6. Variations for harp.*
❀ (M) *** Decca 425 723-2. Marisa Robles, (i) ASMF, Iona Brown – BOIELDIEU; DITTERSDORF: *Harp concertos* etc. *** ❀

Handel's Op. 4/6 is well known in both organ and harp versions. Marisa Robles and Iona Brown make an unforgettable case for the latter by creating the most delightful textures, while never letting the work sound insubstantial. The ASMF accompaniment, so stylish and beautifully balanced, is a treat in itself, and the recording is well-nigh perfect.

The DG recording sounds clear and immediate and the crystalline stream of sound is attractive. Zabaleta's approach is agreeably cool, with imaginative use of light and shade. The Privilege reissue also includes a set of variations by Spohr.

Concerto for 2 lutes in B flat, Op. 4/6.
(M) **(*) RCA 09026 61588-2 [id.]. Julian Bream, Monteverdi O, Gardiner – KOHAUT; VIVALDI: *Concertos.* **(*)

Here the ever-engaging Op. 4/6 appears in Thurston Dart's reconstruction for lute and harp, which Bream has further adjusted and elaborated using a chitarrone for the slow-movement continuo. The performance is a fine one (Bream plays both solo parts) but it suffers from a forward balance for the soloists, so that their dynamic range approaches that of the orchestra with very little contrast. Delectable music-making just the same, and an immaculate CD transfer.

Oboe concertos Nos 1–3, HWV 301, 302a & 287; Concerto grosso, Op. 3/3; Hornpipe in D, HWV 356; Overture in D, HWV 337/8; Sonata à 5 in B flat, HWV 288.
(M) **(*) Ph. 426 082-2 [id.]. Heinz Holliger, ECO, Raymond Leppard.

Holliger, a masterly interpreter, does not hesitate to embellish repeats; his ornamentation may overstep the boundaries some listeners are prepared to accept. His playing and that of the other artists in this collection is exquisite, and the recording is naturally balanced.

Organ concertos, Op. 4/1–6; Op. 7/1–6; in F (The cuckoo and the nightingale), HVW 295; in A, HWV 296; in D min., HWV 304.
(M) *** DG Dig. 435 037-2 (3) [id.]. Simon Preston, E. Concert, Pinnock.

Simon Preston's set of the Handel *Organ concertos* now comes on three discs. On the first, containing the six Op. 4 works, plus the *A major*, though the balance of the solo instrument is not perfect, the playing of both Preston and the English Concert is admirably fresh and lively. Ursula Holliger is outstanding on a baroque harp (taking the place of the organ) in Op. 4, No. 6, and she creates some delicious sounds. The second and third discs, containing the six Op. 7 works, plus the *The cuckoo and the nightingale* and the *D minor*, were recorded on the organ at St John's, Armitage, in Staffordshire, and are even more attractive for the warmth and assurance of the playing, which comes near the ideal for an 'authentic' performance. The *A major* which completes the set was recorded earlier with Op. 4. For those wanting a complete set of the *Organ concertos* this is strongly recommended.

Organ concertos, Op. 4/1–6; Op. 7/1–6.
(M) *** Erato/Warner 4509 91932-2 (2) [id.]. Ton Koopman, Amsterdam Bar. O.
(M) **(*) Teldec/Warner 4509 91188-2 (2) [id.]. Herbert Tachezi, VCM, Harnoncourt.

Ton Koopman's paired sets of Opp. 4 and 7 are a remarkable bargain, complete on two CDs in Erato's Duo Bonsai series. They take precedence over all the competition, both as performances and as recordings. The playing has wonderful life and warmth, tempi are always aptly judged and, although original instruments are used, this is authenticity with a kindly presence, for the warm acoustic ambience of St Bartholomew's Church, Beek-Ubbergen, Holland, gives the orchestra a glowingly vivid coloration and the string timbre is particularly attractive. So is the organ itself, which is just right for the music. Ton Koopman plays imaginatively throughout and he is obviously enjoying himself: no single movement sounds tired and the orchestral fugues emerge with genial clarity. Koopman directs the accompanying group from the keyboard, as Handel would have done, and the interplay between soloist and ripieno is a delight. The sound is first class and the balance could hardly be better.

Herbert Tachezi also concentrates on the twelve concertos which make up Opp. 4 and 7. The ornamentation provided by the soloist was achieved spontaneously at the actual recording sessions and is certainly successful, but Harnoncourt's accompaniments are straightforward, at times even seeming unadventurous and rhythmically positive. But Tachezi's registration and flourishes give constant pleasure, and the chest organ (made by Jürgen Ahrend) is very well chosen for this repertoire. The first concerto of Op. 7 exceptionally requires the use of pedals, and for this a Viennese instrument was used (built by Karl Bucklow in 1858). Both organs contrast well with Harnoncourt's authentic, chamber-sized string group, and his rhythmic pointing is always agreeably lively. Although the more robust and grander qualities of Handel's inspiration are played down somewhat, the recording is fresh, full, transparent and cleanly transferred, and there is much to enjoy here.

Organ concertos, Op. 4/1–6.
(N) (M) *** Virgin Veritas/EMI Dig. VC5 45174-2 [id.]. Bob van Asperen, O of Age of
  Englightenment.

A splendid new set of Op. 4 comes from Bob van Asperen, who uses an organ built by Goetz and Gwynne in 1985 using seventeenth-century models. He directs the Orchestra of the Age of Enlightenment from the keyboard, as Handel would have done, and the results are refreshingly crisp and rhythmic. At the very opening of the first concerto he sets out his colours with an improvisatory flourish of considerable panache, and decoration is wonderfully apt throughout. From the orchestra there is expressive warmth and plenty of weight and grandeur; but it is the sense of buoyant, rhythmic joy that one remembers most: sample the finale of No. 4, the second movement of No. 5 or the piquant opening of No. 6. The recording could hardly be bettered.

Organ concertos, Op. 4/2; Op. 7/3–5; in F (The cuckoo and the nightingale).
(N) (M) *** DG Dig. 447 300-2. Simon Preston, E. Concert, Pinnock.

This is more generous than the previous (full-price) sampler from Preston's series with Pinnock. Both performances and sound are admirably fresh.

Organ concertos, Op. 4/4 & 6; Op. 7/1 & 4; in F (The cuckoo and the nightingale), HWV 295.
(B) *** Erato/Warner 2292 45930-2 [id.]. Marie-Claire Alain (Kern organ of Collegiate Church, Saint-
  Donat, Drôme), Paillard CO, Paillard.

A French view of Handel might be expected to provide a new look, and this bargain selection from Marie-Claire Alain's highly successful (1978) Erato complete set is most enjoyable. The solo playing is consistently alert and imaginative, and the overall effect brings grandeur as well as elegance to this music. The Op. 7 works are particularly enjoyable. Op. 7/1, after an impressively regal opening, has an enchanting closing *Bourrée*. Surely *The cuckoo and the nightingale* can never have been registered more winningly on disc, while its *Siciliano* slow movement is most graciously played. Similarly the registration at the opening of Op. 4/6 (also well known in its version for harp) is memorable. The solo playing is consistently alert and imaginative, and the CD transfers are admirable. With 71 minutes of music, this is a bargain.

Music for the Royal Fireworks (original wind scoring).
*** Telarc Dig. CD 80038 [id.]. Cleveland Symphonic Winds, Fennell – HOLST: *Military band suites.* *** ❀

Music for the Royal Fireworks; 2 Arias for wind band; Concerti a due cori Nos. 1–3.
(Y/B) (M) ** O-L Analogue/Dig. 443 190-2 [id.]. AAM, Hogwood.

Music for the Royal Fireworks; Concerto grosso in C (Alexander's Feast); Overtures: Alceste; Belshazzar; Samson; Saul. Solomon: Arrival of the Queen of Sheba.
(Y/B) (M) *** DG Dig. 447 279-2 [id.]. E. Concert, Trevor Pinnock.

Music for the Royal Fireworks (original version); (i) *Coronation anthems* (see also below).
*** Hyperion Dig. CDA 66350 [id.]. (i) New College, Oxford, Ch.; augmented King's Consort, Robert King.

In 1978, in Severance Hall, Cleveland, Ohio, Frederick Fennell gathered together the wind and brass from the Cleveland Symphony Orchestra and recorded a performance to demonstrate spectacularly what fine playing and digital sound could do for Handel's open-air score. The overall sound-balance tends to favour the brass (and the drums), but few will grumble when the result is as overwhelming as it is on the CD, with the sharpness of focus matched by the presence and amplitude of the sound-image.

Pinnock's performance of the *Fireworks music* has tremendous zest; this is not only the safest but the best recommendation for those wanting a period-instrument version. The account of the *Alexander's Feast concerto* has both vitality and imagination and is no less recommendable. The vigorous and exhilarating performances of five *Overtures*, most of them hardly known at all but full of original ideas, even in the most highly structured pieces, make this a most interesting collection of works, and the Queen of Sheba's arrival is always welcome. All are freshly and cleanly recorded.

King provides the first ever period performance of Handel's *Royal fireworks music* to use the full complement of instruments Handel demanded, assembling no fewer than 24 baroque oboists and 12 baroque bassoonists, 9 trumpeters, 9 exponents of the hand horn and 4 timpanists. It all makes for a glorious noise. King's Handel style has plenty of rhythmic bounce, and the recording in its warmly atmospheric way gives ample scale. The coupled performances of the four *Coronation anthems* are not as incisively dramatic as some but still convey the joy of the inspiration.

Hogwood's version can be counted among the best available and has lively rhythms and keen articulation. Hogwood gives a strong impression of the score, even if no attempt is made to reproduce the forces heard in 1749. The *Concerti a due cori*, sharing musical material taken from familiar works (including *Messiah*), are scored for two groups of wind instruments with an accompanying string orchestra plus continuo. Horns are strongly featured in the two *F major concertos* (Nos. 1 and 3). The present performances are lively enough, but the strings are very thin on top and there is some less than perfect intonation and ensemble. Of course there are some good things, and the resonant sound helps the aural picture (though the violins are obstinately edgy). The two *Arias for wind band* include an arrangement of an actual operatic aria (from *Teseo*) and again are rather spoilt by the inaccurate tuning of the period horns.

Music for the Royal Fireworks; Water music (complete).
(B) *** Erato/Warner 2292 45931-2 [id.]. Paillard CO, Jean-François Paillard.
*** Argo 414 596-2 [id.]. ASMF, Marriner.
(BB) *** Naxos Dig. 8.550109; *4550109* [id.]. Capella Istropolitana, Bohdan Warchal.
(N) (BB) ** RCA Navigator 74321 29236-2. Paillard CO, Jean-François Paillard.

Erato offer a really first-class combination of the complete *Fireworks* and *Water music*, admirably played on modern instruments. There is both vitality and finesse, and a genuine sense of style. The *Fireworks music* is heard in its original wind scoring, and no one could complain about a lack of spectacle – the horns rasp splendidly in the *Overture*, and one can really imagine a fiery backcloth for the grand closing *Minuets*, with the exuberant horns again contrasting well with the oboes. The CD transfer of recordings made in 1973 and 1962 is admirably fresh and modern-sounding.

Marriner, using modern instruments, directs a sparkling account of the complete *Water music* plus the *Fireworks music*. Here Marriner deliberately avoids a weighty manner, even at the magisterial opening of the overture. But with full, resonant recording, this coupling makes sound sense and the remastered Argo recording still sounds both full and fresh. However, it remains at full price.

Bohdan Warchal directs the Capella Istropolitana in bright and lively performances of the complete *Water music* as well as the *Fireworks music*, well paced and well scaled, with woodwind and brass aptly abrasive, and with such points as double-dotting faithfully observed. Textures are clean, with an attractive bloom on the full and immediate sound, to provide a strong bargain recommendation.

Re-recording this music digitally in 1990, Paillard and his Chamber Orchestra fail to match the vitality and sparkle of their earlier, Erato analogue coupling. This is agreeable enough and well recorded, but there is an element of routine in the playing.

(i) *Music for the Royal Fireworks;* (ii) *Water music: suites 1–3* (complete); (i) *Concerto a due cori No. 1 in B flat; Violin concerto in B flat* (arr. from *Sonata à 5*); Marches from: *Atalanta; Joshua; Occasional oratorio.*
(N) (BB) *(*) EMI Seraphim CES5 68523-2 [CDEB 68523] [id.]. (i) Menuhin Festival O, Sir Yehudi Menuhin; (ii) Prague CO, Mackerras.

There are inexpensive couplings of the *Fireworks* and *Water music* on a single CD, which reduces the attractiveness of this Seraphim set, except to admirers of Menuhin. One wonders why EMI did not choose his version of the complete *Water music*, which is in many ways preferable to the Mackerras version. This is lively enough, but there is a heavyweight quality in the string-tone (hardly a question of recording) which at times weighs the music down despite the quality of much of the playing itself. Unfortunately Menuhin's tempi for the *Royal Fireworks music*, using a comparatively new edition by Neville Boyling, are consistently on the slow side, and the main interest of his contribution to this collection is the arrangement of the *Sonata à cinque*, presented under the title of 'Violin concerto in B flat', in which Menuhin himself is the warm-hearted if somewhat romantic soloist. The *Concerto a due cori*, with expansive strings, to present-day ears similarly sounds too ample to seem really stylish.

Music for the Royal Fireworks; Water music (complete); (i) *Oboe concerto No. 2 in B flat.*
(N) (B) **(*) Decca Eclipse Dig. 448 227-2; *448 227-4* [id.]. Stuttgart CO, Karl Münchinger, (i) with Lothar Koch.

Here is a much better way of remembering Münchinger's expertise in baroque repertoire than in the Bach *Orchestral Suites*. His style is a compromise between authenticity and the German tradition. In the complete *Water music* he uses recorders most effectively; the balance, helped by Decca's very transparent sound, is often attractively lightweight. If occasionally tempi seem a shade on the slow side, there is much to enjoy both here and in the *Fireworks music*, where the clarity reveals some shifts of perspective in the *Overture* and *Bourrée*. Some other versions of this music are more buoyant but Münchinger is consistently sympathetic and never dull. With first-class digital recording, the effect is vivid and well focused, and with an oboe concerto (well played by Lothar Koch) thrown in for good measure – and with the additional advantage of economy – this is well worth considering.

Music for the Royal Fireworks: suite; Water music: suite (arr. Harty and Szell); *The Faithful shepherd: Minuet* (ed. Beecham); *Xerxes: Largo* (arr. Reinhardt).
(Y/B) (BB) *** Belart 450 001-2. LSO, Szell.

Many readers will, like us, have a nostalgic feeling for the Handel–Harty suites from which earlier generations got to know these two marvellous scores. George Szell and the LSO offer a highly recommendable coupling of them on a Belart super-bargain issue, with Handel's *Largo* and the *Minuet* from Beecham's *Faithful shepherd suite* thrown in for good measure. The orchestral playing throughout (from the early 1970s) is quite outstanding, and the strings are wonderfully expressive in the slower pieces. The horns excel, and the crisp new transfer seems to add to the sheer zest of the music-making. A splendid bargain.

Water music: Suites Nos. 1–3 (complete).
(Y/B) (BB) *** ASV Dig. CDQS 6152 [id.]. ECO, George Malcolm.
(N) *** Ph. Dig. 434 122 [id.]. E. Bar. Soloists, Gardiner.
*** DG Dig. 410 525-2 [id.]. E. Concert, Pinnock.
(N) (M) **(*) Virgin Veritas/EMI VER5 61240-2 [id.]. Linde Consort, Linde.

Water music: suites Nos. 1–3 (complete); *Concerto grosso in C (Alexander's Feast).*
(M) *** Ph. 434 729-2 [id.]. ASMF, Marriner.

This super-bargain set of the complete *Water music* on the ASV Quicksilva label from George Malcolm and the English Chamber Orchestra tends to sweep the board, except for those insisting on 'authentic instruments'. Indeed in every other sense this is a completely stylish realization of Handel's intentions, with the closing dances of the *Third Suite in G* particularly elegant, while the digital recording approaches demonstration standard. The playing is first class, articulation is deft and detail admirable. There is a sense of delight in the music which makes this version especially appealing.

The 1979 Philips version of the *Water music* brings Sir Neville Marriner's second complete recording, and characteristically he has taken the trouble to correct several tiny textural points wrongly read before. The playing, too, is even finer than on his old Argo disc, helped by full-ranging, refined recording. For anyone wanting a mid-priced version using modern instruments this is highly recommendable, and the coupled *Alexander's Feast concerto grosso* combines energy with polish. However, since this is reissued on Philips's Insignia label, no musical notes are included, only a eulogy of the performers.

Gardiner's set of the *Water music* (with the *F major Suite* played first) brings a characteristically bright and resilient performance, full of vitality and colour – period-intrument playing at its most stimulating. With first-class recording, this is an obvious first choice in its field; but with only 53 minutes on the disc, why did Philips not add the *Royal Fireworks music*?

To offer the *Water music* without the *Fireworks music* at full price now seems ungenerous, but Pinnock's version on DG Archiv remains very enticing. Speeds are consistently well chosen and are generally uncontroversial. One test is the famous *Air*, which here remains an engagingly gentle piece. The recording is beautifully balanced and clear.

Using period instruments, the Linde Consort provides a gentler, more intimate alternative to the outstanding versions of Pinnock and Hogwood. The ensemble is not always so polished, but the easy warmth of the playing is most attractive, not least in the G major movements for flute, recorder, bassoon and strings which Linde (himself the flute-and recorder-player) turns into a separate suite after the groups in F major and D major. First-rate sound backs up bright but unabrasive performances.

CHAMBER MUSIC
Complete chamber music

Volume 1: *Flute sonatas: in E min., Op. 1a/b; in G, Op. 1/5; in B min., Op. 1/9; in D (HWV 378); Halle sonatas Nos. 1–3.*
(Y/B) *** CRD CRD 3373; *CRDC 4073* [id.]. L'Ecole d'Orphée (Stephen Preston, Susan Sheppard, John Toll, Lucy Carolan).

Volume 2: *Oboe sonatas Nos. 1 in B flat (HWV 357); in F (HWV 363a); in C min., Op. 1/8 (HWV 366); Violin sonatas: in D min. (original version of Op. 1/1), HWV 359a; in A, Op. 1/3, HWV 361; in G min., Op. 1/6 (HWV 364a); in D, Op. 1/13 (HWV 371); Allegros for violin and continuo: in A min. (HWV 408); in C min., HWV 412.*
(Y/B) **(*) CRD CRD 3374; *CRDC 4074* [id.]. L'Ecole d'Orphée (David Reichenberg, John Holloway, Susan Sheppard, Lucy Carolan).

The first pair of CDs in CRD's complete survey are very well recorded. The date is given as 1991, but they are analogue and from the early 1980s. Volume 1 contains the seven sonatas for flute (three are the so-called 'Halle' *Trio sonatas*, published in 1730 and thought to be the product of Handel's youth) as well as a sonata recently discovered in Brussels, for flute and continuo in D major (HWV 378). The question of the authenticity and provenance of some of the other music in this set is too complicated to be gone into in these pages but is clearly set out in the insert notes. The playing itself is always spirited and intelligent, and if Stephen Preston's eighteenth-century flute timbre sounds a little watery, that is the nature of the baroque flute, and his phrasing is often beguiling. David Reichenberg's Hailperin oboe is full of ripe colour, and the playing of both artists is immaculate. Indeed there is much to admire in these performances, in both style and execution. However, while those CDs remain available, first choice in this repertoire on original instruments remains with the Camerata Köln on Deutsche Harmonia Mundi at mid-price (see below).

Volume 3: *Trio sonatas, Op. 2: Nos. 1 for flute, violin and continuo in B min.; 2 in G min.; 3 in B flat for 2 violins and continuo; 4 in F for recorder, violin and continuo; 5 in G min.; 6 in G min. for 2 violins and continuo.*
(Y/B) **(*) CRD CRD 3375; *CRDC 4075* [id.]. L'Ecole d'Orphée (John Holloway, Micaela Comberti, Stephen Preston, Philip Pickett, Susan Sheppard, Robert Wooley, John Toll).

Volume 4: *Trio sonatas, Op. 5 for 2 violins and continuo: Nos. 1 in A; 2 in D; 3 in E min.; 4 in G; 5 in G min.; 6 in F; 7 in B flat.*
(Y/B) **(*) CRD 3376; *CRDC 4076* [id.]. L'Ecole d'Orphée (John Holloway, Micaela Comberti, Susan Sheppard, Lucy Carolan).

Volume 5: *Sinfonia in B flat (HWV 338); Trio sonatas: in C min., Op. 2/1a; in F (HWV 392); in G min. (HWV 393); in E (HWV 394); in C (HWV 403).*
(Y/B) **(*) CRD CRD 3377; *CRDC 4077* [id.]. L'Ecole d'Orphée (John Holloway, Micaela Comberti, Susan Sheppard, Lucy Carolan).

The *Trio sonatas* recorded by L'Ecole d'Orphée include the complete Op. 2 set, an alternative version of another sonata of Op. 2 (namely *No. 1 in C minor*, which also appears in its B minor guise for flute, violin and continuo), the seven sonatas of Op. 5, and the three so-called 'Dresden' *Sonatas* (HWV 392–4). Only one of them (in F) is totally authentic, though whoever composed the remaining two was no mean figure. In addition there is a very attractive *Sinfonia in B flat* (HWV 338), which is written in trio sonata form. It is given a splendidly alert and sympathetic performance. There are many musical riches here and no want of accomplishment in the performances. The two violins in use by John Holloway and Micaela Comberti have markedly different tone-quality. Readers unresponsive to the baroque violin may find their pleasure diminished by the raw, thin-edged timbre of the violins here, but those for whom this represents no problems will find much to admire.

As with the flute and oboe sonatas, those who want to make a start on these wonderful works in which Handel's invention seems inexhaustible might begin with Volume 4 of the CRD set, which includes Op. 5. Here Handel frequently borrows from himself, and much of this material is also found in the overtures for the *Chandos anthems* or in the dance music for his operas. The flowing opening theme of the very first *A major Sonata* (HWV 396) has fine Handelian character. No. 6 is familiar, as Handel himself re-used the material of the first and fourth movements for the '*Cuckoo and the Nightingale*' *Organ concerto*. But one of the most exasperating features of these CD transfers, and one which makes them less easy to use than the original LPs, is that individual movements are uncued, only each complete work, so it is very difficult indeed to find one's way about works which often have as many as seven different movements.

Volume 6: *Recorder sonatas, Op. 1: Nos. 2 in G min. (HWV 360); 4 in A min. (HWV 362); 7 in C (HWV 365); 11 in F (HWV 369); in G (HWV 358); in B flat (HWV 377); in D min. (HWV 367a); Trio sonata in F (HWV 405).*

(Y/B) *** CRD 3378; *CRDC 4078* [id.]. L'Ecole d'Orphée (Philip Pickett, Rachel Beckett, Susan Sheppard, Lucy Carolan).

These CRD performances have rightly won much acclaim. There is elegant and finished playing from the two recorder players and, besides the Op.1 *Sonatas*, the programme includes a *G major Sonata*, first published in 1974, and the original D minor version of the *Flute sonata*, Op. 9/1, which has an engaging second movement based on a minor-key variant of a famous allegro in the *Water music*. The *Trio Sonata in F* for two recorders and continuo also represents a recent discovery – by Christopher Hogwood in the Library of Congress – of the second and third movements of a recorder duo and a bass line to go with all three! Excellent, intimate recording, but again with the irritating drawback that individual movements are not cued, and the *D minor Sonata* has seven of them.

Sonatas, Op. 1: Nos. 1 in D min. (HWV 359a) (for violin & continuo); *1a in E min. (HWV 379); 1b in E min. (HWV 359b)* (both for flute & continuo); *2 in G min. (HWV 360)* (for recorder & continuo); *3 in A (HWV 361)* (for violin & continuo); *4 in A min. (HWV 362)* (for recorder & continuo); *5 in G (HWV 363b)* (for flute & continuo); *6 in G min. (HWV 364a)* (for violin & continuo); *7 in C (HWV 365)* (for recorder & continuo); *8 in C min. (HWV 366)* (for oboe & continuo); *9a in D min. (HWV 367a)* (for recorder & continuo); *9b in B min. (HWV 367b)* (for flute & continuo); *11 in F (HWV 369)* (for recorder & continuo); *13 in D (HWV 371)* (for violin & continuo); Halle sonatas Nos. 1–3* (for flute & continuo), *(HWV 374–6); Sonata for oboe & continuo in B flat (HWV 357); Sonata for recorder & continuo in B flat (HWV 377); Sonata for violin & continuo in G (HWV 358).*

(N) *** Hyperion Dig. CDA 66921/3 [id.]. Elizabeth Wallfisch, Lisa Beznosiuk, Rachel Beckett, Richard Tunnicliffe, Paul Nicholson.

As can be seen above, the Hyperion set concentrates on Op. 1, although illogically four of the violin sonatas, previously counted as being part of Handel's opus, have been omitted as spurious (HWV 368, 370 and 372–3), which seems unnecessary when there would have been plenty of room for them (all three discs have a playing time of under an hour). The fine *Halle sonatas* have been included, plus some other miscellaneous works now considered to be authentic. The performances use period instruments and have the advantage of current practice, so both flute and oboe timbres have a strong baroque flavour but the violins are less raw-timbred than the quality offered by L'Ecole d'Orphée; on the other hand the playing itself is mellower and perhaps at times slightly less vital than on the more comprehensive CRD set. It is a case of swings and roundabouts, but for those who enjoy modern instruments the Philips Duo reissue offers the best value of all, and the Harmonia Mundi CD below offers an attractive purchase for authenticists who want the Op. 1 works for flute and recorder.

Flute sonatas (for flute and continuo): *in E min., Op. 1/1a; in D, HWV 378; Halle sonatas* (for flute and continuo) *Nos. 1–3; Oboe sonatas* (for oboe and continuo): *Nos. 1 in B flat (HWV 357); in F (HWV 363a), Op. 1/5; in C min. (HWV 366), Op. 1/8; Recorder sonatas* (for recorder and continuo): *in G min. (HWV 360); in A min. (HWV 362); in C (HWV 365); in F (HWV 369), Op.-1/2, 4, 7 & 11; in B flat*

(HWV 377); in D min. (HWV 367a); Sinfonia in B flat for 2 violins and continuo, HWV 338; Trio sonatas: in E min. for 2 flutes and continuo, HWV 395; in F for 2 recorders and continuo, HWV 405.
(N) (B) *** Ph. Duo 446 563-2 (2) [id.]. ASMF Chamber Ens.

This superb Philips set assembles virtually all the important wind sonatas, plus a single *Trio sonata* for two violins and continuo, on a pair of discs offered for the price of one. William Bennett uses a modern flute very persuasively in the *Flute sonatas* and includes, besides the work from Op. 1 and the three *Halle sonatas*, a more recent discovery from a Brussels manuscript. Nicholas Kraemer and Denis Vigay provide admirable support, and the recording is most realistic and present. In the *Recorder sonatas* Michala Petri plays with her customary virtuosity and flair, and Neil Black is marvellously accomplished in the *Oboe sonatas*. Both artists share an excellent rapport with their continuo players, who include George Malcolm (harpsichord), Denis Vigay (cello) and Graham Sheen (bassoon), and again the sound is exemplary, natural and spacious. Only those seeking original instruments need look elsewhere.

Flute sonatas, Op. 1/1b, 5, 6, 8 & 9; & in D. Oboe sonatas Op. 1/8; in B flat (Fitzwilliam); in F min.
(M) *** HM/BMG Dig. GD 77152 [77152-2-RG]. Camerata Köln.

Recorder sonatas, Op. 1/2, 4, 7 & 11; Recorder sonatas in B flat; in D; in G (Fitzwilliam); Trio sonata in F.
(M) *** HM/BMG Dig. GD 77104 [77104-2-RG]. Camerata Köln.

These two CDs by the Camerata Köln playing on period instruments give very satisfying accounts of this repertoire. Not only is the playing rewarding, but the quality of the 1985 sound has exemplary clarity, yet warmth too.

Sonatas for flute or alto recorder. Op. 1/2, 4, 7, 9 & 11; in B flat.
(N) *** HM Dig. HMU 907151 [id.]. Marion Verbruggen, Ton Koopman, Jaap ter Linden.

Marion Verbruggen uses modern copies of two alto recorders from the early eighteenth century and a similar voice flute in D; the sounds here are appealingly mellow, with the continuo featuring cello, harpsichord and chest organ. The effect is intimate, expressive and lively by turns, but with no attempt at self-conscious bravura. The recording is beautifully balanced.

Frans Brüggen Edition, Volume 9: *Recorder sonatas: in G min., HWV 360; in A min., HWV 362; in C, HWV 365; in F, HWV 369, Op. 1/2, 4, 7 & 11; in F, HWV 389, Op. 2/4. Fitzwilliam sonatas Nos. 1 in B flat, HWV 377; 3 in D min., HWV 367a.*
(Y/B) (M) *** Teldec/Warner 4509 97471-2 [id.]. Frans Brüggen, Alice Harnoncourt, Anner Bylsma, Nikolaus Harnoncourt, Gustav Leonhardt, Herbert Tachezi.

The four sonatas from Op. 1 are those the composer intended for the recorder; the *D minor* and the *B flat Sonatas*, HWV 367a and HWV 377, can be found in the Fitzwilliam collection. The five-movement *Sonata in F*, HWV 389, is designated a trio sonata: the recorder dominates and the violin (here Alice Harnoncourt) is very much a subordinate, shining as a solo instrument only in the third-movement *Adagio* and the following *Allegro*. All these works offer delightfully inventive music, and these performances are outstandingly successful. The spontaneity of the playing is no less striking than the way the scholarship and artistry underpin the style of the music-making. Both the cellist, Anner Bylsma, and the harpsichordist, Gustav Leonhardt, make an equal contribution to this partnership (in HWV 389 Nikolaus Harnoncourt and Herbert Tachezi provide the continuo).

KEYBOARD MUSIC

Chaconne in G, HWV 435; The Harmonious blacksmith (Air and variations from Suite No. 5 in E, HWV 436); Suites Nos. 3 in D min., HWV 346; 4 in E min., HWV 438; 13 in B flat, HWV 434; 14 in G, HWV 441.
(N) (M) ** DG Dig. 447 290-2 [id.]. Trevor Pinnock (harpsichord).

Although Pinnock has undoubted flair and panache, the closeness of the microphones and a fairly uniform *forte* are emphasized by the added presence of CD which, as this 1982 collection proceeds, tends to seem relentless. The result conveys expertise in plenty but rather less in the way of enjoyment; and we must register disappointment at the forward balance. *The Harmonious blacksmith* has been added from a later (1983) recital: it is brilliantly played but the problem of over-projection remains.

Harpsichord suites Nos. 1–8.
(N) (B) *** HM HMA 190447/48 [id.]. Kenneth Gilbert (harpsichord).
*** Erato/Warner Dig. 2292 45452-2 (2). Scott Ross (harpsichord).

Gilbert is a scholar as well as a distinguished player, and his version of the suites, recorded on a copy of a Taskin harpsichord by Bédard, is well worth seeking out, making a fine bargain alternative to Paul Nicholson's more comprehensive (and more expensive) set. Gilbert observes most first-half repeats but not those of the second, and he is as imaginative in the handling of decoration and ornamentation as one would expect. If one were to quibble, it would be merely that some grandeur, some larger-than-life vitality is missing (not a criticism one could apply to his full-priced competitor); but so much else is there that there is no case for qualifying the recommendation. The recording is natural and very well balanced.

Scott Ross plays a copy of a 1733 Blanchet, which suits this repertoire very well, and his performances are in exemplary style. He plays most repeats, but not all – and one wonders why, when the overall playing time is short of two hours. Still, this is a fine set, well though closely recorded.

Harpsichord suites Nos. 1–8, H W V 426/433; 6 Fugues or Voluntarys for organ or harpsichord, H W V 605/ 10; Fugues: in F; E, H W V 611/12.
(Y/B) *** Hyperion Dig. CDA 66931/2 [id.]. Paul Nicholson (harpsichord).

Paul Nicholson gives us Handel's major keyboard *œuvre*, not only the eight splendidly diverse suites of 1720, but also the contrapuntal *Voluntaries*. They are simple, four-part baroque fugal pieces, varied in mood and style according to the key. As an appendix we are offered two miniature fugues, the *F major* from around 1705 and the *E major* from the time of the *Voluntaries*. Paul Nicholson's playing is quite admirable, full of life yet with a degree of intimacy that is very appealing. He has an ideal (unnamed) harpsichord, which is perfect for this repertoire and which is superbly recorded. Nicholson is admirably stylish, his crisp touches of ornamentation are always giving pleasure and are never fussy, and he is generous with repeats. His playing can seem to be improvisational in the preludes, fugues are crystal clear yet never stiff, and the closing *Gigues* have a joyful rhythmic lift. The most famous of the eight is, of course, No. 5 which has the variations known as '*The harmonious blacksmith*' as its finale, here ending in a blaze of bravura. *No. 7 in G minor* has six sharply characterized movements, opening with a flamboyant *Overture*, and its finale is a superb *Chaconne* in which the harpsichord reveals the resources of its lower octaves. Highly recommended, and unlikely to be surpassed in the near future.

VOCAL MUSIC

Gardiner Collection
Dixit Dominus; Coronation anthem: Zadok the Priest. Israel in Egypt: Lamentations of the Israelites for the Death of Joseph; The Ways of Zion do mourn (Funeral anthem); *Semele* (complete).
(N) (B) *** Erato/Warner 4509 99756-2 (5) [id.]. Monteverdi Ch. & O, or E. Bar. Soloists, Gardiner.

Gardiner's collection of Handel choral works from the late 1970s using modern instruments is here joined with *Semele*, recorded (using period instruments) in 1981. At bargain price this set is well worth investigating, even if *Semele* is not absolutely complete. The separate issues are discussed below.

Acis and Galatea (masque).
*** DG 423 406-2 (2) [id.]. Burrowes, Rolfe Johnson, Martyn Hill, Willard White, E. Bar. Soloists, Gardiner.

(i) *Acis and Galatea;* (ii) *Cantata: Look down, harmonious saint.*
*** Hyperion Dig. CDA 66361/2; *KA 66361/2*. (i; ii) Ainsley; (i) McFadden, Covey-Crump, George, Harre-Jones; King's Cons., Robert King.

Robert King directs a bluff, beautifully sprung reading of *Acis and Galatea* that brings out its domestic jollity. Using the original version for five solo singers and no chorus, this may be less delicate in its treatment than John Eliot Gardiner's reading but it is, if anything, even more winning. The soloists are first rate, with John Mark Ainsley among the most stylish of the younger generation of Handel tenors, and the bass, Michael George, characterizing strongly. Claron McFadden's vibrant soprano is girlishly distinctive. This Hyperion issue provides a valuable makeweight in the florid solo cantata, thought to be originally conceived as part of *Alexander's Feast*, nimbly sung by Ainsley.

Certain of John Eliot Gardiner's tempi are idiosyncratic (some too fast, some too slow), but the scale of the performance, using original instruments, is beautifully judged, with the vocal soloists banding together for the choruses. Willard White is a fine Polyphemus. The authentic sounds of the English Baroque Soloists are finely controlled and the vibrato-less string timbre is clear and clean without being abrasive. A thoroughly rewarding pair of CDs.

Marian arias and cantatas: *Ah! Che troppo inequale; Donna, che in ciel; Haec est Regina;* G. B. FER-
RANDINI (attrib. HANDEL): *Il pianto di Maria.*
(Y/B) *** DG Dig. 439 866-2 [id.]. Von Otter, Col. Mus. Ant., Goebel.

Dating from his years in Italy, these Handel works, directly linked to the worship of the Virgin Mary,
inspire von Otter to give radiant performances. Ironically, the longest work, *Il pianto di Maria,* long
attributed to Handel, has been found to be by G. B. Ferrandini; but it has many beauties, not least in a
measured cavatina, *Se d'un Dio.* Both *Haec est Regina* and *Ah! che inequale* are strong, imaginative arias,
and *Donna, che in ciel* is a superb, full-scale cantata with a fine overture and four splendid arias.
Reinhard Goebel and his team give sympathetic support, though the period string-playing is on the
abrasive side. Warm, immediate recording, which captures von Otter's firm mezzo superbly.

(i) *Alceste: Overture and incidental music;* (ii) *Comus: vocal excerpts.*
(M) *** O-L 443 183-2 [id.]. Margaret Cable, David Thomas; (i) Judith Nelson, Emma Kirkby, Christine
    Pound, Margaret Cable, Catherine Denley, Paul Elliott, Rogers Covey-Crump, David Thomas,
    Christopher Keyte; (ii) Patrizia Kwella; AAM, Hogwood.

Handel left us much to enjoy here, with the impressively dramatic *Alceste overture* in D minor and the
Grande entrée for Admetus and Alceste and their wedding guests getting the proceedings off to a fine
start. There follows a series not just of solo items but also some simple tuneful choruses, in which a
small secondary vocal group participates. Hogwood draws lively performances from his usual team and,
as ever, is very well recorded. The music for *Comus* was later used in the *Occasional oratorio*; the five
items offered here show how refreshing was Handel's original. The performances by Patrizia Kwella,
Margaret Cable and David Thomas with the Academy under Hogwood have all the freshness and
vigour one associates with this conductor's earlier series of Purcell theatre music. The transfers of 1979/
80 analogue recordings, made at St Jude's, London, are well up to L'Oiseau-Lyre's usual high standard.

Alexander's Feast (complete).
(N) (M) ** Van. 08.9057.72 (2) [id.]. Heather Harper, Honor Sheppard, Max Worthley, Maurice Bevan,
    Oriana Concert Ch. & O, Alfred Deller.

(i) *Alexander's Feast* (complete). (ii) *Harp concerto, Op. 4/6;* (iii) *Organ concerto, Op. 4/1.*
*** Collins Dig. 7016-2 (2). (i) Argenta, Partridge, George, The Sixteen Ch.; (ii) Lawrence-King,
    Tragicomedia; (iii) Nicholson; (i; iii) The Sixteen O, Christophers.

Alexander's Feast; Concerto grosso in C (Alexander's Feast).
**(*) Ph. Dig. 422 053-2 (2) [id.]. Carolyn Watkinson, Robson, Donna Brown, Stafford, Varcoe,
    Monteverdi Ch., E. Bar. Soloists, Eliot Gardiner.

Alexander's Feast was the first and greatest of the odes by Dryden which Handel set to celebrate St
Cecilia's Day. It was written in 1736 (three years before the less ambitious work he called the *Ode for St
Cecilia's Day*) and was one of the composer's London successes. The invention is consistently on the
highest level, without a single poor number. Not only are the vocal solos and choruses among Handel's
finest, but the orchestra shows many imaginative touches. Handel holds his brass in reserve and the
horns must have made something of a sensation in their colourful entry in praise of Bacchus. The
trumpets, too, make a commanding entry in the opening chorus of Part 2: '*Break his bonds of sleep
asunder*'. In no other work are they used with greater brilliance.

Harry Christophers directs a lively, sympathetic account of Handel's extended cantata, very well sung
and recorded. The three soloists – Nancy Argenta, Ian Partridge and Michael George – are all first rate,
making a more consistent team than the quintet used by Gardiner. The bass, Michael George, is
satisfyingly firm and dark in the two big bass arias. Christophers also provides two of the related Opus 4
concertos instead of Gardiner's one.

Gardiner's version of *Alexander's Feast* was recorded live at performances given at the Göttingen
Festival. The sound is not distractingly dry, but it is still harder than usual on singers and players alike,
taking away some of the bloom. What matters is the characteristic vigour and concentration of
Gardiner's performance. Stephen Varcoe may lack the dark resonance of a traditional bass, but he
projects his voice well. Nigel Robson's tenor suffers more than do the others from the dryness of the
acoustic. The soprano, Donna Brown, sings with boyish freshness, and the alto numbers are divided
very effectively between Carolyn Watkinson and the soft-grained counter-tenor, Ashley Stafford. The
Concerto grosso in C was given with the oratorio at its first performance.

Deller's set first appeared in the UK at the end of the 1960s on the Philips label. Now it reverts to its
original, Vanguard source but it has no coupling and, even at mid-price, is not a very economical
purchase, as the playing time of the second CD is only 34 minutes. However, the solo singing is most
distinguished, the tenor stylish rather than dramatic. Heather Harper is glorious of tone and accurate in

her runs (her melisma on '*shake*' in her first aria is superb). The choral singing is very good, and one can only regret that the very resonant acoustic means that the overall sound, though rich and expansive, lacks bite and sharpness of focus.

Alpestre monte; Mi palpita il cor; Tra le fiamme; Tu fedel? Tu costante? (Italian cantatas).
*** O-L Dig. 414 473-2 [id.]. Emma Kirkby, A A M, Hogwood.

The four cantatas here, all for solo voice with modest instrumental forces, are nicely contrasted, with the personality of the original singer by implication identified with *Tu fedel*, a spirited sequence of little arias rejecting a lover. Even 'a heart full of cares' in *Mi palpita il cor* inspires Handel to a pastorally charming aria, with a delectable oboe obbligato rather than anything weighty, and even those limited cares quickly disperse. Light-hearted and sparkling performances to match.

Aminta e Fillide (cantata).
*** Hyperion CDA 66118 [id.]. Fisher, Kwella, L. Handel O, Darlow.

In writing for two voices and strings, Handel presents a simple encounter in the pastoral tradition over a span of ten brief arias which, together with recitatives and final duet, last almost an hour. The music is as charming and undemanding for the listener as it is taxing for the soloists. This lively performance, beautifully recorded with two nicely contrasted singers, delightfully blows the cobwebs off a Handel work till now totally neglected.

Anthem for the Foundling Hospital; Ode for the birthday of Queen Anne.
*** O-L 421 654-2 [id.]. Nelson, Kirkby, Minty, Bowman, Hill, Thomas, Ch. of Christ Church Cathedral, Oxford, A A M, Preston – HAYDN: *Missa brevis in F.* ***

The *Ode* has its Italianate attractions, but it is the much later *Foundling Hospital anthem* which is the more memorable, not just because it concludes with an alternative version of the *Hallelujah chorus* but because the other borrowed numbers are also superb. An extra tang is given by the accompaniment on original instruments.

Apollo e Dafne (cantata).
**(*) HM HMC 905157 [id.]. Judith Nelson, David Thomas; Hayes, San Francisco Bar. O, McGegan.

Apollo e Dafne is one of Handel's most delightful cantatas, with at least two strikingly memorable numbers, a lovely siciliano for Dafne with oboe obbligato and an aria for Apollo, *Come rosa in su la spina*, with unison violins and a solo cello. Both soloists are first rate, and Nicholas McGegan is a lively Handelian, though the playing of the orchestra could be more polished and the sound more firmly focused.

Athalia (oratorio).
*** O-L Dig. 417 126-2 (2) [id.]. Sutherland, Kirkby, Bowman, Aled Jones, Rolfe Johnson, David Thomas, New College, Oxford, Ch., A A M, Hogwood. .

As Queen Athalia, Dame Joan Sutherland sings boldly with a richness and vibrancy to contrast superbly with the pure silver of Emma Kirkby, not to mention the celestial treble of Aled Jones, in the role of the boy-king, Joas. That casting is perfectly designed to set the Queen aptly apart from the good Israelite characters led by the Priest, Joad (James Bowman in a castrato role), and Josabeth (Kirkby). Christopher Hogwood with the Academy brings out the speed and variety of the score that has been described as Handel's first great English oratorio. The recording is bright and clean, giving sharp focus to voices and instruments alike.

Belshazzar (complete).
*** DG Dig. 431 793-2 (3) [id.]. Rolfe Johnson, Augér, Robbin, Bowman, Wilson-Johnson, E. Concert Ch. & O, Pinnock.
(N) (M) **(*) Teldec/Warner 0630 10275-2 (3) [id.]. Felicity Palmer, Maureen Lehane, Robert Tear, Paul Esswood, Peter van der Bilt, Stockholm Chamber Ch., VCM, Harnoncourt.

Handel modified *Belshazzar* over the years, and Pinnock has opted not for the earliest but for the most striking and fully developed text. The cast is starry, with Arleen Augér at her most ravishing as the Babylonian king's mother, Nitocris, Anthony Rolfe Johnson in the title role, James Bowman as the prophet, Daniel, and Catherine Robbin as King Cyrus, all excellent. Full, well-balanced sound.

With authentic style and instruments set against a relatively intimate acoustic, Harnoncourt's opening of the fine overture to *Belshazzar* on this Teldec recording may initially seem somewhat gruff, but then Harnoncourt's concentration in number after number builds up the high drama of this oratorio. The libretto of Charles Jennens gets near to demanding stage presentation in its echoing of operatic convention, with stage directions at every turn. The drama is the more pointed when the soloists, led by Felicity

Palmer and Robert Tear, keep the story-line clearly in mind with their expressive enunciation of the words. The other soloists, too, are excellent, notably Paul Esswood with his fresh counter-tenor tone, and the bass, Peter van der Bilt. In some ways most enjoyable of all is the singing of the fine Stockholm choir, delectably light and pointed in some of the end-of-scene choruses. Harnoncourt is at his best when given the chance to point a brisk number with lifted rhythms, but he is less effective in warmer music; for the unprejudiced Handelian, this account of a masterpiece should certainly prove stimulating.

Chandos anthems Nos. 1–11 (complete).
*** Chandos Dig. CHAN 0554/7 [id.]. Dawson, Kwella, Partridge, Bowman, George, The Sixteen Ch. & O, Harry Christophers.

It is appropriate that a record label named Chandos should record a complete set of Handel's *Chandos anthems*. This is now available on four CDs in a box (still at full price) and marks one of the most successful and worthwhile achievements of The Sixteen on CD. From the first of these fine works, which Handel based on his *Utrecht Te Deum*, to the last with its exuberant closing *Alleluja* the music is consistently inspired; it has great variety of invention and resourceful vocal scoring. The recordings are well up to the house standard.

Chandos anthems Nos. 1: O be joyful in the Lord; 2: In the Lord put I my trust; 3: Have mercy on me, HWV 246/8.
*** Chandos Dig. CHAN 8600 [id.]. Lynne Dawson, Ian Partridge, The Sixteen Ch. & O, Christophers.

The impact of these performances is affected strongly by the recorded sound, set in a warm acoustic but with rather a close balance; that makes the choir sound bigger. Ian Partridge is the radiant-voiced linchpin of these performances and is superbly matched by Lynne Dawson with her gloriously pure, silvery soprano. The closeness of sound makes the instrumental sonatas which start each *Anthem* more abrasive than they might be, but not uncomfortably so.

Chandos anthems Nos. 4: O sing unto the Lord a new song; 5: I will magnify thee; 6: As pants the hart for cooling streams.
*** Chandos Dig. CHAN 0504 [id.]. Lynne Dawson, Ian Partridge, The Sixteen Ch. & O, Christophers.

The second volume of the Chandos series is hardly less appealing than the first. There are some splendidly vigorous choruses, while in No. 6 there is an equally memorable soprano aria, beautifully sung by Lynne Dawson.

Chandos anthems Nos. 7: My song shall be alway; 8: O come let us sing unto the Lord; 9: O praise the Lord.
*** Chandos Dig. CHAN 0505 [id.]. Patrizia Kwella, James Bowman, Ian Partridge, Michael George, The Sixteeen Ch. & O, Christophers.

Again in this third volume there is splendid singing from the soloists, with Patrizia Kwella joining the team, and there is plenty of interest in the solo writing in these fine, contrasted works, while the choral contribution is well up to standard.

Chandos anthems Nos. 10: The Lord is my light; 11: Let God arise.
*** Chandos Dig. CHAN 0509. Lynne Dawson, Ian Partridge, The Sixteen Ch. & O, Christophers.

The tenor soloist dominates No. 10, and Ian Partridge sings with his customary style and sweetness of timbre. Lynne Dawson makes her entry on the penultimate number. The chorus is again in exhilarating form, especially in the closing *Alleluja*. The recording is spacious while continuing to preserve the music's intimate feeling.

Coronation anthems (1. Zadok the Priest; 2. The King shall rejoice; 3. My heart is inditing; 4. Let Thy hand be strengthened).
(M) *** Decca 436 259-2 [id.]. King's College Ch., ECO, Willcocks – BLOW: *Anthems.* **(*)

(i)*Coronation anthems* (complete); (ii) *Concerti a due cori Nos. 2–3, HWV 333/4.*
(Y/B) (M) *** DG Dig. 447 280-2 [id.]. (i) Westminster Abbey Ch., Preston; (i–ii) E. Concert; (ii) Pinnock.

Coronation anthems (complete); *Judas Maccabaeus; See the conqu'ring hero comes; March; Sing unto God.*
*** Ph. Dig. 412 733-2 [id.]. ASMF Ch., ASMF, Marriner.

The extra weight of the Academy of St Martin-in-the-Fields Chorus compared with the Pinnock version seems appropriate for the splendour of music intended for the pomp of royal ceremonial occasions, and the commanding choral entry in *Zadok the Priest* is gloriously rich in amplitude, without in any way lacking incisiveness. The excerpts from *Solomon* are delightful.

Those who like sparer, more 'authentic' textures will favour Preston in the *Coronation anthems* where, although the overall effect is less grand, the element of contrast is even more telling. To have the choir enter with such bite and impact underlines the freshness and immediacy. The use of original instruments gives plenty of character to the accompaniments. An exhilarating version. The new coupling of the two *Concerti a due cori* is welcome, with the performances full of rhythmic vitality.

The reissued (1961) Argo King's recording of these four anthems makes an admirable mid-priced alternative recommendation, particularly as the extra clarity and presence given to the choir improve the balance in relation to the orchestra. The Blow *Anthems* make a fine bonus.

Dettingen Te Deum; Dettingen anthem.
*** DG Dig. 410 647-2 [id.]. Westminster Abbey Ch., E. Concert, Preston.

The *Dettingen Te Deum* is a splendidly typical work and continually reminds the listener of *Messiah*, written the previous year. Preston's Archiv performance with the English Concert makes an ideal recommendation, with its splendid singing, crisp but strong, excellent recording and a generous, apt coupling. This setting of *The King shall rejoice* should not be confused with the *Coronation anthem* of that name. It is less inspired, but has a magnificent double fugue for finale. The recording is first class.

Dixit Dominus; Coronation anthem: Zadok the Priest.
(N) (M) *** Erato/Warner 4509 99757-2 [id.]. Palmer, Marshall, Brett, Messana, Morton, Thomson, Wilson-Johnson, Monteverdi Ch. & O, Gardiner.

Handel's *Dixit Dominus* dates from 1707 and was completed during his prolonged stay in Italy from 1706 to 1710. It divides into eight sections, and the setting, while showing signs of Handel's mature style in embryo, reflects also the Baroque tradition of contrasts between small and large groups. The writing is extremely florid and requires bravura from soloists and chorus alike. John Eliot Gardiner catches all its brilliance and directs an exhilarating performance, marked by strongly accented, sharply incisive singing from the choir and outstanding solo contributions. In high contrast with the dramatic choruses, the duet for two sopranos, *De torrente*, here beautifully sung by Felicity Palmer and Margaret Marshall, is languorously expressive, but stylishly so. Other soloists match that, and the analogue recording is first rate, proving ideal for CD remastering.

(i) *Dixit Dominus; Laudati pueri;* (ii) *Organ concerto in F (The cuckoo and the nightingale).*
(N) (M) ** Decca Dig. 448 242-2 [id.]. (i) Buchanan, Mackay, Chance, Kendall, Hurford, King's College, Cambridge, Ch., ECO, Cleobury; (ii) Peter Hurford, Concg. CO, Rifkin.

Dixit Dominus; Nisi Dominus; Salve Regina.
*** DG Dig. 423 594-2 [id.]. Augér, Lynne Dawson, Montague, Nixon, Birchall, Westminster Abbey Ch. & O, Simon Preston.

Dixit dominus; Nisi dominus; Silete venti.
*** Chandos Dig. CHAN 0517 [id.]. Dawson, Russell, Brett, Partridge, George, The Sixteen Choir & O, Harry Christophers.

On DG Archiv *Dixit Dominus* is very aptly coupled with fine performances of another – less ambitious – Psalm setting, *Nisi Dominus*, and a votive antiphon, *Salve Regina*, which Handel composed between the two. Preston here draws ideally luminous and resilient singing from the Westminster Abbey Choir, with a fine team of soloists in which Arleen Augér and Diana Montague are outstanding. The playing of the orchestra of period instrumentalists, led by Roy Goodman, in every way matches the fine qualities of the singing.

Christophers' speeds tend to be more extreme, slow as well as fast, and the recorded sound, though full and well detailed, is less immediate. On balance Pinnock with his rather more bouncy rhythms remains the first choice, but the Chandos issue gains significantly from a much more generous third item. *Silete venti* allows the silver-toned Lynne Dawson to shine even more than in the other items, ending with a brilliant *Alleluia* in galloping compound time.

In his King's College Choir version of *Dixit Dominus*, Stephen Cleobury inevitably suffers, in this often elaborate music, from the heavy reverberation of the chapel. It is a fresh and direct reading, well sung but lacking the magic and urgency of the finest versions. The vocal coupling is another of Handel's early Psalm settings, written on his trip to Italy. Peter Hurford's excellent version of a favourite among Handel's organ concertos is a welcome bonus but hardly affects the appeal of the disc when there is so much competition.

Esther (1718 version).
(N) *** Collins Dig. 7040-2 (2) [id.]. Russell, Randle, Padmore, Argenta, Chance, George, Sixteen Ch. & O, Christophers.
**(*) O-L Dig. 414 423-2 (2) [id.]. Kwella, Rolfe Johnson, Partridge, Thomas, Kirkby, Elliott, Westminster Cathedral Boys' Ch., Ch. and AAM, Hogwood.

Esther was the first of Handel's oratorios with a substantial role for the chorus and, like the Hogwood recording on L'Oiseau-Lyre, this period performance opts for the 1718 version of the oratorio. That was originally designed, like the so-called Chandos anthems, for performance at the Duke of Chandos's mansion, Cannons. It may be odd structurally compared with later revisions – with Esther appearing only after the half-way point – but the six compact scenes in a single Act present a crisper experience, and so suit modern taste. Christophers with a slightly smaller choir of 18 singers offers a more intimate view, often lighter and fresher, helped by bright, more immediate recording. One more readily imagines the original setting in a country house. Honours are evenly matched between the two teams of soloists, with Lynda Russell and Nancy Argenta exceptionally sweet and pure in the soprano roles, and with the two tenors sharply contrasted – Thomas Randle more heroic, Mark Padmore purer and finer. Michael George gives fine Handelian thrust to the bass solos.

Like Christophers, Hogwood has opted for the original, 1718 score, and his rather abrasive brand of authenticity goes well with the bright, full recorded sound which unfortunately exaggerates the choir's sibilants. The elaborate passage-work is far too heavily aspirated, at times almost as though the singers are laughing. The vigour of the performance is unaffected and the team of soloists is strong and consistent, with Patrizia Kwella sounding distinctive and purposeful in the name-part.

Funeral anthem for Queen Caroline: The ways of Zion do mourn.
(Y/B) (M) **(*) Erato/Warner 4509 96954-2 [id.]. Norma Burrowes, Charles Brett, Martyn Hill, Stephen Varcoe, Monteverdi Ch. & O, Gardiner.

Queen Caroline – whom Handel had known earlier as a princess in Hannover – was the most cultivated of the royal family of the Georges, and when she died in 1737 he was inspired to write a superb cantata in an overture and eleven numbers including the splendid chorus, *How are the mighty fall'n*. He later used the material for the first Act of *Israel in Egypt*. Gardiner directs a stirring performance which brings out the high contrasts implicit in the music, making the piece energetic rather than elegiac. Excellent work from soloists, chorus and orchestra alike, all very well recorded in the ideal ambience of London's Henry Wood Hall, and most realistically transferred to CD. The only snag is the playing time of 44 minutes: there would have been room for another work here.

Israel in Egypt (oratorio).
(M) **(*) DG 429 530-2 (2) [id.]. Harper, Clark, Esswood, Young, Rippon, Keyte, Leeds Festival Ch., ECO, Mackerras.

(i) *Israel in Egypt;* (ii) *Organ concerto in F (The cuckoo and the nightingale), HWV 295.*
*(**) Collins Dig. 7035-2 (2) [id.]. (i) Nicola Jenkin, Sally Dunkley, Caroline Trevor, Neil MacKenzie, Robert Evans, Simon Birchall, The Sixteen; (ii) Paul Nicholson; O of The Sixteen; Harry Christophers.

(i) *Israel in Egypt;* (ii) *Chandos anthem No. 10: The Lord is my light.*
(Y/B) (B) *** Decca Double 443 470-2 (2) [id.]. (i) Gale, Watson, Bowman, Partridge, McDonnell, Watts, Christ Church Cathedral, Oxford, Ch., ECO, Preston; (ii) Cantelo, Partridge, King's College, Cambridge, Ch., ASMF, Willcocks.

(i) *Israel in Egypt. Coronation anthems: Zadok the Priest; The King shall rejoice.*
(N) (M) *** Ph. Dig. 432 110-2 (2) [id.]. (i) Holton, Priday, Deam, Stafford, Chance, Collin, Kenny, Robertson, Salmon, Tindall, Tusa, Clarkson, Purves; Monteverdi Ch., E. Bar. Soloists, Gardiner.

(i) *Israel in Egypt: Lamentations of the Israelites for the Death of Joseph;* (ii) *The Ways of Zion do mourn* (Funeral anthem).
(N) (M) *** Erato/Warner 4509 99758-2 (2) [id.]. (i) Knibbs, Troth, Greene, Priday, Royall, Stafford, Gordon, Clarkson, Elliott, Kendall, Varcoe, Stewart; (ii) Burrowes, Brett, Hill, Varcoe; Monteverdi Ch. & O, Gardiner.

In his Philips digital version of *Israel in Egypt* Gardiner secures subtler playing from his period instruments, not just more stylish and generally more lightly sprung than in the earlier, Erato version, but conveying more clearly the emotional and dramatic thrust. So the start is more mysterious, and such illustrative numbers as the hopping of the frogs during the plague choruses is even more delightfully pointed than before. As before, first-rate soloists have been chosen from the chorus, and the digital recording is full and well balanced. The *Coronation anthems*, though relatively brief, are also winningly performed.

Using the modern instruments of his Monteverdi Orchestra, Gardiner made his Erato recording in 1978, not long before he decided to adopt period instruments instead. His style here, crisply rhythmic, superbly sprung, with dozens of detailed insights in bringing out word-meaning, is very much what has since become his forte in period performances of Handel and others. The singing both of the chorus and of the twelve soloists chosen from its members is excellent, though, like all other modern recordings, this one slightly falls down in resonance on the most famous number, the duet for basses, *The Lord is a Man of War*. In almost every way Gardiner gains by presenting the *Lamentations* not as an introduction to the main oratorio – which Handel used only at the very first, unsuccessful performance – but as a supplement, with the same music given in its original form, with text unamended: the funeral cantata for Queen Caroline. Excellent, full-bodied, analogue sound.

Simon Preston, using a small choir with boy trebles and an authentically sized orchestra, directs a performance of this great dramatic oratorio which is beautifully in scale. He starts with *The cuckoo and the nightingale organ concerto* – a procedure sanctioned by Handel himself at the first performance – and though inevitably the big plague choruses lack the weight which a larger choir gives them, the vigour and resilience are ample compensation, so that the text is illustrated with extra immediacy. Though Elizabeth Gale is not as firm a soprano as Heather Harper on Mackerras's alternative mid-priced Archiv set, the band of soloists is an impressive one and the ECO is in splendid form. The 1975 recording (originally Argo) is warmly atmospheric, more realistically balanced than the rival Archiv one, and it has been vividly transferred to CD. Moreover this Double Decca (two-for-the-price-of-one) set generously includes the tenth Chandos anthem, *The Lord is my light*, remarkable for some magnificent fugal writing and freshly performed at King's under Sir David Willcocks.

Mackerras's performance represents a dichotomy of styles, using the English Chamber Orchestra sounding crisp, stylish and lightweight and a fairly large amateur choir, impressively weighty rather than incisive. Thus the work makes its effect by breadth and grandiloquence rather than athletic vigour. The solo singing is distinguished, but its style is refined rather than earthy.

Christophers uses the *Lamentations* as a first part to the oratorio, and also – another nod towards Handelian performance-practice – adds the best-known of Handel's organ concertos, the *Cuckoo and the Nightingale*, between Parts One and Two. The playing and singing are even brighter than with Preston, but sadly the Collins recording is so reverberant that there is a serious loss of inner detail.

Jephtha.
*** Ph. Dig. 422 351-2 (3) [id.]. Robson, Dawson, Von Otter, Chance, Varcoe, Holton, Monteverdi Ch., E. Bar. Soloists, Gardiner.
(N) (M) *** Van. 08 5091 73 (3) [id.]. Young, Forrester, Grist, Watts, Lawrenson, Amor Artis Chorale, ECO, Somary.

John Eliot Gardiner's recording was made live at the Göttingen Festival in 1988 and, though the sound does not have quite the bloom of his finest studio recordings of Handel, the exhilaration and intensity of the performance come over vividly, with superb singing from both chorus and an almost ideal line-up of soloists. Nigel Robson's tenor may be on the light side for the title-role, but the sensitivity of expression is very satisfying. Lynne Dawson, with her bell-like soprano, sings radiantly as Iphis; and the counter-tenor, Michael Chance, as her beloved, Hamor, is also outstanding. Anne Sofie von Otter is powerful as Storge, and Stephen Varcoe with his clear baritone, again on the light side, is a stylish Zebul. As for the Monteverdi Choir, their clarity, incisiveness and beauty are a constant delight.

The Vanguard set was the first ever recording of *Jephtha*, made in 1969. It stands up surprisingly well against latterday period performances so that anyone preferring modern instruments need not hesitate. The analogue sound, full, forward and bright, is well transferred, and the freshness and liveliness of Somary's direction, with brisk speeds lightly sprung, are worlds away from the old oratorio tradition. The singers make a formidably starry team with no weak link. Alexander Young, a superb Handel singer, recorded far too little; here he sings most beautifully as Jephtha, not least in *Waft her, angels*. The Canadian mezzo, Maureen Forrester, is caught richly and firmly as Hamor, and the others are first rate too. The relatively small professional chorus is equally assured, producing bright, fresh tone, firmly and forwardly focused.

Joshua (complete).
🏵 *** Hyperion Dig. CDA 66461/2 [id.]. Kirkby, Bowman, Ainsley, George, Oliver, New College, Oxford, Ch., King's Consort, King.

Emma Kirkby is here ideally sparkling and light in the role of Achsa, daughter of the patriarchal leader, Caleb (taken here by the bass, Michael George). Her love for Othniel, superbly sung by James Bowman, provides the romantic interest in what is otherwise a grandly military oratorio, based on the Book of Joshua. The brisk sequence of generally brief arias is punctuated by splendid choruses, with solo numbers often inspiring choral comment. The singing is consistently strong and stylish, with the clear, precise tenor, John Mark Ainsley, in the title-role giving his finest performance on record yet. Robert King and his Consort crown their achievement in other Hyperion issues, notably their Purcell series, with polished, resilient playing, and the choir of New College, Oxford, sings with ideal freshness. Warm, full sound.

Judas Maccabaeus (complete).

(N) (M) *** DG 447 692-2 (3). Felicity Palmer, Janet Baker, Esswood, Ryland Davies, Shirley-Quirk, Keyte, Wandsworth School Ch., ECO, Mackerras.

(N) **(*) Hyperion Dig. CDA 66641/2 (2) [id.]. Kirkby, Denley, Bowman, MacDougall, George, Birchall, Ch. of New College, Oxford, King's Consort, King.

(N) (M) **(*) Van. 08 4072 72 (2) [id.]. Harper, Watts, Young, Shirley-Quirk, Amor Artis Ch., Wandsworth School Boys' Ch., ECO, Somary.

(N) ** HM Dig. HMU 907077/8 [id.] (with appendix). De Mey, Saffer, Spence, D. Thomas, UCLA, Berkeley, Chamber Ch., Philh. Bar. O, McGegan.

Judas Maccabaeus may have a lopsided story, with a high proportion of the finest music given to the anonymous soprano and contralto roles, Israelitish Woman and Israelitish Man; but the sequence of Handelian gems is irresistible, the more so in a performance as sparkling as DG's reissued 1976 recording under Sir Charles Mackerras. Unlike many versions, particularly those which in scholarly fashion attempt to restore Handel's original proportions, this holds together with no let-up of intensity, and though not everyone will approve of the use of boys' voices in the choir (inevitably the tone and intonation are not flawless) it gives an extra bite of character. Hearing even so hackneyed a number as *See, the conqu'ring hero* in its true scale is a delightful surprise. The orchestral group and continuo sound splendidly crisp; when the trumpets enter in *Sound an alarm*, the impact is considerable, just as it must have been for the original Handelian audience. Though some may regret the passing of old-style fruity singing in the great tenor and bass arias, Ryland Davies and John Shirley-Quirk are most stylish, while both Felicity Palmer and Dame Janet crown the whole set with glorious singing, not least in a delectable sequence, towards the end of Act I, on the subject of liberty. The recording quality is outstanding in its CD format, fresh, vivid and clear.

With some superb solo singing and refined instrumental textures, Robert King's performance of what was once Handel's most popular oratorio can be recommended warmly, even though it is not as lively as some of his Purcell recordings. It is partly that the chorus is not as forward or as bright-toned as one wants in Handel; but, that said, there is much to enjoy, with Jamie MacDougall clean and bright if not always ideally firm in the title-role, and with the pure-toned Emma Kirkby well contrasted with the much warmer mezzo of Catherine Denley. Michael George gives splendid weight to the bass arias so central to Handel oratorio.

On Vanguard the solo singing is excellent, with Alexander Young a ringing tenor, and Helen Watts singing the opening aria in Act III exquisitely. Very good recording – the choruses could ideally have a crisper focus, but the effect is wholly natural – and a sense of commitment throughout from all departments.

Like Robert King's Hyperion version, McGegan's rival period performance lacks something of the grandeur which, like other late Handel choral works, this oratorio seems to require. This two-disc set generously offers an appendix, including two arias which Handel added after the first performance in 1747. In a first-rate line-up of soloists Lisa Saffer is outstanding in the key role of the Israelite Woman and, though Guy de Mey in the title-role is hardly idiomatic, his singing is clean and stylish. McGegan tends to be rather more dramatic and incisive than King, but that advantage is offset by the dryness of the recording, typical of the venue in Berkeley, California.

Lucrezia (cantata). Arias: *Ariodante: Oh, felice mio core . . . Con l'ali do constanza; E vivo ancore? . . . Scherza infida in grembo al drudo; Dopo notte. Atalanta: Care selve. Hercules: Where shall I fly? Joshua: O had I Jubal's lyre. Rodelinda: Pompe vane di morte! . . . Dove sei, amato bene? Serse: Frondi tenere e belle . . . Ombra mai fù (Largo).*

(M) *** Ph. 426 450-2. Dame Janet Baker, ECO, Leppard.

Even among Dame Janet's most impressive records this Handel recital marks a special contribution, ranging as it does from the pure gravity of *Ombra mai fù* to the passionate virtuosity in *Dopo notte* from *Ariodante*. Leppard gives sparkling support and the whole is recorded with natural and refined balance. An outstanding disc, with admirable documentation.

Messiah (complete).

*** DG Dig. 423 630-2 (2). Augér, Von Otter, Chance, Crook, J. Tomlinson, E. Concert Ch., E. Concert, Pinnock.

(Y/B) *** HM Dig. HMC 901498.99-2 (2) [id.]. Schlick, Piau, Scholl, Padmore, Berg, Les Arts Florissants, Christie.

*** Ph. Dig. 434 297-2 (2) [id.]. Marshall, Robbin, Rolfe Johnson, Brett, Hale, Shirley-Quirk, Monteverdi Ch., E. Bar. Soloists, Gardiner.

*** Hyperion Dig. CDA 66251/2 [id.]. Lynne Dawson, Denley, Maldwyn Davies, Michael George, The Sixteen Ch. & O, Christophers.

(B) *** Ph. Duo 438 356-2 (2) [id.]. Harper, Watts, Wakefield, Shirley-Quirk, L. Symphony Ch., LSO, Sir Colin Davis.

(B) *** EMI CZS7 62748-2 (2) [Ang. CDMB 62748]. Harwood, J. Baker, Esswood, Tear, Herincx, Amb. S., ECO, Mackerras.

*** Decca Dig. 414 396-2 (2) [id.]. Te Kanawa, Gjevang, Keith Lewis, Howell, Chicago Ch. & SO, Solti.

(B) **(*) CfP CD-CFPD 4718; *TC-CFPD 4718* (2) [id.]. Morison, Thomas, Lewis, Milligan, Huddersfield Ch. Soc., RLPO, Sargent.

(M) **(*) EMI CMS7 63784-2 (2) Trebles from King's, Bowman, Tear, Luxon, King's College, Cambridge, Ch., ASMF, Willcocks.

(BB) **(*) Naxos Dig. 8.550667/8 [id.]. Amps, Davidson, Doveton, Van Asch, Scholars Bar. Ens.

(M) **(*) Erato/Warner Dig. 2292 45960-2 (2) [id.]. Kweksilber, Bowman, Elliott, Reinhardt, The Sixteen, Amsterdam Bar. O, Koopman.

(N) (M) **(*) Van. 08.4019 72 (2) [id.]. Margaret Price, Yvonne Minton, Alexander Young, Justino Diaz, Amor Artis Chorale, ECO, Somary.

(N) (M) **(*) ASV Dig. CDDCS 230 (2) [id.]. Lott, Palmer, Langridge, Lloyd, Huddersfield Ch. Soc., RPO, Mackerras.

(N) (B) ** Decca Double 444 824-2 (2) [id.]. Ameling, Reynolds, Langridge, Howell, ASMF Ch. & O, Marriner.

Pinnock presents a performance using authentically scaled forces which, without inflation, rise to grandeur and magnificence, qualities Handel himself would have relished. The fast contrapuntal choruses, such as *For unto us a Child is born*, are done lightly and resiliently in the modern manner, but there is no hint of breathlessness, and Pinnock (more than his main rivals) balances his period instruments to give a satisfying body to the sound. There is weight too in the singing of the bass soloist, John Tomlinson, firm, dark and powerful, yet marvellously agile in divisions. Arleen Augér's range of tone and dynamic is daringly wide, with radiant purity in *I know that my Redeemer liveth*. Anne Sofie von Otter sustains *He was despised* superbly with her firm, steady voice. Some alto arias are taken by the outstanding counter-tenor, Michael Chance, who in some ways is even more remarkable. The tenor, Howard Crook, is less distinctive but still sings freshly and attractively. With full, atmospheric and well-balanced recording, this is a set not to be missed, even by those who already have a favourite version of *Messiah*.

William Christie and Les Arts Florissants add yet another outstanding account of *Messiah* to the current lists. More than most period performances – but like Trevor Pinnock's – it gives the impression of a live performance caught on the wing, even though it was recorded in the studio. Christie's preference for fast, resilient speeds and light textures, not least in choruses, never prevents him from giving due emotional weight to such key numbers as *He was despised*. That is superbly sung, with touching simplicity, firm tone and flawless intonation, by the counter-tenor, Andreas Scholl. The other singers too sound fresh and young, with the two sopranos, Barbara Schlick and Sandrine Piau, delectably counterpointed, both pure and true, making light of the elaborate divisions in such a number as *Rejoice greatly*. The treble, Tommy Williams, also sings with beautiful, firm clarity in the Angel's narration, *There were shepherds abiding in the fields*. The tenor, Mark Padmore, and the bass, Nathan Berg, complete the pattern, light by old-fashioned standards but fresh and cleanly focused. Christie in his text opts for Handel's later versions of numbers, which generally tallies with what one expects. Excellent sound, though the chorus is placed a little backwardly, so that *Hallelujah* lacks something in impact, with boomy timpani.

Gardiner chooses bright-toned sopranos instead of boys for the chorus and he uses, very affectingly, a solo treble to sing *There were shepherds abiding*. Speeds are fast and light, and the rhythmic buoyancy in the choruses is very striking. There is drama and boldness, too. *Why do the nations* and *The trumpet shall sound* (both sung with great authority) have seldom come over more strongly. The soloists are all first class, with the soprano Margaret Marshall finest of all, especially in *I know that my Redeemer liveth* (tastefully decorated). There are times when one craves for more expansive qualities; the baroque string sound can still give cause for doubts. Yet there are some wonderful highlights, not least Margaret Marshall's angelic version of *Rejoice greatly*, skipping along in compound time.

Christophers consistently adopts speeds more relaxed than those we have grown used to in modern performances and the effect is fresh, clear and resilient. Alto lines in the chorus are taken by male singers; a counter-tenor, David James, is also used for the *Refiner's fire*, but *He was despised* is rightly given to the contralto, Catherine Denley, warm and grave at a very measured tempo. The team of five soloists is at least as fine as that on any rival set, with the soprano, Lynne Dawson, singing with silvery purity to delight traditionalists and authenticists alike. The band of thirteen strings sounds as clean and fresh as the choir. Even the *Hallelujah chorus* – always a big test in a small-scale performance – works well, with Christophers in his chosen scale, through dramatic timpani and trumpets conveying necessary weight. The sound has all the bloom one associates with St John's recordings.

Reissued at bargain price on Philips's Duo label, the LSO recording conducted by Sir Colin Davis has not lost its impact and sounds brightly lit and fresh in its digitally remastered format. Textures are beautifully clear and, thanks to Davis, the rhythmic bounce of such choruses as *For unto us* is really infectious. Even *Hallelujah* loses little and gains much from being performed by a chorus of this size. Excellent singing from all four soloists, particularly Helen Watts who, following early precedent, is given *For He is like a refiner's fire* to sing, instead of the bass, and produces a glorious chest register. The performance is absolutely complete and is excellent value at its new price.

The choruses on EMI have not quite the same zest as on Philips, but they have a compensating breadth and body. More than Davis, Mackerras adopted Handel's alternative versions, so the soprano aria *Rejoice greatly* is given in its optional 12/8 version, with compound time adding a skip to the rhythm. A male alto is also included, Paul Esswood, and he is given some of the bass arias as well as some of the regular alto passages. Among the soloists, Dame Janet Baker is outstanding. Her intense, slow account of *He was despised* – with decorations on the reprise – is sung with profound feeling. The recording is warm and full in ambience and, with the added brightness of CD, sounds extremely vivid.

Sir Georg Solti inspires the most vitally exciting reading on record. The Chicago Symphony Orchestra and Chorus respond to some challengingly fast but never breathless speeds, showing what lessons can be learnt from authentic performance in clarity and crispness. Yet the joyful power of *Hallelujah* and the *Amen chorus* is overwhelming. Dame Kiri Te Kanawa matches anyone on record in beauty of tone and detailed expressiveness, while the other soloists are first rate too, even if Anne Gjevang has rather too fruity a timbre. Brilliant, full sound and great tangibility, breadth and clarity on the CDs.

It is good to have Sir Malcolm Sargent's 1959 recording now restored to the catalogue in full for, apart from the pleasure given by a performance that brings out the breadth of Handel's inspiration, it provides an important corrective to misconceptions about pre-authentic practice. Sargent unashamedly fills out the orchestration (favouring Mozart's scoring where possible). By the side of Davis, his tempi are measured, but his pacing is sure and spontaneous and, with a hundred-strong Huddersfield group, no one will be disappointed with the weight or vigour of the choruses. There is some splendid singing from all four soloists, and Marjorie Thomas's *He was despised* is memorable in its moving simplicity. The success of the CD transfer is remarkable: the old analogue LPs never sounded as clear as this.

Often though *Messiah* may have been recorded, there always seems plenty of room for alternative versions, particularly those which show a new and illuminating view of the work. Willcocks's recording, made in the Chapel at King's in 1971/2, has been described as the 'all-male *Messiah*', since a counter-tenor takes over the contralto solos, and the full complement of the trebles of King's College Choir sings the soprano solos, even the florid ones like *Rejoice greatly*; the result is enchanting, often light and airy. The bigger choruses do not lack robust qualities; however, the engineers have put their microphones fairly close and the resultant added clarity loses some of the normal King's softness of focus. The sound is thus vivid as well as atmospheric, but not quite what one would encounter sitting in the Chapel. A gimmicky version, perhaps, but one that many will find refreshing and involving.

On the bargain Naxos label comes a period performance with a difference. With fresh, immediate sound adding to the impact, the Scholars Baroque Ensemble presents the oratorio on the smallest possible scale, with individual singers from the small chorus coming forward to sing the arias. In keeping with this approach, the performance is directed by one of the basses, David van Asch, and characteristically the booklet seeks as far as possible not to highlight individual contributions like his but to emphasize teamwork. At brisk speeds, with rhythms well sprung, this will please those who fancy such an approach, though the instrumental sound is abrasive in a way one associates with the earliest period performances, and none of the singers has a voice of star quality. By their own definition, these are good choristers rather than great soloists. Given that, there is much to recommend the issue, though many more than traditionalists will prefer an approach that brings out more of Handel's grandeur.

With a small choir, an authentic baroque orchestra and clear-toned, lightweight soloists, Koopman's Erato version provides an intimate view of what is usually presented with grandeur. The ease and relaxation of the approach, not at all abrasive in the way common with authentic performances, are attractive, helped by excellent recording which gives a fine sense of presence – but, inevitably, essential elements in Handel's vision are missing.

Somary directs a crisp, small-scale performance that features sparkling orchestral playing (on modern instruments) and first-rate singing from soloists and chorus alike. His direction is not always consistent but it is never dull, and the recording is first class, warm yet bright and natural. An excellent choice for those wanting a relatively traditional approach and who have a special fondness for all or any of the soloists. The chorus is excellent, its size nicely judged.

The big disappointment of Sir Charles Mackerras's digital set with the Huddersfield Choral Society is that this great choir conveys less weight and bite than many of the small choirs on period recordings. It is largely a question of recording balance, which gives the choral ensemble too little body. The quartet of soloists is a strong and distinctive one – Felicity Lott, Felicity Palmer, Philip Langridge and Robert Lloyd – but hardly traditional-sounding. It is interesting to have Mozart's arrangement used, with its trombones and clarinets, but the traditional cuts are made here; this means that Part 1 comes complete on the first disc and the other two Parts complete on the second. Inconsistently but aptly for a British recording, the original English text is used, not the German actually set by Mozart.

Marriner's conception was to present *Messiah* as nearly as possible in the text followed at the first London performance of 1743. The losses are as great as the gains, but the result has unusual unity, thanks also to Marriner's direction. His tempi in fast choruses can scarcely be counted as authentic in any way: with a small professional chorus he has gone as far as possible towards lightening them and has thus made possible speeds that almost pass belief. Although Anna Reynolds's contralto is not ideally suited to recording, this is otherwise an excellent band of soloists – and in any case Miss Reynolds sings *He was despised* on a thread of sound. Vivid recording.

Messiah (complete; orch. Sir Eugene Goossens).
✵ (M) *** RCA GD 61266-20 (3) [61266-2]. Vyvyan, Sinclair, Vickers, Tozzi, RPO Ch. & O, Sir Thomas Beecham.

This is a performance which at every point radiates the natural flair of the conductor, and Beecham is extraordinarily sensitive to Handel's rhetoric and pathos. The use of the cymbals to cap the choruses *For unto us a child is born* and *Glory to God* is unforgettable. Beecham's tempi are slower than we expect today, but given his expansive view of Handel, they are convincingly appropriate, with the possible exception of the *Hallelujah chorus*, which gathers speed exuberantly as it nears its end. Jennifer Vyvyan and Monica Sinclair both sing freshly. Jon Vickers brings to his tenor arias a heroic quality that is often welcome and effective. Giorgio Tozzi's English is sound and his management of the tricky bass arias (especially *Why do the nations*) compels admiration. But it is above all Beecham's set, and its sense of exultant glory in the riches of Handel's masterpiece is life-enhancing. The 1959 recording of the chorus and orchestra is full and expansive in its CD transfer and the soloists have remarkable presence and immediacy. The third disc with its 17-minute appendix of eight items – normally cut at the time this recording was made – comes as a bonus, as the set is priced as for two mid-range CDs.

Der Messias (sung in German, arr. Mozart): complete.
(M) **(*) DG 427 173-2 (2). Mathis, Finnilä, Schreier, Adam, Austrian R. Ch. & O, Vienna, Mackerras.

Mozart's arrangement of *Messiah* has a special fascination. It is not simply a question of trombones being added but of elaborate woodwind parts too – most engaging in a number such as *All we like sheep*, which even has a touch of humour. *The trumpet shall sound* is considerably modified and shortened. To avoid the use of a baroque instrument, Mozart shares the obbligato between trumpet and horn. Mackerras leads his fine team through a performance that is vital, not academic in the heavy sense. The remastered recording is excellent and a translation is provided.

Messiah (sung in English): highlights.
*** Ph. Dig. 412 267-2 [id.] (from above set, cond. Gardiner).
*** Decca Dig. 417 449-2 [id.] (from above set, cond. Solti).
(M) *** EMI CDM7 69040-2 [id.] (from above set, cond. Mackerras).
(B) **(*) CfP CD-CFP 9007 (from above set, cond. Sargent).

Here Gardiner's collection reigns supreme, with the single caveat that *The trumpet shall sound* is missing. Solti's selection is undoubtedly generous, including all the key numbers and much else besides. The sound is thrillingly vivid and full. At mid-price Mackerras is first choice, while the great and pleasant surprise among the bargain selections is the Classics for Pleasure CD of highlights from Sir Malcolm Sargent's 1959 recording; no one will be disappointed with *Hallelujah*, while the closing *Amen* has a powerful sense of apotheosis.

Messiah: choruses.

(N) (M) **(*) Ph. 446 575-2 [id.]. Monteverdi Ch., E. Bar. Soloists, Gardiner.

Gardiner's complete set of choruses, using sopranos for the treble line, is fresh and pleasing enough; but this CD plays for only 51 minutes, and a selection of highlights would seem a much more sensible choice.

The Occasional oratorio.

(Y/B) *** Hyperion Dig. CDA 66961/2 [id.]. Gritton, Milne, Bowman, Ainsley, George, New College, Oxford, Ch., King's Consort Ch. & Ens., Robert King.

Handel's *Occasional oratorio* may have a slack dramatic structure but, with plentiful borrowings from such works as *Israel in Egypt*, it offers a wonderful showcase of Handel at his most inspired and vigorous. The vigorous choruses in particular, some only a few seconds long, regularly punctuate the work to heighten the effect of the arias, whether lively or beautiful, with some of the solo numbers leading directly into a related chorus with exhilarating effect. The piece culminates in an adaptation of Handel's great coronation anthem, *Zadok the Priest*, with loyal cries of *God save the King* ringing out at the end. The whole performance is fresh and electrifying, with excellent singing from all the soloists. Susan Gritton and Lisa Milne, the clear-toned sopranos, are set against the increasingly dark counter-tenor tones of James Bowman, with John Mark Ainsley and Michael George both clear and fresh Handelian stylists. The chorus fares rather less well in a generally excellent recording for, though the ensemble is first rate, the backward balance takes some of the edge off the more dramatic choruses.

Ode for the birthday of Queen Anne (Eternal source of light divine); Sing unto God (Wedding anthem); Te Deum in D (for Queen Caroline).

*** Hyperion Dig. CDA 66315 [id.]. Fisher, Bowman, Ainsley, George, New College, Oxford, Ch., King's Consort, Robert King.

Handel's *Birthday ode for Queen Anne* combines Purcellian influences with Italianate writing to make a rich mixture. King's performance is richly enjoyable, with warm, well-tuned playing from the King's Consort and with James Bowman in radiant form in the opening movement. The other two items are far rarer. Warmly atmospheric recording, not ideally clear on detail.

Ode for St Cecilia's Day.

*** DG Dig. 419 220-2 [id.]. Lott, Rolfe Johnson, Ch. & E. Concert, Pinnock.

*** ASV Dig. CDDCA 512 [id.]. Gomez, Tear, King's College Ch., ECO, Ledger.

(N) (M) *** Teldec/Warner 0630 12319-2 [id.]. Palmer, Rolfe Johnson, Stockholm Bach Ch., VCM, Harnoncourt.

(M) ** Decca 436 259-2 [id.]. Cantelo, Partridge, King's College Ch., ASMF, Willcocks – BLOW: *Anthems.* **(*)

Trevor Pinnock's account of Handel's magnificent setting of Dryden's *Ode* comes near the ideal for a performance using period instruments. Not only is it crisp and lively, it has deep tenderness too, as in the lovely soprano aria, *The complaining flute*, with Lisa Beznosiuk playing the flute obbligato most delicately in support of Felicity Lott's clear singing. Anthony Rolfe Johnson gives a robust yet stylish account of *The trumpet's loud clangour*, and the choir is excellent, very crisp of ensemble. Full, clear recording with voices vivid and immediate.

Those seeking a version with modern instruments will find Ledger's ASV version a splendid alternative. With superb soloists – Jill Gomez radiantly beautiful and Robert Tear dramatically riveting in his call to arms – this delightful music emerges with an admirable combination of freshness and weight. Ledger uses an all-male chorus; the style of the performance is totally convincing without being self-consciously authentic. The recording is first rate, rich, vivid and clear.

Harnoncourt's Teldec version of the *Ode*, recorded in 1979, comes up well in its digital transfer to CD. It is only slightly less recommendable than Trevor Pinnock's Archiv version, though the non-British choir, for all its fluency, sounds less comfortable than its rival and sings rather less crisply. Anthony Rolfe Johnson is excellent on both versions, while Felicity Palmer as soprano sings most characterfully. One special point in favour of Harnoncourt is his own striking cello playing in the beautiful setting of Dryden's second stanza, *What Passion cannot Musick raise and quell!* Now reissued in Teldec's Das Alte Werk mid-priced series, it is fully competitive.

The CD transfer has improved the impact of what was a very fine 1967 (originally Argo) recording, but the performance is disappointing. It is not the fault of the Academy of St Martin-in-the-Fields, for the *Overture* is one of the highlights of the disc, and there is superb solo playing throughout and a notably warm contribution from the cellos. April Cantelo phrases sensitively and accurately, if with rather a white tone, but her singing seldom beguiles, and it is the tenor who brings the performance fully to life with *The trumpet's loud clangour*.

La resurrezione.
*** O-L Dig. 421 132-2 (2) [id.]. Kirkby, Kwella, C. Watkinson, Partridge, Thomas, AAM, Hogwood.
*** Erato/Warner Dig. 2292 45617-2 [id.]. Argenta, Schlick, Laurens, De Mey, Mertens, Amsterdam Bar. O, Ton Koopman.

Hogwood directs a clean-cut, vigorous performance with an excellent cast. Emma Kirkby is at her most brilliant in the coloratura for the Angel, Patrizia Kwella sings movingly as Mary Magdalene and Carolyn Watkinson as Cleophas adopts an almost counter-tenor-like tone. Ian Partridge's tenor has a heady lightness as St John, and though David Thomas's Lucifer could have more weight he too sings stylishly. Excellent recording.

Koopman's cast of soloists is just as strong, with Barbara Schlick as the Angel outstandingly fine and Klaus Mertens as Lucifer weightier and stronger than his oppposite number. Koopman's approach is lighter and more resilient, allowing more relaxation, though the recording is less well focused, with voices less full and immediate.

Samson (complete).
(N) (M) *** Erato/Warner 2292 45994-2 (3). Tear, J. Baker, Lott, Watts, Shirley-Quirk, Luxon, L. Voices, ECO, Leppard.
*** Teldec/Warner Dig. 9031 74871-2 (2) [id.]. Rolfe Johnson, Alexander, Kowalski, Scharinger, Venuti, Blasi, Arnold Schoenberg Ch., VCM, Harnoncourt.
(N) (M) ** Van. 08 5084 72 (2) [id.]. Peerce, Curtin, Parker, M. Smith, Utah University Symphony Chorale, Utah SO, Abravenel.

Leppard directs a highly dramatic account of Handel's most dramatic oratorio, one which translates very happily to the stage; its culmination, the exultant aria *Let the bright seraphim*, is here beautifully sung by Felicity Lott, but for long was associated with Joan Sutherland at Covent Garden. The moment when the orchestra interrupts a soloist in mid-sentence to indicate the collapse of the temple is more vividly dramatic than anything in a Handel opera, and Leppard handles that and much else with total conviction. Robert Tear as Samson produces his most heroic tones – rather too aggressively so in *Total eclipse* – and the rest of the cast could hardly be more distinguished. Dame Janet Baker – not by nature a seductress in the Dalila sense – yet sings with a lightness totally apt for such an aria as *With plaintive notes*, and the others are in excellent voice. The recording is outstanding, atmospheric and well balanced.

Harnoncourt here conducts a Handel performance where Handelian grandeur shines out from the opening overture with its braying horns and genially strutting dotted rhythms. He is altogether warmer than before, and a fine team of singers, led by Anthony Rolfe Johnson in the title-role, is allowed full expressiveness, with speeds in slow numbers broader than one might expect. So the blind Samson's first aria, *Total eclipse*, is very measured, with Rolfe Johnson using the widest tonal and dynamic range. Though the recording catches some flutter in Roberta Alexander's voice as Dalila, she gives a character-ful performance, well contrasted with Angela Maria Blasi, her attendant, who sings the lovely aria, *With plaintive note*, most beautifully. Maria Venuti in the climactic *Let the bright seraphim* at the end is not ideally pure-toned, but she sings strongly and flexibly. Other fine singers include Alastair Miles, magnifi-cent in the bass role of the giant, Harapha, not least in *Honour and arms*, as well as the rich-toned counter-tenor, Jochen Kowalski as Micah and Christoph Prégardien in the tenor role of the Philistine. With the Schoenberg choir singing incisively, Harnoncourt presents the work not only with period instruments but on a more authentic scale.

Cut to fit on two very well-filled discs, the Vanguard set offers a bright, vigorous performance with strong, forthright singing from Jan Peerce as a heavyweight Samson and the bright-toned soprano, Phyllis Curtin, singing not just Dalila but several incidental roles. In its own traditional terms it is enjoyable enough, with bright choral singing and brisk conducting, but for a modern-instrument ver-sion Raymond Leppard's Erato set with Robert Tear and Dame Janet Baker is far more stylish and better recorded, and it avoids disfiguring cuts.

Saul (complete).
*** Ph. Dig. 426 265-2 (3) [id.]. Miles, Dawson, Ragin, Ainslie, Mackie, Monteverdi Ch., E. Bar. Soloists, Gardiner.
(N) (M) *** DG 447 696-2 [id.]. Armstrong, M. Price, Bowman, Ryland Davies, English, Dean, McIntyre, Winfield, Leeds Festival Ch., ECO, Sir Charles Mackerras.
(Y/B) (M) ** Teldec/Warner Dig. 4509 97504-2 (2) [id.]. Fischer-Dieskau, Rolfe Johnson, Esswood, Varady, Gale, V. State Op. Ch., VCM, Harnoncourt.

(N) (M) ** Van. 08 5088 72 (2) [id.]. Hemsley, Vyvyan, Watts, Handt, Sjöstedt, Copenhagen Boys' Ch., VSO, Wöldike.

Gardiner's performance is typically vigorous in what represents Handel's full emergence as a great oratorio composer, with the widest range of emotions conveyed. The alternation of mourning and joy in the final sequence of numbers is startlingly effective. With Derek Lee Ragin in the counter-tenor role of David, with Alastair Miles as Saul, Lynne Dawson as Michal and John Mark Ainslie as Jonathan, it is not likely to be surpassed on disc for a long time.

With an excellent combination of soloists Mackerras steers an exhilarating course in a work that naturally needs to be presented with authenticity but equally needs to have dramatic edge, and the result is powerful on one hand, moving on yet another. The contrast of timbre between Armstrong and Price, for example, is beautifully exploited, and Donald McIntyre as Saul, Ryland Davies as Jonathan and James Bowman as a counter-tenor David are all outstanding, while the chorus willingly contributes to the drama. An outstanding set, beautifully recorded (at the Leeds Triennial Music Festival in 1972) and vividly transferred to CD.

Harnoncourt's version was recorded live at the Handel tercentenary celebrations in Vienna in 1985 and, whatever the advantages of period performance, the extraneous noises of coughs and creaks, together with the odd slip of execution, seriously reduce its merits. Dietrich Fischer-Dieskau in the name-part is most characterful, but his expressive style is very heavy for Handel, particularly in the recitatives. It is still for the most part a rich and noble performance, and Julia Varady, though not quite idiomatic, is individual too, with tone cleanly focused. The English members of the cast sing stylishly, notably Anthony Rolfe Johnson as Jonathan and Paul Esswood as David. Elizabeth Gale's bright soprano is not always sweetly caught by the microphones, but it is a sympathetic performance. Harnoncourt's direction is lively but he misses much of the grandeur of the work, and some of the cuts he makes are damaging. The Vienna State Opera Concert Choir are responsive, but they never quite sound at home coping with English words.

Dating from well before the Vanguard recordings of Handel made by Johannes Somary, Wöldike's pioneering set of *Saul* involves an earlier tradition, with a large, firmly focused orchestra set in a rather reverberant acoustic. Though recitatives are slow and laboured, Wöldike generally avoids the worst heaviness of that tradition, and there is fine singing from such soloists as Thomas Hemsley, splendid in Saul's brilliant aria *A serpent in my bosom*. Jennifer Vyvyan sings beautifully as Michal and, most moving of all, Helen Watts is superb as David, whose arias are among the highspots of the performance. The most serious snag is that the text is savagely cut, with roughly two-thirds of what you hear on such a rival period recording as John Eliot Gardiner's on Philips.

Solomon.
✹ *** Ph. Dig. 412 612-2 (2) [id]. C. Watkinson, Argenta, Hendricks, Rolfe Johnson, Monteverdi Ch., E. Bar. Soloists, Gardiner.
(N) (M) **(*) Van. 08 5086 72 (2) [id.]. Diaz, Armstrong, Tear, Rippon, Palmer, Amore Artis Chorale, ECO, Somary.

This is among the very finest of all Handel oratorio recordings. With panache, Gardiner shows how authentic-sized forces can convey Handelian grandeur even with clean-focused textures and fast speeds. The choruses and even more magnificent double-choruses stand as cornerstones of a structure which may have less of a story-line than some other Handel oratorios – the Judgement apart – but which Gardiner shows has consistent human warmth. The Act III scenes between Solomon and the Queen of Sheba are given extra warmth by having in the latter role a singer who is sensuous in tone, Barbara Hendricks. Carolyn Watkinson's pure mezzo is very apt for Solomon himself, while Nancy Argenta is clear and sweet as his Queen, but the overriding glory of the set is the radiant singing of Gardiner's Monteverdi Choir. Its clean, crisp articulation matches the brilliant playing of the English Baroque Soloists, regularly challenged by Gardiner's fast speeds, as in *The arrival of the Queen of Sheba*; and the sound is superb, coping thrillingly with the problems of the double choruses.

Somary in this and other recordings for Vanguard did impressive work in the 1960s and 1970s in helping to establish a new, fresher approach to Handel oratorio, well before period performance took over. With a crisp professional chorus and a formidable line-up of soloists, this offers an enjoyable, infectiously sprung performance, marred by the choice of voice for the title-role. Handel himself opted for a mezzo rather than a castrato or a tenor, but here Somary, following now-discredited tradition, has a bass, singing an octave lower than written. Admittedly Justino Diaz sings with satisfyingly dark, firm tone to make the result dramatically very convincing, and the other soloists, drawn from among the finest British singers of the time, are all excellent. For this magnificent pageant of an oratorio, John Eliot Gardiner's period performance remains a firm first choice, but it is good to have this too, at mid-price.

Susanna.
**(*) HM Dig. HMU 907030/2 [id.]. Hunt, Minter, Feldman, Parker, J & D. Thomas, U. C. Berkeley Chamber Ch., Philh. Bar. O, McGegan.

The wealth of arias and the refreshing treatment of the Apocrypha story of Susanna and the Elders make it ideal for records. McGegan's performance does not quite match those of his earlier Handel recordings, made in Budapest. This one was done live with a talented period group from Los Angeles. The main snag is that the dry acoustic brings an abrasive edge to the instrumental sound and takes away bloom from the voices. Yet with fine soloists including Lorraine Hunt (Susanna), Drew Minter (Joacim) and Jill Feldman (Daniel), this is far more than a mere stop-gap.

Theodora (complete).
(N) *** HM Dig. HMU 907060/62 (3) [id.]. D. Thomas, Minter, J. Thomas, Hunt, Lane, Rogers, University of California (Berkeley) Chamber Ch., Philh. Baroque O, McGegan.
(M) **(*) Van. 08.4075.72 (2). Harper, Forrester, Lehane, Young, Lawrenson, Amor Artis Ch., ECO, Somary.
**(*) Teldec/Warner Dig. 2292 46447-2 (2) [id.]. Alexander, Blochwitz, Kowalski, Van Nes, Scharinger, Schönberg Ch., VCM, Harnoncourt.

Theodora was a favourite with Handel himself among his oratorios, and McGegan's spirited, exuberant performance makes one realize why, so many fine numbers does it contain. Unlike previous recordings, this one not only gives the text absolutely complete but also offers alternative numbers not included in the regular Handel edition. The fine team of soloists is impressively headed by Lorraine Hunt, who also shone in McGegan's earlier, prize-winning recording of *Susanna*, with the counter-tenor, Drew Minter, the tenor, Jeffrey Thomas, and the bass, David Thomas, again singing stylishly. They are not helped by the dry acoustic, but the sound is less aggressive than in the earlier set, and it means that words are crystal clear.

The reissued Vanguard account is traditional in style and is directed by an understanding and intelligent Handelian, Johannes Somary. With fresh and sympathetic singing from soloists who are stylistically at home in Handel, the result is most enjoyable. Maureen Forrester in particular sings superbly, but all the singing is at least reliable, and the recording has transferred warmly and vividly to CD.

There is much to enjoy in this lively Teldec account, with fresh, clean textures typical of the Concentus Musicus, and with Harnoncourt thrusting in manner, occasionally to the point of being heavy-handed. The solo casting is strong, though this team of international singers does not always sound at home, either stylistically or in singing English. Roberta Alexander is the finest of the soloists, with the counter-tenor Jochen Kowalski exceptionally warm of tone but hardly sounding Handelian in the role of Didymus. Jard van Nes is warm and fruity as Irene and Hans Peter Blochwitz is light and fresh as Septimius. Bright, full recording.

The Triumph of time and truth.
*** Hyperion CDA 66071/2 [id.]. Fisher, Kirkby, Brett, Partridge, Varcoe, L. Handel Ch. and O, Darlow.

Darlow's performance of Handel's very last oratorio is broad and strong and very enjoyable. The soloists all seem to have been chosen for the clarity of their pitching – Emma Kirkby, Gillian Fisher, Charles Brett and Stephen Varcoe, with the honey-toned Ian Partridge singing even more beautifully than the others, but with a timbre too pure quite to characterize 'Pleasure'. Good atmospheric recording.

Utrecht Te Deum and Jubilate.
(M) *** O-L 443 178-2 [id.]. Kirkby, Nelson, Brett, Elliott, Covey-Crump, D. Thomas, Ch. of Christ Church Cathedral, Oxford, AAM, Simon Preston – VIVALDI: *Gloria.* ***

Using authentic instruments and an all-male choir with trebles, Preston directs a performance which is not merely scholarly but characteristically alert and vigorous, particularly impressive in the superb *Gloria* with its massive eight-part chords. With a team of soloists regularly associated with the Academy of Ancient Music, this can be confidently recommended, especially as this mid-priced reissue is now coupled with a fine account of Vivaldi's best-known *Gloria* setting.

OPERA

Agrippina (complete).
*** HM Dig. HMU 907063/65 (3). Bradshaw, Saffer, Minter, Hill, Isherwood, Popken, Dean, Banditelli, Szilági, Capella Savaria, McGegan.

Agrippina is delightfully light-hearted, magnetic in its fanciful telling of the intrigues between the Emperor Claudius, his wife Agrippina, Nero her son and Poppea, as well as Otho (Ottone) and Pallas (Pallante). Nicolas McGegan is markedly sympathetic and, with a fine bloom on voices and instruments, notably the brass, the performance is exhilaratingly fresh and alert. The cast is first rate, led by the silvery Sally Bradshaw as Agrippina, the bright Nero of Wendy Hill and the seductive Poppea of Lisa Saffer, all well contrasted in their equally stylish ways.

Alcina (complete).
*** EMI Dig. CDS7 49771-2 (3) [Ang. CDCB 49771]. Augér, Della Jones, Kuhlmann, Harrhy, Kwella, Maldwyn Davies, Tomlinson, Opera Stage Ch., City of L. Bar. Sinfonia, Hickox.

(i) *Alcina* (complete); (ii) *Giulio Cesare (Julius Caesar)*: highlights.
(M) **(*) Decca 433 723-2 (3) [id.]. Sutherland, M. Sinclair, (i) Berganza, Alva, Sciutti, Freni, Flagello, LSO; (ii) Elkins, M. Horne, Conrad, New SO; Bonynge.

It would be hard to devise a septet of Handelian singers more stylish than the soloists here. Though the American, Arleen Augér, may not have the weight of Joan Sutherland, she is just as brilliant and pure-toned, singing warmly in the great expansive arias. Even next to her, Della Jones stands out in the breeches role of Ruggiero, with an extraordinary range of memorable arias, bold as well as tender. Eiddwen Harrhy as Morgana is just as brilliant in the aria, *Tornami a vagheggiar*, usually 'borrowed' by Alcina, while Kathleen Kuhlmann, Patrizia Kwella, Maldwyn Davies and John Tomlinson all sing with a clarity and beauty to make the music sparkle. Hickox underlines the contrasts of mood and speed, conveying the full range of emotion, with warm, spacious sound, recorded at EMI's Abbey Road studio.

Although the 1962 Decca *Alcina* is less complete than the newer EMI set, it has the advantage of including some 50 minutes of highlights from *Giulio Cesare*, made a year later, which Sutherland did not undertake in a complete version. *Alcina*, however, represents the extreme point of what can be described as Sutherland's dreamy, droopy period. The fast arias are stupendous. But anything slow and reflective, whether in recitative or aria, has Sutherland mooning about the notes, with no consonants audible at all and practically every vowel reduced to 'aw'. It is all most beautiful of course, but she could have done so much better. Of the others, Teresa Berganza is completely charming in the castrato part of Ruggiero, even if she does not manage trills very well. Monica Sinclair shows everyone up with the strength and forthrightness of her singing. Both Graziella Sciutti and Mirella Freni are delicate and clear in their two smaller parts. Richard Bonynge draws crisp, vigorous playing from the LSO. The 30-year-old Walthamstow recording is vintage Decca, and the CD transfer hints at its age only in the orchestral string sound.

Not surprisingly, the *Giulio Cesare* highlights are used as a vehicle for Sutherland, and her florid elaborations of melodies turn *da capo* recitatives into things of delight and wonder. There is some marvellous singing from Marilyn Horne and Monica Sinclair too, and Bonynge conducts with a splendid sense of style. As a sample, try *V'adoro pupile* – Cleopatra's seduction aria. Full translations are provided in both works.

Alessandro (complete).
(M) **(*) HM/BMG GD 77110 (3) [77110-2-RG]. Jacobs, Boulin, Poulenard, Nirouët, Varcoe, Guy de Mey, La Petite Bande, Kuijken.

Sigiswald Kuijken directs his team of period-performance specialists in an urgently refreshing, at times sharply abrasive, reading of one of Handel's key operas. As a high counter-tenor, René Jacobs copes brilliantly with the taxing role of Alexander himself. His singing is astonishingly free and agile, if too heavily aspirated. Among the others, Isabelle Poulenard at her best sounds a little like a French Emma Kirkby, though the production is not quite so pure and at times comes over more edgily. The others make a fine, consistent team, the more effective when the recording so vividly conveys a sense of presence with sharply defined directional focus.

Amadigi di Gaula (complete).
*** Erato/Warner Dig. 2292 45490-2 (2) [id.]. Stutzmann, Jennifer Smith, Harrhy, Fink, Musiciens du Louvre, Minkowski.

Minkowski's electrifying performance is one of his sharpest, dominated vocally by the magnificent young French contralto (no mere mezzo) of Nathalie Stutzmann in the title-role. She sings Amadigi's gentle arias most affectingly, notably the lovely *Sussurrate, onde vezzose*, and the two women characters, Amadigi's lover Melissa and Princess Oriana, are well taken by Eiddwen Harrhy and Jennifer Smith, with the brilliant arias for Prince Dardano of Thrace superbly sung by Bernarda Fink. Marc Minkowski directs a performance on an intimate scale, and the more involving for that.

Ariodante (complete).

(N) *** HM Dig. HMC 907146/48 (3) [id.]. Hunt, Gondek, Saffer, Lane, Cavallier, Muller, Wilhelmshaven Vocal Ens., Freiburger Bar. O, McGegan.

(Y/B) (M) *** Ph. 442 096-2 (2) [id.]. J. Baker, Mathis, N. Burrowes, Bowman, Rendall, Ramey, L. Voices, ECO, Leppard.

Ariodante, dating from 1735, the same year as *Alcina*, is among the most richly inspired of Handel's operas, as the Raymond Leppard recording with Dame Janet Baker has long borne witness. McGegan's performance on Harmonia Mundi, recorded in Göttingen in 1995 immediately after festival perform-ances on stage, brings clear advantages. Not only is there an exceptionally strong and consistent cast, the text is far fuller and the period-instrument orchestra is full-bodied and sweetly tuned, with the experi-ence of live performing adding to the dramatic bite. McGegan springs rhythms infectiously, making speeds that are faster than Leppard's seem natural, never breathless, letting the music relax where necessary, again influenced by live experience. In the castrato title-role Lorraine Hunt may not have the emotional weight of Janet Baker, but hers is a fresh, clear and firm mezzo, which she uses most charactefully and imaginatively. Her big Act II aria, *Scherza infida*, in its positive strength even brings unexpected echoes of Kathleen Ferrier. The others too, mainly American singers, all have fresh, clean delivery and free flexibility, notably Juliana Gondek as the heroine, Ginevra, Lisa Saffer as Dalinda and Jennifer Lane as Polinesso. Nicolas Cavallier as the King may not have the richness of Samuel Ramey in Leppard's set, but his attack too is clean, and Rufus Muller in the tenor role of Lucanio, clear and firm, like the women sings elaborate divisions with ideal precision, dazzlingly brilliant in his Act II aria, *Il tuo sangue*. Excellent recording with bloom on the voices, aptly intimate and full of presence.

Ariodante has a story which inspired Handel to write an amazing sequence of memorable and intensely inventive arias and duets, with not a single weak link in the chain, a point superbly conveyed in this colourful, urgent performance under Raymond Leppard. The castrato role of Ariodante is a challenge for Dame Janet Baker, who responds with singing of enormous expressive range, from the dark, agon-ized moments of the C minor aria early in Act III to the brilliance of the most spectacular of the three display arias later in the Act. Dame Janet's duets with Edith Mathis as Princess Ginevra, destined to marry Prince Ariodante, are enchanting too, and there is not a single weak member of the cast, though James Bowman as Duke Polinesso is not as precise as usual, with words often unclear. Though this long work is given uncut, it is among the most riveting Handel opera recordings currently available, helped by the consistently resilient playing of the English Chamber Orchestra and the refined, beautifully bal-anced (1978) analogue recording, transferred so successfully to CD.

Flavio (complete).

*** HM Dig. HMC 901312/13 (2) [id.]. Gall, Ragin, Lootens, Fink, *et al.*, Ens. 415, Jacobs.

Based on a staging of this unjustly neglected Handel opera at the 1989 Innsbruck Festival, René Jacobs' recording vividly captures the consistent vigour of Handel's inspiration. Handel's score was brilliantly written for some of the most celebrated singers of the time, including the castrato, Senesino. His four arias are among the highspots of the opera, all sung superbly here by the warm-toned and characterful counter-tenor, Derek Lee Ragin; almost every other aria is open and vigorous, with the whole sequence rounded off in a rousing ensemble. René Jacobs' team of eight soloists is a strong one, with only the strenuous tenor of Gianpaolo Fagotto occasionally falling short of the general stylishness. Full, clear sound.

Giulio Cesare (complete).

*** HM Dig. HMC 901385/7 [id.]. Larmore, Schlick, Fink, Rorholm, Ragin, Zanasi, Visse, Concerto Köln, Jacobs.

(N) *** Astree Auvidis E 8558 (3) [id.]. Bowman, Dawson, Laurens, James, Visse, La Grande Ecurie et la Chambre du Roy, Jean-Claude Malgoire.

The counter-tenor, René Jacobs, now conductor of the German group, Concerto Köln, is a warmly expressive rather than a severe period performer. With a cast of consistently fresh voices, with rhythms sprung infectiously, he also allows the broadest expansion on the great reflective moments. The casting of the pure, golden-toned Barbara Schlick as Cleopatra proves outstandingly successful. Jennifer Larmore too, a fine, firm mezzo, with a touch of masculine toughness in the tone, makes a splendid Caesar. Together they crown the whole performance with the most seductive account of their final duet. Derek Lee Ragin is excellent in the sinister role of Tolomeo (Ptolemy); so are Bernarda Fink as Cornelia and Marianne Rorholm as Sesto, with the bass, Furio Zanasi, as Achille. Jacobs' expansive speeds mean that the whole opera will not fit on three CDs, but the fourth disc, at 18 minutes merely supplementary, comes free as part of the package, and includes an extra aria for the servant, Nireno, delightfully sung by the French counter-tenor, Dominique Visse. Firm, well-balanced sound.

Jean-Claude Malgoire, taking a lighter, less abrasive view of Handel than in his earlier recordings, directs his outstanding cast in a fresh, free-running performance of Handel's most frequently performed (but too rarely recorded) opera. The direct rival here is the Harmonia Mundi set directed by René Jacobs with an equally fine cast, and choice may well depend on preference over the central singer, the counter-tenor, James Bowman, in the Malgoire set strongly contrasted against the firm and purposeful mezzo, Jennifer Larmore. Bowman cannot quite match Larmore in the brilliance of his florid singing, but the timbre is firm and rich at less demanding speeds, and the portrait of a hero is conveyed convincingly. The contrast between Lynne Dawson as Cleopatra and Barbara Schlick is a key one too, for Dawson, following Malgoire's general approach, concentrates on beauty and classical poise, whereas Schlick brings out greater depth of expression. The contrast is similar over Giullemette Laurens as Cornelia as against Bernarda Fink, the one poised, the other more deeply expressive, often at broader speeds. By contrast the counter-tenor, Dominique Visse, is the more actively characterful as the villainous Tolomeo, where Derek Lee Ragin for Jacobs combines sharp characterization with cleaner vocalization. Malgoire's text is not quite as complete as Jacobs', with cuts in recitative, but the three-disc format might be counted more convenient.

Giulio Cesare: highlights.
(M) **(*) Teldec/Warner Dig. 2292 42410 [id.]. Esswood, Alexander, Lipovšek, Murray, Schoenberg Ch., VCM, Harnoncourt.

Instead of issuing Harnoncourt's complete set on CD, Teldec offer just short of an hour of highlights. The opera is strongly cast with Marjana Lipovšek and Ann Murray both making fine contributions. Paul Esswood as Cesare sings pleasingly, especially in *Va tacito e nascosto* with its horn obbligato, but ideally one wants more striking differentiation between the voices. Roberta Alexander takes readily to Cleopatra's coloratura, although curiously she is replaced by Lucia Popp in the closing bourrée, *Ritorni omai*. Harnoncourt directs the proceedings with plenty of rhythmic spirit and makes the most of the *Sinfonia bellica*. Good, bright recording with plenty of resonant atmosphere.

Giustino (complete).
(N) *** HM Dig. HMU 907130/32 [id.]. Chance, Röschmann, Kotoski, Gondek, Lane, Padmore, Minter, Cantamus Halle Chamber Ch., Freiburg Baroque O, McGegan.

First heard in 1737 and never revived until 1967, the opera, *Giustino*, has been consistently underestimated. Based loosely on Roman history, the plot follows the career of the self-made man among emperors, Justinian (or Justin), described in the notes as 'a baroque Dick Whittington'. This splendid, lively set should do much to bring a full reassessment, for McGegan with his fast, crisp manner and fondness for extra decoration in *da capo* repeats brings out the element of sparkle and irony implied in the improbable story, treated refreshingly in dozens of brief arias. It obviously helped that the recording was made in studio conditions immediately after a sequence of stage performances at the Göttingen Festival in 1994. Michael Chance is outstanding in the title-role originally written for a castrato, and Dorothea Röschmann sings most movingly in the key role of Arianna, who in each of the three Acts has the most important and substantial arias. The counter-tenor, Drew Minter, stylish and intelligent as he is, fails to give enough bite to the villainous role of Amanzio; but there are few other disappointments, and the tenor, Mark Padmore, sings with virtuoso flair in the military role of Vitaliano. The German string-players are less sweet-toned and more abrasive than we have latterly come to expect in period recordings but, with clear, well-balanced sound, this is a set to delight all Handelians, filling in an important gap. The three substantial Acts – the middle one much shorter than the other two – are each complete on a single CD.

Hercules (complete).
(N) (M) *** DG Dig. 447 689-2 (2) [id.]. Tomlinson, Sarah Walker, Rolfe Johnson, Jennifer Smith, Denley, Savidge, Monteverdi Ch., E. Bar. Soloists, Gardiner.

Gardiner's generally brisk performance of *Hercules* using authentic forces may at times lack Handelian grandeur in the big choruses, but it conveys superbly the vigour of the writing, its natural drama; and the fire of this performance is typified by the singing of Sarah Walker as Dejanira in her finest recording yet. John Tomlinson makes an excellent, dark-toned Hercules. Youthful voices consistently help in the clarity of the attack – Jennifer Smith as Iole, Catherine Denley as Lichas, Anthony Rolfe Johnson as Hyllus and Peter Savidge as the Priest of Jupiter. Refined playing and outstanding recording quality make this particularly welcome at mid-price.

Orlando (complete).
*** O-L Dig. 430 845-2 (3) [id.]. Bowman, Augér, Robbin, Kirkby, D. Thomas, AAM, Hogwood.

Handel's *Orlando* was radically modified to provide suitable material for individual singers, as for example the bass role of the magician, Zoroastro, specially created for a member of Handel's company. Even so, the title-role seems to have failed to please the celebrated castrato, Senesino, for whom it was intended, probably because of Handel's breaks with tradition, notably in the magnificent mad scene which ends Act II on the aria, *Vaghe pupille*, with the simple ritornello leading to amazing inspirations. That number, superbly done here by James Bowman, with appropriate sound effects, is only one of the virtuoso vehicles for the counter-tenor. For the jewelled sequences of arias and duets, Hogwood has assembled a near-ideal cast, with Arleen Augér at her most radiant as the queen, Angelica, and Emma Kirkby characteristically bright and fresh in the lighter, semi-comic role of the shepherdess, Dorinda. Catherine Robbin assumes the role of Prince Medoro strongly and David Thomas sings stylishly as Zoroastro. This is one of Hogwood's finest achievements on record, taut, dramatic and rhythmically resilient. Vivid, open sound.

Ottone, re di Germania (complete).
*** Hyperion Dig. CDA 66751/3 [id.]. Bowman, McFadden, Jennifer Smith, Denley, Visse, George, King's Consort, Robert King.
**(*) HM Dig. HMU 907073/5 [id.]. Minter, Saffer, Gondek, Spence, Popken, Dean, Freiburg Bar. O, McGegan.

Previously unrecorded, *Ottone* simultaneously prompted these two versions, both of which have their points of advantage. Nicholas McGegan continues his impressive Handel series for Harmonia Mundi in a recording with the Freiburg Baroque Orchestra and with Drew Minter taking the title-role, while Robert King and his King's Consort offer a version on Hyperion with James Bowman as Ottone. When the women principals in McGegan's version have purer, firmer voices than their rivals, there is a strong case for preferring his set. As the heroine, Teofane, Lisa Saffer for McGegan is markedly sweeter and clearer than Claron McFadden for King. When it comes to the key castrato roles taken by counter-tenors, it is quite different. For McGegan, Drew Minter, a stylish singer, no longer has the power to give the many bravura arias the thrust they need, whereas for King, Bowman with his far richer tone continues to sing with enormous panache and virtuoso agility. Dominique Visse as the duplicitous Adalberto on King's set tends to overcharacterize, but again the singing makes the rival version seem colourless. Add to that the extra richness and bloom on the instrumental sound in the Hyperion version, and the balance clearly goes in its favour. This may not be as distinctive as some of Handel's later Italian operas, but as ever the sequence of brief numbers has an irresistible freshness.

Partenope (complete).
(M) *** HM/BMG GD 77109 (3) [77109-2-RG]. Laki, Jacobs, York, Skinner, Varcoe, Müller-Molinari, Hill, La Petite Bande, Kuijken.

With the exception of René Jacobs, rather too mannered for Handel, the roster of soloists here is outstanding, with Krisztina Laki and Helga Müller-Molinari welcome additions to the team. Though ornamentation is sparse, the direction of Sigiswald Kuijken is consistently invigorating, as is immediately apparent in the *Overture*; the 1979 recording sounds quite marvellous in its CD format.

Il pastor fido (complete).
**(*) Hung. Dig. HCD 12912 (2) [id.]. Esswood, Farkas, Lukin, Kállay, Flohr, Gregor, Savaria Vocal Ens., Capella Savaria, McGegan.

Il pastor fido is an unpretentious pastoral piece, which charms gently rather than compelling attention. Nicholas McGegan demonstrates what talent there is in Budapest, among singers as among instrumentalists. Singers better known in much later operatic music translate well to Handel, for example the celebrated bass, József Gregor, but the most stylish singing comes from the British counter-tenor, Paul Esswood, in the castrato role of Mirtillo. Good sound and excellent documentation.

Radamisto (complete).
**(*) HM Dig. HMU 907111/13 [id.]. Popken, Gondek, Saffer, Hanchard, Dean, Cavallier, Freiburger Bar. O, McGegan.

Radamisto is a magnificent work. The best-known aria, the plaintive *Ombra cara*, sung by Radamisto, leads on to a whole sequence of magnificent minor-key numbers in Act II, with some of the arias given to Zenobia, Radamisto's wife, marked by strange, sudden switches of mood. This first complete recording is very welcome in revealing much superb material, even if the period-performance manners are less sympathetic than have become common on disc. The strings of the Freiburg orchestra are very abrasive, and even under the direction of McGegan rhythms are too often square, not sprung as winningly as they might be, while recitative is on the heavy side. Nevertheless, there is some first-rate singing, with the title-role – originally written for the castrato, Senesino – strongly taken by the firm-toned counter-tenor, Ralf Popken, who projects well, even if he is occasionally hooty. It is not his fault that *Ombra cara* sounds rather stodgy, for he shades his tone most beautifully for the reprise. Juliana Gondek sings with full, warm tone as Zenobia, producing crisp trills and ornaments, though most of the others are not quite so successful. The recording, made in Göttingen after a festival production, is on the dry side but has plenty of presence.

Rodelinda, Regina de Langobardi (complete).
**(*) HM/BMG Dig. RD 771927 (3). Schlick, Schubert, Cordier, Wessel, Prégardien, Schwarz, La Stagione, Schneider.

On this German recording from Michael Schneider and La Stagione, the celebrated *Dove sei*, inaccurately translated as 'Art thou troubl'd', is tenderly sung with plaintive tone by the British counter-tenor, David Cordier, matching the rest of the excellent, otherwise all-German cast. Barbara Schlick is pure and golden in the title-role and the tenor, Christoph Prégardien, is also outstanding as the hero, Grimoaldo. Schneider is a lively and fresh Handelian not afraid of expressiveness but often adopting a clipped, abrasive manner. He encourages generous ornamentation in *da capo* repeats. First-rate, clean sound.

Semele (complete).
*** DG Dig. 435 782-2 (3) [id.]. Battle, M. Horne, Ramey, Aler, McNair, Chance, Mackie, Amb. Op. Ch., ECO, John Nelson.
(N) (M) *** Van. 08.5082 72 (2) [id.]. Armstrong, Watts, Palmer, Tear, Diaz, Deller, Fleet, Amor Artis Chorale, ECO, Somary.
(N) (M) **(*) Erato/Warner 4509 99759-2 (2) [id.]. Burrowes, Della Jones, Lloyd, D. Thomas, Rolfe Johnson, Kwella, Penrose, M. Davies, Monteverdi Ch., E. Bar. Soloists, Gardiner.

With its English words, *Semele* stands equivocally between the genres of opera and oratorio, presenting even more interpretative problems than usual. DG's new digital recording turns away from current fashion in using modern rather than period instruments, but the balance of advantage lies very much in its favour, compared with the Erato set of Gardiner; even period fanatics may well find it the better choice. Surprisingly, the Nelson performance is generally crisper and faster than Gardiner's, with rhythms sprung just as infectiously. Most importantly, he opens out the serious cuts made by Gardiner, following the old, bad tradition. If *Semele* – dating from 1744, three years after *Messiah* – is known as a rule only by its most celebrated aria, *Where'er you walk*, it contains many other superb numbers. Handel was aiming to satirize George II's mistress, Lady Yarmouth, in his portrayal of the central character of Semele – a self-regarding princess seduced by Jupiter who through him seeks to become immortal, just as Lady Yarmouth wanted to become queen. The story of *Semele* derives from Ovid's *Metamorphoses*, and Congreve's libretto was written in 1708.

Though at times he favours slow, oratorio-like tempi, Somary still keeps in mind an operatic flavour and the Amor Artis Chorale (a pseudonym for a professional choir very familiar on record) sings splendidly, often with great vigour, and even attempts some attractive if inauthentic corporate ornamentation. Overall the performance has much charm and spirit with superb soloists. Like the rest of this Vanguard series from the 1970s, the fine recording allows excellent detail, yet is full and expansive.

The Erato reissue in the Libretto series of John Eliot Gardiner's 1981 version of *Semele* offers a period performance with the English Baroque Soloists using an excellent cast of British specialist singers. Very well recorded, it has the very practical advantage of coming on only two mid-price discs, and the extensive cuts which make that possible are the traditional ones, some of them sanctioned by Handel himself. Though this was an early EBS recording, not quite as polished as more recent ones, Gardiner's ability to use period performance with warmth and imagination makes it consistently compelling. Norma Burrowes is a sweet, pure Semele, and Anthony Rolfe Johnson is outstanding as Jupiter, singing *Where'er you walk* with a fine sense of line and excellent pacing.

The Sorceress (pasticcio).
**(*) Ph. Dig. 434 992-2 [id.]. Kiri Te Kanawa, AAM, Hogwood.

This pasticcio, with items drawn from a whole range of Handel operas (*Rinaldo, Alcina, Giulio Cesare, Ariodante, Agrippina, Admeto* and *Giustino*) was devised for a Dutch television programme. The CD – like the video version, complete with ballet interludes – is taken from the soundtrack, providing in effect a sequence of seven arias, sung with characteristic poise and sumptuous tone by Dame Kiri, spiced with instrumental pieces, mostly brief. Though the plot is broadly based on the situation in *Alcina*, only one aria is taken from that opera, *Ombre pallide*, which, preceded by an accompanied recitative, makes up by far the longest item. It is made even longer by Dame Kiri's somewhat languid performance. She is not nearly as animated as Arleen Augér was in Richard Hickox's fine complete recording of the opera. Otherwise, even with speeds on the slow side, Dame Kiri sings gloriously, with four of Cleopatra's arias from *Giulio Cesare* – including the seduction aria, *V'adoro pupille* – providing the cornerstones. Hogwood draws fresh sounds from the Academy but he might have sounded even sharper at faster speeds. Clear, well-balanced sound.

Teseo (opera; complete).
*** Erato/Warner Dig. 2292 45806-2 (2) [id.]. James, Della Jones, Gooding, Lee Ragin, Napoli, Gall, Les Musiciens du Louvre, Minkowski.

Dating from December 1712, *Teseo* was only the second opera that Handel wrote for London, and the first after he had established himself here. Using an Italian translation of a French libretto originally written for Lully 40 years earlier, Handel uniquely produced a hybrid between an Italian *opera seria* and a French tragédie lyrique, with the classical story of Theseus and Medea told in a brisk sequence of short arias. Sadly, after its initial run of 13 performances *Teseo* was never produced again until the present century. The score may not contain great Handel melodies, but it is characteristically fresh and imaginative. Marc Minkowski, the liveliest of period performance specialists in France, brings out the inventiveness, helped by an excellent cast, dominated by British and American singers. These include Della Jones as Medea, Eirian James in the castrato role of Teseo, Julia Gooding as Agilea and characterful counter-tenors, Derek Lee Ragin and Jeffrey Gall, as Egeo and Arcane.

COLLECTIONS

Arias: *Aci, Galatea e Polifemo: Qui l'augel di pianta in pianta. Floridante: Bramo te sola; Se dolce m'era già. Giulio Cesare in Egitto: Se in fiorito ameno prato; Va tacito. Orlando: Ah stigie larve | Vaghe pupille; Fammi combattere. Partenope: Furibondo spira il vento. Radamisto: Ombra cara di mi sposa. Rinaldo: Cara sposa, amante cara.*
*** RCA Dig. 09026 61205-2 [id.]. Nathalie Stutzmann, Hanover Band, Goodman.

Nathalie Stutzmann is both characterful and brilliant in this valuable collection of arias from ten Handel operas, recorded in London with Roy Goodman and the Hanover Band. With Stutzmann so positive a singer, each item emerges as a winner, strikingly memorable. Military rhythms are a feature in several, including the opening item, *Fammi combattere* from *Orlando*, which is like a trial run for *Let the bright Seraphim* from *Samson*. The sequence ends with the most tragic of the arias, *Ombra cara* from *Radamisto*, in which Stutzmann and her accompanists give the darkly chromatic writing the fullest expressive weight.

Arias: *Alexander's Feast: The Prince, unable to conceal his pain; Softly sweet in Lydian measures. Atalanta: Care selve. Giulio Cesare: Piangerò. Messiah: Rejoice greatly; He shall feed his flock. Rinaldo: Lascia ch'io pianga. Samson: Let the bright Seraphim.*
**(*) Delos Dig. D/CD 3026 [id.]. Arleen Augér, Mostly Mozart O, Schwarz – BACH: *Arias.* **(*)

Arleen Augér's bright, clean, flexible soprano is even more naturally suited to these Handel arias than to the Bach items with which they are coupled. The delicacy with which she tackles the most elaborate divisions and points the words is a delight.

Opera arias: *Agrippina: Bel piacere. Orlando: Fammi combattere. Partenope: Funbondo spira il vento. Rinaldo: Or la tromba; Cara sposa; Venti turbini; Cor ingrato; Lascia ch'io pianga. Serse: Frondi tenere; Ombra mai fù.*
(M) **(*) Erato/Warner Dig. 2292 45186-2 [id.]. Marilyn Horne, Sol. Ven., Scimone.

Horne gives virtuoso performances. The flexibility of her voice in scales and trills and ornaments of every kind remains formidable, and the power is extraordinary down to the tangy chest register.

Arias: *Judas Maccabaeus: Father of heaven. Messiah: O Thou that tellest; He was despised. Samson: Return O God of Hosts.*
❀ (M) (***) Decca 433 474-2. Kathleen Ferrier, LPO, Boult – BACH: Arias. (***)

Kathleen Ferrier had a unique feeling for Handel; these performances are unforgettable for their communicative intensity and nobility of timbre and line. She receives highly sympathetic accompaniments from Boult, another natural Handelian.

Hanson, Howard (1896–1981)

(i) *Piano concerto in G, Op. 36. Mosaics; Symphonies Nos. 5 (Sinfonia sacra), Op. 43;* (ii) *7 (A Sea symphony)*.
*** Delos Dig. D E 3130 [id.]. (i) Carol Rosenberger; Seattle S O, Schwarz; (ii) with Seattle Symphony Chorale.

Even if none of these works has the concentration of the early symphonies, admirers of the composer will want this collection, for all the music is given ardent advocacy and is superbly recorded. *Mosaics* is in variation form, compressed into an ongoing movement. The single-movement *Sinfonia sacra* – inspired by Christ's Passion – is also very succinct, showing the composer's Nordic inheritance. The *Sea Symphony*, a setting of Walt Whitman, contains some powerful choral writing, and the composer looks back to his most successful piece, the *Romantic Symphony*, in the finale. The four-movement *Piano concerto* (1948) is well made, and has a fine slow movement. Carol Rosenberger is an eloquent soloist.

Symphonies Nos. 1 in E min. (Nordic); 2 (Romantic); Elegy in memory of Serge Koussevitzky.
*** Delos Dig. D/CD 3073 [id.]. Seattle S O, Gerard Schwarz.

Hanson was of Swedish descent and his music has a strong individuality of idiom and colour. The *Second Symphony* is warmly appealing and melodically memorable with an indelible theme which permeates the structure. These Seattle performances have plenty of breadth and ardour, and Schwarz's feeling for the ebb and flow of the musical paragraphs is very satisfying. The recording, made in Seattle Opera House, is gloriously expansive and the balance is convincingly natural.

Symphonies Nos. 1 in E min. (Nordic), Op. 21; 2 (Romantic), Op. 30; (i) *Song of democracy.*
(M) *** Mercury 432 008-2 [id.]. Eastman-Rochester O, composer, (i) with Eastman School of Music Ch.

Hanson's own pioneering stereo recordings of his two best-known symphonies have a unique thrust and ardour. The *Song of democracy* has plenty of dramatic impact and is also very well recorded.

Symphony No. 3; Elegy in memory of my friend Serge Koussevitzky, Op. 44; (i) *Lament for Beowulf.*
(M) *** Mercury 434 302-2 [id.]. Eastman-Rochester O, composer, (i) with Eastman School of Music Ch.

For those familiar with the earlier works, the musical terrain of the *Third Symphony* is familiar: the string threnodies surge purposefully forward, there are similar rhythmic patterns and confident rhetorical gestures. This is highly accessible music. This applies also to the *Elegy*, while the cantata also makes an immediate impression and is very well sung. However, here as in the orchestral works the 1958 Mercury sound is first rate.

(i) *Symphony No. 4 (Requiem), Op. 34;* (ii) *Lament for Beowulf, Op. 25; Merry Mount: suite, Op. 31;* (iii) *Pastorale for oboe, harp and strings, Op. 38; Serenade for flute, harp and strings, Op. 35.*
*** Delos Dig. D E 3105 [id.]. (i) Seattle S O; (ii) with Symphony Ch.; (iii) N Y Chamber Symphony of 92nd Street Y; Gerard Schwarz.

Like so much of Hanson, the *Fourth Symphony* can be described as neo-Sibelian in the way that many Swedish composers of the period such as Atterberg were. The *Lament for Beowulf* is in its way an impressive achievement. Gerard Schwarz proves an even more eloquent exponent of the work than the composer, who recorded it for Mercury in the 1950s, but he has the benefit of a softer-grained, less glassy recording. The *Pastorale for oboe, harp and strings* and the *Serenade for flute, harp and strings* find Hanson at his best; they are both unpretentious and beautifully fashioned.

Harbison, John (born 1938)

(i) *Concerto for double brass choir and orchestra;* (ii) *The Flight into Egypt;* (iii) *The Natural world.*
*** New World Dig. N W 80395-2 [id.]. (i) LAPO, Previn; (ii) Roberta Anderson, Sanford Sylvan, Cantata Singers & Ens., David Hoose; (iii) Janice Felty, Los Angeles Philharmonic New Music Group, Harbison.

These three fine works provide an illuminating survey of the recent work of one of the most communicative of American composers today. The most striking and vigorous is the concerto he wrote as resident composer for Previn and the Los Angeles Philharmonic, and for the orchestra's brass section in particular. The other two works reveal the more thoughtful Harbison, the one a collection of three songs to nature poems by Wallace Stevens, Robert Bly and James Wright. *The Flight into Egypt* is a measured and easily lyrical setting of the story of the Holy Family fleeing from King Herod. Sanford Sylvan and the choir sing the main text, with Roberta Anderson interjecting as the Angel. Excellent performances and recording.

Harris, Roy (1898–1979)

(i) *Violin concerto; Symphonies Nos. 1; 5.*
** Albany AR012 [id.]. (i) Gregory Fulkerston; Louisville O, Leighton Smith; Mester or Whitney.

The *First Symphony* is strong stuff, hardly less impressive than No. 3, but neither No. 5 nor the *Violin concerto* adds greatly to our picture of its composer. Gregory Fulkerston gives a persuasive account of the solo part, but the strings of the enterprising Louisville Orchestra are wanting in body and lustre. The recordings are serviceable rather than distinguished.

Epilogue to profiles in courage; When Johnny comes marching home (An American overture).
** Albany TROY 027-2 [id.]. Louisville O, Jorge Mester – BECKER: *Symphonia brevis;* SCHUMAN: *Symphony No. 4* etc. **

Roy Harris's overture, *When Johnny comes marching home,* is a fresh and attractive piece and, like most of Harris's music of the 1930s, has a vital impulse which by 1964, when he composed the *Epilogue to profiles in courage,* had slackened into self-imitation. Good performances and rather good recording too.

Hartmann, Karl Amadeus (1905–1963)

Concerto funèbre.
(Y/B) *** Teldec/Warner Dig. 4509 97449-2 [id.]. Zehetmair, Deutsche Chamber Philharmonie – BERG; JANACEK: *Violin concertos.* ***

As one of the two couplings for his clean-cut version of the Berg *Concerto,* Zehetmair offers this strong, intense *Concerto funèbre* for violin and strings – very much reflecting in its dark moods the troubled period, 1939, when it was written. Well worth exploring.

Symphony No. 3.
(N) (M) *** EMI Dig. CDM5 55254-2. Bamberg SO, Ingo Metzmacher – IVES: *Robert Browning Overture.* ***

Hartmann's brand of post-expressionism may be a tough nut to crack but it is, generally speaking, a nut worth cracking. The *Third Symphony* comes from 1948–9, though its history is a bit more complicated. It began life as two separate entities, a *Sinfonia tragica,* started at the beginning of the war and revised in 1943, and a *Klagesange,* which occupied the composer on and off during 1944–7. Whatever its genesis, there is no doubting that it is a work of anguish and eloquence, and the Bamberg Symphony Orchestra under Ingo Metzmacher give as persuasive an account as one could imagine. They produce a far more beautiful sound than the rival set under Leitner on Wergo; readers prepared to take the trouble with this music will find it rewarding. Good recording.

Harty, Hamilton (1879–1941)

A Comedy overture; (i) *Piano concerto;* (ii) *Violin concerto;* (iii) *In Ireland (Fantasy). An Irish symphony;* (ii) *Variations on a Dublin air. With the wild geese.* (iv) *The Children of Lir; Ode to a nightingale.* Arrangement: *Londonderry Air.*
(N) (M) *** Chandos Dig. 7035 (3) [id.]. (i) Binns; (ii) Holmes; (iii) Fleming, Kelly; (iv) Harper; Ulster O, Thomson.

Bryden Thomson's box gathers together Harty's major orchestral and concertante works with great success, and each disc is also available separately – see below.

(i) *Piano concerto in B min.;* (ii) *Violin concerto in D.*
(N) (M) *** Chandos Dig. CHAN 7032 [id.]. (i) Malcolm Binns, (ii) Ralph Holmes; Ulster O, Thomson.

Harty's *Piano concerto,* written in 1922, has strong Rachmaninovian influences, but the melodic freshness remains individual in this highly sympathetic performance. Though the *Violin concerto* has no strongly individual idiom, the invention is fresh and often touched with genuine poetry. Ralph Holmes gives a thoroughly committed account of the solo part and is well supported by an augmented Ulster Orchestra under Bryden Thomson.

An Irish symphony; A Comedy overture; (i) *In Ireland* (fantasy for flute, harp and orchestra). *With the wild geese.*
(N) (M) *** Chandos Dig. CHAN 7034 [id.]. Ulster O, Thomson, (i) with Fleming, Kelly.

The *Irish symphony* has won great acclaim for its excellent scoring and good craftsmanship. The Scherzo is particularly engaging. It is extremely well played by the Ulster Orchestra under Bryden Thomson, while the *In Ireland fantasy* is full of delightful Irish melodic whimsy. Melodrama enters the scene in the symphonic poem, *With the wild geese,* but its Irishry asserts itself immediately in the opening theme. Again a splendid performance and a high standard of digital sound.

With the wild geese (symphonic poem).
(B) *** CfP CD-CFP 4635; *TC-CFP 4635.* RSNO, Gibson – GERMAN: *Welsh rhapsody;* MACCUNN: *Land of Mountain and flood;* SMYTH: *Wreckers overture.* ***

With the wild geese is a melodramatic piece about the Irish soldiers fighting on the French side in the Battle of Fontenoy. The ingredients – a gay Irish theme and a call to arms among them – are effectively deployed; although the music does not reveal a strong individual personality, it is carried by a romantic sweep which is well exploited here. The 1968 recording still sounds most vivid, and this anthology makes a first-rate bargain.

VOCAL MUSIC

(i) *The Children of Lir; Ode to a nightingale.* (ii) *Variations on a Dublin air.* Arrangement: *Londonderry Air.*
(N) (M) *** Chandos Dig. CHAN 7033 [id.]. Ulster O, Thomson, with (i) Heather Harper; (ii) Holmes.

Harty's setting of Keats's *Ode to a nightingale* is richly convincing, a piece written for his future wife, the soprano, Agnes Nicholls. The other work, directly Irish in its inspiration, evocative in an almost Sibelian way, uses the soprano in wordless melisma, here beautifully sung by Heather Harper. The performances are excellent, warmly committed and superbly recorded. The *Variations on a Dublin air,* for violin and orchestra, and Harty's arrangement of the *Londonderry Air* have been added for the reissue.

Hasse, Johann (1699–1783)

(i; ii) *Aria 'Ah Dio, ritornate'* from *La conversione di San'Agostino* for viola da gamba and harpsichord; (iii; i–ii) *Flute sonata in B min., Op. 2/6;* (ii) *Harpsichord sonata in C min. Op. 7/6;* (iv; i–iii) Cantatas: *Fille, dolce mio bene; Quel vago seno, O Fille;* Venetian ballads: *Cos e' sta Cossa?; Grazie agli inganni tuoi; No ste' a condanare; Si' la gondola avere', non crie'.*
*** CRD Dig. CRD 3488 [id.]. (i) Erin Headley; (ii) Malcolm Proud; (iii) Nancy Hadden; (iv) Julianne Baird.

Johann Hasse was a remarkable example of a composer who outlived his times and was left behind by the musical course of events – the penalty of surviving until his 85th year. A member of the group of composers centred round the court of Frederick the Great at Potsdam, his career peaked in the 1730s, although his success as an operatic composer continued on and off for another three decades. Finally in his seventies he graciously acknowledged Mozart's superiority; nevertheless he went on producing operas. The cantatas here are written in a pastoral style, with important flute obbligatos (a legacy from Frederick). They show much charm and distinct expressive feeling, and Julianne Baird has exactly the right voice for them, with a freshness of tone and purity of line matched by the right degree of ardour. The *Harpsichord sonata,* alternating fast and slow movements, is inventive and essentially good-humoured and the *Aria* for viola da gamba readily shows the composer's operatic style, while the Venetian ballads which close this elegantly performed and very well-recorded concert are also full of character, cultivated rather than folksy in their more popular idiom. Hasse may not have the strongest musical personality but everything here has a refreshing amiability.

his seventies he graciously acknowledged Mozart's superiority; nevertheless he went on producing operas. The cantatas here are written in a pastoral style, with important flute obbligatos (a legacy from Frederick). They show much charm and distinct expressive feeling, and Julianne Baird has exactly the right voice for them, with a freshness of tone and purity of line matched by the right degree of ardour. The *Harpsichord sonata*, alternating fast and slow movements, is inventive and essentially good-humoured and the *Aria* for viola da gamba readily shows the composer's operatic style, while the Venetian ballads which close this elegantly performed and very well-recorded concert are also full of character, cultivated rather than folksy in their more popular idiom. Hasse may not have the strongest musical personality but everything here has a refreshing amiability.

Haydn, Josef (1732–1809)

Cello concertos in C & D, Hob XVIIb/1–2.
*** Ph. Dig. 420 923-2 [id.]. Heinrich Schiff, ASMF, Marriner.
*** O-L Dig. 414 615-2 [id.]. Christophe Coin, AAM, Hogwood.
(BB) *** Naxos Dig. 8.550059; *4550059* [id.]. Ludovít Kanta, Capella Istropolitana, Peter Breiner –
   BOCCHERINI: *Cello concerto*. ***
(M) **(*) EMI Dig. CDM7 64326-2 [id.]. Lynn Harrell, ASMF, Marriner – VIVALDI: *Concertos*. **

Cello concerto in D, Hob VIIb/2.
*** EMI CDC7 47840-2 [id.]. Jacqueline du Pré, LSO, Barbirolli – BOCCHERINI: *Concerto*. **(*)

Heinrich Schiff produces a beautiful sound, as indeed do the Academy under Marriner. These are impressively fresh-sounding performances with lyrical and affectionate (but not too affectionate) playing from all concerned. The recording has the realistic timbre, balance and bloom one associates with Philips.

Christophe Coin, too, is a superb soloist, and provided the listener has no reservations about the use of original instruments, Hogwood's accompaniments are equally impressive. Excellent sound.

Kanta is a soloist of quality. The excellent Naxos recording is made in a bright, resonant acoustic in which every detail is clearly registered, though the players are perhaps forwardly placed. The accompaniments are alert and fresh. Kanta plays contemporary cadenzas. This record is a genuine bargain.

The attractions of Harrell's coupling are enhanced by the inclusion of two Vivaldi concertos interspersed with Haydn (although the recorded sound is strikingly different). Harrell, rather after the manner of Rostropovich, seeks to turn these elegant concertos into big, virtuoso pieces, helped by Marriner's beautifully played accompaniments. Although touches of romantic expressiveness tend to intrude, the result is enjoyable, even if cadenzas are distractingly long. The digital recording is full and vivid (the analogue Vivaldi transfers are brighter and less smooth).

With Barbirolli to partner her, Jacqueline du Pré's performance of the best-known *D major Concerto* is warmly expressive. The conviction and flair of the playing are extraordinarily compelling, and the romantic feeling is matched by an attractively full, well-balanced recording.

(i) *Cello concerto in C, Hob VIIb/1;* (ii; iv) *Horn concertos Nos. 1–2;* (iii; iv) *Trumpet concerto in D.*
(M) *** Decca 430 633-2 [id.]. (i) Rostropovich, ECO, Britten; (ii) Tuckwell; (iii) Alan Stringer; (iv)
   ASMF, Marriner.

Rostropovich's earlier (1964) stereo recording of the *C major Cello concerto* for Decca is undoubtedly romantic, and some may feel he takes too many liberties in the slow movement. The coupling of first-class 1966 versions of both the *Horn concertos* by Tuckwell in peak form and Stringer's 1967 account of the *Trumpet concerto* is certainly tempting.

(i) *Cello concertos: in C, Hob VIIb/1; in D, Hob VIIb/2;* (ii) *Violin concertos: in C; in A; in G, Hob VIIa/1,
3 & 4;* (ii; iii) *Double concerto for violin and harpsichord in F, Hob XVIII/6.*
(B) *** Ph. Duo 438 797-2 (2) [id.]. ECO with (i) Walevska, De Waart; (ii) Accardo; (iii) Canino.

The three *Violin concertos* are all early; the *C major*, written for Tomasini, is probably the best. The other two have come into the limelight fairly recently. Accardo plays with great elegance and charm, but it would be idle to pretend that this is great music. The same goes for the *Double Concerto for violin and harpsichord*, which is of relatively slender musical interest. The soloists are perhaps a shade forward but the quality and balance are lifelike, and the 1980 recording has been well transferred. The two *Cello concertos* are, of course, much better known; Christine Walevska presents them freshly and she is well partnered by Edo de Waart and the ECO. She has a fairly small solo image and is balanced almost within the orchestra; the effect is to give a chamber-like quality to the music-making which is very agreeable, for the solo playing is not lacking in personality.

Harpsichord concerto in D, Hob XVIII/2; Overture in D, Hob Ia/7.

(M) *** Decca 440 033-2 [id.]. George Malcolm, ASMF, Marriner – ARNE: *Harpsichord concerto No. 5* etc.; C. P. E. BACH: *Harpsichord concerto;* J. C. BACH: *Harpsichord concerto.* ***

This Haydn *D major Concerto* is justly well known and has never sounded better on record. It is expertly played by George Malcolm and the ASMF, both on top form, while the recording is exemplary in both tone-quality and balance. The *Overture* is an alternative finale (version B) to the *Symphony No. 53 in D* (*L'Impériale*) and is a light-hearted piece, dating from the mid-1770s. The couplings will also give much musical satisfaction, particularly given such persuasive advocacy as they are here by these artists.

(i) *Harpsichord concertos: in F, Hob XVIII/3; in G, Hob XVIII/4; in D, Hob XVIII/11;* (i; ii) *Double concerto in F for harpsichord and violin, Hob XVIII/6;* (iii) *Concertini: in C, Hob XIV/3; in C, Hob XIV/ 11; in C, Hob XIV/12; Concertino (Divertimento) in G, Hob XIV/13; Concertino in F, Hob XIV/F2; Divertimenti in C, Hob XIV/4; in C, Hob XIV/7; in C, Hob XIV/8; in F, Hob XIV/9; in C, Hob XIV/C2.*

(N) (B) *** Ph. Duo 446 542-2 (2) [id.]. Ton Koopman; (i) Amsterdam Musica Antiqua or Amsterdam Bar. O; (ii) with Huggett; (iii) Goebel, Stuurop, Medlam.

Ton Koopman's admirable Philips Duo set covers the 14 concertante Haydn keyboard works listed in the Hoboken catalogue now thought to be authentic. (He has recorded the *Organ concertos*, Hob XVIII/ 1, 2, 7, 7, 8 and 10 separately, and no doubt these will reappear during the lifetime of this book.) The present coverage includes the ten small concertos from the 1760s called either *Divertimenti* or *Concertini* which are of little real substance but which still make attractive, undemanding listening. Here the accompanying group is made up of Reinhard Goebel and Alda Stuurop (violins) and Charles Medlam (cello), all playing on period instruments. The four longer concertos, including the rightly famous *D major* (scored for oboes and horns) and the *Double concerto for violin, keyboard and strings*, Hob XVIII/ 6, use a larger accompanying group, which Koopman directs from the keyboard, although it is not clear from the documentation which of the two orchestras is playing in which concerto. As sound, these recordings could hardly be bettered: the balance is finely judged and the acoustic warm, with the performers not on top of the listener. Yet detail registers perfectly. The performances themselves are thoroughly alive and highly accomplished. Though occasionally Koopman might have allowed the music to unfold at a more leisurely pace, no reservations need diminish the strongest recommendation (especially bearing in mind the modest cost), save for the warning that this is not the best Haydn.

Horn concerto No. 1 in D, Hob VIId/3.

(M) *** Decca 417 767-2 [id.]. Barry Tuckwell, ASMF, Marriner – MOZART: *Concertos Nos. 1–4.* ***

Tuckwell's playing throughout is of the highest order, and Marriner's vintage accompaniments are equally polished and full of elegance and vitality. The remastering is admirably fresh.

Horn concertos Nos. 1 in D, Hob VIId3; 2 in D, Hob VIId4.

(M) *** Teldec/Warner Dig. 9031 74790-2 [id.]. Dale Clevenger, Liszt CO, Rolla – M. HAYDN: *Concertino.* ***

Dale Clevenger, principal horn with the Chicago Symphony, gives superb accounts of the two *Horn concertos* attributed to Haydn (the second is of doubtful lineage). The accompaniments are supportive, polished and elegant. The Telefunken recording, made in a nicely judged and warm acoustic, is in the demonstration class.

(i) *Horn concertos Nos. 1–2;* (ii) *Trumpet concerto in E flat;* (i) *Divertimento a 3 in E flat.*

**(*) Nimbus NI 5010 [id.]. (i) Thompson; (ii) Wallace; Philh. O, Warren-Green.

Michael Thompson gives bold, confident accounts of the two *Horn concertos*, with a sprinkling of decoration. John Wallace's trumpet timbre is strikingly brilliant, as recorded, and his playing in the *Trumpet concerto* is full of personality. He too likes to decorate and there are some attractive surprises in the finale. The recording was made in the resonant ambience of All Saints', Tooting.

3 Organ concertos in C, Hob. XVIII/1, 5 & 10.

(B) *** Erato/Warner 4509 94581-2 [id.]. Marie-Claire Alain, Bournemouth Sinf., Guschlbauer – C. P. E. BACH: *Organ concerto, Wq. 34.* **(*)

Marie-Claire Alain offers the three best-known *C major Organ concertos*. They are agreeably lively and inventive, and the baroque orchestration with trumpets adds plenty of extra colour. It is difficult to imagine them being presented more effectively than they are on this Erato reissue from the late 1970s. Marie-Claire Alain's registration is admirable; both solo-playing and accompaniments are alert and sparkling. The sound is fresh and bright: the CD's treble gains from very slight paring back. An enjoyable C. P. E. Bach concerto is offered as a bonus on this bargain-priced Bonsai reissue.

Piano concertos: in F, Hob XVIII/3; in G, Hob XVIII/4; in C, Hob XVIII/5; in F, Hob XVIII/7; in G, Hob XVIII/9; in C, Hob XVIII/10; in D, Hob XVIII/11; in F, Hob XVIII/F2; in C, Hob XIV/12; in G, Hob XIV/13; Divertimenti in C (for piano and strings), *Hob XIV/C2 & XIV/4.*
(N) (B) ** Teldec/Warner 4509 97973-2 (2). Philippe Entremont, VCO.

More than half the concertos here are almost certainly spurious, and the music is pretty thin. Among the authentic concertos, the famous *D major*, Hob XVIII/11, readily stands out and is given a lively, robust account by Entremont and the Vienna Chamber Orchestra. He makes no attempt to emulate period manners, but the playing is bold and unsentimental and the articulation crisp. The recording is good, if rather forward. But the rest of his programmme is less appealing, and in any case the Philips Koopman set is of an entirely different calibre.

Piano concertos: in F, Hob. XVIII/3; in G, Hob. XVIII/4; in D, Hob. XVIII/11.
*** Sony Dig. SK 48383 [id.]. Emanuel Ax, Franz Liszt CO.
(B) **(*) Erato/Warner Dig 4509 94580-2 [id.]. Michèle Boegner, ECO, Garcia.

The popular *D major Concerto* comes with the *F major*, from Haydn's first years at Esterháza, and the *G major*, which is somewhat later but still written with the harpsichord in mind. Emanuel Ax gives them on the modern grand piano and he does so with great elegance and finesse. He evidently enjoys a good rapport with the Franz Liszt Chamber Orchestra, who respond warmly to his direction, and throughout all three concertos the music sounds fresh and sparkling. The quality of the recording is outstanding; the piano sounds particularly real and lifelike, and the balance, too, is well struck. This could well serve as the staple recommendation in this repertoire, given its artistic and technical excellence.

The performances by Michèle Boegner and the ECO under José–Luis Garcia are also enjoyable and offer both modern (1991) digital recording and a very reasonable price. The accounts of the *F major* and *G major Concertos* are fluent and musical, but the best-known *D major* (much the finest work) springs vividly and refreshingly to life and is alone worth the price of the disc. Outer movements sparkle and the slow movement is agreeably warm and expressive. The sound is excellent.

Trumpet concerto in E flat.
🏵 *** Ph. Dig. 420 203-2 [id.]. Håkan Hardenberger, ASMF, Marriner – HERTEL ***; HUMMEL *** 🏵; STAMITZ: *Concertos.* ***
*** Sony CD 37846 [id.]. Marsalis, Nat. PO, Leppard – HUMMEL: *Concerto* *** (with L. MOZART: *Concerto* ***).
(B) *** CfP Dig CD-CFP 4589. Ian Balmain, RLPO, Kovacevich – MOZART: *Horn concertos.* ***

Hardenberger's playing of the noble line of the *Andante* is no less telling than his fireworks in the finale and, with Marriner providing warm, elegant and polished accompaniments throughout, this is probably the finest single collection of trumpet concertos in the present catalogue.

Marsalis is splendid too, his bravura no less spectacular, with the finale a tour de force, yet never aggressive in its brilliance. His way with Haydn is eminently stylish, as is Leppard's lively and polished accompaniment.

With Stephen Kovacevich as conductor, Ian Balmain favours extreme speeds for Haydn's delectable *Trumpet concerto*, playing brilliantly. It makes an apt and attractive coupling for Claire Briggs's fine recordings of all four Mozart *Horn concertos*, very well recorded.

Violin concerto in C, Hob VIIa/1.
(M) *** Teldec/Warner Dig. 9031 74784-2 [id.]. Zehetmair, Liszt CO – M. HAYDN: *Concerto* **(*); SIBELIUS: *Concerto.* **

Haydn's *C major Violin concerto* is given a superb performance by the young Hungarian violinist, Thomas Zehetmair, stylish, strong and resilient. He also directs the accompaniments, which are alert and spirited in outer movements and responsive in the lovely *Adagio*.

24 Minuets, Hob IX/16.
(M) *** Decca 436 220-2 [id.]. Philh. Hungarica, Antal Dorati.

This collection of 24 *Minuets*, amazingly varied and imaginative, was written late in Haydn's career and, though few of them have the symphonic overtones of the minuets in the late symphonies, they represent the composer at his most inspired. It is not recommended to play them all at one sitting, but the set certainly adds point to Haydn's own definition of a good composer as 'one who can write a brand new minuet'. Dorati's performances are characteristically genial, and the excellent (1975) recording is transferred freshly and crisply, yet with plenty of weight in the orchestral sound.

The Seven Last Words of Christ on the Cross (original orchestral version).
(M) ** Van. 08. 2034.71 I Solisti di Zagreb, Antonio Janigro.

It is good to have the orchestral version of Haydn's great sequence of slow movements on disc and it is played eloquently enough by Janigro and his Zagreb group and given full, realistic, late-1960s recording. However, this performance fails to move the listener as do the finest of the string quartet versions – see below.

Sinfonia concertante in B flat for violin, cello, oboe, bassoon and orchestra, Hob I/105.
(Y/B) (BB) **(*) ASV Dig CDQS 6140 [id.]. Frieman, Pople, Anderson, Gambold, L. Festival O, Ross
    Pople – STAMITZ: *Sinfonias concertantes.* **(*)

Directing the players from the solo cello, Ross Pople draws a strong and alert rather than an elegant performance from his London Festival Orchestra, well recorded in bright, firmly focused sound. Though the solo playing is not always ideally refined, there is a winning sense of musicians acting out a drama, at speeds that are comfortable, never exaggerated. The coupling of *Sinfonias concertantes* by Stamitz is very apt and attractive.

SYMPHONIES

Symphonies Nos. 1–104; A; B.
(N)✿ (B) *** Decca 448 531-2 (33) [id.]. Philharmonia Hungarica, Antal Dorati.

Antal Dorati was ahead of his time as a Haydn interpreter when, in the early 1970s, he made his pioneering recording of the complete Haydn symphonies. Superbly transferred to CD in full, bright and immediate sound, the performances are a consistent delight, with brisk allegros and fast-flowing *Andantes*, with textures remarkably clean. The slow, rustic-sounding accounts of Minuets are more controversial, but the rhythmic bounce makes them very attractive too. The discs are packaged simply in a box, and that brings economy in storage space too! Certainly this set is a bargain if ever there was one.

*Symphonies Nos. 1 in D min.; 2 in C; 4 in D; 5 in A; 10 in D; 11 in E flat; 18 in G; 27 in G; 32 in C; 37 in C;
Symphony A (Partita) in B flat.*
**(*) O-L Dig. 436 428-2 (3). AAM, Hogwood.

*Symphonies Nos. 3 in G; 14 in A; 15 in D; 17 in F; 19 in D; 20 in C; 25 in C; 33 in C; 36 in E flat; 108
(Partita) in B flat.*
**(*) O-L Dig. 436 592-2 (3) [id.]. AAM, Hogwood.

*Symphonies Nos. 6 in D (Le Matin); 7 in C (Le Midi); 8 in G (Le Soir); 9 in C; 12 in E; 13 in D; 16 in B
flat; 40 in F; 72 in D.*
**(*) O-L Dig. 433 661-2 [id.]. AAM, Hogwood.

*Symphonies Nos. 21 in A; 22 in E flat (Philosopher); 23 in G; 24 in D; 28 in A; 29 in E; 30 in C
(Allelujah); 31 in D (Horn signal); 34 in D min.*
**(*) O-L Dig. 430 082-2 (3) [id.]. AAM, Hogwood.

*Symphonies Nos. 26 in D; 42 in D; 43 in E flat (Mercury); 44 in E min. (Trauer); 48 in C (Maria
Theresia); 49 in F min. (La Passione).*
**(*) O-L Dig. 440 222-2 (3) [id.]. AAM, Hogwood.

Symphonies Nos. 35 in B flat; 38 in C; 39 in G min.; 41 in C; 58 in F; 59 in A (Fire); 65 in A.
**(*) O-L Dig. 433 012-2 (3) [id.]. AAM, Hogwood.

Symphonies Nos. 45 in F sharp min.; 46 in B; 47 in G; 51 in B flat; 52 in C min.; 64 in A.
(N) *** O-L Dig. 443 777-2 (3) [id.]. AAM, Hogwood.

In his Haydn series Hogwood has mellowed in period-performance manners, compared with his pioneering set of the Mozart *Symphonies.* The playing, too, is now more polished. He uses a small group of strings (about half the size of that chosen by Tafelmusik, who have the benefit of H. C. Robbins Landon's advice in this matter). In particular he avoids abrasiveness in slow movements which, though much leaner than with modern instruments, are sympathetically phrased though sometimes a little stiff. In general his direct, crisply rhythmic approach to these works tends not to convey the charm of Haydn. Even so he offers all repeats! No harpsichord continuo is employed, as in the Goodman project. The finely detailed, firmly focused recording perfectly brings out the transparency of textures, while giving body to the sound. If you are a Hogwood aficionado, these boxes can be acquired with confidence, particularly the most recent collection, appropriately subtitled 'Climax of the *Sturm und Drang*'.

Symphonies Nos. 1 in D; 2 in C; 3 in G; 4 in D; 5 in A.
*** Hyperion Dig. CDA 66524 [id.]. Hanover Band, Roy Goodman.

Symphonies Nos. 6 in D (Le Matin); 7 in C (Le Midi); 8 in G (Le Soir).
*** Hyperion Dig. CDA 66523 [id.]. Hanover Band, Roy Goodman.

Symphonies Nos. 9 in C; 10 in D; 11 in E flat; 12 in E.
*** Hyperion Dig. CDA 66529 [id.]. Hanover Band, Goodman.

Symphonies Nos. 13 in D; 14 in A; 15 in D; 16 in B flat.
*** Hyperion Dig. CDA 66534 [id.]. Hanover Band, Goodman.

Symphonies Nos. 17 in F; 18 in G; 19 in D; 20 in C; 21 in A.
*** Hyperion Dig. CDA 66533 [id.]. Hanover Band, Goodman.

Symphonies Nos. 22 in E flat (Philosopher); 23 in G; 24 in D; 25 in C.
(Y/B) *** Hyperion Dig. CDA 66536 [id.]. Hanover Band, Goodman.

Symphonies Nos. 42 in D; 43 in E flat (Mercury); 44 in E min. (Trauer).
**(*) Hyperion Dig. CDA 66530 [id.]. Hanover Band, Goodman.

Symphonies Nos. 45 in F sharp min. (Farewell); 46 in B; 47 in G.
**(*) Hyperion Dig. CDA 66522 [id.]. Hanover Band, Goodman.

Symphonies Nos. 48 in C (Maria Theresia); 49 in F min. (Passione); 50 in C.
**(*) Hyperion Dig. CDA 66531 [id.]. Hanover Band, Goodman.

Symphonies Nos. 70 in D, 71 in B flat, 72 in D.
*** Hyperion Dig. CDA 66526 [id.]. Hanover Band, Roy Goodman.

Symphonies Nos. 73 in D (La chasse), 74 in E flat , 75 in D.
*** Hyperion Dig. CDA 66520 [id.]. Hanover Band, Roy Goodman.

Symphonies Nos. 76 in E flat; 77 in B flat; 78 in C min.
*** Hyperion Dig. CDA 66525 [id.]. Hanover Band, Roy Goodman.

Symphonies Nos. 82 in C (The Bear); 83 in G min. (The Hen); 84 in E flat.
*** Hyperion Dig. CDA 66527; KA 66527 [id.]. Hanover Band, Goodman.

Symphonies Nos. 90 in C; 91 in E flat; 92 in G (Oxford).
*** Hyperion Dig. CDA 66521; KA 66521 [id.]. Hanover Band, Goodman.

Symphonies Nos. 93 in D; 94 in G (Surprise); 95 in C min.
*** Hyperion Dig. CDA 66532 [id.]. Hanover Band, Goodman.

Symphonies Nos. 101 in D (Clock); 102 in B flat; Overture: Windsor Castle.
*** Hyperion Dig. CDA 66528 [id.]. Hanover Band, Goodman.

From the very outset of his Hyperion project, Goodman, who began at the beginning with the low-numbered symphonies, established a winning manner in early Haydn and, as the series progressed, he showed that his dramatic approach (tougher than Kuijken, for instance, in his COE recordings for Virgin) was being fruitful in the middle-period and later works. The performances offer consistently alert and well-sprung readings, which generally favour fast Allegros and relatively spacious slow movements which, more than in most period performances, give expressive warmth to Haydn's melodies, without overstepping the mark into romanticism. That Goodman is very much the positive director of the group is brought out by the generally close balance given to the harpsichord continuo, which is far more audible than in most versions. The recording is resonant, giving bloom to the strings, yet oboes and horns (and other wind and brass, when used) come through vividly. Altogether, this Hyperion series is achieving a balance of style somewhere between the more plangent Hogwood approach and the fuller scale possible with Dorati, using modern instruments.

Symphonies Nos. 1–20.
(N) (M) **(*) Nimbus Dig. NI 5426/30 [id.]. Austro-Hungarian Haydn O, Adám Fischer.

The Nimbus project of recording all the Haydn symphonies on modern instruments in the Haydnsaal of the Esterházy Palace brings playing which is fresh yet warm, with the considerable reverberation adding to the weight and scale of the earlier symphonies, in a manner that some ears will relish but others will find too opulent. In the accompanying notes the conductor, Adám Fischer, comments that the chosen orchestra, which is made up of players from Vienna and Budapest, carries forward the tradition of

Austro-Hungarian music-making. The playing itself is warm and elegant, and again and again in these early symphonies the ear enjoys the finesse of this music-making and its ripeness of texture, with the rich-toned Viennese horns soaring out over the strings when given an opportunity to do so. The woodwind are sprightly and offer plenty of colour, and in Nos. 6–8 the various orchestral solos are taken with distinction. The conductor's speeds are moderate. Slow movements are gracious and phrasing is cultivated; minuets are courtly and finales lively and resilient, without being rushed. The sound itself is rich in ambience and easy to enjoy, for it does not cloud.

Symphonies Nos. 82 in C (The Bear); 83 in G min. (The Hen); 84 in E flat; 85 in B flat (La Reine); 86 in D; 87 in A (Paris Symphonies).
(N) (M) **(*) Nimbus Dig. NI 5419/20 [id.]. Austro-Hungarian Haydn O, Adám Fischer.

The expansive sound of the Austro-Hungarian Orchestra suits the *Paris Symphonies*. *La Poule* and *La Reine* (with its rhythmically powerful opening movement) both show Fischer and his players at their best, and finest of all is one of the least known, *Symphony No. 84 in E flat* with another remarkably original first movement. Slow movements are warm and poised: the *Largo* of No. 86 is particularly successful, as is the light-hearted trio of its Minuet, with a vigorous finale, lightly articulated, to cap the work off. The sound is always satisfyingly full-bodied, with the violins resonantly rich. The weighty bass is not always absolutely clean, but generally the effect is very believable.

Symphonies Nos. 88 in G; 89 in F; 90 in C; 91 in E flat; 92 in G (Oxford); Sinfonia concertante in B flat for violin, cello, oboe, bassoon and orchestra.
(N) (M) ** Nimbus Dig. NI 5417/8 [id.]. Austro-Hungarian Haydn O, Adám Fischer.

When so much trouble has been taken to record this specially assembled orchestra in the authentic venue of the old Haydnsaal in the Esterházy Palace, it is surprising that in style Fischer's are such old-fashioned readings, apparently little influenced by the example of period performances. As with the other issues in this Nimbus series the recording is full and pleasing, but the warm resonance prevents sharpness of detail and also has the effect of blunting the string articulation. Too often one feels the need for more bite in allegros. Tempi are almost always very relaxed, so that the famous slow movement of No. 88 in G, warmly expressive as it is, very nearly drags, although Fischer brings off the *Adagio* of the *Oxford symphony* beautifully. Throughout Minuets are very stately indeed but finales dance gracefully and opening Adagios are warmly expressive; yet in the end there is an absence of conveyed exhilaration. The *Sinfonia concertante* included on the second disc is a particularly pleasing performance, with most sympathetic solo playing.

Symphonies Nos. 93–104.
(M) **(*) Nimbus Dig. NI 5200/4 [id.]. Austro-Hungarian Haydn O, Adám Fischer.

With three symphonies apiece on the first two discs of the five-disc Nimbus set, Fischer's cycle of all twelve *London symphonies* makes a neat and attractive package, with consistently fresh, resilient and refined performances. Though these works were first given in the intimate surroundings of the Hanover Square Rooms in London, they were very quickly heard in this much grander setting, and the performances reflect the fact, with broad speeds made weightier by the reverberant Nimbus recording, so that in sound the tuttis relate rather to a Karajan or Bernstein performance than to one by a regular chamber orchestra. Only in lightly scored passages does one register the true scale of the orchestra, and such a movement as the lovely *Adagio* of No. 102 with its soaring melody is given added beauty by the ambience and slow speed. The set can be warmly recommended to most who resist period performance when, even at broad speeds, rhythms are light and resilient. Never sounding breathless, Fischer's Haydn consistently brings out the happiness of the inspiration. The first-movement allegro of No. 93 gets the cycle off to a delectable start, with the three-in-a-bar rhythms given a delicious lift. Not everyone will like the reverberance of the Nimbus recording, but these are very much performances to relax with.

Other miscellaneous symphonies

Symphonies Nos. 6 in D (Le Matin); 7 in C (Le Midi); 8 in G (Le Soir).
*** DG Dig. 423 098-2 [id.]. E. Concert, Pinnock.
(BB) *** Naxos Dig. 8.550722 [id.]. N. CO, Ward.

These were almost certainly the first works that Haydn composed on taking up his appointment as Kapellmeister to the Esterházys. Pinnock's performances are polished and refined, yet highly spirited, with infectious allegros and expressive feeling. There is certainly weight here, yet essentially this is a bracing musical experience with the genius of these early works fully displayed.

    A splendid début in these early symphonies from the Northern Chamber Orchestra under Nicholas Ward. Throughout these works the wind players obviously relish their solos, the flute chirps merrily and the bassoon immediately has a chance to shine in the Trio of the Minuet of No. 6; even the double bass has a solo in the comparable movement of No. 7. In the *Andante* of *Le Soir* the strings create a chamber-music atmosphere, and it is the intimate scale of these performances that is so attractive. Modern instruments are used, but textures are fresh and the ambience of the Concert Hall of New Broadcasting House, Manchester, adds the right degree of warmth.

Symphonies Nos. 22 in E flat (Philosopher); 63 in C (La Roxelane); 80 in D min.
*** DG Dig. 427 337-2 [id.]. Orpheus CO.

The Orpheus players give all three symphonies with that sense of style, polish and intelligent commitment we have come to expect from them. Pacing, suppleness of phrase and precision of ensemble again demonstrate that for them a conductor isn't necessary, and the DG sound is first class.

Symphonies Nos. 22 in E flat (Philosopher); 86 in D; 102 in B flat.
(N) *** EMI Dig. CDC5 55509-2 [id.]. CBSO, Sir Simon Rattle.

More than any other Haydn symphony recordings on modern instruments, this triptych establishes a middle path between traditional and period styles of performance. So well has Rattle trained his Birmingham players that you could even mistake them for the Orchestra of the Age of Enlightenment. It is also refreshing to have a coupling of symphonies from different periods of Haydn's career. One of the most striking of the early works, the *Philosopher*, with its trudging chorale on two cor anglais, comes with one of the *Paris Symphonies*, No. 86, and one of the final *London* set. If only No. 102 had a nickname, it would be even more widely appreciated as a supreme masterpiece with its exhilarating outer movements and the most beautiful of all Haydn slow movements. Rattle's speeds are on the fast side but not extreme, though justly he treats the Minuet of No. 102 as a nimble one-in-a-bar Scherzo. Only in the final *Presto* of No. 86 does Rattle opt for a hectic speed, making one marvel at the agility of the Birmingham horns in repeated triplets.

Symphonies Nos. 23 in G; 24 in D; 61 in D.
(Y/B) (BB) *** Naxos Dig. 8.550723 [id.]. N. CO, Nicholas Ward.

The fresh, stylish approach of the Northern Chamber Orchestra seems entirely suited to these three symphonies, and here Nicholas Ward makes a persuasive case for the use of modern instruments. No. 24 includes a leading semi-concertante flute part (nicely managed) and the *G major* has a wistful *Andante* for strings alone, and a vital *Presto* finale, well sprinkled with strongly accented quadruplets. The opening movement of No. 61 is obviously more mature and is presented with both character and charm. Excellent recording.

Symphonies Nos. 26 in D min. (Lamentatione); 35 in B flat; 49 in F min. (La Passione).
(BB) **(*) Naxos Dig. 8.550721 [id.]. N. CO, Ward.

Although enjoyable, the follow-up disc from Nicholas Ward and his Northern Chamber Orchestra is not quite as fresh-sounding as the first. The playing remains elegant and the horns (in B flat alto) are splendid in the Minuet of No. 35. But the opening *Allegro assai con spirito* of the *Lamentatione* could do with a shade more bite, and in the *Adagio* the warm resonance makes the finely played oboe solo almost a cor anglais and the melodic line like a Handel aria. The opening slow movement of No. 49 is not as intense as it might be, though the *Allegro di molto* which follows has plenty of energy, as does the finale, while the horns shine again in the Trio of the Minuet. The resonance of the BBC's Studio 7 in Manchester brings a pleasingly mellow sound-picture, but the string detail is not sharply defined.

Symphonies Nos. 26 (Lamentatione), 35, 38–9, 41–2, 43 (Mercury), 44 (Trauer), 45 (Farewell), 46–7, 48 (Maria Theresia), 49 (La passione), 50–52, 58, 59 (Fire), 65.
(M) *** DG Dig. 435 001-2 (6). E. Concert, Trevor Pinnock.

Pinnock's forces are modest (with 6.5.2.2.1 strings), but the panache of the playing conveys any necessary grandeur. It is a new experience to have Haydn symphonies of this period recorded in relatively dry and close sound, with inner detail crystal clear (harpsichord never obscured) and made the more dramatic by the intimate sense of presence, yet with a fine bloom on the instruments. Some may find a certain lack of charm at times, and others may quarrel with the very brisk one-in-a-bar minuets and – dare one say it! – even find finales a bit rushed.

Symphonies Nos. 26 in D min. (Lamentatione); 48 in C (Maria Theresia); 49 in F min. (La Passione).
(N) (M) *** Sony SMK 66929 [id.]. L'Estro Armonico, Derek Solomons.

The Haydn series by Derek Solomons and L'Estro Armonico remains incomplete, but these stimulating performances of three of the finest *Sturm und Drang* symphonies are most welcome back to the catalogue at mid-price. Recorded in the pleasingly atmospheric acoustic of St Barnabas Church, Woodside

Park, the sense of lively, intimate music-making is most appealing. Solomons keeps his ensemble of period instruments very small, with six violins, but only one each of the other stringed instruments, a scale Haydn himself employed at Esterháza. The ensemble is not always as polished as in some authentic performances, but for the general listener the important point is that Solomons has modified his earlier approach to slow movements, which no longer have the squeezing, bulging style sometimes favoured by the authentic movement. Special mention must be made of the horn playing of Anthony Halstead, especially in the *Adagio* of No. 48, which is hauntingly beautiful. The invigorating opening movement of that same work, bursting with exuberance, brings thrilling sound, and the Minuet is no less impressive. No. 49, too, is a very strong performance, and there is no hint of routine in the playing in all three symphonies.

Symphonies Nos. 26 in D min. (Lamentatione); 52 in C min.; 53 in D (L'Impériale).
(N) (M) *** Virgin Veritas/EMI Dig. VER5 61212-2 [id.]. La Petite Bande, Sigiswald Kuijken.

These are fresh, vital, cleanly articulated performances which wear their authenticity lightly and even indulge in speeds for slow movements that are more expansive and affectionate than many purists would allow.

Symphonies Nos. 30 in C (Alleluja); 45 in F sharp min. (Farewell); 73 in D (La Chasse).
(N) (M) ** Teldec/Warner Dig. 0630 10016-2 [id.]. VCM, Harnoncourt.

Harnoncourt's robust style is invigorating, yet it misses most of the charm of the *Andante* of the *Alleluja Symphony*, while in the *Farewell Symphony* his refined delicacy in the *Adagio* seems coolly uninvolved and, as he is generous with repeats throughout, this stretches to over 12 minutes. Then the Minuet is taken at a brisk one-in-a-bar and will seem very rushed to most listeners, although Harnoncourt slows down for the Trio. The finale is effective enough without being memorable.

Symphonies Nos. 30 in C (Alleluja); 55 in E flat (Schoolmaster); 63 in C (La Roxelane).
(Y/B) (BB) *** Naxos Dig. 8.550757 [id.]. Northern CO, Nicholas Ward.

An entirely winning triptych of named Haydn symphonies, spanning a highly creative period from the three-movement *Alleluja* (1765), with its delightful woodwind contribution in the *Andante*, to *La Roxelane* (1780), where the *Allegretto* paints an engaging portrait of a flirtatious character in a play and the finale fizzes with energy. In between comes *The Schoolmaster*, whose Adagio brings a theme and variations of disarming simplicity. Alert and vivacious playing from all concerned; admirable pacing and first-class sound ensure a welcome for a disc that would be just as recommendable if it cost far more.

Symphonies Nos. 31 in D (Horn signal); 59 in A (Fire); 73 in D (La chasse).
(Y/B) *** Teldec/Warner Dig. 4509 90843-2 [id.]. VCM, Nikolaus Harnoncourt.

This is one of Harnoncourt's very best records. All three symphonies are notable for their spectacular horn parts. The playing here – using natural horns – is superb, with throatily exuberant braying at the opening of the *Horn signal*, an equally striking contribution throughout the *Fire Symphony* (where the horns are crooked in A), and more cheerful hunting-calls in the spirited finale of *La chasse*. In *No. 31 in D*, besides the four important horn parts there are extended solos for violin and cello in the outer movements. The playing is not only extremely vital and polished but even has an element of charm (not something one can always count on from this source). The orchestra communicate their involvement throughout. Few period records of Haydn symphonies are more invigoratingly enjoyable than this, and the recording is splendid.

Symphonies Nos. 41 in C; 42 in D; 43 in E flat (Mercury).
*** Sony Dig. SK 48370 [id.]. Tafelmusik, Weil.

Symphonies Nos. 44 in E min. (Trauer); 51 in F sharp min.; 52 in C min.
*** Sony Dig. SK 48371 [id.]. Tafelmusik, Weil.

Symphonies Nos. 45 in F sharp min. (Farewell); 46 in B; 47 in G.
*** Sony Dig. SK 53986 [id.]. Tafelmusik, Weil.

Symphonies Nos. 50 in C; 64 in A; 65 in A.
*** Sony Dig. SK 53985 [id.]. Tafelmusik, Weil.

This new series from Sony is produced with the estimable H. C. Robbins Landon as musicological and artistic consultant, and he has expressed personal pleasure with the results. In short these recordings set new standards in this repertoire. The size of the group seems just about ideal with 20 strings, 7.6.3.2.2, against which oboes and horns and sometimes trumpets are vividly balanced. There is no harpsichord continuo. All four of these records are a great success and if you want these symphonies performed on period instruments this is the way to play them. Bruno Weil's tempi are apt and Tafelmusik is sensitive to details of phrasing and dynamics and they obviously love Haydn. The effect is admirably spontaneous. The group are very well recorded, too. The sound is full yet admirably transparent. The notes are exemplary and, although competing authentic performances offer different insights, the present series is surpassed by none of them.

Symphonies Nos. 42 in D; 45 in F sharp min. (Farewell); 46 in B.
(Y/B) (M) *** DG 447 281-2 [id.]. E. Concert, Pinnock.

Haydn's famous *Farewell Symphony*, given a vibrant and characterful performance with a very beautiful slow movement, is here coupled with two apparently straightforward but still forward-looking works, No. 42 with its memorably solemn *Andantino e cantabile* and *No. 46 in B major*. Here the ethereal 6/8 *Poco Adagio* contrasts with an invigorating scherzando finale where the high horns (crooked in B alto) produce repeated bursts of hair-raising virtuosity. And Haydn has a characteristic trick up his sleeve for, just before the end, the Minuet returns, only to be swept away by a final rally from the horns.

Symphony No. 44 in E min. (Trauer).
(M) *** Carlton Dig. PCD 820 [id.]. O of St John's, Smith Square, Lubbock – MOZART: *Symphony No. 40.* **(*)

The Orchestra of St John's are on their toes throughout their splendidly committed account of the *Trauersinfonie*. The recording too is in the demonstration class.

Symphonies Nos. 44 in E min. (Trauer); 88 in G; 104 in D (London).
(BB) *** Naxos Dig. 8.550287; *4550287* [id.]. Capella Istropolitana, Barry Wordsworth.

Symphonies Nos. 45 in F sharp min. (Farewell); 48 in C (Maria Theresia); 102 in B flat.
(BB) *** Naxos Dig. 8.550382; *4550382* [id.]. Capella Istropolitana, Barry Wordsworth.

Symphonies Nos. 82 in C (The Bear); 96 in D (Miracle); 100 in G (Military).
(BB) *** Naxos Dig. 8.550139; *4550139* [id.]. Capella Istropolitana, Barry Wordsworth.

Symphonies Nos. 83 in G min. (The Hen); 94 in G (Surprise); 101 in D (The Clock).
(BB) *** Naxos Dig. 8.550114; *4550114* [id.]. Capella Istropolitana, Barry Wordsworth.

Symphonies Nos. 85 in B flat (La Reine); 92 in G (Oxford); 103 in E flat (Drum roll).
(BB) *** Naxos Dig. 8.550387 [id.]. Capella Istropolitana, Barry Wordsworth.

Like Barry Wordsworth's recordings of Mozart symphonies, also with the Capella Istropolitana on the Naxos label, this Haydn collection provides a series of outstanding bargains at the lowest budget price. The sound is not quite as clean and immediate as in the Mozart series, a little boomy at times in fact, and Wordsworth's preference for relatively relaxed speeds is a little more marked here than in Mozart, but the varied choice of works on each disc is most attractive. At their modest cost, these are well worth collecting.

Symphonies Nos. (i) 45 in F sharp min. (Farewell); (ii) 88 in G; (iii) 104 in D (London).
(B) *** DG 439 428-2 [id.]. (i) ECO, Barenboim; (ii) VPO, Boehm; (iii) LPO, Jochum.

A highly stimulating triptych of Haydn performances by three different conductors, all of whom have something positive to say about this repertoire. Barenboim's *Farewell Symphony* has much vitality and there is sensitive playing in the remarkable *Adagio*, one of Haydn's finest. Boehm and the VPO are at their very best in No. 88, with the slow movement gravely expansive. The playing has great polish and refinement, and Boehm's touch instantly charms in the spirited finale. Jochum's is among the most musically satisfying accounts of No. 104 in the catalogue; and all three recordings (from the 1970s) sound first class in their remastered form. A genuine bargain, playing for 77 minutes.

Symphonies Nos. 53 in D (L'Impériale); 73 in D (La Chasse); 79 in F.
*** DG Dig. 439 779-2 [id.]. Orpheus CO.

The Orpheus Chamber Orchestra turn in performances of liveliness, sensitivity and intelligence. For those who do not want period-instrument forces, they prove a consistently reliable alternative and, despite the absence of a conductor, there is no want of personality about their readings. They are also recorded with exemplary clarity, with a comfortable halo of reverberance that lends freshness and bloom to the sound. All three symphonies are thoroughly enjoyable, and we hope the earlier issues, which were originally issued uneconomically with only two symphonies per CD, will now reappear, more generously presented.

Symphonies Nos. 69 in C (Laudon); 89 in F; 91 in E flat.
(M) **(*) Naxos Dig. 8.550769 [id.]. Budapest Nicolaus Esterházy Sinfonia, Béla Drahos.

The resonance of the Reformed Church, Budapest, prevents the sharpest definition here. The orchestra is set back and the internal balance is natural: the strings have bloom without edginess. This is alert, thoroughly musical playing with apt tempi. The *Andante con moto* of No. 89 is elegantly done, and the variations of the *Andante* of No. 91 are neatly handled (with an elegant bassoon solo). All in all this gives pleasure, but a bit more brightness on top would have been welcome.

Symphonies Nos. 72 in D; 93 in D; 95 in C min.
(Y/B) (BB) *** Naxos 8.550797 [id.]. Nicolaus Esterházy Sinfonia, Béla Drahos.

These performances are polished, warm and spirited and, if the Naxos recording is again on the reverberant side, it does not cloud textures. Four horns are featured prominently in No. 72 and provide many bravura flourishes and virtuoso scales in the opening movement; the playing here is first class. The solo flute shares the stage with the principal violin in the concertante *Andante*, and he returns to grace the delightfully elegant variations which make up the finale. All in all, this engaging work is fully worthy to stand alongside its mature companions when played as seductively as this. The orchestral response is equally impressive in the fine slow movements of these later works, and throughout Béla Drahos's pacing is matched by the overall sense of spontaneity and style.

Symphonies Nos. 80 in D min.; 87 in A; 89 in F.
(N) (BB) *** ASV Dig. CDQS 6156 [id.]. LMP, Jane Glover.

Jane Glover conducts the London Mozart Players in strong and energetic performances of these three relatively rare symphonies. No. 87 is the least known of the *Paris symphonies*; but all three of these works show Haydn at his most inventive. *No. 80 in D minor* begins as though it were a throwback to the *Sturm und Drang* period, but then at the end of the exposition Haydn gives a winning smile, as though to say, 'I fooled you!' No. 89 ends with a dance movement which contains delectable *strascinando* (dragging) passages, where the music hesitates before launching into reprises, done with great zest by the LMP. No. 87 also has its delights, notably in the lyrical *Adagio* with lovely flute and oboe solos. Though textures are not as transparent as we are beginning to demand in an age of period performance – largely a question of the ambient recorded sound – these modern-instrument performances are as winning as they are lively, making a very real bargain.

Symphonies Nos. 82–87 (Paris); 93–104 (London Symphonies).
(N) (B) **(*) Sony SX7K 64202 (7). NYPO, Leonard Bernstein.

Bernstein's *Paris Symphonies* are impressive. He obviously enjoys the music, and the playing of the New York Philharmonic is very alive, phrasing is sensitive and dynamic nuances are carefully attended to. The rhythmic jokiness of the finale of *The Bear* is attractively managed and the witty string writing in the first movement, which led to the christening of No. 83 as *The Hen*, is very nicely pointed. The account of *No. 84 in E flat* is particularly impressive. The recordings were made in the Manhattan Center or Avery Fisher Hall between 1962 and 1967, and the CD transfers bring rather shrill violins (though there is plenty of weight), which at times make the allegros sound a bit fierce, as in the first movements of Nos. 86 and 87; but the string ensemble is excellent and, for all one's reservations about the sound, these are performances to be reckoned with: they are eminently felt.

Bernstein offers comparably large-scale performances of the *London Symphonies*, recorded between 1970 and 1975. The sound is again quite full but with a similar problem of a degree of fierceness on the violins. The performances show Bernstein's warmth and the spirited NYPO response to the conductor's often grand manner. But while there are many fine individual moments, like the *Andante* of No. 96 or the *vivace* finale of No. 99, often the phrasing is rather heavily expressive, and this especially applies to the Minuets. The last five symphonies are among the most successful, particularly the *Drum roll*, with slow movements always individual. The *Andante* of *The Clock* is particularly engaging, and the *Allegretto* of the *Military* brings spectacular percussion – no holds barred. No. 104 was the earliest to be recorded (in 1958) and sounds thinner than the others. Whatever one's reservations, this music-making is full of personality and is always committed.

(Paris) Symphonies Nos. 82 in C (The Bear); 83 in G min. (The Hen); 84 in E flat.
⊛ *** Virgin/EMI Dig. VC7 59537-2. O of Age of Enlightenment, Kuijken.
(Y/B) *** Sony Dig. SK 66295 [id.]. Tafelmusik, Bruno Weil.

(Paris) Symphonies Nos. 85 in B flat (La Reine); 86 in D; 87 in A.
⊛ *** Virgin/EMI Dig. VC7 59557-2. O of Age of Enlightenment, Kuijken.
(Y/B) *** Sony Dig. SK 66296 [id.]. Tafelmusik, Bruno Weil.

Symphonies Nos. 82 in C (The Bear); 83 in G min. (The Hen); 84 in E flat; 85 in B flat (La Reine); 86 in D; 87 in A (Paris Symphonies).
(N) (B) *** Decca Double 448 195-2 (2) [id.]. Philharmonia Hungarica, Antal Dorati.
(B) *** Ph. Duo 438 727-2 (2) [id.]. ASMF, Sir Neville Marriner.
(Y/B) (M) ** DG Dig. 445 532-2 (2) [id.]. BPO, Karajan.

The two Virgin discs, well filled, with three symphonies apiece, together present an outstanding set of Haydn's six *Paris Symphonies*, between them offering among the most enjoyable period-performance recordings of Haydn ever. Above all, Kuijken and his players convey the full joy of Haydn's inspiration in every movement.

Notwithstanding the splendid set by the Orchestra of the Age on Enlightenment under Kuijken on Virgin, which remain very recommendable, these Sony Tafelmusik recordings continue to set new standards in this repertoire. For the *Paris Symphonies* the size of the string group has been slightly increased (8,7,5,4,2), against which flute, and pairs of oboes, bassoons, horns and – where scored – trumpets are balanced very effectively. The texture is at once full and transparent. As before, the performances are brimful of character. Minuets are rhythmically energetic, yet the pacing is not exaggerated, while finales have irrepressible spirit without being rushed. In short, if you want these symphonies performed on period instruments, this is the way to play (and record) them.

Dorati's set of *Paris Symphonies* makes a fine Double Decca bargain. These performances are well up to the high standard of his integral Haydn series, freshly stylish performances with plenty of vigour. The sinewy strength of the G minor opening of No. 83 for a moment brings a hint of *Sturm und Drang*, then yields its surprise as it gives way to the clucking of its titular *Hen*, while the variations which form its slow movement are matched in charm by those based on the French folksong ('*La gentille et jeune Lisette*') which make up the *Romance: Allegretto* of No. 85. No. 84 has a first movement of the most delicate fantasy, while No. 87, after its sublime *Adagio*, ends in a mood of lithe high spirits, yet is by no means insubstantial. The only point of controversy here is Dorati's consistently slow tempi for the minuets, nicely pointed as they are.

From Marriner, spirited and well-played accounts of the *Paris Symphonies*, distinguished by excellent ensemble and keen articulation. Nos. 86 and 87 (and perhaps 84) are digital recordings, the remainder being analogue, though this is not indicated in the documentation. The playing has that touch of charm which is so essential in Haydn. It is possible to imagine performances of greater character and personality than these (in the slow movements there is a tendency to blandness) but, generally speaking, they are very lively and musical and a good alternative to the Dorati recordings. They are certainly economically priced.

Karajan's set is big-band Haydn with a vengeance; but of course the orchestra of the *Concert de la Loge Olympique*, for which Haydn wrote these symphonies, was a large band, consisting of forty violins and no fewer than ten double-basses. It goes without saying that the quality of the orchestral playing is superb. However, these are rather heavy-handed accounts, closer to Imperial Berlin than to Paris; generally speaking, the slow movements are kept moving but the Minuets are very slow indeed, full of pomp and majesty – and, at times, too grand. In spite of the clean if slightly cool digital recordings, which have splendid presence, these performances are too charmless and wanting in grace to be wholeheartedly recommended. On CD the early-1980s digital sound has excellent presence but sounds just a little fierce in tuttis.

Symphonies Nos. 83 in G min. (La Poule); 88 in G; 96 in D (Miracle).
(N) (M) (***) Dutton mono CDSJB 1003 [id.]. Hallé O, Sir John Barbirolli.

Barbirolli's recording of No. 83 (*The Hen*), made in 1949, was the very first in the catalogue, originally appearing on three 78-r.p.m. records. Characteristically, he gives it an energetic reading full of fun and high dramatic contrasts. So the clucking of the second subject has rarely been pointed with more wit. The 12/8 finale has splendid swagger, with Barbirolli occasionally pressing ahead of the basic tempo in his eagerness. By latterday standards this is a rugged rather than an elegant performance, but the magnetism and vigour are irresistible. No. 96, with which *The Hen* was originally coupled on LP, has freer, more open sound. The playing is a degree more polished and elegant, with no diminution of energy or wit, and again the flute and oboe emerge as stars in the Hallé team. No. 88 was recorded in 1953 but was never issued, maybe for lack of a coupling. That Barbirolli here observes the repeats in both halves of the first movement (very rare practice at the time) suggests that his criterion for repeating may simply have been how much he liked the music. He sustains the great melody of the *Largo* at a slow speed with elegance as well as warmth, and the fun of the finale is delightfully caught, with the Hallé violins at their best, articulating cleanly. Whatever detailed reservations there may be, the bounce and magnetism of Barbirolli at his peak come over from first to last.

Symphony No. 88 in G.
(N) ✸ (M) (***) DG mono 447 439-2 [id.]. BPO, Furtwängler – SCHUBERT: *Symphony No. 9.* (***)
(M) **(*) Sony SM2K 47563 [id.]. NYPO, Bernstein – *Masses Nos. 10–11.* **(*)

Even those who usually find Furtwängler's interpretations too idiosyncratic will be drawn to this glowing performance. The beauty of his shaping of the main theme of the slow movement is totally disarming, and the detail of the finale, lightly sprung and vivacious, is a constant pleasure. The Berlin Philharmonic plays marvellously well for him, and the 1951 recording, made in the attractive ambience of the Jesus-Christus Kirche in Berlin, needs no apology. In its remastered form it sounds admirably fresh, yet has plenty of body too. Here it is coupled with Schubert's *Ninth Symphony*, an ideal candidate for reissue in DG's 'Originals' series of legendary recordings.

Like the *Paris Symphonies*, Bernstein's New York account of *No. 88 in G* has much to recommend it. The glorious *Largo*, taken expansively, is overtly expressive and some might feel it too heavy, but there is no mistaking Bernstein's personal warmth. The playing in the sparkling finale is most infectious. Good, well-balanced 1963 sound.

Symphonies Nos. 88 in G; 89 in F; 90 in G.
(N) *** Sony Dig. SK 66253-2 [id.]. Tafelmusik, Weil.

Continuing on after the *Paris Symphonies*, Bruno Weil and Tafelmusik offer here another stiumlating triptych from 1787/8. The first movement of No. 88 is not rushed and the noble tune of the slow movement is unerringly paced, so that the energetic Minuet with its robust drone trio is the more telling, and the finale sparkles. No 89 in F is particularly winning, with vivacious outer movements and plenty of charm in the *Andante* (which derives from one of the composer's concertos for lire organizzate, Hob VIIh:5); there is engaging wind playing throughout the work. No. 90 opens grandly but the lively outer movement allegros are lit up by the high horns, unusually crooked in C alto. For all the strength and vigour of these performances Weil never misses the touches of humour and the joke false ending of the G major work, and its continuation after four bars of silence, is neatly managed.

Symphonies Nos. 88 in G; 92 in G (Oxford); 94 in G (Surprise).
(N) (M) **(*) DG Dig. 445 554-2 [id.]. VPO, Bernstein.

All three G major symphonies emanate from concerts at the Musikvereinsaal in the mid-1980s, using the full strings of the Vienna Philharmonic and given a richly upholstered recording. For all his idiosyncrasies, Bernstein is never more winning than in Haydn, and he observes the repeat of the development and restatement in the first movement of No. 88 and gives a romantic and rather beautiful account of the *Largo*. The slow movement of the *Surprise* is also taken relaxedly, and the speed of the finale is challengingly fast. Good sound, and there is no doubt that these are 'live performances'.

Symphonies Nos. 88 in G; 92 in G (Oxford); 95 in C min.; 98 in B flat; 100 in G (Military); 101 in D (Clock); 102 in B flat; 104 in D (London).
(M) ** EMI CMS7 63667-2 (3) [id.]. Philh. O or New Philh. O, Klemperer.

Klemperer, not the likeliest conductor in Haydn, in his broad, measured view yet shows his mastery in structuring and rhythmic pointing. With good analogue sound, an interesting historical document.

Symphonies Nos. 88 in G; 95 in C min.; 101 in D (Clock).
(M) **(*) RCA 09026 60729-2 [id.]. Symphony O or Chicago SO, Fritz Reiner.

Reiner's Haydn is – perhaps not surprisingly – a little Germanic: all three slow movements are measured, although Haydn's markings for both the *Clock* and No. 95 are *Andante*. The leisurely *Largo* in No. 88 is sustained by the beauty of the playing, and the spacious equivalent of No. 95 is also phrased with much care and affection. Finales, though never rushed, are nimble and sprightly. The recording – from 1960 and (in the case of the *C minor Symphony*) 1963 – is certainly full, with more ample textures than we would expect today.

Symphonies Nos. 88 in G; 104 in D (London).
*** CRD CRD 3370; *CRDC 4070* [id.]. Bournemouth Sinf., Ronald Thomas.

Although the orchestra is smaller than the Concertgebouw or LPO, the playing has great freshness and vitality; indeed it is the urgency of musical feeling that Ronald Thomas conveys which makes up for the last ounce of finesse.

Symphony No. 92 in G (Oxford).
(N) (M) (***) Dutton Lab. mono CDEA 5003 [id.] Paris Conservatoire O, Walter – SCHUBERT: *Symphony No. 9.* ***
(N) (**) VAI mono VAIA 1081-2. Paris Conservatoire O, Walter – BERLIOZ: *Symphonie fantastique.* (**)

(N) (M) (**) Sony mono SMK 68446 [id.]. French R. O, Szell – MOZART: *Violin concerto No. 4; Symphony No. 35.* **

Only three months after the Anschluss, Bruno Walter made this Haydn recording in Paris, where he had taken refuge with the Paris Conservatoire Orchestra. These magnetic performances rather contradict the idea of Bruno Walter as the purveyor of sunshine and charm in Schubert and Haydn. One marvels at the whirlwind energy and resilience of allegros in both the Schubert and the Haydn symphonies. Even Walter's broad tempos and expressive phrasing in slow movements are firmly controlled. Despite one or two blips, Dutton's transfer, coupled with the classic account of the *Great C major Symphony* of Schubert (made in London later the same year), is infinitely superior in terms of focus, body and smoothness to the Canadian alternative, which is coupled with Berlioz's *Symphonie fantastique*. Those wanting this fine account of the *Oxford Symphony* should go for the Dutton.

Even more than in the Mozart symphony and concerto with which it is coupled, Szell's live account of the *Oxford Symphony*, recorded in 1959, finds him in relaxed mood, not severe but smiling, bringing out the wit, not least in the finale. Limited, mono sound.

Symphonies Nos. 92 in G (Oxford); 104 in D (London).
(M) *** Carlton IMP Classics Dig. 30367 0035-2. E. Sinfonia, Groves.

Sir Charles Groves's performances are robust yet elegant as well; both slow movements are beautifully shaped, with Haydn's characteristic contrasts unfolding spontaneously. In the last movement of the *Oxford*, the dancing violins are a special delight in what is one of the composer's most infectious finales.

Symphonies Nos. 93 in D; 94 in G (Surprise); 97 in C; 99 in E flat; 100 in G (Military); 101 in D (Clock) (London Symphonies).
(Y/B) ✪ (B) *** Ph. Duo Analogue/Dig. 442 614-2 (2). Concg. O, Sir Colin Davis.

Symphonies Nos. 95 in C min.; 96 in D (Miracle); 98 in B flat; 102 in B flat; 103 in E flat (Drum Roll); 104 in D (London) (London Symphonies).
(Y/B) ✪ (B) *** Ph. Duo Analogue/Dig. 442 611-2 (2). Concg. O, Sir Colin Davis.

Symphonies Nos. 93–104.
(M) *** DG 437 201-2 (4). LPO, Jochum.
(M) (***) EMI mono CMS7 64389-2 (2) (*Nos. 93–98*) [id.]. RPO, Sir Thomas Beecham.
(M) *** EMI CMS7 64066-2 (2) (*Nos. 99–104*) [id.]. RPO, Sir Thomas Beecham.
(N) ** Ph. Dig. 442 788-2 (4) [id.]. O of 18th Century, Brüggen.

This Haydn series (recorded between 1975 and 1981) is one of the most distinguished sets Sir Colin Davis has given us over his long recording career, and its blend of brilliance and sensitivity, wit and humanity gives these two-for-the-price-of-one Duo reissues a special claim on the collector who has not already invested in the performances when they cost far more. There is no trace of routine in this music-making and no failure of imagination. The excellence of the playing is matched by Philips's best recording quality, whether analogue or digital. The Concertgebouw sound is resonant and at times weighty but has good definition, and the warmth and humanity of the readings are especially striking in slow movements. The *Allegretto* of the *Military Symphony* is properly grand and expansive, balanced by vital, sparkling outer movements. Excellent notes from Robin Golding. A bargain in every sense of the word.

The art of phrasing is one of the prime secrets of great music-making, and no detail in Beecham's performances of the *London Symphonies* goes untended. They have also great warmth, drama too, and perhaps a unique geniality. The sound throughout is full and fresh, with plenty of body, sweet violin-timbre and no edge. The first box are mono recordings; they sound admirably full-bodied and have been transferred amazingly successfully. The performances possess an inner life and vitality that put them in a class of their own.

Jochum secures fine, stylish playing from the LPO, challenging them with often very fast tempi in outer movements. Those fast tempi sometimes prevent the music from having quite the lilt it has with Beecham or the gravitas of Sir Colin Davis; but the athletic exuberance of Jochum in Haydn, his ability to mould slow movements with tenderness that never spills over into unstylish mannerism (and to handle the sets of themes and variations to bring great diversity of atmosphere and mood), makes these wonderfully satisfying readings of Haydn's greatest symphonies. In the finale of No. 98 Jochum adds a harpsichord to the texture so that Haydn's charming little joke at the end can make its point all the better. Overall, this set will give much refreshment, and the recording is naturally balanced and clear, with its warm reverberation presenting these works on a somewhat bigger scale, yet with rather less weight than Davis brings. Many will feel this to be a perfect compromise.

Frans Brüggen, so successful in his early career in the world of chamber music and as a recorder virtuoso, has proved disappointing in his more recent search for authenticity on the rostrum. His approach to the last symphonies of Haydn in particular brings remarkable contradictions of style. He is not helped by the resonant acoustic which creates weighty textures and a focus which is not always quite clean in fortissimos. Openings and first-movement allegros are generally portentous and large-scale, generating almost a Beethovenian atmosphere and, while slow movements bring the restrained, 'authentic' string style, the expansive moments again often seem too inflated. Finales are usually snappily rhythmic and the orchestral playing is of high quality with fine wind solos, but the end result fails to convince.

Symphonies Nos. 93 in D; 95 in C min.; 97 in C. (London Symphonies).
(N) (B) *** Sony SBK 67175; *SBT 67175* [id.]. Cleveland O, George Szell.

With superb polish in the playing and precise phrasing it would be easy for performances such as these to sound superficial, but Haydn's music obviously struck a deep chord in Szell's sensibility and there is humanity underlying the technical perfection. Indeed there are many little musical touches from Szell to show that his perfectionist approach is a dedicated and affectionate one. There is also the most delectable pointing and a fine judgement of the inner balance. Szell's minuets have a greater rhythmic spring than Bernstein's. The recordings have been splendidly remastered and the sound is fuller and firmer than it ever was on LP, with the Cleveland ambience well caught: there is still some thinness in the violins in No. 95, but it is not serious. Both Nos. 95 and 97 are strong performances; Szell brings out the maturity of first movements – the slow introduction of No. 97 immediately commands attention – and the beauty of the slow movements, among Haydn's finest (as is the *Largo cantabile* of No. 93). A highly recommendable reissue.

Symphonies Nos. 93 in D; 94 in G (Surprise); 95 in C min.
*** HM/BMG Dig. 05472 77275 [id.]. La Petite Bande, Sigiswald Kuijken.

Sigiswald Kuijken has changed record companies and orchestras, but he still provides polished performances that are at once extremely alive and convey enjoyment in the music's drama and genial craftsmanship. The playing is less earthily robust than with Goodman (who has this same triptych – see above), but the virtuosity here in Allegros is both precise and infectious. The *Largo* slow movement of No. 93 may be pressed on rather strongly for some tastes, but not the slow movement of the *Surprise*, and the minuets have a nice lift. The recording gives a slightly more mellow effect than the Hyperion, without losing transparency.

Symphonies Nos. 94 in G (Surprise); 96 in D (Miracle); 100 in G (Military).
(M) *** Decca 417 718-2 [id.]. Philh. Hungarica, Dorati.
(N) (M) **(*) Teldec/Warner Dig. 0630 10018-2 [id.]. Concg. O, Harnoncourt.

These three symphonies, collected from Dorati's historic complete Haydn cycle, make a delightful group. The only controversial speed comes in the *Andante* of the *Surprise*, much faster than usual, but the freshness of the joke is the more sharply presented.

Harnoncourt's performances, although they bring much dynamic gruffness, yet have great character. Accents are stronger than ever, and in the *Andante* of the *Surprise*, after the orchestra has fined down to a pianissimo for the repetition of the opening phrase, not only is there one loud explosive interuption but others follow, and the climax is spectacular. Then the Minuet whirls along at a forcefully rhythmic one-in-a-bar. There is marvellous orchestral playing throughout, and if one accepts the sheer weight of the fortissimo tuttis, the *Miracle* is an impressive reading; here the Minuet is not pressed so hard, with the fizzing energy unleashed in the finale. Not surprisingly the 'Military' interlude in the *G major Symphony* is sensational, with the timpani and percussion made to sound very like combined canon and musket fire; the finale is pretty explosive too. The recording is full-blooded to suit the musicmaking.

Symphonies Nos. (i) 94 in G (Surprise); (ii) 96 in D (Miracle); (i) 104 in D (London).
(M) **(*) EMI CDM5 65178-2 [id.]. (i) Pittsburgh SO; (ii) LSO; Previn.

Previn offers an attractive triptych for those favouring Haydn on a larger scale. The performances of Nos. 94 and 104 are lively and very well played and recorded. The only reservations concern the slow movements, which sound just a little perfunctory and lacking in poise. No. 96, however, recorded two years earlier with the LSO, shows Previn at his finest, with the pointing and attention to detail matched by the genial atmosphere. Indeed there is a Beechamesque touch to this music-making. The concertante element is a delight and the finale has real wit. The late-1970s recordings have all been very successfully remastered.

Symphonies Nos. 94 in G (Surprise); 98 in B flat; 101 in D (Clock); 104 in D (London).
(B) *** Erato/Warner Dig. 4509 91933-2 [id.]. SCO, Raymond Leppard.

Three favourite Haydn symphonies are offered here at bargain price in an Erato Bonsai Duo reissue, together with the surprisingly rare *No. 98 in B flat*, an unquestioned masterpiece. This attractive pair of discs offers eminently sane, likeable performances from Raymond Leppard and the Scottish Chamber Orchestra. These artists convey a pleasure in what they are doing, and that is more than half the battle. They bring not only geniality and high spirits to these symphonies but also grace and considerable poetic feeling. The recording is agreeably natural and as fresh and warm as the performances themselves. A very useful chamber-sized alternative to the larger orchestras favoured in this repertoire on other labels.

(i) *Symphonies Nos. 94 in G (Surprise)*; (i) *100 in G (Military)*; (ii) *String quartet No. 77 (Emperor), Op. 76/3.*
(N) (BB) ** RCA Navigator Dig./Analogue 74321 24197-2. (i) ECO, Jean-François Paillard; (ii) V. String Qt.

Genial, polished and well-sprung accounts of two favourite Haydn symphonies from Paillard which are enjoyable for their spirited warmth, even if the resonant acoustic slightly inflates the tuttis. The Vienna Quartet then give a lively, sympathetic account of Haydn's most famous string quartet, but here the resonant inflation is much worse, so that in the slow movement the noble melody sounds as if it is being played by a string orchestra.

Symphonies Nos. 94 in G (Surprise); 101 in D (Clock).
(M) *** DG 423 883-2 [id.]. LPO, Jochum.
(N) **(*) DG Gold Dig. 439 038-2 [id.]. BPO, Karajan.

Jochum's are marvellously fresh, crisp accounts of both symphonies, elegantly played and always judiciously paced. The sound remains first class, with added clarity but without loss of bloom, the bass cleaner and only slightly drier.

Two impressive examples of Karajan's big-band Haydn for those who put dignity and weight as a priority in this music, though No. 94 is not without humour. As usual, the remastering brings a firmer outline, and no one could fault the superb playing of the BPO.

Symphonies Nos. 99 in E flat; 100 in G (Military).
(Y/B) **(*) HM/BMG Dig. 05472 77328-2 [id.]. La Petite Bande, Sigiswald Kuijken.

After the success of the Petite Bande's *Paris Symphonies*, this is slightly disappointing. The playing has many virtues but tuttis are just a bit husky and the last touch of spontaneity is missing in slow movements, though the finales of both symphonies are full of lightness and energy. But in any case this is one work too few for a full-priced CD: the overall playing time is only 52 minutes.

Symphonies Nos. 101 in D (Clock); 102 in B flat.
(N) **(*) HM/BMG Dig. 05472 77351-2 [id.]. La Petite Bande, Sigiswald Kuijken.

Kuijken is pretty well back on form for this fine coupling of two of the *London Symphonies*. The *Andante* of the *Clock* is ideally paced, and indeed tempi throughout are apt, with allegros full of life, especially the exuberant finale of No. 102. Here the *Adagio* is presented thoughtfully and with a slight degree of detachment but remains pleasingly spontaneous. Excellent recording, but the 53 minutes' content is ungenerous.

CHAMBER MUSIC

Cassations (Divertimenti): in G, Hob III/1; in G, Hob II/G1; in C (Birthday), Hob II/11; in F, Hob II/20.
(Y/B) (M) **(*) Virgin Veritas/EMI Dig. VER5 61163-2 [id.]. Linde Consort, Hans-Martin Linde.

Haydn's *Cassations* and *Divertimenti* have not the finesse of the best works of Mozart, but they have plenty of imaginative touches, particularly in their instrumentation. Two of those offered here are fairly ambitious (Hob II, Nos. G1 and 20), scored for a nonet (including a pair each of oboes and horns); the remaining two, written around 1765, are scored for a sextet (including flute and oboe), often used with charm and effectively demonstrating the special timbres of the early instruments played here. Overall the performances have plenty of character, although in the hands of, say, the ASMF they would undoubtedly be more winning still. The recording, made in a fairly reverberant acoustic, has a quite large-scale effect, but the result is not unstylish.

Flute trios for 2 flutes and cello (bassoon) Nos. 1–4 (London), Hob IV/1–4; Duo for 2 flutes (arr. of *String quartet in D, Op. 76/5*); *Echo for 2 flutes* (arr. of *Divertimento for 2 string trios in E flat*).
**(*) Sony Dig. SK 48061 [id.]. Rampal, Schulz, Audin.

(i) *Flute trios for 2 flutes & cello Nos. 1–4 (London), Hob IV/1–4;* (ii) *Flute quartets, Op. 5, Nos. 1 in D, Hob II/D9; 2 in G, Hob H/G4; 3 in D, Hob II/D10; 4 in G, Hob II/1; 5 in D, Hob II/D11; 6 in C, Hob II/11.*
(Y/B) *** Accent Dig. ACC 9283/4 (2) [id.]. (i) Bernard Kuijken, Mark Hantaï, Wieland Kuijken; (ii)
   Bernard, Siegfried & Wieland Kuijken, François Fernandez.

The *London Trios* date from 1794 during Haydn's visit to England and the first two include variations on the song, '*Trust not too much*'. They are delightful works and receive felicitous performances from this authentic group on Accent who make the most winning sounds. The *Flute quartets*, Op. 5, in the view of H. C. Robbins Landon may not all be by Haydn. It seems fairly certain, however, that the first two, also known as *Divertimenti*, are authentic, very early works from the 1750s. All the music is engaging when played with such finesse and warmth, although this is a set to be dipped into rather than taken in large doses. The recording is admirably fresh and realistic.

   The arrangement of the *String quartet*, Op. 76/5, for two flutes was the work of a London musician, Samuel Arnold. This is essentially for collectors with a very sweet musical tooth indeed, although undoubtedly the *Presto* finale heard by itself is captivating. On Sony come equally fine performances and excellent recording.

Piano trios (complete).
✸ (M) *** Ph. 432 061-2 (9). Beaux Arts Trio.

It is not often possible to hail one set of records as a 'classic' in quite the way that Schnabel's Beethoven sonatas can be so described. Yet this set can be described in those terms, for the playing of the Beaux Arts Trio is of the very highest musical distinction. The contribution of the pianist, Menahem Pressler, is little short of inspired, and the recorded sound on CD is astonishingly lifelike. The CD transfer has enhanced detail without losing the warmth of ambience or sense of intimacy.

Piano trio in E flat, Hob XV/10.
(N) (M) ** Sony Stern Edition III SM2K 64516 (2) [id.]. Stern, Rose, Istomin – MOZART: *Piano quartet No. 2;* SCHUBERT: *Piano trios Nos. 1–2.* **

This rather over-characterized account of the *E flat Trio*, written in 1784–5, has plenty of vigour and impetus, but the close balance gives the feeling of high-powered music-making, which is not entirely sympathetic.

Piano trios, Hob XV, Nos. 24–27.
(M) *** Ph. 422 831-2. Beaux Arts Trio.

These are all splendid works. No. 25 with its *Gypsy rondos* is the most famous, but each has a character of its own, showing the mature Haydn working at full stretch. The playing here is peerless and the recording truthful and refined.

Piano trios Nos. 42 in E flat, Hob XV/30; 43 in C, Hob XV/27; 44 in E, Hob XV/28; 45 in E flat, Hob XV/ 29.
✸ *** Sony Dig. SK 53120 [id.]. Vera Beths, Anner Bylsma, Robert Levin.

Piano trios Nos. 43–45.
(N) (B) **(*) HM HMC Dig. 901572 [id.]. Patrick Cohen, Erich Höbarth, Christophe Coin.

Outstanding performances in every way. This Sony group plays with immense flair and spirit and conveys the exhilaration of the finale of the *C major Trio* (No. 43, Hob. XV/27) superbly well and the depth and poetry of the middle movements. Infectious in its high spirits and delight in music-making. And how well they are recorded! It is good to have modern digital alternatives to the justly famous Beaux Arts versions. Strongly recommended.

   The Cohen Trio are not quite so successful in Haydn as they were in early Beethoven but their playing is still refreshing. In the *C major Trio* there are a few over-strong accents and an occasional touch of abrasiveness, brought by the close microphones. The remarkable *E major Trio* flows readily, and the strange dark feeling of the *Allegretto* is well caught. Its climbing scale unexpectedly develops as a passacaglia but the sombre mood is dispelled in the jolly finale. Best of all is the *E flat Trio*, which opens winningly. The players capture the *innocentement* of the *Andantino* and are at their finest in the robust vigour of the rustic dance which ends the piece boisterously. However the competing Sony disc offers an extra work and makes an obvious first choice.

String quartets

String quartets: Nos. 1 in B flat (La chasse), Op. 1/1; 32 in C, Op. 20/2; 35 in F min., Op. 20/5; 46 in E flat, Op. 50/3; 57 in G; 58 in C; 59 in E, Op. 54/1–3; 65 in B flat; 66 in G, Op. 64/3–4; 74 in G min. (Rider), Op. 74/3; 77 in C (Emperor), Op. 76/3; 78 in B flat (Sunrise), Op. 77/2.
(Y/B) (**(*)) Testament mono SBT 3055 (3) [id.]. Pro Arte Qt.

String quartets: Nos. 6 in C, Op. 1/6; 16 in B flat; 17 in F (Serenade), Op. 3/4–5 (Hoffstetter); 31 in E flat; 34 in D, Op. 20/1 & 4; 38 in E flat (Joke); 39 in C (Bird); 42 in D (How do you do?), Op. 33/2, 3 & 6; 49 in D (Frog), Op. 50/6; 60 in A; 62 in B flat, Op. 55/1 & 3; 68 in E flat, Op. 64/6; 69 in B flat, Op. 71/1; 72 in C; 73 in F, Op. 74/1–2; 81 in G, Op. 77/1.
(Y/B) (**(*)) Testament mono SBT 4056 (4) [id.]. Pro Arte Qt.

While LP and CD reissues have kept the name of the Busch Quartet alive, the Pro Arte (for whom, incidentally, Bartók composed his *Fourth Quartet*) is a less familiar one to modern collectors. All the players were from the Brussels Conservatoire and enjoyed international repute in the 1920s and '30s, not only for their Viennese classics but for their advocacy of contemporary music. In their hands the Haydn *Quartets* bring us a world of delight, wisdom and sanity, and few groups are better guides. They have great purity of style and an immaculate intonation and technique, while they seem always to hit on exactly the right tempo, which in turn enables phrasing to speak naturally. The interplay between each of the musicians could hardly be more subtle in its responsiveness. However, the actual sound of these recordings calls for a little tolerance. The violin, particularly above the stave, is wanting in real bloom, and one would welcome more space between movements, which would surely not have been beyond the ingenuity of the engineers supervising these transfers, a fault which disfigured the LP versions (remastered by Keith Hardwick). Sometimes there is as little as two or three seconds. Less than perfect sound, perhaps, as might be expected from their recording dates (1931–8), but impeccable Haydn playing. The appearance on CD of these once-famous Haydn performances is a cause for celebration.

String quartets: in E flat, Op. 1/0; Nos. 43 in D min., Op. 42; 83 in B flat, Op. 103.
**(*) Mer. ECD 88117 [id.]. English Qt.

These fine players rise to all the challenges posed by this music, and the recorded sound is eminently truthful. There would have been room for another quartet on this disc, which offers rather short measure at 43 minutes.

String quartets Nos. 1 in B flat; 2 in E flat; 3 in D; 4 in G, Op. 1/1–4.
(BB) **(*) Naxos Dig. 8.550398 [id.]. Kodály Qt.

String quartets Nos. 5 in E flat; 6 in C, Op. 1/5–6; 7 in A; 8 in E, Op. 2/1–2.
(BB) **(*) Naxos Dig. 8.550399 [id.]. Kodály Qt.

Haydn is credited with 'inventing' the string quartet, but he claimed that he had come across the form by accident. The Op. 1 and Op. 2 quartets are in essence five-movement divertimenti scored for four string players. The first four were published in Paris in 1764, together with two other works, under the collective title, '*Six Simphonies ou Quatuors dialogués*'. These earliest works have not quite the unquenchable flow of original ideas that the early symphonies have but, in such fresh performances as these, they make easy and enjoyable listening even if, with the performances generous in observing repeats, some movements outstay their welcome. The resonant ambience of the Unitarian Church in Budapest seems not unsuitable for works which lie midway between divertimenti and quartets, and the focus seems brighter and sharper on the second CD, recorded in June 1991, two months after the first.

String quartets Nos. 1 in B flat, Op. 1/1; 67 in D (Lark), Op. 64/5; 74 in G min., Op. 74/3 (Rider).
*** DG Dig. 423 622-2 [id.]. Hagen Qt.

The Hagen are supple, cultured and at times perhaps a little overcivilized, but in these three Haydn quartets they play flawlessly and are wonderfully alert and intelligent.

String quartets Nos. 1 in B flat, Op. 1/1; 67 in D (Lark), Op. 64/5; 77 in C, Op. 76/3.
(N) (BB) ** Tring Dig. TRP 028 [id.]. RPO Chamber Ens., Jonathan Carey.

In spite of the Tring listing, these are not chamber orchestra performances, although the resonant acoustic does create an almost string-orchestral texture from the four players, led by Jonathan Carey. The performances are warm and polished: they do not find enough variety of dynamic in the repetitions of the famous tune in the slow movement of the *Emperor*, but the *Lark* soars up nicely and the *Vivace* finale is infectious. But the highlight here is the very early, Op. 1 *Quartet*, which is strikingly fresh. In the *Adagio* the leader's extended solo is played most beautifully and creates a memorable level of tension.

String quartet No. 3 in D, Op. 1/3.
(M) ** Decca 433 691-2 [id.]. Weller Qt – *Quartets Nos. 37–39.* **(*)

The Weller Quartet's performance is accurate and musical, but it really springs to life only in the vivacious Scherzo, which is admittedly by far the best movement.

String quartets Nos. 9 in F; 10 in B flat, Op. 2/4 & 6; 35 in D min., Op. 42.
(BB) **(*) Naxos Dig. 8.550732 [id.]. Kodály Qt.

The Unitarian Church, Budapest, continues to provide a warm, flattering tonal blend of much aural beauty, but a texture that is a little too ample for early Haydn, while the fairly close microphones reduce the dynamic range. However, the Kodály's friendly style and elegant finish suit early Haydn. (Both Op. 2 quartets are simple five-movement works, each with a pair of minuets.) These performers find exactly the right degree of expressiveness for the *Adagio* of Op. 2/4 and are equally at home in the engaging *Andante ed innocentemente* which opens the first movement of Op. 42, a splendid work, written a quarter of a century later.

String quartets Nos. 17 in F (Serenade), Op. 3/5; 38 in E flat (Joke), Op. 33/2; 76 in D min. (Fifths), Op. 76/2.
(B) **(*) Discover Dig. DIDCD 920172 [id.]. Sharon Qt.

The Sharon Quartet are an excellent group and they give warm and spirited accounts of these three favourite quartets. They are recorded in the resonant acoustics of St John's Church in Cologne and, like some of the recordings made for Naxos by the Kodály Quartet, the resonance expands the texture, although not seriously enough to prevent enjoyment, for they make a bright, clean sound. They find charm in Hofstetter's famous '*Serenade*' of Op. 3 and are equally good in the *Variations* which form the slow movement of the *Fifths*; at the same time, they find the right approach to the '*Joke*' in the finale of Op. 33/2.

String quartets Nos. 17 in F (Serenade), Op. 3/5; 63 in D (Lark), Op. 64/5; 76 in D min. (Fifths), Op. 76/2.
(M) *** Ph. 426 097-2. Italian Qt.

First-class playing here; although the first movement of the *Lark* is a bit measured in feeling, the *Serenade quartet* is made to sound inspired, its famous slow movement played with exquisite gentleness. The *D minor Quartet* is admirably poised and classical in feeling.

String quartets Nos. 19 in C; 21 in G; 22 in D min., Op. 9/1, 3 & 4.
(BB) *** Naxos Dig. 8.550786 [id.]. Kodály Qt.

String quartets Nos. 20 in E flat; 23 in B flat; 24 in A, Op. 9/2, 5 & 6.
(BB) *** Naxos Dig. 8.550787 [id.]. Kodály Qt.

The Kodály Quartet are in excellent form throughout Opus 9. Their simple eloquence in all three slow movements on the first disc serves Haydn well: the *Largo* of Op. 9/3 is ideally paced and beautifully poised. The players then go on to give a captivating account of the finale. Indeed, all the finales here are superb, showing Haydn at full stretch. The last of the set in A major opens with a very attractive *Presto* in 6/8, which is delightfully buoyant here. It has a beautiful *Adagio*, dominated by a favourite Haydn triplet rhythm and giving much scope to the solo violin, who soars above the texture in a long cantilena and is even given space for a brief cadenza just before the movement ends. Fortunately the Naxos recording team (in December 1992 and January 1993) have mastered the acoustics of the Unitarian Church in Budapest. The microphones are in the right place, the sound is not inflated: in fact the balance brings a vividly realistic impression.

String quartets Nos. 31 in E flat; 32 in C; 33 in G min.; 34 in D; 35 in F min.; 36 in A, Op. 20/1–6.
✿ *** Astrée Dig. E 8784 (2) [id.]. Mosaïques Qt.

String quartets Nos. 31 in E flat; 32 in C; 33 in G min., Op. 20/1–3.
(BB) ** Naxos Dig. 8.550701 [id.]. Kodály Qt.

String quartets Nos. 34 in D; 35 in F min.; 36 in A (Sun quartets), Op. 20/4–6.
(BB) ** Naxos Dig. 8.550702 [id.]. Kodály Qt.

The four players of the Mosaïques Quartet create individual timbres which are pleasing to the ear without any overt opulence, textures which have body and transparency, are perfectly matched and never edgy. There is no squeezed phrasing, and the use of vibrato is as subtle as the control of colour and dynamic. Intonation and ensemble are remarkably exact. The effect, not as genially friendly or casual as the Kodály series on Naxos, is often breathtaking in its rapt concentration. Such is the calibre of this music-making and the strength of insight of these players that the character of these fine, relatively early works is communicated with seemingly total spontaneity. This is playing of rare distinction which is immensely revealing and rewarding, helped by state-of-the-art recording of complete realism and presence within an acoustic that provides the necessary intimacy of ambience.

The Naxos Kodály series continues to bring polished, sympathetic playing of considerable warmth. Allegros are lively, but the acoustics of the Unitarian Church, Budapest, though providing beautifully rich string-textures, here make the effect almost orchestral and bring an element of blandness to the fine *Adagio* slow movements; throughout, the dynamic range of the playing is reduced by the microphone positioning. The *Adagio* of Op. 20/2 brings some fine playing, and the theme and variations of the *Poco adagio e affettuoso* of the *D major Quartet*, Op. 20/4, are attractively characterized but badly need a wider dynamic contrast. This is even more striking in the *Fuga a quattro soggetti* which forms the finale of Op. 20/2.

String quartets Nos. 32 in C, Op. 20/2; 44 in B flat, Op. 50/1; 76 in D min. (Fifths), Op. 76/2.
(Y/B) (BB) *** ASV Dig. CDQS 6144 [id.]. Lindsay Qt.

Obviously, since these are public performances, one has to accept music-making reflecting the heat of the occasion, the odd sense of roughness (the finale of Op. 76, No. 2), for these artists take risks – and this is perhaps a shade faster than it would be in a studio. There is splendid character in these performances and plenty of musical imagination. These readings have a spontaneity which is refreshing in these days of retakes! The recordings are eminently truthful and audience noise is minimal. An excellent bargain.

String quartets Nos. 34 in D, Op. 20/4; 47 in C sharp min., Op. 50/4; 77 in C (Emperor), Op. 76/3.
*** ASV Dig. CDDCA 731 [id.]. Lindsay Qt.

The Lindsay performances were again recorded at public performances, on this occasion in London's Wigmore Hall. The advantages this brings are twofold: higher spontaneity and a greater propensity to take risks. In all three performances the gains outweigh any loss, though the balance tends to cause some coarse-sounding tone in fortissimo passages.

String quartets Nos. 35 in F min., Op. 20/5; 40 in B flat, Op. 33/4; 70 in D, Op. 71/2.
(Y/B) (BB) *** ASV Dig. CDQS 6146 [id.]. Lindsay Qt.

The immediacy of the Lindsays' playing here is just as striking as before, yet at the rather serious opening of the *F minor*, Op. 20/5, the approach is appropriately sober and considered as well as spontaneous. This quartet also has a tender *Siciliano* slow movement which is played with affecting simplicity and grace. The account of the *B flat Quartet*, Op. 33/4, brings a burst of applause at the end, as well it might, with its deeply thoughtful *Largo* and engaging finale. Three marvellous works, recorded with striking presence.

String quartets Nos. 37–42, Op. 33/1–6; 43 in D min., Op. 42.
(Y/B) (B) *** HM Dig. HMA 1903002/3. Festetics Qt.

String quartets Nos. 37 in B min.; 38 in E flat (Joke); 39 in C (Bird), Op. 33/1–3.
*** Kingdom KCLCD 2014 [id.]. Bingham Qt.
(M) **(*) Decca 433 691-2 [id.]. Weller Qt – *Quartet No. 3.* **

String quartets Nos. 37 in B min.; 38 in E flat (Joke); 40 in B flat, Op. 33/1–2 & 4.
(N) **(*) ASV Dig. CDDCA 937 [id.]. Lindsay Qt.

String quartets Nos. 38 in E flat (Joke); 39 in C (Bird); 41 in G, Op. 33/2, 3 & 5.
(N) *** Audivis Astrée Dig. E 8569 [id.]. Mosaïques Qt.

String quartets Nos. 39 in C (Bird); 41 in G; 42 in D, Op. 33/3, 5 & 6.
(N) *** ASV Dig. CDDCA 938 [id.]. Lindsay Qt.

String quartets Nos. 40 in B flat; 41 in G; 42 in D (How do you do), Op. 33/4–6.
*** Kingdom KCLCD 2015 [id.]. Bingham Qt.
(M) **(*) Decca 433 692-2 [id.]. Weller Qt – *Quartet No. 83.* **

String quartets Nos. 37–38 & 41, Op. 33/1–2 & 5.
(Y/B) (BB) **(*) Naxos 8.550788 [id.]. Kodály Qt.

String quartets Nos. 39–40 & 42, Op. 33/3–4 & 6.
(Y/B) (BB) **(*) Naxos 8.550789 [id.]. Kodály Qt.

Although Haydn had written some fine quartets before these were published in 1782, this Op. 33 set proved a watermark. Here he finally established himself as complete master of a new medium with such skill, musical fecundity and wit that he never surpassed them in terms of cultivated musical pleasure, even if later works, Op. 76 for instance, embrace a somewhat wider range of mood and feeling.

Those wanting Op. 33 on period instruments will surely be delighted with this Musique d'Abord set from the Quatuor Festetics. These Hungarians play with great spirit (the finale of the *Joke* has the requisite sense of fun), and their overall lightness of touch and the transparency of texture are very appealing. Slow movements have freshness and just the right combination of gravitas and expressive feeling: the phrasing is smoothly linear without those unattractive bulges that seem to haunt performances on original instruments. Almost every movement has the kind of sparkle and spontaneity that make one want to return to it, and the recording is most naturally balanced in the much-used Unitarian Church of Budapest. For most listeners this will be a clear first choice, for Op. 42 is also excellently played.

So far only one disc has arrived of the Mosaïques' Op. 33 but, when the other follows, this set will surely trump the Festetics versions, for the performances are even more penetrating. Indeed the intensity of this playing is remarkable: like the Lindsays, uncovering hidden depths in these works, even in the *Joke Quartet*. This opens in an amiably leisured fashion, and the Minuet bounces strongly, with the Trio deliciously pointed with exquisite portamenti. The eloquent *Largo* is then comparatively austere, so that the release of tension in the lighthearted finale is the more winning. The *Vivace* opening of the *G major* has real grip and the slow movement subtly combines grace with a hint of melancholy, a whiff of which even strays into the Scherzo's trio. The first movement of the *C major* is hardly less compelling, and again there is a touch of darkness in the *Allegretto*, as distinct from the serenity of the beautiful *Adagio*. The finale then dances with fairy lightness. Marvellous playing and excellent, vivid recording.

The tonal matching and ensemble of the Bingham Quartet are most impressive, with the leader, Stephen Bingham, a remarkably stylish player who really understands how to shape a Haydn phrase. Above all the Binghams convey their pleasure in the music, and every performance here sounds fresh. The recording was made at the Conway Hall, London, in 1990. The balance is a shade close, but the instruments are naturally focused, individually and as a group, the sound rather less robust and mellow than with the Budapest Kodály recordings, although the effect is certainly real. Even if the range of dynamic is a little affected, the playing itself is full of light and shade so that if the volume level is carefully set one soon forgets this reservation in the sheer pleasure this music affords.

The Kodály Quartet play Op. 33 with an easy relaxed warmth. Their style is low-key so that the 'Joke' finale of Op. 33/2 is rather gentle and muted; on the other hand, the reason for the sobriquet of the *Bird Quartet* is affectionately conveyed and the finale is delightfully light-hearted. Slow movements are serene and quietly musical. Minuets are generally full of character, with the trios nicely realized, and this applies especially to the charming middle section of the Scherzo in the *Joke Quartet*. In short these are performances which convey the players' affection for this wonderful music with no possible desire to put their own personalities between composer and listener, and some listeners may feel the approach brings at times just a hint of blandness, unusual in this series. The Naxos recording is wholly natural with the acoustics of the Budapest Unitarian Church beautifully caught without any textural inflation.

If the Kodály Quartet are exceptionally relaxed in Op. 33, the Lindsays are at the opposite end of the scale: vividly alert and with the playing full of tension. This effect is emphasized by the recording, made in Trinity Church, Wentworth, where the microphones are close, giving striking presence and emphasizing the bite on the timbre of the leader, Peter Cropper, the effect only just short of edginess. Fortunately the superb ensemble stands up to such scrutiny but the finale of the *B minor Quartet*, for instance, played with great vigour, has a slightly aggressive feel. No one could say that the Lindsays miss the wit inherent in the finale of the *Joke*; yet, in spite of the gentle ending, the smile is weakened by the vibrant purposefulness. The performances here use the Henle Urtext edition, which differs quite substantially in phrasing and, in places, even in notes from the more familiar Peters Edition, especially at the opening of Op. 33/1. The second disc includes a Rosette-worthy account of Op. 33/3 with Haydn's birdsong exquisitely simulated.

The Weller Quartet offer very polished and lively playing and they are beautifully recorded. They also offer the bonus of two extra works. If the performances are not as penetrating as those of the Festetics Quartet or the young Bingham group, they are sunny and civilized and always enjoyable. In all three performances tempi are generally well considered, even if the finale of the *Joke* is perhaps too fast; on the other hand the last movement of Op. 33/4 is beautifully judged.

String quartets Nos. 43 in D min., Op.42; 67 in D (Lark), Op. 64/5; 79 in D, Op. 76/5.
(Y/B) (BB) *** ASV Dig. CDQS 6145 [id.]. Lindsay Qt.

The Lindsays are given a striking presence here and the spontaneity of their playing is gripping. The presto finales (particularly the moto perpetuo of *The Lark*, which overall is most strikingly done) offer fizzing bravura and the beautiful slow movement of Op. 76/5 is rapt in its quiet intensity. There are remarkably few moments of roughness of ensemble arising from the impetuosity of the playing.

String quartets Nos. 50–56 (The Seven Last Words of our Saviour on the Cross), Op. 51.
✱ *** ASV Dig. CDDCA 853 [id.]. Lindsay Quartet.

String quartets Nos. 50–56 (The Seven Last Words of our Saviour on the Cross), Op. 51; 83 in B flat, Op. 103.
(BB) *** Naxos Dig. 8.550346 [id.]. Kodály Qt.

No work for string quartet, not even late Beethoven, presents more taxing interpretative problems than Haydn's *Seven Last Words of our Saviour on the Cross.* The recording by the Lindsay Quartet, while offering all the devotional gravity that Haydn demands, brings not just an illuminating variety but also a sense of drama. In concert the Lindsays have performed it, as Haydn wanted, with a brief spoken address between movements explaining the title of each. The CD booklet provides the text of just such a commentary by Dr John Taylor, formerly Bishop of Winchester, and the performance makes no compromise for, unlike some others, the Lindsays observe the first-half repeats in each movement, extending the work to a full 70 minutes, instead of under an hour. Their range of expression, in dynamic, tempo and phrasing, is extremely wide, and they intensify the fundamental darkness of Haydn's minor-key inspirations with magical contrasts into the major mode. After the long sequence of slow movements, the Lindsays' account of the final, brief Presto, *Il terremoto,* then conveys the full, elemental force of the earthquake. It is thrilling with so elusive a work to have so complete an answer in a single recording, with sound both well defined and glowingly beautiful, set against an apt church acoustic.

The Kodály Quartet give a memorable performance, strongly characterized and beautifully played, with subtle contrasts of expressive tension between the seven inner slow movements. They also offer an appropriate bonus in Haydn's last, unfinished, two-movement *Quartet.* The recording is first rate, vividly present yet naturally balanced, like the other issues in this attractive Naxos series.

String quartets Nos. 50–56 (The Seven Last Words of Christ); 63–68, Op. 64 1–6 (Tost quartets).
(M) **(*) DG 431 145-2 (3). Amadeus Qt.

It is perhaps a pity that the Amadeus version of *The Seven Last Words of Christ* is linked on CD with Op. 64, for the immaculate Amadeus style, though not lacking in drama, does tend to smooth over the darker side of Haydn. The last six of the twelve *Tost Quartets* are another matter. Here the superb ensemble and cultivated playing are always easy on the ear when the recording is so well balanced and natural. Indeed, overall these performances give much pleasure.

String quartets Nos. 57 in G; 58 in C; 59 in E, Op. 54/1–3; 60 in A; 61 in F min. (Razor); 62 in B flat, Op. 55/1–3.
(M) **(*) DG 437 134-2 (2) [id.]. Amadeus Qt.

These are the first six of the twelve quartets dedicated to a rich, self-made patron, Johann Tost, who was also a violinist, and they include a number of masterpieces. Op. 55/2 acquired its nickname, *The Razor,* from a curious story. 'My best quartet for a decent razor,' Haydn said one day, and an enterprising publisher successfully took up the challenge. Though the Amadeus Quartet does not always play with the fullest intensity in some of the great slow movements, the ensemble is superb and the results are always easy on the ear. The CD transfers of recordings made in Munich in 1971/2 are fresh and clean.

String quartets Nos. 57 in G; 58 in C; 59 in E, Op. 54/1–3.
*** ASV Dig. CDDCA 582 [id.]. Lindsay Qt.
(BB) *** Naxos Dig. 8.550395; 4550395 [id.]. Kodály Qt.
(Y/B) *** Hyperion Dig. CDA 66971 [id.]. Salomon Qt.
(M) *** Virgin/EMI Dig. CUV5 61127-2 [id.]. Endellion Qt.

The present works show Haydn at his most inventive. The playing of the Lindsay Quartet is splendidly poised and vital, and the recording is very fine indeed.

The Kodály players enter animatedly into the spirit of the music; the leader, Attila Falvay, shows himself fully equal to Haydn's bravura embellishments in the demanding first violin writing. The Naxos sound is fresh and truthful.

The Salomon Quartet, led by Simon Standage, play on period instruments, but there is nothing anaemic or edgy about the body of tone they command, and the pervading feeling here is of freshness, with finales spirited without being rushed off their feet. This is one of the very best records from these excellent players and the recording is absolutely first class.

The Endellion Quartet on Virgin are bright-eyed, fresh and vital. The overall sound is beautifully integrated. Yet the Lindsays' insights go deeper, even if at times they have marginally less surface polish.

String quartets Nos. 60 in A; 61 in F min. (Razor); 62 in B flat, Op. 55/1–3 (Tost Quartets).
(Y/B) *** ASV Dig. CDDCA 906 [id.]. Lindsay Qt.
(BB) **(*) Naxos Dig. 8.550397. Kodály Qt.
(N) **(*) Hyperion Dig. CDA 66972 [id.]. Salomon Qt.

Here the Lindsays are heard under studio conditions, but in Holy Trinity Church, Wentworth, and the results, on the second set of *Tost Quartets*, are marginally less chimerical than in their live recordings, but not less dedicated or less vital. There is of course greater polish, as the fizzing finale of Op. 55/3 readily demonstrates. The recording is lifelike and vivid without excessive resonance.

Opus 55 brings playing from the Kodály Quartet which is undoubtedly spirited and generally polished, but the music-making at times seems plainer than usual in the Naxos series. The recording is bright and clear, with a realistic presence.

Generally fine playing from the Salomon Quartet in Op. 55, although this record is not quite as memorable as was Op. 54. The *Razor*, the second of the set, comes off very well indeed; but the slow movements in the two works on either side of it sound a shade too precise. The recording is truthful but rather close.

String quartets Nos. 63–8, Op. 64/1–6.
(N) (B) *** HM Dig. HMA 1903040/1 [id.]. Festetics Qt.

String quartets Nos. 63 in C; 64 in B min.; 65 in B flat, Op. 64/1–3.
(BB) *** Naxos Dig. 8.550673 [id.]. Kodály Qt.

String quartets Nos. 66 in G; 67 in D (Lark); 68 in E flat, Op. 64/4–6.
(BB) *** Naxos Dig. 8.550674 [id.]. Kodály Qt.

The excellent Hungarian Festetics Quartet follow their esteemed recording of Haydn's Op. 33 with an equally perceptive and animated set of Op. 64. Again their readings are very positive, yet the lightness of touch is balanced by buoyant rhythmic feeling and spontaneous impetus. Slow movements are played with a restrained vibrato and nicely judged espressivo, the line not spoilt by exaggerated bulges. Minuets are infectious and finales sparkle; the first movement of Op. 64/3 for example swings along spiritedly and, after the solemn *Adagio*, the rustic charm of the Minuet is appealingly caught. The brio of the first movement of Op. 64/4 gains much from the lightness of texture, while the leader's delicate, soaring line as the *Lark* is exquisite. The exposition repeat is observed, so the listener revels in the theme's many reappearances. The glowing *Adagio – cantabile e sostenuto* is also beautifully played. Indeed the last three quartets of the set continually demonstrate not only the high quality of this music-making, but how much these works can gain from performance on period instruments when the authentic style is unexaggerated and the ensemble and tonal matching are so precise. The recording, made in the Budapest Unitarian Church, is fairly close but could hardly be more beautifully balanced.

These Kodály performances are all enjoyable, but the set seems to get better and better as it progresses. Op. 64/1–3 were recorded on 25–29 April 1992; the last to be done, the *B flat major*, is remarkably successful, with a vigorous opening *Vivace assai* and a rapt *Adagio*. The other three works were taped on 1–3 May, and clearly the group had found its top form. The *Adagio – cantabile e sostenuto* of No. 4 finds them at their most concentrated: the *Lark* has never soared aloft more spontaneously and the Minuet and finale of No. 6 close the set in a winningly spirited fashion. The warm acoustics of the Budapest Unitarian Church provide a mellow and expansive sound-image, but not an orchestral one, and detail remains clear. A most enjoyable set.

String quartets Nos. 67 in D (Lark), Op. 64/5; 74 in G min. (Rider), Op. 74/3; 77 in C (Emperor), Op. 76/ 3.
(Y/B) (B) *** DG 439 479-2 [id.]. Amadeus Qt.

Here is a worthwhile triptych of named quartets for those seeking to sample the Amadeus Quartet in Haydn. Their superb ensemble is immediately noticeable at the opening of the *Lark Quartet*, as is Norbert Brainin's vibrato, giving the Amadeus sound its special stamp. The finale brings spiccato precision that dazzles the ear. The *Largo* of the *Rider Quartet* sounds just a little deliberate but its intensity is no doubt, and the gutsy vibrancy of the playing in the finale is equally remarkable. These date from the 1970s; the *Emperor* was made a decade earlier and the recording is a trifle thinner, though the body of tone the group commands projects impressively. The performance shows these fine musicians in the best possible light. The CD transfers are expertly done, and this Classikon reissue is excellent value.

String quartets Nos. 69 in B flat; 70 in D; 71 in E flat (Apponyi Quartets), Op. 71/1–3; 72 in C; 73 in F; 74 in G min. (Rider), Op. 74/1–3.
(BB) *** Naxos Dig. 8.550394 (*Nos. 69–71*); 8.550396 (*Nos. 72–74*) [id.]. Kodály Qt.

The *Apponyi Quartets* are among the composer's finest. The Naxos recordings by the Kodály Quartet are outstanding in every way and would be highly recommendable even without their considerable price advantage. The digital recording has vivid presence and just the right amount of ambience: the effect is entirely natural.

String quartets Nos. 69 in B flat; 70 in D; 71 in E flat, Op. 71/1–3 (Apponyi).
**(*) Chandos Dig. CHAN 9416 [id.]. Chilingirian Qt.

The Chilingirians' opening of the first of the *Apponyi Quartets* (so named because their 'onlie begetter' was Count Antal Apponyi) is very positive. This is spick-and-span playing, highly musical and full of character. Slow movements are well shaped and expressive and there are moments of wit, notably in the Minuet and Trio of No. 3. The recording is truthful. Yet this playing, although by no means plain, lacks something of the sunny quality the Kodály Quartet brings to this music.

String quartets Nos. 69 in B flat; 70 in D; 71 in E flat, Op. 71/1–3; 72 in C; 73 in F; 74 in G min. (Rider), Op. 74/1–3; 81 in G; 82 in F, Op. 77/1–2; 83 in D min., Op. 103.
(M) *** DG 429 189-2 (3). Amadeus Qt.

This excellent set shows the Amadeus on their finest form; there is a sense of spontaneity as well as genuine breadth to these readings. The recordings have a warm acoustic and plenty of presence.

String quartets Nos. 71 in E flat, Op. 71/3; 72 in C, Op. 74/1.
**(*) Hyperion CDA 66098 [id.]. Salomon Qt.

String quartets Nos. 73 in F; 74 in G min., Op. 74/2–3.
**(*) Hyperion CDA 66124 [id.]. Salomon Qt.

The appropriately named Salomon Quartet use period instruments. They are vibrato-less but vibrant; the sonorities, far from being nasal and unpleasing, are clean and transparent. There is imagination and vitality here, and the Hyperion recording is splendidly truthful. However, each disc offers short measure.

String quartets Nos. 72 in C; 73 in F; 74 in G min. (Rider), Op. 74/1–3.
(N) (BB) *** Naxos Dig. 8.550396 [id.]. Kodály Qt.

The Kodály Quartet are on top form here and give refreshing accounts of these three splendid quartets. Their simplicity of approach to the slow movement of the F major is particularly appealing, and the finale is sheer delight. The *Rider* is another of their most striking performances, including another memorable slow movement and a closing movement combining grace and refined ensemble with plentiful energy. The recording could hardly be bettered, completely natural and with the acoustic perfectly handled.

String quartet No. 74 in G min., Op. 74/3.
(N) (M) *** Cal. CAL 6698 [id.]. Talich Qt – BOCCHERINI: *Quartet, Op. 58/2;* MENDELSSOHN: *Quartet No. 2;* MICA: *Quartet No. 6.* ***

The *Quartet in G minor*, Opus 74, No. 3 (dedicated to Count Apponyi), is one of Haydn's greatest quartets. It brings a very beautiful, serenely introspective *Largo assai* in which, in this searching Talich performance, one has the feeling of eavesdropping on private music-making. After the blithe Minuet, the finale is engagingly light and spirited. Superb playing and most natural recording, and the rest of the performances on this generously filled mid-priced CD (76 minutes) are equally distinguished.

String quartets Nos. 75 in G; 76 in D min. (Fifths); 77 in C (Emperor); 78 in B flat (Sunrise); 79 in D; 80 in E flat, Op. 76/1–6 (Erdödy Quartets).
✲ (BB) *** Naxos Dig. 8.550314; *4550314* (*Nos. 75–77*); 8.550315; *4550315* (*Nos. 78–80*). Kodály Qt.
*** Hung. HCD 12812/3-2 [id.]. Tátrai Qt.
(B) **(*) Sony SB2K 53522 (2). Tokyo Qt.

String quartets Nos. 76 in D min. (Fifths); 77 in C (Emperor); 78 in B flat (Sunrise), Op. 76/2–4.
✲ (BB) *** Naxos Dig. 8.550129; *4550129* [id.]. Kodály Qt.

Haydn's six *Erdödy Quartets*, Op. 76, contain some of his very greatest music, and these performances by the Kodály Quartet are fully worthy of the composer's inexhaustible invention. Their playing brings a joyful pleasure in Haydn's inspiration and there is not the slightest suspicion of over-rehearsal or of routine: every bar of the music springs to life spontaneously, and these musicians' insights bring an ideal combination of authority and warmth, emotional balance and structural awareness.

The Tátrai's performances are unforced and natural, as intimate as if they were playing for pleasure, and as authoritative as one could hope for. The splendours of this set are as inexhaustible as those of the Beaux Arts set of the *Trios*.

The Tokyo Quartet offer superb playing and an immaculate tonal blend, and they are unfailingly intelligent. Yet it is a pity that they do not relax a little more and allow the music to unfold at greater leisure, as do the Kodály players, for they do not convey the humanity and charm that distinguish the Naxos set. The recording is faithful, but they are not as well served by the engineers as they were by DG for their prize-winning Bartók cycle; the sound, though fresh, is a little lacking in bloom at upper dynamic levels.

String quartets Nos. 76 in D min. (Fifths); 77 in C (Emperor); 78 in B flat (Sunrise), Op. 76/2–4.
(M) *** Teldec/Warner Dig. 9031 77602-2 [id.]. Eder Qt.

These are elegant performances that are unlikely to disappoint even the most demanding listener, save perhaps in the finale of the *Emperor*, which is taken a little too quickly. But this is unfailingly thoughtful quartet-playing whose internal balance and tonal blend are practically flawless.

String quartets Nos. 81 in G; 82 in F, Op. 77/1–2; 83 in D min., Op. 103.
*** Astrée Dig. E 8799 [id.]. Mosaïques Qt.
*** Hyperion Dig. CDA 66348 [id.]. Salomon Qt.
(B) **(*) HM Dig. HMA 1903001 [id.]. Festetics Qt.

String quartets Nos. 81 in G; 82 in F, Op. 77/1–2.
(N) (BB) ** Naxos Dig. 8.553146 [id.]. Kodály Qt.

Using original instruments to totally convincing effect, the Mosaïques Quartet give outstanding performances of Haydn's last three quartets. They play with much subtlety of colour and dynamic and bring total concentration to every bar of the music. The crisp, bouncing rhythm of the first movement of Op. 77/1 is engagingly arresting, and the *Adagio* is ideally paced and extremely eloquent; the *presto* Minuet of Op. 77/2 is bracingly crisp in articulation, followed by a rapt *sotto voce* introduction for the following *Andante*. The *E flat Quartet*, Haydn's last, is beautifully judged. The recording is absolutely real: the sound is transparent as well as immediate, within an ideally chosen acoustic. Moreover there is never a hint of acerbity of timbre from any of the four players, nor of the unattractive squeezing of lyrical lines which has spoiled so many authentic performances. This is among the finest of all Haydn quartet records.

The Salomon, recorded in a less ample acoustic, produce an altogether leaner sound but one that is thoroughly responsive to every shift in Haydn's thought. They seem to have great inner vitality and feeling.

Although the opening of Op. 77/1 has a pleasing rhythmic character, there is a coolness about the playing of the Festetics Quartet that lends itself less well to Haydn's expressive slow movement. They are at their best in the last quartet; and the transparency of texture from the use of original instruments brings some refreshing textures elsewhere, but in the last resort the effect is too austere.

The Kodály Quartet give comparatively robust performances of both works, made to seem even more robust by the close balance which reduces the dynamic range – not that the playing is notable for pianissimo contrast. This is warm, friendly music-making and in that respect (and in that respect only) preferable to the Festetics; but the latter's playing has considerably more subtlety, and they offer an extra work.

String quartet No. 83 in B flat, Op. 103.
(M) ** Decca 433 692-2 [id.]. Weller Qt – *Quartets Nos. 40–42*. **(*)

The Weller give an eminently smooth and polished account of the incomplete two-movement quartet of Haydn's old age.

KEYBOARD MUSIC

Piano sonatas Nos. 1–16; 17–19 (Hob Deest) 20; 28, Hob XIV/5; 29–62, Hob XVII/1–52 & G1; XVII/D1; The Seven last words on the Cross; Adagio in F; Capriccio in G on the song 'Acht Sauschneider müssen sein'; Fantasia in C; 7 Minuets from 'Kleine Tänz für die Jugend'; Variations in F min.; 5 Variations in D; 6 Variations in C; 12 Variations in E flat; 20 Variations in A.
(Y/B) (B) *** Decca 443 785-2 (12) [id.]. John McCabe.

John McCabe made the first successful complete survey of the Haydn *Sonatas* for Argo between 1974 and 1977, including also *The Seven last words on the Cross*, an arrangement not made by the composer but approved by him. It is remarkably successful here. Indeed two things shine through John McCabe's performances: their complete musicianship and their fine imagination. In presenting them as he does on a modern piano, McCabe makes the most of the colour and subtlety of the music, and in that respect his style is more expressive, less overtly classical than Jandó's (see below) while the recording is made to sound somewhat softer-grained by the acoustic of All Saints' Church, Petersham. Given phrasing so clearly articulated and alertly phrased, and such varied, intelligently thought-out and wholly responsive presentation, this set can be recommended very enthusiastically. The recordings are of the very highest quality, truthful in timbre and firmly refined in detail, and they must be numbered among the most successful of this repertoire ever to be put on disc, for the piano is notoriously difficult to balance in eighteenth-century music. The set is most reasonably priced and the pianist provides his own extensive and illuminating notes. To sample the calibre of this enterprise, begin with *The Seven last words* – playing of unexaggerated expressive feeling that almost makes one believe this was a work conceived in pianistic terms.

Andante with variations in F min., Hob. XVIII/6; Piano sonatas Nos. 59 in E flat, Hob. XVI/49; 60 in C, Hob. XVI/50; 62 in E flat, Hob. XVI/52.

(N) *** Ph. Brendel Edition Dig./Analogue 446 921-2 [id.]. Alfred Brendel – MOZART: *Piano concertos and sonatas.* **(*)

This disc acts as a mere sampler of Brendel's outstanding Haydn recordings. In Hob. XVI/49 (analogue), the first to be recorded, he observes all the repeats and the sound is first class. The rest of the programme is digital. His playing throughout is of real distinction, aristocratic without being aloof, concentrated without being too intense. Everything is cleanly articulated and finely characterized. He is accorded lifelike and vivid recording.

Piano sonatas Nos. 11 in B flat, Hob XVI/2; 31 in A flat, Hob XVI/46; 39 in D min., Hob XVI/24; 47 in B min., Hob XVI/32.

*** Decca Dig. 436 455-2 [id.]. Sviatoslav Richter.

Richter's crisp, classical style, with sparing use of the pedal and strong rhythmic feeling is immediately noticeable at the opening of the *B minor* work, bringing a feeling almost of a *moto perpetuo*, although the variations of colour and dynamic prevent any hint of monotony. The *Andante* is cool and gentle and the finale brings toccata-like brilliance of execution. So it is with the others here, though the *Adagios* of both the *D minor* and (especially) the *A flat major* are gentle and touching, while the two closing movements of the early *B flat Sonata* have an engaging simplicity. Clear, realistic 1986 sound and not too much applause.

Piano sonatas Nos. 32 in G min., Hob XVI/44; 54 in G, Hob XVI/40; 55 in B flat, Hob XVI/41; 58 in C, Hob XVI/48; 62 in E flat, Hob XVI/52.

*** Decca Dig. 436 454-2 [id.]. Sviatoslav Richter.

Richter's second Decca Haydn CD, made in Mantua in 1987, is undoubtedly the more attractive of the two, the playing no less direct but with less of a sense of classical austerity. The opening of the *G minor Sonata* is very winning indeed, and his softness of approach is carried over to the following *G major* work. Both the *C major* (Hob XVI/48) and the well-known *E flat major* (Hob XVI/52) are among Haydn's finest works for the piano – and that means very fine indeed – and Richter's playing is fully worthy of this marvellous music. Again the sound is vivid and immediate.

Piano sonatas Nos. 33 in C min., Hob XVI/20; 47 in B min., Hob XVI/32; 53 in E min., Hob XVI/34; 50 in D, Hob XVI/37; 54 in G, Hob XVI/40; 56 in D, Hob XVI/42; 58 in C; 59 in E flat; 60 in C; 61 in D; 62 in E flat, Hob XVI/48–52; Adagio in F, Hob XVII/9; Andante with variations in F min., Hob XVII/6; Fantasia in C, Hob XVII/4.

*** Ph. 416 643-2 (4). Alfred Brendel.

This collection offers some of the best Haydn playing on record – and some of the best Brendel, too. The eleven sonatas, together with the *F minor Variations* and the *C major Fantasia*, have been recorded over a number of years and are splendidly characterized and superbly recorded. The first is analogue, the remainder digital.

Piano sonatas Nos. 33 in C min., Hob XVI/20; 58 in C, Hob XVI/48; 60 in C, Hob XVI/50.

*** Denon Dig. C37 7801 [id.]. András Schiff.

Schiff plays with an extraordinary refinement and delicacy; he is resourceful and highly imaginative in his use of tone-colour; his phrasing and articulation are a constant source of pleasure. Superb in every way and beautifully recorded, too.

Piano sonatas: 33 in C min., Hob XVI/20; 60 in C, Hob XVI/50; 62 in E flat, Hob XVI/52; Andante & Variations in F min., Hob XVIII/6.
*** Virgin/EMI Dig. VC5 45254-2 [id.]. Mikhail Pletnev.

Pletnev's reading of the *Sonatas* is full of personality and character. The *C major* is given with great elegance and wit, and the great *E flat Sonata* is magisterial. This playing has a masterly authority, and Pletnev is very well recorded.

Piano sonatas Nos. 36 in C, Hob XVI/21; 37 in E, Hob XVI/22; 38 in F, Hob XVI/23; 39 in D, Hob XVI/24; 40 in E flat, Hob XVI/25; 41 in A, Hob XVI/26.
(Y/B) (BB) **(*) Naxos Dig. 8.553127 [id.]. Jenö Jandó.

Piano sonatas Nos. 48 in C, Hob XVI/35; 49 in C sharp min., Hob XVI/36; 50 in D, Hob XVI/37; 51 in E flat, Hob XVI/38; 52 in G, Hob XVI/39.
(Y/B) (BB) *** Naxos Dig. 8.553128 [id.]. Jenö Jandó.

Jandó seems to have been very slightly below par when he recorded Volume 4 (8.553127) of his ongoing set of Haydn sonatas in May 1993. The playing is as bright and clear as before and the interpretations are well thought out, but just occasionally there is a hint of stiffness and overall there is not always the degree of spontaneity we expect from this artist.

A month later, in June of the same year, he was back on form with all the freshness that marked his earlier records in the series, as the opening of *No. 36 in C* immediately shows. The finale of *No. 37 in E major* is beautifully played, and the following two sonatas with their fine slow movements will not disappoint his admirers. Excellent piano sound, crisp but not too dry.

Piano sonatas Nos. 38 in F, Hob XVI/23; 51 in E flat, Hob XVI/38; 52 in G, Hob XVI/39.
*** Mer. CDE 84155; *KE 77155* [id.]. Julia Cload.

Julia Cload's cool, direct style is heard at its best in her second group of sonatas. The piano image is bright and clear, with just a touch of hardness on *fortes*.

Piano sonatas Nos. 42 in G, Hob XVI/27; 43 in E flat, Hob XVI/28; 44 in F, Hob XVI/29; 45 in A, Hob XVI/30; 46 in E, Hob XVI/31; 47 in B min., Hob XVI/32.
(BB) *** Naxos Dig. 8.550844 [id.]. Jenö Jandó (piano).

The six sonatas offered here (in what is Volume II of Jenö Jandó's ongoing series) were written between 1774 and 1776 and were later grouped together and published by Hummel as Haydn's Op. 14. Although they are all comparatively straightforward three-movement classical sonatas, such a comment is deceptive for Haydn consistently has something individual to contribute. *No. 44 in F*, supposedly influenced by C. P. E. Bach, has a somewhat quirky first movement and a characteristically imaginative final Minuet which goes unexpectedly into the minor and has much of the format of a theme and variations. The last work of the set in B minor opens with perhaps the most striking idea of all and, after the gracious central Minuet, ends in a flurry of precocious virtuosity, with Jandó clearly in his element. He shows himself a complete master of this repertoire, and the recording, crisp and clean but not too dry, is first class.

Piano sonatas Nos. 50 in D, Hob XVI/37; 54 in G, Hob XVI/40; 55 in B flat, Hob XVI/41; Adagio in F, Hob XVIII/9.
*** Mer. ECD 84083; *KE 77083* [id.]. Julia Cload.

Julia Cload's playing is fresh, characterful and intelligent, and will give considerable pleasure. She has the advantage of very truthful recorded sound.

Piano sonatas Nos. 53 in E min., Hob XVI/34; 54 in G, Hob XVI/40; 55 in B flat, Hob XVI/41; 56 in D, Hob XVI/42; 58 in C, Hob XVI/48; Variations in F min. (Sonata, un piccolo divertimento), Hob XVIII/6.
(BB) *** Naxos Dig. 8.550845 [id.]. Jenö Jandó (piano).

These are distinctly appealing performances of the three *Sonatas*, Hob XVI/40–42, dedicated to Princess Marie Esterházy, who had married the grandson of Haydn's princely patron. They are each in two movements, and in the case of the *G major* the first is marked *Allegretto e innocente*, an obvious tribute to feminine charm. But all three are fine works and not as simple as they at first appear. Jandó also gives a splendid account of the more ambitious three-movement *Sonata in E minor*, Hob XVI/34. He is a true Haydn player and this (Volume III of his projected series) is in every way recommendable, particularly as the recording is so vivid and clean: just right for the repertoire.

Piano sonatas Nos. 56 in D, Hob XVI/42; 58 in C; 59 in E flat; 60 in C; 61 in D; 62 in E flat, Hob XVI/48–52.
(M) *(**) Sony Dig. SM2K 52623 [id.]. Glenn Gould.

Gould's clean, classical style in Haydn is often refreshing, but after a while the squeaky-clean articulation, although quite remarkably crisp, becomes a little wearing and the ear craves a less staccato, less percussive approach to allegros. This is not a fortepiano imitation but a pianoforte played with the most sparing sonority. Gould undoubtedly makes a sensitively expressive response to slow movements, but an air of eccentricity remains in the overall shaping of phrases. The digital recording is clear, to match the playing.

Piano sonatas Nos. 58 in C; 59 in E flat; 60 in C; 61 in D; 62 in E flat, Hob XVI/48–52.
*** RCA Dig. RD 77160 [77160-2-RC]. Andreas Staier (fortepiano).

Andreas Staier plays a recent copy by Christopher Clarke of a fortepiano from around 1790 by the Viennese maker, Anton Walter, and proves a highly sensitive and imaginative interpreter. He brings a surprisingly wide dynamic range as well as a diversity of keyboard colour to these pieces and holds the listener throughout. He is very well recorded indeed.

Piano sonatas Nos. 58 in C, Hob XVI/48; 62 in E flat, Hob XVI/52.
(M) **(*) Decca 433 900-2 [id.]. Wilhelm Backhaus – MOZART: *Sonatas.* **(*)

There is some of Haydn's greatest keyboard music here – the *C major* and *E flat Sonatas* are especially fine – and its greatness is not minimized by Backhaus, even though his clean articulation with its light pedalling misses the composer's genial side. The 1957 piano recording is very truthful.

Piano sonatas Nos. 59 in E flat; 60 in C; 61 in D; 62 in E flat, Hob XVI/49–52.
(BB) *** Naxos Dig. 8.550657 [id.]. Jenö Jandó.

Jenö Jandó here shows himself as strong and sympathetic in Haydn as in Beethoven. Although the performances are straighter, Nos. 60 and 62 compare remarkably favourably with Pletnev's masterly accounts. Without allowing himself stylistic idiosyncrasies, Jandó shows himself a thoughtfully imaginative player as well as a bold one, and the finale of the great *E flat Sonata* has splendid, unforced bravura. The recording, made in the Unitarian Church, Budapest, provides an attractive ambience without an excess of ecclesiastical resonance.

VOCAL MUSIC

Arianna a Naxos (cantata).
(N) *** Decca Dig. 440 297-2 [id.]. Cecilia Bartoli, András Schiff – BEETHOVEN: *Che fa il mio bene?* etc.; MOZART: *Ridente la calma;* SCHUBERT: *Da quel sembiante appresi* etc. ***

Arianna a Naxos; Fidelity; The mermaid's song; Pastoral song; Sailor's song; She never told her love; Spirit's song; Der verdienstvolle Sylvius.
(N) *** DG Dig. 447 106-2 [id.]. Anne Sofie von Otter, Melvyn Tan (fortepiano) – MOZART: *Lieder.* ***

To declare a preference between Cecilia Bartoli and Anne Sofie von Otter in Haydn's extended scena is virtually impossible. With its double alternating recitative and aria, the first doubtful concerning a lover's faithfulness, the second expressing the despair and anger of known betrayal, Haydn's setting demands the widest range of mood and identification with the words; both singers rise to the occasion with passion and consummate artistry. Bartoli has the inestimable András Schiff as partner; Von Otter has Melvyn Tan's eloquent fortepiano. So in the end it depends on the couplings: the other Haydn songs on the DG disc are happily varied in mood, to bring either innocent simplicity (*A Pastoral song*), histrionics (*Fidelity*) – with Tan very much rising to the occasion – or touching, unexaggerated pathos (*She never told her love* and *Der verdienstvolle Sylvius*). By comparison, the *Sailor's song* is suitably robust and the melancholy *Spirit's song*, which ends the recital, pensively nostalgic. The recording balance is just about ideal.

The Creation (complete; in English).
*** EMI Dig. CDS7 54159-2 [Ang. CDCB 54159] (2). Augér, Langridge, David Thomas, CBSO & Ch., Simon Rattle.
*** Decca Dig. 430 397-2 (2) [id.]. Kirkby, Rolfe Johnson, George, New College, Oxford, Ch., AAM Ch. & O, Hogwood.

The English version may have its oddities – like the 'flexible tiger' leaping – but it is above all colourful, and Rattle brings out that illustrative colour with exceptional vividness: birdsong, lion-roars and the like. He has plainly learnt from period performance, not only concerning speeds – often surprisingly brisk, as in the great soprano aria, *With verdure clad* – but as regards style too. The male soloists sound none too sweet as recorded, but they characterize positively; and there is no finer account of the soprano's music than that of Arleen Augér. The weight of the Birmingham chorus is impressive, achieved without loss of clarity or detail in a full, well-balanced recording.

Hogwood defies what has become the custom in period performance and opts for large forces. The result, for all its weight, retains fine clarity of detail and an attractive freshness. The choir of New College, Oxford, with its trebles adds to the brightness of choral sound, and the trio of soloists is admirably consistent – Emma Kirkby brightly distinctive, and Anthony Rolfe Johnson sweet-toned. Hogwood may lack some of the flair and imagination of Rattle, but it would be hard to find a period performance to match this. The sound has fine presence and immediacy.

The Creation (Die Schöpfung; in German).
(M) *** DG 435 077-2 (2). Janowitz, Ludwig, Wunderlich, Krenn, Fischer-Dieskau, Berry, V. Singverein, BPO, Karajan.
(Y/B) *** Sony SX2K 57965 (2) [id.]. Monoyios, Hering, Van der Kamp, Tölz Boys' Ch., Tafelmusik, Bruno Weil.
*** DG Dig. 419 765-2 (2) [id.]. Blegen, Popp, Moser, Ollmann, Moll, Bav. R. Ch. & SO, Bernstein.
(Y/B) *** Decca 443 445-2 (2) [id.]. Ziesak, Lippert, Pape, Scharinger, Chicago Ch. & SO, Solti.
(N) (M) **(*) DG Dig. 445 584-2 (2) [id.]. Battle, Winbergh, Moll, Stockholm R. Ch. and Chamber Ch., BPO, Levine.
(Y/B) **(*) Telarc Dig. CD 80298 (2) [id.]. Upshaw, Humphrey, Cheek, Murphy, McGuire, Chamber Ch. & SO, Shaw.
(B) (**(*)) DG Double mono 437 380-2 (2) [id.]. Irmgard Seefried, Richard Holm, Kim Borg, St Hedwig's Cathedral Choir, BPO, Markevitch.
(N) (M) ** Teldec/Warner Dig. 0630 10026-2 (2) [id.]. Gruberová, Protschka, Holl, Schönberg Ch., VSO, Harnoncourt.

(i) *The Creation (Die Schöpfung):* complete (in German); (ii) *Salve regina.*
(B) *** Double Decca 443 027-2 (2) [id.]. (i) Lucia Popp, Werner Hollweg, Kurt Moll, Helena Döse, Benjamin Luxon, Brighton Festival Ch., RPO, Dorati; (ii) Arleen Augér, Alfreda Hodgson, Anthony Rolfe Johnson, Gwynne Howell, L. Chamber Ch., Argo CO, László Heltay.

Among versions of *The Creation* sung in German, Karajan's 1969 set remains unsurpassed and, at mid-price, is a clear first choice despite two small cuts (in Nos. 30 and 32). The combination of the Berlin Philharmonic at its most intense and the great Viennese choir makes for a performance that is not only polished but warm and dramatically strong too. The soloists are an extraordinarily fine team, more consistent in quality than those on almost any rival version.

Bruno Weil conducts a brisk, clean-cut reading, using the period instruments of Tafelmusik and a bright-toned chorus, augmented by the Tölz Boys' Choir. If the intimacy at times seems to reduce the scale of this masterpiece, and Weil at times is fussy over detail, the urgent exuberance of the performance is most winning, with an outstanding trio of cleanly focused soloists. The chorus is finely focused too, providing sharp, dramatic contrasts, and the orchestral sound is so clean that one can hear the fortepiano continuo even in tuttis. A good contrasting approach to Christopher Hogwood's on his large-scale period performance in English.

Dorati, as one would expect, directs a lively and well-sprung account. The very opening is magnetic and its imaginative touches and joyfulness of spirit more than compensate for any minor lapses in crispness of ensemble. The soloists are a splendid team. The chorus is as gusty as you like in *Die Himmel erzählen,* with the soloists nicely balanced. While Karajan is not superseded, Dorati's enjoyably spontaneous 1976 account is certainly well worth considering, especially as it is offered for the cost of a single premium-priced CD. The set opens gloriously with Heltay's lovely 1979 recording of the *Salve regina,* an early work dating from 1771, comparable in its depth of feeling with his finest vocal music. The recording is most realistic and the CD transfer of *The Creation* is strikingly vivid and immediate.

Bernstein's DG version, recorded at a live performance in Munich, uses a relatively large chorus, encouraging him to adopt rather slow speeds at times. What matters is the joy conveyed in the story-telling, with the finely disciplined chorus and orchestra producing incandescent tone, blazing away in the big set-numbers, and the performance is compulsive from the very opening bars. Five soloists are used instead of three, with the parts of Adam and Eve sung by nicely contrasted singers, confirming this as an unusually persuasive version, well recorded in atmospheric sound.

Recorded live in the autumn of 1993, Sir Georg Solti's second recording, made (like the first) with Chicago forces, presents a striking difference. The influence of period performance means that not only does he adopt fast speeds, but his very choice of soloists reflects the new generation of light, clear singers, all excellent. Ornamentation and the use of a fortepiano continuo also give further indication of Sir Georg's new stance on this work, which results in a crisp, buoyant reading, full of dramatic contrasts, which nevertheless is not out of scale with Haydn's vision. If in such a number as the first Adam and Eve duet of Part 3 Solti's speed is excessively fast, making the result trivial, the buoyancy remains, and generally he and his team avoid breathlessness, with splendid choral singing, captured in full, bright sound. However, first choice among modern-instrument performances remains with Rattle, sung in English.

Though James Levine with his weighty forces is occasionally heavy-handed over both dynamics and rhythm, lacking rather in elegance, he conveys the joy of inspiration in this work with characteristic boldness. He is helped not just by the highly polished playing of the orchestra but by characterful singing from all three soloists and fresh, finely disciplined choral singing. The recording, made not in the Philharmonie but in the Jesus-Christus Kirche, is weighty and satisfyingly full, with ample bloom.

Robert Shaw with his keenly disciplined chamber choir conducts a strong, clean-cut performance, using an English translation modified from the traditional one. Though Shaw's generally broad speeds show little influence from period performance, his concern for clarity of texture is very different from old-style performances, and the Telarc engineers help with full, immediate sound, bringing out sharp dynamic contrasts. Dawn Upshaw adopts too romantically expressive a manner, but the solo singing is good, with Heidi Grant Murphy and James Michael McGuire brought in for the Adam and Eve numbers of Part 3.

Markevitch's recording was made at the very end of the mono LP era and was first published in 1958. It shows the extraordinary expertise of the DG engineers at that time, for only the somewhat thin orchestral violins really betray the age of the recording. The soloists are naturally caught and the chorus is brilliantly and cleanly recorded. Markevitch is nothing if not dramatic. The opening *Prelude* is full of electric tension and the choruses have great energy and bite. All three soloists are excellent.

Harnoncourt's version with the Vienna Symphony Orchestra was recorded live. It follows the first printed edition of 1800, using the same size of forces as in performances of that date, with a gentle fortepiano replacing harpsichord in recitatives. Compared with the finest versions the ensemble is on the rough side, and the singing of the male soloists is often rough, too. The tenor, Josef Protschka, shouts Uriel's first entry but settles down after that; while by far the most distinguished singing of the set comes from Edita Gruberová, dazzling and imaginative, with slightly backward balance helping to eliminate the touch of hardness that the microphone often brings out in her voice. The sound otherwise is full and clear.

The Creation: highlights.
(Y/B) (B) *** DG 439 454-2 [id.] (from above recording; cond. Karajan).

Anyone whose budget will not stretch to a complete version of Haydn's masterpiece will find that this 70-minute bargain Classikon highlights disc includes the key solos and choruses.

(i) *The Creation;* (ii) *Mass No. 14 in B flat (Harmoniemesse), Hob XXII/14.*
(M) ** Sony SM2K 47560 (2). (i) Raskin, Young, Reardon, Camerata Singers: (ii) Blegen, Von Stade, Riegel, Estes, Westminster Ch.; NYPO, Bernstein.

Bernstein's first recording of *The Creation* was made in the Avery Fisher Hall in 1966. It is a fine, spontaneous account with bouncy choruses and an excellent team of soloists. The sound is not ideally refined in the upper range but it is reasonably spacious, and the warmth and vigour of the performance carry the day. The *Harmoniemesse* was done in the Manhattan Center in 1973 and the recording is obviously more modern and rather more spacious, though closely balanced. The performance has characteristic energy and pace. Good value, though Bernstein's digital DG set of *The Creation* is preferable on almost all counts, including recording quality (see above).

Masses

Masses Nos. 1a in G (Rorate coeli desuper), Hob XXII/3; (i) 5 in E flat (Grosse Orgelmesse): Missa in honorem Beatissimae Virginis Mariae, Hob XXII/4; (ii) 6 in G (Missa Sancti Nicolai), Hob XXII/6.
*** O-L 421 478-2 [id.]. Christ Church Cathedral, Oxford, Ch., AAM, Preston, with (i) Nelson, Watkinson, Hill, D. Thomas; (ii) Nelson, Minty, Covey-Crump, D. Thomas.

In the early *E flat Mass* Haydn followed the rococo conventions of his time, generally adopting a style featuring Italianate melody which to modern ears inevitably sounds operatic. The *Missa Sancti Nicolai* has a comparable freshness of inspiration. The performance is first rate in every way, even finer than that of the earlier Mass, beautifully sung, with spontaneity in every bar and a highly characterized accompaniment. The little *Missa rorate coeli desuper* was written by Haydn when he was still a choirboy in Vienna, and it may well be his earliest surviving work. Excellent recording ensures that this CD receives a warm welcome.

Mass No. 2 in F (Missa brevis), Hob XXII/1.
*** O-L 421 654-2 [id.]. Kirkby, Nelson, Ch. of Christ Church Cathedral, Oxford, AAM, Preston –
   HANDEL: *Anthem for Foundling Hospital* etc. ***

Haydn's early *Missa brevis* is engagingly unpretentious; some of its sections last for under two minutes
and none takes more than three and a half. The two soprano soloists here match their voices admirably
and the effect is delightful.

Masses No. 2a (1768): *Sunt bona mixta malis* (fragment), *Hob XXII/2; 7 in B flat (Little organ mass):
Missa brevis Sancti Joannis de Deo, Hob XXII/7; Ave Regina, Hob XXIIIb/3; Offertorium: Non nobis,
Domine, Hob XXIIIa/1; Responsorium ad absolutionem: Libera me, Hob XXIIb/1; 4 Responsoria de
Venerabili, Hob XXIIIc/4 a–d; Salve Regina, Hob XXIIIb/1.*
⊛ *** Sony Dig. SK 53368 [id.]. Marie-Claude Vallin, Ann Monoyios, Tölz Boys' Ch., L'Archibudelli,
   Tafelmusik, Bruno Weil.

The Mass fragment, *Sunt bona mixta malis* (consisting of a *Kyrie* and part of the *Gloria* of an
incomplete mass in D minor), was recently discovered in the attic of a country house in Northern
Ireland and establishes that at that time Haydn was composing vocal music in an austere, antique,
contrapuntal style, looking back towards Palestrina. The four *Responsoria de Venerabili* are more extrovert in feeling, but the second is again in the older style. Other works on this record – the *Responsorium
ad absolutionem, Libera me*, and the *Offertorium, Non nobis, Domine* – reflect this same grave contrapuntal idiom and have had to be re-dated in consequence. The collection is completed with a later Mass
and two fine early works from the 1750s, the *Ave Regina*, in which Marie-Claude Vallin sings with the
purity of a boy treble, and the poignant *Salve Regina in E*. Here the soprano solo is superbly and
touchingly sung by Ann Monoyios. It is undoubtedly a profoundly felt work, certainly the finest of
Haydn's youthful period. The *Missa brevis: Sancti Joannis de Deo* features a solo organ which delightfully accompanies the boy treble soloist in the *Benedictus* (sung here by a member of the Tölz Boys'
Choir). This fascinating record cannot be recommended too highly. The performances are admirably
stylish and very fresh and alive.

Mass No. 3 (Missa Cellensis): Missa Sanctae Caeciliae, Hob XXII/5.
*** O-L Dig. 417 125-2 [id.]. Nelson, Cable, Hill, Thomas, Ch. of Christ Church Cathedral, AAM,
   Preston.

The *Missa Cellensis* is Haydn's longest setting of the liturgy. Preston directs an excellent performance
with fine contributions from choir and soloists, set against a warmly reverberant acoustic.

Masses Nos. (i) *7 in B flat (Little organ mass): Missa brevis Sancti Joannis de Deo, Hob XXII/7;* (ii) *8 in C
(Mariazellermesse): Missa Cellensis, Hob XXII/8;* (iii) *Organ concerto No. 1 in C, Hob XVIII/1.*
(M) *** Decca 430 160-2 [id.]. (i) J. Smith; Scott; (ii) J. Smith, Watts, Tear, Luxon; (i; ii) St John's College,
   Cambridge, Ch., Guest; (i–iii) ASMF; (iii) Preston, Marriner.

With excellent singing and fine orchestral playing, this is a very desirable issue in the splendid Guest
series. The CD transfers are admirably fresh and well focused, and for a bonus we are given Simon
Preston's persuasive account of an early organ concerto. Preston's vivid registration and Marriner's
spirited accompaniment ensure the listener's pleasure.

Masses Nos. (i) *7 in B flat: Missa brevis Sancti Joannis de Deo (Little organ mass), Hob XXII/7;* (ii) *9 in B
flat (Heiligmesse): Missa Sancti Bernardi von Offida, XXII/10;* (iii) *11 in D min. (Nelson); Missa in
angustiis, Hob XXII/11;* (iv) *12 in B flat (Theresienmesse), Hob XXII/12.*
(N) (B) ** EMI forte Dig. CZS5 68592-2 (2). (i) Hendricks, Murray, Blochwitz, Hölle; (ii) Vaness,
   Soffel, Lewis, Salomaa; (iii) Marshall, Watkinson, Lewis, Holl; Leipzig R. Ch., Dresden State O,
   Marriner.

Although digitally recorded and presented here economically on an EMI forte double, these Marriner
performances cannot compare with George Guest's series on Decca. In the *Missa brevis* Marriner
favours brisk speeds, defying the weight of his forces, which is increased by the bass-heavy Dresden
recording. Though the Leipzig Radio Chorus is sometimes stressed, as are the soloists, this is an
enjoyably vigorous reading. The *Heiligmesse* and the *Theresienmesse* were recorded together and bring
more vigorous and responsive singing from the Leipzig Chorus. Here these wonderfully disciplined
singers are on top form and rise superbly to Marriner's often challengingly fast speeds; their ensemble in
slow sections is sweeter than that of the soloists or even that of the orchestra. The solo singers are close-
balanced so that the vibrato of the two women is exaggerated and the full quartet makes an ill-matched
ensemble. Heard like this, these are voices not well suited to Haydn, and the reverberation in the
recordings inflates what by latterday standards is too hefty an orchestral sound. The *Nelson mass* brings

a perfectly acceptable performance, with good soloists and the Leipzig Choir still on excellent form. The ample Dresden acoustic does not prevent internal clarity, and this account brings moments which match the companion Masses in vigour; yet overall the effect is essentially cultured, weighty and just a shade bland.

Mass No. 9 in B flat (Heiligmesse): Missa Sancti Bernardi von Offida, Hob XXII/10.
(M) *** Decca 430 158-2 [id.]. Cantelo, Minty, Partridge, Keyte, St John's College, Cambridge, Ch., ASMF, Guest – MOZART: *Litaniae de venerabili.* ***

Of all Haydn's Masses the *Heiligmesse* is one of the most human and direct in its appeal. Its combination of symphonic means and simple vocal style underlines its effectiveness. Like the other records in this series, this is a splendid performance, and the vintage Argo sound has been transferred very successfully to CD.

Mass No. 10 in C (Paukenmesse): Missa in tempore belli, Hob XXII/9.
(M) *** Decca 430 157-2 [id.]. Cantelo, Watts, Tear, McDaniel, St John's College, Cambridge, Ch., ASMF, Guest – MOZART: *Vesperae sollennes.* ***

Guest provides a clean, brightly recorded account with good soloists. The Argo performance sounds very fresh in its remastered format.

Masses Nos. (i) *10 in C (Paukenmesse): Missa in tempore belli, Hob. XXII/9;* (ii) *11 in D min. (Nelson): Missa in angustiis.*
(M) **(*) Sony SM2K 47563 (2). Killebrew, (i) Wells, Devlin, Titus, Norman Scribner Ch., O; (ii) Blegen, Riegel, Estes, Westminster Ch., NYPO; Bernstein – *Symphony No. 88 in G.* **(*)

Bernstein recorded the *Paukenmesse* in Washington National Cathedral in 1973 in connection with a peace demonstration. The result has great emotional intensity, and within the acoustics of the cathedral the choir produces gloriously rich sounds. Stylistically the performance is more questionable, but it certainly has a sense of occasion, and the remastered recording – originally produced for quadrophony – is fuller than usual from this source. The account of the *Nelson Mass*, recorded in the Manhattan Center three years later, has comparable intensity and a striking choral vitality and bite. The soloists are good, and this, too, has the spontaneity of a live occasion. A fine performance of the *Symphony No. 88* is thrown in for good measure – see above.

Mass No. 11 in D min. (Nelson): Missa in angustiis.
(M) *** Decca 421 146-2. Stahlman, Watts, Wilfred Brown, Krause, King's College, Cambridge, Ch., LSO, Willcocks – VIVALDI: *Gloria.* ***
(M) **(*) Decca Dig. 436 470-2 [id.]. Bonney, Howells, Rolfe Johnson, Roberts, L. Symphony Ch., City of L. Sinfonia, Hickox – MOZART: *Coronation mass.* **(*)

Mass No. 11 in D min. (Nelson); Te Deum in C, Hob XXIIIc/2.
*** DG Dig. 423 097-2 [id.]. Lott, C. Watkinson, Maldwyn Davies, Wilson-Johnson, Ch. & E. Concert, Pinnock.

The *Nelson Mass* (*Missa in angustiis*: 'Mass in times of fear') brings a superb choral offering from Trevor Pinnock and the English Concert. With incandescent singing from the chorus and fine matching from excellent soloists, Pinnock brings home the high drama of Haydn's autumnal inspiration. Similarly, the *Te Deum* leaps forward from the eighteenth century all the more excitingly in an authentic performance such as this. Excellent, full-blooded sound, with good definition.

The CD of the famous Willcocks account is admirably full-bodied and vivid; those not wanting to stretch to Pinnock's full-priced digital CD will find this a satisfactory alternative with its very generous Vivaldi coupling.

Hickox conducts a lively, well-sung reading of the most celebrated of Haydn's late Masses, most impressive in the vigorous, outward-going music which – with Haydn – makes up the greater part of the service. What is disappointing is the recessed sound of the choir, with inner parts less well defined than they should be. The soloists are good but, as recorded, Barbara Bonney's soprano has a thinness along with the purity. Enjoyable as this is, it falls short of the superb Argo version of 20 years earlier.

Mass No. 12 in B flat (Theresienmesse), Hob XXII/12.
(M) *** Decca 430 159-2 [id.]. Spoorenberg, Greevy, Mitchinson, Krause, St John's College, Cambridge, Ch., Guest – M. HAYDN: *Ave Regina;* MOZART: *Ave verum corpus.* ***
(M) *** Sony Dig. SM2K 47522 (2). Popp, Elias, Tear, Hudson, London Symphony Ch., LSO, Bernstein – BEETHOVEN: *Choral fantasia* etc. ***

The *Theresa Mass* may be less famous than the *Nelson Mass* but its inspiration is hardly less memorable.

George Guest injects tremendous vigour into the music and the St John's Choir, in splendid form, makes the very most of this fine work. Good solo singing and brilliant, vivid, 1965 recording.

Bernstein's grand manner goes with playing and singing of infectious bounce and resilience, typical of this conductor. The soloists are first rate, and this can be warmly recommended as an enjoyably spontaneous large-scale alternative to Guest's fine version on Decca.

Mass No. 13 in B flat (Schöpfungsmesse), Hob XXII/13.
(M) *** Decca 430 161-2 [id.]. Cantelo, Watts, Tear, Forbes Robinson, St John's College, Cambridge, Ch., ASMF, Guest – MOZART: *Mass No. 12 (Spaur).* ***

Guest again draws an outstanding performance from his own St John's College Choir and an excellent band of professionals, a fresh and direct reading to match the others of his highly successful Argo series.

Mass No. 14 in B flat (Harmoniemesse), Hob XXII/14.
(M) *** Decca 430 162-2 [id.]. Spoorenberg, Watts, Young, Rouleau, St John's College, Cambridge, Ch., Guest – MOZART: *Vesperae de Dominica.* ***

Haydn was over seventy when he started writing this Mass, but his freshness and originality are as striking as in any of the earlier works. The fine performance caps the others in this outstanding series. The quartet of soloists is strong, with Helen Watts in particular singing magnificently. The brilliant and well-balanced 1966 recording has been transferred splendidly to CD, which now offers a substantial bonus in the Mozart *Vespers*, recorded at St John's over a decade later.

Il ritorno di Tobia (oratorio).
(M) *** Decca 440 038-2 (3) [id.]. Hendricks, Zoghby, Della Jones, Langridge, Luxon, Brighton Festival Ch., RPO, Dorati.

Based on a subject from the Apocrypha, the story of Tobias and the Angel, *Il ritorno di Tobia* is the equivalent in oratorio terms of *opera seria*, and though the arias are very long they generally avoid *da capo* form. Most invigorating are the coloratura arias for the Archangel Gabriel (here the dazzling Barbara Hendricks) and the arias for the other soprano, Sara (the radiant Linda Zoghby), which include a lovely meditation, accompanied unexpectedly by antiphonies between oboes and cors anglais in pairs. The other soloists do not quite match the sopranos, but the Brighton Festival Chorus is lively and fresh-toned; except in the rather heavy recitatives, Dorati springs the rhythms beautifully, with the five magnificent choruses acting as cornerstones for the whole expansive structure. The (1979) Kingsway Hall recording is both brilliant and atmospheric.

The Seasons (complete; in English).
(M) *** Ph. 434 169-2 (2) [id.]. Harper, Ryland Davies, Shirley-Quirk, BBC Ch. & SO, Sir Colin Davis.

Like Boehm on DG (see below), Sir Colin Davis directs a tinglingly fresh performance of Haydn's mellow last oratorio. In this work – based with flamboyant freedom on a German translation of James Thomson's poem in English – there is more than usual reason for using a translation, and the excellent soloists and chorus get most of the words across to the listener. Indeed the fine (1968) recording does not sound in the least dated – it is full and clear, with a most pleasing bloom. Those who have a preference for an English text will not find this in any way musically inferior to the recommended German-language recordings.

The Seasons (Die Jahreszeiten; complete; in German).
*** DG Dig. 431 818-2 (2). Bonney, Rolfe Johnson, Schmidt, Monteverdi Ch., E. Bar. Soloists, Gardiner.
(B) *** Ph. Dig. 438 715-2 (2) [id.]. Edith Mathis, Siegfried Jerusalem, Dietrich Fischer-Dieskau, Ch. & ASMF, Marriner.
(Y/B) (B) *** DG Double 437 940-2 (2) [id.]. Janowitz, Schreier, Talvela, V. Singverein, VSO, Karl Boehm.

As in so many of his choral recordings, Gardiner brushes away any cobwebs from the music in Haydn's last oratorio. Gardiner here more than ever rejects the idea prevalent among period performers that slow, measured speeds should be avoided, and almost always gets the best of both worlds in intensity of communication, whatever the purists may say. Even more than usual, this studio performance conveys the electricity of a live event. The silver-toned Barbara Bonney and Anthony Rolfe Johnson at his most sensitive are outstanding soloists, and though the baritone, Andreas Schmidt, is less sweet on the ear, he winningly captures the bluff jollity of the role of Simon.

Sir Neville Marriner directs a superbly joyful performance of Haydn's last oratorio, effervescent with the optimism of old age. Edith Mathis and Dietrich Fischer-Dieskau are as stylish and characterful as one would expect, pointing the words as narrative. The tenor too is magnificent: Siegfried Jerusalem is both heroic of timbre and yet delicate enough for Haydn's most elegant and genial passages. The chorus and orchestra, of authentic size, add to the freshness. The recording, made in St John's, Smith Square, is warmly reverberant without losing detail. The CD virtually transforms the sound, with added definition for both chorus and soloists, with cues for every individual item, and a total playing time of nearly two hours and a quarter. Highly recommended – a remarkable bargain by any standards.

Boehm's performance enters totally into the spirit of the music. The soloists are excellent and character-ize the music fully; the chorus sing enthusiastically and are well recorded. But it is Boehm's set. He secures fine orchestral playing throughout, an excellent overall musical balance and real spontaneity in music that needs this above all else. The CD transfer of the 1967 recording is admirably managed; the sound overall is a little drier, but the chorus have plenty of body and there is an excellent sense of presence.

Stabat Mater.
(M) *** Decca 433 172-2 [id.]. Augér, Hodgson, Rolfe Johnson, Howell, L. Chamber Ch., Argo CO, Laszlo Heltay.

Haydn's *Stabat Mater* is scandalously neglected and it is good that Heltay's reading conveys its essential greatness, helped by excellent soloists and vividly atmospheric recording.

Te Deum in C, Hob XXIIIc/2.
(BB) *** RCA Navigator 74321 29238-2. V. Boys' Ch., Ch. Viennensis, VCO, Gillesberger – MOZART: *Requiem mass.* ***

A fine, vigorous account of the *Te Deum* by these Viennese forces, very vividly recorded, coupled to a not inconsiderable account of Mozart's *Requiem*. At super-bargain price it makes excellent value.

OPERA

Armida (complete).
*** Ph. 432 438-2 (2) [id.]. Norman, Ahnsjö, Norma Burrowes, Ramey, Leggate, Rolfe Johnson, Lausanne CO, Dorati.

More than most of Haydn's works in this form, *Armida* presents a psychological drama, with the myrtle tree the most obvious of symbols. On CD it makes a fair entertainment, with splendid singing from Jessye Norman, even if she scarcely sounds malevolent. Claes Ahnsjö as the indecisive Rinaldo does better than most tenors in coping with the enormous range. Indeed the whole team of soloists is one of the most consistent in Dorati's Haydn opera series, with Norma Burrowes particularly sweet as Zelmira. As well as some advanced passages, *Armida* also has the advantage that there is little *secco* recitative. The 1978 recording quality is outstanding.

La fedeltà premiata (complete).
*** Ph. 432 430-2 (3) [id.]. Valentini Terrani, Landy, Von Stade, Titus, Cotrubas, Alva, Mazzieri, Lövaas, SRO Ch., Lausanne CO, Dorati.

La fedeltà premiata shows its composer on his finest form. It was the first of Dorati's series of Haydn opera recordings for Philips, launched with characteristic effervescence, helped by an excellent Haydn-sized orchestra and a first-rate cast. The proud Aramanta is superbly taken by Frederica von Stade, while Haydn's unconventional allocation of voices brings a fine baritone, Alan Titus, to match her as the extravagant Count Perrucchetto. But the sweetest and most tender singing comes from Ileana Cotrubas as the fickle nymph, Nerina. The recording is intimate but with plenty of atmosphere. It is well trans-ferred to CD, but at times one feels the cueing could be more generous.

(i) *L'incontro improviso* (complete). Arias for: (ii) *Acide e Galatea.* (iii) SARTI: *I finti eredi.* (iv) TRAETTA: *Ifigenia in Tauride.* (ii–iv) Terzetto from: PASTICCIO: *La Circe, ossia L'isola incantata.*
*** Ph. 432 416-2 (3) [id.]. (i; iv) Ahnsjö; (i) Zoghby, Trimarchi, Luxon, M. Marshall, Della Jones, Prescott; (ii) Devlin; (iii) Baldin; Lausanne CO, Dorati.

In eighteenth-century Vienna the abduction opera involving Moorish enslavement and torture became quite a cult. The greatest instance is Mozart's *Entführung*, but this example of the genre from Haydn is worthy of comparison, with its very similar story; the result is musically delightful. The most heavenly number of all is a trio for the three sopranos in Act I, *Mi sembra un sogno*, which, with its high-flown legato phrases, keeps reminding one of *Soave sia il vento* in *Così fan tutte*. The tenor's trumpeting arias are beautifully crisp and the vigorous canzonettas for the two *buffo* basses include a nonsense song or two. Benjamin Luxon and Domenico Trimarchi are delectable in those roles. Claes Ahnsjö is at his finest, resorting understandably to falsetto for one impossible top E flat; the role of the heroine is superbly taken by Linda Zoghby, and she is well supported by Margaret Marshall and Della Jones. The layout places each of the three Acts on a single CD and makes room on the third for two arias which Haydn devised for other men's operas, plus one for his own *Acide e Galatea*. The selection ends with an amazing eating and drinking trio.

L'infedeltà delusa (complete).
*** Ph. 432 413-2 (2) [id.]. Mathis, Hendricks, Baldin, Ahnsjö, Devlin, Lausanne CO, Dorati.
(M) **(*) HM/BMG 05472 77316-2 (2) [id.]. Argenta, Lootens, Prégardien, M. Schäfer, Varcoe, La Petite Bande, Sigiswald Kuijken.

L'infedeltà delusa may not be dramatically the most imaginative of stage works, but by the standards of the time it is a compact piece, punctuated by some sharply noteworthy ideas. The opera brings many memorable numbers, such as a laughing song for Nencio (on Philips the admirable Claes Ahnsjö) and a song of ailments for the spirited and resourceful heroine, Vespina (Edith Mathis, lively and fresh). Dorati draws vigorous, resilient performances from everyone (not least from the delightful Barbara Hendricks). The Philips recording is splendidly full-blooded and neatly transferred on to a pair of CDs, with one Act complete on each.

The plot of the opera is unusual for the time in giving the role of the heavy father to the tenor (well taken on RCA by Christoph Prégardien), reflecting the fact that it was expressly designed for Karl Friberth, literary adviser to Prince Esterházy as well as a singer. This alternative version on period instruments nicely captures the flavour of a semi-domestic performance in the prince's country palace. Both the RCA sopranos, Nancy Argenta and Lena Lootens, are agile and precise, if a little edgy. Both tenors, Markus Schäfer as well as Prégardien, are stressed by the range demanded but, like the bass, Stephen Varcoe, they have clean voices, suitable for Haydn on a small scale. The scale of the whole work, much shorter than was common in the late eighteenth century, makes it the more apt for revival today. *L'infedeltà delusa* may be no *Così fan tutte* but this too is a most enjoyable set, worth considering at mid-price, even if the Dorati version is a pretty clear first choice.

L'isola disabitata (complete).
*** Ph. 432 427-2 (2) [id.]. Lerer, Zoghby, Alva, Bruson, Lausanne CO, Dorati.

Were it not for the preponderance of accompanied recitative over set numbers, *L'isola disabitata* would be an ideal Haydn opera to recommend to the modern listener. As it is, many passages reflect the *Sturm und Drang* manner of middle-period Haydn – and this is hinted at immediately in the overture – often urgently dramatic, with tremolos freely used. But in Act I it is only after twenty minutes that the first aria appears, a delightful piece for the heroine with a hint of *Che farò* in Gluck's *Orfeo*. Vocally, it is the second soprano here, Linda Zoghby, who takes first honours, though the baritone, Renato Bruson, is splendid too. The piece ends with a fine quartet of reconciliation, only the eighth number in the whole piece. The direction of recitatives is unfortunately not Dorati's strong point – here, as elsewhere in the series, rather too heavy – but with excellent recording, very vividly transferred to CD, and with just the right degree of ambience, this makes a fascinating issue. The two Acts are given a CD apiece.

(i) *Il mondo della luna* (complete). (ii) Arias for: Cantata: *Miseri noi, misera patria*; Petrarch's sonnet from *Il Canzoniere: Solo e pensoso*. BIANCHI: *Alessandro nell'Indie*. CIMAROSA: *I due supposti conti*. GAZZANIGA: *L'isola di Alcina*. GUGLIELMI: *La Quakera spiritosa*. PAISIELLO: *La Frascatana*. PASTICCIO: *La Circe, ossia l'Isola incantana*.
*** Ph. 432 420-2 (3) [id.]. (i) (i) Trimarchi, Alva, Von Stade, Augér, Mathis, Valentini Terrani, Rolfe Johnson, Lausanne CO, Dorati ; (ii) Edith Mathis, Lausanne CO, Jordan.

Il mondo della luna ('The world on the moon') is better known (by name at least) than the other Haydn operas that the Philips series has disinterred. Written for an Esterházy marriage, it uses the plot of a naïve but engaging Goldoni comedy. Much of the most charming music comes in the brief instrumental interludes, and most of the arias are correspondingly short. That leaves much space on the discs devoted to *secco* recitative and, as on his other Haydn opera issues, Dorati proves a surprisingly sluggish harpsichord player. Nevertheless, with splendid contributions from the three principal women singers, this is another Haydn set which richly deserves investigation by anyone devoted to opera of the period. The eight substitution arias (including *Solo e pensoso*, the lovely setting of Petrarch's twenty-eighth sonnet – the last Italian aria Haydn wrote) are simply and stylishly sung by Edith Mathis. The 1977 recording is first class throughout, as is the CD transfer; and the layout, with one Act allotted to each of the three CDs, leaves room for the eight substitution arias (recorded three years later) on the last disc.

Orlando paladino (complete).
*** Ph. 432 434-2 (3) [id.]. Augér, Ameling, Killebrew, Shirley, Ahnsjö, Luxon, Trimarchi, Mazzieri, Carelli, Lausanne CO, Dorati.

One might infer from this delightful send-up of a classical story in opera that Haydn in his pieces for

Esterháza was producing sophisticated charades for a very closed society. Though long for its subject-matter, this is among the most delightful of all, turning the legend of Roland and his exploits as a medieval champion into something not very distant from farce. There are plenty of touches of parody in the music: the bass arias of the King of Barbary suggest mock Handel and Charon's aria (after Orlando is whisked down to the Underworld) brings a charming exaggeration of Gluck's manner. Above all the Leperello-like servant figure, Pasquale, is given a series of numbers which match and even outshine Mozart, including a hilarious duet when, bowled over by love, he can only utter monosyllables – cue for marvellous *buffo* singing from Domenico Trimarchi. The overall team is strong, with Arleen Augér as the heroine outstandingly sweet and pure. George Shirley as Orlando snarls too much in recitative, but it is an aptly heroic performance; and Elly Ameling and Gwendoline Killebrew in subsidiary roles are both excellent. The recitatives here, though long, are rather less heavily done than in some other Dorati sets, and the 1976 recording is first rate and splendidly transferred to three CDs, one for each Act.

La vera costanza (complete).
*** Ph. 432 424-2 (2) [id.]. Norman, Donath, Ahnsjö, Ganzarolli, Trimarchi, Lövaas, Rolfe Johnson, Lausanne CO, Dorati.

Like Mozart's *Marriage of Figaro*, *La vera costanza* has serious undertones, if only because it is the proletarian characters who consistently inspire sympathy while the aristocrats come in for something not far short of ridicule. The individual numbers may be shorter-winded than in Mozart, but Haydn's sharpness of invention never lets one down, and the big finales to each of the first two Acts are fizzingly impressive, pointing clearly forward to *Figaro*. Overall, the opera is nicely compact. In every way bar one this is a delectable performance. The conducting of Dorati sparkles, Jessye Norman is superb as the virtuoso fisher-girl, Rosina, while the others make up an excellent team, well cast in often difficult roles designed for the special talents of individual singers at Esterháza. The snag is the continuo playing of Dorati himself, heavy and clangorous, holding up the lively singing of the *secco* recitatives. Apart from some discrepancy of balance between the voices and a touch of dryness in the acoustic, the recorded sound is excellent.

Collections

Ein Magd ein Dienerin (cantilena); *Miseri noi, misera patria!* (cantata). Interpolation arias: *Chi vive amante* (for BIANCHI: *Alessandro nell' Indie*). *La moglie quando è buona* (for CIMAROSA: *Giannina è Bernadone*). *Il meglio mio carattere* (for CIMAROSA: *L'Impresario in Augustie*). *Ah, crudel! poi chè la brami* (for GAZZANIGA: *La Vendemmia*). *Sono Alcina* (for GAZZANIGA: *Lisola di Alcina*). *Son pietosa* (for pasticcio by Naumann).
(Y/B) (M) *** Erato/Warner Dig. 4509 98498-2 [id.]. Teresa Berganza, Scottish CO, Leppard.

Most of the items on this delightful recital disc are 'insertion' arias which Haydn wrote for productions of other composers' operas at Esterháza in the years between 1780 and 1790. They are generally short and tuneful, boasting of the singers' constancy in love or whatever; Berganza with brilliant accompaniment sings them with delicious sparkle. The most substantial item is *Miseri noi, misera patria!*, darker and more deeply expressive: and there, too, Berganza rises superbly to the challenge. Excellent Erato recording, most successfully transferred to compact disc, where both the voice and the accompanying group sound vivid within a natural perspective. Recommended.

Haydn, Michael (1737–1806)

Concertino for horn and orchestra in D.
(M) *** Teldec/Warner Dig. 9031 74790-2 [id.]. Dale Clevenger, Liszt CO, Rolla – J. HAYDN: *Concertos.* ***

Michael Haydn's *Concertino* is played with fine style by Dale Clevenger, whose articulation is a joy in itself. Rolla and his orchestra clearly enjoy themselves and the recording, like the coupled concertos by Josef Haydn, is very realistic indeed.

(i) *2 Flute concertos: in D, MH 81 and MH 105; Symphony in F, MH 25.*
(N) **(*) Nimbus Dig. NI 5392 [id.]. (i) István-Zsolt Nagy, Austro-Hungarian Haydn O, Adam Fischer (with Joseph HAYDN: *Symphony No. 22* **(*))

These two *galant* flute concertos are slight but most engaging. The perky, rhythmically pointed main theme of the first movement of MH 105 (which opens the concert) is immediately inviting, especially when played with such character and finesse as it is by István-Zolt Nagy. The *F major Symphony* is a recently discovered early work, conventional but with a characteristically amiable 'walking' *Andante*. It is a pity another Michael Haydn symphony could not have been recorded to complete the programme, instead of Josef's *Philosopher* which is enjoyable enough, but not especially memorable as a performance. The recording is warmly resonant throughout, with the flute balanced well forward.

Violin concerto in B flat.
(M) **(*) Teldec/Warner Dig. 9031 74784-2 [id.]. Zehetmair, Liszt CO – J. HAYDN: *Concerto* ***; SIBELIUS: *Concerto.* **

A *Violin concerto* from Michael Haydn (written in 1760) makes an enterprising coupling for the better-known work by his brother, Josef. The finale is the weakest part, though not lacking in spirit. The performance with Thomas Zehetmair combining roles of soloist and conductor is strongly characterized and very well recorded.

Symphonies: in A, P.6; in B flat, P.9; in G, P.16; in E flat, P.26; in F, P. 32.
(N) *** Chandos Dig. CHAN 9352 [id.]. L Mozart Players, Mattias Bamert.

At last Chandos bring us some performances of the Michael Haydn Symphonies that really do them full justice. Moreover Bamert's programme only duplicates one work included in Rimbu's serviceable alternative collection on Olympia. P.6 and P 9 are both four-movement works but the others are in three-part Italian overture form. The elegance of the gentle *Andante* of the *A major Symphony* sets the seal on the playing, warm, polished and cultivated, while the *Allegro molto* finale, with its bold horns might almost be by Mozart. The charming *Andantino* of P.9 is no less engaging while the closing Rondo of P 16 has plenty of high spirits. None of this is great music, but all of it is enjoyable and the composer's penultimate F major work (1789) brings a strong, impressively constructed opening movement and a tender *Adagio* where the strings are muted. The recording is pleasingly full and resonant, without detail being blurred.

Symphony in C, P.12.
(M) *** Teldec/Warner Dig. 9031 74788-2 [id.]. Liszt CO, János Rolla – ROSSINI: *String sonatas.* ***

This *Symphony in C major* contains a strikingly beautiful inspiration, the central elegiac *Andante in A minor* for strings with solo oboe. It is very well played throughout and is freshly recorded.

Symphonies: in C, P.12; in F, P.32; in D, P.43; in E, P.44.
** Olympia Dig OCD 435 [id.]. Oradea PO, Romeo Rimbu.

The Oradea Philharmonic are not the world's most polished ensemble, but here they play with lots of spirit in music with which they seem more acclimatized. The conductor is certainly a persuasive advocate of these symphonies of Michael Haydn, another composer who had Oradean associations – although it was called Grosswardein in the eighteenth century. Each is an impressive work, showing the composer with almost as strong a symphonic personality as Joseph. They are well recorded, and this CD is well worth exploring.

Divertimenti: in C, P. 98; in C, P. 115.
*** Denon Dig. C37 7119 [id.]. Holliger, Salvatore Qt – J. C. BACH: *Oboe quartet;* MOZART: *Adagio.* ***

Both these *Divertimenti* contain captivating and original inspirations. The longer of the two, P. 98, has a fizzing first movement and a joyful *Presto* finale, while P. 115 brings unexpected timbres. Well coupled and vividly recorded.

String quintets: in B flat, P.105; in C, P.108; in G, P.109.
**(*) Sony Dig. SK 53897 [id.]. L'Archibudelli.

It is good to have modern recordings of Michael Haydn's *String quintets*. P.108/9 date from 1773, and Mozart knew and admired them. The *C major* with its engaging *Andante cantabile* slow movement was very popular in its day. P.105 is more of a cassation or serenade and has seven movements, including an attractive fourth-movement set of variations and a *marcia* finale. All the works are inventive. Here they are played freshly, elegantly and authentically, without edginess, and the only drawback for some ears may be the modest squeezing of phrases in slow movements plus some rather strong accents in minuets. The recording is fresh with firmly focused yet transparent textures.

Ave Regina.
(M) *** Ph. 430 159-2 [id.]. St John's College, Cambridge, Ch., Guest – J. HAYDN: *Theresienmesse;* MOZART: *Ave verum corpus.* ***

This lovely antiphon, scored for eight-part double choir, looks back to Palestrina and the Venetian school of the Gabrielis and the young Monteverdi. It is beautifully sung and recorded.

Headington, Christopher (1931–96)

Violin concerto.

✹ *** ASV CDDCA 780 [id.]. Xue Wei, LPO, Glover – R. STRAUSS: *Violin concerto.* ***

The Headington *Violin concerto* is a warmly lyrical, unashamedly tonal work in which a fiery central Scherzo is framed by two longer, more reflective movements, both with a vein of melancholy which echoes the comparable movements in the violin concertos of Walton and Prokofiev. The finale is a spacious set of variations in which the last and longest acts as a movingly meditative summary. Xue Wei plays with a passionate commitment to match that in his Brahms and Tchaikovsky recordings, with Jane Glover and the London Philharmonic providing warmly sympathetic accompaniments. Excellent sound. Those looking for twentieth-century music that is accessible and rewards familiarity need not hesitate.

Heath, Dave (born 1956)

The Frontier.

(M) *** Virgin/EMI CUV5 61121-2 [id.]. LCO, Warren-Green – ADAMS: *Shaker loops* *** ✹; GLASS: *Company* etc. ***; REICH: *8 Lines.* ***

Most minimalist composers are American and, although Dave Heath was born in Manchester, the influences on his music are transatlantic. In *The Frontier* the incisive rhythmic astringency is tempered by an attractive, winding lyrical theme which finally asserts itself just before the spiky close. The work was written for members of the LCO, and their performance, full of vitality and feeling, is admirably recorded.

Hebden, John (18th century)

6 Concertos for strings (ed. Wood).

**(*) Chandos Dig. CHAN 8339 [id.]. Cantilena, Shepherd.

Little is known about John Hebden except that he was a Yorkshire composer who also played the cello and bassoon. These concertos are his only known works, apart from some flute sonatas. Although they are slightly uneven, at best the invention is impressive. The concertos usually feature two solo violins and are well constructed to offer plenty of contrast. The performances here are accomplished, without the last degree of polish but full of vitality. The recording is clear and well balanced, and given good presence.

Heinichen, Johann David (1683–1729)

Dresden concerti: in C, S 211; in G, S 213; in G (Darmstadt), S 214; in G (Venezia), S 214; in G, S 215; in F, S 217; in F, S 226, in F, S 231; in F, S 232; in F, S 233; in F, S 234; in F, S 235; Concerto movement in C min., S 240; Serenata di Moritzburg in F, S 204; Sonata in A, S 208.

*** DG Dig. 437 549-2 (2) [id.]. Col. Mus. Ant., Reinhard Goebel.

Dresden concerti: in F, S 231; 233/5; in G, S 213; Concerto movement in C min., S 240; Sonata in A, S 208.

*** DG Dig. 437 849-2 [id.]. Col. Mus. Ant., Reinhard Goebel.

Johann David Heinichen, a contemporary of Bach, was a Dresden court musician and the concertos here were intended for the (obviously excellent) Dresden court orchestra. Their personnel must have included some very good horn players, for the horn parts in the F major concertos are hair-raisingly spectacular. It is the orchestral colour that makes these concertos so appealing rather than their invention, which is more predictable, although often very charming (witness the grace of the oboe theme in the *Larghetto* of the *G major Concerto*, Seibel 213). Goebel's Cologne forces have not always been strong on charm in previous recordings, but they obviously relish the delicacy of Heinichen's wind scoring and his neat and busily vital allegros. The recording is freshly vivid, clean and realistic. Goebel's notes are scholarly if not especially detailed in relation to individual concertos. One would be tempted to recommend the single-disc selection, but DG have cunningly not included therein the lollipop of the set. This is the *Pastorell* second movement of the *C major Concerto*, Seibel 211, with its piquant drone (track 5 of the second CD); the effect for all the world sounds like an unusually refined set of bagpipes. It is immediately followed by a peaceful *Adagio* for flute and strings and a sparkling finale.

Alma mater redemptoris; Beatus vir; De profundis; Lamentations of Jeremiah; Nicht das Band, das dich bestricket (oratorio); *Nisi Dominus aedificaverit; Warum toben die Heiden; Pastorale in A.*
(N) **(*) DG Dig. 447 092-2 (2) [id.]. Mechthild Georg, Axel Köhler, Jörg Dürmüller, Scot Weir, Raimund Nolte, Col. Mus. Ant., Goebel.

Here is a representative selection of Heinichen's vocal music, including an oratorio, *Nicht das Band, das dich bestricket* (which lasts nearly 50 minutes), Latin Psalm settings and three surviving *Lamentations*, each for a solo voice (tenor, bass and alto) and chamber ensemble. These probably contain the most rewarding music. But (unlike Biber) Heinichen is not revealed as a composer of inspired originality here, though he has some individual ideas about orchestration. The singers here are all impressive, but Goebel is less so. He too often favours rhythmic plodding, and one wonders whether in other hands this music would sound more inspiring. The *Pastorale*, a brief instrumental composition, ends the programme.

Helweg, Kim (born 1956)

American fantasy (A tribute to Leonard Bernstein).
(N) ** Chandos Dig. CHAN 9398 [id.]. Safri Duo & Slovak Piano Duo – BARTOK: *Sonata for 2 pianos and percussion;* LUTOSLAWSKI: *Paganini variations.* ***

The notes are uninformative and tell us more about the Slovak Piano Duo and the Danish Safari Duo than about Kim Helweg. His piece was written specifically for these artists and they play it brilliantly. It is a four-movement sonata and at the same time a set of variations on Bernstein's song, *America*, from *West Side Story*. In idiom it pays generous tribute to both Bernstein and Bartók. But although it is obviously the work of a resourceful and intelligent musician, it is of insufficient individuality to reward repeated listening. Stunning recording. The audience goes wild at the end of the performance.

Henze, Hans Werner (born 1926)

Symphonies Nos. (i) *1–5;* (ii) *6.*
(M) *** DG 429 854-2 (2) [id.]. (i) BPO, (ii) LSO, composer.

The Henze *Symphonies* are remarkable pieces which inhabit a strongly distinctive sound-world. The *First* with its cool, Stravinskian slow movement is a remarkable achievement, and there is a dance-like feel to the *Third*. It is rich in fantasy. The *Fourth* is among the most concentrated and atmospheric of his works; there is at times an overwhelming sense of melancholy. The *Fifth* is strongly post-expressionist. The *Sixth Symphony* was composed while Henze was living in Havana. The performances are excellent and the recorded sound amazingly vivid. An important and indispensable set, recommended with enthusiasm.

Symphony No. 7; Barcarola.
*** EMI Dig. CDC7 54762-2 [id.]. CBSO, Rattle.

Rattle conducts his Birmingham orchestra in one of the most powerful recordings of Henze's music. The *Seventh Symphony* is not only the longest he has written, it is also the weightiest and most traditionally symphonic, Beethoven-like in four substantial movements. Rather belying its title, the *Barcarola* presents a similarly weighty and massive structure, an elegiac piece of over 20 minutes, written in memory of Paul Dessau and inspired by the myth of the ferryman, Charon, crossing the Styx. The dramatic bite of both performances, recorded live in Symphony Hall, Birmingham, makes them instantly compelling. Full, colourful recording to bring out the richness of Henze's orchestral writing.

Voices.
(Y/B) *** Berlin Classics 2180-2 BC (2) [id.]. Roswitha Trexler, Joachim Vogt, Leipzig RSO Chamber Ens., Horst Neumann.

Written for the London Sinfonietta in 1973, this massive and wide-ranging song-cycle of 22 numbers, lasting over 90 minutes, is among Henze's most inspired and characterful works. So in his techniques he ranges widely, from highly sophisticated, post-serial structures to jazz, aleatory patterns and music-theatre pieces, notably in ironic songs echoing Kurt Weill, several of them setting poems by Bertolt Brecht. The wonder is that, so far from seeming too disparate a sequence, *Voices* gathers in richness as it progresses, varying not just the moods and themes but the forces used in each song over a very wide span, with instruments including ocarina, accordion, mouth-organ and electric guitar, as well as a large percussion section. Some of the episodes are violent, but the work is rounded off with the most beautiful and most extended piece, a duet, *Blumenfest* ('Carnival of flowers'), in which mellifluous and flexible vocal lines for mezzo and tenor intertwining seem to suggest a final ray of hope, with bitterness gone. This analogue recording, made in Germany in 1980, presents a sharply focused performance, strong and dramatic, with two excellent, clean-cut soloists. It is good that at last it should be made more generally available.

OPERA

Die Bassariden (The Bassarids).
*** Koch Schwann 314 006-2 (2) [id.]. Tear, Schmidt, Armstrong, Riegel, Lindsley, Wenkel, Burt, Murray, Berlin RIAS Chamber Ch. & RSO, Albrecht.

Henze's *The Bassarids*, based on the *Bacchae* of Euripides, presents a contrast of rival philosophies between the Dionysiac and the Apollonian, the sensual and the intellectual. With its meaty musical argument and consciously symphonic shape, it is an opera that has cried out for a complete recording, and this fine account from Berlin fits the bill well, amply confirming the work's power. The cast is first rate, including Kenneth Riegel, Andreas Schmidt, Robert Tear and Karen Armstrong, and the choral writing adds greatly to the impact, splendidly realized here by the RIAS Choir.

Der junge Lord (The Young Lord; complete).
(M) *** DG 445 248-2 (2) [id.]. Mathis, Grobe, McDaniel, Driscoll, Johnson, German Op., Berlin, Christoph von Dohnányi.

As a reaction against his earlier, generally very serious operas, Henze in 1965 completed this piece designed as an *opera buffa*. This is Henze at his most amiable, and it results for much of the time in his Stravinskian side dominating, though he also allows himself a warmer vein of lyricism than usual. The plot in its comedy is consciously cynical, involving a snobbish community duped by a titled Englishman. He introduces an alleged English lord who finally turns out to be an ape. There is an underlying seriousness to the piece, and in this excellent performance, recorded with the composer's approval, the full range of moods and emotions is conveyed. Very good (1967) sound; in this mid-price reissue a full libretto and translation are provided.

Herbert, Victor (1859–1924)

Cello concerto No. 2 in E min., Op. 30.
(N) *** Sony SK 67173 [id.]. Ma, NYPO, Masur – DVORAK: *Cello concerto.* ***
(N) (M) ** Mercury 434 355-2 [id.]. Miquelle, Eastman-Rochester O, Hanson – GROFE: *Grand Canyon suite; Mississippi suite.* **(*)

The Victor Herbert concerto which sparked Dvořák into writing his masterpiece within the year makes an apt and unusual coupling for that superb work. Yo-Yo Ma gives a compelling, high-powered performance, one which does not overload the piece with cloying sentiment, whether in the brilliant and vigorous outer movements or in the warmly lyrical slow movement with its themes like love songs from Herbert's operettas translated. Ma's use of rubato is perfectly judged, with that slow movement made the more tender at a flowing speed. The finale is then given a quicksilver performance, both brilliant and urgent. With the recordings by Lynn Harrell (Decca) and Julian Lloyd Webber (EMI) not currently listed, this magnificent version could not be more welcome.

Georges Miquelle is a very musical soloist, but his tonal image is modest and he is dynamically upstaged by the orchestra everywhere but in the slow movement. He plays the work sympathetically, but Ma's newest version is much more persuasive.

Hérold, Ferdinand (1791–1833)

La Fille mal gardée (ballet, arr. Lanchbery): complete.
(M) *** Decca Dig. 430 849-2 (2) [id.]. ROHCG O, Lanchbery – LECOCQ: *Mam'zelle Angot.* ***

Lanchbery himself concocted the score for this fizzingly comic and totally delightful ballet, drawing primarily on Hérold's music, but interpolating the famous comic *Clog dance* from Hertel's alternative score, which must be one of the most famous of all ballet numbers outside Tchaikovsky. There is much else of comparable delight. Here, with sound of spectacular Decca digital fidelity, Lanchbery conducts a highly seductive account of the complete ballet with an orchestra long familiar with playing it in the theatre, now reissued coupled with Gordon Jacob's equally delicious confection, based on the music of Lecocq.

La Fille mal gardée: extended excerpts.
(N) ❀ (M) *** EMI Dig. CD-EMX 2268 [id.]. RLPO, Wordsworth.
(M) *** Decca 430 196-2 [id.]. ROHCG O, Lanchbery.

Hérold's score also included tunes from Rossini's *Barber of Seville* and *Cenerentola*, together with a Donizetti selection (mainly from *L'elisir d'amore*). That the music is therefore a complete hotch-potch does not prevent it from being marvellously entertaining. The extended selection here is wonderfully persuasive and brilliantly played, displaying both affection and sparkle in ample quantity. The Kingsway Hall recording quality (produced by Ray Minshull and engineered by Arthur Lillie) is of vintage Decca excellence. One cannot believe that it dates from 1962, for the combination of ambient bloom and the most realistic detail still places it in the demonstration bracket. Lanchbery later recorded the complete ballet (see above) and that is also an outstanding set, but it involves two CDs (and includes Lecocq's *Mam'zelle Angot* ballet music as a fill-up).

However, Barry Wordsworth's scintillating account of a generous extended selection from the ballet includes all the important sequences, and the EMI CD offers some eight minutes more music than the Decca. With playing from the Royal Liverpool Philharmonic Orchestra that combines refinement and delicacy with wit and humour, this is even more highly recommendable, especially for those preferring modern, digital sound.

Herrmann, Bernard (1911–75)

(i) *The Devil and Daniel Webster:* suite; (ii) *Obsession* (abridged score); (i) *Welles raises Kane:* suite.
(M) *** Unicorn UKCD 2065 [id.]. (i) LPO; (ii) Nat. SO; composer.

The Devil and Daniel Webster suite is not first-grade Herrmann: the musical material is not always distinguished enough and one or two of the movements outlast their welcome. *Welles raises Kane* is another matter. Beecham himself gave one of its first performances in New York during the war. The music is drawn from both Orson Welles's *Citizen Kane* and *The Magnificent Ambersons*, but the music itself (unlike the atmosphere of those films) is snappily and evocatively extrovert, showing a brilliant flair for orchestral colour. It is superbly played. For the reissue Unicorn have added a brilliant Decca recording of an abridged version of the music Herrmann wrote for *Obsession* (some 39 minutes overall). It offers some of his most spectacular and evocative writing, including choral effects.

Film scores: *Beneath the Twelve-mile Reef;* (i) *Citizen Kane: suite; Hangover Square:* (ii) *Concerto macabre. On Dangerous Ground: Death hunt. White Witch Doctor: suite.*
(M) *** RCA GD 80707 [0707-2-RG]. Nat. PO, Gerhardt, (i) with Te Kanawa, (ii) Achucarro.

Bernard Herrmann's remarkable 1940 score for *Citizen Kane* is well able to stand up on its own and includes a fascinating pastiche aria from a fictitious opera, *Salammbo*, eloquently sung here by Kiri Te Kanawa. The collection opens with an exhilarating example of the composer's ferocious chase music, the *Death hunt* from *On Dangerous Ground*, led by eight roistering horns with the orchestral brass augmented. *Beneath the Twelve-mile Reef* displays Herrmann's soaring melodic gift and his orchestral flair. The Busoni/Liszt-derived *Concerto macabre* is brilliantly played by Joaquin Achucarro. Charles Gerhardt and his splendid orchestra obviously relish the hyperbole and the recording is spectacular.

Symphony; (i) *The Fantasticks* (song-cycle).
(M) *** Unicorn UKCD 2063 [id.]. (London) National PO, composer, (i) with Michael Rippon; Meriel Dickinson; John Amis; Gillian Humphreys; Thames Chamber Ch.

Underlying everything in this eclectic but enjoyable symphony the argument reflects the approach of a dedicated Sibelian and, though the pretensions may not always be supported by equivalent matter, it is good to hear Herrmann extending himself and giving what is in effect a musical self-portrait. Admirable performance and very good recording, made in 1974, not long before the composer's untimely death. The coupled song-cycle – virtually a cantata – set to words by the Elizabethan poet Nicolas Breton, has more of the composer's own personality and is obviously deeply felt music. With its nicely spiced word-imagery, the music communicates readily, and it is perhaps April that brings the most seductive setting of all (written for soprano with exquisite violin obbligato), and here it is a pity that Gillian Humphreys, who is very sympathetic, has such a close vibrato. Otherwise the soloists are excellent and the orchestral playing quite lovely. Most rewarding when the sound is so atmospheric.

(i) *Moby Dick* (cantata); (ii) *For the fallen.*
(M) *** Unicorn UKCD 2061 [id.]. (i) John Amis, Robert Bowman, Kelly, Rippon, Aeolian Singers, LPO; (ii) Nat. PO; composer.

Herrmann's *Moby Dick* is written in an immediately approachable idiom. The present, extremely dramatic and spontaneous performance should recommend it to any listener who can enjoy a setting of the English language by a composer who shows a real feeling for words. The soloists are first rate, and the chorus and orchestra convey their enthusiasm and excitement in such effective and rewarding music. The recording is also outstanding, and so is the CD transfer. *For the fallen* is a short elegiac obituary for the dead of the Second World War. Its pastoral feeling and understatement are gently haunting. It is beautifully played and recorded.

Wuthering Heights (opera): complete.
(M) *** Unicorn UKCD 2050/52 [id.]. Bainbridge, Kelly, Bell, Beaton, Kitchiner, Rippon, Ward, Bowden, Elizabethan Singers, Pro Arte O, composer.

Bernard Herrmann, best known for his film scores and as conductor, spent many years working on his operatic adaption of Emily Brontë's novel, and the result is confident and professional. Though the writing is purely illustrative rather than musically original, this performance, strongly conducted by the composer, makes for a colourful telling of the story. The solo singing is consistently good and the recording beautifully clear.

Hertel, Johann (1727–89)

Trumpet concerto in D.
*** Ph. Dig. 420 203-2 [id.]. Hardenberger, ASMF, Marriner – HAYDN *** ✿; HUMMEL *** ✿; STAMITZ: *Concertos.* ***

Johann Hertel's *Trumpet concerto* is typical of many works of the same kind written in the Baroque era. Håkan Hardenberger clearly relishes every bar and plays with great flair.

Hildegard of Bingen (1098–1179)

Canticles of ecstasy.
(Y/B) ✿*** HM/BMG Dig. 05472 77320-2 [id.]. Sequentia, Barbara Thornton.

Born almost exactly nine centuries ago, Abbess Hildegard of Bingen has over the last decade emerged as one of the great creative figures of medieval times, not just an inspired composer but a poet, dramatist and theologian, a correspondent with emperors and popes. Following on Gothic Voices' best-selling disc for Hyperion (see below), the fine German group, Sequentia, has under Barbara Thornton embarked on a collected recording of her works. This latest instalment is among the most moving and beautiful yet. At speeds more spacious than those of Gothic Voices, with women's voices alone, the elaborate monodic lines soar heavenwards even more sensuously, matching the imagery of Hildegard's poetry. For a meditative mood this outdoes Gregorian chant. Highly recommended.

Ordo virtutum (The Play of the Virtues).
(M) *** HM/BMG Dig. GD 77051 (2) [77051-2-RG]. Köper, Mockridge, Thornton, Laurens, Feldman, Monahan, Lister, Trevor, Sanford, Smith, Sequentia.

The more one learns about Abbess Hildegard of Bingen, the more astonishing her achievement appears. *Ordo virtutum* is a mystery play, and this 90-minute piece includes strikingly dramatic passages, with the Devil himself intervening. This recording, made in collaboration with West German Radio of Cologne, is outstandingly fine.

Hymns and sequences: *Ave generosa; Columba aspexit; O Ecclesia; O Euchari; O Jerusalem; O ignis spiritus; O presul vere civitatis; O viridissima virga.*
*** Hyperion CDA 66039 [id.]. Gothic Voices, Muskett, White, Page.

This record draws on the Abbess Hildegard of Bingen's collection of music and poetry, the *Symphonia armonie celestium revelationum* – 'the symphony of the harmony of celestial revelations'. These hymns and sequences, most expertly performed and recorded, have excited much acclaim – and rightly so. A lovely CD.

Hindemith, Paul (1895–1963)

Concert music for brass and strings, Op. 50; (i) *Viola concerto (Schwanendreher). Nobilissima visione.*
*** Decca Dig. 433 809-2 [id.]. San Francisco SO, Herbert Blomstedt, (i) with Geraldine Walther.

The three substantial works on the disc include his most sensuously beautiful score, *Nobilissima visione.*
Inspired by the frescos of Giotto in Florence, it ends with a noble *Passacaglia.* The *Concert music* is
characteristic of Hindemith's early music, with its chunky tonal contrasts and emphatic rhythms set
against a brief lyrical interlude. *Schwanendreher* is a concerto for viola (Hindemith's own instrument),
based on German folk-themes, ending with a jolly set of variations. As in their previous Hindemith
coupling of *Mathis der Mahler, Trauermusik* and the *Metamorphoses on themes of Weber,* Blomstedt
and the orchestra bring out the warmth as well as the rugged power.

*Concert music for brass and strings, Op. 50; Symphonic metamorphoses on themes of Weber, Symphony in
E flat.*
(M) ** Sony SMK 47566 [id.]. NYPO, Bernstein.

The *Concert music* and the *Symphonic metamorphoses* are much recorded and, although Bernstein's
performances are vital and brilliantly played, the rather coarse (1961) recording of the former is not an
asset to the music's presentation. The 1968 quality in the *Symphonic metamorphoses* is fuller; if not
particularly refined it is acceptable, as is the sound in the *Symphony,* recorded a year earlier, also in the
unflattering Avery Fisher Hall. Bernstein's performance teems with energy in the first movement of this
eloquent and surprisingly little-heard piece. It is very charismatic and triumphs over the shallow sound.

Concerto for orchestra; (i) *Violin concerto; Kammermusik No. 4* (for violin & chamber ensemble).
Ragtime; Suite of French dances.
(N) ** ASV Dig. CDDCA 945 [id.]. (i) Michael Guttman; Philh. O, Serebrier.

The *Concerto for orchestra* is an early work from 1926, vital and inventive. It is well enough played by the
Philharmonia Orchestra, though Serebrier sets a rather galumphing plod at the beginning. However, the
performance overall is acceptably spirited. The Belgian violinist, Michael Guttman, was a pupil of
André Gertler and later went on to the Juilliard to study with Dorothy DeLay. He produces a sweet but
small tone when required, as in the slow movement of the 1939 *Violin concerto,* though there are
occasional insecurities of intonation. There are better versions to be had, though the recording by Brian
Culverhouse is very well detailed and very present – with perhaps a tendency for tutti not to expand. The
1925 *Kammermusik No. 4* is not the equal of the Kulka (Decca) or Rundel (RCA) in terms of artistic
finesse or transparency of texture. The disc also includes the *Suite französischer Tänze,* transcriptions
made in 1958 of dances from the *Livres de Danceries* by Claude Gervaise and Estienne du Terte, which
also inspired Poulenc's *Suite française* and his 1921 bagatelle, *Ragtime.* Hindemithians will find this a
good rather than an indispensable issue.

Cello concerto.
(N) (Y/B) *** RCA Dig. 09026 68027-2 [id.]. Starker, Bamberg SO, Russell Davies – SCHUMANN: *Cello
concerto.* ***

It would be curmudgeonly to withhold a third star from Janos Starker's exemplary account of the *Cello
concerto;* it is played with finesse and elegance, and Dennis Russell Davies gets good results from the
Bamberg orchestra too. However, it is not to be preferred to the Wallfisch–Tortelier account on Chandos
(see below), which has the more logical coupling.

Cello concerto; (i) *Clarinet concerto.*
*** Etcetera KTC 1006 [id.]. Tibor de Machula; (i) George Pieterson; Concg. O, Kondrashin.

The *Cello concerto* is exhilarating and inventive, and Tibor de Machula proves an excellent protagonist.
The *Clarinet concerto* is lyrical and eventful. The recordings (made in the Concertgebouw, Amsterdam)
are public performances and emanate from the Hilversum Radio archives.

(i) *Cello concerto;* (ii) *The Four Temperaments* (Theme and variations for piano and strings).
*** Chandos Dig. CHAN 9124 [id.]. (i) Raphael Wallfisch; (ii) Howard Shelley; BBC PO, Tortelier.

Both the *Cello concerto* and *The Four Temperaments* are vintage Hindemith and well worth adding to
your collection. The four variations of the latter are ingenious and subtle and are splendidly realized by
Howard Shelley and the BBC Philharmonic under Yan Pascal Tortelier. Raphael Wallfisch is the
eloquent soloist in the *Cello concerto.* The Chandos recording is very good indeed. These recordings set
new standards in both works.

Kammermusik Nos. 1 for 12 instruments, Op. 24/1; (i) *2 (Piano concerto), Op. 36/1;* (ii) *3 (Cello concerto), Op. 36/2;* (iii) *4 (Violin concerto), Op. 36/3;* (iv) *5 (Viola concerto), Op. 36/4;* (v) *6 (Viola d'amore concerto), Op. 46/1;* (vi) *7 (Organ concerto), Op. 46/2; Kleine Kammermusik for wind quintet, Op. 24/2.*
*** Decca Dig. 433 816-2 (2). (i) Brautigam; (ii) Harrell; (iii) Kulka; (iv) Kaskkashian; (v) Blume; (vi) van Doeselaar; Concg. O, Chailly.
(N) *** RCA Dig. 09026 61730-2 (2) [id.] (without *Kleine Kammermusik*). (i) Wiget; (ii) Stirling; (iii) Rundel; (iv) Dickel; (v) Just; (vi) Lücker; Ens. Modern, Markus Stenz.

The seven pieces Hindemith called *Kammermusik* were written, as their opus numbers indicate, in three batches. They all come from the 1920s. Described as a kind of twentieth-century equivalent of the *Brandenburg concertos*, they show Hindemith at his most fertile and inventive and are mandatory listening, all highly refreshing and imaginative. The set also includes the delightful little *Wind quintet* (*Kleine Kammermusik*), one of his most frequently performed pieces. This set supersedes its predecessors in every way, not least in the exemplary quality of the Decca recording. The playing of the distinguished soloists and the members of the Concertgebouw is beyond praise.

The RCA set from the Ensemble Modern and Markus Stenz may not have as well-known a line-up of soloists as the Decca set, but the performances are no less zesty and exuberant. In one respect this set of the *Kammermusik* scores over its rival: it is economically packaged with two discs occupying the shelf-space of one; for readers with large collections that may well be a determining factor. Artistically it is a matter of swings-and-roundabouts. Those who already have the Decca set will not feel the need to change, but those who do not should give this new set serious consideration. The *Organ concerto*, the seventh of the set, is recorded in Hindemith's old conservatoire in Frankfurt and comes off no less excellently in Martin Lücker's hands (and feet) than in the Decca with Leo van Doeselaar as soloist. There is a really idiomatic feel to these performances, which have plenty of character and, in the slow movement of No. 2, say, atmosphere. Of course the *Wind quintet*, the *Kleine Kammermusik*, is not included whereas it is in the Decca, which makes a considerable plus factor. The performances are on the whole exhilarating and enjoyable, though overall the Decca recording is more analytical (in the best sense) and retains a slight edge over the newcomer.

Kammermusik No. 5, Op. 36/4; Konzertmusik for viola and orchestra, Op. 48; Viola concerto (Der Schwanendreher).
(N) *** ASV Dig. CDDCA 931 [id.]. Cortese, Philh. O, Brabbins.

This is the first in what is promised to be a complete survey of Hindemith's music for his own instrument, the viola. Paul Cortese is the accomplished soloist in all three works, including the fifth of the *Kammermusik* (available complete in the Decca and RCA editions listed above). The Philharmonia respond with some enthusiasm to Martyn Brabbins's direction, and although there are finer recordings of *Der Schwanendreher* to be had (above all, Tabea Zimmermann on EMI) this disc gives undoubted pleasure. The recording is very good indeed, with great presence and body. There is plenty of detail, though the sound is a bit up-front with less front-to-back depth than is ideal.

(i) *Clarinet concerto;* (ii) *Horn concerto;* (iii) *Concerto for trumpet, bassoon & strings;* (iv) *Concerto for woodwinds, harp & strings.*
(N) **(*) CPO 999 142-2 [id.]. (i; iv) Mehlhart; (ii) Neunecker; (iii) Friedrich; (iii–iv) Wilkening; (iv) Büchsel, Varcol, Cassedanne; Frankfurt RSO, Werner Andreas Albert.

The *Clarinet concerto* was written for Benny Goodman in 1947 and first performed by him and the Philadelphia Orchestra under Ormandy, while the remaining three concertos come from 1949. As far as we can determine, there are no alternative versions of the *Concerto for trumpet, bassoon and strings* or the *Concerto for woodwinds* (flute, oboe, clarinet and bassoon), *harp and strings*. Both are short works, neither longer than a quarter of an hour. The *Concerto for winds and harp* is the more rewarding of the two and more varied in texture. The *Trumpet and bassoon concerto* finds Hindemith in more routine mode. The soloist is rather too forward in the *Clarinet concerto* and, though the recording quality is decent, it is possible to imagine more transparent orchestral textures. The performances throughout are eminently acceptable; although Hindemith aficionados will want this, other collectors will probably be inclined to give it lower priority than other recent Hindemith releases.

(i; iii) *Clarinet concerto.* (ii; iii) *Horn concerto.* (iii) *Concert music for brass and strings, Op. 50; Nobilissima visione: suite; Symphonia serena.* (iv–v) *Scherzo for viola and cello.* (iv) *Sonata for solo viola, Op. 25/1.* (iv–vi) *String trio No. 2.*
(M) *** EMI mono/stereo CDC5 55032-2 (i) Louis Cahuzac; (ii) Dennis Brain; (iii) Philh. O, cond. composer; (iv) composer (viola); (v) Emanuel Feuermann; (vi) Szymon Goldberg.

At last EMI have restored virtually all the records Hindemith made with the Philharmonia Orchestra in

1956, which originally ran to three Columbia blue-label LPs. (The only omission is the *Symphony in B flat for concert band.*) Particularly welcome is the *Clarinet concerto*, played here by the French virtuoso, Louis Cahuzac. A good track to sample is the second movement, which is full of high spirits and wit and which sounds amazingly present and vivid. Dennis Brain's classic account of the *Horn concerto* and the 1956 version of the *Nobilissima visione* suite are both well known, but the *Symphonia serena* has not been reissued in the UK since the 1950s and is a splendid affair, a useful supplement to Yan Pascal Tortelier's newly recorded version with the BBC Philharmonic. Of particular interest to Hindemithians will be the pre-war collectors' items featuring Hindemith's viola playing: the 1934 Abbey Road recordings of the *Sonata for solo viola* and the *String trio No. 2* with Szymon Goldberg and Emanuel Feuermann, along with the *Scherzo for viola and cello*, written between 5 a.m. and 8 a.m. on the day of the recording to fill up the sixth side of the *Trio*! Each of the two discs lasts nearly 80 minutes and offers exceptional value. Recommended to all who like Hindemith, as well as those who think they don't!

Horn concerto.
(N) (***) EMI mono CDC7 47834-2 [id.]. Dennis Brain, Philh. O, composer – R. STRAUSS: *Horn concertos Nos. 1–2.* (***) ✸

Dennis Brain recorded the Hindemith/Richard Strauss coupling just a year before he died, driving overnight from the Edinburgh Festival to his home in London when he fell asleep and crashed into a tree. This record makes a worthy memento. The Hindemith *Concerto* is altogether drier than the Strauss but has a hauntingly original, ruminative finale, in which the soloist declaims a short poem – written by the composer – in such a way that the note values match the syllables of the words. Brain's performance is incomparable and the first-class mono recording has been transferred expertly.

Viola concerto (Der Schwanendreher).
*** EMI Dig. CDC7 54101-2 [id.]. Tabea Zimmermann, Bav. RSO, David Shallon – BARTOK: *Viola concerto.* ***

Record companies are not their own best friends. To encumber such an excellent performance of Hindemith's *Der Schwanendreher* with such meagre playing-time and so reduce its attractiveness to the public is unfair to both the collector, the artists and the engineers. Everything about this performance is excellent – indeed it is arguably the best now before the public – and is certainly better recorded than the rather cool sound Decca get for Geraldine Walther and Blomstedt in San Francisco. If you are prepared to pay full price for such short measure, you will be well rewarded in terms of both artistic and technical quality.

(i) *Viola concerto, 'Der Schwanendreher'*; (ii) *Violin concerto; Kammermusik No. 4 (Violin concerto), Op. 36/3.*
(N) (BB) **(*) RCA Navigator 74321 24219-2. (i) Igor Boguslavsky; (ii) David Oistrakh; USSR RSO, Rozhdestvensky.

David Oistrakh made his Russian recording of the *Violin concerto* the same year as his Decca version with the composer (see below). It is hardly less dazzling, and even if the sound cannot match its London counterpart it is fully acceptable; it is good to have in addition his hardly less charismatic account of the concerto which Hindemith placed fourth in his *Kammermusik*. The violist, Igor Boguslavsky, also makes an impressive solo contribution to another fine performance, of *Der Schwanendreher*, the central movement wonderfully warm. This has somewhat more refined sound, since in the two works for violin the soloist is balanced very forwardly. Rozhdestvensky provides vivid accompaniments and, although the Russian brass coarsens tuttis, this disc is more than worth its modest cost, even though the documentation is totally inadequate.

Violin concerto.
(N) (M) *** Sony Stern Edition II SMK 64507 [id.]. Stern, NYPO, Bernstein – PENDERECKI: *Violin concerto.* ***

When it first appeared, Stern's 1964 recording tended somewhat to be eclipsed by the composer's own Decca record with David Oistrakh. Naturally the performance under Hindemith has an authority that no competitor can match. But this American account is very fine indeed: Stern plays with eloquence, and Bernstein's accompaniment is always sympathetic and at times has something special to offer. In places it scores over the composer's own (towards the end of the slow movement, for example) but the recording is less analytical than the Decca and detail is less in evidence. The new coupling is admirably chosen, and this makes another key record in Box II of Sony's Stern Edition.

(i) *Violin concerto;* (ii) *Mathis der Maler (Symphony);* (iii) *Symphonic metamorphoses on themes of Weber.*

✹ (M) *** Decca 433 081-2 [id.]. (i) David Oistrakh, LSO, composer; (ii) SRO, Kletzki; (iii) LSO, Abbado.

Oistrakh's performance of the Hindemith *Violin concerto* is a revelation. The composer, clearly inspired by the marvellous contribution of his soloist, provides an overwhelmingly passionate accompaniment and the 1962 recording still sounds extraordinarily vivid and spacious. The Rosette is for the concerto but the couplings are well chosen, both also offering vintage late 1960s Decca sound. Abbado's *Symphonic metamorphoses on themes of Weber* is second to none. Kletzki's account of *Mathis der Maler* is also impressive, very well prepared and with a similar attention to detail. He, too has the advantage of finely balanced and truthful recording, and the Suisse Romande Orchestra still plays very well for him. With 77 minutes of music offered, this is an indispensable disc for all Hindemithians, even if some duplication is involved.

(i) *Violin concerto;* (ii) *Symphony in E flat.*

(Y/B) ** Everest EVC 9009 [id.]. (i) Joseph Fuchs, LSO, Sir Eugene Goossens; (ii) LPO, Sir Adrian Boult.

Both performances come from 1958 and were accorded what was thought at the time to be state-of-the-art recording. Joseph Fuchs in fact provided the première recording of the *Violin concerto*, and his account can well withstand comparison with its contemporaries. Sir Adrian's account of the *Symphony in E flat* has appropriate dignity and lucidity, though at full price readers are more likely to be drawn to the marvellously recorded Chandos version from the BBC Philharmonic and Yan Pascal Tortelier.

Der Dämon; (i) *Hérodiade* (two versions).

(Y/B) *** CPO Dig. 999 220-2 [id.]. (i) Annie Gicquel; Siegfried Mauser, Frankfurt RSO, Albert.

Der Dämon (The Demon) (1922) is an early ballet, 'a Dance Pantomime in two scenes', and it comes close to the world of the *Kammermusiken*; it has much delicacy of touch and great resource in matters of colour; and it is full of imaginative, original textures. There is a prominent role for the piano, brilliantly and sensitively played by Siegfried Mauser, whose ethereal cascades afford much delight. *Hérodiade* dates from 1944 and derives its inspiration from Mallarmé's poem. It is an excellent idea to let us have it first with the text, then again without it, and Annie Gicquel speaks it in exemplary fashion. The recording lends it an aural halo, but this is to be preferred to too dry a sound. *Hérodiade* is a beautiful score and Werner Andreas Albert gets excellent results from his Frankfurt forces. The Hessischer Rundfunk engineers produce recordings that are a model of good balance. Strongly recommended.

(i) *The Four Temperaments; Nobilissima visione.*

**(*) Delos Dig. D/CD 1006 [id.]. (i) Carole Rosenberger; RPO, James de Preist.

The Four Temperaments, a set of variations, is one of Hindemith's finest and most immediate works. Carole Rosenberger gives a formidable reading of this inventive and resourceful score. James de Preist also secures responsive playing from the RPO strings and gives a sober, well-shaped account of the *Nobilissima visione* suite, doing justice to its grave nobility.

Mathis der Maler (symphony).

(N) (M) **(*) EMI CDM5 65868-2. Pittsburgh SO, Steinberg – MARTIN: *Petite symphonie concertante;* TOCH: *Symphony No. 3.* ***

Mathis der Maler (symphony); *Concert music, Op. 50; Symphonic metamorphoses on themes by Carl Maria von Weber.*

*** DG Dig. 429 404-2 [id.]. Israel PO, Bernstein.

Mathis der Maler (symphony); *Nobilissima visione; Symphonic metamorphoses on themes by Weber.*

(Y/B) *** EMI Dig. CDC5 55230-2 [id.]. Phd. O, Sawallisch.

(N) *(*) DG Dig. 447 389-2 [id.] BPO, Abbado.

Mathis der Maler (symphony); *Symphonic metamorphoses on themes by Weber; Trauermusik.*

*** Decca Dig. 421 523-2 [id.]. San Francisco SO, Blomstedt.

The Philadelphia Orchestra made a celebrated 78-r.p.m. set of the *Mathis der Maler Symphony* in the days of Ormandy, and the present generation show themselves equally at home with this score. It is good to hear this great orchestra sounding itself again. Sawallisch draws a warm, rich-textured sound from them, and he also gives a performance of the *Nobilissima visione* that does justice to its breadth and dignity. Sawallisch's account of the *Symphonic metamorphoses on themes by Carl Maria von Weber* is not quite as sharp or fleet of foot as the Bernstein set, but it is still very well characterized. The *Mathis* scores over the rival Blomstedt on Decca in depth of characterization and orchestral opulence and, all things considered, should be the preferred recommendation.

Blomstedt has a strong feeling for *Mathis der Maler* and presents a finely groomed and powerfully shaped performance, with lucid and transparent textures. The famous *Trauermusik* has an affecting quiet eloquence and dedication: the solo viola, Geraldine Walther, is exceptionally sensitive. Blomstedt's reading of the *Symphonic metamorphoses on themes of Carl Maria von Weber* is appropriately light in touch; and the recording is exemplary in the naturalness of its balance.

High-voltage Hindemith from Bernstein and the Israel Philharmonic; it was recorded live in the Robert Mann Auditorium in Tel Aviv whose dry acoustic is a handicap. In both the *Concert music for brass and strings* and the *Weber metamorphoses* the playing is exhilarating, and the *Mathis der Maler* performance is thrilling.

Steinberg's pioneering stero recording shows the Pittsburgh orchestra at their finest, with a performance that is tense and well disciplined, yet which never allows the underlying emotion to be obscured. The final movement with its brilliant and exciting fugue comes out as a magnificent culmination. While this cannot perhaps be considered a first choice, the early (1957) stereo is remarkably full and atmospheric to match the brilliance and warmth of the performance. The Toch coupling, too, is especially worth investigating.

Abbado's memorable record of the *Symphonic metamorphoses* which he made for Decca in the late 1960s has been reissued (see above) concurrent with this new, DG version, which is not superior. There is nothing wrong with the playing of the Berlin Philharmonic, but the sound is synthetic and unnatural. There is not enough ambience round the upper strings and they are robbed of the bloom and sonority we associate with them. Readers wanting this triptych should stick with the Sawallisch on EMI.

(i) *Mathis de Maler* (symphony); (ii) *String quartet No. 2, Op. 22;* (iii) *String trio No. 2.*
(**) Koch Schwann mono 3-1134-2 [id.]. (i) BPO, Hindemith; (ii) Amar Qt; (iii) Goldberg, Hindemith, Feuermann.

Hindemith made two records of the *Mathis symphony*, both with the Berlin Philharmonic, one in 1934 and the second in 1955. This is the pioneering account, made only a year after Hitler's advent to power and at the height of the controversy that enveloped the opera right from its inception. The Koch transfer is satisfactory, and the coupling is valuable in that it offers the *Second String quartet*, recorded in 1927 by the Amar Quartet in which Hindemith was the violist and his brother, Rudolph, the cellist. The copy used for the transfer is not without blemish – and nor is the playing. The transfer of the *String trio* is not as good as in the EMI set, but the disc makes a useful supplement to it.

Sinfonia serena; Symphony (Die Harmonie der Welt).
⊛ *** Chandos Dig. CHAN 9217 [id.]. BBC PO, Yan Pascal Tortelier.

The *Sinfonia serena* (1946) is a brilliant and inventive score, full of humour and melody. The scoring is inventive and imaginative, the textures varied and full of genial touches. There is plenty of wit in the Scherzo, which paraphrases a Beethoven march from 1809. The *Symphony, Die Harmonie der Welt* (1951), is another powerful and consistently underrated score. Like *Mathis der Maler*, it is related to an opera, in this case based on the life of the seventeenth-century astronomer, philosopher and musician, Johannes Kepler. These well-prepared and finely shaped performances are given state-of-the-art recording quality. An outstanding issue.

Symphonic metamorphoses on themes by Weber.
*** Ph. Dig. 422 347-2 [id.]. Bav. RSO, C. Davis – REGER: *Mozart variations.* *** ⊛
(N) (M) *** Decca 448 579-2 [id.]. LSO, Abbado – JANACEK: *Sinfonietta;* PROKOFIEV: *Symphony No. 3.* ***
(M) **(*) EMI CDM5 65175-2 [id.]. Phd. O, Ormandy – BARTOK: *Miraculous Mandarin* etc. **(*)

Sir Colin Davis's account of the *Symphonic metamorphoses* is first class, though not perhaps as gutsy as Bernstein (DG). However, the reading has plenty of character and enormous finesse and is given state-of-the art Philips recording. Recommended with enthusiasm.

It is a relief to find a conductor like Abbado who is content to follow the composer's own dynamic markings and who does not give way to the temptation to score interpretative points at the music's expense. The stopped notes on the horns at the beginning of the finale, for example, are marked *piano*, and they are played here so that they add a barely perceptible touch of colour to the texture. The Decca engineers balance this so musically that the effect is preserved. This admittedly unimportant touch is symptomatic of the subtlety of Abbado's approach in a performance that in every respect is of the highest quality, while the vintage (1968) recording is surely worthy to be included in Decca's 'Classic

Sound' series. Readers will note that this performance is also available coupled with the *Violin concerto* –
see above.

The Philadelphia Orchestra play with splendid panache and brilliance, the humour of the second
movement perhaps realized less effectively in their hands than with, say, Blomstedt. In every other
respect this is first class, and the recording is full-bodied and does justice to the Philadelphia sound.

Symphony in E flat; Overture Neues vom Tage; Nobilissima visione.
*** Chandos Dig. CHAN 9060 [id.]. BBC PO, Tortelier.

The *Symphony in E flat* is an inventive and resourceful score and is well worth investigating. Yan Pascal
Tortelier gets excellent results from the BBC Philharmonic. Good, musicianly performances of
Nobilissima visione and the much earlier *Neues vom Tage* Overture complete an admirable addition to
the Hindemith discography.

Trauermusik (for viola and string orchestra).
(M) *** EMI CDM5 65079-2 [id.]. ECO, Daniel Barenboim – BARTOK: *Divertimento for strings*;
SCHOENBERG: *Verklaerte Nacht* ***.

This piece of *Gebrauchsmusik* ('utility music') was written in 24 hours in January 1936 when the composer
was informed of the death of King George V. Its gentle, elegiac quality was highly suitable for the occasion,
and the piece – in four sections – is not too long and is enjoyable for its simple, restrained eloquence. It is
excellently performed and recorded here, and the couplings are equally successful in a quite different way.

CHAMBER MUSIC

(i) *Alto saxophone sonata;* (ii) *Bass tuba sonata;* (iii) *Bassoon sonata;* (iv) *Morgenmusik;* (v) *Trio;* (vi)
Trombone sonata; (vii) *Trumpet sonata.*
** BIS CD159 [id.]. (i) Savijoki, Siirala; (ii) Lind, Harlos; (iii) Sonstevold, Knardahl; (iv) Malmö Brass
Ens.; (v) Pehrsson, Jonsson, Mjönes; (vi) Lindberg, Pöntinen; (vii) Tarr, Westenholz.

(i) *Alto horn sonata in E flat;* (ii) *Bass tuba sonata;* (i) *Horn sonata;* (iii) *Trombone sonata;* (iv) *Trumpet
sonata.*
(M) ** Sony SM2K 52671 (2) [id.]. (i) Mason Jones; (ii) Abe Torchinsky; (iii) Henry Charles Smith; (iv)
Gilbert Johnson; Glenn Gould.

The *Alto saxophone sonata* and the *Alto horn sonata* are one and the same work. The BIS recordings
were made at various times during the mid-1970s and early 1980s and, with the exception of the
Trombone sonata, are analogue. They are for the most part rather closely balanced though not disturbingly so. The Sony recordings are all from 1976 but unfortunately do not offer the *Recorder trio*, expertly
played on the BIS by Claes Pehrsson, Anders-Per Jonsson and Anders Mjönes, or the exhilarating
Morgenmusik for brass – not to mention the inventive *Bassoon sonata*. On the other hand, Sony's mid-
price two-CD set gives you the *Alto horn sonata* with Mason Jones. Glenn Gould has great feeling for
Hindemith and plays with strong personality and commitment throughout, even though the tiresome
vocalise is a strain. Despite the eminence of his soloists and the somewhat forward quality of the BIS
balance, the latter is probably the safer recommendation.

Octet.
(N) **(*) Nimbus Dig. NI 5461 [id.]. BPO Octet – BEETHOVEN: *Septet.* **(*)

The *Octet* is a late work (from 1958) and was written for the Berlin Philharmonic Octet, who gave the
première with Hindemith himself as second viola the following year. They recorded it for DG in the
1960s and on both occasions Rainer Zeppertiz, the double-bass on this recording, took part. The music
is well fashioned but a bit manufactured, and many of the ideas find the composer at his most routine.
The exception is the central slow movement, which has considerable eloquence. The playing is expert,
but the recording is closely balanced and upfront.

Septet.
(N) *** Virgin/EMI Dig. VC5 45056-2. Deutsche Kammerphilharmonie Wind – TOCH: *5 pieces for
wind and percussion;* WEILL: *Violin concerto.* ***

Hindemith's *Septet* dates from 1948 and, save for the finale (which was written in Rome), was composed
in Taormina. There is no alternative version, and any subsequent rival will have its work cut out to
match the present performance by the wind of the Deutsche Kammerphilharmonie, which is outstanding in every way. Hindemith's use of sonority is consistently imaginative and the invention fresher than
in the later *Octet*. Admirers of the composer need not hesitate. Exemplary recording. The Toch and
Weill couplings are both excellent.

String quartet No. 3, Op. 22.

(Y/B) ❀ (***) Testament mono SBT 1052 [id.]. Hollywood Qt – PROKOFIEV: *Quartet No. 2;* WALTON: *Quartet in A min.* (***) ❀

The remarkable Hollywood Quartet version of the *Third Quartet*, which first appeared on these shores in 1952, is pretty stunning. The Hollywood Quartet possessed an extraordinary virtuosity and perfection of ensemble, and it is difficult to imagine more persuasive advocacy. The transfer is excellent and, although the mono sound does not represent the state of the art these days, the performance still sweeps the board.

(i) *Viola sonatas* (for viola and piano) *Op. 11/4; Op. 25/4;* (Unaccompanied) *Viola sonatas: Op. 11/5; Op. 25/1; Op. 31/4.*
*** ECM Dig. 833 309-2 (2) [id.]. Kim Kashkashian, (i) Robert Levin.

The solo *Sonatas* are played with superb panache and flair – and, even more importantly, with remarkable variety of colour – by Kim Kashkashian, who has an enormous dynamic range. The performances of the sonatas with piano are hardly less imaginative and the recording is good.

(Solo) *Viola sonatas Nos. 1; 2, Op. 11/5; 3, Op. 25/1; 4, Op. 31/4.*
(N) *** ASV Dig. CDDCA 947 [id.]. Paul Cortese.

Four sonatas for solo viola are not to be heard straight off and are fare for aficionados rather than for the wider musical public. Paul Cortese is a player of considerable accomplishments and he is persuasive in this forbidding repertoire. He is not perhaps always as imaginative or poetic as Kim Kashkashian (ECM), but the disc is certainly recommendable if you find the latter to be out-of-stock.

PIANO MUSIC

Berceuse; In einer Nacht, Op. 15; Kleines Klavierstück; Lied; 1922 Suite, Op. 26; Tanzstücke, Op. 19.
**(*) Marco Polo Dig. 8.223335 [id.]. Hans Petermandl.

Exercise in three pieces, Op. 31/I; Klaviermusik, Op. 37; Series of little pieces, Op. 37/II; Sonata, Op. 17; Two little piano pieces.
** Marco Polo Dig. 8.223336 [id.]. Hans Petermandl.

Ludus Tonalis; Kleine Klaviermusik, Op. 45/4.
** Marco Polo Dig. 8.223338 [id.]. Hans Petermandl.

Piano sonatas Nos. 1–3; Variations.
** Marco Polo Dig. 8.223337 [id.]. Hans Petermandl.

Hans Petermandl is an expert guide in this repertoire and presents it with real sympathy for, and understanding of, the idiom; his performances are very persuasive. The textures in Hindemith's piano music are often unbeautiful and less than transparent and, although neither the piano nor the acoustic of the Concert Hall of Slovak Radio is outstanding, the sound is perfectly acceptable.

Organ sonatas Nos. 1–3.
*** Chandos Dig. CHAN 9097 [id.]. Piet Kee – REGER: *Four organ pieces.* ***

The *Sonatas* of Hindemith are one of the mainstays of the twentieth-century organ repertoire, and the appearance of this new CD restores them to their rightful place in the catalogue. Piet Kee plays on the Müller organ of St Bavo in Haarlem, an instrument more suited to Hindemith than the somewhat spacious acoustic in which it is recorded. This small point apart, Kee plays with his customary distinction and character. All three sonatas are rewarding, and no one investing in this disc is likely to be disappointed on either artistic or technical grounds.

When lilacs last in the dooryard bloom'd (Requiem).
*** Telarc Dig. CD 80132 [id.]. DeGaetani, Stone, Atlanta Ch. & SO, Robert Shaw.
(M) **(*) Sony/CBS MPK 45881. Louise Parker, George London, NY Schola Cantorum, NYPO, composer.

Robert Shaw commissioned Hindemith to compose this 'Requiem for those we loved' at the end of the 1939–45 war. It is one of the composer's most deeply felt works and one of his best. Shaw gives a performance of great intensity and variety of colour and nuance. Both his soloists are excellent, and there is both weight and subtlety in the orchestral contribution. Splendid recording.

On Sony, Hindemith himself is at the helm, so the performance carries a special authority. The music has surpassing beauty and eloquence. Louise Parker and George London are committed soloists and the recording has a full and realistic acoustic.

(i) *Cardillac* (opera) complete; (ii) *Mathis der Maler*: excerpts.
(M) *** DG 431 741-2 (2) [id.]. Fischer-Dieskau, Grobe, (i) Kirschstein, Kohn, Cologne R. Ch. & SO,
   Keilberth; (ii) Lorengar, Berlin RSO, Ludwig.

Taken from a radio performance, this reissue of *Cardillac* shows Hindemith at his most vigorous.
Fischer-Dieskau as the goldsmith has a part which tests even his artistry, and though the other soloists
are variable in quality the conducting of Keilberth holds the music together strongly. As a generous and
ideal coupling, the second disc contains an hour of excerpts from Hindemith's even more celebrated
opera, *Mathis der Maler*, again with Fischer-Dieskau taking the lead, and with Donald Grobe in a
supporting role. Regina is beautifully sung by Pilar Lorengar. The 1960s recordings of both operas are
excellently transferred, with voices full and fresh. No texts are given, but instead there are detailed
summaries of the plots, with copious quotations.

Mathis der Maler (opera; complete).
(Y/B) (M) *** EMI CDS5 55237-2 (3) [id.]. Fischer-Dieskau, Feldhof, J. King, M. Schmidt, Meven,
   Cochran, Malta, Grobe, Wagemann, Bav. R. Ch. & SO, Kubelik.

There is little doubt that the opera *Mathis der Maler* is Hindemith's masterpiece. Fischer-Dieskau
proves the ideal interpreter of the central role, the painter Mathias Grünewald, who in the troubled
Germany of the sixteenth century joins the cause of the rebellious peasants – a subject with a very clear
relevance to the times when the piece was written, during the rise of the Nazis. The performance
includes other fine contributions from James King as the Archbishop, Donald Grobe as the Cardinal,
Alexander Malta as the army commandant and Manfred Schmidt as the Cardinal's adviser. The women
principals are less happily chosen; Rose Wagemann as Ursula is rather squally. But with splendid
playing and singing from Bavarian Radio forces under Kubelik, this is a highly enjoyable as well as an
important set. Moreover the first-class (1977) analogue recording was made in the famous Munich
Herculessaal. Its warm, glowing acoustics are just as kind to the voices as to the orchestra, with the
balance between soloists, chorus and orchestra very natural, as is immediately apparent in the atmospheric opening scene. The CD transfer (engineered by Simon Gibson at Abbey Road) is a model of its
kind.

Hoddinott, Alun (born 1929)

(i) *Chorales, variants and fanfares* (for brass and organ); *Quodlibet on Welsh nursery tunes; Ritornelli 2,
Op. 100/2.*
(N) *** Nimbus Dig. NI 5466 [id.]. Fine Arts Brass Ens.; (i) with Kevin Bowyer (organ) – MATHIAS:
   Summer dances; Soundings. ***

The most remarkable and original work here is the *Chorales, variants and fanfares*, written in 1992 for
the Swansea Festival. It sub-divides into three sections, each interweaving organ and brass textures in a
highly imaginative interplay, the organ at times taking a concertante role, at others becoming part of the
group, with its pedals effectively extending the lower sonority. The sombrely evocative opening leads to
the virtuoso *Fanfares*, with the organ dancing along in bravura discourse with the brass, but the closing
section of the work is valedictory, with the organ building harmonic blocks for the brass to top for the
pungent apotheosis. The concert opens with Hoddinott's witty scoring of five attractive Welsh nursery
tunes and ends with the second of his three *Ritornelli* (1979) a suite of five sharply characterized pieces
which, though interesting, are rather less rewarding than the other two works. Performances are first
class and the recording in the demonstration bracket, with the balance between organ and brass expertly
managed within the warm ambience of St Mary's Collegiate Church, Warwick.

Holloway, Robin (born 1943)

Second Concerto for orchestra, Op. 40.
*** NMC Dig. D015M [id.]. BBC SO, Oliver Knussen.

Another valuable issue among those CD 'singles' marketed at a special price and devoted to new
music. Holloway's *Second Concerto* made a powerful impression when it was first performed in
1979. The composer tells us that the background inspiration was a visit in 1977–8 to North Africa
with its strong contrasts of colour and texture, opulence and austerity, brilliant light and dense
shadow. It is a richly imaginative score and shows a sensitivity of high quality, as well as a considerable mastery of instrumental resource. The *Concerto* is a work of substance that is well worth
getting to know and is well served by the BBC Symphony Orchestra and Oliver Knussen. The engineers

produce a better sound from the Maida Vale Studios than we have heard on any other occasion.

(i) *Romanza for violin and small orchestra, Op. 31;* (ii) *Sea-surface full of clouds, Op. 28.*
*** Chandos Dig. CHAN 9228 [id.]. (i) Gruenberg; (ii) Walmsley-Clark, Cable, Hill, Brett, Hickox Singers; City of L. Sinfonia, Richard Hickox.

Robin Holloway is one of the most imaginative of contemporary composers, and the two works recorded here show his sensitivity to colour and marvellous feeling for the orchestra. The *Sea-surface full of clouds* begins luminously, rather like Szymanowski, and has an at times magical atmosphere. There is an affecting and consuming melancholy about the *Romanza* for violin and orchestra. A composer of a refined intelligence and real sensibility.

Holmboe, Vagn (born 1909)

(i) *Cello concerto, Op. 120;* (ii) *Brass quintet, Op. 79;* (iii) *Triade, Op. 123;* (iv) *Benedic Domino, Op. 59.*
*** BIS Analogue/Dig. CD-78 [id.]. (i) Bløndahl Bengtsson, Danish RSO, Ferencsik; (ii) Swedish Brass Quintet; (iii) Edward Tarr, Elisabeth Westenholz; (iv) Camerata Ch., Per Enevold.

Vagn Holmboe's magificent *Cello concerto*, along with the Dutilleux *Concerto*, is one of the finest examples of the genre to have appeared in recent years. The textures are transparent, and the music inhabits a distinctive world of its own. An excellent performance of an eloquent work. The choral piece, *Benedic Domino*, is one of a cycle of motets comprising the *Liber canticorum*, composed in the 1950s, that has an austere beauty and elevation of feeling that are rare in contemporary music. The *Brass quintet* (1961) is an effective and stirring piece, written for the New York Brass Quintet; and the *Triade* for trombone and organ comes from the 1970s, as does the *Cello concerto*, and is hardly less striking. Only the *Quintet* is a digital recording but its companions here are also strikingly good as sound.

Symphonies Nos. 1, Op. 4; 3 (Sinfonia rustica), Op. 25; 10, Op. 105.
(Y/B) *** BIS Dig. CD 605 [id.]. Aarhus SO, Arwel Hughes.

The *First Symphony* (*Sinfonia da camera*) comes from 1935. Its general outlook is neo-classical and its proportions are modest (it takes about 15 minutes) but one recognizes the vital current of the later Holmboe, the lucidity of thinking and the luminous textures. The last movement has an infectious delight in life; so, too, has the exhilarating finale of the *Third* (*Sinfonia rustica*), the first of his three wartime symphonies. The *Tenth* (1970–71) is, of course, a piece of much greater substance, commissioned by Sixten Ehrling and the Detroit Orchestra (and recorded by him in the days of LP). It is dark, powerful and imaginative; altogether one of the Danish composer's most subtle and satisfying works. The performances and recordings are altogether first class.

Symphony No. 2, Op. 15; Sinfonia in memoriam, Op. 65.
(N) ❀ *** BIS Dig. CD 695 [id.]. Aarhus SO, Owain Arwel Hughes.

The *Second Symphony* (1938–9) won a competition in 1939 and its success put Holmboe on the map in his native Denmark. Small wonder, you will say, when you hear the imaginative middle movement and its vital companions. (With the prize money the composer bought a plot of land near Ramløse, where he has written the remainder of his output and where he and his wife have planted some 7,000 trees!) The *Sinfonia in memoriam* was commissioned in 1955 by Danish Radio to mark the tenth anniversary of the liberation. Unlike so many commissioned works, this springs from great feeling, for the composer had a number of close friends active in the Resistance. It is a dark work of striking power and imaginative breadth and is masterly in every way. Owain Arwell Hughes and the Aarhus orchestra give a performance that is in every way worthy of it, and the recording is in the demonstration bracket. Only the last three symphonies – above all, the wonderfully imaginative *Eleventh*, along with the *Twelfth* (1989) and the *Thirteenth*, composed in his mid-eighties and first performed in March 1996 – now remain to be be added to the catalogue; and they will be appearing in the lifetime of this volume.

Symphonies Nos. (i) 4 (Sinfonia sacra), Op. 29. 5, Op. 35.
**(*) BIS Dig. CD 572 [id.]. (i) Jutland Op. Ch.; Aarhus SO, Owain Arwel Hughes.

The *Fifth Symphony* makes a good entry point into Holmboe's world. In outlook it is strongly tonal and neo-classical: the Stravinsky of the *Symphony in C* briefly comes to mind, but Holmboe is very much his own man and a distinctive musical landscape is immediately established. The only word to describe its outer movements is exhilarating. The slow movement has a modal character, but an anguished outburst in the middle serves as a reminder that this is a wartime work, composed during the dark days of the Nazi occupation. The *Fourth* (*Sinfonia sacra*) is a six-movement choral piece dedicated to the memory of his brother who perished in a Nazi concentration camp. It encompasses a bracing vigour and underlying optimism alongside moments of sustained grief. Very good performances, though the strings are a little under-strength and the acoustic is on the dry side. But don't let this put you off this inspiriting music.

Symphonies Nos. 6, Op. 43; 7, Op. 50.
**(*) BIS Dig. CD 573. Aarhus SO, Owain Arwel Hughes.

Holmboe's *Sixth Symphony* is a much darker piece than its predecessor. This is a distinctively Nordic world and the brooding, slow-moving fourths of the long introduction prompt astronomical analogies: one seems to be surveying some forces in outer space; and there is writing of great luminosity too. The one-movement *Seventh Symphony* is a highly concentrated score, individual in both form and content, which encompasses great variety of pace and mood. The three intermedia which punctuate it are wonderfully luminous. Owain Arwel Hughes acquits himself very well, and this is music that speaks with so strong and distinctive a voice that it is self-recommending. There are few if any Nordic symphonies post-Nielsen and -Sibelius of this quality.

Symphonies Nos 8, Op. 56 (1951); 9 (1968).
(Y/B) ✹*** BIS Dig. CD 618 [id.]. Aarhus SO, Arwel Hughes.

Only three of Holmboe's symphonies were recorded in the days of vinyl (Nos. 7, 8 and 10), of which perhaps the *Eighth*, available on Turnabout (with the Royal Danish Orchestra under Jerzy Semkow), enjoyed the longest currency. This new version by the Aarhus orchestra under Owain Arwel Hughes is infinitely superior. This conductor has real feeling for the composer and not only penetrates the spirit of the score but is scrupulous in his observance of the letter. Dynamic and agogic markings are meticulously yet unobtrusively followed; one is left with the impression that this symphony has never really had its due until now. The *Ninth Symphony* is wholly unfamiliar. After its first performance in Copenhagen in 1968, which was subsequently broadcast by the BBC, it was revised and this is its première recording. A dark, powerful work, the *Ninth* is among the finest Holmboe has given us: Professor Richard Taruskin recently spoke of him in *The New York Times* as 'possibly the greatest living symphonist' and what he wrote of the *Sixth* certainly applies to the *Ninth*: 'Form and expressive content, in a word, are one. It is every symphonic composer's ideal but very few achieve it so fully.' Taruskin compared it to 'academic discourse of a thrillingly high order . . . if you have ever left a lecture hall haunted and altered, this may offer a comparable cognitive adventure.' Like the *Sixth* and *Seventh Symphonies*, this disc of the *Eighth* and *Ninth* is to be recommended with urgency. This is music which, one can feel with some certainty, future generations will want to hear. The Aarhus orchestra are equally persuasive in the *Ninth* as in the *Eighth*, and the recording is the best so far in the cycle.

String quartets Nos. 1, Op. 46; 3, Op. 48; 4, Op. 63.
*** Marco Polo Dacapo Dig. CDDC 9203 [id.]. Kontra Qt.

These quartets have a certain reserve: nothing is overstated, everything is quietly but cogently argued and, once one has broken through its reticence, its rewards are rich. This issue is the first in a complete survey from the Kontra Quartet, and if all the performances are as committed as this it will be a landmark in the catalogue. This is easily the finest post-war quartet cycle in Scandinavia, and those who respond to the quartets of Shostakovich or Robert Simpson should lose no time in investigating them.

String quartets Nos. 2, Op. 47; 5, Op. 66; 6, Op. 78.
(N) *** Danacord Dig. 8.224026. Kontra Qt.

Holmboe has over 20 string quartets to his credit, and this new CD by the Kontra Quartet is no less successful than its predecessor. The *Second Quartet* from 1949 has a particularly engaging main theme and these artists play it with conviction. The *Fifth* (1955) and *Sixth* (1961) are both finely argued works. What a rewarding composer Holmboe is, and how well played and recorded these quartets are!

Holmès, Augusta (1847–1903)

Andromeda (symphonic poem); *Ireland* (symphonic poem); (i) *Ludus pro patria: Night and love. Overture for a comedy; Poland* (symphonic poem).
(Y/B) *** Marco Polo Dig. 8.223449 [id.]. Rheinland-Pfalz PO, Samuel Friedmann; (i) Patrick Davin.

Augusta Holmès was the inspiring force behind the César Franck *Piano quintet* which embodied much of that master's strong feeling for her. She was from an Anglo-Irish family that had settled in France; Alfred de Vigny was her godfather – and, some maintain, her real father. She was a person of remarkable gifts for, apart from her musical talents, she was an accomplished painter and wrote well. Unable (on account of her sex) to gain admission to the Paris Conservatoire, she received encouragement from both Liszt and Wagner before becoming a pupil of Franck. She composed some 150 songs in all but also tried her hand at larger forms, and she gained the distinction of being commissioned to write a massive work for the centenary of the French Revolution, the *Ode triomphale*, which called for no fewer than 1,200 performers and was heard at the Palais d'Industrie by an audience of 15,000! Although the *Overture for a comedy* (1876) is trite, *Andromeda* is quite striking, rather Lisztian at first and with occasional reminders of Vincent d'Indy, though some of the orchestral textures are more transparent than those of so many of the Franck circle. *Andromeda* is by far the best piece on the disc, and the best scored, though limitations in Augusta Holmès's technique (particularly her reliance on sequence, and the relatively limited development of ideas) are evident. But this is music of much interest – and its composer was obviously no mean talent. She has been well served by the Rheinland-Pfalz Philharmonic under Samuel Friedmann. The recordings too are eminently satisfactory.

Holst, Gustav (1874–1934)

'*The essential Holst*': (i) *Egdon Heath, Op. 47;* (ii) *A Moorside suite;* (iii) *The Perfect Fool, Op. 39;* (iv) *The Planets, Op. 32;* (v) *St Paul's suite, Op. 29/2;* (vi) *Ave Maria, Op. 9b; Choral hymns from the Rig Veda* (Group 3), *Op. 26/3; The Evening watch, Op. 43/1;* (vii) *The Hymn of Jesus, Op. 37;* (vi) *This have I done for my true love, Op. 34/1.*

(N) (B) *** Decca Double Analogue/Dig. 444 549-2 (2) [id.]. (i; iii) LPO, Boult; (ii) Grimethorpe
    Colliery Band, Howarth; (iv) LPO, Solti; (v) St Paul CO, Hogwood; (vi) Purcell Singers, I. Holst;
    (vii) BBC Ch. & SO, Boult.

The brilliant Decca recording of Solti's Chicago version of the *Planets* combined with Boult's vintage accounts of *Egdon Heath* and *The Perfect Fool* ballet music is discussed below in its single-disc format. Boult's distinguished performance of the *Hymn of Jesus* is also available on another Double Decca, joined with music by Delius and Elgar. But if the present compilation is suitable, it could make a splendid basis for a Holst collection. The jolly, folksy *St Paul's suite* for strings, with its delicately etched second-movement '*Ostinato*' and characteristically haunting *Intermezzo*, could hardly be done better. Newcomers to this work will be pleased to welcome the unexpected entry of *Greensleeves* in the *Dargason* finale. *A Moorside suite* sounds splendid in its original, brass-band form (it was written for the National Championship contest at Crystal Palace in 1928) and it is superbly played by the Grimethorpe Colliery Band under Elgar Howarth, with recording approaching demonstration standard. Aptly, the first of the *Rig-Veda Choral hymns* (taken from a Sanskrit source), the *Hymn to the dawn*, brings echoes of *Neptune* from *The Planets*, while the fast and rhythmically fascinating *Hymn to the waters* is even more attractive. The vocal music serves to balance the picture of Holst as a composer, to show the more mystical side of his musical character. Beautifully atmospheric recording to match intense and sensitive performances.

(i) *Beni Mora (oriental suite), Op. 29/1; A Fugal overture, Op. 40/1; Hammersmith – A Prelude and scherzo for orchestra, Op. 52;* (ii) *Japanese suite;* (i) *Scherzo (1933/4); A Somerset rhapsody, Op. 21.*
*** Lyrita SRCD 222 [id.]. (i) LPO; (ii) LSO; Boult.

Beni Mora (written after a holiday in Algeria) is an attractive, exotic piece that shows Holst's flair for orchestration vividly. Boult clearly revels in its sinuosity. *The Japanese suite* is not very Japanese, although it has much charm, particularly the piquant *Marionette dance* and the innocuous *Dance under the cherry tree*. The most ambitious work here is *Hammersmith*, far more than a conventional tone picture, intensely poetic. Although conceived for military band, it was orchestrated a year later (1931). The *Scherzo*, from a projected symphony that was never completed, is strong, confident music. The *Somerset rhapsody* is unpretentious but very enjoyable, and the brief, spiky *Fugal overture* is given plenty of lift and bite to open the concert invigoratingly. As with other records in this Lyrita series the first class analogue recording has been splendidly transferred to CD.

Brook Green suite for strings; Capriccio for orchestra; (i) *Double violin concerto, Op. 49;* (ii) *Fugal concerto for flute, oboe and strings, Op. 40/2. The Golden Goose* (ballet music, arr. Imogen Holst), *Op. 45/ 1;* (iii) *Lyric movement for viola and small orchestra. A Moorside suite: Nocturne* (arr. for strings); *2 Songs without words, Op. 22.*
**(*) Lyrita SRCD 223 [id.]. ECO, Imogen Holst, with (i) Emanuel Hurwitz, Kenneth Sillito; (ii)
    William Bennett, Peter Graeme; (iii) Cecil Aronowitz.

Although not all of this is top-quality Holst, the programme is generous (75 minutes) and there are some interesting rarities here. The *Capriccio* proves an exuberant piece, with some passages not at all capriccio-like. *The Golden Goose* was written as a choral work for St Paul's Girls' School; these orchestral snippets were put together by Imogen Holst and, if comparatively slight, reflect the sharpness of an imagination which was often inspired by the needs of an occasion. The *Double concerto*, with its bi-tonality and cross-rhythms, is grittier and with much less obvious melodic appeal, but it remains an interesting example of the late Holst. The first two movements of the *Fugal concerto* are much more appealing with their cool interplay of wind colour, particularly when the soloists are so distinguished. The *Lyric movement for viola and small orchestra* is certainly persuasive in the hands of Cecil Aronowitz and is one of the most beautiful of Holst's later pieces. The slow movement from the *Moorside suite* – originally written for brass band – is heard here in the composer's own arrangement for strings; and the concert is completed with the comparatively familiar *Brook Green suite* and two *Songs without words*, early works that are tuneful and colourful. All the performances are sympathetically authentic and the recording is well up to Lyrita's usual high standard.

Brook Green suite for string orchestra; (i) *A Fugal concerto, Op. 40/2;* (ii) *Lyric movement for viola and small orchestra; St Paul's suite for string orchestra, Op. 29/2. Arrangements of Morris dance tunes: Bean setting; Constant Billy; Country gardens; How d'ye do; Laudanum bunches; Rigs o'Marlow; Shepherd's hey.*
*** Koch Dig. 3-7058-2 [id.]. New Zealand CO, Nicholas Braithwaite; with (i) Alexa Still, Stephen
      Popperwell; (ii) Vyvyan Yendoll.

The *Fugal concerto* features concertante solos for flute and oboe and is a beautifully crafted triptych of miniatures; the rather more ambitious *Lyric movement* is hardly less appealing and is warmly played here by Vyvyan Yendoll, who has a fine, rich timbre. The New Zealand Chamber Orchestra respond sensitively and persuasively to Nicholas Braithwaite who is thoroughly at home in this repertoire. The textures of the *Brook Green suite* are pleasingly light and airy and in the *St Paul's suite* the gutsy opening *Jig* makes a complete contrast with the pianissimo delicacy of the *Ostinati*. The set of country dances is agreeably spontaneous. The recording is in the demonstration bracket.

Brook Green suite for string orchestra; (i) *Fugal concerto for flute and oboe. The Perfect Fool* (ballet suite), *Op. 39; St Paul's suite for string orchestra, Op. 26/2; A Somerset rhapsody, Op. 21/2.*
(Y/B) (M) *** EMI CD-EMX 2227; *TC-EMX 2227*. ECO, Sir Yehudi Menuhin.

There are a number of collections of Holst's shorter orchestral works currently available on CD, but none better played or recorded than this and none less expensive. It includes warmly characterized performances of both the works Holst wrote for St Paul's Girls' School, not just the *St Paul's suite* but also the *Brook Green suite*, both sounding fresh, while the rarer *Somerset rhapsody* is also very atmospherically presented. There is some delightful solo playing from Jonathan Snowden and David Theodore in the *Fugal concerto*, and many will welcome Menuhin's vivid account of *The Perfect Fool*, Holst's most familiar orchestral suite after *The Planets*. If the programme suits, you need look no further.

Brook Green suite; (i) *Double violin concerto, Op. 49;* (ii) *Fugal concerto for flute, oboe and strings, Op. 40/ 2;* (iii) *Lyric movement for viola and small orchestra; 2 Songs without words, Op. 22; St Paul's suite, Op. 29/ 2.*
*** Chandos Dig. CHAN 9270 [id.]. (i) Ward, Watkinson; (ii) Dobing, Hooker; (iii) Tees; City of L.
      Sinf., Hickox.

Hickox's collection brings together a delightful group of Holst's shorter pieces. The most striking piece of all, a fine example of Holst's later, sparer style, is the *Double concerto* for two violins and small orchestra, very taut and intense. The delicacy of the solo playing in the central *Lament* of this fine work is matched by the ethereal pianissimo from Stephen Tees at the opening of the *Lyric movement*. Tees is satisfyingly rich-toned and, if not absolutely flawless on intonation, clear parallels with Vaughan Williams's viola writing are readily drawn. The woodwind playing is delightful here too, as is the gentle clarinet solo which opens the *Country song*, the first of Holst's two *Songs without words*; the second, appropriately, is more robust. The *Brook Green suite* is wonderfully fresh and there is a comparable lightness of touch at the opening of the delightful *Fugal concerto*, a nice example of early neo-classicism, which does not sound in the least pedagogic. The *St Paul's suite* combines infectious vigour in the outer movements with wistful delicacy in the *Ostinato* and an intensely felt *Intermezzo*. What matters throughout this programme is the surging warmth that Richard Hickox draws from his modest forces. The recording is superb – very real indeed.

Cotswolds Symphony in F (Elegy: In memoriam William Morris), Op. 8; Indra (symphonic poem), Op. 13; (i) *Invocation (for cello and orchestra), Op. 19/2;* (iii) *The Lure (ballet music); The Morning of the year: Dances, Op. 45/2. Sita: Interlude from Act III, Op. 23;* (ii) *A Song of the night (for violin and orchestra), Op. 19/1; A Winter idyll.*
(N) *** Lyrita Dig./Analogue SRCD 209 [id.]. (i) Alexander Baillie; (ii) Lorraine McAslan; LPO or
      (iii) LSO; David Atherton.

The earliest work here, *A Winter idyll*, was written in 1897, the year after his fellow-student's Hurlstone's *Variations on an original theme* when Holst was in his early twenties. Lewis Foreman's informative note speaks of the influence of Stanford, but both in this work and in the *Elegy*, which is a slow movement originally forming part of a *Cotswolds Symphony*, one can detect little of the mature Holst. The familiar fingerprints do surface, however, in *Indra* (1903) and *A Song of the night* (1905), which is among the scores Colin Matthews has edited. *The Lure* (1921) was written at short notice for Chicago and is characteristic, but the inspiration is not of the quality of *The Perfect fool*. When they were first performed at a BBC concert, the *Dances from The Morning of the year* (1926-27) shared the programme with Honegger's *King David*, and they enjoy the distinction of being the very first commission made by the BBC Music Department. Holstians will need no urging to acquire this interesting, well-played and well-recorded disc. None of the music is Holst at his best, but it usefully fills in our picture of him.

Hammersmith: Prelude and scherzo, Op. 52.
(M) *** Mercury 432 009-2 [id.]. Eastman Wind Ens., Fennell – BENNETT: *Symphonic songs* ***; JACOB: *William Byrd suite* ***; WALTON: *Crown Imperial.* *** ✸

Holst's highly original and characteristically individual piece is scored for 25 individual wind instruments (there is no doubling of parts in this recording). Fennell's pioneering stereo recording is superbly played by these expert students from the Eastman School, and the effect is totally spontaneous. The recording remains demonstration-worthy, though it dates from 1958!

Invocation for cello and orchestra, Op. 19/2.
*** RCA RD 70800. Lloyd Webber, Philh. O, Handley – DELIUS: *Concerto;* VAUGHAN WILLIAMS: *Folksongs fantasia.* ***

Holst's *Invocation for cello and orchestra* is a highly attractive and lyrical piece, well worth reviving. Both the performance and recording are of admirable quality. Recommended.

Military band suites Nos. 1 in E flat; 2 in F.
✸ *** Telarc Dig. CD 80038 [id.]. Cleveland Symphonic Winds, Fennell – HANDEL: *Royal Fireworks music.* ***
(M) *** EMI Dig. CDM5 65122-2 [id.]. Central Band of the RAF, Wing Commander Eric Banks – GRAINGER: *Lincolnshire posy* etc.; VAUGHAN WILLIAMS: *English folk songs suite.* ***

Holst's two *Military band suites* contain some magnificent music. Frederick Fennell's new versions have more gravitas though no less *joie de vivre* than his old Mercury set. They are magnificent, and the recording is truly superb – digital technique used in a quite overwhelmingly exciting way. The *Chaconne* of the *First Suite* makes a quite marvellous effect here. The playing of the Cleveland wind group is of the highest quality.

The new EMI/RAF version of the suites is extraordinarily successful. It has a great sense of style and conveys a marvellous projection of high spirits; the only blot is the dead-sounding bass drum at the end of the great *Chaconne* of the *First suite*. Wing Commander Banks could, with advantage, have taken this movement (or at least its closing section) a fraction more slowly, and perhaps next time he is recording for EMI he can persuade the producer, Brian Culverhouse, to borrow an orchestral bass drum and re-record just this movement again. The Vaughan Williams and Grainger couplings are just as distinguished; the recording throughout, made in Watford Town Hall, is in the demonstration bracket: it has crisp, clean transients and fine amplitude.

Military band suites Nos. 1–2. Hammersmith: Prelude and scherzo, Op. 52.
(BB) *** ASV CDQS 6021. L. Wind O, Denis Wick – VAUGHAN WILLIAMS: *English folksong suite* etc. ***

The London performances have great spontaneity, even if they are essentially lightweight, especially when compared with the Fennell versions. The sound is first class.

The Planets (suite), *Op. 32.*
(Y/B) *** DG Dig. 445 860-2; *445 860-4* [id.]. Monteverdi Ch. women's voices, Philh. O, Gardiner – GRAINGER: *The Warriors.* ***
*** Denon Dig. CO 75076 [id.]. King's College Ch., RPO, James Judd. ***
*** Decca Dig. 417 553-2 [id.]. Montreal Ch. & SO, Dutoit. ***
(M) *** EMI CDM7 64748-2 [id.]. LPO, Boult (with G. Mitchell Ch.) – ELGAR: *Enigma variations.* ***
(BB) *** DG 439 446-2 [id.]. Boston SO, Steinberg – ELGAR: *Enigma variations.* ***
*** DG Gold Dig. 439 011-2 [id.]. Berlin Ch., BPO, Karajan.

(Y/B) (B) **(*) BBC Radio Classics BBCRD 9104 [id.]. BBC SO, Sargent – ELGAR: *Enigma Variations.* **(*)

(Y/B) (M) **(*) EMI CDM5 65423-2 [id.]. R. Wagner Chorale women's voices, LAPO, Stokowski – RAVEL: *Alborada* **(*); STRAVINSKY: *Petrushka.* **

(Y/B) (M) **(*) EMI Dig. CDM7 64740-2 [id.]. Philh. O, Rattle – JANACEK: *Sinfonietta.* ***

(Y/B) (M) **(*) Ph. Dig. 442 408-2 [id.]. Berlin R. Ch., BPO, Sir Colin Davis.

(Y/B) (***) EMI mono CDC7 54837-2 [id.]. LSO, composer – ELGAR: *Enigma variations.* (***)

(Y/B) (BB) (***) RCA Navigator 74321 17905-2 [id.]. Phd. Ch. & O, Ormandy – VAUGHAN WILLIAMS: *Fantasias.* ***

(i) *The Planets;* (ii) *Egdon Heath, Op. 47;* (iii) *The Perfect Fool* (suite), *Op. 39.*
(M) *** Decca 440 318-2 [id.]. LPO, cond. (i) Solti, with LPO Ch.; (ii; iii) Boult.

(i) *The Planets;* (ii) *The Perfect Fool* (suite).
(B) *** Decca 433 620-2; *433 620-4* [id.]. (i) LAPO, Mehta; (ii) LPO, Boult.
(M) **(*) Virgin/EMI Dig. CUV5 61257-2 [id.]. RLPO, Mackerras.

(i) *The Planets. St Paul's suite, Op. 29/2.*
(BB) *** Tring Dig. TRP 007. RPO, Vernon Handley, (i) with Ladies of Ambrosian Ch.

Even when branching out from his usual repertory, John Eliot Gardiner has imaginative things to say in his interpretations. *The Planets* offers a performance of high voltage, with plenty of panache and an acute feeling for atmospheric colour. With speeds never exaggerated, he avoids vulgarity – perhaps having taken a lesson from Boult's classic reading – yet with his rhythmic flair he gives the pieces a new buoyancy. Outstandingly enjoyable are the two most extrovert pieces: *Jupiter, the bringer of jollity* has rarely sounded so joyful, with a hint of wildness at the start, and the dancing rhythms of *Uranus* have a scherzando sparkle, with timpani and brass stunningly caught in the full, brilliant recording. The offstage women's chorus at the end of *Neptune* has seldom been more subtly balanced. Gardiner's *Planets* stands alongside the other current highly recommendable versions, Judd on Denon, Dutoit on Decca and Hilary Davon Wetton – all superb in their different ways. But none of these offers a coupling, whereas on DG the unusual Grainger coupling, typically rumbustious, pays tribute to the conductor's great-uncle, the composer Balfour Gardiner, who promoted the first performances of both works. Among bargain versions Handley remains very recommendable on Tring (coupled with the *St Paul's suite*).

The RPO play marvellously under James Judd, while the Denon recording, very much in the demonstration class, is very spectacular, with a wide dynamic range – but not too wide for comfort. The glowing Walthamstow acoustics bring out Holst's many characteristically original touches of colour, and his special effects are superbly realized. *Mars,* taken fast and pungently laced with percussion, is both ferocious and sinisterly evil, and the peaceful *Venus,* translucently beautiful (lovely horn and flute playing), is rich textured yet not voluptuous. *Mercury* sparkles and fizzes across the heavens with exquisitely light woodwind articulation and a delicious pianissimo coda. *Jupiter* blazes boisterously: here Judd unerringly builds the famous central melody to a gloriously expansive climax; then a tremendous splash from the percussion heralds the ebullient reprise. *Saturn* has a desperate melancholy: the string and brass bring a resigned desolation, and the gentle anguish of the clearly defined bass-line is very poignant. After the gleeful impetus of *Uranus, Neptune* makes a haunting conclusion, the King's College Choir entering gently but rapturously and fading into silence at the end.

Charles Dutoit's natural feeling for mood, rhythm and colour, so effectively used in his records of Ravel, here results in an outstandingly successful version, both rich and brilliant, and recorded with an opulence to outshine almost all rivals. It is remarkable that, whether in the relentless build-up of *Mars,* the lyricism of *Venus,* the rich exuberance of *Jupiter* or in much else, Dutoit and his Canadian players sound so idiomatic. The final account of *Saturn* is chillingly atmospheric.

After a sinister opening, Handley builds the climax of *Mars* impressively and the well-separated closing chords have malignant impact. The noble tune of *Jupiter* develops a similar build-up of intensity, well maintained in the spirited reprise of the opening section which has a rumbustious coda. *Saturn,* too, brings a well-graduated, melancholy climax, and the choral diminuendo to silence in *Neptune* is beautifully managed by the Ambrosians. *Venus* is warm and beautiful rather than sensuous or withdrawn, and the resonance provides a lustrous *Mercury,* undoubtedly chimerical if less sharply etched than in some versions. But the sound overall is attractively rich, giving glowing orchestral colour, the horns expansively opulent. What makes this bargain disc especially worth considering is the bracingly fresh account of the *St Paul's suite,* offered as a bonus. The recording of the string body is also very realistic.

The Decca recording for Solti's Chicago version is extremely brilliant, with *Mars* given a vivid cutting edge at the fastest possible tempo. Solti's directness in *Jupiter* (with the trumpets coming through splendidly) is certainly riveting, the big tune red-blooded and with plenty of character. In *Saturn* the spareness of texture is finely sustained and the tempo is slow, the detail precise; while in *Neptune* the coolness is even more striking when the pianissimos are achieved with such a high degree of tension. The CD gives the orchestra great presence, and the addition of Boult's classic versions of *Egdon Heath* and *The Perfect Fool* ballet music makes this reissue very competitive and marginally preferable to the EMI alternative of the same three works.

Sir Adrian Boult gives a performance at once intense and beautifully played, spacious and dramatic, rapt and pointed. The great melody of *Jupiter* is calculatedly less resonant and more flowing than previously but is still affecting, and *Uranus* as well as *Jupiter* has its measure of jollity. The spacious slow movements are finely poised and the recording still stands up well, with added presence and definition.

Mehta's set of *Planets* set a new standard for sonic splendour when it was first issued in 1971. The new ADD transfer still provides outstanding sound, but there is a touch more edge on the strings and the quality has lost just a little of its richness and amplitude; though definition is sharper, the background hiss is fractionally more noticeable. Even so, this is a superb disc and a clear first bargain choice. As on the Solti *Planets*, Boult's splendid account of the ballet suite from *The Perfect Fool* has now been added. This was recorded a decade earlier, but the vintage Decca sound remains spectacular, with the LPO brass hardly less resplendent than their colleagues in Los Angeles.

On this Classikon super-bargain reissue, recorded in 1971, Steinberg's Boston set of *Planets* was another outstanding version from a vintage analogue period. It remains one of the most exciting and involving versions and now sounds brighter and sharper in outline, though with some loss of opulence. *Mars* in particular is intensely exciting. At his fast tempo, Steinberg may get to his fortissimos a little early, but rarely has the piece sounded so menacing on record. The testing point for most will no doubt be *Jupiter*, and here Steinberg the excellent Elgarian comes to the fore, giving a wonderful *nobilmente* swagger.

Karajan's early (1981) digital recording is spectacularly wide-ranging, while the marvellously sustained pianissimo playing of the Berlin Philharmonic – as in *Venus* and the closing pages of *Saturn* – is very telling indeed. *Mars* has great impact, and the sound, full and firm in the bass, gives the performance throughout a gripping immediacy and presence. *Jupiter*, at its climax, still seems a bit fierce: ideally it needs a riper body of tone, although the syncopated opening erupts with joy, the unison horns are superbly robust, and the big melody has a natural flow and nobility. *Venus* brings sensuous string-phrasing, *Mercury* and *Uranus* have beautiful springing in the triplet rhythms, and the climax of that last movement brings an amazing glissando on the organ. In short this is a thrilling performance and highly recommendable, but it remains at full price and without a coupling.

Though the label, incorrectly, suggests the Royal Festival Hall as the venue, Sargent's BBC Radio Classics account of *The Planets* was recorded, like the Elgar, in the Royal Albert Hall. One marvels that no one in the reissuing record company noticed the three-second reverberation confirming the point. Though this was a February performance, not one given at the Proms, the atmosphere is similarly electric, with the sequence of movements building warmly and atmospherically. As in the Elgar, the playing may be a degree less polished than in Sargent's studio recording, but the excitement and tension are markedly greater, and for most that is what will matter. Good, full-bodied if rather opaque sound.

Stokowski's approach to *The Planets* is both brisk and sensuous (*Venus* very much the Goddess of Love rather than the 'bringer of peace'), with every movement except *Mercury* faster than usual. Yet such is Stokowski's magnetism that at a flowing speed *Saturn* conveys rapt stillness and the fast movements have tremendous swagger. This is very early stereo (1956) and the Capitol recording of the Los Angeles Philharmonic was made in so-called 'full-dimensional sound'. It is bright and clear but lacks the allure of RCA's 'Living stereo' of the same period.

For Simon Rattle, EMI's digital recording provides wonderfully atmospheric sound, and the quality in *Venus* and *Mercury* is also beautiful, clear and translucent. Otherwise it is not as distinctive a version as one might have expected from this leading conductor; it is sensibly paced but neither so polished nor so bitingly committed as Karajan or Boult, and *Jupiter* is disappointing, lacking in thrust and warmth.

Sir Colin Davis's *Mars* is menacingly fast, with weighty Berlin brass and barbaric accents adding to the forcefulness. The resonant recording brings sumptuous textures to *Venus*, while even *Saturn* has a degree of opulence. *Mercury*, however, is infectiously spirited, and *Jupiter*, with a grand central tune, is bucolic in its amplitude. *Uranus* brings galumphing brass, and the closing *Neptune* is both ethereal and sensuous, an unusual combination, brought about partly by the warm reverberation. There are more subtle versions than this, but it is easy to enjoy. However, this reissue offers no coupling.

Mackerras's usual zestful approach communicates readily and the Liverpool orchestra bring a lively response, but the over-reverberant recording tends to cloud the otherwise pungently vigorous *Mars*, and both *Venus* and *Saturn* seem a little straightforward and marginally undercharacterized, while again in the powerful climax of *Uranus* there is some blurring from the resonance. *The Perfect Fool*, with its vivid colouring and irregular rhythms, has much in common with *The Planets* and makes a fine coupling, especially when played with such flair.

Holst first recorded *The Planets* in 1922 in the days of acoustic engineering. There are significant differences in his later (1926) electrical recording. Hence it is arguable that under ideal conditions Holst would have taken longer in some passages (as he did in the 1922 recording of *Venus*). Be that as it may, his 1926 version is still pretty amazing – and sounds quite remarkably vivid for its day. Inhibited he may have been by the cramped conditions of the studio and the playing time but one can easily forget that, given the sheer vitality of these performances. This is an indispensable issue.

Ormandy's 1975 RCA recording now reappears on RCA's super-bargain Navigator label, generously coupled with Vaughan Williams string works. It was one of the finest records he made as principal conductor of the Philadelphia Orchestra in the last few years before he retired. The playing has great electricity, and it is a pity that RCA's balancing engineers apparently sought brilliance above all else and endeavoured to make a quite artificial sonic impact. The CD transfer brings a fierce edginess in the treble (caused by placing the microphones much too close). The orchestra does not sound like this in the flesh. Even so, this is a highly compelling reading. Ormandy paces the central tune of *Jupiter* slowly and deliberately. The performance is at its finest in *Uranus* (with crisply vigorous brass articulation) and the restrained melancholy of *Saturn*, deeply felt and somehow personal in its communication. *Neptune* too is beautifully tapered off at the close.

Air and variations; 3 Pieces for oboe & string quartet, Op. 2.
*** Chandos Dig. CHAN 8392 [id.]. Francis, English Qt – BAX: *Quintet;* MOERAN: *Fantasy quartet;* JACOB: *Quartet.* ***

The three pieces here are engagingly folksy, consisting of a sprightly little *March*, a gentle *Minuet* with a good tune, and a *Scherzo*. Performances are first class, and so is the recording.

VOCAL MUSIC

Canons for equal voices: The Fields of sorrow; David's lament for Jonathan; Truth of all truth. Choral folk-songs, Op. 23: The song of the Blacksmith; I sowed the seeds of love; Matthew, Mark, Luke and John; I love my love; Swansea Town. (i) *Choruses for male voices, Op. 53: Good Friday; Love song; Intercession; Before sleep; Drinking song. Choral hymns from the Rig Veda, Op. 26: Hymn to Manas.* (ii) *A Dirge for two veterans. The Homecoming.*
(N) (M) *** EMI CMS5 65123-2 (2) [id.]. Baccholian Singers, Ian Humphris, with (i) ECO; (ii) Philip Jones Brass Ens. – VAUGHAN WILLIAMS: *Folksong arrangements;* ELGAR: *Part-songs* etc. ***

The Baccholian Singers present a beautiful and memorable collection of Holst's smaller choral pieces, including the less-often-heard and darkly compressed *Dirge for two veterans* (a setting of Walt Whitman for male voices, brass and percussion) and the highly original Hardy setting, *The Homecoming*, with its stark narrative and dialogue. The *Six Choruses for male voices*, dating from 1931–2, are hardly less individual and are most stimulating, Warm, atmospheric recording. This is part of an invaluable collection drawn from three different LPs and is strongly recommended to all lovers of English song.

A Choral Fantasia, Op. 51; Choral Symphony, Op. 41.
(N) **(*) Hyperion Dig. CDA 66660 [id.]. Lynne Dawson, Guildford Choral Society, RPO, Hilary Davan Wetton.

Hilary Davan Wetton here offers the ideal and very generous coupling of two related works which together form a culmination of Holst's choral works. Though the ensemble of the Guildford Choral Society is not ideally crisp, and one really wants more weight of sound, the originality of Holst's choral writing and the purposeful nature of the argument are never in doubt, with Lynne Dawson the radiantly beautiful soprano soloist in both works. Holst is nothing if not daring in using well-known texts of Keats in the *Choral Symphony*, adding a new dimension even to the 'Ode on a Grecian urn'. In some ways Boult's earlier version of the *Choral Symphony* with the LPO Choir (awaiting return to the catalogue) is even finer, although that recording is not sharply focused, while Imogen Holst's 1964 account of the *Choral Fantasia* is special – see below.

(i) *A Choral Fantasia, Op. 51;* (ii) *Psalm 86.*
(N) (M) *** EMI CDM5 65588-2 [id.]. (i) Janet Baker; (ii) Ian Partridge, Purcell Singers, ECO, Imogen Holst – FINZI: *Dies natalis;* VAUGHAN WILLIAMS: *5 Mystical songs* etc. ***

Holst's *Choral Fantasia* – a setting of words written by Robert Bridges in commemoration of Purcell – was one of his later works, and probably the unusual combination of performers has prevented more frequent performances. It is not an easy work to grasp, and Holst's extremes of dynamic tend to hinder rather than help. But it is well worth getting to know. Dame Janet Baker once again shows her supreme quality as a recording artist. The recording, though not lacking ambient warmth, is admirably clear (indeed the organ pedals are only too clear). The sound could perhaps be more open, but there is no lack of projection and vividness, and the bloom of the analogue original remains untarnished. The setting of *Psalm 86*, with its expressive tenor part sung beautifully by Ian Partridge, is also included in this generous compilation. The recording here is outstanding, and the success of both these performances owes much to the inspired direction of the composer's daughter.

(i; ii) *A Choral Fantasia, Op. 51;* (ii) *A Dirge for two veterans;* (iii) *Hymn of Jesus; Ode to Death, Op. 38;* (i; ii) *7 Partsongs, Op. 44.*

(N) *** Chandos Dig. CHAN 9437 [id.]. (i) Patricia Rozario; (ii) Joyful Company of Singers; (iii) London Symphony Ch.; City of L. Sinf., Hickox.

Richard Hickox proves a passionate advocate of these shorter choral works of Holst, demonstrating that the two Whitman settings, *A Dirge for two veterans* and the *Ode to Death*, are among his finest pieces for voices. Both were inspired by Holst's response to the First World War, the *Dirge* written just after war had started in 1914, a grim processional for male voices, brass and percussion, and the *Ode* in 1919 when it was over and his disillusion was even more intense. That second work is in very much the same vein of inspiration as his masterpiece, the *Hymn of Jesus* and, with the larger forces of the London Symphony Chorus, brings the most powerful performance here. Both the later works, the *Seven Partsongs* of 1925 as well as the *Choral Fantasia* of 1930, set poems by Robert Bridges, with the choral writing fluently beautiful. Though Patricia Rozario is not in her finest form, the Joyful Company of Singers sing superbly in intense and moving performances, helped by rich and full Chandos sound.

Choral hymns from the Rig Veda (Groups 1–4), *H. 97–100; 2 Eastern pictures for women's voices and harp, H. 112; Hymn to Dionysus, Op. 31/2.*

**(*) Unicorn Dig. DKPCD 9046 [id.]. Royal College of Music Chamber Ch., RPO, Willcocks; Ellis.

The *Choral hymns from the Rig Veda* show Holst writing with deep understanding for voices, devising textures, refined, very distinctively his, to match atmospherically exotic texts. Though performances are not always ideally polished, the warmth and thrust of the music are beautifully caught. The *Hymn to Dionysus*, setting words from the *Bacchae* of Euripides in Gilbert Murray's translation, a rarity antici-pating Holst's *Choral symphony*, makes a welcome and substantial fill-up, along with the two little *Eastern pictures*. Beautifully clean and atmospheric recording.

Choral hymns from the Rig Veda (Group 3), *H. 99, Op. 26/3.*

*** Hyperion CDA 66175 [id.]. Holst Singers & O; Davan Wetton; T. Owen – BLISS: *Lie strewn the white flocks;* BRITTEN: *Gloriana: Choral dances.* ***

The third group of *Choral hymns from the Rig Veda*, like the whole series, reveals Holst in his Sanskritic period at his most distinctively inspired. In this responsive performance, it makes an excellent coupling for the attractive Bliss and Britten items, atmospherically recorded.

The Cloud messenger, Op. 30; The Hymn of Jesus, Op. 37.

*** Chandos Dig. CHAN 8901 [id.]. Della Jones, London Symphony Ch. & LSO, Richard Hickox.

Hickox's account of Holst's choral masterpiece, *The Hymn of Jesus*, dramatic and highly atmospheric, easily outshines even Sir Adrian Boult's vintage version for Decca. Not only does modern digital sound make an enormous difference in a work where the choral sounds are terraced so tellingly, but Hickox secures tauter and crisper ensemble, as well as treating the sections based on plainchant with an aptly expressive freedom. The long-neglected choral piece, *The Cloud messenger*, may lack the concentration of *The Hymn of Jesus* but it brings similarly incandescent choral writing. Warmly and positively realized by Hickox and his powerful forces, with Della Jones a fine soloist, it makes a major discovery, whatever its incidental shortcomings. Rich and ample Chandos recording adds to the involvement.

The Evening watch, H.159; 6 Choruses, H.186; Nunc dimittis, H.127; 7 Partsongs, H.162; 2 Psalms, H.117.

*** Hyperion Dig. CDA 66329 [id.]. Holst Singers & O, Hilary Davan Wetton.

Having given us a splendid set of *Planets*, Hilary Davan Wetton now turns to the often more austere but no less inspired choral music. *The Evening watch* creates a rapt, sustained pianissimo until the very closing bars, when the sudden expansion is quite thrilling. The *Six Choruses* for male voices show the composer at his most imaginative, while the comparable *Partsongs* for women often produce a ravish-ingly dreamy, mystical beauty. The final song, *Assemble all ye maidens*, is a narrative ballad about a lost love, and its closing section is infinitely touching. The performances are gloriously and sensitively sung and unerringly paced.

Hymn of Jesus, Op. 37.
(N) (b) *** Decca Double 443 170-2 (2) [id.]. BBC Ch., BBC SO, Boult – DELIUS: *Sea drift* ***; ELGAR: *Dream of Gerontius.* **(*)

Boult's superb performance of *The Hymn of Jesus*, a visionary masterpiece that brings some of Holst's most searching inspirations, comes as a generous and apt – if unusual – coupling for Elgar's great oratorio and Delius's *Sea drift*. The spatial beauty of Holst's choral writing is vividly caught with fine presence in the 1962 Kingsway Hall recording. A full text is included.

OPERA

(i) *Savitri* (complete); (ii) *Dream city* (song cycle, orch. Matthews).
**(*) Hyperion Dig. CDA 66099 [id.]. (i) Langridge, Varcoe, Palmer, Hickox Singers; (ii) Kwella; City of L. Sinfonia, Hickox.

Felicity Palmer is more earthy, more vulnerable as Savitri than Janet Baker was in the earlier Argo recording, her grainy mezzo well caught. Philip Langridge and Stephen Varcoe both sing sensitively with fresh, clear tone, though their timbres are rather similar. Hickox is a thoughtful conductor both in the opera and in the orchestral song-cycle arranged by Colin Matthews from Holst's settings of Humbert Wolfe poems. Patrizia Kwella's soprano at times catches the microphone rather shrilly.

Holst, Imogen (1907–84)

String quartet No. 1.
*** Conifer Dig. 74321 15006-2. Brindisi Qt – BRIDGE: *3 Idylls;* BRITTEN: *String quartet No. 2.* ***

Imogen Holst's two-movement *Quartet* is a shortish work; although not strongly personal, it is full of interest. Both performance and recording are of high quality.

Holt, Simon (born 1958)

. . . era madrugada . . .; Shadow realm; Sparrow night; (i) *Canciones.*
*** NMC Dig. D008 [id.]. (i) Fiona Kimm; Nash Ens., Lionel Friend.

Among British composers of the younger generation there is none more thoughtful and concentrated than Simon Holt, and, thanks to NMC, it is good to have at last a complete disc of his music. Regularly he has found inspiration in Spanish sources, particularly Lorca, and two of the four pieces are fine examples – . . . *era madrugada*, a sinister evocation of a Lorca poem about a man found murdered in the hour just before dawn (*madrugada*). Like the other three pieces, it was written for the Nash Ensemble, who here under Lionel Friend respond superbly to Holt's virtuoso demands. Fiona Kimm is the formidable mezzo soloist in three Spanish settings, *Canciones;* but rather more approachable are the two highly atmospheric instrumental works, *Shadow realm* and *Sparrow night*, which round the disc off. These two also bring sinister nightmare overtones. The superb recording is engineered by Holt's fellow-composer, Colin Matthews.

Holten, Bo (born 1948)

(i) *Clarinet concerto* (1987); (ii) *Sinfonia concertante for cello and orchestra* (1985–6).
*** Chandos Dig. CHAN 9272 [id.] (i) Jens Schou; (ii) Morten Zeuten; Danish National RSO; (i) Jorma Panula; (ii) Hans Graf.

Bo Holten is a highly talented Danish composer now in his mid-forties and best known in the UK for his work as a choral conductor with the BBC Singers. The *Clarinet concerto* is certainly appealing. The *Sinfonia concertante* comes from a broadcast of 1987 and is long on complexity (36 minutes 6 seconds) and short on substance, but there are sufficient moments of poetic vision to encourage one to return to it. It is played with great zest and conviction by Morten Zeuten (cellist of the Kontra Quartet), and the recording has exemplary presence and clarity.

Honegger, Arthur (1892–1955)

Le chant de Nigamon; Monopartita; Napoleon (film incidental music); *Les hombres. Phaedre: Prelude. Prélude, fugue and postlude; The Tempest: Prelude.*
**(*) Erato/Warner Dig. 2292 45862-2 [id.]. Monte Carlo PO, Constant.

A warm welcome must be given to the music for *Phaedre*, which is highly imaginative and atmospheric. The earliest work recorded here is *Le chant de Nigamon* (1917), a tone-poem concerning the fate of an American Indian chief who is burnt at the stake; and it is both graphic and powerful. The *Monopartita* is Honegger's last orchestral piece, coming from the same period as the *Fifth Symphony*. Again the invention is of the highest quality. Decent performances and acceptable, though not first-class, recorded sound.

Cello concerto.
**(*) Ph. Dig. 432 084-2 [id.]. Julian Lloyd Webber, ECO, Yan Pascal Tortelier – FAURE: *Elégie* **; D'INDY: *Lied* **(*); SAINT-SAENS: *Concerto* etc. **(*)

Honegger's pastoral *Concerto* is a work of immense appeal. Lloyd Webber plays with refined musicianship and conveys the charm and character of this piece very effectively. He is well supported by Yan Pascal Tortelier, and the Philips recording is eminently natural and well balanced.

(i) *Cello concerto;* (ii) *Pastorale d'été.*
(M) (***) EMI mono CDC5 55036-2 (i) Maurice Maréchal, Paris Conservatoire O; (ii) SO; composer – POULENC: *Aubade* etc. (***)

Honegger's 1930 account of the enchanting and atmospheric *Pastorale d'été* is coupled here with a wartime account of the *Cello concerto* by its dedicatee, Maurice Maréchal, made in 1943 and sounding remarkably fresh for its period. A valuable addition to the 'Composer in Person' series.

Horace victorieux; Mermoz: La traversée des Andes; Le vol sur l'Atlantique; Pacific 231; Rugby; Pastorale d'été; La tempête: Prélude.
*** DG Dig. 435 438-2 [id.]. Toulouse Capitole O, Plasson.

Michel Plasson and his fine Toulouse orchestra give excellent performances of these Honegger pieces. *Horace victorieux* is a noisy score but full of imaginative touches, as are the two scenes recorded here for the film *Mermoz*. We are also offered a beautifully languorous account of *Pastorale d'été*, among the best committed to disc, and Plasson's accounts of *Pacific 231* and *Rugby* are full of high spirits. His version of the *Prélude*, composed for a production of Shakespeare's *Tempest* in the late 1920s, is as fierce and violent as the composer's own pioneering Parlophone 78-r.p.m. disc. DG provide a realistic and natural sound-picture with plenty of detail. Strongly recommended.

Nocturne; Pastorale d'été; (i) *La Danse des morts.*
** Calliope CAL 9855 [id.]. (i) Davy, Collart, Piquemal, Lassus Vocal Ens.; Jeune SO de Douai, Vachey.

La Danse des morts is a powerful and imaginative score, concentrated in atmosphere and marked by much depth of feeling. This analogue (1981) performance, performed by the Jeune Orchestre Symphonique de Douai, is first class in terms of youthful commitment and enthusiasm, and the recorded sound is very present. The Ensemble Vocale de Roland de Lassus is not always in tune, and the intonation of the soprano is also vulnerable, although both the baritone and spoken parts are very well done. The *Nocturne for Orchestra* is full of character and harmonic interest. The Douai Youth Orchestra are not quite up to the exposed divided string-writing with which it opens (and which returns in the closing section) and their expertise is strained elsewhere, but they play with real dedication. They do not, alas, possess all the tonal finesse required in the *Pastorale d'été*.

Pacific 231.
(N) (M) *** Decca 448 576-2 [id.]. SRO, Ansermet – CHABRIER: *España* **(*); DEBUSSY: *La Mer* **(*); DUKAS: *L'apprenti sorcier* ***; RAVEL: *Boléro; La Valse.* ***
**(*) Ph. Dig. 432 993-2 [id.]. O de Paris, Semyon Bychkov – MILHAUD: *Le bœuf sur le toit;* POULENC: *Les biches.* **(*)

Ansermet conveys all the grinding power of Honegger's railway evocation, and its surging lyricism too, but some of the detail is clouded by the resonance at the climax. An impressive performance just the same.

Semyon Bychkov gives us a good ride on his train, though there are one or two oddities of balance (bassoons are very forward at one point), puzzling in so splendidly engineered an issue. It comes with goodish accounts of *Les biches* and *Le bœuf sur le toit.*

Symphonies Nos. 1; 2 for strings with trumpet obbligato; 3 (Symphonie liturgique); 4 (Deliciae Basilienses); 5 (Di tre re); Mouvement symphonique No. 3; Pacific 231; The Tempest: Prelude.
(M) *** Sup. 11 1566-2 (2). Czech PO, Baudo.

These performances come from the 1960s, but they are more than merely serviceable. The sound comes up very well indeed and the playing of the Czech Philharmonic for Baudo is totally committed. The performance of the *Fifth Symphony* has never been surpassed (except possibly by the pioneering Munch recording) and has amazing presence and detail for its period.

Symphony No. 1; Pastorale d'été; 3 Symphonic movements: Pacific 231; Rugby; No. 3.
*** Erato/Warner Dig. 2292 45242-2 [id.]. Bav. RSO, Dutoit.

Honegger's *First Symphony* is a highly stimulating and rewarding piece. Charles Dutoit gets an excellent response from the Bavarian Radio Symphony Orchestra, who produce a splendidly cultured sound and particularly beautiful phrasing in the slow movement. Dutoit also gives an atmospheric and sympathetic account of the *Pastorale d'été* and in addition offers the *Three Symphonic movements*, of which *Pacific 231* with its robust and vigorous portrait of a railway engine is by far the best known.

Symphony No. 2 for strings and trumpet.
*** Delos Dig. DE 3121 [id.]. Seattle SO, Gerard Schwarz – R. STRAUSS: *Metamorphosen*; WEBERN, arr. Schwarz: *Langsamer satz.* ***

In terms of recording quality, Schwarz's account can hold its own alongside the very best, and the playing of the Seattle strings is splendidly responsive. He is just a bit too slow at the very beginning (conductors like Karajan and Munch manage to convey a sense of movement as well as darkness and introspection) and the same reservation could be made against the slow movement, but there is plenty of atmosphere. Although it does not displace the Jansons or Karajan accounts or other recommendations, this performance is very fine indeed and will give much pleasure.

Symphonies Nos. 2 for strings with trumpet obbligato; 3 (Symphonie liturgique).
(N) ✿ (M) *** DG 447 435-2 [id.]. BPO, Karajan – STRAVINSKY: *Concerto in D.* ***

Symphonies Nos. 2 for strings and trumpet obbligato; 3 (Liturgique); Pacific 231.
*** EMI Dig. CDC5 55122-2 [id.]. Oslo PO, Jansons.

Karajan's accounts of these magnificent symphonies come from 1973 and still remain in a class of their own. Not even Munch's pioneering recording of the *Symphony No. 2* or its successors comes near to it for sheer poetic intensity, and the *Symphonie liturgique* has likewise never been surpassed. It is luminous, incandescent and moving. The only rival is the Jansons version with the Oslo Philharmonic on EMI, but this is at full price. The Karajan is one of his greatest records and cannot be recommended too strongly, particularly in view of its competitive price and the additional coupling. It certainly deserves its place as one of DG's 'Legendary Recordings', reissued in their Originals series.

Jansons's account of these two symphonies is the first successful challenge to the classic Karajan record from the 1970s. It is arguably the Oslo orchestra's best record to date. The playing has a virtuosity and tonal sophistication that are almost the equal of the Berliners' sumptuous string-tone in the *Symphony for strings*, and superb concentration and control. The recording is magnificently rich and present, detail is splendidly focused. The *Symphonie liturgique* is thrilling in their hands, and there is an excellent account of *Pacific 231* as well. This can now serve as a key recommendation in the Honegger discography, though it does not displace the Karajan.

Symphonies Nos. 2 for strings; 5 (Di tre re).
(M) (***) RCA mono/stereo GD 60685 [60685-2-RG]. Boston SO, Charles Munch – MILHAUD: *La création du monde* etc. ***

Charles Munch made the first recordings of both *Symphonies*; in fact this transfer of the *Fifth* is one of them. The *Second*, made in 1953, is a bit harder-driven than his later version with the Orchestre de Paris. The performance of the *Fifth* is full of character though the sound is a bit dry. The witty and enigmatic middle movement has never been surpassed on record. Some (but relatively little) allowance needs to be made for the actual sound-quality of the 1952 mono recording.

Symphonies Nos. 3 (Symphonie liturgique); 5 (Di tre re); Chant du joie; Pacific 231; Pastorale d'été.
(M) *** Sup. 11 0667-2. Czech PO, Serge Baudo.

Symphonies Nos. 3; 5; Pacific 231.
*** Chandos Dig. CHAN 9176 [id.]. Danish Nat. R. O, Järvi.

Honegger's *Pacific 231* has thundered along the tracks to more striking effect than it does here under Baudo (Honegger himself steered it more briskly into the station in the days of steam), but the two symphonies are splendidly played and recorded. The *Symphonie liturgique* has stiff competition to meet in the classic Karajan account, but Neeme Järvi and the Danish orchestra serve it very well indeed, and the digital Chandos recording is even more detailed and present, and certainly fuller, than the DG version. Järvi's version of the *Fifth Symphony* is also masterly, even if it does not match the hell-for-leather abandon of Baudo's Supraphon set. But that is now over 30 years old and, though it still sounds pretty amazing, this is undeniably superior.

Serge Baudo's 1960s recording of the *Fifth* still remains among the very best versions of the work, superior in sonic terms to the Munch and infinitely more vital than the Dutoit. The *Liturgique* is not quite in the Karajan class but it is very good indeed as are the remaining pieces on offer. Given the modest price of this disc plus the generous playing time, this deserves a very strong recommendation.

Symphony No. 4 (Deliciae Basilienses).
(M) *** Erato/Warner 2292 45689-2 [id.]. French Nat. RSO, Munch – DUTILLEUX: *Métaboles*. ***

Munch's 1967 account of the delightful *Fourth Symphony* remains by far the most characterful on disc – it is to be preferred to any of the full-price rivals and has the right blend of energy and atmosphere. The recording is also eminently acceptable. An additional attraction is the interesting coupling. Strongly recommended.

Les aventures du Roi Pausole.
**(*) MGM Musiques Suisses Dig. CD 6114 (2) [id.]. Bacquier, Sénéchal, Barbaux, Yakar, Basle Madrigalists, Swiss Youth PO, Maro Venzago.

One doesn't associate Honegger with light operetta, but this is exactly what *Les aventures du Roi Pausole* is. Moreover it was very successful in its day and is an almost unqualified delight. The models are Mozart, Chabrier, Messager and Offenbach, and the invention is often piquant and, at its best, memorable. The singing is lively and characterful, though Christine Barbaux's Aline is not flattered by the microphones. The orchestral playing is spirited rather than elegant; but the recording is not distinguished and suffers from inconsistencies of level. At times you have to turn up the dialogue, after which the next musical number is too loud. Hence, some reservations about the third star – but the score is good fun. There are some 45 minutes of spoken dialogue and 75 of music; the set includes a libretto in French and a summary in other languages.

Jeanne d'Arc au bûcher.
✹ *** DG Dig. 429 412-2 [id.]. Keller, Wilson, Escourrou, Lanzi, Pollet, Command, Stutzman, Aler, Courtis, R. France Ch., Fr. Nat. O, Seiji Ozawa.

Honegger's 1935 setting of the Claudel poem is one of his most powerful and imaginative works, full of variety of invention, colour and textures. It is admirably served by these forces, and in particular by the Joan of Marthe Keller. The singers, too, are all excellent and the Choir and the six soloists of the Maîtrise of Radio France are as top-drawer as the orchestra. The DG engineers cope excellently with the large forces and the acoustic of the Basilique de Saint-Denis.

Judith.
**(*) Van. 08 9054 71 [id.]. Devrath, Christiansen, Madeleine Milhaud (nar.), Salt Lake Symphonic Ch., Utah SO, Abravanel.

Judith is a dramatic vocal–orchestral concert work with interspersed narration. In some respects it scores over *Le roi David* in musical concentration, variety of pace and range of musical devices; some passages are marvellously imaginative and atmospheric (the Choral Invocation to protect Judith on her voyage through the valley of fear to cross into the Assyrian lines is quite chilling). The performance dates from 1964 and is totally committed; the only let-down is in some of the choral singing, which could be stronger. The work is short (just under 45 minutes) and it would have added to the competitiveness of the issue to provide a fill-up. But if it is short on quantity, it is long on musical and dramatic interest.

Le Roi David (complete).
(M) *** Erato/Warner 2292 45800-2 [id.]. Eda Pierre, Collard, Tappy, Petel, Valere, De Dailly, Philippe Caillard Ch., Ens. Instrumental, Dutoit.
(M) *** Van. 08.4038.71 [OVC 4038]. Davrath, Sorensen, Preston, Singher, Madeleine Milhaud, Utah University Ch., Utah SO, Abravanel.

Charles Dutoit's *Le Roi David* uses the original instrumental forces and not the full orchestra favoured by most of his rivals. The recording comes from 1970, not that anyone coming to it afresh would guess that. It is a compelling performance of strong dramatic coherence.

The Vanguard version was made in 1961. It is remarkably vivid, well detailed and present, and the playing of the Utah Symphony under Maurice Abravanel is very fine. The recording also stands up well. Netania Davrath is excellent too, and so is Madeleine Milhaud, the composer's wife, as the Witch of Endor. Thoroughly recommendable.

Horneman, Christian Frederik Emil (1840–1906)

Aladdin overture; Ouverture héroïque: Helteliv; (i) *Gurre* (incidental music).

(N) *** Chandos Dig. CHAN 9373 [id.]. (i) Guido Päevatalu, Danish R. Ch.; Danish RSO, Schønwandt.

In his lifetime the Dane, Christian Frederik Emil Horneman, was thought of as the natural successor to Gade and J. P. E. Hartmann. Horneman studied at Leipzig at the same time as Grieg and with Moscheles, but his independence of thought made him the natural link between Gade and Nielsen. Indeed Nielsen himself is said to have acknowledged the influence of Horneman on his harmony and orchestration. Be that as it may, Horneman is an altogether delightful composer, and the music recorded here deserves the widest dissemination. The incidental music to Holger Drachmann's play, *Gurre*, the major work on the disc, dates from 1900-1901, and when it was first staged, at the Royal Theatre, Copenhagen, Nielsen was still a member of the orchestra and probably played on that occasion. It is light-textured and full of charming, gracious invention and is beautifully scored. It is quite enchanting, particularly in such persuasive hands and the baritone, Guido Päevatalu, sings his simple strophic songs with great character. The other two pieces, *Helteliv* ('A Hero's Life') and the *Aladdin overture* are the only purely orchestral works Horneman ever wrote. They come from the 1860s, and indeed the *Aladdin overture* is his first orchestral work; it shows a real flair for colour. It prompted him to work on an opera of the same name for the following 24 years but, although it was produced in Copenhagen, it has never maintained the hold on the repertoire that it apparently deserves. This is a most enjoyable disc, beautifully played and recorded. Strongly recommended.

Hotteterre, Jacques-Martin (1674–1763)

Frans Brüggen Edition, Volume 6: *Suite No. 1 in D minor for 2 treble recorders.*

(Y/B) (M) *** Teldec/Warner 4509 97468-2 [id.]. Frans Brüggen, Kees Boekehardt – DIEUPART: *Suites in G min. & A.* ***

Hotteterre (known as Le Romain) came from a family famous both as composers and as instrument-makers. His suite, written for two treble recorders '*sans basse continue*', offers a charming collection of dances using a germinal idea, common to all, first heard in the opening *Gravement*. The general effect is innocuous until the ambitious five-minute finale, when the theme is developed as a *Passacaille*. The performance on original instruments is expert and pleasing.

Hovhaness, Alan (born 1911)

Symphony No. 2 (Mysterious mountain), Op. 32; And God created great whales; Alleluia and fugue; Celestial fantasy; Prayer of St Gregory; Prelude and quadruple fugue.

*** Delos Dig. DE 3157 [id.]. Seattle SO, Gerard Schwarz.

This music is spacious, amiably melodic and easy to come to terms with. The *Symphony No. 2* begins with pastoral, modal writing, leading to a central fugal climax and returning to rich, expressive serenity. *The Prayer of St Gregory* is essentially a chorale and is rather appealing in its innocence. But the most sensational piece here is *And God created great whales*, which reaches a huge climax and interpolates tapes of the actual song of the humpbacked whale. The effect is really very grandiose indeed, and everybody here rises to the occasion, including both the whales and the recording engineers.

Symphonies Nos. 22 (City of light), Op. 236; 50 (Mount St Helens), Op. 360.

*** Delos Dig. DE 3137 [id.]. Seattle SO, composer.

If you enjoyed the spectacle of Symphony No. 2, you'll really respond to the extravagant *Mount St Helens Symphony* with its haunting *Spirit Lake* central movement and awe-inspiring *Volcano* eruption for a finale, where some of the orchestral effects are quite grotesquely shattering. *City of Light* is more conventional, but agreeable enough. Performances and recording are first class, but this is not a record for a flat with thin walls.

Howells, Herbert (1892–1983)

(i) *Fantasia; Threnody* (both for cello and orchestra). *The King's herald; Paradise Rondel; Pastoral rhapsody; Procession.*
(N) *** Chandos Dig. CHAN 9410 [id.]. (i) Moray Welsh; LSO, Hickox.

This delightful and moving disc offers a whole sequence of orchestral works which, for whatever reason, Howells hid from the world. Herbert Howells was so shy about his orchestral music that only since his death have such pieces as these emerged. The most personal works here are the *Fantasia* and *Threnody*, both for cello and orchestra, together forming a sort of rhapsodic concerto. Howells was reflecting his anguish over the death of his ten-year-old son, with flashes of anger punctuating the elegiac lyricism. The longer and more complex of the two, the *Fantasia*, dates from 1936–7, while *Threnody*, simpler in its lyricism, was sketched rather earlier. Probably planned as the slow movement of a three-movement *Cello concerto*, it is given here in the orchestration made by Christopher Palmer for the Howells centenary concert in 1992. The other major piece is the *Pastoral rhapsody*, written in 1923. This is more conventionally English, except for a radiant climax, with anglicized echoes of *Daphnis et Chloé* and *Petrushka*. Similarly pastoral but predominantly vigorous, the *Paradise Rondel* of 1925, named after a Cotswold village, is full of sharp contrasts, with one passage offering clear echoes of the *Russian dance* from *Petrushka*. The collection opens with the boldly extrovert *King's herald*, bright with Waltonian fanfares. It was arranged for orchestra from a brass band original as a coronation offering in 1937. *Procession*, which closes the sequence, the earliest work here, brings more echoes of *Petrushka*, again reflecting Howells's response to the Diaghilev Ballets Russes' appearances in London. Helped by rich, atmospheric sound, Richard Hickox draws performances that are both brilliant and warmly persuasive from the LSO, with Moray Welsh a movingly expressive soloist in the concertante works.

PIANO MUSIC

The Chosen tune; Cobbler's hornpipe; Gadabout; Lambert's clavichord: Lambert's fireside (Hughes' ballet; De la Mare's pavanne; Sir Hugh's galliard); Musica sine nomine; 3 Pieces, Op. 14; Sarum sketches; Slow dance (Double the Cape); Snapshots, Op. 30; Sonatina.
*** Chandos Dig. CHAN 9273 [id.]. Margaret Fingerhut.

Howells's output for piano is not perhaps among his most important music but, as this survey shows, he has a good feeling for keyboard sonorities and the invention among these works is remarkably high. The high-spirited writing, as in *Gadabout* (1928) and *Jackanapes* (the third of the *Three Pieces*, Op. 14), has a Grainger-like rhythmic exuberance, while Howells can also be touchingly solemn, as in the dark processional which is the last item of Op. 14 or in the second of the *Sarum sketches*. The *Sonatina* is late, written when the composer was nearly eighty. It is astonishingly fresh, one of his very best works, spikily high-spirited and with a thoughtfully tender slow movement marked *serioso ma teneramente*, with something of Ravel in its thinking. Margaret Fingerhut captures its slightly reticent atmosphere perfectly, as she does the mood of the *Musica sine nomine*, a nostalgically beautiful tribute to John Ireland on his eightieth birthday in 1959. Throughout this highly stimulating and enjoyable programme this fine pianist readily catches the composer's moods, light or grave, and she is most realistically recorded.

Howells' clavichord (20 pieces for clavichord or piano): *Books I–II; Lambert's clavichord* (12 pieces for clavichord), *Op. 21.*
** Hyperion Dig. CDA 66689 [id.]. John McCabe (piano).

Howells felt an affinity with the Tudor period of English music. Each of these pieces is short and precise, averaging a duration of two minutes. Just like those Elizabethan works of Byrd, Dowland and others, they have agreeably inconseqential titles like *Samuel's air, H.H. his Fancy, Sir Richard's Toye* and, later, *Goff's fireside*. What is extraordinary is John McCabe's decision to record all of them on the piano. Certainly, as John McCabe suggests, 'the bittersweet harmonies can benefit from the greater tonal range of the modern instrument', but despite his judicious use of the sustaining pedal many of these miniatures could be even more effective on the clavichord or harpsichord. They are very well played and well recorded, but this collection has a question mark hanging over it: 'How would they have sounded if. . .?'

VOCAL MUSIC

3 Children's songs (Eight o'clock, the postman's knock; The days are clear; Mother, shake the cherry-tree); 3 Folksongs (I will give my love an apple; The brisk young widow; Cendrillon); 4 French chansons, Op. 29; A Garland for de la Mare (group of 11 unpublished songs); *In green ways* (song-cycle), *Op. 43; Peacock Pie* (song-cycle), *Op. 33; 2 South African settings (Loneliness; Spirit of freedom); 4 Songs, Op.*

22 (There was a maiden; Madrigal; The widow bird; Girl's song). Miscellaneous songs: *An old man's lullaby; Come sing and dance; Flood; Gavotte; Goddess of the Night; Here she lies; King David; The little boy lost; Lost love; Mally O!; The Mugger's song; O garlands, hanging by the doors; O my deir hert; Old Meg; Old skinflint; The restful branches.*

*** Chandos Dig. CHAN 9185/6 (2) [id.]. Lynne Dawson; Catherine Pierard; John Mark Ainsley; Benjamin Luxon; Julius Drake.

This two-disc collection covers virtually all of Howells's completed songs, most of them previously unrecorded and many still unpublished. One of the driving forces behind the project is the pianist Julius Drake, who plays the accompaniments with a consistent rhythmic spring and a sense of fantasy. Two of the finest songs are among the best known, *King David* and *Come sing and dance*, and such a group of miniatures as *Peacock Pie*, settings of Walter de la Mare written early in Howells's career, have a characteristic point and charm. Far more searching are the 11 much longer settings of de la Mare poems. In this 40-minute sequence, *Garland for de la Mare*, Howells shows what close sympathy he had not just for the child-like, nursery-style poems of *Peacock Pie* but for those which in a subtle way capture a childish sense of mystery and new discovery, so typical of the poet. Among the other fascinating examples are two South African settings to words by the Afrikaans poet, Jan Celliers, including one very topical at the time the discs appeared in May 1994, *Spirit of freedom*. The sopranos, Catherine Pierard and Lynne Dawson, both have aptly fresh, English-sounding voices, with John Mark Ainsley as the thoughtful tenor and Benjamin Luxon the characterful baritone, a fine team, even though the recording brings out some unevenness in the vocal production of both Ainsley and Luxon.

Chichester service: Magnificat; Nunc dimittis. A Hymn for Saint Cecilia; Like as the hart desireth the waterbrooks; My eyes for beauty pine; O salutaris Hostia; Salve Regina.

(*) ASV Dig. CDDCA 851 [id.]. David Went, Ch. of The Queen's College, Oxford, Matthew Owens – LEIGHTON: *Crucifixus pro nobis* etc. *

Whereas some of his orchestral and chamber music has a certain pallor, Howells is at his best in his choral work and the pieces gathered here are all worth having. Neither in terms of ensemble nor intonation is The Queen's College, Oxford, choir in the first league, but the performances are committed and give pleasure, and they are well recorded. The disc has the advantage of coupling rarely heard music of quality by Kenneth Leighton.

Collegium regale: canticles; Behold, O God our defender; Like as the hart; St Paul's service: Canticles. Take him to earth for cherishing. (Organ): *Psalm prelude: De profundis; Master Tallis's testament.*

*** Hyperion Dig. CDA 66260 [id.]. St Paul's Cathedral Ch., Scott; Christopher Dearnley.

All the music here is of high quality and the recording gives it resonance, in both senses of the word, with the St Paul's acoustic well captured by the engineers. A fine representation of a composer who wrote in the mainstream of English church and cathedral music but who had a distinct voice of his own.

Collegium regale: Te Deum and jubilate; Office of Holy Communion; Magnificat and Nunc dimittis. Preces & Responses I & II; Psalms 121 & 122; Take him, earth for cherishing. Rhapsody for organ, Op. 17/ 3.

⊛ *** Decca Dig. 430 205-2 [id.]. Williams, Moore, King's College, Cambridge, Ch., Cleobury.

Here is an unmatchable collection of the settings inspired by the greatest of our collegiate choirs, King's College, Cambridge, presented in performances of heartwarming intensity in that great choir's 1989 incarnation. The boy trebles in particular are among the brightest and fullest ever to have been recorded with this choir. The disc sensitively presents the sequence in what amounts to liturgical order, with the service settings aptly interspersed with responses, psalm-chants, anthems with organ introits and voluntaries all by Howells. Even those not normally attracted by Anglican church music should hear this.

Hymnus Paradisi, An English Mass.

*** Hyperion Dig. CDA 66488 [id.]. Kennard, Ainsley, RLPO Ch., RLPO, Handley.

Hymnus Paradisi is a heartfelt expression of grief over the death of the composer's son at the age of nine; Handley conveys a mystery, a tenderness rather missing from the previous recording, made by Sir David Willcocks for EMI, strong as that is. Handley's soloists bring a moving compassion, as in the haunting setting of the 23rd Psalm which makes up the third movement. The Hyperion digital recording is warm, full and atmospheric. *An English Mass* is simpler yet also hauntingly beautiful.

Missa Sabrinensis.

(Y/B) *** Chandos Dig. CHAN 9348 [id.]. Janice Watson, Della Jones, Martyn Hill, Donald Maxwell, London Symphony Ch., LSO, Rozhdestvensky.

Rozhdestvensky here conducts a passionate account of what in many ways is the most powerful of all the composer's major works. As the title implies, Howells was inspired not just by the liturgy and conventional devotional concerns, but by his deep love of the countryside round the Severn. The result is one of the most full-blooded and sustained expressions of ecstasy to be found in any setting of the Mass. There is little of the restraint that is typical of much of Howells' choral writing. Rather he exploits the lushest, most passionate elements in his richly post-impressionist style, and he hardly lets up over the whole span. This represents a peak in Howells' creative career and, though there is some roughness in the ensemble, it would be hard to imagine a more inspired performance than Rozhdestvensky's. Over the incandescent singing of the choir, the four excellent soloists give radiant performances, with the golden-toned soprano, Janice Watson, regularly crowning the mood of ecstasy in her solos. Full, glowing, atmospheric sound to match.

(Organ) *Psalm prelude, Set 1/1; Paen; Prelude: Sine nomine.* (Vocal): *Behold, O God our defender; Here is the door; Missa Aedi Christi: Kyrie; Credo; Sanctus; Benedictus; Agnus Dei; Gloria. Sing lullaby; A spotless rose; Where wast thou?.*
*** CRD Dig. CRD 3455; *CRDC 4155* [id.]. New College, Oxford, Ch., Edward Higginbottom (organ).

A further collection of the music of Herbert Howells, splendidly sung by Edward Higginbottom's fine choir, while he provides the organ interludes in addition. Among the shorter pieces, the carol-anthem, *Sing lullaby*, is especially delightful, and the programme ends with the motet, *Where wast thou?*, essentially affirmative, in spite of the question posed at the opening. Beautifully spacious sound makes this a highly rewarding collection.

Requiem. Motets: *The House of the Mind; A Sequence for St Michael.*
*** Chandos Dig. CHAN 9019 [id.]. Finzi Singers, Spicer – VAUGHAN WILLIAMS: *Lord thou hast been our refuge* etc. ***

Requiem; Take him, earth, for cherishing.
(Y/B) *** United Recordings Dig. 88033 [id.]. Sally Barber, Julia Field, Mark Johnstone, Andrew Angus, Vasari, Jeremy Backhouse – MARTIN: *Mass.* ***

Howells' *Requiem* is the work which prepared the way for *Hymnus Paradisi*, providing some of the material for it. For unaccompanied chorus, it presents a gentler, compact view of what in the big cantata becomes powerfully expansive. The Finzi singers, 18-strong, give a fresh and atmospheric, beautifully moulded performance, well coupled with two substantial motets with organ by Howells as well as choral pieces by Vaughan Williams.

On United, the soloists and Vasari, a choir conducted by Jeremy Backhouse, are absolutely first class and give a well-nigh exemplary performance, possibly finer than its immediate rival. Doubtless couplings will resolve the matter of choice. The present disc offers the *Requiem* in harness with another Mass from the inter-war years by Frank Martin.

Stabat Mater.
(Y/B) *** Chandos Dig. CHAN 9314 [id.]. Neill Archer, London Symphony Ch., LSO, Rozhdestvensky.

Completed and performed in 1965, when the composer was seventy-three, the *Stabat Mater* was Howells' last major work. This is a setting of the well-known text which outshines almost any other in its passionate involvement. Though the ecstasy is not as consistently sustained as in the earlier *Missa Sabrinensis*, with many more passages of hushed devotion, one registers with new intensity the agony of St John the Divine at the foot of the Cross, the companion of the Virgin Mary. The saint is personified in the tenor solos, here sung superbly by Neill Archer with a clear, heady tone, starting with his first thrilling entry on *O quam tristis*. As in the *Missa*, Rozhdestvensky proves the most passionate advocate, magnetically leading one through the whole rich score. Though ensemble sometimes suffers, it is a small price to pay for such thrusting, spontaneous-sounding conviction. Glowing, rich sound.

Humfrey, Pelham (1647–74)

Verse anthems: *By the waters of Babylon; Have mercy on me, O God; Hear, O Heav'ns; Hear my prayer, O God; Hear my crying, O God; Lift up your heads; Like as the hart; O give thanks unto the Lord; O Lord my God.*
*** HM Dig. HMU 907053 [id.]. Donna Deam, Drew Minter, Rogers Covey-Crump, John Potter, David Thomas, Clare College, Cambridge, Ch., Romanesca, Nicholas McGegan.

Verse anthem: *O Lord my God*.
(M) *** Erato/Warner 4509 99718-2 [id.]. Charles Brett, Martyn Hill, David Thomas, Monteverdi Ch.,
 E. Bar. Sol., Gardiner – Concert: '*Music of the Chapels Royal*'. ***

Pelham Humfrey (or Humphrey) began his career about 1660 as a chorister at the Chapel Royal and
made such an impression that he was sent abroad at the expense of the royal purse of Charles II to study
in France and Italy. He brought back from Italy (and from Lully in France) a thorough absorption of
the operatic style, and his verse anthems are remarkably dramatic and powerfully expressive, using
soloists almost like operatic characters. *By the waters of Babylon* and, especially, *O Lord my God* are very
striking indeed. Nicholas McGegan's fine performances reflect this histrionic dimension, helped by his
soloists who at times approach stylistic boundaries in their performance of what is essentially devotional
music, even if intensely felt. With a highly sensitive instrumental contribution from the excellent
Romanesca, this collection (about half of Humfrey's surviving output) is very freshly recorded and is
strongly recommended to the adventurous collector.

 Those seeking just a single example of Humfrey's unique combination of operatic drama and pathos
should sample John Eliot Gardiner's telling account of one of the very finest of these verse anthems, *O
Lord my God!*, in which the very moving supplication has faint echoes of Purcell's Dido's lament and the
declamation, 'For many dogs are come about me, and the counsel of the wicked lay'th siege against me,'
is very dramatic indeed. This is part of a well-chosen anthology of anthems and motets associated with
the Chapels Royal, including fine examples by Matthew Locke and John Blow, as well as Purcell,
included in the Gardiner Collection.

Hummel, Johann (1778–1837)

Bassoon concerto in F.
*** Denon Dig. CO 79281 [id.]. Werba, V. String Soloists, Honeck – MOZART; WEBER: *Concertos*. ***

A good modern recording of Hummel's engaging *Bassoon concerto* was needed and Michael Werba is a
personable and characterful soloist. He is well accompanied and recorded and the couplings are
attractive.

Piano concertos: in A min., Op. 85; B min., Op. 89.
*** Chandos Dig. CHAN 8505 [id.]. Stephen Hough, ECO, Bryden Thomson.
(B) *** Discover Dig. DICD 920117 [id.]. Dana Protopopescu, Slovak R. New PO, Rahbari.

The *A minor* is Hummel's most often-heard piano concerto, never better played, however, than by
Stephen Hough on this Chandos disc. The coda is quite stunning; it is not only his dazzling virtuosity
that carries all before it but also the delicacy and refinement of colour he produces. The *B minor*, Op. 89,
is more of a rarity, and is given with the same blend of virtuosity and poetic feeling which Hough brings
to its companion. He is given expert support by Bryden Thomson and the ECO – and the recording is
first class.

 At bargain price Discover offers an outstanding alternative coupling. Well accompanied by the Slovak
Radio New Philharmonic, Dana Protopopescu, always sounding fresh and spontaneous, plays with
lightness, point and poetry. On her smaller scale, she even rivals Stephen Hough in his prize-winning
recording of the same two concertos for Chandos at full price, though Hough is more impulsive.

Trumpet concerto in E.
⊛ *** Ph. Dig. 420 203-2 [id.]. Hardenberger, ASMF, Marriner – HAYDN *** ⊛; HERTEL ***;
 STAMITZ: *Concertos*. ***

Trumpet concerto in E flat.
*** Sony CD 37846 [id.]. Marsalis, Nat. PO, Leppard – HAYDN: *Concerto* *** (with L. MOZART:
 Concerto ***).

Hummel's *Trumpet concerto* is usually heard in the familiar brass key of E flat, but the brilliant Swedish
trumpeter, Håkan Hardenberger, uses the key of E, which makes it sound brighter and bolder than
usual. Neither he nor Marriner miss the genial lilt inherent in the dotted theme of the first movement,
the slow-movement cantilena soars beautifully over its jogging pizzicato accompaniment, and the finale
captivates the ear with its high spirits and easy bravura. This is the finest version of the piece in the
catalogue, for Marriner's accompaniment is polished and sympathetic.

 Marsalis gives a fine account of Hummel's *Concerto*, but does not quite catch its full *galant* charm. In
matters of bravura, however, he cannot be faulted; he relishes the sparkling finale.

Clarinet quartet in E flat.
(Y/B) (M) *** O-L 444 167-2 [id.]. Alan Hacker, The Music Party – WEBER: *Clarinet quintet.* ***

A delectable work, played as beautifully as the Weber coupling. Alan Hacker uses a Goulding clarinet *circa* 1880, and this would be the sound Hummel himself would have recognized. Hacker plays allegros with plenty of character and spirit and, at times, a winning bite on the timbre, yet there is plenty of warmth in the lyrical music. The Music Party also use original instruments and their positive approach brings a matching touch of abrasiveness but no lack of feeling. Lovers of the authentic style will find this very stimulating.

Septet in D min., Op. 74.
*** CRD CRD 3344; *CRDC 4044* [id.]. Nash Ens. – BERWALD: *Septet.* ***

Hummel's *Septet* is an enchanting and inventive work with a virtuoso piano part, expertly dispatched here by Clifford Benson. A fine performance and excellent recording make this a highly desirable issue, particularly in view of the enterprising coupling.

String quartets: in C; in G; in E flat, Op. 30/1–3.
*** Hyperion Dig. CDA 66568 [id.]. Delmé Qt.

Hummel wrote his three *String quartets* – his only contribution to the form – in 1803/4. Hummel's works are closer to Haydn than Beethoven, though the first of the set in C major with its impressive opening *Adagio e mesto* in the minor key, fine *Adagio*, and brisk, scherzo-like Minuet, with its forward-looking structure, obviously lean towards the influence of the later composer, while the audacious quotation of *Comfort ye* from Handel's *Messiah* in the preceding *Andante*, brings yet another example of Hummelian sleight of hand. In short these are fascinating works, highly inventive, and crafted with the composer's usual fluent charm. They are splendidly played by the Delmé group, who provide plenty of vitality and warmth. The Hyperion recording is fresh and believable.

Violin sonatas: in E flat, Op. 5/3; in D, Op. 50; Nocturne, Op. 99.
*** Amon Ra CD-SAR 12 [id.]. Ralph Holmes, Richard Burnett.

Ralph Holmes's violin timbre is bright and the Graf fortepiano under the fingers of Richard Burnett has plenty of colour and does not sound clattery. Burnett has a chance to catch the ear in the finale of the *D major Sonata* when he uses the quaintly rasping cembalo device (without letting it outstay its welcome). The *Nocturne* is an extended piece (nearly 16 minutes) in variation form. A thoroughly worthwhile issue, 'authentic' in the most convincing way, which shows this engaging composer at his most assured and inventive.

Mass in B flat, Op. 77; Tantum ergo (after Gluck).
*** Koch Dig. 3-7117-2 [id.]. Westminster Oratorio Ch., New Brunswick CO, John Floreen.

Hummel wrote his *Mass in B flat* while working for the Esterházys. It is an unpretentious work of great charm and a real discovery. The Westminster Choir (from the College of that name in Princeton, New Jersey) give exactly the right kind of modest performance, emphasizing the work's warm lyricism; the conductor, while not lacking vigour, is careful not to be too forceful at climaxes. The orchestral accompaniment is nicely in scale, and the recording, though not crystal clear, has the most agreeable ambience.

Humperdinck, Engelbert (1854–1921)

The Bluebird: Prelude; Star dance. Hänsel und Gretel: Overture. Königskinder: Overture; Preludes to Acts II & III. The Sleeping Beauty: suite.
(Y/B) (M) **(*) Virgin/EMI Dig. CUV5 61128-2 [id.]. Bamberg SO, Karl Anton Rickenbacher.

By far the most memorable piece here is the *Hänsel und Gretel Overture*, although the Introduction to Act III of *Königskinder* is also very touching, characteristically using horns to evoke the Minstrel's last song. The *Overture* to the same opera is significant in demonstrating Humperdinck's characteristic failing – a prolixity of ideas, none of which is quite memorable enough to emerge from the ongoing energy of the writing. His post-Wagnerian orchestration can be too thick and this inhibits his festive pieces, but the lightly scored items have charm, for instance the *Star dance* from *The Bluebird* or the *Ballade* from *The Sleeping Beauty*. Rickenbacher secures warm, cultured playing from his Bambergers, and the Virgin sound is full and pleasing if lacking just a little in sparkle. Worth trying at mid-price.

The Canteen Woman (Die Marketenderin): Prelude. The Merchant of Venice: Love scene. Moorish rhapsody: Tarifa (Elegy of summer); Tangier (A night in a Moorish coffee-house); Tetuan (A night in the desert). The Sleeping Beauty: suite.
**(*) Marco Polo Dig. 8.223369 [id.]. Slovak RSO (Bratislava), Martin Fischer-Dieskau.

The Love scene from *The Merchant of Venice* ('On such a night') is beautiful but rather over-extended, and all three sections of the *Moorish rhapsody* are much too long (the composite piece lasts some 32 minutes). The opening of the *Summer elegy* begins with raptly ethereal writing for the violins, but the jolly Moorish coffee-house sequence sounds as if the restaurant has been leased from the owner of a Bavarian bier-keller. The Slovak performances under Martin Fischer-Dieskau (the famous Lieder singer's grandson) are not ideally polished but have freshness and vitality, while the Marco Polo recording is open and reasonably full.

Hänsel und Gretel (complete).
(Y/B) *** Teldec/Warner Dig.4509 94549-2 (2) [id.]. Larmore, Ziesak, Schwarz, Weikl, Behrens, Tölz Boys' Ch., Bav. RSO, Runnicles.
*** EMI Dig. CDS7 54022-2 (2) [Ang. CDCB 54022]. Von Otter, Bonney, Lipovšek, Schwarz, Schmidt, Hendricks, Lind, Tölz Boys' Ch, Bav. RSO, Tate.
(M) *** EMI CMS7 69293-2 (2) [Ang. CDMB 69293]. Schwarzkopf, Grümmer, Metternich, Ilsovay, Schürhoff, Felbermayer, Children's Ch., Philh. O, Karajan.
(Y/B) *** Ph. Dig. 438 013-2 (2) [id.]. Murray, Gruberová, Ludwig, Gwyneth Jones, Grundheber, Bonney, Oelze, Dresden State O, Sir Colin Davis.
(Y/B) (M) **(*) RCA 74321 25281-2 (2). Moffo, Donath, Fischer-Dieskau, Berthold, Ludwig, Augér, Popp, Bav. R. Ch. & RSO, Eichhorn.

The success of the Teldec version of *Hänsel und Gretel* is largely due to Donald Runnicles, who has a lighter touch than his direct rivals, regularly favouring faster speeds than the others, including Tate. The lightness and refinement of the playing bring transparent textures and the most delicate pianissimos. Runnicles adds to the fantasy by giving his soloists an extra degree of freedom, encouraging individual expressiveness. In the casting the emphasis more than ever is on fresh, youthful voices. So it was too with Barbara Bonney and Anne Sofie von Otter in the Tate set, but here the distinction between boy and girl is if anything even more sharply drawn. Ruth Ziesak as Gretel and Jennifer Larmore as Hänsel are above all natural-sounding, with little or no feeling of mature opera-singers pretending to be children, yet with no sense of strain and none of the edginess. Fresh clarity marks the other voices too, even that of the Witch as taken by Hanna Schwarz. Though aptly she uses a croaking voice, it makes the witch sharply sinister without being too frightening. Hildegard Behrens is strong and characterful, with Bernd Weikl firm and dark as the Father, while Rosemary Joshua makes a welcome recording début in opera as a bright-toned Sandman and Christine Schafer, fuller and firmer, is warmly contrasted as the Dew Fairy. On balance a first recommendation, the set brings incidentally a fascinating supplement in a brief orchestral coda, just over a minute long, which Humperdinck wrote in 1894 for a production of the opera in Dessau with Cosima Wagner as director. Ingeniously he has the Dessau national anthem set in counterpoint against various themes from the opera, with toy trumpets providing a commentary.

Tate brings a Brucknerian glow to the *Overture*, and then launches into a reading of exceptional warmth and sympathy at speeds generally faster than those in rival versions. The Witch of Marjana Lipovšek is firm and fierce, using the widest range of expression and tone. The chill that Lipovšek conveys down to a mere whisper makes one regret, more than usual, that the part is not longer. All the casting matches that in finesse, with no weak link. Barbara Bonney as Gretel and Anne Sofie von Otter as Hänsel are no less fine than the exceptionally strong duos on the rival sets. There is only a slight question mark over the use of the Tölz Boys' Choir for the gingerbread children at the end. Inevitably they sound what they are, a beautifully matched team of trebles, and curiously the heart-tug is not quite so intense as with the more childish-sounding voices in the rival choirs. That is a minimal reservation, however, when the breadth and warmth of the recording add to the compulsion of the performance.

Karajan's classic 1950s set of Humperdinck's children's opera, with Schwarzkopf and Grümmer peerless in the name-parts, is enchanting; this was an instance where everything in the recording went right. The original mono LP set was already extremely atmospheric. In most respects the sound has as much clarity and warmth as rival recordings made in the 1970s. There is much to delight here; the smaller parts are beautifully done and Else Schürhoff's Witch is memorable. The snag is that the digital remastering has brought a curious orchestral bass emphasis, noticeable in the overture and elsewhere, but notably in the *Witch's ride*.

Sir Colin Davis has rarely conducted a more glowing opera performance on record than this. It is his inspired direction, beautifully paced, as though captured live, which above all compels attention.

Though in beauty of timbre neither Edita Gruberová nor Ann Murray can quite match their principal rivals on disc, the contrast of timbre between the bright, sometimes edgy sound of Gruberová and the plainer sound of Murray is always very clearly defined, and their sharp characterization and feeling for words seals that distinction. There is comparable casting for both the Mother and the Witch. Dame Gwyneth Jones could not be more positive as the Mother, singing so as to cut through all textures. And though under pressure the voice acquires a characteristic beat, the pitching is always clear and defined. Christa Ludwig gives a similarly positive and characterful performance as the Witch, putting over both the melodramatic and the comic moments with superb timing. Franz Grundheber makes a clean-toned Father, while Barbara Bonney, Gretel for Tate, here becomes the Sandman, sweetly expressive, and Christiane Oelze's light, bright soprano is most apt for the Dew Fairy. Recorded in the Lukaskirche, the sound gives plenty of bloom on voices and orchestra, though with the focus less sharp than in Runnicles' Teldec version.

There are some fine solo performances on the mid-priced 1971 RCA set, notably from Helen Donath as Gretel and Christa Ludwig as the Witch; and Kurt Eichhorn's direction is vigorous, with excellent orchestral playing and full, atmospheric recording. It is a pity that a more boyish-sounding singer than Anna Moffo could not have been chosen for the role of Hänsel but, all told, this is a colourful and enjoyable account of a unique, eternally fresh opera, well worth considering.

Humphrey, Pelham – see Humfrey, Pelham

Hurlstone, William (1876–1906)

The Magic mirror: suite; Variations on a Hungarian air; Variations on an original theme.
(N) *** Lyrita Dig. SRCD 208 [id.]. LPO, Braithwaite.

As a glance at his dates shows, William Hurlstone only just reached thirty before the ill-health which dogged him during his life claimed him. A pupil of Stanford and Dannreuther, his fellow students at the Royal College of Music included Frank Bridge, John Ireland, Vaughan Williams and Holst as well as Coleridge Taylor, whom he befriended and who also died young. Indeed when he played his piano concerto in 1896, Holst played trombone and Vaughan Williams was among the percussion. The *Variations on an original theme* also date from 1896, though the theme on which they are based comes from a *Trio*, written two years earlier. They show considerable inventive resource and although, like the *Variations on a Hungarian air*, there is also a certain debt to Brahms, they have a lightness of touch and a feeling for the orchestra which is marked. *The Magic mirror suite* of 1900 also offers reminders of the Elgar of *The Wand of youth*. But it is not long before one can sense something quietly individual beginning to surface. The LPO and Nicholas Braithwaite give lively, cultured performances of this eminently well-crafted, immaculately scored and civilized music, and they are beautifully recorded.

Hvoslef, Ketil (born 1937)

(i) *Antigone (1982);* (ii) *Violin concerto.*
*** Aurora Dig. ACD4969 [id.]. (ii) Trond Saeverud; Bergen PO, cond. (i) Eggen; (ii) Kitaienko.

Ketil Hvoslef is the son of Harald Saeverud and one of the brightest and most individual figures in the Norwegian musical firmament. He has the same craggy, salty quality as his father, the same rugged independence of personality and creative resource. This CD offers *Antigone*, which comes from the early 1980s, and the *Violin concerto*, composed almost ten years later, in which the soloist is his son, Trond.

Ibert, Jacques (1890–1962)

Bacchanale; Bostoniana; (i) *Flute concerto. Escales (Ports of call); Hommage à Mozart; Louisville concerto; Paris (suite).*
*** Decca Dig. 440 332-2 [id.]. (i) Timothy Hutchins; Montreal SO, Charles Dutoit.

Dutoit knows exactly where he is going in this repertoire: *Escales* has all the required sensuous, Mediterranean feeling and colour, and Timothy Hutchins is an estimable soloist in the *Flute concerto*. If the unknown music is not quite so indelible as these three best-known works it is still most enjoyable when played with such idiomatic flair. *Bostoniana* is in fact the only finished movement of the composer's second symphony, written for the Boston Symphony; the *Louisville concerto* was commissioned by yet another American ensemble and the Ibertian tribute to Mozart came in time for the bicentennial celebrations of Mozart's birth. Needless to say, the recording with rich, clear textures is yet another example of Decca expertise in St Eustache, Montreal.

Bacchanale; Bostoniana; Divertissement; Louisville concerto; Symphonie marine.
(N) (M) ** EMI CD-EMX 2269 [id.]. CBSO, Frémaux.

Frémaux's account of the *Divertissement* is warm-hearted and vigorous, with genuine exuberance in the 'police-whistle' finale, but the Birmingham recording is somewhat over-reverberant. It suits the *Bacchanale* rather more readily, although this is an empty piece to which Frémaux applies an appropriate degree of frenzy. The three other works are very well played, but the music itself is hardly more distinguished and scarcely does justice to the inventive powers of this often charming composer.

La Ballade de la Geôle de Reading; Féerique; 3 Pièces de Ballet (Les Rencontres); (i) *Chant de Folie; Suite Elisabéthaine.*
**(*) Marco Polo Dig. 8.223508 [id.]. (i) Slovak Ph. Ch.; Slovak RSO (Bratislava), Adriano.

The *Suite Elisabéthaine* is a nine-movement suite taken from the incidental music Ibert composed for Shakespeare's *A Midsummer Night's Dream*. It is largely pastiche and four of the movements draw on Blow, Purcell, Bull and Gibbons. More characteristic is *La Ballade de la Geôle de Reading*, an exercise in neo-impressionism and highly accomplished. The *Chant de Folie* is an effective four-minute choral and orchestral piece inspired by the composer's experiences in the First World War and at one time championed by Koussevitzky. Its brevity has doubtless inhibited modern performances. Good performances and eminently serviceable recording.

Divertissement.
*** Chandos Dig. CHAN 9023 [id.]. Ulster O, Yan Pascal Tortelier – MILHAUD: *Le Bœuf; Création;* POULENC: *Les Biches.* ***
(M) *** RCA 09026 61429-2 [id.]. Boston Pops O, Arthur Fiedler – OFFENBACH: *Collection.* **
(N) (M) *** Decca 448 571-2 [id.]. Paris Conservatoire O, Martinon – BIZET: *Jeux d'enfants* ***; BERLIOZ: *Overtures* **(*); SAINT-SAENS: *Danse macabre* etc. ***

Yan Pascal Tortelier provides at last a splendid, modern, digital version of Ibert's *Divertissement*. There is much delicacy of detail, and the coupled suite from Poulenc's *Les Biches* is equally delectable. Marvellous, top-drawer Chandos sound.

Fiedler's racy account of Ibert's *Divertissement* is as sparkling as you could wish, with genuine Gallic insouciance. The *Valse, Parade* and exuberant *Finale* have tremendous élan. The recording too is splendidly lively and atmospheric. It is a pity that the Offenbach collection which acts as coupling is recorded less successfully.

Martinon's 1960 account has never been surpassed for its sheer fizzing energy and wit, and it is a pity that, as remastered for this reissue in Decca's 'Classic Sound' series, the *Introduction* sounds rather thin and shrill. But after that the sound fills out and the performance has marvellous aplomb. The galloping finale, complete with its uninhibited police-whistle, sounds for all the world like the accompaniment to a farcical police chase from the days of the Keystone Kops.

Escales (Ports of call).
(M) *** RCA 09026 61500-2 [id.]. Boston SO, Munch – DEBUSSY: *La Mer* **(*); SAINT-SAENS: *Symphony No. 3.* *** ❀
(M) **(*) Mercury 432 003-2 [id.]. Detroit SO, Paray – RAVEL: *Alborada* etc. ***

Short though it is, this is a first-rate work. The opening of *Palermo* offers some ravishing textures from the Boston violins (French impressionism at its most seductive); the second evocation has a piquantly oriental favour and the finale, *Valencia*, has gay dance rhythms. Munch's performances are splendid and the 1956 recording, if balanced rather closely, has brilliance and transparency; although it does not sound as rich and sumptuous as the outstanding Saint-Saëns symphony with which it is coupled, the effect is slightly preferable to Paray's fine Mercury version.

Paray's recording catches the Mediterranean exoticism of *Escales* admirably, and the 1962 Mercury recording has plenty of atmosphere as well as glittering detail. The Ravel couplings are very impressive too.

Escales; Ouverture de fête; Tropisms pour des amours imaginaires.
(M) *** EMI CDM7 64276-2 [id.]. Fr. Nat. R. O, Jean Martinon.

The well-known *Escales* have genuine atmosphere in Martinon's exemplary performance, and the 1974 recording is spacious, at times sensuously so, and pleasingly natural. The strings here have more allure than in Paray's Mercury version. *Tropisms* has moments of real imagination and is a piece of greater substance than the *Ouverture de fête* which, though it has a striking principal theme, is rather inflated. All three performances are expert and the CD transfer is most impressive.

Symphonie concertante (for oboe and string orchestra).
(M) *** RCA GD 87989 [7989-2-RG]. John de Lancie, LSO, Previn – FRANCAIX: *L'horloge de flore*
*** ❀; R. STRAUSS: *Oboe concerto*. ***

Ibert's *Symphonie concertante* has vitality and impulse and demands great virtuosity from the orchestra, and the extended *Adagio* has a wan, expressive poignancy. John de Lancie is a first-class soloist. André Previn directs with much conviction and spirit. The sound is very good – its slight lack of opulence suits the music.

d'India, Sigismondo (*c.* 1582–*c.* 1630)

Duets, Laments and Madrigals: *Amico, hai vinto; Ancidetemi pur, dogliosi affanti; Che nudrisce tua speme; Giunto a la tomba; Langue al vostro languir; Occhi della mia vita; O leggiadr' occhi; Quella vermiglia rosa; Son gli accenti che ascolto; Torna il sereno Zefiro.*
(B) **(*) HM HMA 901011 [id.]. Concerto Vocale – CESTI: *Cantatas.* **(*)

Sigismondo d'India was among the vanguard of the new movement founded by Monteverdi at the beginning of the seventeenth century, and his laments show him to be a considerable master of expressive resource. The performances are authoritative, though there are moments of slightly self-conscious rubato that hold up the flow. The recording is fully acceptable and the coupling is also of considerable interest; this is worth exploring.

Amico, hai vinto; Diana (Questo dardo, quest' arco); Misera me (Lamento d'Olympia); Piangono al pianger mio; Sfere fermate; Torna il sereno zefiro.
*** Hyperion CDA 66106 [id.]. Emma Kirkby, Anthony Rooley (chitarone) – MONTEVERDI: *Lamento d'Olympia* etc. ***

Sigismondo d'India's setting of the *Lamento d'Olympia* makes a striking contrast to Monteverdi's and is hardly less fine. This is an affecting and beautiful piece and so are its companions, particularly when they are sung as superbly and accompanied as sensitively as they are here. A very worthwhile CD début.

Il primo Libro de Madrigali (1606): *Interdette speranz'e van desio. Ottavo Libro de Madrigali: Il pastor fido*, Act IV, Scene 9: *Se tu, Silvio crudel, mi saetti* (five madrigal cycle).
(Y/B) ❀ (M) *** Virgin Veritas/EMI Dig. VER5 61165-2 [id.]. Chiaroscuro, L. Baroque, Nigel Rogers –
MONTEVERDI: *Madrigals.* *** ❀

The opening piece, d'India's *Interdette speranz'e van desio* ('Forbidden hopes and vain desire'), is freely set, and is stimulating as well as beautiful, but it is in the cycle from his Eighth Book of Madrigals, *Se tu, Silvio crudel, mi saetti*, that one experiences not only the composer's lyrical originality to the full but also his affinity with the operatic writing of his greater contemporary, Monteverdi. The vocal dialogue (which alternates, often subtly, solo and ensemble singing) expresses disdain and anger, love, pain and fear of death; and d'India's setting is touching and dramatic by turns, and also requires effortless vocal virtuosity. The quality of the performances is superlative, refined without a hint of preciosity, and always alive. The accompaniments on theorbo and harpsichord are delicately balanced, while the recording is immaculately realistic. An outstanding collection in every way.

(i) *Madrigals for 5 voices: Book No. 8* (complete); Solo madrigals and chamber duets: (ii) *Che farai, Meliseo?;* (iii) *Da l'onde del mio pianto;* (iv) *Odi quel rosignuolo;* (ii) *Qual fiera sì crudel?.* Duets: (iv; v) *Alla guerra d'amor, La mia Filli crudel; La Virtù.*
(Y/B) (M) *** O-L Dig. 444 168-2 [id.]. (i) Kirkby, Tubb, Nichols, Cornwell, King, Wistreich; (ii) David Thomas; (iii) Martyn Hill; (iv) Emma Kirkby; (v) Judith Nelson; Cons. of Musicke, Rooley.

The performances of the complete five-part madrigals from Book 8 (1624) are authoritative, though there are moments of slightly self-conscious rubato that hold up the flow. The recording could be more spacious and warmer; despite that qualification, this is thoroughly recommendable, made the more so by the additional, earlier, solo madrigals (from 1609 and 1621) and chamber duets (1615). Those for male voices are essentially melancholy, but Emma Kirkby soon brightens things up with her sparkling, highly decorated nightingale song, and the female duets, '*My cruel Phyllis*' and '*To the war of love*', are very lively indeed. The CD transfers give an excellent natural presence.

d'Indy, Vincent (1851–1931)

(i) *Fantasy on French popular themes* (for oboe and orchestra), *Op. 31. Saugefleurie* (Legend after a tale by Robert de Bonnières); *Tableaux de voyage, Op. 36; L'Etranger: Prelude to Act II. Fervaal: Prelude to Act I.*
(Y/B) ** Marco Polo Dig. 8.223659 [id.]. (i) Philippe Cousu; Württemberg PO, Gilles Nopre, or (i) Jean-Marc Burfin.

The tone-poem, *Saugefleurie,* based on a tale by Robert de Bonnières and dating from 1884, is the earliest piece on this CD and is not otherwise available at present. Not that much of this repertoire suffers from duplication: the *Tableaux de voyage* were once available on an EMI issue under Pierre Dervaux. But the last time the lovely *Prelude to Act I* of *Fervaal* was in the British catalogues was from Munch on a Decca 78-r.p.m. disc, and under Monteux. It is unaccountable that music of this quality, which also has the seeds of popularity, is so parlously neglected. New to the catalogue is the *Fantaisie sur des thèmes populaires françaises* for oboe and orchestra, which should be sought out by players: it has a fervent charm which is very winning. The performances of all these pieces are variable; they fall short of distinction but are more than routine. The recording, too, is eminently satisfactory and aficionados of French music need not hesitate.

Jour d'été à la montagne, Op. 61; (i) *Symphonie sur un chant montagnard français, Op. 25.*
(Y/B) **(*) Erato/Warner Dig. 2292 45821-2 [id.].(i) Catherine Collard; R. France PO, Janowski.

The Erato disc is worth having for the sake of *Jour d'été à la montagne,* one of d'Indy's most inspired pieces. This version is artistically superior to the rival under Pierre Dervaux on EMI, though the late lamented Catherine Collard's version of the *Symphonie sur un chant montagnard français,* sometimes known as the *Symphonie Cévenole,* is handicapped by some unsympathetic accompanying from Janowski and a synthetic balance which does not allow the sound to expand. Good playing from the Orchestre Philharmonique de Radio France.

Jour d'été à la montagne, Op. 61; Tableaux de voyage, Op. 36.
(M) **(*) EMI CDM7 64364-2 [id.]. Loire PO, Pierre Dervaux.

Jour d'été à la montagne was inspired by the beauties of the Vivarais region of central France where d'Indy was born. *Tableaux de voyage* is a delightful suite, written originally for piano. This is a most enjoyable coupling that reveals d'Indy as a far richer and more rewarding composer than most people give him credit for, and the performances are in no sense second-rate, even though the Orchestre Philharmonique des Pays de Loire is scarcely of international standing. The recording is very good and well transferred to CD, but the measure is short (47 minutes): the original LP included also *La forêt enchantée.*

Lied, Op. 19.
**(*) Ph. Dig. 432 084-2 [id.]. Julian Lloyd Webber, ECO, Yan Pascal Tortelier – FAURE: *Elégie* **; HONEGGER: *Concerto* **(*); SAINT-SAENS: *Concerto* etc. **(*)

Vincent d'Indy's *Lied for cello and orchestra* has something of the nobility that always distinguished this composer, and it comes with an interesting coupling in the shape of the Honegger *Concerto.*

Symphonie sur un chant montagnard français (Symphonie cévenole).
*** Decca Dig. 430 278-2 [id.]. Jean-Yves Thibaudet, Montreal SO, Dutoit – FRANCK: *Symphony.* ***
(M) **(*) RCA GD 86805 [6805-2-RG]. Nicole Henriot-Schweitzer, Boston SO, Munch – FRANCK: *Symphony.* **(*) 🏵
(Y/B) (M) **(*) RCA 09026 62582-2 [id.]. Henriot-Schweitzer, Boston SO, Charles Munch – BERLIOZ: *Harold in Italy.* *(*)
(Y/B) (BB) **(*) Naxos 8.550754 [id.]. Thiollier, Nat. SO of Ireland, Antonio de Almeida – FAURE: *Ballade;* FRANCK: *Symphonic variations.* **(*)

Jean-Yves Thibaudet's Decca account is sensitively played and outstandingly well recorded. A clear first choice.

Nicole Henriot-Schweitzer plays the piano part most sympathetically and Munch presents a fresh and crisp performance. The early (1958) stereo recording comes up well. This is now available in an alternative coupling.

On Naxos the French-born but American-trained François-Joël Thiollier gives an intelligent performance of the *Symphonie sur un chant montagnard.* Perfectly acceptable, perfectly well accompanied and decently recorded (though the soloist is rather forwardly placed by the engineers) and with an interesting coupling. It is worth the money, but there are finer accounts to be had, some (like Jean-Yves Thibaudet) at full-price.

(i) *Symphonie sur un chant montagnard français;* (ii) *Symphony No. 2 in B flat, Op. 57.*
(M) *** EMI CDM7 63952-2. (i) Ciccolini, O de Paris, Baudo; (ii) Toulouse Capitole O, Plasson.

Aldo Ciccolini gives a good account of himself in the demanding solo part of the *Symphonie*, and the Orchestre de Paris under Serge Baudo give sympathetic support. The recording is pleasing and with a convincing piano image. In the *Second Symphony* Michel Plasson proves a sympathetic and committed advocate, and his orchestra responds with enthusiasm and sensitivity to his direction. The recording too is spacious, full and well focused.

String quartets Nos. 1 in D, Op. 35; 2 in E, Op. 45.
**(*) Marco Polo Dig. 8.223140 [id.]. Kodály Qt.

The *First Quartet* is a large-scale piece and beautifully crafted. The *Second* (1897) is hardly less ambitious and shows something of the composer's admiration for late Beethoven; it must also be said that greater variety of texture would be welcome. The excellent Kodály Quartet are recorded in the Italian Institute in Budapest, where the rather close balance tends to iron out dynamic extremes.

Ippolitov-Ivanov, Mikhail (1859–1935)

Caucasian sketches (suite), *Op. 10.*
(Y/B) *** Chandos Dig. CHAN 9321 [id.]. BBC PO, Fedor Glushchenko – KHACHATURIAN: *Symphony No. 3* etc. ***
*** ASV Dig. CDDCA 773. Armenian PO, Tjeknavorian – KHACHATURIAN: *Gayaneh* etc. **(*)

Once a popular repertory piece, the colourful *Caucasian sketches* have fallen out of favour; only the final *Procession of the Sardar* is generously represented on CD. The present version by the BBC Philharmonic under Fedor Glushchenko is generally superior to the only other alternative on ASV.

The *Procession of the Sardar*, the hit number from the *Caucasian sketches*, is played by the Armenians with great brio. The other items rely mainly on picaresque oriental atmosphere for their appeal, which Tjeknavorian also captures evocatively in this brightly lit recording.

Liturgy of St John Chrysostom, Op. 37; Vespers, Op. 43.
(Y/B) *** Sony Dig. SMK 64091 [id.]. Lege Artis Chamber Ch., Boris Analyan.

These are beautiful pieces, not as profound, powerful or soulful as either Tchaikovsky's or Rachmaninov's settings, but well worth having. A useful and pleasing addition to the catalogue. The Lege Artis Chamber Choir rise excellently to the not inconsiderable demands made on them, and the recording has an appropriately warm acoustic.

Ireland, John (1879–1962)

Concertino pastorale; Downland suite (arr. composer and Geoffrey Bush); *Orchestral poem; 2 Symphonic studies* (arr. Geoffrey Bush).
(Y/B) *** Chandos Dig. CHAN 9376 [id.]. City of L. Sinfonia, Richard Hickox.

An outstanding disc: the finest recorded collection of Ireland's orchestral music ever. It is beautifully played and gloriously recorded. The valedictory *Threnody* of the *Concertino pastorale* and the lovely *Elegy* from the *Downland suite* show the composer at his most lyrically inspired, and the rapt playing here does them full justice: the *Threnody* is infinitely touching. The early *Orchestral poem* (1904) is a surprisingly powerful work as presented here with great passion, with splendid brass writing at its climax. There is a hint of Vaughan Williams in the quieter central section. The two *Symphonic studies* come from film music Ireland wrote for *The Overlanders*, not incorporated into the concert suites: the brass chromatics in the first have a familiar ring, the second has a wild momentum, recalling the cattle stampede in the film, but both stand up well as independent concert pieces.

Piano concerto in E flat.
*** Conifer Dig. 74321 15007-2 [id.]. Kathryn Stott, RPO, Handley – BRIDGE: *Phantasm;* WALTON: *Sinfonia concertante.* ***
*** Unicorn Dig. DKPCD 9056 [id.]. Tozer, Melbourne SO, Measham – RUBBRA: *Violin concerto.* ***

Piano concerto in E flat; Legend for piano and orchestra; Mai-Dun (symphonic rhapsody).
*** Chandos Dig. CHAN 8461 [id.]. Parkin, LPO, Thomson.
(M) (***) Dutton Laboratories mono CDAX 8001 [id.]. Eileen Joyce, Hallé O, Leslie Heward – MOERAN: *Symphony.* *** ⌾

(i) *Piano concerto in E flat;* (ii; iv) *A London overture;* (iii; iv) *Mai-Dun* (symphonic rhapsody); (v) *Comedy overture;* (vi) *Greater love hath no man;* (vii) *The Sally Gardens;* (viii) *Sea fever.*

(M) (***) EMI mono CDM7 64716-2. (i) Colin Horsley, RPO, Basil Cameron; (ii) LSO; (iii) Hallé O; (iv) Barbirolli; (v) GUS, Kettering, Band, Geoffrey Brand; (vi) Chichester Cathedral Ch., John Birch; (vii) Dame Janet Baker, Gerald Moore; (viii) Robert Lloyd, Nina Walker.

Kathryn Stott gives the most sympathetic reading of Ireland's *Piano concerto* on record since the original interpreter on disc, Eileen Joyce. Spaciously expressive in the lyrical passages and crisply alert in the jazzy finale, Stott plays with a sense of spontaneity, using freely idiomatic rubato. Generously and aptly coupled with the much more neglected Walton and Bridge works, and very well recorded, this version makes an easy first choice for the work.

Eric Parkin gives a splendidly refreshing and sparkling performance and benefits from excellent support from Bryden Thomson and the LPO. They are no less impressive in *Mai-Dun* and the beautiful *Legend for piano and orchestra.*

Geoffrey Tozer also gives a characterful account of Ireland's lyrical and often whimsical *Concerto.* Tozer conveys the poetic feel of the slow movement and, though he takes a rather measured tempo in the finale, the music loses none of its freshness. The recording is a little studio-bound, but too much should not be made of this. Doubtless the coupling will decide matters for most collectors.

Eileen Joyce's 1942 recording of this delightful concerto readily demonstrates the flamboyant romanticism for which she was famous and even a moment or two of fantasy, plus the freshness of discovery. Leslie Heward accompanies with flair, and the orchestral playing is impressive. The superb transfers of the original 78s show the work of Dutton Laboratories at its finest, offering sound that in its body and sense of presence sets new standards in re-creating what it felt like listening to the original 78s, with the one snag that, as the original shellac pressings were the source, there is noticeable wow on the piano tone, especially striking in the central *Lento.* No complaints about the orchestra: the strings are full and warm.

However, many listeners will prefer the later, stereo recording by Colin Horsley with Basil Cameron which retains that initial freshness and has excellent sound. In this performance the slow movement has a serene poise and beauty which are ravishingly memorable. In the finale Eileen Joyce has marginally greater dash, but Colin Horsley still offers plenty of sparkle and Basil Cameron proves a fine partner. The rest of the programme includes both the *London overture* and the brass band piece on which it was based. *Mai-Dun* receives persuasive advocacy from Barbirolli, but this is not Ireland at his finest. The composer's two most famous songs are also very welcome.

A Downland suite; Elegiac meditation; The Holy Boy.
*** Chandos Dig. CHAN 8390 [id.]. ECO, David Garforth – BRIDGE: *Suite for strings.* ***

A Downland suite was originally written for brass band. However, the present version was finished and put into shape by Geoffrey Bush, who also transcribed the *Elegiac meditation.* David Garforth and the ECO play with total conviction and seem wholly attuned to Ireland's sensibility. The recording is first class, clear and naturally balanced.

Epic march; The Overlanders (film incidental music): *suite* (arr. Mackerras).
(M) *** Unicorn UKCD 2062 [id.]. W. Australian SO, David Measham – VAUGHAN WILLIAMS: *On Wenlock Edge.* ***

The Overlanders is not the best of Ireland, but it contains some good ideas (the Scherzo, *The Brumbles,* is particularly effective) and it is persuasively presented here. The *Epic march* is jolly and rhythmically folksy, then presents an almost elegiac grand tune, for which Measham slows in respect but presents grandly at the end. This is all recommendable enough, for the CD transfers are first rate and the Vaughan Williams coupling is most appealing.

A London overture.
(M) *** EMI CDM5 65109-2 [id.]. LSO, Barbirolli – VAUGHAN WILLIAMS: *London symphony.* **(*)

One of Ireland's most immediately attractive works, and Barbirolli's performance of it is a great success, as is the remastering of an outstanding recording: the effect is tangible and real in its crisply vivid focus. The main theme (rhythmically conjuring up the bus conductor's call of 'Piccadilly!') is made obstinately memorable, and the ripe romanticism of the middle section is warmly expansive in Barbirolli's hands. The freshness of the sound makes the performance sound newly minted.

A London overture; Epic march; (i) *The Holy Boy; Greater love hath no man; These things shall be; Vexilla regis.*
*** Chandos Dig. CHAN 8879 [id.]. (i) Bryn Terfel, London Symphony Ch., LSO, Richard Hickox.

Richard Hickox is a sympathetic interpreter of the composer and obtains sensitive results (and good singing) in *The Holy Boy* and *These things shall be*. The disc is of particular interest in that it brings a rarity, *Vexilla Regis* for chorus, brass and organ. First-class recorded sound.

(i) *Cello sonata;* (ii) *Fantasy sonata for clarinet and piano;* (i) *The Holy boy* (for cello and piano); (iii) *Phantasie trio; Piano trios Nos. 2–3;* (iv) *Violin sonatas Nos. 1–2.*
(N) *** Chandos Dig. CHAN 9377/8 [id.]. (i; iii) Karine Georgian; (i; iii–iv) Ian Brown; (ii) Gervase de Peyer, Gwenneth Pryor; (iii–iv) Lydia Mordkovitch.

Few British composers have written with quite such easy lyricism as John Ireland. Though he usually concentrated on small forms, this fine collection of his chamber works shows how effectively he could develop his striking, memorable themes on a larger scale, often using the one-movement Fantasy form devised by W. W. Cobbett in reflection of the Elizabethans. The first two of the *Piano trios*, well contrasted, follow that pattern, but the masterpiece is the four-movement *Piano trio No. 3* of 1938, passionately intense. The two *Violin sonatas* are both superb works too, masterfully played here by Lydia Mordkovitch with Ian Brown, who also accompanies Karine Georgian in the *Cello sonata*. Completing the set, the recording of the *Fantasy sonata* of 1943 for clarinet dates from earlier, with Gervase de Peyer and Gwenneth Pryor playing with equal commitment.

PIANO MUSIC

The Almond tree; Decorations; Merry Andrew; Preludes: (The undertone; Obsession; The Holy Boy; Fire of spring); Rhapsody; Sonata in E min.; Summer evening; The Towing-path.
*** Chandos Dig. CHAN 9056 [id.]. Eric Parkin.

Amberley Wild Woods; Ballad; The darkened valley; Equinox; For remembrance; Greenways; In those days; Leaves from a child's sketchbook; London pieces; 2 Pieces; Prelude in E flat; Sonatina.
*** Chandos Dig. CHAN 9140 [id.]. Eric Parkin.

Ballade of London nights; Columbine; Month's mind; On a birthday morning; 3 Pastels; 2 Pieces (February's child; Aubade); 2 Pieces (April; Bergomask); Sarnia; A Sea idyll; Soliloquy; Spring will not wait.
*** Chandos Dig. CHAN 9250 [id.]. Eric Parkin.

Eric Parkin has now completed another survey on Chandos. It goes without saying that he is completely inside Ireland's idiom and he brings both dedication and sympathy to this repertoire. Moreover the sound is clean, well-rounded and pleasing.

April; The darkened valley; Green Ways (The cherry tree; Cypress; The palm and May); In those days (Daydream; Meridian); London pieces (Chelsea Reach; Ragamuffin; Soho forenoons); 3 Pastels (A Grecian lad; The boy bishop; Puck's birthday); Preludes (The undertone; Obsession; The holy boy; Fire of spring); A Sea idyll; Summer evening; The towing path.
(Y/B) (B) **(*) CfP Dig. CD-CFP 4674; *TC-CFP 4674*. Desmond Wright.

Though Eric Parkin has over the years recorded a far wider range of Ireland's piano music, this selection on CfP brings together most of the favourites, like *Ragamuffin* from the *London pieces* and *The holy boy*, hauntingly lyrical, the third of the four *Preludes*. *The darkened valley* and *The towing path*, too, show Ireland at his most tenderly expressive. Though Desmond Wright is not always gentle enough in his treatment, these are fresh, responsive performances which gather together some of the most appealing English piano music written this century, too long neglected.

Isaac, Heinrich (c. 1450–1517)

Missa de Apostolis. Motets: *Optime pastor; Tota pulchra es; Regina caeli laetare; Resurrexi et adhuc tecum sum; Virgo prudentissima.*
*** Gimell Dig. CDGIM 023; *1585T23* [id.]. Tallis Scholars, Peter Phillips.

The German contemporary of Josquin des Pres, Heinrich Isaac has not until recently been widely appreciated. The Mass setting is glorious, culminating in an ethereal version of *Agnus Dei*, flawlessly sung by the Tallis Scholars. Among the many striking passages is the opening of the six-part setting of *Virgo prudentissima* for two upper voices only, with women's rather than boys' voices all the more appropriate with such a text. Ideally balanced recording.

Ives, Charles (1874–1954)

Calcium light night; Country band march; Largo cantabile: Hymn; 3 Places in New England; Postlude in F; 4 Ragtime dances; Set for theatre orchestra; Yale–Princeton football game.
*** Koch Dig. 37025-2 [id.]. O New England, Sinclair.

This selection of shorter Ives pieces makes an ideal introduction for anyone wanting just to sample the work of this wild, often maddening, but always intriguing composer. Excellent performances and recording.

Central Park in the dark; New England Holidays symphony; The unanswered question (original and revised versions).
*** Sony Dig. MK 42381 [id.]. Chicago Symphony Ch. & O, Tilson Thomas.

The *New England Holidays symphony* comprises four fine Ives pieces normally heard separately. The performance from Michael Tilson Thomas and his Chicago forces is in every way superb, while the wide-ranging CBS recording provides admirable atmosphere. This is now among the most impressive Ives records in the catalogue.

Robert Browning overture.
(N) *** EMI Dig. CDM5 55254-2. Bamberg SO, Igor Metzmacher – HARTMANN: *Symphony No. 3.*
    ***

Ives aficionados are unlikely to want this disc just for the sake of the *Robert Browning overture.* However, those investigating the Hartmann *Symphony* with which it is coupled are unlikely to be disappointed with this performance. Its contours seem smoother and its textures finer and more polished than one recalls from earlier accounts, but it is not beautified. Recommended.

Symphony No. 1 in D min.
*** Chandos Dig. CHAN 9053 [id.]. Detroit SO, Järvi – BARBER: *Essays 1–3.* ***

There is a certain freshness about the melodic invention of the *First Symphony* that is appealing; the idiom is polite and generally conservative with Dvořák as perhaps the strongest influence, but there are already glimpses of iconoclasm in the modulatory shifts. Neeme Järvi gives a very persuasive account of it and there is a fresh and unforced virtuosity from the Detroit orchestra. Excellent, very natural recorded sound, excellently balanced.

Symphonies Nos. 1; 4.
*** Sony Dig. SK 44939 [id.]. Chicago SO, Michael Tilson Thomas.

Tilson Thomas's strong and brilliant Chicago performances make a generous and apt coupling, the more valuable for providing first recordings of the revised editions of the composer's tangled scores, with bright, well-detailed sound and superb playing.

Symphony No. 1 in D min.; Orchestral set No. 2. Robert Browning overture; The unanswered question.
(N) (BB) **(*) RCA Navigator 74321 29246-2. Chicago SO, Morton Gould.

This very first recording of the *First Symphony*, an immediately attractive work, was made in 1965; it has that special quality of freshness almost always found in recording premières, with the mercurial spirit of Ives emerging every so often, so that the result is very enjoyable indeed. The most striking piece in the *Orchestral set No. 2* is the third – with a title too long to quote. With typical Ivesian vividness it tells of an incident on the subway in New York, when the news of the sinking of the *Lusitania* shocked everyone. Someone started singing '*In the sweet by and by*', and gradually the whole crowd on the station platform took the song up – an incident that naturally chimed with Ives's feeling for confused, welling sound. The *Robert Browning overture* (at 20 minutes) has some good ideas but rather outstays its welcome, and the other two pieces of the *Orchestral set* are attractive without achieving quite the degree of sharp memorability which marks both the third and *The unanswered question*, one of the composer's most beautiful and imaginative pieces. Gould's performances are sympathetic and very well played, but they just lack the intensity that Bernstein and others brought to them, although they are still pretty magnetic. Indeed this bargain-basement CD is worth having for the symphony alone, and the mid-1960s recordings are basically warm and atmospheric, even if the violins are very brightly lit, and even fierce at times. But if you are a newcomer to Ives, this is a good (and inexpensive) place to start.

Symphony No. 2.
(N) *** Chandos Dig. CHAN 9390-2. Detroit SO, Järvi – CRESTON: *Symphony No. 2.* ***

Ives' admirers will in all probability have one of the earlier versions of this symphony by Bernstein, Slatkin or Tilson Thomas, but newcomers to the repertoire should consider the claims of this newcomer.

It is a very good performance and has the great advantage of also offering Neeme Järvi's account of Paul Creston's vital and invigorating *Second Symphony*.

Symphony No. 2; Central Park in the dark; The gong on the hook and ladder; Hallowe'en; Hymn for strings; Tone roads No. 1; The unanswered question.
*** DG Dig. 429 220-2 [id.]. NYPO, Bernstein.

Bernstein's disc brings one of the richest offerings of Ives yet put on record, offering the *Symphony No. 2* plus six shorter orchestral pieces. They include two of his very finest, *Central Park in the dark* and *The unanswered question*, both characteristically quirky but deeply poetic too. The extra tensions and expressiveness of live performance here heighten the impact of each of the works. The difficult acoustic of Avery Fisher Hall in New York has rarely sounded more sympathetic on record.

Symphonies Nos. 2; 3 (The Camp meeting).
**(*) Sony Dig. SK 46440 [id.]. Concg. O, Michael Tilson Thomas.

Tilson Thomas's performances may not have the fervour of a Bernstein in this music – perhaps reflecting the fact that this is not an American orchestra – but they are strong and direct, and in No. 3 the revised edition is used on record for the first time.

Symphonies Nos. 2; 3 (The Camp Meeting); (i) Central Park in the dark.
(M) **(*) Sony SMK 47568 [id.]. NYPO, Bernstein; (i) with Seiji Ozawa; Maurice Peress.

Bernstein has re-recorded this music more recently for DG, but these earlier recordings from the 1960s have characteristic conviction and intensity and there is nothing wrong with the remastered sound which is full and atmospheric, if closely balanced. But the dynamics of the playing convey the fullest range of emotion. *Central Park in the dark* is wildly individual in its evocation. The playing of the New York Philharmonic, whether under Bernstein or his younger assistants, is of high quality.

Symphony No. 3 (The camp meeting).
*** Argo 417 818-2 [id.]. ASMF, Marriner – BARBER: *Adagio;* COPLAND: *Quiet City;* COWELL: *Hymn;* CRESTON: *Rumor.* ***
*** Pro Arte Dig. CDD 140 [id.]. St Paul CO, Russell Davies – COPLAND: *Appalachian spring* etc. ***

Symphony No. 3; (i) Orchestral set No. 2.
*** Sony Dig. MK 37823 [id.]. Concg. O, Tilson Thomas; (i) with Concg. Ch.

Tilson Thomas's version of Ives's most approachable symphony is the first to use the new critical edition, prepared with reference to newly available Ives manuscripts. The *Second Orchestral set*, with its three substantial atmosphere pieces, brings performances of a comparable sharpness. First-rate recording to match the fine performances.

Russell Davies does not use the new edition of Ives's score; nevertheless, he gives a fine account of this gentlest of Ives's symphonies, with its overtones of hymn singing and revivalist meetings, and the beauty of the piece still comes over strongly.

Marriner's account is first rate in every way. It does not have the advantage of a digital master, but the 1976 analogue recording has slightly sharper detail in this remastered format.

Symphony No. 3; 3 Places in New England.
(M) *** Mercury 432 755-2 [id.]. Eastman-Rochester O, Howard Hanson – SCHUMAN: *New England triptych* ***; MENNIN: *Symphony No. 5.* **(*)

Symphony No. 3; 3 Places in New England; Set No. 1; A Set of pieces; The unanswered question.
(Y/B) *** DG Dig. 439 869-2 [id.]. Orpheus CO.

The Orpheus Chamber Orchestra never cease to amaze and their playing here is of their usual stunning order of accomplishment and artistry. Their account of the *Third Symphony* is as good as any in the catalogue, and the same goes for their evocative and imaginative accounts of the companion pieces.

Ives's quixotic genius is at its most individual in the *Three places in New England*. Both works are most understandingly presented on Mercury under Howard Hanson, who is equally at home in the folksy imagery of the *Third Symphony*. The acoustics of the Eastman Theatre are less than ideally expansive, but the 1957 recording is remarkably full-bodied and vivid.

(i) *Symphony No. 4; Robert Browning Overture;* (ii) Songs: *An Election, Lincoln the great commoner, Majority, They are There!*
(M) *** Sony MPK 46726 [id.]. (i) NY Schola Cantorum; (ii) Gregg Smith Singers; American SO, Stokowski.

The (originally 1965) recording of the *Fourth Symphony*, made at the same period as the belated première of the work, brings a stunning performance, with sound that is still amazingly full and vivid. Stokowski also brings out the often aggressive vigour of the *Robert Browning Overture*. The choral songs with orchestra provide an attractive makeweight.

Variations on America.
** Teldec/Warner Dig. 9031 74007-2 [id.]. NYPO, Masur – BRAHMS: *Variations on a theme of Haydn;* REGER: *Variations and fugue on a theme of Mozart.* **

Ives' *Variations on America* are the bonus in this all-variations programme, given a musicianly and well-groomed performance without any exaggeration, but ideally calling for more flamboyance.

String quartets Nos. 1–2.
*** DG Dig. 435 864-2 [id.]. Emerson Qt – BARBER: *Quartet.* **(*)

The *First* of Ives' *String quartets* comes from the composer's early twenties and makes liberal use of hymn-tunes in the first movement fugue. The *Second* is made of sterner stuff and its high norm of dissonance prompts one's thoughts to turn to the Bartók of the *Third* and *Fourth quartets*. It is undeniably an extraordinary musical document and is well worth study. The Emerson Quartet give it a performance of stunning efficiency and brilliance. Ensemble is impeccable, the tone carefully nourished and honed, with every detail of dynamic meticulously calculated and in place. Full-blooded and very present DG recording.

Songs: *Autumn; Berceuse; The cage; Charlie Rutlage; Down East; Dreams; Evening; The greatest man; The Housatonic at Stockbridge; Immortality; Like a sick eagle; Maple leaves; Memories: 1, 2, 3; On the counter; Romanzo di Central Park; The see'r; Serenity; The side-show; Slow march; Slugging a vampire; Songs my mother taught me; Spring song; The things our fathers loved; Tom sails away; Two little flowers.*
*** Etcetera Dig. KTC 1020 [id.]. Roberta Alexander, Tan Crone.

Roberta Alexander presents her excellent and illuminating choice of Ives songs in chronological order, starting with one written when Ives was only fourteen, *Slow march*, already predicting developments ahead. Sweet, nostalgic songs predominate, but the singer punctuates them with leaner, sharper inspirations. Her manner is not always quite tough enough in those, but this is characterful singing from an exceptionally rich and attractive voice. Tan Crone is the understanding accompanist, and the recording is first rate.

Jacob, Gordon (1895–1987)

Mini-concerto for clarinet and string orchestra.
*** Hyperion CDA 66031 [id.]. Thea King, NW CO of Seattle, Alun Francis – COOKE; RAWSTHORNE: *Concertos.* ***

Gordon Jacob in his eighties responded to an earlier recording of his music by Thea King by writing this miniature concerto for her, totally charming in its compactness, with not a note too many. Thea King is the most persuasive of dedicatees, splendidly accompanied by the orchestra from Seattle and treated to first-rate 1982 analogue sound, splendidly transferred.

William Byrd suite.
(M) *** Mercury 432 009-2 [id.]. Eastman Wind Ens., Fennell – BENNETT: *Symphonic songs* ***; HOLST: *Hammersmith* ***; WALTON: *Crown Imperial.* *** ✿

Gordon Jacob's arrangement of the music of Byrd is audaciously anachronistic, but it is very entertaining when played with such flair. The recording is up to the usual high Mercury standard in this repertoire.

Divertimento for harmonica and string quartet.
*** Chandos Dig. CHAN 8802 [id.]. Tommy Reilly, Hindar Qt – MOODY: *Quintet; Suite.* ***

Gordon Jacob's set of eight sharply characterized miniatures shows the composer at his most engagingly imaginative and the performances are deliciously piquant in colour and feeling. The recording could hardly be more successful.

Oboe quartet.
*** Chandos Dig. CHAN 8392 [id.]. Francis, English Qt – BAX: *Quintet;* HOLST: *Air and variations* etc.; MOERAN: *Fantasy quartet.* ***

Gordon Jacob's *Oboe quartet* is well crafted and entertaining, particularly the vivacious final Rondo. The performance could hardly be bettered, and the recording is excellent too.

Janáček, Leoš (1854–1928)

Adagio for orchestra; Ballad of Blaník; Cossack dance; (i) *Danube Symphony. The Fiddler's child* (ballad); *Idyll for strings; Jealousy overture; Lachian dances;* (ii) *The Pilgrimage of the soul (Violin concerto);* (iii) *Schluck und Jau* (incidental music): excerpts: *Andante & Allegretto. Serbian Kolo. Sinfonietta; Suite, Op. 3; Suite for strings; Taras Bulba* (rhapsody).
*** Sup. Dig. 11 1834-2 (3) [id.]. Brno State PO, František Jílek, with (i) Karolína Dvořáková; (ii) Ivan Zenatý; (i; iii) Jiří Beneš.

(i) *The Ballad of Blaník;* (ii) *Sinfonietta; Taras Bulba.*
(N) (M) **(*) BBC Radio Classics 15656 91352 [id.]. BBC SO, cond. (i) Mackerras; (ii) Rozhdestvensky
– MARTINU: *Double concerto.* **(*)

Rozhdestvensky gets excellent results from the BBC Symphony Orchestra in the *Sinfonietta* and *Taras Bulba*, the former recorded in the Festival Hall and the latter at a Promenade Concert, both in 1981. Rozhdestvensky seems to have a keen sympathy for the composer and has a good feel for the music's drama and atmosphere. Mackerras's account of the less familiar *Ballad of Blaník* with the same forces, which comes from a Prom two years earlier, is predictably idiomatic. There are better-recorded rivals but as performances these are more than just acceptable. They give pleasure and those for whom state-of-the-art recorded sound is not a primary consideration will find these broadcasts well worth acquiring.

(i) *Danube Symphony. Sinfonietta;* (ii) *The Pilgrimage of the soul (Violin concerto);* (iii) *Schluck und Jau.*
*** Sup. Dig. 11 1422-2 [id.]. Brno State PO, František Jílek, with (i) Karolina Dvořáková; (ii) Ivan Zenatý; (i; iii) Jiří Beneš.

Jílek's performance of the *Sinfonietta* can hold its own with the best in terms of atmosphere and authority, though the recording is admittedly not in the demonstration bracket. The *Danube Symphony* was completed by Osvald Chlubna. This new version, prepared by the scholars Leoš Faltus and Miloš Stědrů, contains only Janáček's text. There is some invention of great imagination here as, indeed, there is in the *Violin concerto (The Pilgrimage of the soul).* Ivan Zenatý is an aristocrat of the violin and his performance is no less poignant than the Teldec alternative by Thomas Zehetmair. The incidental music to *Schluck und Jau* was reconstructed in the 1970s by Jarmil Burghauser and is a two-movement piece about as long as the *Violin concerto* and likewise full of characteristic ideas. Of the other two discs, the first offering the *Lachian dances*, the early *Suite for strings* and its seven-movement companion, the *Idyll*, is well filled, and the other disc brings such valuable scores as *Blaník, The Fiddler's Child* and *Taras Bulba.* Good, idiomatic performances and very good, though not demonstration-quality recordings. The Brno studios are less reverberant than the House of the Artists in Prague, and the results here are much more than just agreeable.

Capriccio for piano left-hand and wind; Concertino for piano and seven instruments.
*** RCA Dig. RD 60781 [60781-2]. Rudolf Firkušný, Czech PO, Václav Neumann – DVORAK: *Piano concerto in G min.* ***

Firkušný himself is now older than Janáček was when he wrote these remarkable pieces, but he conveys a youthful fire which seems to burn almost as brightly as the earlier recordings he made in the 1950s and 1970s. A thoroughly worthwhile coupling with Dvořák.

(i) *Capriccio for piano and wind; Concertino for piano and chamber ensemble;* (ii) *Lachian dances;* (iii) *Sinfonietta;* (iv) *Suite for string orchestra;* (iii) *Taras Bulba;* (v) *Mládí* (suite for wind).
(N) (B) *** Decca Double Analogue/Dig. 448 255-2 (2) [id.]. (i) Paul Crossley, L. Sinf., David Atherton; (ii) LPO, Huybrechts; (iii) VPO, Mackerras; (iv) LAPO, Marriner; (v) Bell, Craxton, Pay, Harris, Gatt, Eastop.

This Double Decca offers much essential Janáček in absolutely first-class performances and recordings. Paul Crossley is the impressive soloist in the *Capriccio* and the *Concertino*, performances that can be put alongside those of Firkušný – and no praise can be higher. This account of *Mládí* is among the finest available; the work's youthful sparkle comes across to excellent effect here, while the late-1970s analogue sound is very truthful and well balanced. Mackerras's VPO coupling of the *Sinfonietta* and *Taras Bulba* is digital (1980). The massed brass of the *Sinfonietta* has tremendous bite and brilliance as well as characteristic Viennese ripeness. *Taras Bulba* is also given more weight and body than usual, the often savage dance-rhythms presented with great energy. The music of the *Lachian dances*, while vividly scored, is on a rather lower level of inspiration, but the performance here under the Belgian conductor, François Huybrechts, is highly idiomatic and effective, and he is helped by fine playing from the LPO and more high-quality Decca sound – using the Kingsway Hall to good effect. The *Suite for string orchestra* was Marriner's first recording with the Los Angeles Chamber Orchestra, made in England during the orchestra's 1974 tour. The recording site was St John's, Smith Square, and the sound is characteristically ripe. The *Suite* is an early and not entirely mature piece but, when played as committedly as it is here, its attractions are readily perceived, and it certainly does not want character.

(i) *Concertino for piano and seven instruments;* (ii) *Sinfonietta; Taras Bulba.*
(B) *** DG 439 437-2 [id.]. (i) Rudolf Firkušný (Bav. RSO (members)); (ii) Bav. RSO; Kubelik.

A quite outstanding bargain triptych that would make a worthwhile addition to any collection, large or small. Kubelik has a special feeling for this repertoire and partners Rudolf Firkušný in a thoroughly idiomatic account of the *Concertino*, with the dialogue between keyboard and sparsely scored accompaniment both plangent and witty. *Taras Bulba* with its unpleasant scenario of death and torture is powerfully evoked, with a discerning balance between passion and subtlety. The organ part is integrated into the texture most delicately in the first section, yet adds grandiloquence to the work's triumphant apotheosis, with its vision of a triumphant Cossack future. Virtuoso playing from the Bavarian orchestra throughout, with much excitement generated in the last two sections. The orchestra is hardly less impressive in the *Sinfonietta* (and particularly so in the central movements), while at the opening and close of the work the spacious acoustic of the Munich Herculessaal is especially suited to the massed brass effects. The vintage (1970) recording has been superbly remastered and sounds amazingly fresh.

Capriccio (for piano left hand & chamber ensemble); *Concertino* (for piano & chamber orchestra); *Mládí (Youth)* for wind sextet; *March of the Blue Boys* for piccolo and piano; (i) *Nursery rhymes (Říkadla)* for chamber choir & chamber ensemble.
(N) *** Chandos Dig. CHAN 9399 [id.]. Berman, Netherlands Wind Ens., Thierry Fischer; (i) with Prague Music Ac. Ch.

The Chandos issue is a valuable addition to the Janáček discography. All these pieces come from his last years (1924–8) and, as well as *Mládí*, include the *March of the Blue Boys*, on which Janáček drew for inspiration in the *vivace* third movement. Though Firkušný remains in a class of his own, Boris Berman is a good soloist in both the *Concertino* and *Capriccio*. The astonishing *Říkadla* are given with great character by the Netherlands Wind Ensemble and the Prague Academy Choir. Thierry Fischer confirms the positive impression he made in his Frank Martin recording for DG: the playing throughout is full of life and sensitivity. Vibrant recorded sound, rather bright and forward (that is meant as a compliment), and every detail tells.

Violin concerto (Pilgrimage of the soul) (reconstructed Faltus & Stědrů).
(Y/B) *** Teldec/Warner Dig. 4509 97449-2 [id.]. Zehetmair, Philh. O, Holliger – HARTMANN: *Concerto funèbre;* BERG: *Violin concerto.* ***

In his last year Janáček worked on his opera, *From the House of the Dead*, based on Dostoevsky, the autograph score of which contains sketches for a violin concerto he had planned to call *Pilgrimage of the soul*. He used some of its ideas in the overture to the opera, but the concerto remained in fragmentary form. On his death, his pupil, Břetislav Bakala, who had seen the opera through the press, prepared a performing version of the piece. The present version, the work of Leoš Faltus and Miloš Stědrů, revived interest in the piece when it was premièred in 1988, and there are two rival accounts currently on the market (from Josef Suk on Supraphon and Christian Tetzlaff on Virgin). This is highly original music, with some delightful lyrical ideas, imaginatively scored, albeit also with moments of top-heavy orchestral writing, searing in its intensity – particularly as played here by Thomas Zehetmair and the Philharmonia under Heinz Holliger. Excellent recorded sound. This is a most rewarding triptych, well worth exploring at mid-price.

The Fiddler's child (ballad for orchestra); *Jealousy: overture; Taras Bulba; The Cunning little vixen* (suite).
*** Chandos Dig. CHAN 9080 [id.]. Czech PO, Bělohlávek.

Bělohlávek is perhaps less at home in *Taras Bulba* than in the nature mysticism of the suite from *Cunning little vixen* or the pathos of *The Fiddler's child*. There are more dramatic and fiery accounts of *Taras*, but the beauty of the orchestral playing and the opulence and detail of the recording still just earn it a three-star rating.

Sinfonietta.
*** EMI Dig. CDC7 47504-2 [id.]. Philh. O, Rattle – *Glagolitic Mass.* ***
(Y/B) (M) *** EMI Dig. CDM7 64740-2 [id.]. Philh. O, Rattle – HOLST: *Planets.* **(*)
(Y/B) (M) *** DG Dig. 445 501-2 [id.]. BPO, Abbado – BARTOK: *The Miraculous Mandarin* etc. ***
(N) (M) *** Decca 448 579-2 [id.]. LSO, Abbado – HINDEMITH: *Symphonic metamorphoses;* PROKOFIEV: *Symphony No. 3.* ***

*** Chandos Dig. CHAN 8897 [id.]. Czech PO, Bělohlávek – MARTINU: *Symphony No. 6;* SUK:
Scherzo. ***

(Y/B) *** Sony Dig. SK 47182 [id.]. LSO, Tilson Thomas – *Glagolitic Mass.* ***

(M) *** DG 437 254-2 [id.]. Bav. RSO, Kubelik – SMETANA: *Symphonic poems.* ***

(M) **(*) Telarc CD 82010 [id.]. LAPO, André Previn – BARTOK: *Concerto for orchestra.* **(*)

Sinfonietta; Lachian dances; Taras Bulba.

(BB) *** Naxos Dig. 8.550411 [id.]. Slovak RSO (Bratislava), Ondrej Lenárd.

(i) *Sinfonietta;* (ii) *Taras Bulba;* (iii) *The cunning little vixen:* suite.

(N) (BB) **(*) RCA Navigator 74321 29251-2. (i) USSR RSO, Bolshoi Theatre Brass O; (ii) USSR
MoC SO; (iiii) Leningrad PO; Rozhdestvensky.

Rattle gets an altogether first-class response from the orchestra and truthful recorded sound from the
EMI engineers; many collectors may find the EMI sound more pleasing. Rattle's coupling with the
Glagolitic Mass is very attractive indeed. It is also available at medium price with a less successful Holst
coupling.

Abbado's DG recording was made in 1987, some two decades after his admirable Decca version with
the LSO. Now he has the advantage of digital recording and the Berlin Philharmonic Orchestra on
splendid form. The Jesus-Christus Kirche provides a superbly spacious sonority for the brass. The
opening of the Berlin performance brings a tautening of the pace, but the interpretation is not greatly
changed and the subtleties of colour are not diminished by the more robust body of the newer version.

In his earlier, Decca recording Abbado gives a splendid account of the *Sinfonietta* and evokes a highly
sympathetic response from the LSO. His acute sensitivity to dynamic nuances and his care for detail are
felt in every bar. The recording balance, too, allows the subtlest of colours to register while still having
plenty of impact.

Jiři Bělohlávek's exultant and imaginative account of the *Sinfonietta* is one of the best currently on offer
and is coupled with an outstanding version of Martinů's *Sixth Symphony*; the recording, made in the
Smetana Hall, Prague, is impressive.

A strong, bold and brassy performance from Tilson Thomas, with the LSO at their virtuoso best,
helped by very full recorded sound, bright as well as weighty. However, fine though this is, it would not
be preferable to Rattle or to Abbado.

On Naxos we have the normal LP coupling of the *Sinfonietta* and *Taras Bulba*, but with the *Lachian
dances* thrown in for good measure, all played by musicians steeped in the Janáček tradition – and all at
a very modest cost. These are excellent performances and well worth the money involved; the recording,
made in a fairly resonant studio, is natural and free from any artificially spotlit balance.

The Bavarian orchestra is in virtuoso form and there is some fine playing here and much vitality. The
recording was made in the Hercules Hall in Munich which is very suited to Janáček's plangent brass
sonorities. Kubelik's performance makes an enjoyably vibrant coupling for the Smetana symphonic
poems, but this performance is also included in an even more attractive bargain collection – see above.

The amiability of Janáček's colourful and brassy work is what dominates Previn's performance rather
than any more dramatic qualities. It matches his relaxed view of the Bartók *Concerto for orchestra*,
which comes as a unique coupling. The Los Angeles Philharmonic has never been recorded with a
warmer and more realistic bloom than here by Jack Renner of Telarc in Royce Hall, UCLA. However,
those looking for more bite and brilliance in this work will probably be happier with either the splendidly vital Mackerras recording, coupled with *Taras Bulba*, or the Rattle version.

The very modestly priced Navigator triptych draws on three different Russian orchestras, all of which
are thoroughly at home in Janáček's special sound-world. In the *Sinfonietta* the Bolshoi brass (with
Slavonic vibrato) are suitably pungent, and especially arresting at the close. The inner movements are
strongly characterized by Rozhdestvensky, and he is equally impressive in the vibrantly atmospheric
account of *Taras Bulba*. This is a live, digital recording from 1985; the others are from 1965 and 1976
respectively, and all offer sound which is both vivid and atmospheric. The suite from *The cunning little
vixen* consists of two 'interludes', each about nine minutes in length. They are beautifully played at
another live concert, but the audience indicates its presence only at the beginning and end. Excellent
value.

Suite for string orchestra.

(Y/B) (B) *** Discover Dig. DICD 920234 [id.]. Virtuosi di Praga, Vlček – SUK: *Serenade for strings* etc.
***

The expanded Virtuosi di Praga give an appropriately ardent and certainly a bravura account of
Janáček's six-movement *Suite for string orchestra*, an early work (1893) yet one full of melodic diversity
and individuality. The recording shows this group of seventeen players (including the leader/director,

Oldřich Vlček) as possessing a vividly full sonority, yet they do not miss the work's more subtle touches, and this inexpensive disc is a welcome addition to the catalogue.

CHAMBER MUSIC

(i; iii) *Allegro; Dumka; Romance; Sonata* (for violin and piano); (ii; iii) *Pohádka (Fairy tale); Presto* (for cello and piano); (iii) (Piano) *In the mists; 3 Moravian dances; On an overgrown path, Series I–II; Paralipomena; Reminiscence; Piano sonata in E flat min. (I. X. 1905); Theme and variations (Zdenka's variations).*
(Y/B) ** BIS Dig. CD 663/664 [id.]. (i) Ulf Wallin; (ii) Mats Rondin; (iii) Roland Pöntinen.

This excellent collection ranges from the *Romance* for violin and piano from the late 1870s, to the *Reminiscence* for piano, written in the last year of his life. Pöntinen is an unfailingly intelligent player. Ulf Wallin proves a strong yet sensitive advocate of the *Violin Sonata*, and the cellist Mats Rondin is no less admirable in the *Pohádka (Fairy tale)* and the *Presto* for cello and piano. Those wanting the set primarily for the piano music would be better served by either of the Firkušný sets or the Andsnes recital (see below), but readers wanting the whole collection may rest assured that both playing and recording are of a generally high standard.

(i; ii) *Concertino;* (ii) *Mládi;* (i) *In the mists.*
(Y/B) (M) **(*) EMI CDM5 65304-2 [id.]. (i) Lamar Crowson; (ii) Melos Ens. – NIELSEN: *Wind quintet.* ***

The Melos Ensemble give a very characterful account of *Mládi*, a remarkable evocation of youth. The analogue recording, made in the late 1960s, is very good indeed, as it is in the *Concertino*. Lamar Crowson is completely inside the idiom here and in sensitivity and imagination is second to none. Likewise *In the mists* is poetic and unfailingly perceptive and withstands comparison with both Firkušný, Andsnes and others, save for one reservation concerning the recording: the piano is not in ideal condition and there could be more space round the sound. This does not apply in the *Concertino*, which sounds suitably vibrant.

String quartet No. 1 (Kreutzer sonata).
*** RCA Dig. 09026 61816-2 [id.]. Vogler Qt – DEBUSSY; SHOSTAKOVICH: *Quartets.* ***

To miss this performance by the Vogler Quartet would be a pity. Taken on its own merits, it is very impressive: intelligent and alive, and well recorded too.

String quartet No. 1 (Kreutzer sonata).
(N) *** Testament SBT 1074 [id.]. Smetana Qt – DVORAK: *Piano quintet* etc. ***

String quartet No. 2 (Intimate letters).
(N) *** Testament SBT 1075 [id.]. Smetana Qt – DVORAK: *String quartet No. 14* etc. ***

String quartets Nos. 1 (Kreutzer); 2 (Intimate letters).
*** ASV Dig. CDDCA 749 [id.]. Lindsay Qt (with DVORAK: *Cypresses* ***).
(N) *** RCA Dig. 09026 68286-2 (3) [id.]. Tokyo Qt – BARTOK: *Quartets Nos. 1–6.* ***
**(*)* HM Dig. HMC 901380 [id.]. Melos Qt.
(N) ** EMI Dig. CDC5 55457-2 [id.]. Alban Berg Qt.

(i) *String quartets Nos. 1–2;* (ii) *Mládi: suite for wind sextet.*
**(*) Koch/Panton 11203-2 [id.]. (i) Vlach Qt; (ii) Foerster Wind Quintet, Josef Horák.

(i) *String quartets Nos. 1–2;* (ii) *On an overgrown path: suite No. 1.*
*** Calliope Dig. CAL 9699 [id.]. (i) Talich Qt; (ii) Radoslav Kvapil.

Pride of place must go to the Talich Quartet on Calliope, not because their recording is the best – it is by no means as vivid as the ASV – but because of their extraordinary qualities of insight. They play the *Intimate letters* as if its utterances came from a world so private that it must be approached with great care. The disc's value is much enhanced by a fill-up in the form of the *First suite, On an overgrown path*. Radoslav Kvapil is thoroughly inside this repertoire.

The Lindsays on ASV are eminently competitive and have the right blend of sensitivity and intensity. Theirs must certainly rank very highly among current recommendations. It is played with the same concentration and sensitivity they bring to all they do, and recorded with great naturalness.

The Tokyo offer both quartets as an appetizer to their Bartók cycle, accommodating them on the first CD before the first Bartók *Quartet*. There is plenty of fire and passion, and they seem fully attuned to Janáček's sensibility. Choice in this repertoire must be dictated by preferred couplings.

These days the two Janáček *Quartets* alone do not really represent the good value for money they represented in the days of LP. The Melos Quartet offer nothing in addition to the two *Quartets*, but theirs are performances of considerable character and fire and, though the playing-time is ungenerous and the recording a bit fierce, they are worth consideration. All the same, the Koch/Panton coupling with the Vlach Quartet, recorded in 1969, and a 1970 version of *Mladi* should not automatically be dismissed on grounds of age. The performances are very idiomatic and appealing, the recording far from inferior; and this record will give pleasure.

The Alban Berg coupling was made at public performances in the Mozartsaal and the Konzerthaus in Vienna in 1993. They play with enormous and at times almost frenzied intensity and are not frightened to produce rough, gutsy sound. Indeed that impression is possibly enhanced by the fierce, strident recording. Heard immediately after the Smetana Quartet's 1960s stereo recordings, one wonders whether the art of recording has progressed. Although not a primary factor, the absence of a fill-up will disincline some collectors from pursuing this disc. To offer a 43½-minute CD at premium price currently seems almost unacceptable; moreover there are better rivals.

Violin sonata.
(N) *** Virgin/EMI Dig. VC5 45122-2. Christian Tetzlaff, Leif Ove Andsnes – DEBUSSY: *Sonata;* NIELSEN: *Sonata No. 2;* RAVEL: *Sonata.* ***
(*) DG Dig. 427 351-2 [id.]. Gidon Kremer, Martha Argerich – BARTOK: *Sonata No. 1;* MESSIAEN: *Theme and variations.* *

Christian Tetzlaff and Leif Ove Andsnes play with commitment and dedication. Theirs is an eloquent – indeed at times inspired – performance, and they are accorded excellent recording.

The *Sonata* is also played with great imaginative intensity and power by Gidon Kremer and Martha Argerich, though it is less selfless here than with on Tetzlaff and Andsnes on Virgin: there is some expressive exaggeration. Excellent DG recording.

Along an overgrown path: Suite No. 1; In the mists; Piano sonata (I.X.1905).
*** Virgin/EMI Dig. VC7 59639-2 [id.]. Leif Ove Andsnes.

Leif Ove Andsnes gives us a very well-thought-out and imaginatively realized recital, including a highly sensitive account of *In the mists*, which is second to none in conveying the pervasive melancholy and evocative atmosphere of these pieces. This is every bit as telling as Mikhail Rudy's EMI account, and beautifully recorded.

Piano sonata (1.X.1905); In the mists; 3 Moravian dances; On an overgrown path: Books 1 & 2; A recollection.
*** EMI Dig. CDC7 54094-2 [id.]. Mikhail Rudy.

Piano sonata (1.X.1905); In the mists; On the overgrown path, Book 2; A recollection; Theme & variations.
(M) *** DG 429 857-2 [id.]. Rudolf Firkušný.

Rudolf Firkušný recorded these pieces for DG in the early 1970s and he produces seamless legato lines, hammerless tone and rapt atmosphere. Given its competitive price, many collectors will opt for this anthology, which still sounds very good and also includes the *Zdenka Theme and variations*.

Mikhail Rudy proves a perceptive and sympathetic guide in this music. His is a fine account of the *Sonata*, and he succeeds in penetrating the world of the *Overgrown path* miniatures to perfection. He conveys their acute sense of melancholy and their improvisatory character with distinction, and the recorded sound is very natural.

VOCAL MUSIC

Coz ta nase bríza (Our birch tree); Elegie na smrt dcery Olgy (Elegy on the death of daughter Olga); Hradcanske písnicky (Song of Hradcany); Holubicka (The dove); Kacena divoká (The wild duck); Kantor Halfar (Schoolmaster Halfar); Potulný silenec (The wondering madman); Ríkadla (Nursery rhymes); Vlci stopa (The wolf's trail).
(N) ***Ph. Dig. 442 534-2 [id.]. Netherlands Chamber Ch., Schoenberg Ens., Reinbert De Leeuw.

While the operas have taken hold in the repertoire, Janáček's choral music, which is extensive, remains to make headway outside his native country. These works contain much that is most deeply characteristic and individual in the Janáček style. They cover a wide range from such straightforward partsongs as *Our birch tree* or *The Dove* to the ingenious, dazzling *Ríkadla* ('Nursery rhymes') of his last years. The affecting *Elegy on the death of daughter Olga* begins as if we are in the middle of *On an overgrown path* and is as every bit as subtle. Nor do these pieces lose their capacity to surprise. The cruel vocal writing sometimes strains the generally perfect intonation of the Netherlands Chamber Choir (as in *The weep-*

ing fountain) but they and members of the Schoenberg Ensemble under Reinbert De Leeuw produce cultured, well-blended results, and the Philips recording is impressive in its clarity and presence. In *Ríkadla* this must yield in terms of character and flair to the Czech choir and to their countrymen, the Netherlands Wind Ensemble. It is possible to imagine wilder and more passionate performances, particularly from Moravian choirs, but in an area of the repertoire which is not generously served this deserves a strong recommendation.

Glagolitic Mass (original version, ed. Wingfield).
(Y/B) *** Chandos Dig. CHAN 9310[id.]. Kiberg, Stene, Svensson, Cold, Danish Nat. R. Ch. & SO, Mackerras – KODALY: *Psalmus hungaricus*. ***

The scholar, Paul Wingfield, has managed to reconstruct Janáček's original score, before it was simplified for the first inadequate performers, and without the unauthorized amendments made in the published score after the composer's death. The added rhythmic complexities of this version, as interpreted idiomatically by Mackerras, often adopting speeds faster than usual, encourage an apt wildness which brings an exuberant, carefree quality to writing which here, more than ever, seems like the inspiration of the moment. The wildness is also reinforced by having the *Intrada* at the very beginning, before the Introduction, as well as at the end. There is no finer Janáček interpreter than Mackerras, and this is among his finest Janáček recordings. The chorus sings incisively with incandescent tone, and the tenor soloist, Peter Svensson, by far the most important of the four, has a trumpet-toned precision that makes light of the high tessitura and the stratospheric leaps that Janáček asks for. The soprano Tina Kiberg, also bright and clear rather than beautiful in tone, makes just as apt a choice. The mezzo, Randi Stene, is excellent, and only a certain unsteadiness in Ulrik Cold's relatively light bass tone prevents this from being an ideal quartet. The coupling is unexpected but very illuminating, again with the choir and tenor soloist aptly cast. Recorded sound of a weight and warmth that convey the full power of the music. Only the organ solo of the penultimate movement lacks a little in bite, thanks to a backward balance, even if it makes up in clarity.

Glagolitic Mass.
*** EMI Dig. CDC7 47504-2 [id.]. Palmer, Gunson, Mitchinson, King, CBSO & Ch., Rattle – *Sinfonietta*. ***
(Y/B) *** Sony Dig. SK 47182 [id.]. Beňačková, Palmer, Lakes, Kotcherga, Scott, London Symphony Ch., LSO, Tilson Thomas – *Sinfonietta*. ***.
(M) **(*) Sony SMK 47569 [id.]. Pilarczyk, Gedda, Gaynes, Westminster Ch., NYPO, Bernstein – POULENC: *Gloria*. ***
(B) ** DG Double 437 937-2 (2) [id.]. Lear, Haefliger, Rössel-Majdan, Crass, Bav. R. Ch. & O, Kubelik – DVORAK: *Stabat Mater*. **

Rattle's performance of the standard published score, aptly paired with the *Sinfonietta*, is strong and vividly dramatic, with the Birmingham performers lending themselves to Slavonic passion. The recording is first class.

Tilson Thomas directs a powerful, virtuoso performance of the normal published score, superbly played and sung, and helped by full, weighty recorded sound. The soprano solos are both idiomatic and beautiful as sung by Beňačková, unsurpassed by any rival; and Gary Lakes, though not quite idiomatic, uses his clean-cut, firm Heldentenor tone in the important tenor solos with no strain whatever. The London Symphony Chorus is magnificent, and the LSO plays brilliantly in every department, not least in the woodwind and brass, with the brightness of the sound adding to the impact. An excellent version if you want the *Sinfonietta* as coupling, though Rattle on EMI is in some ways more individual.

Though Bernstein's reading of the *Glagolitic Mass* is not entirely idiomatic, it is a fine red-blooded performance and one which has the merit of distinguished soloists who add much to the performance. The vivid (1963) recording is one of the best of those Bernstein made in the Avery Fisher Hall.

Kubelik's DG version is fresh and well sung and fully acceptable if you want the Dvořák coupling, but at almost every point the versions by Rattle and Kempe are preferable.

Mass in E flat; (i) *Otčenáš (The Lord's Prayer)*.
(N) (M) *** EMI Dig. CDM5 65587-2 [id.]. King's College, Cambridge, Ch., Cleobury; Stephen Lane; (i) with Arthur Davies, Osian Ellis – KODALY: *Missa brevis*. **(*)

The *Mass* comes from 1907–8 and was never completely finished. It is possible that Janáček used some of it twenty years later in the *Glagolitic Mass*. Janáček's pupil, Vilém Petrželka, discovered the *Kyrie* and *Agnus Dei* and a part of the *Credo*, which he completed. It is a beautiful piece. *Otčenáš (The Lord's Prayer)* is earlier (1901), written originally for tenor, chorus and harmonium (or piano); accompaniment was replaced in 1906 by organ and harp. The singing is generally good, though the sound is (not unnaturally) English rather than Slavonic. There is no alternative version of either work, and they are both valuable additions to the Janáček discography.

OPERA

The Cunning Little Vixen (complete); *Cunning little vixen* (suite, arr. Talich).
*** Decca Dig. 417 129-2 (2) [id.]. Popp, Randová, Jedlická, V. State Op. Ch., Bratislava Children's Ch., VPO, Mackerras.

Mackerras's thrusting, red-blooded reading is spectacularly supported by a digital recording of outstanding, demonstration quality. The inspired choice of Lucia Popp as the vixen provides charm in exactly the right measure: sparkling and coquettish, spiteful as well as passionate. The supporting cast is first rate, too. Talich's splendidly arranged orchestral suite is offered as a bonus in a fine new recording.

(i) *The Cunning Little Vixen* (sung in English); (ii) *Taras Bulba*.
*** EMI CDS7 54212-2 (2) [id.]. (i) Watson, Tear, Allen, ROHCG Ch. & O; (ii) Philh. O; Simon Rattle.

For anyone who wants the work in English, Simon Rattle's recording provides an ideal answer, with Rattle's warmly expressive approach to the score giving strong support to the singers, who equally have gained in expressiveness from singing their roles on stage in the theatre. The cast is outstanding, with Lillian Watson delightfully bright and fresh as the Vixen and Thomas Allen firm and full-toned as the Forester. If Mackerras's Janáček style is more angular and abrasive, bringing out the jagged, spiky rhythms and unexpected orchestral colours, Rattle's is more moulded, more immediately persuasive, if less obviously idiomatic.

The excursions of Mr Brouček (complete).
(Y/B) *** Sup. 11 2153-2 (2) [id.]. Přibyl, Svejda, Jonášová, Czech PO Ch. & O, Jílek.

Though Janáček seems to have intended the opera as a biting satire, this performance comes over more gently and with real charm, thanks to the understanding conducting of Jílek, but also to the characterization of the central character, the bumbling, accident-prone Mr Brouček (literally Mr Beetle). Vilém Přibyl portrays him as an amiable, much-put-upon figure as he makes his excursions. The complicated exchanges are clearly identifiable, thanks to the libretto, while the big team of Czech singers (doubling up roles in the different parts, with Vladimir Krejčik remarkable in no fewer than seven of them) are outstanding, bringing out both the warmth and sense of fun behind the writing. The result is a delight, as sharp and distinctive as any Janáček opera. The analogue recording, made in Prague in 1980, is full and atmospheric with a fine sense of presence on CD.

From the house of the dead (complete).
(Y/B) ** Sup. 10 2941-2 (2) [id.]. Novák, Jirglová, Přibyl, Zídek, Horaček, Souček, Czech PO Ch. & O, Neumann.

(i) *From the house of the dead;* (iii) *Mládí* (for wind sextet); (ii; iii) *Říkadla* (for Chamber Ch. & 10 instruments).
*** Decca Dig. 430 375-2 (2) [id.]. (i) Jedlička, Zahradníček, Zídek, Zítek, V. State Op. Ch., VPO, Mackerras; (ii) L. Sinf. Ch.; (iii) L. Sinf., Atherton.

With one exception, the Decca cast is superb, with a range of important Czech singers giving sharply characterized vignettes. The exception is the raw Slavonic singing of the one woman in the cast, Jaroslav Janska as the boy, Aljeja, but even that fails to undermine the intensity of the innocent relationship with the central figure, which provides an emotional anchor for the whole piece. The chamber-music items added for this reissue are both first rate.

For all its many qualities, for a number of reasons this Czech version of Janáček's last opera is not a serious rival to the Decca set. In the central role of Goryanchikov, Richard Novák is less steady than Jedlička on Decca, and Milada Jirglová, fruity and wobbly, is even less convincing as the boy, Aljeja, than her opposite number. The Supraphon is too reverberant for so claustrophobic a subject. Voices tend to be set well forward of the orchestra, which tends to mask the differences in the version of the score used by Neumann, not the Kubelik edition favoured by Mackerras, which aims at re-creating Janáček's spare original scoring, but the more conventional orchestration of Chlubna and Bakala, if without Chlubna's sentimental ending.

Jenůfa (complete).
✸ *** Decca Dig. 414 483-2 (2) [id.]. Söderström, Ochman, Dvorský, Randová, Popp, V. State Op. Ch., VPO, Mackerras.

(N) (M) **(*) EMI CMS5 64576-2 (2) [id.]. Domanínská, Kniplová, Přibyl, Zídek, Prague Nat. Theatre Ch. & O, Bohumil Gregor.

It was with *Jenůfa* that Janáček scored his first real success in the opera house: the work has a striking and immediate sense of identity, a powerful atmosphere and a strong dramatic argument. This is the warmest and most lyrical of Janáček's operas, and it inspires a performance from Mackerras and his team which is deeply sympathetic, strongly dramatic and superbly recorded. Elisabeth Söderström creates a touching portrait of the girl caught in a family tragedy. The two rival tenors, Peter Dvorský and Wieslav Ochman as the half-brothers Steva and Laca, are both superb; but dominating the whole drama is the Kostelnitchka of Eva Randová. Some may resist the idea that she should be made so sympathetic but, particularly on record, the drama is made stronger and more involving.

The 1969 Prague version was originally issued on the Supraphon label, in a co-production with EMI. Its main strength lies in the fine characterization of the mother, the Kostelnička, the most complex and dominant figure in the action. Though none of the singers may be absolutely first class, and they are not free from Slav vibrato, the company has fine teamwork and Bohumil Gregor directs the performance with genuine imaginative vitality and succeeds in conveying the compelling atmosphere of the score. However, the acoustic of this recording is rather reverberant and, though the CD transfer has improved the focus considerably, detail is inevitably smudged when compared with the later, Decca set. Even so, it remains vibrantly enjoyable and is well documented, with a clearly printed libretto.

Káta Kabanová (complete).
**(*) Sup. 10 8016-2 612 (2) [id.]. Tikalová, Blachut, Komancová, Vích, Mixová, Kroupa, Prague Nat. Theatre Ch. & O, Jaroslav Krombholc.

(i) *Káta Kabanová* (complete); (ii) *Capriccio for piano and 7 instruments; Concertino for piano and 6 instruments.*
*** Decca 421 852-2 (2) [id.]. (i) Söderström, Dvorský, Kniplová, Krejčik, Márová, V. State Op. Ch., VPO, Mackerras; (ii) Paul Crossley, L. Sinf., Atherton.

Káta Kabanová is based on Ostrovsky's play, *The Storm*. Elisabeth Söderström dominates the cast as the tragic heroine and gives a performance of great insight and sensitivity; she touches the listener deeply and is supported by Mackerras with imaginative grip and flair. He draws playing of great eloquence from the Vienna Philharmonic Orchestra. The other soloists are all Czech and their characterizations are brilliantly authentic. But it is the superb orchestral playing and the inspired performance of Söderström that make this set so memorable. The recording has a truthfulness and realism that do full justice to Janáček's marvellous score, vividly transferred to CD, with a double bonus added in the shape of the two concertante keyboard works, in which Paul Crossley is the impressive soloist. These are performances that can be put alongside those of Firkušný – and no praise can be higher.

The alternative Czech performance has the loving authenticity one expects from this source. Something of the original sharpness of sound is lost – in part because of the recording, in part because Vaclav Talich's reorchestration is used. The cast is strong, with a superb performance from the tenor Blachut at the peak of his career. However, Drahomíra Tikalová in the name-role cannot match Söderström in intensity of expression and feeling.

(i) *The Makropulos affair (Věc Makropulos)*: complete; (ii) *Lachian dances.*
*** Decca 430 372-2 (2) [id.]. (i) Söderström, Dvorský, Blachut, V. State Op. Ch., VPO, Mackerras; (ii) LPO, Huybrechts.

Mackerras and his superb team provide a thrilling new perspective on this opera, with its weird heroine preserved by magic elixir well past her 300th birthday. Elisabeth Söderström is not simply malevolent: irritable and impatient rather, no longer an obsessive monster. Framed by richly colourful singing and playing, Söderström amply justifies that view, and Peter Dvorský is superbly fresh and ardent as Gregor. The recording, like others in the series, is of the highest Decca analogue quality. The performance of the *Lachian dances* is highly idiomatic and makes a good bonus.

Osud (complete; in Czech).
(N) *** Orfeo Dig. C 384951A [id.]. Straka, Aghová, Prague Chamber Ch., Czech PO, Albrecht.
(N) ** Sup. 0045-2 611 [id.]. Přibyl, Hajóssyová, Bruno Janáček Op. Ch. & O, Jílek.

As the English National Opera production demonstrated, *Osud* offers a masterly score, rich as well as compact, making a powerful theatrical experience, whatever the oddities of the plot. Gerd Albrecht in his studio recording of 1995 has the benefit of good digital sound, and the Czech Philharmonic is both polished and keenly idiomatic. His cast is first rate, with Peter Straka tackling the high tessitura of the central role of Zivný with no strain, weightier than his Czech rival on Supraphon if less characterful than Philip Langridge on the earlier, EMI version (in English) under Sir Charles Mackerras. Lívia

Aghová is well cast as Míla, bright and clear, sweeter than her Czech rival, though voices are balanced rather distantly. The recording, not as full or rich as the EMI, comes on a single disc in a double jewel-case with notes, libretto and translation.

The Supraphon recording dates from 1975–6, and was made in Brno with the Theatre orchestra and a cast well tuned to the idiom. František Jílek takes an urgent, keenly idiomatic view of the score, but the playing is far less polished than in rival versions, and the sound is more limited. Characterful as he is, the veteran Vilém Přibyl sounds strained in the role of Zivný, the young composer hero, and Magdaléna Hajóssyová as Míla has a bright voice, tending to edginess. Like the Orfeo issue, this one comes on a single disc in a double jewel-case.

Osud (complete; in English).
*** EMI Dig. CDC7 49993-2 [Ang. CDC 49993]. Langridge, Field, Harries, Bronder, Kale, Welsh National Op. Ch. & O, Mackerras.

Janáček's – most unjustly neglected – opera, richly lyrical, more sustained and less fragmented than his later operas, is not just a valuable rarity but makes an ideal introduction to the composer. Philip Langridge is superb in the central role of the composer, Zivny, well supported by Helen Field as Mila, the married woman he loves, and by Kathryn Harries as her mother – a far finer cast than was presented on a short-lived Supraphon set. This performance uses Rodney Blumer's excellent English translation, adding to the immediate impact. Sir Charles Mackerras matches his earlier achievement in the prize-winning series of Janáček opera recordings for Decca, capturing the full gutsiness, passion and impetus of the composer's inspiration. The warmly atmospheric EMI recording, made in Brangwyn Hall, Swansea, brings out the unusual opulence of the Janáček sound, yet it allows words to come over with fine clarity.

Joachim, Joseph (1831–1907)

(i) *Violin concerto in the Hungarian manner, Op. 11. Overtures: Hamlet, Op. 4; Henry IV, Op. 7.*
(M) *** Carlton Dig. MCD 27. (i) Elmer Oliveira; LPO, Leon Bottstein.

Joseph Joachim's fame rests as a legendary performer and the dedicatee of the Brahms *Violin concerto*, rather than as a composer. Nevertheless his concerto is one of the most demanding works written for the instrument in the nineteenth century. Conservative in outlook and indebted to Mendelssohn and Beethoven, it is a very considerable achievement – as, for that matter, is the playing of Elmer Oliveira in this truthful, present and well-balanced recording. The conductor Leon Bottstein also gives committed accounts of the splendid *Henry IV* and *Hamlet Overtures*. An enterprising and rewarding release.

Johansen, David Monrad (1888–1974)

String quartet, Op. 36.
(Y/B) (BB) *** Naxos Dig. 8.550879 [id.]. Oslo String Qt – GRIEG: *String quartets.* ***

David Monrad Johansen was an important figure in Norwegian musical life during the 1930s. His *String quartet*, composed in 1969 when in his early eighties, is persuasively played by the Oslo String Quartet and is impeccably recorded. It is a well-crafted piece but not as distinctively personal as *Pan* or the best of his mature works.

Johnson, Robert (c. 1582–1633)

Lute and Theatre music: *Almans I–III; Corant; Fantasia; Galliard; Pavan;* Ayres: *Adieu, fond love; Arm, arm!; As I walked forth; Away delights; Care-charming sleep; Charon, oh Charon; Come away, Hecate; Come away, thou lady gay; Come, heavy sleep; Come hither, you that love; Full fathom five; Hark! hark! the lark!; Have you seen the white lily grow?; O let us howl; Tell me dearest; 'Tis late and cold; Where the bee sucks; Woods, rocks and mountains.*
❀ *** Virgin/EMI Dig. VC7 59321-2 [id.]. Emma Kirkby, David Thomas, Anthony Rooley.

Robert Johnson was born two decades after Dowland and Campion, and he had the most individual musical personality. In this most engaging recital, Emma Kirkby sings with characteristic freshness and charm in Shakespearean numbers like *Hark! hark! the lark!* and *Where the bee sucks*, and she is utterly ravishing in the poignant *Come, heavy sleep*, and the following, equally beautiful *Care-charming sleep*. David Thomas is hardly less expressive in Ariel's *Full fathom five* from *The Tempest* with its gently tolling bell and *Have you seen the white lily grow?* (Ben Jonson). Like Kirkby, his decoration is felicitous, often florid but never fussy. After the drama of the male solo songs, Thomas is joined by Emma Kirkby in the dialogue interchange of *Come away, Hecate* (from Middleton's *The Witch*) complete with vociferous growls which suggest that the angst is not to be taken too seriously. Anthony Rooley then calms the atmosphere with delicately played lute solos, which demonstrate the composer's ready versatility. Two more duets end the programme, *Come away thou lady gay*, with a garrulous cackling response from Kirkby, and *Tell me dearest*, in which she is altogether more demure. The recording is absolutely natural, the presence of the singers enhanced by the pleasing acoustic, and the lute is never made to seem larger than life. This is a programme that can be listened to straight through with much pleasure, admirably simulating a live recital.

Jolivet, André (1905–74)

Chant de Linos.
*** Koch Dig. 3-7016 [id.]. Atlantic Sinf. – JONGEN: *Concert;* DEBUSSY: *Sonata*. ***

The *Chant de Linos* was originally composed for flute and piano, but Jolivet subsequently made this highly effective transcription for flute, violin, viola, cello and harp. It is played with exemplary taste and effortless virtuosity by Bradley Garner and his colleagues of the Atlantic Sinfonietta and is most beautifully recorded.

Jongen, Joseph (1873–1953)

(i) *Allegro appassionato for viola and orchestra, Op. 79; Suite for viola and orchestra, Op. 48.* (ii) *Symphonie concertante for organ and orchestra, Op. 81.*
**(*) Koch Schwann Dig. CD 315 012 [id.) (i) Therèse-Marie Gilissen, RTBF SO, Brian Priestman; (ii) Hubert Schoonbroodt, Liège SO, René Defossez.

Symphonie concertante for organ and orchestra, Op. 81.
*** Telarc Dig. CD 80096 [id.]. Michael Murray, San Francisco SO, De Waart – FRANCK: *Fantaisie* etc. ***

(M) ** EMI CDM5 65075-2 [id.]. Virgil Fox, Fr. Nat. Theatre Op. O, Prêtre – DE GREEF: *Piano concerto.* **

Anyone who likes the Saint-Saëns *Third Symphony* should enjoy the Jongen *Symphonie concertante*. Even if the music is on a lower level of inspiration, the passionate *Lento misterioso* and hugely spectacular closing *Toccata* make a favourable impression at first hearing and wear surprisingly well afterwards. Michael Murray has all the necessary technique to carry off Jongen's hyperbole with the required panache. He receives excellent support from Edo de Waart and the San Francisco Symphony Orchestra. The huge Ruffatti organ seems custom-built for the occasion and Telarc's engineers capture all the spectacular effects with their usual aplomb. A demonstration disc indeed.

The *Sinfonia concertante* begins fugally, but there is a lot of Franck, d'Indy and Ravel in its writing. Jongen himself was the soloist in its first performance in 1924 and would presumably find the Schoonbroodt–Defossez recording more congenial than the brash and brassy Virgil Fox account recorded at Les Invalides in the 1960s.

The Koch Schwann version comes from 1975 and is less aggressively recorded than the Koch version, although needing greater transparency. It has the advantage of being coupled with the *Suite for viola and orchestra*, Op. 48, whose first movement almost calls to mind the elegiac tone of Lekeu's *Adagio* for quartet and strings. Neither version is top-drawer, and the spectacular Telarc version by Michael Murray remains an easy first choice.

Concert à cinq.
*** Koch Dig. 3-7016-2 [id.]. Atlantic Sinf. – DEBUSSY: *Sonata;* JOLIVET: *Chant de Linos*. ***

The three-movement *Concert à cinq* for flute, harp and string trio is a civilized piece very much in the post-impressionist style. It remains more pleasing than memorable, though these players do their utmost for it.

Joplin, Scott (1868–1917)

Rags: *Bethena (concert waltz); Cascades rag; Country club (ragtime two-step); Elite syncopations; The Entertainer, Euphonic sounds (A syncopated novelty); Fig leaf rag; Gladiolus rag; Magnetic rag (syncopations classiques); Maple leaf rag; Paragon rag; Pine apple rag; Ragtime dance; Scott Joplin's new rag; Solace (Mexican serenade); Stoptime rag; Weeping willow (ragtime two-step).*
(M) *** Nonesuch Elektra/Warner 7559 79159-2. Joshua Rifkin (piano).

Joshua Rifkin is the pianist whose name has been indelibly associated with the Scott Joplin revival, originally stimulated by the soundtrack music of the very successful film, *The Sting*. His relaxed, cool rhythmic style is at times more subtle than Dick Hyman's more extrovert approach and, although the piano timbre is full, there is a touch of monochrome in the tone-colour.

Rags: *A Breeze from Alabama; The Cascades; The Chrysanthemum; Easy winners; Elite syncopations; The Entertainer, Maple leaf rag; Original rags; Palm leaf rag; Peacherine rag; Something doing; The Strenuous life; Sunflower slow drag; Swipesy; The Sycamore.*
(M) *** RCA GD 87993 [7993-2-RG]. Dick Hyman.

Dick Hyman's playing is first rate. His rhythmic spring, clean touch and sensibility in matters of light and shade – without ever trying to present this as concert music – mean that pieces which can easily appear stereotyped remain fresh and spontaneous-sounding throughout. The recording has fine presence; the piano image seems just right.

Treemonisha (opera: arr. and orch. Schuller): complete.
(M) **(*) DG 435 709-2 (2) [id.]. Balthrop, Allen, Rayam, White, Houston Grand Op. Ch. and O, Schuller.

The deliciously ingenuous score will not appeal to all tastes, with its mixture of choral rags, barber's shop quartets, bits of diluted Gilbert and Sullivan, Lehár and Gershwin, and much that is outrageously corny, but – to some ears – irresistibly so. The work has the ethos of the musical rather than of the opera house. But (with the exception of some unlovable singing from Betty Allen as Monisha) the performance and recording are first class and many will find themselves warming to the spontaneity of Joplin's invention.

Josquin des Prés (c. 1450–1521)

Motets: *Ave Maria, gratia plena; Ave, nobilissima creatura; Miserere mei, Deus; O bone et dulcissime Jesu; Salve regina; Stabat mater dolorosa; Usquequo, Domine, oblivisceris me.*
*** HM Dig. HMC 901243 [id.]. Chapelle Royale Ch., Herreweghe.

The Chapelle Royale comprises some nineteen singers, but they still produce a clean, well-focused sound and benefit from excellent recording. Their account of the expressive *Stabat mater* sounds thicker-textured than the New College forces under Edward Higginbottom, but there is a refreshing sense of commitment and strong feeling.

Antiphons, Motets and Sequences: *Inviolata; Praeter rerum serium; Salve regina; Stabat mater dolorosa; Veni, sancte spiritus; Virgo prudentissima; Virgo salutiferi.*
*** Mer. ECD 84093 [id.]. New College, Oxford, Ch., Higginbottom.

The Meridian anthology collects some of Josquin's most masterly and eloquent motets in performances of predictable excellence by Edward Higginbottom and the Choir of New College, Oxford. An admirable introduction to Josquin, and an essential acquisition for those who care about this master.

Missa: L'homme armé super voces musicales.
*** DG 415 293-2 [id.]. Pro Cantione Antiqua, Bruno Turner – OCKEGHEM: *Missa pro defunctis.* ***

This Mass on the *L'homme armé* theme is both one of the most celebrated of all Mass settings based on this secular melody and at the same time one of Josquin's most masterly and admired works. Jeremy Noble's edition is used in the present (1977) performance, which must be numbered among the very finest accounts not only of a Josquin but of any Renaissance Mass to have appeared on record. On CD, the transparency of each strand in the vocal texture is wonderfully clear and the singers are astonishingly present.

Missa Pange lingua; Missa La sol fa re mi.
*** Gimell Dig. CDGIM 009; *1585T-09* [id.]. Tallis Scholars, Peter Phillips.

The Gimell recording of the *Missa Pange lingua* has collected superlatives on all counts and was voted record of the year in the *Gramophone* magazine's 1987 awards. The tone the Tallis Scholars produce is perfectly blended, each line being firmly defined and yet beautifully integrated into the whole sound-picture. Their recording, made in the Chapel of Merton College, Oxford, is first class, the best of the *Missa Pange lingua* and the first of the ingenious *Missa La sol fa re mi*. Not to be missed.

Kabalevsky, Dmitri (1904–87)

Cello concertos Nos. 1 in G min., Op. 49; 2 in C min., Op. 77; (ii) *Improvisato, Op. 21/1; Rondo, Op. 69* (both for violin & piano).
*** Olympia Dig. OCD 292 [id.]. (i) Marina Tarasova, SO of Russia, Veronika Dudarova; (ii) Natalia Likopoi, Ludmila Kuritskaya.

Marina Tarasova has a vibrant intensity, enormous tonal eloquence and a dazzling technique, much of which registers in these performances of the two *Cello concertos*, and this is surely an ideal coupling. She does not bring as much elegance or character to the endearing *First Concerto* as do Yo-Yo Ma and Ormandy on CBS, though the poignant ending of the middle movement comes off beautifully. Nor does her account of the sombre *Second Concerto in C minor* banish memories of Wallfisch. Still she is very good indeed and no one investing in these performances is likely to be disappointed. Viktoria Dudarova gets decent playing from the orchestra and the recording is very good, full and clear. The two violin-and-piano pieces are very well played indeed.

Cello concerto No. 1 in G min.
*** Sony Dig. MK 37840 [id.]. Yo-Yo Ma, Phd. O, Ormandy – SHOSTAKOVICH: *Cello concerto No. 1.* ***

The excellence of Ma's performance is matched by a fine recording which adds considerably to the refinement and presence of the sound, and its vividness is such as to seem to add stature to the music itself.

Cello concerto No. 2, Op. 77.
*** Chandos Dig. CHAN 8579 [id.]. Wallfisch, LPO, Thomson – GLAZUNOV: *Chant du ménestrel;* KHACHATURIAN: *Concerto.* ***

The *Second Cello concerto* is played eloquently – and with the greatest virtuosity – by Raphael Wallfisch, who is well supported by Bryden Thomson and the LPO. Excellent recording too.

Violin concerto in C, Op. 48.
*** Chandos Dig. CHAN 8918 [id.]. Lydia Mordkovitch, SNO, Järvi -KHACHATURIAN: *Violin concerto.* ***

Kabalevsky's *Violin concerto* is most persuasively presented by these artists. Throughout, Lydia Mordkovitch plays with great flair and aplomb and is given first-class Chandos recording.

Symphonies Nos. 1 in C sharp min., Op. 18; 2 in C min., Op. 19.
(Y/B) ** Olympia Dig. OCD 268 [id.]. Szeged PO, Acél.

Kabalevsky's *First Symphony* unfolds naturally and the musical procedures have real dignity, even if some of the material of the finale is banal. The *Second Symphony* is both more individual and tautly argued. Good, though not first-class, performances from the Szeged Philharmonic Orchestra under Erwin Acél (though the opening of the *Second Symphony* is nicely alert); however, the recording is handicapped by a rather cramped and constricted acoustic.

(i) *Symphony No. 4 in C min., Op. 54;* (ii) *Requiem, Op. 72.*
** Olympia OCD 290 (2) [id.]. (i) Leningrad PO; (ii) Valentina Levko, Vladimir Valaitis, Moscow Artistic Educational Institute Ch., Moscow SO; Kabalevsky.

The *Fourth Symphony* is a rather conventional work which goes through the correct motions of sonata form, but the ideas are only intermittently engaging; indeed, many border on the commonplace. Kabalevsky conducts with great abandon and the Leningrad orchestra respond with some enthusiasm to his direction. The *Requiem* is a more rewarding piece, even if much of it is hard work. But the longueurs are offset by some moving passages and a genuine, unforced dignity that grips the listener. The performers are committed and the singing of high standard. It is good to have these performances restored to circulation for, even if they do not reveal a great musical personality at work, the fact remains that Kabalevsky's music is not negligible either. The sound in the *Requiem* is very good indeed for the period – and the place.

24 Preludes, Op. 38; Sonata No. 3, Op. 46; Sonatina in C, Op. 13/1.
(Y/B) *** Olympia Dig. OCD 266 [id.]. Murray McLachlan.

Murray McLachlan makes out a persuasive case for Kabalevsky's *24 Preludes*, Op. 38. There is a similarity to the Chopin *Preludes* in that the cycle contains a prelude in every key, arranged through the cycle of fifths in relative major and minor keys, but there it ends. Each of the preludes is based on a folk tune, mostly drawn from Rimsky-Korsakov's collection, and in *No. 13 in F sharp minor* we encounter the theme made famous by Stravinsky in the closing bars of *Firebird*. McLachlan does the set with great fluency and clarity of articulation. He also gives us two of Kabalevsky's best-known piano pieces, the *Sonatina* (1930) and the *Piano Sonata No. 3* (1946) with its Prokofievian middle movement. In the *Sonata*, Pizarro (see below) is the more imaginative in his handling of tone-colour and dynamic range. The piano-sound is decent but could do with greater transparency and bloom. All the same, it would be invidious to withhold a three-star grading.

Piano sonatas Nos. 1 in F, Op. 6; 2 in E flat, Op. 45; 3 in F, Op. 46; 4 Preludes, Op. 5; Recitative and Rondo, Op. 84.
(Y/B) *** Collins Dig. 1418-2 [id.]. Artur Pizarro.

On the present disc Artur Pizarro collects the three Kabalevsky *Sonatas*, together with the early *Four Preludes*, Op. 5, and a *Recitative and Rondo* dating from 1967, the fiftieth anniversary of the October Revolution. The *Sonata No. 1 in F*, Op. 6, was composed in 1927 while Kabalevsky was still a pupil of Miaskovsky, and its opening reflects not only the latter's influence but, even more so, that of Scriabin. Pizarro makes much more of the *Third Sonata* than McLachlan and gives a highly polished account of all the pieces recorded here and there is much to give pleasure, particularly when it is played with such elegance. The piano-sound is truthful and reasonably fresh, though there is perhaps more resonance than some will like. Recommended.

Piano sonata No. 3, Op. 46.
(M) (***) RCA mono GD 60377 [id.]. Vladimir Horowitz – BARBER; PROKOFIEV: *Sonatas* etc. (***)

Horowitz cannot give Kabalevsky's music the calibre of the Barber or Prokofiev sonatas with which it is coupled, and the 1947 recording is a bit subfusc. But the power of the playing certainly comes through, especially in the brilliant finale.

Colas Breugnon (complete).
*** Olympia OCD 291 A/B (2) [id.]. Boldin, Isakova, Kayevchenko, Maksimenko, Duradev, Gutorovich, Mishchevsky, Stanislavsky & Nemirovich-Danchenko Moscow Music Theatre Ch. & O, Zhemchuzhin.

This complete recording, made in Russia in the 1970s, confirms that the effervescent overture is not just a flash in the pan but part of an exceptionally winning piece, rhythmically inventive and full of good tunes, many of them drawn from French folksong. The snag is that between Acts I and II in the three-Act layout there is a story-gap of 40 years. Enough of the same characters are still around to maintain continuity, but youthful effervescence is less apt for the aged characters in Acts II and III. Nevertheless the Russian performance and recording, made by members of the Moscow Music Theatre, is most convincing, with a cast superbly led by the baritone, Leonid Boldin, in the title-role. The other male singers are first rate too, with splendidly alert singing from the chorus (which, in good proletarian fashion, plays a key part in the opera). The women soloists are raw-toned in a very Russian way, and the whole performance under Georgy Zhemchuzhin reflects the confidence of experience on stage. The 1973 recording, rather dry but with fine presence, catches the voices splendidly, though the orchestra is backwardly placed. But reservations may be put to one side; this is a thoroughly worthwhile set.

Kalinnikov, Vasily (1866–1901)

Intermezzos Nos. 1 in F sharp min.; 2 in G.
*** Chandos Dig. CHAN 8614 [id.]. SNO, Järvi – RACHMANINOV: *Symphony No. 3*. ***
These two colourful *Intermezzos* with a flavour of Borodin are charming.

Symphony No. 1 in G min.
*** Chandos Dig. CHAN 8611 [id.]. SNO, Järvi – GLAZUNOV: *The Sea; Spring*. ***

Kalinnikov's *First Symphony* contains something akin to the flow and natural lyricism of Borodin, and the second movement has something of the atmosphere and character of early Rachmaninov or his almost exact contemporary, Glazunov. Neeme Järvi and the Scottish National Orchestra seem fired with enthusiasm for this appealing work, and the engineers serve them admirably. Strongly recommended.

Symphony No. 2 in A; The Cedar and the palm; Overture: Tsar Boris.
*** Chandos Dig. CHAN 8805 [id.]. SNO, Järvi.

The *Second Symphony*, though not quite as appealing as No. 1, is played by the Scottish orchestra under Neeme Järvi with enthusiasm and commitment, and the Chandos recording is in the demonstration class. Both the *Overture* and *The Cedar and the palm* are worth having on disc.

Kern, Jerome (1885–1945)

Overtures: (i) *The Cat and the fiddle; The Girl from Utah; Have a heart; Leave it to Jane; O, Lady! Lady!;* (ii) *Show Boat;* (i) *Sitting pretty; Sweet Adeline; Very warm for May;* (i, iii) Film music: *Swing Time* (suite).
(N) (B) ** EMI forte Dig. CZS5 68589-2 (2). (i) Nat. PO; (ii) L. Sinf.; (iii) Ambrosian Ch.; McGlinn –
  GERSHWIN: *Broadway and film music* **(*); PORTER: *Overtures.* ***

These Jerome Kern overtures, recorded from the original band-parts of musicals dating from between 1914 (*The Girl from Utah*) and 1939 (*Very warm for May*), are musically unimpressive. They are all played with an infectious sense of style, but really memorable tunes are thin on the ground. In *Sweet Adeline*, instead of his own material, Kern uses a pot-pourri of period songs from the 1890s, including *Daisy, Daisy* and *The Band played on*. By far the most attractive music comes in the film score from *Swing Time*, which includes *The way you look tonight*. For this reissue, the *Overture* from McGlinn's complete recording of *Showboat* has been added, but that is not much more than a pot-pourri.

Songs from musicals: *Centennial Summer: All through the day. Cover Girl: Long ago and far away. High, Wide and Handsome: The folks who live on the hill. Lady be Good: The last time I saw Paris. Music in the Air: The song is you. Roberta: Yesterdays; Smoke gets in your eyes. Sally: Look for the silver lining. Show Boat: Can't help lovin' dat man. Swing Time: The way you look tonight. Very warm for May: All the things you are. You were never Lovelier: I'm old fashioned.*
(N) *** EMI Dig. CDC7 54527-2 [id.]. Dame Kiri Te Kanawa, L. Sinf., Jonathan Tunick.

Kiri Te Kanawa proves completely at home in these luscious and life-enhancing Kern favourites. Her rich vocal line is matched by a nice feeling for the wittier lyrics. But it's the tunes that count, and she revels in them. So does Jonathan Tunick, who has scored the accompaniments; and the London Sinfonietta obviously enjoy themselves too, yet there is also a sense of sophistication and style. Excellent recording.

Showboat (complete recording of original score).
⊛ *** EMI Dig. CDS7 49108-2 (3) [Ang. A23 49108]. Von Stade, Hadley, Hubbard, O'Hara, Garrison, Burns, Stratas, Amb. Ch., L. Sinf., John McGlinn.

In faithfully following the original score, this superb set at last does justice to a musical of the 1920s which is both a landmark in the history of Broadway and musically a work of strength and imagination hardly less significant than Gershwin's *Porgy and Bess* of a decade later. The original, extended versions of important scenes are included, as well as various numbers written for later productions. As the heroine, Magnolia, Frederica von Stade gives a meltingly beautiful performance, totally in style, bringing out the beauty and imagination of Kern's melodies, regularly heightened by wide intervals to make those of most of his Broadway rivals seem flat. The London Sinfonietta play with tremendous zest and feeling for the idiom; the Ambrosian Chorus sings with joyful brightness and some impeccable American accents. Opposite von Stade, Jerry Hadley makes a winning Ravenal, and Teresa Stratas is charming as Julie, giving a heartfelt performance of the haunting number, *Bill* (words by P. G. Wodehouse). Above all, the magnificent black bass, Bruce Hubbard, sings *Ol' man river* and its many reprises with a firm resonance to have you recalling the wonderful example of Paul Robeson, but for once without hankering after the past. Beautifully recorded to bring out the piece's dramatic as well as its musical qualities, this is a heart-warming issue.

Ketèlbey, Albert (1875–1959)

The Adventurers: overture; Bells across the meadow; Caprice pianistique; Chal Romano; The Clock and the Dresden figures; Cockney suite, excerpts: *Bank holiday; At the Palais de Danse. In a Monastery*

garden; In the moonlight; In a Persian market; The Phantom melody; Suite romantique; Wedgewood blue.
** Marco Polo Dig. 8.223442 [id.]. Slovak Philharmonic Male Ch., Slovak RSO (Bratislava), Adrian
   Leaper.

The Marco Polo collection has the advantage of modern digital recording and a warm concert-hall
acoustic, and the effect is very flattering to *In a Monastery garden*. Adrian Leaper's performance is
romantically spacious and includes the chorus. If elsewhere his characterization is not always as apt as
Lanchbery's, this is still an agreeable programme. It offers several novelties and, though some of these
items (for instance *The Adventurers overture*) are not vintage Ketèlbey, there is nothing wrong with the
lively Slovak account of the closing *In a Persian market*, again featuring the chorus.

*Bells across the meadow; Chal Romano (Gypsy lad); The Clock and the Dresden figures; In a Chinese
temple garden; In a monastery garden; In a Persian market; In the moonlight; In the mystic land of Egypt;
Sanctuary of the heart.*
(B) *** CfP CD-CFP 4637; *TC-CFP 4637* [id.]. Vernon Midgley, Jean Temperley, Leslie Pearson
   (piano), Amb. S., Philh. O, Lanchbery – LUIGINI: *Ballet Egyptien.* ***

A splendid collection in every way. John Lanchbery uses every possible resource to ensure that, when the
composer demands spectacle, he gets it. *In the mystic land of Egypt*, for instance, uses soloist and chorus
in canon in the principal tune (and very fetchingly too). In the *Monastery garden* the distant monks are
realistically distant, in *Sanctuary of the heart* there is no mistaking that the heart is worn firmly on the
sleeve. The orchestral playing throughout is not only polished but warm-hearted – the middle section of
Bells across the meadow, which has a delightful melodic contour, is played most tenderly and loses any
hint of vulgarity. Yet when vulgarity is called for, it is not shirked – only it's a stylish kind of vulgarity!
The recording is excellent, full and brilliant.

Khachaturian, Aram (1903–78)

Cello concerto.
*** Chandos Dig. CHAN 8579 [id.]. Wallfisch, LPO, Thomson – GLAZUNOV: *Chant du ménestrel;*
   KABALEVSKY: *Cello concerto No.2.* ***
(M) ** Ph. 434 166-2 [id.]. Walevska, Monte Carlo Opera O, Inbal – PROKOFIEV: *Cello concerto.* **

Khachaturian's *Cello concerto* of 1946 has some sinuous Armenian local colour for its lyrical ideas, but
none of the thematic memorability of the concertos for violin and piano and the *Gayaneh ballet* score,
on which Khachaturian's reputation must continue to rest. Raphael Wallfisch plays with total commitment and has the benefit of excellent and sympathetic support. The recording is of the usual high
standard we have come to expect from Chandos.
    Christine Walevska gives a committed account of the work and she is well accompanied by Inbal, but
the Philips sound is not especially vivid. This CD is issued as a limited edition.

Cello concerto in E min.; Concerto-rhapsody for cello and orchestra in D min.
(Y/B) **(*) Olympia Dig. OCD 539 [id.]. Marina Tarasova, Russian SO, Veronica Dudarova.

The *Concerto-rhapsody for cello and orchestra in D minor* comes from 1963 and was first given by
Rostropovich in London. Marina Tarasova plays both works with great eloquence and expressive
vehemence; she has a big tone and impeccable technique. The orchestral playing is gutsy and sturdy
without, perhaps, the finesse that might have toned down some of the garishness of the orchestral
colours. The recording is bright and breezy – not worth a three-star grading and nor is the orchestral
contribution, though Tarasova certainly is.

Flute concerto (arr. Rampal/Galway); *Gayaneh: Sabre dance. Masquerade: Waltz. Spartacus: Adagio of
Spartacus and Phrygia.*
*** RCA Dig. 07863 57010-2. Galway, RPO, Myung-Whun Chung.

Khachaturian's *Flute concerto* is a transcription of the *Violin concerto*; Galway has prepared his own
edition of the solo part. Needless to say, the solo playing is peerless; if in the finale even Galway cannot
match the effect Oistrakh makes with his violin, the ready bravura is sparklingly infectious. As encores,
he offers three of Khachaturian's most famous melodies.

Piano concerto in D flat.
(Y/B) ❀ (M) (**(*)) RCA mono GD 60921. William Kapell, Boston SO, Koussevitzky – LISZT:
   Mephisto waltz (**(*)); PROKOFIEV: *Piano concerto No. 3.* (**(*)) ❀

(Y/B) (M) **(*) Hyperion Dig. CDA 66293 [id.]. Servadei, LPO, Giunta – BRITTEN: *Piano concerto*.
**(*)

(Y/B) (**) VAI mono VAIA IPA 1027 [id.]. William Kapell, NBC SO, Frank Black – RACHMANI-
NOV: *Piano concerto No. 3*. (*(**))

(i) *Piano concerto in D flat. Dance suite; Polka; Waltz* (both for wind band).
(N) *** ASV Dig. CDDCA 964 [id.]. (i) Dora Serviarian-Kuhn; Armenian PO, Tjeknavorian.

The Armenian partnership of Dora Serviarian-Kuhn and Loris Tjeknavorian provides a clear first
recommendation for Khachaturian's somewhat uneven *Piano concerto*, easily the finest account to have
appeared on disc since the pioneering versions of William Kapell and Moura Lympany. The playing has
all the necessary drive in the first movement but does not lack the necessary weight for the reprise of the
main theme at the very end of the work. The sinuous poetry of the lyrical Armenian folk-themes is well
caught, particularly in the *Andante* where the conductor judiciously balances the flexatone so that it
adds a whistling edge to the texture without seeming too prominent. The Russian dance finale has plenty
of dash, but what makes the performance individual is the sense of quixotic fantasy Serviarian-Kuhn
brings to her cadential bravura. The bright piano-timbre and comparatively lean orchestral textures are
not a disadvantage in a work that can too easily sound inflated. The other pieces on the ASV disc are
very slight but lively enough; easily the most memorable item is the second *Uzbek dance* in the *Dance
suite*, quite extended and touchingly atmospheric as a cor anglais solo brings it to a gentle close.

It is difficult to imagine a better-played account of the *Piano concerto* than that by William Kapell and
the Boston Symphony under Koussevitzky (though not so hard to imagine better recorded sound). This
incandescent performance, which Kapell recorded in his early twenties, should persuade even those who
normally find the Khachaturian concerto irredeemably cheap and tawdry. Koussevitzky gets stunning
results from the orchestra and Kapell's virtuosity and delicacy are remarkable. Even if the sound calls
for lots of tolerance (the recording dates from 1946), the performance soon has a mesmeric effect. One is
reminded of Stravinsky's response on hearing Leonard Bernstein's *Rite of Spring*: 'Wow!'

Annette Servadei makes up in clarity and point for a relative lack of weight in the outer movements,
which she takes at speeds marginally slower than usual. The slow movement brings hushed and intense
playing, sympathetically supported by the LPO under Joseph Giunta in a digital recording that is well
balanced and unaggressive and sounding good. However, ideally this work needs a stronger grip than
these artists exert – the first movement in particular could do with greater thrust.

Kapell's NBC performance with Frank Black conducting comes from May 1945 (a year earlier than his
Boston version), and the sound is abysmal, harsher and more cramped than with Koussevitzky. If you
want the Khachaturian from this artist (and you should), then go for the Boston performance. But you
should also note that the coupling on VAI, the Rachmaninov *Piano concerto No. 3*, is one of the most
extraordinary and electrifying before the public. It is not a commercial recording but is an astonishing
tour de force, second only to Horowitz and Rachmaninov himself.

(i) *Piano concerto in D flat;* (ii) *Violin concerto in D min.;* (iii) *Masquerade suite;* (iv) *Symphony No. 2.*
(N) (B) **(*) Decca Double 448 252-2 (2) [id.]. (i) De Larrocha, LPO, Frühbeck de Burgos; (ii) Ricci,
LPO, Fistoulari; (iii) LSO, Stanley Black; (iv) VPO, composer.

The key performance here is the composer's own – of the *Second Symphony*. His advocacy is passionate
and the recording is spectacular (although the CD remastering does not help its garish qualities). The
slow movement of the *Piano concerto* as interpreted by a Spanish pianist and a Spanish conductor
sounds evocatively like Falla, and the finale is also infectiously jaunty. Not so the first movement, which
is disappointingly slack in rhythm at a dangerously slow tempo. Ricci is a good deal more consistent in
the *Violin concerto*. He does not supply quite the demonic energy which the outer movements ideally call
for, but his lyrical approach has its own attractions, and the closing pages of the slow movement are
wonderfully atmospheric. The late-1950s recording does not have the projection we would expect today,
but Ricci's fine playing is well focused. The *Masquerade suite* is consistently alive and colourful and is
vividly if forwardly recorded.

(i) *Piano concerto in D flat; Gayaneh* (ballet) *suite; Masquerade: suite.*
**(*) Chandos Dig. CHAN 8542 [id.]. (i) Orbelian, SNO, Järvi.

The Chandos recording is splendid technically, well up to the standards of the house. Constantin
Orbelian, an Armenian by birth, plays brilliantly and Järvi achieves much attractive lyrical detail.
Overall it is a spacious account, and though the finale has plenty of gusto, the music-making seems just
a shade too easygoing in the first movement. The couplings, sumptuously played, are both generous and
appealing.

Violin concerto in D min.
*** Chandos Dig. CHAN 8918 [id.]. Lydia Mordkovitch, SNO, Järvi -KABALEVSKY: *Violin concerto.*
***
(*) EMI Dig. CDC7 47087-2 [id.]. Perlman, Israel PO, Mehta – TCHAIKOVSKY: *Méditation.* *
(M) ** Mercury 434 318-2 [id.]. Szeryng, LSO, Dorati – BRAHMS: *Violin concerto.* *(*)

Among recent performances of this attractively inventive concerto, Lydia Mordkovitch is probably the most competitive. She plays with real abandon and fire, and Chandos balance her and the orchestra in a thoroughly realistic perspective. This new version has far superior sound to Oistrakh on Chant du Monde.

Perlman's performance sparkles too – indeed it is superb in every way, lyrically persuasive in the *Andante* and displaying great fervour and rhythmic energy in the finale. He is well accompanied by Mehta (who nevertheless does not match the composer's feeling for detail). However, on CD one's ear is drawn to the very forward balance of the soloist, and the generally bright lighting becomes rather fierce at the opening tutti of the finale – the comparatively dry Israeli acoustic does not provide an ideal bloom on the music-making. The coupling is attractive but offers very short measure.

Although more successful than the coupled Brahms concerto, Szeryng's 1964 recording of the Khachaturian does not measure up to the finest versions of the past, notably those of Leonid Kogan and David Oistrakh and, more recently, Perlman. It is a lightweight account, at its most convincing in the folksy lyricism of the *Andante* and in the sparkle of the finale, where the soloist is on top technical form. The recording is good but does not flatter the solo violin timbre.

(i) *Violin concerto in D min.; Gayaneh* (extended suite); *Masquerade suite.*
(***) EMI mono CDC5 55035-2 [id.]. (i) David Oistrakh; Philh. O, composer.

David Oistrakh's EMI mono recording of the *Violin concerto* was made in the Kingsway Hall in 1954. It has the advantage of first-class recording, and such is the freshness and power of the performance that one adjusts almost immediately to the absence of stereo, for the sound is well balanced and spacious. The slow movement and dancing finale are particularly memorable and, throughout, Oistrakh's reading combines warmth and Slavic intensity with easy brilliance. The couplings on EMI are more obviously attractive than the alternative Russian stereo CD, and again no apologies have to be made for the bright EMI recording with its attractive ambience. The *Masquerade suite* and the eight best numbers from *Gayaneh* bring a refreshing sense of newness and discovery: the lyrical music is full of atmosphere, finding delicacy as well as warmth, while the famous *Sabre dance* bursts at the seams with energy.

Gayaneh (ballet): complete final score.
(Y/B) **(*) Russian Disc RDCD 11 029 (2) [id.]. USSR R. & TV Large SO, Djansug Kakhidze.

Khachaturian's original full score for *Gayaneh*, dating from 1942, is perhaps his finest extended work. Fortunately Tjeknavorian made a complete recording of it for RCA, and this is in urgent need of reissue. The composer later reworked and added to the music in order to fit a new scenario (because the earlier narrative, with its ingenuous wartime moral tone, had become embarrassing to the Soviets). The fresh inspiration of the original is expanded and often vulgarized in the later version about love and jealousy among shepherds dwelling in the mountains. But plenty of striking ideas remain. This Russian recording from 1976 has great verve and energy but does not disguise the shallower invention and the inflation of the louder passages. Nevertheless the recording is vivid and, although brash, is not unacceptably so; and these performers know just how to present the folk dances.

Gayaneh (ballet): extended suite.
(M) **(*) Mercury 434 323-2 [id.]. LSO, Dorati – SHOSTAKOVICH: *Symphony No. 5.* **(*)

Dorati understands this music as well as anyone, and his *Sabre dance* has plenty of energy; and the other dances admirably celebrate Khachaturian's local colour. The 1960 Mercury recording is brilliant, with a tendency to fierceness in the strings, which suits the music well enough. There are eight items here; Dorati omits *Gayaneh's Adagio.*

Gayaneh (ballet): *suite; Masquerade: suite; Spartacus* (ballet): *suite.*
(*) ASV. Dig. CDDCA 773. Armenian PO, Tjeknavorian – IPPOLITOV-IVANOV: *Caucasian sketches.* *

Gayaneh: suite; Spartacus: suite.
(M) **(*) Decca 417 737-2 [id.]. VPO, composer – PROKOFIEV: *Romeo and Juliet.* ***

The composer's own first selection on Decca was recorded in 1962 and offers five items from *Gayaneh* and four from *Spartacus.* Khachaturian achieves a brilliant response from the VPO and everything is most vivid, notably the famous *Adagio* from *Spartacus*, which is both expansive and passionate. It is a pity that the Decca remastering process has brought everything into such strong focus; the massed violins now have an added edge and boldness of attack, at the expense of their richness of timbre.

The Armenians clearly relish the explosive energy of this music. The *Masquerade suite* relies rather more on charm for its appeal, but Tjeknavorian and his players bring a determined gusto, even to the *Waltz* and certainly to the ebullient closing *Galop*. Then the vibrant Spartacus and his ardent lover Phrygia come on stage with a great flair of passion in a melody that is justly famous. One wishes the recording were more sumptuous here, but for the most part its burnished primary colours suit the dynamic orchestral style.

Gayaneh (ballet): highlights; *Spartacus* (ballet): highlights.
(B) *** CfP CD-CFP 4634; *TC-CFP 4634*. LSO, composer (with GLAZUNOV: *The Seasons: Autumn:* Philh. O, Svetlanov ***).

The composer's 1977 pairing for EMI of selections from his two famous ballets offers one more item from *Gayaneh* than on his earlier (1962) Decca coupling. The EMI sound, obviously more modern than the Decca, is a shade reverberant for the more vigorous numbers, but the present remastering presents a firmer focus than on LP. The effect is realistically spectacular with full, rich strings so that the famous *Adagio of Spartacus and Phrygia* expands opulently as well as ardently. The LSO play excitingly throughout. There is a gorgeous response from the violins in the extra item, called *Invention*, from *Gayaneh*. The inclusion of *Autumn*, the most memorable section of Glazunov's *Seasons* – its vigorously thrusting string theme stirringly conducted by Svetlanov – increases the appeal of this CD. At bargain price it is now a best buy for those wanting a suite from the two Khachaturian ballets.

Greeting overture; Festive poem; Lermontov suite; Ode in memory of Lenin; Russian fantasy.
(N) ** ASV Dig. CDDCA 946 [id.]. Armenian PO, Tjeknavorian.

Although it has plenty of characteristic Armenian colour, most of this music is routine Khachaturian, or worse: the *Festive poem* (at nearly 20 minutes) is far too inflated for its content, and the *Ode to Lenin* is an all too typical Soviet tribute. The sub-Rimskian finale of the *Lermontov suite* is by far the best movement. The *Russian fantasy* uses an agreeable folk-like melody, but we hear it repeated too often before the final quickening. Good performances, but the resonant recording is acceptable rather than sparkling.

Spartacus (ballet): *suites Nos. 1–3.*
*** Chandos Dig. CHAN 8927 [id.]. SNO, Neeme Järvi.

The ripe lushness of Khachaturian's scoring in *Spartacus* narrowly skirts vulgarity. Järvi and the SNO clearly enjoy the music's tunefulness and primitive vigour, while the warmly resonant acoustics of Glasgow's Henry Wood Hall bring properly sumptuous orchestral textures, smoothing over the moments of crudeness without losing the Armenian colouristic vividness.

Symphonies Nos. 1 in E min.; 3 in C (Symphonic poem).
*** ASV Dig. CDDCA 858 [id.]. Armenian PO, Loris Tjeknavorian.

Symphony No. 1 in E min.; (i) *Masquerade suite.*
** Russian Disc RDCD11005 [id.]. Moscow R. SO, Alexander Gauk; (i) composer.

The *First Symphony* was Khachaturian's exercise on graduating from Miaskovsky's class in 1934. It is far from negligible and in some ways is superior to some of his later work – certainly to the bombastic *Third*. Now there are two recordings: a modern account from Armenia under Tjeknavorian which enjoys the advantage of good digital recording, and an older one from the redoubtable Alexander Gauk, made in the late 1950s, whose sonic limitations may deter some enthusiasts. It does, however, have the advantage of the composer's performance of the *Masquerade* suite, recorded in stereo. Gauk keeps a stronger grip on proceedings than Tjeknavorian, but the better technical quality will doubtless be more widely preferred. The Armenian orchestra play well for Tjeknavorian, and his is the safer recommendation.

Symphony No. 2 in E min. (The Bell); Battle of Stalingrad (suite).
**(*) ASV Dig. CDDCA 859 [id.]. Armenian PO, Loris Tjeknavorian.

Symphony No. 2 (original version); *Gayaneh: suite* (excerpts).
*** Chandos Dig. CHAN 8945 [id.]. Royal Scottish O, Järvi.

The *Second Symphony* comes from 1943 but the composer subsequently made a number of revisions, the last in 1969, which Tjeknavorian has recorded. It acquired its nickname, '*The Bell*', because of a motive heard on tubular bells, and in the slow movement makes fascinating use of the *Dies irae*. Neeme Järvi and his Scottish forces give a very fine account of themselves and they enjoy the benefit of a superb recording. It runs to some 51 minutes, while Tjeknavorian's final revision prunes the score down to 42 minutes 45 seconds. The suite from *The Battle of Stalingrad* is taken from a score composed for a patriotic film and is empty and inflated.

(i) *Symphony No. 3 (Symphonic poem). Triumphal poem.*
(Y/B) *** Chandos Dig. CHAN 9321 [id.]. BBC PO, Fedor Glushchenko, (i) with Simon Lindley.
   IPPOLITOV-IVANOV: *Caucasian sketches.* ***

If the *Third Symphony* was as strong on musical substance as it is on decibels, it would be something to reckon with. But, alas, it is garish and empty; there are no fewer than eighteen trumpets in all! Analgesics and earplugs will be in brisk demand in its vicinity. The BBC Philharmonic, spurred on by their Russian conductor, play as if they believe in it, and the Chandos recording is in the demonstration category. The three stars are for the performance and the recording – not for the music!

The Valencian Widow (incidental music): *suite; Gayaneh* (ballet): *suite No. 2.*
*** ASV Dig. CDDCA 884 [id.]. Armenian PO, Loris Tjeknavorian (with TJEKNAVORIAN: *Danses
   fantastiques* **(*)).

Khachaturian's early suite from his incidental music to the Spanish comedy, *The Valencian Widow* (1940), is probably his first major score and, brimming over with striking tunes as it is, one is surprised that it has not been discovered by the gramophone before this. This is the Khachaturian of *Gayaneh*, so the coupling of seven lesser-known but indelible excerpts from that fine ballet score – undoubtedly the composer's masterpiece – is very appropriate. Tjeknavorian and his orchestra play this music with great spirit and relish its Armenian flavours; they are equally at home in Tjeknavorian's own suite of *Danses fantastiques*, full of energy and colour if essentially sub-Khachaturian. Splendidly vivid, yet spacious sound.

Clarinet trio.
(N) (B) *** HM Dig.HMA 1901419 [id.]. Walter Boeykens Ens. – PROKOFIEV: *Overture on Jewish
   themes* etc. ***

Khachaturian's *Clarinet trio* is a slight but pleasing work, full of sinuous, Armenian melodic lines. With a *Moderato* finale (in some ways the most striking movement, with the central dance section rather soberly framed), it is without the hyperbole which often distinguishes this composer's orchestral writing. It is very well played and recorded.

PIANO MUSIC

10 Children's pieces; 2 Pieces; Poem; Sonata; Sonatina; Toccata; Waltz (from *Masquerade*).
**(*) Olympia Dig. OCD 423 [id.]. Murray McLachlan.

Apart from the *Toccata* (1932), which is a frequent encore, Khachaturian's piano music rarely features in piano recitals. At 80 minutes, this CD offers all of it with the exception of the *Scenes from childhood* and the *Recitative and fugues*. The early pieces, *Poem* (1927) and the *Valse-Caprice* and *Dance* (1926), are much like the *Toccata*, pretty empty, but the later pieces including the *Sonatina* (1959), the *Ten Children's pieces* (1964) and the *Sonata* (1961) are worth a hearing, even though they are limited in range and rely on a small vocabulary of musical devices. Murray McLachlan is a persuasive guide. His recording, made at All Saints' Church, Petersham, is eminently serviceable though there are times when the attentions of a tuner would not have come amiss (particularly in the garrulous first movement of the *Sonata*).

Klami, Uuno (1900–61)

Kalevala suite, Op. 23; Karelian rhapsody, Op. 15; Sea pictures.
**(*) Chandos Dig. CHAN 9268 [id.]. Iceland SO, Sakari.

The *Kalevala suite* is Klami's best-known work but, like the other two pieces on this disc, it is highly derivative. Ravel and Schmitt mingle with Falla, Sibelius and early Stravinsky; while there are some imaginative and inspired passages (such as the opening of the *Terheniemi* or Scherzo), there is some pretty empty stuff as well. The performances under Petri Sakari are very good indeed. Playback level needs to be high if the recording is to be heard to anywhere near best advantage; there is good perspective and a wide dynamic range.

Lemminkäinen's island adventures; (i) *Song of Lake Kuujärvi; Whirls: suites Nos. 1 & 2.*
(Y/B) *** BIS Dig. CD 656 [id.]. (i) Esa Ruuttunen; Lahti SO, Osmo Vänskä.

Klami was a master of orchestral colour, as one might expect from a composer who had the benefit of Ravel's criticism. *Lemminkäinen's island adventures* dates from 1934 and is more Sibelian than is usual with this composer. He had originally included it in the *Kalevala suite* and then published it separately, but its musical substance does not really sustain its length. There is quite a lot of Prokofiev and Shostakovich in the ballet, *Whirls,* and in *Song of Lake Kuujärvi,* and greater depth in the orchestral song. The performances are good and Esa Ruuttunen is an excellent baritone, and the recording offers wide dynamic range and natural perspective.

Knipper, Lev (1898–1974)

(i) *Concert poem for cello and orchestra; Sinfonietta for strings.*
** Olympia OCD 163 [id.]. (i) Shakhovskaya; Moscow Conservatoire CO, Teryan – MIASKOVSKY: *Symphony No. 7.* **

This *Sinfonietta* is well-fashioned but rather anonymous music, albeit with some moments of beauty. The *Concert poem* opens strikingly and is played magnificently, but is not strongly individual either.

Knussen, Oliver (born 1952)

(i) *Songs without voices, Op. 26;* (ii) *Sonya's lullaby, Op. 16; Variations, Op. 24;* (iii; i) *Hums and songs of Winnie-the-Pooh, Op. 6;* (iii) *4 Late poems and and epigram of Rainer Maria Rilke, Op. 23;* (iv; i) *Océan de terre, Op. 10;* (iv; ii) *Whitman settings, Op. 25.*
*** Virgin/EMI Dig. VC7 59308-2 [id.]. (i) Chamber Music Soc. of Lincoln Center, composer; (ii) Peter Serkin; (iii) Lisa Saffer; (iv) Lucy Shelton.

Some of Oliver Knussen's shorter works, all sharply characterful, here receive superb performances from American musicians, biting and committed, making light of the complexities of argument and texture. Serkin, for whom the solo piano works were written, plays incisively, both warmly responsive and muscular, not just in those works but also as accompanist to Lucy Shelton in the angular Whitman settings. The *Pooh songs,* with Lisa Saffer another bright, clear soprano, reflect Knussen's fascination with children's literature; but they are certainly not music for children, reflecting simply a mood of playfulness. The most complex work is the earliest, *Océan de terre,* but even that is clarified in such a performance as this. Good, well-focused sound. (This CD is available only through EMI's Special Import Service.)

Kodály, Zoltán (1882–1967)

Concerto for orchestra; Dances of Galánta; Dances of Marosszék; Háry János: suite; Symphony in C; Summer evening; Theatre overture; Variations on a Hungarian folksong (The Peacock).
(B) *** Double Decca 443 006-2 (2) [id.]. Philh. Hungarica, Antal Dorati.

This is all music which, though it is always beautifully written and often colourful, is not always as cogent as it might be. The more ambitious pieces like the *Concerto for orchestra* and the three-movement *Symphony in C* are certainly enjoyable, but they lack the sharpness of inspiration that pervades the music of Kodály's friend Bartók. The *Symphony* comes from the composer's last years and lacks real concentration and cohesion. Even so, in Dorati's hands the passionate *Andante* is strong in gypsy feeling and the jolly, folk-dance finale, if repetitive, is colourful and full of vitality. *Summer evening,* too, is warmly evocative, but in the *Theatre overture,* brightly and effectively scored, the invention is thin. The 1973 sound remains of vintage quality and the CD transfers are first rate.

(i) *Dances of Galánta; Dances of Marosszék;* (ii) *Háry János: suite.*
(M) *** Mercury 432 005-2 [id.]. (i) Philharmonia Hungarica; (ii) Minneapolis SO, Dorati – BARTOK: *Hungarian sketches* etc. ***

Dances of Galánta; Dances of Marosszék; Háry János suite; Variations on a Hungarian folksong (The Peacock).
(N) *** Decca Dig. 444 322-2 [id.]. Montreal SO, Charles Dutoit.
(M) *** Decca 425 034-2 [id.]. Philharmonia Hungarica, Dorati.

Dances of Galánta; Dances of Marosszék; Variations on a Hungarian folksong (The Peacock).
(N) (BB) ** Naxos Dig. 8.550520 [id.]. Slovak RSO (Bratislava), Adrian Leaper.

Dances of Galánta; Háry János: suite.
*** Delos Dig. DE 3083 [id.]. Seattle SO, Gerard Schwarz – BARTOK: *Miraculous Mandarin.* **(*)

Charles Dutoit, like Antal Dorati before him on Decca, offers the four most popular of Kodály's orchestral works in richly resonant, purposeful performances, with rhythms crisply sprung and with superb playing from the fine soloists of the Montreal orchestra. Though Dorati and his Hungarian players may at times sound more idiomatic, Dutoit and his Montreal players gain in brilliance, helped by recording of demonstration quality, outstanding even by Montreal standards. The *Peacock variations* benefit most of all from the opulence of the Montreal sound, not least in the glorious climax of the finale, which with Dutoit has tremendous panache.

From sneeze to finale, the Minneapolis orchestral playing in the *Háry János suite* is crisp and vigorous; given the excellent 1956 Mercury stereo, Dorati went on to record the other two sets of dances with the Philharmonia Hungarica in 1958. The playing of the woodwind soloists in the slow dances is intoxicatingly seductive, and the power and punch of the climaxes come over with real Mercury fidelity. An outstanding disc, since the Bartók couplings are equally successful.

The Philharmonia Hungarica performances of the *Galánta dances* and the familiar *Háry János suite* are also first class, and the *Peacock variations* – luxuriantly extended, highly enjoyable and deserving of greater popularity – are equally fine. While the older, Mercury performances have a very special electricity of their own, the 1973 Decca recording is more modern and is of vintage quality.

The Seattle Symphony Orchestra play Kodály's music with great vividness and warmth. The *Háry János suite* is more spaciously romantic in feeling than some versions – helped by the rich acoustics of Seattle Opera House – and there is less surface glitter. But *The Battle and defeat of Napoleon* and the *Entrance of the Emperor and his Court* have all the necessary mock-drama and spectacle, and it is good to hear the cimbalom again balanced so effectively within the orchestra. The *Galánta dances* have splendid dash. The recording is outstandingly real.

The Bratislava players know just what this music is about and they play beautifully, but Adrian Leaper's direction seems a little lacking in temperament; this music should ideally sound more volatile. The recording is very good.

(i–iii; vi) *Háry János* (play with music): complete recording of music, with narration by Peter Ustinov; (iv) *The Peacock* (folksong for unaccompanied chorus); (ii; v–vi) *Psalmus Hungaricus;* (vi) *Variations on a Hungarian folksong (The Peacock).*
(Y/B) (M) **(*) Decca Double 443 488-2 (2) [id.]. (i) Olga Szönyi, Márgit László, Erszébet Komlössy, György Melis, Zsolt Bende, Lásló Palócz; (ii) Wandsworth School Boys' Ch.; (iii) Edinburgh Festival Ch.; (iv) London Symphony Ch.; (v) Lajos Kozma, Brighton Festival Ch.; (vi) LSO; all cond. Kertész.

All of Kodály's music for *Háry János* is included here, and the links are provided by Peter Ustinov in many guises. Whether the comedy stands the test of repetition is another matter, but it is good to have Kodály's full score, including a number of pieces as attractive as those in the well-known suite, and vocal versions of some that we know already. Superb recording. This Double Decca reissue also includes a much-valued performance of the *Psalmus Hungaricus*, Kodály's most vital choral work. The light tenor tone of Lajos Kozma is not ideal for the solo part, but again the authentic Hungarian touch helps. The *Peacock variations* make a marvellous display piece, and it was a happy idea to include the folksong itself, stirringly sung by the London Symphony Chorus. No attempt in the variations to build an intellectual structure: orchestral resource provides the mainspring, and the LSO revels in the virtuoso challenge. The CD transfers are first class throughout.

Háry János suite.
(BB) *** Naxos Dig. 8.550142; *4550142* [id.]. Hungarian State O, Mátyás Antal (with Concert: '*Hungarian festival*' ***).

The Hungarian performance of the *Háry János suite* is wonderfully vivid, with the cimbalom – perfectly balanced within the orchestra – particularly telling. The grotesque elements of *The Battle and defeat of Napoleon* are pungently and wittily characterized and the *Entrance of the Emperor and his Court* also has an ironical sense of spectacle. The brilliant digital sound adds to the vitality and projection of the music-making, yet the lyrical music is played most tenderly.

Variations on a Hungarian theme (The Peacock).
(N) *** EMI Dig. CDC7 54858-2 [id.]. LPO, Welser-Möst – BARTOK: *Miraculous mandarin* etc. **

Welser-Möst is at his most understanding in his refined account of the colourful *Peacock variations*.

Where in the Bartók works his meticulous approach sounds underpowered, the Kodály is made to sound the more purposeful from similar treatment, with warm and polished playing from the LPO.

(Unaccompanied) *Cello sonata, Op. 8; Cello sonata* (for cello and piano), *Op. 4.*
(N) (B) *** HM Dig. HMA 1901325 [id.]. Lluís Claret, (i) with Rose-Marie Cabestany.

On the evidence of this record, the Andorran cellist, Lluís Claret, has a larger-than-life musical personality, and one is sorely tempted to use the word 'vintage' to describe his inspired performance of Op. 8, which has extraordinary power and intensity, while its improvisatory feeling brings the immediacy of 'live' music-making. This is a memorably compulsive account of a work which, until now, Starker has made his own. Moreover the recording is real and tangible within a suitably open acoustic. Rose-Marie Cabestany joins Claret persuasively for the less ambitious but still impressive two-movement *Sonata for cello and piano*, Op. 4, and proves an excellent partner, so that this piece is by no means an anticlimax after the major work. This is one of the finest bargains yet on Harmonia Mundi's Musique d'Abord label.

(Unaccompanied) *Cello sonata, Op. 8;* (i) *Duo for violin and cello.*
*** Delos D/CD 1015 [id.]. Janos Starker, (i) Josef Gingold.

When, not long before the composer's death, Kodály heard Starker playing this *Cello sonata*, he apparently said: 'If you correct the ritard in the third movement, it will be the Bible performance.' The recording is made in a smaller studio than is perhaps ideal; the *Duo*, impressively played by Starker and Josef Gingold, is made in a slightly more open acoustic. There is a small makeweight in the form of Starker's own arrangement of the Bottermund *Paganini variations.*

String quartet No. 2, Op. 10.
*** DG Dig. 419 601-2 [id.]. Hagen Qt – DVORAK: *String quartet No. 12* etc. ***
(N) *** Testament SBT 1072 [id.]. Hollywood Qt – DVORAK; SMETANA: *Quartets.* (***)

The Hagen give a marvellously committed and beautifully controlled performance of the *Second* – indeed as quartet playing it would be difficult to surpass. In range of dynamic response and sheer beauty of sound, this is thrilling playing and welcome advocacy of a neglected but masterly piece. The recording is well balanced and admirably present.

Although American readers will know the Hollywood Quartet's account of this piece, it will be new to collectors on this side of the Atlantic. It was recorded in 1958 and, unlike the Dvořák and Smetana with which it is coupled, is in stereo. Once a frequent item on concert and radio programmes, the Kodály has become something of a rarity. The present performance can only be described as masterly, enhancing the attractions of an already excellent issue.

Budavári Te Deum; Missa brevis.
*** Hung. HCD 11397-2 [id.]. Andor, Ekert, Makkay, Mohácsi, Szirmay, Réti, Gregor, Hungarian R. & TV Ch., Budapest SO, Ferencsik.

The *Budavári Te Deum* is predictably nationalist in feeling. The *Missa brevis* is also one of Kodály's strongest works, almost comparable in stature to the *Psalmus Hungaricus*. The singing is accurate and sensitive, and the playing of the Budapest orchestra under Ferencsik absolutely first class.

Missa brevis.
(N) (M) **(*) EMI Dig. CDM5 65587-2 [id.]. King's College, Cambridge, Ch., Cleobury; Stephen Lane – JANACEK: *Mass* etc. ***

The *Missa brevis*, as its subtitle, *In tempore belli*, suggests, was composed at the height of the Second World War; it was first conceived as an organ Mass; but in 1945, when the Russians were laying siege to Budapest, Kodály transcribed it for voices and organ, subsequently orchestrating it. It is one of Kodály's strongest and most deeply felt works, every bit as powerful as the *Psalmus Hungaricus*. Ferencsik's recording was of the orchestral version, whereas Stephen Cleobury gives it in its earlier form, as did Laszlo Heltay in the 1970s. Some of the treble lines could be more secure, but for the most part this is a good performance, even if it lacks the bite and intensity that Hungarian singers would bring to it.

(i; ii; v) *Missa brevis;* (ii; v) *Pange lingua;* (iii) *Psalmus Hungaricus;* (iv; v) *Psalm 114.*
✪ (M) *** Decca 433 080-2 [id.]. Brighton Festival Ch. with (i) Gale, Le Sage, Francis, Hodgson, Caley, Rippon; (ii) Bowers-Broadbent (organ); (iii) Kozma, Wandsworth School Boys' Ch., LSO, Kertész; (iv) Weir (organ); (v) cond. Heltay.

László Heltay directs all the music except the *Psalmus Hungaricus*, which is splendidly vibrant in the hands of István Kertész and there is no doubt that Heltay's meticulous training contributed to the fluency of that outstanding performance, idiomatically presented in Hungarian. The *Missa brevis* is literally a short setting of the Mass, not one which omits the *Credo*. The *Pange lingua* is a more searching piece, sung here with glorious tone and great intensity. The short setting of *Psalm 114*, from the Geneva Psalter, is also very moving and shows Kodály's relatively gentle art at its most persuasive, and here Gillian Weir makes an impressive contribution. A highly rewarding 70-minute collection, given vintage Decca sound from the mid-to late 1970s.

Psalmus hungaricus, Op. 13.
(Y/B) *** Chandos Dig. CHAN 9310 [id.]. Svensson, Copenhagen Boys' Ch., Danish Nat. R. Ch. & SO, Mackerras – JANACEK: *Glagolitic Mass.* ***

As the unusual but refreshing coupling for the Janáček *Mass*, the *Psalmus hungaricus* is here infected with an element of wildness that sweeps away any idea of Kodály as a bland composer. As in the Janáček, the tenor Peter Svensson is an excellent, clear-toned and incisive soloist, if here rather more backwardly balanced. The glory of the performance lies most of all in the superb choral singing, full, bright and superbly disciplined, with the hushed pianissimos as telling as the great fortissimo outbursts. It is a mark of Mackerras's understanding of the music that the many sudden changes of mood sound both dramatic and natural. Full, warm and atmospheric recording, with plenty of detail.

Koechlin, Charles (1867–1961)

(i) *Ballade for piano and orchestra, Op. 50. 7 Stars Symphony (suite), Op. 13.*
(M) *** EMI Dig. CDM7 64369-2 [id.]. (i) Bruno Rigutto; Monte Carlo PO, Myrat.

The 'stars' of the *Symphony* are terrestrial rather than galactic: Fairbanks and Marlene Dietrich, not Betelgeuse and Sirius. Koechlin is an interesting figure who has been spoken of as a French Charles Ives, though so glib a comparison does not do justice to his individuality of mind. The *Seven Stars Symphony* is not, strictly speaking, a symphony, rather a series of sketches evoking the great personalities of the cinema in the 1920s and '30s, and it is coupled here with an earlier work written for the pianist Henriette Fauré. Koechlin is a stimulating figure and, given the keen advocacy of these artists and the excellence of the CD sound, this enterprising reissue well rewards investigation.

Les Bandar-log (symphonic poem), Op. 176.
(M) *** EMI CDM7 63948-2 [id.]. BBC SO, Dorati – BOULEZ: *Le soleil des eaux;* MESSIAEN: *Chronochromie* etc. ***

Les Bandar-log is a symphonic poem based on the Kipling story, but used to satirize the vagaries of twentieth-century composers with fluent mastery, and the score is aurally fascinating, especially in a performance as finely played and dedicated as this and with a 1964 recording which in its CD transfer approaches the demonstration class.

Les heures persanes, Op. 65.
*** Marco Polo Dig. 8.223504 [id.]. Reinland-Pfalz PO, Segerstam.

Koechlin's powers as an orchestrator are evident in these 16 exotic mood-pictures *d'après Vers Isphahan de Pierre Loti* which were originally composed for the piano in 1913. They evoke a journey recorded by Pierre Loti in 1900. 'He who wants to come with me to see at Isfahan the season of roses should travel slowly by my side, in stages, as in the Middle Ages' (to quote Loti's preface), and the cynic might be tempted to say that we do. The work is generally slow-moving, but this music has tremendous atmosphere and exotic colours and the very titles of the movements (*Les collines au coucher de soleil, A l'ombre près de la fontaine marbre*, for example) conjure up some idea of its character. In the hands of Leif Segerstam and the Reinland-Pfalz Orchestra this music casts a powerful spell. It is also beautifully recorded.

The Jungle Book (Le livre de la Jungle).
*** Marco Polo Dig. 8.223484 [id.]. Reinland-Pfalz PO, Segerstam.

The Jungle Book (Le livre de la Jungle); (i) 3 songs (Seal Lullaby, Night-Song in the Jungle; Song of Kala Nag) for soloists, chorus and orchestra, Op. 18.
(M) *** RCA Dig. 09026 61955-2 (2) [id.]. Berlin RSO, Zinman, (i) with Vermillion, Botha, Lukas & Ch.

Koechlin's lifelong fascination for Kipling's *Jungle Book* is reflected in this extraordinary four-movement tone-poem whose composition extended over several decades. *La course de printemps*, Op. 95, the longest of them, is extraordinarily imaginative and pregnant with atmosphere: you can feel the heat and humidity of the rainforest and sense the presence of strange and menacing creatures. *La loi de la jungle* is the most static and the least interesting. Leif Segerstam is excellent in this repertoire and with his refined ear for texture distils a heady atmosphere. His reading of *Les bandar-log* may not be superior to Dorati's pioneering EMI version with the BBC Symphony Orchestra (see above) but it more than holds its own and, like its companions, is beautifully recorded. Anyone with a feeling for the exotic will respond to this original and fascinating music.

David Zinman and the Berlin Radio Symphony Orchestra on RCA include three Op. 18 songs (*Seal lullaby*, *Night-song in the jungle* and *Song of Kala Nag*) for soloists, chorus and orchestra, and necessitating an additional disc, albeit accommodated economically on a two-for-the-price-of-one Duo set, as in the Double Decca and Philips Duo series. Generally speaking, Zinman's performance is almost as atmospheric, though the texture is more brightly lit and clearly defined. Either can be safely recommended with three stars, but, if your shop stocks both, Segerstam has the stronger atmosphere and would be a first recommendation.

Kohaut, Carl (Joseph) (1736–93)

Lute concerto in F.
(M) **(*) RCA 09026 61588-2. Julian Bream, Monteverdi O, Gardiner – HANDEL; VIVALDI: *Concertos.* **(*)

Kohaut, a Bohemian composer, was himself a lutenist and this is a well-made little work, *galant* in style and with an attractively simple *arioso* forming the slow movement. The performance is excellent and the recording good, except for the larger-than-life solo instrument caused by the forward balance.

Kokkonen, Joonas (born 1921)

(i) *Cello concerto; Symphonic sketches; Symphony No. 4.*
*** BIS Dig. CD 468 [id.]. (i) Torleif Thedéen, Lahti SO, Osmo Vänskä.

The *Fourth Symphony* is the strongest work here: its ideas are symphonic, its structure organic and its atmosphere powerful. The *Cello concerto* is a lyrical piece, very accessible. The Swedish cellist, Torleif Thedéen, gives a performance of great restraint, mastery and sensitivity. Good orchestral playing and recording.

(i) *Cello concerto;* (ii) *Symphony No. 3;* (iii) *Cello sonata.*
(M) *** Finlandia FACD 027 [id.]. (i; iii) Noras; (i) Helsinki PO, Freeman; (ii) Finnish RSO, Berglund; (iii) Heinonen.

There is precious little to choose between Arto Noras's version of the *Cello concerto* and that of the young Swedish cellist, Torleif Thedéen; both play with aristocratic finesse and convey the composer's intentions with admirable fidelity; both were recorded in close collaboration with the composer, though Thedéen on BIS has the advantage of digital recording. Paavo Berglund's excellent recording of the *Third Symphony* was made in the early 1970s and briefly appeared on Decca in the UK. This Finlandia record has the advantage of economy.

(i) *Sinfonia da camera; Il paesaggio* ; (ii) '*. . . durch einen Spiegel . . .*' (iii) *Wind quintet.*
*** BIS Dig. CD 528 [id.]. (i; ii) Lahti SO; (i) Vänskä; (iii) Söderblom; (ii) with Tiensuu; (iii) Lahti Sinf. Wind Quintet.

Those coming new to Kokkonen's musical idiom, should try the pretentiously titled but resourceful and imaginative '*. . . durch einen Spiegel . . .*', subtitled *Metamorphosis* for twelve strings and harpsichord. There are some rewardingly individual sonorities. *Il paesaggio* is an evocative landscape study, and the earlier *Wind quintet* is a lively piece. The early *Sinfonia da camera* is grey general-purpose modern music deriving from Bartókian-Hindemithian roots. Very good performances and splendid recording.

Symphony No. 1; Music for string orchestra; (i) *The Hades of the birds* (song-cycle).
*** BIS Dig. CD 485 [id.]. Lahti SO, Söderblom; (i) Monica Groop.

The *Music for string orchestra* is a rather powerful piece lasting almost half-an-hour, well wrought and its invention finely sustained if slightly anonymous. The colourings are dark. *The Hades of the birds* is a short song-cycle, which shows Monica Groop's talents to strong effect, but it is the *First Symphony* which is the strongest piece on the disc. It is serious in purpose and as far as the orchestra is concerned shows considerable mastery of colour.

Symphony No. 2; Inauguratio; Erekhtheion (cantata); *The Last temptations* (opera): *Interludes*.
**(*) BIS Dig. CD 498 [id.]. Vihavainen, Grönroos, Akateeminen Laulu Ch., Lahti SO, Vänskä.

The *Second Symphony* is a work of some eloquence and its invention has a certain freshness and quality, even if it remains ultimately unmemorable. The interludes from his opera, *The Last temptations*, make a strong impression. Not an essential purchase for admirers of this composer.

Symphony No. 3; (i) *Opus sonorum;* (ii) *Requiem*.
*** BIS Dig. CD 508 [id.]. Lahti SO, Söderblom; (i) with Ilkka Sivonen; (ii) Iskoski, Grönroos, Savonlinna Op. Festival Ch.

Söderblom's account of the *Third Symphony* has detail and atmosphere, and the same must be said of the *Requiem*. In the *Opus sonorum*, written in reaction to the vast battery of percussion so common in the 1960s, Kokkonen assigns all the percussion part to a piano, played with great delicacy here.

(i) *Piano quintet; String quartets Nos. 1–3*.
*** BIS Dig. CD 458 [id.]. (i) Valsta; Sibelius Ac. Qt.

The *Quintet* is a slight but not unpleasing work; the *First Quartet*, which sounds like any chamber work of the period, has more gravitas. Like its companions it is very well played, but even such eloquent advocacy cannot disguise a certain facelessness. But three stars for the performers and the engineers.

The Last Temptations (opera): complete.
**(*) Finlandia FACD 104 (2) [id.]. Auvinen, Ruohonen, Lehtinen, Talvela, Savonlinna Op. Festival Ch. & O, Söderblom.

The Last Temptations tells of a revivalist leader, Paavo Ruotsalainen, from the Finnish province of Savo and of his inner struggle to discover Christ. The opera is dominated by the personality of Martti Talvela, and its invention for the most part has a dignity and power that are symphonic in scale. All four roles are well sung, and the performance under Ulf Söderblom is very well recorded indeed.

Koppel, Herman D. (born 1908)

Cello concerto, Op. 56.
*** BIS CD 80 [id.]. Erling Blondal Bengtsson, Danish Nat. RSO, Schmidt – NORHOLM: *Violin concerto*. ***

Herman D. Koppel's idiom stems from Stravinsky and Bartók, but the opening of his *Cello concerto* has something of the luminous quality of Tippett's *Midsummer Marriage*. Very good recording of an inventive and original piece that deserves to enter the wider international repertoire. It is more satisfying than either the Kokkonen or Sallinen concertos.

Korngold, Erich (1897–1957)

Violin concerto in D, Op. 35.
*** EMI CDC7 47846-2 [id.]. Perlman, Pittsburgh SO, Previn – GOLDMARK: *Concerto*. ***

(i) *Violin concerto;* (ii) *Much Ado About Nothing* (suite), *Op. 11*.
(Y/B) *** DG Dig. 439 886-2 [id.]. Gil Shaham; (i) LSO, Previn; (ii) Previn (piano) – BARBER: *Violin concerto*. ***

The Korngold was written within five years of the Barber *Concerto* and makes a desirable coupling for it. Indeed the conjunction of Barber and Korngold works splendidly, when in the Barber the ripe performance brings out moments that are not too distant from the world of Hollywood music, and the Korngold then emerges as a central work in that genre. The Israeli violinist, Gil Shaham, gives a performance of effortless virtuosity and strong profile. Shaham may not have quite the flair and panache of the dedicatee, Jascha Heifetz, in his incomparable reading, but he is warmer and more committed than Itzakh Perlman in his Pittsburgh recording for EMI, again with Previn conducting. There is greater freshness and conviction than in the Perlman. The recording helps, far clearer and more immediate than Perlman's EMI. It is true that in his cooler way Perlman finds an extra tenderness in such passages as the entry of the violin in the slow movement, but Shaham and Previn together consistently bring out the work's sensuous warmth without making the result soupy. The suite from Korngold's incidental music to *Much Ado About Nothing* provides a delightful and apt makeweight, with Previn as pianist just as understanding and imaginative an accompanist and Shaham yearningly warm without sentimentality, clean and precise in attack.

Film scores: *The Adventures of Robin Hood* (suite); *Captain Blood: Ship in the Night;* (i) *The Sea Hawk* (suite).
(M) *** RCA GD 80912 [0912-2-RG]. Nat. PO, Charles Gerhardt; (i) with Amb. S. – STEINER: *Film scores.* ***

Curiously, although this collection, centring on the swashbuckling movies of Errol Flynn, is entitled *'Captain Blood'*, only a fragment – if a potent one – is included from Korngold's music for this film. Juxtaposed with the more flamboyant Steiner scores for other Flynn vehicles, this makes for one of the very best of these Hollywood anthologies. As in the rest of the series, the dedication of Charles Gerhardt and the superb playing of the National Philharmonic Orchestra, coupled with sumptuous RCA recording, means that these performances communicate strongly.

Film scores: excerpts from: *Another Dawn; Anthony Adverse; Deception:* (i) *Cello concerto in C, Op. 37. Of Human Bondage; The Prince and the Pauper; The Private Lives of Elizabeth and Essex; The Sea Wolf.*
(M) *** RCA GD 80185; *GK 80185* [0185-2-RG; *0185-4-RG*]. Nat. PO, Gerhardt, (i) with Gabarro.

Korngold drew on the attractive, lightweight score for *The Prince and the Pauper* as a basis for the variations in the last movement of the *Violin concerto,* while *Night scene* from *Another Dawn* – very effective in its own right – was to provide the principal theme of the first movement. For *Deception* he invented a miniature cello concerto, which is heard here in its expanded complete format. The performances by Gerhardt and the National Philharmonic are as persuasive as ever, with brilliant, spacious recording to match.

Sinfonietta, Op. 5; Sursum corda, Op. 13.
(Y/B) *** Chandos Dig. CHAN 9317 [id.]. BBC PO, Bamert.

Korngold's *Sinfonietta* is a product of his precocious boyhood, a substantial four-movement work, a symphony in all but name, betraying a prodigious technical expertise both in the management and organization of musical ideas and in the handling of the orchestra; and not only that, the ideas themselves are of real quality and individuality. Moreover it is most skilfully scored, with Respighian pre-echoes in the Scherzo. The waltz-rhythms in the sonata-form first movement are immediately engaging, and even Korngold rarely outshone the lyrical warmth of the slow movement, while the finale brings the most extended structure of all, with more Hollywood anticipations. At 43 minutes, it is an extraordinary achievement for a fourteen-year-old and in its way is comparable (though not quite, perhaps, in quality of inspiration) only with Mendelssohn in the *Octet* and *Midsummer Night's Dream* music – an adolescent composer springing as it were fully equipped on to the musical scene. When in 1938 Korngold was working against time to write the score for the Hollywood epic with Errol Flynn, *The Adventures of Robin Hood,* he thought back to the brilliant symphonic overture he had composed 18 years earlier, *Sursum corda.* At the stroke of a pen the opening fanfare motif provided the motto theme for the hero, and he also borrowed extensively from other passages. The original virtuoso showpiece lasting 20 minutes is finer than one might expect, an extraordinarily sumptuous piece that in its wide range of moods keeps suggesting that it will turn into the *Pines of Rome.* There are alternative versions of the *Sinfonietta,* but the present performance by the BBC Philharmonic Orchestra under Matthias Bamert is a clear front-runner and the Chandos recording is altogether superb in terms of definition and opulence. A ripely enjoyable disc of beautifully played performances, and a valuable addition to the catalogue, with the sumptuous sound-picture a little distant.

Symphony in F sharp, Op. 40; (i) *Abschiedslieder, Op. 14.*
*** Chandos Dig. CHAN 9171 [id.]. (i) Linda Finnie; BBC PO, Downes.

The *Symphony* is a work of real imaginative power. It is scored for large forces – a big percussion section including piano, celeste, marimba, etc., and the orchestra is used with resource and flair. A big, 50-minute work, its opening almost calls to mind Prokofiev's textures, though there is also a fair amount of Mahler. The BBC Philharmonic play with enthusiasm and sensitivity for Edward Downes. The *Abschiedslieder* are much earlier and were completed in 1920; there is a great deal of Strauss, Mahler and Zemlinsky here. Linda Finnie is a persuasive soloist, and the balance is eminently well judged. The Chandos recording is wide-ranging and lifelike.

Piano trio in D, Op. 1.
(Y/B) *** Ph. Dig. 434 072-2. Beaux Arts Trio – ZEMLINSKY: *Piano trio.* ***

Although we have admired the Pacific Arts Trio on the Delos label the present version is both played and recorded better, and must supplant it. The Beaux Arts take a more leisurely and relaxed view of the piece: indeed there will be some who have become accustomed to and who will prefer the greater tautness and urgency of the Delos version. However, the Beaux Arts is now the one to have on all counts, unless a coupling with the *Violin sonata* is wanted – see below.

(i) *Piano trio in D, Op. 1; Violin sonata in G, Op. 6.*
(Y/B) *** EMI CDC5 55401-2 [id.]. Glenn Dicterow, Israela Margalit; (i) with Alan Stepansky.

Written when he was only twelve and dedicated to his father, Julius, the Viennese critic, the *Piano trio*, inventive and distinctive, betrays remarkably few influences, save the occasional echo of Richard Strauss, who promptly praised the boy's work. The *Violin sonata* of three years later, written for Carl Flesch and Artur Schnabel, is even more adventurous, with an extended Scherzo, the longest of the four movements, which develops from its skittish opening into darker moods. The slow movement, marked to be played 'with deep expressiveness', is the most richly lyrical, before the *Allegretto* finale brings an equivocal conclusion. Warmly expressive performances and full, well-balanced recording.

String sextet, Op.10.
*** Hyperion Dig. CDA 66425 [id.]. Raphael Ens. – SCHOENBERG: *Verklaerte Nacht*. ***

The Korngold *Sextet* is an amazing achievement for a seventeen-year-old. Not only is it crafted with musicianly assurance and maturity it is also inventive and characterful. The Raphael Ensemble play it with great commitment and the Hyperion recording is altogether first class.

3 Lieder, Op. 18. Lieder: *Alt-spanisch; Gefasster Abschied; Glückwunsch; Liebesbriefchen; Sonett für Wien; Sterbelied.*
*** DG Dig. 437 515-2 [id.]. Anne Sofie von Otter, Bengt Forsberg – BERG: *7 Early songs;* STRAUSS: *Lieder.* ***

Anne Sofie von Otter and Bengt Forsberg follow up the success of their prize-winning disc of Grieg songs with inspired playing and singing, not just in Berg and Strauss, relatively well known, but in these rare and immediately attractive songs by Erich Korngold. Though a few date from his early, precocious years in Vienna, including some of the most sensuously beautiful, such a charming miniature as *Alt-spanisch* is taken from the film music he wrote in 1940 for the swashbuckling Hollywood film, *The Sea Hawk*. Singer and pianist draw out the intensity of emotion to the full without exaggeration or sentimentality. A fascinating programme.

OPERA

Die tote Stadt (complete).
(M) *** RCA GD 87767 (2) [7767-2-RG]. Neblett, Kollo, Luxon, Prey, Bav. R. Ch., Tölz Ch., Munich R. O, Leinsdorf.

At the age of twenty-three Korngold had his opera, *Die tote Stadt*, presented in simultaneous world premières in Hamburg and Cologne! The score includes many echoes of Puccini and Richard Strauss, but its youthful exuberance carries the day. Here René Kollo is powerful, if occasionally coarse of tone, Carol Neblett sings sweetly in the equivocal roles of the wife's apparition and the newcomer, and Hermann Prey, Benjamin Luxon and Rose Wagemann make up an impressive cast. Leinsdorf is at his finest.

Violanta (complete).
**(*) Sony CD 79229 [MK 35909]. Marton, Berry, Jerusalem, Stoklassa, Laubenthal, Hess, Bav. R. Ch., Munich R. O, Janowski.

Korngold was perhaps the most remarkable composer-prodigy of this century; he wrote this opera at the age of seventeen. Though luscious of texture and immensely assured, the writing lets one down by an absence of really memorable melody but, with a fine, red-blooded performance and with Siegfried Jerusalem a youthfully fresh hero, it makes a fascinating addition to the recorded repertory. Eva Marton, not always beautiful of tone, combines power and accuracy in the key role of the heroine. The recording is quite full if not especially refined.

Das Wunder der Heliane (complete).
*** Decca Dig. 436 636-2 (3) [id.]. Tomowa-Sintow, Welker, De Haan, Runkel, Pape, Gedda, Berlin R. Ch. & RSO, Mauceri.

Like the Decca set of Krenek's *Jonny spielt auf*, this Korngold opera, also first performed in Vienna in 1927, comes in a series devoted to works banned by the Nazis, '*Entartete Musik*', so-called decadent music. The narrative itself is full of overt eroticism. Though the plot, with its tyrannical ruler, his wife and a mysterious stranger, is unconvincing, Decca's magnificent recording amply confirms the view that this is Korngold's masterpiece, musically even richer than his better-known opera, *Die tote Stadt*. The opening prelude, with its exotic harmonies and heavenly choir, will seduce anyone with a sweet tooth, and though in three Acts of nearly an hour each it is overlong, Korngold – who had just emerged from his years as a child prodigy to rival Mozart – sustains the story with a ravishing score. Puccini as well as Strauss is often very close, with one passage in the big Act I love-duet bringing languorous echoes of the end of *Fanciulla del West*. Korngold's lavish Hollywood scores of the 1930s are thin by comparison. John Mauceri draws glorious sounds from the Berlin Radio Symphony Orchestra, and the cast is headed by three outstanding singers, the soprano Anna Tomowa-Sintow at her richest, an impressive American Heldentenor, John David de Haan, as the Stranger and Hartmut Welker as the Ruler.

Kozeluch, Leopold (1747–1818)

Clarinet concerto No. 2 in E flat.
*** ASV Dig. CDDCA 763 [id.]. Emma Johnson, RPO, Herbig – CRUSELL; KROMMER: *Concertos*. ***

The Bohemian composer, Leopold Kozeluch, was the cousin of the slightly better-known Jan (Johann), and his concerto is a highly agreeable work, especially when performed so magnetically by Emma Johnson. There is plenty of Johnsonian magic here to light up even the most conventional passage-work, and the 'naturally flowing melodies' (the soloist's own description), and she is well accompanied and admirably recorded, with the slow movement made to sound recessed and delicate.

Kraft, William (born 1923)

(i) *Concerto for 4 percussion soloists & orchestra; Contextures: Riots – Decade '60.*
(N) **(*) Decca 448 580-2 [id.]. (i) Composer, Goodwin, Delancey, Clark; LAPO, Mehta.

William Kraft's *Contextures* was inspired by the various themes that so disturbed America during the 1960s: the racial turmoil in the cities and the war in Vietnam. The musical invention hardly measures up to the seriousness of these themes and, although the vintage (1968) Decca recording is very impressive, it is not a work of great substance. The *Concerto for four percussion soloists and orchestra* produces some telling effects, and the performance is splendidly efficient.

Kramář, František – see Krommer, Franz
Krása, Hans (1899–1944)

String quartet.
(Y/B) *** Decca Dig. 440 853-2 [id.]. Hawthorne Qt – HAAS: *Quartets Nos. 2 & 3.* ***

Hans Krása and his compatriot, Pavel Haas, were born in the same year and sent to the gas chambers at the Terezin or Teresienstadt camp on the same day. Krása came from Prague and became a pupil of Zemlinsky, but he was influenced by French music as much as by the Viennese school. His *String quartet* is a remarkably mature piece for a twenty-two-year-old and, along with the occasional echoes of Janáček and the French, also burlesques a theme from Smetana's *The Bartered Bride overture*. Although there are rapidly changing moods and colours, the composer holds everything together with a keen and intelligent logic. The Hawthorne Quartet play very persuasively and are excellently recorded. A rewarding issue.

Kreisler, Fritz (1875–1962)

Violin concerto in the style of Vivaldi.
(Y/B) *** DG Dig. 439 933-2 [id.]. Gil Shaham, Orpheus CO – VIVALDI: *The Four Seasons.* ***

An amiable pastiche, which sounds almost totally unlike Vivaldi as we experience his music performed today – indeed the name of Boccherini could well have been substituted in the title credit and, even then, could not disguise the early-twentieth-century provenance of the work. It is warmly played and clearly enjoyed by its performers, and the sumptuousness of the sound is the more striking coming, as it does, immediately after Vivaldi's wintry winds.

Allegretto in the style of Boccherini; Caprice Viennoise; Chanson Louis XIII and Pavane; Liebeslied; Liebesfreud; Minuet; The old refrain; Praeludium and allegro; Recitativo and Scherzo; Rondino on a theme of Beethoven; Schön Rosmarin; Tambourin chinois; Tempo di minuetto.

(N) (M) *** Mercury 434 351-2 [id.]. Henryk Szeryng, Charles Reiner (with LECLAIR: *Violin sonata No. 3 in D;* GLUCK, arr. Kreisler: *Mélodie;* LOCATELLI: *The Labyrinth* **).

It is good to have a reminder of the artistry of Henryk Szeryng, who made many of his best concerto recordings in the earliest days of stereo. His playing of these occasional pieces of Kreisler – not all of them by any means trifles – is superb. The invention of the music is always made to sound spontaneous. How stylishly and lightly he throws off a piece like '*Schön Rosmarin*' and what gentle charm he finds for the *Chanson Louis XIII*. The 1963 recording is firmly focused and truthful. The remaining items are played as virtuoso encores rather than showing any natural sympathy for the baroque style, although no one could fail to be impressed by the bravura of Locatelli's *Labyrinth*. However, in these pieces the Mercury sound brings rather more edge to the violin timbre.

Allegretto in the style of Boccherini; Allegretto in the style of Porpora; Caprice viennoise; Cavatina; La Chasse in the style of Cartier; La Gitana; Grave in the style of W. F. Bach; Gypsy caprice; Liebesfreud; Liebesleid; Praeludium and allegro in the style of Pugnani; Recitative and scherzo; Schön Rosmarin; Shepherd's madrigal; Sicilienne et rigaudon in the style of Francoeur; Toy soldiers' march; Viennese rhapsodic fantasia; arr. of *Austrian National Hymn.*

(BB) **(*) ASV CDQS 6039. Oscar Shumsky, Milton Kaye.

Oscar Shumsky's combination of technical mastery and musical flair is ideal for this music; and it is a pity that the rather dry recording and forward balance – well in front of the piano – makes the violin sound almost too close.

Caprice viennoise; Chanson Louis XIII & Pavane in the style of Couperin; La Gitana; Liebeslied; Liebesfreud; Polinchinelle; La Précieuse in the style of Couperin; Rondino on a theme by Beethoven; Scherzo alla Dittersdorf; Tambourin chinois; Schön Rosmarin. Arrangements: BACH: *Partita No. 3 in E, BWV 1006: Gavotte.* BRANDL: *The old refrain.* DVORAK: *Humoresque.* FALLA: *La vida breve: Danza española.* GLAZUNOV: *Sérénade espagnole.* HEUBERGER: *Midnight bells (Im chambre séparée).* POLDINI: *Poupée valsante.* RIMSKY-KORSAKOV: *Sadko: Chanson hindoue.* SCHUBERT: *Rosamunde: Ballet music No. 2.* SCOTT: *Lotus Land.* TCHAIKOVSKY: *Andante cantabile from Op. 11.* WEBER: *Violin sonata No. 1 in F, Op. 10: Larghetto.* TRAD.: *Londonderry air.*

(M) (***) EMI mono CDH7 64701-2 [id.]. Fritz Kreisler, Franz Rupp or Michael Rachelsein; or (in *Scherzo*) Kreisler String Qt.

Impeccable and characterful performances by Fritz Kreisler of his own lollipops, including those 'in the style of' pieces with which – until he owned up – he fooled his audiences into believing they were actually written by the composers in question. Most of the recordings were made with Franz Rupp in 1936 or 1938, and the transfers offer a convincingly realistic if studio-ish balance and are of excellent technical quality; a few (the *Polinchinelle*, the pieces in the style of Couperin, the Schubert *Rosamunde ballet music*, the Glazunov and Weber arrangements, *The old refrain* (especially) and an indulgent performance of Heuberger's *Im chambre séparée*) date from 1930 and here the piano balance is poor, the piano badly defined. However, these were recorded before Kreisler's accident and the violin timbre is noticeably more opulent. A valuable document.

Caprice viennoise, Op. 2; La Gitana; Liebesfreud; Liebesleid; Polichinelle; La Précieuse; Recitativo and scherzo caprice, Op. 6; Rondo on a theme of Beethoven; Syncopation; Tambourin chinois; Zigeuner (Capriccio). Arrangements: ALBENIZ: *Tango, Op. 165/2.* WEBER: *Larghetto.* WIENIAWSKI: *Caprice in E flat.* DVORAK: *Slavonic dance No. 10 in E min.* GLAZUNOV: *Sérénade espagnole.* GRANADOS: *Danse espagnole.*

(M) *** DG 423 876-2 [id.]. Shlomo Mintz, Clifford Benson.

Shlomo Mintz plays with a disarmingly easy style and absolute technical command, to bring out the music's warmth as well as its sparkle. A very attractive programme, given first-class recording and splendid presence without added edge on CD.

Krenek, Ernst (1900–1991)

Jonny spielt auf (complete).

**(*) Decca Dig. 436 631-2 (2) [id.]. Kruse, Marc, St Hill, Kraus, Posselt, Leipzig Op. Ch., Leipzig GO, Zagrosek.

Ernst Krenek's opera, *Jonny spielt auf* ('Jonny plays on'), was acclaimed as the first jazz opera, even though the composer always resisted that description. Yet it proved a flash in the pan. Paris was unimpressed, and back in Germany it was quickly banned by the Nazi regime, which condemned it as '*Entartete Musik*', decadent music. Hearing the opera now in a fine recording, based on a 1990 Leipzig production – made just before the composer died at the age of ninety – it stands as more than a historical curiosity. Contradicting its reputation, it is a lyrical post-romantic piece. One's first disappointment is that it hardly matches the Kurt Weill operas. The idiom is far milder, with syncopations used more gently in the jazzy passages and with the instrumentation less abrasive. Though the Leipzig Gewandhaus Orchestra under Lothar Zagrosek does not always sound at home in the jazzy sequences, the recording provides the most convincing evidence yet that the piece deserves reappraisal. Heinz Kruse as Max sustains his long monologues impressively, and Krister St Hill as Jonny also sings well, even if the microphone catches an unevenness in their voices. It is Alessandra Marc as the heroine, Anita, who emerges as the main star, relishing lush Krenek melodies that yet never quite stick in the mind.

Kreutzer, Joseph (1778–1832)

Grand Trio.
*** Mer. Dig. CDE 84199 [id.]. Conway, Silverthorne, Garcia – BEETHOVEN: *Serenade;* MOLINO: *Trio.*
***

Joseph Kreutzer, thought to be the brother of Rodolphe Kreutzer, dedicatee of Beethoven's *A major Violin sonata*, wrote many works for the guitar, of which this is a delightful example. The guitar, given at least equal prominence with the other instruments, brings an unusual tang to the textures of this charming piece, ending with a rousing *Alla Polacca*. A nicely pointed performance, very well recorded in warm, faithful sound.

Krommer, Franz (1759–1831)

Clarinet concerto in E flat, Op. 36.
*** ASV Dig. CDDCA 763 [id.]. Emma Johnson, RPO, Herbig – CRUSELL: *Concerto No. 1;* KOZE-
LUCH: *Concerto No. 2.* ***

Emma Johnson is at her most winning in this attractive concerto which is made to sound completely spontaneous in her hands, particularly the engaging finale, lolloping along with its skipping main theme. The *Adagio* is darker in feeling, its mood equally well caught. Excellent accompaniments and warm, refined recording make this a most engaging triptych.

Clarinet concerto in E flat, Op. 36; (i) *Double clarinet concertos in A flat, Opp. 35 & 91.*
(Y/B) (BB) ** Naxos Dig. 8.553178 [id.]. Kálmán Berkes; (i) Kaori Tsutsui; Nicolaus Esterházy Sinfonia.

Both the soloists here are good players and they blend very well together; but slow movements are rather deadpan and not all the music's sense of fun comes over. Neither clarinettists nor orchestra are helped by the reverberant recording which means a forward balance for the soloists and tends to coarsen the tuttis by spreading the sound. Even so, the *Double concerto*, Op. 91, a winner if ever there was one, is very enjoyable, with the first movement swinging along merrily and the *Polacca* finale, with its jaunty duet theme introduced against orchestral pizzicatos, equally fluent.

Symphonies Nos. 2 in D, Op. 40; 4 in C min., Op. 102.
*** Chandos Dig. CHAN 9275 [id.]. LMP, Bamert.

A delightful addition to the representation of Krommer (born František Kramář) in the catalogue. Collectors who acquired the *Harmonien*, played by the Netherlands Wind Ensemble, or the *Octets* (now deleted), which the Sabine Meyer wind ensemble recorded for EMI, will know how infectiously high-spirited this composer is; and they will not be disappointed by the two symphonies played here by the London Mozart Players under Matthias Bamert. They present a different picture of him: the *D major Symphony* (1803) opens in something of the manner of *Don Giovanni*, while much else conveys a distinctly Beethovenian visage. The *C minor*, Op. 102, composed towards the end of the second decade of the nineteenth century, already has a whiff of the changing sensibility that we find in Schubert and Weber. Very interesting and refreshing music, played with evident enthusiasm and well recorded.

Kuhlau, Friedrich (1786–1832)

(i) *Concertino for two horns, Op. 45;* (ii) *Piano concerto in C, Op. 7; Overture Elverhøj (The elves' hill), Op. 100.*
*** Unicorn Dig. DKPCD 9110 [id.]. (i) Ib Lansky-Otto, Frøydis Ree Wekre; (ii) Michael Ponti; Odense SO, Othmar Maga.

The overture *Elverhøj* or *The elves' hill* is probably Kuhlau's best-known work and is certainly the finest piece on this disc. The *Piano concerto in C*, Op. 7, is modelled on Beethoven's concerto in the same key. The *Concertino for two horns* (1821) is full of initially engaging, but eventually unmemorable, ideas. Very good performances from all concerned, and satisfactory recording.

Elverhøj (The elves' hill), Op. 100.
** Dacapo Dig. DCCD 8902 [id.]. Gobel, Plesner, Johansen, Danish R. Ch. & SO, John Frandsen.

Kuhlau's incidental music to J. L. Heiberg's play, *Elverhøj*, is endearingly fresh. Not so the recording however; this sounds really rather dryish, as if recorded in a fully packed concert hall. The music has great charm and the performance too under John Frandsen is very sympathetic.

Lulu (opera): complete.
*** Kontrapunkt/HM 32009/11 [id.]. Saarman, Frellesvig, Kiberg, Cold, Danish R. Ch. & SO, Schönwandt.

This *Lulu* comes from 1824 and is surely too long: the spoken passages are omitted here – but, even so, the music takes three hours. The opening of Act II has overtones of the Wolf's Glen scene in *Der Freischutz* and the dance of the black elves in the moonlight is pure Mendelssohn – and has much charm. The invention is generally fresh and engaging, though no one would claim that it has great depth. The largely Danish cast cope very capably with the not inconsiderable demands of Kuhlau's vocal writing, the Danish Radio recording is eminently truthful and vivid, and Michael Schönwandt draws excellent results from the Danish Radio Chorus and Orchestra.

Kuhnau, Johann (1660–1722)

Der Gerechte kommt um (motet).
(Y/B) (M) *** O-L 443 199-2 [id.]. Christ Church Ch., AAM, Preston – BACH: *Magnificat;* VIVALDI: *Nisi dominus* etc. ***

Kuhnau was Bach's predecessor in Leipzig. He wrote this charming motet with a Latin text; it was later arranged in a German version, and there are signs of Bach's hand in it. The piece makes an excellent makeweight coupling for the original version of Bach's *Magnificat*.

Lachner, Franz Paul (1803–90)

Symphony No. 5 in C min. (Passionata), Op. 52 (Preis-Symphonie).
(Y/B) **(*) Marco Polo Dig. 8.223502 [id.]. Slovak State PO (Košice), Paul Robinson.

Franz Lachner's *Fifth Symphony* is an ambitious work, lasting an hour, lyrical and well crafted. Its ideas unfold naturally and with a certain fluency; its scoring is effective and its idiom is close to the world of Schubert and Mendelssohn. It is a little conventional: phrase structures are rather four-square and predictable. All the same, one can see why the work enjoyed esteem in more conservative circles. It has more than mere curiosity value, and the Slovak orchestra under Paul Robinson play it with obvious enjoyment. Decent recording.

Septet in E flat.
*** Marco Polo Dig. 8.223282 [id.]. Ens. Villa Musica – FUCHS: *Clarinet quintet.* ***

Franz Lachner was a friend of Schubert, and his *Septet* dates from 1824, the same year as the Schubert *Octet*. The *Septet* is not great music but has an easy-going charm that is really quite winning, and it is nicely played and well recorded by this Mainz-based group.

Lajtha, László (1892–1963)

Hortobágy, Op. 21; Suite No. 3, Op. 56; Symphony No. 7, Op. 63 (Revolution Symphony).
(Y/B) **(*) Marco Polo Dig. 8.223667 [id.]. Pécs SO, Nicolás Pasquet.

László Lajtha was one of the leading Hungarian composers and scholars to emerge after the generation of Bartók and Kodály. Indeed, as an exact contemporary of Honegger and Milhaud, he is separated from his compatriots by a mere decade. The *Seventh Symphony* is a well-wrought and eclectic score that is worth hearing. There are echoes of Bartók (the *Music for strings, percussion and celeste*), Kodály and even a reminder of Vaughan Williams. Like the latter's contemporaneous *Ninth Symphony*, Lajtha's *Seventh* makes conspicuous use of the saxophone. The scoring is effective (occasionally one is reminded of the Prokofiev-like moments in Tubin's *Sixth Symphony*) but, although it is finer than the *Fourth* or *Ninth Symphonies*, which appeared on Hungaroton, it does not possess the concentration or profile one expects of a major symphonist. The suite from *Hortobágy*, a memorable film set in the plains of Hungary, and the *Two symphonic portraits* are effectively scored but their material is insufficiently distinctive. Good performances and recording.

3 Berceuses; Contes, Op. 2; Des Ecrits d'un musicien, Op. 1; 6 Piano pieces; Prélude.
** Marco Polo Dig. 8.223473 [id.]. Klára Körmendi.

Lajtha was a highly accomplished pianist. Most of these pieces date from the earlier part of his career (1913–18) and show a responsiveness to the modern music of the period, Bartók and Debussy, and there is also an awareness of Schoenberg. The *Six Piano Pieces* of 1930 are obviously Bartókian and the *Three Berceuses* (1955–7) have a certain charm. A fastidious craftsman and a composer of culture, the piano music is a little too anonymous to make strong claims on the repertoire, though Klára Körmendi plays with evident conviction. The recording is clean and believable.

Lalo, Edouard (1823–92)

Cello concerto No. 1 in D min., Op. 33.
*** ASV Dig. CDDCA 867 [id.]. Sophie Rolland, BBC PO, Gilbert Varga – MASSENET: *Fantaisie;* SAINT-SAENS: *Cello concerto No. 1.* ***
(N) *** EMI CDC5 55528-2 [id.]. Jacqueline du Pré, Cleveland O, Barenboim – R. STRAUSS: *Don Quixote.* *** ✿
(N) (B) *** Decca Eclipse Dig. 448 712-2; *448 712-4* [id.]. Lynn Harrell, Berlin RSO, Chailly – SAINT-SAENS; SCHUMANN: *Concertos.* ***
(Y/B) *** Finlandia/Warner Dig. 4509 95768-2 [id.]. Arto Noras, Finnish RSO, Saraste – ELGAR: *Cello concerto.* ***
*** DG Dig. 427 323-2 [id.]. Matt Haimovitz, Chicago SO, Levine – SAINT-SAENS: *Concerto No. 1;* BRUCH: *Kol Nidrei.* ***
(B) *** DG 431 166-2. Heinrich Schiff, New Philh. O, Mackerras – FAURE: *Elégie;* SAINT-SAENS: *Cello concerto No. 1.* ***
(M) **(*) Mercury 432 010-2 [id.]. Janos Starker, LSO, Skrowaczewski – SAINT-SAENS; SCHUMANN: *Concertos.* ***
(M) **(*) Sony SBK 48278; *SBT 48278* [id.]. Leonard Rose, Phd. O, Ormandy – BLOCH: *Schelomo;* FAURE: *Elégie;* TCHAIKOVSKY: *Rococo variations.* ***

Sophie Rolland's account of the endearing Lalo *Cello concerto in D minor* reveals her as a formidable talent. She plays with effortless eloquence and is given responsive support from the BBC Philharmonic under Gilbert Varga, though he is a little brusque in the *Intermezzo*. An enjoyable and convincing performance, probably the finest to appear since Yo-Yo Ma's Sony account (which is currently withdrawn). The excellence of the BBC/ASV recording makes for a strong recommendation.

Jacqueline du Pré's recorded repertory is thrillingly expanded in previously unpublished recordings of Strauss and Lalo. While the studio recording of *Don Quixote*, dating from 1968, has been pieced together from long-buried tapes, this recording of the Lalo *Concerto* was taken live from a broadcast in Cleveland in January 1973, right at the end of du Pré's playing career in one of her last remissions from multiple sclerosis. It is a masterly performance and is totally involving, even though the cello is balanced rather more backwardly than in du Pré's studio recordings. In spite of that, her fire at the opening grabs the attention, leading on to a performance that is both passionate and poetic, with the slow movement deeply elegiac and the dance rhythms of the finale full of Spanish colour. Excellent background notes are provided by Tully Potter as well as by Andrew Keener.

Lynn Harrell's account is also highly recommendable. There is a yearning intensity in the *Intermezzo*, while the outer movements combine spontaneity and vigour. Chailly's accompaniment is attractively bold and the recording, made in the Berlin Jesus-Christus Kirche, has an attractively warm ambience, while the cello image is very tangible and the orchestra is given plenty of colour and presence. Harrell's couplings are generous in including concertos by both Saint-Saëns and Schumann.

Arto Noras commands impeccable technical address and he has no need to fear comparison with the others listed above. He is an aristocrat among cellists in much the same way as Fournier was (and Haimowitz on DG is not). He receives very responsive support from Saraste and the Finnish Radio Orchestra, and very truthful recording.

An outstandingly impressive début from the young cellist, Matt Haimovitz; the performance throughout combines vitality with expressive feeling in the most spontaneous manner. The recording is very well balanced indeed and highly realistic.

This was Heinrich Schiff's début recording in 1977, made when he was still very young. His account of the Lalo *Concerto* is fresh and enthusiastic and very well recorded for its period. With its excellent coupling it makes a real bargain.

Janos Starker's 1962 recording with the LSO under Stanislaw Skrowaczewski sounds remarkably good for its age. Though the tutti chords are brutal and clipped, Starker plays splendidly, and the famous Mercury recording technique lays out the orchestral texture quite beautifully and with remarkable transparency.

Leonard Rose gives a strong, spontaneous account of this sometimes intractable concerto, bringing out its melodic character as well as its vitality of invention. Ormandy's accompaniment is wonderfully supportive and it is a pity that the orchestral sound has a hint of edginess in the violins and is a bit two-dimensional.

(i) *Cello concerto No. 1 in D min.;* (ii) *Namouna* (ballet): *Rhapsodies Nos.1–2; Valse de la cigarette. Rapsodie norvégien.*
(Y/B) (B) **(*) DG Double 437 371-2 [id.]. (i) Pierre Fournier, LOP; (ii) ORTF; Jean Martinon –
   BIZET: *Symphony* etc. **(*)

Fournier's performance of the *Cello concerto* lends both dignity and nobility to a work whose ideas are in fact of slender substance. Martinon gets a spirited response from the Lamoureux players, but the recording is not top-drawer. There is much engaging music in *Namouna*, a ballet score much admired by Debussy and nicely played here within an atmospheric acoustic. Jean Martinon is a sympathetic exponent throughout and he also gives us the attractively tuneful *Rapsodie norvégienne* in its adapted version for orchestra alone (1879). The original, composed a year earlier, featured a concertante violin.

Namouna (ballet): extended excerpts: *(suites Nos. 1–2 & Allegro vivace; Tambourin; La Gitane; Bacchanale).*
**(*) Audivis Valois Dig. V 4677 [id.]. Monte-Carlo PO, David Robertson.

Namouna (ballet): *suites Nos. 1–2; Valse de la cigarette.*
**(*) ASV Dig. CDDCA 878 [id.]. RPO, Yondani Butt (with GOUNOD: *Mors et Vita: Judex*).

There is no complete version available of Lalo's ballet, but David Robertson has added four more items to the content of Lalo's two suites, plus the charmingly Gallic *Valse de la cigarette* (which the composer extracted as a separate number). He has also re-established the music in ballet-order, whereas in the suites Lalo reassembled the items for concert performance. There is much engaging music here, especially the Beechamesque lollipop, *La Sieste*. Robertson secures sensitive, polished playing from his Monte Carlo orchestra, who resound with warmth, and the recording, if not quite top-drawer, has plenty of colour and ambience.

Yondani Butt achieves performances of the suites and the *Valse de la cigarette* which have comparable colour and finesse, and the RPO play extremely well. Even so, they don't necessarily upstage their French competitors and they offer less music. Where they gain is in the *Prélude*, which is an unashamed crib from Wagner's *Das Rheingold*. Clearly the British players relish the connection and make the most of the rumbustious climax (aided by Brian Culverhouse's vibrantly expansive recording), where the French orchestra tries not to wallow in Wagnerian amplitude. The ASV disc offers a big *religieuse* Gounod tune as an encore, but more of *Namouna* would have been preferable.

Symphonie espagnole (for violin and orchestra), *Op. 21.*
(N) *** EMI Dig. CDC5 55292-2 [id.]. Sarah Chang, Concg. O, Dutoit – VIEUXTEMPS: *Violin concerto
   No. 5.* ***
(Y/B) (M) *** DG Dig. 445 549-2 [id.]. Perlman, O de Paris, Barenboim – SAINT-SAENS: *Concerto No.
   3;* BERLIOZ: *Rêverie et caprice.* ***
*** DG Dig. 427 676-2 [id.]. Mintz, Israel PO, Mehta – SAINT-SAENS: *Introduction & Rondo capric-
   cioso;* VIEUXTEMPS: *Concerto No. 5.* ***
(N) (M) *** Sony Stern Edition II SM2K 64501 (2) [id.]. Stern, Phd. O, Ormandy (with Concert ***).
**(*) RCA Dig. RD 60942 [09026 60942-2]. Anne Akiko Meyers, RPO, López-Cobos – BRUCH:
   Scottish fantasia. ***

(M) **(*) Sony SBK 48274; *SBT 48274* [id.]. Zukerman, LAPO, Mehta – VIEUXTEMPS: *Concerto No. 5.* **(*)

(BB) ** Naxos Dig. 8.550494 [id.]. Marat Bisengaliev, Polish Nat. RSO, Wildner (with: SARASATE: *Zigeunerweisen* ***; SAINT-SAENS: *Havanaise;* RAVEL: *Tzigane* **(*)).

Symphonie espagnole, Op. 21 (omitting *Intermezzo*).

(N) (M) (**(*)) RCA Heifetz Collection mono 09026 61753-2 [id.]. Heifetz, RCA Victor SO, Steinberg – CHAUSSON: *Poème* **(*); SAINT-SAENS: *Havanaise* etc.; SARASATE: *Zigeunerweisen*. (***)

Sarah Chang's dazzling account of Lalo's five-movement feast of Spanish dance-rhythms goes readily to the top of the list. Dutoit provides a vigorous backing and the soloist's seductive lilt in the shimmering malaguena of the first movement is matched by the sparkling seguidilla rhythms of the Scherzo and the bouncing habañera of the Intermezzo, with the music's contrasting languor fully reflecting the Mediterranean sunshine. After a nostalgically songful *Andante* (where the Concertgebouw brass makes itself sonorously felt) the finale scintillates. The orchestra readily echoes Chang's sparkle and the expansively resonant recording (far preferable to the comparatively dry sound which DG provide for Perlman) is ideally balanced. That this is a live recording is apparent from the spontaneous life of the playing, but the audience is not audibly apparent until the enthusiastic applause at the close.

The 1980 DG recording of Lalo's five-movement distillation of Spanish sunshine regularly pops in and out of the catalogue and, although the lively digital sound remains a trifle dry, Perlman's performance easily maintains its place near the top of the list. Barenboim combines rhythmic buoyancy with expressive flair and the richness and colour of Perlman's tone are never more telling than in the slow movement, which opens tenderly but develops a compelling expressive ripeness. The brilliance of the Scherzo is matched by the dancing sparkle of the finale. For the reissue in the Masters series, the Berlioz *Rêverie et caprice* makes an attractive if brief bonus.

Mintz, too, plays with much panache; he is highly seductive in the lilting secondary theme of the first movement, and he brings a comparable touch of restrained voluptuousness to the habañera rhythms of the *Intermezzo*, while the Scherzo is light as thistledown. Mehta opens a bit heavily but provides a satisfactory acccompaniment, while the recording, made live in the Israel Mann Auditorium, is acceptable, full, if not ideally transparent.

Stern's version from the late 1960s has all the rich, red-blooded qualities that have made this artist world-famous. Reservations concerning the close balance are inevitable (although Ormandy's fine accompaniment is not diminished), but the playing makes a huge impact on the listener and, although the actual sound-quality is far from refined, the charisma of this performance is unforgettable.

Anne Akiko Meyers' account offers a genuine alternative view. Her approach to the first movement's secondary theme has a beguilingly light touch, the seductive Spanish lilt pastel-shaded, and her sense of fantasy brings a similar airy lightness to the Scherzo. She introduces the lovely melody of the *Andante* with magically hushed intensity. The finale brings appealing sparkle and delicacy of articulation. López-Cobos does not quite match his young soloist in concentration. However, he has the advantage of really first-class recording, achieving a natural balance with the soloist.

Heifetz's 1951 account has superb panache and there are no complaints about the mono recording. Alas, he omitted the *Intermezzo* (a practice curiously common in his time), which is our loss, but the performance of the rest, like all the music on this CD, is dazzling.

Zukerman's performance is outstandingly successful. He plays with great dash and fire yet brings a balancing warmth. The rhythmic zest of the Scherzo, with its subtle control of dynamic shading, is contrasted with a richly expressive *Andantino*, to be followed by a dazzling display of fireworks in the finale. Mehta accompanies with sympathetic gusto, and the reverberant, larger-than-life recording suits the style of the music-making, the soloist balanced very forwardly indeed. Zukerman's couplings are more generous than Perlman's, but the effect of the DG recording is to give Perlman's account slightly more romantic finesse.

Marat Bisengaliev is an accomplished player with a rich tone and secure technique, and his Slavonic temperament means that Lalo's Spanish ideas are presented with sultry flair. Jonathan Wildner is lively enough in the first movement and manages to make Lalo's quiet woodwind detail register in spite of the resonance. But he takes the *Andante* rather steadily, and the finale again could have used more sheer sparkle from the orchestra. The three encores are very successful. *Zigeunerweisen*, the highlight, has glowing gypsy panache and the luscious lyrical tune sounds properly beguiling, Saint-Saëns's *Havanaise* is stylishly sympathetic, and Ravel's *Tzigane* has real temperament and fire. The reverberant recording acoustic suits these pieces much better than the Lalo.

Piano trios Nos. 1 in C min., Op. 7; 2 in B min.; 3 in A min, Op. 26.
(Y/B) *** ASV Dig. CDDCA 899 [id.]. Barbican Piano Trio.

As always with Lalo, this is the kind of unpretentious, inventive, well-crafted and delightful music which nineteenth-century civilization seemed able to foster and their composers to produce – and of which the late twentieth is conspicuously and lamentably bare. There is little to say about the music (always a good sign) and not much more about the performances, except to note their excellence and poise. A rewarding issue, and well recorded into the bargain.

Lambert, Constant (1905–51)

Aubade héroïque; (i) *The Rio Grande; Summer's last will and testament.*
❀ *** Hyperion Dig. CDA 66565 [id.]. Sally Burgess, Jack Gibbons, William Shimell, Ch. of Opera North and Leeds Festival, (i) with Jack Gibbons; English N. Philh., Lloyd-Jones.

The Rio Grande, Lambert's jazz-based choral concerto setting a poem by Sacheverell Sitwell, is one of the most colourful and atmospheric works from the 1920s. With Sally Burgess a warmly expressive soloist, sharply dramatic choral singing, and Jack Gibbons the brilliant, keenly responsive pianist, Lloyd-Jones gives a totally idiomatic account of music that requires crisp attack combined with a jazzy freedom of rhythm. The *Aubade héroïque* is an evocative tone-poem inspired by Lambert's memory of a beautiful morning in Holland in 1940 when, with the Nazi invasion, it was far from certain whether he and his colleagues would be able to get back to England. Inspired by the death of his friend (and alcoholic evil influence) Peter Warlock/Philip Heseltine, *Summer's last will and testament* is a big, 50-minute choral work setting lyrics by the Elizabethan, Thomas Nashe, on the unpromising subject of the threat of plague. Lloyd-Jones and his outstanding team, mainly from Opera North, bring out the vitality and colour of the writing, with each of the nine substantial sections based on Elizabethan dance-rhythms. The recording in all three works is full, vivid and atmospheric.

(i; ii) *Concerto for piano and nine players*; (i) *Piano sonata*; (iii; i) *8 Poems of Li-Po*; (iv; i) *Mr Bear Squash-you-all-flat.*
(Y/B) *** Hyperion Dig. CDA 66754 [id.]. (i) Ian Brown; (ii) Nash Ens., Lionel Friend; with (iii) Philip Langridge; (iv) Nigel Hawthorne.

Constant Lambert's remarkable qualities are in excellent evidence here in the Nash Ensemble's anthology which brings two of his most powerful works, the *Concerto for piano and nine players* and the *Piano sonata*, as well as one of his most delicately wrought, the *Eight Poems of Li-Po*, in a lovely performance from Philip Langridge. Ian Brown proves an equally exemplary advocate in the *Concerto* and the *Piano sonata*, which is not generously represented on disc. *Mr Bear Squash-you-all-flat* is new to the catalogue: Lambert's first composition, an entertainment written at roughly the same time as Walton's *Façade*, when Lambert was still in his teens, and based on a Russian fairy story. Imaginative and accomplished but, hardly surprisingly, not first-class Lambert. It is not certain whether Lambert meant the text to be spoken, but Nigel Hawthorne speaks it excellently; he is somewhat reticently balanced (a fault on the right side). Nevertheless, a valuable addition to Lambert's representation on disc – speaking of which: when are Lyrita going to restore *Pomona* and *Romeo and Juliet* to circulation?

Horoscope (ballet): *suite.*
❀ *** Hyperion CDA 66436 [id.]. E. N. Philh. O, Lloyd-Jones – BLISS: *Checkmate;* WALTON: *Façade.*
***

The music for *Horoscope* is sheer delight, and it seems incredible that the only previous complete recording of the suite was made in the mid-1950s by Irving for Decca. David Lloyd-Jones is equally sympathetic to its specifically English atmosphere. He wittily points the catchy rhythmic figure which comes both in the *Dance for the followers of Leo* and, later, in the *Bacchanale*, while the third-movement *Valse for the Gemini* has a delectable insouciant charm. Excellent playing and first-class sound, perhaps a shade resonant for the ballet pit, but bringing plenty of bloom.

Lambert, Michel (*c.* 1610–96)

Airs de cour: *Admirons notre jeune et charmante Déesse; Ah! qui voudra desormais s'engager; C'en est fait, belle Iris; D'un feu secret je me sens consumer; Il faut mourir plutost que le changer; Iris n'est plus, mon Iris m'est ravie; Je suis aymé de celle que j'adore; Ma bergere est tendre et fidelle; Ombre de mon amant; Par mes chants tristes et touchants; Pour vos beaux yeux, Iris; Le repos, l'ombre, le silence; Tout l'univers obéit*

à l'amour, Trouver sur l'herbette.
(B) *** HM HMA 1901123 [id.]. Les Arts Florissants, William Christie.

Grove speaks of Michel Lambert's airs as models of elegance and grace, in which careful attention was paid to direct declamation. The 300 or so that survive show his artistry in characterization and dialogue to have been of the highest order. They are beautifully performed and expertly recorded by members of Les Arts Florissants and William Christie and are altogether delightful. Unlike some bargain issues, there is excellent documentation with the original texts and translation.

Lampe, John Frederick (1702/3–51)

(i) *Pyramus and Thisbe* (A mock opera); (ii) *Flute concerto in G (The Cuckoo).*
(Y/B) *** Hyperion Dig. CDA 66759 [id.]. (i) Padmore, Bisatt, Opera Restor'd, Peter Holman; (ii) Rachel Brown.

Pyramus and Thisbe, written in 1745, is a reworking of the entertainment given by the rude mechanicals in Shakespeare's *Midsummer Night's Dream*, with the role of the heroine, Thisbe, taken not by a man but by a soprano. The Opera Restor'd company, with Jack Edwards as stage director, here present it complete with spoken Prologue for several attendant characters. Following the overture come 16 brief numbers, with the score edited and completed by the conductor, Peter Holman. Mark Padmore is outstanding as Pyramus, with Susan Bisatt a fresh-toned Thisbe. The warm, immediate recording brings out the distinctive timbre of the period instruments, notably the braying horns. As an agreeable make-weight, the disc also offers Lampe's only surviving independent orchestral work, the *G major Flute concerto*, with its three crisp movements lasting little more than 5 minutes.

Landowski, Marcel (born 1915)

(i) *Concerto for ondes martenot, strings and percussion;* (ii) *Piano concerto No. 2;* (iii) *Concerto for trumpet, strings and electro-acoustic instruments.*
(Y/B) *** Erato/Warner 4509 96972-2 [id.]. (i) Jeanne Loriod, O de Chambre de Musique Contemporain, Jacques Rondon; (ii) Annie d'Arco, ORTF, Jean Martinon; (iii) Maurice André, Strasbourg PO, Alain Lombard.

Marcel Landowski is little more than a name outside France, where he is much respected – and rightly so, if his symphonies are anything to go by: his handling of complex orchestral textures and orchestral colours is highly imaginative. In the *Piano concerto* of 1963, the balance places the soloist too prominently and the instrument itself sounds tubby. The musical invention can be compared to certain kinds of conversation, civilized and intelligent, which holds you while it goes on but which remains ultimately unmemorable. The *Concerto for ondes martenot* of 1954 is also the finer of the two works, stronger in atmosphere and invention than its companion, and its idiom is a cross between Honegger and Shostakovich. Add Bartókian *Night music* to that mix, and you have the opening of the *Trumpet concerto* (1976). Scored for small forces (no oboes, and two horns and one trombone), it also makes discreet use of magnetic tape. It is even finer than the *Concerto for ondes martenot* and its seriousness of purpose and powerful atmosphere make a strong impression. The 1978 Strasbourg recording is excellent and Maurice André plays it with total commitment. One can only hope now that younger virtuosi like Håkan Hardenberger and Sergei Nakariakov will take it up.

Symphonies Nos. (i) *1 (Jean de la peur);* (ii) *2;* (i) *3 (Des espaces); 4.*
(Y/B) *** Erato/Warner Dig. 4509 96973-2 (2) [id.]. (i) French Nat. O; Georges Prêtre; (ii) ORTF, Jean Martinon.

The *First*, *Third* and *Fourth* of Landowski's symphonies were recorded in 1988 and have been available before. To them Erato have now added an analogue recording from 1970 of the *Second Symphony*, conducted by Jean Martinon (economically packaged in one single jewel-case). Like its companions the musical language and thought processes have their roots in Honegger; the musical argument is well sustained and has a certain dignity. Even if he does not possess a strongly distinctive profile, Landowski has a powerful and fertile imagination, a resourceful sense of orchestration, and a commanding symphonic grip. He holds the listener from the first bar to the last. Martinon proves a wholly sympathetic interpreter and the analogue recording has no lack of warmth and space. The two-movement *Third Symphony* (*Des espaces*), written in the immediate wake of the *Second* in 1965, is very atmospheric: its opening *Grave* casts a powerful spell, while the scurrying activity of the *Allegro deciso* movement is skilfully sustained. Although these are not as strong as the Honegger or Dutilleux symphonies, they are imaginative and rewarding. Prêtre gets exemplary results from the French National Orchestra. If you have the opportunity of sampling this set, try the opening minute or so of the *Fourth Symphony*, and if you respond to its world you will enjoy all these pieces. Generally excellent recorded sound.

Lang, David (born 1957)

(i) *Are you experienced?; Under Orpheus.*
(Y/B) (***) Chandos Dig. CHAN 9363 [id.]. (i) Composer (nar.); Netherlands Wind. Ens., Mosko –
  ADAMS: *Grand pianola music* etc. ***

Are you experienced? is presumably a cult work to which we would not wish to return very often, if at all. It draws its genesis from a Jimi Hendrix song and album, and the narrator/composer acts as guide through such musically illustrated experieces as 'On being hit on the head' and 'On hearing the voice of God'. It opens rather in the manner of 'Are you sitting comfortably' from the BBC's *Listen with Mother*, and very soon we were not sitting comfortably at all. To our ears, it is all pretentious and unappealing. *Under Orpheus* consists of a pair of minimalist crescendos into dissonance, the first, *Aria*, led by piano tremolandos, the second an undulating *Chorale*. Obviously the performances are very well played, and the recording is in the demonstration bracket.

Lange-Müller, Peter Erasmus (1850–1926)

(i) *Albumsblade;* (ii) *Fantasistykker, Op. 39;* (iii) *Piano trio in F min., Op. 53;* (ii) *Romance in G, Op. 63.*
(N) *(*) Kontrapunkt Dig. CD32298 [id.]. (i) Carl Nielsen Qt; (ii) Søren Elbæk, Morten Mogensen; (iii)
  Copenhagen Trio.

Lange-Müller was an interesting figure and one of the greatest masters of Danish song. He was largely self-taught but was tormented by ill-health in the shape of incapacitating headaches which plagued him all his life. The *Piano trio in F minor* is the main work on this disc and owes much to Brahms and Franck; but it is held together well, and the musical ideas are fresh and appealing. The other works are also attractive but the performers, accomplished and efficient though they are, suffer from the handicap of a small acoustic. The aural effect is unpleasing, but the music itself is not without interest – far from it.

Langgaard, Rued (1893–1953)

Symphony No. 1 (Klippepastoraler); Fra Dybet.
*** Chandos Dig. CHAN 9249 [id.]. Danish Nat. RSO & Ch., Segerstam.

Rued Langgaard began this symphony when he was fourteen; he was only eighteen when he finished revising it. Langgaard was a figure of undoubted but flawed talent, but as this banal, five-movement overblown sprawl slowly unwinds its 67 minutes, one realizes that the composer subjected this particular piece to no real critical scrutiny. Not to put too fine a point upon it, he was essentially a windbag. There are some imaginative moments in the finale. *Fra Dybet* ('From the Deep') comes from the other end of his career and was completed not long before his death: it opens rather bombastically but soon lapses into sentimentality at the entrance of the choir. Good recording.

Symphonies Nos. 4 (Løfvald: The falling of the leaf); 5 (Steppelands); 6 (Himmelrivende: The storming of the heavens).
*** Chandos Dig. CHAN 9064 [id.]. Danish Nat. RSO, Neeme Järvi.

Rued Langgaard's *Fourth Symphony*, subtitled *The falling of the leaf* or, rather less romantically, *Defoliation*, has retained little more than a foothold on the repertoire. The *Sixth* (*Himmelrivende* – variously translated as *The storming of the heavens* or, on this CD, as *Heavens asunder*) is another work which hovers on the periphery of the catalogue. In fact this Chandos collaboration with Danish Radio makes a useful introduction to this far from uninteresting composer, for these works have passages that almost persuade one as to the justice of the claims made by his admirers; what is lacking in Langgaard is any real sense of organic growth and ultimately, it must be said, a distinctive and original personality. However, Neeme Järvi makes out a strong case for this music and the Danish Radio Orchestra play with conviction and sympathy. They are given excellent recorded sound.

Symphonies Nos. 4 (Løvfald); 6 (Den Himmelrivande); (i) Sfærernas Musik.
(Y/B) **(*) Danacord DACOCD 340/341 [id.]. (i) Edith Guillaume, Danish R. Ch.; Danish RSO,
  John Frandsen.

Sfærernas musik (*The Music of the spheres*), written in 1918 in between the two symphonies recorded here, is an extraordinary piece of undoubted vision and originality. It has a wild-eyed intensity and a quasi-mystical quality that is unusual in the Nordic music of its time. One has the feeling that it could equally stop earlier or go on longer, but formal coherence is not Langgaard's strong suit. The performances are good and the recording eminently satisfactory without being quite in the Chandos league.

Symphonies Nos. 10 (Yon Dwelling of Thunder); 11 (Ixion); 12 (Helsingeborg); Sfinx (tone-poem).
** Danacord Dig. DACOCD 408 [id.]. Artur Rubinstein PO, Ilya Stupel.

The *Eleventh* and *Twelfth Symphonies* are shorter than they seem; in fact the *Eleventh* lasts less than six minutes but its main theme is of awesome vapidity. It could easily pass muster in some Hollywood feature about a misunderstood and neglected composer. The language is openly neo-romantic, which would not in itself matter were the musical invention tinged with a flicker of real distinction. The Artur Rubinstein Philharmonic Orchestra turns in serviceable performances and are decently enough recorded, but do not dispel the impression that this is music of shadows rather than substance.

Symphonies Nos. 13 (Faithlessness); 16 (The Deluge of Sun); Anti-Christ (opera): *Prelude.*
** Danacord Dig. DACOCD 410. Artur Rubinstein PO, Ilya Stupel.

The *Sixteenth Symphony* opens rather like Strauss, then comes to an abrupt stop, before launching into a short, Schumannesque Scherzo of about 1½ minutes in the same key, and thence into a *Dance of chastisement*. The *Elegy* which follows also has touches of Schumann and there is a short and unconvincing finale. In the *Thirteenth* (*Undertro*, 'Faithlessness') the composer returns to material he had first used in his *Seventh Symphony*, which he had in turn borrowed from his countryman, Axel Gade. What it lacks in substance it makes up for in bombast. Probably the best thing here is the *Prelude* to the opera, *Anti-Christ*, a much earlier piece dating from the 1920s. The performances and recordings are respectable rather than distinguished.

Langlais, Jean (born 1907)

(i) *Messe solennelle;* (i; ii; iii) *Missa Salve regina;* (Organ): (i) *Paraphrases grégoriennes, Op. 5: Te Deum. Poèmes évangéliques, Op. 2: La Nativité. Triptyque grégorien: Rosa mystica.*
*** Hyperion Dig. CDA 66270 [id.]. Westminster Cathedral Ch., David Hill, (i) with J. O'Donnell; (ii) A. Lumsden; (iii) ECO Brass Ens.

Jean Langlais' organ music owes much to Dupré's example, and the two Masses are archaic in feeling, strongly influenced by plainchant and organum, yet with a plangent individuality that clearly places the music in the twentieth century. The style is wholly accessible and the music enjoys fervent advocacy from these artists, who are accorded sound-quality of the high standard one expects from this label.

Larsson, Lars-Erik (1908–86)

(i) *Violin concerto, Op. 42.* (ii) *Förklädd Gud (A god in disguise), Op. 24; Pastoral suite, Op. 19.*
** Sony Dig. SK 64140 [id.]. (i) Arve Tellefsen, Swedish RSO, Esa-Pekka Salonen; (ii) Hillevi Martinpelto, Håkan Hagegård, Erland Josephson, Swedish R. Ch. & O, Salonen.

Like the well-known *Pastoral Suite*, *Förklädd Gud* ('A god in disguise') has charm, and the latter is full of naïve and folk-like but captivating ideas; and it is well done by both the two soloists and the distinguished narrator. Salonen does not let the music speak for itself as Stig Westerberg and Sten Frykberg did on earlier recordings, but his direction is smart and crisp. The recording, made in Stockholm's Berwald Hall, is not state-of-the-art, being very two-dimensional. Frykberg's BIS recording, coupled with the *Third Symphony*, is much better, and Håkan Hagegård's voice was fresher and more youthful then. Larsson's *Violin concerto* is one of his best works, very much in the manner of Walton and Prokofiev, lyrical and atmospheric with a quiet Nordic melancholy all its own. A beautiful piece, very well played by Arve Tellefsen and the Swedish Radio Orchestra, but the recording is again decent and acceptable but no more.

Symphonies Nos. 1 in D, Op. 2; 2, Op. 17.
**(*) BIS Dig. CD 426 [id.]. Helsingborg SO, Hans-Peter Frank.

The *First Symphony* is derivative but a work of obvious promise, fluent and well put together. There are obvious echoes of the Russian post-nationalists as well as Nielsen and Sibelius. Much the same could be said of the more mature *Second Symphony* (1936–7), which is genial and unpretentious. Good performances and recording, but the music itself is not Larsson at his strongest.

Symphony No. 3 in C min., Op. 34; (i) *Förklädd Gud (A God in disguise), Op. 24.*
** BIS CD 96 [id.]. (i) Nordin, Hagegård, Jonsson, Helsingborg Concert Ch.; Helsingborg SO,
    Frykberg.

A God in disguise was a production for Swedish Radio. The choral suite for two soloists and narrator
that Larsson fashioned from it has great freshness and charm. This 1978 performance has some fine
singing from Håkan Hagegård, and the Helsingborg chorus and orchestra give a serviceable account of
the score. It is as diatonic as *A God in disguise* and, though not completely successful, is strong enough to
deserve rescue.

Lassus, Orlandus (c. 1532–94)

Madrigals: *Al dolce suon'; Ben convenne; Bestia curvafia pulices; Ove d'alta montagna; Praesidium sara;
Spent'è d'amor.* Motets: *Beati pauperes/Beati pacifici; Da pacem, Domine; Domine, quando veneris;
Gloria patri et filio.* Chansons: *Lucescit jam o socii; Voir est beaucoup.*
(M) ** Teldec/Warner Dig. 4509 93685-2 [id.]. Alsfelder Vocal Ens., Helbich.

Expertly directed performances with good intonation and tonal blend. Wolfgang Helbich does not vary
the forces here, however; everything is done with full chorus, whereas many of the items would have
benefited from greater variety of vocal texture. Thus, in spite of beautiful recording, the overall impact
of this reissue is less than the sum of its parts.

(i) Motets: *Ave Regina caelorum; O mors, quam amara est; Salve Regina; Penitential Psalms: I, Domine,
ne in furore tuo;* (ii) *III, Domine, ne in furore tuo;* (i) *Miserere mei Deus;* (iii) *Missa super Bell'
Amfitrit'altera;* Motets: *Domine convertere; In convertendo; In monte Oliveti; Lauda Sion Salvatorem;
Tristis est anima mea.*
(M) **(*) DG 439 958-2 (2) [id.]. (i) Pro Cantione Antiqua, Hamburger Bläserkreis, Bruno Turner; (ii)
    Regensburger Domchor, Instrumental Ens., Hans Schrewmsl Aachener Domsingknaben, Krebs,
    Rotzsch, Hudemann, Ens. Rudolf Pohl.

This handsomely produced two-CD set does not offer new material but it is well worth considering
nevertheless. The *Missa super Bell' Amfitrit'altera* and the Motets on the first CD were recorded in 1968,
the third *Penitential Psalm* in 1958; the remaining two and the motets *Ave Regina caelorum, O mors
quam amara est* and the *Salve Regina* in 1974. The *Mass* differs from the slightly later version by Simon
Preston and the Choir of Christ Church, Oxford, now on Decca Ovation (see below) in employing
instrumental support, and the results are more opaque. (The Oxford performance has a sweeter tone,
wider expressive range and greater transparency.) The same reservation may be levelled against the 1974
recordings with the Pro Cantione Antiqua and the Hamburger Bläserkreis and Bruno Turner. They are
eloquent performances, beautifully sung (the singers include James Bowman, Paul Esswood and Ian
Partridge), and accompanied by cornett, trombones etc. (see below).

Motets: *Ave Regina caelorum; O mors, quam amara est; Salve Regina. First Penitential Psalm: Domine,
ne in furore tuo.*
(M) **(*) DG 437 072-2. Pro Cantione Antiqua, Hamburg Wind Ens., Bruno Turner – PALESTRINA:
    Missa Aeterna Christi munera etc. **

We are offered here one of the *Penitential Psalms* plus three motets in expert performances by the
London Pro Cantione Antiqua under Bruno Turner. This is very beautiful music and there is plenty of
historical evidence to support the view that the Psalms were accompanied, though whether the instruments chosen here would be used together is conjectural. The blend between the expressive vocal style
favoured by Turner and his distinguished group (which includes James Bowman, Paul Esswood, Ian
Partridge and others) and the more restrained instrumental style may not convince all listeners, but it
makes for noble, eloquent music-making. The CD transfers of 1974 recordings offer sound of remarkable refinement and realism – even better than in the set above.

Chansons: *Bon jour mon cœur* (ensemble and solo versions); *Fleur de quinz ans; J'ayme la pierre
précieuse; Margot labourez les vignes; La nuict froide et sombre; Pour courir en poste a la ville; Susanne
ung jour* (with ANON.: Intablature for lute from the Wickhambrook Lute Manuscript); Motets: *Cum
natus esset Jesus; In monte Oliveti; Stabat Mater.*
(Y/B) (M) *** Virgin Veritas/EMI Dig. VER5 61166-2 [id.]. Hilliard Ens., Paul Hillier.

One half is devoted to motets, the other to chansons; both are sung one voice to a part. The tonal blend
is as perfect as is usual with this ensemble, intonation is extraordinarily accurate, and there is no vibrato.
The sacred pieces, and in particular the setting of the *Stabat Mater* which opens the first half, are most

impressive. In some of the chansons there is a discreet lute accompaniment to lend variety. Of the chansons, *La nuict froide et sombre* is quite magical and given with great feeling and colour. One of the other songs tells of an unscrupulous friar, in which all suggestions of virtuous behaviour bring the refrain: 'Brother Lubin can't do it'; others include a simple expression of delight in a loved one, a tale of attempted seduction based on the story of Susanna and the Elders, and a hopeful offer to a fifteen-year-old girl to '*vous faire apprendre*' (teach you how it is done!). For all these racier poems, Lassus provides the most refined setting. A useful addition to the Lassus discography and beautifully recorded.

De profundis clamavi; Exaltabo te, Domine; Missa octavi toni; Missa qual donna.
*** Nimbus Dig. NI 5150 [id.]. Christ Church Cathedral Ch., Oxford, Stephen Darlington.

The *Missa qual donna* is a late work, expressive and mellifluous, and very well sung by the choir of Christ Church Cathedral, Oxford. As a pendant, the disc also includes Cipriano de Rore's Petrarch setting, *Qual donna a gloriosa fama*, which the Mass takes as its inspiration. The contrast between this and the *Missa octavi toni*, also known as the *Missa Jäger* (*Hunting Mass*), could hardly be more striking. The motet, *De profundis clamavi*, one of the great penitential Psalms, is almost the most eloquent and expressive of the pieces here. At times one could wish for more ardent tone from the trebles; but unquestionably these are fine performances, and the recording is very good indeed.

Le Lagrime di San Pietro a 7.
(N) (BB) *** Naxos Dig. 8.553311 [id.]. Ars Nova, Bo Holten.
*** HM Dig. HMC 901483 [id.]. Kiehr, Koslowsky, Berridge, Türk, Lamy, Koay, Peacock, Ens. Voc. Européen, Herreweghe.
(M) **(*) O-L 443 197-2 [id.]. Emma Kirkby, Nigel Rogers, Consort of Musicke, Rooley.

Le Lagrime de San Pietro ('The Tears of St Peter') is a late work, a setting of 20 verses of the poet, Luigi Transillo (1510–68), a Neapolitan best known for his lyrical love-sonnets. Like much Renaissance music, it can be performed by a vocal consort or a choir, with or without instruments. The music is rich in variety of expressive means: Howard Mayer Brown calls it a work of 'almost Baroque religious fervour'. The Naxos performance by a first-class Danish choir (6 sopranos, 2 altos, 2 counter-tenors, 4 tenors and 3 basses) is comparatively robust yet offers singing of great sensitivity and a wide range of dynamic. Word meanings are eloquently conveyed (Naxos provides a full text and translation), and Bo Holton shapes the performance to move onwards with gathering intensity towards its climax. The final and twenty-first madrigal, *Vide homo*, for which Lassus himself possibly provided the text, becomes a moving cry of shame and despair as St Peter confronts Christ on the cross, yet the music uplifts the listener on its wave of expressive feeling. The recording, made at the Copenhagen Grundtvigskirken, has a properly spacious ambience, yet is admirably clear.

The *Lagrime di San Pietro* is full of symbolism – seven being the number associated with suffering; the writing is in seven parts, and there are 21 pieces in all (a multiple of seven), the last of which is a Latin motet on the theme of suffering. It is a work of great expressive purity and is performed by Herreweghe's forces with dedication and perfection in the matter of intonation. Excellent recording.

Rooley's performance is given one voice to a part and its impact might have been heightened had the artists permitted themselves an even wider tone-colour. The absence of vibrato produces a whiteness of tone that eventually tires the ear, even though there is every sensitivity to the words and great clarity of texture. Instruments are used in the closing motet, but otherwise much is made of the madrigalian character of this work. There are of course many legitimate approaches to this music and this admirably recorded and well-annotated CD will surely give much satisfaction, despite the noted reservations.

9 Lamentationes Hieremiae.
*** HM Dig. HMC 901299 [id.]. Paris Chapelle Royale Ens., Herreweghe.

9 Lamentationes Hieremiae. Aurora lucis rutilat; Christus resurgens; Magnificat Aurora lucis rutilat; Missa Pro defunctis; Regina coeli; Surgens Jesu.
*** Hyperion Dig. CDA 66321/2 [id.]. Pro Cantione Antiqua, Bruno Turner.

The Harmonia Mundi set of the *Lamentations* enjoys one obvious advantage over its rival on Hyperion in that the nine *Lamentations* are all accommodated on the one disc, while Bruno Turner's 1981 digital recording spills over on to two. However, in addition to the *Lamentations* for Maundy Thursday, Good Friday and Holy Saturday, the Hyperion recording offers music for Easter Sunday including the glorious *Aurora lucis rutilat* for two five-part choirs and the *Magnificat* based on the motet. The performances by the Pro Cantione Antiqua under Bruno Turner are very persuasive, expressive and vital. The recording too is spacious and warm. So, for that matter, is the Harmonia Mundi recording for the Chapelle Royale and Philippe Herreweghe, whose performances are wholly admirable.

Missa Ad imitationem Vinum bonum; Motet: *Vinum bonum; Missa super Quand'io pens'al martire* (with ARCADELT: Madrigal: *Quand'io pens'al martire*). *Missa super triste départ* (with GOMBERT: Chanson: *Triste départ*).
(N) *** Decca Dig. 444 335-2 [id.]. King's College, Cambridge, Ch., Stephen Cleobury.

It is good to welcome the King's College Choir back on Decca with a generous 70-minute programme, superbly sung, offering three of Lassus's finest Masses, together with their secular source-material. The parody Mass in praise of wine was first published in Paris in 1577 and is quite surprisingly extrovert, as is the motet on which it is based, singing the praises of good wine but also referring to the miracle at Cana. The *Missa super Quand'io pens'al martire* is a particularly appealing and beautiful work, and again this is not surprising when Arcadelt's four-part madrigal is such a fine piece. An outstanding addition to the growing Lassus discography.

Missa Osculetur me; Motets: *Alma Redemptoris Mater; Ave regina caelorum; Hodie completi sunt; Osculetur me; Regina caeli; Salve Regina; Timor et tremor.*
*** Gimell Dig. CDGIM 018; *1585T-18* [id.]. Tallis Scholars, Peter Phillips.

Lassus learned the technique of double-choir antiphonal music in Italy. The Mass is preceded by the motet, *Osculetur me* (*Let him kiss me with the kisses of his lips*), which provides much of its motivic substance and is glorious in its sonorities and expressive eloquence. The singing of the Tallis Scholars under Peter Phillips is as impressive as it was on their earlier records, and the recording is beautifully present.

Missa super Bell' Amfitrit'altera; Psalmus penitentialis VII (Psalm 143); Motets: *Alma redemptoris Mater; Omnes de Saba venient; Salve regina, mater misericordiae; Tui sunt coeli.*
❀ (M) *** Decca 433 679-2 [id.]. Christ Church Cathedral, Oxford, Ch., Simon Preston.

The *Mass* is Venetian in style, scored for double choir, each comprising SATB. The seventh *Penitential Psalm* uses a five-part choir with divided tenors, and at *Sicut erat* expands to a six-part choir with divided trebles. The trebles here are firm in line, strong in tone. Indeed, throughout, the singers produce marvellously blended tone-quality and Simon Preston secures magical results. As if this were not enough, the choir conclude with the four eight-part motets, amazingly rich in texture, including a Christmas motet, *Tui sunt coeli*. The acoustic is warm and atmospheric (the recordings were made in Merton College Chapel, Oxford, in 1974/5) and these performances have an admirable vitality and plenty of expressive range. The CD transfer further enhances the sound and the effect is uncannily real and vivid.

Prophetiae Sibyllarum. Settings of Petrarch, Ronsard and du Bellay: Chansons: *Amour donne-moy pays; Bon jour mon coeur; Comme un qui prend; J'ay de vou voir; J'espère et crains; La nuict froide et sombre; O foible esprit; Ronds-moi mon cœur; La terre les eaux va Beuvant; La vita fugge.* Madrigals: *Crudele acerba; I vo piangendo; Mia benigna fortun'e; Soleasi nel mio cor; Standomi un giorno.*
*** HM/BMG Dig. 05472 77304-2 [id.]. Cantus Cölln, Konrad Junghänel.

The *Prophetiae Sibyllarum* ('Sibylline Prophecies') sets a cycle of humanistic Latin verse based on Neapolitan legends that tell how the caves at Cumae were the home of the Sibyls who foretold the coming of God. Jerome Roche in his 1982 monograph writes of the work as 'mysterious, brooding music, but never unsettling emotionally in the manner of Gesualdo'. In addition, we have the madrigal-cycle, *Standomi un giorno*, and five other Petrarch settings, as well as settings by two of *La Pléiade*, Pierre de Ronsard and Joachim du Bellay. It is difficult to imagine these better performed than they are here by the Cantus Cölln and Konrad Junghänel, and they are excellently recorded too.

St Matthew Passion; Exsultet; Visitatio.
**(*) HM Dig. HMU 907076 [id.]. Paul Elliot, Theatre of Voices, Paul Hillier.

This is Lassus at his most austere and devotional, with more chant than polyphony; it is not the best entry-point into his music for those unfamiliar with its opulence. The *Visitatio* (*Easter Dialogue*), which uses the edition by John Stevens, and the *Exsultet* from the Paschal Vigil, are purely chant. In the *Passion* Paul Elliot sings the part of the Evangelist, Paul Hillier that of Christ. The recording, made in California where Hillier now teaches, is exemplary.

Lawes, Henry (1596–1662)

Songs: *Amintor's welladay; The angler's song; Come sad turtle; Fairwell despairing hopes; Hark, shepherd swains; I laid me down; I prithee send me back my heart; The Lark; My soul the great God's praises sings;*

O King of heaven and hell; Sing, fair Clorinda; Sitting by the streams; Slide soft you silver floods; Sweet stay awhile; Tavola; Thee and thy wondrous deeds; This mossy bank.
*** Hyperion CDA 66315 [id.]. Emma Kirkby, Consort of Musicke, Anthony Rooley.

The Lawes songs were enormously popular in their time. Today their direct, declamatory style seems comparatively unsubtle alongside Purcell. The melancholy is tangible, but not overtly expressive. The brief but effective *Tavola* is like an arietta from an Italian opera. The Hyperion collection is fairly wide in its range: the title-number (*Sitting by the streams*) is a verse anthem. There are plenty of secular songs too, notably the engaging *Angler's song*, and admirers of Emma Kirkby – here in radiant voice – and Rooley's immaculately stylish Consort of Musicke will find much to enjoy here.

Leclair, Jean-Marie (1697–1764)

6 Concertos, Op. 7; 6 Concertos, Op. 10.
(N) (M) *** Erato/Warner 0630 11225-2 (3) [id.]. Jarry, Lardé, Paillard CO, Paillard.

Flute concerto in C, Op. 7/3; Violin concertos: in F; in A, Op. 7/4 & 6; in A, Op. 10/2.
(N) *** Chandos Dig. CHAN 0564 [id.]. Rachel Brown; Simon Standage, Coll. Mus. 90.

Violin concertos: in D min., Op. 7/1; in D; F; G min, Op. 10/3–4 & 6.
(N) *** Chandos Dig. CHAN 0589 [id.]. Simon Standage, Coll. Mus. 90.

Violin concertos: Op. 7/2 in D; 7/5 in A min.; Op. 10/1 in B flat; 10/5 in E min.
*** Chandos Dig. CHAN 0551 [id.]. Simon Standage, Coll. Mus. 90.

The twelve concertos of Opp. 7 and 10 make up Leclair's complete orchestral output. Op. 7 was composed in 1737 and Op. 10 in 1743–4; generally speaking, they are underrated and their merits are considerable. Although one cannot include among these a strongly individual lyrical power, the *Aria gracioso* of No. 1 is quite ear-catching, while both the *Adagio* of Op. 7/4 and the *Largo* of Op. 7/5 are distinctly appealing. The *Andante* of Op. 10/3 could well have been written by Vivaldi. Finales too are sprightly in their invention. Op. 7/3 is optionally for flute or oboe, and Rachel Brown makes a pleasing case for the use of a baroque flute, especially in the rather winning slow movement. Simon Standage is a stylish soloist of impeccable technique and Collegium Musicum 90 (4.4.2.2.1) provide authentic, spirited accompaniments. The recordings were made either in St Jude's in north-west London or in All Saints', East Finchley, and textures are transparent and have good sonority.

The performances by the violinist Gérard Jarry and flautist Christian Lardé are of exemplary style and virtuosity. Those who must have the music played with the benefit of period sonorities can turn to the alternative Chandos/Simon Standage ongoing series or to Schröder's selection (see below); but there is nothing in this Erato set that is wanting in stylistic sense or musical verve, and the recording is first class and most naturally transferred to CD. There are excellent and extensive notes by Harry Halbreich.

Violin concertos: in C & A min., Op. 7/3 & 5; in G min., Op. 10/6.
(M) *** Teldec/Warner 4509 92180-2 [id.]. Jaap Schröder, Concerto Amsterdam (with NAUDOT: *Recorder concerto in G, Op. 17/5:* Brüggen, VCM, Harnoncourt **).

Distinguished playing from Jaap Schröder and his colleagues, who make outstanding advocates of these concertos. Leclair is a stronger composer than he is often given credit for. The *G minor Concerto*, Op. 10/6, is a work of real sensibility and imagination, and one only has to sample the slow movements of both the other concertos to discover that Leclair's melodic lines are individual and pleasing. The performances are on period instruments or copies and can be recommended to *aficionados*, as the 1978 analogue sound is both flattering and vivid. The *Recorder concerto* by Jacques-Christophe Naudot (*c.* 1690–1762) which is provided as a bonus is less individual but very well played. However, here the sound of the supporting group is thin and less well focused.

Scylla et Glaucis (opera): complete.
(N) ❀ (M) *** Erato/Warner Dig. 4509 99762-2 (3) [id.]. Donna Brown, Crook, Mellon, Yakar, Monteverdi Ch., E. Bar. Soloists, Gardiner.

A younger contemporary of Rameau, Jean-Marie Leclair regrettably wrote only this one opera. First heard at the Paris Opéra in 1746, it follows the formal pattern of the tragédie lyrique laid down by Lully and developed by Rameau, involving an allegorical prologue and five Acts. The style is more direct, less elaborate than Rameau's, and the speed with which the brief numbers follow each other – some arias as brief as a minute long – give the piece a freshness which easily sustains its length of nearly three hours.

In 1979 John Eliot Gardiner was responsible for the first performance (at St John's, Smith Square, London) anywhere in modern times, followed by a broadcast. Here with a different cast of principals in a production sponsored by Lyon Opéra, of which he is music director, Gardiner crowns that achievement, demonstrating this to be one of the neglected masterpieces of late French baroque, every bit as worthy to be remembered as Rameau's operas. Quite apart from Gardiner's characteristically electrifying direction, the playing and singing can hardly be faulted. Donna Brown makes a sweet-toned Scylla, who yet rises to the extra challenge of her longer numbers. Howard Crook is superb in the tenor role of Glaucus, headily beautiful, never strained by the highest tessitura; while Rachel Yakar characterizes the malevolent role of the sorceress, Circe, without ever transgressing the bounds of classical stylishness. With all these singers, ornamentation becomes a natural point of expression, never clumsy or forced, and the recording, made in St Giles, Cripplegate, is brightly atmospheric, full and clear. The set is doubly attractive, restored to the catalogue at mid-price as part of Gardiner's 'French Baroque Edition', and an excellent booklet with a translation is included.

Lecocq, Alexandre (1832–1918)

Mam'zelle Angot (ballet, arr. Gordon Jacob).
(M) *** Decca 430 849-2 (2) [id.]. Nat. PO, Bonynge – HEROLD: *La Fille mal gardée*. ***

Mam'zelle Angot is a gay, vivacious score with plenty of engaging tunes, prettily orchestrated in the modern French style. Bonynge offers the first recording of the complete score, and its 39 minutes are consistently entertaining when the orchestral playing has such polish and wit. The Kingsway Hall recording is closely observed: the CD brings sharp detail and tangibility, especially at lower dynamic levels.

Le Flem, Paul (1881–1984)

Symphony No. 4; (i) Le grand jardinier de France (film music). *7 Pièces enfantines; Pour les morts (Tryptique symphonique No. 1).*
(Y/B) ** Marco Polo Dig. 8.223655 [id.]. Rhenish PO, James Lockhart, (i) with Gilles Nopre.

Paul Le Flem is another of the French composers who is emerging from the shadows into which he has been so prematurely cast. The *Fourth Symphony* brings an amazing creative vitality, when one thinks that its composer was just ninety years young at the time (1971–2). (As his dates will show at a glance, he lived to be 103.) The *Sept Pièces enfantines* is an orchestral transcription of a set of children's pieces for piano, and *Le grand jardinier de France* is a film score. Both have a certain charm and would have more, had the orchestra been allowed more rehearsal. Wind intonation is not always flawless. Le Flem is not, perhaps, a major personality, but the *Fourth Symphony* is in its way quite remarkable, and had the performance greater finesse, the disc would have rated a three-star recommendation.

Lehár, Franz (1870–1948)

Friederike (complete).
(Y/B) (M) *** EMI CMS5 65369-2 (2). Donath, Dallapozza, Fuchs, Finke, Grabenhorst, Bav. R. Ch., Munich R. O, Wallberg.

The idea of Richard Tauber inspiring Lehár to write an operetta with the poet Goethe as the main character may sound far-fetched, but that is just what *Friederike* is, more ambitious than a genuine operetta and bringing the obvious snag for non-German speakers that there is a great deal of spoken dialogue, the more disruptive because there is no libretto, let alone an English translation. However, there is a track-by-track synopsis of each number, and in every other respect this is a delightful reissue, with Helen Donath charming and sensitive in the name-part. Dallapozza has a light, heady tenor, at times stressed by the weight of the part of Goethe but rising above all to the great Tauber number, *O Mädchen, mein Mädchen!*, based (like other numbers) on a Goethe poem, *Mailied*. Heinz Wallberg is a lively and persuasive director, and the 1980 recording has the bloom one associates with German EMI productions.

Giuditta: highlights.
(Y/B) (M) **(*) Decca 436 900-2 [id.]. Gueden, Kmentt, Loose, Dickie, Czerwenka, Berry, V. State Op. Ch. & O, Rudolf Moralt.

The Decca recording dates from 1958 and, although only highlights are offered, the 76-minute time-span ensures that nothing of great importance is omitted. The performance is affectionately idiomatic in a Viennese way, well sung and vividly presented. Hilde Gueden is in fresh, sparkling form and Waldemar Kmentt makes an excellent Octavio: their duet, *Schön wie die blau Sommernacht*, makes another attract-ive hit to put beside Gueden's delightful *Mein Lippen, sie küssen so heiss*. There is no libretto but a good plot summary details individual numbers. Vivid sound ensures a welcome for this reissue.

Der Graf von Luxemburg: highlights; *Der Zarewitsch:* highlights.
(Y/B) (M) *** Decca 436 896-2 [id.]. Gueden, Kmentt, V. Volksoper O, Max Schönherr.

Unlike the Decca highlights from *Giuditta* and *The Merry Widow*, these selections are not derived from complete sets but were specially recorded together in their present format in the Sofiensaal in 1965. Although the offerings are not especially generous, with less than half an hour from each operetta, the recording itself (produced by Christopher Raeburn) is splendid, as demonstrated by the atmospheric opening scenes, with vivacious support from the chorus and orchestra. The two principals are on top form so that the *Wolgalied* in *Der Zarewitsch* and the charming *Kosende Wellen* are matched by the delightful waltz-duet of *Der Graf von Luxemburg*, *Bist du's, lachendes Glück*, a hit if ever there was one. Brief plot summaries place each number in narrative perspective.

Das Land des Lächelns (The Land of smiles) (complete).
(Y/B) (M) **(*) EMI CMS5 65372-2 (2). Rothenberger, Gedda, Holm, Friedauer, Moeller, Bav. R. Ch., Graunke SO, Willy Mattes.

This 1967 recording has on the whole transferred well to CD. Don't be put off by the sound of the overture, which seems thin because of the relatively small orchestra for the opening scene, but then has plenty of theatrical presence. The recording is atmospheric and real, not only in conveying the songs but also in the spoken dialogue, which is well produced. The cast is strong. Gedda is in excellent form and, besides Anneliese Rothenberger, Renate Holm makes a charming contribution as Mi. The famous tunes, including 'You are my heart's delight', are splendidly done. Yet again there is no libretto, especially desirable in the operetta; but we are offered a track-by-track synopsis of each number.

The Merry Widow (Die lustige Witwe; complete, in German).
(Y/B) *** DG Dig.439 911-2 [id.]. Studer, Skovhus, Bonney, Trost, Terfel, Monteverdi Ch., VPO, Gardiner.
✹ *** EMI CDS7 47178-8 (2) [Ang. CDCB 47177]. Schwarzkopf, Gedda, Waechter, Steffek, Knapp, Equiluz, Philh. Ch. and O, Matačić.
(M) (***) EMI mono CDH7 69520-2 [id.]. Schwarzkopf, Gedda, Kunz, Loose, Kraus, Philh. Ch. & O, Ackermann.
** EMI Dig. CDS5 55152-2 (2). Lott, Hampson, Szmytka, Aler, Dirk Bogarde (nar.), Glyndebourne Ch., LPO, Welser-Möst.

A single-disc version of *The Merry Widow*, with full text and ample dialogue, neatly packaged with libretto, makes an attractive recommendation ahead of any rival. John Eliot Gardiner has the bonus of the Vienna Philharmonic very much on home ground, playing not only with a natural feeling for the idiom but with unrivalled finesse and polish. The characteristic spring which Gardiner brings to the rhythms goes with idiomatic rubato, often daringly extreme. By comparison, such a rival as Welser-Möst, recorded live, seems cautious, with recorded sound lacking the sparkle of this DG alternative. As Hanna Glawari, the widow of the title, Cheryl Studer gives her most endearing performance yet. She may not have quite the vivacity of Elisabeth Schwarzkopf, but Studer's very first entry establishes her authority and charm, and the gentle half-tone on which she opens the soaring melody of the *Vilja-lied* is ravishing. Consistently she sings with sweeter, firmer tone than Felicity Lott on the Welser-Möst set and, though the Swedish baritone, Boje Skovhus, as Danilo cannot match the velvet of Thomas Hampson's voice for Welser-Möst, he makes an even more animated, raffish hero. The second couple, Valencienne and Camille, are delectably taken by Barbara Bonney and Rainer Trost, clear and youthful-sounding, outshining all rivals. The rest make an outstanding team, with Bryn Terfel, ripely resonant, turning Baron Mirko into more than a *buffo* character, while the choristers of Gardiner's Monteverdi Choir, obviously enjoying their Viennese outing, bring to Lehár the point and precision they have long devoted to the baroque repertory.

Matačić provides a magical set, guaranteed to send shivers of delight through any listener with its vivid sense of atmosphere and superb musicianship. It is one of Walter Legge's masterpieces as a recording manager, creating a sense of theatre that is almost without rival in gramophone literature. The CD opens up the sound yet retains the full bloom, and the theatrical presence and atmosphere are something to marvel at.

It was the mono set, of the early 1950s, which established a new pattern in recording operetta. Ten years later in stereo Schwarzkopf was to record the role again, if anything with even greater point and perception, but here she has extra youthful vivacity, and the *Viljalied* – ecstatically drawn out – is unique. Some may be troubled that Kunz as Danilo sounds older than the Baron, but it is still a superbly characterful cast, and the transfer to a single CD is bright and clear.

The live Welser-Möst recording was made at the Royal Festival Hall in July 1993. Much will depend on the listener's response to Dirk Bogarde's narration which punctuates the separate numbers: it aims to be a witty text, written by Tom Stoppard, which Bogarde delivers with an arch knowingness. The music-making is disappointing too, for though Welser-Möst has a fair idea of the idiom, his slowish speeds often diminish the sparkle, as in the *March septet* in Act II, celebrating women. Thomas Hampson makes a handsome, swaggering Danilo, but not even he is vocally at his sweetest, and the other three principals all sing with more uneven production than usual so that their duets – among the most delightful of all the numbers in the piece – lose their charm. Felicity Lott has plenty of charm and dignity as the Widow herself, but her voice too is given an unpleasant edge at times, not nearly as sweet as it can be. As well as the dialogue, the applause is also intrusive.

The Merry Widow (Die lustige Witwe): highlights.
(Y/B) (M) **(*) Decca 436 899-2 [id.]. Gueden, Kmentt, Grunden, Loose, Dönch, V. State Op. Ch. & O, Robert Stolz.

As with *Giuditta*, these highlights come from a complete set, recorded in Vienna in 1958 with character-istic Decca flair. We are taken straight into the salon of the Pontevedrian Embassy, with its multitude of guests, laughter and talk, clinking cocktail glasses and rustling dresses. This extraordinary ambient effect swirls into the room in the most spectacular manner and the *Polonaise* at the beginning of Act II and the entrance of the grisettes in Act III have a similar startling presence. The recording itself is very 'live' throughout and the degree of over-brightness adds to the sparkle. Hilda Gueden gives a melting performance as the Widow and she sings the *Vilja-Lied* most seductively. Per Grunden makes Danilo a heady tenor role (it is usually sung by a baritone); Waldemar Kmentt is an appealing Camille de Rosillon and the other parts are well up to standard. Robert Stolz conducts an entirely authentic performance, missing not a whit of sparkle or allure, with the Vienna State Opera Orchestra adding a characteristic lilt to the music and the chorus adding to the zest of the music-making.

The Merry Widow: (abridged, in an English version by Hassall).
(N) (BB) **(*) CfP Silver Double CDCFPSD 4742 (2). Catherine Wilson, Blanc, Hay, Hillman, Scottish Op. Ch., Philh. O, Gibson – VERDI: *Un ballo in maschera:* highlights. ***

Gibson is at his freshest and most inspired in this magic operetta. The 1976 recording is warm and full and the selection of items is admirable, with several passages included which in the past have often been missed in 'complete' recordings, notably the Act III *Cakewalk*. Much of the singing is pleasing rather than distinguished, but it is the splendid teamwork which makes this such a sparkling entertainment, and it can be warmly recommended at the price, especially as the coupling is also very successful.

Der Zarewitsch (complete).
*** Eurodisc 610 137 (2). Kollo, Popp, Rebroff, Orth, Hobarth, Bav. R. Ch., Munich R. O, Wallberg.

René Kollo may not have the finesse of a Tauber, but he sings with a freshness and absence of manner-ism that bring out the melodic beauty. Lucia Popp as the heroine, Sonya, sings ravishingly, and there is no weak link in the cast elsewhere, and the exhilaration of the entertainment comes over all the more refreshingly in the excellent CD transfer. No text is given, only notes in German.

'Lehar gala': Arias from: (i) *Eva;* (ii) *Friederike; Der Graf von Luxemburg; Das Land des Lächelns; Die lustige Witwe; Paganini; Schön ist die Welt; Der Zarewitsch;* (i) *Zigeunerliebe.*
(Y/B) (M) **(*) Decca 436 897-2 (2) [id.].(i) Pilar Lorengar, V. Op. O, Weller; (ii) Renate Holm, Werner Krenn, V. Volksoper O, Paulik.

Some 53 minutes of this hour-long compilation come from a two-LP set of operetta excerpts which Renate Holm and Werner Krenn made together in the Sofiensaal in December 1970, produced by Christopher Raeburn. They were both in splendid voice, and the opening *Merry widow waltz*, when they first sing the famous melody together and then lovingly hum it as a romantic reprise, is quite delightful. Songs like Krenn's title-number, *Schöne ist die Welt*, and Holm's *Ich bin verliebt*, from the same operetta, are splendidly done, and their charming duet from *The Land of smiles, Bei einem Tee à deux*, is matched by Krenn's heady *Dein ist mein ganzes Herz!*. The seductive *Gern hab'ich die Frau'n geküst* from *Paganini* and the *Wolgalied* from *Der Zarewitsch* are hardly less successful, while the following duet, *Kosende Wellen*, is ravishing, as is the justly famous *Bist du's, lachendes Glück?* from *Der Graf von Luxemburg*. The only slight snag is that there is too little variety in the programme – almost all the music is relaxed and lyrical. However, to end the concert, Pilar Lorengar comes on stage and adds a Hungarian gypsy flavour with a vibrant *Hör'ich Cymbalklänge* from *Zigeunerliebe*. The recording is first class throughout.

Leigh, Walter (1905–43)

Concertino for harpsichord and string orchestra.
(Y/B) (B) *** BBC Radio Classics BBCRD 9119 [id.]. George Malcolm, ASMF, Marriner – FINZI: *Clarinet concerto* **(*) (with Concert ***).

Like Butterworth, whose *Banks of Green Willow* is included on this disc, Walter Leigh was killed in action before his gifts could develop fully. His *Concertino for harpsichord and string orchestra*, with its heavenly slow movement, which dates from 1936, is an inventive and resourceful score, whose delights remain undimmed. It is currently unrepresented in the commercial catalogues and has surely never been played more winningly than it is here by George Malcolm. The balance with Marriner and his Academy is perfectly judged, so that the appearance of so lively a performance (from 1972), expertly engineered by the late James Burnett, usefully fills a gap. This is a highlight of a desirable bargain collection of English music, by Butterworth, Finzi, Vaughan Williams and Warlock – see our Concerts section, below.

Leighton, Kenneth (1929–88)

(i) *Cello concerto;* (ii) *Symphony No. 3 (Laudes Musicae).*
*** Chandos Dig. CHAN 8741 [id.]. (i) Wallfisch; (ii) Mackie; SNO, Bryden Thomson.

The symphony is in part a song-cycle, and its glowing, radiant colours and refined textures are immediately winning. Raphael Wallfisch plays the *Concerto* as if his life depended on it, and the *Symphony* draws every bit as much dedication from its performers. The recording is very immediate, and has stunning clarity and definition.

Veris gratia (for cello, oboe and strings), *Op. 9.*
*** Chandos Dig. CHAN 8471 [id.]. Wallfisch, Caird, RLPO, Handley – FINZI: *Cello concerto.* ***

Finzi is the dedicatee of Kenneth Leighton's *Veris gratia*, and so it makes an appropriate coupling for his *Cello concerto*, more particularly as its English pastoral style nods in his direction. The performance is highly sympathetic, George Caird the excellent oboist, and the naturally balanced recording is first class.

Conflicts, Op. 51; Fantasia contrappuntistica, Op. 24; Household pets, Op. 86; Sonatina No. 1; 5 Studies, Op. 22.
**(*) Abacus Dig. ABA 402-2 [id.]. Eric Parkin.

Kenneth Leighton was one of the most musical of pianists and wrote beautifully for the instrument. The *Household pets* is a sensitive piece, refined in craftsmanship, and the *Fantasia contrappuntistica* is comparably powerful. Eric Parkin plays it with total sympathy, and the recording is eminently serviceable.

Crucifixus pro nobis; Give me the wings of faith; O sacrum convivium; The second service: Magnificat; Nunc dimittis. Solus ad victimam.
*** ASV Dig. CDDCA 851 [id.]. David Went, Ch. of The Queen's College, Oxford, Matthew Owens – HOWELLS: *Chichester service* etc. **(*)

As a chorister in his youth, Kenneth Leighton wrote with an inborn sympathy for the voice and a natural feeling for line. These are beautiful pieces with an occasional reminder of Britten, and they are well sung, too, by the Choir of The Queen's College, Oxford, at which Leighton was a student.

Lekeu, Guillaume (1870–94)

(i) *Piano quartet* (2nd movt ed. d'Indy); (ii) *Cello sonata in F.*
*** Koch Schwann Dig. 310 185 [id.] (i–ii) Blumenthal, (i) Adamopoulos, Desjardins, (i–ii) Zanlonghi.

Lekeu's *Cello sonata* was written when he was a mere eighteen and is a powerful, big-boned piece whose first movement alone takes well over 20 minutes (the whole work lasts just under 50). The *Piano quartet*, composed at the instigation of Ysaÿe, was left incomplete when Lekeu succumbed to typhus; it was finished by d'Indy, who was a supportive figure after the death of Franck. The style is heavily indebted to these masters, but there is a dignity and melancholy at the heart of Lekeu's music which is moving. Excellent performances and vividly present recording.

Piano trio in C min.
**(*) Koch Schwann Dig. 310 060 [id.] Blumenthal, Adamopoulos, Zanlonghi.

The *Piano trio* is an astonishing achievement for a twenty-year-old, secure in its grasp of form and full of expressive intensity. The main influence, apart from that of his master, is Wagner, whose music Lekeu had encountered the previous year. Lekeu is a thoughtful composer and, though the slow movement perhaps outstays its welcome (it lasts 19 minutes), there are relatively few *longueurs*. The performance is dedicated, and the only reservation is the quality of the piano-tone which is thick at the bottom end of the register; the acoustic is a bit over-reverberant. Despite some academic touches, this is music of quality.

Lemba, Artur (1885–1960)

Symphony in C sharp min.
*** Chandos Dig. CHAN 8656 [id.]. SNO, Järvi (with Concert: *'Music from Estonia'*: Vol. 2***).

Lemba's *Symphony in C sharp minor* was the first symphony ever to be written by an Estonian. It sounds as if he studied in St Petersburg: at times one is reminded fleetingly of Glazunov, at others of Dvořák (the scherzo) – and even of Bruckner (at the opening of the finale) and of Elgar. This is by far the most important item in an enterprising collection of Estonian music.

Leoncavallo, Ruggiero (1858–1919)

I Pagliacci (complete).
(N) (M) *** DG 449 727-2 [id.]. Carlyle, Bergonzi, Taddei, Panerai, La Scala, Milan, Ch. & O, Karajan.
(N) *** DG 419 257-2 (3) [id.] cast as above, La Scala, Milan, Ch. & O, Karajan – MASCAGNI: *Cavalleria rusticana*. ***
(M) *** RCA GD 60865 (2) [60865-2]. Caballé, Domingo, Milnes, John Alldis Ch., LSO, Santi – PUCCINI: *Il Tabarro*. **(*)
(***) EMI mono CDS7 47981-8 (3) [Ang. CDCC 47981]. Callas, Di Stefano, Gobbi, La Scala, Milan, Ch. & O, Serafin – MASCAGNI: *Cavalleria rusticana*. (***)
(B) **(*) Naxos Dig. 8.660021 [id.]. Gauci, Martinucci, Tumagian, Dvorsky, Skovhus, Slovak Philh. Ch., Czech RSO, Rahbari.
(M) (**(*)) Nimbus mono NI 7843/4 [id.]. Gigli, Pacetti, Basiola, Nessi, Paci, La Scala Ch. & O, Ghione – MASCAGNI: *Cavalleria rusticana*.

Karajan's *Pagliacci* has dominated the catalogue for three decades alongside its natural operatic partner, *Cavalleria rusticana*, so it is apt that DG have chosen it for separate reissue in their series of 'Originals', freshly remastered. Karajan does nothing less than refine Leoncavallo's melodrama, with long-breathed, expansive tempi and the minimum of exaggeration. Karajan's choice of soloists was clearly aimed to help that – but the passions are still there; and rarely if ever on record has the La Scala Orchestra played with such beautiful feeling for tone-colour. Bergonzi is among the most sensitive of Italian tenors of heroic quality, and it is good to have Joan Carlyle as Nedda, touching if often rather cool. Taddei is magnificently strong, and Benelli and Panerai could hardly be bettered in the roles of Beppe and Silvio. The combined set remains available (and unsurpassed) but on three records at pre-mium price – although, as well as *Cav.*, DG provide a splendid set of performances of operatic inter-mezzi as a filler. However, the separate *Pagliacci* is something of a bargain.

For those who do not want that obvious coupling, the alternative RCA set is a first-rate recom-mendation, with fine singing from all three principals, vivid playing and recording, and one or two extra passages not normally included – as in the Nedda–Silvio duet. Milnes is superb in the Prologue.

It is thrilling to hear *Pagliacci* starting with the Prologue sung so vividly by Tito Gobbi. Di Stefano, too, is at his finest, but the performance inevitably centres on Callas and there are many points at which she finds extra intensity, extra meaning. Serafin's direction is strong and direct. The mono recording is dry, with voices placed well forward but with choral detail blurred, and this set is overpriced.

Alexander Rahbari conducts his Slovak forces in a vigorous, red-blooded reading which with first-rate solo singing makes an excellent bargain recommendation, very well recorded, if with the chorus a little distant. Miriam Gauci is a warmly vibrant Nedda, with plenty of temperament, and Eduard Tumagian is an outstanding Tonio, not only firm and dark of tone but phrasing imaginatively. As Canio, Nicola Martinucci has an agreeable tenor that he uses with more finesse and a better line than many more celebrated rivals, even though his histrionics at the beginning and end of *Vesti la giubba* are unconvincing.

The Nimbus transfer of the classic 1934 recording with Gigli focuses the voices effectively enough, giving them a mellow bloom – though the orchestra, often rather recessed, is relatively muffled. Gigli is very much the centre of attention, with Iva Pacetti as Nedda clear and powerful rather than characterful.

I Pagliacci: highlights.
(Y/B) ** Ph. Dig. 442 482-2 [id.] (from complete recording, with Domingo, Stratas, Pons; cond. Prêtre) –
   MASCAGNI: *Cavalleria rusticana:* highlights. **

This full-priced half-hour set of highlights is strictly for Domingo devotees. It is taken from the sound-track of Zeffirelli's film of the opera, in which the great tenor, in splendid voice, heroically dominates the performance. Juan Pons sings the Prologue impressively, but the rest of the cast is far less impressive and Teresa Stratas's singing becomes very raw under pressure.

Leonin (*c.* 1163–90)

Organa: *Alleluya, Epulemur Azamis; Gaude Maria; Propter veritatem; Viderunt omnes.*
(N) *** Lyrichord LEMS 8002 [id.]. Russell Oberlin, Charles Bressler, Donald Perry – PEROTINUS:
   Organa. ***

Over eight centuries have passed since the construction of the Cathedral of Notre Dame began and Leonin, the cathedral's composer, was writing this music. It is in two parts, with the top voice moving in unison or octaves, or over a sustained or only occasionally moving second part. Sometimes both voices sing in unison. The present performances are extraordinarily convincing and take us back in time to the very beginning of written music. The recording is excellent. This is perhaps the most fascinating disc yet issued by Lyrichord.

Liadov, Anatol (1855–1914)

About olden times, Op. 21b; Baba-Yaga, Op. 56; The enchanted lake, Op. 62; 3 Fanfares; Kikimora, Op. 63; The musical snuff-box, Op. 32; Polonaises, Opp. 49 & 55; 8 Russian folksongs, Op. 58.
**(*) ASV Dig. CDDCA 657 [id.]. Mexico City SO, Bátiz.

Three stars for the ASV recording by Brian Culverhouse – but the performances under Enrique Bátiz fall just short of that rating: the magical world of the finest of these scores could perhaps be conveyed with a more subtle atmosphere.

Baba-Yaga, Op. 56; The Enchanted lake, Op. 62; Kikimora, Op. 63.
(N) *** DG Dig. 447 084-2 [id.]. Russian Nat. O, Pletnev – RIMSKY-KORSAKOV: *Le Coq d'or;*
   TCHEREPNIN: *La Princesse lointaine* etc. ***

(i) *Baba Yaga, Op. 56; The Enchanted lake, Op. 62; Kikimora, Op. 63;* (ii) *8 Russian folksongs.*
(BB) **(*) Naxos Dig. 8.550328 [id.]. Slovak PO, (i) Gunzenhauser; (ii) Kenneth Jean – Concert:
   'Russian Fireworks'.

Anatol Liadov is almost as well known for what he did not write as for what he actually accomplished. It was he whom Diaghilev commissioned to write *The Firebird* and it was his dilatory response that prompted the impresario to turn to Stravinsky. Liadov's lethargy even prompted his teacher, Rimsky-Korsakov, to suspend him from his class. Yet these are exquisite miniatures, full of atmosphere and colour, which owe much to Rimsky but are at the same time distinguished by an individual fantasy and a remarkable feeling for orchestral colour. Mikhail Pletnev and his Russian National Orchestra give evocative performances of them: indeed their account of *The Enchanted lake* is the best since Koussevitzky's magical 78-r.p.m., and there can be no finer tribute. Excellent sound.

It is good to have inexpensive recordings of these key Liadov works, particularly the *Russian folksongs*, eight orchestral vignettes of great charm, displaying a winning sense of orchestral colour. The perform-ances are persuasive, and the digital recording is vivid and well balanced.

Ligeti, György (born 1923)

(i) *Cello concerto; Chamber concerto;* (ii) *Piano concerto.*
*** Sony Dig. S K 58945 [id.]. (i) Miklós Perényi; (ii) Ueli Wiget; Modern Ens., Peter Eötvös.

These three concertos span two decades of Ligeti's output. The *Cello concerto* and the *Chamber concerto*, for 13 instruments, are vivid in colour, complex in detail and undoubtedly full of energy. To some ears their content may not match their undoubted prolixity of surface comment. The *Piano concerto* has five movements. The most striking movement is the second; perhaps the others, exuberant as they are, outlast their welcome. Dedicated Ligetians (are there many, we wonder) will welcome these obviously skilled and committed performances, well recorded, with Wiget a striking advocate of the demanding solo role in the concertante work for piano.

Chamber concerto.
(B) *** DG Dig. 439 452-3 [id.]. Ens. InterContemporain, Boulez – LUTOSLAWSKI: *Chain 3* etc.; SCHNITTKE: *Concerto grosso No. 1.* ***

This bargain DG CD presents a performance of the *Chamber concerto* that is a useful supplement to that offered above, and admirers of this composer's cloudy sound-textures can safely investigate. In this work the specific notes matter less than the washes of colour. Excellent performance and recording.

Bagatelles.
*** Crystal CD 750 [id.]. Westwood Wind Quintet – CARLSSON: *Nightwings;* MATHIAS: *Quintet;* BARBER: *Summer music.* ***

Ligeti's folk-inspired *Bagatelles* are highly inventive and very attractive; and they are played with dazzling flair and unanimity of ensemble by this American group.

Lilburn, Douglas (born 1915)

Symphonies Nos. 1 (1949); *2* (1951); *3 in one movement* (1961).
(Y/B) *** Continuum Dig. 1069 [id.]. New Zealand SO, John Hopkins.

Douglas Lilburn is the doyen of New Zealand composers. The three symphonies collected here on this well-filled disc show an impressive musical mind at work. There is a strong affinity with Scandinavian music, induced perhaps by the similarities of latitude and landscape, and an imposing formal coherence. The opening of the *Third Symphony in one movement* almost suggests an antipodean Holmboe. The musical invention shows a consistently high level of imagination, and the performances by the New Zealand Symphony Orchestra under John Hopkins, to whom the *Third Symphony* is dedicated, are thoroughly committed. Excellent, well-balanced recorded sound enhances the claims of this disc, and mention should be made of the unusually informative and authoritative note by John Thomson. Strongly recommended.

Liszt, Franz (1811–86)

Piano concertos Nos. 1–2; Fantasia on Hungarian folksongs; Fantasia on themes from Beethoven's 'Ruins of Athens'; Grande fantaisie symphonique on themes from Berlioz's 'Lélio'; Malédiction; Polonaise brillante on Weber's Polonaise brillante in E (L'Hilarité); Totentanz (paraphrase on the *Dies Irae*); SCHUBERT/LISZT: *Wanderer fantasia.*
(B) *** EMI CZS7 67214-2 (2) [id.]. Michel Béroff, Leipzig GO, Kurt Masur.

Béroff's account of the two concertos can hold its own with the best of the competition: here there is nothing routine or slapdash, but instead excitement, warmth and spontaneity, along with his remarkable technical prowess. The Leipzig recording, too, sounds first rate in its remastered form and the distinguished orchestral playing under Masur is given plenty of body and weight. This is especially satisfying in the Schubert *Wanderer* arrangement, while the opening of the Beethoven and Berlioz *Fantasias* are full of atmosphere. The piano timbre has plenty of body and colour as well as sparkle. This is an exhilarating and rewarding set which can be given the strongest recommendation on all counts.

(i) *Piano concertos 1–2; Totentanz* (paraphrase on the '*Dies irae*'). *Années de pèlerinage: Book 1: 1st year: Switzerland; Book 2: 2nd year (Italy); Book 3: 3rd Year (Italy) excerpts: Aux cyprès de la Villa d'Este; Sunt lachrimae rerum; Sursum corda* (only). *Sonata in B min.; Concert paraphrase of 'Isolde's Liebestod' from Wagner's 'Tristan'. Csárdás macabre; En rêve (Nocturne); Harmonies poétiques et religieuses (Invocations; Bénédiction de Dieu dans la solitude; Pensée des morts); Funérailles. Klavierstück in F sharp; Légendes Nos.1–2; La lugubre gondola Nos. 1–2; Mosonyis Grabgeleit; Nuages gris; Prelude and fugue on the name, 'BACH'; RW (Venezia); Schlaflos! Frage und Antwort; Unstern (Sinistre); Valse oubliée No. 1; Vexilla regis Prodeunt; Weinachtsbaum (Christmas tree) suite (excerpts); Variations on 'Weinen, Klagen, Sorgen Zagen'.*

(N) (M) *** Ph. Brendel Edition Analogue/Dig. 446 924-2 (5) [id.]. Alfred Brendel, (i) LPO, Haitink.

Brendel's 1972 recordings of the *Concertos* and *Totentanz* have long been among the key versions of these volatile works and Haitink is a persuasive accompanist. Brendel's set of the *Second year* of the *Années de pèlerinage* was recorded that same year and proved no less outstanding. The performances are of superlative quality, the playing highly poetic and brilliant, while the analogue recording offers Philips's most realistic quality. The *First year* (*Switzerland*) came 14 years later and was recorded digitally. It has many impressive moments but also some ugly fortissimi that are not wholly the responsibility of the engineers. Brendel plays the pieces *segue*, without pauses and, although there is some atmospheric playing in the set, the moments of magic are relatively few. The four excerpts from the *Third year* were recorded as part of an outstanding (1979) analogue recital, which included the extraordinary late pieces, many of whose names are unfamiliar. The music is often surprisingly stark and bitter and Brendel's presentation of them is distinguished by a concentration and subtlety of nuance that are wholly convincing, helped by extremely lifelike recording. The *Prelude and fugue on the name 'BACH'* and the *Variations* on *'Weinen, Klagen, Sorgen, Zagen'* are better known as organ pieces but sound no less impressive on the piano when played so masterfully, and the *Harmonies poétiques et religieuses* are hardly less distinguished. However, the *Sonata* is something of a disappointment. Brendel has recorded this work three times and Philips have chosen the most recent version, made in 1991. It was a great pity that his second recording (also digital) was not chosen (voted by the *Gramophone* as 'Piano Record of the Year' in 1983). The newest account brings a similarly wide range of colour, yet there is not the same spontaneity nor a comparable firmness of grip. There is much brilliant pianism, but the overall purpose of the reading seems much less clear and even the recording, though bright and clean, is less impressive than either the 1983 version or even the analogue record, made in the 1960s. But overall this box shows Brendel as a superbly understanding Lisztian.

Piano concertos Nos. 1 in E flat; 2 in A.
(Y/B) (M) **(*) Cziffra Edition, Volume 3: EMI CDM5 65252-2 [id.]. György Cziffra, Philh. O, André Vandernoot – TCHAIKOVSKY: *Piano concerto No. 1.* **

(i) *Piano concertos Nos. 1–2;* (ii) *Hungarian rhapsody No. 2; Liebestraum; Les Préludes.*
(N) (BB) **(*) RCA Navigator 74321 29244-2. (i) Leonard Pennario, RPO, Leibowitz; (ii) Boston Pops O, Arthur Fiedler.

(i) *Piano concertos Nos. 1–2.* Symphonic poems: *Les Préludes; Mazeppa.*
(Y/B) **(*) Chandos Dig. CHAN 9360 [id.]. (i) Geoffrey Tozer; SRO, Järvi.

Piano concertos Nos. 1–2; Totentanz.
⊛ *** DG Dig. 423 571-2 [id.]. Zimerman, Boston SO, Ozawa.
(M) *** Ph. 426 637-2. Alfred Brendel, LPO, Haitink.

Piano concertos Nos. (i) 1 in E flat; (ii) 2 in A. Années de pèlerinage: Sonetto 104 del Petrarca. Hungarian rhapsody No. 6; Valse oubliée.
(M) *** Mercury 432 002-2 [id.]. Byron Janis, (i) Moscow PO, Kondrashin; (ii) Moscow RSO, Rozhdestvensky (also with SCHUMANN: *Romance in F sharp; Novellette in F.* FALLA: *Miller's dance.* GUION: *The harmonica player ***).

Piano concertos Nos. (i) 1 in E flat; (ii) 2 in A. Piano sonata in B min.
(N) (M) *** Ph. 446 200-2 [id.]. Sviatoslav Richter, (i–ii) with LSO, Kirill Kondrashin.
(Y/B) (B) ** BBC Radio Classics BBCRD 9108 [id.]. John Ogdon, with (i) BBC Scottish SO, George Hurst; (ii) BBC SO, C. Davis.

Krystian Zimerman's record of the two *Concertos* and the *Totentanz* is altogether thrilling, and he has the advantage of excellent support from the Boston orchestra under Ozawa. It has poise and classicism and, as one listens, one feels this music could not be played in any other way – surely the mark of a great performance! This record is outstanding in every way, and it now makes a first choice for this repertoire.

However, Sviatoslav Richter's 1961 performances on Philips are very distinguished indeed, and the recent remastering by Wilma Cozart Fine makes the very most of the recording, originally engineered by the Mercury team. It is good that both Wilma and Robert Fine receive a credit in the insert notes for the excellence of the original sound-balance. Richter's playing is unforgettable and so is his rapport with Kondrashin and the LSO, whose playing throughout is of the very highest order. For the current reissue, Richter's electrifying and highly poetic new recording of the *Sonata* has been added; Philips are, however, reluctant to suggest a recording date. The sound is vivid and present but the acoustic is rather dry for full comfort. However, given playing of this calibre, one soon adjusts.

Around the time they were recording Richter's Liszt *Concertos* for Philips in London (1962), the Mercury engineers paid a visit to Moscow to record Byron Janis in the same repertoire, and his is a comparably distinguished coupling. Janis's glittering articulation is matched by his sense of poetry and drama, and there is plenty of dash in these very compelling performances, which are afforded character-istically brilliant Mercury sound, although the piano is too close. The encores which follow the two *Concertos* are also very enjoyable.

Brendel's Philips recordings from the early 1970s hold their place at or near the top of the list. There is a valuable extra work offered here and the recording is of Philips's best. The performances are as poetic as they are brilliant, and those who doubt the musical substance of No. 2 will find their reservations melt away.

The two Liszt concertos suit Cziffra's bold, volatile manner very well indeed and, if there is an element of brutality in the *First Concerto*, there is also great excitement and drive, and the glittering solo playing has enormous panache. The work's lyrical side, too, is persuasively encompassed, as is the scintillating wit of the Scherzo. The *Second Concerto* is even finer. The work's quicksilver moods bring a true feeling of spontaneity and the orchestra is with him to a man, as if together they were extemporizing it all, so that the finale brings great dash and flair. The recordings (made in 1958 and 1961) with bright primary colours and a tendency to harshness of lighting suit the music-making admirably. In spite of the use of the Kingsway Hall, the sound, though basically full, is comparatively two-dimensional.

Pennario's performances are assured and brilliant, yet the slow movement of No. 1 is touchingly wistful. Leibowitz provides excellent support and the opening of the *A major Concerto* is enticingly atmospheric. The recording, though forward, is full and vivid, and the result is sensitive, sparkling and spontaneous, with a thrilling lack of inhibition at the close of the *Second Concerto*. There is nothing much wrong with Fiedler's exciting Boston Pops accounts of the two orchestral works, which are also vividly recorded. It was a pity that the famous *Liebestraum* could not have been provided in its original piano format, though the orchestral version is undoubtedly luscious. This bargain-basement collection is first-class value.

Tozer and Järvi establish a successful partnership. The Suisse Romande Orchestra, too, seems in good form. The performances are enjoyable, but alongside Cziffra they seem lightweight, although they have an attractive element of fantasy. There is nothing special, either, about the performances of the two symphonic poems, which generously increase the playing time to 71 minutes. Karajan is far more impressive in both, and especially in *Mazeppa*. The distant fanfare which heralds Mazeppa's triumphal return at the end of the piece, a frisson-creating moment in the Karajan performance, is here much too close.

It is good to have a memorial of so commanding a Lisztian as John Ogdon in such an enticing and generous coupling. The pity is that the performances are so variable. The *Second Concerto*, recorded at a Prom performance in 1971, is electrifying, a performance which alone makes the disc well worth buying, thanks to the concentration and clarity of both pianist and conductor. After that the *First Concerto*, recorded in Glasgow in 1983, is disappointingly slack, perhaps a reflection of Ogdon's periodic illness. Though the *Sonata*, recorded at the Canterbury Festival in 1987, is not as brilliant in its virtuosity as Ogdon could be at his peak, it is still a powerful and commanding account, helped by full, immediate sound.

Piano concerto No. 1 in E flat.
*** Chesky CD 93 [id.]. Earl Wild, RPO, Sargent – CHOPIN: *Concerto No. 1* **(*); FAURÉ: *Ballade for piano and orchestra.* ***
(N) (M) *** DG 449 719-2 [id.]. Argerich, LSO, Abbado – CHOPIN: *Piano concerto No. 1.* ***

(i; ii) *Piano concerto No. 1 in E flat;* (i) *Piano sonata in B min.; Hungarian rhapsody No. 6;* (iii) *Années de pèlerinage: Vallée d'Obermann; Les jeux d'eau à la Villa D'Este.*
(Y/B) (B) **(*) DG 439 409-2 [id.]. (i) Martha Argerich; (ii) LSO, Abbado; (iii) Lazar Berman.

Earl Wild is in his element and gives a glittering and powerful account of Liszt's famous warhorse, yet one that does not lack either delicacy or warmth. The famous triangle Scherzo is crystalline in its clarity and the full-blooded recording matches the extravagance of Liszt's exciting finale.

For some reason Martha Argerich (in 1968) recorded only Liszt's *First Concerto* and not the *Second*. However, in the *E flat Concerto* there is an excellent partnership between the pianist and Abbado, and this is a performance of flair and high voltage which does not ever become vulgar. It is very well recorded and, in this reissue coupled with Chopin for DG's 'Legendary Recordings' series of

'Originals', it sounds better than ever. The performance is also available on DG's bargain Classikon label, coupled with the *Sonata*, which Argerich recorded three years later. Her account has tremendous assurance and vigour and there is no lack of spontaneity. But the work's lyrical feeling and indeed its breadth are sacrificed to some extent to the insistent forward pulse of the playing. The *Rhapsody* gives no cause for complaint and the recording is clear (if not especially rich), but Lazar Berman's perform-ances of the two excerpts from the *Années de pèlerinage* which complete the CD show how Liszt playing can be controlled as well as seemingly impulsive and poetic.

Piano concerto No. 2 in A.
*** Virgin/EMI Dig. VC7 59613-2 [id.]. Leif Ove Andsnes, Bergen PO, Dmitri Kitaenko – GRIEG:
  Piano concerto etc. ***

Leif Ove Andsnes is a real musician who plays with great tenderness and poetic feeling as well as bravura. Marvellous sound, too, with a piano in perfect condition (not always the case on records) and an excellent balance.

(i) *Dante Symphony;* (ii) *Années de pèlerinage, Book 2: Après un lecture du Dante (Fantasia quasi sonata).*
*** Teldec/Warner Dig. 9031 77340 [id.]. (i) Women's voices of Berlin R. Ch., BPO, Daniel Barenboim;
  (ii) Barenboim (piano).

Liszt's *Dante Symphony* divides naturally into two very expansive, equally balanced halves – *Inferno* and *Purgatorio* – each lasting about 21 minutes, with a relatively short choral *Magnificat* as a finale. The work opens diabolically, with the rasping trombones evoking the gates of Hell, followed by a sustained frenzy of writing for strings and brass; later in a romantic interlude we meet Francesca da Rimini in all her grief. Interestingly, she is introduced by a bass clarinet in a not dissimilar way to her entrance on the clarinet in Tchaikovsky's symphonic poem. A blinding flash of harps introduces the malignant Scherzo, and the movement reaches a tremendous climax. The second movement is calming – some might say becalmed in its spacious paragraphs. Finally the heavenly chorus enters and lusciously proclaims salva-tion. Barenboim really has the measure of this somewhat rambling work and controls its rhapsodic structure admirably, holding the tension throughout the first movement and creating enormous visceral excitement at the close. He is helped by marvellous playing from the BPO, who really sound as if they believe in it all, and the radiant choral effects are superbly brought off. The resonant acoustic of Berlin's Schaulspielhaus lets everything expand with Wagnerian amplitude and the result is very impressive indeed. As an encore, Barenboim leaves the rostrum for the piano and offers the *Dante Sonata*, which has the same literary basis but offers a quite different musical treatment. The performance is flam-boyantly arresting, but the piano recording is curiously shallow.

(i) *Fantasia on Hungarian folk tunes; Hungarian rhapsodies Nos. 2 & 5.*
(B) *** DG 429 156-2 [id.]. (i) Shura Cherkassky; BPO, Karajan (with BRAHMS: *Hungarian dances Nos. 17–20* ***).

(i) *Fantasia on Hungarian folk tunes. Hungarian rhapsodies Nos. 2 & 5; Mephisto waltz No. 2.*
(M) *** DG 419 862-2 [id.]. (i) Cherkassky; BPO, Karajan.

Shura Cherkassky's glittering 1961 recording of the *Hungarian fantasia* is an affectionate performance with some engaging touches from the orchestra, though the pianist is dominant and his playing is superbly assured. The rest of the programme is comparably charismatic.

(i) *Fantasia on Hungarian folk tunes. Hungarian rhapsodies;* Symphonic poems: *Mazeppa; Les Préludes; Tasso, lamento e trionfo. Mephisto waltz No. 2.*
**(*) DG 415 967-2 (2). (i) Shura Cherkassky; BPO, Karajan.

The cellos and basses sound marvellous in the *Fifth Rhapsody* and *Tasso*, and even the brashness of *Les Préludes* is a little tempered. *Mazeppa* is a great performance, superbly thrilling and atmospheric. A superb achievement, showing Karajan and his Berlin orchestra at their finest. However, this set now seems overpriced.

A Faust symphony.
(N) *** DG Dig. 449 137-2 [id.]. Vinson Cole, Dresden State Op. Ch. & State O, Sinopoli.
(Y/B) *** EMI Dig. CDC5 55220-2 [id.]. Peter Seiffert, Ernst-Senff Ch. Male voices, Prague
  Philharmonic Ch., BPO, Rattle.
(N) (M) *** DG 447 449-2 [id.]. Kenneth Riegel, Tanglewood Festival Ch., Boston SO, Bernstein.
**(*) Denon Dig. CO 75634 [id.]. Jianyi Zhang, Berlin R. Ch., RSO, Inbal.
(M) **(*) Carlton Dig. PCD 1071 [id.]. Antonio Necolescu, Hungarian R. Ch., Budapest & State SO,
  Francesco D'Avalos.

Sinopoli's performance generates all the adrenalin one would expect from a live occasion, with the thrusting opening movement particularly exciting. The central portrait of Gretchen, with its delicate oboe solo, has an appealing simplicity and, with a comparably touching contribution from the fine tenor soloist, Vinson Cole, the work's close has a real sense of mystic apotheosis. The recording is strikingly vivid and gives plenty of bite to climaxes, yet it is also spacious and atmospheric, if not as rich as Rattle's EMI version.

Rattle's début recording with the Berlin Philharmonic brings an exceptionally warm and persuasive reading. That it was recorded live is particularly helpful in this expansively episodic work. Rattle's spontaneity of expression, whether in pointing the main melodies or in moulding the all-important transitions, carries the ear on magnetically. He is helped by ravishing playing from the Berlin players, not least the strings, with the central movement representing the heroine, Gretchen, emerging as the high point of the performance. That the recording, made in the Philharmonie, sets the orchestra at a slight distance, notably the brass, prevents tuttis from biting as hard and as dramatically as they can. The impact of Bernstein's masterly (mid-priced) analogue version from Boston is more powerful, but Rattle is closer to Beecham's pioneering stereo set, and on its own terms one quickly adjusts to the balances of the Berlin sound, relishing its beauty. The performance culminates in a rapt account of the choral apotheosis, with the men's chorus clearly focused and with Peter Seiffert singing radiantly, headily beautiful through the range.

Bernstein on DG seems to possess the ideal temperament for holding together grippingly the melodrama of the first movement, while the lovely *Gretchen* centrepiece is played most beautifully. Kenneth Riegel is an impressive tenor soloist in the finale, there is an excellent, well-balanced choral contribution, and the Boston Symphony Orchestra produce playing which is both exciting and atmospheric. While Sinopoli's version remains first choice, the Bernstein account (reissued as one of DG's 'Originals') makes a fine, mid-priced alternative.

The two other digital recordings have individual merits but neither displaces current recommendations. D'Avalos's performance has much vitality and makes up in gutsy spontaneity for any lack of finesse, while the Hungarian orchestral playing is really very good. His tenor soloist, Antonio Necolescu, has a rather wide vibrato, and that offers minor problems in the work's passionate apotheosis, but the Hungarian choir sings with plenty of bite and D'Avalos's reading of the last movement (*Mephistofeles*) has more pungency than Inbal's version. The recording is vivid, but has fullness too.

Where Inbal scores is in his added gravitas and his sense of architecture. Helped by the resonant acoustic, the Berlin Radio Orchestra provides warmly full-bodied textures and the element of vulgarity in Liszt's inspiration is minimized, if some of the music's gusto is simultaneously lost. Gretchen's portrayal in the central movement is poetically refined and *Mephistofeles* is a strong rather than a grotesquely Satanic portrait. But Inbal comes into his own in the closing pages when, with his splendidly ardent soloist and fine chorus, he creates a hugely expansive final climax, anticipating Wagner in its richness of amplitude and drama.

Hungarian rhapsodies Nos. 1–6.
(M) **(*) Mercury 432 015-2 [id.]. LSO, Dorati – ENESCU: *Roumanian rhapsody No. 1.* ***

Hungarian rhapsodies Nos. 1–6; Hungarian battle march; Rákóczy march.
(M) **(*) EMI CDM7 64627-2. Philh. Hungarica or LPO, Boskovsky.

Dorati's is undoubtedly the finest set of orchestral *Hungarian rhapsodies*. He brings out the gypsy flavour and, with lively playing from the LSO, there is both polish and sparkle. The Mercury recording is characteristically vivid.

Boskovsky does not fully catch the mercurial element, the sudden changes of mood which is the gypsy heritage of these pieces, but the Philharmonia Hungarica (who play in Nos. 1, 4 and 6 – *Carnival in Pest*) are obviously at home; and the LPO clearly enjoy the famous No. 2, while the *Third* with its effective use of the cimbalom, has plenty of colour. The *Rákóczy march* (No. 15 for piano) is done spiritedly by the Hungarian group, but the little-known *Hungarian battle march* does not emerge here as a lost masterpiece. The freshly remastered recordings (from 1977/8) sound well and, though Dorati on Mercury takes pride of place in this repertoire, this EMI disc certainly gives pleasure.

Hungarian rhapsodies Nos. 1 in F min.; 4 in D min.; Les Préludes.
(M) **(*) Sony SMK 47572 [id.]. NYPO, Bernstein – ENESCU: *Roumanian Rhapsody No. 1* (with BRAHMS: *Hungarian dances Nos. 5–6* **(*)).

Notable for the vivid coupled performance of the Enescu *Rhapsody*, this collection shows characteristic Bernstein brilliance, with first-rate orchestral playing throughout. The sound is a bit glossy in the violins, but has weight too, especially for the heavy brass in the final peroration of *Les Préludes*, which is wonderfully pontifical. Indeed Bernstein is very much at home in this melodramatic piece, not missing its noble lyricism alongside its excitement. The two Brahms *Hungarian dances* are played with plenty of dash.

Hungarian rhapsodies Nos. 2, 6, 9, 12, 14 & 15 (arr. Peter Wolf).
(Y/B) (B) *** HM Dig. HMA 1903046 [id.]. Franz Liszt CO, János Rolla.

These transcriptions for strings are most enjoyable, giving the rhapsodies a chimerical lightness of texture. They are very well played indeed by this excellent orchestra, and Rolla's performances have nicely calculated rubato and plenty of spirit. Excellent, fresh recording. Not an alternative to the usual full-orchestra versions but a worthwhile bargain supplement.

Mephisto waltz.
(N) (M) *** RCA 09026 61246-2 [id.]. Chicago SO, Reiner – TCHAIKOVSKY: *Symphony No. 6* etc.
   **(*)

Reiner's account of the *Mephisto waltz* is the star item on this CD, unsurpassed on disc. The Chicago playing is superb, exciting and seductive by turns, and the hall ambience gives added lustre throughout, but especially to the woodwind detail in the score's gentler moments.

SYMPHONIC POEMS

Ce qu'on entend sur la montagne; Festklänge; Mazeppa; Orpheus; Les Préludes; Prometheus; Tasso, lamento e trionfo.
(B) **(*) Ph. Duo 438 751-2 (2) [id.]. LPO, Bernard Haitink.

Hamlet; Héroïde funèbre; Hungaria; Hunnenschlacht; Die Ideale; Mephisto waltz No. 1; Von der Wiege bis zum Grabe.
(B) **(*) Ph. Duo 438 754-2 (2) [id.]. LPO, Bernard Haitink.

Apart from *Les Préludes*, the splendid *Mazeppa* and, to a lesser extent, *Tasso*, Liszt's symphonic poems enjoy fairly limited favour. The relatively popular pieces have by no means the monopoly of Liszt's inspiration; some of his earlier efforts, such as *Ce qu'on entend sur la montagne* and *Festklänge*, suffer not only from formal weakness but also from a lack of interesting melodic invention, and many of their pages are let down by rhetorical bursts and by the repetition of melodramatic flourishes. But the final work, *From the cradle to the grave*, has a visionary quality which shows Liszt thinking far ahead of his time. In *Hamlet*, for instance, there is a lot to admire; the *Héroïde funèbre* is nobly conceived, and Haitink's restrained yet powerful performance does it full justice. *Prometheus* is also successful and *Hungaria* has an agreeable gypsy violin sequence to offset its patriotic fervour and brass chorales. *Hamlet* brings great dramatic intensity and plenty of atmosphere; *Festklänge* mixes polonaise dance-rhythms with more romantic sections. *Die Ideale* is based on Schiller's poem and has a pleasing rhap-sodical feeling imbued with melancholy until the self-assurance of its closing pages. It is not an easy work to bring off, and Haitink's direct, dedicated manner does not always catch its changing moods. The performance of *Festklänge* is more successful but, like *Hunnenschlacht* ('The battle of the Huns'), it lacks extrovert bravura, although no one could complain about the impressive organ effects at the close of the latter piece. *Les Préludes* and *Mazeppa* (which sounds marvellous in Karajan's hands), though structurally well conceived, lack that strain of histrionic vulgarity which makes them more ear-catching, and in the familiar *Mephisto waltz* there is a hint of reserve not entirely in the spirit of a Bacchanalian dance. Nevertheless the orchestral playing is first rate throughout these four discs and the recording has never sounded better – far more vivid than on the original LPs. Liszt invented the symphonic poem; here is an inexpensive and, for the most part, rewarding way to sample his achievement overall. There is good documentation.

Hunnenschlacht (symphonic poem).
** Telarc Dig. CD 80079 [id.]. Cincinnati SO, Kunzel – BEETHOVEN: *Wellington's victory.* **

A direct, unsubtle performance of a rarely recorded piece. The Telarc sound, however, is highly spec-tacular. Those wanting the *'Battle' symphony* of Beethoven won't be disappointed with this, although the CD is rather short measure.

Symphonic poems: *Mazeppa; Orpheus; Les Préludes; Tasso, lamento e trionfo. Mephisto waltz No. 2.*
(M) ** EMI CDM7 64850-2 [id.]. Leipzig GO, Kurt Masur.

Masur is not altogether at home in the melodrama of *Les Préludes* and *Mazeppa* – although the latter is excitingly done, if without the panache of Karajan. He breezes through *Orpheus* at record speed and misses the endearing gentleness that Beecham brought to it in the early 1960s. Nevertheless these performances are all strongly characterized and extremely well played and, although the digital remastering has robbed the sound of some of its rich sonority in the lower strings, the brightness of the new sound-balance has a different kind of appeal.

Mazeppa; Les Préludes; Prometheus; Tasso, lamento e trionfo (symphonic poems).
(BB) *** Naxos Dig. 8.550487 [id.]. Polish Nat. RSO (Katowice), Michael Halász.

Michael Halász has the full measure of this repertoire and this is one of the most successful collections of Liszt's symphonic poems to have emerged in recent years. He draws some remarkably fine playing from the Katowice Radio Orchestra. The brass playing is very impressive throughout, especially the trombones and tuba, who have the epic main theme of *Mazeppa*, but its grandiloquence is no less powerful in *Les Préludes*, weighty and never brash. The recording is spacious, with full natural string textures, but it is the resounding brass one remembers most.

Totentanz (for piano and orchestra).
(M) *** RCA 09026 61250-2 [id.]. Byron Janis, Chicago SO, Reiner – Concert: *'The Reiner sound'*. ***

Recorded in 1959, this is still one of the most exciting accounts of Liszt's *Dance of death* in the catalogue. It opens in thrillingly dramatic fashion, but the scherzando element later is no less successful. A powerful partnership between Janis and Reiner ensures that the tension is well held throughout, and the Chicago ambience makes its own evocative contribution. Though the close balance is not as natural as some of the earlier Chicago recordings, the sound here is fuller and more realistic than on the original LP.

Elégies Nos. 1–2; La lugubre gondola; Romance oubliée; Die Zelle in Nonnenwerth.
(N) *** RCA Dig. 09026 68290-2 [id.]. Steven Isserlis, Stephen Hough – GRIEG: *Cello sonata;* RUBIN-STEIN: *Cello sonata No. 1.* ***

The five cello pieces of Liszt, all of them brief and all of them adapted from earlier works, are used to frame two high-romantic cello sonatas by Grieg and Rubinstein, with the latter in danger of neglect. Isserlis and Hough give inspired performances, bringing out the distinctive lyricism of Liszt's writing for cello. The *Romance oubliée* ('Forgotten romance'), adapted from an early song, was originally written for viola, with an added arpeggio passage at the end reflecting Berlioz's *Harold in Italy*, which Liszt had arranged for viola and piano. In the two *Elégies* Isserlis is most persuasive in the improvisation-like passages, while the disc is rounded off by two Liszt pieces that are slightly more substantial than the others: *Die Zelle in Nonnenwerth* is a late adaptation of an early song, spare in texture; and Liszt's tribute to Wagner after his death, *La lugubre gondola*, is only one of Liszt's many different adaptations. Warm, well-balanced sound.

PIANO MUSIC

Complete piano music, Vol. 1: *Albumblatt in waltz form; Bagatelle without tonality; Caprice-valses Nos. 1 & 2; Ländler in A flat; Mephisto waltzes Nos. 1–3; Valse impromptu; 4 Valses oubliées.*
*** Hyperion Dig. CDA 66201 [id.]. Leslie Howard.

Complete piano music, Vol. 2: *Ballades Nos. 1–2; Berceuse; Impromptu (Nocturne); Klavierstück in A flat; 2 Légendes; 2 Polonaises.*
**(*) Hyperion Dig. CDA 66301. Leslie Howard.

Complete piano music, Vol. 3: *Fantasia and fugue on B-A-C-H; 3 Funeral odes: Les morts; La notte; Le triomphe funèbre du Tasse; Grosses Konzertsolo; Prelude on Weinen, Klagen, Sorgen, Sagen; Variations on a theme of Bach.*
** Hyperion Dig. CDA 66302 [id.]. Leslie Howard.

Complete piano music, Vol. 4: *Adagio in C; Etudes d'éxécution transcendante; Elégie sur des motifs de Prince Louis Ferdinand de Prusse; Mariotte.*
** Hyperion Dig. CDA 66357 [id.]. Leslie Howard.

Complete piano music, Vol. 5: Concert paraphrases: BERLIOZ: *L'Idée fixe; Overtures: Les Francs-Juges; Le Roi Lear; Marche des pèlerins; Valse des Sylphes.* CHOPIN: *6 Chants polonais.* SAINT-SAENS: *Danse macabre.*
*** Hyperion Dig. CDA 66346 [id.]. Leslie Howard.

Complete piano music, Vol. 6: Concert paraphrases: AUBER: *3 Pieces on themes from La muette de Portici.* BELLINI: *Réminiscences de Norma.* BERLIOZ: *Benvenuto Cellini: Bénédiction et serment.* DONIZETTI: *Réminiscences de Lucia di Lammermoor; Marche funèbre et Cavatina (Lucia).* ERNST (Duke of Saxe-Coburg-Gotha): *Tony: Hunting chorus.* GLINKA: *Russlan and Ludmilla: Tscherkessen-*

marsch. GOUNOD: *Waltz from Faust.* HANDEL: *Almira: Sarabande and Chaconne.* MEYERBEER: *Illustra-*
tions de L'Africaine. MOZART: *Réminiscences de Don Juan.* VERDI: *Aida: Danza sacra & Duetto finale.*
TCHAIKOVSKY: *Eugene Onegin: Polonaise.* WAGNER: *Tristan: Isoldes Liebestod.* WEBER: *Der Freischütz:*
Overture.
*** Hyperion Dig. CDA 66371/2 [id.]. Leslie Howard.

Complete piano music, Vol. 7: Chorales: *Crux ave benedicta; Jesu Christe; Meine Seele; Nun danket alle*
Gott; Nun ruhen all Wälder; O haupt; O Lamm Gottes; O Traurigkeit; Vexilla Regis; Was Gott tut; Wer
nur den Lieben; Via Crucis; Weihachtsbaum; Weihnachtslied.
** Hyperion Dig. CDA 66388 [id.]. Leslie Howard.

Complete piano music, Vol. 8: *Alleluia and Ave Maria; Ave Marias 1–4; Ave Maria de Arcadelt; Ave*
Maris stella; Harmonies poétiques et religieuses (complete); *Hungarian Coronation Mass; Hymnes;*
Hymne du Pape; In festo transfigurations; Invocation; O Roma nobilis; Sancta Dorothea; Slavimo slavno
slaveni!; Stabat mater; Urbi et orbi; Vexilla regis prodeunt; Zum Haus des Herrn.
** Hyperion Dig. CDA 66421/2 [id.]. Leslie Howard.

Complete piano music, Vol. 9: *6 Consolations; 2 Elégies; Gretchen* (from *Faust Symphony*); *Sonata in B*
min.; Totentanz.
** Hyperion Dig. CDA 66429 [id.]. Leslie Howard (piano).

Complete piano music, Vol. 10: Concert paraphrases: BELLINI: *Hexaméron (Grand bravura variations*
on the March from *I Puritani).* BERLIOZ: *Symphonie fantastique. Un portrait en musique de la Marquise*
de Blocqueville.
**(*) Hyperion Dig. CDA 66433 [id.]. Leslie Howard.

Complete piano music, Vol. 11: *Abschied (Russisches Volkslied); Am Grabe Richard Wagners; Carrousel*
de Madame P-N; Dem Andenken Petöfis; Epithalium; Klavierstück in F sharp; En Rêve; 5 Klavierstücke;
Mosonyis Grabgeleit; Recueillement; Resignazione; Romance oubliée; RW (Venezia); Schlaflos! Frage
und Antwort; Sospiri; Toccata; Slyepoi (Der blinde Sänger); Die Trauergondel (La lugubre gondola);
Trauervorspiel und Trauermarsch; Trübe Wolken (Nuages gris); Ungams Gott; Ungarisches Königslied;
Unstern: Sinistre; Wiegenlied (Chant de berceau).
**(*) Hyperion Dig. CDA 66445 [id.]. Leslie Howard.

Complete piano music, Vol. 12: *Années de pèlerinage, 3rd Year (Italy); 5 Hungarian folksongs; Historical*
Hungarian portraits.
** Hyperion Dig. CDA 66448 [id.]. Leslie Howard.

Complete piano music, Vol. 13: Concert paraphrases: ALLEGRI/MOZART: *A La Chapelle Sistine:*
Miserere d'Allegri et Ave verum corpus de Mozart. BACH: *Fantasia and fugue in G min.; 6 Preludes and*
fugues for organ.
** Hyperion Dig. CDA 66438 [id.]. Leslie Howard.

Complete piano music, Vol. 14: *Christus; Polonaises de St Stanislas; Salve Polonia; St Elizabeth.*
**(*) Hyperion Dig. CDA 66466 [id.]. Leslie Howard.

Complete piano music, Vol. 15: Concert paraphrases of Lieder: BEETHOVEN: *Adelaïde; An die ferne*
Geliebte; 6 Gellert Lieder; 6 Lieder von Goethe; An die ferne Geliebte. DESSAUER: *3 Lieder.* FRANZ: *Er est*
gekommenin Sturm und Regen; 12 Lieder. MENDELSSOHN: *7 Lieder* including *Auf Flügeln des Gesanges.*
CLARA & ROBERT SCHUMANN: *10 Lieder* including *Frülingsnacht; Widmung.*
**(*) Hyperion Dig. CDA 66481/2 [id.]. Leslie Howard.

Complete solo piano music, Vol. 16: Piano transcriptions: DAVID: *Bunte Reihe* (24 character pieces for
violin and piano), *Op. 30.*
*** Hyperion Dig. CDA 66506 [id.]. Leslie Howard.

Complete piano music, Vol. 17: Concert paraphrases: DONIZETTI: *Spirito gentil* from *La Favorita;*
Marche funèbre from *Don Sebastien.* GOUNOD: *Les Sabéennes (Berceuse)* from *La Reine de Saba.*
GRETRY: *Die Rose (Romance)* from *Zémire et Azor.* MEYERBEER: *3 Illustrations du Prophète; Fantasia*
and fugue on Ad nos, ad salutarem undam on a theme from *Le Prophète.* MOSONYI: *Fantasy on Szép*
Ilonka (Mosonyi). WAGNER: *Spinning song and Ballade* from *Der fliegende Holländer; Pilgrims' chorus*
and O du, mein holder Abendstern from *Tannhäuser; Valhalla* from *The Ring; Feierlicher Marsch zum*
heiligen Grail from *Parsifal.*
**(*) Hyperion Dig. CDA 66571/2 [id.]. Leslie Howard.

Complete piano music, Vol. 18: Concert paraphrases: BEETHOVEN: *Capriccio alla turca; Fantasy* from *Ruins of Athens.* LASSEN: *Symphonisches Zwischenspiel zu Calderons Schauspiel über allen Zauber Liebe.* MENDELSSOHN: *Wedding march and dance of the elves* from *A Midsummer night's dream.* WEBER: *Einsam bin ich, nicht alleine from La Preciosa.* HEBBEL: *Nibelungen.*
**(*) Hyperion Dig. CDA 66575 [id.]. Leslie Howard.

Leslie Howard's ambitious project to record the complete music of Liszt proceeds apace and at least two of these issues have already collected a Grand Prix du Disque in Budapest (Volumes 5 and 6). The performances are very capable and musicianly, and there are moments of poetic feeling, but for the most part his playing rarely touches distinction. The kind of concentration one finds in great Liszt pianists such as Arrau, Kempff and Richter (and there are many younger artists whose names also spring to mind) rarely surfaces. Howard's technical equipment is formidable but poetic imagination and the ability to grip the listener are here less developed: his rushed account of the *Sonata* does not really stand up against the current competition. One of the most interesting issues is Volume 16, the *Bunte Reihe* of Ferdinand David (1810–70), a contemporary of Mendelssohn. These are transcriptions of music for violin and piano in which the violin seems hardly to be missed at all. Leslie Howard plays them beautifully. Certainly the coverage so far is remarkable and, if this playing rarely takes the breath away either by its virtuosity or poetic insights, it is unfailingly intelligent and the recordings are first class.

Complete piano music, Vol. 19: *Die Lorelei; 3 Liebesträume; Songs for solo piano, Books 1–2.*
*** Hyperion Dig. CDA 66593 [id.]. Leslie Howard.

Complete piano music, Vol. 20: *Album d'un voyageur: Années de pèlerinage*, 1st, 2nd & 3rd years (first versions); *Chanson du Béarn; Fantaisie romantique sur deux mélodies suisses; Faribolo pastour.*
*** Hyperion Dig. CDA 66601/2 [id.]. Leslie Howard.

Complete piano music, Vol. 21: ROSSINI: *Soirées musicales; Grande fantaisie on motifs from Soirées musicales; 2nd Fantaisie on motifs from Soirées musicales.* DONIZETTI: *Nuits d'été à Pausilippe.* MERCADANTE: *Soirées italiennes. 3 Sonetti di Petrarca* (1st version); *Venezia e Napoli* (1st set).
*** Hyperion Dig. CDA 66661/2 [id.]. Leslie Howard.

Complete piano music, Vol. 22: Concert paraphrases of Beethoven Symphonies: *Symphonies Nos. 1–9.*
** Hyperion Dig. CDA 66671/5 [id.]. Leslie Howard.

Complete piano music, Vol. 23: BERLIOZ: (i) *Harold in Italy.* LISZT: (i) *Romance oubliée.* GOUNOD: *Hymne à Sainte Cécile.* MEYERBEER: *Le moine; Festmarsch.*
**(*) Hyperion Dig. CDA 66683 [id.]. Leslie Howard, (i) with Paul Coletti.

Complete piano music, Vol. 24: Concert paraphrases: BEETHOVEN: *Septet, Op. 20.* MOZART: *Requiem mass, K.626: Confutatis; Lacrimosa. Ave verum corpus, K.618.* VERDI: *Requiem mass: Agnus dei.* ROSSINI: *Cujus animam: Air du Stabat Mater; 3 Chœurs religieux: La Charité.* GOLDSCHMIDT: *7 Tödsunden: Liebesszene und Fortunas Kugel.* MENDELSSOHN: *Wasserfahrt und der Jäger Abschied.* WEBER: *Schlummerlied mit Arabesken; Leyer und Schwert-Heroïde.* HUMMEL: *Septet No. 1 in D min.*
** Hyperion Dig. CDA 66761/2 [id.]. Leslie Howard.

Complete piano music, Vol. 25: *San Francesco: Prelude: The canticle of the sun; Canticle of the sun of St Francis of Assisi. Ave maris stella; Gebet; Ich liebe dich; Il m'aimait tant; O pourquoi donc; Ora pro nobis; O sacrum convivium* (2 versions); *Rezignazione – Ergebung; Salve regina; Von der Wiege bis zum Grabe; Die Zelle in Nonnenwerth.*
**(*) Hyperion Dig. CDA 66694 [id.]. Leslie Howard.

Complete piano music, Vol. 26: *Allegro di bravura; Apparitions; Berceuse; 12 Etudes; Feuilles d'album; Galop de bal; Hungarian recruiting dances; Impromptu brillant on themes of Rossini and Spontini; Klavierstücke (aus der Bonn Beethoven-Kantatej); 2 Klavierstücke; Marche hongroise; Notturno No. 2; Rondo di bravura; Scherzo in G min.; Variation on a waltz of Diabelli; Variations on a theme of Rossini; 5 Variations on a theme from Méhul's Joseph; Waltz in A; Waltz in E flat.*
**(*) Hyperion Dig. CDA 66771/2 [id.]. Leslie Howard.

Complete piano music, Vol. 27: *Canzone napolitana* (2 versions); *La cloche sonne; Gleanings from Woronince; God save the Queen; Hungarian national folk tunes (Ungarische Nationalmelodien); Hussite song; La Marseillaise; Rákóczi march; Szózat and Hungarian hymn; Vive Henri IV.*
*** Hyperion Dig. CDA 66787 [id.]. Leslie Howard.

Complete piano music, Vol. 28: *Bulow-Marsch; Heroischer Marsch im Ungarischer Geschwindmarsch; Csárdás; Csárdás macabre; Csárdás obstiné; Festmarsch zur Goethejubiläumsfeier; Festpolonaise; Festvorspiel; Galop in A min.; Grand galop chromatique; Huldigungsmarsch; Kunstierfestzug zur*

Schillerfeier; Marche héroïque; Mazurka brillante; Mephisto polka; Petite valse; Rákóczy Marsch; Vorn Fels zurn Meer; La favorite; Scherzo and march; Siegesmarsch; Ungarischer Marsch zur Krönungsfeier in Ofen-Pest; Ungarischer Stürmmarsch; Zweite Festmarsch.   .
**(*) Hyperion Dig. CDA 66811/2 [id.]. Leslie Howard.

The two Liszt *Songbooks* offer 12 early Lieder in engagingly simple transcriptions. Leslie Howard plays them beautifully, as he does the three *Liebesträume*, of which only the third is really familiar. Volume 20 centres on what Leslie Howard prefers to call *Album d'un Voyager*, the early edition of what we know as the *Années de pèlerinage* (which the composer tried, unsuccessfully, to suppress). Book I includes a flamboyant extra item, *Lyon*, inspired by a workers' uprising, and only two of the pieces in Book II, *Fleurs mélodiques des Alpes*, were retained in the final set of *Années de pèlerinage*. Apart from the *Paraphrases* in Book III, this collection also includes an unknown major improvisatory work of the same period and inspiration, the 18-minute-long *Fantaisie romantique sur deux mélodies suisses*, with plenty of opportunities for bravura in the latter part. A fascinating collection, very well played indeed. Volume 21 is lightweight, opening with the Rossini *Soirées musicales*, which we know from the much later Britten orchestrations, and *Soirées italiennes*, based on rather less interesting music by Mercadante. For the second disc Howard returns to the initial versions of the *Années de pèlerinage*, including the *Petrarch Sonnets* and *Venezia e Napoli*. The second CD ends with a pair of *Grand fantasias* on themes from the *Soirées* which began the recital.

Volume 22 brings us to Liszt's paraphrases of the nine Beethoven symphonies. Leslie Howard's 'interpretations' are sound throughout; he makes more of some movements than others (the first movement of the *Eroica* could be more compelling) and the resonance of the recording is not ideal for revealing detail. The *Ninth* works impressively, if not as earth-shaking as Katsaris's version on Teldec. Overall, this is surprisingly enjoyable to listen to; without the orchestral colour, one notices the more what is happening in the internal arguments of these inexhaustible works.

Volume 23 is an effective transcription of Berlioz's *Harold in Italy* for viola and piano, and Howard takes the opportunity to include Liszt's own *Romance oubliée* for the same combination. Here Paul Coletti joins the pianist, and the performances are well played and spontaneous, if not earth-shaking. The transcriptions of the Beethoven and Hummel *Septets*, however, do not really work at all. This music either needs the instrumental colour or a much more witty approach (and the resonant recording is not helpful). However, there are some other paraphrases here that are much more effective, notably the excerpts from Goldschmidt's *Die sieben Todsünden* and two transcribed Mendelssohn choruses.

The *Cantico del Sol di San Francesco d'Assisi* is pleasantly based on *In dulci jubilo*. Then comes the chrysalis of the symphonic poem, *From the cradle to the grave*, which was greatly expanded in its orchestral form. Volume 26 is almost entirely devoted to works written when Liszt was a teenager, and the *Variations* show his mettle. Volume 27 offers patriotic songs and airs in a much more interesting and varied programme than it looks at first glance. *God save the Queen* was written for a British tour in 1840/ 41 and the tune is immediately interestingly varied in the opening bars. *La Marseillaise* starts off straightforwardly and the variants come later, but the tune reasserts itself strongly. The *Ungarische Nationalmelodien* is in effect a sketch for the *Sixth Hungarian rhapsody*. But there are plenty of enticing ideas here, notably the three-part suite, *Glanes de Woronince*, and the delightful French folksong arrangements, *Vive Henry IV* and *La cloche sonne*. Howard is at his most imaginative. Volume 28 is essentially a collection of marches and lively extrovert pieces, but they are very well presented.

Complete piano music, Vol. 29: *Hungarian themes and rhapsodies, Nos. 1–22.*
(N) ** Hyperion Dig. CDA 66851/2 [id.]. Leslie Howard.

Here is the source material for Liszt's *Hungarian rhapsodies* and the *Hungarian fantasia* in earlier, more earthy form, before the dances became sophisticated concert repertoire. There is even an early version (subsequently discarded) of the *Consolation No. 3*. Of course not all the music here is equally interesting, but Leslie Howard brings it to life fluently. His playing has convincing rubato but lacks something in flair and adrenalin.

Complete piano music, Vol. 30: Operatic fantasies, concert paraphrases and transcriptions: DONIZETTI: *Valse de concert on 2 motifs of Lucia de Lammermoor and Parisina.* GOUNOD: *Les Adieux (Rêverie on a theme from Roméo et Juliette).* ERKEL: *Schwanengesang and march to Hunyadi László.* MEYERBEER: *Réminscences de Robert le diable; Cavatine; Valse infernale.* MOZART: *Fantasy on themes from Nozze di Figaro and Don Giovanni.* VERDI: *Ernani; Rigoletto; Il Trovatore: Miserere* (concert paraphrases); *Réminiscences de Simon Boccanegra.* WAGNER: *Lohengrin: Elsa's bridal procession; Wedding march; Elsa's dream; Lohengrin's reproof. Fantasy on themes from Rienzi.* WEBER: overture: *Oberon.*
(N) ** Hyperion Dig. CDA 66861/2 [id.]. Leslie Howard.

It is difficult for present-day music-lovers to appreciate that in Liszt's time even a piece as familiar as

Weber's *Oberon overture* was relatively inaccessible outside the opera house, and it must be said that Howard does not make a great deal of it – the allegros sound unpianistic. But of course his operatic paraphrases were designed both to entertain and to remind listeners not only of the tunes that made up the best-known operas of Mozart, Verdi and Wagner but those of lesser composers too. Some of this music ideally needs a Horowitz, but for the most part Leslie Howard is up to the display and pyrotechnics which Liszt's embellishments require. However, Mozart's *Là ci darem* is heavily romanticized and the Verdi paraphrases also need more impetus. The Wagner transcriptions are more successful.

Complete piano music, Vol. 31: 'The Schubert transcriptions' (Vol. 1): *Ave Maria; Der Gondelfahrer; Erlkönig; Märche für das Pianoforte übertragen: Trauermarsch (Grande marche funèbre); Grande marche; Grande marche characteristique. Marche militaire* (concert paraphrase); *Mélodies hongroises; Die Rose; La Sérénade; Soirées de Vienne; 2 Transcriptions for Sophie Menter.*
(N) ** Hyperion Dig. CDA 66951/3 [id.]. Leslie Howard.

Complete piano music, Vol. 32: 'The Schubert transcriptions' (Vol. 2): *Die Forelle; Frühlingsglaube; Marche hongroise* (2 versions); *Meeresstille; 6 Mélodies favorites de la belle meunière; 6 Mélodies of Franz Schubert; 4 Sacred songs; Schuberts Ungarische Melodien; Schwanengesang; 12 Songs from Winterreise; Ständchen (Leise flehen).*
(N) ** Hyperion Dig. CDA 66954/6 [id.]. Leslie Howard.

Complete piano music, Vol. 33: 'The Schubert transcriptions' (Vol. 3): *Die Forelle; Die Gestirne; 2 Lieder; 12 Lieder* (2 versions); *Marche hongroise; Meerestille* (2 versions); *Müllerlieder; Die Nebensonnen; Schwanengesang; Soirées de Vienne: Valse caprice No. 6; 12 songs from Winterreise.*
(N) ** Hyperion Dig. CDA 66957/9 [id.]. Leslie Howard.

Liszt obviously admired Schubert enormously and wanted to champion him as well as play his music. The songs were obvious candidates because of their sheer tunefulness, but he was also attracted to Schubert's lighter dance music. The *Soirées de Vienne* really suit Howard and are played with a pleasantly Schubertian feeling and nicely judged rubato, while the *Valse caprice* is quite charming. And what of the songs? The four *Geistliche Lieder* (*Sacred songs*) which open the collection are made to seem unremittingly sombre, and Howard has a tendency to over-characterize the darker songs elsewhere. *Die Forelle* and some of the other most famous songs are not very imaginatively done, although *Erlkönig* comes off well. But not everyone will want two complete *Schwanengesangs* without a singer. Of course the transcriptions are free – sometimes (but not often) very free – and there is more Liszt than Schubert. Leslie Howard plays them (as Liszt surely would have done) with comparable freedom in matters of phrasing and rubato, and for the most part he is convincing, if at times his tempi seem a little too indulgent.

Complete piano music, Vol. 34: *12 Grandes études; Morceau de salon.*
(N) *** Hyperion Dig. CDA 66973 [id.]. Leslie Howard.

These *Grandes études* were the pilot version of the *Etudes d'exécution transcendente*, which appeared a quarter of a century later, in 1851. This (as with so much of this invaluable series) is their first recording, as the composer expressly forbade their performance. This music demands great bravura, and Leslie Howard surpasses himself in rising to the challenge with remarkable confidence. There is much to tickle the ear here, and all this music is Liszt's own and is not borrowed from others!

Complete piano music, Vol. 35: *Arabesques (2 mélodies russes):* (ALABIEV: *Le rossignol.* P. BULAKHOV: *Chanson bohémienne*). Russian transcriptions: AN AMATEUR FROM ST PETERSBURG: *Mazurka.* (Liszt's) *Prelude à la Polka de Borodin.* BORODIN: (i) *Polka.* K. BULAKHOV: *Galop russe.* CUI; DARGOMIZHSKY: *Tarentelles.* WIELHORSKY: *Autrefois.* Hungarian transcriptions: *Rákóczi-march.* ABRANYI: *Flower song.* FESTETICS: *Spanish Ständchen.* SZECHENYI: *Introduction and Hungarian march.* SZABADI/ MASSENET: *Revive Szegedin!.* VEGH: *Valse de concert.* ZICHY: *Valse d'Adèle.*
(N) *** Hyperion Dig. CDA 66984 [id.]. Leslie Howard, (i) with Philip Moore.

Liszt was especially enthusiastic about new Russian music and, as can by seen from the piece based on the *Mazurka* of 'An Amateur from St Petersburg', he didn't restrict his interest to famous names, although they are all here. He composed his own piano solo introduction to Borodin's engaging four-handed *Polka*, which is included here with the help of Philip Moore. Most of the Hungarian names are unfamiliar but the music itself, if slight, is often delightful. The two opening *Arabesques* are enticing; but everything tickles the ear, especially Abranyi's *Flower waltz*, and no one can say that Leslie Howard does not relish its glittering colours. As usual, good recording. This is a most enjoyable collection.

Complete piano music, Vol. 36: *Consolations Nos. 1–6; Elégie: Entwurf der Ramann; Excelsior! (Prelude to The bells of Strasburg Cathedral); Fanfare for the unveiling of the Carl August memorial; Geharnischte Lieder, National hymn (Kaiser Wilhelm!); Rosario Schlummerlied im Grabe; Die Zelle in Nonnenwerth* (2 versions); *Weimars Volkslieder Nos. 1–2.*
(N) **(*) Hyperion Dig. CDA 66995 [id.]. Leslie Howard.

The first version of the six *Consolations* misses out the most famous *Third in D flat* and substitutes a less memorable piece in *C sharp minor*, but in all other respects these earlier pieces are valid in their own right and are well worth having on disc, although the performances do tend to languish a bit. The rest of the programme consists of novelties, including cathedral bells (celebrated here by the two versions of *Die Zelle in Nonnenwerth* as well as by *Excelsior!*), all unknown, many of them occasional pieces and of no great interest except for *Rosario*, three gentle settings of *Ave Maria* which are persuasively atmospheric.

Complete piano music, Vol. 37: BULOW: *Tanto gentile e tanto onesta.* CONRADI: *Zigeuner polka.* ERNST: *Die Gräberinsel der Fürsten zu Gotha.* HERBECK: *Tanzmomente Nos. 1–8; No. 4* (alternative). LASSEN: *Ich weil' in teifer Einsamkeit; Löse, Himmel meine Seele* (2 versions). LESSMAN: *3 Lieder from Julius Wolff's Tannhäuser.* LISZT/LOUIS FERDINAND: *Elégie sur des motifs du Prince Louis Ferdinand de Prusse.*
(N) ** Hyperion Dig. CDA 67004 [id.]. Leslie Howard.

Liszt's interest in Johann Ritter von Herbeck reflects the latter's importance in Viennese musical life of the time. He was choirmaster as well as composer, and his *Tanzmomente* consists of eight dances, many of them waltzes of some charm. Liszt's transcriptions flatter them agreeably and he expands the finale considerably and to good effect. Otto Lessen was a journalist and theatre manager, and his songs also make agreeable transcriptions, as does Hans von Bülow's *Tanto gentile.* The closing *Zigeuner-Polka* of August Conradi was a pop hit in its day, and Liszt's arrangement adds a bit of spice to the melodic sequence. All this music is exceedingly rare, but its musical interest is frankly limited. The Lassen and Bülow pieces are the highlights.

Complete piano music, Vol. 38: *Concert études and Episodes from Lenau's Faust: Les préludes; 3 Etudes de concert; 2 Concert studies; 2 Episodes from Lenau's Faust.*
(N) *** Hyperion Dig. CDA 67015 [id.]. Leslie Howard.

Volume 38 is a good deal more substantial than its predecessor, starting off with the popular *Les Préludes*, which anticipates the orchestral version fairly closely, with a few minor differences near the end. The transcription is made in pianistic terms and works well. The three *Etudes de concert* continue in familiar territory, especially the third, a Lisztian romantic blossoming better known as '*Un Sospiro*' (which Howard presents boldly). *Waldesrauschen* and *Gnomenreigen* (beautifully done) are equally welcome, as is the opportunity of hearing the two *Faust* pieces together in their piano versions, of which the *Mephisto waltz* is easily the more famous. A rewarding collection, very well played and recorded.

Années de pèlerinage (complete): *Book 1, 1st Year: Switzerland; Book 2, 2nd Year: Italy; Supplément: Venezia e Napoli; Book 3, 3rd Year: Italy.*
(B) *** DG 437 206-2 (3). Lazar Berman.

The *Années de pèlerinage* contain some of Liszt's very finest inspiration, and Lazar Berman's 1977 complete recording is fully worthy of it. Berman's technique is fabulous, more than equal to the demands made by these 26 pieces. The playing is enormously authoritative and quite free of empty display and virtuoso flamboyance, even though its brilliance is never in question. Indeed Berman brings searching qualities to this music: much of the time he is thoughtful and inward-looking in pieces like *Angelus* and *Sunt lachrymae rerum.* The imaginative colour and flair he displays in *Les cloches de Genève* and the simple freshness of *Eglogue* are matched by the felicity of the watery evocations, *Au lac de Wallenstadt* and *Les jeux d'eaux à la Villa d'Este*, while the power of the *Dante sonata* is equalled by the coruscating glitter of his articulation of the *Tarantella* from the *Supplément, Venezia e Napoli.* The recording, made in the Munich Alter Herkulessaal, is excellent. It is firmly and faithfully transferred to CD and does full justice to Berman's range of colour and dynamics. Moreover this box is remarkably inexpensive.

Années de pèlerinage: 1st Year (Switzerland); 2nd (with supplement) & 3rd Years (Italy): complete. *Hungarian rhapsodies Nos. 1–19* (complete).
(M) **(*) EMI CMS7 64882-2 (4) [id.]. Georges Cziffra.

Cziffra's accounts of the complete *Années de pèlerinage* show the same prodigious virtuosity and keyboard command that make his set of *Hungarian rhapsodies* unforgettable. His account of the *Dante sonata* is enormously dramatic and produces the same fabulous digital dexterity that makes the *Tarantella* from the Italian Supplement, *Venezia e Napoli*, so breathtaking. In the more poetic pieces from Book 1, *Au lac de Wallenstadt* and *Au bord d'une source*, he finds more restrained romantic feeling, and in the Third Year *Les jeux d'eau à la Villa d'Este* brings some most delicate articulation. But at times the music's passion takes him over the top (as with *Aux cyprès de la Villa d'Este*) and he is not helped by a degree of hardness on piano timbre that is already somewhat dry. Remarkable pianism just the same. As can be seen below, the *Hungarian rhapsodies* (in which he is in his element) are available separately.

Années de pèlerinage, 1st Year (Switzerland).
*** Decca Dig. 410 160-2 [id.]. Jorge Bolet.
(Y/B) (BB) *** Naxos Dig. 8.550548 [id.]. Jenö Jandó.

This recording of the Swiss pieces from the *Années de pèlerinage* represents Bolet at his very peak, with playing of magical delicacy as well as formidable power. The piano sound is outstandingly fine.

Even remembering his excellent Beethoven and Haydn recordings, Jandó's performances of the Liszt *Années de pèlerinage* represent his most impressive achievement on record to date. The solemn opening of *La chapelle de Guillaume Tell* immediately shows the atmospheric feeling he can generate in this remarkable music, and its later, more grandiose rhetoric is handled with powerful conviction. The recording is first class, and the feeling throughout is very much of the spontaneity of live music-making.

Années de pèlerinage, 2nd Year (Italy) (complete).
*** Decca Dig. 410 161-2 [id.]. Jorge Bolet.

Années de pèlerinage, 2nd year (Italy); Supplement: Venezia e Napoli.
(Y/B) ✹ (BB) *** Naxos Dig. 8.550549 [id.]. Jenö Jandó.

Jandó offers Lisztian playing of the highest order, confirming the *Années de pèlerinage* as being among the supreme masterpieces of the piano. *Sposalizio* is superbly evoked, and the three contrasted *Petrarch Sonnets* bring the most imaginatively varied characterization, with No. 123 especially chimerical. But clearly Jandó sees the *Dante sonata* as the climactic point of the whole series. His performance has tremendous dynamism and power. One has the sense of Liszt himself hovering over the keyboard. Again first-class recording and the feeling of a continuous live recital. This is the disc to try first, and we have awarded it a token Rosette.

The pianistic colourings in this second fine instalment in Bolet's Liszt series are magically caught here, whether in the brilliant sunlight of *Sposalizio* or the visionary gloom of *Il penseroso*. The *Dante sonata* brings a darkly intense performance, fresh and original and deeply satisfying.

Années de pèlerinage, 3rd Year (Italy) (complete).
*** Ph. Dig. 420 174-2 [id.]. Zoltán Kocsis.
(Y/B) (BB) *** Naxos Dig. 8.550550 [id.]. Jenö Jandó.

Zoltán Kocsis gives the most compelling account of these sombre and imaginative pieces; apart from beautiful pianism, he also can convey the dark power of the music without recourse to percussive tone. He is splendidly recorded by the Philips engineers.

The opening *Angelus* shows Jandó at his most imaginatively expansive and commanding, while *Les jeux d'eaux à la Villa d'Este* sparkles and glitters: this is playing of great appeal. The dark power of *Sunt lacrymae rerum* and the *Marche funèbre* bring resounding sonority from the piano's lower octaves, and then Jandó provides more expansive rhetoric for the composer's flamboyant and not entirely convincing spiritual apotheosis, *Sursum corda*. A splendid and satisfying culmination to a set of performances that can be compared with the finest from the past. The secret of Jandó's playing is that he is deeply involved in every note of Liszt's music.

Années de pèlerinage, Book 2; Supplement: Venezia e Napoli (Gondoliera; Canzone; Tarantella); 3rd Year: Les jeux d'eau à la Villa d'Este; Ballade No. 2 in B min.; Harmonies poétiques et religieuses: Bénédiction de Dieu dans la solitude.
*** Decca Dig. 411 803-2 [id.]. Jorge Bolet.

A dazzling pendant to Liszt's Italian *Années de pèlerinage*, and the recital includes two of Liszt's weightiest conceptions, the *Bénédiction* and the *Ballade*, both spaciously conceived and far too little known. Vivid and full piano recording.

Années de pèlerinage, 1st Year: Au bord d'un source. 2nd Year: Sonetto del Petrarca No. 104. 2 Concert studies: Waldesrauschen; Gnomenreigen. Mephisto waltz No. 1; Rhapsodie espagnole.
*** Sony Dig. SK 47180 [id.]. Murray Perahia – FRANCK: *Prélude, choral et fugue.* ***

Murray Perahia's Liszt shows all the keyboard distinction and poetic insight we associate with him. This is memorable and very distinguished Liszt playing, and the Sony engineers do full justice to him.

Années de pèlerinage, 1st Year: Vallée d'Obermann; 2nd Year: Après une lecture du Dante (Dante sonata); Sonetto 104 del Petrárca; 3rd Year: Les jeux d'eau à la Villa d'Este. Ballade No. 2 in B min.; 6 Chants polonais de Chopin; Concert paraphrases on operas by Verdi; 2 Concert studies: Waldesrauschen; Gnomenreigen. 3 Etudes de concert; 12 Etudes d'exécution transcendante; Funérailles; Harmonies poétiques et religieuses: Bénédiction de Dieu dans la solitude; Sonata in B min.; Valse oubliée No. 1 in F sharp.
(M) *** Ph. Dig. 432 305-2 (5) [id.]. Claudio Arrau.

Claudio Arrau's Liszt performances combine an aristocratic finesse with just the proper amount of virtuoso abandon. His rubato is never excessive and always idiomatic. The performances are always completely within the sensibility of the period, yet are completely of our time as well. The excellent Philips recordings do justice to his thoroughly individual sound-world.

Années de pèlerinage, 2nd year: 3 Sonetti di Petrarca (Nos. 47, 104 & 123). Concert paraphrase on the Quartet from Verdi's Rigoletto; Consolations Nos. 1–5; Liebesträume Nos. 1–3.
(M) *** DG 435 591-2 [id.]. Daniel Barenboim.

Daniel Barenboim proves an ideal advocate for the *Consolations* and *Liebestraume*, and he is highly poetic in the *Petrarch sonnets*. His playing has an unaffected simplicity that is impressive and throughout there is a welcome understatement and naturalness, until he arrives at the *Rigoletto paraphrase* which is played with plenty of flair and glitter. The quality of the recorded sound is excellent.

Années de pèlerinage, 2nd Year (Italy): Sposalizio; Il penseroso; Canzonetta del Salvator Rosa; Sonetto del Petrarca Nos. 47, 104 & 123; Supplement: Venezia e Napoli: Gondoliera. 2 Legends: St Francis of Assisi preaching to the birds; St Francis of Paola walking on the water.
(N) (M) *** DG 449 093-2 [id.]. Wilhelm Kempff.

In the early days of mono LP, Kempff made a famous record of Liszt piano music for Decca. He plays much of the same programme here, adding *Sposalizio*, and he had lost none of his magic and sense of poetry in the intervening years. Few listeners will fail to respond to these evocative and masterly performances, and one wonders why DG chose not to reissue this outstanding recital as a 'Legendary Recording' rather than putting it on their mid-priced Galleria label. The recording is excellent.

Années de pèlerinage, 3rd Year: Tarantella. Harmonies poétiques et religieuses: Pensées des morts; Bénédiction de Dieu dans la solitude; Legend: St Francis of Assisi preaching to the birds. Mephisto waltz No. 1; Rhapsodie espagnole.
(Y/B) (M) *** Virgin Dig. CUV5 61129-2 [id.]. Stephen Hough.

Few pianists of the younger generation have quite such a magic touch as Stephen Hough, and this mid-price reissue in Virgin's new Ultraviolet series rescues one of his finest recordings. His performances of these six substantial Liszt pieces are all magnetic. With phenomenal articulation he brings sparkle and wit to the fireworks of the *Mephisto waltz* and the *Tarantella* from the third year of the *Années de pèlerinage*, and plays the extended slow movement of the *Bénédiction* with velvety warmth. The delicate tracery of the birdsong sounds in *St Francis's sermon to the birds* equally displays Hough's love of keyboard sound, beautifully caught in vivid recording. Among the most rewarding of all CDs of Liszt.

Concert paraphrases: Bellini: Réminiscences de Norma. Verdi: Rigoletto; Miserere du Trovatore. Wagner: Tannhäuser overture; Am stillen Herd from Die Meistersinger; Liebestod from Tristan und Isolde; Années de pèlerinage, 2nd Year: Sonnetti del Petrarca Nos. 123 & 124; Consolation No. 3; Hungarian rhapsody No. 12 in C sharp min.
(N) (BB) **(*) CfP Silver Double CDCFPSD 4745 (2). Craig Sheppard – *Sonata* etc. ***

Craig Sheppard was the second prizewinner in the Leeds Piano Competition of 1972, a formidable challenger to the eventual winner, Murray Perahia. Though he lacks Perahia's individuality, Sheppard's playing of Liszt on this record is a fine tribute to his musicianship and technique, especially in the *Concert paraphrases*. He does not manage to disguise the awkwardness of the *Pilgrim's chorus* section of *Tannhäuser* where the pianist is expected to play the big tune and the swirling (string) accompaniment simultaneously with only two hands. But the *Trovatore* scene has fine, red-blooded melodrama, and the passion of the *Liebestod* is excitingly projected. The *Réminiscences de Norma*, too, are stylishly done. The other items come from his début recital in 1973 and are almost equally compelling. The piano tone is bold and clear. It was a happy idea on this Silver Double reissue to couple these performances with a memorable account of the *Sonata* by another celebrated prizewinner, Bernard d'Ascoli – see below.

Concert paraphrases of Schubert Lieder: *Auf den Wasser zu singen; Aufenthalt; Erlkönig; Die Forelle; Horch, horch die Lerch; Lebe wohl!; Der Lindenbaum; Lob der Tränen; Der Müller und der Bach; Die Post; Das Wandern; Wohin.*
*** Decca Dig. 414 575-2 [id.]. Jorge Bolet.

Superb virtuosity from Bolet. He is not just a wizard but a feeling musician, though here he sometimes misses a feeling of fun. First-rate recording.

Concert paraphrase of Verdi's *Rigoletto; Etudes d'exécution transcendante d'après Paganini: La Campanella. Harmonies poétiques et religieuses: Funérailles. Hungarian rhapsody No. 12; Liebestraum No. 3. Mephisto waltz No. 1.*
*** Decca Dig. 410 257-2 [id.]. Jorge Bolet.

Bolet's playing is magnetic, not just because of virtuosity thrown off with ease, but because of an element of joy conveyed, even in the demonic vigour of the *Mephisto waltz No. 1.* The relentless thrust of *Funérailles* is beautifully contrasted against the honeyed warmth of the famous *Liebestraum No. 3* and the sparkle of *La Campanella.* First-rate recording.

3 Concert studies; 2 Concert studies; 6 Consolations; Réminiscences de Don Juan (Mozart).
*** Decca 417 523-2 [id.]. Jorge Bolet.

In the *Concert studies* the combination of virtuoso precision and seeming spontaneity is most compelling in the splendid account of the *Don Juan* paraphrase. The *Consolations* show Bolet at his most romantically imaginative: he plays them beautifully.

Etudes d'exécution transcendante (complete).
**(*) Ph. 416 458-2 [id.]. Claudio Arrau.
**(*) Decca Dig. 414 601-2 [id.]. Jorge Bolet.

Arrau always plays with great panache and musical insight which more than compensate for the occasional smudginess of the recorded sound.

   Bolet is a little disappointing, lacking a little in demonry; but as a searching interpreter of the composer and his musical argument he has few rivals.

Hungarian rhapsodies Nos. 1–19.
(M) *** DG 423 925-2 (2) [id.]. Roberto Szidon.
(B) ** Ph. Duo 438 371-2 (2) [id.]. Michele Campanella.

Roberto Szidon's set of the *Hungarian rhapsodies* is highly recommendable. There is plenty of fire and flair here, and much that will dazzle the listener! The recording, too, sounds excellent.

   Michele Campanella's bargain survey of the Liszt *Hungarian rhapsodies* has no want of technical command or finesse, and there are moments when the bravura provides excitement, as in the closing pages of the famous *No. 2 in C sharp minor.* But for the most part these performances lack the flair and spontaneity of Roberto Szidon's set, where the playing is not only more gripping but also much more imaginatively illuminating. The Philips set is provided with adequate documentation and has characteristically fine recording.

Hungarian rhapsodies Nos. 1–15; Rhapsodie espagnole.
(B) *** EMI CZS5 69003-2 (2) [id.]. György Cziffra.

Cziffra's performances are dazzling. They are full of those excitingly chimerical spurts of energy and languorous rubato that immediately evoke the unreasonably fierce passions of gypsy music. Yet the control is absolute (try the delectably free opening of *No. 12 in C sharp minor,* or the *D minor* (No. 7)). There is plenty of power in reserve and poetry too (the introduction to *No. 5 in E minor* is made to seem very like Chopin). For sheer glitter, sample *No. 10 in E major.* The high degree of temperament in the playing, with hardly two consecutive phrases at an even tempo, makes even Szidon (who has the full measure of the music) seem almost staid. Cziffra with coruscating brilliance sets every bar of the music on fire. Some might find him too impulsive for comfort (and they should turn to the DG alternative), but this is surely the way Liszt would have played them: the *Rákóczy march* (No. 15) is a *tour de force.* The recording, made in the Salle Wagram, Paris, in 1957/8 (or, in the case of Nos. 2, 6, 12 and 15, in the Hungaraton Budapest Studio a year earlier), is a little dry and close but otherwise truthful, and it does not lack sonority. The *Rouge et Noir* reissue offers two discs for the price of one.

Hungarian rhapsodies Nos. 2–3, 8, 13, 15 (Rákóczy march); 17; Csárdás obstinée.
(M) *** Van. 08.4024.71 [OVC 4024]. Alfred Brendel.

Although the Vanguard recording is not a recent one, it sounds very good in this excellent CD transfer, and the playing is very distinguished indeed. There are few more charismatic or spontaneous accounts of the *Hungarian rhapsodies* available, and there is no doubt about the brilliance of the playing nor the quality of musical thinking that informs it.

Mephisto waltz.
(Y/B) (M) (**(*)) RCA mono GD 60921. William Kapell – KHACHATURIAN: *Piano concerto;* PROKOFIEV: *Piano concerto No. 3.* (**(*)) ✸

William Kapell's *Mephisto waltz*, recorded in 1945, must be one of the most dazzling ever, and it ranks alongside the likes of Horowitz, Cziffra, Richter and Pletnev. Moreover it comes with incandescent accounts of the Khachaturian *Piano concerto* (with Koussevitzky, no less), and the Prokofiev *Third Piano concerto.*

Piano sonata in B min.
(M) *** RCA 09026 61614-2 [id.]. Emil Gilels – SCHUBERT: *Sonata No. 17.*
(Y/B) (M) **(*) RCA 09026 62590-2 [id.]. Artur Rubinstein – BACH: *Chaconne;* FRANCK: *Prelude, chorale and fugue.* ***

Piano sonata; Années de pèlerinage, 2nd Year: Après une lecture du Dante (Dante sonata). Mephisto waltz No. 1.
*** Denon Dig. C37 7547 [id.]. Dezsö Ránki.

Piano sonata; 3 Concert studies.
*** Chandos Dig. CHAN 8548 [id.]. Louis Lortie.

Piano sonata; Concert study No. 2 (La Leggierezza).
(N) (BB) *** CfP Silver Double Dig. CDCFPSD 4745 (2). Bernard d'Ascoli – *Concert paraphrases* etc. **(*)

Piano sonata; Grand galop chromatique; Liebesträume Nos. 1–3; Valse impromptu.
*** Decca Dig. 410 115-2. Jorge Bolet.

Piano sonata; 2 Legends; Scherzo and March.
*** Hyperion Dig. CDA 66616 [id.]. Nikolai Demidenko.

Gilels's version of the Liszt *Sonata* is masterly. It has something in common with Curzon's stunning account (at present awaiting restoration to the catalogue) and can be spoken of alongside Pletnev. It is as penetrating in its way as Horowitz's famous pre-war record was virtuosic, and the playing here is equally astonishing technically. The 1964 recording leaves little cause for complaint on CD. It is vividly transferred and is not without body.

Nikolai Demidenko's account of the *Sonata* has won golden opinions, and rightly so. His is a keenly dramatic and powerfully projected account that has the listener on the edge of his or her seat. It must be numbered among the finest performances that this young Russian pianist has given us and is free from the slight mannerisms and the disruptive rubati that sometimes mar his recitals. The excitement and virtuosity are second to none and almost call to mind Horowitz, and his playing can be measured against that of Brendel and Pletnev. He has the advantage of exceptionally vivid recorded sound, and the remainder of the recital goes equally well.

Louis Lortie gives almost as commanding a performance of the Liszt *Sonata* as any in the catalogue; its virtuosity can be taken for granted and, though he does not have the extraordinary intensity and feeling for drama of Pletnev, he has a keen awareness of its structure and a Chopinesque finesse that win one over. The Chandos recording, though a shade too reverberant, is altogether natural.

Bernard d'Ascoli displays classical qualities in his refreshing and intense reading of this most romantic of sonatas. It is the sort of interpretation that one might have expected Wilhelm Kempff to have given, with articulation of pearly clarity, wonderful singing legato in the big melodies and an emphasis on control and concentration rather than thrusting urgency. Yet there is no lack of power, and the result is most satisfying. The delicate account of *La Leggierezza* makes a fine encore. The early (1982) digital recording is dry but faithful, and the coupled recital from Craig Sheppard, another prizewinner, makes this a very recommendable Silver Double.

The power, imagination and concentration of Bolet are excellently brought out in his fine account of the *Sonata*. With the famous *Liebestraum* (as well as its two companions) also most beautifully done, not to mention the amazing *Grand galop*, this is one of the most widely appealing of Bolet's outstanding Liszt series. However, the *Sonata* is also available in a Double Decca set – see below.

Dezsö Ránki's account of the *Sonata* is very impressive indeed and can hold its own with almost any of its rivals. The *Mephisto waltz* and the *Dante sonata* are hardly less powerful in the hands of the young Hungarian master, the latter with real fire and a masterly control of dramatic pace. The Denon recording is absolutely first class.

Rubinstein's performance of the *Sonata* was recorded in 1965, and there is some hardness of timbre in fortissimos. But at *piano* and *mezzo forte* levels (and there is a wider range of dynamic here than on some Rubinstein records) the tone is subtly coloured, and Rubinstein's mercurial approach to the music is wonderfully spontaneous, bringing an astonishing fire and brilliance for a pianist of his age, and considerable poetry to the more thoughtful moments.

Piano sonata in B min.; Concert paraphrase of Mendelsssohn's Wedding march from A Midsummer Night's Dream; Concert study No. 1: Waldesrauschen. Harmonies poétiques et religieuses: Funérailles. Etudes d'éxécution transcendante d'après Paganini: La Campanella; La Chasse.
(Y/B) (M) *(**) Cziffra Edition, Volume 1: EMI CDM5 65250-2 [id.]. György Cziffra.

Cziffra plays with extraordinary virtuosity and temperament, but his reading of the *Sonata* is exasperatingly wilful and self-aware. There are moments of exquisite poetry, but also a feeling of calculation, alternating with wild bursts of bravura. *Funérailles* is prodigiously powerful and has the widest range of mood and colour. *Waldesrauschen* brings fabulous digital dexterity, but Cziffra's impulsiveness runs away with the music's natural flow. The two *Paganini studies* show him at his most captivatingly chimerical; the opening of the paraphrase of the Mendelssohn *Wedding march* has a witty charm, though the grandiose central section is less appealing. The Paris studio recordings, made between 1958 and 1975, are variable, often unflatteringly hard.

Miscellaneous Recitals

Piano sonata; Années de pèlerinage, 1st Year: Au bord d'une source; 2nd Year: Sonetto 104 del Petrarca; 3rd Year: Les jeux d'eau à la Ville d'Este; Concert paraphrases: Die Forelle; Erlkönig (Schubert); Réminiscences de Don Juan (Mozart); Rigoletto (Verdi). Consolation No. 3; Etudes d'exécution transcendante d'après Paganini: La campanella. Etudes de concert: Gnomenreigen; Un sospiro. Harmonies poétiques et religieuses: Funérailles. Hungarian rhapsody No. 12 in C sharp min.; Liebesträume No. 3 in A flat; Mephisto waltz No. 1.
(N) (B) *** Decca Double Dig. 444 851-2 (2). Jorge Bolet.

The full range of the late Jorge Bolet's achievement for Decca in the music of Liszt is admirably surveyed here, ending with his commanding account of the *Sonata*. He can be romantic without sentimentality, as in the *Consolation*, *Un sospiro* or the most famous *Liebesträume*, yet can dazzle the ear with bravura or beguile the listener with his delicacy of colouring, as in the *Années de pèlerinage*. All the recordings here save the Mozart *Concert paraphrase* are digital and are as clear and present as one could wish.

ORGAN MUSIC

Fantasia and fugue on 'Ad nos, ad salutarem undam'; Prelude and fugue on B-A-C-H; Variations on 'Weinen, Klagen, Sorgen, Zagen'.
(BB) *** ASV CDQS 6127 [id.]. Jennifer Bate (Royal Albert Hall organ) – SCHUMANN: *4 Sketches.* ***

Jennifer Bate gives superb performances of the three major Liszt warhorses. The clarity and incisiveness of her playing go with a fine sense of line and structure, and there is plenty of exuberance in the *'Ad nos' Fantasia and fugue*. Even making no allowance for the Royal Albert Hall's acoustic problems, the analogue recording captures an admirable combination of definition and atmosphere, well conveyed on CD. This makes a fine super-bargain alternative to the competing digital versions, which are only marginally more sharply defined.

VOCAL MUSIC

Lieder: Blume und Duft; Der du von dem Himmel bist; Du bist wie eine Blume; Die drei Zigeuner; Einst; Es war ein König in Thule; Freudvoll und leidvoll; Hohe Liebe; Ich möchte hingehn; Ihr Auge; Im Rhein, im schönen Strome; Mignons Lied (Kennst du das Land); O lieb' so lang du dieben kannst; Uber allen Gipfeln ist Ruh; Und wir dachten der Toten; Was Liebe sei; Wieder möcht' ich dir begegnen.
*** Decca Dig. 430 512-2 [id.]. Brigitte Fassbaender, Jean-Yves Thibaudet.

The sensitive poetry of Thibaudet's playing goes with powerful singing from Fassbaender in superb, characterful voice, with each highly individual artist challenging the other in imagination. There are few collections of Liszt songs to match this generous one in either range or intensity. Outstanding in every way, with excellent, helpful sound.

Lieder: *Blume und Duft; Der drei Zigeuner; Der du von dem Himmel bist* (2 settings); *Ein Fichtenbaum steht einsam; Es muss ein Wunderbares sein; Es rauschen die Winde; Der Hirt; Ihr Auge; Ihr Glocken von Marling; Freudvoll und leidvoll; Die Loreley; O komm im Traum; Des Tages laute Stimmen schweigen; Uber allen Gipfeln ist Ruh; Vergiftet sind meine Lieder.*
*** Capriccio Dig. 10 294 [id.]. Mitsuko Shirai, Hartmut Höll.

There are only one or two collections of Liszt songs as searchingly persuasive as this, and none more beautiful. Provocatively the record starts with Shirai at her most vehement in *Vergiftet sind meine Lieder* (My songs are poised), written when Liszt's long relationship with the Countess d'Agoult was breaking up. Regrettably, no English translations are provided with the text, only a commentary.

Lieder: *Comment, disaient-ils; Es muss ein Wunderbares sein; Es rauschen die Winde; Go not happy day; Ihr Auge; Im Rhein, im schönen Strome; Oh, quand je dors; La tombe et la rose; Die Vätergruft; Vergiftet sind meiner Lieder; Wanderers Nachtlied.*
🏵 *** EMI Dig. CDC5 55047-2 [id.]. Thomas Hampson, Geoffrey Parsons – BERLIOZ; WAGNER: *Lieder.* *** 🏵

On his disc of romantic songs, Thomas Hampson ranges wide in his selection of 11 by Liszt, ending magically with one of the best-known, his setting in French of Victor Hugo, *Oh, quand je dors*. Characteristic, in that he finds a wider range of expressiveness and dynamic than almost any of his rivals, building from the drawing-room charm of the opening to a tremendous climax. He is helped by Parsons' accompaniment and the fine, warm recording. Other fascinating songs include Liszt's setting of Tennyson in English, *Go not happy day*, with the words oddly stressed. There is also a still, hushed and intense setting of Goethe's *Wanderers Nachtlied*, best known from Schubert. Magnetic, rich-voiced performances.

Missa choralis; Via crucis.
(M) ** Saga EC 3399-2 [id.]. BBC N. Singers, Gordon Thorne; Francis Jackson.

It was Saga (now a mid-price rather than a bargain label) who pioneered the coupling of Liszt's *Missa choralis* and *Via crucis*, and the performances – especially of the latter – are committed and effective, with Francis Jackson's powerful organ-playing very impressively dramatic. The Saga recording is, however, comparatively studio-ish, with the organ very forward.

Litolff, Henri (1818–91)

Concerto symphonique No. 4: Scherzo.
(Y/B) (M) *** Decca 425 082-2 [id.]. Clifford Curzon, LPO, Sir Adrian Boult – BRAHMS: *Piano concerto;* FRANCK: *Symphonic variations.* ***
*** Ph. Dig. 411 123-2 [id.]. Misha Dichter, Philh. O, Marriner (with Concert of concertante music ***).

Curzon provides all the sparkle Litolff's infectious *Scherzo* requires, and the 1958 Walthamstow Town Hall recording makes a delightful encore for the Brahms *Concerto* and the Franck *Symphonic variations* in this reissue in Decca's Classic Sound series. The fine qualities of the original sound, freshness and clarity, remain impressive.

Misha Dichter gives a scintillating account of Litolff's delicious *Scherzo*, played at a sparklingly brisk tempo. Marriner accompanies sympathetically and the recording is excellent.

Lloyd, George (born 1913)

Piano concerto No. 3.
**(*) Albany Dig. TROY 019-2; *TROY 019-4* [id.]. Kathryn Stott, BBC PO, composer.

The *Third Piano concerto* is very eclectic in style, with flavours of Prokofiev (with diluted abrasiveness) and even of Khachaturian – minus vulgarity – in outer movements which have a toccata-like brilliance and momentum. Kathryn Stott plays with a pleasing, mercurial lightness and makes the most of the music's lyrical feeling. But the slow movement is too long (19½ minutes) and its passionate climax uses material which does not show Lloyd at his best. On the other hand, the wistful tune at the centre of the finale is rather appealing. The composer achieves a fine partnership with his soloist and the performance has undoubted spontaneity.

(i) *Piano concerto No. 4; The lily-leaf and the grasshopper; The transformation of that Naked Ape.*
*** Albany A R 004 [id.]. Kathryn Stott; (i) LSO, composer.

The *Fourth Piano concerto* is a romantic, light-hearted piece with a memorable 'long singing tune' (the composer's words), somewhat Rachmaninovian in its spacious lyricism contrasting with a 'jerky' rhythmic idea. The performance by Kathryn Stott and the LSO under the composer is ardently spontaneous from the first bar to the last. The solo pieces are eclectic but still somehow Lloydian. The recording is first rate.

Symphonies Nos. 1 in A; 12.
*** Albany Dig. TROY 032-2; *TROY 032-4* [id.]. Albany SO, composer.

The pairing of George Lloyd's first and last symphonies is particularly appropriate, as they share a theme-and-variations format. The *First*, written in 1932 but recently revised, is relatively lightweight. The mature *Twelfth* uses the same basic layout but ends calmly with a ravishingly sustained pianissimo, semi-Mahlerian in intensity, that is among the composer's most beautiful inspirations. At the beginning of the work, the listener is soon aware of the noble lyrical theme which is the very heart of the *Symphony*. The Albany Symphony Orchestra gave the work its première and they play it with enormous conviction and eloquence. The concentration of the music-making throughout is that of a live performance, helped by the superb acoustics of the Troy Savings Bank Music Hall, which produces sound of demonstration quality. This record therefore makes an admirable starting point for anyone wishing to begin an exploration of the music of a composer who communicates readily.

Symphonies Nos. 2 and 9.
*** Albany Dig. TROY 055 [id.]. BBC PO, composer.

Lloyd's *Second Symphony* is a lightweight, extrovert piece, conventional in form and construction, though in the finale the composer flirts briefly with polytonality, an experiment he did not repeat. The *Ninth* (1969) is similarly easygoing; the *Largo* is rather fine, but its expressive weight is in scale, and the finale, 'a merry-go-round that keeps going round and round', has an appropriately energetic brilliance. Throughout both works the invention is attractive, and in these definitive performances, extremely well recorded, the composer's advocacy is very persuasive.

Symphony No. 3 in F; Charade (suite).
*** Albany Dig. TROY 90 [id.]. BBC PO, composer.

The *Third Symphony* dates from the composer's nineteenth year, and after some consideration he decided to leave it unrevised. On the whole it works well, its idiom undemanding but agreeable. Although it is described as a one-movement piece, it clearly subdivides into three sections and it is the central *Lento* which has *the* tune, a winding, nostalgic theme that persists in the memory. It is atmospherically prepared and eventually blossoms sumptuously. *Charade* dates from the 1960s and attempts to portray the London scene of the time, from aggressive *Student power* and *LSD* to *Flying saucers* and *Pop song*. The ironic final movement, *Party politics*, is amiable rather than wittily abrasive. The composer is good at bringing his music vividly to life, and he is very well recorded indeed.

Symphony No. 4.
*** Albany A R 002; *A R 002C* [id.]. Albany SO, composer.

George Lloyd's *Fourth Symphony* was composed during his convalescence after being badly shell-shocked while serving in the Arctic convoys of 1941/2. The first movement is directly related to this period of his life, and the listener may be surprised at the relative absence of sharp dissonance. After a brilliant scherzo, the infectious finale is amiable, offering a series of quick, 'march-like tunes', which the composer explains by suggesting that 'when the funeral is over the band plays quick cheerful tunes to go home'. Under Lloyd's direction, the Albany Symphony Orchestra play with great commitment and a natural, spontaneous feeling. The recording is superb.

Symphony No. 5 in B flat.
*** Albany Dig. TROY 022-2; *TROY 022-4* [id.]. BBC PO, composer.

The *Fifth Symphony* is a large canvas, with five strong and contrasted movements, adding up to nearly an hour of music. It was written during a happy period spent living simply on the shore of Lac Neuchâtel, during the very hot summer of 1947. In the finale the composer tells us: 'everything is brought in to make as exhilarating a sound as possible – strong rhythms, vigorous counterpoints, energetic brass and percussion'. The symphony is played with much commitment by the BBC Philharmonic under the composer, who creates a feeling of spontaneously live music-making throughout. The recording is first class.

(i) *Symphonies Nos. 6;* (ii) *10 (November journeys);* (i) *Overture: John Socman.*
**(*) Albany Dig. TROY 15-2; *TROY 15-4* [id.]. (i) BBC PO; (ii) BBC PO Brass, composer.

The bitter-sweet lyricism of the first movement of *November journeys* is most attractive, but the linear writing is more complex than usual in a work for brass. In the finale a glowing *cantando* melody warms the spirit, to contrast with the basic *Energico*. The *Calma* slow movement is quite haunting, no doubt reflecting the composer's series of visits to English cathedrals, the reason for the subtitle. The *Sixth Symphony* is amiable and lightweight; it is more like a suite than a symphony. Lloyd's performances are attractively spontaneous and well played, and the equally agreeable *John Socman overture* also comes off well, although it is rather inconsequential.

Symphony No. 7.
*** Albany Dig. TROY 057 [id.]. BBC PO, composer.

The *Seventh Symphony* is a programme symphony, using the ancient Greek legend of Proserpine. The slow movement is particularly fine, an extended soliloquy of considerable expressive power. The last and longest movement is concerned with 'the desperate side of our lives – "Dead dreams that the snows have shaken, Wild leaves that the winds have taken",' yet, as is characteristic with Lloyd, the darkness is muted; nevertheless the resolution at the end is curiously satisfying. Again he proves an admirable exponent of his own music. The recording is splendid.

Symphony No. 11.
*** Albany Dig. TROY 060 [id.]. Albany SO, composer.

The urgently dynamic first movement of the *Eleventh* is described by the composer as being 'all fire and violence', but any anger in the music quickly evaporates, and it conveys rather a mood of exuberance, with very full orchestral forces unleashed. With the orchestra for which the work was commissioned, Lloyd conducts a powerful performance, very well played. The recording, made in the Music Hall of Troy Savings Bank near Albany, is spectacularly sumptuous and wide-ranging.

PIANO MUSIC

An African shrine; The aggressive fishes; Intercom baby; The road through Samarkand; St Anthony and the bogside beggar.
**(*) Albany Dig. AR 003; *C-AR 003* [id.]. Martin Roscoe.

The most ambitious piece here is *An African shrine*, in which the composer's scenario is linked (not very dissonantly) to African violence and revolution. *The road through Samarkand* (1972) has travellers from the younger generation leaving for the East; while *The aggressive fishes* are tropical and violently moody, changing from serenity to anger at the flick of a fin. The two most striking pieces are the picaresque tale of the *Bogside beggar* and the charming lullaby written for a baby whose mother is in another room listening with the aid of modern technology. Martin Roscoe's performances are thoroughly committed and spontaneous, and the recording is first class.

VOCAL MUSIC

A Symphonic Mass.
✹ *** Albany Dig. TROY 100 [id.]. Brighton Festival Ch., Bournemouth SO, composer.

George Lloyd's *Symphonic Mass* is the composer's masterpiece. Written for chorus and orchestra (but no soloists) on the largest scale, the work is linked by a recurring main theme, a real tune which soon lodges insistently in the listener's memory, even though it is modified at each reappearance. It first appears as a quiet setting of the words *Christe eleison*, nearly four minutes into the *Kyrie*. The climax of the whole work is the combined *Sanctus* and *Benedictus*, with the latter framed centrally. To the words *Dominus Deus* the great melody finds its apotheosis in a passage marked *largamente con fevore*. Then the *Sanctus* reasserts itself dramatically and, after a cry of despair from the violins, the movement reaches its overwhelmingly powerful and dissonant dénouement. Peace is then restored in the *Agnus Dei*, where the composer tells us the words *Dona nobis pacem* became almost unbearably poignant for him.

The performance is magnificent and the recording is fully worthy, spaciously balanced within the generous acoustic of the Guildhall, Southampton, and overwhelmingly realistic, even in the huge climax of the *Sanctus* with its shattering percussion.

The Vigil of Venus (Pervigilium Veneris).
*** Albany Dig. TROY 170 [id.]. Carolyn James, Thomas Booth, Welsh Nat. Op. Ch. & O, composer.

Following up the success of his recordings of his symphonies, George Lloyd here directs Welsh National Opera forces in this ambitious oratorio. Here, as in the symphonies, he thumbs his nose at fashion in a score which both pulses with energy and cocoons the ear in opulent sounds. Delian ecstasy is contrasted against the occasional echo of Carl Orff, an attractive mixture, even if – for all the incidental beauties – there is dangerously little variety of mood in the nine substantial sections. The composer was not entirely happy with what he was able to achieve in that first recording; even so, his performance certainly does not lack intensity and the recording (made by Argo engineers) is excellent, given the inherent problems of the recording venue in Swansea.

Iernin (opera; complete).
(Y/B) *** Albany Dig. TROY 121/3 (3) [id.]. Hill Smith, Pogson, Herford, Rivers, Powell, BBC Singers & Concert O, composer.

George Lloyd was only twenty-one when in the early 1930s he wrote this ambitious opera, and there is an open innocence in the warmly atmospheric, lyrical score. The piece was inspired by an ancient Cornish legend about ten maidens turned into a circle of stones, one of whom, Iernin (pronounced Ee-er-nin), returns in human form. Though this is ostensibly an old-fashioned opera, it deserves revival, and on the recording – taken from a BBC Radio 3 presentation in 1988 – the composer conducts a red-blooded, warmly expressive reading. Though some of the ensemble writing is less distinguished, the offstage choruses of faery folk are most effective. As to the soloists, Marilyn Hill Smith sings brightly in the title-role with all the agility needed, and the tenor, Geoffrey Pogson, copes well with the hero's role, if with rather coarse tone. The most distinguished singing comes from the rich-toned contralto, Claire Powell, as Cunaide. The third disc includes a half-hour interview with the composer, which makes up in part for the absence of background notes in the booklet with the libretto. Excellent, well-balanced BBC sound.

Lloyd Webber, William (1914–82)

(i) *Missa Sanctae Mariae Magdalenae;* (ii) Arias: *The Divine compassion: Thou art the King. The Saviour: The King of Love. 5 Songs.* (iii; iv) *In the half light (soliloquy); Air varié* (after Franck); (iv) *6 Piano pieces.*
*** ASV Dig. CDDCA 584 [id.]. (i) Richard Hickox Singers, Hickox; I. Watson (organ); (ii) J. Graham Hall; P. Ledger; (iii) Julian Lloyd Webber; (iv) John Lill.

William Lloyd Webber was a distinguished academic who, in a few beautifully crafted works, laid bare his heart in pure romanticism. In his varied collection, the *Missa Sanctae Mariae Magdalenae* is both the last and the most ambitious of his works, strong and characterful. John Lill is a persuasive advocate of the *Six Piano pieces,* varied in mood and sometimes quirky, and accompanies Julian Lloyd Webber in the two cello pieces, written – as though with foresight of his son's career – just as his second son was born. Graham Hall, accompanied by Philip Ledger, completes the recital with beautiful performances of a group of songs and arias. Recording, made in a north London church, is warm and undistracting.

Lôbo, Duarte (c. 1565–1646)

Missa pro defunctis.
(Y/B) (BB) *** Naxos Dig. 8.550682 [id.]. Oxford Schola Cantorum, Jeremy Summerly – CARDOSO: *Missa pro defunctis.* ***

Here is another new name from the great age of Renaissance polyphony to conjure with – the Portuguese composer, Duarte Lôbo, Mestre de Capela at Lisbon Cathedral. He was an almost exact contemporary of Manuel Cardoso, whose music we have already discovered and who provides an eloquent coupling for this splendid Naxos CD. As performed here, Lôbo's *Missa pro defunctis* for double choir is a work of beautiful flowing lines (following directly on from Palestrina), bold dramatic contrasts and ardent depth of feeling. The *Agnus Dei* is particularly beautiful. A solo treble briefly introduces each section except the *Kyrie,* which adds to the effect of the presentation. This is another triumph from Jeremy Summerly and his excellent Oxford group (38 singers), who catch both the Latin fervour and the underlying serenity of a work which has a memorably individual voice.

Motets: *Audivi vocem de caelo; Pater peccavi.*
(N) (BB) *** Naxos Dig. 8.553310 [id.]. Ars Nova, Bo Holten (with Concert of Portuguese polyphony ***) – CARDOSO: *Motets;* MAGALHAES: *Missa O Soberana luz* etc. ***

Lôbo's two beautiful motets, *Audivi vocem de caelo* ('I heard a voice from heaven') and *Pater peccavi*

('Father, I have sinned') confirm the individuality of his writing. They are part of an outstandingly sung collection which is among the most desirable records of its kind in the catalogue.

Locatelli, Pietro (1695–1764)

L'Art del violino (12 violin concertos), *Op. 3*.
*** Hyperion Dig. CDA 66721/3 [id.]. Elizabeth Wallfisch, Raglan Bar. Players, Nicholas Kraemer.

Pietro Locatelli was an almost exact contemporary of Handel and Vivaldi. It was in 1733 that he wrote the present set of concertos, in some ways anticipating Paganini by more than half a century. Each concerto is fitted out in both outer movements with an extended *Capriccio*, obviously of enormous technical difficulty to players of the time, with fast, complicated, sometimes stratospheric upper tessitura. Elizabeth Wallfisch not only throws off the fireworks with ease but also produces an appealingly gleaming lyrical line. Although Locatelli has not as strong a melodic personality as his famous contemporaries, the invention here has rhythmic vitality (which at times mirrors Vivaldi) and, in the Largo slow movements, a series of flowing ideas that have an inherent Handelian grace. With excellent, vital and stylish support from Kraemer and his Raglan Baroque Players, this may be counted a stimulating authentic re-creation of a set of concertos which had a profound influence on the violin technique of the time. The very well-balanced recording (the soloist real and vivid) is admirably clear yet has plenty of ambience.

Concerti grossi, Op. 1/1–12.
(N) **(*) Hyperion Dig. CDA 66981/2 [id.]. Raglan Bar. Players, Elizabeth Wallfisch, Nicholas Kraemer.

Locatelli's Op. 1 dates from 1721 and was the work which established him as a major composer. The 12 concertos are in a conventional *concerto grosso* form, with a concertino of two violins and cello, and with the composer occasionally adding a viola. The Corellian influence is striking and, significantly, No. 8 is a *Christmas concerto*, ending with a pastoral slow movement of some charm if of no special individuality. The performances here are lively enough, but there is at times an element of routine, a feeling of jogging along, as if the players recognize that this is not a very distinctive Opus. Elizabeth Wallfisch leads the concertino and is fully up to the bravura demands placed on her, though in the lyrical music her 'authentic' style of phrasing seems slightly more intrusive than usual. The recording is bright and vivid, the ambience spacious. But this is not the work with which to begin an exploration of Locatelli's output.

Concerti grossi, Op. 1/2, 5 & 12; Il Pianto d'Arianna, Op. 7/6; Sinfonia in F min. (composta per le esequie della sua Donna che si celebrarono in Roma).
(Y/B) *** Opus 111 OPS 30-104 [id.]. Europa Galante, Fabio Biondi.

The composer himself set great store by his Opus 1 and they are remarkable works, full of individuality. The very opening of the first concerto in D major brings a *Largo* melody of strong character, and allegros are appealingly sprightly. The last of the set, in G minor, is one of the finest, consisting of five diverse movements, including a vivace *Sarabanda*. The Sonata subtitled *Il Pianto d'Arianna*, from Opus 7, is even more ambitious, with ten brief movements, an occasional whiff of Vivaldi, and plenty of drama. Perhaps most striking of all here is the *Sinfonia 'for the funeral of his lady which took place in Rome'*, which opens with an accented *Lamento* of rare intensity, in which the composer could be suggesting a heartbeat. It has to be said that this is not certainly by Locatelli but, heard in context, it sounds like it. The performances here are full of cleanly articulated, bouncing rhythmic vitality and are also persuasively expressive. Fabio Biondi, who really knows his way about this repertoire, uses a triple rather than a double layout, with the concertino, a further tutti group still made up of soloists, plus the real tutti or ripieno. The organ continuo adds subtle extra colour. The recording is most vividly clear yet not too close, with plenty of natural ambience. Highly recommended.

Concerti grossi: in B flat; in G min., Op. 1/3 & 12; in E flat, Op. 4/10; in F, Op. 7/4; in E flat (Il piano d'Arianna), Op. 7/6.
(N) ** Teldec/Warner Dig. 4509 94551-2 [id.]. Concerto Köln.

Locatelli's dramatic *E flat major Concerto grosso*, Op. 7/6, offers an instrumental paraphrase of the tragedy of Ariadne, abandoned by Theseus, which inspired Monteverdi's famous *Lamento d'Arianna*. There are winds, violin recitativos, tearful laments, moments of histrionic drama, and a touching *Grave* conveying the heroine's despair before her spirited angry outburst when she calls for revenge. The six-movement work ends with an epilogue of resignation. The performance here is certainly strongly characterized; but too often, both here and throughout this generous programme, the tread of the members of Concerto Köln is heavy and, although the playing is polished and expert, and often very lively (especially in finales), the rhythms fail to lift off and the strong accents are abrasive. The resonant recording makes for a broad and very ample spread of sound and slow movements are at times ungainly. This is a disc for aficionados of this particular ensemble; others should be wary.

12 Flute concertos, Op. 2.
(N) (M) ** Van. Dig. 99099 (2) [id.]. Jed Wentz, Musica ad Rhenum.

The Vanguard set is fluent and highly musical, and the continuo group (including organ in Nos. 2, 4, 6, 9 and 11) is very effective; but, alongside Stephen Preston, Jed Wentz's period flute sounds a little pale. Even so, this is offered at mid-price and is very well recorded. Readers will note that the cueing goes wrong for the final double sonata (in which, presumably, Wentz plays a duet with himself), which starts at track 19 (not 18), since the previous sonata has four sub-divisions, not the indicated three.

(i) *6 Introduttioni teatrali, Op. 4: Nos. 1 in D; 2 in F; 3 in B flat; 4 in G; 5 in D; 6 in C.* (ii) *Trio sonatas: in E min., Op. 5/2; in D & A, Op. 8/2 & 10.*
(N) ✿ *** DHM Dig. 0542 77207-2 [id.]. (i) Freiburg Bar. O, Thomas Hengelbrock; (ii) Gottfried von Goltz, Guido Larisch, Torsten Johann.

There is simply no better introduction to the music of Locatelli than this superbly invigorating collection of his six *Theatrical introductions*. They are essentially (highly inventive) small-scale concerti grossi, with a concertino of four players, written in the fast–slow–fast manner of an Italian overture. Indeed the finale of No. 5 reminds one of the fifth concerto grosso of Handel's Op. 6. The fast movements erupt with vitality and bravura in these sparkling accounts from the excellent Freiburg Baroque Orchestra (4;3;2;2;1 plus harpsichord), who use period instruments brightly and freshly, and entirely without edgy acerbity, while the accented chords which are an integral part of Locatelli's allegros are played with gutsy incisiveness. These young players are not intimidated by the expressive writing and, although vibrato is minimal, there is no lack of sunshine. To add diversity, the *Introduttioni* are presented in pairs, and in between the concertino step forward to offer three *Trio sonatas* which are mellower but hardly less inventive. The recording, in an ideal acoustic, is first class. A most rewarding disc.

6 Trio sonatas, Op. 5.
(N) (M) **(*) Van. Dig. 99087 [id.]. Musica ad Rhenum.

Locatalli's Op. 5 *Trio sonatas* are full of agreeable, singing melody and have plenty of lively invention too. It is optional to use a pair of flutes or two violins in their performance, and it might have been a good idea to vary the instrumentation, as two flutes used continually can prove too much of a good thing. However, Jed Wentz and Marion Moonen play with style and they blend nicely together; the continuo group includes a bassoon for added colour. Good performances, without any of the acerbities one associates with period performance, nicely recorded.

Locke, Matthew (c. 1621–77)

Consort of Fower Parts: suites Nos. 1 in D min.; 2 in D min./maj.; 3 & 4 in F; 5 in G min.; 6 in G.
(N) *** Astrée Audivis Dig. E 8519 [id.]. Hespèrion XX.

Consort of Fower Parts: suites Nos. 1–6. Duos for 2 bass viols Nos. 1 in C; 2 in D.
(N) (M) **(*) Virgin Veritas/EMI Dig. VC5 45142-2 [id.]. Fretwork, with Nigel North & Paul Nicholson.

Matthew Locke, born in Devon, was a choirboy at Exeter Cathedral but later moved to work as a musician in London; here in 1660, when Charles II was restored to the throne of England, Locke became Master of the King's Music at the royal court. At that time he had 24 violins at his disposal, but he probably wrote the *Consort of Fower Parts* earlier, in the 1650s. If they are less ambitious in instrumentation, they are much more so in musical achievement. Indeed the remarkably ethereal *Fantazie* opening the *Fifth suite in G minor*, which is magnetically presented in the Hespèrion performance, can be measured against comparable music by Purcell. Each suite opens with a *Fantazie* and then follows a standard sequence of *Courante*, *Ayre* and *Saraband*. Locke's suites were regarded at the time as being composed, 'after the old style', but the music itself is forward-looking and by no means predictable. It seems likely that they would have been performed with continuo, and this practice is followed sparingly in both the Fretwork and Hespèrion performances, the former using archlute and organ, the later preferring a double harp to the lute.

Both sets of performances are highly musical, scholarly and well recorded, but there is a clear first choice. In the dance movements there is a extra rhythmic vigour and buoyancy with Hespèrion, and in the *Ayres* of the *First* and *Second suites*, for instance, there is an extra expressive warmth, compared with a faster tempo and relative austerity of feeling with Fretwork. The latter's playing brings somewhat more refined textures, and the Virgin Veritas programme includes two extra works: a pair of *Duos* (each in six movements) for two bass viols. Of these, it is the second that is obviously the more appealing and it has a subtle organ continuo (although the booklet suggests the reverse – that the organ is involved in the *C major Duo*). But in spite of this bonus, it is the Hespèrion playing which is the more penetrating in this fine music.

Loeffler, Charles (1861–1935)

A Pagan poem, Op. 14.
(M) **(*) EMI CDM5 65074-2 [id.]. SO, Stokowski with Robert Hunter, William Kosinski – GLIERE: *Symphony No. 3.* **(*)

Loeffler's highly eclectic but richly coloured *Pagan poem* is his only claim to fame; it is based on Virgil's *Eighth Eclogue* and tells of a young girl, Thessaly, who tries, with the aid of sorcery, to win back the lover who has left her. The ambitious scoring includes obbligato piano and a cor anglais solo, but it is the brass that carry the day at the triumphant conclusion. Its hyperbole is well understood by Stokowski, who gives a sumptuously exciting performance in the tradition of Hollywood film music. An ideal coupling for Glière with the early (1957) stereo providing plenty of opulent spectacle.

Loewe, Carl (1796–1869)

Frauenliebe (song-cycle) *Op. 60.* Goethe, Heine and Rückert Lieder: *Der du von dem Himmel heist; Erste Liebe; Hinkende Jamben; Ich hab in Traume geweinet; Im Traume sah ich die Geliebte; Irrlichter; Die Lotusblume; Mädchenwünsche; Meine Ruh ist hin; O süsse Mutter; Die Pfarrjüngferchen; Sehnsucht; Süsses Begräbnis; Szene aus Faust; Unber allen Gipfeln ist Ruh.*
(N) (M) *** DG Dig. 445 575-2 [id.]. Brigitte Fassbaender, Cord Garben.

Carl Loewe's songs are much more imaginative than their status as 'interesting historical documents' suggests, and they are full of easy melody. Records of them are so rare that, despite occasional shortcomings, this collection should be snapped up before it succumbs to the deletions axe. *Frauenliebe*, Loewe's cycle of nine songs set to poems of Adelbert von Chamisso, inevitably invites comparison with Schumann, and if it has less depth than *Frauenliebe und Leben* Loewe's sequence remains infinitely touching; Brigitte Fassbaender sings it tenderly and with much charm. There are nine songs in all, although the composer published only seven of them as his Op. 60. Loewe's heroine is impulsive and soon falls deeply in love, and we follow her progress to a Schubertian dream of happiness, the wedding ring and revelling in marital bliss, her lover's sudden death and the poignant epilogue addressed to her daughter who, by the nature of things, will follow in her mother's footsteps. The final words of blessing are not sung but gently spoken. Not all the other songs here suit Fassbaender so well; she is best in the gentler settings. Goethe's *Scene with Faust* is lovely, as is *Uber allen Gipfeln ist Ruh*, while Rückert's *Irrlichter* ('Will-o'-the-wisps'), sung precociously fast, is captivating. But it is a pity that the recital opens with Goethe's *Meine Ruh ist hin*, which brings some repeated ugly upward scoops. Nevertheless this rare CD is not to be missed.

Lotti, Antonio (c. 1667–1740)

Crucifixus.
(Y/B) (B) *** Decca Double 443 868-2 (2) [id.]. Palmer, Langridge, Esswood, Keyte, St John's College, Cambridge, Ch., Philomusica, Guest – BONONCINI: *Stabat Mater* ***; PERGOLESI: *Magnificat in C; Stabat Mater* **(*); D. SCARLATTI: *Stabat Mater;* A. SCARLATTI: *Domine, refugium factus es nobis; O magnum mysterium;* CALDARA: *Crucifixus.* ***

This short *Crucifixus*, which takes less than four minutes, may well have inspired the noble Caldara setting with which it frames Bononcini's beautiful *Stabat Mater* in this highly desirable collection of choral music. The Lotti setting is less elaborate in texture than Caldara's but it is hardly less noble or affecting. Performance and recording are excellent.

Lourié, Arthur (1892–1966)

Concerto da camera; (i) *A little chamber music;* (ii) *Little Gidding.*
*** DG Dig. 437 788-2 [id.]. Gidon Kremer, (i) Thomas Klug; (ii) Kenneth Riegel, Deutsche Kammerphilharmonie.

Arthur Lourié was one of the pioneers of modernism in the early years of the Soviet Union. In the course of time he became disenchanted with modernism and in 1941 settled in the United States. *A little chamber music* comes from the 1920s and in its obvious neo-classicism betrays a certain closeness to Stravinsky's aesthetic, as well as a touch of Shostakovich's sardonic humour. The *Concerto da camera* was written in America and is a six-movement work in a quasi-baroque style. The melodic ideas all tend to be short-breathed but characterful. Lourié's setting of T. S. Eliot's *Little Gidding*, the first of the *Four Quartets*, shows great affinity with Eliot's world and is arguably the most imaginative thing on the disc. Kremer and the Deutsche Philharmonie play with a sense of real discovery and commitment, and Kenneth Riegel is at his usual best. Interesting repertoire rather than great music, but very rewarding all the same, and well worth acquiring, particularly in so fine a recording.

Lovenskiold, Herman (1815–70)

La Sylphide (ballet) complete.
(M) *** Chandos Dig. CHAN 6546; *MBTD 6546* [id.]. Royal Danish O, David Garforth.

La Sylphide (1834) predates Adam's *Giselle* by seven years. It is less distinctive than Adam's score, but it is full of grace and the invention has genuine romantic vitality – indeed the horn writing in the finale anticipates Delibes. The wholly sympathetic playing is warm, elegant, lively and felicitous in its detailed delicacy, yet robust when necessary and always spontaneous. A most enjoyable disc, superbly recorded.

Ludford, Nicholas (1485–1557)

Masses; Magnificat benedicta & Motets (as listed below).
(Y/B) ✿ (M) *** ASV/Gaudeamus CDGAX 426 (4) [id.]. The Cardinall's Musick, Andrew Carwood.

Nicholas Ludford is one of the least familiar of the Tudor masters; he never enjoyed the fame of his older contemporary, Fayrfax, or the much younger Tallis. Ludford has remained outside the repertoire of most cathedral choirs, little more than a name to those with an interest in early music. According to Dr John Bergsagel's *Grove* article, Ludford composed 11 complete Masses and three incomplete, thus making him 'the most prolific of English composers of masses'. This four-CD box gathers together the four splendid discs of Ludford's music performed by Carwood and his excellent group of singers, who are individually as impressive as in the blended whole. This is music of remarkably passionate feeling, and it brings to life a composer who spent much of his working life in St Stephen's Chapel at St Margaret's, Westminster. He was an ardent Catholic and was very happily married – he paid for his wife to have her own pew and gave her an elaborate ceremonial burial. He then married again, and his second wife was instructed to prepare something more modest for his interment alongside his beloved first spouse. His music is little short of extraordinary, and we hope our Rosette will tempt collectors to explore it, either through this comprehensive box, which will retail at just short of £40, or by trying one of the individual issues.

Missa Benedicta et venerabilis; Magnificat benedicta.
(Y/B) *** ASV/Gaudeamus Dig. CDGAU 132 [id.]. The Cardinall's Musick, Andrew Carwood.

Ludford uses the same plainchant for both works, but the voicing has a distinct emphasis at the lower end of the range, not only adding to the weight but also bringing a certain darkness to the sonority. The performance has the same spontaneous feeling that distinguishes this magnificent series throughout, and it confirms Ludford as one of the most emotionally communicative and original musicians of his age. The plainsong propers relate the music to the Feast of the Assumption. Excellent, full recording.

Missa Christi Virgo dilectissima; Motet: Domine Ihesu Christie.
(Y/B) *** ASV/Gaudeamus Dig. CDGAU 133 [id.]. The Cardinall's Musick, Andrew Carwood.

This is music of great beauty, whose expressive eloquence and floating lines quite carry the listener away. Andrew Carwood proves an excellent advocate and the sound is also spacious and well balanced.

Missa Lapidaverunt Stephanum; Ave Maria ancilla trinitatis.
(Y/B) *** ASV/Gaudeamus Dig. CDGAU 140 [id.]. Cardinall's Musick, Andrew Carwood.

This Mass, celebrating St Stephen the Martyr, is thought to have been written soon after he was appointed verger and organist there in 1527. In five-part polyphony the scale is formidable, culminating in a magnificent *Agnus Dei*. The performances, fresh and stylish, are punctuated by apt plainsong.

Missa Videte miraculum; Motet: Ave cuius conceptio.
(Y/B) *** ASV/Gaudeamus Dig. CDGAU 131 [id.]. The Cardinall's Musick, Andrew Carwood.

The six-part *Missa Videte miraculum* brings a remarkable double treble line running together, often in thirds. Overall this work is as fine as the others in the series, and it is gloriously sung.

Luigini, Alexandre (1850–1906)

Ballet Egyptien, Op. 12 (suite).
(B) *** CfP CD-CFP 4637; *TC-CFP 4637*. RPO, Fistoulari – KETELBEY: *Collection.* ***

Because of its bandstand popularity, Luigini's amiable and tuneful *Ballet Egyptien* has never been taken very seriously and there is some sparkling doggerel by Richard Murdoch which snappily fits bizarre words about 'Dame Ella Wheeler Wilcox' neatly to the famous opening rhythm. However, the four-movement suite is highly engaging (both the two central sections have good tunes), especially when played as affectionately and stylishly as here under that master conductor of ballet, Anatole Fistoulari. The 1958 recording has come up remarkably freshly, and this makes an excellent bonus for an outstanding Ketèlbey concert.

Lully, Jean-Baptiste (1632–87)

Dies irae; (i) *Te Deum.*
(N) (M) **(*) Erato/Warner 0630 11226-2 [id.]. Jennifer Smith, Devos; (i) Bessac, Vandersteene, Huttenlocher; Valence Vocal Ens., Paillard CO, Paillard.

Both these works are for double choir, but Paillard makes no attempt to divide his forces, relying mainly on contrast between soloists, singly and in a group, chorus and orchestra. The *Dies irae* is a noble piece encapsulating a mood of dark melancholy, and it makes a strong impression here, with a notably dedicated contribution from the two soloists. The effect has a striking, elegiac beauty. The sudden choral interjections at a faster pace are convincingly managed. Here the choral focus in the CD transfer could be cleaner, but the sound has plenty of body and a most attractive ambience. The better-known *Te Deum* dates from 1677. It opens regally with brilliant high trumpets and is a work of contrasting splendour and breadth rather than the general-purpose pomp often favoured by Lully and his followers. Paillard and his forces give a thoroughly committed and eloquent account of the piece, and the recording is richly expansive, with the choral sound cleaner. Incidentally, it was while conducting this work that Lully vigorously brought down the heavy stick that served to mark the beat on to his right foot; gangrene eventually set in, and a couple of months later he died!

Atys (opera): complete.
*** HM Dig. HMC 901257/9 (3). Guy de Mey, Mellon, Laurens, Gardeil, Semellaz, Rime, Les Arts Florissants Ch. & O, Christie.

Christie and his excellent team give life and dramatic speed consistently to the performance of *Atys*, and there are many memorable numbers, not least those in the sleep interlude of Act III. Outstanding in the cast are the high tenor, Guy de Mey, in the name-part and Agnès Mellon as the nymph, Sangaride, with whom he falls in love.

Le bourgeois gentilhomme (comédie-ballet; complete).
(M) *** HM/BMG GD 77059 (2) [77059-2-RG]. Nimsgern, Jungmann, Schortemeier, René Jacobs, Tölz Ch., La Petite Bande, Leonhardt – CAMPRA: *L'Europe galante.* ***

Lully's score is unmemorable and harmonies are neither original nor interesting; but the performance puts Lully's music into the correct stage perspective and, with such sprightly and spirited performers as well as good 1973 recording, this can hardly fail to give pleasure. The orchestral contribution under the direction of Gustav Leonhardt is distinguished by a splendid sense of the French style.

Phaëton (complete).

(Y/B) *** Erato/Warner Dig. 4509 91737-2 (2) [id.]. Crook, Yakar, J. Smith, Gens, Theruel, Ens. Vocale Sagittarius, Musiciens du Louvre, Marc Minkowski.

Mark Minkowski directs a compelling, consistently fresh and resilient reading of Lully's *tragédie en musique*, which at the time was described as 'the opera of the people'. Not only does Minkowski give the piece dramatic bite but he also brings out the colour and vigour of the many dance movements among much else. The prologue and five compact Acts have an involved plot which leads finally – as the title suggests – to the attempt of Phaëton, son of the Sun God, to drive in the chariot of the sun. This threatens to set fire to the Earth, whereupon Jupiter strikes him dead, to the apparent rejoicing of everyone. When Libye can then be partnered by her beloved Epaphus, it is hardly a tragedy at all, with their love earlier celebrated in two brief but intensely beautiful duets, punctuating the many solo airs. The solo cast is strong – with Véronique Gens most affecting as Libye, with Rachel Yakar and Jennifer Smith impressive too, and Howard Crook clean-focused and stylish in the name-part. The recording, a co-production between Erato and Radio France, is very vivid and immediate.

Lumbye, Hans Christian (1810–74)

Amager polka; Amelie waltz; Champagne galop; Columbine polka mazurka; Copenhagen Steam Railway galop; Dream pictures fantasia; The Guard of Amager (ballet): *Final galop. Helga polka mazurka; Hesperus waltz; Lily polka (dedicated to the ladies); Queen Louise's waltz; Napoli* (ballet): *Final galop. Salute to August Bournonville; Salute to our friends; Sandman galop fantastique.*
✹ *** Unicorn Dig. DKPCD 9089 [id.]. Odense SO, Peter Guth.

This superb Unicorn collection offers 75 minutes of the composer's best music, with wonderfully spontaneous performances demonstrating above all its elegance and gentle grace. It opens with a vigorous *Salute to August Bournonville* and closes with a *Champagne galop* to rival Johann junior's polka. In between comes much to enchant, not least the delightful *Amelie waltz* and the haunting *Dream pictures fantasia* with its diaphanous opening textures and lilting main theme. But Lumbye's masterpiece is the unforgettable *Copenhagen Steam Railway galop*. This whimsical yet vivid portrait of a local Puffing Billy begins with the gathering of passengers at the station – obviously dressed for the occasion in a more elegant age than ours. The little engine then wheezingly starts up and proceeds on its journey, finally drawing to a dignified halt against interpolated cries from the station staff. Because of the style and refinement of its imagery, it is much the most endearing of musical railway evocations, and the high-spirited lyricism of the little train racing through the countryside, its whistle peeping, is enchanting. This is a superbly entertaining disc, showing the Odense Symphony Orchestra and its conductor, Peter Guth, as naturally suited to this repertoire as are the VPO under Boskovsky in the music of the Strauss family. The recording has a warm and sympathetic ambience and gives a lovely bloom to the whole programme.

Amelie waltz; Britta polka; Champagne galop; Columbine polka mazurka; Concert polka (for 2 violins and orchestra); *Copenhagen Steam Railway galop; Dream pictures* (fantasy); *The Lady of St Petersburg* (polka); *The Guards of Amager: Final galop. My salute to St Petersburg* (march); *Napoli* (ballet): *Final galop. Polonaise with cornet solo; Queen Louise's waltz; Salute to August Bournonville; St Petersburg champagne galop.*
*** Chandos Dig. CHAN 9209 [id.]. Danish Nat. RSO, Rozhdestvensky.

This new Chandos disc opens with an arresting fanfare and sets off into the *Champagne galop* with much brio. Throughout his programme, Rozhdestvensky's approach is altogether more extrovert than Guth's on Unicorn, and the Royal Danish Orchestra, without loss of finesse, play almost everything here with great gusto. The Copenhagen Steam Railway engine becomes a mainline express and reaches an exhilarating momentum before slamming on its brakes, to be vociferously welcomed by the Danish porters as it arrives at its destination. One cannot but respond to the energy and vivacity of the playing here, while the lovely *Dream pictures* creates a total contrast and is most poetically done. Incidentally, the lively *Britta polka* (unwittingly?) quotes Sullivan's *A magnet hung in a hardware shop* (from *Patience*). This is one of five items not duplicated on the Unicorn disc, but collectors who already have this will surely want the new Chandos collection as a supplement, if only to experience the exuberance of Rozhdestvensky's response to some splendidly entertaining music. The recording is spectacularly resonant and adds to the impact.

Britta polka; Canon galop; Cecilie waltz; Dancing tune from Kroll Waltz; Indian war dance; King Christian IX March of honour; King George I March of honour; Manoeuvre galop; Memories from Vienna waltz; Nordic brotherhood; Pegasus galop; Sommernight at Møns Cliff galop; Sophie waltz; Velocipedes galop; Victoria quadrille; Welcome mazurka; Les Zouaves galop.
*** Unicorn Dig. DKPCD 9143. Odense SO, Peter Guth.

A further, essentially energetic selection of sparkling Lumbye repertoire, splendidly played with much spirit by the excellent Odense orchestra under Guth. The *Velocipedes galop* makes an engaging and vivacious opener, and the *Canon galop* which closes the concert has properly spectacular effects, plus a final bang to make the listener jump. The *Memories from Vienna waltz* has a particularly winning lilt, but there is nothing here that quite matches the *Copenhagen Steam Railway galop*.

Lutoslawski, Witold (1916–94)

(i) *Chain II. Chain III; Novelette;* (i; ii) *Partita.*
(N) (M) *** DG Dig. 445 576-2 [id.]. (i) Mutter, (ii) Philip Moll; (i; ii) BBC SO, composer.

Chain III; Novelette.
(B) *** DG Dig. 439 452-3 [id.]. BBC SO, composer – LIGETI: *Chamber concerto;* SCHNITTKE: *Concerto grosso No. 1.* ***

Chain II, a 'dialogue for violin and orchestra', follows up the technique of *Chain I* (of which at present there is no really satisfactory recording), contrasting fully written sections with *ad libitum* movements, where chance plays its part within fixed parameters. *Chain III* then makes a sustained contrast with its ear-catching orchestral colours. The *Partita* is a development of a piece for violin and piano which Lutoslawski originally wrote for Pinchas Zukerman, with the first, third and fifth movements now scored for violin and orchestra. With Mutter and the composer the most persuasive advocates, both concertante pieces establish themselves as among the finest examples of Lutoslawski's latterday work. *Novelette*, an attractive, scherzo-like piece, full of incandescent energy, is common to both the main, mid-priced programme and the Classikon reissue, coupled with other stimulating works by Ligeti and Schnittke. DG here are obviously treading water to see if they can sell this kind of *avant-garde* music in a wider marketplace at budget price.

Cello concerto.
*** EMI CDC7 49304-2 [id.]. Rostropovich, O de Paris, composer – DUTILLEUX: *Cello concerto.* ***

The *Cello concerto* was written in response to a commission by Rostropovich, whose 1975 recording is now reissued at full price, retaining the original catalogue number and still sounding extremely vivid. As in some other Lutoslawski pieces, there are aleatory elements in the score, though these are carefully controlled. The sonorities are fascinating and heard to good advantage on the EMI CD. The soloist is rather forward, but in every other respect the recording is extremely realistic. Rostropovich is in his element and gives a superb account of the solo role, and the composer's direction of the accompaniment is grippingly authoritative.

Concerto for orchestra.
*** Decca Dig. 425 694-2. Cleveland O, Dohnányi (with BARTOK: *Concerto for orchestra* **(*)).

Lutoslawski's brilliant showpiece is played on Decca with a thrust and precision to bring out the full colour and energy of the work. Dohnányi's dedicated performance is recorded with a fullness and brilliance outstanding even by Decca standards. However, the Bartók coupling is less impressive.

(i) *Concerto for orchestra;* (ii) *Paganini variations* (for piano and orchestra); (iii) *Musique funèbre;* (iv) *Paroles tissées.*
(N) (B) **(*) Decca Double Analogue/Dig. 448 258-2 (2) [id.]. (i) SRO, Kletzki; (ii) Jablonski, RPO, Ashkenazy; (iii) Cleveland O, Dohnányi; (iv) Peter Pears, LSO, composer – SZYMANOWSKI: *Violin concerto No. 2; Symphonies Nos. 2–3.* **(*)

Kletzki directs a brilliant account of the *Concerto for orchestra*, and the Swiss orchestra play very well for him; moreover they are given vintage Decca sound from 1968. The slight snag is that Kletzki makes a small cut in the second movement, though with the composer's permission. However, this is an exciting perfomance and only the most dedicated admirer of the composer will cavil at being short-changed, if that is indeed the case. *Musique funèbre* (not perhaps one of the composer's most inspired pieces) is very well played and recorded, but it does not generate the last degree of tension. The *Paganini variations* for two pianos is very successful indeed, however: it is one of Lutoslawski's earliest and most readily appealing works. Peter Jablonski plays it in the much later transcription for piano and orchestra, and his pleasure and delight will surely be shared by the listener. The digital recording is first class. The *Paroles tissées* were written for Peter Pears, who sings the cycle here, and Lutoslawski's writing shows extraordinary understanding of that singer's special qualities and the colour of his voice. The texts are from poems of Jean-François Chabrun, with haunting imagery recurring in a manner mirrored exactly by the composer's finely textured, sharply conceived writing. Performances and recording are ideal.

(i) *Piano concerto. Chain 3; Novelette.*
*** DG Dig. 431 664-2 [id.]. (i) Krystian Zimerman; BBC SO, composer.

The *Piano concerto* is full of imaginative ideas and opens with some shimmering, sensitively laid-out textures. It is sympathetically written for the piano, Lutoslawski's own instrument (although he has composed rather little for it) and is marvellously played by Zimerman and the BBC Symphony Orchestra under the composer. It is beautiful to listen to, but for all its diversity of aural incident and activity one is left wondering whether there is much of enduring substance. The two remaining works are also very convincingly presented. Absolutely first-rate recording.

Dance preludes (for clarinet and orchestra).
*** Hyperion Dig. CDA 66215 [id.]. Thea King, ECO, Litton – BLAKE: *Clarinet concerto;* SEIBER: *Concertino.* ***
*** Chandos Dig. CHAN 8618 [id.]. Janet Hilton, SNO, Bamert – COPLAND; NIELSEN: *Concertos.* ***

Lutoslawski's five folk-based vignettes are a delight in the hands of Thea King and Andrew Litton, who give sharply characterized performances, thrown into bold relief by the bright, clear recording. Janet Hilton also emphasizes their contrasts with her expressive lyricism and crisp articulation in the lively numbers. Excellent recording.

(i) *Postlude No. 1;* (ii) *Preludes and fugues for 13 solo strings;* (iii) *Paroles tissées;* (iv) *3 Poèmes d'Henri Michaux.*
(N) (M) *** EMI CDM5 65865-2 [id.]. (i) Polish Nat. RSO; (ii) Polish CO; (iii) Louis Devos; (iv) Krakow R, Ch.; all cond. composer.

The searching *Preludes and fugues for thirteen solo strings* (1970–72) shows the mature Lutoslawski; the choral *Poèmes* were written a decade earlier. With their variety of effects, including whispering and syllabic monotones, the writing readily contrasts with the atmospheric *Paroles tissées* ('woven words') with its mystical feeling and remarkable word-imagery. Together with the elliptical *Postlude* this programmes offers a well-planned demonstration of the composer's breadth of achievement. Performances and recordings are of a high standard, as is the recording from the late 1970s.

Symphonies Nos. 1–2; Symphonic variations.
(M) *** EMI CDM5 65076-2 [id.]. Polish R. Nat. SO, composer.

The wholly beguiling *Symphonic variations*, with its Szymanowskian palette and luminosity, is an early work (1938); the symphonies date from 1947 and 1966/8, respectively. The latter consolidates the new language the composer formed after his change of style in the mid-1950s; the *First* is written against a musical background influenced by Hindemith, Bartók and Prokofiev and perhaps by Stravinsky too. But the work has its own individuality and is well worth hearing. The composer is an eloquent advocate, and the 1976/7 recordings are spacious and full-bodied with bright detail.

Symphonies Nos. 3–4; (i) *Les espaces du sommeil.*
(Y/B) *** Sony Dig. SK 66280 [id.]. LAPO, Esa-Pekka Salonen; (i) with John Shirley-Quirk.

Sony have now added a brand-new recording of the *Fourth Symphony* to Salonen's previous coupling of No. 3 and *Les espaces du sommeil*. The format of the *Fourth*, Lutoslawski's culminating symphony, is elliptical, its broodingly atmospheric opening building to an almost Waltonian lyrical cantilena and a darkly passionate climax. This slowly disintegrates until a brief, emphatically rhythmic coda produces a sudden resolution. It is a remarkable piece, aurally fascinating as well as gripping. Salonen gives deeply committed, passionate accounts of both this and the dramatic *Third Symphony*, also built in one continuous span. Here he challenges the composer's own interpretation, and in *Les espaces du sommeil* Salonen provides a different slant from the composer himself, making it – with the help of John Shirley-Quirk as an understanding soloist – much more evocative and sensuous in full and well-balanced sound.

Paganini variations (arr. Ptasazynska).
(N) *** Chandos Dig. CHAN 9398 [id.]. Safri Duo & Slovak Piano Duo – BARTOK: *Sonata for 2 pianos and percussion* ***; HELWEG: *American fantasy.* **

A slight piece from Lutoslawski's youth, dressed up by Marta Ptasazynska for the same forces as the

Bartók *Sonata*. It is brilliantly played and no less remarkably recorded at a Danish Radio concert. There is enthusiastic applause, which is understandable, and whistling, which is unfortunate.

String quartet.
*** Olympia OCD 328 [id.]. Varsovia Qt – SZYMANOWSKI: *Quartets;* PENDERECKI: *Quartet No. 2.* ***

Lutoslawski tells us that in his *String quartet* he uses 'chance elements to enrich the rhythmic and expressive character of the music without in any way limiting the authority of the composer over the final shape of the piece'. Whatever its merits, it has a highly developed and refined feeling for sonority and balance and, generally speaking, succeeds in holding the listener.

Lyatoshynsky, Boris (1895–1968)

Symphony No. 1 in A min., Op. 2; Overture on 4 Ukrainian themes, Op. 20; Poem of reunification, Op. 40.
(Y/B) *** Russian Disc Dig. RDCD 11055 [id.]. Ukrainian State SO, Vladimir Gnedash.

Symphonies Nos. 2, Op. 26; 3 in B min., Op. 50.
(Y/B) *** Marco Polo Dig. 8.223540 [id.]. Ukrainian State SO, Theodore Kuchar.

Symphonies Nos. 4 in B flat min., Op. 63; 5 in C ('Slavonic'), Op. 67.
(Y/B) *** Marco Polo Dig. 8.223541 [id.]. Ukrainian State SO, Theodore Kuchar.

Symphony No. 4 in B flat min., Op. 63; (i) *On the banks of the Vistula, Op. 59;* (ii) *Lyric poem.*
(Y/B) ** Russian Disc Dig. RDCD 11062 [id.]. Ukrainian State SO, Igor Blazhkov; (i) Viktor Sirenko;
    (ii) Fedor Glushchenko.

Lyatoshynsky began writing his *First Symphony* immediately after the First World War, while he was still studying with Glière in Kiev, and it is a well-crafted, confident score that inhabits the world of Russian post-nationalism, Strauss and Scriabin. It abounds in contrapuntal elaboration and abundant orchestral rhetoric. The *Second Symphony* followed in 1936, but its air of pessimism did not sit well in post-*Lady Macbeth* Russia and it was not premièred until 1964 and was, generally speaking, still out of tune with the prevailing Soviet ideological climate. The *Third Symphony*, with which Marco Polo couple it, is a decade later and was composed in 1951, some three years after the Zhdanov affair had plunged Soviet composers into temporary paralysis. Lyatoshynsky was still denounced during this period for his 'formalism, decadence, aggression, sadism and cacophony' – not bad going. Although the *Third Symphony* tries hard to be a good Soviet symphony, it does not wholly convince – and it does not quite ring true either as a more personal statement. (Incidentally, Mravinsky's recording of it, coupled with the Shostakovich *Festival overture*, Liadov's *Enchanted lake* and *Baba-Yaga*, is available on Russian Disc RD CD10900.)

The *Fourth Symphony* (1963) reflects something of the cultural thaw in the Soviet Union and is more directly Shostakovichian than its predecessors. Its middle movement depicts what must be a mysterious, chimerical city to a Ukrainian, just as it is a source of wonder to everyone else: namely, Bruges. There is striking use of bells and celesta, and at times a suggestion of Messiaen. The *Fifth Symphony* certainly pays tribute to his master in using the Rus theme, *Il'ya Mourametz*, as well as a wide variety of Russian, Bulgarian and Serbian liturgical melodies. It aspires to explore the common roots of the Slavonic peoples; hence its title. There are many touches of colour and some token modernity, but basically this looks back to earlier masters – Glière, Rimsky-Korsakov and the Russian post-nationalists.

Those with exploratory tastes will find much to satisfy them in these symphonies, provided they are not expecting masterpieces. As far as performances are concerned, the Ukraine orchestra obviously is inside this music, and none of the playing is second rate. The Marco Polo recordings are more than marginally superior to the Russian Disc, and the performances sound much better rehearsed than is usually the case with this label, while the odd fillers on the Russian Discs are not of sufficient interest to tip the scales in their favour.

MacCunn, Hamish (1868–1916)

The Land of the mountain and the flood (concert overture).
(B) *** CfP CD-CFP 4635; *TC-CFP 4635*. RSNO, Gibson – GERMAN: *Welsh rhapsody;* HARTY:
    With the wild geese; SMYTH: *Wreckers overture.* ***

MacCunn's descriptive overture is no masterpiece, but it has a memorable tune, is attractively atmospheric and is constructed effectively. Sir Alexander Gibson's performance is quite outstanding in its combination of warmth, colour and drama, and the recording is excellent. So is the CD transfer, and this enterprising collection is a real bargain.

MacDowell, Edward (1861–1908)

Piano concertos Nos. 1 in A min., Op. 15; 2 in D min., Op. 23.
⚛ *** Olympia Dig. OCD 353 [id.]. Donna Amato, LPO, Paul Freeman.

Of MacDowell's two *Piano concertos* the *First* is marginally the lesser of the two: the melodic content, though very pleasing, is slightly less memorable than in the *Second*. This is a delightful piece, fresh and tuneful, redolent of Mendelssohn and Saint-Saëns. Donna Amato's scintillating performance is entirely winning, and she is equally persuasive in the *A minor*. This music needs polish and elegance as well as fire, and Paul Freeman's accompaniments supply all three. The recording, made in All Saints', Tooting, has an agreeable ambient warmth. A highly rewarding coupling in all respects.

Piano concerto No. 2 in D min., Op. 23.
*** Chesky CD 76 [id.]. Earl Wild, RCA Victor SO, Freccia – RACHMANINOV: *Piano concerto No. 3.* ***

Earl Wild never played more brilliantly or more appealingly on record than in these coupled recordings of MacDowell and Rachmaninov, engineered by Decca in the mid-1960s. The performance of the finer of the two MacDowell concertos is technically dazzling, and so assured and sympathetic is Wild's style that the concerto is almost made to sound a masterpiece. Massimo Freccia and the so-called RCA Victor Symphony Orchestra (probably including members of the RPO) provide excellent support, and Wild is much better balanced and recorded than his RCA competitor, Van Cliburn.

(i) *Piano concerto No. 2 in D min., Op. 23. Woodland sketches: To a wild rose, Op. 51/1.*
(M) **(*) RCA [60420-2-RG]. Van Cliburn, (i) Chicago SO, Hendl – SCHUMANN: *Concerto.* **(*)

Van Cliburn is not helped by a recording balance which consistently makes him sound rather too loud; but the performance otherwise has the advantage of warm Chicago acoustics, and Walter Hendl's vigorous and sympathetic support, with its fire and spontaneity, triumph over the technical problems. The Scherzo is superb. MacDowell's most famous solo piano piece makes a pleasing encore, though the performance is a trifle cool. (This record is currently available in the USA only.)

PIANO MUSIC

Fireside tales, Op. 61; New England idylls, Op. 62; Sea pieces, Op. 55; Woodland sketches, Op. 51.
**(*) Marco Polo Dig. 8.223631 [id.]. James Baragallo.

MacDowell's most famous piano piece opens this recital: *To a wild rose* (named by his wife) is the first of the ten *Woodland sketches*. They are all pleasant if not distinctive vignettes, most lasting a little over a minute. The other three suites are very similar. The *Sea pieces* are without any striking oceanic evocation: the thoughtful suggestion of the composer's response to *Starlight* is perhaps most memorable. Of the *Fireside tales*, the opening *An old love story* immediately sets the cosy atmosphere, and *From a German forest* brings another simple evocation that is engaging in its simplicity. This is certainly not a CD to listen to all at once but to be dipped into; one can appreciate that James Baragallo is a thoroughly sympathetic exponent, and he is well recorded too.

McEwen, John Blackwood (1868–1948)

A Solway Symphony; (i) Hills o'heather; Where the wild thyme blows.
(Y/B) *** Chandos Dig. CHAN 9345 [id.]. (i) Moray Welsh; LPO, Mitchell.

Sir John McEwen wrote his highly evocative *Solway Symphony* in 1911, a triptych of seascapes marked by magically transparent orchestration and crisply controlled argument. McEwen was influenced by the folksong movement – notably here in *Hills o'heather* with its hints of reels – but the flavour is quite individual, with occasional echoes of Sibelius in the sparer moments. Above all, this is warm-hearted music. The first of the three movements of the symphony, *Spring tide*, is built on a striking motif, argued with clean-cut directness. The second movement, *Moonlight*, is developed, Sibelius-like, over a gently nagging ostinato, while the finale, *The sou'west wind*, opens with brassy exuberance in galloping compound time, and only later develops a stormy side, before ending darkly in F sharp minor. *Hills o'heather* is a charming movement for cello and orchestra, while *Where the wild thyme blows* uses slow pedal points to sustain harmonically adventurous arguments. The performances, conducted by Alasdair

Mitchell, who edited the scores, are outstanding, a well-deserved tribute to a neglected composer who was far more than an academic. The recording is sumptuously atmospheric.

Mackenzie, Alexander (1847–1935)

Benedictus, Op. 37/3; Burns – 2nd Scottish rhapsody, Op. 24; Coriolanus (incidental music): *suite, Op. 61; The cricket on the hearth: Overture, Op. 62; Twelfth Night* (incidental music): *Overture/suite, Op. 40.*
(Y/B) *** Hyperion Dig. CDA 66764 [id.]. BBC Scottish SO, Martyn Brabbins.

Sir Alexander Mackenzie wrote in the Stanford/Elgar/Parry tradition rather than showing any strong Scottish traits. However, in the *Burns rhapsody* he gets round the problem by using three Scottish folk tunes quite felicitously, notably '*Scots! wha hae*' which is very emphatic. The second movement has charm, and indeed Mackenzie's own lyrical gift is quite striking in the jolly, at times Sullivanesque *Cricket on the hearth overture* (which also shows his deft orchestral skill), and of course the *Benedictus* with a melody typical of its time. The incidental music for *Twelfth night* is in the form of an overture, subdivided into six sections, with a Shakespeare quotation for each to identify its mood. These vignettes are attractively scored and have considerable character. The whole programme is presented with commitment and polish by the BBC Scottish Symphony Orchestra and makes a very agreeable hour and a quarter of not too demanding listening. The recording is excellent.

MacMillan, James (born 1959)

(i). *. . as others see us; 3 Dawn rituals; Untold;* (ii) *Veni, veni, Emmanuel (concerto for percussion and orchestra);* (iii) *After the Tryst (miniature fantasy for violin and piano).*
✪ *** RCA Catalyst Dig. 09026 61916-2 [id.]. (i) Scottish CO (members), composer; (ii) Evelyn Glennie, SCO, Saraste; (iii) Ruth Crouch, composer.

Veni, veni, Emmanuel, written for Evelyn Glennie, instantly reveals the composer's rare gift of communicating with electric intensity to a wide audience, rare in new music today. His dedication, strongly motivated by his devout Catholicism and his equally passionate left-wing stance, invariably colours what he writes, making us share not his precise beliefs but the spiritual intensity that goes with them. In *Veni, veni, Emmanuel* MacMillan has written a concerto for percussion that in its energy as well as its colour consistently reflects both the virtuosity and the charismatic personality of Evelyn Glennie. Taking the Advent plainsong of the title as his basis, he reflects in his continuous 26-minute sequence the theological implications behind the period between Advent and Easter. The five contrasted sections are in a sort of arch form, with the longest and slowest section in the middle. The very close of the work brings a crescendo of chimes intended to reflect the joy of Easter in the Catholic service and the celebration of the Resurrection. In this superb recording the orchestra as well as Evelyn Glennie play with both brilliance and total commitment, if not with quite the extra thrill that at the end is experienced in live performances. In the fill-up works – brief pieces marked by the same dramatic intensity – MacMillan himself as conductor inspires strong, positive performances from various groups of SCO players. With first-rate, atmospheric sound – *Veni, veni, Emmanuel* recorded in Usher Hall, Edinburgh, the rest in City Hall, Glasgow – this is an outstanding first issue on BMG's Catalyst label.

The Confession of Isobel Gowdie; Tryst
*** Koch/Schwann Dig. 3-1050-2 [id.]. BBC Scottish SO, Maksymiuk.

Inspired by the horrific execution in 1662 of Isobel Gowdie, tortured into confessing herself a witch, MacMillan has used the story as a metaphor for twentieth-century witch-hunting, including what he sees as resurgent fascism today. The result is rather like Vaughan Williams's *Tallis fantasia* updated and then invaded by Stravinsky's *Rite of spring*. The other piece on the disc, *Tryst* – marginally longer at 28 minutes – has similar qualities. In juxtaposition it emerges as the obverse of *Isobel Gowdie*, similarly a massive single movement in arch form. This time the music works from violence at the beginning and end to a long slow meditation in the middle, again with echoes of ecclesiastical chant a basic element. Maksymiuk proves a dedicated interpreter.

(i) *Seven last words from the Cross* (for choir and string orchestra); (ii) *Cantos sagrados* (for choir and organ).
(Y/B) *** RCA Catalyst Dig. 09026 68125-2 [id.]. Polyphony, with (i) LCO, composer; (ii) Christopher Bowers-Broadbent.

Seven last words from the Cross is a modern choral counterpart of Haydn's masterpiece. On one level it is just another of the slow-moving, easily mellifluous expressions of religious devotion that have had such spectacular success on CD. Each of these seven movements for chorus and strings intensifies each message from the Cross in dramatic contrasts and illustration. In four of them the title-words are amplified by liturgical texts in Latin or English, with the layering of musical ideas matching that of the words. Consistently they bring out the meaning so as to make one share Christ's suffering. *Cantos sagrados* illustrates the layering device again. In each of the three movements he juxtaposes poems by Spanish-American authors (in translation) alongside traditional Latin texts, setting the violence and tragedy of political persecution against the consolations of faith. So the last and most poignant of the three, about a firing-squad, resolves on the words, ever gentler, of one of the executioners, 'Forgive me, *companero.*' The idiom is clear and approachable, but hardly conventional. The performances, vividly recorded, are electrifying, with the players of the London Chamber Orchestra and the organist Christopher Bowers-Broadbent (in *Cantos sagrados*), as well as the fine singers of Stephen Layton's group, Polyphony, consistently inspired by the music and its composer-conductor. Characteristically, MacMillan's notes are terse, clear and helpful.

Maconchy, Elizabeth (born 1907)

Concertinos Nos. 1 (1945); 2 (1984).
*** Hyperion Dig. CDA 66634 [id.]. Thea King, ECO, Wordsworth – ARNOLD: *Clarinet concertos* etc.;
     BRITTEN: *Clarinet concerto movement.* ***

The two Maconchy *Concertinos*, each in three movements and under ten minutes long, have a character-istic terseness, sharp and intense, that runs no risk whatever of seeming short-winded. Not only Thea King but the ECO under Barry Wordsworth bring out the warmth as well as the rhythmic drive, as in the other attractive works on the disc.

String quartets Nos. 1–4.
*** Unicorn Dig. DKPCD 9080 [id.]. Hanson Qt.

String quartets Nos. 5–8.
*** Unicorn Dig. DKPCD 9081 [id.]. Bingham Qt.

String quartets Nos. 9–13.
(N) *** Unicorn Dig. DKPCD 9082 [id.]. Mistry Qt.

All these works testify to the quality of Maconchy's mind and her inventive powers. She speaks of the quartet as 'an impassioned argument', and there is no lack of either in these finely wrought and compelling pieces. Even if there is not the distinctive personality of a Bartók or a Britten, her music is always rewarding. Though the playing may occasionally be wanting in tonal finesse, both groups play with total commitment and are well recorded.

Madetoja, Leevi (1887–1947)

Symphonies Nos. 1 in F, Op. 29; 2 in E flat, Op. 35.
*** Chandos Dig. CHAN 9115 [id.]. Iceland SO, Petri Sakari.

Sibelius had only three pupils: Leevi Madetoja, Toivo Kuula and Bengt de Törne. Madetoja was the most important, and his three symphonies and the opera, *Pohjalaisia*, are well worth investigating. Apart from Sibelius himself, the *First Symphony* is indebted to various contemporaries; there is a dash of Strauss and of the Russian post-nationalists, a touch of Reger and, above all, of the French. The *Second Symphony* is an almost exact contemporary of Sibelius's *Fifth* and is expertly fashioned and appealing. The slow movement is very Sibelian, but all the same there are distinctive accents too. Petri Sakari is a first-rate exponent of these pieces and he secures an excellent response from his Icelandic players. The Chandos recording is very naturally balanced and difficult to flaw.

Symphony No. 3 in A, Op. 55; Huvinäytelmäalkusoitto (Comedy overture), *Op. 53; Okon Fuoko: suite No. 1, Op. 58; Pohjalainen sara (The Ostrobothnians): suite, Op. 52.*
*** Chandos Dig. CHAN 9036 [id.]. Iceland SO, Petri Sakari.

Symphony No. 3; Okon Fuoko: suite, Op. 58; Pohjolaisia suite, Op. 52.
(Y/B) *** Finlandia Dig. 4509-96867-2 [id.]. Finnish RSO, Saraste.

The *Third Symphony* is both Finnish, in its modality and melancholy, and Gallic, in its clarity of line and elegant orchestration. Its only failing, perhaps, is in its finale where invention flags a little but otherwise it is a first-rate score which ought to enjoy wide appeal. So, too, should the Chandos coup-lings, the delightfully high-spirited and attractive *Comedy Overture* and the imaginative suites. The Iceland orchestra give dedicated and persuasive accounts of both scores.

Jukka-Pekka Saraste's CD with the Finnish Radio Symphony Orchestra comes into direct competition with the Chandos issue from the Iceland Symphony Orchestra and Petri Sakari. The opera *Pohjolaisia* (*The Ostrobothnians*) and the ballet-pantomime *Okon Fuoko*, shows a strong feeling for colour and atmosphere. The performances and recording are both good and there is no reason to deny them a three-star rating. All the same, Sakari gets more imaginative and sensitive performances from his Reykjavik forces, and his disc has the added and important bonus of offering the delightful *Comedy Overture* as well. Where a choice between the two is presented, do not hesitate – go for the Chandos version.

The Ostrobothnians (Pohjalaisa) (opera in 3 Acts).
*** Finlandia 511002 (2). Hynninen, Erkkila, Lokka, Finnish Nat. Op. Ch. & O, Panula.

Madetoja's opera is an adaptation by the composer himself of a play by Artturi Järviluoma. The setting is the western Finnish plains of Ostrobothnia (which Madetoja knew well) and its central theme is the Bothnian farmer's love of personal liberty and his abhorrence of all authoritarian restraints. The nationalist tone of the original play was prompted by the growing Russification of Finland in the period leading up to and including the First World War. The opera is interspersed with humorous elements that lighten the mood and lend the work variety. Madetoja's language is not ahead of its time: it springs from much the same soil as most Scandinavian post-nationalists. However, the score makes often imaginative use of folk material, and Madetoja's sense of theatre and lyrical gift are in good evidence. Although it is unlikely to find a place on the international opera circuit, *Pohjalaisa* is a good work that well rewards attention, and this 1975 performance has the benefit of excellent teamwork from the soloists, and keen and responsive playing from the orchestra. The analogue recording is very good indeed.

Magalhães, Filipe de (1571–1652)

Missa O Soberana luz; Motets: *Commissa mea pavesco; Vidi aquam.*
(N) (BB) *** Naxos Dig. 8.553310 [id.]. Ars Nova, Bo Holten – CARDOSO; LOBO *Motets.* ***

Filipe de Magalhães was the youngest of the three great Portuguese composers who all became pupils of Manuel Mendes (*c.* 1547–1605) at Evora in eastern Portugal. The others, Cardoso and Lobo, are also represented in this outstanding concert, but Magalhães was reputedly the favourite pupil. One can see why, listening to his highly individual writing in both the Mass *O Soberana luz* and the two hardly less memorable motets, *Vidi aquam* ('I beheld the water') and *Commissa mea pavesco* ('I tremble at my sins') with its instantly poignant opening. The flowing perfection of the linear writing and the imaginative contrasts of tempo between sections of the Mass are striking enough, but the ravishing beauty of the chorale-like, 'harmonized' passages is even more remarkable. In the Mass the *Sanctus* soars radiantly and the lovely *Benedictus* is equally affecting, only to be capped by the *Agnus Dei*. The Danish perform-ances are wonderfully eloquent and the recording, made at Kasterskirken, Copenhagen, has an ideal ambience and is beautifully clear.

Mahler, Gustav (1860–1911)

Symphonies Nos. 1–9.
(B) *** Decca Dig./Analogue 430 804-2 (10). Buchanan, Zakai, Chicago Ch. (in No. 2); Dernesch, Ellyn Children's Ch., Chicago Ch. (in No. 3); Te Kanawa (in No. 4); Harper, Popp, Augér, Minton, Watts, Kollo, Shirley-Quirk, Talvela, V. Boys' Ch., V. State Op. Ch. & Singverein (in No. 8); Chicago SO, Solti.

Symphonies Nos. 1–9; 10 (Adagio).
(B) **(*) Ph. 442 050-2 (10). Concg. O, Haitink (with Ameling, Heynis & Netherlands R. Ch. in No. 2; Forrester, Netherlands R. Ch. & St Willibrord Boys' Ch. in No. 3; Ameling in No. 4; Cotrubas, Harper, Van Bork, Finnila, Dieleman, Cochran, Prey, Sotin, Amsterdam Choirs in No. 8).

Symphonies Nos. 1–10.
(M) **(*) DG 435 162-2 (13) [id.]. Hendricks, Ludwig, Wittek, M. Price, Blegen, Zeumer, Baltsa, Schmidt, Reigel, Prey, Van Dam, Brooklyn Boys' Ch., Westminster Ch., N Y Choral Artists, V. Boys' Ch., V. Singverein, V. State Op. Ch., Concg. O, NYPO, or VPO, Bernstein.

Symphonies Nos. 1–10; (i) *Kindertotenlieder.*
(B) ** Sony Dig. S14K 48198 (14) [id.]. Marton, Norman, Battle, Sweet, Coburn, Quivar, Fassenbaender, Leech, Nimsgern, Estes, V. Boys' Ch., V. State Op. Konzertvereinigung, Schönberg Ch.; (i) Baltsa; VPO, Maazel.

Solti's achievement in Mahler has been consistent and impressive, and this reissue is a formidable bargain that will be hard to beat. Nos. 1–4 and 9 are digital recordings, Nos. 5–8 are digitally remastered analogue. Solti draws stunning playing from the Chicago Symphony Orchestra, often pressed to great virtuosity, which adds to the electricity of the music-making; if his rather extrovert approach to Mahler means that deeper emotions are sometimes understated, there is no lack of involvement; and his fiery energy and commitment often carry shock-waves in their trail. All in all, an impressive achievement.

It is a measure of Bernstein's greatness as a Mahler interpreter and the electricity he consistently conveys in these edited live recordings that, despite obvious shortcomings, they so readily add up to more than the sum of their parts. The wilfulness of some of the readings, the heaviness of underlining, the exaggeratedly slow speeds, notably in Nos. 3 and 9, even seem to enrich the total experience. This is a personal statement by one great musician on another, and represents a monumental achievement.

Haitink's set of Mahler *Symphonies* comes at bargain price and offers characteristically refined and well-balanced Philips recording. The performances bring consistently fine playing from the Concertgebouw Orchestra, but Haitink is not by nature an extrovert Mahlerian. While he is always sensitive and thoughtful – and this works well enough in Nos. 1 (his earlier recording is included) and 4 (with Elly Ameling a freshly appealing soloist) and they have an attractive simplicity of approach – Nos. 2 and 8 lack the necessary sense of occasion, and No. 8 also needs greater overall grip and a more expansive recording. No. 5 is fresh and direct (the *Adagietto* a little cool) but No. 6 has more refinement than fire. The finest of the set are the deeply satisfying accounts of No. 3 (with fine contributions from both Maureen Forrester and the choristers) and the finely wrought and intensely convincing perform- ance of No. 7. However, the series is capped by an outstanding performance of No. 9. Here Haitink is at his most inspirational and the last movement has a unique concentration, with its slow tempo main- tained to create the greatest intensity of feeling. As usual from Philips, the original recordings are consistently enhanced by the CD transfers, and only No. 8 is technically disappointing.

Maazel's cycle of the Mahler symphonies with the Vienna Philharmonic brings generally broad, spa- cious readings, digitally recorded and generally well played. Yet these studio performances tend not to convey the full dramatic impact of these massive works, as they might have done with an audience in the concert-hall. When they are considered as a cycle, that reservation becomes all the more noticeable. On 14 discs, even at bargain price it is not an inexpensive package, even though the recorded sound is generally very impressive. The pick of the set is the *Fourth* and that shows Maazel at his most inspir- ational. Apart from No. 8 these recordings are not now available separately.

Symphonies Nos. 1–4.
(M) **(*) EMI CMS7 64471-2 (4). Mathis, Soffel (in *No. 2*); LPO Ch. (in *Nos. 2 & 3*); Wenkel, Southend Boys' Ch. (*in No. 3*); Lucia Popp (*in No. 4*), LPO, Klaus Tennstedt.

Tennstedt's complete Mahler cycle is offered, spread over three separate mid-priced boxes, and will be a perfect antidote for those who find Solti's view of Mahler over-intense to the point of neurosis and the Chicago sound too massively voluptuous and brightly lit. No. 1 – the first to be recorded, in Abbey Road in 1977 – sets the style of Tennstedt's approach, with textures fresh and neat, the opening evoca- tion of spring comparatively gentle and the style of phrasing less moulded than we have come to expect. The precision and directness, however, do not preclude coaxing use of rubato in the slow movement, while the big string melody in the finale (which comes after a powerfully dramatic opening) is both spacious and passionate at its climax. The analogue recording is first class, warm and vividly coloured and transferred admirably. In the *Resurrection Symphony*, however, most Mahlerians will prefer a more tinglingly dramatic performance than this, though Tennstedt's account is consistently dedicated, and especially so in the finale, conveying Mahlerian certainties in the light of day, underplaying neurotic tensions. The digital recording is excellent. No. 3, with its arrestingly powerful introduction, is one of the finest of the cycle. Tennstedt gives an eloquent reading, spaciousness underlined, with measured tempi. With Ortrud Wenkel a fine soloist and the Southend Boys adding lusty freshness to the bell music in the fifth movement, this performance with its movingly noble finale is very impressive, again splen- didly recorded, digitally. No. 4 is hardly less successful. Again the reading conveys spaciousness and strength, yet Tennstedt's agreeably light touch in the outer movements brings an innocence entirely in keeping with this most endearing of the Mahler symphonies. He makes the argument seamless in his easy transitions of speed, yet here he never deliberately adopts a coaxing, overtly charming manner, and in that he is followed most beautifully by Lucia Popp, the pure-toned soloist in the finale. The peak of the work as Tennstedt presents it lies in the long slow movement, here taken very slowly and intensely.

The 1982 digital recording, made in the Kingsway Hall, is among EMI's finest, full and well balanced.

Symphony No. 1 in D (Titan).
(M) *** Decca 417 701-2 [id.]. LSO, Solti.
*** DG Dig. 429 228-2 [id.]. Philh. O, Sinopoli.
(Y/B) *** DG Dig. 431 769-2 [id.]. BPO, Claudio Abbado.
(M) *** Unicorn UKCD 2012. LSO, Horenstein.
(N) (BB) *(*) Tring Dig. TRP 029 [id.]. RPO, Yuri Simonov.

(i) *Symphony No. 1 in D (Titan); (ii) Symphony No. 10: Adagio.*
(N) (M) ** DG Dig. 445 565-2 [id.]. (i) Chicago SO; (ii) VPO; Abbado.

The London Symphony Orchestra under Solti play Mahler's *First* like no other orchestra. They catch the magical opening with a singular evocative quality, at least partly related to the peculiarly character-istic blend of wind timbres, and throughout there is wonderfully warm string-tone. The remastering for CD has improved definition without losing the recording's bloom.

Sinopoli's, too, is a warmly satisfying reading, passionately committed, with refined playing from the Philharmonia. The sound is rich and refined to match.

Abbado's Berlin reading, like others in his Mahler series, was recorded live and, though one or two coughs intrude, the sound is fresh and full, bringing out the beauty and clarity of the Berlin strings. Though Abbado occasionally exaggerates the pointing of rhythms and speed-changes (as in the Laendler), the high voltage of the whole performance makes it most compelling, if not an obvious first choice.

Horenstein's version has a freshness and concentration which put it in a special category among the many rival accounts. Fine recording from the end of the 1960s, though the timpani is balanced rather too close.

Abbado's alternative, Chicago reading of the *First Symphony* is consistently well paced and recorded in impressive digital sound in 1981. By rights it should be an easy first choice – yet he misses some of the natural tension which should communicate naturally from such music-making. In the *Wunderhorn* inspirations of the first two movements, too rarely does the music smile. The funeral march of the slow movement is wonderfully hushed, more spontaneous-sounding than the rest, with superb playing from the Chicago orchestra. The *Adagio* from the *Tenth*, recorded four years later, was taken from a live concert. However, Abbado is not a conductor who seems to benefit greatly from such a choice. The microphones are comparatively close, the sound is refined, but there is surprisingly little feeling of a live occasion, although the beauty of the Vienna string-playing is never in doubt.

Simonov's performance is nothing if not impulsive, and its ethos is Slavic rather than German, espe-cially in the slow movement. The peasant dance of the second movement is forcefully unidiomatic. In the outer movements there are enormously dramatic contrasts. In the first, Simonov holds back until the coda, then unleashes an explosive fortissimo, and he does the same thing twice in the finale. The free-running adrenalin cannot be doubted and there is a thrilling contribution from the RPO brass, but the result is too idiosyncratic for general recommendation despite the fine playing and spectacular digital sound.

Symphony No. 1 in D (with Blumine).
(Y/B) **(*) HM Dig. HMU 907118-2 [id.]. Florida PO, Judd.
(Y/B) ** EMI Dig. CDC7 54647-2 [id.]. CBSO, Rattle.

James Judd demonstrates the virtuoso qualities of the Florida Philharmonic in a warm, well-pointed, spontaneous-sounding performance, slightly marred by a slow and rather heavy reading of the second-movement Laendler, which yet includes a most delicate account of the central Trio. The atmospheric recording sets the orchestra at a slight distance, which may take away some of the bite but enhances the beauty of the string-tone, not least in a dedicated performance of *Blumine*, which comes as a supple-ment after the symphony.

Recorded live in Symphony Hall, Birmingham, Rattle's account with the CBSO is rather lacking in the spontaneity one expects. Speed-changes in the first movement sound self-conscious, as do the exagger-ations of dotted rhythms, as in the Laendler second movement. It remains an acceptable reading, well recorded, but hardly matches Rattle's achievement in other Mahler recordings. As a preface to the main work, the *Blumine* movement, which Mahler excised from the original version of the symphony, is given with a freshness and spontaneity that rather shows up the rest.

Symphony No. 1 in D min.; (i) Lieder eines fahrenden Gesellen.
(Y/B) *** Teldec/Warner Dig. 9031 74868-2 [id.]. (i) Håkan Hagegård; NYPO, Masur.
(B) **(*) DG 439 446-2 [id.]. Bav. RSO, Kubelik, (i) with Dietrich Fischer-Dieskau.

Masur's live recording offers a fresh, unsentimental reading of the symphony with the generous and apt coupling of the related song-cycle, *Lieder eines fahrenden Gesellen*, all very well recorded with fine presence and atmosphere. The New York Philharmonic is in outstanding form, with crisp ensemble and clean attack. Masur underplays the irony in such characterful passages as the 'Jewish wedding' episode of the slow movement, but then allows himself a spaciously moulded account of the great melody in the finale, which contrasts with his bold, swaggering view of the main sections. Håkan Hagegård, balanced well forward, gives a clear, firm reading of the cycle, bringing word-meaning out into sharp focus. There may be even finer accounts of the symphony available, but the present coupling is still very much worth considering.

On DG Classikon, Kubelik gives an intensely poetic reading. He is here at his finest in Mahler and though, as in later symphonies, he is sometimes tempted to choose a tempo on the fast side, the result could hardly be more glowing. The rubato in the slow funeral march is most subtly handled. In its bargain CD reissue the quality is a little dry in the bass and the violins have lost some of their warmth, but there is no lack of body. In the *Lieder eines fahrenden Gesellen* the sound is fuller, with more atmospheric bloom. No one quite rivals Fischer-Dieskau in these songs, and this is a very considerable bonus, especially at bargain price.

Symphonies Nos. (i) *1;* (ii) *2 (Resurrection).*
(N) (B) *** Decca Double 448 921-2 (2) [id.]. (ii) Harper, Watts, London Symphony Ch.; LSO, Solti.
(M) ** Sony SM2K 47573 (2) [id.]. (i) NYPO; (ii) J. Baker, S. Armstrong, Edinburgh Festival Ch., LSO; Bernstein.

Solti's 1964 LSO account of No. 2 remains a demonstration of the outstanding results Decca were securing with analogue techniques at that time, although on CD the brilliance of the fortissimos may not suit all ears. Helen Watts is wonderfully expressive, while the chorus has a rapt intensity that is the more telling when the recording perspectives are so clearly delineated. Coupled with his outstanding version of No. 1, it makes a genuine bargain at Double Decca price.

Bernstein's earlier (1966) account of the *First Symphony* is an excellent, red-blooded version but, when competition is so intense in this work, it falls below a top recommendation because of the close-up (originally CBS) sound. Similarly the *Resurrection Symphony*, recorded in Ely Cathedral in September 1973 and concluded in George Watson's College, Edinburgh, a few months later, is far too badly balanced for the discs to have a general recommendation. The performance is idiosyncratic but deeply felt and has superb contributions from the two soloists, not to mention the chorus and the orchestra.

Symphonies Nos. (i) *1 (Titan);* (ii) *2 (Resurrection);* (iii) *Lieder eines fahrenden Gesellen.*
(N) (M) *** Sony SMK 64447 (2) [id.]. (i) Columbia SO; (ii) Emilia Cundari, Maureen Forrester, Westminster Ch., NYPO; (iii) Mildred Miller, Columbia SO; Bruno Walter.

As part of the initial volume of Sony's Bruno Walter Edition, his stereo recordings of the *First* and *Second Symphonies* are now economically coupled on a pair of discs together with the *Lieder eines fahrenden Gesellen*. The *First Symphony* was recorded in Hollywood in 1961 with a specially assembled orchestra of first-class musicians; in its newly remastered form the recording sounds better than ever, richer and fuller at the bottom end of the spectrum, and the dynamic range seemingly extended. The ambient warmth emphasizes the Viennese character of the reading, with glowing detail – especially during the evocative opening section – and with the final apotheosis drawn out spaciously and given added breadth and impact. Even more than the *First Symphony*, the 1958 set of the *Resurrection Symphony* is among the gramophone's indispensable classics. In the first movement there is a restraint and in the second a gracefulness which provide a strong contrast with a conductor like Solti. The recording was one of the last Walter made in New York – in Carnegie Hall – before his series with the Columbia Symphony Orchestra; it was remarkably good for its period and the dynamic range is surprisingly wide. In the newest remastering, detail registers more clearly; while the sound is not sumptuous, in the finale the balance with the voices still gives the music an ethereal resonance, with the closing section thrillingly expansive. In the 1960 recording of the *Lieder eines fahrenden Gesellen* the superb orchestral detail glows as never before. Mildred Miller is perhaps not an inspirational soloist, but she sings well enough, and Walter ensures that the performance is dramatically alive. The tangibility of both voice and orchestra is striking and the balance is first class.

Symphonies Nos. (i) *1 in D (Titan);* (ii) *10: Adagio* (arr. Krenet, ed. Jokl).
(B) **(*) Sony Dig./Analogue SBK 53259 [id.]. (i) NYPO, Mehta; (ii) Cleveland O, Szell.

Mehta's Sony/CBS digital version of the *First Symphony*, successfully recorded in the Avery Fisher Hall in 1980, is far preferable to his later, Israeli, Decca CD. It has no less urgency and drama, but here Mehta's Viennese training comes out in the lilt of the Ländler second movement while his freely expressive rubato in the third, after the dark opening, is very appealing. While the strings lack a genuine pianissimo in the slow introduction, detail is attractively colourful and the reading overall has undoubted spontaneity. Many will also welcome the reissue of Szell's 1958 recording of the *Adagio* from the *Tenth Symphony* in Jokl's edition. Although today we are used to hearing the whole work in Deryck Cooke's completion, the Cleveland orchestral playing is stylish as well as eloquent. The sound, too, is very good.

Symphony No. 2 in C min. (Resurrection).
⚜ *** EMI CDS7 47962-8 (2) [Ang. CDCB 47962]. Augér, J. Baker, CBSO Ch., CBSO, Rattle.
*** Ph. Dig 438 935-2 (2) [id.]. McNair, Van Nes, Ernst Senff Ch., BPO, Haitink.
(M) *** EMI CDM7 69662-2 [id.]. Schwarzkopf, Rössl-Majdan, Philh. Ch. & O, Klemperer.
(M) *** Chandos CHAN 6595/6 [id.]. Lott, Hamari, Latvian State Ac. Ch., Oslo Philharmonic Ch., Oslo PO, Jansons.
(B) *** Double Decca 440 615-2 (2) [id.]. Ileana Cotrubas, Christa Ludwig, V. State Op. Ch., Mehta – SCHMIDT: *Symphony No. 4.* ***
*** DG 439 953-2 (2) [id.]. Studer, Meyer, Arnold Schoenberg Ch., VPO, Abbado.
(Y/B) (M) **(*) Decca Dig. 443 350-2 (2). Ziesak, Hellekant, San Francisco Ch. & SO, Blomstedt.
(M) **(*) Carlton Dig. DPCD 910 (2) [MCA MCAD 11011]. Valente, Forrester, London Symphony Ch., LSO, Kaplan.

(i) *Symphony No. 2 in C min. (Resurrection);* (ii) *Lieder eines fahrenden Gesellen;* (iii) *Lieder und Gesang aus der Jugendzeit:* excerpts.
(N) (M) *** DG Dig. 445 587-2 (2) [id.]. (i) Fassbaender, Plowright, Philh. Ch.; (ii) Fassbaender; (iii) Weikl; Philh. O, Sinopoli.

Simon Rattle's reading of Mahler's *Second* is among the very finest records he has yet made, superlative in the breadth and vividness of its sound and with a spacious reading which in its natural intensity unerringly sustains generally slow, steady speeds to underline the epic grandeur of Mahler's vision. The playing of the CBSO is inspired. The choral singing, beautifully balanced, is incandescent, while the heart-felt singing of the soloists, Arleen Augér and Dame Janet Baker, is equally distinguished and characterful.

Bernard Haitink's 1993 version with the Berlin Philharmonic also brings one of his very finest Mahler recordings, weighty and bitingly powerful. The sound of the Berlin Philharmonic in the Philharmonie is caught with a vividness and sense of presence rarely matched. Above all Haitink conveys the tensions of a live occasion, even though this was a studio performance, leading up to a glorious apotheosis in the Judgment Day finale. The soloists are outstanding, and the chorus immaculately expands from rapt, hushed singing to incandescent splendour. Outstanding in every way, this can be placed alongside Rattle's superb CBSO set.

Sinopoli's version of the *Resurrection* has the additional advantage that the two CDs also include two Mahler song-cycles: the *Lieder eines fahrenden Gesellen*, beautifully sung by Brigitte Fassbaender, and the *Songs of Youth 'aus der Jugendzeit'*, skilfully orchestrated by Harold Byrns and well sung by Bernd Weikl, bringing extra anticipations of the mature *Des Knaben Wunderhorn* songs. In the symphony Sinopoli has meticulous concern for detail, yet he still conveys consistently the irresistible purposefulness of Mahler's writing, fierce at high dramatic moments and intense too, rarely relaxed, in moments of meditation, with *Urlicht* beautifully sung with warmth and purity by Fassbaender. The recorded sound, though not quite as full and vivid as that for Rattle, is among the most brilliant of any in this work. Rosalind Plowright is a pure and fresh soprano soloist, contrasting well with the equally firm, earthier-toned mezzo of Fassbaender.

Klemperer's performance – one of his most compelling on record – comes on a single CD, and the remastered sound is impressively full and clear, with the fullest sense of spectacle in the closing pages. The first movement, taken at a fairly fast tempo, is intense and earth-shaking, and though in the last movement some of Klemperer's speeds are designedly slow, he conveys supremely well the mood of transcendent heavenly happiness in the culminating passage, with chorus and soloists themselves singing like angels.

The crisp attack at the start of the opening funeral march sets the pattern for an exceptionally refined and alert reading of the *Resurrection Symphony* from Jansons and his Oslo orchestra. During the first four movements, this may seem a lightweight reading, but the extra resilience and point of rhythm bring out the dance element in Mahler's *Knaben Wunderhorn* inspirations rather than ruggedness or rusticity, while at the finale the whole performance erupts in an overwhelming outburst for the vision of Resurrection. That transformation is intensified by the breathtakingly rapt and intense account of the song, *Urlicht*, which precedes it. In the finale, power goes with precision and meticulous observance of markings, when even Mahler's surprising diminuendo on the final choral cadence is observed. With the Oslo Choir joined by singers from Jansons's native Latvia, the choral singing is heartfelt, to crown a version which finds a special place even among the many distinguished readings on a long list.

Zubin Mehta sounds a different conductor, not at all like his NYPO self, when he is drawing as sympathetic a Mahler performance as this from the Vienna Philharmonic. The refinement of the playing, recorded with vivid clarity and warmth, puts this among the finest versions of the symphony. The second movement has *grazioso* delicacy and, though the third movement begins with the sharpest possible timpani strokes, there is no hint of brutality, and the *Wunderhorn* rhythms have a delightful lilt. After that comes *Urlicht*, pianissimo in D flat after the Scherzo's final cadence in C minor, and Christa Ludwig is in superb form. The enormous span of the finale brings clarity as well as magnificence, with fine placing of soloists and chorus and glorious atmosphere in such moments as the evocation of birdsong over distant horns, as heavenly a moment as Mahler ever conceived. The CD transfer has brightened the analogue sound somewhat, but there is still plenty of ambient warmth.

Abbado's recording with the Vienna Philharmonic was made live in 1992 in the Musikverein, offering a predictably fine, beautifully paced performance, but one that rather suffers, compared both with his Berlin version of the *Fifth*, recorded live six months later, and with Haitink's Berlin account of the *Second*, issued simultaneously. The Vienna Philharmonic's ensemble is less refined than that of the Berliners, even in the strings, and the sound is less immediate and involving. Tensions are not helped when the audience is so noisy. Yet with powerful soloists and a superb choir, it is still a strong reading.

Very well recorded in full and detailed sound and played with fine point and polish, Blomstedt's San Francisco version comes in a package of two discs at a special price – originally two for the price of one – and so makes a good bargain. The dramatic bite and rhythmic point go with keen control of tension, so that Blomstedt's slow speed for the second-movement *Andante* and fast speed for the third-movement Laendler (almost a waltz) are well sustained. In the many sections of the outer movements too, Blomstedt maintains concentration, even if at the very end of the Judgement Day scene his is an urgent and impulsive rather than a weighty reading or one with a sense of occasion. Excellent choral and solo singing.

Under Gilbert Kaplan the LSO plays with a biting precision and power to shame many an effort on record under a world-renowned conductor. Added to that, the sound is exceptionally brilliant and full, bringing home the impact of the big dramatic moments, which are what stand out in the performance. Valente and Forrester, as well as the fine chorus, sing with a will, crowning a performance that is never less than enjoyable, thanks above all to the playing and to superb sound.

Symphony No. 3 in D min.
*** Ph. Dig. 432 162-2 (2) [id.]. Jard van Nes, Tölz Boys' Ch., Ernst-Senff Ch., BPO, Haitink.
*** DG Dig. 410 715-2 (2) [id.]. J. Norman, V. State Op. Ch., V. Boys' Ch., VPO, Abbado.
(M) *** Unicorn UKCD 2006/7 [id.]. Procter, Wandsworth School Boys' Ch., Amb. S., LSO, Horenstein.

(i) *Symphony No. 3. Kindertotenlieder.*
(Y/B) **(*) Chandos Dig. CHAN 9117/18 [id.]. Finnie, Royal Scottish O, Järvi; (i) with R. Scottish Ch. & Junior Ch.

(i) *Symphony No. 3;* (ii) *Kindertotenlieder; Des Knaben Wunderhorn: Das irdische Leben. 3 Ruckert Lieder: Ich atmet' einem linden Duft; Ich bin der Welt abhanden gekommen; Um Mitternacht.*
(M) *** Sony SM2K 47576 (2) [id.]. (i) Martha Lipton, Schola Cantorum Ch., Boys' Ch. of Church of Transfiguration; (ii) Jennie Tourel; NYPO, Bernstein.

Symphony No. 3; 5 Rückert Lieder.
(M) *** Sony M2K 44553 (2) [id.]. Janet Baker, London Symphony Ch., LSO, Tilson Thomas.

Michael Tilson Thomas inspires the orchestra to play with bite and panache in the bold, dramatic passages and to bring out the sparkle and freshness of the *Knaben Wunderhorn* ideas; but what crowns the performance is the raptness of his reading of the noble, hymn-like finale, hushed and intense, beautifully sustained. There is a formidable bonus in Dame Janet Baker's searching performances of the five *Rückert Lieder*. Excellent CBS sound, both warm and brilliant.

With the Berlin Philharmonic producing glorious sounds, recorded with richness and immediacy, Haitink conducts a powerful, spacious reading. It culminates in a glowing, concentrated account of the slow finale, which gives the whole work a visionary strength often lacking. The mystery of *Urlicht* is then beautifully caught by the mezzo soloist Jard van Nes.

With sound of spectacular range, Abbado's performance is sharply defined and deeply dedicated. The range of expression, the often wild mixture of elements in this work, is conveyed with extraordinary intensity, not least in the fine contributions of Jessye Norman and the two choirs. The recording has great presence and detail on CD.

Horenstein is at his most intensely committed. The manner is still very consistent in its simple dedication to the authority of the score and its rejection of romantic indulgence; but with an extra intensity the result has the sort of frisson-creating quality one knew from live Horenstein performances and the recording quality is both full and brilliant. Fine vocal contributions from Norma Procter, the Ambrosian Singers and the Wandsworth School Boys' Choir.

Bernstein's 1961 account of Mahler's *Third Symphony*, strong and passionate, has few of the stylistic exaggerations that sometimes overlaid his interpretations. Here his style in the slow movement is more heavily expressive than Horenstein's, but many will respond to his extrovert involvement. The remastered recording, made in New York's Manhattan Center, the venue of so many of the best of his early records, has added spaciousness and body in this very successful remastering for CD; it is rather less refined than the Unicorn sound but is better balanced. The vocal contributions from Martha Lipton and the two choirs contribute to the success of this venture and the generous Lieder coupling is well worth having, and Jennie Tourel is in excellent voice.

Järvi conducts a warmly expressive, spontaneous-sounding reading which brings out the joy behind Mahler's inspiration rather than any tragedy. This makes light of the epic qualities in this massive work. Though the ensemble of the Royal Scottish Orchestra is not as immaculate as that of some distinguished rivals, the bite of communication is always intense, helped by full, atmospheric Chandos recording. Järvi brings out the folk-like elements in the second and third movements, and Linda Finnie is a dedicated soloist in the hushed Nietzsche setting of the fourth movement, warm here rather than ominous; and she gives a felt, expressive reading of the *Kindertotenlieder*, beautifully shaded in the second song. This again concentrates on warmth rather than tragedy, with the storm of the final song rather underplayed and with Finnie's tight vibrato exaggerated at times by the microphone.

Symphony No. 4 in G.
(Y/B) *** DG Dig. 437 527-2 [id.]. Edita Gruberová, Philh. O, Sinopoli.
(M) *** EMI Dig. CD-EMX 2139; *TC-EMX 2139*. Felicity Lott, LPO, Welser-Möst.
(M) *** DG 419 863-2 [id.]. Edith Mathis, BPO, Karajan.
(M) *** EMI CDM5 65179-2 [id.]. Elly Ameling, Pittsburgh SO, Previn (with SCHUBERT: Lieder: *An die Musik;* (i) *Der Hirt auf dem Felsen; Ständchen* – Ameling, Irwin Gage or Joerg Demus; (i) with George Pieterson ***).
(Y/B) (BB) *** Naxos Dig. 8.550527 [id.]. Lynda Russell, Polish Nat. RSO, Antoni Wit.
*** Denon Dig. C37 7952 [id.]. Helen Donath, Frankfurt RSO, Inbal.
(Y/B) (BB) **(*) RCA Navigator 74321 21286-2. Lisa Della Casa, Chicago SO, Reiner – R. STRAUSS: *Burleske*. **(*)
(Y/B) (M) ** Ph. 442 394-2 [id.]. Elly Ameling, Concg. O, Haitink.

(i) *Symphony No. 4 in G;* (ii) *Lieder eines fahrenden Gesellen.*
⊛ (B) *** Sony SBK 46535; *SBT 46535* [id.]. (i) Judith Raskin, Cleveland O, Szell; (ii) Frederica von Stade, LPO, Andrew Davis.

(i) *Symphony No. 4 in G;* (ii) *Lieder und Gesang aus der Jugendzeit.*
(N) (M) (***) Sony mono SMK 64450 [id.]. Desi Halban; (i) NYPO, Bruno Walter; (ii) Walter (piano).

George Szell's 1966 record of Mahler's *Fourth* represented his partnership with the Cleveland Orchestra at its highest peak and the digital remastering for CD brings out the very best of the original recording. The performance remains uniquely satisfying: the music blossoms, partly because of the marvellous attention to detail (and the immaculate ensemble), but more positively because of the committed and radiantly luminous orchestral response to the music itself. In the finale Szell found the ideal soprano to match his conception. An outstanding choice, generously coupled. In contrast with most other recorded performances, Frederica von Stade insinuates a hint of youthful ardour into her highly enjoyable account of the *Wayfaring Lad* cycle.

Sinopoli's is a positive, characterful reading which in the first movement draws an extreme contrast between the clucking opening theme – brisker than usual – and the broadly lyrical second subject – played slowly with extreme tenutos. What keeps such disparate elements together is Sinopoli's concentration, which never lets the performance fall into routine, the feeling of a run-through. The rustic elements of the second-movement Laendler, not least the bright scordatura violin, are enhanced by a delicious lilt. Though at the opening of the slow movement Sinopoli's moulding draws attention to itself, this is a rapt performance, naturally sympathetic, and Gruberová at her sweetest amd freshest makes a charming soloist in the child-heaven finale, with Sinopoli jauntily exaggerating the dotted rhythms. Superb recording, as in the rest of the series.

Welser-Möst's outer movements are fresh and beautifully shaped, with Felicity Lott a youthful-sounding soloist, and the Laendler second movement clean-cut and crisp. It is the third movement *Adagio* that crowns the performance, hushed and intense from the start, with the emotional outbursts strongly controlled. At mid-price with excellent modern digital sound, spacious like the performance, it makes an outstanding mid-priced recommendation, a fine alternative to Szell.

Karajan's refined and poised, yet undoubtedly affectionate account remains among the finest versions of this lovely symphony, and Edith Mathis's sensitively composed contribution to the finale matches the conductor's meditative feeling. With glowing sound, this makes another outstanding mid-priced recommendation alongside Szell's renowned Cleveland CD.

Previn starts the first movement more slowly than usual, underlining the marked speed-changes very clearly, and the second movement is unusually light and gentle. But it is the spaciousness of the slow movement, at a very measured pace, that provides total fulfilment, followed by a light and playful account of the finale, with Ameling both sweet-toned and characterful. The 1978 recording, made in Heinz Hall, Pittsburgh, has fine depth and range. It was a happy idea then to give Elly Ameling three Schubert songs as encores. She sings *An die Musik* and *Ständchen* quite simply and is even more eloquent in *Der Hirt auf dem Felsen* ('The shepherd on the rock'). Here the contribution of the clarinet-tist, George Pieterson, is sensitive, if without any special magic.

Antoni Wit conducts a fresh, spontaneous-sounding reading, beautifully played and recorded, that can be warmly recommended at Naxos's bargain price. This is more enjoyable than many full-priced issues, with easy manners at well-chosen speeds, so that the rustic *Wunderhorn* element is sharply brought out. The flowing speed for the slow movement means that there is no suspicion of self-consciousness in the warm expressiveness. Lynda Russell is a pure-toned soprano soloist in the finale, both fresh and warm, with Wit giving a good lilt to the rhythm. Excellent sound, which gives a good bite and focus to the woodwind, so important in Mahler, though the Katowice horn favours a touch of East European tone.

There is a pastoral element in Inbal's approach all through, reflecting the *Wunderhorn* basis, and even the spacious slow movement is easily songful rather than ethereal. Helen Donath brings boyish, Hansel-like timbre to her solo in the finale.

Walter's glowingly radiant reading suffers from the fairly limited mono sound (especially at the climax of the slow movement). But the remastering of the 1945 recording has worked wonders, and orchestral textures are clear and yet warm. Desi Halban's contribution is refreshingly individual, dramatic as well as touching, and she is comparably impressive in the songs, which Walter accompanies discreetly at the piano. Her account of *Ich ging mit Lust durch einen grünen Wald* is enchanting.

Reiner's version was made – like most of his famous recordings – in Orchestra Hall, Chicago (in 1958). The recording has been digitally remastered, with great improvement to the sound, which remains brightly lit but has attractively vivid detail, naturally glowing within the acoustic bloom of the hall. The performance is wayward, but lovingly so; and everything Reiner does sounds spontaneous. There is a mercurial quality in the first movement and plenty of drama, too; the second is engagingly pointed but with a balancing warmth, the Viennese influence strong. The slow movement has striking intensity, with its rapt closing pages leading on gently to the finale in which Lisa della Casa, in ravishing voice, matches Reiner's mood.

Haitink's earlier, late-1960s Concertgebouw version is predictably well played and the recording has come up very well indeed on the mid-priced CD reissue. The performance is sober, but it has an attractive simplicity, and Elly Ameling matches Haitink's approach in her serene contribution to the finale. Although it lacks drama, this is an easy version to live with; but the later, digital, Concertgebouw account with Roberta Alexander is preferable, a most winning performance, but it is currently withdrawn. In his latest version (Philips 434 123-2) Haitink conducts the Berlin Philharmonic in a warm, highly polished reading that can hardly be faulted, except that it rather misses the innocent freshness lying behind this of all Mahler's symphonies. The child-heaven finale too is smoother than usual, with Sylvia McNair the light and boyish soloist. Full, well-balanced sound.

Symphony No. 5 in C sharp min.
*** DG Dig. 437 789-2 [id.]. BPO, Abbado.
(M) *** EMI Dig. CD-EMX 2164; *TC-EMX 2164*. RLPO, Mackerras.
❀ (M) *** EMI CDM7 64749-2 [id.]. New Philh. O, Barbirolli.
(N) (M) *** DG 447 450-2 [id.]. BPO, Karajan.
*** EMI Dig. CDC7 49888-2 [id.]. LPO, Tennstedt.
*** DG Dig. 415 476-2 [id.]. Philh. O, Sinopoli.
*** Denon Dig. CO 1088 [id.]. Frankfurt RSO, Inbal.
(N) (BB) **(*) RCA Navigator 74321 29249-2. Boston SO, Erich Leinsdorf.
(M) ** Sony SMK 47580 [id.]. NYPO, Bernstein.

(M) ** Carlton PCD 1033 [id.]. Symphonica of L., Wyn Morris.
(B) ** Belart 450 135-2. LAPO, Zubin Mehta.

Abbado's is an outstanding new version, recorded live in the Philharmonie, Berlin, with the dramatic tensions of a concert performance vividly captured. Abbado's view is clean-cut and taut, bringing out the high contrasts between movements, pointing rhythms not just precisely but with often-Viennese seductiveness. The great *Adagietto* is raptly done, wistful rather than openly romantic at a flowing tempo, and the *Wunderhorn* finale is at once refined and exuberant. With excellent sound, there are few versions to match this, presenting Abbado at his peak.

Mackerras in his well-paced reading sees the work as a whole, building each movement with total concentration. There is a thrilling culmination on the great brass chorale at the end, with polish allied to purposefulness. Barbirolli in his classic reading may find more of a tear-laden quality in the great *Adagietto*; but Mackerras, with fewer controversial points of interpretation and superb modern sound, makes an excellent first choice.

Barbirolli's famous 1969 version on any count is one of the greatest, most warmly affecting performances ever committed to disc, expansive, yet concentrated in feeling: the *Adagietto* is very moving. The recording was made in Watford Town Hall and has been remastered most successfully. A classic version, and still a fine bargain.

Karajan's 1973 recording (previously available on DG's bargain label) now reverts to mid-price as a 'Legendary Performance' in DG's series of 'Originals'. Karajan's characteristic emphasis on polish and refinement goes with sharpness of focus. His is at once one of the most beautiful and one of the most intense versions available, starting with an account of the first movement which brings more biting funeral-march rhythms than any rival. Radiant playing from the Berlin Philharmonic and full, atmospheric recording, made in the Berlin Jesus-Christus-Kirche. However, the CD transfer is very brightly lit and some softening of the brilliance on top is needed for complete comfort.

Tennstedt's later, digital recording of the *Fifth* was also made live, at the Festival Hall. The emotional tension of the occasion is vividly captured. As a Mahler interpretation, it is at once more daring and more idiosyncratic than Tennstedt's earlier, studio recording, but the tension is far keener. The experience hits one at full force.

Sinopoli's version draws the sharpest distinction between the dark tragedy of the first two movements and the relaxed *Wunderhorn* feeling of the rest. Sinopoli seems intent on not overloading the big melodies with excessive emotion. This comes out the more clearly in the central movements, where relaxation is the keynote, often with a pastoral atmosphere. The celebrated *Adagietto* brings a tenderly wistful reading, songful and basically happy, not tragic. Warmly atmospheric recording, not lacking brilliance, but not always ideally clear on detail.

Inbal brings out the *Wunderhorn* element in the *Fifth* very convincingly. He may not be as exciting as some rivals, but, with superb playing and beautifully balanced sound, full and atmospheric, it is an exceptionally sympathetic reading. The second and third movements, unusually relaxed, lead to an account of the *Adagietto* that is warmly songful yet hushed and sweet, while the finale conveys the happiness of pastoral ideas leading logically to a joyful, triumphant close.

Leinsdorf is predictably less gentle than some in the famous *Adagietto* – indeed he brings out its underlying neurosis – but elsewhere his directness makes for an unexpectedly strong and convincing result. The relentlessness adds to the strength and not to any sense of the music's byways being trampled over. The recording from 1963 has the advantage of warm Boston acoustics, and this characterful performance with first-class playing from the great Boston orchestra is the least expensive recommendable version of the Mahler *Fifth* in the catalogue, though it is by no means a first choice.

The *Adagietto* is the highlight of Bernstein's earlier performances, reissued on Sony. It brings a heady beauty so delicate that one holds one's breath. Elsewhere Bernstein's care for detail means that he never seems quite to plumb the depths of Mahler's inspiration. The first movement, for example, seems too careful, for all the virtuosity of the playing. The recording, too, made in the Avery Fisher Hall in 1963, is not entirely flattering. Fortunately he re-recorded the work digitally with the VPO for DG and this record – also at mid-price – is one of the very finest of his last series of records and includes an equally elegiac account of the *Adagietto* – the music he conducted at the funeral of President Kennedy.

Wyn Morris starts with a strikingly commanding account of the *Funeral march*, but then the second movement is more cautious with the ensemble less crisp than elsewhere. In the third movement Morris captures the Viennese lilt very winningly; he takes the *Adagietto* at a flowing tempo and the finale in a broad, expansive sweep, not quite as sharply focused as it might be. In many ways it is a sympathetic reading, but not consistent in its success. The recording is both atmospheric and brightly lit, not absolutely refined in its definition at climaxes.

Brilliant as the 1977 recording is of Mehta's Los Angeles version, and the playing too, yet it misses the natural warmth of expression that the same conductor found in his reading of No. 2 with the Vienna Philharmonic (see above). Most impressive is the virtuoso Scherzo, but in their different ways the opening Funeral march and the beautiful *Adagietto* both lack the inner quality which is essential if the faster movements are to be aptly framed. The animation of the finale is exaggerated by Mehta's very fast tempo, missing the *Wunderhorn* overtones of this most optimistic of Mahler's conclusions.

Symphonies Nos. 5; 9; 10 (Adagio).
(M) *** EMI CMS7 64481-2 (3). LPO, Klaus Tennstedt.

Rather like Barbirolli, Tennstedt takes a ripe and measured view of the *Fifth* and, though his account of the lovely *Adagietto* lacks the full tenderness of Barbirolli's (starting with a slightly intrusive balance for the harp), this is an outstanding performance, on the one hand thoughtful, on the other warm and expressive. The *Ninth* brings another performance of warmth and distinction, characteristically underlining nobility rather than any neurotic tension, so that the outer movements, spaciously drawn, have architectural grandeur. The second movement is gently done, and the third, crisp and alert, lacks just a little in adrenalin. The playing is excellent both here and in the *Adagio* of the *Tenth*, and the CD transfers are exemplary. These 1978/9 analogue recórdings were made at Abbey Road and the effect is full and spacious. A highly recommendable set.

Symphony No. 6 in A min.
*** DG 415 099-2 (2) [id.]. BPO, Karajan – *5 Rückert Lieder.* **(*)
(Y/B) *** DG Dig. 445 835-2 [id.]. VPO, Boulez.
(M) *** Sony SBK 47654 [id.]. Cleveland O, Szell.
*** Ph. Dig. 426 257-2 [id.]. BPO, Haitink – *Lieder eines fahrenden Gesellen.* ***
(Y/B) (B) *** Naxos Dig. 8.550529 (2) [id.]. Polish Nat. RSO (Katowice), Antoni Wit.
(Y/B) (B) *** Decca Double 444 871-2 (2) [id.]. Concg. O, Chailly – ZEMLINSKY: *Maeterlinck Lieder.* ***
(M) *** Unicorn UKCD 2024/5. Stockholm PO, Jascha Horenstein.
(M) **(*) Decca 425 040-2 [id.]. Chicago SO, Solti.
(N) (B) **(*) EMI forte CZS5 69349-2. New Philh. O, Barbirolli – R. STRAUSS: *Ein Heldenleben.* ***
(Y/B) (B) **(*) EMI CZS7 67816-2 (2). New Philh. O, Barbirolli – R. STRAUSS: *Metamorphosen.* **(*)
**(*) EMI Dig. CDS7 54047-2 [Ang. CDCB 54047]. CBSO, Simon Rattle.

With superlative playing from the Berlin Philharmonic, Karajan's reading of the *Sixth* is a revelation, above all in the slow movement, which emerges as one of the greatest of Mahler's slow movements, and the whole balance of the symphony is altered. Though the outer movements firmly stamp this as the darkest of the Mahler symphonies, in Karajan's reading their sharp focus makes them both compelling and refreshing. The superb DG recording, with its wide dynamics, adds enormously to the impact. Christa Ludwig's set of the *Five Rückert Songs* has been added as a bonus.

Boulez in his first Mahler symphony recording for DG conducts a performance of the most enigmatic symphony which in its power and sharpness of focus transcends almost any rival. Rarely if ever has the Vienna Philharmonic been recorded with such fullness and immediacy in the Musikvereinsaal as here. Boulez's control of speeds is masterful, never rushed, even though this is a performance squeezed on to a single disc, and the slow movement brings hushed, ravishingly beautiful playing of a refinement it would be hard to match. The finale is rugged and weighty, with crisp pointing of rhythms, making this an outstanding recommendation alongside Karajan who, on two discs, also includes Christa Ludwig's five *Rückert Lieder*. Though RL found this a performance observed rather than felt at white heat, EG was totally involved.

Szell's powerful outer movements are masterfully shaped and unerringly paced, with the second-movement scherzo beautifully sprung to bring out the grotesquerie. The *Andante moderato* then brings a uniquely delicate and moving account, hauntingly wistful, tender without a hint of sentimentality. The CD transfer gives a fuller, more atmospheric impression of what the orchestra sounded like in Severance Hall, Cleveland, than most of the studio recordings of the time. At budget price, squeezed on to a single disc, this is buried treasure and a fine counterpart to Szell's classic reading of Mahler's *Fourth*.

Haitink conducts a noble reading of this difficult symphony, underplaying the neurosis behind the inspiration, but, in his clean-cut concentration and avoidance of exaggeration, making the result the more moving in its degree of reticence, yet intensely committed. Jessye Norman's rich-toned account of *Lieder eines fahrenden Gesellen* makes a powerful bonus. Excellent sound, both full-blooded and refined.

The excellent quality of the Katowice Orchestra of Polish Radio is impressively demonstrated in all four movements of this difficult symphony. The ensemble can hardly be faulted, hardly less polished than that of Dohnányi's Cleveland Orchestra, and the full, atmospheric recording enhances that quality with string-sound that is fresh, radiant and full of bloom, thanks in part to the helpful acoustic. Wit conducts a spacious performance, clean and well sprung, with the varying moods sharply contrasted. Above all, he conveys the tensions behind the notes, with the beauty of the slow movement warmly conveyed with easy, unexaggerated rubato and with the strings coping confidently with the occasional controlled portamento. On two full discs it becomes less of a super-bargain than some Naxos issues, but it stands comparison with any rival.

Chailly's version with the Concertgebouw offers brilliant playing and spectacular sound in a reading remarkable for the broad, rugged approach in the outer movements. There is relentlessness in the slow speed for the first movement, with expressive warmth giving way to a square purposefulness, tense and effective. The third movement brings a comparably simple, direct approach at a genuine flowing *Andante*. In its open songfulness it rouses Wunderhorn echoes. Anyone fancying the unexpected but attractive Zemlinsky coupling need not hesitate.

In the first movement, Horenstein finds extra weight by taking a more measured tempo than most conductors. It is a sober reading that holds together with wonderful concentration, yet the slow movement brings the most persuasive rubato. The finale brings another broad, noble reading. Yet some will feel that 33 minutes is short measure for the second CD.

Solti draws stunning playing from the Chicago orchestra. The sessions were in March and April 1970, and this was the first recording he made with them after he took up his post as principal conductor; as he himself said, it represented a love-affair at first sight. The electric excitement of the playing confirms this, with brilliant, immediate but atmospheric sound. Solti's rather extrovert approach is here at its most impressive. His fast tempi may mean that he misses some of the deeper emotions, and the added brightness of the CD transfer perhaps emphasizes this, but it is still a very convincing and involving performance.

Barbirolli gives a characteristically expansive account of Mahler's *Sixth Symphony*, and there are many of the same fine qualities as in his version of the *Fifth*, recorded with the same orchestra a year later. But, particularly in the first movement, the slow tempo is allowed to drag a little, so that tension falls. Such wavering of concentration will not trouble everyone, but the 1967 Kingsway Hall recording has now lost some of its bloom. Moreover there is nothing like the same illusion of a live Barbirolli performance as there is with the *Fifth*. There is a choice of couplings, and the pairing with *Ein Heldenleben* is to be preferred as it has a superior CD transfer. The alternative brings one of the most beautiful performances of Strauss's *Metamorphosen* ever recorded; but again the sound is less full than on the original LPs.

At spacious speeds Rattle directs a thoughtful, finely detailed reading of what has become a favourite symphony for him. The performance yet lacks the electric tension which usually marks his work with this orchestra, with ensemble less crisp. One admires without being involved in the way Mahler demands, even in Rattle's tender and hushed account of the slow movement, which he places second in the scheme instead of third, following Mahler's last thoughts on the work rather than what is published. The sound is full and warm, but in its diffuseness it undermines tension further compared with the finest versions.

Symphonies Nos. 6, 7 & 8.

(M) *** EMI Dig. CMS7 64476-2 (4) [id.]. LPO, Klaus Tennstedt (with, in *No. 8*, Connell, Wiens, Lott, Schmidt, Denize, Versalle, Hynninen, Sotin, Tiffin School Boys' Ch., LPO Ch.).

While the *Eighth* marks a superb culmination the finest of Tennstedt's cycle, and is magnificently recorded, Nos. 6 and 7 are also a very considerable achievement, and this four-CD digital box is a real bargain. Tennstedt's reading of the *Sixth* is characteristically strong, finding more warmth than usual, even in this dark symphony. So the third-movement *Andante* is warmly beautiful, open and song-like, almost Schubertian in its sweetness, though there is never any question of Tennstedt taking a sentimental view of Mahler. His expressiveness tends towards conveying joy rather than Mahlerian neurosis, and for some that may make this too comfortable a reading. Karajan has more power and bite; his scale is bigger and bolder and the Berlin playing is more brilliant. Yet the EMI digital recording brings extra range and impact in the famous hammer-blows of fate in the finale and the result overall is most satisfying. The *Seventh* is even finer. Tennstedt is predictably spacious, and the first movement's architectural span is given the kind of expansive structural unity that one associates with Klemperer; but the concentration of the LPO playing under Tennstedt brings much greater success here than Klemperer found in his disappointing New Philharmonia version. In the central movements Tennstedt is not as imaginative as Solti, who is more mercurial in the second *Nachtmusik*, but the former is again at his most impressive in the finale, showing his directness and strength, and with vigorous support from the LSO players, who are on top form throughout the symphony. The digital recording is full, yet beautifully clear in detail. As for the *Eighth*, Tennstedt's broader, grander view makes at least as powerful an impact as Solti's Decca set; even though the playing does not always have the searing intensity of the Chicago orchestra, the singing of the LPO Choir combined with the Tiffin School Boys' Choir is unforgettable, with concentrated pianissimos matched by the expansive climaxes, where the opulent sound of the Westminster Cathedral organ adds to the feeling of weight and power.

Symphonies Nos. 6 in A min; 7 in E min.
(Y/B) **(*) EMI Dig. CDS5 55294-2 (3) [id.]. LPO, Tennstedt.

Not to be confused with Tennstedt's studio recordings of these symphonies in his Mahler cycle (see above), the separate box from EMI offers live recordings made at the Royal Festival Hall in November 1991 and May 1993, among the last performances he conducted there before his retirement. Though they hardly replace the studio recordings, what makes them special is the extra warmth of expressiveness they offer, notably in the slow movement of No. 6 and in the two *Nachtmusik* movements of No. 7. Regularly speeds are a degree slower in both works, with Tennstedt in a live concert allowing himself greater flexibility, with more extreme tenutos, always with an expressive purpose. The downside is that ensemble is not as crisp, notably in No. 6 and in the slow introduction to the finale of No. 7. The recording of No. 6 is thin on string-tone, with too little Mahlerian bite and less detail than in the studio recording. The sound in No. 7 is good, with plenty of atmosphere as well as bite. Nevertheless, under the circumstances these reservations are of comparatively little consequence and this makes a valuable addition to the Tennstedt discography.

Symphonies Nos. (i) *6 in A min.;* (ii) *8 in E flat (Symphony of 1000).*
(M) *(**) Sony SM3K 47581 [id.]. (i) NYPO; (ii) Spoorenberg, Gwyneth Jones, Annear, Reynolds, Procter, Mitchinson, Ruzdjak, McIntyre, Leeds Festival Ch., London Symphony Ch., Orpington Junior Singers, Highgate School Boys' Ch., Finchley Children's Music Group, LSO; Bernstein.

Bernstein's first CBS recording of the *Sixth* was made in the Avery Fisher Hall in 1967. Like the *Third*, it stood out from the others in the set, but the bright, close-up sound remains a drawback. Like the later, digital version with the VPO, one can argue that his tempi are inclined to be too fast (particularly in the first movement, which no longer sounds like a funeral march) but the searing intensity of the performance – like a live concert – comes over readily. The later version brings more refinement of expression, but not more concentration, and involves two full-priced CDs (DG 427 697-2). The New York recording is reissued on three mid-priced CDs but includes also the *Eighth Symphony*, recorded at Walthamstow in 1966. The Leeds Festival Chorus is strongly stiffened by professional choristers, and the result is splendidly incisive. The unfortunate point, undermining much of the superb achievement in the performance, is the closeness of sound and the resultant lack of atmosphere in the recording quality.

Symphony No. 7 in E min.
*** DG Dig. 419 211-2 (2) [id.]. NYPO, Bernstein.
(M) *** Decca 425 041-2 [id.]. Chicago SO, Solti.
(Y/B) (M) *** DG Dig. 445 513-2 [id.]. Chicago SO, Abbado.
*** Denon Dig. CO 1553/4 [id.]. Frankfurt RSO, Inbal.
**(*) EMI Dig. CDC7 54344-2 [id.]. CBSO, Rattle.
(Y/B) (BB) **(*) Naxos Dig. 8.550531 [id.]. Polish Nat. RSO, Michael Halász.

Symphony No. 7; (i) *Kindertotenlieder.*
(Y/B) *** DG Dig. 437 851-2 (2) [id.]. (i) Bryn Terfel; Philh. O, Sinopoli.

Leonard Bernstein's *Seventh* for DG was recorded from live performances. It is a riveting performance from first to last, ending with a searingly exciting account of the finale which triumphantly flouts the idea of this as a weak conclusion. It is a performance to send you off cheering – a splendid example of Bernstein's flair in Mahler. The recording is a little harsh at times, next to the finest modern digital sound.

Sinopoli, always a very positive Mahlerian, is here at his most personal in presenting a colourful, sharply characterized reading. Even more than usual with Sinopoli it is a performance of extremes, controversial but powerful to a degree that makes the whole experience disturbing. In each section Sinopoli immediately establishes an individual approach, usually far slower than usual, sometimes much faster. The first *Nachtmusik*, shimmering and atmospheric, is as evocative as the lyrical second, in which Sinopoli at very slow speed uses extreme rubato in his careful moulding of phrase. In between, the third-movement Scherzo at high speed becomes a nightmare fantasy, while the vast finale is delivered with fine panache, at the end pushed to the verge of hysteria. The vivid recording which marks the whole series is here at its most involving, with the brass gloriously rich. Bryn Terfel's magnificent interpretation of the *Kindertotenlieder*, heartfelt and intense, crowns the issue.

In interpretation, Solti's version is as successful as his fine account of the *Sixth Symphony*, extrovert in display but full of dark implications. The tempi tend to be challengingly fast – at the very opening, for example, and in the Scherzo (where Solti is mercurial) and in the finale (where his energy carries shock-waves in its trail). The second *Nachtmusik* is enchantingly seductive, and throughout the orchestra plays superlatively. This is one of Solti's finest Mahler records and the recording is brilliant and full – the CD transfer increases the brightness.

Abbado's command of Mahlerian characterization has never been more tellingly displayed than in this most problematic of the symphonies; even in the loosely bound finale Abbado unerringly draws the threads together. The contrasts in all its movements are superbly brought out, with the central interludes made ideally atmospheric, as in the eeriness of the Scherzo and the haunting tenderness of the second *Nachtmusik*. The precision and polish of the Chicago orchestra go with total commitment, and the recording is one of the finest DG has made with this orchestra. A clear first choice in the mid-price range.

Inbal's account of the *Seventh* is one of the high points of his Mahler series, masterfully paced, relaxed and lyrical where appropriate, but incorporating all the biting tensions that are missing in his version of the *Sixth*, the other dark, middle symphony. The recording is outstandingly fine in its vivid, natural balances.

Rattle, as ever, proves a sensitive and persuasive Mahlerian, in this most equivocal Mahler symphony. He made this recording live in The Maltings at Snape, disappointed with an earlier, studio version, which he did not want to have issued. Sadly, live or not, this performance does not have the biting tension and thrust that makes Rattle's recording of the *Second Symphony* so compelling, and the sound is not as full. The first movement suffers most, and the finale is the most successful. But as a single-disc version of the symphony – when most other versions take two CDs – this is still well worth considering.

Very well played and treated to refined and well-balanced digital recording, the Naxos version offers excellent value on a single disc at super-bargain price. With well-chosen speeds, often brisk but unhurried, with crisp ensemble and good rhythmic point, the only snag is that, by the standards of the finest versions, it is undercharacterized, lacking both flamboyance and tragic weight. Even there one has an advantage in the haunting melody of the second *Nachtmusik*, which is the more moving for being treated in a restrained way.

Symphonies Nos. 7; 9; 10 (Adagio).
(M) **(*) Sony SM3K 47585 (3) [id.]. NYPO, Bernstein.

In 1965 Bernstein drew a performance of the *Seventh* of characteristic intensity and beauty from the New York Philharmonic; his love of the music is evident in every bar. The playing is fabulous, yet there are also reservations. His warmth of phrasing in the second subject makes Bernstein's pointing sound self-conscious and tense, and in the *Night music* of the second and fourth movements, where the New York orchestra produces playing of heavenly refinement, the same feeling is present. Even in the finale, where Bernstein's thrusting dynamism holds the disparate structure together, there is the feeling that he is unable to relax into simplicity. The recording, made in the Avery Fisher Hall, is vivid and forward, not as full-bodied or refined as the later, DG version, which on two full-priced discs costs far more but is worth the extra outlay. The New York *Ninth* – a lucky symphony on records – is undoubtedly a great performance. Here Bernstein's sense of urgency has its maximum impact, though in the finale he does not quite achieve the visionary intensity of his later recording for DG with the Berlin Philharmonic. In the *Adagio* from the *Tenth*, recorded a decade after the others in 1975, Bernstein uses the old, fallible edition, but again the passionate commitment of his performance is hard to resist, with contrasts underlined between the sharpness of the *Andante* passages and the free expressiveness of the main *Adagio*. The recording is characteristically close but quite full, and for Bernstein admirers with limited budgets this box is certainly good value.

Symphony No. 8 (Symphony of 1000).
(Y/B) ✪ *** DG Dig. 435 433-2 (2) [id.]. Studer, Blasi, Jo, Lewis, Meier, Nagai, Allen, Sotin, Southend Boys' Ch., Philh. Ch. & O, Sinopoli.
(N) *** Decca 448 293-2 [id.]. Harper, Popp, Augér, Minton, Watts, Kollo, Shirley-Quirk, Talvela, V. Boys' Ch., V. State Op. Ch. & Singverein, Chicago SO, Solti.
*** EMI Dig. CDS7 47625-8 (2) [Ang. CDCB 47625]. Connell, Wiens, Lott, Schmidt, Denize, Versalle, Hynninen, Sotin, Tiffin School Boys' Ch., LPO Ch., LPO, Tennstedt.
(Y/B) (B) *** Sony SBK 48281; *SBT 48281* [id.]. Robinson, Marshall, Heichele, Wenkel, Laurich, Walker, Stilwell, Estes, Frankfurt Kantorei, Singakademie, Limburger Boys' Ch., Op. & Museum O, Gielen.
(Y/B) **(*) DG Dig. 445 843-2; *445 843-4* (2) [id.]. Studer, McNair, Rost, Von Otter, Lang, Seiffert, Terfel, Rootering, Tölz Boys' Ch., Berlin R. & Prague Philharmonic Ch., BPO, Abbado.

(N) (M) ** Ph. 446 195-2 [id.]. Cotrubas, Harper, Van Borkh, Finnila, Dieleman, Cochran, Prey, Sotin, Amsterdam Choirs, Conc. O, Haitink.

(i) *Symphony No. 8 (Symphony of 1000). Symphony No. 10: Adagio.*
**(*) DG 435 102-2 (2) [id.]. VPO, Bernstein, (i) with Price, Blegen, Zeumer, Schmidt, Baltsa, Riegel, Prey, Van Dam, V. Op. Ch., V. Boys' Ch.

Giuseppe Sinopoli crowns his Mahler cycle with the Philharmonia in a ripely passionate account of this most extravagant of the series, recorded with a richness and body that outshine any digital rival. In vividness of atmosphere it is matched only by Solti's magnificent analogue version, recorded in Vienna, which has the added advantage of now being available on a single CD. Sinopoli, highly analytical in his methods and flexible in his approach to speed, here conveys a warmth of expression that brings joyful exuberance to the great outburst of the opening *Veni creator spiritus*. It builds into one of the most thrilling accounts ever, helped by a superb team of soloists and incandescent choral singing, recorded with fine weight and body. In the long second movement and its setting of the closing scene of *Faust*, Sinopoli's approach is almost operatic in its dramatic flair, magnetically leading from one section to another, with each of the soloists characterizing strongly. As in the first movement, the chorus sings with fine control and incandescent tone, from the hypnotic first entry through to a thrilling final crescendo on '*Alles vergangliche*'.

Though it does not always have the searing intensity that marks Solti's overwhelming Decca version, Tennstedt's broader, grander view makes at least as powerful an impact, and with the extra range and richness of the modern EMI recording, coping superbly with even the heaviest textures, for most listeners it will be equally satisfying. It is the urgency and dynamism of Solti which make his reading irresistible, ending in an earth-shattering account of the closing hymn. Tennstedt, both there and elsewhere, finds more light and shade. His soloists, though a strong, characterful team, are not as consistent as Solti's. The great glory of the EMI set is the singing of the London Philharmonic Choir, assisted by Tiffin School Boys' Choir. The chorus may be rather smaller than in live performance, but diction and clarity are aided, with no loss of power.

Bernstein's DG version of the *Eighth* is more compelling and better recorded (in 1975) than his earlier, CBS/Sony recording; but at full price it is hardly a primary recommendation, even though the sound is quite full and atmospheric.

Recorded live at the opening of the Alte Oper in Frankfurt in August 1981, Gielen's version offers a direct, fresh reading, full of atmosphere, in which brisk speeds allow ample weight. Far more than the Abbado Berlin version, it vividly conveys the atmosphere of a great event. The analogue recording is less full than some, but it is naturally balanced with plenty of presence, if with brass a little distant. The chorus sings with heartfelt intensity, and the soloists make a distinguished team, except that the ringing Heldentenor, Mallory Walker, develops a beat in the voice under stress as Dr Marianus. On a single disc at budget price in Sony's Essential Classics series, it makes an outstanding bargain.

Claudio Abbado's 1994 recording, keenly analytical and precisely balanced, fails to capture the very quality one would expect in a live account: a sense of atmosphere. Except in the final chorus, '*Alles vergangliche*', where the tension and slow momentum are irresistible, making a magnificent climax, this is too often a detached-sounding reading, clear and transparent rather than intense, relating the music more than usual to Mahler's *Knaben Wunderhorn* inspirations. The chorus in this live performance sings powerfully, but ensemble is not always ideally crisp. The soloists make a fine, expressive team. Cheryl Studer, who sings Magna peccatrix in the Sinopoli version, is here the Penitent Woman instead, and Sylvia McNair instead sings Magna peccatrix with fresh, light tone.

Haitink's 1971 analogue version, characteristically thoughtful and direct, also lacks the biting intensity needed to convey the work's epic purpose to the full. The solo singing has its blemishes, but on CD the recording, originally rather dull and limited, has come up very freshly, with balances cleanly registered.

Symphony No. 9 in D min.
(N) *** DG Gold Dig. 439 024-2 (2) [id.]. BPO, Karajan.
(Y/B) *** DG Dig. 445 817-2 [id.]. Philh. O, Sinopoli.
*** DG 435 378-2 [id.]. BPO, Leonard Bernstein.
(M) *** EMI CDM7 63115-2 [id.]. BPO, Barbirolli.
(M) *** EMI CMS7 63277-2 (2) [Ang. CDMB 63277]. New Philh. O, Klemperer – WAGNER: *Siegfried idyll.* **(*)
(N) (B) (***) Dutton Lab. mono CDEA 5005 [id.]. VPO, Bruno Walter.

Symphony No. 9 (with rehearsal & conversation between Bruno Walter and Arnold Michaelis).
(N) (M) *** Sony SMK 64452 (2) [id.]. Columbia SO, Bruno Walter.

Symphony No. 9; Symphony No. 10: Adagio.
*** Nuova Era Dig. 6906/7 (2). Mahler-Jugend O, or European Community Youth O, James Judd.
*** Denon Dig. CO 1566/7 [id.]. Frankfurt RSO, Inbal.

Symphony No. 9; (i) Kindertotenlieder; 5 Rückert Lieder.
(Y/B) (B) *** DG Double 439 678-2 (2) [id.]. BPO, Karajan; (i) with Christa Ludwig.

Fine as Karajan's other Mahler recordings have been, his two accounts of the *Ninth* transcend them. In the earlier analogue version it is the combination of richness and concentration in the outer movements that makes for a reading of the deepest intensity, while in the middle two movements there is point and humour as well as refinement and polish. Helped by full, spacious recording, the sudden pianissimos which mark both movements have an ear-pricking realism such as one rarely experiences on record, and the unusually broad tempi are superbly controlled. In the finale Karajan is not just noble and stoic; he finds the bite of passion as well, sharply set against stillness and repose.

Yet within two years Karajan went on to record the work even more compulsively at live performances in Berlin. The major difference in that later recording is that there is a new, glowing optimism in the finale, rejecting any Mahlerian death-wish and making it a supreme achievement. The 'original-image' bit-processing has added to the projection, but the strings have plenty of body.

The earlier (1980) analogue performance makes a remarkable bargain alternative, reissued as a DG Double and costing half as much as the later, digital recording. Moreover the performances of the *Kindertotenlieder* and *Rückert Lieder* have a distinction and refinement of playing which stand out above all. Ludwig's singing is characterful too, with the poise and stillness of the songs beautifully caught. Even if the microphone conveys some unevenness in the voice, the recording is rich and mellow to match the performances.

Those who want an unbuttoned, overtly emotional reading of Mahler's last completed symphony will find Sinopoli's version an excellent choice. He may occasionally nudge speeds and phrases this way and that, but always in the interests of expressive warmth; and the full, glowing sound, with radiant brass and a vivid sense of presence, adds to the impact. Few versions match this in the weight and power of the great climaxes in the massive, measured outer movements, while the crisp pointing of the middle two movements brings out their grotesquerie very vividly. If the slow finale is passionate rather than spiritual, Sinopoli pursues that approach to the end, with the final hushed pianissimo still retaining warmth, instead of disappearing into nothingness.

Bernstein's version of Mahler's *Ninth*, made live in 1979, was the solitary occasion when he was permitted to conduct Karajan's own orchestra, and the response is electric, with playing not only radiant and refined but also deeply expressive in direct response to the conductor. Highly spontaneous, with measured speeds superbly sustained in a tautly concentrated reading. Bernstein conveys a comparably hushed inner quality.

Walter's Sony (originally CBS) performance was recorded in late January and early February 1961, and the producer, John McClure, took the opportunity to record a working portrait of the occasion. That is supplemented here by a 16-minute conversation between the conductor and Arnold Michaelis, dating from five years earlier. Walter's performance lacks mystery at the very start, but through the long first movement he unerringly builds up a consistent structure, controlling tempo more closely than most rivals, preferring a steady approach. The middle two movements similarly are sharply focused rather than genial, and the finale, lacking hushed pianissimos, is tough and stoically strong. A fine performance, quite different from his famous (1934) VPO account which (courtesy of Mike Dutton) is now available in a really first-class transfer.

Barbirolli greatly impressed the Berliners with his Mahler performances live, and this recording reflects the players' warmth of response. He opted to record the slow and intense finale before the rest, and the beauty of the playing makes it a fitting culmination. The other movements are strong and alert too, and the sound remains full and atmospheric, though now more clearly defined. An unquestionable bargain.

Klemperer's performance was recorded in 1967 after a serious illness. His refusal to languish pays tribute to his spiritual defiance, and the physical power is underlined when the sound is full-bodied and firmly focused. The sublimity of the finale comes out the more intensely, with overt expressiveness held in check and deep emotion implied rather than made explicit.

Inbal's reading may not have the epic power or the sweeping breadth of Karajan, but his simple dedication brings a performance just as concentrated in its way, simulating the varying tensions of a live performance and leading to a wonderfully hushed culmination, not tragic as with Karajan, but in its rapt ecstasy looking forward to the close, on murmurs of '*Ewig*', of *Das Lied von der Erde*. As a logical fill-up, the *Adagio* from the *Tenth Symphony* brings a similarly natural and warm reading. The sound in both works is excellent in its natural balance, a fine example of the Denon engineers' work.

Judd conducts the brilliant young players of the Mahler-Jugend Orchestra in a deeply moving account

of the *Ninth*, recorded live in Bratislava in April 1990. With recording of spectacular range and vividness, this makes one of the most appealing of all versions. The searing emotional commitment of the
players comes out consistently, and no allowance whatever need be made on technical grounds for their
youth. The performance of the *Adagio* from *No. 10* is not quite so distinguished, though warmly
satisfying; it was recorded in August 1987 by the rival band from EEC countries, the European
Community Youth Orchestra.

Bruno Walter's 1938 version with the Vienna Philharmonic was the first recording of this symphony
ever issued. The opening is not promising, with coughing very obtrusive; but then, with the atmosphere
of the Musikvereinsaal caught more vividly than in most modern recordings, the magnetism of Walter
becomes irresistible in music which he was the first ever to perform. Ensemble is often scrappy in the first
movement, but intensity is unaffected; even at its flowing speed, the finale brings warmth and repose
with no feeling of haste. The new Dutton transfer (transferred direct from 78-r.p.m. shellac discs) can do
little about the audience noises, but the sound-balance is further enhanced over the EMI transfer
(CDH7 63029-2), and the last movement in particular offers amazingly natural and believable string-
sound.

Symphony No. 10 in F sharp (Unfinished) (revised performing edition by Deryck Cooke).
*** EMI Dig. CDC7 54406-2 [id.]. Bournemouth SO, Rattle.
(Y/B) (B) **(*) Decca Double Dig. 444 872-2 (2) [id.]. Berlin RSO, Chailly – SCHOENBERG: *Verklärte
Nacht*. **

With digital recording of outstanding quality, Simon Rattle's vivid and compelling reading of the
Cooke performing edition has one convinced more than ever that a remarkable revelation of Mahler's
intentions was achieved in this painstaking reconstruction. The Bournemouth orchestra plays with
dedication, marred only by the occasional lack of fullness in the strings.

Reissued at bargain price on this Double Decca, Chailly's Decca version is superbly recorded and his
grasp of the musical structure is keen. The Berlin Radio Orchestra is highly responsive, although the
internal tension of the music-making is not as high as in Rattle's version.

LIEDER AND SONG-CYCLES

7 frühe Lieder (with piano); *11 frühe Lieder* (arr. Berio); *Lieder eines fahrenden Gesellen*.
*** Teldec/Warner Dig. 9031 74002-2. Thomas Hampson, David Lutz or Philh. O, Berio.

Thomas Hampson is in magnificent voice for his unusual collection of Mahler songs. He does the first
seven of the early songs and the *Wayfaring Lad* songs with piano accompaniment by David Lutz. He
then turns to the remaining early songs in the distinctive orchestral arrangements made by Luciano
Berio. Though Berio follows Mahlerian practice in many of his orchestral colourings, notably in the
woodwind, his instrumentation overall is far thicker and weightier, making it harder for the voice.
Though these arrangements are far less 'authentic' than those made of a group of the same songs by
Colin and David Matthews (see below), they have their fascination when sung as warmly and sensitively
as by Thomas Hampson. First-rate sound.

*7 early Lieder: Ablosung im Sommer; Fruhlingsmorgen; Hans und Grete; Nicht Wiedersehen!;
Selbstgefühl; Starke Einbildungskraft; Zu Strassburg Auf der Schanz'* (orch. D. and C. Matthews).
*** Unicorn Dig. DKPCD 9120 [id.]. Jill Gomez, Bournemouth Sinf., Carewe – MATTHEWS: *Cantiga,
Introit; September music*. ***

Some years before they took on the task of helping Deryck Cooke with the performing edition of
Mahler's *Tenth Symphony*, David and Colin Matthews made this orchestration of Mahler's so-called
'Youth' songs. As is shown in this sensitive performance from Jill Gomez and the Bournemouth
Sinfonietta under John Carewe, their feeling for the Mahler sound is unerring, making these a most
rewarding addition to the tally of regular Mahler song-cycles with orchestra. It proves a very apt
coupling for the warmly sympathetic works of David Matthews on the disc, notably the dramatic scena,
Cantiga, powerful and immediately attractive.

Kindertotenlieder.
(M) (**) Decca mono 425 995-2 [id.]. Kathleen Ferrier, Concg. O, Klemperer – BRAHMS: *Liebeslieder
Waltzes*. (***)

Kindertotenlieder; Des Knaben Wunderhorn: 3 songs; *Leider eines fahrenden Gesellen; 4 Rückert Lieder*.
**(*) Decca Dig. 425 790-2 [id.]. Brigitte Fassbaender, Deutsches SO, Berlin, Chailly.

Kindertotenlieder; Lieder eines fahrenden Gesellen.
(Y/B) (M) **(*) Decca 440 491-2 [id.]. Kirsten Flagstad, VPO, Boult – WAGNER: *Wesendonck Lieder.*
***

(i) *Kindertotenlieder; Lieder eines fahrenden Gesellen;* (ii) *5 Rückert Lieder.*
*** EMI CDC7 47793-2 [id.]. Dame Janet Baker, (i) Hallé O; (ii) New Philh. O, Barbirolli.

Dame Janet Baker's collaboration with Barbirolli represents the affectionate approach to Mahler at its warmest, intensely beautiful, full of breathtaking moments. The spontaneous feeling of soloist and conductor for this music comes over as in a live performance and brings out the tenderness to a unique degree. An indispensable CD.

Fassbaender gives fearless, vividly characterized performances of Mahler's three shorter orchestral song-cycles, adding for good measure three songs from *Des Knaben Wunderhorn,* including *Urlicht,* usually heard as part of the *Symphony No. 2.* In that last, her voice is not quite as even as usual, and the orchestra in *Kindertotenlieder* is slacker than elsewhere; but otherwise this is an issue to recommend to anyone who fancies these songs with a woman's voice, though Dame Janet Baker's vintage perform-ances with Barbirolli are more beautiful, with gentleness part of the mixture.

Flagstad sings masterfully in these two most appealing of Mahler's orchestral cycles, but she is unable to relax into the deeper, more intimate expressiveness that the works really require. The voice is magnifi-cent, the approach always firmly musical (helped by Sir Adrian's splendid accompaniment), but this recording is recommendable for the singer rather than for the way the music is presented.

The Ferrier version with Klemperer is a live recording taken from a broadcast in July 1951, some two years after her EMI recording with Bruno Walter. Though the voice is caught vividly and the richness of her interpretation has, if anything, intensified, the surface-hiss is daunting. Unusually coupled with the Brahms in which Ferrier's role is only incidental.

(i) *Kindertotenlieder;* (ii) *Lieder eines fahrenden Gesellen;* (i) *4 Rückert Lieder (Um Mitternacht; Ich atmet' einen linden Duft; Blicke mir nicht in die Lieder; Ich bin der Welt).*
*** DG 415 191-2 [id.]. Dietrich Fischer-Dieskau, (i) BPO, Boehm; (ii) Bav. RSO, Kubelik.

Only four of the *Rückert Lieder* are included (*Liebst du um Schönheit* being essentially a woman's song), but otherwise this conveniently gathers Mahler's shorter and most popular orchestral cycles in perform-ances that bring out the fullest range of expression in Fischer-Dieskau at a period when his voice was at its peak.

Das klagende Lied: complete *(Part 1, Waldmärchen; Part 2: Der Spielmann; Part 3, Hochzeitsstücke).*
*** Decca Dig. 425 719-2 [id.]. Susan Dunn, Markus Baur, Fassbaender, Hollweg, Schmidt, Düsseldorf State Musikverein, Berlin RSO, Chailly.
(M) **(*) Sony SK 45841 [id.]. Hoffman, Söderström, Haefliger, Nienstedt, Lear, Burrows, LSO, Boulez.

The strength of the Chailly version lies with the splendid singing of the Düsseldorf Choir and the demonstration-worthy Decca recording, full of presence. While not quite upstaging Simon Rattle in revealing the music's marvellously imaginative detail, Chailly pulls one special trick out of the hat in *Waldmärchen* by using a boy alto (Markus Baur) to represent the voice from the grave, a tellingly sepulchral effect, and again after the off-stage band sequence.

Boulez is a distinctive Mahlerian. His clear ear concentrates on precision of texture, but the atmospheric ambience adds warmth despite the forward balance, which also ensures very little difference in sound between the two recordings. Certainly the chill at the heart of this gruesome story of the days of chivalry and knights in armour is the more sharply conveyed. *Waldmärchen* is less effective than the rest. Good singing from the chorus, less good from the soloists.

Des Knaben Wunderhorn.
*** EMI CDC7 47277-2. Schwarzkopf, Fischer-Dieskau, LSO, Szell.
(M) **(*) Sony SMK 47590-2 [id.]. Christa Ludwig, Walter Berry, NYPO, Bernstein.

Szell's warmth and tenderness, coupled with the most refined control of pianissimo in the orchestra matches the tonal subtleties of his two incomparable soloists. Wit and dramatic point as well as delicacy mark these widely contrasted songs, and the device of using two voices in some of them is apt and effective.

It is arguable that orchestral Lieder need a more robust approach than comparable Lieder with piano, and there is a strong case to be made for Bernstein's rich, robust account of these endlessly fascinating songs. Full-blooded sound from 1969.

(i) *Des Knaben Wunderhorn;* (ii) *Lieder eines fahrenden Gesellen.*

(Y/B) (B) **(*) Carlton IMP PCD 2020 [id.]. (i) Dame Janet Baker, Sir Geraint Evans, LPO; (ii) Roland Hermann, Symphonica of L.; (i; ii) Wyn Morris.

Des Knaben Wunderhorn; Lieder eines fahrenden Gesellen; 11 Lieder Aus der Jugendzeit; 4 Rückert Lieder.

(M) **(*) Sony SM2K 47170 (2) [id.]. Christa Ludwig, Walter Berry, Dietrich Fischer-Dieskau, Leonard Bernstein (piano).

Dame Janet and Sir Geraint recorded Mahler's cycle in 1966 for Delysé, long before they both received the royal accolade. This was also Wyn Morris's first major essay in the recording studio; though he secures crisp playing from the LPO, the orchestral phrasing could ideally show more affection and be less metrical in charming songs that need some coaxing. Dame Janet in particular turns her phrases with characteristic imagination, and her flexibility is not always matched by the orchestra. Baker could hardly be more ideally cast, but Sir Geraint is more variable. However, it is good to have this recording available again at mid-price. Roland Hermann's performance of the *Lieder eines fahrenden Gesellen* is fresh, committed and intelligent, though his baritone is not always flattered by the otherwise atmospheric stereo.

Where the *Wunderhorn* songs with Christa Ludwig and Walter Berry keep constantly in touch with the folk-inspiration behind them, the other groups with Fischer-Dieskau bring an even subtler and more sophisticated partnership between pianist and singer. It is true that, even in the *Wunderhorn* songs, Bernstein allows himself the most extreme rubato and tenuto on occasion, and with the Fischer-Dieskau performances both singer and pianist adopt a far more extreme expressive style all through.

Des Knaben Wunderhorn (excerpts): *Verlor'ne Müh; Rheinlegendchen; Wo die schönen Trompeten blasen; Lob des hohen Verstandes; Aus! Aus!. Lieder: Erinnerung; Frühlingsmorgen; Ich ging mit Lust durch einen grünen Wald; Phantasie aus Don Juan; Serenade aus Don Juan.*

*** DG Dig. 423 666-2 [id.]. Anne Sofie von Otter, Rolf Gothoni – WOLF: *Lieder.* ***

The Mahler half of Anne Sofie von Otter's brilliant recital is just as assured and strongly characterized as the formidable group of Wolf songs. Rolf Gothoni's sparkling and pointed playing makes this a genuinely imaginative partnership, bringing out the gravity as well as the humour of the writing. Excellent, well-balanced recording.

Lieder eines fahrenden Gesellen.

*** Ph. Dig. 426 257-2 [id.]. Jessye Norman, BPO, Haitink – Symphony No. 6. ***

Jessye Norman is a joy to the ear, with Haitink, in his accompaniment for the jaunty second song, providing the necessary lightness. The stormy darkness of the third song fits the soloist more naturally, always a magnetic singer. It makes a valuable extra for Haitink's deeply satisfying version of the *Sixth Symphony.*

Lieder eines fahrenden Gesellen; Lieder und Gesänge (aus der Jugendzeit); Im Lenz; Winterlied.

(✖) *** Hyperion CDA 66100 [id.]. Dame Janet Baker, Geoffrey Parsons.

Dame Janet presents a superb collection of Mahler's early songs with piano, including two written in 1880 and never recorded before, *Im Lenz* and *Winterlied*; also the piano version of the *Wayfaring Lad* songs in a text prepared by Colin Matthews from Mahler's final thoughts, as contained in the orchestral version. The performances are radiant and deeply understanding from both singer and pianist, well caught in atmospheric recording. A heart-warming record.

Das Lied von der Erde.

(Y/B) (M) *** BBC Radio Classics BBCRD 9120 [id.]. J. Baker, Mitchinson, BBC Northern SO, Leppard.

(M) *** Ph. 432 279-2 [id.]. Dame Janet Baker, James King, Concg. O, Haitink.

(M) *** DG 419 058-2 [id.]. Ludwig, Kollo, BPO, Karajan.

*** DG Dig. 413 459-2 [id.]. Fassbaender, Araiza, BPO, Giulini.

(N) (M) **(*) Sony SMK 64455 [id.]. Mildred Miller, Ernst Haefliger, NYPO, Bruno Walter.

(Y/B) (B) **(*) DG 439 471-2 [id.]. Nan Merriman, Ernst Haefliger, Concg. O, Jochum.

(**) Decca mono 414 194-2. Ferrier, Patzak, VPO, Walter.

(i) *Das Lied von der Erde;* (ii) *Des Knaben Wunderhorn;* (iii) *Kindertotenlieder; Lieder eines fahrenden Gesellen.*

(N) (B) *** Ph. Duo 454 014-2 (2) [id.]. (i) J. Baker, King; (ii) J. Norman, Shirley-Quirk; (iii) Hermann Prey; Concg. O, Haitink.

Taken from a performance for radio in the Free Trade Hall, Manchester, the Leppard version offers Dame Janet Baker at her very peak in 1977, giving one of the most moving and richly varied readings of the contralto songs ever. The final *Abschied* has a depth and intensity, a poignancy and, at the end, a feeling of slipping into the unconscious, that set it above even Dame Janet's earlier recording with Haitink. John Mitchinson may not have the most beautiful tenor, but his voice focuses ever more securely through the work, with many cleanly ringing top notes. Raymond Leppard defies any idea that he is just a baroque specialist, finding wit as well as weight and gravity. He draws fine playing from the orchestra, now renamed the BBC Philharmonic, though the body of strings is thin for Mahler. Acceptable BBC sound, with the voices naturally placed, not spotlit: with any reservations, this remains an essential purchase for admirers of Dame Janet and Mahler.

The combination of this most deeply committed of Mahler singers with Haitink, the most thoughtfully dedicated of Mahler conductors, also produces radiantly beautiful and moving results, helped by refined and atmospheric recording. James King cannot match his solo partner, often failing to create fantasy, but his singing is intelligent and sympathetic. This must now take second place to the BBC recording. However, this version – vividly re-transferred – is now additionally offered on a Philips Duo set, coupled with Mahler's three other key song-cycles, and as such is very tempting. In *Des Knaben Wunderhorn* the singing of both Jessye Norman and John Shirley-Quirk brings out the purely musical imagination of Mahler at his finest, while Haitink's accompaniments are refined and satisfying, especially when the 1976 analogue sound is vividly atmospheric. Hermann Prey's performances of *Kindertotenlieder* and the *Lieder eines fahrenden Gesellen* are fresh and intelligent, and the colour of the baritone voice brings a darkness of timbre which is especially poignant, as in the third song of the *Wayfaring lad* cycle. Haitink's accompaniments are again understanding, yet they create urgency through the briskness of the chosen tempi. If in the last instance Prey cannot quite match Fischer-Dieskau or indeed Dame Janet Baker (see above) in intensity of expression, these performances are still estimable, and the Philips recording (from 1970) is of very high quality – the effect is most beautiful.

Karajan presents *Das Lied* as the most seductive sequence of atmospheric songs, combining character-istic refinement and polish with a deep sense of melancholy. He is helped enormously by the soloists, both of whom have recorded this work several times, but never more richly than here. The sound on CD is admirably vivid and does not lack a basic warmth.

Giulini conducts a characteristically restrained reading. With Araiza a heady-toned tenor rather than a powerful one, the line *Dunkel ist das Leben* in the first song becomes unusually tender and gentle, with rapture and wistfulness keynote emotions. In the second song, Fassbaender gives lightness and poign-ancy rather than dark tragedy to the line *Mein Herz ist müde*; and even the final *Abschied* is rapt rather than tragic, following the text of the poem; and the playing of the Berlin Philharmonic could hardly be more beautiful.

Though Bruno Walter's 1960 New York version does not have the tear-laden quality in the final *Abschied* that made his earlier Vienna account (in mono) with Kathleen Ferrier unique, that is the only serious shortcoming. Haefliger sparkles with imagination and Miller is a warm and appealing mezzo soloist, lacking only the last depth of feeling you find in a Ferrier or Janet Baker; and the maestro himself has rarely sounded so happy on record, even in Mahler. The remastered recording has been freshly remastered for the Bruno Walter Edition and now has even more vivid detail.

Generally Jochum avoided conducting Mahler – as a Brucknerian, underlining the point that these massive masters of symphony are totally contrasted. His reading of *Das Lied*, beautiful and compelling as it is, helps to explain why, for it speaks of the radiant calm of the Bruckner temperament rather than of Mahlerian tensions. Excellent solo singing and fine, clean recording, vivid and kind to the voices: worth considering at bargain price.

It is a joy to have the voice of Kathleen Ferrier so vividly caught on CD – not to mention that of the characterful Patzak – in Bruno Walter's classic Vienna recording for Decca. The sad thing is that the violin tone in high loud passages has acquired a very unattractive edge, not at all like the Vienna violins, and this makes for uncomfortable listening.

Das Lied von der Erde. (arr. Schoenberg & Riehn).
(Y/B) *** RCA Dig. 09026 68043-2 [id.]. Jean Rigby, Robert Tear, Premiere Ens., Mark Wigglesworth.

For the performing society he founded in Vienna, Schoenberg sparked off a whole series of chamber arrangements of works by Mahler and others. This one of *Das Lied* was left unfinished, but, as com-pleted by the scholar, Rainer Riehn, the clarification of an already transparent score brings many bonuses, not least a balance that allows the soloists to sing without stress even in the heaviest climaxes. Robert Tear's tenor tone has not sounded so free in years, and Jean Rigby movingly sustains the slowest possible speed for the long final *Abschied*, helped by the unfailing concentration of Mark Wigglesworth and the ensemble he created. In a superb instrumental team the oboe of Alison Alty is outstanding.

(i) *Das Lied von der Erde;* (ii) *5 Rückert Lieder.*
(Y/B) (B) **(*) Sony SBK 53518; *SBT 53518* [id.]. (i) Lilli Chookasian, Richard Lewis, Philadelphia O,
    Ormandy; (ii) Frederika von Stade, LPO, Andrew Davis.

A coupling for *Das Lied* is rare enough, but so generous a one as the *Rückert Lieder* on a bargain-label
issue is worth investigating. Ormandy conducts a purposeful, superbly played reading, dating from
1966, that may lack something in Mahlerian magic but which, with fine solo singing, carries you
magnetically through to the final climax. Richard Lewis is by his standards sometimes a little rough in
tone, but his perception is unfailing, and Lilli Chookasian's warm, weighty mezzo, with vibrato well
controlled, brings poise and gravity to her songs, not least the final *Abschied.* Frederika von Stade makes
a characterful soloist in the *Rückert Lieder,* sometimes colouring the voice too heavily; but, with fine
bloom on the 1976 sound, she brings out ravishing tonal contrasts, helped by Andrew Davis's sympathetic accompaniment.

5 Rückert Lieder.
(*) DG 415 099-2 (2) [id.]. Christa Ludwig, BPO, Karajan – *Symphony No. 6.* *

Christa Ludwig's *Rückert Lieder* are fine, positive performances, but it is the distinction and refinement
of the orchestral playing and conducting that make this reissue valuable.

Malipiero, Gianfrancesco (1882–1973)

String quartets Nos. 1–8.
*** ASV Dig. CDDCD 457 (2) [id.]. Orpheus Qt.

Malipiero's eight *String quartets* are all modest in length: the longest being the *First* (*Rispetti e stram-
botti*) (1920), which runs to twenty minutes, while the *Eighth* (1963–4), written when the composer was
in his early eighties, takes only twelve. None falls below a certain level of distinction, all are beautifully
crafted and there is much freshness and fertility of invention. They are all played with expertise and
conviction by the Orpheus Quartet, and very well recorded indeed.

Marais, Marin (1656–1728)

*L'Arabesque; Le Badinage; Le Labyrinthe; Prélude in G; La Rêveuse; Sonnerie de Sainte Geneviève du
Mont de Paris; Suite in G; Tombeau pour Monsieur de Sainte-Colombe.*
(BB) *** Naxos Dig. 8.550750 [id.]. Spectre de la Rose – SAINTE-COLOMBE: *Le Retour* etc. ***

Naxos have stepped in enterprisingly and chosen a programme that is not only most attractive in its own
right, but which also includes the key items used in the fascinating conjectural film about the relationship between Marin Marais and his reclusive mentor, Sainte-Columbe (*Tous les matins du monde*).
Spectre de la Rose consists of a first-rate group of young players using original instruments (not that a
viola da gamba could be anything else), led by Alison Crum, who plays in a dignified but austere style
which at first seems cool but which is very effective in this repertoire. *Le Badinage* is perhaps a little stiff
and unsmiling, but the key item, Marais' eloquent lament for his teacher, *Tombeau pour Monsieur de
Sainte-Colombe,* is restrained and touching. Good, bright, forward recording, vividly declaiming the
plangent viola da gamba timbre. But be careful not to play this record at too high a volume setting.

La Gamme en forme de petit opéra; Sonata à la marésienne.
(B) *** HM HMA 1901105 [id.]. L. Baroque.

La Gamme is a string of short character-pieces for violin, viola de gamba and harpsichord that takes its
inspiration from the ascending and descending figures of the scale. Although it is *en forme de petit opéra,*
its layout is totally instrumental and the varied pieces and dramatic shifts of character doubtless inspire
the title. The *Sonata à la marésienne* also has variety and character. The London Baroque is an excellent
group, and they are well recorded too.

6 Recorder suites (in B flat; C; E min.; F; 1–2 in G min.).
(M) **(*) Teldec/Warner 9031 77617-2 (2) [id.]. Quadro Hotteterre.

Marin Marais is a sophisticated and subtle composer whose music deserves more than just specialist
attention. He was a great master of the gamba, in which his innate melancholy found a natural outlet.
These recorder suites form a collection of *Pièces en trio pour le flute, violon et dessus de viole avec b.c.*
(basso continuo) and are played throughout by two recorders, cello and harpsichord. The performances
are of the highest sensitivity and virtuosity. The music is often doleful in its expressive feeling, but it

would be idle to pretend that it always sustains attention. Unlike some of Marais's gamba writing, these suites are of limited interest and belong among that repertoire which is more rewarding to play than to hear. Aficionados can be assured of the excellence of both performance and recording, although the close balance limits the dynamic range.

Suites for viols: in D min.; in G; Tombeau de Mr Meliton.
*** HM/BMG Dig. RD 77146 [77146-2-RC]. Kenneth Slowik, Jaap ter Linden, Konrad Junghänel.

The viol music of Marin Marais is, like certain white wines, an acquired taste; however, once acquired, it is quite addictive. The present artists, Kenneth Slowik and Jaap ter Linden, alternate between bass viol and gamba in the two suites, with Konrad Junghänel on theorbo, and they give vibrant, spirited performances that are most persuasive. The recording needs to be played at a lower than usual level-setting if a realistic result is required.

Marcello, Alessandro (1669–1747)

6 Oboe concertos (La Cetra).
(M) *** DG 427 137-2 [id.]. Heinz Holliger, Louise Pellerin, Camerata Bern, Füri.

The six concertos of *La Cetra* reveal a pleasing mixture of originality and convention; often one is surprised by a genuinely alive and refreshing individuality. These performances are vital and keen, full of style and character, and the recording is faithful and well projected.

Oboe concerto in D min.
(BB) **(*) Naxos Dig. 8.550556 [id.]. József Kiss, Ferenc Erkel CO – C. P. E. BACH: *Concertos.* **(*)

This enjoyable concerto, once attributed (in a different key) to Benedetto Marcello, is given a good performance here by József Kiss and is very well recorded. One might have preferred more dynamic contrast from the soloist, but his timbre is right for baroque music and he plays with plenty of spirit. This disc is well worth its modest cost for the C. P. E. Bach couplings.

Marenzio, Luca (1553–99)

Madrigals: *Come inanti de l'alba; Crudele acerba; Del cibo onde il signor; Giunto a la tomba; Rimanti inpace; Sola angioletta* (sestina); *Strider faceva; Tirsi morir volea; Venuta era; Vezzosi augelli.*
(B) *** HMA 1901065 [id.]. Concerto Vocale, René Jacobs.

Luca Marenzio enjoyed an enormous reputation during his lifetime, particularly in England, and this record gives an altogether admirable picture of his breadth and range. There are poignant and expressive pieces such as *Crudele, acerba*, from the last year of his life, which is harmonically daring, and lighter pastoral madrigals such as *Strider faceva* and the more ambitious sestina, *Sola angioletta*, which this excellent group of singers, occasionally supported by theorbo and lute, project to striking effect. Fine singing and recording and a modest price serve to make this a most desirable issue.

Markevitch, Igor (1912–83)

(i) *The Flight of Icarus;* (ii) *Galop;* (iii) *Noces;* (iv) *Serenade.*
(N) *** Largo Dig. 5127 [id.]. (i) Lyndon-Gee, Lang, Gagelmann, Haeger; (ii) Markevitch Ens., Köln; (i; iii; iv) Lessing; (iv) Meyer, Jensen.

Born in Kiev, the son of the pianist, Boris Markevitch, the young Igor moved with his family to Switzerland and, after the war, became a pupil of Cortot at the Paris Conservatoire. *Noces*, for piano, was composed in 1925 when Markevitch was only thirteen, and it was on the strength of this and a *Sinfonietta* that Diaghilev was prompted to take him up. Indeed it was with a *Piano concerto* commissioned by Diaghilev that he made his London début in 1929. The young composer-conductor was only twenty when he composed *L'Envol d'Icare* which Lifar commissioned but subsequently never produced. It is heard here not in its orchestral form but in the transcription for two pianos and percussion. *Noces*, neatly played by Kolja Lessing, is close to the world of Poulenc and Satie, and it is obvious that Markevitch knew his Ravel. The *Serenade* is akin to the Milhaud of the *Petites symphonies*, and there is tremendous energy and a lot of Stravinsky in *L'Envol di'Icare*. This disc does not reveal Markevitch to be a great composer, but it gives an insight into his talent and musicianship which will be of interest to all those who care about the Diaghilev years and Paris between the wars.

Marsh, John (1752–1828)

Symphonies Nos. 1 in B flat (ed. Robins); *3 in D; 4 in F; 6 in D; A Conversation Symphony for 2 Orchestras* (all ed. Graham-ones).
** Olympia Dig. OCD 400 [id.]. Chichester Concert, Ian Graham-Jones.

John Marsh was essentially a musical amateur (in the best sense). In his way he was innovative: because of the continuing influence of Handel the symphony format was not fashionable in England at that time. For the most part they each consist of three short movements and, while the tunes sometimes have a whiff of Handel, there is a strong element of the English village green. The *Conversation Symphony* does not divide into two separate ensembles but makes contrasts between higher and lower instrumental groupings. Five of his works are presented here with enthusiasm by an aptly sized authentic Baroque group; they play well and are quite effectively recorded.

Martin, Frank (1890–1974)

Ballades for: (i) *cello & small orchestra;* (ii) *flute, strings & piano;* (iii) *piano & orchestra;* (iv) *saxophone & small orchestra;* (v) *viola, wind, harpsichord, timpani & percussion;* (vi) *trombone & piano.*
(Y/B) *** Chandos Dig. CHAN 9380 [id.]. (i) Peter Dixon; (ii) Celia Chambers; (ii–iii; v–vi) Roderick Elms; (iv) Martin Robertson; (v) Philip Dukes, Rachel Masters; (vi) Ian Bousfield; LPO, Matthias Bamert.

The *Ballades* are among Martin's most personal utterances. Only three are otherwise currently available; there are no alternative versions of the *Saxophone ballade* or the *Ballade for cello*, except in the version with piano. The only other recording of the *Ballade for viola and wind* was by Menuhin and has long been out of circulation. So the present issue is a most valuable addition to the Martin discography, particularly in view of the excellence and commitment of the performances. Subtle, state-of-the-art recording with no false 'hi-fi' brightness, but a natural and unobtrusive presence. An indispensable disc for admirers of this subtle and rewarding master.

Ballades for: (i) *flute, strings & piano;* (ii) *piano & orchestra;* (iii) *saxophone & small orchestra;* (iv) *trombone, piano & strings. Concerto for 7 wind instruments.*
(N) **(*) Decca Dig. 444 455-2 [id.]. (i) Jacques Zoon; (ii) Ronald Brautigan; (iii) John Harle; (iv) Christian Lindberg; Concg. O, Chailly.

Taken in isolation, this collection from the Royal Concertgebouw Orchestra and Riccardo Chailly of four of the *Ballades* plus the *Concerto for seven wind instruments* is an enjoyable, worthwhile issue. The playing is very alive and virtuosic, the recording clear and well lit, and, as a glance at the titling will show, the roster of soloists is impressive. But the *Ballades* are much better served on the Chandos collection, and in Amsterdam the *Concerto* has none of the subtlety of the Chamber Orchestra of Europe on DG and little of its atmosphere. Atmosphere is all-important in Frank Martin's music, and in this respect the Chailly set falls just a little short.

(i) *Ballade for piano and orchestra;* (ii) *Ballade for trombone and orchestra;* (iii) *Concerto for harpsichord and small orchestra.*
**(*) Jecklin-Disco JD 529-2. (i) Sebastian Benda; (ii) Armin Rosin; (iii) Christiane Jaccottet; Lausanne CO, composer.

The *Harpsichord concerto* is a highly imaginative and inventive piece, arguably the most successful example of the genre since the Falla *Concerto*. The orchestral texture has a pale, transparent delicacy that is quite haunting, and the atmosphere is powerful – as, indeed, it is in the fine *Ballade*. Christiane Jaccottet is a committed advocate and her performance has the authority of the composer's direction.

(i) *Piano concerto No. 2;* (ii) *Violin concerto.*
** Jecklin-Disco JD 632-2 [id.]. (i) Badura-Skoda; (ii) Schneiderhan; Luxembourg RSO, composer.

The *Violin concerto* is a score of great subtlety and beauty. Don't be put off by the less than lustrous sound, for this is a masterpiece and has the benefit of having Martin himself at the helm. The *Second Piano concerto* is not as lyrical as the *Violin concerto* but is still worth investigation for its thoughtful slow movement.

(i; ii) *Violin concerto;* (ii) *Concerto for 7 wind instruments, timpani, percussion & strings; Etudes for strings;* (iii) *Passacaglia for strings;* (ii; iv) *Petite symphonie concertante for harp, harpsichord, piano & double string orchestra;* (ii; v) *In terra pax* (oratorio).
(N) (B) (***) Decca Double mono/stereo 448 264-2 (2) [id.]. (i) Schneiderhan; (ii) SRO, Ansermet; (iii)

Stuttgart CO, Münchinger; (iv) Jamet, Vaucher-Clerc, Rossiaud; (v) Buckel, Höffgen, Haefliger, Mollet, Stämpfli, Union Ch. & Lausanne Women's Ch.

This set contains not only the pioneering record of the *Petite symphonie concertante* but also Schneiderhan's superb (1955) performance of the *Violin concerto*, often ethereal in its beauty. Both performances have a concentration and atmosphere that have rarely been matched since. The 1951 recording of the *Petite symphonie concertante* brings a thin edge to the upper string timbre, which seems to be emphasized by the CD transfer; the *Violin concerto*, however, sounds much better, with Schneiderhan's gloriously pure timbre captured very naturally. The other orchestral recordings are vivid enough, and Münchinger's shaping of the powerful, 12-minute *Passacaglia* shows him at his most concentrated and the Stuttgart strings in excellent form. *In terra pax* is a 1963 stereo recording. The oratorio was commissioned by the Swiss Radio in preparation for the end of the 1939–45 war and it was first performed by Ansermet. Martin's music has an appropriate eloquence and spirituality, and he is admirably served by his fine soloists. The score falls into four short sections, all with biblical texts, and its sincerity and sense of compassion leave a strong impression. No complaints about the sound here.

Concerto for 7 wind instruments, percussion and strings; (i) *Erasmi monumentum* (for organ and orchestra); *Etudes for strings.*
*** Chandos Dig. CHAN 9283 [id.]. (i) Leslie Pearson; LPO, Matthias Bamert.

Erasmi monumentum is a substantial piece of some 25 minutes. The first movement, *Homo pro se* ('The independent man'), alludes to the name given to Erasmus by his contemporaries; the second is *Stulticiae Laus* ('In praise of folly'), and the third is *Querela Pacis* ('A plea for peace'). The outer movements are pensive and atmospheric; the middle movement is less convincing. Matthias Bamert's account of the *Concerto for seven wind instruments* is very assured, more relaxed and less keenly animated than either the highly imaginative Thierry Fischer on DG or Armin Jordan on Erato, but thoroughly persuasive all the same. He makes rather heavy weather of the *Etudes*, which are not as strongly characterized as Fischer's; neither the concerto nor the *Etudes* displaces the DG, which fully deserves its Rosette.

Concerto for 7 wind instruments, percussion and strings; Etudes; (i) *Polyptique for violin and two string orchestras.*
✹ *** DG Dig. 435 383-2 [id.]. (i) Marieke Blankestijn; COE, Thierry Fischer.

This is a remarkable record and quite in a class of its own. The *Polyptique* is a work of serene profundity, inspired by a polyptych, a set of very small panels depicting scenes from the Passion which Martin saw in Siena. It is a work of great power and is played with rapt concentration and dedication by Marieke Blankestijn and the European Chamber Orchestra under Thierry Fischer. In the *Concerto for seven wind instruments, percussion and strings* there is a lightness of accent and refinement of tone and dynamics that are quite exceptional, and the *Etudes pour cordes* similarly outclasses its predecessors. The tone is pure and there is the widest possible range of timbre, colour and dynamics without ever the slightest hint of self-consciousness. Music of great quality, playing of great artistry, and recording to match.

The Four elements; (i) *In terra Pax.*
(N) *** Chandos Dig. CHAN 9465 [id.]. (i) Judith Howarth, Della Jones, Martyn Hill, Roderick Williams, Stephen Roberts, Brighton Festival Ch.; LPO, Bamert.

Les quatre éléments, written for Ansermet's eightieth birthday in 1967, is a highly imaginative work which exhibits to striking effect Martin's feeling for the orchestra and his subtle mastery of texture. This is its first recording since Haitink's in the late 1960s, coupled with the roughly contemporaneous *Cello concerto*, and this supersedes it. *In terra Pax* is a noble work, and this makes a distinguished addition to the growing Martin discography. The singers are not perhaps quite as impressive as in the Ansermet set, but in every other respect the new recording is superior.

Petite symphonie concertante.
(N) (M) **(*) EMI CDM5 65868-2. SO, Stokowski – HINDEMITH: *Mathis der Maler* **(*); TOCH: *Symphony No. 3.* ***

Stokowski's preoccupation with sonorities pays good dividends here as this work contains an attractive diversity of themes and, although the early stereo lacks something in opulence, he still manages to spin a full texture in the slow movement, whereas elsewhere detail is very clear. The sound is spacious too, and there is no lack of intensity. But the main interest of this CD is the splendid Toch *Symphony*.

Symphonie concertante (arr. of *Petite symphonie concertante* for full orchestra); *Symphony; Passacaglia.*
(Y/B) ✹*** Chandos Dig. CHAN 9312 [id.]. LPO, Matthias Bamert.

The *Symphony* is new to the gramophone and is a haunting and at times quite magical piece. It has all the subtlety of colouring of the mature Martin and is a piece of great imaginative resource. The slow movement in particular has an other-worldly quality, suggesting some verdant, moonlit landscape, strongly related in its muted colouring to the world of Debussy's *Pelléas et Mélisande*. The two pianos are effectively used and though, as in the *Petite symphonie concertante*, lip service is paid to the twelve-note system, the overall effect is far from serial. Its main companion here is the transcription Martin made for full orchestra of the *Petite symphonie concertante* the year after its first performance, without the harp, harpsichord and piano soloists and with an ample complement of wind, brass and other instruments. Harp and piano are in fact used for colouristic effects but completely relinquish any hint of soloist ambitions. The *Passacaglia* is the only modern digital recording of Martin's 1962 transcription for full orchestra of his much (and rightly) admired (1944) organ piece. Sensitive playing from the LPO under Matthias Bamert and exemplary Chandos recording.

Piano quintet; String quintet (Pavane couleur de temps); String trio; Trio sur des mélodies populaires irlandaises.
*** Jecklin-Disco JD 646-2 [id.]. Zurich Ch. Ens.

The *Piano quintet* has an eloquence and an elegiac dignity that are impressive; the short string quintet, subtitled *Pavane couleur de temps* (the title is taken from a fairy story in which a young girl wishes for 'a dress the colour of time'), is a beautiful piece. The *Piano trio on Irish popular themes* is full of imagination and rhythmic life. The *String trio* is a tougher nut to crack; its harmonies are more astringent and its form more concentrated. To summarize: altogether a most satisfying disc, offering very good performances and recordings.

VOCAL MUSIC

Der Cornet.
*** Orfeo Dig. S 164881A [id.]. Marjana Lipovšek, Austrian RSO, Zagrosek.
(N) *** Ph. Dig. 442 535-2 [id.]. Jard van Nes, Amsterdam Nieuw Sinf., Reinbert de Leeuw.

Der Cornet or, to give it its full title, *Die Weise von Liebe und Tod des Cornets Christoph Rilke* ('The Lay song of the love and death of Cornet Christoph Rilke'), is one of Martin's most profound and searching works. It sets all but four of the 27 stanzas of Rainer Maria Rilke's poem, which tells of a youthful ensign who dies in 1660 'under the sabres of the Turks into an ocean of flowers'. Each of the prose-poems gives a different aspect of the narrative, from the ensign's homesick adolescence and enforced maturity to his discovery of youthful love and early death. Though Rilke's poem sold only 300 copies when it first appeared in 1899, it became a best-seller once the 1914–18 war broke out. Martin's setting for contralto and small chamber orchestra was written at the height of the war and in the immediate wake of *Le vin herbé*, his oratorio on the Tristan legend. The shadowy, half-real atmosphere often reminds one of the world of *Pelléas*; and Martin's responsiveness to the rhythm and music of the words is as idiomatic as Debussy's, even though German was not his native tongue. All his fingerprints are there, and the restrained, pale colourings provide an effective backcloth to the vivid and poignant outbursts which mark some of the settings. It would feature more often in concert performances were singers able to sustain it. It is demanding for the soloist and emotionally exhausting for the listener. The performance by Jard van Nes is no less remarkable than that of Marjana Lipovšek on Orfeo – and honours are equally divided. Sensitive orchestral playing under Reinbert de Leeuw and faithfully balanced, well-recorded sound. This music casts a powerful spell and is strongly atmospheric. Whether you get this or the Orfeo rival does not matter, so long as you do not miss this wonderful work.

The performance by the contralto, Marjana Lipovšek, is also a *tour de force*, and the orchestral playing under Lothar Zagrosek is highly sympathetic. The recording is very faithful, and the performance certainly puts one completely under the spell of this strongly atmospheric work.

Mass for double choir.
(Y/B) *** United Recordings 88033 [id.]. Vasari, Jeremy Backhouse – HOWELLS: *Requiem* etc. ***
*** Koch Bayer Dig. BR 100084 [id.]. Frankfurt Vocal Ens., Ralf Otto – REGER: *Geistliche Gesänge.* ***
(*) Nimbus Dig. NI 5197 [id.]. Christ Church Cathedral Ch., Oxford, Stephen Darlington – POULENC: *Mass in G* etc. *

The Martin *Mass* is one of his purest and most satisfying utterances. Irrespective of competition, the present account is quite masterly in every respect and Vasari, a choir conducted by Jeremy Backhouse, get remarkably fine results. A very convincing performance, and an exemplary recording.

Ralf Otto's fine Frankfurt choir also have a great understanding of and feeling for this work, and convey its poignancy and depth. Their performance is quite a powerful and moving experience, and they produce a refined and expressive tonal blend as well as a wide dynamic range, which are well captured by the engineers.

The Choir of Christ Church Cathedral, Oxford, under Stephen Darlington also give a good account of themselves: their tone is clean and beautifully balanced. The boys' voices are moving in a different way from that of the Frankfurt choir, but the English performance does not add up to quite as impressive or richly imaginative a musical experience. The Nimbus disc is eminently well recorded.

(i) *6 Monologues from Everyman;* (ii) *Maria triptychon;* (i) *The Tempest:* 3 excerpts.
(N) *** Chandos Dig. CHAN 9411 [id.]. (i) David Wilson-Johnson (ii) Linda Russell; LPO, Bamert.

Only three excerpts from Frank Martin's opera, *The Tempest* (1953–5), have so far been recorded (on both occasions by Fischer-Dieskau, once with the composer himself and on another occasion under Ansermet), and such is their quality that the appetite is whetted for the whole work. As with the present Chandos CD, Fischer-Dieskau's DG recording coupled them with the *Everyman monologues,* one of the most powerful song-cycles of the twentieth century; it is a measure of David Wilson-Johnson's artistry here that in both instances one forgets the exalted comparison that the appearance of this new record excites. He sings with intense – but not excessive – dramatic feeling and total commitment and conviction. The extra rarity on this disc is the *Maria triptychon,* which Martin wrote in response to a commission from Wolfgang Schneiderhan for a work that he could perform together with his wife, the soprano Irmgaard Seefried. The central movement, *Magnificat,* originally stood on its own and was first given in 1968 under Haitink, but Martin subsequently added the two outer movements, *Ave Maria* and *Stabat Mater.* The former is one of his most inspired pieces, and Linda Russell and the violinist Duncan Riddell give a totally dedicated account of it. This is a most beautiful work, and Bamert and the LPO give a thoroughly sympathetic account of it. They generate a keen sense of atmosphere, and the Chandos recording is every bit as good as the other issues in this splendid series.

Requiem.
*** Jecklin-Disco JD 631-2 [id.]. Speiser, Bollen, Tappy, Lagger, Lausanne Women's Ch., Union Ch., SRO, composer.

This is arguably the most beautiful *Requiem* to have been written since Fauré's and, were the public to have ready access to it, would be as popular. The recording, made at a public performance that the (then 83-year-old) composer conducted in Lausanne Cathedral, is very special. The analogue recording is not in the demonstration class, but this music and performance must have three stars.

Le vin herbé (oratorio).
*(**) Jecklin-Disco JD 581/2-2 [id.]. Retchitzka, Tuscher, Comte, Morath, De Montmollin, Diakoff, De Nyzankowskyi, Tappy, Jonelli, Rehfuss, Vessières, Olsen, composer, Winterthur O (members), Desarzens.

Martin's oratorio on the Tristan legend is laid out for a madrigal choir of twelve singers, who also assume solo roles, and a handful of instrumentalists, including the piano, played here by the septuagenarian composer himself. It is powerful and hypnotic, and there is some fine singing here from Tuscher, Tappy and Rehfuss. The instrumental playing, though not impeccable, is dedicated (and the same must be said for the choral singing). The 1960s sound is much improved in the CD format.

Martinez, Marianna (1744–1812)

Dixit dominus; In exitu Israel.
(N) * Koch Schwann Aulos Dig. 3-1788-2 [id.]. Lippitz, Bieber, Mavrák, De Vries, Cologne Kurrende & Clara Schumann O, Elke Mascha Blankenburg.

Marianna Martinez was a Viennese prodigy. She was fortunate to be the daughter of the papal nuncio; the librettist, Pietro Metastasio, a friend of the family, took an interest in her and arranged for the young Haydn to give her singing and keyboard lessons and also to instruct her in composition, She caused a sensation when her first Mass was performed: she was just sixteen. One would like to welcome her as an important discovery, and her music undoubtedly has fair craftsmanship and Viennese charm. The *Dixit dominus* opens brightly with trumpets and a lively chorus, but overall the work suffers from a very homely style of performance, with more enthusiasm than polish. The soprano and contralto soloists who sing the florid duet, *Virgam virtulis,* are technically very insecure and, although the flutes provide an engaging obbligato, one winces every now and then at their poor intonation. The *Juravit Dominus* brings another impressive fugal chorus but shows up the inadequacies of the Kölner Kurrende, and *Dominus a dextris,* a vocal quartet nicely decorated with oboes, again needs far more secure solo singing. *In exitu Israel* also opens vigorously and freshly; its main components are a series of four amiable vocal quartets, which seem to be Martinez's speciality. They are operatic in style (with a Mozartian flavour, if without that master's subtle skill in part-writing) with the third, *Orechie e nari*, and the fourth, *V'ha quei che l'orme*, particularly attractive. The closing chorus is telling but – here and throughout – Blankenburg's conducting is flabby and one senses that, given a much higher standard of performance, these works could emerge in a far better light.

Martinů, Bohuslav (1890–1959)

La Bagarre; Half-time; Intermezzo; The Rock; Thunderbolt.
*** Sup. SUP 001669 [id.]. Brno State O, Vronsky.

La Bagarre and *Half-time* are early evocations, the latter a Honeggerian depiction of a roisterous half-time at a football match that musically doesn't amount to a great deal. The three later works are much more interesting – *Intermezzo* is linked to the *Fourth Symphony* – and the collection as a whole will be of great interest to Martinů addicts, if perhaps not essential for other collectors. All the performances are alive and full of character, and the recording is vividly immediate.

(i) *Concertino in C min. for cello, wind instruments and piano;* (ii) *Harpsichord concerto;* (iii) *Oboe concerto.*
*** Sup. Dig. 11 0107-2 031 [id.]. (i) Alexandr Večtomov, Vladimir Topinka, members of Czech PO; (ii) Zuzana Růžičková, Václav Rehák; (iii) Jiří Krejči; (ii; iii) Czech Philharmonic Chamber O; (i, iii) Petr Skvor; (ii) Václav Neumann.

Zuzana Růžičková has made a number of recordings of the *Harpsichord concerto* but this is her most successful. The sound is agreeably spacious, though the balance is synthetic and the piano has equal prominence with the solo harpsichord. However, the playing is spirited and sympathetic; and the *Oboe concerto* is heard to excellent advantage too, with very good playing and a well-laid-out sound-picture. The early *Concertino for cello with piano, wind and percussion* is more than acceptably played and recorded.

(i) *Concerto for double string orchestra, piano and timpani;* (ii) *Concerto for string quartet and orchestra;* (iii) *Sinfonia concertante for oboe, bassoon, violin, cello and orchestra.*
*** Virgin/EMI Dig. VC7 59575-2 [id.]. (i) Alley, Fullbrook; (ii) Endellion Qt; (iii) Daniel, Reay, Watkinson, Orton; City of L. Sinfonia, Hickox.

The *Double concerto* has splendid vitality in Hickox's hands and he has obvious sympathy for this repertoire. The *Sinfonia concertante* is more rewarding than the neo-Baroque *Concerto for string quartet and orchestra*, which is very manufactured. However, this is a useful addition to the growing Martinů discography, and Richard Hickox is an enthusiastic and expert guide in this terrain.

Concerto for double string orchestra, piano and timpani; 3 Frescoes of Piero della Francesca. (i) *Rhapsody-concerto for viola and orchestra.*
*(**) BIS Dig. CD 501 [id.]. (i) Nobuko Imai; Malmö SO, James DePreist.

Nobuko Imai's performance of the *Rhapsody-concerto* is quite special. It has the feel of live music-making, as if the musicians were all swept along by the current this all generates. She is excellently supported by the Malmö orchestra, who play very well indeed throughout. The *Double concerto* receives a dignified reading, but the acoustic unfortunately lets things down: it is far too reverberant; nor is the balance ideal in the *Frescoes*, where wind and brass come dangerously close to swamping the strings.

Concerto for double string orchestra, piano and timpani; (i) *Sinfonietta giocosa for piano and orchestra;* (ii) *Rhapsody-concerto for viola and orchestra.*
**(*) Conifer Dig. 76505 51210-2. Brno State PO, Mackerras; (i) Dennis Hennig, Australian CO, Mackerras; (ii) Rivka Golani, Berne SO, Peter Maag.

Rivka Golani's unaffected account of the *Rhapsody-concerto*, all the more eloquent for being under-stated, is here added to the *Double concerto* reviewed below, and the delightful *Sinfonietta giocosa*, both previously coupled with music by different composers. The wartime but apparently carefree *Sinfonietta giocosa* gets a delightfully fresh performance and an acceptable recording, though the balance is a bit synthetic with little back-to-front depth.

Concerto for double string orchestra, piano and timpani; Spalíček – ballet suites.
*** Conifer Dig. 74321 17919-2 [id.]. Brno State PO, Mackerras.

The ballet *Spalíček* is an engaging score, based on traditional Czech fairytale tunes and nursery rhymes.

The music is delightful and some of the numbers, particularly the *Dance of the Ladies of Honour*, captivating. If you enjoy the Dvořák of the *Slavonic dances*, you will respond to this fresh and open-hearted music. Mackerras also includes the powerful *Concerto for double string orchestra, piano and tympani*, again well played and recorded, though the pianist produces some less-than-elegant tone at climaxes. Eminently recommendable though in the *Double concerto*, Bělohlávek perhaps gives the more concentrated reading.

Concerto for double string orchestra, piano and tympani; Symphony No. 1.
*** Chandos Dig. CHAN 8950 [id.]. Czech PO, Jiří Bělohlávek.

Jiří Bělohlávek's dedicated and imaginative account of the *First Symphony* is very good indeed. Bělohlávek is totally inside this music, and the recording, made in the agreeably resonant Spanish Hall of Prague Castle, is very natural. The *Double concerto* is one of the most powerful works of the present century, and its intensity is well conveyed in this vital, deeply felt performance. Strongly recommended for both works.

Cello concertos Nos. 1–2.
(Y/B) **(*) Sup. 1110 3901-2 [id.]. Angelica May, Czech PO, Václav Neumann.

Cello concertos Nos. 1–2; Concertino in C min. for cello, wind instruments, piano & percussion.
(Y/B) *** Chandos Dig. CHAN 9015 [id.]. Raphael Wallfisch, Czech PO, Bělohlávek.

The *Cello concerto No. 1* was composed in 1930 but has been revised twice, in 1939 and 1955. It is in this third form that both artists have recorded it. The *Cello concerto No. 2*, written in New York at the turn of the year 1944–5, is the bigger of the two, some 36 minutes in all, and had to wait until Saša Večtomov performed it in 1965, six years after Martinů's death. It opens with a very characteristic and infectiously memorable B flat tune, and there is much of the luminous orchestral writing one associates with the *Fourth* and *Fifth Symphonies*. It is a warm-hearted, lyrical score with a Dvořák-like radiance.

   The fine German cellist Angelica May, a Casals pupil, gives a good account of both scores and, in the absence of the Wallfisch, this is perfectly recommendable. But as both performance and recording, her version is outclassed by the Chandos, which has much greater definition and presence and also has the advantage of offering the *Concertino for cello, wind, piano and percussion* (1924).

Oboe concerto.
*** Nimbus Dig. NI 5330 [id.]. John Anderson, Philh. O, Simon Wright – FRANCAIX: *L'horloge de flore;* R. STRAUSS: *Concerto.* ***

The newest Nimbus account, by John Anderson, principal of the Philharmonia, is outstanding in every way, with the *Andante* quite ravishing when the soloist's timbre is so rich. The recording is first class and the couplings particularly attractive.

Piano concertos Nos. 2; 3; 4 ('Incantation').
(Y/B) ✿*** RCA Dig. 09026 61934 [id.]. Rudolf Firkušný, Czech PO, Libor Pešek.

The present set by Rudolf Firkušný, who premièred all three concertos and was the dedicatee of No. 3, was well worth waiting for. The finest of them is *Incantation* (*Piano concerto No. 4*), which here receives a performance that is unlikely ever to be surpassed. Its exotic colourings and luminous, other-worldly landscape with its bird-like cries and extraordinary textures have never been heard to better advantage. It is a work of strong atmosphere and mystery, and Firkušný is its ideal advocate. He makes a stronger case for the *Second Piano concerto* than any previous pianist, and the brightly optimistic *Third* is hardly less persuasive. It is astonishing to think that he was over eighty when these performances were recorded. There are none of the tell-tale signs of age that distinguished many of his older contemporaries: indeed the performances radiate youthful vitality. Part of the success of these performances is the quality of the orchestral support. In the *Fourth Concerto* nothing is hurried and every phrase is allowed to breathe – and the same goes for its two companions. The recording is very good indeed.

Violin concertos Nos. 1–2; Rhapsody concerto for viola and orchestra.
(N) (M) **(*) Sup. 11 1969-2 [id.] Josef Suk, Czech PO, Václav Neumann.

The *Second Violin concerto* was written for Mischa Elman, who had heard and liked the *First Symphony* and immediately commissioned a concerto. It is an appealing and inventive score and of greater substance than its predecessor from the 1930s, which came to light only in the early 1970s; it finds Martinů very much in concerto-grosso mode. It is resourceful nevertheless, and Josef Suk is the only violinist so far to record it. By far the most poignant and eloquent of these three works is the *Rhapsody-concerto* for viola and orchestra, in which Suk is also the soloist and which dates from the period of the *Fantaisies symphoniques*. Suk is a masterly player, of course, and the Czech Philharmonic play with obvious pleasure. The recordings are analogue and inner detail is not quite as sharply focused as in the very best discs from the 1970s; at mid-price, however, this is quite competitive.

Double concerto for two string orchestras, piano & timpani.
(N) (M) **(*) BBC Radio Classics 15656 91352 [id.]. BBC SO, Mackerras – JANACEK: *Sinfonietta* etc.
   **(*)

Mackerras has recorded the *Double concerto* for Supraphon more than once and he is totally inside this idiom. His is a vividly characterized and exhilarating performance which comes from a 1979 Promenade Concert. The texture is not so transparent and perhaps lacks the full presence of the coupled Janáček *Sinfonietta*, recorded in the Festival Hall. There are one or two inconsistencies in balance (the opening of the second movement sounds more recessed than the last bars of the first), but the performance has such strong personality and atmosphere that many will be tempted to overlook the rather opaque sound. The excellent pianist is Harold Lester. Recommended to those for whom sound is not the foremost concern.

Spaliček (ballet; complete); *Dandelion* (Romance); *5 Duets on Moravian folksongs.*
*** Sup. Dig. 11 0752-2 (2). Soloists, Kantilena Children's Ch., Kühn Mixed Ch., Brno State PO, František Jílek.

The original of Martinů's engaging ballet, *Spaliček*, dates from 1931–2 and must in some sense have been a reaction against the sophistication of life in Paris. This is the first recording of the complete score and it makes an even more positive impression than the more conventionally scored suites (see above). The dances familiar from the suites are interspersed with vocal episodes, both solo and choral, and there is inevitably far greater variety of texture and pace than is evident from the suites. Its three Acts last some 97 minutes and, although there are some longueurs, they are very few. For the most part this music is quite captivating, particularly given the charm of this performance. Two shorter works complete the set: *Dandelion Romance* for mixed chorus and soprano, and *Five Duets on Moravian folksong texts* for female voices, violin and piano, both of which come from his last years. All in all, a delightful addition to the Martinů discography.

Symphonies Nos. 1–6 (Fantaisies symphoniques).
(M) *** Sup. 11 0382-2 (3) [id.]. Czech PO, Václav Neumann.

Symphonies Nos. 1–6.
(Y/B) **(*) Chandos Dig. CHAN 9103/5 [id.]. Royal Scottish Nat. O, Bryden Thomson.

Symphonies Nos. 2; 6 (Fantaisies symphoniques).
(Y/B) **(*) Chandos Dig. CHAN 8916 [id.]. Royal Scottish Nat. O, Bryden Thomson.

Symphonies Nos. 1–4.
*** BIS Dig. CD 362-3 [id.]. Bamberg SO, Järvi.

Martinů always draws a highly individual sound from his orchestra and secures great clarity, even when the score abounds in octave doublings. He often thickens his textures in this way, yet, when played with the delicacy these artists produce, they sound beautifully transparent. On hearing the *First*, Virgil Thomson wrote, 'the shining sounds of it sing as well as shine', and there is no doubt this music is luminous and life-loving. The BIS recording is in the demonstration class yet sounds completely natural, and the performances under Neeme Järvi are totally persuasive and have a spontaneous feel for the music's pulse.

   Neumann's set was recorded in the Dvořák Hall of the House of Artists, Prague, between January 1976 (No. 6) and 1978 (No. 5). The transfers to CD are excellently done: the sound is full, spacious and bright; it has greater presence and better definition than the original LPs, yet with no edginess in the strings. Václav Neumann's performances have an impressive breadth and, though there could be more urgency and fire in places, the readings have life, colour and impetus, and are thoroughly compelling when the Czech orchestra play so vividly.

   Bryden Thomson's set of the Martinů symphonies have a robust spirit and an enthusiasm which cannot be gainsaid, and they are accorded very good Chandos sound. The *Sixth Symphony* (the *Fantaisies symphoniques*) is not quite as subtle or as imaginative as the Bělohlávek on the same label, coupled with the *Concerto for double string orchestra* (see above), though the recording is every bit as good.

Symphonies Nos. 1; 3; 5.
*** Multisonic 31 0023-2 (2). Czech PO, Ančerl.

This is the real thing. Whether or not you have modern versions of these Martinů symphonies, you should obtain these powerful, luminous performances; they come from Czech Radio recordings made in

1963, 1966 and 1962 respectively. They are such superb and convincing readings that readers should not hesitate. The music glows in Ančerl's hands and acquires a radiance that quite belies its date.

Symphonies Nos. 3–4.
(N) (M) **(*) Sup. 11 1967-2 011 [id.]. Czech PO, Václav Neumann.

The Supraphon recordings were made in the 1970s and are analogue. No harm in that, of course, though the sound is a little diffuse and wanting in detail. The performances are good though they are neither better nor more imaginative than those by Neeme Järvi (BIS 363: same coupling) or, in the case of the *Fourth Symphony* alone, Bělohlávek (Chandos). Both of those are full price and the present issue retails at mid-price. Those not wanting to pay more will find these (as one would expect) thoroughly idiomatic accounts. However, if sound is not a primary concern, Ančerl's mono account of No. 3 has stronger artistic claims.

Symphony No. 4; Memorial to Lidice; (i) *Field Mass.*
*** Chandos Dig. CHAN 9138 [id.]. (i) Ivan Kusjner, Czech Ph. Ch.; Czech PO, Jiří Bělohlávek.

Despite its wartime provenance the *Fourth Symphony* is one of the composer's sunniest works; the infectious high spirits of the Scherzo and the luminous, glowing textures of the slow movement and its harmonic resource are irresistible. There is a radiance about this work that is quite special, and Bělohlávek's account of it is quite the best that has appeared in recent years. It is better played than the Järvi, though perhaps the latter scores in the eloquence of the slow movement. The *Memorial to Lidice,* composed in response to a Nazi massacre, is a powerful and haunting piece, and so is the *Field Mass,* which receives its best performance until now – by far. The soloist is excellent and the choral singing has an appropriate ardour. Thoroughly convincing performances and an indispensable item in any Martinů discography.

Symphony No. 5; Les Fresques de Piero della Francesca; Memorial to Lidice; The Parables.
(Y/B) **(*) Supraphon mono/stereo 11 1931–2 [id.]. Czech PO, Ančerl.

Most of these are pioneering recordings. The *Fifth Symphony* comes from 1955 and the *Memorial to Lidice* from 1957 and, although the sound is naturally constricted in range, it never detracts for one moment from the stature of these performances. They have great radiance and give enormous pleasure. The *Three Frescoes* and *The Parables* are in stereo and were made in 1959 and 1961 respectively. The *Three Frescoes* are given a marvellously glowing performance and, though it has still not been possible to remove the slight glassiness and shrillness in the string-tone above the stave, there is rather more detail and body than in the LP. *The Parables,* never released in stereo on LP in the UK, sound better, and the performances have tremendous authority, conveying that luminous quality that make the Martinů sound-world so special. An indispensable element in any Martinů collection.

Symphonies Nos. 5; 6 (Fantaisies symphoniques).
*** BIS Dig. CD 402 [id.]. Bamberg SO, Järvi.

The *Fifth* is a glorious piece and Järvi brings to it that mixture of disciplined enthusiasm and zest for life that distinguishes all his work. Wonderfully transparent, yet full-bodied sound, in the best BIS manner.

Symphony No. 6 (Fantaisies symphoniques).
*** Chandos Dig. CHAN 8897 [id.]. Czech PO, Bělohlávek – JANACEK: *Sinfonietta;* SUK: *Scherzo.*
***

(i) *Symphony No. 6 (Fantaisies symphoniques); Les Fresques de Piero della Francesca; Memorial to Lidice.* (ii) *Vigilie for organ.*
(Y/B) **(*) Chant du Monde PR 254 050 [id.]. (i) Prague RSO, Vladimír Válek; (ii) Václav Uhlíř.

Symphony No. 6 (Fantaisies symphoniques); (i) *Bouquet of flowers.*
(Y/B) (**(*)) Sup. mono 11 1932-2901 [id.]. Czech PO, Ančerl; (i) with Domaníská, Cervená, Havlak, Mráz, Kühn Children's Ch., Czech Philharmonic Ch.

This Chandos reading has the inestimable benefit of the Czech Philharmonic. Moreover the interpretation has great dramatic strength and is fully characterized; undoubtedly these players believe in every note. It is an outstanding performance that does full justice to the composer's extraordinarily imaginative vision and is very well recorded.

Ančerl's 1960 recording of the *Fantaisies symphoniques* has now been superseded in some ways by the Bělohlávek version, but there is a visionary feel to the earlier, Supraphon account that is more easily recognized than defined. It comes with *Bouquet of flowers,* the cycle of settings of folk texts for mixed and children's chorus which charms, captivates and touches. Some allowances have to be made for the mono recording, but they are few and are more than compensated for by this inspiring music-making.

On Chant du Monde these are live Czech Radio recordings: the *Memorial to Lidice* comes from 1992, the *Sixth Symphony* from 1986 and the *Frescoes* from 1993. The sound is very resonant but there is no lack of detail; the performance of the symphony is very good indeed and, though sonically both Bělohlávek and Järvi are superior, the playing has plenty of spirit and imagination. The *Memorial to Lidice* is very moving. Válek takes a broader tempo in the first two of the three *Frescoes* than Ančerl and, though there is an added sense of space, some may feel a slight loss of urgency. While recognizing this, we warmed to this performance very much. The short makeweight, the *Vigilie*, is one of Martinů's last works, written only four months before his death and left unfinished. It was completed by the organist, Bedřich Janáček. A recommendable disc which is worth the money.

CHAMBER MUSIC

Cello sonatas Nos. 1 (1939); 2 (1942); 3 (1952).
(Y/B) *** RCA Dig. 09026 61220-2 [id.]. Janos Starker, Rudolf Firkušný.
*** Hyperion Dig. CDA 66296 [id.]. Steven Isserlis, Peter Evans.

The *Cello sonatas* are well served in the catalogue. The RCA version with Starker and Firkušný is, perhaps predictably, the more impressive of the two. Firkušný's authority in this repertoire is unchallenged, and Starker has a natural eloquence though his tone is small. They are given the benefit of very good recorded sound and, at full price, are to be preferred to their British rivals.

Steven Isserlis and Peter Evans also offer very good playing and very acceptable recording, but Starker and Firkušný are first choice.

Duo for violin and cello; Piano trio No. 1 (5 Pièces brèves).
(N) * Chandos Dig. CHAN 9452 [id.]. Bekova Sisters – RAVEL: *Piano trio etc.* *

A well-planned and, on the face of it, attractive disc. The *Piano trio No. 1* (or *Cinq pièces brèves*) and the *Duo*, the first of two, are not so generously represented in the catalogue for us to look askance at any newcomer. But the performances are not special enough to prompt one to replay this disc. Good recorded sound.

Flute sonata.
*** RCA Dig. 07863 57802-2 [7802-2-RC]. James Galway, Phillip Moll – DVORAK: *Sonatina;* FELD: *Sonata.* ***

With the outer movements generally jolly and extrovert, bringing distinctive Martinů touches, the main weight of the *Flute sonata* comes in the central *Adagio*. Galway is characteristically individual but without mannerism in his performance, and is most sympathetically accompanied by Moll. Relatively dry recording, with a fine sense of presence.

4 Madrigals for oboe, clarinet and bassoon; 3 Madrigals for violin and viola; Madrigal sonata for piano, flute and violin; 5 Madrigal stanzas for violin and piano.
*** Hyperion Dig. CDA 66133 [id.]. Dartington Ens.

These delightful pieces exhibit all the intelligence and fertility of invention we associate with Martinů's music. The playing of the Dartington Ensemble is accomplished and expert, and the recording, though resonant, is faithful.

Nonet; Trio in F for flute, cello and piano; La Revue de cuisine.
*** Hyperion CDA 66084 [id.]. Dartington Ens.

A delightful record. Only one of these pieces is otherwise available on CD and all of them receive first-class performances and superb recording. The sound has space, warmth, perspective and definition. An indispensable issue for lovers of Martinů's music.

Piano quintet No. 2.
*** ASV Dig. CDDCA 889 [id.]. Peter Frankl, Lindsay Qt – DVORAK: *Piano quintet.* ***

Martinů's *Second Piano quintet* is a remarkably successful piece, characteristically original in its content and rhythmic style. The Lindsays with Peter Frankl have its full measure and – as in the coupled Dvořák *Quintet* – after the impulsive opening movement it is the central movements which bring playing of striking insight and subtlety, with rapt concentration at the opening of the finale. The recording is lively and present, with the piano well integrated, although there is just a touch of thinness on the strings. An outstanding coupling.

Sonata for 2 violins and piano.
**(*) Hyperion Dig. CDA 66473 [id.]. Ososowicz, Kovacic, Tomes – MILHAUD: *Violin duo etc.* **(*);
PROKOFIEV: *Violin sonata.* ***

Martinů's *Sonata for two violins and piano* finds him full of invention and vitality. Krsyia Osostowicz, Ernst Kovacic and Susan Tomes play it with all the finesse and sensitivity you could want and are excellently recorded. The disc would be even more recommendable if it had a longer playing time than 46 minutes.

String quartets Nos. 1–7.
(Y/B) **(*) Sup. 110 994-2 (3) [id.]. Panocha Qt.

The Panocha Quartet's recordings of the Martinů cycle were made at various times between 1979 and 1982. The *First* of the quartets is both the longest and the most derivative; it is heavily indebted to the world of Debussy and Ravel. The *Third* is by far the shortest (it takes barely 12 minutes) and has the nervous energy and rhythmic vitality characteristic of the mature composer. The *Fourth* and *Fifth* are close to the *Double Concerto for two string orchestras, piano and timpani*. The *Fifth* is the darkest of the quartets and in its emotional intensity is close in spirit to Janáček's *Intimate Letters*. The *Sixth* – and in particular its first movement – is a powerful and disturbing piece, and there is a sense of scale and a vision that raise it above its immediate successor, which is fluent, well crafted and nicely fashioned but wanting in the freshness and spontaneity that distinguishes, say, the *Sinfonietta giocosa*. To be frank, the quartets do not show Martinů at his most consistently inspired but are still worth investigating. The Panocha set is eminently recommendable, even though it is a bit steep to ask full price for it, and the recordings are a bit two-dimensional.

Violin sonatas Nos. 2–3; 5 Madrigal sonatas.
** Sup. Dig. 11 0099-2 [id.]. Josef Suk, Josef Hála.

The *Second Violin sonata* is a short and attractive work, while the bigger-boned *Third* speaks much the same language as the symphonies. Josef Suk and Josef Hála give excellent acounts of all three pieces, though the 1987 recording is less than appealingly balanced. The sound is rather synthetic and too close.

VOCAL MUSIC

The Butterfly that stamped (ballet): 5 scenes (arr. Rybár).
(Y/B) ** Sup. Dig. 11 0380-2 [id.] Women's voices of Kühn Ch., Prague SO, Bělohlávek.

Martinů's choral ballet, *The Butterfly that stamped*, is an early work from his Paris years, based on one of Kipling's *Just-So* stories. Unfortunately Kipling's publisher demanded payment for the copyright, and Martinů, who was eking out a penurious existence, had to abandon the project. The five scenes have been put into a performing edition by Jaroslav Rybár. The score has a great deal of Gallic charm and does not follow the avant-garde line of *La Bagarre*. A pity that Supraphon market this slight but charming score (lasting only 41 minutes 47 seconds) at full price – without the addition of a fill-up. (One of his other works of the period could easily have been accommodated on it.) Recommended to collectors with a penchant for Martinů all the same.

The Epic of Gilgamesh (oratorio).
(❀) *** Marco Polo Dig. 8.223316 [id.]. Depoltová, Margita, Kusnjer, Vele, Karpílšek, Slovak Ph. Ch. & O, Zdeněk Košler.
(Y/B) *** Sup. 11 1824 [id.]. Machotková, Zahradníček, Zítek, Prôša, Brousek, Czech Philh. Ch., Prague SO, Bělohlávek.

The Epic of Gilgamesh comes from Martinů's last years and is arguably his masterpiece. It evokes a remote and distant world, full of colour and mystery. Gilgamesh is the oldest poem known to mankind: it predates the Homeric epics by 1,500 years, which places it at 7000 BC or earlier. The work abounds with invention of the highest quality and of consistently sustained inspiration. The performance is committed and sympathetic and the recording very natural in its balance.

Bělohlávek's version can almost hold its own artistically with the excellent Marco Polo account. The latter was intended to underline the inspired quality of the music itself as much as the quality of performance and recording. This does not displace the Marco Polo but it can certainly be recommended alongside it.

(i) *Hymn to St James;* (ii) *Mount of three lights;* (iii) *The Prophecy of Isaiah.*
** Sup. Dig. 11 0751-2 (2). (i) Doležal, Novák, Haničinec; (i; ii) Kuhn Mixed Ch., Prague SO, Pavel Kühn; (ii; iii) Romanová, Drobková; (iii) Kozderka, Pěruška, Haničinec, Boguna, Kiezlich, Prague R. Ch., Hora.

This disc gathers three cantatas Martinů composed towards the end of his life. The *Mount of three lights* is a rarity and new to the catalogue in this country. It is based on a bizarre mixture of Czech folksong, bits of H. V. Morton's book, *In the Steps of the Master*, and *The Gospel according to St Matthew*! Though it is not quite as concentrated or haunting as *The Epic of Gilgamesh* or *The Prophecy of Isaiah*, it is powerful stuff and well worth the attention of all admirers of the composer. It is well performed by these forces, save perhaps for the bass, Richard Novák, whose wobble may prove too much for some listeners. The *Hymn of St James* has moments of a disarming simplicity of utterance; generally speaking, though, it is not top-drawer Martinů. However, *The Prophecy of Isaiah* is; it is a work of great substance and depth. Its austere sound-world and seriousness resonate in the mind, though the performance is less impressive than the old LP under Karel Ančerl, which deserves reissue; and readers should be cautioned that the bass has a terribly wide vibrato. The recording comes in an uneconomical two-CD format, though it lasts less than an hour.

OPERA

Ariane.
** Sup. Dig. 10 4395-2. Lindsley, Phillips, Doležal, Novák, Czech PO, Vaclav Neumann.

Ariane is a slight work to which Martinů turned as a relaxation from *The Greek Passion*. It is based on the play, *Le voyage de Thésée*, by Georges Neveux. Apparently the demanding role of Ariane was inspired by Callas; it is all quite engaging and high-spirited without being Martinů at his very best. Written in the course of a month, it is a short piece, no longer than 43 minutes, though it is housed in a two-CD format so as to accommodate a multi-lingual booklet and libretto. The singers (and in particular Celina Lindsley) are very good indeed: only Richard Novák's wide vibrato is problematic. Decent rather than outstanding recording quality.

The Greek Passion (sung in English).
*** Sup. Dig. 10 3611/2 [id.]. Mitchinson, Field, Tomlinson, Joll, Moses, Davies, Cullis, Savory, Kuhn Children's Ch., Czech PO Ch., Brno State PO, Mackerras.

Written with much mental pain in the years just before Martinů died in 1959, this opera was the work he regarded as his musical testament. It tells in an innocent, direct way of a village where a Passion play is to be presented; the individuals – tragically, as it proves – take on qualities of the New Testament figures they represent. This extraordinarily vivid recording – almost stereoscopic in its clear projection of the participants – was made by a cast which had been giving stage performances for the Welsh National Opera in what in effect is the original language of Martinů's libretto, English. The combination of British soloists with excellent Czech choirs and players is entirely fruitful. Mackerras makes an ideal advocate, and the recording is both brilliant and atmospheric. With the words so clear, the absence of an English libretto is not a serious omission, but the lack of any separate cues within the four Acts is a great annoyance.

Julietta (complete).
*** Sup. 10 8176-2 (3) [id.]. Tauberová, Zídek, Zlesák, Otava, Bednářr, Mixová, Jedenáctík, Procházková, Hanzalíková, Soukupová, Jindrák, Veverka, Svehla, Zlesák, Lemariová, Berman, Prague Nat. Theatre Ch. & O, Jaroslav Krombholc.

Described by the composer as a Dreambook, *Julietta* was given first in Prague in March 1938. This vintage Supraphon recording, made in 1964, captures that surreal quality vividly. You would never guess the date of the recording, for the ear is mesmerized from the very start, when the howling of a high bassoon introduces the astonishingly original prelude. The voices as well as the orchestra are then presented with a bright immediacy which reinforces the power and incisiveness of Krombholc's performance. The sharpness of focus adds to the atmospheric intensity, as when in the first Act The Man in the Window plays his accordion. Ivo Zídek gives a vivid portrait of the central character, Michel, perplexed by his dream-like search, and there is no weak link in the rest of the cast. The snag is that the set stretches extravagantly to three discs, when the opera could have been fitted on to two, though that layout brings the advantage of having each Act complete on a single disc. Informative notes and libretto come with multiple translations.

Martucci, Giuseppe (1856–1909)

(i) *Piano concerto No. 1 in D min.;* (ii) *La canzone dei Ricordi*.
** ASV Dig. CDDCA 690 [id.]. (i) Caramiello; (ii) Yakar; Philh. O, D'Avalos.

The *First Piano concerto* (with Francesco Caramiello a capable soloist) is inevitably derivative, and it is the song-cycle that is the chief attraction here: Rachel Yakar sings beautifully and is particularly affecting in the Duparc-like *Cantavál ruscello la gaia canzone*. The recording is generally faithful.

(i) *Piano concerto No. 2 in B flat min., Op. 66. Canzonetta, Op. 55/1; Giga, Op. 61/3; Minuetto, Op. 57/2; Momento musicale, Op. 57/3; Serenata, Op. 57/1; Tempo di gavotta, Op. 55/2.*
** ASV Dig. CDDCA 691 [id.]. Francesco Caramiello; (i) Philh. O, D'Avalos.

The *Second Piano concerto* is a big, 40-minute piece in a Brahmsian mould but is nevertheless full of individual touches. Caramiello copes very successfully with its very considerable demands, and the results all round are eminently acceptable. The fill-ups derive mainly from piano pieces and are wholly delightful. The recording is good.

Giga, Op. 61/3; Notturno, Op. 70/1; Novelletta, Op. 82.
*** Sony Dig. SK 53280 [id.]. La Scala PO, Muti – BUSONI: *Turandot suite;* CASELLA: *Paganiniana.*
***

The three Martucci pieces are played with infinitely greater sensitivity and finesse than in the ASV survey of Martucci's symphonies and concertos by D'Avalos. They were all composed at about the turn of the century and have the gentleness and elegiac quality of Fauré and Elgar with a touch of Wagner (Martucci conducted the Italian première of *Tristan*). This is altogether a most valuable issue and can be strongly recommended.

Symphony No. 1 in D min., Op. 75; Notturno, Op. 70/1; Novelletta, Op. 82; Tarantella, Op. 44.
** ASV Dig. CDDCA 675 [id.]. Philh. O, D'Avalos.

The *First Symphony* is greatly indebted to Brahms, but elsewhere there is a vein of lyricism that is more distinctive. The *Notturno* has the nobility and eloquence of Elgar or Fauré and deserves to be much better known. The performances by the Philharmonia under Francesco D'Avalos are serviceable rather than distinguished, but the recording is very truthful and well balanced.

Symphony No. 2 in F, Op. 81; Andante in B flat, Op. 69; Colore orientale Op. 44/3.
** ASV Dig. CDDCA 689 [id.]. Philh. O, D'Avalos.

The *Second Symphony* is a relatively late work. Though the performance falls short of distinction, it leaves the listener in no doubt as to Martucci's quality as a composer and the nobility of much of his invention. The *Colore orientale* is an arrangement of a piano piece; the beautiful *Andante*, a work of depth, has a Fauréan dignity. The recording is a bit too closely balanced.

Le canzone dei ricordi; Notturno, Op. 70/1.
*** Hyperion Dig. CDA 66290 [id.]. Carol Madalin, ECO, Bonavera – RESPIGHI: *Il tramonto.* ***

Le canzone dei ricordi is a most beautiful song-cycle, and its gentle atmosphere and warm lyricism are most seductive. At times Carol Madalin has a rather rapid vibrato, but she sings the work most sympathetically and with great eloquence. The *Notturno* is beautifully played. Recommended with all possible enthusiasm.

Mascagni, Pietro (1863–1945)

Cavalleria rusticana (complete).
*** RCA RD 83091. Scotto, Domingo, Elvira, Isola Jones, Amb. Op. Ch., Nat. PO, Levine.
*** DG 419 257-2 (3) [id.]. Cossotto, Bergonzi, Guelfi, Ch. & O of La Scala, Milan, Karajan – LEONCAVALLO: *I Pagliacci* *** (also with collection of Operatic intermezzi ***).
(***) EMI mono CDS7 47981-8 (3) [Ang. CDCC 47981]. Callas, Di Stefano, Panerai, Ch. & O of La Scala, Milan, Serafin – LEONCAVALLO: *I Pagliacci.* (***)
(M) **(*) Decca 425 985-2 [id.]. Tebaldi, Bjoerling, Bastianini, Maggio Musicale Fiorentino Ch. & O, Erede.
(M) (***) RCA mono GD 86510 [RCA 6510-2-RG]. Milanov, Bjoerling, Merrill, Robert Shaw Chorale, RCA O, Cellini.
(B) **(*) Naxos Dig. 8.660022 [id.]. Evstatieva, Aragall, Tumagian, Di Mauro, Michalková, Slovak Philh. Ch., Czech RSO, Rahbari – LEONCAVALLO: *I Pagliacci.* **(*)
(M) (**) Nimbus mono NI 7843/4 [id.]. Gigli, Bruna Rasa, Marcucci, Bechi, Simionato, La Scala Ch. & O, composer – LEONCAVALLO: *I Pagliacci.* (**(*))

On balance, in performance the RCA issue stands as the best current recommendation, with Domingo giving a heroic account of the role of Turiddù, full of defiance. Scotto is strongly characterful too, and James Levine directs with a splendid sense of pacing, by no means faster than his rivals (except the leisurely Karajan) and drawing red-blooded playing from the National Philharmonic. The recording is very good, strikingly present in its CD format.

Karajan pays Mascagni the tribute of taking his markings literally, so that well-worn melodies come out with new purity and freshness, and the singers have been chosen to match that. Cossotto quite as much as Bergonzi keeps a pure, firm line that is all too rare in this much-abused music. Not that there is any lack of dramatic bite. The CD transfer cannot rectify the balance, but voices are generally more sharply defined, while the spacious opulence is retained.

Dating from the mid-1950s, Callas's performance as Santuzza reveals the diva in her finest form, with edginess and unevenness of production at a minimum and with vocal colouring at its most characterful. The singing of the other principals is hardly less dramatic and Panerai is in firm, well-projected voice.

The early (1957) Decca recording with Tebaldi offers a forthright, lusty account of Mascagni's piece of blood and thunder and has the distinction of three excellent soloists. Tebaldi is most moving in *Voi lo sapete*, and the firm richness of Bastianini's baritone is beautifully caught. As always, Bjoerling shows himself the most intelligent of tenors, and it is only the chorus that gives serious cause for disappointment; they are very undisciplined. The CD sound is strikingly bright and lively.

Admirers of Milanov will not want to miss her beautiful singing of *Voi lo sapete*, and in the duet Merrill's dark, firm timbre is thrilling. Bjoerling brings a good measure of musical and tonal subtlety to the role of Turiddù, normally belted out, while Cellini's conducting minimizes the vulgarity of the piece.

As in his parallel recording of *Pag.*, Alexander Rahbari conducts a red-blooded reading of *Cav.*, making it a first-rate super-bargain choice. Stefka Evstatieva is a warmly vibrant Santuzza, well controlled, no Slavonic wobbler, and Giacomo Aragall as Turiddù, not quite as fresh-sounding as he once was, yet gives a strong, characterful performance, with Eduard Tumagian excellent as Alfio, firm and dark. Well-focused digital recording. This set is a real bargain.

EMI's vintage (1940) version of *Cav.*, conducted by the composer with Gigli as Turiddù, came out on CD in an ungenerous two-disc package from EMI, and we await its reissue. It is good to have it again available on CD from Nimbus, along with the curious little speech of introduction that Mascagni himself recorded. Yet the composer's sluggish speeds mean that this opera has to start awkwardly at the end of the *Pag.* disc. Nimbus's transfer captures the voices well, giving them a mellow bloom, though the focus is not nearly as sharp as on the old EMI transfer, and the orchestral sound becomes muzzy.

Cavalleria rusticana (highlights).
(Y/B) ** Ph. Dig. 442 482-2 [id.] (from complete recording, with Domingo, Obraztsova, Bruson; cond. Prêtre) – LEONCAVALLO: *I Pagliacci*: highlights. **

Like its Leoncavallo coupling, this full-priced set of highlights (rather more than half-an-hour in length) comes from the soundtrack of a film. It stands or falls by the listener's allegiance to Domingo, who is undoubtedly in fine voice. His supporting cast is less impressive, with Obraztsova's somewhat unwieldy mezzo robustly characterful rather than melting.

Iris (complete).
*** Sony Dig. M2K 45526 (2) [id.]. Domingo, Tokody, Pons, Giaiotti, Bav. R. Ch., Munich R. O, Patanè.

Musically, *Iris* brings a mixture of typical Mascagnian sweetness and a vein of nobility often echoing Wagner. With a strong line-up of soloists including Domingo, and with Giuseppe Patanè a persuasive conductor, this recording makes as good a case for a flawed piece as one is ever likely to get. Domingo's warm, intelligent singing helps to conceal the cardboard thinness of a hero who expresses himself in generalized ardour. The Hungarian soprano, Ilona Tokody, brings out the tenderness of the heroine, singing beautifully except when under pressure. Juan Pons, sounding almost like a baritone Domingo, is firm and well projected as Kyoto, owner of a geisha-house, and Bonaldo Giaiotti brings an authentically dark Italian bass to the role of Iris's father. Full, atmospheric recording.

Lodoletta (complete).
*** Hung. Dig. HCD 31307/8 [id.]. Maria Spacagna, Kelen, Szilágyi, Polgár, Kálmándi, Hungarian State Op. Children's Ch., Hungarian R. & TV Ch. & State O, Charles Rosekrans.

In vivid sound and with some excellent singing, this valuable first recording from Hungaroton makes a persuasive case for Mascagni's unashamed mixture of charm and sentimentality. As the little Dutch girl, Lodoletta, Maria Spacagna sings most sensitively, even if the voice is too warm and full to suggest extreme youth. As the dissolute painter who unwittingly drives her to her death Péter Kelen proves a stylish and heady-toned lyric tenor. The American, Charles Rosekrans, makes a very sympathetic conductor, in charge of a strong cast from the Hungarian State Opera.

Mason, Benedict (born 1954)

Lighthouses of England and Wales.
**(*) Collins Dig. Single 2004-2 [id.]. BBC SO, Zagrosek.

Mason's piece is based on the distinctively rhythmic light signals of dozens of specific lighthouses (plus a fog-signal or two). It then develops into an evocative seascape, in its way a descendant of Debussy's *La mer*. Lothar Zagrosek directs a finely concentrated performance, and the recorded sound is outstanding.

Massenet, Jules (1842–1912)

Le Carillon (ballet): complete.
(N) (B) *** Decca Double Dig. 444 836-2 (2) [id.]. SRO, Richard Bonynge – DELIBES: *Coppélia*. ***

Le Carillon was written in the same year as *Werther*. The villains of the story who try to destroy the bells of the title are punished by being miraculously transformed into bronze jaquemarts, fated to continue striking them for ever! The music of this one-act ballet makes a delightful offering – not always as lightweight as one would expect. With his keen rhythmic sense and feeling for colour, Bonynge is outstanding in this repertory, and the (1984) Decca recording is strikingly brilliant and colourful. A fine bonus (37 minutes) for a desirable version of Delibes' *Coppélia*, at the cheapest possible price.

Le Cid: ballet suite.
(N) (B) *** Decca Double 448 095-2 (2) [id.]. New Philh. O, Richard Bonynge – DELIBES: *Sylvia* (complete). ***
(Y/B) (M) *** Decca Dig. 444 110-2 [id.]. Nat. PO, Bonynge – MEYERBEER: *Les Patineurs* (with DELIBES: *Naïla*, LSO, Bonynge; THOMAS: *Hamlet: ballet music* ***).

Over the years, Decca have made a house speciality of recording the ballet music from *Le Cid* and coupling it with Constant Lambert's arrangement of Meyerbeer (*Les Patineurs*). Bonynge's version is the finest yet, with the most seductive orchestral playing, superbly recorded, with the remastering for CD adding to the glitter and colour of Massenet's often witty scoring, and made the more attractive at Double Decca price. For the reissue in Decca's Ballet Gala series, Delibes' charming *Naïla Intermezzo* (a dainty little valse) and the lively, easily melodic – if less distinctive – ballet from Act IV of Thomas's *Hamlet* have been added, played with characteristic flair.

(i) *Piano concerto in E flat. Papillons noirs, Papillons blancs; Devant la Madone; 10 Pièces de genre, Op. 10; Eau dormante; Eau courante; Musique pour 'bercer les petits enfants'; Toccata; Valse folle; Valse triste.*
(M) ** EMI CDM7 64277-2 [id.]. Aldo Ciccolini, (i) Monte Carlo Nat. Op. O, Cambreling.

Massenet's *Piano concerto in E flat* has perhaps the manners of the Saint-Saëns but none of the flair, and though some of the genre pieces and certainly the two impromptus, *Eau dormante* and *Eau courante*, have a certain charm, this has greater curiosity than musical value. Aldo Ciccolini plays with conviction and is well supported in the concerto by Sylvain Cambreling and the Monte Carlo Opera Orchestra. The sound is a bit shallow, and the piano pieces are recorded rather closely in the Salle Wagram.

Don Quichotte: 2 Interludes; Scènes alsaciennes; Scènes pittoresques.
(Y/B) (M) ** Erato/Warner 4509 99771-2 [id.]. Monte Carlo Op. O, Gardiner.

Scènes de féerie; Scènes dramatiques; La Vierge: The last sleep of the Virgin.
(Y/B) (M) ** Erato/Warner 4509 99770-2 [id.]. Monte Carlo Op. O, Gardiner.

This pair of CDs, recorded in 1978, gathers together four of Massenet's seven orchestral suites, plus a few encores, including one of Sir Thomas Beecham's favourites, *The last sleep of the Virgin*. In fact this is all music which would respond to the Beecham touch. John Eliot Gardiner secures quite impressively characterized performances. The strings play sensitively in *Le sommeil de Desdémone*, the central movement of the *Scènes dramatiques* (which all have Shakespearean connotations) while the violins are also impressive in the *Apparition*, the most memorable movement of *Scènes de féerie*. The *Scènes pittoresques* are bright and fresh, the horns tolling in the *Angelus* with resonant impact. The *Scènes alsaciennes* also come off colourfully. The Monte Carlo orchestra play well enough, and the full recording – just a little studio-ish in acoustic – disguises any deficiencies, for the wind solos are well taken. But the reissue on two discs, playing for 45 and 41 minutes respectively, is ungenerous, even at mid-price. The four suites could easily have been fitted on to a single CD.

Fantaisie.
*** ASV Dig. CDDCA 867 [id.]. Sophie Rolland, BBC PO, Gilbert Varga – LALO: *Cello concerto;*
SAINT-SAENS: *Cello concerto No. 1.* ***

Massenet composed his three-movement *Fantaisie for cello and orchestra* in 1897 while on holiday in
Aix-les-Bains. Music for the sweet-toothed (and none the worse for that), though its ideas are not
anywhere near as memorable as those of its two companions on this disc. The Canadian cellist, Sophie
Rolland, and the BBC forces under Gilbert Varga play it with total commitment and fervour as if they
believe every note. Excellent recording.

Hérodiade (ballet) *suite; Orchestral suites Nos. 1; 2 (Scènes hongroises); 3 (Scènes dramatiques).*
(Y/B) (BB) ** Naxos Dig. 8.553124 [id.]. New Zealand SO, Jean-Yves Ossonce.

The ballet suite from *Hérodiade* comes in the final scene of the opera and the five movements are nicely
scored, including flutes and harp, delicate dancing strings, a luscious tune in the middle strings, decorated by chirpy woodwind, and a vigorous dance finale. The other orchestral suites are also well worth
hearing, offering a further series of sharply memorable vignettes, demonstrating Massenet's ready store
of tunes and his charmingly French orchestral palette. In the *Scènes hongroises* the charming *leggiero*
second movement is followed by characteristic *risoluto* brass writing. The more histrionic *Scènes dramatiques* (with a Shakespearean inspiration) brings a touching and very balletic central *Mélodrame*, originally entitled *Le sommeil de Desdémone*. The playing of the New Zealand orchestra is first class, polished
and vivid, and it is a pity that the microphones are somewhat close. The wind have plenty of colour, but
the string tuttis are made to sound a bit tight and fierce.

Orchestral suite No. 1, Op. 13; Cendrillon (opera): *suite. Esclarmonde* (opera): *suite.*
** Marco Polo Dig. 8.223354 [id.]. Hong Kong PO, Kenneth Jean.

The delicate atmosphere of *L'île magique* and *Hymenée* from *Esclarmonde*, and the charming *Nocturne*
from the *Suite*, Op. 13, is matched by the vigour of the finales from both, the *Marche et Strette* of Op. 13
and *La Chasse*, with its hunting horns in the operatic suite. The charming *Cendrillon* vignettes also have
plenty of sparkle. The playing does not find the degree of Beechamesque finesse that makes for totally
memorable results in such repertoire, but this remains an enjoyable collection.

Mélodies: Berceuse; Elégie; Les mains; La mort de la cigale.
**(*) EMI Dig. CDC7 54818-2 [id.]. José van Dam, Jean-Philippe Collard – GOUNOD; SAINT-SAENS:
Songs.

As in Gounod and Saint-Saëns, José van Dam's firm, dark tone brings out the beauty of these five
Massenet songs, with the celebrated *Elégie* enhanced by the cello solo of Guy Rogé. Except in *Les
mains*, Collard is heavier-handed here than in his solo playing. Altogether an unusual and enjoyable
recital.

OPERA

Cendrillon (complete).
**(*) Sony CD 79323 (2) [M2K 35194]. Von Stade, Gedda, Berbié, Welting, Bastin, Amb. Op. Ch.,
Philh. O, Rudel.

Julius Rudel directs a winning performance of Massenet's Cinderella opera. The Fairy Godmother is
the bright-toned Ruth Welting and Cendrillon a soprano. Von Stade gives a characteristically strong and
imaginative performance, untroubled by what for her is high tessitura. The pity is that the role of the
prince, originally also written for soprano, is here taken by a tenor, Gedda, whose voice is no longer
fresh-toned. Jules Bastin sings most stylishly as Pandolfe, and the others make a well-chosen team. The
recording is vivid, but spacious too. Worth exploring, even at full price.

Chérubin (complete)
⊛ *** RCA/BMG Dig. 09026 60593-2 (2) [60593-2]. Von Stade, Ramey, Anderson, Upshaw, Bav. State
Op. Ch., Munich RSO, Steinberg.

What Massenet did in this delightful *comédie chantée* of 1903 (he was sixty at the time) was to follow up
what happened to Cherubino after the *Marriage of Figaro*. There is none of the social comment of
Beaumarchais, or of da Ponte or Mozart, just a frothy entertainment, one brimming with ear-tickling
ideas, from the dazzlingly witty overture onwards. In this superb RCA recording the cast is both starry
and ideal, with June Anderson powerful and flamboyant as the dancer with whom Cherubino has a
fling, Dawn Upshaw sweet and pure as Nina, his faithful sweetheart, and Samuel Ramey warm and firm
as the Philosopher. Yet finest of all is Frederica von Stade in the title-role. Cherubino is a perky figure,
much more self-confident and pushy than in Mozart, master of his own household, though still full of

youthful high spirits. What seals this as an exhilarating experience is the conducting of Pinchas Steinberg with the Munich Radio Symphony Orchestra, strong and thrustful yet responsive to the dramatic subtleties, plainly a conductor who should be used more often in recordings. The sound is fresh and atmospheric, bringing out the sparkle and fantasy of the piece.

Le Cid (complete).
** Sony CD 79300 (2) [M2K 34211]. Bumbry, Domingo, Bergquist, Plishka, Gardner, Camp Chorale, NY Op. O, Queler.

The CBS recording is taken from a live performance in New York and suffers from boxy recording quality. Only with the entrance of Domingo in the second scene does the occasion really get going, and the French accents are often comically bad. Domingo, not always as stylish as he might be, is in heroic voice and Grace Bumbry as the proud heroine responds splendidly. The popular ballet music is given a sparkling performance. But this should have been reissued at mid-price.

Cléopâtre (complete).
**(*) Koch/Schwann Dig. 3 1032-2 (2) Harries, Streiff, Olmeda, Henry, Maurette, Hacquard, Festival Ch., Nouvel O de Saint-Étienne, Fournillier.

Cléopâtre was the very last of Massenet's operas, written in 1912, the year he died. With exotic choruses, fanfares, dances and marches, it makes one regret that Massenet – unlike Erich Korngold – did not live to become a Hollywood composer: *Cléopâtre* has much of the easy opulence of a film spectacular. This première recording was taken from a live performance at the Massenet Festival in Saint-Etienne in 1990, with Patrick Fournillier conducting. The cast has no serious weakness, and the two principal roles are splendidly taken, with Didier Henry firm and responsive as Mark Antony and with Kathryn Harries demonstrating what a rich role for a singing actress this Cléopâtre is. Miss Harries with her rich mezzo should be used more on record, when her expressive intensity here in her big solos is magnetic. That is particularly so in the concluding scenes. Antony's death-throes bring first an extended love-duet leading to what becomes a Massenet equivalent of Isolde's *Liebestod*. The Koch live recording is not helped by the dryness of the orchestral sound, though only the brass is seriously affected, and the voices are vividly caught.

Don Quichotte (complete).
*** EMI Dig. CDS7 54767-2 (2) [id.]. Van Dam, Fondary, Berganza, Toulouse Capitole Ch. & O, Plasson.

(i) *Don Quixote* (complete); (ii) *Scènes alsaciennes*.
(M) *** Decca 430 636-2 (2) [id.]. (i) Ghiaurov, Bacquier, Crespin, SRO Ch. & O, Kord; (ii) Nat. PO, Bonynge.

Massenet's operatic adaptation of Cervantes' classic novel gave him his last big success. There is genuine nobility as well as comedy in the portrait of the knight, and that is well caught here by Ghiaurov, who refuses to exaggerate the characterization. Bacquier makes a delightful Sancho Panza, but it is Régine Crespin as a comically mature Dulcinée, who provides the most characterful singing, flawed vocally but commandingly positive. Kazimierz Kord directs the Suisse Romande Orchestra in a performance that is zestful and electrifying, and the recording is outstandingly clear and atmospheric.

Michel Plasson conducts a sumptuous account of Massenet's charming Cervantes-based opera, with José van Dam singing gloriously as the Don, producing consistently firm and velvety tone. Alain Fondary as Sancho Panza is equally strong and firm vocally, shadowing and matching his master instead of contrasting, never indulging in exaggeratedly comic effects. Teresa Berganza as Dulcinée adds to the sensuousness of the performance, with the Toulouse acoustic bringing out the richness and beauty of Massenet's orchestral writing. No one will be disappointed, but the 1977 Decca set still has clear advantages. With Ghiaurov and Bacquier, the two central roles are more aptly characterized as well as more clearly contrasted, and Régine Crespin too is a formidably characterful Dulcinée. The Decca analogue sound is more clearly focused than the EMI digital, with the chorus full and immediate and with stage effects creating a vivid atmosphere. At mid-price the Decca set also comes with an attractive fill-up, the *Scènes alsaciennes*, brightly and colourfully presented by Bonynge and the National Philharmonic Orchestra.

Esclarmonde (complete).
(M) *** Decca 425 651-2 (3) [id.]. Sutherland, Aragall, Tourangeau, Davies, Grant, Alldis Ch., Nat. PO, Bonynge.
(Y/B) **(*) Koch Schwann Dig. 3-1269-2 (3) [id.]. Gavazzeni-Daviola, Sempere, Parraguin, Tréguier, Courtis, Gabelle, Massenet Festival Ch., Budapest Liszt SO, Fournillier.

Joan Sutherland is the obvious diva to encompass the demands of great range, great power and brilliant coloratura of the central role of *Esclarmonde*, and her performance is in its way as powerful as it is in Puccini's last opera. Aragall proves an excellent tenor, sweet of tone and intelligent, and the other parts are well taken too. Richard Bonynge draws passionate singing and playing from chorus and orchestra, and the recording has both atmosphere and spectacle to match the story, based on a medieval romance involving song-contests and necromancy.

Recorded live at concert performances in October/November 1992, the Koch set is among the most successful sets to have come from the Massenet Festival in Saint-Etienne. The digital recording is full and clear, coping very well with the massed forces, giving plenty of detail, and Patrick Fournillier as a specialist interpreter of this composer persuades singers and players alike to perform with sympathy for the Massenet idiom. The Italian soprano, Denia Gavazzeni-Daviola, with a voice bright and clear at the top but which has fair weight down below, tackles here the weightiest of the Massenet roles and, though she cannot match Sutherland in the warmth and weight of her singing in this music, the element of vulnerability in the princess with magic powers is more readily conveyed than with Sutherland. The Spaniard, José Sempere, sings freshly and clearly as the hero, Roland, if less ringingly and with less warmth than Giacomo Aragall, the tenor who sings opposite Sutherland on her Decca recording. Reissued on CD at mid-price, that remains the first recommendation.

Grisélidis (complete).
(Y/B) *** Koch Schwann Dig. 3-1270-2 [id.]. Command, Viala, Larcher, Desnoues, Courtis, Henry, Treguier, Sieyès, Lyon Ch., Franz Liszt SO of Budapest, Fournillier.

Grisélidis is a curious opera, one which, against his usual practice, took Massenet several years to complete. One reason may be that the subject – a medieval morality found in Plutarch, Boccaccio and Perrault – fits awkwardly with a broadly realistic style representing high romanticism. To suggest the medieval atmosphere and the purity of the heroine, Griselidis, Massenet exceptionally dallies with modal writing, if not very consistently, and the introduction of the Devil as a comic figure, henpecked by his wife, gets in the way of one taking the threat to Griselidis and her virtue seriously. Michèle Command sings warmly as the heroine and Jean-Luc Viala sings splendidly in the incidental tenor role of the shepherd, Alain, in love with Griselidis, but pushed aside by the Marquis, who sweeps her off her feet, only to prove an over-possessive husband. As the Marquis, Didier Henry is in rather gritty voice, and it is a pity that Jean-Philippe Courtis does not bring out the comedy of the Devil's role more positively, though he sings well enough. Clear, generally well-balanced 1992 'live' recording.

Hérodiade (complete).
(N) *** EMI Dig. CDC5 55378-2 (3) [CDCC 55378]. Studer, Denize, Heppner, Hampson, Van Dam, Capitole Toulouse Ch. & O, Plasson.
(N) ** Sony Dig. S2K 66847 (2) [id.]. Fleming, Zajick, Domingo, Pons, Cox, San Francisco Op. Ch. & O, Gergiev.

Massenet's opera about Salome and John the Baptist, completed in 1880, has little in common with either the Bible story or the violent Strauss opera based on Oscar Wilde's play. The title itself is misleading, for *Hérodiade*, mother of Salome and wife of Herod, is in no way the central figure. To illustrate the idiosyncratic approach, one merely notes that the final scene, so far from involving Salome in asking for John's head, has an ecstatic duet for them both, 'hymning the chaste flame of their immortal love' – as the EMI synopsis graphically puts it. When John is executed, Salome then kills herself. What matters is that the opera offers five fat parts for well-contrasted voices, and it is good to have two fine new recordings, each offering leading singers.

Michel Plasson on the EMI set has almost every advantage, when his studio recording offers well-balanced sound, opulent and firmly focused, with none of the snags inevitable in a live recording made during a stage performance. His text is complete too, using the final and fullest version of a work which Massenet revised several times. Add to that a more consistent cast, in which you have not only outstanding singers in the roles of Salome and John (Jean) but also in the three other main roles. As Hérodiade herself, Nadine Denize sings with gloriously rich, firm tone, and Thomas Hampson's portrait of Hérode could hardly be richer either vocally or dramatically, with words brought out vividly. It would be hard too to imagine a finer Phanuel than José van Dam, with his well-contrasted bass-baritone incisive in attack. As for Cheryl Studer as Salome, she has rarely sung with such expressive range and beauty of tone, with words crystal-clear. Sam Heppner as Jean confirms in his clear, firmly focused delivery earlier impressions of his development as a genuine heroic tenor with few rivals today. There are first-rate singers too in the small roles, and the Toulouse orchestra plays with glowing warmth and intensity, helped by the acoustic of the Halle-aux-Grains, far less washy than the Capitole where EMI recordings used to be made. A warmly enjoyable set from first to last, admirably filling a major gap in the catalogue.

But for the simultaneous arrival of the EMI version, the Sony set offering a live recording from the San Francisco Opera would have been very welcome indeed. Valery Gergiev, if not quite as idiomatic as Plasson, is also warmly sympathetic, holding concentration with passionate intensity over the four substantial Acts. The cuts in Acts II, III and IV mean that the opera is offered on two discs instead of three, and some will not be worried by the omissions, though it is odd, when Plácido Domingo is a major glory of the set, that one of them, albeit tiny, comes in Jean's one big aria at the beginning of Act IV. Others involve the incidental ballet music in Act IV. Domingo is in powerful voice, singing with great flair, even though the microphone catches an uncharacteristic roughness. Renée Fleming makes a most sympathetic Salome, singing her first aria with ravishing beauty, but after that rarely matching Studer in word-pointing or characterization. The others are disappointing, even Dolora Zajick, a noted Amneris who here makes Hérodiade into a closely related character, with powerful singing which nevertheless is spoilt by uneven, at times wobbly, tone. Juan Pons as Hérode is clear and direct, but dull and unimaginative next to Hampson, and Kenneth Cox as Phanuel is unsteady. Live recording means that voices are sometimes too distant, and the orchestra lacks body.

Le Roi de Lahore (complete).
❀ (M) *** Decca Dig. 433 851-2 (2) [id.]. Sutherland, Lima, Milnes, Ghiaurov, Morris, Tourangeau, L. Voices, Nat. PO, Bonynge.

Le Roi de Lahore was Massenet's first opera for the big stage of L'Opéra in Paris and marked a turning point in his career, even introducing the supernatural, with one Act set in the Paradise of Indra. The characters may be stock figures out of a mystic fairytale, but in the vigour of his treatment Massenet makes the result red-blooded in an Italianate way. This vivid performance under Bonynge includes passages added for Italy, notably a superb set-piece aria which challenges Sutherland to some of her finest singing. Sutherland may not be a natural for the role of the innocent young priestess, but she makes it a magnificent vehicle with its lyric, dramatic and coloratura demands. Luis Lima as the King is somewhat strained by the high tessitura, but his is a ringing tenor, clean of attack. Sherrill Milnes as the heroine's wicked uncle sounds even more Italianate, rolling his 'r's ferociously; but high melodrama is apt, and with digital recording of demonstration splendour and fine perspective this shameless example of operatic hokum could not be presented more persuasively on CD.

Thaïs (complete).
(N) (M) ** EMI CMS5 65479-2 (2) [id.]. Sills, Milnes, Gedda, Van Allan, John Alldis Ch., New Philh. O, Maazel.

Thaïs is an exotic period-piece, set in Egypt in the early Christian era, the story of a monk who seeks to save a beautiful courtesan and is himself destroyed. Sentimental as the plot is, it inspired Massenet to some of his characteristically mellifluous writing, with atmospheric choruses and sumptuous orchestration. Maazel's conducting is crisply dramatic (and he plays the violin solo himself most tastefully in the famous *Meditation*). The casting is good, except for the heroine. Beverly Sills has a bright, almost brittle voice, and here it sounds neither seductive nor idiomatic, for the unevenness of the production, already noticeable in earlier recordings, has grown more obtrusive. She is at her best as the reformed *Thaïs* in the later scenes. Sherrill Milnes is a powerful but conventional Athanaël and, though Nicolai Gedda as Nicias sings with his usual intelligence, it is not a young enough voice for the role. A good, warm recording, well transferred on to CD, and with a complete text and translation.

Werther (complete).
*** Ph. 416 654-2 (2) [id.]. Carreras, Von Stade, Allen, Buchanan, Lloyd, Children's Ch., ROHCG O, C. Davis.
(M) **(*) EMI CMS7 63973-2 (2) [Ang. CDMB 63973]. Gedda, De los Angeles, Mesplé, Soyer, Voix d'Enfants de la Maîtrise de l'ORTF, O de Paris, Prêtre.

Sir Colin Davis has rarely directed a more sensitive or more warmly expressive performance on record than his account of *Werther*, based on a stage production at Covent Garden. Frederica von Stade makes an enchanting Charlotte, outshining all current rivals on record. Carreras uses a naturally beautiful voice freshly and sensitively. Thomas Allen as Charlotte's husband Albert and Isobel Buchanan as Sophie, her sister, are excellent, too. The CD transfer on to a pair of discs has been highly successful, with a single serious reservation: the break between the two CDs is badly placed in the middle of a key scene between Werther and Charlotte, just before *Ah! qu'il est loin ce jour!*

Victoria de los Angeles's golden tones, which convey pathos so beautifully, are ideally suited to Massenet's gentle melodies and, though she is recorded too closely (closer than the other soloists), she makes an intensely appealing heroine. Gedda makes an intelligent romantic hero, though Prêtre's direction could be subtler.

Mathias, William (1934–92)

(i) *Clarinet concerto;* (ii) *Harp concerto;* (iii) *Piano concerto No. 3.*

(Y/B) *** Lyrita SRCD 325 [id.]. (i) Gervase de Peyer; (ii) Osian Ellis; (iii) Peter Katin; LSO or New
Philh. O, Atherton.

Helped by vividly immediate recording, the *Clarinet concerto* with its clean-cut, memorable themes
sparks off an inspired performance from Gervase de Peyer, not just in the lively outer movements, but in
the poignant *Lento espressivo* in the middle. The *Harp concerto* (1970) is less outward-going, but it
prompts Mathias to create evocative, shimmering textures, very characteristic of him. The harp,
superbly played by the dedicatee, Osian Ellis, is set alongside exotic percussion, with the finale a snappy
jig that delightfully keeps tripping over its feet. In the *Piano concerto No. 3* of 1968 the outer movements
bring jazzily syncopated writing, like Walton with a difference, here incisively played by Peter Katin.
They frame an atmospheric central *Adagio* with echoes of Bartókian 'night music', like Bartók with a
difference.

Summer dances; Soundings.

(N) *** Nimbus Dig. NI 5466 [id.]. Fine Arts Brass Ens. – HODDINNOTT: *Chorales, variants and
fanfares* etc. ***

Mathias's seven *Summer dances* (1990) bring witty rhythmic quirkiness but, if the writing is consistently
skilful, the invention is at times rather conventional. His *Soundings* (commissioned by the Philip Jones
Brass and first performed in 1988) is much more entertaining with its kinky *March* (its humour agreeably lugubrious), a darkly nostalgic *Elegy* and a catchy but unpredictable final *Capriccio*. Fine playing
and splendid recording in an ideal acoustic that brings plenty of sonority but provides firmly focused
detail.

String quartets Nos. 1–3.

(N) *** Metier Dig. MSVCD 92005 [id.]. Medea Qt.

Spanning the years 1967–86, Mathias's three string quartets make a fine sequence, illuminating his
whole achievement. The *First Quartet*, in a single 20-minute movement, pithily argued, has a
Stravinskian directness. The idiom brings momentary echoes of Britten, but might best be described as
music by a composer who has thoroughly digested the Bartók quartets. The *Second Quartet* dates from
1980–81, and in each of its four compact movements Mathias echoes medieval music in different ways.
The result is stylistically as individual as the *First Quartet*, never sounding merely derivative. The *Third
Quartet*, dating from 1986, brings together elements of both the earlier works, with the first of its three
movements developing from a deceptively light opening into a taut, large-scale structure comparable
with the *Quartet No. 1*. All three quartets, very well recorded, are outstandingly well performed by the
young Medea Quartet, formed as recently as 1991 at the Royal Academy of Music.

Wind quintet.

*** Crystal CD 750 [id.]. Westwood Wind Quintet – CARLSSON: *Nightwings;* LIGETI: *Bagatelles;*
BARBER: *Summer music.* ***

Of the five movements of this spirited *Quintet* the Scherzo is particularly felicitous and there is a rather
beautiful *Elegy*. The playing of the Westwood Wind Quintet is highly expert and committed, and the
recording is very good indeed.

Lux aeterna, Op. 88.

*** Chandos Dig. CHAN 8695 [id.]. Felicity Lott, Cable, Penelope Walker, Bach Ch., St George's
Chapel Ch., Windsor, LSO, Willcocks; J. Scott (organ).

Just as Britten in the *War Requiem* contrasted different planes of expression with Latin liturgy set
against Wilfred Owen poems, so Mathias contrasts the full choir singing Latin against the boys' choir
singing carol-like Marian anthems, and in turn against the three soloists, who sing three arias and a trio
to the mystical poems of St John of the Cross. Overall, the confidence of the writing makes the work far
more than derivative, an attractively approachable and colourful piece, full of memorable ideas, especially in this excellent performance, beautifully sung and played and atmospherically balanced.

Matthews, Colin (born 1946)

(i) *Cello concerto;* (ii) *Sonata No. 5 (Landscape), Op. 17.*

(M) *** Unicorn Dig. UKCD 2058 [id.]. (i) Alexander Baillie, L. Sinf.; (ii) Berlin RSO, John Carewe.

Colin Matthews' *Sonata No. 5*, subtitled *Landscape*, is one of the most powerful and ambitious orchestral works to have been written by a British composer of the younger generation, in effect a large-scale symphony in a single movement, richly and evocatively scored. This is a formidable achievement and, though the Berlin live performance conducted by John Carewe is not as strong or committed as that which the BBC broadcast earlier, this is a splendid celebration of a fast-growing talent. The *Cello concerto* too is an impressive piece, again confidently argued on a broad scale. It is a pity that, with this of all instruments, Matthews does not allow himself a warmer lyricism; but with Alexander Baillie brilliantly bringing out the power of the declamatory writing and intensifying the underlying darkness of the piece, this too emerges as a fine, ambitious work, warm in its emotions. On this CD it is as well recorded as it is dedicatedly played.

Matthews, David (born 1942)

Symphony No. 4, Op. 52.
**(*) Collins Single Dig. 2008-2 [id.]. East of England O, Malcolm Nabarro.

David Matthews is a gifted and imaginative composer with a good musical mind, whose work deserves wider exposure. There is a lot of Britten, Stravinsky and Tippett (on whose music he has written a book) in his musical thinking, but all the same he is his own man. His *Fourth Symphony* takes 27 minutes 17 seconds and is well worth hearing. The orchestral playing is spirited, though the strings are not world class; but the recording is very vivid and well detailed.

Matthus, Siegfried (born 1936)

Nachtlieder, for baritone, string quartet and harp.
*(*) EMI Dig. CDC7 54520-2 [id.]. Fischer-Dieskau, Graf, Cherubini Qt – SCHOECK: *Notturno.* *(*)

Nachtlieder, dedicated to Fischer-Dieskau, sets for baritone, string quartet and harp various texts on the theme of Night from Herder's *Alte ägyptische Philosophie* through to Heine and Morgenstern. It is a most imaginative and atmospheric work (not wholly uninfluenced by Schoeck as well as by the example of Ravel's *Mallarmé* settings). It is very well played here and deserves the attention of all connoisseurs of song; but Fischer-Dieskau was in his mid-sixties when he made this recording, and it finds the voice wanting in timbre and bloom.

Maunder, John (1858–1920)

Olivet to Calvary (cantata).
(B) **(*) CfP CD-CFP 4619. John Mitchinson, Frederick Harvey, Guildford Cathedral Ch., Barry Rose; P. Morse (organ).

It is easy to be patronizing about music like this but, provided one accepts the conventions of style in which it is composed, the music is effective and often moving. The performance has an attractive simplicity and genuine eloquence. Frederick Harvey is particularly moving at the actual moment of Christ's death; in a passage that, insensitively handled, could be positively embarrassing, he creates a magical, hushed intensity. The choir sing beautifully, and in the gentler, lyrical writing (the semi-chorus *O Thou whose sweet compassion*, for example) sentimentality is skilfully avoided. The 1964 recording is first class in every way, and it has been admirably transferred to CD.

Maw, Nicholas (born 1935)

Odyssey.
*** EMI Dig. CDS7 54277-2 (2) [Ang. CDCB 54277]. CBSO, Simon Rattle.

Spanning an hour and 40 minutes, Nicholas Maw's *Odyssey* has been counted the biggest continuous orchestral piece ever written. As in Mahler, if not so readily, one comes to recognize musical landmarks in the six substantial movements. The slow movement alone lasts over half an hour, while the allegros bring a genuine sense of speed, thrusting and energetic. It was at Rattle's insistence that this superb recording was made at live concerts. The result is astonishingly fine, with the engineers totally disguising the problems of recording in Birmingham Town Hall.

(i) *Flute quartet;* (ii) *Piano trio.*
(Y/B) *** ASV Dig. CDDCA 920 [id.]. Monticello Trio; with (i) Judith Pearce; (ii) Paul Coletti.

Commissioned by the Koussevitzky Foundation, the *Piano trio* is among Maw's most impressive and ambitious chamber works. It was written in 1991 for the Monticello Trio, who here record it in a warmly expressive performance, fiery where necessary. Between them the two massive movements encompass the traditional four movements of classical form, with a spectral Scherzo emerging in the middle of the broadly lyrical first movement, aptly marked *un poco inquieto.* The first half of the even longer second movement, thoughtful and slow, leads to the vigorous, easily striding finale section, which finally relapses into meditation. Maw's *Flute quartet* of 1981 was written for Judith Pearce of the Nash Ensemble, who plays it most beautifully here; it is another fine example of Maw's broad romanticism, powerful and lyrical, often sensuous, approachable yet clearly contemporary. Though the central slow movement opens as a fugue, it develops emotionally to become an atmospheric nocturne, leading to a scurrying finale. Excellent performances and sound.

Maxwell Davies, Peter (born 1934)

Ave maris stella; Image, reflection, shadow; (i) *Runes from a holy island.*
(M) *** Unicorn UKCD 2038. Fires of London, (i) cond. composer.

This is a CD compilation of key Maxwell Davies works. *Ave maris stella*, essentially elegiac, finds the composer at his most severe and demanding. The second piece, *Image, reflection, shadow*, is a kind of sequel. *Runes*, conducted by the composer, is much shorter yet just as intense in its rapt slowness. Ideal performances, well recorded, from the group for which all this music was written.

The Boyfriend; The Devils (film-scores): suites. (i) *Seven in nomine.*
*** Collins Dig. 1095-2 [id.]. (i) Mary Thomas; Aquarius, Nicholas Cleobury.

In 1971 Maxwell Davies did the sharply imagined scores for two Ken Russell films. Maxwell Davies's distorting lens works surprisingly well in both. Nicholas Cleobury draws alert playing from Aquarius, though in *The Boyfriend* the distant recording takes away some of the necessary bite. From the same crisply economical period *Seven in nomine* is a series of rather severe reworkings of the *In nomine* theme of John Taverner, which somewhat obsessed Maxwell Davies while writing his opera on that Tudor composer.

Caroline Mathilde – concert suite
*** Collins Dig. Single 2002-2. BBC PO, composer.

The composer conducts the BBC Philharmonic in these vivid performances, brilliantly recorded. A valuable addition to Collins's 20th-Century Plus series of CD singles.

(i) *Trumpet concerto;* (ii) *Symphony No. 4.*
*** Collins Dig. 1181-2 [id.]. (i) John Wallace, SNO; (ii) SCO; composer.

Inspired by the dazzling and poetic playing of the Philharmonia principal, John Wallace, the soloist on the record, the *Trumpet concerto*, written in 1988, is one of the most rewarding of Maxwell Davies's later works. Another source of inspiration has been St Francis, and the slow movement links with the saint's sermon to the birds, deeply meditative; the final coda in its Messiaenic jangling represents sublime glorification when St Francis receives the stigmata. The *Fourth Symphony* of 1984 brings similarly striking landmarks. Though it uses chamber forces, this four-movement work is texturally the thorniest of the composer's symphonies, not an easy piece but one with a powerful physical impact. The playing both of the SNO in the concerto and of the SCO in the symphony is strongly committed, with excellent recorded sound.

Violin concerto.
(M) *** Sony Dig. SMK 58928 [id.]. Isaac Stern, RPO, Previn – BRITTEN: *Cello symphony.* ***
(N) (M) *** Sony Stern Edition II Dig. SMK 64506 [id.]. Stern, RPO, Previn – BARBER: *Violin concerto.* ***

Maxwell Davies wrote this massive *Violin concerto* (over half an hour long) specifically with Isaac Stern in mind, to a commission from the RPO to celebrate its fortieth anniversary. There are parallels here with the Walton *Violin concerto* of over 40 years earlier. The composer was inspired to draw on a more warmly lyrical side that he has displayed rarely. Davies claims to have been influenced by his favourite violin concerto, Mendelssohn's, but there is little of Mendelssohnian lightness and fantasy here; for all its beauties, this is a work which has a tendency to middle-aged spread, not nearly as taut in expression as the Walton. Stern, understandably, seems less completely involved here than in the inspired Barber coupling.

Renaissance and Baroque realisations: (PURCELL: *Fantasia & 2 pavans; Fantasia upon one note.* BACH: *Well-tempered Clavier: Preludes & fugues in C sharp major and min.* (i) GESUALDO: *Tenebrae super Gesualdo.* DUNSTABLE: *Veni sancte – Veni creator spiritus.* KINLOCH: *His fantaisie. 3 Early Scottish motets*).
(M) *** Unicorn UKCD 2044 [id.]. Fires of London, (i) with Mary Thomas; composer.

These pieces mainly represent the composer in the 1960s abrasively distorting into foxtrot and other dance rhythms pieces by Purcell, Bach, Dunstable and others. It is like painting a moustache on the Mona Lisa, only more fun.

Sinfonia; Sinfonia concertante.
(M) *** Unicorn Dig. UKCD 2026 [id.]. SCO, composer.

In his *Sinfonia* of 1962 Peter Maxwell Davies took as his inspirational starting point Monteverdi's *Vespers* of 1610, and the dedication in this music, beautifully played by the Scottish Chamber Orchestra under the composer, is plain from first to last. The *Sinfonia concertante* is a much more extrovert piece for strings plus solo wind quintet and timpani. In idiom this is hardly at all neo-classical and, more than usual, the composer evokes romantic images, as in the lovely close of the first movement. Virtuoso playing from the Scottish principals, not least the horn. Well-balanced recording.

Sinfonia accademica; (i) *Into the labyrinth.*
(M) *** Unicorn UKCD 2022. (i) Neil Mackie; SCO, composer.

Into the labyrinth, in five movements, might be regarded more as a song-symphony than as a cantata, a prose-poem inspired by the physical impact of Orkney. The fine Scottish tenor, Neil Mackie, gives a superb performance, confirming this as one of Maxwell Davies's most beautiful and moving inspirations. The *Sinfonia accademica* provides a strong and attractive contrast, and again evokes the atmosphere of Orkney. Strong, intense performances under the composer, helped by first-rate recording.

Symphony No. 2.
*** Collins Dig. 1403-2 [id.]. BBC PO, composer.

Written for the centenary of the Boston Symphony Orchestra, the *Second* represents the composer's search for a latter-day equivalent, personal to him, of the traditional conflicts of symphonic form. He sets out his aims lucidly in the notes. Though the textures are complex, he hopes in the four conventionally balanced movements to make the musical logic speak for itself. Like Sibelius, he has also taken inspiration directly from nature, the seascape near his Orkney home which has been an important force in many of his later works. The outer, most obviously symphonic, movements are the ones that benefit most from repetition on disc, but the whole work, with its reposeful slow movement and shadowy Scherzo, makes an immediate impact, though under the composer the playing of the BBC Philharmonic is not as taut as it might be. Excellent sound.

(i) *Symphony No. 5;* (ii) *Chat Moss; Cross Lane Fair;* (i) *5 Klee pictures.*
(Y/B) *** Collins Dig. 1460-2 [id.]. (i) Philh. O; (ii) BBC PO; composer.

Maxwell Davies's *Fifth Symphony* is in a single movement lasting only 25 minutes, half the length of his previous symphonies. The 34 sections, some lasting several minutes and others only a few seconds, convey the tautness of a passacaglia, with groups of sections linked to produce a structure which, like Sibelius's *Seventh,* echoes the contrasted movements of a conventional symphony. Davies has sharpened his idiom too, making it more approachable and lyrical, with an underlying reliance on two plainchants from the *Liber Usualis.* Just as strikingly, his instrumental writing has a new beauty, not least in the rapt slow passages, and in the concertante passages for flute, trumpet, timpani and other instruments. A bold climax leads finally to a deeply reflective coda, confirming this as the most memorable yet of Davies's symphonies. The other works here, much lighter, all reflect in different ways the composer's preoccupation with childhood and youth. *Chat Moss,* which provided material for the symphony, evokes a childhood memory of a neighbouring heath and, more light-heartedly, *Cross Lane Fair* in 11 cleanly divided sections presents a picture of an old-fashioned fair with jugglers and roundabouts, using Northumbrian pipes set against the full orchestra, often led by brass. The *Klee portraits* were written at the beginning of Davies's career in connection with his teaching at Cirencester Grammar School, sharply establishing his distinctive tone of voice. The composer draws intense performances from both the Philharmonia (in the *Symphony*) and the BBC Philharmonic.

(i) *Vesalii Icones; The Bairns of Brugh; Runes from a Holy Island.*
(Y/B) (M) *** Unicorn-Kanchana Analogue/Dig. UKCD 2068 [id.]. (i) Jennifer Ward Clarke, Fires of
    London, composer.

Maxwell Davies has the great quality of presenting strikingly memorable visions, and *Vesalii Icones* is
certainly one, an extraordinary cello solo with comment from a chamber group. It was originally written
to accompany a solo dancer in a fourteen-fold sequence, each dance based on one of the horrifying
anatomical drawings of Vesalius (1543) and each representing one of the Stations of the Cross.
Characteristically, the composer has moments not only of biting pain and tender compassion but also
of deliberate shock tactics – notably when the risen Christ turns out to be Antichrist and is represented
by a jaunty fox-trot. This is difficult music, but the emotional landmarks are plain from the start, and
that is a good sign of enduring quality. Jennifer Ward Clarke plays superbly, and so do the Fires of
London, conducted by the composer. The 1970 recording is excellent. The two shorter pieces, digitally
recorded more than a decade later, make a valuable fill-up, *The Bairns of Brugh* a tender lament (viola
over marimba) and *Runes* a group of brief epigrams.

Resurrection.
(N) ** Collins Dig. 7034-2 (2) [id.]. Della Jones, Robson, Martyn Hill, Jenkins, Herford, Finley, J. Best,
    Blaze, BBC PO, composer.

Resurrection is an oddity, a musical autobiography in stylized operatic form offering a ragbag of situations and experiences. The Hero is a stuffed dummy who, through the Prologue and long single Act, is
consistently humiliated to make him conform with the prejudices of today. The composer's aim of
satirizing society should have sparked off a whole series of the kind of parodistic pieces which he
conceived so brilliantly in the 1960s. Yet the edge here is blunted, and the deliberate banality of TV
jingles and the like falls into its own trap. The introduction of a Rock Band (Blaze) and an Electronic
Vocal Quartet merely adds to the impression of the composer flailing about, unselfcritically throwing in
every idea that occurs to him. What makes the discs exciting to hear is the quality of the performance,
featuring an excellent team of soloists, with the composer drawing fine, incisive playing from the BBC
Philharmonic, helped by superb sound. The characterful Della Jones in particular is outstanding both
as the Elder Sister and at the end as the Antichrist.

OPERA

The Lighthouse (chamber opera; complete).
(Y/B) *** Collins Dig. 1415-2 [id.]. Mackie, Keyte, Comboy, BBC PO, composer.

The Lighthouse, one of the most successful of recent chamber operas, tells the story of three lighthouse
keepers who mysteriously disappeared without explanation from a solitary lighthouse off the coast of
the Outer Hebrides in 1900. The first half consists of a long Prologue involving the Court of Inquiry,
where three officials are questioned wordlessly by the solo horn. The second, main section, *The Cry of
the Beast*, goes back to the lighthouse itself, presenting the three keepers, taken by the same singers, who
are introduced in characteristic songs, a vulgar music-hall song for Blaze, a sentimental love-ballad for
Sandy, and – most significantly – a vehement revivalist song about God's revenge on the Children of
Israel for Arthur, a rabble-rousing Evangelical. It is Arthur's obsession that infects all three, insisting
that the Beast is coming, and the climax comes in a storm when they are all convinced that the
Antichrist has arrived. The coda presents the arrival of three more keepers, the same figures transformed. It is a powerful story, simply and directly told, and though in a recording one misses the
atmospheric help of a stage set, this fine performance, conducted by the composer – with the tenor, Neil
Mackie, outstanding among the three soloists, undaunted by the high tessitura – brings the story home
powerfully, with all its overtones, aided by the printed text.

The Martyrdom of St Magnus.
*** Unicorn Dig. DKPCD 9100 [id.]. Dives, Gillett, Thomson, Morris, Kelvin Thomas, Scottish
    Chamber Op. Ens., Michael Rafferty.

With Gregorian chant providing an underlying basis of argument, Davies has here simplified his regular
idiom. The musical argument of each of the nine compact scenes is summarized in the interludes which
follow. The story is baldly but movingly presented, with St Magnus translated to the present century as a
concentration camp victim, finally killed by his captors. Outstanding among the soloists is the tenor,
Christopher Gillett, taking among other roles that of the Prisoner (or saint).

Mayerl, Billy (1902–59)

Aquarium suite; Autumn crocus; Bats in the belfry; Busybody; Fireside fusiliers; Four Aces suite; From a Spanish lattice; A Lily pond; Marigold; Minuet by candlelight; Parade of the sandwich-board men; Pastoral sketches; Waltz for a lonely heart.
(Y/B) ** Marco Polo Dig. 8.223514 [id.]. Andrew Ball, Slovak RSO, Bratislava, Gary Carpenter.

Aquarium suite; Autumn crocus; Bats in the belfry; Four Aces suite: Ace of Clubs; Ace of Spades. 3 Dances in syncopation, Op. 73; Green tulips; Hollyhock; Hop-o'-my-thumb; Jill all alone; Mistletoe; Parade of the sandwich-board men; Sweet William; White heather.
**(*) Chandos Dig. CHAN 8848 [id.]. Eric Parkin.

Billy Mayerl left an indelible legacy of light pieces of high quality, with writing that is often much more complex and sophisticated than the rags of Joplin and his contemporaries. Mayerl's most famous lyrical numbers, such as *Marigold* and *Autumn crocus*, combine 'a blend of elegance, wistfulness, nonchalance and high spirits – qualities which stamped his whole output'. The best of his pieces sound surprisingly undated. Eric Parkin obviously enjoys this repertoire and plays the music with much sympathy and vivacious rhythmic freedom, even if his shoulders are not quite as loose as those of Susan Tomes, whose Virgin collection has been withdrawn. His programme is well chosen to suit his own approach to Mayerl's repertoire, and this Chandos record is certainly very enjoyable as he is very well treated by the recording engineers.

Marigold gains nothing from the addition of the orchestra (especially when the tempo is so laid back), and nor do the few other examples here, such as *Bats in the belfry* and *Busybody*, with its Stravinskian allusions. Mayerl's rather watery mood-pieces are pleasant, often nicely scored (sometimes but not always by the composer – full details given here), but are instantly forgettable. They are well enough played and recorded.

Medtner, Nikolai (1880–1951)

(i) *Piano concertos Nos. 1 in C min., Op. 33; 2 in C min., Op. 50; 3 in E min. (Ballade), Op. 60.* (Piano) *Sonata-Ballade in F sharp, Op. 27.*
*** Chandos Dig. CHAN 9040 (2) [id.]. Geoffrey Tozer; (i) LPO, Järvi.

(i) *Piano concerto No. 1 in C min., Op. 33; Sonata-Ballade in F sharp, Op. 27.*
*** Chandos Dig. CHAN 9038 [id.]. Tozer, (i) LPO, Järvi.

(i) *Piano concerto No. 1 in C min., Op. 33;* (ii) *Piano quintet in C, Op. posth.*
(Y/B) **(*) Hyperion Dig. CDA 66744 [id.]. Dmitri Alexeev, with (i) BBC SO, Lazarev; (ii) New Budapest Qt.

Piano concertos Nos. 2 in C min., Op. 50; 3 in E min., Op. 60.
*** Hyperion Dig. CDA 66580 [id.]. Nikolai Demidenko, BBC Scottish SO, Jerzy Maksymiuk.
*** Chandos Dig. CHAN 9039 [id.]. Tozer, LPO, Järvi.

After some years of neglect, the recording industry is taking more interest in Medtner, this Russian aristocrat of the piano who spent his last years in London. Chandos offer the three concertos together as a package or separately. Their soloist is the Australian Geoffrey Tozer, who also plays the *Sonata-Ballade*, Op. 27, for good measure. In the *Second* and *Third Concertos* they come into direct competition with Hyperion with Nikolai Demidenko as soloist. Tozer has obvious feeling for this composer and his playing has no lack of warmth and virtuosity. He has the advantage over his rival of a richer, more transparent recording and a more sympathetic and responsive accompanist in Järvi and the London Philharmonic. Demidenko, on the other hand, has the greater fire and dramatic flair, and his performance with the BBC Scottish Orchestra under Jerzy Maksymiuk has one very much on the edge of one's chair. He is by no means as well recorded as Tozer: the sound of the piano is shallow and the orchestra lacks real transparency and is a bit two-dimensional in terms of front-to-back perspective. All the same, many will feel that this is a small price for playing of such thrilling quality.

Dmitri Alexeev plays the *First Piano concerto* with virtuosity, flair and sympathy, and the BBC Symphony Orchestra under Alexander Lazarev give excellent support. The recording is very good and generally well balanced, and overall gives better results than the coupling, the late *Piano quintet in C major*. Alexeev plays it with dedication, but the New Budapest Quartet are conscientious rather than committed or inspired partners. The two-dimensional and rather congested recording does not help.

Piano concertos Nos. 2 in C min., Op. 50; 3 in E min., Op. 60 (Ballade); Arabesque in A min., Op. 7/2; Tale in F min., Op. 26/3.
(***) Testament mono SBT 1027 [id.]. Composer, Philh. O, Dobrowen.

At last we have two of the celebrated set of Medtner concerto recordings which the Maharajah of Mysore funded in the late 1940s. Medtner was then in his sixties but his playing is still pretty magisterial. These two concertos and the early miniatures that make up the disc still possess an aristocratic allure and a musical finesse that it is difficult to resist. The performances were never reissued in the UK in the days of LP, and their reappearance at long last is as welcome as it is overdue. Good transfers.

(i) *Piano quintet in C, Op. posth.;* (ii) *Violin sonata No. 2 in G, Op. 44.*
(Y/B) ** Russian Disc RDCD 11019 [id.]. Svetlanov, with (i) Borodin Qt; (ii) Labko.

The *Piano quintet*, on which Medtner laboured for so long, is played with much greater variety of tone and dynamics by Svetlanov and the Borodin Quartet than in the more recent Hyperion issue (see above). They prove far more persuasive than their modern rivals, where one is more aware of Medtner's thick textures. The 1968 recording calls for tolerance, but it is worth extending for the sake of some fine music-making. Alexander Labko plays the *Second Violin sonata* with conviction and eloquence. He is generally well partnered by Yevgeni Svetlanov, who proves a sensitive pianist even if he is not perhaps the equal of the greatest virtuosi. Unfortunately the 1968 recording is not good, even for its age, and is wanting in frequency range.

Violin sonatas Nos. 1 in B min., Op. 21; 2 in G, Op. 44; 3 in E min., Op. 57 (Epica); Canzonas and Dances, Op. 43; 3 Nocturnes, Op. 16.
**(*) Russian Disc MK Dig. 417109 (2) [id.]. Alexander Shirinsky, Dmitri Galynin.

Violin sonatas Nos. 1–2.
(Y/B) *** Chandos Dig. CHAN 9293 [id.]. Lydia Mordkovitch, Geoffrey Tozer.

The two Russian CDs comprise Medtner's complete output for violin and piano – indeed his entire chamber music save for the *Piano quintet*. The *Second* and *Third Sonatas* are both big-boned works, lasting almost 50 minutes apiece, and despite their apparent air of rhapsody are held together closely. They are not easy listening and call for keen concentration; more approachable is the much shorter *First Sonata* which has genuine charm. The *Nocturnes* and their lyrical companions on this disc should be repertoire pieces. The performances are good and the recorded balance decently judged and sonically acceptable but not top-drawer.

The first two of Medtner's three *Violin sonatas* also come on a well-recorded Chandos release. Lydia Mordkovitch proves a most imaginative and thoughtful advocate of the sonata. Apart from his not inconsiderable support at the keyboard, Geoffrey Tozer also contributes committed liner-notes hailing the *Second Sonata* in somewhat extravagant terms: 'It is one of Medtner's finest compositions and is one of the grandest chamber works in existence.' As far as the *G major Sonata* is concerned, the Chandos issue must remain the preferred recommendation among the three now available; Lydia Mordkovitch betrays an effortless expressive freedom, and both she and her partner are well recorded too.

PIANO MUSIC

(Piano, four hands) (i) *Russian round dance, Op. 58/1;* (Piano) *Forgotten melody: Danza festivo, Op. 38/3; 2 Tales, Op. 20; 3 Tales, Op. 51/1–3.* Songs: (ii) *Down in the garden;* (iii) *The Muse; The Rose;* (ii) *The Ravens; Serenade; To a dreamer, The wagon of life;* (iii) *When roses fade;* (ii) *The willow; Winter evening.* (iii) *Goethe Lieder; Aus Lila; Einsamkeit; Elfenliedchen; Glückliche Fahrt; Selbstbetrug; Im Vorübergehn; 3 Lieder, Op. 46: Praeludium; Die Quelle; Winternacht.*
(***) EMI mono EMI CDC7 54839-2 [id.]. Composer, with (i) Moiseiwitsch; (ii) Oda Slobodskaya; (iii) Elisabeth Schwarzkopf.

Apart from the pieces from Opp. 20, 51 and 58, which were recorded in 1936, these recordings all date from 1946–7 and 1950. They add a further dimension to the picture of the composer's music-making that we have from the concertos. Both Slobodskaya and Schwarzkopf give finely characterized accounts of these songs, all too few of which have been recorded since. There is nearly 80 minutes of Medtner playing either as solo pianist, as accompanist or, with his friend Benno Moiseiwitsch, as duo-pianist, and no one with an interest in Russian music should be without them.

Russian round dance; Knight errant, Op. 58/1–2.
*** Hyperion Dig. CDA 66654 [id.]. Nikolai Demidenko, Dmitri Alexeev – RACHMANINOV: *Suite* etc. ***

The Russian round-dance or *khorovod* was written in 1946 and Medtner and Moiseiwitsch recorded it the same year for EMI. Here it is given with great lightness of touch, though this partnership lose beauty of tone-production above fortissimo.

Canzona matinata, Op. 39/4; Canzona serenata, Op. 38/6; Dithyrambe, Op. 10/2; Fairy tale, Op. 20/1; Sonata elegia in D min., Op. 11/2; Sonata reminiscenza in A min., Op. 38/1; Sonata tragica in C min., Op. 39/5; Theme and variations in C sharp min., Op. 55.
** Hyperion Dig. CDA 66636 [id.]. Nikolai Demidenko.

No one who has heard Medtner's own playing, which is simple, direct and totally free of any affectation, or who recalls Gilels's account of the *Sonata reminiscenza* will find Demidenko's perfumed account entirely acceptable. By their side Demidenko sounds posturing and self-regarding. As a guide to Medtner, the less glamorous Hamish Milne (CRD) remains the truer interpreter. Demidenko's formidable pianism is not in question but some of his artistic judgements are less sound, and the quality of the Hyperion recording has also been overpraised. It is good without being distinguished and there is a lack of transparency, particularly in the middle range.

Dancing fairy tale, Op. 48/1; Fairy tale (1915); Fairy tales in D min., Op. 51/1; in E min., Op. 34/2; in F min., Op. 26/3; in G sharp min., Op. 31/3. Funeral march, Op. 31/2; The Organ grinder, Op. 54/3; Russian fairy tale, Op. 42/1; Sonata in G min., Op. 22; Sonata reminiscenza in A min., Op. 38/1.
*** Chandos Dig. CHAN 9050 [id.]. Geoffrey Tozer.

Tozer takes much less time over the *Sonata reminiscenza* than Demidenko but creates the illusion of unhurried calm. His playing has the classic virtues of being truthful to the letter (and the spirit) of the score and he allows the music to speak for itself without recourse to ostentation or flamboyance. The lifelike recording enhances the claims of this issue and bodes well for the enterprise (a complete survey of the keyboard music) as a whole.

Dithyramb, Op. 10/2; Elegy, Op. 59/2; Skazki (Fairy tales): No. 1 (1915); in E min., Op. 14/2; in G, Op. 9/3; in D min. (Ophelia's song); in C sharp min., Op. 35/4. Forgotten melodies, 2nd Cycle, No. 1: Meditation. Primavera, Op. 39/3; 3 Hymns in praise of toil, Op. 49; Piano sonata in E min. (The Night Wind), Op. 25/2; Sonata Triad, Op. 11/1–3.
*** CRD CRD 3338/9 [id.]. Hamish Milne.

Improvisation No. 2 (in variation form), Op. 47; Piano sonata in F min., Op. 5.
*** CRD Dig. CRD 3461 [id.]. Hamish Milne.

3 Novelles, Op. 17; Romantic sketches for the young, Op. 54; Piano sonatas in G min., Op. 22; A min., Op. 30; 2 Skazki, Op. 8.
*** CRD Dig. CRD 3460 [id.]. Hamish Milne.

Medtner's art is subtle and elusive. He shows an aristocratic disdain for the obvious, a feeling for balance and proportion, and a quiet harmonic refinement that offer consistent rewards. There is hardly a weak piece here, and Milne is a poetic advocate whose technical prowess is matched by first-rate artistry. The recording too is very truthful and vivid.

Méhul, Etienne-Nicolas (1763–1817)

Symphonies Nos. 1–4; Overtures: La chasse de jeune Henri; Le trésor supposé.
*** Nimbus Dig. NI 5184/5 [id.]. Gulbenkian Foundation O, Swierczewski.

Méhul was a contemporary of Cherubini and flourished during the years of Napoleon. He was enormously prolific and wrote no fewer than 25 operas in the period 1790–1810. The four symphonies recorded here come from 1808–10 (Nos. 3 & 4 have been discovered only in recent years by David Charlton, who has edited them) and are well worth investigating. The invention is felicitous and engaging, and in *No. 4 in E major* Méhul brings back a motif of the *Adagio* in the finale, a unifying gesture well ahead of its time. The performances are eminently satisfactory even if the strings sound a shade undernourished.

Melartin, Erkki (1875–1937)

Symphonies Nos. 5, Op. 90 (Sinfonia brevis); 6, Op. 100.
** Ondine Dig. ODE 799-2 [id.]. Tampere PO, Leonid Grin.

Erkki Melartin's dates coincide exactly with those of Ravel and he, too, has a good feel for orchestral colour though he was less responsive to French influence than his fellow-countrymen, Madetoja and

Klami. There is an *art nouveau* feel to his music (Glière, Scriabin and Mahler) and, though some of his ideas are empty and overblown, his was obviously a considerable talent. The *Fifth* (1915) has an extremely attractive *Intermezzo* and the melodramatic *Sixth* (1924) is also worth investigating. One can see why these symphonies have not made their way into the repertoire (though there are worse that have), but they are the product of an intelligent mind. Well-conducted performances and goodish recording.

Mendelssohn, Fanny (1805–47)

Piano trio in D, Op. 11.
*** Hyperion Dig. CDA 66331 [id.]. Dartington Piano Trio – Clara SCHUMANN: *Trio in G min.* ***

Like Clara Schumann's *G minor Trio* with which it is coupled, the *Piano trio* has impeccable craftsmanship and great facility. Its ideas are pleasing, though not strongly individual. The Dartington Piano Trio play most persuasively and give much pleasure. Excellent recording.

3 Pieces for piano, 4 hands.
*** Sony Dig. SK 48494 [id.]. Tal & Groethuysen – Felix MENDELSSOHN: *Andante and allegro* etc. ***

Yaara Tal and Andreas Groethuysen are a wonderful duo and have the capacity to transform dust into gold – not that Fanny Mendelssohn's *Pieces* are inferior. They have charm, and seem even more charming than they are in this duo's hands.

Mendelssohn, Felix (1809–47)

Capriccio brillant for piano and orchestra, Op. 22.
(N) (B) ** Sony SBK 48166; *SBT 48166* [id.]. Rudolf Serkin, Phd. O, Ormandy – BRAHMS: *Concerto No. 1;* SCHUMANN: *Intro. and allegro appassionato.* **(*)

Serkin is on good form here. This is a brilliant performance, not without panache, if not especially strong on charm. The recording is a little shallow, but otherwise good.

(i) *Piano concerto in A min.* (for piano and strings); (ii) *Piano concertos Nos. 1–2; Capriccio brillant, Op. 22.*
(M) *** Teldec/Warner Dig. 9031 75860-2 [id.]. Cyprien Katsaris; (i) Franz Liszt CO, Rolla; (ii) Leipzig GO, Masur.

It was a happy idea to pair the early *A minor Piano concerto* with the two mature works in this form. The former is an extended piece, lasting over half an hour, far longer than the two numbered concertos, an amazing work for a thirteen-year-old, endlessly inventive. It is impossible not to respond to Katsaris's vitality, even if at times there is a feeling of his rushing his fences. He plays with enormous vigour in the outer movements and receives strong support from Masur. There is nothing heavy, yet the music is given more substance than usual, while the central slow movements bring a relaxed lyrical *espressivo* which provides admirable contrast. The full, well-balanced recording has attractive ambience and sparkle.

(i) *Piano concerto in A min.* (for piano and strings); (i; ii) *Double piano concerto in E. String symphony No. 12 in G min.*
(M) *** Decca 433 729-2 [id.]. (i) John Ogdon; (ii) Brenda Lucas; ASMF, Marriner.

Here is a highly attractive (and generous: 74 minutes) compilation from Mendelssohn's precocious teenage years. The remarkably ambitious and successful *A minor Concerto* was written when he was thirteen and the *Double Concerto* and *String Symphony* (in which the flowing tranquillity of the *Andante* is most appealing) come from approximately two years later. The delightful concertante rarities both have engaging ideas and are played with great verve and spirit by John Ogdon and his wife. The orchestral playing is equally lively and fresh throughout the disc, and the vivid (originally Argo) Kingsway Hall recording from the late 1960s has hardly dated.

Piano concertos Nos. 1 in G min., Op. 25; 2 in D min., Op. 40; Capriccio brillant in B min., Op. 22.
⊛ *** Chandos Dig. CHAN 9215 [id.]. Howard Shelley, LMP.

Piano concertos Nos. 1–2; Capriccio brillant, Op. 22; Rondo brillant in E flat, Op. 29.
(BB) *** Naxos Dig. 8.550691-2 [id.]. Benjamin Frith, Slovak State PO (Košice), Robert Stanovsky.

Howard Shelley offers marvellous playing in every respect: fresh, sparkling and dashing in the fast movements, poetic and touching in the slower ones. The London Mozart Players are a group of exactly the right size for these works and they point rhythms nicely and provide the necessary lift. Shelley is particularly good in the finales and certainly conveys the scherzando quality in the closing *Presto* of No. 2. He despatches the *Capriccio brillant* with similar aplomb, and the recording-balance is admirably judged, with rich, truthful recorded sound.

But Howard Frith on Naxos is a hardly less personable and nimble soloist: he is sensitively touching in the slow movements and makes much of the fine *Adagio* of No. 2. The Slovak orchestra accompany with vigour and enthusiasm, and if the effect is at times less sharply rhythmic this is partly the effect of a somewhat more reverberant acoustic. The piano balance here is bolder, more forward, although the orchestra certainly makes a strong impression. What gives the Naxos disc an extra edge (apart from its price) is the inclusion of the *Rondo brillant*, which Frith despatches with admirable vigour and sparkle. This disc is enjoyable in every way and is undoubtedly very good value indeed.

(i) *Piano concertos Nos. 1–2. Prelude and fugue, Op. 35/1; Rondo capriccioso, Op. 14; Variations sérieuses, Op. 54.*
(Y/B) (M) *** Sony SMK 42401 [id.]. Murray Perahia; (i) ASMF, Marriner.

Perahia's playing catches the Mendelssohnian spirit with admirable perception. There is sensibility and sparkle, the slow movements are shaped most beautifully and the partnership with Marriner is very successful, for the Academy give a most sensitive backing. The recording could be more transparent but it does not lack body, and the piano timbre is fully acceptable. At mid-price, a very recommendable issue.

Double piano concertos: in A flat; in E.
*** Hyperion Dig. CDA 66567 [id.]. Coombs, Munro, BBC Scottish SO, Maksymiuk.

Mendelssohn's *Double concerto in A flat* is the most ambitious of all his concertante works, and the work in E brings an expansive first movement too; they provide formidable evidence of the teenage composer's fluency and technical finesse. Stephen Coombs and Ian Munro prove ideal advocates, playing with delectable point and imagination, finding a wit and poetry in the writing that might easily lie hidden, with even the incidental passagework magnetizing the ear. The recording of the pianos is on the shallow side, and the string-tone is thin too, but that is not inappropriate for the music.

Double piano concerto in E.
**(*) Ph. Dig. 432 095-2 [id.]. Katia and Marielle Labèque, Philh. O, Bychkov – BRUCH: *Double concerto.* **(*)

Mendelssohn's ambitious *E major Double concerto* is not an early masterpiece but is well crafted (if a bit long) and enjoyable. The Labèques play it with enthusiasm and flair, and Bychkov accompanies manfully. But, partly because of the resonant acoustic, the effect is rather inflated and the ear looks for more transparency and lightness of texture in such an amiable piece.

Violin concertos: in D min. (for violin & strings); in E min., Op. 64.
(Y/B) *** RCA Dig. 09026 62512-2 [id.]. Kyoko Takezawa, Bamberg SO, Claus Peter Flor.
*** Ph. Dig. 432 077-2 [id.]. Viktoria Mullova, ASMF, Marriner.

Kyoko Takezawa gives winning accounts of both the great Mendelssohn *Violin concerto in E minor* and the youthful D minor work, resurrected over 40 years ago by Yehudi Menuhin. With a dedicated Mendelssohnian conductor, Claus Peter Flor, these are performances which consistently reflect the joy of the performers in the music. Takezawa's reading of the *D minor* is full of fantasy, with each movement sharply characterized to make the piece seem more mature than it is.

Purity is the keynote of Mullova's fresh and enjoyable readings of both concertos, the early *D minor* as well as the great *E minor* which is tenderly expressive rather than flamboyant in the expression of emotion, yet with concentration keenly maintained. So the central *Andante* is sweet and songful and the finale, light and fanciful, conveys pure fun in its fireworks. The early work follows a similar pattern, with youthful emotions given full rein and with the finale turned into a headily brilliant Csardas. The Philips recording is admirably natural and beautifully balanced, but Takezawa is now a first choice for this coupling.

Violin concerto in E min., Op. 64.
(Y/B) (M) *** Sony Dig. SMK 64250 [id.]. Cho-Liang Lin, Philh. O, Tilson Thomas – BRUCH: *Concerto;* VIEUXTEMPS: *Concerto No. 5.* ***
(BB) *** Naxos Dig. 8.550153 [id.]. Nishizaki, Slovak PO, Jean – TCHAIKOVSKY: *Concerto.* ***
(Y/B) *** Denon Dig. CO 78913 [id.]. Chee-Yun, LPO, Lopez-Cóboz – VIEUXTEMPS: *Concerto No. 5.* ***

(Y/B) (M) *** DG Dig. 445 515-2 [id.]. Anne-Sophie Mutter, BPO, Karajan – BRAHMS: *Violin concerto.* ***

*** RCA Dig. 09026 61700-2. Anne Akiko Meyers, Philh. O, Andrew Litton (with DVORAK: *Romance, Op. 11;* MASSENET: *Thaïs: Méditation* ***) – VAUGHAN WILLIAMS: *Lark ascending.* ***

*** EMI Dig. CDC7 49663-2 [id.]. Nigel Kennedy, ECO, Tate – BRUCH: *Concerto No. 1;* SCHUBERT: *Rondo.* ***

*** ASV CDDCA 748 [id.]. Xue-Wei, LPO, Ivor Bolton – BRAHMS: *Violin concerto.* ***

(Y/B) (M) *** Carlton IMP Dig. PCD 2005 [id.]. Jaime Laredo, SCO – BRUCH: *Concerto No. 1.* ***

(M) *** EMI CDM7 69003-2 [id.]. Menuhin, Philh. O, Kurtz – BRUCH: *Concerto No. 1.* ***

(M) *** DG 419 067-2 [id.]. Milstein, VPO, Abbado – TCHAIKOVSKY: *Concerto.* ***

**(*) RCA 09026 61743-2 [RCA 61743-2-RC]. Heifetz, Boston SO, Munch – TCHAIKOVSKY: *Concerto* etc. **(*)

(***) Testament mono SBT 1037 [id.]. Martzy, Philh. O, Kletzki – BRAHMS: *Concerto.* (***)

(M) (***) EMI mono CDH7 69799-2 [id.]. Yehudi Menuhin, BPO, Furtwängler – BEETHOVEN: *Concerto.* (***)

(Y/B) (***) Beulah mono 1PD 10 [id.]. Alfred Campoli, LPO, Boult – ELGAR: *Violin concerto.* (***)

(N) (M) **(*) Sony Stern Edition I SMK 66827 [id.]. Stern, Phd. O, Ormandy – DVORAK: *Violin concerto; Romance.* **

(B) **(*) Discover Dig. DICD 920122 [id.]. Evgeny Bushkov, Slovak New PO, Rahbari – TCHAIKOVSKY: *Concerto.* **

(M) (***) EMI mono CDH7 64562-2 [id.]. Szigeti, LPO, Beecham – MOZART: *Violin concerto No. 4;* PROKOFIEV: *Violin concerto No. 1.* (***)

(N) (M) **(*) Sup. SU 1939-2 011 [id.]. Josef Suk, Czech PO, Karel Ančerl – BERG: *Concerto* ***; BRUCH: *Concerto.* **

Cho-Liang Lin's vibrantly lyrical account now reappears with the Bruch *G minor* plus the Vieuxtemps No. 5, to make an unbeatable mid-priced triptych. They are all three immensely rewarding and poetic performances, given excellent, modern, digital sound, and Michael Tilson Thomas proves a highly sympathetic partner in the Mendelssohn *Concerto.*

Takako Nishizaki gives an inspired reading of the *Concerto*, warm, spontaneous and full of temperament. The central *Andante* is on the slow side, but well shaped, not sentimental, while the outer movements are exhilarating, with excellent playing from the Slovak Philharmonic. Though the forwardly placed violin sounds over-bright, the recording is full and warm. A splendid coupling at super-bargain price.

The young South Korean fiddler, Chee-Yun, joins the list of players to give inspirationally fresh accounts of Mendelssohn's lovely *Concerto*, full of sparkle and imagination. Her tone is full and sweet and the pianissimo introduction of the second subject of the opening movement is exquisite. The graceful *Andante*, played very gently at first but with a strong central climax, is capped by a vivacious finale, with Lopez-Cóboz and the LPO providing admirable support throughout. However, the relatively short Vieuxtemps coupling, although equally enticing, is not as generous as with Lin's competing Sony disc, which offers the Max Bruch as well.

In the Mendelssohn E minor, even more than in her Brahms coupling, the freshness of Anne-Sophie Mutter's approach communicates vividly to the listener, creating the feeling of hearing the work anew. Her gentleness and radiant simplicity in the *Andante* are very appealing, and the light, sparkling finale is a delight. Mutter is given a small-scale image, projected forward from the orchestral backcloth; the sound is both full and refined.

As her previous discs for RCA have demonstrated, Anne Akiko Meyers is a thoughtful rather than a flamboyant virtuoso, and the four items suit her exceptionally well. This is a small-scale reading of the Mendelssohn, but she compensates in sweetness and poetry. At a flowing speed her sweetly lyrical account of the *Andante* completely avoids sentimentality. The Dvořák then emerges as far more than just a salon piece with a Slavonic flavour. The Massenet too, which can seem all too sweet, is played with natural gravity. Though there are many other versions of the Mendelssohn, this one, offering an unusual sequence of other items, all played with compelling dedication and poetry and recorded in vivid sound, clearly has its place.

Kennedy establishes a positive, masculine view of the work from the very start, but fantasy here goes with firm control. The slow movement brings a simple, songful view of the haunting melody, and the finale sparkles winningly, with no feeling of rush. With a bonus in the rare Schubert *Rondo* and clear, warm recording, it makes an excellent recommendation.

Xue-Wei's version, clean and fresh if a little reticent emotionally, makes a generous and attractive coupling for his equally recommendable version of the Brahms. There are more strongly characterized readings than this but, with its pastel-shaded lyricism, this is undoubtedly satisfying, helped by first-rate recording.

Laredo's version on a mid-price CD brings an attractively direct reading, fresh and alert but avoiding mannerism, marked by consistently sweet and true tone from the soloist. The orchestral ensemble is amazingly good when you remember that the soloist himself is directing. The recording is vivid and clean.

The restrained nobility of Menuhin's phrasing of the famous principal melody of the slow movement has long been a hallmark of his reading with Efrem Kurtz, who provides polished and sympathetic support. The sound of the CD transfer is bright, with the soloist dominating but the orchestral texture well detailed.

Milstein's DG version comes from the early 1970s. His is a highly distinguished performance, very well accompanied. His account of the slow movement is more patrician than Menuhin's, and his slight reserve is projected by DG sound which is bright, clean and clear in its CD remastering.

Campoli's sweet, perfectly formed tone and polished, secure playing are just right for the Mendelssohn Concerto, and this is a delightful performance, notable for its charm and disarming simplicity. The 1958 recording has been impeccably transferred and, although this record is in the premium-price range, with its fine Elgar coupling it is a splendid reminder of a superb violinist.

As one might expect, Heifetz gives a fabulous performance. His speeds are consistently fast, yet in the slow movement his flexible phrasing sounds so inevitable and easy that it is hard not to be convinced. The finale is a tour de force, light and sparkling, with every note in place. The recording has been digitally remastered with success and the sound is smoother than before.

It is not just the perfect sweetness and purity of Martzy's tone that is so impressive, coupled with flawless intonation, but also her natural imagination in phrasing. So her freely flexible rubato always sounds spontaneous, and the hushed tenderness of her pianissimo playing is breathtaking, as in the link into the second subject of the first movement and in the central Andante. The performance is also remarkable for the quicksilver energy of the finale and, with the soloist well forward, the mono sound is full and clear.

Menuhin's unique gift for lyrical sweetness has never been presented on record more seductively than in his classic, earlier version of the Mendelssohn Concerto with Furtwängler. The digital transfer is not ideally clear, yet one hardly registers that this is a mono recording from the early 1950s.

Another totally memorable performance by Stern from the late 1950s. It has great bravura, culminating in a marvellously surging account of the finale. The slow movement too is played with great eloquence and feeling but, when pianissimos are non-existent – partly, but not entirely, the fault of the close recording-balance – the poetic element is diminished, even though there is a full flood of romanticism.

The latest bargain digital recording from Discover introduces a brilliant young Russian soloist, Evgeny Bushkov, a pupil of Leonid Kogan. His small, sweet, silvery timbre suits the Mendelssohn concerto admirably, and he prepares and plays the secondary theme of the opening movement with appealing tenderness. The Andante, too, has a matching simplicity and the finale no lack of bravura and fire. He is well accompanied, and the recording, made in the Concert Hall of Slovak Radio, Bratislava, is full and well balanced. Not a first choice, however, for the coupled Tchaikovsky Concerto sounds less spontaneous.

It is good to have Szigeti's wonderfully intense performance of the Mendelssohn Violin concerto back in circulation, together with the other classic records he did in the 1930s with Sir Thomas Beecham. The EMI transfer is the one to have.

Suk's small, sweet timbre is particularly suited to the Mendelssohn concerto and his intonation is immaculate. This is a highly congenial performance, not as individual as some, with a straightforwardly lyrical slow movement and a finale which gains from not being rushed off its feet. An excellent CD transfer, firm and full.

(i) Violin concerto in E min.; (ii) Symphony No. 4 (Italian); Overtures: The Hebrides (Fingal's Cave); A Midsummer Night's Dream; Ruy Blas.
(Y/B) (BB) *** EMI Seraphim CES5 68524-2 (2) [CEDB 68524]. LSO, with (i) Sir Yehudi Menuhin, cond. Rafael Frühbeck de Burgos; (ii) Previn – BRUCH: Violin concerto No. 1. ***

Menuhin's second stereo recording, with Rafael Frühbeck de Burgos, has its moments of roughness, but it has magic too: at the appearance of the first movement's second subject and in the slow movement, even if the timbre itself is a little spare. The recording sounds fuller than the earlier account with Kurtz, and this makes a good bargain on EMI's new Seraphim label, coupled with the Bruch Concerto and Previn's highly recommendable 1979 version of the Italian Symphony, plus the three most popular overtures. Previn, always an inspired Mendelssohnian, gives exuberant performances. In the symphony the outer movements are urgent, without sounding at all breathless, and are finely sprung; the essential first-movement exposition repeat is included. Recording balance has the strings a little less forward than usual, but the overall effect is agreeably full.

(i) *Violin concerto in E min.;* (ii) *A Midsummer Night's Dream: Overture, Op. 21; Scherzo; Nocturne; Wedding march. Overtures: Fingal's Cave (The Hebrides);* (iii) *Ruy Blas;* (ii) *Symphony No. 4 (Italian), Op. 90;* (iv) *Rondo capriccioso, Op. 14; Songs without words, Opp. 19/1–2; 30/4 & 6; 62/1 & 6; 67/4–6; Variations sérieuses, Op. 54.*
(Y/B) (B) **(*) Ph. Duo 444 302-2 (2) [id.]. (i) Accardo, LPO, Dutoit; (ii) Boston SO or BBC SO, Sir Colin Davis; (iii) New Philh. O, Sawallisch; (iv) Werner Haas.

Accardo's account of the *Violin concerto* is lithe and sparkling in the outer movements, and the slow movement, taken slower than usual, is expressive in a natural, unforced way. But some ears will find his phrasing here too restrained to capture Mendelssohn's romantic inspiration in full bloom. There are no reservations about Sir Colin Davis's coupling of an exhilarating but never breathless account of the *Italian Symphony* (complete with exposition repeat) with the four most important items from *A Midsummer Night's Dream*, and the mid-1970s recording is warm and refined. The ripeness of the Boston playing is persuasive. There is no lack of drama or evocation from the BBC Symphony Orchestra in *Fingal's Cave*, and Sawallisch opens the programme with a robust account of *Ruy Blas*. Werner Haas provides the piano interludes very musically and manages to include both the *Spring song* and *Spinning song* in his well-chosen collection of *Songs without words*. He is well recorded. But what a pity room was not found for the *Scottish Symphony*.

Symphonies for string orchestra Nos. 1 in C; 2 in D; 3 in E min.; 4 in C min.; 5 in B flat; 6 in E flat.
*** Nimbus Dig. NI 5141 [id.]. E. String O, William Boughton.

Symphonies for string orchestra Nos. 7 in D min.; 8 in D; 10 in B min.
*** Nimbus Dig. NI 5142 [id.]. E. String O, William Boughton.

Symphonies for string orchestra Nos. 9 in C; 11 in F; 12 in G min.
*** Nimbus Dig. NI 5143 [id.]. E. String O, William Boughton.

Mendelssohn's twelve *String symphonies*, written for family performance by one of the most brilliant boy-geniuses in the history of music, contain delectable inspirations by the dozen. William Boughton conducts the English String Orchestra in winningly energetic readings of these delightful works, not as polished in ensemble as some rivals, but with warmly atmospheric recording helping to make them very persuasive.

Symphonies for strings Nos. 2 in D; 3 in E min.; 9 in C; 10 in B min.
*** BIS Dig. CD 643 [id.]. Amsterdam New Sinf., Lev Markiz.

The recordings by the Amsterdam New Sinfonietta are the first instalment of a new, complete survey. They are very well if resonantly recorded, but the playing, both vital and expressive, is of high quality and the sound is clearly textured as well as full. Recommendable, alongside the current alternatives, and on grounds of recording a possible first choice.

Symphonies for string orchestra, Nos. 9 in C min.; 10 in B min.; 12 in G min.
*** Hyperion CDA 66196 [id.]. L. Festival O, Ross Pople.

Ross Pople achieves performances that are as polished and spirited as they are lyrically responsive. No. 9 has a particularly gracious slow movement following the drama of its opening, but No. 12 with its clear debt to Bach is also most impressive. Excellent sound.

Symphonies Nos. 1–5.
(M) *** DG 429 664-2 (3). Mathis, Rebman, Hollweg, German Op. Ch., BPO, Karajan.
(Y/B) (B) **(*) RCA 74321 20286-2 (3). Casapietra, Stolte, Schreier, Leipzig R. Ch. (in *No. 2*); Leipzig GO, Masur.

Symphonies Nos. 3 (Scottish); 4 (Italian), Op. 90.
(Y/B) (BB) ** RCA Navigator 74321 17891-2. Leipzig GO, Masur.

Symphonies Nos. 1–5; Overtures: Fair Melusina, Op. 32; The Hebrides (Fingal's Cave), Op. 26; A Midsummer Night's Dream, Op. 21; Octet, Op. 20: Scherzo.
*** DG Dig. 415 353-2 (4) [id.]. LSO, Abbado (with Connell, Mattila, Blochwitz and London Symphony Ch. in Symphony No. 2).

Abbado's is a set to brush cobwebs off an attractive symphonic corner; in the lesser-known symphonies it is his gift to have you forgetting any weaknesses of structure or thematic invention in the brightness and directness of his manner. So the youthful *First* has plenty of C minor bite. The toughness of the piece makes one marvel that Mendelssohn ever substituted the scherzo from the *Octet* for the third movement (as he did in London), but helpfully Abbado includes that extra scherzo, so that on CD, with a programming device, you can readily make the substitution yourself. Good, bright recording, though not ideally transparent.

Karajan's distinguished set of the Mendelssohn *Symphonies* was recorded in 1971/2 in the Berlin Jesus Christus Kirche. The early C minor work sounds particularly fresh, and the *Hymn of praise* brings the fullest sound of all; the very fine choral singing is vividly caught. The soloists make a good team, rather than showing any memorable individuality; but overall Karajan's performance is most satisfying. The *Scottish Symphony* is a particularly remarkable account and the *Italian* shows the Berlin Philharmonic in sparkling form: the only drawback is Karajan's characteristic omission of both first-movement exposition repeats. There are few reservations to be made about the *Reformation Symphony*, and the sound has been effectively clarified without too much loss of weight.

Recorded by Eurodisc in 1971/2, the earlier of Masur's two Mendelssohn *Symphony* cycles, reissued in RCA's Symphony Edition, makes an excellent bargain-priced alternative to the strongly characterized later set for Teldec. The recording is warmer and more immediate, and Masur's preference for flowing speeds in slow movements is not so marked, often with more affectionate moulding of phrase. The performances are often more vivid and more spontaneous-sounding, notably that of No. 2, the *Hymn of Praise*, where the forward focus of the voices adds to the impact of a most refreshing reading. Sadly, the two most popular symphonies, the *Scottish* and *Italian*, are the least successful, with generally slow speeds and slacker ensemble than in the rest. Masur here observes the exposition repeat in the *Italian* but not in the *Scottish*. These are also available separately on RCA's super-bargain Navigator label, but this is a case where Masur's mid-priced Teldec alternative coupling of these two key works is clearly preferable. The symphonies in the RCA set have also been issued separately at mid-price: *Symphonies Nos. 1 and 3* (74321 20287-2); *Symphony No. 2* (74321 20288-2); *Symphonies Nos. 4 and 5* (74321 20289-2).

Symphonies Nos. 1 in C min., Op. 11; 5 in D (Reformation), Op. 107.
(Y/B) **(*) Decca Dig. 444 428-2 [id.]. Berlin RSO, Ashkenazy.

Symphonies Nos. 1; 5; Hebrides overture (Fingal's cave), Op. 26.
*** Chandos Dig. CHAN 9099 [id.]. Philh. O, Weller.

Weller plays the *First Symphony* as if it were a mature work, not the inspiration of a fifteen-year-old, making the strongest contrast between the fast outer movements and the *Andante* which is spaciously moulded. In the *Reformation Symphony* and in *Fingal's Cave* there is an emotional thrust that is very involving, leading to a joyfully exultant conclusion in the finale. The Chandos recording is richly full-bodied, though not sharply defined.

Ashkenazy conducts the former Radio Symphony Orchestra in fresh, finely moulded readings of both symphonies, the first instalment in a projected Mendelssohn cycle. At generally spacious speeds in slow movements, Ashkenazy phrases affectionately, with very gentle pianissimos. He brings out the tenderness of the *Andante* of No. 1 without sentimentality and finds mystery in the slow introduction of the *Reformation Symphony*. By contrast, allegros are taken fast, with the Minuet of No. 1 becoming almost a Scherzo, as does the second movement of the *Reformation*. There are moments in the first movements of both symphonies when Ashkenazy comes near to sounding too hectic, but he compensates in his springing of rhythms. As recorded, the string sound is thinner than usual with this orchestra, but otherwise the quality is excellent.

Symphony No. 2 in B flat (Hymn of praise), Op. 52.
(M) *** DG 431 471-2. Mathis, Rebmann, Hollweg, German Op. Ch., BPO, Karajan.
*** Opus 111 OPS 30-98. Soile Isokoski, Mechthild Bach, Frieder Lang, Chorus Musicus Köln, Das neue Orchester, Christoph Spering.
*** DG Dig. 423 143-2 [id.]. Connell, Mattila, Blochwitz, London Symphony Ch., LSO, Abbado.
(Y/B) **(*) EMI Dig. CDC7 49764-2 [id.]. Laki, Shirai, Seiffert, Düsseldorf Musikverein Ch., BPO, Sawallisch.
(Y/B) **(*) Chandos Dig. CHAN 8995 [id.]. Haymon, Hagley, Straka, Philh. Ch. & O, Weller.

We have already praised the 1972 Karajan recording of the *Hymn of praise* within the context of his complete set of Mendelssohn symphonies above. In some ways Abbado's full-price digital version is even finer, if not more clearly recorded, brushing aside all sentimentality, both fresh and sympathetic and, though the recording is not ideally clear on inner detail, the brightness reinforces the conductor's view. The chorus, well focused, is particularly impressive, and the sweet-toned tenor, Hans-Peter Blochwitz, is outstanding among the soloists.

It is timely that Spering, following up the success of Herreweghe's Harmonia Mundi version of *Elijah*, here presents a performance of the *Hymn of Praise* in period style. Spering is relaxed in his choice of tempos, but in no way does he let the music drag or become sentimental. With clean, crisp textures this is a most refreshing performance, full of incidental beauties. For example, the once-celebrated duet for the two soprano soloists, *Ich harrete des Herrn* ('I waited for the Lord'), is intensely beautiful in its simplicity, with Soile Isokoski (also in Herreweghe's *Elijah*) and Mechthild Bach both angelically sweet yet nicely contrasted. The tenor soloist, Frieder Lang, is also exceptionally sweet-toned, though his projection is keen enough to make the *Huter, ist die Nacht bald hin?* ('Watchman, what of the night?') episode very intense and dramatic. Though not always clear in inner definition, the freshness of the choral singing matches that of the whole performance.

Recorded live in the Philharmonie, Berlin, Sawallisch's EMI version consistently conveys dramatic bite. Mendelssohn's arguments, not always his most cogent, are made to seem fresh and immediate, with warmly affectionate phrasing in slower passages never running the risk of sounding sentimental. The sense of occasion is most telling in the choral movements, with the Düsseldorf Chorus adding powerfully to the thrust of the performance, and with excellent solo singing. Balances are not always ideal and there is some thinness in the strings; but this can be recommended to anyone wanting a live account.

The great merit of Weller's Chandos version is the warmth and weight of the recorded sound, with a large chorus set against full-bodied, satisfyingly string-based orchestral sound. Though Weller's speeds are sometimes dangerously slow, as in the lovely duet for the two sopranos, *Ich harrete des Herrn*, the sense of spontaneity in the performance makes it compelling throughout, even if ensemble is not always ideally crisp. Cynthia Haymon and Alison Hagley are warm-toned soloists, with Peter Straka an expressive, if slightly fluttery, tenor.

Symphony No. 3 in A min. (Scottish), Op. 56; A Midsummer Night's Dream: Overture, Op. 21 and excerpts, Op 61; Overture: The Hebrides (Fingal's Cave).
(Y/B) (M) **(*) Decca 443 578-2 [id.]. LSO, Peter Maag.

Under Maag, the *Scottish Symphony* is played most beautifully, and its pastoral character, occasioned by Mendelssohn's considerable use of strings throughout, is amplified by a Kingsway Hall recording of great warmth. The response of the LSO has quite remarkable freshness in this highly spontaneous performance. The opening string cantilena is poised and very gracious and thus sets the mood for what is to follow. Unfortunately the first-movement exposition repeat is not observed, but to do so was not unusual in those days. One other small complaint: Maag is too ponderous in the final *Maestoso*, but there is a compensating breadth and the effect is almost Klempererian. The remastered sound is first class, with a natural balance and glowing woodwind detail. Only a degree of thinness of timbre in the violins when playing above the stave betrays the age of the original. *Fingal's Cave* is no less successful. Maag's *Overture* and excerpts from a *A Midsummer Night's Dream* derive from a more extended LP selection, dating from the earliest days of stereo (1957). The fairy string music is beautifully translucent, and if Maag's treatment of the *Overture*'s forthright second subject strikes the ear as rhythmically mannered, the recording includes a strong contribution from a fruity bass wind instrument which might possibly be Mendelssohn's ophicleide but which is probably a well-played tuba. The recording is clean and well projected; in the remastering, the luminous quality one remembers in the original has been retained. These vintage recordings play for 76 minutes.

Symphony No. 3 in A min. (Scottish), Op. 56; Overtures; Calm sea and a prosperous voyage; The Hebrides (Fingal's Cave); Ruy Blas.
(BB) **(*) Naxos Dig. 8.550222; 4.550222 [id.]. Slovak PO, Oliver Dohnányi.

Oliver Dohnányi conducts a joyful account of the *Scottish Symphony* on Naxos, given the more impact by forward recording. Mendelssohn's lilting rhythms in all the fast movements are delightfully bouncy, and though the slow movement brings few hushed pianissimos, its full warmth is brought out without sentimentality. The three overtures, also very well done, not least the under-appreciated *Ruy Blas*, make an excellent coupling.

Symphonies Nos. 3 in A min. (Scottish); 4 in A (Italian), Op. 90.
*** Decca Dig. 433 811-2 [id.]. San Francisco SO, Herbert Blomstedt.
(N) *** Mer. Dig. CDE 84261 [id.]. Apollo CO, Chernaik.
(M) *** DG Dig. 427 810-2 [id.]. LSO, Abbado.
(BB) *** ASV CDQS 6004. O of St John's, Lubbock.
(M) *** Teldec/Warner Dig.4509 92148 [id.]. Leipzig GO, Kurt Masur.
(Y/B) *** Ph. Dig. 442 130-2 [id.]. ASMF, Sir Neville Marriner.
*** Teldec/Warner Dig. 9031 72308-2 [id.]. COE, Harnoncourt.
*** EMI CDC7 54000-2 [id.]. L. Classical Players, Norrington.
**(*) Chandos Dig. CHAN 9032 [id.]. Philh. O, Weller.
(Y/B) (M) **(*) DG 439 980-2 [id.]. Israel PO, Bernstein.

Of all the many discs coupling Mendelssohn's two most popular symphonies, the *Scottish* and the *Italian*, there is none finer than Blomstedt's. Not only does he choose ideal speeds – not too brisk in the exhilarating first movement of the *Italian* or sentimentally drawn out in slow movements – he conveys a feeling of spontaneity throughout, springing rhythms infectiously. The sound is outstandingly fine, outshining any direct rival.

The dynamic young American conductor, David Chernaik, gives performances of these two symphonies which in their vitality and freshness are second to none. Although the recording is live, the audience is notably quiet and shows its presence only by clapping perfunctorily at the end of each work, a distraction which could and should have been edited out. The London-based Apollo Chamber Orchestra, on its toes throughout, is exactly the right size for these two symphonies, and the recording (in St John's, Smith Square) has been beautifully balanced so that detail is transparently clear, yet a warm ambience remains. Wind and string playing alike are consistently fresh. The *Scottish* is particularly fine, with a vigorous opening movement, a vivaciously buoyant Scherzo, a songful *Adagio* (ideally paced) and a particularly satisfying final coda, exuberant but not rushed. Chernaik includes the essential exposition repeats in both symphonies, and in the *Italian* the light, sparkling string articulation in the outer movements bounces infectiously, the *Saltarello* finale particularly joyful with its chortling woodwind vying with scintillating bravura from the violins, particularly neat in their pianissimos.

Abbado's fine digital recordings of the *Scottish* and *Italian Symphonies*, coupled together from his complete set, make a splendid mid-price bargain. The recording is admirably fresh and bright – atmospheric, too – and the ambience, if not absolutely sharply defined, is very attractive. Both first-movement exposition repeats are included.

Lubbock's coupling of the *Scottish* and *Italian Symphonies* makes an outstanding super-bargain issue, offering performances of delightful lightness and point, warmly and cleanly recorded. The string section may be of chamber size but, amplified by a warm acoustic, the result sparkles, with rhythms exhilaratingly lifted. The slow movements are both on the slow side but flow easily with no suspicion of sentimentality, while the *Saltarello* finale of No. 4, with the flute part delectably pointed, comes close to Mendelssohnian fairy music.

Masur observes exposition repeats in both symphonies, and his choice of speeds brings out the freshness of inspiration judiciously, avoiding any suspicion of sentimentality in slow movements which are taken at flowing tempi. Conversely, the allegros are never hectic to the point of breathlessness. The one snag is that the reverberant Leipzig recording tends to obscure detail in tuttis; the Scherzo of the *Scottish*, for example, becomes a blur, losing some of its point and charm. Otherwise, the sound of the orchestra has all the characteristic Leipzig bloom and beauty. Indeed the orchestral sound is glorious and the cultured playing always a joy to listen to, while at the climax of the first movement, by bringing out the timpani strongly, Masur finds a storm sequence almost to match *Fingal's Cave*. This disc is not a first choice, but as an alternative coupling it can be strongly recommended, for the effect has a natural concert-hall feel and the performances are very satisfying.

Marriner in his 1994 Philips version offers direct and sensitive readings of both symphonies, generally a fraction faster than those he recorded earlier for Decca. This time too he observes the exposition repeats in both symphonies. In the slow movements, the more flowing speeds bring a clear advantage, particularly when the Academy violins are even sweeter and purer than before, helped by recording that is a degree more refined. In the fast movements there are also many gains – as in the Scherzo of the *Scottish*, which is lighter and more transparent – but also some disadvantages, as in the first movement of the *Italian* which, though clean and clear, is rather hard-driven, not able to relax as readily as the joyful earlier reading. The coda to the finale of the *Scottish* reverses the trend, and Marriner chooses a slower speed, making the passage a fraction heavier and less buoyant, leading up to the great whoops of joy on the unison horns. All in all, an enjoyable disc, but not a first choice for this coupling.

As in Beethoven and Schubert, Nikolaus Harnoncourt's happy relationship with the Chamber Orchestra of Europe brings performances which on modern instruments might be counted 'historically aware', with shortened phrasing, limited string vibrato, rasping horns and clean-cut timpani. The cleanness of texture is enhanced by Harnoncourt's generally relaxed speeds, which allow Mendelssohnian rhythms to have an infectious spring. Natural, well-balanced sound.

As in his Schumann, Norrington opts for unexaggerated speeds in the outer movements, relatively brisk ones for the middle movements. The results are similarly exhilarating, particularly in the clipped and bouncy account of the first movement of the *Italian*. The *Scottish Symphony* is far lighter than usual, with no hint of excessive sweetness. The scherzo has rarely sounded happier, and the finale closes in a fast gallop for the 6/8 coda with the horns whooping gloriously. Good, warm recording, only occasionally masking detail in tuttis.

Walter Weller conducts the Philharmonia in refreshingly spontaneous-sounding performances full of vitality. The sense of live performances caught on the wing compensates for the occasional lack of crispness in the ensemble. The reverberant Chandos recording, warmly atmospheric, at times obscures inner detail in orchestral tuttis, but these are warm, amiable readings which build excitingly to climaxes as in live performance. The only speeds that might be counted controversial are those for the slow movements in both symphonies, as well as for the introduction to the *Scottish*. More expansive than usual, Weller sustains them well, avoiding sentimentality.

Bernstein and the Israel orchestra, recorded live in Munich in 1979, give a loving performance of the *Scottish Symphony* but their expansive tempi run the risk of overloading Mendelssohn's fresh inspiration, with the heavy expressiveness making the slow introduction and slow movement sound almost Mahlerian, as if especially for the German audience. The rhythmic lift of the Scherzo and finale makes amends; but it is a performance to bring out for an interesting change, rather than a version to recommend for repeated listening. The recording is well balanced and full. The sparkling account of the *Italian* was made a year earlier in the Mann Auditorium, Tel Aviv, but remains convincingly atmospheric if not ideally clear. It is also available at bargain price, coupled with the *Midsummer Night's Dream* incidental music – see below.

Symphonies Nos. 3 in A min. (Scottish); 4 in A (Italian); Octet, Op. 30: Scherzo.
**(*) ASV Dig. CDDCA 700 [id.]. SCO, Serebrier.

Serebrier offers a chamber-sized version in bright, close-up sound, which has plenty of power, with relatively more weight given to the wind. Some minor imperfections of ensemble are exposed but, with speeds generally thrustful and urgent, these are positive, enjoyable readings. In the horn passage of the third-movement Trio of the *Italian*, Serebrier compensates for any lack of magic in rustic directness. He observes the exposition repeat in the *Italian*, but not in the *Scottish*, though he provides a makeweight in the *Scherzo* from the *Octet* in the composer's orchestral arrangement.

Symphony No. 4 in A (Italian), Op. 90.
(Y/B) (M) *** DG Dig. 445 514-2 [id.]. Philh. O, Sinopoli – SCHUBERT: *Symphony No. 8.* *** ❀
(B) *** DG 429 158-2. BPO, Karajan – SCHUMANN: *Symphony No. 1.* ***
(Y/B) **(*) Decca Dig. 440 476-2 [id.]. VPO, Sir Georg Solti – SHOSTAKOVICH: *Symphony No. 5.* **(*)
(Y/B) (**) Sir Thomas Beecham Trust mono BEECHAM 6 [id.]. NYPO, Beecham – SIBELIUS:
    Symphony No 7; TCHAIKOVSKY: *Capriccio italien.* (**)

Sinopoli's great gift is to illuminate almost every phrase afresh. His speeds tend to be extreme – fast in the first movement but with diamond-bright detail, and on the slow side in the remaining three. Only in the heavily inflected account of the third movement is the result at all mannered but, with superb playing from the Philharmonia and excellent Kingsway Hall recording, this rapt performance is most compelling. For refinement of detail, especially at lower dynamic levels, the CD is among the most impressive digital recordings to have come from DG.

Karajan's performance of the *Italian* is superbly polished and well paced. The reading is straighter than usual, notably in the third movement, though the effect of Karajan's slower pace is warm, never bland. The recording is very brightly lit in its remastered transfer and has lost some of its depth. The coupling with Schumann comes at bargain price.

In the *Italian Symphony* you would never recognize this live performance with the Vienna Philharmonic as the work of the same conductor as Solti's earlier, Chicago recording. Though in the first movement the speed is even faster than before, if only fractionally, the lightness and resilience of the Viennese players make it seem far less tense and far more buoyant. In the finale too, the Vienna performance is lighter and more resilient, and in the middle two movements the contrasts are even more extreme, with speeds kept flowing, so avoiding the heaviness of the Chicago performance. The recording is acceptable, though it could be fuller-bodied.

Sir Thomas recorded the *Italian Symphony* only twice: once with the New York Philharmonic in 1942 and subsequently, in 1951, with the RPO. The present account does not have quite as much grace and poise as the later version; but it still has admirable freshness, and the New York orchestra play with real zest. The recording is opaque but perfectly acceptable for its period.

(i) *Symphony No. 4 in A (Italian), Op. 90; Overture The Hebrides (Fingal's Cave);* (ii) *A Midsummer Night's Dream: Overture, Op. 21; Scherzo; Nocturne; Wedding march, Op. 61.*
(B) *** DG 439 411-2 [id.]. (i) Israel PO, Bernstein; (ii) Bav. RSO, Kubelik.
(Y/B) (M) **(*) Virgin/EMI CUV5 61131-2 [id.]. LSO, Barry Wordsworth.

(i) *Symphony No. 4 in A (Italian); Overtures: The Hebrides (Fingal's Cave);* (ii) *Ruy Blas; A Midsummer Night's Dream: Overture; Scherzo; Intermezzo; Nocturne; Wedding march.*
(N) (B) **(*) Decca Dig. 448 237-2 [id.]. (i) VPO, Dohnányi; (ii) Montreal SO, Dutoit.

Bernstein's performance of the *Italian Symphony* (exposition repeat included) is sparkling and persuasive. The 1978 recording was made at a public concert and, though speeds are often challengingly fast in outer movements, they never fail to convey the exhilaration of the occasion. *Fingal's Cave* is also a live recording, made a year later, and while it has plenty of romantic warmth and Bernstein is slightly more indulgent, it too sounds spontaneously alive. In the items from *A Midsummer Night's Dream* the Bavarian orchestra are on top form, especially in the *Overture* which is beautifully played. The *Scherzo*, too, has the lightest touch from the woodwind, the *Nocturne* brings a fine horn solo and the *Wedding march* is suitably vigorous. The 1964 recording, made in the Herkules-Saal, Munich, still sounds excellent, and this bargain Classikon CD would grace any collection.

Wordsworth combines a sparkling version of the *Italian Symphony* (with attractively light articulation in the bracing outer movements and the essential first-movement exposition repeat included), with the four most important items from *A Midsummer Night's Dream* and a very lively performance of *Fingal's Cave*. If the programme is suitable, this is certainly enjoyable and the recording is first class.

Dohnányi's is a refreshing account of the *Italian*, never pushed too hard, although the *Saltarello* is taken exhilaratingly fast. It is a pity that the first-movement exposition repeat is omitted so that one misses the extended lead-back passage. However, the CD is generously full for, besides Dohnányi's slow and romantic account of the *Hebrides overture*, there is Dutoit's splendidly vital *Ruy Blas* with its commanding brass opening ringing out superbly and the scurrying violins very vivid and tangible. Indeed both this and the 32-minute selection from the *Midsummer Night's Dream* incidental music are marvellously recorded. The acoustics of Saint-Eustache in Montreal are ideal, giving a wonderful bloom to the dancing strings and a very convincing, concert-hall illusion to the whole programme. However, the playing in the incidental music is altogether more routine: the very brisk *Scherzo* conveys little charm, although the *Wedding march* is grand without being pompous.

Symphony No. 4 in A (Italian); A Midsummer Night's Dream: Overture, Op. 21; Incidental music, Op. 61: Scherzo; 'You spotted snakes'; The Speels; Intermezzo; 'What hempen homespuns'.
(Y/B) (M) *** Virgin Veritas/EMI Dig. VER5 61183-2 [id.]. O of Age of Enlightenment, Mackerras.

Mackerras directs fresh, resilient, 'authentic'-style performances of both the *Symphony* and the *Midsummer Night's Dream* music. The middle two movements of the *Symphony* are marginally faster than usual but they gain in elegance and transparency, beautifully played here, as is the *Midsummer Night's Dream* music. It is particularly good to have an ophicleide instead of a tuba for Bottom's music in the *Overture*, and the boxwood flute in the *Scherzo* is a delight.

(i) *Symphony No. 4 (Italian);* (ii) *A Midsummer Night's Dream: Overture, Op. 21; Incidental music, Op. 61: Scherzo; Intermezzo; Nocturne; Wedding march; Fanfare & funeral march; Dance of the rustics.*
(BB) *** LaserLight Dig. 15 526 [id.]. (i) Philh. O, János Sándor; (ii) Budapest PO, Kovacs.

A first-class coupling in the super-bargain range from LaserLight. Sándor gives a fresh and exhilarating account of the *Italian Symphony*, with particularly elegant Philharmonia playing, and the digital sound is excellent. The performance of a generous selection from the *Midsummer Night's Dream* incidental music also shows the Budapest orchestra on top form: this is most beguiling and is recorded in a pleasingly warm acoustic which does not cloud detail.

Symphony No. 4 (Italian); Overtures: Fair Melusina, Op. 32; The Hebrides (Fingal's Cave), Op. 26; Son and stranger (Die Heimkehr aus der Fremde), Op. 89.
(Y/B) (M) *** Carlton IMP Dig. PCD 2003 [id.]. Berne SO, Peter Maag.

Peter Maag, making a welcome return to the recording studio with his Berne orchestra, here offers a winningly relaxed performance of the *Italian Symphony* (including exposition repeat), plus an attractive group of overtures, which once more confirms him as a supreme Mendelssohnian. *The Hebrides* receives a spacious reading and the two rarer overtures are a delight too, particularly *Son and stranger*, which in Maag's hands conveys radiant happiness. At bargain price, with full and brilliant recording, it is first rate.

Symphony No. 5 in D min. (Reformation), Op. 107.
(N) (M) *** DG 449 720-2 [id.]. BPO, Maazel – FRANCK: *Symphony in D min.* ***

The *Reformation Symphony* springs grippingly to life in Maazel's hands. The Berlin Philharmonic brass make an immediate impact in the commanding introduction and the orchestral playing throughout continues on this level of high tension. The finale is splendidly vigorous, the chorale, *Ein' feste Burg is unser Gott*, ringing out resplendently. If ever one were choosing a 'best buy' for this individual symphony, Maazel's interpretation would rank very high on the list. It was aptly chosen for reissue in DG's series of 'Legendary Recordings', and the Franck coupling is hardly less impressive. The recording is spacious and has been vividly enhanced by the DG CD transfer.

CHAMBER AND INSTRUMENTAL MUSIC

Cello sonatas Nos. 1 in B flat, Op. 45; 2 in D, Op. 58; Assai tranquillo; Song without words, Op. 109; Variations concertantes, Op. 17.
*** Hyperion Dig. CDA 66478 [id.]. Richard Lester, Susan Tomes.

Cello sonatas Nos. 1 in B flat, Op. 45; 2 in D, Op. 58; Songs without words, Op. 19/1; Op. 109; Variations concertantes, Op. 17.
(Y/B) *** RCA Dig. 09026 62553-2 [id.]. Steven Isserlis, Melvyn Tan (fortepiano).

There are few cello sonatas so exhilarating as the second of the two written by Mendelssohn. Susan Tomes, the inspired pianist of the group, Domus, and her cellist colleague, Richard Lester, give a performance full of flair on this ideally compiled disc of Mendelssohn's collected works for cello and piano, brimming with charming ideas. As well as the works with opus number they include a delightful fragment, *Assai tranquillo*, never previously recorded.

Steven Isserlis and Melvyn Tan convey a freshness, delight and authenticity in music-making that rekindles enthusiasm for this delightful repertoire. They pace both sonatas expertly and are faithfully served by the RCA engineers. Like their colleagues, Richard Lester and Susan Tomes on Hyperion, they command poetry as well as virtuosity.

Octet in E flat, Op. 20.
*** Hyperion Dig. CDA 66356 [id.]. Divertimenti – BARGIEL: *Octet.* ***
** Sony Dig. SK 48307 [id.]. L'Archibudelli, Smithsonian Chamber Players – GADE: *Octet in F.* **

Divertimenti give a very natural and unforced account of the celebrated *Octet* which, though it may not be the most distinguished in the catalogue, still gives great pleasure. Excellent recorded sound.

In their performance of the *Octet*, L'Archibudelli and the Smithsonian Chamber Players give a spirited but hurried and not always cleanly articulated account of Mendelssohn's ravishing score. They offer an interesting rarity in the form of Gade's essay in the same genre, clearly modelled on the Mendelssohn, and are well recorded; but this is not enough to put this in a commanding position in the *Octet* lists!

Octet in E flat, Op. 20; Symphonies for string orchestra Nos. 6 in E flat; 10 in B min.
*** Denon Dig. CO 73185 [id.]. I Solisti Italiani.

I Solisti Italiani are none other than the old Virtuosi di Roma, and they play with all the finesse and grace you would expect from them. The *Octet* is delightful and could be a first choice, were the acoustic not quite so resonant. The two early *Symphonies* are given with not only elegance but also a conviction that is very persuasive indeed.

Octet in E flat, Op. 20; String quintet No. 1 in A, Op. 18.
(Y/B) *** Virgin Veritas/EMI Dig. VC5 45168-2. Hausmusik.

Using period instruments, the British-based group, Hausmusik, gives a most refreshing performance of the *Octet* and couples it with another miraculous masterpiece of Mendelssohn's boyhood. The period performance gives extra weight to the lower lines compared with the violins, with the extra clarity intensifying the joyfulness of the inspiration. Most revealing of all is the way that the last two movements of the *Octet*, the feather-light *Scherzo* and the dashing finale, with their similar figuration, are presented in contrast, the one slower and more delicately pointed than usual, the other more exhilarating at high speed. At mid-price, a clear first choice for the *Octet*.

Octet in E flat, Op. 20; String quintet No. 2 in B flat, Op. 87.
*** Ph. 420 400-2 [id.]. ASMF Chamber Ens.
(N) (BB) *(*) ASV Dig. CDQS 6168 [id.]. Primavera Chamber Ens.

This Philips successor comes from just over a decade after the Academy's earlier record of Mendelssohn's *Octet* and the playing has greater sparkle and polish. The recorded sound is also superior and sounds extremely well in its CD format. The *Second Quintet* is an underrated piece and it too receives an elegant and poetic performance that will give much satisfaction.

With athletic opening movements, these performances by the Primavera Chamber Ensemble are efficient and well played, but fail to charm. They are acceptably recorded.

Piano quartets Nos. 1 in C min.; 2 in F min.; 3 in B min., Op. 1–3.
(Y/B) (M) *** Virgin/EMI Dig. CUV5 61203-2 [id.]. Domus.

Piano quartet No. 1 in C min., Op. 1; Piano sextet in D, Op. 110.
(BB) **(*) Naxos Dig. 8.550966 [id.]. Bartholdy Piano Qt (augmented).

Piano quartets Nos. 2 in F min., Op. 2; 3 in B min., Op. 3.
(BB) **(*) Naxos Dig. 8.550967 [id.]. Bartholdy Piano Qt.

The *Piano quartet No. 1 in C minor* was the composer's first published composition and was succeeded the following year by another, dedicated to '*Monsieur le Professeur Zelter par son élève Felix Mendelssohn-Bartholdy*', equally fluent and accomplished. However, none of the ideas of this *F minor* work is as remarkable as those of its successor in *B minor* of 1825. All three pieces have charm, vitality and musicianship, particularly in the hands of Domus, who play with the taste and discernment we have come to expect from them. Excellent recording.

The Bartholdy Quartet have an excellent pianist in Pier Narciso Masi, and his mercurial style is just right for these early works. The string players are always fluent and show a light-hearted vivacity in Mendelelssohn's scherzos (especially in the very winning *Allegro molto* of No. 3) and finales, and they play the simple slow movements gracefully. The *Piano sextet* also comes from the composer's youth and, like the other works, it has an engaging immediacy. The recording was made in the fairly resonant Clara Wieck Auditorium in Heidelberg, which means that the microphones are fairly close to the strings and the balance is slightly contrived. Nevertheless the sound is good and the piano well caught. While Domus remain a clear first choice, this Naxos set is worth considering.

Piano trios Nos. 1 in D min., Op. 49; 2 in C min., Op. 66.
(N) **(*) Sony Dig. SK 66351 [id.]. Wanderer Trio.
**(*) Chandos Dig. CHAN 8404 [id.]. Borodin Trio.
**(*) Teldec/Warner Dig. 2292 44947-2. Trio Fontenay.
(N) (M) ** Sony Stern Edition III SMK 64519 [id.]. Stern, Rose, Istomin.

The Sony recordings follow the style of their predecessors by being much too resonant. But these are strong and ardent readings, with notably fine playing in both slow movements and with the cellist, Raphael Pidoux, standing out, although the pianist, Vincent Coq, also makes a very considerable contribution. Marginally a first choice on performance grounds.

The Borodin Trio are also recorded in a very resonant acoustic and are rather forwardly balanced. They give superbly committed but somewhat overpointed readings. All the same, there is much musical pleasure to be found here.

The Trio Fontenay are rather brightly recorded and they play with passionate commitment and great virility. Undoubtedly powerful and keenly alive though both performances are, they do not communicate much charm.

This coupling is not one of the highlights of the third Box in Sony's Stern Edition. The playing is of course expert, and Eugene Istomin's pianism is pleasingly light-fingered and fluent. The Scherzo of the *C minor Trio* brings great brilliance from all three artists. But the studio acoustic is relatively dry and unflattering; the ear craves a softer ambience and more charm of the kind that comes intermittently in the *Andante con moto tranquillo* of the *D minor Trio*. Outer-movement allegros are extremely lively but a bit hard-pressed; the players don't readily convey the fact that they are enjoying themselves.

String quartets: in E flat; Nos. 1 in E flat, Op. 12; 2 in A min., Op. 13; 3–5, Op. 44/1–3; 6 in F min., Op. 80; 4 Pieces, Op. 81.
*** Hyperion Dig. CDS 44051/3 [id.]. Coull Qt.

String quartets Nos. 1–6.
*** EMI CDS7 54514-2 (3) [id.]. Cherubini Qt.

The young Mendelssohn in Berlin in his teens was able to study the scores of late Beethoven quartets even before he had a chance to hear the music performed. His own youthful quartets reflect that influence from what at the time was the most avant-garde music imaginable. For those wanting a complete set, the Coull survey is eminently satisfactory, the playing alive and spontaneous, well paced and musically penetrating. Moreover they bring the advantage of both freshness and completeness (including the early (1823) *Quartet*, written a year before the *C minor First Symphony*). The quietly intense playing in the slow movements of the later works – and indeed in Op. 13 – and the charming, graceful *Intermezzo* of this same quartet show the group's affinity with this repertoire, while the *Canzonetta* of Op. 12 introduces Mendelssohn's fairies, tripping in gracefully. The Scherzo of Op. 44/3 is another highlight, and the opening of Op. 44/2 is particularly warm and well paced. The recording is realistic and well balanced.

A new set of the six regular Mendelssohn *Quartets* is most welcome from the young members of the Cherubini Quartet who consistently play with warmth as well as intensity. Here with a light touch they bring out the mercurial charm of Mendelssohn as well as his vigour and high spirits. The pity is that, unlike the set from the Coull Quartet, this one does not include two works from opposite ends of

Mendelssohn's career that provide an extra insight into his development: the early *E flat Quartet* (without opus number), written when he was only fourteen, and the collection of four movements, Op. 81, that in shape and sequence group themselves satisfyingly together. One only wishes that the Cherubinis, consistently imaginative, had been persuaded to do the extra items as well.

String quartets Nos. 1 in E flat, Op. 12; 2 in A min., Op. 13; 2 Pieces, Op. 81.
*** Hyperion Dig. CDA 66397 [id.]. Coull Qt.

For those wanting the first two *Quartets* only, the Coull Quartet give fresh and unaffected accounts of both and have the benefit of very good recorded sound. Tempi are well judged and everything flows naturally. The Coull offer the additional inducement of two of the *Four pieces*, Op. 81, which were published after Mendelssohn's death.

String quartet No. 2 in A min., Op. 13.
(N) (M) *** Cal. CAL 6698 [id.]. Talich Qt – BOCCHERINI: *Quartet, Op. 58/2;* HAYDN: *Quartet No. 74;*
    MICA: *Quartet No. 6.* ***

Mendelssohn's *Quartet in A minor*, Op. 13, has a serene and remarkably searching slow movement, before its charmingly memorable 'Intermezzo' which is linked to the lively but lyrical *Presto* finale, which has something of the character of a Mendelssohn Scherzo. A most enjoyable work, played with spirit, warmth and cultivated elegance by this superb group, who are most naturally recorded. The couplings are all equally recommendable.

String quartet No. 2 in A min., Op. 13; String quintet No. 2 in B flat, Op. 87.
(Y/B) *** Virgin/EMI Dig. VC5 45104-2 [id.]. Hausmusik.

This makes an interesting and musically satisfying alternative to most of the current versions of this music on offer. Hausmusik give very well-characterized readings of both the *A minor Quartet* and the much later *Second Quintet*. Phrasing is alert and articulate; they have finely blended tone and transparency of texture; above all, they communicate delight in this music. Excellent recording, too.

String quintets Nos. 1 in A, Op. 18; 2 in B flat, Op. 87.
(M) *** Sony/CBS CD 45883. Laredo, Kavafian, Ohyama, Kashkashian, Robinson.

Laredo and his ensemble achieve good matching of timbre, and they give lively accounts of both these neglected works, lacking neither warmth nor finesse. The 1978 recording has responded well to remastering, and has body and presence.

Violin sonata in F min., Op. 4.
(M) *** O-L 443 196-2 [id.]. Jaap Schröder, Christopher Hogwood (fortepiano) – SCHUBERT: *Violin sonatinas.* ***

As the early opus number indicates, this Mendelssohn *Violin sonata* is an early piece. It is not the most memorable of his early works, though it has many endearing moments, and it is here presented most persuasively on period instruments. Jaap Schröder plays a Stradivarius of 1709 and Christopher Hogwood a fortepiano of the mid-1820s. Alive and natural recording.

Violin sonatas: in F min., Op. 4; in F (1838).
*** DG Dig. 419 244-2 [id.]. Shlomo Mintz, Paul Ostrovsky.

Mendelssohn was only fourteen when he composed the *F minor Sonata*, but the 1838 *Sonata* comes from Mendelssohn's productive Leipzig period. The performances are beyond reproach; the playing of both artists is a model of sensitivity and intelligence, and the recording is absolutely first class. Strongly recommended.

ORGAN MUSIC

Organ sonatas Nos. 2 in C min.; 3 in A; 6 in D min., Op. 65/2–3 & 6; Preludes and fugues: in C min.; in G; in D min., Op. 37/1–3.
(N) ✷ (M) *** Decca Dig. 444 570-2 [id.]. Peter Hurford (organ of Ratzeburg Cathedral) – BRAHMS: *Chorale preludes.* ***

Hurford's performances of Mendelssohn bring the same freshness of approach which made his Decca Bach series so memorable. Indeed the opening of the *Prelude and fugue in C minor* is given a baroque exuberance, and he finds a similar identification in his magnificent account of the *Sixth Sonata*. Here Mendelssohn more than pays homage to Bach in his splendidly imaginative set of choral variations (and fugue) on *Vater unser* ('Our Father'). Throughout the recital the throaty reeds of the characterful Ratzeburg organ prevent any possible hint of blandness, yet in the *Andantes* – essentially songs without words for organ – the registration has engaging charm. The recording is superb, as the majestic opening of the *Third Sonata* immediately demonstrates, with the organ given marvellous presence. For this reissue as Volume IV of Hurford's 'Organ masterpieces' series, the Brahms *Chorale preludes* have been added – another fine example of a later master paying his own tribute to Bach.

PIANO MUSIC

Andante and allegro brilliant in A, Op. 92; Andante and variations in B flat, Op. 83a; Piano trio No. 2 in C min., Op. 66.
*** Sony Dig. SK 48494 [id.]. Tal & Groethuysen – Fanny MENDELSSOHN: *3 Pieces for piano, 4 hands.*
***

Playing of exceptional quality from this remarkable duo. Everything, including the transcription of the *C minor Piano trio*, sparkles, and the recording does them full justice.

Andante and rondo capriccioso in E min., Op. 14; Prelude and fugue in E minor/major, Op. 35/1; Sonata in E, Op. 6; Variations sérieuses in D min., Op. 53.
*** Sony Dig. MK 37838 [id.]. Murray Perahia.

Perahia is perfectly attuned to Mendelssohn's sensibility and it would be difficult to imagine these performances being surpassed. The quality of the CBS recording is very good indeed.

Etude in F min.; Preludes & 3 Etudes, Op. 104; 6 Preludes & fugues, Op. 35; Prelude & fugue in E min.
**(*) Nimbus NI 5071 [id.]. Martin Jones.

Fantasy in F sharp min., Op. 28; 3 Fantaisies et caprices, Op. 16; Fantasy on 'The last rose of summer', Op. 15; Variations: in E flat, Op. 82; in B flat, Op. 83; Variations sérieuses in D min., Op. 53.
**(*) Nimbus NI 5072 [id.]. Martin Jones.

Sonatas: in E, Op. 6; in G min., Op. 105; in B flat, Op. 106; Kinderstücke, Op. 72.
**(*) Nimbus NI 5070 [id.]. Martin Jones.

In his collection of Mendelssohn piano music, Martin Jones provides a fascinating slant on the composer, particularly his youthful inspirations. In many ways the disc of sonatas is the most interesting of all, reflecting Mendelssohn's devotion to Beethoven and his sonatas. The *Preludes and fugues* inevitably reflect his even deeper devotion to Bach, then still under-appreciated. The sets of variations on the third disc were mostly written later in his career, examples of his high skill and love of the keyboard, rather than works of genius. Martin Jones is an excellent advocate, playing dedicatedly and persuasively, not always immaculately but without mannerism. The recordings, made in the 1970s, come up very well in the CD transfers, with the atmosphere of a small hall realistically conveyed.

Preludes and fugues Nos. 1–6, Op. 35; 3 Caprices, Op. 33; Perpetuum mobile in C, Op. 33.
(Y/B) (BB) *** Naxos Dig. 8.550939 [id.]. Benjamin Frith.

In the first of what is obviously going to be a distinguished series, Benjamin Frith offers a highly imaginative set of the Op. 35 *Preludes and fugues*, full of diversity, from the flamboyant opening *Prelude in E minor* to the expansive *Prelude No. 6 in B flat*. The Fugues are sometimes bold, sometimes thoughtful, sometimes quite light-hearted, yet they are never made to sound trivial. The three *Caprices* are equally varied in mood and colour and are most sensitively presented, with the last one opening solemnly and then providing characteristically light-hearted Mendelssohnian dash. The *Perputuum mobile* makes a scintillating encore. Acceptably full if not remarkable piano sound, recorded in St Martin's Church, East Woodhay. But the playing promises well for what is to follow.

Rondo capriccioso, Op. 14; Songs without words: in G; in A (Spring song), Op. 62/1 & 6; in C (Spinning song), Op. 67/4.
(M) *** Decca 433 902-2 [id.]. Wilhelm Backhaus – SCHUBERT: *Impromptus* etc. **(*)

Perhaps surprisingly, Backhaus is at his most persuasive in this well-planned and expertly played miniature Mendelssohn programme. The 1955 recording, too, is remarkably good.

Scherzo from A Midsummer Night's Dream, Op. 61 (trans. Rachmaninov).
*** Hyperion CDA 66009 [id.]. Howard Shelley – RACHMANINOV: *Variations* etc. ***

Howard Shelley, with fabulously clear articulation and delectably sprung rhythms, gives a performance of which Rachmaninov himself would not have been ashamed.

Songs without words, Books 1–8 (complete).
**(*) Hyperion Dig. CDA 66221/2 [id.]. Lívia Rév.

Songs without words, Books 1–8 (complete); *Albumblatt, Op. 117; Gondellied; Kinderstücke, Op. 72; 2 Klavierstücke.*
(B) *** DG Double 437 470-2 (2) [id.]. Daniel Barenboim.

Songs without words (complete); *Andante and variations in E flat, Op. 82; Andante cantabile e presto agitato in B; Variations in B flat, Op. 83.*
(B) *** Ph. Duo 438 709-2 (2) [id.]. Ilse von Alpenheim.

This 1974 set of Mendelssohn's complete *Songs without words*, which Barenboim plays with such affectionate finesse, has dominated the catalogue for nearly two decades. For this reissue, the six *Kinderstücke* (sometimes known as 'Christmas pieces') have been added, plus other music, so that the second of the two CDs plays for 73 minutes. The sound is first class. At Double DG price (two CDs for the price of one) this sweeps the board in this repertoire, although it is a pity that there is no back-up documentation except for a list of titles.

Ilse von Alpenheim's set of *Songs without words* may not have quite the distinctive character of Barenboim, but she plays this music with an appealing spontaneous simplicity. Her sensibility is at times a little solemn, and just occasionally in the faster pieces she has a slight tendency to rush her fences. But these are performances which show individuality without self-conscious idiosyncrasy: the famous *Spring song*, for instance, brings an attractively light chimerical touch, and elsewhere there are many agreeable moments of poetic tranquillity. Of the encores, the *Andante and variations in E flat* is particularly appealing in this respect. The (1980) recording of the piano is first class, well up to Philips's usual high standard. Not a first choice, perhaps, but an undoubted bargain.

Lívia Rév is a thoughtful, sensitive and aristocratic artist. Her survey of the *Songs without words* has charm and warmth, and she includes a hitherto unpublished piece. The set is handsomely presented and the recording is warm and pleasing; it is, however, somewhat bottom-heavy. Yet the slightly diffuse effect suits the style of the playing.

VOCAL MUSIC

Lieder: *Allnächtlich im Traume; Altdeutsches Liede; And'res Maienlied; An die Entfernte; Auf der Wanderschaft; Auf Flügeln des Gesanges ('On wings of song'); Bei deder Wiege; Der Blumenkranz; Da lieg' ich unter den Bäumen; Entelied; Erster Verlust; Das erste Veilchen; Es lauschte das Lamb; Frühlingslied* (3 versions: Lenau, Lichtenstein and Klingemann settings); *Grüss; Hirtenlied; Jagdlied; Minnelied* (Deutsches Volkslied); *Minnelied* (Tieck); *Der Mond; Morgengruss; Nachtlied; Neue Liebe; O Jugend; Pagenlied; Reiselied* (2 versions: Heine and Ebert); *Scheindend; Schiflied; Schlafloser Augen Leuchte; Tröstung; Venetianisches Gondellied; Volkslied (Feuchtersleben); Das Waldschloss; Wanderlied; Warnung vor dem Rhein; Wenn sich zwei Herzen scheiden; Winterlied.*
(M) **(*) EMI CMS7 64827-2 (2) Fischer-Dieskau, Sawallisch.

Though Mendelssohn generally reserved his finest song-like inspirations for the *Songs without words*, the lyrical directness of these settings of Heine, Eichendorff, Lenau and others assures him of a niche of his own among contemporary composers of Lieder. Fischer-Dieskau conveys the joy of fresh discovery but in some of the well-known songs – *Grüss* or *On wings of song* – he tends to overlay his singing with heavy expressiveness. Lightness should be the keynote, and that happily is wonderfully represented in the superb accompaniments of Sawallisch. Excellent, natural recording.

Elijah (oratorio), *Op. 70.*
*** Chandos Dig. CHAN 8774/5 [id.]. White, Plowright, Finnie, A. Davies, London Symphony Ch., LSO, Hickox.
(N) (B) *** EMI forte CZS5 68601-2 (2). Gwyneth Jones, Janet Baker, Gedda, Fischer-Dieskau, Woolf, Wandsworth School Boys' Ch., New Philh. Ch. & O, Frühbeck de Burgos.
**(*) Teldec/Warner Dig. 9031 73131-2 (2) [id.]. Alastair Miles, Helen Donath, Jard van Nes, Donald George, Leipzig MDR Ch., Israel PO, Masur.
**(*) Ph. Dig. 432 984-2 (2) [id.]. Kenny, Dawson, Von Otter, Rigby, Rolfe Johnson, Begley, Allen, Connell, Hopkins, ASMF Ch., ASMF, Marriner.
**(*) HM Dig. HMC 901463/4. Petteri Salomaa, Soile Isokoski, Monica Groop, John Mark Ainsley, Delphine Collot, La Chapelle Royale, Coll. Voc., O des Champs-Elysées, Herreweghe.

Richard Hickox with his London Symphony Chorus and the LSO secures a performance that both pays tribute to the English choral tradition in this work and presents it dramatically as a kind of religious opera. Willard White may not be ideally steady in his delivery, sometimes attacking notes from below, but he sings consistently with fervour, from his dramatic introduction to the overture onwards. Rosalind Plowright and Arthur Davies combine purity of tone with operatic expressiveness, and Linda Finnie, while not matching the example of Dame Janet Baker in the classic EMI recording (still not available), sings with comparable dedication and directness in the solo, *O rest in the Lord*. The chorus fearlessly underlines the high contrasts of dynamic demanded in the score. The Chandos recording, full and immediate yet atmospheric too, enhances the drama.

Frühbeck proves an excellent Mendelssohnian, neither a callous driver nor a romantic meanderer. The choice of Fischer-Dieskau to take the part of the prophet is more controversial. His pointing of English words is not always idiomatic, but his sense of drama is infallible and goes well with this Mendelssohnian new look. Gwyneth Jones and Nicolai Gedda similarly provide mixed enjoyment, but the splendid work of the chorus and, above all, the gorgeous singing of Dame Janet Baker, dominant whether in hushed intensity or commanding fortissimo, make this a memorable and enjoyable set, very well recorded (in the late 1960s) and spaciously and realistically transferred to CD. Offered in EMI's forte double series it makes a remarkable bargain.

Masur as a Mendelssohnian consistently eliminates any hint of sentimentality, but in *Elijah* his determination to use a new broom involves many fast speeds that fail to let this dramatic music blossom, not least in the exuberant final chorus. Yet anyone wanting a fine, modern, digital recording using the German text, crisply and urgently done, should not be too disappointed, particularly when Alastair Miles sings so freshly and intelligently in the title-role.

Marriner in his line-up of soloists may look unmatchable, and there is much fine singing; but with the mellifluous Elijah of Thomas Allen balanced rather backwardly in the live recording, less dominant than he should be, the result is refined rather than dramatically powerful. Marriner and his splendid forces are in danger of sounding too well-mannered. He gives the quartets and double-quartets to the soloists, whereas Hickox, following the English tradition, has the chorus singing them.

Herreweghe's reading, using period forces, recorded live in Metz in February 1993, is predictably clean, fresh and light-textured. With a German text, this is as far removed from the English choral tradition as could be, and probably far removed too from the first performance in Birmingham in 1846. Yet in its way it is quite compelling, thanks to the bright, clear choral singing. Petteri Salomaa is a lightweight Elijah, occasionally fluttery in timbre, and Soile Isokoski is less sweet-toned than in the Opus 111 recording of the *Hymn of Praise*, but John Mark Ainsley and Monica Groop are both excellent. Clear, atmospheric recording.

A Midsummer Night's Dream: Overture, Op. 21; Incidental music, Op. 61 (complete).

*** EMI CDC7 47163-2 [id.]. Watson, Wallis, Finchley Children's Music Group, LSO, Previn.

*** RCA Dig. 07863 57764-2 [7764-2-RC]. Popp, Lipovšek, Bamberg Ch. & SO, Flor.

(B) *** CfP Dig. CD-CFP 4593; *TC-CFP 4593*. Wiens, Walker, LPO Ch. & O, Litton.

(M) *** DG 415 840-2 [id.]. Mathis, Boese, Bav. R. Ch. & SO, Kubelik – WEBER: *Overtures: Oberon; Der Freischütz.* ***

(M) (***) RCA mono GD 60314. Eustis, Kirk, University of Pennsylvania Women's Glee Club, Phd. O., Toscanini – BERLIOZ: *Romeo and Juliet: Queen Mab scherzo.* (**)

On EMI, Previn offers a wonderfully refreshing account of the complete score; the veiled pianissimo of the violins at the beginning of the Overture and the delicious woodwind detail in the Scherzo certainly bring Mendelssohn's fairies into the orchestra. Even the little melodramas which come between the main items sound spontaneous here, and the contribution of the soloists and chorus is first class. The *Nocturne* (taken slowly) is serenely romantic and the *Wedding march* resplendent. The recording is naturally balanced and has much refinement of detail.

Claus Peter Flor's account omits the little melodramas, which is a pity; but for those who require the major items only, this beautiful RCA CD could well be a first choice. Recorded in the warmly resonant acoustics of the Dominikanerbau, Bamberg, the orchestra is given glowingly radiant textures; but Flor's stylish yet relaxed control brings the kind of intimacy one expects from a chamber group. Lucia Popp's vocal contribution is delightful, especially when she blends her voice so naturally with that of Marjana Lipovšek in *You spotted snakes*.

Andrew Litton also includes the melodramas and, like Previn, he uses them most effectively as links, making them seem an essential part of the structure. He too has very good soloists; in the *Overture* and *Scherzo* he displays an engagingly light touch, securing very fine wind and string playing from the LPO. The wide dynamic range of the recording brings an element of drama to offset the fairy music. Both the *Nocturne*, with a fine horn solo, and the temperamental *Intermezzo* are good examples of the spontaneity of feeling that permeates this performance throughout and makes this disc a bargain.

Although Kubelik omits the melodramas, this makes room for an appropriate coupling of the two finest Weber overtures (both also associated with magic) with *Oberon* drawing an obvious parallel with Mendelssohn. They are marvellously played and the sound and 1965 recording are strikingly fresh.

Toscanini's Philadelphia recording offers the seven most popular numbers from the *Midsummer Night's Dream* music, including the song with chorus, *You spotted snakes*, and the final melodrama. In sparkling performances it offers a fine example of his more relaxed manners in his one Philadelphia season.

A Midsummer Night's Dream: Overture, Op. 21 (incidental music): suite.
(M) *** Sony SBK 48264; *SBT 48264* [id.]. Cleveland O, Szell – BIZET: *Symphony;* SMETANA: *Vltava.* ***

Seldom can Mendelssohn's score have been played so brilliantly on record as under Szell. The orchestral ensemble is superb, the fairies dance with gossamer lightness in the violins, yet the tension is high so that the listener is gripped from the first bar to the last of the *Overture*. The *Scherzo* is infectious and in the *Nocturne* the solo horn is cool but very sensitive. This may not be everyone's idea of Mendelssohn but of its kind it is first class, and the 1967 recording sounds smoother and fuller than on the old LP.

3 Psalms, Op. 78.
**(*) Nimbus Dig. NI 5171 [id.]. Oslo Cathedral Ch., Terje Kvam – GRIEG: *4 Psalms.* **(*)

All three *Psalms* have considerable beauty and dignity, especially the first, a setting of Psalm 11 with its ingenious four-part canon. Good performances by the Oslo Cathedral Choir, and eminently serviceable recording. However, at under 45 minutes, the CD offers short measure.

Psalms Nos. 98: Singet dem Herrn ien neues Lied; 114: Da Israel aus Aegypten Zog; (i) *Lass', O Herr, mich Hülfe finden, Op. 96;* (ii) *Lauda Sion, Op. 73.*
*** Erato/Warner Dig. 4509 94359-2 [id.]. (i) Stutzmann; (ii) Brunner, Ihara, Ramirez, Huttenlocher, Gulbenkian Foundation Ch. & O, Lisbon, Corboz.

These two Psalm settings inspire Mendelssohn to some of his most effectively Bach-like writing. The text of Psalm 98 inspired Bach too and, though austerity periodically turns into sweetness, both pieces are welcome in performances as fresh and alert as these. *Lauda Sion* is less varied in its expression, a persistent hymn of praise, but *Lass', O Herr* ('Let me find your help, O Lord'), a paraphrase of Psalm 13, is set in four contrasted sections featuring contralto and chorus and ending with a Fugue. Excellent performances and fine recording.

St Paul, Op. 36.
**(*) Ph. 420 212-2 (2). Janowitz, Lang, Blochwitz, Stier, Polster, Adam, Leipzig R. Ch. & GO, Masur.

Masur, always a persuasive interpreter of Mendelssohn, here directs a performance which, without inflating the piece or making it sanctimonious, conveys its natural gravity. Theo Adam is not always steady, but otherwise the team of soloists is exceptionally strong, and the chorus adds to the incandescence, although placed rather backwardly. The Leipzig recording is warm and atmospheric.

Mennin, Peter (1923–83)

Symphony No. 5.
(M) **(*) Mercury 432 755-2 [id.]. Eastman-Rochester O, Howard Hanson – IVES: *Symphony No. 3* etc.; SCHUMAN: *New England triptych.* ***

Peter Mennin is not as individual a musical personality as William Schuman, let alone Charles Ives; but the *Canto* central movement of his *Fifth Symphony* has a piercing melancholy which is slightly reminiscent of the Barber *Adagio for strings*. The outer movements develop plenty of polyphonic energy, but the toccata-like linear writing lacks real memorability. Hanson's performance is persuasive and vital, and the 1962 Mercury sound makes the very most of the relatively unexpansive acoustics of the Eastman Theatre.

Menotti, Gian-Carlo (born 1911)

Piano concerto in F.
(M) **(*) Van. 08.4029.71 [OVC 4071]. Earl Wild, Symphony of the Air, Jorge Mester – COPLAND: *Concerto.* ***

Menotti's *Piano concerto*, like most of his music, is easy and fluent, never hard on the ear. Its eclectic style brings a pungent whiff of Shostakovich at the opening, and there are hints of Khachaturian elsewhere. Even if it is unlikely to bear repeated listening, the charisma and bravura of Earl Wild's playing make the music sound more substantial than it is.

Amahl and the Night Visitors (opera): complete.
*** That's Entertainment CDTER 1124. Lorna Haywood, John Dobson, Curtis Watson, Christopher Painter, James Rainbird, ROHCG Ch. & O, David Syrus.

Recorded under the supervision of the composer himself, this is a fresh and highly dramatic perform-ance, very well sung and marked by atmospheric digital sound of striking realism. Central to the success of the performance is the astonishingly assured and sensitively musical singing of the boy treble, James Rainbird, as Amahl, while Lorna Haywood sings warmly and strongly as the Mother, with a strong trio of Kings.

Amahl and the night visitors: Introduction; March; Shepherd's dance. Sebastian (ballet): suite.
*** Koch Dig. 3-7005-2 [id.]. New Zealand SO, Schenck – BARBER: *Souvenirs.* ***

This seven-movement suite from *Sebastian* is beautifully crafted and expertly scored music whose attrac-tions are strong, as are the three movements from *Amahl and the night visitors*. The players under Andrew Schenck, who sound as if they are enjoying themselves, are well recorded.

Mercadante, Saverio (1795–1870)

Flute concertos: in D; E; E min.
*** RCA Dig. 09026 61447-2 [id.]. James Galway, Sol. Ven., Scimone.

These three *Flute concertos* show Mercadante to be an excellent craftsman with a nice turn for lyrical melody in the slow movements with their simple, song-like cantilenas. Both the *Andante alla siciliana* of the *D major Concerto* and the *Largo* of the *E minor* are appealing, especially with Galway as soloist, while the *Rondo Russo* or *Polacca* finales are inventively spirited. Scimone makes the most of the often exuberantly florid tuttis of the opening movements, and elsewhere he accompanies Galway's silvery melodic line, sparkling and delicate by turns, with style and polish. The sound is excellent.

Merikanto, Aarre (1893–1958)

(i) *Violin concertos Nos. 2; 4;* (ii) *10 Pieces;* (iii) *Genesis.*
*** Finlandia Dig. FACD 387 [id.]. (i) Saatikettu, Helsinki PO, James De Priest; (ii) Avanti CO, Angervo; (iii) Mattila, Savonlinna Op. Festival Ch., Lahti SO, Söderblom.

Merikanto's *Second Violin concerto* is quite a find, a most imaginative work which will appeal to anyone who likes the exoticism of Szymanowski and the nature mysticism of Janáček. The expressionist *Ten Pieces* and in particular the first, the *Largo misterioso*, cast a strong spell. The *Fourth Violin concerto* – he burned the *Third* – has a folksy Prokofiev-like character but has no lack of astringency. Merikanto's works emanate from an altogether distinctive sound-world. Very good performances and recording. Strongly recommended.

(i) *Fantasy for orchestra; Largo misterioso;* (ii) *Notturno;* (i) *Pan; Symphonic study.*
*** Finlandia Dig. FACD 349 [id.]. Finnish RSO, (i) Segerstam; (ii) Saraste.

The *Fantasy for orchestra* is a work of an extraordinarily rich imagination. Both the *Fantasy* and the tone-poem, *Pan*, are sensitively conducted by Leif Segerstam, who successfully conveys their haunting, other-worldly atmosphere. The *Notturno* and *Largo misterioso* are also beautiful pieces that immediately cast a strong spell.

Juha (opera) complete.
**(*) Finlandia FACD 105 (2) [id.]. Lehtinen, Kostia, Krumm, Kuusoja, Finnish Nat. Op. Ch. and O, Ulf Söderblom.

The musical language of *Juha* reflects the composer's international sympathies and yet the music is far more than merely eclectic. It is atmospheric and highly expert in scoring and, in its way, bears a quite distinctive stamp. The singing on the whole is more than respectable, and Matti Lehtinen in the title-role is outstanding. The opera is not long – under two hours – and is very well worth investigating.

Messager, André (1853–1929)

Les deux pigeons (ballet) complete.
*** Decca Dig. 433 700-2 [id.]. Welsh Nat. Op. O, Richard Bonynge.

Messager's charming gypsy ballet was premièred at the Paris Opéra in 1886 on the same bill as Donizetti's *La Favorita*, but it swiftly established its independence. We are familiar with the suite, but this is the first complete recording. The music is slight but cleverly scored, after the manner of Delibes; agreeably tuneful, it does not wear out its welcome. Bonynge secures playing from the Wesh Opera Orchestra that is consistently graceful and sparkling. The recording, made in the slightly intractable Brangwyn Hall, Swansea, is vivid and naturally balanced, if not quite Decca's very best.

Messiaen, Olivier (1908–92)

Des canyons aux étoiles; Couleurs de la cité céleste; Oiseaux exotiques.
*** Sony Dig. MK 44762 [id.]. Paul Crossley, L. Sinf., Salonen.

The power of the writing in Messiaen's vast symphonic cycle, *Des canyons aux étoiles*, comes out vividly in Esa-Pekka Salonen's CBS version, with Paul Crossley as soloist both incisive and deeply sympathetic. Salonen's performance is not obviously devotional in the first five movements; but then, after Michael Thompson's virtuoso horn solo, in the sixth movement Salonen and his players increasingly find a sharper focus, with the playing of the London Sinfonietta ever more confident and idiomatic. *Oiseaux exotiques* find Crossley in inspired form as soloist, and with *Couleurs de la cité céleste* made tough rather than evocative. The recording is sharply focused, but has good presence and atmosphere.

(i) *Chronochromie;* (ii) *Et exspecto resurrectionem mortuorum.*
(M) *** EMI CDM7 63948-2 [id.]. (i) BBC SO, Dorati; (ii) O de Paris & Ens. de Percussion, Baudo – BOULEZ: *Le soleil des eaux;* KOECHLIN: *Les Bandar-log.* ***

Messiaen's *Chronochromie* characteristically has its inspiration in nature, the composer's long-established preoccupation with birdsong, and the culminating *Epode*, readily understandable as a climactic representation of the birds' dawn chorus. This fine performance and immensely vivid recording are worthy of the music, and for the reissue EMI have added Serge Baudo's excellent 1968 recording of *Et exspecto resurrectionem mortuorum*. Baudo conducted its first performances in Paris and Chartres.

(i) *Hymne au Saint-sacrement; Les offrandes oubliées;* (ii) *Visions de l'amen.*
(M) **(*) Erato/Warner 4509 91707-2 [id.]. (i) O de l'ORTF, Marius Constant; (ii) Katia and Marielle Labèque.

Constant gives atmospheric yet passionate accounts of these two early works, catching also their rich vein of mysticism. The recordings, from the beginning of the 1970s, have a pleasingly warm ambience and do not sound too dated. The Labèque duo play the *Visions de l'amen* brilliantly, their performance bolder in profile and less withdrawn in atmosphere than rival versions, but compelling nevertheless.

Turangalîla Symphony.
*** Decca Dig. 436 626-2 [id.]. Jean-Yves Thibaudet, Takashi Harada, Concg. O, Chailly.
*** DG Dig. 431 781-2 [id.]. Yvonne & Jeanne Loriod, Bastille O, Chung.

(i) *Turangalîla symphony;* (ii) *Quartet for the end of time.*
*** EMI Dig. CDS7 47463-8 [id.] (2). (i) Donohoe, Murail, CBSO, Rattle; (ii) Gawriloff, Deinzer, Palm, Kontarsky.

Among the new generation of one-disc versions of *Turangalîla*, Chailly's powerful, dramatic reading with the Concertgebouw makes an outstanding first choice. The richness of the sound goes with beautiful balance, fine clarity and a keen sense of presence, heightening the impact of Chailly's clean-cut, brilliant interpretation. Chailly's sharpness at a fast tempo in the catchy fifth movement, *Joie du sang des étoiles*, conveys its joy with a jazzy lilt, and the following *Jardin du sommeil d'amour* conveys sensuousness rather than spiritual intensity, taken at a flowing tempo. In the seventh movement, *Turangalîla II*, the wit and point of Thibaudet's playing heighten the sharpness of focus and, though some will prefer a warmer reading, no one will fail to appreciate the concentration and intensity of Chailly's performance. The Decca recording is in the demonstration class.

Chung's reading with the Bastille Orchestra was recorded in 1990 in the composer's presence, not long before he died. Messiaen's endorsement is confirmed when the soloists are his wife and his sister-in-law, at times less precise than rivals, but bringing a unique, expressive intensity. Their contributions, particularly the pointed piano-playing of Yvonne Loriod, heighten the natural warmth of Chung's reading, less high-powered and at times less precise than Chailly's rival one-disc version, and less cleanly recorded, but very persuasive.

Simon Rattle conducts a winning performance of *Turangalîla*, not only brilliant and dramatic but warmly atmospheric and convincing. It is not just that his rendering of the love music is ripely sensuous: in his rhythmic control of the fast dramatic movements he is equally understanding. The recording is warm and richly co-ordinated while losing nothing in detail. Peter Donohoe and Tristan Murail play with comparable warmth and flair. Led by Aloys Kontarsky, the performance of the *Quartet for the end of time* provides a contrasted approach to Messiaen from Rattle's, when atmospheric warmth is only an incidental.

(i) *Colours de la Cité céleste;* (ii) *Et exspecto resurrectionem mortuorum.*
(N) (M) ** Sony SMK 68332 [id.]. Groupe Instrumental à percussion de Strasbourg, with (i) Yvonne Loriod; (ii) O du Domaine Musical; Boulez (with STRAVINSKY: *Symphonies of wind instruments;* with NYPO **).

In Messiaen's own words, his *Colours de la Cité céleste* 'turns on itself like a rose-window', bringing together, with astonishing assurance, elements from plainsong, Greek and Hindu music, not to mention the persistent birdsong which runs through so much of this composer's writing. Boulez's account, helped by close microphones, centres on sharpness of detail rather than atmosphere; the result seems literal and fails to be seductive. Similarly, in the larger scale of *Et exspecto resurrectionem* the concentration of a series of clearly differentiated sounds and sonorities brings a negative effect. One cannot help feeling here that the musical content is spread rather thin, with too meandering a tempo predominating – pregnant pauses repeated overmuch lose their pregnancy. The Stravinsky encore makes a rather more positive impression, but this is essentially a reissue for Boulez aficionados rather than for the general collector.

Quatuor pour la fin du temps.
*** Delos Dig. D/CD 3043 [id.]. Chamber Music Northwest – BARTOK: *Contrasts.* ***
(M) *** Ph. 422 834-2. Beths, Pieterson, Bylsma, De Leeuw.

(i) *Quatuor pour la fin du temps (Quartet for the end of time);* (ii) *Le merle noir.*
(M) *** EMI CDM7 63947-2 [id.]. (i) Gruenberg, De Peyer, Pleeth, Béroff; (ii) Zöller, Kontarsky.

Messiaen's visionary and often inspired piece was composed during his days in a Silesian prison camp. Among his fellow-prisoners were a violinist, a clarinettist and a cellist who, with the composer at the piano, made its creation possible. The 1968 EMI account, led by Erich Gruenberg and with Gervase de Peyer the inspirational clarinettist, is in the very highest class, the players meeting every demand the composer makes upon them, and the fine, clear Abbey Road recording gives the group striking presence while affording proper background ambience. The bonus, *Le merle noir*, exploits the composer's love of birdsong even more overtly and is splendidly played and recorded here.

We already know the calibre of David Shifrin's playing from his recording of Copland's *Clarinet concerto*. Here, like his colleagues, he fully captures the work's sensuous mysticism, while the solos of Warren Lash (cello) and Williams Doppmann have a wistful, improvisatory quality: both *Louange à l'éternité de Jésus* and the closing *Louange à l'immortalité de Jésus* are played very beautifully. The Delos recording is naturally balanced and very realistic, while the ambience is suitably evocative.

The Dutch team on Philips are also given the benefit of very good recording which has transferred well to CD; moreover their account has the merit of outstanding team-work and Reinbert de Leeuw has a keen sense of atmosphere, though he does not dominate the proceedings. There is also some superbly eloquent playing from George Pieterson and Anner Bylsma.

(i) *Quatuor pour la fin du temps;* (ii) *Cinq rechants* (for 12 voices).
(M) *** Erato/Warner 4509 91708 [id.]. Fernandez, Deplus, Neilz, Petit; (ii) Solistes des Chœurs de l'ORTF, Marcel Couraud.

The French Ensemble on Erato give a strong, powerfully integrated performance, well held together by the pianist, Marie-Madeleine Petit. Among her colleagues, Jacques Neilz, the cellist, is raptly inspirational in the fifth movement (*Louange à l'Eternité de Jésus*) and is all but matched by the playing of his violinist colleague, Huguette Fernandez; the clarinettist, Guy Deplus, does not quite manage to achieve an opening crescendo out of nothingness but still makes a sensitive contribution. The recording is very good, clear and well balanced. The coupling is the extraordinary vocal work, *Cinq rechants*, written for a choir of twelve soloists. The composer's inspiration of human passion brings both lyrical intensity and extraordinary irregular rhythmic effects (some of which have an Indian source) and the various bursts and cascades of vocal tone give the work a stimulatingly original vitality. The performance is remarkably assured and full of ardent spontaneity, and the group are vividly recorded. Excellent notes are provided by the composer.

Theme and variations.
*** DG Dig. 427 351-2 [id.]. Gidon Kremer, Martha Argerich – BARTOK: *Sonata No. 1* ***; JANACEK:
  Sonata. **(*)

Messiaen's *Theme and variations* is an early work and the music's fervour is well captured here.

PIANO MUSIC

Catalogue d'oiseaux (complete); *La fauvette des jardins.*
**(*) DG Dig. 439 214-2 (3) [id.]. Anatol Ugorski.

It is good to have such a bold, powerful, obviously deeply felt and essentially Slavonic approach to
Messiaen's multi-faceted evocations of birdsong heard against graphically depicted landscapes, often
rough-hewn, with all the extravagance of nature. It is impossible not to respond to such vivid pictorialism, even if Ugorski's response is essentially extrovert and at times almost melodramatic in its dynamism and sense of contrast. This would make a spectacular impression at a live performance, but under
domestic circumstances the greater intimacy and the less flamboyant, more subtle approach of Peter
Hill on Unicorn is the more satisfying. And the DG recording is very immediate, not necessarily an
advantage when the playing creates its own presence.

Catalogue d'oiseaux, Books 1–3.
*** Unicorn Dig. DKPCD 9062 [id.]. Peter Hill.

Catalogue d'oiseaux, Books 4–6: L'alouette calandrelle; La bouscarle; La merle de roche; La rousserolle
effarvatte.
*** Unicorn Dig. DKPCD 9075 [id.]. Peter Hill.

These scores derive their inspiration from Messiaen's beloved birdsong. Little of the piano writing is
conventional and the music is vivid and colourful to match the plumage of the creatures which Messiaen
depicts so strikingly. Peter Hill prepared this music in Paris with the composer himself and thus has his
imprimatur. He evokes the wildlife pictured in this extraordinary music to splendid effect, and is
recorded with the utmost clarity and definition.

Catalogue d'oiseaux, Book 7; Supplement: La fauvette des jardins.
*** Unicorn Dig. DKPCD 9090 [id.]. Peter Hill.

In addition to the last book of the *Catalogue d'oiseaux* we have here *La fauvette des jardins*, which the
sleeve annotator describes as the perfect parergon to the cycle. The composer himself has spoken with
great warmth of this artist and, given what we hear on this disc, he has every reason to.

Préludes (complete); *Vingt regards sur l'enfant Jésus.*
(B) **(*) EMI CMS7 69161-2 (2) [id.]. Michel Béroff.

The *Préludes* are early works but, like *Vingt regards*, show Béroff at his most inspired, generating the
illusion of spontaneous creation. Clean, well-focused sound – but, even though the venue was the Salle
Wagram, the close balance brings a lack of rich sonority.

Vingt regards sur l'enfant Jésus.
(N) *** Collins Dig. 7033-2 [id.]. Joanna MacGregor.
(M) *** Erato/Warner 4509 91705-2 (2) [id.]. Yvonne Loriod.
(BB) *** Naxos Dig. 8.550829/30 [id.]. Håkon Austbø.

Joanna MacGregor's powerful and highly atmospheric new Collins set of *Vingt regards* now takes its
place as a primary recommendation for Messiaen's remarkable, visionary and often uncompromising
work. She does not shirk the percussive Bartókian pianism of a movement like *La parole toute-puissante*
('The all-powerful word') and is equally impressive in evoking the 'fiery flames' of *Regard des Anges*. Yet
in the *Regard du silence* the quiet evocation is compelling and the contemplative *Je dors, mais mon cœur*
veille ('I sleep, but my heart is awake') has comparable concentration. The closing section, *Regard de*
l'Eglise d'Amour, brings a superb sense of apotheosis. The recording is very fine indeed, with just the
right degree of ambient warmth.

  The 1973 recording by Yvonne Loriod – the composer's second wife – of *Vingt regards* has long been
considered very special in its understanding and feeling for the composer's mystical sound-world. The
piano recording is full but is otherwise acceptable rather than outstanding – yet the magnetism of the
playing overcomes the lack of the sharpest focus.

  Håkon Austbø as one-time prize-winner of the Olivier Messiaen Competition for Contemporary Music
in Royan has excellent credentials for performing this repertoire, and his is an individual view, with a
wider range of tempi and dynamic than Loriod. His account of the opening *Regard du Père* and the

later *Regard du Fils sur le Fils* is paced much more slowly, but his playing has great concentration and evocative feeling so that he readily carries the slower tempo, and in *Par lui tout a été fait* articulation is bolder, giving the music a stronger profile, helped by the clearer, Naxos digital focus. This is undoubtedly a performance that grips the listener and can be strongly recommended as an alternative view.

Visions de l'Amen.
*** EMI CDC7 54050-2 [id.]. Alexandre Rabinovitch, Martha Argerich.
*** New Albion Dig. NA 045 CD [id.]. Double Edge (Edmund Niemann & Nurit Tilles).

Messiaen's *Visions de l'Amen* for two pianos is a long, eloquent work in seven sections with a powerful sense of mystery, and is played with uncommon conviction by the Russian pianist-composer, Alexandre Rabinovitch, with Martha Argerich at the second piano.

The performance from Edmund Niemann and Nurit Tilles is hardly less arrestingly spontaneous. They capture the work's colour and atmosphere powerfully and evocatively – it is Messiaen at his most compelling – and some may prefer the sound of the New Albion recording. The two pianists are set back in a fairly reverberant but not blurring acoustic, which enhances the work's plangent palette.

ORGAN MUSIC

Complete works for organ: *Apparition de l'Eglise éternelle; L'Ascension (4 Méditations); Le banquet céleste; Le corps glorieux (7 Visions de la vie des ressuscités); Diptyque (Essai sur la vie terrestre et l'éternité religieuse); Livre d'Orgue (Reprises par interversion; Première pièce en trio; Les mains de l'abîme; Chants oiseaux; Deuxième pièce en trio; Les yeux dans les roues; Soixante-quatre durées). Messe de la Pentecôte; La Nativité du Seigneur (9 Méditations).*
(M) *** EMI mono CZS7 67400-2 (4) [id.]. Composer (Cavaillé–Coll organ de L'Eglise de la Sainte-Trinité, Paris).

In an intensive series of sessions which began at the end of May and continued through June and July 1956, Olivier Messiaen returned to the organ in Sainte-Trinité, with which all his music is associated, and recorded everything he had written and published before that date. These performances not only carry the imprint of the composer's authority, but also the inspiration of the occasion. The large-scale works have a concentration and compelling atmosphere that are unforgettable. No apologies at all need be made for the range, breadth and faithfulness of the recording, although some must be made for the organ itself, which is not always perfectly tuned. There is minor background hiss, which is not troublesome, and technically the CD transfers are a remarkable achievement.

Livre du Saint Sacrement.
*** Unicorn Dig. DKPCD 9067/8 [id.]. Jennifer Bate (organ of Sainte-Trinité, Paris).

What a sound! This is a quite spectacular recording and carries the composer's imprimatur. Jennifer Bate makes an impressive and compelling case for these hypnotic pieces, and the recording is in the demonstration bracket.

(i) *Méditations sur le mystère de la Sainte Trinité;* (ii) *3 Petites Liturgies de la Presence Divine.*
(M) *** Erato/Warner 4509 92007-2 [id.]. (i) composer (Cavaillé-Coll organ, L'Eglise de la Sainte-Trinité, Paris); (ii) Yvonne & Jeanne Loriod, ORTF Ch. & CO, Couraud.

The composer's own performance of the *Méditations* is uniquely powerful, and the Sainte-Trinité organ is very well recorded. The performance is vital and spontaneous; the sensuousness of the more luscious choral sections and the spectacular oriental percussion in Part II come over splendidly. The *Trois Petites Liturgies* has an immediate appeal, and this would be a good starting-point for newcomers to this composer's music. The recording is not always absolutely refined but it has great immediacy and impact.

La Nativité du Seigneur (9 meditations); Le banquet céleste.
★ *** Unicorn Dig. DKPCD 9005 [id.]. Jennifer Bate (organ of Beauvais Cathedral).

'*C'est vraiment parfait!*' said Messiaen after hearing Jennifer Bate's Unicorn recording of *La Nativité du Seigneur*, one of his most extended, most moving and most variedly beautiful works. For the CD issue, *Le banquet céleste* also provides an intense comment on the religious experience which has inspired all of the composer's organ music. The recording of the Beauvais Cathedral organ is of demonstration quality.

VOCAL MUSIC

Chants de terre et de ciel; Harawi (Chants d'amour et de mort). 3 Mélodies (Pourquoi; Le sourire; La fiancée); Poèmes pour Mi.
(M) *** EMI CMS7 64092-2 (2). Michèle Command, Marie-Madeleine Petit.

Michèle Command is here most characterful and firmly focused, with her accompanist just as warmly idiomatic. The three early songs of 1930 lead naturally to the two cycles from the late 1930s, more complex in their melodic lines. It is then that the ambitious Harawi cycle of 1945 reveals the full scope of the mature Messiaen's style, with its echoes of birdsong. This hour-long cycle belongs to what the composer regarded as his 'Tristan and Isolde' trilogy, along with the *Turangalîla Symphony* and the choral cycle, *Cinq Rechants*. Clear, undistracting sound.

Meyerbeer, Giacomo (1791–1864)

Les Patineurs (ballet suite, arr. & orch. Lambert).
(Y/B) (B) *** Decca Dig. 444 110-2 [id.]. Nat. PO, Richard Bonynge – MASSENET: *Le Cid* etc. ***
(M) *** Decca 425 468-2 (3). Nat. PO, Bonynge – TCHAIKOVSKY: *Sleeping Beauty*. **(*)

Les Patineurs was arranged by Constant Lambert using excerpts from two of Meyerbeer's operas, *Le Prophète* and *L'Etoile du Nord*. Bonynge's approach is warm and comparatively easy-going but, with such polished orchestral playing, this version is extremely beguiling. The sound too is first rate. There are alternative couplings.

Il Crociato in Egitto (complete).
*** Opera Rara OR 10 (4). Kenny, Montague, Della Jones, Ford, Kitchen, Benelli, Platt, Geoffrey Mitchell Ch., RPO, David Parry.

This was the sixth and last opera which the German-born Meyerbeer wrote for Italy. The musical invention may not often be very distinctive, but the writing is consistently lively, notably in the ensembles. With one exception – Ian Platt, ill-focused in the role of the Sultan – the cast is a strong one, with Dianna Montague outstanding in the castrato role of the Crusader-Knight, Armando. Della Jones, too, in the mezzo role of Felicia, whom Armando has abandoned in favour of Palmide, the Sultan's daughter, sings superbly with agile coloratura and a rich chest register. Yvonne Kenny is brilliant as Palmide. Bruce Ford, with his firm, heroic tone, and Ugo Benelli are very well contrasted in the two tenor roles. Though the chorus is small, the recording is clear and fresh.

Les Huguenots (complete).
(M) *** Decca 430 549-2 (4) [id.]. Sutherland, Vrenios, Bacquier, Arroyo, Tourangeau, Ghiuselev, New Philh. O, Bonynge.

Sutherland is predictably impressive, though once or twice there are signs of a 'beat' in the voice, previously unheard on Sutherland records. The rest of the cast is uneven, and in an unusually episodic opera, with passages that are musically less than inspired, that brings disappointments. Gabriel Bacquier and Nicola Ghiuselev are fine in their roles and, though Martina Arroyo is below her best as Valentine, the star quality is unmistakable. The tenor, Anastasios Vrenios, copes with the extraordinarily high tessitura and florid diversions. Vrenios sings the notes, which is more than almost any rival could. Fine recording to match this ambitious project, well worth investigating by lovers of French opera. The work sounds newly minted on CD.

Le Prophète (complete).
**(*) Sony M3K 79400 (3) [id.]. Horne, Scotto, McCracken, Hines, Dupony, Bastin, Boys' Ch. of Haberdasher's Aske's School, Amb. Op. Ch., RPO, Henry Lewis.

This recording anticipated the 1977 production at the New York Met. with the same conductor and principal soloists. None of the soloists is quite at peak form, though they all sing more than competently. Nevertheless, with vigorous direction by Henry Lewis – rather brutal in the Coronation scene – there is much to enjoy. The recording is vividly transferred to CD but would have benefited from a more atmospheric acoustic.

Miaskovsky, Nikolay (1881–1950)

Cello concerto in C min., Op. 66.
(Y/B) ❀ (M) *** EMI CDM5 65419-2 [id.]. Rostropovich, Philh. O, Sargent – TANEYEV: *Suite de concert*. ***

*** Ph. Dig. 434 106-2 [id.]. Julian Lloyd Webber, LSO, Maxim Shostakovich (with SHOSTAKOVICH: *The Limpid Stream: Adagio*) – TCHAIKOVSKY: *Rococo variations.* ***

(i) *Cello concerto;* (ii) *Cello sonatas Nos. 1 in D, Op. 12; 2 in A min., Op. 81.*

(Y/B) *** Olympia Dig. OCD 530 [id.]. Marina Tarasova, with (i) Moscow New Op. O, Yevgeny Samoilov; (ii) Alexander Polezhaev.

The Miaskovsky *Cello concerto* has an overwhelming sense of nostalgia and an elegiac atmosphere that is quite individual. Its very directness of utterance and diatonic simplicity can easily mask its depths. Although it does not encompass as wide a range as does the Elgar, it has a similarly powerful expressive impact. Marina Tarasova earns praise for coupling it so logically with the two *Cello sonatas.* The *Sonata in D major*, Op. 12 (1911, revised 1930), does not differ in idiom from its much later companion, *No. 2 in A minor*, Op. 81. Tarasova has a strong musical personality and produces a magnificent tone; she receives sympathetic support from her accompanists, and decent recording.

All credit to Julian Lloyd Webber for championing this piece and doing so with eloquence, and to Philips for recording it so impressively. Highly recommended, if the Tchaikovsky coupling is suitable.

However, Rostropovich's pioneering account with Sir Malcolm Sargent is still in a class of its own. It could not be played with greater eloquence and restraint, and the (1956) Abbey Road recording is amazingly full and fresh – one would never guess its age.

(i) *Lyric concertino for flute, clarinet, horn, bassoon, harp and string orchestra, Op. 32/3; Salutation overture in C, Op. 48; Serenade for chamber orchestra in E flat, Op. 32/1; Sinfonietta for string orchestra in B min., Op. 32/2.*
*** Olympia Dig. OCD 528 [id.]. Moscow New Op. O, Samoilov.

The *Serenade* has great charm and strong lyrical appeal; the *Lyric concertino*, and particularly its slow movement, has considerable harmonic subtlety. The performance under Yevgeny Samoilov is much finer than the earlier account by Vladimir Verbitzky (see below), and he gives a sensitive reading of the *Sinfonietta for strings*. These are endearing pieces; not so the *Salutation overture*, written for Stalin's 60th birthday, which is worth giving a miss. Very good recording.

Sinfonietta for strings in B min., Op. 32/2; Theme and variations; 2 Pieces, Op. 46/1; Napeve.
(Y/B) *** ASV Dig. CDDCA 928 [id.]. St Petersburg CO, Roland Melia.

The *Sinfonietta for strings* will appeal to anyone of a nostalgic disposition. The players give an affectionate, well-prepared account of it and convey the wistful, endearing nature of the slow movement to perfection. The *Theme and variations* (on a theme of Grieg) also has the same streak of melancholy. The first of the *Two Pieces*, Op. 46, No. 1, is a transcription and reworking for strings of the inner movements, reversing their order, of Miaskovsky's *Symphony No. 19 for military band*, composed in 1939. The St Petersburg Chamber Orchestra is an expert and responsive ensemble, and the ASV recording does them proud.

Symphonies Nos. (i) 1 in C min., Op. 3; (ii) 19 in E flat for wind band, Op. 46.
**(*) Russian Disc RDCD 11 007 [id.]. (i) USSR Ministry of Culture SO, Gennady Rozhdestvensky; (ii) Russian State Brass O, Nikolai Sergeyev.

Miaskovsky's *First Symphony* is a student work, very much in the received tradition, observing all the conventions one would expect to find in a symphonist of the post-nationalist Russian school. All the same, if the thematic ideas may not be highly individual, they betray (as so often with this composer) an endearing generosity of feeling, and there is a strongly Russian atmosphere throughout. It is obvious from the very start of the work that Miaskovsky was a composer who could think on a big scale. The *Nineteenth Symphony in B flat* for military band was written in 1939 for the 21st anniversary of the Red Army and is a slighter piece, worth hearing for its inner movements, a wistful *Moderato* and a well-written *Andante.* The *First Symphony* is well played by the Ministry of Culture Orchestra under Gennady Rozhdestvensky, though the brass sound a bit raw, as indeed do the upper strings. The *Nineteenth* is played with great brio and genuine affection. The less-than-three-star recording-quality should not deter collectors from investigating this work.

Symphonies Nos. 5 in D, Op. 18; 9 in E min., Op. 28.
*** Marco Polo Dig. 8.223499 [id.]. BBC PO, Downes.

The *Fifth Symphony* is a sunny, pastoral score dating from 1918, very much in the tradition of Glazunov and Glière. Downes's recording with the BBC Philharmonic, recorded in an admittedly over-resonant venue in Derby, is to be preferred both artistically and sonically to its earlier rival by the USSR Symphony Orchestra under Ivanov on Olympia (now deleted). The *Ninth Symphony* is somewhat better served than No. 5 so far as the sound is concerned. It is vintage Miaskovsky, more cogently argued and more interesting in thematic substance than the *Eighth.* Very good performances and good enough recording to make three stars.

Symphony No. 6 in E flat min. (Revolutionary), Op. 23.
(Y/B) (**(*)) Russian Disc mono RDCD 15008 [id.]. Yurlov Russian Ch., USSR SO, Kirill
    Kondrashin.
** Olympia Dig. OCD 510. Anima Moscow Chamber Ch., Russian SO, Veronika Dudarova.

Here, at long last on CD, is the première recording of the mammoth *Sixth Symphony* with choral finale,
which alerted many collectors to Miaskovsky's real stature. It is his most ambitious symphony; the
ravages and privation of the First World War and then the October Revolution, as well as private
tragedies, served to make this a symphony both of tragic dimensions and of dramatic vigour. There are
echoes of Miaskovsky's master, Glière, and also of Scriabin but, in the trio of the Scherzo, Miaskovsky
strikes that note of nostalgia and lost innocence he was to make so much his own in the *Cello concerto*
(and at times in the *Violin concerto* too). It is a highly individual and often masterly score, although let
down a little by its (somewhat inflated) choral finale, which employs folk and revolutionary songs,
including the *Carmagnole*, which earned the symphony its nickname, *The Revolutionary*. Though the
present recording is not of recent provenance, this is the one to have.

The Olympia version under Veronika Dudarova is inside the idiom and also offers stereo recording. If
the strings are lacking in weight (they are distinctly vinegary above the stave in the first movement and
less than opulent elsewhere) and the brass sound a bit raw, the essential character of the work is
conveyed well enough. The recording is not top-drawer but is more than acceptable.

Symphony No. 7 in B min., Op. 24.
** Olympia OCD 163 [id.]. USSR RSO, Ginsburg – KNIPPER: *Concert poem* etc. **

The *Seventh Symphony* (1922) is one of Miaskovky's finest symphonies, a much shorter work than its
vast predecessor. The pastoral writing in the *Andante* movement has great beauty, and the performance
under Leo Ginsburg is very persuasive. The sound is very agreeable and better balanced than the
Knipper with which it is coupled.

Symphony No. 8 in A, Op. 26.
** Marco Polo Dig. 8.223297 [id.]. Slovak RSO (Bratislava), Robert Stankovsky.

Although the *Eighth* is not one of Miaskovsky's finest symphonies, it is still worth investigating. There
are some characteristic ideas, and initially unfavourable impressions are soon dispelled as one comes
closer to it. Neither the performance nor the recording is distinctive, but both are thoroughly acceptable;
there is a lack of subtlety here, but not of vitality and commitment.

Symphony No. 12 in G min., Op. 35; Silence (symphonic poem after Poe), *Op. 9.*
**(*) Marco Polo Dig. 8.223302 [id.]. Slovak RSO (Bratislava), Robert Stankovsky.

The *Twelfth Symphony* is endearingly old-fashioned and has strong appeal. Although some of the big
rhetorical gestures of the *Sixth Symphony* are to be found in the second movement, there are also some
pre-echoes of things to come in the later symphonies. It is highly enjoyable, particularly when it is as well
played as it is here by the Bratislava Radio Orchestra under their gifted young conductor, Robert
Stankovsky. The tone-poem *Silence* draws for its inspiration on Edgar Allan Poe's *The Raven* and has a
strongly atmospheric quality with a distinctly *fin-de-siècle* air: if you enjoy Rachmaninov's *Isle of the
dead*, you should investigate it. The orchestra play with enthusiasm and they are decently recorded.

CHAMBER MUSIC

String quartets Nos. 1 in A min., Op. 33/1; 4 in F min., Op. 33/4.
(Y/B) ** Russian Disc RDCD 11013 [id.]. Taneyev Qt.

The Taneyev Quartet of Leningrad recorded all the Miaskovsky *Quartets* on LP during the course of
the 1980s, and their release on CD is warmly to be welcomed. Although Miaskovsky composed half as
many quartets as symphonies (thirteen as opposed to twenty-seven), they are hardly less important,
always finely crafted and possessing moments of real depth. Like so much of Miaskovsky's music, they
are conservative in idiom but their ideas are often memorable. The *First Quartet* finds him more among
the avant-garde of Russian composers than the conservative figure he became, and it has a far higher
norm of dissonance than we are used to. It is a surprisingly fascinating and powerful score. The *Fourth*,
in F minor, is less challenging and more overtly lyrical and traditional in outlook. These imaginative and
thought-provoking works are eminently well played, but the recording lets things down. The players are
forwardly balanced, the sound is hard and vinegary and needs to be tamed above the stave. All the same,
such is the interest of this disc that it must have a strong recommendation.

PIANO MUSIC

Piano sonatas Nos. 1 in D min., Op. 6; 2 in F sharp min., Op. 13; 3 in C min., Op. 19; 6 in A flat, Op. 64/2.
**(*) Olympia Dig. OCD 214 [id.]. Murray McLachlan.

In its way, the *First Sonata* is an oddity; its opening, like that of the Balakirev *B flat minor Sonata* written two years earlier, is fugal, but much of the second movement is more akin to the early Scriabin sonatas. So, too, is the *Second*, though Taneyev, Glazunov and Medtner also spring to mind. The pianist, Murray McLachlan, possesses a very considerable talent. An enterprising issue in every way, and well recorded.

Piano sonatas Nos. 4 in C min., Op. 27; 5 in B, Op. 64/1; Sonatine in E min., Op. 57; Prelude, Op. 58.
*** Olympia Dig. OCD 217 [id.]. Murray McLachlan.

The middle movement of the *Sonatine*, marked *Narrante e lugubre*, is dark and pessimistic, and quite haunting. McLachlan speaks of the 'enormous tactile pleasure' it gives to the performer, and his playing is both authoritative and persuasive. Perhaps this is the record to try first, since both *Sonatas*, not just the more 'radical' *Fourth*, are of interest and substance. Good recording.

Piano sonatas Nos. 6 in A flat, Op. 62/2; 7 in C, Op. 82; 8 in D min., Op. 83; 9 in F, Op. 84.
**(*) Marco Polo Dig. 8.223178 [id.]. Endre Hegedüs.

Piano sonatas Nos. 7 in C, Op. 82; 8 in D min., Op. 83; 9 in F, Op. 84; Reminiscences, Op. 29; Rondo-Sonata in B flat min., Op. 58; String quartet No. 5: Scherzo (trans. Aliawdina): Yellowed Leaves, Op. 31.
**(*) Olympia Dig. OCD 252 [id.]. Murray McLachlan.

The sonatas on the Olympia disc are all from 1949. The music is of the utmost simplicity but has an endearing warmth. As in the earlier discs, McLachlan provides scholarly and intelligent notes. The recording is good though the acoustic ambience is perhaps not absolutely ideal.

The Marco Polo disc brings the last four sonatas. The young Hungarian pianist, Endre Hegedüs, is often the more imaginative interpreter: he colours the second theme of the *Barcarolle* section of the *Eighth Sonata* with greater tenderness and subtlety than Murray McLachlan on Olympia, though the latter has great freshness. The sound is a little wanting in bloom. On balance, then, honours are fairly even between these two artists.

Mica, Jan Adam Franisek (1746–1811)

String quartet No. 6 in C.
(N) (M) *** Cal. CAL 6698 [id.]. Talich Qt – BOCCHERINI: *Quartet, Op. 58/2;* HAYDN: *Quartet No. 74;* MENDELSSOHN: *Quartet No. 2.* ***

The Bohemian composer, Jan Mica (1746–1811), writes elegantly in the *galant* style, and this *C major Quartet* (his sixth) brings an enticing opening theme, then continues in a cultivated and courtly style. Yet the *Rondo* finale produces a quite touching central interlude and one is reminded of Boccherini. Throughout, the warmth and finesse of the Talich playing ensure our enjoyment of what is a slight but well-crafted little work.

Milán, Luis de (c. 1500–c. 1561)

El Maestro: Fantasias Nos. 7, 8, 9 & 16; Pavanas Nos. 1, 4, 5 & 6; Tento No. 1.
(M) *** RCA 09026 61606-2. Julian Bream (lute) (with MUDARRA: *Fantasia*) – NARVAEZ: *Collection.*
***

This music was originally written for the vihuela, a hybrid instrument popular in sixteenth-century Spain, looking like a guitar but tuned like a lute. It was Milán who produced the first published book of this music in 1535, calling it *El Maestro* and including also instruction. Julian Bream seeks and achieves nobility of feeling in this repertoire and often chooses slow, dignified tempi. It all sounds splendid here on a proper lute, especially when so beautifully recorded.

Milhaud, Darius (1892–1974)

L'Apothéose de Molière, Op. 286; Le bœuf sur le toit, Op. 58; (i) Le carnaval d'Aix, Op. 83b. Le carnaval de Londres, Op. 172.
*** Hyperion Dig. CDA 66594 [id.]. (i) Jack Gibbons; New L. O, Ronald Corp.

Le carnaval d'Aix is a work full of carefree high spirits and is bathed in Mediterranean sun with the occasional poignant moment of nostalgia – a delight from start to finish, and very expertly played by Jack Gibbons and the New London Orchestra under Ronald Corp. They also convey the Satie-like circus-music character of *Le bœuf sur le toit* to excellent effect. What delightful music this is, and so expertly fashioned by this lovable composer. The Molière pastiche and the arrangement of melodies from *The Beggar's Opera* are not top-drawer Milhaud, but they are still worth having. Very good recording from the Hyperion team.

Ballade, Op. 61; Le carnaval d'Aix; Piano concertos Nos. 1 & 4; 5 Etudes, Op. 63.
*** Erato/Warner Dig. 2292 45992-2 [id.]. Claude Heffler, O Nat. de France, David Robertson.

Claude Heffler's account of Milhaud's delightful *Le carnaval d'Aix* with the Orchestre National must rank high in terms of easy-going charm and Mediterranean-like atmosphere, an altogether delightful performance. All the pieces on this disc, incidentally, are for piano and orchestra. The *Ballade* was composed for Roussel, and Milhaud made his piano début at its première in New York: its languorous opening seems to hark back to his days in Brazil. The first of the *Cinq Etudes* shows Milhaud in window-breaking, polytonal mode, as does the third, *Fugues*, while the fourth, *Sombre*, also has a high norm of dissonance; on the other hand, the second, *Doucement*, has a beguiling charm. The *First Piano concerto* is a relaxed, charming work not dissimilar to, though more complex in texture than, Jean Françaix's well-known *Concertino*. The *Fourth Piano concerto*, Op. 295 (1949), is an inventive piece of some substance with a particularly imaginative, dream-like slow movement. Of the new CDs to have appeared in the wake of the Milhaud centenary this is among the very best, and it is beautifully and naturally recorded.

Le bœuf sur le toit.
(M) *** Mercury 434 335-2 [id.]. LSO, Dorati – AURIC: *Overture;* FETLER: *Contrasts;* FRANCAIX: *Piano concertino;* SATIE: *Parade.* ***
**(*) Ph. Dig. 432 993-2 [id.]. Ch & O de Paris, Bychkov – HONEGGER: *Pacific 231;* POULENC: *Les biches.* **(*)

Dorati's reading, effervescent and light-hearted, catches the idiom splendidly and the music's lilt is infectiously conveyed. The LSO are obviously enjoying themselves and their playing, subtle as well as vivid, catches the audacious mood of a piece which is a trifle long for its content but which still entertains. The (1965) Mercury recording is perfectly judged, giving the music both transparency, vibrant colour and its proper edge.

A highly proficient account of *Le bœuf sur le toit* from the Orchestre de Paris, which plays with appropriate brilliance under Bychkov. But the performance does not have the abandon and *joie de vivre* which distinguish the Dorati LSO account which is now happily restored to circulation and which still sounds pretty amazing.

Le bœuf sur le toit, Op. 58; (i) *Harp concerto, Op. 323. La création du monde, Op. 81.*
*** Erato/Warner Dig. 2292 45820 [id.]. (i) Frédérique Cambreling; Lyon Op. O, Kent Nagano.

Kent Nagano and the Orchestra of the Opéra de Lyon give a splendid account of themselves in both the ballets. In *La création* the playing is full of character (the jazz fugue comes off marvellously) and the opening has splendid atmosphere; and much the same may be said of Nagano's exhilarating account of the Cocteau-inspired *Le bœuf sur le toit*: the playing is first rate and so, too, is the digital recording. The 1953 *Harp concerto* was written in America for Nicanor Zabaleta. It is not top-drawer Milhaud; there is more activity than substance for much of the time, but the slow movement has many beautiful things and Cambreling makes out a very good case for the high-spirited finale. Recommendable – eminently so in the case of the ballets.

Le bœuf sur le toit, Op. 58; La création du monde, Op. 81.
*** Chandos Dig. CHAN 9023 [id.]. Ulster O, Yan Pascal Tortelier – IBERT: *Divertissement;* POU-LENC: *Les Biches.* ***

A most engaging account of *Le bœuf sur le toit* from Tortelier and his Ulster players, full of colourful detail, admirably flexible, and infectiously rhythmic. Perhaps *La création du monde* is without the degree of plangent jazzy emphasis of a French performance, but its gentle, desperate melancholy is well caught, and the playing has plenty of colour and does not lack rhythmic subtlety. The Chandos recording, although resonant, is splendid in every other respect, and so are the couplings.

(i) *Le bœuf sur le toit;* (ii) *La création du monde;* (iii) *Saudades do Brasil; Suite provençale;* (iv) *Scaramouche* (for 2 pianos).
(***) EMI mono/stereo CDC7 54604-2 [id.]. (i) Champs-Elysées Theatre O; (ii) Ens. of 19 soloists; (iii) Concert Arts O, composer; (iv) Marcel Meyer, composer.

Milhaud's own account of *La création du monde* has a certain want of abandon but is otherwise well played, and this *Scaramouche* has an altogether special charm. Older collectors will recall the Capitol mono LP coupling of the captivating *Suite provençale* and the carefree and catchy *Saudades do Brasil*, which now appears for the first time in stereo sounding very sprightly indeed. The Hollywood players who comprised the 'Concert Arts' orchestra respond to the composer with evident delight, and they make this a most desirable issue. In addition there is *Le bœuf sur le toit* that Milhaud made with a Champs-Elysées orchestra in 1958 which will be new to most collectors and which makes a welcome makeweight to an altogether delightful (and, for lovers of this composer, indispensable) issue. However, it was curmudgeonly of EMI to put the disc in the full-price range.

La création du monde.

(Y/B) (M) *** Virgin/EMI Dig. CUV5 61206-2 [id.]. Lausanne CO, Zedda – DEBUSSY: *Danse; Sarabande;* PROKOFIEV: *Sinfonietta.* ***

La création du monde; Suite provençale.

(M) *** RCA GD 60685 [60685-2-RG]. Boston SO, Charles Munch – HONEGGER: *Symphonies Nos. 2 & 5.* (***)

Both Munch performances come from the early 1960s and are full of all the style and spirit you would expect from this combination. Munch's account of *La création du monde* has great virtuosity and panache, though the Boston recording always sounded a bit too reverberant, and still does. The *Suite provençale*, based on tunes by another Provençal composer, André Campra, is one of Milhaud's most captivating pieces. A thoroughly enjoyable disc.

Milhaud's ballet, with its mixture of yearning melancholy and jazzy high spirits, comes off splendidly in Alberto Zedda's highly spontaneous account, its witty syncopations and brassy exuberance bringing an unbridled effervescence to offset the restrained blues feeling of the main lyrical theme. The performance doesn't miss the Gershwin affinities, and the very vivid recording makes a bold dynamic contrast between the work's tender and abrasive moments.

Suite française.

(M) *** CDWHL 2067. L. Wind O, Wick – GRAINGER: *Irish tune from County Derry* etc.; POULENC: *Suite française.*

Milhaud's *Suite française* for wind is an enchanting piece, full of Mediterranean colour and vitality. It would be difficult to imagine a more idiomatic or spirited performance than this one, which has excellent blend and balance. Vivid recording.

Symphonies for chamber orchestra Nos. 1 (Le Printemps); 2 (Pastoral); 3 (Serenade); 5 (Dixtour d'instruments).

** Koch Dig. 3-7067-2 [id.]. Sinfonia O of Chicago, Barry Faldner (with DEBUSSY: *Symphony in B min.;* GOUNOD: *Petite symphonie for winds* **).

Barry Faldner and his Chicago Sinfonia, drawn from principals and other winds of the Chicago Symphony, give expert accounts of four of the little symphonies Milhaud composed in the 1920s. It would have made better sense (as well as rendering them more competitive) to have recorded all six rather than offering Faldner's orchestral transcription of Debussy's 10-minute symphony, a piece of little significance and not very characteristic of the composer. The performances of the Milhaud are very alert, characterful and polished – and very well recorded indeed. They give much pleasure.

Symphonies Nos. 1 (1939); 2 (1944); Suite provençale.

⊛ *** DG Dig. 435 437-2 [id.]. Toulouse Capitole O, Michel Plasson.

The *Second Symphony* is richly imaginative, melodically inventive and rewarding. Sample the fourth movement, *Avec sérénité*, and you will see just how sunny, relaxed and easy-going this music is; try also the slow movement of the *First* for its powerful, nocturnal atmosphere. The Orchestre du Capitole de Toulouse and Michel Plasson play these melodious scores with total commitment and convey their pleasure in rediscovering this music. The recording is very natural with a refined tone and well-balanced perspective. The delightful *Suite provençale* is as good as a holiday in the south of France – and cheaper!

Symphonies Nos. 4, Op. 281; 8 (Rhodanienne), Op. 362.

(M) *** Erato/Warner 2292 45841-2 [id.]. O Philh. RTF, cond. composer.

The *Fourth Symphony* is scored for unusually large forces, including two saxophones and a vast array of percussion, all heard to good effect in the first movement, which depicts the French uprising of 1848 with massive polytonal and dissonant clashes; the second laments the fallen, the third describes liberty rediscovered and the finale is almost festive. The *Eighth Symphony*, Op. 362, is subtitled *Rhodanienne* and evokes the course of the river Rhône from its beginnings in the Alps down to the Camargue. Rich in instrumental resource, it is full of imaginative colours and textures, and the playing of the Orchestre Philharmonique de l'ORTF for Milhaud himself is absolutely first rate. Both performances date from 1968; the sound is much cleaned up for this CD, which commands an unqualified recommendation.

Symphonies Nos. 6, Op. 343; 7, Op. 344; Ouverture méditerranéenne.
(Y/B) *** DG. Dig. 439 939-2 [id.].Toulouse Capitole O, Michel Plasson.

The *Sixth* is among the most relaxed and purely beautiful of the Milhaud symphonies, and Michel Plasson and the Orchestre du Capitole de Toulouse play it with evident affection. As with the glorious pastoral first movement of the *Sixth*, Plasson also lingers rather too much over the slow movement of the *Seventh* (he takes 12 minutes 27 seconds as opposed to Alun Francis' 8 minutes 52 seconds – see below). The problems posed by the exposed string writing above the stave are not helped by this tempo. The recording quality is very good, though not as finely detailed or as beautifully placed as in the earlier coupling of the *First* and *Second Symphonies* by the same artists.

Symphonies Nos. 7, Op. 344; 8 (Rhôdanienne), Op. 362; 9, Op. 380.
(Y/B) *** CPO Dig. CPO 999 166-2 [id.]. Basel RSO, Alun Francis.

The *Seventh* and *Ninth* are both three-movement works with their centre of gravity being their slow movements. Alun Francis actually makes more sense of the slow movement of the *Seventh* than does Plasson, holding it together in an altogether more realistic tempo. It is a powerful and often searching movement, even if there is a fair amount of note-spinning in the outer movements. For that matter, so there is in the *Ninth*, though it begins splendidly with a short and lively *Modérément animé*. If the *Eighth Symphony* is full of colour, the scoring is also open to the charge of being a bit too dense. The acoustic is drier than that of the Salle aux Grains in Toulouse, which is why the tempi are more taut and detail better defined. The Basel Radio Orchestra is a far from second-rate ensemble and in the *Seventh Symphony* hold up well against their French colleagues. Recommended.

(i) *Symphony No. 8 (Rhôdanienne), Op. 362;* (i; ii) *Scaramouche for saxophone, Op. 165c;* (iii) *La Cheminée du Roi René, Op. 205;* (iv) *Organ preludes, Op. 231b/3, 7–8;* (v) *Cantique du Rhône, Op. 155.*
** Praga PR 250 013 [id.]. (i) Czech PO, Neumann, (ii) with Neidenbach-Rahbari; (iii) Mihule, Vaček, Hůlka, Uher, Svárovsky; (iv) Tvrzský; (v) Czech R. Mixed Ch., Kühn.

The 1966 performance of the *Eighth Symphony* (*Rhôdanienne*) is not superior to the composer's own on Erato, but the disc is well worth acquiring even if it involves duplication. (The *Cantique du Rhône* for a cappella choir, a setting of words by Claudel in praise of the Rhône, composed in Aix in 1936, is a beautiful piece, well sung here by the Pavel Kühn Choir and, like *Scaramouche*, recorded in 1987.) The saxophone version of *Scaramouche* is played with plenty of character and a certain artful charm by Sohre Neidenbach-Rahbari and the Czech Philharmonic and was recorded at a live performance. *La Cheminée du Roi René* for wind quintet has an abundant charm, much of which is conveyed in this 1979 studio performance.

(i; ii) *Symphony No. 10, Op. 382;* (i; iii) *Concertino d'hiver for trombone and strings, Op. 327;* (iv) *Music for Prague, Op. 415;* (i; v) *Hommage à Comenius, Op. 421.*
** Praga PR 250 012 [id.]. (i) Prague R.O; (ii) Košler; (iii) Pulec, cond. Krombholc; (iv) Czech PO, composer; (v) Zikmundová, Jindrák, Hrnčíř.

The *Concertino d'hiver* comes from the set of 'Four Seasons' that Milhaud composed over a period of two decades and subsequently linked together. Not as inventive as the pre-war *Concertino de printemps*, it is given a very good performance by Zdenek Pulec and the Prague Radio Orchestra under Jaroslav Krombholc (1976). The quality in the 1970 performance of the *Tenth Symphony* with Zdenek Košler conducting is sonically superior to Milhaud's own account on Koch. *Musique pour Prague* was commissioned for the Prague Spring Festival in 1966, and this performance under Milhaud's own baton sounds a little better than the Koch rival. The textures are occasionally thick and hyperactive, but on the whole it is more rewarding than the symphony itself. Also associated with Prague is the cantata for soprano and baritone Milhaud composed in honour of the Czech philosopher and bishop Comenius (1592–1670), a pioneer of universal education, which is new to the catalogue. This, like the symphony, is a studio performance from 1970, though the soprano, Eva Zikmundová, has a characteristic Slavonic vibrato.

Symphony No. 10, Op. 382; Musique pour l'Indiana; (i) *L'Homme et son désir.*
(N) (M) **(*) BBC Radio Classics 15656 91512 [id.]. BBC SO, composer, (i) with Dodd, Newman, Barrett, Holt – SATIE: *Jack in the Box.* **(*)

These performances were recorded at the BBC Maida Vale studios when Milhaud made a guest appearance with the BBC Symphony Orchestra in 1970, when he would have been in his late seventies. This was an all-Milhaud concert, save for his transcription of Satie's *Jack in the Box*. (He had conducted his *Sixth Symphony* in 1957 but had never been invited back during the 1960s.) Neither the *Musique pour l'Indiana* nor the *Tenth Symphony* finds his inspiration as fresh or as generous as in the youthful *L'Homme et son désir*. All the same, this disc is a valuable historic document, the kind of thing the BBC should be unearthing from its archives. Milhaud conducted the symphony in Prague, a performance that has appeared commercially, but this has somewhat better-detailed sound. A disc of special interest to admirers of French music in general and of Milhaud in particular.

CHAMBER MUSIC

Caprice, Op. 335a; Duo concertant, Op. 351; Petit concert, Op. 192; Le printemps, Op. 18; Violin sonata No. 2, Op. 40; Sonatine, Op. 100; Le voyageur sans bagage (suite) *Op. 157b*.
(Y/B) ** Schwann Dig. 3-1310-2 [id.]. Trio Bellerive.

Very bright, up-front recording in the suite from the music to *Le voyageur sans bagage* (1936) for clarinet, violin and piano, though it is very well played. The sound is better in the *Violin sonata No. 2* and *Le printemps*, though the balance rather favours Robert Hairgrove's piano than Sandra Goldberg's violin. The performance of the former does not have as much charm as Zimmermann and Lonquich (see below). The pieces for clarinet and piano, the *Petit concert*, the *Sonatine*, Op. 100, and the two pieces from the mid-1950s (the *Caprice*, Op. 335a, and the *Duo concertant*, Op. 351) are played with spirit, but one could imagine them being more winning. The close, unrelieved recording is a handicap.

Duo for 2 violins, Op. 243; (i) *Sonata for 2 violins and piano, Op. 15*.
(*) Hyperion Dig. CDA 66473 [id.]. Osostowicz, Kovacic, (i) Tomes – MARTINU: *Violin sonata* **(*); PROKOFIEV: *Violin sonata*. *

The *Sonata for two violins and piano* of 1914 is beautifully crafted and has a charming slow movement but is very slight. Not as slight, though, as the *Duo*, the first two movements of which were composed at a dinner party; the finale was written the following morning. Musically it is all rather like having *canapés* and *petits fours* and missing out the meal! Elegant performances from Krysia Osostowicz and Ernst Kovacic – and in the *Sonata* Susan Tomes.

Music for wind: *La Cheminée du Roi René, Op. 105; Divertissement en trois parties, Op. 399b; Pastorale, Op. 47; 2 Sketches, Op. 227b; Suite d'après Corette, Op. 161b*.
(M) **(*) Chandos CHAN 6536 [id.]. Athena Ens., McNichol.

Though none of this is first-class Milhaud, it is still full of pleasing and attractive ideas, and the general air of easy-going, life-loving enjoyment is well conveyed by the alert playing of the Athena Ensemble. One's only quarrel with this issue is the somewhat close balance. However, this can be remedied a little by a lower-level setting; even if the overall playing time is not very generous, this is an excellent entertainment.

Sonatina for clarinet and piano; Sonatina for flute and piano; Sonata for flute, oboe, clarinet and piano; Sonatina for oboe and piano.
*** Orfeo Dig. CO 60831A [id.]. Brunner, Nicolet, Holliger, Maisenberg.

The *Sonata* is an ingenious and delightful piece, most expertly played here. The later *Sonatinas* have no less charm and polish, and are beautifully played and very naturally recorded. A strong recommendation for a very attractive concert.

(i) *Oboe sonatina, Op. 337;* (ii) *Suite après Corette, Op. 161b;* (iii) *Violin sonata No. 1, Op. 240;* (iv) *4 Visages, Op. 238;* (v) *Organ pastorale, Op. 229;* (vi) *3 Chansons de Négresse, Op. 148b;* (vii) *2 Poems by Blaise Cendrars, Op. 113*.
*** Praga PR 250 008 [id.].(i) Adamus, Bogunia; (ii) Hedba, Nechvatal, Zedník; (iii) Spelina, Friesl; (iv) Christ, Klánský; (v) Grubich; (vi) Fassbaender, Gage; (vii) Smíšený, Kühn Mixed Ch., Kühn.

Another compilation from Prague to honour the Milhaud centenary. All are live performances, made in Prague between 1981 and 1990, and are of decent to excellent quality. The two choral settings of poems by Blaise Cendrars, which open the CD, are of striking quality and are very well sung by Pavel Kühn's choir. The *Trois Chansons de Négresse* hark back to Milhaud's years in Rio, where he served as secretary to Paul Claudel at the French Embassy, and are sung with great character and charm by Brigitte Fassbaender. The *Pastorale*, Op. 229, for organ is a rather lovely and meditative piece. Wolfram Christ is the excellent soloist in the *Sonata No. 1*, based on eighteenth-century French tunes, and the *Quatre Visages* for viola and piano, the latter a portrait of four ladies from California, Wisconsin, Brussels and Paris. Like Jean Françaix's *Cinq Portraits de jeunes filles* for piano, it has character and a winning charm

– as, for that matter, have most of the other pieces. The *Suite d'après Corette* for oboe, clarinet and bassoon is elegantly played and sounds more persuasive here than in some French performances we have heard. A welcome issue and a valuable addition to the Milhaud discography.

String quartets Nos. 1, Op. 5; 2, Op. 16.
(N) (B) *** Discover Dig. DICD 920290 [id.]. Arriaga Qt.

The *First Quartet* comes from 1912 and is dedicated to the memory of Milhaud's fellow-Provencal, Cézanne; it is among the most diatonic of all his works. It is unusual in having two slow movements, both of which find him at his most serene. There are occasional hints of the Debussy *Quartet* and even a faint shadow of Franck in the *Grave* movement. The *Second* was composed during the first of the war years (1914–15) at about the time Milhaud was embarking on that key work in his development, *Les choéphores*, and there are signs of an emergent fascination with polytonality. The Arriaga Quartet are even more persuasive than their rivals on the Cybella label. They produce some real *pianopianissimo* tone when required and communicate their feeling for the music. Try the middle movement (there are five movements in all), whose silky textures (much of it is *con sord*) come over beautifully.

String quartets Nos. 1, Op. 5; 7 in B flat, Op. 87; 10, Op. 218; 16, Op. 303.
*** Cybella Dig. CY 804 [id.]. Aquitaine National Qt.

The *First Quartet* is a beautifully relaxed, sunny work, rather Debussian in feel. The *Seventh* speaks Milhaud's familiar, distinctive language; its four short movements are delightful, full of melody and colour. The *Tenth* is attractive too, while the *Sixteenth* was a wedding anniversary present for the composer's wife: its first movement has great tenderness and warmth. The Aquitaine Quartet has excellent ensemble, intonation is good and their playing is polished. The recording has a wide dynamic range and a spacious tonal spectrum.

String quartets Nos. 5, Op. 64; 8, Op. 121; 11, Op. 232; 13, Op. 268.
*** Cybella Dig. CY 805 [id.]. Aquitaine National Qt.

The *Fifth Quartet* is not one of Milhaud's most inspired; the *Eighth*, on the other hand, has much to commend it, including a poignant slow movement. No. 11 has a splendid pastoral third movement and a lively jazzy finale; No. 13 has overtones of Mexico in its finale and a beguiling and charming *Barcarolle*. Both performance and recording are very good.

Violin sonata No. 2, Op. 40.
(Y/B) *** EMI Dig. CDC7 54541-2 [id.]. Frank Peter Zimmermann, Alexander Lonquich – AURIC:
   Sonate; FRANCAIX: *Sonatine;* POULENC: *Sonata;* SATIE: *Choses vues.* ***

Listen to Zimmermann and Lonquich play Milhaud's *Second Sonata* after hearing Sandra Goldberg and Robert Hairgrove, and it is as if one were hearing a completely different piece. There is much greater character and variety of tonal colour than in the Schwann rival, and both artists bring sparkle and charm to this piece. Beautifully present and lively recording, though the piano is slightly favoured in preference to the violin.

PIANO MUSIC

Piano sonata No. 1; L'automne; Printemps, Books 1 & 2; 4 Sketches (Esquisses); Sonatine.
(Y/B) (B) ** Discover Dig. DICD 920 167 [id.]. Billi Eidi.

Milhaud was a capable pianist. Here is a good cross-section of his output for solo piano covering four decades from the *Première Sonate* to the *Sonatine*. Some of the music, such as the first book of *Printemps* or the *Quatre Esquisses*, is charming; none of it makes great demands on either the pianist or the listener, and some of it is pretty inconsequential. All the same, taken in small doses, there is much that gives pleasure – and would give more if the recording were not quite so bottom-heavy or wanting in transparency. Billi Eidi's playing is fluent, sensitive and totally committed.

Minkus, Léon (1826–1917)

La Bayadère (complete; arr. Lanchbery)
*** Decca Dig. 436 917-2 (2) [id.]. ECO, Richard Bonynge.

Lanchbery has provided the present score, and though officially he is responsible for the orchestration, who knows, perhaps he had a hand in its content, as in his vintage arrangement of Hérold's *La fille mal gardée*. Whatever the case, the result is highly engaging. Unlike Adam's rather disappointing *Le Corsaire* (also recorded by the same forces), this work is full of attractive melody and sparkling orchestral effects. If you like late-nineteenth-century ballet music, then here is nearly two hours of it, played with much vivacity, elegance and drama, and given Decca's top-quality sound.

Moeran, Ernest J. (1894–1950)

(i) *Cello concerto. Sinfonietta.*
*** Chandos Dig. CHAN 8456 [id.]. (i) Raphael Wallfisch; Bournemouth Sinf., Del Mar.

Raphael Wallfisch brings an eloquence of tone and a masterly technical address to the *Cello concerto* and he receives responsive orchestral support from Norman Del Mar and the Bournemouth players. The well-crafted *Sinfonietta* is among Moeran's most successful pieces: its invention is delightfully fresh, and there is that earthy, unpretentious musicality that makes Moeran so appealing a composer. The recording is a little on the reverberant side but well balanced and present.

(i) *Violin concerto. 2 Pieces for small orchestra: Lonely waters; Whythorne's shadow.*
*** Chandos Dig. CHAN 8807 [id.]. (i) Lydia Mordkovitch; Ulster O, Vernon Handley.

The *Violin concerto* is strongly lyrical in feeling. The first movement is ruminative and rhapsodic, its inspiration drawn from Moeran's love of the west coast of Ireland; the middle movement makes use of folk music; while the finale, a ruminative elegy of great beauty, is the most haunting of the three. Lydia Mordkovitch plays with great natural feeling for this music and, quite apart from his sensitive support in the *Concerto*, Vernon Handley gives an outstanding (and affecting) account of *Lonely waters*. Superb recording.

Serenade in G (complete original score); (i) *Nocturne.*
*** Chandos Dig. CHAN 8808 [id.]. Ulster O, Vernon Handley, (i) with Mackey, Renaissance Singers –
   WARLOCK: *Capriol suite* etc. ***

The *Serenade in G* is a welcome addition to the catalogue, a work which has a good deal in common with Warlock's *Capriol suite* in its orchestral dress. Both use dance forms from a previous age and transform them with new colours and harmonic touches. Handley and the Ulster Orchestra present it with striking freshness and warmth in its original version. Handley also offers the lovely *Nocturne*, a setting of a poem by Robert Nichols for baritone solo and eight-part chorus, which was much admired by Britten. It is given a wholly sympathetic performance and recording here, and the resonant acoustics of the Ulster Hall, Belfast, provide a warmly atmospheric ambient glow.

Symphony in G min.
⚜ *** Dutton Laboratories mono CDAX 8001 [id.]. Hallé O, Leslie Heward – IRELAND: *Piano concerto.* (***)

There is always something special about first recordings, but this is remarkable in more than one respect. First, it is a wonderful performance of a great British symphony. Secondly, it celebrates a great British conductor, working at white-hot intensity, who died (so prematurely) just over a year after the original 78s appeared. Walter Legge produced the sessions in Manchester's Houldsworth Hall, and his mono sound-balance was completely natural, using the slightly dry hall acoustics to maximum advantage. Finally, no praise can be too great for Michael Dutton's CD transfer, made direct from the 78-r.p.m. shellac pressings, using the Cedar system to suppress the surface noise, yet providing sound for which no apologies whatsoever need to be made, with no edginess to ruin the strings: the violins sound particularly fresh. The composer was present at the sessions and gave his imprimatur. This CD is fully worthy of it. The Ireland coupling is hardly less indispensable.

Symphony in G min.; Overture for a masque.
*** Chandos Dig. CHAN 8577 [id.]. Ulster O, Vernon Handley.

Moeran's superb *Symphony in G minor* is in the best English tradition of symphonic writing and worthy to rank with the symphonies of Vaughan Williams and Walton. But for all the echoes of these composers (and Holst and Butterworth, too) it has a strong individual voice. Vernon Handley gives a bitingly powerful performance, helped by superb playing from the Ulster Orchestra, totally committed from first to last. The *Overture for a masque*, a brash, brassy piece in its fanfare opening and Waltonian cross-rhythms, makes an attractive and generous fill-up. The recording is superb.

Fantasy quartet for oboe and strings.
*** Chandos Dig. CHAN 8392 [id.]. Francis, English Qt – BAX: *Quintet;* HOLST: *Air and variations* etc.; JACOB: *Quartet.* ***

Moeran's folk-influenced *Fantasy quartet*, an attractively rhapsodic single-movement work, is played admirably here, and the recording is excellent, well balanced too.

(i) *String quartet in A min.;* (ii) *Violin sonata in E min.*
*** Chandos Dig. CHAN 8465 [id.]. (i) Melbourne Qt; (ii) Donald Scotts, John Talbot.

There is a strong folksong element in the *Quartet*, and some French influence too; these pieces are stronger than they have been given credit for. Good performances and recording.

String trio in G.
(N) (M) (***) Dutton Lab. CDAX 8014 [id.]. Pougnet, Riddle, Pini – BAX: *Nonet;* FERGUSON: *Octet;* DELIUS: *Violin sonata No. 3.* (***)

This is an only recording of the work, and it would be hard to imagine a better performance of this lyrical and resourceful piece, which is full of imagination. The recording sounds remarkably fresh in this fine transfer.

Molino, Francesco (1775–1847)

Trio, Op. 45.
*** Mer. Dig. CDE 84199 [id.]. Conway, Silverthorne, Garcia – BEETHOVEN: *Serenade;* JOSEPH KREUTZER: *Grand Trio.* ***

Italian-born, Molino first settled in Spain, before going on to London and Paris, where he built a reputation as a violinist and guitarist. Undemanding music to complete a charming disc for a rare combination. First-rate playing and recording.

Molter, Johann (1696–1765)

Trumpet concertos Nos. 1–3 in D, MWV IV/12–14; (i) *Double trumpet concertos in D, MWV IV/7, 8, 10–11.*
*** RCA Dig. 09026 61200-2. Guy Touvron; (i) Guy Messler; Württemberg CO, Heilbronn, Joerg Faerber.

Johann Molter is well remembered for his concertos, especially those for the trumpet, for which he wrote with innate skill, even though he was not a brass player himself. His melodic lines lie high in the clarino range, and the brilliantly felicitous bravura writing makes the utmost demands on his soloists. In all four double concertos here, both trumpeters are thoughtfully left resting in the engaging *Andante* slow movements, which are usually for strings alone. MWV IV/10 is an exception, bringing a divertimento-like interlude, scored for woodwind alone. In the solo concertos, although outer movements are hardly less brilliant, and rewardingly so, the trumpeter also has a central slow melody in the highest tessitura. The performances here are persuasively accomplished, and Joerg Faerber and his excellent Württemberg players provide alert and spirited accompaniments and are particularly sympathetic in the serene *Andantes*. The recording is most realistic.

Mompou, Federico (1893–1987)

Escenas infantiles (orch. Tansman); *Suburbis* (orch. Rosenthal); (i) *Combat del Sueño;* (ii) *Los Improperios.*
*** HM Dig. HMC 901482 [id.]. O of Cambra Theatre, Lliure, Josep Pons, with (i; ii) Virginia Parramon; (ii) Jerzy Artysz, Valencia Ch.

The two orchestral works were scored by other hands, but the writing itself has much charm and the pastel-shaded colouring is inherent in the music itself. Not surprisingly, the flavour and impressionistic influences are both Spanish and French, with whiffs of Ravel and the Debussy of *Ibéria*. The oratorio, *Los Improperios*, is much more ambitious and – although there are reminders of Poulenc and even of Delius – the music has an individual voice, both orchestrally and in its serene, gleaming choral writing. *Combat del Sueño* is a triptych of ardent yet poignant love songs – somewhat like Ravel's *Shéhérazade* – combining memorable melodic lines with spare and delicate orchestration. They are seductively sung here by Virginia Parramon. Jerzy Artysz joins her in the oratorio, and the excellent choral and orchestral contributions under the persuasive Josep Pons, plus warm yet vividly atmospheric recording, ensure a strong recommendation for this very rewarding collection. Mompou may be eclectic, but he is also very personable.

Suite compostellana (for guitar).

(M) *** RCA Dig. 09026 61596-2 [id.]. Julian Bream – RECITAL: *'Twentieth-century guitar'*. ***

Mompou's *Suite compostellana* is his only work for guitar – and very fine it is, beautifully written for the instrument and with a prevailing mood of wistful melancholy. Bream's performance is wonderfully sympathetic and spontaneous and the digital recording is first class.

14 Cançons i dansas; Preludes Nos. 5; 6 (for the left hand); 7 (Fireworks).

(Y/B) ✿*** RCA Dig. 09026 62554-2 [id.]. Alicia de Larrocha.

Alicia de Larrocha has previously recorded a group of the *Cançons i dansas* for Decca as part of a recital of *'Musica española'* (see below). Now she offers the whole set and is given first-class, modern, digital recording. The sense of repose in No. 5, the delicate loveliness of No. 7 and the wistful charm of No. 11 are characteristic of the intimacy of feeling of this playing. The performances have much warmth and grace, and we have transferred our Rosette from the earlier record. The present recital also includes four *Preludes*, of which No. 11 is aptly dedicated to the pianist. Mompou could surely not hope to find a more understanding advocate.

7 Cançons i dansas; Impresiones íntimas; Música callada IV; Preludio VII a Alicia de Larrocha.

(M) *** Decca 433 929-2 (2) [id.]. Alicia de Larrocha – Recital: *'Musica española'*. ***

This is gentle, reflective music which brings peace to the listener. Its quiet ruminative quality finds an eloquent exponent in Alicia de Larrocha, to whom Mompou dedicated one of his preludes. The *Impresiones íntimas* date from 1911–14 and is his first work of note. Like Falla and Turina, Mompou was drawn to Paris, and these pieces have absorbed something of the delicacy of Debussy in their poetic feeling, fine detail and well-calculated proportions. Alicia de Larrocha plays these poetic miniatures *con amore*, and the Decca recording is quite superb. This is reissued as part of a generous and stimulating recital of piano music by Mompou's Spanish contemporaries.

8 Canciones i danzas; Escenas de niños; Fiestas lejanas; Paisajes; Pessebres; Suburbis.

(M) *** EMI CDM7 64470-2 [id.]. Gonzalo Soriano or Carmen Bravo.

Gonzalo Soriano plays these reflective miniatures simply and with the right degree of restrained eloquence. Mompou is the very antithesis of a gaudy impressionist; his musical pictures are restrained and delicately delineated. Carmen Bravo also finds poetry in the rest of the programme and is charmingly perceptive in his portrayal – in *Suburbis* – of *L'home de l'aristo* (the *aristo* was a cross between a hand-held miniature barrel-organ and a hurdy-gurdy). The *Escenas de niños* are gentle children's pictures, while the *Fiestas lejanas* are a series of brief vignettes, echoes and memories of past festivities. The two closing *Paisajes* with evocations of fountain, bell and lake are delightful, and the playing here catches well their delicately picaresque understatement. A rewarding and generous recital, given remarkably good recording, even though it dates from the early days of stereo.

Jeunes filles au jardin; El carrer, el guitarrista i el vell cavall; Canción y danza Nos. 5, 6 & 8; La fuente y la compaña.

(M) (***) EMI mono CDC7 54836-2 [id.]. (i) Composer – FALLA: *Harpsichord concerto* etc.; GRANA-DOS: *Danzas españolas* etc.; NIN: *Cantos populares españolas*. (***)

One of the most valuable of the marvellously documented and beautifully restored 'Composers in Person' CDs that EMI have recently published. Federico Mompou was the most long-lived of the Spanish composers recorded on this disc. (When R.L. was in Barcelona, some years before the composer's death, he was told that Mompou claimed never to have gone to bed before 3 o'clock in the morning during the whole of his life!) He remains the most intimate and the most intensely private of Spanish composers. He recorded these six pieces while in London in 1950, though unaccountably they were never published until now. They are slight but beautiful and enhance what is a highly interesting disc.

Mondonville, Jean-Joseph Cassanea de (1711–72)

Titon et L'Aurore (complete).

*** Erato/Warner Dig. 2292 45715-2 (2) [id.]. Fouchécourt, Napoli, Huttenlocher, Smith, Monnoyios, Les Musiciens du Louvre, Minkowski.

Described as a 'heroic-pastoral', *Titon et L'Aurore* fluently pours forth a sequence of crisp ideas in each of the three acts of this formal classical tale of the mortal Titon who has the temerity to fall in love with Aurora, goddess of the dawn. Some of the instrumental effects are most vivid and the work is full of charming ideas, presented with freshness and vigour. Marc Minkowski proves an ideal interpreter, directing a performance of the highest voltage, which yet allows the singers a full range of expressiveness. Jean-Paul Fouchécourt proves an outstanding example of the French *haute-contre*, sustaining stratospheric lines with elegance and no strain. Catherine Napoli is bright and clear, if shallow at times as Aurore, while Anne Monnoyios sings with ideal sweetness as L'Amour. Highlights are available on 4509 98520-2.

Montéclair, Michel de (1667–1737)

Cantatas: *Pan et Syrinx; Le Triomphe de la Constance*.
(Y/B) (M) *** O-L 444 169-2 [id.]. Judith Nelson, Huggett, Preston, Coin, Hogwood – François
  COUPERIN: *Leçons de Ténèbres*. ***

Michel Pignolet de Montéclair held no court appointment; he was a *basse de violon* player at the Opéra and is best known as the teacher of Couperin's daughters. It is not surprising that his instrument plays a prominent part in the accompaniment of these two classical cantatas, of which *Le Triomphe* has a charming pastoral lyricism, while *Pan et Syrinx*, though not less appealingly melodic, is more dramatic, with many imaginative touches in the lively accompaniment. Judith Nelson is surely an ideal soloist, freshly appealing in the pastoral flow, and dealing with the considerable bravura of the upper tessitura in the latter piece with captivating aplomb. She is very touching in Pan's melancholy recitative and lament, after Syrinx has perished in the waters of the Erynmanthus; with its flute obbligato, this brings a remarkable depth of chromatic expressive feeling. Here Stephen Preston's contribution is most sensitive and, throughout, the stylish and lively accompaniments add much to this most enjoyable and stimulating music.

Monteverdi, Claudio (1567–1643)

Ab aeterno ordinata sum; Confitebor tibi, Domine (3 settings); *Deus tuorum militum sors et corona; Iste confessor Domini sacratus; Laudate Dominum, O omnes gentes; La Maddalena: Prologue: Su le penne de venti. Nisi Dominus aedificaverit domum.*
⊛ *** Hyperion Dig. CDA 66021 [id.]. Kirkby, Partridge, Thomas, Parley of Instruments.

There are few records of Monteverdi's solo vocal music as persuasive as this. The three totally contrasted settings of *Confitebor tibi* (Psalm 110) reveal an extraordinary range of expression, each one drawing out different aspects of word-meaning. Even the brief trio, *Deus tuorum militum*, has a haunting memorability – it could become to Monteverdi what *Jesu, joy of man's desiring* is to Bach – and the performances are outstanding, with the edge on Emma Kirkby's voice attractively presented in an aptly reverberant acoustic. The accompaniment makes a persuasive case for authentic performance on original instruments. The CD sounds superb.

Madrigals, Book I (complete); Book 7: *Tempro la cetra; Tirsi e Clori.*
(N) (M) *** Virgin Veritas/EMI VC5 45143-2 [id.]. Consort of Musick, Anthony Rooley.

With the arrival of Book I, Rooley's distinguished survey of this extraordinarily diverse madrigal repertoire is all but complete, and no doubt Book VII will arrive during the lifetime of this volume. At the time of this first collection Monteverdi was just nineteen years of age and already beginning to explore a world which he was to make very much his own. Two-thirds of his chosen texts here are concerned with love's disappointments, the words full of torments and aching hearts, which gives him plenty of opportunity for expressive dolour. Though these early madrigals are usually brief and without the sharp poignancy of later examples (it was not until the Third Book that his originality began to make itself felt to the full) there is much here that is imaginative and there is consistent lyrical beauty. The simple presentation, with good tuning and fine blending, seems just right for this repertoire. Rooley ends his programme with two rather more ambitious pieces from Book VII, with instrumental accompaniment – the engaging introductory sonnet, where the poet tunes his lyre and finds it will respond only to themes of love, and the charming pastoral ballet, *Tirsi e Clori*, written for the Mantua Court, about the joy of requited love and faithfulness. With good soloists, the performances readily capture the music's happiness. The recording is first class.

Madrigals, Book 2 (complete).
(N) (M) *** Virgin Veritas/EMI Dig. VC7 59282-2 [id.]. Cons. of Musicke, Rooley.

It is good that Rooley is turning to the earlier Books of the Monteverdi madrigals, including the very effective Tasso settings. Much of this music is simpler in its appeal and imagery than the later writing, but it all comes to life with great freshness here. Immaculate recording.

Madrigals, Book 3 (complete).
(N) (M) *** Virgin Veritas/EMI Dig. VC7 59283-2 [id.]. Cons. of Musicke, Rooley.

This is a livelier, more vibrant collection than Book 2, and Rooley and his group respond accordingly. A most stimulating concert.

Madrigals, Book 4 (complete).
*** O-L Dig. 414 148-2 [id.]. Cons. of Musicke, Anthony Rooley.

With Book 4 we move on to some of Monteverdi's finest settings. Under Anthony Rooley the excellent, well-integrated singers of the Consort of Musicke give masterly performances of this dazzling collection of madrigals. The flexibility and control of dramatic contrast, conveying consistent commitment, make this one of this group's finest records, helped by atmospheric but aptly intimate recording.

Madrigals, Book 6 (complete).
(M) *** Virgin Veritas/EMI Dig. VC7 59605-2 [id.]. Consort of Musicke, Anthony Rooley.

Il sesto libro de madrigali (1614) includes the five-part transcription of the *Lamento d'Arianna* and *Zefiro torno*, and also pieces from Monteverdi's years at Mantua. The Consort of Musicke maintain the high standards of taste and artistry with which we associate them. Excellent recording.

Madrigals from Books 7 and 8: *Amor che deggio far; Altri canti di Marte; Chiome d'oro; Gira il nemico insidioso; Hor ch'el ciel e la terra; Non havea Febo ancora – Lamento della ninfa; Perchè t'en fuggi o Fillide; Tirsi e Clori (ballo concertato for 5 voices and instruments).*
(B) *** HM HMA 1901068 [id.]. Les Arts Florissants, Christie.

The singing of this famous group is full of colour and feeling and, even if intonation is not absolutely flawless throughout, it is mostly excellent. Much to be preferred to the bloodless white tone favoured by some early-music groups. Good recording. A bargain.

Madrigals, Book 8: *Madrigali guerrieri et amorosi (Madrigals of love and war).*
❀ (M) *** Ph. 432 503-2 (2) [id.]. Armstrong, Bostock, Fuller, Harper, Howells, Watson, Hodgson, Collins, Alva, Davies, Oliver, Tear, Wakefield, Dean, Grant, Glyndebourne Ch. (members), ECO, Leppard.

This set provided a richly enjoyable start to a magnificent project of the early 1970s, nothing less than the complete recording by Leppard and his varied forces of Monteverdi's enormous total output of madrigals. With his star-studded cast Leppard ensures that there is nothing earnest or pedestrian about the results. Some – used to more acerbic textures – may complain at the warmth and richness, not only of the opening *Sinfonia* but also of the pair of magnificent six-part choruses which open each set (both *guerrieri* and *amorosi*), but here as elsewhere Leppard is demonstrating the enormous variety of expression of the composer's three described musical styles, *concitato*, *temperato* and *molle*, and the string accompaniments on modern instruments sound very much in place. First-class, atmospheric recording and CD transfers of the very highest Philips quality.

Madrigals, Book 8: Madrigali amorosi.
(M) *** Virgin Veritas/EMI Dig. VC7 59621-2 [id.]. Consort of Musicke, Anthony Rooley.

Monteverdi published his *Eighth Book* in 1638 after a long gap in his madrigal output. One of the very greatest of the songs is *Lamento della ninfa* (which Nadia Boulanger so memorably recorded) in what Monteverdi called the *stile rappresentativo* or theatre style, and that is affectingly done here.

Madrigals: *Addio Florida bella; Ahi com'a un vago sol; E così a poco a poco torno farfalla; Era l'anima mia; Luci serene e chiare; Mentre vaga Angioletta ogn'anima; Ninfa che scalza il piede; O mio bene, a mia vita; O Mirtillo, Mirtill'anima mia; Se pur destina; Taci, Armelin deh taci; T'amo mia vita; Troppo ben può questo tiranno amore.*
(B) *** HM HMA 1901084 [id.]. Concerto Vocale.

A highly attractive collection of generally neglected items, briskly and stylishly performed. The most celebrated of the singers is the male alto, René Jacobs, a fine director as well as soloist. With continuo accompaniment, the contrasting of vocal timbres is achieved superbly. Excellent recording and very good value.

Madrigals: *A Dio, Florinda bella; Altri canti d'amour; Amor che deggio far; Hor che'l ciel e la terra; Presso un fiume tranquillo; Questi vaghi concenti; Quio rise, O Tirsi.*
(M) ** Teldec/Warner 4509 93268-2 [id.]. Jacobeit, Förster-Dürlich, Van t'Hoff, Runge, Villisech, Hamburg Monteverdi Ch., Leonhardt Consort.

Highly regarded when first issued, this 1963 recording now brings some problems in its CD transfer, caused by the generous acoustics of the Christ-König-Kirche, Hamburg. The choral focus is somewhat blurred and the resonance also affects the accompanying group. However, many of these items are dialogue madrigals with the interplay of excellent soloists (*A Dio, Florida bella* is a delightful example), and in *Hor che'l ciel e la terra* the solemn choral section is undoubtedly enhanced by the reverberations. The Hamburg Monteverdi Choir is a splendid ensemble and throughout these performances are as stylish as they are sensible. But the measure is short: 43½ minutes.

Madrigals: *Altri canti di Marte; Ardo avvampo; Hor che'l ciel e la terra; Ballo: Movete al mio bel suon; O ciecchi, ciecchi; Questi vaghi concenti.* (i) *Sestina: Lagrime d'amante al sepolcro dell'amata.*
(M) *** Decca 433 174-2 [id.]. Palmer, Holt, Bowen, Evans, Elwes, Thomas, Heinrich Schütz Ch., Norrington; (i) Schütz Cons.

These fine madrigals are given crisp, well-drilled performances by Norrington, not as relaxedly expressive as Leppard's outstanding Philips set, but most refreshing. The ample acoustic of St John's, Smith Square, adds agreeable atmosphere. The eloquent and moving *Sestina* is one of Monteverdi's most unusual and original extended settings.

Madrigals: *'Batto', qui pianse Ergasto; Gira, il nemico insidioso amore; Hor che'l ciel e la terra; O come sei gentile; Ogni amante è guerrir; Zefiro torna.*
(Y/B) ❀ (M) *** Virgin Veritas/EMI Dig. VER5 61165-2 [id.]. Chiaroscuro, L. Baroque, Nigel Rogers – D'INDIA: *Madrigals.* *** ❀

A hand-picked half-dozen of Monteverdi's finest madrigals, superlatively sung, consistently bringing out the expressive originality and the extraordinary variety of the settings, to say nothing of their inherent vocal bravura. *Zefiro torna* is justly famous, but *'Batto', qui pianse Ergasto* is hardly less remarkable, and the two *Madrigali guerrieri et amorosi* are very telling indeed. The engagingly lyrical *O come sei gentile* follows immediately after the d'India dramatized cycle from *Il pastor Fido* and makes a fascinating comparison. Accompaniments are nicely balanced and the recording has an exceptionally real and vivid presence.

Madrigali erotici: Chiome d'oro; Come dolci hoggi l'auretta; Con che saovita; Mentre vaga Angioletta; Ogni amante e guerrier; Ohimè, dov'è il mio ben?; Parlo misero, o taccio; S'el vostro cor, Madonna; Tempro la cetra; Vorrei baciarti o Filli.
*** O-L Dig. 421 480-2 [id.]. Emma Kirkby, Nelson, Holden, Elliot, King, Thomas, Cons. of Musicke, Rooley.

Most of the madrigals on this CD come from the Seventh Book of 1619, very much a watershed in Monteverdi's output. In many instances they are for virtuoso singers and make a break with the past in that they call for instrumental accompaniment. The recording is excellently balanced. Strongly recommended.

Madrigals (Duets and solos): *Chiome d'oro, bel thesoro; Il son pur vezzosetta pastorella; Non è di gentil core; O come sei gentile, caro augellino; Ohimè dov'è il mio ben?; Se pur destina e vole il cielo, partenza amorosa.* Sacred music: *Cantate Domino; Exulta, filia Sion; Iste confessoe II; Laudate Dominum in sanctis eius; O bone Jesu, o piissime Jesu; Sancta Maria, succurre miseris; Venite, siccientes ad aquas Domini.* (Opera) *Il Ritorno d'Ulise in patria: Di misera regina (Penelope's lament).*
(M) *** Carlton 30365 0016-2 [id.]. Emma Kirkby, Evelyn Tubb, Consort of Musicke, Rooley.

Those who have enjoyed the Hyperion disc listed above, also featuring the delightful artistry of Emma Kirkby, will surely revel in this bargain collection, mostly of duets in which she is joined by Evelyn Tubb. The two voices are admirably matched and both artists ornament their lines attractively and without overdoing it. Evelyn Tubb is given a solo opportunity in Penelope's lament from *Il ritorno d'Ulise*, which she sings dramatically and touchingly. Anthony Rooley's simple accompaniments with members of the Consort of Musicke are also imaginatively stylish. It is a pity that the documentation is inadequate; otherwise this collection is a genuine bargain.

Con che soavità; Lamento d'Arianna; Lettera amorosa: Se i languidi mieie sguardi. Excerpts from: (i) *L'incoronazione di Poppea;* (ii) *L'Orfeo.*
(N) (M) **(*) Teldec/Warner 0630 10032-2 [id.]. Cathy Berberian, VCM, Harnoncourt; with (i) Paul Esswood; (ii) Nigel Rogers, Günther Theuring, Lajos Kozma.

It must have seemed a good idea to combine Cathy Berberian's contributions to Harnoncourt's complete recordings of two major Monteverdi operas with three other key vocal solos, notably the touching *Lamento d'Arianna* which she recorded only a few years before her death. In the event, however, it makes a rather bitty collection, even though she was at her finest as the Messenger in *Orfeo* and as *Ottavia* in *L'incoronazione di Poppea*, and the third excerpt from the latter opera, *A Dio Roma*, although movingly sung, finishes quite abruptly and leaves the listener rather in mid-air.

Lamento d'Olympia; Maladetto sia l'aspetto; Ohimè ch'io cado; Quel sdengosetto; Voglio di vita uscia.
*** Hyperion CDA 66106 [id.]. Emma Kirkby, Anthony Rooley (chitarone) – D'INDIA: *Lamento d'Olympia* etc. ***

A well-planned recital from Hyperion contrasts the two settings of *Lamento d'Olympia* by Monteverdi and his younger contemporary, Sigismondo d'India. The performances by Emma Kirkby, sensitively supported by Anthony Rooley, could hardly be surpassed; her admirers can be assured that this ranks among her best records.

Motets and madrigals: *Adoramus te; Cantate Domino; Domine, ne in furore tuo; Era l'anima mia; Ohimè se tanto amate; Zefiro torna.*
(M) ** Decca 440 032-2 [id.]. Monteverdi Ch., John Eliot Gardiner – GESUALDO: *Motets.* **

These performances are marked by excellent singing, with firm tone and intonation, but there is an element of interpretative exaggeration that looks forward to Eliot's later 'authentic' style and is not always wholly convincing here. Dynamics and tempi are rather extreme but there is no lack of life and vitality, and the really excellent recording – firm and clearly focused – will undoubtedly tempt many collectors.

Motets: *Ego flos campi; Ego sum pastor bonus; Exulta, filia Sion; Fuge, fuge anima mea, mundum; Iusti tulerunt spolia; Lapidabant Stephanum; Lauda, Jerusalem; Laudate Dominum; Nigra sum; O bone Jesu, illumina oculos meos; O bone Jesu, O piissime Jesu; O quam pulchra es; Pulchra es; Salve regina; Spuntava al dì; Sugens Jesus, Dominus noster; Surge propera, amica mea; Veni in hortum meum* (with PICCININI: *Toccata X*).
*** Virgin/EMI Dig. VC7 59602-2 [id.]. Brigitte Lesne, Gérard Lesne, Josep Benet, Josep Cabré, Il Seminario Musicale, Tragicomedia.

The music on this disc encompasses all periods of Monteverdi's career; the earliest comes from his first published collection, the *Sacrae Canticulicae* (1582) composed when he was only fifteen. Other pieces, such as the *Salve Regina*, come from the *Selva Morale* (1640), while *Pulchra es* and *Nigra sum* are performed on instruments alone. The solo motet *O quam pulchra es* is preceded by a *Toccata* by Alessandro Piccinini about which the excellent notes are silent. The performances here are expert and totally committed. Excellent recording.

Missa de cappella a 4; Missa de cappella a 6 (In illo tempore); Motets: *Cantate domino a 6; Domine ne in furore a 6.*
*** Hyperion Dig. CDA 66214 [id]. The Sixteen, Christophers; M. Phillips.

Harry Christophers draws superb singing from his brilliant choir, highly polished in ensemble but dramatic and deeply expressive too, suitably adapted for the different character of each Mass-setting, when the four-part Mass involves stricter, more consistent contrapuntal writing and the six-part, in what was then an advanced way, uses homophonic writing to underline key passages. Vivid, atmospheric recording.

Vespro della Beata Vergine (Vespers).
✱ *** DG Dig. 429 565-2 (2) [id.]. Monoyios, Pennicchi, Chance, Tucker, Robson, Naglia, Terfel, Miles, H. M. Sackbutts & Cornetts, Monteverdi Ch., London Oratory Ch., E. Bar. Soloists, Gardiner.
*** Hyperion Dig. CDA 66311/2 [id.]. The Sixteen, Harry Christophers.
*** EMI Dig. CDS7 47078-8 [Ang. CDCB 47077] (2). Kirkby, Nigel Rogers, David Thomas, Taverner Ch., Cons. & Players, Canto Gregoriano, Parrott.
(M) **(*) Teldec/Warner Dig. 4509 92629-2 (2) [id.]. Marshall, Palmer, Langridge, Equiluz, Hampson, Korn, Tölz Boys' Ch., V. Hofburg Ch. Choral Scholars, Schoenberg Ch., VCM, Harnoncourt.
(M) **(*) Teldec/Warner 4509 92175-2 (2) [id.]. Hansmann, Jacobeit, Rogers, Van t'Hoff, Van Egmond, Villisech, V. Boys' Ch. soloists, Hamburg Monteverdi Ch., Plainsong Schola of Munich Capella Antiqua, VCM, Jürgen Jürgens.
(N) (B) *(*) EMI forte CZS5 68631-2 (2). Ameling, Burrowes, Brett, Tear, Rolfe Johnson, Hill, Knapp, Noble, King's College Ch., Early Music Cons. of L., Ledger – SCHUTZ: *Psalm 150;* G. GABRIELI: *Motets.* **(*)

Gardiner's second recording of the *Vespers* vividly captures the spatial effects that a performance in the Basilica of St Mark's, Venice, made possible. Gardiner made his earlier recording for Decca in 1974 using modern instruments (see below). Here, with the English Baroque Soloists and a team of soloists less starry but more aptly scaled, all of them firm and clear, he directs a performance even more compellingly dramatic. It would be hard to better such young soloists as the counter-tenor Michael Chance, the tenor Mark Tucker and the bass Bryn Terfel. Without inflating the instrumental accompaniment – using six string-players only, plus elaborate continuo and six brass from His Majesties Sackbutts and Cornetts – he combines clarity and urgency with grandeur. Gardiner's version more than any other conveys the physical thrill which above all has established this long-neglected work as music for today, bringing it into the central repertory alongside the choral masterpieces of later centuries. Gardiner (as before) does not include plainchant antiphons, and so has room on the two discs for the superb alternative setting of the *Magnificat*, in six voices instead of seven, in another dedicated performance.

The Sixteen's version of Monteverdi's 1610 *Vespers* on Hyperion, beautifully scaled, presents a liturgical performance of what the scholar, Graham Dixon, suggests as Monteverdi's original conception. As it is, with a liturgical approach, the performance includes not only relevant Gregorian chant but antiphon substitutes, including a magnificent motet of Palestrina, obviously relevant, *Gaude Barbara*. The scale of the performance is very satisfying, with The Sixteen augmented to 22 singers (7.4.6.5) and with members of the group taking the eight solo roles.

Though Andrew Parrott uses minimal forces, with generally one instrument and one voice per part, so putting the work on a chamber scale in a small church setting, its grandeur comes out superbly through its very intensity. Brilliant singing here by the virtuoso soloists, above all by Nigel Rogers, whose distinctive timbre may not suit every ear but who has an airy precision and flexibility to give expressive meaning to even the most taxing passages. Fine contributions too from Parrott's chosen groups of players and singers, and warm, atmospheric recording.

Harnoncourt's admirers may well be attracted to his 1986 recording, particularly now that it is reissued at mid-price. It was recorded live and gives a keen sense of occasion, with the grandeur of the piece linked to a consciously authentic approach. There is a ruggedness in the interpretation, entirely apt, which is lightened by the characterful refinement of the solo singing from an exceptionally strong team of soloists, not to mention the fine singing from all three choirs. Ample, atmospheric recording.

Recorded in Vienna in 1966/67 the Jürgens set is scholarly yet not without warmth. The liturgical sequence is respectful, and authentic instruments are used. The continuo tends to be somewhat lightweight, but there is a sure sense of style. The opening chorus is vivid with the colour of renaissance trumpets and recorders, but the CD transfer cannot disguise a lack of sharpness of focus here and in the more complex analogue choral textures. At mid-price this is fair value, for the soloists are all fine artists and the choral singing is committed and polished. Documentation is excellent.

On paper it may seem that the King's performance under Ledger presents an excellent midway course between Gardiner's larger-scale dramatic performance using original instruments and Schneidt's reflective, intimate one, but in practice there are disappointments. In the first instance the CD transfer brings distortion with the full panoply of brass in the opening chorus and, although the sound improves later, Ledger's tempi are often disturbingly fast yet lacking in the rhythmic exuberance which makes the rival versions so compelling. The solo singing is good, but there is a perfunctory element which prevents this glorious music from flowering as it should.

Vespro della Beata Vergine (with *Magnificat II*); *Missa in illo tempore*.
(N) (B) *** DG 447 719-2 (2) [id.]. Paul Esswood, Kevin Smith, Ian Partridge, John Elwes, David Thomas, Christopher Keyte, Instrumental soloists, Regensburg Cathedral Ch., Schneidt.

When Schneidt's DG Archiv set was issued on LP in 1975, we gave it a Rosette as the most dedicated and beautiful performance of Monteverdi's choral masterpiece yet put on record, finer than Gardiner's first Decca set, which was also a landmark in its day. In its excellent transfer to CD it comes up as freshly as ever. With male voices alone – soloists as well as choir – and a small, authentic band of instrumentalists (the cornetti squeaking delightfully), its intimacy is set against a gloriously free church acoustic which yet allows clarity. The Regensburg Choir uses young voices, and the tenor and bass singing is not always as incisive as it might be, but the rest is superbly sensitive, not just the bright-sounding trebles but also the superb team of soloists, all of them from Britain. In live performance it may not be possible for two male altos to take the solo parts in *Pulchra es*, but here Paul Esswood and Kevin Smith sing radiantly, while Ian Partridge in *Nigra sum* excels even his standards of expressiveness and beautiful tone-colour. Not the least attraction of this inexpensive reissued set is that, besides including (like Gardiner in his latest version) the alternative and scarcely less elaborate setting of the *Magnificat*, Schneidt adds the superb *Missa in illo tempore*.

(i) *Vespro della Beata Vergine (Vespers);* (ii) Motet: *Exultent coeli.*

(Y/B) (B) *** Decca Double 443 482-2 (2) [id.]. (i) Gomez, Palmer, Bowman, Tear, Langridge, Shirley-Quirk, Rippon, Monteverdi Ch. & O, Salisbury Cathedral Boys' Ch., Philip Jones Brass Ens., Munrow Recorder Consort; (ii) Monteverdi Ch., Philip Jones Brass & Wind Ens.; Gardiner (with (ii) Christmas motets: G. GABRIELI: *Angelus ad pastores; Audite principes; O magnum mysterium; Quem vidistis pastores?; Salvator noster.* BASSANO: *Hodie Christus natus est* ***).

Gardiner's earlier Decca recording was made before he had been won over entirely to the claims of the authentic school. Modern instruments are used and women's voices, but Gardiner's rhythms are so resilient that the result is exhilarating as well as grand. Singing and playing are exemplary, and the recording is one of Decca's most vividly atmospheric, with relatively large forces presented and placed against a helpful, reverberant acoustic. Now issued as a Double Decca (two CDs for the price of one), this set is well worth considering, with the addition to the *Vespers* of a collection of Christmas motets, mostly by Giovanni Gabrieli, first issued in 1972. The rich, sonorous dignity of Gabrieli's *Sonata pian'e forte* sounds resplendent, and in the choral numbers the vocal and instrumental blend is expert. The most impressive work here is Gabrieli's glorious *Quem vidistis pastores?*. Monteverdi's *Exultent caeli* is shorter, but one is again amazed by the range of expressive contrast. Then there is Gabrieli's fine *Salvator noster*, a motet for three five-part choirs, jubilantly rejoicing at the birth of Christ. The CD transfer is admirable.

OPERA AND OPERA-BALLET

Il ballo dell'Ingrate; Il combattimento di Tancredi e Clorinda; Tirsi e Clori (opera-ballets).

(Y/B) ✪*** O-L Dig. 440 637-2 [id.]. Bott, King, Ainsley, Bonner, George, New London Consort, Pickett.

The star of this outstanding Monteverdi disc is Catherine Bott, as she is of so many discs from Pickett and the New London Consort. It is both apt and attractive that for once one has all three of these inspired opera-ballets, a generous triptych. Pickett characterically presents them with a sharp clarity and concern for dramatic bite, to match and outshine any of the various rivals in each work. The voices are especially well chosen for contrast as well as for clarity. So the narration in *Tancredi*, the most substantial contribution, is taken by John Mark Ainsley with his clean-cut tenor that is yet darker and weightier than that of Andrew King, who sings Tancredi. Yet it is Catherine Bott who more than anyone brings the narrative to life, with delectably pointed and finely shaded singing, using a wider tonal range than is common in Monteverdi. Similarly in the *Ballo dell'Ingrate* she, an exceptionally animated Venus, is well contrasted with Tessa Bonner as Amore and Michael George as a sepulchral Plutone. The third work is much shorter but presents the simple dialogue of the lovers in similarly dramatic terms, with Bott partnered by Andrew King as Tirsi, joined at the end by the chorus of other soloists. First-rate, well-balanced sound.

Alfred Deller Edition: (i) *Il ballo delle ingrate;* (ii) *Lamento d'Arianna.*

(Y/B) (M) **(*) Van. 08.5063.71 [id.]. (i) Alfred Deller, McLoughlin, Ward, Cantelo, Amb. S., L. Chamber Players, Denis Stevens; (ii) Shepppard, Le Sage, Worthley, Todd, Deller, Bevan, Deller Consort, Deller.

Denis Stevens's pioneering stereo version of Monteverdi's *Il ballo delle ingrate* dates from 1956 and has an impressive cast, well backed up by the Ambrosian Singers and London Chamber Players. Although the orchestral sound seems rather ample to ears used to original instruments, this account rings true and there is much that is authentic, not least the decoration of the vocal line, especially by Deller himself who is most moving as Venus. Eileen McLoughlin makes a delightful Amor, and David Ward is suitably stentorian as Pluto. Readers will remember that Monteverdi wrote his early opera-ballet for performance at the wedding celebrations of Duke Francesco Gonzaga of Mantua. The Duke was to marry the young Infanta Margherita of Savoy, and the message of the opera is that she should be passionately generous in the arms of her husband-to-be. In *Il ballo* the ungrateful ladies have been confined to Hades for refusing their lovers' advances and at the end of the opera they sing a touching chorus of penitence for their unfortunate lack of ardour, followed by a plea from their leader (the sweet-voiced April Cantelo) that the noble ladies of the court should learn from their experience! It is all emotively communicated here and the recording is vivid, if rather close. In addition Deller directs a performance of the famous *Lamento d'Arianna*, sung by a vocal sextet comprising Honor Sheppard, Sally le Sage, Max Worthley, Philip Todd, Maurice Bevan and Deller himself. Here the individual voices, while having plenty of character, do not always match ideally in consort. Nevertheless a thoroughly worthwhile reissue in the Alfred Deller Edition.

Il ballo delle ingrate; Sestina: Lagrime d'amante al sepolcro dell'amata.
**(*) HM Dig. HMC 901108 [id.]. Les Arts Florissants, Christie.

William Christie directs refreshingly dramatic accounts of both *Il ballo delle ingrate* and the *Sestina*. His singers have been chosen for character and bite rather than for beauty of tone, and the final lament of *Il ballo* is spoilt by exaggerated plaintiveness, but (particularly in the *Sestina*) the boldness of Christie's interpretation makes for very compelling performances, beautifully recorded. The note on the CD version irritatingly omits details of the soloists.

(i) *Il combattimento di Tancredi e Clorinda. Lamento della Ninfa; Mentre vaga Angioletta; Ogni amante e guerrier.*
(M) *** Teldec/Warner Dig. 4509 92181-2 [id.]. (i) Equiluz, Schmidt, Hollweg, Murray, Langridge, Hartman, Perry, Palmer, Mühle, Franzden; VCM, Harnoncourt.'

Harnoncourt directs sharply characterized readings of substantial items from Monteverdi's eighth Book of Madrigals plus two *Canti amorosi*. The substantial scena telling of the conflict of Tancredi and Clorinda is made sharply dramatic in a bald way. *Ogni amante e guerrier*, almost as extended, is treated with similar abrasiveness, made attractively fresh but lacking subtlety. The two *Canti amorosi* are treated quite differently, in a much warmer style, with the four sopranos of *Mentre vaga Angioletta* producing sensuous sounds. *Lamento della Ninfa*, perhaps the most celebrated of all Monteverdi's madrigals, brings a luscious performance with the solo voice (Ann Murray) set evocatively at a slight distance behind the two tenors and a bass. On CD the recording is extremely vivid, with voices and instruments firmly and realistically placed. The documentation is first class in every way, with full translations and the composer's own fascinatingly detailed instructions as to how *Il Combattimento* should be staged.

L'Incoronazione di Poppea.
(N) *** DG Dig. 447 088-2 (3) [id.]. McNair, Von Otter, Hanchard, Chance, D'Artegna, E. Bar. Soloists, Gardiner.
(Y/B) *** Virgin/EMI Dig. VCT5 45082-2 (3) [id.]. Arleen Augér, Della Jones, Linda Hirst, James Bowman, Gregory Reinhart, City of L. Bar. Sinfonia, Hickox.
(M) **(*) Teldec/Warner 2292 42547-2 (4) [id.]. Donath, Söderström, Berberian, Esswood, VCM, Harnoncourt.
(N) (M) **(*) Teldec/Warner 0630 10027-2 (2) [id.]. Yakar, Esswood, T. Schmidt, Tappy, Salminen, Perry, Zurich Opera House Monteverdi Ens., Harnoncourt.

With an exceptionally strong and consistent cast in which even minor roles are taken by star singers like Catherine Bott and Nigel Robson, Gardiner presents a purposeful, strongly characterized performance. He is helped by the full and immediate sound of the live recording, made in concert at the Queen Elizabeth Hall, London. Sylvia McNair is a seductive Poppea and Anne Sofie von Otter a deeply moving Ottavia, both singing ravishingly. Francesco d'Artegna, a robustly Italian-sounding bass, makes a stylish Seneca, and there are clear advantages in having a counter-tenor as Nero instead of a mezzo-soprano, particularly one with a slightly sinister timbre like Dana Hanchard. So in the sensuous duet which closes the opera, the clashing intervals of the voices are given a degree of abrasiveness, suggesting that, though this is a happy and beautiful ending, the characters still have their sinister side. The text has been modified with newly written ritornellos by Peter Holman, using the original, authentic bass line, and aiming to be 'closer to what Monteverdi would have expected' than the usual flawed text.

The tender expressiveness of Arleen Augér in the title-role of Monteverdi's elusive masterpiece goes with a very spare accompaniment of continuo instruments, contrasting not just with the opulent score presented at Glyndebourne by Raymond Leppard, but with the previous period performance on record, that of Nikolaus Harnoncourt and the Concentus Musicus of Vienna, who has a far wider, more abrasive range of instrumental sound. Hickox overcomes the problems of that self-imposed limitation by choosing the widest possible range of speeds. The purity of Augér's soprano may make Poppea less of a scheming seducer than she should be, but it is Monteverdi's music for the heroine which makes her so sympathetic. Taking the castrato role of Nero, Della Jones sings very convincingly with full, rather boyish tone, while Gregory Reinhart is magnificent in the bass role of Seneca. James Bowman is a fine Ottone, with smaller parts taken by such excellent young singers as Catherine Denley, John Graham-Hall, Mark Tucker and Janice Watson.

Nikolaus Harnoncourt's well-paced and dramatic version makes a welcome reappearance at mid-price in Teldec's Harnoncourt series. First issued in 1974, it offers a starry cast, with Elisabeth Söderström as Nero (imaginative but not always ideally steady), Helen Donath pure-toned as Poppea and Cathy Berberian as the most characterful and moving Ottavia on disc. Others include Paul Esswood and Philip Langridge, and Harnoncourt's bold and brassy instrumentation adds to the bite. The snag is that, unnecessarily, the set stretches to four discs instead of three, which cancels out the price advantage over the excellent rival set from Richard Hickox.

Recorded in June 1978, only four years after his Vienna version with its very full text, Harnoncourt's Zurich recording is very different, done as it was in connection with a staged production and recorded here – not in the opera house – with stage noises and movement, presumably part of a video version. The text is cut by over an hour, which allows the whole opera to be fitted on two CDs instead of four, and the non-specialist will be little worried. The extra sensuousness of the approach is instantly established in the harp flourishes of the introduction, guaranteed to seduce the listener's ear, and the aim at a wide audience is confirmed in the choice of a tenor for the role of Nero instead of a soprano. Eric Tappy is a most stylish singer but his voice, as recorded, is rather edgy, which means that the rejoicing duet with Lucano after Seneca's death is bluff and hearty rather than pointed, and the final duet with Poppea loses some of its heavenly beauty. Rachel Yakar sings most beautifully as Poppea, while the role of Seneca is taken by the resonant, black-voiced Matti Salminen. The recording is vivid but suffers from high tape-hiss.

Orfeo (opera): complete.
*** O-L Dig. 433 545-2 (2) [id.]. Ainsley, Gooding, Bott, Bonner, George, Grant, New L. Cons., Pickett.
*** DG Dig. 419 250-2 (2) [id.]. Rolfe Johnson, Baird, Lynne Dawson, Von Otter, Argenta, Robson, Monteverdi Ch., E. Bar. Soloists, Gardiner.
(M) *** EMI Dig. CMS7 64947-2 (2). Rogers, Kwella, Kirkby, J. Smith, Chiaroscuro, L. Bar. Ens., L. Cornett & Sackbutt Ens., Charles Medlam.
(N) (M) **(*) DG 447 703-2 [id.]. Rogers, Petrescu, Reynolds, Partridge, Bowman, Hamburg Monteverdi Ch., Hamburg Instrumental Ens., Jürgens.
(M) ** Teldec/Warner 2292 42494-2 (2). Kozma, Hansmann, Berberian, Katanosaka, Villisech, Van Egmond, Munich Cappela Antiqua, VCM, Harnoncourt.
(N) ** Lyrichord Dig. LEMS 9002 (2) [id.]. Jeffrey Thomas, Dana Hanchard, Jessica Tranzillo, Jennifer Lane, Timothy Leigh Evans, Michael Brown, Paul Shipper, Artek, Gwendolyn Toth.
(N) ** Erato/Warner Dig. 4509 96958-2 (2) [id.]. Quilico, Michael, C. Watkinson, Voutsinos, Tappy, Le Roux, De Mey, Ledroit, Alliot-Lugaz, Borst, Whittingham, La Chapelle Royale Vocal Ens., Lyon Opéra O, Michel Corboz.

Pickett has not tried to treat *Orfeo* with kid gloves but has aimed above all to bring out its freshness. Compared with John Eliot Gardiner, whose DG Archiv recording combines precision and alertness in presenting the drama, Pickett is rougher, not caring quite so much about pinpoint ensemble, preferring less extreme speeds and characteristically relying more on dramatic contrasts in instrumentation. So, in the dark *Sinfonia* with its weird chromatic writing which at the opening of Act III represents Orfeo's arrival in the underworld, Pickett cuts out strings and uses brass instruments alone. He has the cornetts, sackbutts and a rasping regal organ playing at a lower pitch than usual, deducing that transposition from Monteverdi's use of high clefs. The result is all the more darkly menacing. As Orfeo, John Mark Ainsley may have a less velvety tenor than Anthony Rolfe Johnson on the Gardiner set, but his voice is more crisply flexible in the elaborate decorations of *Possente spirto*, Orfeo's plea to Charon. Outstanding among the others, establishing the characterful style of the solo singing from the start, is Catherine Bott. In *Orfeo* she not only sings the elaborate role given to La Musica in the Prologue, sensuously beautiful and seductive in her coloration, but also the part of Proserpina and the key role of the Messenger, who graphically describes the death of Euridice. Excellent among the others are Julia Gooding as Euridice, the counter-tenor Christopher Robson as Hope and Tessa Bonner as the Nymph.

John Eliot Gardiner very effectively balances the often-conflicting demands of authentic performance – when this pioneering opera was originally presented intimately – and the obvious grandeur of the concept. So the 21-strong Monteverdi Choir conveys, on the one hand, high tragedy to the full, yet sings the lighter commentary from nymphs and shepherds with astonishing crispness, often at top speed. However, Gardiner is strong on pacing. He gives full and moving expansion to such key passages as the messenger's report of Euridice's death, sung with agonizing intensity by Anne Sophie von Otter. Lynne Dawson is also outstanding as the allegorical figure of Music in the *Prologue*, while Anthony Rolfe Johnson shows his formidable versatility in the title-role. This is a set to take you through the story with new involvement. Though editing is not always immaculate, the recording on CD is vivid and full of presence.

Nigel Rogers – who recorded the role of Orfeo ten years earlier for DG Archiv – in the EMI version has the double function of singing the main part and acting as co-director. Rogers has modified his extraordinarily elaborate ornamentation in the hero's brilliant pleading aria before Charon and makes the result all the freer and more wide-ranging in expression, with his distinctive fluttering timbre adding character. With the central singer directing the others, the concentration of the whole performance is all the greater, telling the story simply and graphically; and Euridice's plaint, beautifully sung by Patrizia

Kwella, is the more affecting for being accompanied very simply on the lute. The other soloists make a good team, though Jennifer Smith as Proserpina, recorded close, is made to sound breathy. The brightness of the cornetti is a special delight, when otherwise the instrumentation used – largely left optional in the score – is modest. Excellent, immediate recording, making for a fine mid-priced alternative to Gardiner.

The earlier Archiv version with Nigel Rogers as Orfeo still has its place in the catalogue, especially within a lively, atmospheric performance like Jürgens'. Even in this first performance of the massive aria in which Orfeo pleads with Charon, Rogers treats the florid writing not as a technical obstacle race but as a test of expressiveness, giving the character extra depth. His fine virtuoso performance is matched by the singing of such artists as James Bowman and Ian Partridge. Alexander Malta as Charon and Stafford Dean as Pluto are wonderfully dark and firm in bass tone, while Emilia Petrescu as Euridice and Anna Reynolds as Sylvia equally combine stylishness and expressive strength. The chorus and orchestra are outstanding. The 1973 recording has an ample acoustic, simulating a performance in a nobleman's hall; but it is well focused in the CD transfer and the amplitude is agreeably rich. The sound of the plucked instruments is especially beguiling.

In Harnoncourt's version, the ritornello of the Prologue might almost be by Stravinsky, so sharply do the sounds cut. He is an altogether more severe Monteverdian than John Eliot Gardiner. In compensation, the simple and straightforward dedication of this performance is most affecting, and the solo singing, if not generally very characterful, is clean and stylish. One exception to the general rule on characterfulness comes in the singing of Cathy Berberian as the Messenger. She is strikingly successful and, though slightly differing in style from the others, she sings as part of the team. Excellent recording. The extra clarity and sharpness of focus – even in large-scale ensembles – add to the abrasiveness from the opening *Toccata* onwards, and the 1968 recording certainly sounds immediate, with voices very realistic. A highlights disc might be the best choice, and this is available (75 minutes) on Teldec 0630 13807-9.

The Lyrichord issue offers the first American performance of this opera, a fresh account, well sung and played, which is seriously marred by absurdly reverberant recording. The opening Toccata sounds as though it was recorded in a swimming-bath. The singers are then placed close within the same acoustic, which encourages speeds marginally broader than in other period performances. The chorus is made up of solo voices only, which makes the large-scale acoustic all the more inexplicable.

Corboz's digital version was recorded – 17 years after his pioneering version of 1968 – in connection with a successful staging of the piece at the Aix-en-Provence Festival, with an approach – using modern instruments – more conventionally operatic than in period performances. The oddity is to have a baritone rather than a tenor as Orfeo, but Gino Quilico is a most stylish singer, and among the others Colette Alliot-Lugaz as La Musica and Carolyn Watkinson as the Messenger are both outstanding. Clear, well-balanced sound.

Il ritorno d'Ulisse in patria (complete).
*** HM Dig. HMC 90 1427/9 [id.]. Prégardien, Fink, Högeman, Hunt, Visse, Tucker, D. Thomas, Concerto Vocale, René Jacobs.
(M) **(*) Teldec/Warner 2292 42496-2 (3) [id.]. Eliasson, Lerer, Hansen, Baker-Genovesi, Hansmann, Equiluz, Esswood, Wyatt, Walters, Van Egmond, Mühle, Junge Kantorei, VCM, Harnoncourt.

Il ritorno d'Ulisse in patria is here treated to a most enjoyable version by René Jacobs with the same cast as in the Montpellier Festival. It offers a scholarly performance that is not afraid of being warmly expressive. Jacobs as a singer himself is most understanding of the need to give his soloists free rein, and they make a first-rate team, with the clear-toned German tenor Christoph Prégardien splendid as Ulisse, firm and heroic but light enough to cope with the elaborate ornamentation. Bernarda Fink with her rich, firm mezzo gives full weight to Penelope's agony, and it is encouraging to find such excellent British singers as the tenors Martyn Hill and Mark Tucker and the baritone David Thomas taking character roles. The French counter-tenor Dominique Visse is also excellent, both as Human Frailty in the Prologue and as one of Penelope's suitors, with Guy de Mey in the comic role of the glutton, Iro. Jacobs explains that with the surviving manuscripts raising dozens of textual questions, he decided to return to the original five-Act division of the text which, as he suggests, is better-balanced. He also inserts music by Rossi and Caccini for the choruses included in the text but missing from the score, all adding to the impact of the whole piece.

Harnoncourt's 1971 recording of *Il ritorno d'Ulisse* brings a sympathetic performance, generally not quite as brisk as Jacobs in his recording from the Montpellier Festival, and rather more square in rhythm, but bringing a keener sense of repose, important in Monteverdi. The solo singing is not as characterful as that on the Jacobs set, nor as Harnoncourt's *Poppea*, though Norma Lerer makes a touching Penelope, with Sven Olaf Eliasson a stylish Ulisse, not ideally pure of timbre.

Ballet e balletti: *Tirsi e Clori* (complete). *Il ballo delle ingrate: ballet. Orfeo:* excerpts: *Lasciate i monti; Vieni imeneo; Ecco pur ch'a voi ritorno; Moresca. Madrigali guerrieri e amorosi: Volgendo il ciel* (ballet); *Scherzi musicali: De la Belleza* (ballet).

(N) (M) **(*) Gardiner Collection: Erato/Warner Dig. 4509 99716-2 [id.]. Kwella, Rolfe Johnson, Dale Woodrow, Monteverdi Ch., E. Bar. Soloists, Gardiner.

This is in effect a Monteverdi sampler; while the mosaic from *Orfeo*, for instance, may not suit the specialist listener, it makes delightful listening when the singing is so fresh. The music from the famous *Il ballo delle ingrate* is very short (about 3½ minutes) and seems pointless out of context; but all the rest, notably the choral ballet, *Tirsi e Clori*, is most engaging with its changes of mood: sometimes dolorous, sometimes gay and spirited. Gardiner's direction, as always, is vivid and his pacing lively; there is much to titillate the ear in the spicy vocal and orchestral colouring. The balance is fairly close but the overall perspective is well defined, within a warm acoustic. However, at 46½ minutes the content is not generous.

Moody, James (born 1907)

(i) *Quintet for harmonica and string quartet;* (ii) *Suite dans le style français.*
*** Chandos Dig. CHAN 8802 [id.]. Tommy Reilly; (i) Hindar Qt; (ii) Skaila Kanga – JACOB: *Divertimento.* ***

James Moody's *Suite in the French style* may be pastiche but its impressionism is highly beguiling. The *Quintet* is more ambitious, less charming perhaps, but likely to prove even more rewarding on investigation, especially the very diverse theme and variations of the finale, the longest movement. The performance and recording are hardly likely to be bettered.

Mosonyi, Mihály (1815–70)

(i) *Piano concerto in E min.;* (ii) *Symphony No. 1 in D.*
(Y/B) ** Marco Polo Dig. 8.223539 [id.]. (i) Körmendi, Slovak State Philh. O (Košice); (ii) Slovak RSO (Bratislava); Stankovsky.

Mihály Mosonyi is hardly a household name in this country and his representation on disc is meagre. Originally Michael Brand and born in Bradford, he adopted Hungarian nationality and changed his name in 1859, some years after settling in Pest. Despite his origins, Mosonyi is thought of as one of the most representative nineteenth-century Hungarian composers – apart, of course, from the more obvious major figures, Liszt and Erkel. The *Symphony No. 1 in D* is an early work, composed in his late twenties and modelled on the Viennese classics in general and Beethoven in particular. The *Piano concerto in E minor*, which comes from about the same time, shows the influence of Chopin and Weber. If, like the symphony, it is not strong on individuality, it is at least well-crafted, well-bred music and well worth an occasional airing. Klára Körmendi is the fluent soloist and receives decent orchestral support from Robert Stankovsky and his Slovak forces.

Moszkowski, Moritz (1854–1925)

Air de ballet, Op. 36/5; Albumblatt, Op. 2; Au Crépuscule, Op. 68/3; Barcarolle from *Offenbach's Tales of Hoffmann; Chanson bohème* from *Bizet's Carmen; Danse Russe; En Automne, Op. 36/4; Expansion, Op. 36/3; La Jongleuse, Op. 52/4; Minuetto, Op. 68/2; Nocturne, Op. 68/1; Poème de Mai; Près de berceau; Rêverie, Op. 36/2; Serenata, Op. 15/1; Tarantella, Op. 27/2; Valse Mignonne.*
**(*) Collins Dig. 1412-2. Seta Tanyel.

The composer/pianist Moszkowski once came to London to conduct his *Spanish dances* at a Henry Wood Promenade Concert. Famous in their day, they are all but forgotten now, and his piano music seems faded too. Pieces like *Au Crépuscule* have a certain sub-Lisztian charm, and *La Jongleuse* is an engaging *moto perpetuo*, while *Près de berceau* is the epitome of a salon piece. Seta Tanyel characterizes the music well enough, but she is hard put to sustain interest through a 69-minute recital of genre pieces that are heard most effectively as encores at the end of a more substantial programme. The *Air de ballet* is an ideal example with its brilliant filigree at the close which sparkles readily in her hands. Good recording.

Mourant, Walter (born 1910)

The Pied Piper.
*** ASV Dig. CDDCA 568 [id.]. MacDonald, N. Sinfonia, Bedford – COPLAND; FINZI: *Concertos.*
***

Walter Mourant's *Pied Piper* is a catchy, unpretentious little piece for clarinet, strings and celeste, which in a gently syncopated style effectively contrasts 3/4 and 6/8 rhythms. It makes an attractive filler after the Copland *Concerto.*

Mozart, Leopold (1719–87)

Cassation in G: Toy symphony (attrib. Haydn). (i) *Trumpet concerto in D.*
*** Erato/Warner Dig. 2292 45199-2. (i) Touvron; Paillard CO, Paillard – W. A. MOZART: *Musical Joke.*
***

One could hardly imagine this *Cassation* being done with more commitment from the effects department directed by Paillard, while the music itself is elegantly played. After this, the more restrained approach to the excellent two-movement *Trumpet concerto* seems exactly right. The recording has plenty of presence and realism.

Mozart, Wolfgang Amadeus (1756–91)

Adagio and fugue in C minor: see also below, in VOCAL MUSIC, under Complete Mozart Edition, Volume 22.
Complete Mozart Edition, Volume 3: *Cassations Nos. 1 in G, K.63; 2 in B flat, K.99; Divertimento No. 2 in D, K.131; Galimathias musicum, K.32; Serenades Nos. 1 in D, K.100 (with March in D, K.62); 3 in D, K.185 (with March in D, K.189); 4 in D (Colloredo), K.203 (with March in D, K.237); 5 in D, K.204 (with March in D, K.215); 6 in D (Serenata notturna), K.239; 7 in D (Haffner), K.250 (with March in D, K.249); 8 in D (Notturno for 4 orchestras), K.286; 9 in D (Posthorn), K.320 (with Marches in D, K.335/ 1–2); 13 in G (Eine kleine Nachtmusik), K.525.*
(M) *** Ph. Dig. 422 503-2 (7) [id.]. ASMF, Sir Neville Marriner.

Marriner and his Academy are at their very finest here and make a very persuasive case for giving these works on modern instruments. The playing has much finesse, yet its cultivated polish never brings a hint of blandness or lethargy; it is smiling, yet full of energy and sparkle. In the concertante violin roles Iona Brown is surely an ideal soloist, her playing full of grace. Throughout this set the digital recording brings an almost ideal combination of bloom and vividness.

Cassations Nos. 1 in G, K.63; 2 in B flat, K.99; Adagio and fugue in C min., K.546.
*** Capriccio Dig. 10 192 [id.]. Salzburg Camerata, Végh.

These excellent performances of the early *Cassations*, so full of attractive invention, can be strongly recommended. The playing combines vitality with finesse and, to make a proper contrast, the Camerata find plenty of drama in the *Adagio and fugue*. Very good recording.

CONCERTOS

Complete Mozart Edition, Volume 9: (i) *Bassoon concerto;* (ii) *Clarinet concerto;* (iii) *Flute concertos Nos. 1–2; Andante in C for flute & orchestra;* (iii; iv) *Flute and harp concerto;* (v) *Horn concertos Nos. 1–4; Concert rondo in E flat for horn and orchestra;* (vi) *Oboe concerto. Sinfonia concertante in E flat, K.297b; Sinfonia concertante in E flat, K.297b* (reconstructed R. Levin).
(M) **(*) Ph. Dig. 422 509-2 (5) [id.]. (i) Thunemann; (ii) Leister; (iii) Grafenauer; (iv) Graf; (v) Damm; (vi) Holliger; ASMF, Marriner (except (vi) Holliger).

The principal wind concertos here are recent digital versions. They are all well played and recorded. However, there is a slightly impersonal air about the accounts of the *Bassoon* and *Clarinet concertos,* well played though they are; and there are more individual sets of the works for horn. The *Sinfonia concertante* is offered both in the version we usually hear (recorded in 1972, with the performance attractively songful and elegant) and in a more modern recording of a conjectural reconstruction by Robert Levin, based on the material in the four wind parts.

Bassoon concerto in B flat.
*** Denon Dig. CO 79281 [id.]. Werba, V. String Soloists, Honeck – HUMMEL; WEBER: *Concertos.* ***
*** Caprice Dig. CAP 21411. Knut Sönstevold, Swedish RSO, Comissiona – PETTERSSON: *Symphony No. 7.* ***

Though not quite as individual as some versions, Michael Werba's account does not lack character or geniality and he is well accompanied and recorded. He features the cadenzas by Eusebius Mandyczewski to good effect. If the couplings are suitable, this is recommendable.

Knut Sönstevold's performance of Mozart's concerto is good enough to compete in an already crowded market, but Mozartians are likely to turn elsewhere in search of a more logical coupling. A good, big-band performance, which does give pleasure, and very well recorded.

(i) *Bassoon concerto in B flat, K.191;* (ii) *Clarinet concerto in A, K.622;* (iii) *Flute concerto No.1 in G, K.313; Andante in C, K.315;* (iii; iv) *Flute and harp concerto in C, K.299;* (v) *Horn concertos Nos. 1–4;* (vi) *Oboe concerto in C, K.314; Sinfonia concertante in E flat, K.197b.*
(M) *** DG Dig. 431 665-2 (3). (i) Morelli; (ii) Neidlich; (iii) Palma; (iv) Allen; (v) Jolley or Purvis; (vi) Wolfgang; Orpheus CO.

Randall Wolfgang's plaintive, slightly reedy timbre is especially telling in the *Adagio* of the *Oboe concerto* and he plays the finale with the lightest possible touch, as does Susan Palma the charming Minuet which closes the *Flute concerto.* The *Sinfonia concertante* for wind is pleasingly fresh. All the works are given excellent modern recordings and this is a very persuasive collection, probably a 'best buy' for those wanting all the music in a digital format.

(i) *Bassoon concerto;* (ii) *Clarinet concerto;* (iii) *Oboe concerto, K.314.*
(N) *** Decca Dig. 443 176-2 (i) David McGill; (ii) Franklin Cohen; (iii) John Mack; Cleveland Orchestra, Dohnányi.
(BB) **(*) Naxos Dig. 8.550345 [id.]. (i) Turnovský; (ii) Ottensamer; (iii) Gabriel; V. Mozart Academy, Wildner.
(M) ** EMI CDM7 64355-2 [id.]. (i) Günter Piesk; (ii) Karl Leister; (iii) Lothar Koch; BPO, Karajan.

In this favourite trio of Mozart concertos for reed instruments, Christoph von Dohnányi and the Cleveland Orchestra successfully follow up their record of the *Flute and harp concerto* and *Sinfonia concertante for violin, viola and orchestra* (see below) with an impressive showcase disc using three more soloists from the orchestra. It is beautifully recorded and attractively balanced. Franklin Cohen steals the limelight with his mastery and polish in the *Clarinet concerto.* He is especially touching when, with a cadential flourish, he reintroduces the lovely melody of the *Adagio* very gently and adds elaborate decorations. Then later he teases the ear with extra ornamentation in the finale, but the result remains a little strait-laced rather than exuberant. The oboist, John Mack, has an appealingly sweet (but not too sweet) timbre; he plays most stylishly and his sprightly closing rondo is a delight. Yet he too uses unusually long and elaborate cadenzas which never sound quite like improvisations. Then the woody bassoonist, David McGill, in the third work instantly establishes keener individuality, matching the high polish of his colleagues but readily assuming the central role ahead of the conductor. He does not overdo the humour in the finale. Even if the overall impression here is very much of orchestral principals stepping forward under the conductor, this remains very enjoyable music-making by musicians who are clearly at one with Mozart.

In the *Oboe concerto* the soloist on Naxos, Martin Gabriel, is excellent. The clarinettist, Ernst Ottensamer, is also a sensitive player, his slow movement is full of feeling; and there is an accomplished performance of the *Bassoon concerto* from Stepan Turnovský, who has the measure of the work's character and wit. Recommendable, particularly at the price.

The three performances on this EMI reissue come from a series of recordings of Mozart's concertante wind works that Karajan made in 1971. Günter Piesk gives a predictably fine account of the *Bassoon concerto,* but the *Clarinet concerto* is a little bland and, while Koch is also an estimable soloist in the work for oboe, the richly homogeneous orchestral accompaniments without much analytical detail, although pleasingly warm and elegantly phrased, tend to rob the music of vitality. No complaints about the CD transfers.

(i) *Bassoon concerto in B flat, K.191;* (ii) *Clarinet concerto in A, K.622;* (iii) *Violin concerto No. 3 in G, K.216.*
(M) *** EMI stereo/mono CDM7 63408-2 [id.]. (i) Brooke; (ii) Brymer; (iii) De Vito; RPO, Beecham.

Beecham's romantically expansive reading of the Mozart *Clarinet concerto* with Jack Brymer the glowing soloist is a 1958 classic recording, totally individual in every phrase, with conductor and soloist inspiring each other. The account of the *Bassoon concerto* has equal magic, thanks to the comparable partnership between Beecham and Gwydion Brooke. But the surprise here is the equally inspired and highly personal 1949 mono account of the *G major Violin concerto*, with Gioconda de Vito as soloist. She too conveys magic comparable to Beecham's own, with the slow movement again luxuriantly expansive.

Clarinet concerto in A, K.622.
(M) *** Decca 433 727-2 [id.]. Gervase de Peyer, LSO, Maag – SPOHR; WEBER: *Concertos.* ***
*** Denon Dig. CO 75289 [id.]. Paul Meyer, ECO, Zinman – BUSONI: *Adagio* ***; COPLAND: *Concerto.* **(*)

Gervase de Peyer made his Decca recording in the Kingsway Hall in 1959, and the performance is as fine as any available. De Peyer's timbre is succulent, his control of colour subtle, and the playing is fluent and lively, with masterly phrasing in the slow movement and a vivacious finale. The couplings, too, are thoroughly worthwhile.

An enjoyably bracing performance from Paul Meyer and David Zinman, cool and elegant and given refined, truthful recording of Denon's best quality. This is not to say that the playing lacks warmth, but the heart is not worn on the sleeve and the lovely slow movement is refreshing and touching, without having sensuous overtones. The finale is delightfully spirited. Excellent recording, too.

Clarinet concerto; Flute concerto No. 1, K.313; Andante for flute & orchestra, K.315; Flute & harp concerto; Oboe concerto; Horn concertos Nos. 1–4; Rondo for horn & orchestra, K.371.
(B) *** Ph. 426 148-2 (3). Brymer, Claude Monteux, Ellis, Black, Civil, ASMF, Marriner.

Jack Brymer's Philips recording of the *Clarinet concerto* is the third he has made; in some ways it is his best, for he plays with deepened insight and feeling. The *Flute* and *Oboe concertos* are hardly less recommendable and the *Flute and harp concerto* is delightful, even if the instruments are made to seem jumbo-sized! Alan Civil's third recording of the *Horn concertos* was made in 1973, and the performances are highly enjoyable, with Sir Neville Marriner's polished and lively accompaniments giving pleasure in themselves.

(i) *Clarinet concerto in A, K.622;* (ii) *Flute concerto No. 1 in G, K.313;* (iii) *Oboe concerto in C, K.314.*
(N) (B) ** DG 439 508-2 [id.]. (i) Leister, BPO, Kubelik; (ii) Linde, Munich CO, Stadlmair; (iii) Turetschek, VPO, Boehm.

Karl Leister gives a thoughtfully sensitive and musical performance of the *Clarinet concerto*, but with his gentle, introvert style and lack of a forceful personality the effect is rather too self-effacing. However, Kubelik's attention to detail and gracious phrasing mean that the orchestral contribution gives great pleasure. Impeccably played and neatly phrased, Linde's performance of the *Flute concerto* has a hint of rhythmic stiffness in the outer movements. The highlight is the slow movement, where the playing is beautifully poised and the melody breathes in exactly the right way. In both works the mid-1960s recording is of good quality but shows its age a little in the string timbre. The recording of the *Oboe concerto* is from a decade later, though the sonic difference is minimal. Gerhard Turetschek proves an appealingly delicate and sweet-timbred soloist and this is very civilized music-making.

(i) *Clarinet concerto;* (ii) *Flute and harp concerto in C, K.299.*
*** ASV Dig. CDDCA 532 [id.]. (i) Emma Johnson; (ii) Bennett, Ellis; ECO, Leppard.
(Y/B) (B) *** Carlton IMP Dig. PCD 2011 [id.]. (i) Campbell; (ii) Davies, Masters; City of L. Sinfonia, Hickox.

Emma Johnson's account of the *Clarinet concerto* has a sense of spontaneity, of natural magnetism which traps the ear from first to last. There may be some rawness of tone in places, but that only adds to the range of expression, which breathes the air of a live performance. Leppard and the ECO are in bouncing form, as they are too for the *Flute and harp concerto*, though here the two excellent soloists are somewhat on their best behaviour, until the last part of the finale sends Mozart bubbling up to heaven. First-rate recording.

David Campbell's agile and pointed performance of the clarinet work brings fastish speeds and a fresh, unmannered style in all three movements. His tonal shading is very beautiful. The earlier flute and harp work is just as freshly and sympathetically done, with a direct, unmannered style sounding entirely spontaneous.

(i) *Clarinet concerto in A;* (ii) *Oboe concerto in C, K.314;* (i; ii; iii) *Sinfonia concertante, K.297b.*
*** ASV Dig. CDCDO 814 [id.]. (i) Richard Hosford; (ii) Douglas Boyd; (iii) O'Neill, Williams; COE, Schneider.

It would be hard to imagine a performance of the *Oboe concerto* that conveys more fun in the outer movements, infectiously pointed and phrased, both by the ever-imaginative Douglas Boyd and by his colleagues. The wind soloists in this live recording of the *Sinfonia concertante* are four COE artists who each know when to take centre stage and when to hold back in turn. The variations of the finale are pure delight. Richard Hosford in his reading of the *Clarinet concerto* uses a basset clarinet with its extended lower range, allowing Mozart's original intentions to be realized. At slowish speeds he leans towards the lyrical rather than the dramatic, even in the first movement, and ends with a delightfully bouncy account of the finale. Full, atmospheric recording.

(i) *Clarinet concerto;* (ii) *Clarinet quintet in A, K.581.*
*** Hyperion Dig. CDA 66199 [id.]. Thea King, (i) ECO, Tate; (ii) Gabrieli Qt.
(Y/B) (M) **(*) Ph. 442 390-2 [id.]. Jack Brymer, with (i) LSO, Sir Colin Davis; (ii) Allegri Qt.

Thea King's coupling brings together winning performances of Mozart's two great clarinet master-pieces. She steers an ideal course between classical stylishness and expressive warmth, with the slow movement becoming the emotional heart of the piece. The Gabrieli Quartet is equally responsive in its finely tuned playing. For the *Clarinet concerto* Thea King uses an authentically reconstructed basset clarinet such as Mozart wanted. With Jeffrey Tate an inspired Mozartian, the performance – like that of the *Quintet* – is both stylish and expressive, with the finale given a captivating bucolic lilt. Excellent recording.

Jack Brymer's (1964) Philips account of the *Clarinet concerto* with Sir Colin Davis has an eloquent autumnal serenity and the reading a soft lyricism that is very appealing. However, the leisurely (1970) interpretation of the *Quintet* is more controversial. Generally the very slow tempi throughout are well sustained, although in the finale the forward flow of the music is reduced to a near-crawl. Good transfers.

(i) *Flute concertos Nos. 1–2; Andante in C, K.315;* (ii) *Flute and harp concerto, K.299;* (iii) *Sinfonia concertante for flute, oboe, horn & bassoon, K.297b* (reconstructed R. Levin); (iv) *4 Flute quartets, K.285, K.285a, K.285b; K.298.*
(B) **(*) Ph. Duo 442 299-2 [id.]. (i) Aurèle Nicolet, Cong. O, Zinman; (ii) Hubert Barwahser, Osian Ellis, LSO, C. Davis; (iii) Nicolet, Holliger, Baumann, Thunemann, ASMF, Marriner; (iv) William Bennett, Grumiaux Trio.

Aurèle Nicolet's performances of the *Flute concertos* and *Andante for flute and orchestra* are very positive, and the solo playing throughout is expert and elegantly phrased. Barwahser and Ellis give a sparkling account of the *Flute and harp concerto* and Sir Colin Davis accompanies them with the greatest sprightliness and sympathy. If these are not a top choice in this repertoire, the William Bennett accounts of the four *Flute quartets* with the Grumiaux Trio certainly are. They are, to put it in a nutshell, exquisitely played and very well recorded. The wind *Sinfonia concertante* in which the oboe and clarinet parts are replaced by flute and oboe respectively, is an interesting conjectural experiment rather than an essential part of a Mozart collection. The recordings throughout are smoothly remastered and sound fine.

Flute concertos Nos. (i) *1 in G, K.313;* (ii) *2 in D, K.314.*
(N) (B) *** Carlton IMP PCD 2036 [id.]. Judith Hall, Philh. O, Peter Thomas.
(M) *** Carlton PCD 807. Galway, New Irish Chamber Ens., Prieur.

Flute concertos Nos. 1 in G, K.313; 2 in D, K.314; Andante in C, K.315.
(BB) **(*) Naxos Dig. 8.550074; *4550074* [id.]. Herbert Weissberg, Capella Istropolitana, Sieghart.

Judith Hall produces a radiantly full timbre. Moreover she is a first-class Mozartian, as she demon-strates in her cadenzas as well as in the line of the slow movements, phrased with a simple eloquence that is disarming. There is plenty of vitality in the allegros, and Peter Thomas provides polished, infectious accompaniments to match the solo playing. The balance is good and the 1987 sound is bright and clear. However, at 45 minutes 30 seconds, the offering is not particularly generous.

Galway's performances are also very enjoyable. The accompaniments, ably directed by André Prieur, are reasonably polished and stylish, and the recording (although it gives a rather small sound to the violins) is excellent, clear and with good balance and perspective. It might be argued that Galway's vibrato is not entirely suited to these eighteenth-century works and that his cadenzas, too, are slightly anachronistic. But the star quality of his playing disarms criticism.

The Naxos record by Herbert Weissberg and the Capella Istropolitana under Martin Sieghart can hold its head quite high alongside the competition. Weissberg does not have the outsize personality of some of his rivals but he is a cultured player, and the quality of the recording is excellent. In short, good value for money and very pleasant sound.

(i) *Flute concerto No. 1 in G, K.313; Andante in C, K.315;* (ii) *Flute and harp concerto in C, K.299.*
(M) *** RCA GD 86723 [6723-2-RG]. James Galway; (i) Lucerne Festival O, Baumgartner; (ii) with
    Marisa Robles, LSO, Mata.
(M) *** Erato/Warner 2292 45832-2 [id.]. Rampal, (i) VSO, Guschlbauer; (ii) Lily Laskine, Paillard CO,
    Paillard.

James Galway's silvery timbre seems as unlike an original instrument as could possibly be imagined.
Galway is well supported by the Lucerne orchestra, rather reverberantly recorded, with the solo flute
placed well forward. The coupled *Flute and harp concerto* has seldom sounded more lively than it does
here, with an engaging element of fantasy in the music-making, a radiant slow movement and a very
spirited finale. Marisa Robles makes a characterful match for Galway and they are well accompanied.
    Rampal and Lily Laskine also create a genuine symbiosis in the *Flute and harp concerto*: their interplay
has great charm and delicacy, and the slow movement is a delight. The solo concerto and *Andante* find
Rampal in equally good form and he is well accompanied in both instances. With well-transferred
recordings from the mid-1960s, this CD is well worth its mid-price.

(i) *Flute concertos Nos. 1–2, K.313/4;* (ii) *Flute and harp concerto in C, K.299.*
(M) *** Decca 440 080-2 [id.]. (i) William Bennett, ECO, Malcolm; (ii) Werner Tripp, Hubert Jellinek,
    VPO, Münchinger.

William Bennett gives a beautiful account of the concertos, among the finest in the catalogue. Every
phrase is shaped with both taste and affection, and the playing of the ECO under George Malcolm is
fresh and vital. The earlier Vienna recording of the *Flute and harp concerto* has also stood the test of
time, and again the recording is smooth, full, nicely reverberant and with good detail. Refinement and
beauty of tone and phrase are a hallmark throughout, and Münchinger provides most sensitive accompaniments. A first-rate (75 minutes) compilation.

(i) *Flute concerto No. 1 in G, K.313;* (ii) *Flute and harp concerto in C, K.299;* (iii) *Oboe concerto in C,
K.314;* (iv) *Sinfonia concertante in E flat, K.297b.*
(N) (BB) **(*) CfP Silver Double Dig. CDCFPSD 4808 (2). (i; ii) Snowden; (ii) Thomas; (iii) Hunt; (iv)
    Theodore, Hill, Price, Busch; LPO, (i; iv) Mackerras; (ii–iii) Litton.

Jonathan Snowden's account of the *Flute concerto* is attractive, sprightly, stylish and polished (though
some might not take to his comparatively elaborate cadenzas). The performance of the *Flute and harp
concerto* is even more winning. Where Gordon Hunt in the *Oboe concerto* seems a less natural concerto
soloist, Snowden, in collaboration with Caryl Thomas on the harp, is both sparkling and sensitive,
regularly imaginative in his individual phrasing. In the first movement of the *Sinfonia concertante* for
wind, Mackerras is characteristically brisk, and his performance has plenty of life throughout, and
charm too, in the closing variations. The solo playing here (by a different group) is of high quality; the
Adagio is persuasive, if with no striking individuality. With excellent digital recording, this makes an
enjoyable if not a distinctive collection.

(i) *Flute & harp concerto, K.299. Serenade in G (Eine kleine Nachtmusik), K.525;* (ii) *Sinfonia concertante
in E flat for violin, viola & orchestra, K.364.*
(Y/B) *** Decca Dig. 443 175-2 [id.]. Cleveland O, Christoph von Dohnányi, with (i) Joshua Smith, Lisa
    Wellbaum; (ii) Daniel Majeske, Robert Vernon.

Here are two more eminently acceptable performances of both the *Concerto for flute, harp and orchestra*
and the *Sinfonia concertante in E flat*, K.364, the latter coming as a memorial to Daniel Majeske, the
distinguished and long-serving concert master of the Cleveland Orchestra, about whom Dohnányi
writes movingly. The *Sinfonia concertante* is very well paced and completely free from any interpretative
egocentricity. A musicianly, rather aristocratic performance, free from any playing to the gallery. The
recording reproduces very faithfully and freshly. The *Concerto for flute, harp and orchestra* comes off
nicely and has an appropriate *joie de vivre*. Not necessarily a first choice in either work, but worth
considering alongside the best, and eminently recommendable if you want this particular coupling.

(i) *Flute and harp concerto in C, K.299; Sinfonia concertante in E flat, K.297b.*
(BB) *** Naxos Dig. 8.550159; *4550159* [id.]. (i) Jiri Válek, Hana Müllerová; Capella Istropolitana,
    Richard Edlinger.

Richard Edlinger's account of the *Flute and harp concerto* is thoroughly fresh and stylish, and the two
soloists are excellent. Although the *Sinfonia concertante in E flat*, K.297b, is not quite so successful, it is
still very impressive, and it gives much pleasure. Both performances are very decently recorded; in the
lowest price-range they are a real bargain.

(i) *Flute and harp concerto;* (ii) arr. of *Violin sonatas Nos. 17 in C, K.296; 24 in F, K.376* (for flute and piano).
** RCA Dig. 09026 61789-2 [id.]. James Galway, (i) Marisa Robles, LSO, Tilson Thomas; (ii) with Phillip Moll.

Apart from the excellence of the modern, digital recording, there seems no reason to prefer James Galway's newest recording of the *Flute and harp concerto* to his earlier version with the same partner, Marisa Robles (GD 86723). That was more appropriately coupled, whereas the transcription of some *Violin sonatas* seems a less valuable exercise when there is ample flute repertoire available. In any case, when the second subject of the first movement of the concerto appears, Galway produces a mannered slowing of tempo which could become irritating on repetition.

Horn concertos Nos. 1 in D, K.412; 2–4 in E flat, K.417, 447 & 495.
(M) *** Decca 417 767-2. Barry Tuckwell, LSO, Maag – HAYDN: *Concerto No. 1.* ***
(B) *** CfP Dig. CD-CFP 4589. Claire Briggs, RLPO, Stephen Kovacevich – HAYDN: *Trumpet concerto.* ***

Horn concertos Nos. 1 in D, K.412 (with alternative versions of Rondo); *2–4 in E flat, K.417, K.447 & K.495; Allegro, K.370b & Concert rondo in E flat* (ed. Tuckwell); *Fragment in E, K.494a.*
*** Collins Dig. 1153-2 [id.]. Barry Tuckwell, Philh. O.

Horn concertos Nos. 1–4; Concert rondo in E flat, K.371 (ed. Civil or E. Smith).
*** Sony Dig. SK 53369 [id.]. Ab Koster, Tafelmusik, Bruno Weil.
*** Chandos Dig. CHAN 9150 [id.]. Frank Lloyd, N. Sinfonia, Richard Hickox.
(Y/B) (M) *** Ph. 442 397-2 [id.]. Alan Civil, ASMF, Marriner.
(BB) *** Naxos Dig. 8.550148; *4.550148* [id.]. Miloš Stevove, Capella Istropolitana, Josef Kopelman.
(Y/B) (B) **(*) Carlton IMP Dig. PCD 2013. Richard Watkins, City of L. Sinfonia, Hickox.

Horn concertos Nos. 1–4; Concert rondo in E flat, K.371 (arr. Tuckwell).
(M) *** EMI Dig. CDM7 64851-2 [id.]. Radovan Vlatković, ECO, Tate – R. STRAUSS: *Horn concerto No. 1.* ***

Horn concertos Nos. 1–4; Concert rondo, K.371 (ed. Tuckwell); *Fragment, K.494a.*
*** Virgin/EMI Dig. VC7 59558-2 [id.]. Timothy Brown (hand horn), O of Age of Enlightenment, Kuijken.
(M) *** EMI CDM7 69569-2. Barry Tuckwell, ASMF, Marriner.

Barry Tuckwell's Collins CD, his fourth recording of the Mozart *Horn concertos*, remains a first choice for those wanting these works in a modern-instrument performance with first-class, digital sound. They are fresh, without a suspicion of routine, and are played with rounded tone and consistently imaginative phrasing. Moreover the Collins collection is unusually complete. Besides the *Fragment*, K.494a, Tuckwell includes both the familiar *Concert Rondo*, K.371, plus an *Allegro* first movement which Mozart wrote to go with it. Tuckwell also includes his own alternative *Rondo* finale of the *Concerto in D*, K.412, which is called No. 1 but which was the last to be written. This is based directly on Mozart's autograph, and the two alternative finales are placed side by side on this 71-minute CD.

We must also give the most cordial welcome to a splendid authentic set from Tafelmusik, which makes a very tempting alternative. Ab Koster is a very personable soloist and he plays on an Austrian hand-horn, built by Ignaz Lorenz of Linz. His plump timbre is very different from Tuckwell's – obviously very like the sound Mozart would have recognized, with stopped notes neatly incorporated into the melodic line. Melodic lines are allowed to breathe in the most attractive way while allegros are as spirited as one would wish, and the fresh, transparent textures of the accompanying Tafelmusik group (a sizeable band: 9.8.4.3.2, plus wind) are equally refreshing. Splendid recording, but this CD includes only the four *Concertos* plus the *Rondo*, K.371.

The other performance on original instruments is hardly less enjoyable. Timothy Brown also uses an open hand-horn without valves. He uses stopped notes with especially smart effect in the Rondos, and more sparingly and more subtly in the lyrical music. His control of the upper range of the instrument is remarkably free and even, yet the ear is often subtly aware that certain notes are being contrived. Far from being a drawback, this tends to increase the range of colour. Brown's lyrical line is very persuasive. In short these performances sound delightfully fresh, and give constant pleasure. Timothy Brown includes the additional *Rondo* and also the *Fragment*, which (like Tuckwell) he leaves in mid-air, at the point at which the composer abandoned his manuscript. Kuijken's accompaniments, while light, bright and transparent, are also pleasingly smooth and cultivated. With first-rate recording this is also highly recommendable.

Among the more recent versions is a fine set by Frank Lloyd, an outstanding soloist of the new generation. He plays these works with great character and poetic warmth; his phrasing is supple and his tone full, though never suave. Like Tuckwell, he uses a modern German double horn with great skill and sensitivity. Hickox provides admirable accompaniments, and the Chandos recording is well up to the high standards of the house.

Miloš Stevove is principal horn with the Slovak Philharmonic Orchestra, and with his Bohemian background he is naturally at home in this genial music. He uses the slightest trace of vibrato but it is never obtrusive, and one has only to listen to the *Larghetto* of K.447 or the *Andante cantabile* of K.495 to discover his naturally warm feeling for a Mozartian phrase. Allegros are lively and the Rondos have agreeable lift. In short, with excellent, stylish accompaniments from the Capella Istropolitana this is enjoyably spontaneous. The recording is very good too; though not quite as beautiful as the Chandos, it has a compensating freshness.

Radovan Vlatković's tone is very full, with the lower harmonics telling more resonantly than is characteristic of a British soloist; there is also at times the slightest hint of vibrato, but it is applied with great discretion and used mostly in the cadenzas. His performances are full of imaginative touches and he has the perfect partner in Jeffrey Tate, who produces sparkling accompaniments. All in all, another outstanding set, most winningly different from the playing of the British generation. Moreover Vlatković includes both the *Concert rondo*, K.371, and, very appropriately, a quite outstanding account of the *First Horn concerto* of Richard Strauss which, although more romantic, has so much in common with the spirit of the Mozart concertos.

Tuckwell's first (1960) stereo recording of the *Horn concertos* re-emerges freshly on Decca's mid-price label, now shorn of the *Fragment*, K.494a, but offering instead Haydn's best concerto to make it more competitive. Peter Maag's accompaniments are admirably crisp and nicely scaled, giving his soloist buoyant support, and the vintage recording still sounds astonishingly well. However, EMI have also effectively remastered Tuckwell's second set with Marriner, and the 1972 recording sounds fuller, with slightly more body to the violins. This CD has the advantage of including not only the *Concert rondo* but also the *Fragment in E*.

Alan Civil's Philips set was made in 1973. The recording is obviously modern and the performances are highly enjoyable, with Sir Neville Marriner's polished and lively accompaniments giving pleasure in themselves. The balance has the effect of making the horn sound slightly larger than life.

Claire Briggs here gives brilliant performances of all four *Concertos*, with the celebrated finale of No. 4 taken exceptionally fast. Even that is superbly articulated without any feeling of breathlessness, though it lacks some of the fun that others have brought.

Richard Watkins has the advantage of first-class modern digital recording on a bargain-priced label. He is an expert player and shows a genuine Mozartian sensibility. But this easy lyrical flow does mean that slow movements are very limpid and relaxed, and even the Rondos, articulated lightly, take wing more gently than usual. Hickox's accompaniments, on the other hand, are efficient and positive. But generally there is a somewhat self-effacing quality to the solo performances which detracts from the music's projection, and Barry Tuckwell's Collins set has an altogether stronger profile.

(i) *Horn concertos Nos. 1–4;* (ii) *Piano and wind quintet in E flat, K.452.*
(***) EMI mono CDC5 55087-2 [id.]. Dennis Brain; (i) Philh. O, Karajan; (ii) Colin Horsley & members of Dennis Brain Wind Ens.

EMI have reissued Dennis Brain's famous (1954) mono record of the concertos with Karajan, and the remastering has been done with great orchestral body and warmth resulting. Brain's horn timbre was unique. As for the playing, Brain's glorious tone and phrasing – every note is alive – is life-enhancing in its warmth; the *espressivo* of the slow movements is matched by the joy of the Rondos, spirited, buoyant, infectious and smiling. Karajan's accompaniments, too, are a model of Mozartian good manners and the Philharmonia at their peak play wittily and elegantly. Brain's distinguished earlier recording of the *Piano and wind quintet* has been added, with Colin Horsley making a fine contribution on the piano. However, the CD has now reverted to full price.

Oboe concerto in C, K.314.
*** ASV Dig. CDCOE 808 [id.]. Douglas Boyd, COE, Berglund – R. STRAUSS: *Oboe concerto.* ***

Douglas Boyd is never afraid to point the phrasing individually, spontaneously and without mannerism. Others may be purer in their classicism, but this is a very apt reading next to Strauss. Recorded in Henry Wood Hall, the sound is full and vivid.

Piano concertos

Complete Mozart Edition, Volume 7: (i) *Piano concertos, K.107/1–3;* (ii) *Nos. 1–4;* (iii) *5, 6, 8, 9, 11–27; Concert rondos 1–2;* (iii; iv) *Double piano concertos, K.242 & K.365;* (v) *Triple concerto in F, K.242.*
(M) **(*) Ph. Analogue/Dig. 422 507-2 (12) [id.]. (i) Ton Koopman, Amsterdam Bar. O; (ii) Haebler, Vienna Capella Academica, Melkus; (iii) Brendel, ASMF, Marriner; (iv) Imogen Cooper; (v) Katia and Marielle Labèque, Bychkov, BPO, Bychkov.

Piano concertos Nos. 1–6; 8–9; 11–27; Rondo in D, K.382.
(M) *** EMI CZS7 62825-2 (10). Daniel Barenboim, ECO.

Piano concertos Nos. 1–6; 8–9; 11–27; Rondos Nos. 1–2, K.382 & 386.
(N) ✹ (M) *** Sony Analogue/Dig. SX12K 46441 (12). Murray Perahia, ECO.

(i) *Piano concertos Nos. 1–6; 8, 9, 11–27; Concert rondos Nos. 1 in D, K.382;* (ii) *2 in A, K.386;* (iii) *Double piano concerto in E flat, K.365;* (iii; iv) *Triple piano concerto in F, K.242.*
(Y/B) (B) *** Decca Analogue/Dig. 443 727-2 (10) [id.]. Ashkenazy, (i) with Philh. O; (ii) LSO, Kertész; (iii) Barenboim, ECO; (iv) Fou Ts'ong.

Piano concertos Nos. 1 in F, K.37; 8 in C, K.246; 9 in E flat, K.271.
(Y/B) (M) **(*) Decca Dig. 425 089-2 [id.]. Vladimir Ashkenazy, Philh. O.

Piano concertos Nos. 2 in B flat, K.39; 16 in D, K.451; 17 in G, K.453.
(Y/B) (M) *** Decca Dig./Analogue 425 092-2 [id.]. Vladimir Ashkenazy, Philh. O.

Piano concertos Nos. 3 in D, K.40; 18 in B flat, K.456; 19 in F, K.459.
(Y/B) (M) *** Decca Dig./Analogue 425 093-2 [id.]. Vladimir Ashkenazy, Philh. O.

Piano concertos Nos. 4 in G, K.41; 21 in C, K.467; 23 in A, K.488.
(Y/B) (M) *** Decca Dig./Analogue 425 095-2 [id.]. Vladimir Ashkenazy, Philh. O.

(i) *Piano concertos Nos. 5 in D, K.175; 6 in B flat, K.238;* (ii) *Triple concerto in F, K.242.*
(Y/B) (M) **(*) Decca Dig./Analogue 425 088-2 [id.]. Vladimir Ashkenazy, with (i) Philh. O; (ii) Barenboim & Fou Ts'ong, ECO.

(i) *Piano concertos Nos. 11 in F, K.413; 12 in A, K.414;* (ii) *Double concerto in E flat, K.365.*
(Y/B) (M) **(*) Decca Dig./Analogue 425 090-2 [id.]. Vladimir Ashkenazy, with (i) Philh. O; (ii) Barenboim, ECO.
Piano concertos Nos. 13 in C, K.415; 14 in E flat, K.449; 15 in B flat, K.450.
(M) *** Decca Dig. 425 091-2 [id.]. Vladimir Ashkenazy, Philh. O.

Piano concertos Nos. 20 in D min., K.466; 22 in E flat, K.482.
(Y/B) (M) *** Decca Dig./Analogue 425 094-2 [id.]. Vladimir Ashkenazy, Philh. O.

Piano concertos Nos. 24 in C min., K.491; 25 in C, K.503; Rondo No. 1 in D, K.382.
(Y/B) (M) *** Decca Dig./Analogue 425 096-2 [id.]. Vladimir Ashkenazy, Philh. O.

(i) *Piano concertos Nos. 26 in D ('Coronation'), K.537; 27 in B flat, K.595;* (ii) *Rondo No. 2 in A, K.386.*
(Y/B) (M) *** Decca Dig./Analogue 425 097-2 [id.]. Vladimir Ashkenazy, with (i) Philh. O; (ii) LSO, Kertész.

By omitting the four early concertos after J. C. Bach, Sony have been able to reissue the Perahia set on twelve mid-priced CDs. The cycle is a remarkable achievement; in terms of poetic insight and musical spontaneity, the performances are in a class of their own. There is a wonderful singing line and at the same time a sensuousness that is always tempered by spirituality. About half the recordings are digital and of excellent quality and, we are glad to report, the earlier, analogue recordings have been skilfully remastered with first-class results, both in this complete set and in the separate issues below. The strings now sound smooth and full (the previously noticed edginess has disappeared) and the balance gives no cause for complaint. This is an indispensable set in every respect.

Those wanting a modern digital set of the Mozart concertos and for whom the flatteringly resonant sound of the Schiff/Végh series offers problems (see below) can readily turn to Ashkenazy, where the Decca recording is more crisply focused, with bright, athletic strings against a warm backgound ambience. Ashkenazy's set with the Philharmonia appeared over more than a decade: the early *Concertos* are the most recent (1987), while the *G major*, K.453, and the *C major*, K.467, come from 1977. The account of the *E flat Concerto*, K.365, with Barenboim and the ECO and the *Triple concerto* with Fou Ts'ong to complete the trio, is earlier still (1972). These performances have won golden opinions over the years, and the clarity of both the performances and the recordings is refreshing: indeed the fine Decca sound is one of their strongest features. With their latest remastering Decca have been able to squeeze the recordings on to ten generously full, bargain-priced CDs, which make a very attractive proposition. The

CDs are also available separately at mid-price on Decca's Ovation label. If their insights do not always seem to strike quite as deeply as Perahia's, the latter's complete box on Sony suffers from less than congenial remastering of the earlier, analogue recordings. No such complaint can be made about the Decca transfers, which are remarkably fresh and natural. Many of these performances are among the finest available, combining refreshing spontaneity with an overall sense of proportion and balance. *Nos. 12 in A* and *13 in C* are particularly striking; with their natural, expressive feeling and sparkle, they convey real enjoyment, and the slow movement of the *A major*, K.414, is given memorable depth. These are digitally recorded and the sound is well defined and transparent, the ambience very attractive. Nos. 15 and 16 again show characteristic sensibility: both slow movements are played very beautifully yet without a trace of narcissism, and the finales sparkle. In *No. 17 in G* there is a fine sense of movement, yet nothing is hurried; *No. 19 in F* is hardly less successful, both subtle and sparkling. *No. 23 in A* – again with fine digital recording – is beautifully judged, alive, fresh and warm, while in *No. 24 in C minor* Ashkenazy has the full measure of the music's breadth and emotional power; and his playing, while showing all the elegance and poise one could desire, never detracts from the coherence of the whole. The first movement of No. 25 is on the grandest scale, and the opening movement of the *Coronation* (No. 26) is also appropriately magisterial, yet brings some exquisitely shaded playing in the *Larghetto*, while No. 27 caps the cycle impressively. The recording of these last three concertos is again digital and very lifelike: no orchestral detail is masked and the woodwind glow, while the piano timbre is most beautiful.

The sense of spontaneity in Barenboim's performances of the Mozart concertos, his message that this is music hot off the inspiration line, is hard to resist, even though it occasionally leads to over-exuberance and idiosyncrasies. These are as nearly live performances as one could hope for on record, and the playing of the English Chamber Orchestra is splendidly geared to the approach of an artist with whom the players have worked regularly. They are recorded with fullness, and the sound is generally freshened very successfully in the remastering.

The Philips Mozart Edition *Piano concertos* box is based on Brendel's set with the ASMF under Marriner. Throughout, his thoughts are never less than penetrating. The transfers are consistently of the very highest quality, as is the playing of the Academy of St Martin-in-the-Fields under Sir Neville Marriner. To make the set complete, Ingrid Haebler gives eminently stylish accounts of the first four *Concertos* on the fortepiano, accompanied by Melkus and his excellent Vienna Capella Academica; the sound is admirably fresh. However, on disc two the ear gets rather a shock when Ton Koopman presents the three works after J. C. Bach. Convincing though these performances are, it seems a strange idea to offer an authentic approach to these three concertos alone, particularly as at the end of the disc we return to a delightfully cultured performance on modern instruments of the alternative version for three pianos of the so-called *Lodron Concerto*, K.242, provided by the Labèque duo.

Piano concertos Nos. 1 in F, K.37; 2 in B flat, K.39; 3 in D, K.40; 4 in G, K.41.
(BB) ** Naxos Dig. 8.550212. Jenö Jandó, Concentus Hungaricus, Idikó Helgi.

These early concertos are given crisp, direct performances by Jandó, well accompanied. But the resonance of the Italian Institute in Budapest does not provide as sharp a focus as with the best of his other recordings of this repertoire.

Piano concertos Nos. 5–6, 8–9, 11–27.
(N) (M) *** Decca Dig. 448 140-2 (9) [id.]. András Schiff, Salzburg Mozarteum Camerata Academica, Végh.

András Schiff's cycle with the Salzburg Mozarteum Camerata Academica under Sándor Végh proves to be one of the most satisfying of recent years and – along with the new Shelley series on Chandos – arguably the finest since Murray Perahia's cycle of the late 1970s. Not all these records have been discussed by us individually, so we have gained pleasure in encountering the performances together as a set. Schiff plays a Bösendorfer piano and its relatively gentle, cleanly focused timbre has something of the precision of a fortepiano without any loss of the colour which comes with a more modern instrument. The recording is consistently more beautiful than in Perahia's Sony set, with sweet strings and glowing woodwind and the piano usually balanced naturally and integrated with the orchestra. For some listeners in certain works the warm resonance may offer a problem. This is immediately apparent in the orchestral tutti of the first concerto included here, No. 5 in D major, K.175. The rather diffuse opening of the *Coronation concerto*, K.537, is another example, yet the slighty misty focus certainly adds an air of mystery to the opening of the *D minor*, K.466. There is a comparably evocative anticipation of drama at the beginning of the *C minor*, K.491, while in the famous string passage which gently ushers in the slow movement of No. 21 in C, K.467, the effect is both warm and ethereal. The lovely A major, K.488, also gains much from the glowing ambience, particularly the beautifully played *Adagio*. The recordings were made in a variety of Viennese venues between 1984 and 1990, including the Mozarteum, the Grosser Saal of the Konzerthaus, the Viersen Festhalle, and the Millstatt Kirche, although the balance and warm ambience seem fairly consistent. This is agreeably relaxed music-making, though not in the least lacking in intensity or weight. Just occasionally Schiff dots his 'i's and crosses his 't's a little too precisely, but for the most part he is so musicianly and perceptive that this seems unimportant. In short, these are lovely performances, enhanced by the quality of the accompaniment under Végh, who is unfailingly supportive. For the most part Schiff plays his own cadenzas, but in the first movement of K.466 he uses a cadenza by Beethoven, and the finale of K.488 brings one by George Malcolm. There is an accompanying booklet which includes two essays: 'A performer's approach' by Schiff himself, and a general survey by Jeremy Siepmann called 'Mozart's Utopian visions'. All these records are also available separately in their original couplings.

Piano concertos Nos. 5–6; 8–9; 11–27; Rondo in D, K.382.
**(*) Ph. Dig. 438 207-2 (9) [id.]. Mitsuko Uchida, ECO, Jeffrey Tate.

Mitsuko Uchida, following up her stylish and sensitive accounts of the *Piano sonatas*, began a cycle of the concertos in 1985 with Nos. 20 and 21, which set the style for the series (recorded over a period of nearly five years) with playing of considerable beauty and performances guaranteed never to offend and most likely to delight. But on the highest level their degree of reticence – despite the superb orchestral work of the ECO under Tate – makes them often less memorable than the very finest versions. The earlier concertos are neatly and elegantly done, although at times one would welcome more extrovert sparkle. There is some lovely playing, although her cultured approach at times offers more than a glimpse of Dresden china. She is unfailingly elegant but a little over-civilized; some will find a faint hint of preciosity here and there. Uchida is eminently alive and imaginative, although at times one would welcome a greater robustness of spirit, a lively inner current, and this applies particularly to the last two concertos, K.537 and K.595. Throughout, Jeffrey Tate draws splendid playing from the ECO, and these artists have the benefit of exceptionally good recorded sound; although the perspective favours the piano, the timbre of the solo instrument is beautifully captured.

Piano concertos Nos. 5–6, 8–9, 11–27; (i) *Double piano concerto, K.365;* (i; ii) *Triple piano concerto, K.242. Concert Rondos 1–2.*
(M) *** DG Dig. 431 211-2 (9) [id.]. Malcolm Bilson (fortepiano), E. Bar. Soloists, Gardiner, (i) with Robert Levin; (ii) Melvyn Tan.

Malcolm Bilson's complete set of the Mozart *Piano concertos* appears on nine mid-price CDs. Bilson is an artist of excellent musical judgement and good taste, and his survey is the only one at present available on the fortepiano, though we gather that one is under way from Melvyn Tan, who features here in the *Triple concerto*. For the most part, there is little to quarrel with here and much to enjoy.

Piano concertos Nos. 5 in D, K.175; 25 in C, K.503.
(N) *** Sony Dig. SK 37267 [id.]. Perahia, ECO.

Murray Perahia has the measure of the strength and scale of the *C major*, K.503, as well as displaying tenderness and poetry; while the early *D major*, K.175, has an innocence and freshness that are completely persuasive. The recording is good, but the upper strings are a little fierce and not too cleanly focused.

Piano concertos Nos. 6 in B flat, K.238; 8 in C, K.246; 19 in F, K.459.
(BB) *** Naxos Dig. 8.550208; *4550208* [id.]. Jenö Jandó, Concentus Hungaricus, Mátyás Antal.

No. 19 in F is a delightful concerto and it receives a most attractive performance, aptly paced, with fine woodwind playing, the finale crisply sparkling. No. 6 is hardly less successful; if No. 8 seems plainer, it is still admirably fresh. With excellently balanced recording this is a genuine bargain.

Piano concertos Nos. 6 in B flat, K.238; 13 in C, K.415.
*** Sony SK 39223 [id.]. Murray Perahia, ECO.

Perahia brings a marvellous freshness and delicacy to the *B flat Concerto*, K.238, but it is in the *C major*, with its sense of character and subtle artistry, that he is at his most sparkling and genial. Even if the acoustic ambience is less than ideally spacious, the CBS sound is still good.

Piano concertos Nos. 6 in B flat, K.238; 17 in G, K.453; 21 in C, K.467.
(N) (M) *** DG 447 436-2 [id.]. Géza Anda, Salzburg Mozarteum Camerata Academica.

It is proper that Géza Anda's Mozart concerto series from the 1960s should find a place in DG's 'Originals' series. His poetic account of the *C major Concerto*, K.467, is one of the most impressive from his cycle, notably for a beautifully poised orchestral introduction to the famous slow movement (a picture of 'Elvira Madigan' appears on the front of the CD). In the *G major*, K.453, Anda, who is soloist and conductor throughout the disc, errs a little on the side of heaviness of style, but again there is both strength and poetry, while the DG recording is excellent in both balance and clarity. The *B flat Concerto*, K.238, which also has a most beautiful slow movement, is played simply and eloquently, although perhaps the finale could have had a lighter touch in the orchestra (and this applies too to K.467). The recording is not quite so cleanly transferred in the early work. It comes last on the CD and is by no means of lesser appeal, and this remains a most enjoyable triptych.

Piano concertos Nos. 8 in C (Lützow), K.246; 9 in E flat (Jeunehomme), K.271; Concert rondo No. 2 in A, K.386.
(Y/B) 🏵 (M) *** Decca 443 576-2 [id.]. Ashkenazy, LSO, Kertész.

Ashkenazy's earlier, 1966 coupling with Kertész, which includes also the *A major Concert rondo*, has now been appropriately reissued in Decca's Classic Sound series and the recorded quality remains beautifully fresh and realistic. The magnificent performances originally earned the LP a Rosette and we see no reason not to carry it forward. Ashkenazy has the requisite sparkle, humanity and command of keyboard tone, and his readings can only be called inspired. He is very well supported by the LSO under Kertész, and they make an excellent case for a partnership with a sympathetic conductor, rather than having the soloist direct the proceedings from the keyboard.

Piano concertos Nos. 8 in C, K. 246; 13 in C, K. 415; 25 in C, K. 503.
(Y/B) (B) **(*) HMA 1903022 [id.]. Kocsis, Franz Liszt CO, János Rolla.

Robust and thoroughly lively and musical accounts of Mozart's three C major concertos, a unique (75-minute) coupling. The slow movement of K.503 comes off especially well and the finale is infectious. Fine, modern, digital recording and a good balance ensure the appeal and value of the disc; even if the sound is a shade resonant, everything is clearly focused.

Piano concertos Nos. 8 in C, K.246; 23 in A, K.488; 24 in C min., K.491; 27 in B flat, K.595.
(Y/B) (B) *** DG Double 439 699-2 (2) [id.]. Wilhelm Kempff, Bamberg SO or BPO, Ferdinand Leitner.

Nothing Kempff recorded was without a degree of magic, and so it is here. His separate coupling of Nos. 23 and 24 with the Bamberg orchestra offered playing that was uniquely poetic and inspired, but his introvert delicacy is controversial in K.246 and K.595. Much of the playing is very dreamy and gentle (some of the detail in the piano part of K.246 is exquisite), its 'inner' quality producing a very relaxed manner, perhaps too much so in the rondo of K.595. The earlier concerto is undoubtedly livelier. The music-making is never self-admiring and the recordings are naturally balanced. With two discs offered for the price of one, many will find this well worth trying.

(i) *Piano concerto No. 9 in E flat, K.271. Symphony No. 41 (Jupiter).*
(N) (M) (**(*)) Sony mono SMK 68445 [id.]. (i) Firkušný; Concg. O, George Szell.

In the concerto, the thinness of the strings, as recorded in mono (in 1959) in the relatively intimate setting of the Mozarteum in Salzburg, gives little idea of the Concertgebouw sound, but the clarity of the piano from top to bottom is a bonus, with Firkušný's diamond-bright articulation beautifully caught and with the lightness of bass bringing similarities to fortepiano sound. The rapt intensity of Firkušný's playing, his readiness to scale down the volume of sound to a thread of pianissimo (like Casadesus in his Mozart recordings in Cleveland) makes the result the more magnetic in a way that contrasts with the robust sound which regularly marked Szell's Cleveland recordings, not least in concertos. In the symphony as well, his stylishness as a Mozartian shines out here more clearly than in his Cleveland recordings. Speeds are hardly different at all in the *Jupiter* as compared with the Cleveland studio performance of 1963, but the manner is a degree more relaxed, allowing a measure of charm, helped by the extra lightness and clarity. Szell observes the exposition repeat in the first movement, but not in the finale.

(i) *Piano concertos Nos. 9 in E flat, K.271; 14 in E flat, K.449.*
(M) *** Van. 8.4015.71 [OVC 4015]. Alfred Brendel; (i) I Solisti di Zagreb, Janigro.

Brendel's 1968 performance of No. 9 is quite outstanding, elegant and beautifully precise. The classical-sized orchestra is just right and the neat, stylish string-playing matches the soloist. The performance of K.449 is also first rate, with a memorably vivacious finale. Altogether this is an outstanding reissue with natural sound which hardly shows its age in the clean remastering.

Piano concertos Nos. 9 in E flat, K.271; 15 in B flat, K.450; 22 in E flat, K.482; 25 in C, K.503; 27 in B flat, K.595.

(Y/B) (B) *** Ph. Duo 442 571-2 (2) [id.]. Alfred Brendel, ASMF, Marriner.

A first-class follow-up to Brendel's first Duo collection of Mozart piano concertos (see below). The account of the opening *Jeunehomme* is finely proportioned and cleanly articulated, with a ravishing account of the slow movement. The finale has great sparkle and finesse and the recording has exemplary clarity. Brendel is hardly less fine in K.450, and the *E flat Concerto* has both vitality and depth. Brendel's first movement has breadth and grandeur as well as sensitivity, while the *Andante* has great poetry. No. 25 (there is well-deserved applause at the close) was recorded at a live performance and has life and concentration, and a real sense of scale. Here as elsewhere the playing of the ASMF under Marriner is alert and supportive. K.595 is also among Brendel's best Mozart performances, with a beautifully poised *Larghetto* and a graceful, spirited finale. The recordings were made between 1974 and 1981 (No. 15 is digital) and offer characteristically fresh and natural sound. Highly recommended.

Piano concertos Nos. 9 in E flat, K.271; 17 in G, K.453.
(M) *** Chandos Dig. CHAN 9068 [id.]. Howard Shelley, LMP.
**(*) Teldec/Warner Dig. 9031 73128-2 [id.]. Daniel Barenboim, BPO.

Piano concertos Nos. 9 in E flat (Jeunehomme), K.271; 17 in G, K.453; Rondo in D, K.382.
(N) (M) *** DG Dig. 447 291-2 [id.]. Malcolm Bilson (fortepiano), E. Bar. Soloists, Gardiner.

Howard Shelley is the latest to embrace the challenge of directing Mozart concertos from the keyboard. Shelley's playing is a delight and is possessed of a refreshing naturalness which should win many friends. There is spontaneity and elegance, a strong vein of poetic feeling and extrovert high spirits. His *G major concerto* belongs in the most exalted company and can withstand comparison with almost any rival. But both performances are touched by distinction, and they are beautifully recorded too.

This is a recoupling on DG. *Piano concerto No. 9*, K.271, was the first to be recorded (in 1983) in Malcolm Bilson's cycle; No. 17 came three years later. Bilson shows himself a lively and imaginative artist, well matched by the ever-effervescent Gardiner. The CD catches the lightness and clarity of the textures, with the fortepiano sound not too twangy and with wind balances often revelatory. The darkness of the C minor slow movement of K.271 is eerily caught; K.453, as ever, is a delight, with Bilson allowing himself a natural degree of expressiveness, within the limits of classical taste. The lightness of the keyboard action encourages the choice of fast allegros, but never at the expense of Mozart. The *Rondo*, K.382, makes a pert encore.

Barenboim in the same coupling as Shelley is free from affectation and self-indulgence. His playing is in exemplary taste without any trace of the tendency to beautify and italicize this or that phrase which one recalls from some of his old ECO cycle, good though that was in so many other respects. The orchestral sonority may be a little overnourished for those accustomed to period-instrument groups, but this will not worry most collectors. The engineers serve both pianist and orchestra well; these are satisfying accounts which will not disappoint.

Piano concertos Nos. 9 in E flat (Jeunehomme), K.271; 23 in A, K.488; Concert rondo in A, K.386.
(B) **(*) Erato/Warner 2292 45935-2 [id.]. Maria-João Pires, Gulbenkian Foundation CO of Lisbon, Guschlbauer.

(i) *Piano concertos Nos. 20 in D min., K.466;* (ii) *21 in C, K.467. Rondo in A min., K.511.*
(B) ** Erato/Warner 2292 45933-2 [id.]. Pires; (i) Lausanne CO, Jordan; (ii) Gulbenkian Foundation CO of Lisbon, Guschlbauer.

(i) *Piano concertos Nos. 26 in D min. (Coronation), K.537;* (ii) *27 in B flat, K.595;* (i) *Concert rondo in D, K.382.*
(B) **(*) Erato/Warner 2292 45934-2 [id.]. Pires; (i) Gulbenkian Foundation CO of Lisbon, Guschlbauer; (ii) Lausanne CO, Jordan.

Erato are reissuing on the bargain Bonsai label some of Maria-João Pires's recordings from the mid-to late 1970s. She plays here with evident spirit and taste as well as immaculate fingerwork. Her playing reminds one a little of Ingrid Haebler's early Vox accounts (before her Mozart acquired some of the gentility and rectitude that have sometimes eroded the freshness of her playing, much though one admires it in many respects). Miss Pires is at her best in the *Jeunehomme*, K.271 (she is especially sensitive in the middle section of the closing Rondo). The coupling of K.466 and K.467 has less individuality, though neither performance is without atmosphere. Greater dash and fire in outer movements would have been welcome, but Miss Pires offers many insights and she is impressive in the *Coronation concerto*. Guschlbauer gives her most musical support; so too does Armin Jordan, although he is inclined to display a less striking profile. Smooth transfers of well-balanced analogue sound. Good value, but in the last resort not distinctive.

Piano concertos Nos. 9 in E flat, K.271; 21 in C, K.467.
(N) *** Sony SK 34562 [id.]. Murray Perahia, ECO.

Perahia's reading of K.271 is wonderfully refreshing and delicate, with diamond-bright articulation, urgently youthful in its resilience. The famous *C major Concerto* is given a more variable, though still highly imaginative performance. Faithful, well-balanced recording.

Piano concertos Nos. 11 in F, K.413; 12 in A, K.414; 14 in E flat, K.449.
(N) *** Sony SK 42243 [id.]. Murray Perahia, ECO.

These performances remain in a class of their own. When it first appeared, we thought the *F major*, K.413, the most impressive of Perahia's Mozart concerto records so far, its slow movement wonderfully inward; and the *E flat Concerto*, K.449, is comparably distinguished. The current remastering is very successful.

Piano concertos Nos. 12 in A, K.414; 14 in E flat, K.449; 21 in C, K.467.
(BB) *** Naxos Dig. 8.550202; *4550202* [id.]. Jenö Jandó, Concentus Hungaricus, András Ligeti.

In Jandó's hands the first movement of K.449 sounds properly forward-looking; the brightly vivacious K.414 also sounds very fresh here, and its *Andante* is beautifully shaped. The excellent orchestral response distinguishes the first movement of K.467: both grace and weight are here, and some fine wind playing. An added interest in this work is provided by Jandó's use of cadenzas provided by Robert Casadesus. Jandó is at his most spontaneous throughout these performances and this is altogether an excellent disc, well recorded.

Piano concertos Nos. 12 in A, K.414; 19 in F, K.459.
(M) *** Chandos Dig. CHAN 9256 [id.]. Howard Shelley, LMP.

Another fine disc in Howard Shelley's musically rewarding and beautifully recorded series. Admirers of this artist need not hesitate in investing here, with the music's expressive range fully encompassed without mannerism, slow movements eloquently shaped and outer movements aptly paced and alive with vitality.

Piano concertos Nos. 12 in A, K.414; 20 in D min., K.466; Rondo in D, K.382.
*** RCA Dig. 09026 60400 [id.]. Kissin, Moscow Virtuosi, Spivakov.

The *D major Rondo*, K.382, has an elegance and delicacy worthy of the greatest Mozart players of the day. The *A major Concerto* shows the same immaculate technical finesse and musical judgement (save, perhaps, in the slow movement, which some could find a little oversweet). There are perhaps greater depths in the *D minor Concerto* than Kissin finds but, even so, the playing is musical through and through and gives unfailing pleasure. The recorded sound is very good and the disc as a whole deserves the attention of any Mozartian.

Piano concertos Nos. 13 in C, K.415; 24 in C min., K.491.
(Y/B) (M) *** Chandos Dig. CHAN 9326 [id.]. Howard Shelley, LMP.

Like Perahia before him, Howard Shelley directs from the keyboard and this, the fifth in his ongoing series, is as distinguished as its predecessors. He has immaculate keyboard manners and his strong, natural musicianship is always in evidence. An instinctive yet thoughtful Mozartian whose consummate artistry places his cycle among the very finest now on the market.

Piano concertos Nos. 14 in E flat, K.449; 15 in E flat, K.450; 16 in D, K.451.
(M) *** EMI CDM7 69124-2 [id.]. Barenboim, ECO.

Barenboim's playing is spontaneous and smiling, while the orchestra respond with genuine vitality and sparkle. K.451 is particularly enjoyable, with a brisk, jaunty account of the first movement, a flowing, expressive slow movement and an exuberant finale. Good recording.

(i) *Piano concertos Nos. 14 in E flat, K.449; 15 in B flat K.450; 19 in F, K.459; 21 in C, K.467; 26 in D (Coronation), K.537; 27 in B flat, K.595; (i; ii) Double piano concerto in E flat, K.365. Adagio in B min., K.540; Piano sonatas Nos. 8 in A min., K.310; 11 in A, K.331; 13 in B flat, K.333; 14 in C min., K.457; Fantasia in C min., K.475; Rondo in A min., K.511.*
(N) (M) **(*) Ph. Brendel Edition Analogue/Dig. 446 921-2 (5) [id.]. Alfred Brendel, with (i) ASMF, Marriner; (ii) Imogen Cooper – HAYDN: *Andante & variations in F min.; Piano sonatas.* ***

Among Brendel's many fine recordings of the Mozart concertos, the *E flat major*, K.449, ranks highly, distinguished by beautifully clean and alive passage-work, while there is superb control and poise. The main ideas are well shaped without being overcharacterized. Tempi are wisely chosen and perfectly related. He is hardly less impressive in K.450. In K.467 the outer movements are brisk, but tempo is not in itself a problem. Each detail of a phrase is meticulously articulated, every staccato and slur carefully observed in an almost didactic fashion. But it is curmudgeonly to dwell on reservations when there is so much to delight in these performances. The playing is very impressive indeed, and so, too, is the recording. In the *Coronation concerto*, as always, Brendel's articulation and intelligence excite admiration. Only in the slow movement does one feel a trace of didacticism. There are no such reservations about No. 27, which is in every way distinguished and is beautifully recorded. The playing is immaculate: everything is deeply thought out but retains its spontaneity. Similarly the *Double concerto* (with Imogen Cooper) is elegant and poised, combining vigour with tonal refinement, and here as elsewhere Marriner's accompaniments are comparably polished. The *Sonatas*, however, bring a few reservations. The pianism is masterly, as one would expect from this great artist, but the performances of Nos. 8 and 14 strike one as the product of excessive ratiocination. There is no want of inner life, the texture is wonderfully clean and finely balanced, but the listener is all too aware of the mental preparation that has gone into the interpretations. The staccato markings in the slow movement of K.310 are exaggerated and the movement as a whole is unsmiling and strangely wanting in repose. Self-conscious playing, immaculately recorded. Both Nos. 11 and 13, however, are a joy, and beautifully recorded too. Very distinguished playing indeed.

Piano concertos Nos. 14 in E flat, K.449; 23 in A, K. 488; 24 in C min., K.491.
(N) (M) *** DG Dig. 447 295-2 [id.]. Malcolm Bilson (fortepiano), E. Bar. Soloists, Gardiner.

Here are three key Mozart concertos in a generous triptych, with the tough *E flat Concerto* coming last. The much-loved *A Major*, K.488, is as fresh as you could wish for, with plenty of zing in outer movements – the horns ringing through the texture – the *Adagio* very poised. Here the ear notices the comparative lack of the darker sonority of a modern instrument, but this is still most sensitive playing, not over-elaborated. Gardiner and the English Baroque Soloists provide vigorous, large-scale orchestral tuttis, matching Bilson's expressiveness on the one hand, while on the other relishing the fast speeds he prefers in the finales and bringing wit to the last movement of K.488. The *Larghetto* of the *C minor* brings no reservations and this is a performance which combines drama with poetry; here the tempo of the finale is a moderate *Allegretto*, allowing the detail to register admirably. Excellent recording, fresh and full-bodied, yet clear.

Piano concertos Nos. 14 in E flat, K.449; 27 in B flat, K.595.
(M) *** Chandos Dig. CHAN 9137 [id.]. Howard Shelley, LMP.

Admirable performances, stylish and with a fine Mozartian sensibility. This is altogether most refreshing, and the recording is very good indeed.

(i) *Piano concerto No. 15 in B flat, K.450; Symphony No. 36 in C (Linz), K.425.*
(N) (M) **(*) Decca 448 570-2 [id.]. (i) Leonard Bernstein (piano); VPO, Bernstein.

An enjoyably light-hearted Mozartian coupling. In the performance of the *Linz Symphony* one relishes the carefree quality in the playing. The *Concerto*, even more than the *Symphony*, conveys the feeling of a conductor enjoying himself on holiday. Bernstein's piano playing may not be poised in every detail, but every note communicates vividly – so much so that in the slow movement he even manages to make his dual tempo convincing – faster for the tuttis than for the more romantic solos. The finale is taken surprisingly slowly, but Bernstein brings it off. The sound projects vividly enough, but it is not clear why Decca chose to include this reissue in their 'Classic Sound' series.

Piano concertos Nos. 15 in B flat, K.450; 16 in D, K.451.
(N) *** Sony Dig. SK 37824 [id.]. Perahia, ECO.

Perahia's are superbly imaginative readings, full of seemingly spontaneous touches and turns of phrase very personal to him, which yet never sound mannered. His version of the *B flat Concerto* has sparkle, grace and intelligence; both these performances are very special indeed. The recording is absolutely first rate, intimate yet realistic and not dry, with the players continuously grouped round the pianist.

Piano concertos Nos. 16 in D, K.451; 25 in C, K.503; Rondo in A, K.386.
(BB) *** Naxos Dig. 8.550207; 4550207 [id.]. Jenö Jandó, Concentus Hungaricus, Mátyás Antal.

Jenö Jandó gives a very spirited and intelligent account of the relatively neglected *D major Concerto*, K.451, in which he receives sensitive and attentive support from the excellent Concentus Hungaricus under Mátyás Antal. The performance has warmth. The players sound as if they are enjoying themselves and, although there are greater performances of the *C major Concerto*, K.503, on record, they are not at this extraordinarily competitive price.

Piano concertos Nos. 17 in G, K.453; 18 in B flat, K.456.
(N) *** Sony Dig. SK 36686 [id.]. Perahia, ECO.
(BB) *** Naxos Dig. 8.550205; *4550205* [id.]. Jenö Jandó, Concentus Hungaricus, Mátyás Antal.

The *G major Concerto* is one of the most magical of the Perahia cycle and is on no account to be missed. The *B flat*, too, has the sparkle, grace and finesse that one expects from him. Even if you have other versions, you should still add this to your collection, for its insights are quite special.

This is also one of the finest in Jandó's excellent super-bargain series. Tempi are admirably judged and both slow movements are most sensitively played. The variations which form the *Andante* of K.456 are particularly appealing in their perceptive use of light and shade, while the very lively *Allegro vivace* finale of the same work is infectiously spirited. Jandó uses Mozart's original cadenzas for the first two movements of K.453 and the composer's alternative cadenzas for K.546. Excellent sound.

Piano concertos Nos. 17 in G, K.453; 21 in C, K.467.
(N) *** DG Dig. 439 941-2 [id.]. Maria-João Pires, COE, Abbado.

We admired Maria-João Pires's Mozart concertos, recorded with the Lisbon orchestra way back in the 1970s, and are pleased to see that DG have (we presume) embarked on a complete survey with her. If it is as good as the two concertos recorded here, it will be worth having. Her playing, both in the mercurial *G major Concerto* and in its more ceremonial *C major* companion, is elegant, searching and intelligent. She has taste and fine musicianship, and the Chamber Orchestra of Europe under Abbado give excellent support. In the *C major* we would not necesarily recommend her in preference to Perahia, Shelley or Brendel, but there is none of the preciosity that marred Uchida's cycle with Jeffrey Tate. Good recording.

Piano concertos Nos. 18 in B flat, K.456; 19 in F, K.459.
(N) *** HM Dig. HMU 907138 [id.]. Melvyn Tan, Philh. Bar. O, McGegan.

No one is more convincing on the fortepiano than Melvyn Tan, who is now undertaking a new series of Mozart concertos for Harmonia Mundi. This record makes an auspicious start. The pointedly rhythmic main theme of the *F major Concerto* suits the fortepiano particularly well – which is not to say that the *Allegretto* isn't equally winning, with some delightful wind playing from these characterful period instrumentalists, who shine again in the perky finale. The *B flat Concerto* is hardly less successful: the gentle melancholy of its G minor slow movement has an engaging fragility, and the superb finale – one of Mozart's most ambitious – is given its full character. McGegan and his players are clearly completely at one with their soloist. The recording is more intimate, slightly drier than in Malcolm Bilson's DG series, and the result is most persuasive. There are only 54 minutes of music here, but they are certainly addictive.

Piano concertos Nos. 19, K.459; 20, K.466; 21, K.467; 23, K.488; 24, K.491; Concert rondos Nos. 1–2, K.382 & 386.
✤ (B) *** Ph. Duo 442 269-2 [id.]. Alfred Brendel, ASMF, Marriner.

This must be the Mozartian bargain of all time, five piano concertos and two concert rondos – all for the cost of one premium-price CD. A Rosette then for generosity, to say nothing of the distinction of the performances. Indeed, throughout, the playing exhibits a sensibility that is at one with the composer's world. With Brendel, K.459 sparkles all the way through and the playing of the ASMF could hardly be improved on. The slow movement is quite magical and the finale again has great zest and brilliance. The two minor-key concertos (*20 in D minor, 24 in C minor*) are also superbly played and recorded, though perhaps they miss the last ounce of tragic intensity. There are minor qualms about K.467. The finale sounds over-rehearsed, and some of the joy and high spirits are sacrificed in the sense of momentum. Yet there remains much to delight. There are no reservations whatsoever about Brendel's account of K. 488, which is among the best in the catalogue. The decoration of the solo part in the slow movement is never obtrusive, always in style. The two *Concert rondos* – the first (K.382) is the Viennese alternative to the *Salzburg concerto* (K.175) – are no less elegantly performed, and throughout the set the Philips sound-balance is impeccable.

Piano concertos Nos. 19 in F, K.459; 23 in A, K.488.
(N) ✤ *** Sony Dig. SK 39064 [id.]. Murray Perahia, ECO.

Murray Perahia gives highly characterful accounts of both *Concertos* and a gently witty yet vital reading of the *F Major*, K.459. As always with this artist, there is a splendidly classical feeling allied to a keenly poetic sensibility. His account of K.488 has enormous delicacy and inner vitality, yet a serenity that puts it in a class of its own.

Piano concerto No. 20 in D min., K.466.

(Y/B) (BB) **(*) EMI Seraphim Dig. CES5 68520-2 (2) [CDEB 68520]. Youri Egorov, Philh. O,
Sawallisch – BEETHOVEN: *Piano concerto No. 5; Violin concerto.* **(*)

A generous coupling for an imaginative if slightly controversial account of the *Emperor* and *Violin
concerto* in EMI's bargain-basement, two-disc series. The Mozart performance, though well played, is
less distinctive, even though Egorov is stylish and Sawallisch finds plenty of drama in the outer movements and begins the finale, the most striking of the three, with great energy and bustle. The slow
movement, too, is elegantly shaped. Good, bright (1985) EMI digital recording, made at Abbey Road.

Piano concerto No. 20 in D min., K.466; Rondo in D, K.382.

(N) (M) (**) DG mono 447 976-2 [id.]. Kempff, Dresden PO, Van Kempen – BEETHOVEN: *Concerto No.
3.* (**)

Despite the crumbly orchestral recording with heavy surface hiss (transferred from 78s recorded in
1942), the Mozart is remarkable for the transparency of Kempff's playing, full of the sparkling qualities
that mark his later Mozart concerto recordings. In the first movement he plays his own cadenza, which is
full of romantic progressions. The *Rondo* is similarly magnetic.

Piano concertos Nos. 20 in D min., K.466; 21 in C, K.467.

✧ *** DG Dig. 419 609-2 [id.]. Malcolm Bilson (fortepiano), E. Bar. Soloists, Gardiner.

(M) *** RCA GD 87967 [7967-2-RG]. Rubinstein, RCA Victor SO, Wallenstein (with HAYDN:
Andante & variations in F min. ***).

(i) *Piano concertos Nos. 20 in D min., K.466; 21 in C, K.467.* (ii) *Serenade No. 13 in G (Eine kleine
Nachtmusik), K.525.*

(Y/B) (BB) *** RCA Navigator 74321 17888-2. (i) Géza Anda, VSO; (ii) Bamberg SO, Jochum.

These are vital, electric performances by Bilson and the English Baroque Soloists, expressive within
their own lights, neither rigid nor too taut in the way of some period Mozart, nor inappropriately
romantic. This is a disc to recommend even to those who would not normally consider period performances of Mozart concertos, fully and vividly recorded with excellent balance between soloist and orchestra – better than you would readily get in the concert hall.

Rubinstein has seldom been caught so sympathetically by the microphones, and the remastered 1961
recording has the orchestral sound admirably freshened. In each concerto the slow movement is the
kernel of the interpretation. Rubinstein's playing is melting. Altogether Wallenstein is an excellent
accompanist, for finales have plenty of sparkle. The Haydn *Andante and variations*, a substantial bonus
recorded a year earlier, again demonstrates Rubinstein's aristocratic feeling for a classical melodic line:
it is played most beautifully.

Both performances by Anda have an attractive simplicity and are admirably spontaneous, with slow
movements sensitive and graciously phrased. The delicacy of the solo playing entirely avoids any suggestions of Dresden china, while the orchestral introduction to the *D minor* has plenty of atmosphere. For a
bonus, Jochum provides an agreeable account of Mozart's most famous serenade. Here the full-bodied
string-sound brings robustness rather than transparency, but the finale has an appropriate rhythmic
lightness. Excellent value.

(i) *Piano concertos Nos. 20 in D min., K.466; 21 in C, K.467;* (ii) *22 in E flat, K.482; 23 in A, K.488.*

(Y/B) (BB) *** EMI Seraphim CES5 68529-2 (2) [CEDB 68529]. Annie Fischer, Philh. O; (i)
Sawallisch; (ii) Boult.

This is one of the real bargains on EMI's Seraphim (two-for-the-price-of-one-medium-price-CD) label
and well worth having, even if duplication is involved. Annie Fischer's coupling of Nos. 21–22 was very
highly regarded when it first appeared in 1959 (mono only) on Columbia CX 1630. Fischer's gentle,
limpid touch, with its frequent use of half-tones, gives a great deal of pleasure. The slow movements of
both these concertos are beautifully done, and the pianist's intimate manner is often shared by the
Philharmonia's wind soloists, who offer playing of polish and delicacy. In the *C major Concerto* she uses
cadenzas by Busoni and in the *E flat Concerto* the first-movement cadenza is by Hummel, which adds
another point of interest to this coupling. Her coupling of the *D minor* and *A major* followed, a year
later. In the *D minor Concerto* Boult's tempi are sensible and the orchestral playing is again felicitous,
particularly from the wind. The reading perhaps misses the ultimate in breadth and dramatic fire, but it
is a very good performance all the same. In K.488, Fischer plays with liveliness of feeling and refinement
of touch, and the passage-work is deft, and in any event this is a thoroughly enjoyable and often
perceptive performance. Beethoven's cadenzas are used in the *D minor Concerto*.

(i) *Piano concertos Nos. 20 in D min., K.466; 21 in C, K.467; 23 in A, K.488; 27 in B flat, K.595. Piano sonata No. 17 in D, K.576; Rondo in A min., K.511.*
✵ (B) *** Double Decca Analogue/Dig. 436 383-2 (2). Vladimir Ashkenazy, Philh. O.

This set – with two CDs offered for the price of one – deserves to be successful and is highly recommendable on all counts. With the three favourite Mozart piano concertos included, plus a splendid *Sonata* and a charming *Rondo*, this is real bounty. Ashkenazy's performance of the famous *C major Concerto* combines a refreshing spontaneity with an overall sense of proportion and balance. His *A major*, too, is beautifully judged, alive and fresh, yet warm – one of the most satisfying accounts yet recorded, even finer than Brendel's. No quarrels either with the *B flat*, which is as finely characterized as one would expect. The recording focuses closely on the piano, yet no orchestral detail is masked and the overall impression is very bright and lifelike. The *Sonata* and *Rondo* were recorded earlier (in 1967); the playing is equally fine.

Piano concertos Nos. 20 in D min., K.466; 23 in A, K.488.
(M) *** Chandos Dig. CHAN 8992 [id.]. Howard Shelley, LMP.

Those wanting this coupling with modern instruments will find Howard Shelley's performances no less rewarding. Characterization is strong, yet the slow movement of K.488 is very beautiful and touching. Splendid Chandos recording.

(i) *Piano concertos Nos. 20 in D min., K.466; 23 in A, K.488. Symphonies Nos. 36 in C (Linz), K.425; 38 in D (Prague), K.504.*
(N) (BB) **(*) CfP Silver Double CDCFPSD 4781 (2). (i) Allan Schiller; LPO, Mackerras.

This record is dominated by Mackerras and he provides a strong, dramatic account of the first movement of the *D minor Concerto* in which Allan Schiller responds spiritedly. The slow movement acts as an interlude of cool simplicity before the comparably vigorous finale, in which Schiller's digital dexterity adds to the sparkle without detracting from his seriousness of purpose. Vigour is also the keynote of the outer movements of the *A major*, K.488, and the freshness is striking. But again the *Adagio* offers a direct, unadorned approach which is on the plain side, although better this than romantic idiosyncrasy. Mackerras then proceeds to give fine stylish performances of both symphonies, generous with repeats and splendidly played. Though the inclusion of harpsichord continuo will not please everyone, these performances are refreshingly invigorating and throughout the disc the recording (from the mid-1970s) is excellent.

Piano concertos Nos.20 in D min., K.466; 27 in B flat, K.595.
(N) *** Sony SK 42241 [id.]. Murray Perahia, ECO.

Perahia produces wonderfully soft colourings and a luminous texture in the *B flat Concerto*, yet at the same time he avoids underlining too strongly the valedictory sense that inevitably haunts this magical score. In the *D minor Concerto* none of the darker, disturbing undercurrents go uncharted, but at the same time we remain within the sensibility of the period. An indispensable issue, well recorded and excellently transferred.

Piano concertos Nos. 21 in C, K.467; 22 in E flat, K.482.
(N) *** Chandos Dig. CHAN 9404 [id.]. LMP, Howard Shelley.

Howard Shelley's cycle continues to delight, and his survey of the Mozart canon survives the most exalted comparisons. The *C major* has dignity, intelligence and poetic feeling. The *E flat* has poise and breadth, and the winds of the London Mozart Players are heard to good advantage. These performances can be confidently recommended alongside the very finest rivals, such as Perahia (Sony) and Andras Schiff/Sándor Végh (Decca).

Piano concertos Nos. 21 in C, K.467; 23 in A, K.488.
(Y/B) (M) *** Virgin/EMI Dig. CUV5 61123-2 [id.]. Jean-Bernard Pommier, Sinfonia Varsovia.

A suprisingly rare coupling of what are now arguably the two favourite Mozart piano concertos here works very well indeed. Both performances have plenty of sparkle in outer movements – the first movement of K.467 is particularly arresting – and both slow movements are played simply and beautifully. Jean-Bernard Pommier's *Adagio* in K.488 compares favourably with Brendel's, and the string playing at the famous opening of the *Andante* of K.467 is ravishing in its transparent delicacy and gentle warmth. The finale of the same work is brisk but never sounds rushed. The sound is first class.

Piano concertos Nos. 21 in C, K.467; 24 in C min., K.491.
(Y/B) (M) *** Carlton IMP Dig. PCD 2006 [id.]. Howard Shelley, City of L. Sinfonia.

Howard Shelley gives delightfully fresh and characterful readings of both the popular *C major* and the great *C minor* concertos, bringing out their strength and purposefulness as well as their poetry, never overblown or sentimental. His Carlton (formerly Pickwick) disc makes an outstanding digital bargain, with accompaniment very well played and recorded.

Piano concertos Nos. 21 in C, K.467; 25 in C, K.503.
❀ (B) *** Ph. 426 077-2. Kovacevich, LSO, C. Davis.

The partnership of Kovacevich and Davis almost invariably produces inspired music-making. Their balancing of strength and charm, drama and tenderness, make for performances which retain their sense of spontaneity but which plainly result from deep thought, and the weight of both these great C major works is formidably conveyed. The 1972 recording is well balanced and refined.

(i) *Piano concertos Nos. 21 in C, K.467; 26 in D (Coronation), K.537;* (ii) *12 Variations on 'Ah, vous dirai-je, Maman', K.265.*
(N) ❀ (B) *** Sony SBK 67178; *SBT 67178* [id.]. (i) Robert Casadesus, Columbia SO or Cleveland O, Szell; (ii) André Previn (piano).

The ravishing slow movement of K.467 has never sounded more magical than here, and Casadesus then takes the finale at a tremendous speed; but, for the most part, this is exquisite Mozart playing, beauti-fully paced and articulated. Although the orchestra tends to dwarf the pianist in tuttis, the subtleties of the solo playing are well caught. For the *Coronation concerto* the balance tends to favour the soloist, but the smaller orchestral scale is telling and the accompaniment could hardly be more stylish. Casadesus and Szell are again inspired to a totally memorable performance, and again the slow movement is captivating: Casadesus's Mozart may at first seem understated, but the imagination behind his readings is apparent in every phrase. And as if this were not enough for a bargain reissue, Sony have added a superb account of the *'Ah, vous dirai-je' variations* ('Twinkle, twinkle, little star') from the young André Previn, recorded in Hollywood in 1962. The crisp articulation and stylish overview are a joy, and the end result is wonderfully spontaneous.

Piano concertos Nos. 21 in C, K.467; 27 in B flat, K.595.
*** Sony Dig. SK 46485 [id.]. Murray Perahia, COE.
(M) **(*) Carlton MCD 74 [id.]. Fou Ts'ong, Sinfonia Varsovia.

Murray Perahia gives performances of characteristic understanding and finesse with the Chamber Orchestra of Europe. There are new and different insights into both works though neither reading necessarily displaces his earlier accounts with the ECO, which may have a slight edge on the newcomer in terms of freshness and spontaneity.

Fou Ts'ong and the Sinfonia Varsovia give us very musical playing and have the advantage of exemplary recording, well balanced and in a warm, beautifully spacious acoustic. There is much to admire, though the occasional mannerism must be noted, and there are times in both works when one feels that the vital sense of flow is not quite vital enough. All the same there is a great deal to enjoy here and, were it at bargain price, it would be competitive. The pianist-conductor's humming is occasionally audible and, though less obtrusive than Glenn Gould in this respect, is unwelcome.

(i) *Piano concerto No. 22 in E flat, K.482. Serenade No. 13 in G (Eine kleine Nachtmusik), K.525; Symphony No. 40 in G min., K.550.*
(Y/B) (M) ** BBC Radio Classics BBCRD 9112 [id.]. (i) Michael Roll; BBC SO, Sir John Pritchard.

Michael Roll's account of the great *E flat Concerto*, K.482, comes from a 1971 Prom and is a reading of much pianistic finesse and musical elegance. The sound is a bit thick and tubby – and there are some restive coughs. Sir John Pritchard's *G minor Symphony* is a 1981 Prom performance; it is warm and musicianly and is untouched by routine. Big-band, old-fashioned Mozart, it nevertheless has a certain style. *Eine kleine Nachtmusik* is lighter in touch, and the players appear to be enjoying themselves. The sound is a bit heavy and opaque but, for all its its sonic limitations, this is worth considering at its modest price – in particular for the sake of Michael Roll.

Piano concertos Nos. 22 in E flat, K.482; 23 in A, K.488.
*** Ph. Dig. 420 187-2 [id.]. Mitsuko Uchida, ECO, Tate.

In balance, fidelity and sense of presence, few recordings of Mozart piano concertos can match Uchida's fine coupling of the late *E flat*, K.482, with its immediate successor, the beautiful *A major*, and Uchida's thoughtful manner, at times a little understated, is ideally set against outstanding playing from the ECO with its excellent wind soloists.

Piano concertos Nos. 22 in E flat, K.482; 24 in C min., K.491.
(N) *** Sony SK 42242 [id.]. Perahia, ECO.
(M) **(*) Carlton Dig. MCD 79 [id.]. Fou Ts'ong, Sinfonia Varsovia.

Not only is Perahia's contribution inspired in the great *E flat Concerto*, but the wind players of the ECO are at their most eloquent in the slow movement. Moreover the *C minor Concerto* emerges here as a truly Mozartian tragedy, rather than as foreshadowing Beethoven, which some artists give us. Both recordings are improved in focus and definition in the CD transfer.

Like his coupling of Nos. 21 and 27, Fou Ts'ong gives accomplished, highly musical accounts of these two concertos, the playing lacking in neither style nor vividness. On the whole, K.482 is more memorable than K.491, with expressive and bracing playing in good balance, but there are more deeply searching readings of the *C minor*, and one again wishes that this record was in their bargain range when it would have been far more competitive.

Piano concertos Nos. 22 in E flat, K.482; 26 in D (Coronation), K.537.
(Y/B) (M) *** DG Dig. 447 283-2 [id.]. Malcolm Bilson (fortepiano), E. Bar. Soloists, Gardiner.

The *Coronation concerto* is presented strongly as well as elegantly, with the authentic timpani cutting dramatically through the textures in the first movement. Full and spacious recording in a helpful acoustic. The earlier concerto is hardly less vibrant and lyrically convincing, with the contrasts of the finale particularly effective.

Piano concertos Nos. 23 in A, K.488; 24 in C min., K.491.
(M) *** DG 423 885-2 [id.]. Kempff, Bamberg SO, Leitner.
**(*) Virgin/EMI Dig. VC7 59280-2 [id.]. Mikhail Pletnev, Deutsche Kammerphilharmonie.
(Y/B) (M) **(*) Ph. Dig. 442 648-2 [id.]. Mitsuko Uchida, ECO, Tate.

(i) *Piano concertos Nos. 23 in A, K.488;* (ii) *24 in C min., K.491; Rondo in A, K.511.*
(M) *** RCA GD 87968 [7968-2-RG]. Rubinstein, RCA Victor SO, (i) Alfred Wallenstein; (ii) Josef Krips.

Kempff's outstanding performances of these concertos are uniquely poetic and inspired, and Leitner's accompaniments are comparably distinguished. The 1960 recording still sounds well, and this is strongly recommended at mid-price.

Rubinstein brings characteristic finesse and beauty of phrasing to his coupling; K.488 is especially beautiful. In K.491 the crystal-clear articulation is allied to the aristocratic feeling characteristic of vintage Rubinstein: the slow movement is memorable in its poise. Krips's accompaniment acts as a foil to the tragic tone of this great and wonderfully balanced work. The recordings, from 1958 and 1961 respectively, sound fresh, and the *Rondo*, recorded in 1959, is equally distinguished.

Pletnev and the Deutsche Kammerphilharmonie have obviously established a close rapport and there is great personality here – whether you like everything about it or not. In Pletnev's hands the slow movement of the *A major Concerto* is among the most beautiful on record, the finale the most rushed – many may find it unacceptable. In the *C minor Concerto* he is intensely dramatic, Beethovenian in feeling and powerful in conception: his own first-movement cadenza looks even more forward into the nineteenth century. There is nothing bland here: commanding playing from all concerned, but not to all tastes.

It a pity that for this reissue Philips abandoned the original coupling (K.482 and K.488) which made a fascinating match, presenting illuminating contrasts rather than similarities. In No. 23, Uchida's thoughtful manner, at times a little understated, is ideally set against outstanding playing from the ECO with its excellent wind soloists. In No. 24, in spite of a dramatic opening from Jeffrey Tate, her tonal refinement and delicacy are sometimes in stronger evidence than her sense of scale, and that applies especially to the reticent slow movement and finale.

Piano concertos Nos. 23 in A, K.488; 26 (Coronation), K.537.
(M) **(*) Teldec/Warner Dig. 4509 92150-2 [id.]. Friedrich Gulda, Concg. O, Harnoncourt.

Friedrich Gulda discreetly participates in the orchestral *ritornelli*. The playing of the Concertgebouw Orchestra is careful in handling both balance and nuances, and Nikolaus Harnoncourt is particularly successful in conducting the *Coronation concerto*. Gulda gives an admirably unaffected and intelligent account of the *A major*, which is enjoyable – as, for that matter, is his reading of the *Coronation* – but it does not constitute a challenge to such rivals as Perahia or Brendel or Ashkenazy in K.488.

Piano concertos Nos. 23 in A, K.488; 27 in B flat, K.595.
(Y/B) (M) *** Ph. 442 391-2 [id.]. Alfred Brendel, ASMF, Marriner.

On Philips, two of the best of Brendel's Mozart concertos. However, these performances are included in

Brendel's two Duo sets of Mozart concertos (one in each) and these represent marvellous value; the present disc remains of interest to those requiring only this particular coupling.

(i) *Piano concerto No. 26 in D, K.537;* (ii) *Piano and wind quintet in E flat, K.452.*
(Y/B) *** Decca Dig. 443 877-2 [id.]. András Schiff, (i) Camerata Ac. Mozarteum, Salzburg, Végh; (ii) Holliger, Schmid, Thunemann, Vladkovic.

Musically the Schiff–Végh survey of the Mozart concertos, now nearing its end, has proved a great success, though the acoustic of the Grosser Saal of the Salzburg Mozarteum may be a shade too resonant for some tastes. Not in any doubt is the quality of his playing or the musicianship of Sándor Végh. The coupling, the *Quintet for piano and wind,* made in the Mozartsaal of the Konzerthaus, is marvellously done, though some may feel Schiff's instrument is a trifle reticently balanced in relation to the wind.

Piano concerto No. 27 in B flat, K.595; (i) *Double piano concerto in E flat, K.365.*
❀ (M) *** DG 419 059-2 [id.]. Emil Gilels, VPO, Boehm, (i) with Elena Gilels.

Gilels's is supremely lyrical playing that evinces all the classical virtues. No detail is allowed to detract from the picture as a whole; the pace is totally unhurried and superbly controlled. All the points are made by means of articulation and tone, and each phrase is marvellously alive, while Boehm and the Vienna Philharmonic provide excellent support. The performance of the marvellous *Double concerto* is no less enjoyable. Its mood is comparatively serious, but this is not to suggest that the music's sunny qualities are not brought out. The quality on CD is first class, refining detail yet not losing ambient warmth.

(i) *Piano concerto No. 27 in B flat, K.595. Piano sonatas Nos. 11 in A, K.331; 14 in C min., K.457.*
(M) **(*) Decca 433 898-2 [id.]. Backhaus, (i) VPO, Karl Boehm.
(M) **(*) Decca 448 600-2 [id.] (without *Sonatas*). Backhaus, VPO, Boehm – BRAHMS: *Piano concerto No. 2.* ***

Backhaus is magisterial and, if he is rhythmically rather uneven and the performance of the concerto does not always flow smoothly, the performance, very well accompanied by Boehm, has great character. The two *Sonatas* are also welcome. The manner is a little unsmiling in its directness, but the classicism is appealing in its total lack of romantic overlay. There is something very compelling about this music-making, for Backhaus's personality projects strongly in every bar. The early (1955) stereo is remarkably truthful. (This is also available coupled with Brahms's *Second Concerto* in Decca's Classic Sound series.)

Violin concertos

Complete Mozart Edition, Volume 8: (i) *Violin concertos Nos 1–5; 7 in D, K.271; Adagio in E, K.261; Rondo in B flat, K.269; Rondo in C, K.373.* (i; ii) *Concertone, K.190;* (iii; iv) *Double Concerto in D for violin, piano and orchestra, K.315f;* (iii; v; vi) *Sinfonia concertante in A, for violin, viola, cello and orchestra, K.320e.* (iii; v) *Sinfonia concertante in E flat, K.364.*
(M) **(*) Ph. Analogue/Dig. 422 508-2 (4). (i) Szeryng; (ii) with Poulet, Morgan, Jones; New Philh. O, Gibson; (iii) Iona Brown, with (iv) Shelley; (v) Imai; (vi) Orton; ASMF, Marriner.

Philip Wilby has here not only completed the first movement of an early *Sinfonia concertante for violin, viola and cello* (Mozart's only music with concertante cello) but also, through shrewd detective work, has reconstructed a full three-movement *Double concerto* from what Mozart left as 'a magnificent torso', to use Alfred Einstein's description; it is for violin, piano and orchestra. The result here is a delight, a full-scale 25-minute work which ends with an effervescent double-variation finale, alternately in duple and compound time. That is superbly done with Iona Brown and Howard Shelley as soloists; and the other ASMF items are very good too, with Iona Brown joined by Nobuko Imai most characterfully on the viola in the great *Sinfonia concertante*, K.364. What is a shade disappointing is to have Henryk Szeryng's readings of the main violin concertos from the 1960s instead of the Grumiaux set. Szeryng is sympathetic but a trifle reserved and not as refreshing as Grumiaux.

Violin concertos Nos. 1–5; Adagio in E, K.261; Rondo in C, K.373.
(N) (B) **(*) Sony SBK 46539/40; *MBK 46539/40* [id.]. Zukerman, St Paul CO.

Zukerman's set has the advantage of excellent digital recording and a good balance, the violin forward but not distractingly so. The playing of outer movements is agreeably simple and fresh, and in slow movements Zukerman's sweetness of tone will appeal to many, although his tendency to languish a little in his expressiveness, particularly in the *G major*, K.216, rather less so in the *A major*, K.219, may be counted a less attractive feature, and he is not always subtle in his expression of feeling. Nevertheless this is still enjoyably spontaneous music-making and his admirers will certainly not be disappointed with K.219. The shorter pieces are played with some flair, the *Adagio* most appealingly. The St Paul Chamber Orchestra accompanies with stylish warmth. This set is excellent value and the two discs (and cassettes) are available separately, with concertos 1–3 together on the first.

Violin concertos Nos. (i) *1 in B flat, K.207;* (ii) *2 in D, K.211;* (iii) *3 in G, K.216;* (ii) *4 in D, K.218;* (i) *5 in A (Turkish), K.219;* (ii) *Adagio in E, K.261; Rondo in C, K.373.* (iv) *Concertone for 2 violins and orchestra in C, K.190; Sinfonia concertante in E flat for violin, viola and orchestra, K.364.*
(N) (M) **(*) Sony Stern Edition I SM3K 66475 (3) [id.]. Isaac Stern, with (i) Columbia SO, Szell; (ii) ECO, Schneider; (iii) Cleveland O, Szell; (iv) Zukerman, ECO, Barenboim.

It goes without saying that Stern's solo playing is always splendid; it is simply that he is not always as sensitive on detail as his rivals, and this especially applies to No. 1 and rather less so to No. 5 where the accompaniment is provided by the Columbia Symphony Orchestra under Szell. The interpretation of No. 3, however, displays Stern's qualities of sparkling stylishness at their most intense in a very satisfying reading, with a beautifully poised and pointed accompaniment from the same conductor but now with the splendid Cleveland Orchestra. In Nos. 2 and 4, Stern has the benefit of rather fuller recording and his playing, as always, is full of personality. The great *Sinfonia concertante* stands among the finest available and is certainly the jewel in this set, presenting as it does two soloists of equally strong musical personality, and listening to the solo concertos again, so impressively remastered, is to relish the sheer beauty of Stern's tone and phrasing. The *Concertone* is attractive enough, if not one of Mozart's most inspired pieces, and here the dryness of the acoustic rather detracts from the charm of a work which on any count goes on too long for its material. Stern, Zukerman and Barenboim pay the central *Andantino grazioso* the compliment of a really slow tempo, and though this makes a very long movement the concentration is superb. Whatever the shortcomings of the recording, the artistry of the soloists shines out through every bar.

Violin concertos Nos. 1 in B flat, K.207; 2 in D, K.211; 5 in A (Turkish), K.219.
(Y/B) (M) *** Virgin/EMI Dig. VC5 45010-2 [id.]. Monica Huggett, O of Age of Enlightenment.

Violin concertos Nos. 3 in G, K.216; 4 in D, K.218; Adagio in E, K.261; Rondo in B flat, K.269.
(Y/B) (M) *** Virgin/EMI Dig. VC5 45060-2 [id.]. Monica Huggett, O of Age of Enlightenment.

Violin concertos Nos. 1–5; Adagio in E, K.261; Rondo in C, K.373; Rondo concertante in B flat, K.269.
(B) *** Double Decca 440 621-2 (2). Mayumi Fujikawa, RPO, Weller.
(Y/B) (M) **(*) DG Dig. 445 535-2 (2) [id.]. Itzhak Perlman, VPO, Levine.
(Y/B) (BB) **(*) RCA Navigator 74321 21277-2 (*Nos. 1–3 & Rondo, K.373*); 74321 21278-2 (*Nos. 4–5; Adagio, K.261 & Rondo K. 269*). Josef Suk, Prague CO, Libor Hlaváček.

(i) *Violin concertos Nos. 1–5;* (ii) *Adagio in E, K.261; Rondo in C, K.373;* (i; iii) *Sinfonia concertante in E flat, K.364.*
(B) *** Ph. Duo 438 323-2 (2) [id.]. Arthur Grumiaux, (i) LSO, C. Davis; (ii) New Philh. O, Leppard; (iii) with Arrigo Pellicia.

Violin concertos Nos. 1–5; (i) *Sinfonia concertante in E flat for violin, viola and orchestra, K.364.*
(Y/B) (BB) **(*) EMI Seraphim CES5 68530-2 (2) [CDEB 68530]. Sir Yehudi Menuhin, Bath Festival O; (i) with Rudolph Barshai.

Grumiaux's accounts of the Mozart *Violin concertos* come from the early 1960s and are among the most beautifully played in the catalogue at any price. The orchestral accompaniments have sparkle and vitality, and Grumiaux's contribution has splendid poise and purity of tone. For this generous reissue on their bargain Duo label, Philips have added the *Adagio*, K.261, and *Rondo*, K.373, recorded later in 1967, and also a fine performance of the great *Sinfonia concertante*, K.364, with Arrigo Pellicia proving a sensitive partner for Grumiaux, especially in the *Andante*. The new CD transfers are brightly lit but still faithful.

Mayumi Fujikawa has the advantage of admirably stylish and sympathetic accompaniments from Walter Weller, who secures consistently warm and polished playing from the RPO. Throughout there is much evidence of the soloist's musicianship and imagination, and every one of these performances comes sparklingly to life. Of course this set comes into direct competition with Grumiaux, also at bargain price, which must still remain a first choice. Yet the 1979/80 Decca recording is much warmer than the Philips, the violin is caught with complete naturalness and the orchestra is recorded so beautifully that this Double Decca set certainly holds its place.

If you want performances on original instruments, this Virgin set can be strongly recommended. Monica Huggett directs from the bow and she is a superb soloist: spontaneous, vital, warm and elegant.

She plays her own cadenzas, and very good they are too. Orchestral textures are fresh and transparent, ensemble is excellent, and the solo playing is without even a drop of vinegar; indeed the violin timbre, if not opulent, is firm, well focused and sparkling.

Perlman gives characteristically assured, virtuoso readings of these concertos of Mozart's youth, which, with Levine as a fresh and undistracting Mozartian, bring exceptionally satisfying co-ordination of forces. The virtuoso approach sometimes involves a tendency to hurry, and the power is emphasized by the weight and immediacy of the recording. Warmth is here rather than charm; but Perlman's individual magic makes for magnetic results all through, not least in the intimate intensity of slow movements. Those of the first two concertos are particularly graceful, but at times (and notably in the two most popular concertos, Nos. 3 and 5) he treats the works rather more as bravura showpieces than is common. However, Perlman's virtuosity is effortless and charismatic, and the orchestral playing is first class. The DG recording is well balanced, with the soloist close but not too excessively so, and the perspective is on the whole well judged.

However, the alternative set (available on two separate CDs) on RCA's super-bargain Navigator label is by no means upstaged. Josef Suk's recordings date from 1972. The solo playing has character, warmth and humanity, and its unaffected manner is especially suited to the first two concertos. The last three concertos have an agreeable simplicity and a freedom from histrionic gestures that is most welcome, and the recording, though not as vividly detailed as the DG, is agreeably smooth and natural. Hlaváček does not always make enough of the dynamic contrasts and, throughout, this music-making is dominated by Suk. This is partly a matter of the recording balance. But with any reservations noted, these are delightful performances and very good value.

Menuhin's recordings date from the early 1960s, a fruitful period for this fine artist, when he was closely associated with the Bath Festival. Most violinists use cadenzas by Joachim, but in all but No. 3 (where he chooses those by Franco) Menuhin uses cadenzas of his own, and many may feel that they are not Mozartian. Otherwise the style is sensibly exploited, and these performances give an engaging sense of musicians making intimate music together for the joy of it. There is plenty of warmth and colour. First movements are sufficiently ebullient, without loss of dignity and grace, due to a nice choice of tempi. The solo playing is not always immaculate, and compared, say, with Grumiaux it is romantic, yet in slow movements Mozart's melodies are floated gracefully and effortlessly. One is always conscious that this is the phrasing of a master musician who can also provide the lightest touch in finales, which are alert and extrovert. In the *Sinfonia concertante* Menuhin and Barshai comprise a splendid team with happily similar views. Throughout, the stereo has a bright sheen and, with the remastering, the orchestral violins are made to sound glassy above the stave, but the ear adjusts when the music-making is so distinctive and the acoustic is basically warm.

Violin concertos Nos. 1 in B flat, K.207; 2 in D, K.211; Rondo No. 1 in B flat, K.269.
*** Denon Dig. C37 7506 [id.]. Jean-Jacques Kantorow, Netherlands CO, Hager.

Violin concertos Nos. 1 in B flat, K.207; 2 in D, K.211; Rondo in B flat, K.269; Andante in F (arr. Saint-Saëns from *Piano concerto No. 21, K.467*).
(BB) **(*) Naxos Dig. 8.550414 [id.]. Takako Nishizaki, Capella Istropolitana, Johannes Wildner.

Kantorow's coupling makes an excellent start to his Mozart series. He is given alert, stylish accompaniments by Leopold Hager and the Netherlands Chamber Orchestra, and the recording is eminently realistic. The *B flat Rondo* makes an excellent bonus. Kantorow plays his own cadenzas – and very good they are.

This was the last disc to be recorded (in 1990) of Takako Nishizaki's fine survey of the violin concertos. The opening movement of K.207 is brisk and fresh, although this is the least individual of Nishizaki's readings. The *Second Concerto*, K.211, has rather more flair, the *Andante* touchingly phrased, and the finale has a winning lightness of touch. The *Rondo* is also an attractively spontaneous performance, and as an encore we are offered Saint-Saëns's arrangement of the famous '*Elvira Madigan*' theme from the *C major Concerto*, K.467.

Violin concertos Nos. 2 in D, K.211; 4 in D, K.218.
*** EMI Dig. CDC7 47011-2 [id.]. Anne-Sophie Mutter, Philh. O, Muti.

Anne-Sophie Mutter is given very sensitive support from the Philharmonia under Muti. Her playing combines purity and classical feeling, delicacy and incisiveness, and is admirably expressive. The EMI recording is very good; the images are sharply defined, but the balance is convincing.

Violin concerto No. 3 in G, K.216.
(N) (B) *** EMI forte CZS5 69331-2 (2) [id.]. David Oistrakh, Philh. O – BEETHOVEN: *Triple concerto;* BRAHMS: *Double concerto;* PROKOFIEV: *Violin concerto No. 2.* ***

(N) *** EMI Dig. CDC5 55426-2 [id.]. Frank Peter Zimmermann, BPO, Sawallisch – BRAHMS: *Violin concerto*. **(*)

David Oistrakh was at his finest in this beautiful 1958 performance of Mozart's *G major Concerto*. His supple, richly toned yet essentially classical style suits the melodic line of this youthful work and gives it the stature of maturity. The orchestral contribution is directed by the soloist himself and is surprisingly polished. EMI provide admirably smooth yet vivid sound, and this is just one of four marvellous performances which make up this forte compilation, one of the finest concertante bargains in the catalogue.

With the the string complement of the Berlin Philharmonic aptly reduced, and with Sawallisch at his most sparkling, Zimmermann's studio recording of Mozart's *G major Concerto* is a delight, with a quicksilver lightness in the outer movements, very different from the traditional big bow-wow approach, and a compelling repose and concentration in the central *Adagio*. In its own right this is superb music-making, but it was perverse to couple it with Brahms rather than other violin concertos by Mozart.

(i) *Violin concertos Nos. 3 in G, K.216; 4 in D, K.218;* (ii) *Duo for violin and viola in G, K.423.*
(M) **(*) DG Dig. 439 525-2 [id.]. Gidon Kremer; (i) VPO, Harnoncourt; (ii) Kim Kashkashian.

Kremer and Harnoncourt make a characterful partnership in the Mozart violin concertos, although Harnoncourt is nothing if not eccentric. In the *G major*, K.216, the first movement flows at just the right pace, and then in the *Andante* a comma is placed to romanticize the climbing opening phrase of the main theme slightly. But with Kremer playing sweetly throughout, such individual touches may be found very acceptable (including a long cadenza in the first movement of No. 3) when there is plenty of vitality and Harnoncourt's tuttis are always strong. The *Duo* (quite substantial at 17 minutes) makes an interesting bonus, with skilful playing and a good balance between Kremer and Kashkashian. But there is more to this music than these players find.

(i) *Violin concertos Nos. 3 in G, K.216; 4 in D, K.218. Serenade: Eine kleine Nachtmusik, K.525.*
(Y/B) (M) **(*) Sony stereo/mono SMK 64468 [id.]. (i) Zino Francescatti; Columbia SO, Walter.

Francescatti's coupling of the *Third* and *Fourth* Mozart *Concertos* is probably his best record, and in their remastered CD format these fine performances from 1958, recorded in California, are given a new lease of life. The playing is at times a little wayward, but Bruno Walter accompanies throughout with his usual warmth and insight and falls into line sympathetically with his soloist. Both slow movements are beautifully played, albeit with an intensity that barely stops short of romanticism. In some ways the *D major* suits Francescatti's opulent style of playing best. The whole atmosphere of this music-making represents the pre-authentic approach to Mozart at its most rewarding. The 1954 New York recording of the *Night music* is no great asset. The playing is acceptable but the string recording is harsh and ill-focused.

Violin concertos Nos. 3 in G, K.216; 5 in A (Turkish), K.219.
(BB) *** Naxos Dig. 8.550063 [id.]. Takako Nishizaki, Capella Istropolitana, Stephen Gunzenhauser.

This is the finest of Nishizaki's three discs of the Mozart violin concertos on Naxos. The readings are individual and possess the most engaging lyrical feeling and the natural response of the soloist to Mozartian line and phrase. A good balance, the soloist forward, but convincingly so, and the orchestral backcloth in natural perspective. A real bargain.

Violin concerto No. 4 in D, K.218.
(***) EMI mono CDH7 64562-2 [id.]. Szigeti, LPO, Beecham – MENDELSSOHN: *Violin concerto;* PROKOFIEV: *Violin concerto No. 1.* (***)
(**) Pearl mono GEMM CDS 9996 [id.]. Kreisler, LSO, Sir Landon Ronald – BACH: *Double violin concerto;* BEETHOVEN; BRAHMS; MENDELSSOHN; *Violin concertos.* (**)

Szigeti recorded the *D major Concerto* with that consummate Mozartian, Sir Thomas Beecham, a decade after the Kreisler version, and the combination produces music-making of a high order. It comes with a magical account of the Prokofiev *D major Concerto* and a fine Mendelssohn. Of the two transfers of the same coupling now on offer, the EMI is far smoother and more revealing.

The Kreisler account with Sir Landon Ronald comes from 1924 and his thrilling, glorious tone survives acoustic technique and the inevitable surface noise which Pearl have not fully succeeded in taming. It comes in harness with a host of other remarkable performances.

Violin concerto No. 4 in D, K.218; (i) *Sinfonia concertante in E flat, for violin, viola and orchestra, K.364.*
(BB) **(*) Naxos Dig. 8.550332 [id.]. Takako Nishizaki, (i) Ladislav Kyselak; Capella Istropolitana, Stephen Gunzenhauser.

A fine account of No. 4, with Takako Nishizaki's solo playing well up to the high standard of this series and with Stephen Gunzenhauser's perceptive pacing adding to our pleasure. The *Sinfonia concertante* is very enjoyable too, if perhaps slightly less distinctive. The finale is infectious in its liveliness, its rhythms buoyantly pointed. Again, a good balance and excellent sound.

Violin concertos Nos. 4, K.218; 5 (Turkish), K.219.
*** Nimbus Dig. NI 5009. Oscar Shumsky, SCO, Yan Pascal Tortelier.

Shumsky's performances with the Scottish Chamber Orchestra have the advantage of being totally unaffected, natural and full of character. Yan Pascal Tortelier secures a very alive and thoroughly musical response from the orchestra. The recording is nicely balanced.

Violin concertos Nos. 4 in D, K.218; 5 in A (Turkish), K.219; Adagio in E, K.261; Rondos Nos. 1 in B flat, K.269; 2 in C, K.373.
(M) **(*) EMI CDM7 64868-2 [id.]. David Oistrakh, BPO.

David Oistrakh's performances come from his complete set, recorded in 1970/71. The slow movement of K.219 is particularly fine, and so too is the finale. The three shorter concertante works also show the soloist at his finest; though the accompaniment for the *Adagio*, K.261, remains richly upholstered, this is played very beautifully. With 77 minutes of music this is excellent value, for the soloist is truthfully caught and the balance is convincing.

Violin concerto No. 5 in A (Turkish), K.219.
(M) *** RCA 09026 61757-2 [61757-2-RG]. Heifetz with CO – *String quintet, K.516* etc. ***
(Y/B) (M) *** DG 447 403-2 [id.]. Wolfgang Schneiderhan, BPO, Jochum – BEETHOVEN: *Violin concerto*. *** ⊛

Marvellously exhilarating Mozart from Heifetz, though his actual entry in the first movement is quite ethereal. He directs the accompanying group himself, the only time he did so on record. The early (1954) stereo is fully acceptable and the performance memorable, with the crystalline clarity of articulation matched by warmth of timbre and aristocratic phrasing.

This was perhaps the finest of the complete set of Mozart's violin concertos which Schneiderhan recorded with the Berlin Philharmonic in the late 1960s. He plays with effortless mastery and a strong sense of classical proportion, and the Berlin orchestra support him well. The recording is realistically balanced, and this makes a generous coupling for his famous record of the Beethoven, made six years earlier.

(i) *Violin concerto No. 5 in A (Turkish), K.219; Symphony No. 35 in D (Haffner).*
(N) (M) (**) Sony mono SMK 68446. (i) Erica Morini; French R. O, George Szell – HAYDN: *Symphony No. 92.* (**)

The French orchestra is a degree less polished than Szell's own Cleveland Orchestra in his studio recording, but greater relaxation in the slow movement, taken at a slower speed, makes the result more winning, less severe. The violinist, Erica Morini, too little recorded, is a soloist who responds positively to an intimate setting, the opposite of a showy virtuoso. In places the edginess of violin tone in this 1959 recording makes the intonation suspect, but this is a poetic and felt performance.

(i) *Concertone in C, K.190;* (ii) *Sinfonia concertante in E flat, for violin, viola and orchestra, K.364.*
⊛ *** DG 415 486-2 [id.]. Perlman, Zukerman, Israel PO, Mehta.
*** Sony Dig. SK 47693 [id.]. Cho-Liang Lin, Jaime Laredo, ECO, Leppard.
**(*) RCA Dig. 09026 60467-2 [id.]. Vladimir Spivakov, with (i) Boris Garlitski; (ii) Shlomo Mintz; Moscow Virtuosi.

The DG version of the *Sinfonia concertante* was recorded in Tel Aviv at the Huberman Festival in December 1982. It is balanced with the soloists a fraction too near the microphones. The performance is in a special class and is an example of 'live' recording at its most magnetic, with the inspiration of the occasion caught on the wing. Zubin Mehta is drawn into the music-making and accompanies most sensitively. The *Concertone* is also splendidly done; the ear notices the improvement in the sound-balance of the studio recording of this work. But the *Sinfonia concertante*, with the audience incredibly quiet, conveys an electricity rarely caught on record.

Cho-Liang Lin's outstanding performance of the *Sinfonia concertante* is also mandatory listening. The playing has great finesse and style, and Lin makes a natural partnership with Laredo. Neil Black (oboe) and Charles Tunnell (cello) add to the distinction of the *Concertone*. The recording is reverberant, which brings a large-scale orchestral image, but it is fuller and smoother than the DG alternative.

Highly accomplished playing from Vladimir Spivakov and Shlomo Mintz on the viola, eminently vital and musicianly, as is the playing of the Moscow Virtuosi both in the *Sinfonia concertante* and in the

Concertone. Boris Garlitski is Spivakov's excellent partner in the latter, and the oboist Mikhail Evstigoreev is worth special mention for his purity of tone and style. Both performances give pleasure but do not resonate in the memory in the way that classic accounts do. The recordings, made in the Herkulessaal in Munich, are clean and well focused.

Dances and Marches

Contredanses: La Bataille, K.535; Das Donerwetter, K.534; Les filles malicieuses, K.610; Der Sieg vom Helden Koburg, K.587; Il trionfo delle donne, K.607. Gallimathias musicum (quodlibet), K.32; 6 German dances, K.567; 3 German dances, K.605; German dance: Die Leyerer, K.611. March in D, K.335/1. A Musical joke, K.522.
*** DG Dig. 429 783-2 [id.]. Orpheus CO.

A splendid sampler of the wit and finesse, to say nothing of the high quality of entertainment, provided by Mozart's dance music, which kept people on their feet till dawn at masked balls in the 1780s and early 1790s. The playing of the Orpheus group is winningly polished, flexible and smiling, and they bring off the *Musical joke* with considerable flair, both in the gentle fun of the *Adagio cantabile*, which is exquisitely played, and in the outrageous grinding dissonance of the 'wrong notes' at the end. First-class sound, fresh, transparent and vividly immediate.

Complete Mozart Edition, Volume 6: La Chasse, KA.103/K.299d; Contredanses, K.101; K.123; K.267; K.269b; K.462; (Das Donnerwetter) K.534; (La Bataille) K.535; 535a; (Der Sieg vom Helden Koburg) K.587; K.603; (Il trionfo delle donne) K.607; (Non più andrai) K.609; K.610; Gavotte, K.300; German dances, K.509; K.536; K.567; K.571; K.586; K.600; K.602; K.605; Ländler, K.606; Marches, K.214; K.363; K.408; K.461; Minuets, K.61b; K.61g/2; K.61h; K.94, 103, 104, 105; K.122; K.164; K.176; K.315g; K.568; K.585; K.599; K.601; K.604; Minuets with Contredanses, K.463; Overture & 3 Contredanses, K.106.
🏵 (M) *** Ph. 422 506-2 (6). V. Mozart Ens., Willi Boskovsky.

Much of the credit for this remarkable undertaking should go to its expert producer, Erik Smith, who, besides providing highly stylish orchestrations for numbers without Mozart's own scoring, illuminates the music with some of the most informative and economically written notes that ever graced a record. The CD transfers preserve the excellence of the mid-1960s sound. The collector might feel that he or she is faced here with an *embarras de richesses* with more than 120 *Minuets*, nearly 50 *German dances* and some three dozen *Contredanses*, but Mozart's invention is seemingly inexhaustible, and the instrumentation is full of imaginative touches.

2 Contredanses, K.603; Contredanse, K.610; 19 German Dances, K.571/1–6; K.600/1–6; K.602/1–4; K.605/1–3; Marches: in D, K.335/1; in C & D, K.408/1–3; 10 Minuets, K.599/1–6; K.601/1–4.
(M) *** Decca 430 634-2 [id.]. V. Mozart Ens., Willi Boskovsky.

A self-recommending single-disc selection from Boskovsky's admirable survey of Mozart's dance music. The selection, of course, includes the famous *Sleigh ride* (within K.605) which has some superb post-horn playing, and there are other special effects, notably the charming hurdy-gurdy of K.602. The transfers are impeccable.

German dances, K.509/1–6; K.536/1–6; K.567/1–6; K.571/1–6; 12 German dances, K. 586.
(Y/B) *** Sony Dig. SK 46696 [id.]. Tafelmusik, Bruno Weil.

Of period-instrument ensembles, Tafelmusik must be numbered among the most persuasive. They bring the advantages of authentic instruments (clarity of texture and lightness of articulation) without the attendant aural discomfort. Bruno Weil directs light and refreshing accounts of all these pieces and is very truthfully and cleanly recorded. Readers will find most of them enjoyable and some altogether captivating.

12 German dances, K.586; 6 German dances, K.600; 4 German dances, K.602; 3 German dances, K.605.
(BB) *** Naxos Dig. 8.550412 [id.]. Capella Istropolitana, Johannes Wildner.

Fresh, bright, unmannered performances of some of the dance music Mozart wrote right at the end of his life. The playing is excellent and the recording is bright and full. An excellent super-bargain alternative to the Boskovsky Decca CD.

Complete Mozart Edition, Volume 45: 'Rarities and curiosities': Contredanses in B flat & D (completed Smith); *The London Sketchbook:* (i) *3 Contredanses in F; 2 Contredanses in G; 6 Divertimenti.* (ii) *Wind divertimenti* arr. from operas: *Don Giovanni* (arr. Triebensee); *Die Entführung aus dem Serail* (arr. Wendt) & (i) *March, K 384.* (i; iii) *Rondo in E flat for horn and orchestra, K 371* (completed Smith); (iv) *Larghetto for piano and wind quintet, K 452a;* (v) *Modulating prelude in F/E min.* (vi) *Tantum ergo in B flat, K 142; in D, K 197;* (vii) *Idomeneo: Scene & rondo.* (viii) *Musical dice game, K.516.*

(M) *** Ph. 422 545-2 (3) [id.]. (i) ASMF, Marriner; (ii) Netherlands Wind Ens.; (iii) Timothy Brown; cond. Sillito; (iv) Uchida, Black, King, Farrell, O'Neil; (v) Erik Smith (harpsichord); (vi) Frimmer, Leipzig R. Ch. & SO, Schreier; (vii) Mentzler, Hendricks, Bav. RSO, C. Davis; (viii) Marriner & Smith.

The first CD includes the innocent little piano pieces from the child Mozart's 'London Notebook'. Erik Smith has orchestrated them and, if the results may not be important, they charm the ear at least as much as Mozart's early symphonies, with many unexpected touches. Marriner and the Academy are ideal performers and the 1971 recording is warm and refined. Then come the arrangements for wind of selections from two key operas, elegantly played by the Netherlands Wind Ensemble. Finally come the rarities and curiosities, the *Rondo for horn and orchestra* with the missing 60 bars (discovered only in 1989) now added, and the other music made good by Erik Smith. There is a curious finale in which Erik Smith and Sir Neville Marriner participate (with spoken comments) in a *Musical dice game* to decide the order of interchangeable phrases in a very simple musical composition. The result, alas, is something of a damp squib.

Divertimenti and Serenades

Divertimenti Nos. 2 in D, K.131; 15 in B flat, K.287.
(Y/B) (BB) *** Naxos Dig. 8.550996 [id.]. Capella Istropolitana, Harald Nerat.

If this is the start of a new Naxos series of Mozart *Divertimenti* from the Capella Istropolitana under Harald Nerat, then we are in for a treat. The playing is beautifully turned and polished. The string group seems just the right size, and they phrase elegantly; the sound is full and transparent, bringing the sweetest modern violin timbre, yet the effect is as refreshing as any period performance. The *D major Divertimento* is charmingly scored for flute, oboe, bassoon, four horns and strings, with woodwind adding frequent touches of colour, but it has a gracious second-movement *Adagio* cantilena of disarming simplicity for strings alone. The *B flat Divertimento* was written five years later, in Salzburg, and is scored more simply for two horns and strings. The lovely E flat major *Adagio* has that touch of gentle pathos that is Mozart's very own, and the finale brings a recitativo from the principal violin before its lighthearted conclusion, with a feather-light response from the violins.

Complete Mozart Edition, Volume 4: *Divertimenti for strings Nos. 1–3, K.136/8; Divertimenti for small orchestra Nos. 1 in E flat, K.113; 7 in D, K.205* (with *March in D, K.290*); *10 in F, K.247* (with *March in F, K.248*); *11 in D, K.251; 15 in B flat, K.287; 17 in D, K.334* (with *March in D, K.445*); *A Musical joke, K.622; Serenade (Eine kleine Nachtmusik), K.525.*
(M) *** Ph. Dig. 422 504-2 (5) [id.]. ASMF CO.

This is one of the most attractive of all the boxes in the Philips Mozart Edition. The music itself is a delight, the performances are stylish, elegant and polished, while the digital recording has admirable warmth and realistic presence and definition.

Divertimenti for strings Nos. 1–2, K.136/7; Serenades Nos. 6 (Serenata notturna), K.239; 13 (Eine kleine Nachtmusik), K.525.
*** Capriccio 10185 [id.]. Salzburg Mozarteum Camerata Academica, Végh.

Delightfully bold, fresh and characterful performances from the Salzburg group, very well recorded. Only in the slow movement of *Eine kleine Nachtmusik*, taken rather slowly, is the playing a shade less refined. Curiously, Végh changes the regular order of movements in K.137, making it a conventional fast-slow-fast piece, though neither the label nor the note recognizes the change.

Complete Mozart Edition, Volume 5: *Divertimentos for wind Nos. 3 in E flat, K.166; 4 in B flat, K.186; 6 in C, K.188; 8 in F, K.213; 9 in B flat K.240; 12 in E flat, K.252; 13 in F, K.253; 14 in B flat, K.270; 16 in E flat, K.289; in E flat, K.Anh. 226; in B flat, K.Anh. 227; Divertimentos for 3 basset horns, K.439b/1–5; Duos for 2 horns, K.487/1–12; Serenades for wind No. 10 in B flat, K.361; 11 in E flat, K.375; 12 in C min., K.388; Adagios: in F; B flat, K.410–11.*
(M) *** Ph. Analogue/Dig. 422 505-2 (6) [id.]. Holliger Wind Ens. (or members of); Netherlands Wind Ens., De Waart (or members of); ASMF, Marriner or Laird.

Mozart's wind music, whether in the ambitious *Serenades* or the simpler *Divertimenti*, brings a naturally felicitous blending of timbre and colour unmatched by any other composer. It seems that even when writing for the simplest combination of wind instruments, Mozart is incapable of being dull. The playing of the more ambitious works is admirably polished and fresh, and it is interesting to note that

Holliger's group provides a stylishly light touch and texture with the principal oboe dominating, while the blending of the Netherlanders is somewhat more homogeneous, though the effect is still very pleasing.

Divertimenti Nos. 10 in F, K.247; 11 in D, K.331.
**(*) Capriccio 10 203 [id.]. Salzburg Mozarteum Camerata Academica, Végh.

The playing, as in Végh's previous issues, has striking freshness and vitality; these are chamber orchestral performances on modern instruments, but the scale is admirable and the resonance adds a feeling of breadth. Although slow movements tend to be on the slow side, while not lacking grace, allegros sparkle and have dash without ever seeming hurried, even if ensemble isn't always absolutely immaculate.

Divertimenti Nos. 10 in F, K.247; 11 in D, K.251; 15 in B flat, K.287; 17 in D, K.334.
(N) (M) ** DG 449 094-2 (2). BPO, Karajan.

Needless to say, these are beautifully played performances (especially the slow movement and finale of K.287) and as such they prompt the liveliest admiration. At the same time there is a predictably suave elegance that seems to militate against spontaneity. Each phrase is exquisitely moulded, perfumed and powdered, and the result, although beguiling in its way, is just too much of a good thing. Cultured and effortless readings, smoothly recorded and well balanced, they somehow leave one untouched. There is too much legato and too little sparkle.

Divertimento No. 11 in D, K.251; Serenade No. 9 in D (Posthorn), K.320; 2 Marches in D, K.335/1–2.
**(*) Sony Dig. SK 53277 [id.]. BPO, Claudio Abbado.

Abbado uses a modest chamber group from the orchestra for the *Divertimento* and larger forces for the *Posthorn Serenade*. The playing is lively and cultivated, with plenty of rhythmic character and much finesse from the strings and a charming delicacy from the woodwind in the *concertante* movement of the *Serenade*. In the first Trio of the second Minuet of the latter work, Andrea Blau plays what sounds very like a treble recorder, a curious but effective change of colour. This is an enjoyable concert, very well recorded (the serenade at a live performance), but a smaller scale can be even more effective in this repertoire.

Divertimento No. 17; Divertimento for strings No. 1, K.136.
*** Denon Dig C37 7080 [id.]. Augmented Berlin Philh. Qt.

On Denon, a successful account from the augmented Berlin Philharmonia Quartet. The music-making is polished, spirited and full of warmth. The *String divertimento* is equally attractive but makes a less substantial encore than the ASMF programme. The digital recording is fresh and believable.

Complete Mozart Edition, Volume 25: (i) *Idomeneo* (ballet music), *K.367;* (ii) *Les petits riens* (ballet), *K.299b; Music for a pantomime (Pantalon und Colombine), K.446* (completed and orch. Beyer); *Sketches for a ballet intermezzo, K.299c* (completed and orch. Erik Smith); (iii) *Thamos, King of Egypt* (incidental music), *K.345.*
(M) *** Ph. 422 525-2 (2) [id.]. (i) Netherlands CO, David Zinman; (ii) ASMF, Marriner; (iii) Eickstädt, Pohl, Büchner, Polster, Adam, Berlin R. Ch. & State O, Klee.

This volume collects together Mozart's theatre music and makes a particularly enticing package. Zinman and his Netherlanders give a neatly turned account of the ballet from *Idomeneo*, musical and spirited. Marriner takes over with modern digital sound for *Les petits riens* and the two novelties, and the ASMF playing has characteristic elegance and finesse. The *Sketches for a ballet intermezzo* survive only in a single-line autograph, but Erik Smith's completion and scoring provide a series of eight charming vignettes, most with descriptive titles, ending with a piquant *Tambourin*. The music for *Pantalon and Columbine* (more mime than ballet) survives in the form of a first violin part, and Franz Beyer has skilfully orchestrated it for wind and strings, using the first movement of the *Symphony*, K.84, as the overture and the last movement of *Symphony*, K.120, as the finale. Beautifully played as it is here, full of grace and colour, this is a real find and the digital recording is first rate. *Thamos, King of Egypt* is marvellous music which it is good to have on record, particularly in such persuasive hands as these. The choral singing is impressive and the orchestral playing is excellent.

Masonic funeral music: see below, in VOCAL MUSIC, under Complete Mozart Edition, Volume 22
A Musical joke, K.522.
*** Erato/Warner Dig. 2292 45199-2 [id.]. Paillard CO, Paillard – L. MOZART: *Cassation* etc. ***

Happily paired with a high-spirited version of Leopold Mozart's *Toy symphony*, Paillard's account of Mozart's fun piece makes the most of its outrageous jokes, with the horns in the opening movement boldly going wrong and the final discordant clash sounding positively cataclysmic; yet it takes into account the musical values, too.

Overtures: *Apollo et Hyacinthus; Bastien und Bastienne; La clemenza di Tito; Così fan tutte; Don Giovanni; Die Entführung aus dem Serail; La finta giardiniera; Idomeneo; Lucio Silla; Mitridate, rè di Ponto; Le nozze di Figaro; Il rè pastore; Der Schauspieldirektor; Die Zauberflöte.*
(BB) *** Naxos Dig. 8.550185; *4550185* [id.]. Capella Istropolitana, Barry Wordsworth.

Wordsworth follows up his excellent series of Mozart symphonies for Naxos with this generous collection of overtures, no fewer than 14 of them, arranged in chronological order and given vigorous, stylish performances. In Italian overture form, *Mitridate* and *Lucio Silla*, like miniature symphonies, have separate tracks for each of their three contrasted sections. Very well recorded, the disc is highly recommendable at super-bargain price.

Overtures: *La clemenza di Tito; Così fan tutte; Don Giovanni; Die Entführunbg aus dem Serail; Idomeneo; Le nozze di Figaro; Der Schauspieldirektor; Die Zauberflöte. Serenade No. 13 (Eine kleine Nachtmusik).*
(Y/B) *** Sony Dig. SK 46695 [id.]. Tafelmusik, Bruno Weil.

Alert and vital performances by this Canadian period-instrument group under Bruno Weil. Mozart overtures do not come much fresher than this, and the players convey pleasure and delight in what they are doing. Very clean recording quality from the Sony team of engineers.

Serenades Nos. 1 in D, K.100; 7 in D (Haffner), K.250; 9 in D (Posthorn), K.320; 13 in G (Eine kleine Nachtmusik), K.525; Serenata notturna, K.239.
(Y/B) (B) **(*) Decca Double 443 458-2 (2) [id.]. Vienna Mozart Ens., Willi Boskovsky.

Boskovsky and the Vienna Mozart Ensemble play with elegance and sparkle, and these performances still sound outstandingly bracing and vivid. The recordings were made in the Sofiensaal over a decade between 1968 and 1978. The account of *Eine kleine Nachtmusik*, one of the freshest and most attractive on disc and dating from 1968, now has a somewhat astringent treble, while Boskovsky's 1973 *Posthorn Serenade*, which has a natural musicality and is very well balanced, seems rather dry in the matter of string-timbre, though the bloom remains on the wind and the posthorn is tangible in its presence. Like the *Haffner serenade*, it is marvellously alive, full of the sparkle and elegance we associate with this group, with admirable phrasing and feeling for detail, yet the *Haffner* (dating from 1972) has a distinctly warmer ambience. The very engaging earliest *Serenade in D*, K.100, has the greatest glow of all, although it was recorded in 1970. Nevertheless many will count this excellent value for money in Decca's two-for-the-price-of-one series, offering 159 minutes of music on the pair of CDs.

Serenades Nos. 3 in D, K.185; 4 in D (Colloredo), K.203.
(BB) *** Naxos Dig. 8.550413; *4550413* [id.]. Salzburg CO, Harald Nerat.

Well-played, nicely phrased and musical accounts on Naxos, recorded in a warm, reverberant acoustic, but one in which detail clearly registers. The Salzburg Chamber Orchestra has real vitality, and most readers will find these accounts musically satisfying and very enjoyable.

Serenades Nos. 3 in D, K.185; 13 in G (Eine kleine Nachtmusik), K.525.
(Y/B) (M) **(*) O-L Dig. 443 185-2 [id.]. Schröder, AAM, Hogwood.

Mozart's first large-scale *Serenade* dates from 1773. In this work Mozart established the feature of including a miniature violin concerto as part of the structure, though here its movements are interspersed with others. This presents the drawback to the present recording, for Schröder's account of the solo violin role in the *Andante* is rather too straight and direct, though he offers more charm later on when he contributes to the Trio of the Minuet. The performance overall is brimming with vitality, the finales especially neat and infectious, and those who do not object to the pervasive astringency of 'original' string timbres in a piece essentially intended to divert will find that the variety of Mozart's invention is fully characterized. In *Eine kleine Nachtmusik* Hogwood follows Thurston Dart's earlier example by adding the missing minuet to restore the original five-movement format. However – unlike Dart, who transcribed a minuet from a piano sonata – Hogwood uses a minuet which Mozart composed in collaboration with his English pupil, Thomas Attwood. All the repeats in every movement but one are observed – which is perhaps too much of a good thing, giving an overall playing time of 26 minutes! The performance is given with one instrument to a part and is sprightly and alive. The recording is first rate, although the upper string-sound is very brightly etched.

Serenades Nos. 6 in D (Serenata notturna), K.239; 7 in D (Haffner), K.250.
*** Telarc Dig. CD 80161 [id.]. Prague CO, Mackerras.

In Mackerras's coupling the playing is lively and brilliant, helped by warm recorded sound, vivid in its sense of presence, except that the reverberant acoustic clouds the tuttis a little. The violin soloist, Oldrich Viček, is very much one of the team under the conductor rather than a virtuoso establishing his individual line. By omitting repeats in the *Haffner*, Mackerras leaves room for the other delightful *Serenade*, just as haunting, with the terracing between the solo string quartet (in close focus) and the full string band aptly underlined.

Serenades Nos. 6 in D (Serenata notturna), K.239; 13 in G (Eine kleine Nachtmusik), K.525.
(B) *** Carlton Dig. PCD 861 [id.]. Serenata of London – ELGAR: *Serenade;* GRIEG: *Holberg suite.* ***

The performance of the *Night music* by the Serenata of London is as fine as any available. There is not a suspicion of routine here; indeed the players, for all the excellence of their ensemble, give the impression of coming to the piece for the first time. The *Serenata notturna* is perhaps not quite so inspired a work, but these excellent players make a good case for it and are agreeably sprightly whenever given the opportunity. The recording has striking naturalness and realism; this is an outstanding CD bargain.

Serenades Nos. 6 in D (Serenata notturna), K.239; 13 (Eine kleine Nachtmusik), K.525; Serenade for wind No. 12 in C min., K.388.
(M) **(*) DG Dig. 439 524-2 [id.]. Orpheus CO.

The *Serenata notturna*, which can easily sound bland, has a fine sparkle here. The famous *Night music*, however, is rather lacking in charm with a very brisk opening movement, alert enough and very polished, but somewhat unbending. The *Wind serenade* restores the balance of excellence, alert and sympathetic and full of character. The digital recording is first class throughout.

Serenade No. 9 in D (Posthorn), K.320; 2 Marches in D, K.335/1–2.
(M) ** Teldec/Warner Dig. 4509 92149-2 [id.]. Dresden State O, Harnoncourt.

Serenades Nos. 9 in D (Posthorn); 13 (Eine kleine Nachtmusik), K.525.
**(*) Telarc CD 10108 [id.]. Prague CO, Mackerras.

(i) *Serenades Nos. 9 in D (Posthorn), K.320; 13 in G (Eine kleine Nachtmusik), K.525;* (ii) *6 German dances, K.509; Minuet in C, K.409.*
(M) **(*) Sony SBK 48266; *SBT 48266* [id.]. (i) Cleveland O, George Szell; (ii) LSO, Leinsdorf.

Serenades Nos. 9 in D (Posthorn); 13 in G (Eine kleine Nachtmusik); Symphony No. 32 in G, K.318.
(N) (M) ** DG Dig. 445 555-2 [id.]. VPO, Levine.

The Prague strings have great warmth and Mackerras gets vital results from his Czech forces. Rhythms are lightly sprung and the phrasing is natural in every way. The Telarc acoustic is warm and spacious with a wide dynamic range (some might feel it is too wide for this music), and most ears will find the effect agreeable.

Marvellously vivacious playing from the Clevelanders in the *Posthorn Serenade*, especially in the exhilarating *presto* finale, yet there is no lack of tenderness in the *concertante* third movement marked *Andante grazioso*. *Eine kleine Nachtmusik* is similarly polished and vital, and in both works the Severance Hall acoustic provides a full ambience, but it is a pity that the close balance means a reduced dynamic range. Even so, this is music-making of great character. Leinsdorf's *German dances* make a lively bonus, if not as distinctive as the Szell performances.

In the *Posthorn Serenade* Levine's tempi are well judged and the Vienna Philharmonic play with distinction. This performance is certainly among the best now available, and the coupling is no less persuasive. The recording is clean and well balanced, if lacking something in warmth. Indeed, there is a sharpness of outlines on the DG compact disc which suggests that the microphones were placed a shade too close to the musicians. For the reissue a spirited account of the Italian overture, *Symphony No. 32*, has been added.

The Dresden State Orchestra, not surprisingly, play well for Harnoncourt and produce a certain overt charm, but the ample Dresden acoustic helps to inflate the performances, which are quite unlike those we are used to from this conductor. Boskovsky is altogether fresher and offers a much more substantial coupling (see above).

Serenade No. 10 in B flat for 13 wind instruments, K.361.
*** ASV Dig. CDCOE 804 [id.]. COE Wind Soloists, Schneider.
*** Ph. Dig. 412 726-2 [id.]. ASMF, Marriner.
**(*) Accent ACC 68642D [id.]. Octophorus, Kuijken.

Serenade No. 10 in B flat for 13 wind instruments, K.361; Divertimento in F (for 2 oboes, 2 horns & 2 bassoons), K.213.
(M) **(*) Chandos Dig. CHAN 6575. SNO Wind Ens., Paavo Järvi.

The brilliant young soloists of the Chamber Orchestra of Europe, inspired by the conducting of Alexander Schneider, give an unusually positive, characterful reading. Right at the start, the flourishes from the first clarinet are far more effective when played as here, not literally, but with Schneider leading them on to the first forte chord from the full ensemble. From then on the individual artistry of the players is most winning. The sound is exceptionally vivid and faithful.

The Marriner version fits very stylishly in the Academy's series of Mozart wind works, characteristically refined in its ensemble, with matching of timbres and contrasts beautifully judged, both lively and graceful with rhythms well sprung and speeds well chosen, yet with nothing mannered about the result. Full, warm recording that yet allows good detail.

On period instruments Barthold Kuijken directs his talented team in an authentic performance where the distinctive character of eighteenth-century instruments brings a sparer, lighter texture, as it should. Speeds tend to be on the cautious side but the liveliness of the playing makes up for that. The recording adds to the clarity.

The SNO Wind Ensemble's version under Paavo Järvi (son of a famous father) is enjoyably spontaneous-sounding, though ensemble is not quite as polished as in the finest versions. Speeds are well chosen, and the recording is warm, though the detail is sometimes masked by the lively acoustic. The little *Divertimento* makes an attractive bonus. Not a first choice but, at mid-price and with digital recording, worth considering.

Serenades Nos. 10 in B flat; 12 in C min., K.388.
(B) *** HM Dig. HMA 1903051 [id.]. Budapest Wind Ens., Zoltán Kocsis.

The Budapest wind players blend beautifully in slow movements and phrase with pleasingly simple, expressive warmth; allegros are infectiously buoyant, especially the Rondo finale of the so-called *Grand Partita in B flat*, which also has a satisfyingly full sonority. Both works contain a notable set of variations: in K.361 it is the penultimate movement, in K.388 the finale, and the colour and diversity of the playing make a high point in each work. Kocsis himself composes a brief oboe cadenza for the latter and a clarinet cadenza for the lovely *Romance* in K.361.

Serenades for wind Nos. 11 in E flat, K.375; 12 in C min., K.388.
*** ASV Dig. CDCOE 802 [id.]. COE, Schneider.

Serenades Nos. 11 & 12; Adagio in B flat, K.411; Adagio in C, K.Anh94.
(Y/B) ** Chandos Dig. CHAN 9284 [id.]. Netherlands Wind Ens.

With Schneider as a wise and experienced guide, the COE Wind give performances which combine brilliance and warmth with a feeling of spontaneity. K.375 in particular is a delight, as genial as it is characterful, conveying the joy of the inspiration. K.388 might have been more menacing at the C minor opening, but the result is most persuasive, with excellent digital sound set against a warm but not confusing acoustic.

To those familiar with the Netherlands Wind Ensemble's accounts of the Mozart serenades, directed by Edo de Waart (and still available in the Philips Mozart Edition: 422 505-2), these new versions may well disappoint – not so much on account of the recording, which is bright and lifelike, but because of the performances. They are eminently musical and well prepared, and it would be an exaggeration to call them workmanlike; they are, as one would expect, highly accomplished but not as fresh or spontaneous as the earlier set.

Serenade No. 13 in G (Eine kleine Nachtmusik), K.525.
*** Ph. Dig. 410 606-2 [id.]. I Musici (with concert of Baroque music***).

I Musici play the music with rare freshness, giving the listener the impression of hearing the work for the first time. The playing is consistently alert and sparkling, with the *Romanze* particularly engaging. The recording is beautifully balanced.

Sinfonia concertante for violin, viola and orchestra in E flat, K.364.
(M) ** EMI CDM7 64632-2 [id.]. David & Igor Oistrakh, BPO, D. Oistrakh – BRAHMS: *Violin concerto.* **(*)

Although the solo playing is rich-timbred and beautifully matched, the orchestral accompaniment polished and the recording full and pleasing, there is a curiously literal approach to the music-making here, and the imaginative spark which can bring this glorious work fully to life is missing.

(i) *Sinfonia concertante in E flat for violin, viola and orchestra, K.364;* (ii) *Sinfonia concertante in E flat for oboe, clarinet, horn, bassoon and orchestra, K.297b.*
(Y/B) (B) *** Virgin/EMI Dig. CUV5 61205-2 [id.]. (i) Warren-Green, Chase; (ii) Hunt, Collins, Thompson, Alexander; LCO, Warren-Green.

(Y/B) (BB) **(*) ASV Dig. CDQS 6139 [id.]. (i) McAslan, Inque; (ii) Anderson, Hacker, Gambold, Taylor; L. Festival O, Ross Pople.

In the ideal coupling of Mozart's paired *Sinfonias concertantes*, Christopher Warren-Green is joined by Roger Chase to provide a characteristically vital account of Mozart's inspired work for violin and viola. The *Andante* is slow and warmly expressive, yet without a trace of sentimentality. This is very satisfying, with its full-timbred sound from soloists and orchestra alike. The coupling, K.297b, is even more delectable and it would be hard to imagine a more persuasive team of wind players than those here. The full-bodied recording has plenty of space and atmosphere and the soloists in both works remain real and tangible.

The outer movements of K.364 have a fine rhythmic spring on ASV, and the *Andante* with a warm response from both soloists is touchingly expressive in a pleasingly restrained manner. Lorraine McAslan is rather near the microphone, which is not entirely flattering to her upper range in the first movement, but the viola is not too backward, and the recording projects vividly. The account of the work with wind soloists also brings a lively, alert performance with speeds relaxed enough to allow a winning lift to rhythms, making it a genial, affectionate reading which yet never falls into sentimentality. Only in the finale is the result a little heavy, but the 6/8 coda becomes all the more playful. Alan Hacker's distinctive reedy clarinet provides an extra tang, and the way the soloists appear in turn as protagonists in the variations finale is delightfully done. The sound is bright, firm and realistic. Good value.

Complete Mozart Edition, Volume 21: (i) *Sonatas for organ and orchestra (Epistle sonatas) Nos. 1–17* (complete). *Adagio & allegro in F min., K.594; Andante in F, K.616; Fantasia in F min., K.608.*
(M) **(*) Ph. 422 521-2 (2). Daniel Barenboim (organs at Stift Wilhering, Linz, Austria; Schlosspfarrkirche, Obermarchtal, Germany – K.594; K.608); (i) German Bach Soloists, Helmut Winschermann.

The *Epistle sonatas* derive their name from the fact that they were intended to be heard between the Epistle and Gospel in the Mass. Admittedly they are not great music or even first-class Mozart; however, played with relish they make a strong impression. The final *Sonata*, K.263, becomes a fully fledged concerto. The set is completed with the other works by Mozart which are usually heard on the organ, and here Barenboim's registration is particularly appealing.

Sonatas Nos. 1–17 (Epistle sonatas) for organ and chamber orchestra.
(BB) **(*) Naxos Dig. 8.550512 [id.]. János Sebestyén, Budapest Ferenc Erkel CO.

While it is understood that, apart from No. 16 in C, K.329, which has a specific solo part, the organ is not intended as a solo instrument in these *Chiesa sonatas*, it seems perverse to balance the instrument so that it blends in completely with the orchestral texture, as the Naxos engineers have done. Otherwise these alert, polished and nicely scaled performances could hardly be improved on and, apart from the controversial matter of the relationship of the organ to the orchestra, the recording is first class.

SYMPHONIES

Symphonies Nos. 1 in E flat, K.16; in F, K.19a; 4 in D, K.19; 5 in B flat, K.22; in G, K.45a; 6 in F, K.43; 7 in D, K.45; 8 in D, K.48; 9 in C, K.73; in F, K.76; in B flat, K.45b; in D, K.81; in D, K.97; in D, K.95; 11 in D, K.84; in B flat, K. Anh. 214; in F, K.75; in C, K.96; 10 in G, K.74; 12 in G, K.110; 13 in F, K.112; 14 in A, K.114; 15 in G, K.124.
*** DG Dig. 437 792-2 (4) [id.]. E. Concert, Pinnock.

This is repertoire that Hogwood pioneered on original instruments in a most arresting way. But Pinnock's Mozartian enterprise has the advantage of some years' experience of authentic performance, and certain exaggerated elements have been absorbed into a smoother but not less vital playing style. Moreover players have accommodated themselves to 'authentic' manners, and intonation has improved very considerably. So in these new performances we have greater polish, smoother and less edgy violins, and even a hint of vibrato. Slow movements have more lyrical feeling. These four discs explore early Mozartian symphonic territory and show the remarkable advance from the childhood works, which are often rather engaging, to those symphonies written at the beginning of the 1770s when a recognizable Mozartian personality was formed. A clear first choice for authenticists.

Symphonies Nos. 1 in E flat, K.16; 4 in D, K.19; in F, K.19a; 5 in B flat, K.22; in G, K.45a; 6–36; 38–41.
(N) (M) **(*) DG 435 360-2 (11) [id.]. VPO, Levine.

James Levine was the players' own surprising choice of conductor when the Vienna Philharmonic agreed to record the complete Mozart symphonies for the bicentenary year, and though the perform- ances may sometimes be heavy-handed and may lack charm, there is no lack of energy, and no risk of

Mozart being sentimentalized. The string forces used are modest, even though slow movements such as that of the *Jupiter* have a Viennese smoothness. The recording is full-bodied but in places bright to the point of edginess, particularly on string-tone in allegros. Mackerras on Telarc may offer a complete Mozart cycle with more finesse and exhilaration, but all these Levine performances are enjoyable and never boring. The set comes out somewhere between mid-and bargain-price.

Complete Mozart Edition, Volume 1: *Symphonies Nos. 1 in E flat, K.16; 4 in D, K.19; in F, K.19a; 5 in B flat, K.22; 6 in F, K.43; 7 in D, K.45; in G (Neue Lambacher), G.16; in G (Alte Lambacher), K.45a; in B flat, K.45b; 8 in D, K.48; 9 in C, K.73; 10 in G, K.74; in F, K.75; in F, K.76; in D, K.81; 11 in D, K.84; in D, K.95; in C, K.96; in D, K.97; 12 in G, K.110; 13 in F, K.112; 14 in A, K.114; 15 in G, K.124; 16 in C, K.128; 17 in G, K.129; 18 in F, K.130; 19 in E flat, K.132* (with alternative slow movement); *20 in D, K.133; in D, K.161 & 163; in D, K.111 & 120; in D, K.196 & 121; in C, K.208 & 102. Minuet in A, K.61g/1.*
(M) *** Ph. 422 501-2 (6) [id.]. ASMF, Marriner.

The reissue, in the Philips Complete Mozart Edition, of Marriner's recordings of the early symphonies confirms the Mozartian vitality of the performances and their sense of style and spontaneity. There are some important additions, notably the *Symphony in F*, K.19a, written when the composer was nine. Also now included are alternative Minuets for the Salzburg *Symphony No. 14 in A*, K.114. The layout remains on six compact discs and the ear is again struck by the naturalness and warm vividness of the transfers. Except perhaps for those who insist on original instruments, the finesse and warmth of the playing here is a constant joy.

Complete Mozart Edition, Volume 2: *Symphonies Nos. 21–36; 37: Adagio maestoso in G, K.44* (Introduction to a symphony by M. Haydn); *38–41; Minuet for a Symphony in C, K.409.*
(M) **(*) Ph. 422 502-2 (6) [id.]. ASMF, Marriner.

As with the early works, the later symphonies in the Marriner performances, as reissued in the Philips Mozart Edition, are conveniently laid out on six mid-priced CDs, offered in numerical sequence, without a single symphony having to be divided between discs. However, the over-resonant bass remains in the recording of No. 40 and the *Haffner* (both of which date from 1970, nearly a decade before the rest of the cycle was recorded). Otherwise the transfers are of Philips's best quality, and the performances generally give every satisfaction, even if their style does not show an awareness of the discoveries made – in terms of texture and balance – by the authentic school.

Symphonies Nos. 1 in E flat, K.16; 2 in B flat, K.17 (attrib. Leopold MOZART); *3 in E flat, K.18* (written by Carl ABEL); *4 in D, K.19; 5 in B flat, K.22.*
(Y/B) (BB) ** Naxos Dig. 8.550871 [id.]. Northern CO, Nicholas Ward.

Symphonies Nos. 6 in F, K.43; 7 in D, K.45; 8 in D, K.48; 9 in C, K.73; 10 in G, K.74.
(Y/B) (BB) ** Naxos Dig. 8.550872 [id.]. Northern CO, Nicholas Ward.

Naxos are here starting another complete series – of the Mozart symphonies. These first two discs cover the juvenile works, including K.17, now attributed to the composer's father, and K.18, which was Wolfgang's own copy of a work written by Carl Abel. The performances are well played, spirited and warmly recorded. On the second disc the playing of *Molto allegro* finales is very energetic and Nicholas Ward accents strongly, to give the music as much rhythmic character as possible. The recording, made in the BBC's Manchester studio Concert Hall, is attractively warm and naturally balanced, and this is enjoyable if not distinctive music-making.

Symphonies Nos. 1 in E flat, K.16; 4 in D, K.19; in F, K.19a; 5 in K.22; in G, K.45a; 6–36; 38–41.
(M) *** Telarc Dig. CD 80300 (10) [id.]. Prague CO, Mackerras.

Mackerras's is an outstanding series, with electrifying performances of the early as well as the later symphonies. Even in the trivial boyhood works there is not a suspicion of routine, with the playing full of dramatic contrasts in rhythm, texture or dynamic. Mackerras has a keen feeling for Mozart style, not least in the slow movements and minuets, which he regularly takes faster than usual. His flowing andantes are consistently stylish too, with performances on modern instruments regularly related to period practice. An outstanding instance comes in the G minor *Andante* of *No. 5 in B flat*, K.22, where Mackerras, fastish and light, makes others seem heavy-handed in this anticipation of romanticism, underlining the harmonic surprises clearly and elegantly. Consistently Mackerras finds light and shade in Mozart's inspirations, both early and late, though some may feel that, with warm reverberation characteristic of this Prague orchestra's recording venue, the scale is too large, particularly in the early symphonies. Harpsichord continuo, where used, is usually well balanced.

Symphonies Nos. 11 in D, K.84; 12 in G, K.110; 13 in F, K.112; 14 in A, K.114.
(Y/B) (BB) ** Naxos Dig. 8.550873 [id.]. Northern CO, Nicholas Ward.

The performances here are warm and polished and, although in the earlier works one would have liked a bit more bite in the allegros (original instruments are an advantage in this respect), Nicholas Ward rises to the occasion in the A major work, which receives a strong and (in the slow movement) expressive response from his excellent players. Well-balanced, natural sound, except that in the finale of the A major work the horns don't pierce the texture as brightly as they might.

Symphonies Nos. 13–24; 48, K.111a, 50, K.141a, 51, K.207a & 523, K.213a.
(N) *** EMI Dig. CDS5 55480-2 (3) [CDCC 55480]. ECO, Jeffrey Tate.

The choice of 16 early Mozart symphonies in Jeffrey Tate's collection may not be quite consistent, but on three well-filled discs it makes an attractive package for those who do not want a more complete collection such as Sir Charles Mackerras (Telarc) and James Levine (DG) provide. All but the last two of the 16 symphonies span the years 1771, when Mozart was fifteen, to 1773, when he produced the *G minor*, No. 25, his first out-and-out masterpiece among the symphonies. The four extra symphonies, given supplementary numbers between 48 and 52, are adaptations Mozart made of early opera over-tures, the last two dating from 1775–6, all of them colourful pieces. Incidentally, none of those extras is included in either the Mackerras or the Levine box.

Comparing Tate with Mackerras, one can broadly say that Tate is lighter and sweeter, and both are less weighty than Levine. Superb ECO oboists are rightly credited in two expressive slow movements, Gordon Hunt in No. 22 and Neil Black in No. 52, a transcription of Aminta's aria in *Il rè pastore*. Warm, well-balanced sound.

Symphonies Nos. 13 in F, K.112; 14 in A, K.114; 15 in G, K.124; 16 in C, K.128; 23 in D, K.181; 24 in B flat, K.182.
(M) *** Decca 436 223-2 [id.]. ASMF, Marriner.

Brisk, fresh, yet gracefully sympathetic performances of four early symphonies, plus two slightly later ones. Nos. 13–16 come from the period after Mozart's initial essays, when he was beginning to imitate rather than to express his own untrammelled if immature genius. Nos. 23 and 24 belong to the last symphonies that Mozart wrote before the sequence of really great works starts (with Nos. 25 and 29), but they have plenty of spirited invention and both performances are effervescent and finely detailed in their lightness and understanding. Any interpretative freedoms are a positive addition to enjoyment and, with an aptly sized group, splendidly recorded in the late 1960s, the bright CD transfers make a very good case for using modern instruments in these works.

Symphonies Nos. 14 in A, K.114; 15 in G, K.124; 16 in C, K.128; 17 in G, K.129; 18 in F, K.130.
*** Telarc Dig. CD 80242 [id.]. Prague CO, Mackerras.

No. 14 in A is a particularly fine work (as indeed are all Mozart's A major symphonies) and, like the others here, it receives an invigorating account with brisk Allegros and a strong, one-in-a-bar tempo for the Minuet (this suits the Minuet of *No. 18 in F* even better as it is very folksy). Slow movements, however, are very direct and are pressed onwards, slightly unbending; here some might find Mackerras's approach too austere. The bright recording is resonant, which prevents absolute clarity, but the clean lines of the playing ensure plenty of stimulating impact.

Symphonies Nos. 16 in C, K.128; 17 in G, K.129; 18 in F, K.130; 19 in E flat, K.132; 20 in D, K.133; 21 in A, K.134; 22 in C, K.162; 23 in D, K.181; 24 in B flat, K.182; 25 in G min., K.183; 26 in E flat, K.184; 27 in G, K.199; 28 in C, K.200; 29 in A, K.201.
(Y/B) *** DG Dig. 439 915-2 (4). E. Concert, Trevor Pinnock.

This invigorating DG box of the Salzburg Symphonies is a splendid follow-up to Pinnock's collection of the earlier juvenile works. The playing has polish and sophistication, fine intonation and spontaneity and great vitality, balanced by warm, lyrical feeling in slow movements. Indeed the account of *No. 29 in A major* is among the finest available (on either modern or original instruments) and the earlier A major work (No. 21) is very impressive too, as is the G minor, K.183, and the very 'operatic' *No. 23 in D major*. Another clear first choice, and not only for authenticists.

Symphonies No. 19 in E flat, K.132; 20 in D, K.133; 21 in A, K.134; 22 in C, K.162; 23 in D, K.162b.
*** Telarc Dig. CD 80217 [id.]. Prague CO, Mackerras.

Mackerras, having had great success with his Telarc recordings of the later symphonies, is equally lively in these early works from Mozart's Salzburg period. The surprising thing is how fast his speeds tend to be. In one instance the contrast is astonishing, when at a very brisk *Andantino grazioso* Mackerras turns the slow middle movement of No. 23 into a lilting Laendler, quite different from other performances.

The recording is reverberant, as in the later symphonies, giving relatively weighty textures; with such light scoring, however, there is ample clarity, with braying horns riding beautifully over the rest.

Symphonies Nos. 21 in A, K.134; 22 in C, K.162; 23 in D, K.181; 24 in B flat, K.182; 26 in E flat, K.184.
(N) (BB) ** Naxos Dig. 8.550876 [id.]. Northern CO, Nicholas Ward.

The three *Salzburg Symphonies*, K.181–2 and K.184, all written in 1773 with the young Mozart felicitously using woodwind solos within their *grazioso Andantes*, are most successful in Ward's elegant and sprightly performances, and the recording is lively to match. However, the sound is duller and less transparent in K.134 and K.162, and the playing too seems to have less zest, though it is still nicely turned.

Symphonies Nos. 24 in B flat, K.173; 26 in E flat, K.161a; 27 in G, K.161b; 30 in D, K.202.
*** Telarc Dig. CD 80186 [id.]. Prague CO, Mackerras.

Where in later symphonies Mackerras chooses more relaxed speeds, here he tends to be more urgent, as in the finale of No. 26 or the *Andantino grazioso* slow movement of No. 27, where he avoids the questionable use of muted strings. The reverberation of the recording gives the impression of a fairly substantial orchestra, without loss of detail, and anyone fancying this particular group of early Mozart symphonies need not hesitate.

Symphonies Nos. 25–36 (Linz); 38 (Prague); 39–40; 41 (Jupiter).
(M) *** EMI Dig. CMS7 63857-2 (6) [Ang. CDC 63857]. ECO, Jeffrey Tate.

Tate is generally smoother in style than Mackerras, but the characterization is marked, with fine detail and clean articulation freshening the result. In all these works he provides a winning combination of affectionate manners, freshness and elegance. Like Mackerras in his brighter, more thrustful account of the *Paris*, Tate provides the alternative *Andante* slow movement, an interesting curiosity, and on CD you can readily programme whichever you prefer. Tate's account of the *Jupiter* has an apt scale which yet allows the grandeur of the work to come out. On the one hand it has the clarity of a chamber orchestra performance, but on the other, with trumpets and drums, its weight of expression never underplays the scale of the argument which originally prompted the unauthorized nickname. In both Nos. 40 and 41 exposition repeats are observed in outer movements, particularly important in the *Jupiter* finale. Tate's keen imagination on detail, as well as over a broad span, consistently conveys the electricity of a live performance. The recording is well detailed, yet has pleasant reverberation, giving the necessary breadth. A fine set overall.

Symphonies Nos. 25 in G min., K.183; 26 in E flat, K.184; 27 in G, K.199; 29 in A, K.201; 32 in G, K.318.
(M) *** Decca 430 268-2. ASMF, Marriner.

With an aptly sized group, very well balanced by the engineers, Marriner secures effervescent performances of the earlier symphonies, especially the little *G minor*, the first of the sequence of really great works. The scale of No. 29 is broad and forward-looking, yet the continuing alertness is matched by lightness of touch, while the imaginative detail of any interpretative freedoms adds positively to the enjoyment.

Symphonies Nos. 25 in G min., K.183; 26 in E flat, K.184; 28 in C, K.200.
(N) (M) ** Teldec/Warner Dig. 4509 97485-2 [id.]. Concg. O, Harnoncourt.

Symphonies Nos. 29 in A, K.201; 30 in D, K.202; 31 in D (Paris), K.297.
(N) (M) ** Teldec/Warner Dig. 4509 97486-2 [id.]. Concg. O, Harnoncourt.

Symphonies Nos. 32 in G, K.318; 33 in B flat, K.319; 34 in C, K.338.
(N) (M) **(*) Teldec/Warner Dig. 4509 97487-2 [id.]. Concg. O, Harnoncourt.

Symphonies Nos. 35 in D (Haffner), K.385; 36 in C (Linz), K.425.
(N) (M) **(*) Teldec/Warner Dig. 4509 97488-2 [id.]. Concg. O, Harnoncourt.

Symphonies Nos. 38 in D (Prague), K.504; 39 in E flat, K.543.
(N) (M) **(*) Teldec/Warner Dig. 4509 97489-2 [id.]. Concg. O, Harnoncourt.

Symphonies Nos. 40 in G min., K.550; 41 in C (Jupiter), K.551.
(N) (M) ** Teldec/Warner Dig. 4509 97490-2 [id.]. Concg. O, Harnoncourt.

Nikolaus Harnoncourt's Mozart, for all its merits, is nothing if not wilful. He made his survey of the later Mozart symphonies over the period between 1983 and 1988, turning from conducting an ensemble of original instruments to the glories of the Concertgebouw Orchestra and establishing his personality immediately, with strong, even gruff accents, yet at times with an approach which (notably in slow movements, with speeds rather slower than usual) is relatively romantic in its expressiveness. He constantly secured fine playing, and the Teldec engineers rewarded him with bright, clear, yet resonant recording, very different from the sound the Philips engineers get from this orchestra. Overall the results are of mixed appeal. No. 25 is very puposeful indeed: it opens aggressively and the lovely slow movement lacks serenity. The unsuppressed energy in the finale brings guttural tuttis. The opening of No. 26 is comparably pungent, tuttis emphatic and heavy, and the first movement of No. 28 is more *Molto* than *Allegro spiritoso*; although here the gentle, muted string-playing in the *Andante* is beautiful, there is a feeling of restlessness. The last two movements are also crisp and fast: the finale combines lightness of articulation and great energy. No. 29 brings erratic tempi and very bold contrasts in the first movement; in the slow movement there is the most delicate string-playing, but the steady momentum reduces the feeling of repose. No. 30 is certainly exhilarating, though the bursts from the trumpets in the finale are explosive. Alternative slow movements are given for the *Paris Symphony*, the second one much lighter in weight. Both this and *No. 33 in B flat* are among Harnoncourt's most successful performances, with beautiful, cleanly articulated playing. In No. 33 Harnoncourt overdoes his slowness in the *Andante* but adds to the breadth of the finale by giving the repeats of both halves. The performances of Nos. 34 and the *Haffner* are refreshingly direct, certainly dramatic, marked by relatively unforced tempi; but charm is somewhat missing. *No. 32 in G* again shows Harnoncourt at his best, although it is made to sound weightier than usual. In the *Linz* he observes even more repeats than are marked in the regular scores, making it, like K.318, a more expansive work than usual. The *Prague* is generally very successful, superbly played, and Harnoncourt is again very generous with repeats (it runs for 38 minutes). Tempi are again erratic in No. 39 (the Minuet is rushed), although the first movement of this symphony is well judged; *No. 40 in G minor* has an unsettled mood overall (hardly Mozartian), with the slow movement very brisk. The *Jupiter* offers superbly disciplined playing, although the results are on the heavy side and the inclusion of all repeats gives an overall playing time of nearly 42 minutes.

Symphonies Nos. 25 in G min., K.183; 26 in E flat, K.184; 29 in A, K.201; 32 in G, K.318.
(Y/B) (M) *** Dig. O-L 444 161-2 [id.]. AAM, Hogwood.

In Hogwood's view, the *G minor Symphony* (No. 25) is not a 'little G minor' after all, for with all repeats observed (even those in the minuet the second time round) it acquires extra weight; in so lively and fresh a performance as this, the extra length from repetition proves invigorating, never tedious. The *A major* – another 'big symphony' – also has an incisiveness and clarity without losing anything in rhythmic bounce. The style of the playing with its non-vibrato tang is very bright on top, and clean. Though authenticity in Mozart has moved on since these recordings were made, between 1979 and 1981 (so that Pinnock's newest DG survey is less severe in its upper range of string-timbre and has greater polish and more precise intonation), these pioneering recordings still stimulate the ear and the recording has plenty of ambient warmth (so important in the slow movement of K.201, which is beautifully played) as well as transparency. The offering here is exceptionally generous: 76 minutes.

Symphonies Nos. 25 in G min., K.183; 32 in G, K.318; 41 in C (Jupiter), K.551.
(BB) *** Naxos Dig. 8.550113; 4550113 [id.]. Capella Istropolitana, Barry Wordsworth.

Symphonies Nos. 27 in G, K.199/161b; 33 in B flat, K.319; 36 in C (Linz), K.425.
(BB) *** Naxos Dig. 8.550264; 4550264 [id.]. Capella Istropolitana, Barry Wordsworth.

Symphonies Nos. 28 in C, K.200; 31 in D (Paris), K.297; 40 in G min., K.550.
(BB) *** Naxos Dig. 8.550164; 4550164 [id.]. Capella Istropolitana, Barry Wordsworth.

Symphonies Nos. 29 in A, K.201; 30 in D, K.202; 38 in D (Prague), K.504.
(BB) *** Naxos Dig. 8.550119; 4550119 [id.]. Capella Istropolitana, Barry Wordsworth.

Symphonies Nos. 34 in C, K.338; 35 in D (Haffner), K.385; 39 in E flat, K.543.
(BB) *** Naxos Dig. 8.550186; 4550186 [id.]. Capella Istropolitana, Barry Wordsworth.

Symphonies Nos. 40 in G min., K.550; 41 in C (Jupiter), K.551.
(BB) *** Naxos Dig. 8.550299 [id.]. Capella Istropolitana, Barry Wordsworth.

Barry Wordsworth's series of 15 symphonies on the Naxos super-bargain-priced label brings consistently refreshing and enjoyable performances. The Capella Istropolitana consists of leading members of the Slovak Philharmonic Orchestra of Bratislava; though their string-tone is thinnish, it is very much in scale with the clarity of a period performance but tonally far sweeter. The recording is outstandingly good, with a far keener sense of presence than in most rival versions and with less reverberation to obscure detail in tuttis. Wordsworth observes exposition repeats in first movements, but in the finales only in such symphonies as Nos. 38 and 41, where the movement particularly needs extra scale. In slow movements, as is usual, he omits repeats. He often adopts speeds that are marginally slower than we expect nowadays in chamber-scale performances; but, with exceptionally clean articulation and infectiously sprung rhythms, the results never drag, even if No. 29 is made to sound more sober than usual. In every way these are worthy rivals to the best full-priced versions, and they can be recommended with few if any reservations. Anyone wanting to sample might try the coupling of Nos. 34, 35 and 39 – with the hard-stick timpani sound at the start of No. 39 very dramatic. The *Linz* too is outstanding. For some, the option of having the last two symphonies coupled together will be useful.

Symphonies Nos. 25 in G min., K.183; 28 in C, K.200; 29 in A, K.201.
*** Telarc Dig. CD 80165 [id.]. Prague CO, Mackerras.

If you want performances on modern (as opposed to period) instruments, these are at least as fine as any, fresh and light, with transparent textures set against a warm acoustic and with rhythms consistently resilient. Mackerras's speeds are always carefully judged to allow elegant pointing but without mannerism, and the only snag is that second-half repeats are omitted in slow movements, and in the finale too of No. 29.

Bruno Walter Edition
(i) *Symphonies Nos. 25 in G min., K.183; 28 in C, K.200; 29 in A, K.201;* (ii) *35 in D (Haffner), K.385.*
(N) (M) (***) Sony mono SMK 64473 [id.]. (i) Columbia SO; (ii) NYPO, Bruno Walter.

'The birth of a performance' (recorded rehearsals of *Symphony No. 36*); (i) *Symphonies Nos. 36 in C (Linz) K.425;* (ii) *38 in D (Prague), K.504.*
(N) (M) (***) Sony mono SM2K 64474 (2) [id.]. (i) Columbia SO; (ii) NYPO, Bruno Walter.

Symphonies Nos. 39 in E flat, K.543; 40 in G min., K.550; 41 in C (Jupiter), K.551.
(N) (M) (**) Sony mono SMK 64477 [id.]. NYPO, Bruno Walter.

Walter's recordings were made in the 1950s and have been impressively transferred. The early symphonies on the first CD show his touch at its lightest (especially in K.201) and there is some lovely playing, both graceful and delicate, from the New York violins in slow movements. The *Haffner* sparkles with vitality; this and the *Linz* (offered together with its justly famous rehearsal sequence) and the *Prague* all show Walter at his finest – stylish and vital yet always making the music sing. *No. 39 in E flat* is a strong performance, but the *G minor*, K.550, is curiously heavy and unspontaneous, while the *Jupiter*, more appropriately weighty, lacks incandescence.

Symphonies Nos. 25 in G min., K.183; 31 in D (Paris), K.297; Symphony in D (The Posthorn), after K.320; Masonic funeral music (Maurerische Trauermusik), K.477.
(Y/B) *** Sony Dig. SK 48385-2 [id.]. BPO, Abbado.

Claudio Abbado and the Berlin Philharmonic defy the fashion for period performance in exhilarating accounts of Mozart using modern instruments. Like his other Mozart recordings made for Sony in Berlin, this is warmly recommended to those who want to hear Mozart playing which marries sweetness and purity to crisp rhythms and dramatic bite. Although the string band is substantial, the purity and clarity of the playing aerates textures. Woodwind doubling is always clearly audible. The recording also captures very tellingly the lugubrious timbres of the *Masonic funeral music*, made dark with extra weight of wind set against a string section without cellos.

Symphonies Nos 26 in E flat, K.184; 27 in G, K.199; 28 in C, K.200; 30 in D, K.202; 32 in G, K.318.
*** ASV Dig. CDDCA 762 [id.]. LMP, Jane Glover.

Glover's generous coupling of five early symphonies brings typically fresh and direct readings, marked by sharp attack and resilient rhythms, at speeds on the fast side. With tuttis a little weightier than with most rivals, these are brightly enjoyable performances.

Symphonies Nos. 28 in C, K.200; 29 in A, K.201; 30 in D, K.202; 40 in G min., K.550; 41 in C (Jupiter), K.551.
(B) **(*) EMI Dig. CZS7 67564-2 [id.]. ASMF, Marriner.

In his continuing series for EMI, Marriner secures warm and gracious playing from the Academy in the three early symphonies but, with articulation that brings neat rather than sharp rhythmic incisiveness, the effect is somewhat more bland than with Marriner's earlier, Argo (Decca) recordings. Slow movements are very persuasive, in both their delicacy of touch and elegant contours. In No. 29 Marriner observes more repeats than before and the performance has an affectionate breadth, with plenty of energy reserved for the last movement. Marriner is at his very best in No. 40, a work he always did very sympathetically. In the last two movements he is strikingly dramatic, with crisper articulation and faster speeds than in his earlier recording for Philips, and this time in the slow movement he observes the first-half repeat. The *Jupiter* is also very well done, but the effect is less charismatic – though, as in the others in this digital series, the recording is first rate.

Symphonies Nos. 28 in C, K.200; 29 in A, K.201; 35 in D (Haffner).
*** Sony Dig. SK 48063 [id.]. BPO, Claudio Abbado.

Though Abbado's Berlin sound is weighty, the results are not just big-scaled but elegant too, with horns whooping out brightly. Abbado is never mannered and his phrasing and pointing of rhythm are delicately affectionate, conveying an element of fun and with speeds never allowed to drag. Slow movements are kept flowing, and finales are hectically fast, but played with such verve and diamond-bright articulation that there is no feeling of breathlessness. The Sony engineers have coped splendidly with the acoustic problems of the Philharmonie to give a full and forward sound, with good presence.

Symphonies Nos. 29–36; 38–41; Divertimento No. 7 in D, K.205; 2 Marches, K.335.
(M) **(*) EMI CZS7 67301-2 (4). ECO, Barenboim.

Barenboim's recordings were made at Abbey Road over a five-year span, between 1966 and 1971. With fine rhythmic pointing and consistently imaginative phrasing, these performances certainly have a place in the catalogue. Nos. 29 and 34 are particularly successful, and the *Paris* (No. 31) is also given an outstanding performance, the contrasts of mood in the first movement underlined and the finale taken at a hectic tempo that would have sounded breathless with players any less brilliant than the ECO. The box also includes the *D major Serenade*, K.205, which responds well to Barenboim's affectionate treatment, while the two *Marches* are attractively jaunty and colourful.

Symphonies Nos. 29 in A, K.201; 31 in D (Paris), K.297; 32 in G, K.318; 33 in B flat, K.319; 34 in C, K.338; 35 in D (Haffner), K.385; 36 in C (Linz), K.425; 38 in D (Prague), K.504; 39 in E flat, K.543; 40 in G min., K.550; 41 in C (Jupiter), K.551.
(N) **(*) Ph. Dig. 442 604-2 (5) [id.]. E. Bar. Soloists, Gardiner.

Recorded between 1984 and 1989, these performances originally appeared on five separate discs, offering period performances which lean towards nineteenth-rather than eighteenth-century manners, with dark-toned, weighty tuttis set in high contrast to transparent treatment of lightly scored passages. Had Gardiner made the recordings a year or so later, he would probably have used fewer agogic hesitations and underlinings for, by his standards, they sometimes lack a little in spontaneity. But anyone fancying late Mozart symphonies with a Beethovenian tinge and with extreme dynamic contrasts need not hesitate, for the playing avoids the abrasiveness of earlier period performances, and the recordings are generally full and weighty. However, the set remains at full price.

Symphonies Nos. 29 in A, K.201; 32 in G, K.318; 33 in B flat, K.319; 35 (Haffner); 36 (Linz); 38 (Prague); 39 in E flat, K.543; 40 in G min., K.550; 41 (Jupiter).
(M) *** DG 429 668-2 (3) [id.]. BPO, Karajan.

With Nos. 29, 32 and 33 added to the original LP box, these are beautifully played and vitally alert readings; and the recordings, made between 1966 and 1979, are well balanced and given full, lively transfers to CD. There are details about which some may have reservations, and the opening of the *G minor*, which is a shade faster than in Karajan's earlier, Vienna performance for Decca, many not be quite dark enough for some tastes. But the *Jupiter*, although short on repeats, has weight and power as well as surface elegance.

Symphonies Nos. 29 in A, K.201; 40 in G min., K.550; 41 (Jupiter), K.551.
(M) ** EMI CDM7 64327-2 [id.]. BPO, Karajan.

Karajan's EMI recordings are separated by a decade. No. 29 – by far the most impressive – was made in the Grünewaldkirche in 1960. It is a warm, polished performance, realized with much finesse, and it has plenty of life. Nos. 40 and 41 were made in the Jesus-Christus Kirche in 1970; the sound is thicker, the effect more resonant and less sharply focused. The playing of the orchestra remains a joy in itself and the interpretations are purposeful and considered, but Karajan's earlier performances with the VPO for Decca sound fresher and were made not long after the EMI version of K.201.

Symphonies Nos. 31 in D (Paris), K.297; 32 in G, K.318; 33 in B flat, K.319; 34 in C, K.338; 35 in D (Haffner), K.385; 36 in C (Linz), K.425; 38 in D (Prague), K.504; 39 in E flat, K.543; 40 in G min., K.550; 41 in C (Jupiter), K.551.
(N) *** DG Dig. 447 043-2 (4). English Concert, Pinnock.

Among period performances of Mozart symphonies Pinnock's stand out above all others, and this four-disc collection covering the masterpieces from the *Paris* to the *Jupiter* can be warmly recommended not just to period enthusiasts but also to non-specialist collectors. It is the joy and exhilaration in Mozart's inspiration that consistently bubble out from these performances, even from the dark *G minor* or the weighty *Jupiter*. The rhythmic lift which Pinnock consistently finds is infectious throughout, magnetizing the ear from the start of every movement, and few period performances are as naturally and easily expressive as these. Allegros are regularly on the fast side but never hectically so, and it is a measure of Pinnock's mastery that when in a slow movement such as that of the *Prague* he chooses an unusually slow speed, there is no feeling of dragging. Where Gardiner in these same works exaggerates the dynamic contrasts, Pinnock keeps them firmly in the eighteenth-century tradition, with textural contrasts more clearly integrated. The performances are all billed as being 'directed from the harpsichord', but that continuo instrument is never obtrusive, and one can only register surprise that such subtlety and exuberance have been achieved without a regular conductor. Clear, well-balanced sound, with the orchestra in some symphonies set more distantly than in others.

Symphonies Nos. 31 in D (Paris), K.297; 33 in B flat, K.319; 34 in C, K.338.
**(*) Telarc Dig. CD 80190 [id.]. Prague CO, Mackerras.

Mackerras and the Prague Chamber Orchestra give characteristically stylish and refined performances, clean of attack and generally marked by brisk speeds. As in their accounts of the later symphonies, all repeats are observed – even those in the *da capos* of minuets – and the only snag is that the reverberant Prague acoustic, more than in others of the Telarc series, clouds tuttis: the Presto finale of the *Paris* brings phenomenal articulation of quavers at the start, which then in tuttis disappear in a mush.

(i) *Symphonies Nos. 31 in D (Paris), K.297; 36 in C (Linz), K.425;* (ii) *Overture: Le nozze di Figaro.*
(BB) *** ASV CDQS 6033. (i) LSO; (ii) RPO, Bátiz.

After a sprightly account of the *Figaro overture* from the RPO, the LSO under Bátiz provide two spirited and polished accounts of favourite named symphonies. Tempi in outer movements are brisk, but the *Presto* finale of the *Linz* (for instance) produces some sparkling playing from the strings; and in both slow movements the phrasing is warm and gracious. With excellent digital recording, this makes an enjoyable super-bargain pairing.

Symphonies Nos. 31 in D (Paris), K.297; 36 in C (Linz), K.425; 38 in D (Prague), K.504.
*** ASV Dig. CDDCA 647 [id.]. LMP, Jane Glover.

Jane Glover and the London Mozart Players offer a particularly attractive and generous coupling in the three Mozart symphonies associated with cities. Happily, exposition repeats are observed in the outer movements. The performances are all fresh and vital in traditional chamber style, with little influence from period performance. Tuttis are not always ideally clear on inner detail; but the result is nicely in scale, not too weighty, with the delicacy beautifully light and airy.

Symphonies Nos. 32 in G, K.318; 33 in B flat, K.319; 35 in D (Haffner), K.385; 36 in C (Linz), K.425.
(M) *** DG 435 070-2 [id.]. BPO, Karajan.

Here is Karajan's big-band Mozart at its finest. Although there may be slight reservations about the Minuet and Trio of the *Linz*, which is rather slow (and the other minuets are also somewhat stately), overall there is plenty of life here and slow movements show the BPO at their most graciously expressive. The remastered sound is clear and lively, full but not over-weighted.

Symphonies Nos. 32 in G, K.318; 35 in D (Haffner), K.385; 39 in E flat, K.543.
*** Telarc Dig. CD 80203 [id.]. Prague CO, Mackerras.
(BB) *** ASV Dig. CDQS 6071. ECO, Mackerras.

On Telarc, Mackerras is fresh rather than elegant, yet with rhythms so crisply sprung that there is no sense of rush. His whirling one-in-a-bar treatment of Minuets may disconcert traditionalists, but brings exhilarating results. The third movements of both the *Haffner* and No. 39 become scherzos, not just faster but fiercer than regular minuets, and generally his account of No. 39 is as commanding as his outstanding versions of the last two symphonies. The clanging attack of harpsichord continuo is sometimes disconcerting, but this music-making is very refreshing.

Mackerras's ASV version was recorded digitally, in 1985, before he moved on to make his integral set for Telarc. Mackerras here anticipates the urgent style of the later recordings, especially in the Minuets and, with generally brisk speeds, the ASV readings are attractively fresh and full of momentum. Mackerras rarely seeks to charm, but unfussily presents each movement with undistractingly direct manners. The strong character of the music-making is in no doubt, and the sound is appealingly bright and vivid; at super-bargain price this undoubtedly remains competitive.

Symphonies Nos. 34 in C, K.338; 35 in D (Haffner), K.385; 39 in E flat, K.543.
*** ASV Dig. CDDCA 615 [id.]. LMP, Jane Glover.

Tackling three major works, Jane Glover provides freshly imaginative performances that can compete with any in the catalogue, given the most vividly realistic recorded sound; Nos. 34 and 39 are especially striking. This collection can be recommended with enthusiasm.

Symphonies Nos. 35 (Haffner); 36 (Linz); 38 (Prague); 39 in E flat; 40 in G min.; 41 (Jupiter).
(Y/B) (B) **(*) EMI CZS5 68351-2 (2). BPO, Karajan.
(Y/B) (M) **(*) DG 447 416-2 (2) [id.]. BPO, Boehm.

Karajan offers large-orchestra Mozart, the fairly reverberant acoustic giving considerable breadth and impact to the orchestra. The interpretations too have plenty of weight, notably in the *Jupiter*, although Karajan also shows poise and grace: the opening of No. 36 is especially fine. Yet in the last analysis this music-making is wanting in the final touch of spontaneity and fire and, for all the magnificent orchestral playing, the listener is sometimes left vaguely unsatisfied and not only by the lack of transparency in the orchestral textures. The recordings were made in the Berlin Jesus-Christus Kirche in 1970.

Karl Boehm's way with Mozart in the early 1960s was broader and heavier in texture than we are used to nowadays, and the exposition repeats are the exception rather than the rule; but these Berlin Philharmonic performances are warm and magnetic, with refined and strongly rhythmic playing, and there is an attractive honesty and strength about them. The *Linz*, for instance, is an example of Boehm at his finest, with an agreeable, fresh vitality; but overall there is a comfortable quality of inevitability here, perpetuating a long Mozart tradition. The recordings sound full, vivid and well-balanced in the new transfers.

(i) *Symphonies Nos. 35 in D (Haffner), K.385; 36 in C (Linz);* (ii) *Rondo for violin and orchestra in B flat, K.269.*
(M) *** Sony Dig. MDK 44647 [id.]. (i) Bav. RSO, Kubelik; (ii) Zukerman, St Paul CO.

First-class performances from Kubelik and the Bavarian Radio orchestra, well paced and alive in every bar. The *Haffner* is particularly strong, and Kubelik's spacious presentation of the *Linz* is also satisfying. Both slow movements are beautifully played. At the end, Zukerman provides a sparkling encore. The CBS recording is admirable, full, yet clear and well balanced.

(i) *Symphonies Nos. 35 in D (Haffner), K.385; 36 in C (Linz), K.425;* (ii) *Divertimento No. 1 for strings, K.136; Serenade No. 6 (Serenata notturna).*
(Y/B) (M) *** Virgin/EMI Dig. CUV5 61204-2 [id.]. (i) Sinfonia Varsovia; (ii) Lausanne CO, Sir Yehudi Menuhin.

As in Menuhin's winning versions of the last four Mozart symphonies, Mozart is again presented with a smile on his face. Though modern instruments are used, the scale is intimate, with textures beautifully clear. There is elegance and charm as well as energy in outer movements, and in the slow movements Menuhin moulds the phrasing with Beechamesque magic, yet never adopts excessively slow speeds or over-romantic manners. The *Serenata notturna* and the *Divertimento* make a generous coupling. Performances are similarly fresh and elegant, though, as recorded, the strings of the Lausanne Chamber Orchestra are a degree less sweet, and the acoustic is bigger and more reverberant.

Symphonies Nos. 35 in D (Haffner), K.385; 36 in C (Linz); 38 in D (Prague).
(N) (BB) *** RCA Navigator 74321 24198-2. ECO, Jean-François Paillard.
(N) (B) (***) Dutton Lab. mono CDEA 5001 [id.]. LPO, Sir Thomas Beecham.

Stylish, excellently paced performances from Paillard and the ECO, with warmly expressive slow movements – that for the *Linz* is particularly fine – and sparkling finales. Those enjoying these works in lively, traditional performances will find there is both polish and warmth here, and plenty of vitality. The recording is resonant but not so much as to obscure detail. An excellent bargain-basement triptych.

It was Beecham's advocacy in the early years of the century which led to the late Mozart symphonies finally achieving their rightful position among the greatest masterpieces of the symphonic repertoire. These recordings, which were to dominate the catalogue until the arrival of LP, were made in 1939–40, either at Abbey Road or Kingsway Hall. The *Haffner* used both venues, and the ear can detect the change of acoustic 4½ minutes into the first movement. Beecham's dictum was to present Mozart with 'the maximum of virility coupled with the maximum of delicacy', coupled also with loving care with phrasing and subtle attention to dynamic nuance. The first movement of the *Linz* is endearingly characteristic of his boldness of style, steadily paced, without any loss of vitality. Beecham's way with Minuets, however, was to present them with genial stateliness to contrast with the brilliant articulation of the dancing finales. (He even includes the exposition repeat in the finale of No. 36, as there was room for it on the 78 side.) These Dutton transfers come into direct competition with those of EMI. The contrasts are not quite consistent. In the *Haffner* and *Prague*, the Dutton sound is marginally warmer and more rounded, with the boxiness gone, where the EMI sound is brighter and more immediate, with a hint of harshness. In the slow movement of the *Haffner* it is astonishing how different the woodwind solos sound, with the balance somehow altered. Curiously, in the *Linz* the contrasts between Dutton and EMI are rather the other way about. As to the subtly pointed magic of Beecham in Mozart, that hardly needs commendation, readily defying this purist age. Highly recommended at bargain price.

Symphonies Nos. 35 in D (Haffner), K.385; 40 in G min., K.550; 41 in C (Jupiter), K.551.
(M) *** Sony SBK 46333; *SBT 46333* [id.]. Cleveland O, Szell.

As in his companion triptych of late Haydn symphonies, Szell and his Clevelanders are shown at their finest here. The sparkling account of the *Haffner* is exhilarating, and the performances of the last two symphonies are equally polished and strong. Yet there is a tranquil feeling to both *Andantes* that shows Szell as a Mozartian of striking sensibility and finesse. He is at his finest in the *Jupiter*, which has great vigour in the outer movements and a proper weight to balance the rhythmic incisiveness; in spite of the lack of repeats, the work's scale is not diminished. Here the sound is remarkable considering the early date (late 1950s), and the remastering throughout is impressively full-bodied and clean.

Symphonies Nos. 36 in C (Linz); 38 in D (Prague); 39 in E flat, K.543; 40 in G min., K.550; 41 in C (Jupiter).
(B) *** Ph. Duo 438 332-2 (2) [id.]. ASMF, Marriner.

This is an inexpensive way of acquiring first-class performances of Mozart's last five symphonies. The recordings are of high quality, all being made in 1978 or 1980, except for No. 40, which dates from a decade earlier (1970). Here the bass is a shade over-resonant, but the present transfer has made it seem firmer than previously. In terms of finesse and elegance of phrasing, the orchestral playing is of very high quality and Marriner's readings are satisfyingly paced, full of vitality and warmth. There is not a whiff of original-instrument style here, but those who enjoy the sound of Mozart in a modern orchestra of a reasonable size should be well satisfied.

Symphonies Nos. 37 in G, K.444: Introduction (completed by M. Haydn); *40 in G min., K.550; 41 in C (Jupiter), K.551.*
*** ASV Dig. CDDCA 761 [id.]. LMP, Jane Glover.

This is an excellent example of Jane Glover's work with the LMP. Anyone who fancies this generous coupling need hardly hesitate, particularly when in the two last Mozart symphonies Glover does not skimp on repeats, as she might have done. She omits them – as most versions do – in the slow movements, but includes exposition repeats in the finales as well as in first movements, particularly important in the *Jupiter*, with its grandly sublime counterpoint. There Glover's speed is exceptionally fast, with ensemble not quite so refined or crisp as in some rival versions, but still making for a strong and enjoyable reading.

Symphonies Nos. 38 in D (Prague), K.504; 39 in E flat, K.543.
*** Virgin/EMI Dig. VC7 59561-2 [id.]. Sinfonia Varsovia, Sir Yehudi Menuhin.
(M) *** Sony Dig. MDK 44648 [id.]. Bav. RSO, Rafael Kubelik.
**(*) Ph. Dig. 426 283-2 [id.]. E. Bar. Soloists, Gardiner.

Menuhin's Mozart with this hand-picked orchestra – of which he is the Principal Conductor – has a clear place for those who, resisting period instruments, yet want many of the benefits of an authentic approach without sacrificing sweetness of string sound. It may be surprising to some that Menuhin is such a complete classicist here, with speeds on the fast side. Yet he does not sound at all rushed. He treats the third-movement trio of No. 39 as a brisk Laendler, almost hurdy-gurdy-like, refusing – after consultation with the autograph – to allow a rallentando at the end. Otherwise the only other oddity is his omission of the exposition repeat in the first movement when as a rule he is generous with repeats. The fresh, immediate sound highlights the refined purity of the string-playing.

Kubelik has the advantage of first-class, modern, digital recording. The playing has verve and is highly responsive. No. 39 is especially invigorating in its racy finale but has plenty of strength too.

For many listeners, Gardiner represents a happy medium in period performance. He is able to relax while at the same time preserving sparkle and plenty of rhythmic character. Here he is cooler than usual, and slow movements seem marginally less penetrating. Even so, there is an inherent vitality that it is difficult to resist, and the playing is wonderfully polished, far smoother and indeed with a more human profile than Hogwood shows.

Symphony No. 40 in G min., K.550.

(Y/B) *** RCA Dig. 09026 68032-2 [id.]. N. German RSO, Wand – TCHAIKOVSKY: *Symphony No. 5.* ***

(M) **(*) Carlton Dig. PCD 820; *CIMPC 820* [id.]. O of St John's, Smith Square, Lubbock – HAYDN: *Symphony No. 44.* ***

(M) (**) RCA mono GD 60271 [60271-2-RG]. NBC SO, Toscanini – BEETHOVEN: *Symphony No. 3.* (***)

Unexpected as this pairing of Mozart and Tchaikovsky may be, Wand in live recordings brings them together with a radiant consistency. Though in Mozart Wand follows many of the performing manners of an earlier generation, notably with a very slow, lovingly moulded account of the second-movement *Andante*, the remarkable point is how transparent he makes the textures. Also remarkable in Wand's performance is the lightness and speed of the Minuet, a whirling one-in-a-bar to match any authenticist. The refinement of approach means that, even in the first-movement development, he seems reluctant to find menace in the music; rather he concentrates on beauty, and that without any lack of intensity. A fascinating coupling for a unique account of the Tchaikovsky, vividly recorded.

   Lubbock's is a pleasingly relaxed account of Mozart's *G minor Symphony*, well played – the Minuet particularly deft – and nicely proportioned. The last ounce of character is missing from the slow movement, but the orchestra is responsive throughout, and the recording is in the demonstration class.

   Dating from March 1950, Toscanini's version was recorded in the notoriously dry Studio 8-H in Radio City, New York; though the sound is uncomfortable, the high voltage of the interpretation makes considerable amends, with expressive warmth tempering the conductor's characteristic urgency. The slow movement is elegantly done, and even though the finale brings a measure of fierceness, Toscanini eases lovingly into the second subject.

Symphonies Nos. 40 in G min., K.550; 41 in C (Jupiter), K.551.

(Y/B) ✿ (M) *** DG Dig. 445 548-2 [id.]. VPO, Bernstein.

(M) *** Virgin/EMI Dig. CUV5 61133-2 [id.]. Sinfonia Varsovia, Sir Yehudi Menuhin.

*** Ph. Dig. 426 315-2 [id.]. E. Bar. Soloists, Gardiner.

*** Telarc Dig. CD 80139 [id.]. Prague CO, Mackerras.

(B) *** CfP CD-CFP 4253; *TC-CFP 40243*. LPO, Mackerras.

(M) **(*) O-L Dig. 443 180-2 [id.]. AAM, Schröder (leader), Hogwood (continuo).

(i) *Symphonies Nos. 40–41;* (ii) *Serenade: Eine kleine Nachtmusik, K.525.*

(Y/B) (B) **(*) DG 439 472-2 [id.]. (i) BPO; (ii) VPO; Boehm.

Symphonies Nos. 40–41; Overture: The Marriage of Figaro.

(B) *** RPO TRP 004 [id.]. RPO, Glover.

Bernstein's electrifying account of No. 40 is keenly dramatic, individual and stylish, with the finale delightfully airy and fresh. If anything, the *Jupiter* is even finer: it is exhilarating in its tensions and observes the repeats in both halves of the finale, making it almost as long as the massive first movement. Bernstein's electricity sustains that length, and one welcomes it for establishing the supreme power of the argument, the true crown in the whole of Mozart's symphonic output. Pacing cannot be faulted in any of the four movements and, considering the problems of making live recordings, the 1984 sound is first rate, lacking only the last degree of transparency in tuttis. This mid-price reissue on DG's Masters label now takes its place again at the top of the list of recommendations for this coupling.

   Recorded in exceptionally vivid, immediate sound, Menuhin's versions of both symphonies with the Sinfonia Varsovia find a distinctive place in an overcrowded field, with playing of precision, clarity and bite which is consistently refreshing, giving a feeling of live music-making. Menuhin reveals himself again as very much a classicist, preferring speeds on the fast side, rarely indulging in romantic tricks. He is generous with repeats – observing exposition repeats in both first movement and finale of the *Jupiter*, for example. With such vivid sound, this is the best current recommendation for this favourite pairing.

   Gardiner's coupling is also very impressive indeed and, for those wanting period instruments, this is a clear first choice. These are both large-scale conceptions with the strings fuller and with less edge than usual, and there are no eccentric tempi. Allegros are strongly motivated and slow movements spacious, that of the *Jupiter* strikingly so, and played with great eloquence. The finale has great vitality and purpose yet certainly does not lack weight. The second repeat is not taken here, which is a pity; but these remain powerful and stimulating readings, very well played and recorded.

   On Telarc, with generally fast speeds, so brisk that he is able to observe every single repeat, Mackerras takes a fresh, direct view which, with superb playing from the Prague Chamber Orchestra, is also characterful. The speeds that might initially seem excessively fast are those for the Minuets, which – with fair scholarly authority – become crisp country dances, almost Scherzos. On the question of repeats, the doubling in length of the slow movement of No. 40 makes it almost twice as long as the first movement, a dangerous proportion – though it is pure gain having both halves repeated in the magnificent finale of the *Jupiter*.

On Classics for Pleasure, Mackerras directs excellent, clean-cut performances which can stand comparison with any at whatever price. He observes exposition repeats in the outer movements of the *G minor* but not the *Jupiter*, which is a pity for so majestic a work.

At super-bargain price in the Royal Philharmonic Collection, Jane Glover conducts fresh, urgent performances, stylishly moulded, which include exposition repeats that generally outshine her own earlier, smaller-scale readings with the London Mozart Players on ASV. With rhythms crisply sprung in fast movements and with slow movements warmly lyrical and relaxed without becoming over-romantic, these performances, brightly recorded, stand comparison with almost any version, and the *Figaro overture* provides a welcome makeweight, though on ASV the *Symphony No. 37* (mainly by Michael Haydn) was even more generous.

The separate issue of Nos. 40 and 41 from Hogwood's collected edition makes an alternative recommendation for those wanting period performances: brisk and light, but still conveying the drama of No. 40 and the majesty of the *Jupiter*.

By its side Boehm sounds mellow and cultivated but still magnetic and strong. He, of course, is much less generous in the matter of repeats, but the Berlin Philharmonic play very beautifully and the recording is agreeably warm and full, the reissue inexpensive. *Eine kleine Nachtmusik* was recorded a decade and a half later, and the VPO playing is polished and fresh, with a neat, lightly pointed finale.

CHAMBER MUSIC

Complete Mozart Edition, Volume 14: (i) *Adagio in C for glass harmonica, K.356;* (i; ii) *Adagio in C min. & Rondo in C for glass harmonica, flute, oboe, viola & cello;* (iii) *Clarinet trio in E flat (Kegelstatt), K.498;* (iv; v) *Piano quartets Nos. 1–2;* (iv) *Piano trios Nos. 1–6; Piano trio in D min., K.442;* (vi) *Piano and wind quintet in E flat, K.452.*

(M) *** Ph. Dig./Analogue 422 514-2 (5) [id.]. (i) Bruno Hoffmann; (ii) with Nicolet, Holliger, Schouten, Decroos; (iii) Brymer, Kovacevich, Ireland; (iv) Beaux Arts Trio, (v) with Giuranna; (vi) Brendel, Holliger, Brunner, Baumann, Thunemann.

This compilation of Mozart's chamber music with piano has no weak link. The last three discs contain the complete set of the Mozart *Piano trios* recorded by the Beaux Arts Trio in 1987, a first-rate cycle which includes not only the six completed trios but also the composite work, put together by Mozart's friend, the priest Maximilian Stadler, and listed by Köchel as K.442. The Beaux Arts' teamwork – with the pianist Menahem Pressler leading the way – brings consistently fresh and winning performances, as it also does in the two great *Piano quartets* where, in recordings made in 1983, they are joined by the viola-player, Bruno Giuranna. The *Piano and wind quintet*, K.452, recorded in 1986, subtly contrasts the artistry of Alfred Brendel at the piano with that of the oboist, Heinz Holliger, leading a distinguished team of wind-players. The only non-digital recordings are those of the *Kegelstatt trio*, characterfully done by Stephen Bishop-Kovacevich with the clarinettist Jack Brymer and the viola-player Patrick Ireland, and of the two shorter works involving glass harmonica. Those last are conveniently included here as an extra, both with Bruno Hoffmann playing that rare instrument, so titillating to the ear if heard in fairly brief spans.

Adagio in C for cor anglais, 2 violins & cello, K.580a.
*** Denon Dig. C37 7119 [id.]. Holliger, Salvatore Qt – M. HAYDN: *Divertimenti;* J. C. BACH: *Oboe quartet.* ***

Though the shortest of the four works on Holliger's charming disc, this Mozart fragment is in a world apart, deeply expressive. Excellent performances and recording.

Canons for strings; Canons for woodwind: see below, under VOCAL MUSIC: Complete Mozart Edition, Volume 23

Complete Mozart Edition, Volume 10: (i; vi) *Clarinet quintet;* (ii) *Flute quartets Nos. 1–4;* (iii; vi) *Horn quintet;* (iv; vi) *Oboe quartet;* (v) *Sonata for bassoon and cello, K.292.* (vi) Fragments: *Allegro in F, K.App. 90/580b for clarinet, basset horn, & string trio; Allegro in B flat. K.App. 91/K.516c for a clarinet quintet; Allegro in F, K.288 for a divertimento for 2 horns & strings; String quartet movements: Allegro in B flat, K.App. 72/464a; Allegro in B flat, K.App. 80/514a; Minuet in B flat, K.68/589a; Minuet in F, K.168a; Movement in A, K.App. 72/464a. String quintet No. 1 in B flat, K.174: 2 Original movements: Trio & Finale. Allegro in A min., K.App. 79 for a string quintet. Allegro in G, K.App. 66/562e for a string trio* (completed, where necessary, by Erik Smith).

(M) *** Ph. Analogue/Dig. 422 510-2 (3) [id.]. (i) Pay; (ii) Bennett, Grumiaux Trio; (iii) Brown; (iv) Black; (v) Thunemann; Orton; (vi) ASMF Chamber Ens.

These are highly praised performances of the major chamber works featuring modern wind instruments (Antony Pay uses a normal clarinet). The rest of the items are by no means inconsequential offcuts but provide music of high quality, notably the *String quartet movement*, K.514a. The *Minuet in B flat*, K.589a, in the rhythm of a polonaise and possibly the first draft for the finale of the *Hunt quartet*, is a real charmer which, had it received more exposure, might well have become a Mozartian lollipop like the famous and not dissimilar Minuet in the *D major Divertimento*, K.334. The two pieces with solo clarinet are also very winning. The performances here are all polished and spontaneous and beautifully recorded.

(i) *Clarinet quartet in E flat, K.347a; Clarinet quintet in A, K.581;* (ii) *Quintet for clarinet, basset horn and string trio.*
(BB) ** Naxos Dig. 8.550390 [id.]. József Balogh; (i) Béla Kovács; Danubius Qt (members).

(i) *Clarinet quartets: in B flat, K.317d; in F, K.496;* (ii) *Clarinet trio (Kegelstatt) for clarinet, viola and piano, K.498.*
(BB) **(*) Naxos Dig. 8.550439 [id.]. József Balogh; (i) Daniubius Qt (members); (ii) Jenö Jandó, György Konrád.

Mozart's *Clarinet quartets* are arrangements, with the first two based on violin sonatas (K.378 and K.380) while the third is a version of the piano trio, K.496. They were published posthumously in 1799 and it seems unlikely that Mozart made the arrangements himself. Never mind, they are most enjoyable in this form and suit the clarinet very well. They are most persuasively presented here, and very well recorded. Unfortunately József Balogh, who plays so sympathetically in the *Quartets*, is less memorable in the *Quintet*, where he paces the famous *Larghetto* a shade too fast. However, he makes up a good team with Jandó and Konrád for the fine *Kegelstatt trio*. Here the performance is relaxed but enjoyable (it could have used a shade more momentum in the first movement).

Clarinet quintet in A, K.581.
(N) (B) *** Decca Eclipse Dig. 448 232-2; *448 232-4* [id.]. Peter Schmidl, Vienna Octet (members) –
   BEETHOVEN: *Septet in E flat, Op. 20.* ***

Peter Schmidl, using a basset clarinet, is sometimes just a little cool, but his intimate approach has its own appeal. He phrases gently and beautifully, with imagination in his nuancing and much delicacy in matters of light and shade. Of course these Viennese players use modern instruments, and the sound they make is consistently full and smooth. The closing section of the finale is sheer joy, with some delicious chortling articulation from the soloist. The 1989 Decca recording is state-of-the-art, and while this would not necessarily be a clear first choice for the *Quintet*, it is very distinguished, and the splendid Beethoven coupling makes this Eclipse reissue an oustanding bargain.

(i) *Clarinet quintet in A, K.581; Divertimento No. 1 for strings in D, K.136* (quartet version).
(M) *** Saga EC 3387-2. (i) Thea King; Aeolian Qt.

Clarinet quintet in A, K.581; Clarinet quintet fragment in B flat, K.516c; (i) *Quintet fragment in F for clarinet in C, basset-horn and string trio, K.580b* (both completed by Duncan Druce).
*** Amon Ra/Saydisc CD-SAR 17 [id.]. Alan Hacker, Salomon Qt, (i) with Lesley Schatzberger.

Leading the CD versions of the *Clarinet quintet* (alongside Thea King's outstanding coupling with the *Clarinet concerto* on Hyperion – see above) is a superb recording by Alan Hacker with the Salomon Quartet, using original instruments. Hacker's gentle sound on his period instrument is displayed at its most ravishing in the *Larghetto*. He is matched by the strings, and especially by the leader, Simon Standage, who blends his tone luminously with the clarinet. Tempi are wonderfully apt throughout the performance, the rhythms of the finale are infectiously pointed, the music's sense of joy fully projected. The recording balance is near perfect. Hacker includes a fragment from an earlier projected *Quintet* and a similar sketch for a work featuring C clarinet and basset-horn with string trio. Both are skilfully completed by Duncan Druce.

   With great refinement in matters of tonal shading, and consistently beautiful phrasing, this Saga recording remains among the most attractive versions of the *Quintet*. Miss King's articulation in the third-movement solos and in the delightfully pointed finale is a joy. The closing pages of the work are especially beautiful. This is all helped by excellent support from the Aeolian Quartet and a most realistically balanced recording from Saga. The ungenerous filler is bright and breezy, with very fast tempi for the outer movements and a graceful, if matter-of-fact account of the *Andante*.

(i) *Clarinet quintet in A, K.581;* (ii) *Horn quintet in E flat, K.407;* (iii) *Oboe quartet in F, K.370.*
(M) *** Ph. 422 833-2. (i) Antony Pay; (ii) Timothy Brown; (iii) Neil Black; ASMF Chamber Ens.

It is a delightful idea to have the *Clarinet quintet*, *Oboe quartet* and *Horn quintet* on a single CD. Here, Antony Pay's earlier account of the *Clarinet quintet*, played on a modern instrument, with the Academy of St Martin-in-the-Fields players must be numbered among the strongest now on the market for those not insisting on an authentic basset clarinet. Neil Black's playing in the *Oboe quartet* is distinguished, and again the whole performance radiates pleasure, while the *Horn quintet* comes in a well-projected and lively account with Timothy Brown. The recording, originally issued in 1981, is of Philips's best.

(i) *Clarinet quintet;* (ii) *Oboe quartet in F, K.370.*
(B) *** CfP CD-CFP 4377; *TC-CFP 4377.* (i) Andrew Marriner; (ii) Gordon Hunt, Chilingirian Qt.
(M) *** Carlton Dig. PCD 810 [id.]. (i) Puddy; (ii) Boyd, Gabrieli Qt.

On the bargain-priced CfP version, recorded in 1981, the young Andrew Marriner's persuasive account occupies the front rank, quite irrespective of price. Marriner's playing in the *Quintet* is wonderfully flexible; it reaches its apex in the radiantly beautiful reading of the slow movement, although the finale is also engagingly characterized. The *Oboe quartet* is delectable too, with Gordon Hunt a highly musical and technically accomplished soloist. The CfP issue was recorded in the Wigmore Hall and the sound-balance is most believable.

The alternative mid-priced Carlton CD brings a reading of the *Clarinet quintet* which is clean and well paced and, if lacking the last degree of delicacy in the slow movement, is never less than stylish. The young oboist, Douglas Boyd, then gives an outstanding performance in the shorter, less demanding work, with the lilting finale delectably full of fun. The digital recording is vividly immediate and full of presence, with even the keys of the wind instruments often audible.

(i) *Clarinet quintet in A, K.581; String quartet No. 20 in D (Hoffmeister), K.499.*
(M) **(*) Whitehall Associates Dig. MQCD 6001 [id.]. (i) Jack Brymer; Medici Qt.

The Medici String Quartet have set up their own label. Jack Brymer joins them for their first Mozart CD and has a benign influence in a fine, mellifluous performance of the *Clarinet quintet*. He plays the *Adagio* as a sustained half-tone and conjures from the strings comparably soft playing. Perhaps a little more dynamic variety would have been an advantage, but the concentration is sustained right through. The finale is delightful; there is an attractive improvisational feeling in the lyrical variation before the main theme makes its joyful return. The recording is truthful, but the close balance is more noticeable in the coupled *Hoffmeister quartet*, which is a lively, well-integrated performance, if without the individuality of the *Quintet*. However, at mid-price this coupling is certainly worth considering.

(i) *Clarinet quintet in A, K.581;* (ii) *String quintets Nos. 1 in B flat, K.174; 2 in C min., K.406.*
*** Cal. Dig. CAL 9232 [id.]. Talich Qt, with (i) Bohuslav Zahradnik; (ii) Karel Rehak.

The Talich performances here are of the highest quality: just sample the delicacy of the playing in the lovely *Adagio* of K.174 or the energy of the simple yet spirited finale. The *C minor Quintet* is of course the composer's transcription of the *Serenade for wind*, K.388, and the players make the very most of the splendid variations which form the finale. The *Clarinet quintet* is exquisitely done. Bohuslav Zahradnik's contribution has much delicacy of feeling and colour; he is highly seductive in the slow movement, and even in the finale the effect is gentle in the most appealing way without any loss of vitality. The recording balance is exemplary in all three works and the acoustic admirably chosen. A rewarding triptych in every way – and a playing time of 80 minutes 17 seconds!

(i) *Clarinet quintet in A, K.581; String quintet No. 4 in G min., K.516.*
(Y/B) (B) ** DG 439 460-2 [id.]. Amadeus Qt, with (i) Gervase de Peyer; (ii) Cecil Aronowitz.

It was a happy idea to pair what are perhaps Mozart's two greatest *Quintets* on this bargain Classikon reissue. Gervase de Peyer gives a warm, smiling lead in the *Clarinet quintet*, with a sunny opening movement, a gentle, expressive *Larghetto* and a delightfully genial finale. The Amadeus accompany with sensibility, and the 1975 recording is flawless. The recording of the *String quintet* (with its Elysian slow movement) was made six years earlier but the CD transfer shows its age by a degree of edginess on top which is emphasized by the accented playing at higher dynamic levels. This performance has also been admired, and there is no question about the refinement and polish of the playing, although the effect is not as fresh and pleasing as with K.581 because of the sound-quality.

Complete Mozart Edition, Volume 13: (i) *Divertimento in E flat for string trio, K.563;* (ii) *Duos for violin and viola Nos. 1–2, K.423/4;* (i) *6 Preludes and fugues for string trio, K.404a;* (iii) *Sonata (String trio) in B flat, K.266.*
(M) *** Ph. 422 513-2 (2) [id.]. (i) Grumiaux, Janzer, Szabo; (ii) Grumiaux, Pelliccia; (iii) ASMF

Chamber Ens.
(N) (B) *** Ph. Duo 454 023-2 (2). As above.

Grumiaux's 1967 recorded performance of the *Divertimento in E flat* remains unsurpassed; he is here joined by two players with a similarly refined and classical style. The recording has been remastered again: the balance still favours Grumiaux but he also dominates the performance artistically (as he does also in the *Duos*) and the result is now fully acceptable. In the *Duos*, which are ravishingly played, the balance is excellent, and Arrigo Pelliccia proves a natural partner in these inspired and rewarding works. The *Sonata for string trio* is well played by the ASMF Chamber Ensemble and it has a modern, digital recording. Of the six *Preludes and fugues*, the first three derive from Bach's *Well-tempered clavier*, the fourth combines an *Adagio* from the *Organ sonata*, BWV 527, with *Contrapunctus 8* from the *Art of fugue*, the fifth is a transcription of two movements from the *Organ sonata*, BWV 526, and the sixth uses music of W. F. Bach. The performances here are sympathetic and direct, the recorded sound bold, clear and bright. As can be seen, this set has now been issued on a Duo, with a resulting saving in cost.

Divertimento in E flat for string trio, K.563.
*** Sony Dig. MK 39561 [id.]. Kremer, Kashkashian, Ma.

Gidon Kremer, Kim Kashkashian and Yo-Yo Ma turn in an elegant and sweet-toned account on Sony/ CBS and are excellently recorded. Indeed, the sound is fresh and beautifully realistic. There are many perceptive insights, particularly in the *Adagio* movement which is beautifully done.

Flute quartets Nos. 1 in D, K.285; 2 in G, K.285a; 3 in C, K.285b; 4 in A, K.298.
(N) *** Sony Dig. SK 66240 [id.]. Irena Grafenauer, Gidon Kremer, Veronika Hagen, Clemens Hagen.
(M) *** Van. 08.4001.71 [OVC 4001]. Paula Robinson, Tokyo Qt (members).
*** Accent ACC 48225D. Bernhard and Sigiswald Kuijken, Van Dael, Wieland Kuijken.
*** Sony Dig. MK 42320 [id.]. Rampal, Stern, Accardo, Rostropovich.
(BB) ** ASV CDQS 6099. Richard Adeney, Melos Ens. (members).

Mozart professed an aversion for the flute (partly because at the time its intonation was suspect and its timbre could be watery), yet he wrote some delightful music for it, none more so than these delicious, lightweight quartets. This new Sony CD is second to none. Irene Grafenauer's playing is in every way memorable, with the most elegant phrasing and an appealing timbre (try the captivating second movement of the *D major Quartet*) and the accompanying group, led by Kremer, are highly supportive. Of course the flute dominates throughout, and this is reflected in the recording balance, which is very natural in all respects. Nevertheless this highly musical soloist always allows the string detail to come through when it takes precedence, as in some of the delightfully ingenuous variations which open the A major work.

The Vanguard recording of the *Flute quartets* (presumably from the 1960s – no date is given) is most winning. Paula Robinson displays a captivating lightness of touch and her silvery timbre seems eminently suited to Mozart. Needless to say, the Tokyo Quartet provide polished accompaniments which combine warmth with much finesse, and the recording is most naturally balanced.

Readers normally unresponsive to period instruments should hear these performances by Bernhard Kuijken, for they have both charm and vitality; they radiate pleasure and bring one close to this music. This record is rather special and cannot be recommended too strongly. The playing is exquisite and the engineering superb.

It would be hard to dream up a more starry quartet of players than that assembled on the CBS disc. But the recording was made in a relatively dry studio, and the acoustic emphasizes the dominance of Rampal's flute in the ensemble, with the three superstar string-players given little chance to shine distinctively except in the finale of K.285. A delectable record none the less.

The performances by Richard Adeney with distinguished members of the Melos Ensemble (Hugh Maguire, Cecil Aronowitz, Terence Weill) date from 1978. The balance treats the flute very much in a solo capacity and is vividly close, although the characterful playing of Adeney's colleagues is not masked. The effect is undoubtedly lively and spontaneous but has not the imaginative insight or persuasive charm of the best versions. However, this excellently transferred CD is in the lowest price-range and represents good value.

Flute quartets Nos. 1–4; Oboe quartet (arr. for flute, Galway), K.370.
**(*) RCA Dig. 09026 60442-2 [id.]. James Galway, Tokyo Qt.

James Galway is an impeccable soloist and the Tokyo Quartet provide admirable support. The recording too is fresh and well balanced and, if Galway dominates, that is partly the result of Mozart's writing and the use of a modern instrument. Some may feel that in slow movements his sweet, silvery timbre and individual vibrato are too much of a good thing, and this is particularly noticeable in the famous cantilena of the *G major* work. But this is perhaps carping – if Galway brings this music to the attention of a wider public, well and good. The transcription of the *Oboe quartet* is more questionable, although it must be admitted that here the *Adagio* sounds refreshingly different on the flute, and the performance cannot be faulted.

Horn quintet in E flat, K.407.
(Y/B) (M) *** Teldec/Warner Dig. 4509 97451-2 [id.]. Radovan Vlatkovič, Berlin Soloists – BEETHOVEN: *Septet*. ***

Radovan Vlatkovič has a plumper, more resonant horn-timbre than we are used to in the UK, and he also judiciously uses a touch of vibrato in the East European manner. But he is a most musical Mozartian and his big sound is balanced with a matching sumptuous sound from the accompanying string-group. This is certainly enjoyable, with the finale as nimble as you like.

(ii) *Horn quintet in E flat, K.407;* (ii) *Oboe quartet in F, K.370; A Musical Joke, K.522.*
(BB) **(*) Naxos Dig. 8.550437 [id.]. (i) József Kiss; (ii) Jenö Keveházi; Kodály Qt.

Highly musical if not especially individual performances of the *Horn quintet* and *Oboe quartet*; in the latter the oboe is balanced forwardly and seems a bit larger than life; but no matter, the recordings have a pleasingly resonant bloom. The *Musical Joke* really comes off well: the horn players have a great time with their wrong notes.

Piano quartets Nos. 1 in G min., K.478; 2 in E flat, K.493 (see also above, under Complete Mozart Edition, Volume 14).
*** Ph. Dig. 410 391-2 [id.]. Beaux Arts Trio with Giuranna.
(Y/B) *** Decca Dig. 444 115-2 [id.]. András Schiff, Shiokawa, Höbarth, Perényi.

The Beaux Arts group provide splendidly alive and vitally sensitive accounts that exhilarate the listener, just as does the Curzon–Amadeus set (see below), and they have the advantage of first-class digital recording. The Beaux Arts play them not only *con amore* but with the freshness of a new discovery, and the sound (particularly that of the piano) is exceptionally lifelike.

Not only does András Schiff play Mozart's fortepiano, an Anton Walter of about 1780, but Yuuko Shiokawa plays his violin, a mid-eighteenth-century instrument from Mittenwald in Bavaria (as is Miklós Perényi's 1770 cello), while Erich Höbarth uses a viola made by Carlo Antonio Testore of Milan, also believed to have belonged to Mozart. The stringed instruments produce real warmth in the acoustic of the Wienersaal of the Salzburg Mozarteum, though the fortepiano sounds somewhat papery and wanting in timbre. Generally, these are articulate and affectionate performances which will give pleasure, though this should not be an only recommendation in this repertoire. The Beaux Arts, using modern instruments, are rather special.

(i) *Piano quartets Nos. 1–2;* (i) *Horn quintet in E flat, K.407.*
❀ (M) *** Decca mono 425 960-2 [id.]. (i) Clifford Curzon, Amadeus Qt; (ii) Dennis Brain, Griller Qt.

All versions of the Mozart *Piano quartets* rest in the shadow of the recordings by Clifford Curzon and members of the Amadeus Quartet. No apologies need be made for the 1952 mono recorded sound. The performances have a unique sparkle, slow movements are elysian. One's only criticism is that the *Andante* of K.478 opens at a much lower dynamic level than the first movement, and some adjustment of the controls needs to be made. The *Horn quintet* coupling was recorded in 1944 and the transfer to CD is even more miraculous. The slight surface rustle of the 78-r.p.m. source is in no way distracting and Dennis Brain's performance combines warmth and elegance with a spirited spontaneity, and the subtleties of the horn contribution are a continuous delight. A wonderful disc that should be in every Mozartian's library.

Piano quartet No. 1 in G min., K.478.
(N) *** Ph. Dig. 446 001-2 [id.]. Alfred Brendel, Thomas Zehetmair, Tabea Zimmermann, Richard Duven – SCHUBERT: *Trout quintet*. ***

Brendel's performance of the *G minor Piano quartet* has vigour and sensitivity and, not surprisingly, an admirable sense of style. It very well recorded too and, although most collectors will prefer a disc containing both piano quartets, this is a sizeable bonus for an outstanding account of Schubert's *Trout quintet*.

Piano quartet No. 2 in E flat, K.493.
(N) (M) ** Sony Stern Edition III SM2K 64516 (2) [id.]. Stern, Katims, Schneider, Istomin – HAYDN: *Piano trio;* SCHUBERT: *Piano trios*. **

A perfectly respectable account from Stern and his colleagues, not very flatteringly recorded (Stern's violin sounds wiry) during the 1957 Casals Festival in Puerto Rico. There is plenty of life here, but a lack of charm until the finale, which goes well.

Piano trios Nos. 1–6 (see also above, under Complete Mozart Edition, Volume 14)
*** Chandos Dig. CHAN 8536/7 (2). Borodin Trio.

Piano trios Nos. 1–6; Piano trio in D min., K.442.
*** Ph. Dig. 422 079-2 (3). Beaux Arts Trio.

(i) *Piano trios Nos. 1 in B flat, K.254; 2 in G, K.496; 3 in B flat, K.502; 4 in E, K.542; 5 in C, K. 548; 6 in G, K.564;* (ii) *Clarinet trio (Kegelstatt) in E flat, K. 498.*
(Y/B) (B) *(**) Ph. Duo 446 154-2 (2) [id.]. (i) Beaux Arts Trio; (ii) Brymer, Kovacevich, Ireland.

Apart from including an extra work, the Beaux Arts are more generous with repeats, which accounts for the extra disc in their digital version. Their performances are eminently fresh and are no less delightful and winning. There is a somewhat lighter touch here compared with the Chandos alternative, thanks in no small degree to the subtle musicianship of Menahem Pressler. The Philips recording is strikingly realistic and present.

The Borodin Trio are slightly weightier in their approach and their tempi are generally more measured than the Beaux Arts', very strikingly so in the *Allegretto* of the *G major*. All the same, there is, as usual with this group, much sensitive playing and every evidence of distinguished musicianship. The balance in the Philips set tends to favour the piano a little; the Chandos, recorded at The Maltings, Snape, perhaps produces the more integrated sound.

The Beaux Arts Trio's earlier performances, made in the late 1960s, still sound vivid and fresh. As music-making, this has almost equal artistic claims on the listener and, though the timbre of Daniel Guilet's violin is noticeably much thinner than the ear would expect in a more modern recording, if pinched it is well focused. Different ears and different reproducers will react to this with varying degrees of dissatisfaction; but Menahem Pressler's piano playing is most naturally caught. In the *Clarinet trio* the balance is such that Jack Brymer's clarinet dominates and Stephen Kovacevich's piano is slightly recessed, but the overall effect is beautiful, warmer than in the *Piano trios*. But the later, digital set of the *Piano trios* is well worth the extra cost.

Piano and wind quintet in E flat, K.452.
(Y/B) (M) *** Sony Dig. SMK 42099 [id.]. Perahia, members of ECO – BEETHOVEN: *Quintet.* ***
(M) *** Decca 421 151-2. Ashkenazy, L. Wind Soloists – BEETHOVEN: *Quintet.* ***

An outstanding account (now at mid-price) of Mozart's delectable *Piano and wind quintet* on CBS, with Perahia's playing wonderfully refreshing in the *Andante* and a superb response from the four wind soloists, notably Neil Black's oboe contribution. Clearly all the players are enjoying this rewarding music, and they are well balanced, with the piano against the warm but never blurring acoustics of The Maltings at Snape.

Ashkenazy's performance in Mozart's engaging *Quintet* is also outstandingly successful, polished and urbane, yet marvellously spirited. His wind soloists are a distinguished team and their playing comes fully up to expectations. The balance and sound-quality are of the highest order and the CD sounds very natural, although the balance is forward. A first-class mid-priced alternative to the full-price versions led by Perahia and Lupu.

String quartets

Complete Mozart Edition, Volume 12: *String quartets Nos. 1–23.*
(M) *** Ph. 422 512-2 (8) [id.]. Italian Qt.

The earliest recordings by the Italians now begin to show their age (notably the six *Haydn Quartets*, which date from 1966): the violin timbre is thinner than we would expect in more modern versions. But the quality is generally very satisfactory, for the Philips sound-balance is admirably judged. As a set, the performances have seen off all challengers for two decades or more; one is unlikely to assemble a more consistently satisfying overview of these works, or one so beautifully played. They hold a very special place in the Mozartian discography.

String quartets Nos. 1 in G, K.80; 2 in D, K.155; 3 in G, K.156; 4 in C, K.157; 5 in F, K.158; 6 in B flat, K.159; 7 in E flat, K.160; 8 in F, K.168; 9 in A, K.169; 10 in C, K.170; 11 in E flat, K.171; 12 in B flat, K.172; 13 in D min., K.173; Divertimenti: in D, K.136; in B flat, K.137; in F, K.138.
*** DG Dig. 431 645-2 (3) [id.]. Hagen Qt.

This set of three CDs presents all of Mozart's music for string quartet up to the age of seventeen and it is played with much charm and polish. Unlike the Quartetto Italiano, the Hagens include the

Divertimenti, K.136–8. In this present set they strike an excellent balance between naturalness of utterance and sophistication of tone, and the DG recording is first class.

String quartets Nos. 1 in G, K.80; 2 in D, K.155; 4 in C, K.157.
(N) (BB) ** Naxos Dig. 8.550541 [id.]. Eder Qt.

String quartets Nos. 3 in G, K.156; 5 in F, K.158; 6 in B flat, K.159; 17 in B flat (Hunt), K.458.
(N) (B) ** Naxos Dig. 8.550542 [id.]. Eder Qt.

String quartets Nos. 7 in E flat, K.160; 8 in F, K.168; 9 in A, K.169; 22 in B flat (Prussian No. 2), K.589.
(N) (BB) **(*) Naxos Dig. 8.550544 [id.]. Eder Qt.

String quartets Nos. 10 in C, K.170; 11 in E flat, K.171; 15 in D min., K.421.
(N) (BB) **(*) Naxos Dig. 8.550546 [id.]. Eder Qt.

String quartets Nos. 12 in B flat, K.172; 13 in D min., K.173; 21 in D (Prussian No. 1), K.575.
(N) (BB) **(*) Naxos Dig. 8.550545 [id.]. Eder Quartet.

String quartets Nos. 16 in E flat, K.428; 18 in A, K.464.
(N) (BB) ** Naxos Dig. 8.550540 [id.]. Eder Qt.

String quartet No. 19 in C (Dissonance), K.465; Divertimenti: in D, K.136; in B flat, K.137; in F, K.138.
(N) (BB) ** Naxos Dig. 8.550543 [id.]. Eder Qt.

String quartets Nos. 20 in D (Hoffmeister), K.499; 23 in F (Prussian No. 3), K.590; Adagio and fugue in C min., K.546.
(N) (BB) **(*) Naxos Dig. 8.550547 [id.]. Eder Qt.

There is nothing cheap about the Naxos recordings except the asking price. The Eder Quartet are an extremely fine ensemble with an admirable sense of style and exemplary musicianship. The snag is the venue, the Sashalom Reformed Church in Budapest, which affords the group the most beautiful sound, but the effect overall is almost orchestral and too often loses the intimacy of the medium. However, it seems to affect some performances more than others, and the three early quartets (K.160 and K.168–9) on the third disc, which in their first-movement allegros keep reminding us of the Salzburg *Divertimenti* (K.136–8), are not affected too adversely. The slow movement of the F major, K.168, is very touching, and it is beautifully played. The *Second Prussian Quartet* is also elegantly done, although once again the resonant acoustic gives an unwanted expansion of tone and takes some of the edge off the playing. The fourth and fifth discs include five of the amazingly mature Viennese quartets of 1773, with their portents of the later Mozart, notably the touching *Un poco Adagio* of K.170 and the remarkable opening movement of the *D minor*, K.173, which also has an engagingly courtly *Andantino grazioso*. They are played most sympathetically and the warmth of the sound is undoubtedly agreeable. The *Dissonance* opens with the Eder group creating considerable atmospheric tension; then the Allegro sets off rather determinedly. The fairly close balance prevents a real pianissimo, but the effect is real if inflated. The three Salzburg *Divertimenti* (which we also often hear in chamber-orchestra presentation), which are better suited by the acoustic, are given sympathetic, lively performances, if lacking the last ounce of sparkle. The later *Hoffmeister* and the two *Prussian Quartets* show the composer at full stretch, and the Eder performances will not disappoint. The players bring a potent intensity to the climax of the *Adagio and fugue* and, although they could perhaps have achieved more attack at the opening of the fugue, this effect is partly caused by the warm resonance. For those with limited budgets, this series is worth considering.

String quartet No. 1 in G, K.80.
(B) *** Discover Dig. DICD 920171 [id.]. Sharon Qt – BEETHOVEN: *Harp quartet;* RAVEL: *Quartet in F.*
**(*)

The Sharon Quartet give an excellent account of Mozart's *First* divertimento-like *Quartet*, which he wrote in Italy at the age of fifteen. The playing has life and finesse and, although the recording (made in a Cologne Church) is reverberant, detail is clear; indeed the acoustic rather suits the music.

String quartets Nos. 8 in F, K.168; 9 in A, K.169; 10 in C, K.170; 11 in E flat, K.171; 12 in B flat, K.172.
*** Cal. Dig. CAL 9247 [id.]. Talich Qt.

One has only to listen to the *Andante* of K.168 (introducing the mute) or the nostalgic lyricism of the *Adagio* in K.170 to realize that these quartets marked a step forward for the young composer. K.171 then opens with an *Adagio* of real depth, which is recapitulated at the movement's close, while its *Andante* (again using mutes) brings a quiet nocturnal atmosphere. The Talich players are the soul of finesse and bring the intimacy of familiarity. They play with expressive simplicity, while bringing vitality to allegros and conveying a consistent feeling of spontaneous liveliness throughout. They are naturally if forwardly balanced, and beautifully recorded. There are few records of Mozart's earlier quartets to match this collection.

String quartets Nos. 14 in G, K.387; 15 in D min., K.421; 16 in E flat, K.428; 17 in B flat (Hunt), K.458; 18 in A, K.464; 19 in C (Dissonance), K.465 (Haydn Quartets); 20 in D (Hoffmeister), K. 499; 21 in D, K.575; 22 in B flat, K.589; 23 in F, K.590 (Prussian Quartets Nos. 1–3).
(Y/B) (M) *** Teldec/Warner 4509 95495-2 (4). Alban Berg Qt.

The Teldec recordings were made by the Alban Berg in the latter half of the 1970s; the performances have not since been surpassed, and now they make one of the most distinguished sets of Mozart's late quartets currently available, with the additional advantage of economy. The playing is thoroughly stylish and deeply musical; it is entirely free from surface gloss and there are none of the expressive exaggerations of dynamics and phrasing that marred this group's later records of Beethoven's *Rasumovsky Quartets* for EMI. The *Haydn Quartets* are consistently successful; the *Hunt* (1979) is still possibly the finest on the market and the *Dissonance* too is first class, with a wonderfully expressive account of the slow movement. Although dynamic gradations are steep, there is no sense of exaggeration – on the contrary these are wholly excellent performances, which are recommended with enthusiasm. The account of the *First Prussian Quartet* has much style and character, and the group are at their very best in Mozart's last two quartets. Their readings have an honesty and a directness that are enhanced by polish and finesse. Ensemble cannot be faulted and, though competition is strong, their claims still rank very high. The recordings have been transferred impeccably. The sound is rather more brightly astringent in the treble than the Chilingirians on CRD (CRD 3362/4), and is obviously less modern but does not lack underlying warmth. The disc coupling K.464 and K.465 offers slightly more expansive sound than the earlier recordings.

String quartets Nos. 14 in G, K.387; 15 in D min., K.421; 16 in E flat, K.428; 17 in B flat (Hunt), K458; 18 in A, K.464; 19 in C (Dissonance), K.465 (Haydn Quartets).
✪ *** CRD CRD 3362; CRD C 4062 (Nos. 14–15); 3363; 4063 (Nos. 16–17); 3364; 4064 (Nos. 18–19) [id.]. Chilingirian Qt.
*** Hyperion Dig. CDS 44001/3 [id.]. Salomon Qt.
(Y/B) *** Denon Dig. CO 75850/2 [id.]. Kuijken Qt.

String quartets Nos. 14–19; Fragment, K.464a.
(Y/B) ** DG Dig. 431 797-2 (3) [id.]. Emerson Qt.

String quartets Nos. 14 in G, K.387; 15 in D min., K.421.
(M) **(*) Whitehall Associates Dig. MQCD 6004 [id.]. Medici Qt.
(Y/B) ** Decca Dig. 440 076-2 [id.]. Ysaÿe Qt.
(Y/B) ** DG Dig. 439 861-2 [id.]. Emerson Qt.

String quartets Nos. 14 in G, K.387; 15 in D min., K.421; 3 in G, K.156.
*** Cal. CAL 9241 [id.]. Talich Qt.

String quartets Nos. 16 in E flat, K.428; 17 in B flat (Hunt), K.458.
*** Cal. CAL 9242 [id.]. Talich Qt (with HAYDN: *String quartet No. 74 in G min., Op. 74/3* **(*)).
(Y/B) **(*) Decca Dig. 440 077-2 [id.]. Ysaÿe Qt.

String quartets Nos. 16 in E flat, K.428; 18 in A, K.464; Fragment (Rondo), K.464a.
(Y/B) **(*) DG Dig. 439 914-2 [id.]. Emerson Qt.

String quartets Nos. 16 in E flat, K.428; 19 in C (Dissonance), K.465.
(M) **(*) Whitehall Associates Dig. MQCD 6002 [id.]. Medici Qt.

String quartets Nos. 17 in B flat (Hunt), K.458; 18 in A, K.464.
(Y/B) *** Hyperion Dig. CDA 66234 [id.]. Salomon Qt.
(M) **(*) Whitehall Associates Dig. MQCD 6003 [id.]. Medici Qt.

String quartets Nos. 18 in A, K.464; 19 in C (Dissonance), K.465.
(Y/B) ** Decca Dig. 440 078-2 [id.]. Ysaÿe Qt.

(i) *String quartets Nos. 18 in A, K.464; 19 in C, K.465;* (ii) *Violin sonata No. 18 in G, K.301.*
*** Cal. CAL 9243 [id.]. (i) Talich Qt; (ii) Peter Messiereur, Stanislav Bogunia.

The set of six quartets dedicated to Haydn contains a high proportion of Mozart's finest works in the genre. The Chilingirian Quartet plays with unforced freshness and vitality, avoiding expressive mannerism but always conveying the impression of spontaneity, helped by the warm and vivid recording.

Unlike most quartets, they never sound superficial in the elegant but profound slow movements. The three CDs are packaged separately and offer demonstration quality.

These performances by the Talich Quartet are immaculate in ensemble and the performances have a special kind of shared intimacy which is yet immediately communicative. There is complete understanding of what Mozart is trying to say and a warmth and elegance of phrasing which is totally appealing. The analogue recordings are beautiful, very smooth on top, the balance slightly middle-and bass-orientated, more noticeably so on CAL 9242. After the finale of K.421 and a pause of about twelve seconds, the Haydn Op. 74/3 begins with the level disconcertingly higher and the transfer much brighter. This too is a very fine performance – but be prepared! Perhaps the *Dissonance* could have a stronger profile but it, too, is beautifully played and recorded.

The playing of the Salomon Quartet is highly accomplished and has a real sense of style; they do not eschew vibrato, though their use of it is not liberal, and there is admirable clarity of texture and vitality of articulation. There is no want of subtlety and imagination in the slow movements. The recordings are admirably truthful and lifelike, and those who seek 'authenticity' in Mozart's chamber music will not be disappointed.

There are also very impressive performances by the Kuijken Quartet on Denon, again using original instruments. One is struck how at the opening of the *Dissonance Quartet*, which comes first on disc 1, the sparer textures add to the sense of the music's originality. Certainly slow movements sound leaner than with modern instruments, but finales dance with increased lightness. For us the Chilingirians and Talich are both special in these works, but for those wanting period performances the Kuijkens can be strongly recommended alongside the Salomon Quartet on Hyperion.

The Medici provide a polished, well-integrated set of 'Haydn' quartets, fresh and alert, if without always the touch of extra individuality that appears in their account of the *Clarinet quintet*. The studio recordings are rather closely balanced (although they are not airless) and the leader is obviously near the microphone. These records are competitively priced and certainly give pleasure.

There is no question as to the power and brilliance of the Emersons' playing: the quality of their technical finish, unanimity of thought, impeccable intonation and spot-on ensemble is hardly in question. However, they do not seem fully attuned to the sensibility of the period. They play wonderfully and with great intelligence, but there is little sense of repose or relaxation in the slow movements and too much power in the outer movements. Those wanting to sample this series could try the separate CD which couples K.428, one of the most felt performances, with K.464, where the variations of the *Andante* show the players at their most articulate but less able to charm the ear. This disc also includes Mozart's projected original finale of the latter, an engaging 6/8 movement which, nevertheless, ends in mid-air where the composer abandoned it.

With the Ysaÿe Quartet the *G major*, K.387, is more closely balanced than the *D minor*, K.421, and on the second disc this also seems to apply, if to a lesser extent, when comparing K.458 with K.428. The playing in K.387 is what the French call *nerveux* and there is little sense of space in the faster movements or repose in the slow movement. In the first movement of the *D minor*, K.421, the players' feelings do not seem to be engaged, and there is a similar impression in the *Andante con moto* of K.428, although they are at their most impressive in the calm atmosphere of the *Adagio* of K.458. The *Dissonance Quartet* opens well, but the slow movement is bland and here, as in K.464, the resonant sound gives inflated textures. The playing is most enjoyable in the finale of the A major work, which is very spirited.

String quartet No. 14 in G, K.387; (i) String quintet No. 4 in G min., K.516.
(Y/B) *** ASV Dig. CDDCA 923 [id.]. Lindsay Qt, (i) with Patrick Ireland.

This is what chamber-music playing is about. The Lindsays radiate a delight in their music and judge the character of each piece of music exactly. There is none of the chromium-plated perfection of the Emersons, and one has only to compare the finale of K.387, played with enormous vitality and sparkle (even with an element of risk in the virtuosity), with that of the Quatuor Ysaÿe on Decca to sense immediately that the music-making is a world apart. The slow movement of the *G minor String quintet* is very touching in its gentle intensity. These are among the very finest modern recordings of either work. They were made in All Saints', Petersham, and the fairly close microphones are in no way intrusive, capturing the players against a very attractive ambience. The disc must be recommended with enthusiasm and we hope it will be the first of a series.

String quartets Nos. 15 in D min., K.421; 17 in B flat (Hunt), K.458.
*** Denon C37 7003 [id.]. Smetana Qt.

The Smetana find just the right tempo for the first movement of the *D minor*, unhurried but forward-moving. *The Hunt*, which is placed first on the disc, is given a spirited performance and is rather more polished than most of its CD rivals; it is a pleasure to report with enthusiasm on these well-paced accounts.

String quartets Nos. 17 in B flat (Hunt), K.458; 19 in C (Dissonance), K.465.
❀ *** Teldec/Warner 2292 43037-2 [id.]. Alban Berg Qt.

The Alban Berg version of the *Hunt quartet* dates from 1979 and is still possibly the finest account on the market. It has great polish and freshness and well withstands all the competition that has come since. The *Dissonance* is of similar vintage. It, too, is first class, with a wonderfully expressive account of the slow movement; there is a sense of total dedication about these wholly excellent performances, which are recommended with enthusiasm. No reservations about the transfers.

String quartets Nos. 20 in D (Hoffmeister), K.499; 21 in D, K.575; 22 in B flat, K.589; 23 in F, K.590 (Prussian Quartets Nos. 1–3).
*** CRD CRD 3427/8; *CRD C 4127/8* [id.]. Chilingirian Qt.

The Chilingirian Quartet give very natural, unforced, well-played and sweet-toned accounts of the last four *Quartets*. They are very well recorded too, with cleanly focused lines and a warm, pleasing ambience; indeed in this respect these two discs are second to none.

(i) *String quartets Nos. 20 in D, K.499; 21 in D, K.575;* (ii) *Violin sonata No. 17 in C, K.296.*
*** Calliope CAL 9244 [id.]. (i) Talich Qt; (ii) Peter Messiereur, Stanislav Bogunia.

The Talich coupling of K.499 and K.575 is digital and the recording brighter and more present than in the *Haydn Quartets*. The playing has comparable sensibility and plenty of vitality.

String quartets Nos. 21 in D, K.575; 22 in B flat, K.589.
*** Nimbus Dig. NI 5351 [id.]. Franz Schubert Qt.

The Franz Schubert Quartet play with refreshing lack of affectation and great sweetness of tone. There is perhaps more sweetness than depth in the slow movements; but at the same time it must be said that there is nothing narcissistic about the playing, and the listener is held from start to finish. They are very well recorded too. At 51 minutes 46 seconds there would be room for another quartet, but, as a glance above and below will confirm, this is a criticism that can be widely levelled.

String quartets Nos. 21 in D, K.575; 23 in F, K.590.
(Y/B) **(*) Arcana Dig. A 9 [id.]. Festetics Qt.

The Hungarian Quatuor Festetics, who play '*sur instruments d'époque*', as the French so engagingly put it, approach Mozart with a degree of severity that not all will take to. The opening of K.575 is superbly poised, and the *Andante* is most eloquent. But never a suspicion of a smile until the arrival of the Minuet, and even this is very purposeful. Strong accents abound, and there is something a bit spare about the finale too, vital though it is. There is some marvellous playing throughout both quartets, and the performances have much strength and gravitas, to say nothing of superb ensemble and the most careful control of light and shade. A record to be greatly admired, but not one to fall in love with. The recording is made in an unlikely venue, the Zögernitz Casino in Vienna, and is vividly faithful, if a bit close.

Complete Mozart Edition, Volume 11: *String quintets Nos. 1–6.*
(M) *** Ph. 422 511-2 (3). Grumiaux Trio, with Gerecz, Lesueur.

(i) *String quintets Nos. 1–6;* (ii) *Clarinet quintet in A, K.581.*
(N) ❀ (M) *** Cal. CAL 9231/3 [id.]. Talich Qt, with (i) Bohuslav Zahradnik; (ii) Karel Rehak.
(M) *** Sony M3YK 45827 (3). (i) Juilliard Qt with John Graham; (ii) Harold Wright, Marlboro Ens. (Alexander Schneider, Isidore Cohen, Samuel Rhodes, Leslie Parnas).

String quintets (Nos. 5) in D, K.593; (6) in E flat, K.614.
(N) *** Cal. Dig. CAL 9233 [id.]. Talich Qt, Karel Rehak.

Glorious performances from the augmented Talich Quartet, with both the *C major* and *G minor* (together on the first disc), unforgettable in their expressive warmth, matching of timbre and easy, unforced spontaneity. The *Adagio* of the *G minor* is raptly beautiful. The second disc, which includes the *Clarinet quintet* in a gently radiant account featuring Bohuslav Zahradnik as the soloist, has been praised above in its separate issue; suffice it to say that the third disc, containing K.593 and K.614, is equally rewarding. The playing time is only 49 minutes 26 seconds, but this is still a disc to treasure. The recording balance is exemplary throughout and the acoustic admirably chosen. Everything is clear and naturally projected without any digital exaggeration. The three discs are currently offered for the price of two. The set has already been awarded a Diapason D'or.

The Grumiaux ensemble's survey of the *String quintets* offers immensely civilized and admirably conceived readings. Throughout the set the vitality and sensitivity of this team are striking, and in general this eclipses all other recent accounts. The remastering of the 1973 recordings for CD is very successful indeed.

While the Grumiaux box remains preferable, the Juilliard set on the Sony makes a very good alternative. The performances are finely shaped and very alive, and even those who do not always warm to this ensemble will find them both alive and responsive here. There is depth in slow movements and plenty of spirit elsewhere. The first movement of the *D major*, K.593, for example, is a delight. The recordings, which emanate from the late 1970s, have come up very well and the set has the additional inducement of offering a very musical account of the *Clarinet quintet* from 1970.

String quintets (Nos. 1) in B flat, K.174 (with original version of *Trio of the Minuet* and *Finale*); *(2) in C, K.515*.
(N) (BB) **(*) Naxos Dig. 8.553103 [id.]. Eder Qt, with János Fehérvári.

String quintets (Nos. 4) in C min., K.406; (3) in G min., K.516.
(N) (BB) *(*) Naxos Dig. 8.553104 [id.]. Eder Qt, with János Fehérvári.

The augmented Eder Quartet move on to what is obviously going to be a complete set of the *String quintets*, and the first disc again displays their unexaggerated Mozartian style, a fine blend of tone and musicianship. The *Andante* of the *C major Quintet* is particularly eloquent, the finale as lively as it is graceful. The recording (again using the Budapest Unitarian Church) is full and natural, with the resonance adding ambient bloom without too much inflation. While not a match for the Talich or Hausmusik, these performances are eminently recommendable to those with limited budgets. But after the success of the first disc, the second is disappointing. The playing is still thoughtful and ensemble is clean, but there is an element of routine, and neither performance really takes off. It is not until the opening *Adagio* of the finale of the *G minor Quartet* that the Eder account achieves real concentration.

String quintets (Nos. 2) in C, K.515; (3) in G min., K.516; 5 in D, K.593; 6 in E flat, K.614.
(N) (M) *** Virgin Veritas/EMI Dig. VCD 45169-2 (2). Hausmusik.

String quintets (Nos. 2) in C, K.515; (3) in G min., K.516.
(N) **(*) Sony Dig. SK 66259 [id.]. L'Archibudelli.
** RCA Dig. 09026 60940-2 [id.]. Tokyo Qt, Pinchas Zukerman.

Those seeking period performances of the four finest of the Mozart *Quintets* should be more than satisfied with the playing of Hausmusik. These recordings were made in 1991/2, and for some reason the set was not completed. But as the very opening of the *C major* readily demonstrates, this playing brings a wonderfully light rhythmic touch and is remarkably airy in texture. The first movement of the *G minor* is managed no less beautifully, while the allegros of both the *D major* and *E flat major Quintets* burst with energy. Slow movements have a movingly restrained espressivo, withdrawn but without a feeling of austerity, and the *Adagio* of the *G minor* is hauntingly dark in its gentle melancholy. Finales bounce along joyfully and, although quite different in character, these performances are every bit as rewarding as those on modern instruments by the Talich. The EMI recording is very distinguished in its fine balance and naturalness.

With L'Archibudelli, allegros (including Minuets) have a pleasing lilt and rhythmic lift, and the fresh, transparent textures avoid edginess. Some might find the accents in the slow movement of the *C major* a shade too forceful; but in the beautiful *Adagio* of the *G minor*, where a minimum of vibrato creates a somewhat austere beauty, the concentration is in no doubt The tension is carried over to the sustained opening of the finale, which then takes off infectiously when the allegro arrives. Excellent vivid recording within an open acoustic. But there is less grace and charm here than with Hausmusik.

In terms of unanimity of ensemble, technical finesse and tonal blend, the Tokyo is one of the finest quartets now before the public and their accounts of both these great works is marked by impeccable technical address. But feeling resides on the surface and there is too little sense of spontaneity or the depth and poignancy this great music must have. Compare the humanity and naturalness of the Talich set or the Grumiaux on Philips, and one is in a different world.

Complete Mozart Edition, Volume 15: *Violin sonatas Nos. 1–34; Sonatinas in C & F, K.46d & 46e; Sonatina in F (for beginners), K.547; Sonata in C, K.403* (completed Stadler); *Adagio in C min., K.396; Allegro in B flat, K.372; Andante & allegretto in C, K.404; Andante in A & Fugue in A min., K.402* (completed Stadler); *12 Variations on 'La bergère Célimène', K.359; 6 Variations on 'Hélas, j'ai perdu mon amant', K.360.*
(M) **(*) Ph. Analogue/Dig. 422 515-2 (7). Gérard Poulet, Blandine Verlet; Arthur Grumiaux, Walter Klien; Isabelle van Keulen, Ronald Brautigan.

The early sonatas, from K.6 through to K.31, were recorded in the mid-1970s by Gérard Poulet with Blandine Verlet on harpsichord. The various fragments, sonatinas, sonatas (K.46d, K.46e, K.403 and K.547) and variations were recorded in 1990 by Isabelle van Keulen and Ronald Brautigan. For the remaining four CDs, Philips have turned to the set by Arthur Grumiaux and Walter Klien, recorded digitally in the early 1980s. There is a great deal of sparkle and some refined musicianship in these performances, and pleasure remains undisturbed by the balance which, in the 1981 recordings, favours the violin. The later recordings, from 1982 and 1983, are much better in this respect.

Violin sonatas Nos. 1–16, K.6–15 & 26–31.
(B) *** Ph. Duo 438 803-2 (2) [id.]. Gérard Poulet, Blandine Verlet.

These early *Violin sonatas* include the young Mozart's first works to appear in print. It seems impossible to determine how much there is of Mozart's father, Leopold, in their composition; certainly he master-minded the project (and the music of J. C. Bach was also a probable influence), but the precociously sprightly invention is consistently ear-catching and, even if the keyboard dominates the musical argu-ment, the violinist is always making attractive comments. The performances here are most persuasive in their vitality and freshness, and they are very well balanced and recorded (in 1975). This set derives from Volume 15 of Philips's Complete Mozart Edition and is well worth having as a separate issue. There is much to delight and fascinate the ear, although these are records to dip into rather than to play all through!

Clara Haskil: The Legacy, Volume 1: Chamber music

Violin sonatas Nos. 18; 21; 24; 26; 32; 34.
(Y/B) (M) (***) Ph. mono 442 625-2 (5) [id.]. Arthur Grumiaux, Clara Haskil – BEETHOVEN: *Violin sonatas Nos. 1-10.* (***)

Violin sonatas Nos. 18 in C, K.301; 21 in E min., K.304; 24 in F, K.376; 26 in B flat, K.378.
(Y/B) (M) (***) Ph. mono 442 629-2. Arthur Grumiaux, Clara Haskil.

Violin sonatas Nos. 32 in B flat, K.454; 34 in A, K.526.
(Y/B) (M) (***) Ph. mono 442 630-2. Arthur Grumiaux, Clara Haskil.

These six sonatas come – coupled with the complete *Violin sonatas* of Beethoven – as Volume One of Philips's so-called 'Clara Haskil Legacy'. This was a celebrated partnership and these classic accounts, which have excited much admiration over the years (and which doubtless will continue to do so), have been excellently transferred. The original mono recordings come from the late 1950s, yet the sound is remarkably vivid and true, and background noise has been virtually vanquished. The performances represent the musical yardstick by which all later versions were judged and are highly recommendable. The discs currently are not available separately.

Violin sonatas Nos. 26 in B flat, K.378; 28 in E flat, K.380; 32 in B flat, K.454; Violin sonatina in F, K.457.
*** Olympia OCD 125 [id.]. Igor Oistrakh, Natalia Zertsalova.

Igor Oistrakh has not as assertive a personality as his father, and he makes a very real partnership here with Zertsalova, who is an excellent Mozartian. These are all splendid works and they are played with fine classical feeling and impetus; the Rondo finale of K.380 is a demonstrable example of the sparkle of this music-making. The recording, too, is truthful.

PIANO MUSIC
Piano duet

Complete Mozart Edition, Volume 16: (i) *Andante with 5 variations, K.501; Fugue in C min., K.426; Sonatas for piano duet in C, K.19d; D, K.381; G, K.357; B flat, K.358; F, K.497; C, K.521; Sonata in D for two pianos, K.448;* (ii) *Larghetto and Allegro in E flat* (reconstructed Badura-Skoda).
(M) ** Ph. 422 516-2 (2) [id.]. (i) Haebler, Hoffman; (ii) Demus, Badura-Skoda.
(N) [B] *** Ph. Duo 454 026-2 (2) [id.]. Haebler, Hoffmann; Demus, Badura-Skoda (as above)

This two-CD set includes all the music Mozart composed for piano duet or two pianos, in elegant (if at times a little too dainty) performances by Ingrid Haebler and Ludwig Hoffman in recordings dating from the mid-1970s. Also included is a Mozart fragment, the *Larghetto and Allegro in E flat*, probably written in 1782–3 and completed by Paul Badura-Skoda, who recorded it in 1971 for the Amadeo label with Jörg Demus. Despite the occasional distant clink of Dresden china, all these performances give pleasure and are very decently recorded. They are also now available on an inexpensive Duo set.

Andante with 5 variations, K.501; Sonata in D for 2 pianos, K.448.
*** Chandos Dig. CHAN 9162 [id.]. Louis Lortie, Hélène Mercier (with SCHUBERT: *Fantasia in F min.* ***).

The Louis Lortie–Hélène Mercier partnership give one of the most sensitive accounts of the *D major Sonata*, K.448, currently available on disc, and their account of the *Andante and variations* is equally fine. The Schubert coupling is also recommendable. Very good recording.

Sonata in D, K.448.
*** Sony SK 39511 [id.]. Murray Perahia, Radu Lupu – SCHUBERT: *Fantasia in D min.* ***

With Perahia taking the primo part, his brightness and individual way of illuminating even the simplest passage-work dominate the performance, producing magical results and challenging the more inward Lupu into comparably inspired playing. Pleasantly ambient recording made at The Maltings, Snape, and beautifully caught on CD.

Sonatas: in F, K.497; in C, K.521; Pieces for mechanical organ: *Adagio and allegro in F min., K.594; Adagio and allegro in F min., K.608.*
✹ *** Ottavio Dig. OTR C129242. Imogen Cooper and Anne Queffélec.

Above all, these performances convey a sense of joy in the music. The *Sonatas* – both highly inspired – are framed by the two works for mechanical clock, which here sound both thoughtful and unusually commanding: the opening *Adagio* of K.594 is wonderfully serene. The first movement of the *C major Sonata* sets off with great spirit, yet detail is always imaginatively observed; the *Andante* which follows is delightfully poised, and the finale has the lightest touch. The slow movement of K.497 reminds the listener immediately of the horn concertos, a lovely, flowing melody, so persuasively presented, while the finale has a most engaging lilt. Altogether this is playing of great distinction. Everything is marvellously fresh and there is never the least suspicion of Dresden china. Very strongly recommended.

Solo piano music

Piano sonatas Nos. 1–18; Fantasia in C min., K.475.
✹ (M) *** Ph. Dig. 422 517-2 (5) [id.]. Mitsuko Uchida.
(N) (B) *** Decca 443 717-2 (5). András Schiff (piano).

Piano sonatas Nos. 1–18; Sonatas in C, K.46d; in F, K.46e.
(B) *** DG 419 445-2 (5) [id.]. Christoph Eschenbach.

On Philips, Mitsuko Uchida's collection, with beautiful and naturally balanced digital recording made in the Henry Wood Hall, London, has now been reissued on 5 mid-priced CDs by omitting the shorter pieces, except for the *C minor Fantasia*. Miss Uchida's set of the Mozart *Sonatas* brings playing of consistently fine sense and sound musicianship. There is every indication that this will come to be regarded as a classic series to set alongside those of Gieseking and Walter Klien. Every phrase is beautifully placed, every detail registers, and the early *Sonatas* are as revealing as the late ones. The piano recording is completely realistic, slightly distanced in a believable ambience.

András Schiff's earlier, Decca recordings now also reappear, in a bargain box. Schiff, without exceeding the essential Mozartian sensibility, takes a somewhat more romantic and forward-looking view of the music. His fingerwork is precise yet mellow, and his sense of colour consistently excites admiration. He is slightly prone to self-indulgence in the handling of some phrases, but such is the inherent freshness and spontaneity of his playing that one accepts the idiosyncrasies as a natural product of live perform-ance. The piano is set just a little further back than in the Philips/Uchida recordings, and the acoustic is marginally more open, which suits his slightly more expansive manner.

Christoph Eschenbach gives consistently well-turned, cool and elegant performances without affect-ation or mannerism. Those looking for an unidiosyncratic, direct approach to Mozart should find this poised, immaculate pianism to their taste. The famous *Andante grazioso* variations which form the first movement of the *Sonata in A*, K.331, are entirely characteristic, played very simply and directly. Other pianists are gentler, more romantic, but Eschenbach's taste cannot be faulted and the clean precision of the *Rondo Alla Turca* finale is very impressive.

Piano sonatas Nos. 1–18; Fantasias: in D min., K.397; C min., K.475.
*** DG Dig. 431 760-2 (6). Maria João Pires.

Piano sonatas Nos. 1 in C, K.279; 2 in F, K.280; 9 in D, K.311; 18 in D, K.576.
*** DG Dig. 435 882-2 [id.]. Maria João Pires.

Piano sonatas Nos. 3 in B flat, K.281; 4 in E flat, K.282; 15 in F: Andante and allegro, K.533; Rondo, K.494.
*** DG Dig. 437 546-2 [id.]. Maria João Pires.

Piano sonatas Nos. 5 in G, K.283; 6 in D, K.284; 10 in C, K.330.
*** DG Dig. 437 791-2 [id.]. Maria João Pires.

Piano sonatas Nos. 7 in C, K.309; 12 in F, K.332; 17 in B flat, K.570.
*** DG Dig. 439 769-2 [id.]. Maria João Pires.

Piano sonatas Nos. 8 in A min., K.310; 13 in B flat, K.333; 16 in C, K.545.
*** DG Dig. 427 768-2 [id.]. Maria João Pires.

Piano sonatas Nos. 11 in A, K.331; 14 in C min., K.457; Fantasias: in C min., K.475; in D min., K.397.
*** DG Dig. 429 739-2 [id.]. Maria João Pires.

Maria João Pires is a stylist and a fine Mozartian, as those who have heard any of her cycle on Denon will know. But this splendid new DG set marks a step forward over her earlier interpretations. Pires is always refined yet never wanting in classical feeling, and she has a vital imagination. In these new readings there is even more life: she strikes an ideal balance between poise and expressive sensibility, conveying a sense of spontaneity in everything she does. Moreover, the DG recording is fuller, with greater depth than the Denon set, and the slight dryness to the timbre suits the interpretations, which are expressively fluid and calm without a trace of self-consciousness. With allegros always alert and vital yet never too predictable in their expressive contrasts, this is playing to stimulate the listener consistently – even the hackneyed *C major Sonata*, K.545, sounds freshly minted. While Uchida's much-praised versions are full of personal intimacy, Pires's more direct style with its tranquil eloquence is no less satisfying.

Piano sonatas Nos. 2 in F, K.280; 4 in E flat, K.282; 14 in C min., K.457; Fantasia in C min., K.475.
(B) ** Discover Dig. DICD 920144 [id.]. Aldo Ciccolini.

Piano sonatas Nos. 3 in B flat, K.281; 12 in F, K.332; 13 in B flat, K.333.
(B) ** Discover Dig. DICD 920148 [id.]. Aldo Ciccolini.

Piano sonatas Nos. 7 in C, K.309; 10 in C, K.330; 16 in C, K.545.
(B) ** Discover Dig. DICD 920145 [id.]. Aldo Ciccolini.

Aldo Ciccolini's new digital survey of the Mozart *Sonatas* is strikingly well recorded: the presence of the piano is very tangible. However, the forwardness emphasizes the playing style, which is very strong, even percussive, in its directness of articulation. That is not to suggest a lack of sensibility, only that (for some ears) the effect may seem too forceful for this repertoire. When Ciccolini relaxes and plays lightly, he can readily charm the ear, but the fortissimos are very strongly accented indeed.

Piano sonatas Nos. 3 in B flat, K.281; 10 in C, K.330; 13 in B flat, K.333; Adagio in B min., K.540; Rondo in D, K.485.
(Y/B) (M) *** DG Dig. 445 517-2 [id.]. Vladimir Horowitz.

Playing of such strong personality from so great an artist is self-recommending. With Horowitz there were astonishingly few reminders of the passage of time and the artistry and magnetism remain undiminished. The recordings were made in the pianist's last vintage period, between 1985 and 1989, in either a New York studio, the pianist's home, or an Italian studio in Milan (K.333). As usual, the piano is tightly tuned and the sound is slightly shallow, though very suitable for Mozart. Remarkable playing, not always completely free from affectation; but for variety of articulation just sample the *Allegretto grazioso* finale of K.333 and, for simply expressed depth of feeling, the *Adagio*, K. 540.

Piano sonatas Nos. 4 in E flat, K.282; 5 in G, K.283; 10 in C, K.330; 12 in F, K.332.
(M) **(*) Decca 433 900-2 [id.]. Wilhelm Backhaus – HAYDN: *Sonatas.* **(*)

Backhaus was always magisterial and here his playing, strongly classical in style, commands the listener's interest. The rhythmic control is not always exact, but the whole effect is far removed from the scented periwig style of Mozart pianism, and if the sonatas are taken one at a time the spontaneous quality of the playing is enjoyable for its sheer strength of personality. However, listening to the recital as a whole, one is conscious that rather more lightening of the texture is needed in slow movements. The recording, from the 1960s, is faithful and clear.

Piano sonatas No. 8 in A min., K.310; 11 in A, K.331; 15 in F, K.533.
✪ *** Sony Dig. SK 48233 [id.]. Murray Perahia.

Murray Perahia celebrates his return to the recording studios with this recital, which is easily the finest Mozart sonata record for some years. Such is his artistry that one is never consciously aware of it. Again we have the old story of the search for truth producing beauty almost as a by-product. Nothing is beautified, nor does he shrink from conveying that hint of pain that fleetingly disturbs the symmetry of the slow movements. The Sony engineers provide excellent sound. Here is one of the records that will be reissued in 2010 or thereabouts as a 'Great Recording of the Last Century'.

Piano sonatas Nos. 12 in F, K.332; 13 in B flat, K.333; 14 in C min., K.457; Fantasy in C min.
*** Sony Dig. SK 46748 [id.]. Andreas Haefliger.

The Swiss-born, Juilliard-trained Andreas Haefliger is still in his twenties and shows himself to be an impressive Mozartian. These are finely poised and well-integrated performances with plenty of sensitivity. The Sony recording is very clean and firm. Eminently recommendable.

Complete Mozart Edition, Volume 18: *8 Variations in G, K.24; 7 Variations in D, K.25; 12 Variations in C, K.179; 6 Variations in G, K.180; 9 Variations in C, K.264; 12 Variations in C, K.265; 8 Variations in F, K.352; 12 Variations in E flat, K.353; 12 Variations in E flat, K.354; 6 Variations in F, K.398; 10 Variations in G, K.455; 12 Variations in B flat, K.500; 9 Variations in D, K.573; 8 Variations in F, K.613; Adagio in B min., K.540; Eine kleine Gigue in G, K.574; Fantasia in D min., K.397; Minuet in D, K.355; Rondos: in D, K.485; in A min., K.511; 21 Pieces for keyboard, K.1, K.1a–1d;1f; K.2–5; K.5a; K.33b; K.94; K.312; K.394–5; K.399–401; K.408/1; K.453a; K.460.*
(M) ** Ph. Analogue/Dig. 422 518-2 (5) [id.]. Ingrid Haebler or Mitsuko Uchida (both piano), Ton Koopman (harpsichord).

Although the gentle clink of Dresden china can occasionally be heard, Ingrid Haebler is an intelligent and perceptive artist who characterizes these variations with some subtlety. The quality of the sound is very good indeed: there is both warmth and presence. Mitsuko Uchida gives us various short pieces, such as the *A minor Rondo*, K.511, and the *B minor Adagio*, K.540, which she plays beautifully – though at less than 40 minutes her disc offers rather short measure. However, Haebler and Koopman make up for that, the latter offering 21 short pieces, including some juvenilia, which he dispatches with some degree of brusqueness. He is very brightly recorded.

VOCAL MUSIC

Complete Mozart Edition, Volume 22: (i) *Adagio and fugue in C min., K.546; Maurerische Trauermusik, K.477.* (ii) *La Betulia liberata (oratorio), K.118.* (iii) *Davidde penitente (cantata), K.469.* (iv) *Grabmusik (Funeral music), K.42.* (v; i) Masonic music: *Dir, Seele des Weltalls, K.429; Ihr unsre neuen Leiter, K.484; Die ihr unermesslichen Weltalls Schöpfer, ehrt, K.619; Lasst uns mit geschlung'gnen Händen, K.623; Laut verkünde unsre Freude, K.623; Lied zur Gesellenreise, K.468; Lobgesang auf die feierliche Johannisloge, K.148; Die Maurerfreude, K.471; Zerfliesset heut, geliebte Brüder, K.483.* (vi) *Passionslied: Kommet her, ihr frechen Sünder, K.146.* (vii) *Die Schuldigkeit des ersten Gebots (Singspiel), K.35.*
(M) **(*) Ph. Analogue/Dig. 422 522-2 (6) [id.]. (i) Dresden State O, Schreier; (ii) Schreier, Cotrubas, Berry, Fuchs, Zimmermann, Salzburg Chamber Ch. & Mozarteum O, Hagen; (iii) M. Marshall, Vermillion, Blochwitz; (iv) Murray, Varcoe; (v) Schreier, Blochwitz, Schmidt, Leipzig R. Ch.; (vi) Murray; (vii) M. Marshall, Murray, Nielsen, Blochwitz, Baldin; (iii; iv; vi; vii) Stuttgart RSO, Marriner.

The two big oratorios are both early works, *La Betulia liberata* and (even earlier, dating from his twelfth year) *Die Schuldigkeit des ersten Gebots* ('The Duty of the First Commandment'). *Davidde penitente* is the cantata largely derived from the torso of the *C minor Mass*, while the sixth disc, in many ways the most inspired of all, contains the Masonic music, vividly done in Dresden under the direction of Peter Schreier. For convenience that disc also includes the purely instrumental Masonic music, the *Maurerische Trauermusik* and the *Adagio and fugue in C minor*. Directed by Leopold Hager, *La Betulia liberata* is a plain, well-sung performance that does not quite disguise the piece's excessive length. Sir Neville Marriner is the conductor both of *Die Schuldigkeit* and of *Davidde penitente*, giving sparkle to the early oratorio and vigour to the cantata, a fine piece. Full texts are given, and informative notes on individual works.

Complete Mozart Edition, Volume 20: (i) *Alma Dei creatoris, K.277;* (ii) *Ave verum corpus, K.618;* (i) *Benedictus sit Deus Pater, K.117; Cibavit eos ex adipe frumenti, K.44;* (iii) *Dixit et Magnificat, K.193;* (i) *Ergo interest, an quis, K.143;* (ii) *Exsultate jubilate, K.165;* (i) *God is our refuge (motet), K.20; Inter natos Mulierum, K.72;* (iii) *Litaniae de B M V (Lauretanae), K.109 & K.195;* (i) *Kyries, K.33; K.90–91; K.322–3;* (ii) *Kyrie, K.341;* (iii) *Litaniae de venerabili altaris sacramento, K.125 & K.243;* (i) *Miserere mei, Deus, K.85; Misercordias Domini, K.222; Quaerite primum regnum Dei, K.86; Regina coeli, laetare, K.108;*

K.127; K.276; Sancta Maria, mater Dei, K.273; Scande coeli limina, K.34; Sub tuum praesidium, K.198; Te Deum laudamus, K.141; Veni, Sancte Spiritus, K.47; Venite, populi, venite, K.260; (ii) *Vesperae solennes de confessore, K.339;* (iii) *Vesperae solennes de Domenica, K.321.*

(M) *** Ph. 422 520-2 (5) [id.]. (i) Nawe, Reinhardt-Kiss, Schellenberger-Ernst, Selbig, Burmeister, Lang, Büchner, Eschrig, Ribbe, Pape, Polster; (ii) Te Kanawa, Bainbridge, Ryland Davies, Howell, London Symphony Ch. & LSO, Sir Colin Davis; (iii) Frank-Reinecke, Shirai, Burmeister, Riess, Büchner, Polster, (i; iii) Leipzig R. Ch. & SO, Kegel.

It is fascinating to find that the boy Mozart's very first religious piece is an unaccompanied motet, written in London to an English text, *God is our refuge* – which here the Leipzig singers very forgivably pronounce 'reefuge'. Herbert Kegel with the Dresden Staatskapelle and his Leipzig Radio Choir are responsible for the great majority of the pieces here, fresh and alert if on occasion rhythmically too rigid. The big exception is the great setting of the *Solemn vespers*, K.339, for which Sir Colin Davis's 1971 version has understandably been preferred, when the young Kiri Te Kanawa sings the heavenly soprano setting of *Laudate Dominum* so ravishingly. She is also the soloist in the early cantata *Exsultate jubilate* with its brilliant *Alleluia*. Those 1971 recordings, made in London, are bass-heavy, but the rest brings very fresh and clean recording, with the choir generally more forwardly placed than in the recordings of Mozart's Masses, made by the same forces.

Complete Mozart Edition, Volume 23: (i) *2 Canons for strings; 14 Canons for woodwind; 10 Interval canons for woodwind;* (ii) *6 Canons for female voices; 3 Canons for mixed voices; 13 Canons for male voices; 4 puzzle canons for mixed voices.* (iii) *53 Concert arias. Aria* (with ornamentation by Mozart) for: J. C. BACH: *Adriano in Siria.* (iv) *8 Vocal Duets, Trios and Quartets.* (v) Alternative arias and duets for: *Così fan tutte; Don Giovanni; Die Entführung aus dem Serail; La finta semplice; Idomeneo; Lucio Silla; Mitridate; Le nozze di Figaro.*

(M) *** Ph. 422 523-2 (8) [id.]. (i) Bav. RSO (members); (ii) Ch. Viennensis, Mancusi or Harrer; (iii) Moser, Schwarz, Popp, Mathis, Gruberová, Sukis, Araiza, Ahnsjö, Lloyd, Berry, Kaufmann, Blochwitz, Lind, Burrows, Eda-Pierre; (iv) Blochwitz, Schariner, Pape, Kaufmann, Lind, Jansen, Schreier; (v) Blochwitz, Szmytka, Wiens, Gudbjörnson, Vermillion, Schreier, Mathis, Burrows, Tear, Terfel, Kaufmann, Lind, Scharinger.

This Philips set offers not just a collection of a dozen or so ensembles and a whole disc of 35 canons (some of them instrumental) but also some fascinating alternative versions and substitute arias for different Mozart operas, from *La finta semplice* and *Mitridate* through to the three Da Ponte master-pieces. It is fascinating to have Bryn Terfel, for example, as Figaro in a varied recitative and slightly extended version of the Act I aria, *Non piu' andrai*. Eva Lind is vocally a less happy choice for the items involving Susanna and Zerlina, and generally the sopranos chosen for this collection, stylish Mozartians as they are, have less sumptuous voices than those on the Decca set.

Complete Mozart Edition, Volume 24: (i) Lieder: *Abendempfindung; Als Luise die Briefe ihres ungetreuen Liebhabers; Die Alte; An Chloe; An die Freude; An die Freundschaft; Die betrogene Welt; Dans un bois solitaire; Geheime Liebe; Der Frühling; Gessellenreise; Die grossmütige Gelassenheit; Ich würd' auf meinem Pfad; Das Kinderspiel; 2 Kirchenlieder (O Gottes Lamm; Als aus Agypten); Des kleinen Friedrichs Geburtstag; Die kleine Spinnerin; Komm, liebe Zither, komm; Lied der Freiheit; Das Lied der Trennung; Un moto di gioia; Oiseaux, si tous les ans; Ridente la calma; Sehnsucht nach dem Frühling; Sei du mein Trost; Das Traumbild; Das Veilchen; Verdankt sei es dem Glanz der Grossen; Die Verschweigung; Warnung; Wie unglücklich bin ich nit; Der Zauberer; Die Zufriedenheit (2): (Was frag' ich viel nach Geld und Gut; Wie sanft, wie ruhig fühl' ich hier); Die Zufriedenheit im niedrigen Stande.* (ii) *6 Notturni for voices and woodwind, K.346; K.436/9 & K.549.*

(M) *** Ph. 422 524-2 (2) [id.]. Elly Ameling, (i) with Dalton Baldwin (piano or organ) or Benny Ludemann (mandolin); (ii) with Elisabeth Cooymans, Peter van der Bilt, Netherlands Wind Ens. (members).

Elly Ameling is the ideal soprano for such fresh and generally innocent inspirations, with her voice at its purest and sweetest when she made the recordings in 1977. In the 1973 recordings of the *Notturni* (setting Italian texts by Metastasio) she is well matched by her soprano and baritone partners, though these are mostly plainer, less distinctive miniatures. Included are two hymns with organ and two tiny songs with mandolin, while aptly the very last of the series, K.598, is one of the lightest of all, *Children's games*, sparklingly done. The recordings come up with fine freshness and presence.

Songs: *Abendempfindung; Als Luise die Briefe; An Chloe; Die betrogene Welt; Dans un bois solitaire; Komm, liebe Zither; Oiseaux, si tous les ans; Sehnsucht nach dem Frühling; Der Zauberer.*

(N) *** DG Dig. 447 106-2 [id.]. Anne Sofie von Otter, Melvyn Tan (fortepiano) – HAYDN: Songs. ***

A delightful recital in all respects. There is a winning charm in the opening *Komm, liebe Zither*, and *Oiseaux, si tous les ans* (with its curious rhythmic reminder of Sullivan's *Iolanthe*) is hardly less appealing. The disillusioned heroine of *Die betrogene Welt* ('The world deceived') has plenty of spunk, while *Abendempfindung* (Mozart at his most inspired) is tenderly moving. *An Chloe* sparkles, sounding for all the world like Schubert, while the spring-fresh *Sehnsucht nach dem Frühling* brings a captivating lilt. Melvyn Tan accompanies most sensitively and – as so often with this artist – makes one feel that nothing other than a fortepiano could have been used to give these songs the right lift. The balance seems just about ideal, and the Haydn couplings are equally pleasing.

Concert arias: *Ah! lo previdi . . . Ah t'invola, K.272; Bella mia fiamma . . . Resta oh cara, K.528; Chi sa, K.582; Nehmt meinen Dank, ihr holden Gönner, K.383; Non più, tutto ascolta . . . Non temer, amato bene, K.490; Oh temerario Arbace! . . . Per quel paterno amplesso, K.79/K.73d; Vado, ma dove?, K.583*. Opera arias: (ii) *Le nozze di Figaro: Porgi amor; E Susanna non vien! . . . Dove sono*. (iii) *Der Schauspieldirektor: Bester Jüngling!*
(M) *** Decca 440 401-2 [id.]. Kiri Te Kanawa: (i) V. CO, György Fischer; (ii) LPO, Solti; (iii) VPO, Pritchard.

Kiri Te Kanawa's Decca set of Mozart's concert arias for soprano, recorded in 1982, makes a beautiful and often brilliant recital. Items range from one of the very earliest arias, *Oh temerario Arbace*, already memorably lyrical, to the late *Vado, ma dove*, here sung for its beauty rather than for its drama. Atmospheric, wide-ranging recording, which has transferred well to CD. The arias from *Figaro* and *Schauspieldirektor* come from the complete Decca sets and show the singer at her finest.

Concert arias: *Alma grande e nobil core, K.578; Ch'io mi scordi di te?, K.505; Nehmt meinen Dank, K.383; Vado, ma dove?, K.583*. Lieder: *Abendempfindung; Als Luise die Briefe; Die Alte; An Chloë; Dans un bois solitaire; Im Frühlingsanfang; Das Kinderspiel; Die kleine Spinnerin; Das Lied der Trennung; Oiseaux, si tous les ans; Ridente la calma; Sehnsucht nach dem Frühling; Das Trumbild; Das Veilchen; Der Zauberer; Die Zuhfriedenheit*.
(M) *** EMI mono/stereo CDH7 63702-2 [id.]. Schwarzkopf, Gieseking; Brendel; LSO, Szell.

Schwarzkopf's classic series of the Mozart songs with Gieseking makes a splendid reissue at mid-price; it includes the most famous one, *Das Veilchen*. As a generous coupling, the disc also includes Schwarzkopf's much later recordings, with Szell conducting four concert arias – including the most taxing of all, *Ch'io mi scordi di te?*, with Brendel playing the piano obbligato. Though the voice is not quite so fresh in the concert arias, the artistry and imagination are supreme, and stereo recording helps to add bloom.

Concert arias: *A questo seno . . . Or che il cielo, K.374; Basta, vincesti . . . An non lasciarmi, K.486a; Voi avete un cor fedele, K.217. Exsultate, jubilate* (motet), *K.165. Litaniae de venerabili altaris sacramento, K.243: Dulcissimum convivium. Vesperae de Dominica, K.321: Laudate dominum*.
(B) *** Ph. 426 072-2. Elly Ameling, ECO, Leppard.

Elly Ameling's singing, besides being technically very secure, has a simple radiance in the phrasing which is very beautiful. She is equally happy in the concert arias, sung with delightful flexibility of phrase, and in the ecclesiastical music, where the style has a serene simplicity, while *Exsultate, jubilate* has an infectious sense of joy.

Concert arias: *Bella mia fiamma . . . Resta, o cara!, K.528; Ch'io mi scordi di te?, K.505*. Arias: *Don Giovanni: Or sai chi l'onore; Crudele! Ah, no, mio bene; Non mi dir. Idomeneo: Se il padre perdei; O smania! . . . D'Oreste e d'Ajace. Le nozze di Figaro: Porgi, amor; Deh vieni non tardar; E Susanna non vien! . . . Dove sono. Il rè pastore: L'amerò, sarò costante. Die Zauberflöte: Ach, ich fühl's*.
(M) *** RCA 09026 61357-2 [id.]. Leontyne Price, New Philh. O, Adler or Santi; RCA Italiana Op. O, Molinari-Pradelli; LSO, Downes.

This record is an adjunct to Leontyne Price's four-disc miscellaneous 'Prima donna' collection (see Recitals, below) and the items here make an equally outstanding representation of her art. One does not think of her primarily as a Mozartian, yet the very opening concert aria, *Ch'io mi scordi*, shows the extra dimension of drama in her vocal personality, never at the expense of the vocal line. She is thrilling as Electra and *Or sai chi l'onore* (*Don Giovanni*) is scarcely less vehement. The glorious legato line is heard at its most ravishing in the major *Figaro* arias, whether as Susanna (*Deh vieni*) or the Countess (*Dove sono*), and the excerpt from *Il rè pastore*, *L'amerò, sarò costante*, with its weaving violin obbligato, is radiant. Nearly all these recordings were made in the late 1960s, when the voice was at its freshest. Accompaniments are highly sympathetic and the vocal quality is most natural and vivid, and with lovely orchestral sound.

Concert arias: *Il burbero di buon cuore: Chi sà. Vado, ma dove, K.583. Exsultate, jubilate, K.165.* Arias: *La clemenza di Tito: Parto, parto. Idomeneo: Ch'io mi scordi . . . Non temer, amato bene. Le nozze di Figaro: Al desio di chi t'adore; Un moto di gioia mi sento.*
(Y/B) (M) *** Erato/Warner Dig. 4509 98497-2 [id.]. Dame Janet Baker, Scottish CO, Leppard.

In a Mozart programme, recorded in 1984, which extends well beyond the normal mezzo-soprano repertoire, Dame Janet sings with all her usual warmth, intensity and stylishness, hardly if at all stretched by often high tessitura. The biggest challenge is the most taxing of all Mozart's concert arias, *Ch'io mi scordi di te?*, with Leppard a brilliant exponent of the difficult obbligato part. There Baker, so far from being daunted by the technical problems, uses them to intensify her detailed rendering of words. The two *Figaro* items are alternative arias for Susanna, both of them delightful. Sesto's aria from *Clemenza di Tito* presents another challenge, magnificently taken, as does the early cantata, *Exsultate, jubilate*, with its famous *Alleluia*. The other two arias were written for Louise Villeneuve – Dorabella to be – as an enrichment of her part in an opera by Soler, more delightful rarities. Excellent sound with wonderful presence, and warmly sympathetic accompaniment.

Concert arias: (i) *Ch'io mi scordi di te . . . Non temer, K.505;* (ii) *Misero me! . . . Misero pergoletto, K.77; Ombra felice! . . . Io ti lascio, K.255.* Arias: (iii) *La clemenza di Tito: Parto, parto;* (iv) *Deh per questo istante solo.* (iii) *Così fan tutte: Temerari! . . . Come scoglio; E Amore un ladroncello; Ei parte . . . Per pietà;* (v) *Ah! Scostati! . . . Smanie implacabili.* (iii) *Le nozze di Figaro: Non so più; Voi che sapete;* (ii) (Replacement aria): *Giunse alfin il momento . . . Al desio di chi t'adora.*
(M) *** Decca 421 899-2 [id.]. Teresa Berganza, with (i) Geoffrey Parsons; (ii) VSO, György Fischer; (iii) LSO, Pritchard; (iv) V. State Op. O, Kertész; (iv) LPO, Solti.

The greater part of this CD represents Berganza's Mozart début recital, which received universal praise when it first appeared in 1962, her tone-colour unfailingly beautiful and the sense of style immaculate. Now the collection has been made more up to date by the inclusion of an excerpt from her complete set, *La Clemenza di Tito* of 1967, and *Smanie implacabili* from the 1973 *Così fan tutte* with Solti. To complete the picture, two more concert arias and a replacement aria which Mozart composed in 1789 for a revival of *Figaro* are added. Here one notices the extra vocal maturity, but throughout it is the consistency that is so striking, the rich voice controlled with the sort of vocal perfection one associates with her compatriot, Victoria de los Angeles. Bright, vivid transfers throughout.

Ave verum corpus, K.618.
(M) *** Decca 430 159-2 [id.]. St John's College, Cambridge, Ch., Guest – J. HAYDN: *Theresienmesse;* M. HAYDN: *Ave regina.* ***

This simple and eloquent account of Mozart's choral lollipop is beautifully recorded and, it is to be hoped, may introduce some collectors to the inspired late Haydn Mass with which it is coupled.

Ave verum corpus, K.618; Exsultate, jubilate, K.165; Kyrie in D minor, K.341; Vesperae solennes de confessore in C, K.339.
**(*) Ph. 412 873-2 [id.]. Te Kanawa, Bainbridge, Ryland Davies, Howell, London Symphony Ch., LSO, C. Davis.

This disc could hardly present a more delightful collection of Mozart choral music, ranging from the early soprano cantata, *Exsultate, jubilate*, with its famous setting of *Alleluia*, to the equally popular *Ave verum*. Kiri Te Kanawa is the brilliant soloist in the cantata, and her radiant account of the lovely *Laudate Dominum* is one of the highspots of the *Solemn vespers*, here given a fine, responsive performance. The 1971 recording has been remastered effectively, although the choral sound is not ideally focused.

(i–ii) *Ave verum corpus, K.618;* (iii–iv) *Exsultate, jubilate, K.165; Masses Nos.* (i–iii; v) *10 in C (Missa brevis): Spatzenmesse, K.220;* (ii–iii; vi) *16 in C (Coronation), K.317.*
(M) *** DG 419 060-2. (i) Regensburg Cathedral Ch.; (ii) Bav. RSO, Kubelik; (iii) Edith Mathis; (iv) Dresden State O, Klee; (v) Troyanos, Laubenthal, Engen; (vi) Procter, Grobe, Shirley-Quirk, Bav. R. Ch.

Kubelik draws a fine, vivid performance of the *Coronation Mass* from his Bavarian forces and is no less impressive in the earlier *Missa brevis*, with excellent soloists in both works. Then Edith Mathis gives a first-class account of the *Exsultate, jubilate* as an encore. The concert ends with Bernard Klee directing a serenely gentle account of the *Ave verum corpus* (recorded in 1979).

(i) *Ave verum corpus, K.618;* (ii) *Exsultate jubilate, K.165;* (i–iii) *Masses Nos. 10 in C (Spatzenmesse; 'Sparrow Mass');* (iv) *16 in C (Coronation), K.317;* (i) *Offertorium de tempore (Misericordias Domine), K.222;* (iv) *Vesperae de Domenica, K.321;* (i–iii) *Vesperae solennes de confessore, K.339.*

(B) **(*) Erato/Warner Duo 4509 95362-2 (2) [id.]. (i) Philippe Caillard Chorale; (ii) Rotraud Hansmann; (iii) Annie Bartelloni, Michel Sénéchal, Roger Soyer; V. Bar. Ens.; (iv) Patricia Wise, Monika Bürgener, Michael Cousins, Heinz Ecker, Lisbon Gulbenkian Foundation Ch. & O; all cond. Guschlbauer.

A splendid Erato Bonsai Duo collection of Mozart church music that is much more than the sum of its parts. Throughout, Theodor Guschlbauer knows just where he is going and his pacing always feels right. The choral contributions, whether of the Lisbon Chorus or the smaller, Philippe Caillard group, have both discipline and commitment: these singers really rise to the occasion. The performance of the *Spatzenmesse* is particularly attractive. It is full of high spirits and is a remarkably concise piece (the *Kyrie* lasts only 1 minute 44 seconds and the *Sanctus* is a burst of joy merely 57 seconds long). The *Benedictus* provides a fine ensemble for the solo team. Before that, we have heard the excellent soprano soloist, Rotraud Hansmann, showing her mettle in the *Exsultate jubilate*, where the famous *Alleluia* sparkles, and she is no less impressive in the more demanding and equally well-known *Laudate Dominum* of the *Solemn Vespers*, which she sings with serene radiance. In the *Laudate Dominum* of the *Vesperae de Domenica*, Patricia Wise is not her match. This is a more florid piece, much more difficult technically; it is well enough managed, but one feels that the singer is under pressure. But she leads the solo team confidently in the *Bendictus* of the *Coronation Mass*, another very lively performance, and seems altogether more at ease in the final *Agnus Dei*, where she is joined at the end by her colleagues; then the chorus closes the work vigorously in a glorious culmination, very operatic in feeling. These reservations are of minor account: all this music is greatly enjoyable, and the analogue recordings, all from the late 1960s (except K.317 and K.321, which are a decade later), are of good quality and excellently transferred. This is well worth exploring – but be warned: no documentation is provided about the music except for the cued list of tracks.

Exsultate, jubilate, K.165 (Salzburg version); Motets: *Ergo interest, K.143; Regina coeli* (2 settings), *K.108, K.127.*
*** O-L Dig. 411 832-2 [id.]. Emma Kirkby, Westminster Cathedral Boys' Ch., AAM Ch. and O, Hogwood.

The boyish, bell-like tones of Emma Kirkby are perfectly suited to the most famous of Mozart's early cantatas, *Exsultate, jubilate*, culminating in a dazzling account of *Alleluia*. With accompaniment on period instruments, that is aptly coupled with far rarer but equally fascinating examples of Mozart's early genius, superbly recorded.

(i) *Exsultate jubilate, K.165;* (ii) *Litaniae Lauretanae in D, K.195; Mass No. 16 (Coronation), K.317;* (iii) *Requiem mass (No. 19) in D min., K.626.*
(B) **(*) Double Decca 443 009-2 (2) [id.]. (i) Erna Spoorenberg; (ii; iii) Cotrubas, Watts, Tear, Shirley-Quirk; (ii) Oxford Schola Cantorum; (iii) ASMF Ch; (i–iii), ASMF, Marriner.

It is good to have Marriner's 1971 (Argo) recordings of two of Mozart's most appealing early choral works, the *Litaniae Lauretanae* and the *Coronation Mass*, back in the catalogue on this Double Decca set. The solo work is particularly good (notably Ileana Cotrubas in the two lovely *Agnus Dei* versions) and the Academy Choir is on its best form. Erna Spoorenberg's impressive *Exsultate jubilate* was recorded earlier (1966). However, Marriner generates less electricity than usual in the coupled (1977) *Requiem Mass*. It is interesting to have a version which uses the Beyer Edition and a text which aims at removing the faults of Süssmeyer's completion. Solo singing is good, and some of the choruses (the *Dies irae*, for instance) are vibrant, but at other times they are less alert and the tension slackens. The sound is excellent, well balanced and vivid.

Litaniae de venerabili altaris sacramento, K.243.
(M) *** Decca 430 158-2 [id.]. Marshall, Cable, Evans, Roberts, St John's College, Cambridge, Ch., Wren O, Guest – HAYDN: *Heiligmesse.* ***

Mozart made four settings of the Litany, of which this is the last, written in 1776. It is ambitiously scored for an orchestra of double wind, two horns and three trombones – used to add sonorous gravity to many of the choral passages and to bring point and drama to the choral fugue, *Pignus futurae gloriae*; in the beautiful *Dulcissimum convivium* the solo soprano is accompanied with flutes added to the orchestra in place of the oboes. It is Mozart at his most imaginative and vital; the artists here rise to the occasion and give a highly responsive performance, with Margaret Marshall outstanding among the soloists. Excellent 1980 sound.

Masonic music (see also above, in Complete Mozart Edition, Volume 22)

Masonic music: *Masonic funeral music (Maurerische Trauermusik), K.477; Die ihr des unermesslichen Weltals Schöpfer ehrt* (cantata), *K.619; Die ihr einen neuen Grade, K.468; Dir, Seele des Weltalls* (cantata), *K.429; Ihr unsre neuen Leiter* (song), *K.484; Lasst uns mit geschlungnen Händen, K.623a; Laut verkünde unsre Freude, K.623; O heiliges Band* (song), *K.148; Sehen, wie dem starren Forscherange, K.471; Zerfliesset heut', geliebte Brüder, K.483.*

(M) *** Decca 425 722-2. Werner Krenn, Tom Krause, Edinburgh Festival Ch., LSO, Kertész.

This Decca reissue contains the more important of Mozart's masonic music in first-class performances, admirably recorded. Most striking of all is Kertész's strongly dramatic account of the *Masonic funeral music*; the two lively songs for chorus, *Zerfliesset heut'* and *Ihr unsre neuen Leiter*, are sung with warm humanity and are also memorable. Indeed the choral contribution is most distinguished throughout, and Werner Krenn's light tenor is most appealing in the other items which he usually dominates.

Complete Mozart Edition, Volume 19: *Masses Nos. 1 in G (Missa brevis), K.49; 2 in D min. (Missa brevis), K.65; 3 in C ('Dominicus'), K.66; 4 in C min. (Weisenhaus), K.139; 5 in G (Pastoral), K.140; 6 in F (Missa brevis), K.192; 7 in C (Missa in honorem Ssmae Trinitatis), K.167; 9 in D (Missa brevis), K.194; 10 in C (Spatzenmesse; 'Sparrow Mass'), K.220; 11 in C ('Credo'), K.257; 12 in C (Spaur-Messe), K.258; 13 in C ('Organ solo'), K.259; 14 in C (Missa longa), K.262; 15 in B flat (Missa brevis), K.275; 16 in C ('Coronation'), K.317; 17 in C (Missa solemnis), K.337; 18 in C min. (Great), K.427; 19 in D min. (Requiem), K.626.*

(M) **(*) Ph. Analogue/Dig. 422 519-2 (9) [id.]. Mathis, Donath, M. Price, McNair, Montague, Shirai, Casapietra, Trudeliese Schmidt, Lang, Schiml, Markert, Burmeister, Knight, Schreier, Araiza, Heilmann, Baldin, Ryland Davies, Rolfe Johnson, Ude, Jelosits, Adam, Polster, Andreas Schmidt, Hauptmann, Rootering, Grant, Eder; Leipzig R. Ch.; Monteverdi Ch.; V. Boys' Ch.; John Alldis Ch.; Ch. Viennensis; Leipzig RSO; E. Bar. Soloists; Dresden State O; LSO; VSO; Dresden PO; Kegel; C. Davis; Gardiner; Schreier; Harrer.

Only the *C minor Mass* has period performers. John Eliot Gardiner's inspired reading, with superb soloists as well as his Monteverdi Choir and English Baroque Soloists, has rightly been chosen, and the *Requiem* comes in another outstanding modern version, with the Dresden Staatskapelle and Leipzig Radio Choir conducted by Peter Schreier, as imaginative a conductor as he is a tenor. That same choir and orchestra under the choir's regular conductor, Herbert Kegel, is responsible for the great bulk of the rest of the Masses. With the chorus tending to be placed a little backwardly, it does not always sound its freshest, but performances – with consistently clean-toned soloists, including latterly Mitsuko Shirai – are bright and well sprung. Sir Colin Davis and the LSO in the earliest recording here, dating from 1971, take a weightier view than any in the *Credo Mass*, K.257, with sound bass-heavy, but again his vigour and freshness are very compelling. Two favourite Masses, the *Coronation Mass* and the *Spatzenmesse* (Sparrow Mass), come in performances conducted by Uwe Christian Harrer with the Vienna Symphony Orchestra and the Vienna Boys' Choir; boys also distinctively take the soprano and alto solos. Though Harrer's speeds tend to be slow, the rhythmic buoyancy is most compelling, with choral sound full and forward.

Mass No. 3 in C (Dominicus), K.66; Vesperae de Domenica, K.321.
(Y/B) (M) *** Teldec/Warner Dig. 2292 46469-2 [id.]. Margiono, Bonney, Von Magnus, Heilmann, Cachemaille, Arnold Schoenberg Ch., V. Hofburgkapelle Choral Scholars, VCM, Harnoncourt.

Harnoncourt is at his finest in this splendidly lively Mass which the thirteen-year-old Mozart wrote for a personal friend ten years his senior when he took holy orders. It has sixteen brief jewels of movements, and the direct Harnoncourt style with its strong accents and positive characterization brings every one of them vividly to life. The bright tempi too are apt and the soloists equally strong. The more ambitious *Vesperae de Domenica*, written a decade later, with its plainsong introduction to each of six sections, forms a neat and joyful *Missa brevis*, here refreshingly alive and brimful of variety of invention. Again the singing of chorus and soloists alike is highly stimulating, and Harnoncourt's affection brings a committed and vivacious approach which is entirely successful. The recording is first rate.

Mass No. 4 in C min. (Weisenhausmesse), K.139.
(M) *** DG 427 255-2. Janowitz, Von Stade, Moll, Ochman, V. State Op. Ch., VPO, Abbado.

(i; ii) *Mass No. 4 in C min. (Weisenhaus), K.139;* (i) *Exsultate jubilate, K.165.*
(Y/B) (M) **(*) Teldec/Warner Dig. 2292 44180-2 [id.]. (i) Barbara Bonney; (ii) Rappé, Protschka, Hagegård, Arnold Schoenberg Ch., VCM, Harnoncourt.

By any standards this is a remarkably sustained example of the thirteen-year-old composer's powers, with bustling allegros in the *Kyrie, Gloria* and *Credo*, as well as at the end of the *Agnus Dei*, while the *Gloria* and *Credo* end with full-scale fugues. This far from negligible piece sounds at its very best in

Abbado's persuasive hands.

This lively early work responds to strong characterization and, with excellent soloists and vibrant choral singing, is another refreshing example of Harnoncourt's view of authenticity. Barbara Bonney's *Exsultate jubilate* is enjoyably bracing, though it is sung a semitone lower than in modern instrument performances. The sound is satisfactory. However, for those not insisting on original instruments Abbado's DG recording remains a more obvious first choice.

Mass No. 12 in C (Spaur), K.258.
(M) *** Decca 430 161-2 [id.]. Palmer, Cable, Langridge, Roberts, St John's College, Cambridge, Ch., Wren O, Guest – HAYDN: *Schöpfungsmesse.* ***

The *Spaur Mass* is not among Mozart's most inspired, but its directness is appealing and the *Benedictus* offers a fine Mozartian interplay of chorus and soloists. In a vigorous performance like this, it is most enjoyable.

Mass No. 16 in C (Coronation), K.317.
(Y/B) (M) **(*) DG Dig. 445 543-2 (2) [id.]. Battle, Schmidt, Winbergh, Furlanetto, V. Singverein, VPO, Karajan – BEETHOVEN: *Missa solemnis.***(*)
(M) **(*) Decca Dig. 436 470-2 [id.]. Margaret Marshall, Murray, Covey-Crump, Wilson-Johnson, King's College Ch., ECO, Cleobury – HAYDN: *Nelson Mass.* **(*)

Mass No. 16 in C (Coronation), K.317; Vesperae solennes de confessore, K.339.
(Y/B) (M) ** Teldec/Warner Dig. 4509 95990-2 [id.]. Rodgers, Von Magnus, Protschka, Polgár, Arnold Schoenberg Ch., V. Hofburgkapelle Choral Scholars, VCM, Harnoncourt.

(i) *Mass No. 16 in C (Coronation), K.317; Vesperae solennes de confessore, K.339;* (ii) *Epistle sonata in C, K.278/271e.*
(N) *** O-L Dig. 436 585-2 [id.]. AAM, Hogwood, with (i) Kirkby, Robbin, Ainsley, George, Winchester Quiristers and Cathedral Ch.; (ii) Alastair Ross.

Oiseau-Lyre offers easily the finest CD, a coupling of the *Coronation Mass* and the *Vespers*, and indeed it is one of Hogwood's most succesful records. In using boy trebles he quite upstages Harnoncourt, and the choral singing has both vitality and a sense of joy. The soloists are an excellent team overall, but it is Emma Kirkby's glorious contributions one remembers especially, not least her radiant *Laudate Dominum* in the *Solemn vespers*. The organ sonata is an attractive if not essential bonus, and the recording is spacious and naturally balanced as well as vivid.

Karajan's 1985 recording of Mozart's *Coronation Mass* is certainly vibrant, with fine choral singing and good soloists. Kathleen Battle sings beautifully in the *Agnus Dei*, and the recording is bright, if not ideally expansive.

Though in terms of its rhythms Cleobury's performance is not as lively as the finest versions of K.317, this performance can be recommended warmly, with its excellent soloists and fresh choral singing all beautifully recorded. It is generously coupled to an even more vibrant account of Haydn's *Nelson Mass*.

Harnoncourt is not entirely logical in using period instruments, but women rather than boy trebles in the choir. As usual, accents are strong, dynamic contrasts are exaggerated and phrasing is somewhat eccentrically moulded, although Joan Rodgers is a fine soprano soloist in both works, her line eloquent and without exaggerations. As with the *C minor Mass*, the recording has plenty of atmosphere but could be more clearly defined.

Masses Nos. (i; ii) *16 in C (Coronation), K.317;* (i; iii) *18 in C min. (Great), K.427;* (i; iv) *Requiem Mass, K.626.*
(B) **(*) Ph. Duo 438 800-2 (2) [id.]. (i) Helen Donath, Ryland Davies; (ii) Gillian Knight, Stafford Dean; John Alldis Ch., LSO; (iii) Heather Harper, Stafford Dean, L. Symphony Ch., LSO; (iv) Yvonne Minton, Gerd Nienstedt, Alldis Ch., BBC SO; Sir Colin Davis.

These very successful CD transfers demonstrate the best features of the original recordings, which date from between 1967 and 1971. Sir Colin Davis's vital account of the *Coronation Mass* is given with a fine team of soloists; and in the so-called *'Great' Mass in C minor* the use of the Robbins Landon edition – which rejects the accretions formerly used to turn this incomplete torso of a work into a full setting of the liturgy – prompts him to a strong and intense performance which brings out the darkness behind Mozart's use of the C minor key. Again he is helped by fine soprano singing from Helen Donath, and from Heather Harper too. The *Requiem*, with a smaller choir, is more intimate and the soloists are more variable, yet with his natural sense of style Davis finds much beauty of detail. While the scale is authentic and the BBC orchestra is in good form, this reading, enjoyable as it is, does not provide the sort of bite with which a performance on this scale should compensate for sheer massiveness of tone.

Masses Nos. (i) *16 in C (Coronation), K.317;* (ii) *19 in D min. (Requiem Mass), K.626.*
(N) (M) ** Teldec/Warner Dig. 0630 10019-2 [id.]. (i) Rodgers, Von Magnus, Protschka, Polgár, Arnold
Schönberg Ch.; Choral Scholars of V. Hofburgkapelle; (ii) Yakar, Wenkel, Equiluz, Holl, V. State
Op. Konzertvereinigung; VCM, Harnoncourt.

Harnoncourt's is a distinctive view of the Mozart Masses, with strong accents adding a rhythmic
forcefulness to an otherwise freshly sung performance of the *Coronation Mass.* The acoustic is resonant
but not unattractively so in flattering the fine solo team in the *Benedictus.* However, in the *Requiem,*
while the fortissimo choral declarations come through with pungent force, in the gentler moments
(especially the *Lacrimosa* and the *Hostias*) the chorus might almost be performing in a swimming bath,
and though the ambience again adds glamour to the solo voices (another fine group) it is disconcertingly
inconsistent to have an orchestra of original instruments set against vocal sound so vague.

Mass No. 18 in C min. (Great), K.427.
*** DG Gold Dig. 439 012-2 [id.]. Hendricks, Perry, Schreier, Luxon, V. Singverein, BPO, Karajan.
*** Ph. Dig. 420 210-2 [id.]. McNair, Montague, Rolfe Johnson, Hauptmann, Monteverdi Ch., E. Bar.
Soloists, Gardiner.
*** Decca Dig. 425 528-2. Augér, Dawson, Ainsley, D. Thomas, Winchester Cathedral Ch. &
Winchester College Quiristers, AAM, Hogwood.
(Y/B) (M) **(*) Teldec/Warner Dig. 4509 95991-2 [id.]. Láki, Dénes, Equiluz, Holl, V. State Op. Ch. Soc.,
VCM, Harnoncourt.

Mass No. 18 in C min., K.427; Kyrie in D min., K.341.
(Y/B) (M) **(*) Virgin Veritas/EMI Dig. VER5 61167-2 [id.]. Barbara Schlick, Monika Frimmer,
Christoph Prégardien, Klaus Mertens, Cologne Chamber Ch., Collegium Cartusianum, Neumann.

(i) *Mass No. 18 in C min., K.427;* (ii) *Vesperae solennes de confessore, K.339.*
(N) (M) ** Ph. 446 197-2 [id.]. (i) Marshall, Palmer, Rolfe Johnson, Howell, ASMF & Ch., Marriner; (ii)
Burmeister, Büchner, Polster, Leipzig R. Ch. & SO, Kegel.

In his (1982) digital recording of the *C minor Mass* Karajan gives Handelian splendour to this greatest
of Mozart's choral works and, though the scale is large, the beauty and intensity are hard to resist. Solo
singing is first rate, particularly that of Barbara Hendricks, the dreamy beauty of her voice ravishingly
caught. Woodwind is rather backward, yet the sound is both rich and vivid – though, as the opening
shows, the internal balance is not always completely consistent. Nevertheless this digitally remastered
CD in the Karajan Gold series sounds more vivid than ever, and the chorus is tangibly present.

John Eliot Gardiner, using original instruments, gives an outstandingly fresh performance of high dramatic contrasts, marked by excellent solo singing – both the sopranos pure and bright-toned and
Anthony Rolfe Johnson in outstandingly sweet voice. With the recording giving an ample scale without
inflation, this too can be warmly recommended.

Hogwood's version can be considered alongside the fine Gardiner account, even though his control of
rhythm is less resilient and often squarer. The soloists if anything are even finer, and many Mozartians
will prefer having boy trebles in the chorus and German pronunciation of Latin. Hogwood also opts for
an edition by Richard Maunder which, among other things, adds appropriate instruments to the
incomplete orchestrations of the *Credo* and *Et incarnatus est.* This is particularly impressive in the
Credo, where trumpets and timpani bring an aptly festive flavour, adding to the panache of the opening.
The sound has a vivid sense of presence, with treble tone cutting through very freshly.

Peter Neumann's account of the *C minor Mass* has a great deal going for it: fine soloists – with Barbara
Schlick always fresh and captivating in the *Laudamus te* – spacious choral singing, gloriously if somewhat backwardly recorded, and excellent playing from an authentic-sized orchestra on original instruments. The *Sanctus* is properly expansive and the overall conception warmly persuasive in its relaxed
way. But in the last resort the chorus lacks the bite to make the performance really gripping. The rather
solemn *Kyrie* has plenty of character with the performance darkly lyrical rather than dramatic.

Harnoncourt's emphatic rhythmic style in both slow and fast passages will not please everyone but, with
a well-chosen quartet of soloists and responsive choral singing, this will suit Harnoncourt admirers,
though the reverberant recording is not always helpful to detail. Gardiner's Philips version is a safer,
more general recommendation for those wanting an 'authentic' version, and the recording, too, is
clearer.

In the *C minor Mass* Marriner secures a good response from his artists in a well-thought-out and
conscientious reading, and there is some fine singing. But this performance falls short of being really
inspired and does not quite communicate the sense of stature that this music calls for. Similarly the
Leipzig Radio Chorus sings impressively under Kegel and the soloists are good, but in the last resort this
performance lacks the kind of compulsive individuality to make it memorable.

Masses Nos. (i) *18 in C min. (Great), K.427;* (ii) *19 in D min. (Requiem), K.626.*
(b) (**(*)) DG Double stereo/mono 437 389-2 (2) [id.]. (i) Stader, Töpper, Haefliger, Sardi, St Hedwig's
   Cathedral Ch., Berlin RSO, Fricsay; (ii) Seefried, Pitzinger, Holm, Borg, V. State Op. Ch., VPO,
   Jochum.

Fricsay's powerful 1960 recording of the *C minor Mass* brings often bitingly dramatic choral singing.
The performance is not without its eccentricities (the accelerando at the close of the *Osanna*, for
instance) but the conductor's volatile approach adds to the feeling of freshness. Maria Stader distinguishes herself in the *Laudamus te* and concludes the *Credo* most beautifully. Hertha Töpper, however, is less satisfactory and in the *Domine Deus* she tends to mar the duet she shares with Stader by
conveying a lack of comfort in certain high passages where a similar phrase passes from one singer to
the other. But even with such blemishes, this music-making communicates very directly, and the focus is
remarkably clear on CD, with plenty of depth to back up the bright upper range. The coupling,
Jochum's 1956 mono recording of the *Requiem Mass*, is a characteristically inspirational account with
powerfully committed choral singing (witness the fervour of the *Dies irae* and *Sanctus*), capped by the
splendid closing *Lux aeterna*. There are good soloists who work well together as a team and Kim Borg is
particularly strong. No apologies need be made for the mono sound, which is forward, vivid and well
focused.

Requiem Mass (No. 19) in D min., K.626.
(m) *** Virgin/EMI Dig. CUV5 61260-2 [id.]. Yvonne Kenny, Alfreda Hodgson, Arthur Davies,
   Gwynne Howell, N. Sinfonia Ch., London Symphony Ch., N. Sinfonia, Richard Hickox.
(n) *** DG Dig. Gold 439 023-2 [id.]. Tomowa-Sintow, Müller Molinari, Cole, Burchuladze, V.
   Singverein, VPO, Karajan.
*** Ph. Dig. 411 420-2 [id.]. Margaret Price, Schmidt, Araiza, Adam, Leipzig R. Ch., Dresden State O,
   Schreier.
(bb) *** RCA Navigator 74321 29238-2. Equiluz, Eder, Vienna Boys' Ch., V. State Op. Ch. & O,
   Gillesberger – HAYDN: *Te Deum.* ***

Requiem Mass, K.626; Kyrie in D min., K.341.
*** Ph. Dig. 420 197-2 [id.]. Bonney, Von Otter, Blochwitz, White, Monteverdi Ch., E. Bar. Soloists,
   Gardiner.

John Eliot Gardiner with characteristic panache gives one of the most powerful performances ever, for
while the lighter sound of the period orchestra makes for greater transparency, the weight and bite are
formidable. The soloists are an outstanding quartet, well matched but characterfully contrasted too, and
the choral singing is as bright and luminous as one expects of Gardiner's Monteverdi Choir. The superb
Kyrie in D minor makes a very welcome and generous fill-up, to seal a firm recommendation.

   Richard Hickox's excellent version of the *Requiem Mass* on the Virgin Ultraviolet label matches any in
the catalogue. With generally brisk speeds and light, resilient rhythms, it combines gravity with authentically clean, transparent textures in which the dark colourings of the orchestration, as with the basset
horns, come out vividly. All four soloists are outstandingly fine, and the choral singing is fresh and
incisive, with crisp attack. The voices, solo and choral, are placed rather backwardly; otherwise the
recording is excellent.

   Karajan's 1987 digital version of the *Requiem* is a large-scale reading, but one that is white-hot with
intensity and energy. The power and bite of the rhythm are consistently exciting. The solo quartet is first
rate, though Helga Müller Molinari is on the fruity side for Mozart. Vinson Cole, stretched at times, yet
sings very beautifully, and so does Paata Burchuladze with his tangily distinctive, Slavonic bass tone.
The close balance adds to the excitement. As with all these reprocessed Karajan Gold CDs, the sound is
made marginally firmer by the remastering, but readers will note that this CD in consequence now
reverts from mid-to full price.

   Peter Schreier's is a forthright reading of Mozart's valedictory choral work, bringing strong dramatic
contrasts and marked by superb choral singing and a consistently elegant and finely balanced accompaniment. The singing of Margaret Price in the soprano part is almost finer than any other yet heard on
record, and the others make a first-rate team, if individually more variable. Only in the *Kyrie* and the
final *Cum sanctis tuis* does the German habit of using the intrusive aitch annoy. Altogether this is most
satisfying.

   The surprise version is Gillesberger's. Using treble and alto soloists from the Vienna Boys' Choir, who
sing with confidence and no little eloquence, this performance also has the advantage of a dedicated
contribution from Kurt Equiluz. Gillesberger's pacing is well judged and the effect is as fresh as it is
strong and direct. The 1982 recording is excellent, vivid yet full, and the result is powerful but not too
heavy. This is very well sung indeed, as is the rare Haydn coupling. This is a real bargain.

Requiem mass (No. 19) in D min. (ed. Maunder).
**(*) O-L Dig. 411 712-2 [id.]. Emma Kirkby, Watkinson, Rolfe Johnson, David Thomas, Westminster Cathedral Boys' Ch., A A M Ch. and O, Hogwood.

Hogwood's version cannot be compared with any other, using as it does the edition of Richard Maunder, which aims to eliminate Süssmayr's contribution to the version of Mozart's unfinished masterpiece that has held sway for two centuries. So the *Lacrimosa* is completely different, after the opening eight bars, and concludes with an elaborate *Amen*, for which Mozart's own sketches were recently discovered. This textual clean-out goes with authentic performance of Hogwood's customary abrasiveness, very fresh and lively to underline the impact of novelty.

Ridente la calma, K.152.
(N) *** Decca Dig. 440 297-2 [id.]. Cecilia Bartoli, András Schiff – BEETHOVEN: *Che fa il mio bene?* etc.; HAYDN: *Arianna a Naxos;* SCHUBERT: *Da quel sembiante appresi* etc. ***

Ridente la calma is invested with much innocent charm by Cecilia Bartoli within an interesting collection of Italian songs by German composers.

Vesperae de domenica, K.321.
(M) *** Decca 430 162-2 [id.]. Marshall, Cable, Evans, Roberts, St John's College, Cambridge, Ch., Wren O, Guest – HAYDN: *Harmoniemesse.* ***

Aptly coupled with Haydn's *Harmoniemesse*, Mozart's vibrant *Vesperae de domenica* opens with a series of brilliant choral settings (with contrasting solo quartet), accompanied by trumpets and strings. Margaret Marshall is appropriately agile in the lively soprano solo of the *Laudate Dominum*, and the work closes with an ambitious *Magnificat* in which all the participants are joined satisfyingly together. The St John's performance is full of vigour and the 1980 recording is full and vivid.

Vesperae solennes de confessore, K.339.
(M) *** Decca 430 157-2 [id.]. Palmer, Cable, Langridge, Roberts, St John's College, Cambridge, Ch., Wren O, Guest – HAYDN: *Paukenmesse.* ***

Although Guest's version of Mozart's masterpiece does not always match the full-price recording by Sir Colin Davis for Philips (see above under *Ave verum corpus*) – with Felicity Palmer a less poised soloist than Kiri Te Kanawa – the Decca account has the advantage of authenticity in the use of boys in the chorus. Moreover the CD transfer of the 1979 Argo recording is preferable to the less well-defined Philips sound.

OPERA

Complete Mozart Edition, Volume 26: *Apollo et Hyacinthus* (complete).
(M) *** Ph. 422 526-2 (2) [id.]. Augér, Mathis, Wulkopf, Schwarz, Rolfe Johnson, Salzburg Chamber Ch. & Mozarteum O, Hager.

The opera was written when Mozart was eleven, with all but two of the parts taken by schoolchildren. The style of the writing and vocalization is rather simpler than in other dramatic works of the boy Mozart, but the inspiration is still remarkable, astonishingly mature. The orchestration is assured and full of imaginative touches. The performance here is stylish and very well sung. Excellent, clear and well-balanced recording, admirably transferred to CD.

Complete Mozart Edition, Volume 30: *Ascanio in Alba* (complete).
(M) **(*) Ph. 422 530-2 (3) [id.]. Sukis, Baltsa, Mathis, Augér, Schreier, Salzburg Chamber Ch., Salzburg Mozarteum O, Hager.

Ascanio in Alba (complete).
(N) (B) *** Naxos Dig. 8.660040-2 (2). Windsor, Chance, Feldman, Milner, Mannion, Paris Sorbonne University Ch., Budapest Concerto Armonico, Jacques Grimbert.

Mozart at the age of fifteen wrote this charming, ever-inventive 'festa teatrale' for the coronation of the Archduke Ferdinand to an Italian princess in Milan in 1771. A court entertainment rather than an opera proper, it designedly identifies characters in a classical story, with the bride and bridegroom taking part in a delightful and original closing trio. The Naxos version, squeezing the dozens of arias and choruses on to two 79-minute discs, easily outshines previous recordings with a lightly sprung, stylishly conducted performance featuring an outstanding cast. The counter-tenor, Michael Chance, sings flawlessly in the castrato role of Ascanio, son of Venus, even-toned and brilliantly flexible. The others are fresh-toned too. Lorna Windsor, bright and clear as Venus, is nicely contrasted with the girlish-sounding Silvia of Jill Feldman, who sings with fine assurance in one of the two extended arias.

The other, even more extended and demanding, is given to Fauno, with Rosa Mannion arguably the most accomplished soloist of all. The excellent tenor taking the role of Aceste is Howard Milner. Well recorded with transparent textures, if with chorus backwardly balanced, this makes an outstanding bargain in every way, rare Mozart that for most will be a delightful discovery.

Hager makes an excellent start with an exceptionally lively account of the delightful overture, but then the choruses seem relatively square, thanks to the pedestrian, if generally efficient singing of the Salzburg choir. Hager's speeds are sometimes on the slow side, but the singing is excellent, with no weak link in the characterful cast, though not everyone will like the distinctive vibrato of Lilian Sukis as Venus. The 1976 analogue recording is full and vivid. But this set is now completely upstaged by the new Naxos version.

Bastien und Bastienne (complete). Concert arias: *Mentre ti lascio, o figlia, K.513; Misero! o sogno . . . Aura, che intorno spiri, K.431. Le nozze di Figaro: Giunse alfin il momento . . . Deh vieni; Un moto di gioia.*
*** Sony Dig. SK 45855 [id.]. Gruberová, Cole, Polgar, Liszt CO, Leppard.

Complete Mozart Edition, Volume 27: *Bastien und Bastienne* (complete); Lieder: *Komm, liebe Zither, komm; Die Zufriedenheit.*
(M) *** Ph. Dig. 422 527-2 [id.]. Dominik Orieschnig, Georg Nigl, David Busch, V. Boys' Ch., VSO, Harrer.

Leppard conducts a near-ideal performance of the eleven-year-old Mozart's charming little one-Acter, very well recorded. Edita Gruberová is delectably fresh and vivacious as the heroine, Vinson Cole is a sensitive and clean-voiced Bastien and Laszlo Polgar is full of fun in the buffo role of Colas. The Liszt Chamber Orchestra of Budapest plays with dazzling precision. As a generous fill-up, the three soloists sing Mozart arias, including the big scena for tenor, *Misero! o sogno*, and a replacement aria for Susanna, especially written for the 1789 production of *Le nozze di Figaro*: *Un moto di gioia*.

On Philips, the opera is performed by boy trebles instead of the soprano, tenor and bass originally intended. Members of the Vienna Boys' Choir give a refreshingly direct performance under Uwe Christian Harrer, missing little of the piece's charm. The two songs with mandolin accompaniment, also sung by one of the trebles, make an attractive fill-up. First-rate 1986 digital sound.

Complete Mozart Edition, Volume 44: *La clemenza di Tito* (complete).
(M) *** Ph. 422 544-2 (2) [id.]. Dame Janet Baker, Minton, Burrows, Von Stade, Popp, Lloyd, ROHCG Ch. & O, Sir Colin Davis.

La clemenza di Tito (complete).
(N) *** EMI Dig. CDS5 55489-2 (2) [id.]. Winbergh, Vaness, Ziegler, Senn, Barbaux, V. State Op. Ch., VPO, Muti.
*** DG Dig. 431 806-2 (2). Rolfe Johnson, Von Otter, McNair, Varady, Robbin, Hauptmann, Monteverdi Ch., E. Bar. Soloists, Gardiner.
*** Teldec/Warner Dig. 4509 90857-2 (2) [id.]. Langridge, Popp, Ziesack, Murray, Ziegler, Polgár, Zurich Op. Ch. & O, Harnoncourt.
(M) *** DG 429 878-2 (2) [id.]. Berganza, Varady, Mathis, Schreier, Schiml, Adam, Leipzig R. Ch., Dresden State O, Boehm.
(Y/B) **(*) O-L Dig. 444 131-2 (2) [id.]. Heilman, Bartoli, Della Jones, Montague, Bonney, Ch. & AAM, Christopher Hogwood.

Sir Colin Davis's superb set is among the finest of his many Mozart recordings. Not only is the singing of Dame Janet Baker in the key role of Vitellia formidably brilliant; she actually makes one believe in the emotional development of an impossible character, one who progresses from villainy to virtue with the scantiest preparation. The two other mezzo-sopranos, Minton as Sesto and Von Stade in the small role of Annio, are superb too, while Stuart Burrows has rarely if ever sung so stylishly on a recording as here. Davis's swaggering manner transforms what used to be dismissed as a dry *opera seria*. Excellent recording.

Recorded live on stage at the 1988 Salzburg Festival, Muti's version is vividly dramatic, full of expressiveness of a kind underplayed in period performance, with the Vienna Philharmonic producing traditional, consistently beautiful, orchestral sound. The tension of the live performance is powerfully conveyed, underlining the emotional thrust behind a piece long dismissed as uninvolving. The cast is a strong one, with Carol Vaness as Vitellia and Delores Ziegler as Sesto intense and characterful, two singers who built their Mozartian reputations at Glyndebourne, although Vaness comes under strain by the end of this live event. Gösta Winbergh makes a noble Tito, heroic of tone and never strained, and the others are good if not always ideally sweet of tone. A good alternative to the Colin Davis version, if you want a recording on modern instruments, though in this Muti set live performance involves interruption from stage noises and audience applause. Atmospheric sound, despite oddities of balance for voices.

Again, with his vitality and bite, Gardiner turns the piece into a genuinely involving drama. Though the team of soloists is not quite as consistent as on Sir Colin Davis's 1977 recording, Anthony Rolfe Johnson is outstanding in the title-role, matching the vivid characterization of both Anne Sofie von Otter as Sesto and Julia Varady as Vitellia. Sylvia McNair is an enchanting, pure-toned Servilia and Catherine Robbin a well-matched Annio, though the microphone catches an unevenness in the voice, as it does with Cornelius Hauptmann in the incidental role of Publio. More seriously, DG's vivid, immediate recording picks up a distracting amount of banging and bumping on stage in the Süssmayr recitatives.

Nikolaus Harnoncourt is expansively romantic. In keeping with this approach, he uses modern, not period instruments. Even so, he has not forgotten his early devotion to period performance, making this a very viable account for anyone wanting a half-way approach. Though recorded in association with Zurich Opera, this is a studio, not a live, recording like Gardiner's. It gains from not having stage noises in recitative. Ann Murray is at her finest as Sesto, if not quite as firm or dominant as von Otter for Gardiner. Philip Langridge is a splendid Tito, and it is good to have Lucia Popp so affecting in her very last recording. Ruth Ziesak and Delores Ziegler complete a strong team which will not disappoint anyone, even if it cannot quite compare with Gardiner's, singer for singer.

Boehm gave the work warmth and charm, presenting the piece more genially than we have grown used to. The atmospheric recording helps in that, and the cast is first rate, with no weak link, matching at every point that of Sir Colin Davis on his full-price Philips set. Yet, ultimately, even Julia Varady for Boehm can hardly rival Dame Janet Baker for Davis, crisper and lighter in her coloratura. Davis's incisiveness, too, has points of advantage; but, to summarize, any Mozartian can safely leave the preference to his feelings about the two conductors, the one more genial and glowing, the other more urgently dramatic.

With clean, crisp manners Hogwood draws transparent textures from the players in the Academy, pointing rhythms and phrases more lightly and almost as imaginatively as Gardiner. Sesto as portrayed by the characterful Cecilia Bartoli is clearly established as the central figure in the drama, with Della Jones as Vitellia comparably positive, though neither of them produces quite such beautiful and even, cleanly focused tone as their opposite numbers for Gardiner, the magnificent Anne Sofie von Otter and Julia Varady. Diana Montague as Annio and Barbara Bonney as Servilia both weigh in favour of Hogwood, but Uwe Heilmann with his slightly fluttery tenor conveys nothing like the heroic strength of Anthony Rolfe Johnson in the title-role for Gardiner. Clean, well-balanced studio sound.

Complete Mozart Edition, Volume 42: *Così fan tutte* (complete).
(M) *** Ph. 422 542-2; *422 542-4* (3/2) [id.]. Caballé, Dame Janet Baker, Cotrubas, Gedda, Ganzarolli, Van Allan, ROHCG Ch. & O, Sir Colin Davis.

Così fan tutte (complete).
(N) *** Decca Dig. 444 174-2 (3). Renée Fleming, Anne Sofie von Otter, Frank Lopardo, Olaf Bär, Adelina Scarabelli, Michele Pertusi, COE, Solti.
(Y/B) ✿ (M) *** EMI CMS7 69330-2 (3) [Ang. CDMC 69330]. Schwarzkopf, Ludwig, Steffek, Kraus, Taddei, Berry, Philh. Ch. & O, Boehm.
*** Ph. Dig. 422 381-2 (3) [id.]. Mattila, Von Otter, Szmytka, Araiza, Allen, Van Dam, Amb. Op. Ch., ASMF, Marriner.
✿ (M) (***) EMI mono CHS7 69635-2 (3) [Ang. CDHC 69635]. Schwarzkopf, Otto, Merriman, Simoneau, Panerai, Bruscantini, Philh. Ch. & O, Karajan.
(Y/B) *** DG Dig. 437 829-2 (3) [id.]. Roocroft, Mannion, Gilfry, Trost, James, Feller, E. Bar. Soloists, Gardiner.
*** EMI Dig. CDS7 47727-8 (3) [Ang. CDCC 47727]. Vaness, Ziegler, Watson, Aler, Duesing, Desderi, Glyndebourne Ch., LPO, Haitink.
(M) *** Erato/Warner 2292 45683-2 (3) [id.]. Te Kanawa, Stratas, Von Stade, Rendall, Huttenlocher, Bastin, Rhine Op. Ch., Strasbourg PO, Lombard.
(M) (***) EMI mono CHS7 63864-2 (2) [Ang. CDHB 63864]. Souez, Helletsgruber, Nash, Domgraf-Fassbaender, Brownlee, Eisinger, Glyndebourne Festival Ch. & O, Fritz Busch.
** Telarc Dig. CD 80360 (3) [id.]. Lott, McLaughlin, Focile, Hadley, Corbelli, Cachemaille, Edinburgh Festival Ch., SCO, Mackerras.

In contrast to his prickly and straight-faced recording of the early 1970s, Solti's digital *Così*, recorded live at the Royal Festival Hall in 1994, is as sparkling and full of humour as you could want. With the youthful and starry cast acting the story out on stage so as to sharpen the dramatic point, Solti takes a fast and light approach which yet has none of his old fierceness. The speeds may challenge the singers, notably in the many ensembles, but Solti gives his performers every consideration in moulding the arch of phrases or in allowing time for elaborate decorations. Though such meditative passages as the lovely little trio, *O soave sia il vento*, and the opening of Fiordiligi's aria, *Per pietà*, are taken at flowing speeds, faster than usual, they have a poise that holds one rapt. Much is owed to the superb playing of the Chamber Orchestra of Europe and, though the Festival Hall acoustic means that violin-tone has an edge on it, the Decca engineers have managed to overcome the snags of that notoriously difficult venue brilliantly. Renée Fleming as Fiordiligi, brought in as substitute at the last minute, yet proves a central focus among the soloists. She excels even over her performances in the role at Glyndebourne, singing with a firm, full voice that is yet brilliant and flexible, ranging down to a satisfyingly strong chest register. Dazzling as her *Come scoglio* is in Act I, *Per pietà* in Act II brings even greater emotional depth, poised and commanding, intensified by contrasts of dynamic more daringly extreme than in rival versions. Frank Lopardo too, as Ferrando, most sensitively uses his distinctive tenor over an unusually wide dynamic range, so that in the lovely aria, *Un aura amorosa*, he sings the reprise in a gentler, more beautiful half-tone than anyone else on disc. Anne Sofie von Otter predictably makes a characterful Dorabella, well contrasted with Fleming, and Olaf Bär a keenly intelligent Guglielmo, while two Italian singers, less well known but well chosen, Adelina Scarabelli and Michele Pertusi, complete the team in the manipulative roles of Despina and Alfonso. Altogether Solti's finest Mozart recording yet, outshining even his *Figaro*.

Boehm's classic set has been handsomely repackaged and remains a clear alternative choice, despite the attractions of the new Gardiner version. Its glorious solo singing is headed by the incomparable Fiordiligi of Schwarzkopf and the equally moving Dorabella of Christa Ludwig; it remains a superb memento of Walter Legge's recording genius and still bears comparison with any other recordings made before or since.

Marriner directs a fresh and resilient performance, beautifully paced, often with speeds on the fast side, and with the crystalline recorded sound adding to the sparkle. Though the women principals make a strong team, the men are even finer: Francisco Araiza as Ferrando, Thomas Allen as Guglielmo and José van Dam as Alfonso all outstanding so that, though the reading is lighter in weight than those of Boehm, Karajan, Haitink or Davis, it has more fun in it, bringing out the laughter in the score.

Commanding as Schwarzkopf is as Fiordiligi in the 1962 Boehm set, the extra ease and freshness of her singing in the earlier (1954) version under Karajan makes it even more compelling. Nan Merriman is a distinctive and characterful Dorabella, and the role of Ferrando has never been sung more mellifluously on record than by Leopold Simoneau. The young Rolando Panerai is an ideal Guglielmo, and Lisa Otto a pert Despina; while Sesto Bruscantini in his prime brings to the role of Don Alfonso the wisdom and artistry which made him so compelling at Glyndebourne. Karajan has never sparkled more naturally in Mozart than here, for the high polish has nothing self-conscious about it. Though the mono recording is not as clear as some others of this period, the subtleties of the music-making are very well caught.

John Eliot Gardiner chooses voices that are both fresh and well focused, with the roles of all four of the lovers taken by young singers – Amanda Roocroft, Rosa Mannion, Rainer Trost and Rodney Gilfry. For this comedy, Gardiner, more controversially, opted to get the engineers to record a live performance not in concert but on stage. Stage noises are often intrusive, with laughter and applause punctuating the performance, not always helpfully. Whatever the snags, the full flavour of *Così*, its effervescence as well as its deeper qualities, comes over the more intensely as a result and Gardiner secures ensemble as crisp as you would expect in a studio recording. Though Roocroft and Mannion do not sound quite as sweet and even as they can, few tenors on disc can rival the German, Rainer Trost, in the heady beauty of his voice, above all in Ferrando's aria, *Una aura amorosa*. The poise and technical assurance of all the singers, not least Rodney Gilfry as Guglielmo, put this among the very finest versions of *Così*, outshining many with far starrier (and older) casts. DG offers the alternative of a video version (072 436-31), also made on stage, but at the Théâtre du Châtelet in Paris instead of Ferrara, and with Claudio Nicolai instead of Carlos Feller as Alfonso. The unscripted noises are here explained in the detail of Gardiner's own (sometimes excessive) staging, but with delectably pretty scenery. The crowning achievement on both CD and video is that the dénouement in the long Act II finale has a tenderness and depth rarely matched.

With speeds often more measured than usual, Haitink's EMI version still conveys the sparkle of live performances at Glyndebourne. The excellent teamwork, consistently conveying humour, makes up for a cast-list rather less starry than that on some rival versions. This is above all a sunny performance, sailing happily over any serious shoals beneath Da Ponte's comedy. Claudio Desderi as Alfonso helps to establish that Glyndebourne atmosphere, with recitatives superbly timed and coloured. If Carol Vaness and Delores Ziegler are rather too alike in timbre to be distinguished easily, the relationship becomes all the more sisterly when, quite apart from the similarity, they respond so beautifully to each other. John Aler makes a headily unstrained Ferrando, beautifully free in the upper register; and Lilian Watson and Dale Duesing make up a strong team. The digital recording gives fine bloom and an impressive dynamic range to voices and orchestra alike.

The energy and sparkle of Sir Colin Davis are set against inspired and characterful singing from the three women soloists, with Montserrat Caballé and Janet Baker proving a winning partnership, each challenging and abetting the other all the time. Cotrubas equally is a vivid Despina, never merely arch. Though Gedda has moments of rough tone and Ganzarolli falls short in one of his prominent arias, they are both spirited, while Richard van Allan sings with flair and imagination. Sparkling recitative, and recording which has you riveted by the play of the action.

On Erato, Kiri Te Kanawa's voice sounds radiant, rich and creamy of tone; she is commanding in *Come scoglio*, and tenderly affecting in *Per pietà*, which is more moving here than with Levine. Lombard is a sympathetic accompanist, if not always the most perceptive of Mozartians; some of his tempi are on the slow side, but his sextet of young singers make up a team that rivals almost any other, giving firm, appealing performances. With warm recording of high quality, this is most enjoyable and could be a first choice for any who follow the singers in question.

The legendary Glyndebourne performance, the first ever recording of *Così fan tutte*, is the finest of the three pioneering sets recorded on 78s in the mid-1930s with the newly founded Glyndebourne company. The sound in the CD transfer, though limited, is amazingly vivid, with voices very well focused and with a keener sense of presence than on many recordings of the 1990s. Busch at the time was a progressive Mozartian, preferring athletic treatment, and nowadays even the use of a piano for the recitatives instead of a harpsichord seems less outlandish with the emergence of the fortepiano. John Brownlee as Don Alfonso is very much the English aristocrat, with 'fruffly-fruffly' English vowels instead of Italianate ones, but he is a fine, stylish singer. Ina Souez and Luise Helletsgruber are technically superb; and Heddle Nash and Willi Domgraf-Fassbaender as their lovers are at once stylish and characterful, with Irene Eisinger as a delightfully soubrettish Despina. Cuts are made in the recitatives according to the custom of the time and, more seriously, four numbers disappear – including, amazingly, Ferrando's *Tradito, schernito* and Dorabella's *E amore un ladroncello*. The bonus is that, with those cuts, the opera fits on to only two mid-price CDs.

Mackerras aims to present a performance on modern instruments which echoes the practices and manner of a period performance, heightening dramatic moments, making ensembles brisk and exciting. Unfortunately, as in the previous recording, the sound is too reverberant, which is even less apt for this frothy comedy. It inflates the scale of the performance, with recitative sounding as though delivered in a church. It blunts the crispness and undermines the clarity of ensembles. The cast is strong but, whether or not affected by the acoustic and the recording, Mozart manners are on the rough side. A flawed set, but enjoyable if you can adjust to the acoustic.

Così fan tutte (excerpts).
(***) Testament mono SBT 1040 [id.]. Jurinac, Thebom, Lewis, Kunz, Borriello, Glyndebourne Festival O, Fritz Busch; Alda Noni, Philh. O, Susskind.

The superb Testament transfer of excerpts from *Così fan tutte* in the 1950 Glyndebourne production gives a vivid idea of the way that even in the first year when the re-established Glyndebourne Festival was recovering its pre-war format, standards were never higher. Fritz Busch in his penultimate season was as incisive as before the war, directing performances at once superbly disciplined yet easy and amiable. Sena Jurinac as Fiordiligi, clear and vibrant, provides the central glory, with both her two big arias included, as well as six of her ensemble numbers, and three substantial rehearsal 'takes'. Blanche Thebom too, as Dorabella, sings with clarity and freshness, and the others make a splendid team. Alda Noni, the Despina, was not recorded at the Glyndebourne sessions but later, at Abbey Road, with Susskind and the Philharmonia. The recording brings out a flutter in her voice, less steady than the others. As in pre-war days, a piano is used instead of harpsichord for recitatives.

Così fan tutte: highlights.
(Y/B) *** DG Dig. 437 994-2 [id.] (from above recording, cond. Gardiner).

The Gardiner highlights offers a generous selection (73 minutes) of key items, including the Overture. It will be especially useful to those collectors who have chosen Boehm's set and want a reminder of a splendid 'authentic' performance using original instruments.

Complete Mozart Edition, Volume 41: *Don Giovanni* (complete).
(M) *** Ph. 422 541-2; *422 541-4* (3/2) [id.]. Wixell, Arroyo, Te Kanawa, Freni, Burrows, Ganzarolli, ROHCG Ch. & O, Sir Colin Davis.

Don Giovanni (complete).

*** EMI CDS7 47260-8 (3) [Ang. CDCC 47260]. Waechter, Schwarzkopf, Sutherland, Alva, Frick, Sciutti, Taddei, Philh. Ch. & O, Giulini.

(Y/B) *** DG Dig. 445 870-2 (3) [id.]. Gilfry, Orgonosova, Margiono, James, d'Arcangelo, Prégardien, Clarkson, Silvestrelli, Monteverdi Ch., E. Bar. Soloists, Gardiner.

(M) *** Decca 411 626-2 (3). Siepi, Danco, Della Casa, Corena, Dermota, V. State Op. Ch., VPO, Krips.

*** DG Dig. 419 179-2 (3) [id.]. Ramey, Tomowa-Sintow, Baltsa, Battle, Winbergh, Furlanetto, Malta, Burchuladze, German Op. Ch., Berlin, BPO, Karajan.

*** EMI Dig. CDS7 47037-2 (3) [Ang. CDCC 47036]. Allen, Vaness, Ewing, Gale, Lewis, Van Allan, Rawnsley, Kavrakos, Glyndebourne Ch., LPO, Haitink.

(Y/B) (M) *** EMI CMS7 63841-2 (3) [Ang. CDMC 63841]. Ghiaurov, Claire Watson, Ludwig, Freni, Gedda, Berry, Montarsolo, Crass, New Philh. Ch. & O, Klemperer.

(M) (***) EMI mono CHS7 63860-2 (3) [Ang. CDHB 63860]. Siepi, Schwarzkopf, Berger, Grümmer, Dermota, Edelmann, Berry, Ernster, V. State Op. Ch., VPO, Furtwängler.

**(*) O-L Dig. 425 943-2 (3) [id.]. Hagegård, Cachemaille, Augér, Della Jones, Van der Meel, Bonney, Terfel, Sigmundsson, Drottningholm Court Theatre Ch. & O, Ostman.

(M) (***) EMI mono CHS7 61030-2 (3) [Ang. CDHB 61030]. Brownlee, Souez, Von Pataky, Helletsgruber, Baccaloni, Henderson, Mildmay, Glyndebourne Fest. Ch. & O, Fritz Busch.

(M) **(*) DG 437 341-2 (3) [id.]. Fischer-Dieskau, Jurinac, Stader, Seefried, Haefliger, Kohn, Sardi, Kreppel, Berlin RIAS Chamber Ch. & R.O, Fricsay.

(N) (M) ** Decca 444 594-2 (3) [id.]. Siepi, Corena, Nilsson, L. Price, Ratti, Valletti, Blankenburg, Van Mill, V. State Op. Ch., VPO, Leinsdorf.

The classic Giulini EMI set, lovingly remastered to bring out even more vividly the excellence of Walter Legge's original sound-balance, sets the standard by which all other recordings have come to be judged. Elisabeth Schwarzkopf, as Elvira, emerges as a dominant figure to give a distinctive but totally apt slant to this endlessly invigorating drama. The young Sutherland may be relatively reticent as Anna but, with such technical ease and consistent beauty of tone, she makes a superb foil. Taddei is a delightful Leporello, and each member of the cast – including the young Cappuccilli as Masetto – combines fine singing with keen dramatic sense.

John Eliot Gardiner's set was recorded mainly live but with tidying sessions afterwards. As in his *Figaro*, the result is vividly dramatic, beautifully paced and deeply expressive, with little or none of the haste associated with period practice. The performance culminates in one of the most thrilling accounts ever recorded of the final scene, when Giovanni is dragged down to hell, presented in sound of spine-tingling immediacy. Stage noises are minimally intrusive, and much is gained from having the music paced in relation to live performances. Gardiner opts for a text that is neither that of the original Prague version nor the usual amalgam of Prague and Vienna. Dramatically the result is tauter, and the numbers omitted are here included in an appendix. Sometimes lightness goes too far, as when Charlotte Margiono as Donna Elvira sings '*Ah fuggi il traditor*' in a half-tone, but increasingly Gardiner encourages his soloists, particularly Anna and Elvira, to sing expansively, bringing out the full weight of such arias as '*Mi tradi*' and Anna's '*Non mi dir*'. Fine as Margiono is, Luba Orgonosova is even more assured and characterful as Anna, and the agility of both is exemplary. Rodney Gilfry excels himself, on one side tough and purposeful, on the other a smooth seducer, with the clean-toned voice finely shaded. Ildebrando d'Arcangelo is suitably darker-toned as Leporello, lithe and young-sounding, hardly a *buffo*. Julian Clarkson makes a crotchety Masetto, and Eirian James a warmer, tougher Zerlina than usual, aptly so for her extra scene. The Commendatore of Andrea Silvestrelli, though recessed on the recording, is magnificently dark and firm, not least in the final confrontation. A recording that sets new standards for period performance, and vies with the finest of traditional versions.

Sir Colin Davis has the advantage of a singing cast that has fewer shortcomings than almost any other on disc and much positive strength. Martina Arroyo controls her massive dramatic voice more completely than one would think possible, and she is strongly and imaginatively contrasted with the sweetly expressive Elvira of Kiri Te Kanawa and the sparkling Zerlina of Mirella Freni. As in the Davis *Figaro*, Ingvar Wixell and Wladimiro Ganzarolli make a formidable master/servant team with excellent vocal acting, while Stuart Burrows sings gloriously as Don Ottavio, and Richard Van Allan is a characterful Masetto. Davis draws a fresh and immediate performance from his team, riveting from beginning to end, and the recording is now better defined and more vivid than before.

Krips's recording of this most challenging opera has kept its place as a mid-priced version that is consistently satisfying, with a cast of all-round quality headed by the dark-toned Don of Cesare Siepi. The women are not ideal, but they form an excellent team, never overfaced by the music, generally characterful, and with timbres well contrasted. To balance Siepi's darkness, the Leporello of Corena is even more saturnine, and their dramatic teamwork is brought to a superb climax in the final scene – quite the finest and most spine-tingling performance of that scene ever recorded. The 1955 recording – genuine stereo – still sounds remarkably well.

Even if ensemble is less than perfect at times in the Karajan set and the final scene of Giovanni's descent to Hell goes off the boil a little, the end result has fitting intensity and power. Though Karajan was plainly thinking of a big auditorium in his pacing of recitatives, having Jeffrey Tate as continuo player helps to keep them moving and to bring out word-meaning. The starry line-up of soloists is a distinctive one. Samuel Ramey is a noble rather than a menacing Giovanni, consistently clear and firm.

Haitink's set superbly captures the flavour of Sir Peter Hall's memorable production at Glyndebourne, not least in the inspired teamwork. The only major change from the production on stage is that Maria Ewing comes in as Elvira, vibrant and characterful, not ideally pure-toned but contrasting characterfully with the powerful Donna Anna of Carol Vaness and the innocent-sounding Zerlina of Elizabeth Gale. Keith Lewis is a sweet-toned Ottavio, but it is Thomas Allen as Giovanni who – apart from Haitink – dominates the set, a swaggering Don full of charm and with a touch of nobility when, defiant to the end, he is dragged down to hell – a spine-chilling moment as recorded here. Rarely has the Champagne aria been so beautifully sung, with each note articulated – and that also reflects Haitink's flawless control of pacing, not always conventional but always thoughtful and convincing. Excellent playing from the LPO – well practised in the Glyndebourne pit – and warm, full recording, far more agreeable than the dry sound in the old auditorium at Glyndebourne.

The lumbering tempo of Leporello's opening music will alert the listener to the predictable Klemperer approach and at that point some may dismiss his performance as 'too heavy' – but the issue is far more complex than that. Most of the slow tempi which Klemperer regularly adopts, far from flagging, add a welcome breadth to the music, for they must be set against the unusually brisk and dramatic interpretation of the recitatives between numbers. Added to that, Ghiaurov as the Don and Berry as Leporello make a marvellously characterful pair. In this version the male members of the cast are dominant and, with Klemperer's help, they make the dramatic experience a strongly masculine one. Nor is the ironic humour forgotten with Berry and Ghiaurov about, and the Klemperer spaciousness allows them extra time for pointing. Among the women, Ludwig is a strong and convincing Elvira, Freni a sweet-toned but rather unsmiling Zerlina; only Claire Watson seriously disappoints, with obvious nervousness marring the big climax of *Non mi dir*. It is a serious blemish but, with the usual reservations, for those not allergic to the Klemperer approach, this stands as a good recommendation – at the very least a commanding experience. The set now reappears at mid-price, its catalogue number unchanged, but the presentation more stylish.

The historic Furtwängler performance was recorded live by Austrian Radio at the 1954 Salzburg Festival, barely three months before the conductor's death. Though speeds are often slow by today's standards, his springing of rhythm never lets them sag. Even the very slow speed for Leporello's catalogue aria is made to seem charmingly individual. With the exception of a wobbly Commendatore, this is a classic Salzburg cast, with Cesare Siepi a fine, incisive Don, dark in tone, Elisabeth Schwarzkopf a dominant Elvira, Elisabeth Grümmer a vulnerable Anna, Anton Dermota a heady-toned Ottavio and Otto Edelmann a clear and direct Leporello. Stage noises often suggest herds of stampeding animals, but both voices and orchestra are satisfyingly full-bodied in the CD transfer, and the sense of presence is astonishing.

Ostman follows up his earlier recordings of *Così fan tutte* and *Le nozze di Figaro* with this period performance of *Don Giovanni*. This time, with a far darker score, he has modified his stance. Though speeds are still often fast, this time they rarely seem breathless. Håkan Hagegård as Giovanni could be sweeter-toned, but his lightness and spontaneity, particularly in exchanges with the vividly alive Leporello of Gilles Cachemaille, are most winning, with recitative often barely vocalized. Arleen Augér is a radiant Donna Anna, while Della Jones is a full-toned Elvira and Bryn Terfel a resonant Masetto. Understandably, the original Prague text is used. Such essential additions as Ottavio's *Dalla sua pace* (beautifully sung by Nico van der Meel) and Elvira's *Mi tradi* are given in an appendix on the third disc.

The early Glyndebourne set shows Fritz Busch an inspired Mozartian, pointing the music with a freshness and absence of nineteenth-century heaviness rare at the time. A piano is used for the *secco* recitatives; but the interplay of characters in those exchanges has never been caught more infectiously on disc. John Brownlee as Giovanni may have a rather British-stiff-upper-lip Italian accent but his is a noble performance, beautifully sung, and he is brilliantly set against the lively, idiomatically Italian Leporello of Salvatore Baccaloni. Audrey Mildmay as Zerlina makes a delightful foil for the excellent, if otherwise little-known Ina Souez and Luise Helletsgruber. Koloman von Pataky uses his light, heady tenor well as Ottavio, and David Franklin and Roy Henderson are first rate as the Commendatore and Masetto respectively. Keith Hardwick's digital transfers are astonishingly vivid, with very little background noise.

As he has shown in his recording of *Die Zauberflöte*, Fricsay is a forceful, dramatic Mozart conductor, but here the absence of charm is serious. This is mainly felt in some ridiculously fast speeds. Zerlina, Masetto and their rustic friends are hustled unmercifully along in 6/8, and poor Zerlina has an even worse time when it comes to her aria, *Batti batti*. Seefried being the superb artist she is, her charm comes through. The cast is generally strong, but unfortunately there is a serious blot in the Donna Elvira of Maria Stader; she is made to sound shrill and some of her attempts to get round the trickier florid passages leave a good deal to be desired. Yet most of the singing is very stylish. Haefliger shows himself as one of the finest Mozart tenors of the time, Karl Kohn is a fine, incisive Leporello, Ivan Sardi an exceptionally rich-voiced Masetto, and Seefried a truly enchanting Zerlina. As so often on records, Sena Jurinac is not quite as thrilling here as one remembers her in the flesh. Fischer-Dieskau is a particularly interesting choice of Don; his characterization proves powerful and forwardly projected. Yet with all these plus points, the set does not quite add up to the sum of its parts, even though there is much to enjoy. The 1958 recording was made in the Berlin Jesus-Christus Kirche, so the stereo is remarkably atmospheric.

The Leinsdorf set from the early 1960s was uncut and very well recorded. It originally appeared on RCA but now reverts to its home label. The excellent Don of Cesare Siepi, already established in the Krips version, is if anything even more impressive here. Leontyne Price is a fine Elvira, but Birgit Nilsson is rather miscast as Anna: she makes very gusty noises in trying to get round some of the more difficult passages. Valletti and Corena are both very good, but in the last resort it is the conducting of Leinsdorf which makes one qualify a recommendation. This is far preferable to his *Marriage of Figaro* (see below), but there is something of the same inflexibility.

Don Giovanni: highlights.

(M) *** EMI CDM7 63078-2 (from above recording, with Sutherland, Schwarzkopf, Waechter; cond. Giulini).

*** DG Dig. 449 139-2 (from above recording, with Gilfry, Orgonasova; cond. Gardiner).

(Y/B) (M) **(*) DG 445 463-2 [id.] (from complete recording, with Milnes, Tomowa-Sintow, Schreier; cond. Boehm).

(N) (BB) ** CfP Silver Double CDCFPSD 4739 (2). Shirley-Quirk, Armstrong, Tear, Mathes, Dean, Garrard, Murray, Jackson, SCO, Gibson – R. STRAUSS: *Der Rosenkavalier*. ***

Not surprisingly, the Giulini EMI selection concentrates on Sutherland as Donna Anna and Schwarzkopf as Donna Elvira, so that the Don and Leporello get rather short measure, but Sciutti's charming Zerlina is also given fair due. The selection from the Gardiner set is at full price but runs to 73 minutes.

Boehm's selection is very generous (76 minutes) and is taken from live performances at Salzburg (recorded in 1977). It makes a welcome representation of a set centring round Sherrill Milnes's unusually heroic assumption of the role of the Don, and he sings with a richness and commitment to match his swaggering stage presence. The rest of the cast give stylish performances without being deeply memorable but, unlike *Così* where ensembles were less than ideally crisp, this live *Giovanni* presents strong and consistently enjoyable teamwork. The balance again favours the voices but is especially vivid in the culminating scene. For this reissue (which includes the *Overture*) an adequate cued synopsis, linked to the narrative, has been provided.

This collection of highlights from the Scottish Opera's 1975 production is welcome enough on a bargain Silver Double with some enjoyable singing. John Shirley-Quirk is an intelligent rather than a flamboyant Don, singing his serenade in delightful half-tones and almost coping with Gibson's impossibly fast tempo for the *Champagne aria*. Rachel Mathes as Donna Anna brings a powerful recording voice, but none of the others is presented at peak form. This may be the fault of the conductor, who misses some of the bite of dramatic tension. The selection, which includes the *Overture*, is not particularly generous, and the recording could be more refined and atmospheric.

Die Entführung aus dem Serail (complete).

*** DG Dig. 435 857-2 (2) [id.]. Orgonasova, Sieden, Olsen, Peper, Hauptmann, Mineti, Monteverdi Ch., E. Bar. Soloists, Gardiner.

(M) *** DG 429 868-2 (2) [id.]. Augér, Grist, Schreier, Neukirch, Moll, Leipzig R. Ch., Dresden State O, Boehm.

(N) (M) *** Teldec/Warner Dig. 0630 10025-2 (2) [id.]. Kenny, Watson, Schreier, Gamlich, Salminen, Zurich Op. Ch. & Mozart O, Harnoncourt.

Unlike Gardiner's *Idomeneo* and *La clemenza di Tito*, *Entführung* was not recorded live but in the studio immediately after a concert performance. With a comedy like this, studded with spoken dialogue, that was a wise decision. The overture immediately establishes the extra zest of the performance, with wider dynamic contrasts, more body in the sound, and with more spring in the rhythm and a keener sense of fun. So Konstanze's great heroic aria, *Martern aller Arten*, has tremendous swagger; thanks also to glorious singing from Luba Orgonasova, at once rich, pure and agile, the close is triumphant. Curiously, Gardiner exaggerates the *ad lib.* markings in the first half of that climactic aria. Orgonasova sounds far richer than Lynne Dawson, the outstanding Konstanze for Hogwood; and in the other great aria, *Traurigkeit*, she is warmer too, less withdrawn. As Belmonte, Stanford Olsen for Gardiner is firmer and more agile than the fluttery Uwe Heilmann for Hogwood, and though Cornelius Hauptmann, Gardiner's Osmin, lacks a really dark bass, he too is firmer and more characterful than the unsteady Günther von Kannen for Hogwood. Add to that a recording which gives a clearer idea of staging, and you have a version of *Entführung* to be recommended as first choice even for those who would not normally go for a period performance.

Boehm's is also a delectable account, superbly cast and warmly recorded. Arleen Augér proves the most accomplished singer on record in the role of Constanze, girlish and fresh, yet rich, tender and dramatic by turns, with brilliant, almost flawless coloratura. The others are also outstandingly good, notably Kurt Moll whose powerful, finely focused bass makes him a superb Osmin, one who relishes the comedy too. The warm recording is beautifully transferred, to make this after Gardiner easily the most sympathetic version of the opera on CD, with the added attraction of being at mid-price.

Harnoncourt's version establishes its uniqueness at the very start of the overture, tougher and more abrasive than any previous recording, with more primitive percussion effects than we are used to in his Turkish music. It is not a comfortable sound, compounded by Harnoncourt's often fast allegros racing singers and players off their feet. Slow passages are often warmly expressive, but the stylishness of the soloists prevents them from seeming excessively romantic. The men are excellent: Peter Schreier singing charmingly, Wilfried Gamlich both bright and sweet of tone, Matti Salminen outstandingly characterful as an Osmin who, as well as singing with firm dark tone, points the words with fine menace. Yvonne Kenny as Constanze and Lilian Watson as Blonde sound on the shrill side, partly a question of microphones. Readers will note that this has now been reissued on two (instead of three) CDs and at mid-price. There is also a highlights disc (75 minutes) on Teldec 0630 13811-9.

Complete Mozart Edition, Volume 33: *La finta giardiniera* (complete).
(M) *** Ph. 422 533-2 (3) [id.]. Conwell, Sukis, Di Cesare, Thomas Moser, Fassbaender, Ihloff, McDaniel, Salzburg Mozarteum O, Hager.

Leopold Hager has a strong vocal team, with three impressive newcomers taking the women's roles – Jutta-Renate Ihloff, Julia Conwell (in the central role of Sandrina, the marquise who disguises herself as a garden-girl) and Lilian Sukis (the arrogant niece). Brigitte Fassbaender sings the castrato role of Ramiro, and the others are comparably stylish. It is a charming – if lengthy – comedy, which here, with crisply performed recitatives, is presented with vigour, charm and persuasiveness. The recording, made with the help of Austrian Radio, is excellent.

Complete Mozart Edition, Volume 28: *La finta semplice* (complete).
(M) *** Ph. Dig. 422 528-2 (2) [id.]. Hendricks, Lorenz, Johnson, Murray, Lind, Blochwitz, Schmidt, C. P. E. Bach CO, Schreier.

Schreier's version replaces the earlier, Orfeo full-priced set from Leopold Hager, particularly when it comes at mid-price on two discs instead of three. The digital recording is wonderfully clear, with a fine sense of presence, capturing the fun of the comedy. Ann Murray has never sung more seductively in Mozart than here as Giacinta, and the characterful Barbara Hendricks is a delight in the central role of Rosina.

Idomeneo (complete).
(✹) *** DG Dig. 431 674-2 (3) [id.]. Rolfe Johnson, Von Otter, McNair, Martinpelto, Robson, Hauptmann, Monteverdi Choir, E. Bar. Soloists, Gardiner.
(M) *** DG 429 864-2 (3) [id.]. Ochman, Mathis, Schreier, Varady, Winkler, Leipzig R. Ch., Dresden State O, Boehm.
*** Decca Dig. 411 805-2 (3) [id.]. Pavarotti, Baltsa, Popp, Gruberová, Nucci, V. State Op. Ch., VPO, Pritchard.
(M) ** Ph. 422 537-2 (3) [id.]. Francisco Araiza, Susanne Mentzer, Barbara Hendricks, Roberta Alexander, Uwe Heilmann, Werner Hollweg, Harry Peeters, Bav. R. Ch. & RSO, Sir Colin Davis.

With its exhilarating vigour and fine singing, Gardiner's revelatory recording, taken from live performances, will please many more than period-performance devotees. Gardiner's aim has been to include all the material Mozart wrote for the original 1781 production, whether it was finally used or not, and he recommends the use of the CD programming device for listeners to select the version they prefer, with supplementary numbers put at the end of each disc. Gardiner's Mozartian style is well sprung and subtly moulded rather than severe, and his choice of singers puts a premium on clarity and beauty of production rather than weight. Even Hillevi Martinpelto, the young soprano chosen to sing the dramatic role of Elettra, keeps a pure line in her final fury scene, avoiding explosiveness – a passage given in alternative versions. The other principals sing beautifully too, notably Anne Sofie von Otter as Idamante and Sylvia McNair as Ilia, while Anthony Rolfe Johnson, a tenor on the light side for the role of Idomeneo in a traditional performance, is well suited here, with words finely projected. The electrifying singing of the Monteverdi Choir adds to the dramatic bite, and the sound is excellent, remarkably fine for a live performance in a difficult venue.

Boehm's conducting is a delight, often spacious but never heavy in the wrong way, with lightened textures and sprung rhythms which have one relishing Mozartian felicities as never before. As Idomeneo, Wieslaw Ochman, with tenor tone often too tight, is a comparatively dull dog, but the other principals are generally excellent. Peter Schreier as Idamante also might have sounded more consistently sweet, but the imagination is irresistible. Edith Mathis is at her most beguiling as Ilia, but it is Julia Varady as Elettra who gives the most compelling performance of all, sharply incisive in her dramatic outbursts, but at the same time precise and pure-toned, a Mozartian stylist through and through.

In the Decca version, spaciously conducted by Sir John Pritchard, Pavarotti is the only tenor among the principal soloists. Not only is the role of Idamante given to a mezzo instead of a tenor – preferable, with what was originally a castrato role – but that of the High Priest, Arbace, with his two arias is taken by a baritone, Leo Nucci. The wonder is that though Pavarotti reveals imagination in every phrase, using a wide range of tone colours, the result remains well within the parameters of Mozartian style. Casting Baltsa as Idamante makes for characterful results, tougher and less fruity than her direct rivals. Lucia Popp as Ilia tends to underline expression too much, but it is a charming, girlish portrait. Gruberová makes a thrilling Elettra, totally in command of the divisions, as few sopranos are; owing to bright Decca sound, the projection of her voice is a little edgy at times.

To have a major new opera-set like this, issued from the start on a mid-priced label, is generous, but Sir Colin Davis's second version of Mozart's great *opera seria* was designed as part of the Philips Complete Mozart Edition and is priced accordingly. It comes with the fine qualities of presentation associated with the series; the text aims at completeness, with an appendix on the third disc containing major numbers like Arbace's two arias, omitted in the main text, as well as the ballet music designed to be performed after the drama is over. It also has the advantage over Davis's previous recording that the role of Idamante is given to a mezzo instead of a tenor, following Mozart's original Munich text. Such a number as the great Quartet of Act III benefits much by that – but unfortunately, as in Davis's previous version, there are flaws in the casting; his reading has also grown smoother and less incisive, less fresh than before, if now at times grander.

Francisco Araiza's efforts to produce the heroic tone needed often sound strained, and he is not clean enough in his attack; while Barbara Hendricks as Ilia adopts an even less apt Mozartian style, with too much sliding and under-the-note attack, missing the purity needed for this character. Uwe Heilmann as Arbace is also disappointing, and it is as well that his arias are left to the appendix. Others in the cast are far finer, but the total result is less than completely satisfactory, particularly arriving so soon after John Eliot Gardiner's brilliant and dramatic full-priced version for DG Archiv using period instruments. The Philips recording is full and warm, but the Gardiner set is well worth its extra cost.

Complete Mozart Edition, Volume 32: *Lucio Silla* (complete).
(M) *** Ph. 422 532-2 (3) [id.]. Schreier, Augér, Varady, Mathis, Donath, Krenn, Salzburg R. Ch. & Mozarteum Ch. & O, Hager.

Lucio Silla (slightly abridged).
*** Teldec/Warner Dig. 2292 44928-2 (2). Schreier, Gruberová, Bartoli, Kenny, Upshaw, Schoenberg Ch., VCM, Harnoncourt.

The sixteen-year-old Mozart wrote his fifth opera, on the subject of the Roman dictator Sulla (Silla), in double quick time. There are many pre-echoes of later Mozart operas, not just of the great *opera seria*, *Idomeneo*, but of *Entführung* and even of *Don Giovanni*. On Philips the castrato roles are splendidly taken by Julia Varady and Edith Mathis, and the whole team could hardly be bettered. The direction of Hager is fresh and lively, and the only snag is the length of the *secco* recitatives. However, with CD one can use these judiciously.

What Harnoncourt has done is to record a text which fits on to two generously filled CDs, not just trimming down the recitatives but omitting no fewer than four arias, all of them valuable. Yet his sparkling direction of an outstanding, characterful team of soloists brings an exhilarating demonstration of the boy Mozart's genius, with such marvels as the extended finale to Act I left intact. As in the earlier set, Schreier is masterly in the title-role, still fresh in tone, while Dawn Upshaw is warm and sweet as Celia, and Cecilia Bartoli is full and rich as Cecilio. The singing of Edita Gruberová as Giunia and Yvonne Kenny as Cinna is not quite so immaculate, but still confident and stylish. The Concentus Musicus of Vienna has rarely given so bright and lightly sprung a performance on record. Excellent digital sound.

Complete Mozart Edition, Volume 29: *Mitridate, rè di Ponto* (complete).
(M) **(*) Ph. 422 529-2 (3) [id.]. Augér, Hollweg, Gruberová, Baltsa, Cotrubas, Salzburg Mozarteum O, Hager.

Hager's fresh and generally lively performance (the rather heavy recitatives excepted) brings splendid illumination to the long-hidden area of the boy Mozart's achievement. Two of the most striking arias (including an urgent G minor piece for the heroine, Aspasia, with Arleen Augér the ravishing soprano) exploit minor keys most effectively. Ileana Cotrubas is outstanding as Ismene, and the soloists of the Salzburg orchestra cope well with the often important obbligato parts. The CD transfer is vivid and forward and a little lacking in atmosphere.

Complete Mozart Edition, Volume 40: *Le nozze di Figaro* (complete).
(M) *** Ph. 422 540-2 (3) [id.]. Freni, Norman, Minton, Ganzarolli, Wixell, Grant, Tear, BBC Ch. & SO, Sir Colin Davis.

Le nozze di Figaro (complete).
*** Decca Dig. 410 150-2 (3). Te Kanawa, Popp, Von Stade, Ramey, Allen, Moll, LPO & Ch., Solti.
(Y/B) (M) *** EMI CMS7 63266-2 (2) [Ang. CDMB 63266]. Schwarzkopf, Moffo, Cossotto, Taddei, Waechter, Vinco, Philh. Ch. & O, Giulini.
❀ (B) *** CfP CD-CFPD 4724; *TC-CFPD 4724* (2). Sciutti, Jurinac, Stevens, Bruscantini, Calabrese, Cuénod, Wallace, Sinclair, Glyndebourne Ch. & Festival O, Gui.
(Y/B) *** DG Dig. 439 871-2 (3) [id.]. Terfel, Hagley, Martinpelto, Gilfry, Stephen, McCulloch, Feller, Egerton, Backes, Monterverdi Ch., E. Bar. Soloists, Gardiner.
(Y/B) *** Teldec/Warner Dig. 4509 90861-2 (3) [id.]. Scharinger, Bonney, Margiono, Hampson, Lang, Moll, Langridge, Netherlands Op. Ch., Concg. O, Harnoncourt.
(M) **(*) Decca 417 315-2 (3) [id.]. Gueden, Danco, Della Casa, Dickie, Poell, Corena, Siepi, V. State Op. Ch., VPO, Erich Kleiber.
(N) (M) *** DG 449 728-2 (3) [id.]. Janowitz, Mathis, Troyanos, Fischer-Dieskau, Prey, Lagger, German Op. Ch. & O, Boehm.
(N) **(*) DG Dig. 445 903-2 (3) [id.]. McNair, Gallo, Studer, Skovhus, Bartoli, V. State Op. Ch., VPO, Abbado.
(Y/B) **(*) Telarc CD-80388 (3) [id.]. Miles, Focile, Vaness, Corbelli, Mentzer, Murphy, Ryland Davies, Rebecca Evans, SCO and Ch., Mackerras.
**(*) EMI Dig. CDS7 49753-2 (3) [Ang. CDCC 49753]. Desderi, Rolandi, Stilwell, Lott, Esham, Glyndebourne Ch., LPO, Haitink.
(M) (**(*)) EMI mono CMS7 69639-2 (2) [Ang. CDMB 69639]. Schwarzkopf, Seefried, Jurinac, Kunz, Majkut, London, V. State Op. Ch., VPO, Karajan.
(N) (M) *(*) Decca 444 602-2 [id.]. Tozzi, Peters, Della Casa, London, Elias, Corena, V. State Op. Ch., VPO, Leinsdorf.

Solti opts for a fair proportion of extreme speeds, slow as well as fast, but they rarely if ever intrude on the quintessential happiness of the entertainment. Samuel Ramey, a firm-toned baritone, makes a virile Figaro, superbly matched to the most enchanting of Susannas on record, Lucia Popp, who gives a sparkling and radiant performance. Thomas Allen's Count is magnificent too, tough in tone and characterization but always beautiful on the ear. Kurt Moll as Dr Bartolo sings an unforgettable *La vendetta* with triplets very fast and agile 'on the breath', while Robert Tear far outshines his own achievement as the Basilio of Sir Colin Davis's amiable recording. Frederica von Stade is a most attractive Cherubino, even if *Voi che sapete* is too slow; but crowning all is the Countess of Kiri Te Kanawa, challenged by Solti's spacious tempi in the two big arias, but producing ravishing tone, flawless phrasing and elegant ornamentation throughout. With superb, vivid recording this now makes a clear first choice for a much-recorded opera. However, in view of the strong competition, Decca should find a way of reducing its price.

Like others in EMI's series of Mozart operas, Giulini's set has been pleasingly re-packaged and has a cleanly printed, easy-to-read libretto, giving an advantage over the competing CfP set. It remains a classic, with a cast assembled by Walter Legge that has rarely been matched, let alone surpassed. Taddei with his dark bass-baritone makes a provocative Figaro; opposite him, Anna Moffo is at her freshest and sweetest as Susanna. Schwarzkopf as ever is the noblest of Countesses, and it is good to hear the young Fiorenza Cossotto as a full-toned Cherubino. Eberhard Waechter is a strong and stylish Count. On only two mid-priced discs it makes a superb bargain, though – as in the other EMI two-disc version, the Gui on CfP – Marcellina's and Basilio's arias are omitted from Act IV.

The effervescent 1955 stereo Glyndebourne recording makes a bargain without equal on only two CDs from CfP. The transfer on CD brings sound warmer, more naturally vivid and with more body than on many modern recordings. Just as Sesto Bruscantini is the archetypal Glyndebourne Figaro, Sena Jurinac is the perfect Countess, with Graziella Sciutti a delectable Susanna and Risë Stevens a well-contrasted Cherubino, vivacious in their scenes together. Franco Calabrese as the Count is firm and virile, if occasionally stressed on top; and the three character roles have never been cast more vividly, with Ian Wallace as Bartolo, Monica Sinclair as Marcellina and the incomparable Hugues Cuénod as Basilio. The only regret is that Cuénod's brilliant performance of Basilio's aria in Act IV has had to be omitted (as it so often is on stage) to keep the two discs each within the 80-minute limit. There is no libretto; instead a detailed synopsis is provided, with cueing points conveniently indicated. But this set costs little more than a third the price of the Decca/Solti version.

Gardiner's version was recorded live in concert performances at the Queen Elizabeth Hall in London in 1993, and this brings disadvantages in occasional intrusive stage noises, but it also offers a vividly dramatic and involving experience. In one instance the effect of the moment goes too far, when Cherubino (Pamela Helen Stephen) sings 'Voi che sapete' for the Countess in a funny, nervous voice. That is very much the exception, for Gardiner's approach is lively and often brisk, with period manners made more genial and elegant than on the rival period recording from Drottningholm on Oiseau-Lyre. One of the most consistent and characterful of modern casts is led superbly by Bryn Terfel as Figaro, already a master in this role, with the enchanting, bright-eyed Alison Hagley as Susanna. Rodney Gilfry and Hillevi Martinpelto are fresh and firm as the Count and Countess, aptly younger-sounding than usual. Carlos Feller is a characterful buffo Bartolo, and Francis Egerton a wickedly funny Basilio. In Act III Gardiner adopts the revised order, suggested by Robert Moberly and Christopher Raeburn, with the Countess's aria placed earlier. More controversially, in Act IV he divides the recitative for Figaro's aria so that part of it comes logically before Susanna's 'Deh vieni'. A fine addition to Gardiner's Mozart opera series for DG Archiv.

The pacing of Sir Colin Davis has a sparkle in recitative that directly reflects experience in the opera house, and his tempi generally are beautifully chosen to make their dramatic points. Vocally the cast is exceptionally consistent. Mirella Freni (Susanna) is perhaps the least satisfying, yet there is no lack of character and charm. It is good to have so ravishingly beautiful a voice as Jessye Norman's for the Countess. The Figaro of Wladimiro Ganzarolli and the Count of Ingvar Wixell project with exceptional clarity and vigour, and there is fine singing too from Yvonne Minton as Cherubino, Clifford Grant as Bartolo and Robert Tear as Basilio. The 1971 recording has more reverberation than usual, but the effect is commendably atmospheric and on CD the voices have plenty of presence.

Harnoncourt on Teldec makes the Royal Concertgebouw Orchestra produce fresh, light and transparent sounds close to period style. Speeds are relaxed, bringing out the fun and sparkle of the piece. The excellent cast has Thomas Hampson as a dominant Count, Charlotte Margiono as a tenderly sweet Countess, with Barbara Bonney a charmingly provocative Susanna and Anton Scharinger a winning Figaro, both tough and comic. Recitative at flexible speeds conveys the dramatic confrontations and complications vividly. A version that gets the best of both interpretative worlds, new and old.

Kleiber's famous set was one of Decca's Mozart bicentenary recordings of the mid-1950s. It remains an attractively strong performance with much fine singing. Few sets since have matched its constant stylishness. Gueden's Susanna might be criticized but her golden tones are certainly characterful and her voice blends with Della Casa's enchantingly. Danco and Della Casa are both at their finest. A dark-toned Figaro in Siepi brings added contrast and, if the pace of the recitatives is rather slow, this is not inconsistent within the context of Kleiber's overall approach. It is a pity that the Decca remastering, in brightening the sound, has brought a hint of edginess to the voices, though the basic atmosphere remains. Also, the layout brings a less than felicitous break in Act II. In this respect the cassettes were superior – and they had smoother sound, too.

Boehm's version of Figaro, reissued by DG as a 'Legendary Recording', is also among the most consistently assured performances available. The women all sing most beautifully, with Janowitz's Countess, Mathis's Susanna and Troyanos's Cherubino all ravishing the ear in contrasted ways. Prey is an intelligent if not very jolly-sounding Figaro, and Fischer-Dieskau gives his dark, sharply defined reading of the Count's role. All told, a great success, with fine playing and recording, here impressively remastered. This and Abbado's version of Verdi's Macbeth are the first two opera recordings – and the first multi-CD sets – to be included in DG's 'Originals' series.

Drawing beautiful sounds from the Vienna Philharmonic, Claudio Abbado with a cast of mainly young singers turns the opera into an immaculate recital. At generally brisk speeds and with recitatives trippingly delivered, the plot moves speedily but with little sparkle or sense of fun. The basic reason is that Abbado adopts a surprisingly metrical, unyielding approach, failing to bend rhythms and phrases to suit the needs of words or plot or the natural expressiveness of singers. Sylvia McNair as Susanna, Cheryl Studer as the Countess and Cecilia Bartoli as Cherubini are all characterful and musically imaginative enough to overcome much of the dulling effect of this, but the character-roles of Dr Bartolo, Marcellina and Basilio are all displayed colourlessly, with young voices unable to present the characters convincingly. Lucio Gallo is a dark-voiced Figaro who finds it hard to point comedy, similar in tone to the Count of Boje Skovhus, who however has a less pleasing, grittier voice. Most disappointing of all are the big ensembles, the Act III sextet as well as the finales to Acts II and IV, where with unexpectedly slow speeds and metrical rhythms the comedy evaporates. Happily, the final resolution on '*Contessa perdono*' is done ravishingly, with Cheryl Studer crowning a totally radiant performance. McNair also sings enchantingly and Bartoli is ideally cast. It is worth hearing the set for these three alone. The recording, faithful to voices, is slightly cavernous.

The big advantage of the Telarc version is that Sir Charles Mackerras with the Scottish Chamber Orchestra provides some 34 minutes of alternative items and variants. It is fascinating, for example, to have two alternative versions of the Count's Act III aria, with the difficult triplets largely removed, and there is also a heavily ornamented version of Cherubino's '*Voi che sapete*'. Mackerras also encourages his singers to provide ornamentation in their arias and, more than his rivals, he inserts appoggiature, avoiding 'blunt endings'. Like Harnoncourt, Mackerras aims to get the best of both interpretative worlds, but with the balance more towards period performance, using modern instruments but in a small orchestra and with speeds generally brisker and bowing lighter. Orchestrally, this is an exceptionally characterful reading, more so than for the singing of the arias and ensembles. Alastair Miles as Figaro sings superbly with clean focus but, next to his main rivals, he is straight-faced, and similarly the Susanna of Nuccia Focile is a little lacking in charm and humour, while Carol Vaness as the Countess is perhaps stressed by Mackerras's slow speeds (an exception) for her two big arias. The Count of Alessandro Corbelli is rather rough in tone, and Alfonso Antoniozzi is too light and unsteady as Bartolo, but Ryland Davies is a superb Basilio and Susanne Mentzer a strong Marcellina, both given their arias in Act IV, which comes complete on disc 3, along with the appendices. Any reservations are made relative to only the finest rivals; with warm sound, the set can be strongly recommended, particularly to anyone who wants to hear the extra material.

As in his other Glyndebourne recordings, Haitink's approach to Mozart is relaxed and mellow, helped by beautifully balanced orchestral sound. Where in *Così* the results were sunny, here in *Figaro* there is at times a lack of sparkle. There is much fine singing and excellent ensemble, and the set is well worth hearing, in particular for Claudio Desderi's idiomatically pointed and characterful Figaro, a vintage Glyndebourne performance. Yet next to the finest versions – as, for example, Solti's – this falls short in the line-up of soloists. That even applies to Felicity Lott as the Countess. Though she sings *Dove sono* with melting simplicity, the voice is not caught as well as it can be, and she does not match such a rival as Kiri Te Kanawa. Gianna Rolandi as Susanna and Faith Esham as Cherubino are both stylish without being specially characterful, and the microphone gives an edge to their voices.

Recorded in 1950, Karajan's first recording of *Figaro* offers one of the most distinguished casts ever assembled; but, curiously at that period, they decided to record the opera without the secco recitatives. That is a most regrettable omission when all these singers are not just vocally immaculate but vividly characterful – as for example Sena Jurinac, later the greatest of Glyndebourne Countesses, here a vivacious Cherubino. The firmness of focus in Erich Kunz's singing of Figaro goes with a delightful twinkle in the word-pointing, and Irmgard Seefried makes a bewitching Susanna. Schwarzkopf's noble portrait of the Countess – not always helped by a slight backward balance in the placing of the microphone for her – culminates in the most poignant account of her second aria, *Dove sono*. The sound, though obviously limited, presents the voices very vividly.

Vocally the 1960 Leinsdorf set is impressive. Giorgio Tozzi makes a fine Figaro, with a rich, dark voice (weaker admittedly at either end of the register) which is flexible enough to cope with all the vocal acting that a really comic and convincing Figaro should display. The Susanna of Roberta Peters is attractive if not always quite as stylish as one would ideally ask. There is much sparkle in her singing and, if anything, her tone-colour is too rich, for when she comes up against the Countess of Lisa della Casa there is a risk of confusion, even if in the 'Letter duet' the result is most beautiful. Della Casa displays genuinely patrician qualities with some lovely mezza voce in *Dove sono*. The Cherubino of Rosalind Elias is not quite ideal but is still impressive, and Fernando Corena is a magnificent Dr Bartolo. One could continue with the list of vocal felicities, but the snag is the ham-fisted conducting of Leinsdorf. The ridiculously fast speed in the Overture results in some scrambled playing even from the Vienna Philharmonic, and then in number after number he chooses speeds that are much too fast, and – even more serious – manages to eliminate all the charm from Mozart's score in an interpretation notable for its graceless qualities. We need a highlights disc from this set to rescue some of the more successful numbers from an excellent cast.

Le nozze di Figaro: highlights.
(B) *** DG 439 449-2 (from above set, with Janowitz, Mathis, Prey, Fischer-Dieskau; cond. Boehm).
(N) **(*) Telarc Dig. CD 80449 [id.] (from above set with Milnes, Focile, Vaness, Corbelli, Mentzner; cond. Mackerras).

Boehm's selection includes many of the key numbers, but with a little over an hour of music it is less than generous and inadequately documented; but the singing is first class and the sound vivid.

A well-selected 77 minutes from the Mackerras Scottish set, with most of the key items, will be useful as this is not likely to be a first choice for the complete opera, except for those with a special interest in the singers or the additional items which Mackerras includes (but which are not offered here). There is a good synopsis, but it is not cued.

Complete Mozart Edition, Volume 39: *L'Oca del Cairo* (complete).
(M) *** Ph. Dig. 422 539-2 [id.]. Nielsen, Wiens, Coburn, Schreier, Johnson, Fischer-Dieskau, Scharinger, Berlin R. Ch. (members), C. P. E. Bach CO, Schreier – *Lo sposo deluso*. ***

We owe it to the Mozart scholar and Philips recording producer, Erik Smith, that these two sets of Mozartian fragments, *L'Oca del Cairo* and *Lo sposo deluso*, have been prepared for performance and recorded. *L'Oca del Cairo* ('The Cairo goose'), containing roughly twice as much music as *Lo sposo deluso*, involves six substantial numbers, most of them ensembles, including an amazing finale to the projected Act I, with contrasted sections following briskly one after the other. It is very well conducted by Peter Schreier, who also takes part as one of the soloists. Dietrich Fischer-Dieskau takes the *buffo* old-man role of Don Pippo, and Anton Scharinger is brilliant in the patter aria in tarantella rhythm for the major-domo, Chichibio, bringing a foretaste of Donizetti. Fresh, bright digital recording.

Complete Mozart Edition, Volume 35: *Il rè pastore* (complete).
(M) **(*) Ph. Dig. 422 535-2 (2) [id.]. Blasi, McNair, Vermillion, Hadley, Ahnsjö, ASMF, Marriner.

Il rè pastore, the last of Mozart's early operas, is best known for the glorious aria, *L'amero*, one of the loveliest he ever wrote for soprano. The whole entertainment is among the most charming of his early music, a gentle piece which works well on record. This version by Marriner and the Academy, with a first-rate cast and with plenty of light and shade, and superbly played, does not efface memories of the 1979 DG version conducted by Leopold Hager, which offered even purer singing. Here Angela Maria Blasi, despite a beautiful voice, attacks notes from below, even in *L'amero*. Excellent sound.

Complete Mozart Edition, Volume 36: *Der Schauspieldirektor* (complete).
(M) **(*) Ph. 422 536-2 (2) [id.]. Welting, Cotrubas, Grant, Rolfe Johnson, LSO, Sir Colin Davis – *Zaïde*. ***

Der Schauspieldirektor (The Impresario): complete.
(M) *** DG 429 877-2; *429 877-4 (3/2)* [id.]. Grist, Augér, Schreier, Moll, Dresden State O, Boehm – *Die Zauberflöte*. **(*)

The DG performance of *Der Schauspieldirektor* is without dialogue, so that it is short enough to make a fill-up for Boehm's *Zauberflöte*. Reri Grist's bravura as Madame Herz is impressive, and Arleen Augér is pleasingly fresh and stylish here. The tenor and bass make only minor contributions, but Boehm's guiding hand keeps the music alive from the first bar to the last.

There is no contest whatsoever between the two rival prima donnas presented in the Philips recording. *Ich bin die erste Sängerin* ('I am the leading prima donna'), they yell at each other; but here Ileana Cotrubas is in a world apart from the thin-sounding and shallow Ruth Welting. Davis directs with fire and electricity a performance which is otherwise (despite the lack of spoken dialogue) most refreshing and beautifully recorded (in 1975) in a sympathetic acoustic.

Complete Mozart Edition, Volume 31: *Il sogno di Scipione* (complete).
(M) *** Ph. 422 531-2 (2) [id.]. Popp, Gruberová, Mathis, Schreier, Ahnsjö, Thomas Moser, Salzburg Chamber Ch. & Mozarteum O, Hager.

Il sogno di Scipione presents an allegorical plot with Scipio set to choose between Fortune and Constancy. Given the choice of present-day singers, this cast could hardly be finer, with Edita Gruberová, Lucia Popp and Edith Mathis superbly contrasted in the women's roles (the latter taking part in the epilogue merely), and Peter Schreier is joined by two of his most accomplished younger colleagues. Hager sometimes does not press the music on as he might, but his direction is always alive.

With fine recording, vividly and atmospherically transferred to CD, the set is not likely to be surpassed in the immediate future.

Complete Mozart Edition, Volume 39: *Lo sposo deluso.*
(M) *** Ph. 422 539-2 [id.]. Palmer, Cotrubas, Rolfe Johnson, Tear, Grant, LSO, Sir Colin Davis – *L'Oca del Cairo.* ***

The music presented here from *Lo sposo deluso* is the surviving music from an unfinished opera written in the years before *Figaro*, and it contains much that is memorable. The *Overture*, with its trumpet calls, its lovely slow middle section and recapitulation with voices, is a charmer, while the two arias, reconstructed by the recording producer and scholar, Erik Smith, are also delightful: the one a trial run for Fiordiligi's *Come scoglio* in *Così*, the other (sung by Robert Tear) giving a foretaste of Papageno's music in *The Magic Flute*.

Complete Mozart Edition, Volume 36: *Zaïde.*
(M) *** Ph. 422 536-2 (2) [id.]. Mathis, Schreier, Wixell, Hollweg, Süss, Berlin State O, Klee – *Der Schauspieldirektor.* **(*)

Zaïde, written between 1779 and 1780 and never quite completed, was a trial run for *Entführung*. Much of the music is superb, and melodramas at the beginning of each Act are strikingly effective and original, with the speaking voice of the tenor in the first heard over darkly dramatic writing in D minor. Zaïde's arias in both Acts are magnificent: the radiantly lyrical *Ruhe sanft* is hauntingly memorable, and the dramatic *Tiger aria* is like Constanze's *Martern aller Arten* but briefer and more passionate. Bernhard Klee directs a crisp and lively performance, with excellent contributions from singers and orchestra alike – a first-rate team, as consistently stylish as one could want.

Die Zauberflöte (complete).
*** Ph. Dig. 426 276-2 (2) [id.]. Te Kanawa, Studer, Lind, Araiza, Bär, Ramey, Van Dam, Amb. Op. Ch., ASMF, Marriner.
(N) *** Erato/Warner Dig. 0630 12705-2 (2) [id.]. Mannion, Blochwitz, Dessay, Hagen, Scharinger, Les Arts Florissants, William Christie.
✸ (M) (***) DG mono 435 742-2 (2). Stader, Streich, Fischer-Dieskau, Greindl, Haefliger, Berlin RIAS Ch. & SO, Fricsay.
(Y/B) *** EMI CDS5 55173-2 (2). Janowitz, Putz, Popp, Gedda, Berry, Frick, Schwarzkopf, Ludwig, Hoffgen (3 Ladies), Philh. Ch. & O, Klemperer.
(M) *** EMI mono CHS7 69631-2 (2) [Ang. CDHB 69631]. Seefried, Lipp, Loose, Dermota, Kunz, Weber, V. State Op. Ch., VPO, Karajan.
*** EMI Dig. CDS7 47951-8 (3) [Ang. CDCC 47951]. Popp, Gruberová, Lindner, Jerusalem, Brendel, Bracht, Zednik, Bav. R. Ch. & SO, Haitink.
*** Telarc Dig. CD-80302 (2). Hadley, Hendricks, Allen, Anderson, Lloyd, SCO & Ch., Mackerras.
(B) *** Naxos Dig. 8 660030/31 (2) [id.]. Norberg-Schulz, Kwon, Lippert, Leitner, Tichy, Rydl, Hungarian Festival Ch., Failoni O, Budapest, Halász.
**(*) O-L Dig. 440 085-2 (2) [id.]. Bonney, Sumi Jo, Streit, Cachemaille, Sigmundsson, Drottningholm Court Theatre Ch. & O, Ostman.
(M) **(*) DG 429 877-2; *429 877-4* (3/2) [id.]. Lear, Peters, Otto, Wunderlich, Fischer-Dieskau, Hotter, Crass, Berlin RIAS Chamber Ch., BPO, Boehm – *Der Schauspieldirektor.* ***
(N) (M) **(*) RCA 74321 32240-2 [id.]. Donath, Geszty, Schreier, Adam, Hoff, Leib, Vogel, Leipzig R. Ch., Dresden State O, Suitner.
(M) (**(*)) Pearl mono GEMMCDS 9371 (2). Lemnitz, Roswaenge, Berger, Hüsch, Strienz, Ch. & BPO, Beecham.
(Y/B) (B) ** Ph. Duo Dig. 442 568-2 (2) [id.]. Margaret Price, Serra, Schreier, Moll, Melbye, Venuti, Tear, Dresden Kreuzchor, Leipzig R. Ch., Dresden State O, Sir Colin Davis.

Marriner directs a pointed and elegant reading of *Zauberflöte*, bringing out the fun of the piece. It lacks weight only in the overture and finale, and the cast is the finest in any modern recording. Dame Kiri lightens her voice delightfully, while Olaf Bär, vividly characterful, brings the Lieder-singer's art to the role of Papageno. Araiza's voice has coarsened since he recorded the role of Tamino for Karajan, but this performance is subtler and conveys more feeling. Cheryl Studer's performance as Queen of the Night is easily the finest among modern recordings; and Samuel Ramey gives a generous and wise portrait of Sarastro. This is now the finest digital version, superbly recorded, with the added advantage that it comes on only two discs instead of the three used for most other recent recordings.

Based on a production at the Aix-en-Provence Festival, and recorded in 1995 in collaboration with Radio France, William Christie's Erato set sweeps the board for recordings using period instruments.

Arnold Ostman's Drottningholm set similarly re-creates the sparkle and exuberance of a live perform-ance, but that is a small-scale reading, and the very opening of the overture under Christie instantly demonstrates that this is a performance which, along with lighter qualities, can where necessary convey the full weight of Mozart's masonic inspiration, with the instruments of Les Arts Florissants firm and full. More than his rivals, Christie wears his period manners easily and amiably, with fast speeds crisp and light, and with some numbers – such as Papageno's first aria – relaxedly expansive. There is no weak link in the cast, with Rosa Mannion a warm, touching Pamina, able to bring out deeper feelings as in *Ach, ich fühls*, and Blochwitz is an imaginative, sweetly expressive Tamino, while Natalie Dessay as Queen of the Night is unusually warm-toned for the role, not so much a frigid figure as a fully rounded character, with the coloratura display dazzlingly clear. Scharinger is a genial, rich-toned Papageno, and Hagen a Sarastro satisfyingly clean of focus. Above all, the joyful vigour of Mozart's inspiration captures one from first to last, making this a strong contender, even if you would normally choose a modern-instrument version.

From the early LP era Fricsay's is an outstandingly fresh and alert *Die Zauberflöte*, marked by generally clear, pure singing and well-sprung orchestral playing at generally rather fast speeds. In some ways Fricsay anticipates the Mozart tastes of a later generation, even if his approach to ornamentation is hardly in authentic-period style. Maria Stader and Dietrich Fischer-Dieskau phrase most beautifully, but the most spectacular singing comes from Rita Streich as a dazzling Queen of the Night – the finest on record – and the relatively close balance of the voice gives it the necessary power such as Streich generally failed to convey in the opera house. It is this unique contribution which nudges us towards a Rosette; but Ernst Haefliger, too, is at his most honeyed in tone as Tamino, and only the rather gritty Sarastro of Josef Greindl falls short – and even he sings with a satisfyingly dark resonance. This was the first version to spice the musical numbers with brief sprinklings of dialogue, just enough to prevent the work from sounding like an oratorio. Even including that, DG has managed to put each of the Acts complete on a single disc. The transfer of the original 1954 mono recording (made in the Berlin Jesus-Christus-Kirche) is remarkably full-bodied, with a pleasant ambience and sense of presence.

Klemperer's conducting of *The Magic Flute* is one of his finest achievements on record; indeed he is inspired, making the dramatic music sound more like Beethoven in its breadth and strength. But he does not miss the humour and point of the Papageno passages, and he gets the best of both worlds to a surprising degree. The cast is outstanding – look at the distinction of the Three Ladies alone – but curiously it is that generally most reliable of all the singers, Gottlob Frick as Sarastro, who comes nearest to letting the side down. Lucia Popp is in excellent form, and Gundula Janowitz sings Pamina's part with a creamy beauty that is just breathtaking. Nicolai Gedda too is a firm-voiced Tamino. The transfer to a pair of CDs, made possible by the absence of dialogue, is managed expertly. However, like Klemperer's set of Beethoven's *Fidelio*, this recording has reverted to full price and, even though it has been re-packaged, such an increase in cost seems in no way justifiable.

Apart from the Fricsay set with Rita Streich which includes some spoken dialogue, there has never been a more seductive recording of *Zauberflöte* than Karajan's mono version of 1950. The Vienna State Opera cast here has not since been matched on record: Irmgard Seefried and Anton Dermota both sing with radiant beauty and great character, Wilma Lipp is a dazzling Queen of the Night, Erich Kunz as Papageno sings with an infectious smile in the voice, and Ludwig Weber is a commanding Sarastro. There is no spoken dialogue; but on two mid-priced CDs instead of three LPs, it is a Mozart treat not to be missed, with mono sound still amazingly vivid and full of presence.

Haitink directs a rich and spacious account of *Zauberflöte*, superbly recorded in spectacularly wide-ranging digital sound. The dialogue – not too much of it, nicely produced and with sound effects adding to the vividness – frames a presentation that has been carefully thought through. Popp makes the most tenderly affecting of Paminas and Gruberová has never sounded more spontaneous in her brilliance than here as Queen of the Night: she is both agile and powerful. Jerusalem makes an outstanding Tamino, both heroic and sweetly Mozartian; and though neither Wolfgang Brendel as Papageno nor Bracht as Sarastro is as characterful as their finest rivals, their personalities project strongly and the youthful freshness of their singing is most attractive. The Bavarian chorus too is splendid.

Though the recording puts a halo of reverberation round the sound, Mackerras and the Scottish Chamber Orchestra find an ideal scale for the work. His speeds are often faster than usual, not least in Pamina's great aria of lament, *Ach, ich fühl's*, but they always flow persuasively. This is the version among recent ones which best conveys the fun of the piece, as well as its power. Jerry Hadley makes a delightfully boyish Tamino, with Thomas Allen the most characterful Papageno, singing beautifully. Robert Lloyd is a noble Sarastro, and though June Anderson is a rather strenuous Queen of the Night, it is thrilling to have a big, dramatic voice so dazzlingly agile. Barbara Hendricks is a questionable choice as Pamina, not clean enough of attack, but the tonal quality is golden. Among modern recordings this is a set to put beside Haitink's very enjoyable EMI version, despite the reverberant sound.

Though Kurt Rydl is the only established recording artist among the soloists, the Naxos set offers a very satisfying performance, well conducted and well recorded, with some very stylish solo singing. At budget price with a fair measure of German dialogue included (but on separate tracks to allow it to be programmed out if preferred), this makes a first-rate recommendation, competitive with some of the classic sets. As Tamino, Herbert Lippert is a good, clean-cut Germanic tenor, hardly ever strained, with fine legato in *Dies Bildnis*. The young Norwegian, Elisabeth Norberg-Schulz, is a bright, girlish Pamina, who sustains a slow speed for *Ach, ich fühl's* very effectively, tenderly making it an emotional high point. Rydl is a powerful Sarastro, if not always perfectly steady, and Tichy is a delightful Papageno, defying Halász's uncharacteristically stodgy tempo for his first aria, and from there consistently conveying characterful humour without vocal exaggeration. Perhaps the most exciting newcomer is Hellen Kwon, an outstanding Queen of the Night, using full, firm tone with bright attack in her two big arias. The recording is clear and well balanced, with the Queen's thunder vividly caught.

In contrast with his earlier Drottningholm recordings of Mozart operas, often rushed and brittle, Ostman in his Oiseau-Lyre series offers a far more sympathetic set of *Zauberflöte*. It may lack weight but it rarely sounds rushed, for consistently Ostman gives a spring to the rhythms. That was something which disappointingly is missing from Roger Norrington on EMI, a rival recording using period forces. Ostman's cast too is markedly preferable to Norrington's, with no weak link. Barbara Bonney is a charming Pamina, with Kurt Streit a free-toned Tamino and with Gilles Cachemaille as Papageno both finely focused and full of fun. Sumi Jo is a bright, clear Queen of the Night and, though the Sarastro of Kristian Sigmundsson is lightweight, that matches the overall approach.

One of the glories of Boehm's DG set is the singing of Fritz Wunderlich as Tamino, a wonderful memorial to a singer much missed. Fischer-Dieskau, with characteristic word-pointing, makes a sparkling Papageno on record and Franz Crass is a satisfyingly straightforward Sarastro. The team of women is well below this standard – Lear taxed cruelly in *Ach, ich fühl's*, Peters shrill in the upper register (although the effect is exciting), and the Three Ladies do not blend well – but Boehm's direction is superb, light and lyrical, but weighty where necessary to make a glowing, compelling experience. Fine recording, enhanced in the CD set, which has also found room for Boehm's admirable account of *Der Schauspieldirektor*, a very considerable bonus to this mid-priced reissue.

The RCA (originally Eurodisc) set is well cast, directed with breadth and spirit, and vividly recorded. Indeed, considering that the recording was made at the beginning of the 1970s, it sounds remarkably well, although with a forward balance there is not the subtlety of perspective one finds in more modern sets. There are no real flaws here. The finest performances come from Peter Schreier, an outstanding Tamino, ardent and stylish; Sylvia Geszty's Queen of the Night is fierce to the point of shrillness, but it is a forceful projection and balances with Donath's somewhat ingenuous portrayal of Pamina, prettily sung. Theo Adam is a commanding Sarastro and Renata Hoff and Günther Leib make an attractive team as Papagena and Papageno; while the orchestral playing is first rate, the contribution of the Leipzig Radio Choir is less impressive. There is a minimum of dialogue and it is separately cued. Not a top choice, but enjoyable just the same. The accompanying libretto is in German with no translation.

Recorded in Berlin between November 1937 and March 1939, Beecham's recording of *Zauberflöte* was also the first opera set produced by Walter Legge. It brings a classic performance. Beecham was at his peak, pacing each number superbly, and the vocal delights are many, not least from Tiana Lemnitz as a radiant Pamina, Erna Berger as a dazzling Queen of the Night, and Gerhard Hüsch as a delicately comic Papageno, bringing the detailed art of the Lieder-singer to the role. Of the three currently available transfers of this Beecham recording to CD, the Pearl is the one which captures the original 78 recording most naturally, with the keenest sense of presence for the voices, even if it leaves it with plentiful surface hiss. The disappointment of the EMI alternative is the dryness of the sound, with a limited top, little sense of presence and no bloom on the voices. The Nimbus attempt finds that company's re-recording process, using an acoustic gramophone, less effective than it can be. The orchestral sound is made thin, almost disembodied, and though the voices have bloom on them, they often jangle.

The last of Sir Colin Davis's recordings of Mozart's major operas, and the only one made outside Britain, is also the least successful. With speeds often slower than usual and the manner heavier, it is a performance of little sparkle or charm, one which seems intent on bringing out serious, symbolic meanings. Thus, although Margaret Price produces a glorious flow of rich, creamy tone, she conveys little of the necessary vulnerability of Pamina in her plight. Luciana Serra sings capably but at times with shrill tone and not always with complete security; while Peter Schreier is in uncharacteristically gritty voice as Tamino, and Mikael Melbye as Papageno is ill-suited to recording, when the microphone exaggerates the throatiness and unevenness of his production. The greatest vocal glory of the set is the magnificent, firm and rich singing of Kurt Moll as Sarastro. The recording is excellent. Although this Duo reissue is inexpensive, it is upstaged by the competing Halász Naxos set from Budapest.

Die Zauberflöte: highlights.
*** Ph. Dig. 438 495-2 [id.] (from above recording, with Te Kanawa, Studer, Araiza, Bär, Ramey; cond.
    Marriner).
(M) *** EMI CDM7 63451-2; *EG 763451-4* (from above recording, cond. Klemperer).
(M) (***) EMI mono CD-EMX 2220; *TC-EMX 2220* [id.] (from above recording with Seefried, Lipp;
    cond. Karajan).
(Y/B) (B) **(*) DG Classikon 449 845-2 [id.] (from above recording, with Lear, Peters, Wunderlich,
    Fischer-Dieskau, Crass; cond. Boehm).

First choice goes to Marriner with his outstanding cast and first-class, modern, digital recording. The
selection includes the *Overture* and plays for 69 minutes. Otherwise, those looking for a first-rate set of
highlights from *Die Zauberflöte* will find the mid-priced Klemperer disc hard to beat. It makes a good
sampler of a performance which, while ambitious in scale, manages to find sparkle and humour too. A
synopsis details each individual excerpt, and in this case the inclusion of the *Overture* is especially
welcome. The remastered sound has plenty of presence, but atmosphere and warmth too.

The Karajan Vienna State Opera selection on Eminence will be a good way for many to sample a highly
enticing mono set with a superb cast, all on the top of their form. The selection lasts 68 minutes, but
seven of these are taken up by the Overture, a less than sensible idea, even if it is superbly played. It is
disgraceful, though, that the front of this CD – aimed at a popular market – does not make it absolutely
clear that the sound is mono.

The hour of excerpts from Boehm's recording is not obviously directed towards bringing out its special
qualities, although there would have been room on the CD (which includes the *Overture*) for at least
another quarter of an hour of music, to measure up with the companion selection from *Don Giovanni*.
One would have liked more of Wunderlich's Tamino, one of the great glories of the set. However, the
key arias are all included and the sound is fresh and full. This is now on DG's bargain Classikon label,
which means that the synopsis is not cued.

Recitals

Arias from: *La clemenza di Tito; Così fan tutte; Don Giovanni; Die Entführung aus dem Serail; Idomeneo;
Le nozze di Figaro; Die Zauberflöte.*
(Y/B) (M) *** Ph. Dig. 442 410-2 [id.]. Cheryl Studer, ASMF, Marriner.

This is a very impressive recital indeed. Only the aria from *Idomeneo* could be considered a little undercharacterized – and that is a marginal criticism; the Queen of the Night's arias from *Die Zauberflöte* are
superbly done, as is the opening *Martern aller Arten* (from *Die Entführung*) and the excerpts from *Così*
and *Don Giovanni* are hardly less memorable in a quite different way. Excellent accompaniments and
recording, but the measure is fairly short (55 minutes).

Arias: *La clemenza di Tito: S'altro che lagrime. Così fan tutte: Ei parte . . . Sen . . . Per pietà. La finta
giardiniera: Crudeli fermate . . . Ah dal pianto. Idomeneo: Se il padre perdei. Lucio Silla: Pupille amate. Il
rè pastore: L'amerò, sarò costante. Zaïde: Ruhe sanft, mein holdes Leben. Die Zauberflöte: Ach ich fühl's
es ist verschwunden.*
*** Ph. Dig. 411 148-2 [id.]. Kiri Te Kanawa, LSO, C. Davis.

Kiri Te Kanawa's is one of the loveliest collections of Mozart arias on record, with the voice at its most
ravishing and pure. One might object that Dame Kiri concentrates on soulful arias, ignoring more
vigorous ones; but with stylish accompaniment and clear, atmospheric recording, beauty dominates
all.

Arias: *Don Giovanni; Die Entführung aus dem Serail; Idomeneo; Le nozze di Figaro; Die Zauberflöte.*
(M) (***) EMI mono CDH7 63708-2. Elisabeth Schwarzkopf (with various orchestras & conductors,
    including John Pritchard).

Just how fine a Mozartian Schwarzkopf already was early in her career comes out in these 12 items,
recorded between 1946 and 1952. The earliest are Konstanze's two arias from *Entführung*, and one of
the curiosities is a lovely account of Pamina's *Ach ich fühl's*, recorded in English in 1948. The majority,
including those from *Figaro* – Susanna's and Cherubino's arias as well as the Countess's – are taken
from a long-unavailable recital disc conducted by John Pritchard. Excellent transfers.

ANTHOLOGIES

'*Fifty Years of Mozart singing on record*': (i) *Concert arias;* Excerpts from: (ii) *Mass in C min., K.427;* (iii)
La clemenza di Tito; (iv) *Così fan tutte;* (v) *Don Giovanni;* (vi) *Die Entführung aus dem Serail;* (vii) *La
finta giardiniera;* (viii) *Idomeneo;* (ix) *Le nozze di Figaro;* (x) *Il rè pastore;* (xi) *Zaïde;* (xii) *Die
Zauberflöte.*

(M) (***) EMI mono CMS7 63750-2 (4) [id.]. (i) Rethberg, Ginster, Francillo-Kaufmann; (ii) Berger; (iii) Kirkby-Lunn; (iv) V. Schwarz, Noni, Grümmer, Hahn, Kiurina, Hüsch, Souez, H. Nash; (v) Vanni-Marcoux, Scotti, Farrar, Battistini, Corsi, Leider, Roswaenge, D'Andrade, Pinza, Patti, Maurel, Renaud, Pernet, McCormack, Gadski, Kemp, Callas; (vi) Slezak, L. Weber, Tauber, Lehmann, Nemeth, Perras, Ivogün, Von Pataky, Hesch; (vii) Dux; (viii) Jurinac, Jadlowker; (ix) Stabile, Helletsgruber, Santley, Gobbi, Lemnitz, Feraldy, Schumann, Seinemeyer, Vallin, Rautawaara, Mildmay, Jokl, Ritter-Ciampi; (x) Gerhart; (xi) Seefried; (xii) Fugère; Wittrisch; Schiøtz, Gedda, Kurz, Erb, Kipnis, Galvany, Hempel, Sibiriakov, Frick, Destinn, Norena, Schöne, Kunz.

This is an astonishing treasury of singing, recorded over the first half of the twentieth century. It begins with Mariano Stabile's resonant 1928 account of Figaro's *Se vuol ballare*, snail-like by today's standards, while Sir Charles Santley in *Non piu andrai* a few tracks later is both old-sounding and slow. The stylistic balance is then corrected in Tito Gobbi's magnificently characterful 1950 recording of that same aria. Astonishment lies less in early stylistic enormities than in the wonderful and consistent purity of vocal production, with wobbles – so prevalent today – virtually non-existent. That is partly the result of the shrewd and obviously loving choice of items, which includes not only celebrated marvels like John McCormack's 1916 account of Don Ottavio's *Il mio tesoro* (breaking all records for breath control, and stylistically surprising for including an appoggiatura), but many rarities. The short-lived Meta Seinemeyer, glorious in the Countess's first aria, Germaine Feraldy, virtually unknown, a charming Cherubino, Johanna Gadski formidably incisive in Donna Anna's *Mi tradi*, Frieda Hempel incomparable in the Queen of the Night's second aria – all these and many dozens of others make for compulsive listening, with transfers generally excellent. There are far more women singers represented than men, and a high proportion of early recordings are done in languages other than the original; but no lover of fine singing should miss this feast. The arias are gathered together under each opera, with items from non-operatic sources grouped at the end of each disc. Helpfully, duplicate versions of the same aria are put together irrespective of date of recording, and highly informative notes are provided on all the singers.

Muffat, Georg (1653–1704)

Armonico tributo cioè sonata da camera: Nos. 2 in G min.; 5 in G.
**(*) HM/BMG Dig. 05472 77303-2 [id.]. Freiburg Bar. Cons. – BIBER: *Sonatae tam Aris.* **(*)

Muffat's sonatas (1682) are almost exactly contemporary with the Biber sonatas with which they are coupled but they are much more conventional works. Yet they attractively provide a touch of gravitas between the chimerical Biber pieces. They are played authentically and with spirit, and are well recorded. But with a playing time of 59 minutes there would have been room here for yet another work by each composer.

Mundy, William (c. 1529–c. 1591)

Vox Patris caelestis.
*** Gimell CDGIM 339 [id.]. Tallis Scholars, Phillips – ALLEGRI: *Miserere;* PALESTRINA: *Missa Papae Marcelli.* ***

Mundy's *Vox Patris caelestis* was written during the short reign of Queen Mary (1553–8). The work is structured in nine sections in groups of three, the last of each group being climactic and featuring the whole choir, with solo embroidery. Yet the music flows continuously, like a great river, and the complex vocal writing creates the most spectacular effects, with the trebles soaring up and shining out over the underlying cantilena. The Tallis Scholars give an account which balances linear clarity with considerable power. The recording is first class and the digital remastering for CD improves the focus further.

Mussorgsky, Modest (1839–81)

The Capture of Kars (Triumphal march); St John's night on the bare mountain (original score); *Scherzo in B flat. Khovanshchina: Prelude to Act I;* (i) *Introduction to Act IV. The Destruction of Sennacherib.* (i; ii) *Joshua.* (i) *Oedipus in Athens: Temple chorus. Salammbô: Priestesses' chorus* (operatic excerpts all orch. Rimsky-Korsakov).
✹ (M) *** RCA 09026 61354-2 [id.]. (i) London Symphony Ch.; (ii) Zehava Gal; LSO, Abbado.

To commemorate the centenary of Mussorgsky's death, in 1981 Abbado and the LSO came up with this very attractive and revealing anthology of shorter pieces. The *Khovanshchina Prelude*, very beautifully played indeed, is well enough known, but it is good to have so vital and pungent an account of the original version of *Night on the bare mountain*, different in all but its basic material from the Rimsky-Korsakov arrangement. Rimsky was right to prune it: at 12 minutes, without the slow end-piece, it is a shade over-long, but Mussorgsky's scoring is so original and imaginative that the ear is readily held. Best of all are the four choral pieces; even when they are early and untypical (*Oedipus in Athens*, for example), they are immediately attractive and very Russian in feeling, and they include such evocative pieces as the *Chorus of Priestesses* (intoning over a pedal bass) from a projected opera on Flaubert's novel. The recording is first rate and the CD transfer enhances the original considerably, giving the chorus greater presence without loss of atmosphere or perspective. This is one of the most attractive Mussorgsky records in the catalogue and is not to be missed: the performers are on their toes throughout.

Night on the bare mountain (orch. Rimsky-Korsakov).
(N) (M) *** EMI CDM5 65715-2 [id.]. O de Paris, Rostropovich – RIMSKY-KORSAKOV: *Scheherazade;* *Capriccio espagnol.* **(*)
(M) *** Mercury 432 004-2 [id.]. LSO, Dorati – PROKOFIEV: *Romeo and Juliet suites.* ***

A bold, exciting account from Rostropovich, emphasizing the richness of Rimsky-Korsakov's orchestration rather than the starkness of Mussorgsky's original conception – but not necessarily the worse for that, when the recording is full-blooded to match.

Dorati's fine 1960 account of *Night on the bare mountain* comes as an encore for Skrowaczewski's outstanding Prokofiev, and it is interesting at the end of *Romeo and Juliet* to note the subtle shift of acoustic from the Minneapolis auditorium to Wembley Town Hall.

Night on the bare mountain (original version); *Pictures at an exhibition* (orch. Ravel).
(M) ** Teldec/Warner Dig. 9031 77600-2 [id.]. Cleveland O, Christoph von Dohnányi.

Dohnányi's coupling of the *Pictures* with *Night on the bare mountain* fails to match the electrifying impact of the famous earlier Telarc record of these same two works (CD 80042). Well, not quite the same, since Dohnányi chooses Mussorgsky's original score of the latter piece rather than the Rimsky-Korsakov arrangement. His somewhat cultivated approach tends to smooth over the music's crudities; Kaspryzk makes a much better case for this work. Although the Cleveland acoustics add considerably to the sound of the new record and there is some very fine orchestral playing in the various *Pictures* (the *Unhatched chicks* and *The Tuileries* both offer superb, restrained instrumental virtuosity), the more dramatic and grotesque elements of the score are less effectively characterized.

(i) *Night on the bare mountain* (arr. Rimsky-Korsakov); (ii) *Pictures at an exhibition* (orch. Ravel).
*** DG Dig. 429 785-2 [id.]. NYPO, Sinopoli – RAVEL: *Valses nobles et sentimentales.* **(*)
*** Telarc Dig. CD 80042 [id.]. Cleveland O, Maazel.
(M) *** RCA [id.]. 09026 61958-2 [id.]. Chicago SO, Reiner – *Concert of Russian showpieces.* ***
(N) (B) **(*) Decca Eclipse Dig. 448 233-2; *448 233-4* [id.]. Montreal SO, Dutoit – RIMSKY-KORSAKOV: *Capriccio espagnole* etc. **(*)
(BB) **(*) Naxos 8.550051 [id.]. Slovak PO, Nazareth – BORODIN: *In the Steppes of Central Asia* etc. **(*)
(Y/B) (M) ** Virgin/EMI Dig. CUV5 61135-2 [id.]. Royal Liverpool PO. Ch. & O, Mackerras – BORODIN: *Prince Igor: Overture and Polovtsian dances.* ***

Sinopoli's electrifying New York recording of Mussorgsky's *Pictures at an exhibition* not only heads the list of modern digital versions but also it again displays the New York Philharmonic as one of the world's great orchestras, performing with an epic virtuosity and panache that recall the Bernstein era of the 1960s. The playing of violins and woodwind alike is full of sophisticated touches, so well demonstrated by their colourful, brilliant articulation in *Tuileries Gardens* and *Limoges*, the wittily piquant portrayal of the *Unhatched chicks*, and the firm, resonant line of the lower strings in *Samuel Goldenberg and Schmuyle*. But it is the brass that one rememembers most, from the richly sonorous opening *Promenade*, through the ferocious bite and subtle grotesquerie of *Gnomus*, the bleating trumpet of *Schmuyle*, the stabbing sforzandos at the opening of *Catacombs*, to the malignantly forceful rhythms of *The hut on fowl's legs*, with the playing of the trombones and tuba often assuming an unusual yet obviously calculated dominance of the texture. The finale combines power with dignified splendour, and the bells toll out from their tower to emphasize the Byzantine character of Hartmann's picture of the *Kiev Gate. A Night on the bare mountain* is comparably vibrant, with the Rimskian fanfares particularly vivid and the closing pages full of Russian nostalgia. The splendid digital recording, made in New

York's Manhattan Center, has breadth and weight, and its fullness comes with a believable overall perspective and excellent internal definition.

The quality of the Telarc Cleveland recording is apparent at the very opening of *Night on the bare mountain* in the richly sonorous presentation of the deep brass and the sparkling yet unexaggerated percussion. With the Cleveland Orchestra on top form, the *Pictures* are strongly characterized; this may not be the subtlest reading available, but each of Mussorgsky's cameos comes vividly to life. After a vibrantly rhythmic *Baba-Yaga*, strong in fantastic menace, the closing *Great Gate of Kiev* is overwhelmingly spacious in conception and quite riveting as sheer sound, with the richness and amplitude of the brass which make the work's final climax unforgettable. Unfortunately the *Pictures* are not cued separately.

Reiner's RCA *Pictures* (recorded in 1957) is another demonstration of vintage stereo using simple microphone techniques to achieve a natural concert-hall balance. The sound-balance is full and atmospheric and Reiner's approach is evocative to match – the sombre picture of *The old castle*, the lumbering *Ox-wagon*, the unctuous picture of *Samuel Goldenberg* (powerfully drawn in the strings) and the superb brass playing in the *Catacombs* sequence are all memorable. The final climax of *The Great Gate of Kiev* is massively effective, if not quite matching the Cleveland Telarc version in sheer spectacle. The Chicago brass is again very telling in *Night on a bare mountain*, made two years later, a performance just as strongly characterized. The current CD transfers are very impressive indeed.

Dutoit's *A Night on the bare mountain* is strong and biting, but again the adrenalin does not flow as grippingly as in, say, Solti's version. Dutoit's *Pictures* have each movement strongly characterized and there is a sense of fun in the scherzando movements. But overall this is less involving than with Reiner, and the brilliant recording is not as sumptuous as some other versions, although it has the bloom characteristic of the Montreal sound.

The super-bargain Naxos coupling is vividly played and recorded and is well worth its modest price. *A night on the bare mountain* is played flexibly, yet does not lack excitement. The *Pictures*, too, have plenty of character. The climax of *Bydlo* is dramatically enhanced by a fortissimo contribution from the timpanist, and the detail throughout is well observed, from the bleating Schmuyle to the chirping chicks. *Tuileries* and *Limoges* bring lightly etched orchestral bravura, while the closing picture of the Kiev Gate has architectural grandeur and a sense of majesty. Enjoyable, if lacking the last touch of individuality.

Mackerras surprisingly comes over at a lower voltage than usual. Although his opening *Promenade* is fairly brisk, the first few pictures, though well played, are almost bland and, while *Bydlo* reaches a fairly massive climax, it is not until *Limoges* that the performance springs fully to life; then *The Hut on fowl's legs* is powerfully rhythmic, with an impressive tuba solo. *The Great Gate of Kiev* is not as consistently taut as in some versions, but it is properly expansive at the close, with the recording, always full-bodied, producing an impressive breadth of sound. Perhaps the tam-tam might ideally have been placed a fraction nearer (as it is in the famous Telarc/Cleveland recording: CD 80042). *Night on the bare mountain*, although vivid enough, lacks Satanic bite, and the closing pages fail to wring the heartstrings.

(i) *Night on the bare mountain* (arr. Rimsky-Korsakov); *Pictures at an exhibition* (arr. Funtek). (ii) *Songs and dances of death* (arr. Aho).

*** BIS Dig. CD 325 [id.]. (i) Finnish RSO, (i) Leif Segerstam; (ii) Järvi, with Talvela.

This fascinating CD offers an orchestration by Leo Funtek, made in the same year as Ravel's (1922); it is especially fascinating for the way the different uses of colour change the character of some of Victor Hartman's paintings: the use of a cor anglais in *The old castle*, for instance, or the soft-grained wind scoring which makes the portrait of *Samuel Goldenberg and Schmuyle* more sympathetic, if also blander. The performances by the Finnish Radio Orchestra under Leif Segerstam both of this and of the familiar Rimsky *Night on the bare mountain* are spontaneously presented and very well recorded. The extra item is no less valuable: an intense, darkly Russian account of the *Songs and dances of death* from Martti Talvela with the orchestral accompaniment plangently scored by Kalevi Aho.

Night on a bare mountain (trans. Tchernov).

(N) ❀ *** Teldec/Warner Dig. 4509 96516-2 [id.]. Boris Berezovsky – BALAKIREV: *Islamey*. *** ❀

This remarkable transcription by Konstantin Tchernov sounds hardly less dazzling in Berezovksy's hands than the outstanding *Islamey* with which it is coupled. The engineers capture very good piano sound.

(i) *Night on the bare mountain* (arr. and orch. Stokowski); (ii) *Boris Godunov: symphonic synthesis* (arr. Stokowski).

(N) (M) ** Decca Phase 4 443 896-2 [id.]. (i) LSO; (ii) SRO; Stokowski – BORODIN: *Polovtsian dances* ***; TCHAIKOVSKY: *1812 overture* etc. **(*)

Pictures at an exhibition. (arr. and orch. Stokowski).

(N) (M) ** Decca Phase 4 443 898-2 [id.]. New Phil. O, Stokowski – SCRIABIN: *Poème de l'extase;*
STRAVINSKY: *Firebird suite* etc. **(*)

Stokowski's *Night on the bare mountain* opens with a grotesque balance at the opening, with the heavy
brass to the fore. This is Stokowski's own orchestration, so gauche emphasis is fair enough. Few records
have more noise on them at climaxes, but the bizarre orchestral effects are telling in a crude way, and the
gentle coda is beautifully done in Stokowski's romantically drenched, ecstatic manner. Stokowski's
arrangement omits the familiar brass fanfare motif which Rimsky added in his more sophisticated
version.

The extended symphonic synthesis from *Boris Godunov* has a technicolor flavour; yet, for all the hyperbole of the presentation, Stokowski's magnetism ensures that the music's power communicates, even if
the stark austerity of Mussorgsky's original is missing.

Similarly Stokowski's arrangement of *Pictures at an exhibition* is not notable for its subtlety. The
pictures are blown up with Phase Four immediacy, so that the orchestra sounds right on top of the
listener. With a restricted dynamic range, the sound is very coarse and the inner tension is stretched to
breaking point. The closing climax is harsh. Even so, the sheer personality of this music-making makes
its impact.

Pictures at an exhibition (orch. Ravel).

(Y/B) (M) *** DG 447 426-2 [id.]. BPO, Karajan – DEBUSSY: *La Mer;* RAVEL: *Boléro.* ***

(Y/B) ❀ (M) *** RCA 09026 61401-2 [id.]. Chicago SO, Fritz Reiner – RESPIGHI: *The Fountains of
Rome; The Pines of Rome.* *** ❀

*** DG Gold Dig. 439 013-2 [id.]. BPO, Karajan – RAVEL: *Boléro* etc. ***

*** Sony Dig. SK 45935 [id.]. BPO, Giulini – STRAVINSKY: *Firebird suite.* **(*)

(N) (M) *** DG Dig. 445 556-2 [id.]. LSO, Abbado – RAVEL: *Une barque sur l'océan* etc. ***

(M) *** DG 415 844-2 [id.]. Chicago SO, Giulini – RAVEL: *Ma mère l'Oye; Rapsodie espagnole.* ***

(M) *** EMI Dig. CDM7 64516-2 [id.]. Phd. O, Muti – STRAVINSKY: *Rite of spring.* ***

(M) *** Decca Dig. 417 754-2 [id.]. Chicago SO, Solti – BARTOK: *Concerto for orchestra.* ***

(M) (***) RCA mono 09026 61392-2 [id.]. Boston SO, Koussevitzky (with DEBUSSY: *Saraband*) –
RAVEL: *Boléro, Daphnis et Chloé* etc. (***)

(N) (BB) **(*) EMI Seraphim Dig. CES5 68539-2 (2) [CDEB 68539]. Philh. O, Maazel – DEBUSSY: *La
Mer; Nocturnes* ***; RAVEL: *Alborada* etc. **(*)

(B) **(*) Belart 450 081-2. New Philh. O, Lorin Maazel – PROKOFIEV: *Piano concerto No. 3.* **(*)

(M) (**) RCA mono GD 60287 [60287-2-RG]. NBC SO, Toscanini – ELGAR: *Enigma variations.* (***)

Pictures at an exhibition (orch. Ravel); *Khovanshchina: Prelude; Persian dance; Prince Golitsin's departure into exile* (orch. Shostakovich).

(B) **(*) Erato/Warner Dig. 4509 92870-2 [id.]. Rotterdam PO, James Conlon.

Among the many fine versions of Mussorgsky's *Pictures* on CD, Karajan's 1966 record stands out. It is
undoubtedly a great performance, tingling with electricity from the opening Promenade to the spaciously conceived finale, *The Great Gate of Kiev*, which has real splendour. Other high points are the
ominously powerful climax of *Bydlo* as the Polish ox-wagon lumbers into view very weightily, and the
venomously pungent bite of the brass – expansively recorded – in the sinister *Catacombs* sequence,
which is given a bizarre majesty. Detail is consistently pointed with the greatest imagination, not only in
the lighter moments but, for instance, in *The hut on fowl's legs*, where the tuba articulation is sharp and
rhythmically buoyant. Throughout, the glorious orchestral playing, and especially the brass sonorities,
ensnare the ear; even when Karajan is relatively restrained, as in the nostalgic melancholy of *The old
castle*, the underlying tension remains. The remastered analogue recording still sounds marvellous, and
this reissue, in DG's 'Originals' series of legendary recordings, includes a uniquely evocative performance of Debussy's *La Mer* as well as a very exciting account of Ravel's *Boléro*.

Reiner's 1957 Chicago performance was orginally issued in the UK in October 1958 (as RCA SB 2001),
around the same time as Karajan's Philharmonia account. With the advantage of the rich acoustics of
Symphony Hall, the RCA sound-balance is more atmospheric than the EMI recording, if less sharply
focused. The finale climax of *The Great Gate of Kiev* shows the concentration of the playing. The
remastering is fully worthy, and there is excellent documentation.

Karajan's 1986 recording is one of the most impressive of DG's digital recordings remastered by their
Original-image-bit processing. The tangibility of the sound is remarkable, with the opening brass
Promenade and the massed strings in *Samuel Goldenberg and Schmuyle* notable in their naturalness of
sonority. The power of *Bydlo* is as impressive as the tension in the pianissimo tremolando strings in *Cum
mortuis in lingua mortua*. With superb Berlin Philharmonic playing and the weight of the climaxes

contrasting with the wit of *Tuileries* and the exhilaration of *The market at Limoges*, this is certainly now among the top recommendations. Even the spacious finale, where Karajan fails to detach the massive chords – if not quite as electrifying as his earlier, analogue version – is given greater impact by the added weight and makes a fittingly grandiose culmination.

Giulini's newest, Sony account of Mussorgsky's *Pictures* can also be counted among the finest recent versions. Recorded in the Jesus Christus Kirche, Berlin, the sound is rich and spacious, the orchestral playing superb. The reading has a pervading sense of nostalgia which haunts the delicate portrayal of *The old castle* and even makes the wheedling interchange between the two Polish Jews more sympathetic than usual. A powerful and weighty *Baba Yaga*, yet with the bizarre element retained in the subtle rhythmic pointing of the middle section, leads naturally to a majestic finale, with the Berlin brass full-bloodedly resplendent, and the tam-tam flashing vividly at the climax.

Abbado takes a straighter, more direct view of Mussorgsky's fanciful series of pictures than usual. He is helped by the translucent and naturally balanced digital recording; indeed, the sound is first class, making great impact at climaxes yet also extremely refined, as in the delicate portrayal of the unhatched chicks. Abbado's speeds tend to be extreme, with both this and *Tuileries* taken very fast and light, while *Bydlo* and *The Great Gate of Kiev* are slow and weighty. This now reappears at mid-price, coupled with Ravel.

Giulini's 1976 Chicago recording has always been among the front runners. He is generally more relaxed and often more wayward than Karajan, but this is still a splendid performance and the finale generates more tension than Karajan's most recent, digital version, though it is not as overpowering as the earlier, analogue recording.

Muti's reading, given the excellence of its recorded sound, more than holds its own, although the balance is forward and perhaps not all listeners will respond to the brass timbres at the opening. The lower strings in *Samuel Goldenberg and Schmuyle* have extraordinary body and presence, and *Baba-Yaga* has an unsurpassed virtuosity and attack, as well as being of a high standard as a recording. The coupling is no less thrilling. This can be recommended even to those readers who have not always responded to later records from this conductor.

Solti's performance is fiercely brilliant rather than atmospheric or evocative. He treats Ravel's orchestration as a virtuoso challenge, and with larger-than-life digital recording it undoubtedly has demonstration qualities, and the transparency of texture, given the forward balance, provides quite startling clarity.

From Koussevitzky comes the Ravel orchestration of *Pictures at an exhibition* conducted by the man who commissioned it and recorded it in 1930. The shallow sound should not deter readers from hearing this, for it is superbly characterized and splendidly played. Moreover it comes with what is arguably the best *Daphnis et Chloé* suite ever made.

Maazel has the advantage of first-class playing from the 1962 Philharmonia Orchestra, and all these pictures spring to life colourfully, even if the characterization is not as sharp as with Karajan. After a comparatively subtle portrait of *Baba-Yaga*, Maazel draws out the final climax of *The Great Gate of Kiev* very spaciously indeed.

Maazel's Belart account from 1972 offers an immensely vivid reading, brilliantly recorded, with only a touch of brashness at the end. Moreover, this bargain CD has an unexpected and attractive coupling.

Conlon uses Ravel's orchestration but makes a few changes in the light of studying Mussorgsky's piano manuscript (to which Ravel had no direct access). The changes are only slightly more than cosmetic, although two extra bars have been added effectively to the coda of the *Ballet of the unhatched chicks* and two – added by Ravel – have been removed from *Baba-Yaga*. But the most striking change is with the vehement performance of *Bydlo* at one unrelenting dynamic level – which may be what Mussorgsky wrote but which in practice works less well than Ravel's opening crescendo. Otherwise this is a strongly characterized, very well-played performance, which could have clearer detail, for the acoustic of Rotterdam's empty De Doelen Concert Hall is very resonant. However, the closing *Great Gate of Kiev* has much breadth and dignity, even if the tam-tam strokes at the end are clouded by the reverberation. The couplings are what make this record really distinctive, with excerpts from *Khovanshchina*, orchestrated by Shostakovich, who (unlike Rimsky-Korsakov) leaves Mussorgsky's music untouched. The wonderfully evocative *Prelude* has never sounded more beautiful than here.

Toscanini was no colourist, and his regimented view of the exotic Mussorgsky–Ravel score is at its least sympathetic in the opening statement of the opening *Promenade*, not just rigidly metrical but made the coarser by the cornet-like trumpet tone. Many of the individual movements are done with greater understanding – for example, the *Ballet of the unhatched chicks* – but too often Toscanini's lack of sympathy undermines the character of this rich score. Clean, bright transfer.

(i) *Pictures at an exhibition* (orch. Ravel); (ii) *Pictures at an exhibition* (original piano version).
(Y/B) (M) **(*) Ph Dig. 442 650-2 [id.]. (i) VPO, Previn; (ii) Brendel.

Previn's Philips version was recorded during live performances in Vienna. Obviously the Philips engineers had problems with the acoustics of the Musikvereinsaal, as the bass is noticeably resonant and inner definition is far from sharp. Otherwise the balance is truthful; but the performance, though not lacking spontaneity, is not distinctive, and there is a lack of the kind of grip which makes Karajan's version so unforgettable.

Brendel's performance of the original piano score has its own imaginative touches and some fine moments: the *Ballet of the Unhatched Chicks* is delightfully articulated, and both the *Bydlo* and *Baba-Yaga* are powerful, the latter coming after a darkly evocative *Catacombs/Cum mortuis* sequence. Brendel keeps the music moving but effectively varies the style of the Promenades. The closing pages, however, need to sound more unbuttoned: Brendel is weighty, but fails to enthral the listener. The recording is faithful.

Pictures at an exhibition; St John's night on the bare mountain (original version); (i) *The destruction of Sennacherib;* (ii) *Joshua; Oedipus in Athens: Chorus of people in the temple. Salambô: Chorus of priestesses.*
(Y/B) *** DG Dig. 445 238-2 [id.]. BPO, Abbado; with (i) Prague Philharmonic Ch.; (ii) and Elena Zaremba.

Abbado included the four choral items on an outstanding mid-priced RCA record (see above). This was coupled with other short orchestral pieces besides *St John's night on the bare mountain* and is splendidly played and sung. This new CD offers an equally vivid account of *St John's night on the bare mountain*. The choral pieces are richly sung and the short cantata, *Joshua*, is particularly successful with its central solo, *The Amorite women weep*, movingly sung by Elena Zaremba. There is also much to praise in the spacious performance of the *Pictures* with its individually observed detail. It is not as electrifying as Karajan's analogue version or Sinopoli's highly recommendable digital account, but it is notable for the refinement of its colouring and evocation, often more gently evocative than usual. One of the most telling portraits is of *Goldenberg and Schmuyle*, the one so opulently self-aware, the other obsequiously bleating; the rich Berlin brass are sonorously compelling in *Catacombs*, and *Baba-Yaga* is savagely rhythmic, while the *Great Gate of Kiev* is steadily built to a very impressive climax, with the contrasting chorale hushed, almost vocal in effect, and the tam-tam adding splendour to the final culmination.

Pictures at an exhibition (original piano version).
❀ *** Virgin/EMI Dig. VC7 59611-2 [id.]. Mikhail Pletnev – TCHAIKOVSKY: *Sleeping Beauty*: excerpts. *** ❀

Pictures at an exhibition (piano version, ed. Horowitz).
(M) (***) RCA mono GD 60321. Vladimir Horowitz – TCHAIKOVSKY: *Piano concerto No. 1*. (***) ❀

Pictures at an exhibition (piano version, ed. Horowitz); *Sunless: On the river* (arr. Horowitz).
(M) (***) RCA mono GD 60449 [60449-2-RG]. Horowitz – TCHAIKOVSKY: *Piano concerto No. 1*. (***)

There are remarkable effects of colour and of pedalling in Pletnev's performance – easily the most commanding to have appeared since Richter and, one is tempted to say, a re-creation rather than a performance. Pletnev does not hesitate to modify the odd letter of the score in order to come closer to its spirit. *The Ballet of the unhatched chicks* has great wit and the *Great Gate of Kiev* is extraordinarily rich in colour. An altogether outstanding issue.

Horowitz's famous 1951 recording, made at a live performance at Carnegie Hall, is as thrilling as it is perceptive. Mussorgsky's darker colours are admirably caught and the lighter, scherzando evocations are dazzlingly articulated. But it is the closing pictures which are especially powerful, the pungent *Baba-Yaga*, and the spectacular *Great Gate of Kiev*, where Horowitz has embroidered the final climax to add to its pianistic resplendency. This has now been reissued as Volume 44 in the Toscanini Edition, admirably paired with his equally devastating account of Tchaikovsky's *First Piano concerto*, recorded at a live concert in 1943. This is an indispensable coupling and no admirer of great pianism should be without this record. RCA have also reissued this version of the *Pictures*, plus Horowitz's arrangement of *On the river* from Mussorgsky's song-cycle, *Sunless*, coupled with the 1941 *studio* recording of the Tchaikovsky concerto, a performance which we find less satisfying.

(i) *Pictures at an exhibition* (arr. Leonard for piano and orchestra). *3 Pictures from the Crimea* (orch. Goehr); *Night on the bare mountain* (arr. & orch. Rimsky-Korsakov); *Scherzo in B flat* (orch. Rimsky-Korsakov); *From my tears* (orch. Kindler); *Khovanshchina: Prelude* (orch. Rimsky-Korsakov); *Golitsyn's*

journey (orch. Stokowski); *Sorochinsky Fair: Gopak* (orch. Liadov).
*** Cala Dig. CACD 1012; *CAMC 1012*. (i) Tamás Ungár; Philh. O, Geoffrey Simon.

Lawrence Leonard's arrangement of Mussorgsky's *Pictures* for piano and orchestra is remarkably effective and very entertaining. The concertante format works admirably, especially powerful in *Gnomus* and *The hut on fowl's legs*, charmingly depicting the *Unhatched chicks* (a piquant mixture of keyboard and woodwind, spiced with xylophone). There are many added touches of colour and the wind whistles round *The Old Castle*, to the discomfiture of the melancholy troubadour, and sinisterly accompanies the witch as she flies in on her broomstick at the close of the menacing *Baba-Yaga*. *The Tuileries*, where piano and woodwind alternate, is another delightful variation, and *Samuel Goldenberg* is portentously depicted as the heavy brass joins the strings, with the piano bleating Schmuyles' sycophantic response. After leading the way through the *Catacombs*, the piano dominates the spectacular portrayal of *The Great Gate of Kiev* just like the finale of a grand romantic concerto. The other pieces are all well worth having, notably Rimsky's chimerical scoring (following the composer's orchestral sketch) of the *Scherzo in B flat*. The three *Pictures from the Crimea* are darkly nostalgic, and the lively *Gopak*, like the *Khovanshchina* excerpts (Stokowski's arrangement of *Golitsyn's journey* is sombrely characterful), are very welcome. Hans Kindler's scoring of the Tchaikovskian melody, *From my tears*, is also adeptly managed. All Geoffrey Simon's performances have plenty of life, and Tamás Ungár makes an exciting contribution and is fully equal to all the technical demands of the revised piano-part. The recording is warm, full and expansive, but not always sharply defined.

Song-cycles: The nursery; Songs and dances of death. Songs: Darling Savishna; Forgotten; The He-Goat; The Puppet-show; Mephistopheles' Song of the flea.
(Y/B) ✹ *** Conifer Dig. 7605 51229-2 [id.]. Sergei Leiferkus, Semion Skigin.

These are impressive performances; not only does Sergei Leiferkus make a beautiful sound, but his singing has immense character and power. He can be passionate, earthy and yet aristocratic, touching and then magisterial by turn. He seems to command an unlimited range of colour and to be able to draw forth all the drama and variety of vocal timbre these songs demand. In Semion Skigin he has a pianist of commanding dramatic talent and, at the same time, exemplary restraint. This is the only Mussorgsky song-recital of recent times that can rank alongside the classic pre-war records of Kipnis or the majestic 1950s Christoff set. The Conifer recording is first class, too.

The Complete Songs.
✹ (M) (***) EMI mono CHS7 63025-2 (3) [Ang. CHS 63025]. Boris Christoff, Alexandre Labinsky, Gerald Moore, French R. & TV O, Georges Tzipine.
(Y/B) ** Chandos Dig. CHAN 9336-8 [id.]. Aage Haugland, Poul Rosenblom.

Boris Christoff originally recorded these songs in 1958; they then appeared in a four-LP mono set with a handsome book, generously illustrated with plates and music examples, giving the texts in Russian, French, Italian and English, and with copious notes on each of the 63 songs. Naturally the documentation cannot be so extensive in the CD format – but, on the other hand, one has the infinitely greater ease of access that the new technology offers. The Mussorgsky songs constitute a complete world in themselves, and they cast a strong spell: their range is enormous and their insight into the human condition deep. Christoff was at the height of his vocal powers when he made the set with Alexandre Labinsky, his accompanist in most of the songs; and its return to circulation cannot be too warmly welcomed. This was the first complete survey, and it still remains the only really recommendable set.

It must be conceded that the fine Danish bass, Aage Haugland, and his partner, Poul Rosenblom, do not banish memories of Christoff. Haugland is cultured, but the dramatic intensity, the larger-than-life characterization of the Bulgarian is simply not there. Compare, say, the first two of the *Songs and dances of death* – or, in fact, any of the songs – with Leiferkus, and you are in a totally different world. These are well recorded but much less gripping and involving.

Songs and dances of death (orch. Shostakovich).
(Y/B) *** EMI Dig. CDC7 55232-2 [id.]. Lloyd, Phd. O, Jansons – SHOSTAKOVICH: *Symphony No. 10.*
***

Robert Lloyd gives a commanding and sonorous account of the Shostakovich transcription of Mussorgsky's gripping *Songs and dances of death* as a fill-up to Jansons' intense and powerful reading of the Shostakovich *Tenth Symphony*.

OPERA

Boris Godunov (original version; complete).
*** Sony Dig. S3K 58977 (3) [id.]. Kotcherga, Leiferkus, Lipovšek, Ramey, Nikolsky, Langridge, Slovak
 Philharmonic Ch., Bratislava, Tölz Boys' Ch., Berlin RSO, Abbado.
**(*) EMI CDS7 54377-2 (3) [id.]. Talvela, Gedda, Mróz, Kinasz, Haugland, Krakow Polish R. Ch.,
 Polish Nat. SO, Semkow.

Claudio Abbado recorded *Boris Godunov* in its original version in conjunction both with live concert
performances in Berlin and with the subsequent stage production at the Salzburg Festival. The result
may initially seem to dilute the essential ruggedness of this work but, with speeds which regularly press
ahead, the urgency of the composer's inspiration is conveyed as never before on disc, without reducing
the epic scale of the work or its ominously dark colouring. Abbado inserts the beautiful scene in front of
St Basil's at the start of Act IV, but then omits from the final Kromy Forest scene the episode about the
Simpleton losing his kopek, which would otherwise come in twice – as it does in the Semkow (EMI) set.
Vocally, the performance centres on the glorious singing of Anatoly Kotcherga as Boris. Rarely has this
music been sung with such firmness and beauty as here and, so far from losing out dramatically
compared with rivals who resort to *parlando* effects for emphasis, the performance gains in intensity.
Kotcherga may not have as weighty a voice as Talvela on EMI, but with Abbado encouraging high
contrasts, the darkly meditative depth of the performance is enhanced without loss of power. The other
principal basses, Samuel Ramey as the monk, Pimen, and Gleb Nikolsky as Varlaam, are well contrasted, even if Ramey's voice sounds un-Slavonic. The tenor, Sergei Larin, sings with beauty and clarity
up to the highest register as the Pretender, not least in the Polish act, while Marjana Lipovšek is a
formidably characterful Marina, if not quite as well focused as usual. Having Philip Langridge as
Shuisky and Sergei Leiferkus as Rangoni reinforces the starry strength of the team. The sound is
spacious, more atmospheric than usual in recordings made in the Philharmonie in Berlin, and allowing
high dynamic contrasts, with the choral ensembles – so vital in this work – full and glowing.
 Though the EMI version offers (at full price) only an analogue recording of 1977, its warmth and
richness go with a forward balance and a high transfer level that many will prefer to digital rivals. The
voices have an extra bite, not least the firm, weighty bass of Martti Talvela as Boris or of Aage
Haugland, magnificent as Varlaam. Nicolai Gedda is excellent as the Pretender, if not as free on top as
Larin in the Abbado set. The other soloists, as well as the chorus, make up a formidable Polish team,
with hardly a weak link. Bozena Kinasz as Marina is particularly impressive. Jerzy Semkow may not
convey such bite and beauty as Abbado, but in his rugged, measured way he conveys more intensity at
moments of high drama than the other Sony rival, Tchakarov, helped by the firm, full sound. If this
were reissued at mid-price it would be a strong contender.

Boris Godunov (arr. Rimsky-Korsakov).
*** Decca 411 862-2 (3) [id.]. Ghiaurov, Vishnevskaya, Spiess, Maslennikov, Talvela, V. Boys' Ch., Sofia
 R. Ch., V. State Op. Ch., VPO, Karajan.

With Ghiaurov in the title-role, Karajan's superbly controlled Decca version, technically outstanding,
comes far nearer than previous recordings to conveying the rugged greatness of Mussorgsky's masterpiece. Only the Coronation scene lacks something of the weight and momentum one ideally wants.
Vishnevskaya is far less appealing than the lovely non-Slavonic Marina of Evelyn Lear on EMI, but
overall this Decca set has much more to offer. However, Abbado's Sony recording of the original version
now makes a clear first choice for this opera, and Decca need to reissue the Karajan at mid-price, when it
would still be competitive.

Khovanshchina (complete).
*** DG Dig. 429 758-2 (3) [id.]. Lipovšek, Burchuladze, Atlantov, Haugland, Borowska, Kotscherga,
 Popov, V. State Op. Ch. & O, Abbado.
**(*) Ph. Dig. 437 147-2 (3) [id.]. Minjelkiev, Galusin, Steblianko, Ohotnikov, Borodina, Kirov Theatre
 Ch. & O, Gergiev.

Abbado's live recording brings the most vivid account of this epic Russian opera yet on disc. He uses the
Shostakovich orchestration (with some cuts), darker and harmonically far more faithful than the old
Rimsky-Korsakov version. Yet Abbado rejects the triumphant ending of the Shostakovich edition and
follows instead the orchestration that Stravinsky did for Diaghilev in 1913 of the original subdued
ending as Mussorgsky himself conceived it. When the tragic fate of the Old Believers, immolating
themselves for their faith, brings the deepest and most affecting emotions of the whole opera, that close,
touching in its tenderness, is far more apt. Lipovšek's glorious singing as Marfa, the Old Believer with
whom one most closely identifies, sets the seal on the whole performance. Aage Haugland is a rock-like
Ivan Khovansky and, though Burchuladze is no longer as steady of tone as he was, he makes a noble

Dosifei. Stage noises sometimes intrude and voices are sometimes set back, but this remains a magnificent achievement.

Gergiev does not disguise the squareness of much of the writing and his performance lacks the flair and brilliance of Abbado. He stays faithful to the Shostakovich version of the score to the very end. There he simply adds a loud version of the *Old Believers' chorale* on unison brass – hardly a subtle solution! The Kirov soloists make a fine team, but on almost all counts Abbado is more persuasive.

Mysliveček, Josef (1737–81)

Violin concerto in C.
(N) (B) *** Discover Dig. DICD 920265 [id.]. Ivan Zenaty, Virtuosi di Praga, Oldrich Vlček (with DVORAK: *Romance; Mazurka ***) – VANHAL: *Violin concerto*. ***

Born in Bohemia almost a generation before Mozart, Mysliveček wrote fresh, vigorous music, of which this violin concerto is a fine examples, its central slow movement a brief, gentle interlude. The Vanhal coupling is a comparable work, equally attractive. On this well-recorded bargain issue Ivan Zenaty with his clean, full tone proves an outstanding advocate, with the Virtuosi di Praga providing lively support on modern instruments. In the two shorter concertante works of a century later, Zenaty and the orchestra readily adapt their style to the romanticism of Dvořák, tender in the *Romance*, flamboyant in the *Mazurka*.

Narváez, Luys de (1500–*c.* 1555)

El Delphin de Musica, Book 1: *Fantasia No. 5.* Book 2: *Fantasias Nos. 5–6;* Book 3: *La canción del Emperor.* Book 4: *O gloriosa domina (Seys differencias).* Book 5: *Arde coracón, arde; Ye se asiente el Rey Raminor.* Book 6: *Conde claros; Guárdame las vacas; Tre diferencias por otra parte; Baxa de contrapunto.*
(M) *** RCA 09026 61606-2. Julian Bream (lute) – MILAN: *Collection.* ***

The collection Bream plays here is more diverse than the coupled Milán pieces and he includes some arrangements of the popular songs of the time and some of the earliest-known *differencias* (variations). Bream is in his element in this repertoire and each piece is eloquently felt and strongly characterized; the music's nobility is readily conveyed. The recording is first class.

Nevin, Arthur (1871–1943)

From Edgeworth Hills.
(Y/B) *** Altarus Dig. AIR-CD 9024 [id.]. Donna Amato – Ethelbert NEVIN: *A Day in Venice* etc. ***

Arthur Nevin was without his older brother's melodic individuality, but he wrote spontaneously and crafted his pieces nicely. The most striking number of *From Edgeworth Hills* is the tripping *Sylphs*, very characteristic of its time, while *As the moon rose* has an agreeably sentimental tune, and the picaresque *Firefly* sparkles nicely here. *Toccatella* is rhythmically a bit awkward but is quite a showpiece, and Donna Amato plays it with real dash. Excellent recording.

Nevin, Ethelbert (1862–1901)

A Day in Venice (suite), *Op. 25; Etude in the form of a Romance; Etude in the form of a scherzo, Op. 18/1–2; May in Tuscany* (suite), *Op. 21; Napoli (En passant), Op. 30/3; Mighty lak' a rose* (after the transcription by Charles Spross); *O'er hill and dale* (suite); *The Rosary* (arr. Whelpley); *Water scenes, Op. 13.*
(Y/B) *** Altarus Dig. AIR-CD 9024 [id.]. Donna Amato – Arthur NEVIN: *From Edgeworth Hills.* ***

Ethelbert Nevin was born in Edgeworth, Pennsylvania (on the outskirts of Pittsburgh), in 1862. Nevin scored his first great success when *Narcissus* became a world-wide hit. Even today its melody is recognizable by most older listeners, if perhaps not so readily identified. Donna Amato grew up in the area where he was born, and she takes care not to sentimentalize these genre pieces, which can be just a little trite but also quite engaging. Perhaps she might have let herself go a little more in *Narcissus*, but elsewhere she hits the spot, notably in the closing *Barcarolle* of the *Water scenes* and in the Italian set, *A Day in Venice*. *The Rosary* was Nevin's other big hit, with the sheet music selling over a million copies in the decade following its publication in 1898. It sounds pretty ordinary now, but of course was intended to be sung. *Mighty lak' a rose* retains all its charm. The manuscript was found on the composer's desk after his death, and it makes a good epitaph – quite as memorable as MacDowell's *To a wild rose*. The recording is clear and natural in a pleasing acoustic.

Nicolai, Carl Otto (1810–49)

The merry wives of Windsor (Die lustigen Weiber von Windsor): complete.
(Y/B) (M) *** Decca 443 669-2 (2) [id.]. Ridderbusch, W. Brendel, Malta, Ahnsjö, Sramek, Donath, T. Schmidt, Sukis, Bav. R. Ch. & SO, Kubelik.
(M) **(*) EMI CMS7 69348-2 (2) [Ang. CDMB 69348]. Frick, Gutstein, Engel, Wunderlich, Lenz, Hoppe, Putz, Litz, Mathis, Ch. & O of Bav. State Op., Heger.

Kubelik's performance may be slightly lacking in dramatic ebullience, but its extra subtlety has perceptive results – as in the entry of Falstaff in Act I, where Kubelik conveys the tongue-in-cheek quality of Nicolai's *pomposo* writing. Ridderbusch portrays a straight and noble Falstaff. Although as an opera this may not have the brilliant insight of Verdi or all the atmosphere of Vaughan Williams, it has its own brand of effervescence which is equally endearing and is well caught here. The dialogue is crisply edited, and the recording, while fairly reverberant, is vividly atmospheric. *Faute de mieux*, it should receive a strong recommendation.

The great glory of the fine EMI set is the darkly menacing Falstaff of Gottlob Frick in magnificent voice, even if he sounds baleful rather than comic. It is good too to have the young Fritz Wunderlich as Fenton opposite the Anna Reich of Edith Mathis. Though the others hardly match this standard – Ruth-Margret Putz is rather shrill as Frau Fluth – they all give enjoyable performances, helped by the production, which conveys the feeling of artists who have experienced performing the piece on stage. The effectiveness of the comic timing is owed in great measure to the conducting of the veteran, Robert Heger. From the CD transfer one could hardly tell the age of the recording, with the voices particularly well caught. Alas, this enjoyable set is withdrawn as we go to press.

Nielsen, Carl (1865–1931)

Clarinet concerto, Op. 57.
*** Chandos Dig. CHAN 8618 [id.]. Janet Hilton, SNO, Bamert – COPLAND: *Concerto;* LUTOSLAW-SKI: *Dance preludes.* ***

Janet Hilton gives a highly sympathetic account of the Nielsen *Concerto*, but it is characteristically soft-centred and mellower in its response to the work's more disturbing emotional undercurrents than Olle Schill's splendid account on BIS – see below. However, those who prefer a record offering other clarinet works will not be disappointed by Janet Hilton's alternative programme. The Chandos recording is first class.

(i) *Clarinet concerto, Op. 57;* (ii) *Flute concerto;* (iii) *Maskarade:* excerpts.
(Y/B) (M) (***) Dutton Lab. mono CDLXT 2505 [id.]. (i) Ib Erikson; (ii) Holger Gilbert-Jespersen; Danish State RSO, (i; iii) Jensen; (ii) Wöldike.

Like the Jensen account of the symphonies (see below), this excellent transfer from Dutton Laboratories offers us a link with Nielsen's own times. Holger Gilbert-Jespersen gave the first performance of the *Flute concerto* in Paris in 1926 and was its dedicatee. This 1954 recording gives as good an indication of Nielsen's intentions as we will ever have. The *Clarinet concerto* with Ib Erikson is no less masterly – and what good sound!

(i) *Clarinet concerto, Op. 57;* (ii) *Flute concerto;* (iii) *Violin concerto, Op. 33.*
*** Chandos Dig. CHAN 8894 [id.]. (i) Thomsen; (ii) Christiansen; (iii) Sjøgren; Danish RSO, Schønwandt.

Niels Thomsen's powerfully intense account of the late *Clarinet concerto* is completely gripping. Michael Schønwandt gives sensitive and imaginative support, both here and in the two companion works. Toke Lund Christiansen is hardly less successful in the *Flute concerto*. Kim Sjøgren and Schønwandt give a penetrating and thoughtful account of the *Violin concerto*; there is real depth here, thanks in no small measure to Schønwandt. The recording is first class.

(i) *Clarinet concerto;* (ii) *Flute concerto. An Imaginary journey to the Faeroe Islands; Saul and David: Prelude.* (iii) *Springtime in Fünen, Op. 42.*
**(*) Sony Dig. SK 53276 [id.]. Swedish RSO, Salonen, with (i) Håkan Rosengren; (ii) Per Flemström; (iii) Asa Bäverstam, Kjell Sandve, Per Høyer, Linnéa Ekdale, Andréas Thors, Swedish R. Ch. & Boys' Ch.

Håkan Rosengren has the measure of the *Clarinet concerto*, which he plays with considerable flair, and he receives excellent support from Salonen. The *Flute concerto* fares equally well. The *Prelude* to *Saul and David* comes off well, but the earthy (yet seraphic) innocence and simplicity of *Springtime in Fünen* elude Salonen altogether. The singers do not banish memories of earlier and rival versions. The concertos, though not first recommendations, deserve three stars but the cantata falls well short of that. Good recording, as one would expect from this source.

(i) *Clarinet concerto, Op. 57;* (ii) *Symphony No. 3 (Sinfonia espansiva). Maskarade overture.*
*** BIS Dig. CD 321 [id.]. (i) Olle Schill; (ii) Pia Raanoja, Knut Skram; Gothenburg SO, Myung-Whun Chung.

Olle Schill brings brilliance and insight to what is one of the most disturbing and masterly of all modern concertos. The young Korean conductor secures playing of great fire and enthusiasm from the Gothenburgers in the *Third Symphony* and he has vision and breadth – and at the same time no want of momentum. Two soloists singing a wordless vocalise are called for in the pastoral slow movement, and their contribution is admirable. Myung-Whun Chung also gives a high-spirited and sparkling account of the *Overture* to Nielsen's comic opera, *Maskarade*. The BIS recording is marvellous, even by the high standards of this small company.

(i) *Clarinet concerto, Op. 57;* (ii) *Serenata in Vano;* (iii) *Wind quintet, Op. 43.*
(***) Clarinet Classics mono CC 002 [id.]. (i) Cahuzac, Copenhagen Op. O, Frandsen; (ii) Oxenvad, Larsson, Sorensen, Jensen, Hegner; (iii) Royal Chapel Wind Quintet.

These are pioneering recordings and an essential part of any Nielsen collection. The *Clarinet concerto* was to have been recorded by its dedicatee, Aage Oxenvad, who is heard in both the *Quintet* and the *Serenata in Vano*, but death intervened and the eminent French clarinettist Louis Cahuzac filled the breach. This lovely performance of the *Quintet* is so full of character that in some ways it remains unsurpassed. These transfers are a great improvement on the earlier ones on Danacord LPs, a bit dry but eminently clean and well detailed in the case of the *Concerto*, which Cahuzac plays with great feeling.

(i) *Flute concerto; Symphony No. 1; Rhapsody overture: An imaginary journey to the Faeroe Islands.*
*** BIS Dig. CD 454 [id.]. (i) Patrick Gallois; Gothenburg SO, Myung-Whun Chung.

The *Flute concerto* is given a marvellous performance by Patrick Gallois, and Myung-Whun Chung and the Gothenburg orchestra have an instinctive feeling for Nielsen. They play with commendable enthusiasm and warmth, and Chung shapes the *Symphony* with great sensitivity to detail and a convincing sense of the whole. The *Rhapsody overture: An imaginary journey to the Faeroe Islands* is not the composer at his strongest, but it has a highly imaginative opening.

Violin concerto, Op. 33.
⊛ *** Sony Dig. SK 44548 [id.]. Cho-Liang Lin, Swedish RSO, Salonen – SIBELIUS: *Violin concerto.* *** ⊛

(i) *Violin concerto, Op. 33. Symphony No. 5, Op. 50.*
*** BIS Dig. CD 370 [id.]. (i) Dong-Suk Kang, Gothenburg SO, Myung-Whun Chung.

Cho-Liang Lin brings as much authority to Nielsen's *Concerto* as he does to the Sibelius and he handles the numerous technical hurdles with breathtaking assurance. His perfect intonation and tonal purity excite admiration, but so should his command of the architecture of this piece; there is a strong sense of line from beginning to end. Salonen is supportive here and gets good playing from the Swedish Radio Symphony Orchestra.

Dong-Suk Kang is more than equal to the technical demands of this concerto and is fully attuned to the Nordic sensibility. He brings tenderness and refinement of feeling to the searching slow movement and great panache and virtuosity to the rest. The *Fifth Symphony* is hardly less successful and is certainly the best-recorded version now available. Myung-Whun Chung has a natural feeling for Nielsen's language and the first movement has real breadth.

En aften paa Giske: Prelude (1889); Bøhmiske-dansk folketone; Helios, Overture, Op. 17; Paraphrase on 'Nearer my God, to thee', for wind band; Rhapsodic overture: An imaginary journey to the Faeroe Islands; Saga-drøm, Op. 39; Symphonic rhapsody (1888).
**(*) Chandos Dig. CHAN 9287 [id.]. Danish Nat. RSO, Rohzdestvensky.

The *Paraphrase on the Psalm, 'Nearer, my God, to thee', for wind band* is both noble and individual. Rozhdestvensky gives musicianly, well-prepared and often poetic accounts of the more familiar pieces, though his *Helios, Overture* must be the slowest ever – over 14 minutes! His account of *Saga-drøm* ('The

Dream of Gunnar') is also spacious. Very good recording, but in the last analysis these performances are a little deficient in zest.

Hagbarth and Signe; Ebbe Skammelsen; Sankt Hansaftenspil (incidental music).
(Y/B) ** Kontrapunkt Dig. 32188 [id.]. Henriette Bonde-Hansen, Lars Thodberg Bertelsen, Lane Lind, Nils Bank Mikkelsen; Funen Ac. Children's Ch., Odense Philharmonic Ch., Odense SO, Tamas Vetö.

The incidental music collected here is pretty routine stuff. All three scores are for wind (in the case of *Hagbarth and Signe* four bronze lurs), voices and percussion. There are altogether some forty-five fragments, many of them simple horn-calls or short scraps of melody, few of them giving us much of a glimpse of the real Nielsen. Good performances and recording.

Symphonies Nos. (i) *1 in G min., Op. 7;* (ii) *2 (Four Temperaments), Op. 16;* (iii) *3 (Sinfonia espansiva), Op. 27;4 (Inextinguishable), Op. 29;* (i) *5, Op. 50;* (iii) *6 (Sinfonia semplice).*
(Y/B) *** Decca Dig. 443 117-2 (3) [id.]. San Francisco SO, Blomstedt (with Kromm, McMillan in No. 3).
(Y/B) (B) *** RCA Dig. 74321 20290–2 (3) [id.]. Royal Danish O, Paavo Berglund.
*** Chandos Dig. CHAN 9163/5 [id.]. Royal Scottish O, Thomson.
(Y/B) (**(*)) Danacord mono DACOCD 351/3 [id.]. Danish RSO; (i) Erik Tuxen; (ii) Launy Grøndahl; (iii) Thomas Jensen.

Symphonies Nos. 1 in G min. Op. 7; 2 in B min., Op. 16.
**(*) DG Dig. 439 775-2 [id.]. Gothenburg SO, Neeme Järvi.

Symphonies Nos. (i) *3 (Espansiva), Op. 27; 4 (Inextinguishable), Op. 29.*
**(*) DG Dig. 439 776-2 [id.]. Gothenburg SO, Neeme Järvi, (i) with Hynninen.

Symphonies Nos. 5, Op. 50; 6 (Sinfonia semplice).
**(*) DG Dig. 439 777-2 [id.]. Gothenburg SO, Neeme Järvi.

Blomstedt's complete Decca set appears at a modest discount – three discs for rather more than the cost of two – and is pretty well self-recommending. Individual verdicts on the performances are to be found below. All six are among the finest available, and the reservation concerning No. 6, where a broader tempo would have helped generate greater evocation in the opening movement, is relatively insignificant against the overall success of this series. All Decca have now done is to assemble the three CDs into one slipcase. To put it briefly, they remain the best all-round modern set and can be purchased with confidence, though individual symphonies in the BIS set score very highly – and the DG recordings with the Gothenburg orchestra are a model of what a good recording should be. The performances are generally speaking not the equal of the Blomstedt, and the present box holds its own.

Berglund's set with the Royal Danish Orchestra, in which Nielsen once served, was recorded between 1987 and 1989. The ever-fresh *First Symphony* is given a thoroughly straightforward account and Berglund holds the architecture of the work together in a most convincing way. Berglund's account of the *Sinfonia espansiva* (No. 3) is perhaps the finest of his cycle. The playing of the Royal Danish Orchestra is beautifully prepared and full of vitality. His two soloists, though unnamed, are very good and the general architecture of the work is well conveyed. The *Fourth (Inextinguishable)* is more problematic. Generally speaking, Berglund stays close to the tempo markings but, in his desire to convey the sense of drama and urgency, he tends to be impatient to move things on, particularly in the closing paragraphs. The playing is spirited enough, but even the Royal Danish Orchestra sounds a little out of breath at the end!The *Fifth* opens with a strong sense of atmosphere. The second movement's complex structure is well controlled and satisfyingly resolved. Apart from some loss of focus at the climax of the first movement, the recording encompasses the wide dynamic range with impressive sonority and colour. In the *Sinfonia semplice* (No. 6) Berglund again proves a perceptive guide. His performance matches Blomstedt's in integrity and insight and is obviously the product of much thought. Here as elsewhere, the RCA engineers produce a recording of splendid body and presence. In the event, Berglund's set can be strongly recommended alongside (though not in preference to) Blomstedt, and it also has a distinct price advantage. Three CDs have been reissued separately at mid-price: *Symphonies Nos. 1–2* (74321 20291-2); *Symphonies Nos. 3–4* (74321 20292-2); *Symphonies Nos. 5–6* (74321 20293-2).

Generally speaking Bryden Thomson's Nielsen symphonies are eminently sound and straightforward, without the extra ounce of finish that we find with the Blomstedt set. If they are not as beautifully recorded as Järvi on DG, they still sound impressive and as performances have the merit of being totally unmannered and unfussy, with generally well-chosen tempi. Thomson's version of the *Sixth* is arguably the best now on the market, and his *Fourth* has great fire. The set can hold its own with most of the first recommendations without displacing any of them – except in the two cases mentioned.

Neeme Järvi's Nielsen cycle as a whole has much going for it – absolutely first-class recording with a completely natural balance which enables the strings to sound rich and sonorous in fortissimo passages, delicate and transparent in lightly scored writing; the wind are ideally placed, with no hint of spotlighting yet with every detail registering clearly; and the brass and percussion are equally successfully captured. The Gothenburg orchestra play with great enthusiasm and responsiveness. At the same time, not all the performances can be wholeheartedly recommended. Järvi does not allow the atmosphere and mystery of the *Fifth Symphony*'s first movement to register fully. He is far too intent to move things on. In the *First Symphony* he is a shade too brisk in the outer movements though not unacceptably so, and the inner movements are played with real eloquence. The inner movements of the *Second Symphony* have plenty of character, though Järvi does make a little too much of the *allargando* markings in the third, which becomes a little overblown. Again the finale is rather rushed off its feet, particularly at the very end. The *Sinfonia espansiva* is well paced, and the slow movement features some particularly sensitive singing from Hynninen. The finale is let down by some uncharacteristic moments of bombast.

The Danacord set of three CDs tells us more about Nielsen than almost any later performances and these mono broadcasts are the nearest we can come to Nielsen's own intentions. Only one commercial disc is included: Jensen's masterly account of the *Sixth Symphony*. Launy Grøndahl's version of the *Second Symphony* (*The Four Temperaments*) has tremendous fire, and Jensen's accounts of the *Third* (*Sinfonia espansiva*) and *Fourth* (*Inextinguishable*) are pretty electrifying. There are many better recordings of these symphonies but few that come closer to their spirit; although allowances must be made for the poor quality of sound in some instances, these performances radiate an authenticity of atmosphere and love of the scores that is quite infectious.

Symphonies Nos. (i) *1 in G min. Op. 7; 2 in B min., Op. 16;* (i & ii) *3 (Espansiva), Op. 27;* (iii) *4 (Inextinguishable), Op. 29;* (i) *5, Op. 50;* (iii) *6 (Sinfonia semplice);* (i; iv) *Clarinet concerto, Op. 57;* (i; v) *Flute concerto;* (i; vi) *Violin concerto, Op. 33.*

(M) *** BIS Dig. CD 614/6 (4) [id.]. Gothenburg SO, (i) Myung-Whun Chung; (ii) with Raanoja, Skram; (iii) Neeme Järvi; (iv) with Olle Schill; (v) Patrick Gallois; (vi) Dong-Suk Kang.

Myung-Whun Chung's accounts of the *First* and *Second Symphonies* can hold their own against the very best, and his version of the *Sinfonia espansiva* is one of the very best – and can be recommended alongside Blomstedt (Decca). It has the inestimable advantage of the Gothenburg Hall acoustic and warm, splendidly present recording. The concertos are all excellent – some may even prefer them to the rival collection on Chandos. Dong-Suk Kang's reading of the *Violin concerto* is eloquent in every respect and a worthy alternative to Cho-Liang Lin on Sony; and both Patrick Gallois and Olle Schill are magnificent soloists. The package as a whole with four records for the price of three is eminently competitive.

Symphonies Nos. 1 in G min., Op. 7; 2 in B min., Op. 16 (The 4 Temperaments).
*** Chandos Dig. CHAN 8880 [id.]. Royal Scottish O, Bryden Thomson.

Strong, vigorous accounts of both symphonies from the Royal Scottish Orchestra under Bryden Thomson, with a particularly well-characterized reading of *The Four Temperaments*. The second movement is perhaps a shade too brisk, but in most respects these performances are difficult to fault.

(i) *Symphonies Nos. 1 in G min., Op. 7; 5, Op. 50;* (ii) *Helios overture, Op. 17.*
(Y/B) ✪ (M) *** Dutton Lab. mono CDLXT 2502 [id.]. Danish State RSO; (i) Thomas Jensen; (ii) Erik Tuxen.

These are exemplary transfers of the première recording of the *First Symphony* and the first LP recordings of the *Fifth* (the very first was on 78s under Tuxen) and the *Helios Overture*. Jensen and Tuxen both played under Nielsen, and their performances have a special authenticity. The quality of these Decca recordings is captured with absolute fidelity in these stunning transfers; the engineers of the day, working in the pleasingly warm yet crisp acoustic of the Danish Radio concert hall produced remarkably truthful results. An indispensable issue that belongs in every Nielsen collection.

Symphonies Nos. 1 in G min., Op. 7; 6 (Sinfonia semplice).
*** Decca Dig. 425 607-2 [id.]. San Francisco SO, Blomstedt.
(N) (BB) **(*) Naxos Dig. 8.550826 [id.] Nat. SO of Ireland, Leaper.

Blomstedt's record of the *First Symphony* has vitality and freshness, and there is a good feel for Nielsen's natural lyricism. He inspires the San Francisco orchestra to excellent effect and the lean, well-focused string sound and songful wind playing are lovely. In the *Sixth Symphony* he has no want of intensity, though a broader tempo would have helped generate greater atmosphere in the first movement. However, the performance is undeniably impressive and enjoys the advantage of far better recording.

Very good performances indeed of Nielsen's first and last symphonies from Adrian Leaper and the National Symphony Orchestra of Ireland. The sound is exceptionally well balanced, with exemplary detail and good perspective. The playing is well prepared, full of vitality, and phrasing is always intelligent. Blomstedt on Decca and Berglund with the Danish Orchestra on RCA are finer still (these players have the music in their blood), but the Naxos disc remains very good value for money.

Symphony No. 2 (The Four Temperaments), Op. 16; Aladdin suite, Op. 34.
*** BIS CD 247 [id.]. Gothenburg SO, Myung-Whun Chung.

Symphonies Nos. 2 (The Four Temperaments); (i) 3 (Espansiva), Op. 27.
*** Decca Dig. 430 280-2 [id.]. (i) Kromm, McMillan; San Francisco SO, Blomstedt.
(Y/B) ** Chandos Dig. CHAN 9300 [id.]. (i) Kringelborn, Frederiksson; Royal Stockholm PO, Rozhdestvensky.

This coupling is possibly the finest of Blomstedt's cycle: he finds just the right tempo for each movement and nowhere is this more crucial than in the finale of the *Espansiva*. The two soloists are good and the orchestra play with all the freshness and enthusiasm one could ask for. The recording, though not quite in the demonstration bracket, is very fine indeed.

Myung-Whun Chung has a real feeling for this repertoire and his account of the *Second Symphony* is also very fine. The Gothenburg Symphony Orchestra proves an enthusiastic and responsive body of players. The recording is impressive, too, and can be recommended with enthusiasm.

Rozhdestvensky's Swedish coupling offers cultured and urbane playing, very well recorded and thoroughly idiomatic in its way, but wanting in the fire and character that distinguish rival Nielsen performances. Not a first recommendation.

Symphonies Nos. 2 (The Four Temperaments), Op. 16; 4 (The Inextinguishable), Op. 29.
(M) ** Sony SMK 47597-2. NYPO, Bernstein.

(i) Symphonies Nos. 3 (Sinfonia espansiva), Op. 27; (ii) 5, Op. 50.
(M) **(*) Sony SMK 47598-2. (i) Ruth Guldbaeck, Niels Moller, Royal Danish O; (ii) NYPO, Bernstein.

Bernstein, who had an undoubted feeling for this composer, gives the *Second Symphony* a fine, powerful reading with plenty of fire in the first movement. But the inner movements are too slow and expressive, detail too heavily underlined to be wholly satisfactory. Bernstein's performance of the genial *Espansiva* with the Royal Danish Orchestra also has a lot going for it. And yet, for all the excellence of the orchestral playing, this performance misses something of the music's innocence. In the *Fourth*, at times Nielsen's finely drawn lines again quiver with an expressive emphasis that strikes a jarring note. But it would be churlish to concentrate on the defects in these performances; they have many merits: liveliness, enthusiasm and admirable orchestral playing. Furthermore Bernstein conveys a genuine love for the music, for all the overstatement in which he occasionally indulges. Bernstein is at his finest in the *Fifth*, giving an immensely powerful reading, and the passion of the string cantilena and the following movement through into the finale are indicative of the spontaneous feeling which pervades the whole symphony. The well-detailed, resonant recording adds to the impact of the performance.

(i) Symphonies No. 2 (The Four Temperaments), Op. 16; (ii) 5, Op. 50; (i) Symphonic rhapsody in F.
(N) (M) ** BBC Radio Classics 15656 91462 [id.]. (i) BBC Welsh SO, Bryden Thomson; (ii) New Philh. O, Horenstein.

The *Second Symphony* was recorded some time during the 1970s and does not have the vitality or crispness of Bryden Thomson's relatively recent commercial recording on Chandos. The *Fifth*, recorded rather drily, comes from a broadcast made two years after the Horenstein/New Philharmonia partnership recorded the work for Unicorn. In short, these are serviceable performances but not as good as the commercial recordings.

(i) Symphony No. 3 (Sinfonia espansiva), Op. 27. Movements for string orchestra; Maskarade (suite).
(N) * Kontrapunkt Dig. 32203 [i.d]. (i) Eva Hess Thaysen, Lars Thodberg Bertelsen; Odense SO, Serov.

Eduard Serov has a good natural feeling for Nielsen, though his judgement in matters of tempi is controversial. The Scherzo is too judicious and measured, and the finale too slow. The first two movements are admirably paced. Good though the playing is, the balance at the beginning of the finale is quite impossible, with a weak string line and unmusical perspective (unimportant inner parts are too prominent). Generally speaking, the sound is a bit opaque at the bottom end of the spectrum. The juvenilia, transcriptions for strings of early quartet movements, are hardly characteristic and do not tip the balance in the record's favour any more than do the *Maskarade* pieces.

(i) *Symphonies No. 3 (Sinfonia espansiva). 5.*
*** Chandos Dig. CHAN 9067 [id.]. (i) Bott, Roberts; Royal Scottish O, Bryden Thomson.

Bryden Thomson's chosen tempi in the *Sinfonia espansiva* are just right, particularly in the finale which has posed difficulties for so many interpreters. In the slow movement Catherine Bott and Stephen Roberts are excellent, and the performance has a refreshing directness that is most likeable. The *Fifth Symphony* is equally committed and satisfying. Thomson draws a vibrant response from his players in the second movement and there is much beauty of detail in the first. The recordings are very good indeed, though one feels the need for heavily scored passages to open out a little more. Recommended, albeit not in preference to Blomstedt, who is differently coupled.

Symphony No. 4 (Inextinguishable), Op. 29.
(Y/B) (M) *** DG Dig. 445 518-2 [id.]. BPO, Karajan – SIBELIUS: *Tapiola.* ***

One of the very finest performances of Nielsen's *Fourth* comes from Karajan. The orchestral playing is altogether incomparable; there is both vision and majesty in the reading and a thrilling sense of commitment throughout. The wind playing sounds a little over-civilized – but what exquisitely blended, subtle playing this is. It is also excellently recorded, although there is an editing error in the finale.

Symphony No. 4 (Inextinguishable); Pan and Syrinx.
(M) *** EMI CDM7 64737-2 [id.]. CBSO, Rattle – SIBELIUS: *Symphony No. 5.* ***

Simon Rattle's version of the *Inextinguishable* dates from the late 1970s and is also very fine indeed, though it is perhaps a shade judicious when put alongside his live broadcast (with the Philharmonia) dating from the same period. All the same, it deserves a strong recommendation, particularly given the fact that it is at mid-price and comes with an altogether outstanding account of *Pan and Syrinx* (the best ever on record) and his classic account of Sibelius's *Fifth Symphony.* Excellent sound.

Symphonies Nos. 4 (Inextinguishable); 5, Op. 50.
*** Decca Dig. 421 524-2 [id.]. San Francisco SO, Blomstedt.
(Y/B) (BB) ** Naxos Dig. 8.550743 [id.]. Nat. SO of Ireland, Adrian Leaper.

The opening of Blomstedt's *Fourth* has splendid fire: this must sound as if galaxies are forming. Blomstedt conveys Nielsen's image about the soaring string-lines in the slow movement ('like the eagle riding on the wind') most strikingly. The finale is exhilarating, yet held on a firm rein. The *Fifth Symphony*, too, is impressive: it starts perfectly and is almost as icy in atmosphere as those pioneering recordings of the 1950s. The desolate clarinet peroration also comes off most successfully. The recording balance could not be improved upon.

There is nothing to grumble at in the Naxos coupling of these two symphonies – but nothing to get excited about either, though Leaper is a fine musician with a good feel for this repertoire. The *Fourth* is well prepared but neither highly charged nor tautly held together. Similarly, the *Fifth Symphony* is decently played but does not cast as strong a spell as the classic accounts from Jensen or Blomstedt. The recorded sound is more than acceptable.

Symphonies Nos. 4 (Inextinguishable); 6 (Sinfonia semplice).
✹ *** Chandos Dig. CHAN 9047 [id.]. Royal Scottish O, Bryden Thomson.
**(*) BIS Dig. CD 600 [id.]. Gothenburg SO, Neeme Järvi.

The late Bryden Thomson's coupling of the *Fourth* and *Sixth Symphonies* is by far the most successful of his Nielsen cycle and possibly the finest recording of his career. The *Fourth Symphony* has great sweep and excitement, and though Blomstedt and the San Francisco orchestra on Decca have the greater polish, there is the same directness that has distinguished earlier issues in the cycle but with greater fire. Bryden Thomson's account of the *Sixth Symphony* is quite simply the finest version now before the public, and arguably the most penetrating since Thomas Jensen's first recording. Moreover he strikes just the right tempo for the first movement, a fraction broader than Blomstedt, and gets to the heart of the eloquent *Proposta seria* too: indeed no one brings us closer to the spirit of this music than Thomson, and the recording is very good too. Recommended with enthusiasm.

Neeme Järvi's accounts of the *Fourth* and *Sixth Symphonies* are good performances that are beautifully played and most naturally recorded, even if Järvi's readings do not go quite as deeply as do those of Thomson and Blomstedt. All the same, this disc has much going for it and readers investing in it should not be disappointed.

Symphonies Nos. 5, Op. 50; 6 (Sinfonia semplice).
(N) (M) **(*) EMI CDM5 65867-2 [id.]. Danish RSO, Blomstedt.
(Y/B) ** Chandos Dig. CHAN 9367 [id.]. Stockholm PO, Rozhdestvensky.

Blomstedt's recordings with the Danish Radio Orchestra were much respected in the 1970s and they stand up well to the test of time. His later, San Francisco performances are perhaps superior and deeper in some respects, though the Copenhagen acoustic is warmer. In any event no one investing in them will find cause for disappointment.

Rozhdestvensky does not give us the whole picture, even if he comes close to it at times. He carefully displays details of the terrain without actually bringing the landscape before one's eyes; its mystery eludes him. The music is in these Swedish players' blood, but Rozhdestvensky does not have his finger on its pulse.

CHAMBER MUSIC

Canto serioso; Fantasias for oboe and piano, Op. 2; The Mother (incidental music), Op. 41; Serenata in vano; Wind quintet, Op. 43.
**(*) Chandos CHAN 8680 [id.]. Athena Ens.

This reissue gathers together Nielsen's output for wind instruments in chamber form, with everything played expertly and sympathetically. The recording is balanced very close; nevertheless much of this repertoire is not otherwise available, and this is a valuable disc.

String quartets Nos. 1 in G min., Op. 13; 2 in F min., Op. 5; 3 in E flat, Op. 14; 4 in F, Op. 44. 5 quartet movements, FS2.
*** Kontrapunkt Dig. 32150-1 [id.]. Danish Qt.

The new set from the Danish Quartet is the best since the Copenhagen Quartet's LPs: these players are sensitive to the shape of the phrase, they produce a wide dynamic range, including really soft pianissimo tone when required. They are not always the last word in polish, but everything they do is musical and leaves one marvelling at the freshness of invention Nielsen commanded, which makes one forgive the occasional rough edge and the somewhat dry quality and rather close balance of the recording. This shortcoming should not be overstressed but deserves mention. The set also includes five short movements that Nielsen wrote in his late teens and early twenties, emphatically not great music but of undoubted interest for students of the composer. Recommended.

String quartets Nos. 1 in G min., Op. 13; 2 in F min., Op. 5; 3 in E flat, Op. 14; 4 in F, Op. 44. (i) *String quintet in G* (1888); (ii) *Andante lamentoso (At the bier of a young artist)* (1910).
*** BIS Dig. CD 503/4 [id.]. Kontra Qt, (i) Philipp Naegele; (ii) Jan Johansson.

There is an ardour and temperament to the playing here, which most listeners will find very persuasive. In addition we are given by far the finest account yet recorded of the *G major String quintet*, where the Kontra Quartet are joined by the American violist Philipp Naegele, and the only current account of the *Andante lamentoso* (*At the bier of a young artist*) in its chamber form. The BIS recordings, made in the Malmö Concert Hall, have plenty of presence and clarity, and are rather forwardly (but not unpleasingly) balanced. Recommended, alongside the Danish Quartet.

String quintet in G (1888), FS5.
*** Chandos Dig. CHAN 9258 [id.]. ASMF Ens. – SVENDSEN: Octet. ***

The *String quintet in G major* is very well fashioned and owes more to Svendsen, under whose baton the composer was to play, than to his teacher, Gade. It makes both an agreeable and an appropriate companion for Svendsen's early and delightful *Octet*. It receives a three-star performance and recording.

Violin sonata No. 2 in G min., Op. 35.
(N) *** Virgin/EMI Dig. VC5 45122-2. Christian Tetzlaff, Leif Ove Andsnes – DEBUSSY; JANACEK; RAVEL: *Sonatas*. ***

Nielsen's *G minor Sonata* is a transitional work in which Nielsen emerges from the geniality of the *Sinfonia espansiva* into the darker and more anguished world of the *Fourth Symphony*. It has much of the questing character of the latter and much of its muscularity. Christian Tetzlaff and Leif Ove Andsnes give a very distinguished – at times inspired – performance, and are accorded excellent recording.

Wind quintet, Op. 43.
*** Sony Dig. CD 45996. Ens. Wien-Berlin – TAFFANEL: *Quintet*. ***
(Y/B) (M) *** EMI CDM5 65304-2 [id.]. Melos Ens. – JANACEK: *Concertino* etc. **(*)

The Ensemble Wien-Berlin gives one of the best accounts of the Nielsen *Wind quintet* to have appeared in years. Their tonal blend and purity of intonation are beyond praise and there are too many felicities of characterization in the variation movement to enumerate. They are also beautifully recorded, and the only reservation must be that, at 50 minutes, this disc gives short measure.

The Melos account of the *Wind quintet* was made in the 1960s but still sounds fresh and vibrant. In its day it was a first recommendation and it still ranks among the very best. It comes, too, with a valuable Janáček coupling that includes *Mládi* and the *Concertino*.

PIANO MUSIC

Chaconne, Op. 32; Humoresque-bagatelles, Op. 11; 5 Pieces, Op. 3; 3 Pieces, Op. 59; Suite luciferique, Op. 45.
(N) ❀ *** Virgin/EMI Dig. VC5 45129-2 [id.]. Leif Ove Andsnes.

How is it that Nielsen's piano music has never attracted the attention of pianists of international standing? Although the *Suite*, Op. 45, was dedicated to Schnabel, he never played it in public. Yet this music is quite wonderful; the early pieces have great charm and the later *Suite* and the *Three Pieces*, Op. 59, great substance. Although their finest exponent up to now, the Danish pianist Arne Skjold Rasmussen, committed them to disc, he never enjoyed the international exposure to which his gifts entitled him. But now at last they have found a princely interpreter in the Norwegian, Leif Ove Andsnes, who has a natural feeling for and understanding of this music. Indeed these are performances of eloquence and nobility that are unlikely to be surpassed for some years to come, and the recorded sound is vivid and lifelike.

VOCAL MUSIC

Amor and the Poet; An evening at Giske; Cosmus; Sir Oluf he rides; Tove; Willemoes (incidental music).
(N) **(*) BIS Dig. CD 641 [id.] Henriette Bonde-Hansen, Susanne Persson; Jan Lund; Jesper Vigant, Danish Nat. Op. Ch.; Aalborg SO, Tamas Vetö.

This is of greater musical interest than the anthology of incidental music on the Kontrapunkt label, though it would be idle to pretend that all of it is fully worthy of the Danish master. The music to *Herr Oluf han rider* (*Sir Oluf he rides*) occupies almost half the CD. It was written for a play by Holger Drachmann which, apart from the incidental music, proved to be a flop. Produced in 1906, the year of *Maskarade*, it was composed at high speed (in one number Nielsen even presses one of his early piano pieces, Op. 3, into service). The overture is very imaginative and deserves to enter the repertoire, but for the most part the music is slight. There are 12 numbers in all, comprising only about half of Nielsen's complete score. *An evening at Giske* (*En aften paa Giske*), the earliest piece on the disc, is better held together than Rozhdestvensky's Stockholm Philharmonic version on Chandos. The Overture, *Love and the Poet* (*Amor og Digtaren*) is not dissimilar in style or quality to *An imaginary journey to the Færoe Islands* and comes from the last years of Nielsen's life. More engaging than the Kontrapunkt collection with *Hagbarth og Signe*, but of specialist rather than general interest.

(i) *Hymnus amoris, Op. 12;* (ii) *3 Motets, Op. 55; The sleep, Op. 18;* (iii) *Springtime in Fünen, Op. 43.*
*** Chandos Dig. CHAN 8853 [id.]. Soloists; (i) Copenhagen Boys' Ch.; (ii–iii) Danish Nat. R. Ch.; (iii) Skt. Annai Gymnasium Children's Ch., Danish Nat. RSO; (i; iii) Segerstam; (ii) Parkman.

Hymnus amoris is full of glorious music whose polyphony has a naturalness and freshness that it is difficult to resist, and which is generally well sung. The harsh dissonances of the middle *Nightmare* section of *Søvnen* ('The Sleep') rather shocked Danish musical opinion at the time and still generate a powerful effect. Segerstam gets very good results both here and in the enchanting *Springtime in Fünen*, and the solo singing is good. The three motets actually contain a Palestrina quotation. Generally excellent performances and fine recorded sound.

(i) *Springtime in Fünen. Aladdin suite, Op. 34.*
*** Unicorn Dig. DKPCD 9054 [id.]. (i) Ingo Nielsen, Von Binzer, Klint, Lille Muko University Ch., St Klemens Children's Ch.; Odense SO, Veto.

Springtime in Fünen is one of those enchanting pieces to which everyone responds when they hear it, yet which is hardly ever performed outside Denmark. The engaging *Aladdin* orchestral suite is well played by the Odense orchestra. This disc is a little short on playing time – but no matter, it is well worth its cost and will give many hours of delight.

STAGE WORKS

Aladdin (complete incidental music), *Op. 34*.
*** Chandos Dig. CHAN 9135 [id.]. Ejsing, Paevatalu, Danish R. Chamber Ch. & SO, Rozhdestvensky.

Until now the *Aladdin* music has been known only from the 20–minute, seven-movement suite, but the complete score runs to four times its length. And so this CD gives us an additional hour of Nielsen that has never been available before. The four oriental dances were conceived almost symphonically with an appropriate contrast of tonality and pace. Some numbers are choral, and there are songs and a short piece for solo flute. Thirteen of the movements are designed to accompany spoken dialogue and, although not all of it is of equal musical interest and substance, most of it is characteristically Nielsenesque, and much of it is delightful. The two soloists, Mette Ejsing and Guido Paevatalu, are very good and the Danish Radio forces respond keenly to Rozhdestvensky's baton. This is not top-drawer Nielsen but, given such a persuasive performance and excellent recording, one is almost lulled into the belief that it is.

Aladdin suite; Maskarade Overture.
(Y/B) **(*) Decca Dig. 425 857-2 [id.]. San Francisco Ch. & SO, Blomstedt – GRIEG: *Peer Gynt suites.* **(*)

Blomstedt is an eminently reliable guide to this repertoire, though both Myung-Whun Chung (BIS) and Rozhdestvensky (Chandos) are more atmospheric in the *Aladdin* music, the latter in the complete score. Well played and recorded, but not quite a full three-star recommendation all the same.

OPERA

Maskarade (complete).
**(*) Unicorn DKPCD 9073/4 [id.]. Hansen, Plesner, Landy, Johansen, Serensen, Bastian, Brodersen, Haugland, Danish R. Ch. & SO, Frandsen.

Maskarade is a buoyant, high-spirited score, full of strophic songs and choruses, making considerable use of dance and dance-rhythms, and having the unmistakable lightness of the *buffo* opera. It is excellently proportioned. The performance here is delightful, distinguished by generally good singing and alert orchestral support. The disappointment is the CD transfer which, in trying to clarify textures, has in fact made the focus less clean.

Saul and David (complete).
⊛ *** Chandos Dig. CHAN 8911/12 [id.]. Haugland, Lindroos, Kiberg, Westi, Ch. & Danish Nat. RSO, Järvi.

Nielsen's first opera is here sung in the original language, which is as important with Nielsen as it is with Janáček, and it has the merit of an outstanding Saul in Aage Haugland. The remainder of the cast is very strong and the powerful choral writing is well served by the Danish Radio Chorus. The opera abounds in wonderful and noble music, the ideas are fresh and full of originality. It convinces here in a way that it rarely has before, and the action is borne along on an almost symphonic current that disarms criticism. A marvellous set.

Nietzsche, Friedrich (1844–1900)

(i) Music for piano duet: *Manfred (meditation); Nachklang einer Sylvesternacht.* (ii) Lieder: *Aus der Jugendzeit; Beschwörung; Da geht ein Bach; Es winkt und neigt sich; Gebet an das Leben; Gern und gerner; Junge Fischerin; Das Kind an die erloschene Kerze; Mein Platz vor der Tür; Nachspiel; Ständchen; Unendlich; Ungewitter; Verwelkt; Wie sich Rebenranken en schwingen.* Melodrama for voice and piano: *Der zerbrochene Ringlein.*
(N) **(*) Ph. Dig. 426 863-2 [id.]. (i) Dietrich Fischer-Dieskau, Elmar Budd (piano duet); (ii) Fischer-Dieskau, Aribert Reimann.

What, one wonders, did Wagner and his wife, Cosima, think, when at their Tribschen home their young philosopher friend, Nietzsche, exactly a year after the *Siegfried idyll*, presented Frau Wagner with a 15-minute piano-duet piece, *Nachklang einer Sylvesternacht*, ('Echo of a New Year')? Might Wagner's response have set the seeds for the celebrated and bitter rift? Cosima at least was diplomatic in wondering whether it was intended to be orchestrated; but the sequence of ideas is impossibly gauche in its presentation, and the other duet, *Manfred-Meditation*, almost as long, is no more competent. This is the eager work of an amateur, but at least in the songs, spattered with banal progressions as they are, there are some amiable ideas which, with such an interpreter as Fischer-Dieskau, communicate warmly, though the one melodrama is no more effective than most such speech-songs.

Nin, Joaquín (1879–1949)

Cantos populares españoles Nos. 3, 4, 6, 7, 19 & 20.
(M) (***) EMI mono CDC7 54836-2 [id.]. Ninon Vallin, composer – FALLA: *Harpsichord concerto* etc.;
    GRANADOS: *Danzas españolas* etc.; MOMPOU: *Piano pieces.* (***)

Although Joaquín Nin was born and died in Cuba, he spent the better part of his life in Paris and Berlin, where he was active as a virtuoso pianist and teacher. His *Cantos populares españoles* are rather similiar in character to the celebrated Falla set. The incomparable Ninon Vallin sings six of them with great simplicity and Nin proves himself a charming accompanist. The recordings, made in Paris in 1929, when Vallin was at the height of her powers, sound remarkably good. They come with highly interesting couplings.

Norby, Erik (born 1936)

The Rainbow snake.
*** BIS CD 79 [id.]. Danish Nat. RO, Frandsen – BENTZON: *Feature on René Descartes;* JORGENSON:
    To love music. **

The Rainbow snake is an American Indian fable which tells how drought had produced infertility in the land. The snake heard of this and let itself be thrown, coiled up, into the sky where it uncoiled until it touched the earth at both ends. It then arched its back and scraped down the blue ice which had given rise to the drought, thus restoring life to the earth. Every time the sun and rain meet, the snake stretches its luminous body across the heavens. The scoring is highly colourful, the harmonic language impressionist. All highly atmospheric, with kaleidoscopic changes of harmony against an almost static rhythmic background. It is very well played and recorded.

Nørholm, Ib (born 1931)

Violin concerto, Op. 60.
*** BIS CD 80 [id.]. Leo Hansen, Danish Nat. RSO, Herbert Blomstedt – KOPPEL: *Cello concerto.*
    ***

Ib Nørholm's *Violin concerto* not only evinces considerable imaginative powers but contains some music of real beauty and is expertly laid out for the orchestra. The Danish Radio recording, while not state of the art, is more than acceptable, and it comes with a rewarding coupling.

(i) *Symphonies Nos. 4 (Décreation), Op. 76. 5 (The 4 Elements), Op. 80.*
(N) ** Kontrapunkt Dig. CD 32212 [id.]. (i) Pavlovski, Dahlberg, Høyer, Ib Nørholm, Danish Nat. R.
    Ch.; Danish Nat. RSO, Serov.

Like Per Nørgård, Ib Nørholm was a pupil of Holmboe and his early music is very much in the tradition of the lyric Nordic style of Nielsen and Holmboe. In the 1960s and '70s his musical personality was more responsive to trends in the European avant-garde. Some feel that he embraced the 'new internationalism' too enthusiastically. The *Fourth Symphony* (*Décreation*) is highly self-conscious – the subtitle itself, *Moralities* or *There may be many miles to the nearest spider*, puts you in the picture. The symphony takes as its theme the genesis of man and of the universe, and there are many imaginative touches during its course. Sadly, inspiration is intermittent and the work as a whole is deficient in thematic vitality. There is a lot going on but very little actually happens. The *Fifth Symphony* (*The Four Elements*) is better, though again its neo-expressionism outstays its welcome. The performances under Eduard Serov are obviously committed, and in the *Fourth* the composer himself is the narrator. Decent recording.

Novák, Vitězslav (1870–1949)

(i) Symphonic poems: *About the Eternal longing, Op. 33; In the Tatras, Op. 26;* (ii) *Moravian-Slovak suite, Op. 32.*
(M) **(*) Sup. 11 0682-2 [id.]. (i) Czech PO; (ii) Brno State PO, Karel Sejna.

In the Tatras (1902), an opulent Straussian tone-poem, and *About the Eternal longing* (1903/4) were inspired by unrequited love for a beautiful young pupil, Růžena. The *Slovak suite* is a heavenly score. *Two in love*, its third movement, could well become as widely popular as any piece of music you care to think of. *In the church*, the opening movement, has something in common with Mozart's *Ave verum corpus*, though more obviously romantic, and the closing *At night* is beguilingly atmospheric. All three works here are persuasively played. The recording of the two symphonic poems is atmospheric and clear but a bit pale in the more expansive tuttis; the suite has slightly more body and colour.

De profundis, Op. 67; Overture, Lady Godiva, Op 41; South Bohemian suite, Op. 64.
(N) (***) Sup. mono 11 1873-2 011 [id.]. Brno State PO, Jaroslav Vogel.

Born at the time of the Franco-Prussian war, Novák lived long enough to see the end of the Second World War and the Communist takeover in Czechoslovakia. These classic performances all come from 1960, except for the *De profundis*, which Jaroslav Vogel recorded two years later. The recordings still sound very good for their period and the performances are unlikely to be surpassed. What attractive music it is, too. Recommended.

Pan (symphonic poem), *Op. 43.*
*** Marco Polo Dig. 8.223325 [id.]. Slovak PO, Zdeněk Bílek.

Novák's five-movement symphonic poem, *Pan*, has some lovely music in it. Novák belonged to the generation of composers (Delius, Mahler, Debussy, Janáček, Sibelius etc.) for whom Nature was still central, and there is a pantheistic sensibility here. The scoring has great delicacy and imaginative resource, and there is a distinctly Gallic feeling to much of it. Lyrical, often inspired (occasionally a bit overlong – particularly the last movement) and rewarding, this score is beautifully played by the Slovak Philharmonic under Zdeněk Bílek, and no less beautifully recorded.

Nyman, Michael (born 1948)

(i) *Piano concerto;* (ii) *MGV.*
(Y/B) *** Argo Dig. 443 382-2; *443 382-4* [id.]. (i) Kathryn Stott, Royal Liverpool PO; (ii) Michael Nyman Band, O; composer.

Michael Nyman's *Piano concerto*, representing minimalist music at its most haunting, became a run-away hit, partly thanks to its being used on the soundtrack of Jane Campion's film, *The Piano*. As Nyman explains, the solo piano music was written first, and only later was it developed into this four-movement concerto. *Musique à grande vitesse* was commissioned for the inauguration of the high-speed TGV train from Paris to Lille. Not surprisingly, it relies on train rhythms, with all their unexpected syncopations. The Michael Nyman Band, heavily amplified, is set as a ripieno group alongside the orchestra, giving the piece what the composer thinks of as concerto grosso associations. Powerful, forward recording.

The convertibility of lute strings; For John Cage; Self-laudatory hymn of Inanna and her omnipotence; Time will pronounce.
(Y/B) *** Argo Dig. 440 282-2 [id.]. James Bowman, Fretwork, Trio of London, Virginia Black, London Brass.

Inspired by the first onslaught of the war in Bosnia, *Time will pronounce* uses a piano trio alternately to evoke the pain of war and the violence. In typical Nyman fashion it is a string of linked sections, emotionally unrelenting but with more slow music than is usual with this highly charged, self-indulgent composer. At the end the music fades inconclusively to nothing. The *Self-laudatory hymn* is a weird but magnetic piece for the odd combination of counter-tenor and consort of viols, setting an ancient Near Eastern text with biblical overtones. It should not work, but with such performers as James Bowman and Fretwork, for whom it was written, it does. The least appealing piece is *The convertibility of lute strings*, in which Nyman exploits his aggressive vein in heavy, jangling writing for solo harpsichord. The only piece with jollity in it is *For John Cage*, using the ten instruments of London Brass with wit as well as colour, ending with a slow, chorale-like section with a crescendo at the end, leaving one hanging in mid-air. Whatever reservations have to be made about such minimalist inspirations, the individuality is undeniable, and performances and recording are vividly colourful.

Noise, sounds and sweet airs.
(Y/B) *** Argo Dig. 440 842-2 [id.]. Bott, Summers, Bostridge, Ensemble Instrumental de Basse-Normandie, Dominique Debart.

Rarely has Nyman's brand of minimalism been so strikingly compelling as here, and the magnetism is hard to resist. The musical material is drawn from his opera-ballet, *La princesse de Milan*, with new vocal lines superimposed over the top, setting a text drawn from Shakespeare's *The Tempest*, 'very heavily and idiosyncratically edited', as Nyman says himself. The oddest idiosyncrasy is that the three different voices keep switching roles, so that the words of Prospero, Miranda and other characters are divided among all three singers. The performance and recording are superb, as vivid as any Nyman on disc, giving the result a hypnotic fascination. The three soloists in particular sing magnificently, each with clear, firm, richly focused voice. Catherine Bott, always compelling, is well matched by the alto, Hilary Summers and the clear-toned young tenor, Ian Bostridge.

Nystroem, Gösta (1890–1966)

(i) *Viola concerto (Hommage à la France). Ishavet (Arctic Sea);* (ii) *Sinfonia concertante for cello and orchestra.*
(Y/B) *** BIS Dig. CD 682 [id.]. (i) Nobuko Imai; (ii) Niels Ullner; Malmö SO, Paavo Järvi.

Niels Ullner is a fine cellist with an opulent tone and eloquent phrasing and his is a thoughtful, well-integrated performance of the *Sinfonia concertante*. This is not a concerto but rather a reflective exchange between soloist and orchestra, and the music has both quality and depth. The *Viola concerto* was composed after the Nazi invasion of 1940; hence its subtitle *Hommage à la France*. This is its first complete recording and it has a neo-classical and eminently Gallic *joie de vivre*, as well as poignancy. Nobuko Imai plays it superbly and, throughout the whole programme, the Malmö orchestra are in excellent form under Neeme Järvi's son, Paavo. The recording is transparent and has excellent presence and definition.

Ockeghem, Johannes (*c.* 1410–97)

Alma redemptoris mater; Missa Mi-Mi; Salve Regina.
(Y/B) *** ASV Dig. CD GAU 139 [id.]. The Clerks' Group, Edward Wickham (with motets by BUSNOIS, ISAAC and OBRECHT).

Ockeghem's *Salve Regina*, the motet *Alma redemptoris mater* and the *Missa Mi-Mi* are contrasted here with motets by three of his contemporaries. The *Missa Mi-Mi* is so named because of the recurring descending fifth, both named 'mi' in the natural and soft hexachords. These performances have a refreshing enthusiasm and the approach to rhythm is remarkably free. The Clerks' Group and Edward Wickham, who specialize in the music of the late Middle Ages and early Renaissance, promise us more Ockeghem, including the *Requiem* – and if the others are as good as this, readers can invest in the series with confidence.

Masses for 3 voices: Missa sine nomine; Missa quinti toni.
(N) *** Lyrichord Dig. LEMS 8010 [id.]. Schola Discantus, Kevin Moll.

Here is a natural follow-up to the superb Lyrichord CD of organa by Leonin and Perotinus. The very austerity of Ockeghem's part-writing, with its serenely flowing polyphony, adds to the potency of his music for modern ears. It is very beautifully sung by a vocal quartet of high quality whose tonal matching and fine tuning are ideal. The recording, too, is clear yet has a perfectly judged ambience.

Requiem (Missa pro defunctis).
*** DG 415 293-2 [id.]. Pro Cantione Antiqua, Hamburger Bläserkreis für alte Musik, Turner – JOSQUIN DES PRES: *Missa – L'homme armé.* ***

The DG Archiv version of the *Missa pro defunctis* was originally recorded in Hamburg in 1973. The Pro Cantione Antiqua was unmatched at this period (with such artists as James Bowman and Paul Esswood as their counter-tenors, this is hardly surprising), and Bruno Turner's direction has both scholarly rectitude and musical eloquence to commend it.

Requiem (Missa pro defunctis); Missa Mi-Mi (Missa quarti toni).
(N) (M) *** Virgin Veritas/EMI Dig. VER5 61219-2 [id.]. Hilliard Ens., Hillier.

Ockeghem's *Missa pro defunctis* is the first surviving polyphonic *Requiem*. The *Missa Mi-Mi* is his most widely performed Mass and survives in three different sources in the Vatican Library; in one it is called *Missa Quarti Toni* and in another *My-My*, which is assumed to derive from the short motif that appears in the bass section at the beginning of each main section and consists of a descending fifth. These performances, reissued on Virgin Veritas, have the expertise, secure intonation, blend and ensemble that one expects from these singers, and the music itself has an austere and affecting simplicity. Although it has had a qualified welcome from specialists in this field and despite a certain blandness, it would be curmudgeonly not to welcome such generally persuasive accounts of both works. At mid-price these make an eminently serviceable introduction to the sacred music of this composer and they are very well recorded, too.

Offenbach, Jacques (1819–80)

Cello concerto.
*** RCA RD 71003. Ofra Harnoy, Cincinnati SO, Kunzel – SAINT-SAENS: *Concerto No. 1;* TCHAI-
    KOVSKY: *Rococo variations.* ***

Offenbach's *Cello concerto* is a delight, with all the effervescence and tunefulness of his operettas. It is played with verve and brio and a full range of colour by Ofra Harnoy and did much to establish her reputation, while the accompaniment from Kunzel and his Cincinnati players is just as lively and sympathetic. Excellent recording throughout.

Gaîté parisienne (ballet, arr. Rosenthal): complete.
✹ (M) *** RCA 09026 61847-2 [id.]. Boston Pops O, Arthur Fiedler – ROSSINI/RESPIGHI: *Boutique
    fantasque.* ***

Fiedler's *Gaîté parisienne* is irresistible – one of his very finest records. The orchestra are kept exhilarat-ingly on their toes throughout and are obviously enjoying themselves, not least in the elegantly tuneful waltzes and in the closing *Barcarolle*, which Fiedler prepares beautifully and to which the generous acoustic of Symphony Hall affords a pleasing warmth without in any way blunting or coarsening the brilliance. The percussion, including bass drum in the exuberant *Can-Can*, adds an appropriate condi-ment and John Pfeiffer's superb new transfer makes the recording sound remarkably fresh and full. Unbelievably it dates from 1954, one of the very first of RCA's 'Living Stereo' records and still one of the finest.

(i) *Gaîté parisienne* (ballet, arr. Rosenthal; complete); (ii) *Overtures and suites* from: *Orpheus in the
    Underworld* (1874 version, with *Pastoral ballet*); *Le voyage dans la lune* (with *Snowflakes ballet*).
(Y/B) (M) *** Ph. 442 403-2 [id.]. (i) Pittsburgh SO, Previn; (ii) Philh. O, Almeida.

An outstanding coupling. In *Gaîté parisienne* Previn realizes that tempi can remain relaxed and the music's natural high spirits will still bubble to the surface. The orchestral playing is both spirited and elegant, with Previn obviously relishing the score's delightful detail. This is mirrored by the Philips digital sound-balance, which has substance as well as atmosphere and brilliance. Perhaps the tuba thumping away in the bass is a shade too present, but it increases one's desire to smile through this engagingly happy music. The *Snowflakes ballet* from *Le voyage dans la lune* is a charmer, and the ballet from *Orpheus in the Underworld* is hardly less delectable. The other surprise is the *Orpheus overture*, not the one we know – which, it must be admitted, is a better-crafted piece – but a more extended work in pot-pourri style, with some good tunes. Almeida is no less high-spirited than Previn, and the Philharmonia's response is both polished and elegant. Excellent recording too.

Gaîté parisienne (ballet, arr. Rosenthal): extended excerpts.
(B) *** DG Double 437 404-2 (2) [id.]. BPO, Karajan – CHOPIN: *Les Sylphides* *** ✹; DELIBES:
    Coppélia: suite ***; GOUNOD: *Faust* etc. **(*); RAVEL: *Boléro* ***; TCHAIKOVSKY: *Sleeping Beauty*
    (suite). **(*)

Karajan's selection is generous. On the DG disc, only Nos. 3–5, 7 and 19–21 are omitted. The remaster-ing of the 1972 recording is highly successful, although the sound is very brightly lit. However, textures have been lightened to advantage and the effect is to increase the raciness of the music-making, while its polish and sparkle are even more striking. This now comes in a generous compilation of ballet music, all in performances showing characteristic Karajan panache.

Gaîté parisienne (ballet music, arr. Rosenthal): excerpts; *Overture: Orpheus in the Underworld.*
(M) ** Sony SMK 47532 [id.]. NYPO, Bernstein (with SUPPE: *Overture: Beautiful Galathea* ***) –
    BIZET: Symphony. **(*).

Bernstein's suite includes a good deal of the raciest part of the score and then closes with the *Barcarolle*. The playing is characteristically effervescent, but the rather hard light of the 1969 CBS sound – the recording was made in the Avery Fisher Hall – makes everything seem brittle, and the ear is easily tired, unless a modest volume level is chosen. The Overtures are characteristically boisterous: Bernstein is warmly elegant as well, in Suppé's *Beautiful Galathea*.

(i) *Musette (Air de ballet)*. Overtures: *La Belle Hélène; La Grande-Duchesse de Gérolstein; Orpheus in the Underworld. Les belles Américaines: Waltz* (orch. Robert Russell Bennett). *Contes d'Hoffmann: Intermezzo; Introduction; Minuet; Barcarolle. Geneviève de Brabant: Galop. La Périchole:* Pot-pourri.
(M) ** RCA 09026 61429-2 [id.]. Boston Pops O, Arthur Fiedler – IBERT: *Divertissement.* ***

For once the CD transfer of this RCA 'Living Stereo' recording from 1956 is disappointing. The Boston resonance intrudes on the music-making and tends to blunt the effect of the playing, so that one has the impression that Fiedler is fielding a second team. But the selection is interesting and generous, and Samuel Mayes is a sympathetic cello soloist in the *'Air de ballet from the 17th Century'*. Curiously, the Ibert *Divertissement* which acts as coupling and which was recorded a month later, is as racy as you could wish, and the recorded sound is comparably lively.

Overtures: *La Belle Hélène; Bluebeard; La Grande-Duchesse de Gérolstein; Orpheus in the Underworld; Vert-vert. Barcarolle from Contes d'Hoffmann.*
**(*) DG Dig. 400 044-2 [id.]. BPO, Karajan.

Other hands besides Offenbach's helped to shape his overtures. Most are on a pot-pourri basis, but the tunes and scoring are so engagingly witty as to confound criticism. Karajan's performances racily evoke the theatre pit. The Berlin playing is very polished and, with so much to entice the ear, this cannot fail to be entertaining; however, the compact disc emphasizes the dryness of the orchestral sound; the effect is rather clinical, with the strings lacking bloom.

Le Papillon (ballet; complete).
(N) (B) *** Decca Double 444 821-2 (2) [id.]. Nat. PO, Bonynge – TCHAIKOVSKY: *Nutcracker.* ***

Le Papillon is Offenbach's only full-length ballet and it dates from 1860. The quality of invention is high and the music sparkles from beginning to end. In such a sympathetic performance, vividly recorded (in 1972 in the Kingsway Hall), it cannot fail to give pleasure.

Cello duos, Op. 54: Suites Nos. 1–2.
(B) *** HM 1901043. Roland Pidoux and Etienne Péclard.

Offenbach was himself a very accomplished cellist, and these two works are tuneful and imaginatively laid out to exploit the tonal possibilities of such a duo. Offenbach's natural wit is especially apparent in the *First Suite in E major*. The performances are excellent and so is the recording.

OPERA

Les brigands (complete).
**(*) EMI Dig. CDS7 49830-2 (2). Raphanel, Alliot-Lugaz, Raffalli, Trempont, Le Roux, Lyon Opera Ch. & O, Gardiner.

Les brigands has a Gilbertian plot about brigands and their unlikely association with the court of Mantua, with the carabinieri behaving very like the police in *The Pirates of Penzance*. The tone of the principal soprano, Ghislaine Raphanel, is rather edgily French, but the rest of the team is splendid. Outstanding as ever is the characterful mezzo, Colette Alliot-Lugaz, in another of her breeches roles. Warm, well-balanced recording. (This recording has been deleted as we go to press.)

Les Contes d'Hoffmann (The Tales of Hoffmann): complete.
✹ *** Decca 417 363-2 (2) [id.]. Sutherland, Domingo, Tourangeau, Bacquier, R. Suisse Romande and Lausanne Pro Arte Ch., SRO, Bonynge.
**(*) Ph. 422 374-2 (3) [id.]. Francisco Araiza, Eva Lind, Cheryl Studer, Jessye Norman, Anne Sofie von Otter, Samuel Ramey, Dresden Ch. & State O, Tate.
(Y/B) (M) ** EMI CMS7 63222-2 (2) [Ang. CDMB 63222]. Gedda, D'Angelo, Schwarzkopf, De los Angeles, Benoit, Faure, Ghiuselev, London, Sénéchal, Blanc, Chœurs René Duclos, Paris Conservatoire O, Cluytens.

On Decca Joan Sutherland gives a virtuoso performance in four heroine roles, not only as Olympia, Giulietta and Antonia but also as Stella in the *Epilogue*. Bonynge opts for spoken dialogue, and puts the Antonia scene last, as being the more substantial. His direction is unfailingly sympathetic, while Sutherland is impressive in each role, notably as the doll Olympia and in the pathos of the Antonia scene. As Giulietta she hardly sounds like a *femme fatale*, but still produces beautiful singing. Domingo gives one of his finest performances on record, and so does Gabriel Bacquier. It is a memorable set, in every way, much more than the sum of its parts.

Jeffrey Tate in this textually troubled work uses a new edition prepared by Michael Kaye that takes account of the discovery of 350 more manuscript pages in addition to those which expanded the Oeser edition to Wagnerian lengths. One big difference here from the complete Oeser edition is that dialogue replaces all the recitatives written by Ernest Guiraud. The Prologue is more extended, showing the transformation of the Muse into Nicklausse, with extra material in the Olympia and Antonia Acts too, such as the striking trio for Hoffmann, Nicklausse and Coppélius. Also, Tate points out that 'the Giulietta act contains music that shows conclusively that Offenbach would have wanted a single voice to embody all of Hoffmann's female infatuations'. It is a pity that the logic of the project was not carried through, with a single singer chosen for all the heroines, as in the Bonynge/Sutherland set. As it is, Jessye Norman, the Antonia of the new set, cunningly lightens her voice, making it sound as girlish as she can, and she urges the music on at a brisker speed than usual in the charming duet, *C'est une chanson d'amour*, but it is still hard to imagine her as the fragile young girl destined to die. Tate's determination to adopt an authentic text leads him to reject the septet, based on the *Barcarolle* theme, not even including it in an appendix. Nor is Dapertutto's *Scintille, diamant* included, drawn originally from another Offenbach work, when the authentic *Tourne, tourne miroir*, is restored at that point. The new set uses the sour alternative ending to the Venice Act, with Giulietta accidentally taking poison. Samuel Ramey sings very well in all four villainous roles, with satisfyingly firm, dark tone, even if he finds it hard to sound really sinister, but principal vocal honours go to Anne Sofie von Otter as a superb Muse and Nicklausse, making one relish all the extra music given the character in this version. Eva Lind is bright and clear, if a little edgy and shallow, as Olympia, perfectly doll-like in fact; and Cheryl Studer is technically very strong and confident, even if she does not quite sound in character. Francisco Araiza makes an agreeable Hoffmann, but he lacks the flair of his finest rivals, and the voice tends to lose its focus under pressure. Even with reservations, there is a very strong textual case for this set, and admirers of the opera will surely want to have it alongside the first choice with Sutherland, Domingo and Bacquier.

Several bad mistakes in casting prevent the mid-1960s EMI set from being the rare delight it should have been. It has some marvellous moments, and the whole of the *Barcarolle* scene with Schwarzkopf is a delight, but the very distinction of the cast-list makes one annoyed that the result is not better. André Cluytens surprisingly proved quite the wrong conductor for this sparkling music, for he has little idea of caressing the music and rarely fails to push on regardless. Gianna d'Angelo's Olympia is pretty but shallow, George London's Coppelius and Dr Miracle unpleasantly gruff-toned and, most disappointing of all, Victoria de los Angeles is sadly out of voice, with the upper register regularly turning sour on her. But with such artists even below their best there are characterful moments which take the listener along well enough. Cluytens in his ruthlessness has a certain demonic energy which has its dramatic side. The recording is atmospheric and the CD transfer has given it added liveliness.

Les Contes d'Hoffmann: highlights.
(M) *** Decca 421 866-2 (from above set, cond. Bonynge).

The Decca highlights disc is one of the finest compilations of its kind from any opera. With over an hour of music, it offers a superbly managed distillation of nearly all the finest items and is edited most skilfully.

Orpheus in the Underworld: highlights of English National Opera production (in English).
**(*) That's Entertainment Dig. CDTER 1134. Kale, Watson, Angas, Squires, Bottone, Pope, Belcourt, Styx, Burgess, E. Nat. Op. Ch. & O, Mark Elder.

The sparkling English National Opera production depends a lot for its fun on the racy new adaptation and translation by Snoo Wilson and the ENO producer, David Pountney. Offenbach devotees should be warned: there is little of Parisian elegance in this version and plenty of good knockabout British fun, brilliantly conveyed by the whole company, including Bonaventura Bottone's hilariously camp portrait of a prancing Mercury. Bright, vivid recording to match the performance.

La Périchole (complete).
(M) *** Erato/Warner 2292 45686-2 (2) [id.]. Crespin, Vanzo, Bastin, Lombard, Friedmann, Trigeau, Rhine Op. Ch., Strasbourg PO, Lombard.

Though both Régine Crespin in the title-role and Alain Vanzo as her partner, Piquillo, were past their peak at that time, their vocal control is a model in this music, with character strongly portrayed but without any hint of vulgar underlining. Crespin is fresh and Vanzo produces heady tone in his varied arias, some of them brilliant. Jules Bastin is characterful too in the subsidiary role of Don Andres, Viceroy of Peru. Lombard secures excellent precision of ensemble from his Strasbourg forces, only occasionally pressing too hard. The recorded sound is vivid and immediate, and the libretto provides a detailed synopsis of the action between the texts and translations of numbers.

Robinson Crusoe (sung in English).
*** Opera Rara ORC 7 (3) [id.]. Brecknock, Kenny, Kennedy, Hartle, Hill Smith, Oliver, Browne,
   Geoffrey Mitchell Ch., RPO, Alun Francis.

More ambitious than Offenbach's operettas, *Robinson Crusoe* offers a sequence of fresh and tuneful
numbers with many striking ensembles. The plot is derived less from Daniel Defoe than from the British
pantomime tradition, which in the middle of last century turned regularly to Crusoe as a story.
Characterization is strong and amusing, with a secondary couple shadowing Crusoe and his beloved
Edwige. The casting is also from strength, with John Brecknock and Yvonne Kenny outstanding as
Crusoe and Edwige, while Man Friday, as in the original Paris production, is sung by a mezzo, Sandra
Browne. On the three discs are 3¾ hours of music, covering numbers which the composer cut even from
the original production. The witty English translation, very freely adapted from the French text, with
some changes of plot, is by Don White, and words are admirably clear.

Arias and excerpts: *Barbe Bleu: Overture; Couplets de Boulette et de la Rosière. La Belle Hélene: Amours
divins. La Fille du tambour-major: Chanson de la Fille. La Grande-Duchesse de Gérolstein: Overture;
Dites-lui; Ah! que j'aime les militaires! Madame l'Archiduc; Couplets de l'alphabet. Orphée aux enfers:
Couplets du berger joli. La Périchole: Overture and excerpts. Pomme d'api: Overture; Couplet de pomme;
J'en prendrai un deux, trois. La Romance de la Rose: Overture. La Vie parisienne: Rondeau et Valse.*
(N) *(*) RCA Dig. 09026 68116-2 [id.]. Frederica von Stade, SCO, Almeida.

An enticing programme, let down by poor casting. Frederica von Stade looks handsome enough in the
picture on the front of the CD, with her short hair-style, and she could certainly bring off some of these
roles with a stage presence. But on record her voice is simply too old-sounding for this repertoire. Even
as the Grande-Duchesse, her *Dites-lui* is too mature and, though she brings off the engaging *Valse* from
La Vie parisienne appealingly enough, elsewhere too often the champagne-like soubrette sparkle which
these couplets need above all else eludes her. Moreover Almeida could ideally provide a lighter touch
with the orchestra.

Onslow, Georges (1784–1853)

String quintets: in C min. (The Bullet), Op. 38; in E, Op. 39; in B min., Op. 40.
(N) **(*) Sony Dig. SK 64308 [id.]. L'Archibudelli & Smithsonian Chamber Players.

Georges Onslow, the son of an English lord, suffered a similar fate to Oscar Wilde, being banished to
France after a homosexual scandal, and so returned to the place of his birth in the Auvergne, but he
later travelled to Germany. He produced 34 string quintets, of which his fifteenth is nicknamed *The
Bullet*. It is associated with a very serious hunting accident, in which he was struck in the head by a
bullet intended for a wild boar. He was severely injured but survived to finish the work with its highly
descriptive, indeed spectacular, Minuet describing his suffering and subsequent fever and delirium. The
group here go over the top in this movement, with their anguished sforzandos and glissandos; but they
play the peaceful *Andante sostenuto* (subtitled *Convalescena*) very beautifully. The energetic and optimistic finale describes his recovery, and it is presented here with appropriate spirited vitality. The other
two *Quintets* are not quite so striking, though the *E major* has an expressive *Adagio grandioso* and the
composer obviously still remembers his catastophe with instructions to play it *con espressione e un
accento di malinconia*. The *B minor Quintet* has a strong opening movement and yet another unusually
rhythmic Minuet. Its *Adagio*, like the *E major*, has something of the dignity of Haydn. In short these
quintets are well worth getting to know; if the 'authentic' sounds here are on the astringent side, this is
still first-class quartet playing.

Orff, Carl (1895–1982)

Carmina Burana.
*** Decca Dig. 430 509-2; *430 509-4* [id.]. Dawson, Daniecki, McMillan, San Francisco Boys' & Girls'
   Choruses, San Francisco Symphony Ch. & SO, Blomstedt.
*** Ph. Dig. 422 363-2 [id.]. Gruberová, Aler, Hampson, Shinyukai Ch., Knaben des Staats & Berlin
   Cathedral Ch., BPO, Ozawa.
⊛ (M) *** Sony SBK 47668 [id.]. Harsanyi, Petrak, Presnell, Rutgers University Ch., Phd. O, Ormandy.
*** EMI CDC7 47411-2 [id.]. Armstrong, English, Allen, St Clement Danes Grammar School Boys'
   Ch., London Symphony Ch., LSO, Previn.
(N) (M) *** DG 447 437 [id.]. Janowitz, Stolze, Fischer-Dieskau, Schöneberger Boys' Ch., Berlin

German Op. Ch. & O, Jochum.

(Y/B) (BB) *** RCA Navigator Dig. 74321 17908-2. Hendricks, Aler, Hagegård, St Paul's Cathedral Boys' Ch., L. Symphony Ch., LSO, Mata.

(M) *** Carlton Dig. PCD 855 [id.]. Walmsley-Clark, Graham-Hall, Maxwell, Southend Boys' Ch., London Symphony Ch., LSO, Hickox.

(Y/B) *** RCA Dig. 09026 61673-2 [id.]. McNair, Aler, Hagegård, St Louis Ch. & SO, Slatkin.

**(*) Teldec/Warner Dig. 9031 74886-2 [id.]. Sumi Jo, Jochen Kowalski, Boje Skovhus, LPO Ch., Southend Boys' Ch., LPO, Mehta.

(N) (M) ** Decca Phase 4 444 105-2 [id.]. Burrowes, Devos, Shirley-Quirk, Brighton Festival Ch., RPO, Dorati.

Blomstedt's is the finest modern version of Orff's exhilaratingly hedonistic cantata. Throughout the choral singing, men, boys, and girls, all enjoy themselves hugely – as they should, with such stimulating words to sing. They generate great passion and energy and all three soloists are equally outstanding. John Daniecki's use of vocal colouring is entertainingly diverse, while Kevin McMillan is a splendidly unctuous Abbot, and Lynne Dawson portrays the girl in the red tunic with sensuous innocence. Blomstedt's reading is full of imaginative touches of light and shade, yet the flow of passionate energy is paramount. He is helped by the remarkable range and sonority of the Decca recording, very much in the demonstration bracket.

Ozawa's digital recording of Orff's justly popular cantata carries all the freshness and spontaneity of his earlier successful Boston version. The *Cours d'amours* sequence is the highlight of his reading, with the soprano, Edita Gruberová, highly seductive; Thomas Hampson's contribution is also impressive. Ozawa's infectious rubato in *Oh, oh, oh, I am bursting out all over*, interchanged between male and female chorus towards the end of the work, is wonderfully bright and zestful, with the contrast of the big *Ave formosissima* climax which follows made to sound spaciously grand. Taken overall, this Philips version readily goes to the top of the list alongside Blomstedt.

Ormandy and his Philadelphians have just the right panache to bring off this wildly exuberant picture of the Middle Ages by the anonymous poets of former days, and there is no more enjoyable analogue version. It has tremendous vigour, warmth and colour and a genial, spontaneous enthusiasm from the Rutgers University choristers, men and boys alike, that is irresistible. The soloists are excellent, but it is the chorus and orchestra who steal the show; the richness and eloquence of the choral tone is a joy in itself. This is quite splendid, one of Ormandy's most inspired recordings and, even if you already have the work in your collection, this exhilarating version will bring additional delights.

Previn's 1975 analogue version, vividly recorded, is even more sharply detailed than Ozawa's. It is strong on humour and rhythmic point. The chorus sings vigorously, the men often using an aptly rough tone; and the resilience of Previn's rhythms, finely sprung, brings out a strain not just of geniality but of real wit. This is a performance which swaggers along and makes you smile. Among the soloists, Thomas Allen's contribution is one of the glories of the music-making, and in their lesser roles the soprano and tenor are equally stylish. The digital remastering is wholly successful: the choral bite is enhanced, yet the recording retains its full amplitude. But this should be reissued at mid-price.

Jochum's 1968 recording of *Carmina Burana* has never sounded better than it does in this reissue in DG's 'Originals' series. The choral pianissimos lack the very last degree of immediacy, but the underlying tension of the quiet singing is very apparent. The recording has a wide dynamic range and when the music blazes it has real splendour and excitement. Fischer-Dieskau's singing is refined but not too much so, and his first solo, *Omnia Sol temperat*, and later *Dies, nox et omnia* are both very beautiful, with the kind of tonal shading that a great Lieder singer can bring; he is suitably gruff in the Abbot's song – so much so that for the moment the voice is unrecognizable. Gerhard Stolze too is very stylish in his falsetto *Song of the roasted swan*. The soprano, Gundula Janowitz, finds a quiet dignity for her contribution and this is finely done. The closing scene is moulded by Jochum with wonderful control, most compelling in its restrained power.

Mata's splendid 1980 digital recording now comes at super-bargain price and is highly recommendable on all counts. It is a joyously alive and volatile reading, not as metrical in its rhythms as most; this means that at times the London Symphony Chorus is not as clean in ensemble as it is for Previn. The choristers of St Paul's Cathedral sing with purity and enthusiasm but are perhaps not boyish enough, though the soloists are first rate (with John Aler coping splendidly, in high, refined tones, with the Roast Swan episode). There is fine warmth of atmosphere and no lack in the lower range; indeed in almost every respect the sound is superb. This is unbeatable value for those wanting a bargain-priced version.

Richard Hickox, on his brilliantly recorded Carlton CD, like Previn uses the combined London Symphony forces, but adds the Southend Boys' Choir who make sure we know they understand all about sexual abandon – their *Oh, oh, oh, I am bursting out all over* is a joy. Penelope Walmsley-Clark, too, makes a rapturous contribution: her account of the girl in the red dress is equally delectable. The other soloists are good but less individual, and the chorus rises marvellously to climaxes, while the sharp articulation of consonants when the singers hiss out the words of *O Fortuna* in the closing section is a highlight. The documentation provides a vernacular narrative for each band but no translation.

Slatkin's new RCA recording was made in St Louis in 1992 and is notable for an unbeatable trio of soloists, two of whom are featured on Mata's earlier recording. But one especially remembers Sylvia McNair's ravishing portrayal of the girl in the red tunic, whose final submission is so seductively sweet. The choral singing is enjoyably rhythmic and vigorously crisp. Slatkin's reading is spacious and certainly brings out the grandeur of the opening and closing sections, but in the Court of Love his trebles are very chaste; their racily knowing '*Oh, Oh, Ohs*' are without the pubescent sexual abandon of the British performances variously under Previn, Hickox and Mata. But this remains overall a very convincing performance, if not a first choice. The acoustic of St Louis Powell Symphony Hall is suitably rich and expansive but the chorus is not very sharply defined when singing softly.

Mehta's newest Teldec version is often enjoyably vigorous, it has good soloists and an excellent choral response, with the Southend boys throatily enjoying their pubescent spree. Sumi Jo is a seductive if rather knowing Girl in the Red Shift who submits willingly, rising nimbly up her ascending scale to a spectacularly floated pianissimo. But Boje Skovhus makes a strongly vibrant rather than a subtle contribution. The recording, made at The Maltings, Snape, is resonantly spectacular, especially in the matter of the orchestral percussion, but the quieter choral passages are a little recessive. In the last resort this is not a first choice, for Mehta's direction is not as imaginative or as spontaneously exuberant as that of his finest competitors.

Dorati's version was recorded in the Kingsway Hall in 1976 in Decca's Phase Four system. The result is a beefy, vibrant account with good singing and playing. Despite some eccentric speeds, Dorati shows a fine rhythmic sense, but the performance cannot match the best available. The remastered recording brings a bold impact in fortissimos, but the quieter, more atmospheric passages are less cleanly defined.

Catulli Carmina.
(N) (M) *** DG 449 097-2 [id.]. Arleen Augér, Wieslaw Ochman, Berlin Op. Ch., 4 pianos & percussion, Jochum – EGK: *The Temptation of St Anthony*. ***

Though in sheer memorability it cannot match *Carmina burana*, Orff's sequel (using much the same formula) has its nagging attractions. For anyone hypnotized by the earlier and more popular work, *Catulli Carmina* is the Orff piece to recommend next. Jochum's version has never been surpassed. His chorus sings with sharp, rhythmic point and, if imagination is called for in such music, Jochum matches flexibility with a spark of humour in his control of mechanistic rhythms. His soloists are individual and sweet-toned. The recording is very fine, although even on CD evocative pianissimos sound a little recessed.

(i) *Die Kluge;* (ii) *Der Mond.*
(M) *** EMI CMS7 63712-2 (2) [Ang. CDMB 63712]. (i) Cordes, Frick, Schwarzkopf, Wieter, Christ, Kusche; (ii) Christ, Schmitt-Walker, Graml, Kuen, Lagger, Hotter; Philh. Ch. & O, Sawallisch.

Sawallisch's pioneering Orff recordings of the mid-1950s are vivid and immediate on CD, with such effects as the thunderbolt in *Der Mond* impressive still. Elisabeth Schwarzkopf is characterful and dominant as the clever young woman of the title in *Die Kluge*. It is good too to hear such vintage singers as Gottlob Frick and Hans Hotter in unexpected roles. Musically, these may not be at all searching works, but both short operas provide easy, colourful entertainment, with Sawallisch drawing superb playing from the Philharmonia. No texts are provided, but the discs are very generously banded. (This set has currently been withdrawn.)

Pachelbel, Johann (1653–1706)

Canon in D.
(M) *** Virgin/EMI Dig. CUV5 61145-2 [id.]. LCO, Warren-Green – ALBINONI: *Adagio;* VIVALDI: *Four seasons*. ***

A lovely performance of the *Canon* from Christopher Warren-Green and his excellent London Chamber Orchestra, with a delicately graceful opening and a gorgeous climax and with radiant violins. With splendid sound this is as fine as any version in the catalogue. Other enjoyable performances are listed in the Concerts section.

Pacius, Fredrik (1809–91)

Kung Karls Jakt (King Charles's Hunt) (opera): complete.
(M) *** Finlandia Dig. FACD 107. Törnqvist, Lindroos, Krause, Grönroos, Jubilate Ch., Finnish Nat.
Op. O, Söderblom.

Fredrik Pacius became known as 'the father of Finnish music', for he brought the Finnish capital, then a provincial backwater, into contact with the mainstream of European music. His opera *King Charles's Hunt* brings pretty simple musical ideas. Some are pleasant but there is little evidence of much individuality. There is some fine singing from Pirkko Törnqvist as the fisherman's daughter, Leonora, Peter Lindroos as her fiancé, and from Walton Grönroos as the coup leader, Gustaf Gyllenstjerna. The young King is a speaking role. Much care has been lavished on the production and Ulf Söderblom holds things together admirably. No masterpiece is uncovered but it will be of interest to collectors with a specialist interest in the beginnings of opera in the northern countries.

Padilla, Juan Gutierrez de (c. 1590–1664)

Missa: Ego flos campi. Stabat Mater.
(M) *** Carlton Dig. PCD 970 [id.]. Mixolydian, Piers Schmidt – VICTORIA: *Missa surge propera* etc.
***

Juan Gutierrez de Padilla's Mass, *Ego flos campi*, for double choir is more homophonic than much of his other music. The Mass is nevertheless full of interest, though of course the comparison which the sleeve-writer makes between the two composers on the disc is not to Victoria's disadvantage. Padilla's setting of the *Stabat Mater* lacks the expressive depth of that Renaissance master. Dedicated performances and excellent recording.

Paganini, Niccolò (1782–1840)

Andante amaroso; Balletto campestre (Variations on a comic theme; orch. Tamponi); *Larghetto con passione; Moto perpetuo in C, Op. 11; Polacca with variations in A; Sonata for grand viola; Sonata Maria Luisa in E; Sonata Varsavia; Variations on The Carnival of Venice; Variations on a theme from Rossini's Mosè.*
(B) *** EMI CZS7 67567-2 (2). Salvatore Accardo, COE, Tamponi.

Salvatore Accardo here explores the by-ways of Paganini's concertante music for violin and orchestra (with one piece for viola), and much of the virtuosity is stunning – sample the *Moto perpetuo*. As can be seen from the listing, Paganini's favourite device was a set of variations on a simple, often ingenuous theme, alternating *galant* lyricism with fiendish bravura. Accardo is equally at home in both. The orchestral accompaniments are of minimal interest but they are warmly supportive; the flattering ambience of the recording and the good balance ensure that the sounds reaching the listener are pleasingly believable: the CD transfers are admirably faithful. The two discs are offered for the price of one. There are, however, no notes about the music.

Violin concertos Nos. 1–6.
(M) *** DG 437 210-2 (3) [id.]. Accardo, LPO, Dutoit.

Violin concertos Nos. 1 in D, Op. 6; 2 in B min. (La Campanella), Op. 7.
*** DG 415 378-2 [id.]. Accardo, LPO, Dutoit.

Violin concertos Nos. 3 in E; 4 in D min.
*** DG 423 370-2 [id.]. Accardo, LPO, Dutoit.

Violin concerto No. 5 in A min.; Maestosa sonata sentimentale; La primavera in A.
*** DG 423 578-2 [id.]. Accardo, LPO, Dutoit.

Violin concerto No. 6 in E min., Op. posth.; Sonata with variations on a theme by Joseph Weigl; Le streghe (Variations on a theme of Süssmayr), Op. 8; Variations of Non più mesta from Rossini's La Cenerentola.
*** DG 423 717-2 [id.]. Accardo, LPO, Dutoit.

Paganini's concertos can too often seem trivial and long-winded; it is a tribute to the virtuosity and artistry of Salvatore Accardo that they reveal so much musical interest in his hands. But – as we have observed before – Accardo's technique is formidable and his intonation marvellously true; these qualities, blended with good taste, make this series of performances distinctive. Apart from No. 5 (which, like No. 6, was orchestrated by Federico Mompellio), these are all genre works written to a formula in which the composer produced a series of contrasting lyrical operatic melodies to offset the fireworks of the outer movements. Having said this, Paganini's invention holds up well throughout these works. Tuttis are stereotyped but have plenty of impulse, the lyrical tunes are all very engaging, and the violinistic display is consistently ear-tickling when presented with such panache. Accardo is beautifully accompanied by Dutoit who always keeps even the most conventional passage-work alive. The recordings were made in Barking Town Hall in 1974/5 and the remastering preserves the hall ambience, yet has a cleaner orchestral bass than the LPs.

Violin concerto No. 1 in D, Op. 6.
⚠ *** EMI CDC7 47101-2 [id.]. Itzhak Perlman, RPO, Foster – SARASATE: *Carmen fantasy.*** ⚠
*** DG Dig. 429 786-2 [id.]. Gil Shaham, NYPO, Sinopoli – SAINT-SAENS: *Concerto No. 3.* ***
(Y/B) **(*) EMI Dig. CDC5 55026-2 [id.]. Sarah Chang, Phd. O, Sawallisch – SAINT-SAENS: *Havanaise; Intro & Rondo capriccioso.* **(*)

(i) *Violin concerto No. 1 in D, Op. 6. Caprices for solo violin Nos. 1, 3–4, 9–11, 14, 16–17, 24.*
(Y/B) (B) *** DG 439 473-2 [id.]. Salvatore Accardo; (i) LPO, Charles Dutoit.

Violin concerto No. 1 in D, Op. 6; I Palpiti; Perpetuela; Sonata napoleone.
(Y/B) (M) *** DG 439 981-2 [id.]. Accardo, LPO, Dutoit.

Itzhak Perlman demonstrates a fabulously clean and assured technique and, with the help of the EMI engineers, he produces a gleamingly rich tone, free from all scratchiness. Lawrence Foster matches the soloist's warmth with an alive and buoyant orchestral accompaniment. Provided one does not feel strongly about Perlman's traditional cuts, there has been no better record of the *D major Concerto.*

Although Perlman's EMI version of Paganini's *First Concerto* is special, otherwise Accardo's account is second to none in its sense of lyrical style, finesse and easy bravura. The selection of solo *Caprices*, too, is well made, including the most famous of all, which so many other composers have used for variations of their own. Accardo presents his selection with an eloquence far beyond mere display. Excellent recording.

Accardo's account is also available, recoupled at mid-price with attractive, shorter concertante pieces, of which the *Perpetuela* is quite dazzling and *I Palpiti* is like an operatic air with variations.

Gil Shaham's technical ease in the histrionics of Paganini's stratospheric tessitura, harmonics and all, is breathtaking, and he can phrase an Italianate lyrical melody – and there are some good ones in this *Concerto* – with disarming charm and ravishing timbre. His dancing spiccato in the finale is a joy and, however high he ascends, there is never a hint of scratchiness. Sinopoli's finely graduated and often dramatic accompaniment could hardly be more sympathetic.

Sarah Chang made her début with this famous bravura concerto in the Avery Fisher Hall at the age of eight and now, at the relatively mature age of twelve (!), she has recorded it in Philadelphia. The slow movement is fresh and direct rather than romantic, but she knows how to charm the ear gently. The finale is dazzling. While Perlman remains supreme in this work, Chang can bounce her bow with aplomb and never fails to entice the ear. Sawallisch gives her admirable support, but the recording is flattering neither to soloist (balanced close) nor to orchestra, which lacks sumptuousness.

Violin concertos Nos. 1 in D, Op. 6; 2 in B min. (La Campanella), Op. 7.
*** Denon Dig. CO 77611 [id.]. Kantorow, Auvergne O.
(BB) *** Naxos Dig. 8.550649 [id.]. Ilya Kaler, Polish Nat. RSO, Gunzenhauser.
(B) *** DG 429 524-2 [id.]. Shmuel Ashkenasi, VSO, Esser.

Kantorow plays superbly and he is very naturally recorded (the microphones in exactly the right place). In both concertos his lyrical line is very appealing indeed and the fireworks are dazzling, especially in the *La Campanella* finale of No. 2. The Denon recording is digital, but the acoustics have a slightly studio-ish feeling.

The young Russian virtuoso, Ilya Kaler, was a pupil of Leonid Kogan and is fully equal to Paganini's once devilish technical demands and the phrasing of warm Italianate melody. His bouncing staccato in the sparkling spiccato finales of both concertos is managed adeptly and in every respect his technique is commandingly secure. Stephen Gunzenhauser is a sympathetic accompanist throughout, and the Polish Radio Orchestra play with suppleness and bring a sense of elegance and style to this music. There is no lack of dazzle in the fireworks, and no damp squibs here. With very good notes, this is an excellent example of a Naxos super-bargain at its best.

At bargain price on CD, Ashkenasi's coupling of the two favourite Paganini *Concertos* is also very good value. He surmounts all the many technical difficulties in an easy, confident style and, especially in the infectious *La Campanella* finale of No. 2, shows how completely he is in control. The microphone is close, but his timbre is sweet and the high tessitura and harmonics are always cleanly focused.

Allegro di concert (Moto perpetuo) in C, Op. 11; Cantabile in D, Op. 17; Centone si sonate: in D; in A, Op. 64/2 & 4; Guitar and violin sonatas: in A; A min.; E min., Op. 3/1, 4 & 6; Grand sonata for violin & guitar in A, Op. posth.; Sonata concertata in A, Op. 61; Sonata a preghiera (arr. Hannibal).
*** DG Dig. 437 837-2 [id.]. Gil Shaham, Göran Söllscher.

The atmosphere of much of this repertoire is comparatively intimate, something these artists readily appreciate, and their playing is immaculate and amiably easy-going. Perhaps at times here the style of performance could with advantage have been more extrovert, but the present hour-long recital will make attractive late-evening entertainment (not taken all at once, of course). The recording has a realistic balance and fine presence.

Cantabile for violin and guitar; 6 Centone di sonate, Lettera A (for violin and guitar); *12 Sonatas for violin and guitar, Op. 2/1–6; Op. 3/1–6; Sonata concertata in A; Grand sonata in A; Fantasia on a theme from Rossini's 'Mosè in Egitto'; Tarantella in A min.* (all for violin and guitar).
(N) (B) *** Teldec/Warner 4509 97974-2 (2). György Terebesi, Sonja Prunnbauer.

This valuable collection contains works that came to light only in 1910 when Paganini's effects were auctioned; a substantial number of pieces for violin and guitar were discovered, all highly accomplished. If they are lightweight and undemanding, they are also tuneful and entertaining. In the sets of sonatas, the violin is very much predominant and the guitar part is designed so that almost any reasonably proficient accompanist would have no trouble at all in giving support to the violin line. Most of them are very short, almost always with only two movements, although sometimes with a mid-movement change of tempo. The *Sonata concertata* is aptly named, giving the guitar a fair share of the limelight, and the *Grand sonata* bristles with bravura for that instrument. Both these works are in three movements and are altogether more substantial. György Terebesi is a most appealing player, with a sweet timbre, and he is well supported by Sonja Prunnbauer. The recording is excellent, and this set is in no way inferior to the DG selection below; it costs very little more and offers more than twice as much music. There are no back-up notes included, but this is music simply meant for light-hearted enjoyment, to be dipped into and not played all at once.

Violin and guitar: Cantabile; Centone di sonate No. 1 in A; Sonata in E min., Op. 3/6; Sonata concertata in A.
*** Sony M K 34508 [id.]. Itzhak Perlman, John Williams – GIULIANI: *Sonata.* ***
Superb playing from Perlman and John Williams, and a good balance; the music-making here gives much pleasure, and this is a generally distinguished disc.

Cantabile and valse; 6 Sonatas for violin and guitar, Op. 2; Sonata for gran viola and guitar; Variations di bravura on Caprice No. 24.
(N) (B) **(*) Naxos Dig. 8.550759 [id.]. Scott St John, Simon Wynberg.

Cantabile in D; 6 Sonatas for violin and guitar, Op. 3; Sonata concertata in A; Variations on Barucabà, Op. 14.
(N) (B) **(*) Naxos Dig. 8.550690 [id.]. Scott St John, Simon Wynberg.

As can be seen, Naxos are planning a complete edition of Paganini's music for violin and guitar. Scott St John plays with flair and considerable virtuosity: his approach has more extrovert dazzle and rather less charm than the performances on Teldec, and he dominates the performances strongly. The recording venue is resonant, which means close microphones, but the violin timbre is bright without being edgy.

Centone di sonate for violin and guitar, Nos. 1–12.
(N) (BB) **(*) Naxos Dig. 8.553141 (Nos. 1–6); 8.553142 (Nos. 7–12) (available separately). Moshe Hammer, Norbert Kraft.

Moshe Hammer plays with plenty of character and an agreeable cantabile line: his style lies somewhere between those of Scott St John and Terebesi on Teldec. He is truthfully recorded in a resonant ecclesiastical acoustic, and the effect is slightly smoother in Volume II (*Sonatas Nos. 7–12*), made three months after Volume I. But both records reproduce realistically and offer enjoyable music-making.

24 Caprices, Op. 1.
(M) *** DG 429 714-2; *429 714-4* [id.]. Salvatore Accardo.
*** EMI CDC7 47171-2 [id.]. Itzhak Perlman.
(BB) *** Naxos Dig. 8.550717 [id.]. Ilya Kaler.
(M) *** Decca 440 034-2 [id.]. Ruggiero Ricci.

(м) **(*) Teldec/Warner Dig. 9031 76259-2 [id.]. Thomas Zehetmair.

Accardo succeeds in making Paganini's most routine phrases sound like the noblest of utterances and he invests these *Caprices* with an eloquence far beyond the sheer display they offer. There are no technical obstacles and, both in breadth of tone and in grandeur of conception, he is peerless. He observes all the repeats and has an excellent CD transfer.

Perlman's playing is also flawless, wonderfully assured and polished, yet not lacking imaginative feeling. Such is the magnetism of his playing that the ear is led on spontaneously from one variation to the next. The transfer to CD of the 1972 recording is extremely natural. But this is at full price.

Those looking for a bargain will surely not be disappointed with the Russian fiddler, Ilya Kaler, on Naxos. He studied under Kogan and in 1981 won the Grand Prize at the Genoa Paganini competition. His playing is technically very assured, the lyrical bowing vibrant in a Slavic way, and, like Ricci, he projects a strong profile. The 1992 Naxos recording, truthful and real, is very well balanced: the violin is present but the engineers also convey the acoustic of Orum Hall, Valparaiso, Indiana. How attractively this colours the opening of the famous *No. 9 in E major*, which has superb variety of bowing!

Ricci's Decca recording dates from 1959 but it is remarkably real, with a vivid presence. Ricci's playing often offers a breathtaking display of bravura and, oddly enough, his very occasional imperfections (usually minor slips of intonation) come at points where they are least expected – in the easier rather than the more difficult parts. The playing has great personality and the quicksilver articulation is often dazzlingly precise, conveying enormous dash, for instance in *No. 5 in A minor*. A most enjoyable and stimulating set, and the violin sounds life-size. However, Perlman and Accardo are even more polished.

Thomas Zehetmair has a somewhat more reticent personality and seems to want to avoid blazing virtuosity for its own sake. His style of articulation in the faster passages at times has an almost throwaway quality, but he soars most agreeably in the lyrical writing and his timbre above the stave is richly caught by the recording. There is much to appreciate and enjoy in these performances, but in the last resort Zehetmair projects less charisma than his competitors.

Paine, John Knowles (1839–1906)

Symphony No. 1 in C min., Op. 23; Overture, As you like it.
*** New World Dig. NW 374-2 [id.]. NYPO, Mehta.

Paine's symphonies were milestones in the history of American music, and it is good that at last Mehta's fine recordings of both of them will allow them to be appreciated more widely. Paine consciously inspires echoes of Beethoven, with little feeling of dilution – though, after his dramatic C minor opening, he tends to relax into sweeter, more Mendelssohnian manners for his second subject and the three other movements. What is striking is the bold assurance, and the overture is also full of charming ideas. Mehta is a persuasive advocate, helped by committed playing and full, well-balanced recording.

Symphony No. 2 in A, Op. 34.
*** New World Dig. NW 350-2 [id.]. NYPO, Mehta.

Written four years after the *First Symphony*, this magnificent work is both more ambitious and more memorable than its predecessor and, far more remarkably, anticipates Mahler. The idiom is notably more chromatic than that of the *First*, and the other movements – introduced by an extended slow introduction – bring an element of fantasy, as in the fragmented rhythms and textures of the Scherzo. Mehta draws a strongly committed performance from the New York Philharmonic, and the sound is first rate.

Paisiello, Giovanni (1740–1816)

Piano concertos Nos. 1–8.
(N) **(*) ASV Dig. CDDCS 229 (2) [id.]. Monetti, ECO, Gonley.

Piano concertos Nos. 1 in C; 5 in D; 7 in A; 8 in C.
*** ASV Dig. CDDCA 873 [id.]. Monetti, ECO, Gonley.

Piano concertos Nos. 2 in F; 3 in A; 4 in G min.; 6 in B flat.
**(*) ASV Dig. CDDCA 872 [id.]. Monetti, ECO, Gonley.

Mariaclara Monetti reveals herself to be an artist who can produce a silk purse out of more humble material, for her playing here is both sparkling and elegant. Paisiello obviously was primarily an opera composer, and these concertos, though not wanting grace or fluency, are often very conventional in most other respects. But with a ready facility Paisiello could certainly spin an expressive cantilena. As it happens, the *First Concerto* is one of the finest of the set in this respect, but so is No. 4 on the second disc. Nos. 5, 7 (especially) and 8 all have agreeably melodic slow movements. Paisiello was distinctly better at rondo finales than first movements, and those of both Nos. 1 and 7 stand out for their catchy ideas. There are some good moments elsewhere of course, but this repertoire would be more attractive on a bargain label. No complaints about the recording, and on the whole the first of the two discs is the one to go for. As can be seen, the eight concertos are also available as a boxed set, though with no saving in cost. (The two discs come in a slipcase.)

Il barbiere di Siviglia (opera): complete.
*** Hung. Dig. HCD 12525/6-2 [id.]. Laki, Gulyás, Gregor, Gati, Sólyom-Nagy, Hungarian State O, Adám Fischer.

Paisiello's *Barbiere di Siviglia* for many generations has been remembered only as the forerunner of Rossini's. The musical inspiration may too often be short-winded, but the invention is full of vitality, and that is reflected captivatingly in this Hungarian performance under Adám Fischer. Jószef Gregor is a vividly characterful Bartolo, a role more important here than in Rossini, while István Gati is a strong, robust Figaro. Krisztina Laki is a brilliant Rosina and Dénes Gulyás a clean, stylish Almaviva, relishing his Don Alonso imitation. Full, vivid recording.

Palestrina, Giovanni Pierluigi di (1525–94)

(i) *Good Friday Liturgy: Improperia (Reproaches). Lamentations of Jeremiah: No. 9, Incipit oratorio Jeremiae prophetae:* (iii) original and (ii) revised versions. (i) *Mass and Motet: Dum complerentur; Mass and motet: Tu es Petrus;* (iv) *Missa Papae Marcelli.* Motets: (ii) *Illumina oculos meos; Jubilate Deo; Laudate dominum omnes gentes; Pueri Hebraeorum.*
(M) ** DG Analogue/Dig. 439 961-2 (2). (i) Regensburger Domchor, Hans Schrems; (ii) cond. Theobald Schrems; (iii) Pro Cantione Antiqua, Bruno Turner; (iv) Westminster Abbey Ch., Simon Preston.

An interesting and well-planned Palestrina collection, if not one to laud to the skies, except for the Westminster Abbey performance of the *Missa Papae Marcelli.* The Regensburg Choristers sing wonderfully well in the works of Mozart and Haydn, but they have not quite the same fluency in music of the sixteenth century. Although the music flows well, the Mass singing is inclined to be square and here, as in the motets, the singers are not always careful to give the music plenty of light and shade. On the first CD *Incipit oratio Jeremiae prophetae* is heard from the Regensburgers, richly textured, in its shorter, revised version – although it is not absolutely sure that Palestrina himself made the revision. Then on the second disc Bruno Turner and his excellent Pro Cantione Antiqua give the original version containing a longer ending for the section, *Aquam nostram*, with a full repetition of the final phrase '*Lassis non dabatur*'. Performance tempi are very similar, but the latter takes over three minutes longer. Moreover Bruno Turner performs the work with a small vocal consort, with no more than two or three voices to each part. Its more limited sonority undoubtedly suits the *Lamentation*, which is beautifully sung. All this music is given good analogue recording from the early 1960s, although the definition of the words is misty. The second of the CDs opens with Simon Preston's digital recording of Palestrina's most famous work, the *Missa Papae Marcelli.* The account by the Westminster Abbey choristers transcends any such stylistic limitations. The digital recording is first class. All Saints', Tooting, was used rather than the Abbey, and the acoustics are both intimate and expansive, while detail is beautifully caught – a model of how to manage this repertoire on CD.

Ave Regina Caelorum; Lamentations of Jeremiah I–III; Gloriosi principes terrae; Missa in duplicibus minoribus II.
(Y/B) *** HM/BMG Dig. 05472 77317-2 [id.]. Maîtrise de Garçons de Colmar, Ens. Gilles Binchois, Cantus Figuratus, Dominique Vellard.

This ensemble produce singing of exceptional purity and quality. The Marian antiphon, *Ave Regina Caelorum*, is for two choruses, one high and one low, and was printed in 1575. The *Missa in duplicibus minoribus*, which belongs to the Mantuan repertory, was discovered in Milan as late as 1950 and is not otherwise available. All this material is sung with impressive control, a wonderfully integrated balance and great beauty of tone. Those who find Palestrina too bland should investigate this eloquent and beautifully recorded disc.

Canticum canticorum Salomonis (Fourth Book of Motets for 5 voices from the *Song of Songs*).
(Y/B) *** Hyperion Dig. CDA 66733 [id.]. Pro Cantione Antiqua, Bruno Turner.

The *Canticum canticorum Salomonis* is one of Palestrina's most sublime and expressive works, possibly wider in its range than anything else he composed, and certainly as deeply felt. His disclaimer in the dedication to Pope Gregory XIII, which Bruno Turner quotes at the beginning of his notes ('There are far too many poems with no other subject than love of a kind quite alien to the Christian faith'), cannot disguise the fervour which he poured into these 29 motets. The ten members of the Pro Cantione Antiqua under Bruno Turner bring an appropriate eloquence and ardour, tempered by restraint. They are accorded an excellently balanced and natural-sounding recording. This music is not generously represented on disc, but no one acquiring this is likely to be disappointed.

Canticum canticorum; Madrigals for 5 voices, Book I: 8 Madrigali spirituali.
(Y/B) (M) *** Virgin Veritas/EMI Dig. VED5 61168-2 (2) [id.]. Hilliard Ens., Paul Hilliard.

The Hilliard Ensemble provide beautifully shaped performances, with refined tonal blend and perfect intonation, but they are more remote and ultimately rather cool in emotional temperature. The second CD includes eight Petrarch settings from the First Book of Madrigals. Excellent recording.

Missa Aeterna Christi munera; Missa Papae Marcelli.
(Y/B) (BB) **(*) Naxos Dig. 8.550573 [id.]. Oxford Camerata, Jeremy Summerly.

Summerly's are bold, flowing performances, lacking something in mysticism and ethereal dynamics, but sung very confidently, with textures clear and the performances alive and compelling. The Oxford Camerata consists of twelve singers, of whom a third are female, and the blend is impressive. The account of the lesser-known *Missa Aeterna Christi munera* is particularly compelling. The recording was made in Dorchester Abbey, so the ambience is flattering, although the balance is fairly close.

Missa: Assumpta est Maria; Missa: Sicut lilium.
*** Gimell Dig. CDGIM 020; *1585T-20* [id.]. Tallis Scholars, Peter Phillips.

After the *Missa Papae Marcelli*, the *Missa: Assumpta est Maria* is one of Palestrina's most sublime works. Its companion on this CD is based on the motet, *Sicut lilium inter spinas* ('Like a lily among thorns'). As is their practice, the Tallis Scholars record the Masses together with the motets on which they are based, and sing with their customary beauty of sound and well-blended tone. They are superbly recorded in the Church of St Peter and St Paul in Salle, Norfolk.

Antiphon: Assumpta est Maria; Missa: Assumpta est Maria. Antiphon, Motet and Missa: Veni sponsa Christi. Magnificat VI toni.
(M) *** Decca 433 678-2 [id.]. St John's College, Cambridge, Ch., Guest.

The older St John's record of *Assumpta est Maria* sounds splendid on CD, if perhaps not so refined in texture as its digital competitor, and the St John's performance is thoroughly persuasive. The Decca couplings are even more generous (70 minutes) than on the Gimell CD and equally attractive. Some may find the presentation a little lacking in Latin fervour: the trebles sound distinctly Anglican. But this is fine singing by any standards, and has great purity of tone and beauty of phrasing.

Hodie Beata Virgo; Litaniae de Beata Virgine Maria in 8 parts; Magnificat in 8 parts (Primi Toni); Senex puerum portabat; Stabat Mater.
(M) *** Decca 421 147-2 [id.]. King's College Ch., Willcocks – ALLEGRI: *Miserere*. ***

The flowing melodic lines and serene beauty which are the unique features of Palestrina's music are apparent throughout this programme, and there is no question about the dedication and accomplishment of the performance. Argo's recording is no less successful, sounding radiantly fresh and clear.

Missa: Benedicta es (with *Plainchant*).
*** Gimell CDGIM 001; *1585T-01* [id.]. Tallis Scholars, Peter Phillips (with JOSQUIN: *Motet: Benedicta es*).

Palestrina's Mass is coupled with the Josquin motet, *Benedicta es*, on which it is based, together with the plainchant sequence on which both drew. It would seem that this Mass was the immediate predecessor of the *Missa Papae Marcelli* and was composed while the music of *Benedictus es* was still at the forefront of the composer's mind. The Tallis Scholars and Peter Phillips sing with impressive conviction and produce an expressive, excellently blended sound.

Missa brevis; Missa: Nasce la gioia mia (with PRIMAVERA: *Madrigal: Nasce la gioia mia*).
*** Gimell Dig. CDGIM 008; *1585T-08* [id.]. Tallis Scholars, Phillips.

The *Missa: Nasce la gioia mia* is a parody Mass, modelled on the madrigal, *Nasce la gioia mia* by Giovan Leonardo Primavera. The Tallis Scholars and Peter Phillips give expressive, finely shaped accounts of both the *Missa brevis* and the *Mass*, which they preface by the madrigal itself. A most rewarding disc: no grumbles about the recording.

Missa: Nigra sum (with motets on *Nigra sum* by LHERITIER; VICTORIA; DE SILVA).
*** Gimell Dig. CDGIM 003; *1585T-03* [id.]. Tallis Scholars, Phillips.

Palestrina's *Missa: Nigra sum* is another parody Mass, based on a motet by Jean Lheritier, and follows its model quite closely; its text comes from the Song of Solomon. On this record, the plainchant and the Lheritier motet precede Palestrina's *Mass*, plus motets by Victoria and Andreas de Silva, a relatively little-known Flemish singer and composer who served in the Papal chapel and later in Mantua. The music is inspiring and the performances exemplary. This is a most beautiful record and the acoustic of Merton College, Oxford, is ideal.

Missa Papae Marcelli.
*** Gimell CDGIM 339; *1585T-39* [id.]. Tallis Scholars, Phillips – ALLEGRI: *Miserere;* MUNDY: *Vox Patris caelestis.* ***

Missa Papae Marcelli; Missa brevis.
(Y/B) *** Hyperion Dig. CDA 66266 [id.]. Westminster Cathedral Choir, David Hill.

Missa Papae Marcelli; Tu es Petrus (motet).
*** DG 415 517-2 [id.]. Westminster Abbey Ch., Preston (with ANERIO: *Venite ad me omnes;* NANINO: *Haec dies;* GIOVANNELLI: *Jubilate Deo* ***) – ALLEGRI: *Miserere.* **(*)

David Hill and the Westminster Cathedral Choir give an imposing and eloquent *Missa Papae Marcelli* that many collectors may prefer to the finely sung Gimell issue from the Tallis Scholars. They, too, have the advantage of a spacious acoustic and excellent recording, and those for whom the visual element on the Tallis videotape and laserdisc offers no appeal may well prefer these fine performances.

The account by the Westminster Abbey choristers is a performance of great fervour, married to fine discipline, rich in timbre, eloquent both at climaxes and at moments of serenity. The singing is equally fine in the hardly less distinctive motet, *Tu es Petrus.* Felice Anerio, Giovanni Bernardino Nanino and Ruggiero Giovannelli represent the following generation of composers. Their contributions to this collection are well worth having, particularly Giovannelli's *Jubilate Deo* which makes a splendid closing item. The digital recording is first class.

The Gimell alternative is an analogue recording from 1980. The singing has eloquence, purity of tone, and a simplicity of line which is consistently well controlled.

Missa Papae Marcelli; Alma redemptoris Mater; Magnificat 1 toni; Nunc dimittis. Stabat mater; Surge illuminare.
(Y/B) *** Gimell Dig. CDGIM 994 [id.]. Tallis Scholars (with ALLEGRI: *Miserere* ***).

The Tallis Scholars are here recorded in the Basilica of Maria Maggiore in Rome, where Palestrina was a choirboy and, later, master of the choristers. The most celebrated of Palestrina's masses, *Missa Papae Marcelli*, receives as eloquent a performance as any in the catalogue. The Tallis Scholars have wonderful fluidity and the sense of movement never flags in this finely tuned, well-paced reading. Much the same goes for the remaining motets here and, of course, for the Allegri *Miserere*, which had a unique association with the Sistine Chapel until Mozart heard it and wrote it down from memory for performance elsewhere. As the recording was made before an audience, there is applause, which is quite inappropriate and very tiresome. In every other respect this is a first-class issue and can be warmly recommended. It should be noted that it is also available on videotape (GIMVP 994) and laserdisc (GIMLD 994). The cameras explore the rich artistic inheritance of the Basilica and enhance the sense of atmosphere and of occasion the performances engender; in its LD form, the sound is as impressive as on CD, but the VT is remarkably firm and wide-ranging tonally. Those with suitable players may well find this an inducement which sways them in its favour; those who strongly dislike applause will doubtless turn to the many excellent rival versions.

Missa Papae Marcelli; Alma Redemptoris Mater (antiphon); *Peccantem me quotidie* (motet); *Stabat Mater.*
(BB) **(*) ASV CDQS 6086. L. Pro Cantione Antiqua, Bruno Turner.

Bruno Turner uses small forces throughout his well-conceived programme (the concert opens with the Mass), and these are most beautiful performances of all four pieces, offering both intelligence and sensitivity in the handling of each line. Partly because of the recording balance, which is rather forward, one can hear the inner parts with uncommon clarity and, although this is not achieved at the expense of the overall sonority, some might feel that the clear and precise acoustic robs the music of some of its mystic atmosphere. This is not the only way of performing and recording Palestrina, but it is none the less impressive, and it makes one listen to the linear detail with fresh ears.

Missa Papae Marcelli; Stabat Mater.
(M) *** Carlton PCD 863 [id.]. Pro Cantione Antiqua, Mark Brown.

With an all-male choir and no boy trebles, and with one voice per part, the Pro Cantione Antiqua chamber choir yet sings with power and resonance against a warm and helpful church acoustic. The authentic atmosphere is enhanced by the inclusion of relevant plainchants between the sections of the *Mass*. The magnificent eight-part *Stabat Mater* also receives a powerful performance, warm and resonant.

Palmgren, Selim (1878–1951)

Barcarolle, Op. 14; Finnish rhythms, Op. 31; Illusion, Op. 1/2; Intermezzo Op. 3/4; 3 Piano pieces, Op. 54; Snowflakes, Op. 57/2; Sonette, Op. 4/3; Spring, Op. 27; Spring, Op. 47: 2 Pieces; Youth, Op. 28.
(N) *** Finlandia Dig. 4509-98991-2 [id.]. Izumi Tateno.

During the First World War the Finnish public found it easier to assimilate Palmgren's *Second* and *Fourth Piano concertos* and his piano miniatures than the more severe and challenging *Fourth* and *Fifth Symphonies* of Sibelius. Indeed, at one time in his homeland Palmgren was thought to be threatening Sibelius's pre-eminence. Palmgren will be remembered here by the older generation of piano students brought up on pieces like *May night* and *Moonlight*. He was spoken of as the 'Chopin of the north' for he wrote more idiomatically for the piano than Sibelius; but his music is limited both in its emotional range and in its repertory of pianistic devices. The present disc collects some of his early and middle-period music, from *Illusion* (which comes from his first published collection of 1899) through to the *Three Piano pieces*, Op. 54, of 1918. There is a certain poetic feeling, tinged at times by a hint of gentility. Palmgren was influenced by impressionism, though his melancholic sensibility is undoubtedly Nordic. Izumi Tateno is Japanese-born but has lived in Finland since his student days. He plays these pieces with great sympathy and is very well recorded.

Pandolfi Mealli, Giovanni Antonio (fl. 1660–69)

Violin sonatas: La cesta; La castella; La Clemente; La Sabbatina, Op. 3/2, 4, 5 & 6; La Bernabea; La Biancuccia; La vinciolina, Op. 4/1, 4 & 6; (i) Anon.: *Harpsichord suites in A, C & D.*
(Y/B) *** Channel Dig. CCS 5894 [id.]. Andrew Manze, (i) Richard Egarr, Fred Jacobs.

Giovanni Antonio Pandolfi Mealli's reputation rests on a single surviving copy of two sets of violin sonatas, six sonatas in each. Seven are recorded here, interspersed with three anonymous, French-influenced harpsichord suites, very different in style. The notes suggest the possibility that the composer was Christian Flor (1626–97). These are all rewarding and interesting scores, marvellously played by all concerned, and very well recorded too.

Panufnik, Andrzej (1914–91)

(i) *Arbor Cosmica;* (ii) *Symphony No. 3 (Sinfonia sacra).*
*** Elektra Nonesuch/Warner Dig. 7559 79228-2 [id.]. (i) NY Chamber Symphony; (ii) Concg. O; composer.

The *Sinfonia sacra* is one of Panufnik's most warmly and immediately communicative works, and here receives a magnificent performance from the Concertgebouw under the composer. As the title implies, *Arbor Cosmica* directly reflects a visual concept, this time the branches of a tree. The 12 'evocations' are all generated from a single three-note chord, each with the structure mapped out like a tree. The composer draws dedicated performances both from the Concertgebouw and the New York Chamber Symphony, with the former inevitably sounding richer and fuller.

(i) *Autumn music; Heroic overture;* (i, ii) *Nocturne;* (iii) *Sinfonia rustica;* (i) *Tragic overture.*
(M) *** Unicorn UKCD 2016. (i) LSO, Horenstein; (ii) with Anthony Peebles; (iii) Monte Carlo Op. O, composer.

The *Autumn music* and *Nocturne* may strike some listeners as musically uneventful, but the opening of the *Nocturne* is really very beautiful indeed and there is a refined feeling for texture and a sensitive imagination at work here. The *Sinfonia rustica* is the most individual of the works recorded here and has plenty of character. The performance under the composer is thoroughly committed. The LSO under Horenstein play with conviction and they are very well recorded.

(i) *Bassoon concerto;* (ii) *Violin concerto;* (iii) *Hommage à Chopin.*
*** Conifer Dig. 74321 16188-2 [id.]. (i) Thompson; (ii) Smietana; (iii) K. Jones; L. Musici, Stephenson.

The *Violin concerto* is a strongly atmospheric piece and is well worth a place in the repertory; it is beautifully played here by Krzysztof Smietana. The *Hommage à Chopin* owes its origin to a commission from Unesco. Panufnik composed five vocalises for voice and piano that make use of folk music from Masovia, in 1966 transcribing them for flute and orchestra; they could not have more persuasive advocacy than they do from Karen Jones and the London Musici. The *Bassoon concerto* (1985) is a darker piece, dedicated to the memory of the Polish priest, Jerzy Popieluszko, who was murdered that year; Robert Thompson plays it with great sensitivity. The London Musici under Mark Stephenson play with dedication throughout and, as the recording was made in the presence of the composer, it can be assumed to be authoritative. The Conifer sound, very well balanced at The Maltings, Snape, is first class.

Cello concerto.
*** NMC Dig. Single D 0105 [id.]. Rostropovich, LSO, Hugh Wolff.

The *Cello concerto* of Sir Andrzej Panufnik, his very last work, completed only days before his death in September 1991, is here presented by Rostropovich. The recording is even more successful at conveying the purposefulness of the writing than the first performance, bringing out the tautness of the palindromic structure, with the two movements, each in arch form, a mirror-image of the other, slow then fast. The result is not a drily schematic work, as one might expect, but a piece that in its warmth reflects the player who inspired it, strong and eventful with a more open lyricism than in many previous Panufnik compositions.

(i) *Piano concerto. Symphony No. 9 (Sinfonia della speranza).*
*** Conifer Dig. 74321 16189-2 [id.]. (i) Ewa Poblocka; LSO, composer.

In a massive single movement of 41 minutes Panufnik's *Ninth Symphony* brings a formidable example of the composer's fascination with translating geometric concepts into notes. The visual analogy here is with light travelling through a prism, and the accompanying booklet provides a diagram illustrating how the formula works, using a three-note cell refracted in various ways. The result has similarities with a gigantic passacaglia and there is no denying the symphony's strength. Panufnik's *Piano concerto* is not so extended, but carries comparable weight. The opening *Entrata* has a neo-classical flavour in its ostinatos for the solo instrument, leading to a bald, spare central slow movement. The mood is rather like that of some of Bartók's night music. By contrast, the finale is violently rhythmic with jazzy syncopations. Though the piano writing gives the soloist relatively little chance for conventional keyboard display, her playing adds to the power of the composer's purposeful interpretation. The piano tone is a degree too clangy, but otherwise the recording is spacious and full.

(i) *Concerto festivo;* (ii) *Concerto for timpani, percussion and strings; Katyń epitaph; Landscape;* (iii) *Sinfonia sacra (Symphony No. 3).*
(M) *** Unicorn UKCD 2020. (i) LSO, (ii) with Goedicke & Frye; (ii) Monte Carlo Op. O, composer.

This splendidly recorded collection might be a good place for collectors to begin exploring Panufnik's output. The *Concertos* are both readily communicative and the *Katyń epitaph* is powerfully eloquent. The best of this music is deeply felt. The *Sinfonia sacra* serves to demonstrate the spectacular quality of the vividly remastered recording, with its compelling introductory 'colloquy' for four trumpets, followed by a withdrawn section for strings alone. In the finale of the second part of the work, Hymn, the trumpets close the piece resplendently.

(i) *Concerto for timpani, percussion and strings. Harmony* (a poem for chamber orchestra); (ii) *Sinfonia concertante for flute, harp and strings.*
*** Conifer Dig. 75605 51217-2 [id.]. L. Musici, Mark Stephenson, with (i) Richard Benjafield, Graham Cole; (ii) Karen Jones, Rachel Masters.

The *Concertino* is a highly effective work based on a four-note motif, F-G-B-C; Panufnik creates an imaginative sound-world using both tuned and untuned percussion. The *Sinfonia concertante* is highly atmospheric, often hauntingly so, but somewhat more static. Karen Jones and Rachel Masters make a highly persuasive solo partnership. By far the most impressive work here is *Harmony*, written for the composer's wife, but as a celebration of their 25th wedding anniversary. Opening with a poignantly ethereal pianissimo on the violins, this distinctive 16-minute piece alternates passages for strings and wooodwind; then they finally join together and move to a passionately piercing climax. The performance here has great intensity and, given greater exposure, this piece could become really popular, after the manner of Barber's *Adagio*, though thematically it is more diffuse. Performance and recording throughout are first class.

Symphony No. 8 (Sinfonia votiva).
*** Hyperion Dig. CDA 66050 [id.]. Boston SO, Ozawa – SESSIONS: *Concerto for orchestra.* ***
(N) (M) **(*) BBC Radio Classics BBCRD 9124 [id.]. BBC SO, composer – SZYMANOWSKI: *Symphonies Nos. 3–4.* **(*)

The *Sinfonia votiva* has a strongly formalistic structure, but its message is primarily emotional. Though Panufnik's melodic writing may as a rule reflect the formalism of his thought rather than tapping a vein of natural lyricism, the result is most impressive, particularly in a performance of such sharp clarity and definition as Ozawa's, very well recorded.

Andrzej Panufnik conducting his own *Eighth Symphony* makes a useful alternative to Ozawa's full-price version on Hyperion. While it does not in any way displace the latter, it carries obvious advantages. Opinions may be divided on the music itself, not so much on the treatment of the material as on the quality of the ideas. The vein of lyricism is pretty thin, and he makes the ideas themselves last a long time.

Paray, Paul (1886–1979)

Mass for the 500th anniversary of the death of Joan of Arc.
(M) **(*) Mercury 432 719-2 [id.]. Yeend, Bible, Lloyd, Yi-Kwei-Sze, Rackham Ch., Detroit SO, Paul Paray – SAINT-SAENS: *Symphony No. 3.* ***

Paray's *Mass*, much admired by the composer, Florent Schmitt, could hardly have a more eloquent performance. The soloists are good and the choir are inspired to real fervour by their conductor, who at the close (in a brief recorded speech) expresses his special satisfaction with the singing of the closing, very romantic *Agnus Dei*. Excellent (1957) Mercury stereo, using the Ford Auditorium in Detroit.

Parry, Hubert (1848–1918)

(i) *The Birds: Bridal march;* (ii) *English suite; Lady Radnor's suite* (both for strings); *Overture to an unwritten tragedy; Symphonic variations.*
*** Lyrita SRCD 220 [id.]. (i) LPO; (ii) LSO; Boult.

The *Bridal march* comes from Parry's equivalent to Vaughan Williams's *Wasps*, a suite of incidental music for *The Birds*, also by Aristophanes. Here the rich, *nobilmente* string melody asserts itself strongly over any minor contributions from the woodwind aviary. The two *Suites* of dances for strings have some charming genre music and the *Overture* is very strongly constructed. But best of all is the set of variations, with its echoes of Brahms's *St Anthony* set and its foretastes of *Enigma*: a big work in a small compass. Boult's advocacy is irresistible. and the CD transfer demonstrates the intrinsic excellence of the analogue recordings, with gloriously full string sound.

Piano concerto in F sharp min.
(N) *** Hyperion Dig. CDA 66820 [id.]. Piers Lane, BBC Scottish SO, Martyn Brabbins – STANFORD: *Piano concerto.* ***

The *Piano concerto in F sharp minor* may at first seem rather naïve in the way it embraces a grand manner but, written in 1880, it is a relatively early work which appeals openly with its directness and lyricism. The Brahmsian echoes are supplemented in the finale by clear if momentary echoes of Bizet's *Carmen*, then a very new work. Piers Lane plays with feeling and brilliance, helped by beautiful sound.

Lady Radnor's suite.
*** Nimbus Dig. NI 5068 [id.]. E. String O, Boughton – BRIDGE: *Suite;* BUTTERWORTH: *Banks of green willow* etc. ***

Parry's charming set of pastiche dances, now given an extra period charm through their Victorian flavour, makes an attractive item in an excellent and generous English collection, one of Nimbus's bestsellers. Warm, atmospheric recording, with refined playing set against an ample acoustic.

Symphonies Nos. 1–5; Symphonic variations in E min.
*** Chandos Dig. CHAN 9120-22 [id.]. LPO, Matthias Bamert.

The rehabilitation of Parry has been long overdue; Chandos have now done this remarkable British nineteenth-century 'English Renaissance' musician full justice by recording the complete set of the symphonies. Bamert proves a masterly interpreter and takes us convincingly through the symphonic terrain of a highly influential composer about whom Elgar declared, 'He is our leader – no cloud of formality can dim the healthy sympathy and broad influence he exerts upon us. Amidst all the outpourings of modern English music the work of Parry remains supreme.' Bamert's set, discussed in detail below, is offered here complete on three CDs and includes also Parry's best-known orchestral work, the *Symphonic variations*.

Symphony No. 1 in G; Concertstück in G min.
*** Chandos Dig. CHAN 9062 [id.]. LPO, Bamert.

Symphony No. 1 in G; From death to life.
** Nimbus Dig. NI 5296 [id.]. English SO, Boughton.

Parry began work on his *First Symphony* in December 1880. Only a few weeks previously he had made his acquaintance with Brahms's *First*, and it had an obvious influence on him, not least in the grand main theme of his own finale. Bamert immediately demonstrates his response to the composer's muse in the way the opening *Con fuoco* sails off with a powerful thrust in the first movement. His control of the overall structure with its interrelated thematic material is most convincing, through the eloquent *Andante* and the Scherzo with its double trio, until he brings the finale to an impressively up-beat conclusion. He offers the earlier *Concertstück for orchestra* as coupling, almost equally convincingly performed, even though here the Wagnerian influences remain incompletely absorbed. The spacious Chandos recording seems exactly right for this pre-Elgarian opulence of symphonic thought.

William Boughton starts with the disadvantage of the very reverberant acoustic of the Great Hall of Birmingham University, which brings even greater opulence but a less clean focus and, at times, ill-defined orchestral detail. Boughton's reading displays a less firm grip on Parry's overall symphonic scheme and the resulting performance has altogether less cogency. His coupling, the symphonic poem, *From Death to Life*, is well played but not made to sound really memorable.

Symphony No. 2 in F (Cambridge); Symphonic variations.
*** Chandos Dig. CHAN 8961 [id.]. LPO, Matthias Bamert.

The *Second Symphony* opens confidently (with distinct Mendelssohnian associations) and Brahms's influence reappears in the main lyrical idea of the finale. In between there is a reminder of Dvořák in the Scherzo and of Schumann in the romantic warmth of the *Andante*. But for all its eclecticism and occasional longwindedness, notably in the finale, Parry finds his own voice and the music has a genuinely vital flow. Bamert's advocacy certainly holds the listener's attention and the orchestra responds with obvious relish. The *Symphonic variations* is certainly worth having on disc, even if it is nothing like as memorable as Elgar's *Enigma*. Excellent, full-bodied sound of the best Chandos vintage.

Symphonies Nos. 3 in C (English); 4 in E min.
*** Chandos Dig. CHAN 8896 [id.]. LPO, Matthias Bamert.

No. 3 is the most immediately approachable of the symphonies, with its bold melodies, often like sea-shanties, and its forthright structure. Yet it is No. 4 which proves even more rewarding, a larger-scale and more ambitious work which, amazingly, was never performed at all between the first performance of the revised version in 1910 and the present recording. The bold opening, in its dark E minor, echoes that of Brahms's *First Piano concerto*, leading to an ambitious movement lightened by thematic transformation that can take you in an instant into infectious waltz-time. The elegiac slow movement and jolly and spiky scherzo lead to a broad, noble finale in the major key. Bamert again proves a masterly interpreter, bringing out the warmth and thrust of the writing, akin to that of Elgar but quite distinct. The sound is rich and full to match the outstanding playing.

Symphony No. 5 in B min.; Symphonic variations; Elegy to Johannes Brahms; (i) *Blest pair of Sirens.*
(M) *** EMI CDM5 65107-2 [id.]. LPO, Boult, (i) with LPO Ch.

Symphony No. 5 in B min.; Elegy for Brahms; From death to life.
*** Chandos Dig. CHAN 8955 [id.]. LPO, Bamert.

The *Fifth* and last of Parry's symphonies is in four linked movements, terser in argument than the previous two in the series and often tougher, though still with Brahmsian echoes. After the minor-key rigours of the first movement, *Stress*, the other three movements are comparably subtitled *Love*, *Play* and *Now*, with the Scherzo bringing echoes of Berlioz and the optimistic finale opening with a Wagnerian horn-call. The *Elegy for Brahms* conveys grief, but its vigour rises above passive mourning into an expression of what might almost be anger. *From death to life* consists of two connected movements, exuberantly melodic, with a theme in the second which echoes Sibelius's *Karelia*. It would be hard to imagine finer, more committed performances than those on Chandos, or richer sound.

This was the last record made by Sir Adrian Boult, whose recording of the slow movement is particularly beautiful here. Equally impressive is the *Elegy*, not merely an occasional piece but a full-scale symphonic movement which builds to a powerful climax. The sharply inventive *Symphonic variations* fills out the Parry portrait. Recording and performances are exemplary, a fitting coda to Sir Adrian's recording career. To make the CD even more representative, it is good to welcome so enjoyably professional a motet as Parry's *Blest pair of Sirens*. The performance by the London Philharmonic Choir should be more incisive, but it still conveys much of the right atmosphere. Throughout, the digital remastering has been wholly beneficial.

Nonet in B flat.
*** Hyperion Dig. CDA 66291 [id.]. Capricorn – STANFORD: *Serenade (Nonet)*. ***

Parry's *Nonet* is for flute, oboe, cor anglais and two each of clarinets, bassoons and horns. Although the finale is perhaps a little lightweight, it is a delight from beginning to end. If one did not know what it was, one would think of early Strauss, for it is music of enormous accomplishment and culture as well as freshness. An excellent performance and recording.

(i) *Piano quartet in A flat; Piano trio No. 1 in E min.*
**(*) Mer. Dig. CDE 84248 [id.]. Deakin Piano Trio, (i) with Yuko Inoue.

After the success of the Chandos series of the Parry symphonies, it is good to have his chamber music appearing in a comparable Meridian series. In his actual idiom, Brahms and Schumann were still the more important influences, with diatonic melody providing clear-cut thematic material, well argued. The *E minor Piano trio*, the first of three that Parry wrote, is both shorter and more direct than the *Piano quartet*, which is more ambitious, with a darkly meditative slow introduction echoing late Beethoven. That leads to a clear-cut and happy main theme, and from then on introspection plays little part in the argument until the very end of the work. Though the performance on the disc is not as polished as one would like, Parry's melodic writing is more than distinctive enough to rebut the charge of mere imitation, with such a movement as the dashing tarantella-like Scherzo of the *Piano quartet* very effective indeed. The recording, made in a helpful acoustic at St Olave's School, Orpington, balances the piano rather behind the rest, which is a pity when Catherine Dubois so often takes the lead.

Piano trios Nos. 2 in B min.; 3 in G.
*** Mer. Dig. CDE 84255 [id.]. Deakin Piano Trio.

In the two *Piano trios* the English element in Parry's invention is more clearly identifiable, with some themes bringing anticipations of Elgar. Equally, the healthy outdoor feel of the triple-time main themes of the finales of both trios has a hint of English folk-music, while the folky element in the third-movement Scherzo of No. 2 is like a cross between Dvořák and Stanford, with Czech and Irish elements attractively intermingled. Both works are richly enjoyable, with the warm, open lyricism of the slow movement of No. 2 particularly attractive. The players of the Deakin Piano Trio seem more happily adjusted to the rigours of recording than in the first volume, with rather better matching and intonation.

Violin sonata in D, Op. 103; Fantasie-sonata in B, Op. 75; 12 short pieces.
*** Hyperion CDA 66157 [id.]. Erich Gruenberg, Roger Vignoles.

The *Fantasie-sonata* provides a fascinating example of cyclic sonata form, earlier than most but also echoing Schumann. The three-movement *Sonata in D* is another compact, meaty piece, the strongest work on the disc. The *Twelve short pieces*, less demanding technically, are delightful miniatures. Gruenberg and Vignoles prove persuasive advocates, and the recording is first rate.

VOCAL MUSIC

Blest pair of sirens; I was glad (anthems).
*** Chandos Dig. CHAN 8641/2 [id.]. London Symphony Ch. & LSO, Hickox – ELGAR: *Dream of Gerontius*. ***

Parry's two finest and most popular anthems make an attractive coupling for Hickox's fine, sympathetic reading of Elgar's *Dream of Gerontius*. The chorus for Parry is rather thinner than in the main work but is very well recorded.

Evening Service in D (Great): Magnificat; Nunc dimittis. Hear my words, ye people; I was glad when they said unto me; Jerusalem; Songs of farewell.

*** Hyperion CDA 66273 [id.]. St George's Chapel, Windsor, Ch., Christopher Robinson; Roger Judd (organ).

Everyone knows *Jerusalem*, which highlights this collection resplendently. In the *Songs of farewell* trebles are used and the effect is less robust than in Marlow's version, but undoubtedly very affecting. Perhaps the stirring coronation anthem, *I was glad*, needs the greater weight of an adult choir, but it is still telling here. The excerpts from the *Great Service in D* are well worth having on record, as is the anthem, *Hear my words, ye people*. Excellent recording, the chapel ambience colouring the music without blunting the words.

Songs of farewell.

*** Conifer Dig. 75605 51155-2 [id.]. Trinity College, Cambridge, Ch., Richard Marlow – STANFORD: *Magnificat* etc. ***

Parry's *Songs of farewell* represent his art at its deepest. Finest and most searching of the set is the Donne setting, *At the round earth's imagined corners*, with its rich harmonies poignantly intense and beautiful. Richard Marlow with his splendid Trinity Choir, using fresh women's voices for the upper lines instead of trebles, directs thoughtful, committed performances, very well recorded, which capture both the beauty and the emotion.

The Soul's ransom (sinfonia sacra); The Lotos eaters.

*** Chandos Dig. CHAN 8990 [id.]. Jones, Wilson-Johnson, LPO and Ch., Bamert.

Using a biblical text *The Soul's ransom*, with its sequence of solos and choruses, forms a broadly symphonic four-movement structure with references back not only to Brahms and the nineteenth century but to much earlier choral composers, notably Schütz. This 45-minute piece is generously coupled with *The Lotos eaters*, a setting for soprano, chorus and orchestra of eight stanzas from Tennyson's choric song of that name, with Della Jones again the characterful soloist. Full and atmospheric recording to match the incandescent performances.

Pärt, Arvo (born 1935)

(i) *Arbos* (two performances); (ii) *Pari Intervallo;* (iii) *An den Wassern zu Babel; De Profundis;* (iv; v) *Es sang vor langen Jahren;* (iii) *Summa;* (iii; v; vi) *Stabat Mater.*

*** ECM Dig. 831 959-2 [id.]. (i) Brass Ens., Stuttgart State O, Davies; (ii) Bowers-Broadbent; (iii) Hilliard Ens., Hillier; (iv) Bickley; (v) Kremer, Mendelssohn; (vi) Demenga.

All the music recorded here gives a good picture of Pärt's musical make-up with all its strengths and limitations. *Arbos*, which is heard in two different versions, 'seeks to create the image of a tree or family tree'. It does not modulate and has no development, though pitch and tempi are in proportional relationships. Like the *Cantus in memory of Benjamin Britten*, the *Stabat Mater* (1985) for soprano, counter-tenor, tenor and string trio is distinguished by extreme simplicity of utterance and is almost totally static. This music relies for its effect on minimal means and invites one to succumb to a kind of mystical, hypnotic repetition rather than a musical argument. The artists performing here do so with total commitment and are excellently recorded.

(i) *Cantus in memory of Benjamin Britten; Festina lente; Summa;* (i; ii) *Tabula rasa;* (ii) *Fratres; Spiegel im Spiegel.*

(M) *** EMI Dig. CD-EMX 2221; *TC-EMX 2221*. (i) Bournemouth Sinf., Richard Studt; (ii) Tasmin Little, Martin Roscoe.

An admirable and enterprising compilation from EMI Eminence to tempt those who have not yet sampled this composer's highly individual sound-world with its tintinnabulation (ringing bells). *Summa* is another version of the vocal *Creed* and is certainly effective, if not superior in its new costume. In the two chamber works Tasmin Little holds the listener's attention by the intensity of her commitment and the powerful projection of her playing. But most striking of all is the ambitious *Tabula rasa* with strong contrasts between the erupting energy of the opening *Ludus* and the aptly named second-movement *Silentium* which, of course, isn't silent but spins a compulsive atmospheric web. Fine performances and evocative sound, spread within an ecclesiastical acoustic, and first-rate recording combine to give this programme persuasive advocacy, if not to convince the listener that Pärt is one of the greatest composers of our time.

Collage on B-A-C-H; Cantus in memory of Benjamin Britten.
(Y/B) *** RCA Dig. 09026 68061-2 [id.]. Moscow Virtuosi, Vladimir Spivakov – SHOSTAKOVICH: *Chamber symphony No. 2;* DENISOV: *Variations;* SHCHEDRIN: *Stalin cocktail.* ***

These intense and very well-played performances show Pärt at his most imaginatively approachable. The three brief, neo-baroque movements (a spiccato *Toccata,* lyrical *Sarabande* – with engaging oboe solo, interrupted by saturated chords for strings and piano – and the dissonantly contrapuntal *Ricercar finale*) are like Bach seen through a distorting prism. The result is both inventive and colourful, while the Britten work uses descending scales against a tolling bell yet creates both brilliant textures and an intense climax. First-class recording and stimulating couplings.

Fratres (6 versions); *Cantus in memory of Benjamin Britten; Festina lente.*
(N) *** Telarc Dig. CD 80387 [id.]. Jane Manning, France Springuel, Mireille Gleizes, I Fiamminghi, Rudolph Werthen.

For all the repetitions involved in Pärt's minimalist progressions there are no more hypnotic examples of his curiously compelling, ritualistic writing than this sequence of six settings of a very simple monastic chorale which he calls *Fratres.* We hear it first slowly swelling up from a *piano-pianissimo* on strings, with unobtrusive decorative percussion, then sinking away again. Then follow variants featuring first a solo violin, then for a carefully blended wind octet, for eight cellos used in their higher register, then returning to a string group and quickening to achieve the flavour of an elegant baroque dance, further adapted to the more economical texture of a string quartet, and finally rustling on the cello with the piano tolling a bell-like accompaniment until a closing climax builds and abates. The Britten tribute and *Festina lente for strings and harp ad libitum* are used as interludes. The playing here has great atmosphere and concentration, while Telarc's glowing sound adds to the sensuous physical beauty.

Fratres; Summa (string quartet versions).
*** Virgin/EMI Dig. VC5 45023-2 [id.]. Chilingirian Qt – TAVENER: *Last Sleep of the Virgin* etc. ***

Like the Tavener works with which they are generously coupled on this 74-minute CD, these are both atmospheric works with a liturgical basis, using sparse basic material, which try to convey a sense of eternity. The performances here, obviously felt, make an interesting comparison with the alternative versions discussed above. But it must be admitted that, as music, they are less potent than the Tavener pieces.

Passio Domini Nostrum Jesu Christi secundum Joannem.
*** ECM Dig. 837 109-2 [id.]. Michael George, John Potter, Hilliard Ens., Western Wind Chamber Ch. (Instrumental group), Paul Hillier.

Pärt's *Passion of our Lord Jesus Christ according to St John* was composed in a bleak narrative style that reminds one of a mixture of Stravinsky and Schütz. It repeats the same scraps of ideas over and over again; it takes 70 minutes and never seems to leave the Aeolian mode, and it ought to be intolerable; yet in its way it is a strangely impressive experience, albeit not a wholly musical one. Impeccable recording and a dedicated performance.

Penderecki, Kryszstof (born 1933)

(i) *Anaklasis;* (ii; iii) *Capriccio for violin and orchestra;* (iii) *De natura sonoris I & II; The dream of Jacob; Fonogrammi; Threnody for the victims of Hiroshima;* (iv) *Canticum canticorum Salomonis.*
(M) *** EMI CDM5 65077-2 [id.]. (i) LSO; (ii) Wanda Wilkomirska; (iii) Polish Nat. RSO; (iv) Krakow Philharmonic Ch.; composer.

A splendid anthology and an admirable introduction to Penderecki's music. The longest work is the setting of a text from the *Song of Solomon* for large orchestra and sixteen solo voices. The other, shorter pieces will probably have a more lasting impact. The beautiful and touching *Threnody* for 53 strings (1959–61) is the best-known piece and originally made the composer's name internationally; it is here given a magnificent performance. So is the ambitious *Capriccio* in which Wilkomirska proves a superb soloist. *Anaklasis,* an inventive piece for strings and percussion, and *De natura sonoris* are more obviously brilliant in their use of contrasts, while *The dream of Jacob* of 1974 is as inventive as the rest but sparer and more cogent. Performances are definitive and the recordings, a co-production between EMI and Polish Radio, are of a very high standard.

The Awakening of Jacob; (i) *Cello concerto No. 2;* (ii) *Viola concerto. Paradise Lost: Adagietto.*
*** Polski Nagrania PNCD 020 [id.]. (i) Monighetti; (ii) Kamasa; Polish Nat. RSO, Antoni Wit.

The *Cello concerto No. 2* was written for Rostropovich, and this 1984 recording is impressively played by Ivan Monighetti. The *Viola concerto* is rather like skimmed Bartók; it brings masterly playing from Stefan Kamasa and the Polish Radio Orchestra. One cannot escape the suspicion that behind the mask of colour and orchestral trickery there is little real substance. However, these mid-1980s performances have plenty of ardour and commitment and are well recorded.

Violin concerto.
(N) (M) *** Sony Stern Edition II SMK 64507 [id.]. Stern, Minnesota O, Skrowaczewski – HINDEMITH: *Violin concerto.* ***

This concerto, written for Isaac Stern in 1977, marked Penderecki's return to a more conservative idiom. Even so, his fingerprints are clearly identifiable and the compression of thematic material, combined with spare, clean textures, makes for memorable results. The single movement, which lasts nearly 40 minutes, contains within it the traces of a funeral march, a Scherzo and a meditative adagio. The performance here is passionately committed, with Stern at his most inspired, and the recording is splendidly detailed. With its hardly less valuable Hindemith coupling, this is a key reissue in the second Box of Sony's Stern Edition.

String quartet No. 2.
*** Olympia OCD 328 [id.]. Varsovia Qt – SZYMANOWSKI: *Quartets;* LUTOSLAWSKI: *Quartet.* ***

Penderecki's *First quartet* lasts seven minutes; the *Second* is not much longer and is hardly more substantial. It is full of the gimmicks and clichés of the period. Whatever its merit, it is extremely well played.

Penella, Manuel (1880–1939)

El gato montes.
(Y/B) *** DG Dig. 435 776-2 (2) [id.]. Domingo, Villarroel, Pons, Berganza, Madrid SO, Miguel Roa.

This is a red-blooded performance of a melodramatic piece half-way between opera and zarzuela, which Plácido Domingo has a special affection for. He sings the role of the bullfighter, Rafael, in love with the heroine Soleá, who still keeps her affection for the bandit, Juanillo, *El gato montes,* 'The wildcat'. The writing is fluent and lyrical, with scenes punctuated by attractive orchestral pieces, notably the most celebrated, a paso doble. The musical invention may not be distinguished, but in such beefy performances, with Juan Pons in the title-role a genuine rival for Domingo, it is certainly attractive. The casting of the women principals is strong too, with Veronica Villarroel fresh and bright as the heroine and Teresa Berganza as characterful as ever as the Gypsy. Full, forward sound.

Pepping, Ernst (1901–81)

Passionsbericht des Matthäus.
** Chandos Dig. CHAN 8854 [id.]. Danish Nat. R. Ch., Parkman.

Ernst Pepping's style derives mainly from Reger, Distler and Hindemith, but he is a composer of quality. The *St Matthew Passion* is a rather extraordinary piece: a motet passion of the kind that flourished in the late Renaissance and early Baroque from Lassus through to Schütz but which was subsequently replaced by the dramatic settings of Bach. The Danish Radio Choir under Stefan Parkman rise to the challenge and give a generally good account of the piece, though the choral tone is not always cleanly focused. The music has integrity and beauty, and it improves as one comes closer to it, and the Danish Radio recording is good.

Pergolesi, Giovanni (1710–36)

Miserere II in C min.
(M) *** Decca 430 359-2. Wolf, James, Covey-Crump, Stuart, Magdalen College, Oxford, Ch., Wren O, Bernard Rose – A. and G. GABRIELI: *Motets.* **(*)

Pergolesi's *Miserere* is both ambitious and moving. The singers are all of quality, particularly Richard Stuart, and Bernard Rose secures expressive and persuasive results from the Magdalen College Choir and the Wren Orchestra. The (originally Argo) recording sounds magnificently real and vivid in its CD format.

(i) *Magnificat in C;* (ii) *Stabat Mater.*

(Y/B) (B) **(*) Decca Double 443 868-2 (2) [id.]. (i) Vaughan, J. Baker, Partridge, Keyte, King's College Ch., ASMF, Willcocks; (ii) Palmer, Hodgson, St John's College, Cambridge, Ch., Argo CO, Guest – BONONCINI: *Stabat Mater;* D. SCARLATTI: *Stabat Mater;* A. SCARLATTI: *Domine, refugium factus es nobis; O magnum mysterium;* CALDARA: *Crucifixus;* LOTTI: *Crucifixus.* ***

This well-planned Double Decca collection centres on three different settings of the *Stabat Mater dolorosa.* Pergolesi's version dates from 1735 and, subsequently, settings were made by many other composers, including Vivaldi and Haydn. Pergolesi conceived a work which has secular and even theatrical overtones, and its devotional nature is unexaggerated. George Guest directs a sensible, unaffected performance, simple and expressive, with relaxed tempi, not overladen with romantic sentiment. He has very good soloists, Felicity Palmer and Alfreda Hodgson blending very well together. It is a performance that does not emphasize the music's dramatic variety, and the choral singing, though felt, is not particularly vibrant. The *Magnificat* – doubtfully attributed, like so much that goes under this composer's name – is a comparatively lightweight piece, notable for its rhythmic vitality. The King's College Choir under Willcocks gives a sensitive and vital performance, and the recording matches it in intensity of atmosphere.

Stabat Mater.
*** DG 415 103-2 [id.]. Margaret Marshall, Valentini Terrani, LSO, Abbado.

(i; ii) *Stabat Mater;* (ii) *In coelestibus regnis;* (i) *Salve Regina in A.*
*** Hyperion Dig. CDA 66294 [id.]. (i) Gillian Fisher; (ii) Michael Chance; King's Consort, Robert King.

Abbado's account brings greater intensity and ardour to this piece than any rival, and he secures marvellously alive playing from the LSO – this without diminishing religious sentiment. The DG recording has warmth and good presence and the perspective is thoroughly acceptable. This is now a clear first choice.

The Hyperion recording makes a very good case for authenticity in this work. The combination of soprano and male alto blends well together yet offers considerable variety of colour. Gillian Fisher's *Salve Regina* is quite a considerable piece in four sections, whereas Michael Chance's motet is brief but makes an engaging postlude. Excellent sound.

Perotinus Magister (c. 1160–25)

Organa: *Alleluya, Nativitas; Sederunt principes.*
(N) *** Lyrichord LEMS 8002 [id.]. Russell Oberlin, Charles Bressler, Donald Perry, Seymour Barab – LEONIN: *Organa.* ***

Perotinus extended the simple polyphony of Leonin from two to three and four parts, and the ear is very aware of the intervals which characterize the organum: unison, octave, fourths and fifths. This music is more florid, freer than the coupled works written several decades before. The performances here are totally compelling and the recording excellent.

Pettersson, Allan (1911–80)

(i) *Viola concerto. Symphony No. 5.*
*** BIS Dig. CD 480 [id.]. (i) Nobuko Imai; Malmö SO, Moshe Atzmon.

Allan Pettersson's *Fifth* is a one-movement work and begins well. However, invention flags and the brooding, expectant atmosphere and powerful ostinatos arouse more promise of development than fulfilment. The *Viola concerto* comes from the last year of Pettersson's life and is pretty amorphous. Both pieces lack the concentration and quality of Tubin or Holmboe. The three stars are for the performers and the recording team.

Symphony No. 7.
*** Caprice Dig. CAP 21411. Swedish RSO, Comissiona – MOZART: *Bassoon concerto.* ***

Allan Pettersson's *Seventh Symphony* established him in the 1960s after a long period of neglect. A Swedish public, nourished on lashings of Blomdahl and a diet of serial and post-serial music, warmed to his tonal, post-Mahlerian language. The *Seventh* is a long, dark work which wears an anguished visage and packs a considerable emotional punch. Its musical substance is less weighty than appears to be the case on first acquaintance, and the ideas seem static and thinly spread; but it has a strong emotional appeal for many music-lovers and its atmosphere is quite powerful. Those who dismiss its composer impatiently as a self-pitying windbag should hear this work, which has an undoubted eloquence. Sergiu Comissiona gives a dedicated and sensitive account of the score that is every bit as fine as Dorati's première recording. The rather bizarre coupling is unlikely to sway the collector one way or the other.

Pfitzner, Hans (1869–1949)

(i) *Das Christ-Elflein: Overture, Op. 20. Palestrina: Preludes, Acts I, II and III.* (i; ii) *Duo for Violin, Cello and Small Orchestra, Op. 43;* (iii) Lieder: *Abbitte; Die Einsame; Der Gartner; Hast du von den Fischerkindern; Herbstgefühl; Hussens Kerker; In Danzig; Leuchtende Tage; Michaelskirchplatz; Nachts; Säerspruch; Zum Abschied meiner Tochter.*
(Y/B) (M) (***) EMI mono CDC5 55225-2 [id.] (i) Berlin State Opera O, composer; (ii) with Max Strub, Ludwig Hoelscher; (iii) Gerhard Hüsch; composer (piano).

Pfitzner recorded relatively little of his own music. The present, generously filled disc runs to 75 minutes and brings the 1931 Polydor recording of the three *Palestrina Preludes* and the 1927 *Christ-Elflein Overture.* The *Duo* was recorded much later, in 1938, but is a rather feeble piece; as Robin Holloway nicely puts it in the sleeve or liner-note, 'the overall impression is lacklustre, with flashes of impotent fire'. The *Lieder*, though by no means the equal of Schoeck in musical inspiration or poetic feeling, are worth having for the incomparable artistry and diction of Gerhard Hüsch. Pfitzner himself was by this time nearly seventy and given to overpedalling. (The songs were also available in a Preiser transfer, which includes the *Symphony in C* and the *Duo*, but neither of the other pieces.)

Palestrina (opera) complete.
(M) *** DG 427 417-2 (3) [id.]. Gedda, Fischer-Dieskau, Weikl, Ridderbusch, Donath, Fassbaender, Prey, Tölz Boys' Ch., Bav. R. Ch. & SO, Kubelik.
(Y/B) ** Berlin Classics Dig. BC 1001-2 (3) [id.]. Schreier, Lang, Lorenz, Wlaschiha, Hübner, Ketelsen, Peter Jürgen Schmidt, Nossek, German Op., Berlin, Ch., Berlin State O, Suitner.

Though Pfitzner's melodic invention hardly matches that of his contemporary, Richard Strauss, his control of structure and drawing of character through music make an unforgettable impact. It is the central Act, a massive and colourful tableau representing the Council of Trent, which lets one witness the crucial discussion on the role of music in the church. The outer Acts – more personal and more immediately compelling – show the dilemma of Palestrina himself and the inspiration which led him to write the *Missa Papae Marcelli*, so resolving the crisis, both personal and public. At every point Pfitzner's response to this situation is illuminating, and this glorious performance with a near-ideal cast, consistent all through, could hardly be bettered in conveying the intensity of an admittedly offbeat inspiration. This CD reissue captures the glow of the Munich recording superbly and, though this is a mid-price set, DG has not skimped on the accompanying booklet.

Recorded live at concert performances given in Berlin – Acts I and III in 1986, Act II in 1988 – the Berlin Classics issue of Pfitzner's epic opera is chiefly distinguished by the animated, characterful singing of Peter Schreier in the title-role. In almost every other way, even in the recorded sound, this set, worthy as it is, cannot quite match Kubelik's magnificent version, but Schreier's portrait of the much-troubled polyphonic master is well worth hearing, even more thoughtful and intense than that of Nicolai Gedda for Kubelik.

Pierné, Gabriel (1863–1937)

Les Cathédrales: Prelude (No. 1); Images, Op. 49; Paysages franciscains, Op. 43; Viennoise (suites de valses et cortège blues), Op. 49 bis.
(M) *** EMI CDM7 63950-2. Loire PO, Pierre Dervaux.

The opening *Prélude* to *Les Cathédrales* is an evocation of the desolation caused by war; while *Images* is full of touches of pastiche – a reference to Dukas's *La Péri* in the opening, an allusion to Debussy's *Gigues*, and so on – and there follows a set of pieces, *Viennoise*, in which Pierné developed two of the numbers in the divertissement as 'valses et cortège blues'. The three picturesque *Paysages franciscains* betray the composer's love of Italy. All of this is rewarding music in the best French tradition, extremely well played, and the recording has plenty of warmth and atmosphere.

Pijper, Willem (1894–1947)

String quartets Nos. 1–5.
(Y/B) *** Olympia Dig. OCD 457 [id.]. Schönberg Qt.

Willem Pijper was a dominant force in Dutch music between the wars. This CD collects all five of his *String quartets*. The post-war *Fifth Quartet* (1946) was left unfinished at his death, though two movements were completed. Pijper's music is concentrated and thoughtful, eminently civilized and predominantly gentle in outlook, even if it falls short of having that unmistakable and distinctive voice betokening a great composer. The Schönberg Quartet is one of the finest Dutch ensembles, and they are beautifully recorded. A rewarding disc, well worth investigating.

Pinto, George Frederick (1785–1806)

Piano sonatas Op. 3/1–2; Fantasia and sonata in C min.; Grand sonata in C min. (To his friend, John Field).
(N) ** Olympia OCD 494 [id.]. Riko Fukuda (fortepiano).

Pinto was a musical prodigy in London at the turn of the eighteenth century and these works date from between 1801 and 1808. They show Pinto to be a conventional composer, although undoubtedly he anticipates the style of early Beethoven. He has a few good ideas (as at the very opening of the *Sonata*, Op. 3/1, or the *Adagio* of Op. 3/2), but his allegros seldom mine any deep level of argument. Riko Fukuda's performances are robust but sympathetic. Truthful recording.

Piston, Walter (1894–1976)

(i; ii) *Capriccio for harp and strings;* (ii) *3 New England sketches;* (iii) *Serenata;* (ii) *Symphony No. 4.*
🏵 *** Delos Dig. DE 3106 [id.]. (i) Wunrow; (ii) Seattle SO; (iii) NY CO; Gerard Schwarz.

Piston's *Fourth* is arguably the finest American symphony, as powerful in its forward sweep as the Harris *Third* and better held together than either Barber's *First* or Copland's *Third*. The remaining pieces, not only the *New England sketches* but also the inventive *Capriccio for harp and strings*, are well worth seeking out. The fine recording and Gerard Schwarz's natural and unforced direction make this a most desirable CD. The slow movement of the *Serenata*, equally well played by New York forces, is quite inspired.

The Incredible flutist (ballet; complete); *New England sketches; Symphony No. 6* (1955).
*** RCA Dig. RD 60798 [60798-2-RC]. St Louis SO, Leonard Slatkin.

Walter Piston's ballet, *The Incredible flutist*, is one of the most refreshing and imaginative of all American scores. The most powerful work on Slatkin's disc is the *Sixth Symphony*, about which Piston wrote rather disarmingly, 'It seemed as though the melodies were being written by the instruments themselves as I just followed along,' and there is an inexorable sense of logic and inevitability. Piston is a cultivated, refined symphonist who does not wear his heart on his sleeve. The playing of the St Louis orchestra under Leonard Slatkin both here and in the *New England sketches* is sensitive and brilliant, and the RCA engineers give them excellent quality.

Symphonies Nos. 5; (i) *7 and 8.*
** Albany AR 011 [id.]. Louisville O, Whitney, (i) Mester.

The *Fifth Symphony* has a sureness of purpose and feeling for organic growth that are the hallmark of the true symphonist. The *Seventh* and *Eighth Symphonies*, though not quite the equal of the finest Piston, are powerful and rewarding works which will speak to those who are more concerned with substance than with surface appeal. The Louisville performances are thoroughly committed and good, without being outstanding. The recordings sound better than they did on LP.

(i) *Piano quintet. Passacaglia; Piano sonata; Toccata.*
**(*) Northeastern/Koch Int. Dig. NR 232-CD [id.]. Leonard Hokanson; (i) Portland Qt.

The *Piano quintet* must be numbered among the finest post-Second World War piano quintets; it is a work of great vitality and integrity. These artists give a more than respectable account of it, and Leonard Hokanson proves no less convincing and responsive in the early *Piano sonata*. The recording is fully acceptable.

String quartets Nos. 1–3.
** Northeastern/Koch Dig. NR 9001-CD [id.]. Portland Qt.

Piston's five *String quartets* are finely crafted pieces, sinewy and Hindemithian at times (the first movement of No. 1), thoughtful and inward-looking at others (the Lento opening of No. 2 and the slow
movement of No. 3). His music never wears its heart on its sleeve, but if its emotional gestures are
restrained there is no real lack of warmth. The Portland Quartet play well and the recordings are clear,
although the acoustic is a little on the small side.

Pizzetti, Ildebrando (1880–1968)

*Messa di Requiem. Due composizioni corali: Il giardino di Afrodite; Piena sorgeva la luna. Tre compo-
sizioni corali: Cade la sera; Ululate; Recordare, Domine.*
*** Chandos Dig. CHAN 8964 [id.]. Danish Nat. R. Chamber Ch., Stefan Parkman.

Pizzetti wrote with exceptional sympathy for voices, and his *Requiem* is a work of striking beauty and
purity of utterance. In his note John Waterhouse speaks of it as occupying something of the same
position in Italian music as the Vaughan Williams *Mass in G minor* does in English music. This Chandos
issue has the merit of offering two other Pizzetti rarities in performances of high quality by the Danish
Radio Chamber Choir, and there is no doubt that this is a most rewarding issue, one of the finest choral
records of recent years.

Pleyel, Ignaz (1757–1831)

(i) *Sinfonia concertante for violin, cello and strings in D. Symphony in A; Flute quartet in B.*
(Y/B) (BB) ** Discover Dig. DICD 920130 [id.]. (i) Bushkov, Kozodov; Moscow Concertino (members), Evgueni Bushkov.

The name of Ignaz Pleyel is famous as a French manufacturer of pianos but, around the time that
Haydn was visiting London for the Salomon concerts, Pleyel was far better known as a composer and
his easily tuneful, facile music was enormously popular. His writing is a bit like Boccherini without the
pathos. Here the *Flute quartet* (for flute, violin, viola and cello) has surface charm and the *Symphony* is
fluent, if rather too long. It has a catchy theme for its closing *Rondo*, and the *Sinfonia concertante* –
easily the best work here, and half as long as the *Symphony* – is full of similarly neat invention and again
brings an engaging finale. The whole programme is given persuasive advocacy by this excellent Russian
group who are thoroughly within the style of the music and play with expert precision and much vitality.
The snag is that they are forwardly balanced and rather dryly recorded, and the dynamic contrast of
their playing is reduced by the close microphones. Even so, this inexpensive disc gives a fascinating
glimpse of an interesting and distinctly talented musician.

Ponce, Manuel (1882–1948)

Folia de España (Theme and variations with fugue).
(M) *** Sony SBK 47669; SBT 47669 [id.]. John Williams (guitar) – BARRIOS: *Collection.* ***

Ponce's *Variations on 'Folia de España'* are subtle and haunting, and their surface charm often conceals
a vein of richer, darker feeling. The performance is first rate and the sound admirably clean and finely
detailed, yet at the same time warm.

Ponchielli, Amilcare (1834–86)

La Gioconda (complete).
*** Decca Dig. 414 349-2 (3) [id.]. Caballé, Baltsa, Pavarotti, Milnes, Hodgson, L. Op. Ch., Nat. PO,
Bartoletti.
*** EMI CDS7 49518-2 (3) [Ang. CDCC 49518]. Callas, Cossotto, Ferraro, Vinco, Cappuccilli,
Companeez, La Scala, Milan, Ch. & O, Votto.
(N) (M) ** Decca 444 598-2 (3) [id.]. Milanov, Elias, Di Stefano, Warren, Santa Cecilia Ac., Rome, Ch. &
O, Previtali.

The colourfully atmospheric melodrama of this opera gives the Decca engineers the chance to produce
one of their most vivid opera recordings. Caballé is just a little overstressed in the title-role but produces

glorious sounds. Pavarotti has impressive control and heroic tone. Commanding performances too from Milnes as Barnaba, Ghiaurov as Alvise and Baltsa as Laura, firm and intense all three. Bartoletti proves a vigorous and understanding conductor, presenting the blood and thunder with total commitment but finding the right charm in the most famous passage, the *Dance of the hours*.

Maria Callas gave one of her most vibrant, most compelling, most totally inspired performances on record in the title-role of *La Gioconda*, with flaws very much subdued. The challenge she presented to those around her is reflected in the soloists – Cossotto and Cappuccilli both at the very beginning of distinguished careers – as well as the distinctive tenor Ferraro and the conductor Votto, who has never done anything finer on record. The recording still sounds well, though it dates from 1959.

The Previtali set is worth hearing for a vintage performance from Zinka Milanov, rather past her best, with raw tone both above and below, but she floats a glorious top B flat on *Come t'amo*. Leonard Warren was another favourite singer at the Met., but his somewhat woolly baritone did not always record well. Di Stefano, however, produces much heroic tone, and the recording is fair for its late-1950s vintage.

Popov, Gavril (1904–1972)

(i) *Symphonies Nos. 1, Op. 7;* (ii) *2 (Motherland), Op. 39.*
(N) **(*) Olympia Dig./Analogue OCD 576 [id.]. (i) Moscow State SO; (ii) USSR R. & TV SO;
    Gennady Provatorov.

Along with Shostakovich, Prokofiev and Miaskovsky, Gavril Popov was singled out for condemnation at the Soviet composers' conference, presided over by Zhdanov in 1948. An accomplished all-round musician and a pupil of Vladimir Shcherbachov in Leningrad, Popov appeared as a pianist with Shostakovich in the Mozart *E flat Concerto*, K.365, and was a prolific composer for the cinema, providing music for 38 films, including some by Eisenstein. He gave us six symphonies in all, plus a good deal of chamber music as well as an opera on *Alexander Nevsky*. His *First Symphony* occupied him during 1928–34 and not long before the *Lady Macbeth* affair was denounced as formalistic and 'ideologically alien to Soviet order'. He had established himself sufficiently in early 1930s Germany with his *Septet* for Malko, Klemperer, Scherchen and Erich Kleiber to compete with one another for the first performance of the *First Symphony*. The first movement is over 20 minutes long, inventive and powerful, though indebted to Shostakovich, his junior by two years. The wartime *Second Symphony* (1943) opens with a long and expansive slow movement, not without overtones of the cinema, while the lively *Presto* sounds as if it has strayed out of *Petrushka*. Perhaps the most eloquent movement is the third, a soulful and powerfully sustained threnody. Small wonder Shostakovich admired his music, which is finely paced, expertly constructed and brilliantly scored. The performances under Gennady Provatorov are totally committed, though the recordings are not wholly satisfactory. The *First* was made in 1989 and is digital; the *Second* dates from 1961 and is perhaps a little shallow but perfectly acceptable. This should not, however, deter readers from investigating this interesting music which is every bit as rewarding as Vainberg, Kancheli and Schnittke (and probably more).

Porter, Cole (1891–1964)

Overtures: *Anything goes; Can-Can; Gay divorce; Kiss me, Kate. Night and day* (from *Gay divorce*).
(N) (B) *** EMI forte Dig. CZS5 68589-2 (2). L. Sinf., McGlinn – GERSHWIN: *Broadway and film
    music* **(*); KERN: *Overtures.* **

These overtures were not put together or scored by the composer but by the professionals of the day. As *Gay divorce* does not include the most famous number from the show, a separate arrangement of *Night and day* has been included, richly scored. The performances here are definitive and the bright recording fits the music like a glove.

Song arrangements for orchestra: *Anything goes; Begin the beguine; Blow, Gabriel blow; In the still of the night; It's de-lovely; I've got you under my skin; My heart belongs to Daddy; Night and day; It's all right with me; Ridin' high; So in love; You'd be so nice to come home too* (all orch. Ray Wright).
(M) **(*) Mercury 434 327-2 [id.]. O, Frederick Fennell – GERSHWIN: *Song arrangements.* **(*)

The lyrics are missed more than most with orchestral arrangements of Cole Porter songs and, though Ray Wright's scoring is imaginative and admirably sophisticated, this is essentially a CD to use as a pleasing background for a dinner party, rather than for concentrated listening. Unusually for this label, the recording is multi-miked, so the stereo effects are unashamedly directional. But the sound is silky-smooth as well as being clearly defined and, of its kind, this is very good indeed.

Kiss me Kate (musical).
*** EMI Dig. CDS7 54033-2 (2). Barstow, Hampson, Criswell, Dvorsky, Burns, Evans, Amb. Ch., L. Sinf., John McGlinn.

Having two opera-singers, Josephine Barstow and Thomas Hampson, in the principal roles of the ever-argumentative husband-and-wife team who play Kate and Petruchio in *The Taming of the Shrew* works excellently, both strong and characterful. Kim Criswell is delectable as Lois Lane, brassy but not strident in *Always true to you, darling, in my fashion*. Strong characterization too from George Dvorsky, Damon Evans and Karla Burns, with the London Sinfonietta playing their hearts out. The recording is full and vivid with enough atmosphere to intensify the sense of presence.

Songs: *After you; Don't look at me that way; Ev'ry time we say goodbye; I concentrate on you; I love Paris; In the still of the night; It's all right with me; I've got you under my skin; Just one of those things; Let's misbehave; Night and day; Ridin' high; So in love; True love; You'd be so nice to come home to.*
(Y/B) ** EMI Dig. CDC5 55050-2 [id.]. Kiri Te Kanawa, New World PO, Peter Matz.

A disappointment. Kiri's rich vocal-line cannot fail to make an effect in a song like *Night and day*, and her sensuous allure is suitable for some other numbers, like *In the still of the night*. But overall the effect is blandly sensuous with not enough sparkle. Good arrangements and sumptuous sound.

Songs: *Begin the Beguine; Bring me back my butterfly; Bull Dog; Don't fence me in; Drink; Easy to love; A fool there was; How's your romance?; I concentrate on you; In the still of the night; It was written in the stars; I've got you under my skin; My cozy little corner in the Ritz; Night and day; Two little babes in the wood; When I had a uniform on; When my baby goes to town; Who said Gay Paree?.*
*** EMI Dig. CDC7 54203-2 [id.]. Thomas Hampson, Ambrosian Ch., LSO, McGlinn.

Thomas Hampson proves an ideal baritone for this repertory, totally inside the idiom, yet bringing to it a gloriously firm, finely controlled voice. The selection is a delightful one, including not just popular 'standards' but unexpected rarities. Excellent sound.

Let's do it; Miss Otis regrets; My heart belongs to Daddy; The physician; Night and day.
(*) Unicorn Dig. DKPCD 9138 [id.]. Jill Gomez, Martin Jones, Instrumental Ens. – BRITTEN: *Songs.* *

Though the accompanist, Martin Jones, is too stiff and deadpan in these five classic Cole Porter songs, Jill Gomez is so warmly expressive a singer that the dry backing serves to add to the poignancy of songs like 'Miss Otis Regrets'. Despite the reservations, a good coupling for the Britten items.

Poulenc, Francis (1899–1963)

(i) *Les animaux modèles;* (ii; iii) *Les biches* (complete ballet); (ii) *Bucolique;* (i; iv) *Concert champêtre (for harpsichord & orchestra);* (i; v) *Double piano concerto in D min.;* (vi) *2 Marches et un intermède (for chamber orchestra); Les mariés de la Tour Eiffel (La baigneuse de Trouville; Discourse du Général).* (ii) *Matelote provençale; Pastourelle;* (vi) *Sinfonietta; Suite française.*
(B) *** EMI Analogue/Dig. CZS7 62690-2 (2). (i) Paris Conservatoire O; or (ii) Philh. O; (iii) with Amb. S.; (iv) with Van de Wiele, or (v) composer and Février; (vi) O de Paris; all cond. Prêtre.

Les biches comes here in its complete form, with the choral additions that Poulenc made optional when he came to rework the score. The music is a delight, and so too is the group of captivating short pieces, digitally recorded at the same time (1980): *Bucolique, Pastourelle* and *Matelote provençale*. High-spirited, fresh, elegant playing and sumptuous recorded sound enhance the claims of all this music. The *Suite française* is another highlight. It is well played and recorded in a pleasing, open acoustic. Poulenc himself was a pianist of limited accomplishment, but his interpretation (with partner) of his own skittish *Double concerto* is infectiously jolly. In the imitation pastoral concerto for harpsichord, Aimée van de Wiele is a nimble soloist, but here Prêtre's inflexibility as a conductor comes out the more, even though the finale has plenty of high spirits. The *Sinfonietta*, too, could have a lighter touch, but it does not lack personality. *Les animaux modèles* is based on the fables of La Fontaine, with a prelude and a postlude, but here the recording is rather lacking in bloom, and the *Deux Marches* are also a trifle overbright. With nearly 156 minutes' playing time, these CDs are well worth exploring.

Les animaux modèles; Les biches (ballet): *suite; Les mariés de la Tour Eiffel: 2 Marches et un intermède.*
** Claves Dig. CD 50-9111[id.]. SW German RSO, Baden-Baden, Viotti.

Marcello Viotti gets a more Gallic sound from his Baden-Baden orchestra and more stylish results too in *Les biches* than Bychkov does from the Orchestre de Paris. But neither good playing nor decent recording make for a really strong recommendation, given the brevity of the programme on offer, a mere 48 minutes 39 seconds. Uneconomic, given the fact that this is at full price.

(i) *Aubade (Concerto chorégraphique);* (ii) *Concert champêtre for harpsichord and orchestra;* (iii) *Organ concerto in G min.;* (i) *Piano concerto in C sharp min.;* (i; iv) *Double piano concerto in D min.*
✸ (B) *** Erato/Warner Duo Dig. 4509 95303-2 (2) [id.]. Rotterdam PO, James Conlon, with (i) Duchable; (ii) Koopman; (iii) Alain; (iv) Collard.

(i) *Aubade; Piano concerto;* (i; ii) *Double piano concerto.*
(M) *** Erato/Warner Dig. 0630 13738-2 [id.]. Rotterdam PO, Conlon, with (i) Duchable; (ii) Collard.

This Erato Bonsai Duo is one of the most attractive of all Poulenc issues. The *Aubade* is an exhilarating work of great charm. It dates from the late 1920s and is a send-up of Mozart, Stravinsky etc. The *Piano concerto* has a most beguiling opening theme and evokes the faded charms of Paris in the '30s. The skittish *Double concerto* is infectiously jolly. One could never mistake the tone of voice intended. The performances of two of the solo works by François-René Duchable and the Rotterdam orchestra have a certain panache and flair that are most winning. The *Double concerto* too captures all the wit and charm of the Poulenc score, with the 'mock Mozart' slow movement particularly elegant. Perhaps in these two solo works Duchable is a shade too prominent, but not sufficiently so to disturb a strong recommendation, for the sound is otherwise full and pleasing. The *Organ concerto*, too, has never come off better on record than in Marie-Claire Alain's performance using the excellent Flenthrop organ in Rotterdam's concert hall, the Doelen. The *Concert champêtre* always offers problems of balance as it is scored for a full orchestra, but the exaggerated contrast was clearly intended by the composer. The performance is most perceptive, with a particularly elegant and sparkling finale. James Conlon provides admirable accompaniments throughout a highly recommendable pair of discs. As can be seen, three of these works are also available separately at mid-price, but the Duo is well worth its small extra cost.

Aubade (Concerto chorégraphique); Piano concerto in C sharp min.; (i) *Double piano concerto in D min.*
(M) **(*) EMI CDM7 64714-2 [id.]. Tacchino, (i) Paris Conservatoire O; (ii) Ringeissen, Monte Carlo PO; Prêtre.

On EMI the performance of the *Aubade* is nicely pointed, and the *Concerto* too receives a finely poised and brilliantly executed performance. However, the *Double concerto*, where Gabriel Tacchino is joined by Bernard Ringeissen, is disappointing, with the result brash and hard-driven. It was a great pity that EMI didn't choose the composer's own version of this work with Jacques Février. Poulenc may have been only an amateur pianist, but his interpretation (with partner) had an agreeable lightness of touch, bringing out all the humour.

Aubade; Sinfonietta.
*** Hyperion Dig. CDA 66347 [id.]. New London O, Corp – HAHN: *Le bal de Béatrice d'Este.* ***

The *Sinfonietta* is a fluent and effortless piece, full of resource and imagination, and Ronald Corp and the New London Orchestra do it proud. This performance has a real sense of style and Gallic elegance. Julian Evans is an alert soloist in the *Aubade*: his is a performance of real character and, though less well balanced than the *Sinfonietta*, he can hold his own artistically with the best. The Hahn rarity with which it is coupled enhances the interest and value of this release.

(i) *Aubade. Improvisations; Mouvements perpétuels; 2 Novelettes; Nocturnes;* (ii) *Trio for oboe, bassoon and piano.*
(***) (M) EMI mono CDC5 55036-2 [id.]. Composer, with (i) Straram CO, Walther Straram; (ii) Roger Lamorlette, Gustave Dhérin – HONEGGER: *Cello concerto* etc. (***)

While he was not the most elegant or finished of pianists, Poulenc's playing had plenty of character, nowhere more so than in the 1930 recording of the *Aubade for piano and eighteen instruments* which sounds remarkably fresh, save, perhaps, for the rather papery timbre of the solo instrument. The solo pieces generally come off well, though the composer occasionally sounds as if another hour's practice wouldn't have come amiss! Splendid playing from the Walther Straram players (there is a striking period flavour here) and in particular from Roger Lamorlette and Gustave Dhérin, the two wind players in the *Trio*, recorded in 1928. Allowances have to be made for variable quality – but, for all that, this disc is not to be missed.

Les biches (ballet; complete).
**(*) Ph. Dig. 432 993-2 [id.]. Ch. & O de Paris, Semyon Bychkov – HONEGGER: *Pacific 231;* MILHAUD: *Le bœuf sur le toit.* **(*)

Semyon Bychkov and the Orchestre de Paris offer us the complete choral version of *Les biches* – though, to be fair, the chorus are heard in only three movements. Bychkov gives a goodish account of the score, though it is not quite as light or as Parisian as the Prêtre version, which is to be preferred (see above). At times Bychkov makes slightly heavy weather of one or two of the numbers. Perhaps the beefier recording and the thicker sonority at the bottom end of the range are to blame.

Les biches (ballet suite).
*** Chandos Dig. CHAN 9023 [id.]. Ulster O, Yan Pascal Tortelier – IBERT: *Divertissement*; MILHAUD: *Le bœuf; La création.* ***

Yan Pascal Tortelier and the Ulster Orchestra give an entirely winning account of Poulenc's ballet suite. Here the opening has delightfully keen rhythmic wit, and the playing is equally polished and crisply articulated in the gay *Rag-Mazurka* and infectious *Final*. The lovely *Adagietto* is introduced with tender delicacy, yet reaches a suitably plangent climax. Top-drawer Chandos sound and splendid couplings ensure the overall success of this admirable compilation.

(i) *Concert champêtre; Concerto in G min. for organ, strings and timpani;* (ii) *Piano concerto in C sharp min.;* (iii; iv) *Double piano concerto;* (v) *Sextet for piano, flute, oboe, clarinet, bassoon & horn;* (iii) *Sonata for 2 pianos;* (vi) *Gloria.*
(N) (B) *** Decca Double Analogue/Dig. 448 270-2 (2) [id.]. (i) Malcolm (harpsichord or organ), ASMF, Iona Brown; (ii) Rogé, Philh. O, Dutoit; (iii) Eden & Tamir; (iv) SRO, Comissiona; (v) Rogé, Gallois, Bourgue, Portal, Wallez, Cazalet; (vi) Greenberg, Lausanne Pro Arte Ch., SRO, López-Cobos.

George Malcolm pairs an excellent account of the *Organ concerto* with the *Concert champêtre*; in the latter he changes over to the harpsichord with equal felicity. In this work the engineers did not succumb to the temptation to make the solo instrument sound larger than life. Some might feel that in the finale Malcolm rushes things a bit, but the music effervesces and in every other respect this is an exemplary account. Pascal Rogé is completely attuned to the spirit and sensibility of this still-underrated master and there is much tenderness in his account of the *Piano concerto* as well as a gamin-like *joie de vivre* that is also shared by Eden and Tamir in their twinklingly light-hearted account of the *D minor Double piano concerto*. They are less successful in the *Sonata for two pianos*. This relatively late work (1953) should not be confused with the more popular two-piano sonata which they have also recorded. Here again they bring their formidable technique to bear on tricky music, but the result lacks the lighter, more sparkling qualities they found so readily in the *Concerto*. Pascal Rogé takes over at the keyboard again for the *Sextet*, a disarmingly fresh performance, its only slight drawback being the reverberance of the Salle Pleyel. A generous and inexpensive anthology, mainly of the highest calibre. López-Cobos's excellent account of the *Gloria* is discussed below.

Concerto in G min. for organ, strings and timpani.
(*) Chandos Dig. CHAN 9271 [id.]. Ian Tracey (organ of Liverpool Cathedral), BBC PO, Yan Pascal Tortelier – GUILMANT: *Symphony No. 1;* WIDOR: *Symphony No. 5.* *

The wide reverberation period of Liverpool Cathedral produces gloriously plushy textures (the orchestra strings are radiantly rich in colour) but little plangent bite, and some may feel that the effect is too overwhelmingly sumptuous for Poulenc's *Concerto*. Yet it is easy to wallow in the gloriously full sounds, and the performance itself, spacious to allow for the resonance, is certainly enjoyable.

Double piano concerto in D min.
(Y/B) (M) *** Teldec/Warner Dig. 4509 97445-2 [id.]. Güher and Süher Pekinel, French R. PO, Janowski – SAINT-SAENS: *Carnival of the animals.* ***

The Pekinel Duo come from mixed Spanish/Turkish parentage and their account of Poulenc's *Double concerto* is second to none. They play with great dash and sparkle, relishing the Mozartian pastiche of the *Larghetto* and the sensuous Ravelian/Satiesque nostalgia of the other lyrical ideas. Janowski provides a lively and thoroughly supportive accompaniment, and the recording balance is excellent. The only drawback is the brief time-span of this coupling (38 minutes overall), but the Saint-Saens zoological fantasy is equally enticing, so this is still a very attractive disc.

Suite française.
(M) *** ASV CDWHL 2067. L. Wind O, Wick – GRAINGER: *Irish tune from County Derry* etc.; MILHAUD: *Suite française.* ***

This engaging suite is based on themes by the sixteenth-century composer, Claude Gervaise. Poulenc scored them for a small ensemble of wind instruments and they come up very freshly in these artists' hands. Excellent recording and couplings. Thoroughly recommended.

CHAMBER MUSIC

(i) *Elégie for horn and piano;* (ii) *Violin sonata;* Music for 2 pianos: *Le Bal masqué (Capriccio); Elégie; L'Embarquement pour Cythère; Sonata; Sonata for piano* (4 hands).
(N) *** Decca Dig. 443 968-2 [id.]. (i) Cazalet; (ii) Juillet; Rogé, Collard.

Poulenc has the capacity to charm and enchant and, at the same time, speak to the listener. His lightness of touch and elegance often mask a vein of deeper feeling into which he can briefly move to striking and original effect. No one is more closely attuned to Poulenc's world than Pascal Rogé, and his presence ensures the authenticity of feeling that distinguished his earlier Poulenc. His masterly compatriot, Jean-Philippe Collard, is no less superb. In the *Elégie* for horn, written in memory of Dennis Brain, André Cazalet is an eloquent player and so, too, is Chantal Juillet in the *Violin sonata*. An outstanding issue.

(i) *L'invitation au château (for clarinet, violin & piano);* (ii) *Mouvements perpétuels for flute, oboe, clarinet, bassoon, horn, violin, viola, cello & bass;* (iii) *Rapsodie nègre for flute, clarinet, string quartet, baritone & piano;* (iv) *Sextet for flute, oboe, clarinet, bassoon, horn & piano;* (v) *Sonata for clarinet; Sonata for clarinet & bassoon;* (vi) *Sonata for 2 clarinets;* (vii) *Sonata for flute and piano;* (viii) *Oboe sonata;* (ix) *Trio for oboe, bassoon & piano;* (x) *Villanelle for piccolo & piano.*
(Y/B) (B) *** Cala Dig. CACD 1018 (2) [id.]. (i–vi) James Campbell; (i–ii) Peter Carter; (i) John York; (ii–iv; vii; x) William Bennett; (ii; iv; viii; ix) Nicholas Daniel; (ii; iv–v; ix) Rachel Gough; (ii; iv) Richard Watkins; (ii) Roger Tapping, Bruno Schrecker, Chris West; (iii) Allegri Qt (Peter Carter, David Roth, Roger Tapping, Bruno Schrecker), Peter Sidhom; (iii; viii–ix) Julius Drake; (iv; vii; x) Clifford Benson; (vi) David Campbell – RAVEL: *Introduction and allegro* etc. ***

These Cala discs are a terrific bargain. The Poulenc accounts for the bulk of the two CDs (two hours' music in fact), all of it full of sparkle and freshness of invention. The discs comprise the complete chamber music for woodwind by Ravel and Poulenc, with the exception of works written primarily for the voice. The performances have great elegance and finesse. There are rarities, such as the *Rapsodie nègre* and *L'invitation au château* for clarinet, violin and piano which Cala claim as a first recording. Poulenc has this rare gift of being able to move from the most flippant high spirits to the deepest poignancy, as in the *Oboe sonata*, expressively played by Nicholas Daniel. His pianist, Julius Drake, is highly sensitive, though the piano is not always ideally focused in the excessively resonant acoustic. Elsewhere, in the captivating incidental music to a play by Jean Cocteau and Raymond Radiguet, *L'invitation au château*, the playing is expert, tasteful and stylish. The *Mouvements perpétuels*, the *Sextet* and the various wind sonatas are beautifully played with great relish and spirit. This is a most attractive set, which deserves the widest dissemination. Had the piano been as well balanced as it is played, this would have earned a Rosette.

Sextet for piano & wind; Trio for piano, oboe & bassoon; (i) *Le Bal masqué; Le Bestiaire.*
*** CRD Dig. CRD 3437; *CRD C 4137* [id.]. (i) Thomas Allen; Nash Ens., Lionel Friend.

Thomas Allen is in excellent voice and gives a splendid account of both *Le Bal masqué* and *Le Bestiaire*. The Nash play both the *Trio* and the *Sextet* with superb zest and character. The wit of this playing and the enormous resource, good humour and charm of Poulenc's music are well served by a recording of exemplary quality and definition. Not to be missed.

Violin sonata.
(Y/B) *** EMI Dig. CDC7 54541-2 [id.]. Frank Peter Zimmermann, Alexander Lonquich – AURIC: *Sonate;* FRANCAIX: *Sonatine;* MILHAUD: *Sonata;* SATIE: *Choses vues.* ***

Frank Peter Zimmermann and Alexander Lonquich give a zestful account of Poulenc's wartime *Sonata* and convey its *gamin*-like character to perfection. They have charm and vitality. The recording is beautifully present, though it slightly favours the piano.

Piano duet

Capriccio; Elégie; L'embarquement pour Cythère; Sonata for piano, four hands; Sonata for two pianos.
*** Chandos Dig. CHAN 8519 [id.]. Seta Tanyel, Jeremy Brown.

These two artists have a very close rapport and dispatch this repertoire with both character and sensitivity. The Chandos recording is excellent, very vivid and present.

Solo piano music

Badinage; Bourrée au pavillon d'Auvergne; Feuillets d'album; Française; Humoresque; 6 Impromptus, Nos. 1–5; 15 Improvisations; 3 Intermezzi; Mélancolie; 3 Mouvements perpétuels; Napoli; 8 Nocturnes; 3

Novelettes; Pastourelle; 3 Pièces; Pièce brève sur le nom d'Albert Roussel; Presto in B flat; Promenades; Les soirées de Nazelles; Suite in C; Suite française; Thème varié; Valse in C; Valse-improvisation sur le nom de Bach; Villageoise.
**(*) Sony Dig. M3K 44921 (3). Paul Crossley.

Paul Crossley is a perceptive guide in this repertoire, fleet-fingered and unfailingly intelligent, though he does not really have the grace and charm of Pascal Rogé. Good recording quality.

Badinage; Les Biches: Adagietto; Intermezzo No. 3 in A flat; 3 Mouvements perpétuels; Napoli; 3 Pièces; Les soirées de Nazelles; Suite in C; Valse-improvisation sur le nom de Bach.
*** Chandos Dig. CHAN 8637 [id.]. Eric Parkin.

Humoresque; 15 Improvisations; Intermezzi Nos. 1 in C; 2 in D flat; Mélancolie; 3 Novelettes; Presto in B flat; Suite française d'après Claude Gervaise; Thème varié; Villageoises (Petites pièces enfantines).
*** Chandos Dig. CHAN 8847 [id.]. Eric Parkin.

Eric Parkin is an artist of instinctive taste and a refined musical intelligence who is completely inside this idiom: he has plenty of spirit and character and abundant sensitivity. Perhaps Rogé has the greater pianistic finesse plus a gamin-like charm, but Parkin too has charm and, in many of the pieces where they overlap, there is often little to choose between them. The Chandos recording is rather more resonant, though not unacceptably so.

Humoresque; Improvisations Nos. 4, 5, 9–11 & 14; 2 Intermezzi; Intermezzo in A flat; Nocturnes; Presto in B flat; Suite; Thème varié; Villageoises.
*** Decca Dig. 425 862-2 [id.]. Pascal Rogé.

Pascal Rogé's second Poulenc recital is every bit as captivating as his earlier disc (see below). The acoustic is somewhat reverberant but not excessively so. Elegant playing, responsive to all the rapidly changing shifts of tone in Poulenc's music, and strongly recommended.

Improvisations Nos. 1–3; 6–8; 12–13; 15; Mouvements perpétuels; 3 Novelettes; Pastourelle; 3 Pièces; Les soirées de Nazelles; Valse.
✹ *** Decca Dig. 417 438-2 [id.]. Pascal Rogé.

This music is absolutely enchanting, full of delight and wisdom; it has many unexpected touches and is teeming with character. Rogé is a far more persuasive exponent of it than any previous pianist on record; his playing is imaginative and inspiriting, and the recording is superb.

CHORAL MUSIC

Ave verum corpus; Exsultate Deo; Laudes de Saint-Antoine de Padoue; (i) Litanies à la Vierge Noire; 4 Motets pour le temps de Noël; 4 Motets pour le temps de pénitence; Salve Regina.
(M) *** EMI CDM5 65156-2 [id.]. Groupe Vocale de France, John Alldis; (i) with Marie-Claire Alain.

An outstanding collection. This is music that ideally needs French voices, and John Alldis has trained his French group splendidly so that they combine precision and fervour with a natural feeling for the words. The soaring *Ave verum* is matched by the exhilaration of the *Exsultate Deo* and the originality of the *Litanies* with its stabbing bursts of organ tone. The *Salve Regina* is very fine too, and the four *Christmas motets* have the right extrovert joyfulness and sense of wonder. The recording is made within an ecclesiastical ambience, yet definition is admirable.

Figure humaine; Laudes de Saint Antoine de Padoue; 4 Motets pour le temps de Noël; 4 Motets pour un temps de pénitence; 4 Petites prières de Saint François d'Assise.
*** Virgin/EMI Dig. VC7 59192-2 [id.]. The Sixteen, Harry Christophers.

A lovely record which assembles the cantata for double choir, *Figure humaine*, with some of the composer's most celebrated *a cappella* motets. These performances can be recommended strongly, both on artistic grounds and for the excellence of the sound.

Gloria.
(M) *** Sony SMK 47569 [id.]. Judith Blegen, Westminster Ch., NYPO, Bernstein – JANACEK: *Glagolitic Mass.* ***
(N) (B) *** Decca Eclipse 448 711-2; *448 711-4* [id.]. Greenberg, SRO Ch., Lausanne Pro Arte Ch., SRO, López-Cobos – DURUFLE: *Requiem;* FAURE: *Pavane.* ***.
(M) *** Decca 425 077-2 [id.]. Sylvia Greenberg, SRO Ch., Lausanne Pro Arte Ch., SRO, López-Cobos – SAINT-SAENS: *Messe.* **(*)

The *Gloria* is one of Poulenc's last compositions and is among his most successful. Bernstein perhaps underlines the Stravinskian springs of its inspiration and produces a vividly etched and clean-textured account which makes excellent sense in every way and is free from excessive sentiment. Judith Blegen is an appealing soloist, and the 1976 recording, made in New York's Manhattan Center, though not the last word in refinement, is clear, well detailed and spacious. With its vibrant Janáček coupling, this is one of the most attractive reissues in the Bernstein Edition.

López-Cobos gives a fine account of the *Gloria*, expansive yet underlining the Stravinskian elements in the score. The recording is first class, full-bodied and with clean definition. This is available coupled either with Duruflé and Fauré or with the rarer *Mass* by Saint-Saëns.

(i; ii) *Gloria; Ave verum corpus; Exultate Deo;* (ii) *Litanies à la Vierge Noire; 4 Motets pour le temps de Noël; 4 Motets pour un temps de pénitence; Salve regina.*
*** Coll. COLCD 108. (i) Donna Deam, Cambridge Singers, (ii) City of L. Sinfonia, John Rutter.

A generous selection of Poulenc's choral music, much of it of great beauty and simplicity, in very fresh-sounding performances and well-focused sound.

Mass in G; 4 petites prières de Saint François d'Assise; Salve regina.
*** Nimbus Dig. NI 5197 [id.]. Christ Church Cathedral Ch., Oxford, Stephen Darlington – MARTIN: *Mass for double choir.* **(*)

The *Mass in G* is a work of strong appeal and greater dramatic fire than the *Salve Regina* or the more intimate *Quatre petites prières de Saint François d'Assise* for men's voices. The choir of Christ Church Cathedral, Oxford, under Stephen Darlington sing with clean tone and excellent balance, and the Nimbus recording is very good indeed.

(i) *Mass in G. Exultate Deo;* (ii) *Litanies à la Vierge Noire. Salve Regina.*
(B) *** Double Decca 436 486-2 (2) [id.]. St John's College, Cambridge, Ch., Guest; (i) with Jonathon Bond; (ii) Stephen Cleobury – FAURE; DURUFLE: *Requiems.* ***

As an extraordinarily generous bonus for the two great *Requiems* of Fauré and Duruflé, this Double Decca set offers the Poulenc *Mass in G* together with two motets, *Exultate Deo* and *Salve Regina*, finely wrought pieces in performances of great finish. Then, together with Stephen Cleobury, they give us the cool, gently dissonant *Litanies à la Vierge Noire*, a dialogue between voices and organ in which the voices eventually take dominance. It is beautifully done and the St John's College forces cope with the delicacy and sweetness of Poulenc's chromatic harmony throughout. The (originally Argo) recording is eminently realistic and truthful.

Stabat Mater; Litanies à la vierge noire; Salve Regina.
*** HM Dig. HMC 905149 [id.]. Lagrange, Lyon Nat. Ch. and O, Baudo.

In the *Stabat Mater* Serge Baudo certainly makes the most of expressive and dynamic nuances; he shapes the work with fine feeling and gets good singing from the Lyon Chorus. Michèle Lagrange has a good voice and is an eminently expressive soloist. The coupling offers the short *Salve Regina* and the *Litanies à la Vierge Noire*, an earlier and somewhat more severe work.

SONGS

Mélodies: Banalités: Hôtel; Voyage à Paris. Bleuet. C; Calligrammes: Voyage. 4 Chansons pour enfants: Nous voulons une petite soeur. Les chemins de l'amour. Colloque; Hyde Park; Métamorphoses; Miroirs brûlants: Tu vois le feu du soir. Montparnasse; 2 Poèmes de Louis Aragon; 3 Poèmes de Louise Lalanne; Priez pour paix; Tel jour, telle nuit; Toréador.
*** Hyperion Dig. CDA 66147 [id.]. Songmakers' Almanac: Lott, Rolfe Johnson, Murray, Johnson.

Felicity Lott sings the great majority of the songs here, joyful and tender, comic and tragic by turns. The other soloists have one song apiece, done with comparable magnetism, and Richard Jackson joins Felicity Lott (one stanza each) in Poulenc's solitary 'song for two voices', *Colloque*. First-rate recording, though Lott's soprano is not always as sweetly caught as it can be.

Le bestiaire; Chansons gaillardes: La belle jeunesse; Invocation aux Parques. Métamorphoses: C'est ainsi que tu es; Paganini; Reine des mouettes. 2 Poèmes de Guillaume Apollinaire: Dans le jardin d'Anna; Montparnasse. 2 Poèmes de Louis Aragon: 'C'; Fêtes galantes. Tel jour, telle nuit.
(***) EMI mono CDC7 54605-2 [id.]. Pierre Bernac, Francis Poulenc – BRITTEN: *Song cycles.* (***)

It is apt for EMI's 'Composers in Person' series to celebrate two unique partnerships, with Francis Poulenc accompanying Pierre Bernac and Benjamin Britten accompanying Peter Pears. The distinctive voice of each singer was the direct inspiration for most of these songs. That is so, not just with Britten's two sonnet-cycles, but with most of the two-dozen Poulenc songs as well. To hear Bernac performing Poulenc's most moving song, 'C', as well as his other Aragon setting, the cabaret-inspired *Fêtes galantes*, is to have a new, more intense insight into the two contrasted sides of Poulenc's genius, now dedicated, now flippant. Documentation is good and with complete texts but, like all the other issues in this series, the discs come at full price.

Dialogue des Carmélites (complete).
*** Virgin/EMI Dig. VCD7 59227-2 (2). Dubosc, Gorr, Yakar, Fournier, Van Dam, Viala, Dupuy, Lyon Opéra O, Kent Nagano.

The opening of Poulenc's *Dialogue des Carmélites* with its very Stravinskian ostinatos for a moment suggests a minimalist opera, written before its time. Much is owed to the dynamic Nagano, who gives an extra momentum and sense of contrast to a work that with its measured speeds and easily lyrical manner can fall into sameness. That the male casting is so strong, with the principal roles taken by José van Dam and the tenor, Jean-Luc Viala, compensates for any lack of variety in having women's voices predominating in an opera about nuns. Catherine Dubosc in the central role of the fear-obsessed, self-doubting Blanche is fresh and appealing, with Brigitte Fournier charming as the frivolous nun, Constance, and the veteran Rita Gorr as the old Prioress and Rachel Yakar as the new Prioress both splendid. The vivid recording, helped by a stage production in Lyon, culminates in a spine-chilling rendering of the final execution scene, with the sound of the guillotine ever more menacing.

Praetorius, Michael (1571–1621)

Dances from Terpsichore (extended suite).
*** Decca Dig. 414 633-2 [id.]. New L. Cons., Philip Pickett.

Terpsichore is a huge collection of some 300 dance tunes used by the French-court dance bands of Henri IV. They were enthusiastically assembled by the German composer, Michael Praetorius, who also harmonized them and arranged them in four to six parts; however, any selection is conjectural in the matter of orchestration. Philip Pickett's instrumentation is sometimes less exuberant than that of David Munrow before him; but many will like the refinement of his approach, with small instrumental groups, lute pieces and even what seems like an early xylophone! There are also some attractively robust brass scorings (sackbuts and trumpets). The use of original instruments is entirely beneficial in this repertoire; the recording is splendid.

Christmas music: *Polyhymnia caduceatrix et panegyrica Nos. 9–10, 12 & 17. Puericinium Nos. 2, 4 & 5. Musae Sionae VI, No. 53: Es ist ein Ros' entsprungen. Terpsichore: Dances Nos. 1; 283–5; 310.*
*** Hyperion Dig. CDA 66200 [id.]. Westminster Cathedral Ch., Parley of Instruments, David Hill.

Praetorius was much influenced by the polychoral style of the Gabrielis; these pieces reflect this interest. The music is simple in style and readily accessible, and its performance on this atmospheric Hyperion record is both spirited and sensitive.

Christmas music: *Polyhymnia caduceatrix et panegyrica Nos. 10, Wie schön leuchtet der Morgenstern; 12, Puer natus in Bethlehem; 21, Wachet auf, ruft uns die Stimme; 34, In dulci jubilo.*
*** EMI Dig. CDC7 47633-2 [id.]. Taverner Cons., Ch. & Players, Parrott – SCHUTZ: *Christmas oratorio*. ***

This is the finest collection of Praetorius's vocal music in the current catalogue. The closing setting of *In dulci jubilo*, richly scored for five choirs and with the brass providing thrilling contrast and support for the voices, has great splendour. Before that comes the lovely, if less ambitious *Wie schön leuchtet der Morgenstern*. Both *Wachet auf* and *Puer natus in Bethlehem* are on a comparatively large scale, their combination of block sonorities and florid decorative effects the very essence of Renaissance style. The recording is splendidly balanced, with voices and brass blending and intertwining within an ample acoustic.

Previn, André (born 1929)

'*A Different kind of blues*' (*Look at him go; Little face; Who reads reviews?; Night thoughts; A different kind of blues; Chocolate apricot; The five of us; Make up your mind*).
(M) **(*) EMI Dig. CDM7 64319-2 [id.]. Perlman, Previn, Manne, Hall, Mitchell.

Perlman, unlike his colleagues here, is no jazz musician, and he had to have the 'improvisations' written out for him; but the challenge of this project with Previn's colourful and appealing pieces dividing sharply between brilliant and sweet, is very clear from first to last. There are (for E. G.) not many better examples of 'middle-of-the-road' records, and the haunting *Chocolate apricot* could become a classic. No information is given on which critic gave rise to *Who reads reviews?*. The 1981 digital recording is vivid and immediate: the artists have great presence, but in the Editor's view this is a record to sample first. It plays for only 37 minutes.

'It's a breeze' (It's a breeze; Rain in my head; Catgut your tongue; It's about time; Bowing and scraping; A tune for Heather; Quiet diddling; The red bar).
(M) **(*) EMI Dig. CDM7 64318-2 [id.]. Perlman, Previn, Manne, Hall, Mitchell.

If you enjoyed the first collection, you may well find the second (recorded in Pittsburgh as a relaxed supplement to more serious sessions) even more persuasive, although, with only 43 minutes of music included, it would have been more generous of EMI to have combined both programmes on a single CD, if necessary omitting a single piece. No prizes are offered by the Editor for the choice. However, a sweet number like *A tune for Heather* is certainly attractive, with a tinge of Walton. As with the first programme, the digital recording presents balances that are closer to pop than to those one would expect in a semi-classical issue, but the sound is very vivid.

Prokofiev, Serge (1891–1953)

Andante for strings, Op. 50 bis; Autumn (symphonic sketch), *Op. 8; Lieutenant Kijé: suite, Op. 60; The Stone flower: suite, Op. 118; Wedding suite, Op. 126.*
*** Chandos Dig. CHAN 8806 [id.]. SNO, Järvi.

The *Andante* is a transcription for full strings of the slow movement of the *First String quartet*, and its eloquence is more telling in this more expansive format. *Autumn*, on the other hand, is an early piece, much influenced by Rachmaninov, in particular his symphonic poem, *The Isle of the dead*, and is full of imaginative touches. Järvi takes it at a fairly brisk tempo but it remains appropriately atmospheric. The *Wedding suite* is drawn from *The Stone flower* and complements the Op. 118 suite from Prokofiev's last full-length ballet. *The Stone flower* has some engaging lyrical invention, and the music recorded here is still full of appeal. The performances and recording are in the best traditions of the house.

(i; ii) *Autumn, Op. 8;* (i; iii) *Chout* (ballet): *suite;* (iv) *Lieutenant Kijé* (suite); (v; vi) *The Prodigal Son: suite; Scythian suite;* (v; vii) *The Stone flower: suite.*
(N) (B) ** Decca Double 448 273-2 (2) [id.]. (i) LSO; (ii) Ashkenazy; (iii) Abbado; (iv) Netherlands R. PO, Dorati; (v) SRO; (vi) Ansermet; (vii) Varviso.

Autumn is the earliest work here, an atmospheric orchestral sketch written in 1910 and well worth having when Ashkenazy's performance is so sympathetic. Abbado's version of the suite from *Chout*, again with the LSO, offers a generous part of the score and reveals a characteristically sensitive ear for balance of texture. The analogue recording, made in the Kingsway Hall in 1966, was a model of its kind. Dorati's *Lieutenant Kijé* brings a complete contrast. The up-front recording was made in Decca's hi-fi-conscious Phase 4 system (ensuring that every detail is clear, yet with a reasonably wide dynamic range and plenty of ambience). The result is not subtly refined, indeed it is very boldly characterized. But Dorati secures excellent playing from the Netherlands orchestra. Ansermet then takes over for *The Prodigal Son* and the *Scythian suite*, and he is undoubtedly sympathetic, though the Suisse Romande Orchestra has neither the polish nor the opulence of tone to do either score real justice. The mid-1960s Decca recording, however, is well up to standard and captures with admirable clarity the detail of Prokofiev's scoring, especially the brutal complexities of the *Scythian suite*. If only the playing had more panache (the third movement seriously lacks sensuousness), this would have been more strongly recommendable. As it happens, Silvio Varviso has rather greater success in this respect. The Swiss orchestra seems to respond enthusiastically to some guest conductors and here they are at their best, while the recording remains faithful and vivid. Any confirmed Prokofievian will enjoy this.

Boris Godunov, Op. 70 bis: Fountain scene; Polonaise. Dreams, Op. 6. Eugene Onegin, Op. 71: Minuet, Polka, Mazurka. 2 Pushkin waltzes, Op. 120. Romeo and Juliet (ballet): *suite No. 2, Op. 64.*
*** Chandos Dig. CHAN 8472 [id.]. SNO, Järvi.

Järvi's second suite from *Romeo and Juliet* has sensitivity, abundant atmosphere, a sense of the theatre, and is refreshingly unmannered. A fuller selection of the music Prokofiev wrote for a production of *Eugene Onegin* is available – see below – but what is offered here, plus the *Two Pushkin waltzes*, are rather engaging lighter pieces. The performances are predictably expert, the balance finely judged and detail is in exactly the right perspective.

Chout (ballet): *suite, Op. 21a; Love for 3 Oranges: suite, Op. 33a; Le pas d'acier: suite, Op. 41a.*
*** Chandos Dig. CHAN 8729 [id.]. SNO, Järvi.

Järvi has a natural affinity for this repertoire and gets splendid results from the SNO; and the recording is pretty spectacular.

Cinderella (ballet; complete), *Op. 87.*
*** Decca Dig. 410 162-2 (2) [id.]. Cleveland O, Ashkenazy.

Cinderella (ballet; complete), *Op. 87; Summer night: suite, Op. 123.*
(Y/B) ✹ *** DG Dig. 445 830-2 (2) [id.]. Russian Nat. O, Mikhail Pletnev.

Cinderella (ballet; complete), *Op. 87; Symphony No. 1 in D (Classical), Op. 25.*
(N) (B) *** EMI Dig./analogue. forte CZS5 68604-2 (2) LSO, Previn.

Pletnev produces playing of terrific life, lightness of touch, poetic feeling and character. Quite simply the best-played, most atmospheric and affecting *Cinderella* we have ever had on disc. We found its effect tremendously exhilarating, and have had difficulty in stopping playing it! Don't hesitate – on every count this is one of the best recordings, not only of the year but the 1990s.

Otherwise artistic honours are very evenly divided between the Ashkenazy and Previn recordings of Prokofiev's *Cinderella.* Some dances come off better in Previn's EMI version and there is an element of swings and roundabouts in comparing them. Detail is more closely scrutinized by the Decca engineers; Ashkenazy gets excellent results from the Cleveland Orchestra. There are many imaginative touches in this score – as magical indeed as the story itself – and the level of invention is astonishingly high. On CD, the recording's fine definition is enhanced, yet not at the expense of atmosphere, and the bright, vivid image is given striking projection. However, the EMI engineers have a more spacious acoustic within which to work and yet lose no detail. Moreover this now comes on EMI's very economical two-for-the-price-of-one forte series, and the CD reissue adds a splendid account of the *Classical Symphony*, sunlit and vivacious and hardly less well recorded five years previously.

(i) *Cinderella:* excerpts; (ii) *Romeo and Juliet:* excerpts.
(M) *** EMI CD-EMX 2194. (i) RPO, Irving; (ii) Philh. O, Kurtz.

Kurtz's *Romeo and Juliet* comes from the mid-1960s, but Irving's performances are from 1958, yet it would be difficult to guess the dates of either from the sound here, which is admirable in its definition and body. Irving secures very fine playing from the RPO, crisply rhythmic and sympathetic. In *Romeo and Juliet* Kurtz's performances are slightly lacking in dramatic tension in the longer movements, but the shorter dances come off superbly. But what beautifully shaped phrasing the Philharmonia give us and what full timbre.

Cinderella (ballet): *suites Nos. 1 & 2, Op. 107–8:* excerpts. (i) *Peter and the wolf, Op. 67.*
*** Chandos Dig. CHAN 8511 [id.]. (i) Lina Prokofiev; SNO, Järvi.

Peter and the wolf is very slow, but the magnetism of Madame Prokofiev (the composer's first wife), with many memorable lines delivered in her tangily Franco-Russian accent, makes up for that leisurely manner, with beautiful, persuasive playing from the Scottish National Orchestra. Järvi's compilation of eight movements from the two *Cinderella suites* has even more persuasive playing, with the sensuousness of much of the writing brought out. Warmly atmospheric recording, with the narration realistically balanced.

Cinderella: suite No. 1, Op. 107; Lieutenant Kijé (suite); The Love for 3 Oranges: March; Scherzo; The Prince and Princess. Romeo and Juliet: Madrigal; Dance of the girls with lilies.
(BB) *** Naxos Dig. 8.550381 [id.]. Slovak State PO, (Košice), Andrew Mogrelia.

The calibre of this excellent Slovak orchestra is well demonstrated here, and its perceptive conductor, Andrew Mogrelia, is at his finest in his gently humorous portrait of *Lieutenant Kijé*, the three 'best bits' from *The Love for Three Oranges* and the charming items from *Romeo and Juliet*. Excellent recording.

Concertino in G min. for cello and orchestra, Op. 132 (completed and orch. Kabalevsky & Rostropovich); *Sinfonia concertante in E min. for cello and orchestra, Op. 125.*
*** Decca Dig. 436 233-2 [id.]. Lynn Harrell, RPO, Ashkenazy.
(*(**)) Russian Disc mono RDCD 11103 [id.]. Rostropovich, USSR SO, Rozhdestvensky.

Lynn Harrell gives a very impressive account of the *Sinfonia concertante* and Vladimir Ashkenazy gets strongly characterized playing from the RPO, which does full justice to its sardonic humour. A fresh, totally committed and well-prepared performance which blends enthusiasm and spontaneity. The *Concertino* is a much slighter piece but is equally well played. Two other plus points: the Decca recording is very truthful and vivid; and Christopher Palmer's useful notes give a detailed comparison of Op. 125 with its earlier incarnation, the *Cello concerto*, Op. 58. Rostropovich's own performances with the USSR Symphony Orchestra under Rozhdestvensky naturally have a very special authority. They were made at public concerts in 1964 and appear in the UK for the first time. Some allowance must be made for the rather raw sound.

(i) *Flute concerto* (orch. Palmer); (ii) *Humoresque scherzo, Op. 12 bis; Overture on Hebrew themes, Op. 34 bis; Sonata for unaccompanied violins, Op. 115; Symphony No. 1 in D (Classical), Op. 25.*
**(*) Conifer Dig. 74321 15910-2 [id.]. (i) Jonathan Snowden; (ii) Alexander, Gatt, Mackie, Orford; L. Musici, Mark Stephenson.

The *Flute concerto* is an arrangement of the *Sonata in D major*, expertly scored by Christopher Palmer but is in no sense a concerto, the orchestra's role being confined to that of accompaniment. The *Humoresque scherzo* is in Prokofiev's own transcription for four bassoons, and the *Sonata*, Op. 115, was originally intended to be heard played by violins in unison, and sounds effective in this form. The *Overture on Hebrew themes* is well played and recorded, and so is the *Classical Symphony*, though it is rather on the slow side. Jonathan Snowden gives an excellent account of the arrangement of the *D major Sonata* and the recordings are well balanced, natural and realistic.

Piano concertos Nos. 1–5.
*** Chandos Dig. CHAN 8938 (2) [id.]. Boris Berman (in Nos. 1, 4 & 5); Horacio Gutiérrez (in Nos. 2 & 3), Concg. O, Järvi.
(M) **(*) Decca 425 570-2 (2) [id.]. Ashkenazy, LSO, Previn.

Piano concertos Nos. 1 in D flat, Op. 10; 3 in C, Op. 26; 4 in B flat, Op. 53.
(BB) *** Naxos Dig. 8.550566 [id.]. Kun Woo Paik, Polish Nat. RSO (Katowice), Antoni Witt.

Piano concertos Nos. 2 in G min., Op. 16; 5 in G, Op. 55.
(BB) *** Naxos Dig. 8.550565 [id.]. Kun Woo Paik, Polish Nat. RSO (Katowice), Antoni Witt.

(i) *Piano concertos Nos. 1–5;* (ii) *Overture on Hebrew themes. Visions fugitives, Op. 22.*
(B) *** EMI CMS7 62542-2 (2). Michel Béroff; (i) with Leipzig GO, Masur; (ii) with Portal, Parrenin Qt.

The merits of the Berman single discs are discussed below. As a package, their claims are strong, both artistically and in terms of recording quality.

Honours are more evenly divided between Ashkenazy and Béroff than one might expect. Ashkenazy's virtuosity is often challenged by the young Frenchman, and he too plays masterfully; indeed, both sets of performances prove remarkably distinguished on closer acquaintance. However, the remastered Decca recording has a top-heavy balance and the upper strings tend to sound shrill at higher dynamic levels. The EMI CD transfer brings a fairly spiky sound to the violins – one would not guess that this was the Leipzig Gewandhaus Orchestra in the opening tutti of the *First Concerto*, which is bright rather than rich-textured. Nevertheless there is plenty of ambience and the somewhat acerbic sounds are not inappropriate for Prokofiev. Slow movements have plenty of atmosphere. Generous bonuses are offered by the EMI set. Béroff's account of the *Visions fugitives* is particularly distinguished, and the piano recording gives little cause for complaint.

Kun Woo Paik's playing throughout these five concertos has exhilarating bravura. Tempi are dangerously fast at times and occasionally he has the orchestra almost scampering to keep up with him, but they do, and the result is often electrifying. The famous theme and variations central movement of the *Third concerto* is played with great diversity of mood and style and the darkly expressive *Larghetto* of No. 5 is very finely done. The *First concerto*, which comes last on the first CD has great freshness and compares well with almost any version on disc. In short, with vivid recording in the Concert Hall of Polish Radio, which has plenty of ambience, this set is enormously stimulating and a remarkable bargain. It has far better sound than the remastered Decca recording for Ashkenazy.

(i) *Piano concerto No. 1 in D flat. Suggestion diabolique, Op. 4/4.*
(M) *** EMI CDM7 64329-2 [id.]. Gavrilov, (i) LSO, Rattle – BALAKIREV: *Islamey;* TCHAIKOVSKY: *Piano concerto No. 1.* ***

A dazzling account of the *First Piano concerto* from Andrei Gavrilov. This version is second to none for virtuosity and sensitivity. Apart from its brilliance, this performance scores on other fronts too; Simon Rattle provides excellent orchestral support and the EMI engineers offer most vivid recording, while the *Suggestion diabolique* makes a hardly less dazzling encore after the concerto.

Piano concertos Nos. 1 in D flat, Op. 10; 3 in C, Op. 26.
(Y/B) *** DG Dig. 439 898-2 [id.]. Kissin, BPO, Abbado.

(i) *Piano concertos Nos. 1 in D flat, Op. 10; 3 in C, Op. 26. Piano sonata No. 7 in B flat, Op. 83.*
*** ASV Dig. CDDCA 786 [id.]. Mari Kodama, (i) with Philh. O, Kent Nagano.

Yevgeni Kissin gives a virtuosic, dashing account of both concertos and is given highly sensitive and responsive support from the Berlin Philharmonic under Abbado. It is unfailingly brilliant, aristocratic in feeling and wonderfully controlled pianism. After the big theme in the *First Piano concerto*, Kissin does not dash away in quite the same way as did Richter (in his mono recording from the late 1950s on Supraphon, which sounds pretty marvellous even as sound), and in the *Third* there is none of the wild abandon of William Kapell (see below). But this is playing of the greatest artistry and distinction; and the recording is very good. It is a pity that DG did not offer a fill-up, for example one of the sonatas from Kissin, as this CD offers only 42 minutes 27 seconds of playing time. All the same, it is very highly recommendable.

ASV's coupling should win great favour since it brings performances of real panache and style, together with a highly competitive account of the *Seventh Sonata*. Mari Kodama is a vital and imaginative player and the performances are wonderfully alert and fresh-eyed; there is splendid rapport between soloist and conductor (not surprisingly since they are husband and wife) and they benefit from first-class recording. A strong recommendation not only for newcomers to Prokofiev but for the experienced collector.

Piano concertos Nos. 1 in D flat, Op. 10; 3 in C, Op. 26; 5 in G, Op. 55.
*** Sony SK 52483 [id.]. Yefim Bronfman, Israel PO, Zubin Mehta.

Yefim Bronfman's Sony recording offers the *Fifth Piano concerto* instead of the *Sonata* (as on ASV), which makes a more logical and (for the collector) competitive choice – and the recording is similarly excellent in quality. Bronfman is hardly less remarkable or sensitive than Mari Kodama; indeed he is a player of subtlety and possesses a formidable technique and a cultured restraint. The Israel orchestra under Mehta gives good, well-phrased and athletic support. Existing recommendations are not displaced, but for those wanting this particular coupling this deserves a three-star recommendation.

Piano concertos Nos. 1 in D flat, Op. 10; 4 in B flat for the left hand, Op. 53; 5 in G, Op. 55.
*** Chandos Dig. CHAN 8791 [id.]. Boris Berman, Concg. O, Järvi.

On Chandos, very fine performances of all three *Concertos*, and the orchestral playing is very distinguished. Boris Berman has established an enviable reputation as interpreter of this composer, and he plays with great panache and (at times) dazzling virtuosity. He holds the music on a taut rein and has the nervous energy and ebullience this music needs. The superb recording quality will sway many collectors in his favour.

Piano concerto No. 1 in D flat; Piano sonata No. 5 in C, Op. 38.
*** ASV Dig. CDDCA 555 [id.]. Osorio, RPO, Bátiz – RAVEL: *Left-hand concerto etc.* ***

Jorge Federico Osorio is a thoroughly perceptive interpreter. He is accompanied well by Bátiz, and readers wanting this coupling need not fear that it is second best; they are excellently recorded. ASV offer an interesting fill-up in the form of the Prokofiev *Fifth Sonata*, which Osorio does in its post-war, revised form.

Piano concerto No. 3 in C, Op. 26.
(N) (M) *** DG 447 438-2 [id.]. Martha Argerich, BPO, Abbado – RAVEL: *Piano concerto in G* etc. ***
(M) *** Mercury 434 333-2 [id.]. Byron Janis, Moscow PO, Kondrashin (with PROKOFIEV: *Toccata;*
    SCHUMANN: *Sonata No. 3;* MENDELSSOHN: *Songs without words, Op. 61/1;* PINTO: *3 Scenes from childhood* ***) – RACHMANINOV: *Piano concerto No. 3.* ***
(N) (M) **(*) RCA 09026 62691-2 [id.]. Van Cliburn, Chicago SO, Reiner – SCHUMANN: *Piano concerto.* ***
(BB) **(*) Belart 450 081-2. Israela Margalit, New Philh. O, Maazel – MUSSORGSKY: *Pictures.* **(*)
(Y/B) ✦ (M) (**(*)) RCA mono GD 60921 [id.]. William Kapell, Dallas SO, Dorati – KHACHATU-
    RIAN: *Piano concerto* (**(*)) ✦; LISZT: *Mephisto waltz.* (**(*))

This is another ideal choice for reissue in DG's 'Originals' series of 'Legendary Recordings'. Martha Argerich made her outstanding record of the Prokofiev *Third Concerto* in 1968, while still in her twenties, and this record helped to establish her international reputation as one of the most vital and positive of women pianists. There is nothing ladylike about the playing, but it displays countless indications of feminine perception and subtlety. The *C major Concerto* was once regarded as tough music but here receives a sensuous performance, and Abbado's direction underlines that from the very first, with a warmly romantic account of the ethereal opening phrases on the high violins. When it comes to the second subject, the lightness of Argerich's pointing has a delightfully infectious quality, and surprisingly a likeness emerges with the Ravel *G major Concerto*, which was written more than a decade later. This is a much more individual performance of the Prokofiev than almost any other available and brings its own special insights. The 1967 recording, made in the Berlin Jesus-Christus Kirche, always excellent, sounds even more present in this new transfer.

Byron Janis's record with Kondrashin has a certain historical éclat in containing the first recordings made in the Soviet Union (in 1962) by non-Russian recording engineers. The result was a triumphant success, artistically and technically. Janis's account of the Prokofiev *Third Concerto* is outstanding in every way, soloist and orchestra plainly challenging each other in a performance full of wit (particularly in the delightfully managed slow-movement variations), drama and warmth. Even though it was made three decades ago, the Mercury recording sounds amazingly clean and faithful. The recital (recorded in Russia the following year – except for the Schumann, which was made in the USA) is comparatively low-key, except perhaps for the captivating *Scenes from childhood* of Octavio Pinto, which combine charm with glittering yet unostentatious bravura.

Van Cliburn plays with both sympathy and astonishing digital brilliance. However, the 1960 recording is closely balanced, as if the producer, Richard Mohr, decided to counteract the richness of the Chicago ambience with his microphone placing. With a very forward (indeed at times too forward) piano-image and a relatively sharp focus for the violins, he has certainly made his point, and there is no doubting the strong projection of the music-making. We wonder whether he realized that this concerto had its first performance in this very hall (with the composer as pianist) in December 1921, and that the work makes its greatest effect in an expansive acoustic, as is shown by alternative recordings. Nevertheless this remains a distinctive and immensely stimulating account, and the background resonance still adds its warmth.

The performance by Israela Margalit and Maazel is not the most poised available but it has a splendid feeling of spontaneity and enjoyment, and there is no lack of wit in the central theme and variations. The recording balance is somewhat contrived, the resonance of the acoustic competing with the microphone spotlighting, but the end-result is unfailingly vivid and the piano image is tangible. It is not unlikely that those who buy this disc for the Mussorgsky may find themselves turning just as readily to the concerto, for the personality and colour of the score emerge strongly here.

William Kapell's account of the *Third Piano concerto* is dazzlingly brilliant, and the Dallas orchestra under Antal Dorati rise to the occasion too. Indeed this is arguably the most incandescent and vital performance of this concerto ever committed to disc. It comes with an equally remarkable performance of the Khachaturian with the Boston Symphony under Koussevitzky, a powerhouse of vitality. Playing like this silences any criticism one might voice about the recorded sound, which admittedly is pretty grim.

(i) *Piano concerto No. 3 in C, Op. 26;* (ii; iii) *Violin concerto No. 1 in D, Op. 19;* (iii) *Lieutenant Kijé (suite), Op. 60.*

(B) *** DG Analogue/Dig. 439 413-2 [id.]. (i) Martha Argerich, BPO; (ii) Shlomo Mintz; (iii) Chicago SO; all cond. Abbado.

Martha Argerich's highly individual performance of Prokofiev's *C major Concerto* (see above) is here coupled with the *First Violin concerto*, which also has a magical opening, and once again Abbado's accompaniment is peerless, while Mintz phrases with imagination and individuality. *Lieutenant Kijé* is hardly less successful and also sounds splendid; Abbado gets both warm and wonderfully clean playing from the Chicago orchestra. This compilation is one of the very finest reissues on DG's bargain Classikon label.

(i) *Piano concerto No. 3 in C, Op. 26. Symphony No.1 in D, 'Classical', Op. 25: Gavotte* (only; arr. for piano). *Piano sonata No. 4 in C min., Op. 29: Andante assai* (only). *Gavotte, Op. 32/3; Suggestion diabolique, Op. 4/4; Visions fugitives, Op. 22:* excerpts: *Nos. 3, Allegretto; 5, Molto giocoso; 6, Con eleganza; 9, Allegretto tranquillo; 10, Ridiculosamente; 11, Con vivacita; 16, Dolente; 17, Poetico; 18, Con una dolce lentezza.*

(Y/B) (***) EMI mono CDC5 55223-2 [id.]. Composer (piano); (i) LSO, Piero Coppola – GLAZUNOV: *The Seasons.* (***)

Prokofiev's pioneering account of the *Third Piano concerto* has appeared many times since the 1930s. This transfer supersedes them all: not only is the sound smoother and richer, the disc offers Glazunov's remarkable recording of *The Seasons*. At 79 minutes, this is not to be missed.

Piano concerto No. 4 in B flat for the left hand, Op. 53.

*** Sony Dig. SK 47188 [id.]. Fleisher, Boston SO, Ozawa – BRITTEN: *Diversions;* RAVEL: *Left-hand concerto.* ***

(M) (***) Sony mono MPK 46452 [id.]. Rudolph Serkin, Phd. O, Ormandy – REGER: *Piano concerto.* **

The *Fourth Piano concerto* was commissioned, like the Ravel, for Paul Wittgenstein who lost his right hand during the First World War. He did not like it, however, and the piece remained long neglected (its first UK performance was by Malcolm Binns in 1960). It is a powerful and resourceful piece which Fleisher performs with great sympathy and skill. Although his does not necessarily eclipse earlier versions by Michel Béroff and Ashkenazy, it is an interpretation of strong character and comparable stature, and is well accompanied by Ozawa and the Boston orchestra, and is splendidly recorded.

Serkin's recording was made in 1958 and the performance is not likely to be bettered. His mastery helps to disguise some of the work's defects, though even he cannot quite conceal the fact that the vivace finale is far too short to balance the rest properly. The mono recording is excellent.

Piano concerto No. 5 in G, Op. 55.

*** DG 415 119-2 [id.]. Sviatoslav Richter, Warsaw PO, Witold Rowicki – RACHMANINOV: *Piano concerto No. 2.* ***

(N) (B) *(*) EMI forte CZS5 68637-2 (2). Sviatoslav Richter, LSO, Maazel – BARTOK: *Piano concerto No. 2* *(*); TCHAIKOVSKY: *Piano concertos Nos. 1–3.* **

Richter's 1959 account of the *Fifth Piano concerto* is a classic and it cannot be recommended too strongly to all admirers of Richter, Prokofiev and great piano playing.

Richter is his own keenest rival in the 1970 EMI recording of this last of the Prokofiev concertos, which is presented in far sharper focus – not just a question of recording acoustic (here the Kingsway Hall).

Violin concertos Nos. 1 in D, Op. 19; 2 in G min., Op. 63.

(Y/B) ✹ *** Sony SK 53969 [id.]. Cho-Liang Lin, LAPO, Esa-Pekka Salonen – STRAVINSKY: *Violin concerto.* ***

(M) *** Decca 425 003-2. Kyung Wha Chung, LSO, Previn – STRAVINSKY: *Concerto.* ***

**(*) DG Dig. 410 524-2 [id.]. Mintz, Chicago SO, Abbado.

(Y/B) **(*) Denon Dig. CO-75891 [id.]. Boris Belkin, Zürich Tonhalle O, Stern.

(N) (M) **(*) Sony Stern Edition II Dig. SMK 64503 [id.]. Isaac Stern, NYPO, Mehta – BARTOK: *Rhapsodies.* **

The two Prokofiev concertos are among the composer's most richly lyrical works, and Lin brings out their romantic warmth as well as their dramatic bite. Salonen's understanding support, helped by sound more refined than this orchestra usually gets, if with weighty bass, culminates in ravishing accounts of the outer movements of No. 1 and the central slow movement of No. 2. In the Stravinsky, Salonen terraces the accompaniment dramatically, with woodwind and brass bold and full. That goes with another powerful and warmly expressive reading from Lin, confounding the composer's pronouncements on emotion in music.

In this same coupling, Chung on mid-price Decca offers equally compelling Prokofievian readings in excellent analogue sound, more overtly emotional if not quite so commanding. Her performances emphasize the lyrical quality of these *Concertos*, with playing that is both warm and strong, tender and full of fantasy. Previn's accompaniments are deeply understanding, while the Decca sound has lost only a little of its fullness in the digital remastering, and the soloist is now made very present.

Mintz phrases with imagination and individuality and there is an attractive combination of freshness and lyrical finesse. He has the advantage of Abbado's sensitive and finely judged accompaniments. In short, this partnership casts the strongest spell on the listener and, with recording on CD which is both refined and full, this would receive the strongest advocacy, except for the shortness of measure.

On the Denon disc, helped by cleaner, refined sound with good presence, Belkin offers warm, strong readings with many individual insights, notably in his very measured, yearningly tender account of the slow movement of No. 2, but his disc suffers in practical terms by providing no makeweight.

In his digital recordings, made in the Avery Fisher Hall in 1982, Stern's are warmly and boldly extrovert readings, a degree freer in expression and more spontaneous-sounding than his 1965 versions, recorded in Philadelphia, even if Ormandy offered riper accompaniments than Mehta does here. Stern may here lack the depth of poetry of Chung and the fearless brilliance of Perlman, but his accounts are full of character and not without distinction in their own right.

(i) *Violin concertos Nos. 1–2. The Love for 3 oranges:* suite.

(N) *** Decca Dig. 440 331-2 [id.]. (i) Bell; Montreal SO, Dutoit.

Employing a measure of emotional restraint and an exceptionally pure tone, Joshua Bell gives ravishingly beautiful accounts of both concertos, heightening in the great lyrical passages the light and shade contrasts with the formidable bravura writing, which finds him at his most commanding. Others like Chung may find darker emotions here but, with recording outstanding even by Decca's Montreal standards and with an unusual coupling in the arrangement of six pieces from *The Love for Three Oranges*, this is warmly recommendable.

Violin concerto No. 1 in D, Op. 19.
(Y/B) *** Sony SK 66567 [id.]. Julian Rachlin, Moscow RSO, Vladimir Fedoseyev – TCHAIKOVSKY: *Violin concerto.* ***
(***) EMI mono CDH7 64562-2 [id.]. Szigeti, LPO, Beecham – MENDELSSOHN: *Violin concerto;* MOZART: *Violin concerto No. 4.* (***)

The yearning, hushed beauty of Rachlin's treatment of the great opening melody recalls Philip Hope-Wallace's description of Galli-Curci's singing: 'like a nightingale half asleep'. This is not only a movingly poetic performance, with the lyrical outer movements both lighter and faster-flowing than usual, but one which consistently brings out the wit and fun in the writing. It may not be everyone's first choice, but there is no more distinctive reading on disc than this, and anyone who wants this unusual coupling need not hesitate, with the Tchaikovsky also more meditative than usual.

Szigeti's classic (1934) account of Prokofiev's *D major Concerto* with Beecham and the LPO may have been matched but it has hardly been surpassed. It has a virtuosity, a sense of character, an astringency and magic which are quite special. The EMI CD transfer is definitely the one to have: quite smooth and refined.

Violin concerto No. 2 in G min., Op. 63.
(N) (M) *** RCA 09026 61744-2 [61744-2-RG]. Heifetz, Boston SO, Munch – GLAZUNOV; SIBELIUS: *Concertos.* ***
(N) (B) *** EMI forte CZS5 69331-2 (2) [id.]. David Oistrakh, Philh. O, Galliera – BEETHOVEN: *Triple concerto;* BRAHMS: *Double concerto;* MOZART: *Violin concerto No. 3.* ***

In the *arioso*-like slow movement, Heifetz chooses a faster speed than is usual, but there is nothing unresponsive about his playing, for his expressive rubato has an unfailing inevitability. In the spiky finale he is superb, and indeed his playing is glorious throughout. The recording is serviceable merely, though it has been made firmer in the current remastering. But no one is going to be prevented from enjoying this ethereal performance because the technical quality is dated.

David Oistrakh's account of Prokofiev's *G minor Concerto*, made in 1958, occupies a place of honour in the catalogue. In some respects it has never been surpassed, though Heifetz's recordings with Koussevitzky and Munch fall into a special category. Oistrakh's is a beautifully balanced reading which lays stress on the lyricism of the concerto, and the orchestral support he receives could hardly be improved upon. The 1958 recording is admirably spacious and atmospheric, with finely focused detail and great warmth. The CD transfer is immaculate. An altogether marvellous performance, and this forte compilation of four very distinguished concertante recordings is extraordinary value for money.

Divertimento, Op. 43; The Prodigal Son, Op. 46; Symphonic song, Op. 57; Andante (Piano Sonata No. 4).
*** Chandos Dig. CHAN 8728 [id.]. SNO, Järvi.

The *Divertimento* is a lovely piece: its first movement has an irresistible and haunting second theme. Its long neglect is puzzling since it is highly attractive and ought to be popular. So, for that matter, should *The Prodigal Son*, some of whose material Prokofiev re-used the following year in the *Fourth Symphony*. Another rarity is the *Symphonic song*, a strange, darkly scored piece. The recording is first class – as, indeed, are the performances. An indispensable item in any Prokofiev collection.

The Gambler: 4 Portraits, Op. 49; Semyon Kotko: Symphonic suite, Op. 81 bis.
*** Chandos Dig. CHAN 8803 [id.]. SNO, Järvi.

Prokofiev's *Four Portraits* enshrine the best of the opera and are exhilarating and inventive. *Semyon Kotko*, though not top-drawer Prokofiev, is still thoroughly enjoyable. Järvi gives a thoroughly sympathetic reading in vivid and present sound.

Lieutenant Kijé (incidental music): *suite, Op. 60.*
(M) *** EMI Dig. CD-EMX 2214. LPO, Takuo Yuasa – RIMSKY-KORSAKOV: *Scheherazade.* ***

There are many fine accounts of Prokofiev's *Lieutenant Kijé* currently available, but this ranks among the best, the performance beguiling in its affectionate geniality and sense of nostalgia, yet with the *Troika* strongly rhythmic but without heaviness. The full, warm recording helps in this impression, slightly softer in focus than in the vivid coupling.

(i) *Lieutenant Kijé* (suite); *Love for three oranges:* suite; (ii) *Peter and the wolf;* (iii) *Romeo and Juliet* (ballet): excerpts; (iv) *Scythian suite, Op. 20;* (i) *Symphony No. 1 (Classical).*
(B) ** Ph. Duo 442 278-2 (2) [id.]. (i) LSO, Marriner; (ii) Alec McCowen, Concg. O, Haitink; (iii) Rotterdam PO, Edo de Waart; (iv) LAPO, Previn.

Marriner's LSO accounts of the *Lieutenant Kijé* and *Love for three oranges suites* and the *Classical Symphony* are all lively, well played and naturally recorded; but one only has to compare the symphony with his earlier, Decca/Argo version (currently withdrawn) to discover an extra dimension in that performance. In *Peter and the wolf* Alec McCowen uses a new text by Erik Smith which is intelligently prepared to give a fresh look at the story. However, the addition of bird imitations, including the duck quacking 'Let me out!' inside the wolf's stomach at the end, is rather twee and seems designed to appeal to the youngest of listeners. Yet taken as a whole the presentation is vivid, and undoubtedly children will enjoy its liveliness. Perhaps the finest performance comes from the Rotterdam Philharmonic, who play (and very well too) 11 well-chosen numbers from Prokofiev's great Shakespearean ballet score. The recording is full and atmospheric. But the most vivid sound of all comes in Previn's *Scythian suite*, which approaches the demonstration bracket. However, the performance does not quite match this degree of drama: for some reason Previn was not on his best form on this occasion.

The Love for three oranges: suite.
(B) ** Sony SBK 53621; *SBT 53621* [id.]. Phd. O, Ormandy – SHOSTAKOVICH: *Symphony No. 5* etc. **(*)

(i) *Love for three oranges* (suite), *Op. 33a; Scythian suite, Op. 20;* (ii) *Symphony No. 5, Op. 100.*
(M) **(*) Mercury 432 753-2 [id.]. (i) LSO; (ii) Minneapolis SO, Antal Dorati.

Dorati's account of Prokofiev's powerful and atmospheric *Scythian suite* was recorded at Watford Town Hall in 1957; the remastering confirms the excellence of the original engineering. The suite from the *Love for three oranges* is similarly striking in its characterization and vivid primary colours, with the resonance not blunting the rhythms. The CD is worth considering for these two performances; but the *Fifth Symphony*, recorded in Minneapolis two years later, is less successful. Dorati's reading is similarly forceful but the effect is hard and often unsympathetic.

Superb orchestral playing of course, but Ormandy's view of the score is larger than life, spectacle seemingly more important than subtlety, which the close recording tends to emphasize. The excitement is undeniable, but the famous *March* seems rather inflated and heavy.

On the Dnieper (ballet), *Op. 51; Le pas d'acier* (ballet), *Op. 41.*
*** Olympia Dig. OCD 103 [id.]. USSR MoC SO, Rozhdestvensky.

Le pas d'acier is full of vitality and – apart from one or two numbers – highly attractive, very much in the *ballet mécanique* style; *On the Dnieper* is a lyrical work not dissimilar to *The Prodigal Son*. Colourful performances and recordings. Lovers of Prokofiev's ballets should not miss this welcome addition to the discography.

Peter and the wolf, Op. 67 (see also above, under *Cinderella*).
✪ (M) *** Virgin/EMI Dig. CU5 61137-2 [id.]. Gielgud, Ac. of L., Richard Stamp – SAINT-SAENS: *Carnival.* ***
(BB) *** ASV CDQS 6017. Angela Rippon, RPO, Hughes – SAINT-SAENS: *Carnival.* ***
(N) (BB) **(*) Tring Dig. TRP 046 [id.]. Sir John Gielgud, RPO, Andrea Licata – BIZET: *Jeux d'enfants;* ** SAINT-SAENS: *Carnival.* **(*)
(M) **(*) EMI Dig. CD-EMX 2165; *TC-EMX 2165.* William Rushton, LPO, Sian Edwards – BRITTEN: *Young person's guide* ***; RAVEL: *Ma Mère l'Oye.* **
**(*) EMI Dig. CDC7 54730-2 [id.]. Phillip Schofield, Toulouse Capitole O, Plasson (with BRITTEN: *Young person's guide to the orchestra* **(*)) – SAINT-SAENS: *Carnival of the animals.* **
(N) ** Cala Dig. CACD 1022 [id.]. Ben Kingsley, LSO, Mackerras – BRITTEN: *Young person's guide to the orchestra;* DUKAS: *L'apprenti sorcier.* **

(i) *Peter and the wolf;* (ii) *Violin concerto No. 1 in D. Symphony No. 1 in D (Classical).*
**(*) Nimbus NI 5192 [id.]. (i) Christopher Lee; (ii) Hu Kun; E. String O, Sir Yehudi Menuhin.

(i; ii) *Peter and the wolf;* (iii) *Lieutenant Kijé: suite;* (iv) *Love for 3 oranges: suite;* (ii) *Symphony No. 1 in D (Classical).*
✪ (B) *** Decca 433 612-2 [id.]. (i) Sir Ralph Richardson, (ii) LSO, Sargent; (iii) Paris Conservatoire O, Boult; (iv) LPO, Weller.

Sir John Gielgud's highly individual presentation of Prokofiev's masterly narrative with orchestra brings a worthy successor to our previous favourite version, by Sir Ralph Richardson for Decca; moreover Richard Stamp and the Academy of London have the advantage of a superb, modern, digital recording, warmly atmospheric but with a strikingly wide dynamic range. At the end, Sir John, who has presided over these events with a wonderfully benign involvement, becomes Grandfather himself with his restrained moral questioning of Peter's youthful bravado. Throughout, his obvious relish for the colour as well as the narrative flow of the text has been splendidly matched by the detail and impetus of Richard Stamp's accompaniment.

Sir Ralph Richardson brings a great actor's feeling for words to the narrative; he dwells lovingly on their sound as well as their meaning, and this genial preoccupation with the manner in which the story is told matches Sargent's feeling exactly. Sir Malcolm Sargent's direction of the accompaniment shows his professionalism at its very best. The original coupling, Sargent's amiable, polished account of the *Classical Symphony*, has now been restored. All the tempi, except the finale, are slow but Sir Malcolm's assured elegance carries its own spontaneity. The sound is vivid. Boult's Paris recording of *Lieutenant Kijé* offers more gusto than finesse, but the result is exhilaratingly robust and the very early (1955) stereo comes up remarkably well. Weller's *Love for three oranges* is a first-class performance, given top-drawer 1977 recording. But our Rosette is for *Peter and the wolf*.

Angela Rippon narrates with charm yet is never in the least coy; indeed she is thoroughly involved in the tale and thus also involves the listener. The accompaniment is equally spirited, with excellent orchestral playing, and the recording is splendidly clear, yet not lacking atmosphere. This makes an excellent super-bargain recommendation.

Sir John Gielgud made his second recording of *Peter and the wolf* six years after the first, which is orchestrally superior. In this new version the narrative may be more mature but the manner is just as friendly and avuncular; Gielgud becomes increasingly caught up in the story as it progresses, and so do we. The moment when the wolf catches its prey is vividly exciting (and the oboe soloist here responds poignantly) and at the end of the story Gielgud's pleasure in discovering that the duck is still alive bubbles over with merriment. The Italian conductor directs competently and there is some good solo playing from the RPO, but it is the enthusiastic participation of Gielgud and his wonderfully varied vocal inflexions that make this performance so enjoyable. Voice and orchestra are recorded in different acoustics but are quite well edited together.

Although narrative and orchestral commentary were recorded separately on the Eminence recording, it is remarkable how well the two fit together. William Rushton was able to add his story-telling to a vividly colourful orchestral tapestry which had its momentum already established. He is a personable narrator, adding touches of his own like a 'vast' grey wolf and 'nothing to report' from the bird; and this remains a direct, sparkling presentation, brightly and realistically recorded, which cannot fail to entertain children of all ages.

Christopher Lee's is a very relaxed performance, with Menuhin and his orchestra following the narrative rather lazily, but Lee's resonant, richly coloured voice keeps the action going agreeably. With the resonant recording making everything sound somewhat larger than life, it is good that the whimsical pace of the narrative does not preclude excitement and, after the capture, Grandfather's dusty comment is illustrated by some appropriate grumbling from the bassoon. The final procession is grandly expansive, surely the slowest on record, but then Lee delivers the final twist in the story, about the duck's survival, rather neatly. Menuhin's account of the *Classical Symphony* is again very relaxed until the sparkling finale (the *Gavotte* is heavy as well as slow) and Hu Kun's account of the *Violin concerto* is enjoyable rather than distinctive.

Phillip Schofield's narration is bright and enters into the story with enthusiastic, youthful aplomb. His pacing is a bit erratic, quickening at moments of excitement, and the effect will surely appeal to younger TV addicts. While the closing processional is less ambitious than with Menuhin, the oboe is ethereal in resurrecting the duck – almost as if he were a ghost. The couplings are both old analogue recordings. Sir Charles Groves's performance of Britten's *Variations and fugue on a theme of Purcell* (from 1977) is lively and genial; if it lacks the last degree of finesse, it has both high spirits and a fine sense of pace. The analogue recording is first class, colourful and vivid, and younger listeners should certainly respond to it. (There is no narrative.)

Ben Kingsley's narration is a disappointment, very laid back and not very spontaneous-sounding at the opening. His finest moment is his sinister evocation of the wolf 'looking at them with greedy eyes'. Although played and recorded well, there are more spirited versions available than this.

Romeo and Juliet (ballet), *Op. 64* (complete).
(N) (B) *** EMI forte CZS5 68607-2 (2). LSO, Previn.
*** Decca 417 510-2 (2) [id.]. Cleveland O, Maazel.
*** DG Dig. 423 268-2 (2) [id.]. Boston SO, Ozawa.
(N) (BB) **(*) Naxos Dig. 8.553184/5 [id.]. Ukraine Nat. SO, Mogrelia.

(Y/B) ** Royal Opera House Dig. ROH 309–10 [id.]. ROHCG O, Mark Ermler.
(Y/B) ** Chandos Dig. CHAN 9322/3 [id.]. Danish Nat. RSO, Dmitri Kitajenko.

Almost simultaneously in 1973 two outstanding versions of Prokofiev's complete *Romeo and Juliet* ballet appeared, strongly contrasted to provide a clear choice on grounds of interpretation and recording. Previn and the LSO made their recording in conjunction with live performances at the Royal Festival Hall, and the result reflects the humour and warmth which went with those live occasions. Previn's pointing of rhythm is consciously seductive, whether in fast, jaunty numbers or in the soaring lyricism of the love music. The Kingsway Hall recording quality is full and immediate, yet atmospheric too.

Maazel by contrast will please those who believe that this score should above all be bitingly incisive. The rhythms are more consciously metrical, the tempi generally faster, and the precision of ensemble of the Cleveland Orchestra is little short of miraculous. The recording is one of Decca's most spectacular, searingly detailed but atmospheric too. However, the reissue of the Previn set, vividly transferred, at bargain price as a forte double gives it – for the moment – an unbeatable price advantage.

Immediately at the opening, one notices Ozawa's special balletic feeling in the elegance of the string phrasing and the light, rhythmic felicity. Yet he can rise to the work's drama and in the love-music his ardour is compulsive, even if the element of pungency which Maazel brings to the score is almost entirely missing in Boston. But this music-making is very easy to enjoy and the actual playing is very fine indeed, while Ozawa has the advantage of outstanding modern digital recording, full of atmosphere.

Mogrelia's fine Naxos version has drama, irony, delicacy and passionate romantic feeling. His tempi are not always conventional but he secures playing of the highest quality from the first-rate Ukrainian orchestra, and there is plenty of atmosphere. The recording is excellent: spacious, vivid and transparent. The snag is that the synopsis is not related to the 52 separate cues, which are unidentified with titles.

If recording was the sole criterion, then the Royal Opera House's own recording of *Romeo and Juliet* with its fine orchestra and Mark Ermler would sweep the board. This is simply magnificent sound, with sumptuous tone and splendid body and presence. Also usually magnificent is the playing of the Opera House Orchestra, but here it is distinctly under-vitalized and wanting in zest and sparkle. Not recommended except perhaps to audio buffs who specialize in demonstration sound.

Kitajenko's account is very well recorded too, without being quite in the demonstration class of the Ermler. The performance is a very good one but without all the imaginative drive, dramatic fire or sense of atmosphere that are so essential in this wonderful score.

Romeo and Juliet (ballet): extended excerpts.
**(*) RCA Dig. 09026 61388-2 [id.]. Philh. O, Flor.

The new RCA selection (made from all three ballet suites) is intensely felt and the Philharmonia playing is of the highest calibre, exquisite in *Romeo and Juliet before parting* and the delightful *Aubade*. Flor is often warmly attentive to lyrical detail, while the dramatic moments are histrionically arresting. But mostly it is the beauty of the orchestral playing one remembers and the full, expansive sound, deriving from EMI's No. 1 Studio at Abbey Road. This is very rewarding; however, what finally makes the disc uncompetitive is the measure: only 58 minutes.

Romeo and Juliet (ballet), *Op. 64:* highlights.
*** Sony Dig. MK 42662 [id.]. BPO, Salonen.
*** Virgin/EMI Dig. VC7 59278-2 [id.]. RLPO, Libor Pešek.

With magnificent playing from the Berlin Philharmonic Orchestra, Esa-Pekka Salonen's set seems marginally a first choice for those wanting merely a full-priced single disc of excerpts from Prokofiev's masterly score. The Berlin Philharmonic playing has an enormous intensity and a refined felicity in the score's more delicate moments. One is touched and deeply moved by this music-making, while the selection admirably parallels the work's narrative. The recording, made in the Philharmonie, matches sumptuousness with a potent clarity of projection, and the dynamic range is dramatically wide.

Like Salonen, Pešek's selection follows the narrative line, and one feels that the conductor and his players are highly involved in the course of events; in the closing numbers Pešek tightens the screws so that the *Death of Juliet* is devastating. The Royal Liverpool Philharmonic Orchestra play very well indeed and achieve great freshness and spontaneity; they are given a satisfying concert-hall balance. This Virgin CD offers 71 minutes from Prokofiev's inspired score, and every minute is stimulating and enjoyable; but it has to be said that the Berlin Philharmonic playing for Salonen is quite superb and the Sony recording is even more lavish.

Romeo and Juliet (ballet): *suites Nos. 1 & 2, Op. 64.*
(M) *** Mercury 432 004-2 [id.]. Minneapolis SO, Skrowaczewski – MUSSORGSKY: *Night.* ***
(Y/B) (B) **(*) Decca Double 440 630-2 (2) [id.]. SRO, Ansermet – TCHAIKOVSKY: *Swan Lake.* **(*)

Skrowaczewski's recording of the two ballet suites was made in 1962. The playing of the Minneapolis orchestra is on a virtuoso level. The crystal-clear acoustic of the hall in Edison High School, with its backing ambience, seems ideally suited to the angular melodic lines and pungent lyricism of this power-ful score, to underline the sense of tragedy without losing the music's romantic sweep. The fidelity and spectacle of the Mercury engineering reach a zenith in the powerful closing sequence of *Romeo at Juliet's tomb.* At mid-price this is highly recommendable.

Ansermet's performances have both atmosphere and passion (notably *Romeo with Juliet before his departure*). After the ominous introduction, the playing is rhythmically a bit sluggish. But *Juliet as a young girl* and the *Madrigal* are charming, and the love scene of *Romeo and Juliet* is genuinely touching; the *Death of Tybalt* bursts with energy, and *Masks* is nicely pointed. If the Suisse Romande Orchestra in 1961 was not one of the world's greatest ensembles, Ansermet was very persuasive and he brings everything vividly to life. The dramatically vibrant recording is well up to Decca's vintage standard of the early 1960s.

Romeo and Juliet: suite No. 1.
(N) (M) ** DG Dig. 445 577-2 [id.]. Nat. SO of Washington, Rostropovich – SHOSTAKOVICH: *Symphony No. 5.* **

Rostropovich gives a carefully prepared account, thoroughly attentive to details of dynamic markings and phrasing, but symphonic rather than balletic in approach. At no time does the listener feel tempted to spring into dance. Nevertheless the effect is atmospheric in a non-theatrical way, and to some ears the feeling of listening almost to an extended tone-poem is most rewarding, though to others the effect of Rostropovich's approach is ponderous at times. To be fair, some movements give no cause for com-plaint, and the sound, with sharply focused detail undoubtedly makes a vivid impact.

Romeo and Juliet: suites Nos. 1 & 2: excerpts.
*** Telarc Dig. CD 80089 [id.]. Cleveland O, Yoel Levi.
(M) **(*) Sony SBK 48169; *SBT 48169* [id.]. NYPO, Mitropoulos – STRAVINSKY: *Rite of spring.* *

Levi seems to have a special affinity with Prokofiev's score, for pacing is unerringly apt and characteriza-tion is strong. There are some wonderfully serene moments, as in the ethereal introduction of the flute melody in the first piece (*Montagues and Capulets*). The quicker movements have an engaging feeling of the dance and the light, graceful articulation in *The child Juliet* is a delight; but the highlights of the performance are the *Romeo and Juliet love scene* and *Romeo at Juliet's before parting,* bringing playing of great intensity, with a ravishing response from the Cleveland strings. The rich Telarc recording is in the demonstration class, but this offers less music than several of its competitors.

Under Mitropoulos, the New York Philharmonic played with tremendous conviction and dramatic flair. His *Romeo,* though not in every respect representative of the great conductor, should be investigated by all who admire this score. It is handicapped by its coupling, a very ordinary *Rite* under Mehta.

Romeo and Juliet (ballet): *suites Nos. 1 & 3.*
(Y/B) *** DG Dig. 439 870-2 [id.]. Concg. O, Myung-Whun Chung.

Myung-Whun Chung gets playing of great atmosphere, virtuosity and dramatic fire from the Royal Concertgebouw Orchestra, and DG provide a recording of great range and presence, comparable with the very best now in currency. A pity that they did not include the second suite, for which there would have been time, a self-inflicted wound which handicaps a record that should enjoy and certainly deserves the widest exposure. Those who invest in it will not be disappointed.

Romeo and Juliet (ballet): *suite.*
(M) *** Decca 417 737-2 [id.]. Cleveland O, Maazel – KHACHATURIAN: *Gayaneh; Spartacus.* **(*)

An intelligently chosen selection of six pieces (including *Juliet as a young girl,* the *Balcony scene* and *The last farewell*) makes a generous coupling for Decca's Khachaturian ballet scores.

Russian overture, Op. 72; Summer night: suite from *The Duenna, Op. 123; War and Peace* (suite, arr. Christopher Palmer).
*** Chandos Dig. CHAN 9096 [id.]. Philh. O, Järvi.

The *Russian overture* is determinedly popular in appeal, and it teems with ideas, both lyrical and grotesque, and has plenty of vitality. It is played here in a slightly reduced scoring. The *Summer night suite* is notable for its delicate *Serenade* and a charmingly romantic movement called *Dreams.* But the finest music here is Christopher Palmer's suite of interludes from *War and Peace,* full of splendid ideas.

It ends triumphantly with the magnificent patriotic tune associated with Marshal Kutuzov, the architect of the Russian victory. Järvi and the Philharmonia Orchestra are thoroughly at home in these scores, and the Chandos recording is characteristically spectacular. This is well worth exploring.

Sinfonia concertante in E min., Op. 125: see above, under *Concertino*
Sinfonietta in A, Op. 48 (see also below, under *Symphony No. 7*)
(Y/B) (M) *** Virgin/EMI Dig. CUV5 61206-2 [id.]. Lausanne CO, Zedda – DEBUSSY: *Danse* etc.;
MILHAUD: *Création du monde.* ***

Prokofiev could not understand why the early *Sinfonietta* failed to make an impression on the wider musical public, and neither can we. Alongside the *Classical Symphony* the *giocoso* outer movements have a more fragile geniality but they are highly delectable, as are the somewhat angular *Andante*, the brief *Intermezzo* and the witty Scherzo. The use of the orchestral palette is as subtle as it is engaging and, with Alberto Zedda's affectionately light touch and fine Lausanne playing, the piece emerges here with all colours flying. The fairly resonant sound, with the orchestra slightly recessed, adds to the feeling of warmth without blunting the orchestral articulation.

The Stone Flower (ballet): complete.
(Y/B) *** Russian Disc CD 11 022 (2) [id.]. Bolshoi Theatre O, Rozhdestvensky.

The Stone Flower is grievously (if understandably) neglected in favour of its two full-length companions, *Romeo and Juliet* and *Cinderella*. It is not as distinguished, characterful or inventive as they, but Prokofiev at second-best is still worth more than a lot of composers firing on all cylinders. There is much that is imaginative in this score, even if it is not the equal of its two companions in terms of consistency and inspiration. Rozhdestvensky's Bolshoi performance dates from 1968 and still sounds pretty good on CD, but in any case has no current competitors.

SYMPHONIES

Symphonies Nos. 1–7.
*** Chandos Dig. CHAN 8931/4 [id.]. SNO, Järvi.

Symphonies Nos. 1–7; Overture russe, Op. 72; Scythian suite, Op. 20.
(B) **(*) Decca 430 782-2 (4). LSO or LPO, Walter Weller.

These Chandos recordings from the mid-1980s are of the highest quality. They have been shorn of their couplings in this box, the only important loss being the delightful *Sinfonietta*. Both versions of the *Fourth Symphony* are included: the 1947 revision appears with the *Classical* on the first disc, while the 1930 original is coupled with the *Third*. Nos. 2 and 6 are on the third disc, and 5 and 7 on the last, so that no side-breaks are involved. As performances, these are the equal of the best.

Weller began his 1970s Kingsway Hall recordings with the LSO (Nos. 1, 5 and 7) then turned to the LPO. The performances are polished and very well played, though at times they are emotionally a little earthbound. Transfers are well managed, though there is some loss of naturalness in the upper range. The finest of the set is No. 2. Elsewhere, the bitter tang of Prokofiev's language is again toned down and the hard-etched lines smoothed over. The *Seventh* suits Weller's approach readily and he catches the atmosphere of its somewhat balletic second movement particularly well. The *Russian overture* has plenty of energy but the *Scythian suite*, too, needs more abrasiveness. However, those who normally find Prokofiev's orchestral writing too pungent could well be won over by these performances.

Symphony No. 1 in D (Classical), Op. 25.
*** DG Dig. 423 624-2 [id.]. Orpheus CO – BIZET: *Symphony;* BRITTEN: *Simple symphony.* ***

The Orpheus performance has freshness and wit – the droll bassoon solo in the first movement against sparkling string figurations is delightful. In the cantilena of the *Larghetto*, some ears might crave a greater body of violin tone; but the playing has a fine poise, and the minuet and finale have equal flair. Excellent, truthful recording to make this a highly desirable triptych.

Symphonies Nos. 1 in D (Classical), Op. 25; 3 in C min., Op. 44.
*** Ph. Dig. 432 992-2 [id.]. Phd. O, Muti.

Riccardo Muti's account of the *Third Symphony* is strongly characterized and atmospheric, and it has the edge on Neeme Järvi (Chandos) in this respect. Indeed this is the most thrilling account since Abbado's Decca version (see below). It casts a strong spell and is superbly recorded with rich, present and well-detailed sonority – real state-of-the-art sound. The Philadelphia Orchestra may not sound as special as they did in the days of Ormandy or Stokowski, but they remain a first-class ensemble. The

Classical Symphony is one of the best around – and even offers the occasional reminder of Koussevitzky's pioneering recording from the 1930s – there is no higher praise!

Symphonies Nos. 1 in D (Classical); 4 in C, Op. 112 (revised 1947 version).
*** Chandos Dig. CHAN 8400 [id.]. SNO, Järvi.

Järvi succeeds in making out a more eloquent case for the revision of the *Fourth Symphony* than many of his predecessors. He also gives an exhilarating account of the *Classical Symphony*, one of the best on record. The slow movement has real douceur and the finale is wonderfully high-spirited. On CD, the recording has fine range and immediacy, but in the *Fourth Symphony* the upper range is a little fierce in some of the more forceful climaxes.

Symphonies Nos. 1 in D (Classical), Op. 25; 5 in B flat, Op. 100.
(M) *** DG 437 253-2 [id.]. BPO, Karajan.
(Y/B) (M) *** Ph. Dig. 442 399-2 [id.]. LAPO, André Previn.
*** Sony Dig. SK 48239 [id.]. LSO, Tilson Thomas.
(M) *** RCA Dig. 09026 61350-2 [id.]. LPO, Slatkin.
(M) **(*) Sony SBK 53260; *SBT 53260* [id.]. Phd. O, Ormandy.
(M) *(**) Sony SMK 47602 [id.]. NYPO, Bernstein.

Karajan's 1979 recording of the *Fifth* is in a class of its own. The playing has wonderful tonal sophistication and Karajan judges tempi to perfection so that proportions seem quite ideal. The recording has an excellent perspective and allows all the subtleties of orchestral detail to register; however, the digital remastering has overtly brightened the upper range, while the bass response is drier. Nevertheless this remains among the most distinguished *Fifths* ever recorded, and it is coupled with Karajan's 1982 digital recording of the *Classical Symphony*, in which his performance is predictably brilliant and the playing beautifully polished, with grace and eloquence distinguishing the slow movement.

In the first movement of the *Fifth*, Previn's pacing seems exactly right: everything flows so naturally and speaks effectively. The Scherzo is not as high-voltage as some rivals, but Previn still brings it off well; and in the slow movement he gets playing of genuine eloquence from the Los Angeles orchestra. He also gives an excellent account of the perennially fresh *Classical Symphony*. The recording is beautifully natural, with impressive detail, range and body. Although Karajan reigns supreme in this coupling, his analogue recording does not match this Philips competitor, and those wanting modern, digital sound will find Previn an ideal mid-priced alternative.

Tilson Thomas gives a very well-thought-out reading of the *Fifth* and enjoys the benefit of first-class Sony recording. There is a sense of scale and strong character here, though the tenderness that surfaces from time to time in the slow movement eludes him and there could be a more carefree virtuosity in the finale. But these are quibbles and there is no reason not to give this three stars. It is a very lively and intelligent performance, and the recording has much going for it. All the same it does not offer any real challenge to the Karajan, which remains our first recommendation.

Ultimately the same holds for Slatkin's St Louis performance on RCA at mid-price. It is eminently well shaped, spacious and characterful, and there is no want of virtuosity or lyricism. Thoroughly recommendable, without being a first choice.

The Philadelphia Orchestra play superbly and with much wit in the *Classical Symphony*. Ormandy's expansive warmth in the *Adagio* and the easy brilliance of the orchestral articulation in the second and fourth movements make for splendid results in the *Fifth*. Although the early stereo recording could be more opulent and less brightly lit, it still conveys impressively the ample body of tone this great orchestra was creating in the late 1950s.

In the first two movements, Bernstein's homage to the *Classical Symphony*'s eighteenth-century ancestry produces a slightly self-conscious stiffness of manner, but even so the bassoonist manages a gentle smile in his solo and the poise of the strings in the slow movement's upper cantilena is superb. The finale is exhilarating, yet played with admirable precision. In No. 5 he draws more exciting and at times affectionate playing from the NYPO. Bernstein certainly has an ear for the kind of sonority that Prokofiev wanted, and the atmosphere is often well captured (the second subject of the first movement is presented very effectively). Yet, for all its excitement and undoubted commitment, this performance may be found too idiosyncratic for repeated listening, although there are no complaints about the vividness of the recording, made in the Avery Fisher Hall in the mid-1960s.

Symphonies Nos. 1 in D (Classical), Op. 25; 5 in B flat, Op. 100; Romeo and Juliet: excerpts; Chout: final dance.
(Y/B) ❀ (M) (***) RCA mono 09026 61657-2 [id.]. Boston SO, Koussevitzky.

Koussevitzky's *Fifth Symphony* and the four movements from *Romeo and Juliet* are quite simply breathtaking and have never been equalled, except perhaps by Karajan's 1969 record with the Berlin Philharmonic. Yet this has even more fire, zest and virtuosity, and the recordings, made in 1945–6, are remarkably good. The *Classical Symphony* is not to be confused with Koussevitzky's sparkling account on 78-r.p.m. records. Both the *Classical Symphony* and the *Danse finale* from *Chout* come from 1947 and were recorded when the orchestra were on a visit to Carnegie Hall, New York. Likewise these are thrilling performances on which it would be very difficult to improve and, again, few allowances have to be made for the sound-quality. An outstanding issue in every way.

Symphonies Nos. 1 (Classical); 7, Op. 131; Love for 3 oranges (opera): *suite*.
(B) *** CfP CD-CFP 4523. Philh. O, Malko.

All the performances here are quite excellent, and the *Seventh Symphony*, of which Malko conducted the UK première, is freshly conceived and finely shaped. What is so striking is the range and refinement of the 1955 stereo recording: the excellence of the balance and the body of the sound are remarkable.

Symphony No. 2 in D min., Op. 40; Romeo and Juliet (ballet): *suite No. 1, Op. 64.*
**(*) Chandos Dig. CHAN 8368 [id.]. SNO, Järvi.

The *Second Symphony* reflects the iconoclastic temper of the early 1920s; the violence and dissonance of its first movement betray Prokofiev's avowed intention of writing a work 'made of iron and steel'. Neeme Järvi produces altogether excellent results from the Scottish National Orchestra and the Chandos recording is impressively detailed and vivid. The *Romeo and Juliet* suite comes off well; the SNO play with real character.

Symphony No. 3 in C min., Op. 44.
(N) (M) *** Decca 448 579-2 [id.]. LSO, Abbado – HINDEMITH: *Symphonic metamorphoses on themes of Weber*. JANACEK: *Sinfonietta*. ***

In the *Third Symphony* Abbado penetrates the atmosphere and mystery of the highly imaginative inner movements most successfully. These movements exert quite a powerful spell, and their impact is all the greater for Abbado's total lack of exaggeration. The outer movements are slightly less successful, needing a shade more bite and momentum. But the Decca recording has fine body and presence, and if the couplings are suitable this is still very recommendable.

Symphonies Nos. 3; 4 in C, Op. 47 (original, 1930 version).
*** Chandos Dig. CHAN 8401 [id.]. SNO, Järvi.

Neeme Järvi's account of the *Third* is extremely successful. In many ways the original of the *Fourth Symphony* seems more like a ballet suite than a symphony: its insufficient tonal contrast tells – yet the Scherzo, drawn from the music for the Temptress in *The Prodigal Son* ballet, is particularly felicitous.

Symphony No. 5 in B flat, Op. 100.
*** Chandos Dig. CHAN 8576 [id.]. Leningrad PO, Jansons.

(i)*Symphony No. 5;* (ii) *Lieutenant Kijé* (suite).
(N) (M) **(*) Sony SMK 66933 [id.]. (i) Israel PO, Bernstein. (ii) Nat. O of France, Maazel.

Symphony No. 5 in B flat, Op. 100; Waltz suite, Op. 110.
*** Chandos Dig. CHAN 8450 [id.]. SNO, Järvi.

Mariss Jansons's reading with the Leningrad Philharmonic was recorded at a live concert in Dublin. Needless to say, the playing is pretty high voltage, with firm, rich string-tone, particularly from the lower strings, and distinctive wind timbre. Jansons goes for brisk tempi – and in the slow movement he really is too fast. The Scherzo is dazzling and so, too, is the finale, which is again fast and overdriven. An exhilarating and exciting performance, eminently well recorded, recommended to those willing to accept the ungenerous measure.

Järvi's credentials in this repertoire are well established and his direction unhurried, fluent and authoritative. His feeling for the music is unfailingly natural. The three *Waltzes* which derive from various sources are all elegantly played. The Chandos recording is set just a shade further back than some of its companions in the series, yet at the same time every detail is clear.

It would be easy to underestimate Bernstein's version of the *Fifth Symphony*. Edited from live performances, it is a consistently powerful reading, but with the romantic expressiveness underlined. Bernstein is superb at building climaxes, and the playing has great concentration, but for some ears there is too much emotional weight. The recording is bold and full (made in 1979) with a strong, firm bass line.

Maazel, too, gives an exceptionally dramatic and strongly characterized account of Prokofiev's colourful suite, recorded two years later. Though he does not miss the nostalgia of *Lieutenant Kijé*, it is the pungency of the rhythms and the sharp pointing of detail that register most strongly, helped by the resonant acoustic, which adds an effective degree of edge to Prokofiev's bolder scoring. Inner detail registers vividly at all dynamic levels; while Maazel is clearly seeking a strong projection rather than refinement, the committed orchestral response is exhilarating.

Symphonies Nos. 5 in B flat, Op. 100; 7 in C sharp min., Op. 131.
(M) *** EMI CDM5 65181-2 [id.]. LSO, Previn.

In No. 5 Previn takes a weighty view of a wide-spanning symphony. His first-movement tempo is spacious, and the contrasts are strongly underlined, with Prokofiev's characteristic use of heavy brass, notably the tuba, superbly brought out by the LSO players, not to mention the EMI engineers. The slow movement too is firmly placed in the grand tradition of Russian symphonies. The Scherzo and later the finale have fractionally less brilliance than one expects from this source but, with full recording, the effect is still formidably powerful. In the *Seventh*, too, Previn produces much inner vitality and warmth, and again the EMI engineers provide a realistic and integrated sound.

Symphony No. 6 in E flat min., Op. 111. Waltz suite, Op. 110, Nos. 1, 5 and 6.
*** Chandos Dig. CHAN 8359 [id.]. SNO, Järvi.

Though it lags far behind the *Fifth* in popularity, the *Sixth Symphony* goes much deeper than any of its companions; indeed it is perhaps the greatest of the Prokofiev cycle. Neeme Järvi has an instinctive grasp and deep understanding of this symphony; he shapes its detail as skilfully as he does its architecture as a whole. These artists have the measure of the music's tragic poignancy more than almost any of their predecessors on record. The fill-up, as its title implies, is a set of waltzes, drawn and adapted from various stage works.

Symphonies Nos. 6 in E flat min., Op. 111; 7 in C sharp min., Op. 131.
(Y/B) ** Decca Dig. 443 325-2 [id.]. Cleveland O, Ashkenazy.

Ashkenazy's account of the *Sixth Symphony* is quite easily the best recorded in the current catalogue, and the same goes for the *Seventh*. But the actual performances here are less remarkable. In the *Sixth Symphony* Ashkenazy sometimes loses the vital current that flows through its first movement, relaxing the tension a little too much. On the other hand, the *Largo* is really too fast to make the requisite contrast with the *Allegro* movement, and the opening of the finale is far too fast. The opening of the *Seventh Symphony* is phrased rather fussily, though further into the first movement the music is allowed to adopt its natural flow. Generally speaking this is not quite the artistic success which one had every reason to expect.

Symphony No. 7 in C sharp min., Op. 131; Sinfonietta in A, Op. 5/48.
*** Chandos Dig. CHAN 8442 [id.]. SNO, Järvi.

Neeme Järvi's account of the *Seventh Symphony* is hardly less successful than the other issues in this cycle. He draws very good playing from the SNO and has the full measure of this repertoire. The early *Sinfonietta* is a highly attractive coupling (what a sunny and charming piece it is!). The digital recording has great range and is excellently balanced.

CHAMBER AND INSTRUMENTAL MUSIC

Cello sonata in C, Op. 119.
*** Chandos Dig. CHAN 8340 [id.]. Yuli Turovsky. Luba Edlina – SHOSTAKOVICH: *Sonata.* ***

Yuli Turovsky and Luba Edlina are eloquent advocates of this *Sonata*. A finely wrought and rewarding score, it deserves greater popularity, and this excellent performance and recording should make it new friends. The balance is particularly lifelike on CD.

Overture on Jewish themes (for clarinet, piano & string quartet), *Op. 34; Quintet* (for oboe, clarinet, violin, viola & cello), *Op. 39.*
(N) (B) *** HM Dig.HMA 1901419 [id.]. Walter Boeykens Ens. (with KOKAI: *Clarinet quartettino* ***)
  – KHACHATURIAN: *Clarinet trio.* ***

Prokofiev composed his *Overture on Jewish themes* in 1919 at the request of a Jewish commission from a small ensemble of musical refugees in New York (hence the instrumentation). He warmed to a pair of melodies taken from a collection provided by the commission, and the result is a delightful work, at first nostalgic, then energetic and jocular. The *Quintet* was written to accompany a ballet commissioned by a Russian dancer whom the composer had met while working with Diaghilev. It has a wide range of moods: gentle, sardonic, burlesque; while highly characteristic of its composer, it also brings clear rhythmic influences from Stravinsky. Both works are performed here with vigour, affection and wit; indeed they are beautifully played and recorded. The *Quartetettino* (for clarinet and string trio) by Rezsö

Kókai (1906–62) provided as a bonus is deliciously flimsy in texture (suggesting Françaix with Hungarian inflexions) but with a touching folk-tune-like *Canzonetta* for its slow movement.

String quartets Nos. 1 in B min., Op. 50; 2 in F, Op. 92.
*** Olympia Dig. OCD 340 [id.]. American Qt.

The American Quartet play the *First Quartet* far more persuasively than any earlier version and reveal it to be a work of some appeal as well as substance. The *Second* incorporates folk ideas from Kabarda in the Caucasus, to highly characteristic ends. Although the performance does not have quite the bite and zest of the Hollywood Quartet, it does not fall far short of it, and the recording is absolutely first class. A rewarding issue.

String quartet No. 2 in F, Op. 92.
(Y/B) 🅖 (***) Testament mono SBT 1052 [id.]. Hollywood Qt – HINDEMITH: *Quartet No. 3;* WALTON: *Quartet in A min.* *** 🅖

There have been innumerable recordings of Prokofiev's *Second Quartet* since the pioneering Hollywood Quartet version first appeared on these shores in 1952. Not one has matched let alone surpassed this stunning performance, which has an extraordinary precision and intensity (as well as repose when this is required). The transfer sounds excellent and, although the mono sound does not represent the state of the art these days, the performance surely does.

Violin sonata (for solo violin), Op. 115; Sonata for two violins.
*** Chandos Dig. CHAN 8988 [id.]. Mordkovitch, Young – SCHNITTKE: *Prelude;* SHOSTAKOVICH: *Violin sonata.* ***

Sonata for 2 violins, Op. 56.
*** Hyperion Dig. CDA 66473 [id.]. Osostowicz, Kovacic – MARTINU: *Violin sonata;* MILHAUD: *Violin duo* etc. **(*)

The solo *Violin sonata in D*, Op. 115, is a crisply characteristic piece in three short movements. The *Sonata in C for two violins*, written much earlier, is just as effective, played – as here – by solo violins. The warmth of Lydia Mordkovitch is well matched by her partner, Emma Young.

The *Sonata for two violins* gives the impression of being vintage Prokofiev, as performed by Krysia Osostowicz and Ernst Kovacic. The slow movement is played with exceptional imagination and poetry.

Violin sonatas Nos. 1 in F min., Op. 80; 2 in D, Op. 94a.
(N) (M) *** DG Dig. 445 557-2 [id.]. Shlomo Mintz, Yefim Bronfman – RAVEL: *Violin sonata in G.* ***

(i) *Violin sonatas Nos. 1–2;* (ii) *Violin concerto No. 2 in G min., Op. 63.*
(M) *** RCA 09026 61454-2 [id.]. Itzhak Perlman; (i) Vladimir Ashkenazy; (ii) Boston SO, Leinsdorf.

Violin sonatas Nos. 1–2; 5 Mélodies, Op. 35a.
(Y/B) **(*) Decca 440 926-2 [id.]. Joshua Bell, Olli Mustonen.

Both the *Violin sonatas* date from the years immediately after Prokofiev returned to the Soviet Union. The *F minor Sonata* is one of his very finest works, and the *D major*, originally written for the flute and sometimes heard in that form, has a winning charm and melodiousness. Both works are masterly and rewarding.

Shlomo Mintz made a great impression with his coupling of the two *Concertos*, and his recording of the *Sonatas* is hardly less successful. Mintz has a wonderful purity of line and immaculate intonation, and his partner, Yefim Bronfman, is both vital and sensitive. These are commanding performances, imaginative in phrasing and refined in approach. The DG recording is excellent. This is a clear first choice.

Perlman and Ashkenzy also play both works superbly, and the 1969 recording is well balanced, slightly dry in timbre but otherwise truthful. Their coupling is the *Second Violin concerto*, recorded three years earlier. It is an enjoyably fresh and spontaneous account and, even if Leinsdorf provides an accomplished rather than a highly individual accompaniment, the finale comes off particularly vividly. Good recording, with the soloist balanced well forward.

Joshua Bell and Olli Mustonen give a highly intelligent reading of both pieces and the charming *Cinq Mélodies*. Their playing is worth a full three-star rating: both artists have keen and sensitive responses, but they are rather let down by the recording. Although made in one of the best of venues, St George's, Brandon Hill, in Bristol, it favours the piano very much at the expense of the violin. Perlman and Ashkenazy, now restored to circulation on RCA, are to be preferred.

Violin sonata No. 2 in D.
** Ph. Dig. 426 254-2. Viktoria Mullova, Bruno Canino – RAVEL: *Sonata in G;* STRAVINSKY: *Divertimento.* ***

The *Second Sonata* is given a brilliant performance by Mullova and Canino, even if the lyrical charm and tenderness of the first movement elude them and the scherzo is rather rushed. This is musically not as impressive as the Stravinsky or the Ravel with which it is coupled. The recording is quite superb.

PIANO MUSIC

Piano sonatas 1–9 (complete); *Lieutenant Kijé* (suite, transcribed Chiu).
**(*) HM Dig. HMU 907086/8 (3) [id.]. Frederic Chiu.

Frederic Chiu is a brilliant young Chinese-American pianist who has just turned thirty. This is exciting playing and, though there may be a number of interpretative decisions which may not persuade all listeners, this is a set that should be heard. His tempi can be a little extreme, and there are greater extremes of dynamics and colours. The *Seventh* is brilliant and can be ranked along with the best, and the *Sixth*, though not superior to either of the Kissin accounts, is pretty dazzling. Throughout the cycle he impresses with his marvellous fingers, abundant energy and good musical taste. Unfortunately the recording lets him down: the tone is shallow and the balance a bit too close. Otherwise this would have been a strong three-star recommendation.

Piano sonata No. 1 in F min., Op. 1; 4 Pieces, Op. 4; Prelude and Fugue in D min. (Buxtehude, arr. Prokofiev); *2 Sonatinas, Op. 54; Gavotte (Hamlet, Op. 77bis); 3 Pieces, Op. 96.*
*** Chandos Dig. CHAN 9017 [id.]. Boris Berman.

Piano sonata No. 2 in D min., Op. 14; Cinderella: 3 Pieces, Op. 102; Dumka; 3 Pieces, Op. 69; Waltzes (Schubert, arr. Prokofiev).
(Y/B) *** Chandos Dig. CHAN 9119 [id.]. Boris Berman.

Piano sonata No. 3 in A min., Op. 28; Cinderella: 6 pieces, Op. 95; 10 Pieces, Op. 12; Thoughts, Op. 62.
(Y/B) *** Chandos Dig. CHAN 9069 [id.]. Boris Berman.

Piano sonata No. 4, Op. 29; Music for children, Op. 65; 6 Pieces, Op. 52.
*** Chandos Dig. CHAN 8926 [id.]. Boris Berman.

Piano sonata No. 5 in C, Op. 38/135; 4 Pieces, Op. 32; Love for three oranges: Scherzo and March; Romeo and Juliet: 10 Pieces, Op. 75.
*** Chandos Dig. CHAN 8851 [id.]. Boris Berman.

Piano sonatas Nos. 5 in C, Op. 38; 6 in A, Op. 82; 10 in E min., Op. 137 (fragment); *Gavotte (Classical Symphony, Op. 25); Juvenilia; Toccata, Op. 11.*
(Y/B) *** Chandos Dig. CHAN 9361 [id.]. Boris Berman.

Boris Berman's survey of the complete Prokofiev piano music is proving the most satisfactory all-round set of the sonatas so far. Berman always plays with tremendous concentration and control. He commands a finely articulated and vital rhythmic sense as well as a wide range of keyboard colour. The first CD brings some transcriptions. He does not play these with quite the same elegance and distinction that mark the *Sonatinas*, which are beautifully characterized and splendidly recorded. In the *Second Sonata in D minor* Berman is quite magnificent and full of panache. The *Third* is coupled with the inventive but unaccountably neglected *Ten Pieces*, Op. 12. This also has the *Pensées*, Op. 62, and remains one of the most desirable of the set.

The *Fourth Sonata*, like its predecessor, takes its inspiration from Prokofiev's earlier notebooks. The Op. 52 *Pieces* are transcriptions of movements from other works: the ballet *The Prodigal Son*, the *Andante* from the *First Quartet*, the Scherzo from the *Sinfonietta* and one of the *Songs without words*, Op. 35. Berman plays them incisively, with marvellous articulation and wit. On CHAN 8851 he plays the post-war revision of the *Fifth Sonata*, and its crisp, brittle inner movement is heard to splendid advantage. The other works are presented with equal perception. State-of-the-art recording from Chandos, made at The Maltings, Snape. Of course with the *Sixth Sonata* Berman is traversing hotly contested ground. Although Kissin's Sony recital, recorded in Tokyo, generates a level of excitement that Berman does not match, and he takes more risks, Berman's cooler and more collected reading remains eminently recommendable. He then gives us the original (1923) version of the *Fifth Sonata* (generally to be preferred to the revision) but also the minute or so that survives of a *Tenth Sonata* (otherwise only available on Murray McLachlan's Olympia disc).

Piano sonatas Nos. 3 in A min., Op. 28; 7 in B flat, Op. 83; 8 in B flat, Op. 84.
*** DG Dig. 435 439-2 [id.]. Andrei Gavrilov.

Gavrilov's account of the *Seventh Sonata* is exciting and exhilarating, and in this work totally devoid of any exaggeration. In the *Eighth* he is equally if not more successful, and can withstand the most exalted comparisons. He rushes his fences in the *Third*, though as virtuoso playing it is pretty dazzling. Moreover he is given impressive recorded sound.

Piano sonatas Nos. 4 in C min., Op. 29; 5 in C, Op. 38/135; 6 in A, Op. 82; Pastoral sonatina.
(Y/B) ** ASV Dig. CDDCA 754 [id.]. John Lill.

Good though he is, John Lill does not really match or surpass the competition here: In the *Sixth Sonata* he certainly does not command the flair and abandon of Kissin or Pogorelich, or the impressive playing of Boris Berman. Taken on its own merits, there is much that would give satisfaction, but the Lill Prokofiev cycle is not a first choice.

Piano sonata No. 6 in A, Op. 82.
★ *** DG Dig. 413 363-2 [id.]. Pogorelich – RAVEL: *Gaspard de la nuit.* ***

Pogorelich's performance of the *Sixth Sonata* is quite simply dazzling; indeed, it is by far the best version of it ever put on record. It is certainly Pogorelich's most brilliant record so far and can be recommended with the utmost enthusiasm in its CD format.

Piano sonata No. 7 in B flat, Op. 83.
(Y/B) (M) *** DG 447 431-2 [id.]. Maurizio Pollini – *Recital.* ***

This is a great performance by Pollini, well in the Horowitz or Richter category. It is part of a generous CD of twentieth-century music.

Piano sonata No. 7; Toccata in C, Op. 11.
(M) (***) RCA mono GD 60377 [id.]. Vladimir Horowitz – BARBER; KABALEVSKY: *Sonatas* etc. (***)

Horowitz's account of the *Seventh Sonata* is justly legendary. When he had recorded it in 1945 he sent a copy of the disc to the composer, who returned an autographed score to express his admiration. The better-known *Toccata* is hardly less electrifying, and the somewhat confined mono sound is never distracting with playing of this degree of magnetism.

Piano sonatas Nos. 7 in B flat, Op. 83; 8 in B flat, Op. 84.
*** Sony Dig. MK 44680 [id.]. Yefim Bronfman.

Yefim Bronfman has a formidable technique and his clarity of articulation and tonal finesse are unfailingly impressive. The opening of No. 8 has a good sense of forward movement. Highly accomplished playing throughout, though it is distinctly short measure these days. All the same, it is very recommendable.

Piano sonatas Nos. 7 in B flat, Op. 83; 8 in B flat, Op. 84; 9 in C, Op. 103.
*** ASV Dig. CDDCA 755 [id.]. John Lill.

This disc, coupling the last three *Sonatas*, offers exceptionally good value, and the excellent ASV recording was made in Henry Wood Hall. All three performances are of high quality, and John Lill is never less than a thoughtful and intelligent guide in this repertoire.

Piano sonata No. 7; Sarcasms, Op. 17; Tales of an old grandmother, Op. 31; Visions fugitives, Op. 22.
*** Chandos Dig. CHAN 8881 [id.]. Boris Berman.

Piano sonata No. 8; Cinderella: 10 Pieces, Op. 97; 4 Pieces, Op. 3.
*** Chandos Dig. CHAN 8976 [id.]. Boris Berman.

Piano sonata No. 9; Choses en soi, Op. 45; Divertissement, Op. 43 bis; 4 Etudes, Op. 2.
*** Chandos Dig. CHAN 9211 [id.]. Boris Berman.

Berman is completely inside the astringent idiom and subtle character of the *Seventh Sonata*, and his playing in the *Sarcasms* could scarcely be bettered. He gives altogether outstanding performances of all four works, and the superbly vivid recording greatly enhances the sheer musical satisfaction this disc gives.

In the expansive *Eighth Sonata*, there is more pianistic refinement in Berman's account than in the Lill reviewed above, though it is in the ten numbers from *Cinderella* and the Op. 3 *Pieces* that Berman's command of atmosphere and character tells most. The quality of the recorded sound is excellent.

Berman plays the *Ninth Sonata* with tremendous concentration and control. His finely articulated and vital rhythms are matched by a good command of keyboard colour; aided by the clean, well-balanced (though rather forward) recording, he presents this sonata in the most persuasive light. The *Choses en soi* ('Things in themselves') come from the period of the *Third Symphony*, though there is a momentary hint of *The Prodigal Son*. The *Divertissement* is a delightful piece in Prokofiev's most acerbic manner which derived from the ballet, *Trapeze*. Berman couples them with the brilliant Op. 2 *Etudes* of 1909 with which Prokofiev made his Moscow début. A very satisfying recital.

Romeo and Juliet (suite), *Op. 75; Prelude, Op. 12/7; Suggestion diabolique, Op. 4/4*.
**(*) DG Dig. 437 532-2 [id.]. Andrei Gavrilov – RAVEL: *Gaspard* etc. **

Andrei Gavrilov has been here before, on the EMI label. And although there is abundant evidence of pianistic mastery, there is no real need to replace those earlier versions, particularly as – despite the intervening years – these are not better recorded.

VOCAL MUSIC

(i) *Alexander Nevsky* (cantata), *Op. 78;* (ii) *Ivan the Terrible, Op. 116* (film music, arr. Lankester).
*** Sony Dig. S2K 48387 (2) [id.]. (i) Dolora Zajic; (ii) Christopher Plummer (nar.), Sinyavskaya, Leiferkus; L. Symphony Ch., LSO, Rostropovich.

Rostropovich's set offers not the usual cantata version of Prokofiev's music for the Eisenstein film but one, more comprehensive, prepared by Michael Lankester, which tells the story of the Tsar by way of an elaborate narration, dotted with biblical quotations. Having snatches of music joined by spoken narration suits this subject well, though having so much speech means that the piece spreads to a second disc. Particularly moving is the humming chorus which starts the second of the two discs, a hushed and meditative version of the great surging melody which later became a central theme in Prokofiev's epic opera, *War and Peace*, representing General Kutuzov's patriotic defiance. Christopher Plummer is the oratorical narrator, with Sergei Leiferkus and the fruity-toned Tamara Sinyavskaya the excellent soloists, and the London Symphony Chorus both powerful and refined. As a fill-up on the second disc comes the *Alexander Nevsky* cantata. Dolora Zajic is the moving mezzo soloist in the great *Lament for the dead* after the *Battle on the ice*, with Rostropovich again drawing an inspired performance from the LSO and Chorus.

Alexander Nevsky (cantata), Op. 78.
(M) *** EMI CDM7 63114-2. Anna Reynolds, London Symphony Ch., LSO, Previn – RACHMANINOV: *The Bells*. ***

(i) *Alexander Nevsky, Op. 78. Lieutenant Kijé (suite), Op. 60*.
(M) *** RCA GD 60176 [60176-2-RG]. (i) Rosalind Elias, Chicago SO Ch.; Chicago SO, Reiner – GLINKA: *Ruslan Overture*. ***

(i) *Alexander Nevsky, Op. 78;* (ii) *Lieutenant Kijé, Op. 60; Scythian suite, Op. 20*.
(Y/B) (M) *** DG 447 419-2 [id.]. (i) Elena Obraztsova; London Symphony Ch., LSO; (ii) Chicago SO; Claudio Abbado.

(i) *Alexander Nevsky, Op. 78. Scythian suite, Op. 20*.
*** Chandos Dig. CHAN 8584 [id.]. (i) Linda Finnie, SNO Ch.; SNO, Järvi.

Abbado's performance of *Alexander Nevsky* culminates in a deeply moving account of the tragic lament after the battle (here very beautifully sung by Obraztsova), made the more telling when the battle itself is so fine an example of orchestral virtuosity. The chorus is as incisive as the orchestra. The digital remastering of the 1980 recording has been all gain, and the sound is very impressive indeed. A fine account of *Lieutenant Kijé* and what is probably the best version of the *Scythian suite* to appear in many years make this a desirable reissue in DG's Legendary Recordings series. Abbado gets both warm and wonderfully clean playing from the Chicago orchestra and he is accorded excellent engineering. The *Scythian suite* has drive and fire: in the finale – and even in the second movement – Abbado could bring greater savagery and brilliance than he does but, given the power that the Chicago orchestra do bring to this score and the refined colouring that Abbado achieves in the atmospheric *Night* movement, there need be no real reservation in recommending this strongly.

The bitter chill of the Russian winter can be felt in the orchestra at the very opening of Järvi's reading and the melancholy of the choral entry has real Slavic feeling. His climactic point is the enormously spectacular *Battle on the ice*, with the recording giving great pungency to the bizarre orchestral effects and the choral shouts riveting in their force and fervour. Linda Finnie sings the final lament eloquently and Järvi's apotheosis is very affecting, but at the close Obraztsova and Abbado create an even graver valedictory feeling which is unforgettable. As coupling, Järvi chooses the ballet *Ala and Lolly*, which subsequently became the *Scythian suite*. Its motoric rhythms are characteristic of the composer at his most aggressive, but the lyrical music is even more rewarding.

All the weight, bite and colour of the score are captured by Previn, and though the timbre of the singers' voices may not suggest Russians, they cope very confidently with the Russian text; Previn's direct and dynamic manner ensures that the great *Battle on the ice* scene is powerfully effective. Anna Reynolds sings the lovely *Lament for the dead* most affectingly. The sound is sharply defined, with plenty of bite; just a little of the old analogue ambient fullness has gone.

Reiner's version, recorded in 1959, was another of the astonishingly vivid early achievements of the RCA stereo catalogue. The performance is gripping from the first bar to the last, with choral singing of great fervour and a movingly eloquent contribution from Rosalind Elias in the great *Lament*. The *Lieutenant Kijé suite*, recorded two years earlier, is another colourful example of the Chicago orchestra at their peak, the sound again full and atmospheric.

Cantata for the 20th anniversary of the October Revolution, Op. 74.
*** Chandos Dig. CHAN 9095 [id.]. Rozhdestvensky (speaker), Philh. Ch. & O, Järvi – *Stone Flower suite.* ***

Even Prokofiev rarely wrote so wild and totally original a piece as this cantata, designed to celebrate the twentieth anniversary of the 1917 Revolution. The key movement, centrally placed and the longest, uses such exotic percussion as rattles and sirens, with shouting from the chorus, in a graphic description of the revolution in St Petersburg. Järvi, here with his fellow-conductor Gennadi Rozhdestvensky as narrator, has made a first complete recording with the Philharmonia Chorus and Orchestra. A performance by a Russian chorus might have been even more bitingly uninhibited, but it is good to have so sharply original and refreshingly dramatic a piece complete on disc at last, an occasional work that rises far above its first inspiration. As a valuable fill-up comes a suite of excerpts from the folk-tale ballet of 1948, *The Stone Flower*.

Eugene Onegin (incidental music), *Op. 71; Hamlet* (incidental music), *Op. 77; Lieutenant Kijé* (suite), *Op. 60.*
*** Chant du Monde Dig. LDC 288 027/8 (2) [id.]. Koroleva, Stetsenko, Blagovest Ch., Maly Moscow SO, Vladimir Ponkin.

Prokofiev's incidental music for *Eugene Onegin* proves to be a major find, with an inspiration comparable to *Romeo and Juliet* in lyric fervour and melodic sweep. *Hamlet* is less ambitious, offering ten vignettes, but including three engaging songs for Ophelia charmingly sung here by Ludmilla Koroleva. The orchestral playing in both scores is fresh and ardent, and the Russian wind and brass playing is suitably vibrant. The performance of *Lieutenant Kijé* brings out the music's laconic melancholy in a specially Russian way. Excellent, modern, digital recording throughout. This is an indispensable set for any true Prokofievian.

5 Poems of Anna Akhmatova, Op. 27; 2 Poems, Op. 9; 5 Poems of Konstantin Balmont, Op. 36; 3 Romances, Op. 73.
**(*) Chandos Dig. CHAN 8509 [id.]. Carole Farley, Arkady Aronov.

Rare and valuable repertoire. The songs are powerful and full of resourceful and imaginative touches. The Akhmatova settings are quite beautiful. The *Three Romances*, Op. 73, to words of Pushkin, are full of the wry harmonic sleights of hand that are so characteristic of his musical speech. The American soprano, Carole Farley, responds to the different moods and character of the poems and encompasses a rather wide range of colour and tone, although at times her voice is rather edgy and uneven in timbre. The accompaniments of Arkady Aronov are highly sensitive and perceptive. The recording is completely truthful.

OPERA

L'amour des trois oranges (The Love for 3 oranges): complete.
**(*) Virgin/EMI Dig. VCD7 59566-2 (2) [id.]. Bacquier, Bastin, Dubosc, Gautier, Viala, Lyon Opera Ch. & O, Kent Nagano.

French was the language used when the opera was given its first, lavish production in Chicago in December 1921. It inevitably brings a degree of softening in vocal texture, but the brilliant young conductor, Kent Nagano, and his Lyon Opera House team make up for any loss in knife-edged precision of ensemble. Gabriel Bacquier as the King and Jules Bastin as the monstrous Cook, guardian of the three oranges, are well matched by the others, including Jean-Luc Viala as an aptly petulant Prince and Catherine Dubosc as a sweetly girlish Princess Ninette. A snag with the recorded sound is that the commenting chorus – very much a part of the action in *commedia dell'arte* style – is focused too vaguely, a pity when the timing is so crisp. Happily, the focus for the solo voices is clearer. However, it is irritating that there are so few cueing points on the CDs (just one for each scene), even if this is very much an ensemble opera, with few set solos.

The Fiery Angel (complete).

(N) ✹ *** Ph. Dig. 446 078-2 (2) [id.] (Video 070 198-3; LD 070 198-1). Gorchakova, Leiferkus, Pluzhnikov, Ognovanko, soloists; Kirov Op. Ch. & O, Gergiev.

*** DG Dig. 431 669-2 (2) [id.]. Secunde, Lorenz, Zednik, Moll, Gothenburg SO, Järvi.

Impressive as Neeme Järvi's 1990 recording for DG of this elusive but powerful opera is, Gergiev's with Kirov forces is even finer. Based on a novel by Valery Bryusov, *The Fiery Angel* is set in and around Cologne in the 1520s. The opera centres on Renata's obsession with the vision of Madiel, a fiery angel who consumed her thoughts in childhood but who left her when, on reaching puberty, she asked him to consummate their relationship. His image possesses her, and she marries the Count Heinrich, believing that in him Madiel has returned to earth. From the very outset the style is declamatory in a way that recalls Mussorgsky. The vocal line is largely heightened speech, but Prokofiev does provide a series of leitmotivs which are identified with characters or situations in the opera. Indeed, in terms of fantasy and sheer imaginative vision, *The Fiery Angel* reaches heights which Prokofiev never surpassed, and its atmosphere resonates for a long time.

This is the finest of the Philips Kirov series yet, a live recording which, with full, forward sound, avoids most of the snags of a recorded stage-performance. Above all, it offers in the singing and acting of Elena Gorchakova in the central role of Renata, the hysterical woman obsessed by demons, one of the most compelling operatic performances in years. It was she who, when this production was given at Covent Garden, magnetized the audience; here, with experience, the intensity is if anything even greater, with the timbre of the voice often sensuously beautiful, even when stretched to the limit. Sergei Leiferkus as Ruprecht with his clear, firm baritone is also ideally cast; the remainder of the cast, from the Landlady of Evgenia Perlasova to the resonant Inquisitor of Vladimir Ognovanko, are absolutely first class, while the Kirov team provides outstanding, always idiomatic and individual performances in smaller roles. Gergiev proves an inspired conductor who secures orchestral playing of great dramatic eloquence: the players sound as though they have the music in their blood, bringing out the full power of this weird score. There are the inevitable stage noises and not all the voices in big ensembles are properly balanced, but any snag is quickly forgotten.

The presence of vision in the finely directed video tape and laserdisc serves to underline an implicit ambiguity in the opera – whether Madiel and the spirits conjured up in Act II are real or are just Renata's paranoid delusions. Here the use of mimed figures, unseen by the protagonists but perceived by the audience, was a brilliant solution. The frenetic, highly charged atmosphere of the final Convent scene, in which Renata confronts the Inquisitor, and the mass possession to which the nuns succumb, benefits by vision particularly in this splendid production. The sound in the laserdisc version has marvellous presence and detail.

With Järvi, the final scene with the Inquisitor (Kurt Moll ever sinister) and chattering nuns does not quite rise to the expected climax. Nadine Secunde sings passionately as Renata and she is well supported by Siegfried Lorenz as Ruprecht. With such warm advocacy one can fully appreciate the work's mastery, even if the reasons for its failure to get into the repertory remain very clear.

War and peace (complete).

✹ (M) *** Erato/Warner 2292 45331-2 (4) [id.]. Vishnevskaya, Miller, Ciesinski, Tumagian, Ochman, Ghiuselev, Smith, Paunova, Petkov, Toczyska, Zakai, Gedda, Fr. R. Ch. & Nat. O, Rostropovich.

*** Ph. Dig. 434 097-2 (3) [id.]. Gergalov, Prokina, Gregoriam, Borodina, Gerelo, Bogachova, Okhotnikov, Morozov, Kirov Theatre Ch. & O, Gergiev.

War and Peace is not just epic in scale but warmly approachable, with a fund of melody rarely matched this century. Moreover a really complete rendering of Prokofiev's text – never heard by the composer in its finished form – shows triumphantly how the components cohere into an opera of epic achievement. Rostropovich's complete account on record, flawed in some of the casting, nevertheless confirms equally that this is one of the great operatic masterpieces of the century. However, no one should be deceived by the ease of listening into thinking that the writing lacks strength or intensity; rather, Prokofiev, in his game with the Soviet authorities, was submitting to the impossible restrictions of writing a 'people's opera' and succeeding masterfully, knowing that only he could have done it.

In Rostropovich's powerful reading one revels – thanks also to the lively Erato recording – in the vividness of the atmosphere, both in the evocative love scenes and ball scenes of the first half (Peace) and in the high tensions of the battle scenes in the second (War). The opera culminates in a great patriotic chorus, using the most haunting tune of all, earlier sung by General Kutuzov after the Council of Fili, and the emotional thrust is overwhelming. The French Radio Choir sings that chorus with real Russian fervour – though anyone remembering the ENO production will be disconcerted to find the opera starting, not with the shattering choral epigraph which hit so hard at the Coliseum, but with a pot-pourri overture airing some of the main themes. Prokofiev wrote it as an option, and what

Rostropovich has done, with fair logic, is to reserve the choral epigraph – telling of the invasion of Russia – for the beginning of the second half and the scenes of war. It was natural that Rostropovich's wife, Galina Vishnevskaya, should sing the central role of Natasha, as she did in the earlier, much-cut, Bolshoi recording. It is extraordinary how convincingly this mature soprano in her early sixties characterizes a young girl; there may be raw moments, but she is completely inside the role. The Hungarian baritone, Lajos Miller, not flawless either, is a clear-voiced Andrei, and Wieslaw Ochman is a first-rate Pierre, with the veteran, Nicolai Gedda, brought in as Kuragin. Katherine Ciesinski is a warm-toned Sonya, but Dimiter Petkov is disappointingly unsteady as Natasha's father, Count Rostov. The small role of Napoleon is strongly taken by Eduard Tumagian, while Nicola Ghiuselev is a noble Kutuzov, in some ways the most impressive of all. The libretto contains French and English translations, but no Russian transliteration, only the Cyrillic text in a separate section.

The Kirov performance under Valery Gergiev, at rather more urgent speeds than Rostropovich's, may be less warmly expressive and atmospheric, but it brings the advantage of having in the principal roles younger voices. Many will prefer the Kirov Natasha, Yelena Prokina, to the controversially cast Vishnevskaya on the Rostropovich set. The voice is fresher as well as younger-sounding, though the tone becomes hard under pressure, losing any sweetness. Alexandr Gergalov, Prince Andrei in the Kirov performance, is attractively young-sounding too, lighter and more lyrical than Rostropovich's principal, also good, the Hungarian baritone, Lajos Miller. Otherwise the Kirov principals, including Nikolai Okhotnikov as Kutuzov, are almost all as characterful and assured as their generally starrier rivals on Erato, and the sense of purpose from a very large company, well drilled in the music, counterbalances in part, though not entirely, the unhelpful dryness of the sound. The economical layout on three CDs may seem to favour Philips, but there is no price-advantage, when Rostropovich's Erato comes at mid-price in the Libretto series. The three-disc format on Philips is made possible by Gergiev's faster speeds and a briefer text for the final patriotic chorus, though the breaks between discs come awkwardly in the middle of scenes.

Puccini, Giacomo (1858–1924)

Capriccio sinfonico; Crisantemi; Minuets Nos. 1–3; Preludio sinfonico; Edgar: Preludes, Acts I & III. Manon Lescaut: Intermezzo, Act III. Le Villi: Prelude; La Tregenda (Act II).
(Y/B) (M) *** Decca Dig. 444 154-2 [id.]. Berlin RSO, Ricardo Chailly.

In a highly attractive collection of Puccinian juvenilia and rarities, Chailly draws opulent and atmospheric playing from the Berlin Radio Symphony Orchestra, helped by outstandingly rich and full recording. The CD is of demonstration quality. The *Capriccio sinfonico* of 1876 brings the first characteristically Puccinian idea in what later became the opening Bohemian motif of *La Bohème*. There are other identifiable fingerprints here, even if the big melodies suggest Mascagni rather than full-blown Puccini. *Crisantemi* (with the original string quartet scoring expanded for full string orchestra) provided material for *Manon Lescaut*, as did the three little *Minuets*, pastiche eighteenth-century music.

Crisantemi for string quartet.
*** CRD CRD 3366 [id.]. Alberni Qt – DONIZETTI: *Quartet No. 13;* VERDI: *Quartet.* ***

Puccini's brief essay in writing for string quartet dates from the late 1880s; three years later he used the main themes in his first fully successful opera, *Manon Lescaut*. The piece is given a warm, finely controlled performance by the Alberni Quartet and makes a valuable makeweight for the two full-scale quartets by fellow opera-composers. The sound is excellent.

(i) *Crisantemi; Minuets Nos. 1–3; Quartet in A min.: Allegro moderato; Scherzo in A min.;* (ii) *Foglio d'album; Piccolo tango;* (iii; ii) *Avanti Urania; E l'uccellino; Inno a Diana; Menti all'avviso; Morire?; Salve regina; Sole e amore; Storiella d'amore; Terra e mare.*
*** Etcetera KTC 1050. (i) Raphael Qt; (ii) Tan Crone; (iii) Roberta Alexander.

It is fascinating to find among early, rather untypical songs like *Storiella d'amore* and *Menti all'avviso* a charming little song, *Sole e amore*, written jokingly for a journal, 'Paganini', in 1888, which provided, bar for bar, the main idea of the Act III quartet in *La Bohème* of eight years later. The two piano pieces are simple album-leaves; among the six quartet pieces, *Crisantemi* is already well known; the rest are student pieces, including a delightful fragment of a Scherzo. Performances are good, though Roberta Alexander's soprano is not ideally Italianate. The recorded sound is vivid and immediate against a lively hall ambience.

Messa di Gloria.

(Y/B) (M) *** Erato/Warner Dig. 4509 96367-2 [id.]. Carreras, Prey, Amb. S., Philh. O, Scimone.

(M) *** Ph. 434 170-2 [id.]. Lövaas, Hollweg, McDaniel, West German R. Ch., Frankfurt RSO, Inbal (with MOZART: *Vesperae solennes, K.339: Laudate Dominum:* Te Kanawa, LSO, C. Davis ***).

Puccini's *Messa di Gloria,* completed when he was twenty, rebuts any idea that this composer was a late developer. Very much under the influence of Verdi (hearing *Aida* was a profound formative experience), Puccini still showed his positive character as a composer, writing bold melodies with just a hint here and there of individual fingerprints and using the orchestra with astonishing maturity. The various parts were written at different times and even for different purposes; but with the exception of an over-sweet setting of *Agnus Dei* (later used in *Manon Lescaut*) the work stands well together. Best of all is the ambitious and strong setting of the *Gloria,* the longest section and the earliest written. It has a cheeky recurring march theme which may be doubtfully apt for church but which is richly enjoyable. The section ends with a formidable fugue, echoing Beethoven's *Missa solemnis,* no less.

The return of Scimone's second (1983) digital recording of the Puccini *Messa di gloria* at mid-price makes this version much more competitive, even though it has no fill-up. He and a fine team are brisker and lighter than their predecessors on record, yet effectively bring out the red-bloodedness of the writing. José Carreras turns the big solo in the *Gratias* into the first genuine Puccini aria. His sweetness and imagination are not quite matched by the baritone, Hermann Prey, who is given less to do than usual, when the choral baritones take on the yearning melody of *Crucifixus.* Excellent, atmospheric sound.

This 1975 Philips version, available as a limited edition, is excellent value at mid-price. It has stylish soloists, a fine choral contribution and clean, well-balanced recording. Kiri Te Kanawa's ravishing account of the *Laudate Dominum* from Mozart's *Solemn Vespers* is thrown in as an enticing encore.

OPERA

La Bohème (complete).

(***) EMI mono CDS7 47235-8 (2) [Ang. CDCB 47235]. De los Angeles, Bjoerling, Merrill, Reardon, Tozzi, Amara, RCA Victor Ch. & O, Beecham.

*** Decca 421 049-2 (2) [id.]. Freni, Pavarotti, Harwood, Panerai, Ghiaurov, German Op. Ch., Berlin, BPO, Karajan.

❀ (B) (***) Decca Double mono 440 233-2 (2) [id.]. Tebaldi, Prandelli, Gueden, Inghilleri, Corena, Arié, Luise, Santa Cecilia Ac., Rome, Ch. & O, Erede.

(M) *** Decca 425 534-2 (2). Tebaldi, Bergonzi, Bastianini, Siepi, Corena, D'Angelo, St Cecilia Ac. Ch. & O, Serafin.

(***) EMI mono CDS7 47475-8 (2) [Ang. CDCB 47475]. Callas, Di Stefano, Moffo, Panerai, Zaccaria, La Scala, Milan, Ch. & O, Votto.

(Y/B) (M) **(*) EMI CMS7 69657-2 (2) [Ang. CDMB 69657]. Freni, Gedda, Adani, Sereni, Mazzoli, La Scala, Milan, Ch. & O, Schippers.

(Y/B) (B) ** Ph. Duo 442 260-2 (2) [id.]. Ricciarelli, Carreras, Putnam, Wixell, Lloyd, ROHCG Ch. & O, Sir Colin Davis.

(N) (B) ** EMI CZS5 69380-2 (2). Scotto, Kraus, Milnes, Neblett, Plishka, Manuguerra, Amb. Op. Ch., Trinity Boys' Ch., Nat. PO, Levine.

Beecham's is a uniquely magical performance with two favourite singers, Victoria de los Angeles and Jussi Bjoerling, challenged to their utmost in loving, expansive singing. The voices are treated far better by the CD remastering than the orchestra, which is rather thinner-sounding than it was on LP, though as ever the benefits of silent background are very welcome in so warmly atmospheric a reading. With such a performance one hardly notices the recording, but those who want fine modern stereo can turn readily to Karajan.

Karajan too takes a characteristically spacious view of *Bohème,* but there is an electric intensity which holds the whole score together as in a live performance. Pavarotti is an inspired Rodolfo, with comic flair and expressive passion, while Freni is just as seductive as Mimì. Elizabeth Harwood is a charming Musetta. Fine singing throughout the set. The reverberant Berlin acoustic is glowing and brilliant in superb Decca recording, with the clean placing of voices enhancing the performance's dramatic warmth.

The very early Decca set, one of the very first complete operas to appear on LP. Recorded in 1951, it immediately won glowing praise, above all for Tebaldi's radiant and rich-voiced portrayal of Mimì. The effect is still extraordinarily atmospheric in its sense of stage perspective, with sound effects mostly adding to the realism and not overdone. Like the companion early Decca *Die Fledermaus,* the one drawback was the whistly sound of the violins (something to do with the microphones in use at Decca at that time). The CD transfer has improved the violin focus, but the effect is still emaciated above the stave. Yet one soon adjusts to this, for the acoustic is basically warm and evocative. It is still a lovely performance, and there are no appreciable weaknesses in the cast: Gueden (if not always completely Italianate in style) an exceptionally characterful Musetta (a part that fitted her like a glove), Pradelli a most likeable Rodolfo, engagingly light-voiced yet stirring at climaxes, Inghilleri rather old-sounding but still interesting as Marcello. Erede keeps the music flowing: he is not a great conductor but he controls the great love duet of Act I spaciously. The atmospheric opening of Act III at the Paris toll-gate is remarkably evocative, with the kind of production values that were to lead on to the vintage Decca opera recordings of the stereo era already apparent. Indeed, at times here one could almost think stereo had already arrived.

Tebaldi's second Decca set with Bergonzi dominated the catalogue in the early days of stereo. Vocally the performance achieves a consistently high standard, with Tebaldi as Mimi the most affecting. Carlo Bergonzi is a fine Rodolfo; Bastianini and Siepi are both superb as Marcello and Colline, and even the small parts of Benoit and Alcindoro (as usual taken by a single artist) have the benefit of Corena's magnificent voice. The veteran Serafin was more vital here than on some of his records. The recording has its striking vividness and sense of stage perspective enhanced on CD.

Callas, flashing-eyed and formidable, may seem even less suited to the role of Mimi than to that of Butterfly, but characteristically her insights make for a vibrantly involving performance. Though Giuseppe di Stefano is not the subtlest of Rodolfos, he is in excellent voice here, and Moffo and Panerai make a strong partnership as the second pair of lovers. Votto occasionally coarsens Puccini's score but he directs with energy. The comparatively restricted dynamic range means that the singers appear to be 'front stage', but there is no lack of light and shade in Act II.

The engineers placed Freni rather close to the microphone, which makes it hard for her to sound tentative in her first scene, but the beauty of the voice is what one remembers, and from there to the end her performance is conceived as a whole, leading to a supremely moving account of the Death scene. Nicolai Gedda's Rodolfo is not rounded in the traditional Italian way, but there is never any doubt about his ability to project a really grand manner of his own. Thomas Schippers' conducting starts as though this is going to be a hard-driven, unrelenting performance, but after the horseplay he quickly shows his genuinely Italianate sense of pause, giving the singers plenty of time to breathe and allowing the music to expand. The resonant, 1964 recording has transferred vividly to CD and the set has been attractively re-packaged with an excellently printed libretto.

As in *Tosca*, Sir Colin Davis here takes a direct view of Puccini, presenting the score very straight, with no exaggerations. The result is refreshing but rather lacking in wit and sparkle; pauses and hesitations are curtailed. Ricciarelli's is the finest performance vocally. Carreras gives a good generalized performance, wanting in detail and in intensity, and rather failing to rise to the big moments. Wixell makes an unidiomatic Marcello, rather lacking in fun, and Robert Lloyd's bass sounds lightweight as Colline. Ashley Putnam makes a charming Musetta. However, in this Duo reissue, with two CDs offered for the price of one, many will feel this is good value, although it includes a synopsis rather than a libretto.

Reissued to celebrate the opera's centenary, as a bargain double Levine's 1979 set is worth considering, when the recording has plenty of warmth and atmosphere. Alfredo Kraus's relatively light tenor sets the pattern at the very start for a performance that is strong on comedy. One registers the exchanges more sharply than usual on record, and though Kraus (no longer as sweet of timbre as he was) tends to over-point in the big arias, it is a stylish performance. Scotto – who first recorded the role of Mimi for DG in 1962 – is not recorded flatteringly here, for the rawness and unevenness which affect her voice at the top of the stave are distracting, marring an affectionate portrait. Milnes makes a powerful Marcello and Neblett a strong Musetta, a natural Minnie in *Fanciulla* transformed into a soubrette. Levine, brilliant in the comic writing of Acts I and IV, sounds less at home in the big melodies.

La Bohème: highlights.
*** Decca 421 245-2; *421 245-4* [id.] (from above recording with Freni and Pavarotti; cond. Karajan).

It is a pity to cut anything from so taut an opera as *La Bohème*; but those who feel they can make do with a single CD instead of two will find this selection from the Karajan set ideal.

La Fanciulla del West (The Girl of the Golden West) complete.
❀ (M) *** Decca 421 595-2 (2) [id.]. Tebaldi, Del Monaco, MacNeil, Tozzi, St Cecilia Ac., Rome, Ch. & O, Capuana.
**(*) DG 419 640-2 (2) [id.]. Neblett, Domingo, Milnes, Howell, ROHCG Ch. and O, Mehta.
** RCA Dig. 09026 60597-2 (2) [id.]. Marton, Fondary, O'Neill, Planté, Rootering, Ivaldi, Bav. R. Ch., Munich R. O, Slatkin.

The Decca set of *La Fanciulla del West* has been remastered for CD with spectacular success. Tebaldi gives one of her most warm-hearted and understanding performances on record, and Mario del Monaco displays the wonderfully heroic quality of his voice to great – if sometimes tiring – effect. Cornell MacNeil as the villain, Sheriff Rance, sings with great precision and attack, but unfortunately has not a villainous-sounding voice to convey the character fully. Jake Wallace's entry and the song *Che faranno i viecchi miei* is one of the high spots of the recording, with Tozzi singing beautifully. Capuana's expansive reading is matched by the imagination of the production, with the closing scene wonderfully effective.

On DG, Mehta's manner – as he makes clear at the very start – is on the brisk side, not just in the cakewalk rhythms but even in refusing to let the first great melody, the nostalgic *Che faranno i viecchi miei*, linger into sentimentality. Sherrill Milnes as Jack Rance makes that villain into far more than a small-town Scarpia, giving nobility and understanding to the first-Act arioso. Domingo, as in the theatre, sings heroically, disappointing only in his reluctance to produce soft tone in the great aria *Ch'ella mi creda*. The rest of the team is excellent, not least Gwynne Howell as the minstrel who sings *Che faranno i viecchi miei*; but the crowning glory of a masterly set is the singing of Carol Neblett as the Girl of the Golden West herself, gloriously rich and true and with formidable attack on the exposed high notes. Full, atmospheric recording to match, essential in an opera full of evocative offstage effects, but the slight drying-out process of the digital sound adds some stridency in tuttis, readily acceptable with so strong a performance.

Leonard Slatkin conducts a strong and well-paced performance of Puccini's wild-west opera, taking a spacious, sympathetic view. It is good to have Dennis O'Neill taking the principal tenor-role in a major international recording, bringing out the lyrical side of Dick Johnson's role very persuasively. He also rises well to the challenge of the final scene, with the aria, *Ch'ella mi creda*, and the hero's disappearance with Minnie into the sunset. Alain Fondary's firm, dark baritone makes Sheriff Rance less of a villain than usual, conveying wronged nobility. For much of the time Eva Marton manages to sing far more gently than she usually does on disc, and she copes well with the big dramatic moments, but it is still a voice that quickly grows raw, with too many loud, unpitched notes. For all its qualities, this is not among the most recommendable versions.

La Fanciulla del West: highlights.
(Y/B) (M) *** DG 445 465-2 [id.] (from above recording, with Neblett, Domingo, Milnes; cond. Mehta).

This is most welcome as the only current set of highlights from *Fanciulla del West*, covering the whole opera generously with 75 minutes of music. No libretto, but a good track synopsis.

Gianni Schicchi (complete).
(Y/B) (M) *** RCA Dig. 74321 25285-2. Panerai, Donath, Seiffert, Bavarian R. Ch., Munich R. O, Patanè.
(N) *(*) Decca Dig. 444 395-2 [id.]. Nucci, Freni, Alagna, Maggio Musicale Fiorentino O, Bartoletti.

The RCA (formerly Eurodisc) recording of *Gianni Schicchi* brings a co-production with Bavarian Radio, and the recording is vivid and well balanced. Central to the performance's success is the vintage Schicchi of Rolando Panerai, still rich and firm. He confidently characterizes the Florentine trickster in every phrase, building a superb portrait, finely timed. Peter Seiffert as Rinuccio gives a dashing performance, consistently clean and firm of tone, making light of the high tessitura and rising splendidly to the challenge of the big central aria. Helen Donath would have sounded even sweeter a few years earlier, but she gives a tender, appealing portrait of Lauretta, pretty and demure in *O mio babbino caro*. Though Italian voices are in the minority, it is a confident team. In its reissued form, access to the disc has been greatly improved and there are now seven cues.

Bartoletti's *Gianni Schicchi* comes from a complete Decca set of *Il Trittico*, recorded in 1991 but not issued until 1994 (436 261-2), with Mirella Freni common to all three operas. It proved disappointing, partly because Bartoletti's conducting lacked tension but also because Freni was below her vocal best. *Gianni Schicchi* suffers most from Bartoletti's limpness, and Freni is not remotely young-sounding in *O mio babbino caro*. Roberto Alagna gives a clean, trumpet-toned performance as Rinuccio but, though Leo Nucci sings well enough in the title-role, he conveys nothing of the ironic humour behind this magic manipulator. The full Decca recording does little to remedy the shortcomings of the performance.

Madama Butterfly (complete).
*** DG Dig. 423 567-2; *447 774-4* (3/2) [id.]. Freni, Carreras, Berganza, Pons, Amb. Op. Ch., Philh. O, Sinopoli.
**(*) Decca 417 577-2 (3) [id.]. Freni, Ludwig, Pavarotti, Kerns, V. State Op. Ch., VPO, Karajan.
(M) *** RCA GD 84145 (2) [4145-2-RG]. Moffo, Elias, Valletti, Cesari, Catalani, Rome Op. Ch. & O, Leinsdorf.

(M) *** EMI CMS7 69654-2 (2) [Ang. CDMB 69654]. Scotto, Bergonzi, Di Stasio, Panerai, De Palma, Rome Op. Ch. & O, Barbirolli.

(M) **(*) EMI CMS7 63634-2 (2) [Ang. CDMB 63634]; *TC-CFPD 4446*. De los Angeles, Bjoerling, Pirazzini, Sereni, Rome Op. Ch. & O, Santini.

(***) EMI mono CDS7 47959-8 (2) [id.]. Callas, Gedda, Borriello, Danieli, La Scala, Milan, Ch. & O, Karajan.

(B) (**(*)) Decca Double mono 440 230-2 (2) [id.]. Tebaldi, Campora, Inghilleri, Rankin, Santa Cecilia Academy, Rome, Ch. & O, Alberto Erede.

However expansive his speeds, Sinopoli is never sentimental or self-indulgent. Puccini's honeyed moments are given, not sloppily, but with rapt intensity. They are then set the more movingly against the biting moments, from the opening fugato of Act I, sharply incisive, through to the final aria, tough and intense. As she was for Karajan in his classic Decca set, Freni is a model Butterfly; though the voice is no longer so girlish, she projects the tragedy even more weightily than before. José Carreras is similarly presented as a large-scale Pinkerton. Juan Pons is a virile Sharpless and Teresa Berganza an equally positive, unfruity Suzuki. This is a set which in its spacious but intensely concentrated way brings a unique and unforgettable experience. But it is on three CDs.

Karajan's set is also extravagantly laid out on three discs instead of two as for most of the rival sets – slow speeds partly responsible. However, he inspires singers and orchestra to a radiant performance which brings out all the beauty and intensity of Puccini's score, sweet but not sentimental, powerfully dramatic but not vulgar. Freni is an enchanting Butterfly, consistently growing in stature from the young girl to the victim of tragedy, sweeter of voice than any rival on record. Pavarotti is an intensely imaginative Pinkerton, actually inspiring understanding for this thoughtless character, while Christa Ludwig is a splendid Suzuki. The recording is one of Decca's most resplendent, with the Vienna strings producing glowing tone. Recommended, alongside Sinopoli.

Anna Moffo's Butterfly proves delightful, fresh and young-sounding, and the *Flower duet* with Rosalind Elias is enchanting. Valletti's Pinkerton has a clear-voiced, almost Gigli-like charm – preferable to most rivals – and with Corena as the Bonze the only blot on the set vocally is the unimaginative Sharpless of Renato Cesari. Leinsdorf is efficient and undistracting and, with vivid recording (balanced in favour of the voices), this makes a first-class mid-priced recommendation, costing less than half the price of the Decca Karajan set with Freni, Ludwig and Pavarotti.

Under Sir John Barbirolli, players and singers perform consistently with a dedication and intensity rare in opera recordings made in Italy, and the whole score glows more freshly than ever. There is hardly a weak link in the cast. Bergonzi's Pinkerton and Panerai's Sharpless are both sensitively and beautifully sung; Anna di Stasio's Suzuki is more than adequate, and Renata Scotto's Butterfly has a subtlety and perceptiveness in its characterization that more than make up for any shortcoming in the basic beauty of tone-colour.

Victoria de los Angeles' 1960 recording displays her art at its most endearing, her range of golden tone-colour lovingly exploited. Opposite her, Jussi Bjoerling produces a flow of rich tone to compare with that of the heroine. Mario Sereni is a full-voiced Sharpless, but Miriam Pirazzini is a disappointingly wobbly Suzuki; Santini is a reliable, generally rather square and unimaginative conductor who rarely gets in the way. With recording quality freshened, this fine set is most welcome either on a pair of mid-priced CDs or in its CfP cassette format.

Callas's view, aided by superbly imaginative and spacious conducting from Karajan, gives extra dimension to the Puccinian little woman, and with some keenly intelligent singing too from Gedda as Pinkerton this is a set which has a special compulsion. The performance projects the more vividly on CD, even though the lack of stereo in so atmospheric an opera is a serious disadvantage.

Astonishingly, this Decca mono set was made (in 1951) before Tebaldi ever sang the part in the opera house. In the last resort she lacks temperament but there is much magnificent singing. Campora is a fine Pinkerton and the fresh young voices of the two lovers are particularly convincing in Act I. Erede's conducting is stong and dramatic, and there is much to relish, not least the amazingly atmospheric Decca recording, which is very kind to the voices. The orchestra sounds thinner, but the violins have more body here than on those old Ace of Clubs LP pressings. The two CDs come in a single jewel-case with an independent plot summary unrelated to the 40 cues.

Madama Butterfly: highlights.
*** Decca 421 247-2; *421 247-4* [id.] (from above recording with Freni and Pavarotti; cond. Karajan).

Karajan's disc offers an obvious choice for a highlights CD from *Butterfly* if you are willing to pay full price.

Madame Butterfly: highlights (sung in English).
(B) **(*) CfP CD-CFP 4600; *TC-CFP 4600*. Collier, Craig, Robson, Griffiths, Sadler's Wells O, Brian Balkwill.

This 1960 recording was the first of a series of Sadler's Wells highlights discs of opera in English. There are few better examples, for the clear recording lets the listener hear almost every word, and this is achieved without balancing things excessively in favour of the voices. Marie Collier got inside the part very well; she has a big, full voice and she sings most movingly. Charles Craig is a splendid Pinkerton: his singing achieves international standards and he was in particularly fresh voice when this record was made. As to the choice of extracts, the one omission which is at all serious is the entry of Butterfly. As it is, the duet of Pinkerton and Sharpless cuts off just as she is about to come in. The recording wears its years lightly; just occasionally the bright CD transfer brings a touch of peakiness in the vocal climaxes, but the performance remains very involving.

Manon Lescaut (complete).
*** Decca Dig. 440 200-2 (2) [id.]. Freni, Pavarotti, Croft, Taddei, Vargas, Bartoli, NY Met. Op. Ch. & O, Levine.
*** DG Dig. 413 893-2 (2) [id.]. Freni, Domingo, Bruson, ROHCG Ch., Philh. O, Sinopoli.
*** Decca Dig. 421 426-2 (2) [id.]. Kiri Te Kanawa, Carreras, Paolo Coni, Ch. & O of Teatro Comunale di Bologna, Chailly.
*** Naxos Dig. 8.660019/20 (2) [id.]. Gauci, Sardinero, Kaludov, BRT Philh. Ch. & O, Rahbari.
(M) (***) RCA mono GD 60573 (2) [60573-2-RG]. Albanese, Bjoerling, Merrill, Rome Op. Ch. & O, Perlea.
(M) (***) EMI mono CDS7 47393-8 (2) [Ang. CDCB 47392]. Callas, Di Stefano, Fioravanti, La Scala, Milan, Ch. and O, Serafin.
(Y/B) (M) **(*) EMI CMS7 64852-2 (2) [Ang. CDMB 64852]. Caballé, Domingo, Amb. Op. Ch., New Philh. O, Bartoletti.

With Luciano Pavarotti as a powerful Des Grieux, James Levine conducts a comparably big-boned performance of *Manon Lescaut*, bringing out the red-blooded drama of Puccini's first big success, while not ignoring its warmth and tender poetry. The impact is enhanced by exceptionally full, vivid sound, with the voices balanced close, well in front of the orchestra in a way one associates with opera recordings of the 1950s. It represents an opposite view to that taken by the DG engineers when in one of the last Kingsway Hall sessions they recorded the Sinopoli version. There too the title-role was taken by Mirella Freni and, though the closeness of balance on the newer set exposes some inevitable blemishes of age in the voice, its fullness and warmth are more faithfully captured in a performance even warmer and more relaxed. It culminates in an account of the big Act IV aria, *Sola, perduta, abbandonata*, more involving and passionate than any in recent years, with the voice showing no signs of wear. Consistently, Levine conveys the tensions and atmosphere of a stage performance in a way that plainly owes much to his experience at the Met., avoiding the feeling of a studio performance.

Pavarotti's contribution as Des Grieux is more controversial. He tackles his little opening aria challenging the girls to make him fall in love, *Tra voi belle*, with a beefy bravado that misses the subtlety and point of Domingo, for example. But then he characteristically points word-meaning with a bright-eyed intensity that compels attention. The closeness of balance means that in volume his singing rarely drops below mezzo-forte, and as a vocal demonstration Domingo's performance is consistently more refined, but there is little harm in having so passionate a portrait of Des Grieux as Pavarotti's. The rest of the cast is strong too, with Dwayne Croft a magnificent Lescaut who brings out the character's wry humour. The veteran Giuseppe Taddei is superbly cast as Geronte, very characterful and still full-throated, while Cecilia Bartoli makes the unnamed singer in the Act II entertainment into far more than a cipher. One incidental advantage over most rivals is that the break between discs comes after Act II, avoiding any break within an Act.

Plácido Domingo's portrait of Des Grieux on DG is far subtler and more detailed, with finer contrasts of tone and dynamic, than in his earlier, EMI recording opposite Caballé. Freni proves an outstanding choice: her girlish tones in Act I rebut any idea that she might be too mature. Of the others, a first-rate team, Renato Bruson nicely brings out the ironic side of Lescaut's character, and having Brigitte Fassbaender just to sing the *Madrigal* adds to the feeling of luxury, as does John Tomlinson's darkly intense moment of drama as the ship's captain. The voices are more recessed than is common, but they are recorded with fine bloom, and the brilliance of the orchestral sound comes out impressively.

Dame Kiri also gives an affecting characterization, at times rather heavily underlined but passionately convincing in the development from innocent girl to fallen woman. The playing from Chailly's Bologna orchestra cannot quite match that of the Philharmonia, yet Chailly is a degree more idiomatic in his pacing. Both tenors are good but Carreras sounds a little strained at times. The Decca sound, with voices further forward, is the more vivid.

On the bargain Naxos issue, Miriam Gauci gives one of the most sensitive performances of this role on any set. Her Act II aria, *In quelle trine morbide*, is beautifully poised and her monologue in the death scene, *Sola, perduta, abbandonata*, is the more moving for being restrained at the start, building from there in intensity without sacrificing musical values. The young Bulgarian, Kaludi Kaludov, is a clean-cut, virile Des Grieux, opening up impressively in his big moments. Vincente Sardinero makes a power-ful Lescaut, and Rahbari, as in his Bratislava recordings of *Cav.* and *Pag.*, is a red-blooded interpreter of Italian opera, generally pacing well, even if at the very start he is disconcertingly hectic. Though the Brussels orchestra plays with refinement – the strings in particular – the sound is thinner than in the Slovakian recordings, with the orchestra set slightly back. This is the least expensive *Manon Lescaut* in the catalogue but, even if it cost more, it would still be very recommendable.

In Perlea's 1954 recording, the mono sound may be limited, but no Puccinian should miss it, when Jussi Bjoerling gives the finest ever interpretation on record of the role of Des Grieux. Robert Merrill too is superb as Manon's brother, giving delightful irony to the closing scene of Act I, which has rarely sounded so effervescent. The Manon of Licia Albanese is sensitively sung, but the voice is not at all girlish.

It is typical of Callas that she turns the final scene into the most compelling part of the opera. Serafin, who could be a lethargic recording conductor, is here electrifying, and Di Stefano too is inspired to one of his finest complete opera recordings. The cast-list even includes the young Fiorenza Cossotto, impressive as the singer in the Act II *Madrigal*. The recording – still in mono, not a stereo transcription – minimizes the original boxiness and gives good detail.

The EMI version, conducted by Bartoletti, is chiefly valuable for the performance of Montserrat Caballé as the heroine, one of her most affecting, with the voice alluringly beautiful. Otherwise the set is disappointing, with Plácido Domingo unflattered by the close acoustic, not nearly as perceptive as in his much later, DG performance under Sinopoli. Bartoletti's conducting is also relatively coarse, with the very opening forced and breathless. The new transfer to CD, however, has improved the sound, which is now more vivid and atmospheric; the presentation, with a clearly printed libretto, is also attractive.

Manon Lescaut: highlights.
(Y/B) (M) *** DG Dig. 445 466-2 [id.] (from above recording, with Freni, Domingo; cond. Sinopoli).

Most of the key items are included in this well-chosen mid-price selection of highlights from the brilliant Sinopoli set which is a strong alternative recommendation for this opera. An adequate synopsis with track cues is provided in lieu of a libretto. The playing time is 66 minutes.

La Rondine (complete).
*** Sony Dig. M2K 37852 [id.]. Te Kanawa, Domingo, Nicolesco, Rendall, Nucci, Watson, Knight, Amb. Op. Ch., LSO, Maazel.

La Rondine has never caught on, and a recording like this will almost certainly surprise anyone at the mastery of the piece, with a captivating string of catchy numbers. Maazel's is a strong, positive reading, crowned by a superb and radiant Magda in Dame Kiri Te Kanawa, mature yet glamorous. Domingo, by age too mature for the role of young hero, yet scales his voice down most effectively in the first two Acts, expanding in heroic warmth only in the final scene of dénouement. Sadly, the second pair are far less convincing, when the voices of both Mariana Nicolesco and David Rendall take ill to the microphone.

Il Tabarro (complete).
(M) **(*) RCA GD 60865 (2) [60865-2]. Leontyne Price, Domingo, Milnes, John Alldis Ch., New Philh. O, Leinsdorf – LEONCAVALLO: *I Pagliacci*. ***

Leontyne Price may not be ideally cast as the bargemaster's wife, but she is fully in character. Sherrill Milnes is rather young-sounding for the bargemaster, but he sings memorably in the climactic aria. Plácido Domingo makes a fresh-voiced and well-characterized young bargee, while Leinsdorf is at his most sympathetic.

Tosca (complete).
⊛ *** EMI mono CDS7 47175-8 (2) [Ang. CDCB 47174]. Callas, Di Stefano, Gobbi, Calabrese, La Scala, Milan, Ch. and O, De Sabata.
*** DG Dig. 431 775-2 (2). Freni, Domingo, Ramey, Terfel, ROHCG Ch., Philh. O, Sinopoli.
(M) *** Decca 421 670-2 (2) [id.]. Leontyne Price, Di Stefano, Taddei, V. State Op. Ch., VPO, Karajan.
*** DG 413 815-2 (2) [id.]. Ricciarelli, Carreras, Raimondi, Corena, German Op. Ch., BPO, Karajan.
(B) (***) Decca Double mono 440 236-2 (2) [id.]. Tebaldi, Campora, Mascherini, Santa Cecilia Academy, Rome, Ch. & O, Alberto Erede.

**(*) Decca Dig. 414 597-2 (2) [id.]. Te Kanawa, Aragall, Nucci, Welsh Nat. Opera Ch., Nat. PO, Solti.

There has never been a finer recorded performance of *Tosca* than Callas's first, with Victor de Sabata conducting and Tito Gobbi as Scarpia. Gobbi makes the unbelievably villainous police chief into a genuinely three-dimensional character, and Di Stefano as the hero, Cavaradossi, was at his finest. The conducting of De Sabata is spaciously lyrical as well as sharply dramatic, and the mono recording is superbly balanced in Walter Legge's fine production. Though there is inevitably less spaciousness than in a stereo recording, the voices are caught gloriously.

Even more than the Puccini operas he had previously recorded – always with spacious, finely moulded treatment – *Tosca* seems to match Sinopoli's musical personality, helped by DG recording of spectacular weight and range. Ramey's is not a conventional portrait of the evil police-chief, but the role has rarely been sung with more sheer beauty, with such a climax as the *Te Deum* at the end of Act I sounding thrilling in its firmness and power. Domingo's heroic power is formidable too, and unlike many of his opera recordings for DG this one presents him in close-up, not distanced. Freni's is not naturally a Tosca voice, but it is still a powerful, heartfelt performance.

On Decca, Karajan deserves equal credit with the principal singers for the vital, imaginative performance, recorded in Vienna. Taddei himself has a marvellously wide range of tone-colour, and though he cannot quite match the Gobbi snarl he has almost every other weapon in his armoury. Leontyne Price is at the peak of her form and Di Stefano sings most sensitively. The sound of the Vienna orchestra is enthralling – both more refined and richer than usual in a Puccini opera – and it sounds quite marvellous in its digitally remastered format, combining presence with atmosphere and making a superb bargain at mid-price.

On Karajan's DG version the police chief, Scarpia, seems to be the central character, and his unexpected choice of singer, a full bass, Raimondi, helps to show why, for this is no small-time villain but a man who in full confidence has a vein of nobility in him. Katia Ricciarelli is not the most individual of Toscas, but the beauty of singing is consistent. Carreras gives a powerful, stylish performance. The recording is rich and full, with the stage picture clearly established and the glorious orchestral textures beautifully caught.

Tosca was one of Tebaldi's finest parts, and her earlier Decca mono set showed her at her most moving. In addition, Campora and Ezo Mascherini gave far more satisfying support as Cavaradossi and Scarpia respectively than did del Monaco and George London in the later Decca stereo set. The 1951 recording too stands the test of time remarkably well, the orchestra a little distant but the whole effect satisfyingly atmospheric. The choral climax with Scarpia in the *Te Deum* at the end of Act I is remarkably effective, even without the advantage of stereo. Erede's conducting is fittingly full-blooded, and Tebaldi admirers should not hesitate at the very reasonable price, even if there is no libretto/translation, only a synopsis.

Rarely has Solti phrased Italian melody so consistently *con amore*, his fiercer side subdued but with plenty of power when required. Even so, the timing is not always quite spontaneous-sounding, with transitions occasionally rushed. But the principal *raison d'être* of the set must be the casting of Dame Kiri as the jealous opera-singer. Her admirers will relish the glorious sounds, but the jealous side of Tosca's character is rather muted.

Tosca: highlights.
(Y/B) (B) *** DG 439 461-2 [id.] (from above recording, with Ricciarelli, Carreras, Raimondi; cond. Karajan).
(M) ** Decca 421 888-2; *421 888-4* [id.]. Freni, Pavarotti, Milnes, Wandsworth School Boys' Ch., L. Op. Ch., Nat. PO, Rescigno.

The new bargain Classikon 70-minute selection from Karajan's powerful, closely recorded Berlin version is welcome. The breadth of Karajan's direction is well represented in the longer excerpts; there is also Tosca's *Vissi d'arte* and Carreras's two famous arias from the outer Acts. Now Scarpia's music in Act II is much better represented, essential when Raimondi is such a distinctive Scarpia with his dark, bass timbre.

A not especially generous (63 minutes) selection from Rescigno's 1978 Decca set is mainly notable for offering a sampler of Pavarotti's assumption of the role of Cavaradossi; but it is only in Act III that the voice acquires its full magic, and *E lucevan le stelle* is undoubtedly the highlight. As Tosca, Freni sounds rather taxed so that even *Vissi d'arte* produces her stressed tone rather than even, lyrical sound. Milnes is quite well represented in the Act II excerpts: his Scarpia is fresh and direct, with words finely enunciated, a fine characterization. The Decca sound has characteristic brilliance and atmosphere.

Il Trittico: (i) *Il Tabarro;* (ii) *Suor Angelica;* (iii) *Gianni Schicchi.*
(M) *** EMI mono/stereo CMS7 64165-2 (3). (i; iii) Gobbi; (i) Pradelli, Mas; (ii–iii) De los Angeles; (ii) Barbieri; (iii) Canali, Del Monte, Montarsolo; Rome Op. Ch. & O; (i) Bellezza; (ii) Serafin; (iii) Santini.
**(*) Sony CD 79312 (3) [M3K 35912]. (i; ii) Scotto; (i; iii) Domingo; (i) Wixell, Sénéchal; (ii) Horne; (ii; iii) Cotrubas; (iii) Gobbi, Amb. Op. Ch.; (ii) Desborough School Ch.; (i; ii) Nat. PO; (iii) LSO, Maazel.

The classic EMI set of *Il Trittico* has dominated the catalogue since the earliest days of LP, with Tito Gobbi giving two of his ripest characterizations. The central role of the cuckolded bargemaster, Michele, in *Il Tabarro* inspires him to one of his very finest performances on record. Though this version of Puccini's *grand guignol* opera, set on a barge on the Seine in Paris, is a mono recording, not stereo, it conveys the sense of horror far more keenly than any, with Gobbi's voice vividly caught on CD. The central leaf of the triptych, *Suor Angelica*, brings a glowing performance from Victoria de los Angeles, giving a most affecting portrayal of Angelica, the nun ill-treated by her noble family, with Fedora Barbieri formidable as her unfeeling aunt, the Zia Principessa. De los Angeles reappears, charmingly girlish as Lauretta, in *Gianni Schicchi*, where the high comedy has never fizzed so deliciously outside the opera house. She and Gobbi come together just as characterfully in this final opera. Though Gobbi's incomparable baritone is not by nature comic-sounding, he is unequalled as Schicchi, sardonically manipulating the mourning relatives of Buoso Donati, as he frames a new will for them. Puccini, the master of tragedy, here emerges a supreme master of comic timing too. Only *Gianni Schicchi*, recorded last in 1958, is in genuine and excellent stereo; *Il Tabarro* (1955) and *Suor Angelica* (1957) are mono, but all the transfers are expert, clear and convincingly balanced.

Il Tabarro may most seriously lack atmosphere in Maazel's version, but his directness is certainly refreshing, and in the other two operas it results in powerful readings; the opening of *Gianni Schicchi*, for example, has a sharp, almost Stravinskian bite. In the first two operas, Scotto's performances have a commanding dominance, presenting her at her finest. In *Gianni Schicchi* the veteran Tito Gobbi gives an amazing performance, in almost every way as fine as his EMI recording of twenty years earlier – and in some ways this is even more compelling. The only snag is the lack of cueing; CBS provide only one track for the whole of *Il Tabarro* and only two each for *Gianni Schicchi* and *Suor Angelica*, the second in each case being used to indicate the main soprano aria.

Turandot (complete).
*** Decca 414 274-2 (2) [id.]. Sutherland, Pavarotti, Caballé, Pears, Ghiaurov, Alldis Ch., Wandsworth School Boys' Ch., LPO, Mehta.
(M) *** EMI CMS7 69327-2 (2) [Ang. CDMB 69327]. Nilsson, Corelli, Scotto, Mercuriali, Giaiotti, Rome Op. Ch. & O, Molinari-Pradelli.
*** DG Dig. 423 855-2; *423 855-4* (2) [id.]. Ricciarelli, Domingo, Hendricks, Raimondi, V. State Op. Ch., V. Boys' Ch., VPO, Karajan.
(***) EMI mono CDS7 47971-8 (2) [id.]. Callas, Fernandi, Schwarzkopf, Zaccaria, La Scala, Milan, Ch. & O, Serafin.
(Y/B) (M) **(*) EMI CMS5 65293-2 (2) [Ang. CDMB 65293]. Caballé, Carreras, Freni, Plishka, Sénéchal, Maîtrise de la Cathédrale, Ch. of L'Opéra du Rhin, Strasbourg PO, Lombard.

Joan Sutherland gives an intensely revealing and appealing interpretation, making the icy princess far more human and sympathetic than ever before, while Pavarotti gives a performance equally imaginative, beautiful in sound, strong on detail. To set Caballé against Sutherland was a daring idea, and it works superbly well; Pears as the Emperor is another imaginative choice. Mehta directs a gloriously rich and dramatic performance, superlatively recorded, still the best-sounding *Turandot* on CD, while the reading also remains supreme.

The EMI set brings Nilsson's second assumption on record of the role of Puccini's formidable princess. As an interpretation it is very similar to the earlier, RCA performance, but its impact is far more immediate, thanks to the conducting of Molinari-Pradelli. Corelli may not be the most sensitive prince in the world, but the voice is in glorious condition. Scotto's Liù is very beautiful and characterful too. With vividly remastered sound, this makes an excellent mid-priced recommendation, though the documentation, as yet, does not include an English translation.

In Karajan's set, Hendricks is almost a sex-kitten with her seductively golden tone, and one wonders how Calaf could ever have overlooked her. This is very different from the usual picture of a chaste slave-girl. Ricciarelli is a far more vulnerable figure than one expects of the icy princess, and the very fact that the part strains her beyond reasonable vocal limits adds to the dramatic point, even if it subtracts from the musical joys. By contrast, Plácido Domingo is vocally superb, a commanding prince; and the rest of the cast present star names even in small roles.

With Callas, the character seems so much more believably complex than with others, and this 1957 recording is one of her most thrillingly magnetic performances on disc. Schwarzkopf provides a comparably characterful and distinctive portrait as Liù, far more than a Puccinian 'little woman', sweet and wilting. Eugenio Fernandi sounds relatively uncharacterful as Calaf, but his timbre is pleasing enough. By contrast, Serafin's masterly conducting exactly matches the characterfulness of Callas and Schwarzkopf, with colour, atmosphere and dramatic point all commandingly presented. With such a vivid performance, the 1957 mono sound hardly seems to matter, although the choral passages tend to overload at climaxes.

Having earlier sung Liù opposite Joan Sutherland for Decca, Caballé went on to assume the more taxing role of Turandot. With Mirella Freni as Liù there is again a powerful confrontation, not between black and white but between subtler, less fixed characters. So from the very start Caballé conveys an element of mystery while Freni underlines the dramatic rather than the lyrical side of Liù's role. The pity is that the recording is unflattering to the voices – allowing Caballé less warmth and body of tone than usual, while setting Freni so close that a flutter keeps intruding. Lombard, so alert and imaginative in French music, proves a stiff and unsympathetic Puccinian so that the tenor, José Carreras, for example is prevented from expanding as he should in the big arias. Nor is the Strasbourg Philharmonic a match for the LPO on Decca. A good CD transfer and excellent back-up documentation.

Turandot: excerpts.
(M) (***) EMI mono CDH7 61074-2 [id.]. Dame Eva Turner, Martinelli, Albanese, Favero, Tomei, Dua, ROHCG Ch., LPO, Barbirolli.

The excerpts were recorded at two separate 1937 performances and fascinatingly duplicate most of the items, with the second performance in each pair marginally more spacious and helpful in sound, and generally warmer and more relaxed as a performance. Martinelli's heroic timbre may be an acquired taste, but he is stirringly convincing, and Dame Eva Turner gloriously confirms all the legends, even more commanding than in her earlier studio accounts of the big aria, *In questa reggia*. Keith Hardwick's excellent transfers, for all the obvious limitations of recording on stage at Covent Garden, give a superb sense of presence. (This is another important EMI reissue currently withdrawn.)

Turandot: highlights.
(M) *** Decca 433 438-2 [id.] (from above recording, with Sutherland, Pavarotti; cond. Mehta).
(M) *** DG Dig. 435 409-2; *435 409-4* [id.] (from above set, with Ricciarelli, Domingo; cond. Karajan).

A generous and shrewdly chosen collection of excerpts from the glorious Decca set of *Turandot. Nessun dorma*, with Pavarotti at his finest, is here given a closing cadence for neatness. The vintage Decca sound is outstandingly full and vivid.

Domingo is at his very finest on the DG alternative CD, and he is exceptionally well represented in this 70-minute selection of highlights, as indeed is the chorus.

Le Villi: complete.
*** Sony MK 76890 [MK 36669]. Scotto, Domingo, Nucci, Gobbi, Amb. Op. Ch., Nat. PO, Maazel.

Maazel directs a performance so commanding, with singing of outstanding quality, that one can at last assess Puccini's first opera on quite a new level. Scotto's voice tends to spread a little at the top of the stave but, like Domingo, she gives a powerful performance, and Leo Nucci avoids false histrionics. A delightful bonus is Tito Gobbi's contribution reciting the verses which link the scenes; he is as characterful a reciter as he is a singer. The recording is one of CBS's best.

COLLECTIONS

'The Essential Puccini': Preludio sinfonico; Famous arias, duets and choruses from: *La Bohème; La Fanciulla del West; Gianni Schicchi; Madama Butterfly; Manon Lescaut; La Rondine; Suor Angelica; Tosca; Turandot.*
(N) (B) **(*) Decca Double Analogue/Dig. 444 555-2 (2) [id.]. Caballé, Chiara, Freni, Te Kanawa, Sutherland, Tebaldi, Bergonzi, Bjoerling, Carreras, Pavarotti, Corena, Ghiaurov, Krause, Milnes, Siepi (with various orchestras & conductors).

Many collectors will welcome a sampler of the vintage set of *La Bohème* with Tebaldi and Bergonzi at the height of their powers. Five items are included here, including the love scene from Act I. Tebaldi is also at her most seductive in *Madama Butterfly*, which is generously represented with well over half an hour of excerpts, including the whole of the Act I Love duet. She also provides the key arias from *Gianni Schicchi* and *La Rondine*, while Suor Angelica's ravishing *Senza mamma, o bimbo, tu sei morto* comes from Maria Chiara's glorious 1971 début recital, which Decca should urgently restore to the catalogue. Dame Kiri gives a movingly passionate if comparatively unsubtle characterization of *Manon Lescaut;*

with three numbers included, her partner, Carreras, recorded just before his illness, sounds a little strained. It was a pity that Rescigno's recording was chosen for the 30 minutes of so of *Tosca* excerpts, especially as a highlights disc from that set is already available. Freni as Tosca is below her best form and, though Sherrill Milnes does not disappoint as Scarpia, Pavarotti's *E lucevan le stelle* is the high point. Joan Sutherland's assumption of the role of the formidable *Turandot* is justly esteemed, as is Caballé's melting Liù, while Pavarotti delivers a splendid *Nessun dorma*. With Bjoerling on hand to provide a superb *Ch'ella mi creda* from *Fanciulla del West*, this is something of a (143-minute) Puccini feast, with the ripely expansive Decca sound fairly consistent throughout (although the early Tebaldi recordings give some indication of their age in the violin tone). The snag is that the documentation is totally inadequate.

'*Puccini heroines*'; *La Bohème: Sì, mi chiamano Mimì; Donde lieta uscì; Musetta's waltz song. Edgar: Addio, mio dolce amor. La Fanciulla del West: Laggiù nel Soledad. Gianni Schicchi: O mio babbino caro. Madama Butterfly: Bimba, bimba non piangere (Love duet, with Plácido Domingo); Un bel dì. Manon Lescaut: In quelle trine morbide; Sola, perduta, abbandonata. La Rondine: Ore dolci a divine. Tosca: Vissi d'arte. Turandot: In questa reggia. Le Villi: Se come voi piccina.*
*** RCA RD 85999 [RCA 5999-2-RC]. Leontyne Price, New Philh. O or LSO, Downes; Santi.

This collection is a formidable demonstration of the art of Leontyne Price at the very peak of her career, still marvellously subtle in control (the end of Tosca's *Vissi d'arte* for example), powerfully dramatic, yet able to point the *Rondine* aria with delicacy and charm. The *Love duet* from *Butterfly* in which she is joined by Domingo is particularly thrilling, and there is much else here to give pleasure. The remastering is extremely vivid and the voice is given fine bloom and presence. A Puccinian feast!

'*Favourite Puccini*': (i) *La Bohème: Mi chiamano Mimì; Donde lieta uscì;* (ii) *Musetta's waltz song. Gianni Schicchi: O mio babbino caro. Madama Butterfly: Un bel dì;* (iii; iv) *Spira sul mare; Flower duet; Con onor muore . . . Tu, tu.* (ii) *Manon Lescaut: In quelle trine morbide;* (iii) *Sola, perduta, abbandonata.* (ii) *La Rondine: Chi il bel sogno di Doretta.* (iii) *Suor Angelica: Senza mamma, O bimbo, tu sei morto.* (i) *Tosca: Vissi d'arte. Turandot: Tu, che di gel sei cinta;* (i; v) *In questa reggia. Le Villi: Se come voi.*
(M) *** Sony analogue/Dig. SMK 48094 [id.]. (i) Eva Marton; (ii) Kiri Te Kanawa; (iii) Renata Scotto; (iv) with Wixell and Knight; (v) with Carreras.

Kiri Te Kanawa's six ravishing contributions are the highlight of this collection – there is currently no more luscious Puccini singing than this – but the others are very characterful too, even if Eva Marton's Mimì is a shade forceful; she is better suited to the role of Turandot. However, *In questa reggia*, which ends the disc excitingly, delivers a damp squib by fading out. Before that there is much to enjoy, not least Scotto's beautiful *Senza mamma* from *Suor Angelica* and the two moving excerpts (Butterfly's entrance and the opera's climax) from Maazel's complete set of *Madama Butterfly*. The sound is excellent throughout, although sometimes the vocal balance is very forward. There is no back-up documentation, apart from a list of titles and performers.

Arias: *La Bohème: Quando m'en vo' soletta. Gianni Schicchi: O mio babbino caro. Madama Butterfly: Un bel dì. Manon Lescaut: In quelle trine morbide. La Rondine: Chi il bel sogno di Doretta. Tosca: Vissi d'arte. Le Villi: Se come voi piccina.*
*** Sony Dig. MK 37298 [id.]. Kiri Te Kanawa, LPO, Pritchard – VERDI: *Arias.* ***

The creamy beauty of Kiri Te Kanawa's voice is ideally suited to these seven lyrical arias, including such rarities as the little waltz-like song from *Le Villi*, well recorded and sounding especially believable on CD.

Arias: *La Bohème; Sì, mi chiamano Mimì; Donde lieta usci. Gianni Schicchi: O mio babbino caro. Madama Butterfly: Un bel dì; Tu, tu piccolo Iddio. Manon Lescaut: In quelle trine morbide; Sola, perduta, abbandonata. La Rondine: Chi il bel sogno di Doretta. Tosca: Vissi d'arte. Turandot: Signore, ascolta!; Tu che di gel sei cinta. Le Villi: Se come voi piccina.*
*** EMI CDC7 47841-2 [id.]. Montserrat Caballé, LSO, Mackerras.

Montserrat Caballé uses her rich, beautiful voice to glide over these great Puccinian melodies. The effect is ravishing, with lovely recorded sound to match the approach. This is one of the loveliest of all operatic recital discs and the comparative lack of sparkle is compensated for by the sheer beauty of the voice. The CD transfer is extremely successful, vivid yet retaining the full vocal bloom.

Purcell, Henry (1659–95)

Archiv Purcell Collection

'*Purcell Edition*' (complete in slipcase).
(Y/B) (M) **(*) DG 447 147-2 (8) [id.] (all the records are also available separately – see below).

(i) *3 Fantasias for 5 Viols; 9 Fantasias for 4 Viols; Fantasia on one note for 5 viols; In nomine for 6 viols; In nomine for 7 viols;* (ii) Duet: *How pleasant is this flowery plain;* Verse anthem: *In thee, O Lord, do I put my trust;* Song: *Oh! what a scene does entertain my sight;* Drinking song: '*Tis wine was made to rule the day;* Trio: *When the cock begins to crow*.
(Y/B) (M) *** DG mono 447 156-2 [id.]. (i) Schola Cantorum Basiliensis, August Wenzinger; (ii) Saltire Singers, Instrumental Ens., Hans Oppenheim.

(i) *3 Fantasias for 3 Viols; 9 Fantasias for 4 Viols; Fantasia on one note for 5 viols; In nomine for 6 viols; In nomine for 7 viols;* (ii) *Chacony in G min*.
(Y/B) (M) **(*) DG 447 153-2 [id.]. (i) VCM, Alice Harnoncourt; (ii) E. Concert, Pinnock.

(i) *Harpsichord suites Nos. 1–8;* (ii) *Organ voluntaries: in G; for double organ in D min*.
(Y/B) (M) *** DG 447 154-2 [id.]. (i) Colin Tilney (spinet); (ii) Simon Preston (organ).

Anthems: *Man that is born of woman; O God, thou has cast us out; Lord, how long wilt thou be angry?; O God, thou art my God; O Lord God of hosts; Remember not, Lord, our offences; Thou knowest, Lord, the secrets of our hearts.* Verse anthems: *My beloved spake; My heart is inditing; O sing unto the Lord; Praise the Lord, O Jerusalem; They that go down to the sea in ships. Morning Service in B flat: Benedicte omnia opera; Cantate Domino; Deus miscreatur; Magnificat; Nunc dimittis. Evening service in G min.: Magnificat; Nunc dimittis. Latin Psalm: Jehovah, quam multi sunt hostes mei. Te Deum and Jubilate in D.*
(Y/B) (M) *** DG 447 150-2 (2) [id.]. David Thomas, Christ Church Cathedral, Oxford, Ch., E. Concert, Simon Preston.

(i) *Ode on St Cecilia's Day (Hail! bright Cecilia);* (ii) *The Married Beau: suite for strings in D min*.
(Y/B) (M) **(*) DG 447 149-2 [id.]. (i) Simon Woolf, Esswood, Tatnell, Young, Rippon, Shirley-Quirk, Tiffin Ch., Amb. S., ECO, Mackerras.

Dido and Aeneas (opera; complete).
(Y/B) (M) **(*) DG 447 148-2 [id.]. Troyanos, McDaniel, Armstrong, Johnson, Rogers, Hamburg Monteverdi Ch., N. German R. CO, Mackerras.

'*Coronation music for King James II*': BLOW: *God spake sometimes in visions; Behold, O God our defender*. LAWES: *Zadok the Priest*. PURCELL: *My heart is inditing; I was glad*. CHILD: *O Lord, grant the King a long life*. TURNER: *The King shall rejoice*.
(Y/B) (M) **(*) DG Dig. 447 155-2 [id.]. Westminster Abbey Ch., O, Simon Preston.

This well-planned survey has the double advantage not only of showing Purcell's diverse genius but also of demonstrating the riches of DG's Archiv catalogue, ranging over nearly 50 years. The first disc here offers distinguished early recordings by the legendary Schola Cantorum Basiliensis, directed by August Wenzinger, who broke new ground in instrumental musical authenticity in the 1950s, and the talented Scottish Saltire Singers (a vocal quartet as impressive individually as in consort), who record their highly spontaneous accounts of a collection of Purcell's songs and a movingly intimate verse-anthem, happily adding a first-class accompanying group of German musicians.

The Purcell *Fantasias* and *In nomines* are among the most searching and profound works in all music, and the inspired performances by Wenzinger's group have never been supassed: ethereal, infinitely touching in their refined delicacy of texture. Although this first disc is mono, in no way is it technically inferior, and its natural balance and ambience almost bring an illusion of stereo. On the companion CD, the 1963 Vienna Concentus, led by Alice Harnoncourt (with Nikolaus at the time playing 'second fiddle'), provide a second (stereo) set of performances of these wonderful pieces, darkly sombre in colour, using original instruments with a minimum of vibrato. Then at track 16 there is a splash of cold water in the face as Trevor Pinnock and his English Concert (recorded two decades later) demonstrate modern ideas of authenticity of style and pitch with a brightly astringent and strikingly vital account of the famous *Chacony in G minor*. This transition is not entirely comfortable, and it is better to listen to this piece as a separate item.

Colin Tilney (recorded in 1978) uses a spinet (dating from the end of the seventeenth century) which seems particularly suitable for the *Harpsichord suites*. He is in excellent form and the effect is intimate without losing the music's scale. As a bonus, Simon Preston provides two organ pieces, the first piquantly registered on the instrument at Knole Chapel, Sevenoaks, and the more flamboyant *Double organ voluntary* using the organ at Lübeck Cathedral.

The admirable Christ Church two-disc collection of anthems, verse-anthems and excerpts from service settings was recorded in the London Henry Wood Hall in 1980 and lies at the very kernel of the DG-Archiv Purcell Collection. With some of the music not otherwise available, it is self-recommending. Apart from David Thomas's fine contribution (in the verse-anthems) the soloists come from the choir – and very good they are too, especially the trebles. The performances are full of character, vigorous yet with the widest range of colour and feeling, well projected in a recording which simulates a cathedral ambience yet is naturally focused and well detailed – analogue sound at its best.

A splendid all-male performance of Purcell's joyous *Ode on St Cecilia's Day* (1692) comes from Mackerras with an exceptionally incisive and vigorous choral contribution, matched by fine solo singing. Simon Woolf is ideally cast here, and the 1969 recording is excellent, although the balance between soloists and tutti does not make enough distinction in volume between the smaller and larger groups. This is supplemented by a recording of a suite for strings from *The Married Beau*, played pleasingly enough on modern instruments under Baumgartner, but in no way distinctive. The recording dates from ten years earlier but is fully acceptable.

Mackerras returns to direct a 1967 Hamburg recording of *Dido and Aeneas*. Besides being a scholarly account, it is very vital, with tempi varied more widely and more authentically than usual. There is also the question of ornamentation, and on the whole Mackerras manages more skilfully than most of his rivals. He adds a few brief extra items from suitable Purcellian sources to fill in the unset passages of the printed libretto. As to the singing, Tatiana Troyanos makes an imposing, gorgeous-toned Dido, and Sheila Armstrong as Belinda, Barry McDaniel as Aeneas and Patricia Johnson all outshine most rival versions. Generally a fine performance, and Troyanos's account of the famous lament is undoubtedly moving. The 1967 recording is excellent.

Finally comes a collection of music by Purcell's contemporaries and successors, in refined if not always vibrant performances, with the three works of John Blow among the most impressive pieces, alongside the two Purcell contributions. Blow's extended anthem, *God spake sometimes in visions*, opens the proceedings, and here one feels the music-making needs more vigour and thrust, although the choir rises to the closing '*Alleluias*'. Henry Lawes' *Zadok the Priest* is a brief (1 minute 16 seconds) but strong setting, not as memorable as Handel's famous coronation anthem, but here projecting impresssively. William Turner's elaborate symphony-anthem in praise of the king opens and closes with trumpets, but it is essentially an intimate work, with plenty of fine opportunities for the choir's soloists, both individually and grouped. This piece is a real discovery and shows Turner as a composer of distinct personality. Fine, atmospheric, digital recording throughout.

Gardiner Purcell Collection

'*Gardiner Purcell Collection*'.
(Y/B) (M) *** Erato/Warner 4509 99773-2 (8) [id.]. Soloists, Monteverdi Ch. & O, Equale Brass Ens., E. Bar. Soloists, Gardiner.

To commemorate the tercentenary of Purcell's death, the following reissued Erato recordings, all directed with distinction by John Eliot Gardiner, are also available together in a slip-case (at a slightly reduced price); they would make a splendid basis for any Purcell collection. Readers will note that the catalogue numbers have changed since we listed them in our most recent *Yearbook*.

Come, ye sons of art away; Funeral music for Queen Mary (1695).
(Y/B) (M) *** Erato/Warner 4509 99775-2 [id.]. Lott, Brett, Williams, Allen, Monteverdi Ch. & O, Equale Brass Ens., Gardiner.

Come, ye Sons of Art, the most celebrated of Purcell's birthday odes for Queen Mary, is splendidly coupled here with the unforgettable funeral music he wrote on the death of the same monarch. With the Monteverdi Choir at its most incisive and understanding the performances are exemplary, and the recording, though balanced in favour of the instruments, is clear and refined. Among the soloists Thomas Allen is outstanding, while the two counter-tenors give a charming performance of the duet, *Sound the trumpet*. The *Funeral music* includes the well-known *Solemn march* for trumpets and drums, a *Canzona* and simple anthem given at the funeral, and two of Purcell's most magnificent anthems setting the *Funeral sentences*. Recording made in 1976 in Rosslyn Hill Chapel, London.

Ode on St Cecilia's day (Hail! bright Cecilia).
(Y/B) (M) *** Erato/Warner Dig. 4509 99776-2 [id.]. Jennifer Smith, Stafford, Gordon, Elliott, Varcoe, David Thomas, Monteverdi Ch., E. Bar. Soloists, Gardiner.

Gardiner's characteristic vigour and alertness in Purcell come out superbly in this delightful record of the 1692 *St Cecilia Ode* – not as well known as some of the other odes he wrote, but a masterpiece. Soloists and chorus are outstanding even by Gardiner's high standards, and the recording excellent. Recording made in 1982 in the Barbican Concert Hall, London.

Dioclesian; Timon of Athens.
(Y/B) (M) *** Erato/Warner Dig. 4509 99777-2 (2) [id.]. Dawson, Fisher, Covey-Crump, Elliott, George, Varcoe, Monteverdi Ch., E. Bar. Soloists, Gardiner.

The martial music, shining with trumpets, is what stands out in *Dioclesian*, adapted from a Jacobean play first given in 1622. Gardiner is such a lively conductor, regularly drawing out the effervescence in Purcell's inspiration, that the result is delightfully refreshing, helped by an outstanding team of soloists. The incidental music for *Timon of Athens* offers more buried treasure, including such enchanting inventions as *Hark! how the songsters of the grove*, with its 'Symphony of pipes imitating the chirping of birds', and a fine *Masque for Cupid and Bacchus*, beautifully sung by Lynne Dawson, Gillian Fisher and Stephen Varcoe. Excellent Erato sound. Recordings made in Rosslyn Hill Chapel, London, in 1987.

The Indian Queen (incidental music; complete).
(Y/B) (M) *** Erato/Warner 4509 99778-2 [id.]. Hardy, Fisher, Harris, Smith, Stafford, Hill, Elwes, Varcoe, Thomas, Monteverdi Ch., E. Bar. Soloists, Gardiner.

The reissued Erato version is fully cast and uses an authentic accompanying baroque instrumental group. The choral singing is especially fine, with the close of the work movingly expressive. John Eliot Gardiner's choice of tempi is apt and the soloists are all good, although the men are more strongly characterful than the ladies; nevertheless the lyrical music comes off well. The recording is spacious and well balanced. Recording made in 1979 in Henry Wood Hall, London.

King Arthur (complete).
(Y/B) (M) *** Erato/Warner Dig. 4509 99774-2 (2) [id.]. Jennifer Smith, Gillian Fischer, Priday, Ross, Stafford, Elliot, Varcoe, Monteverdi Ch., E. Bar. Soloists, Gardiner.

Gardiner's solutions to the textual problems carry complete conviction, as for example his placing of the superb *Chaconne in F* at the end instead of the start. Solo singing for the most part is excellent, with Stephen Varcoe outstanding among the men. *Fairest isle* is treated very gently, with Gill Ross, boyish of tone, reserved just for that number. Throughout, the chorus is characteristically fresh and vigorous, and the instrumentalists beautifully marry authentic technique to pure, unabrasive sounds. Digital recording, made in 1983 in St Giles, Cripplegate, London.

The Tempest (incidental music).
(Y/B) (M) *** Erato/Warner 4509 99779-2 [id.]. Jennifer Smith, Hardy, Hall, Elwes, Varcoe, David Thomas, Earle, Monteverdi Ch. & O, Gardiner.

Whether or not Purcell himself wrote this music for Shakespeare's last play (the scholarly arguments are still unresolved), Gardiner demonstrates how delightful it is, a masterly collection, in performances both polished and stylish and with excellent solo and choral singing. At least the overture is clearly Purcell's, and that sets a pattern for a very varied collection of numbers, including three *da capo* arias and a full-length masque celebrating Neptune for Act V. The 1979 recording, made in London's Henry Wood Hall, is full and atmospheric; the words are beautifully clear, and the transfer to CD is admirably natural.

INSTRUMENTAL MUSIC

3 Fantasias for 5 viols; 9 Fantasias for 4 viols; Fantasia on one note for 5 viols; In nomine for 6 viols; In nomine for 7 viols.
(Y/B) (M) *** Virgin Veritas/EMI Dig. VC5 45062-2 [id.]. Fretwork.

Purcell wrote these *Fantasias* in 1680 at the time of his twenty-first birthday, consciously adopting what was then considered an archaic style, but displaying not only an astonishing contrapuntal skill but also a harmonic and structural adventurousness which leaps the centuries, sounding to us amazingly modern still in its daring chromaticisms. The players of Fretwork use viols with a concern for matching, tuning and balance which is quite exceptional, and their natural expressiveness matches the deeper implications of these masterpieces in microcosm. This makes a superb modern successor to the earlier recordings by Wenzinger and his Schola Cantorum Basiliensis and by Harnoncourt, both included in DG's Archiv Purcell Collection, above.

Pavans 1–4; Beati omnes qui timent Dominum; In guilty night (Saul and the Witch of Endor); Jehova, quam multi sunt hostes mei; My beloved spake; Te Deum & Jubilate (for St Cecilia's Day, 1694); Te Deum; When on my sick bed I languish.
(Y/B) *** Virgin/EMI Dig. VC5 45061-2 [id.]. Taverner Ch., Consort & Players, Andrew Parrott.

Starting with an exceptionally brisk and compelling account of the *Te Deum and Jubilate*, Parrott and his team provide a refreshing and illuminating survey of Purcell's vocal music, punctuated by four of the adventurous, intense *Pavans* which Purcell wrote in his youth, at about the same time as the great sequence of string *Fantasias*. In the relatively brief span of 70 minutes Parrott ranges wide, with the elaborately contrapuntal Latin anthem, *Jehova, quam multi sunt*, one of Purcell's finest, made the more moving, if less grand, with one voice per part, and with the scena about the Witch of Endor, *In guilty night*, thrillingly dramatic. Well-matched singing and playing, atmospherically recorded.

Sonatas of 3 Parts Nos. 1–12, Z.790/801; Sonatas of 4 Parts Nos. 1–10, Z.802/810; Chacony in G min., Z.730; Pavans, Z.438/52; Three parts upon a ground in D, Z.731.
(Y/B) *** Chandos Dig. CHAN 0572/3 [id.]. Purcell Qt.

Sonatas of 3 parts Nos. 1–7, Z.790–6; Pavans: in A min.; B flat; G min., Z.749, Z.750, Z.752.
*** Chandos Dig. CHAN 8591 [id.]. Purcell Quartet.

Sonatas of 3 Parts Nos. 8–12, Z.797–801; Sonatas in 4 Parts Nos. 1–2, Z.802–3; Chacony in G min., Z.751; Fantasia on a Ground in D & F; Pavans in A, Z.748; G min., Z.751.
*** Chandos Dig. CHAN 8663 [id.]. Purcell Quartet.

Sonatas of 4 Parts Nos. 3–10, Z.804–811; Prelude for solo violin in G min., Z.773; Organ voluntaries Nos. 2 in D min.; 4 in G, Z.718 & 710.
*** Chandos Dig. CHAN 8763 [id.]. Purcell Quartet.

Sonatas of 4 Parts Nos. 1–10, Z.802–11.
*** O-L 433 190-2 [id.]. Mackintosh, Huggett, Coin, Hogwood (chamber organ or spinet).

In these *Sonatas* Purcell turned to the new, concerted style which had been developed in Italy. Interspersed among the *Sonatas* are three earlier and highly chromatic *Pavans*, composed before Purcell embraced the sonata discipline. If anything, the second volume is more attractive than the first, for it includes the indelible *Chacony in G minor*. The third leaves room for a solo violin *Prelude* and two organ *Voluntaries*, both admirably presented and, like the *Sonatas*, offering very realistic sound. The Purcell Quartet give a first-class account of themselves: their playing is authoritative and idiomatic, and the artists are firmly focused in a warm but not excessively reverberant acoustic. Strongly recommended. These authoritative and thoroughly enjoyable accounts of Purcell's *Sonatas* have now been gathered together on two CDs without the miscellaneous items which filled out a third. Whichever format is chosen, this set can be thoroughly recommended.

The Oiseau-Lyre recording has the advantage of including all the four-part works on a single CD, and the playing is authoritative in style and feeling and the recording exemplary.

Sonatas in 3 parts: Nos. 1 in G min.; 2 in B flat; 3 in D min. Sonatas in 4 parts: Nos. 2 in E flat; 3 in A min.; 5 in G min.; 6 in G min.: Chacony; 9 in F (Golden).
(N) (B) *(*) Discover Dig. DICD 920251 [id.]. Slovak Radio Qt.

The Slovak Radio Quartet is an excellent ensemble using modern instruments, and this is a well-chosen programme of marvellous music. The recording is close but truthful; the snag is the almost total absence of dynamic contrast in the playing.

KEYBOARD MUSIC

Harpsichord suites Nos. 1–8, Z.660/663; 666–9; Ground in G min., Z.221; A new Ground in E min., Z.682; Hornpipe, Z.685.
(Y/B) **(*) HM Dig. HMC 901496 [id.]. Kenneth Gilbert (harpsichord).

Not surprisingly, Kenneth Gilbert gives authoritative, stylish and completely spontaneous accounts of these fine suites. He plays a Couchet-Taskin of 1671. The snag is the reverberant recording, which spreads the harpsichord sound so that it tends to become aurally tiring after a while.

'The Purcell Manuscript': *Suites: in A min. & C; Prelude; 3 Minuets; 3 Airs; Thus happy and free; Trumpet minuet; Minuet; 3 Hornpipes.*
(Y/B) *** Virgin/EMI Dig. VC5 45166-2 [id.]. Davitt Moroney (virginals or harpsichord) (with Giovanni DRAGHI: *Suites: in A; C min.; G; G min.;* GIBBONS: *Prelude in G* ***).

This charming disc presents the complete contents of a keyboard lesson-book, discovered in London towards the end of 1993, one of only 15 or 16 Purcell manuscripts to have survived. In his own hand he copied out pieces evidently for a pupil to play. Of the 20 Purcell pieces here, mostly miscellaneous but including *Suites in A minor* and *C major*, five were previously unknown, and six more are arrangements of theatre-pieces unique to this book. Tiny as they are, between them they significantly amplify the picture we have of Purcell's keyboard music. The manuscript also includes a favourite keyboard piece of Orlando Gibbons, the *Prelude in G*, and four suites by Purcell's contemporary, Giovanni Batista Draghi (*c.* 1640–1708), a rival teacher who may well have taken over the pupil's lessons after Purcell's early death. Crisp and bright, Davitt Moroney uses a virginals for the Purcell and two different harpsichords for the more elaborate Draghi pieces.

VOCAL MUSIC

Anthems & Services, Vol. 1: *It is a good thing to give thanks; Let mine eyes run down with tears; My beloved spake; O give thanks unto the Lord; O praise God in his holiness; O sing unto the Lord; Praise the Lord, O Jerusalem.*
*** Hyperion Dig. CDA 66585 [id.]. Witcomb, Finnis, Hallchurch, Bowman, Daniels, George, Evans, King's Cons., Robert King.

Anthems & Services, Vol. 2: *Behold now praise the Lord; Blessed are they that fear the Lord; I will give thanks unto Thee, O Lord; My song shall be alway; Te Deum and Jubilate.*
*** Hyperion Dig. CDA 66609 [id.]. Bowman, Covey-Crump, George, New College, Oxford, Ch., King's Cons., Robert King.

Anthems & Services, Vol. 3: *Begin the song, and strike the living lyre; Blessed Virgin's expostulation: Tell me, some pitying angel. Blow up the trumpet in Zion; Hear my prayer, O Lord; Hosanna to the highest; Lord, I can suffer thy rebukes; The Lord is King, be the people never so impatient; O God, Thou has cast us out; O Lord, our governor; Remember not Lord our offences; Thy word is a lantern unto my feet.*
*** Hyperion Dig. CDA 66623 [id.]. Dawson, Bowman, Daniels, George, Evans, King's Cons. Ch., King's Cons., Robert King.

Anthems & Services, Vol. 4: *Awake ye dead; Behold I bring you glad tidings; Early, O Lord, my fainting soul; The earth trembled; Lord, not to us but to thy name; Lord, what is man?; My heart is inditing of a good matter; O all ye people, clap your hands; Since God so tender a regard; Sing unto God; Sleep, Adam and take thy rest; The way of God is an undefiled way.*
*** Hyperion Dig. CDA 66644 [id.]. Witcomb, Finnis, Hallchurch, Kennedy, O'Dwyer, Gritton, Bowman, Covey-Crump, Daniels, George, Varcoe, R. Evans, New College, Oxford, Ch., King's Cons., Robert King.

Anthems & services, Vol. 5: *Awake, and with attention hear; How long, great God; Let the night perish (Job's Curse); O God, the king of glory; O God, Thou art my God; O, I'm sick of life; O Lord, rebuke me not; Praise the Lord, O my soul, and all that is within me; Rejoice in the Lord alway; We sing to him, whose wisdom form'd the ear; When on my sick bed I languish; With sick and famish'd eyes.*
*** Hyperion Dig. CDA 66656 [id.]. Witcomb, Finnis, Hallchurch, Kennedy, Gritton, Bowman, Covey-Crump, Daniels, George, Evans, King's Cons. Ch., King's Cons., Robert King.

Anthems & Services, Vol. 6: *Great God and just; Hear me, O Lord, the great support; I will love Thee, O Lord; Lord, who can tell how oft he offendeth?; My heart is fixed, O God; O Lord, grant the King a long life; O praise the Lord, all ye heathen; Plung'd in the confines of despair; Thou wakeful shepherd that dost Israel keep; Who hath believed our report?; Why do the heathen so furiously rage together?*
*** Hyperion Dig. CDA 66663 [id.]. Witcomb, Kennedy, O'Dwyer, Bowman, Covey-Crump, Daniels, Agnew, George, New College, Oxford, Ch., King's Cons., Robert King.

Anthems & Services, Vol. 7: *Beati omnes qui timent; In the black dismal dungeon of despair; I was glad* (2 settings: coronation anthem & verse anthem); *Jubilate in B flat; O consider my adversity; Music for the funeral of Queen Mary; Save me O God; Te Deum in B flat; Thy way O God is holy.*
❀ *** Hyperion Dig. CDA 66677 [id.]. Kennedy, O'Dwyer, Goodman, Gritton, Bowman, Short, Covey-Crump, Daniels, Milhofer, George, R. Evans, King's Cons. Ch., King's Cons., Robert King.

Anthems & Services, Vol. 8: *Be merciful unto me; Benedicte in B flat; Blessed is the man that feareth the Lord; Bow down thine ear, O Lord; Full of wrath, his threatening breath; In Thee, O Lord, do I put my trust; Jehova, quam multi sunt hostes mei; Magnificat and Nunc Dimittis in G min.; They that go down to the sea in ships.*

*** Hyperion Dig. CDA 66686 [id.]. O'Dwyer, Kennedy, Bowman, Covey-Crump, Daniels, Padmore, Milhofer, George, King's Cons. Ch., King's Cons., Robert King.

Robert King follows up the success of his collection of Purcell's Odes and Welcome songs (see below) with an equally illuminating collection of the church music. The different categories of work, Services, Verse Anthems, Motets (or Full Anthems) and devotional songs, cover the widest range of style and expression, with King's own helpful and scholarly notes setting each one in context. Generally the most adventurous in style are the Full Anthems, with elaborate counterpoint often bringing amazingly advanced harmonic progressions. Yet the Verse Anthems too include some which similarly demonstrate Purcell's extraordinary imagination in contrapuntal writing. So though Volume 6 is confined to Verse Anthems and devotional songs, they too offer passages of chromatic writing which defy the idea of these categories as plain and straightforward. As the title suggests, the devotional song, *Plung'd in the confines of despair*, is a particularly fine example. Although all the earlier volumes are full of good things, Volume 7 (to which we award a token Rosette for the extraordinary achievement of this series) is the one to recommend first to anyone simply wanting to sample Purcell's church music. Not only does it contain the *Music for the Funeral of Queen Mary* in 1695, with drum processionals, the solemn *March* and *Canzona for brass* and *Funeral sentences*, it has the *B flat Morning service*, two settings of the Coronation anthem, *I was glad*, (one of them previously unrecorded), a magnificent Full Anthem, three Verse Anthems and two splendid devotional songs. Robert King's meticulous notes include a detailed account of Queen Mary's funeral, providing evidence for his view that the *March* was not played with drums accompanying, but on its own. Volume 8, too, is full of fine music. The opening Verse Anthem, *In Thee, O Lord, do I put my trust*, opens with a very striking, slightly melancholy *Sinfonia*, with a six-note figure rising up from a ground bass, which sets the expressive mood. The closing anthem, so appropriate from an island composer, *They that go down to the sea in ships*, is characteristically diverse, with Purcell helping the Lord 'maketh the storm to cease' and at the end providing a joyful chorus of praise. It is astonishing how many of the pieces have never appeared on record before, and that includes some of the finest. King's notes and documentation closely identify each item, adding to one's illumination. An outstanding series, full of treasures, with King varying the scale of forces he uses for each item. Often he uses one voice per part, but he regularly expands the ensemble with the King's Consort Choir or turns to the full New College Choir, which includes trebles.

Anthems & Verse anthems: (i) *Behold, I bring you glad tidings; In Thee, O Lord do I put my trust;* (ii) *Jehova, quam multi sunt hostes mei; Lord, how long wilt thou be angry; My beloved spake;* (ii) *O sing unto the Lord a new song; They that go down to the sea in ships; Who hath believed our report.*
(Y/B) (M) *** Decca 444 525-2 [id.]. Soloists, St John's College, Cambridge, Ch., George Guest; (i) with John Scott (organ) (ii) ASMF.

This selection of eight superb ceremonial pieces, intended for Charles II's Chapel Royal, comes from two Argo LPs, recorded a decade apart but with the sound remarkably consistent. On the first occasion the late Inia te Wiata was outstanding, showing his sense of style in *They that go down to the sea in ships*, especially when he combines in duet with Charles Brett; on the second (of which only two out of five anthems are included) it was Paul Esswood and Ian Partridge who stood out.

Anthems: *O sing unto the Lord; Praise the Lord, O Jerusalem; They that go down to the sea in ships.* Ode: *My heart is inditing; Te Deum and Jubilate Deo in D.*
(M) *** DG 427 124-2. Ch. of Christ Church Cathedral, Oxford, E. Concert, Preston.

The performances in this mid-priced collection are full of character, vigorous yet with the widest range of colour and feeling. The recording, made in London's Henry Wood Hall, is both spacious and well detailed.

Ayres, Theatre music and Sacred songs: *Awake awake, ye dead (Hymn for the Day of Judgement); Birthday ode for Queen Mary: Strike the viol. Dioclesian: O how happy's he; Chaconne. The earth trembled (A hymn on our Saviour's Passion). The Fairy Queen: One charming night. How plaisant is this flow'ry plain and grove (ode). The Indian Queen: Ye twice ten hundred deities; Wake Quivera. Ode for St Cecilia: Raise, raise the voice; Oedipus: Hear, ye sullen pow'rs below; Come away, do not stay. The Old Bachelor: Thus to a ripe consenting maid. Olinda: There ne'er was so wretched a lover as I* (duet). *Timon of Athens: Hark how the songsters. Pavane and Trio.*
(B) **(*) HM HMA 190214 [id.]. Deller Cons. & Ens., Deller.

Deller has put together what one might regard as a sampler of Purcell's vocal music, a varied collection which includes some of his finest inspirations. Always fresh and often lovely performances, given good if not outstanding recording.

Benedicte: O all ye works of the Lord. Coronation music for King James II: I was glad. Funeral music for Queen Mary: Man that is born of woman; In the midst of life; Thou knowest, Lord, the secrets of our hearts. Anthems: Blow up the trumpet in Sion; Hear my prayer, O Lord; I will sing unto the Lord; Jubilate; Lord, how long wilt Thou be angry; O God, Thou art my God; O God, Thou hast cast us out; O Lord God of Hosts; Remember not, Lord, our offences; Save me, O God.

*** Conifer Dig. 74321 16849-2 [id.]. Trinity College Ch., Cambridge, Marlow; Matthews; G. Jackson (organ).

Richard Marlow gets good results from his singers; such expressive anthems as *Remember not, Lord, our offences* and *Hear my prayer, O Lord* are eloquently done and beautifully recorded. Excellent performances from all concerned – not least the Conifer recording team.

Alfred Deller Edition: (i) *Come ye sons of art (Ode on the birthday of Queen Mary, 1694);* Anthems: (ii) *My beloved spake;* (iii) *Rejoice in the Lord alway (Bell anthem);* (iv) *Welcome to all the pleasures (Ode on St Cecilia's Day, 1683).*

(Y/B) (M) **(*) Van. 08.5060 71 [id.]. Alfred Deller, Deller Consort; (i) Mark Deller, Mary Thomas, Bevan, Oriana Concert Ch. & O; (ii) Cantelo, English, Bevan; (iii; iv) Kalmar O; (iii) Thomas, Sheppard, Tear, Worthley; Oriana Concert O; (iv) Cantelo, McLoughlin, English, Grundy, Bevan.

An enjoyable anthology, now reissued as part of the Alfred Deller Edition, showing Deller at his finest. The other soloists are good too, especially the tenor, Gerald English. The two anthems make a fine centrepiece, responding to the demand of Charles II for composers 'not to be too solemn' and to 'add symphonies, etc., with instruments' to their sacred vocal music. The *Bell anthem* is so called because of the repeated descending scales in the introduction. The warm, expressively played accompaniments are rather different from the effect one would achieve today with original instruments. The recording is closely balanced; although made at either Walthamstow or Cricklewood Church, the effect is not quite as spacious as one would expect, though pleasingly full.

Come, ye sons of art away; Ode on St Cecilia's day: Welcome to all pleasures. Funeral music for Queen Mary; Funeral sentences.

(Y/B) (M) **(*) Virgin/EMI Veritas Dig. VC5 45159-2 [id.]. Taverner Consort, Ch. & Players, Parrott.

Come, ye sons of art away; Ode on St Cecilia's Day: Welcome to all the pleasures. Of old when heroes thought it base (Yorkshire Feast song).

*** DG Dig. 427 663-2 [id.]. J. Smith, Priday, Amps, Chance, Wilson, Ainsley, George, Richardson, E. Concert Ch., E. Concert, Pinnock.

Pinnock directs exuberant performances. The weight and brightness of the choral sound go with infectiously lifted rhythms, making the music dance. The soloists are all outstanding, with the counter-tenor duetting of Michael Chance and Timothy Wilson in *Sound the trumpet* delectably pointed. The coupling, the neglected *Yorkshire Feast song*, is full of wonderful inspirations, like the tenor and counter-tenor duet, *And now when the renown'd Nassau* – a reference to the new king, William III.

Though Parrott cannot quite match his rival, Trevor Pinnock, in the *St Cecilia* and *Queen Mary* odes, with speeds generally slower and rhythms rather less alert, his are still very fine performances, sounding more intimate as recorded. Parrott takes the view that Purcell would have used a high tenor and not a second counter-tenor in *Sound the trumpet*, and it works well, with John Mark Ainsley joining the counter-tenor, Timothy Wilson. The coupling is not generous but is apt and well contrasted. In his pursuit of authenticity Parrott has eliminated the timpani part from the well-known solemn march for slide trumpets (performed here on sackbutts) in the *Queen Mary Funeral music* – a pity when it becomes far less effective. The central anthem is beautifully done, and it is good also to have the three *Funeral sentence anthems*, written a few years earlier.

Funeral music for Queen Mary: March, Anthem and Canzona; 3 Funeral sentences; 2 Elegies; 2 Coronation anthems; Anthem for Queen Mary's birthday, 1688: Now does the glorious day appear.

(Y/B) *** Sony Dig. SK 66243 [id.]. Kirkby, Tubb, Chance, Bostridge, Richardson, Birchall, Westminster Abbey Ch., New London Consort, Martin Neary (with music by TOLLETT; PAISIBLE; MORLEY; BLOW).

Funeral music for Queen Mary: March, Anthem and Canzona; 3 Funeral sentences; 2 Elegies; Anthem for Queen Mary's birthday, 1692: Love's goddess sure was blind.

(Y/B) *** Collins Dig. 1425-2 [id.]. The Sixteen, Harry Christophers (with MORLEY: *Funeral sentences;* TOLLETT; PAISIBLE: *Marches*).

Funeral music for Queen Mary: March & canzona in C min.; Funeral sentences; Anthems: Give sentence with me, O Lord; Hear my prayer, O Lord; Jehova, quam multi sunt hostes mei; My beloved spake; O God, Thou art my God; O, I'm sick of life; Rejoice in the Lord alway (Bell anthem); Remember not, Lord, our offences; Organ voluntaries: in C; in G.
**(*) Argo Dig. 436 833-2 [id.]. Winchester Cathedral Ch., David Dunnett (organ), L. Bar. Brass, Brandenburg Cons., Hill.

With the help of the scholar, Bruce Wood, Harry Christophers was here the first on disc to restore the original sequence of musical numbers given at the funeral of Queen Mary in 1695. The well-known *March* and *Canzona*, as well as the beautiful anthem, *Thou know'st, Lord, the secrets of our hearts*, are presented along with the settings of the remaining funeral sentences by Thomas Morley, equally inspired, as well as marches by James Paisible and Thomas Tollett. Authentic military drums are used on their own, so that the marches are less atmospheric than usual, but, with superb, crisply precise singing from the Sixteen in the choral numbers, the whole programme is electric in its intensity. Not least of the delights is the performance of the 1692 Birthday ode, *Love's goddess sure was blind*, given in Bruce Wood's authentically revised text with tenor replacing soprano, as well as two magnificent elegiac anthems to Latin words. Excellent sound, both atmospheric and clear.

In the ample acoustic of Westminster Abbey, where the music was first performed in 1695, Martin Neary, Purcell's latterday successor as master of music there, gives the same sequence of funeral music as Harry Christophers on his excellent Collins disc, plus an even more generous collection of other works inspired by Queen Mary. The result is less polished, less clear, with the sound of traffic murmuring in from outside, but undeniably more atmospheric, conveying a weightier devotional intensity. One has a genuine sense of a great ceremonial, not just in the funeral music but in the other works too, including the glorious 1688 Birthday ode, *Now does the glorious day appear*, the first that Purcell composed for the new Queen. Preference between this and the Collins disc might be left to a choice between fresh soprano voices, as used in The Sixteen's disc, and the boy trebles of the Abbey Choir, more authentic and beautifully tuned but not quite so precise. The soloists are outstanding, notably the counter-tenor, Michael Chance, and the tenor, Ian Bostridge.

David Hill and the Winchester Choir plus instrumentalists provide an interesting alternative to Robert King (see below) in the *Queen Mary funeral music*, opting – like most previous interpreters, but unlike King – to have the drum recessionals simultaneously with the *March*. Though the boy-trebles are attractively fresh-toned, the Winchester ensemble is markedly less polished than King's. The choice of other items includes a number of Purcell's most celebrated anthems, as well as the *Organ Voluntary in C*. Good, atmospheric sound.

In guilty night (Saul and the Witch of Endor); Man that is born of woman (Funeral sentences); Te Deum and Jubilate Deo in D.
(B) **(*) HM HMA 190207 [id.]. Deller Cons., Stour Music Festival Ch. & O, Deller.

In guilty night is a remarkable dramatic scene depicting Saul's meeting with the Witch of Endor. The florid writing is admirably and often excitingly sung by Alfred Deller himself as the King and Honor Sheppard as the Witch. The *Te Deum and Jubilate* are among Purcell's last and most ambitious choral works; the *Funeral sentences* from early in his career are in some ways even finer in their polyphonic richness. The chorus here is not the most refined on record but, with sensitive direction, this attractive collection is well worth hearing. The recording is good.

Odes and Welcome songs Vols. 1–8 (complete).
*** Hyperion Dig. CDS 44031/8 [id.]. Soloists, New College, Oxford, Ch., King's Cons., Robert King.

Odes & Welcome songs, Vol. 1: *Arise my muse (1690); Now does the glorious day appear (1689) (Odes for Queen Mary's birthday); Ode for St Cecilia's Day: Welcome to all pleasures (1683).*
*** Hyperion Dig. CDA 66314 [id.]. Fisher, Bonner, Bowman, Chance, Daniels, Ainsley, George, Potts, King's Cons., Robert King.

Odes & Welcome songs, Vol. 2: *Ode on St Cecilia's Day (Hail! bright Cecilia!) (1692). Ode for the birthday of the Duke of Gloucester: Who can from joy refrain (1695).*
*** Hyperion Dig. CDA 66349 [id.]. Fisher, Bonner, Bowman, Covey-Crump, Ainsley, George, Keenlyside, New College, Oxford, Ch., King's Cons., King.

Odes & Welcome songs, Vol. 3: *Ode for Queen Mary's birthday: Celebrate this festival (1693). Welcome song for Charles II (1683): Fly, bold rebellion (1683). Welcome song for James II: Sound the trumpet, beat the drum (1687).*
*** Hyperion Dig. CDA 66412 [id.]. Fisher, Bonner, Bowman, Kenny, Covey-Crump, Müller, George, Pott, King's Cons., King.

Odes & Welcome songs, Vol. 4: *Ode for Mr Maidwell's School: Celestial music did the gods inspire* (1689). *Ode for the wedding of Prince George of Denmark and Princess Anne: From hardy climes and dangerous toils of war* (1683). *Welcome song for James II: Ye tuneful muses* (1686).
*** Hyperion Dig. CDA 66456 [id.]. Fisher, Bonner, Bowman, Kenny, Covey-Crump, Daniels, George, Pott, King's Cons., Robert King.

Odes & welcome songs, Vol. 5: *Ode for the birthday of Queen Mary: Welcome, welcome, glorious morn* (1691). *Ode for the Centenary of Trinity College, Dublin: Great parent, hail to thee* (1694). *Welcome song for King Charles II: The Summer's absence unconcerned we bear* (1682).
*** Hyperion CDA 66476 [id.]. Fisher, Tubb, Bowman, Short, Covey-Crump, Ainsley, George, Pott, King's Cons., Robert King.

Odes & Welcome songs, Vol. 6: *Ode for Queen Mary's birthday: Love's goddess sure was blind* (1692). *Ode for St Cecilia's Day: Laudate Ceciliam* (1683). *Ode for St Cecilia's Day: Raise, raise the voice* (*c.* 1685). *Welcome song for Charles II: From those serene and rapturous joys* (1684).
*** Hyperion Dig. CDA 66494 [id.]. Fisher, Seers, Bowman, Short, Padmore, Tusa, George, Evans, King's Cons., King.

Odes & Welcome songs, Vol. 7: *Welcome song for Charles II: Swifter Isis, swifter flow* (1681). *Welcome song for the Duke of York: What shall be done in behalf of the man?* (1682). *Yorkshire feast song: Of old, when heroes thought it base* (1690).
*** Hyperion Dig. CDA 66587 [id.]. Fisher, Hamilton,, Bowman, Short, Covey-Crump, Daniels, George, Evans, King's Cons., King.

Odes & welcome songs, Vol. 8: *Ode for the birthday of Queen Mary: Come ye sons of Art, away* (1694). *Welcome song for Charles II: Welcome, viceregent of the mighty king* (1680). *Welcome song for King James: Why, why are all the Muses mute?*
*** Hyperion Dig. CDA 66598 [id.]. Fisher, Bonner, Bowman, Chance, Padmore, Ainsley, George, Evans, Ch. of New College, Oxford, King's Cons., King.

Just what a wealth of inspiration Purcell brought to the occasional music he wrote for his royal and noble masters comes out again and again in Robert King's splendid collection of the Odes and Welcome songs. It is sad that for three centuries this fine music has been largely buried, with just a few of the Odes achieving popularity. In those, King's performances do not always outshine the finest of previous versions, but with an outstanding team of soloists as well as his King's Consort the performances achieve a consistently high standard, with nothing falling seriously short. Being able to hear previously unrecorded rarities alongside the well-known works sets Purcell's achievement vividly in context, helped by informative notes in each volume, written by King himself. Volume 1 includes the shorter of the two *St Cecilia odes* and immediately – among the fine team of soloists – it is a delight to hear such superb artists as the counter-tenors James Bowman and Michael Chance in duet. Volume 3 with the 1693 *Birthday ode* and Volume 7 with the fascinating *Yorkshire feast song* are two more CDs that would make good samplers. Those who want to dive in at the deep end should invest in the complete set, where all eight CDs are offered in a slip-case. First-rate sound throughout.

Ode on St Cecilia's Day (Hail! bright Cecilia).
(Y/B) (M) *** Virgin/EMI Dig. VC5 45160-2 [id.]. Kirkby, Chance, Kevin Smith, Covey-Crump, Elliott, Grant, George, Thomas, Taverner Ch. & Players, Parrott.

Though Parrott's Virgin/EMI version lacks the exuberance of Gardiner's outstanding Erato issue (see above), in a more reticent way it brings a performance full of incidental delights, particularly vocal ones from a brilliant array of no fewer than twelve solo singers, notably five excellent tenors. With pitch lower than usual, some numbers that normally require counter-tenors can be sung by tenors. Interestingly, Parrott includes the *Voluntary in D minor* for organ before the wonderful aria celebrating that instrument and St Cecilia's sponsorship of it, *O wondrous machine*. It holds up the flow, but at least on CD it can readily be omitted.

(i) *Odes for Queen Mary's birthday: Come ye sons of art; Love's Goddess sure.* (ii) *Funeral music for Queen Mary (March; Canzone;* Funeral sentences: *Man that is born of woman; In the midst of life; Thou knowest, Lord; March;* Anthems: *Hear my prayer, O Lord; Remember not, Lord, our offences).* Anthems: *Blessed are they that fear the Lord; My beloved spake; Rejoice in the Lord alway.* (iii) (Organ) *The Queen's doleur; Trumpet minuet in C* (including *March* from *The Married Beau); Trumpet tunes in C & D; Voluntary in A.*
(B) *** EMI CZS7 67524-2 (2) [id.]. (i) Burrowes, Bowman, Lloyd, Brett; Ch.; York Skinner, Hill, Shaw, Lloyd; L. Early Music Cons., Munrow; (ii) Cockerhan, King, Hayes, Chilcott, Morell, Castle,

Byram-Wigfield, Robarts, Grier, King's College Ch., ASMF, Philip Jones Brass Ens., Ledger; (iii) Jean-Patrice Brosse (organ of Cathedral of Sainte Marie de Saint Bertrand de Comminges).

Purcell wrote a series of ceremonial odes for the birthdays of Queen Mary, and rarely has a courtier writing occasional pieces been so deeply and genuinely inspired. *Come ye sons of art* is the richest of the sequence, with its magnificent overture or symphony (no doubt intended to outdo those French at Versailles), and such memorable pieces as the duet, *Sound the trumpet. Love's goddess sure*, though not quite so grand, brings more Purcellian delights. The late David Munrow inspires fine playing and singing from his excellent forces and gives sensitive, intelligent performances of both works, which deliberately opt for an intimate scale, using old instruments and an authentic style of string playing; the results are entirely congenial to the ear. The intimacy clearly detracts from the sense of grandeur and panoply which are apt for this music but, with refined yet full sound to match, this alternative approach is equally satisfying. The coupling, made around the same time (1976/7), at King's is hardly less stimulating. As can be seen from the listing above, *Queen Mary's funeral music* consists of far more than the unforgettable *March* for lugubrious trombones (sackbuts) with punctuating timpani (later repeated without timpani), which still sounds so modern to our ears. Philip Ledger has the advantage of spacious sound (the original LP was issued in quadraphony) and his account of the *March* is darkly memorable. The anthems are well sung too, if slightly less alertly. The organ pieces, very well played, are particularly characterful heard on a comparatively pungent French organ. They are used as a postlude for the two birthday odes, while the voluntary (on disc 2) becomes an overture to introduce the three great verse anthems. The trumpet ayres are jolly, with a hurdy-gurdy effect in the Minuet framing a march from *The Married Beau*; the *Voluntary in C* is dark in timbre to match the dolorous piece specifically dedicated to the Queen.

Duets and solos for counter-tenor: *Bonduca: Sing, sing ye Druids. Come, ye sons of art: Sound the trumpet. Elegy on the death of Queen Mary: O dive custos Auriacae domus. The Maid's last prayer: No, resistance is but vain. Ode on St Cecilia's Day: In vain the am'rous flute. O solitude, my sweetest choice. The Queen's epicedium: Incassum, Lesbia rogas. Timon of Athens: Hark how the songsters.*
*** Hyperion Dig. CDA 66253 [id.]. James Bowman, Michael Chance, King's Cons., King – BLOW: *Ode* etc. ***

A sparkling collection of solos and duets which show both the composer and these fine artists in inspirational form. The performances are joyous, witty and ravishing in their Purcellian melancholy, with often subtle response to word meanings, and King's accompaniments have plenty of character in their own right. Excellent recording.

Songs: *Ah! How sweet it is to love; The earth trembled; An evening hymn; If music be the food of love; I'll sail upon the dog star; I see she flies me ev'rywhere; Let the night perish; Lord, what is man; Morning hymn; A new ground.* Arias: *Birthday ode for Queen Mary: Crown the altar. Bonduca: Oh! Lead me to some peaceful gloom. History of Dioclesian: Since from my dear Astrea's sight. The Indian Queen: I attempt from love's sickness to fly. The Mock marriage: Man that is for woman made. Oedipus: Music for a while. Pausanias: Sweeter than roses. The Rival sisters: Take not a woman's anger ill.*
(N) (BB) *** ASV CDQS 6172 [id.]. Ian Partridge, Jennifer Partridge – BRITTEN: *Winter words.* ***

Appropriately entitled 'Sweeter than Roses', this is a warmly sympathetic collection of favourite Purcell songs from a tenor whose honeyed tones are ideally suited to recording. The style smoother than we have come to expect latterly – this is a reissue of an earlier Enigma issue – but with ever-sensitive accompaniment from George Malcolm, who also contributes one brief solo, this is an excellent recommendation for those who resist the style of authenticity. Atmospheric recording, with the voice well forward. The CD transfer is very faithful, with the voice caught in its presence and natural bloom and the harpsichord image believable and nicely focused.

Songs and airs: *Bess of Bedlam; Evening hymn; If music be the food of love; Lovely, lovely Albina; Not all my torments; Olinda in the shades unseen; The Plaint; O, urge me no more; When first Amintas sued for a kiss.* Arias: *Birthday ode for Queen Mary: Crown the altar. The Fairy Queen: Hark! hark!; O, O let me weep; Ye gentle spirits of the air. The Indian Queen: I attempt from love's sickness to fly. Pausanias: Sweeter than roses. The Tempest: Dear pritty youths. Timon of Athens: The cares of lovers.*
*** O-L Dig. 417 123-2 [id.]. Emma Kirkby, Rooley, Hogwood.

The purity of Emma Kirkby's soprano suits this wide-ranging collection of Purcell songs splendidly, though you might argue for a bigger, warmer voice in the *Bess of Bedlam* song. The *Evening hymn* is radiantly done, and so are many of the less well-known airs which regularly bring new revelation. Excellent recording.

Songs: *Come, let us drink; A health to the nut brown lass; If ever I more riches; I gave her cakes and I gave her ale; Laudate Ceciliam; The miller's daughter; Of all the instruments; Once, twice, thrice I Julia tried; Prithee ben't so sad and serious; Since time so kind to us does prove; Sir Walter enjoying his damsel; 'Tis women makes us love; Under this stone; Young John the gard'ner.*
*** HM HMC 90242 [id.]. Deller Cons., Deller.

One section of this charming and stylish collection has a selection of Purcell's catches, some of them as lewd as rugby-club songs of today, others as refined as *Under this stone* – all of which the Deller Consort take in their stride. The final two pieces are extended items; *If ever I more riches*, a setting of Cowley, has some striking passages. The remastering for CD has greatly improved the sound, with voices fresh and first-rate recording of the instruments.

Songs: *Cupid, the slyest rogue alive; Dear pretty youth; From silent shades; The fatal hour comes on apace; If music be the food of love; Incassum Lesbia; Not all my torments; Now that the sun hath veil'd his light; O solitude* (2 versions); *Stripp'd of their green; Tell me, some pitying angel.* Theatre songs: *Dioclesian: Let us dance; Don Quixote: From rosy bow'rs. The Indian Queen: I attempt from love's sickness to fly. King Arthur: Fairest isle. The Massacre of Paris: Beneath a poplar's shadow. Pausanias: Sweeter than roses. Tyrannic Love: Ah! how sweet it is to love.*
*** Virgin/EMI Dig. VC7 59324-2 [id.]. Nancy Argenta, Nigel North, Richard Boothby, Paul Nicholson.

All but two of these songs were published in Henry Playford's celebratory Purcell collection, *Orpheus Britannicus*, and every one is inspired, offering a remarkable variety of mood and expression. Nancy Argenta's voice seems exactly suited to the repertoire, her tone consistently beautiful but never bland, her feeling for the words matched by her skill at not-too-elaborate ornamentation. The opening and closing soliloquy, *O solitude*, readily shows the beauty of her line, and the poignant melancholy of *Now that the sun hath veil'd his light* and the ravishing account of the familiar *Fairest isle* help to make this a distinctive recital. The infinite variety of the remarkable *From rosy bow'rs* shows her at her most imaginative, and she is fully equal to the range of the extended *Tell me, some pitying angel.* The accompaniments are most beautifully managed, judiciously using archlute, viola da gamba and harpsichord and, in *Now that the sun hath veil'd his light*, a chamber organ. The recording is most natural and realistic.

Songs: *The fatal hour comes on apace; Lord, what is man?; Love's power in my heart; More love or more disdain I crave; Now that the sun hath veiled his light; The Queen's epicedium; Sleep, Adam, sleep; Thou wakeful shepherd; Who can behold Florella's charms.* Arias: *History of Dioclesian: Since from my dear Astrea's sight. Indian Queen: I attempt from love's sickness to fly. King Arthur: Fairest isle. Oedipus: Music for a while. Pausanias: Sweeter than roses. The Rival Sisters: Take not a woman's anger ill. Rule a wife and have a wife: There's not a swain.*
*** Etcetera Dig. KTC 1013 [id.]. Andrew Dalton; Uittenbosch; Borstlap.

Andrew Dalton has an exceptionally beautiful counter-tenor voice, creamy even in its upper register to make the extended 'Hallelujahs' of *Lord, what is man?* and *Now that the sun* even more heavenly than usual. A delightful disc, well recorded.

Songs and dialogues: *Go tell Amynta; Hence fond deceiver; In all our Cinthia's shining sphere; In some kind dream; Lost is my quiet; Stript of their green; What a sad fate is mine; What can we poor females do; Why my poor Daphne, why complaining.* Theatre music: *Amphitryon: Fair Iris and her swain. Dioclesian: Tell me why. King Arthur: You say 'tis love; For love every creature is formed by his nature. The Old Bachelor: As Amoret and Thyrsis lay.*
*** Hyperion CDA 66056 [id.]. Kirkby, Thomas, Rooley.

This nicely planned Hyperion collection has one solo apiece for each of the singers, but otherwise consists of duets, five of them from dramatic works. These near-ideal performances, beautifully sung and sensitively accompanied on the lute, make a delightful record, helped by excellent sound.

Collections

(i) *Abdelazar: suite;* (i; ii) *Cibell for trumpet and strings;* (i) *Dioclesian: Dances from the Masque; Overtures: in D min.; G min.;* (i; ii) *Sonata for trumpet and strings;* (i) *Staircase overture; Suite in G, Z.770; Timon of Athens: Curtain tune;* (Keyboard): (iii) *New Irish tune; New Scotch tune; Sefauchi's farewell; Suite No. 6 in D;* Songs: (iv; i) *Hark how all things; If Love's sweet passion;* (iv; iii) *If music be the food of love; Lord what is man (Divine hymn);* (iv; i) *See even night is here; Thus the ever grateful Spring.*
(Y/B) *** Chandos CHAN 0571 [id.]. (i) Purcell Qt; (ii) Mark Bennett; (iii) Robert Woolley; (iv) Catherine Bott.

Catherine Bott opens this 72-minute concert with a glorious account of one of Purcell's most famous Shakespearean settings, most artfully decorated: *If music be the food of love*; if anything, the later song, *See, even Night herself is here*, is even more ravishing, given an ethereal introduction by the string group. The instrumental items are most rewarding, notably the attractive unpublished suite of dances in G, while the three Overtures are full of plangent character. Robert Woolley's harpsichord contribution is most infectious (the *New Irish tune*, incidentally, is 'Lilliburlero') and he is beautifully recorded, the harpsichord set back in an intimate acoustic and perfectly in scale. There are few better Purcell anthologies than this, and overall the CD gives an ideal introduction to the music of one of the very greatest English composers. The Chandos recording is first class, well up to the standards of the house.

'Music for England, my England': *Sonata for trumpet and strings in D; Abdelazar: Rondeau. The Married beau: Overture. Come ye sons of art (Birthday Ode, 1694): Sound the trumpet. Music for Funeral of Queen Mary: March; Canzona; 3 Funeral sentences. Saul and the Witch of Endor. Dido and Aeneas: Dido's lament. The Indian Queen: Adagio. King Arthur: Fairest Isle; Upon a quiet conscience; Act III* (complete).
(N) *** Erato/Warner 0630 10700-2 [id.]. Chance, Bowman, Dawson, Graham, Argenta, Varcoe, Monteverdi Ch., E. Bar. Soloists, Gardiner

Tony Palmer's film on Purcell to a provocative script by the late John Osborne prompted John Eliot Gardiner to make these fine recordings of music for the sound-track. This generous selection provides an excellent sampler of the composer's work. Not only does it offer favourites like *Fairest isle* (Lynne Dawson in radiant voice) and *Dido's lament* (Susan Graham equally sweet of tone) but also rarities like the dramatic motet, *Saul and the Witch of Endor*, a brilliant *Sonata for trumpet and strings* and a moving *Adagio* from *The Indian Queen*. The *Funeral music for Queen Mary* comes in a sequence with the three *Funeral sentences* – all heard complete in the film. The disc ends with the whole of Act III of *King Arthur* with its frost scene, though from the paltry documentation you would never gather that.

'Pocket Purcell': *Fantasia VIII; Three parts upon a ground;* Anthem: *Rejoice in the Lord, alway.* Funeral sentences: *Man that is born of woman; In the midst of life; Thou knowest Lord.* (Keyboard) *Ground in Gamut; Organ voluntary in D min.* Songs: *Close thine eyes; If music be the food of love;* Duets: *Close thine eyes; Of all the instruments. Suite of theatre music.*
(Y/B) **(*) Virgin/EMI VC5 45116-2 [id.]. Taverner Consort Ch. & Players, Andrew Parrott.

This attempt at an authentic 'Pocket Purcell' nearly comes off. If perhaps it tries to do too many different things in the space of one 66-minute CD, it certainly shows the composer's breadth and variety of achievement. Opening with a four-movement *Suite of theatre music* brightly played (and including the inevitable *Rondeau* from *Abdelazar* which Britten borrowed for his *Young person's guide*). There is also a touching *Fantasia for viols*, a delightful set of keyboard divisions on a *Ground in Gamut*, admirably played by John Toll, and an equally engaging joke-duet for two tenors, *Of all the instruments that are*. The single famous solo song is a welcome inclusion, but Emily Van Evera, for all her agility, does not display quite the charm of Emma Kirkby; the anthem, however, is very fresh in the refined Taverner manner, and the *Funeral sentences* have genuine atmosphere. But the highlight of the collection is the closing item, the *Masque of the Four Seasons* from *The Fairy Queen*, showing Purcell not only at his most exuberant but also at his most melancholy and darkly imaginative, with Jeremy White's splendidly sonorous performance of the great bass aria, *Next, winter comes slowly*. Fine, vivid recording; but this would be far more attractive at mid-price.

Anthems: *Blow up the trumpet in Zion; Hear my prayer, O Lord; I will sing unto the Lord as long as I live; Lord, how long wilt thou be angry?; O God, the King of glory; O God, thou art my God; O God, thou hast cast me out; Remember not, Lord, our offences. Funeral music for Queen Mary (March; Canzone; Funeral sentences: Man that is born of woman; In the midst of life; Thou knowest Lord; March; Queen's Epicideum; Thou Knowest, Lord, the secrets of our hearts; March). Organ voluntaries: in C; D min.; G.*
(Y/B) (BB) ** Naxos Dig. 8.553129 [id.]. Oxford Camerata, Jeremy Summerly; Laurence Cummings.

A worthy attempt to provide a single, budget-priced CD for the tercentenary, celebrating Purcell's church music but also including his *Funeral music for Queen Mary*. In the latter work, a modest brass group appears for the *Marches*, but otherwise the vocal music is organ-accompanied by Laurence Cummings, who also provides acceptable accounts of three solo voluntaries. Although the anthems are sung with warmth and eloquence, the most impressive performance here is the Latin motet, *Jehova, quam multi sunt hostes mei*, with excellent solo contributions from Andrew Carwood and Michael McCarthy. Similarly, it is a soloist who stands out at the centre of the *Funeral music*, with the girl treble Carys-Anne Lane's touching account of *Incassum Lesbia* (the *Queen's Epicedium*). Translations are provided for both works. Pleasing, spacious recording in the Chapel of Hertford College, Oxford. Good value, but this is not in the same class as the two-disc Christ Church collection, above, or indeed the excellent St John's collection of anthems on Decca (444 525-2 – see above).

Songs of welcome and farewell: *O dive custos Auriacae domus (Elegy on the death of Queen Mary); Incassum, Lesbia rogas (The Queen's Epicedium); Raise, raise the voice (Ode for St Cecilia's day); Welcome, vicegerent of the mighty king (Welcome song for Charles II); Why, why are all the Muses mute? (Elegy on the death of Thomas Farmer); Young Thirsis' fate, ye hills and groves, deplore (Elegy on the death of Thomas Farmer); The Fairy Queen: O let me ever, ever weep.*
(Y/B) *** Teldec/Warner Dig. 4509 95068-2 [id.]. Suzie le Blanc, Barbara Borden, Steve Dugardin, Douglas Nasrawi, Harry van der Kamp, Simon Grant, Tragicomedia, Stephen Stubbs & Erin Headley.

Tragicomedia here involves eight talented singers from America and Europe who, with clean, firm voices, sharp attack and precise ensemble, give refreshing performances of a well-varied selection of seven of Purcell's occasional pieces. Those who resist the idea of following Robert King's outstanding series for Hyperion (see above) might opt for this disc, very well recorded. As well as well-known items like the two magnificent *Elegies* for Queen Mary's Funeral, it includes several rarities to cherish. Clean, forward sound to match.

STAGE WORKS AND THEATRE MUSIC

Instrumental suites from: *Dioclesian; The Fairy Queen; The Indian Queen; King Arthur.*
(Y/B) **(*) Sony Dig. SK 66169 [id.]. Tafelmusik, Jean Lamon.

Although Purcell's standard of invention is high and these period performances are vital and alive, if not always strong on expressive charm, it seems perverse to offer 71 minutes of mostly instrumental snippets from essentially vocal works. When the trumpets enter, there is an element of grandeur, certainly, but this is not a disc to play all at once. The bright recording has great immediacy.

Dido and Aeneas (complete).
❀ (M) *** Decca 425 720-2. Dame Janet Baker, Herincx, Clark, Sinclair, St Anthony Singers, ECO, Anthony Lewis.
(Y/B) *** Erato/Warner Dig. 4509-98477-2 [id.]. Gens, Berg, Marin-Degor, Brua, Fouchécourt, Les Arts Florissants, William Christie.
*** Teldec/Warner Dig. 4509 91191-2 [id.]. Della Jones, Harvey, Donna Dean, Bickley, Murgatroyd, St James's Singers & Baroque Players, Ivor Bolton.
(N) *** Chandos Dig. CHAN 0586 [id.]. Ewing, Daymond, MacDougall, R. Evans, Burgess, Bowman, Coll. Mus. 90, Hickox.
*** Ph. Dig. 416 299-2 [id.]. Jessye Norman, McLaughlin, Kern, Allen, Power, ECO and Ch., Leppard.
*** Chandos Dig. CHAN 0521 [id.]. Kirkby, Thomas, Nelson, Noorman, Rees, Taverner Ch. & Players, Parrott.
(M) (***) EMI mono CDH7 61006-2 [id.]. Flagstad, Schwarzkopf, Hemsley, Mermaid Theatre Singers & O, Geraint Jones.
(N) (M) ** EMI CDM5 65664-2 [id.]. De los Angeles, Glossop, Harper, Johnson, Amb. S., ECO, Barbirolli.

Janet Baker's 1962 recording of *Dido* is a truly great performance. The radiant beauty of the voice is obvious enough, but the emotion is implied, as it should be in this music, not injected in great uncontrolled gusts. Listen to the contrast between the opening phrase of *When I am laid in earth* and its repeat a few bars later: it is a model of graduated mezza voce. Then with the words *Remember me!*, delivered in a monotone, she subdues the natural vibrato to produce a white tone of hushed, aching intensity. Anthony Lewis and the ECO (Thurston Dart a model continuo player) produce the crispest and lightest of playing, which never sounds rushed. The other soloists and chorus give very good support. Herincx is a rather gruff Aeneas, but the only serious blemish is Monica Sinclair's Sorceress. She overcharacterizes in a way that is quite out of keeping with the rest of the production. Like most vintage Oiseau-Lyre recordings, this was beautifully engineered.

On Erato the scale is intimate, with one instrument per part, and one voice per part in choruses, yet the emotions conveyed are the opposite of miniature. Christie cunningly varies the pace to intensify the drama. Though speeds are generally fast, with tripping rhythms and light textures, bringing out the joy of so many numbers, Christie points an extreme contrast in Dido's two big arias, giving them full expressiveness at measured speeds. In the final exchanges between Dido and Aeneas the hastening speed of the recitative directly reflects the mounting tensions. What then sets this above other period performances is the tragic depth conveyed by Veronique Gens in Dido's great *Lament*, taken very slowly, with the voice drained and agonized in a way that Janet Baker supremely achieved. Though not all the other French singers match Gens in her fine English pronunciation, this is an exceptionally strong and well contrasted team of singers with cleanly focused voices. The young Canadian baritone, Nathan Berg, dark and heroic of tone, is outstanding as Aeneas, making this thinly drawn character for once more than a wimp. Textually this version is interesting for supplying two very brief extra numbers to fill in the music missing from the end of Act II, as indicated in the suriviving libretto, a *Chorus of triumph* for the witches – a capable pastiche of Purcell to fit Nahum Tate's text – plus a *Grove's dance*, taken from the *Magicians' dance* written for the play, *Circe*. Together they last less than 90 seconds.

Ivor Bolton and the St James's Singers and Players present a period performance, intimately scaled, which avoids the snags of earlier versions, with Della Jones as Dido giving her finest recorded perform-ance yet. She has a weightier mezzo than her rivals in other period performances, yet her flexibility over ornamentation is greater, and *Dido's Lament* is the more moving when, unlike Von Otter on DG Archiv, she is restrained over expressive gestures, keeping a tender simplicity. She shades her voice tonally very much as Dame Janet Baker did in her classic recording with Sir Anthony Lewis and the ECO, made in 1961, long before period manners were adopted. Ivor Bolton's team, recorded with bright immediacy, has no weak link, with Peter Harvey as Aeneas, Susan Bickley as a clear-toned Sorceress, Donna Dean as a characterful Belinda, and Andrew Murgatroyd as the Sailor, a tenor who plays no stylistic tricks. Setting the seal on the performance's success, the choir is among the freshest and liveliest, and the use of a guitar continuo as well as brief guitar interludes (suggested by the original libretto) enhances the happy intimacy of the presentation.

Richard Hickox's version was linked to a striking television presentation marking the Purcell tercenten-ary in 1995. That revolved round the magnetically characterful portrayal of the central role by Maria Ewing, not a singer one normally associates with baroque music. In the event her performance, as recorded, is both distinctive and stylish. Combined with Hickox's lively direction, unmarred by intrusive re-allocation of voices, it makes an impressive version, with Karl Daymond making Aeneas a more complex character than usual, with Rebecca Evans a radiant Belinda, matching Ewing in emotional intensity, and with Sally Burgess a characterful, unexaggerated Sorceress. Add the excellent contribu-tions of James Bowman and Jamie MacDougall, and it makes a strong contender, certainly for admirers of Maria Ewing.

Authenticists should keep away, but the security and dark intensity of Jessye Norman's singing make for a memorable performance, heightened in the recitatives by the equally commanding singing of Thomas Allen as Aeneas. The range of expression is very wide – with Norman producing an agonized whisper in the recitative just before *Dido's Lament*. Marie McLaughlin a pure-toned Belinda, Patrick Power a heady-toned Sailor, singing his song in a West Country accent, while Patricia Kern's performance as the Sorceress uses conventionally sinister expression. Leppard's direction is relatively plain and direct, with some slow speeds for choruses. Excellent recording.

Andrew Parrott's concept of a performance on original instruments has one immediately thinking back to the atmosphere of Josias Priest's school for young ladies where Purcell's masterpiece was first given. The voices enhance that impression, not least Emma Kirkby's fresh, bright soprano, here recorded without too much edge but still very young-sounding. It is more questionable to have a soprano singing the tenor role of the Sailor in Act III; but anyone who fancies the idea of an authentic performance need not hesitate. The CD is exceptionally refined, the sound well focused, with analogue atmosphere yet with detail enhanced.

Though Flagstad's magnificent voice may in principle be too weighty for this music, she scales it down superbly in her noble reading, which brings beautiful shading and masterly control of breath and tone. Schwarzkopf is brightly characterful as Belinda, and though Thomas Hemsley is not ideally sweet-toned as Aeneas, he sings very intelligently; even in this age of period performance, this traditional account under Geraint Jones sounds fresh and lively still, not at all heavy. The mono sound, obviously limited, yet captures the voices vividly, and this above all is Flagstad's set.

Barbirolli – not the most likely conductor in this opera – takes some trouble with his text, using the Neville Boyling Edition that Mackerras, on DG Archiv, also prefers. But on questions of authenticity most other versions have considerable advantages, and Barbirolli finds fewer moments of high emo-tional intensity, such as would justify a 'personality' reading, than one would expect. The tempi are generally perverse, with slow speeds predominating – sometimes grotesquely slow – but with Dido's '*When I am laid in earth*' taken equivalently fast. Victoria de los Angeles makes an appealing Dido, but she does not have the dramatic weight of Janet Baker and the tone sometimes loses its bloom on top. The other singers are good, and the 1965 recording is fresh and immediate, but with keen competition this version commands only a very qualified recommendation.

Dido and Aeneas (complete); *Ode for St Cecilia's Day: Welcome to all pleasures* (1683).
**(*) Ph. Dig. 432 114-2 [id.]. C. Watkinson, Moseley, Monteverdi Ch., E. Bar. Soloists, Gardiner.

Gardiner's version of *Dido* generously couples the opera with the celebrated *St Cecilia's Day ode* of 1683. Characteristically he often chooses brisk speeds for the ensembles, springing rhythms infectiously; like Ivor Bolton, he includes guitar interludes in Acts I and II. His scale is a little larger than Bolton's, generally with more than one instrument per part, but that highlights the fact that the string sound comes near to the abrasive style of early period performances. Carolyn Watkinson is a sensitive Dido, but not as involving as the finest (as for example Della Jones for Ivor Bolton or Dame Janet Baker) with the voice at times suggesting a counter-tenor. Good as Gardiner's team is, it does not quite match Bolton's, singer for singer. Recording is good, though not always ideally balanced, as when the Sailor (Paul Tindall) sings his rollicking song as though off-stage.

Dioclesian; Timon of Athens: Masques only.
(N) *** Chandos Dig. CHAN 0568 [id.]. Pierard, Bowman, Ainsley, Padmore, George, Coll. Mus. 90, Hickox.

Dioclesian; Timon of Athens (Masque).
(N) *** DG Dig. 447 071-2 (2) [id.]. Argenta, Monoyios, Agnew, Edgar-Wilson, Gadd, Birchall, Wallington, Bannatyne-Scott, Foster, E. Concert & Ch., Pinnock.
(N) *** Chandos Dig. CHAN 0569/70 [id.]. Pierard, Bowman, Ainsley, George, Coll. Mus. 90, Hickox.

Following John Eliot Gardiner on Erato, both Trevor Pinnock on DG Archiv and Richard Hickox on Chandos offer the same apt coupling of *Dioclesian* and *Timon of Athens*, both sets of theatre music involving masques. All three versions can be warmly recommended, and choice might well be left to a preference over soloists in each. Gardiner (who has a considerable price advantage) in his 1988 recording is rather more abrasive than his more recent rivals, but that helps to sharpen the focus, with his rhythmic thrust second to none. Hickox takes a lighter view, at times more detached, often adopting faster speeds and using on balance the most consistent team of soloists, including in smaller roles such outstanding younger singers as Ian Bostridge and Nathan Berg. On the other hand, he does not include the overture to *Timon* which both Gardiner and Pinnock do offer, and Pinnock has more repeats.

Pinnock presents both works on a slightly larger (but not inflated) scale than his rivals, often more weighty to match a bigger, warmer though not over-reverberant acoustic. In keeping with this, he is more warmly expressive and often adopts broader speeds, which allow him to spring rhythms the more infectiously, more clearly introducing an element of sparkle and humour. All three include the extra song in Act III of *Dioclesian*, 'When first I saw', though Hickox has it as an appendix, using a tenor (Bostridge), not a soprano. But whichever version is chosen, the effervescence of Purcell's inspiration in two of his finest collections of theatre music is consistently compelling.

The single Chandos CD contains the masque music only.

The Fairy Queen (complete).
*** DG Dig. 419 221-2 (2) [id.]. Harrhy, Jennifer Smith, Nelson, Priday, Penrose, Stafford, Evans, Hill, Varcoe, Thomas, Monteverdi Ch., E. Bar. Soloists, Gardiner.
*** HM Dig. HMC 901308/9; *HMC 401308/9* [id.]. Argenta, Dawson, Daniels, Loonen, Correas, Les Arts Florissants, William Christie.
(Y/B) (B) *** Naxos Dig. 8.550660-1 (2) [id.]. Diane Atherton, Kym Amps, Angus Davidson & Soloists, The Scholars Bar. Ens., led by David van Asch.
(M) *** Decca 433 163-2 (2) [id.]. Vyvyan, Bowman, Pears, Wells, Partridge, Shirley-Quirk, Brannigan, Norma Burrowes, Amb. Op. Ch., ECO, Britten.
(Y/B) **(*) EMI Dig. CDS5 55234-2 (2). Bickley, Hunt, Pierard, Crook, Padmore, Wilson-Johnson, Wistreich, L. Schütz Ch., L. Classical Players, Norrington.
(BB) **(*) HM HMP 390257/8 [id.]. Sheppard, Knibbs, Bevan, Platt, Alfred Deller, Jenkins, Mark Deller, Buttrey, Clarke, Stour Music Ch. & O, A. Deller.
(Y/B) **(*) Erato/Warner Dig. 4509 98507-2 (2) [id.]. Bott, Thomas, Schopper, Amsterdam Bar. Ch. & O, Koopman.

Purcell's setting of Shakespeare's *Midsummer Night's Dream*, written in 1692, followed in the wake of the great success of *Dido and Aeneas*. The music takes the form of five masques, each symbolizing one aspect of the play. Gardiner's performance is a delight from beginning to end, for, though authenticity and completeness reign, scholarship is worn lightly and the result is consistently exhilarating, with no longueurs whatever. The fresh-toned soloists are first rate, while Gardiner's regular choir and orchestra excel themselves, with Purcell's sense of fantasy brought out in each succeeding number. Beautifully clear and well-balanced recording.

William Christie uses a far bigger team of both singers and instrumentalists than John Eliot Gardiner on the rival, DG Archiv set, allowing a wider range of colours. The bite of the performance is increased by the relative dryness of the recorded sound. Among Christie's soloists, Nancy Argenta and Lynne Dawson are outstanding, and the whole team is a strong one. The number of singers in solo roles allows them to be used together as chorus too – an authentic seventeenth-century practice. This makes a vigorous and refreshing alternative to the fine Gardiner set; but the Harmonia Mundi booklet is inadequate.

For Naxos at bargain price the Scholars Baroque Ensemble offer an outstanding version of Purcell's semi-opera, not always quite as beautifully sung as the finest rivals, but stylishly presented with a refreshing vigour in its scholarly approach. The recording too is exceptionally bright and immediate, regularly giving the illusion of a dramatic entertainment on stage. Logically this version, unlike previous ones, presents the purely instrumental numbers designed as interludes for *A Midsummer Night's Dream* as an appendix, rather than including them during the course of the musical entertainment of five separate masques. So the performance starts with the very brief Overture instead of the First Musick Prelude, and the variety of expression throughout is well caught and contrasted. The humour of the Scene of the Drunken Poet is touched in delightfully without exaggeration, thanks to David van Asch, as is the Dialogue between Corydon and Mopsa, though the counter-tenor, Angus Davidson, has a flutter in the voice that the recording exaggerates. One or two of the others are not always quite steady either. Outstanding among the sopranos are Diane Atherton, singing most beautifully in the Night solo of Act II, and Kym Amps, not only bright and agile in *Hark! The ech'ing air* but making the plaint, *O ever let me weep*, of Act V into the emotional high-point of the whole performance. In the edition specially prepared for the Ensemble it is made the more affecting with lamenting oboe obbligato. Instrumental playing on period instruments is first rate, and the chorus sings consistently with bright, incisive attack.

Britten's version from the early 1970s used a newly reshaped arrangement of the music made by Britten himself in collaboration with Imogen Holst and Peter Pears. The original collection of individual pieces is here grouped into four satisfying sections: *Oberon's birthday*, *Night and silence*, the *Sweet passion* and the *Epithalamium*. The cast is consistently satisfying.

Roger Norrington recorded *The Fairy Queen* following a 'Purcell Experience' weekend, culminating in a concert performance of this inspired but disjointed semi-opera. There is a refinement and polish about the solo singing and the ensemble which reflects that intensive preparation. Where William Christie's earthier reading with Les Arts Florissants reflects experience of stage production, bold, jolly and intense, Norrington's wears its polished manners in a crisp, lightly rhythmic way, helped by the finely honed playing of the London Classical Players. Speeds are often brisk, with rhythms lightly sprung, and the impressive line-up of soloists brings distinctive characterization from such singers as David Wilson-Johnson as the Drunken Poet, Mark Padmore in the tenor songs of Act IV and Lorraine Hunt in *Hark! The ech'ing air*, taken very fast and lightly. There is less fun and less dramatic bite here than in Christie's or Gardiner's versions but, recorded in a spacious acoustic, Norrington's light, clean approach never diminishes Purcell's bubbling inspiration.

Deller's set was recorded – very well too – at the Stour Music Festival in 1972 and, although the balance is rather forward, the acoustic is pleasingly warm and the voices and orchestra combine effectively. All the solo singing is of a high standard, with Honor Sheppard particularly memorable as Night in Act II, well matched by Jean Knibbs's Mystery in some of Purcell's most evocative writing. Norman Platt is a suitably bucolic Drunken Poet in Act I and becomes one of a pair of West Country haymakers (Alfred Deller obviously enjoying himself as his companion, Mopsa) in Act III. The many ensembles are eloquently sung and, although this has not quite the sophistication of Gardiner's set, its robust warmth and Deller's considerable concern for detail make for an enjoyable entertainment, well worth its modest price when so smoothly and vividly transferred to CD.

Ton Koopman's version is generally rather mellower than its period-performance rivals, starting with a very spacious account of the opening of the overture. Koopman's approach to each successive number is strongly characterized, at times idiosyncratic, but always convincing, and he offers some fine solo singing from the three billed soloists, notably from Catherine Bott whose accounts of *Ye gentle spirits*, taken very slowly, and of *Hark! The ech'ing air* have an unsurpassed richness and intensity. The soloists billed in small print are less consistent, but Koopman's understanding of this enigmatic Purcell master-piece is never in doubt, including its humour, as in his bluff account of the dialogue of Corydon and Mopsa. He is helped by excellent singing and playing from the Amsterdam Choir and Orchestra.

The Indian Queen (complete).
(N) *** O-L Dig. 444 339-2 [id.]. Kirkby, Bott, Ainsley, D. Thomas, Finley, Williams, AAM Ch. & O, Hogwood.

The Indian Queen (incidental music; complete).
*** HM HMC 90243 [id.]. Knibbs, Sheppard, Mark and Alfred Deller, Elliot, Bevan, Deller Singers, King's Musick, Deller.

Hogwood's recording of Purcell's fourth and last semi-opera, left incomplete at his death, is the first to include the Wedding cantata which the composer's brother, Daniel, wrote to round off the entertainment. It makes an attractive if inconsistent addition to a score which, despite the oddity of the play that inspired the music, contains vintage Purcell inspirations, notably the solo with chorus, *All dismal sounds*, which was the last part of the work completed by Purcell himself. The elaborate chromatics in that confirm the continuing vigour of Purcell's genius to the end. With John Mark Ainsley, Emma Kirkby and Catherine Bott all making outstanding solo contributions, and with clean-cut period playing from the orchestra, this performance on a relatively grand scale is consistently convincing, by turns lively and moving. The rival Gardiner version at mid-price on Erato (made in 1979, soon after he turned to period instruments) lacks the final masque and is more abrasive in sound, though the bass, David Thomas, is firmer than in the later set.

Deller's group is at its liveliest and most characterful in *The Indian Queen. Ye twice ten hundred deities* is sung splendidly by Maurice Bevan; and the duet for male alto and tenor, *How happy are we* (with Deller himself joined by Paul Elliot), as well as the best-known item, the soprano's *I attempt from love's sickness to fly* (Honor Sheppard), are equally enjoyable.

(i) *The Indian Queen* (incidental music); (ii) *King Arthur* (complete).
✪ (M) *** Decca 433 166-2 (2) [id.]. (i) Cantelo, Wilfred Brown, Tear, Partridge, Keyte, St Anthony Singers, ECO, Mackerras; (ii) Morison, Harper, Mary Thomas, Whitworth, Wilfred Brown, Galliver, Cameron, Anthony, Alan, St Anthony Singers, Philomusica of L., Lewis.

This Decca Serenata (originally Oiseau-Lyre) version of *The Indian Queen* dates from 1966 and the recording, from a vintage era, remains first rate. With stylish singing and superb direction and accompaniment (Raymond Leppard's harpsichord continuo playing must be singled out), this is an invaluable reissue. Charles Mackerras shows himself a strong and vivid as well as scholarly Purcellian. The Rosette, however, is for the pioneering 1959 set (also Oiseau-Lyre) of *King Arthur*, fully worthy to stand alongside the companion recording of *Dido and Aeneas*, made three years later – see above. Here the success of the interpretation does not centre on the contribution of one inspired artist, but rather on teamwork among a number of excellent singers and on the stylish and sensitive overall direction of Anthony Lewis. Oiseau-Lyre's excellent stereo also plays a big part. A very happy example is the chorus *This way, that way*, when the opposing spirits (good and evil) make a joint attempt to entice the King, while the famous freezing aria will surely send a shiver through the most warm-blooded listener.

King Arthur (complete).
(Y/B) ✪ *** Erato/Warner Dig. 4509 98535-2 (2) [id.]. Gens, McFadden, Padmore, Best, Salomaa, Les Arts Florissants, William Christie.
*** DG Dig. 435 490-2 (2) [id.]. Argenta, Gooding, Perillo, MacDougal, Tucker, Bannatyne-Scott, Finley, Ch. & E. Concert, Pinnock.

Recorded at sessions immediately after Christie's spectacular production of *King Arthur* in Paris in February 1995 – complete with the Dryden play – this Erato recording of the musical numbers consistently reflects stage experience. Some may not like the crowd noises in the more rollicking numbers but, more than his rivals, Christie brings out the jollity behind much of the piece. Even the pomposo manner of some of the Act Tunes (or interludes) has fun in it, with the panoply of the ceremonial music swaggering along genially. Few will resist the jollity of *Your hay it is mow'd* when the chorus even includes 'gentlemen of the orchestra' in the last verse. Unlike the earlier, Gardiner version (also Erato), this one does not in that character number have the bass soloist (Petteri Salomaa) singing in a broad Mummerset dialect, but it is still earthy enough. Christie's soloists are generally warmer and weightier than Gardiner's, notably Véronique Gens as Venus, sustaining Christie's exceptionally slow speed for *Fairest isle*. Otherwise speeds are generally on the fast side, with *Shepherd, shepherd, cease decoying* deliciously light and brisk. The vigour of Purcell's inspiration in this semi-opera has never been more winningly conveyed in a period performance on disc, with full-bodied instrumental sound set against a helpful but relatively dry acoustic, giving immediacy to the drama.

Pinnock opens with the *Chaconne*, which is placed before the *Overture*. His performance is consistently refreshing and can be recommended alongside, though not in preference to Gardiner's. Linda Perillo makes a charming Philidel. Brian Bannatyne-Scott is superb in Aeolus's *Ye blust'ring brethren*, and in his *Frost aria* he achieves an unusual if controversial effect by beginning his series of shakes from slightly under the note. Not surprisingly, Nancy Argenta sings beautifully in the double roles of Cupid and Venus and her *Fairest isle* will not disappoint; both chorus and orchestra sing and play throughout with consistent vitality. The DG recording is first class, but why no coupling? The second CD plays for only 39 minutes.

King Arthur: highlights.
(M) *** Erato/Warner Dig. 2292 45919-2 (from above complete set; cond. Gardiner).

A well-chosen 64-minute selection from John Eliot Gardiner's complete version (see Gardiner Purcell collection, above), this can be strongly recommended for it contains a great deal of the music, including the famous stereophonic chorus, 'Hither this way'.

Theatre music (collection).
Disc 1: *Abdelazar: Overture and suite. Distressed Innocence: Overture and suite. The Gordian Knot Untied: Overture and suite; The Married Beau: Overture and suite. Sir Anthony Love: Overture and suite.*
Disc 2: *Bonduca: Overture and suite. Circe: suite. The Old Bachelor: Overture and suite. The Virtuous Wife: Overture and suite.*
Disc 3: *Amphitrion: Overture and suite; Overture in G min.; Don Quixote: suite.*
Disc 4: *Overture in G min. The Double Dealer: Overture and suite. Henry II, King of England: In vain, 'gainst love, in vain I strove. The Richmond Heiress: Behold the man. The Rival Sisters: Overture; 3 songs. Tyrannic Love: Hark my Damilcar!* (duet); *Ah! how sweet it is to love. Theodosius:* excerpts. *The Wives' Excuse:* excerpts.
Disc 5: *Overture in D min.; Cleomenes, the Spartan Hero: No, no, poor suff'ring heart. A Dialogue between Thirsis and Daphne: Why, my Daphne, why complaining?. The English Lawyer: My wife has a tongue:* excerpts. *A Fool's Preferment:* excerpts. *The History of King Richard II: Retir'd from any mortal's sight. The Indian Emperor: I look'd and saw within. The Knight of Malta: At the close of the ev'ning. The Libertine:* excerpts. *The Marriage-hater Match'd: As soon as the chaos . . . How vile are the sordid intregues. The Massacre of Paris: The genius lo* (2 settings). *Oedipus:* excerpts. *Regulus: Ah me! to many deaths. Sir Barnaby Whigg: Blow, blow, Boreas, blow. Sophonisba: Beneath the poplar's shadow. The Wives' Excuse:* excerpts.
Disc 6: *Chacony; Pavans Nos. 1–5; Trio sonata for violin, viola da gamba & organ. Aureng-Zebe: I see, she flies me. The Canterbury Guests: Good neighbours why?. Epsom Wells: Leave these useless arts. The Fatal Marriage: 2 songs. The Female Virtuosos: Love, thou art best. Love Triumphant: How happy's the husband. The Maid's Last Prayer:* excerpts. *The Mock Marriage: Oh! how you protest; Man is for the woman made. Oroonoko: Celemene, pray tell me. Pausanius: Song (Sweeter than roses) and duet. Rule a Wife and Have a Wife: There's not a swain. The Spanish Friar: Whilst I with grief.*
(M) *** O-L 425 893-2 (6). Kirkby, Nelson, Lane, Roberts, Lloyd, Bowman, Hill, Covey-Crump, Elliott, Byers, Bamber, Pike, David Thomas, Keyte, Shaw, George, Taverner Ch., AAM, Hogwood.

Most of the music Purcell wrote for the theatre is relatively little heard and much of the music comes up with striking freshness in these performances using authentic instruments. As well as the charming dances and more ambitious overtures, as the series proceeds we are offered more extended scenas with soloists and chorus, of which the nine excerpts from *Theodosius*, an early score (1680), are a particularly entertaining example. Before that, on Disc 3 we have already had the highly inventive *Overture and incidental music* for *Don Quixote*, with much enchanting singing from both the soprano soloists, Emma Kirkby and Judith Nelson. Disc 4 also includes a delightful duet from *The Richmond Heiress*, representing a flirtation in music. There are other attractive duets elsewhere, for instance the nautical *Blow, blow, Boreas, blow* from *Sir Barnaby Whigg*, which could fit admirably into *HMS Pinafore* (Rogers Covey-Crump and David Thomas) and the jovial *As soon as the chaos* from *The Marriage-hater Match'd*. In *Ah me! to many deaths* from *Regulus*, Judith Nelson is at her most eloquent while, earlier on Disc 5, she sings charmingly the familiar *Nymphs and shepherds*, which comes from *The Libertine*, a particularly fine score with imaginative use of the brass. The equally famous *Music for a while*, beautifully sung by James Bowman, derives from *Oedipus*. The last disc also includes a splendidly boisterous *Quartet* from *The Canterbury Guests*. The collection is appropriately rounded off by members of the Academy giving first-class performances of some of Purcell's instrumental music, ending with the famous *Chacony*. The discs are comprehensively documented and with full texts included.

Quantz, Joseph Joachim (1697–1773)

Flute concertos: in C; in D (For Potsdam); G; G min.
*** RCA Dig. RD 60247; *RK 60247* [60247-2-RC; *60247-4-RC*]. James Galway, Württemberg CO, Heilbron, Faerber.

Quantz was a skilled musician and all four concertos here are pleasing, while their slow movements show a genuine flair for melody. The *Arioso mesto* of the *G major* is particularly charming but the *Amoroso* of the *C major* is appealing too. Quantz also wrote well-organized allegros, and the opening *Allegro assai* of the *G major* shows him at his most vigorous, even if perhaps the *Potsdam concerto* is overall the best of the four works here. The thoroughly musical James Galway is most winning in the lyrical cantilenas, and the Württemberg group accompany with polish and much vitality. Excellent sound.

Quilter, Roger (1877–1953)

A Children's overture; Country pieces; 3 English dances; As you like it: suite; The Rake: suite; Where the Rainbow ends: suite.
**(*) Marco Polo Dig. 8.223444. Slovak RSO (Bratislava), Adrian Leaper.

Adrian Leaper plays Roger Quilter's enchanting *Children's overture* with the lightest touch, and the transparency of the recording ensures that all the woodwind detail comes through nicely, and the little fugato on 'A frog he would a-wooing go' is delightfully handled, even if his performance could ideally have had a shade more momentum. One might also have wished for a bigger band with a more opulent string sheen, but the texture here well suits the suites of incidental music, an agreeable mixture of the styles of Edward German (especially the *Country dance* from *As you like it*), Eric Coates and sub-Elgar of the *Nursery suites*. All this nicely scored and amiably tuneful music is freshly and spontaneously presented and the recording is nicely resonant.

Rachmaninov, Sergei (1873–1943)

Piano concertos Nos. (i) *1;* (ii) *2* (2 versions); (i) *3–4;* (ii) *Rhapsody on a theme of Paganini;* (iii) *The Isle of the Dead; Symphony No. 3; Vocalise.* (piano, 4 hands): (iv) *Polka italienne.* (Solo piano): *Barcarolle, Op. 10/3; Daisies* (song transcription); *Etudes-tableaux, Op. 33/2 & 7 & Op. 39/6; Humoresque, Op. 10/5; Lilacs* (song transcription; 2 versions); *Mélodie, Op. 3/3; Moment musical, Op. 16/2; Oriental sketch; Polichinelle, Op. 3/4; Polka de W. R.* (3 versions). *Preludes: in C sharp min., Op. 3/2* (3 versions); *in G min.; in G flat, Op. 23/5 & 10; in E, G, F min., F, G sharp, Op. 32/3, 5–7, 12; Serenade, Op. 3/5* (2 versions); (v) BEETHOVEN: *Violin sonata No. 8 in G, Op. 30/3.* SCHUBERT: *Violin sonata in A, D.574.* GRIEG: *Violin sonata in C min., Op. 45.* BACH: *Partita No. 4, BWV 828: Sarabande.* HANDEL: *Suite No. 5: Air and variations (The Harmonious blacksmith).* MOZART: *Piano sonata in A, K.331: Theme and variations; Rondo alla Turca.* BEETHOVEN: *32 Variations in C min. WoO 80.* LISZT: *Concert paraphrase of Chopin: Polish songs (Return home; The maiden's wish). Concert paraphrases of Schubert: Das Wandern; Serenade. Polonaise No. 2; Concert study: Gnomenreigen; Hungarian rhapsody No. 2.* MENDELSSOHN: *Song without words: Spinning song, Op. 67* (2 versions). *Etudes, Op. 104b/2–3.* SCHUBERT: *Impromptu in A flat, Op. 90/4.* GLUCK: *Orfeo ed Euridice: Mélodie.* SCHUMANN: *Der Kontrabandiste* (arr. Tausig); *Carnaval, Op. 9.* PADEREWSKI: *Minuet, Op. 14/1.* CHOPIN: *Sonata No. 2 (Funeral march); Nocturnes, Op. 9/2; Op. 15/2; Waltzes: Op. 18 (Grand valse brillante), Op. 34/3; Op. 42; Op. 64/1* (2 versions); *Op. 64/ 2; Op. 64/3* (2 versions); *Op. 69/2; Op. 70/1; in E min., Op. posth.; Ballade No. 3; Mazurkas, Op. 63/3, Op. 68/2; Scherzo No. 3.* BORODIN: *Scherzo in A flat.* TCHAIKOVSKY: *The Seasons: November (Troika;* 2 versions). *Humoresque, Op. 10/2; Waltz, Op. 40/8.* SCRIABIN: *Prelude, Op. 11/8.* Johann STRAUSS Jnr: *Man lebt nur einmal (One lives but once;* arr. Tausig). DAQUIN: *Le coucou.* SAINT-SAENS: *Le Cygne* (arr. Siloti). GRIEG: *Lyric pieces: Waltz; Elfin dance.* DOHNANYI: *Etude, Op. 28/6.* HELSELT: *Etude, Op. 2/6 (Si oiseau j'étais).* MOSZKOWSKI: *Etude, Op. 52/4 (La jongleuse).* DEBUSSY: *Children's corner: Dr Gradus ad Parnassum; Golliwog's cakewalk.* Domenico SCARLATTI: *Pastorale* (arr. Tausig). Transcriptions: KREISLER: *Liebesfreud* (3 versions). BACH: (Unaccompanied) *Violin Partita No. 3, BWV 1003: Preludio; Gavotte & Gigue.* MENDELSSOHN: *A Midsummer Night's Dream: Scherzo.* SCHUBERT: *Wohin?.* MUSSORGSKY: *Gopak.* TCHAIKOVSKY: *Lullaby, Op. 16/1.* RIMSKY-KORSAKOV: *Flight of the bumble bee.* BEETHOVEN: *Ruins of Athens: Turkish march.* BIZET: *L'Arlésienne: Minuet.* TRAD.: (vi) *Powder and Paint.*
✲ (M) (***) RCA mono 09026 61265-2 (10) [id.]. Sergei Rachmaninov (piano); with Phd. O, (i) Ormandy; (ii) Stokowski; (iii) cond. composer; (iv) with Natalie Rachmaninov; (v) Fritz Kreisler; (vi) Nadejda Plevitskaya.

(i) *Piano concerto No. 2; Rhapsody on a theme of Paganini;* (ii) *Vocalise.*
(M) (***) Carlton mono GLRS 104 [id.]. Rachmaninov, Phd. O, Stokowski; (ii) composer, Phd. O.

Spurred by the 50th anniversary of Rachmaninov's death, RCA has issued a ten-disc box at mid-price collecting all the recordings the composer made from 1919, the time he arrived in America, until 1942, the year before his death. These include all four of his *Piano concertos* (No. 3 irritatingly cut) as well as the *Paganini rhapsody*, the *Third Symphony* and the tone-poem, *The Isle of the Dead* (also with cuts). Among Rachmaninov's many solo piano recordings it is fascinating to compare his different readings of the most celebrated piece of all, the *Prelude in C sharp minor*. The stiff performance of 1919 (made for Edison) leads to a much freer and subtler reading in 1921, while the 1928 version, using the new electrical process, remains free and subtle but is emotionally less charged. The acoustic recordings, made between 1920 and 1925, are on balance the most cherishable of all, with the sound astonishingly full and the readings sparkling and spontaneous. That is true even of his 1924 recording of the *Piano Concerto No. 2*, now for the very first time issued complete. As in his classic electrical recording of five years later, he is partnered by Stokowski and the Philadelphia Orchestra, but the earlier one has a more volatile quality, with the fingerwork even clearer. Interpreting Chopin, Rachmaninov was also at his freshest and most imaginative in the early recordings, yet dozens of items here bear witness to the claim often made that he was the greatest golden-age pianist of all, bar none. The delicacy of his playing in Daquin's little piece, *Le coucou*, shows how he was able to scale down his block-busting virtuosity and, though in Beethoven's *32 Variations in C minor* he omitted half-a-dozen variations so as to fit the piece on two 78 sides, it is full of flair. There is magic too in his collaborations with Fritz Kreisler, not just in Beethoven but also in the Grieg and Schubert sonatas, and in the private recordings, when he accompanies a gypsy singer in a traditional Russian song or plays a piano duet, the *Polka italienne*, with his wife, Natalie. Transfers are commendably clean but with high background hiss. The ten discs come in a box at mid-price.

For those who want just the two electrical concertante recordings made with Stokowski, the Pickwick CD serves admirably. The transfers are slightly less sharp in detail but agreeably full. Both here and in the RCA version of the second recording of the *C minor Concerto* the woodwind triplets which accompany the reprise of the main theme of the slow movement come out vividly as in no other recording. Even in a live performance these very effective decorations tend to become buried.

Piano concertos Nos. 1–4.
(N) (B) *** Decca Double 444 839-2 (2) [id.]. Vladimir Ashkenazy, LSO, Previn.
(B) *** EMI CZS7 67419-2 (2) [id.]. Collard, Capitole Toulouse O, Plasson.

Piano concertos Nos. 1; 4; Rhapsody on a theme of Paganini, Op. 43.
(N) (M) ** Ph. 446 582-2 (2) [id.]. Zoltán Kocsis, San Francisco SO, Edo de Waart.

(i) *Piano concertos Nos. 2–3. Vocalise, Op. 34/14.*
(N) (M) ** Ph. 446 582-2 (2) [id.]. (i) Zoltán Kocsis; San Francisco SO, Edo de Waart.

Piano concertos Nos. (i) *1 in F sharp min;* (ii) *2 in C min;* (iii) *3 in D min.;* (i) *4 in G min.;* (ii) *Rhapsody on a theme of Paganini, Op. 43.*
(N) (B) **(*) EMI forte CZS5 68619-2 (2). Anievas, New Philh. O; (i) Frühbeck de Burgos; (ii) Atzmon; (iii) Ceccato.

Piano concertos Nos. 1 in F sharp min., Op. 1.; 4 in G min., Op. 40; Rhapsody on a theme of Paganini, Op. 43.
(Y/B) (M) *** Chandos CHAN 6605 [id.]. Earl Wild, RPO, Horenstein.
**(*) Chandos Dig. CHAN 9192 [id.]. Howard Shelley, RSNO, Thomson.

Piano concertos Nos. 2 in C min., Op. 18; 3 in D min., Op. 30.
(M) *** Chandos CHAN 6507; *MBTD 6507* [id.]. Earl Wild, RPO, Horenstein.
**(*) Chandos Dig. CHAN 9192 [id.]. Howard Shelley, RSNO, Thomson.

The new Double Decca set of the four Rachmaninov concertos now tends to sweep the board. The current transfers (unlike the previous, mid-priced incarnation) are admirable, fully capturing the Kingsway Hall ambient warmth yet not lacking brilliance and clarity, and with the *Third Concerto* better focused than when it first appeared on LP. The vintage 1972 performances, with their understanding partnership between Askenazy and Previn, have achieved classic status. The *Second Concerto*'s slow movement is particularly beautiful; it is almost matched by the close of the first movement of the *Third* and the restrained passion of the opening of the following *Adagio*. The individuality and imagination of the solo playing throughout, combined with the poetic feeling of Previn's accompaniments and the ever-persuasive response of the LSO, provide special rewards. An outstanding bargain is every way.

Jean-Philippe Collard's recordings of the four Rachmaninov concertos date from the late 1970s. Collard is completely at home in this repertoire; his account of the *First* has splendid fire and can hold its own with all comers (even Pletnev and Ashkenazy, though the former is incomparable in the slow movement); and much the same goes for its companions. Perhaps the *Third Piano concerto* is the least incandescent in his hands, but readers wanting an inexpensive set (all four concertos for the price of one CD) need look no further, for this is playing of quality, and the recording, though not outstanding, is fully acceptable, and avoids the artificial edginess of the Decca transfers.

The Earl Wild set with Horenstein originally derived from RCA. It was produced by Charles Gerhardt and was recorded at the Kingsway Hall in 1965. They worked marvellously together, with Horenstein producing an unexpected degree of romantic ardour from the orchestra and both artists finding the natural feeling for the ebb and flow of phrases, so readily demonstrated in the composer's own perform-ances, and which has now become a hallmark of Rachmaninovian interpretation. Earl Wild's technique is prodigious and sometimes (as in the first movement of the *Fourth Concerto*) he almost lets it run away with him. What is surprising is how closely the interpretations here seem to be modelled on the com-poser's own versions – not slavishly, but in broad conception. This applies strikingly to the *First Concerto* and the *Rhapsody*. The first movement of the *C minor Concerto* is faster than usual, but the expressive fervour is in no doubt; the *Adagio*, too, blossoms readily. In terms of bravura, the *Third Concerto* is in the Horowitz class. The digital remastering is a great success, the overall balance is truthful and the hall ambience brings a rich orchestral image and plenty of brilliance. However, unfortunately there are three cuts in the *Third Concerto*, one in the second movement and two in the third, a total of 55 bars. Horenstein does not quite match Stokowski's flair, although his rather straight-er approach is still idiomatically sensitive and is helped by the rich body given to the strings by the Kingsway ambience. All in all, this is a first-class and very rewarding set, and the sumptuousness of the sound belies the age of the recording.

Anievas cannot match Ashkenazy as a searching and individual interpreter of Rachmaninov, but his youthful freshness makes all these concerto performances highly enjoyable. With three Mediterranean conductors to help him, and with bright, vivid EMI recording, not as atmospheric as the quality Decca provide for Ashkenazy, the result brings a combination of brilliance and romanticism which never lets go, even if it rarely produces the moments of magical illumination that mark the most inspired inter-pretations. Like Ashkenazy, Anievas gives the *Third Concerto* absolutely uncut and uses the longer, more difficult version of the first-movement cadenza. It is a strong, direct interpretation, though at the very end of the finale the presentation of the big melody nearly goes over the top.

Howard Shelley's recordings, previously available only in a box, are now issued on two separate CDs – still at full price. The recording, made in Caird Hall, Dundee, is certainly sumptuous, almost overwhelm-ingly so at climaxes, with rich strings and powerfully resonant brass and a bold, truthful piano-image projected way out in front. The performances do not lack adrenalin either, although their ebb and flow of tension is not consistent, and at times the music-making almost tends to run away with itself, notably in the *Third Concerto*. The first-movement climax of the *Second Concerto* is very powerful, and there is some lovely playing from the orchestra at the end of the slow movement. The finales have great dash and much charisma from Shelley, but Bryden Thomson at times seems less assured in the idiom. Just after the opening of the *Rhapsody on a theme of Paganini* he produces a curious echo effect (in which his soloist joins), while his *Eighteenth variation* could have more fervour. In the finale of the *First Concerto* his caressing of the lyrical string-tune is too cosy. Moreover he fails to match exactly his soloist's ardour in the big statement of the great melody at the climax of the finale of the *Second Concerto*. The *Fourth Concerto* has some spectacular moments but lacks a really firm profile. Even so, there is much to enjoy here, and Howard Shelley's contribution is consistently distinguished.

Kocsis has fleet fingers and he dashes through the first two concertos with remarkable panache and striking brilliance. But in No. 2 he gives the listener all too little time to savour incidental beauties or to surrender to the melancholy of the slow movement. He takes the first movement of the *Third Concerto* at express speed; undoubtedly there is some exciting playing here and he earns at least one listener's thanks for opting for the shorter cadenza in the first movement, which he plays with electrifying bra-vura. The *Fourth Concerto* is a good deal less rushed, though it is full of excitement and virtuosity when this is required, and the *Rhapsody* brings more thrilling playing. But there are moments, both here and in the concertos, when Kocsis should perhaps rein in his fiery high spirits. He is carried away just a little too far by his own virtuosity and, although this can be very exciting, it is not the whole story. The Philips recording places him rather forward but there is no lack of orchestral detail, and there is plenty of range. Readers should note that the two discs are available separately, one coupling the *First* and *Fourth Concertos* with the *Paganini variations*, the other the *Second* and *Third Concertos* with the orchestral *Vocalise*.

Piano concertos Nos. 1 in F sharp min., Op. 1; 2 in C min., Op. 18.
(***) Olympia mono OCD 190 [id.]. Moura Lympany, Philh. O, Nicolai Malko – PROKOFIEV: *Piano concerto No. 1.* **(*)

Piano concerto No. 3 in D min., Op. 30.

(***) Olympia mono OCD 191 [id.]. Moura Lympany, New SO, Anthony Collins – PROKOFIEV: *Piano concerto No. 3.* **(*)

Moura Lympany's recording of the *Third* comes from a 1952 Decca LP; it sounds simply amazing for its age. Her EMI account of the *First* yields nothing in terms of virtuosity or panache to many bigger names on the international circuit, and the mono sound is very good, though it is not quite as impressive as in the Decca *Third.* In No. 3, as was the custom in the 1950s, she plays Rachmaninov's later cadenza. These are very fine performances which will give pleasure, and Olympia must be congratulated on restoring them to circulation in such excellent transfers.

Piano concerto No. 1 in F sharp min., Op. 1.

(M) *** Mercury 434 333-2 [id.]. Byron Janis, Moscow PO, Kondrashin – PROKOFIEV: *Piano concerto No. 3.* ***

As in the Prokofiev coupling, on the occasion of the first Western-engineered recordings made in the USSR, soloist and orchestra plainly challenged each other to the limit, and the American technical team brilliantly captured the warmly romantic and chimerical interpretation which resulted. The solo playing stands alongside that of Horowitz in this repertoire, scintillating in the finale, yet never offering virtuosity simply for its own sake. Even now the recording is impressive for its clarity of texture and subtle detail within a warm acoustic. The CD represents one of Wilma Cozart Fine's most successful transfers.

(i) *Piano concerto No. 1 in F sharp min., Op. 1;* (ii) *Rhapsody on a theme of Paganini, Op. 43.*

*** Virgin/EMI Dig. VC7 59506-2 [id.]. Pletnev, Philh. O, Pešek.

*** Decca Dig. 417 613-2; *417 613-4* [id.]. Ashkenazy, (i) Concg. O; (ii) Philh. O, Haitink.

Mikhail Pletnev's accounts of the *F sharp minor Concerto* and the *Rhapsody on a theme of Paganini* with the Philharmonia Orchestra under Libor Pešek are very fine indeed. The *Paganini rhapsody* is distinguished not only by quite stunning virtuosity and unobtrusive refinement but also by great feeling. This is playing of classic status, strong in personality and musicianship. The CD sounds especially vivid.

This coupling also finds Ashkenazy in excellent form. The *Paganini variations* are, if anything, even better than his earlier LP with Previn. Haitink gets splendid sound from the Philharmonia in the *Variations* and Decca provides excellent recording. The *First Concerto* is no less impressive, and the Concertgebouw Orchestra under Haitink offer luxurious support.

Piano concertos Nos. 1 in F sharp min., Op. 1; 3 in D min., Op. 30.

(N) **(*) Decca Dig. 448 219-2 [id.]. Thibaudet, Cleveland O, Ashkenazy.

Piano concerto No. 2 in C min., Op. 18; Rhapsody on a theme of Paganini, Op. 43.

(N) **(*) Decca Dig. 440 653-2 [id.]. Thibaudet, Cleveland O, Ashkenazy.

Jean-Yves Thibaudet gives an immaculate account of the *D minor Concerto* with the Cleveland Orchestra under Ashkenazy, himself a formidable exponent of the solo part; and one can only say much the same about the *Second Concerto*, which similarly fails to be really memorable. There are numerous felicities to report throughout the set, and one is never in any doubt as to the pianist's musicianship and intelligence. However, the playing is cultured rather than displaying the high-voltage exhilaration we have from, say, Argerich, Rachmaninov himself, Horowitz, Collard or (in No. 1) Pletnev. Transparent, well-detailed orchestral sound, and well balanced. Thoroughly recommendable, without quite being a first choice. The *Pagagnini Rhapsody* is the most striking performance here, with the 18th variation blossoming rapturously in the orchestra.

Piano concerto No. 2 in C min., Op. 18.

(M) *** RCA 09026 61961-2 [id.]. Van Cliburn, Chicago SO, Reiner – BEETHOVEN: *Concerto No. 5.* ***

(Y/B) (M) *** DG 447 420-2 [id.]. Sviatoslav Richter, Warsaw PO, Stanislaw Wislocki – TCHAIKOVSKY: *Piano concerto No. 1.* (**)

(N) (B) *** Decca Eclipse Dig. 448 221-2; *448 221-4* [id.]. Cristina Ortiz, RPO, Moshe Atzmon – TCHAIKOVSKY: *Piano concerto No. 1.* *(*)

(B) **(*) Erato/Warner Dig. 4509 92872-2 [id.]. Duchable, Strasbourg PO, Guschlbauer – GRIEG: *Concerto.* *(*)

With Reiner making a splendid partner, Van Cliburn's 1958 account of the Rachmaninov *C minor Concerto* is second to none. The pacing of the first movement is comparatively measured, but the climax is unerringly placed, remaining relaxed yet enormously telling. The finale too does not seek to demonstrate runaway bravura but has sparkle and excitement, with the lyrical element heart-warming to match the very beautiful account of the central *Adagio*, full of poetry and romantic feeling. The recording is wonderfully rich, with the Chicago acoustic adding a glorious ambient glow, while the piano, though forwardly placed, has an unexpected body and fullness of timbre. In the finale the cymbals demonstrate an excellent upper range, and the enhancement of the digital remastering almost makes this seem as if it were made yesterday. The coupling with Beethoven's *Emperor* is unusual but stimulating, with Reiner again participating impressively.

With Richter the long opening melody of the first movement is taken abnormally slowly, and it is only the sense of mastery that he conveys in every note which prevents one from complaining. The slow movement too is spacious – with complete justification this time – and the opening of the finale lets the floodgates open the other way, for Richter chooses a hair-raisingly fast allegro. He does not, however, let himself be rushed in the great secondary melody, so this is a reading of vivid contrasts. The sound is very good. It's a great pity that the performance chosen as the new coupling for DG's series of Legendary Recording performances should be Tchaikovsky's *First Concerto*, with Karajan and the Berlin Philharmonic. The Rachmaninov readily fits this description, but the Tchaikovsky certainly does not, except as an example of a performance where two great artists pull simultaneously in different directions.

Cristina Ortiz's account has the advantage of rich Decca digital sound. The performance is warmly romantic, the first-movement climax satisfyingly expansive and the *Adagio* glowingly poetic, while the finale brings sparklingly nimble articulation from Ortiz and a fine expressive breadth from the strings in the famous lyrical melody. However, the Postnikova version of the Tchaikovsky *B flat minor Concerto* which acts as coupling is too eccentric to be recommendable.

A fine, bold, romantic performance from François-René Duchable, well paced and involving. Guschlbauer provides good support, and the modern, digital sound is full-blooded and well balanced. Not a subtle account but an enjoyable one. Unfortunately, it is coupled with a barnstorming account which is inappropriate for the more elusive Grieg *Concerto*.

Piano concertos Nos. 2 in C min., Op. 18; 3 in D min., Op. 30.
(M) **(*) Decca 425 047-2 [id.]. Ashkenazy, (i) Moscow PO, Kondrashin; (ii) LSO, Fistoulari.

Piano concertos Nos. (i) 2 in C min, Op. 18; (ii) 3 in D min., Op. 30. Preludes: in C sharp min., Op. 3/2; in E flat, Op. 23/6.
(❀) (M) *** Mercury 432 759-2 [id.]. Byron Janis; (i) Minneapolis SO; (ii) LSO, Antal Dorati.

Byron Janis has the full measure of this music: his shapely lyrical phrasing and natural response to the ebb and flow of the melodic lines is a constant source of pleasure. In the finale there is all the sparkling bravura one could ask for, but the great lyrical tune is made beguilingly poetic. Although the 1960 recording has plenty of ambience, the Minneapolis violins lack the richness of the LSO strings, recorded at Watford in 1961. The simple opening of the *Third Concerto* benefits from the extra warmth, and Janis lets the theme unwind with appealing spontaneity, and in the great closing climax of the finale the passion is built up – not too hurriedly – to the greatest possible tension. Janis makes two cuts (following the composer's own practice), one of about ten bars in the second movement and a rather longer one in the finale. Two favourite *Preludes*, with the *E flat* coming first, most persuasively played, make some compensation.

Ashkenazy's first (1963) recording of the *C minor Concerto* is more successful than his much later, digital account with Haitink, but less compelling than his second version with Previn, which remains uniquely beautiful. But the performance with Kondrashin offers superb Walthamstow sound and, though Kondrashin does not hold the first movement at a consistent level of tension and its climax is almost over-stated in its accented emphasis, the close of the *Andante* is ravishing (if not quite as fine as with Previn) and no one should be disappointed with the passionate climax of the finale. The *Third Concerto* is another matter. Anatole Fistoulari proved a splendid partner, and this reading is the freshest and most spontaneous of his four recordings of this elusive work. Both CD transfers are outstandingly successful and the vintage (again Walthamstow) sound-balance is very satisfying, present, full-bodied and vivid.

(i) *Piano concerto No. 2;* (ii) *Rhapsody on a theme of Paganini.*
(M) *** Decca 417 702-2 [id.]. Ashkenazy, LSO, Previn.
(BB) *** Naxos Dig. 8.550117; 4550117 [id.]. Jandó, Budapest SO, Lehel.
(B) *** CfP Dig. CD-CFP 9017; TC-CFP 4383. Tirimo, Philh. O, Levi.
(N) (M) (***) Dutton mono CDLXT 2504 [id.]. Julius Katchen; (i) New SO of L., Fistoulari; (ii) LPO, Boult – DOHNANYI: *Variations on a nursery theme.* (***)

For those not investing in the two-disc set, below, which includes the *Third Concerto* played by the same artists, Decca's recoupling of Ashkenazy's earlier recordings with Previn is a very desirable CD indeed. At mid-price it makes a first choice. In the *Concerto*, the gentle, introspective mood of the *Adagio* is among the most beautiful on record. The finale is broad and spacious rather than electrically exciting, but the scintillating, unforced bravura provides all the sparkle necessary. The *Rhapsody* too is outstandingly successful. The Kingsway Hall sound is rich and full-bodied in the best analogue sense. Detail is somewhat sharper in the *Rhapsody*; in the *Concerto*, however, atmosphere rather than clarity is the predominating factor.

Jenö Jandó's performances of both works are strongly recommendable. Jandó has the full measure of the ebb and flow of the Rachmaninovian phraseology, and the slow movement is romantically expansive, the reprise particularly beautiful, while the finale has plenty of dash and ripe, lyrical feeling. The *Rhapsody* is played brilliantly, as fine as any performance in the catalogue. The digital recording is satisfyingly balanced, with a bold piano image and a full, resonant orchestral tapestry.

Concentrated and thoughtful, deeply expressive yet never self-indulgent, Tirimo is outstanding in both the *Concerto* and the *Rhapsody*, making this another of the most desirable bargain versions of this favourite coupling, irrespective of price. Speeds for the outer movements of the *Concerto* are on the fast side, yet Tirimo's feeling for natural rubato makes them sound natural, never breathless, while the sweetness and repose of the middle movement are exemplary. The digital recording is full, clear and well balanced.

This vivid Dutton transfer helps to explain why Julius Katchen's coupling of the Rachmaninov and Dohnányi *Variations* was a classic of the mono LP catalogue, surviving well into the stereo era. The very opening (both musically and sonically) is enormously commanding: Katchen and Boult together capture a sense of new discovery that keeps one riveted from one variation to the next, each one sharply characterized. Katchen's muscular purposefulness in Rachmaninov's virtuoso variations gives way to a most poetic account of the great eighteenth variation, with the entry of the melody magically prepared in the subdued seventeenth. Katchen's rubato is extreme but tenderly spontaneous-sounding. The piano sound is full and firm with fine presence, yet (as in so many early Decca transfers) there is a degree of thinness on exposed high violins, and that shortcoming is more noticeable in the transfer of the *Concerto*, a recording dating from three years earlier, in 1951, with shallower piano tone but with compensating warmth of atmosphere. Katchen's is again a fine reading and, if it is not quite as magnetic or individual as that of the *Rhapsody*, for IM (who wrote the notes accompanying the CD, but not the preceding comments) it was the performance from which he came to discover and love the work, and it remains special, most notably for the fine contribution of the conductor, Anatole Fistoulari. .

(i) *Piano concertos Nos. 2–3; Rhapsody on a theme of Paganini. Preludes: in C sharp min., Op. 3/2; in B flat & G min., Op. 23/2 & 5; in B min. & D flat, Op. 32/10 & 13; Etudes-tableaux, Op. 39/1, 2 & 5.*
(B) *** Double Decca 436 386-2 (2) [id.]. Ashkenazy, (i) LSO, Previn.

This pair of Decca CDs – offered for the cost of a single premium-price disc – includes outstanding performances of Rachmaninov's three greatest concertante works for piano and orchestra, plus five favourite *Preludes* and three of the Op. 39 *Etudes-tableaux*. The digital remastering offers first-class transfers, full and well-balanced, with the Kingsway Hall ambience casting a pleasing glow over the proceedings. This is very highly recommendable, including as it does Ashkenazy's outstanding version of the *C minor Piano concerto*, where the slow movement is memorably beautiful.

(i) *Piano concerto No. 2 in C min., Op. 18; Etudes-tableaux, Op. 39/1–2, 4–6 & 9.*
*** RCA Dig. 07863 57982 [7982-2-RC]. Evgeny Kissin, (i) LSO, Valentin Gergiev.

Evgeny Kissin phrases intelligently and resists the temptation to play to the gallery in any way. He produces a beautiful sound throughout and it is a compliment to him that any comparisons that spring to mind are with great pianists. The LSO under Valentin Gergiev give him every support. The six *Etudes tableaux* are imaginatively played and impressively characterized. The recording is well balanced and truthful.

Piano concerto No. 3 in D min., Op. 30.
(N) *** Ph. 446 673-2 [id.]. Martha Argerich, Berlin RSO, Chailly – TCHAIKOVSKY: *Piano concerto No. 1.* ***
*** Chesky CD 76. Earl Wild, RPO, Horenstein – MACDOWELL: *Piano concerto No. 2.* *** ✿
**(*) Decca Dig. 417 239-2 [id.]. Ashkenazy, Concg. O, Haitink.
(***) Testament mono SBT 1029 [id.]. Gilels, Paris Conservatoire O, Cluytens (with SHOSTAKOVICH: *Prelude and fugue in D*) – SAINT-SAENS: *Piano concerto No. 2.* (***)
*(**) RCA 09026 61564 [id.]. Horowitz, NYPO, Ormandy.
(Y/B) (*(**)) VAI mono VAIA IPA 1027 [id.]. William Kapell, Toronto SO, Sir Ernest MacMillan – KHACHATURIAN: \Piano concerto. (**)

(i) *Piano concerto No. 3. Etudes tableaux, Opp. 33/1–3 & 6; 39/6.*
(N) **(*) EMI/Virgin Dig. VC5 45173-2 [id.]. Leif Ove Andsnes, (i) Oslo PO, Paavo Berglund.

(i) *Piano concerto No. 3. Prelude in B flat, Op. 23/2; Vocalise, Op. 34/14.*
** RCA Dig. 09026 61548-2 [id.]. Kissin; (i) Boston SO, Ozawa.

(i) *Piano concerto No. 3. Sonata No. 2 in B flat min., Op. 36; Moment musical in E flat min., Op. 16/2; Polka; Prelude in C, Op. 32/5.*
(M) (***) RCA (mono) GD 87754 [7754-2-RC-]. Vladimir Horowitz; (i) with RCA SO, Reiner.

There are few finer examples of live recording than Martha Argerich's electrifying performance of Rachmaninov's *Third concerto*, recorded in Berlin in 1982. Her volatility and dash are entirely at one with the romantic spirit of this music, and her interpretation is so commanding that individual eccentricities seem a natural part of the chimerical musical flow. Moreover she plays with great tenderness (well supported by Chailly) in the *Adagio* and the lyrical theme of the finale. Throughout the concerto her bursts of scintillating bravura are quite hair-raising (comparison with Horowitz is not to her disadvantage), yet at the end of the last movement there is a touching pause before she dashes into the final straight with coruscating brilliance. The rush of romantic adrenalin at the close (well supported by the orchestra) is thrilling and brings forth a well-deserved response from the audience in which the listener is tempted to join. The recording is very good; the strings might have been better flattered in the studio but the overall sound-picture satisfyingly demonstrates the skill of the Philips engineering team.

Earl Wild's *Third Concerto* is also among the very finest versions of this work on record. Wild favours the less elaborate version of the first-movement cadenza and plays it with compelling bravura. Horenstein proves a most understanding partner. This alternative coupling on Chesky of the *Third Concerto* with the MacDowell *Second Concerto* is very attractive, but it is a full-priced CD, whereas the Chandos Rachmaninov pairing of the *Second* and *Third Concertos* (see above) is at mid-price.

Horowitz's RCA account with Reiner dates from 1951. As a performance it is full of poetry, yet electrifying in its excitement. In spite of its dated sound and a less than ideal balance, its magic comes over and it is to be preferred to his later performance with Ormandy. The *Sonata* comes from live concerts in 1980 and is also pretty electrifying. He plays the conflation he made (and which Rachmaninov approved) of the 1913 original and the 1931 revision plus a few further retouchings he subsequently added. An indispensable part of any Rachmaninov collection which, in its digitally remastered form, sounds better than it has before.

In January 1978 Horowitz was persuaded to re-record the work in stereo, this time at a live concert, with Ormandy drawing a committed and romantically expansive accompaniment from the New York Philharmonic Orchestra. Perhaps just a little of the old magic is missing in the solo playing, but it remains prodigious and Horowitz's insights are countless. The snag is the recording, which was originally very dry and clinical, the piano timbre lacking bloom. For CD, the remastering has altered the sound-picture radically, considerably softening the focus to bring a more romantic aura to the music-making. The result is that at lower dynamic levels the image appears to recede. The effect is disconcerting – but one can adjust to it, and certainly the effect is more agreeable than the 'bare bones' of the original LP sound-quality.

Gilels's classic account of the *Concerto* with André Cluytens and the Paris Conservatoire Orchestra comes from 1955 and belongs among the 'greats'. The piano-sound is a bit shallow and at times the balance favours the soloist unduly – but what lovely playing. Rachmaninov's own account cannot be displaced, nor, for that matter, the Horowitz/Reiner version, but this should still be in the collections of all who have an interest in Rachmaninov and piano playing.

During his short life William Kapell was closely identified with this concerto, and this performance was recorded in Toronto at a public concert in 1948 when he would have been in his mid-twenties. It is obvious that he knew Rachmaninov's own recording, and equally obvious that he is also very much his own man. He is one of the very few pianists who can be compared to Horowitz and Rachmaninov himself. He plays the same cadenza as they did. The sound is very poor indeed, but the playing is absolutely electrifying. If only some of the more recent performances the companies have been offering had a tenth its level of energy, sheer abandon and poetic ardour.

Ashkenazy has recorded this concerto four times; as a work, it seems to prove elusive for him. On his Decca digital disc he is beautifully recorded and there is unfailing sensitivity and musicianship, but one needs a greater sense of impact and focus – his very first recording with Fistoulari had more ardour and spontaneity.

Leif Ove Andsnes offers cultivated playing in the *D minor Concerto*, which is recorded at a public concert in Oslo. As always, he brings finesse and a refined musicianship to all he does, and the *Etudes tableaux* are touched with distinction. Berglund is supportive and free from egotism, but he does not draw from the Oslo players the refined sonority which Jansons commands. Nevertheless the many admirers of the young Norwegian pianist need not hesitate.

Yevgeni Kissin's opening is very measured and low-voltage. Yet there are a number of poetic insights which almost persuade the listener that the slow tempo is justified. The record is assembled from live performances and the piano is at times discoloured. Ozawa gets decent rather than distinguished results from the orchestra. The recording is curiously veiled and badly wanting in transparency at the top. Nothing this remarkable pianist does is without interest, but this cannot be a first recommendation.

Piano concerto No. 4 in G min., Op. 40 (see also below, under *Monna Vanna*).
⊛ *** EMI CDC7 49326-2 [id.]. Michelangeli, Philh. O, Gracis – RAVEL: *Piano concerto in G.* *** ⊛

This is one of the most brilliant piano records ever made. It puts the composer's own recorded performance quite in the shade, and the Ravel coupling is equally illuminating. The recording does not quite match the superlative quality of the playing but still sounds pretty good.

The Isle of the dead, Op. 29.
(M) *** RCA 09026 61250-2. Chicago SO, Reiner – Concert: *'The Reiner sound'.* ***
(N) (M) *** DG Dig. 445 558-2 [id.]. BPO, Maazel – RIMSKY-KORSAKOV: *Scheherazade.* **

Reiner builds the arch-like span of the music to an impassioned climax and manages the return to the sombre opening mood with equal distinction. The recording, made in 1957, is fairly closely balanced and, although the Chicago ambience remains, the upper strings lose some of their tonal weight at the climax and the range of dynamic is slightly reduced. Nevertheless this shows Reiner at his finest and there are other good things in this compilation.

At a fast speed Maazel's powerful reading of *The Isle of the dead* is less sombre and brooding than usual; but the climaxes have real fervour, and the result is intensely compelling. The 1981 recording is strikingly vivid and full, and it is a pity that the Rimsky-Korsakov coupling is far less recommendable.

The Isle of the dead, Op. 29; Symphonic dances, Op. 45.
(M) *** Decca Dig. 430 733-2. Concg. O, Ashkenazy.
(BB) **(*) Naxos Dig. 8.550583 [id.]. RPO, Enrique Bátiz.

Ashkenazy's is a superb coupling, rich and powerful in playing and interpretation, *The Isle of the dead* relentless in its ominous build-up, while the *Symphonic dances* have extra darkness and intensity too. The splendid digital recording highlights both the passion and the fine precision of the playing.

Bátiz gives the *Symphonic dances* an attractively spontaneous performance, full of lyrical intensity, with some splendid playing from the RPO strings. The vivid recording helps give the feeling that Bátiz almost goes over the top in his extremely passionate climax for *The Isle of the dead*. The performance certainly does not lack darker feelings, and at super-bargain price this remains well worth considering.

Symphonic dances, Op. 45.
(Y/B) *** Everest EVC 9002 [id.]. LSO, Sir Eugene Goossens – STRAVINSKY: *Rite of spring* **

Symphonic dances, Op. 45; (i) Vocalise, Op. 34/14.
(Y/B) (M) *** Sony SMK 57660 [id.]. Novosibirsk PO, Arnold Kaz; (i) with Nelly Lee – STRAVINSKY: *Jeu de cartes.* **(*)

Sir Eugene Goossens conducts a particularly attractive performance of the three *Symphonic dances*. The lyrical secondary theme of the first movement, introduced by the saxophone, is hauntingly nostalgic and the same bitter-sweet lyricism is felt in the '*valse triste*' of the second movement. The burst of passionate feeling and the underlying hint of foreboding are convincingly resolved in the finale. The LSO playing is first class; there is ardour and exuberance, yet ensemble holds crisply together. The recording from the late 1950s is one of the finest of those which Everest made at Walthamstow: full-bodied, clear and with just the right degree of brilliance. But at full price this reissue is uncompetitive.

Arnold Kaz is not a household name and Novosibirsk is not on the common tourist trail, but there is nothing offbeat about this performance. Indeed the *Symphonic dances* get a more than respectable performance; the playing of the Novosibirsk Philharmonic is warm and musical, and Arnold Kaz draws imaginative and sensitive phrasing from his players. A far more enjoyable performance than many from better-known orchestras and glossier maestros – and very well recorded. Without disrespect to Nelly Lee, who trained (and now teaches) at St Petersburg, it would have been better to have had the purely instrumental version of *Vocalise*.

SYMPHONIES

Symphonies Nos. 1–3.
(N) (B) *** Decca Double Dig. 448 116-2 [id.]. Concg. O, Ashkenazy.

Symphonies Nos. 1–3; The Isle of the dead, Op. 29; Symphonic dances, Op. 45; Vocalise, Op. 34/14; Aleko: Intermezzo & Women's dance.
(M) *** EMI CMS7 64530-2 (3) [id.]. LSO, André Previn.

Symphonies Nos. 1–3; The Rock, Op. 7.
(N) (M) **(*) DG Dig. 445 590-2 (2) [id.]. BPO, Maazel.

Reissued at Double Decca price, the Ashkenazy digital set, made between 1980 and 1982, sweeps the board; it can be given an unqualified recommendation, even if a break between the two discs is necessary at the centrepoint of the *Second Symphony*. The performances, passionate and volatile, are intensely Russian; the only possible reservation concerns the slow movement of the *Second*, where the clarinet solo is less ripe than in some versions. Elsewhere there is drama, energy and drive, balanced by much delicacy of feeling, while the Concertgebouw strings produce great ardour for Rachmaninov's long-breathed melodies. The vivid Decca sound within the glowing Concertgebouw ambience is ideal for the music. The three symphonies are also available separately at mid-price with various couplings (436 479/480/481-2).

While Ashkenazy's digital Double Decca set of the three Rachmaninov symphonies with the Concertgebouw Orchestra will probably remain first choice for many collectors, Previn's LSO set at mid-price offers some alternative couplings. His 1973 account of the *Second Symphony* – the most passionately committed performance on record, with a glorious response from the LSO strings – has been remastered for CD a second time, with improvement in the body of the string timbre. This remains a classic account, unlikely to be surpassed. No. 1 is a forthright, clean-cut performance, beautifully played and very well recorded. It may lack some of the vitality that one recognizes in Russian performances (Ashkenazy is more volatile and remains first choice in this work) but is still very enjoyable. Previn's account of the *Third*, however, is outstanding and the LSO's playing again has enormous bravura and ardour. This, like *The Isle of the dead* and *Symphonic dances*, has been remastered very successfully and the performances of the two shorter works have plenty of atmosphere and grip. With the *Aleko* excerpts and the *Vocalise* also included, this EMI box remains very competitive.

Maazel's set is also very impressive and offers superb playing from the Berlin Philharmonic. However, the DG engineers secured a less sumptuous sound in the Berlin Philharmonie than their Decca colleagues, and this emphasizes Maazel's fiercer way with Rachmaninov's passionate impulse. The climaxes of the *Second Symphony* in particular would have been enhanced by a warmer middle and lower range. Maazel's readings are not to be dismissed: the *First Symphony* is particularly fine, with Rachmaninov's often thick orchestration beautifully transparent. The *Third* too is distinctive, unusually fierce and intense. The result is sharper and tougher than one expects, less obviously romantic, and the finale is made to sound rather like a Walton comedy overture at the start, brilliant and exciting; but at the end it lacks joyful exuberance. Exhilaration is the keynote throughout and there is an abundance of adrenalin, yet the lack of expansive romantic warmth is undoubtedly a drawback. Moreover (although it also includes *The Rock*) this is at mid-price, while the Ashkenazy recordings are on a Double Decca – two discs for the cost of one premium-priced CD.

Symphony No. 1 in D min.; The Isle of the dead, Op. 29.
*** Virgin/EMI Dig. VC7 59547-2 [id.]. RPO, Andrew Litton.

Symphony No. 1 in D min.; The Rock (fantasy), Op. 7; Vocalise, Op. 34/14; Aleko: Intermezzo.
(M) *** DG Dig. 435 594-2 [id.]. BPO, Maazel.

With a darkly intense account of *The Isle of the dead* as a generous fill-up, Litton's version of the *Symphony* brings exceptionally beautiful sound which captures the RPO strings in luminous form. This is a powerful performance, as the very opening indicates, but it is just as remarkable for its refinement and gentler qualities, with Litton persuasive in his free use of rubato.

Maazel's is a superb performance, beautifully transparent and consistently clarifying detail. He may lack something in Slavonic passion but, with generous fill-ups, the positive strength of the reading stands well against any rival. The 1984 recording is drier than Ashkenazy's Decca.

Symphony No. 1 in D min.; Etudes-tableaux, Op. 39/2, 6, 7 & 9 (orch. Respighi).
(Y/B) *** Nimbus Dig. NI 5311 [id.]. BBC Welsh SO, Tadaaki Otaka.

Tadaaki Otaka's is a characterful and excellently shaped reading of the *First Symphony*. The recording, too, is very acceptable, though detail is not as well defined or as cleanly laid out as in some other three-star versions, thanks no doubt to the resonance of the acoustic. Respighi's masterly transcriptions of the four *Etudes-tableaux* comprise an appealing makeweight and may sway many collectors. This Nimbus disc is not a first choice but still merits three stars.

Symphony No. 2 in E min., Op. 27.
(M) *** Carlton Dig. PCD 904 [id.]. LSO, Rozhdestvensky.
(BB) *** ASV CDQS 6107 [id.]. Philh. O, Ling Tung.
(Y/B) (M) **(*) Chandos Dig. CHAN 6606 [id.]. SNO, Sir Alexander Gibson.
**(*) Ph. Dig. 438 864-2 [id.]. Kirov O, Gergiev.

Symphony No. 2 in E min., Op. 27; The Rock, Op. 7.
**(*) DG Dig. 439 888-2 [id.]. Russian Nat. O, Pletnev.

Symphony No. 2 in E min., Op. 27; Scherzo in D min.; Vocalise, Op. 34/14.
*** EMI Dig. CDC5 55140-2 [id.]. St Petersburg PO, Jansons.

Symphony No. 2; (i) *Vocalise, Op. 34/14.*
*** Virgin/EMI Dig. VC7 59548-2 [id.]. RPO, Andrew Litton.
**(*) Telarc Dig. CD 80312 [id.]. (i) Sylvia McNair; Baltimore SO, David Zinman.

Rozhdestvensky gives a very Tchaikovskian reading of Rachmaninov's *E minor Symphony*. There is plenty of vitality but, with the big string melodies blossoming voluptuously, the slow movement, after a beguiling opening clarinet solo, has a climax of spacious intensity, its power almost overwhelming. The finale is flamboyantly broadened at the end, and the feeling of apotheosis is very much in the Tchaikovsky mould. With the LSO responding superbly, this is a most satisfying account, and the richness, brilliance and weight of the recording add to the compulsion of the music-making.

Refinement is the mark of Litton's well-paced reading, with the RPO caught in glowing form by the engineers as in the rest of the cycle. There is power in plenty, and Litton readily sustains his observance of the exposition repeat in the first movement, making it a very long movement indeed at over 23 minutes. But the moments of special magic are those where, as in his lightly pointed account of the Scherzo or, most of all, the lovely clarinet melody of the slow movement, subtlety of expression gives Rachmaninov's romanticism an extra poignancy.

Jansons's newest St Petersburg account offers a strong, warm reading in which climaxes are thrust home powerfully, with full dramatic impact. Phrasing is warmly idiomatic, even if occasionally over-moulded, and the recording gives fine body and immediacy to the sound, outshining most latter-day rivals. In Russian fashion the clarinet in the slow movement sounds like an organ stop. A warm, exciting reading which stands among the best modern versions. The coupling is generous, when in addition to *Vocalise*, beautifully done, it offers the early orchestral *Scherzo* of 1887.

Ling Tung's reading is refined but he knows just how to mould the sweeping lines necessary to bring out the rapture inherent in this lovely symphony, notably at the climax of the slow movement and at the very satisfying close. This is a case where the CD transfer brings a striking improvement in the vividness of a 1978 recording which is backwardly balanced. One needs to play back at a fairly high level, then the Philharmonia strings emerge with a warmly natural, radiant sheen of tone. At super-bargain price this is well worth considering.

Gibson and the Scottish National Orchestra have the advantage of an excellent digital recording, made in the Henry Wood Hall in Glasgow. The brass sounds are thrilling, but the slightly recessed balance of the strings is a drawback and there is not the body of tone demonstrated by the best version recommended above. But this is a freshly spontaneous performance and overall the sound is admirably natural, even if it includes some strangely unrhythmic thuds at climaxes (apparently the conductor in his excitement stamping on the podium).

Pletnev brings a fresh mind to this symphony, with his approach very much controlled, giving a strong sense of onward current and producing none of the heart-on-sleeve emotion that can often afflict the slow movement, which seems to be conceived in one long paragraph. The clarity and lightness of articulation that distinguish his piano playing seem to be in ample evidence and, throughout the work, feeling is held in perfect control. It is a performance of quality, though the recording, while good, could be cleaner-detailed in the lower end of the range. Ensemble is endangered by some frenetically fast speeds – as in the finale. *The Rock*, inspired by Lermontov, makes a generous coupling.

As in his opera recordings, Gergiev gives a strong and well-paced reading, if lacking a little in individuality. Although he takes what one might think of as a more traditional approach, he brings an appropriate warmth and also possesses considerable command of the architecture. His first movement (with repeat) is very spacious (22½ minutes). Like Litton, Temirkanov and Zinman, Gergiev observes the exposition repeat in the first movement.

After a slack start Zinman builds the symphony persuasively, if with less character than some, helped by first-rate playing from the Baltimore orchestra. Good, clean sound. The coupling is an attraction when, unlike most rivals, Zinman has *Vocalise* with soprano soloist, the radiant Sylvia McNair. Even with that extra, Zinman manages to observe the exposition repeat in the first movement of the symphony.

Symphony No. 3 in A min., Op. 44.
(M) *** EMI CDM7 69564-2. LSO, Previn – SHOSTAKOVICH: *Symphony No. 6.* ***
*** Chandos Dig. CHAN 8614 [id.]. LSO, Järvi – KALLINIKOV: *Intermezzos.* ***

Symphony No. 3 in A min.; Isle of the dead, Op. 29.
*** Nimbus Dig. NI 5344 [id.]. BBC Welsh SO, Tadaaki Otaka.

Symphony No. 3 in A min.; Symphonic dances, Op. 45.
*** Virgin/EMI Dig. VC7 59549-2 [id.]. RPO, Andrew Litton.

Previn's EMI CD brings an outstanding performance; the digital remastering brings plenty of body alongside the sharpened detail. Previn conveys the purposefulness of the writing at every point, revelling in the richness, but clarifying textures. The LSO has rarely displayed its virtuosity more brilliantly in the recording studio, and, with its generous Shostakovich coupling, this is first choice for this symphony.

The gentleness of Litton's treatment of the great second-subject melody in the *Third Symphony* means that the transparent beauty of Rachmaninov's scoring is brought out superbly. The slow movement has rarely been done so tenderly and, though the opening of the finale may sound not urgent enough, it is crisply pointed and leads on to a superbly brisk, tense conclusion. In the *Symphonic dances* the refinement and beauty go with sharp, clean attack, making an ideal and generous coupling for the *Symphony*.

Tadaaki Otaka's performance of the *Third Symphony* unfolds with complete naturalness and unfailing musical instinct that reflect great credit on their gifted Japanese conductor. There is no trace of unwelcome showmanship, but no lack of panache either. Tempi in all three movements are eminently well judged and phrases are well shaped. Apart from excellent orchestral playing, the technical side of the recording is also handled expertly. A natural concert-hall perspective with plenty of warmth from the acoustic but no lack of detail. The *Isle of the dead* is no less well served and this can be recommended along with the very best on the market.

Järvi in his weighty, purposeful way misses some of the subtleties of this symphony, but with superb playing from the LSO – linking back to André Previn's unsurpassed reading with them – the intensity is magnetic, with even a very slow *Adagio* for the outer sections of the middle movement made to sound convincing, and with the finale thrusting on at an equivalently extreme tempo.

CHAMBER AND INSTRUMENTAL MUSIC

Trios élégiaques Nos. 1 in G min., Op. 8; 2 in D min., Op. 9.
*** Chandos Dig. CHAN 8431 [id.]. Borodin Trio.

The *Trios* are both imbued with lyrical fervour and draw from the rich vein of melancholy so characteristic of Rachmaninov. The performances by the Borodin Trio are eloquent and masterly, and the recording is admirably balanced.

PIANO MUSIC

Music for 2 pianos: (i) *Suites Nos. 1–2, Opp. 5 & 17; Symphonic dances, Op. 45; Russian rhapsody;* (Solo piano) *Etudes-tableaux, Op. 33; Variations on a theme by Corelli, Op. 42.*
(N) (B) *** Decca Double 444 845-2 (2) [id.]. Vladimir Ashkenazy, (i) with André Previn.

The colour and flair of Rachmaninov's writing in the two *Suites* (as inspired and tuneful as his concertos) are captured with wonderful imagination – reflective of a live performance by Ashkenazy and Previn in the summer of 1974. The two-piano version of the *Symphonic dances* was written not as an arrangement of the orchestral score but as a preparation for it. The ingenuity of Rachmaninov's handling of a difficult medium produced a work which in pianistic detail as well as sharpness of argument is masterly. Ashkenazy and Previn are challenged to a dazzling performance, and they are hardly less persuasive in the coupled *Russian rhapsody*, an early piece, musically rather naïve but well worth hearing in a performance as fine as this. Ashkenazy's superb solo performances of the *Etudes-tableaux* and the *Corelli variations* (a rarity and a very fine work) cap the appeal of this bargain Double. The recording throughout is superb, with a natural presence and a most attractive ambience.

Barcarolle in G min., Op. 10/3; Etudes-tableaux, Op. 39/4 & 6; Humoresque in G, Op. 10/5; Lilacs, Op. 21/ 5; 5 Morceaux de fantaisie, Op. 3: (Elégie in E flat min.; Prelude in C sharp min.; Mélodie in E; Polichinelle in F sharp min.; Sérénade in B flat min.); Polka de W. R.; Prelude in G min., Op. 23/5.

Transcriptions: MUSSORGSKY: *Hopak*. SCHUBERT: *Wohin?*. RIMSKY-KORSAKOV: *Flight of the bumble-bee*. KREISLER: *Liebeslied; Liebesfreud. The Star-spangled banner*.
(M) *** Decca 425 964-2 [id.]. Sergei Rachmaninov (Ampico Roll recordings, 1919–29).

Daisies, Op. 38/3; Etudes-tableaux, Op. 33/2 & 7; Op. 39/6; Humoresque, Op. 10/5; Lilacs, Op. 21/5; Mélodie, Op. 3/5; Moment musical, Op. 16/2; Oriental sketch; Polka de W. R.; Preludes: in C sharp min., Op. 3/2; in G flat, Op. 23/10; in E, F min. & F, Op. 32/3, 6 & 7; Serenade, Op. 3/5. Transcriptions: BACH: *Violin partita No. 2: Prelude; Gavotte; Rondo; Gigue*. MENDELSSOHN: *Midsummer Night's Dream: Scherzo*. KREISLER: *Liebesfreud*. SCHUBERT: *Wohin?*. MUSSORGSKY: *Gopak*. TCHAIKOVSKY: *Lullaby, Op. 16/11*. RIMSKY-KORSAKOV: *The Flight of the bumble-bee*.
(M) (***) RCA mono GD 87766 [7766-2-RG]. Sergei Rachmaninov.

These two records make a fascinating comparison. The RCA collection includes virtually all Rachmaninov's solo electric 78–r.p.m. recordings, made between 1925 and 1942, with most dating from 1940. The second offers the composer's Ampico piano-roll recordings, made during a shorter time-span, between 1919 and 1929, when Rachmaninov was at his technical peak. The Ampico recordings were reproduced on a specially adapted Estonia concert grand in the Kingsway Hall and recorded in stereo in 1978/9. On CD the sound is outstandingly real and the impression on the listener is quite uncanny when the recital opens with the *Elégie in E flat minor*, which was put on roll in October 1928 yet has all the spontaneity and presence of live music-making. A number of items are common to both discs, so it is possible to make direct comparisons. The Ampico system at that time could accurately reflect what was played, including note duration and pedalling, but the *strength* at which the notes were struck had to be edited on to the roll afterwards by a skilled musician/technician. It can only be said that listening to these Ampico recordings never brings a feeling of any mechanical tone graduation, and in pieces like the *Humoresque in G major* or the *Polka de W. R.* not only does Rachmaninov's scintillating bravura sound absolutely natural, but also his chimerical use of rubato is more convincing on the earlier recordings. *The Flight of the bumble-bee*, a *tour de force* of exuberant articulation, brings only one second's difference in playing time between the two versions.

Etudes-tableaux, Opp. 33 & 39; Fragments; Fughetta in F; Mélodie in E; Moments musicaux; Morceaux de fantaisie; Morceaux de salon; 3 Nocturnes; Oriental sketch; 4 Pieces; Piece in D min.; 25 Preludes (complete); *Sonatas 1–3* (including original & revised versions of *No. 2*); *Song without words; Transcriptions* (complete); *Variations: on a theme of Chopin ; on a theme of Corelli*.
(M) *** Hyperion Dig. CDS 44041/8 (8). Howard Shelley.

Hyperion have collected Howard Shelley's exemplary survey of Rachmaninov into a mid-price, eight-CD set, and very good it is, too. Shelley can hold his own against most rivals not only in terms of poetic feeling (as you would expect from a distant descendant of the great poet) but in keyboard authority and virtuosity. The recordings are variable in quality but are mostly excellent.

Elégie, Op. 3/1; Etudes-tableaux, Op. 39/3 & 5; Moments musicaux, Op. 16/3–6; Preludes, Op. 23/1, 2, 5 & 6; Op. 32/12.
(Y/B) (M) *** EMI CD-EMX 2237. Andrei Gavrilov – SCRIABIN: *Preludes*. ***

There is some pretty remarkable playing here, especially in the stormy *B flat major Prelude*, while the *G sharp minor* from Op. 32 has a proper sense of fantasy. More prodigious bravura provides real excitement in the *F sharp minor Etude-tableau*, Op. 39/3, and in the *E minor Moment musical*, while Gavrilov relaxes winningly in the *Andante cantabile* of Op. 16/3 and the *Elégie*. Sometimes his impetuosity almost carries him away, and the piano is placed rather near the listener so that we are nearly taken with him, but there is no doubt about the quality of this recital.

Etudes-tableaux, Opp. 33 & 39.
*** Hyperion CDA 66091 [id.]. Howard Shelley.

The conviction and thoughtfulness of Shelley's playing, coupled with excellent modern sound, make this convenient coupling a formidable rival to Ashkenazy's classic versions, which in any case are not coupled together on CD.

Moments musicaux, Op. 16; Morceaux de salon, Op. 10.
*** Hyperion Dig. CDA 66184 [id.]. Howard Shelley.

Howard Shelley has a highly developed feeling for Rachmaninov and distinguishes himself here both by masterly pianism and by a refined awareness of Rachmaninov's sound-world. The recording is eminently realistic and natural.

Moments musicaux, Op. 16; Variations on a theme of Corelli, Op. 42. Transcriptions: *Daisies, Op. 38/3; Lilacs, Op. 21/5;* arr. of KREISLER: *Liebesleid; Liebesfreud.*
** Nimbus Dig. NI 5292 [id.]. Martin Jones.

Exemplary playing from this underrated artist, marred by less than satisfactory recording. The *Variations on a theme of Corelli* and the *Moments musicaux* are analogue recordings dating from 1977, while the four transcriptions are recorded digitally in 1991. The latter are more distantly balanced and the excessive reverberance does not flatter the piano tone. The pianist is still recorded from afar in the bigger works, but the results are nevertheless far more acceptable. The *Corelli variations* are particularly sensitive and idiomatic.

24 Preludes (complete).
*** Erato/Warner Dig. 4509 91714-2 (2) [id.]. Dame Moura Lympany.
(N) (B) ** Carlton IMP Dig. PCD 2052 [id.]. Peter Katin.

24 Preludes; Preludes in D min. and F; Morceaux de fantaisie, Op. 3.
*** Hyperion CDA 66081/2 (available separately) [id.]. Howard Shelley.

24 Preludes (complete); Piano sonata No. 2 in B flat min., Op. 36.
(Y/B) (BB) *** Decca Double 443 841-2 (2) [id.]. Vladimir Ashkenazy.

There is superb flair and panache about Ashkenazy's playing. Perhaps the stormy *B flat major Prelude*, Op. 23/2, is even more hair-raising in Sviatoslav Richter's hands but, as the *G minor Prelude* demonstrates, Ashkenazy's poetic feeling is second to none. At Double Decca price this sweeps the board. As a bonus, the compact discs offer the *Second Piano sonata*, with Ashkenazy generally following the 1913 original score but with some variants. He plays with great virtuosity and feeling, and the result is a *tour de force*.

Moura Lympany's new Erato recording of the Rachmaninov *Preludes* repeats an early success. While the pieces that need bravura seem to offer her no problems, she is at her finest in the lyrical pieces, which truly blossom in her hands, and the famous *G minor* and *A flat major* from Op. 23 are memorable. The whole set moves forward spontaneously, and this make a genuine alternative to the Decca Ashkenazy set, with fine, full and vivid recording of the piano. If you want the utmost bravura, then Ashkenazy would be first choice (and he isn't lacking in poetic feeling), but for romantic warmth the new set is hard to beat. The snag is that the two CDs play for barely 81 minutes: the whole set might just have been squeezed on a single CD.

Shelley is a compellingly individual interpreter of Rachmaninov. Each one of the *Preludes* strikes an original chord in him. These are very different readings from those of Ashkenazy but their intensity is well caught in full if reverberant recording.

Peter Katin's performances are neatly fitted on to a single CD, just seconds short of 80 minutes. The recording was made in 1972 but the bold, clear image itself lends a certain romantic splendour to these performances. Katin has the measure of lyrical music, and it is only in the pieces which make their full effect by sheer bravura that he is at times less than completely convincing.

Preludes: Op. 3/2; Op. 23/1–2, 4–6; Mélodie, Op. 3/3; Polichinelle, Op. 3/4; Variations on a theme of Corelli, Op. 42.
*** Conifer Dig. 75605 51159-2 [id.]. Kathryn Stott.

Kathryn Stott has a good feeling for Rachmaninov and gives well-considered accounts of all the pieces on this generously filled CD; there is a strong rhythmic grip and her phrasing is keenly articulate.

13 Preludes, Op. 32.
*** DG Dig. 427 766-2 [id.]. Lilya Zilberstein – SHOSTAKOVICH: *Sonata No. 1.* ***

Lilya Zilberstein faces rather more formidable competition in the Rachmaninov *Preludes* than in the Shostakovich *Sonata*, but she has technique, style and finesse, and the recording is excellent.

Piano sonatas Nos. 1 in D min., Op. 28; 2 in B flat min., Op. 36 (revised 1931).
*** Hyperion CDA 66047 [id.]. Howard Shelley.

Howard Shelley offers here the 1931 version of the *B flat Sonata*. He has plenty of sweep and grandeur and an appealing freshness, ardour and, when required, tenderness. He is accorded an excellent balance by the engineers.

Piano sonata No. 2 in B flat min., Op. 36 (original version); *Etudes-tableaux, Op. 33/1, 39/4 & 7; Morceaux de fantaisie, Op. 3/3 & 5; Preludes, Op. 23/1 & 7; 32/2, 6, 9 & 10.*
(N) 🏵 *** Ph. Dig. 446 220-2 [id.]. Zoltán Kocsis.

This is one of the finest Rachmaninov recital discs to have come out in recent years. Be it in the smaller, reflective pieces or in the bigger-boned *B flat minor Sonata*, Zoltán Kocsis's piano speaks with totally idiomatic accents, effortless virtuosity and a keen poetic feeling. This is a most distinguished offering and is recommended with enthusiasm. Excellent recording.

Piano sonata No. 2 in B flat min., Op. 36 (original version); *Fragments in A flat; Fughetta in F; Gavotte in D; Mélodie in E; Morceau de fantaisie in G min.; Nocturnes Nos. 1–3; Oriental sketch in B flat; Piece in D min.; 4 Pieces; Prelude in E flat min.; Romance in F sharp min.; Song without words in D min.*
*** Hyperion CDA 66198 [id.]. Howard Shelley.

Howard Shelley now gives us the original version of Op. 36 and his performances here show unfailing sensitivity, intelligence and good taste. They have the merit of excellent recorded sound. A valuable issue.

Suites Nos. 1–2, Opp. 5 & 17; Symphonic dances, Op. 45.
*** Hyperion Dig. CDA 66375 [id.]. Howard Shelley, Hilary Macnamara.

Howard Shelley and Hilary Macnamara give strong performances of both the *Suites* and the *Symphonic dances*. In the *Suites* their responses are not quite as imaginative as those of Ashkenazy and Previn, but there is plenty of dramatic fire in the *Symphonic dances* in this generously filled disc.

Suite No. 2, Op. 17; Russian rhapsody, Op. posth.; Symphonic dances, Op. 45.
*** Hyperion Dig. CDA 66654 [id.]. Nikolai Demidenko, Dmitri Alexeev – MEDTNER: *Russian round dance* etc. **(*)

There are some beautiful things on the Alexeev–Demidenko disc. They shape the second group of the first of the *Symphonic dances* with exquisite sensitivity and colour, and there are many other felicities elsewhere. However, even allowing for the hazards of two pianos, there is some ugly fortissimo tone, which one never finds in a Kissin or a Pletnev recording. There is much to delight the listener all the same, even though Previn and Ashkenazy are to be preferred in this repertoire.

Transcriptions: *Daisies; Lilacs; Polka de W. R.; Vocalise.* BACH: *Prelude; Gavotte; Gigue.* BIZET: *Minuet from L'Arlésienne.* KREISLER: *Liebesleid; Liebesfreud.* MENDELSSOHN: *Midsummer Night's Dream: Scherzo.* MUSSORGSKY: *Sorochinsky Fair: Gopak.* RIMSKY-KORSAKOV: *Flight of the bumble-bee.* SCHUBERT: *Wohin?.* TCHAIKOVSKY: *Lullaby.*
*** Hyperion Dig. CDA 66486 [id.]. Howard Shelley.

Shelley plays with an authority and sensitivity that is wholly persuasive and dispatches the virtuoso transcriptions to the manner born. The transcription of the *Vocalise* is by Zoltán Kocsis, but otherwise all are Rachmaninov's own.

Piano transcriptions: J. S. BACH: *Partita in E min., for unaccompanied violin (Preludio; Gavotte; Gigue).* BIZET: *Minuet from l'Arlésienne.* KREISLER: *Liebesleid; Liebesfreud.* MENDELSSOHN: *Midsummer Night's Dream: Scherzo.* MUSSORGSKY: *Sorochinsky Fair: Gopak.* RACHMANINOV: *Lilacs, Op. 21/5; Daisies, Op. 38/3.* RIMSKY-KORSAKOV: *Flight of the bumble-bee.* SCHUBERT: *Wohin?.* SMITH: *The Star-Spangled Banner.* TCHAIKOVSKY: *Lullaby.*
(N) (BB) ** CfP Silver Double CD CFPSD 4748 (2). Ian Hobson – CHOPIN: *Etudes, Opp. 10 & 25.* **

Ian Hobson's formidable virtuosity is heard to remarkable effect here, but even so one feels he should learn to relax more. His clean articulation suits the Bach transcriptions and Bizet's *Minuet* and is suitably brilliant, if at times less precise, in the famous Mendelssohn display piece. He plays Mussorgsky's *Gopak* boldly with wilful rubato, the coda not entirely convincing, but the *Flight of the bumble-bee* dazzles. The two famous Rachmaninov songs are affectionate, but Schubert's *Wohin?* brings a too insistent staccato; not all will respond to his forcefulness in the Kreisler pieces, and *Liebesfreud*, for all its chimerical bravura, would have benefited from more poise.

Song transcriptions: *Dreams; Floods of spring; In the silent night; The little island; Midsummer eve; The Muse; O, cease thy singing; On the death of a linnet; Sorrow in springtime; To the children; Vocalise; Where beauty dwells.*
**(*) Dell'Arte CD DBS 7001 [id.]. Earl Wild (piano).

Earl Wild is a pianist all too often taken for granted as a virtuoso pure and simple, rather than the great artist that he is. Of course his virtuosity is dazzling – but so too is his refinement of colour and his musicianship. The recording is not of comparable distinction but is acceptable enough.

Variations on a theme of Chopin, Op. 22; Variations on a theme of Corelli, Op. 42; Mélodie in E, Op. 3/3.
*** Hyperion CDA 66009 [id.]. Howard Shelley – MENDELSSOHN: *Scherzo.* ***

Howard Shelley gives dazzling, consistently compelling performances, full of virtuoso flair. The grouping of the more expansive *Chopin variations* brings a kind of sonata balance, with the climax of the final section built superbly by Shelley, helped by first-rate piano sound.

VOCAL MUSIC

The Bells, Op. 35.
(M) *** EMI CDM7 63114-2. Sheila Armstrong, Robert Tear, John Shirley-Quirk, London Symphony Ch., LSO, Previn – PROKOFIEV: *Alexander Nevsky*. ***

The Bells, Op. 35; 3 Russian songs, Op. 41.
(M) *** Decca Dig. 436 482-2 [id.]. Natalia Troitskaya, Ryszard Karczykowski, Concg. Ch. & O, Ashkenazy.

The Bells, Op. 35; 3 Russian songs, Op. 41; Spring, Op. 20.
*** Decca Dig. 440 355-2 [id.]. Alexandrina Pendachanska, Kaludi Kaludov, Sergei Leiferkus, Choral Arts Society, Phd. O, Dutoit.

Ashkenazy's volatile Russian style is eminently suitable for Rachmaninov's masterly cantata. His tenor soloist has just the right touch of temperament, and in the slow movement Natalia Troitskaya's contribution combines Slavonic feeling with freshness. The chorus respond readily to the black mood of the Scherzo and bring a melancholy intensity to the finale. The Decca recording is superb, wide in range, spacious and clear. At mid-price this is a clear first choice.

In *The Bells*, as in Previn's equally fresh and direct account of the other Russian choral work included on his CD, Prokofiev's *Alexander Nevsky*, the London Symphony Chorus sings convincingly in the original language. Previn's concentration on purely musical values as much as on evocation of atmosphere produces powerful results, even when the recording as transferred to CD has lost just a little of its ambient warmth in favour of added presence and choral brilliance.

Charles Dutoit's disc with the Philadelphia Orchestra conveniently couples all three of Rachmaninov's choral works with orchestra. Compared with other versions, the performances are remarkable for subtle pianissimos and half-tones rather than for their dramatic bite. In *The Bells*, for example – much the longest work – Previn is more passionate and Ashkenazy more sparkling and volatile, and with both the recording gives greater sense of presence. *Spring*, the rarest work here, is not as striking in its musical material but it builds up in Dutoit's fine performance to a magnificent climax. The Russian soloists sing with idiomatic bite and, though the chorus is backwardly placed, the dynamic range is impressive. Well worth having, alongside its competitors, if only at last to hear a great orchestra, so often ill-treated by the engineers, recorded properly by the Decca recording team.

Liturgy of St John Chrysostom, Op. 31.
(N) ✪ (B) *** EMI forte CZS5 68664-2 (2). Maximova, Zorova, Vidov, Stoytsov, Petrov, Bulgarian R. Ch., Milkov.
(N) *** Hyperion Dig. CDA 66703 [id.]. Corydon Singers, Matthew Best.

Rachmaninov's *Liturgy of St John Chrysostom*, written in 1910, is an even fuller setting than Tchaikovsky's (of 1878), on which to some extent it was modelled, and it had no more success than its predecessor in convincing the church dignitaries that the powerful emotional feeling so readily projected by its music was not too secular in feeling for use within the context of a religious service. (One must remember that Rachmaninov – like Tchaikovsky – was somewhat equivocal in his allegiance to the Christian faith.) Yet listening to this glorious performance by the Chorus of Bulgarian Radio, recorded in the spacious acoustics of the Alexander Nevsky Memorial Cathedral in Sofia, one can be in no doubt that the work's powerful expressive feeling has an underlying deep spirituality, while the performance itself conveys great religious fervour. Apart from the continuing dialogue between cantor (Ivan Petrov) and chorus (in which the soloists also participate), there are moments of overwhelming simple beauty, as in the sublime, sustained *Cheroubikon* ('Cherubic hymn') which comes immediately before the *Litany of supplication* and is wonderfully celestial here. This makes a complete contrast with the powerful declamation of the *Credo* and the affirmation of the *Mercy of peace*. The setting of *Our Father*, with its almost minimalist simplicity, is hardly less moving. Indeed it would be difficult to imagine this superbly recorded performance being bettered and, although the spacious tempi (which are sustained with continuing concentration) mean that the performance, which takes 97 minutes, stretches to a pair of CDs, the set is offered in EMI's forte series so that the two discs are offered for the price of one. It is a pity that a full text with translation is not included, but the presentation is otherwise fully acceptable.

The fine Hyperion alternative (which has a notable cantor in Peter Scorer) is a sharper, more cleanly enunciated account – the choral sound is without that misty focus which is so much part of the character of Slavic *a capella* singing. It is immensely stimulating, and very well recorded and documented.

However, the Corydons curiously omit the prayer dialogue which is the centrepiece of the *Cherubic hymn* and which in Sofia brings such a strikingly exhilarating response from the chorus. There are various other versions in the catalogue, including a superbly sung and deeply moving account from a Russian Choir (the St Petersburg Chamber Choir under Nikolai Korniev) on Philips (442 776-2). But this has been cut to fit on to a single CD, so choice remains between the two recordings listed above. If you have already succumbed to the *Vespers*, you won't be disappointed with *St John Chrysostom's Liturgy*.

6 Songs, Op. 4; 6 Songs, Op. 8; 12 Songs, Op. 14; 12 Songs, Op. 21; 15 Songs, Op. 26 (including (i) *Two partings*); *14 Songs, Op. 34; 6 Songs, Op. 38; Again you leapt, my heart; April! A festive spring day; By the gates of the holy dwelling; Did you hiccup?; Do you remember that evening?; A flower fell; From St John's Gospel; I shall tell you nothing; Letter to Konstantin Stanislavsky; Night; Powdered paint* (folksong); *Song of disappointment; Twilight has fallen.* (Piano solo): *Daisies; Lilacs.*
(M) *** Decca 436 920-2 (3) [id.]. Elisabeth Söderstrom, Vladimir Ashkenazy, (i) with John Shirley-Quirk.

Recorded between 1974 and 1979, Elisabeth Söderström's set of the major Rachmaninov songs is a glittering jewel in the Decca catalogue. She is a fluent and radiant soloist, often inspired by her accompanist to performances of pure poetry, ranging over the wide span of Rachmaninov's career as well as his whole emotional range, so that you find, for instance, the highly characteristic *Brooding*, or the richly intense *O do not grieve*, alongside a comic skit on a drinking song, *Did you hiccup, Natasha?*. Sonia's final speech in Chekhov's *Uncle Vanya* becomes a song which nicely skirts sentimentality, and there is also a letter in music sent to Stanislavsky on the tenth anniversary of the Moscow Arts Theatre. John Shirley-Quirk joins the team for the wry dialogue, *Two partings*, and Ashkenazy allows himself two solo items in the composer's transcriptions of *Daisies* and *Lilacs*. The recording is vivid in its immediacy and presence. Full translations are provided.

Songs: *Child, you are beautiful like a flower; How I languish; Morning; Spring waters.*
(Y/B) ** Ph. Dig. 442 536-2 [id.]. Dmitri Hvorostovsky, Mikhail Arkadiev (with BORODIN: *For the shores*) – RIMSKY-KORSAKOV; TCHAIKOVSKY: *Songs.* **

Dmitri Hvorostovsky has captured a wide public following since he won the 'Cardiff Singer of the World Competition', some years back, and he undoubtedly makes a glorious sound. His admirers will want this disc, though the recital as a whole falls short at times in terms of characterization. Good recording.

Vespers, Op. 37.
✪ *** HM Chant du Monde Russian Season Dig. LDC 288050 [id.]. St Petersburg Capella, Chernuchenko.
*** Hyperion Dig. CDA 66460 [id.]. Corydon Singers, Matthew Best.

Rachmaninov's *Vespers* – more correctly the 'All-night vigil' – rank not only among his most soulful and intensely powerful music but are also the finest of all Russian choral works. The St Petersburg Capella is in fact the Mikhail Glinka Choir and their lineage goes back to the fifteenth century. Their earlier recording of the piece was pretty impressive. Even so, this newcomer surpasses it and offers singing of an extraordinarily rapt intensity. The dynamic range is enormous, the perfection of ensemble and blend and the sheer beauty of tone such as to exhaust superlatives. Vladislav Chernuchenko gets performances of complete conviction from them, and it is hard to imagine that their singing can be surpassed. The recording does them justice and is made in a suitably atmospheric acoustic.

Though Matthew Best's British choir, the Corydon Singers, lacks the dark timbres associated with Russian choruses and though the result could be weightier and more biting, this is a most beautiful performance, very well sung and recorded in an atmospheric, reverberant setting very apt for such church music.

Vocalise, Op. 34/14 (arr. Dubensky).
(M) *** RCA GD 87831 [7831-2-RG]. Anna Moffo, American SO, Stokowski – CANTELOUBE: *Songs of the Auvergne;* VILLA-LOBOS: *Bachianas Brasileiras No. 5.* ***

Rachmaninov's *Vocalise* was a favourite showpiece of Stokowski, usually in a purely orchestral arrangement; but here with Moffo at her warmest it is good to have the vocal version so persuasively matching the accompaniment.

OPERA

(i) *Monna Vanna* (incomplete opera: Act I, orch. Buketoff); (ii) *Piano concerto No. 4* (original version).
**(*) Chandos Dig. CHAN 8987 [id.]. (i) Milnes, McCoy, Walker, Karoustos, Thorsteinsson, Blythe;
   (ii) William Black; Iceland SO, Buketoff.

Monna Vanna is the fragment of an opera based on Maeterlinck which Rachmaninov wrote around the inspired period of his *Second Symphony*. He thought so well of the fragment that it was the one score he brought away from Russia after the Revolution. Igor Buketoff, who knew the composer, has rescued this Act I score and orchestrated it very sensitively to make an interesting curiosity. In its ripely romantic manner the writing has lyrical warmth and flows freely, thrusting home climactic moments with the same sureness as Rachmaninov's symphonies. Buketoff's performance with the Iceland Symphony is warmly convincing, but the singing is flawed, with Sherrill Milnes, as Monna Vanna's jealous husband, standing out from an indifferent team, otherwise thin-toned and often wobbly. Buketoff's resurrection of the original score of the *Fourth Piano concerto* is rather more expansive than the text we know. William Black is the powerful soloist, though the piano sound, unlike that of the orchestra, lacks weight.

Raff, Joachim (1822–82)

Symphony No. 1 in D (An das Vaterland), Op. 96.
(Y/B) ** Marco Polo Dig. 8.223165 [id.]. Rhenish PO, Friedman.

Symphony No. 2 in C, Op. 140; Overtures: Macbeth; Romeo and Juliet.
(Y/B) ** Marco Polo Dig. 8.223630 [id.]. Slovak State PO (Košice), Urs Schneider.

Symphonies Nos. 3 in F (Im Walde), Op. 153; 10 in F min. (Zur Herbstzeit), Op. 213.
(Y/B) ** Marco Polo Dig. 8.223321 [id.]. Slovak State PO (Košice), Urs Schneider.

Symphonies Nos. 3 in F; 4 in G min., Op. 167.
(Y/B) **(*) Hyperion Dig. CDA 66638 [id.]. Milton Keynes CO, Hilary Davan Wetton.

Symphonies Nos. 4 in G min.; 11 in A min. (Der Winter), Op. 214.
(Y/B) *(*) Marco Polo Dig. 8.223529 [id.]. Slovak State PO (Košice), Urs Schneider.

Symphony No. 5 in E (Lenore), Op. 177.
(M) *** Unicorn UKCD 2031. LPO, Bernard Herrmann.

Symphony No. 5 in E; Overture, Ein feste Burg ist unser Gott, Op. 127.
(Y/B) *(*) Marco Polo Dig. 8.223455 [id.]. Slovak State PO (Košice), Urs Schneider.

Raff was Liszt's assistant at Weimar during the early 1850s and helped prepare his orchestral scores. He enjoyed enormous standing during his lifetime: Ebenezer Prout was not alone in ranking him alongside Wagner and Brahms. His stock fell after his lifetime and he is best remembered for a handful of salon pieces. However, he composed no fewer than eleven symphonies between 1864 and 1883, some of which have excited extravagant praise. (The composer-conductor Bernard Herrmann called No. 5, which he recorded for Unicorn, 'one of the finest examples of the Romantic Programme school – it deserves a place alongside the *Symphonie fantastique* of Berlioz, the *Faust Symphony* of Liszt and the *Manfred Symphony* of Tchaikovsky'.) Yet generally speaking Raff's music is pretty bland, though far from unambitious. The *First Symphony* (*An das Vaterland*), takes itself very ser-iously and runs to over 70 minutes. To be frank, it places some strain on the listener's concentration, and many will not stay the course. Though it won a prize during the composer's lifetime, it can seem hard work from a modern perspective! Although the well-played and -recorded *Symphony No. 2 in C* has a certain charm, it is predominantly Mendelssohnian and, although outwardly attractive, it remains pretty insubstantial. Sampling the performances listed above, one is left in no doubt that they are conscientious in approach but are recommendable to the initiate rather than to the unconverted.

Of the eleven symphonies it is the *Fifth* (*Lenore*) which has captured the imagination of many. No doubt this may be accounted for by the somewhat macabre programme that inspired its finale (the eponymous heroine gallops on horseback with the ghost of her dead lover and is herself abandoned in an open grave). Although the symphony itself is more inspired than some of its companions (it has a particularly eloquent slow movement), it does need rather better advocacy than it receives from the Slovak Philharmonic under Urs Schneider. The Unicorn-Kanchana version by the LPO under Bernard Herrmann, made over a quarter of a century ago, has greater polish and allure, and the recording holds up well against this digital newcomer. The Overture, *Ein feste Burg ist unser Gott*, is hardly sufficient to tip the scales in its favour.

The *Eleventh Symphony in A minor* was left incomplete on Raff's death in 1882 and is not otherwise available; the *Fourth* of 1871, available on the Hyperion version under Hilary Davan Wetton, is not sufficiently persuasive. This music has moments of charm but is essentially second-rate and it must have the most expert advocacy and opulent recorded sound if it is to be persuasive; neither of these two versions is really first class. One needs a Beecham to work his magic on these scores. In these performances they are merely amiable, if insignificant.

Raid, Kaljo (born 1922)

Symphony No. 1 in C min.
*** Chandos Dig. CHAN 8525 [id.]. SNO, Järvi – ELLER: *Dawn; Elegia* etc. ***

Raid's *First Symphony* shows a genuine feel for form and a fine sense of proportion, even though the personality is not fully formed. Well worth hearing. Neeme Järvi gets very committed playing from the Scottish National Orchestra and the recording is warm and well detailed.

Rameau, Jean Philippe (1683–1764)

Les Boréades: orchestral suite; Dardanus: orchestral suite.
*** Ph. Dig. 420 240-2 [id.]. O of 18th Century, Brüggen.

The orchestral suite from *Les Boréades* occupies the larger part of the disc. The invention is full of resource and imagination, and the playing here of both this and *Dardanus* is spirited and sensitive and will provide delight even to those normally unresponsive to authentic instruments.

6 Concerts en sextuor (for strings).
(N) (M) ** Cal. CAL 6838 [id.]. Caen CO, Dautel – BOISMORTIER: *Première suite de clavecin.* **

The anonymous arrangement of Rameau's five suites of *Pièces de clavecin en concert* for string sextet is a novelty and a pleasing one. The arranger used Rameau's instrumental version for harpsichord and two violins: the two violin parts are retained, the upper voice of the harpsichord is given to the third violin, its middle voice to the viola, and the cello follows the bass line. However, these two instruments are not always divided, and the music becomes a true sextet only when the bass has a separate part. The additional *Sixth Suite* is a further transcription of four pieces taken from the third book for the harpsichord, published in 1728, and is very effective, including the famous *La Poule* (clucking realistically on violins to anticipate Saint-Saëns). The music is played spiritedly on modern instruments by the Caen Chamber Orchestra under Jean-Pierre Dautel; if, as recorded, the violins seem a shade pallid, this approaches the sound (if not always the degree of polish) we expect from a period group.

Dardanus: orchestral suite.
(N) (M) *** Erato/Warner 4509 99764-2 [id.]. E. Bar. Soloists, Gardiner.

John Eliot Gardiner offers a substantial selection from the orchestral music of both versions of Rameau's opera (the 1739 score and the score for the 1744 revival which involved radical rewriting of the last two Acts). There is plenty of variety here, from lightly scored dance music to the powerful closing *Chaconne*. Some of the music is slight and, out of context, does not make its full effect; but as a sampler this might tempt some listeners to try the whole work (available only on LP). The CD offers fine if not remarkable sound, with good presence but without the depth of perspective of the best recordings from this source.

Dardanus: suite; *Les Indes galantes:* suite.
(N) (BB) *** DHM Baroque Esprit 05472 77420-2 [id.]. Coll. Aur.

This early example of authentic performance dates from the 1960s. Any abrasiveness deriving from the use of original instruments is countered by the generous acoustics of the Cedernsaal in the Schloss Kirchheim. But the playing has both life and elegance and the sound, though warm and full, is by no means bland: the flutes and oboes (and trumpets in *Les Indes galantes*) bring plenty of added colour. The selection from *Les Indes galantes* is shorter than that provided by Herreweghe, but many will welcome the coupling with *Dardanus*, and the overall playing time is quite generous: 69 minutes. At super-barain price this is very recommendable.

Hippolyte et Aricie: orchestral suite.
(M) *** HM/BMG GD 77009 [77009-2-RG]. La Petite Bande, Kuijken.

This record collects virtually all the orchestral music from *Hippolyte et Aricie*; the melodic invention is fresh and its orchestral presentation ingenious. Sigiswald Kuijken gets delightful results from his ensemble. In every way an outstanding release – and not least in the quality of the sound.

Les Indes galantes: suites for orchestra.
(B) *** HM HMA 1901130 [id.]. Chappelle Royale O, Philippe Herreweghe.
(Y/B) **(*) Ph. Dig. 438 946-2 [id.]. O of 18th Century, Frans Brüggen.

Besides the harpsichord arrangements listed below, Rameau also arranged his four 'concerts' of music from *Les Indes galantes* for orchestra. The result makes nearly three-quarters of an hour of agreeable listening, especially when played so elegantly – and painlessly – on original instruments, and very well recorded (in 1984) by Harmonia Mundi.

Brüggen's performance of the Prologue and four suites from *Les Indes galantes* is alive and responsive. However, the total playing time of this CD is barely 44 minutes.

Naïs: orchestral suite. Le Temple de la Gloire: orchestral suite.
(Y/B) *** HM Dig. HMU 907121 [id.]. Philharmonia Bar. O, Nicholas McGegan.

There is much delightful music here and the playing by the Philharmonia Baroque Orchestra has ravishing finesse, showing original instruments at their most persuasively delicate, textures always transparent; the ear is continually beguiled by this warm and polished playing, beautifully recorded. A quite lovely disc, and at 71 minutes not a morsel too long.

Les Paladins (comédie-ballet): *orchestral suite.*
*** Ph. Dig. 432 968-2 [id.]. O of Age of Enlightenment, Leonhardt.

Gustav Leonhardt's recording of the ballet numbers with the Orchestra of the Age of Enlightenment is little short of a triumph. There is a liveliness, freshness and delight in the colours and rhythms of this inventive score that will captivate the listener and lay to rest any fears of scholarly caution. There is more than an hour's music here, all of it of quality and all played with a panache and style that will win many friends for this composer. The recording, made at St Giles', Cripplegate, is equally crisp and well detailed. Strongly recommended.

Pièces de clavecin en concert Nos. 1–5.
(M) *** Teldec/Warner 9031 77618-2. Brüggen, Sigiswald and Wieland Kuijken, Leonhardt.
*** Virgin/EMI Dig. VC7 59154-2 [id.]. Trio Sonnerie.

The *Cinq pièces de clavecin en concert* are for harpsichord but are more familiar in ensemble versions: in addition to the harpsichord parts, Rameau included additional parts for violin or flute, second violin and bass viol. These pieces, published in 1741, are played on Teldec with a sure sense of style and a real understanding of the niceties of the period. They are recorded on period instruments – but, rest assured, this is no dull, pedantic performance full of musicological rectitude and little musical life. On the contrary, it is scholarly but has genuine liveliness and authenticity of feeling. The music, of course, is delightful, and very much helped by the admirably fresh, transparent recording.

The Trio Sonnerie are also perfectly attuned to the sensibility of the period and its requirements. Theirs is a performance which exhibits a sense of style and a quality of feeling that outweigh any shortcomings. The most notable of these is the fact that they choose to limit the instrumental colours available to them by confining themselves to string instruments and exclude the flute, usual in this repertoire. The Virgin recording is of great naturalness and presence, and this is a strong contender.

KEYBOARD MUSIC

Les Indes galantes: excerpts (harpsichord transcriptions).
*** HM HMC 1901028. Kenneth Gilbert.

These transcriptions are Rameau's own, including not only dance numbers and orchestral pieces but arias as well. Kenneth Gilbert, playing a fine instrument in contemporary tuning, reveals these miniatures as the subtle and refined studies they are. He could not be better served by the recording engineers.

Music for harpsichord: *Book 1* (1706); *Pièces de clavecin* (1724); *Nouvelles suites de pièces de clavecin* (*c.* 1728); *5 Pièces* (1741); *La Dauphine* (1747).
*** O-L Dig. 425 886-2 (2) [id.]. Christophe Rousset (harpsichord).
(M) *** DG 427 176-2 (2). Kenneth Gilbert (harpischord).

Rousset's playing is marvellously persuasive and vital, authoritative and scholarly, yet fresh and completely free from the straitjacket of academic rectitude. He plays a Hemsch in a perfect state of preservation and a 1988 copy of a 1636 Ruckers harpsichord, modified by Hemsch. The sound is excellent.

Kenneth Gilbert, too, is not just a scholar but an artist of genuine insight and stature. He uses three harpsichords, all from the Paris Conservatoire and all from the period: a Goujon and a Hemsch and one by Dumont, restored by Pascal Taskin in 1789. They are superb instruments and are excellently recorded too (in 1977).

Pièces de clavecin: Suite (No. 1) in A min.; L'Agaçante; La Dauphine; L'Indiscrète; La Livri; La Pantomime: La Timide.
*** CRD CRD 3320; *CRDC 4020* [id.]. Trevor Pinnock.

Trevor Pinnock chose a mellow instrument here, making his stylish, crisply rhythmic performances even more attractive. The selection includes *La Dauphine*, the last keyboard piece which Rameau wrote, brilliantly performed. Excellent recording.

Harpsichord suites: in A min. (1728); *in E min.* (1724).
*** CRD CRD 3310; *CRDC 4010* [id.]. Trevor Pinnock.

Harpsichord suites: in D min./maj. (1724); *in G maj./min.* (1728).
*** CRD CRD 3330; *CRDC 4030* [id.]. Trevor Pinnock.

Trevor Pinnock is restrained in the matter of ornamentation, but his direct manner is both eloquent and stylish. The harpsichord is of the French type and is well recorded.

Grand motets: *In convertendo; Quam dilecta laboravi.*
*** HM HM 1901078 [id.]. Gari, Monnaliu, Ledroit, De Mey, Varcoe, Chapelle Royale Ch., Ghent Coll. Vocale, Herreweghe.

These two motets are among Rameau's finest works. The Ghent Collegium Vocale is stiffened by forces from La Chapelle Royale in Paris. They produce excellent results and the soloists are also very fine indeed. The instrumental ensemble includes several members of La Petite Bande and so its excellence can almost be taken for granted.

OPERA-BALLET AND OPERA

Anacréon (complete).
(B) *** HM HMA 190190 [id.]. Schirrer, Mellon, Feldman, Visse, Laplénie, Les Arts Florissants, Christie.

The music here has charm; the performance is as authoritative and stylish as one would expect from William Christie's group. It is not essential Rameau, but it has moments of great appeal. The recording is admirable and this reissue is a genuine bargain.

Les Boréades (complete).
(N) (M) *** Erato/Warner 4509 99763-2 (3) [id.]. Jennifer Smith, Rodde, Langridge, Aler, Lafont, Monteverdi Ch., E. Bar. Soloists, Gardiner.

It was John Eliot Gardiner who in April 1975 conducted the first-ever public performance of this last opera of Rameau, written after he had reached his eighties. The composer died during the rehearsal at the Paris Opéra, and the piece was never staged, until in 1982 Gardiner presented it with enormous success at the Aix-en-Provence Festival with the same cast as here. Though the story – involving the followers of Boreas, the storm god – is highly artificial in a classical way, the music, involving many crisp and brief dances and arias, is as vital and alive as anything Rameau ever wrote, completely contradicting any idea of classical opera as static or boring. Gardiner here directs an electrifying performance with generally first-rate singing, except that Jennifer Smith's upper register, in the central role of Alphise, Queen of Baltria, is not sweet. Chorus and orchestra are outstanding and the recording excellent. Bizarre copyright problems prevented a libretto from being included, which makes it hard to follow the plot because the synopsis is not cued. However, the set is very welcome on CD as part of the Gardiner 'French Baroque Edition'.

Castor et Pollux (complete).
(Y/B) (M) **(*) Erato/Warner Dig. 4509 95311-2 (2) [id.]. Jeffes, Huttenlocher, Jennifer Smith, Buchan, Wallington, Parsons, Rees, E. Bach Festival Singers & Bar. O, Charles Farncombe.

Farncombe – with a cast which gave this tragédie lyrique at Covent Garden and in Paris – uses the revised edition of 1754 and though, after a brisk and refreshing account of the Overture, he fails to spring rhythms brightly enough, this is an admirable mid-priced set, marked by an agreeably authentic orchestral contribution and some stylish singing, notably from Huttenlocher as Pollux, who was not in the stage performances. Excellently clear, 1982 digital recording with a most attractive ambience, made at All Saints', Tooting. The documentation, too, is admirable.

Dardanus (complete).

(Y/B) (M) **(*) Erato/Warner 4509 95313-2 (2) [id.]. Gautier, Eda-Pierre, Von Stade, Devlin, Teucer, Soyer, Van Dam, Paris Op. Ch. & O, Raymond Leppard.

Though the French chorus and orchestra (using modern instruments) here fail to perform with quite the rhythmic resilience that Leppard usually achieves on record, the results are refreshing and illuminating, helped by generally fine solo singing and naturally balanced (if not brilliant) 1980 analogue recording, smoothly transferred to CD, with the choral sound quite vivid. José van Dam as Ismenor copes superbly with the high tessitura, and Christiane Eda-Pierre is a radiant Venus. The story may be improbable (as usual), but Rameau was here inspired to some of his most compelling and imaginative writing. Well documented and well worth exploring.

Les Fêtes d'Hébé: 3rd Entrée: *La Danse.*

(N) (M) *** Erato/Warner 4509 99765-2 [id.]. Jill Gomez, Anne-Marie Rodde, Jean-Claude Orliac, Monteverdi Ch. & O, Gardiner.

Les Fêtes d'Hébé was first staged in 1739 in Paris; it was the fourth major work Rameau had composed for the lyric stage and his second in the opera-ballet genre, *Les Indes galantes* being the first. In its complete form *Les Fêtes d'Hébé* consists of a prologue and three Acts dedicated to poetry, music and, finally, the dance. This last is a pastoral interspersed with dances in which Mercury courts the shepherdess Eglé.

Few people have done more in recent years for Rameau's music than John Eliot Gardiner, and this performance is distinguished by his great feeling for this composer and an alive sensitivity. He secures excellent playing and singing from his forces, and the music itself is inventive and delightful. In short, this is a record not to be missed, particularly if you are a newcomer to Rameau. It is beautifully recorded and the CD transfer is smooth, with lovely textures, choral and orchestral, both warm and transparent, with the soloists most naturally balanced.

Hippolyte et Aricie (complete).

(N) *** DG Dig. 445 853-2 (3). Gens, Fouchécourt, Fink, Feighan, Massis, Naouri, Smythe, Sagittarius Vocal Ens., Les Musiciens du Louvre, Minkowski.

(N) (M) ** Decca 444 526-2 (2) [id.]. Tear, Hickey, J. Baker, Shirley-Quirk, Rhys-Thomas, St Anthony Singers, ECO, Anthony Lewis.

For his first major recording on the DG Archiv label, Mark Minkowski conducts an outstanding account of the first of Rameau's great tragédies-lyriques, a performance that firmly holds together the many jewelled fragments which make up the allegorical Prologue and five extended Acts. He is helped by an excellent cast, with the two young lovers of the title ideally taken by the sweet, silver-toned Véronique Gens, enchantingly girlish, and the light, very French-sounding tenor, Jean-Paul Fouchécourt, similarly conveying depth of feeling in formal melodic lines. Also central to the set's success is the powerful performance of Bernarda Fink as Phèdre, firm and rich, well contrasted with Gens, as memorable in its way as Dame Janet Baker's on the original Argo set conducted by Anthony Lewis, which yet omitted the Prologue. Though in the other major role of Thesée Russell Smythe's baritone is not always sweet, he sings with clear focus and expression, with Luc Coadou aptly sinister as Tisifone and Laurent Naouri sepulchral as Pluton. In the formal scheme the longest, most sustained aria which comes at the very end, celebrating the nightingale, is given to an incidental character, a shepherdess, and is sung here sweetly and charmingly by Annick Massis. Minkowski also draws crisp, alert performances from his chorus and well-tuned orchestra. In an opera for which the composer provided many alternatives, he chooses the original, 1733 text with the first cuts restored, but with minor amendments for which he provides detailed reasons.

This early-1965 Decca (originally Argo) set still sounds well. Lewis, as usual, secures playing of liveliness and feeling and the St Anthony Singers do not disappoint. Of the soloists, both Dame Janet Baker and John Shirley-Quirk give pleasure, though the rest of the cast is uneven and their French is not uniformly good. The snag is that Angela Hickey as Aricie does not always seem to be secure, and her very opening aria, after the Overture, *Temple sacré séjour tranquille*, brings fluttery vibrato. The recording has admirable clarity and detail.

Les Indes galantes (complete).

(Y/B) (M) *** Erato/Warner 4509 95310-2 (3) [id.]. Jennifer Smith, Hartman, Elwes, Devos, Huttenlocher, Ens. Vocale à Cœur Joie de Valence, Paillard O, Valence, Paillard.

The plot of *Les Indes galantes* is complicated but brings opportunities for a splendid tempest and sailors' chorus in Act I, which is set in Turkey. Act II moves to Peru, with a Sun Festival and a volcano erupting (admittedly not as spectacular as the tempest), and Act III with its floral festival is appropriately pastoral and picturesque. Finally we are taken to an Amazonian forest, where the two principal European characters are courting an Indian girl, Zima. She chooses one of her own tribe instead, but a pipe of peace ensures a final reconciliation; there are spectacular trumpets and a triumphant aria from the heroine before the closing ballet. The work is full of lyrical inspiration, and Jennifer Smith sings ravishingly in the roles of Phani, Fatime and Zima, while John Elwes as Tacmas and Adario brings a headily beautiful light-tenor response. Gerda Hartman as Hébé, Emilie and Zaire is charmingly light-weight, if not always quite as secure as Smith, and Philippe Huttenlocher sings all his roles with distinction. The duets and ensembles are often inspired, and the quartet, *Tendre amour*, in Scene 7, which comes before the ballet divertissement of Act III, is fully worthy of Mozart. Paillard directs the proceedings with much flair and warmth, and the 1974 recording is vividly atmospheric. With first-class documentation and a full translation, this is a set to cherish.

Naïs (complete).
(Y/B) (M) *** Erato/Warner 4509 98532-2 (2) [id.]. Russell, Caley, Caddy, Tomlinson, Jackson, Parsons, Ransome, E. Bach Festival Ch. and Bar. O, McGegan.

Rameau's opera *Naïs* tells of Neptune's courtship of the water-nymph Naïs and is full of bold invention. The overture has some astonishing dissonances and syncopations, and the opening battle scenes in which the Heavens are stormed by the Titans and Giants are quite striking. The performance, based on the 1980 English Bach Festival production, is full of spirit and uses authentic period instruments to good effect. The work is not long, and the rewards of the music are such as to counterbalance any reservations one might have as to imperfections in ensemble or the like. Admirers of Rameau will need no prompting to acquire this attractive reissue. The unconverted should sample the opening, which will surely delight and surprise. The sound of this 1980 recording is strikingly well balanced, vivid and present. Highly recommended.

Platée (complete).
** Erato/Warner Dig. 2292 45028-2 (2) [id.]. Ragon, Jennifer Smith, Guy de Mey, Le Texier, Gens, Ens. Vocale Françoise Herr, Musiciens du Louvre, Minkowski.

Platée, written in 1745 and described as a '*ballet bouffon*', is in fact a comic opera, based on a classical theme. With such a send-up of classical tradition, the performers here understandably adopt comic expressions and voices, which in a recording, as opposed to a stage performance, become rather wearing on the listener. Also almost all the soloists aspirate heavily in florid passages. Within that convention this is a lively, brisk performance, very well conducted by Marc Minkowski, but marred by the dryness of the recording. As a work, *Platée* certainly provides a fascinating side-glance at Rameau's mastery.

La Princesse de Navarre (complete).
(N) (M) *** Erato/Warner 0630 12986-2 (3) [id.]. Hill-Smith, Harrhy, Chambers, Rees, Goldthorpe, Caddy, Wigmore, Savidge, E. Bach Festival Singers and Bar. O, McGegan.

La Princesse de Navarre is a collection of dance movements which Rameau used in other works, as well as interludes for the Voltaire comédie. The finest is a chaconne of some magnificence, in which dancers and singers participate. This edition is the first to incorporate all the music Rameau composed for the work. He made substantial revisions, probably more than once and possibly as late as 1763 when Voltaire added a new Prologue for a performance at Bordeaux. There is some altogether delightful music here and those older readers who saw the Covent Garden staging in 1976 will not need reminding as to its quality. Of course, listening to 55 minutes of dances (even though some of them are choral) in close proximity is not the ideal way of enjoying Rameau, but a cued CD recording gives one the opportunity to pick and choose. Very good performances, and excellent recording too.

Pygmalion (complete).
(M) **(*) HM/BMG GD 77143 [77143-2-RG]. Elwes, Van der Sluis, Vanhecke, Yakar, Paris Chapelle Royal Ch., La Petite Bande, Leonhardt.

Leonhardt's 1980 account with John Elwes as Pygmalion and Mieke van der Sluis as Céphise is rather leisurely, but his soloists make a good team, while the use of period instruments brings attractive transparency of texture. The documentation (including full translation) is first class.

Zoroastre (complete).
(M) **(*) HM/BMG GD 77144 (3) [77144-2-RG]. Elwes, De Reyghere, Van der Sluis, Nellon, Reinhart, Bona, Ghent Coll. Vocale, La Petite Bande, Kuijken.

Though Kuijken's characteristically gentle style with his excellent authentic group, La Petite Bande, fails to give the piece all the bite and urgency it needs, this is nevertheless a fine presentation of a long-neglected masterpiece, with crisp and stylish singing from the soloists, notably John Elwes in the name-part and Gregory Reinhart as Abramane. The Ghent Collegium Vocale, placed rather close, sing with vigour in the choruses, but the individual voices fail to blend. The excellent documentation (144 pages, including translations) puts the mid-priced issues of many of the large international companies to shame.

Rangström, Ture (1884–1947)

Symphony No. 1 in C sharp min. (August Strindberg in memoriam); Dithyramb; Spring hymn.
(N) **(*) CPO Dig. CPO999 367-2 [id.]. Norrköping SO, Michail Jurowski.

Symphonies Nos. 1 in C sharp min. (August Strindberg in memoriam); (i) 3 in D sharp (Song under the stars).
(N) ** Sterling CDS 1014-2 [id.]. Swedish RSO, Leif Segerstam; (i) Helsingborg SO, Janos Fürst.

The Swedish conductor, Tor Mann, recorded Rangström's *First Symphony* for Decca in the early 1950s, but it has never maintained itself in the catalogue for any length of time. The work dates from 1914, two years after the death of Strindberg, to whose memory it is dedicated, as indeed is the *Vårhymn (Spring hymn)* of 1942 on the CPO disc. This also includes his very first orchestral work, the *Dithyramb* of 1909. To be frank, it is not in the same league, either in terms of musical substance or craftmanship, as the symphonies of Alfvén and Atterberg. Rangström studied briefly with Pfitzner, though he was basically self-taught, and the prime influences are Franck and early Sibelius. There are some individual things in the slow movement but elsewhere, and particularly in the finale, the rhetoric is overblown and the ideas second-rate. For sheer banality the second group of the finale has to be heard to be believed. It is strange that a composer who could write with such artlessness and inspiration in his songs or in the *Divertimento elegiaco* should exhibit such lapses of taste.

Of the two performances, Michail Jurowski is the more persuasive and he gets very good playing from the Norrköping orchestra. Not that Leif Segerstam's 1979 account with the Swedish Radio Orchestra is in any way negligible; indeed he draws an accomplished performance from his players and is decently recorded in good analogue sound. It is difficult to work up much enthusiasm for the Sterling coupling, the *Third Symphony (Sång under stjärnorna* – 'Song under the stars'), which is also rather corny. All the same, those who greatly warm to, say, Alfvén may find that they respond more positively to this music. No grumbles about the playing of the Helsingborg Symphony Orchestra under Janos Fürst. Whether or not you decide to investigate either of these recordings, do not pass over the collection of songs by Anne Sofie von Otter and Bengt Forsberg which includes *Vingar i natten* ('Wings in the Night'), one of his most beautiful songs which lends its name to the collection DG have recorded (see Vocal Recitals, below).

Rautavaara, Einojuhani (born 1928)

Symphonies 1–3.
*** Ondine Dig. ODE 740-2 [id.]. Leipzig RSO, Max Pommer.

Einojuhani Rautavaara has been overshadowed outside Finland by Joonas Kokkonen and Aulis Sallinen, but the present disc shows him to be a symphonist to reckon with. Ideas never outstay their welcome and there is a sense of inevitability about their development. Those with a taste for Shostakovich or Simpson should find these pieces congenial. Good performances by the Leipzig Radio Orchestra under Max Pommer and very decent recorded sound too.

Symphony No. 6 (Vincentiana); (i) Cello concerto, Op. 41.
(Y/B) *** Ondine Dig. ODE 819-2 [id.]. (i) Marko Ylönen; Helsinki PO, Max Pommer.

The *Sixth Symphony* comes from 1992 and is a large-scale work of over 42 minutes. Like Hindemith's *Mathis der Maler Symphony* or Norman Dello Joio's *Triumph of St Joan*, it draws on material from the opera, *Vincent* (1985–7), based, as its title implies, on the life of van Gogh. There is, appropriately enough, no lack of colour, though the score tends to be both eclectic and amorphous. The orchestral scoring itself is quite sumptuous and there is no lack of incident. However, the invention is hardly symphonic and the canvas does not fully sustain interest. It comes with a much earlier and more cogently argued piece, the *Cello concerto* of 1968, which is expertly played by Marko Ylönen. The recording is very impressive, well detailed and present, and is in the demonstration bracket.

Ravel, Maurice (1875–1937)

Alborada del gracioso.

(Y/B) (M) **(*) EMI CDM5 65423-2 [id.]. French Nat. R. O, Stokowski – HOLST: *The Planets* **(*); STRAVINSKY: *Petrushka.* **

Stokowski's idiomatic account from the French National Orchestra dances infectiously and the 1958 recording sounds fuller than the coupled *Planets*; but the fortissimos remain rather harsh, if extremely vivid.

Alborada del gracioso; Une barque sur l'océan; Boléro; (i) *Piano concerto in G; Piano concerto for the left hand. Daphnis et Chloé* (complete ballet); *L'Eventail de Jeanne: Fanfare. Menuet antique; Ma Mère l'Oye* (complete); *Pavane pour une infante défunte; Rapsodie espagnole; Le tombeau de Couperin; La valse; Valses nobles et sentimentales.*

(❀) (M) *** Decca 421 458-2 (4). Montreal SO with Ch. and (i) Pascal Rogé; Dutoit.

(i) *Alborada del gracioso;* (ii) *Une barque sur l'océan; Boléro;* (i; iii) *Piano concerto for the left hand;* (ii; iv) *Daphnis et Chloé* (complete ballet); (ii) *Fanfare pour L'Eventail de Jeanne; Menuet antique; Ma Mère l'Oye* (complete ballet); (i) *Pavane pour une infante défunte; Rapsodie espagnole;* (ii) *Shéhérazade: Ouverture de féerie. Le tombeau de Couperin; La valse; Valses nobles et sentimentales.*

(M) **(*) Sony SM3K 45842 (3) [id.]. (i) Cleveland O; (ii) NYPO; Boulez; (iii) with Entremont; (iv) Camerata Singers.

Anyone coming new to this repertoire will find Dutoit's four-disc mid-price box unbeatable value: the orchestral playing is wonderfully sympathetic and the recording ideally combines atmospheric evocation with vividness of detail. In the concertos, Pascal Rogé finds gracefulness and vitality for the *G major* work and, if there is less dynamism in the *Left-hand concerto*, there is no lack of finesse. The balance is very realistic and the recording throughout is in the demonstration class.

Boulez's distinguished Sony set offers a glitteringly iridescent account of the *Ouverture de féerie*, which is omitted by Dutoit. Entremont's account of the *Left-hand concerto* is strong and characterful and not lacking in poetic colour; but the CBS sound is a little fierce and does not altogether flatter the piano timbre. On the whole, however, the remastering makes the most of recordings which were originally among the best of their period (1972–5). The *Alborada* is quite brilliant and, throughout, Boulez allows all the music ample time to breathe; gentler textures have the translucence for which this conductor is admired. *Une barque sur l'océan* has a genuine magic, while the complete *Daphnis et Chloé* has a sense of ecstasy. Boulez is also at his very best in *Ma Mère l'Oye* with its luminous textures, and his *Rapsodie espagnole* is equally distinctive: it is beautifully shaped and atmospheric in an entirely different way from Karajan's; Boulez's Spain is brilliant, dry and well lit. Both *Boléro* and *La valse* generate considerable tension and have powerful climaxes. There is no doubt that this music-making with its cleanly etched sound is immensely strong in character, and many listeners will respond to it very positively.

Alborada del gracioso; Une barque sur l'océan; Boléro; Ma Mère l'Oye (complete); *Menuet antique; Ouverture de féerie; Pavane pour une Infante défunte; Rapsodie espagnole; Le tombeau de Couperin; La valse; Valses nobles et sentimentales.*

(N) (B) *** EMI forte CZS5 68610-2 (2) [id.]. O de Paris, Martinon.

Like his version of *Daphnis et Chloé*, Martinon's *Ma Mère l'Oye* is exquisite, among the finest ever put on record (and one does not forget Dutoit and Previn). Although the *Valses nobles et sentimentales* and *La valse* do not eclipse the 1961 Cluytens versions (see below) and the present *La valse* has a rather harsh climax, there is much ravishing delicacy of orchestral playing, notably in *Le tombeau de Couperin* and the rare *Ouverture de féerie* (*Shéhérazade*) with its Rimskian associations – a major 14-minute piece which is not included in most other comparable collections. The CD transfers of mid-1970s analogue recordings, originally made quadraphonically and which were remarkably lifelike and natural on LP, bring a degree of glare on fortissimos, but otherwise the sound is warm and luminously coloured and, throughout, the refined virtuosity of the Orchestre de Paris is a constant source of delight. Excellent value.

Alborada del gracioso; Une barque sur l'océan; Boléro; Ma Mère l'Oye (complete ballet); *Menuet antique; Pavane pour une infante défunte; Rapsodie espagnole; Le tombeau de Couperin; La valse; Valses nobles et sentimentales.*

(M) *** EMI CZS7 67897-2 (2) [id.]. Paris Conservatoire O, Cluytens.

These 1961 performances, made in the Salle Wagram, Paris, are as good as any in the catalogue. They have a strongly idiomatic and atmospheric feel; the *Rapsodie espagnole*, *La valse* and the *Valses nobles* are exceptionally good, and so too is the complete *Ma Mère l'Oye*. The only snag is the wide vibrato of the horn in *Pavane pour une infante défunte*. The recordings still sound remarkably realistic, and not just for the period: they are very good by present-day standards. The two-disc set makes a genuine bargain.

Alborada del gracioso; Boléro; Daphnis et Chloé (ballet): *Suite No. 2; Menuet antique; Ma Mère l'Oye* (complete ballet); *Pavane pour une infante défunte; Rapsodie espagnole; Le tombeau de Couperin; La valse; Valses nobles et sentimentales.*
(B) **(*) Ph. Duo 438 745-2 (2) [id.]. Concg. O, Bernard Haitink.

Although Haitink's Ravel collection, recorded in the early 1970s, is not as magnetic as the superb companion Debussy set on Philips Duo, these are still fine performances, distinguished by instinctive good judgement and taste. The playing of the Amsterdam orchestra is eminently polished and civilized, even if the heady, intoxicating qualities of the music are missed. The *Rapsodie espagnole* lacks the last ounce of dash in the *Feria*, but the *Habañera* is lazily appealing when the orchestral playing is so sleek and refined. There is perhaps not quite enough atmosphere in *Le tombeau de Couperin*, and Haitink's *La valse* fails to captivate or excite the listener as do the finest versions of this piece. Yet the orchestral playing seduces the ear with its refinement and finish, and the engineers produce a sound to match: the perspective is truthful and the overall effect on CD most pleasing, with the remastered recordings improved in firmness of outline without loss of atmosphere or bloom.

(i) *Alborada del gracioso; Boléro; Pavane pour une infante défunte; La valse;* (ii) *Valses nobles et sentimentales.*
(N) (BB) **(*) EMI Seraphim Analogue/Dig. CES5 68539-2 (2) [CDEB 68539]. (i) New Philh. O, Maazel; (ii) RPO, Previn – DEBUSSY: *La Mer; Nocturnes ***; MUSSORGSKY: *Pictures at an exhibition.* **(*)

This is an attractive package. Previn's coupled Debussy is magnetically distinguished, and he gives here a provocatively languorous account of the *Valses nobles et sentimentales*, lazy of tempo and affectionately indulgent, and afforded glowing (1985) digital sound. Maazel, who also offers an enjoyably colourful version of Mussorgsky's *Pictures*, directs the rest of this Ravel collection which offers more first-class orchestral playing. His are brilliant, extrovert performances, with plenty of glitter in the *Alborada* and the *Pavane* played gently and beautifully. The climaxes of both *Boléro* and *La valse* are rhythmically mannered, but there is no lack of adrenalin; the sound, from the early 1970s, is spectacular, if a bit brash.

Alborada del gracioso; Boléro; Rapsodie espagnole; Le tombeau de Couperin; La valse.
(Y/B) (BB) *** RCA Navigator Dig. 74321 17902-2. Dallas SO, Eduardo Mata.

Mata's *Le tombeau de Couperin* has elegance and finesse, while the expansive climaxes of *Boléro* and *La valse* are very compelling. The recording has the most spectacular dynamic range; indeed it is in the demonstration class for its period, especially for those who like glittering percussion, while the Dallas hall provides plenty of atmosphere. The *Alborada* flashes, the *Rapsodie* shimmers and there is a balmy underlying patina of sensuous colour. At super-bargain price, this is highly recommendable.

(i) *Alborado del gracioso; Boléro; Rapsodie espagnole; Le tombeau de Couperin;* (ii) *Valses nobles et sentimentales.*
(N) (B) **(*) Sony SBK 48163; *SBT 48163* [id.]. Phd. O, (i) Ormandy; (ii) Munch.

Ormandy was a first-class Ravel conductor, as those who can recall his wartime *Daphnis et Chloé* (and, for that matter, its successors) can testify. These performances are eminently well worth the money at bargain price, even if the recording is not three-star by 1990s standards.

Alborada del gracioso; Boléro; Rapsodie espagnole; La valse.
*** Decca 410 010-2 [id.]. Montreal SO, Dutoit.

The playing of the Montreal orchestra under Charles Dutoit is absolutely first class and thoroughly atmospheric, and the recorded sound defines the state of the art and, apart from the sumptuous music-making, has impressive refinement and a most musically judged and natural balance.

(i) *Alborada del gracioso;* (ii) *Boléro;* (i) *La valse.*
(M) *** EMI CDM7 64357-2 [id.]. (i) O de Paris; (ii) BPO; Karajan – DEBUSSY: *La Mer.* ***

Karajan's digitally remastered 1978 EMI Berlin Philharmonic *Boléro* has fine presence and a splendid forward impetus. The Paris *Alborada* and *La valse* have been tacked on for this reissue. They were recorded in 1974 as part of an outstanding French concert of Ravel's orchestral music (now withdrawn).

Alborada del gracioso; Fanfare for L'Eventail de Jeanne; Ma Mère l'Oye (complete ballet); *Miroirs: La vallée des cloches* (arr. Percy Grainger); *La valse;* (i) *Shéhérazade* (song-cycle).
*** EMI Dig. CDC7 54204-2 [id.]. (i) Maria Ewing; CBSO, Simon Rattle.

The recording of the CBSO, made in the Arts Centre of Warwick University, is extraordinarily spectacular, with a state-of-the-art sound-balance of the widest range and amplitude. The performances too have great magnetism and electricity, and the orchestral playing is superb. Rattle captures the lambent allure of Percy Grainger's orchestration of the last of the *Miroirs* and gives an equally glowing account of *Ma Mère l'Oye*; *La valse* sounds gorgeous too, climaxing with alarming power. At the beginning of the programme, Maria Ewing's *Shéhérazade* is matched in voluptuous intensity by Rattle and his players; in the aching yearning of *La flûte enchantée* the atmosphere becomes more impressionistic. But it is essentially a dramatic performance, and the shimmering *Alborada* is well placed to follow on afterwards.

Alborada del gracioso; Pavane pour une infante défunte; Rapsodie espagnole; Le tombeau de Couperin; La valse.
(M) *** Mercury 432 003-2 [id.]. Detroit SO, Paray – IBERT: *Escales*. **(*)

Paray's Ravel performances enjoyed a high reputation in the 1960s. His *Rapsodie espagnole* can be spoken of in the same breath as the Reiner/RCA and Karajan/EMI versions, with its languorous, shimmering textures and sparkling *Feria*. His *Alborada* glitters and the *Pavane* is glowingly elegiac. *La valse*, too, is impressively shaped and subtly controlled. *Le tombeau de Couperin* has great refinement and elegance: the solo oboist plays beautifully. All have been excellently remastered.

Alborada del gracioso; Pavane pour une infante défunte; Rapsodie espagnole; Valses nobles et sentimentales.
❀ (M) *** RCA GD 60179 [60179-2-RG]. Chicago SO, Reiner – DEBUSSY: *Ibéria*. *** ❀

These performances are in an altogether special class. In the *Rapsodie espagnole*, the *Prélude à la nuit* is heavy with fragrance and atmosphere; never have the colours in the *Feria* glowed more luminously, while the *Malagueña* glitters with iridescence. In the three and a half decades since it first appeared, this is the recording we have turned to whenever we wanted to hear this work for pleasure. No one captures its sensuous atmosphere as completely as did Reiner, and the recorded sound with its natural concert-hall balance is greatly improved in terms of clarity and definition.

Alborada del gracioso; Rapsodie espagnole.
*** Chandos Dig. CHAN 8850 [id.]. Ulster O, Yan Pascal Tortelier – DEBUSSY: *Images*. ***

Yan Pascal Tortelier gives very good performances of both works and has the advantage of excellent Chandos sound. His *Rapsodie espagnole* is not quite as gripping as some celebrated accounts (Reiner, Karajan, Giulini and others) but it is highly atmospheric all the same, and some collectors may be swayed by the claims of the outstanding digital recording.

Une barque sur l'océan; Rapsodie espagnole; La valse.
(N) (M) *** DG Dig. 445 556-2 [id.]. LSO, Abbado – MUSSORGSKY: *Pictures at an exhibition*. ***

Abbado has impeccable taste in this repertoire, and it goes without saying that the LSO plays superbly throughout. No complaints about the 1986 digital recording either.

Boléro.
(B) *** DG Double 437 404-2 (2) [id.]. BPO, Karajan – CHOPIN: *Les Sylphides* *** ❀; DELIBES: *Coppélia: suite* ***; GOUNOD: *Faust* etc. **(*); OFFENBACH: *Gaîté parisienne:* excerpts; TCHAIKOVSKY: *Sleeping Beauty* (suite). **(*)
(Y/B) (M) *** DG 447 426-2 [id.]. BPO, Karajan – DEBUSSY: *La Mer;* MUSSORGSKY: *Pictures*. ***

Karajan's 1964 *Boléro* is a marvellously controlled, hypnotically gripping performance, with the Berlin Philharmonic at the top of its form. It is available either with a superb suite from *Daphnis et Chloé*, or within a collection of ballet music, almost all of which shows Karajan in top form, or in an outstanding reissue among DG's Legendary Recordings series of 'Originals'; the couplings on the latter both show Karajan at his very finest.

(i) *Boléro;* (ii) *Piano concerto in G;* (iii) *Piano concerto for the left hand;* (i) *Menuet antique;* (iv; i) *Don Quichotte à Dulcinée; Ronsard à son âme.*
(N) (***) EMI mono CDH5 65499-2 [id.]. (i) O, Coppola; (ii) Marguerite Long, O, De Freitas Branco; (iii) Alfred Cortot, Paris Conservatoire O, Munch; (iv) Martial Singher.

A disc of special documentary interest, since it brings us the very first recordings of Ravel's music to be made. When the *Boléro* first appeared in 1930, Ravel's own name was given as the conductor, as indeed was the case with the *Piano Concerto in G major*. Ravel was in fact present in the Salle Pleyel for the former and in the Studio Albert for the latter, but he supervised rather than conducted. It is good to have the 1939 Cortot–Munch version of the *Concerto for the left hand* rather than the earlier and insensitive recording by Paul Wittgenstein, who commissioned it. Piero Coppola is an underrated conductor and his pre-war Debussy *Nocturnes*, *La Mer* and *Le martyre* stand up against the most exalted competition. He conducts everything on this disc, apart from the *Left-hand concerto*, and, since his performances carry the imprimatur of the composer, no admirer of Ravel will want to be without them. The transfers do the best possible for the recordings and are unlikely to sound better.

Boléro; Daphnis et Chloé: suite No. 2.
(M) *** DG 427 250-2. BPO, Karajan – DEBUSSY: *La mer; Prélude.* ***

Karajan's 1964 *Boléro* is a very characteristic performance, marvellously controlled, hypnotic and gripping, with the Berlin Philharmonic at the top of its form. The 1965 *Daphnis et Chloé* suite is outstanding, even among all the competition. He has the advantage of the Berlin Philharmonic at their finest and it would be difficult to imagine better or more atmospheric playing. The CD has opened up the sound spectacularly although now there is a touch of glare.

Boléro; (i) *Daphnis et Chloé: suite No. 2; Ma Mère l'Oye (suite); Valses nobles et sentimentales.*
(BB) *** Naxos Dig. 8.550173; *4550173* [id.]. (i) Slovak Philharmonic Ch.; Slovak RSO (Bratislava), Kenneth Jean.

The Slovak Radio Orchestra, which is a fine body and is superbly recorded, respond warmly to Kenneth Jean. At the price, this is very good value indeed; the *Ma Mère l'Oye* can hold its own alongside all but the most distinguished competition: indeed *Les entretiens de la belle et de la bête* is as keenly characterized as Dutoit at mid-price, and *Le jardin féerique* is enchanting. For those wanting these pieces this is a real bargain.

Boléro; (i) *Daphnis et Chloé: suite No. 2; Pavane pour une infante défunte; La valse.*
(M) *** Decca Dig. 430 714-2; *430 714-4* [id.]. Montreal SO, Dutoit; (i) with chorus.

A further permutation of Dutoit's beautifully made Montreal recordings, warmly and translucently recorded at St Eustache, now reissued at mid-price.

Boléro; Daphnis et Chloé: suite No. 2; La valse.
(M) (***) RCA mono 09026 61392-2. Boston SO, Koussevitzky (with DEBUSSY: *Sarabande*) – MUSSORGSKY: *Pictures.* (***)

Koussevitzky's *Boléro*, *La valse* and the transcription of the Debussy *Sarabande* all come from 1930. Oddly enough, the earlier recordings, certainly his marvellously atmospheric *La valse*, sound fresher and better focused. The second *Daphnis et Chloé* suite is much later (1944–5) and, though the performances could not be more vivid and vibrant, the sound-quality is not really good; there is some discoloration affecting climaxes. His *Lever du jour* feels a shade faster than usual, and the remaining two movements have just the right sense of rapture. There is an inaccurate index-point for the stunning *Danse générale*. Intoxicating stuff despite the sonic limitations.

Boléro; Ma Mère l'Oye (complete); *Pavane pour une infante défunte; Rapsodie espagnole; La valse.*
(N) (M) *** Ph. 442 542-2 [id.]. LSO, Pierre Monteux.

For this Philips reissue Polygram have taken the opportunity to combine recordings from two separate sources. Monteux's 1964 version of the complete *Ma Mère l'Oye* is a poetic, unforced reading, given naturally balanced sound. *La valse* is impressive too, and *Boléro* has well-sustained concentration, even though some will raise an eyebrow at the slight quickening of pace in the closing pages. These three recordings are taken from a Philips original which has responded well to its digital remastering, retaining its warmth while obtaining a clearer profile. The *Pavane* and *Rapsodie espagnole*, however, come from a Decca source and date from two years earlier, yet the sound has strikingly more range and an added lustre. The *Pavane* is warm and poised; the *Rapsodie espagnole* can be spoken of in the same breath as Reiner's version. Monteux moves naturally and spontaneously from the exotic nocturnal atmosphere of the opening *Prélude à la nuit* to the flashing brilliance of the closing *Feria*.

Boléro; Rapsodie espagnole.
*** DG Gold Dig. 439 013-2 [id.]. BPO, Karajan – MUSSORGSKY: *Pictures.* ***

Karajan's later versions of *Boléro* and *Rapsodie espagnole* find the Berlin Philharmonic in characteristically brilliant form, recorded in very wide-ranging digital sound; the thrust of *Boléro* and the sensuousness of the *Rapsodie* are conveyed with unerring power and magnetism, and the close of the *Feria* of the *Rapsodie espagnole* is spectacular indeed!

Boléro; Le tombeau de Couperin; (i) *Tzigane;* (ii) *Shéhérazade* (song-cycle).
(B) *** DG Classikon Dig. 439 414-2 [id.]. (i) Salvatore Accardo; (ii) Margaret Price; LSO, Abbado.

Abbado is on excellent form and brings out all the subtle colourings of Ravel's orchestration, in which he is greatly helped by the excellent DG recording. There is some lovely oboe playing in *Le tombeau de Couperin* and Accardo is superb in *Tzigane*. Margaret Price's singing is ravishingly ecstatic in both *Asie* and *La flûte enchantée*, even if she does not always seem to be quite inside the sensibility of the music. Only in *Boléro* is there any idiosyncrasy: near the climax Abbado makes a perceptible gear-change, pressing the tempo forward somewhat; his involvement is also conveyed in his vocal contributions to the closing pages. The recording here is spectacular. A genuine bargain.

Boléro; La valse.
(N) (M) *** Decca 448 576-2 [id.]. SRO, Ansermet – CHABRIER: *España* **(*); DUKAS: *L'apprenti sorcier* ***; DEBUSSY: *La Mer* **(*); HONEGGER: *Pacific 231.* ***
** Chandos Dig. CHAN 8996 [id.]. Detroit SO, Järvi – ROUSSEL: *Bacchus; Symphony No. 3.* **(*)

Outstanding 1963 performances from Ansermet, very well recorded. Nearly all the music included here shows the Swiss conductor at his best.

Neeme Järvi's *La valse* is brisk and not without its moments of exaggeration – indeed affectation unusual in this conductor. Very natural recorded sound, though not a first choice for either Ravel piece.

Piano concerto in G.
❀ *** EMI CDC7 49326-2 [id.]. Michelangeli, Philh. O, Gracis – RACHMANINOV: *Concerto No. 4.* *** ❀

Piano concerto in G; Piano concerto in D for the left hand.
(*) Chandos Dig. CHAN 8773 [id.]. Louis Lortie, LSO, Frühbeck de Burgos – FAURE: *Ballade.* *

(i) *Piano concerto in G; Piano concerto for the left hand. Une barque sur l'océan; L'Eventail de Jeanne: Fanfare; Menuet antique.*
**(*) Decca Dig. 410 230-2. (i) Rogé; Montreal SO, Dutoit.

(i–ii) *Piano concerto in G; Piano concerto for the left hand;* (ii) *La valse;* (i) (Piano) *Valses nobles et sentimentales.*
(Y/B) (B) *** CfP CD-CFP 4667; *TC-CFP 4667.* (i) Philip Fowke; (ii) LPO, Baudo.

(i) *Piano concerto in G; Gaspard de la nuit.*
(M) *** DG 447 438-2 [id.]. Martha Argerich, (i) BPO, Abbado – PROKOFIEV: *Piano concerto No. 3.* ***

Michelangeli plays with superlative brilliance which yet has great sympathy for the tender moments. The exquisite playing in the slow movement makes up for any deficiencies of dimensional balance. The recording has been remastered very successfully and is of high quality: clear, with bold piano timbre and excellent orchestral detail.

Argerich's half-tones and clear fingerwork give the *G major Concerto* unusual delicacy, but its urgent virility – with jazz an important element – comes over the more forcefully by contrast. Other performances may have caught the uninhibited brilliance in the finale more fearlessly, but in the first movement few other versions can match Argerich's playing. The compromise between coolness and expressiveness in the slow minuet of the middle movement is tantalizingly sensual. Her *Gaspard de la nuit* abounds in character and colour, even if certain touches may disturb the perspective. The remastered recordings (the concerto comes from 1967, *Gaspard* from 1975) sound first class; the concerto balance is very successful and there is crisp detail, while the solo piano has fine presence and no want of colour. The reissue is rightly part of DG's 'Originals' series of 'Legendary Recordings'.

The performances of the *Concertos* by Philip Fowke with Baudo and the LPO are particularly attractive in the way they bring out the jazzy side of Ravel's inspiration, treating the misplaced accents and syncopations less strictly than some, but with winning results. In the slow movement of the *G major Concerto* the Spanish overtones also come out strongly, and Fowke's solo playing in the *Valses nobles et sentimentales* is clean, bright and rhythmic in a muscular way, without ever becoming brutal or unfeeling; nor does he lack poetry. Baudo and the orchestra also give a strongly characterized reading of *La valse*, brisker than some, with waltz rhythms powerfully inflected. Excellent 1988 recording, made in St Augustine's, Kilburn, vivid and attractively atmospheric; this disc and tape are irresistible at bargain price.

Pascal Rogé brings both delicacy and sparkle to the *G major Concerto*, which he gives with his characteristic musical grace and fluency. He brings great poetry and tenderness to the slow movement; but in the *Left-hand concerto* he is a good deal less dynamic, even though there is much to admire in the way of pianistic finesse – and charm. The Decca recording offers excellent performances of three short orchestral pieces as a makeweight.

Louis Lortie's account of the two *Concertos* on Chandos has the advantage of altogether outstanding recording. In the *G major* he is often highly personal without becoming unduly idiosyncratic, with a fastidious sense of colour at his command. In the *Left-hand concerto* he really takes his time over the cadenzas and his agogic hesitations are sometimes over-indulgent. Immaculate playing as such, and superb recording.

(i) *Piano concerto in G; Piano concerto for the left hand in D. A la manière de Borodine; A la manière de Chabrier; Gaspard de la nuit; Jeux d'eau; Menuet antique; Menuet sur le nom de Haydn; Miroirs; Pavane pour une infante défunte; Prélude; Sonatine; Le tombeau de Couperin; Valses nobles et sentimentales.*
(B) **(*) Ph. Duo 438 353-2 (2) [id.]. Werner Haas; (i) Monte-Carlo Opéra O, Galliera.

This well-recorded pair of CDs offers virtually all Ravel's piano music at a bargain price. Werner Haas has a genuine Ravel sensibility and he plays with delicacy and a fine feeling for the music's colour and its moments of gentle rapture. His tempi are consistently apt and he is fully equal to the technical demands of *Gaspard de la nuit*. His crisp articulation in the *Toccata* of *Le tombeau de Couperin* and the *Alborada* from *Miroirs* shows how a ready technical facility is always placed at the service of the composer. Faster passages are very slightly blurred by the resonant acoustic, but otherwise the recording is lifelike and very pleasing. The performances of the two *Concertos* match the rest, refined and satisfying. Perhaps the playing here is a little strait-laced (elsewhere Haas is often pleasingly flexible) but Galliera's fine accompaniments add to the authority of these performances, and the 1968 recording is well balanced. These are performances one could live with, and this set is excellent value.

Piano concerto for the left hand in D.
(BB) *** ASV Dig. CDQS 6092. Osorio, RPO, Bátiz – FRANCK: *Symphonic variations* **(*); SAINT-SAENS: *Wedding-cake* ***; SCHUMANN: *Concerto.* ***
*** Sony Dig. SK 47188 [id.]. Fleisher, Boston SO, Ozawa – BRITTEN: *Diversions;* PROKOFIEV: *Concerto No. 4.* ***

Jorge Federico Osorio's account of the *Left-hand concerto* can hold its own with the best and it is very well recorded. With its tempting bargain couplings, about which there are only minor reservations, this disc is a genuine bargain. He also gives a crisp and colourful performance of the *Alborada* in an alternative, full-price coupling with Prokofiev.

Leon Fleisher's account of the Ravel *Concerto for the left hand* is strongly characterized and full of life and colour. Apart from its general artistic excellence, the strength of his CD also lies in the interest of the coupling. All three works share a common origin in that they were commissioned by the one-armed Austrian pianist, Paul Wittgenstein. Fleisher's account of the Ravel deserves to rank high among current recommendations, and choice will inevitably depend upon couplings. Both the orchestral support and the Sony recording are very good indeed.

Daphnis et Chloé (ballet; complete).
❀ (M) *** RCA 09026 61846-2 [id.]. New England Conservatory & Alumni Ch., Boston SO, Munch.
❀ *** Decca Dig. 400 055-2. Montreal SO and Ch., Dutoit.
(N) *** Decca Dig. 443 934-2 [id.]. Het Groot Ch., Conc. O, Chailly – DEBUSSY: *Khamma.* ***

(i) *Daphnis et Chloé* (ballet; complete); *Alborada del gracioso; Boléro.*
(Y/B) (M) **(*) DG Dig. 445 519-2 [id.]. LSO, Abbado; (i) with L. Symphony Ch.

(i) *Daphnis et Chloé* (complete); (ii) *Ma Mère l'Oye: suite.*
(N) (BB) *** RCA Navigator 74321 29257-2. (i) Dallas Ch. & SO, Mata; (ii) Boston SO, Munch.

Daphnis et Chloé (complete); *Pavane pour une infante défunte; Rapsodie espagnole.*
(M) *** Decca 448 603-2 [id.]. ROHCG Ch., LSO, Pierre Monteux.

(i) *Daphnis et Chloé* (ballet; complete); (ii) *Shéhérazade.*
(M) **(*) Sony SMK 47604 (i) Schola Cant., NYPO; (ii) Horne, Fr. Nat. R. O; Bernstein.

Charles Munch's Boston account is one of the great glories of the 1950s, superior in every way to his later version from the 1960s. The playing in all departments of the Boston orchestra is simply electrifying. The sound here may not be as sumptuous as the Monteux on Decca, but the richness of colour lies in the playing, and there is a heady sense of intoxication that at times sweeps you off your feet, and the integration of the chorus is impressively managed. Try the *Danse de supplication de Chloé* (track 15) and the ensuing scene in which the pirates are put to flight, and you will get a good idea of how dazzling this is, with the ballet ending in tumultous orchestral virtuosity.

Dutoit adopts an idiomatic and flexible style, observing the minute indications of tempo change but making every slight variation sound totally spontaneous. The final *Danse générale* finds him adopting a dangerously fast tempo, but the Montreal players – combining French responsiveness with transatlantic polish – rise superbly to the challenge, with the choral punctuations at the end adding to the sense of frenzy. The digital recording is wonderfully luminous, with the chorus ideally balanced at an evocative half-distance.

Monteux conducted the first performance of *Daphnis et Chloé* in 1912; Decca's 1959 recording, a demonstration disc in its day, captured his poetic and subtly shaded reading in vivid colours in the most agreeably warm ambience. The performance was one of the finest things Monteux did for the gramophone. Decca have added his 1962 recording of the *Pavane*, wonderfully poised and played most beautifully, and the highly spontaneous *Rapsodie espagnole*. A worthy addition to the Classic Sound series.

Riccardo Chailly conducts a remarkably fine complete *Daphnis*. Perhaps the last ounce of magic is missing, but there is plenty of colour and no lack of atmosphere. The excellence of the orchestral playing can be taken for granted, and the same goes for the luminous Decca recording, perhaps the finest the work has received. Not necessarily a first recommendation, but a choice that is unlikely to disappoint.

In the late 1970s Eduardo Mata helped to build the Dallas orchestra into a splendid band, and here he directs a warmly atmospheric and magnetic reading of *Daphnis et Chloé* for which RCA (in 1979) produced one of the finest of their early digital recordings. Two decades later it remains near the demonstration bracket for its clarity and allure (helped by the splendid acoustics of the Dallas auditorium). The closing pages with chorus are particularly impressive. The orchestral response here is comparable to the playing the Boston orchestra gave Munch 21 years earlier in their *Ma Mère l'Oye* suite. This has plenty of lustre, helped by the even warmer Boston resonance which, with a forward balance, robs Ravel's scoring of some of its subtlety. But this is still one of the very best reissues on the Navigator bargain-basement label.

Bernstein's *Daphnis et Chloé* dates from 1964 and comes with an altogether seductive *Shéhérazade* with Marilyn Horne, one of the most sensuous accounts committed to disc. Bernstein is at his very best here and each movement is characterized to perfection. The sound, too, is very good. Horne's *Shéhérazade* weaves the most erotic tales, and while one is under its spell the claims of the incomparable Suzanne Danco and Régine Crespin are almost (though not quite) forgotten. By comparison, Bernstein's 1961 *Daphnis* is less successful; there are good things, of course – most notably the last part, which comprises the second suite, but there are moments of less-than-perfect intonation which diminish its appeal. The sound is a vast improvement on the CBS original – but then it needed to be. In spite of the *Daphnis*, this record is a must.

The brilliant playing of the LSO under Abbado is helped by an exceptionally analytical DG recording which has the widest possible dynamic range – so much so that the pianissimo at the very opening is barely audible for almost thirty seconds. For all its refinement and virtuosity, this is a performance to admire rather than love, lacking the atmospheric warmth that marks, say, the Dutoit version.

(i; ii) *Daphnis et Chloé* (ballet): *suites Nos. 1–2*; (iii) *Ma Mère l'Oye (Mother Goose) suite;* (i; iv) *La valse;* (i; iv; v) *Shéhérazade* (song-cycle).
(N) ❀ (M) *** Dutton Lab. CDK 1201 [id.]. (i) Paris Conservatoire O; (ii) Munch; (iii) Nat. SO, Sidney Beer; (iv) Ansermet; (v) with Suzanne Danco.

Despite an apology about the opening – 'Noise at start of Track 1 as original master' – the detail and depth of focus of the early *ffrr* 78 recording for *Daphnis* are remarkable, with *Daybreak* matching later Munch readings in warmth – indeed its sense of ecstasy has never been surpassed on disc – and with the final *Danse générale* given tremendous thrust. The recording was made at Walthamstow in October 1946, and *La valse* under Ansermet at Kingsway Hall followed a year later. The sound is fuller in bass with even greater clarity, but under Ansermet the ensemble is rougher in a work that cries out for virtuoso treatment. Ansermet is far stronger in *Shéhérazade*, recorded with the same orchestra in Paris in May 1948. With the bright-toned, very French-sounding Danco enunciating the text to bring out every word, it is a taut and purposeful rather than an atmospheric reading, but it still has a flavour all its own. The conductor in *Ma Mere l'Oye* is Sidney Beer, with the orchestra he himself assembled from among London's leading players of the time, many still in the armed forces. Though he sounds rather matter-of-fact at the start after Munch or Ansermet, there is plenty of charm later, with excellent solo work and with the final *Le jardin féerique* rapt in concentration. This Kingsway Hall recording is so luminous that one can hardly believe it is mono, or that the uncannily present and vivid transfers are made direct from 78 shellac discs dating from 1945. The Rosette, however, is for Munch's *Daphnis et Chloé*.

Daphnis et Chloé: suites 1 & 2; Pavane pour une infante défunte.
** DG Gold Dig. 439 008-2 [id.]. BPO, Karajan – DEBUSSY: *La Mer* etc. **

As in the case of *La Mer*, this digital Karajan performance does not have the magic and sense of rapture and intoxication that informed his earlier Berlin account of the second *Daphnis* suite – surely one of the greatest performances of this glorious score ever committed to disc (see above). The remastered digital recording sounds very impressive, but is less atmospheric in effect.

Daphnis et Chloé: suite No. 2; Pavane pour une infante défunte.
(***) Testament mono SBT1017 [id.]. Philh. O, Cantelli – CASELLA: *Paganiniana;* DUKAS: *L'apprenti sorcier,* FALLA: *Three-cornered hat.* (***)

Cantelli's account of *Daphnis* was among his last – and finest – records. It sounds remarkably good in this splendid transfer. Along with Koussevitzky, Ormandy and Karajan, this has classic status.

Ma Mère l'Oye (complete ballet).
(Y/B) (M) *** Mercury 434 343-2 [id.]. Detroit SO, Paray – DEBUSSY: *Ibéria* etc. ***
*** Ph. Dig. 400 016-2 [id.]. Pittsburgh SO, Previn – SAINT-SAENS: *Carnival of the Animals.* ***

Ma Mère l'Oye (complete); *Le tombeau de Couperin; Valses nobles et sentimentales.*
✷ *** Decca Dig. 410 254-2 [id.]. Montreal SO, Dutoit.

Ma Mère l'Oye (complete); *Rapsodie espagnole.*
(M) *** DG 415 844-2 [id.]. LAPO, Giulini – MUSSORGSKY: *Pictures.* ***

A few bars of this Decca record leave no doubt as to its excellence. This offers demonstration quality, transparent and refined, with the textures beautifully balanced and expertly placed. The performances too are wonderfully refined and sympathetic. *Ma Mère l'Oye* is ravishingly beautiful, its special combination of sensuousness and innocence perfectly caught.

Paray's gently evocative *Ma Mère l'Oye* is most beautifully played and recorded. The score's calm innocence with its undercurrent of quiet ecstasy is caught perfectly and the translucence of the sound, recorded in Detroit's Ford Auditorium, offers rather more transparency than with the hardly less fine Debussy couplings. *Laideronette, Empress of the Pagodas* with its impressive stroke on the tam tam is thoroughly exotic, and the closing portrayal of the *Fairy garden* is exquisite. So lustrous is the sound that it is almost impossible to believe the early recording date: 1957.

In Previn's version, played and recorded with consummate refinement, the quality of innocence shines out. The recording is superb, with the Philips engineers presenting a texture of luminous clarity.

The Giulini Los Angeles performance conveys much of the sultry atmosphere of the *Rapsodie espagnole.* Indeed some details, such as the sensuous string responses to the cor anglais tune in the *Feria,* have not been so tenderly caressed since the intoxicating Reiner version. The *Ma Mère l'Oye* suite is also sensitively done; though it is cooler, it is still beautiful.

Ma Mère l'Oye (ballet): *suite.*
(B) *** CfP CD-CFP 4086; *TC-CFP 40086.* SNO, Gibson – BIZET: *Jeux d'enfants;* SAINT-SAENS; *Carnival.* ***
(M) ** EMI Dig. CD-EMX 2165; *TC-EMX 2165.* LPO, Sian Edwards – BRITTEN: *Young person's guide* ***; PROKOFIEV: *Peter and the wolf.* **(*)

Ma Mère l'Oye (ballet): *suite; Pavane pour une infante défunte.*
(M) *** Sony SMK 47545 [id.]. NYPO, Bernstein – DEBUSSY: *Images* etc. **(*)

The New York Philharmonic play Ravel's *Ma Mère l'Oye suite* with exquisite gentleness and much atmosphere. One can sense Bernstein's feeling for the music in every bar, yet he is never mannered. The *Pavane,* too, is given a tender dignity and the horn solo is restrained and beautiful. The recording of the ballet suite was made in the Manhattan Center in 1965, and the sound is pleasing.

Gibson is highly persuasive, shaping the music with obvious affection and a feeling for both the innocent spirit and the radiant textures of Ravel's beautiful score. The orchestral playing is excellent and, with excellent couplings, this is very recommendable.

Warm and beautiful orchestral playing from the LPO under Sian Edwards, but Ravel's magical score does not yield all its secrets here; its sense of gentle, innocent ecstasy is missing.

Rapsodie espagnole.
(Y/B) (B) **(*) BBC Radio Classics BBCRD 9107 [id.]. New Philh. O, Stokowski (with Concert) – BRAHMS: *Symphony No. 4;* VAUGHAN WILLIAMS: *Tallis Fantasia.* **(*)

This Stokowski performance, from an Albert Hall concert in May 1974, comes with a Brahms *Fourth* of the highest voltage. The *Rapsodie espagnole* would no doubt cast a spell under concert conditions, but it is by no means as magical or as atmospheric as Reiner's recording of the previous decade, and is by no means as well recorded. The sound has warmth but is wanting in transparency. All the same, this is a disc well worth considering for the sake of a thrilling Brahms *Fourth*.

Tzigane (for violin and orchestra).
*** EMI Dig. CDC7 47725-2 [id.]. Perlman, O de Paris, Martinon – CHAUSSON: *Poème;* SAINT-SAENS: *Havanaise* etc. ***
(N) (M) *** DG Dig. 447 445-2 [id.]. Itzhak Perlman, NYPO, Mehta – BERG; STRAVINSKY: *Concertos.* ***

Perlman's classic (1975) account of Ravel's *Tzigane* for EMI is marvellously played; the added projection of the CD puts the soloist believably at the end of the living-room. The opulence of his tone is undiminished by the remastering process and the orchestral sound retains its atmosphere, while gaining in clarity.

Perlman's later, digital version is very fine and the recording is obviously modern. But the earlier EMI performance has just that bit more charisma.

La valse.
(M) ** Ph. Dig. 434 733-2 [id.]. VPO, Previn – RIMSKY-KORSAKOV: *Scheherazade*. **(*)

Previn's performance is well played and recorded, though his rubato is not always absolutely convincing. The record was made with an audience present.

Valses nobles et sentimentales.
(*) DG Dig. 429 785-2 [id.]. NYPO, Sinopoli – MUSSORGSKY: *Night* etc. *

With Sinopoli Ravel's *Valses nobles et sentimentales* is perhaps a shade too idiosyncratic, even though it is played superbly by the New York Philharmonic; in the last three sections he takes Ravel's markings to an extreme, with the music almost coming to a halt in the middle of the *Moins vif*.

CHAMBER MUSIC

Berceuse; Pièce en forme de habañera; Tzigane.
(N) *** DG Dig. 445 880-2 [id.]. Dumay, Pires – DEBUSSY; FRANCK: *Violin sonatas*. ***

Polished and elegant performances of these Ravel pieces. There would, of course, have been room on this disc for the 1922 *Sonata*, which at premium price would have made better sense as well as value for money. However, no complaints about these performances or the recording quality.

Introduction and allegro for harp, flute, clarinet and string quartet.
⊛ (M) *** Decca 421 154-2. Osian Ellis, Melos Ens. – DEBUSSY; FRANCK: *Sonatas*. *** ⊛
(Y/B) (***) Testament mono SBT 1053 [id.]. Gleghorn, Lurie, Stockton, Hollywood Qt – CRESTON: *Quartet;* DEBUSSY: *Danse sacrée* etc. TURINA: *La Oración del torero;* VILLA-LOBOS: *Quartet No. 6.* (***)

The beauty and subtlety of Ravel's sublime septet are marvellously realized by this 1962 Melos account. The interpretation has great delicacy of feeling, and the recording hardly shows its age at all.

The Hollywood Quartet's version of the *Introduction and allegro* gives us an example of the exquisite flute playing of Arthur Gleghorn as well as the artistry of Mitchell Lurie and Ann Mason Stockton. A fine performance, sounding remarkably fresh for a 1951 recording.

(i) *Introduction and allegro;* (ii) *Pièce en forme de habañera*.
(Y/B) (B) *** Cala Dig. CACD 1018 (2) [id.]. James Campbell; (i) William Bennett, Ieuan Jones, Allegri Qt; (ii) John York – POULENC: *L'invitation au château* etc. ***

These Cala performances are recommendable in their own right, but they come in a particularly valuable two-CD set for the price of one, which includes over two hours of music for wind instruments by Poulenc. It is sheer delight from start to finish and cannot be too strongly recommended.

Piano trio in A min.
*** Ph. Dig. 411 141-2 [id.]. Beaux Arts Trio – CHAUSSON: *Piano trio*. ***
*** Carlton Dig. MCD 41 [id.]. Solomon Trio – DEBUSSY; FAURE: *Piano trios*. ***
*** Chandos Dig. CHAN 8458 [id.]. Borodin Trio – DEBUSSY: *Violin and Cello sonatas*. ***
(Y/B) ** RCA Dig. 09026 68062-2 [id.]. Previn, Rosenfeld, Hoffman – DEBUSSY: *Piano trio*. **
(N) *(*) Decca Dig. 444 318-2 [id.]. Perlman, Harrell, Ashkenazy – DEBUSSY: *Cello sonata* etc. *(*)

The most recent Beaux Arts account of the Ravel *Trio* is little short of inspired and is even finer than their earlier record of the late 1960s. The recording, too, is of high quality, even if the piano is rather forward.

The Solomon Trio's account of the Ravel is very fine indeed and has the advantage of an excellently balanced recording. It is thoroughly recommendable and has fine couplings, too, and a price advantage.

The Borodin Trio are excellently recorded and their playing has great warmth and is full of colour. Some may find them too hot-blooded by the side of the Beaux Arts.

RCA would have been better advised to have insisted on a more substantial coupling from Previn, Rosenfeld and Hoffman than the early Debussy *G major Trio*, offered here, which is slight and uncharacteristic of the master. However, fine as this is – and its quality is not in doubt – it is handicapped by the coupling and the fact that the playing time is only 48 minutes.

This Perlman/Askenazy/Harrell performance is strongly projected but (like its couplings) wanting that intimacy of feeling and *tendresse* which this most magical of scores calls for. There are many more idiomatic accounts around, and at less than 50 minutes this is not good value.

Piano trio in A min.; Sonata for violin and cello.
(N) * Chandos Dig. CHAN 9452 [id.]. Bekova Sisters – MARTINU: *Duo* etc. *

A well-planned and not unattractive coupling. The *Sonata for violin and cello* is a comparative rarity, but most collectors will want this for the *Piano trio*, one of Ravel's greatest works. But the performances are pretty indifferent and, given the excellent accounts that are already in the catalogue, this is uncompetitive. Good recorded sound.

Piano trio in A min.; Sonata for violin and cello; (i) Chansons madécasses; 3 Poèmes de Stéphane Mallarmé.
**(*) Virgin/EMI Dig. VC5 45016-2 [id.]. (i) Sarah Walker; Nash Ens.

The *Sonata for violin and cello* is expertly played by Marcia Crayford and Christopher van Kampen – as good an account as any – and in the *Piano trio* Ian Brown joins them in what is a performance of real stature and eloquence. In the *Chansons madécasses* and the exquisite *Trois poèmes de Stéphane Mallarmé* Sarah Walker is *primus inter pares* rather than a soloist, though she is not balanced as reticently by the Andrew Keener team as their Debussy *Chansons de Bilitis* with Delphine Seyrig. A pity, since this detracts from what would otherwise be an outstanding record.

String quartet in F.
*** Denon Dig. CO 75164 [id.]. Carmina Qt – DEBUSSY: *Quartet.* ***
*** DG Dig. 437 836-2 [id.]. Hagen Qt – DEBUSSY; WEBERN: *Quartets.* ***
*** Sony Dig. SK 52554 [id.]. Juilliard Qt – DEBUSSY; DUTILLEUX: *Quartets.* ***
(M) *** DG 435 589-2 [id.]. LaSalle Qt – DEBUSSY: *Quartet.* ***
(M) *** Ph. 420 894-2. Italian Qt – DEBUSSY: *Quartet.* ***
(B) *** CfP Dig. CD-CFP 4652; *TC-CFP 4652* [id.]. Chilingirian Qt – DEBUSSY: *Quartet.* ***
(N) **(*) ASV Dig. CDDCA 930 [id.]. Lindsay Qt – DEBUSSY: *String quartet* **(*); STRAVINSKY: *3 Pieces.* ***
(B) **(*) Discover Dig. DICD 920171 [id.]. Sharon Qt – BEETHOVEN: *Harp quartet* **(*); MOZART: *Quartet No. 1.* ***
(M) **(*) Carlton Dig. 3036 70105-2 [id.]. New World Qt – DEBUSSY: *Quartet* **(*); DUTILLEUX: *Ainsi la nuit.* ***

String quartet in F; (i) Introduction & allegro for harp, flute, clarinet and string quartet.
(BB) *** Naxos Dig. 8.550249 [id.]. Kodály Qt, (i) with Maros, Gyöngyössy, Kovács – DEBUSSY: *Quartet.* **(*)
(Y/B) **(*) RCA Dig. 09026 62552-2 [id.]. Tokyo Qt, (i) with Galway, Stolzman, Lehwalder – DEBUSSY: *Quartet.* **(*)

The Carmina Quartet give a splendid account of this elusive masterpiece. The recording is fresh and wide-ranging (perhaps a trace fierce right at the very top) and the playing is of the highest quality. There is plenty of ardour when required, and some moments of impetuousness, but these are small idiosyncrasies in a performance distinguished by good taste and impeccable ensemble. Dynamic contrasts are strong without being excessive, and their playing has what one might call a narrative quality that holds the listener throughout, and the recording is very impressive. The one drawback to this issue is the absence of any additional work besides the usual Debussy coupling.

The equally impressive Hagen Quartet, by adding the Webern, are perhaps even more competitive They give a performance of great finesse and tonal refinement, and are beautifully recorded to boot, very well served by an excellent balance from one of DG's best engineers, Wolfgang Mitelehner.

The Juilliard are very impressive too, not quite so youthful, elegant and fresh in their approach but eminently polished and sensitive. This Sony disc is to be recommended primarily to those attracted to the fine Dutilleux bonus. However, the earlier (and less expensive) versions remain very competitive.

There is little to choose between the DG LaSalle performance and the Italian Quartet on Philips. If the latter have perhaps the greater immediacy and sense of vitality, the former create a superb feeling of atmosphere and bring great freshness and delicacy of feeling to this score.

For many years the Italian Quartet held pride of place in this coupling. Their playing is perfect in ensemble, attack and beauty of tone, and their performance remains highly recommendable, one of the most satisfying chamber-music records in the catalogue.

The Chilingirian recording has plenty of body and presence, and also has the benefit of a warm acoustic. The players give a thoroughly committed account, with well-judged tempi and very musical phrasing. The Scherzo is vital and spirited, and there is no want of poetry in the slow movement. At mid-price this is fully competitive and the sound is preferable to that of the Italian Quartet on Philips.

The Naxos version can more than hold its own. Artistically and technically this is a satisfying performance which has the feel of real live music-making. The *Introduction and allegro* is not as magical or as atmospheric as that of the Melos Ensemble from the 1960s, nor is it as well balanced (the players, save for the harp, are a bit forward), but it is still thoroughly enjoyable.

The Tokyo Quartet are also very impressive, and although their performance is not entirely free from some self-regarding touches its tonal finesse is a joy in itself. In the *Introduction and allegro*, the balance tends to favour Galway, to put it mildly, and there is at times a danger of it becoming a flute concerto!

A highly accomplished and finely etched performance from the Lindsays, who play with their usual aplomb and panache. There are splendid things here, notably the youthful fire of the opening movement and the vivid finale. They do not always match the poetic feeling and the *douceur* which some rivals find, but this is not a neglible account, and it is well recorded.

The Sharon Quartet are completely at home in this music and play with ardour and sensitivity. The resonant acoustic (a Cologne church) suits the work better than the Beethoven coupling. It certainly does not cloud the Scherzo or the energetic account of the finale (which also has much delicacy of feeling) and adds warmth and atmosphere to the *très lent*. Very good playing: if the couplings are suitable, this is a bargain.

The Harvard-based New World Quartet give an admirable account of the Ravel, a shade overprojected at times, and the leader's expressive rubato and that of the violist may not be to all tastes. Well recorded though it is, it does not displace existing recommendations though it offers the inducement of a Dutilleux rarity.

Violin sonata in G.

(N) *** Virgin/EMI Dig. VC5 45122-2. Tetzlaff, Andsnes – DEBUSSY: *Sonata;* JANACEK: *Sonata;* NIELSEN: *Sonata No. 2.* ***

(N) (M) *** DG Dig. 445 557-2 [id.]. Shlomo Mintz, Yefim Bronfman – PROKOFIEV: *Violin sonatas.* ***

*** Ph. Dig. 426 254-2. Viktoria Mullova, Bruno Canino – PROKOFIEV: *Sonata* **; STRAVINSKY: *Divertimento.* ***

The Ravel *Violin sonata* has come into its own in recent years. The performance from Christian Tetzlaff and Leif Ove Andsnes proves as characterful and imaginative as any available, and an additional attraction is the interest of the couplings, in particular the Nielsen *Second Sonata*. Excellent recording too. However, McAslan, Mullova and Mintz also offer highly recommendable versions, so choice can be dictated by the coupling required.

Shlomo Mintz and Yefim Bronfman's account offers highly polished playing, even if it is not so completely inside Ravel's world in the slow movement. The glorious sounds both artists produce are a source of unfailing delight and they are beautifully recorded too. At mid-price, coupled with outstanding versions of the two Prokofiev *Sonatas*, this is very recommendable.

Mullova and Canino also give a beguiling performance. It is played with diamond-like precision and great character. The Philips recording is marvellous. However, the couplings are not as successful as McAslan's.

PIANO MUSIC
Piano duet

Boléro; Introduction and allegro; Ma Mère l'Oye; Rapsodie espagnole; La valse.

✪ *** Chandos Dig. CHAN 8905 [id.]. Louis Lortie and Hélène Mercier.

Lortie's recital for piano (four hands and two pianos) with his Canadian partner, Hélène Mercier, is quite magical; these artists command an exceptionally wide range of colour and dynamic nuance. The acoustic is that of The Maltings, Snape, and the result is quite outstanding sonically: you feel that you have only to stretch out and you can touch the instruments. Ravel's transcriptions are stunningly effective in their hands, even, surprisingly, *Boléro*.

Daphnis et Chloé: suite No. 2; Introduction and allegro; Ma Mère l'Oye; Rapsodie espagnole; La valse.
(N) ** Mer. Dig. CDE 84300 [id.]. Abbott O'Gorman Duo.

There is much that is sensitive here, notably the openings of the *Introduction and allegro* and *Ma Mère l'Oye*. But there is a lack of panache at the climax of *La Valse* and, although the *Feria* which closes the *Rapsodie espagnole* brings exuberance, the opening of *Daphnis and Chloé* lacks evocative magic. In general these performances are no match for those offered by their Chandos competitor.

Ma Mère l'Oye.
*** Ph. Dig. 420 159-2 [id.]. Katia and Marielle Labèque – FAURE: *Dolly;* BIZET: *Jeux d'enfants.* ***

The Labèque sisters give an altogether delightful performance of Ravel's magical score, which he later orchestrated and expanded. The recording could not be more realistic and present.

Ma Mère l'Oye; Rapsodie espagnole (arr. Peter Sadlo).
(Y/B) *** DG Dig. 439 867-2 [id.]. Martha Argerich, Nelson Freire, Peter Sadlo, Edgar Guggeis – BARTOK: *Sonata for 2 pianos & percussion.* ***

This is not Ravel's own transcription of *Rapsodie espagnole* or his original *Ma Mère l'Oye* but an arrangement for two pianos and two percussion players to match up with their account of the Bartók *Sonata for two pianos and percussion*. After saying that, it must be added that the additional parts are done with eminently good taste, restraint and musical imagination (they are drawn and adapted from Ravel's own orchestral version) – but, all the same, is there a need for them at all? A disc which it is more interesting to hear once or twice than to repeat.

Solo piano music

A la manière de Borodine; A la manière de Chabrier; Gaspard de la nuit; Jeux d'eau; Menuet antique; Menuet sur le nom de Haydn; Miroirs; Pavane pour une infante défunte; Prélude; Sérénade grotesque; Sonatine; Le tombeau de Couperin; Valses nobles et sentimentales.
*** Decca Dig. 433 515-2 (2) [id.]. Jean-Yves Thibaudet.
*** CRD Dig. CRD 3383/4; *CRDC 4083/5* [id.]. Paul Crossley.
(Y/B) (M) *** Chandos Dig. CHAN 7004/5 [id.]. Louis Lortie.

Jean-Yves Thibaudet's collected Ravel has won golden opinions everywhere, for this is quite outstanding playing on all counts; Thibaudet exhibits flawless technique, perfect control, refinement of touch and exemplary taste. He distils just the right atmosphere in *Oiseaux tristes* and *Une barque sur l'océan* – but then, one might as well choose any other piece from *Miroirs*, and his *Gaspard* can hold its own with any in the catalogue. The recording is of real distinction too.

  Paul Crossley's accounts of all these works are beautifully fashioned. He is aristocratic, with an admirable feeling for tone-colour and line, and rarely mannered (the end of *Jeux d'eau* is an exception). His version of *Le tombeau de Couperin* has a classical refinement and delicacy that are refreshing. The CRD recording is very good indeed, and this fine set deserves the warmest welcome.

  Chandos have now put Louis Lortie's two Ravel discs together. The first, including *Le tombeau de Couperin, Jeux d'eau, La valse* and the *Valses nobles et sentimentales*, was warmly welcomed in our 1992 edition and we found his *Gaspard de la nuit* with its chilling and atmospheric account of *Le gibet* particularly impressive. Now that these are repackaged at mid-price, let us hope that they will gain the wider dissemination to which their merits entitle them. The Chandos sound, which emanates from The Maltings, Snape, is very realistic and truthful.

A la manière de Borodine; A la manière de Chabrier; Menuet antique; Menuet sur le nom de Haydn; Miroirs; Pavane pour une infante défunte; Prélude; Sérénade grotesque; Sonatine.
*** ASV Dig. CDDCA 809 [id.]. Gordon Fergus-Thompson.

Gaspard de la nuit; Jeux d'eau; Le tombeau de Couperin; Valses nobles at sentimentales.
*** ASV Dig. CDDCA 805 [id.]. Gordon Fergus-Thompson.

Turning to Gordon Fergus-Thompson's Ravel immediately after Thibaudet is to enter a different imaginative world. There is not quite the same concentration that distinguishes Thibaudet's set, nor quite the same keyboard control. Indeed he does not hold the listener in the same grip as the French pianist. However, this is still distinguished playing: there is an ample and rich colour-palette, and his presentation exhibits considerable personality and imagination, which is probably why it has attracted some adverse criticism. Not to be preferred to the Decca set, though readers considering it can be assured that it is very well recorded.

A la manière de Borodine; A la manière de Chabrier; Gaspard de la nuit; Jeux d'eau; Menuet antique; Menuet sur le nom d'Haydn; Miroirs; Pavane pour une infante défunte; Prélude; Sonatine; Le tombeau de Couperin; Valses nobles et sentimentales; (i) *Ma mère l'Oye.*
(B) ** Decca Double 440 836-2 (2). Pascal Rogé, (i) with Denise Françoise.

Pascal Rogé made these recordings in 1973/4 at the beginning of his Decca contract. He is well recorded (though the effect is a little cool) and his playing is sensitive. His performances of the *Sonatine, Le tombeau* and the *Valses nobles et sentimentales* were widely praised on their first appearance, but we have heard more imaginative accounts of *Le tombeau*: the *Forlane* is not keenly delineated and characterized. He produces some finely coloured tone in *Miroirs,* but overall it is a shade pallid and under-characterized, and he does not match either Ashkenazy or Argerich – and certainly not Pogorelich in *Gaspard de la nuit* in terms of authority or panache. Yet there is much that is good here, and the set certainly indicated his natural gifts in this repertoire, which were to be realized more fully in later records.

A la manière de Borodine; A la manière de Chabrier; Gaspard de la nuit; Jeux d'eau; Menuet sur le nom de Haydn; Prélude; Sérénade grotesque; Sonatine; Valses nobles et sentimentales.
**(*) Virgin/EMI Dig. VC7 59322-2 [id.]. Anne Queffélec.

Pavane pour une infante défunte; Menuet antique; Miroirs; Le tombeau de Couperin.
**(*) Virgin/EMI Dig. VC7 59233-2 [id.]. Anne Queffélec.

No quarrels with Anne Queffélec's playing, which is alert, intelligent and vital, as one would expect from so excellent a stylist. There are some masterly and enjoyable interpretations here, but it is all far too closely observed, as if one were in the front row in the concert hall; as a result, not all the atmosphere registers to full effect once the dynamics rise above *mf.*

A la manière de Borodine; A la manière de Chabrier; Menuet antique; Prélude; Le tombeau de Couperin; Valses nobles et sentimentales.
**(*) Nimbus NI 5011 [id.]. Vlado Perlemuter.

Gaspard de la nuit; Jeux d'eau; Miroirs; Pavane.
**(*) Nimbus NI 5005 [id.]. Vlado Perlemuter.

Though Perlemuter's technical command is not as complete as it had been, he gives delightful, deeply sympathetic readings; the sense of spontaneity is a joy. There may be Ravel recordings which bring more dazzling virtuoso displays, but none more persuasive. Nimbus's ample room acoustic makes the result naturally atmospheric on CD.

Gaspard de la nuit.
*** DG Dig. 413 363-2 [id.]. Pogorelich – PROKOFIEV: *Sonata No. 6.* *** ❀

Pogorelich's *Gaspard* is out of the ordinary. In *Le gibet,* we are made conscious of the pianist's refinement of tone and colour first, and Ravel's poetic vision afterwards. But for all that, this is piano playing of astonishing quality. The control of colour and nuance in *Scarbo* is dazzling and its eruptive cascades of energy and dramatic fire have one sitting on the edge of one's seat.

Gaspard de la nuit; Pavane pour une infante défunte; Valses nobles et sentimentales.
(M) *** Decca Dig. 425 081-2 [id.]. Vladimir Ashkenazy (with DEBUSSY: *L'isle joyeuse* ***) – SCRIABIN: *Danses* etc. ***

Ashkenazy's earlier (1965) analogue version of *Gaspard* in its day was a yardstick by which others were judged. His new, digital account is hardly less impressive than the old and is in no way narcissistic. It remains a distinguished alternative to Pogorelich. His *Valses nobles* are splendidly refined and aristo-cratic. The recording has excellent range and is extremely vivid and open. Debussy's *L'isle joyeuse* was recorded at the time of the analogue *Gaspard* and is also a fine performance.

VOCAL MUSIC

3 Chansons.
(Y/B) *** Ph. Dig. 438 149-2 [id.]. Monteverdi Ch., O Révolutionnaire et Romantique, Gardiner – FAURE: *Requiem;* DEBUSSY; SAINT-SAENS: *Choral songs.* ***

With his superb choir, Gardiner lightly and crisply touches in the wit and humour behind the two outer songs with their sixteenth-century overtones, and he draws out the lyrical beauty of the central one. A welcome addition to the fascinating group of works chosen by Gardiner as coupling for his expressive reading of the Fauré *Requiem*.

(i) *Chansons madécasses;* (ii) *Don Quichotte à Dulcinée; 5 mélodies populaires grêcques;* (iii) *3 poèmes de Stéphane Mallarmé.*

(Y/B) (M) *** Sony SMK 64107 [id.]. (i) Norman, Ens. InterContemporain; (ii) José van Dam; (iii) Jill Gomez; BBC SO, Boulez – ROUSSEL: *Symphony No. 3.* **(*)

With three characterful and strongly contrasted soloists, Boulez's collection of Ravel songs with orchestra (including arrangements) makes a delightful mid-priced collection and is especially valuable as the *Don Quichotte* and the *Greek popular songs* are rarely heard in this orchestral form. Van Dam may not be as relaxed here as he was with piano accompaniment (on the HMV recording with Dalton Baldwin which is currently withdrawn), but the dark, firm voice is just as impressive. Excellent sound, full and atmospheric, with translations provided; the addition of Boulez's impressive (1975) version of Roussel's *Third Symphony* makes this reissue all the more desirable.

Shéhérazade (song-cycle).
*** Decca 417 813-2 [id.]. Régine Crespin, SRO, Ansermet (with *Recital of French songs* ***).

Crespin is right inside these songs and Ravel's magically sensuous music emerges with striking spontaneity. She is superbly supported by Ansermet who, aided by the Decca engineers, weaves a fine tonal web round the voice. Her style has distinct echoes of the opera house; but the richness of the singer's tone does not detract from the delicate languor of *The enchanted flute*, in which the slave-girl listens to the distant sound of her lover's flute playing while her master sleeps.

OPERA

L'enfant et les sortilèges (complete).
(Y/B) ✿ (***) Testament mono SBT 1044 [id.]. Nadine Sautereau, André Vessières, Solange Michel, Denise Scharley, Yvon Le Marc'Hadour, Joseph Peyron, Martha Angelici, French Nat. R. Ch. and O, Ernest Bour.
(Y/B) (M) *** EMI Dig. CD-EMX 2241 [id.]. Wyner, Augér, Berbié, Langridge, Bastin, Amb. S., LSO, Previn.

Testament here offer a superlative transfer of the unsurpassed first recording of Ravel's charming one-Acter under Ernest Bour. There is a magic about this performance that completely captivates the listener. Each part, from Nadine Sautereau's Child, Yvon Le Marc'Hadour's Tom-Cat and Clock and Solange Michel's touching squirrel, to Denise Scharley as the Dragonfly and the Mother, could not be improved upon in character, subtlety and style. The singing and playing of the French Radio forces are vital and imaginative. Ravel's exquisite score is heard to best advantage in this extraordinary transfer, in which every detail in the recording comes across to perfection. Though the 1947 mono sound is short on mystery, the sharpness of focus, with voices firm and immediate, heightens the authentic Frenchness of the reading, both jewelled and purposeful. With no stars but with no weak link, the singers make an outstanding team, helped by sound which, with background hiss eliminated, has astonishing presence. No other version casts quite such a strong spell.

Previn's dramatic and highly spontaneous reading of *L'Enfant* certainly brings out the refreshing charm of this still neglected masterpiece. Helped by a strong and stylish team of soloists, this makes superb entertainment. On CD, the precision and sense of presence of the digital recordings come out the more vividly, with subtle textures clarified and voices – including the odd shout – precisely placed. That precision goes well with Previn's performance, crisply rhythmic rather than atmospherically poetic. Those wanting a modern, digital recording should be well satisfied with this at mid-price, for a full libretto with translation is included.

L'enfant et les sortilèges (complete).
*** DG 423 718-2 [id.]. Ogéas, Collard, Berbié, Gilma, RTF Ch. & Boys' Ch., RTF Nat. O, Maazel.

L'heure espagnole (complete).
*** DG 423 719-2 [id.]. Berbié, Sénéchal, Giraudeau, Bacquier, Van Dam, Paris Op. O, Maazel.

Maazel's recordings of the two Ravel one-Act operas were made in the early 1960s and, though the solo voices in the former are balanced too close, the sound is vivid and the performances are splendidly stylish. Neo-classical crispness of articulation goes with refined textures that convey the tender poetry of the one piece, the ripe humour of the other. The CD remastering has been very successful and both performances are given striking presence, without loss of essential atmosphere. Full librettos are included. However, these records are surely now due for mid-price reissue.

(i; ii) *L'enfant et les sortilèges* (complete). *Shéhérazade: Ouverture de féerie* & (ii) *song-cycle*.
(N) **(*) Decca Dig. 440 333-2 [id.]. (i) Alliot-Lugaz, Lefort, Beaupré, Carlson, Gautier, Henry, Sarrazin; (ii) Catherine Dubosc; Ch., Montreal SO, Dutoit.

Dutoit offers a poetic reading of Ravel's fantasy piece on childhood, helped by warm, evocative sound. Voices are balanced forwardly on the sound-stage, which lets words be heard, and the delicacy and point of Colette's offbeat libretto is nicely caught but, compared with Maazel's vivid and immediate reading – let alone Ernest Bour's original recording – this is a version for those who are looking for the beauty of the score to be brought out rather than the sharper qualities. Colette Alliot-Lugaz is superb as the Child, with the rest of the French-speaking cast equally idiomatic, though voices are not always ideally pure or firm. The coupling is most generous, with Catherine Dubosc a fresh-voiced, girlish-sounding soloist in *Shéhérazade*, characterful but not sensuous; the rare *Ouverture de féerie* (also available from Martinon – see above) makes a welcome extra.

L'heure espagnole (complete).
(Y/B) (M) (***) EMI mono CDM5 65269-2 [id.]. Duval, Giraudeau, Vieuille, Herent, Clavensy, O. du Théâtre Nat. de l'Opéra-Comique, André Cluytens.

This recording, with Denise Duval as Concepcion and Jean Giraudeau as Gonzalve, was recorded at the Théâtre des Champs-Elysées in 1952 and makes its first appearance in Britain. Denise Duval is altogether superb, as is the rest of the cast for that matter. Apart from the quality of the singing, the artists of this period understood the importance of diction and acting. The sound comes up very well indeed, and the set should give much pleasure.

Rawsthorne, Alan (1905–71)

Clarinet concerto.
*** Hyperion CDA 66031 [id.]. Thea King, NW CO of Seattle, Alun Francis – COOKE: *Concerto;* JACOB: *Mini-concerto.* ***

Though the *Clarinet concerto* is an early work of Rawsthorne's it already establishes the authentic flavour of his writing with a certain gritty and angular quality masking the obvious depth of feeling behind. That constraint makes for musical strength, the more obviously so in a performance as persuasive as this from soloist and orchestra alike. Excellent 1982 analogue recording, expertly transferred.

Piano concertos Nos. 1–2; (i) *Double piano concerto.*
*** Chandos Dig. CHAN 9125 [id.]. Tozer, (i) with Cislowski; LPO, Bamert.

The *First Piano concerto* was a wartime work – vintage Rawsthorne, with its witty *Chaconne* – and the *Second* (1951) was composed for the Festival of Britain and is also rewarding, though the finale with its cheap opening idea is a bit of a let-down. The *Concerto for two pianos* is likewise stimulating. Tozer gives a good account of the concertos, not perhaps as compelling or understanding as the (now deleted) Malcolm Binns version on Lyrita or Moura Lympany's pioneering disc. The opening of No. 1 is a bit rushed; Tamara-Anna Cislowski is an excellent partner in the 1968 concerto. Matthias Bamert and the LPO are very supportive and the recording is in the best traditions of the house.

Madame Chrysanthème (ballet suite); *Street corner overture.*
(M) *** EMI CDM7 64718-2 [id.]. Pro Arte O, composer – ADDISON: *Carte blanche;* ARNELL: *Great Detective;* BLISS: *Checkmate;* ARNOLD: *Grand grand overture.* (***)

The energetically pithy *Street corner overture* is deservedly one of Rawsthorne's more familiar short pieces: succinct, melodic, rumbustious. *Madame Chrysanthème* was composed for the Sadler's Wells ballet and takes place in nineteenth-century Nagasaki. The music is sharply characterized; the *Hornpipe* owes something to Lord Berners, but it is only the final, rather touching *Les Mousmès* that brings a hint of orientalism. The composer's direction is vivid, and musically these are among the most interesting pieces in this anthology of British music, very well played and brightly recorded in 1960.

Symphonies Nos. (i) *1;* (ii) *2 (Pastoral);* (iii) *3.*
(N) *** Lyrita Analogue/Dig. SRCS 291 [id.]. (i) LPO, Pritchard, or (ii) Nicholas Braithwaite; with Tracey Chadwell, (iii) BBC SO, Norman Del Mar.

Here is a chance to get to grips with the symphonies of another neglected Britsh composer whose music is distinguished by impeccable craftsmanship and first-rate invention, as is readily demonstrated by the *First*, played with such evident enjoyment by the LPO under Sir John Pritchard. But, of the three, the *Second (Pastoral) Symphony* is the most readily approachable, since its thematic material catches the ear, especially in the expressive ideas of the *Poco lento* and the gay country-dance Scherzo. Like Vaughan Williams (and Mahler), Rawsthorne uses a soprano soloist in the finale, with a succinct text by Henry Howard, Earl of Surrey (1516–47), giving brief impressions of three of the four seasons: spring, summer and winter. The music has a powerful atmosphere, and Tracey Chadwell copes successfully with the rather angular vocal-line to catch the essential melancholy of the poem.

Though the actual thematic material of the *Third Symphony* is initially hard to identify (it is possibly too consistent in style and cut for conventional ideas of sonata form), the formal layout is never in doubt. The first movement culminates in a calm recapitulation which resolves earlier tensions most satisfyingly, and the separate sections of the *Sarabande* slow movement build up into one of the most passionate climaxes that Rawsthorne ever wrote. A Scherzo with nebulous, rather Waltonian motifs flying around is followed by a finale that daringly keeps changing gear between fast and slow. It is questionable whether Rawsthorne maintains the flow of argument with sufficient momentum in this movement, but there is no doubt whatever of the beauty and effectiveness of the hushed epilogue. All three works receive superb performances and the recording is outstanding with the sense of space and splendid detail we expect from Lyrita.

Clarinet quartet.
(N) *** Redcliffe Dig. RR 010 [id.]. Nicholas Cox, Redcliffe Ens. – BLISS; ROUTH: *Clarinet quintets.* ***

Rawsthorne's *Clarinet quartet* is more ambivalent in feeling than the Bliss *Quintet*, but its quirky opening movement is appealing and the darker *Poco lento* hardly less striking. In the finale, a purposeful *Allegro risoluto* leads to a slower section before the movement's tensions are resolved by the effective return of the main theme of the opening movement. With Nicholas Cox a most winning soloist, the performance here could hardly be improved upon, and the recording is first class.

Rebelo, João Lourenço (1610–61)

Lamentations for Maundy Thursday; Vesper Psalms.
*** Sony Dig. SK 53115 [id.]. Huelgas Ens., Paul van Nevel.

João Lourenço Rebelo was court composer to John (João) IV of Portugal, and indeed fostered the King's interest in music and his gifts as a composer. Rebelo's leaning was towards the polychoral Venetian style of Giovanni Gabrieli rather than the polyphony of Palestrina. Rebelo was one of the first to compose specific parts for instruments in his polyphonic works. The *Vesper Psalms* and the *Lamentations* recorded here are of striking expressive power and are both played and recorded marvellously with vivid realism. Those who admire Gabrieli and Schütz will find this a congenial yet distinctive voice.

Reger, Max (1873–1916)

Ballet suite; Variations on a theme of Hiller, Op. 100.
*** Orfeo C 090841 [id.]. Bav. RSO, C. Davis.

The *Hiller variations* (1907) is one of Reger's greatest works, full of wit, resource and, above all, delicacy. It culminates, as do so many Reger pieces, in a double fugue. The *Ballet suite* is a delightful piece, scored with great clarity and played, as is the *Hiller variations*, with charm and commitment. Sir Colin Davis emerges as a thoroughly *echt*-Reger conductor and the Bavarian orchestra is in excellent form.

(i) *Concerto in olden style, Op. 123; (ii) Sinfonietta, Op. 90.*
**(*) Koch Dig. 31354-2 [id.]. (i) Harald Orlovsky; (i; ii) Peter Rosenberg; Bamberg SO, Horst Stein.

The *Concerto in olden style* is Reger's tribute to the great Baroque masters, though his Op. 123 is scored for somewhat larger forces! The *Sinfonietta in A major* is an ambitious work, full of luxuriant invention, and richly and at times thickly scored; at others, it is a model of delicacy. The *Largo* is absolutely inspired. Horst Stein gets very good playing from the Bamberg orchestra and the recording is very warm and sonorous, perhaps not transparent enough at the top end of the spectrum.

Piano concerto in F min., Op. 114.
(M) ** Sony MPK 46452 [id.]. Rudolf Serkin, Phd. O, Ormandy – PROKOFIEV: *Piano concerto No. 4.* (***)

Reger's *Piano concerto* is a remarkable and powerful composition. No one but Reger could have conceived the rugged, Brahmsian piano writing. The slow movement is a contemplative, rapt piece that touches genuine depths. Serkin gives a magisterial performance and is well supported by the Philadelphia Orchestra under Ormandy, even though the early-1960s sound is not very inviting.

(i) *Symphonic prologue to a tragedy, Op. 108;* (ii) *2 Romances for violin and orchestra, Op. 50.*
**(*) Schwann CD311 076. (i) Berlin RSO, Albrecht; (ii) with Maile; cond. Lajovic.

The tragedy in question is Sophocles' *Oedipus Rex,* and Reger's *Symphonic prologue* is one of his very finest and most powerful works. Inspiration runs consistently high. The violin *Romances* are beautiful pieces and are very well played by Hans Maile and the Berlin Radio Orchestra. Strongly recommended, it must be said that the 1982 recording is serviceable rather than distinguished.

4 Tone poems after Böcklin, Op. 128; Variations on a theme by Hiller, Op. 100.
*** Chandos Dig. CHAN 8794 [id.]. Concg. O, Järvi.

Those who still think of Reger's music as densely contrapuntal and turgidly scored will be amazed by the delicacy and refinement of his orchestration. Of the four *Tone poems,* textures in *Der geigende Eremit* ('Hermit playing the violin') are wonderfully transparent, and *Im spiel der Wellen* has something of the sparkle of the *Jeu de vagues* movement of *La Mer* photographed in sepia; while the *Isle of the dead* is a lovely and often very touching piece. The *Hiller variations* are gloriously inventive. These works are beautifully recorded and Neeme Järvi's performances have the combination of sensitivity and virtuosity that this composer needs.

Variations and fugue on a theme by Mozart, Op. 132.
⊛ *** Ph. Dig. 422 347-2 [id.]. Bav. RSO, C. Davis – HINDEMITH: *Symphonic metamorphoses.* ***

Sir Colin Davis's account of Reger's *Variations and fugue on a theme by Mozart* has great subtlety and the strings produce a particularly cultured sound. The whole performance has a radiance and glow that does full justice to this masterpiece, which is not only scored with great delicacy but has wit and tenderness in equal measure. The Philips recording is state of the art. Recommended with enthusiasm.

ORGAN WORKS

Aus tiefer Not schrei ich zu dir, Op. 67/3; Intermezzo in F min., Op. 129/7; Introduction and Passacaglia in D min., Op. posth.; Prelude in D min., Op. 65/7.
*** Chandos Dig. CHAN 9097 [id.]. Piet Kee – HINDEMITH: *Organ sonatas.* ***

The four pieces Piet Kee offers on this CD are well chosen, well wrought and inventive. The Müller organ of St Bavo in Haarlem seems ideally suited to this repertoire, as is the slightly reverberant acoustic which rather softens the textures and contours of the Hindemith. Piet Kee plays with his customary authority and distinction. A rewarding and satisfying issue.

Chorale fantasia on Straf' mich nicht in deinem Zorn, Op. 40/2; Chorale preludes, Op. 67/4, 13, 28, 40, 48; Introduction, passacaglia and fugue in E min., Op. 127.
*** Hyperion Dig. CDA 66223 [id.]. Graham Barber (Klais organ of Limburg Cathedral).

The *Introduction, passacaglia and fugue* is bold in conception and vision and is played superbly on this excellently engineered Hyperion disc by Graham Barber. The five *Chorale preludes* give him an admirable opportunity to show the variety and richness of tone-colours of this instrument.

PIANO MUSIC

Variations and fugue on a theme of Bach, Op. 81.
(BB) **(*) Naxos Dig. 8.550469 [id.]. Wolf Harden – SCHUMANN: *Humoreske.* **(*)

Wolf Harden's account of the Reger *Variations and fugue on a theme of Bach,* Op. 81, is very fine. Unfortunately there is far less air or sense of space round the piano here and the instrument sounds much drier than in the Schumann coupling. Yet such is the compelling quality of his playing that it would be curmudgeonly to withhold a recommendation on this count.

VOCAL MUSIC

8 Geistliche Gesänge, Op. 138.
*** Koch Bayer Dig. BR 100084. Frankfurt Vocal Ens., Ralf Otto – MARTIN: *Mass for double choir.* ***

These eight spiritual songs are simple homophonic settings of various sacred texts; all of them have a gravely expressive beauty that is conveyed well by this excellent Frankfurt choir. Excellent recording.

Reich, Steve (born 1936)

8 Lines.
(M) *** Virgin/EMI Dig. CUV5 61121-2 [id.]. LCO, Warren-Green – ADAMS: *Shaker loops* *** ⊛;
GLASS: *Company* etc. ***; HEATH: *Frontier*. ***

Steve Reich's *8 Lines* is minimalism in its most basic form, and, although the writing is full of good-humoured vitality, the listener without a score could be forgiven for sometimes thinking that the music was on an endless loop. The performance is expert.

(i) *Six Pianos;* (ii) *Music for mallet instruments;* (iii) *Variations for winds, strings and keyboards.*
(B) *** DG Analogue/Dig. 439 431-2 [id.]. (i–ii) Chambers, Preiss, Hartenberger, Becker, Velez, composer; (ii) Ferchen, Harms, Jarrett, LaBarbara, Clayton; (iii) San Francisco SO, De Waart.

This collection – which might be entitled 'Stuck in a groove' – admirably charts the progress of Reich's minimalism. Both the first two pieces exploit the composer's technique of endlessly repeating a very brief fragment which gradually becomes transformed, almost imperceptibly, by different emphases being given to it. The *Variations* mark a new departure, using a large orchestra. The recording throughout is of high quality and the San Francisco (digital) sound is easy to wallow in.

Tehillim.
** ECM 827 411-2 [id.]. Steve Reich & musicians, George Manahan.

Steve Reich is listed among the percussion players in *Tehillim*, with Manahan conducting. The central focus, in this Hebrew setting of Psalms 19 and 18 (in that order), is on the vocal ensemble of four voices, a high soprano, two lyric sopranos and an alto. The minimalist technique is the same as in the purely instrumental works, but the result – with clapping and drumming punctuating the singing – has an element of charm rare in minimalist music. With jazzy syncopations and Cuban rhythms, the first of the two movements sounds like Bernstein's *Chichester Psalms* caught in a groove. The second starts slowly but speeds up for the verses of praise to the Lord and the final *Hallelujahs*. Clear, forward, analogue recording.

Variations for winds, strings & keyboard.
*** Ph. 412 214-2 [id.]. San Francisco SO, De Waart – ADAMS: *Shaker loops*. ***

Reich's *Variations* uses a large orchestral rather than a small chamber scale. The repetitions and ostinatos, which gradually get out of phase, are again most skilfully used to produce a hypnotic kind of poetry, soothing rather than compelling.

Reicha, Antonín (1770–1836)

Oboe quintet in F, Op. 107.
*** Hyperion CDA 66143 [id.]. Sarah Francis, Allegri Qt – CRUSELL: *Divertimento;* R. KREUTZER: *Grand quintet*. ***

Antonín Reicha's *F major Quintet* is spectacularly unmemorable but always amiable. The present performance is of high quality and very well recorded.

Wind quintets: in E flat, Op. 88/2; in F, Op. 91/3.
*** Hyperion Dig. CDA 66268 [id.]. Academia Wind Quintet of Prague.

Czech wind playing in Czech wind music has a deservedly high entertainment rating and the present performances are no exception. The music itself has great charm and geniality; it is ingenuous yet cultivated, with some delightful, smiling writing for the bassoon. The players are clearly enjoying themselves, yet they play and blend expertly. The sound too is admirable.

Reindl, Constantin (1738–99)

Sinfonia concertante in D for violin, two flutes, two oboes, bassoon, two horns and strings.
*** Novalis Dig. 150 031-2 [id.]. ECO, Griffiths – STALDER: *Symphony No. 5; Flute concerto*. ***

The *Sinfonia concertante* is fresh and inventive, and the finale has a most attractive (and obstinately memorable) main theme. A delightful performance by the ECO under Howard Griffiths and an excellent, natural and well-balanced recording.

Reinecke, Carl (1824–1910)

Fantasiestücke, Op. 43.
(Y/B) *** EMI Dig. CDC5 55166-2 [id.]. Caussé, Duchable – BEETHOVEN: *Notturno* ***; SCHUBERT: *Arpeggione sonata.* **

Reinecke's musical language is Schumannesque and the *Fantasiestücke*, Op. 43, owe an obvious debt to Schumann's *Märchenbilder*. They are very slight, but Caussé and Duchable make out the best possible case for them.

Respighi, Ottorino (1879–1936)

(i) *Adagio con variazioni* (for cello and orchestra); *The Birds; 3 Botticelli pictures;* (ii) *Il tramonto.*
*** Chandos Dig. CHAN 8913 [id.]. (i) Wallfisch; (ii) Linda Finnie; Bournemouth Sinf., Vásáry.

Respighi's *Adagio* is pleasant, but not distinctive, though Raphael Wallfisch is very persuasive. *The Birds* is an enchanting aviary of orchestral colour and the lovely playing and luminous recording give much pleasure. Dorati's Mercury version is not entirely upstaged, but the softer focus of the Chandos digital sound brings added warmth and atmosphere. The lambent Italianate evocation of the *Three Botticelli pictures* is also aurally bewitching. But what caps the success of this Chandos Respighi anthology is Linda Finnie's ravishing account of *Il tramonto*, even finer than Carol Madalin's on Hyperion – see below. Her vocal timbre is fresh yet has an element of gentle voluptuousness just right for this ecstatic setting of Shelley. Again very responsive orchestral playing and the recording is in the demonstration class throughout this CD.

Ancient airs and dances: suites Nos. 1–3; Berceuse for strings; Suite for flute and strings No. 2: Aria.
(N) ** Chandos Dig. CHAN 9215 [id.]. Sinfonia 21, Richard Hickox.

Ancient airs and dances: suites Nos. 1–3; The Birds (suite).
*** Van./Omega Dig. 08.1007.71. Australian CO, Gee.

Ancient airs and dances: suites Nos. 1–3; The Birds (suite); 3 Botticelli pictures (Trittico Botticelliano).
(N) *** Teldec/Warner Dig. 4509 91729-2 [id.]. St Paul CO, Hugh Wolff.

Ancient airs and dances: suites Nos. 1–3; 3 Botticelli pictures (Trittico Botticelliano).
*** Telarc Dig. CD 80309 [id.]. Lausanne CO, Jesús López-Cobos.

Ancient airs and dances: suites Nos. 1 & 3; The Birds (Gli uccelli); 3 Botticelli pictures (Trittico Botticelliano).
(Y/B) ✪ *** DG Dig. 437 533-2 [id.]. Orpheus CO.

These pieces are stunningly played by this remarkable, conductorless ensemble. Their ensemble is terrific, rhythms wonderfully articulate and the music has a sense of joy and vitality. Sensitive accounts of the *Trittico Botticelliano* and an exhilarating, songful one of *The Birds*. Very fine recording, too.

Christopher Gee's performance of *The Birds* is a complete delight, opening and closing vigorously, yet providing the most refined portraits of the dove, nightingale and cuckoo, with particularly lovely oboe playing in *The dove*. The opening of the *First suite* of *Ancient airs and dances* has a comparable grace and delicacy of feeling; throughout, Lyndon Gee's response to Respighi's imaginative orchestration is wonderfully fresh. The strings produce lovely translucent textures at the beginning of the *Third suite*; yet when a robust approach is called for, the players provide it admirably. The recording, made at the ABC Studio at Chatsworth, Sydney, is in the demonstration class. However, the equally admirable Orpheus DG version offers also the *Botticelli pictures*.

No need to withhold a third star here. The recording is bright but spacious. The playing of the St Paul Chamber Orchestra is excellent and they are responsive to dynamic contrasts and changes of colour. Hugh Wolff gets sympathetic and spirited playing throughout and, although the *Ancient airs and dances* do not displace the Orpheus Chamber Orchestra (DG), which is remarkable by any standards, the disc can be recommended to anyone attracted by this particular coupling.

Opening brightly and comparatively robustly, the Lausanne performance yet has both warmth and finesse. The rhythmic pulse is lively without being heavy, and there is much engaging woodwind detail; at the graceful beginning of the *Third suite* textures are agreeably light and transparent. The Telarc recording is first rate and even more impressive in the *Botticelli pictures*, with *La primavera* burgeoning with the extravagantly exotic spring blossoming, and *The birth of Venus* rapt in its radiantly expansive ecstasy.

Hickox's version is a disappointment. The recording is very resonant and, although there is some fine orchestral playing, the effect is overblown at climaxes. The two very pleasing short pieces (not previously recorded) are used as entr'actes between the suites, which are played with No. 3 coming before No. 2.

(i) *Ancient airs and dances: suite No. 3 for strings;* (ii) *The Birds; The Fountains of Rome; The Pines of Rome.*
(N) (M) ** Ph. Analogue/Dig. 446 573-2 [id.]. (i) I Musici; (ii) San Francisco SO, Edo de Waart.

Ancient airs and dances: suite No. 3 for strings; The Fountains of Rome; The Pines of Rome.
(N) (M) *** DG 449 724-2 [id.]. BPO, Karajan (with BOCCHERINI: *Quintettino*; ALBINONI: *Adagio in G min.* (arr. Giazotto) ***).

Karajan's highly polished, totally committed performances of the two most popular Roman pieces are well supplemented by the *Third suite* of *Ancient airs and dances*, brilliantly played and just as beautifully transferred, more impressive in sound than many more recent Karajan recordings. In the symphonic poems Karajan is in his element, and the playing of the Berlin Philharmonic is wonderfully refined. The opening of the *Ancient airs* brings ravishing tone from the Berlin Philharmonic strings, and they sound even more lavish in Giazotto's famous arrangement of Albinoni's *Adagio*. That has been added as a bonus for this remastered reissue in DG's 'Legendary Recordings' series of 'Originals', while Boccherini's *Quintettino* makes an engaging additional lollipop.

De Waart conducts brilliant and sympathetic performances of the two symphonic poems, but an unnatural balance in the early (1983) digital recording, with unrealistic placing of instruments, is underlined on the finest reproducers. Conversely, I Musici's set of *Ancient airs and dances*, recorded two decades earlier, is pleasant but rather characterless. It is no match for Karajan's version in elegance.

Le astuzie di Colombina; La pentola magica; Sèvres de la vieille France.
*** Marco Polo Dig. 8.223346 [id.]. Slovak RSO (Bratislava), Adriano.

Sèvres de la vieille France is based on seventeenth-and eighteenth-century airs, scored with great elegance and charm; *La pentola magica* makes use of Russian models. *Le astuzie di Colombina*, described as a 'Scherzo Veneziano', uses popular Venetian melodies among other things. The scores contain some winning and delightful numbers. Not top-drawer by any manner of means but second-class Respighi is better than many other composers at their best. Decent performances and good recording.

Ballata delle Gnomidi; (i) *Concerto gregoriano; Poema autunnale.*
*** Chandos Dig. CHAN 9232 [id.]. (i) Lydia Mordkovitch; BBC PO, Downes.

The *Concerto gregoriano* is a meditative, lyrical outpouring making free use of Gregorian modes. Respighi thought of the soloist as the cantor and the orchestra as the congregation, so there is little of the dramatic tension between them that is an essential ingredient in concerto writing. Lydia Mordkovitch is a committed advocate and has the measure of its restrained, expressive eloquence. Apart from some moments of brilliant display, the slightly later *Poema autunnale* for violin and orchestra is also predominantly lyrical and has moments of a Delius-like mysticism. Again Lydia Mordkovitch gives a most affecting account of the piece and is very well supported by Downes and the BBC Philharmonic. The *Ballata delle Gnomidi* (1920) finds Respighi in his most exotic *Roman trilogy* mode: it is a dazzling exercise in colour and orchestration. This issue is one of the high points in the current Chandos survey of the composer.

Belfagor overture; 3 Corali; (i) *Fantasia slava for piano and orchestra; Toccata for piano and orchestra.*
(Y/B) *** Chandos Dig. CHAN 9311 [id.]. (i) Geoffrey Tozer; BBC PO, Downes.

The best thing here is the *Toccata for piano and orchestra*, in which Respighi himself was soloist at its New York première in 1928. It is better argued and structured, more inventive and novel, as well as more musically rewarding, than either of the piano concertos, and its appearance on disc cannot be too warmly welcomed. Tozer plays with considerable bravura and panache and the BBC Philharmonic under Sir Edward Downes are admirably supportive. The *Fantasia slava* is shorter and less interesting, and the same goes for the three chorale arrangements. The *Belfagor* is a re-composition based on themes from his opera, and not the curtain-raiser heard in the theatre. Excellent in every way, and with recording of first-class quality.

Belkis, Queen of Sheba: suite. Metamorphoseon modi XII.
*** Chandos Dig. CHAN 8405 [id.]. Philh. O, Simon.

The ballet-suite *Belkis, Queen of Sheba*, is a score that set the pattern for later Hollywood biblical film music; but *Metamorphoseon* is a taut and sympathetic set of variations. It has been ingeniously based on a medieval theme, and though a group of cadenza variations relaxes the tension of argument in the middle, the brilliance and variety of the writing have much in common with Elgar's *Enigma*. Superb playing from the Philharmonia, treated to one of the finest recordings that even Chandos has produced, outstanding in every way.

(i) *The Birds;* (ii) *3 Botticelli pictures (Trittico Botticelliano)*.
(N) (M) ** BBC Radio Classics 15656 91372 [id.]. (i) BBC PO, Patrick Thomas; (ii) LSO, Mackerras –
   BUSONI: *Comedy overture;* CHERUBINI: *Symphony.* **

The BBC recording of *The Birds* is relatively recent, emanating from the BBC's Northern studios in 1984, while the recording of the *Botticelli pictures* was made in 1969 at Walthamstow Town Hall. The latter is obviously part of a concert recorded by Mackerras and the LSO for the BBC Transcription Service, which used to mount enterprising programmes for sale to foreign radio stations. Both are decent performances and worth the money – but, even if they were not, the disc would be worth having for the sake of the Busoni and Cherubini couplings.

(i) *The Birds* (suite); *Brazilian impressions;* (ii) *The Fountains of Rome; The Pines of Rome*.
(M) **(*) Mercury 432 007-2 [id.]. (i) LSO; (ii) Minneapolis SO, Antal Dorati.

The Minneapolis Northrop Auditorium – for all the skill of the Mercury engineers – never produced a web of sound with quite the magical glow which Orchestral Hall, Chicago, could provide in the late 1950s. Nevertheless, in Dorati's hands the opening and closing evocations of the *Fountains of Rome* have a unique, shimmering brightness which certainly suggests a sun-drenched landscape, although the turning-on of the Triton fountain brings a shrill burst of sound that almost assaults the ears. The tingling detail in the companion *Pines of Rome* is again matched by Dorati's powerful sense of atmosphere, while the finale has an overwhelming juggernaut forcefulness. The coupling of *The Birds* and *Brazilian impressions* was made in the smoother, warmer acoustics of Watford Town Hall in 1957, and here the vividness of detail particularly suits Dorati's spirited account of *The Birds*, bringing pictorial piquancy of great charm and strongly projected dance-rhythms. *Brazilian impressions* recalls Debussy's *Ibéria*, though it is much less subtle. The finale, *Canzone e danza*, certainly glitters in Dorati's hands even if overall this work does not represent Respighi at his finest.

The Birds (suite); *The Fountains of Rome; The Pines of Rome*.
(BB) *** Belart 450 110-2; *450 110-4* [id.]. LSO, István Kertész.

It is good to have Kertész's vintage (1969) triptych back in the catalogue on Polygram's Belart bargain label. It still sounds pretty spectacular and makes a fine bargain. *The Birds* is very engaging in its spirited elegance; seldom before has the entry of the nightingale's song been so beautifully prepared in the central section of *The Pines of Rome*, where Kertész creates a magical, atmospheric frisson. The iridescent brilliance of the turning-on of the Triton Fountain in the companion-piece is matched by the grandeur of the Trevi processional, when Neptune's chariot is imagined to be seen crossing the heavens. In sharpening detail the remastering loses only a little of the original ambient warmth and depth.

3 Botticelli pictures; (i) *Aretusa;* (ii) *Lauda per la Nativita del Signore;* (i) *Il tramonto*.
✺ *** Collins Dig. 1349-2 [id.]. (i) Dame Janet Baker; (ii) Patricia Rosario, Louise Winter, Lynton Atkinson, Hickox Singers; City of L. Sinfonia, Hickox.

This collection is crowned by the contributions of Dame Janet Baker, who gives ravishing performances of two of Respighi's warm and sensitive settings of Shelley poems. *Aretusa* was the first work in which Respighi established his mature style, with lightly surging fountain music that anticipates the *Fountains* and *Pines of Rome*. *Il tramonto* ('The sunset') evokes a mood remarkably similar to *Beim Schlafengehen* from Strauss's *Four Last Songs* and, with Dame Janet Baker as soloist, is just as beautiful. *Lauda* is a nativity cantata which touchingly presents the story as a simple pastoral sequence, with the tenderly expressive woodwind accompaniment suggesting rustic pipe music. The *Trittico Botticelliano* establishes its seductiveness in the shimmering sounds at the very opening of the first movement, *Primavera*. Refined playing and recording.

Brazilian impressions; Church windows (Vetrate di chiesa).
*** Chandos Dig. CHAN 8317 [id.]. Philh. O, Simon.

Respighi's set of musical illustrations of church windows is not among his finest works but is well worth having when the recording is impressively spacious and colourful. Geoffrey Simon is sympathetic and he secures very fine playing from the Philharmonia. On CD, the wide dynamic range and a striking depth of perspective create the most spectacular effects.

Burlesca; Overture Carnevalesca; Prelude, chorale & fugue; Suite in E; Symphonic variations.
**(*) Marco Polo Dig. 8.223348 [id.]. Slovak RSO (Bratislava), Adriano.

The *Symphonic variations*, an early work, is very well crafted, with a lot of Brahms and Franck – though the scoring already betrays Respighi's future expertise. In the *Suite in E major* the influences are mainly Slavonic; primarily Dvořák and Rimsky-Korsakov, but in the *Burlesca* of 1906 with its whole-tone scale one can discern a whiff of Debussy. The release discovers no masterpieces but does afford a valuable insight into Respighi's creative development. Good performances from Adriano and the Slovak Radio Orchestra and decent recording.

Concerto Gregoriano; Poema Autunnale.
(N) *** Decca Dig. 443 324-2 [id.]. Pierre Amoyal, Fr. Nat. O, Dutoit – SAINT-SAENS: *Violin concerto No. 3.* ***

It is good that other soloists are taking up Respighi's beautiful *Concerto Gregoriano*, though readers who already have Lydia Mordkovitch's Chandos recording need not feel prompted to make the change. She has the advantage of an all-Respighi coupling, whereas Pierre Amoyal and Charles Dutoit offer more conventional repertoire in the form of the Saint-Saëns *B minor Concerto*. Amoyal is every bit as well accompanied and recorded – in fact Dutoit and the Orchestre National probably offer a more sensitive accompaniment than does Downes. Downes has the *Ballata delle Gnomidi*, which is an extraordinary piece. If you already have the Saint-Saëns *Concerto*, the Chandos is the one to go for, but if the Decca coupling appeals this can be enthusiastically recommended alongside it.

Piano concerto in A min.; Concerto in modo misolidio.
(Y/B) **(*) Chandos Dig. CHAN 9285 [id.]. Geoffrey Tozer, BBC PO, Downes.

Respighi wrote his *Piano concerto in A minor* in 1902, just after graduating, with the result that the influence of Rachmaninov and other Russians is strong. Grieg is echoed in the scherzando writing for the piano, with the very key of the work hinting at the influence of Schumann too. In three movements, lasting 24 minutes, it makes a welcome addition to the catalogue. It is aptly coupled with a much later and more ambitious concertante work with piano, the *Concerto in modo misolidio* ('in the mixolydian mode'), which, like Respighi's *Concerto gregoriano* (with violin), reflects Respighi's fascination with early Church music. Though the slow movement has echoes of Vaughan Williams's *Tallis fantasia*, and the Passacaglia finale brings some much-needed tautness, it remains too diffuse a work, too extended for its material. The impact of Geoffrey Tozer's playing in both works is undermined by the backward balance of the piano, with only the A minor work taking fire.

Piano concerto in A min.; Fantasia slava for piano and orchestra; Toccata for piano and orchestra.
(N) (BB) *** Naxos Dig. 8.553207 [id.]. Konstantin Scherbakov, Slovak RSO (Bratislava), Howard Griffiths.

An enterprising Naxos CD offers three concertante piano works of Respighi, missing out the *Concerto in modo misolidio* and including instead the more rhetorical *Toccata*, written in 1928, three years after the former piece. At 22 minutes it is too long for its content but has some attractive lyrical writing. The much more concise and rather engaging *Fantasia slava* suddenly surprises the listener by quoting a tune familiar from a Dvořák *Slavonic dance*. The Russian pianist, Konstantin Scherbakov, is a persuasive and at times dazzlingly brilliant soloist and he is accompanied persuasively by the Slovak Radio Symphony Orchestra (Bratislava) under Howard Griffiths. The recording is excellent and this disc, if not preferable to Tozer's Chandos coupling, is well worth its modest cost.

Feste romane; The Fountains of Rome; The Pines of Rome (symphonic poems).
(BB) *** Naxos Dig. 8.550539 [id.]. RPO, Bátiz.
(M) *** Decca Dig. 430 729-2 [id.]. Montreal SO, Dutoit.
*** EMI Dig. CDC7 47316-2 [id.]. Phd. O, Muti.
(B) **(*) Sony SBK 48267; *SBT 48267* [id.]. Phd. O, Ormandy.
(N) (BB) **(*) RCA Navigator 74321 24208-2 [09026 61401-2]. Phd. O, Eugene Ormandy.
(M) (**(*)) RCA mono GD 60262; *GK 60262* [60262-2-RG; *60262-4–RG*]. NBC SO, Toscanini.

The Fountains of Rome; The Pines of Rome.
(Y/B) ✪ (M) *** RCA 09026 61401-2 [id.]. Chicago SO, Fritz Reiner – MUSSORGSKY: *Pictures at an exhibition.* *** ✪
(Y/B) ✪ (M) *** RCA 09026 68079-2 [id.]. Chicago SO, Fritz Reiner – DEBUSSY: *La Mer.* ***

(i) *The of Fountains Rome; The Pines of Rome;* (ii) *Rossiniana* (suite after Rossini).
(N) (M) ** Decca Phase 4 444 106-2 [id.]. (i) New Philh. O, Charles Munch; (ii) RPO, Dorati.

Reiner's legendary recordings of *The Pines* and *Fountains of Rome* were made in Symphony Hall, Chicago, on 24 October 1959, and the extraordinarily atmospheric performances have never been surpassed since. The opening of the *Fountain of Valle Giulia at dawn* captures a sultry Italian warmth, and the slightly recessed orchestral image in the glowing hall acoustics adds to the magic, both here and in

The pines of the Janiculum, where there is exquisitely rapturous response from the strings. The turning on of the Triton fountain brings an unforced cascade of orchestral brilliance, while the triumphal procession of Neptune's chariot across the heavens which forms the powerful centrepiece of the Trevi portrait has an overwhelmingly spacious grandeur. Similarly the climax of *The pines of the Appian Way* is prepared with subtle control, and when the big moment comes it is electrifying. The marvellous orchestral playing is matched by the skill of RCA's technical team, led by Dick Mohr, and indeed by the new generation of transfer engineers, who have put it all on CD with complete fidelity. Reiner's performances are available with two alternative couplings, Debussy's *La Mer* and his equally riveting (1957) recording of the Mussorgsky/Ravel *Pictures at an exhibition*.

The Naxos recording, engineered by Brian Culverhouse in St Barnabas, Mitcham, is also in the demonstration bracket. The climax of *The Fountain of Trevi at mid-day*, when Neptune parades across the heavens, is enormously spectacular, and here a computer organ was used to provide the underlying sustained pedal (the church organ was out of pitch), and effectively clean and weighty it is. The *Pines* and *Fountains* bring extremely fine playing with much warmth and finesse from the RPO, while the cascading waters of the *Triton fountain* become a positive torrent. The focus of the Naxos recording is sharp, and this brings an extra degree of brazen splendour to the tumultuous popular crowd sequences in the *Circus* and *Jubilee* scenes of the *Feste romane*, while at the close of the *October festival* the mandolin serenade emerges more tangibly.

Dutoit, as in other brilliant and colourful pieces, draws committed playing from his fine Montreal orchestra. Where many interpreters concentrate entirely on brilliance, Dutoit finds a vein of expressiveness too, which – for example in the opening sequence of *The Pines of Rome* – conveys the fun of children playing at the Villa Borghese. The recorded sound is superlative on CD, where the organ pedal sound is stunning. At mid-price, this is now very competitive, especially for those who enjoy the Montreal ambience.

Muti gives warmly red-blooded performances of Respighi's Roman trilogy, captivatingly Italianate in their inflexions. With brilliant playing from the Philadelphia Orchestra and warmly atmospheric recording, far better than EMI engineers have generally been producing in Philadelphia, these are exceptional for their strength of characterization.

Ormandy's Sony/CBS *Feste romane* dates from the early days of stereo. The performance has great electricity and enormous surface excitement, and it is a pity that the sound-quality is fiercely brilliant. In the other two works the effect is more opulent, and the Philadelphia playing is fabulous, while the recording has come up astonishingly well. The atmospheric central movements of the *Pines* are ravishing (as is the *Villa Medici Fountain*) and the final evocation of the Roman troops on the Appian Way is overtly sinister. It is a pity that such electrifying performances need some technical indulgence because of the microphone balance, but this is still a very exciting example of the Ormandy/Philadelphia regime at its most spectacularly compelling.

On Navigator, Ormandy again plays all three works with enormous gusto and panache, and the orchestral virtuosity is thrilling, with the robust vulgarity of *Feste romane* breathtaking in its unbuttoned zest. The cascade at the turning on of the Triton fountain is like a dam bursting, and all the pictorial effects spring vividly to life. The 1973–4 recording is immensely spectacular. It is atmospheric too, but brightly lit to the point of garishness, and not all ears will respond to the tingling brilliance. But the performances make an unforgettable impact.

Toscanini's recordings of the Roman trilogy are in a class of their own; they (and Reiner in the *Pines* and the *Fountains*) are the yardstick by which all others are measured. This is electrifying playing, which comes over well in this transfer – though, to be fair, the old LPs had a rounder, fuller (less acidulated) tone on the strings above the stave.

Munch's Phase Four coupling is made artificially spectacular by the microphone placing. The instrumental spotlighting is done with some panache; the treble glitters, though the effect is unrefined, and the 1966 Kingsway Hall recording adds ambient warmth. The sense of spectacle is tangible and to some extent redeems the comparative lack of subtlety in the presentation. Those who regard these scores as 'picture-postcard music' will find that this is what the Decca sound-balance conveys. Respighi's *Rossiniana suite*, arranged from piano pieces taken from Rossini's *Quelques riens pour album*, is not as inspired a score as *La Boutique fantasque*, but it is beautifully played and Dorati's affection is persuasive. The recording, made a decade later, is smoother too.

Feste romane; The Pines of Rome.
(M) *** Decca 425 052-2 [id.]. Cleveland O, Maazel – VERDI: *Le quattro stagioni*. ***

Maazel's 1976 account of *Feste romane* is a remarkable example of vintage Decca recording. The orchestral playing shows matching virtuosity, and the final festival scene ('The night before Epiphany in the Piazza Navona'), with its riotous clamour of trumpets and snatches of melody from the local organ-grinder, is projected with a kaleidoscopic imagery which fascinates the ear. *The Pines of Rome* has comparable electricity and plenty of glamour, and again the sound has a breathtaking sense of presence in the sharply defined CD transfer. The Verdi coupling (the *Four seasons ballet music* from *I vespri siciliani*) is also very successful.

Sinfonia drammatica.
*** Chandos Dig. CHAN 9213 [id.]. BBC PO, Downes.

Respighi's *Sinfonia drammatica* (1914) is a work of ambitious proportions: epic in scale, it lasts just over an hour, the first movement alone taking 25 minutes. Mahler, Strauss and even early Schoenberg are obvious models and, on first hearing, the work might give the impression of being inflated and overblown. Yet it proves rich in incident and lavish in its orchestral colours and virtuosity; even if it is not organic in conception or symphonic in the classical sense, it is an immensely worthwhile addition to the catalogue. If you enjoy the *Alpine Symphony*, you should try this. An excellent performance and outstanding recording.

Violin sonata in B min.
*** DG Dig. 427 617-2 [id.]. Kyung Wha Chung, Krystian Zimerman – R. STRAUSS: *Sonata.* ***

Kyung Wha Chung is at her best and Krystian Zimerman brings an enormous range of colour and dynamics to the piano part – the clarity of his articulation in the *Passacaglia* is exceptional. This is undoubtedly the finest performance to appear on record since the Heifetz version.

VOCAL MUSIC

(i) *Deità silvane;* (i; ii) *Lauda per la Nativitá del Signore. 3 Botticelli pictures (Trittico botticelliano).*
(N) (B) *** Decca Double 444 842-2 (2) [id.]. (i) Robert Tear; (ii) Jill Gomez, Meriel Dickinson; L. Chamber Ch.; Argo CO, Heltay – ROSSINI: *Petite messe solennelle.* **

The two rarities here are most appealing. The *Lauda per la Nativitá del Signore* is a setting of words attributed to Jacapone da Todi, a Franciscan of the thirteenth century, and is ingeniously scored for two flutes, piccolo, oboe, cor anglais, two bassoons, piano (four hands) and triangle, while the voices are wonderfully handled. The *Deità silvane* was originally for soprano and piano, but the composer scored it in 1926 for single wind, horn, percussion, harp and strings – to great effect. All this music, including the much better-known *Botticelli pictures*, shows great skill in the handling of pastel colourings, and the performances reflect credit on all concerned, including the recording team. It is a pity that the coupling is less readily recommendable.

La Primavera; (i) *4 Liriche su poesie popolari armene (1921)* (arr. Adriano).
(Y/B) **(*) Marco Polo Dig. 8.223595 [id.]. Henrietta Lednárová, Jana Valásková, Beata Geriová, Miroslav Dvorský, Richard Haan, Vladimir Kubovčic, Slovak Ph. Ch., Slovak RSO (Bratilava); (i) Denisa Slepkovská, Ens., Adriano.

La Primavera is an ambitious cantata for six soloists, chorus and orchestra. It takes 45 minutes and is not vintage Respighi. But, although it has moments of bombast and periodically finds his muse on automatic pilot, it has some music of real quality and in particular the sixth of the seven movements; there are evocative and opulently scored orchestral interludes. The *Quattro liriche su poesie popolari armene*, which Respighi wrote for his wife, are simple and affecting. They are given here in Adriano's arrangement for flute, oboe, clarinet, bass clarinet, bassoon, trombone and harp. The performances throughout are more than adequate and are acceptably recorded.

La sensitiva.
(M) *** Virgin/EMI CUV5 61118-2 [id.]. J. Baker, City of L. Sinf., Hickox – BERLIOZ: Mélodies (including *Nuits d'été*). ***

Tautly structured over its span of more than half an hour, Respighi's setting of Shelley's poem is a most beautiful piece, which Dame Janet and Richard Hickox treat to a glowing first recording. An unexpected but very enjoyable and generous coupling for the Berlioz items.

Il tramonto.
*** Hyperion Dig. CDA 66290 [id.]. Carol Madalin, ECO, Bonavera – MARTUCCI: *Le canzone dei ricordi; Notturno.* ***

Respighi's *Il tramonto* (*The sunset*) is a glorious work which at times calls to mind the world of late Strauss. A most lovely record. Recommended with all possible enthusiasm.

OPERA

Semirama (complete).
*** Hung. Dig. HCD 31197/98 (2) [id.]. Marton, Bartolini, Kincses, Miller, Polgar, Hungarian State O, Gardelli.

Very differently from Rossini in *Semiramide*, Respighi treats the story as a sort of reverse Oedipus: the lascivious Queen Semirama seduces the young Babylonian general, Merodach, and then finds that he is her son. Respighi offers consistently sumptuous sounds, along with an almost endless flow of melody. The surprise is that this highly accomplished score dates from well before any of the works for which Respighi is usually known, including *The Pines of Rome* (1924). He also anticipates Puccini. One passage, when the Queen questions her victim with an imperiously repeated '*Rispondi!*', is so like the riddle scene in *Turandot* that plainly Puccini was the one who copied, not the young Respighi. This recording, like so many previous opera sets from Budapest, offers splendid playing from the Hungarian State Orchestra, with fine singing from the Radio and Television Chorus and a strong cast of soloists. Eva Marton makes a powerful Queen, and the voice, so often unsteady and ill-focused in recordings, is here firmer than usual in the soaring melodies. Lando Bartolini produces clear, heroic tone as Merodach, though he is reluctant to scale the voice down. Veronika Kincses as the Chaldean princess, Susiana, caresses the Respighi melodies with her sweet, pure tone, but then grows rather edgy for the more dramatic moments. The booklet looks skimpy, but efficiently provides libretto, translation and the necessary background.

Revueltas, Silvestre (1899–1940)

Caminos; Musica para charlar; Ventanas.
*** ASV Dig. CDDCA 653 [id.]. Mexico City PO, Bátiz – CHAVEZ: *Sinfonia de Antigona; Symphony No. 4.* ***

The music on this record is highly colourful, with moments of considerable vulgarity rubbing shoulders with very evocative and imaginative episodes, such as the depiction of *Twilight* in the second *Musica para charlar*. Excellent playing from the Mexican orchestra under Bátiz and sound of demonstration quality, with great impact, detail and presence.

Rheinberger, Joseph (1839–1901)

Organ concerto No. 1 in F, Op. 137.
*** Telarc Dig. CD 80136 [id.]. Michael Murray, RPO, Ling – DUPRE: *Symphony*. ***

Rheinberger's *Concerto* is well made, its invention is attractive and it has suitable moments of spectacle that render it admirable for a coupling with the Dupré *Symphony*, with its use of the massive Albert Hall organ. The performance here is first rate. A fine demonstration disc.

Rihm, Wolfgang (born 1952)

Gesungene Zeit (Time chant).
*** DG Dig. 437 093-2 [id.]. Mutter, Chicago SO, Levine – BERG: *Violin concerto.* ***

Under the title *Gesungene Zeit* ('Time Chant'), Rihm has written what in effect is an extended lyrical meditation for the soloist, heightened and illustrated by the orchestra in the most discreet way. As he says, 'In essence this is monophonic music. And it is always song, even where beat and pulse shorten the breath and press it hard.' As in the Berg, Mutter is inspired, playing with an inner hush that used only rarely to mark her recordings.

Rimsky-Korsakov, Nikolay (1844–1908)

Capriccio espagnol, Op. 34; Le Coq d'or: suite; May night overture; Russian Easter festival overture; Sadko (musical picture), *Op. 5; Symphony No. 2 (Antar), Op. 9;* (i) *The Snow Maiden: suite; The Tale of Tsar Saltan: suite.*
(Y/B) (B) ** Ph. Duo 442 605-2 (2) [id.]. Rotterdam PO, David Zinman; (i) with Roberta Alexander & Women's Ch.

This is an exceptionally generous and attractive compilation, including most of Rimsky's short orchestral works, plus *Antar*. The Rotterdam orchestra plays with appealing freshness and the recording is pleasingly rich and atmospheric. Zinman secures quite lustrous playing in the *Capriccio*, and he finds plenty of atmosphere and colour in *Sadko* and the *May night overture*, with its languorous opening horn solo. *Antar* again brings beauty and warmth in the orchestral playing, with the central movements appealingly done. But here, as in the *Russian Easter festival overture*, more zest would have been welcome, and in the famous Spanish caprice the adrenalin begins to run only at the end. In the *Snow Maiden suite* the *Dance des oiseaux* brings an effective vocal contribution, but the *Tumblers* are not very boisterous fellows. The sinuously sentient qualities of *Le Coq d'or* are somewhat over-refined, and in *Tsar Saltan* the bumble-bee buzzes gently. Generally there is a lack of charisma here, not helped by recording which, though full and rich, lacks sparkle.

Capriccio espagnol, Op. 34; Le coq d'or: suite; Russian Easter festival overture, Op. 36.
(M) *** Mercury 434 308-2 [id.]. LSO, Antal Dorati – BORODIN: *Prince Igor: Polovstian dances.* **(*)

Dorati's 1959 *Capriccio espagnol* brings glittering bravura and excitement from the LSO players, and the *Russian Easter festival overture*, recorded at Walthamstow at the same sessions, is equally dynamic and colourful. Even more remarkably, the rich-hued and vibrant *Le coq d'or* dates from as early as 1956, yet hardly sounds dated. The playing has plenty of allure in its evocation of Queen Shemakha, yet has drama and well defined detail.

Capriccio espagnol; Russian Easter festival overture.
(N) (B) **(*) Decca Eclipse Dig. 448 233-2; *448 233-4* [id.]. Montreal SO, Dutoit – MUSSORGSKY: *Night on the bare mountain* etc. **(*)

Dutoit's *Capriccio espagnol* is comparatively genial and relaxed; the *Russian Easter festival overture* is strong, with a fine climax . In both works the Montreal recording is full, with iridescent detail.

Christmas eve (suite); Le Coq d'or: suite; Legend of the invisible city of Kitezh: suite; May night: overture; Mlada: suite; The Snow Maiden: suite; The Tale of the Tsar Saltan: suite.
*** Chandos Dig. CHAN 8327/9 (3) [id.]. SNO, Järvi.

The *Prelude* to *The invisible city of Kitezh* is described as a hymn to nature, while the delights of the *Christmas eve suite* include a magical evocation of the glittering stars against a snow-covered landscape and, later, a flight of comets. Apart from the feast of good tunes, the composer's skilful and subtle deployment of the orchestral palette continually titillates the ear. Neeme Järvi draws the most seductive response from the SNO; he consistently creates orchestral textures which are diaphanously sinuous. Yet the robust moments, when the brass blazes or the horns ring out sumptuously, are caught just as strikingly and the listener is assured that here is music which survives repetition uncommonly well.

Christmas eve: suite; Le coq d'or: suite; The Tale of Tsar Saltan: suite; Flight of the bumble bee.
*** ASV Dig. CDDCA 772 [id.]. Armenian PO, Tjeknavorian.

Tjeknavorian and his fine Armenian Orchestra are completely at home in Rimsky's sinuous orientalism. There is a first-rate trumpeter to play the arresting fanfares which open each movement of the *Tsar Saltan suite* and articulate the pungently bizarre warnings of *The Golden cockerel*, matched elsewhere by glittering, iridescent wind-colouring. The racy vigour and sparkle of the playing brings a jet-setting bumble bee and the carolling horns and bold brass add to the vividness. The Tchaikovskian *Polonaise* music from *Christmas eve* exudes similar sparkling vitality within a glowing palette. In short this is one of the most desirable and generous Rimsky-Korsakov collections in the current catalogue, and only a degree of thinness in the violin timbre above the stave prevents the use of the adjective, sumptuous. In all other respects this is in the demonstration bracket.

Christmas Eve (suite); Dubinushka, Op. 62; May night overture; Russian Easter Festival overture, Op. 36; Sadko (musical picture), Op. 5; (i) Scheherazade, Op. 35; The Snow Maiden (suite). Tsar Saltan (suite), Op. 57; Tsar Saltan (opera): The Flight of the bumblebee.
(Y/B) (B) **(*) Decca Double 443 464-2 (2) [id.]. SRO, Ansermet, (i) with Geneva Motet Ch.

This is all repertoire for which Ansermet was famous in the early stereo era, and *Scheherazade* must be counted a historic recording. It dates from 1960, and the sound is very impressive for its period, the sonorous rasp of the brass at the start and the weighty spectacle of the shipwreck sequence in the finale, with its splashing tam tam, offers quality regarded as of demonstration standard in its day and not very far short of it now in this newly remastered CD transfer which has a greatly improved focus. Ansermet's skill as a ballet conductor comes out persuasively. The outer movements with their undoubted sparkle are the finest: the first is dramatic and the last is built steadily to a climax of considerable impact. The music's sinuous qualities are not missed and every bar of the score is alive. *May Night* was recorded a year earlier and the strings have far less lustre; but the *Tsar Saltan suite*, also made in 1959, shows Ansermet and the Decca engineers in glittering form, especially in the recording of brass and woodwind and, if again the upper strings are rather thin, the third movement is certainly vibrant in its colourful detail. The *Flight of the bumblebee* is rather leisurely, but perhaps we are too used to this piece being used as a virtuoso show-off.

The second disc opens with a characteristic (1959) account of the *Russian Easter Festival overture*. The whole performance is warmly coloured rather than specially vital, although it is by no means dull. Ansermet is at his finest in the *Christmas Eve suite*; Rimsky's scenario is particularly delightful. This is most enjoyable music and it is played with much affection and that mixture of spontaneity and remarkably graphic orchestral palette which made Ansermet's performances special. It is a great pity that the separate movements of this 24-minute suite are not separately cued. *Dubinushka* is an engaging if repetitive arrangement of the radical song, *The little oak stick*, treated in polonaise style, and it has some typical brass fanfare writing. Ansermet is (again in 1958) well served here by the engineers, as he is in *Sadko*, an exotic fairy-tale handled with characterisic aplomb. The earliest recording offered here is *The Snow Maiden suite* (1957) and if the best item turns out to be our old friend, the *Dance of the tumblers*, the choral *Dance of the birds* is also an attractive trifle (although the choral singing could be more refined). Once again the sound is remarkably warm and richly coloured, and once again Decca omit to provide cues for individual movements. Yet even allowing for such reservations, this set can certainly be recommended at Double Decca price: the performances and recordings have far more character than David Zinman's Rotterdam compilation on Philips discussed above.

Piano concerto in C sharp min., Op. 30.
*** Hyperion Dig. CDA 66640 [id.]. Malcolm Binns, E. N. Philh. O, Lloyd-Jones – BALAKIREV: *Concertos Nos. 1–2.* ***

Malcolm Binns proves a sensitive and intelligent exponent in the Rimsky-Korsakov concerto, which comes coupled with Balakirev's two essays in the form. The Northern Philharmonia under David Lloyd-Jones give excellent support and the Hyperion recording is altogether superior to its Melodiya rival. Moreover the Hyperion disc has the advantage of a Balakirev rarity, the *Second Piano concerto*, which is not otherwise available.

Le Coq d'or (suite).
(N) *** DG Dig. 447 084-2 [id.]. Russian Nat. O, Pletnev – TCHEREPNIN: *La Princesse lointaine* etc; LIADOV: *Baba-Yaga* etc. ***

Rimsky-Korsakov's enchanting opera, his last, is not currently represented on CD, and the orchestral suite is the only chance we have of hearing any of it. Mikhail Pletnev and the Russian National Orchestra, which he founded in 1990, give it a performance of exemplary atmosphere and colour, and theirs is likely to remain in a class of its own for a long time. The coupling is of particular interest in that it brings music by two Rimsky pupils, Liadov and Nikolai Tcherepnin, the latter otherwise currently unrepresented in the catalogue. An outstanding issue.

Scheherazade (symphonic suite), *Op. 35.*
*** EMI CDC7 47717-2 [id.]. RPO, Beecham – BORODIN: *Polovtsian dances.* ***
*** DG Dig. 437 818-2 [id.]. O de l'Opéra Bastille, Chung – STRAVINSKY: *Firebird suite.* ***
(M) *** EMI CD-EMX 2214; *TC-EMX 2214.* LPO, Takuo Yuasa – PROKOFIEV: *Lieutenant Kijé.* ***
(M) *** RCA GD 60875 [60875-2-RG]. Chicago SO, Fritz Reiner – DEBUSSY: *La Mer.* ***
(B) *** CfP CD-CFP 4341; *TC-CFP 4341.* Philh. O, Kletzki – TCHAIKOVSKY: *Capriccio italien.* ***
(M) *** DG 419 063-2; *419 063-4* [id.]. BPO, Karajan – BORODIN: *Polovtsian dances.* ***
(Y/B) **(*) Decca Dig. 443 703-2 [id.]. Concg. O, Chailly (with STRAVINSKY: *Scherzo fantastique*).
(M) **(*) Ph. Dig. 434 733-2 [id.]. VPO, Previn – RAVEL: *La valse.* **
(N) (M) ** DG Dig. 445 558-2 [id.]. BPO, Maazel – RACHMANINOV: *Isle of the dead.* ***

Scheherazade; Capriccio espagnol, Op. 34.
❀ *** Telarc Dig. CD 80208 [id.]. LSO, Sir Charles Mackerras.
(Y/B) **(*) EMI Dig. CDC7 55227-2 [id.]. LPO, Jansons.
(Y/B) (B) **(*) DG Analogue/Dig. 439 443-2 [id.]. (i) Boston SO, Ozawa; (ii) Gothenburg SO, Neeme Järvi.
(BB) **(*) Tring Dig. TRP 003 [id.]. RPO, Barry Wordsworth.
(N) (M) **(*) EMI CDM5 65715-2 [id.]. O de Paris, Rostropovich – MUSSORGSKY: *Night on the bare mountain.* ***

(i–ii) *Scheherazade;* (iii–iv) *Capriccio espagnol;* (i; iv) *Russian Easter festival overture, Op. 36.*
(Y/B) (M) *** Ph. 442 643-2 [id.]. (i) Concg. O; (ii) Kondrashin; (iii) LSO; (iv) Markevitch.

Scheherazade; Fairy tale (Skazka), Op. 29; Sadko, Op. 5; Song of India, from Sadko (arr. Tjeknavorian).
*** ASV Dig. CDDCA 771 [id.]. Armenian PO, Tjeknavorian.

Scheherazade; Russian Easter festival overture.
**(*) RCA Dig. 09026 61173-2. NYPO, Yuri Temirkanov.

Scheherazade; Russian Easter festival overture; The Maid of Pskov: Hunt and storm.
(M) (***) Biddulph mono WHL 010 [id.]. Phd. O, Stokowski.

Scheherazade; Tsar Saltan: orchestral suite.
(BB) *** Naxos Dig. 8.550726. Philh. O, Bátiz.

Mackerras's reading combines gripping drama with romantic ardour, subtlety of colour with voluptuousness; he is helped by a wonderfully beguiling portrait of Scheherazade herself, provided by his
orchestral leader, in this case Kees Hulsmann. Scheherazade's presence is felt at the very opening
through the vivid kaleidoscoping colours of the second movement, blossoming in the ravishing slow
movement, which recalls Beecham in its elegant sumptuousness. The charming closing reverie, with the
Sultan lying peacefully satiated in the arms of his young wife, their themes blissfully intermingled, is
unforgettable. After an appropriate pause, Mackerras then delivers a thrilling bravura account of
Capriccio espagnol, lushly opulent in the variations, glittering in the exotic *Scena e canta gitano*, and
carrying all before it in the impetus of the closing *Fandango asturiano*. Telarc's digital recording is very
much in the demonstration class.

Kondrashin's version of *Scheherazade* with the Concertgebouw Orchestra has the advantage of splendid (1980) analogue recorded sound, combining richness and sparkle within exactly the right degree of
resonance. Hermann Krebbers' gently seductive portrayal of Scheherazade's narrative creates a strong
influence on the overall interpretation. His exquisite playing, especially at the opening and close of the
work, is cleverly used by Kondrashin to provide a foil for the expansively vibrant contribution of the
orchestra as a whole. Kondrashin creates an irresistible forward impulse, leading to a huge climax at the
moment of the shipwreck. On CD one notices that inner detail is marginally less sharp than it would be
with a digital recording, but the analogue glow and naturalness more than compensate, and the richness
of texture is just right for the music. The couplings are generous, giving an overall playing time of 74
minutes. Markevitch gives an excellent account of the *Russian Easter festival overture* with the same
orchestra, with fine orchestral playing to bring out the score's glowing colours in the Amsterdam
acoustic. The *Capriccio espagnol*, too, is brilliantly played by the LSO, and here the sound also has
considerable allure, with the present CD transfer much more vivid than the original LP.

Beecham's 1957 *Scheherazade* is a performance of extraordinary drama and charisma. Alongside the
violin contribution of Stephen Staryk, all the solo playing has great distinction; in the second movement
Beecham gives the woodwind complete metrical freedom. The sumptuousness and glamour of the slow
movement are very apparent and the finale has an explosive excitement, rising to an electrifying climax.
However, this is surely due for a mid-price reissue.

On ASV a refreshing and totally gripping new-look recording of *Scheherazade* from Eastern Russia.
Yuri Boghosian immediately presents a seductively slight and sinuous image for the heroine-narrator
and the first movement brings the strongest attack and thrust from the strings. Throughout the central
movements one is made aware of the lustrous oriental character of Rimsky's melodies. The finale, with
its spectacular storm and shipwreck, has exhilarating animation and bite. Tjeknavorian shows great
imaginative flair in realizing the vivid orchestral effects in the two shorter folk tales and also offers his
own gently luscious arrangement of Rimsky's most famous melody, better known as the *Chant hindue*,
which caresses the ear beguilingly. The brilliant recording has great vividness and projection, but relatively little sumptuousness. But it suits the performances admirably.

On EMI's mid-priced label, Eminence, comes another romantically compulsive account, with the sinuously supple contribution of the orchestral leader, Stephen Bryant, in the role of the heroine believably
placed in the orchestral texture. Takuo Yuasa's reading is more spacious, less urgent than Mackerras's,
but the central movements are full of colour and warmth, and the finale brings grippingly animated
orchestral virtuosity and a powerful climax, with the tam-tam flashing out at the moment of the
shipwreck. The poetic close has a lustrous rapture, even if it is not quite as enchanting as on the
Mackerras disc. At mid-price, with a splendid Prokofiev coupling, no one will be disappointed with this,
for the sound is full-bodied and brilliant, with an attractive ambient glow.

There is a certain freshness about the newest Paris account under Myung-Whun Chung; nothing is
routine and the playing has a certain enthusiasm. Very fast and effective tempo in the finale. The sound
has warmth and perspective, thanks to Wolfgang Mitlehner, one of DG's best *Tonmeister*, though the
timpani resonate perhaps a bit too much. All the same, a very enjoyable newcomer.

Reiner's first movement opens richly and dramatically and has a strong forward impulse. The unnamed orchestral leader, naturally balanced, plays most seductively. Reiner's affectionate individual touches have much in common with Beecham's (full-price) version and sound comparably spontaneous and the finale, brilliant and very exciting, has a climax of resounding power and amplitude. The Chicago Hall ambience makes up in body and spaciousness for any lack of internal clarity.

With highly distinguished violin solos from Hugh Bean, Kletzki's reading is broad in the first movement (with less bite and thrust than with Tjeknavorian), but he makes the second glow and sparkle (the famous brass interchanges having the most vivid projection). The elegantly sinuous finesse of the Philharmonia string playing in the third movement is matched by the exhilaration of the finale. The admirably balanced recording has been enhanced by the CD transfer, and at bargain price this remains very competitive.

Bátiz's reputation for spontaneity in the recording studio is demonstrated at its most telling. His performance is impulsive, full of momentum and seductively volatile. David Nolan's picture of Scheherazade is rhapsodically evanescent and in the key second movement the lilting Philharmonia wind solos are a constant pleasure. The slow movement combines refinement with its sensuous patina, and the finale has fine zest and excitement. The colourful *Tsar Saltan suite* is comparably dramatic and vivid. In short, with first-class recording, both clear in detail and full-bodied, at super-bargain price this is hard to beat.

Jansons gives us a very well-played and warmly distinctive version of Rimsky-Korsakov's *Scheherazade* with much to recommend it. Good characterization and dramatic feeling; perhaps the slow movement has one or two mannerisms, but these are convincing enough in context. After the big brassy opening, Jansons keeps power in reserve, building up more slowly than usual. What then comes out in all four movements is the way he points rhythms, lilting, bouncy and affectionate, to distinguish this from most other versions, bringing a satisfying resolution at the great climax towards the end of the finale, with Joakim Svenheden a warmly expressive soloist. The *Capriccio espagnol* brings a similar combination of expressive warmth and exuberance, with the brilliant *Alborada* at the beginning played with such springy rhythms that it is made to sound relaxed, jolly rather than fierce. Not that there is any shortage of biting excitement in either work. But the recorded sound has less bloom and transparency than others made in Abbey Road Studio No. 1; climaxes are tight and do not open out enough. It is a bit lacking in front-to-back depth.

Karajan's 1967 recording is greatly enhanced in its CD format. The added presence increases the feeling of ardour from the glorious Berlin strings in the *Andante*. The outer movements have great vitality and thrust, and the bright percussion transients add to the feeling of zest. Yet Michel Schwalbé's sinuously luxuriant violin solos are still allowed to participate in the narrative. The fill-up is a sizzling account of the Borodin *Polovtsian dances*, with no chorus, but managing perfectly well without.

Chailly's new Decca *Scheherazade* has sound out of Decca's top drawer, with all the glowing lustre one expects from the Concertgebouw acoustics. Jaap van Zweden's assumption of the role of voluptuous storyteller, though sweetly sinuous, does not have a strong enough profile to dominate the narrative, especially at the opening and close of the work. Chailly's reading is spacious rather than electrifying. But it is in the sensuous grace of the two central movements, with their translucent detail, that the performance is at its most appealing. The brief Stravinsky encore is beautifully played and has never been recorded more richly.

Ozawa's earlier (1977) Boston *Scheherazade* is an attractive performance, richly recorded. The first movement is strikingly spacious, building to a fine climax; if the last degree of vitality is missing from the central movements, the orchestral playing is warmly vivid. The finale is lively enough, if not earth-shaking in its excitement; the reading as a whole has plenty of colour and atmosphere, however, and is certainly enjoyable. Moreover Järvi's digital *Capriccio espagnol* is a distinctive and worthwhile bonus, brilliantly recorded.

Barry Wordsworth's RPO version is offered in the lowest price-range and is certainly recommendable. As the dramatic opening shows, the digital recording is spectacularly full and wide-ranging and, while the solo violin (Jonathan Carney) is rather forwardly balanced, it means that 'Scheherazade' immediately takes a dominating role. The first movement has a fine, spacious sweep and, if the wind solos in the second movement are made to seem rather less spontaneous, the slow movement has an agreeable allure at the opening, and the finale brings plenty of orchestral bravura and excitement. What makes this disc particularly attractive is the outstanding coupling. *Capriccio espagnol* is an elusive work on disc but here vitality is the keynote. The variations are sumptuous but provide plenty of glitter. Then with stabbing brass the *Scena e canto gitano* prepares the way for a vibrant close. The Tring recording was made in All Saints' Church, Petersham, and to counter the resonance the microphones are fairly close, which adds to the brilliance and produces a vivid orchestral presence.

The highlight of the Temirkanov account lies in the richly languorous slow movement, with the warmest, most sensuous string playing at the opening and a delightfully wistful, almost elegiac close. But the spacious opening movement lacks real tension, and the colourful events of the second movement are also very relaxed. The finale brings alert playing and vivid detail and an explosive climax. Overall this cannot compete with current top recommendations, and the *Russian Easter festival overture*, too, takes a while to warm up properly, though again the climax is impressive.

Rostropovich's 1974 account with the Orchestre de Paris (now reissued as part of the Rostropovich Edition) offers glowingly rich sound. The performance of the first movement, spacious and opulent, is very convincing, but in the second the conductor's flexibility in the matter of rubato is not entirely matched by precision in the orchestral playing. This is perhaps a small matter when there is so much lambent allure in the central movements and in the performance as a whole; there is much infectious rhythmic pointing, while the finale is splendidly exciting. The *Capriccio espagnol*, recorded four years later, is similarly sumptuous and appealing.

This collection of Leopold Stokowski's recordings of Rimsky-Korsakov centres on the first of his five versions of *Scheherazade*. Made in 1927, it is wilder and more passionate than later ones; fascinatingly, an alternative version of the first movement, never issued before, is included as a supplement. At a slightly broader speed, spreading to an extra 78-r.p.m. side, it is even more persuasive, and Stokowski's Philadelphia Orchestra, unlike British ones of the time, plays with high polish as well as passion. Equally impressive is Stokowski's intense, volatile account of the *Russian Easter festival overture*, dating from 1929, while the *Hunt and storm* sequence from the *The Maid of Pskov* comes from ten years later, with the sound drier and marginally less full. The Biddulph transfers are excellent, with plenty of body.

Previn in his 1981 Vienna version opts for spacious speeds and a direct, unsentimental view. With his characteristic rhythmic flair and with sumptuous playing from the Vienna Philharmonic the result is certainly enjoyable, if more restrained than usual. Excellent, finely balanced sound, but there are more impressive mid-priced versions for those not insisting on digital sound. The Insignia reissue omits any notes about the music.

There is nothing to detain the collector in the performance by Maazel. The playing of the Berlin Philharmonic Orchestra is, of course, peerless, and in the slow movement they make some gorgeous sounds (though the acoustics of the Philharmonie are not entirely flattering on CD). But Maazel's reading is essentially spacious and the outer movements are wanting in electricity. The main attraction here is the compelling Rachmaninov performance of the coupling.

Symphonies Nos. 1 in E min., Op. 1; 2 (Antar), Op. 9; 3 in C, Op. 32; Capriccio espagnol, Op. 35; Russian Easter festival overture, Op. 36.
*** DG Dig. 423 604-2 (2). Gothenburg SO, Järvi.

Whatever Rimsky-Korsakov's symphonies may lack in symphonic coherence they make up for in colour and charm. Some of the material is a little thin but there is some highly attractive invention as well. *Antar* is not quite as strong as some of its protagonists would have us believe, but it should surely have a stronger presence in the concert and recorded repertoire than it has. The performances under Neeme Järvi have considerable merit and the Gothenburg orchestra is excellently recorded; moreover the addition of the *Capriccio espagnol* and the *Russian Easter festival overture* makes the set a very attractive proposition.

Symphonies Nos. 1 in E min., Op. 1; 2 (Antar), Op. 9; Capriccio espagnol, Op. 34.
*** Chandos Dig CHAN 9178 [id.]. Bergen PO, Dmitri Kitaienko.

The *First Symphony*, composed while Rimsky-Korsakov was still in the navy, is not great music but, like much of his mature output, is full of colour. Kitaienko makes the most of it, as he does of *Antar*, more suite than symphony as its composer freely conceded. Indeed he draws very good playing from the Bergen Philharmonic and the exoticism of the latter is very well conveyed. Kitaienko holds the piece together well and gets very lively results in *Capriccio espagnol*. The recording is very good without being quite in the demonstration class.

Symphony No. 2 (Antar), Op. 9.
(N) (M) *** DG Dig. 445 568-2 [id.]. Gothenburg SO, Järvi – BORODIN: *Symphony No. 2* etc. ***
(M) *** Telarc Dig. CD 82011 [id.]. Pittsburgh SO, Maazel – TCHAIKOVSKY: *Symphony No. 2.* ***

Symphony No. 2 (Antar), Op. 9; Russian Easter festival overture, Op. 36.
**(*) Hyperion Dig. CDA 66399 [id.]. Philh. O, Svetlanov.

On Telarc's mid-price label, Bravo!, *Antar* makes a particularly attractive coupling with Tchaikovsky's *Little Russian Symphony*. Maazel's taut yet sympathetic reading holds together a work which, structurally at least, might more aptly be counted as a suite (as *Scheherazade* is) but which, with strong and colourful yet refined treatment like this, is fittingly regarded as belonging to Rimsky's symphonic canon. Excellent playing – notably in the finale, where the Pittsburgh woodwind excel themselves in delicacy –

and brilliant, finely balanced recording. The richness of the strings and bloom on the woodwind add lustre to Rimsky's sinuous oriental colouring.

As with the Borodin coupling, Järvi's account is essentially spacious. Glorious playing from the Gothenburg strings and warm, lustrous DG recording combine to make the most of Rimsky's languor, and the central movements are by no means lacking in vitality.

It goes without saying that the Philharmonia Orchestra and Svetlanov produce an excellent account of Rimsky-Korsakov's colourful score and there is no want of atmosphere or spirit in their playing. Moreover they are given excellent recorded sound by the Hyperion team. However, even with a fill-up, the playing time is still a mite under 50 minutes, which is short measure for a full-price record these days, even one as good as this. The performances in themselves are not superior to those on the two-CD set on DG from the Gothenburg Orchestra under Neeme Järvi: indeed, if anything, the latter are more atmospheric. Were Hyperion to reissue this, either more competitively priced or with an additional work, it would warrant an unreserved recommendation.

Symphony No. 3 in C, Op. 32; Sadko (Tableau musical), Op. 5; Mlada: Procession of the Nobles. The Maid of Pskov: Overture. The Tsar's Bride: Overture. The Tale of Tsar Saltan: Three Miracles.
(N) *** RCA Dig.09026 62684-2 [id.]. State SO of Russia, Svetlanov.

Rimsky-Korsakov was a harsh self-critic and an inveterate reviser of his scores. The tone-poem *Sadko* was composed in 1867, revised two years later and then again in 1892, not long before he began working on the opera of the same name. The first version of the *Third Symphony* occupied him over several years (1867–73) and then also was overhauled in 1886, when the composer had become something of a virtuoso orchestrator. Yevgeni Svetlanov is ideally at home in this repertoire and this will for most people supersede the rival versions (Butt on ASV and Kitaienko on Chandos). Choice resides between the new, excellently recorded Svetlanov and Neeme Järvi on DG.

Tsar Saltan, Op. 57: March.
(Y/B) (M) *** Telarc Dig. CD 82015 [id.]. RPO, André Previn – TCHAIKOVSKY: *Symphony No. 5.* ***

The crisp, stylized *March* from *Tsar Saltan*, a fairy-tale piece, makes a delightful bonne-bouche, a welcome if ungenerous fill-up to Previn's fine account of the Tchaikovsky *Fifth Symphony*.

Piano and wind quintet in B flat.
*** Hyperion CDA 66163 [id.]. Capricorn – GLINKA: *Grand Sextet.* ***
*** CRD CRD 3409; CRD C 4109 [id.]. Ian Brown, Nash Ens. – ARENSKY: *Piano trio No. 1.* ***

Rimsky-Korsakov's youthful *Quintet for piano, flute, clarinet, horn and bassoon* is a thoroughly diverting piece. It is like a garrulous but endearing friend whose loquacity is readily borne for the sake of his charm and good nature. The main theme of the finale is pretty brainless but singularly engaging, and the work as a whole leaves a festive impression. Capricorn's account has great vivacity and is very well recorded.

The Nash Ensemble give a spirited and delightful account of it on CRD that can be warmly recommended for its dash and sparkle and full, naturally balanced sound. The CD transfer retains all the analogue warmth but is not made at a high level; though those used to digital records might like sharper inner definition, the effect is very pleasing with no lack of presence.

Songs: *The clouds begin to scatter; The Octave; The Wave breaks into spray.*
(Y/B) ** Ph. Dig. 442 536-2 [id.]. Dmitri Hvorostovsky, Mikhail Arkadiev – RACHMANINOV; TCHAIKOVSKY: *Songs.* **

Rimsky-Korsakov wrote over 80 songs, but they are seldom to be heard in the concert hall. Dmitri Hvorostovsky has captivated the public with his glamorous profile and good looks, and he makes a glorious sound in the three songs on his new anthology called '*My restless soul*'. His admirers will want this disc, but the Tchaikovsky and Rachmaninov songs, strong on beauty of sound though they are, are short on characterization. Good recording.

OPERA

Sadko (complete).
(Y/B) *** Ph. Dig. 442 138-2 (3) [id.]. Galusin, Tsidipova, Tarassova, Minjelkiev, Gergalov, Grigorian, Alexashin, Diadkova, Boitsov, Bezzubenkov, Ognovenko, Gassiev, Putilin, Kirov Op. Ch. & O, Gergiev.

Sadko is full of melodic inspiration and atmosphere. Rimsky called it an *opera bilina* and was at pains to stress that it was not so much drama as a sequence of epic scenes. The *biliny* are epic tales of folk origin dealing with half-legendary heroes, not dissimilar in fact to the *Kalevala*. Indeed there is something of the feeling of a pageant about the opera: there are seven tableaux, unfolding a simple story in a series of set numbers, scenes and dances. Whatever its dramatic weaknesses, the score is full of glorious musical invention, sumptuously orchestrated, which puts the listener completely under its spell. The Sadko of Vladimir Galusin is very good, though his handling of dynamic nuance is not always subtle; and the vibrato to which one is long accustomed in Russian sopranos is not worrying in Valentina Tsidipova's portrayal of the Sea Princess, Volkhova. Indeed most of the roles are well sung, with the possible exception of Gegam Grigorian's rather tight-throated Hindu merchant. The conducting of Valery Gergiev is one of the highlights of the performance: he brings great warmth and feeling for colour to the opera. The recording is very good, though there are some stage noises, inevitable in stage performances. There is an excellent video (070 439-1 for the laserdisc; 070 439-3 for the VHS cassette), well directed for the cameras by Brian Large; both sound and vision are particularly impressive on Laserdisc. Thoroughly recommended.

The Tsar's Bride (complete).
** Chant du Monde Dig. LDC 288 056/7 [id.]. Glouboky, Kudriavchenko, Nizienko, Michenkine, Terentieva, Sveshnikov Russian Ac. Ch., Bolshoi Theatre O, Chistiakov.

The Chant du Monde set of *The Tsar's Bride* provides a fair stop-gap, an unhelpfully dry recording of a performance by a Bolshoi cast. Rimsky, ever attentive to musical fashion, was in part reflecting the then recent arrival of Puccini and others, for his heroine, Marfa, is as vulnerable as Mimì or Butterfly. Yet Rimsky's easy, colourful music hardly reflects the darkness of this story of conspiracy, betrayal and poison set in the days of Ivan the Terrible. For him, it seems, writing operas was all too easy, and he here showed little or none of Puccini's power to involve. The Bolshoi performance under Andrei Chistiakov is amiable to match, conveying few stage tensions. As Marfa, Ekaterina Kudriavchenko is firmer than most Russian sopranos but has moments of rawness, and is rather upstaged by the fine mezzo, Nina Terentieva, in the villainous role of Lubacha. Unlike most of the others, she produces beautiful tone despite the dryness. The four Acts are squeezed on to two very well-filled CDs.

Rochberg, George (born 1918)

Violin concerto.
(N) (M) *(**) Sony Stern Edition II SMK 64505 [id.]. Stern, Pittsburgh SO, Previn – STRAVINSKY: *Violin concerto.* (***)

For many years George Rochberg wrote in the twelve-note idiom, then he subsequently rediscovered tonality. His *Violin concerto* instantly proclaims that it is earnest and modern, opening with a suitably astringent gesture from the soloist before relapsing into a neo-romanticism redolent of Bartók and Szymanowski. This is therefore a work which fails to be structurally convincing and which also mixes rather hollow avant-garde dissonance with real music. Nevertheless it has some appealing moments, but it is rather like the rhyme about the little girl with 'a little curl right in the middle of her forehead'. It is beautifully played by Isaac Stern and the Pittsburgh orchestra under Previn, who approach it as if it were a concerto of the very first order. Every now and again they almost manage to convince us that it is better than in fact it is! No complaints about the 1977 recording, which has fine detail and a good balance.

Rodrigo, Joaquín (born 1902)

A la busca del más allá; (i) *Concierto Andaluz* (for 4 guitars); (ii) *Concierto de Aranjuez* (for guitar); (iii) *Concierto de estío* (for violin); (iv) *Concierto en modo galante* (for cello); (v) *Concierto heroico* (for piano); (vi) *Concierto madrigal* (for 2 guitars); (vii) *Concierto pastoral* (for flute); (viii) *Concierto serenata* (for harp). (ii) *Fantasia para un gentilhombre. Música para un jardín; Per la flor del Iliri blau; 5 Piezas infantiles; Soleriana; Zarabanda lejana y villancico.*
(M) *** EMI Dig. CDZ7 67435-2 (4) [id.]. (i) Moreno, Garibay, López, Ruiz; (ii) Alfonso Moreno; (iii) Augustín Léo Ara; (iv) Robert Cohen; (v) Jorge Osorio; (vi) Moreno, Mariotti; (vii) Lisa Hansen; (viii) Nancy Allen; LSO; Mexico State PO; RPO, Enrique Bátiz.

The only missing concertos are the second *Guitar concerto* (*Concierto para una Fiesta*) and the later *Cello concerto* (*Concierto como un divertimento*) commissioned by Julian Lloyd Webber. The present EMI recordings were made between 1980 and 1985, many of them in Watford Town Hall, and are of excellent quality, although the early digital technique often brings an overlit sound to the treble, perhaps appropriate for music drenched in Spanish sunshine. The *Summer concerto* for violin ('conceived in the manner of Vivaldi') is the composer's own favourite, and Augustin Léo Ara catches its neo-classical vitality admirably. The *Cello concerto* is given a masterly performance by Robert Cohen; he combines elegance of phrasing with warm beauty of timbre. The *Concierto serenata* for harp, a favourite of ours, has an unforgettable piquancy and charm. Nancy Allen consistently beguiles the ear with her gentleness. The *Concierto pastoral* is a spikier piece than usual from this composer and its brilliant introduction is far from pastoral in feeling, but Rodrigo's fragmented melodies soon insinuate themselves into the consciousness. Rodrigo's *Piano concerto* has a programmatic content, with the four movements written 'under the sign of the Sword, the Spur, the Cross and the Laurel'. The performers give a strong, extrovert account of the piece.

The *Concierto Andaluz* has its weaknesses but remains engaging if a trifle inflated. A similar comment might be made about the effect of the duo *Concierto madrigal*, with its set of twelve delightful vignettes, many with a medieval flavour, but the four guitar soloists here do not achieve the strongest profile, and this is also one reason why Alfonso Moreno's account of the famous *Concierto de Aranjuez*, though bright and sympathetic, is in no way outstanding. The symphonic poem, *A la busca del más allá*, is evocative and powerfully scored; *Música para un jardín* is a quartet of cradle songs, originally conceived for the piano and scored with all the piquancy at the composer's command. The *Five Children's pieces* are delightful, while the two neo-classical evocations of eighteenth-century Spain (*Soleriana*) are also unostentatiously appealing. *Per la flor del Iliri blau* is based on a Valencian legend, and Rodrigo is more impressive in moments of gently atmospheric detail than in the melodrama. The *Zarabanda lejana* was Rodrigo's first work for guitar. He later orchestrated it and added the *Villancico* to make a binary structure, the first part nobly elegiac, the second a gay dance movement.

(i) *Concierto Andaluz* (for 4 guitars); (ii) *Concierto de Aranjuez;* (ii; iii) *Concierto madrigal* (for 2 guitars); (ii) *Concierto para una fiesta; Fantasia para un gentilhombre*. Solo guitar pieces: *Bajando de la Meseta; En los trigales; Fandango; Junto al Generalife; 3 Little Pieces; Romance de Durandarte; Sonata a la española; Tiento antiquo.*
(M) *** Ph. 432 581-2 (3) [id.]. (i) Los Romeros; (ii) Pepe Romero; (iii) Angel Romero; ASMF, Marriner.

This distinguished set gathers together all Rodrigo's major concertante guitar works in first-class performances and adds a rewarding recital of solo works as a postlude, all played with natural spontaneity and complete authority by an artist who feels this music from his innermost being. The *Sonata* is no less strongly Spanish in character and the genre pieces are comparably picturesque in evoking Mediterranean atmosphere and local dance-rhythms. If the *Concierto para una fiesta* does not quite repeat the success of the *Concierto de Aranjuez*, it still has plenty of Andalusian colour, and Pepe Romero's performance has all the freshness of new discovery. He is equally magnetic in the solo items. Throughout, Marriner and the Academy provide accompaniments which are thoroughly polished and have much warmth, and the Philips sound is most natural and beautifully balanced.

Concierto de Aranjuez (for guitar and orchestra).
✷ (M) *** Decca Dig. 430 703-2; *430 703-4* [id.]. Carlos Bonell, Montreal SO, Dutoit – FALLA: *El amor brujo* etc. *** ✷
(BB) *** Naxos Dig. 8.550729 [id.]. Norbert Kraft, N. CO, Nicholas Ward – CASTELNUOVO-TEDESCO: *Concerto ***; VILLA-LOBOS: *Concerto. **(*)

Concierto de Aranjuez; (i) *Concierto madrigal* (for 2 guitars); *Fantasia para un gentilhombre.*
(M) *** Ph. 432 828-2 [id.]. Pepe Romero; (i) Angel Romero; ASMF, Marriner.

(i) *Concierto de Aranjuez;* (ii) *Fantasia para un gentilhombre.*
(N) (B) *** Decca Eclipse Dig. 448 243-2; *448 243-4* [id.]. Carlos Bonell, Montreal SO, Dutoit – ALBENIZ: *Rapsodia española*; TURINA: *Rapsodica sinfónica. ***
(M) *** Decca Dig. 417 748-2 [id.]. Carlos Bonell, Montreal SO, Dutoit (with FALLA: *Three-cornered hat ***).
*** Sony Dig. SK 37848. John Williams, Philh. O, Frémaux.
(N) (B) *** Sony SBK 58168; *SBT 58168* [id.]. John Williams, (i) Phd. O (members), Ormandy; (ii) ECO, Sir Charles Groves – GIULIANI: *Concerto, Op. 30;* VIVALDI: *Concerto, RV 93. ***

(i) *Concierto de Aranjuez; Fantasia para un gentilhombre. En los trigales; Pastoral; Sonata a la española.*
(B) *** CfP Dig. CD-CFP 4614; *TC-CFP 4614* [id.]. Ernesto Bitetti, (i) Philh. O, Antoni Ros-Marba.

(i) *Concierto de Aranjuez; Fantasia para un gentilhombre. En los trigales; Pequeña Sevillana; Sonata a la española.*
(N) (B) ** Tring Dig. TRP 0050 [id.]. Carlos Bonell; (i) RPO, Kaspszyk.

The Bonell/Dutoit *Concierto* was originally paired with the *Fantasia para un gentilhombre*. Decca made this issue even more attractive by adding a bonus of three dances from Falla's *Three-cornered hat* (taken from Dutoit's complete set). In the *Fantasia*, the balance between warmly gracious lyricism and sprightly rhythmic resilience is no less engaging. There is now a third, even more generous coupling on Decca's Eclipse bargain label which is well worth considering, as the Albéniz and Turina concertante works for piano are given dazzling, sultry performances by De Larrocha and Frühbeck de Burgos.

Decca then reissued the much-praised Bonell/Dutoit recording of the *Concierto* a second time, now recoupled with Alicia de Larrocha's splendid digital recording of Falla's *Nights in the gardens of Spain* plus Dutoit's outstanding complete *El amor brujo*. This is a very attractive pairing and the reasons for the success of the Rodrigo performance remain unaltered: an exceptionally clear, atmospheric and well-balanced digital recording plus Bonell's imaginative account of the solo part, and the strong characterization of the orchestral accompaniments by Charles Dutoit and his excellent Montreal orchestra.

Pepe Romero's performance of the *Concierto de Aranjuez* has plenty of Spanish colour, the musing poetry of the slow movement beautifully caught. The account of the *Fantasia* is warm and gracious, with the Academy contributing quite as much as the soloist to the appeal of the performance. Angel joins Pepe for the Renaissance-inspired duet, *Concierto madrigal*, which is very attractive indeed, making this a very viable alternative to the Decca couplings.

Norbert Kraft is a soloist of personality and he receives spirited, sensitive accompaniments from the Northern Chamber Orchestra under Nicholas Ward. Indeed the work sounds remarkably fresh using a smaller-sized orchestral group, which can bring a degree of intimacy yet produce sufficient body of violin-tone for the rapturous tutti near the end of the *Adagio*. This Naxos CD deserves a place near the very top of the list. The recording is very well balanced, with the guitar given a most convincing relationship with the orchestra and the sound itself vividly realistic.

An excellent bargain anthology from CfP, vividly recorded. Rodrigo's two favourite concertante guitar works are combined with some worthwhile solo items which are very well played by Ernesto Bitetti; indeed the *Sonata a la española*, which ends the programme, is dedicated to him. He gives a rather introspective performance of it, but the *Concierto* is bright-eyed while still finding a languorous intimacy in the slow movement. The performance of the *Fantasia*, too, is especially successful, with Ros-Marba and the Philharmonia providing a brilliantly coloured orchestral backing, full of bracing rhythmic vitality. They are helped by the lively yet atmospheric digital sound.

John Williams's newest version of the *Concierto* (his third) also has the advantage of first-class digital recording. The acoustic, however, is a little dry compared with the Decca issue, while the woodwind is a shade too forward. Nevertheless, this is technically superior to Williams's previous, analogue partnership with Barenboim and the performance is even finer.

John Williams made his first stereo recording of the *Concierto de Aranjuez* in 1965 with the estimable Eugene Ormandy, and followed with the *Fantasia* two years later, when Sir Charles Groves was hardly less sympathetic, especially in the expressive music. The performance of the *Concierto* has an agreeably ruminative, improvisatory quality, especially in the slow movement, and Ormandy provides a chamber-scaled background tapesty which nevertheless has a vivid palette; only in the finale does one feel that the relaxed mood loses some of the music's sparkle. The balance is near ideal, with the guitar nicely placed in relation to the orchestra in a pleasingly atmospheric ambience (in fact a pair of town halls, one in Philadelphia, the other in Barking!). Williams was to record the *Concierto* again with greater charisma, but this early, more intimate account remains very appealing, and the couplings are good, too.

Carlos Bonell's new recording of the *Concierto* for Tring does not begin to match his earlier, Decca account with Dutoit. Kaspszyk's accompaniments are comparatively limp and, although there is a pleasing intimacy in the scale of the music-making, it fails to spring vividly to life. Of the solo pieces easily the finest performance is of the *Sonata a la española*.

The Julian Bream Edition
Concierto de Aranjuez.
(M) *** RCA 09026 61598-2. Julian Bream, Melos Ens., Colin Davis – ARNOLD: *Concierto;* BENNETT: *Concierto* ***.
(M) *** RCA Dig. 09026 61605-2 [id.]. Julian Bream, COE, Gardiner – BERKELEY; BROUWER: *Concertos.* ***
*** EMI Dig. CDC7 54661-2 [id.]. Julian Bream, CBSO, Rattle – ARNOLD: *Concierto;* TAKEMITSU: *To the edge of dream.* ***

(i) *Concierto de Aranjuez;* (ii) *Fantasia para un gentilhombre. Invocation and dance (Hommage à Manuel de Falla); 3 Piezas españolas.*
(M) *** RCA Dig. 09026 61611-2. Julian Bream, (i) COE, Gardiner; (ii) RCA Victor CO, Leo Brouwer.

The differences between Bream's two earlier RCA readings of the *Concierto*, the first (analogue) with Colin Davis in 1963, the second (digital) with Gardiner in 1982, are almost too subtle to analyse and perhaps depend as much on the personalities of the two conductors as on that of the soloist. Certainly neither account is upstaged by the most recent version with Rattle. Colin Davis's direction is at its best in the opening movement, as crisply rhythmic as you could like, and in the slow movement Bream is raptly inspirational. Maybe the Gardiner version has a little extra dash and, for those who prefer an all-Rodrigo programme, this could be a good choice and the famous *Adagio* is played in a very free, improvisatory way, with some highly atmospheric wind solos in the orchestra. The *Fantasia para un gentilhombre* is mellower at its noble opening, but Leo Brouwer, himself a guitarist, brings plenty of orchestral vitality to the later sections of the score. The *Tres Piezas españolas* add to the value of the disc: the second piece, a Passacaglia, is one of Rodrigo's finest shorter works, and both this and the *Homage to Falla* show Bream at his most inspirationally spontaneous. The alternative coupling is with concertos by Berkeley and Brouwer.

The later, E M I recording of the *Concierto* with Rattle is also hugely enjoyable in a slightly more relaxed way. This is not to suggest a lack of point and alertness but, with warmer, somewhat more modern digital sound, the effect is more opulent. The glorious cor anglais solo by Peter Walden at the opening of the *Adagio* immediately creates a more romantic atmosphere, although Bream maintains his ruminative, improvisatory style convincingly. The finale is engagingly spirited and lighthearted. In the end choice will depend on couplings.

Fantasia para un gentilhombre.
(N) (M) ** DG 449 098-2 [id.]. Narciso Yepes, Spanish R. & TV O, Alonso – CASTELNUOVO-TEDESCO: *Concerto* **(*); HALFFTER: *Concerto.* **

Yepes plays impressively, as usual, but Alonso's accompaniment is merely serviceable. These artists have been recorded in a studio with a dry acoustic, which hardly adds glamour to Rodrigo's colourful orchestral palette.

SOLO GUITAR MUSIC

Tres Piezas españolas.
(Y/B) 🏵 (BB) *** RCA Navigator Dig. 74321 17903-2. Julian Bream (guitar) – ALBENIZ: *Collection;* GRANADOS: *Collection.* *** 🏵

Rodrigo's *Three Spanish pieces* are characteristically inventive, the central *Passacaglia* quite masterly and the closing *Zapateado* attractively chimerical in Julian Bream's nimble figers. This 1983 recording has been added to what was already one of the finest of all recorded guitar recitals of Spanish music. An outstanding bargain in every way.

PIANO MUSIC

Music for 2 pianos: (i) *5 Piezas infantiles* (piano, 4 hands): *Atardecer; Gran marcha de los subsecretarios; Sonatina para dos Muñecas;* (solo piano): *Air de ballet sur le nom d'une jeune fille; Album de Cecilia; A l'ombre de Torre Bermeja; Bagatela; Berceuse d'automne; Berceuse de printemps; Danza de la Amapola; 3 Danzas de españa; 4 Estampas andaluzas; 3 Evocaciones; Pastorale; 4 Piezas (Caleseras: Homenaje a Chueca; Fandango del Ventorrillo; Plegaria de la Infanta de Castilla; Danza Valenciana); Preludio de Añoranza; Preludio al Gallo mañanero; Serenata española; Sonada de adiós (Hommage à Paul Dukas); 5 Sonatas de Castilla, con Toccata a modo de Pregón: Nos. 1–2 in F sharp min.; 3 in D; 4 in B min. (como un tiento); 5 in A. Suite: Zarabanda lejana.*
🏵 *** Bridge BCD 9027 A/B [id.]. Gregory Allen (i) with Anton Nel.

Rodrigo's keyboard music is all but unknown and, as this first-class and comprehensive survey shows, for all its eclecticism it is well worth exploring. In his earliest piano work, the *Suite* of 1923, with its sprightly *Prelude*, cool *Sicilienne* and Satie-ish minuet, the link with the French idiom is obvious, while the glittering brilliance of the *Preludio al Gallo mañanero* is unmistakably Debussian. If here the influences are unassimilated, later Rodrigo's use of French impressionism is entirely conscious. The soft melancholy of the last piano piece Rodrigo wrote, in 1987, *Preludio de Añoranza* poignantly recalls the refined delicacy of atmosphere one finds in Ravel. There are other influences too. The *Cinq Sonatas de Castilla* look back further in time and draw continually on the keyboard writing of Scarlatti. But they are spiced with piquant dissonances which the Italian composer would have disowned. The *Serenata española* marks Rodrigo's positive adoption of an overtly Andalusian style, while the *Cuatro Piezas* and the *Cuatro estampas andaluzas* are as sharply Spanish in character as any of the similarly picaresque miniatures of Granados or Albéniz. Rodrigo's children's pieces have especial charm. The delectable

Sonatina para dos Muñecas (two puppets) was designed for four very small hands, those of his grand-children, Cecilia and Patty, who gave the première at the tender ages of nine and twelve respectively! The darker side of Rodrigo's nature, sometimes brooding, sometimes nostalgic, is at its most expressive in the nocturne, *Atardecer*, an ambitious piece for two players; but it also colours some of the mini-atures, not least the austere yet deeply felt *Plegaria de la Infanta de Castilla* from the *Cuatro Piezas*. The recording is uncommonly real and has great presence. In the duo works Allen is admirably partnered by Anton Nel.

A l'ombre de Torre Bermeja; 2 Berceuses; 4 Estampas Andaluzas; 3 Evocaciones (Homenaje a Joaquin Turina); 4 Piezas; 5 Piezas del Siglo XVI (Diferencias sobre Antonio de Cabezón's Canto del Caballero; 2 Pavans of Muis de Milan; Pavan of Enríquez de Valderrábano; Fantasia que contrahace la harpa de Ludovico of Alonso Mudarra).
(Y/B) *** Collins Dig. 1434-2 [id.]. Artur Pizarro.

It is good to have a highly recommendable single-CD representation of Rodrigo's evocative and sharply characterized piano music, opening with five pieces in which the composer draws on earlier Spanish musicians of the sixteenth century – after the fashion of Ravel's *Le tombeau de Couperin*. Of the two gentle *Berceuses*, the *Berceuse d'Automne*, with its sombre, tolling-bell-like figure, is particularly haunt-ing, while the *Turina Evocations* and the even more overtly Spanish *Estampas Andaluzas* glitteringly demonstrate a wide palette of pianistic colour, especially the brilliant closing *Barquitos de Cádiz*. Artur Pizarro (1990 Leeds prize-winner) is thoroughly at home in this repertoire and plays with panache, demonstrating a striking Spanish sensibility and feeling for dynamic nuance. His account of the last piece on this disc, *A l'ombre de Torre Bermeja* is a *tour de force* of spontaneous pianistic flair. He is splendidly recorded.

Roger-Ducasse, Jean-Jules (1873–1954)

Au jardin de Marguérite: Interlude; Epithalame; Prélude d'un ballet; Suite française.
(Y/B) *** Marco Polo Dig. 8.223641 [id.]. Rheinland-Pfalz Philh. O, Segerstam.

Le joli jeu de furet: Scherzo; Marche française; Nocturne de printemps; Orphée: 3 fragments sympho-niques; Petite suite.
(Y/B) *** Marco Polo Dig. 8.223501 [id.]. Rheinland-Pfalz Philh. O, Segerstam.

Those who wish that Ravel and Roussel had been more prolific should investigate these releases. Not that the music of Roger-Ducasse matches Ravel in sheer perfection or strength of personality, or Roussel in terms of inventive vitality or imagination; but he has an elegance and feeling for atmosphere that distinguish Gallic *petits-maîtres*. The *Nocturne de printemps* and the fragmentary but imaginative *Prélude d'un ballet* show a post-impressionist, Debussy-like figure with a refined feeling for the orches-tra; elsewhere, in *Orphée* for example, the influence of d'Indy can be discerned. There are touches of Ravel and in the *Epithalame* something of the high spirits of Les Six. Segerstam has a good feeling for this repertoire and gets atmospheric and sensitive performances from his Baden-Baden forces and good, serviceable recordings from the Marco Polo and radio engineers.

Roman, Johan Helmich (1694–1758)

(i) *Violin concertos: in D min.; E flat; F min.; Sinfonias: in A; D and F.*
*** BIS Dig. CD 284 [id.]. (i) Nils-Erik Sparf; Orpheus Chamber Ens.

None of the *Sinfonias* have appeared on disc before. Of the five *Violin concertos*, the three recorded here are certainly attractive pieces, particularly in such persuasive hands as those of Nils-Erik Sparf and the Orpheus Chamber Ensemble, drawn from the Stockholm Philharmonic. Very stylish and accomplished performances that are scholarly in approach.

Suites: in D (Lilla Drottningholmsmusiquen); G min. (Sjukmans-musiquen); (i) Piante amiche.
*** Musica Sveciae Dig. MSCD 417 [id.]. (i) Pia-Maria Nilsson; Stockholm Nat. Museum CO, Claude Génetay.

The *Drottningholm Music* is familiar from various earlier recordings, but the D major suite of dances known as the *Little Drottningholm Music* consists of 17 dances, none of which appear in the larger collection. They have all the grace and charm we associate with this genial and attractive composer, and the somewhat earlier *Sjukmans-musiquen* has no less appeal. The performances by the Stockholm National Museum Orchestra under one of the pioneers of the early-music revival in the 1950s, the late

Claude Génetay, convey real pleasure in the music-making. The disc includes a short cantata probably (but not certainly) by Roman, *Piante amiche*, which is attractive whatever its authenticity, and nicely sung too by Pia-Maria Nilsson. The recorded sound is well balanced and truthful.

(i) *Assaggi for violin in A, in C min. and in G min., BeRI 301, 310 & 320;* (i; ii) *Violin and harpsichord sonata No. 12 in D, BeRI 212;* (ii) *Harpsichord sonata No. 9 in D min., BeRI 233.*
*** Cap. CAP 21344 [id.]. (i) Jaap Schröder; (ii) Johann Sönnleitner.

The *Assaggi* (essays) recorded here often take one by surprise, particularly when played with such imagination as they are by Jaap Schröder. The harpsichord sonata is also more inward-looking than many others of Roman's pieces, and the only work that one could possibly describe as fairly predictable is the opening *Sonata for violin and continuo*. Excellent performances and recording, as well as exemplary presentation.

Ropartz, Joseph Guy (1864–1955)

Symphony No. 3 (for soloists, chorus and orchestra).
(M) *** EMI Dig. CDM7 64689-2 [id.]. Pollet, Stutzman, Dran, Vassar, Orféon Donostiarra Ch., Toulouse Capitole O, Plasson.

Like the Magnard symphonies, the *Third Symphony* of Ropartz has much nobility and there is a sense of scale and grandeur. There is much in the pantheistic vision of its opening pages that one cannot fail to respond to, and some felicitous harmonic invention. There is a certain unrelieved thickness of texture, particularly in the finale. However, there is a personality here, and all lovers of French music will find it rewarding. Even if the recording (and some of the solo singing) is not of the very highest order, the orchestral playing under Michel Plasson is thoroughly committed.

Rore, Cipriano da (c. 1515–65)

Missa Praeter rerum seriem. Motets: *Ave regina; Descendit in hortum meum; Infelix ego; Parce mihi.*
*** Gimell Dig. CDGIM 29; *1585T-29* [id.]. Tallis Scholars, Peter Phillips (with JOSQUIN DES PRES: Motet: *Praeter rerum seriem* ***).

Cipriano da Rore was Josquin's successor at the Italian Court d'Este at Ferrara. His *Missa Praeter rerum seriem* is appropriately preceded by the richly textured six-part Josquin motet based on the same melodic sequence. There is no doubt that the two works are connected, so perhaps Rore's piece was intended as a tribute to his illustrious predecessor. It is a worthy accolade, lyrically powerful, contrapuntally fascinating, spiritually serene and beautifully sung by these highly experienced singers, whose director knows just how to pace and inflect its linear detail and shape its overall structure. The four motets are hardly less impressive, and Gimell's recording, as ever, is virtually flawless.

Rosenberg, Hilding (1892–1985)

Orfeus i sta'n (Orpheus in town): ballet suite; (i) *Sinfonia concertante for violin, viola, oboe, bassoon and orchestra;* (ii) *Violin concerto No. 1. Symphony Nos. 3 (The Four Ages of Man;* 1939 version); (iii) *4 (Johannes Uppenbarelse: The Revelation of St John the Divine):* excerpts; (iv) *5 (Ortagårdsmästaren);* (v) *Den heliga natten (The Holy Night);* (vi) *Suite in D: Pastorale.*
(***) Caprice mono CAP 21510 (3) [id.]. Swedish RO or Stockholm PO, composer; with (i) Barter, Berglund, Lännerholm, Lavér; (ii) Charles Barkel; (iii) Anders de Wahl, Swedish R. Ch.; (iv) Lorri Lail, Swedish R. Ch.; (v) Björker, Lail, Lindberg-Torlind, Nilsson, Ohlson, Saedén, Widgren, Chamber Ch.; (vi) Lotte Andriesson.

The majority of these Archive recordings were made between 1940 and 1947. The suite from the ballet, *Orpheus in Town*, shows the sophisticated man-about-town side of the composer and is inventive and witty, while his inspiration in the oratorio, *The Holy Night*, is spread rather thin – despite some memorable singing from the baritone, Erik Saedén. There is nothing thin about the *Third Symphony*, based on Romain Rolland's *The Four Ages of Man* and interspersed with narration before each of the four movements. (On this CD, which the composer himself recorded in the 1970s, he reads the narrative.) Its Scherzo also included an elaborate fugal section. The composer's own pacing, particularly in the first movement, is expansive and, above all, convincing, and the same measured style emerges in the excerpts from the *Fourth Symphony* (*The Revelation of St John the Divine*), recorded in 1940 with narrator rather than baritone. The revelation for most collectors will not be *St John the Divine* but the *Fifth Symphony*, for soprano, chorus and orchestra. Like the *Fourth*, it is based on a mixture of biblical texts and Hjalmar Gullberg, but it has a serenity, eloquence and strength which are very striking. For the most part it finds Rosenberg at his most deeply characteristic best. The *Sinfonia concertante* is a good piece in neo-classical idiom (sounding like a Swedish Martinů) but the *Violin concerto No. 1* is of lesser interest and finds the composer in manufactured mode. It is good to hear him as pianist, accompanying Lotte Andriesson in 1935 in the *Pastorale* movement from his *Suite in D* for violin and piano. The documentation could not be more comprehensive or researched more scrupulously, and there is an excellent article by Carl-Gunnar Ahlen. A valuable issue of great documentary interest.

Symphony No. 4 (Johannes Uppenbarelse: The Revelation of St John the Divine).
*** Caprice Dig. CAP 21429. Håkan Hagegård, Swedish R. Ch., Pro Musica Ch., Rilke Ens., Gothenburg SO, Ehrling.

Rosenberg's remarkable 80-minute symphony-oratorio to texts from the Bible and by the Swedish poet, Hjalmar Gullberg, is for large forces and is a powerful work of real vision. Its opening fourths recall the world of Walton's *Belshazzar's feast* or of Hindemith, and one's thoughts occasionally turn to Honegger's *King David*. The biblical text inspires the most vividly expressive music, while the Gullberg poems are in an archaic and often serene style. Despite occasional longueurs, the overall impact of this score is very powerful. A splendid performance, very well recorded, though it needs to be played at a slightly higher level setting than usual.

Rossini, Gioacchino (1792–1868)

Ballet music from: *Mosè; Otello; Le siège de Corinthe; William Tell.*
(Y/B) (B) **(*) Ph. Duo 442 553-2 (2) [id.]. Monte Carlo Op. O, Antonio de Almeida – DONIZETTI: *Ballet music.* ***

Not all these items are lightweight, and Almeida draws positive and vigorous performances from the Monte Carlo orchestra. The strings often play with finesse, notably in the famous *William Tell ballet*, but the orchestra cannot quite provide the colour and degree of zestful brilliance which makes the Philharmonia Donizetti coupling so attractive. The sound in Monte Carlo, although agreeable, is less vivid than in London. Even so, this is very enjoyable.

La boutique fantasque (ballet, arr. Respighi) complete.
(Y/B) (B) *** Decca Dig. 444 109-2 [id.]. Nat. PO, Bonynge – BRITTEN: *Matinées musicales; Soirées musicales.* ***

Bonynge goes for sparkle and momentum above all in Respighi's brilliant arrangement of Rossini. The Decca recording has great brilliance and the orchestral colours glitter within the Kingsway Hall ambience. This account is not as atmospheric at the opening as some versions have been, but it remains infectiously enjoyable and is appropriately part of Decca's Ballet Gala series.

La boutique fantasque: extended suite.
(M) *** RCA 09026 61847-2 [id.]. Boston Pops O, Arthur Fiedler – OFFENBACH: *Gaîté parisienne.* *** ✪

Fiedler offers nearly half an hour of the ballet, not missing out much of importance. The performance sparkles, the playing has warmth and finesse and the Boston acoustics add the necessary atmosphere at the magically evocative opening. John Pfeiffer's remastering of this 1956 recording leaves little to be desired and the coupling is indispensable.

La boutique fantasque (ballet, arr. Respighi): *suite.*
(M) **(*) Chandos CHAN 6503 [id.]. SNO, Gibson – DUKAS: *L'apprenti sorcier;* SAINT-SAENS: *Danse macabre.* **(*)
(M) **(*) Sony SBK 46340 [id.]. Phd. O, Ormandy – TCHAIKOVSKY: *Sleeping Beauty:* highlights. **

Gibson's version of the suite is strikingly atmospheric. Helped by the glowing acoustics of Glasgow's City Hall, the opening has much evocation. The orchestra is on its toes and plays with warmth and zest, and the 1973 recording has transferred vividly to CD.

Ormandy presents Respighi's glittering orchestration with much brilliance and dash, and the Philadelphia Orchestra has all the sumptuousness one could ask for. This is more extrovert music-making than Gibson's and it is undoubtedly exhilarating, even if the effect of the recording is less refined.

Introduction, theme and variations in C min. for clarinet and orchestra.
*** ASV Dig. CDDCA 559 [id.]. Emma Johnson, ECO, Groves – CRUSELL: *Concerto No. 2* *** ⊛;
   BAERMANN: *Adagio* ***; WEBER: *Concertino*. ***

As in all her recordings, Emma Johnson's lilting timbre and sensitive control of dynamic bring imaginative light and shade to the melodic line. Brilliance for its own sake is not the keynote, but her relaxed
pacing is made to sound exactly right. Vivid recording.

String sonatas Nos. 1–6 (complete).
(Y/B) (BB) *** Decca Double 443 838-2 (2) [id.]. ASMF, Marriner (with CHERUBINI: *Etude No. 2 for
   French horn and strings* (with Barry Tuckwell); BELLINI: *Oboe concerto in E flat* (with Roger Lord)
   ***) – DONIZETTI: *String quartet*. ***
*** ASV CDDCA 767 [id.]. Serenata of London (members).
*** Hyperion Dig. CDA 66595 [id.]. O of Age of Enlightenment (members).
(B) *** Ph. Duo 434 734-2 (2). I Musici.

String sonatas Nos. 1 in G; 4 in B flat; 5 in E flat; 6 in D.
(M) *** Teldec/Warner 9031 74788-2 [id.]. Liszt CO, János Rolla – M. HAYDN: *Symphony, P.12*. ***

We have a very soft spot for the sparkle, elegance and wit of these ASMF performances of the Rossini
String sonatas, amazingly accomplished products for a twelve-year-old. The parts were only discovered
in the Library of Congress just after the Second World War. The music corresponds with previously
known works for wind quartet and early string quartets, but there is no doubt that the original scoring
was for two violins, cello and double-bass which takes a genuine solo role in the *Third Sonata*. Marriner
offers them on full orchestral strings but with such finesse and precision of ensemble that the result is all
gain. The 1966 recording still sounds remarkably full and natural, and the current CD transfer adds to
the feeling of presence. The overall playing time of just over 80 minutes means that the six sonatas will
not comfortably fit on a single CD, so the new Double Decca two-for-the-price-of-one format is ideal,
with other music added. Apart from the Donizetti *Quartet*, which has an appropriately Rossinian
flavour, the two minor concertante works are well worth having, with both Barry Tuckwell (in what is in
essence a three-movement horn concertino) and Roger Lord in excellent form.

   Almost simultaneously, Serenata of London, working as a string quartet, and a comparably sized group
from the Orchestra of the Age of Enlightenment, playing period instruments, each manage to include
all six of the *String sonatas* on one CD. As might be expected, the Serenata, playing modern instruments and led by the easily brilliant Barry Wilde, give the warmer, more sunny bouquet to Rossini's
string textures; their competitors, led by the dazzling Elizabeth Wallfisch, offer a slightly drier vintage,
though their approach is by no means unsmiling. Indeed their bass player, ChiChi Nwanoku, brings
added sharpness of attack to his moments of bravura, where Michael Brittain, with comparable virtuosity, at times sounds rather deadpan. On both discs the recording is truthful and naturally balanced.

   On the Philips Duo, I Musici play all six works spiritedly and with plenty of Italian sunshine warming
the phrasing, which is already pleasingly elegant. There is not the degree of wit that is present in the
ASMF/Marriner set, but there is no lack of genial vitality, and the refined naturalness of the early
1970s sound is considerable compensation.

   The merits of the Liszt Chamber Orchestra and János Rolla, who directs from the first desk, are by now
well known. They are virtuosic and polished, and they have the advantage of very natural digital sound.
Moreover the attractive Michael Haydn coupling is considerable compensation for the two missing
sonatas, and the disc comes at mid-price.

PIANO MUSIC

*Sins of old age (Péchés de Vieillesse): Album de Château: Nos. 2–3; Album pour les enfants adolescents:
Nos. 1 & 9; Compositions diverses et esquisses: No. 5. Quelques riens pour album Nos. 3, 5, 12, 16 & 24.
Book 9 (Untitled), Nos. 2–3, 5 & 7 (Marche et réminiscences pour mon dernier voyage).*
(Y/B) ** ASV Dig. CDDCA 901 [id.]. Alberto Portugheis.

Rossini wrote his '*Sins of old age*' (there are more than 150 of them) during the last decade of his life and
he favoured bizarre titles after the manner of Satie half a century later, although the writing itself is not
usually quirky. The pieces are pleasing enough and some of the best ideas have been borrowed by others
(notably the third of the *Riens – Danse sibérienne*, which Respighi used in *La boutique fantasque*). The
most ambitious included here is the final item of the programme (*Marche et réminiscences pour mon
dernier voyage*), which is a kind of witty pastiche of a funeral march, quoting from eight of Rossini's
best-known operas. Alberto Portugheis plays simply and musically but in a deadpan manner, and one
feels the need for more sparkle and a sense of whimsy, particularly in the operatic interpolations (the

arrival of the *William Tell* galop should surely bring a smile). The recording is of good quality.

VOCAL MUSIC

Cantata: *Giovanna d'Arco*. Songs: *L'âme délaissée; Ariette à l'ancienne; Beltà crudele; Canzonetta spagnuola (En medio a mis colores); La grande coquette (Ariette pompadour); La légende de Marguerite; Mi lagnerò tacendo* (5 settings including *Sorzico* and *Stabat Mater*); *Nizza; L'Orpheline du Tyrol (Ballade élégie); La pastorella; La regata veneziana* (3 songs in Venetian dialect); *Il risentimento; Il trovatore*.
*** Decca Dig. 430 518-2 [id.]. Cecilia Bartoli, Charles Spencer.

The songs of Rossini's old age were not all trivial, and this brilliantly characterized selection – with the pianist as imaginative as the singer – gives a delightful cross-section. Bartoli's artistry readily encompasses such a challenge, a singer who, even at this early stage of her career, is totally in command both technically and artistically. The recording, too, has splendid presence.

Petite messe solennelle.
(N) (M) **(*) Decca Dig. 444 134-2 (2) [id.]. Dessì, Scalchi, Sabbatini, Pertusi, Bologna Teatro Comunale Ch. & O, Chailly.
(N) (B) ** Double Decca 444 842-2 (2) [id.]. Marshall, Hodgson, Tear, King, Holford & Constable (pianos), Birch (harmonium), L Chamber Ch., Heltay – RESPIGHI: *Botticelli pictures* etc. ***

(i) *Petite messe solennelle;* (ii) *Stabat Mater*.
(N) (B) **(*) EMI forte Dig. CZS5 68658-2 (2). (i) Popp, Fassbaender, Gedda, Kavrakos, King's College Ch., Katia & Marielle Labèque, Briggs, Cleobury; (ii) Malfitano, Baltsa, Gambill, Howell, Maggio Musicale Fiorentino Ch. & O, Muti.

Rossini's *Petite messe solennelle* must be the most genial contribution to the church liturgy in the history of music. The description '*Petite*' does not refer to size, for the piece is comparable in length to Verdi's *Requiem*; rather it is the composer's modest evaluation of the work's 'significance'. But what a spontaneous and infectious piece of writing it is, bubbling over with characteristic melodic, harmonic and rhythmic invention. The composer never overreaches himself. 'I was born for *opera buffa*, as well Thou knowest,' Rossini writes touchingly on the score. 'Little skill, a little heart, and that is all. So be Thou blessed and admit me to paradise.'

Sawallisch's recording of Rossini's original score of this work – originally Ariola, later Eurodisc – would surely merit the granting of the composer's wish, but perversely it remains out of the catalogue. However, the EMI/King's version provides a different and contrasting view from Sawallisch's. Recorded, not in King's College Chapel – which would have been much too reverberant for Rossini's chamber textures – but in the Music Faculty at Cambridge, this is very enjoyable in its own right. The use of the refined trebles of King's College Choir brings a timbre very different from what Rossini would have expected from boys' voices – but, arguably, close to what he would have wanted. That sound is hard to resist when the singing itself is so movingly eloquent. The work's underlying geniality is not obscured, but here there is an added dimension of devotional intensity from the chorus which, combined with outstanding singing from a fine quartet of soloists and beautifully matched playing from the Labèque sisters, makes for very satisfying results. The recording, too, attractively combines warmth with clarity.

Rossini loses nothing of his natural jauntiness in his setting of the coupled *Stabat Mater*, but Muti's view is a dramatic one, and it is sad that he did not record it with the Philharmonia or with the Vienna Philharmonic, with whom he gave a memorable reading at the 1983 Salzburg Festival. As it is, the Florence Festival forces are sometimes rough – notably the orchestra – and the singing at times unpolished, though the solo quartet is a fine one. Warm but rather unrefined recording.

Chailly chooses Rossini's orchestral version (made in 1867), although Rossini himself preferred his original, as do we. Nevertheless, with a fine solo team, Daniella Dessì and Gloria Scalchi both singing beautifully (and ravishing in their *Qui tollis* duet), and with the bass rising to the occasion in the *Quoniam tu solus sanctus*, this is a very considerable account. The Bologna Chorus are not helped by a somewhat backward balance which, within the warmly resonant acoustic, does not provide an ideal sharpness of focus. But they sing with much ardour, especially in the *Gloria* and *Credo*, and Chailly ensures that the *Et resurrexit* caps the performance ebulliently. Apart from the choral balance (and that is not a real problem when the performers are so committed), the recording is glowing and vivid.

Heltay's 1977 Decca version is given a recording of striking realism and presence (the choral entry in the *Gloria* is arresting in its impact) but, although it does not lack drama, the reading misses the composer's whimsical geniality. Both Margaret Marshall and Alfreda Hodgson sing eloquently; there is some finely shaped and expressive choral singing and good support from the two pianists, with John Birch on the harmonium. But the music-making does not fully catch the music's spirit and can give only limited satisfaction.

Stabat Mater.

✪ *** Chandos Dig. CHAN 8780 [id.]. Field, Della Jones, A. Davies, Earle, London Symphony Ch.,
City of L. Sinfonia, Hickox.

(Y/B) (B) (***) DG Double mono 439 684-2 (2) [id.]. Stader, Radev, Haefliger, Borg, Berlin RIAS
Chamber Ch., St Edwige's Cathedral Ch., Berlin RIAS SO, Fricsay – VERDI: *Requiem.* (***)

(N) (B) ** Sony SB2K 53252 (2) [id.]. Arroyo, Wolff, Bianco, Diaz, Camerata Singers, NYPO,
Schippers – VERDI: *Requiem.* **

Richard Hickox rightly presents Rossini's *Stabat Mater* warmly and with gutsy strength. This is a most
winning account which has one marvelling that a work written piecemeal should have such consistently
memorable invention, much of it anticipating – or reflecting – early Verdi. All four soloists here are first
rate, not Italianate of tone but full and warm, and the London Symphony Chorus sings with fine attack
as well as producing the most refined pianissimos in the unaccompanied quartet, here as usual given to
the full chorus rather than to the soloists. Full-bodied and atmospheric sound.

It is the vitality and drama that come over most strongly in Fricsay's strong and spontaneous account
of a work that can easily sound lightweight. Even the tenor's *Cujus animam*, jaunty as the rhythm may
be, has a warm, lyrical resilience, and the fervour of the choral singing is matched by the soloists. The
effect is very much of compellingly live music-making; and this makes a worthy coupling for Fricsay's
electrifying account of the Verdi *Requiem*. The mono recording from the mid-1950s has astonishing
vividness and the conveyed atmosphere means that no apologies whatever need be made for the
sound.

Schippers conducts a strong and enjoyable performance with fine choral singing. But the soloists are
uneven. Beverly Wolff and Justino Diaz are often impressive, but Martina Arroyo, though confident,
sounds too gusty when the voice is under fortissimo pressure. The remastering is excellent and the sound
is pleasingly full-bodied and clear.

OPERA

Overtures: *Armida; Il barbiere di Siviglia; Bianca e Faliero; La cambiale di matrimonio; La Cenerentola;
Demetrio e Poblibio; Edipo a Colono; Edoardo e Cristina;* (i) *Ermione. La gazza ladra; L'inganno felice;
L'Italiana in Algeri; Maometto II; Otello.* (i) *Ricciardo e Zoraide. La scala di seta; Semiramide; Le siège
de Corinthe; Il Signor Bruschino; Tancredi; Il Turco in Italia; Torvaldo e Dorliska; Il viaggio a Reims;
William Tell. Sinfonia al Conventello; Sinfonia di Bologna.*

(M) *** Ph. 434 016-2 (3) [id.]. ASMF, Marriner; (i) with Amb. S.

Marriner's three discs span all Rossini's overtures, but one must remember that the early Neapolitan
operas, with the exception of *Ricciardo e Zoraide* and *Ermione*, make do with a simple Prelude, leading
into the opening chorus. *Ricciardo e Zoraide*, however, is an extended piece (12 minutes 25 seconds),
with the choral entry indicating that the introduction is at an end. *Maometto II* is on a comparable scale,
while the more succinct *Armida* is an example of Rossini's picturesque evocation, almost like a miniature tone-poem. Twenty-four overtures plus two sinfonias make a delightful package in such sparkling
performances, which eruditely use original orchestrations. Full, bright and atmospheric recording, spaciously reverberant, admirably transferred to CD, with no artificial brilliance.

Overtures: *Il barbiere di Siviglia; La cambiale di matrimonio; La gazza ladra; L'Italiana in Algeri; Otello;
La scala di seta; Semiramide; Le siège de Corinthe; Il signor Bruschino; Tancredi; Torvaldo e Dorliska; Il
Turco in Italia; Il viaggio a Reims; William Tell.*

(Y/B) (B) *** Decca Double 443 850-2 (2) [id.]. Nat. PO, Riccardo Chailly.

In 1981 Chailly and the National Philharmonic made the first compact disc of Rossini overtures (in the
Kingsway Hall) and these performances are now combined with their further compilation, recorded at
Walthamstow Assembly Hall in 1984, to make a desirable bargain double, with each collection presented on a separate disc. The balance of the recordings is truthful, with the orchestral layout very
believable. At times on the first disc there is a degree of digital edge on tuttis, but the bustle from the
cellos is particularly engaging. The solo playing is fully worthy of such clear presentation: the cellos at
the opening of *William Tell* and the principal oboe and horn in *The Italian girl* and *Il Turco in Italia*
respectively all demonstrate that this is an orchestra of London's finest musicians. Just occasionally
elsewhere the ensemble slips when Chailly lets the exhilaration of the moment triumph over absolute
discipline and poise. But under Chailly the spirit of the music-making conveys spontaneous enjoyment
too, especially in *The thieving magpie* and the nicely paced account of *William Tell*. Incidentally, *Il
viaggio a Reims* had no overture at its first performance, but one was cobbled together later, drawing on
the ballet music from *Le siège de Corinthe*. The other novelties, *Otello* – played with great dash – and
Torvaldo e Dorliska, with its witty interchanges between woodwind and strings, are among the high-

lights. *Semiramide* is also elegantly played and *The Barber* is nicely elegant, and overall the performances are undoubtedly as infectious as they are stylish.

Overtures: *Il barbiere di Siviglia; La Cenerentola; La gazza ladra; L'Italiana in Algeri; La scala di seta;
Semiramide; Il Signor Bruschino; Il Turco in Italia; William Tell.*
(N) (M) *** Ph. 446 196-2 [id.]. ASMF, Sir Neville Marriner.

This generous (76-minute) collection of nine overtures is drawn from two separate LPs, originally
published in 1974 and 1976. All the performances are vivacious and, for the earlier record (*Il Barbiere*,
L'Italiana in Algeri, *La scala di seta*, *Il Signor Bruschino* and *Il Turco in Italia*), Marriner resurrected the
original and lighter orchestrations (*sans* heavy brass and bass-drum). They emerge the more sparkling,
and *Il Signor Bruschino* brings the tapping of a triangle stick, not the usual bows (although the writer of
the excellent notes for this reissue was obviously not told of this change). However, no one need fear that
William Tell is minus trombones or lacks an enthusiastic closing *galop*. There is no shortage of recommendable anthologies of Rossini overtures at mid-and bargain-price, but this is certainly among them.

Overtures: *Il barbiere di Siviglia; La Cenerentola; La gazza ladra; L'Italiana in Algeri; Le siège de
Corinthe; Il Signor Bruschino.*
(M) *** DG 419 869-2 [id.]. LSO, Abbado.

Brilliant playing, with splendid discipline, vibrant rhythms and finely articulated phrasing – altogether
invigorating and bracing. There is perhaps an absence of outright geniality here, but these are superb
performances and this remains one of the very finest collections of Rossini overtures ever, for the wit is
spiced with a touch of acerbity, and the flavour is of a vintage dry champagne which retains its bloom,
yet has a subtlety all its own.

Overtures: *Il barbiere di Siviglia; La Cenerentola; La gazza ladra; La scala di seta; Il Signor Bruschino;
William Tell.*
✸ (M) *** RCA GD 60387 [60387-2-RG]. Chicago SO, Fritz Reiner.

As with the others in RCA's remastered Reiner/Chicago series, the 1958 sound-quality has been
improved phenomenally; they are preferable to most digital collections. The blaze of brass tone, supported by a rich orchestral backcloth and resonant bass drum, at the galop in the *William Tell overture*,
is all-engulfing, a thrilling moment indeed; at the same time the scurrying violins display the utmost
virtuosity. But it is the sparkle and vivacity of these performances that one remembers above all – and,
in *La Cenerentola*, the wit, as well as fizzing orchestral bravura. One would have liked the opening
flourish of *La scala di seta* to be neater – it is presented too lavishly here – but this is the solitary
reservation over a magnificent achievement.

Overtures: *Il barbiere di Siviglia; La gazza ladra; L'Italiana in Algeri; La scala di seta; Semiramide; Le
siège de Corinth; William Tell.*
(N) *** RCA Dig. 09026 68139-2 [id.]. Hanover Band, Goodman.

This is a delight; it has an exuberance and pace which are quite captivating. If you want period-
instrument performances, it will be difficult to beat these.

Overtures: *Il barbiere di Siviglia; La gazza ladra; L'Italiana in Algeri; La scala di seta; Semiramide;
William Tell.*
(B) **(*) DG 439 415-2 [id.]. BPO, Karajan.

Karajan's virtuoso performances are polished like fine silver. The main allegro of *La scala di seta*
abandons all decorum when played as fast as this, and elsewhere bravura often takes precedence over
poise. However, with the Berlin Philharmonic on sparkling form, there is wit as well as excitement. The
1971 recording was made (like so many other vintage Karajan recordings) in the Berlin Jesus-Christus-
Kirche, but the remastering casts very bright lighting on the upper range, which makes sonic brilliance
approach aggressiveness in some climaxes.

Overtures: *Il barbiere di Siviglia; La gazza ladra; L'Italiana in Algeri; La scala di seta; Il Signor
Bruschino; Semiramide; William Tell.*
✸ *** EMI Dig. CDC7 54091-2 [id.]. L. Classical Players, Norrington.

It is the drums that take a star role in Norrington's Rossini collection. They make their presence felt at
the beginning and end of an otherwise persuasively styled reading of *Il barbiere*; at the introduction of
La gazza ladra, where the snares rattle spectacularly and antiphonally; creating tension more distinctly
than usual at the beginning of *Semiramide*, and bringing tumultuous thunder to the Storm sequence in
William Tell. Of course the early wind instruments are very characterful too, with plenty of piquant
touches: the oboe colouring is nicely spun in *L'Italiana in Algeri* and properly nimble in *La scala di seta*,

a particularly engaging performance, mainly because of the woodwind chirpings. The brass also make their mark, with the stopped notes on the hand horns adding character to the solo quartet in *Semiramide*, and both horns and trumpets giving a brilliant edge to the announcement of the galop in *William Tell*. The strings play with relative amiability and a proper sense of line and are obviously determined to please the ear as well as to stimulate; altogether these performances offer a very refreshing new look over familiar repertoire. The recording is first class.

Overtures: *La gazza ladra; L'Italiana in Algeri; Semiramide; Il Signor Bruschino; William Tell.*
(N) (B) **(*) EMI forte CZS5 69364-2 (2) [id.]. RPO, Sir Colin Davis – BEETHOVEN: *Symphony No. 7*
*** ⊛; SCHUBERT: *Symphony No. 9.* ***

Sir Colin Davis's 1962 collection, recorded at Abbey Road, brings playing that is admirably stylish with an excellent sense of nuance. *Semiramide* is superb, reminding one of Beecham, as does the spunky opening of *The Thieving Magpie. William Tell* is pretty good too, the opening beautifully played. In *Il Signor Bruschino* it seems as if the bow-tapping device is done by the leader alone, which is rather effective. The CD transfer is vivid, but very brightly lit, with some loss of the body of the original; but the orchestral balance is natural.

Semiramide: Overture.
(***) Testament mono SBT 1015 [id.]. BBC SO, Toscanini – BRAHMS: *Symphony No. 2* (***); MEN-DELSSOHN: *Midsummer Night's Dream* excerpt. (**)

Toscanini's famous concerts with the BBC Symphony Orchestra were obviously very special. This overture from a 1935 concert has one on the edge of one's seat. Quite electrifying. The sound calls for tolerance – but what playing!

Armida (complete).
*** Koch Europa Dig. 350211 [id.]. Gasdia, Merritt, Matteuzzi, Ford, Furlanetto, Workman, Amb. Op. Ch., I Sol. Ven., Scimone.
(Y/B) **(*) Sony Dig. S3K 58968 (3) [id.]. Fleming, Kunde, Francis, Kaasch, Bosi, Zennaro, Fowler, D'Arcangelo, Zadvorny, Teatro di Bologna Ch. & O, Gatti.

Armida is one of the most distinctive of the serious operas that Rossini wrote for Naples in the years after the *Barber of Seville*. Armida has some marvellous fire-eating moments of display, particularly in the last act, when the knight, Rinaldo, finally manages to resist her magic and escape. Her realization of defeat, dramatically conveyed on a repeated monotone, is intensely human. As Armida, Cecilia Gasdia may not be strikingly characterful (Maria Callas knew the role) but her singing is both powerful and agile, firm and bold in Rossini's brilliant coloratura. As for the problem of finding three high *bel canto* tenors capable of tackling elaborate ornamentation, William Matteuzzi and Bruce Ford more than match Chris Merritt as Rinaldo. Though the principal, he is the least gainly of the three, but still impressive, notably in the love duets with Armida. Ferruccio Furlanetto is excellent in two bass roles, and a fourth tenor, Charles Workman, might well have stood in for any of the others. The booklet includes an introduction in English, but no translation of the Italian libretto.

Under Daniele Gatti the Sony performance, recorded live in Bologna in upfront sound with a noisy audience, is lusty rather than subtle, but Renée Fleming (the much-admired Countess in 1974's *Figaro* at Glyndebourne) sings commandingly in the title-role, with the voice both golden and flexible, extending down to a ripe chest-register. The four tenors, with three of them singing a splendid trio in Act III, make a generally stylish team, strongly led by Gregory Kunde as Rinaldo. However, first choice for this opera rests with the Koch Europa set, conducted by Scimone.

L'assedio di Corinto (*The siege of Corinth;* complete).
(M) **(*) EMI CMS7 64335-2 (3). Sills, Verrett, Diaz, Theyard, Howell, Lloyd, Amb. Op. Ch., LSO, Schippers.

Thomas Schippers made this recording in London in 1974 in preparation for a production at the Met. in New York with virtually the same cast. The pity is that he has encouraged the coloratura prowess of the prima donna, Beverly Sills, at the expense of the composer's final thoughts, with display material from Rossini's earlier version. Some of the most striking passages are the patriotic choruses, recognizably Rossinian but not at all in the usual vein. Sills, as so often on record, is variable, brilliant in coloratura but rarely sweet of tone, and she is completely upstaged by Shirley Verrett, singing magnificently as Neocle. Some strong singing too among the others, though not all the men are very deft with ornamentation. The recording, made at All Saints', Tooting, has plenty of atmosphere and has achieved a very satisfactory CD transfer.

Il barbiere di Siviglia (complete).

*** Decca Dig. 425 520-2 (3) [id.]. Bartoli, Nucci, Matteuzzi, Fissore, Burchuladze, Ch. & O of Teatro Comunale di Bologna, Patanè.

(Y/B) *** Ph. Dig. 446 448-2 (2) [id.]. Baltsa, Allen, Araiza, Trimarchi, Lloyd, Amb. Op. Ch., ASMF, Marriner.

*** Teldec/Warner Dig. 9031 74885-2 (2) [id.]. Larmore, Hagegård, Giménez, Corbelli, Ramey, Lausanne CO, López-Cobos.

*** EMI CDS7 47634-8 (2) [Ang. CDCB 47634]. Callas, Gobbi, Alva, Ollendorff, Philh. Ch. & O, Galliera.

(Y/B) (M) *** EMI CMS7 64162-2 (2) [id.]; (B) CfP *TC-CFPD 4704*. De los Angeles, Alva, Cava, Wallace, Bruscantini, Glyndebourne Festival Ch., RPO, Gui.

(B) *** Naxos Dig. 8.660027/29 [id.]. Ganassi, Serville, Vargas, Romero, De Grandis, Hungaria R. Ch., Failoni CO, Budapest, Will Humburg.

(M) *** RCA GD 86505 (3) [RCA 6505-2-RG]. Roberta Peters, Valletti, Merrill, Corena, Tozzi, Met. Op. Ch. & O, Leinsdorf.

**(*) DG Dig. 435 763-2 (3) [id.]. Battle, Domingo, Lopardo, Raimondi, Ch. & COE, Abbado.

(Y/B) (B) (**) Decca Double mono 443 536-2 (2) [id.]. Simionato, Misciano, Bastianini, Corena, Siepi, Maggio Musicale Fiorentino Ch. & O, Erede.

Cecilia Bartoli made this recording when she was still in her early twenties, a mezzo with a rich, vibrant voice who not only copes brilliantly with the technical demands but who also gives a winningly provocative characterization. In her big Act I aria, *Una voce poco fa*, she even outshines the memorable Agnes Baltsa on the excellent Marriner set. Like the conductor, Bartoli is wonderful at bringing out the fun. So is Leo Nucci, and he gives a beautifully rounded portrait of the wily barber. Burchuladze, unidiomatic next to the others, still gives a monumentally lugubrious portrait of Basilio, and the Bartolo of Enrico Fissore is outstanding, with the patter song wonderfully articulated at Patanè's sensible speed.

Il Barbiere was Sir Neville's first opera recording and he finds a rare sense of fun in Rossini's witty score. His characteristic polish and refinement – beautifully caught in the clear, finely balanced recording – never get in the way of urgent spontaneity, the sparkle of the moment. Thomas Allen as Figaro – far more than a *buffo* figure – and Agnes Baltsa as Rosina – tough and biting too – manage to characterize strongly, even when coping with florid divisions, and though Araiza allows himself too many intrusive aitches he easily outshines latterday rivals, sounding heroic, not at all the small-scale tenorino, but never coarse either. Fine singing too from Robert Lloyd as Basilio.

López-Cobos conducts a scintillating performance, helped by brilliant ensembles, generally taken at high speed, with rhythms sprung delectably. Though Håkan Hagegård is a dry-toned Figaro, the recording sets him in a helpful ambience, which equally helps to enhance the comic atmosphere, with the interplay of characters well managed. There are few more stylish Rossini tenors today than Raúl Giménez and, though his voice is not as youthful as some, his musical imagination goes with fine flexibility and point. As for Jennifer Larmore, she is an enchanting Rosina, both firm and rich of tone and wonderfully agile. Crisply consistent, it makes a strong contender among modern digital versions, even next to the delectable Decca version featuring Cecilia Bartoli, particularly when it comes (like Marriner's Philips version) on two discs instead of three.

Gobbi and Callas were here at their most inspired and, with the recording quality nicely refurbished, the EMI is an outstanding set, not absolutely complete in its text, but so crisp and sparkling it can be confidently recommended. Callas remains supreme as a minx-like Rosina, summing up the character superbly in *Una voce poco fa*. The early stereo sound comes up very acceptably on a pair of CDs, clarified to a degree, presenting a uniquely characterful performance with new freshness and immediacy.

Victoria de los Angeles is as charming a Rosina as you will ever find: no viper this one, as she claims in *Una voce poco fa*, and that matches the gently rib-nudging humour of what is otherwise a 1962 recording of the Glyndebourne production. It does not fizz as much as other Glyndebourne Rossini on record but, with a characterful line-up of soloists, it is an endearing performance which in its line is unmatched. The recording still sounds well. Tape collectors should be very well satisfied with the CfP equivalent, issued at bargain price on two cassettes in a chunky box, with synopsis instead of libretto. The CDs have been handsomely re-packaged and the documentation is freshly printed.

Though the cast is not as starry as with most full-price rivals, the Naxos set makes a first-rate bargain. The singing is hardly less stylish, with Sonia Ganassi a rich-toned Rosina, controlling vibrato well, and with Ramon Vargas an agile and attractively youthful-sounding Almaviva. Roberto Serville as Figaro conveys the fun of the role brilliantly. The *buffo* characters are strongly cast too, with Basilio's *La calunnia* (Franco de Grandis) delightfully enlivened by comments from Bartolo (Angelo Romero), both very much involved in their roles. Will Humburg's often brisk speeds, with crisp recitative matched by dazzling ensembles, never prevent the music (and the singers) from breathing. The only reservation is that the glowing Glyndebourne version under Gui with Victoria de los Angeles as Rosina comes (on only two discs) at an even more reasonable price, though with a text not quite so complete.

Roberta Peters is a sparkling Rosina, a singer too little known in Europe, who here lives up to her high reputation at the Met., dazzling in coloratura elaborations *in alt*. Robert Merrill may not be a specially comic Figaro, but the vocal characterization is strong, with the glorious voice consistently firm and well focused. Valletti, Corena and Tozzi make up a formidable team, and Leinsdorf conducts with a lightness and relaxation rare for him on record. Good, clear sound of the period, set against a reverberant, helpful acoustic.

Domingo heads a cast that would be hard to beat today, including Kathleen Battle, Frank Lopardo and Ruggero Raimondi, with Claudio Abbado conducting the Chamber Orchestra of Europe. Domingo is the set's biggest success. Abbado is free and spontaneous-sounding, but his touch, as conveyed in dry, close-up sound, is much heavier-handed, missing much of the sparkle of his earlier DG set, with ensemble-work surprisingly rough. Even Raimondi as Basilio in his big aria, *La calunnia*, is relatively undisciplined, if spontaneous-sounding, and the big bangs at the climax are completely miscalculated. Kathleen Battle makes a minx of a Rosina, coy but full of flair, and Frank Lopardo is a stylish Almaviva, though not well contrasted with Domingo.

Recorded in 1956, the Double Decca mono set of *Il barbiere*, well transferred, is well worth hearing for the characterful portrayals of the principal characters, all from vintage Italian singers at their peak. As Rosina, Simionato may not be ideally flexible in her ornamentation, but her rich, robust mezzo could not be more firmly distinctive, and Bastianini offers a comparably strong, purposeful and clean-cut Figaro. Fernando Corena as Bartolo and Cesare Siepi as Basilio make a classic pair of *buffo* basses, even if Siepi's massive *La calunnia* is astonishingly slow. Alvinio Misciano, the least well-known of the principals, is a clear-toned *tenore di grazia*, only occasionally ungainly as Almaviva. Erede conducts a warmly idiomatic reading.

Il barbiere di Siviglia: highlights.
(Y/B) *** Teldec/Warner Dig. 4509 93693-2 [id.] (from above recording, with Hagegård, Larmore; cond. López-Cobos).
(M) *** EMI CDM7 63076-2 (from above recording, with Gobbi, Callas; cond. Galliera).
**(*) DG Dig. 437 841-2 [id.] (from above recording, with Domingo, Battle; cond. Abbado).
**(*) Ph. Dig. 438 498-2 [id.] (from above recording, with Allen, Baltsa; cond. Marriner).

Teldec offers a generous and comprehensive 76-minute selection from a performance which is outstanding in every way. Jennifer Larmore is an enchanting Rosina; the dry-toned Figaro, Håkan Hagegård, brings out the opera's humour, and Raúl Giménez makes a stylishly attractive hero. López-Cobos directs zestfully and the ensembles are as infectious as they are spirited.

On EMI, Callas remains supreme as a minx-like Rosina. The highlights disc offers most of the key solo numbers from Act I, while in Act II it concentrates on Rossini's witty ensembles, including the extended Second Act *Quintet*. The *Overture* is included and, while it is stylishly played, it would have been better to have offered more of the vocal music.

Abbado's DG selection is more generous (73 minutes) and will be valuable for those wanting to sample Domingo's highly successful assumption of the title-role.

The Philips highlights are well chosen and admirably reflect the qualities of Marriner's complete set, the sound particularly sparkling in the delightful Act II finale. However, the selection omits the Overture and is not particularly generous (57 minutes).

The Barber of Seville (sung in English).
(N) **(*) Chandos Dig. CHAN 7023/4 [id.]. Della Jones, Ford, Opie, Rose, ENO Ch. & O, Bellini.

The dearth of opera in English on disc stems from the big companies' need to target more than just the English-speaking world. Boldly, with help from the Peter Moores Foundation, long devoted to this cause, Chandos here offers at mid-price this *Barber* in English, using the bright translation of Amanda and Anthony Holden. Strongly cast, it is a genial performance, very well played and recorded. The only reservation is over the relaxed conducting of Gabriele Bellini which lacks dramatic bite. Compensating for that, the principal singers not only characterize vividly but together form a lively ensemble. Alan Opie is a strong, positive Figaro, while Della Jones as Rosina both exploits her rich mezzo tones and brings sparkle to the coloratura. It is good too to have so accomplished a Rossini tenor as Bruce Ford singing Almaviva. Peter Rose as Basilio and Andrew Shore as Dr Bartolo, both young-sounding for these roles, are fresh and firm too.

La cambiale di matrimonio (complete).
* Claves Dig. CD 50-9101 [id.]. Praticò, Rossi, Comencini, De Simone, Facini, Baiano, ECO, Viotti.

This was the first of the Claves series to be recorded in London, and unfortunately the venue chosen was the reverberant All Saints', Tooting. The voices have fair bloom on them, but the orchestra, rather recessed, sounds washy, a significant flaw in such intimately jolly music, with ensembles suffering in particular. Viotti is a relaxedly stylish Rossinian, drawing pointed playing from the ECO, but the singing is poor. The tenor Maurizio Comencini sounds unsteady and strained, while Alessandra Rossi as the heroine, agile enough, is too shrill for comfort. The best singing comes from the buffo baritone, Bruno Praticò, as the heroine's father.

La Cenerentola (complete).
*** Decca Dig. 436 902-2 (2) [id.]. Bartoli, Matteuzzi, Corbelli, Dara, Costa, Banditelli, Pertusi, Teatro
    Comunale (Bologna) Ch. & O, Chailly.
(Y/B) *** Teldec/Warner Dig. 4509 94553-2 (2). Larmore, Giménez, Quilico, Corbelli, Scarabelli,
    ROHOCG Ch. & O, Rizzi.
*** Ph. Dig. 420 468-2 (2) [id.]. Baltsa, Araiza, Alaimo, Raimondi, Amb. Op. Ch., ASMF, Marriner.
(M) (***) EMI mono CMS7 64183-2 (2) [Ang. CDMB 64183]. Gabarain, Oncina, Bruscantini, Noni,
    Glyndebourne Festival Ch. & O, Gui.

Chailly's version has the effervescence of a live performance, with none of the disadvantages of a live recording. Cecilia Bartoli, one of the most vibrantly exciting singers of the younger generation, makes an inspired Cenerentola. Her tone-colours are not just more sensuous than those of her rivals: her imagination and feeling for detail add enormously to her vivid characterization, culminating in a stunning account of the final rondo, *Non più mesta*. The rest of the cast has been just as carefully chosen, with William Matteuzzi as an engaging prince, sweeter of tone and more stylish than his direct rivals, while the contrasting of the bass and baritone roles is ideal between Alessandro Corbelli as Dandini, Michele Pertusi as the tutor, Alidoro (substitute for the fairy godmother in the Cinderella story), and Enzo Dara as Don Magnifico. Few Rossini opera-sets have such fizz as this, and the recording is one of Decca's most vivid. The video was recorded more recently at the Houston Grand Opera with Bartolli, Corbelli, Dara and Pertusi continuing in the principal roles and Bruno Campanella conducting with fine spirit. Visually the production is a delight. Subtitled in English, this is very highly recommended (Decca 071 444-3).

On Carlo Rizzi's Teldec version with Covent Garden forces, Jennifer Larmore makes an enchanting heroine, with her creamily beautiful mezzo both tenderly expressive in cantilena and flawlessly controlled through the most elaborate coloratura passages. She may not be the fire-eating Cenerentola the vibrant Cecilia Bartoli is on Chailly's outstanding Decca version, but this is a more smiling character, not least in the final exuberant rondo, *Non più mesta*, which sparkles deliciously, more relaxed than with Bartoli. As Ramiro, Raúl Giménez sings with a commanding sense of style, less youthful but more assured than his rival, while Alessandro Corbelli is far more aptly cast here as Don Magnifico than as Dandini in the Decca set. Here the Dandini of Gino Quilico is youthful and debonair, and Alastair Miles is a magnificent Alidoro. Though the Covent Garden forces cannot quite match the close-knit Bologna team in underlining the comedy as in a live performance, as directed by Carlo Rizzi they are consistently more refined, with more light and shade, bringing out the musical sparkle all the more. Excellent, well-balanced sound.

Marriner's set of *Cenerentola* conveys Rossinian fun to the full. As in *Il barbiere*, the role of heroine is taken by the formidable Agnes Baltsa – not so aptly cast this time in a vulnerable Cinderella role – and that of the hero by Francisco Araiza, sweet and fresh of tone, though still allowing too many aspirants in passage-work. Ruggero Raimondi's commanding and resonant singing as Don Magnifico is very satisfying, and there is no weak link in the rest of the cast. The sound is first class in all respects, nicely resonant with plenty of atmosphere.

Gui's 1953 recording of *Cenerentola* has mono sound of amazing clarity and immediacy. Sadly the text is seriously cut, but the effervescence of Gui's live performances at Glyndebourne has been infectiously caught. Juan Oncina produces the most sweet-toned singing as the Prince, with the vintage baritone, Sesto Bruscantini, a vividly characterful Dandini, almost another Figaro. The title role is sung by the Spanish mezzo, Marina de Gabarain, a strikingly positive singer with a sensuous flicker in the voice, very much in the style of the legendary Conchita Supervia.

Le Comte Ory (complete).
✹ (M) (***) EMI mono CMS7 64180-2 (2) [Ang. CDMB 64180]. Oncina, Roux, Jeannette and
    Monica Sinclair, Glyndebourne Festival Ch. & O, Gui.
✹ *** Ph. Dig. 422 406-2 (2) [id.]. Sumi Jo, Aler, Montague, Cachemaille, Quilico, Pierotti, Lyon Op.
    Ch. & O, Gardiner.

Gui's classic recording of *Le Comte d'Ory*, with the same Glyndebourne forces who gave this sparkling opera on stage, brings pure delight. In limited but clearly focused mono sound, Gui conveys an extra sparkle and resilience, even over Gardiner's brilliant Philips version. There is a natural sense of timing here that regularly has you laughing in joy, as in the dazzling finale of Act I, one of the most infectiously witty of all recordings of a Rossini ensemble. Juan Oncina in his prime as the Count, the Hungarian Sari Barabas as the Countess Adèle and Michel Roux as the Count's friend are superbly matched by Monica Sinclair as the Countess's housekeeper and Ian Wallace as the Count's tutor. Some 10 minutes of text have been cut, but that allows the complete opera to be fitted on two CDs, each containing a complete act.

On Philips, with musical argument more sustained than in other comic pieces of the period, Rossini's mastery is matched by the performance here, beautifully sung and with ensembles finely balanced, as in the delectable Act II trio. Gardiner tends to be rather more tense than Gui was, with speeds on the fast side, and he allows too short a dramatic pause for the interruption to the Nuns' drinking choruses. But the precision and point are a delight. Though John Aler hardly sounds predatory enough as the Count, the lightness of his tenor is ideal, and Sumi Jo as Adèle and Diana Montague as the page, Isolier, are both stylish and characterful. So is the clear-toned Gino Quilico as the tutor, Raimbaud. With the cuts of the old Glyndebourne set opened out and with good and warm, if not ideally crystal-clear, recording, this set takes its place as a jewel of a Rossini issue.

La Donna del Lago (complete).
*** Sony Dig. M2K 39311 (2) [id.]. Ricciarelli, Valentini Terrani, Gonzalez, Raffanti, Ramey, Prague Philharmonic Ch., COE, Pollini.

Maurizio Pollini, forsaking the keyboard for the baton, draws a fizzing performance from the Chamber Orchestra of Europe. Katia Ricciarelli in the title-role of Elena, Lady of the Lake, has rarely sung so stylishly on record, the voice creamy and very agile in coloratura. Lucia Valentini Terrani is no less impressive in the travesti role of Elena's beloved, Malcolm; while Samuel Ramey as Elena's father, Douglas, with his darkly incisive singing makes you wish the role was far longer. Of the two principal tenors, Dalmacio Gonzalez, attractively light-toned, is the more stylish; but Dano Raffanti as Rodrigo Dhu copes with equal assurance with the often impossibly high tessitura. The recording is clear and generally well balanced and given added immediacy in the new format.

Elisabetta Regina d'Inghilterra (complete).
(M) *** Ph. 432 453-2 (2) [id.]. Caballé, Carreras, Masterson, Creffield, Benelli, Jenkins, Amb. S., New Philh. O, Masini.

The first surprise in this lively operatic setting of the Elizabeth and Leicester story comes in the overture, which turns out to be the one which we know as belonging to *Il barbiere di Siviglia*. It is one of a whole sequence of self-borrowings which add zest to a generally delightful score. In a well-sprung performance like this, with beautiful playing from the LSO and some very fine singing, it is a set for any Rossinian to investigate. Of the two tenors, José Carreras proves much the more stylish as Leicester, with Ugo Benelli, in the more unusual role of a tenor-villain, singing less elegantly than he once did. Caballé produces some ravishing sounds, though she is not always electrifying. Lively conducting and splendid recording.

Ermione (complete).
(M) *** Erato/Warner Dig. 2292 45790-2 (2) [id.]. Gasdia, Zimmermann, Palacio, Merritt, Matteuzzi, Alaimo, Prague Philharmonic Ch., Monte Carlo PO, Scimone.

Ermione begins very strikingly with an off-stage chorus, introduced in the slow section of the overture, singing a lament on the fall of Troy. The use of dramatic declamation, notably in the final scene of Act II, also gives due weight to the tragedy; however, not surprisingly, Rossini's natural amiability keeps bursting through, often a little incongruously. Though the three tenors in this Monte Carlo set from Erato are good by modern standards – Ernesto Palacio (Pirro), Chris Merritt (Oreste) and William Matteuzzi (Pilade) – they are uncomfortably strained by the high tessitura and the occasional stratospheric top notes. Cecilia Gasdia makes a powerful Ermione, not always even enough in her production but strong and agile; while Margarita Zimmermann makes a firm, rich Andromaca. Scimone, not always imaginative, yet directs a strong, well-paced performance. The recording is rather dry on the voices, but the hint of boxiness is generally undistracting and this set is a must for true Rossinians.

Guglielmo Tell (*William Tell:* complete, in Italian).
*** Decca 417 154-2 (4) [id.]. Pavarotti, Freni, Milnes, Ghiaurov, Amb. Op. Ch., Nat. PO, Chailly.

Rossini wrote his massive opera about William Tell in French, but Chailly and his team here put forward a strong case for preferring Italian, with its open vowels, in music which glows with Italianate lyricism. Chailly's is a forceful reading, particularly strong in the many ensembles, and superbly recorded. Milnes makes a heroic Tell, always firm, and though Pavarotti has his moments of coarseness he sings the role of Arnoldo with glowing tone. Ghiaurov too is in splendid voice, while subsidiary characters are almost all well taken, with such a fine singer as John Tomlinson, for example, ripely resonant as Melchthal. The women singers too are impressive, with Mirella Freni as the heroine Matilde providing dramatic strength as well as sweetness. The recording, made in 1978 and 1979, comes out spectacularly on CD. The *Pas de six* is here banded into its proper place in Act I.

Guillaume Tell (William Tell) (sung in French).
(M) *** EMI CMS7 69951-2 (4). Bacquier, Caballé, Gedda, Mesplé, Amb. Op. Ch., RPO, Gardelli.

The interest of the 1973 EMI set is that it is sung in the original French. Gardelli proves an imaginative Rossini interpreter, allying his formidable team to vigorous and sensitive performances. Bacquier makes an impressive Tell, developing the character as the story progresses; Gedda is a model of taste, and Montserrat Caballé copes ravishingly with the coloratura problems of Mathilde's role. While Chailly's full-price Decca set puts forward a strong case for using Italian with its open vowels, this remains a fully worthwhile alternative, with excellent CD sound. Indeed the current remastering is first class in every way and the choral passages, incisively sung, are among the most impressive; moreover the set now comes with full translation.

L'inganno felice (complete).
*(*) Claves Dig. CD 50-9211 [id.]. De Carolis, Felle, Zennaro, Previato, Serraiocco, ECO, Viotti.

L'inganno felice is stylishly and energetically conducted by Viotti with sprung rhythms and polished playing, but with a flawed cast. As the heroine, Amelia Felle is agile but too often raw-toned, even if on occasion she can crown an ensemble with well-phrased cantilena. As the hero, Bertrando, Iorio Zennaro has an agreeable natural timbre, but his tenor is not steady enough and strains easily. The buffo, Fabio Previato, is the soloist who comes closest to meeting the full challenge. The recorded sound has a pleasant bloom on it, but the orchestra is too recessed, and though the recitatives are briskly done, with crisp exchanges between the characters, the degree of reverberation is a serious drawback.

L'Italiana in Algeri (complete).
⊛ *** DG 427 331-2 (2) [id.]. Baltsa, Raimondi, Dara, Lopardo, V. State Op. Konzertvereinigung, VPO, Abbado.
*** Sony Dig. M2K 39048 (2) [id.]. Valentini Terrani, Ganzarolli, Araiza, Cologne R. Ch., Capella Coloniensis, Ferro.
(M) *** Erato/Warner 2292 45404-2 (2) [id.]. Horne, Palacio, Ramey, Trimarchi, Battle, Zaccaria, Prague Ch., Sol. Ven., Scimone.

Abbado's brilliant version was recorded in conjunction with a new staging by the Vienna State Opera, with timing and pointing all geared for wit on stage to make this the most captivating of all recordings of the opera. Agnes Baltsa is a real fire-eater in the title-role, and Ruggero Raimondi with his massively sepulchral bass gives weight to his part without undermining the comedy. The American tenor, Frank Lopardo, proves the most stylish Rossinian, singing with heady clarity in superbly articulated divisions, while both buffo baritones are excellent too. Like the CBS set, this uses the authentic score, published by the Fondazione Rossini in Pesaro.

The fine Sony version not only uses the critical edition of the score, it goes further towards authenticity in using period instruments, including a fortepiano instead of harpsichord for the recitatives (well played by Georg Fischer). Lucia Valentini Terrani here gives her finest performance on record to date, with her seductively rich, firm voice superbly agile in coloratura. Francisco Araiza as Lindoro peppers the rapid passage-work with intrusive aitches – but not too distractingly – and the strength of the voice makes the performance heroic with no suspicion of the twittering of a tenorino. Ganzarolli treats the role of the Bey, Mustafa, as a conventional buffo role, with a voice not ideally steady but full of character; the rest of the cast is strong, too.

Scimone's highly enjoyable version is beautifully played and recorded with as stylish a team of soloists as one can expect nowadays. The text is complete and alternative versions of certain arias are given as an appendix. Marilyn Horne makes a dazzling, positive Isabella, and Samuel Ramey is splendidly firm as Mustafa. Domenico Trimarchi is a delightful Taddeo and Ernesto Palacio an agile Lindoro, not coarse, though the recording does not always catch his tenor timbre well. Nevertheless the sound is generally very good indeed.

L'Italiana in Algeri: highlights.
(Y/B) (M) *** Sony SMK 53504 [id.] (from above recording, with Terrani, Araiza; cond. Ferro).
*** DG Dig. 429 414-2 [id.] (from above set, with Baltsa, Raimondi; cond. Abbado).

On Sony a set of highlights (72 minutes) from a first-rate version, with Lucia Valentini Terrani seductively leading a consistently strong cast.

This 67-minute selection of highlights from Abbado's complete set on DG provides a sparkling sampler, but the measure is comparatively short and this is a full-price CD.

Maometto II (complete).
*** Ph. Dig. 412 148-2 (3) [id.]. Anderson, Zimmermann, Palacio, Ramey, Dale, Amb. Op. Ch., Philh. O, Scimone.

Claudio Scimone's account of *Maometto II* has Samuel Ramey magnificently focusing the whole story in his portrait of the Muslim invader in love with the heroine. The other singing is less sharply characterized but is generally stylish, with Margarita Zimmermann in the travesti role of Calbo and June Anderson singing sweetly as Anna. Laurence Dale is excellent in two smaller roles, while Ernesto Palacio mars some fresh-toned singing with his intrusive aitches. Excellent recording.

Mosè in Egitto (complete).
(M) *** Ph. 420 109-2 (2) [id.]. Raimondi, Anderson, Nimsgern, Palacio, Gal, Fisichella, Amb. Op. Ch., Philh. O, Scimone.

Scimone here justifies his claim that the 1819 version is dramatically more effective than both the earlier Italian one and the later Paris one. Rossini's score brings much fine music and, among the soloists, Raimondi relishes not only the solemn moments like the great invocation in Act I and the soaring prayer of Act III, but also the rage aria in Act II, almost like Handel updated if with disconcerting foretastes of Dr Malatesta in Donizetti's *Don Pasquale*. The writing for the soprano and tenor lovers (the latter the son of Pharaoh and in effect the villain of the piece) is relatively conventional, though the military flavour of their Act I cabaletta is refreshingly different. Ernesto Palacio and June Anderson make a strong pair, and the mezzo, Zehava Gal, is another welcome newcomer as Pharaoh's wife. Siegmund Nimsgern makes a fine Pharaoh, Salvatore Fisichella an adequate Arone (Aaron). The well-balanced recording emerges most vividly on CD.

L'occasione fa il ladro (complete).
(M) **(*) Claves Dig. CD 50-9208/9 [id.]. Bayo, De Carolis, Zennaro, Provvisionato, Previati, Massa, ECO, Viotti.

On two discs, this is one of the longer one-Acters in the Claves series, bringing one of the more recommendable performances, with Viotti at his most relaxed. Maria Bayo as the heroine sings warmly and sweetly, with no intrusive aspirates in the coloratura. The soubrette role of Ernestina is also charmingly done, and the buffo characters sing effectively, though the tenor, Iorio Zennaro, is hardly steady enough for Rossinian cantilena. The two discs come in a single hinged jewel-box at upper mid-price.

Otello (complete).
(M) *** Ph. 432 456-2 (2) [id.]. Carreras, Von Stade, Condò, Pastine, Fisichella, Ramey, Amb. S., Philh. O, López-Cobos.

The libretto of Rossini's *Otello* bears remarkably little resemblance to Shakespeare – virtually none at all until the last Act. It is some tribute to this performance, superbly recorded, and brightly and stylishly conducted by López-Cobos, that the line-up of tenors is turned into an asset, with three nicely contrasted soloists. Carreras is here at his finest – most affecting in his recitative before the murder, while Fisichella copes splendidly with the high tessitura of Rodrigo's role, and Pastine has a distinct timbre to identify him as the villain. Frederica von Stade pours forth a glorious flow of beautiful tone, well-matched by Nucci Condò as Emilia. Samuel Ramey is excellent too in the bass role of Elmiro.

La pietra del paragone (complete).
(M) **(*) Van. 08 9031 73 (3) [id.]. Carreras, Wolff, Bonazzi, Elgar, Reardon, Foldi, Diaz, Murcell, Clarion Concerts Ch. & O, Jenkins.

This recording of the *opera buffa*, *La pietra del paragone*, made by Vanguard in New York in 1972, presents the young José Carreras in an incidental role, just one in an attractively fresh-voiced cast of soloists. It is given a vigorous, if occasionally hard-pressed performance under Newell Jenkins with what is called the Clarion Concerts Orchestra and Chorus. The plot of disguises and deceit is a throwback to artificial eighteenth-century conventions, involving a house-party with a couple of poets and a venal critic brought in. For modern performance the problem is the length, though on disc that evaporates when Rossini's invention is at its peak in number after number.

La scala di seta (complete).
*** Claves Dig. 50-9219/20 [id.]. Corbelli, Ringholz, Vargas, De Carolis, Provvisionato, Massa, ECO, Viotti.

The overture is among the best known of all that Rossini wrote, and here Viotti establishes his individuality with an unusually expansive slow introduction leading to a brisk and well-sprung allegro, scintillatingly played by the ECO. The cast here is stronger vocally than those in the rest of the Claves series, with Teresa Ringholz delightful as the heroine, Giulia, warm and agile, shading her voice seductively. She and the buffo, sung by Alessandro Corbelli, have the biggest share of the solo work, and he is also first rate. The tenor Ramon Vargas sings without strain – rare in this series – and the mezzo, Francesca Provvisionato, sings vivaciously as the heroine's cousin, with a little aria in military rhythm a special delight. Warm sound with good bloom on the voices.

Semiramide (complete).
*** DG Dig. 437 797-2 (3). Studer, Larmore, Ramey, Lopardo, Amb. Op. Ch., LSO, Ion Marin.

Semiramide (complete, but with traditional cuts).
(M) *** Decca 425 481-2 (3) [id.]. Sutherland, Horne, Rouleau, Malas, Serge, Amb. Op. Ch., LSO, Bonynge.

Rossini concentrates on the love of Queen Semiramide for Prince Arsace (a mezzo-soprano), and musically the result is a series of fine duets, superbly performed here by Sutherland and Horne (in the mid-1960s when they were both at the top of their form). In Sutherland's interpretation, Semiramide is not so much a Lady Macbeth as a passionate, sympathetic woman and, with dramatic music predominating over languorous cantilena, one has her best, bright manner. Horne is well contrasted, direct and masculine in style, and Spiro Malas makes a firm, clear contribution in a minor role. Rouleau and Serge are variable but more than adequate, and Bonynge keeps the whole opera together with his alert, rhythmic control of tension and pacing. The vintage Decca recording has transferred brilliantly to CD.

On this DG version, Marin opens out many traditional cuts, notably in the role of the tenor, Idreno. Lopardo sings Idreno's splendid Act I aria magnificently, a scene omitted on Decca; and the newer performance, even at speeds generally faster, altogether lasts almost 40 minutes longer, though most of the extra material – recitative, repeats, introductions – is not of major importance. Though Cheryl Studer cannot match Sutherland in command or panache as the Babylonian queen, hers is still a strong, aptly agile performance. Jennifer Larmore sings superbly in the breeches role of Arsace, less powerful than Marilyn Horne but even more convincing in character, with the voice more youthfully fresh. What above all prevents Semiramide and Arsace's great duet, *Serbami ognor*, from sounding so seductively idiomatic is the conducting of Ion Marin, strong and purposeful but often too mechanical, generally missing the helpful rubatos that mark the Bonynge reading. The role of Assur is strongly sung by Samuel Ramey, but he gives little idea of the character's villainous side. The mid-'60s sound of the Decca, transferred to CD at mid-price, is still very vivid, but the digital DG recording provides extra brilliance and range.

Il Signor Bruschino (complete).
(Y/B) *** DG Dig. 435 865-2 [id.]. Battle, Ramey, Lopardo, Desderi, Larmore, ECO, Ion Marin.

You could hardly devise a starrier cast for this 'comic farce in one act' than that assembled by DG, with even the tiny role of the maid, Marianna, taken by Jennifer Larmore. Ion Marin springs rhythms very persuasively, with the first Cavatina of Gaudenzio, the tutor, so delectably pointed in the introduction that one registers the character even before Samuel Ramey enters. Kathleen Battle makes a provocative heroine and the tenor, Frank Lopardo, sings sweetly and freshly as Sofia's lover, Florville. He is delightfully agile in his patter duet with Filiberto, the innkeeper, taken by Michele Pertusi. Excellent, well-balanced sound. The single disc (76 minutes) comes complete with libretto, translation and notes in a double-disc jewel-case.

Tancredi (complete).
(Y/B) (B) *** Naxos Dig. 8.660037/8 [id.]. Podles, Jo, Olsen, Spagnoli, Di Micco, Lendi, Capella Brugensis, Brugense Coll. Instrumentale, Alberto Zedda.
** Sony S3K 39073 (3) [id.]. M. Horne, Cuberli, Palacio, Zaccaria, Di Nissa, Schuman, Ch. and O of Teatro la Fenice, Weikert.

The enterprise of Naxos in recording one of the rarer operas of Rossini is triumphantly rewarded, for this set completely displaces the only rival version from Sony. That came on three full-priced discs against the two here, and the eminent Rossini scholar and conductor, Alberto Zedda, proves a far more resilient, generally brisker and lighter Rossini interpreter than his counterpart. Sumi Jo completely outshines Lella Cuberli as the heroine, Amenaide,in dazzlingly clear coloratura, as well as imaginative pointing of phrase, rhythm and words. The mezzo, Ewa Podles, is less characterful, yet the voice is firm and rich as well as flexible; but it is the tenor, Stanford Olsen, previously heard as Belmonte on John Eliot Gardiner's recording of *Entführung*, who offers some of the freshest, most stylish and sweetly tuned singing from a Rossini tenor in recent years. The recording is a little lacking in body, but that partly reflects the use of a small orchestra, and the voices come over well. Having a studio rather than a live recording (like the Sony) means that ensembles are crisper and better focused. An Italian libretto is provided but no translation. Instead, a helpful synopsis is geared to the different tracks on the discs; had there been a libretto, this could well have received a Rosette.

The chief glory of the live Sony recording from Venice is the enchanting singing of Lella Cuberli as the heroine, Amenaide. The purity and beauty of her tone, coupled with immaculate coloratura and tender expressiveness, make it a memorable performance, confirming the high opinions she won from the DG set of *Il viaggio a Reims*. Marilyn Horne, though not quite as fresh-sounding as earlier in her career, gives a formidable performance in the breeches role of Tancredi, relishing the resonance of her chest register, but finding delicacy too in her big aria, *Di tanti palpiti*. Ernesto Palacio is an accomplished Rossini tenor, commendably agile in the role of Argirio, but the tone tends to grow tight; and Zaccaria as Orbazzano sings with fuzzy, sepulchral tone. The conducting is efficient rather than inspired, failing to make the music sparkle or to bring the drama to life. The recording gives a realistic idea of a dryish theatre acoustic.

Il Turco in Italia (complete).
*** Ph. Dig. 434 128-2 (2) [id.]. Sumi Jo, Alaimo, Fissore, Giménez, Mentzer, Corbelli, Bronder, Amb. Op. Ch., ASMF, Marriner.

On Philips, Sumi Jo as Fiorilla, the sharp-tongued heroine, unhappily married to old Don Geronio, is no fire-eater, as Callas was in her vintage recording, but she sparkles delightfully, a most believable young wife. What seals the success of the Philips version is the playing of the St Martin's Academy under Sir Neville Marriner, consistently crisp and light, wittily bringing out the light and shade in Rossini's score and offering a full text. The big snag with the old Callas set was that it was severely cut by half an hour and more of music. As for the rest of the Philips cast, Simone Alaimo as the visiting Turkish prince, Selim, may lack the sardonic weight of Samuel Ramey on Sony, but it is a fine voice, and the buffo role of Geronio finds Enrico Fissore agile and characterful in his patter numbers. Raúl Giménez is the stylish tenor in the relatively small role of Narciso, which happily acquires an extra aria. Altogether a most welcome follow-up to Marriner's excellent set of the *Barber*.

Il Turco in Italia: highlights.
(Y/B) (M) **(*) Sony Dig. SMK 53505 [id.]. Ramey, Caballé, Dara, Palacio, Berbié, Amb. Op. Ch., Nat. PO, Chailly.

Chailly's recording is very well conducted, with a good feeling for theatrical timing. His cast is strong. Montserrat Caballé as Fiorilla is less girlish than she might be, and Samuel Ramey is a rather straight-laced Selim, but his singing is splendid; and this makes an enjoyable selection, brightly recorded. However, for the complete opera one turns to Marriner's Philips version.

Il viaggio a Reims (complete).
🏵 *** DG Dig. 415 498-2 (2) [id.]. Ricciarelli, Valentini Terrani, Cuberli, Gasdia, Araiza, Giménez, Nucci, Raimondi, Ramey, Dara, Prague Philharmonic Ch., COE, Abbado.
**(*) Sony Dig. S2K 53336 (2) [id.]. McNair, Valentini Terrani, Serra, Studer, Giménez, Matteuzzi, Ramey, Raimondi, Berlin R. Ch., BPO, Abbado.

This DG set is one of the most sparkling and totally successful live opera recordings available, with Claudio Abbado in particular freer and more spontaneous-sounding than he generally is on disc, relishing the sparkle of the comedy, and the line-up of soloists here could hardly be more impressive, with no weak link. Apart from the established stars the set introduced two formidable newcomers in principal roles, Cecilia Gasdia as a self-important poetess and, even finer, Lella Cuberli as a young fashion-crazed widow. Abbado's brilliance and sympathy draw the musical threads compellingly together with the help of superb, totally committed playing from the young members of the Chamber Orchestra of Europe.

It seems strange that Sony should so soon make a new recording of so rare – if delightful – an opera as this in competition with DG's prize-winning version, particularly when Claudio Abbado is again the conductor and the cast features many of the same singers. Again it is a live recording but, with more distanced sound and voices less clear, it sparkles less. The Berlin Philharmonic is less attuned to Rossini

than the Chamber Orchestra of Europe. Though the Sony cast is strong, no individual singer significantly outshines any predecessor, and most are less impressive.

Zelmira (complete).
*** Erato/Warner Dig. 2292 45419-2 (2) [id.]. Gasdia, Fink, Matteuzzi, Merritt, Amb. S., Sol. Ven.,
   Scimone.

Zelmira has always had a bad press, but this recording, well sung (with one notable exception) and
very well recorded, lets us appreciate that Rossinian inspiration had certainly not dried up. Scimone
takes a generally brisk view of both the arias and the ensembles but never seems to race his singers. In
this performance the choice of singers underlines the contrast between the two principal tenor-roles.
Chris Merritt combines necessary agility with an almost baritonal quality as the scheming Antenore,
straining only occasionally, and William Matteuzzi sings with heady beauty and fine flexibility in
florid writing as Ilo. Star of the performance is Cecilia Gasdia in the name-part, projecting words and
emotions very intensely in warmly expressive singing. She is well matched by the mezzo, Barbara
Fink, as her friend, Emma, and only the wobbly bass of José Garcia as the deposed Polidoro mars the
cast.

COLLECTIONS

Arias from *L'assedio di Corinto; Bianca e Faliero; Elisabetta, Regina d'Inghilterra; Guglielmo Tell;
Otello; Semiramide; Tancredi*.
(Y/B) (M) **(*) Virgin/EMI CUV5 61139-2 [id.]. Katia Ricciarelli, Lyon Op. Ch. & O, Ferro.

Admirers of this artist will surely want this recital, even if Ricciarelli was past her peak when it was
recorded in 1989. There is rare material here, sung with much character and at times (as the opening
excerpt from *L'assedio di Corinto* and the *Romanza* from *William Tell* readily show) her line is beautifully spun. But elsewhere, when under stress, she sounds less comfortable, although her vigorous sense
of dramatic style often carries the day. Ferro conducts sympathetically and the Lyon Opera Chorus
gives good support. The recording is vivid, too.

*L'assedio de Corinto: Avanziam' . . . Non temer d'un basso affetto! . . . I destini tradir ogni speme . . .
Signormche tutto puio . . . Sei tu, che stendi; L'ora fatal s'appressa . . . Giusto ciel. La Donna del lago:
Mura Felici; Tanti affetti. Otello: Assisa a pie d'un salice. Tancredi: Di tanti palpiti.*
✳ (M) *** Decca 421 306-2 [id.]. Marilyn Horne, Amb. Op. Ch., RPO, Henry Lewis.

Marilyn Horne's generously filled recital disc brings one of the most cherishable among all Rossini aria
records ever issued. The voice is in glorious condition, rich and firm throughout its spectacular range,
and is consistently used with artistry and imagination, as well as brilliant virtuosity in coloratura. By
any reckoning this is thrilling singing, and the sound is full and brilliant, showing its age hardly at all.

Arias: *La Cenerentola: Non piu mesta. La Donna del Lago: Mura felici . . . Elena! O tu, che chiamo.
L'Italiana in Algeri: Cruda sorte! Amor tiranno! Pronti abbiamo . . . Pensa all patria. Otello: Deh! calma,
o ciel. La Pietra del Paragone: Se l'Italie contrade . . . Se per voi lo care io torno. Tancredi: Di tanti palpiti.
Stabat Mater: Fac ut portem.*
*** Decca Dig. 425 430-2; *425 430-4* [id.]. Cecilia Bartoli, A. Schoenberg Ch., V. Volksoper O, Patanè.

Cecilia Bartoli's first recital of Rossini showpieces brings a formidable demonstration not only of
Bartoli's remarkable voice but of her personality and artistry, bringing natural warmth and imagination
to each item without ever quite making you smile with delight. Yet there are not many Rossini recitals of
any vintage to match this. Vocally, the one controversial point to note is the way that Bartoli articulates
her coloratura with a half-aspirate, closer to the Supervia 'rattle' than anything else, but rather obtrusive. Accompaniments are exemplary, and Decca provided the luxury of a chorus in some of the items,
with hints of staging. Full, vivid recording. Recommended.

'Rossini heroines': Arias from: *La donna del lago; Elisabetta, Regina d'Inghilterra; Maometto II; Le
nozze di Teti e Peleo; Semiramide; Zelmira*.
*** Decca Dig. 436 075-2 [id.]. Cecilia Bartoli, Ch. & O of Teatro la Fenice, Marin.

Cecilia Bartoli follows up the success of her earlier Rossini recital-disc with this second brilliant collection of arias, mostly rarities. The tangy, distinctive timbre of her mezzo goes with a magnetic projection
of personality to bring to life even formal passage-work, with all the elaborate coloratura bright and
sparkling. The rarest item of all is an aria for the goddess Ceres from the classically based entertainment, *Le nozze di Teti e Peleo*, making a splendid showpiece. The collection is crowned by a formidably
high-powered reading of *Bel raggio* from *Semiramide*, with Bartoli excitingly braving every danger.

Rott, Hans (1858–84)

Symphony in E.
*** Hyperion Dig. CDA 66366 [id.]. Cincinnati Philh. O, Gerhard Samuel.

It is astonishing to encounter in Hans Rott's *Symphony* ideas that took root in Mahler's *First* and *Fifth Symphonies*. Structurally the work is original, each movement getting progressively longer, the finale occupying nearly 25 minutes. But the music is full of good ideas and, anticipations of Mahler apart, has a profile of its own. The Cincinnati Philharmonia is a student orchestra who produce extraordinarily good results under Gerhard Samuel. The recording is good. Readers should investigate this issue without delay.

Roussel, Albert (1869–1937)

Bacchus et Ariane (complete ballet), *Op. 43; Le festin de l'araignée (The spider's feast): symphonic fragments.*
(M) *** EMI Dig. CDM7 64690-2 [id.]. O Nat. de France, Prêtre.

This is a particularly valuable mid-priced reissue from 1986. *Bacchus et Ariane* teems with life and is full of rhythmic vitality and richness of detail. It has perhaps less of the poetic feeling of *Le festin* but is nevertheless an exhilarating score. The recording, made in the generous acoustic of the Salle Wagram, is a shade too reverberant at times, but no essential detail is masked. Georges Prêtre obtains an excellent response from the Orchestre National de France in both scores. This supersedes Martinon's albeit excellently balanced earlier version on Erato which contained merely the two suites (or Acts) of the ballet and had no fill-up. The CD freshens detail a little, although the resonance means that the improvement is relatively limited. However, the background silence is certainly an asset in *The spider's feast*.

Le festin de l'araignée (ballet): *suite, Op. 17;* (i) *5 mélodies: Amoureux séparés; Invocation; Le jardin mouillé; Light; Sarabande.*
(M) (***) EMI mono CDC7 54840-2 [id.]. (i) O, composer; (ii) Claire Croïza, composer – SCHMITT: *La tragédie de Salomé* etc. (***)

The composer's own account of the suite from the ballet *Le festin de l'araignée* ('The Spider's feast') has plenty of atmosphere and the benefit of very good recorded sound for its period. The orchestra is uncredited, but the performance evokes a sense of theatre and a strong, imaginative atmosphere. Roussel's recording has already appeared before, together with the songs he recorded with Croïza on Philips and also including some rather less special (relatively modern) performances of the piano music (see our 1990 edition). But this new EMI disc offers by far the more economical and better-transferred version, and it comes with a splendid coupling, Florent Schmitt's *La tragédie de Salomé*.

Sinfonietta; Symphony No. 4, Op. 53.
** Chandos Dig. CHAN 9072 [id.]. Detroit SO, Järvi – DEBUSSY: *La Mer;* MILHAUD: *Suite provençale.*
**

Neeme Järvi gives a spirited and generally idiomatic account of the *Fourth Symphony*, though, as is occasionally his wont, he is far too fast in the slow movement. Roussel's textures can easily sound too dense and the contrapuntal detail is not always clearly delineated. An attractive enough programme in all conscience, but, despite its strong artistic merits and musically balanced recording, not a front-runner in any of the four works.

Suite in F, Op. 33.
(M) **(*) Mercury 434 303-2 [id.]. Detroit SO, Paul Paray – CHABRIER: *Bourrée fantasque* etc. ***

The outer movements of Roussel's *Suite in F* have a compulsive drive which also infects the harmonically complex, bittersweet central *Sarabande*. The scoring is rich (some might say thick), and the resonance of the Detroit Ford Auditorium makes it congeal a little. It is well played and alive, with Paray at his best in the closing *Gigue*.

Symphonies Nos. 1 (La poème de la forêt), Op. 7; 2 in B flat, Op. 23; 3 in G min., Op. 42; 4 in A, Op. 53.
(N) *** RCA Dig. 09026 61511-2 (2) [id.]. R. France PO, Janowski.

The Roussel symphonies have not been ideally served on disc, and Dutoit's (now deleted) set with the Bavarian Radio Orchestra was never much more than a stop-gap. There are plenty of good performances of the *Third*, not the least of which is Raymond Leppard's BBC recording, though the *Fourth* is less well served at present. Karajan's post-war recording remains unsurpassed as a performance but it is hard to get hold of. The present set is a source of celebration and is well worth having. On this showing the Orchestre Philharmonique is the equal of the French Radio's premier ensemble, the Orchestre National, and Marek Janowski has a natural feel for the Roussel idiom. His version of the *First* (*La poème de la forêt*) is the best to appear so far and his *Second*, though it does not obliterate fond memories of Jean Martinon's record with the Orchestre National, is still very good indeed and far more idiomatic than the Dutoit. The *Third* is very good, though the Scherzo is a shade too fast, and the *Fourth* receives a very fine performance. The set is neatly packaged (two discs in the space of one) and the recording, made in the Salle Olivier Messiaen of Radio France, has plenty of body, presence and detail. This is now the standard recommendation for these rewarding and resourceful scores.

Symphony No. 3 in G min., Op. 42.
(Y/B) (M) **(*) DG Dig. 445 512-2 [id.]. O Nat. de France, Bernstein – FRANCK: *Symphony.* **(*)
(Y/B) (M) **(*) Sony SMK 64107 [id.]. NYPO, Boulez – RAVEL: *Chansons.* ***
(N) (M) **(*) BBC Radio Classics 15656 91362 [id.]. BBC N. SO, Leppard – DEBUSSY: *Images;* FAURE: *Ballade for piano and orchestra.* **(*)

Symphony No. 3; Bacchus et Ariane (ballet): *suite No. 2, Op. 43.*
**(*) Chandos Dig. CHAN 8996 [id.]. Detroit SO, Järvi – RAVEL: *Boléro; La valse.* **

Symphonies Nos. 3; 4 in A, Op. 53; Bacchus et Ariane, suite No. 2; Sinfonietta for string orchestra, Op. 52.
(Y/B) **(*) Chandos Dig. CHAN 7007 [id.]. Detroit SO, Neeme Järvi.

This is a much less comfortable symphony than the Franck, with which it is coupled on DG, and Bernstein compulsively brings out all its energy and pungent dissonance, and yet he lightens the mood attractively for the high-spirited finale. The 'live' recording is extremely vivid but a shade harsh.

Neeme Järvi's account of the *Third Symphony* has an engaging vitality and character, and the playing of the Detroit orchestra is highly responsive. In the slow movement he indulges in a rather steep *accelerando* after the fugal section. Likewise his finale feels too fast. But it is a committed performance. His account of the second suite from *Bacchus et Ariane* is both vivid and atmospheric. Some may find the acoustic a shade too resonant, given the complexity of Roussel's textures, but the overall balance is very natural and pleasing. CHAN 7007 offers a more logical coupling with previously available material. Not absolutely ideal performances, perhaps, but better than most of the alternatives, and certainly very recommendable, given the good sound and Järvi's obvious enthusiasm for this repertoire.

Boulez's first movement is surprisingly slow (it is still pungent but has less electricity and brilliance than Bernstein's CBS disc, just reissued). The slow movement, however, has great warmth and humanity. Unfortunately, the recording, made in the Manhattan Center in 1975, is not as first rate as the performance: the acoustic is reverberant and there is plenty of body, but the upper strings are rather shrill. Nevertheless, with the splendid Ravel couplings, this makes an alternative mid-priced recommendation.

This BBC version of the Roussel *Third Symphony* emanates from a 1976 concert at the Free Trade Hall in Manchester, before the orchestra became the BBC Philharmonic. It is an excellent performance in every way and is held together very well, with well-chosen tempi and taut rhythms. The sound is a bit dry and opaque, otherwise it would have had three stars.

CHAMBER MUSIC

(i) *Divertissement for wind quintet & piano, Op. 6;* (ii) *Piano trio in E flat, Op. 2;* (iii) *Violin sonata No. 1, Op. 11.*
(N) **(*) Olympia Dig. OCD 458-2 [id.]. (i–iii) Jet Röling; (i) Paul Verhey, Hans Roerade, Frank van den Brink, Herman Jeurissen, Jos de Lange; (ii–iii) Jean-Jacques Kantorow, (ii) Herre-Jan Stegenga.

(i) *Aria No.2 for oboe & piano;* (ii) *2 Poèmes de Ronsard for flute & soprano, Op. 26;* (iii) *Duo for bassoon & double bass;* (iv) *Impromptu for harp solo, Op. 21;* (v) *Joueurs de flûte for flute & piano, Op. 27;* (vi) *Segovia for guitar, Op. 29;* (vii) *Sérénade for flute, string trio & harp;* (viii) *Sonata No. 2 for piano & violin, Op. 28.*
(N) **(*) Olympia Dig. OCD 459-2 [id.]. (i) Hans Roerade, Jet Röling; (ii) Paul Verhey, Irene Maessen; (iii) Jos de Lange, Quirijn van Regteren Altena; (iv) Erika Waardenburg; (v) Paul Verhey, Jet Röling; (vi) Jan Goudswaard; (vii) Paul Verhey, Schönberg Qt (members), Erika Waardenburg; (viii) Jet Röling, Jean-Jacques Kantorow.

(i) *Andante and Scherzo for flute & piano, Op. 51;* (ii) *Andante from an unfinished wind trio for oboe, clarinet & bassoon (1937);* (iii) *String trio, Op. 58;* (iv) *String quartet, Op. 45;* (v) *Trio for flute, viola & cello, Op. 40;* (vi) *Music from Elpénor, poème radiophonique (1937).*
(N) **(*) Olympia Dig. OCD 460-2 [id.]. (i) Paul Verhey, Jet Röling; (ii) Hans Roerade, Van den Brink,

Jos de Lange; (iii) Van der Meer, Guittart, de Hoog; (iv) Schönberg Qt; (v) Verhey, Stegenga, Guittart; (vi) Paul Verhey, Schönberg Qt (members).

Roussel's chamber music is not so well represented on CD that we can afford to be too unwelcoming to the present set. Indeed there is no need to be. These are good performances, well presented here by these fine Dutch artists. This is eminently civilized music and, without going into too much detail, artistically these would carry a three-star rating. The recordings are eminently serviceable but not wholly ideal. The *Sérénade* for flute, string trio and harp, a lovely piece – and very well played indeed – is not as finely focused as on the old Melos recording (Decca), and the piano in the *Joueurs de flûte* seems to be in a slightly more resonant acoustic than the flute. All the same this is as economical a way as any of exploring this interesting repertoire. Although the ideas are not always as memorable as are the symphonies, the writing is always intelligent and expert. The second of the three discs is probably the best entry-point into the set, all of which are, of course, available separately; if you respond to the music, the performances and the sound, you can proceed from there.

(i) *Evocations, Op. 15;* (ii) *Résurrection (Prélude symphonique d'après Tolstoi), Op. 4.*
(N) (M) *** EMI Dig. CDM5 65564-2 [id.]. (i) Gedda, Stutzmann, Van Dam, Orféon Donostiarra, Anton Ayestaran; (ii) Toulouse Capitole O, Plasson.

It is good to see this coupling returning to the catalogue at mid-price. *Évocations* dates from 1910–11 and reflects something of the impression that Roussel's travels in the Far East and, more particularly, India made on him. It is full of exotic colours and atmosphere, which come splendidly to life in this eminently satisfactory (1986) recording. Plasson directs an excellent performance and adds *Résurrection*, the very first orchestral piece Roussel composed while still under the tutelage of Vincent d'Indy.

Padmâvatî (opera; complete).
*** EMI Dig. CDS7 47891-8 (2) [id.]. M. Horne, Gedda, Van Dam, Berbié, Burles, Dran, Dale, Orféon Donostiarra, Toulouse Capitole O, Plasson.

Padmâvatî was the wife of the Prince of Chitoor who, rather than submit to being given to the soft-speaking but predatory Mogul sultan, Alla-uddin, stabs her beloved and commits *suttee*. That simple plot gives Roussel the opportunity to write colourful, richly atmospheric music. It is a heady mixture, with Plasson drawing warmly sympathetic playing from the Toulouse orchestra. In an excellent cast, José van Dam is superb as the evil, deceptive Sultan and, though Marilyn Horne sounds rather too mature for the name-part, hers is a powerful, convincing performance. One remarkable feature of the opera is the profusion of principal tenors required, and here Gedda as the Prince is splendidly matched with contrasted soloists in smaller roles, Charles Burles, Thierry Dran and Laurence Dale. Warm, convincingly balanced sound. This is well worth exploring.

Routh, Francis (born 1927)

Clarinet quintet.
(N) *** Redcliffe Dig. RR 010 [id.]. Redcliffe Ens. – BLISS: *Clarinet quintet;* RAWSTHORNE: *Clarinet quartet.* ***

Routh's *Quintet* was written for Nicholas Cox, who plays it with great skill and understanding. Its variety of mood makes up for the melodic fragmentation, and its invention is lively throughout. Excellent recording.

Royer, Pancrace (1705–55)

Pièces de clavecin (1746): *La majestueuse; La Zaïde; Les matelots; Tambourins 1–2; L'incertaine; L'aimable; La bagatelle; Suite de la bagatelle; La remouleuse; Les tendres sentiments; Le vertigo; Allemande; La sensible; La marche des Scythes. La chasse de Zaïde.*
⊛ *** O-L Dig. 436 127-2 [id.]. Christophe Rousset (harpsichord).

Royer's *Pièces de clavecin*, his only collection to appear in print, had their origins in his stage works but, unlike Rameau, who transcribed instrumental dances for the keyboard, Royer drew on arias and choral pieces as well. Similarly, *La chasse de Zaïde* comes from his *ballet-héroïque*, *Zaïde* (1739). All these pieces show flashes of real imagination and a refined and developed sensibility. Rousset plays a harpsichord from 1751 by Henri Hemsch which once belonged to Rameau's patron *fermier general*, La Poupelinière, and was in all probability played by Rameau himself. Rousset plays with great flair and poetic imagination and he is impeccably recorded; he also provides the useful and scholarly notes.

Rózsa, Miklós (1907–94)

Symphony in 3 movements, Op. 6a (ed. Palmer); *The Vintner's daughter, Op. 23a.*
*** Koch Dig. 37244-2 [id.]. New Zealand SO, James Sedares.

Rózsa's early attempt in 1930 to write a large-scale symphony proved abortive, and the present structure, minus a Scherzo and heavily edited by Christopher Palmer, relies on an incomplete manuscript. However, as we know from his film scores, Rózsa had no difficulty finding memorable musical ideas and in the first movement uses them cogently and with intensity. The second-movement *Andante* is highly evocative and the finale does not lack fire and energy, even if structurally it remains the least convincing part of the work. *The Vintner's daughter*, a picturesque set of variations, again shows the composer's melodic appeal, and again he uses the orchestral palette as seductively as in his film music. James Sedares and his New Zealand players are obviously caught up in the music and present it persuasively, with the conductor showing a notably firm grip on the first movement of the symphony. The recording has plenty of body and colour.

Rubbra, Edmund (1901–86)

(i) *Viola concerto, Op. 75;* (ii) *Violin concerto, Op. 103.*
(Y/B) *** Conifer Dig. 75605 51225-2 [id.]. (i) Rivka Golani; (ii) Tasmin Little; RPO, Vernon Handley.

The *Viola concerto* is a work of euphony and depth, and Rivka Golani's account is a first recording. Tasmin Little's version of the *Violin concerto* has an effortless and masterly virtuosity; she is well recorded and the RPO under Vernon Handley give excellent support.

Symphonies Nos. (i) *2 in D, Op. 45;* (ii) *7 in C, Op. 88;* (i) *Festival overture, Op. 62.*
*** Lyrita SRCD 235 [id.]. (i) New Philh. O., Handley; (ii) LPO, Boult.

The *Second Symphony* dates from 1937 and, like its predecessor, showed Rubbra to be a symphonist of a rather special order. It is the slow movement that offers the deepest musical experience here. We have writing of a deep originality which has evolved from Holst and Sibelius, which inhabits a northern (but not a Scandinavian) landscape, and which is unlike anything else in the British music of its time. This and the finale are the most successful movements; the latter is inventive and original and has overtones of the *Perigourdine* movement of the *First Symphony*, though its accents are very English. Not the most flawless of Rubbra's symphonies, perhaps, for the score is undoubtedly overladen with contrapuntal detail, and the orchestration is still thick in the first movement. Good performances from Handley of both symphony and the overture which bears an adjacent opus number to the *Fifth*.

The *Seventh Symphony* is also a very considerable piece. The longest and most ambitious of its three movements – perhaps the most enigmatic, too – is the finale, an extended passacaglia and fugue displaying the composer's naturally contrapuntal mode of thought at its most typical. The first movement brings a cogent argument based on a simple four-note motif, and the second a rhythmic Scherzo that leads to a more lyrical, noble climax. Boult's performance is outstandingly successful and the 1970 recording, like that of the *Second* (made eight years later), is up to the high standards of realism one expects from this label. A thoroughly worthwhile and generous coupling (78 minutes).

Symphonies Nos. 3, Op. 49; 4, Op. 53; Resurgam overture, Op. 149; A Tribute, Op. 56.
*** Lyrita Dig. SRCD 202 [id.]. Philh O, Norman Del Mar.

The opening of the *Fourth Symphony* is of quite exceptional beauty and has a serenity and quietude that silence criticism; there is a consistent elevation of feeling and continuity of musical thought. Rubbra's music is steeped in English polyphony and it could not come from any time other than our own. Unquestionably both symphonies have a nobility and spirituality that is rare in any age. The fine *Resurgam overture* is a late work.

Symphonies Nos. 4, Op. 53; 10 (Sinfonia da camera), Op. 145; 11, Op. 153.
(N) *** Chandos Dig. CHAN 9401 [id.]. BBC Nat. O of Wales, Hickox.

This triptych is the first in a new cycle of the Rubbra symphonies which will doubtless be completed during the lifetime of this volume. Richard Hickox is a thoroughly dedicated and sympathetic advocate of Edmund Rubbra's music, and he offers a particularly imaginative account of the *Eleventh Symphony* in one movement (1979), which is new to the catalogue. Like so much of Rubbra's music, it has an organic continuity and inner logic that are immediately striking. And in common with the *Tenth Symphony*, also in one movement, its textures are spare and limpid. The *Fourth Symphony* (1940–42), a wartime work, has great serenity and tranquillity. Its opening is among the most beautiful in all English music of our time. In his notes Robert Saxton speaks tellingly of the timelessness of Rubbra's music: the symphonies 'emanate from within and, as with the work of the best artists, are neither new nor old – they exist, they are what they are'. Hickox's account of the *Fourth* is totally convincing and perhaps marginally to be preferred to Norman Del Mar's version with the Philharmonia Orchestra on Lyrita. The Chandos recording is excellent in every respect, with plenty of warmth and transparency of detail.

Symphony No. 5 in B flat, Op. 63.
(M) *** Chandos CHAN 6576 [id.]. Melbourne SO, Schönzeler – BLISS: *Checkmate* ***; TIPPETT: *Little music.* **(*)

Rubbra's *Fifth Symphony* is a noble work which grows naturally from the symphonic soil of Elgar and Sibelius. Although the Melbourne orchestra is not in the very top division, they play this music for all they are worth, and the strings have a genuine intensity and lyrical fervour that compensate for the opaque effect of the octave doublings. Altogether, though, this is an imposing performance which reflects credit on all concerned. The recording is well balanced and lifelike; but the ear perceives that the upper range is rather restricted.

(i) *Symphonies Nos. 6, Op. 80; 8 (Hommage à Teilhard de Chardin), Op. 132;* (ii) *Soliloquy for cello and orchestra, Op. 57.*
*** Lyrita SRCD 234 [id.]. (i) Philh. O, Norman Del Mar; (ii) Rohan de Saram, LSO, Handley.

The *Sixth* is one of the most admired of Rubbra's symphonies and its slow movement is arguably the most beautiful single movement in all of Rubbra's output. The *Eighth* pays tribute to Teilhard de Chardin, a Jesuit and palaeontologist (1881–1955) who fell out with the Church over his approach to evolution. It has something of the mystical intensity that finds its most visionary outlet in the *Ninth Symphony*. In Norman Del Mar's hands Rubbra's music speaks here with directness and without artifice; the Philharmonia play marvellously and the composer's sound-world is very well served by the recording balance. The *Soliloquy* has been described by Ronald Stevenson as 'a saraband, symphonically developed in flexible tempo . . . a meditation with flashes of interior drama', and its grave beauty exerts a strong appeal. Rohan de Saram plays with a restrained eloquence that is impressive and he has excellent support from the LSO under Vernon Handley.

(i) *Symphony No. 9 (Sinfonia sacra), Op. 140. The Morning Watch for chorus and orchestra, Op. 55.*
(N) ✪ *** Chandos Dig. CHAN 9441 [id.]. (i) Lynne Dawson, Della Jones, Stephen Roberts; BBC Nat. Ch. of Wales, BBC Nat. O of Wales, Hickox.

At long last the *Ninth Symphony*, arguably Rubbra's greatest work, has arrived on CD, and in a magnificent performance and recording. Its stature has long gone unrecognized but there is no doubt that this is Rubbra's most visionary utterance. This is an unqualified masterpiece whose eloquence is of the order of Elgar's *Dream of Gerontius*, Britten's *War Requiem* and Tippett's *A Child of our time*. Indeed it is a work which can withstand the most exalted comparisons and emerge unscathed. The first ideas for it came in 1961, after the *Seventh Symphony*, when Rubbra had thought of it in terms of an oratorio. It was finally completed in 1972, by which time its symphonic character had emerged. Subtitled *The Resurrection*, it was inspired by a painting of Donato Bramante and has something of the character of the Passion, which the three soloists relate in moving fashion. Apart from a BBC performance in the 1980s, this wonderful score has remained unperformed and unrecorded since its first performance in 1973! *The Morning Watch*, a setting of Henry Vaughan for chorus and orchestra, which was originally to have formed part of a choral fifth symphony, is another score of great nobility, which has taken even longer (half a century) to be recorded. Both works are superbly served here by all these fine musicians, and the Chandos recording is no less magnificent.

Symphony No. 10 (Sinfonia da camera), Op. 145; Improvisations on virginal pieces by Giles Farnaby, Op. 50; A tribute to Vaughan Williams on his 70th birthday (Introduction and danza alla fuga), Op. 56.
(M) *** Chandos CHAN 6599. Bournemouth Sinf., Schönzeler.

Rubbra's *Tenth Symphony* is a short, one-movement work, whose opening has a Sibelian seriousness and a strong atmosphere that grip one immediately. Schönzeler is scrupulously attentive to dynamic nuance and internal balance, while keeping a firm grip on the architecture as a whole. The 1977 recording has been impressively remastered. It has a warm acoustic and reproduces natural, well-placed orchestral tone. The upper range is crisply defined. The *Farnaby variations* is a pre-war work whose charm Schönzeler uncovers effectively, revealing its textures to best advantage. *Loath to depart*, the best-known movement, has gentleness and vision in this performance. Strongly recommended. Even though this CD plays for only 40 minutes, it remains indispensable.

String quartets Nos. 1 in F min., Op. 35; 2 in E flat, Op. 51; 3, Op. 112; 4, Op. 150.
(N) (M) ** Conifer Dig. 75605 51260-2 (2) [id.]. Sterling Qt.

It is a source of astonishment that only one of Edmund Rubbra's quartets, the *Second*, has so far been recorded commercially. The *First*, written in 1933 before the *First Symphony* but substantially revised in 1946, half a century ago, was inscribed to Vaughan Williams, who took a personal interest in its development, and the *Fourth* of 1977 is dedicated to Robert Simpson, another master of the quartet medium. These are impressive quartets and have been hailed as masterpieces; they deserve the most dedicated, subtle and persuasive advocacy. The Sterling Quartet have the dedication, but the sound they produce is wanting in bloom and is at times raw and unpleasant. No doubt the close balance is partly to blame. Nor, in the *First Quartet*, do they produce as wide a dynamic range as the music demands. This music is important, so the set must perforce be recommended *faute de mieux*.

(i) *Magnificat and Nunc dimittis in A flat, Op. 65. Missa in honorem Sancti Dominici, Op. 66; 3 Hymn tunes, Op. 114; 3 Motets, Op. 78.*
*** ASV Dig. CDDCA 881 [id.]. Gonville & Caius College, Cambridge, Ch., Geoffrey Webber; (i) Phillips (organ) – HADLEY: *Lenten cantata* etc. ***

The most important work here is the *Missa in honorem Sancti Dominici* (1948), written at about the time of the *Fifth Symphony* and one of the most beautiful of twentieth-century *a cappella* choral pieces written in this or any other country. None of the other works on the disc is its equal. The performance by the Choir of Gonville & Caius College, Cambridge, under Geoffrey Webber is dedicated and sensitive, though it does not altogether banish memories of Richard Hickox's RCA version from the 1970s. Excellent balance, though the organ is obtrusive, particularly so in the first of the Op. 78 *Motets*.

Rubinstein, Anton (1829–94)

Piano concertos Nos. 1 in E, Op. 25; 2 in F, Op. 35.
(Y/B) ** Marco Polo Dig. 8.223456 [id.]. Joseph Banowetz, Czech State PO, Alfred Walter.

Piano concertos Nos. 3 in G, Op. 45; 4 in D min., Op. 70.
** Marco Polo Dig. 8.223382 [id.]. Banowetz, Slovak State PO (Košice), Stankovsky.

Piano concerto No. 5 in E flat, Op. 94; Caprice russe, Op. 102.
(Y/B) **(*) Marco Polo Dig. 8.223489 [id.]. Joseph Banowetz, Slovak RSO (Bratislava), Stankovsky.

Rubinstein was the first composer of concertos in Russia and was enormously prolific. His *First Piano concerto in E major*, dating from 1850, is greatly indebted to Mendelssohn though it is more prolix. As David Brown puts it, Rubinstein's 'enormous facility was unhindered by originality, and he was unashamedly eclectic and conservative'. The *Third Piano concerto in G* (1853–4) is more concentrated, and there is a recording of the *Fourth in D minor* (1864) by his pupil, Josef Hofmann (see Recitals, below); no later pianist has equalled that. By the mid-1860s Rubinstein's perspective had broadened (rather than deepened), and the *Fifth Piano concerto in E flat* (1874) is an ambitious piece, longer than the *Emperor* and almost as long as the Brahms *D minor*. No less a pianist than Joseph Levinne championed it during the early years of the century and no doubt its prodigious technical demands (it was not dedicated to Alkan for nothing) have stood in the way of its wider dissemination. It has all the fluent lyricism one expects of Rubinstein, though most of its ideas, attractive enough in themselves, overstay their welcome.

Joseph Banowetz has now recorded all the concertos for Marco Polo and, although the orchestral support and the recording do not rise much above routine, there is nothing ordinary about Banowetz's pianism. The *Fifth*, at least, is worth investigating (for the *Fourth*, one should turn to Hofmann.) The *Caprice russe* was written four years after the concerto, but the fires were obviously blazing less fiercely. All the same, this is an issue of some interest, and the solo playing has conviction.

Piano concerto No. 4 in D min., Op. 70; Melody in F.
(N) *** Decca Dig. 448 063-2 [id.]. Cherkassky, RPO, Ashkenazy (with encores by TCHAIKOVSKY; GLAZUNOV; MOSZKOWSKI; GODOWSKY).

Cherkassky was eighty-five when he recorded the *Fourth* and, by common consent, best of the *Piano concertos*. It is a performance of distinction and, though not quite as dazzling as the famous 1937 Josef Hofmann performance, is stamped with much the same ring of authenticity. The encores are all taken from an analogue 1974 recital, previously issued on a Oiseau-Lyre LP. Some remarkable pianism there, too, particularly in the Godowsky pieces.

Symphony No. 1 (Ivan the Terrible).
(Y/B) * Marco Polo Dig. 8.223277 [id.]. CSS PO, Stankovsky.

Symphony No. 2 in C (Ocean), Op. 42.
(Y/B) * Marco Polo Dig. 8.220449 [id.]. Slovak PO, Gunzenhauser.

Symphony No. 3 in A, Op. 56; Eroica fantasia, Op. 110.
(Y/B) * Marco Polo Dig. 8.223576 [id.]. Slovak RSO (Bratislava), Robert Stankovsky.

Symphony No. 4 in E flat (Dramatic).
(Y/B) * Marco Polo Dig. 8.223319 [id.]. CSS PO, Stankovsky.

Symphony No. 5 in G min., Op. 107; Overture, Dmitri Donskoi; Faust, Op. 68.
(Y/B) * Marco Polo Dig. 8.223320 [id.]. Georges Enescu State PO, Andreescu.

Symphony No. 6 in A min., Op. 111.
(Y/B) ** Marco Polo Dig. 8.220489 [id.]. Philh. Hungarica O, Varga.

In the words of David Brown, 'Insofar as a Rubinstein style can be identified, it is a compound of Mendelssohn and Schumann, the more radical of mid-century composers like Liszt and Berlioz being firmly excluded.' The symphonies are certainly of less interest than the piano concertos, and readers who don't know the Balakirev, Kalinnikov or Arensky symphonies should explore those first. The *Ocean Symphony* was popular in its day and in its final form runs to seven movements. Professor Brown calls it 'a watery Mendelssohnian piece' and it is not easy to sustain unwavering attention over the course of its 72+ minutes. The Slovak Philharmonic Orchestra of Bratislava under Stephen Gunzenhauser do their best, and the 1986 recording is more than adequate.

Music of lesser stature calls for interpreters of quality and flair if it is to have a chance of convincing the listener. The *Third Symphony* is not endowed with ideas of interest or even with personality and, although it is not entirely without merit, it is mostly predictable stuff. The playing by the Bratislava Radio Symphony Orchestra is fairly routine and Robert Stankovsky brings few insights to the score. The *Eroica Fantasia*, as its high opus number suggests, is a later and, if anything, even less inspired work.

The *Fourth Symphony*, the *Dramatic*, of 1874 runs to some 65 minutes and is not a strong work. Its thematic substance is pretty thin and, despite its epic pretensions, there is little sense of sweep or consistency of inspiration. The *Fifth* of 1880 sprawls less; it lasts under 40 minutes and its ideas, some of them folk-inspired, are held together better. The playing of the Georges Enescu Philharmonic Orchestra of Bucharest under Horia Andreescu is more persuasive than that of its companions. The *Symphony No. 6 in A minor*, composed in 1886, has much stronger material but, despite a relatively strong first movement, the work disintegrates towards the end. However, of the six symphonies this is the one to investigate. The performance and recording are not earth-shattering but are perfectly acceptable.

Cello sonata No. 1 in D, Op. 18.
(N) *** RCA Dig. 09026 68290-2 [id.]. Steven Isserlis, Stephen Hough – GRIEG: *Cello sonata;* LISZT: *Elégies* etc. ***

In these exhilarating performances Isserlis and Hough challenge each other in spontaneously imaginative interplay to bring out all the high-romantic qualities of the music while keeping firmly disciplined control. The Rubinstein sonata has the lyrical directness and honest, four-square construction which make the Mendelssohn cello sonatas so attractive. After a strongly characterized first movement, Isserlis and Hough adopt a genuine flowing *allegretto* for the siciliana rhythms of the central movement, made charmingly fresh; and the exuberant finale finds Hough at his most brilliant in the shimmering pianowriting. Warm, full sound.

Piano sonatas Nos. 1 in F min., Op. 12; 3 in F, Op. 41.
*** Hyperion Dig. CDA 66017 [id.]. Leslie Howard.

Piano sonatas Nos. 2 in C min., Op. 20; 4 in A min., Op. 100.
*** Hyperion Dig. CDA 66105 [id.]. Leslie Howard.

Leslie Howard copes with the formidable technical demands of these *Sonatas* manfully. He proves highly persuasive in all four works, though the actual invention is scarcely distinguished enough to sustain interest over such ambitious time-spans. Rubinstein wrote these pieces for his own use, and doubtless his artistic powers and strong personality helped to persuade contemporary audiences. The 1981 recordings sound excellent.

Ruders, Poul (born 1949)

(i) *Concerto for clarinet and twin orchestra;* (ii) *Violin concerto No. 1;* (iii) *Drama trilogy No. 3 for cello and orchestra 'Polydrama'.*
*** Unicorn Dig. DKPCD 9114 [id.]. (i) Thomsen; (ii) Hirsch; (iii) Zeuten; Odense SO, Tamás Vetö.

Poul Ruders is one of the most naturally talented of the younger Danish composers. His *Violin concerto* is a tribute to the sunny atmosphere of Italian baroque music in general and Vivaldi's *Four Seasons* in particular. Apart from its neo-classicism there is a whiff of minimalism about much of it. The *Clarinet concerto* is strong stuff; to quote Ruders himself, the soloist is a 'Pierrot-like *vox humana* caught in a vice of orchestral onslaught', and the effect is often disturbing and almost surrealistic. He is an imaginative composer with a vein of lyrical feeling and melancholy that surfaces in the *Cello concerto*. A rewarding and interesting figure.

Rutter, John (born 1943)

(i; ii) *The Falcon;* (ii) *2 Festival anthems: O praise the Lord in heaven; Behold, the tabernacle of God;* (ii; iii) *Magnificat.*
*** Coll. Dig. COLCD 114; *COLC 114* [id.]. (i) St Paul's Cathedral Choristers; (ii) Cambridge Singers, City of L. Sinfonia; (iii) with Patricia Forbes; all cond. composer.

The Falcon was Rutter's first large-scale choral work. Its inspiration was a medieval poem, which is linked to the Crucifixion story, but the core of the piece is the mystical central *Lento*. The *Magnificat* has the usual Rutter stylistic touches, with a syncopated treatment of the opening *Magnificat anima mea*, and a joyous closing *Gloria Patri*. The two anthems are characteristically expansive and resplendent with brass. Fine performances and recording in the best Collegium tradition.

(i) *Gloria;* (ii) Anthems: *All things bright and beautiful; For the beauty of the earth; A Gaelic blessing; God be in my head; The Lord bless you and keep you; The Lord is my Shepherd; O clap your hands; Open thou my eyes; Praise ye the Lord; A prayer of St Patrick.*
*** Coll. Dig. COLCD 100; *COLC 100* [id.]. Cambridge Singers, (i) Philip Jones Brass Ens.; (ii) City of L. Sinfonia, composer.

John Rutter has a genuine gift of melody and his use of tonal harmony is individual and never bland. The resplendent *Gloria* is a three-part piece, and Rutter uses his brass to splendid and often spectacular effect. The anthems are diverse in style and feeling and, like the *Gloria*, have strong melodic appeal – the setting of *All things bright and beautiful* is delightfully spontaneous. It is difficult to imagine the music receiving more persuasive advocacy than under the composer, and the recording is first class in every respect.

3 Musical fables: (i) *Brother Heinrich's Christmas;* (ii) *The Reluctant Dragon; The Wind in the Willows.*
**(*) Coll. COLCD 115; *COLC 115* [id.]. City of L. Sinf.; with (i) Brian Kay, Cambridge Singers, composer; (ii) Richard Baker, King's Singers, Hickox.

John Rutter's name is readily associated with carols, and *Brother Heinrich's Christmas* is a musical narrative with choir, telling the story of how one of the most famous of all carols was introduced late at night by the angels to Brother Heinrich, just in time for it be included in the monks' Christmas Day service. It is all highly ingenuous but engagingly presented, and should appeal to young listeners who have enjoyed Howard Blake's *The Snowman*. The settings of the two famous Kenneth Grahame stories are no less tunefully communicative and include simulations of pop music of the 1940s (among other derivations), notably a Rodgers-style ballad which sentimentalizes the end of *The Wind in the Willows* episode, after Toad's escape from prison. All the music is expertly sung and played and blends well with the warmly involving narrative, splendidly done by Richard Baker.

(i) *Requiem; I will lift up mine eyes.*
*** Coll. Dig. COLCD 103; *COLC 103* [id.]. (i) Ashton, Dean; Cambridge Singers, City of L. Sinfonia, composer.

John Rutter's melodic gift, so well illustrated in his carols, is here used in the simplest and most direct way to create a small-scale *Requiem* that is as beautiful and satisfying in its English way as the works of Fauré and Duruflé. The penultimate movement, a ripe setting of *The Lord is my Shepherd* with a lovely oboe obbligato, sounds almost like an anglicized Song of the Auvergne; while Caroline Ashton's performance of the delightful *Pié Jesu* is wonderfully warm and spontaneous, most beautifully recorded on CD, and *I will lift up mine eyes* makes a highly effective encore piece.

Sæverud, Harald (1897–1993)

5 Capricci, Op. 1; Easy Pieces for piano, Opp. 14 & 18; Siljuslåtten, Op. 17.
(Y/B) **(*) Victoria Dig. VCD 19084 [id.]. Smebye.

Sæverud's piano music has a fresh, naïve directness which is touching and, like so much else by Sæverud, is full of character. Pieces like the Silkesokk-slåtten (Silk-sock dance), composed on the birth of the composer's son, Ketil Hvoslef, and the Småfuglsvals (Little bird's waltz) are quite captivating. The pianist Einar Henning Smebye plays with intelligence and subtlety, though the recording is too close to be ideal.

Songs and dances from Siljustøl (Slåtter og stev fra Siljustøl), Opp. 21–22, 24 & 25.
(Y/B) **(*) Victoria Dig. VCD 19085 [id.]. Smebye.

Siljustøl was the name of Sæverud's home outside Bergen. All these pieces are short and most are delightful, but they are best dipped into, rather than heard straight off. Smebye plays with style and relish and, apart from the rather close balance (one hears him stamping the pedals at one point), the recording is very clear and clean.

Sainte-Colombe (died c. 1700)

Concerts à deux violes: Bourrasque; La dubois; La raporté; Le retour; Tombeau les regrets.
*** Astrée Audivis Dig. E 7729 [id.]. Jordi Savall, Wieland Kuijken.

Concerts à deux violes: La conférence; Dalain; Le figuré; La rougeville; Le tendre.
*** Astrée Audivis Dig. E 8743 [id.]. Jordi Savall, Wieland Kuijken.

Le Retour; Tombeau les Regrets.
*** Naxos Dig. 8.550750 [id.]. Spectre de la Rose – MARAIS: Tombeau pour M. de Sainte-Colombe etc.
***

The popular success of the fascinating conjectural film (Tous les matins du monde) about this mysterious, reclusive composer and his relationship with his brilliantly talented young pupil, Marin Marais, has led to the soundtrack album becoming a bestseller. However, this enterprising and inexpensive Naxos recital includes the 'hits' from the film. The two Saint-Colombe works included are austerely but certainly touchingly played by a fresh-sounding 'authentic' group led by Alison Crum (viola da gamba) and Marie Knight (baroque violin). The Naxos recording is vivid, but its forward balance means that for a realistic effect a modest setting of the volume control should be chosen.

Those who are then tempted to explore the music of Saint-Colombe further might invest in the pair of excellent Audivis CDs featuring Jordi Savall, who was associated with the film soundtrack. They are performed by artists who have this music in their bones, and the playing is more subtle and has even greater emotional depth. The two CDs are excellently recorded and are available separately; the second duplicates nothing on the Naxos CD.

Saint-Saëns, Camille (1835–1921)

'The essential Saint-Saëns': (i) Carnival of the animals; (ii) Piano concerto No. 2 in G min., Op. 22; (iii) Violin concerto No. 3 in B min., Op. 61; (iv) Danse macabre, Op. 40; (v) Havanaise, Op. 83; Introduction and rondo capriccioso, Op. 28; (vi) Symphony No. 3 in C min. (Organ), Op. 78; Samson et Dalila: (vii) Air et danse bacchanale; (viii) Mon cœur s'ouvre à ta voix.
(N) (B) **(*) Decca Double 444 552-2 (2) [id.]. (i) Ortiz; (i; ii) Rogé; (iii) Bell; (v) Kyung Wha Chung; (vi) Priest; (viii) Horne; (i) L. Sinf.; (ii; v) RPO; (iii; vii) Montreal SO; (iv) Philh. O; (i–v; vii) cond. Dutoit; (vi) LAPO, Mehta.

Mehta's Los Angeles recording of the Third Symphony opens this programme spectacularly. It is among the more recommendable versions of this much-recorded work, for he draws a well-disciplined and exuberant response from all departments of the orchestra, and the recording certainly does not lack flamboyance in the finale. Joshua Bell's performance of the Violin concerto is very attractive indeed, with the Montreal sound casting a glow over the proceedings so that even the brass chorale sounds genial. The pianissimo opening is full of atmosphere and the Andantino has a pleasingly lyrical simplicity, with the work's romanticism blossoming throughout. The snag to this otherwise fairly enticing Double Decca compilation is that Dutoit's Carnival of the animals – in a crisp, clean, digital recording with very bright sound – is a sad disappointment, lacking genial charactization and charm. The Swan is played in a very matter-of-fact way. However, Charles Dutoit shows himself in a better light in his deft account of the *Danse macabre*, while Kyung Wha Chung is on top imaginative form, playing with flair in both the famous violin showpieces. Marilyn Horne's ripe characterization of Saint-Saëns's most famous aria, 'Softly awakes my heart', will not disappoint: the excerpts from *Samson et Dalila*, including the roistering *Bacchanale*, end the first disc, while Pascal Rogé's account of the favourite Saint-Saëns *Second Piano concerto*, which is second to none, closes the concert. The two discs play for 149 minutes.

(i) *Africa fantasy for piano and orchestra, Op. 89. Ascanio: Valse-finale; Parysatis: Airs de ballet. Sarabande et Rigaudon, Op. 93; Suite algérienne, Op. 60: Marche militaire française.* (ii) *Tarantelle for flute, clarinet and orchestra, Op. 6;* (iii) *Messe de Requiem, Op. 54.*
**(*) Cala Dig. CACD 1015; *CAMC 1015* [id.]. LPO, Geoffrey Simon, with (i) Gwendolyn Mok; (ii) Susan Milan, James Campbell; (iii) Olafimihan, Wyn-Rogers, Roden, Kirkbride, Hertfordshire Ch., Harlow Ch., East London Ch.

La jota aragonesa, Op. 64; (i) *La muse et le poète. La princesse jaune: Overture;* (ii) *Symphony No. 3 in C min.;* (iii) *Danse macabre* (original vocal version). *Grande fantaisie on themes from Samson et Dalila* (arr. Luigini).
** Cala Dig. CACD 1016; *CAMC 1016* [id.]. LPO, Geoffrey Simon, with (i) Stephanie Chase, Robert Truman; (ii) James O'Donnell; (iii) Anthony Roden.

Geoffrey Simon is an amiably persuasive advocate of these Saint-Saëns novelties, even if his affectionate approach emphasizes the music's surface elegance. The resonant acoustics of All Hallows Church, Gospel Oak, cast a warm glow over the proceedings, and detail could be sharper. However, the nicely scored *Airs de Ballet*, which come from the incidental music for *Parysatis*, are certainly enticing. The gracious *Sarabande* and genial *Rigaudon* certainly tickle the ear, as does the tuneful *Valse-finale* from *Ascanio*. But it is the lively and charming *Tarantelle* for flute, clarinet and orchestra which is the vivacious highlight of the first CD. It is winningly played by Susan Milan and James Campbell. The rich sonority of the sound suits the melodically catchy *Marche militaire française*, with its resplendent brass, but the exotically oriental *Africa fantasy for piano and orchestra* loses some of its point and glitter when the acoustic is so resonant. Even so, the performance is full of charm, and Gwendolyn Mok plays with affectionate flair. The *Messe de Requiem* is a real find, even if here the focus of the choral sound needs to be sharper. In its unpretentious, expressive style this work is a kind of French equivalent of Rossini's *Petite messe solennelle*. Pretty good choral singing, a well-matched team of soloists, and the recording gives the work a fine, sonorous impact, even if more bite is needed.

The undoubted highlight of the second disc is the fascinating original vocal version of *Danse macabre*, very much shorter than the familiar tone-poem. It lasts for only 2 minutes 52 seconds; indeed it seems almost to be cut off, but the result is a chrysalis for the orchestral piece. The words are from the poem by Henri Cazalis and make one understand the genial atmosphere of the orchestral work: 'Zig-a-zig-a-zig, Death is tapping at the tomb with his heel at midnight, playing an air on his out-of-tune fiddle – zig-a-zig-a-zag.' The effect is semi-operatic, interrupted by the cock-crow. *La muse et le poète* is an extended (15 minutes 19 seconds) salon duo for violin and cello with orchestra. It opens dreamily, but as it becomes more passionate it also becomes technically demanding. Stephanie Chase and, especially, the cellist Robert Truman are good if not distinctive soloists. The CD opens with the *Jota aragonesa*, which is very like the Glinka fantasy and needs a recording with more glitter. The *Grande fantaisie on Samson et Dalila* arranged by Luigini is rather inflated but is not helped by Geoffrey Simon's very leisurely tempo for *Softly awakes my heart*, even though there is some lovely warm Philharmonia string-playing. The *Overture La princesse jaune* with its oriental flavour and pretty scoring is presented with real charm. But Geoffrey Simon then chooses to end his second CD with the *Organ Symphony* – an agreeable account, but no more than that. The Scherzo with its piano filigree is poorly focused, and in the finale the massive organ entry is without quite enough edge. The close is exciting but not compulsive.

Carnival of the animals.
(Y/B) (M) *** Teldec/Warner Dig. 4509 97445-2 [id.]. Güher and Süher Pekinel, French R. PO, Janowski – POULENC: *Double piano concerto.* ***
(M) *** Virgin/EMI Dig. CUV7 61137-2 [id.]. Anton Nel, Keith Snell, Ac. of L., Richard Stamp – PROKOFIEV: *Peter.* *** ✿
*** Ph. Dig. 400 016-2 [id.]. Villa, Jennings, Pittsburgh SO, Previn – RAVEL: *Ma Mère l'Oye.* ***
(B) *** CfP CD-CFP 4086; *TC-CFP 40086.* Katin, Fowke, SNO, Gibson – BIZET: *Jeux d'enfants; RAVEL: *Ma Mère l'Oye.* ***
(BB) *** ASV CDQS 6017. Goldstone, Brown, RPO, Hughes – PROKOFIEV: *Peter.* ***
(N) (BB) **(*) Tring Dig. TRP 046 [id.]. RPO, Andrea Licata – BIZET: *Jeux d'enfants;* ** PROKOFIEV: *Peter.* **(*)

The piano duo, Güher and Süher Pekinel – of mixed Turkish/Spanish parentage – make a sparklingly spontaneous contribution to Saint-Saëns's zoological fantasy, readily dominating the performance with their scintillating pianism. Janowski and the French Radio Orchestra provide admirable support, and Saint-Saëns's portrait gallery comes vividly and wittily to life. The gentle dignity of Eric Levionnais's *Le Cygne* makes a touching highlight, leading on to an exhilarating finale. The performance is beautifully recorded and naturally balanced within an attractively warm ambience; although the playing time (38 minutes) is short, this mid-priced CD remains highly recommendable.

Richard Stamp directs an outstanding version of Saint-Saëns's witty zoology, full of affectionate humour. After Robert Bailey's gentle, slightly recessed image of *The Swan*, the finale bursts on the listener with infectious vigour, the two pianists producing flourishes of great bravura. Throughout, one responds to the polished overall presentation and sense of fun; although some may feel that the recording is rather resonant, it adds a genial warmth to the vitality of the proceedings.

Previn's version makes a ready alternative. The music is played with infectious rhythmic spring and great refinement. It is a mark of the finesse of this performance – which has plenty of bite and vigour, as well as polish – that the great cello solo of *Le Cygne* is so naturally presented. Fine contributions too from the two pianists, although their image is rather bass-orientated, within a warmly atmospheric recording.

On CfP the solo pianists, Peter Katin and Philip Fowke, enter fully into the spirit of the occasion, with Gibson directing his Scottish players with affectionate, unforced geniality. The couplings are attractive and the CD transfer confirms the vivid colourfulness and presence of the mid-1970s recording.

The two pianists on ASV also play with point and style, and the accompaniment has both spirit and spontaneity. *The Swan* is perhaps a trifle self-effacing, but otherwise this is very enjoyable, the humour appreciated without being underlined. The recording is excellent, and this makes a good super-bargain CD recommendation.

With a pair of unnamed pianists who play brilliantly and enjoy their wrong notes in the self-portrait, this is a vivid performance on Tring, with the solo orchestral instruments closely miked, with the effect of changing the balance in each portrait. The double-bass sounds lugubriously larger-than-life, but the cello plays his famous portrayal of *The swan* in a very melancholy fashion.

(i) *Carnival of the animals;* (ii) *Le Cygne; Piano concertos Nos.* (iii) *2 in G min., Op. 22;* (iv) *4 in C min., Op. 44;* (v) *Violin concerto No. 3 in B min., Op. 61;* (vi) *Danse macabre, Op. 40;* (v) *Introduction and Rondo capriccioso, Op. 28;* (vii) *Symphony No. 3 in C min. (Organ), Op. 78.*

(Y/B) (B) **(*) Ph. Duo 442 608-2 (2) [id.]. (i) Villa, Jennings, Pittsburgh SO, Previn; (ii) Gendron, Gallion; (iii) Davidovich, Concg. O, Järvi; (iv) Campanella, Monte Carlo Op. O, Ceccato; (v) Szeryng, Monte Carlo Op. O, Remoortel; (vi) Concg. O, Haitink; (vii) Chorzempa, Rotterdam PO, Edo de Waart.

This inexpensive Duo collection is described as 'The Best of Saint-Saëns' and indeed it does include good and sometimes fine performances of many of the composer's most attractive orchestral and concertante works. Notable here is Previn's (1980) digital recording of the *Carnival of the animals*, as fine as almost any available (see above). And, to please everyone, Philips have also included a second performance of *Le Cygne* by the inestimable Maurice Gendron, when this famous piece is treated to a more assertively romantic but no less elegant presentation. Bella Davidovich then gives a most sympathetic account of the *G minor Piano concerto* and she draws pleasing tone-quality from the instrument, even if she lacks the last degree of brilliance and flair, notably in the Scherzo. Yet she has the advantage of excellent orchestral support from the Concertgebouw Orchestra (who also give a lively account of the *Danse macabre* under Haitink) and again natural digital recording. In the *C minor Concerto* (which is analogue) the effect is harder, partly because Michele Campanella is a more boldly extrovert soloist; but this account has undoubted vitality and no lack of *espressivo*. Henryk Szeryng gives clean, immaculate performances of the *B minor Violin concerto* and the *Introduction and Rondo capriccioso*. His approach is aristocratic rather than seductive, though in the encore the bravura and sense of style make for impressive results. The contribution of the Monte Carlo orchestra is adequate. De Waart's 1976 recording of the famous *Organ Symphony* cannot be said to be among the most exciting versions available but, with polished orchestral playing and refined Philips sound, it is certainly enjoyable, with a warm *Poco adagio*, and the organ glories at the end of the symphony are given plenty of breadth and impact by the recording.

(i) *Carnival of the animals;* (ii) *Danse macabre, Op. 40; Suite algérienne, Op. 60: Marche militaire française. Samson et Dalila: Bacchanale.* (ii; iii) *Symphony No. 3 in C min., Op. 78.*

(M) *** Sony SBY 47655; *MBK 47655* [id.]. (i) Entremont, Gaby Casadesus, Régis Pasquier, Yan Pascal Tortelier, Caussé, Yo-Yo Ma, Lauridon, Marion, Arrignon, Cals, Cerutti; (ii) Phd. O, Ormandy; (iii) with E. Power Biggs.

(i) *Carnival of the animals;* (ii) *Danse macabre;* (iii) *Symphony No. 3;* (iv) *Wedding-cake* (caprice-valse for piano and orchestra), *Op. 76.*
**(*) ASV Dig CDDCA 665 [id.]. (i) Guillermo Salvador Snr & Jnr, Mexico City PO; (ii) Mexicana State SO; (iii) Noel Rawsthorne, LPO; (iv) Osorio, RPO; Bátiz.

It would be churlish to bracket the third star for this very generous Sony collection (75 minutes 35 seconds) because the *Carnival of the animals* – performed in its original chamber version – strikes the listener as somewhat lacking in lustre at the opening. The ear adjusts to the rather dry effect. It is a starry cast: Yo-Yo Ma personifies *The Swan* gently and gracefully, and the finale is extremely spirited. Ormandy and his splendid orchestra play the other orchestral lollipops with fine panache – the exuberance at the end of the *Samson et Dalila Bacchanale* is overwhelming, with thundering drums. The catchy *French military march* also goes with a swing. No complaint about the 1962 sound in the *Symphony*. The performance is fresh and vigorous, with the conductor's affection fully conveyed. The alert, polished Philadelphia playing brings incisive articulation to the first movement and Scherzo. E. Power Biggs has the full measure of the hall's Aeolian-Skinner organ, and he makes a spectacular contribution to the finale, which Ormandy structures most excitingly.

The *Carnival of the animals* and *Danse macabre* have plenty of genial vitality on ASV but are less strong on finesse, and the forwardly balanced recording adds to the robust feeling. Jorge Federico Osorio, however, dispatches the charming *Wedding-cake caprice-valse* with a winning sparkle. Bátiz's version of the spectacular *Organ symphony* was the first digital success for this work. The orchestral playing is exhilarating in its energy, while the *Poco Adagio* balances a noble, elegiac feeling with romantic warmth. The organ entry is an impressive moment and the sense of spectacle persists in the closing pages.

Cello concerto No. 1 in A min., Op. 33.
*** ASV Dig. CDDCA 867 [id.]. Sophie Rolland, BBC PO, Gilbert Varga – LALO: *Cello concerto in D min.;* MASSENET: *Fantaisie.* ***
*** DG Dig. 427 323-2 [id.]. Matt Haimovitz, Chicago SO, Levine – LALO: *Concerto;* BRUCH: *Kol Nidrei.* ***
*** RCA Dig. RD 71003. Harnoy, Cincinnati SO, Kunzel – OFFENBACH: *Concerto;* TCHAIKOVSKY: *Rococo variations.* ***
(N) (B) *** Decca Dig. Eclipse 448 712-2; *448 712-4* [id.]. Lynn Harrell, Cleveland O, Marriner – LALO; SCHUMANN: *Concertos.* ***
(M) *** Mercury 432 010-2 [id.]. Janos Starker, LSO, Dorati – LALO: *Concerto* **(*); SCHUMANN: *Concerto.* ***
(B) *** DG 431 166-2. Heinrich Schiff, New Philh. O, Mackerras – FAURE: *Elégie;* LALO: *Cello concerto.* ***
**(*) Ph. Dig. 432 084-2 [id.]. Julian Lloyd Webber, ECO, Yan Pascal Tortelier – FAURE: *Elégie* **; D'INDY: *Lied* **(*); HONEGGER: *Concerto.* **(*)

Sophie Rolland's performance of the *A minor Cello concerto* demonstrates a formidable talent. She takes its technical hurdles in her effortless stride and is very well supported by the BBC Philharmonic under Gilbert Varga. Perhaps their opening is marginally too fast for an *Allegro non troppo*, but the performance is in every respect a highly enjoyable one. The excellence of the BBC/ASV recording makes for a strong recommendation.

Haimovitz and Levine also open the *Concerto* with a vigorous surge of passionate feeling, and the second subject is tenderly contrasted, with lovely warm timbre from Haimovitz. This strongly characterized account, full of spontaneity, is extremely realistically recorded.

Ofra Harnoy's is another first-rate account, the opening full of fervour and impulse, played with full tone, while later the timbre is beautifully fined down for the *Adagietto* minuet. The orchestral response is equally refined here; and this well-recorded account is in every way recommendable for its unexpected and attractive Offenbach coupling.

Harrell's reading of the Saint-Saëns, altogether more extrovert than Yo-Yo Ma's (see below), makes light of any idea that this composer always works on a small scale. The opening is positively epic, and the rest of the performance is just as compelling, with the minuet-like *Allegretto* crisply neo-classical. The addition of the Lalo *Concerto* makes this reissue very competitive.

Starker plays the Saint-Saëns *A minor* with charm and grace, and Dorati provides first-class support. The 1964 recording comes up amazingly well and is excellently (and naturally) balanced.

Schiff gives as eloquent an account of this concerto as any on record. He sparks off an enthusiastic response from Mackerras, and the recorded sound and balance are excellent. At bargain price, this deserves the strongest recommendation.

Julian Lloyd Webber plays both Saint-Saëns pieces with considerable virtuosity, though he does not command the range of sonority or colour possessed by some of his rivals. He has the advantage of first-class accompaniment, impressively natural recorded sound and couplings of special interest.

(i) *Cello concerto No. 1, Op. 33;* (ii) *The swan;* (iii) *Allegro appassionato, Op. 43; Cello sonata No. 1, Op. 32; Chant saphique, Op. 91; Gavotte, Op. posth.; Romances Nos. 1 in F, Op. 36; 2 in D, Op. 51;* (iv) *Prière* (for cello & organ).

(Y/B) *** RCA Dig. 09026 61678-2 [id.]. Steven Isserlis; (i) LSO, Tilson Thomas; (ii) Tilson Thomas, Dudley Moore; (iii) Pascal Devoyon; (iv) Stephen Grier.

Steven Isserlis's record of the *Cello concerto in A minor* is among the finest on record and RCA have made some valuable additions to the concerto. Of particular interest is the *Cello sonata No. 1 in C minor,* composed in the same year, in which he is accompanied with elegance and finesse by Pascal Devoyon. Isserlis himself plays with the musicianship and virtuosity one has come to expect from him. Most of the remaining pieces are both worthwhile and entertaining, particularly the *Allegro appassionato.* The *Prière,* Op. 159, for cello and organ was written as late as 1919 and is a small but affecting addition to the composer's representation on CD. The recorded sound is very good indeed and the disc is thoroughly recommendable on all counts.

(i) *Cello concerto No. 1 in A min., Op. 33;* (ii) *Piano concerto No. 2 in G min., Op. 22;* (iii) *Violin concerto No. 3, Op. 61.*

(N) ✪ (M) *** Sony Dig. SMK 66935 [id.]. (i) Yo-Yo Ma, O Nat. de France, Maazel; (ii) Cécile Licad, LPO, Previn; (iii) Cho-Liang Lin, Philh. O, Tilson Thomas.

Three outstanding performances from the early 1980s are admirably linked together in this highly desirable CBS mid-price reissue. Yo-Yo Ma's performance of the *Cello concerto* is distinguished by fine sensitivity and beautiful tone, while Cécile Licad and the LPO under Previn turn in an eminently satisfactory reading of the *G minor Piano concerto* that has the requisite delicacy in the Scherzo and seriousness elsewhere. Cho-Liang Lin's account of the *B minor Violin concerto* with the Philharmonia Orchestra and Michael Tilson Thomas is exhilarating and thrilling; indeed, this is the kind of performance that prompts one to burst into applause; his version is certainly second to none and is arguably the finest yet to have appeared.

Piano concertos Nos. 1 in D, Op. 17; 2 in G min., Op. 22; 3 in E flat, Op. 29; 4 in C min., Op. 44; 5 in F, Op. 103.

(Y/B) (B) *** Decca Double 443 865-2 [id.]. Pascal Rogé, Philh. O, RPO or LPO, Charles Dutoit.

Played as they are here, these concertos can exert a strong appeal: Pascal Rogé brings delicacy, virtuosity and sparkle to the piano part and he receives expert support from the various London orchestras under Dutoit. Altogether delicious playing and excellent piano-sound from Decca, who secure a most realistic balance. On CD the five *Concertos* are successfully accommodated on two discs and the digital remastering is wholly successful, retaining the bloom of the analogue originals, yet producing firmer detail and splendid piano-sound. Now reissued as a Double Decca set (two records for the price of one) the value is obvious.

Piano concerto No. 2 in G min., Op. 22.

(M) *** RCA 09026 61863-2 [id.]. Rubinstein, Phd. O, Ormandy – FALLA: *Nights in the gardens of Spain* etc. **(*); FRANCK: *Symphonic variations for piano and orchestra.* ***

(***) Testament mono SBT 1029 [id.]. Gilels, Paris Conservatoire O, Cluytens (with SHOSTAKOVICH: *Prelude and fugue in D, Op. 87/5*) – RACHMANINOV: *Piano concerto No. 3.* (***)

Rubinstein's version was made in 1969, and he is partnered by that most understanding of accompanists, Eugene Ormandy. Rubinstein's secret is that, though he appears sometimes to be attacking the music, his phrasing is full of little fluctuations so that his playing never sounds stilted. The recording of the piano is rather dry, even hard at times, but the glitter seems just right for the centrepiece.

Gilels's celebrated account of the Saint-Saëns *G minor concerto* comes from 1954 and is masterly in every respect. Its delicacy and refinement still come across in spite of the limitations of the recording, and Gilels gets marvellous support from the Paris orchestra under André Cluytens. Excellent transfers.

Violin concertos Nos. 1 in A, Op. 20; 2 in C, Op. 58; 3 in B min., Op. 61; Caprice andalou, Op. 122; Le Déluge, Op. 45: Prélude. Havanaise, Op. 83; Introduction and Rondo capriccioso, Op. 28; Morceau de concert, Op. 62; Romances: in D, Op. 37; in C, Op. 48; (i) *La Muse et le Poète, Op. 132.* (Also includes: YSAYE: *Caprice d'après l'Etude en forme de valse, Op. 52/6.*)

(M) **(*) EMI CMS7 64790-2 (2) [id.]. Ulf Hoelscher, New Philh. O, Pierre Dervaux; (i) with Ralph Kirshbaum.

This two-CD box collects all Saint-Saëns's music for violin and orchestra (with a short bonus from

Ysaÿe) in performances of excellent quality. Ulf Hoelscher is an extremely accomplished soloist who plays with artistry as well as virtuosity, and he uncovers music of genuine worth and much charm which is not as well-known as the *Third Violin concerto*. The *Second*, incidentally, has a most attractive *Andante* and a catchy *Allegro scherzando* finale, while the first of the two *Romances* deserves to be much better known. The aptly named *Morceau de concert* is most engaging, and the relatively ambitious extended duo concertante piece, *La Muse et le Poète*, in which Hoelscher is admirably partnered by Ralph Kirschbaum, seems much more substantial here than it does in Geoffrey Simon's anthology on Cala (see above). In this EMI set Pierre Dervaux directs excellent accompaniments, and the recording (made at Abbey Road in 1977) is basically of excellent quality. The slight snag is the forward balance of the solo violin, which means that, with the CD remastering, Hoelscher's timbre in the upper range is made to sound just a bit thin. This is also noticeable in the orchestral violins in the closing *Le Déluge Prélude*.

Violin concerto No. 3 in B min., Op. 61.
(Y/B) (M) *** DG Dig. 445 549-2 [id.]. Perlman, O de Paris, Barenboim – LALO: *Symphonie espagnole;*
    BERLIOZ: *Rêverie et caprice.* ***
(N) *** Decca Dig. 443 324-2 [id.]. Pierre Amoyal, Fr. Nat. O, Dutoit – RESPIGHI: *Concerto Gregoriano*
    etc. ***
*** DG Dig. 429 786-2 [id.]. Gil Shaham, NYPO, Sinopoli – PAGANINI: *Concerto No. 1.* ***
*** ASV Dig. CDDCA 680 [id.]. Xue Wei, Philh. O, Bakels – BRUCH: *Concerto No. 1.* ***

(i) *Violin concerto No. 3 in B min., Op. 61;* (ii) *Introduction and rondo capriccioso, Op. 28.*
(N) (M) *** Sony Stern Edition II SM2K 64501 (2) [id.]. Isaac Stern, with (i) O de Paris, Barenboim; (ii)
    Philadelphia O, Ormandy (with Concert ***).

On DG, Perlman achieves a fine partnership with his friend, Barenboim, in a performance that is both tender and strong, while Perlman's verve and dash in the finale are dazzling. The forward balance is understandable in this work, but orchestral detail could at times be sharper. The Berlioz *Rêverie et caprice* has been added for this reissue.

Pierre Amoyal's account of the *B minor Concerto* belongs among the very best in the catalogue and can be recommended alongside Perlman, Lin, etc. Readers who do not know the Respighi *Concerto Gregoriano* with which it is coupled will find that it is something of a discovery, and both Amoyal and Dutoit make out a strong case for it. Excellent recording, too.

One only has to sample the delectable way Gil Shaham presents the enchanting *Barcarolle*, which forms the principal theme of Saint-Saëns's *Andante*, to discover the distinction of his performance, which balances elegant *espressivo* with great dash and fire: neither the soloist nor the conductor lets even the slightest suspicion of routine into a reading which dazzles and charms in equal measure. The recording is first class.

Stern's violin is for once balanced naturally against the orchestra, and paradoxically it gives his splendid performance of the Saint-Saëns more strength than close-up sound does. Though this is not as persuasively affectionate as with Gil Shaham, it remains among the finest versions, and the *Introduction and rondo capriccioso* is dazzling.

Xue Wei's account is full of flair from the very first entry onwards. The orchestral accompaniment is strongly characterized as well, while the soloist creates an ideal mixture of ruminative lyricism and dash, especially in the slow movement. The sound is vivid, even if the balance, within a church acoustic, seems artificially contrived.

Danse macabre, Op. 40.
*** Denon Dig. DC 8097 [id.]. Tokyo Metropolitan SO, Jean Fournet – BERLIOZ: *Symphonie fantas-
    tique.* ***
(M) **(*) Chandos CHAN 6503; *MBTD 6503* [id.]. SNO, Gibson – DUKAS: *L'apprenti sorcier,*
    ROSSINI/RESPIGHI: *La boutique fantasque.* **(*)

Jean Fournet's 1987 performance of *Danse macabre* is a very persuasive reading, well recorded. Gibson's performance is also well played and vividly recorded, but this CD offers rather short measure (37 minutes), even at mid-price.

Danse macabre, Op. 40; (i) *Havanaise, Op. 83; Introduction and Rondo capriccioso, Op. 28. Le jeunesse d'Hercule, Op. 50; Marche héroïque, Op. 34; Phaéton, Op. 39; Le rouet d'Omphale, Op. 31.*
(M) *** Decca 425 021-2 [id.]. (i) Kyung Wha Chung, RPO; Philh. O; Charles Dutoit.

A splendidly conceived anthology. The symphonic poems are beautifully played, and the 1979 Kingsway Hall recording lends the appropriate atmosphere. Charles Dutoit shows himself an admirably sensitive exponent, revelling in the composer's craftsmanship and revealing much delightful orchestral detail in the manner of a Beecham. Decca have now added Kyung Wha Chung's equally charismatic and individual 1977 accounts of what are perhaps the two most inspired short display-pieces for violin and orchestra in the repertoire.

Danse macabre; Le rouet d'Omphale.
(N) (M) *** Decca 448 571-2 [id.]. Paris Conservatoire O, Martinon – BIZET: *Jeux d'enfants* ***; BERLIOZ: *Overtures* **(*); IBERT: *Divertissement.* ***

Martinon's are delightful, Beechamesque performances, offering excellent orchestral playing and a characteristic sense of delicacy and style. The 1960 recording is excellent, and this collection of French music, reissued in Decca's 'Classic Sound' series, is well worth exploring.

Havanaise, Op. 83; Introduction and Rondo capriccioso, Op. 28.
*** EMI Dig. CDC7 47725-2 [id.]. Perlman, O de Paris, Martinon – CHAUSSON: *Poème;* RAVEL: *Tzigane.* ***
(N) (M) (***) RCA Heifetz Collection mono 09026 61753-2 [id.]. Heifetz, RCA Victor SO, Steinberg – CHAUSSON: *Poème* **(*); LALO: *Symphonie espagnole* (**(*)); SARASATE: *Zigeunerweisen.* (***)
(Y/B) **(*) EMI Dig. CDC5 55026-2 [id.]; *EL5 55026-4.* Sarah Chang, Phd. O, Sawallisch – PAGANINI: *Violin concerto No. 1.* **(*)

Perlman plays these Saint-Saëns warhorses with splendid panache and virtuosity on EMI; his tone and control of colour in the *Havanaise* are ravishing. The digital remastering brings Perlman's gorgeous fiddling right into the room, at the expense of a touch of aggressiveness when the orchestra lets rip; but the concert-hall ambience prevents this from being a problem.

The Heifetz performances have quite extraordinary panache: his chimerical bowing in the coda of the *Havanaise* is utterly captivating. Indeed this dazzling playing is unsurpassed on record and the 1951 mono recording, if closely balanced, is very faithful. Even if you have these works in more modern versions, this marvellous disc should not be passed by.

Although she misses some of the sultry seductiveness in the *Havanaise*, the twelve-year-old Sarah Chang still captures the gleaming Spanish sunshine. She is well supported by Sawallisch but is not flattered by the close recording-balance.

Henry VIII: ballet music.
(N) (BB) *** Naxos Dig. 8.553338/9 [id.]. Razumovsky Sinfonia, Mogrelia – DELIBES: *Sylvia.* ***

This ballet-divertissement, described as a '*fête populaire*', comes in Act II of the opera, and in the outer movements Saint-Saëns wittily introduces first a Scottish reel then an Irish jig with Gallic insouciance. But all six numbers, which are enjoyably tuneful, unashamedly incorporate a great many airs from both countries, and Mogrelia presents them affectionately and vividly. With excellent recording, this is a genuine bonus to a pleasing account of Delibes's *Sylvia.*

Introduction and Rondo capriccioso.
*** DG Dig. 427 676-2 [id.]. Mintz, Israel PO, Mehta – LALO: *Symphonie espagnole;* VIEUXTEMPS: *Concerto No. 5.* ***

Mintz dazzles the ear with Saint-Saëns's fireworks, yet playing with elegance and finesse.

Symphonies in A; in F (Urbs Roma); Symphonies Nos. 1–3.
(B) *** EMI CZS7 62643-2 (2) [Ang. CDMB 62643]. French Nat. R. O, Martinon (with Bernard Gavoty, organ de l'église Saint-Louis des Invalides in *No. 3*).

The A and F major works were totally unknown and unpublished at the time of their recording and have never been dignified with numbers. Yet the A major, written when the composer was only fifteen, is a delight and may reasonably be compared with Bizet's youthful work in the same genre. Scored for strings with flute and oboe, the charming Scherzo is matched by the *moto perpetuo* finale, and the whole work makes delightful gramophone listening. More obviously mature, the *Urbs Roma Symphony* is perhaps a shade more self-conscious, but more ambitious too, showing striking imagination in such movements as the darkly vigorous scherzo and the variation movement at the end.

The first of the numbered symphonies is a well-fashioned and genial piece, again much indebted to Mendelssohn, and to Schumann too, but with much delightfully fresh invention. The *Second* is full of excellent ideas. Martinon directs splendid performances of the whole set, well prepared and lively. The account of the *Third* ranks with the best: freshly spontaneous in the opening movement, and the threads knitted powerfully together at the end of the finale. Here the recording could do with rather more sumptuousness. Elsewhere the quality is bright and fresh, with no lack of body, and it suits the Saint-Saëns textures very well.

Symphony No. 2 in A min., Op. 55; Phaéton, Op. 39; Suite algérienne, Op. 60.
*** ASV Dig. CDDCA 599 [id.]. LSO, Butt.

The *Second Symphony* is very well played here with the freshness of an orchestra discovering something unfamiliar and enjoying themselves; Yondani Butt's tempi are apt and he shapes the whole piece convincingly. He is equally persuasive in the picaresque *Suite algérienne*, the source of the justly famous *Marche militaire française*, and indeed in *Phaéton*. Warmly atmospheric recording.

Symphonies Nos. 2 in A min., Op. 55; (i) 3 in C min., Op. 78.
*** Chandos Dig. CHAN 8822 [id.]. Ulster O, Yan Pascal Tortelier; (i) with Gillian Weir.

Yan Pascal Tortelier's performances are very enjoyable and very well recorded. But in the *Second Symphony* Yondani Butt's account has greater freshness, and the slightly less reverberant ASV recording contributes to this. If your interest is primarily in this work, Butt's version is first choice, but if you need both *Symphonies* on one CD, then the Chandos issue has much in its favour. Certainly the hall resonance suits the *Organ symphony* and the work moves to an impressive dénouement.

Symphony No. 3 in C min., Op. 78.
✿ (M) *** RCA 09026 61500-2. Berj Zamkochian, Boston SO, Munch – DEBUSSY: *La Mer* **(*);
    IBERT: *Escales.* ***
*** DG Dig. 419 617-2 [id.]. Simon Preston, BPO, Levine – DUKAS: *L'apprenti sorcier.* ***
(Y/B) (B) *** Carlton Dig. PCD 2010 [id.]. Chorzempa, Berne SO, Maag.
(M) *** Mercury 432 719-2 [id.]. Marcel Dupré, Detroit SO, Paray – PARAY: *Mass.* **(*)

(i; ii) *Symphony No. 3; (ii) Danse macabre, Op. 40; Samson et Dalila: Bacchanale; (i) 3 Rhapsodies sur des cantiques bretons, Op. 7.*
*** BIS Dig. CD 555 [id.]. (i) Hans Fagius; (ii) Royal Stockholm PO, James DePreist.

(i) *Symphony No. 3; (ii) Danse macabre; Le Déluge: Prélude, Op. 45; Samson et Dalila: Bacchanale.*
(M) *** DG 415 847-2 [id.]. (i) Litaize, Chicago SO, Barenboim; (ii) O de Paris, Barenboim.

Munch's Boston recording dates from 1960 (three years after Paray's Detroit version), yet in its currently remastered form it sounds overwhelmingly spectacular. While the resonance enhances the blend of organ and strings in the *Poco adagio*, which has an enveloping warmth, and projects the huge and thrilling organ entry in the finale, the balance allows sparkling detail and represents one of the most successful and most believable recordings ever made in Symphony Hall. The performance is stunning, full of lyrical ardour and moving forward in a single sweep of great intensity. The couplings, showing Munch and his Bostonians at their peak, are equally valuable, if not quite so outstandingly recorded.

With the Berlin Philharmonic in cracking form, Levine's is a grippingly dramatic reading, full of imaginative detail. The great thrust of the performance does not stem from fast pacing: rather it is the result of incisive articulation, while the clarity of the digital recording allows the pianistic detail to register crisply. The thunderous organ entry in the finale makes a magnificent effect, and the tension is held at white heat throughout the movement. The Dukas coupling is equally memorable, and this remains first choice among modern, digital versions of the symphony.

From Stockholm comes another outstanding performance of the *Third Symphony* that is competitive even in a well-stocked market. DePreist is straight and unmannered, completely at the service of the music, and proves very persuasive in this repertoire. Hans Fagius plays the Stockholm Concert Hall organ so that, unlike some performances in which the organist is tacked on afterwards, this is a genuine performance. He plays the *Trois Rhapsodies sur des cantiques bretons* on the splendid Marcussen instrument of St Jakobs Kyrka in Stockholm to striking effect. The recording of all these items is full-blooded and has plenty of impact yet it is beautifully and naturally balanced.

Barenboim's inspirational 1976 version has long dominated the catalogue. Among the reissue's three attractive bonuses is an exciting account of the *Bacchanale* from *Samson et Dalila*. The performance of the *Symphony* glows with warmth from beginning to end. A brilliant account of the Scherzo leads into a magnificently energetic conclusion, with the Chicago orchestra excelling itself with radiant playing in every section. The digital remastering is not wholly advantageous: while detail is sharper, the massed violins sound thinner and the bass is drier. In the finale, some of the bloom has gone, and the organ entry has a touch of hardness.

Maag's extremely well-recorded Berne performance has a Mendelssohnian freshness and the sprightly playing in the Scherzo draws an obvious affinity with that composer. The closing pages have a convincing feeling of apotheosis and, although this is not the weightiest reading available, it is an uncommonly enjoyable one in which the sound is bright, full and suitably resonant.

The fine Paray/Mercury recording dates, astonishingly, from 1957. The early date brings just a hint of shrillness to the violins in the first movement; otherwise the sound remains bold, full and remarkably well detailed. Marcel Dupré's weighty organ entry introduces a finale which is powerfully co-ordinated, building to an impressive climax. However, not everyone may want the coupling, enjoyable as it is.

Wedding-cake (Caprice-valse), Op. 76.
(BB) *** ASV Dig. CDQS 6092. Osorio, RPO, Bátiz – FRANCK: *Symphonic variations* **(*); RAVEL: *Left-hand concerto* ***; SCHUMANN: *Concerto.* **(*)

A delightfully lightweight performance of Saint-Saëns's frothy but engaging *morceau de concert*, infectious and sparkling. Nicely recorded, too.

CHAMBER MUSIC

Bassoon sonata, Op. 168; Clarinet sonata, Op. 167; Caprice on Danish and Russian airs for flute, oboe, clarinet and piano, Op. 79; Feuillet d'album, Op. 81 (arr Taffanel); *Oboe sonata, Op. 166; Odelette for flute and piano, Op. 162; Romance in D flat for flute and piano, Op. 37; Tarantelle for flute, clarinet and piano, Op. 6.*
(Y/B) (B) *** Cala Dig. CACD 1017 (2) [id.]. William Bennett, Nicholas Daniel, James Campbell, Rachael Gough, & Ens. – DEBUSSY: *Chamber music.* ***

The *Sonatas for clarinet, for oboe* and *for bassoon*, Opp. 166–168, are elegantly finished but surprising pieces, with an unaccustomed depth of feeling. The *Caprice* is a diverting kind of pot-pourri, inspired by the composer's visit to Russia in 1876, when he met Tchaikovsky and returned to Paris with the score of *Boris Godunov*, thus kindling the flame of interest in Mussorgsky that burned so brightly in later years. Paul Taffanel's arrangement of the *Feuillet d'album*, Op. 81, for flute, oboe and two each of clarinets, bassoons and horns, is a first recording and, like almost everything on this record, refreshing and elegant. That goes for the performances too, which are well recorded though the piano is occasionally overpowering. Strongly recommended – and outstanding value, considering that one gets two CDs for the price of one, economically packaged and liberally annotated.

Carnival of the animals (chamber version); *Piano trio in F, Op. 18; Septet in E flat, for trumpet, strings & piano, Op. 65.*
*** Virgin/EMI Dig. VC7 59514-2 [id.]. Nash Ens.

This is a highly persuasive account of the first of Saint-Saëns's two *Piano trios*, while the Nash Ensemble capture the humour of the *Septet* and the *Grand fantaisie zoölogique* excellently. The acoustic has warmth and the balance between the instruments, particularly in the *Carnival of the animals*, is admirably judged.

Piano trio No. 1 in F, Op. 18.
(Y/B) **(*) Ara. Dig. Z 6643 [id.]. Golub–Kaplan–Carr Trio – DEBUSSY; FAURE: *Trios.* ***

David Golub, Mark Kaplan and Colin Carr give a very good account of themselves in the *Piano trio in F major*. They are intelligent and imaginative, though in the variation movement Kaplan is not as commanding or full-bodied tonally as his opposite number in the Beaux Arts Trio (currently withdrawn). The piano dominates in the right way, and David Golub makes a particularly strong and vital impression. They are very well recorded too.

Romance for horn and piano, Op. 67.
(M) *** Decca 433 695-2 [id.]. Barry Tuckwell, Vladimir Ashkenazy – BRAHMS: *Horn trio;* FRANCK: *Violin sonata;* SCHUMANN: *Adagio & allegro.* ***

Saint-Saëns's unexpectedly sombre *Romance* is beautifully played by Tuckwell and Ashkenazy, who find exactly the right element of restraint. Excellent 1974 Kingsway Hall recording.

Violin sonata No. 1 in D min., Op. 75.
*** Essex CDS 6044 [id.]. Accardo, Canio – CHAUSSON: *Concert.* ***

The performance by Accardo and Canio is marvellously played, selfless and dedicated. The recording too is very good, and this can be recommended strongly, if the coupling is suitable.

VOCAL MUSIC

Choral songs: *Calme des nuits; Des pas dans l'allée; Les fleurs et les arbres.*
(Y/B) *** Ph. Dig. 438 149-2 [id.]. Monteverdi Ch., O Révolutionnaire et Romantique, Gardiner – FAURE: *Requiem;* DEBUSSY; RAVEL: *Choral works.* ***

Three charming examples of Saint-Saëns's skill and finesse in drawing inspiration from early sources in a way remarkable at the time he was writing. Gardiner and his team give ideal performances, adding to the valuable list of rarities which he provides as coupling for the Fauré *Requiem*.

Mélodies: *Clair de lune; Les cloches de la mer; Danse macabre; Extase; Le lever de la lune; Le pas d'armes du Roi Jean; Rêverie; Si vous n'avez rien à me dire; Sonnet.*
**(*) EMI Dig. CDC7 54818-2 [id.]. José van Dam, Jean-Philippe Collard – GOUNOD; MASSENET: *Mélodies.* **(*)

The velvet legato of José van Dam, with his firm, dark tone, is very satisfying in all but two of this group of Saint-Saëns songs, gentle inspirations which he transforms. The exceptions are the two livelier songs – *Danse macabre* (which prompted the orchestral piece of that name) and *Le pas d'armes du Roi Jean* – which are coarser and rather heavy-handed, not helped by Collard's accompaniments. A valuable recital nevertheless, coupled with Massenet and Gounod songs.

Messe à quatre voix, Op. 4.
(M) **(*) Decca 425 077-2 [id.]. Simon Colston, Anthony de Rivaz, John Vickers, Trevor Owen, Brian Harvey, Worcester Cathedral Ch., Roy Massey & Paul Trepte (grand et petit organs) – POULENC: *Gloria.* ***

Donald Hunt directs an enjoyable performance of an early rarity of Saint-Saëns. Written when he was only twenty-one, this *Mass* shows how well he had learnt his academic lessons for, at various points, he uses with total freshness what at the time were archaic techniques, as in the beautiful *Agnus Dei* at the end. The organ writing is characteristically fresh, and though one finds few signs of deep feeling the piece is well worth hearing. The soloists here are variable, but the choir is excellent and the recording suitably atmospheric.

OPERA

Samson et Dalila (opera): complete.
*** EMI CDS7 54470-2 (2) [Ang. CDCB 54470]. Domingo, Meier, Fondary, Courtis, L'Opéra-Bastille Ch. & O, Myung-Whun Chung.
(M) **(*) DG 413 297-2 (2) [id.]. Obraztsova, Domingo, Bruson, Lloyd, Thau, Ch. & O de Paris, Barenboim.
(N) (M) (**(*)) EMI Classics mono CMS5 65263-2 (2). Luccioni, Bouvier, Cabanel, Cambon, Medus, Paris Opéra Ch. & O, Fourestier.
(N) * Koch-Schwann 3-1774-2 Y6 (2) [id.]. Marjana Lipovšek, Cossutta, Fondary, Vienna Voksoper & Bregenz Festival Choruses, Vienna SO, Cambreling.

In the newer, EMI set, Domingo with Chung gives a deeper, more thoughtful performance than on DG, broader, with greater repose and a sense of power in reserve. When the big melody appears in Dalila's seduction aria, *Mon cœur s'ouvre*, Chung's idiomatic conducting encourages a tender restraint, where others produce a full-throated roar. Meier may not have an ideally sensuous voice for the role, with some unwanted harshness in her expressive account of Dalila's first monologue, but her feeling for words is strong and the characterization vivid. Generally Chung's speeds are on the fast side, yet the performance does not lack weight, with some first-rate singing in the incidental roles from Alain Fondary, Samuel Ramey and Jean-Philippe Courtis. Apart from backwardly placed choral sound, the recording is warm and well focused.

Barenboim proves as passionately dedicated an interpreter of Saint-Saëns here as he did in the *Third Symphony*, sweeping away any Victorian cobwebs. It is important, too, that the choral passages, so vital in this work, be sung with this sort of freshness, and Domingo has rarely sounded happier in French music, the bite as well as the heroic richness of the voice well caught. Renato Bruson and Robert Lloyd are both admirable too; sadly, however, the key role of Dalila is given an unpersuasive, unsensuous performance by Obraztsova, with her vibrato often verging on a wobble. The recording is as ripe as the music deserves.

EMI's 1946 recording from the Paris Opéra provides a formidable showcase for outstanding singers, little known outside France, who represented a singing tradition that largely fell into ruins in following decades. José Luccioni was a favourite in Paris, his voice combining lyric beauty with heroic timbre that made him an outstanding choice as Samson. His diction and command of style are as sure as his vocal production, and so it is with Hélène Bouvier, boasting a rich mezzo, rock-steady throughout its range, and again a perfect command of style. Sadly, her career was cut short by polio. Paul Cabanel as the High Priest was also at the end of his career but is impressive too. Choral singing and orchestral playing are often ragged, and the sound from 78–r.p.m. discs is very limited; but this is a performance with plenty of feeling, well worth investigating.

The Koch-Schwann set was recorded live at the Bregenz Festival in 1988, and it can be recommended only to admirers of individual singers. Carlo Cossutta as Samson uses his big, heroic tenor boldly, but the results are coarse and unstylish, with the microphone catching a judder in the production. Even

Marjana Lipovšek's rich mezzo sounds uneven, as recorded, and she hardly conveys the picture of sensuous seductress. Cambreling, often a sensitive interpreter of French opera, is here stodgy in rhythm and choice of tempo, and the live recording is too variable to offer much competition for the finest digital versions.

Salieri, Antonio (1750–1825)

Fortepiano concertos: in B flat and C.
(Y/B) *** Teldec/Warner Dig. 4509 94569-2 [id.]. Andreas Staier, Concerto Köln – STEFFAN: *Fortepiano concerto*. ***

These two attractive works show Salieri as quite a dab hand at a keyboard concerto with a distinct personality of his own. The rising arpeggio opening of the *C major Concerto* is a bit square, but its ideas are deftly handled and it has a charming minor-key serenade for its *Larghetto* that reminds one a little (at first) of the slow movement of the Mozart *A major*, K.488, but then later produces an unusual and effective pizzicato accompaniment; the spirited finale is in contrast to its sad little coda. The *B flat Concerto* opens strongly and has most agreeable secondary material; the *Adagio* brings the more conventional device of an Alberti bass, and then closes with a winningly cheerful Minuet, almost a lollipop, with simple but effective variations, giving Staier plenty of opportunities to show the fortepiano's paces, contributing his own creative cadenzas which the concertos clearly need. Overall, the performances here could hardly be more persuasive, with the bold, slightly abrasive tuttis from the Concerto Köln adding to the strength of characterization. The recording is first class.

Falstaff (opera): complete.
*** Hung. Dig. HCD 21789/91 [id.]. Gregor, Zempléni, Gulyás, Gáti, Pánczél, Csura, Vámossy, Salieri Chamber Ch. & O, Tamás Pál.

Like Verdi, Salieri and his librettist ignore the Falstaff of the histories. They tell the story within the framework of the conventional two-Act opera of the period. None of the ideas, however charming or sparkling, is developed in the way one would expect in Mozart, but it is all great fun, particularly in a performance as lively and well sung as this. Jószef Gregor is splendid in the name-part, with Dénes Gulyás equally stylish in the tenor role of Ford. Maria Zempléni as Mistress Ford and Eva Pánczél in the mezzo role of Mistress Slender (not Page) are both bright and lively. The eponymous chorus and orchestra also perform with vigour under Tamás Pál; the recording is brilliant, with a fine sense of presence.

Sallinen, Aulis (born 1935)

(i) *Cello concerto, Op. 44; Shadows (Prelude for Orchestra), Op. 52; Symphony No. 4, Op. 49.*
*** Finlandia Dig. FACD 346 [id.]. (i) Arto Noras; Helsinki PO, Kamu.

The *Cello concerto* of 1977 is the most commanding piece here. Sallinen's ideas and his sound-world resonate in the mind. Arto Noras has its measure and plays with masterly eloquence. The middle movement of the *Fourth Symphony* is marked *Dona nobis pacem*; throughout the finale, bells colour the texture, as is often the case in his orchestral writing. *Shadows* is an effective short piece which reflects or 'shadows' the content of the opera, *The King goes forth to France*. The performances under Okko Kamu are very impressive and the recording quite exemplary.

(i) *Violin concerto, Op. 18;* (ii) *Nocturnal dances of Don Juanquixote, Op. 58; Some aspects of Peltoniemi Hintrik's funeral march, Op. 19; Variations for orchestra (Juventas variations), Op. 8.*
*** BIS Dig. CD 560 [id.]. (i) Koskinen; (ii) Thedéen; Tapiola Sinf., Vänskä.

The *Variations for orchestra* is an imaginative and inventive piece which shows remarkable command of the orchestra. It is tonally ambiguous without being serial; indeed at one point there is a reminder of Britten. The *Violin concerto* is also rewarding and in the slow movement often beautiful; one can see that its lyrical impulse is not quite strong enough for it to become part of the standard repertoire, but it is nevertheless an arresting piece and finds a powerful advocate in Eeva Koskinen. *Some aspects of Peltoniemi Hintrik's funeral march* is a transcription for full strings of his *Third Quartet*, a one-movement work in five variations that never lose sight of the basic folk-inspired idea; not one of his strongest works. Nor is *The Nocturnal Dances of Don Juanquixote*, though the *Dances* enjoy excellent advocacy from Torleif Thedéen and the Tapiola Sinfonietta under Osmo Vänskä and a vivid, well-lit but not overbright BIS recording.

(i) *Symphonies Nos. 1; 3;* (ii) *Chorali;* (iii) *Cadenze for solo violin;* (iv) *Elegy for Sebastian Knight;* (v) *String quartet No. 3.*
*** BIS CD 41 [id.]. (i) Finnish RSO, Kamu; (ii) Helsinki PO, Berglund; (iii) Paavo Pohjola; (iv) Frans Helmerson; (v) Voces Intimae Qt.

The *First Symphony*, in one movement, is diatonic and full of atmosphere, as indeed is the *Third*, a powerful, imaginative piece which appears to be haunted by the sounds and smells of nature. The performances under Okko Kamu are excellent. *Chorali* is a shorter piece, persuasively done by Paavo Berglund; and there are three chamber works, albeit of lesser substance. The recordings are from the 1970s and are all very well balanced. Highly recommended.

Symphonies Nos. 2 (Symphonic dialogue for solo percussion player and orchestra), Op. 29; 6 (From a New Zealand Diary), Op. 65; Sunrise Serenade, Op. 63.
(Y/B) *** BIS Dig. CD 511 [id.]. Malmö SO, Okko Kamu.

The *Second Symphony*, like the *First*, is a one-movement affair lasting a quarter of an hour. Its sub-title, *Symphonic dialogue for solo percussion player and orchestra*, gives an accurate idea of its character, pitting the fine soloist, Gerd Mortensen, against the remaining orchestral forces. The main work is the ambitious *Sixth Symphony*. Like the *Third Symphony*, it is powerfully evocative of natural landscape; indeed it is one of the strongest and most imaginative of all Sallinen's symphonies. Okko Kamu gets very responsive playing from the Malmö Symphony Orchestra in both symphonies and in the slight but effective *Sunrise Serenade*. The recording is excellent.

Symphonies Nos. 4, Op. 49; 5 (Washington mosaics), Op. 57; Shadows (Prelude for orchestra), Op. 52.
(Y/B) *** BIS Dig. CD 607 [id.]. Malmö SO, James DePreist.

Suffice it to say that these new performances by the Malmö Symphony Orchestra under James DePreist are every bit as good as the Helsinki rivals listed above and below; if anything, the recording has more impressive range and definition.

Kullervo (opera).
*** Ondine Dig. ODE 780-3T. Hynninen, Sallinen, Jakobsson, Silvasti, Vihavainen, Finnish Nat. Op. Ch. & O, Ulf Söderblom.

Although the theme will be familiar from Sibelius's early symphony of the same name, Sallinen has based his *Kullervo* on the play by Aleksis Kivi and he wrote the libretto himself. The plot emerges from a mixture of narration, in which the chorus plays a central role, and dreams. The opera is a compelling musical drama, far more atmospheric and musically effective than its immediate predecessor, *The King goes forth to France*. Sallinen's musical language has debts to composers as diverse as Britten (shadows of the 'Sunday morning' interlude in *Peter Grimes* briefly cross the score in Kullervo's Dream at the beginning of Act II), Puccini, Debussy even, though they are synthesized into an effective vehicle for a vivid theatrical imagination. There is impressive variety of pace and atmosphere, and the black voices of the Finnish Opera Chorus resonate in the memory. So, too, do the impressive performances of Jorma Hynninen as Kullervo and Anna-Lisa Jakobsson as the smith's young wife and, indeed, the remainder of the cast and the Finnish National Opera Orchestra under Ulf Söderblom. While *Kullervo* may not be a great opera, it is gripping and effective musical theatre, and the Ondine recording has excellent presence and detail.

Sammartini, Giovanni Battista (1700–75)

Symphonies in D; G; String quintet in E.
(B) *** HM HMA 1901245 [id.]. Ens. 145, Banchini – Giuseppe SAMMARTINI: *Concerti grossi* etc. ***

Giovanni Battista was the younger of the two Sammartini brothers; he spent his whole life in Milan. On this record, the Ensemble 145, led by Chiara Banchini, offer two of his symphonies; although neither attains greatness, they have genuine appeal. Good recording.

Sammartini, Giuseppe (c. 1693–1750)

Concerti grossi Nos. 6 & 8; (i) *Recorder concerto in F.*
(B) *** HM HMA 901245 [id.]. (i) Conrad Steinmann; Ens. 145, Banchini – Giovanni SAMMARTINI: *Symphonies* etc. ***

Giuseppe settled in England in the 1720s and he was a refined and inventive composer. The Ensemble

145 is a period-instrument group; they produce a firmly focused sound, even though the textures are light and the articulation lively. Excellent playing from Conrad Steinmann in the *Recorder concerto*.

Sarasate, Pablo (1844–1908)

Carmen fantasy, Op. 25.
❀ *** EMI CDC7 47101-2 [id.]. Itzhak Perlman, RPO, Foster – PAGANINI: *Concerto No. 1.**** ❀

Played like this on EMI, with superb panache, luscious tone and glorious recording, Sarasate's *Fantasy* almost upstages the concerto with which it is coupled. The recording balance is admirable, with the quality greatly to be preferred to many of Perlman's more recent digital records.

Zigeunerweisen, Op. 20.
*** DG Dig. 431 815-2 [id.]. Gil Shaham, LSO, Lawrence Foster – WIENIAWSKI: *Violin concertos Nos. 1 & 2 etc.* ***
(N) (M) (***) RCA Heifetz Collection mono 09026 61753-2 [id.]. Heifetz, RCA Victor SO, Steinberg –
  CHAUSSON: *Poème* **(*); LALO: *Symphony espagnole* (**(*)); SAINT-SAENS: *Havanaise* etc. (***)

Gil Shaham plays Sarasate's sultry and dashing gypsy confection with rich timbre, languorous ardour and a dazzling display of fireworks at the close.

What can one say about the Heifetz performances except that they are unsurpassed: they are dazzling in the fireworks and with the most luscious tone and sophisticated colouring in the lyrical melody. The recording is dry but faithful. This is a marvellous disc.

Sarum Chant

Missa in gallicantu; Hymns: A solis ortus cardine; Christe Redemptor omnium; Salvator mundi, Domine; Veni Redemptor omnium.
*** Gimell Dig. CDGIM 017; *1585T-17* [id.]. Tallis Scholars, Peter Phillips.

Filling in our knowledge of early church music, the Tallis Scholars under Peter Phillips here present a whole disc of chant according to the Salisbury rite – in other words *Sarum chant* – which, rather than the regular Gregorian style, was what churchgoers of the Tudor period and earlier in England heard at their devotions. The greater part of the record is given over to the setting of the First Mass of Christmas, intriguingly entitled *Missa in gallicantu* or *Mass at cock-crow*. Though this is simply monophonic (the men's voices alone are used), it is surprising what antiphonal variety there is. The record is completed with four hymns from the Divine Offices of Christmas Day. The record is warmly atmospheric in the characteristic Gimell manner.

Satie, Erik (1866–1925)

Les aventures de Mercure (ballet); *La belle excentrique: Grand ritournelle. 5 Grimaces pour 'Un songe d'une nuit d'été'; Gymnopédies Nos. 1 & 3; Jack-in-the-box* (orch. Milhaud); *3 Morceaux en forme de poire; Parade* (ballet); *Relâche* (ballet).
(M) **(*) Van. 08.4030.71 [OVC 4030]. Utah SO, Maurice Abravanel.

A generous budget collection of Satie's orchestral music, well played and given full, vivid recording from the beginning of the 1970s; if Abravanel fails to throw off some of the more pointed music with a fully idiomatic lightness of touch, these are still enjoyable performances; the ballet scores have plenty of colour and rhythmic life.

Jack in the Box.
(N) (M) **(*) BBC Radio Classics 15656 91512 [id.]. BBC SO, Milhaud – MILHAUD: *Symphony No. 10* etc. **(*)

Milhaud included his transcription of Satie's piece in a BBC studio concert of his own music that he conducted in 1970, and it makes a fresh and lively start to an all-Milhaud programme. This disc is self-recommending to all who care about French music in general and this composer in particular.

Parade.
(M) *** Mercury 434 335-2 [id.]. LSO, Dorati – AURIC: *Overture;* FETLER: *Contrasts;* FRANCAIX: *Piano concertino;* MILHAUD: *Le bœuf sur le toit.* ***

Satie's *Parade* is the most audacious piece in an excellent Mercury compilation of (mostly) twentieth-century French music, its scoring including several extra-musical effects. Dorati makes it all fit together wittily and entertainingly, and the LSO make the most of the vivid scoring, with the brass obviously relishing their slightly vulgar theme which is somewhat reminiscent of Kurt Weill. The necessary atmosphere and colour are given to the more restrained sections of the score, and the Mercury recording team excel themselves in presenting Satie's kaleidoscopic circus colours with the utmost vividness.

Choses vues à droit et à gauche (sans lunettes).
(Y/B) *** EMI Dig. CDC7 54541-2 [id.]. Frank Peter Zimmermann, Alexander Lonquich – AURIC: *Sonate;* FRANCAIX: *Sonatine;* MILHAUD: *Sonata No. 2;* POULENC: *Sonata.* ***

Satie's only piece for violin and piano, the *Choses vues à droit et à gauche (sans lunettes)* bears charming titles: (1) *Choral hypocrite* ('*My chorales are like those of Bach's, with the difference that they are fewer in number and less pretentious*'); (2) *Fugue a tâtons*; and (3) *Fantaisie musculaire*. They are only moderately amusing but are played with splendid elegance by these two artists.

PIANO MUSIC

Avant-dernières pensées; Chapitres tournés en tous sens; Croquis et agaceries d'un gros bonhomme en bois; Descriptions automatiques; Deux rêveries nocturnes; Heures séculaires et instantanées; Nocturnes Nos. 1– 3, 5; Nouvelles pièces froides; Pièces froides; Prélude de la porte héroïque du ciel; Les trois valses distinguées du précieux dégoûté; Véritables préludes flasques.
*** Decca Dig. 421 713-2 [id.]. Pascal Rogé.

Pascal Rogé's choice of repertoire on this well-filled disc ranges from the Rose-Croix pieces through to the *Nocturnes.* As with the earlier recital, his playing has an eloquence and charm that are altogether rather special, and the recorded sound is very good indeed.

Avant-dernières pensées; Chapitres tournés en tous sens; Le fils des étoiles; Gnossiennes Nos. 2–3; 5 Grimaces pour 'Un songe d'une nuit d'été'; Je te veux (valse); Nocturnes Nos. 2–3 & 5; Les Pantins dansent; Pièces froids (Airs à faire fuir 1–3); Le Piège de Méduse; Première pensée rose & croix; Prélude de la porte héroïque du ciel; Rêverie du pauvre; 2 Rêveries nocturnes; 3 Valses distinguées du précieux dégoûté; Valse-ballet.
(M) *** Saga EC 3393-2 [id.]. John McCabe.

This entertaining and attractive anthology gets better and better as it proceeds. John McCabe has the full measure of Satie's understated melancholy and cool, lyrical nostalgia. The programme ranges from neglected early works like the simple, almost Chopinesque *Valse-ballet,* Satie's first published piano piece dating from 1885, to the quietly nostalgic elegy of the *Rêverie du pauvre* and the thoughtfully ambivalent *Deux Rêveries nocturnes.* The hauntingly simple *Je te veux* and the two sets of pieces, *Le Piège de Méduse* and *Le fils des Etoiles,* are particularly memorable, while the *Cinq Grimaces* end the recital with quirky good humour. The intelligent planning of this 62–minute recital and the penetrating response of the pianism places this CD among the finest Satie collections, and the recording, though not vividly present, is natural within a highly suitable ambience.

(i) *Avant-dernières pensées; Embryons desséchés; Gnossiennes Nos. 1–5; Gymnopédies Nos. 1–3; Nocturne No. 1; Sarabandes Nos. 1–3; Sonatine bureaucratique; 3 Valses distinguées du précieux dégoûté;* (ii) *Croquis et agaceries d'un gros bonhomme en bois; Descriptions automatiques; Je te veux; Poudre d'or.*
(B) **(*) Sony SBK 48283 [id.]. (i) Daniel Varviso; (ii) Philippe Entremont.

Both recitals here were recorded in 1979. Daniel Varviso has the measure of these pieces and plays admirably. Perhaps the first of the *Embryons desséchés* could have greater delicacy and wit, and there could be greater melancholy in the second of the *Gymnopédies.* But there are many good things here and one's main reservation concerns the closely balanced recording of the piano and the slightly dry sound. Entremont, too, is placed forwardly, but he brings charm to the two waltzes, *Je te veux* and *Poudre d'or,* while the *Descriptions automatiques* are engagingly crisp and witty. The collection is generous (71 minutes).

Avant-dernières pensées; Embryons desséchés; 6 Gnossiennes; 3 Gymnopédies; Pièces froides; Sarabande No. 3; Sonatine bureaucratique; 3 Valses distinguées du précieux dégoûté; 3 Véritables préludes flasques (pour un chien).
*** BIS Dig. CD 317 [id.]. Roland Pöntinen.

Roland Pöntinen is a young Swedish pianist, still in his early twenties when this recording was made. He seems perfectly in tune with the Satiean world, and his playing is distinguished by great sensibility and tonal finesse. He is very well recorded too.

Chapitres tournés en tous sens: 1: Celui qui parle trop. Croquis et agaceries: 3: Españaña. Embryons desséchés; Gnossiennes Nos. 1–3; Gymnopédies Nos. 1–3; Nocturne No. 3: Un peu mouvementé. Le piège de Méduse; Premier minuet; Sports et divertissements; Véritables préludes flasques; Vieux séquins et vieilles cuirasses: 2: Danse cuirassée.
(N) (BB) *** RCA Navigator 74321 24214-2. William Masselos – DEBUSSY: *Children's corner* etc. (*)

William Masselos made his reputation with the piano music of Charles Ives, but he proves equally at home with another musical eccentric and this is an outstanding and well-chosen selection of Satie's piano music, beautifully played and well recorded (in 1968), which makes this the least expensive recommendable Satie CD in the catalogue. Alas, the Debussy couplings are played by Alexis Weissenberg, who is altogether less sensitive.

Embryons desséchés; 6 Gnossiennes; 3 Gymnopédies; Heures séculaires et instantanées; Nocturnes Nos. 1–5; Sonatine bureaucratique; Sports et divertissements.
*** Hyperion Dig. CDA 66344 [id.]. Yitkin Seow.

The Singapore-born pianist Yitkin Seow is a good stylist; his approach is fresh and his playing crisp and marked by consistent beauty of sound. Seow captures the melancholy of the *Gymnopédies* very well and the playing, though not superior to Rogé or Queffélec in character or charm, has a quiet reticence that is well suited to this repertoire. The recording is eminently truthful.

Embryons desséchés; 6 Gnossiennes; 3 Gymnnopédies; Je te veux; Nocturnes Nos. 1–5.
(N) (B) *(*) Tring Dig. TRP 069. Ronan O'Hora.

After the success of his Grieg *Lyric pieces* Ronan O'Hora's Satie collection is a great disappointment. The melancholy half-light of this music eludes him and, instead of conveying *tristesse*, the performances are merely limp, as is demonstrated at the very beginning of the recital by the three *Gymnopédies*.

Embryons desséchés; 6 Gnossiennes; 3 Gymnopédies; Je te veux; Nocturne No. 4; Le Picadilly; 4 Préludes flasques; Prélude en tapisserie; Sonatine bureaucratique; Vieux séquins et vieilles cuirasses.
*** Decca Dig. 410 220-2. Pascal Rogé.

Rogé has real feeling for this music and conveys its bitter-sweet quality and its grave melancholy as well as he does its lighter qualities. He produces, as usual, consistent beauty of tone, and this is well projected by the recording. Very well recorded, this remains the primary recommendation on CD for this repertoire, together with its companion above.

Sauguet, Henri (1901–89)

Mélodie concertante for cello and orchestra.
*** Russian Disc RDCD 11108 [id.]. Rostropovich, USSR SO, composer – BRITTEN: *Cello Symphony*. **(*)

Sauguet belongs at the heart of the Gallic tradition, and the opening of his *Mélodie concertante* has a dream-like, pastoral quality that is reminiscent of the Honegger *Cello concerto*. Its source of inspiration was an old, persistent memory of a young cellist from Bordeaux, and the 'warm, urgent sonorities with which she sought to interpret Debussy's music'. It is an extended improvisation, based on a haunting, introspective theme heard at the beginning of the piece. The performance is, of course, authoritative in every way, and the 1964 analogue recording sounds every bit as good as it did in its fine LP format.

Scarlatti, Alessandro (1660–1725)

Concerti grossi Nos. 1 in F min.; 2 in C min.; 3 in F; (i) Sinfonie di concerti grossi for flute and strings Nos. 7 in G min.; 8 in G; 9 in G min.; 10 in A min.; 11 in C; 12 in C min.
(M) *** Ph. Dig./Analogue 434 160-2 [id.]. (i) William Bennett; I Musici.

These noble and elevated works, though not radical in style, have invention of real quality to commend them. I Musici give performances of much eloquence and warmth and great transparency; the latter is welcome in the fugal movements, especially as the 1979 analogue recording is of the very first rank. The *Sinfonie di concerti grossi* feature a flute soloist, in this instance the excellent William Bennett, who plays fluently and in fine style. The performances are lively and attractive, and eminently freshly recorded in Philips's best digital sound.

Dixit Dominus.
*** DG Dig. 423 386-2 [id.]. Argenta, Attrot, Denley, Ashley Stafford, Varcoe, Ch. & E. Concert, Pinnock – VIVALDI: *Gloria.* ***

Pinnock, as so often, inspires his performers to sing and play as though at a live event. This Scarlatti Psalm-setting, very well recorded, makes an attractive coupling for the better known of Vivaldi's settings of the *Gloria.*

Missa, Ad usum Capellae Pontificale. Motets: *Ad te, Domine, levavi; Domine vivifica me; Exaltabo e Domine quoniam; Exultate Deo adjutori; Intellige clamorem meum; Salvum fac populum tuum.*
(N) (M) **(*) Erato/Warner 0630 11229-2 [id.]. Lausanne Vocal Ens., Michel Corboz.

The *Missa, Ad usum Capellae Pontificale* is a fine example of Scarlatti's ready homage to the *stilo antico*. Written in Rome, it was dedicated to Pope Innocent XIII in 1721. The atmosphere is restrained, never overtly dramatic. The polyphony is in four parts; in the *Sanctus* there is a homophonic section, while the brief *Benedictus*, like the melismatic closing *Agnus Dei*, is made simple by the composer's restricting himself to two-part writing throughout. Overall, if not ambitious, the Mass is a moving work, never austerely withdrawn, and Corboz's refined performance catches its restrained mood; even if perhaps he could have produced more dramatic contrast at times, the peaceful atmosphere is very affecting. Each of the six *a capella* motets is short (between two and four minutes); they were also almost certainly written in Rome in the first decade of the eighteenth century. The first four, with their gentle linear flow and serene atmosphere, are again very much in the inherited Palestrina tradition. In the fifth, *Ad te, Domine, levavi* the composer more strongly asserts his own harmonic style; but all five are beautiful and Corboz's performances are worthy of them. The final motet, *Exultate Deo adjutori*, understandably brings a change of mood, and the result is quite light-hearted, very like a madrigal. The reissue is well documented, but it is a pity there are no translated texts.

Motets: *De tenebroso lacu; Infirmata, vulnerata;* (i) *Salve Regina. Totus amore languens.*
(Y/B) (M) *** Virgin Veritas/EMI VC5 45103-2 [id.]. Gérard Lesne; (i) Véronique Gens; Il Seminario Musicale.

The remarkably gifted alto, Gérard Lesne, together with the refreshingly stylish instrumental group, Il Seminario Musicale, are rediscovering baroque repertoire that has been virtually forgotten for two centuries. Lesne has already given us an outstanding collection of motets of Baldassare Galuppi (see above); now he turns to Alessandro Scarlatti, who wrote about a hundred such works. Often strikingly original, in many ways they are like vocal concerti grossi, contrasting slow and fast movements to suit the text; at the same time they combine an Italianate expressive melodic cantilena with an operatic feeling for drama. *De tenebro lacu* evokes a vision of souls in hell and the highly imaginative string introduction (a simple but spiky falling arpeggio) creates the mood for the opening words, 'From the depths of the dark lake'. The profound melancholy of *Infirma, vulnerata* is revealed with touching eloquence. Lesne is right inside the music's expressive world and it is difficult to imagine this being better (or more authentically) sung. In the setting of *Salve Regine* he is joined by the fresh-voiced (and, when necessary, spirited) Véronique Gens, and their voices blend admirably. Perhaps most moving of all is the solemnly tragic *Totus amore languens*, whose mood then lifts joyfully in the final section: 'What could be more delectable than this heavenly ardour?' Throughout, the accompaniments are creative, vital and warmly supportive – stimulating and beautiful in their own right. This is period-instrument performance at its most revealing. The recording is vivid, yet has just the right degree of warmth and spaciousness. Full translations are provided.

Motets: *Domine, refugium factus es nobis; O magnum mysterium.*
(Y/B) (B) *** Decca Double 443 868-2 (2) [id.]. Schütz Ch. of L., Roger Norrington – BONONCINI: *Stabat Mater* ***; PERGOLESI: *Magnificat in C; Stabat Mater* **(*); D. SCARLATTI: *Stabat Mater;* CALDARA: *Crucifixus;* LOTTI: *Crucifixus.* ***

These two motets are fine pieces that show how enduring the Palestrina tradition was in seventeenth-century Italy. They are noble in conception and are beautifully performed here and, given first-class sound, make a fine bonus for this enterprising Double Decca collection of Italian baroque choral music.

(i) *St Cecilia Mass;* (ii) Motets: *Domine, refugium factus et nobis; O magnum mysterium.*
(M) *** Decca 430 631-2 [id.]. (i) Harwood, Eathorne, Cable, Eans, Keyte, St John's College Ch., Wren O, Guest; (ii) Schütz Ch. of L., Norrington.

This is far more florid in style than Scarlatti's other Masses and it receives from Guest a vigorous and fresh performance. The soloists cope with their difficult fioriture very confidently and they match one another well. The two motets are noble in conception and are beautifully performed under Roger Norrington.

Scarlatti, Domenico (1685–1757)

Keyboard sonatas (complete).
*** Erato/Warner 2292 45309-2 (34) [id.]. Scott Ross, Huggett, Coin, Henry, Vallon.

The tercentenary of Domenico Scarlatti's birth prompted the production of an integral recording of Scarlatti's 555 *Keyboard sonatas*, including the three intended for organ, others for violin and continuo, and two for the unlikely combination of violin and oboe in unison. Scott Ross, who, with the participation of Monica Huggett (violin), Christophe Coin (cello), Michel Henry (oboe) and Marc Vallon (bassoon), is primarily responsible, plays five different harpsichords plus the organ, and he is very well recorded throughout in varying acoustics. Scarlatti's invention shows an inexhaustible resourcefulness, and Ross's playing is fully worthy: he is lively, technically assured, rhythmically resilient and, above all, he conveys his enjoyment of the music, without eccentricity. We cannot claim to have heard all thirty-four CDs, but all the evidence of sampling suggests that for the Scarlatti addict they will prove an endless source of satisfaction. The documentation is ample, providing a 200-page booklet about the composer, his music and the performers. The overall cost of this set is somewhere in the region of £200.

Keyboard sonatas, Kk. 1, 3, 8–9, 11, 17, 24–5, 27, 29, 87, 96, 113, 141, 146, 173, 213–14, 247, 259, 268, 283–4, 380, 386–7, 404, 443, 519–20, 523.
(N) *** Virgin/EMI Dig. VCD5 45123-2 (2) [id.]. Mikhail Pletnev (piano).

What a happy idea to record a carefully chosen selection of some of Scarlatti's finest and most adventurous sonatas, stretching over two CDs, giving the fullest opportunity to demonstrate the extraordinary range of this music in a recital-length programme playing for 140 minutes. In the opening *D major Sonata*, Kk. 443, Pletnev establishes a firm pianistic approach, yet the staccato articulation reminds us that the world of the harpsichord is not so far away. However, in the *G major Sonata*, Kk. 283, and in the following Kk. 284 with its fuller piano sonority transforms the effect of the writing. The second CD opens with the almost orchestral Kk. 96 *in D*, with its resonant horn calls, and later the lovely, flowing *C minor Sonata* and the even more expressive Kk. 11 *in F sharp minor* bring a reflective poetic feeling, which could not have been matched in colour by the plucked instrument. The performances throughout are in the very front rank, played very freely and with consistent imagination, not least the dazzling closing work in *D major*, Kk. 29, with its contrasts of mood and semi-improvisatory feeling. Pletnev is beautifully recorded.

Keyboard sonatas, Kk. 1, 8–9, 11, 13, 20, 87, 98, 119, 135, 159, 380, 450, 487 & 529.
*** DG Dig. 435 855-2 [id.]. Ivo Pogorelich (piano).

Pogorelich plays with captivating simplicity and convinces the listener that this is music which sounds far more enjoyable on the piano than on the harpsichord. His dazzling execution, using the lightest touch, consistently enchants the ear with its subtle tonal colouring, and the music emerges ever sparkling and fresh. These performances can be measured against those of Horowitz and not found wanting. Moreover Pogorelich is beautifully recorded in an ideal acoustic, and the hour-long programme is admirably chosen to provide maximum variety.

Keyboard sonatas: Kk. 1, 9, 30, 69, 113, 127, 132–3, 141, 159, 175, 215, 380, 430, 481, 492 & 502.
*** Collins Dig. 1322-2 [id.]. Joanna MacGregor (piano).

Joanna MacGregor has a lively intelligence and exemplary taste; she plays all these sonatas with flawless technical address and flair. Pianistic narcissism seems foreign to her nature and her interpretations are quite properly conceived in pianistic terms and do not strive to imitate the terrace dynamics of the harpsichord. Moreover she is very well recorded.

Keyboard sonatas: Kk. 7, 33, 49, 54, 87, 96, 105–7, 159, 175, 206–7, 240–41, 347–8, 380–81, 441–4, 518–19, 524–5.
(BB) *** HM HMP 90 1164/5 [id.]. Rafael Puyana (harpsichord).

Rafael Puyana gives eminently red-blooded performances of these *Sonatas*, which are refreshing and invigorating. He uses a three-manual harpsichord from 1740 by Hass of Hamburg, restored by Andrea Goble, which makes a splendidly rich sound, present and lively. Authoritative playing, though he tends, with some exceptions, to concentrate on the more outgoing and brilliant rather than the inward-looking *Sonatas*.

Keyboard sonatas, Kk. 8, 11, 52, 87, 159, 169, 202, 206, 208–9, 215, 337, 380, 415, 430 & 446.
*** EMI Dig. CDC7 54483-2 [id.]. Bob van Asperen (harpsichord).

Bob van Asperen's Scarlatti recital is exhilarating and dashing; its high spirits delight and invigorate, even when Van Asperen is inclined to opt for too dizzy a tempo. His instrument is a copy of a Dulcken and it is heard to excellent effect in this EMI recording. But it is not only in the dazzling virtuoso pieces that he is so impressive; he is equally persuasive in the more inward-looking and searching pieces which are included here. In short, this is one of the best Scarlatti recitals on the harpsichord to have appeared for some years and is warmly recommended. It has, alas, been withdrawn as we go to press.

Keyboard sonatas, Kk. 8, 20, 32, 107, 109, 124, 141, 159, 234, 247, 256, 259, 328, 380, 397, 423, 430, 440, 447, 481, 490, 492, 515 & 519.
⊛ (M) (***) EMI mono CHS7 64934-2 [id.]. Wanda Landowska (harpsichord).

Landowska led the revival of interest in the harpsichord at a time when it was a relative rarity both in the recital room and in the recording studio. She used a thunderous Pleyel that was specially built to withstand the rigours of 1920s and '30s travel; but her playing has more character than most modern players put together; it is electrifying in its sheer vitality and imagination. Lionel Salter's excellent notes quote her as saying she was 'sensitive to Scarlatti's bucolic mind, his rustic jauntiness . . . the elemental strength, the richness of his rhythmical power, as well as all that is Moorish in them. He has the genuine nobility, the heroism and the audacity of Don Quixote.' The first batch of sonatas was recorded in 1934 and the others in 1939 and 1940. Indispensable.

Keyboard sonatas, Kk. 9, 27, 33, 69, 87, 96, 159, 193, 247, 427, 492, 531; Fugue in G min., K.30.
(Y/B) (M) *** Erato/Warner 4509 96960-2 [id.]. Anne Queffélec (piano).

Anne Queffélec employs a modern Steinway with great character and apomb. She immediately captures the listener in the dashing opening of the *D major Sonata*, Kk. 96, with its lively fanfares and, in the gentler *B minor*, Kk. 27, her rippling passage-work is Bach-like in its simplicity. She alternates reflective works with those sonatas calling for sparkling bravura and her choice is unerringly effective. The recital closes with a *Fugue* which unfolds with calm inevitability. The 1970 recording is first class; the piano is naturally focused and has plenty of space, without any resonant blurring.

Keyboard sonatas, Kk. 25, 33, 39, 52, 54, 96, 146, 162, 197–198, 201, 303, 466, 474, 481, 491, 525, 547.
(Y/B) **(*) Sony SK 53460 [id.]. Vladimir Horowitz (piano).

Provided you are prepared to accept sometimes less than flattering and often rather dry recorded sound, this is marvellous playing which sweeps away any purist notions about Scarlatti having to be played on the harpsichord. The eighteen sonatas were chosen by Horowitz after he had recorded nearly twice as many throughout 1964. The very opening, staccato *D major*, Kk. 33, is made to sound very brittle by the close balance, but in the following *A minor*, Kk. 54, the pianist's gentle colouring is fully revealed. Here, as in the two slow *F minor sonatas*, Kk. 466 and Kk. 481, the music is particularly beautiful in a way not expected of Scarlatti. The playing time has been extended to 72 minutes by the addition of six more sonatas to the content of the original CD.

Keyboard sonatas, Kk. 46, 87, 99, 124, 201, 204a, 490–92, 513, 520–21.
*** CRD CRD 3368; *CRDC 4068* [id.]. Trevor Pinnock (harpsichord).

No need to say much about this: the playing is first rate and the recording outstanding in its presence and clarity. There are few better anthologies of Scarlatti in the catalogue, although the measure is not particularly generous.

Keyboard sonatas, Kk. 108, 118–19, 141, 198, 203, 454–5, 490–92, 501–2, 516–19.
*** HM/BMG Dig. RD 77224 [77224-2]. Andreas Staier (harpsichord).

Andreas Staier characterizes each of these Scarlatti sonatas vividly and with real imagination. Playing (and recording) of this quality has no need to fear even the most exalted comparisons. A strongly recommended issue.

Keyboard sonatas: Kk. 115–16, 144, 175, 402–3, 449–50, 474–5, 513, 516–17, 544–5.
**(*) Decca Dig. 421 422-2 [id.]. András Schiff (piano).

Exquisite and sensitive playing, full of colour and delicacy. As always, András Schiff is highly responsive to the mood and character of each piece. At times one wonders whether he is not a little too refined: in some, one would have welcomed more abandon and fire. However, for the most part this is a delightful recital, and the Decca recording is exemplary in its truthfulness.

Keyboard sonatas, Kk. 213–14; 318–19; 347–8; 356–7; 380–81; 454–5; 478–9; 524–7.
(N) (B) *** DG 439 438-2 [id.]. Ralph Kirkpatrick (harpsichord).

At the beginning of the 1970s, when this recital first appeared on LP, Ralph Kirkpatrick's monumental study of Domenico Scarlatti was the standard work on the subject, and it remains an enormously readable and erudite book. These performances, paired according to his theory, have all the panache and scholarship one would expect from this artist, in addition to a welcome degree of freedom and poetry. Some of his Bach playing has seemed pedantic, so it is a pleasure to welcome this brightly recorded bargain collection back to the catalogue without reservation.

Stabat Mater.
*** Erato/Warner Dig. 2292 45219-2 [id.]. Monteverdi Ch., E. Bar. Soloists, Gardiner – Concert: *'Sacred choral music'*. ***
(Y/B) (B) **(*) Decca Double 443 868-2 (2) [id.]. Schütz Ch. of L., Roger Norrington – BONONCINI: *Stabat Mater* ***; PERGOLESI: *Magnificat in C; Stabat Mater* **(*); A. SCARLATTI: *Domine, refugium factus es nobis; O magnum mysterium;* CALDARA: *Crucifixus;* LOTTI: *Crucifixus*. ***

The *Stabat Mater* shows Scarlatti to be a considerable master of polyphony; though it falls off in interest towards the end, it still possesses eloquence and nobility – and it is far less bland than Pergolesi's setting. Gardiner's fine performance couples three motets of interest, by Cavalli, Gesualdo and Clément, which are also splendidly done. The recording is very good indeed, notably fresh in its CD format.

    Norrington's performance is admirable, though not always impeccable in matters of tonal balance; and the recording is very good. Overall this well-designed Double Decca set combines three fine *Stabat Mater* settings with other comparable baroque choral music, all well performed and impressively recorded.

Schillings, Max von (1868–1933)

(i) *Violin concerto, Op. 23. King Oedipus (tone-poem), Op. 11; Moloch: Harvest festival scene.*
*** Marco Polo Dig. 8.223324 [id.]. (i) Ernö Rozsa; Czecho-Slovak RSO (Bratislava), Alfred Walter.

Max von Schillings' *Violin concerto* is a beautifully crafted and highly accomplished score in the post-Romantic idiom with echoes of Wagner, Richard Strauss, Reger and Pfitzner. It is a long work whose first movement alone runs to 23 minutes. Although it reveals no strong individuality, it has a certain rhetorical command and lyrical warmth to commend it, and its masterly handling of the orchestra will make a strong appeal to those with a taste for turn-of-the-century music. Its attractions are considerable and they are well conveyed in this passionate and committed performance. The eloquent soloist is the twenty-year-old Romanian-born Hungarian, Ernö Rozsa, who plays marvellously and inspires the Kosice Orchestra under Alfred Walter to great heights. Neither the excerpt from the opera *Moloch* (1906) nor the *Symphonic Prologue to the Oedipus Tyrannus of Sophocles* (1900) makes anywhere near as strong an impression. The Marco Polo recording is very well detailed and has plenty of warmth and presence.

Schmelzer, Johann (c. 1620–80)

Sonata natalitia a 3 chori; Sonata II a 8 chori; 3 Sonatas a 3; Sonata a 4; Sonata a 5; Sonata IV a 6; Sonata I a 8.
(Y/B) (M) ** Teldec/Warner 4509 95989-2 (2) [id.]. VCM, Harnoncourt – FUX: *Concentus musico instrumentis*. ***

While the *Sonata natalitia,* using recorders, piffari (early oboes), trombones and strings, certainly creates aurally fascinating and intricate textures, some of the other works, especially those for brass (where the clarinos produce a curious throttled tone), are less successful. It is when we come to the *Sonata IV a 6* (for two violins, three viols and continuo), the *Sonata a 3* (for violin, viola (violetta), viol and continuo), and the *Sonata a 3* (for three violins and continuo) that the composer begins really to stimulate the listener properly, and it is a pity that these were not added on to the Fux programme to make a single CD instead of giving Schmelzer a 48-minute disc to himself. No complaints about the recording, which is excellent.

Schmidt, Franz (1874–1939)

Symphony No. 1 in E.
(N) *** Chandos Dig. CHAN 9357 [id.]. Detroit SO, Neeme Järvi – R. STRAUSS: *Intermezzo excerpts.*
***

Franz Schmidt's *First Symphony* was composed during his early to mid-twenties and, as one might expect, is derivative. He was fleetingly a pupil of Bruckner before passing into the hands of Robert Fuchs, who taught such dissimilar figures as Mahler, Sibelius and Hugo Wolf. As befits an orchestral player (he was a cellist in the Vienna Philharmonic), his orchestration is masterly and the influences he encountered range from Bruckner to Brahms, Wagner, Strauss and – in his woodwind writing – Dvořák. The ideas are delightful (often captivating) and the whole work, though no masterpiece, offers evidence of considerable mastery. It leaves one in no doubt that Schmidt was a born symphonic composer with a real feeling for the long-breathed line and the natural growth and flow of ideas. The Detroit Symphony Orchestra under Neeme Järvi play with a freshness and enthusiasm which are totally persuasive. They sound Viennese, and the recording is very good, though perhaps lacking in the transparency and front-to-back depth which mark the very finest Chandos records. Strongly recommended.

Symphony No. 2 in E flat.
*** Chandos Dig. CHAN 8779 [id.]. Chicago SO, Järvi.

The *Second Symphony* owes much to Strauss and Reger and, if it is not as individual as his later works, like the noble *Fourth Symphony*, it shows the fertility of his invention and his command of the orchestra. The Chicago orchestra play magnificently for Järvi and are very well recorded.

Symphony No. 4 in C.
(B) *** Decca 440 615-2 (2) [id.]. VPO, Zubin Mehta – MAHLER: *Symphony No. 2 (Resurrection).* ***

Symphony No. 4 in C min.; Variations on a Hussar's song.
(N) *** EMI Dig. CDC5 55518-2 [id.]. LPO, Welser-Möst.

One of Schmidt's greatest and most personal works, coupled with one of his most genial. This neglected symphony is in one long movement, whose material all derives from the inspired, long-breathed trumpet theme with which it opens. Schmidt's music has an elegiac feel to it and a nobility of utterance which places him almost as the natural successor to Bruckner. The orchestration is masterly and the chromaticism, though occasionally reminiscent of Reger, is never cloying. Mehta's impressive recording of it with the Vienna Philharmonic from the early 1970s, easily one of his most memorable discs, has recently been reissued by Decca as the coupling for his Mahler *Second* (see above); but this newcomer from the LPO and Franz Welser-Möst completely supersedes it. Like many Austrians, Welser-Möst obviously has great feeling for the composer and manages to convey this to his players. The delightful *Variations on a Hussar's song*, written two years before the symphony in 1931, comes off with equal conviction.

Mehta also finds a dignity that reminds one a little of Elgar. The brightened recording gains in vividness in its CD transfer but loses a little of its fullness, though the Vienna ambience remains very telling.

(i) *Clarinet quintet No. 1 in B flat* (for clarinet, piano & strings); (ii) *3 Phantasiestücke on Hungarian national themes;* (iii) (Piano) *Romance in A; Toccata in D min.*
** Marco Polo Dig. 8.223415 [id.]. (i) Aladár Jánoska, Frantisek Török, Alexander Lakatos; (i; ii) Ján Slávik; (i–iii) Daniela Ruso.

The *B flat Quintet* for clarinet, piano, violin, viola and cello is predominantly elegiac; it was composed after the death of his daughter and can best be described as having something of the autumnal feeling of late Brahms, the subtlety of Reger and the dignity and nobility of Elgar or Suk. The players sound pretty tentative at the very start but soon settle down, though their tempo could with advantage have been slower. All the same, this is a thoroughly sympathetic, recommendable account. The *Drei Phantasiestücke* and the two piano pieces, the *Romance* and the *D minor Toccata*, are early and less interesting, though they are well enough played.

Clarinet quintet No. 2 in A (for clarinet, piano & strings).
*** Marco Polo Dig. 8.223414 [id.]. Jánoska, Mucha, Lakatos, Slávik, Ruso.

The *Quintet in A major for clarinet, piano and strings* is unusual: it begins like some mysterious other-worldly scherzo which immediately introduces a pastoral idea of beguiling charm. The second movement is a piano piece in ternary form; there is a longish scherzo, full of fantasy and wit, and there is an affecting trio, tinged with the melancholy of late Brahms. The fourth movement sets out as if it, too, is going to be a long, meditative piano piece, but its nobility and depth almost put one in mind of the Elgar *Quintet*. The fifth is a set of variations on a theme of Josef Labor, and is sometimes played on its own. In all, the piece takes an hour and, of the two performances now before the public, the Slovak account on Marco Polo is the one to go for. The recording has freshness and bloom, though it could benefit from a bigger recording venue. This is a glorious work.

String quartets Nos. 1 in A; 2 in G.
(N) *** Nimbus Dig. NI 5467 [id.]. Franz Schubert Qt of Vienna.

The Schmidt quartets come from 1925 and 1929 and inhabit much the same world as Reger, early Schoenberg and Strauss. The Franz Schubert Quartet of Vienna succeed in handling the dense, chromatic part-writing that opens the *Second Quartet* with rock-steady intonation. There are earlier accounts (one of them transferred to CD) by the Vienna Konserthaus Quartet, but this completely supersedes them both artistically and in terms of recorded sound. Those who respond to the *Fourth Symphony* will find much to delight them here.

Das Buch mit sieben Siegeln (The Book with 7 seals): oratorio.
**(*) Orfeo Dig. C 143862H (2). Schreier, Holl, Greenberg, Watkinson, Moser, Rydl, V. State Op. Ch., Austrian R SO, Zagrosek.

Das Buch mit sieben Siegeln has much music of substance and many moments of real inspiration. Peter Schreier's St John is one of the glories of this set, and there are fine contributions from some of the other soloists. This performance was recorded in the somewhat unappealing acoustic of the ORF studios and is wanting in the transparency that the score deserves; however, the sound is more than acceptable.

Schmitt, Florent (1870–1958)

Etude pour Le palais hanté (The haunted palace) after Edgar Allan Poe.
(M) *** EMI Dig. CDM7 64687-2 [id.]. Monte Carlo PO, Prêtre – CAPLET: *Masque* **(*); DEBUSSY: *Chute de la maison Usher.* ***

Like Debussy and Caplet in the works used for coupling in this well-planned CD, Schmitt found the inspiration for his *Etude* in Edgar Allan Poe. It is a richly evocative piece, some 12 minutes in length, and is given an enthusiastic performance under Prêtre. The recording is excellent; the work undoubtedly adds to the interest of an issue which is an indispensable acquisition for all Debussians.

Symphony No. 2, Op. 137; La danse d'Abisag, Op. 75; (i) *Habeyssée* (suite for violin and orchestra), *Op. 110. Rêves, Op. 65.*
(Y/B) *** Marco Polo Dig. 8.223689 [id.].(i) Hannele Segerstam; Rheinland-Pfalz PO, Leif Segerstam.

La danse d'Abisag, like the much earlier *Tragédie de Salomé*, has a biblical theme: unlike Salome, Abisag, despite her erotic dancing, fails to arouse the ageing monarch (King David). The *Symphony No. 2*, Op. 137, so numbered to distinguish it from the *Symphonie concertante for piano and orchestra*, was a work of Schmitt's advanced age – and no mean achievement for a composer in his eighty-eighth year! In terms of orchestral expertise and flair, it is second to none, and the opulence of its palette and imaginative vitality is remarkable. *Rêves* is an early piece, inspired by a poem by Léon-Paul Fargue and appropriately atmospheric; and *Habeyssée*, said to be inspired by an Islamic legend, is a three-movement suite for violin and orchestra. This is a rewarding issue which offers some good playing from the Rheinland-Pfalz Orchestra under Segerstam, who excels in this repertoire. Good recording too.

La tragédie de Salomé (ballet; complete).
*** Marco Polo Dig. 8.223448 [id.]. Fayt, Rheinland-Pfalz PO, Davin.

The full score of the original hour-long ballet now emerges from its long slumber to make its first appearance since 1907. Although the scoring is for fewer players, Schmitt's skill as an orchestrator is such that the heady, exotic draft he prepared is hardly less potent than the more sumptuously scored, 1908 version. The piece is as long again as the more familiar ballet, and much of the music that was lost in the process is every bit as atmospheric and colourful. Patrick Davin and the Rheinland-Pfalz Philharmonic Orchestra cast a strong spell, and Marie-Paule Fayt is the off-stage nymphet. The Marco Polo recording has a good, spacious acoustic and plenty of detail. This is a valuable addition to the catalogue, almost worthy of a Rosette insofar as the music really deserves to be heard and appreciated, and these performers do it justice. The documentation is of unusual interest and gives a detailed account of the action of the ballet.

(i) *La tragédie de Salomé, Op. 50;* (ii) *Piano quintet in B min., Op. 51: Lent.*

(***) EMI mono CDC7 54840-2 [id.]. Composer (cond./piano), with (i) O des Concerts Straram; (i) Calvet Qt – ROUSSEL: *Le festin de l'araignée* etc. (***)

La tragédie de Salomé has been neglected on record (Martinon recorded it in the 1970s and, more recently, Janowski) but none makes so strong an effect in terms of sheer atmosphere as this old (1930) account which, with its more leisurely tempi, allows the heady, exotic atmosphere to register far more effectively than do later records. The engineers have done wonders with the sound, which is making its first appearance since the original 78s. The account of the slow movement of the contemporaneous *Piano quintet* (1908) has appeared on LP and, though it is less memorable, at least it gives an opportunity for hearing the composer as pianist as well as conductor.

Schnittke, Alfred (born 1934)

Concerto grosso No. 1.

(B) *** DG Dig. 439 152-2 [id.]. Kremer, Grindenko, Smirnov, COE, Schiff – LIGETI: *Chamber concerto;* LUTOSLAWSKI: *Chain 3* etc. ***

With his semi-baroque pastiche, the *Concerto grosso No. 1*, Schnittke has provided the nearest he can get to a popular hit, so it will be interesting to see whether this budget Classikon reissue provides it with a large market; certainly the *Toccata* second movement and the *Rondo* are very striking. The soloists are balanced very forwardly in relation to the ripieno, but they can certainly stand up to the aural scrutiny, and the performance overall makes a strong impact.

Concerto grosso No. 1; Quasi una sonata; Moz-Art à la Haydn; A Paganini.

(Y/B) (M) *** DG Dig. 445 520-2 [id.]. Kremer, Smirnov, Grindenko, COE, Schiff.

The *Concerto grosso* is already available at bargain price on Classikon in this very performance. If, however, you want to jump in at the deep end of the Schnittke repertoire, the present collection offers the formidable, at times even ferocious, *Quasi una sonata* with its extraordinary scratchings and abrasions, the pastiche *Moz-Art à la Haydn*, which is almost humorous, and the virtuoso solo violin piece, *A Paganini*. The performances here are expert, very committed and brilliantly recorded.

(i) *Cello concerto No. 2. In memoriam . . .*

*** Sony Dig. SK 48241 [id.]. (i) Rostropovich; LSO, Ozawa.

Schnittke has a strong feeling for the cello, and his *Second Cello concerto* is conceived on a large scale, the main emotional weight residing in the fifth and last movement, a passacaglia lasting a quarter of an hour. Its powerful, concentrated atmosphere resonates long in the mind and leaves what one could describe as a strong aftertaste. So, for that matter, does *In memoriam . . .*, a transcription and re-working of the *Piano quintet*, written on the death of his mother. Something of the very private grief and spare, hollow textures of the quintet is lost but there are gains in colour in the highly imaginative use of the orchestra. The recording has exceptional richness, detail and depth and the performance of the concerto has all the authority and panache one might expect.

Violin concertos Nos. 1–2.

*** BIS Dig. CD 487 [id.]. Mark Lubotsky, Malmö SO, Eri Klas.

The *First Violin concerto* inhabits a post-romantic era. Its lyricism is profoundly at variance with its successor of 1966, commissioned by Mark Lubotsky, the soloist on this record. Here the central concept is what Schnittke calls 'a certain drama of tone colours', and there is no doubt that much of it is vividly imagined and strongly individual. The double-bass is assigned a special role of a caricatured 'anti-soloist'. There is recourse to the once fashionable aleatoric technique, but this is all within carefully controlled parameters. The Malmö orchestra under Eri Klas play with evident feeling in both works and are very well recorded. This is an altogether highly satisfactory coupling.

(i) *Gogol suite* (compiled Rozhdestvensky); *Labyrinths.*

*** BIS Dig. CD 557 [id.]. Malmö SO, Lev Markiz; (i) with Anton Kontra.

There is a surrealistic quality to the *Gogol suite* reminiscent of Gogol's own words quoted in Jürgen Köchel's note, 'The world hears my laughter; my tears it does not see nor recognise.' *Labyrinths* is a ballet score composed in 1971, thin in development and musical ideas but sufficiently strong in atmosphere to survive the transition from stage to concert hall. The Malmö Orchestra under Lev Markiz play very well and the recording is in the demonstration class.

Cello sonata.
*** BIS Dig. CD 336 [id.]. Torleif Thedéen, Roland Pöntinen – STRAVINSKY: *Suite italienne;*
SHOSTAKOVICH: *Sonata.* ***

The *Cello sonata* is a powerfully expressive piece, its avant-garde surface enshrining a neo-romantic soul.
Torleif Thedéen is a refined and intelligent player who gives a thoroughly committed account of this
piece with his countryman, Roland Pöntinen.

Prelude in memoriam Shostakovich (for 2 solo violins).
*** Chandos Dig. CHAN 8988 [id.]. Mordkovitch, Young – PROKOFIEV; SHOSTAKOVICH: *Violin
sonatas.* ***

The Schnittke *Prelude* for two solo violins is the shortest of the works on Lydia Mordkovitch's excellent
disc of Soviet violin music, but it is among the most moving in its intense, elegiac way. She is well
matched by her partner, Emma Young.

String quartet No. 2.
(N) **(*) Collins Dig. 1450-2 [id.]. Duke Qt – SHOSTAKOVICH: *String quartet No. 8;* TCHAIKOVSKY:
String quartet No. 1. **(*)

Schnittke's *First Quartet* dates from 1966, but he waited 14 years before returning to the medium in
1980. It was written as a memorial to the film director, Larissa Shepitko, who died in a car accident the
previous year. Its four movements convey pain and anguish and, even for those who find Schnittke's
music more shadow than substance, it makes a strange and disturbing impact. The recording is a bit too
closely balanced to warrant a full three-star recommendation but artistically this is a success.

Violin sonata No. 1; Sonata in the olden style.
*** Chandos Dig. CHAN 8343 [id.]. Dubinsky, Edlina – SHOSTAKOVICH: *Violin sonata.* ***

Schnittke's *First sonata* is a well-argued piece that seems to unify his awareness of the post-serial musical
world with the tradition of Shostakovich. On this version it is linked with a pastiche of less interest,
dating from 1977. Excellent playing from both artists, and very good recording too.

Piano sonata.
(Y/B) *** Chandos Dig. CHAN 8962 [id.]. Boris Berman – STRAVINSKY: *Serenade* etc. ***

Berman gives as persuasive an account of Schnittke's *Piano sonata* as it is possible to imagine. He is very
well recorded, too, and the three Stravinsky pieces with which it comes are also given with great pianistic
elegance.

OPERA

Leben mit einem Idioten (Life with an idiot): complete.
*** Sony Dig. S2K 52495 (2) [id.]. Duesing / Bischoff, Ringholz, Haskin, Zimnenko, Leggatte, Vocal
Ens. & Rotterdam PO, Rostropovich.

This is a live recording, with Mstislav Rostropovich conducting, of the world première production of
Schnittke's first opera, *Life with an idiot*, staged by Netherlands Opera in Amsterdam in the spring of
1992. Predictably, the piece defies operatic convention, which means that it is at least as effective on disc
as when seen in the theatre. This is an adaptation not of Dostoevsky but of a story by a fellow dissident,
Victor Erofeyev, who like Schnittke spent some of his youth in the West. It is an allegory of Soviet
oppression. As an opera it hardly works, but Schnittke's often violent, always energetic score characteristically heightens nerve-jangling situations to make it an involving personal cantata, with incidental
musical echoes of Stravinsky's comparably stylized domestic cantata, *The Wedding*. Rostropovich draws
a vigorous performance from the Rotterdam Philharmonic, with Dale Duesing and Teresa Ringholz as
the central character and his wife, both excellent, and with Howard Haskin providing peremptory
interjections as the central character, Vova.

Schoeck, Othmar (1886–1957)

3 Lieder, Op. 35; 6 Lieder, Op. 51; Das Wandsbecker Liederbuch, Op. 52; Im Nebel; Wiegenlied.
** Jecklin Dig. JD677-2 [id.]. Juliane Banse, Dieter Henschel, Wolfram Rieger.

Das Wandsbecker Liederbuch is a latterday equivalent of the Hugo Wolf Songbooks; they offer a
portrait of a poet (in this case Mathius Claudius) rather than a thematically connected cycle, and the
songs, though highly conservative in idiom, are full of subtleties and depth, as indeed are the remaining
songs on this CD. They are decently sung and recorded, and admirers of Schoeck's art need not

hesitate.

Der Sänger (The Singer), Op. 57.

(Y/B) ** Koch-Schwann Dig. 310921 [id.]. Frieder Lang, Ruth Lang-Oester.

Der Sänger is a setting of twenty-six poems by the nineteenth-century Swiss poet, Heinrich Leuthold, to whose work Schoeck's friend, Hermann Hesse, had introduced him. Its sentiment harmonized with Schoeck's own feelings of melancholia and the feeling that he had been denied the recognition to which his talents entitled him. Like the other late song-cycles *Unter Sternen* (*Under the stars*) and *Das stille Leuchten* (*The silent light*) it contains songs of great beauty.

OPERA

Penthesilea, Op. 39.

(Y/B) *** Orfeo C 364942 B [id.]. Helga Dernesch, Jane Marsh, Mechthild Gesendorf, Marjana Lipovšek, Theo Adam, ORF SO, Albrecht.

Like Strauss's *Elektra*, *Penthesilea* is set in the Ancient World, is in one Act and has a high norm of dissonance – hardly surprising, given the action. So gripping is it, so masterly its sense of pace and dramatic contrast, that one is on the edge of one's seat throughout. Despite its kinship with Strauss's expressionism, its sound-world is quite distinctive. Its scoring is quite unusual: four violins only; a huge wind section, including ten clarinets at various pitches; brass and two pianos. At times the writing almost looks forward to Britten. The present production was recorded by Oesterreichischer Rundfunk (ORF) at the 1982 Salzburg Festival and has performances of thrilling intensity from Helga Dernesch in the title-role and Theo Adam as Achilles, as well as Jane Marsh (Prothoe) and Marjana Lipovšek (the High Priestess). The recording has ample detail and presence and is in every way satisfactory.

Venus (complete).

(Y/B) *** MGB Musikszene Schweiz CD 6112 (2) [id.]. Lang, Popp, O'Neal, Fassbender, Skovhus, Alföldi, Heidelberg Kammer Ch., Basle Boys' Ch., Swiss Youth PO, Venzago.

Venus is based on a libretto by Schoeck's school-friend, Armin Rüeger, who drew on two sources for his text: Prosper Mérimée's *La Vénus d'Ille* and a short story by Eichendorff called *Das Marmorbild*. The basic argument is simple and comes from Ovid, though Rüeger sets the action in a country castle in the south of France. The tenor role is particularly demanding and may have hampered the work reaching the international stage. Venzago's conducting radiates total dedication, and so does the playing of the young Swiss orchestra. The opening scene almost prompts one's thoughts to turn to the Strauss of *Ariadne*, but as the opera unfolds Venzago's view of the work as partly 'an enormous orchestral poem (exposition, development, Scherzo and recapitulation) with obbligato voices' seems more and more valid. The sheer quality of the invention is notable amd many of the ideas, particularly the Venus motive, have great tenderness and delicacy. Schoeck's scoring is superb, and those who know *Penthesilea* should lose no time in acquiring this glorious score. The performance may not be absolutely ideal vocally, but it is worth putting up with that for the sake of such a beautiful work. Good and atmospheric recording.

Schoenberg, Arnold (1874–1951)

'*Arnold Schoenberg Exposition*'.

(N) (M) **(*) Sony SM4K 62364 (4) [id.].

This four-CD survey gives the listener an opportunity to investigate Schoenberg's development and also to make an assessment of his atonal explorations. In making a powerful contribution to the influence of the Second Viennese School, Schoenberg left a trail of wreckage behind in the field of traditional writing. Other composers, less individually suited to the straitjacket of the atonal system, climbed aboard the bandwagon, often with disastrous results (for them and us), and the onward progress of tonal diatonic writing was forced into a musical backwater. Fortunately times are changing, and it will be interesting to see how much of Schoenberg's output survives to become part of the major repertoire of the twenty-first century.

'*The Early tonal years*': (i) *Chamber symphony No. 1, Op. 9;* (ii) *Verklaerte Nacht (String sextet), Op. 4;* (iii) *Friede auf Erden, Op. 13;* (iv) *Gurrelieder: Song of the wood-dove.*

(N) (M) *** Sony SMK 62019 [id.]. (i) Marlborough Festival O (members); (ii) Trampler, Ma, Juilliard String Qt; (iii) BBC Singers; (iv) Jessye Norman, Ens. InterContemporain (members), Boulez.

The first disc, not unexpectedly, opens with Schoenberg's post-Wagnerian *Verklaerte Nacht* with its erotically potent, Tristanesque chromaticism, written in 1902. The Juilliard performance of what is in effect a symphonic poem for string sextet is highly charged but rather over-characterized, especially at the opening, so that the composer's volatile but seamless, sensuous flow does not proceed as evenly as would be ideal. Nevertheless, technically it is marvellously played and richly and atmospherically recorded. Schoenberg then reacted against himself, and in 1906 took a new path with the polyphonically complex *First Chamber Symphony* for 15 instruments. In spite of the work's formal and textural compression, its diaphanous scoring for the string quintet at times almost returns to the 'transfigured' mood of the earlier work. The Marlborough performance is committed and highly spontaneous. *Friede auf Erden* ('Peace on earth') for unaccompanied chorus was written the following year, its part-writing even more thornily complex. Here its vocal difficulties, which inhibited early performances, are readily surmounted by the BBC Singers under Boulez and they make it sound almost mellifluous. In the lovely *Lied der Waldtaube* ('Song of the wood dove') from *Gurrelieder* (1911), which closes the programme, Jessye Norman is a radiant soloist, crowning her performance with a thrilling top B flat.

'The Expressionist years': (i) *String quartet No. 2 in F sharp min., Op. 10;* (ii) *6 Small pieces for piano, Op. 19;* (iii) *Pierrot lunaire, Op. 21;* (iv) *Die glückliche Hand, Op. 18.*

(N) (M) **(*) Sony SMK 62020 [id.]. (i) Valente, Juilliard String Qt; (ii) Glenn Gould; (iii) Yvonne Minton (reciter), Debost, Pay, Zukerman, Harrell, Barenboim; (iv) Nimsgern, BBC Singers and SO; (iii; iv) Boulez.

The *Second String quartet* (1907–8) is individual and powerful; its last two movements (both slow) are intensified by the contribution of a soprano, here Benita Valente, who is given settings of a prayerful Litany and its answer. The Juilliards are less sympathetic than they were in *Verklaerte Nacht*: there is no lack of intensity but there is a want of real pianissimo, not helped by the close balance. Glenn Gould displays a ready grasp of the six minuscule piano *Pieces* (1911). But the key work here is *Pierrot lunaire* (1912), a setting of 21 poems by Albert Giraud for recitalist and modest-sized instrumental ensemble, which brings many technical and interpretative problems. As can be seen from the cast-list here, the performance gathers together a distinguished group of instrumentalists, but the result is lacking in the expressive intensity one expects of Boulez in this music. With Yvonne Minton eschewing sing-speech, the vocal line is precisely pitched, with frequent recourse to half-tones. It is a musical result, but it hardly conveys the cabaret associations which are important in this highly coloured, melodramatic work. However, Boulez's approach places Schoenberg's score within the mainstream of vocal writing, and many listeners will relish the comparative lack of difficulty in coming to terms with its highly original language. *Die glückliche Hand* (which the composer translated as 'The hand of Fate') is much more successful, with Nimsgern an impressive bass soloist. The disc ends with a six-minute interview with Halsey Stephens, 'Schoenberg the painter', recorded in 1949.

'Dodecaphony': (i) *Variations for orchestra, Op. 31;* (ii) *Suite for piano, Op. 25;* (iii) *Moses und Aron: Act II, scene 3.*

(N) (M) ** Sony SMK 62021 [id.]. (i; iii) BBC SO, Boulez; (ii) Glenn Gould; (iii) Palmer, Knight, Manning, Watts, Cassilly, Winfield, Hermann, Orpheus Boys' Ch.

Boulez's strong, compulsive account of the orchestral *Variations*, composed between 1926 and 1928, is also available coupled with a matching orchestral version of *Verklaerte Nacht* (see below). Here it is supplemented by a recorded talk by the composer, made by Radio Frankfurt in 1931. Gould's 1964 recording of the piano *Suite,* Op. 25, has the expected concentration. But it was a curious idea to select just the third scene of the second Act of *Moses and Aron* (1932), effective though is, when the complete recording of the opera from which it comes is readily available. It is certainly well performed and recorded.

'Schoenberg in America': (i) *Piano concerto in C, Op. 42;* (ii) *Phantasy for violin with piano accompaniment, Op. 47;* (iii) *String trio, Op. 45;* (iv) *Dreimal tausend Jahre, Op. 50a;* (v) *Kol Nidre, Op. 39;* (vi) *Psalm 130, Op. 50b;* (vii) *A survivor from Warsaw, Op. 46.*

(N) (M) *** Sony SMK 62022 [id.]. (i) Ax, Philh. O, Salonen; (ii) Menuhin, Gould; (iii) Juilliard Qt (members); (iv; vi) BBC Singers; (vii) Günther Reich; (v; vii) Shirley-Quirk, BBC Ch. & SO; (iv–vii) Boulez.

With Schoenberg's *Piano concerto* we take a jump of a decade to 1942. It is a work which consciously echoes the world of the romantic concerto in twelve-note serial terms, but the thick and (at times) glutinous textures favoured by the composer tend to obscure the focus of the argument rather than making it sweeter on the ear. The soloist, Emanuel Ax, immediately displays an engaging lyrical feeling at the opening, and his performance is warmly sympathetic (the *Giocoso* finale very attractively handled). But despite flatteringly luminous (1992) recording, made in Watford Town Hall, Salonen does not convince the listener that the work is orchestrally a complete success. Of Schoenberg's final two chamber works, the intractable *String trio* was begun in 1946 when the composer was in hospital, recovering from a heart attack; Schoenberg suggested that its restless progress reflected the course of his illness, treatment and convalescence. It is confidently played by the Juilliard group and the 1985 recording is very well balanced. The *Phantasy for violin and piano* (1949), though not opening very invitingly, is perhaps marginally more approachable. This distinguished account by Menuhin and Gould is a mono recording from 1965, made by CBC in Toronto, and it is of first-class quality. But perhaps the most striking music here, apart from *A survivor from Warsaw* with its extraordinary opening so vividly and dramatically projected, is the remaining triptych of vocal pieces from the BBC Singers. In such choral works, particularly when inspired by a Jewish theme, as in the magnificent *Kol Nidre* of 1938 for narrator, mixed chorus and orchestra, the composer's full romanticism broke out. Fine performances and excellent sound.

(i) *Accompaniment to a motion picture scene, Op. 34;* (ii) *Chamber symphony No. 1, Op. 9;* (i; iii) *Die Jakobsleiter* (oratorio fragments, completed Zillig).
(M) *** Sony SMK 48462 [id.]. (i) BBC SO; (ii) Ens. InterContemporain (members); (iii) Nimsgern, Bowen, Partridge, Hudson, Shirley-Quirk, Rolfe Johnson, Wenkel, Mesplé, BBC Singers; Boulez.

It is good to see the reappearance of Boulez's first Schoenberg survey on Sony at mid-price, even if, as seems likely, he re-records the repertory. The performance of the film scene is as atmospheric as one would expect, if not as emotionally involved as the *Chamber Symphony*, given a strong, warmly enjoyable account. (The second *Chamber Symphony* is coupled with *Moses und Aron* – see below.) *Die Jakobsleiter* is an ambitious oratorio, which he left fully sketched out. It was completed and orchestrated by Winifried Zillig, revealing an exceptionally powerful piece. Strongly cast, the performance has passion and commitment and the recording projects it vividly.

Chamber symphonies Nos. 1, Op. 9; 2, Op. 38; Verklaerte Nacht.
*** DG Dig. 429 233-2 [id.]. Orpheus CO.

The Orpheus Chamber Orchestra couple their fine account of *Verklaerte Nacht* with the two *Chamber symphonies*. Their *Verklaerte Nacht* is swift-moving and a bit overheated; it does not have the subtle range of colouring and dynamics that marks the classic Karajan version. Both the *Chamber symphonies* come off well and the disc is worth acquiring solely for their sake. A rather brightly lit but very good recording.

(i) *Chamber Symphony No. 1 , Op. 9;* (ii) *5 Pieces for orchestra;* (i) *Variations, Op. 31; Verklaerte Nacht;* (iii) *Ewartung, Op. 17; 6 Songs, Op. 8.*
(N) (B) **(*) Double Decca Analogue/Dig. 448 279-2 (2). (i) LAPO, Mehta; (ii) Cleveland O, or (iii) VPO, with Anja Silja, Dohnányi.

It was to Los Angeles that Schoenberg moved to live out his last years, and it would have gladdened him that his local orchestra had achieved a degree of brilliance to match that of any orchestra in America. The *First Chamber Symphony* is given a rich performance under Mehta, arguably too fast at times but full of understanding for the romantic emotions which underlie much of the writing. The Op. 31 *Variations*, among the most taxing works Schoenberg ever wrote, somehow reveal their secrets and their unmistakable greatness more clearly when the performance has such a sense of drive, while Mehta's *Verklaerte Nacht* has warmth and intensity yet is free of schmalz; it is sympathetically recorded and the Los Angeles strings play with great virtuosity and opulence of tone. The Cleveland Orchestra are comparably at home in Schoenberg's seminal *Five Pieces*. Their perfection of ensemble goes with a remarkable depth of feeling, and the digital recording, full, rich and weighty, is of demonstration standard, not as brightly lit as the quality the Decca engineers provide for Mehta. Schoenberg's searingly intense monodrama, *Ewartung*, makes an apt bonus. Silja is at her most committed. The sound under pressure may be raw, but the self-tortured questionings of the central character come over grippingly; again the digital sound is outstandingly vivid.

(i) *Chamber Symphony No. 1, Op. 9;* (ii; iii) *Erwartung;* (iii) *Variations for orchestra, Op. 31.*
(Y/B) *** EMI Dig. CDC5 55212-2 [id.]. (i) Birmingham Contemporary Music Group; (ii) Bryn-Julson; (iii) CBSO; Sir Simon Rattle.

With Rattle there is no question of missing the heart behind the composer's severe intellectual argument. In the *Chamber Symphony No. 1* Rattle, with fifteen players from the Birmingham Contemporary Music Group, springs rhythms infectiously, relaxedly bringing out the thrust of argument. The playing may not be as bitingly crisp as in some rival versions but it has far more character, thanks to both conductor and players. By contrast, he is daringly expansive in the *Variations* of 1928, even more so than Karajan in his classic recording with the Berlin Philharmonic. The Birmingham players may not always be quite so refined as the Berliners, but they play with even greater emotional thrust and with a keener sense of mystery, while heightened dynamic contrasts add to the dramatic bite. Equally in Schoenberg's taxing atonal vocal lines, Phyllis Bryn-Julson sings with a clarity and definition to coax the ear instead of assaulting it. She may not be as dominant or powerful as Jessye Norman in her Philips recording (see below), but, bright and clear, she gives a more vulnerable portrait, tender and compelling, with Rattle more urgent than James Levine for Norman. Superb sound.

Chamber Symphony No. 2.
(N) (M) **(*) EMI CDM7 65869-2 [id.]. New Philh. O, Prausnitz – BUSONI: *Berceuse élégiaque* ***; WEILL: *Symphonies Nos. 1–2.* **

The two movements of Schoenberg's *Chamber Symphony No. 2* were composed 23 years apart, the first elegiac and passionate, the second begining vivaciously but ending in a darker mood. Prausnitz's account has plenty of character and feeling, and is well played and recorded, but it is not distinctive.

Chamber Symphony No. 2; Music to a motion-picture scene; Verklaerte Nacht.
(Y/B) *** Teldec/Warner Dig. 9031 77314-2 [id.]. COE, Holliger.

Holliger and the Chamber Orchestra of Europe give one of the most passionate performances of Schoenberg's *Verklaerte Nacht* on disc, reflecting 'the glow of inmost warmth' in the Richard Dehmel poem which inspired it. It is imaginatively coupled with representative works from later periods, the atmospheric *Incidental music to a motion-picture scene* and the *Chamber Symphony No. 2*. Holliger and the COE are more expansive, as well as more committed, than the Orpheus Chamber Orchestra on their DG disc, bringing out a lilting Viennese quality in the second of the two movements of the *Chamber Symphony No. 2*. First-rate sound.

Piano concerto, Op. 42.
(N) *** Chandos Dig. CHAN 9375. Malling, Danish Nat. RSO, Schønwandt – SCHUMANN: *Piano concerto.* *(*)

Amalie Malling proves an intelligent and sympathetic soloist who, if not more persuasive than some of her better-known rivals such as Pollini and Brendel, is every bit as convincing. Michael Schønwandt gets very good results from the Danish orchestra and the texture is lucid and transparent, and splendidly recorded. The coupling is, however, not completely logical or particularly successful. This needs a reissue with the pairing better thought out.

Pelleas und Melisande (symphonic poem), *Op. 5.*
(M) **(*) EMI CDM7 65078-2 [id.]. New Philh. O, Barbirolli – R. STRAUSS: *Metamorphosen.* **(*)

It was Richard Strauss who suggested to Schoenberg the subject of Maeterlinck's drama as an opera. Schoenberg opted for a Straussian symphonic poem, and this he completed before he ever knew that Debussy had turned the same subject into an opera. What Barbirolli underlines is the red-bloodedness of the emotions portrayed, and his account is full of passion. The recording is expansive to match, though the tuttis are vibrant rather than refined.

Pelleas und Melisande, Op. 5; Variations for orchestra, Op. 31; Verklaerte Nacht (orchestral version), *Op. 4.*
(M) *** DG 427 424-2 (3) [id.]. BPO, Karajan – BERG: *Lyric suite; 3 Pieces;* WEBERN: *Collection.* ***

The Straussian opulence of Schoenberg's early symphonic poem has never been as ravishingly presented as by Karajan and the Berlin Philharmonic in this splendidly recorded version. The gorgeous tapestry of sound is both rich and full of refinement and detail, while the thrust of argument is powerfully conveyed. These are superb performances which present the emotional element at full power but give unequalled precision and refinement. The Op. 31 *Variations*, the most challenging of Schoenberg's orchestral works, here receives a reading which vividly conveys the ebb and flow of tension within the phrase and over the whole plan. Superb recording, excellently remastered.

Pelleas und Melisande, Op. 5; Verklaerte Nacht, Op. 4.
(Y/B) *** DG Dig. 439 942-2 [id.]. Philh. O, Sinopoli.

In *Pelleas* Sinopoli, broad and expansive, cannot quite match the biting passion and sharp characterization of Karajan in his superb Berlin performance, but he finds an impressionistic beauty to this richly varied score which for once relates it to the Debussy masterpiece on the same subject. In *Verklaerte Nacht* Sinopoli does not draw such weight of sound from the Philharmonia strings as do some other versions which use the 1943 string orchestra score, but in his refinement he relates it more clearly to the chamber scale of the original sextet. Glowing sound to match.

3 Pieces for chamber orchestra (1910); *Suite, Op. 29; Verklaerte Nacht* (string sextet version), *Op. 4.*
(M) *** Sony Analogue/Dig. SMK 48465 [id.]. Ens. InterContemporain (members), Boulez.

Boulez first recorded *Verklaerte Nacht* in the version for full strings – see below – but this beautifully played account for solo strings is even more impressive. The neo-classical *Suite* – with Boulez this time conducting a mere seven players – reveals a totally different side of the composer, a spiky piece presented at its sharpest in this reading. There is no lack of intimacy and expressive feeling, and the CBS recording is first class. The *Three Pieces for chamber orchestra* were found after Schoenberg had died and date from 1910. They are atonal and the third piece was unfinished. This is an earlier analogue recording but of good quality.

5 Pieces for orchestra, Op. 16.
*** EMI Dig. CDC7 49857-2 [id.]. CBSO, Rattle – BERG: *Lulu: suite;* WEBERN: *6 Pieces.* ***
*** DG Dig. 419 781-2 [id.]. BPO, Levine – BERG: *3 Pieces;* WEBERN: *5 Pieces.* ***
(M) *** Mercury 432 006-2 [id.]. LSO, Dorati – BERG: *3 Pieces; Lulu suite;* WEBERN: *5 Pieces.* ***

Rattle and the CBSO give an outstanding reading of this Schoenberg masterpiece, bringing out its red-blooded strength, neither too austere nor too plushy. With sound of demonstration quality and an ideal coupling, it makes an outstanding recommendation.

The colour and power of Schoenberg's Opus 16 *Pieces* also come over superbly in Levine's purposeful, concentrated reading. This is an interpretation designed to relate Schoenberg to his predecessors rather than to the future. Warm, full-toned recording, with some spotlighting.

Dorati, in his pioneering coupling with other works written at the same period by Schoenberg's emergent pupils, used the version the composer made in 1949, with a slightly reduced orchestra. The performance is strong; the 1962 sound is admirably vivid and clear.

(i) *5 Pieces for orchestra, Op. 16;* (ii) *Ode to Napoleon Buonaparte, Op. 41* (for string quartet, piano and reciter); (iii) *Serenade, Op. 24* (for clarinet, bass clarinet, mandolin, guitar, violin, viola, cello and bass voice).
*** Sony SMK 48463 [id.]. (i) BBC SO; (ii) David Wilson-Johnson; (iii) John Shirley-Quirk; (ii; iii) Ens. InterContemporain (members), Boulez.

With Boulez, the *Five Pieces for orchestra* emerge as colourfully expressive, hardly more elusive than Debussy when played as strongly as this. The Abbey Road recording has plenty of body and atmosphere. The *Serenade* finds Schoenberg in rather crustily neo-classical mood, and even Boulez with his team (including Shirley-Quirk) cannot bring out all the lightness the composer seems to have intended. With David Wilson-Johnson a characterfully ironic narrator, the Byron setting of the *Ode to Napoleon* is more warmly memorable. Both are very clearly recorded and, if the balance is close, there is plenty of ambient warmth.

Variations for orchestra, Op. 31; Verklaerte Nacht, Op. 4.
✲ *** DG 415 326-2 [id.]. BPO, Karajan.

(i) *Variations for orchestra, Op. 31;* (ii) *Verklaerte Nacht, Op. 4;* (i; iii) *Die glückliche Hande, Op. 18.*
(M) **(*) Sony SMK 48464 [id.]. (i) BBC SO; (ii) NYPO; (iii) Siegmund Nimsgern, BBC Singers; Boulez.

Karajan's version of *Verklaerte Nacht* is altogether magical and very much in a class of its own. There is a tremendous intensity and variety of tone and colour: the palette that the strings of the Berlin Philharmonic have at their command is altogether extraordinarily wide-ranging.

Boulez's account of the thornily immediate *Variations* and the coupled New York Philharmonic performance of *Verklaerte Nacht* may lack the warmth, final polish and subtlety of Karajan's celebrated versions, but Boulez's earthiness, unrelentingly forceful, is compelling in the former, while in the latter he has the full measure of Schoenberg's poetry and secures responsive playing from the New York Philharmonic. The Sony recording is vivid but not as richly beautiful as the Berlin sound. There is also a bonus here in the 'psychological pantomime', *Die glückliche Hande*, which is sharply observed, with Nimsgern a fine soloist.

Verklaerte Nacht.
*** Denon Dig. CO 79442 [id.]. Sinfonia Varsovia, Krivine – R. STRAUSS: *Metamorphosen;* WAGNER: *Siegfried idyll.* ***
(N) (BB) *** RCA Navigator 74321 29243-2. Georgian State CO, Liana Isakadze – BERG: *Violin concerto;* WEBERN: *Passacaglia for orchestra.* ***
(M) *** EMI CDM5 65079-2 [id.]. ECO, Daniel Barenboim – BARTOK: *Divertimento for strings;* HINDEMITH: *Trauermusik.* ***

(Y/B) (B) ** Decca Double Dig. 444 872-2 (2) [id.]. Berlin RSO, Chailly – MAHLER: *Symphony No. 10.* **(*)

Emmanuel Krivine draws playing of refined sonority from his excellent Polish string ensemble, who play as if their lives are at stake. It is a performance of strong contrast both in dynamic range and in dramatic character, and is of a high emotional temperature. This is one of the most powerful and convincing of recent recordings and, though it does not displace Karajan's celebrated account, it is as deeply felt and in its way almost as subtle. It has the merit of excellent digital recorded sound.

On the evidence of this CD, the Georgian State Chamber Orchestra has a first-class string section, and they play Schoenberg's sensuous string work with a uniquely Slavonic ardour to grip the listener in the intensity of the final climax. Isakadze controls the emotional ebb and flow unerringly, and there is refinement here as well as passion. The recording is admirably full and vivid, and this comes at the lowest possible price with two other key twentieth-century works.

Barenboim is a most persuasive advocate of this score and receives a warmly immediate response from his players. He is given very good (1967) Abbey Road sound, lacking only a very little in refinement in the extreme upper range, and with plenty of body. This is highly involving, and interestingly coupled.

Chailly's version of Schoenberg's work is very well played and recorded, but it is in no way distinctive.

(i) *Verklaerte Nacht, Op. 4; 5 Orchestral pieces, Op. 16;* (ii) (Piano): *3 Pieces, Op. 11; 6 Little Pieces, Op. 19.* arr. BUSONI: *Piece, Op. 11/2 (Konzertmässige interpretation).*
(Y/B) *** Teldec/Warner Dig. 4509 98256-2 [id.]. (i) Chicago SO, Barenboim; (ii) Barenboim (piano).

Barenboim's Teldec reading of *Verklaerte Nacht* in the 1943 string orchestra version is weighty and passionate, with the Chicago strings playing superbly, while the *Five Orchestral pieces* are comparably purposeful and sharply characterized. They lead naturally to the miniatures for piano, which Barenboim interprets with persuasive warmth, treating them rather like Brahms 'with the wrong notes'. He concludes with a fascinating rarity, an elaborate rearrangement of the second of the Op.11 *Pieces* which Busoni made in 1909, turning it into something close to late Liszt. The notes are excellent, with copious musical illustrations. Warm sound, if not ideally detailed in the orchestral works.

Verklaerte Nacht, Op. 4 (string sextet version).
⊛ (***) Testament mono SABT 1031 Hollywood Qt, with Alvin Dinkin, Kurt Reher – SCHUBERT: *String quintet.* (***) ⊛
*** Hyperion Dig. CDA 66425 [id.]. Raphael Ens. – KORNGOLD: *Sextet.* ***

The 1950 Hollywood account was the first version of *Verklaerte Nacht* in its original sextet form ever to appear on records, and arguably it remains unsurpassed and possibly unequalled. This almost flawless performance enjoyed the imprimatur of Schoenberg himself, who supplied the sleeve-note for it (reproduced in the excellent booklet), the only time he ever did so. The sound is remarkably good and very musical. Recommended with enthusiasm.

For those wanting a modern, digital version, the Raphael Ensemble have the advantage of very good recorded sound and give a fine account of Schoenberg's score. They also have the advantage of a rarity in their coupling, the youthful *Sextet* of Korngold.

OTHER CHAMBER MUSIC

String quartets Nos. 1 in D min., Op. 7; (i) *2 in F sharp min., Op. 10. 3, Op. 30; 4, Op. 37.*
(***) Archiphon ARC mono 103/4 [id.]. Kolisch Qt, (i) with C. Gifford.

No quartet has ever been more closely associated with these pieces than the Kolisch, and the present recordings were made at the turn of 1936-7. The Hollywood composer, Alfred Newman, who was studying with Schoenberg at the time, brought the quartet into the film studio and recorded the whole cycle as a present for the composer. They were straight performances with no re-takes, though the Kolisch always played these works (and other repertoire) by heart – with the exception of the *Fourth*, which was new. They recorded this work just before giving its première. It is well worth putting up with surface noise (which one soon barely notices anyway) for the sake of *real* music-making. Indeed, given phrasing of this quality, one is tempted to say that even the sceptic will be persuaded that there is more to the rigorously disciplined *Third* and *Fourth Quartets* than later ensembles have found; and never have the two earlier *Quartets* sounded so eloquent. The set contains a short speech of thanks by Schoenberg.

String quartet No. 2 in F sharp min., Op. 10.
(N) *** EMI CDC5 55289-2 [id.]. Roocroft, Britten Qt – SCHUBERT: *String quartet in A min.* ***

If Amanda Roocroft's current popularity leads collectors to this repertoire, this EMI issue will have performed a valuable service. Her performance of the Stefan Georg settings in the last two movements is impressive, while the playing of the Britten Quartet has eloquence and warmth, and the recording gives no grounds for complaint. Those seeking this particular coupling will not be disappointed.

Piano music: *3 Pieces, Op. 11; 6 Small Pieces, Op. 19; 5 Pieces, Op. 23; 3 Pieces, Op. 33a & b; Suite, Op. 25.*
(M) *** DG 423 249-2 [id.]. Maurizio Pollini.

This CD encompasses Schoenberg's complete piano music. Pollini plays with enormous authority and refinement of dynamic nuance and colour, making one perceive this music in a totally different light from other performers. He is accorded excellent sound (very slightly on the dry side), extremely clear and well defined.

VOCAL MUSIC

Erwartung, Op. 17.
*** Decca Dig. 417 348-2 (2) [id.]. Anja Silja, VPO, Dohnányi – BERG: *Wozzeck.* ***

Schoenberg's searingly intense monodrama makes an apt and generous coupling for Dohnányi's excellent version of Berg's *Wozzeck.* As in the Berg, Silja is at her most passionately committed, and the digital sound is exceptionally vivid.

(i) *Erwartung.* (ii) Cabaret songs: *Arie aus dem Spiegel von Arcadien; Einfältiges Lied; Galathea; Der genügsame Liebhaber; Jedem das Seine; Mahnung; Nachtwandler* (with trumpet, piccolo & snare drum).
*** Ph. Dig. 426 261-2 [id.]. Jessye Norman; (i) Met. Op. O, Levine; (ii) James Levine (piano).

The monodrama, *Erwartung* – 'Expectation' – may be among the least appealing of Schoenberg's formidable *œuvre,* but Jessye Norman and James Levine present it on a Philips disc which could well win the composer more friends than any ever issued before. She herself has said that Erwartung is 'technically the most difficult thing I have ever sung' but that, having learnt it, she found it 'immensely singable'. That clearly accounts for the warmth, intensity, range of expression and sheer beauty that she and Levine bring to this score. Levine draws ravishing sounds from the Metropolitan Opera Orchestra; Jessye Norman's singing, beautiful and totally secure over the widest range of expression and dynamic, is a revelation too. Compare this with Anja Silja, accompanied by Christoph von Dohnányi on their fine Decca issue, and the extra depth, range of emotion and refinement of the New York performance come out at every point. The impact of this *Erwartung* is brilliantly heightened by the total contrast of the Schoenberg coupling. Accompanied by Levine at the piano – a sparkily individual partner – Jessye Norman sings all eight of the cabaret songs that Schoenberg wrote when he was working in Berlin. In these witty, pointed, tuneful songs Schoenberg was letting his hair down in a way that to his detractors must be almost unimaginable. These are art-songs that yet completely belong to the half-world of cabaret and Jessye Norman projects her personality as masterfully as a latterday Marlene Dietrich.

(i) *Erwartung, Op. 17;* (ii) *Gurrelieder: Song of the Wood-dove;* (iii) *Pierrot lunaire, Op. 21.*
(M) ** Sony SMK 48466 [id.]. (i) Janis Martin, BBC SO; (ii) Jessye Norman, Ens. InterContemporain (members); (iii) Minton, Barenboim, Debost, Pay, Zukerman, Harrell; Boulez.

The monodrama *Erwartung* contrasts well with the lovely *Lied der Waldtaube* in its chamber scoring with Jessye Norman a radiant soloist, crowning her performance with a thrilling top B flat. Boulez brings passionate feeling to both, and the recording is full and immediate. As can be seen from the cast list, the performance of *Pierrot lunaire* gathers together a distinguished group of instrumentalists, but here the result lacks the expressive intensity one expects of Boulez in this music. With Yvonne Minton eschewing sing-speech, the vocal line is precisely pitched, with frequent recourse to half-tones. It is a most musical result but hardly conveys the cabaret associations which are important in this highly coloured, melodramatic work.

Gurrelieder.
(Y/B) *** DG Dig. 439 944-2 (2) [id.]. Sweet, Jerusalem, Lipovšek, Wekler, Langridge, Sukowa, Vienna State Op. Ch., Schoenberg Ch., Slovak Phil Ch., BPO, Abbado.
*** Decca Dig. 430 321-2 (2) [id.]. Jerusalem, Dunn, Fassbaender, Brecht, Haage, Hotter, St Hedwig's Cathedral Ch., Berlin, Düsseldorf State Musikverein, Berlin RSO, Chailly.

(i) *Gurrelieder;* (ii) *4 Orchestral songs.*
(M) *** Sony SM2K 48459 (2) [id.]. (i) Jess Thomas, Napier, Nimsgern, Bowen, Reich, BBC Singers & Ch. Soc., Goldsmith's Ch. Union, Men's voices of LPO Ch.; (i; ii) Yvonne Minton, BBC SO; Boulez.

Recorded live in the Philharmonie, Berlin, Abbado's version begins magnetically with the most delicate tracery of sound, immediately capturing both atmosphere and dramatic intensity. Though Siegfried Jerusalem as Waldemar is not quite as firmly focused as he was on Riccardo Chailly's Decca set, he conveys more passion, and regularly Abbado's reading is freer and more volatile than Chailly's, with a sense of wonder enhanced by the very atmosphere of a concert. Susan Dunn as Tove in Chailly's version is firmer and truer than Abbado's Sharon Sweet, whose tight vibrato is often intrusive, but this is a strong, characterful reading, and Marjana Lipovšek is deeply moving as the Wood-Dove, with the hushed tension behind her big solo tellingly conveyed. Philip Langridge is outstanding as Klaus-Knarr and Hartmut Welker makes a bluff if slightly unsteady Peasant. The only soloist who is controversial is the woman speaker, Barbara Sukowa, whose use of sliding *Sprech-Stimme*, chattering in the style of *Pierrot Lunaire*, comes near to being comic. With the Berlin Philharmonic's playing richly and atmospherically caught, this must now stand as a first choice among live recordings, though the extra weight and detail of the sound in Chailly's studio version will for many make that still preferable.

Chailly's magnificent recording of Schoenberg's massive *Gurrelieder* remains highly recommendable. Siegfried Jerusalem as Waldemar is not only warm and firm of tone, but imaginative too. Susan Dunn makes a sweet, touchingly vulnerable Tove, while Brigitte Fassbaender gives darkly baleful intensity to the message of the Wood-dove. Hans Hotter is a characterful Speaker in the final section. The impact of the performance is the more telling with sound both atmospheric and immediate, bringing a fine sense of presence, not least in the final choral outburst.

Boulez's warm, expressive style using slow, luxuriating tempi brings out the operatic quality behind Schoenberg's massive score. With Boulez, the Wagnerian overtones are richly expressive and, though Marita Napier and Jess Thomas are not especially sweet on the ear, they show the big, heroic qualities which this score ideally demands, while Yvonne Minton is magnificent in the *Song of the Wood-dove*. Boulez builds that beautiful section to an ominous climax and, at mid-price, remains competitive, for the CBS/Sony recording has attractively vivid and atmospheric sound, and this set also offers a generous coupling of Yvonne Minton's fine account of the *Orchestral songs*.

Music for chorus: *2 Canons; 3 Canons, Op. 28; Dreimal Tausend Jähre, Op. 50a; Friede auf Erden, Op. 13; 3 Folksongs, Op. 49; 3 German folksongs; Kol Nidrei, Op. 39; 4 Pieces, Op. 27; 6 Pieces, Op. 35; Psalm 130, Op. 50b; Modern Psalm No. 1, Op. 50 C; A Survivor from Warsaw, Op. 46.*
(M) *** Sony S2K 44571 (2) [id.]. John Shirley-Quirk, Günther Reich, BBC Singers, BBC SO, Pierre Boulez.

With passionately committed performances from the BBC Singers, this superb collection of choral music explodes any idea that Schoenberg was a cold composer. His adoption of an idiom far removed from abrasive atonality in most of these pieces makes this one of the most approachable of Schoenberg sets, with the use of a narrator in three of the works adding spice to the mixture. The later works, written in America, use twelve-note technique with astonishingly warm, rich results. First-rate recording. Translations are given of the full texts.

Pierrot lunaire, Op. 21 (see also above, under *The Book of the Hanging Gardens*).
(M) *** Chandos CHAN 6534 [id.]. Jane Manning, Nash Ens., Rattle – WEBERN: *Concerto.* ***

Jane Manning is outstanding among singers who have tackled this most taxing of works, steering a masterful course between the twin perils of, on the one hand, actually singing and, on the other, simply speaking; her sing-speech brings out the element of irony and darkly pointed wit that is an essential. Rattle draws strong, committed performances from the members of the Nash Ensemble and, apart from some intermittently odd balances, the sound is excellent.

OPERA

Moses und Aron.
*** Decca Dig. 414 264-2 (2) [id.]. Mazura, Langridge, Bonney, Haugland, Chicago Ch. and SO, Solti.

(i) *Moses und Aron* (complete); (ii) *Chamber Symphony No. 2, Op. 38.*
(M) *** Sony SM2K 48456 (2). (i) Reich, Cassilly, Palmer, Knight, BBC Singers, Orpheus Boys' Ch., BBC SO; (ii) Ens. InterContemporain; Boulez.

Solti gives Schoenberg's masterly score a dynamism and warmth which set it firmly – if perhaps surprisingly – in the grand romantic tradition, yet finds an element of fantasy and, in places – as in the *Golden Calf* episode – a sparkle such as you would never expect from Schoenberg. The Moses of Franz Mazura may not be as specific in his sing-speech as was Gunter Reich in the two previous versions – far less sing than speech – but the characterization of an Old Testament patriarch is the more convincing. As Aaron, Philip Langridge is lighter and more lyrical, as well as more accurate, than his predecessor with Boulez, Richard Cassilly. Aage Haugland with his firm, dark bass makes his mark in the small role of the Priest;

Barbara Bonney too is excellent as the Young Girl. Above all, the brilliant singing of the Chicago Symphony Chorus matches the playing of the orchestra in virtuosity. More than ever the question-mark concluding Act II makes a pointful close, with no feeling of a work unfinished. The brilliant recording has an even sharper focus on CD.

Pierre Boulez is helped not just by the passionately committed singing and playing (with Günter Reich expansive in his fully rounded characterization of Moses) but also by the rich, atmospheric recording, so that the operatic qualities are allowed to blossom. It is typical of Boulez that in the final scene Moses' mounting frustration in the face of the glib, articulate Aron is superbly built up, so that the final words – *O Wort, du Wort das mir fehlt* – come with a compelling sense of tragedy. Though the composer planned a third Act, such a moment makes a telling conclusion. Richard Cassilly makes a big-scaled Aron, a worthy brother-adversary to the central tragic figure. The *Second Chamber Symphony*, given an equally committed performance, follows the end of the opera to make a good bonus on the second CD.

Schreker, Franz (1878–1934)

(i) *Chamber symphony for 23 solo instruments;* (ii) *Nachtstück;* (i) *Prelude to a drama;* (ii) *Valse lente.*
**(*) Koch Int. Dig. CD 311 078. Berlin RSO, (i) Gielen, (ii) Rickenbacher.

Schreker's *Chamber symphony* is quite magical, scored with great delicacy and feeling for colour. The other works are not quite so seductive but they, too, have a heady art-nouveau atmosphere. A most rewarding disc, with good performances and very acceptable, though not out of the ordinary, recording. But don't miss this issue.

Die Gezeichneten (opera): complete.
(Y/B) *** Decca Dig. 444 442-2 (3) [id.]. Kruse, Connell, Pederson, Muff, Berlin R. Ch. & O, Zagrosek.
(Y/B) *(*) Marco Polo Dig. 8.223328/30 [id.]. Soloists, Dutch R. & TV Ch. & O, De Waart.

The opening prelude of this opera with its magic, shimmering sounds, using the most exotic orchestration, establishes the hothouse atmosphere of a story which in its melodrama can indeed be regarded as decadent, if hardly more so than Strauss's *Salome*. What Zagrosek's gloriously recorded version demonstrates is the range of atmospheric beauty in the score. Ripe echoes of composers from Scriabin to Puccini intensify the story of a dying woman painter, Carlotta, who deserts her faithful, ugly lover, Alviano, in favour of the physical love of Tamare, finally giving herself to him with fatal consequences. The Decca cast has no weak link, with Heinz Kruse fresh and clear-toned in the taxing tenor role of Alviano and Elizabeth Connell conveying with sharp clarity the positive yet vulnerable character of the heroine. Monte Pederson in cleanly focused singing conveys the animal quality of Tamare, while Alfred Muff is well contrasted as the older figure of Duke Adorno. Zagrosek draws dedicated playing and singing from the massive ensemble, and the beautifully balanced sound is of demonstration quality.

Irrelohe (opera; complete).
(N) *** Sony Dig. S2K 66850 (2) [id.]. Pabst, DeVol, Randová, V. Singverein, VSO, Gülke.

Ten years ago Schreker was barely represented on record, but now *Die Gezeichneten* and *Der Schatzgräber* are both available on CD. *Irrelohe* comes immediately after *Der Schatzgräber*, being first produced in 1924. Hailed after the First World War as the finest musical-dramatist after Wagner, Schreker was subjected to increasing denigration. His musical language is lush and overripe in the manner of Strauss and Puccini. The idiom is a cross between the Strauss of *Elektra* and Korngold, albeit with a higher norm of dissonance. *Irrelohe* was attacked by the press, but this was as much the result of resentment at his success and of growing anti-semitism. The opera is set in the eighteenth century. Count Heinrich (Michael Pabst) lives as a recluse in Irrelohe castle, fearing hereditary madness should he give way to sexual passion. His love for Eva (Luana DeVol) inspires the jealousy of her suitor, Peter, as well as the enmity of Christobald, whose own fiancée had been raped by Heinrich's father. Peter attempts to prevent their wedding but is killed in the ensuing struggle; in the meantime, Christobald sets fire to Irrelohe. (Echoes of Valhalla's fate in *Götterdämmerung*.) Eva finally sings of the redemptive power of love. Although Wolfgang Molkow's note speaks of it having 'quite an inventory of horror-film clichés', *Irrelohe* holds the listener almost from start to finish. The characters and the vocal lines are finely drawn and the orchestral sound is sumptuous. It is imaginative music, highly sophisticated in its use of the orchestra, but in a succession of effectively realized atmospheres rather than being strongly melodic in inspiration. There are inspired passages – the Prelude to Act III is one, though the Act is probably the least interesting musically. The performance under Peter Gülke is thoroughly committed and the cast is strong. The set derives from a concert performance at the Grosser Musikvereinsaal in Vienna and, although the singers are a bit forward, there is excellent orchestral detail. The break at the end of the first CD (in the middle of Act II, scene 8) is ugly. Those who know *Der Schatzgräber* will need no prompting to investigate this set. This *is* gripping and masterly stuff, and Schreker's score is well served by the cast, orchestra and all involved in this production.

Der Schatzgräber (opera): complete.
**(*) Capriccio Dig. 60010-2 (2) [id.]. Protschka, Schnaut, Stamm, Haage, Hamburg State O, Gerd
   Albrecht.

The attractions of Schreker's sweet-sour treatment of a curious morality fairy-story are fairly well conveyed in this first recording, made live at the Hamburg State Opera in 1989, though there are very few signs of the audience's presence, with no applause, even at the end. Josef Protschka sings powerfully as Elis, hardly ever over-strenuous, but Gabriele Schnaut finds it hard to scale down her very bright and powerful soprano and seems happiest when she is scything your ears with loud and often unsteady top notes; yet she is certainly dramatic in this equivocal role. Outstanding among the others is Peter Haage as the court jester. *Der Schatzgräber* may be hokum, but it is enjoyable hokum, and, with Albrecht drawing committed performances from the whole company, this well-made recording is most welcome.

Schröter, Johann (1752–88)

Piano concerto in C, Op. 3/3.
*** Sony Dig. MK 39222 [id.]. Murray Perahia, ECO – MOZART: *Piano concertos Nos. 1–3, K.107.* ***

Johann Samuel Schröter was a highly accomplished pianist, and this sparkling little *Concerto* explains why he was so successful. Murray Perahia gives it all his care and attention without overloading it with sophistication. His account is delightful in every way, and beautifully recorded.

Schubert, Franz (1797–1828)

Rondo in A for violin and strings, D.438.
*** EMI Dig. CDC7 49663-2 [id.]. Nigel Kennedy, ECO, Tate – BRUCH; MENDELSSOHN: *Concertos.*
   ***

The ideas in Schubert's *Rondo* flow very sweetly with Kennedy, making this an attractive bonus to the usual Bruch–Mendelssohn coupling.

Symphonies Nos. 1–6; 8–9.
**(*) Teldec/Warner Dig. 4509 91184-2 (4) [id.]. Concg. O, Harnoncourt.
(B) **(*) Nimbus Dig. NI 5270/3 [id.]. Hanover Band, Roy Goodman.

Symphonies Nos. 1–6; 8 (Unfinished); 9 (Great); Overtures: Fierabras; In the Italian style in C; Des Teufels Lustschloss.
(B) **(*) Decca 430 773-2 (4). VPO, István Kertész.

Symphonies Nos. 1–6; 8–9; Grand Duo in C, D.812 (orch. Joachim); *Rosamunde overture (Die Zauberharfe), D.644.*
*** DG Dig. 423 651-2 (5) [id.]. COE, Abbado.

Symphonies Nos. 1 in D, D.82; 4 in C (Tragic), D.417; Overture in the Italian style in C, D.591.
(Y/B) *** Teldec/Warner Dig. 4509 97509-2 [id.]. Concg. O, Harnoncourt.

Symphonies Nos. 2 in B flat, D.125; 6 in C, D.589.
(Y/B) ** Teldec/Warner Dig. 4509 97510-2 [id.]. Concg. O, Harnoncourt.

Symphonies Nos. 3 in D, D.200; 5 in B flat, D.485; 8 in B min. (Unfinished).
(Y/B) *** Teldec/Warner Dig. 4509 97511-2 [id.]. Concg. O, Harnoncourt.

Symphony No. 9 in C (Great), D.944.
(Y/B) **(*) Teldec/Warner Dig. 4509 97512-2 [id.]. Concg. O, Harnoncourt.

(i) *Symphonies Nos. 1 in D, D.82; 2 in B flat, D.125; 3 in D, D.200; 4 in C min. (Tragic), D.417; Overtures in the Italian style Nos. 1 in D; 2 in C, D.590/1;* (ii) *Overtures: in B flat, D.470; in E min., D.648.*
(N) (B) **(*) Ph. Duo 446 536-2 (2) [id.]. (i) Dresden State O, Sawallisch; (ii) LPO, Leppard.

Symphonies Nos. 5 in B flat, D.485; 6 in C, D.589; 8 in B min. (Unfinished); 9 in C (Great).
(N) (B) **(*) Ph. Duo 446 539-2 (2) [id.]. Dresden State O, Sawallisch.

Abbado's is an outstanding set. Rarely has he made recordings of the central Viennese classics which find him so naturally sunny and warm in his expression. Speeds are often on the fast side but never feel breathless, and the recording is refined, with fine bloom on the string-sound. Textually too, the Abbado set takes precedence over its rivals and there are certain fascinating differences from what we are used to. The five CDs are now also available separately – see below.

Kertész began with Nos. 8 and 9 and the overtures (which are well worth having), and these two symphonies are the finest performances in the cycle. The *Ninth* is fresh, dramatic and often very exciting, the *Unfinished* highly imaginative and comparably dramatic in its wide dynamic contrasts. In the two early symphonies Kertész scores with the spirited VPO playing and a light touch, and this also applies to Nos. 3 and 6, even if they are without the last ounce of character and distinction. The playing of the VPO is beyond reproach throughout, and it has a pervading freshness, helped by the transparent yet full Decca sound.

It is a pity that Harnoncourt in his Schubert cycle did not turn to the Chamber Orchestra of Europe instead of to the Concertgebouw. Had he done so, it would have been even more fascinating to compare Harnoncourt's Schubert with Abbado's, also featuring the COE. As it is, Harnoncourt takes a relatively severe view, and significantly he is at his finest in the darkness of the *Tragic Symphony*. There is little of Schubertian charm here, with his eccentrically slow tempo for the finale of No. 6 in its lumbering gait missing the pure sunlight of the piece. Echoing period practice, Harnoncourt's preference for short phrasing also tends to make slow movements less songful, though equally it adds to the bite and intensity of other movements, notably Scherzos with their sharp cross-rhythms. Not that any reservations detract seriously from a most refreshing cycle, direct and unmannered. Though the reverberance of the Amsterdam Concertgebouw hall obscures detail in tuttis, as well as reinforcing the weight of sound, the recording is warm and otherwise helpful. Harnoncourt, like Abbado, has used specially prepared texts, but they avoid the radical changes that spice the Abbado set. The two Harnoncourt discs to go for are the pairing of the *Tragic* with No. 1 and the generous triptych of Nos. 3, 5 and the *Unfinished*. No. 1 is given a very strong performance and sounds more mature than usual, though the *Andante* has no lack of grace, and the same comment might be applied to Nos. 3 and 5. The *Allegretto* of the *D major Symphony* is not pointed as wittily as with Beecham, but it still has charm. The *Unfinished* brings evocative atmosphere combined with high drama, and all these works show Harnoncourt at his most characterful; moreover Harnoncourt and his players obviously relish the Rossinian touches in the *Italian overture* which comes as an encore to the superb account of the *Tragic Symphony*. Like the *Fifth Symphony*, the overture sounds relatively weighty but has plenty of zest and a brilliant close.

As in his Beethoven cycle, also recorded for Nimbus, Goodman draws lively, beautifully sprung performances of the Schubert symphonies from the players of the Hanover Band. For anyone wanting period performances of these works, they can be warmly recommended as a mid-priced set, with the reservation that the characteristic Nimbus balance is more damaging here than it is in Beethoven. The strings are attractively caught in a warm acoustic, but the reverberation tends to obscure detail in tuttis, with the woodwind set so far backwards that it is often barely audible, and even the rasp of the natural horns is underplayed. Nos. 1 and 4 (*Tragic*) have also been issued separately on NI 5158, and the *Unfinished* is available coupled with the *Overture and incidental music from Rosamunde* (NI 5274), both at full price.

The price of the Sawallisch set is very competitive indeed, and the late-1960s recording is of Philips's best Dresden quality, full, weighty and resonant without undue clouding, while the strings and woodwind have plenty of bloom. Where Sawallisch excels is in the way he can command attention with the gentlest pianissimo at the beginning of a movement; when all but two of the symphonies (Nos. 5 and 8) have slow introductions, and even the *Unfinished* has its introductory phrase, that is very important. It is characteristic that in the *Unfinished* Sawallisch's tempi for both movements are very slow, but they are beautifully sustained by the hushed intensity of the playing, and it is the same in the sustained tread of the first movement of the *Ninth*. Here Sawallisch's reading is both dramatic and refreshingly direct, and the range of sonority commanded by the Dresden orchestra is heard at its most impressive, particularly in the beautifully played *Andante*, while the finale has fine impetus. What the conductor proves again and again in the mature symphonies is his mastery in pointing a Schubert phrase without seeming to do so and without blunting its essential simplicity. Because of this, the *Fifth* is a most endearing performance, warm and graceful yet with plenty of vigour in the last two movements. Where Sawallisch is rather less successful is in conveying the high spirits of the very early symphonies. His accounts of Nos. 1 and 2 could be lighter and fresher, although finales go with a swing. But by No. 3 conductor and orchestra are working very happily together and the playing is stylish and elegant, the *Allegretto* very winning. By comparison the first movement of the *Tragic* is weighty and No. 6 is by no means lightweight either, although the *Andante* is graceful and the Scherzo bursts with energy. However, comparison with Kertész in the earlier symphonies is by no means to Sawallisch's disadvantage, and in the later works the Dresden sound undoubtedly brings an added gravitas. The first of the two Philips Duos includes the pair of engaging *Overtures in the Italian style*, of which the first, in its introduction, quotes the lovely lyrical tune also used by Schubert in his *Rosamunde (Die Zauberharfe) overture*, although with its contour slightly different. Two other overtures, almost completely unknown, are admirably played by Leppard and the LPO, making a useful bonus as all four make a natural link with the spirit of one or other of the symphonies.

Symphonies Nos. 1–3; 4 (Tragic); 5–7; 8 (Unfinished); 9 in C (Great); 10 in D, D.936a; Symphonic fragments in D, D.615 and D.708a (completed and orch. Newbould).
*** Ph. Dig. 412 176-2 (6) [id.]. ASMF, Marriner.

Marriner's excellent set gathers together not only the eight symphonies of the regular canon but two more symphonies now 'realized', thanks to the work of Professor Brian Newbould of Hull University. For full measure, half a dozen fragments of other symphonic movements are also included, orchestrated by Professor Newbould. The set brings sparkling examples of the Academy's work at its finest, while the bigger challenges of the *Unfinished* (here completed with Schubert's Scherzo filled out and the *Rosamunde B minor Entr'acte* used as finale) and the *Great C major* are splendidly taken. These are fresh, direct readings, making up in rhythmic vitality for any lack of weight. The recordings, all digital, present consistent refinement and undistractingly good balance. But this set now seems expensive.

Symphonies Nos. 1 in D, D.82; 2 in B flat, D.125.
*** DG Dig. 423 652-2 [id.]. COE, Abbado.
(Y/B) (BB) **(*) Naxos Dig. 8.553093 [id.]. Failoni O of Budapest, Michael Halász.

The coupling of the two earliest *Symphonies* on DG brings bright and sparkling performances, reflecting the youthful joy of both composer and players. Abbado brings out the sunny relaxation of the writing, most exhilaratingly of all in the light-hearted finales. The recording of both captures the refined playing of the COE very vividly.

Michael Halász and the Failoni Orchestra are affectionately easy-going rather than overtly dramatic, but they play both these works most winningly, finding all the delicacy of Schubert's inspiration. The recording too is full and naturally balanced, and one's only reservation is that the resonance of the Italian Institute in Budapest makes the tuttis spread and lose some of the sharpness of focus. But this is a most enjoyable disc nevertheless and well worth its modest cost.

Symphony No. 3 in D, D.200.
*** RCA Dig. 09026 61876-2. N. German RSO, Wand – SCHUMANN: *Symphony No. 3.* ***

Günter Wand's Schubert *D major* is eminently acceptable: very well played and vital, though 56 minutes for a full-price CD is not particularly generous these days. The recording, made at the Musikhalle in Hamburg, has warmth and presence. Not a first recommendation, perhaps, but worth three stars.

Symphonies Nos. 3 in D, D.200; 4 in C min. (Tragic), D.417.
*** DG Dig. 423 653-2 [id.]. COE, Abbado.

Crisp, fast and light, No. 3 is given a delectable performance by Abbado. In No. 4, the *Tragic*, Abbado makes the slow C minor introduction bitingly mysterious before a clean, elegant *Allegro*, and with this conductor the other movements are also elegant and polished as well as strong. Textually, No. 4 eliminates the extra bars in the slow movement which had been inserted originally by Brahms. The slow movement is outstandingly beautiful, with the oboe solo – presumably COE's Douglas Boyd – most tenderly expressive.

Symphonies Nos. 3 in D, D.200; 5 in B flat, D.485; 6 in C, D.589.
⊛ (M) *** EMI CDM7 69750-2. RPO, Beecham.

Beecham's are magical performances in which every phrase breathes. There is no substitute for imaginative phrasing and each line is shaped with affection and spirit. The *Allegretto* of the *Third Symphony* is an absolute delight. The delicacy of the opening of the *Fifth* is matched by the simple lyrical beauty of the *Andante*, while few conductors have been as persuasive as Beecham in the *Sixth* 'little' *C major Symphony*. The sound is now just a shade drier in Nos. 3 and 6 than in their last LP incarnation but is generally faithful and spacious. This is an indispensable record for all collections and a supreme bargain in the Schubert discography.

Symphonies Nos. 3 in D, D.200; 6 in C, D.589.
(Y/B) (BB) *** Naxos Dig. 8.553094 [id.]. Failoni O of Budapest, Michael Halász.

These are entirely delightful performances, fully capturing the innocent charm of these youthful symphonies. The Failoni strings play with airy grace and the woodwind bring a similar delicacy of colour to their solos and gentle chording. Michael Halász is most sensitive and in the *Allegretto* second movement of No. 3 – Schubert at his most endearingly ingenuous – the conductor's style is Beechamesque in its affectionate elegance. The economy of Schubert's scoring means that the resonant acoustic affects the clarity of the tuttis only marginally and it certainly lends an attractive bloom to the proceedings.

Symphonies Nos. 3 in D, D.200; 8 in B min. (Unfinished), D.759.
(M) *** Carlton Classics Dig. PCD 848 [id.]. City of L. Sinfonia, Hickox.

Hickox's coupling makes a first-rate bargain recommendation on the Carlton IMP label. These are fresh and direct readings, never putting a foot wrong, very well recorded, with a chamber orchestra sounding full and substantial. Others may find more individuality and charm, but the crisp resilience of the playing is consistently winning.

Symphony No. 4 in C min. (Tragic), D.417; Grand duo in C, D.812 (orch. Joachim).
(Y/B) (BB) **(*) Naxos 8.553095 [id.]. Failoni O of Budapest, Michael Halász.

Halász presents the *Tragic Symphony* – Schubert himself gave the work its title – sympathetically and, though this is not a strongly dramatic reading, the resonant acoustic adds a certain weight, and the *Andante* is warmly and expressively played. This inexpensive disc is valuable for its coupling, the orchestration of the large-scale *Grand Duo* for piano duet, written in 1824 and orchestrated by the violinist Josef Joachim. The work is convincingly played, with gravitas and freshness nicely balanced. The warm resonancy of the Budapest Italian Institute suits this work very well.

Symphonies Nos. 4 in C min. (Tragic); 5 in B flat; Rosamunde overture.
(N) (M) **(*) DG 449 099-2 [id.]. BPO, Karl Boehm.

A good (if, in the last analyisis, not outstanding) version of the *Tragic* from Boehm, with splendid, disciplined playing from the Berlin Philharmonic, who are recorded well, if resonantly. The *Fifth* is a different matter, the first movement wonderfully light and relaxed; the slow movement, though also relaxed, never seems to outstay its welcome, and in the last two movements the Berlin playing makes for power as well as lightness. The *Rosamunde overture* tops off a generally enjoyable disc.

(i) *Symphonies Nos. 4 (Tragic); 8 (Unfinished);* (ii) *9 in C (Great).*
(N) (BB) ** EMI Seraphim CES5 68534-2 (2). (i) VPO, Kubelik; (ii) Hallé O, Barbirolli (with BRAHMS: *Variations on a theme by Haydn:* VPO, Barbirolli ***).

Here is a case where a super-bargain two-disc set falls down seriously by the mis-matching of performances of an entirely different calibre. Barbirolli's 1966 account of the *Great C major Symphony* is a warm, lyrical reading, with its speeds perfectly chosen to solve all the notorious interpretative traps with the minimum of fuss. The Hallé playing may miss the last degree of polish but it is far more important that the Barbirollian magic is conveyed at its most intense. Barbirolli is completely consistent and although, characteristically, he may always indulge in affectionate phrasing, he is usually steady in maintaining tempi broadly throughout each movement. The second subject of the first movement, for example, brings no 'gear-change' but equally no sense of the music being forced; and again with the tempo changes at the end of the movement, Barbirolli's solution is very satisfying. The recording is full and vivid, as it is in the coupled Brahms *St Anthony variations*, where the VPO playing is first class and Barbirolli is again at his finest. Alas, the only thing to praise on the second of these paired CDs is the warm and pleasing sound. Kubelik's VPO performance of the *Tragic Symphony* opens dramatically enough and is well played, but there is an element of routine throughout until the temperature picks up in the finale. The *Unfinished* is even more run-of-the-mill, lapsing into downright dullness in the second movement.

Symphony No. 5 in B flat, D.485.
(N) (M) *** DG 447 433-2 [id.]. VPO, Boehm – BEETHOVEN: *Symphony No. 6.* ***
(Y/B) (M) *** RCA 09026 61793-2 [id.]. Chicago SO, Fritz Reiner (with MENDELSSOHN: *Hebrides overture* ***) – BRAHMS: *Symphony No. 3.* ***

Boehm's recording of the *Fifth Symphony* dates from the very end of his career. In his eighties he preferred a tauter, more incisive view than he had given in his 1967 Berlin performance, weightier, but still with a light rhythmic touch, while the slow movement is not lacking grace. The finale is strong and purposeful and this is Boehm at his finest, with superbly polished and responsive VPO playing in repertoire they know and love. The 1980 recording is full and warm, taken from a live performance at the Hohenems Schubertiade, and rightly reissued now in DG's 'Legendary Recordings' series of 'Originals'.

Reiner's is a most attractive performance, brightly and clearly recorded, yet with a glowing ambience. This reading of No. 5, essentially sunny and with an easy-going *Andante*, brings a strongly vigorous finale, following a third movement where Reiner indulges the trio with an affectionate rallentando. Mendelssohn's famous Hebridean overture comes as an exciting encore: its storm has seldom sounded more dramatic, yet the lyrical warmth is not missed. Again, fresh sound.

Symphonies Nos. 5 in B flat, D.485; 6 in C, D.589.
*** DG Dig. 423 654-2 [id.]. COE, Abbado.

Abbado brings out the happy songfulness of the slow movements in these works, as well as the rhythmic resilience of the *Allegros*. As in No. 4, so also in No. 6 Abbado eliminates the extra bars added by Brahms in his original Schubert Edition. Excellent recording, with fine bloom and good, natural contrasts.

Symphonies Nos. 5 in B flat, D.485; 6 in C, D.589; 8 in B min. (Unfinished).
(Y/B) (M) (***) Dutton Lab. mono CDLX 7014 [id.]. LPO, Sir Thomas Beecham.

Sir Thomas Beecham's legendary earlier Schubert recordings were made in 1937 (the *Unfinished*), 1939 (No. 5) and 1944 (No. 5), with the LPO. No. 5 was always greatly admired; No. 6, recorded when Beecham returned to England from America, apparently brought ensemble problems and a number of re-takes, but the results in the end were well up to form. The *Unfinished*, as dramatic as it is seamless, is surely among the greatest of all recordings of this much-recorded symphony. The ear is astonished by the breadth of dynamic range possible in the 78–r.p.m. era and the warmth of the sound overall, recorded at Abbey Road or Kingsway Hall (No. 5). The documentation observes in No. 5: 'second movement swish as on original master', but the surface background generally is so diminished by the CEDAR process that it ceases to be a consideration.

Symphonies Nos. 5 in B flat, D.485; 8 in B min., (Unfinished).
(N) (M) *** Sony Bruno Walter Edition SMK 64487 [id.]. Columbia SO or NYPO, Walter (with: BEETHOVEN: *Overture Leonora No. 3* ***).

Bruno Walter brings special qualities of warmth and lyricism to the *Unfinished*. Affection, gentleness and humanity are the keynotes of this performance; while the first movement of the *Fifth* is rather measured, there is much loving attention to detail in the *Andante*. The 1961 recording emerges fresh and glowing in its CD format and, like the rest of the Walter series, completely belies its age. The sound is richly expansive as well as clear, and the CD is in every way satisfying.

Symphonie Nos. 5 in B flat, D.485; 8 in B min., (Unfinished); Overtures: In the Italian style in C; Rosamunde (Die Zauberharfe).
(N) (B) ** Decca Eclipse Dig. 448 707-2; *448 707-4* [id.]. San Francisco SO, Blomstedt.

Blomstedt seldom disappoints, but his account of the *Fifth*, played on a chamber scale with plenty of finesse, nevertheless lacks Schubertian charm. The *Unfinished*, too, is relatively uneventful until the second movement, when at last the performance begins to glow luminously. Nothing wrong with the overtures or the excellent Decca recording, but this remains a coupling that for the most part fails to be memorable, at least partly the result of the weighty sound.

Symphonies Nos. 5 in B flat, D.485; 9 in C, D.944 (The Great).
(M) (**) RCA mono GD 60291 [60291-2-RG]. NBC SO, Toscanini.

In his 1947 performance of No. 9, Toscanini is tauter and faster than either his earlier or later recording. A useful antidote for it serves to remind one that Schubert was still a young man when this was composed with what was a bright future ahead and that the valedictory halo which came to surround it was a nineteenth-century phenomenon.

Symphonies Nos. (i) 6 in C; (ii) 9 in C (Great).
(N) (M) **(*) Mercury 434 354-2 [id.]. (i) LSO, Schmidt-Isserstedt; (ii) Minneapolis SO, Skrowaczewski.

A unique coupling of the two C major symphonies – each completely different in character – and two most interesting readings. One could not mistake this account of the *Sixth* as a Beecham performance – Schmidt-Isserstedt is after all a more deliberately matter-of-fact conductor. But helped by the warm, glowing ambience of Watford Town Hall, which in turn underlines the bubbling gaiety of the work, all is joy until the finale, when one does perhaps begin to feel the *Allegro moderato* to be a little too moderate. In the *Ninth* Skrowaczewski is attractively straightforward and animated. He manages to maintain a steady speed through the whole of the coda in the first movement without sounding ruthless and, after a sympathetic *Andante*, the Scherzo and finale have compelling impetus. This performance certainly fills an interpretative gap and and again reveals the strength of the conductor's personality. The 1961 Minneapolis recording is full-bodied but (as so often in the Northtrop Auditorium) the violins are made to sound fierce.

'*The essential Schubert':* (i) *Symphonies Nos. 8 in B min. (Unfinished), D.759; 9 in C (Great) D.944;* (ii; iii) *Piano quintet in A (Trout), D.667;* (ii) *Impromptu in G flat, D.899/3; Moment musical, D.780/3; Rosamunde:* (iv) *Jägerchor; Ballet music in G.* Lieder: (v) *An Sylvia;* (vi) *Ave Maria;* (vii) *Die Forelle;* (v) *Heidenröslein.*
(N) (B) *** Decca Double Analogue/Dig. 444 546-2 (2) [id.]. (i) VPO, Solti; (ii) Clifford Curzon; (iii) V. Octet (members); (iv) V. State Op. Ch., VPO, Münchinger; (v) Hermann Prey, Karl Engel; (vi) Leontyne Price, VPO, Karajan; (vii) Gabriele Fontana, György Fischer.

Whatever constitutes the 'essential' Schubert (and there is a great deal more of it than can be included on a pair of CDs), the *Unfinished* and *Great C major Symphonies* are certainly indispensable, and Solti does these marvellous works full justice. Both bring superb VPO playing. The *Unfinished* has great concentration and atmosphere and there are few accounts of No. 9 that are more glowingly resilient, lyrically fresh and sunny, yet with plenty of drama. The Decca recording too is outstanding in its richness and detail. Clifford Curzon's vintage recording of the *Trout* is hardly less distinguished, a good-natured reading with an admirable rapport between the pianist and the excellent Viennese players. Again vigour and freshness go hand in hand. The recording is beautifully balanced and has a pleasingly warm ambience. Curzon's performances of the most beautiful of Schubert's *Impromptus* and a favourite *Moment musical* are hardly less winning, while Hermann Prey and Gabriele Fontana (who is delightfully innocent-sounding in *Die Forelle*) give fine accounts of three famous songs. The inclusion of the *Hunting chorus* from *Rosamunde* alongside the familiar *Ballet music* is a pleasant surprise and, if so much else is missing (notably the *String quintet* and great final *Piano sonata in B flat*), this is still a thoroughly worthwhile set in its own right, playing for 148 minutes.

Symphony No. 8 in B min. (Unfinished), D.759.
(Y/B) ❀ (M) *** DG Dig. 445 514-2 [id.]. Philh. O, Sinopoli – MENDELSSOHN: *Symphony No. 4 (Italian).* ***
(Y/B) *** DG Dig. 439 862-2 [id.]. NY Met. O, Levine – BEETHOVEN: *Symphony No.3.* ***
(M) *** DG 415 848-2 [id.]. BPO, Karajan – MENDELSSOHN: *Symphony No. 4.* ***

Sinopoli secures the most ravishingly refined and beautiful playing; the orchestral blend, particularly of the woodwind and horns, is magical. It is a deeply concentrated reading of the *Unfinished*, bringing out much unexpected detail, with every phrase freshly turned in seamless spontaneity. The contrast, as Sinopoli sees it, is between the dark – yet never histrionic – tragedy of the first movement, relieved only partially by the lovely second subject, and the sunlight of the closing movement, giving an unforgettable, gentle radiance. The exposition repeat is observed, adding weight and substance. This takes its place among the recorded classics. The warmly atmospheric recording, made in Kingsway Hall, is very impressive.

Levine in his strong, dramatic reading demonstrates the prowess of his own opera orchestra in the regular orchestral repertory. After the sombre opening motif, the brightness of the first subject leads on to a performance full of bold contrasts, with the crescendo at the beginning of the development bringing a frisson of excitement, as a live performance would. Full-bodied sound, set against greater reverberance than you normally find in Manhattan Center recordings. A good recommendation for anyone wanting this in the attractive and generous but unusual coupling with Beethoven's *Eroica.*

Karajan's 1965 DG recording of the *Unfinished* sounds fresher still in remastered form. Its merits of simplicity and directness are enhanced by the extraordinary polish of the orchestral playing, lighting up much that is often obscured. The first movement is extremely compelling in its atmosphere; the slow movement too brings tinglingly precise attack and a wonderful sense of drama.

Symphony No. 8 in B min. (Unfinished); Grand Duo in C, D.812 (orch. Joachim).
*** DG Dig. 423 655-2 [id.]. COE, Abbado.

Abbado's outstandingly refined and sensitive version comes with an unusual and valuable coupling, the orchestral arrangement of the piano-duet *Grand Duo* made by Joachim, once erroneously thought to be the missing *Symphony No. 7.* The second subject in the *Unfinished* brings some slightly obtrusive agogic hesitations at the beginning of each phrase; but with such responsive playing they quickly sound fresh and natural.

Symphonies Nos. 8 (Unfinished); 9 in C (Great).
(N) (B) *** DG 439 475-2 [id.]. BPO, Karl Boehm.
(M) **(*) Sony SBK 48268; *SBT 48268* [id.]. Cleveland O, Szell.
(M) **(*) EMI CDM7 64628-2 [id.]. BPO, Karajan.
(N) (M) **(*) Erato/Warner Dig. 4509 99611-2 (2). Lyon Op. O, Gardiner.
(Y/B) ** DG Dig. 437 689-2 [id.]. Dresden State O, Sinopoli.

Boehm's mid-1960s version of the *Unfinished Symphony* with the Berlin Philharmonic combines deep sensitivity and great refinement, and the points of detail as well as the overall warmth keep this version among the very finest on record. The opening of the development – always a key point – is magically done, and, throughout, the superb recording quality gives unusual clarity while allowing the Berlin Philharmonic ensemble its natural opulence. Boehm's performance of the *Ninth*, recorded three years earlier, stands in the lyrical Furtwängler tradition rather than in the forceful Toscanini stream, but it is the balance between the conflicting interests in this symphony which distinguishes Boehm's reading. His modification of tempo in the various sections of the first movement is masterly in its finesse, often so subtle that it requires close attention to spot it. In the slow movement, the rhythmic spring to the repeated quavers is delectable, with the Berlin players really on their toes. Nor is there any lack of drama in the performance, for the playing is marvellous throughout. Only in the finale, taken rather fast, is the playing slightly less gripping, and even there one has excitement in plenty. The recording is very good indeed and in its CD transfer sounds fresh, warm and full. An outstanding reissue – this is surely a coupling that deserved a place in DG's 'Legendary Performances' series; at Classikon price it is a real bargain.

Szell's, too, is a splendid performance of the *Unfinished*, strong yet sensitive. Phrasing and general discipline are so immaculate, one would expect the result to seem cold but, on the contrary, Szell never lacks warmth here, and drama and beauty walk hand in hand in the second movement. Apart from the lack of a real pianissimo, the 1960 recording is very good for its time. The *Ninth* dates from the previous year. Szell's control of tempo in the first movement brings a convincing onward flow, and the performance is notable for the alertness and rhythmic energy of the playing, yet there is no lack of resilience in the *Andante*. The Scherzo has great brio and leads naturally to the brilliant finale, where few rivals can match the precision of the hectic triplet rhythms. The sound is fuller in this remastered form than it was originally on LP, although the finale is a little lacking in weight, especially in the closing pages.

Karajan recorded a complete set of Schubert *Symphonies* for EMI towards the end of the 1970s and its culmination came, not in No. 9, but in the *Unfinished*, which, with Berlin refinement at its most ethereal, has an other-worldly quality, rapt and concentrated. The *Great C major* is compelling too, but here some may find that the reverberant acoustic gives the impression of too much weightiness. But this is not a superficial reading: it has plenty of impetus and power, while the *Andante* has freshness too. The finale has undoubted thrust, although tuttis bring a degree of heaviness, caused as much by the sound itself as by the playing.

Gardiner made these recordings in 1986 and 1987, before he had espoused the cause of original instruments. In the opening movement of the *Great C major* he negotiates all the problems inherent in the tempo changes with consummate ease: indeed the coda of the first movement is particularly satisfying. The *Andante* is certainly *con moto* but is elegantly handled, and it is surprising, considering that the performance was recorded live, that the reading overall lacks the last degree of compulsive zest, although the warm acoustic does tend to blunt some of its attack and the bite of the modern string instruments. The resonance suits the *Unfinished*, which is most impressive and dramatic, yet with the second movement glowingly lyrical. But one feels that this is not Gardiner's last word on either symphony.

Sinopoli recorded the *Unfinished* before, with the Philharmonia, in an exceptionally spacious, intense reading (see above). The 1992 Dresden recording is not only markedly faster, the speeds are more flexible and Sinopoli's observance of dynamic markings is also freer. Nevertheless the radiant playing of the Dresden orchestra helps to make it convincing, but in the *Great C major* the instability of tempo is more damaging to overall cohesiveness. The result lacks the strength and purposefulness of the finest readings.

Symphony No. 9 in C (Great), D.944.
(N) (M) *** Virgin Veritas/EMI Dig. VER5 61245-2 [id.]. O of Age of Enlightenment, Mackerras.
(M) *** Decca 430 747-2 [id.]. VPO, Solti.
(N) (M) (***) DG mono 447 439-2 [id.]. BPO, Furtwängler – HAYDN: *Symphony No. 88.* (***) ✸
(N) (B) *** EMI forte CZS5 69364-2 (2) [id.]. Cleveland O, George Szell – BEETHOVEN: *Symphony No. 7* *** ✸; ROSSINI: *Overtures.* **(*)

**(*) EMI Dig. CDC7 49949-2. L. Classical Players, Norrington.
(Y/B) (BB) *(*) Naxos Dig. 8.553096 [id.]. Failoni O of Budapest, Michael Halász.

Symphony No. 9 in C (Great); Rosamunde: Overture (Die Zauberharfe), D.644.
*** DG Dig. 423 656-2 [id.]. COE, Abbado.

Symphony No. 9 in C (Great); Rosamunde: Overture; Ballet music; Entr'acte No. 3.
(N) (M) **(*) Bruno Walter Edition: Sony SMK 64478 [id.]. Columbia SO, Bruno Walter.

Symphony No. 9 in C (Great); Rosamunde: Overture; Entr'acte No. 2; Ballet No. 2.
(N) (M) **(*) DG Dig. 445 559-2 [id.]. Chicago SO, James Levine.

Symphony No. 9 in C (Great); Rosamunde: Ballet music Nos. 1–2.
(N) (B) (***) Dutton Lab. mono CDEA 5003 [id.]. LSO, Bruno Walter – HAYDN: *Symphony No. 92.*
(***)

Though the COE is by definition an orchestra of chamber scale, the weight of Abbado's version, taken from his complete cycle, is ample, while allowing extra detail to be heard, thanks also to the orchestra's outstandingly crisp ensemble. Speeds are very well chosen, and the expressive detail is consistently made to sound natural. This version is important too for including textual amendments, and the Scherzo has four extra bars that were originally cut by Brahms in his early edition. The sound is beautifully refined, to match the point and polish of the playing. The *Rosamunde* (*Zauberharfe*) *overture* makes a valuable and generous fill-up.

In the first recording to use period instruments, Sir Charles Mackerras and the Orchestra of the Age of Enlightenment on the Virgin Classics label give a winning performance, one that will delight both those who prefer conventional performance and devotees of the new authenticity. The characterful rasp and bite of period brass instruments and the crisp attack of timpani are much more striking than any thinness of string-tone. It is a performance of outstanding freshness and resilience. With every single repeat observed, the heavenly length is joyfully as well as powerfully sustained and the warm, atmospheric recording gives a fine sense of presence. Now at mid-price, it is even more recommendable.

Sir George Solti is not the first conductor one thinks of as a Schubertian, but the *Great C major symphony* prompted him to one of the happiest and most glowing of all his many records, an outstanding version, beautifully paced and sprung in all four movements and superbly played and recorded. Now reissued at mid-price, this is an unbeatable bargain and would be first choice, irrespective of cost, for I.M.

Coupled with a unique version of Haydn's *Symphony No. 88*, also recorded in the Jesus-Christus Kirche in Berlin, this makes a perfect candidate for reissue in DG's 'Legendary Performances' series. As with the Haydn, Furtwängler gives the *Great C major* a glowing performance, if a highly individual one. The first movement brings an outstanding example of his wizardry, when he takes the recapitulation at quite a different speed from the exposition and still makes it sound convincing. In the beautifully played *Andante*, his very slow tempo is yet made resilient by fine rhythmic pointing. The mono recording dates from 1951 and the sound is remarkably fresh and very well balanced, with the dynamic range in the slow movement strikingly wide.

Szell's Cleveland account was his second in stereo with that orchestra (the first is discussed above, paired with the *Unfinished*). It was made in Severance Hall by an EMI team led by Peter Andry and – although subsequently issued on the CBS Epic label – it has the hallmarks of an HMV recording from the beginning of the 1970s, with a wider dynamic range than Szell usually enjoyed and better overall balancing. It sounds remarkably good in this new CD transfer. Szell's powerful reading provides a reminder that the parallels between him and another great disciplinarian conductor, Toscanini, were sometimes significant. Szell's approach is similarly direct, but lyrical feeling underlies the surface brightness and the crisply sprung rhythms are exhilarating. With superb playing from the Cleveland Orchestra the result is certainly dramatic, and the seemingly spontaneous return of the opening horn tune in the coda of the first movement is manipulated with masterly skill. The slow movement is refreshingly unindulgent but by no means without warmth. But it is in the hectic triplets of the finale that the orchestra is unmatched in precision, with a sparkling lightness of articulation that is a joy to the ear.

Bruno Walter's classic account of the *Great C major*, recorded in London in September 1938, enjoyed great celebrity in the 1940s and early 1950s, and is in many respects a more vital performance than his later version for CBS/Sony, enjoyable though that is. The cosily charming Walter glows from the *G major Rosamunde ballet*, but the vitality and resilience of allegros in the *Great C major* are what really strike the listener. Walter's relaxed tempos and expressive phrasing in the slow movement seem just right, with the speed variations in the first movement far less free than with many conductors since. Excellent transfers. A fine addition to the new Dutton bargain-price series.

Roger Norrington's version is by far the most provocative of the period-performance versions of the *Great C major*. The first movement brings splendid snap and swagger, exhilaratingly presented with Mendelssohnian lightness. But it will take most listeners some time to adjust to the total absence of the usual slowings in the final coda, which here sounds perfunctory. Yet in his crisp, brisk reading of the slow movement Norrington does allow himself a relaxation in the cello melody after the big climax, rightly so. Only in the finale is the speed relatively conventional, with triplets clarified. All repeats are observed, even those in the da capo return of the Scherzo.

Bruno Walter's 1959 CBS recording has been impressively enhanced on CD; the warm ambience of the sound – yet with no lack of rasp on the trombones – seems ideal for his very relaxed reading. The performance has less grip than Furtwängler's, while Solti shows greater spontaneity; but in the gentler passages there are many indications of Walter's mastery, not least in the lovely playing at the introduction of the second subject of the *Andante*. There is much to admire, even if this never quite achieves the distinction of the conductor's earlier recordings of this symphony. Needless to say, the *Rosamunde* music makes an endearing bonus.

Levine conducts a refined performance, beautifully played and excellently recorded, which is commendably free from mannerism yet which may on that account seem under-characterized. He omits the exposition repeats in the outer movements (just as was universally done until recently). Conversely, all the repeats in the Scherzo are observed, which unbalances the structure.

The *Ninth* is the one disappointment of the Halász Naxos cycle. His control of tempo in the first movement is not always convincing, and the *Andante* does not avoid a suspicion of routine. The Scherzo goes well, but the conductor's grip on the finale is not always taut enough, and the listener is made conscious of its length.

CHAMBER AND INSTRUMENTAL MUSIC

Arpeggione sonata, D.821 (arr. for cello) (see also under *Trout quintet*).
*** Ph. Dig. 412 230-2 [id.]. Maisky, Argerich – SCHUMANN: *Fantasiestücke* etc. ***
(Y/B) (M) **(*). Decca 443 575-2 [id.]. Rostropovich, Britten – BRIDGE: *Cello sonata.* ***
(Y/B) **(*) EMI Dig. CDC5 55166-2 [id.]. Caussé, Duchable – BEETHOVEN: *Notturno;* REINECKE: *Fantasiestücke.* ***

Mischa Maisky and Martha Argerich make much more of the *Arpeggione sonata* than any of their rivals. Their approach may be relaxed, but they bring much pleasure through their variety of colour and sensitivity. The Philips recording is in the very best traditions of the house.

Rostropovich gives a curiously self-indulgent interpretation of Schubert's slight but amiable *Arpeggione sonata*. The playing of both artists is eloquent and it is beautifully recorded, but it will not be to all tastes. However, the 1968 recording is particularly valuable for its coupling of the Bridge *Sonata*. The reissue is part of Decca's Classic Sound series.

Gérard Caussé gives a refined account of the *Arpeggione sonata* with François-René Duchable. His viola sounds closer to the original instrument than does the modern cello. Though he is the opposite of insensitive, Duchable is not always the most imaginative partner.

Arpeggione sonata, D.821 (arr. in G min. for clarinet & piano).
*** Chandos Dig. CHAN 8506 [id.]. Gervase de Peyer, Gwenneth Pryor – SCHUMANN: *Fantasiestücke; 3 Romances;* WEBER: *Silvana variations.* ***

So persuasive is the performance of Gervase de Peyer and Gwenneth Pryor that the listener is all but persuaded that the work was actually written for this combination.

Arpeggione sonata in A min. (arr. for flute); *Introduction and variations on Trock'ne Blumen* from *Die schöne Müllerin; Schwanengesang: Ständchen, D.957/4.*
**(*) RCA Dig. 07863 55303-2. James Galway, Phillip Moll.

The *Arpeggione sonata* also transcribes surprisingly well for the flute and is played with skill and some charm by this partnership. The *Introduction and variations on Trock'ne Blumen* are as neatly played. Not distinctive, but a pleasing and well-recorded recital.

(i) *Fantasy in C, D.934;* (i; ii) *Piano trio No. 2 in E flat, D.929;* (iii) *String quartets Nos. 8 in B flat, D.112 (Op. 168); 14 in D min. (Death and the Maiden), D.810; 15 in G, D.887 (Op. 161).*
(Y/B) (***) Pearl mono GEMMCDS 9141 (2) [id.]. (i) Adolf Busch, Rudolf Serkin; (iii) with Hermann Busch; (iii) Busch Qt.

Some have spoken of the Busch Quartet's Schubert as the greatest ever committed to disc. Certainly the

G major Quartet has never had so searching and powerful a reading, and the early *B flat Quartet*, which used to be known as Op. 168, sounds every bit as captivating as one remembers it from the days of shellac. The *E flat Trio* and the *C major Fantasy* are also in the highest class, and the Pearl transfers are very good indeed. These two CDs, packed economically in one jewel-case, encompass three LPs and are really excellent value for money. A lovely set.

Octet in F, D.803.
*** EMI Dig. CDC7 54118-2. Hausmusik.
*** Chandos Dig. CHAN 8585 [id.]. ASMF Chamber Ens.
(M) *** Teldec/Warner 4509 91448-2 [id.]. Berlin Soloists.
(M) *** O-L Dig. 444 160-2 [id.]. AAM Chamber Ens.
(M) *** DG 437 318-2 [id.]. V. Chamber Ens.
*** ASV Dig. CDDCA 694 [id.]. Gaudier Ens.

Octet in F, D.803; Eine kleine Trauermusik (for wind nonet), D.79.
(N) *** Praga Dig. PR 250 087 [id.]. Czech Nonet.

(i) *Octet in F, D.803;* (ii) *Minuet and Finale in F for wind octet, D.72.*
(N) ✪ (B) *** Decca Eclipse Dig. 448 715-2; *448 715–4* [id.]. (i) Vienna Octet; (ii) Vienna Wind Soloists.

As a companion disc to their equally delectable version of the Beethoven *Septet*, the Vienna Octet give a gloriously warm-hearted and sparkling account of Schubert's *Octet*. The *Andante with variations* has great charm and the high spirits of the finale are bucolic in their joy, with the coda managed superbly. This is quite irresistible, and the two charming miniatures from Schubert's youth make a delightful encore. Demonstration sound-quality and the lowest possible price take this straight to the top of the list.

Hausmusik's performance of Schubert's *Octet* on period instruments is so winning that it can be recommended warmly even to those who do not normally follow the authenticity cult. Speeds are rarely extreme, allowing full, open expressiveness, as in the *Adagio*; and allegros are generally easy enough to allow a delectable rhythmic spring. The pointing is the more infectious when period string-playing allows textures to be so transparent. There are few Schubert records that so consistently convey the joys of spring.

The new Chandos version brings a performance just as delightful as the earlier one by the ASMF, less classical in style, a degree freer in expression, with Viennese overtones brought out in Schubert's sunny invention. It has the benefit of excellent modern digital sound, cleaner on detail than before.

The Berlin Soloists give a strong and stylish performance which, on a bigger scale than most, designedly brings out the symphonic power of a piece lasting over an hour. Every single repeat is observed, and with such distinguished playing that length is readily sustained. This is very well characterized, not just in the big, symphonic movements but in the charming *Andante variations* too.

The members of the Czech Nonet give a characteristically infectious and engaging performance, never more so than in the finale which, after a dramatic opening, continues with rustic high spirits, often winningly bucolic in feeling. But the playing throughout combines refinement of blending and ensemble with spirited warmth. The *Trauermusik*, which opens with solemn horns, makes an unusual prelude for the main work. The recording is beautifully balanced within a spacious but not over-resonant acoustic.

The Academy's Chamber Ensemble using period instruments brings out the open joyfulness of Schubert's inspiration, with excellent matching and vivid recording. The reading is not at all stiff or pedantic, but personal and relaxed. Lightness is the keynote, with speeds never eccentrically fast.

The Vienna Chamber Ensemble do not overlap in personnel with the New Vienna Octet, who have recorded this work for Decca, though their performance has a similar polish and urbane Viennese warmth. This is mellifluous Schubert, and very engaging it is: fresh and elegant. This dates from 1980, and the CD transfer maintains the smoothness and realism of the LP. Very enjoyable.

The Gaudier Ensemble give an entirely winning account of the *Octet*, essentially spontaneous yet very relaxed and catching all the ingenuous Schubertian charm. Excellent sound, vivid yet well balanced within a pleasing acoustic which gives a feeling of intimacy. An ideal record for a warm summer evening.

Piano quintet in A (Trout), D.667.
(N) *** Ph. Dig. 446 001-2 [id.]. Alfred Brendel, Thomas Zehetmair, Tabea Zimmermann, Richard
     Duven, Peter Riegelbauer – MOZART: *Piano quartet No. 1.* ***
*** Decca Dig. 411 975-2 [id.]. András Schiff, Hagen Qt.
(N) (M) **(*) Decca 448 602-2 [id.]. Curzon, Vienna Octet (members) – DVORAK: *Piano quintet.* ***
(M) ** Ph. 434 146-2 [id.]. Beaux Arts Trio (augmented) – BEETHOVEN: *Piano trio No. 5.* ***

Piano quintet in A (Trout); Adagio and rondo concertante in F, D.487.
(N) (BB) **(*) Naxos Dig. 8.550658 [id.]. Jenö Jandó, Kodály Qt, with István Tóth.

(i; ii; iii) *Piano quintet in A (Trout);* (i; iii) *Arpeggione sonata, D.821;* (iv; i). *Die Forelle.*
(N) **(*) Sony Dig. SK 61964 [id.]. (i) Ax; (ii) Frank, Young, Meyer; (iii) Ma; (iv) Barbara Bonney.

(i) *Piano quintet in A (Trout);* (ii) *String quartet No. 14 (Death and the Maiden).*
(M) **(*) Decca 417 459-2 [id.]. (i) Curzon, Vienna Octet (members); (ii) VPO Qt.
(M) **(*) Sony SBK 46343; *SBT 46343* [id.]. (i) Horszowski, Budapest Qt (members), Julius Levine; (ii) Juilliard Qt.
(B) ** DG 439 416-2 [id.]. (i) Demus, Schubert Qt; (ii) Amadeus Qt.

(i) *Piano quintet in A (Trout);* (ii) *String trios, D.471 & D.581.*
(M) *** Ph. 422 838-2. (i) Haebler, Grumiaux, Janzer, Czako, Cazauran; (ii) Grumiaux String Trio.

(i) *Piano quintet in A (Trout);* (ii) *Die Forelle;* (iii) *Der Hirt auf dem Felsen.*
**(*) ASV Dig. CDDCA 684 [id.]. (i) Yitkin Seow, Prometheus Ens.; (ii; iii) Ann Mackay; (iii) Christopher Craker.

(i) *Piano quintet in A (Trout);* (ii) *Der Hirt auf dem Felsen.*
(M) **(*) Carlton IMP Classics PCD 868 [id.]. (i) Nash Ens.; (ii) Lott, Collins, Brown.

The new Brendel performance is superbly recorded, the imagery rich and tangible, especially the piano, with Thomas Zehetmair's violin sweetly caught and the string bass gently resounding at the bottom. Like Brendel's previous Cleveland performance, which it easily displaces, this lacks something in trad-itional Viennese charm, but it has a compensating warmth and weight and certainly plenty of natural impetus. It is a reading which grows on one, with Brendel consistently persuasive. The very opening is arresting: one welcomes the exposition repeat, and there are many individual imaginative touches to follow. The simplicity at the beginning of the second movement is endearing, and there is a delightfully graduated ritardando towards the end of the first section, which is repeated in the coda. Similarly in the third movement, the famous *Trout* is given the gentlest presentation, before being sent off on its travels. Then, after all energy has been expended, the delicate fifth variation has an engagingly soft intimacy, before the bright-eyed return of the theme. The finale is the more telling for being extended by the exposition repeat. The inclusion of a substantial Mozart coupling gives this Philips account a distinct advantage over the competing Decca version, which is in some ways even more endearing.

András Schiff and the Hagen Quartet give a delectably fresh and youthful reading of the *Trout quintet*, full of the joys of spring, but one which is also remarkable for hushed concentration, as in the exceptionally dark and intense account of the opening of the first movement. The Scherzo brings a light, quick and bouncing performance, and there is extra lightness too in the other middle movements. Alongside Brendel (but no other current rivals), this version observes the exposition repeat in the finale, and with such a joyful, brightly pointed performance one welcomes that.

Clifford Curzon's 1958 recording of the *Trout* sounds its age in the thin violin timbre, although the piano tone has plenty of colour. It remains a classic performance, with a distinguished account of the piano part and splendidly stylish support from the Vienna players. The Vienna Philharmonic perform-ance treats *Death and the Maiden* with comparable affection; the playing is peerless, Boskovsky, the leader, showing all his skill and musicianship in the variations. Both recordings have a warm ambience and in the string quartet the upper range is full. The *Trout* is additionally available, impressively remastered, coupled to Dvořák's Op. 81 *Piano quintet* in Decca's Classic Sound series.

There is some admirably unassertive and deeply musical playing from Miss Haebler and from the incomparable Grumiaux. These artists do not try to make 'interpretative points' but are content to let the music speak for itself. The quality of the recorded sound is good. Philips have added a pair of *String trios*, given characteristically refined performances by Grumiaux and his companions, delightful music superbly played.

Horszowski's contribution to the *Trout* is undoubtedly distinguished and his clean, clear playing dom-inates the performance which, although full of imaginative detail, is a little on the cool side – though refreshingly so, for all that. The Juilliard Quartet are far from cool in the *Death and the Maiden quartet*, the unanimity of ensemble consistently impressive. In both works the sound is a little dry, but not confined.

Emanuel Ax leads an impressive ensemble in this invigorating Sony account of the *Trout quintet* which opens every bit as freshly as the new Brendel version. But, alas, there is a constant tendency to move onwards too quickly. This does not affect the famous theme and variations, which is done most imagina-tively, but the Scherzo is very fast indeed, and the finale sounds rushed. A pity, as Yo-Yo Ma's perform-ance of the *Arpeggione sonata* is totally endearing, with all the warmth, joy and innocent Schubertian charm one could ask for. To include the song associated with Schubert's quintet is always a happy idea, but Barabara Bonney's account is direct rather than innocently beguiling. No complaints about the recording balance or the generous measure.

The Jandó/Kodály *Trout* is above all bracing. The first movement is soon moving along briskly and at a concert one could well be swept along by the momentum of the performance, for there is relaxation in the *Andante* and the famous *Variations* are mellow and strongly characterized. The polish and impetus of this playing is never in doubt and the recording is excellent, but this account obviously comes from east of Vienna. The *Adagio and rondo concertante* sounds a stronger work here than usual and the rondo is spirited and jolly.

On DG Classikon, Demus dominates, partly because the piano recording and balance are bold and forward, and the string timbre is thinner. Nevertheless the transfer brings very acceptable sound and there is – as befits the eponymous quartet – a real feeling for Schubertian lyricism here, and the performance has spontaneity. The earlier of the Amadeus's two stereo versions of the *Death and the Maiden quartet* gives a wonderful impression of unity as regards the finer points of phrasing, for example at the very beginning of the variations, even if this account has not the depth of the very finest versions. The DG transfer is well managed, although the sound is a little dated.

The Prometheus Ensemble turn in a very enjoyable and fresh account of the *Trout* on ASV. There are two bonuses in the shape of the equivalent song, charmingly done by Ann Mackay, and *The Shepherd on the rock*. The playing in the *Quintet* is alert and well shaped, and well recorded, too.

The account by the Nash Ensemble on Carlton also brings a fill-up in the shape of *The Shepherd on the rock*. They are rather forwardly recorded here and their account is just a little wanting in the spontaneity that distinguishes the finest of the current versions. Ian Brown is, as always, a sensitive artist.

The Beaux Arts *Trout* is a delightfully fresh performance. Every phrase is splendidly alive, there is no want of vitality or sensitivity, and the recording is basically well balanced. The snag is the digital remastering, which gives undue prominence to Isidore Cohen's violin, lighting it up brightly and thinning down the timbre.

(i; ii) *Piano quintet in A (Trout); (i; iii) Piano trios Nos. 1 in B flat, D.898; 2 in E flat, D.929; Notturno in E flat, D.897; Sonata in B flat, D.28* (both arr. for piano trio).
(B) **(*) EMI CZS7 62742-2 (2) [id.]. (i) Hephzibah Menuhin; (ii) Amadeus Qt, J. Edward Merrett; (iii) Sir Yehudi Menuhin & Maurice Gendron.

The 1958 Hephzibah Menuhin/Amadeus *Trout* has a pleasingly domestic sense of scale and considerable charm, even though the bright recording creates a balance in favour of the upper register of the piano and the upper strings. The Amadeus Quartet play with nicely judged feeling. Intimacy is also the keynote of the works for piano trio, and in the *Trios* Menuhin relaxes with his pianist sister and cellist friend to produce delightfully spontaneous-sounding performances. The atmosphere of the *Second Trio* is caught perceptively and the unassertive music-making captures the music's spirit very appealingly. These recordings are cleanly remastered; the sound lacks something in fullness but the focus is natural and the balance realistic.

Piano trios Nos. 1 in B flat, Op. 99; 2 in E flat, Op. 100.
(N) (M) ** Sony Stern Edition III SM2K 64516 (2) [id.]. Stern, Rose, Istomin – HAYDN: *Piano trio;* MOZART: *Piano quartet No. 2.* **

The Sony performances of the two Schubert *Piano trios* (recorded in 1964 and 1969 respectively) cannot compare with the Stern/Rose/Istomin accounts of the Beethoven and Brahms *Trios*. Although there is a lively impetus, there is also an element of fierceness in the way these artists approach both first-movement allegros. Inner movements come off much better. They cannot help but respond to the beautiful *Andante* of the *E flat Trio*, with Leonard Rose's fine cello playing well in evidence; and finales do not lack sparkle. But overall this is music which calls for a more relaxed, more intimate response. The recording is clear, but the New York studio ambience is not flattering.

(i) *Piano trios Nos. 1–2; Adagio in E flat ('Notturno')* (for piano trio), *D. 897; Sonata in B flat* (for piano trio), *D. 28;* (ii) *String trios: in B flat* (in one movement), *D. 471; in B flat, D. 581.*
(B) *** Ph. Duo 438 700-2 (2) [id.]. (i) Beaux Arts Trio; (ii) Grumiaux Trio.

The Beaux Arts set of the Schubert *Piano trios* from the late 1960s is another of the extraordinary bargains now offered on the Philips Duo label. The performances provide impeccable ensemble with the pianist, Menahem Pressler, always sharply imaginative and the cellist, Bernard Greenhouse, bringing simple dedication to such key passages as the great slow-movement melody of the *Trio No. 2 in E flat*. Written during Schubert's student days, the attractive early *Sonata in B flat* has the same kind of fluency as Beethoven's *First Piano trio*, though the lyrical flow has the unmistakable ring of

Schubert. The *Notturno*, played here with great eloquence, recalls the rapt, hushed intensity of the glorious slow movement of the *String quintet*. The recording is naturally balanced, a little dry in the treble, which means that Daniel Guilet's violin timbre is sometimes a little ungenerous; but the CD transfer never makes it sound edgy. What makes the set doubly attractive is the inclusion of the two much rarer *String trios*, also early works from 1816/17. The four-movement *B flat Trio* is a sheer delight with that quality of innocence which lets Schubert's music stand apart, obviously post-Mozartian yet with a simplicity all its own. Given such persuasive advocacy, both pieces cannot fail to make a strong impression. The Grumiaux performances are deeply musical, unforced and well shaped, while the 1969 recording has vividness and presence as well as a natural, lifelike sound-quality.

Piano trio No. 1 in B flat; Sonata movement in B flat.
(BB) **(*) Naxos Dig. 8.550131; 4550131 [id.]. Stuttgart Piano Trio.

The Stuttgart Piano Trio may be at budget price but this is not a bargain-basement performance; the playing is musicianly and intelligent and there are many sensitive touches. Although the sound is somewhat less than ideal, there is a reasonable amount of air round the three instruments.

Piano trio No. 2 in E flat, D.929; Notturno, D.897.
(N) * Chandos Dig. CHAN 9414 [id.]. Bekova Sisters.

There is no particular reason to prefer the Bekova Sisters in the *E flat Trio* to the many rival versions on the market. Their playing is run-of-the-mill, and the first movement is so slow and deliberate as to call for more tolerance than we suspect many readers will be willing to extend. Good recording, as is usual from this source, but a disappointment artistically.

String quartets Nos. 1–15.
(M) ** DG 419 879-2 (6) [id.]. Melos Qt of Stuttgart.

The early quartets have an altogether disarming grace and innocence, and some of their ideas are most touching. The Melos are an impressive body whose accounts of this repertoire are unmannered and on the whole sympathetic. They are let down by recording quality that is less than distinguished, but the remastering has brought added presence.

String quartets Nos. 4 in C, D.46; 14 in D min. (Death and the Maiden), D.810.
*** RCA Dig. RD 87990 [id.]. Tokyo Qt.

Among newer recordings, the Tokyo give a keenly felt and beautifully phrased account of *Death and the Maiden*, and they are persuasive advocates of the charming, early *C major Quartet*; moreover the RCA recording is first class. They make a very beautiful sound (which some might find too sweet) and in this respect are to be preferred to the Lindsays, though the latter go deeper into the music. But this is undoubtedly worth ranking among the top recommendations, for those looking for a modern version.

String quartet No. 8 in B flat, D.112.
(Y/B) (M) (***) EMI mono CHS5 65308-2 (4) [id.]. Busch Qt (with MENDELSSOHN: *Capriccio in E min.*) – BEETHOVEN: *String quartets.* *** ✺

The excellence and lightness of spirit the Busch communicate in this quartet is exhilarating. There is an alternative transfer available on Pearl (see above).

String quartets Nos. 8 in B flat, D.112; 13 in A min., D.804.
*** ASV Dig. CDDCA 593 [id.]. Lindsay Qt.

In the glorious *A minor* the Lindsays lead the field. It would be difficult to fault their judgement in both these works so far as tempi and expression are concerned, and dynamics are always the result of musical thinking. The recording team has done them much credit.

String quartets Nos. 11 in E, D.353; 14 in D min. (Death and the Maiden), D.810.
(N) (M) ** DG 447 531-2 [id.]. Melos Qt.

It is a pity that the quality of the mid-1970s recorded sound is not more appealing in this coupling. Generally speaking, the Melos Quartet's playing is expert enough but, though the comparatively rare *E major Quartet* is welcome, their account of the *Death and the Maiden* would not be a first recommendation. The performance certainly has intensity but the players occasionally wear their hearts a little too much on their sleeves.

String quartets Nos. 11 in E, D.353; 15 in G, D.887.
(M) *** Decca 433 693-2 [id.]. Allegri Qt.

The Allegri are recorded in a somewhat reverberant acoustic (the Church of St George the Martyr,

London) but their account of the *G major Quartet* is most rewarding. The *E major*, composed a decade earlier, is if anything even finer, fresh and spontaneous and with excellent judgement in the matter of tempi. The analogue recordings date from the late 1970s and have been most realisically transferred to CD.

String quartets Nos. 12 in C min. (Quartettsatz), D.703; 13 in A min., D.804; 14 in D min. (Death and the Maiden); 15 in G, D.887.
(Y/B) ✪ (B) *** Ph. Duo 446 163-2 (2) [id.]. Italian Qt.

The Italian Quartet's 1965 coupling of the *Quartettsatz* and the *Death and the Maiden quartet* was counted the finest available in its day, with the famous variations played with great imagination and showing a notable grip in the closing pages. Technically the playing throughout is remarkable. There is just a hint of edge on the sound at times, but the original recording was very well balanced, and the CD adds to the immediacy. These players' understanding of Schubert is equally reflected in their performance of the *A minor Quartet*, recorded a decade later. Originally the long exposition repeat was omitted to get the work on a single LP side; now it has been restored. The familiar '*Rosamunde*' slow movement is (to our ears) beautifully paced – though some may find it a bit slow – and again has an impressive command of feeling. The 1976 sound, too, is first class. The *G major Quartet* is, if anything, even finer. The conception is bold, the playing is distinguished by the highest standards of ensemble, intonation and blend, and the recording is extremely vivid, making this – even after nearly two decades – one of the most thought-provoking accounts of the *Quartet* now before the public. The 1977 recording still sounds remarkably real and present. The CD transfers throughout this set are a great credit to the Philips engineers.

String quartets Nos. 12 in C min. (Quartettsatz), D.703; 14 in D min. (Death and the Maiden), D.810.
*** ASV Dig. CDDCA 560 [id.]. Lindsay Qt.
(BB) **(*) Naxos Dig. 8.550221; 4550221 [id.]. Mandelring Qt.

String quartet No. 14 in D min. (Death and the Maiden), D.810.
(M) *** Ph. 420 876-2. Italian Qt – DVORAK: *Quartet No. 12* *** (with BORODIN: *Nocturne* *).

The Lindsays' intense, volatile account of the *Death and the Maiden quartet* is played with considerable metrical freedom and the widest range of dynamic, and the *Quartettsatz*, which acts as the usual filler, is unusually poetic and spontaneous in feeling. The recording is excellent.

The Italian Quartet offer a fine coupling with Dvořák, and the Borodin *Nocturne* is thrown in for good measure. They bring great concentration and poetic feeling to this wonderful score. The sound of the reissue is vivid and clear.

The Mandelring Quartet are very good indeed. The performances are sensitively and sensibly played and very decently recorded, and anyone tempted by this Naxos disc will not be disappointed for so modest an outlay.

String quartet No. 13 in A min., D.804.
(N) *** EMI CDC5 55289-2. Britten Qt – SCHOENBERG: *String quartet No. 2.* ***

Although the Britten are not to be preferred to the Brandis in the Schubert, they offer an enterprising coupling in the form of the *Second Quartet* of Schoenberg, with Amanda Roocroft singing the Stefan Georg settings in the last two movements. The experience and wisdom of the Brandis tell, but the Brittens have a youthful appeal too, which may make choice difficult for collectors.

String quartets Nos. 13 in A min., D.804; 14 (Death and the Maiden).
(N) *** Nimbus Dig. NI 5438 [id.]. Brandis Qt.

The Brandis Quartet have warmth and bring a natural eloquence to these quartets that is all the more potent for being free of interpretative point-making. They are decently recorded, too. Recommended.

String quartets Nos. 13 in A min.; 14 in D min. (Death and the Maiden); 15 in G, D.887.
*** Nimbus NI 5048/9 [id.]. Chilingirian Qt.

In their two-disc set of the last three *Quartets*, the Chilingirians give strongly committed, characterful and spontaneous-sounding readings, warmly recorded and full of presence. On the upper-mid-priced Nimbus label, they make a most attractive recommendation.

String quartet No. 14 in D min. (Death and the Maiden).
(N) (BB) *** CfP Silver Double CDCFPSD 4772 (2). Gabrieli String Qt – BORODIN: *String quartet No. 2* ***; BRAHMS: *Clarinet quintet* **(*); DVORAK: *String quartet No. 12.* ***

Like the other performances on this Classics for Pleasure Silver Double, the Gabrielis give a direct, sensitive and polished account of Schubert's great *D minor Quartet*, not wearing their hearts on their sleeves but genuinely touching in the slow movement. The recording, from the beginning of the 1970s, is first class and has been smoothly transferred to CD. For those collectors wanting all four works, this is excellent value.

String quartets Nos. 14 in D min. (Death and the Maiden); 15 in G.
(M) (***) EMI (mono) CDH7 69795-2 [id.]. Busch Qt.

The Busch Quartet's account is more than fifty years old, but it brings us closer to the heart of this music than almost any other. The slow movement of the *Death and the Maiden quartet* is a revelation, and the same must be said of the *G major*, which has enormous depth and humanity. For its age, the sound is still amazing.

String quintet in C, D.956.
*** ASV Dig. CDDCA 537 [id.]. Lindsay Qt, Douglas Cummings.
✸ (M) *** Saga EC 3368-2. Aeolian Qt, Bruno Schreker.
(N) (M) *** Sony Dig. SMK 39134. Cleveland Qt, Yo-Yo Ma.
✸ (***) Testament mono SBT 1031 Hollywood Qt, Kurt Reher – SCHOENBERG: *Verklaerte Nacht.* (***) ✸
(Y/B) *** Channel Classics Dig. CCS 6794 [id.]. Orpheus Qt, Peter Wispelwey.
(Y/B) *** Teldec/Warner Dig. 4509 94564-2 [id.]. Borodin Qt, Misha Milman.
(Y/B) (***) Biddulph mono LAB 093 [id.]. Pro Arte Qt, Anthony Pini – BRAHMS: *String sextet No. 1.* (***)

(i) *String quintet in C; String quartet No. 12 (Quartettsatz), D.703.*
*** Decca Dig. 436 324-2 [id.]. Takács Qt, (i) with Miklós Perényi.

String quintet in C; String trio in B flat, D.581.
(BB) *** Naxos Dig. 8.550388 [id.]. Villa Musica Ens.

The Lindsay version gives the impression that one is eavesdropping on music-making in the intimacy of a private concert. They observe the first-movement exposition repeat and the effortlessness of their approach does not preclude intellectual strength. In the ethereal *Adagio* they effectively convey the sense of it appearing motionless, suspended, as it were, between reality and dream, yet at the same time never allowing it to become static. Their reading must rank at the top of the list; it is very well recorded.

The augmented Aeolian Quartet give a strong, virile performance. It might seem bald, were it not for the depth of concentration that the players convey in every bar. In the slow movement the Aeolians daringly adopt the slowest possible *Adagio*, and the result might have seemed static but for the inner tension which holds one breathless through hushed pianissimos of the most intense beauty. The analogue recording, though not of the clearest in terms of individual definition of instruments, has been transferred to CD with remarkable presence and the body of tone has not been lost. This is a clear first bargain choice, and there are few premium-priced issues which approach, let alone match, its intensity.

The Cleveland Quartet and Yo-Yo Ma have won golden opinions for their account of the *Quintet* on Sony. They are scrupulous in observing dynamic markings (the second subject is both restrained and *pianissimo*) and they also score by observing all repeats. Their performance has feeling and eloquence, as well as a commanding intellectual grip. Moreover they are admirably recorded and thus present a strong challenge at mid-price.

The Hollywood Quartet's 1951 version of the *Quintet* with Kurt Reher as second cello stands apart. Over 40 years on, its qualities of freshness and poetry, as well as an impeccably confident technical address, still impress as deeply as ever. This is the product of consummate artistry and remains very special indeed.

The Villa Musica players tackle the great *C major Quintet* with a freshness and concentration that are consistently compelling, even if the finale is neat and clean rather than urgently dramatic. The little *String trio* makes an attractive and generous fill-up, another assured and stylish performance. With clear, well-balanced recording this super-budget issue makes an outstanding bargain and offers an excellent alternative to the Saga version for those wanting digital sound.

The Takács Quartet with Miklós Perényi on Decca (very well recorded), taking a freely expressive view and sounding spontaneous, regularly find Schubertian magic, as when the leader plays with the most withdrawn half-tone at the start of the *Adagio* slow movement. Particularly when the Takács disc also offers the *Quartettsatz* as a bonus, the Decca issue remains competitive, with the jollity of the Scherzo and finale set against the spacious strength of the first two massive movements.

The Orpheus Quintet offer a performance of communicated warmth and feeling, both in the slow movement and in the remarkable *Andante* central section of the Scherzo. The playing is fresh and feels alive, and the recording has striking body and realism.

On Teldec, the augmented Borodin Quartet command the listener's rapt attention throughout a performance which demonstrates both their emotional involvement and their almost unique unanimity of ensemble. The *Adagio* is beautifully played, but its special, almost unearthly intensity is not experienced to the full, as the players strive – with great success – to create the most beautifully blended sound. The recording is superbly balanced, and it is impossible for the listener not to respond to music-making of this calibre.

The Pro Arte Quartet's 1935 account of the Schubert *Quintet*, with Anthony Pini as second cello, dominated the pre-war catalogues. Its humanity and warmth still tell, particularly in the slow movement. It comes with a fine account of the Brahms *B flat Sextet*, made in the same year. Needless to say, some allowance has to be made for the recording, eminently well transferred though it is.

Violin sonatinas Nos. 1–3, D.384/5 & D.408.
(M) *** O-L 443 196-2 [id.]. Jaap Schröder, Christopher Hogwood (fortepiano) – MENDELSSOHN: *Violin sonata.* ***

This makes a clear choice for those wanting these works on original instruments. However, the inclusion of repeats (bringing a total playing time of 55 minutes) means that there was apparently no room for the *Duo*, D.574, and an early Mendelssohn sonata has been added instead. Jaap Schröder uses a Stradivarius and Christopher Hogwood a piano from about 1825 by Georg Haschka. It does not produce the range of nuance and tonal subtlety of which the modern piano is capable, but its lightness of colour has its own special charm. Jaap Schröder plays with fine artistry, and both artists are truthfully recorded. Modern performances will enjoy a wider appeal – probably rightly – but this is undoubtedly a set to hear.

PIANO MUSIC FOR FOUR HANDS

Andantino variè in B min., D.823; Duo in A min., D.947; Fantasia in F min., D.940; Grand duo sonata in C, D.812; 3 Marches militaires, D.733; 6 Polonaises, D.824; Rondo in A, D.951; Variations on an original theme in A flat, D.813.
(N) (M) *** Erato/Warner 0630 11231-2 (2). Anne Queffélec & Imogen Cooper.

It is good to have a thoroughly recommendable mid-priced set of Schubert's music for piano/four hands, including the greatest work ever written for the genre, the *F minor Fantasia*. Some of this music (including that piece) has also been recorded by Gilels and his daughter Elena for DG, and that shorter survey will no doubt resurface before too long; but the playing of Anne Queffélec and Imogen Cooper is hardly less eloquent than their rivals', and they also offer a commanding account of the *Grand duo sonata*. The slighter pieces also come off well: the *Variations* are beautifully played and have an engaging innocence, while the most famous *Marche militaire* sparkles. Its two lesser-known companions are also worth having on disc when played (like the six *Polonaises*) so brightly and spontaneously. The 1978 analogue recording is well balanced, clear and natural, the acoustic neither over-reverberant nor too confined.

Allegro in A min., Lebenstürme, D.947; Divertissement, D.823; Grandes marches, D.819; 4 Polonaises, D.599; Rondo in A, D.951; Variations in E min. on a French song, D.624.
(N) *** Sony S2K 66256 (2) [id.]. Tal, Groethuysen.

Tal and Groethuysen are about the best duo-partnership currently before the public and almost any of their records can be recommended to those who care for intelligent and sensitive playing. This set is no exception and brings much pleasure. They play with a genuine Schubertian sensibility and the widest range of dynamic: the delicacy of their pianissimos is most impressive. Their opening *Lebenstürme* ('Storms of life') is appropriately volatile, and the *Variations on a French song* are most engaging. The recording is resonant, but they are not too closely balanced.

Divertissement à l'hongroise in G min., D.818; Fantaisie in F min., D.940; Introduction and 4 variations on an original theme and finale in B flat, D.603; 3 Marches héroïques, D.602; Overture in F, D.675; 6 Polonaises, D.824; 8 Variations on a theme from Hérold's opera Marie in C, D.908.
**(*) Sony S2K 58955 [id.]. Duo Tal and Groethuysen.

This is interesting and rare repertoire, and the Duo Tal and Groethuysen play it with lively vigour. They are at their best in the glorious *Fantaisie in F minor*, and they find charm in the *Introduction and four variations on an original theme*. But elsewhere they often seem too loud, in the *Overture* for instance and in the *Divertissement* (and the recording is not entirely flattering to their fortissimos).

Fantasia in F min., D.940.
*** Sony Dig. SK 39511 [id.]. Murray Perahia, Radu Lupu – MOZART: *Double piano sonata.* ***
(Y/B) *** Chandos Dig. CHAN 9162 [id.]. Lortie, Mercier – MOZART: *Andante with variations* etc. ***

Recorded live at The Maltings, the performance of Lupu and Perahia is full of haunting poetry, with each of these highly individual artists challenging the other in imagination. Warmly atmospheric recording.

The Louis Lortie–Hélène Mercier partnership is as impressive here as it is elsewhere. The Schubert holds its own even against such illustrious competition as the Lupu–Perahia recording on Sony, also coupled with Mozart. Very good recording.

PIANO MUSIC

Allegretto in C min., D.915; 3 Klavierstücke (Impromptus), D.946.
(Y/B) (M) ** Carlton IMP Classics Dig. 30367 00902 [id.]. Joeres – VORISEK: *Impromptus.* **

It was an intelligent idea to couple these Schubert *Impromptus* with the Voříšek pieces that inspired them (and indeed the whole genre). The German pianist, Dirk Joeres, is a sensitive and imaginative player, and his playing will give pleasure, though his recording is just a shade bass-heavy.

Allegretto in C min., D.915; Moments musicaux Nos. 1–6, D.780; 2 Scherzi, D.593; 12 Valse nobles, D.969.
(M) **(*) DG 435 072-2. Daniel Barenboim.

Some of the finest playing here comes in the two *Scherzi*. The *Allegretto in C minor* is given an effective, improvisatory quality, but the twelve *Valses nobles* are played too forcefully for their full charm to be revealed. In the *Moments musicaux* there is much to admire, yet there is an element of calculation that robs the impact of freshness. The piano-tone on DG has impressive presence and weight.

Fantasia in C (Wanderer), D.760.
*** Sony Dig. MK 42124 [id.]. Murray Perahia – SCHUMANN: *Fantasia in C.* ***
*** EMI CDC7 47967-2. Sviatoslav Richter – DVORAK: *Piano concerto.* ***
(M) *** Ph. 420 644-2. Alfred Brendel – *Sonata No. 21.* ***
(N) (M) *** DG 447 451-2 [id.]. Maurizio Pollini – SCHUMANN: *Fantasia, Op. 17.* ***

Murray Perahia's account of the *Wanderer* stands alongside the finest. In his hands it sounds as fresh as the day it was conceived, and its melodic lines speak with an ardour and subtlety that breathe new life into the score. The recording is more than acceptable.

Richter's 1963 performance is masterly in every way. The piano timbre is real and the remastering gives the great pianist a compelling presence; the coupling is hardly less outstanding.

Brendel's playing is of a high order, and he is truthfully recorded and coupled with what is perhaps Schubert's greatest *Sonata*, so this is excellent value at mid-price.

Pollini's account is outstanding and, though he is not ideally recorded and the piano timbre is shallow, the playing still shows remarkable insights. Moreover the Schumann coupling is equally fine.

Fantasia in C (Wanderer), D.760; Impromptus, D.899/3 & 4; Piano sonata No. 21 in B flat, D.960.
(✪) *** RCA RD 86257 [RCA 6257-2-RC]. Artur Rubinstein.

Rubinstein plays the *Wanderer fantasia* with sure magnificence and, particularly in the variations section, he is electrifying. The two *Impromptus* are played with the most subtle shading of colour and delectable control of rubato, and the superb account of the *Sonata* shows Rubinstein as a magically persuasive Schubertian. The 1965 sound is remarkably real, with fine presence and little shallowness.

Impromptus Nos. 1–4, D.899; 5–8, D.935.
*** Sony Dig. SK 37291 [id.]. Murray Perahia.
*** DG Dig. 435 788-2 [id.]. Andrei Gavrilov.
*** Decca Dig. 411 711-2 [id.]. Radu Lupu.

Impromptus Nos. 1–4, D.899; 5–8, D.935; Allegretto in C min., D.915; 11 Ecossaises, D.781; Hungarian melody in B min., D.817.
(N) (M) *** Ph. 442 543-2 [id.]. Alfred Brendel.

Perahia's account of the *Impromptus* is very special indeed and falls barely short of greatness. Directness of utterance and purity of spirit are of the essence here. The CBS recording is very good, truthful in timbre.

Andrei Gavrilov's playing has something of the divine simplicity for which this music calls. No expressive excesses and a wide dynamic range. Surprisingly, perhaps, this is quite selfless playing which serves Schubert well. So, too, does the admirably balanced DG recording. One of the best, even in a strongly competitive field, and highly recommendable.

Brendel's analogue set of *Impromptus* is also magical. It is difficult to imagine finer Schubert playing than this; to find more eloquence, more profound musical insights, one has to go back to Edwin Fischer – and even here comparison is not always to Brendel's disadvantage. In its newest remastering the sound is enhanced: the piano image is slightly firmer and clearer, without appreciable loss of sonority. Also an attractive batch of encores have been added: the *Ecossaises* are particularly winning.

Lupu's account of the *Impromptus* is of the same calibre as the Brendel analogue version, and he is most beautifully recorded on CD. Indeed, in terms of natural sound this is a most believable image.

Impromptus 1–4, D.899; Moments musicaux 1–6, D.780; 6 German dances, D.820; Grazer Galopp, D.925; Hungarian melody in B min., D.817.
(Y/B) *** Decca Dig. 430 425-2 [id.]. András Schiff.

Impromptus Nos. 5–8, D.935; 3 Klavierstücke, D.946; Allegretto in C min., D.915; 12 Ländler, D.790.
(Y/B) *** Decca Dig. 425 638-2 [id.]. András Schiff.

It was with this pair of 1990 discs that András Schiff laid the foundations for his Schubertian odyssey. The playing is idiomatic, intelligent and humane, and the recording more than acceptable. It is impossible to recommend his *Impromptus* over and above those of Brendel or Lupu, but no one who has found satisfaction in his current survey of the sonatas will be disappointed with them. We had hoped the arrangement of repertoire would have been reordered by Decca so that (as with major competitors) the eight *Impromptus* would have been placed on a single CD, and that may yet happen, as 425 638-2 has just been withdrawn as we go to press.

Impromptus Nos. 1–4, D.899; Piano sonata No. 21 in B flat, D.960.
*** Calliope Dig. CAL 9689 [id.]. Inger Södergren.

Inger Södergren's account of the first four *Impromptus* belongs in exalted company, and the *B flat Sonata* is hardly less fine. Her playing is marked throughout by sensitivity and a selfless and unostentatious dedication to Schubert. The recording is acceptable rather than outstanding.

4 Impromptus, D.899; Impromptu in B flat, D.935/3; Moments musicaux, D.780/1, 2 & 6.
(B) *** LaserLight Dig. 15609 [id.]. Jenö Jandó.

At last Jenö Jandó is heard recorded in an acoustic that does justice to his talent. The sound, at least in the opening *B flat major Impromptu* of D.935, is fresh and truthful, the ambience is warm, and the playing is very good. The balance is not as good in the three *Moments musicaux* or in the D.899 *Impromptus*: it is closer and marginally drier.

Impromptus: Nos. 6 in A flat; 7 in B flat, D.935/2–3; 6 Moments musicaux, D.780; Valses nobles, D.969; SCHUBERT/LISZT: *Soirée de Vienne No. 6.*
(M) **(*) Decca stereo/mono 433 902-2 [id.]. Wilhelm Backhaus – MENDELSSOHN: *Rondo capriccioso* etc. *** (with SCHUMANN: *Fantasiestück, Op. 12: Warum? **(*)*).

Backhaus's almost peremptory manner in Schubert, strongly classical in feeling, is quite different from the style of players like Perahia and Lupu, yet this remains magnetic music-making. Even if it is not the most subtle Schubert interpretation, there is much character, and considerable brilliance too, in the *B flat major Impromptu*. There is, however, less sweetness than usual in the equally famous *A flat Impromptu*, taken fairly briskly. This, like Schumann's *Warum?*, derives from a mono recording of an unidentified live recital. The recordings from 1955/6 are good.

Moments musicaux Nos. 1–6, D.780; 3 Klavierstücke, D. 946.
(Y/B) (M) *** Virgin Veritas/EMI Dig. VER5 61161-2 [id.]. Melvyn Tan (fortepiano) – BEETHOVEN: *Allegretto in C min.* etc. ***

These pieces sound very effective indeed on Melvyn Tan's fortepiano (a modern instrument by Derek Adlam, modelled on an 1814 Viennese instrument). Tan finds a remarkable range of colour and, though the effect is less mellow than with a modern instrument, one's ears adjust almost immediately, so strongly does his playing project. Indeed, with textures clear but by no means bare, the music's inner emotional feeling is conveyed the more readily, while the perky *No. 3 in F minor* has a most engaging character when articulated with such precison.

Moments musicaux, D.780; 2 Scherzi, D.593; Piano sonata No. 14 in A min., D.784.
*** DG Dig. 427 769-2 [id.]. Maria João Pires.

Maria João Pires gives masterly accounts of the *Moments musicaux* and the *A minor Sonata*, distinguished throughout by thoughtful and refined musicianship, and she is fully aware of the depth of feeling that inhabits the *Moments musicaux*, without ever indulging in the slightest expressive exaggeration. The digital recording is exceptionally present and clear.

Piano sonatas Nos. 1 in E, D.157; 2 in C, D.279; 3 in E, D.459; 4 in A min., D.537; 5 in A flat, D.557; 6 in E min., D.566; 7 in E flat, D.568; 9 in B, D.575; 11 in F min., D.625; 13 in A, D.664; 14 in A min., D.784; 15 in C, D.840 (Relique); 16 in A min., D.845; 17 in D, D.850; 18 in G, D.894; 19 in C min., D.958; 20 in A, D.959; 21 in B flat, D.960.
(M) *** DG 423 496-2 (7) [id.]. Wilhelm Kempff.

Wilhelm Kempff's cycle was recorded over a four-year period (1965–9) and elicited much admiration in our earlier editions. DG has now collected the sonatas into a seven-CD box and those wanting a comprehensive survey of this repertoire need look no further at present. There have been performances of comparable stature: Gilels in the *A minor*, D.784, and *D major*, D.850, Lupu (*G major*, D.894), Perahia (*A major*, D.960) and Richter, but there is no individual overview of the whole cycle that has been musically as consistently satisfying as Kempff's. The recordings are not state of the art (there is an occasional hint of shallowness) but they are very acceptable indeed and there is a wisdom about his playing which puts it in a special category.

Piano sonatas Nos. 1 in E, D.157; 14 in A min., D.784; 20 in A, D.959.
(M) *** Decca 425 033-2 [id.]. Radu Lupu.

Lupu is sensitive and poetic throughout. In the *A major* work he strikes the perfect balance between Schubert's classicism and the spontaneity of his musical thought, and at the same time he leaves one with the impression that the achievement is perfectly effortless, with an inner repose and depth of feeling that remain memorable long after the record has ended. Excellent vintage Decca recording, made in the Kingsway Hall in the late 1970s.

Piano sonata No. 4 in A min., D.537.
** DG Dig. 400 043-2 [id.]. Michelangeli – BRAHMS: *Ballades.* ***

Michelangeli's Schubert is less convincing than the Brahms coupling. His playing, though aristocratic and marvellously poised, is not free from artifice, and the natural eloquence of Schubert eludes him. Splendid recording.

Piano sonatas Nos. 1 in E, D.157; 3 in E, D.459; 13 in A, D.664.
(N) *** Decca Dig. 430 311-2 [id.]. András Schiff.

Piano sonatas Nos. 2 in C, D.279; 11 in F min., D.625; 21 in B flat, D.960.
(Y/B) *** Decca Dig. 440 310-2 [id.]. András Schiff.

Piano sonatas Nos. 4 in A min., D.537; 20 in A, D.959.
(Y/B) *** Decca Dig. 440 309-2 [id.]. András Schiff.

Piano sonatas Nos. 5 in A flat, D.557; 9 in B, D.575; 18 in G, D.894.
*** Decca Dig 440 307-2 [id.]. András Schiff.

Piano sonatas Nos. 6 in E min., D.566; 14 in A min., D.784; 17 in D, D.850.
*** Decca Dig. 440 306-2 [id.]. András Schiff.

Piano sonatas Nos. 7 in E flat, D.568; 19 in C min., D.958.
(Y/B) *** Decca Dig. 440 308-2 [id.]. András Schiff.

Piano sonatas Nos. 8 in F sharp min., D.571; 15 in C (Relique), D.840; 16 in A min., D.845.
*** Decca Dig. 440 305-2 [id.]. András Schiff.

With the collection including the *First Sonata*, D.157 (written when the composer was eighteen), András Schiff sets the seal on his seven-CD survey for Decca which has excited golden opinions. In his note he calls them 'among the most sublime contributions written for the piano' – and he plays them as if they are, too. The simplicity of Schiff's approach in the E major work (D.459) is most winning, particularly in the gentle melancholy of the *Andante*, while the first movement of the *A major*, D.664, brings all the warmth, subtlety and feeling for Schubert that have distinguished the earlier issues in his series, while the beautiful slow movement and sparkling finale do not disappoint either. Schiff has some distinguished rivals, including Imogen Cooper, but mostly in individual sonatas: Brendel, Perahia in the *A major*, Lupu, Ashkenazy, Richter and others; and the complete set from Wilhelm Kempff is still in currency. Schiff's is a survey that blends pianistic finesse with keen human insights, and readers considering adding a new cycle to their collection need have no serious qualms about starting here. He has a good feeling for the architecture of these pieces, so often looked down upon as discursive, and he invests detail with just the right amount of feeling. The recordings, made in the Brahms-Saal of the Musikverein in Vienna, are eminently satisfying.

Piano sonatas Nos. 14–21; German dances; Impromptus; Moments musicaux; Wanderer fantasia.
*** Ph. Dig. 426 128-2 (7) [id.]. Alfred Brendel.

Piano sonatas Nos. 14 in A min., D.784; 17 in D, D.850.
*** Ph. Dig. 422 063-2 [id.] Alfred Brendel.

Piano sonatas Nos 15 in C (Relique), D.840; 18 in G, D.894.
*** Ph. Dig. 422 340-2 [id.]. Alfred Brendel.

Piano sonata No. 16 in A min., D.845; 3 Impromptus, D.946.
*** Ph. Dig. 422 075-2 [id.]. Alfred Brendel.

Piano sonata No. 19 in C min., D.958; Moments musicaux Nos. 1–6, D.780.
*** Ph. Dig. 422 076-2 [id.]. Alfred Brendel.

Piano sonata No. 20 in A, D.959; Allegretto in C min., D.915; 16 German dances, D.783; Hungarian melody in B min., D.817.
**(*) Ph. Dig. 422 229-2 [id.]. Alfred Brendel.

Piano sonata No. 21 in B flat, D.960; Wanderer fantasia, D.760.
*** Ph. Dig. 422 062-2 [id.]. Alfred Brendel.

Brendel's new digital set is perhaps more intense than his last cycle of recordings for Philips, though there was a touching freshness in the earlier set, and he has the benefit of clean, well-focused sound. Generally speaking, these are warm performances, strongly delineated and powerfully characterized, which occupy a commanding place in the catalogue. Their separate availability is also noted, and all of them can be confidently recommended to Brendel's admirers.

'The last six years, 1823–1828', Vol. 1: Piano sonatas Nos. 14 in A min., D.784; 18 in G, D.894; 12 German dances (Ländler), D.790.
*** Priory/Ottavo Dig. OTR C68608 [id.]. Imogen Cooper.

Vol. 2: *Piano sonatas Nos. 15 in C, D.840; 20 in C, D.959; 11 Ecossaises, D.781.*
*** Priory/Ottavo Dig. OTR C58714 [id.]. Imogen Cooper.

Vol. 3: *Piano sonata No. 16 in A min., D.845; 4 Impromptus, D.935.*
*** Priory/Ottavo Dig. OTR C88817 [id.]. Imogen Cooper.

Vol. 4: *Piano sonata No. 17 in D, D.850; 6 Moments musicaux, D.780.*
*** Priory/Ottavo Dig. OTR C128715 [id.]. Imogen Cooper.

Vol. 5: *Piano sonata No. 21 in B flat, D.960; Allegretto in C min., D.915; 3 Impromptus (Klavierstücke), D.946.*
*** Priory/Ottavo Dig. OTR C88821 [id.]. Imogen Cooper.

Vol. 6: *Piano sonata No. 19 in C min., D. 958; 4 Impromptus, D.899.*
*** Priory/Ottavo Dig. OTR C78923 [id.]. Imogen Cooper.

We are indebted to a reader for drawing our attention to Imogen Cooper's outstanding set of the late Schubert sonatas on the Dutch Ottavo label. Miss Cooper has a true Schubertian sensibility; her feeling for this composer's special lyricism is second to none, yet her playing has both strength and a complete understanding of the music's architecture. The recordings were made in the London Henry Wood Hall over a period of three years, between June 1986 and July 1989, using a Steinway for the first three volumes and a fine-sounding Yamaha for the later records. The balance is admirable and the sound full, with a convincing natural resonance. The playing has the spontaneity of live music-making, and the warm colouring and fine shading of timbre are as pleasing to the ear as the many subtle nuances of phrasing, which are essentially based on a strong melodic line. These performances can be recommended alongside those by artists with the most illustrious names, and they do not fall short. With their fine, modern, digital recording these CDs will give much delight and refreshment.

Piano sonatas Nos. 4 in A min., D.537; 13 in A, D.664; 14 in A min., D.784; 15 in C, D.840; 16 in A min. (Relique), D.845; 19 in C min., D.958; 20 in A, D.959; 21 in B flat, D.960; Allegretto in C min., D.915; 11 Ecossaises, D.781; Fantasia in C (Wanderer), D.760; 12 German dances, D.790; 16 German dances, D.783; Hungarian melody in B min., D.817; 6 Moments musicaux, D.780.
(N) (M) *** Ph. Brendel Edition Analog/Dig. 446 923-2 (5) [id.]. Alfred Brendel.

Four out of the five records here come from Brendel's earlier, analogue set of Schubert recordings, but the first, pairing Nos. 4 and 13, is digital. Here Brendel's account of the *A minor Sonata*, D.537, sounds a little didactic: the gears are changed to prepare the way for the second group, and this sounds unconvincing on the first hearing and more so on the repeat. He also broadens on the modulation to F major towards the end of the exposition, only to quicken the pulse in the development. The result is curiously inorganic. The *A major*, D.664, is also given with less simplicity and charm than one expects from this great artist. There is some disruptive and studied agogic fluctuations which are not always convincing. No complaints about the sound, which is clear, well focused and natural. The analogue recordings which Brendel made in the early 1970s are noticeably more naturally flexible, even if his approach to tempo is that of a romantic, often making accelerandi to heighten climaxes. Both in *Sonatas 14 in A minor* and *15 in C major* he manages to convey romantic feeling within a relatively taut framework; indeed in the *C major* his eloquence and poetry leave nothing to be desired. No. 16, D.845, is one of the very finest of the series, with a searching reading of the first movement, free in expression, but direct too. The variations of the slow movement are given heavenly length, while the Scherzo and finale have strength and urgency. *No. 20 in A major*, however, suffers from rather more agogic changes than is desirable, and the *C minor Sonata*, D.958, is also not free from this charge. But one does not want to make too much of this, for the result is nearly always made to seem convincing. Brendel's performance of the final *B flat major Sonata* is as impressive and full of insight as one would expect; his playing of the *Wanderer fantasia* is also of a high order, and throughout he is truthfully recorded. The *German dances* are delightful and particularly beautifully played, while the *Moments musicaux* are given wonderfully poetic performances and rank very highly indeed in Brendel's Schubert discography. The slightly soft-grained recording is exemplary.

Piano sonatas Nos. 13 in A, D.664; 14 in A min., D.784; Hungarian melody, D.817; 12 Waltzes, D.145.
(Y/B) ✺ (M) *** Decca 443 579-2 [id.]. Ashkenazy.

A magnificent record in every respect. Ashkenazy is a great Schubertian who can realize the touching humanity of this giant's vision as well as his strength. There is an astonishing directness about these performances and a virility tempered by tenderness. This matches Ashkenazy's own high standards, and Decca have risen remarkably to the occasion. The 1966 analogue recording, reissued in Decca's Classic Sound series, has splendid range and fidelity. We gave the original LP a Rosette and see no reason to withhold it now.

Piano sonatas Nos. 13 in A, D.664; 21 in B flat, D.960.
(Y/B) *** Decca Dig. 440 295-2 [id.]. Radu Lupu.
(N) **(*) Conifer Dig. 75605 51254-2 [id.]. Mikhail Kazakevich.

Notwithstanding their ongoing series of Schubert *Sonatas* from András Schiff, Decca have celebrated Radu Lupu's first return to the studios in over a decade with new recordings of two Schubert *Sonatas*. It is one of the most searching of all new Schubert recordings and finds this masterly pianist at his most eloquent and thoughtful. Not as well recorded as Schiff – but don't let that worry you. This is rather special playing.

 Mikhail Kazakevich is also an impressive Schubertian, playing these two masterpieces with thoughtful understanding and the great *B flat Sonata* (in which he includes the exposition repeat) with commanding boldness. He is very well recorded. At a recital these performance would certainly be very well received, but in terms of recording he faces considerable competition and it must be conceded that Ashkenazy and Schiff both bring a finer sensibility to the *A major*, while for the *B flat* one would more readily turn to Kovacevich or Kempff (among others).

Piano sonatas Nos. 15 in C (Unfinished), D.840; 19 in C min., D.958; 16 German Dances, D.783.
(M) *** Van. 08.4026.71 [OVC 4026]. Alfred Brendel.

Brendel was at his finest and most spontaneous in the l960s. The *C minor Sonata* is particularly fine, with a thoughtful, improvisatory feeling in the slow movement which is consistently illuminating. The two-movement *C major Sonata* also has a memorable *Andante*, and the *German Dances* are an endless delight. The recording is full and bold.

Piano sonatas Nos. 15 in C (Relique), D.840; 21 in B flat, D.960.
(N) (M) **(*) DG 445 716-2 [id.]. Daniel Barenboim.

To say that Barenboim gives a Kempff-like reading of Schubert's greatest sonata, D.960, is not to deny his characteristic individuality but to point out that his is a reflective, lyrical view of the work, marked by clean semi-quaver work and sharp dynamic contrasts. Yet the slightest sense of artifice is destructive in this composer, and Barenboim's delivery of the first movement's opening statement is just a shade self-conscious. The artless grace and Blake-like innocence of this idea do not quite come across here. The second movement is slow and concentrated, the Scherzo light and sparkling with a real sense of joy. The finale is sharpened with clear-cut contrasts, yet there is curious inelegance in the second subject, an obtrusive left-hand staccato at the end of the first half of the theme. But this issue remains attractive for its imaginative coupling, the unfinished *C major Sonata*, a formidably large-scale argument, presented in its full stature by Barenboim. The recording is truthful, bold and clear.

Piano sonata No. 17 in D, D.850.
(M) *** RCA 09026 61614-2 [id.]. Emil Gilels – LISZT: *Sonata.* ***

Like the Liszt *Sonata* with which it is coupled, Gilels's highly perceptive account captures the music's Schubertian spirit in a somewhat similar way to Curzon's very persuasive account. If in his own way Gilels is authoritative and commanding, like Curzon he finds a special magic to engage the ear in the delightful finale.

Piano sonata No. 17 in D, D.850; Impromptus in A flat; in G flat, D.899/3–4; Moments musicaux Nos. 1–6, D. 780.
(Y/B) (M) *** Decca 443 570-2 [id.]. Clifford Curzon.

Some who know more forceful interpretations may find this too wayward, but Schubert surely thrives on some degree of coaxing. Curzon could hardly be more convincing – the spontaneous feeling of a live performance captured better than in many earlier discs. Curzon also gives superb performances of the *Moments musicaux*. These readings are among the most poetic in the catalogue, and the recording throughout is exemplary. The *Impromptus* make an attractive bonus (the *G flat major* particularly magical) in this reissue in Decca's Classic Sound series, and they too are beautifully played. The recording remains of Decca's finest analogue quality.

Piano sonatas Nos. 17 in D, D.850; 20 in A, D.959; 21 in B flat, D.960; March in E, D.606; Moments musicaux, D.780.
(M) (***) EMI mono CHS 764259-2 (2). Artur Schnabel.

It was thanks to Schnabel's championship that the *Piano sonatas* re-entered the repertory for they were rarities in the recital rooms of the 1920s and early 1930s. Both the *A major* and *B flat Sonatas* sound as well as they are ever likely to, for neither was state-of-the-art piano-sound. The *Moments musicaux* sound remarkably full-bodied. The playing is full of characteristic insights, though it must be admitted that later recordings of the *B flat* from Kempff and Curzon surpassed Schnabel technically. But as always with this artist there is imagination of a remarkable order. These recordings are now fifty years old, but some of the playing Schnabel offers – at the opening of the *B flat* and in the slow movements of all three *Sonatas* – will never be less than special.

Piano sonata No. 19 in C min., D.958; Moments musicaux Nos. 1–6, D.780.
(M) *** Decca Dig. 417 785-2 [id.]. Radu Lupu.

Lupu's performance has a simple eloquence that is most moving. His *Moments musicaux* are very fine indeed. The Decca recording is very natural and, at mid-price, this is extremely competitive.

Piano sonatas Nos. 19 in C min., D.958; 20 in A, D.959.
*** DG Dig. 427 327-2 [id.]. Maurizio Pollini.

Piano sonata No. 21 in B flat, D.960; Allegretto in C min., D.915; Klavierstücke, D.946.
*** DG Dig. 427 326-2 [id.]. Maurizio Pollini.

In Pollini's hands these emerge as strongly structured and powerful sonatas, yet he is far from unresponsive to the voices from the other world with which these pieces resonate. Perhaps with his perfect pianism he does not always convey a sense of human vulnerability, as have some of the greatest Schubert interpreters.

Piano sonatas Nos. 19 in C min., D.958; 20 in A, D.959.
**(*) Sony Dig. SK 46690 [id.]. Mark Swatzentruber.

Mark Swatzentruber makes a generally positive impression in his début record in the UK. He is a good player and allows the music to unfold without too much interpretative intrusion. Although they have some impressive moments, these are essentially decent rather than distinguished accounts, and the recorded sound is really not of three-star standard.

Piano sonatas Nos. 19 in C min., D. 958; 20 in A, D. 959; 21 in B flat, D. 960; 3 Impromptus (Klavierstücke), D. 946/1–3.
(B) **(*) Ph. Duo 438 703-2 [id.]. Alfred Brendel.

Brendel's analogue recordings of the Schubert late *Sonatas* were among the finest of his records made in the early 1970s and would seem an obvious recommendation on Philips's Duo bargain label. But the *A major* suffers from rather more agogic changes than is desirable. Some listeners may find these interferences with the flow of the musical argument a little too personal. The *C minor Sonata* is not free from this charge but it remains an impressive performance. Brendel's account of the *B flat Sonata* is characteristically imposing and full of insight, as one would expect. Here his mood is both serious and introspective, and he is not unduly wayward; moreover he is at his very finest in the *Klavierstücke*. This is eloquent and profoundly musical playing. Throughout, the recording is well up to Philips's high standard of realism and the CD transfers are impeccable, with the background hiss a problem only for eagle ears.

Piano sonata No. 20 in A, D.959.
*** Sony Dig. M K 44569 [id.]. Murray Perahia – SCHUMANN: *Piano sonata No. 2.* ***

Perahia's combination of intellectual vigour and poetic insight shows that awareness of proportion and feeling for expressive detail which distinguish the greatest interpreters. As always with this artist, every phrase speaks and each paragraph breathes naturally.

Piano sonatas Nos. 20 in A, D.959; 21 in B flat, D.960.
(N) (M) *** Virgin Veritas/EMI VER5 61272-2 [id.]. Melvyn Tan (fortepiano).

Melvyn Tan uses a fortepiano that was much admired by Beethoven. He is a compelling artist of keen musical intelligence who makes you listen, even when you might not agree with every expressive or agogic hesitation. Generally speaking, tempi are well judged, though the *Andantino* of the *A major* and the slow movement of the *B flat* are far too fast. However, by the end of each movement he almost convinces you that he is right and, in the case of the *B flat*, he succeeds. His account of this sonata is very impressive: there is depth of feeling as well as many felicities of sonority. Whether or not you are completely persuaded, these performances will make you think afresh about this music. The recording is first class.

Piano sonata No. 21 in B flat, D.960.
(N) (M) *** Decca 448 578-2 [id.]. Clifford Curzon – BRAHMS: *Piano sonata No. 3* etc. ***
(M) *** Ph. 420 644-2. Alfred Brendel – *Wanderer fantasia.* ***

Curzon's is among the finest accounts of the *B flat Sonata* in the catalogue. Tempi are aptly judged and everything is in fastidious taste. Detail is finely drawn but never emphasized at the expense of the architecture as a whole. It is beautifully recorded, and the piano sounds very truthful in timbre. For the reissue in Decca's 'Classic Sound' series, the Brahms *F minor Sonata* has been added, an equally perceptive account, plus a pair of *Intermezzi*, to make this quite outstanding value.

Brendel's earlier analogue performance is as impressive and full of insight as one would expect. He is not unduly wayward, for his recording has room for the *Wanderer fantasy* as well, and he is supported by excellent Philips sound.

Piano sonata No. 21 in B flat, D.960; Allegretto in C min., D.915; 12 Ländler, D.790.
(Y/B) ✿ *** EMI Dig. CDC5 55359-2 [id.]. Kovacevich.

Stephen Kovacevich made a memorable recording of the great *B flat major Sonata* for Hyperion which (in our 1988 edition) we called 'one of the most eloquent accounts on record of this sublime sonata and one which is completely free of expressive point-making. It is an account which totally reconciles the demands of truth and the attainment of beauty.' One could well say the same of the present version, though, if anything, it explores an even deeper vein of feeling than its predecessor. Indeed it is the most searching and penetrating account of the work to have appeared in recent years and, given the excellence and truthfulness of the recording, must carry the strongest and most enthusiastic recommendation.

Piano sonata No. 21 in B flat, D.960; Impromptus: in G flat; in E flat, D.899/2 & 3; in B flat, D.935/3; Moments musicaux: in A flat; in F min., D.780/2 & 5.
(Y/B) ✿ (B) *** DG 439 462-2 [id.]. Wilhelm Kempff.

It is a tribute to Kempff's inspirational artistry that with the most relaxed tempi he conveys such consistent, compelling intensity in Schubert's greatest sonata. Kempff's long-breathed expressiveness is hypnotic, so that here quite as much as in the *Great C major Symphony* one is bound by the spell of the heavenly length. Rightly, Kempff observes the first-movement exposition repeat with the important nine bars of lead-back and, though the overall manner is less obviously dramatic than is common, the range of tone-colour is magical, with sharp terracing of dynamics to plot the geography of each movement. This remarkable performance belongs to a tradition of pianism that has almost disappeared, and we must be eternally grateful that its expression has been so glowingly captured. After the sonata we are offered an attractively diverse mini-recital of *Moments musicaux* and *Impromptus*, opening with the treasurable *G flat Impromptu*, D.899/2. This is perhaps the very finest of all the distinguished reissues on DG's Classikon bargain label so far.

VOCAL MUSIC

Dietrich Fischer-Dieskau: The EMI Recordings

The First Recital (1951): *Der Atlas; Ihr Bild; Fischermädchen; Die Stadt; Am Meer; Der Doppelgänger; Erlkönig; Nacht und Träume; Du bist die Ruh; Ständchen.*

Volume I (1955): *Der Wanderer an den Mond; Uber Wildemann; Der Einsame; Auflösung; Der Kreuzzug; Totengräbers Heimweh; Nachtviolen; Frühlingssehnseht; Geheimnes; Rastlose Liebe; Liebesbotschaft; Im Abendrot; Abschied.*

Volume II (1957): *Dem Unendlichen; Die Sterne; An die Musik; Wehmut; Kriegers Ahnung; Der Zwerg; Der Wanderer; Frühlingsglaube; Die Taubenpost; An Silvia; Im Frühling; Auf der Bruck.*

Volume IIIa (1958): *Ständchen; Alinde; Nähe des Geliebten; Normanns Gesang; In der Ferne.*

Volume IIIb (1958): *Aufenthalt; Lied des gefangenen Jägers; Greisengesang; Erlkönig; Nachtstück.*

(all with Gerald Moore).

Volume IV (1959): *Gruppe aus dem Tartarus; Die Götter Griechenlands; Ewartung; Sehnsucht; Der Taucher.*

Volume V (1959): *Der Sänger; Die Bürgschaft; Der Fischer; Einsamkeit.*

Volume VIa (1959): *Am Strome; Der Alpenjäger; Erlafsee; Wie Ulfru fischt; Beim Winde; Trost; Auf der Donau* (1959).

Volume VIb (1959): *Abendstern; Liedesend; Sehnsucht; Heliopolis; Zum Punsche; Der Sieg; An die Freunde.*

(Volumes IV–VIb with Karl Engel).

Volume VII (1962): *Der Atlas; Ihr Bild; Das Fischermädchen; Die Stadt; Am Meer; Der Doppelgänger; Lachen und Weinen; Dass sie hier gewesen; Sei mir gegrüsst; Du bist die Ruh; Im Walde (Waldesnacht).*

Volume VIII (1965): *Seligkeit; Heidenröslein; Ständchen; Des Fischers Liebesglück; Fischerweise; Der Jüngling an der Quelle; An die Laute; Die Forelle; Auf der Riesenkoppe.*

Volume IX (1965): *An die Entfernte; Auf dem Wasser zu singen; Der Schiffer; Der Wanderer; Nachtgesang; Das Zügenglöcklein; Der Jüngling und der Tod; Das Heimweh; Das Lied im Grünen; Der Tod und das Mädchen; Der Winterabend; Der zürnende Barde; Der Strom; Litanei auf das Fest Aller Seelen.*

(all with Gerald Moore).

(N) (M) *** EMI mono/stereo CMS5 65670-2 (6) [CDMF 65670]. Dietrich Fischer-Dieskau, Gerald Moore or Karl Engel.

This HMV set makes an admirable survey of Fischer-Dieskau's Schubert recordings for EMI over a decade and a half before he moved to Deutsche Grammophon to make the extensive survey listed below. It is particularly interesting to compare the earliest recordings (the first in mono), with the voice and manner still youthfully fresh, to the second generation, again with Gerald Moore but also with Karl Engel. The contrast is fascinating, with the voice still younger than on DG. The transfers are superbly managed and full translations are provided to make this an indispensable supplement to the DG sets.

Lieder, Volume 1 (1811–17); Volume 2 (1817–28); Song cycles: *Die schöne Müllerin; Schwanengesang; Die Winterreise.*

(B) *** DG 437 214-2 (21). Fischer-Dieskau, Gerald Moore (as below).

Fischer-Dieskau's monumental survey of all the Schubert songs suitable for a man's voice (some of the longer ones excepted) was made over a relatively brief span, with the last 300 songs concentrated on a period of only two months in 1969, yet there is not a hint of routine. The two big boxes of nine discs come at bargain price, whereas the smaller box, containing the song-cycles, comes at mid-price. Nor has the background information been skimped. Each box contains complete German texts and English translations (plus summaries in French) as well as introductory essays. The one serious omission is an alphabetical list of titles. It makes it unnecessarily hard to find a particular song – much the most likely way of using so compendious a collection.

This collection of 21 CDs is offered at bargain price, as are the two separate 9-disc collections of Lieder listed below. The three great song-cycles – also included here – cost more if purchased separately.

Lieder, Volume I (1811–17): *Ein Leichenfantasie; Der Vatermörder* (1811); *Der Jüngling am Bache* (1812); *Totengräberlied; Die Schatten; Sehnsucht; Verklärung; Pensa, che questo istante* (1813); *Der Taucher* (1813–15); *Andenken; Geisternähe; Erinnerung; Trost, An Elisa; Die Betende; Lied aus der Ferne; Der Abend; Lied der Liebe; Erinnerungen; Adelaide; An Emma; Romanze: Ein Fräulein klagt' im finstern Turm; An Laura, als sie Klopstocks Auferstehungslied sang; Der Geistertanz; Das Mädchen aus der Fremde; Nachtgesang; Trost in Tränen; Schäfers Klagelied; Sehnsucht; Am See* (1814); *Auf einen Kirchhof; Als ich sie erröten sah; Das Bild; Der Mondabend* (1815); *Lodas Gespenst* (1816); *Der Sänger*

(1815); *Die Erwartung* (1816); *Am Flusse; An Mignon; Nähe des Geliebten; Sängers Morgenlied; Amphiaraos; Das war ich; Die Sterne; Vergebliche Liebe; Liebesrausch; Sehnsucht der Liebe; Die erste Liebe; Trinklied; Stimme der Liebe; Naturgenuss; An die Freude; Der Jüngling am Bache; An den Mond; Die Mainacht; An die Nachtigall; An die Apfelbäume; Seufzer; Liebeständelei; Der Liebende; Der Traum; Die Laube; Meeres Stille; Grablied; Das Finden; Wandrers Nachtlied; Der Fischer; Erster Verlust; Die Erscheinung; Die Täuschung; Der Abend; Geist der Liebe; Tischlied; Der Liedler; Ballade; Abends unter der Linde; Die Mondnacht; Huldigung; Alles um Liebe; Das Geheimnis; An den Frühling; Die Bürgschaft; Der Rattenfänger; Der Schatzgräber; Heidenröslein; Bundeslied; An den Mond; Wonne der Wehmut; Wer kauft Liebesgötter?* (1815); *Der Goldschmiedsgesell* (1817); *Der Morgenkuss; Abendständchen: An Lina; Morgenlied: Willkommen, rotes Morgenlicht; Der Weiberfreund; An die Sonne; Tischlerlied; Totenkranz für ein Kind; Abendlied; Die Fröhlichkeit; Lob des Tokayers; Furcht der Geliebten; Das Rosenband; An Sie; Die Sommernacht; Die frühen Gräber; Dem Unendlichen; Ossians Lied nach dem Falle Nathos; Das Mädchen von Inistore; Labetrank der Liebe; An die Geliebte; Mein Gruss an den Mai; Skolie – Lasst im Morgenstrahl des Mai'n; Die Sternenwelten; Die Macht der Liebe; Das gestörte Glück; Die Sterne; Nachtgesang; An Rosa I: Warum bist du nicht hier?; An Rosa II: Rosa, denkst du an mich?; Schwanengesang; Der Zufriedene; Liane; Augenlied; Geistes-Gruss; Hoffnung; An den Mond; Rastlose Liebe; Erlkönig* (1815); *Der Schmetterling; Die Berge* (1819); *Genügsamkeit; An die Natur* (1815); *Klage; Morgenlied; Abendlied; Der Flüchtling; Laura am Klavier; Entzückung an Laura; Die vier Weltalter; Pflügerlied; Die Einsiedelei; An die Harmonie; Die Herbstnacht; Lied: Ins stille Land; Der Herbstabend; Der Entfernten; Fischerlied; Sprache der Liebe; Abschied von der Harfe; Stimme der Liebe; Entzückung; Geist der Liebe; Klage: Der Sonne steigt; Julius an Theone; Klage: Dein Silber schien durch Eichengrün; Frühlingslied; Auf den Tod einer Nachtigall; Die Knabenzeit; Winterlied; Minnelied; Die frühe Liebe; Blumenlied; Der Leidende; Seligkeit; Erntelied; Das grosse Halleluja; Die Gestirne; Die Liebesgötter; An den Schlaf; Gott im Frühling; Der gute Hirt; Die Nacht; Fragment aus dem Aeschylus* (1816); *An die untergehende Sonne* (1816/17); *An mein Klavier; Freude der Kinderjahre; Das Heimweh; An den Mond; An Chloen; Hochzeitlied; In der Mitternacht; Trauer der Liebe; Die Perle; Liedesend; Orpheus; Abschied; Rückweg; Alte Liebe rostet nie; Gesänge des Harfners aus Goethes Wilhelm Meister: Harfenspieler I: Wer sich der Einsamkeit ergibt; Harfenspieler II: An die Türen will ich schleichen; Harfenspieler III: Wer nie sein Brot mit Tränen ass. Der König in Thule; Jägers Abendlied; An Schwager Kronos; Der Sänger am Felsen; Lied: Ferne von der grossen Stadt; Der Wanderer; Der Hirt; Lied eines Schiffers an die Dioskuren; Geheimnis; Zum Punsche; Am Bach im Frühling* (1816); *An eine Quelle* (1817); *Bei dem Grabe, meines Vaters; Am Grabe Anselmos; Abendlied; Zufriedenheit; Herbstlied; Skolie: Mädchen entsiegelten; Lebenslied; Lieden der Trennung* (1816); *Alinde; An die Laute* (1827); *Frohsinn; Die Liebe; Trost; Der Schäfer und der Reiter* (1817); *Lob der Tränen* (1821); *Der Alpenjäger; Wie Ulfru fischt; Fahrt zum Hades; Schlaflied; Die Blumensprache; Die abgeblühte Linde; Der Flug der Zeit; Der Tod und das Mädchen; Das Lied vom Reifen; Täglich zu singen; Am Strome; Philoktet; Memnon; Auf dem See; Ganymed; Der Jüngling und der Tod; Trost im Liede* (1817).

(B) *** DG 437 215-2 (9). Dietrich Fischer-Dieskau, Gerald Moore.

This remarkable project, with Volume 1 recorded between 1966 and 1968 and Volume 2 over two months of intensive sessions in 1969, is an astonishing achievement in bringing together the greatest Schubertian of our time and the finest accompanist in a wide survey of the Lieder for solo voice. Already in 1811, as a boy in his early teens, Schubert was writing with astonishing originality, as is shown in the long (19 minutes) opening Schiller setting, a *Funeral Fantasy* with its rough, clashing intervals of a second and amazing harmonic pointers to the future. Drama comes very much to the fore in the second song here, *Der Vatermörder* ('A father died by his son's hand'), while the composer's endearing, flowing lyricism makes both *Der Jüngling am Bache* and *Die Schatten* sound remarkably mature. *Totengräberlied* ('Dig, spade, dig on!') brings a characteristically light touch to a gravedigger's soliloquy as he reflects that rich and poor alike, handsome and noble, are all in the end reduced to bones. Throughout these nine well-filled CDs the diversity of Schubert's imagination holds the listener, and his melodic gift almost never disappoints, especially when the performances are so completely at home with the music. The songs are presented in broadly chronological order and the arrangement of items ensures that each disc of the nine makes a satisfying recital in its own right. The CD transfers are impeccable, adding a little in presence to what were originally very well-balanced recordings.

Lieder, Volume II (1817–28): *An die Musik; Pax vobiscum; Hänflings Liebeswerbung; Auf der Donau; Der Schiffer; Nach einem Gewitter; Fischerlied; Das Grab; Der Strom; An den Tod; Abschied; Die Forelle; Gruppe aus dem Tartarus; Elysium; Atys; Erlafsee; Der Alpenjäger; Der Kampf; Der Knabe in der Wiege* (1817); *Auf der Riesenkoppe; An den Mond in einer Herbstnacht; Grablied für die Mutter; Einsamkeit; Der Blumenbrief; Das Marienbild* (1818); *Litanei auf das Fest Allerseelen* (1816); *Blondel zu Marien; Das Abendrot; Sonett I: Apollo, lebet noch dein Hold verlangen; Sonett II: Allein, nachdenken wie gelähmt vom*

Krampfe; Sonett III: Nunmehr, da Himmel, Erde schweigt; Vom Mitleiden Mariä (1818) ; *Die Gebüsche; Der Wanderer; Abendbilder; Himmelsfunken; An die Freunde; Sehnsucht; Hoffnung; Der Jüngling am Bache; Hymne I: Wenige wissen das Geheimnis der Liebe; Hymne II: Wenn ich ihn nur hab; Hymne III: Wenn alle untreu werden; Hymne IV: Ich sag es jedem; Marie; Beim Winde; Die Sternennächte; Trost; Nachtstück; Prometheus; Strophe aus Die Götter Griechenlands* (1819); *Nachthymne; Die Vögel; Der Knabe; Der Fluss; Abendröte; Der Schiffer; Die Sterne; Morgenlied* (1820); *Frühlingsglaube* (1822); *Des Fräuleins Liebeslauschen* (1820); *Orest auf Tauris* (1817); *Der entsühnte Orest; Freiwilliges Versinken; Der Jüngling auf dem Hügel* (1820); *Sehnsucht* (1817); *Der zürnenden Diana; Im Walde* (1820); *Die gefangenen Sänger; Der Unglückliche; Versunken; Geheimnes; Grenzen der Menschheit* (1821); *Der Jüngling an der Quelle* (1815); *Der Blumen Schmerz* (1821); *Sei mir gegrüsst; Herr Josef Spaun, Assessor in Linz; Der Wachtelschlag Ihr Grab; Nachtviolen; Heliopolis I: Im kalten, rauhen Norden; Heliopolis II: Fels auf Felsen hingewälzet; Selige Welt; Schwanengesang: Wie klage'ich's aus; Du liebst mich nicht; Die Liebe hat gelogen; Todesmusik; Schatzgräbers Begehr; An die Leier, Im Haine; Der Musensohn; An die Entfernte; Am Flusse; Willkommen und Abschied* (1822); *Wandrers Nachtlied: Ein Gleiches; Der zürnende Barde* (1823); *Am See* (1822/3); *Viola; Drang in die Ferne; Der Zwerg; Wehmut; Lied: Die Mutter Erde; Auf dem Wasser zu singen; Pilgerweise; Das Geheimnis; Der Pilgrim; Dass sie hier gewesen; Du bist die Ruh; Lachen und Weinen; Greisengesang* (1823); *Dithyrambe; Der Sieg; Abendstern; Auflösung; Gondelfahrer* (1824); *Glaube, Hoffnung und Liebe* (1828); *Im Abendrot; Der Einsame* (1824); *Des Sängers Habe; Totengräbers Heimwehe; Der blinde Knabe; Nacht und Träume; Normans Gesang; Lied des gefangenen Jägers; Im Walde; Auf der Bruck; Das Heimweh; Die Allmacht; Fülle der Liebe; Wiedersehn; Abendlied für die Entfernte; Szene I aus dem Schauspiel Lacrimas; Am mein Herz; Der liebliche Stern* (1825); *Im Jänner 1817 (Tiefes Leid); Am Fenster; Sehnsucht; Im Freien; Fischerweise; Totengräberweise; Im Frühling; Lebensmut; Um Mitternacht; Uber Wildemann* (1826); *Romanze des Richard Löwenherz* (1827); *Trinklied; Ständchen; Hippolits Lied; Gesang (An Silvia); Der Wanderer an den Mond; Das Zügenglöcklein; Bei dir allein; Irdisches Glück; Wiegenlied* (1826); *Der Vater mit dem Kind; Jägers Liebeslied; Schiffers Scheidelied; L'incanto degli occhi; Il traditor deluso; Il modo di prender moglie; Das Lied im Grünen; Das Weinen; Vor meiner Wiege; Der Wallensteiner Lanznecht beim Trunk; Der Kreuzzug; Das Fischers Liebesglück* (1827); *Der Winterabend; Die Sterne; Herbst; Widerschein* (1828); *Abschied von der Erde* (1825/6).

(B) *** DG 437 225-2 (9) [id.]. Dietrich Fischer-Dieskau, Gerald Moore.

Volume II of this great project brings the mature songs; performances and recording are just as compelling as in Volume 1. In their Berlin sessions Fischer-Dieskau and Moore adopted a special technique of study, rehearsal and recording most apt for the project. The sense of spontaneity and new discovery is unfailing, since each take was in fact a performance. On a later occasion, both artists might have taken a different view but, using the ease of access possible with CD, this collection is a unique way of sampling the many different aspects of Schubert's genius. The collection opens appropriately with *An die Musik* of 1817 and, as before, the songs in this volume are laid out chronologically with certain obvious exceptions – on disc 4, for instance, *Orest auf Tauris* (1817) is placed alongside the highly contrasted *Der entsühnte Orest*, 'Orestes purified' (1820) – and the closing recital on disc 9 is suitably concluded with *Abschied von der Erde* ('Farewell to the Earth'), dating from 1825/6. Once again there is much unfamiliar repertory to discover: the four *Hymnes* grouped together on the second disc are little known but show the composer's imaginative diversity in a specifically religious connotation, while the unexpected song dedicated to *Herr Josef Spaun, Assessor in Linz*, which closes the fourth CD, is strikingly operatic. Both booklets offer full translations and each includes also brief essays by Fischer-Dieskau and Walther Dürr on the composer.

Lieder, Volume III: Song-cycles: *Die schöne Müllerin; Schwanengesang; Die Winterreise.*
(M) *** DG 437 235-2 (3) [id.]. Dietrich Fischer-Dieskau, Gerald Moore.

Fischer-Dieskau and Moore had each recorded these great cycles of Schubert several times already before they embarked on this set in 1971/2 as part of DG's Schubert song series. It was no mere repeat of earlier triumphs. If anything, these performances – notably that of the darkest and greatest of the cycles, *Winterreise* – are even more searching than before, with Moore matching the hushed concentration of the singer in some of the most remarkable playing that even he has put on record. As in the extensive recitals listed above, Fischer-Dieskau is in wonderfully fresh voice, and the transfers to CD have been managed very naturally.

Lieder: *Abendbilder; Am Fenster; Auf der Bruck; Auf der Donau; Aus Heliopolis; Fischerweise; Im Frühling; Liebeslauschen; Des Sängers Habe; Der Schiffer; Die Sterne; Der Wanderer; Wehmut; Das Zügenglöcklein.*
(N) (M) *** DG 445 717-2 [id.]. Dietrich Fischer-Dieskau, Sviatoslav Richter.

Recorded live in 1977, this beautifully balanced selection of Schubert songs displays the singer's enormous range of expression, as well as the acute sensitivity of the pianist in responding. The songs have been grouped almost in a cycle, starting with a biting expression of self-torment (*Des Sängers Habe*, translated colloquially as 'Break my luck to smithereens'). This is sung perhaps too aggressively here (understandably so) but gradually the mood lightens from melancholy (*Wehmut*) to brighter thoughts (*Das Zügenglöcklein* – 'The little bell'). Not many of these songs are well known, but it is a programme to delight aficionado and newcomer alike, atmospherically recorded with remarkably little interference from audience noises.

Elly Ameling collection ('The early years'): Disc 1: *An die Laute; An die Nachtigall* (2 settings); *An Sylvia; Der Blumenbrief; Du bist die Ruh'; Du Liebst mich nicht; Das Lied im Grünen; Der Einsame; Fischerweise; Die Gebüsche; Im Abendrot; Im Freien; Im Haine; Die Liebe hat gelogen; Der liebliche Stern; Das Mädchen; Die Männer sind méchant; Minnelied; Nacht und Träume; Nachtviolen; Rosamunde: Romanze. Schlummerlied; Der Schmetterling; Seligkeit; Die Sterne; Die Vögel; Der Wachtelschlag.* Disc 2: *Ave Maria; Gretchen am Spinnrade; Gretchens Bitte; Heidenröslein; Jäger, ruhe von der Jagd; Der König in Thule; Die junge Nonne; Die Liebende schreibt; Liebhabner in allen Gestalten; 4 Mignon Lieder (Kennst du das Land; Nur wer die Sehnsucht kennt; Heiss mich nicht reden; So lass mich scheinen); Nähe des Geliebten; Raste, Krieger!; Scene aus Faust; Suleika I & II.* Disc 3: *Abendbilder; An die Musik; An den Mond; Bertas Lied in der Nacht; Die Blumensprache; Erster Verlust; Frühlingssehnsucht; Der Knabe; Nachthymne; Schwestergruss; Sei mir gegrüsst; Die Sterne; Wiegenlied.* Disc 4: *Am Bach im Frühling; An den Tod; An die Entfernte; An die untergehende Sonne; Auf dem Wasser zu singen; Die Forelle; Fülle der Liebe; Ganymed; Die Götter Griechenlands; Im Abendrot; Im Frühling; Der Musensohn; Der Schiffer; Schwanengesang: Sehnsucht; Sprach der Liebe.*
(M) *** Ph. Analogue/Dig. 438 528-2 (4) [id.]. Elly Ameling, Dalton Baldwin (CDs 1–3); Rudolf Jansen (CD 4).

Elly Ameling appeared on the international scene in the mid-1960s. These records cover her period of maturity from 1972 until 1984. Her lovely voice with its diamond purity is consistently appealing and she is a persuasive interpreter, whether in the engaging *Mignon* songs or in the most familiar favourites: the poised freshness of *Nacht und Träume*, the innocence of *Nachtviolen* or the more emotionally fraught *Die Liebe hat gelogen*. These, like so much else, are most affecting; the analogue recordings on the first two discs show her at the peak of her form, with Dalton Baldwin most sensitive in support. The third disc, digitally recorded in 1982, had the distinction of being the first Lieder recital to appear on compact disc and readily deserved its accolade. It is a typically characterful and enchanting collection, starting with *An die Musik* and including other favourites like the *Cradle song* as well as lesser-known songs that admirably suit the lightness and sparkle of Ameling's voice. The fourth CD offers a 1984 digital recital with Rudolf Janson accompanying. It brings more delights, even if the voice is not quite as fresh and agile as in the earlier collections, notably the 1972 recordings included on the second disc. Yet she is able to bring new depths to such a song as *An die Entfernte* and her breath control remains immaculate – as in the opening *Ganymed* – while she still brings delightful bounce to the ever-popular *Der Musensohn*. Her voice is caught naturally by the engineers and the balance is excellent. A treasurable collection, marred only by the absence of translations: only the German texts are given.

The Graham Johnson Schubert Lieder Edition

When it comes to background information, the rival project to record all Schubert's songs – Graham Johnson's for Hyperion using some of the greatest singers of the day – sets standards it would be hard for anyone to match in whatever field. With each disc devoted to a group of songs on a particular theme, Johnson provides notes that add enormously to the enjoyment, heightening the experience of hearing even the most familiar songs.

Lieder Vol. 1: *Der Alpenjäger; Amalia; An den Frühling; An den Mond; Erster Verlust; Die Ewartung; Der Fischer; Der Flüchtling; Das Geheimnis; Der Jüngling am Bache; Lied; Meeres Stille; Nähe des Geliebten; Der Pilgrim; Schäfers Klagelied; Sehnsucht; Thekla; Wanderers Nachtlied; Wonne der Wehmut.*
*** Hyperion Dig. CDJ 33001 [id.]. Dame Janet Baker, Graham Johnson.

Hyperion's complete Schubert song edition, master-minded by the accompanist, Graham Johnson, is planned to mix well-known songs with rarities. Dame Janet's whole collection is devoted to Schiller and Goethe settings, above all those he wrote in 1815, an exceptionally rich year for the 18-year-old; one marvels that, after writing his dedicated, concentrated setting of *Wanderers Nachtlied*, he could on that same day in July write two other equally memorable songs, *Der Fischer* and *Erster Verlust (First loss)*. Dame Janet is in glorious voice, her golden tone ravishing in a song such as *An den Mond* and her hushed tone caressing the ear in *Meeres Stille* and *Wanderers Nachtlied*. Presented like this, the project becomes a voyage of discovery.

Lieder Vol. 2: *Am Bach im Frühling; Am Flusse; Auf der Donau; Fahrt zum Hades; Fischerlied* (two settings); *Fischerweise; Der Schiffer; Selige Welt; Der Strom; Der Taucher; Widerschein; Wie Ulfru fischt.*
*** Hyperion Dig. CDJ 33002 [id.]. Stephen Varcoe, Graham Johnson.

Graham Johnson with the baritone, Stephen Varcoe, devises a delightful collection of men's songs, culminating in the rousing strophic song, *Der Schiffer*, one of the most catchily memorable that Schubert ever wrote, here exhilaratingly done. Otherwise the moods of water and wave, sea and river, are richly exploited. The last 28 minutes of the collection are devoted to the extended narrative, *Der Taucher* (*The Diver*), setting a long poem of Schiller which is based on an early version of the Beowulf saga. Varcoe and Johnson completely explode the long-accepted idea that this is overextended and cumbersome, giving it a thrilling dramatic intensity.

Lieder Vol. 3: *Abschied; An die Freunde; Augenlied; Iphigenia; Der Jüngling und der Tod; Lieb Minna; Liedesend; Nacht und Träume; Namenstagslied; Pax vobiscum; Rückweg; Trost im Liede; Viola; Der Zwerg.*
*** Hyperion Dig. CDJ 33003 [id.]. Ann Murray, Graham Johnson.

This is one of Ann Murray's finest records with the intimate beauty of the voice consistently well caught and with none of the stress that the microphone exaggerates on record. Like the songs that Johnson chose for Ann Murray's husband, Philip Langridge, these too represent Schubert in his circle of friends, with their poems his inspiration, including a long flower ballad, *Viola*, by his close friend, Franz von Schober, which Murray and Johnson sustain beautifully.

Lieder Vol. 4: *Alte Liebe rostet nie; Am See; Am Strome; An Herrn Josef von Spaun (Epistel); Auf der Riesenkoppe; Das war ich; Das gestörte Glück; Liebeslauschen; Liebesrausch; Liebeständelei; Der Liedler; Nachtstück; Sängers Morgenlied* (2 versions); *Sehnsucht der Liebe.*
*** Hyperion Dig. CDJ 33004 [id.]. Philip Langridge, Graham Johnson.

Philip Langridge brings a collection to illustrate Schubert's setting of words by poets in his immediate circle, ending with *Epistel*, a tongue-in-cheek parody song addressed to a friend who had left Vienna to become a tax collector, extravagantly lamenting his absence. It is Johnson's presentation of such rarities that makes the series such a delight. Langridge has rarely sounded so fresh and sparkling on record.

Lieder Vol. 5: *Die Allmacht; An die Natur; Die Erde; Erinnerung; Ferne von der grossen Stadt; Ganymed; Klage der Ceres; Das Lied im Grünen; Morgenlied; Die Mutter Erde; Die Sternenwelten; Täglich zu singen; Dem Unendlichen; Wehmut.*
*** Hyperion Dig. CDJ 33005 [id.]. Elizabeth Connell, Graham Johnson.

Thanks in part to Johnson's choice of songs and to his sensitive support at the piano, Connell has rarely sounded so sweet and composed on record, yet with plenty of temperament. The collection centres round a theme – this one, Schubert and the countryside, suggested by the most popular song of the group, *Das Lied im Grünen*. As ever, the joy of the record is enhanced by Johnson's brilliant, illuminating notes.

Lieder Vol. 6: *Abendlied für die Entfernte; Abends unter der Linde* (two versions); *Abendstern; Alinde; An die Laute; Des Fischers Liebesglück; Jagdlied; Der Knabe in der Wiege (Wiegenlied); Lass Wolken an Hügeln ruh'n; Die Nacht; Die Sterne; Der Vater mit dem Kind; Vor meiner Wiege; Wilkommen und Abschied; Zur guten Nacht.*
*** Hyperion Dig. CDJ 33006 [id.]. Anthony Rolfe Johnson, Graham Johnson (with chorus).

The theme of Anthony Rolfe Johnson's contribution is 'Schubert and the Nocturne'. Two items include a small male chorus, a group of individually named singers. *Jagdlied* is entirely choral, and the final *Zur guten Nacht*, a late song of 1827, has the 'Spokesman' answered by the chorus, ending on a gentle *Gute Nacht*. Rolfe Johnson's voice has never sounded more beautiful on record, and the partnership of singer and accompanist makes light even of a long strophic song (i.e. using essentially the same music for each verse) like *Des Fischers Liebesglück*, beautiful and intense.

Lieder Vol. 7: *An die Nachtigall; An den Frühling; An den Mond; Idens Nachtgesang; Idens Schwanenlied; Der Jüngling am Bache; Kennst du das Land?; Liane; Die Liebe; Luisens Antwort; Des Mädchens Klage; Meeres Stille; Mein Gruss an den Mai; Minona oder die Kunde der Dogge; Naturgenuss; Das Rosenband; Das Sehnen; Sehnsucht* (2 versions); *Die Spinnerin; Die Sterbende; Stimme der Liebe; Von Ida; Wer kauft Liebesgötter?.*
*** Hyperion Dig. CDJ 33007 [id.]. Elly Ameling, Graham Johnson.

An extraordinarily rewarding sequence of 24 songs, all written in the composer's *annus mirabilis*, 1815. With Ameling both charming and intense, Johnson's robust defence in his ever-illuminating notes of the first and longest of the songs, *Minona*, is amply confirmed, a richly varied ballad. Here too is a preliminary setting of *Meeres Stille*, less well-known than the regular version, written a day later, but just as clearly a masterpiece, sung by Ameling in a lovely intimate half-tone at a sustained pianissimo. It is fascinating too to compare the two contrasted settings of Mignon's song, *Sehnsucht*, the first of five he ultimately attempted.

Lieder Vol. 8: *Abendlied der Fürstin; An Chloen; An den Mond; An den Mond in einer Herbstnacht; Berthas Lied in der Nacht; Erlkönig; Die frühen Gräber; Hochzeitslied; In der Mitternacht; Die Mondnacht; Die Nonne; Die Perle; Romanze; Die Sommernacht; Ständchen; Stimme der Liebe; Trauer der Liebe; Wiegenlied.*
*** Hyperion Dig. CDJ 33008 [id.]. Sarah Walker, Graham Johnson.

For Sarah Walker, with her perfectly controlled mezzo at its most sensuous, the theme is 'Schubert and the Nocturne', leading from the first, lesser-known version of the Goethe poem, *An den Mond*, to two of the best-loved of all Schubert's songs, the delectable *Wiegenlied*, 'Cradle-song', and the great drama of *Erlkönig*, normally sung by a man, but here at least as vividly characterized by a woman's voice.

Lieder Vol. 9: *Blanka; 4 Canzonen, D.688; Daphne am Bach; Delphine; Didone abbandonata; Gott! höre meine Stimme; Der gute Hirt; Hin und wieder Fliegen Pfeile; (i) Der Hirt auf dem Felsen. Ich schleiche bang und still (Romanze). Lambertine; Liebe Schwärmt auf allen Wegen; Lilla an die Morgenröte; Misero pargoletto; La pastorella al prato; Der Sänger am Felsen; Thekla; Der Vollmond strahlt (Romanze).*
*** Hyperion Dig. CDJ 33009 [id.]. Arleen Augér, Graham Johnson; (i) with Thea King.

'Schubert and the theatre' is the theme of Arleen Augér's contribution, leading up to the glories of his very last song, the headily beautiful *Shepherd on the rock*, with its clarinet obbligato. The *Romanze*, *Ich schleiche bang* – adapted from an opera aria – also has a clarinet obbligato. Notable too are the lightweight Italian songs that the young Schubert wrote for his master, Salieri, and a lovely setting, *Der gute Hirt* ('The good shepherd'), in which the religious subject prompts a melody which anticipates the great staircase theme in Strauss's *Arabella*.

Lieder Vol. 10: *Adelwold und Emma; Am Flusse; An die Apfelbäume, wo ich Julien erblickte; An die Geliebte; An Mignon; Auf den Tod einer Nachtigall; Auf einen Kirchhof; Harfenspieler I; Labetrank der Liebe; Die Laube; Der Liebende; Der Sänger; Seufzer; Der Traum; Vergebliche Liebe; Der Weiberfreund.*
*** Hyperion Dig. CDJ 33010 [id.]. Martyn Hill, Graham Johnson.

Graham Johnson here correlates the year 1815 with what has been documented of his life over those twelve months, which is remarkably little. So the songs here form a kind of diary. The big item, overtopping everything else, is the astonishing 38–stanza narrative song, *Adalwold and Emma*, with Hill ranging wide in his expression. It is almost half an hour long, from the bold march-like opening to the final happy resolution.

Lieder Vol. 11: *An den Tod; Auf dem Wasser zu singen; Auflösung; Aus 'Heliopolis' I & II; Dithyrambe; Elysium; Der Geistertanz; Der König in Thule; Lied des Orpheus; Nachtstück; Schwanengesang; Seligkeit; So lasst mich scheinen; Der Tod und das Mädchen; Verklärung; Vollendung; Das Zügenglöcklein.*
*** Hyperion Dig. CDJ 33011 [id.]. Brigitte Fassbaender, Graham Johnson.

Starting with a chilling account of *Death and the maiden*, the theme of Brigitte Fassbaender's disc is 'Death and the composer'. Fassbaender's ability precisely to control her vibrato brings baleful tone-colours, made the more ominous by the rather reverberant, almost churchy, acoustic. So in *Auf dem Wasser zu singen* the lightly fanciful rippling-water motif presents the soul gliding gently 'like a boat' up to heaven, and the selection ends astonishingly with what generally seems one of the lightest of Schubert songs, *Seligkeit*. This, as Johnson suggests, returns the listener from heaven back to earth. In this, as elsewhere, Fassbaender sings with thrilling intensity, with Johnson's accompaniment comparably inspired.

Lieder, Vol. 12: *Adelaide; An Elise; An Laura, als sie Klopstocks Auferstehungslied sang; Andenken; Auf den Sieg der Deutschen; Ballade; Die Betende; Don Gayseros I, II, III; Der Geistertanz; Lied an der Ferne; Lied der Liebe; Nachtgesang; Die Schatten; Sehnsucht; Trost; Trost in Tränem; Der Vatermörder.*
** Hyperion Dig. CDJ 33012 [id.]. Adrian Thompson, Graham Johnson.

Adrian Thompson's disc brings the only disappointment so far in Graham Johnson's outstanding Schubert series. As recorded, the voice sounds gritty and unsteady, with the tone growing tight and ugly under pressure, yet this collection of early songs, all teenage inspirations, still illuminates the genius of Schubert at this earliest period of his career. But it is a pity a sweeter voice was not used.

Lieder, Vol. 13: (i) *Eine altschottische Ballade. Ellens Gesang I, II & III (Ave Maria); Gesang der Norna; Gretchen am Spinnrade; Gretchens Bitte; Lied der Anna Lyle; Die Männer sind méchant; Marie; Das Marienbild;* (i) *Normans Gesang; Szene aus Faust. Shilrik und Vinvela; Die Unterscheidung.*
*** Hyperion Dig. CDJ 33013 [id.]. Marie McLaughlin, Graham Johnson; (i) with Thomas Hampson.

The theme for Marie McLaughlin's contribution to the Hyperion Schubert edition is broadly a survey of Schubert's inner conflicts and contradictions. The Goethe settings are crowned by one of the most celebrated of all Schubert songs, *Gretchen am Spinnrade*. McLaughlin gives a fresh and girlish portrait, tenderly pathetic rather than tragic. Fascinatingly the selection also includes *Gretchens Bitte*, an extended song that Schubert left unfinished and for which Benjamin Britten in 1943 provided a completion of the final stanzas. The translations of Scottish ballads cover a wide range. *Eine altschottische Liede* is one of the three dramatic items involving the baritone, Thomas Hampson, which also include a sinister dialogue for Gretchen and an evil spirit, *Szene aus Faust*. McLaughlin's voice comes over sweetly, with brightness and much charm.

Lieder, Vol. 14: *Amphiaraos; An die Leier;* (i) *Antigone und Oedip. Der entsühnte Orest; Freiwilliges Versinken; Die Götter Griechenlands; Gruppe aus dem Tartarus; Fragment aus dem Aeschylus;* (i) *Hektors Abschied. Hippolits Lied; Lied eines Schiffers an die Dioskuren; Memnon; Orest auf Tauris; Philoktet; Uraniens Flucht; Der Zürnenden Diana.*
*** Hyperion Dig. CDJ 33014 [id.]. Thomas Hampson, Graham Johnson; (i) with Marie McLaughlin.

Thomas Hampson's theme here is 'Schubert and the classics', mainly Ancient Greece. Matching the hushed intensity of the opening song, *Die Götter Griechenlands*, singer and accompanist give a rapt performance, and Hampson's ecstatically sweet tone, with flawless legato, contrasts with the darkly dramatic timbre – satisfyingly firm and steady – that he finds for later songs and dialogues, including the finale *Hektors Abschied*. In that dialogue Marie McLaughlin sings the part of Andromache to Hampson's Hector.

Lieder, Vol. 15: *Am Fenster; An die Sonne; An die untergehende Sonne; Der blinde Knabe; Gondelfahrer; Im Frieien; Ins stille Land; Die junge Nonne; Klage an den Mond; Kolmas Klage; Die Mainacht; Der Mondabend; Der Morgenkuss; Sehnsucht; Der Unglückliche; Der Wanderer an den Mond; Der Winterabend.*
❀ *** Hyperion Dig. CDJ 33015 [id.]. Dame Margaret Price, Graham Johnson.

In the fifteenth disc of his Hyperion series, Graham Johnson, accompanying Dame Margaret Price in songs on the theme of 'Night', achieves a new peak. One song that was new to us is *Klage an den Mond* ('Lament to the Moon'), gloriously fresh and lyrical. Price and Johnson find here a distinctive magic so that its simple melody rings through the memory for hours. The other Holty setting on Margaret Price's disc is of *Die Mainacht*, much better known in Brahms's raptly beautiful setting. The young Schubert simply lets his lyricism flower as no one else could. Johnson and Dame Margaret match that with folk-like freshness, concealing art. In the best-known song, *Der Wanderer an den Mond*, Price is light and crisp, but she finds extra mystery in the moonlight scene of *Am Fenster*, poignantly reflecting the lover's sadness.

Lieder, Vol. 16: *An die Freude; An Emma; Die Bürgschaft; Die Entzückung an Laura I & II; Das Geheimnis; Der Jüngling am Bache; Laura am Clavier; Leichenfantasie; Das Mädchen aus der Fremde; Die vier Weltalter; Sehnsucht; Der Pilgrim.*
*** Hyperion Dig. CDJ 33016 [id.]. Thomas Allen, Graham Johnson.

Following the pattern of Graham Johnson's unique Schubert series, Thomas Allen in Schiller settings is challenged to some of his most sensitive singing, using the widest tonal range. They include two extended narrative songs that are a revelation, one of them, *Leichenfantasie* ('Funereal fantasy'), written when Schubert was only fourteen. As before, Johnson's notes and commentaries greatly heighten one's understanding both of particular songs and of Schubert generally.

Lieder, Vol. 17: *Am Grabe Anselmos; An den Mond; An die Nachtigall; An mein Klavier; Aus 'Diego Manazares' (Ilmerine); Die Einsiedelei; Frühlingslied; Geheimnis; Der Herbstabend; Herbstlied; Die Herbstnacht; Klage; Klage um Ali Bey; Lebenslied; Leiden der Trennung; Lied; Lied in der Absehenheit; Litanei; Lodas Gespenst; Lorma; Minnelied; Pflicht und Liebe; Phidile; Winterlied.*
*** Hyperion Dig. CDJ 33017 [id.]. Lucia Popp, Graham Johnson.

It was fitting that one of the last recordings which Lucia Popp made, only months before her tragic death in the autumn of 1993, was her contribution to Graham Johnson's Schubert series. These songs, written in 1816 and almost all of them little known, inspire all her characteristic sweetness and charm. They include an extended narrative song to a text from Ossian, *Lodas gespent*, which, like others resurrected by the indefatigable Johnson, defies the idea that long equals boring. She also relishes two of Schubert's rare comic songs, pointing them deliciously. As ever, Johnson's notes are a model of fascinating scholarship.

Lieder, Vol. 18: *Abendlied; An den Schlaf; An die Erntfernte; An die Harmonie; An mein Herz; Auf den Tod einer Nachtigall; Auf der Bruck; 'Die Blume und der Quell'; Blumenlied; Drang in die Ferne; Erntelied; Das Finden; Das Heimweh* (2 versions); *Im Frühling; Im Jänner 1817 (Tiefes Lied); Im Walde; Lebensmut; Der Liebliche Stern; Die Nacht; Uber Wildemann; Um Mitternacht.*
*** Hyperion Dig. CDJ 33018 [id.]. Peter Schreier, Graham Johnson.

This eighteenth disc in Graham Johnson's masterly series represents the halfway point, with Peter Schreier providing a keenly illuminating supplement to his prize-winning recordings with András Schiff of the great Schubert song-cycles for Decca. The challenge is just as great here, when this particular group centres on strophic songs. The first nine songs are all early ones, dating from 1816, leading to just one extended non-strophic song, *Das Heimweh*, D.851, of 1825. Its weight and complexity come over the more powerfully after such a preparation. Johnson then delivers a master-stroke by devising for Schreier what amounts to a new Schubert song-cycle, presenting in sequence ten settings of poems from the *Poetisches Tagebuch* ('Poetic Diary'), by the obsessive, unstable poet, Ernst Schulze, all written in 1825 and 1826. Quoting the first song, Johnson calls the cycle *Auf den wilden Wegen* ('On the wild paths'), with the sequence following the poet's madly fanciful love-affair with a beloved who in real life rejected him as a mere stranger. Schreier and Johnson in their imaginative treatment present clear parallels with *Winterreise*, offering one momentary haven of happiness, instantly shattered. That comes in the best-known song, *Im Frühling*, among the most haunting that even Schubert ever wrote. Johnson's very detailed notes, as in previous discs of the series, intensify enjoyment enormously.

Lieder, Vol. 19: *Abendlied; Am See; Auf dem See; Auf dem Wasser zu singen; Beim Winde; Der Blumen Schmerz; Die Blumensprache; Gott im Frühling; Im Haine; Der liebliche Stern; Nach einem Gewitter; Nachtviolen; Die Rose; Die Sterne; Suleika I & II; Die Sternennächte; Vergissmeinicht.*
*** Hyperion Dig. CDJ 33019 [id.]. Felicity Lott, Graham Johnson.

Graham Johnson's theme for Felicity Lott's disc is 'Schubert and flowers', prompting a sequence of charming, ever-lyrical songs, mostly neglected but including such a favourite as *Nachtviolen* (raptly sung) and – less predictably – *Auf dem Wasser zu singen*, all enchantingly done. Lott's soprano is not caught quite at its purest, but the charm and tender imagination of the singer consistently match the inspired accompaniments. In his detailed notes Johnson manages to include a 'Schubertian florilegium', listing several hundred of the songs inspired by particular flowers.

Lieder, Vol. 20: *'Schubertiad'* (1815) Songs and part-songs: *Abendständchen (An Lina); Alles um Liebe; Als ich sie erröten sah; Begräbnislied; Bergknappenlied; Der erste Liebe; Die Frölichkeit; Geist der Liebe; Grablied; Heidenröslein; Hoffnung; Huldigung; Klage um Ali Bey; Liebesrausch; Die Macht der Liebe; Das Mädchen von Inistore; Der Morgenstern; Nachtgesang; Ossians Lied nach dem Falle Nathos; Osterlied; Punschlied (Im Norden su singen); Schwertlied; Schwangesang; Die Tauschung; Tischerlied; Totenkranz für ein Kind; Trinklied* (2 versions); *Trinklied vor der Schlacht; Wiegenlied; Winterlied; Der Zufriedene.*
*** Hyperion Dig. CDJ 33020 [id.]. Patricia Rozario, John Mark Ainsley, Ian Bostridge, Michael George, Graham Johnson; L. Schubert Chorale, Stephen Layton.

The twentieth volume of the Hyperion Schubert series brings a different kind of recital disc, with a range of singers performing no fewer than 32 brief songs and ensemble numbers, all written in 1815. Johnson conceives that this might well have been the sort of Schubertiad to take place towards the end of that year and, aptly for the opening and closing numbers, chooses drinking songs. In between, the vigorous and jolly songs are effectively contrasted with a few darker ones, such as a burial song. The team of singers has the flair one expects of Johnson as founder of the Songmakers' Almanac, with the young tenor, Ian Bostridge, making a welcome first appearance, potentially an outstanding singer. More Schubertiads are planned for later on in the Hyperion series.

Lieder, Vol. 21: Songs from 1817–18: *Die abgeblühte Linde; Abschied von einem Freunde; An die Musik; An eine Quelle; Erlafsee; Blondel zu Marien; Blumenbrief; Evangelium Johannes; Der Flug der Zeit; Die Forelle; Grablied für die Mutter; Häbflings Liebeswerbung; Impromptu; Die Liebe; Liebhaber in allen Gestalten; Lied eines Kind; Das Lied vom Reifen; Lob der Tränen; Der Schäfer und der Reiter; Schlaflied; Schweizerlied; Sehnsucht; Trost; Vom Mitleiden Mariä.*
(Y/B) *** Hyperion Dig. CDJ 33021 [id.]. Edith Mathis, Graham Johnson.

Instead of adopting a particular theme for this sequence, sung with characteristic sweetness by the Swiss soprano, Edith Mathis, Graham Johnson has devised a delectable group of 24 songs written in 1817–18, including a high proportion of charmers. Two of them are among the best known of all Schubert's songs, *Die Forelle* ('The trout') and *An die Musik*, here sung with disarming freshness and given extra point through Johnson's inspired playing. The songs in swinging compound or triple time are particularly delightful, as are the often elaborately decorative accompaniments which Johnson points with winning delicacy.

Lieder, Vol. 22: *'Schubertiad II': Der Abend; Das Abendroth; An die Sonne; An Rosa I & II; An Sie; Das Bild; Cora an die Sonne; Cronnan; Die drei Sänger; Die Erscheinung; Furcht der Geliebten; Gebet wahrend der Schlacht; Genugsamkeit; Das Grab; Hermann und Thusnelda; Das Leben ist ein Traum; Lob des Tokayers; Lorma; Das Mädchen aus der Fremde; Morgenlied; Punschlied; Scholie; Selma und Selmar; Die Sterne; Trinklied; Vaterlandslied.*
(Y/B) *** Hyperion Dig. CDJ 33022 [id.]. Lorna Anderson, Catherine Wyn-Rogers, Jamie MacDougall, Simon Keenlyside; Graham Johnson.

The year 1815 was an *annus mirabilis* for Schubert, and Graham Johnson here, from the wealth of songs written in those twelve months, devises a sequence such as the composer might have performed with friends in an intimate Schubertiad. So the solo items are punctuated by three male-voice quartets and one trio for female voices in which the main soloists, listed above, are joined by four other distinguished singers: Patricia Rozario, Catherine Denley, John Mark Ainsley and Michael George. Though most of the 28 items are brief, they include one more-extended song, *Die drei Sänger* ('The three minstrels'), in which Schubert adventurously illustrates the narrative in an almost operatic way. The final page is missing from the manuscript, which is here sensitively completed by Reinhard von Hoorickx.

Lieder, Volume 23: Songs from 1816: *Abendlied; Abschied von der Harfe; Am ersten Maimorgen; An Chloen; Bei dem Grabe meines Vater; Edone; Der Entfernten; Freude der Kinderjahre; Die frühe Liebe; Geist der Liebe; Gesänger des Harfners aus 'Wilhelm Meister' (Wer sich der Einsamkeit ergibt; Wer nie sein Brot mit Tränen ass; An die Türen will ich schleichen); Das Grab; Der Hirt; Julius an Theone; Der Jüngling an der Quelle; Klage; Die Knabenzeit; Der Leidende (2 versions); Die Liebesgötter; Mailied; Pflügerlied; Romanze; Skolie; Stimme der Liebe; Der Tod Oscars; Zufriedenheit.*
(Y/B) *** Hyperion Dig. CDJ 33023 [id.]. Christoph Prégardien, Graham Johnson.

The German lyric tenor, Christoph Prégardien, uses his lovely voice with its honeyed tone-colours through a wide, expressive range in a very varied selection of songs from 1816. It is his artistry as well as Johnson's that makes the opening item so riveting, a long narrative song to words by Ossian in translation, which Prégardien's feeling for word-meaning helps to bring to life. That is followed by a brief chorus, *Der Grab*, sung by the London Schubert Chorale, which Johnson intends as a comment on that narrative. The poet is Johann von Salis-Seewis, who is also represented by four solo songs, including the ravishing *Der Jungling an der Quelle*, one of the most haunting that Schubert ever composed. In that year Schubert was expanding the range of poets he chose to set, including Johann Mayrhofer for the first time, here represented by the little-known *Der Hirt* ('The shepherd'). The selection of 19 items is rumbustiously rounded off by a drinking-song, *Skolie*.

Lieder, Vol. 25: (i) *Die schöne Müllerin* (song-cycle); (ii) with additional poems by Wilhelm Müller.
(N) ❀ *** Hyperion Dig. CDJ 33025 [id.]. (i) Ian Bostridge, Graham Johnson; (ii) read by Dietrich Fischer-Dieskau,

For this first of the big song-cycles in his comprehensive Schubert edition for Hyperion, Graham Johnson could not have chosen his singer more shrewdly. It is a delight to have in Ian Bostridge a tenor who not only produces youthfully golden tone for this young man's sequence but who also gives an eagerly detailed account of the 20 songs, mesmeric at the close, to match even the finest rivals. With the help of Johnson's keenly imaginative accompaniment, Bostridge's gift for changing face and conveying mood makes the story-telling exceptionally fresh and vivid. The bonus is also to have Dietrich Fischer-Dieskau (now retired from singing) reciting the Müller poems which Schubert failed to set. Johnson is at his most inspired too in his detailed notes, which will be a revelation even to experienced Schubertians.

Miscellaneous vocal recitals

'A Schubert evening': (i) *Abendstern; Am Grabe Anselmos; An die Nachtigall; An die untergehende Sonne'; Berthas Lied in der Nacht; Delphine; Ellen's Gesang from The Lady of the Lake (Raste Krieger; Jäger von der Jagd; Ave Maria); Epistel an Herrn Josef von Spaun; Gondelfahrer; Gretchen am Spinnrade; Hin und wieder, Iphigenia; Die junge Nonne; Kennst du das Land; Liebe schwärmt; Das Mädchen; Das Mädchens Klage; Die Männer sind méchant; Mignon Lieder I–III (Heiss mich nicht reden; So lasst mich scheinen; Nur wer die Sehnsucht kennt); Schlummerlied; Schwestergruss; Strophe von Schiller (Die Götter Griechenlands); Suleika songs I–II (Was bedeutet die Bewegung; Ach, um deine feuchten Schwingen); Wiegenlied; Wiegenlied (Schlafe, schlafe).* 'Favourite Lieder': (ii) *An die Musik; An Sylvia; Auf dem Wasser zu singen; Du bist die Ruh'; Die Forelle; Frühlingslaube; Heidenröslein; Litanei; Der Musensohn; Nacht und Träume; Rastlose Lied; Der Tod und das Mädchen.*

(N) ✻ (B) *** EMI CZS5 69389-2 (2) [id.]. Dame Janet Baker, with (i) Gerald Moore; (ii) Geoffrey Parsons.

This astonishingly generous collection, offered on EMI's two-for-the-price-of one forte label, combines a pair of recitals recorded by Dame Janet at two different stages in her career, in 1970 and a decade later. The first collection ranges wide in an imaginative *Liederabend* of Schubert songs that includes a number of comparative rarities. They move from the delectably comic *Epistel* to the ominous drkness of *Die junge Nonne.* The two cradle songs are irresistible, the Seidl setting even more haunting than the more famous one; and throughout Baker consistently displays the breadth of her emotional mastery and her range of tone-colour. With Gerald Moore (who returned to the studio out of retirement especially for the occasion) still at his finest, this is a rarely satisfying collection. Only the opening *Gretchen am Spinnrade* brings a performance which one feels Baker could have intensified on repetition. Yet it has an attractive simplicity and shows the lovely freshness of the voice to perfection. As it happens, this song was also included in the later (1980) recital with Geoffrey Parsons, and there it is sung with heartfelt expression, together with an equally moving account of *Die junge Nonne.* But these duplicate versions have both been omitted here. What remains is treasurable. Take a poll of favourite Schubert songs and a high proportion of these would be in the dozen offered in the 1980 group. With a great singer treating each with loving, detailed care, the result is a charmer of a recital. The very first item, Dame Janet's strongly characterized reading of *Die Forelle*, makes it a fun song, and similarly Parsons' naughty, springing accompaniment to *An Sylvia* (echoed later by the singer) gives a twinkle to a song that can easily be treated too seriously. One also remembers the ravishing *subito piano* for the second stanza of *An die Musik.* The later recording is of fine EMI vintage and catches the more mature voice naturally and with rather more presence than a decade earlier. It is a pity that, because the set is so economically priced, there are no translations, but this remains an unmissable reissue.

Lieder: *Alinde; Am Tage aller Seelen; An die Entfernte; An die Laute; Auf dem Wasser zu singen; Auf der Riesenkoppe; Die Bürgschaft; Du bist die Ruh'; Der Fischer; Der Fischers Liebesglück; Fischerweise; Die Forelle; Die Götter Griechenlands; Greisengesang; Heidenröslein; Das Heimweh; Im Walde; Der Jüngling an der Quelle; Der Jüngling und der Tod; Lachen und Weinen; Lied des gefangenen Jägers; Das Lied im Grünen; Nachtgesang; Nachtstück; Nähe des Geliebten; Normans Gesang; Der Schiffer; Sei mir gegrüsst; Seligkeit; Das sie hier gewesen; Ständchen; Strophe aus Die Götter; Der Strom; Der Tod und das Mädchen; Der Wanderer; Der Winterabend; Das Zügenglöcklein; Der zürnende Barde.*

(M) *** EMI CMS7 63566-2 (2) [Ang. CDMB 63566]. Dietrich Fischer-Dieskau, Gerald Moore; Karl Engel.

Dating from 1965, most of the items in this collection of Schubert songs superbly represent the second generation of Fischer-Dieskau recordings with Gerald Moore, deeper and more perceptive than his mono recordings, yet with voice and manner still youthfully fresh. The contrast is fascinating, if subtle, between that main collection and the last nine songs on the second disc: they were recorded six years earlier, with three of them accompanied by Karl Engel, and with the voice still younger but presented in drier sound. (Alas, this set has just been withdrawn.)

Lieder: *Die Allmacht; An die Natur; Auf dem See; Auflösung; Erlkönig; Ganymed; Gretchen am Spinnrade; Der Musensohn; Rastlose Liebe; Suleika I; Der Tod und das Mädchen; Der Zwerg.*
*** Ph. Dig. 412 623-2 [id.]. Jessye Norman, Philip Moll.

Jessye Norman's characterization of the four contrasting voices in *Erlkönig* is powerfully effective, and the reticence which once marked her Lieder singing has completely disappeared. The poignancy of *Gretchen am Spinnrade* is exquisitely touched in, building to a powerful climax; throughout, the breath control is a thing of wonder, not least in a surpassing account of *Ganymed.* Fine, sympathetic accompaniment from Philip Moll, and first-rate recording.

Lieder: *Am Flusse; An den Mond; Der Fischer; Erster Verlust; Erlkönig; Ganymed; Geheimnes; Gesänge des Harfners I, II & III; Heidenröslein; Hoffnung; Liebhaber in alten Gestalten; Meeres Stille; Mignon; Lied der Mignon I, II & III; Der Musensohn; Rastlose Liebe; Der Sänger; Schäfers Klagenlied; Wanderers Nachtlied I & II.*
** Sony Dig. SK 53104 [id.]. Brigitte Fassbaender, Cord Garben.

Fassbaender's Sony disc of Schubert songs, including many favourites, is marred by the ham-fisted playing of Cord Garben. Rich as her mezzo is, it comes near to being drowned under the busy piano-parts of *Erlkönig* and *Musensohn* when played and recorded so heavily. Yet the characterfulness of Fassbaender in everything she does transforms each song, making even the best-known of them fresh and individual.

Lieder: *An die Laute; An die Leier; An die Musik; An Silvia; Auf der Bruck; Du bist die Ruh'; Erlkönig; Das Fischermädchen; Die Forelle; Ganymed; Gruppe aus dem Tartarus; Heidenröslein; Lachen und Weinen; Litanei auf das Fest; Meeres Stille; Der Musensohn; Rastlose Liebe; Schäfers Klagelied; Ständchen; Die Taubenpost; Der Tod und das Mädchen; Der Wanderer; Wandrers Nachtlied.*
(Y/B) *** DG Dig. 445 294-2 [id.]. Bryn Terfel, Malcolm Martineau.

Bryn Terfel's DG disc of Schubert confirms how this young Welsh bass-baritone has an exceptional gift to project his magnetic personality with comparable intensity, whether in opera or in Lieder, whether live or on disc. Terfel emerges as a positive artist, giving strikingly individual and imaginative readings of these 23 favourite songs. As you immediately realize in three favourite songs common to both collections, *Heidenröslein, An Silvia* and *Du bist die Ruh'*, Terfel is daring in confronting you face to face, very much as the young Fischer-Dieskau did, using the widest range of dynamic and tone. You might argue that Terfel's characterization of the different characters in *Erlkönig* is too extreme, but it is a measure of his magnetism that the result is so dramatically compelling. Full, firm sound.

Lieder: *An die Musik; An Sylvia; Auf dem Wasser zu singen; Ave Maria; Du bist die Ruh'; Die Forelle; Ganymed; Gretchen am Spinnrade; Heidenröslein; Im Frühling; Die junge Nonne; Litanei; Mignon und der Harfner; Der Musensohn; Nacht und Träume; Sei mir gegrüsst; Seligkeit.*
(Y/B) (M) *** Carlton Classics Dig. PCD 2016 [id.]. Felicity Lott, Graham Johnson.

At mid-price, Felicity Lott's collection brings an ideal choice of songs for the general collector. With Graham Johnson the most imaginative accompanist, even the best-known songs emerge fresh and new, and gentle songs like *Litanei* are raptly beautiful.

Lieder: *An die Musik; An Sylvia; Auf dem Wasser zu singen; Ganymed; Gretchen am Spinnrade; Im Frühling; Die junge Nonne; Das Lied im Grünen; Der Musensohn; Nachtviolen; Nähe des Geliebten; Wehmut.*
(M) (***) EMI mono CDH7 64026-2 [id.]. Elisabeth Schwarzkopf, Edwin Fischer.

Schwarzkopf at the beginning of her recording career and Fischer at the end of his make a magical partnership, with even the simplest of songs inspiring intensely subtle expression from singer and pianist alike. Though Fischer's playing is not immaculate, he left few records more endearing than this, and Schwarzkopf's colouring of word and tone is masterly.

Lieder: *An die Nachtigall; An mein Klavier; Auf dem Wasser zu singen; Geheimnis;* (i) *Der Hirt auf dem Felsen; Im Abendrot; Ins stille Land; Liebhaben in allen Gestalten; Das Lied im Grünen; Die Mutter Erde; Romanze; Der Winterabend.*
*** HM Orfeo C 001811 A [id.]. Margaret Price, Sawallisch; (i) with H. Schöneberger.

Consistent beauty of tone, coupled with immaculately controlled line and admirably clear diction, makes Margaret Price's Schubert collection a fresh and rewarding experience. Sawallisch as ever shows himself one of the outstanding accompanists of the time, readily translating from his usual role of conductor.

Lieder: *An Sylvia; Auf der Bruck; Bei dir allein; Du bist die Ruh'; Der Einsame; Freiwilliges Versinken; Gondelfahrer; Die Götter Greichenlands; Gruppe aus dem Tartarus; Heidenröslein; Himmelsfunken; Im Haine; Der Jüngling an der Quelle; Lied eines Schiffers; Nachtviolen; Prometheus; Ständchen; Die Sterne; Waldesnacht; Der Wanderer an den Mond.*
(Y/B) (M) *** EMI Dig. CD-EMX 2224; *TC-EMX 2224*. Simon Keenlyside, Malcolm Martineau.

The velvety beauty of Keenlyside's cleanly focused baritone goes with fresh, thoughtful readings of 20 favourite songs, perfectly judged, with ever-sensitive accompaniment from Martineau. At mid-price it makes another outstanding recommendation for a Schubert disc which includes one or two unusual songs among many favourites.

Lieder: *Auf dem Wasser zu singen; Ave Maria; Die Forelle; Du bist die Ruh; Ganymed; Gretchen am Spinnrade; Gretchens Bitte; Heidenröslein; Heiss mich nicht reden;* (i) *Der Hirt auf dem Felsen. Im Abendrot; Kennst du das Land; Liebhaber in allen Gestalten; Nahe des Geliebten; Nur wer die Sehnsucht kennt; So lasst mich scheinen; Ständchen.*
(N) *** Teldec/Warner Dig. 4509 90873-2 [id.]. Barbara Bonney, Geoffrey Parsons; (i) with Sharon Kam.

There is always a place in the catalogue for a really first-rate recital of Schubert lieder, and this just missed inclusion in our last edition. Barbara Bonney here is at her freshest, and who better to accompany her than Geoffrey Parsons? The generous programme (well over an hour) includes many firm favourites, and Bonney not only sings with much beauty of tone and a flowing Schubertian line but with real concern for word-meanings. Songs like *Die Forelle, Auf dem Wasser zu singen* and the lovely *So lasst mich scheinen* sound especially fresh; and it is always good to have 'The shepherd on the rock' (*Der Hirt auf dem Felsen*) with its fluid obbligato clarinet (here the persuasive Sharon Kam). Throughout the recital one has a real sense of spontaneity and a natural partnership between these two fine artists.

Songs: *Da quel sembiante appresi; Guarda, che bianca luna; Io vuo'cantar di Cadmo; Mi batte'l cor!; Mio ben ricordati; Non t'accostar all'urna; La pastorella; Pensa, che questo istante; Se dall'Etra; Vedi quanto adoro ancora ingrato!.*
(N) *** Decca Dig. 440 297-2 [id.]. Cecilia Bartoli, András Schiff – BEETHOVEN: *Che fa il mio bene?* etc.; HAYDN: *Arianna a Naxos;* MOZART: *Ridente la calma.* ***

Bartoli is at her finest here in *Dido's lament*, but the other rare songs are also fresh and enjoyable, helped by sensitive accompaniments from András Schiff.

Lieder: *Erlkönig; Erster Verlust; Fischerweise; Die Forelle; Ganymed; Gesang des Harfners I (Wer sich der Einsamkeit ergibt); Ihr Bild; Der Jungling und der Tod; Liebesbotschaft; Nacht und Träume; Der Schiffer; Seligkeit; Der Wanderer an den Mond.*
(Y/B) (M) (***) Decca mono 440 065-2 [id.]. Souzay, Bonneau – SCHUMANN: *Dichterliebe.* (***)

Gérard Souzay recorded the majority of these songs in 1956, though three of them, *Gesang des Harfners, Erlkönig* and *Fischerweise*, were recorded in 1950 at the outset of his international career. The voice possesses a wonderful freshness and poignancy; and 'the beauty of timbre and evenness of production' to which John Steane alludes in his authoritative notes is strikingly in evidence. Souzay's command of legato is matched by an ability to characterize that is second to none and it is a matter for celebration that Philips have now restored his *Winterreise* and *Die schöne Müllerin* to circulation (see below), yet the early Schubert discs he made for Decca are to be cherished and their reissue could not be more timely or welcome.

Lieder: *Schwanengesang: Liebesbotschaft; Abschied; Die Stadt; Die Taubenpost. Winterreise: Der Lindenbaum. An den Mond; An eine Quelle.* (i) *Auf dem Strom. Auf dem Wasser zu singen; Auf der Bruck; Die Forelle; Im Abendrot; Im Freien; Im Frühling; Der Musensohn; Rastlose Liebe; Das Rosenband; Der Schiffer; Wandrers Nachtlied II.*
(N) *** Ph. Dig. 438 932-2 [id.]. Hans-Peter Blochwitz, Rudolf Jansen; (i) with Marie-Luise Neunecker.

This recital is notable not only for highly rewarding performances but also for a particularly felicitous choice of programme. It is good to have the items from *Schwanengesang* and the more melancholy excerpts from *Winterreise*, but there is not a single song here that does not show the composer at his most inspired or Hans-Peter Blochwitz in less than top form. His fresh tenor voice and simple lyrical style do not preclude a sense of the dramatic, as in *Auf dem Strom*, where the horn obbligato is splendidly played by Marie-Luise Neunecker. Rudolph Jansen's accompaniments are flawless and the recording is excellent. But why only 64 minutes? There was certainly room for one or two encores.

(i; ii) Duets: *Antigone und Oedip; Cronnan; Hektors Abschied; Hermann und Thusnelda; Licht und Liebe (Nachtgesang); Mignon und der Harfner; Selma und Selmar; Sing-Ubungen;* (vi) *Szene aus Goethes Faust.* (ii; iii; iv; v) Trios: *Die Advokaten; Gütigster, Bester, Weisester; Die Hochzeitsbraten; Kantata zum Geburtstag des Sängers Johann Michael Vogl; Punschlied; Trinklied; Verschwunden sind die Schmerzen (a cappella).* (i–iv) Quartets: *An die Sonne; Gebet; Die Geselligkeit (Lebenslust); Gott der Weltschöpfer; Gott im Ungewitter; Hymne an den Undenlichen; Nun lasst uns den Leib begraben (Begräbnislied); Des Tages Weihe; Der Tanz.*
(M) *** DG 435 596-2 (2) [id.]. (i) Dame Janet Baker; (ii) Fischer-Dieskau; (iii) Ameling; (iv) Schreier; (v) Laubenthal; Gerald Moore; (vi) with Berlin RIAS Chamber Ch.

Not all these duets are vintage Schubert – some of the narrative pieces go on too long – but the artistry of Baker and Fischer-Dieskau makes for magical results. Gerald Moore, who is at his finest throughout the set, relishes the magic too. The trios are domestic music in the best sense. Specially delightful are the two contrasted drinking songs, but *The wedding feast (Die Hochzeitsbraten)* is even more remarkable, a 10½-minute scena in the style of *opera buffa*. The quartets, like the trios, were written for various domestic occasions, but the use of four voices seems to have led the composer regularly to serious or religious subjects. These are sweet and gentle rather than intense inspirations, but one could hardly ask for more polished and inspired performances than these. Fine recording from 1973/4, giving the singers a vivid presence on CD.

6 Antiphons for the Blessings of the Branches on Psalm Sunday; Auguste jam coelestium in G, D.488; Deutsche Messe, D.872 (with Epilogue, The Lord's Prayer); Graduale in C, D.184; Hymn to the Holy Ghost, D.964; Kyries: in D min., D.31; F, D.66; Lazarus, D.689; Magnificat in C, D.486; Offertorium (Totus in corde) in C, D.136; Offertorium (Tres sunt) in A min., D.181; 2 Offertoriums (Salve Regina) in F, D.223 & A, D.676; Psalm 23, D.706; Psalm 92, D.953; Salve Reginas: in B flat, D.106; in C, D.811; Stabat Mater in G min., D.175; Tantum ergo (3 settings) in C, D.460/1 & D.739; Tantum ergo in D, D.750.
(M) *** EMI Dig./Analogue CMS7 64783-2 (3) [id.]. Popp, Donath, Rüggerberg, Venuti, Hautermann, Falk, Fassbaender, Greindl-Rosner, Dallapozza, Araiza, Protschka, Tear, Lika, Fischer-Dieskau, Capella Bavariae, Bav. R. Ch. & SO, Sawallisch.

Volume two of Sawallisch's great and rewarding Schubertian survey has much glorious music, sung with eloquence and richly recorded in the Munich Hercules Hall. Even some of the shortest items – such as the six tiny *Antiphons*, allegedly written in half an hour – have magic and originality in them. Plainer, but still glowing with Schubertian joy, is the so-called *Deutsche Messe*. The *Magnificat*, too, is a strongly characterized setting, and even the three settings of St Thomas Aquinas's *Tantum ergo* (all in C) have their charm. There are other surprises. The lovely setting of the *Offertorium in C (Totus in corde)* is for soprano, clarinet and orchestra, with the vocal and instrumental lines intertwining delectably, while the no less appealing *Auguste jam coelestium* is a soprano-tenor duet. The *Salve Regina in C*, D.811, is written for four male voices, *a cappella*, and they again contribute to the performance of *Psalm 23*, where Sawallisch provides a piano accompaniment. The religious drama, *Lazarus*, has the third CD to itself. Schubert left it unfinished and, though no more dramatic than his operas, it contains much delightful music. With Robert Tear in the name-role, Helen Donath as Maria, Lucia Popp as Jemima, Maria Venuti as Martha, Josef Protschka as Nathanael and Fischer-Dieskau as Simon, it is very strongly cast and the performance is splendid; indeed the singing is outstanding from chorus and soloists alike throughout this set, and the warm, well-balanced recording adds to one's pleasure.

Kyries: in B flat, D.45; D min., D.49; Masses Nos. 1 in F, D.105; 2 in G, D.167; 3 in B flat, D.324; 4 in C, D.452; 5 in A flat, D.678; 6 in E flat, D.950; Offertorium in B flat, D.963; Salve Reginas: in F, D.379; in B flat, D.386; Stabat Mater in F min., D.383; Tantum ergo in E flat, D.962.
(M) *** EMI Dig./Analogue CMS7 64778-2 (4) [id.]. Popp, Donath, Fassbaender, Dallapozza, Schreier, Araiza, Protschka, Fischer-Dieskau, Bav. R. Ch. & SO, Sawallisch.

Sawallisch's highly distinguished survey of Schubert's church music was recorded in the early 1980s. This first volume is centred on his major Mass settings, especially his masterpiece in this form, the *E flat Mass*. Though the chorus is not flawless here, the performances are warm and understanding. The earlier Mass settings bring superb, lively inspirations, not to mention the separate *Kyries* and *Salve Reginas*. Excellent, cleanly focused sound, for the most part digital, with the benefit of the ambience of the Munich Herkulessall.

(i) *Lazarus* (cantata); (ii) *Mass in G, D.167.*
(Y/B) (M) *** Erato/Warner 4509 98533-2 (2) [id.].(i) Armstrong, Welting; (i–ii) Chamonin, Rolfe Johnson; (i) Hill; (i–ii) Egel, Ch. and New French R. PO, Guschlbauer.

About 80 minutes of *Lazarus* survive, and then the work comes to an abrupt end in the middle of a soprano solo! Some of it is as touching as the finest Schubert, and other sections are little short of inspired; there are some thoroughly characteristic harmonic colourings and some powerful writing for the trombones. Much of it is very fine indeed; though it would be idle to pretend that its inspiration is even, no Schubertian would want to be without it, for the best of it is quite lovely. The singers and the French Radio forces are thoroughly persuasive, and it would be difficult to fault Theodore Guschlbauer's direction or the warm quality of the sound achieved by the engineers. The *G major Mass*, an earlier piece written when Schubert was only eighteen, has less depth and subtlety than the best of *Lazarus*; but there are some endearing moments and the *Agnus Dei* is poignant. Again the performance and recording here are excellent.

Magnificat, D.486; Offertorium, D.963; Stabat Mater, D.383.
(Y/B) (M) *** Erato/Warner 4509 96961-2 [id.]. Armstrong, Schaer, Ramirez, Huttenlocher, Goy, Lausanne Vocal Ens. & CO, Corboz.

Schubert's strikingly fresh setting of the *Stabat Mater* dates from the composer's nineteenth year, yet it shows him at the height of his early powers and has many anticipations of later music, especially in the Terzetto for soprano, tenor, bass and chorus (No. 11) and the fine chorus, *Wer wird Zähren sanften Mitleids* (No. 5), with its superb horn-writing. There is a lovely, Bach-like tenor aria, with oboe obbligato, in which Alejandro Ramirez is very stylish; and the bass aria, *Sohn des Vaters*, recalls the Mozart of *Die Zauberflöte*. Here Philippe Huttenlocher may not be quite dark enough but his pure-sounding baritone remains very appealing. The chorus is incisive, both in counterpoint in Schubert's lively if somewhat pedagogic fugues, and in the simple chordal writing. The other, lesser pieces make a good coupling, also persuasively directed by Corboz, and the recording, although not crystal clear, has transferred vividly.

Mass No. 6 in E flat, D.950.
(B) *** Erato/Warner Duo Dig. 4509 95307-2 (2) [id.]. Michael, Balleys, Baldin, Homberger, Brodard, Swiss R. Chamber Ch., Lausanne Pro Arte Ch., SRO, Jordan – SCHUMANN: *Mass.* ***

In every way this *Mass* is a richly rewarding work, product of the last year of Schubert's short life. The chorus is far more important than the soloists; nevertheless they are a good team, well led by the soprano, Audrey Michael. The Swiss and Lausanne choirs blend well together and sing with ardour and discipline. The digital sound is well focused and the acoustic expansive, and the results are powerful and satisfying. Coupled with a rare Mass of Schumann, this is a valuable reissue, the more attractive for being reissued in Erato's Bonsai series (two CDs for the price of one) and it is a great pity that there is no proper documentation offering information about the music itself.

Rosamunde Overture (Die Zauberharfe, D.644) and incidental music, D.797 (complete).
*** DG Dig. 431 655-2 [id.]. Anne Sofie von Otter, Ernst Senff Ch., COE, Abbado.

Abbado and COE give joyful performances of this magical incidental music. It is a revelation to hear the most popular of the entr'actes played so gently: it is like a whispered meditation. Even with a slow speed and affectionate phrasing, it yet avoids any feeling of being mannered. Glowing recording to match. Anne Sofie von Otter is an ideal soloist.

Song-cycles

Song-cycles: *Die schöne Müllerin, D.795; Schwanengesang, D.957; Winterreise, D.911.* Lieder: *Du bist die Ruh'; Erlkönig; Nacht und Träume.*
(M) (***) EMI mono CMS7 63559-2 (3) [Ang. CDMC 63559]. Dietrich Fischer-Dieskau, Gerald Moore.

Fischer-Dieskau's early mono versions may not match his later recordings in depth of insight, but already the young singer was a searching interpreter of these supreme cycles. Gerald Moore was, as ever, the most sympathetic partner.

Die schöne Müllerin (song-cycle), *D.795* (see also above, under Graham Johnson Schubert Lieder Edition, Volume 25).
*** DG 415 186-2 [id.]. Dietrich Fischer-Dieskau, Gerald Moore.
*** Decca Dig. 430 414-2 [id.]. Peter Schreier, András Schiff.
*** Capriccio Dig. 10 082 [id.]. Josef Protschka, Helmut Deutsch.
(Y/B) (M) *** CfP CD-CFP 4672; *TC-CFP 4672* [id.]. Ian and Jennifer Partridge.
(Y/B) **(*) Decca Dig. 440 354-2 [id.]. Uwe Heilmann, James Levine.

Die schöne Müllerin (complete); *An die Laute; Der Einsame; Die Taubenpost.*
(M) **(*) Decca 436 201-2. Peter Pears, Benjamin Britten.

Die schöne Müllerin (complete); *Die Forelle; Frühlingsglaube; Heidenröslein.*
(N) (M) ** DG 447 452-2 [id.]. Fritz Wunderlich, Hubert Geisen.

(i) *Die schöne Müllerin, D.795*; (ii) *Ständchen*; (i) *Der Musensohn, D.764.*
(N) (BB) ** RCA Navigator 74321 29241-2. Fritz Wunderlich; (i) Kurt Heinz Stolze; (ii) Rolfe Reinhardt.

Fischer-Dieskau's classic 1972 version on DG remains among the very finest ever recorded, combining as it does his developed sense of drama and story-telling, his mature feeling for detail and yet spontaneity too, helped by the searching accompaniment of Gerald Moore. It is a performance with premonitions of *Winterreise*.

András Schiff brings new illumination in almost every phrase, to match the brightly detailed singing of Schreier, here challenged to produce his most glowing tone. Schreier, matching his partner as he did in their earlier, prize-winning recording of *Schwanengesang* (see below), transcends even his earlier versions of this favourite cycle, always conveying his response so vividly that one clearly registers his changes of facial expression from line to line. Outstandingly warm and well-balanced recording.

Josef Protschka gives an intensely virile, almost operatic reading, which is made the more youthful-sounding in the original keys for high voice. As recorded, the voice, often beautiful with heroic timbres, sometimes acquires a hint of stridency, but the positive power and individuality of the performance make it consistently compelling, with all the anguish behind these songs caught intensely. The timbre of the Bösendorfer piano adds to the performance's distinctiveness, well if rather reverberantly recorded.

Ian Partridge's is an exceptionally fresh and urgent account. Rarely if ever on record has the dynamic quality of the cycle of Schubert songs been so effectively conveyed, rising to an emotional climax at the end of the first half with the song *Mein!*, expressing the poet's ill-found joy welling up infectiously. Partridge's subtle and beautiful range of tone is a constant delight, and he is most imaginatively accompanied by his sister, Jennifer. The balance of the 1973 recording is forward and present: this is an outstanding bargain reissue and should win many new friends for Lieder.

With James Levine a sensitive accompanist, the tenor, Uwe Heilmann, gives a deeply felt reading, often headily beautiful but at times too heavily pointed both in detail of word-meaning and in musical phrase. The last two songs about the brook are finely sustained at spacious speeds, giving a foretaste of the darkness of *Die Winterreise*. The recording – made in the Margrave's opera house in Bayreuth in August 1992 – captures the distinctive voice well but, with lightness in the bass, makes the piano too clattery.

Fischer-Dieskau may find more drama in the poems, and Gerald Moore matches his subtlety of inflexion at every point; but Pears is imaginative too, if for once in rather gritty voice, and Britten brings a composer's insight to the accompaniments so that, while Fischer-Dieskau provides more charm in this most sunny of song-cycles, the Pears/Britten partnership remains uniquely valuable.

Fritz Wunderlich's recording was made in 1966 and won both a Grand Prix des Discophiles and L'Orphée d'Or when it appeared the following year. It now reappears as one of DG's 'Legendary Originals'. Wunderlich had one of the most headily beautiful voices among German tenors and that alone makes his record cherishable. But when he recorded the cycle (and the three favourite songs which are also included here), he had still to develop as a Lieder singer, and for so subtle a cycle the performance lacks detail. Moreover he was handicapped by a rather unimaginative accompanist, and the recording is unflattering to the piano.

Recorded in 1957, the earlier of Wunderlich's two recordings of the cycle has him at his freshest and most eager, with the voice full and forward. Sadly the accompaniments are stodgily played. However, his admirers will find that this Navigator reissue is very inexpensive.

Song-cycles: *Die schöne Müllerin, D.795* (complete); *Schwanengesang* (excerpts): *Liebesbotschaft; Kriegers Ahnung; Frühlingssehnsucht; Abschied; Der Atlas; Ihr Bild; Das Fischermädchen; Die Taubenpost* (only). *Winterreise, D.911* (complete). Lieder: *An die Laute; An die Musik; An Sylvia; Auf der Bruck; Dithyrambe; Der Doppelgänger; Erlkönig; Erster Verlust; Des Fischers Liebesglück; Die Forelle; Frühlingsglaube; Ganymed; Heidenröslein; Im Abendrot; Der Jüngling an der Quelle; Die Liebe hat gelogen; Lied eines Schiffers an die Dioskuren; Meeres Stille; Der Musensohn; Nacht und Träume; Normans Gesang; Rastlose Liebe; Der Schiffer; Ständchen; Der Tod und das Mädchen; Dem Unendlichen; Der Wanderer; Wandrers Nachtlied; Der Zwerg.*
(M) *** Ph. 438 511-2 [id.]. Gérard Souzay, Dalton Baldwin.

Souzay's sunny style is particularly suited to *Die schöne Müllerin*, the most sunny of song-cycles. Fischer-Dieskau may find more drama in the poems, but Souzay's concentration on purely musical values makes for one of the most consistently attractive versions ever recorded, with the words never neglected and Dalton Baldwin giving one of his most imaginative performances on record. This dates from 1964; *Wintereisse* is earlier (1961/2), when Souzay also recorded his incomplete selection from *Schwanengesang* (one or two of the missing songs are included in the two recitals which follow). Once again the singing is intense and the cycle is firmly held together, with musical values paramount. But in *Winterreise* Souzay hardly outshines Peter Pears or Fischer-Dieskau.

The 29 miscellaneous Lieder combine the contents of two recitals, recorded in 1961 and 1967. The earlier collection, which includes many top favourites, is ideal in all respects. Souzay's style is wonderfully sympathetic, superbly dramatic in the *Erlkönig*, for instance – one of the finest performances of this song on record – and he spins his tone exquisitely in the quieter songs; *Wandrers Nachtlied* is a particularly fine example. In the later recordings one feels that his mood is too unvaryingly introspective at times. Of course, many of Schubert's greatest songs are melancholy and inward-looking, but on a record the careful placing of a happy song can lighten the mood. Here, even though Souzay's contrasts between *An die Laute* and the following *Der Tod und das Mädchen* are beautifully made and the ear delights in *Der Musensohn*, there is some lack of variety overall. Dalton Baldwin's accompaniments are often superb: the ripples of the lute, or the brook in *Der Jüngling an der Quelle*, are delightfully characterized, while the strong, rhythmic mood of *Normans Gesang* (one of Schubert's most dramatic ballad songs) is an artistic highlight. But Baldwin participates actively in every song and he is helped by the excellent recording balance.

Schwanengesang (Lieder collection), *D.957;* Lieder: *An die Musik; An Sylvia; Die Forelle; Heidenröslein; Im Abendrot; Der Musensohn; Der Tod und das Mädchen.*
*** DG 415 188-2 [id.]. Dietrich Fischer-Dieskau, Gerald Moore.

Schwanengesang. Am Fenster; Bei dir allein; Herbst; Der Wanderer an den Mond.
*** Decca Dig. 425 612-2. Peter Schreier, András Schiff.

Schwanengesang; 5 Lieder: *Am Fenster; Herbst; Sehnsucht; Der Wanderer an den Mond; Wiegenlied, D.867.*
❀ *** DG Dig. 429 766-2 [id.]. Brigitte Fassbaender, Aribert Reimann.

Schwanengesang. Im Freien; Der Wanderer an den Mond; Das Zügenglücklein.
*** EMI Dig. CDC 749997-2. Olaf Bär, Geoffrey Parsons.

Brigitte Fassbaender gives a totally distinctive and compelling account of *Schwanengesang*, proving stronger and more forceful than almost any rival. She turns what was originally a relatively random group of late songs into a genuine cycle, by presenting them in a carefully rearranged order and adding five other late songs. Her magnetic power of compelling attention is intensified by the equally positive accompaniment of Aribert Reimann. The celebrated Schubert *Serenade* to words by Rellstab is far more than just a pretty tune, rather a passionate declaration of love; and Fassbaender builds her climax to the cycle round the final Heine settings, heightening their dramatic impact by the new ordering.

Fischer-Dieskau's DG version with Moore, though recorded ten years before his CD with Brendel (currently withdrawn), brings excellent sound in the digital transfer, plus the positive advantages, first that the voice is fresher, and then that the disc also contains seven additional songs, all of them favourites.

Schreier's voice may no longer be beautiful under pressure, but the bloom on this Decca recording and the range of tone and the intensity of inflexion over word-meaning make this one of the most compelling recordings ever of *Schwanengesang*. Enhancing that are the discreet but highly individual and responsive accompaniments of András Schiff. Like Bär on his fine EMI version, Schreier makes up a generous CD-length by including not just the 14 late songs published together as *Schwanengesang*, but four more, also from the last three years of Schubert's life. The recording is vividly real.

Olaf Bär also amplifies the collection of late songs posthumously published as *Schwanengesang* with well-chosen extra items from the same period, notably (like Schreier) *Der Wanderer an den Mond*. Where Schreier is confidential in that song at a brisk speed, Bär brings out the agony and weariness of the traveller addressing the moon. In *Ständchen*, where Schreier is light and charming, Bär is strong and passionate.

Winterreise (song cycle), *D.911.*
*** DG 415 187-2 [id.]. Dietrich Fischer-Dieskau, Gerald Moore.
(N) *** Ph. Dig. 446 407-2 [id.]. Wolfgang Holzmair, Imogen Cooper.
*** Ph. Dig. 411 463-2 [id.]. Dietrich Fischer-Dieskau, Alfred Brendel.
(Y/B) (M) *** DG 447 421-2 [id.]. Dietrich Fischer-Dieskau, Joerg Demus.
❀ (M) *** Decca 417 473-2 [id.]. Peter Pears, Benjamin Britten.
(B) *** DG 439 432-2 [id.]. Fischer-Dieskau, Barenboim.
*** EMI Dig. CDC7 49334-2 [id.]. Olaf Bär, Geoffrey Parsons.
(N) **(*) Decca Dig. 436 122-2 [id.]. Peter Schreier, András Schiff.
(Y/B) *** Virgin/EMI Dig. VC5 45070-2 [id.]. Thomas Allen, Roger Vignoles.
*** EMI Dig. CDC7 49846-2 [id.]. Brigitte Fassbaender, Aribert Reimann.
(Y/B) (M) **(*) DG Dig. 445 521-2 [id.]. Christa Ludwig, James Levine.
(BB) ** ASV CDQS 6085 [id.]. Robert Tear, Philip Ledger.

In the early 1970s Dietrich Fischer-Dieskau's voice was still at its freshest, yet the singer had deepened and intensified his understanding of this greatest of song-cycles to a degree where his finely detailed and thoughtful interpretation sounded totally spontaneous, and this DG version is now freshened on CD. However, the collaboration of Fischer-Dieskau with one of today's great Schubert pianists, Alfred Brendel, brings endless illumination in the interplay and challenge between singer and pianist, magnetic from first to last. With incidental flaws, this may not be the definitive Fischer-Dieskau reading, but in many ways it is the deepest and most moving he has ever given. The recording is excellent.

Wolfgang Holzmair gives an exceptionally beautiful reading of this most taxing song-cycle, using his fresh, firm, youthful voice to present a vivid portrait of the tragic lover strikingly different from those which find weight and darkness from the start. Here, with the songs flowing more freely than usual, the traveller sets out in hope and eagerness, only later finding disillusion. The last two songs, *Die Nebensonnen* and *Der Leiermann*, are then the more moving for being understated, presented with daring simplicity, to make this a young man's tragedy. Holzmair, with a baritone full of tenor-like timbres, never rests content with sheer beauty of tone but consistently uses his many colourings to intensify word-meaning without exaggeration, often tenderly, never forcing the voice even in powerful fortissimos. Imogen Cooper proves the most sympathetic accompanist, searching and imaginative.

There are those who regard Fischer-Dieskau's third recording of *Winterreise* as the finest of all, such is the peak of beauty and tonal expressiveness that the voice had achieved in the mid-1960s, and the poetic restraint of Demus' accompaniment. The recording still sounds well, and as a mid-price reissue in DG's Legendary Recordings series it certainly makes an excellent alternative recommendation.

What is so striking about the Pears performance is its intensity. One continually has the sense of a live occasion and, next to it, even Fischer-Dieskau's beautifully wrought singing sounds too easy. As for Britten, he re-creates the music, sometimes with a fair freedom from Schubert's markings, but always with scrupulous concern for the overall musical shaping and sense of atmosphere. The sprung rhythm of *Gefror'ne Tränen* is magical in creating the impression of frozen teardrops falling, and almost every song brings similar magic. The recording and the CD transfer are exceptionally successful in bringing a sense of presence and realism.

Fischer-Dieskau's fifth recording of Schubert's greatest cycle, made in 1979, has now appeared on DG's Classikon bargain label, with the voice still in superb condition. Prompted by Barenboim's spontaneous-sounding, almost improvisatory accompaniments, it is highly inspirational. In expression this is freer than the earlier versions, and though some idiosyncratic details will not please everyone the sense of concentrated development is irresistible. The recording is very natural and beautifully balanced, and full translations are included.

Bär, with Geoffrey Parsons a masterly accompanist, is both intensely dramatic and deeply reflective, while finding a beauty of line and tone to outshine almost anyone. The darkness of the close is given the intensity of live communication, and the sound is outstanding, with voice and piano given intimacy in a helpful atmosphere.

As in *Die schöne Müllerin* and *Schwanengesang*, the partnership of Schreier and Schiff brings much new revelation, with the pianist as individual in his imagination as the singer, rather as Britten is with Pears. Schreier's voice is not always perfectly steady, but the focus is clean, and only occasionally is there a roughening of tone, and that to intensify the drama. With Schreier's facial expression instantly apparent, this is an intensely involving reading, with changes of mood vividly conveyed, positive, electrifying, often confidential, though the full, immediate recording does not help pianissimos.

Thomas Allen's concentration on purely musical qualities, far from watering down word-meaning, is used to intensify the tragic emotions of the wandering lover. Allen uses a wider dynamic range than most of his direct rivals, shading the voice down to a half-tone for intimate revelations, then expanding dramatically, using the art of the opera-singer. In the two final songs, *Die Nebensonnen* and *Der Leiermann*, he is very restrained, keeping them hushed instead of underlining expressiveness. The poignancy of Schubert's inspiration is allowed to speak for itself.

Brigitte Fassbaender gives a fresh, boyishly eager reading of *Winterreise*, marked by a vivid and wide range of expression; she demonstrates triumphantly why a woman's voice can bring special illumination to this cycle, sympathetically underlining the drama behind the tragic poet's journey rather than the more meditative qualities. Reimann, at times a wilful accompanist, is nevertheless spontaneous-sounding like the singer. Excellent sound.

With James Levine a concentrated and often dramatic accompanist, consistently adding to the sense of spontaneous and immediate communication, Christa Ludwig gives a warmly satisfying performance, making use of the mature richness of the voice rather than bringing any striking new insights. Though the different sections of *Frühlingstraum*, for example, are beautifully contrasted, it is the extra darkness of the piano in low keys that adds most to the tragedy. Full, natural recording.

It is good to have a super-bargain version of *Die Winterreise*, but the account by Robert Tear and Philip Ledger is disappointing from two artists who might have been expected to follow in the inspired tradition of Pears and Britten. It is partly the dryness and lack of bloom on the voice in the studio recording – with the piano sounding too close – which underlines a degree of squareness in the slower songs. The vigorous songs go much better, and the CD transfer has undoubtedly improved the sound, but the basic reservations remain.

OPERA

Fierrabras (complete).
*** DG Dig. 427 341-2 (2) [id.]. Protschka, Mattila, Studer, Gambill, Hampson, Holl, Polgár, Schoenberg Ch., COE, Abbado.

Few operas by a great composer have ever had quite so devastatingly bad a press as *Fierrabras*. Schubert may often let his musical imagination blossom without considering the dramatic effect, but there are jewels in plenty in this score. Many solos and duets develop into delightful ensembles, and the influence of Beethoven's *Fidelio* is very striking, with spoken melodrama and offstage fanfares bringing obvious echoes. A recording is the ideal medium for such buried treasure, and Abbado directs an electrifying performance. Both tenors, Robert Gambill and Josef Protschka, are on the strenuous side, but have a fine feeling for Schubertian melody. Cheryl Studer and Karita Mattila sing ravishingly, and Thomas Hampson gives a noble performance as the knight, Roland. Only Robert Holl as King Karl (Charlemagne) is unsteady at times. The sound is comfortably atmospheric, outstanding for a live recording.

Schulhoff, Erwin (1894–1942)

Flammen (opera; complete).
(N) *** Decca Dig. 444 630-2 (2). Westi, Eaglen, Vermillion, Prein, Wolff, Soloists, Berlin RIAS Chamber Ch., Deutsches SO, Berlin, John Mauceri.

Flammen is another impressive offering in Decca's remarkable Entartete Musik series of works condemned by the Nazis, this time featuring the Czech-Jewish composer, Erwin Schulhoff, who died in internment in 1942. First heard in Brno in 1932 with the Czech title, '*Plameny*', this opera is a curiosity, a rich and exotic score inspired by a stylized story and characters, with long, purely instrumental passages which in a stage presentation would involve ballet and mime. The central figure is Don Juan, condemned to eternal life amid the hell-flames of the title, loved by the symbolic figure of Death (a woman) who is yet unable to claim him. The other principal women's roles are taken by a single singer (here the rich-voiced and formidable Jane Eaglen), with Donna Anna turning into Margarethe when the stylized story implies that Don Juan and Faust are linked. Dramatically, it is variably successful, but the concluding scenes are most moving, and the richness of the sounds in a score with echoes of Busoni, Korngold, Weill and even Mahler will delight those with a sweet tooth. The performance is outstanding in every way, with John Mauceri drawing bitingly intense playing and singing from his excellent team. Kurt Westi is superb in the central role of Don Juan, clear, firm and fresh, and both Jane Eaglen and Iris Vermillion as Death sing with power and passion. Recording of demonstration quality.

Schuman, William (1910–92)

Judith; New England triptych; Symphony for strings; Variations on America.
*** Delos Dig. DE 3115 [id.]. Seattle SO, Gerard Schwarz.

The composer himself heard these performances and spoke of their combination of 'intellectual depth, technical superiority and emotional involvement' – and who are we to dissent! The *Symphony for strings*, his Fifth, is one of his strongest and most beautiful works. This Seattle account has the advantage of fresh recorded sound. The ballet, *Judith*, was written for Martha Graham. Powerful and atmospheric music, here given a performance with both these qualities. The *New England triptych* makes use of New England themes by the Bostonian, William Billings (1746–1800), whose music served to fuel the cause of the American Revolution. This present account is superior to the version by Howard Hanson on Mercury.

New England triptych.
(M) *** Mercury 432 755-2 [id.]. Eastman-Rochester O, Howard Hanson – IVES: *Symphony No. 3* etc. ***; MENNIN: *Symphony No. 5.* **(*)

William Schuman is not as outrageously original as Ives, but his sound-world is individual and wholly American. Each of the three pieces is an orchestral anthem, the first a thrustingly vibrant *Hallelujah*; the second is in the form of a round, and the finale features a marching song. Splendidly alive playing and excellent (1963) Mercury recording, admirably transferred to CD.

Symphony No. 10 (American Muse); American Festival overture; New England triptych. IVES, arr. SCHUMAN: *Variations on America.*
(Y/B) *** RCA Dig. 09026 61282-2 [id.]. St Louis SO, Slatkin.

It is difficult to escape the impression that Schuman's symphonic muse slumbered a little after the *Sixth*, which Ormandy recorded so eloquently in the 1950s. All (save Nos. 1 and 2, which he suppressed) have been recorded, though not all are currently available. His *Tenth Symphony* was composed in 1975 for the United States Bicentennial; it is a three-movement piece whose centre of gravity resides in its big, contemplative middle movement with the usual polytonal choral harmonies. But splendid though much of it is, Schuman's inspiration is touched a little by routine, the gestures sound just a little too much like self-imitation when put alongside the more spontaneous eloquence of symphonies 3–6. There is plenty of excitement in the outer movements and the St Louis orchestra play with enormous conviction. Their performance of the *American Festival overture* is pretty dazzling, too, and yields little to Bernstein's DG account. Both the *New England triptych* and the Ives transcription, *Variations on America*, fare equally well. Those who have been bitten by the Schuman bug will be grateful for this excellent première recording, but for those coming to his music afresh, the *Third* and *Fifth Symphonies* make a better entry point into his world.

String quartets Nos. 2, 3 & 5.
(N) *** HM Dig. HMU 907114 [id.]. Lydian String Qt.

The *Third Quartet* (1939) serves as a reminder of what a powerful composer William Schuman is. Less accessible, perhaps, than Aaron Copland or his exact contemporary, Samuel Barber, Schuman's music has sinew and a toughness that is bracing. It demands persuasive and committed playing from its interpreters, which it receives from the fine Lydian Quartet, and concentration from its listeners. The *Second Quartet* (1937) is slighter than the *Third* but is a strong piece nevertheless. The latter has something of the volcanic energy and drive of the *Third Symphony*, Schuman's best-known work, as well as its sense of line and momentum; it is one of the great American quartets. The *Fifth Quartet* is a relatively late piece, coming from 1987, and its opening is among Schuman's most inward and searching inspirations. Some may find his quartets a hard nut to crack but they are well worth taking trouble over. All three are beautifully played and recorded.

Schumann, Clara (1819–96)

Piano trio in G min., Op. 17.
*** Hyperion Dig. CDA 66331 [id.]. Dartington Piano Trio – Fanny MENDELSSOHN: *Trio.* ***

Clara's *Piano trio* moves within the Mendelssohn–Schumann tradition with apparently effortless ease and, when played as persuasively as it is here, makes a pleasing impression. If it does not command the depth of Robert, it has a great deal of charm to commend it. Excellent recording.

Schumann, Robert (1810–56)

Cello concerto in A min., Op. 129.
(Y/B) *** BIS Dig. CD 486 [id.]. Torleif Thedéen, Malmö SO, Markiz – ELGAR: *Concerto.* ***
(M) *** Mercury 432 010-2 [id.]. Janos Starker, LSO, Skrowaczewski – LALO: *Concerto* **(*); SAINT-SAENS: *Concerto.* ***
(N) *** RCA Dig. 09026 68027-2 [id.] Starker, Bamberg SO, Russell Davies – HINDEMITH: *Cello concerto.* ***
(N) (BB) *** Naxos Dig. 8 550 938 [id.]. Maria Kliegel, Nat. SO of Ireland, Andrew Constantine – BRAHMS: *Double concerto.* ***
(N) (B) *** Decca Eclipse Dig. 448 712-2; *448 712-4* [id.]. Lynn Harrell, Cleveland O, Marriner – LALO; SAINT-SAENS: *Concertos.* ***
(N) ** Finlandia 4509 98886-2 [id.]. Arto Noras, Finnish RSO, Sakari Oramo – DVORAK: *Cello concerto.* **(*)
(N) (M) * DG Dig. 445 574-2 [id.]. Maisky, VPO, Bernstein – DVORAK: *Concerto.*

The young Swedish virtuoso, Torleif Thedéen, is splendidly recorded on BIS, and the Malmö orchestra give him sympathetic support. He plays with a refreshing ardour, tempered by nobility and a reticence that is strongly appealing. He couples it with an account of the Elgar that is every bit as attuned to the latter's sensibility as any in the catalogue. Strongly recommended.

The Schumann *Cello concerto* is not generously represented at the mid-price or bargain end of the catalogue; Janos Starker gives a persuasive account of it that is thoroughly sensitive to the letter and spirit of the score. Skrowaczewski accompanies with spirit and without the rather explosive, clipped tutti chords that rather disfigure the Lalo with which it is coupled. The 1962 recording is amazing for its age: people make great claims for these early Mercury recordings and, judging from this expertly engineered disc, rightly so!

On RCA, playing of finesse from Starker, who has recorded the Schumann *Concerto* many times. He is well accompanied by Russell Davies and the Bambergers, and very decently recorded. For those wanting a hybrid coupling this can be recommended, but the Hindemith may not be a first choice of coupling for those primarily interested in Schumann, and Starker's earlier, Mercury version will seem a better choice for most of his admirers, particularly as it is offered at mid-price.

The Schumann *Cello concerto* makes an apt coupling for the Brahms *Double concerto* and is the more attractive for coming on the Naxos super-budget label in a warmly spontaneous-sounding performance, very well recorded. Kliegel takes a spacious, lyrical view of the first movement, using a soft-grained tone at the start, with wide vibrato. The simple, dedicated approach to the central *Langsam* also brings dedicated playing, while the finale is wittily pointed, not least in the second subject.

Harrell's is a big-scale reading, strong and sympathetic, made the more powerful by the superb accompaniment from the Cleveland Orchestra. Its controversial point is that he expands the usual cadenza with a substantial sequence of his own. The digital recording is outstandingly fine.

Arto Noras in the Finlandia version suffers from backward balance, even though there is plenty of body in the Finlandia sound, making his playing less involving. He is not helped by occasional sluggishness in the accompaniment, though the finale brings compensation in its crispness and swagger. A fair if not outstanding recommendation for this coupling with the Dvořák.

Like the coupled Dvořák *Concerto*, Maisky's recording was taken from live performances. Bernstein seems reluctant to let the music speak for itself, and this affects the eloquent, generous-toned soloist, who similarly has moments of self-indulgence. This is not as perversely eccentric as the coupling, but even in its own right it can hardly be recommended for repeated listening.

(i) *Cello concerto in A min.;* (ii) *Piano concerto in A min.*
(N) (M) **(*) DG 449 100-2 [id.]. (i) Rostropovich, Leningrad PO, Rozhdestvensky; (ii) Argerich, Nat. SO of Washington, Rostropovich.

Rostropovich's DG performance of the *Cello concerto* is superbly made, introspective yet at the same time outgoing, with a peerless technique at the command of a rare artistic imagination. The sound is vivid. In the *Piano concerto* Rostropovich moves to the rostrum and Argerich takes on the role of soloist. The partnership produces a performance which is full of contrast – helped by a recording of wide dynamic range – and strong in temperament. There is an appealing delicacy in the *Andantino* and the outer movements have plenty of vivacity and colour. Yet in the last analysis the work's special romantic feeling does not fully blossom here, although the playing is not without poetry. The recording is admirably lifelike and well balanced.

(i) *Cello concerto in A min., Op. 129;* (ii) *Piano concerto in A min., Op. 54; Introduction and allegro appassionato, Op. 92.*
(M) ** EMI CDM7 64626-2 [id.]. (i) Jacqueline du Pré, New Philh. O, Barenboim; (ii) Barenboim, LPO, Dietrich Fischer-Dieskau.

The most attractive performance here is Jacqueline du Pré's 1968 recording of the *Cello concerto*. Her spontaneous style is strikingly suited to this most recalcitrant of concertos and the slow movement is particularly beautiful. She is ably assisted by Daniel Barenboim, and the only snag is the rather faded orchestral sound, unflattered by the present transfer, though the cello timbre is realistically focused. The coupling was recorded in the mid-1970s; the sound is somewhat firmer and the balance lets the piano dominate but, with the LPO below its best under Fischer-Dieskau (a good but not outstanding conductor), this is probably just as well. Barenboim is brisk and not particularly poetic, and these performances lack what he usually achieves on record: a sense of spontaneity, a simulation of a live performance.

(i) *Cello concerto;* (ii) *Piano concerto in A min.;* (iii) *Violin concerto in D min.;* (ii) *Introduction and allegro appassionata;* (iv) *Konzertstück in F for four horns and orchestra, Op. 86.*
(B) **(*) EMI Analogue/Dig. CZS7 67521-2 (2) [id.]. (i) Paul Tortelier, RPO, Yan Pascal Tortelier; (ii) Barenboim, LPO, Fischer-Dieskau; (iii) Kremer, Philh. O, Muti; (iv) Hauptmann, Klier, Kohler, Seifert, BPO, Tennstedt.

This is a useful collection of Schumann's concertante works and it is a pity that it is let down somewhat by Barenboim's rather too direct account of the works for piano (see above). Tortelier's is a characteristically inspirational performance of the *Cello concerto*, at its most concentrated in the hushed rendering of the slow movement. The *Violin concerto* comes off pretty well in the hands of Gidon Kremer. Its vein of introspection seems to suit him and he gives a generally sympathetic account of it and has very good support from the Philharmonia under Riccardo Muti. The (digital) recording was made in the Kingsway Hall in 1982 and is vivid and convincingly balanced. What makes this two-disc set well worth considering in EMI's Rouge et Noir series (offering two CDs for the price of one) is the inclusion of the exuberant *Konzertstück* with its brilliant horn playing. The four soloists from the Berlin Philharmonic play with superbly ripe virtuosity and Tennstedt's direction is both urgent and expansive. The 1978 recording is admirably full-blooded.

Piano concerto in A min., Op. 54.
(N) [M] *** Ph. 446 192-2 [id.]. Kovacevich, BBC SO, Sir Colin Davis – GRIEG: *Concerto; Sonata.* ***
*** EMI Dig. CDC7 54746-2 [id.]. Lars Vogt, CBSO, Rattle – GRIEG: *Concerto.* ***
*** Sony Dig. MK 44899 [id.]. Perahia, Bav. RSO, Colin Davis – GRIEG: *Concerto.* ***
*** CfP Dig. CD-CFP 4574. Pascal Devoyon, LPO, Maksymiuk – GRIEG: *Concerto.* ***
*** Ph. 412 251-2 [id.]. Brendel, LSO, Abbado – WEBER: *Konzertstück.* ***
(M) (***) EMI mono CDH7 69792-2. Lipatti, Philh. O, Karajan – MOZART: *Piano concerto No. 21.* (*(**))
(M) **(*) Decca 417 728-2 [id.]. Radu Lupu, LSO, Previn – GRIEG: *Concerto.* **(*)
(M) *** RCA [60420-2-RG]. Van Cliburn, Chicago SO, Reiner – MACDOWELL: *Concerto No. 2.* **(*)
(N) (M) *** RCA 09026 62691-2 [id.]. Van Cliburn, Chicago SO, Reiner – PROKOFIEV: *Piano concerto No. 3.* **(*)
(B) **(*) Decca 433 628-2 [id.]. Gulda, VPO, Andrae – FRANCK: *Symphonic variations* *** ✪; GRIEG: *Concerto.* ***
(M) **(*) Sony/CBS CD 44849 [id.]. Fleisher, Cleveland O, Szell – GRIEG: *Concerto.* **(*)
(BB) **(*) ASV Dig. CDQS 6092. Osorio, RPO, Bátiz – FRANCK: *Symphonic variations* **(*); RAVEL: *Left-hand concerto* ***; SAINT-SAENS: *Wedding-cake.* ***
(N) (B) *(*) Decca Eclipse Dig. 448 235-2; *448 235-4* [id.]. Jorge Bolet, Berlin RSO, Chailly – GRIEG: *Piano concerto.* *
(N) *(*) Chandos Dig. CHAN 9375-2. Malling, Danish Nat. RSO, Schønwandt – SCHOENBERG: *Piano concerto.* ***
(Y/B) * Sony Dig. SK 52567 [id.]. Kissin, VPO, Giulini (with GRIEG: *Carnival scene, Op. 19/3; I love you, Op. 41/3;* LISZT: *Concert paraphrases of Schubert's Erlkönig; Die Forelle; Soirées de Vienne: Valse caprice No. 6* ***).

(i; ii) *Piano concerto in A min.;* (i; iii) *Introduction and allegro appassionato, Op. 92. Novellette in F, Op. 21/1; Toccata in C, Op. 7; Waldszenen, Op. 82.*
(N) (M) **(*) DG stereo/mono 447 440-2 [id.]. Sviatoslav Richter, with (i) Warsaw Nat. PO, (ii) Witold Rowicki, (iii) Stanislaw Wislocki.

(i) *Piano concerto in A min. Arabeske in C, Op. 18.*
(M) *** Mercury 432 011-2 [id.]. Byron Janis, Minneapolis SO, Skrowaczewski – TCHAIKOVSKY: *Piano concerto No. 1.* **(*)

(i) *Piano concerto in A min. Arabeske; Etudes symphoniques, Op. 13.*
(M) *** RCA 09026 61444-2 [id.]. Rubinstein; (i) RCA Victor SO, Krips.
(Y/B) (M) **(*) DG Dig. 445 522-2 [id.]. Pollini; (i) BPO, Abbado.

(i) *Piano concerto in A min.; Carnaval; Kinderszenen (Scenes from childhood), Op. 15.*
(Y/B) (B) **(*) DG 439 476-2 [id.]. Wilhelm Kempff; (i) Bav. RSO, Kubelik.

Our primary recommendation for this favourite Romantic concerto remains with the successful symbiosis of Stephen Kovacevich and Sir Colin Davis, who give an interpretation which is both fresh and poetic, unexaggerated but powerful in its directness and clarity, and the spring-like element of the outer movements is finely presented by orchestra and soloist alike. The sound has been admirably freshened, and this is even more attractive at mid-price.

Lars Vogt was the Second Prize winner at the 1990 Leeds International Piano Competition when he impressed by his sensitivity and innate sense of style. Both these attributes, and a keen imagination, are strongly in evidence in this account of the Schumann, in which he is well supported by Simon Rattle and the CBSO. There is stiff competition, of course, from Lipatti, Curzon, Kovacevich and Lupu, but among modern recordings Vogt acquits himself with honour. The Grieg coupling is very fine indeed.

Perahia's version also benefits from having the guiding hand of Sir Colin Davis directing the orchestra. The recording is live. The confident bravura in the performances presents Perahia in a rather different light from usual. He is never merely showy, but here he enjoys displaying his ardour and virtuosity as well as his ability to invest a phrase magically with poetry. With its full and spacious sound, the Perahia is among the finest recent versions of this favourite coupling.

It is good to have Rubinstein's early (1958) New York (Manhattan Center) recording of the *A minor Piano concerto* restored to the catalogue as it is clearly preferable to his later, Chicago version, which suffered from a more restricted dynamic range, and few apologies have to be made for the sound. Rubinstein takes the allegros of these two interconnected movements (separated by the charming

Intermezzo) at comparatively modest speeds and he achieves the ideal compromise between an impression of spontaneous poetry in quieter passages (his rubato is marked but most natural) and a firm overall control. It is interesting that the conductor here, Josef Krips, was also the conductor on Kempff's old mono recording, which was also notable for its relaxed allegros, and one wonders what influence he had in the matter. As couplings, we are offered Rubinstein's 1969 recording of the *Arabeske*, aristocratic in feeling and with nuances of rubato to remind us of his Chopin. The *Etudes symphoniques* were recorded at a live recital in Carnegie Hall in 1961, and the commanding playing is made the more gripping by the communication with the audience – witness the burst of adrenalin at the *Allegro marcato* (*Etude No. 4*) and the variations which follow.

Kempff, after a rather positive account of the opening chords of the *Piano concerto*, proceeds characteristically to produce an unending stream of poetry. The dialogue of the *Intermezzo* is like an intimate conversation overheard. Tempi are generally leisurely, notably so in the finale where, with fine support from the Bavarian Radio Orchestra under Kubelik, the main theme has an engaging lilt. Good early-1970s recording. Of the solo recordings neither is among Kempff's more compelling Schumann performances. The comparatively extrovert style of *Carnaval* does not seem to suit him too well and there is no special degree of illumination such as we expect from this artist either here or in the *Scenes from childhood*. Good rather than outstanding piano recording, made in the same period as the concerto.

Pascal Devoyon is aristocratic without being aloof, pensive without being self-conscious, and brilliant without being flashy. Natural musicianship and artistry are always in evidence, and at bargain price this is very competitive, with excellent playing from the LPO under Jerzy Maksymiuk.

Byron Janis's Schumann *Concerto* is a lovely performance, and the 1962 recording sounds amazingly improved over its previous incarnations, especially in regard to the orchestra. Janis's reading finds an almost perfect balance between the need for romantic ardour and intimacy in the *Concerto* – the exchanges between the piano and the woodwind soloists in the first movement are most engagingly done. Skrowaczewski provides admirable support throughout, and this is highly recommendable too.

Brendel's is a thoroughly considered, yet fresh-sounding performance, with meticulous regard to detail. There is some measure of coolness, perhaps, in the slow movement, but on the whole this is a most distinguished reading.

Dinu Lipatti's celebrated EMI recording has acquired classic status and will more than repay study. The transfer is excellent. A splendidly aristocratic account in very acceptable sound.

Lupu's clean boldness of approach to the first movement is appealingly fresh, but the fusing together of the work's disparate masculine and feminine Romantic elements has not been solved entirely. The digital CD transfer is especially telling in the quieter moments, but tuttis are less transparent than with a digital recording.

Van Cliburn's performance is very persuasive, the first movement rhapsodical in feeling, certainly poetic but exciting too. The *Intermezzo* is pleasingly fresh and the finale admirably buoyant and spirited. Altogether this is most attractive, and so is the unusual MacDowell coupling. However, this also comes with an alternative coupling of Prokofiev, a brilliant performance but with a less naturally balanced recording, drawing one's attention to the well-integrated sound-picture offered in the Schumann *Concerto*, where the Chicago ambience adds characteristic warmth. This version is available only in the USA.

Gulda's account is refreshingly direct yet, with light, crisp playing, never sounds rushed. The *Intermezzo* remains delicate in feeling, with nicely pointed pianism. The finale is just right, with an enjoyable rhythmic lift, and the early stereo (1956), though a little dated, is fully acceptable.

Fleischer's 1960 account with Szell is also distinguished, the reading combining strength and poetry in a most satisfying way, yet with a finale that sparkles, in spite of a very bold, upfront orchestral recording, which tends to sound a little fierce.

Pollini's account of the concerto is not without tenderness and poetry (witness the slow movement), but he is at times rather business-like and wanting in freshness. He is handicapped by rather unventilated recording and an inconsistent balance. (The piano seems much further back in the slow movement by comparison with the first.) The coupled piano pieces, however, are in every way successful. His account of the *Symphonic studies* has a symphonic gravitas and concentration; it also has the benefit of excellent recorded quality. Pollini includes the five additional variations that Schumann omitted from both the editions published during his lifetime, placing them as a group between the fifth and sixth variations.

This reissue in DG's 'Originals' series does not always represent Richter at his very finest. The performance of the concerto is not as interesting as one would expect. Its opening speed is fast and the interpretation is in the main without idiosyncrasy, but only in the finale does one really feel that vibrant quality in his playing which marks Richter out among even the great virtuosos. One might hypothesize that the comparative sluggishness of the orchestra affected Richter's concentration. Not that the concerto and the *Introduction and allegro appassionato* (one of Schumann's less interesting works) lack style, but the tension could be greater, particularly in the latter. The focus of the late-1950s Polish recording has been improved in the concerto but in Opus 92 remains a little fuzzy around the edges, not quite up to the standard one expects from DG. The *Novellette* and *Toccata* are fabulous performances, full of hair-raising virtuosity, but shaped with an unerring sense of style and musical as well as technical control. The piano tone is dry but clear. The *Waldszenen* is a mono recording, taken from an earlier LP collection, recorded in 1956. It is beautifully played, Richter very much the poet of the forest, and the mono sound gives no cause for complaint.

Jorge Federico Osorio's account of the Schumann *Concerto* is boldly romantic yet in no way lacking in poetry. The central *Intermezzo* is beautifully in scale, but in the first movement, with Bátiz bringing strong support in the tuttis, he presses on impulsively, and the finale has similar urgency. Some may prefer a more relaxed romanticism, but there is no lack of spontaneity here and the result is undoubtedly fresh and involving. Excellent recording and recommendable couplings make this disc a genuine bargain.

Jorge Bolet's Schumann is rather more successful than his Grieg, but he does not show any true feeling for this repertoire. The performance is agreeably relaxed – the short central movement comes off best – but the interplay between wind soloists and pianist in the first movement seems disappointingly matter-of-fact and the finale tends towards heaviness. The recording is admirable.

Given the formidable array of rival entries in the current catalogue, Amalie Malling stands little chance of being competitive. A Schumann concerto that is short on poetic feeling is hardly worth giving serious consideration. Her Schoenberg is excellent, and it would have been more sensible for her to have recorded other repertoire of the second Viennese school.

Evgeny Kissin sounds inhibited and ill at ease in his recording with Giulini and the Vienna Philharmonic. Although he can produce a wide range of pianissimo colour, we do not hear it. Giulini's soggy accompaniment does not help either. Instead of the normal Grieg coupling, we have a couple of miniatures, the *Carnival scene*, Op. 19/3, and a transcription of his most famous song, *Jeg elsker Dig*, as well as some Liszt paraphrases, including Schubert's *Erlkönig* and *Die Forelle*. All these are played with a spontaneity and poetry that are so elusive in the concerto and they need recoupling.

(i) *Piano concerto in A min., Op. 54;* (ii) *Violin concerto in D min.*
(Y/B) *(**) Teldec/Warner Dig. 4509 90696-2 [id.]. (i) Argerich; (ii) Kremer; COE, Harnoncourt.

In her live recording of the *Piano concerto*, Martha Argerich gives a vividly compelling, characteristically volatile reading, at once poetic and full of fancy, powerful and often wildly individual, culminating in an account of the finale so daring one wants to cheer at the end, so freely does the adrenalin flow. Though the orchestra is hard pressed to keep up with her at her fast basic speed, there is a splendid swing to the rhythm and no sense of haste. Kremer's performance of the still-neglected *Violin concerto* is disappointing in comparison with the warmth and bravura of his earlier version, recorded for EMI with Riccardo Muti and the Philharmonia Orchestra (see below). In neither concerto is the recorded sound ideally warm or full-bodied, with tuttis rather muddy in texture.

(i) *Piano concerto in A min., Op. 54;* (ii) *Abendlied, Op. 85/12; Adagio and Allegro in A flat, Op. 70; Fantasiestücke, Op. 73; 3 Romances, Op. 94; 5 Stücke im Volkston, Op. 102.* (Piano) *Etudes symphoniques, Op. 13. Fantasia in C, Op. 17; Fantasiestücke, Op. 12; Kinderszenen, Op. 15; Kreisleriana, Op. 16.*
(N) (M) *** Ph. Brendel Edition Analogue/Dig. 446 925-2 (5) [id.]. Alfred Brendel, with (i) LSO, Abbado; (ii) Heinz Holliger – BRAHMS: *Piano concertos; Ballades* etc. ***

Brendel's is a fresh, thoughtful account of the *Piano concerto*, missing something of the work's delicate romantic feeling in the slow movement; but on the whole this is a satisfying reading, not lacking in poetry. Neither the orchestral response under Abbado nor the Philips recording will seriously disappoint. It was a curious idea to include the series of pieces with oboe, beautifully though Holliger plays. They are available separately – see below. But the piano music is all well chosen. The very opening of the *Fantasiestücke*, Op. 12, demonstrates magically spontaneous playing; both this and the *Fantasia in C* are full of imaginative touches of colour, strong as well as poetic. The digital sound is rather more forward than one would encounter in the recital room, but it serves Brendel well and truthfully conveys the depth of timbre. *Kinderszenen* and *Kreisleriana* bring more thoughtful and poetically characterized playing from Brendel, and he is again very well recorded, while the *Etudes symphoniques* are ardent and yet beautifully controlled, again given first-class digital sound.

Violin concerto in D min.
(N) *** Decca Dig. 444 811-2 [id.]. Joshua Bell, Cleveland O, Christoph von Dohnányi – BRAHMS: *Violin concerto.* ***
(M) *** Teldec/Warner Dig. 4509 91444-2 [id.]. Zehetmair, Philh. O, Eschenbach – DVORAK: *Concerto* etc. **(*)

(N) (M) *(*) Teldec/Warner Dig. 06030 10015-2 [id.]. Gidon Kremer, COE, Harnoncourt –
BEETHOVEN: *Violin concerto.* *** ✦

With Dohnányi and the Cleveland Orchestra adding to the weight and drama, Joshua Bell in a commanding performance defies the old idea of this as an impossibly flawed piece, bringing out charm as
well as power. The central slow movement has a rapt intensity rarely matched, and the dance-rhythms of
the finale have fantasy as well as jauntiness and jollity. With full-bodied, well-balanced recording, this is
a disc which offers an apt and generous coupling, with both concertos in versions not easily surpassed.

Thomas Zehetmair is also perfectly cast for the Schumann *Concerto*. He understands the central
European tradition and makes the very most of the comparatively weak first movement. The *Langsam*
slow movement is glorious (Schumann seemingly at his most inspired) and even the erratic finale is made
to sound jolly and not too disjointed. Eschenbach accompanies sympathetically and the recording is
excellent. This can also be strongly recommended, although Zehetmair's coupling is not as enticing as
that of Joshua Bell.

Kremer first recorded the Schumann *Violin concerto* very successfully with Muti, but this is now deleted.
His newer account with Harnoncourt is much less appealing. Not only is the speed of the first movement slower, Kremer sounds heavy and over-emphatic to the point of self-consciousness. The slow
movement lacks the magic it had before, beautiful as Kremer's playing still is. When it comes to the
finale, the choice of speed is wildly eccentric, a half-speed such as you would use for a rehearsal, dull and
plodding. The recording does not help, with its lack of sharpness of orchestral focus at higher dynamic
levels.

Violin concerto in A min., Op. 129 (arr. from *Cello concerto* by the composer and orch. Shostakovich).
(Y/B) **(*) DG Dig. 439 890-2 [id.]. Kremer; Boston SO, Ozawa – SHOSTAKOVICH: *Violin concerto
No. 2.* **(*)

Gidon Kremer's coupling is ingeniously conceived. Schumann himself made an arrangement of the solo
part of his *Cello concerto* for solo violin; this performance combines that with the orchestral version of
the *Cello concerto* which Shostakovich made, aiming to improve on Schumann's own orchestration. As
Kremer demonstrates, there is much to be said for the solution of using the Shostakovich scoring as an
accompaniment for the violin version, when the main result of Shostakovich's tinkerings is to give more
edge to the orchestral part, making the tuttis cleaner and bolder. Kremer in this live recording performs
the piece with his usual flair and imagination, adopting speeds rather faster than those usual in the cello
version, and the orchestra sounds fuller-bodied than in the genuine Shostakovich *Concerto*, which
comes as coupling.

Introduction and Allegro appassionato in G, Op. 92.
(N) (B) **(*) Sony SBK 48166; *SBT 48166* [id.]. Rudolf Serkin, Phd. O, Ormandy – BRAHMS: *Concerto
No. 1* **(*); MENDELSSOHN: *Capriccio brillant.* **

Serkin plays this somewhat elusive work with his accustomed panache and he is given excellent support
from Ormandy. The piano-tone could be fuller in timbre but the overall effect has considerable warmth,
and those looking for a recording of this relatively unfamiliar piece will find much here to arrest them.
The Brahms coupling also shows Serkin at his finest.

Overture, scherzo and finale in E, Op. 52.
(B) *** DG 431 161-2. BPO, Karajan – BRAHMS: *Symphony No. 1.* ***

This serves merely as a bonus for Karajan's fine 1964 recording of the Brahms *First Symphony* and this
performance is second to none.

Symphonies Nos. 1 in B flat (Spring); 2 in C; 3 (Rhenish); 4 in D min. (original Leipzig version);
Overture, scherzo and finale, Op. 52.
(Y/B) ✦ *** RCA Dig. 09026 61931–2 (2) [id.]. Hanover Band, Goodman.

Roy Goodman's versions on period instruments are a revelation, not just an academic exercise. Few
period performances of nineteenth-century works can match these refreshing accounts, either for the
vigour and electricity of the playing or for the new perceptions given. Convincingly Goodman shows
how these works are far more cohesive in their often volatile inspiration than many used to think.
Textures are clarified, but never to reduce the impact of the music, rather to give them exceptionally
clean-cut terracing of sound, thanks also to the satisfyingly beefy recording. Most thrilling are the
antiphonal contrasts of the brass choirs, setting the braying timbre of period horns (two of the four
natural valveless instruments in Nos. 1 and 4, as the composer wanted) against the brightness of the
trumpets. The sharp accenting of woodwind comment, often syncopated, is also enhanced, with
Goodman securing superb ensemble. The strings are naturally thinner, with violins and cellos unable to

expand over the wide dynamic range of modern instruments, but Goodman compensates in encouraging a warmly espressivo style in slow movements, with *Andantes* flowing easily, never trivialized. The first disc contains the three works dating from 1841, not just the *Spring Symphony* (No. 1) and the *Overture, scherzo and finale* but the original Leipzig version of the *Symphony No. 4*, usually heard in the revision of ten years later. Not only is the scoring lighter, the slow transitions into the Allegros of the outer movements are both more compact, with each sequence made very convincing by Goodman, particularly the big crescendo into the finale. Brahms preferred this earlier version, and here one registers why.

Symphonies Nos. 1–4.
(M) *** DG 429 672-2 (2) [id.]. BPO, Karajan.
(N) *** DG Dig. 439 923-2 (2) [id.]. Dresden State O, Sinopoli.
(Y/B) (B) *** RCA 74321 20294-2 (2). Phd. O, James Levine.
(Y/B) (M) ** Teldec/Warner Dig. 4509 95501-2 (2) [id.]. LPO, Kurt Masur.
(N) (B) ** Decca Double Dig. 452 214-2 (2). Cleveland O, Dohnányi.

Symphonies Nos. 1–4; Overtures: Genoveva; Manfred.
(B) *** DG Double 437 395-2 (2). BPO, Kubelik.

Symphonies Nos. 1 in B flat (Spring), Op. 38; 2 in C, Op. 61.
(B) *** Sony SBK 48269; SBT 48269 [id.]. Bav. RSO, Kubelik.

Symphonies Nos. 3 in E flat (Rhenish), Op. 97; 4 in D min., Op. 120; Overture Manfred, Op. 115.
(B) *** Sony SBK 48270; SBT 48270 [id.]. Bav. RSO, Kubelik.

Symphonies Nos. 1–4; Overture, scherzo and finale, Op. 52.
(M) *** EMI CMS7 64815-2 (2) [id.]. Dresden State O, Sawallisch.

Symphonies Nos. 1–4; Scenes from Goethe's Faust: Overture.
(M) ** EMI CMS7 63613-2 (2) [id.]. New Philh. O or Philh. O, Klemperer.

The Dresden CDs of the Schumann *Symphonies* under Sawallisch are as deeply musical as they are carefully considered; the orchestral playing combines superb discipline with refreshing naturalness and spontaneity. Sawallisch catches all Schumann's varying moods, and his direction has splendid vigour. These recordings have dominated the catalogue, alongside Karajan's, for some years and they are most welcome on CD. Although the reverberant acoustic brought a degree of edge to the upper strings, the sound-picture has the essential fullness which the Karajan transfers lack, and the remastering has cleaned up the upper range to a considerable extent. The set now appears in a mid-priced box and the individual CDs have been restored: CDM7 69471-2 (*Symphonies Nos. 1 & 4; Overture, scherzo and finale*) and CDM7 69472-2 (*Symphonies Nos. 2–3*).

Karajan's interpretations of the Schumann *Symphonies* stand above all other recordings on modern instruments. No. 1 is a beautifully shaped performance, with orchestral playing of the highest distinction; No. 2 is among the most powerful ever recorded, combining poetic intensity and intellectual strength in equal proportions; and No. 3 is also among the most impressive versions ever commited to disc: its famous fourth-movement evocation of Cologne Cathedral is superbly spacious and eloquent, with quite magnificent brass playing. No. 4 can be classed alongside Furtwängler's famous record, with Karajan similarly inspirational, yet a shade more self-disciplined than his illustrious predecessor. However, the reissued complete set brings digital remastering which – as with the Brahms symphonies – has leaner textures than before, while in tuttis the violins above the stave may approach shrillness.

In vivid sound, warm yet finely detailed, Sinopoli directs the Dresden Staatskapelle in powerful, immediately compelling performances of all four symphonies, No. 2 being taken from a live performance. Sinopoli's way of moulding phrases and varying tempi is here consistently convincing, with the Dresden players responding warmly, not least in the slow movements of Nos. 1 and 2 and in the weighty, intense account of the Cologne cathedral-inspired fourth movement of No. 3. Speeds are extreme at times in both directions – weighty and slow in the Scherzo of No. 4, athletically brisk in the finale – but the conviction of each reading is never in doubt, and the recording is particularly rich and full on brass, most important in the outer movements of the *Rhenish*. There is no finer digital cycle using modern instruments, though Roy Goodman's RCA version on period instruments is even more revelatory.

The RCA bargain 'Symphony Edition' brings a splendid set of Schumann to cap the series. Recorded in a glowingly warm acoustic, the Philadelphia Orchestra has seldom sounded so rich-textured over recent years. The strings expand gloriously in the *Adagio* of No. 2; the brass produce the most expansive sonorities in the *Rhenish*. The performances are as vital as they are warm, and Levine usually produces accelerandos at the ends of outer movements to increase the excitement. The series is capped with a superb version of No. 4, where the powerful link into the finale brings brass playing to remind one not only of Wagner but of the *Ring*, and the very flexible account of the finale itself is not only thrilling but in its control of tempo shows that Levine has listened to the famous Furtwängler interpretation, absorbed its detail and made it his own. The two discs are available separately at mid-price: *Symphonies Nos. 1 and 3* (74321 20295-2) and *Symphonies Nos. 2 and 4* (74321 20296-2).

Kubelik's earlier set on DG is beautifully played and well recorded. The readings have not the drive of Karajan, notably in No. 4, but have both eloquence and warmth. They are straightforward, unmannered and recorded in a spacious acoustic with good CD transfers. With the two overtures also very well played as a bonus, this is another bargain on the Double DG label.

Kubelik's fine Sony set also remains fully competitive. The recording was made in the Hercules-Saal, Munich, in 1979, and the advantages of that glowing acoustic can be felt in the great cathedral evocation of the fourth movement and the famous link to the finale of the *Fourth*, where the Bavarian brass is very impressive. The orchestral playing is generally very fine (if not quite as polished as the Berlin Philharmonic) and is especially eloquent in the spacious slow movements. These are strongly character-ized readings with plenty of life and vitality which display the same bright and alert sensitivity to Schumann's style as did his earlier set for DG. But the Sony recording is obviously more modern, and the latest CD transfer brings plenty of body to the sound and a better focus to the violins than in the Sawallisch set. That more logically includes the *Overture, scherzo and finale*, but many will count the *Manfred overture* an equally desirable alternative.

The Masur set, well played as it is and given full-blooded digital sound, is less convincing. The perform-ances have boldness and strength, but slow movements do not match Levine's in romantic expansiveness and the second movement of the *Rhenish* is comparatively brusque. In the *Fourth Symphony* Masur uses the original (1841) Leipzig version of the score favoured by Brahms, where the differences are most marked in the finale.

There is not much that is springlike about Klemperer's reading of No. 1. The opening is tremendously spacious and unsmiling, though the allegro itself has plenty of affectionate touches and a lightish rhythm. Needless to say, the orchestral playing is of high quality with the woodwind particularly distinguished. The lack of geniality is a drawback but it would be wrong to give the impression that the performance is merely heavy-handed. There are many touches that underline the strength of Schumann's thinking in a way that other conductors fail to do. It certainly emerges as a weightier document than it does in either the Kubelik or Levine versions, even though they both display greater fire and urgency. Klemperer's determinedly measured approach is much less effective in No. 2 and the slow movement refuses to take off, while the *Rhenish* is again massively individual. Here the perform-ance misses far too much of the exhilaration of Schumann's inspiration. The *Fourth Symphony* is a different matter and needs a separate reissue. It is a masterly performance, giving the symphony a special stature. Klemperer's slow introduction has a weight and consequence that immediately command atten-tion, and for the finale Klemperer's speed is faster than many and he makes the conclusion most exciting. Plainly the Philharmonia players were on their toes throughout: the intensity of Klemperer's conviction comes over in shaping of phrases that is often quite breathtaking.

Dohnányi's Cleveland versions are superbly played and equally splendidly recorded. Thus the *Rhenish Symphony*, with its rich sonorities, cannot fail to make an impression. But overall these performances, although affectionately shaped, are seriously lacking in fire and impetus, so that inner movements come off much better than outer ones.

Symphony No. 1 in B flat (Spring), Op. 38.
(Y/B) (M) *** DG 447 408-2 [id.]. BPO, Karajan – BRAHMS: *Symphony No. 1.* ***
(B) *** DG 429 158-2 [id.]. BPO, Karajan – MENDELSSOHN: *Symphony No. 4.* ***

Karajan is totally attuned to Schumann's sensibility and he provides a strong yet beautifully shaped performance of the *Spring Symphony*. The very opening is electrifying with the Berlin Philharmonic giving of their finest, and this unsurpassed reading makes a highly appropriate coupling with Brahms in DG's Legendary Performances series of 'Originals'. The sound is an obvious improvement on the previous CD incarnation of this well-balanced analogue recording from the early 1970s, adding body and weight to the clear, fresh detail; it is also available at bargain price, coupled with Mendelssohn's *Italian Symphony*.

Symphonies Nos. 1; 3 in E flat (Rhenish), Op. 97.
(BB) *** ASV Dig. CDQS 6073 [id.]. RLPO, Janowski.

Janowski's pairing of the *Spring* and *Rhenish symphonies* is particularly successful. The pacing through-out both symphonies is most convincing, with a good deal of the inspirational pull that makes the Karajan readings so telling. In the Cologne Cathedral evocation of the *Rhenish*, the Liverpool brass rise sonorously to the occasion and the recording is altogether first class, bright, clear and full, with a concert hall ambience. At super-bargain price, this is strongly competitive.

Symphonies Nos. 1; 4 in D min.
(N) (M) *** DG 445 718-2 [id.]. BPO Karajan.

As we go to press, Karajan's recording of the *Spring Symphony* is additionally available coupled with the splendid account of the *Fourth Symphony* at mid-price, in which the current transfer seems somewhat fuller than in the boxed set.

Symphony No. 2 in C, Op. 61.
(M) *** DG 435 067-2 [id.]. BPO, Karajan – BRAHMS: *Symphony No. 2.* ***

Karajan's powerful account of Schumann's *C major Symphony* has great eloquence and is marvellously played. The recording here sounds rather more expansive than in the boxed set.

Symphony Nos. 2; 3 in E flat (Rhenish), Op. 97.
*** DG Dig. 423 625-2 [id.]. BPO, Levine.
(B) *** DG 429 520-2 [id.]. BPO, Kubelik.

Levine conducts warm and positive readings of both *Symphonies*, drawing superb playing from the Berlin Philharmonic. Though the Berlin recording is warm and full to match – allowing thrilling crescendos in the Cologne Cathedral movement of the *Rhenish* – the inner textures are not ideally clear. The compensation is that the modern digital recording gives a satisfyingly full body to the sound.

An excellent alternative bargain coupling from Kubelik. No. 2 is beautifully played and eloquently shaped, and in the *Rhenish* Kubelik's straightforward, unmannered approach, coupled to a natural warmth, provides a musical and thoroughly enjoyable account.

Symphonies Nos. 2; 4 in D min., Op. 120.
(BB) ** ASV CDQS 6084 [id.]. RLPO, Janowski.

This is a less successful coupling than Janowski's companion recordings of Nos. 1 and 3. No. 2 comes off better than No. 4, with some fine, expressive playing from the Liverpool strings in the *Adagio* and an exciting finale. There is no lack of freshness elsewhere. No. 4 is fast. Janowski does not relax enough to let the first movement's lyrical blossoming take the fullest effect. There is more poise in the *Romanze* (and some fine wind playing too), but the finale is pushed forward rather aggressively and the accelerandos at the end of both outer movements sound unspontaneous.

Symphony No. 3 in E flat (Rhenish), Op. 97.
(Y/B) (M) *** DG Dig. 445 502-2 [id.]. LAPO, Giulini – BEETHOVEN: *Symphony No. 5.* ***
*** RCA Dig. 09026 61876-2. N. German RSO, Wand – SCHUBERT: *Symphony No. 3.* ***

Giulini's *Rhenish* is completely free of interpretative exaggeration and its sheer musical vitality and nobility of spirit are beautifully conveyed. The Los Angeles players produce a very well-blended, warm and cultured sound that is a joy to listen to in itself. The 1980 recording is also extremely fine and, with its superb Beethoven coupling, this is very highly recommendable.

Günter Wand's account of the *Rhenish* has integrity; it is straightforward and direct and in the Cologne Cathedral movement has no want of dignity. Wand is in excellent form, and the recordings are both spacious and present. A firm recommendation if you want this particular coupling, but he does not displace Karajan, Sawallisch, Levine or Kubelik in Schumann.

Symphonies Nos. 3 (Rhenish); 4 in D min. (first (1841) version).
(N) * Teldec/Warner Dig. 4509 90867-2 [id.]. COE, Harnoncourt.

These are as near perfunctory performances as Harnoncourt has ever drawn from the brilliant and dedicated young players of the Chamber Orchestra of Europe. Tension is missing in almost every movement, with ensemble relatively slack, and recording a little hazy. On the same label Masur offers a far finer version of the 1841 version of No. 4.

Symphonies Nos. 3 in E flat (Rhenish); 4 in D min., Op. 120.
*** EMI CDC7 54025-2 [id.]. L. Classical Players, Norrington.

Norrington not only clarifies textures, with natural horns in particular standing out dramatically, but, at unexaggerated speeds for the outer movements – even a little too slow for the first movement of No. 3 – the results are often almost Mendelssohnian. Middle movements in both symphonies are unusually brisk, turning slow movements into lyrical interludes. Warm, atmospheric recording.

Symphony No. 4 in D min., Op. 120.
(N) (M) *** DG 447 666-2 [id.]. Dresden State O, Karajan – BARTOK: *Piano concerto No. 3.* ***

A most lyrical and powerful account of the *Fourth Symphony* from the 1972 Salzburg Festival with the Staatskapelle, Dresden, in tremendous form. Karajan's reading does not differ greatly from his Berlin version from the 1970s or the later account with the Vienna Philharmonic. A marvellous performance and good recording.

CHAMBER MUSIC

Abendlied, Op. 85/2; Adagio and allegro in A flat, Op. 70; Fantasiestücke, Op. 73; 3 Romances, Op. 94; 3 Pieces in Folk style, Op. 102/2–4.
(M) *** Ph. 426 386-2. Heinz Holliger, Alfred Brendel.

The three *Romances* are specifically for oboe, but Holliger suggests that the others too are suitable for oboe, since the composer himself gave different options. One misses something by not having a horn in the *Adagio and allegro*, a cello in the folk-style pieces, or a clarinet in the *Fantasiestücke* (the oboe d'amore is used here); but Holliger has never sounded more magical on record and, with superbly real recording and deeply imaginative accompaniment, the result is an unexpected revelation.

Adagio and allegro for horn and piano, Op. 70.
(M) *** Decca 433 695-2 [id.]. Barry Tuckwell, Vladimir Ashkenazy – BRAHMS: *Horn trio;* FRANCK: *Violin sonata;* SAINT-SAENS: *Romance.* ***

Schumann's *Adagio and allegro* requires ripe romantic feeling and considerable virtuosity from the horn soloist. Needless to say, both these requirements are readily met by Barry Tuckwell and Vladimir Ashkenazy, and these artists create a fine artistic partnership. The 1974 Kingsway Hall recording cannot be faulted.

Clarinet sonatas (arr. of *Violin sonatas*) *Nos. 1 in A min., Op. 105; 2 in D min., Op. 121; 3 Romanzen, Op. 94.*
(Y/B) ** Sony SK Dig. 48035 [id.]. Neidich, Hokanson.

Charles Neidich plays the two violin sonatas in a transcription for his instrument along with the *Three Romances*, Op. 94, originally written for the oboe. The sonatas do not really work in this medium (the clarinet sonority at the top of the register is shrill and insufficiently sustained), though Neidich is a sensitive enough player and Leonard Hokanson a wonderful partner. His piano is not ideally balanced (there is too much resonance and the instrument is not in perfect condition).

Fantasiestücke, Op. 73.
(Y/B) *** Decca Dig. 430 149-2 [id.]. Cohen, Ashkenazy – BRAHMS: *Clarinet sonatas.* ***

Fantasiestücke, Op. 73; 3 Romances, Op. 94.
*** Chandos Dig. CHAN 8506 [id.]. Gervase de Peyer, Gwenneth Pryor – SCHUBERT: *Arpeggione sonata;* WEBER: *Silvana variations.* ***

With warmth of tone and much subtlety of colour, Gervase de Peyer gives first-class performances and is well supported by Gwenneth Pryor. The recording is most realistic.

A thoroughly recommendable alternative account by Franklin Cohen and Vladimir Ashkenazy of these lovely pieces; if you want them on clarinet, this version is as good as any. It is well recorded, too.

Fantasiestücke, Op. 73; 5 Stücke in Volkston, Op. 102.
*** Ph. Dig. 412 230-2 [id.]. Maisky, Argerich – SCHUBERT: *Arpeggione sonata.* ***

Mischa Maisky and Martha Argerich give relaxed, leisurely accounts of these pieces that some collectors may find almost self-indulgent. Others will luxuriate in the refinement and sensitivity of this playing.

Märchenbilder, Op. 113.
*** Virgin/EMI Dig. VC7 59309-2 [id]. Lars Anders Tomter, Leif Ove Andsnes – BRAHMS: *Viola sonatas.* *** ⓦ
**(*) Chandos Dig. CHAN 8550 [id.]. Imai, Vignoles – BRAHMS: *Viola sonatas.* **(*)

The young Norwegian duo bring great sensitivity and freshness to bear on the *Märchenbilder*, and their playing gives great pleasure, as does the Brahms coupling.

The *Märchenbilder* are pleasing miniatures, persuasively played here by Nobuko Imai and Roger Vignoles. The recording acoustic is not ideal, but this does not seriously detract from the value of this coupling.

Piano quartets: in C min.; in E flat, Op. 47.
**(*) RCA Dig. 09026 61384-2 [id.]. André Previn, Young Uck Kim, Heichiro Ohyama, Gary Hoffman.

The present issue unearths a rarity in the form of the *C minor Quartet*, written in 1829 when Schumann was still in his teens. It is not the strongest Schumann and, given the fact that at 47 minutes this CD represents short measure, any recommendation is inevitably qualified. It is a pity that the accomplished team could not have found time to fit an additional work into their sessions.

Piano quartet in E flat, Op. 47; (i) *Piano quintet in E flat, Op. 44.*
*** Ph. 420 791-2 [id.]. Beaux Arts Trio, Rhodes, (i) with Bettelheim.
**(*) CRD CRD 3324; *CRD C 4024* [id.]. Rajna, members of the Alberni Qt.

The Beaux Arts Trio (with associates) give splendid performances of both these fine chamber works. The vitality of inspiration is consistently brought out, and with that goes the Beaux Arts' characteristic concern for fine ensemble and refined textures. The recording is beautifully clear and clean.

Though not quite so flawlessly polished in their playing, Rajna and the Alberni give performances that in their way are as urgent and enjoyable as those on the Philips disc. The recording is brighter and crisper, which gives an extra (and not unlikeable) edge to the performances.

Piano quartet in E flat, Op. 47; Piano quintet in E flat, Op. 44; Adagio and allegro in A flat, Op. 70; Andante & variations in B flat, Op. 46; Fantasiestücke, Op. 73; Märchenbilder, Op. 113; Violin sonata No. 2 in D min., Op. 121.
(N) *** EMI Dig. CDS5 55484-2 (2) [CDCB 55484]. Argerich, Schwarzenberg, Hall, Imai, Maisky, Neunecker, Gutman, Rabinovitch.

These recordings were made at a series of informal concerts at Nijmegen, and they radiate a spontaneity and life that are more difficult to capture under studio conditions. The *Piano quintet* with Argerich, Dora Schwarzenberg, Lucy Hall, Nobuko Imai and Mischa Maisky must be numbered among the most vibrant on record, and the *Piano quartet*, with Natalia Gutman replacing Maisky and with Alexandre Rabinovitch at the piano, is hardly less fine. Although this is an arbitrary collection, those whose needs are met by this particular compilation are unlikely to find any disappointment here. The *Andante and variations*, Op. 46, is more of a rarity on records, though there are alternatives to be found.

Piano quintet in E flat, Op. 44.
(BB) *** Naxos Dig. 8.550406; *4550406* [id.]. Jenö Jandó, Kodály Qt – BRAHMS: *Piano quintet.* ***
(N) (***) Testament mono SBT 3063 [id.]. Victor Aller, Hollywood Qt – BRAHMS: *Piano quartets* etc. (***)

A strongly characterized performance of Schumann's fine *Quintet* from Jenö Jandó and the Kodály Quartet. This is robust music-making, romantic in spirit, and its spontaneity is well projected by a vivid recording, made in an attractively resonant acoustic. With its comparable Brahms coupling, this makes an excellent bargain.

Exhilarating and masterly, this Testament CD comes from the compilation of Brahms chamber music, recorded by the Hollywoods in the mid-1950s. A performance of some stature which transcends sonic limitations.

(i) *Piano quintet in E flat, Op. 44; String quartet No. 1 in A min., Op. 44/1.*
(N) *(*) DG Dig. 447 111-2 [id.]. (i) Paul Gulda; Hagen Qt.

Paul Gulda and the Hagen Quartet are not particularly competitive in the *Piano quintet*. They are neither idiomatic nor particularly sensitive to its subtle change of moods, and they rush the first movement off its feet. Nor does the *A minor Quartet* fare very much better. It is curiously overheated and, by comparison with such classic versions as the Quartetto Italiano or the Vogler, it sounds almost febrile.

Piano trios Nos. 1–3; Fantasiestücke in A min., Op. 88.
(Y/B) *** Ph. Dig. 432 165-2 (2) [id.]. Beaux Arts Trio.
**(*) Chandos Dig. CHAN 8832/3 (2) [id.]. Borodin Trio.

Piano trio No. 1 in D min., Op. 63.
**(*) CRD CRD 3433; *CRD C 4133* [id.]. Israel Piano Trio – BRAHMS: *Piano trio No. 2.* **(*)

Piano trios Nos. 2 in F, Op. 80; 3 in G min., Op. 110; Fantasiestücke, Op. 88.
(Y/B) ** CRD Dig. CRD 3458 [id.]. Israel Piano Trio.

The Beaux Arts are probably the safest bet in this repertoire, an instance of the most obvious recommendation being the best. Not that competition is exactly legion, but none that we have heard can outclass the Beaux Arts in terms of musicianship and finesse. Cultured playing, matched by truthful and present recording.

On Chandos are full-hearted performances that give undoubted pleasure – and would give more, were it not for some swoons from Rostislav Dubinsky who, at the opening of the *D minor Trio*, phrases with a rather ugly scoop. While too much should not be made of this, greater reticence would have been more telling throughout. The Chandos recording is vivid and faithful.

The Israel Piano Trio give a powerfully projected account of the *D minor Trio*; the pianist is at times rather carried away, as if he were playing a Brahms concerto. There are, however, some sensitive and intelligent touches, and the recording is first class.

The Israel performance of Nos. 2 and 3 is much the same as that of No. 1: lively, articulate playing with a sometimes over-forceful pianist. Not in the same class as the Beaux Arts.

Piano trios Nos. 2 in F, Op. 80; 3 in G min., Op. 110.
(N) ** Teldec/Warner Dig. 4509 90864-2 [id.]. Trio Fontenay.

Musicianly performances from the Trio Fontenay, but a trifle brightly lit and hard. There is no want of youthful drive and musical intelligence to be found here, but there is room – at least on the part of the pianist – for greater tenderness. The Beaux Arts get closer to the Schumann sensibility.

String quartets Nos. 1–3.
**(*) DG Dig. 423 670-2 (3). Melos Qt – BRAHMS: *String quartets 1–3* **(*).

String quartet No. 1 in A min., Op. 41/1.
(Y/B) *** RCA Dig. 09026 61438-2 [id.]. Vogler Qt – BRAHMS: *String quartet No. 3.* ***

String quartet No. 3 in A, Op. 41/3.
(Y/B) *** RCA Dig. 09026 61866-2 [id.]. Vogler Qt – BRAHMS: *String quartet No. 2.* ***

Fine accounts of both *Quartets* from the Vogler, an extremely fine quartet who have recently recorded the quartets of both Brahms and Schumann. If the coupling meets your particular needs, it would really be difficult to improve on them. They have the advantage of a rich and beautifully blended sonority and refined musicianship. Moreover the RCA recording is very good indeed. If the *F major Quartet*, Op. 41/2, when it arrives, is their equal, this is likely to be a first recommendation for some years to come.

The Melos performances, for all their ardour, do not seem completely at one with Schumann's world: there is a certain want of tenderness and introspection. Perhaps the brightly lit and forward recording militates against them and, like the Vogler, they come linked only with Brahms.

String quartets Nos. 1 in A min.; 2 in F, Op. 41/1–2.
*** CRD CRD 3333; CRDC 4033 [id.]. Alberni Qt.

These well-recorded and sympathetic performances by the Alberni Quartet have plenty of finesse and charm and are guided throughout by sound musical instinct.

Violin sonatas Nos. 1 in A min., Op. 105; 2 in D min., Op. 121.
*** DG Dig. 419 235-2 [id.]. Gidon Kremer, Martha Argerich.

The *Violin sonatas* both date from 1851 and are 'an oasis of freshness' in his last creative period. Kremer and Argerich are splendidly reflective and mercurial by turn and have the benefit of an excellent recording.

PIANO MUSIC

Abegg variations, Op. 1; Davidsbündlertänze, Op. 6.
*** Ottavio Dig. OTRC 39027 [id.]. Imogen Cooper – BRAHMS: *Fantasias, Op. 116.* ***

Imogen Cooper plays the *Abegg variations* with a rare combination of iridescent brilliance and poetic feeling, and she characterizes the *Davidsbündlertänze* with consistent imagination and colour. She is gently ravishing in the gentler numbers like *Innig* and the lovely closing *Nicht Schnell*, yet catches the robust geniality of *Mit Humour* without a hint of heaviness. The playing is spontaneous from first to last, and the recording most realistic.

Abegg variations, Op. 1; Fantasiestücke, Op. 12; March in G min., Op. 76/2; Novellette in F, Op. 21/1; Toccata in C, Op. 7; Waldszenen, Op. 82.
(M) (***) DG mono 435 751-2 [id.]. Sviatoslav Richter.

It was his 1956 DG mono LP of the *Waldszenen*, six of the *Fantasiestücken* and the *G minor March*, Op. 76, which served as Richter's visiting card in the West. Alec Robertson hailed his triumphant entry on the scene in the *Gramophone* magazine, and other great discs soon followed including the *Toccata* (1959) and the *Abegg variations* (1962). His supreme pianism shines through the years and, although the sound shows its age, it is an improvement over the original LP. The three stars are for the performances; some allowance must be made for the sound-quality.

Albumblätter, Op. 99; Arabeske, Op. 18; Etudes symphoniques, Op. 13.
(BB) *** Naxos Dig. 8.550144 [id.]. Stefan Vladar.

Stefan Vladar intersperses the additional studies that Schumann published as an appendix into the *Etudes symphoniques*. His account is quite simply superb in every respect and deserves recording of comparable excellence. His account of the *Albumblätter* is hardly less masterly. Artistically this rates three stars, with the compelling quality of the playing transcending the sonic limitations of the recording.

Allegro, Op. 8; Gesänge der Frühe, Op. 133; Novelletten, Op. 21; 3 Fantasiestücke, Op. 111.
**(*) Olympia Dig. OCD 436 [id.]. Ronald Brautigam.

As the opening *Allegro* shows, this is strong, spontaneously impulsive playing and in the *Novelletten* some might wish for less passion and more poise. However, there is poetry too: the second and, especially, the third of the *Fantasiestücke* are very appealing. The *Gesänge der Frühe* ('Morning songs') brings the most responsive playing of all and is most touchingly done. Clear, bold piano recording.

Arabeske in C, Op. 18; Blumenstück, Op. 19; Carnaval, Op. 9; Davidsbündlertänze, Op. 6; Fantasia in C, Op. 17; 8 Fantasiestücke, Op. 12; 3 Fantasiestücke, Op. 111; Faschingsschwank aus Wien, Op. 26; Humoresque in B flat, Op. 20; Kinderszenen, Op. 15; 4 Nachtstücke, Op. 23; Novelletten, Op. 21; Papillons, Op. 2; 3 Romances, Op. 28; Piano sonatas Nos. 1 in F sharp min., Op. 11; 2 in G min., Op. 22; Waldszenen, Op. 82.
(M) **(*) Ph. 432 308-2 (7) [id.]. Claudio Arrau.

Claudio Arrau's playing has warmth, poise and the distinctive, aristocratic finesse that graced everything this artist touched. Arrau has the measure of Schumann's impulsive temperament and is almost always perfectly attuned to his sensibility. Not all the rubati ring true and there are moments that seem a little self-conscious. But there is a very great deal to admire in this compilation, and few collectors will be greatly disappointed.

Arabeske in C, Op. 18; Faschingsschwank aus Wien, Op. 26; Kreisleriana, Op. 16.
(BB) *(*) Naxos Dig. 8.550783 [id.]. Jenö Jandó.

Carnaval, Op. 9; Kinderszenen, Op. 15; Papillons, Op. 2.
(BB) ** Naxos Dig. 8.550784 [id.]. Jenö Jandó.

After his successful Beethoven and Haydn recordings, Jandó's Schumann is disappointing. He is inclined to fast tempi and is too impulsive by half, and the result – not helped by the bold, bright piano-sound – often becomes aggressive. *Kinderszenen* and *Carnaval* both have moments of poetry and display considerable virtuosity, but the former hardly ever seems to inhabit the innocent world of children. The opening of *Kreisleriana* and the *Finale* of *Faschingsschwank aus Wien* bring much dash but not nearly enough poise, and *Papillons*, too, needs a less forthright approach.

Arabeske in C, Op. 18; Etudes symphoniques, Op. 13.
(N) **(*) Decca Dig. 444 338-2 [id.]. Thibaudet – BRAHMS: *Paganini variations.* **(*)

Jean-Yves Thibaudet is a cultured player who offers good taste and refined pianism. His technical command is second to none, but in terms of poetic insight he must yield to Lupu in the *Arabesque* and to Perahia in the *Symphonic studies*. Those who invest in this disc will find much to satisfy them but, despite good Decca sound, there is not enough to disturb earlier recommendations for this coupling.

Arabeske, Op. 18; 3 Romanzen; Faschingsschwank aus Wien; Waldszenen.
(Y/B) **(*) DG Dig. 437 538-2 [id.]. Maria João Pires.

Maria João Pires is an artist of insight and temperament. Her Schumann recital, though not in the same league as Lupu's, is well worth hearing. She is a musician of intuition who is thoroughly inside Schumann's world and though in none of these pieces would her version be a first choice, it is still deserving of recommendation.

Blumenstück, Op. 19; 4 Fugues, Op. 72; March No. 2, Op. 76/2; Nachtstücke, Op. 23; Toccata, Op. 7.
*** Decca Dig. 436 456-2 [id.]. Sviatoslav Richter.

A superb recital, recorded, with great fidelity, in Mantua in 1986. The programme makes a particularly satisfying whole, opening with the four diverse *Fugues*, on through the ebullient *March*, to the exhilaratingly joyful *Toccata*, and the meltingly characteristic *Blumenstück* – where Richter is at his most magically poetic. The recital ends with the comparatively rare *Nachtstücke*, in four sections ranging over the widest range of mood. This is Schumann playing of the highest distinction.

Carnaval; Faschingsschwank aus Wien, Op. 26; Kinderszenen, Op. 15.
(B) *** DG 431 167-2. Daniel Barenboim.

Barenboim's 1979 reading of *Carnaval* is one of his finest recording achievements in his role as pianist rather than as conductor. His lively imagination lights on the fantasy in this quirkily spontaneous sequence of pieces and makes them sparkle anew. *Carnival jest from Vienna* is more problematic, but the challenge inspires Barenboim, and here too he is at his most imaginative and persuasive, bringing out the warmth and tenderness as well as the brilliance. The recital opens with a tender and charismatic reading of *Kinderszenen*. The 1979 recording is bold and truthful, but the CD transfer has lost a little of the fullness in the bass.

Carnaval, Op. 9; Kreisleriana, Op. 16.
(N) * Chandos Dig. CHAN 9388 [id.]. Miceál O'Rourke.

Miceál O'Rourke's Chandos coupling is hardly likely to raise much enthusiasm. The playing is mostly pedestrian and earthbound, though there are intermittent flashes of poetic feeling. No quarrels with the recording quality.

Davidsbündertänze, Op. 6; Fantasiestücke, Op. 12.
(Y/B) (BB) *(*) Naxos Dig. 8.550493 [id.]. Benjamin Frith.

Benjamin Frith, who is also undertaking a Mendelssohn survey for Naxos, is an impressive if rather impulsive interpreter of Schumann. Yet he can be touchingly poetic, as in the opening *Des Abends*, *Warum?* and *Fabel* from the *Fantasiestücke*. However, Naxos had not, in 1991, solved their studio problem for recording the piano, and the results here in the Clara Wieck Auditorium, Heidelberg, fail to bring enough depth of sonority for this repertoire.

Davidsbündlertänze, Op. 6; Sonata No. 2 in G min., Op. 22; Toccata, Op. 7.
*** Teldec/Warner Dig. 9031 77476 [id.]. Boris Berezovsky.

Boris Berezovsky is a keyboard lion of the first order. Everything we have so far heard of his has been of exceptional artistry and great finesse. His formidable musicianship is allied to a technique of magisterial calibre, and this coupling is very impressive indeed.

5 Etudes, Op. posth.; Etudes symphoniques, Op. 13; Papillons, Op. 2.
**(*) Sony CD 76635 [MK 34539]. Murray Perahia.

Murray Perahia has a special feeling for the *Symphonic studies*. He also plays the additional five studies, which Schumann omitted from the published score, as an addendum. The *Papillons* are unlikely to be surpassed but the engineers give Perahia too close a balance to be ideal.

Etudes symphoniques, Op. 13; Fantasie in C, Op. 17.
(N) (M) (**(*)) DG mono 447 977 [id.]. Wilhelm Kempff.

Kempff's Schumann disc, issued to celebrate his centenary in 1995, offers two mono recordings dating from the mid-1950s. Kempff proves far happier in the dozen jewelled sections that make up the *Etudes symphoniques*, here given a rare clarity and sparkle, than in the broad span of the *C major Fantasie*, where he is less inspired. Whatever reservations one may make, however, the magnetically individual personality of the pianist rides triumphant.

Etudes symphoniques, Op. 13; Intermezzi, Op. 4; Sonata No. 2 in G min., Op. 22; Toccata, Op. 7.
*** Conifer Dig. 75605 51227-2 [id.]. Mikhail Kazakevich.

Mikhail Kazakevich has a natural feeling for both the virtuosic pianism and the fervour of Schumann together with inwardness and poetic insight. Indeed his is one of the finest accounts of the *G minor Sonata* and the *Etudes symphoniques* to have appeared in recent years. In terms of technical address and subtlety of colouring, Kazakevich is most impressive. The recording is good though just a trifle shallow at times.

Fantasia in C, Op. 17.
(N) (M) *** DG 447 451-2 [id.]. Maurizio Pollini – SCHUBERT: *Wanderer fantasia*. ***
*** Sony Dig. MK 42124 [id.]. Murray Perahia – SCHUBERT: *Wanderer fantasia*. ***

This is among the most distinguished Schumann performances in the catalogue. Pollini's playing throughout has a command and authority on the one hand and deep poetic feeling on the other that hold the listener spellbound. The recording is good but not outstanding. A welcome mid-priced reissue in DG's series of 'Originals'.

Murray Perahia's account of the *C major Fantasy* is a performance of vision and breadth, immaculate in its attention to detail and refinement of nuance. The recording is good, even if it does not wholly convey the fullest range of sonority and dynamics.

Fantasia in C, Op. 17; Faschingsschwank aus Wien (Carnival jest from Vienna), Op. 26; Papillons, Op. 2.
(M) *** EMI CDM7 64625-2 [id.]. Sviatoslav Richter.

Richter's 1961 account of the *Fantasia in C* is a wonderfully poetic performance. Richter's phrasing, his magnificent control of dynamics, his gift for seeing a large-scale work as a whole – all these contribute towards the impression of unmatchable strength and vision. The recording is faithful, with genuine presence. The other two works included on this CD were recorded live during Richter's Italian concert tour a year later. The piano sound inevitably is somewhat less sonorous, shallower at fortissimo level, but fully acceptable. The account of *Papillons* is beguilingly subtle in control of colour.

Fantasia in C, Op. 17; Kreisleriana, Op. 16.
(M) *** RCA 09026 61264-2 [id.]. Artur Rubinstein.

Rubinstein's account of the *Fantasia in C* is wonderfully subtle in its control of tempo and colour, and the poetry of the outer sections is quite magical. In spite of the close balance, Rubinstein achieves exquisite gradations of tone; the recording, made in 1965, is among the best he received during this period. *Kreisleriana* is hardly less compelling, with the great pianist at his most aristocratic, although the impetuous opening is recorded rather shallowly.

Fantasiestücke, Op. 12; Kinderszenen, Op. 15; Kreisleriana, Op. 16.
(M) *** Ph. Dig. 434 732-2 [id.]. Alfred Brendel.

Fantasiestücke is strong as well as poetic. The *Kinderszenen* is also one of the finest performances of the 1980s and is touched with real distinction. Brendel's *Kreisleriana* is intelligent and finely characterized. He is better recorded (in 1981/2) than most of his rivals and, though certain details may strike listeners as less spontaneous, the overall impression is highly persuasive.

Humoreske in B flat, Op. 20.
(BB) **(*) Naxos Dig. 8.550469 [id.]. Wolf Harden – REGER: *Variations.* **(*)

Wolf Harden's performance of the Schumann *Humoreske* is highly imaginative, idiomatic and full of sensitive touches. There is plenty of air round the aural image.

Humoreske, Op. 20; Kinderszenen, Op. 15; Kreisleriana, Op. 16.
(Y/B) *** Decca Dig. 440 496-2 [id.]. Radu Lupu.

This is Schumann playing of quite exceptional insight and naturalness. Lupu is one of the few Schumann interpreters whose understanding of the composer can be measured alongside that of Murray Perahia. His account of the *Humoreske*, Op. 20, is the most poetic and spontaneous since the famous Richter version (issued over here in the 1950s on Parlophone), and the *Kreisleriana* are hardly less magical. This is playing of great poetry and authority. The recording is excellent, albeit resonant, and although there are odd occasions where twangy notes disturb they are of small moment in playing of such distinction. The Schumann piano disc of the year.

Kinderszenen, Op. 15; Sonata No. 1 in F sharp min., Op. 11; Waldszenen, Op. 82.
*** Decca Dig. 421 290-2 [id.]. Vladimir Ashkenazy.

Ashkenazy has his finger(s) on the pulse of Schumann's inspiration. The playing is very natural and all the more impressive for that. He proves a sound guide in the *Waldszenen*, and his *Kinderszenen* is one of the most appealing in the catalogue, again with a naturalness and directness that are attractive. The Decca recording is excellent.

Piano sonata No. 2 in G min., Op. 22.
*** Sony Dig. MK 44569 [id.]. Murray Perahia – SCHUBERT: *Piano sonata No. 20.* ***

Perahia's account of the Schumann *G minor Sonata* is fresh, ardent and vital; every phrase is beautifully moulded yet somehow seems spontaneous in feeling – and spontaneity was the essence of Schumann's youthful genius. The recording places the listener fairly near the piano but is eminently truthful.

ORGAN MUSIC

4 Sketches, Op. 58 (ed. Bate).
(BB) *** ASV CDQS 6127 [id.]. Jennifer Bate (Royal Albert Hall organ) – LISZT: *Organ music.* ***

The *Four Sketches* were originally written for a piano with pedal attachment and are here arranged for organ by E. Power Biggs. Each of the pieces is in 3/4 time, but the writing is attractively diverse; they are pleasant trifles. Rich, atmospheric recording with fair detail, impressively transferred to CD. Generously coupled with Liszt's three major organ warhorses, this makes a very tempting super-bargain reissue.

VOCAL MUSIC

Lieder from *Album für die Jugend, Op. 79; Gedichte der Königen Maria Stuart, Op. 135; Myrthen Lieder, Op. 25:* excerpts. *Abends am Strand; Die Kartenlegerin; Ständchen; Stille Tränen; Veratine Liebe.*
*** CRD CRD 3401; *CRD C 4051* [id.]. Sarah Walker, Roger Vignoles.

Sarah Walker's 1982 Schumann collection is most cherishable, notably the five Mary Stuart songs which, in their brooding darkness, are among Schumann's most memorable. With superb accompaniment and splendid recording, this is an outstanding issue.

Dichterliebe, Op. 48.
(Y/B) (M) (***) Decca mono 440 065-2 [id.]. Souzay, Bonneau – SCHUBERT: *Lieder*. ***

Gérard Souzay and Jacqueline Bonneau were recorded in 1953 at the beginning of his international career. Souzay's voice possesses a wonderful freshness and poignancy; and 'the beauty of timbre and evenness of production' to which John Steane alludes in his authoritative notes is strikingly in evidence. The command of legato is matched by an ability to characterize that is second to none.

(i) *Dichterliebe, Op. 48;* (ii) *Frauenliebe und Leben, Op. 42.*
(B) ** Analogue/Dig. DG 439 417-2 [id.]. (i) Dietrich Fischer-Dieskau, Christophe Eschenbach; (ii) Brigitte Fassbaender, Irwin Gage.

Fischer-Dieskau's earlier DG *Dichterliebe* (recorded between 1973 and 1977) is not quite as emotionally plangent as his later, digital version on Philips, but the contrasts between expressive warmth and a darker irony are still apparent. Eschenbach's accompaniment is always imaginative and the recording has fine presence. Fassbaender's account of the deeply moving female cycle is certainly strongly characterized, with a wide range of expression and fine detail, but she conveys little sense of vulnerability and there is little attempt to beautify the voice – though it is a fine and consistent instrument. If the underlying sentimentality of the poems is here concealed, so is much else. Irwin Gage is an excellent accompanist and the digital recording is very vivid.

Dichterliebe, Op. 48; 6 Gedichte, Op. 90; Liederkreis, Op. 39; Myrthen, Op. 25: Aus den östlichen; Widmung (only). *Requiem, Op. 90.* Lieder: *Auf den Sonnenschein; Die beiden Grenadiere; Dein Angesicht; Nichts Schöneres; Romanze; Der Schätzgräber; Des Sennen Abschied; Der Spielmann; Ständchen.*
(N) (M) *** Ph. 442 741-2 (2) [id.]. Gérard Souzay, Dalton Baldwin – BEETHOVEN: *An die ferne Geliebte* etc.; BRAHMS: *Lieder*. ***

Although this set, which includes a veritable feast of Lieder, is described as 'The Early Years', Souzay had made an earlier mono recording of the *Dichterliebe* for Decca with Jacqueline Bonneau which remains treasurable – see above. However, the later, mature version with Dalton Baldwin, made nine years later in 1962 (alonside the *Sechs Gedichte*, *Requiem* and two *Myrthen Lieder*), also shows exceptional insight and accomplishment, and the same may be said of the *Liederkreis* (and the miscellaneous songs), which date from 1966. Comparison with Fischer-Dieskau in this wonderful song-cycle proves endlessly illuminating (what marvellous songs they are!). Both singers are, in their way, equally fine, bringing to each of the songs great imaginative feeling as well as their familiar vocal accomplishment. Fischer-Dieskau has recorded the cycle several times, yet in every instance there are many details in which Souzay's artistry and humanity will seem of such an order as to silence criticism, and his sympathy with Schumann's sensibility is extraordinary. For many listeners Souzay's comparative reticence – compared with the German baritone's intense expressive feeling – will carry the day, and few who hear Souzay's account of *Mondnacht* will deny the French singer's exceptional insight and accomplishment, while Dalton Baldwin provides wonderfully sensitive support. The recital ends with a group of (mostly) popular songs, beautifully sung, of which the closing *Dein Angesicht* is quite ravishing. The only drawback to this indispensable set is the absence of full translations – only the German texts are provided.

Dichterliebe, Op. 48; Liederkreis, Op. 39.
*** Ph. Dig. 416 352-2 [id.]. Dietrich Fischer-Dieskau, Alfred Brendel.
(B) *** CfP CD-CFP 4651; *TC-CFP 4651*. Ian Partridge, Jennifer Partridge.

Fischer-Dieskau, in inspired collaboration with Alfred Brendel, brings an angry, inconsolable reading, reflecting the absence of fulfilment in the poet's love. The Op. 39 *Liederkreis* also brings inspired, spontaneous-sounding performances, with the voice here notably fresher.

Ian and Jennifer Partridge recorded this coupling in 1974. Blessed with a radiantly beautiful light voice, Ian's thoughtfulness illuminates every line, helped by superbly matched accompaniments. The recording is well balanced and truthful and is transferred most naturally to CD. A real bargain.

Dichterliebe (song-cycle), *Op. 48; Liederkreis* (song-cycle), *Op. 39; Myrthen Lieder, Op. 25.*
*** DG 415 190-2 [id.]. Dietrich Fischer-Dieskau, Christoph Eschenbach.

An outstandingly fine *Dichterliebe* plus the magnificent Op. 39 *Liederkreis*, made the more attractive on CD by the generous addition of seven of the *Myrthen* songs. Eschenbach is imaginative on detail without ever intruding distractingly. Very good sound for the period.

Dichterliebe, Op. 48; Liederkreis, Op. 24. Lieder: *Der arme Peter (I; II; III); Du bist wie eine Blume; Lehn deine Wang'; Die Lotusblume; Mein Wagen rollet langsam; Tragödie (I; II); Was will die einsame Träne.*
(N) *** Ph. Dig. 446 086-2 [id.]. Wolfgang Holzmair, Imogen Cooper.

Holzmair, with his light, tenorish baritone, proves a perfect poet in *Dichterliebe*. Not many recordings so happily combine consistent beauty of tone over a wide range with such ardour, intensity and fine detail, and Imogen Cooper is an inspired accompanist. That cycle to poems by Heine is then perfectly complemented by Schumann's other, more disparate and varied Heine cycle, the *Liederkreis*, Opus 24, as well as seven other Heine items. Here too Holzmair proves a masterly interpreter, alert and intense but finely controlled, as in the extreme contrast between the two songs grouped as *Tragödie*, the one out-going, the other inward. Excellent sound.

Frauenliebe und Leben (song-cycle), *Op. 42.*
(Y/B) ✸ (M) *** Saga EC 3361-2 [id.]. Dame Janet Baker, Martin Isepp (with Lieder recital ***).

Janet Baker's range of expression in her earlier, Saga recording of the Schumann cycle runs the whole gamut from a joyful golden tone-colour in the exhilaration of *Ich kann's nicht fassen* through an ecstatic half-tone in *Süsser Freund* (the fulfilment of the line *Du geliebter Mann* wonderfully conveyed) to the dead, vibrato-less tone of agony at the bereavement in the final song. Martin Isepp proves a highly sensitive and supportive partner, and the recording balance – originally curiously artificial – has been immeasurably improved by the CD transfer.

Frauenliebe und Leben, Op. 42; 5 Lieder, Op 40 (Märzveilchen; Muttertraume; Der Soldat; Der Spielmann; Verratene Liebe). Lieder: *Abendlied; Dein Angesicht; Die Kartenlegerin; Die Löwenbraut; Lust der Sturmnacht; Mein schöner Stern; Die Meersee; Rose, Meer und Sonne; Der Schatzgräber Schneeglöckchen; Des Sennen Abscheid; Die Soldatenbraut; Stille Liebe; Volksliedchen; Vom Schlaraffenland.*
(N) *** DG Dig. 445 881-2 [id.]. Anne Sofie von Otter, Bengt Forsberg.

Anne Sofie von Otter characterizes the contrasting songs in *Frauenliebe* with exceptional intensity, presenting a character, as in an opera, developing from youthful, eager girl to bereaved widow. By creating a character outside herself, von Otter may for some seem a shade detached compared with other, more personally involved singers, but that strengthens the cycle, minimizing the sentimentality of the poems. This is an exceptionally generous recital (79 minutes) and other songs on the disc are then characterized commandingly, with dramatic contrasts heightened. Try the beautiful Heine setting, *Dein Angesicht* ('Your face'), sung with poise and flawless legato. Excellent sound and fine accompaniment from Forsberg. Highly recommended.

Liederkreis, Op. 39; 12 Kerner-Lieder, Op. 35.
*** Hyperion Dig. CDA 66596 [id.]. Margaret Price, Graham Johnson.

Graham Johnson partners Margaret Price in a superb Schumann disc, coupling the sequence of 12 settings of Justinus Kerner, Op. 35, with the Eichendorff *Liederkreis*, Op. 39. The singer's presence, magnetism and weight of expression are superbly caught, and the tonal beauty and immaculate sense of line go with detailed imagination in word-pointing. So Price may underplay the horror of such a song from Opus 39 as *Waldesgespräch* about meeting the Lorelei, but the moment of confrontation is sharply pointed when legato is suddenly abandoned. The lesser-known *Kerner-Lieder* also contain many treasures. First-rate sound.

Mass in C min., Op. 147; Requiem für Mignon, Op. 98b.
(B) *** Erato/Warner Dig. Duo 4509 95307-2 [id.]. Michael, Bizimeche-Elsinger, Silveira, Teiseira, Schoeffler, Brodard, Lisbon Gulbenkian Foundation Ch. & O, Corboz – SCHUBERT: *Mass No. 6.* ***

Schumann's *Mass in C minor* is a powerful work in which the chorus is all-important. The Lisbon singers rise to the challenge eloquently under Corboz, who is a persuasive exponent. He has good soloists, and Audrey Michael is particularly touching in the *Offertorium*, where she sings with a treble-like purity. The *Sanctus* which follows is also very fine. The less ambitious *Requiem für Mignon* is also very attractively done, with the matching of the female solo voices particularly pleasing. Excellent digital recording gives a natural projection and focus to the performers, and the only drawback to this excellent Erato Bonsai Duo set is the absence of documentation about the music, so necessary with rare repertoire of this kind.

Das Paradies und die Peri, Op. 50 (oratorio; complete).
(Y/B) *** RCA/Eurodisc Dig. RD 69105 (2) [69105-2-RC]. Büchner, Schiml, Kaufmann, Planté, Schopper, Sweet, Schmiege, Bamberg Ch. & SO, Kuhn.

(i) *Das Paradies und die Peri. Overture, Scherzo and Finale, Op. 52.*
(N) *** DG Dig. 445 875-2 (2) [id.]. (i) Faulkner, Murphy, Quivar, Wilke, Lewis, Swensen, Hale, Dresden State Op. Ch.; Dresden State O, Sinopoli.

Das Paradies und die Peri; 9 Romances and ballads for mixed choir, Opp. 59, 67, 75 & 145.
(N) (M) *** EMI CMS7 69447-2 (2) [id.]. Edda Moser, Marheineke, Fassbaender, Gedda, Tripp, Wewel, Düsseldorf State Musikverein Ch., Düsseldorf SO, Henryk Czyz.

Though Clara Schumann described this secular oratorio as the most beautiful work that her husband had yet written, it cannot in lyrical invention match the songs that he was writing at the same time (in the early 1840s). Even so, this morality on the theme of salvation has many beauties. Sinopoli is the most persuasive advocate in this curious, enigmatic work, moulding phrases warmly to give the impression of a live event. He draws from his Dresden forces performances both rich and refined, to outshine rival versions both in the playing and in the full and opulent recorded sound, with solo voices fresh and clear. The *Overture, Scherzo and Finale* makes a welcome and generous fill-up, another strong and sympathetic performance, as impressive as Sinopoli's fine readings of the numbered symphonies.

Gustav Kuhn also offers a fine team of soloists and bright, well-balanced recording. The two most important soloists are certainly characterful, Sharon Sweet powerful if not always ideally firm as the Peri and Eberhard Büchner clear, fresh and keenly idiomatic as the first tenor.

Recorded in full, well-balanced analogue sound in the mid-1970s, Henryk Czyz's Dusseldorf perform-ance is very well cast and offers a fresh, direct performance, not as subtle as Sinopoli's, not as well recorded as Kuhn's Bamberg version, but always convincing. At mid-price and with a generous and unusual fill-up, it makes a good alternative recommendation.

(i) *Requiem in D flat, Op. 148;* (ii) *Requiem für Mignon, Op. 98b.*
(B) *** EMI Dig. CZS7 67819-2 (2) [id.]. (i) Helen Donath, Doris Soffel, Nicolai Gedda; (i; ii) Dietrich Fischer-Dieskau; (ii) Brigitte Lindner, Andrea Andonian, Mechthild George, Monika Weichhold; Düsseldorf Musical Soc. Ch., Düsseldorf SO, Klee – BRAHMS: *German Requiem.* **(*)

Like Mozart, Schumann was unable to shake off the conviction that the *Requiem* was for himself. The opening *Requiem aeternam* is affecting and dignified, and the final *Benedictus* has a haunting eloquence. Bernhard Klee extracts a very sympathetic response from his distinguished team of soloists and the fine Düsseldorf chorus and orchestra. They also give an attentive and committed account of the 1849 *Requiem for Mignon*, Op. 98b. The EMI recording is natural and well balanced. This now comes in harness with Tennstedt's impressively spacious account of the Brahms *Requiem*.

Der Rose Pilgerfahrt, Op. 112.
(Y/B) *** Chandos Dig. CHAN 9350 [id.]. Inga Nielsen, Deon van der Walt, Annemarie Møller, Guido Paevatalu, Danish Nat. R. Ch. and SO, Gustav Kuhn.

Schumann wrote his cantata, *Der Rose Pilgerfahrt* ('The Pilgrimage of the rose'), in 1851 towards the end of his career, and the pity is that such a charming, fresh inspiration is so little known, for it defies the usual verdict that Schumann's later music lacks the spark which fired him earlier. The very opening has the lyrical openness of Schubert, its freshness enhanced by the interplay of solo voices and women's chorus. The idiom, as well as recalling Schubert, often suggests the folk-based writing of Humperdinck in *Hänsel und Gretel*, similarly innocent-seeming, but in fact subtle. Gustav Kuhn conducts an aptly bright and atmospheric performance, very well recorded, with the warm-toned Inga Nielsen and the clear-toned tenor, Deon van der Walt, in the two principal roles of the heroine, Rosa, and the tenor narrator. The chorus and orchestra are first rate, with colourful genre numbers including a chorus of elves and a drinking song. The recording, sponsored by Danish Radio, is full-bodied and atmospheric. A valuable rarity. Sadly, the booklet contains no translation alongside the German text, though Richard Wigmore's note and summary are very helpful.

Scenes from Goethe's Faust.
✹ (M) *** Decca 425 705-2 (2). Harwood, Pears, Shirley-Quirk, Fischer-Dieskau, Vyvyan, Palmer, Aldeburgh Festival Singers, ECO, Britten.
(Y/B) **(*) Sony Dig. SK 66308 (2) [id.]. Terfel, Mattila, Rootering, Bonney, Wottrich, Vermillion, Poschner-Klebel, Graham, Blochwitz, Peeters, BPO, Abbado.
(Y/B) (M) **(*) EMI Dig. CMS7 69450-2 (2) [id.]. Fischer-Dieskau, Mathis, Berry, Gedda, Daniels, Lövas, Schwarz, Sharp, Gramatzki, Stamm, Düsseldorf Music Soc. Ch., Tölz Boys' Ch., Düsseldorf SO, Klee.

Though the episodic sequence of scenes is neither opera nor cantata, the power and imagination of much of the music, not least the delightful garden scene and the energetic setting of the final part, are immensely satisfying. In 1972, soon after a live performance at the Aldeburgh Festival, Britten inspired his orchestra and his fine cast of singers to vivid performances, which are outstandingly recorded against the warm Maltings acoustic. This is magnificent music, and readers are urged to explore it – the rewards are considerable.

Abbado's recording was taken live from concert performances in June 1994, using a cast, headed by Bryn Terfel in the title-role and with Karita Mattila as Gretchen, that could hardly be bettered at the time. Abbado's direction is strong and sympathetic, and the singing good; but one has only to go back to Benjamin Britten's inspired Decca recording of 1972 to find even keener imagination, not just in the conducting but in the singing too. Bryn Terfel is thoughtful and expressive as Faust, but Fischer-Dieskau was far more illuminating and detailed, while Elizabeth Harwood as Gretchen sang even more radiantly than Mattila here, bringing out the heroine's tenderness and vulnerability. Equally, Jan-Hendrik Rootering as Mephistopheles here is not as characterful as John Shirley-Quirk. The analogue 1972 sound is also rather cleaner than the 1994 digital, but, were the Decca set to become unavailable, this Sony will always provide a most enjoyable recording of an all-too-rare work.

Klee takes a sharply dramatic view of Schumann's strange collection of Goethe portraits and with bright, atmospheric, digital recording the score is made to seem less wayward than it can. The cast of singers is strong, but Fischer-Dieskau is here not as steady as he was in Britten's recording of ten years earlier. Nor – particularly in the final scene – does Klee have the imaginative insights that gave that recording such compelling magic and earned it a Rosette.

Spanische Liebeslieder, Op. 138.
(N) *** EMI CDC5 55430-2 [id.]. Bonney, Von Otter, Streit, Bär, Deutsch, Forsberg – BRAHMS: *Liebeslieder waltzes* etc. **

Despite the similarity of name, Schumann's set is quite different from Brahms's well-known pieces, far less festive. In the Schumann, five of the ten numbers are solos, two are duets and two more are for piano duet only, with only a single quartet at the end. With some charming ideas and very well performed, it makes an apt and generous coupling for EMI's live recording of the Brahms (not nearly as successful as a performance) and is otherwise unavailable on CD.

Schurmann, Gerard (born 1928)

6 Studies of Francis Bacon for large orchestra; Variants for small orchestra.
*** Chandos CHAN 9167 [id.]. BBC SO, composer.

Inspired by the fantastic, often violent or painful paintings of Francis Bacon, Schurmann here writes a virtuoso orchestral showpiece, full of colourful effects. The vigour of the writing is admirably caught both in this performance and in the often spiky writing of the *Variants* for a rather smaller orchestra, set against passages of hushed beauty. First-rate 1979 recording, made in the warm acoustics of All Saints', Tooting, and admirably transferred to CD.

Schütz, Heinrich (1585–1672)

Christmas oratorio (Weihnachtshistorie).
*** EMI Dig. CDC7 47633-2 [id.]. Kirkby, Rogers, Thomas, Taverner Cons., Taverner Ch., Taverner Players, Parrott – PRAETORIUS: *Christmas motets.* ***

There is no sense of austerity here, merely a sense of purity, with the atmosphere of the music beautifully captured by these forces under Andrew Parrott. One is soon gripped by the narrative and by the beauty and simplicity of the line.

Christmas oratorio; Easter oratorio (Historia der Auferstehung Jesus Christi).
*** Sony Dig. SK 45943 [id.]. Prégardien, Van der Sluis, Egeler, Kendall, Müller, Robson, Spägele, Stuttgart Chamber Ch., Cologne Musici Fiata, Stuttgart Bar. O, Bernius.

Bernius's fine account of the *Christmas oratorio* on Sony is certainly as good as any available, if not better, and enjoys the advantage of another major Schütz coupling, the *Historia der Auferstehung Jesus Christi*, a performance of exceptionally gripping quality. Schütz's second liturgical work after *The Psalms of David*, this *Easter oratorio* dates from 1623 and draws on both the text and the musical procedures of the *Easter Historia* by Antonio Scandello, one of Schütz's predecessors at Dresden. The work is one of grave, expressive beauty and a moving purity of utterance, and the performance here is excellent. It is more strongly projected than the inward and reposeful performance by René Jacobs and the Concerto Vocale on Harmonia Mundi (HMC 90 1311). On Sony Christopher Prégardien is an excellent Evangelist and Frieder Bernius has the advantage of first-rate soloists in Mieke van der Sluis, Andrea Egeler and Mona Spägele. Christoph Robson's Jesus is also moving. Bernius maintains an excellent sense of pace through both works and the instrumentalists are excellently balanced and recorded. Artistically and as a recording, this is among the finest of Schütz issues.

Italian Madrigals (complete).
(B) *** HM HMA 1901162 [id.]. Concerto Vocale, René Jacobs.
(M) **(*) HM/BMG Dig. GD 77118 [77118-2-RG]. Consort of Musicke, Rooley.

Schütz's first and only *Book of Italian Madrigals* reflects his encounter with the music of Giovanni Gabrieli and Monteverdi. The Concerto Vocale, led by the counter-tenor, René Jacobs, employ a theorbo which provides added variety of colour, and at times they offer great expressive and tonal range. They omit the very last of the madrigals, the eight-part *Vasto mar*.

Anthony Rooley and the Consort of Musicke are perhaps less varied (no instruments are used) but style and intonation are impeccable, though there are occasional discrepancies of pitch between some madrigals.

Motets: *Auf dem Gebirge; Der Engel sprach; Exultavit cor meum; Fili mi Absolon; Heu mihi Domine; Hodie Christus natus est; Ich danke Dir, Herr; O quam tu pulchra es; Die Seele Christi, helige mich; Selig sind die Todten.*
(BB) *** ASV CDQS 6105 [id.]. Pro Cantione Antiqua, L. Cornett & Sackbut Ens., Restoration Ac., Edgar Fleet.

An eminently useful and well-recorded super-bargain anthology of Schütz motets that offers such masterpieces as *Fili mi Absolon* (for bass voice, five sackbuts, organ and violone continuo) and the glorious *Selig sind die Todten* in well-thought-out and carefully prepared performances under Edgar Fleet. These accounts have a dignity and warmth that make them well worth considering. Moreover the CD transfer is excellently managed, the sound rich and clear.

Musicalische Exequien. Motets: *Auf dem Gebirge; Freue dich des Weibes Jugend; Ist nicht Ephraim mein teurer Sohn; Saul, Saul, was verfolgst du mich.*
*** DG Dig. 423 405-2 [id.]. Monteverdi Ch., E. Bar. Soloists, His Majesties Sackbutts & Cornetts, Gardiner.

Schütz's *Musical Exequien* contains music that is amazing for its period. The Monteverdi Choir responds with fiery intensity, making light of the complex eight-part writing in the second of the three *Exequies.* Four more superb motets by Schütz make an ideal coupling, with first-rate recorded sound.

O bone Jesu, fili Mariae.
(N) (M) *** DG Dig. 447 298-2 [id.]. Monteverdi Ch., E. Bar. Soloists, Gardiner – BUXTEHUDE: *Membra Jesu nostri.* ***

A wonderfully eloquent performance of this *Spiritual concerto* by one of the greatest of baroque masters. Schütz juxtaposes stanzas of a poem ascribed to St Bernard of Clairvaux with prose passages of Latin devotional literature, treating the latter as recitative and the former set homophonically, and ending the cantata in *concertato* style. Beautifully recorded.

The Psalms of David (Psalmen Davids).
*** Sony Dig. S2K 48042 (2) [id.]. Stuttgart Chamber Ch. & Soloists, Cologne Musica Fiata, Wilson & Bernius.

The Psalms of David (1619) was the first work Schütz composed on his return to northern Europe after his years in Venice with Giovanni Gabrieli. The Sony version, recorded in 1991, is complete and the Stuttgart Chamber Choir and the Musica Fiata Köln under Frieder Bernius give both lively and expressive accounts; all the pieces were recorded in the course of a few days and the performances in some cases are a little routine. For the most part, however, this is a very fine and recommendable set, very thoroughly annotated and a considerable advance over the Archiv set made in 1971–2 by the Regensburger Domspätzen and the Hamburger Bläserkreis under Hans Martin Schneidt.

Psalm 150.
(N) (B) **(*) EMI forte CZS5 68631-2 (2). Cambridge University Musical Soc., Bach Ch., King's College Ch., Wilbraham Brass Soloists, Willcocks – G. GABRIELI: *Motets* etc. **(*); MONTEVERDI: *Vespers.* *(*)

Schütz's setting of *Psalm 150* is for double choirs and soloists, each used in juxtaposition against the others, with built-in antiphony an essential part of the composer's conception. The majesty of Schütz's inspiration certainly comes over vividly here, the closing *Alleluja* having remarkable weight and richness, though the overall focus of the recording is not absolutely clean.

Sacred choral music (1648).
(M) **(*) HM/BMG Dig. GD 77171 (2) [id.]. Knabenchor Hannover, Heinz Hennig.

The Hanover recording of the Schütz *Geistliche Chormusik* comes from the early 1980s and was made in collaboration with Westdeutsche Rundfunk. It is of particular value in that it offers not only all 29 motets of the collection but also alternative versions of seven of them, two in more than one form. The notes are scholarly and helpful, and at mid-price it remains an attractive proposition. On the whole the singing is very good, though the tone of the Knabenchor of Hanover is not always perfectly focused; the recording, while generally acceptable, is at times a little opaque. However, there is at the time of writing no alternative version, and the set is to be recommended. Readers will derive much satisfaction from it.

Sinfoniae sacrae, Op. 66/2–13, 15, 17–19 (SWV 258–269, 271, 273–5).
(Y/B) (M) *** Erato/Warner Dig. 4509 96964-2 [id.]. Dietschy, Bellamy, Laurens, Zaepfel, Elwes, De Mey, Fabre-Garrus, Les Saqueboutiers de Toulouse.

Schütz's twenty *Sinfoniae sacrae* of 1629, of which sixteen are included here, are the result of the Dresden composer's second visit to Italy in 1628, when he was strongly influenced by Monteverdi and the Italian *concertato* style. These pieces fascinatingly combine voices and instruments in a single texture, usually with an interweaving interplay, and rarely with the instruments acting just as an obbligato. Here the collection is framed by the lively opening *Buccinate in neomenia tuba* (No. 19), which is complex and colourful, with its paired tenors, cornet, bass-trumpet and bassoon, and the equally joyful *Veni dilecte mi* (No. 18), where the voices of two sopranos and two tenors intermingle with a pair of sackbutts. The latter dialogue of a Shulamite and her lover, together with Nos. 9–10 (where tenor and bass are joined by two violins), are expressive settings from the *Song of Songs*. Perhaps the most famous is the tragic *Fili mi, Absalon* (No. 13), David's lament, in which the eloquent bass-line is amplified by magnificent interludes for four sackbutts, which are here gloriously sonorous and the effect very moving. The performances are eminently stylish and freshly spontaneous, and the instrumentalists are expert – and, moreover, play in tune. The balance is beautifully judged, with voices and instruments within the same perspective, and the digital recording is wholly realistic.

Schwantner, Joseph (born 1943)

From afar (fantasy for guitar and orchestra).
(N) ** Virgin/EMI Dig. CDC5 55083-2 [id.]. Sharon Isbin, St Paul CO, Hugo Wolff – CORIGLIANO: *Troubadours* **(*); FOSS: *American landscapes.* ***

Schwantner's *Fantasy* is just that, a kaleidoscope of colour and contorted rhythms. It opens with a strong flavour of Spanish flamenco strumming which returns later, but for the most part it depends more on sound and texture than on musical content. The performance has plenty of life and the recording certainly does not lack atmosphere, but this is the kind of avant-garde writing that comes off best at a live performance.

Scriabin, Alexander (1872–1915)

(i) *Piano concerto in F sharp min., Op. 20;* (ii) *Poème de l'extase, Op. 54;* (i) *Prometheus – The poem of fire, Op. 60.*
*** Decca 417 252-2 [id.]. (i) Ashkenazy, LPO; (ii) Cleveland O; Maazel.

Ashkenazy plays the *Piano concerto* with great feeling and authority. *Prometheus* too, powerfully atmospheric and curiously hypnotic, is given a thoroughly poetic and committed reading and Ashkenazy copes with the virtuoso obbligato part with predictable distinction. Maazel's 1979 Cleveland recording of *Le Poème de l'extase* is a shade too efficient to be really convincing. The playing is often brilliant and the recording is very clear but the trumpets are rather forced and strident. However, it can be regarded as a bonus for the other two works.

Symphonies Nos. 1–3; Poème de l'extase; (i) *Prometheus.*
*** EMI CDS7 54251-2 (3) [id.]. Toczyska, Myers, Westminster Ch. (in *No. 1*), Phd. O, Muti, (i) with Alexeev.

Symphonies Nos. (i) *1 in E, Op. 26; 2 in C min., Op. 29; 3 in C min. (Le divin poème); 4 (Poème de l'extase), Op. 54;* (ii) *5 (Prometheus), Op. 60;* (iii) *Piano concerto in F sharp min., Op. 20. Rêverie.*
(Y/B) (B) ** RCA 74321 20297-2 (3). Frankfurt RSO, Kitajenko, with (i) Siniawskaia, Fedin; (ii) Figuralchor, Krainev; (iii) Oppitz.

Muti's complete set of the Scriabin *Symphonies* can be recommended almost without reservation. True, in No. 3 the recording could be more refined, but overall the sound is as vivid and richly coloured as the performances. With the two additional symphonic poems (*Le Poème de l'extase* white-hot with passionate intensity, yet masterfully controlled) now added, in the place of the original, less appropriate Tchaikovsky couplings, this is an impressive achievement.

The set from the Frankfurt Radio forces is in its way desirable, though it would be idle to pretend that it offers a serious challenge to Riccardo Muti's set with the Philadelphia Orchestra on EMI. That however does not offer the early, Chopinesque *Piano concerto in F sharp minor* as part of the package; nor does it come at so competitive a price. Be warned, however, that Dmitri Kitajenko does not shrink from adding to the percussion and adding cymbal clashes at will. Not content with that, he goes even further and adds a chorus at the closing section of *Poème de l'extase*. One does not have to be a purist to find this unacceptable in the absence of any supporting documentary evidence as to Scriabin's own wishes. If the *Poème de l'extase* cannot be recommended, the *Prometheus* has much in its favour, including some impressive pianism from Vladimir Krainev. It is not however to be preferred to the Ashkenazy–Maazel version on Decca, nor is Gerhard Oppitz's account of the concerto as subtle or imaginative as the Ashkenazy. However, the discs can be purchased separately, and the first three symphonies are certainly recommendable at the price. Not only are the performances thoroughly idiomatic but the recorded sound has much going in its favour too; it is rich in detail and has plenty of air round the aural image. For the record, the *First Symphony* is coupled with *Le poème de l'extase* on the first disc (74321 20298-2); the *Second* with the *Piano concerto* (74321 20299-2) and the *Third* with *Prometheus* and the *Rêverie* (74321 20300-2). The third disc carries the strongest recommendation. All the same, even here the Muti remains far superior.

Symphony No. 1 in E, Op. 26.
*** Olympia Dig. OCD 159 [id.]. Gorokhovskaya, Pluzhnikov, Glinka State Ac. Ch. of Leningrad, USSR RSO, Fedoseyev.

The digital recording from the Soviet Union is relaxed and unforced and the two soloists, Yevgenia Gorokhovskaya and Konstantin Pluzhnikov, are every bit as fine as their EMI rivals, Stefania Toczyska and Michael Myers. This can be recommended with confidence.

(i) *Symphony No. 1 in E, Op. 26;* (ii) *Prometheus, Op. 60.*
(N) **(*) Decca Dig. 444 517-2 [id.]. (i) Balleys, Larin, Berlin R. Ch.; (ii) Jablonski; Berlin Deutsches SO, Ashkenazy.

If recording were the sole criterion, Ashkenazy's account of the *First Symphony* with Birgitte Balleys and Sergei Larin as soloists, the Berlin Radio Chorus and Berlin Deutsches Symphony Orchestra would be a first choice. The sound is sumptuous, extraordinarily well detailed and with superb presence – altogether in the demonstration bracket. The performance does not perhaps have quite the sheer grip and magnetism of Muti's Philadelphia account, but it is far from negligible. Both here and in *Prometheus*, in which Peter Jablonski is the fine soloist, one misses that wild-eyed, demonic fire that is so strong an ingredient in Scriabin's make-up. Not that there is anything routine, but the overall impression is a shade too cultured and judicious. It deserves a three-star rating for the outstanding sound-quality, but be warned that the performance is not three-star. The earlier *Prometheus* in which Ashkenazy takes part as the pianist is still the best (see above).

Symphony No. 2 in C min., Op. 29.
*** Chandos Dig. CHAN 8462 [id.]. SNO, Järvi.

Although it is less amorphous than its predecessor, the *Second Symphony* needs the most fervent advocacy if the listener is to be persuaded. This splendid account from Järvi, with its richly detailed Chandos recording, can be recommended strongly.

Symphony No. 3 in C min. (Le divin poème), Op. 43.
*** Chandos Dig. CHAN 8898 [id.]. Danish Nat. RSO, Järvi – ARENSKY: *Silhouettes.* ***

Symphony No. 3 (Le divin poème); Le Poème de l'extase, Op. 54; Rêverie, Op. 24.
*** Decca Dig. 430 843-2 [id.]. Berlin RSO, Ashkenazy.

Scriabin's mammoth *Third Symphony* calls for vast forces, but there is no doubt that it is original, both in layout and in substance. There is something refreshingly unforced and natural about Järvi's version which puts this score in a far better light than those conductors who play it for all they are worth. One of the special attractions of the Chandos issue is its rather endearing coupling, Arensky's *Silhouettes*, which are not otherwise available.

   Vladimir Ashkenazy has the advantage of the more logical coupling, an all-Scriabin programme, and good engineering from the Decca team. The Berlin Radio forces are very good and there is a highly charged feel to the performances, particularly that of *Le Poème de l'extase.*

Le Poème de l'extase, Op. 54.
(Y/B) (M) *** Sony SM2K 64100 (2) [id.]. NYPO, Boulez – BARTOK: *Wooden Prince* etc. **(*)
(N) (M) **(*) Decca Phase 4 443 898-2 [id.]. Czech PO, Stokowski – MUSSORGSKY: *Pictures at an exhibition* **; STRAVINSKY: *Firebird suite; Pastorale.* **(*)

Boulez's electrifying account of *Le Poème de l'extase* (not previously released) is surely unsurpassed on record for its ardour and the way Boulez controls the overall shaping of its climaxes and balances the orchestra so that the all-important trumpet part emerges from within a texture that is inherently voluptuous, even if the sound-quality itself could be more alluring. The recording, made in the Avery Fisher Hall, is, however, full and atmospheric and the work's final orgasmic culmination is almost overwhelming, with superb playing from the NYPO. This needs to be recoupled more appropriately on a single CD.

   Stokowski's version of the *Poème de l'extase* was recorded live when the nonagenarian conductor visited Prague. The result, tactfully edited from more than one performance, has all the passionate commitment of a concert-hall performance, with the ebb and flow of tension and the flexibiity of phrasing the more compellingly captured. The Phase Four recording highlights individual instruments, but not disastrously so.

PIANO MUSIC

2 Danses, Op. 73; 4 Morceaux, Op. 51; 4 Morceaux, Op. 56; 2 Poèmes, Op. 32.
(M) *** Decca Analogue/Dig. 425 081-2 [id.]. Vladimir Ashkenazy – RAVEL: *Gaspard* etc. ***

Ashkenazy is as thoroughly at home in these miniatures as he is in the *Sonatas*, readily finding their special atmosphere and colour, and the recording is first class. The recordings were made in 1977, with the exception of the Op. 51 *Morceaux*, which are later (1982) and digital.

Etudes (complete): *in C sharp min., Op. 2/1; 12 Etudes, Op. 8; 8 Etudes, Op. 42 (1903); in E flat, Op. 49/1; Op. 56/4 (1908); 3 Etudes, Op. 65.*
**(*) Hyperion Dig. CDA 66607 [id.]. Piers Lane.

Piers Lane makes light of the various technical problems in which these pieces abound and he plays with an admirable sense of style. Yet he does not give us the whole picture. He has sensibility and produces a good sonority, aided in no small measure by an excellently balanced recording; but one misses the nervous intensity, the imaginative flair and the feverish emotional temperature that the later pieces call for. At the time of writing there is no alternative view of the complete *Etudes* to be had on CD, so that this fills an important gap in the catalogue.

12 Etudes, Op. 8; 2 Nocturnes, Op. 5; Piano sonatas Nos. 2 in G sharp min. (Sonata fantasy), Op. 19; 3 in F sharp min., Op. 23.
(Y/B) ** ASV Dig. CDDCA 882 [id.]. Gordon Fergus-Thompson.

Preludes: in B, Op. 2/2; C sharp min., Op. 9/1; 24 Preludes, Op. 11; 6 Preludes, Op. 13; 5 Preludes, Op. 15; 5 Preludes, Op. 16; 7 Preludes, Op. 17.
(Y/B) ** ASV Dig. CDDCA 919 [id.]. Gordon Fergus-Thompson.

Although Gordon Fergus-Thompson is almost totally inside the Scriabin world, one crucial ingredient eludes him: a sense of manic possession. Naturally there is always a fear that finesse and polish will suffer if too many risks are taken, but without demonic fire and rapt absorption something essential is lost. Fergus-Thompson's account of the massive *Third Sonata* does not really surpass the earlier version he made in the late 1980s (see below), nor does it eclipse memories of broadcast performances he has given. The smaller-scale *Etudes*, Op. 8, are generally very much better. A greater range of keyboard colour and subtlety in the handling of dynamic nuance shadings is needed at times even on the second disc, devoted to the *Preludes*. On the whole there are better things here, and playing of considerable atmosphere and refinement – though he pulls some of the *Preludes*, Op. 11, hopelessly out of shape. The recordings are generally lifelike and present, but neither of these CDs does this fine artist as much justice as his earlier set of the *Sonatas Nos. 4, 5, 9* and *10*.

12 Etudes, Op. 8; Piano sonatas Nos. 3–5, Opp. 23; 30; 53.
*** Pianissimo Dig. PP 10394 [id.]. Yuki Matsuzawa.

Yuki Matsuzawa is a gifted young Japanese player with a remarkable feel for Scriabin. Whether in the Chopinesque *Etudes* or the bigger-boned *Third Sonata* she seems wholly attuned to the Scriabin sensibility; the opening of the *Third* is perhaps not as commanding or dramatic as Horowitz, but hers is a thoughtful and powerful reading too, and she is very persuasive in the *Fourth* and *Fifth Sonatas*, too.

Etudes, Op. 8/7 & 12; Op. 42/5. Preludes, Op. 11/1, 3, 9, 10, 13, 14, 16; Op. 13/6; Op. 15/2; Op. 16/1 & 4; Op. 27/1; Op. 48/3; Op. 51/2; Op. 59/2; Op. 67/1. Sonatas Nos. 3, Op. 23; 5, Op. 53.
(M) (***) RCA mono/stereo GD 86215 [6215-2-RC]. Vladimir Horowitz.

The RCA engineers have done wonders to these recordings from the 1950s though some of the original shallowness and clatter remains. The *Preludes* and the legendary account of the *Third Sonata* come from 1956. The *Fifth* is much later, coming from the mid-1970s, and has more bloom. The performances form an essential part of any good Horowitz collection.

Mazurkas, Op. 3/1–10; Op. 25/1–9; Op. 40/1–2.
*** Collins Dig. 1394-2 [id.]. Artur Pizarro.
(N) * Nimbus Dig. NI 5446 [id.]. Marta Deyanova.

Apart from Chopin, Scriabin is the only composer to have raised the mazurka to an art-form. These are often exquisite miniature tone-poems, and they are splendidly played and recorded. Artur Pizarro is a Leeds Competition Prizewinner, and listening to this record one sees why his artistry was so much admired.

Marta Deyanova is a Bulgarian pianist who made a strong impression on Menuhin and Szeryng in the 1960s and whom we recall hearing with pleasure on earlier occasions. The present set of *Mazurkas* is largely a disappointment. In terms of finesse and elegance it does not compare with Pizarro's fine set (Collins) and her wide dynamic range is constricted, although it is adequately recorded; she conveys little charm or magic.

Preludes, Op. 11, Nos. 2, 4–6, 8–14, 16; 18, 20, 22 & 24.
(Y/B) (M) *** EMI CD-EMX 2237. Andrei Gavrilov – RACHMANINOV: *Elégie* etc. ***

Gavrilov's selection from Opus 11 is arbitrary. At times his approach is impetuous, and dynamics can be exaggerated; but playing of this order is still pretty remarkable. The balance is not too close, yet the CD brings a tangible presence and the piano timbre is well caught.

Piano sonatas Nos. 1–10.
(M) *** Decca 425 579-2 (2) [id.]. Vladimir Ashkenazy.

Piano sonatas Nos. 1–10; Piano sonata in E flat min. (1887–9); Sonata fantaisie in G sharp min.
(M) **(*) DG 431 747-2 (3). Roberto Szidon.

Piano sonatas Nos. 1–10; Sonate-fantaisie in G sharp min.
(N) *** Hyperion Dig. CDA 67131/2 [id.]. Marc-André Hamelin.

The Scriabin sonatas are well served at present. There are several fine versions, including those by Vladimir Ashkenazy (Decca) and Roberto Szidon (DG), both at medium price. However, they must both yield to the newcomer by Marc-André Hamelin on this excellently recorded set. He commands the feverish intensity, the manic vision, wide dynamic range and fastidious pedalling that Scriabin must have. There are other fine Scriabin cycles and, of course, celebrated accounts of single sonatas from Horowitz, Richter and Sofronitzky, but of newer cycles Hamelin's must now be a first recommendation.

Ashkenazy is clearly attuned to this repertoire, though he is at his finest in the earlier sonatas. The last three are given with brilliance and vision, and there is no lack of awareness of the demonic side of Scriabin's musical personality. These are fine performances and are well recorded.

Roberto Szidon's DG reissue offers the whole set. Szidon seems especially at home in the later works. His version of the *Black Mass sonata* (No. 9) conveys real excitement. At medium price this is an attractive reissue and can be considered alongside Ashkenazy's series. The DG recording is good but not ideal and the tone tends to harden at climaxes.

Piano sonata No. 3 in F sharp min., Op. 23; 2 Poèmes, Op. 32; Vers la flamme, Op. 72.
**(*) Kingdom Dig. KCLCD 2001. Gordon Fergus-Thompson – BALAKIREV: *Piano sonata.* **(*)

Gordon Fergus-Thompson here gives a splendid account of Scriabin's overheated *F sharp minor Sonata* and sensitive, atmospheric performances of the other pieces here. A reverberant but good recording.

Piano sonatas Nos. 4, Op. 30; 5, Op. 53; 9 (Black Mass), Op. 68; 10, Op. 70. Etude in C sharp min., Op. 2/ 1; 8 Etudes, Op. 42.
**(*) ASV Dig. CDDCA 776 [id.]. Gordon Fergus-Thomson.

Fergus-Thomson is thoroughly inside this idiom. At the same time it must be conceded that his performances are not as manic or high-voltage as those of Richter and Horowitz and in the cruelly competitive world of recorded music would not be a first choice. Nevertheless there is much musical nourishment here to satisfy the collector.

Piano sonatas Nos. 8, Op. 66; 9, Op. 68; 10, Op. 70; 2 Danses, Op. 73; 2 Poèmes, Op. 69; 2 Poèmes, Op. 71; 2 Preludes, Op. 67; 5 Preludes, Op. 74; Vers la flamme, Op. 72.
*(**) Altarus Dig. AIR-CD 9020 [id.]. Donna Amato.

Donna Amato seems wholly attuned to Scriabin's sensibility and plays all his late music (Opp. 66–74), including the last three *Sonatas*, to the manner born. Scriabin's world is claustrophobic – but unfortunately so is the recording, which sounds as if it was made in a small acoustic environment but with some echo added. The sound-quality diminishes the pleasure this CD gives but not of course Amato's artistry.

Sculthorpe, Peter (born 1929)

(i) *Nourlangie* (for solo guitar, strings and percussion). *From Kakadu; Into the dreaming.*
(Y/B) *** Sony Dig. SK 53361 [id.]. John Williams; (i) Australian CO, Richard Hickox – WESTLAKE: *Antartica suite.*

Peter Sculthorpe, born in Tasmania, finds much of his inspiration in the physical nature of the Australian landscape. *Nourlangie* is an extraordinarily imaginative and evocative piece, inspired by the composer's first sight of the enormous monolithic rock of that name in the Kakadu National Park. The music fuses evocation (the opening, with sounding gongs, is very compelling) and local dance song, which are effectively and naturally integrated into the texture to give a strong underlying melodic vein. The central climax brings a great burst of 'birdsong' and later bird-calls decorate the closing section. The piece has moments of serenity yet demonstrates the power of nature to send the spirit soaring. The performance here is superb, with John Williams's guitar heard in a concertante role, admirably balanced within the overall sound-picture. The other two pieces are for solo guitar. *From Kakadu* is an intimate, improvisatory piece, somewhat minimalist in conception, in four changing sections, *Grave, Comodo, Misterioso* and *Cantando*, which sustains its ten-minute length admirably. *Into the dreaming* was inspired by a quiet solitary walk in the Valley of Winds at Katajuta in Uluru National Park. It opens mystically but generates much energy in its central section before returning to the restrained mood of the opening. John Williams plays both pieces with total spontaneity and complete improvisational freedom. He is most naturally, if forwardly, recorded. With its stimulating coupling, this whole concert is highly recommendable.

Segerstam, Leif (born 1942)

Symphonies Nos. (i) *11;* (ii) *14.*
** BIS Dig. CD 483 [id.]. (i) Swedish RSO, Leif Segerstam; (ii) Finnish RSO, Mikael Samuelson.

This gifted Finnish conductor is a prolific composer, and the symphonies recorded here exhibit something of the same mixture of flair and self-indulgence that is to be found in his conducting. There are flashes of imagination alongside long stretches of seemingly random activity. Those who are looking for symphonic writing in any real sense of the term will be disappointed, as will those expecting to encounter any strong or significant creative personality. Two stars for the recording and the expertise of the fine orchestras involved; for the composer none!

Seiber, Mátyás (1905–60)

Clarinet concertino.
*** Hyperion Dig. CDA 66215 [id.]. Thea King, ECO, Litton – BLAKE: *Concerto;* LUTOSLAWSKI: *Dance preludes.* ***

Mátyás Seiber's highly engaging *Concertino* was sketched during a train journey (in 1926, before the days of seamless rails) and certainly the opening *Toccata* has the jumpy, rhythmic feeling of railway line joints and points. Yet the haunting slow movement has a touch of the ethereal, while the Scherzo has a witty jazz element. Thea King has the measure of the piece; she is accompanied well by Litton, and very well recorded. Recommended.

Four French folk songs: Réveillez-vous; J'ai descendu; Le Rossignol; Marguerite, elle est malade.
(M) *** RCA 09026 61601-2. Peter Pears, Julian Bream (guitar) – BRITTEN: *Songs from the Chinese* etc; WALTON: *Anon in love.* ***

Mátyás Seiber's arrangements of four French folksongs are enchantingly simple and, as Bream says, the accompaniments 'use the guitar adroitly'. They bring ravishing tone and line from Pears. Vivid recording, made by a Decca team, but it was unconscionable of RCA not to provide translations, even if one can enjoy the songs without them.

Seixas, José António Carlos de (1704–42)

Harpsichord concerto in A; Sinfonia in B flat; Keyboard sonatas Nos. 1, 16, 32–3, 42, 46–7, 57, 71 & 79.
(N) *** Virgin Veritas/EMI Dig. VC5 45114-2 [id.]. Ketil Haugsand, Norwegian Bar. O.

The Portuguese composer, Carlos Seixas, spent his life as an organist in Lisbon, also teaching harpsichord at the Court. He is revealed here as having a distinct musical personality, and the jolly outer movements of his *A major Concerto* – separated by only a brief Adagio – are enjoyably spirited in the hands of Ketil Haugsand, who also conducts the excellent period orchestral group. The *Sinfonia* is essentially an Italian overture with a fast closing minuet, and the *Keyboard sonatas* also show Italian influences. The earlier works are in a single movement, but the last three are more ambitious. This is not great music but always inventive and very personable, and it is effectively presented here and very well recorded.

Sessions, Roger (1896–1985)

Concerto for orchestra.
*** Hyperion Dig. CDA 66050 [id.]. Boston SO, Ozawa – PANUFNIK: *Symphony No. 8.* ***

Sessions's *Concerto for orchestra* finds him at his thorniest and most uncompromising, with lyricism limited to fleeting fragments of melody; but the playful opening leads one on finally to a valedictory close, sharply defined. Ozawa makes a powerful advocate, helped by superb playing from the Boston orchestra.

Symphony No. 4; Symphony No. 5; Rhapsody for orchestra.
*** New World Dig. NW 345 [id.]. Columbus SO, Badea.

Roger Sessions shares with Walter Piston, his tonal contemporary, a highly developed sense of structure and an integrity that remained unshaken by changes of fashion. His musical language is dense and his logic is easier to sense than to follow. The performances by the Columbus Symphony Orchestra under Christian Badea appear well prepared, and there is no doubt as to their commitment and expertise. The sound ideally needs a larger acoustic, but every strand in the texture is well placed and there is no feeling of discomfort.

Shapero, Harold (born 1920)

Symphony for classical orchestra; Nine-minute overture.
**(*) New World Dig NW 373-2 [id.]. LAPO, Previn.

Harold Shapero's *Symphony for classical orchestra* has a propulsive energy and moves with complete assurance. This work seems to derive its inspiration from Beethoven and Stravinsky's *Symphony in C* and is a highly stimulating piece. Previn gets good results from the Los Angeles orchestra but does not bring the sheer vitality that distinguished Bernstein's pioneering record.

Shchedrin, Rodion (born 1933)

(i) *Carmen* (ballet; arr. from Bizet): *suite; Concerto for orchestra (Naughty limericks).*
(N) (BB) **(*) Naxos Dig. 8.553038 [id.]. Ukrainian State O, Theodor Kuchar.

(i) *Carmen* (ballet; arr. from Bizet): *suite; Humoresque. In imitation of Albéniz; Stalin cocktail.*
*** Chandos Dig. CHAN 9288 [id.]. I Musici de Montréal, Yuli Turovski; (i) with Ens. Répercussion –
  TURINA: *La oración del torero.* ***

Rodion Shchedrin's free adaptation of Bizet's *Carmen* music uses Bizet's tunes, complete with harmony,
and reworks them into a new tapestry using only strings and percussion (including vibraphone). The
whole thing is brilliantly done and wears surprisingly well. There have been previous recordings of
Shchedrin's score but this new Chandos version by I Musici de Montréal sweeps the board. Recorded in
the richly resonant acoustic of the Eglise de la Nativité de la Sainte-Vierge, La Prairie, Quebec, the
sound is very much in the demonstration bracket, with glittering percussion effects (marimba and
vibraphone particularly well caught) and dramatic use of side drum snares. Yuli Turovski's performance
opens evocatively and is highly dramatic, winningly expressive and subtle in its use of the wide range of
string colour and dynamic. The pastiche, *In imitation of Albéniz*, and the grotesque, Shostakovich-like
Humoresque are offset by a malignant parody-evocation of Stalin, full of creepy special effects and with
a shout of horror at the end. They are very well presented here, but one would not want to return to
them very often.

Kuchar's version is also vividly played, with wit as well as high drama and atmosphere. The Naxos
recording is excellent. The brief (8½-minute) *Concerto for orchestra* with its curious subtitle is a kaleidoscopic scherzando, a whirlwind presentation of Russian folk-motives over a minimalist ostinato. It is
played with great verve but rather outstays its welcome.

(i) *The Lady and the lapdog* (ballet); (ii) *Music for the city of Köthen.*
*** Olympia OCD 262 [id.]. (i) Bolshoi Theatre O, Lazarev; (ii) Moscow Virtuosi Chamber O,
  Spivakov.

Shchedrin's 50-minute ballet after Chekhov's *The Lady and the lapdog* is a haunting and atmospheric
score that casts a powerful spell. As in his celebrated *Carmen ballet*, Shchedrin shows great imagination
in the use of the orchestra. The invention is strong and, although its balletic origins are obvious, the
music itself has a discernible narrative thread that makes for compelling listening. The fill-up, *Music for
the city of Köthen*, brings something of the same orchestral flair and resourcefulness; it makes inventive
use of baroque forms and conventions. The analogue recordings have admirable body, clarity and
warmth. The Bolshoi Orchestra under Alexander Lazarev produce excellent and responsive playing in
the ballet, and the Moscow Virtuosi are hardly less impressive in the companion-piece.

Stalin cocktail.
(Y/B) *** RCA 09026 68061-2 [id.]. Moscow Virtuosi, Vladimir Spivakov – SHOSTAKOVICH: *Chamber
  symphony No. 2;* PART: *Collage on B-A-C-H* etc.; DENISOV: *Variations.* ***

Shchedrin's *Stalin cocktail* was written as a celebratory encore piece for Spivakov and his excellent
chamber group. A nightmare-like presentation of a very famous Russian folksong cocks a snook at
Stalin for whom the tune was once adapted with sycophantic lyrics. The cocktail is dashed to the ground
at the close with a piercing vocal splash from all members of the orchestra.

Shebalin, Vissarion (1902–63)

Symphonies Nos. (i) *1 in F min., Op. 6;* (ii) *3 in C, Op. 17.*
(N) **(*) Olympia OCD 577 [id.]. USSR RSO, (i) Mark Ermler; (ii) Valery Gergiev.

Shebalin was four years older than Shostakovich and their first symphonies appeared in the same year,
1925. Shebalin has been scantily represented in the UK catalogues and the only work we can recall
hearing from the LP era is his *Eighth String quartet* which, superficially at least, sounds very much like
Shostakovich. Shebalin's *First Symphony in F minor*, Op. 6, is heavily indebted to his mentor,
Miaskovsky, and there are strong echoes of the latter's *Sixth Symphony*, composed two years earlier.
Shebalin's craftsmanship is hardly less distinguished than Miaskovsky's: the orchestral writing is
assured and the thematic invention is intelligent though not as memorable and characterful as in
Shostakovich's No. 1. The *Third Symphony*, Op. 17, which comes from the 1930s, was dedicated to

Shostakovich but, for all its moments of eloquence and undoubted expertise, its substance is not distinctive enough to sustain its length. Those with an interest in Shostakovich should investigate these symphonies, for they are well worth hearing.

Sheppard, John (c. 1515–c. 1559)

Christe Redemptor omnium; In manus tuas; Media vita; Reges Tharsis; Sacris solemniis; Verbum caro.
*** Gimell Dig. CDGIM 016; *1585T-16* [id.]. Tallis Scholars, Peter Phillips.

All the music here is based on chant, and much of it is for the six-part choir, which produces a particularly striking sonority. The *Media vita* ('In the midst of life we are in death') is a piece of astonishing beauty, and it is sung with remarkable purity of tone by the Tallis Scholars under Peter Phillips. Glorious and little-known music: the recording could hardly be improved on.

Gaude virgo Christiphera; In manus tuas; Libera nos, salva 1–2; Reges Tharsis.
*** Proudsound Dig. PROUCD 126; *PROU 126* [id.]. Clerkes of Oxenford, David Wulstan – TYE:
   Mass Euge bone. ***

The Clerkes of Oxenford under David Wulstan produce a very different sonority from the Tallis group, wonderfully blended and balanced, with a tonal sophistication that is remarkable. They overlap only minimally with the Gimell disc, so both can be recommended to the enthusiast. They are placed rather more distantly than the Tallis Scholars but are splendidly recorded in a spacious but not over-reverberant acoustic.

Motets: *Filiae Hierusalem venite; Haec dies; In manus tuas Domine I; In pacem in idipsum; Justi in perpetuum vivent; Laudem dicite Deo; Libera nos, salva nos I; Paschal Kyrie; Regis Tharsis et insulae; Spiritus sanctus procedens I; Verbo caro factum est.*
⊛ *** Hyperion Dig. CDA 66259 [id.]. The Sixteen, Christophers.

Here in eleven superb responsories The Sixteen consistently convey the rapturous beauty of Sheppard's writing, above all in ethereal passages in the highest register, very characteristic of him. Even there The Sixteen's sopranos seem quite unstressed by the tessitura. There are not many more beautiful records of Tudor polyphony than this.

Motets: *Gaude, gaude, gaude Maria; In manus tuas* (1st setting); *Laudem dicite Deo; In pace; Verbum caro.*
(B) **(*) CfP CD-CFP 4638; *TC-CFP 4638* [id.]. Clerkes of Oxenford, David Wulstan – TALLIS:
   Motets. **(*)

The performances by the Clerkes of Oxenford under Davis Wulstan are full of fervour, particularly in the inspired *Gaude, gaude, gaude Maria* and the closing *Verbum caro*. Wulstan presses on very strongly, and some might feel there is a lack of contrasting repose and not enough subtlety in the sheer thrust of his direction. But the commitment of the singing will surely convince anyone who buys this CD on impulse that this is great music and that its composer's name should be more familiar. The 1978 analogue recording has plenty of body and atmosphere.

Shostakovich, Dmitri (1906–75)

Ballet suites Nos. 1–5; Festive overture, Op. 96; Katerina Ismailova: suite.
(Y/B) *** Chandos Dig. CHAN 7000/1 [id.]. RSNO, Järvi.

This highly entertaining set generally represents Shostakovich in light-hearted, often ironic mood, throwing out *bonnes-bouches* like fireworks and with a sparkling vividness of orchestral colour. The *Ballet suites* were the composer's way of satirically but anonymously re-using material from earlier works which lay unperformed for political reasons. There are plenty of good tunes. The *Fifth suite* draws entirely on music from a 1931 ballet, *The Bolt* (see below). This is the most extended of the five suites, offering nearly half an hour of music, full of wry, quirky ideas, typical of the young Shostakovich. The *Suite* from *Katerina Ismailova* (*Lady Macbeth of Mtsensk*) consists of entr'actes from between the scenes which effectively act as emotional links, and the writing is both illuminating and characterful. Järvi is entirely at home in all this music and clearly relishes its dry humour. The playing is equally perceptive and full of flair. The recording is spectacular and resonantly wide-ranging in the Chandos manner.

The Bolt (ballet; complete recording).
(Y/B) *** Chandos Dig. CHAN 9343/4 (2) [id.]. Royal Stockholm PO, Stockholm Transport Band, Rozhdestvensky.

Dating from 1931, *The Bolt* is a massive ballet-score that in its original form sank without trace, largely thanks to the feeble, cumbersome propagandist libretto. Yet the dances are so sharp and colourful in their inspiration that over the years suites of movements have been heard, and now Rozhdestvensky in this vivid, full-blooded recording resurrects the complete score of 43 movements, lasting two and a half hours. The music readily demonstrates how dazzlingly inventive the young Shostakovich was, even when faced with an indifferent subject. Rozhdestvensky plainly believes passionately in this score, and he draws an electrifying performance from the Swedish orchestra of which he is music director. In demonstration sound, it makes a most attractive box of delights, even if it is hardly a masterpiece.

Chamber symphony in C min. Op. 110a (arr. Barshai from *String quartet No. 8); Symphony for strings, Op. 118a* (arr. Barshai from *String quartet No. 10).*
*** DG Dig. 429 229-2. COE, Rudolf Barshai.

The *Chamber symphony* is an arrangement for full strings of the *Eighth Quartet*, and the *Symphony for strings* is a similar transcription of the *Tenth*. Both were made by Rudolf Barshai and he directs them with the authority of the composer and bears his imprimatur. These are strong performances of real eloquence and power, which are excellently recorded and can be confidently recommended to those who prefer the dark, brooding transcriptions to the inward-looking originals.

Chamber symphony No. 2.
(Y/B) *** RCA Dig. 09026 68061-2 [id.]. Moscow Virtuosi, Vladimir Spivakov – DENISOV: *Variations.* PART: *Collage on B-A-C-H* etc. SHCHEDRIN: *Stalin cocktail.* ***

Vladimir Milman's arrangement of the *Third String quartet* as the *Chamber symphony No. 2* is every bit as effective as No. 1, transcribed by Barshai from the *Eighth*. The *F major Quartet* ranges enigmatically wide in mood, opening skittishly in folksong style and with a strongly rhythmic Scherzo. At its heart is a powerful *Adagio* passacaglia which is to return to cap the passionate climax of the finale, which then moves towards a final *piano-pianissimo* of bleak oblivion. The piece is played marvellously here, and the bright yet spacious recording seems just right for the music.

Cello concerto No. 1 in E flat, Op. 107.
*** Sony Dig. MK 37840 [id.]. Yo-Yo Ma, Phd. O, Ormandy – KABALEVSKY: *Cello concerto No. 1.* ***
*** Chandos Dig. CHAN 8322 [id.]. Raphael Wallfisch, ECO, Geoffrey Simon – BARBER: *Cello concerto.* ***

(i) *Cello concerto No. 1 in E flat, Op. 107;* (ii) *Symphony No. 5 in D min., Op. 47.*
(N) (M) *** Sony Dig. MYK 44903 [id.]. (i) Yo-Yo Ma, Phd. O, Ormandy; (ii) NYPO, Bernstein.

Yo-Yo Ma plays with an intensity that compels the listener, and the Philadelphia Orchestra give eloquent support. This has been reissued at mid-price, generously coupled with Bernstein's exciting (1979) account of the *Fifth Symphony*, recorded in Tokyo when Bernstein and the New York Philharmonic were on tour there. Unashamedly Bernstein treats the work as a Romantic symphony. The slow movement is raptly beautiful and the finale is brilliant and extrovert, with no hint of irony. On CD the bass is made to sound full and rich, and the slight distancing of the sound places the orchestra within a believable ambience.

Wallfisch handles the first movement splendidly, though there is not quite the same sense of momentum as in Yo-Yo Ma's account. However, he gives a sensitive account of the slow movement and has thoughtful and responsive support from the ECO. The Chandos recording is outstandingly fine.

(i) *Cello concerto No. 1 in E flat, Op. 107;* (ii) *Piano concertos Nos. 1 in C min. for piano, trumpet and strings, Op. 35; 2 in F, Op. 102.*
(N) (BB) *** RCA Navigator 74321 29254-2. USSR RSO, with (i) Mikhail Khomitser, cond. Rozhdestvensky; (ii) Eugene List, cond. Maxim Shostakovich.

Eugene List plays the *First Piano concerto* with splendid dash and brilliance, underlining its brittle sonorities and brash swagger. He opens the *Second* with comparably crisp, rhythmic vigour and takes the finale very much up to speed; throughout there is plenty of character and spirit. Though the sound is vivid, the strings of the USSR Radio Symphony Orchestra are somewhat wanting in bloom. But both slow movements have plenty of atmosphere and List has the advantage of the authority of Maxim Shostakovich's direction. Rostropovich notwithstanding, his Russian colleague Mikhail Khomitser is a formidable soloist in the *Cello concerto*. The forward balance means that he dominates the performance, yet Rozhdestvensky provides a strong, concentrated backing. The first movement has very positive impetus and the *Andantino* develops a haunting, improvisational nostalgia. The orchestral recording could ideally be more refined but there is no lack of atmosphere. A real bargain,.

Cello concertos Nos. 1 in E flat, Op. 107; 2, Op. 126.
*** Ph. Dig. 412 526-2 [id.]. Heinrich Schiff, Bav. RSO, Maxim Shostakovich.
**(*) BIS Dig. CD 626 [id.]. Torleif Thedéen, Malmö SO, James DePreist.
(N) **(*) Virgin/EMI Dig. VC5 45145-2 [id.]. Truls Mørk, LPO, Jansons.
(N) ** DG 445 821-2 [id.]. Maisky, LSO, Tilson Thomas.

Schiff's superbly recorded account does not displace Yo-Yo Ma in the *First*, but it can hold its own. The *Second Concerto* is a haunting piece, essentially lyrical; it is gently discursive, sadly whimsical at times and tinged with a smiling melancholy that hides deeper troubles. The recording is enormously impressive.

The gifted young Swedish cellist, Torleif Thedéen, has a lot going for him and his passionately committed performances would honour any collection. He has the advantage of excellent engineering, which gives a very alive sound, plus good orchestral support from the Malmö Orchestra under James DePreist.

The Norwegian cellist, Truls Mørk, is an eminently forthright Shostakovich interpreter, and his account of both concertos also ranks among the very best. He is not afraid of allowing the music to speak for itself, and the amazingly present and vivid recording weighs heavily in Virgin's favour.

By the side of Mischa Maisky, Truls Mørk seems a model of sobriety and understatement. The Russian-born Israeli cellist tends to wear his heart very much on his sleeve, and many may find his fervour a little unrelenting. However, he has the advantage of splendid orchestral playing under Michael Tilson Thomas, who gets a more powerful atmosphere even than Mariss Jansons.

(i) *Cello concerto No. 1 in E flat, Op. 107; Piano concertos Nos.* (ii) *1 in C min., Op. 35;* (iii) *2 in F, Op. 102.*
(M) *** Sony MPK 44850 [id.]. (i) Rostropovich, Phd. O, Ormandy; (ii) Previn; (iii) Bernstein; NYPO, Bernstein.

Rostropovich made this recording of the *Cello concerto No. 1* within a few months of the first performance in Russia. Shostakovich himself attended the recording session in Philadelphia and gave his approval to what is a uniquely authoritative reading. Sony have now shrewdly made an attractive triptych for CD by including Bernstein's radiant account of the *Second Piano concerto*, along with Previn's equally striking account of No. 1. Though these New York performances bring somewhat dated recording, both pianists have a way of turning a phrase to catch the imagination, and a fine balance is struck between Shostakovich's warmth and his rhythmic alertness.

Cello concerto No. 2, Op. 126.
(B) *** DG Double 437 952-2 (2) [id.]. Rostropovich, Boston SO, Ozawa – BERNSTEIN: *3 Meditations* etc.; BOCCHERINI: *Cello concerto No. 2;* GLAZUNOV: *Chant du Ménestrel;* TARTINI: *Cello concerto;* TCHAIKOVSKY: *Andante cantabile* etc.; VIVALDI: *Cello concertos.* ***

(i) *Cello concerto No. 2, Op. 126. Symphony No. 5 in D min., Op.47.*
(Y/B) (B) ** DG 439 481-2 [id.]. (i) Rostropovich, Boston SO, Ozawa; (ii) Nat. SO of Washington, Rostropovich.

Rostropovich plays with beautifully controlled feeling, and Seiji Ozawa brings sympathy and fine discipline to the accompaniment, securing admirably expressive playing from the Boston orchestra. The analogue recording is first class. As can be seen, this is part of a remarkably generous DG Double anthology, showing Rostropovich's art over the widest range, and which is far more recommendable than the alternative bargain coupling offering a vibrant but highly idiosyncratic account of the *Fifth Symphony*. Although the finale is intense and exciting, there is also a hectoring quality which is distinctly unappealing.

Piano concertos Nos. (i) *1 in C min. for piano, trumpet and strings, Op. 35;* (ii) *2 in F, Op. 102.*
(M) *** SMK 47618-2. [id.]. (i) André Previn, William Vacciano; (ii) Leonard Bernstein; NYPO, Bernstein (with: POULENC: *Double piano concerto:* Arthur Gold & Robert Fizdale (pianos) ***).

(i) *Piano concertos Nos. 1–2. 3 Fantastic dances, Op. 5; 24 Preludes & fugues, Op. 87/1, 4–5, 23–24.*
**(*) EMI mono CDC7 54606-2 [id.]. Composer; (i) L. Vaillant, Fr. Nat. RSO, Cluytens.

Piano concertos Nos. 1–2; The Unforgettable year 1919, Op. 89; The Assault on beautiful Gorky (for piano and orchestra).
(B) *** CfP Dig. CD-CFP 4547; *TC-CFP 4547.* Alexeev, Philip Jones, ECO, Maksymiuk.

Alexeev is a clear first choice in both *Concertos*, and his record would sweep the board even at full price. The digital recording is excellent in every way and scores over its rivals in clarity and presence. There is a fill-up in the form of a miniature one-movement *Concerto* from a film-score called *The Unforgettable year 1919*.

This shrewd pairing of Bernstein's radiant account of the *Second Concerto* with Previn's equally strik-ing reading of No. 1 makes an attractive disc when coupled with a spiky yet genial version of the Poulenc *Double concerto*. The Shostakovich recordings are far from recent but sound most vivid. The Poulenc concerto, too, is both witty and abrasive, with an excellent contribution from the piano duo, Arthur Gold and Robert Fizdale. It was recorded at about the same time (1961) and the CD transfer of a not particularly smooth original is thoroughly satisfactory. This is one of the most winning discs in the Bernstein Royal Edition.

The two piano concertos were recorded, albeit in mono only, with the French Radio Orchestra under André Cluytens in 1958 for French Columbia. Shostakovich's technical address and rhythmic vitality are not in question, though by this time he was just beginning to lose some of the finesse in matters of keyboard colour and dynamic nuance which he must obviously have commanded in his youthful days. However, both concertos are very well supported by Cluytens, and the trumpeter Ludovic Vaillant proves a high-spirited fellow-soloist. In addition to the early *Fantastic dances*, we have some of the Op. 87 *Preludes and fugues* that he recorded in the late 1950s. They admirably convey his intentions and have a special sense of concentration, even if they do not possess subtlety of colouring. An indispensable document for all admirers of the great composer. However, this should have been issued at mid-price.

Piano concerto No. 1 in C min. for piano, trumpet and strings, Op. 35.
(N) (M) *** Decca 448 577-2 [id.]. John Ogdon, John Wilbraham, ASMF, Marriner – BARTOK: *Divertimento; Music for strings, percussion and celesta.* ***

Ogdon, on top form, gives a clean, stylish performance which encompasses both the humour and the hints of romanticism in the *First Concerto*. He remains a little more detached than his accompanists in the tender slow movement, and the trumpet playing of John Wilbraham is masterly. In addition, the early 1970s recorded quality is most vivid. The comparatively backward balance of the strings gives the work a chamber quality to match that of the Bartók works, an unexpected but attractive coupling. The result is fully worthy of Decca's Classic Sound series, even if the recordings were all originally made by an Argo team!

(i) *Piano concerto No. 1 in C min., Op. 35. Jazz suites 1–2; Tahiti trot, Op. 16.*
(N) **(*) Decca Dig. 433 702-2 [id.]. (i) Ronald Brautigam, Peter Masseurs; Concg. O, Chailly.

A perfectly enjoyable account of the *Piano and trumpet concerto* from Brautigam and his excellent trumpet partner, Peter Masseurs, vividly accompanied by Chailly; but in the last resort this is not really memorable. The main point of interest here is the pair of *Jazz suites* from the 1930s, hitherto unrecorded. The scoring is modest, naturally using a saxophone and also a less likely accordion. Often witty music, played with considerable élan under Chailly: the Concertgebouw players sound unexpect-edly at home. But all this is upstaged by the *Tahiti trot*, Shostakovich's instantaneous arrangement of Youmans's 'Tea for two', which is irresistible.

(i) *Piano concerto No. 1 in C min., Op. 35. Symphony No. 1 in F, Op. 10.*
(N) ** EMI Dig. CDC5 55361-2 [id.]. (i) Mikhail Rudy, Ole Edvard Antonsen; BPO, Jansons.

In Mikhail Rudy's hands, the *Concerto for piano, trumpet amd strings* starts off very slowly for an *Allegro moderato*, and the effect is ponderous. He does proceed at a more normal tempo at the second *Più mosso* marking. In the slow movement Jansons is also a shade slower than most rivals, but he draws ravishing sound from the Berlin Philharmonic strings. Ole Edvard Antonsen plays with impeccable musicianship and taste. All in all, a well-thought-out but not wholly convincing performance; and much the same verdict must be returned on the *First Symphony*. Wonderful playing from the Berliners, but the overall impression is a little studied, a little wanting in spontaneity. There would have been room for the *Second Symphony* too; at 54 minutes this is short measure for a full-price disc.

(i) *Piano concerto No. 2 in F, Op. 102;* (ii) *Violin concerto No. 1 in A min., Op. 99.*
*** Decca Dig. 425 793-2 [id.]. (i) Ortiz; (ii) Belkin; RPO, Ashkenazy.

Cristina Ortiz gives a sparkling account of the jaunty first movement of the *Piano concerto No. 2*, and she also brings out the fun and wit of the finale with fluent, finely pointed playing, not least in the delicious interpolated bars of 7/8. Boris Belkin in the first and more popular of the violin concertos plays immaculately and with consistently sweet, pure tone, but he misses some of the work's darker, deeper undertones. Decca sound is full and well balanced, not as distanced as other recordings in Ashkenazy's series. A satisfying coupling.

Violin concertos Nos. 1 in A min., Op. 99; 2 in C sharp min., Op. 129.
*** Virgin/EMI Dig. VC7 59601-2 [id.]. Sitkovetsky, BBC SO, Andrew Davis.
*** Chandos Dig. CHAN 8820. Lydia Mordkovitch, SNO, Järvi.

Virgin's coupling by Sitkovetsky and the BBC Symphony Orchestra under Andrew Davis is impressive and intense; there is no doubt as to its excellence, it has tremendous bite. It is also splendidly recorded, and takes its place at the top of the list.

Mordkovitch's concentrated reading of No. 2 is matched by Järvi and the orchestra in their total commitment. She even outshines the work's dedicatee and first interpreter, David Oistrakh, in the dark reflectiveness of her playing, even if she cannot quite match him in bravura passages. In the better-known concerto (No. 1) the meditative intensity is magnetic, with a fullness and warmth of tone that have not always marked her playing on record before.

Violin concerto No. 1 in A min., Op. 99.
*** EMI Dig. CDC7 49814-2 [id.]. Perlman, Israel PO, Mehta – GLAZUNOV: *Violin concerto.* ***

Perlman's version of the Shostakovich *First Violin concerto* was recorded live in the Mann Auditorium in Tel Aviv. There is no violinist in the world who in sheer bravura can quite match Perlman, particularly live, and the ovation which greets his dazzling performance of the finale is richly deserved. Yet some of the mystery and the fantasy which Russian interpreters have found – from David Oistrakh onwards – is missing, and the close balance of the solo instrument, characteristic of Perlman's concerto recordings, undermines hushed intensity.

Violin concerto No. 2 in C sharp min., Op. 129.
(Y/B) ** DG Dig. 439 890-2 [id.]. Gidon Kremer, Boston SO, Ozawa – SCHUMANN: *Violin concerto* (arr. of *Cello concerto*). **

Gidon Kremer's DG account of the Op. 129 concerto with Ozawa and the Boston Symphony is played with his customary aplomb and mastery, though the recording is not really in the demonstration bracket. Both as a performance and as a recording this would have to have something very special to offer to displace the more logical coupling of the two Shostakovich concertos.

Five days, five nights (suite), Op. 111a; Hamlet (suite), Op. 116a (film music); *King Lear (suite), Op. 137.*
*** RCA RD 87763 [7763-2-RC]. Belgian R. O, Serebrier.

Hamlet obviously generates powerful resonances in Shostakovich's psyche and prompts responsive and committed playing from the Belgian Radio Orchestra, while much of the score for *Five days, five nights* inhabits the bleak world of the *Eleventh Symphony*.

The Gadfly (film music): *suite, Op. 97a.*
(B) **(*) CfP CD-CFP 4463; *TC-CFP 4463.* USSR Cinema SO, Emin Khachaturian.

The Gadfly (suite), *Op. 97a; Hamlet* (film incidental music), *Op. 116:* excerpts; *King Lear* (suite), *Op. 58a.*
(Y/B) **(*) Koch Dig. 3-7274-2. [id.]. Korean Broadcasting System SO, Vakhtang Jordania.

The Gadfly (suite), *Op. 97a; Hamlet* (suite), *Op. 116.*
(Y/B) ** Cap. Dig. 10 298 [id.]. Berlin RSO, Leonid Grin.

The score for *The Gadfly* is quite pleasing but at times is wholly uncharacteristic. On CfP, a musically committed and well-recorded issue, although the brightening of the sound in the digital remastering has lost some of the smoothness of the original LP.

The Korean Radio forces offer *The Gadfly* and *King Lear* suites and the first, third and fourth movements of the *Hamlet* music, while the Capriccio disc opts for all eight movements of the latter. Neither offers short change in that both discs run to nearly 80 minutes. The Koch disc is to be preferred for the greater intensity and discipline of the orchestral response, and the three movements from *Hamlet* are keenly felt. Both are eminently recommendable discs.

The Golden Age (ballet; complete).
**(*) Chandos Dig. CHAN 9251/2 [id.]. Royal Stockholm PO, Rozhdestvensky.

This is the first complete recording of Shostakovich's first ballet, with its extraordinary plot of Soviet and capitalist sportsmen and women. The famous *Polka* is meant to satirize a disarmament meeting in Geneva. The music as a whole is remarkably potent and full of succulent ideas (even *Tea for two* arrives during Act II) and with the big set-pieces expansively and sometimes darkly symphonic. The score is well played in Stockholm, but the warm orchestral style does not always readily bring out the music's plangent character and moments of barbed wit. Rozhdestvensky directs idiomatically as far as possible, but at times his tempi suggest that he is not directing a virtuoso group or one composed of musicians who can take naturally to the abrasive Slavonic idiom. But, with very good recording, this is fascinatingly more than a stop-gap.

Hamlet (1932 production; complete incidental music), *Op. 32;* (1954 production; incidental music); *King Lear* (1941 production; complete incidental music), *Op. 58a.*
(N) *** Cala Dig. CACD 1021 [id.]. Winter, Wilson-Johnson, CBSO, Mark Elder.

An enterprising release, which offers Shostakovich's music for Nikolai Akimov's 1932 production of *Hamlet.* Akimov altered and extended Shakespeare's conception, even interpolating bits of Erasmus; Hamlet appeared as 'an obese glutton who in outward appearance resembled Falstaff, Claudius was a timorous neurasthenic, and Ophelia was a dissolute, tipsy wench'. The play lasted five hours, and a whole hour had to be cut after the dress rehearsal. Shostakovich's score has many biting and sarcastic episodes, and listening to the 30 short numbers – some only a few seconds long – makes for unsettled listening. There are spoken interpolations from the player-king and queen. Also included here is a a a Gigue and finale from a 1954 production of *Hamlet*, and the Fool's songs, brilliantly sung by David Wilson-Johnson, from a 1941 production of *King Lear*, full of inventive things. This is not top-drawer Shostakovich, but congratulations are in order for Cala's enterprise in recording all this and to the City of Birmingham Orchestra under Mark Elder for the vital and alert performances. The recording too is expertly and tastefully balanced.

Symphonies Nos. 1–15; (i; ii) *From Jewish folk poetry;* (ii) *6 Poems of Marina Tsvetaeva.*
(Y/B) (B) *** Decca Dig./Analogue 444 430-2 (11) [id.]. Varady, Fischer-Dieskau, Rintzler; (i) Söderström, Karczykowski; (ii) Wenkel; Ch. of LPO or Concg. O; LPO or Concg. O, Haitink.

No one artist or set of performances holds all the insights into this remarkable symphonic canon, but what can be said of Haitink's set is that the playing of both the London Philharmonic and the Concertgebouw orchestras is of the highest calibre and is very responsive; moreover the Decca recordings, whether analogue or digital, are consistently of this company's highest standard, outstandingly brilliant and full. If without the temperament of a Mravinsky, Haitink proves a reliable guide to this repertoire, often much more than that, and sometimes inspired. All in all, a considerable achievement. The eleven discs are now offered together at bargain price, but they also remain available separately at mid-price – see below.

Symphonies Nos. 1 in F min., Op. 10; 12 in D min. (The Year 1917), Op. 112.
(Y/B) (M) ** BMG/Melodiya 74321 19848-2 [id.]. Moscow PO, Kondrashin.

Symphonies Nos. (i) *2 in B (October Revolution), Op. 14;* (ii) *14 in G min., Op. 135.*
(Y/B) (M) *** BMG/Melodiya 74321 19844-2 [id.]. (i) Russian Republic Ch.; (ii) Tselovalnik, Nestorenko; Moscow PO, Kondrashin.

Symphonies Nos. (i) *3 in E flat (The First of May), Op. 20; 5 in D min., Op. 47.*
(Y/B) (M) ** BMG/Melodiya 7432 119845-2 [id.]. (i) Russian Republic Ch.; Moscow PO, Kondrashin.

Symphony No. 4 in C min., Op. 43.
(Y/B) (M) *** BMG/Melodiya 74321 19840-2 [id.]. Moscow PO, Kondrashin.

Symphonies Nos. 6 in B min., Op. 54; 10 in E min., Op. 93.
(Y/B) (M) *(*) BMG/Melodiya 74321 19847-2 [id.]. Moscow PO, Kondrashin.

Symphony No. 7 in C (Leningrad), Op. 60.
(Y/B) (M) ** BMG/Melodiya 74321 19839-2 [id.]. Moscow PO, Kondrashin.

Symphony No. 8 in C min., Op. 65.
(Y/B) (M) *(*) BMG/Melodiya 74321 19841-2 [id.]. Moscow PO, Kondrashin.

Symphonies Nos. 9, Op. 70; 15 in A, Op. 103.
(Y/B) (M) **(*) BMG/Melodiya 74321 19846-2 [id.]. Moscow PO, Kondrashin.

Symphony No. 11 (The Year 1905), Op. 103.
(Y/B) (M) ** BMG/Melodiya 74321 19843-2 [id.]. Moscow PO, Kondrashin.

Symphony No. 13 in B flat min. (Babi Yar), Op. 113.
(Y/B) (M) *** BMG/Melodiya 74321 19842-2 [id.]. Eisen, Russian Republic Ch., Moscow PO, Kondrashin.

Kirill Kondrashin's cycle was made over a long period of time: the *Fourth Symphony* dates from 1962, not long after its first performance at the end of the previous year, while the last to appear (in the mid-1970s) were Nos. 7 (*Leningrad*), 14 and 15. The set is of importance in that Shostakovich himself expressed confidence in this conductor, and it is clear that in many instances he comes closer than most to the spirit of this music. Not all the performances strike us as *sans pareil*. In none of them is the playing of the Moscow Philharmonic as distinguished or as finely disciplined as in many rival accounts. Nor, to be fair, are Kondrashin's insights deeper than those of Mravinsky or (in the case of Nos. 5, 6, 7 and 11) Stokowski. It is rare to find one cycle that fulfils the aspirations with which it embarks and, although Haitink and the Concertgebouw have strong merits, there is no single survey that is absolutely ideal in every respect. Nos. 4, 13 and 14 make the strongest impression in Kondrashin's hands. Despite the sonic limitations inevitable over the course of over 30 years, the *Fourth* is almost indispensable. It has that sense of discovery, raw intensity and sheer eloquence which silence criticism – or should do. And the 1967 account of the *Thirteenth* has an authentic feel to it that makes its claims on the collector strong. Both the *Fourteenth*, song-cycle-cum-symphony and the enigmatic *Fifteenth Symphony* have much to recommend them.

Elsewhere the cycle is less even. The brisk tempi Kondrashin adopts for the first movement of both the *Sixth* and *Eighth* symphonies diminish their intensity of feeling and directness of effect and, though he makes out a stronger case for the *Third* than some rivals, he is no match for Mravinsky in the *Twelfth*. The Moscow Philharmonic strings are by no means as sumptuous as those of the USSR State Academic Symphony (or the 'USSR Symphony' as it was known at one time), nor as responsive as those in Pletnev's Russian National Orchestra; and they do not sound quite as warm or smooth as on the LP. It is difficult to generalize, but the bass is sometimes firmer and definition is keener. There are roughnesses on the originals that are not quite smoothed out.

Symphony No. 1 in F min., Op. 10; (i) Piano concerto No. 1 in C min., Op. 35.
(N) *** EMI Dig. CDC5 55361-2 [id.]. (i) Mikhail Rudy; BPO, Jansons.

Drawing superb playing from the Berlin Philharmonic, Jansons conducts a finely detailed reading of the *First Symphony* which is both precise and intense. So the second-movement scherzando, despite a very fast speed, is never breathless, and the oboe solo at the start of the slow movement could not be more tender in its refinement, while even the hectic close is perfectly controlled, both exciting and sharply focused. Mikhail Rudy in the concerto brings out new poetry, and the *Lento* slow movement has rarely been so yearningly beautiful, with the Berlin strings radiant. If in the outer movements Rudy does not bite as sharply as some pianists, his sensitivity is heightened by Jansons's idiomatic conducting, full of humour in the finale. Excellent sound.

Symphonies Nos. 1 in F min., Op. 10; 3 (The First of May), Op. 20.
(M) *** Decca Dig. 425 063-2 [id.]. LPO Ch., LPO, Haitink.
(N) **(*) Olympia Dig. OCD 161 [id.]. USSR MoC SO, Rozhdestvensky
(BB) ** Naxos Dig. 8.550623 [id.]. Slovak RSO (Bratislava), Ladislav Slovák.

In this now popular coupling, Haitink still leads the field, when the Decca recording is outstandingly clear and brilliant. His account of No. 1 is strong and very well played. It may lack something in youthful high spirits but not in concentration. No. 3 is not one of Shostakovich's finest works but is worth having when played as committedly as here.

On Naxos, Slovák conducts energetic performances of both Nos. 1 and 3, even if some of the playing is rough. In this coupling, Haitink offers more pointed and sharply focused readings, better played and recorded, while Rozhdestvensky is both stronger and earthier, despite less refined recording.

Symphonies Nos. (i) 1 in F min.; (ii) 5 in D min.
(Y/B) **(*) Sup. 11 1951-2 [id.]. Czech PO, Karel Ančerl.
(N) (M) **(*) BBC Radio Classics 15656 91542 [id.]. (i) RPO, Horenstein; (ii) LSO, Stokowski.

Both performances on Supraphon are good and the *Fifth* is excellent. In their day they were highly recommendable (the *First* dates from 1964 and the *Fifth* from 1961). The sound has less body and presence than in more modern recordings but Ančerl shapes the slow movement of the *Fifth* with a powerful eloquence. It is to be preferred to many modern, glossier performances with brightly lit, state-of-the-art recording.

Stokowski was the first conductor to record Shostakovich's *Fifth Symphony*, back in the 1930s, but this live Prom performance of 1964 brings an even more urgently electrifying account, a fine example of the maestro's work late in his career. Speeds are consistently on the fast side, adding to the cogency, and Stokowski avoids letting his natural expressiveness turn into sentimentality. Fast as the speed of the Scherzo is, it conveys all the wry humour needed, and the thrilling finale rightly draws a tremendous cheer at the end. Microphone placing means that here you get a good hall atmosphere, but with rather intrusive audience noise. Stokowski's much earlier studio recording for Everest (see below) has comparable intensity and no audience intrusions, but that is more expensive and has no coupling. However,

Horenstein's account of No. 1 is disappointing for, though he conveys energy, the ensemble in this live performance, given at Nottingham in 1970, is too slack to sustain frequent repetition.

Symphonies Nos. 1 in F min., Op. 10; 5 in D min., Op. 47; (i) 7 in C, Op. 60; Prelude No. 14 in E flat min., Op. 34 (arr. Stokowski).
(***) Pearl GEMM CDS9044 [id.]. Phd. O; (i) NBC SO, Stokowski.

Stokowski's *First Symphony* was recorded in 1934, less than a decade after its première under Malko. The sound is dryish and, among the perfect ensemble and attack, the playing has one or two slight blemishes. But there is tremendous atmosphere and concentration, and the transfers are excellent. Stokowski's (1939) pioneering *Fifth* is an electrifying performance, impeccably played and splendidly transferred. The slow movement has a gripping intensity that is quite exceptional. But this is now available in a superior Dutton transfer, coupled with the *Sixth Symphony* (see below). The famous transcription of the *E flat minor Prelude*, Op. 34, has a brooding, Mussorgskian menace all its own, while Stokowski's *Leningrad Symphony* is hardly less gripping. This *Leningrad* for all its sonic defects makes for exciting listening.

Symphonies Nos. 1 in F min.; 6 in B min., Op. 54.
*** Chandos Dig. CHAN 8411 [id.]. SNO, Järvi.

Järvi's account of the *First Symphony* is strikingly more volatile than Haitink's in the outer movements – there is no lack of quirkiness in the finale, while the *Largo* is intense and passionate. The *Sixth* has comparable intensity, with an element of starkness in the austerity of the first movement. The Scherzo is skittish at first but, like the finale, has no lack of pungent force.

Symphonies Nos. 1 in F min., Op. 10; 7 in C (Leningrad), Op. 60.
(N) ** DG Dig. 427 632-2 (2) [id.]. Chicago SO, Bernstein.

A two-disc set for these two symphonies is extravagant, but Bernstein's expansive treatment of both works demands it. The Chicago orchestra plays superbly for him, but the full bite and ruthlessness of the *Leningrad Symphony* are largely missing, with the celebrated ostinato of the first movement dragging at a slow speed. The soft-grained quality extends to Bernstein's view of No. 1, though the maniacally energetic sequences of the second and fourth movements spark him to performances of characteristically high voltage. Full-bodied sound.

Symphonies Nos. 1 in F min., Op. 10; 9 in E flat, Op. 70.
*** Teldec/Warner Dig. 4509 90849-2 [id.]. Nat. SO of Washington, Rostropovich.

In Rostropovich's hands the youthful *First Symphony* begins very promisingly indeed and continues well. Indeed there is plenty of fulfilment. This *First* is a very good account, free from exaggeration, even if he rushes the Scherzo off its feet. Rostropovich is also given a decently balanced recording. The *Ninth*, too, is well served; fears that the slow movement might be pulled out of shape prove generally groundless, though there is one moment of agogic exaggeration. Generally, this can be recommended to those looking for this particular coupling.

Symphonies Nos. 1 in F min., Op. 10; 15 in A, Op. 141.
(N) ** Decca Dig. 436 838-2 [id.]. Montreal SO, Dutoit.

Helped by rich, full recording, Dutoit's generous coupling of Nos. 1 and 15 brings clean, lucid readings of both works that take few risks, lacking something in Russian thrust. It is welcome when, at the end of the fourth movement of No. 1 (too well-mannered earlier), the final pages bring a performance of manic excitement. However, in No. 15 the quotations from the death-motif in Wagner's *Ring* lack menace. Haitink is unsurpassed in this quixotic work.

Symphonies Nos. 2 in B (October Revolution), Op. 14; 3 in E flat (The First of May), Op. 20.
(Y/B) *** Teldec/Warner Dig. 4509 90853-2 [id.]. London Voices, LSO, Rostropovich.

Although Rostropovich is often prone to excessive expressive vehemence and tends on occasion to italicize and point-make, these two performances, like his accounts of the *First* and *Ninth*, have a natural eloquence that is very persuasive. The LSO respond to his playing with real fervour; everything is well prepared and well thought out, and he has the advantage of very well-engineered sound. Perhaps it could be objected that the two symphonies do not offer enough playing-time for a premium-priced disc, but the quality of this issue is not in doubt. Recommended.

Symphonies Nos. 2 (October Revolution), Op. 14; 10 in E min., Op. 93.
(M) **(*) Dig./Analogue 425 064-2 [id.]. LPO Ch., LPO, Haitink.

Haitink's performance of No. 2 is admirable, and it is given excellently balanced sound with great presence and body. No. 10 is a masterpiece, and Haitink really has the measure of the first movement, whose climaxes he paces with an admirable sense of architecture. He secures sensitive and enthusiastic playing from the LPO, both here and in the malignant Scherzo. In the third movement he adopts a slower tempo than usual, which would be acceptable if there were greater tension or concentration of mood; but here and in the slow introduction to the finale the sense of concentration falters. The 1977 analogue recording (like the digital *Second*, made in the Kingsway Hall) is outstandingly realistic.

Symphonies Nos. 2 in B (October Revolution), Op. 14; 15 in A, Op. 141.
(N) (BB) ** Naxos Dig. 8.550624 [id.]. Slovak RSO (Bratislava), Ladislav Slovák.

Slovák's version of No. 2 on Naxos begins disconcertingly with muffled growling, but then opens up well on the Allegro, with the choral second half fresh and dramatic. No. 15 may not match Haitink's version in tension but it is played and recorded well.

Symphony No. 4 in C min., Op. 43.
(N) *** EMI Dig. CDC5 55476-2 [id.]. CBSO, Rattle (with BRITTEN: *Russian funeral* ***).
*** Chandos Dig. CHAN 8640 [id.]. SNO, Järvi.
(M) **(*) Decca 425 065-2 [id.]. LPO, Haitink.
(N) (BB) ** Naxos Dig. 8.550625 [id.]. Slovak RSO (Bratislava), Ladislav Slovák.
(N) ** RCA Dig. RD 60887 [09026 60887-2]. St Louis SO, Leonard Slatkin.

Rattle conducts his Birmingham orchestra in a revelatory performance of the elusive *Fourth Symphony*, sustaining the expansive movements masterfully, bringing out the biting irony and humour of much of the writing, presented with Russian swagger, while never forgetting the underlying darkness. Above all, the orchestra plays incandescently, with an unstoppable thrust to convey the impression of a live, tensely dramatic event, with the full-bodied sound (recorded in Birmingham's Symphony Hall) adding to the weight and impact. The rare Britten piece is a valuable and generous makeweight.

Järvi draws from the SNO playing which is both rugged and expressive, consistently conveying the emotional thrust of the piece and making the enigmatic ending, with its ticking rhythm, warmer than usual, as though bitterness is finally evaporating. He is helped by exceptionally rich, full recording.

Haitink brings out an unexpected refinement in the *Symphony*, a rare transparency of texture. He is helped by recording of Decca's finest quality, vividly remastered. Detail is caught superbly; yet the earthiness and power, the demonic quality which can make this work so compelling, are underplayed.

Despite some technical accidents, the Slovak version on Naxos can be recommended as a bargain for strong and purposeful playing of an enigmatic work, well recorded in immediate sound.

Slatkin conducts the St Louis orchestra in a plain, well-played reading of a work that requires sharper tensions and drama, not helped by slightly distanced recording.

Symphony No. 5 in D min., Op. 47 (see also under *Cello concerto No. 1*).
*** EMI Dig. CDC7 49181-2 [id.]. Oslo PO, Jansons.
(M) *** Erato/Warner 2292 45752-2 [id.]. Leningrad PO, Mravinsky.
(M) *** Telarc Dig. CD 82001 [id.]. Cleveland O, Maazel – STRAVINSKY: *Rite of spring.* **(*)
(N) **(*) Everest EVC 9030 [id.]. NY Stadium SO, Stokowski.
(M) **(*) Mercury 434 323-2 [id.]. Minneapolis SO, Skrowaczewski – KHACHATURIAN: *Gayaneh ballet suite.* **(*)
(Y/B) **(*) Decca Dig. 440 476-2 [id.]. VPO, Solti – MENDELSSOHN: *Symphony No. 4.* **(*)
(N) (M) ** DG Dig. 445 577-2 [id.]. Nat. SO of Washington, Rostropovich – PROKOFIEV: *Romeo and Juliet: suite No. 1.* **

Symphony No. 5; Age of gold: Polka.
(B) **(*) Sony SBK 53261; *SBT 53261* [id.]. Phd. O, Ormandy – PROKOFIEV: *Love for 3 oranges: suite.* **

Symphony No. 5; 5 Fragments, Op. 42.
*** Decca Dig. 421 120-2 [id.]. RPO, Ashkenazy.

(i) *Symphony No. 5;* (ii) *Hamlet* (film incidental music), *suite, Op. 116.*
(Y/B) (BB) *** RCA Navigator 74321 24212-2 [id.]. (i) LSO, Previn; (ii) Belgian RSO, José Serebrier.

Ashkenazy's account of Shostakovich's most popular symphony is an exceptionally searching and intense reading, bitingly dramatic, yet finding an element of wry humour in the second and fourth movements to outshine any rival. Ashkenazy conveys in the slow movement's spareness a rare sense of desolation, hushed and refined, with the woodwind solos adding to the chill. The Decca fill-up, the very rare *Five Fragments*, sharp little inventions, like the main work are given demonstration sound quality.

Previn's RCA version, dating from early in his recording career (1965), remains at the top of the list of bargain recommendations. This is one of the most concentrated and intense readings ever, superbly played by the LSO at its peak. In the third movement he sustains a slower speed than anyone else, making it deeply meditative in its dark intensity, while his build-up in the central development section brings playing of white heat. The bite and urgency of the second and fourth movements are also irresistible. Only in the hint of analogue tape-hiss and a slight lack of opulence in the violins does the sound fall short of the finest modern digital recordings – and it is more vividly immediate than most. The new coupling is appropriate. *Hamlet* obviously generated powerful resonances in Shostakovich's psyche and produced vivid incidental music: the opening Ball scene is highly reminiscent of *Romeo and Juliet*. The playing of the Belgian Radio Orchestra under Serebrier is eminently serviceable without being really distinguished, but with atmospheric recording this 28-minute suite makes a considerable bonus.

Jansons' EMI version with the Oslo orchestra on top form brings a tautly incisive, electrically intense reading, marked by speeds notably faster than usual that yet have the ring of authenticity. The development section in the first movement, for example, builds up bitingly into a thrilling climax, with the accelerando powerfully controlled. Not a first choice, but an exciting one.

Mravinsky conducted the première of the *Fifth Symphony* in 1937, and so brings a special authority to this work. The present version is not free from the odd untidiness but there is still evidence of a commanding personality, and even though the recording itself is not in the luxury bracket, this CD must figure high on any list.

Brilliant in performance, spectacular in recorded sound, like all of Maazel's Cleveland recordings for Telarc, this Shostakovich reading is also warm, with the Cleveland violins sweet and pure in the long-legged melody of the second subject in the first movement. Though Maazel is faster than is common in the exposition section, he allows himself less stringendo than usual in the build-up of the development. The other three movements are also on the fast side, with little feeling of Ländler rhythm in the Scherzo and a sweet rather than rarefied reading of the *Largo* slow movement. This fits neatly between the spacious but rather severe reading of Haitink and the boldly expressive Bernstein.

The Philadelphia Orchestra made the very first recording of the *Fifth Symphony* (under Stokowski), and they play it marvellously here: the strings produce the most opulent tone and generate considerable eloquence in the slow movement; the solo flute, too, makes a highly distinguished contribution. Ormandy has always shown a special feeling for Shostakovich and he is direct and straightforward, but neither here (in 1965) nor in his later, RCA disc does one sense the degree of commitment that marked his earlier recording of the *First Symphony*. *The Age of gold polka* makes a witty encore after the Prokofiev coupling.

Stokowski gave us the first recording of this symphony in the 78 era. The Stadium Symphony Orchestra of New York is neither as flexible nor as virtuosic an ensemble as the superb instrument Stokowski created in Philadelphia during the first decade of electric recording, but the Stokowski electricity is here as intensely as ever and it makes this performance an unforgettable experience. There is less subtlety in the individual wind solos than in the old 78 set, but the strings re-create that 'drenched radiance' of texture in the upper register that Stokowski made his own and which makes the lyrical climaxes of the first and third movements so memorable. The sound itself is surprisingly good, though there is background hiss.

Skrowaczewski's Minneapolis account of Shostakovich's *Fifth* was one of the first really successful stereo recordings, with great concentration in the pianissimo string-playing in the *Largo* and a finale which, after an exhilarating *Allegro*, brings a trenchant, ponderous coda, anticipating much later performances, after the composer had revealed that his closing section was not intended to be an ingenuous triumphant celebration. The first movement has a fast opening speed, but the conductor understands Shostakovich's melodic line and, although this is a wilful reading, it is also an exciting one. The recording was made in the Northrop Auditorium in 1961 and is full yet astonishingly clear, but the upper strings have that curious thinness which was characteristic of Mercury's Minneapolis ventures at that time. However, the ear soon adjusts, and this performance is very compelling.

In Shostakovich's *Fifth Symphony* Solti adopts a more espressivo style than in his previous Shostakovich recordings, with the *Largo* slow movement beautifully moulded at a flowing speed, conveying warmth in a movement which is often treated with emotional reserve. The great soaring second-subject theme of the first movement too is given the warmth of the Vienna strings, and in both the Scherzo and finale Solti brings out Shostakovich's wry humour rather than his more brutal qualities. When the live recording, made in the Musikverein, is not very full-bodied, this is hardly a first choice, but both the Mendelssohn and the Shostakovich provide a welcome slant on the works themselves and on the conductor.

Rostropovich's account is too idiosyncratic to be recommended without qualification. He secures a refined, cultured string-tone, capable of searing intensity and strength, and all sections of the orchestra play with excellent attack and ensemble. The opening is given with hushed *ppp* intensity (the marking is in fact *piano*) and all promises well until, as is so often the case with this great Russian musician, he disturbs the natural musical flow for the sake of expressive effect. The brakes are abruptly applied in the Scherzo (at fig. 56), just before the horn figure is repeated, and he also pulls other phrases around. He wrings the last ounce of intensity out of the finale, which is undoubtedly imposing, but there is also a hectoring quality which is distinctly unappealing. The recording is on the whole good, even if it is a multi-mike, somewhat synthetic balance.

Symphonies Nos. 5 in D min.; 6 in B min., Op. 54.
(N) 🏵 (B) (***) Dutton Lab mono CDAX 8017 [id.]. Phd. O, Stokowski.

Stokowski's electrifying première of the *Fifth* has never been surpassed on record, notably for the intensity and beauty of the string playing in the first and third movements. The new Dutton transfer is little short of miraculous in its vividness and presence, and the quality of the recording is astonishing. Stokowski's *Sixth* was made in 1940, only a few months after the work was premièred, and it brings one face to face not only with this symphony but also with the bleak, harsh times during which it came into being. It is powerfully atmospheric, the lines wonderfully sustained and the playing at times frighteningly intense. This performance has a special ring of authenticity.

Symphonies Nos. 5 in D min.; 9 in E flat, Op. 70.
(M) *** Decca Dig. 425 066-2 [id.]. (i) Concg. O; (ii) LPO, Haitink.
(BB) *** Naxos Dig. 8.550427 [id.]. Belgian R. & T V O, Alexander Rahbari.
(M) **(*) Sony SMK 47615-2. NYPO, Bernstein.
(N) *(*) Decca Dig.448 122-2. Montreal SO, Dutoit.
(N) (BB) * Naxos Dig. 8.550632 [id.]. Slovak RSO (Bratislava), Ladislav Slovák.

In No. 5 Haitink is eminently straightforward, there are no disruptive changes in tempo, and the playing of the Concertgebouw Orchestra and the contribution of the Decca engineers are beyond praise. There could perhaps be greater intensity of feeling in the slow movement but, whatever small reservations one might have, it is most impressive both artistically and sonically. The coupled No. 9 is superb. Without inflation Haitink gives it a serious purpose, both in the poignancy of the waltz-like second movement and in the equivocal emotions of the outer movements. The recording is outstanding in every way.

   Both in the hushed intensity of the lyrical passages and in the vigour and bite of Shostakovich's violent allegros Rahbari's reading is most convincing, with dramatic tensions finely controlled in a spontaneous-sounding way. In No. 9 Rahbari opts for a controversially slow *Moderato* second movement but sustains it well, and the outer movements are deliciously witty in their pointing. The playing of all sections is first rate, and the sound is full and brilliant. An outstandingly generous coupling makes this a most attractive issue, even with no allowance made for the very low price.

   This was Bernstein's first recording of the *Fifth*, made in 1959; he re-recorded it later digitally. His view of the work was admired by the composer, perhaps because the finale opens so ferociously. Bernstein revels in the high spirits of the *Ninth*, and he also manages the alternation of moods very successfully. The sound has been greatly improved in both symphonies.

   Despite rich Montreal sound and beautiful playing, Dutoit's reading of No. 5 lacks the thrust and power needed and, though No. 9 is more successful, it lacks something in bite and tension. In this coupling Haitink is preferable, with Decca sound just as vivid.

   Slovák's version of No. 5 on Naxos is not as well played as most in this series, making it a doubtful recommendation, even as a bargain. The earlier, Rahbari coupling on the same label is the one to go for in this price-range.

Symphony No. 6 in B min., Op. 54.
(M) *** EMI CDM7 69564-2. LSO, Previn – RACHMANINOV: *Symphony No. 3.* ***

Here Previn shows his deep understanding of Shostakovich in a powerfully drawn, unrelenting account of the opening movement, his slow tempo adding to the overall impact. After that the offhand wit of the central Scherzo comes over the more delicately at a slower tempo than usual, leaving the hectic finale to hammer home the deceptively joyful conclusion to the argument. Excellent recording, impressively remastered.

(i) *Symphonies Nos. 6 in B min., Op. 54;* (ii) *9 in E flat, Op. 70.*
(N) **(*) DG Dig. 419 771-2 [id.]. VPO, Bernstein.
(N) **(*) EMI Dig. CDC7 54339-2 [id.]. Oslo PO, Mariss Jansons.
(Y/B) **(*) Everest EVC 9005 [id.]. (i) LPO, Boult; (ii) LSO, Sargent.

Perversely slow as Bernstein is in most movements of both symphonies, with the first movement of No. 6 and the *Moderato* (more like *Adagio*) of No. 9 minutes longer than any rival, the performances, recorded live, are electrifying, rhythmically alert to counter any slowness, helped by superb playing and spectacular recording.

Jansons in No. 6 is purposeful and strong, if emotionally restrained in the first movement, lithe and resilient in the Scherzo and finale, consistently adopting speeds on the fast side. No. 9 is then light and resilient, again with speeds on the fast side and with brilliant playing from the Oslo orchestra. Full, well-balanced recording, not as forward as the sound for most other Jansons Shostakovich discs.

Boult secures very good playing from the LPO and the late-1950s Walthamstow recording is excellent. But he is not as intense as he might be and this inevitably detracts from the sense of symphonic architecture. Sargent's account of the *Ninth* is lyrical and attractive, with infectious vitality in the odd-numbered of the five movements. One is at times reminded of Prokofiev's *Classical Symphony*, which Sargent also did well. Again the recording is very good indeed, approaching the demonstration class. This is undoubtedly an enjoyable coupling. However, these accounts are upstaged by Previn's *Sixth* and Haitink's *Ninth* – both differently coupled.

Symphonies Nos. 6 in B min., Op. 54; 12 in D min. (The Year 1917), Op. 112.
(M) *** Decca Dig. 425 067-2 [id.]. Concg. O, Haitink.

Haitink's structural control, coupled with his calm, taut manner, is particularly impressive in the slow movement of No. 6. As a work, No. 12 is more problematic. There is much of the composer's vision and grandeur here but also his crudeness. However, the sheer quality of the sound and the superb responsiveness and body of the Concertgebouw Orchestra might well seduce many listeners. As with the *Sixth* the slow movement has a marvellous sense of atmosphere, which is well conveyed in this Decca performance; the Amsterdam orchestra play as if they believe every crotchet and, though not even their eloquence can rescue the finale, overall the performance is very successful.

Symphony No. 7 in C (Leningrad), Op. 60.
*** Chandos Dig. CHAN 8623 [id.]. SNO, Järvi.
(M) **(*) Decca Dig. 425 068-2 [id.]. LPO, Haitink.
(M) **(*) Sony SMK 47616-2. NYPO, Bernstein.
(M) (***) RCA mono GD60293 [60293-2-RG]. NBC SO, Toscanini.
(N) (BB) * Naxos 8.550627 [id.]. Slovak RSO (Bratislava), Ladislav Slovák.

Järvi's is a strong, intense reading, beautifully played and recorded, which brings out the full drama of this symphony in a performance that consistently gives the illusion of spontaneity in a live performance, as in the hushed tension of the slow, expansive passages. There have been more polished versions than this, but, with its spectacular Chandos sound, it makes an excellent choice as a single-disc version.

Haitink is here eminently straightforward. There could perhaps be greater intensity of feeling in the slow movement, and the long first-movement *ostinato* is not presented histrionically; but the deep seriousness which Haitink finds in the rest of the work challenges comparisons with the other wartime symphony, the epic *Eighth*. The playing of the Concertgebouw Orchestra is beyond praise, and the splendid contribution of the Decca engineers ensures the success of this CD.

Bernstein brings a certain panache and fervour to his reading, particularly in the inspired slow movement, so that one is tempted to look indulgently at its occasional overstatements.

Toscanini and the NBC Orchestra bring an urgency and fervour that is altogether special and an intensity that shines through the primitive recorded sound. There is a special feeling of authenticity that conveys the flavour of the period and the vividness of the experience more effectively than many modern recordings. Be warned, however, the 1942 sound does call for some tolerance.

Slovák's Naxos version is variably successful, with the massive first movement too lacking in tension to sustain it with its deliberate banality. Fast movements are far more successful, but the ominous strength of the work is missing. Recording drier than in most of the series.

Symphony No. 8 in C min., Op. 65.
*** Ph. Dig. 422 442-2 [id.]. Leningrad PO, Mravinsky.
(M) *** Decca Dig. 425 071-2 [id.]. Concg. O, Haitink.
*** Teldec/Warner Dig. 9031 74719-2 [id.]. Nat. SO of Washington, Rostropovich.
(N) **(*) Ph. Dig. 446 062-2 [id.]. Kirov O, Gergiev.
(N) **(*) Denon Dig. CO 78910 [id.]. VSO, Inbal.
(N) (BB) *(*) Naxos Dig. 8.550628 [id.]. Slovak RSO (Bratislava), Ladislav Slovák.

Mravinsky's live recording in full, clear, digital sound gives a superb idea of the magnetism of his reading, demonstrating the firm structural strength while plumbing the deep personal emotions in this stressed wartime inspiration. Most significantly, Mravinsky's flowing speed for the elusive *Allegretto* finale makes the close of the work less equivocal than usual. It is a great performance and, though ensemble is inevitably not always quite as polished as in the finest studio recordings, discrepancies are minimal.

Haitink characteristically presents a strongly architectural reading of this war-inspired symphony, at times direct to the point of severity. After the massive and sustained slow movement which opens the work, Haitink allows no lightness or relief in the Scherzo movements, and in his seriousness in the strangely lightweight finale (neither fast nor slow) he provides an unusually satisfying account of an equivocal, seemingly uncommitted movement.

With Rostropovich, his intensity and that of his players does not spill over into excess. This is a gripping account that can rank alongside the best performances one has heard on or off record – Mravinsky, Rozhdestvensky, Kondrashin and the excellent Haitink – and it is very well recorded too.

Recorded in Holland in 1994, Gergiev's reading is remarkable for its concentration, with the massive span of the first movement held firmly together, leading to towering climaxes. Though the third-movement Scherzo is warmer and less tough than it might be, it erupts thrillingly when the brilliant trumpet solo enters and then resolves after the climax at the end on to a very slow, sustained *Largo*. The culminating resolution is tenderly achieved on the seemingly inevitable transition into the relative ease of the last, hushed movement. The sound is full-bodied but slightly cloudy, not as vivid and immediate as in such outstanding versions as Haitink's, now at mid-price.

Inbal's version on Denon opens in a restrained, withdrawn way, and much of the performance seems a degree understated but, helped by recording with an exceptionally wide dynamic range, the impact is shattering at the big climaxes. Though the third-movement Scherzo at a slowish speed lacks excitement, it erupts thrillingly at the end, and the consistent refinement of the playing makes this an excellent version for those looking for some restraint in this epic work.

Slovák on Naxos takes a rugged view of this powerful work, with the opening, weighty and purposeful, setting the pattern. Though tension is not always sustained in the middle movements, the weight of the sound helps to convey the brutal strength of the big climaxes, resolving in a genial account of the gentle fifth movement. Sound on the dry side but vivid.

Symphony No. 9 in E flat.
(N) **(*) Decca Dig. 444 458-2 [id.]. Carnegie Hall Project O, Solti – BRAHMS: *Variations on a theme of Haydn* **(*); R. STRAUSS: *Don Juan* *** (with Concert **(*)).

Solti's account of the *Ninth Symphony* was recorded at the end of a special workshop in which gifted instrumentalists were assembled in Carnegie Hall and given the opportunity to work with the maestro. The results are exhilarating; though he keeps things on a taut rein, there is plenty of wit and high spirits. The Scherzo and the last pages of the finale are played at a tremendous pace which some ears will take to more than others.

Symphony No. 9 in E flat, Op. 70; Festive overture, Op. 96; Katerina Ismailova (Lady Macbeth of Mtsensk): 5 Entr'actes. Tahiti trot (arr. of Youmans's *Tea for two*), *Op. 16.*
*** Chandos Dig. CHAN 8567 [id.]. SNO, Järvi.

Järvi's version of the *Ninth* brings a warmly expressive, strongly characterized reading in superb, wide-ranging sound. The point and wit of the first movement go with bluff good humour, leading on to an account of the second-movement *Moderato* that is yearningly lyrical yet not at all sentimental, contrasted with the fun and jokiness of the final *Allegretto*. The mixed bag of fill-up items is both illuminating and characterful, ending with the jolly little chamber arrangement that Shostakovich did in the 1920s of Vincent Youmans's *Tea for two*, the *Tahiti trot*.

Symphonies Nos. (i) *9 in E flat;* (ii) *10 in E min.*
(M) (***) Sony mono MPK 45698 [id.]. NYPO, (i) Efrem Kurtz; (ii) Dmitri Mitropoulos.

Dmitri Mitropoulos's pioneering account of the *Tenth Symphony* with the New York Philharmonic penetrates more deeply into the heart of this score than any of the recent newcomers; only Karajan's mid-1960s version can be put alongside it. It comes with Efrem Kurtz's 1949 version of the *Ninth* with the same orchestra, playing with great virtuosity. The sound is remarkably good for its period (an edit has removed one note from the opening phrase of the scherzo), but apart from that hiccup this is a stunning performance.

Symphony No. 10 in E min., Op. 93.
(N) *** DG Gold Dig. 439 036-2 [id.]. BPO, Karajan.
(Y/B) *** EMI Dig. CDC5 55232-2 [id.]. Phd. O, Jansons – MUSSORGSKY: *Songs and dances of death.* ***

(N) (B) *** Carlton IMP Dig. PCD 2043 [id.]. Hallé O, Skrowaczewski.
(M) (***) Saga mono EC 3366-2. Leningrad PO, Mravinsky.

(M) ** EMI Dig. CDM7 64870-2 [id.]. Philh. O, Simon Rattle – BRITTEN: *Sinfonia da Requiem.* ***
(N) ** RCA Dig. RD 60448 [09026 60448-2]. Concg. O, Claus Peter Flor.
(N) * Decca Dig. 433 073-2 [id.]. Chicago SO, Solti.

Symphony No. 10 in E min., Op. 93; Ballet suite No. 4.
*** Chandos Dig. CHAN 8630 [id.]. SNO, Järvi.

Already in his 1967 recording Karajan had shown that he had the measure of this symphony; this newer version is, if anything, even finer. In the first movement he distils an atmosphere as concentrated as before, bleak and unremitting, while in the *Allegro* the Berlin Philharmonic leave no doubts as to their peerless virtuosity. Everything is marvellously shaped and proportioned, and the early (1981) digital sound is made firmer by this 'original-image' bit re-processing.

Mariss Jansons's account of the *Tenth Symphony* is the finest of his series and the best version of this work we have had for some time. He draws a splendid response from the Philadelphia Orchestra, and the playing has tremendous fervour. It is obvious that this performance is the result of real feeling and much thought. There are some minor idiosyncrasies in the reading but reservations are small and, with recording which is very vivid and present, this must receive the strongest recommendation. Karajan's interpretation remains pre-eminent, but the EMI sound is generally preferable and Jansons offers a substantial coupling.

Järvi, too, conducts an outstandingly strong and purposeful reading in superb sound, full and atmospheric. In the great span of the long *Moderato* first movement he chooses an ideal speed, which allows for moments of hushed repose but still builds up relentlessly. The curious little *Ballet suite No. 4*, with its sombre *Prelude* leading to a bouncy *Waltz* and a jolly *Scherzo tarantella*, makes a delightful bonus.

Recorded in full, brilliant and weighty sound, Skrowaczewski's version of the *Tenth* is also a top recommendation. Above all, the spacious *moderato* of the long first movement has a natural power and concentration which put it among the finest versions, with the Hallé brass superbly focused at the climaxes.

Mravinsky conducted the work's première, but his mono LP was originally let down by dim recording. The sound has been improved on CD. In the long first movement Mravinsky captures the doleful melancholy of the opening and he moves to the bitter desperation of the climax with great eloquence. The Leningrad Philharmonic plays the Scherzo with staggering virtuosity and the work is satisfyingly resolved in the finale.

Rattle's Philharmonia version is curiously wayward in the two big slow movements, first and third in the scheme. In the first, Rattle is exceptionally slow, and though in principle such a view might yield revelatory results tension slips too readily. So too in the third movement. The Scherzo and energetic finale are much more successful. The recording does not help, with the strings sounding thin and lacking body.

Very well played and recorded, Flor's version lacks the flair and intensity of the finest rivals and, unlike the outstanding Jansons version on EMI, offers no coupling.

Recorded live in Chicago in 1990, Solti's version, uncoupled and with harsh, rather dry sound, is uncompetitive, particularly when the performance is often too relentless. In any case it has just been withdrawn as we go to press.

Symphony No. 11 (The Year 1905), Op. 103.
*** Delos Dig. D/CD 3080 [id.]. Helsinki PO, James DePreist.
(M) *** Decca Dig. 425 072-2 [id.]. Concg. O, Haitink.
**(*) DG Dig. 429 405-2 [id.]. Gothenburg SO, Järvi.
(N) (M) **(*) BBC Radio Classics 15656 91422 [id.]. BBC SO, Pritchard.

1905 was the year of the first Russian uprising, which foreshadowed the revolution to come rather more than a decade later. The result is a programme symphony conceived on a fairly large scale and, as in the *Leningrad Symphony*, its style is sometimes repetitive. The DePreist version won golden opinions: it certainly has the benefit of magnificent recording. The Helsinki orchestra may lack the weight and richness of sonority of the greatest orchestras but it plays with great intensity and feeling. A performance that has striking atmosphere and expressive power.

Haitink's sense of architecture is as impressive as always, even if at times he seems almost detached, lacking the last degree of tension. However, the Concertgebouw Orchestra plays superbly, and the Decca sound is as brilliant and realistic as ever.

Neeme Järvi's account of the *Eleventh Symphony* has much to recommend it, including good orchestral playing and very fine recorded sound. Good though it is, the performance misses the last ounce of intensity that made the old LP accounts of Mravinsky and Stokowski so extraordinarily powerful.

The BBC Radio Classics issue comes from a relay from London's Royal Festival Hall in April 1985 and is an eminently presentable performance. Sir John Pritchard drew playing of some eloquence from the BBC Symphony Orchestra, but when put alongside, say, the DePreist version one notes the greater intensity and atmosphere. The recording sounds very good, considering the problems posed by the venue, and the audience is quieter than on many records from this source. Not a first choice, but it is well worth the money.

Symphony No. 12 in D min. (The Year 1917), Op. 112.
(M) *** Erato/Warner 2292 45754-2 [id.]. Leningrad PO, Mravinsky.

The *Twelfth Symphony* is one of Shostakovich's more problematic essays in the genre. However, when a conductor of Mravinsky's quality is at the helm and drawing playing of electrifying intensity from the Leningrad Philharmonic, that impression is almost dispelled. Mravinsky's first version appeared in the early 1960s and long reigned supreme, but this Erato account, taken from a concert performance in 1984, is even higher in voltage, and the recording does ample justice to their playing.

Symphony No. 13 in B flat min. (Babi-Yar), Op. 113.
(M) *** Decca Dig. 425 073-2 [id.]. Marius Rintzler, Concg. Male Ch. & O, Haitink.
(N) *** Sup. SU 0160-2 231. Peter Mikuláš, Prague Philharmonic Ch., Prague SO, Maxim Shostakovich.
*** Teldec/Warner Dig. 4509-90848-2 [id.]. Yevtushenko, Leiferkus, New York Ch. Arts, NYPO, Masur.
(N) ** Olympia Dig. OCD 132 [id.]. Anatoly Safiulin, Yurlov State Chamber Ch., USSR MoC SO, Rozhdestvensky.
(N) (BB) ** Naxos Dig. 8.550630 [id.]. Peter Mikuláš, Slovak Philharmonic Ch. and RSO (Bratislava), Ladislav Slovák.
(N) ** Decca Dig. 444 791-2 [id.]. Aleksashkin, Sir Anthony Hopkins, Chicago SO, Sir Georg Solti.

The often brutal directness of Haitink's way with Shostakovich works well in the *Thirteenth Symphony*, particularly in the long *Adagio* first movement, whose title, *Babi-Yar*, gives its name to the whole work. That first of five Yevtushenko settings, boldly attacking anti-semitism in Russia, sets the pattern for Haitink's severe view of the whole. Rintzler with his magnificent, resonant bass is musically superb but, matching Haitink, remains objective rather than dashingly characterful. The resolution of the final movement, with its pretty flutings surrounding a wry poem about Galileo and greatness, then works beautifully. Outstandingly brilliant and full sound, remarkable even for this series.

Maxim Shostakovich's Supraphon version, with sound so vivid you hear some alien noises, is menacingly atmospheric, one of the finest of his recordings of his father's symphonies. Helped by the immediate sound, he sustains each movement with fine concentration, with each movement heightened by characterful singing from the superb Czech bass, Peter Mikuláš, even more individual than in his Naxos recording. So in the second movement, '*Humour*', brutal and tense, he conveys a gleam of manic menace in the music and brings out the full chilling horror of the third movement with its picture of women queueing. The chorus with its Slavonic timbres sounds totally idiomatic too, not balanced too close, making this one of the most convincing versions of this moving and atmospheric song-cycle symphony.

Kurt Masur's reading of the *Babi-Yar Symphony* is very powerful indeed, full of atmosphere and intensity. It has the benefit of Sergei Leiferkus and the Men of the New York Choral Artists and very clean and well focused recording. Another point of interest is Yevtushenko's readings which flank the performance. It does not sweep the board, but it is certainly among the best versions we have had to date.

With beefy, unrefined yet immediate recording, Rozhdestvensky's Olympia version offers an idiomatic performance, helped by very Russian-sounding singers, chorus as well as soloist. In the second movement, '*Humour*', the power cannot match the finest versions, among them Maxim Shostakovich's, and the playing is not always as crisp as in the rest of this series.

Slovák's version on Naxos is marred by the roughness of the choral sound, not helped by the closeness of the voices, but once the ruggedness of the reading is accepted there is much to enjoy, with Mikuláš a firm and characterful bass soloist. Sadly, Slovák's *Allegretto* for the last movement with its gentle opening is so fast it sounds trivial. Dryish recording which yet atmospherically captures withdrawn string pianissimos.

Polished and refined as the playing is in Sir Georg Solti's live recording, made in Chicago, it lacks the earthiness which this work needs to make its full impact. It is too well-mannered, and the device of having English translations of the poems spoken by Sir Anthony Hopkins before the first, second and third movements is not a success, with the reciter again suggesting emotional restraint. Nor is the Decca recording a match in its range and body for Haitink's from the same stable.

Symphony No. 14 in G min., Op. 135.
(N) (BB) *** Naxos Dig. 8.550631 [id.]. Hajóssyová, Mikuláš, Slovak RSO (Bratislava), Ladislav
Slovák.
(M) **(*) Sony SMK 47617-2. Teresa Kubiak, Isser Bushkin, NYPO, Bernstein.

(i) *Symphony No. 14, Op. 135;* (ii) *6 Poems of Marina Tsvetaeva, Op. 143a.*
(M) *** Decca Dig. 425 074-2 [id.]. (i) Varady, Fischer-Dieskau; (ii) Wenkel; Concg. O, Haitink.

The *Fourteenth* is Shostakovich's most sombre and dark score, a setting of poems by Lorca, Apollinaire,
Rilke, Brentano and Küchelbecker, all on the theme of death; Haitink's version gives each poem in its
original language. It is a most powerful performance, and the outstanding recording is well up to the
standard of this fine Decca series. The song-cycle, splendidly sung by Ortrun Wenkel, makes a fine
bonus.

Slovák's account of No. 14 is one of the finest in his Shostakovich series for Naxos, strongly characterized in each of the eleven contrasted movements with the help of two superb soloists. Mikuláš is just as
strong and individual as in No. 13, and Hajóssyová with her firm, Slavonic mezzo is equally idiomatic.
Regularly, Slovák and his performers bring out the menace behind the composer's inspiration on the
theme of death, with the fourth song, '*The Suicide*', particularly moving in its tenderness. The booklet
gives a summary of each poem, but no texts or translations. Full, immediate sound.

Bernstein's version with Teresa Kubiak and Isser Bushkin, recorded in 1976, does not have the benefit of
such excellent sound as the Haitink, yet, taken in its own right, it is perfectly acceptable and the
performance is both powerful and deeply felt without underlining expressive points to excess.
Shostakovich's bleak ruminations on the theme of death exercise a compelling fascination, for Bernstein
gets good playing from the New Yorkers and there is a Mussorgskian atmosphere here which eludes the
Decca performance. A pity there is no coupling: this plays for only 51 minutes.

(i) *Symphony No. 15 in A, Op. 141;* (ii) *From Jewish folk poetry* (song-cycle), *Op. 79.*
⊛ (M) *** Decca Analogue/Dig. 425 069-2 [id.]. (i) LPO; (ii) Söderström, Wenkel, Karczykowski,
Concg. O; Haitink.

Early readings of the composer's last symphony seemed to underline the quirky unpredictability of the
work, with the collage of strange quotations – above all the *William Tell* galop, which keeps recurring in
the first movement – seemingly joky rather than profound. Haitink by contrast makes the first movement sound genuinely symphonic, bitingly urgent. He underlines the purity of the bare lines of the
second movement; after the Wagner quotations which open the finale, his slow tempo for the main
lyrical theme gives it heartaching tenderness, not the usual easy triviality. The playing of the LPO is
excellent, with refined tone and superb attack, and the recording is both analytical and atmospheric.
The CD includes a splendidly sung version of *From Jewish folk poetry*, settings which cover a wide
range of emotions including tenderness, humour and even happiness as in the final song. Ryszard
Karczykowski brings vibrant Slavonic feeling to the work which, with its wide variety of mood and
colour, has a scale to match the shorter symphonies.

CHAMBER AND INSTRUMENTAL MUSIC

Cello sonata in D min., Op. 40.
*** Chandos Dig. CHAN 8340 [id.]. Turovsky, Edlina – PROKOFIEV: *Sonata.* ***
*** BIS Dig. CD 336 [id.]. Thedéen, Pöntinen – SCHNITTKE: *Sonata;* STRAVINSKY: *Suite italienne.*
***

Yuli Turovsky and Luba Edlina play the *Cello sonata* with great panache and eloquence, if in the finale
they almost succumb at times to exaggeration in their handling of its humour – no understatement here.

The Swedish cellist, Torleif Thedéen, has a real feeling for its structure and the vein of bitter melancholy
under its ironic surface. Roland Pöntinen gives him excellent support and the BIS recording does justice
to this partnership.

Cello sonata in D min., Op. 40; (i) *Piano trio No. 2 in E min., Op. 67.*
**(*) Sony Dig. MK 44664 [id.]. Yo-Yo Ma, Emanuel Ax; (i) with Isaac Stern.

The *Trio* receives a deeply felt performance, one which can hold its own with any issue, past or present.
The *Sonata* is another matter; the playing is as beautiful as one would expect, but here Ma's self-
communing propensity for reducing his tone is becoming a tiresome affectation. Ax plays splendidly and
the CBS recording is very truthful.

Piano quintet in G min., Op. 57.
(N) (***) Testament mono SBT 1077 [id.] Victor Aller, Hollywood Qt – FRANCK: *Piano quintet.* (***)
(*) CRD CRD 3351; *CRDC 4051* [id.]. Clifford Benson, Alberni Qt – BRITTEN: *Quartet No. 1.* *

Piano quintet, Op. 57; Piano trio No. 2 in E min., Op. 67.
**(*) Chandos Dig. CHAN 8342; *A BTD 1088* [id.]. Borodin Trio, Zweig, Horner.

Piano quintet in G min.; Piano trio No. 2; 4 Waltzes for flute, clarinet & piano.
(N) *** Virgin/EMI Dig. VC7 59312-2 [id.]. Nash Ens. (members).

The Nash Ensemble on Virgin offer the ideal coupling – plus an interesting makeweight – of two of Shostakovich's key chamber works, written before his quartet series developed, when he completed only the first, relatively trivial work. The *Piano trio* is a particularly painful and anguished work, dedicated to the memory of a close friend, Ivan Sollertinsky, who died in the year of its composition. Both the *Piano quintet* and the *Trio* point the way forward, and the Nash players bring out the dedicated intensity in this very personal writing, with refined readings which can be warmly recommended, even if they are not quite as characterfully individual as the very finest. Excellent sound.

On Testament a magisterial account of the *Piano quintet* if ever there was one, this belongs among the finest of interpretations. Its praises were sung by the authors of *The Record Guide* in the mid-1950s when they spoke of it in their down-to-earth manner as 'a dazzling performance and their tone, though often extremely delicate, is never skinny'. Readers who care about Shostakovich should find it an indispensable issue and need make few allowances for the 1952 sound.

The Chandos version is bold in character and concentrated in feeling. Alternatively, there is a vigorous and finely conceived account from Clifford Benson and the Alberni Quartet, vividly recorded; if the Britten coupling is wanted, this will be found fully satisfactory. All three accounts of the *Quintet* are very satisfactory.

Piano trio No. 1, Op. 8.
*** EMI Dig. CDC7 49865-2 [id.]. Chung Trio – TCHAIKOVSKY: *Piano trio.* ***

The Op. 8 *Piano trio* is an early work, written when Shostakovich was only seventeen, convalescing from tuberculosis and recovering from the death of his father. It is a short piece, some 12 minutes long, but is deeply felt and well worth getting to know. Readers will recognize some ideas that resurface later in the *First Symphony*. The Chungs play with great dedication and are most truthfully recorded.

2 Pieces for string octet, Op. 11.
*** Chandos Dig. CHAN 9131 [id.]. ASMF Chamber Ens. – ENESCU: *Octet in C;* R. STRAUSS: *Capriccio: Sextet.* ***

The Academy of St Martin-in-the-Fields Chamber Ensemble play splendidly and with conviction; they are beautifully recorded and also offer a highly recommendable version of the Enescu *Octet*.

String quartets

String quartets Nos. 1–15.
(M) *** Decca 433 078-2 (6). Fitzwilliam Qt.

The Shostakovich *Quartets* thread through his creative life like some inner odyssey and inhabit terrain of increasing spiritual desolation. The Fitzwilliam Quartet played to Shostakovich himself and gave the UK premières of his last three quartets, and they bring to the whole cycle complete and total dedication. One has only to sample the first two quartets to discover the sustained and often hushed intensity of this playing, which so consistently has the spontaneity of live music-making. They are given first-class recording too, with great presence and natural body. The recordings were made in All Saints' Church, Petersham, Surrey between 1975 and 1977; a rather forward balance was chosen, perhaps because of the ecclesiastical acoustic, and this is slightly emphasized by the CD transfer, yet there is a natural transparency and a firm focus throughout. There are minor criticisms, but they are too trivial to weigh in the balance, for this set is by any standards a formidable achievement.

String quartets Nos. 1–15; (i) Piano quintet in G min.
(M) *** EMI CMS5 65032-2 (6) [id.]. Borodin Qt, (i) with Sviatoslav Richter.

String quartets Nos. 1 in C, Op. 49; 9 in E flat, Op. 117; 12 in D flat, Op. 133.
*** EMI CDC7 49266-2 [id.]. Borodin Qt.

String quartets Nos. 5 in B flat, Op. 92; 15 in E flat min., Op. 144.
*** EMI CDC7 49270-2 [id.]. Borodin Qt.

String quartets Nos. 7 in F sharp min., Op. 108; 8 in C min., Op. 110; (i) *Piano quintet, Op. 57.*
*** EMI Dig. CDC7 47507-2 [id.]. Borodin Qt, (i) with Sviatoslav Richter.

String quartets Nos. 10 in A flat, Op. 118; 13 in B flat min., Op. 138; 14 in F sharp, Op. 142.
*** EMI CDC7 49269-2 [id.]. Borodin Qt.

EMI offer the Borodin Quartet's second complete cycle. They are available separately, at full price. We hope they remain available in this individual format, but the complete set is a more economical invest- ment. The present recordings are made in a generally drier acoustic than their predecessors, and Nos. 3 and 5 suffer noticeably in this respect. However, the ears quickly adjust and the performances can only be described as masterly. The Borodins possess enormous refinement, an altogether sumptuous tone and a perfection of technical address that is almost in a class of its own – and what wonderful inton- ation! These and the Bartók six are the greatest quartet cycles produced in the present century and are mandatory listening. The *Piano quintet* was recorded at a public concert at the Moscow Conservatoire, and it goes without saying that with Richter at the helm the account is a powerful one, although the quality of the sound here is noticeably dry and forward.

String quartets Nos. 1 in C, Op. 49; 2 in A, Op. 68; 4 in D, Op. 83.
(N) (***) Koch/Consonance mono 81-3005 [id.]. Beethoven Qt.

String quartets Nos. 3 in F, Op. 73; 6 in G, Op. 101.
(N) *** Koch/Consonance 81-3007 [id.]. Beethoven Qt.

String quartets Nos. 7 in F sharp min., Op. 108; 8 in C min., Op. 110; 15 in E flat min., Op. 144.
(N) *** Koch/Consonance 81-3006 [id.]. Beethoven Qt.

String quartets Nos. 9, in E flat, Op. 117; 10 in A flat, Op. 118; 11 in F min., Op. 122.
(N) *** Koch/Consonance 81-3009 [id.]. Beethoven Qt.

String quartets Nos. 12 in D flat, Op. 133; 13 in B flat min., Op. 138; 14 in F sharp, Op. 142.
(N) *** Koch/Consonance 81-3008 [id.]. Beethoven Qt.

While the symphonies span the best part of half a century (1926–71), Shostakovich turned to the quartet medium only after the *Fifth Symphony* and his rehabilitation into Soviet favour. The greater intimacy of the medium enables him to touch on private depths that would have been inappropriate in the more public world of the symphonies, though the canvas is too small to encompass the epic power and tragic sweep of the *Eighth* and *Tenth Symphonies*. Right from the *First Quartet* of 1938 through to the last, finished not long before his death, the Beethoven Quartet were closely associated with them and gave the first performances of nearly all. Since they collaborated so closely with him, their view of this cycle carries special authority. Collectors who were lucky enough to get to know this often inspiring music from the old Melodiya LPs from the 1950s and '60s and who still treasure them, will welcome their reappearance in this cleaned-up form. With a few exceptions (Nos. 8, 10 and 13), theirs were also first recordings – and no other group was closer to Shostakovich's mind. Nos. 9, 10 and 11, for example, were made in 1965 and 1969, when the works were fresh from the composer's pen. Even if you have the fine cycles by the Borodins and the Fitzwilliams, this set is an important documentary record. In some of the earlier recordings allowances must be made for the sound; No. 3 is a later performance (1960) than the old mono LP, which used to be coupled to the *Piano quintet* on Parlophone.

String quartets Nos. 1 in C, Op. 49; 8 in C min., Op. 110; 9 in E flat, Op. 117.
(N) (BB) *** Naxos Dig. 8.550973 [id.]. Eder Qt.

If the Naxos disc is not necessarily a first choice, no one investing in it need fear they are getting short- changed. The Eder Quartet is a very distinguished ensemble and have a very good feeling for this repertoire. They are actually better recorded than the Borodins on EMI, and those for whom economy is a primary concern should consider this.

String quartets Nos. 2 in A, Op. 68; 12 in D flat, Op. 133.
*** Virgin/EMI Dig. VC7 59281-2 [id.]. Borodin Qt.

String quartets Nos. 3 in F, Op. 73; 7 in F sharp min., Op. 108; 8 in C min., Op. 110.
*** Virgin/EMI Dig. VC7 59041-2 [id.]. Borodin Qt.

The new Borodin accounts have the benefit of far better and more refined recording than their earlier, Melodiya versions on EMI. The sound is richer and cleaner and has a pleasing bloom, as one would expect from the Snape Maltings. As far as the performances are concerned, some things come off better than others so that on balance there is little to choose between the earlier and newer sets; those who have the former need not make a change. This is one of the greatest quartets now before the public and they are completely inside this music. Those coming new to these works will probably opt for the newer, Virgin, digital versions.

String quartets Nos. 2 in A, Op. 68; 5 in B flat, Op. 92; 7 in F sharp min., Op. 108.
**(*) Olympia OCD 532 [id.]. Shostakovich Qt.

String quartets Nos. 6 in G, Op. 101; 8 in C min., Op. 110; 9 in E flat, Op. 117.
**(*) Olympia OCD 533 [id.]. Shostakovich Qt.

String quartets Nos. 12 in D flat, Op. 133; 13 in B flat min., Op. 138; 14 in F sharp, Op. 142.
**(*) Olympia OCD 535 [id.]. Shostakovich Qt.

The Shostakovich Quartet recordings emanate from the 1970s and from Moscow Radio tapes; they offer eminently serviceable performances in decent, analogue sound. We have responded to their cycle with appreciation; theirs are the kind of performances one would be perfectly happy with if they were the only ones available; and the recordings are very satisfactory indeed.

String quartets Nos. 2 in A, Op. 68; 12 in D flat, Op. 133.
(N) (BB) *** Naxos Dig. 8.550975 [id.]. Eder Qt.

If anything, the Eder coupling of Nos. 2 and 12 is even more impressive than their first disc. The account of the third-movement *Adagio: Recitativo and Romance* of No. 2 with its intense, improvisatory feeling is particularly fine, and the closing *Theme and variations* is strongly characterized. Similarly the extended *Allegretto* second movement of No. 12 is powerfully argued and these performances have compelling concentration throughout. The recording too is excellent.

String quartets Nos. 4 in D, Op. 83; 8 in C min., Op. 110; 11 in F min., Op. 122.
*** ASV Dig. CDDCA 631 [id.]. Coull Qt.

The *Fourth quartet* is a work of exceptional beauty and lucidity, one of the most haunting of the cycle; the *Eleventh Quartet* is a puzzling, almost cryptic work in seven short movements. The Coull are one of the most gifted of the younger British quartets and give eminently creditable accounts of all three pieces. A very good (if slightly overlit) recording on CD.

String quartets Nos. 4 in D, Op. 83; 11 in F min., Op. 122; 14 in F sharp, Op. 142.
(N) *** DG Dig. 445 864-2 [id.]. Hagen Qt.

The Hagen Quartet is as impeccable an ensemble as any now before the public, and if the appearance of this disc heralds a complete cycle it is very good news. There is a stark austerity about the Beethoven Quartet's versions that the newcomers do not always achieve but, generally speaking, these are among the most beautifully played and thoughtful readings of these *Quartets* to have appeared in recent years.

String quartet No. 8, Op. 110.
(M) **(*) Decca 425 541-2 [id.]. Borodin Qt – BORODIN; TCHAIKOVSKY: *Quartets.* **(*)
(N) **(*) Collins Dig. 1450-2 [id.]. Duke Qt – SCHNITTKE: *String quartet No. 2;* TCHAIKOVSKY: *String quartet No. 1.* **(*)

The Borodins' Decca performance is outstanding and the recording real and vivid, although the balance means that in the CD transfer the effect is very forward, almost too boldly immediate.

The Duke Quartet have collected golden opinions for their concert performances and for their earlier record of quartets by Barber and Dvořák. This hybrid collection of Russian quartets can also be recommended. They are unquestionably a fine ensemble with keen, alert responses and remarkable unanimity of mind. Their version joins the extensive discography of the *Eighth Quartet* (there are about 20 currently available); few are less than serviceable, most are very good indeed, and this is among them. As with their earlier CD, the upfront balance does not do them any favours and brings the listener uncomfortably near (sometimes it seems one is actually on) the platform. With this proviso, if the coupling meets your needs, you can invest in it with some confidence.

String quartets Nos. 12 in D flat, Op. 133; 13 in B flat min., Op. 138; 14 in F sharp, Op. 142.
(N) *** Koch/Consonance 81-3008 [id.]. Beethoven Qt.

This completes the series by the Beethoven Quartet. Even if you have the fine cycles by the Borodins and the Fitzwilliams, this set is an important documentary record. In some of the earlier recordings allowances must be made for the sound; No. 3 is a later performance (1960) than the old, mono LP, which used to be coupled to the *Piano quintet* on Parlophone.

String quartets Nos. (i) 14, Op. 142; (ii) 15, Op. 144.
*** HM/Praga PR 254043 [id.]. (i) Glinka String Qt; (ii) Beethoven Qt.

The Praga recordings date from 1976–7 and come from the Czech Radio archives. The Glinka Quartet is a first-rate ensemble and their intense account of the *Fourteenth Quartet*, recorded only a year after the composer's death, is deeply felt. The Beethoven Quartet's account of the *Fifteenth* (they also recorded it commercially for Melodiya) penetrates deeply into this death-haunted music and this can be recommended.

Viola sonata, Op. 147.
*** EMI Dig. CDC7 54394-2 [id.]. Tabea Zimmermann, Hartmut Höll – BRITTEN: *Lachrymae;* STRAVINSKY: *Elégie.* ***

Shostakovich's *Viola sonata* is perhaps his most bleak and comfortless work, a true song of sorrow, ruminating on the imminence of death. Tabea Zimmermann and her partner, Hartmut Höll, give as powerful and chilling an account of it as one could imagine. The recording is of striking clarity and presence.

Violin sonata, Op. 134.
*** Chandos Dig. CHAN 8988 [id.]. Mordkovitch, Benson – PROKOFIEV: *Sonatas;* SCHNITTKE: *In memoriam.* ***
*** Chandos Dig. CHAN 8343 [id.]. Dubinsky, Edlina – SCHNITTKE: *Sonata No. 1* etc. ***

The *Violin sonata* can seem a dry piece, but Mordkovitch's natural intensity, her ability to convey depth of feeling without sentimentality, transforms it. Clifford Benson is the understanding pianist. In first-rate sound it makes a fine central offering for Mordkovitch's well-planned disc of Soviet violin music.

Rostislav Dubinsky's account is undoubtedly eloquent, and Luba Edlina makes a fine partner. The recording is excellent too, although it is balanced a shade closely.

PIANO MUSIC

24 Preludes, Op. 34.
*** Decca Dig. 433 055-2 [id.]. Olli Mustonen – ALKAN: *25 Preludes.* ***

Of the recordings of the Shostakovich *Preludes*, Op. 34, currently listed in the catalogue the Decca version by the young Finnish pianist, Olli Mustonen, is the strongest contender both artistically and technically. This is the best record of the *Preludes* since Menahem Pressler's old LP from the 1950s.

24 Preludes, Op. 34; Piano sonata No. 2, Op. 61; 3 Fantastic dances, Op. 5.
*** Hyperion Dig. CDA 66620 [id.]. Tatiana Nikolayeva.

Here are the most important Shostakovich piano works *not* inspired by Tatiana Nikolayeva, played by one of the composer's most trusted exponents and very well recorded indeed. She is one of the authentic advocates of Shostakovich, and her CD will be a must for most collectors. Recommended alongside Mustonen.

24 Preludes and fugues, Op. 87.
(Y/B) ✿ (M) *** BMG/Melodiya 74321 19849-2 (3) [id.]. Tatiana Nikolayeva.
*** Hyperion Dig. CDA 66441/3 [id.]. Tatiana Nikolayeva.

In this repertoire, the first choice must inevitably be Tatiana Nikolayeva, 'the onlie begetter', as it were, of the *Preludes and fugues*. Her reading has enormous concentration and a natural authority that is majestic. There is wisdom and humanity here, and she finds depths in this music that have eluded most other pianists who have offered samples. No grumbles about the Hyperion recording, which is very natural. However, her Melodiya set, made in 1987, is if anything cleaner and better focused (if a bit dry). In neither reading will readers be disappointed.

Piano sonata No. 1.
*** DG Dig. 427 766-2 [id.]. Lilya Zilberstein – RACHMANINOV: *Preludes.* ***

The early *Sonata* is a radical piece, with something of the manic, possessed quality of Scriabin and the harmonic adventurousness of Berg. Lilya Zilberstein rises triumphantly to its formidable demands, and she makes a strong case for it; she is recorded with striking immediacy and impact. As piano sound, this is state of the art.

OPERA

Lady Macbeth of Mtsensk (complete).
✿ *** EMI CDS7 49955-2 (2) [Ang. CDCB 49955]. Vishnevskaya, Gedda, Petkov, Krenn, Tear, Amb. Op. Ch., LPO, Rostropovich.

*** DG Dig. 437 511-2 (2) [id.]. Ewing, Haugland, Larin, Langridge, Kristine Ciesinski, Moll, Kotcherga, Zednik, Paris Bastille Op. Ch. & O, Myung-Whun Chung.

Rostropovich, in his finest recording ever, proves with thrilling conviction that this first version of Shostakovich's greatest work for the stage is among the most original operas of the century. Vishnevskaya is inspired to give an outstanding performance and provides moments of great beauty alongside aptly coarser singing; and Gedda matches her well, totally idiomatic. As the sadistic father-in-law, Petkov is magnificent, particularly in his ghostly return, and there are fine contributions from Robert Tear, Werner Krenn, Birgit Finnilä and Alexander Malta.

If ever Rostropovich's classic EMI recording of this opera is unavailable, then Chung's provides an alternative not quite so violent or powerful, but even more moving. The sound is more atmospheric, not quite so immediate, which enhances the gentler, lyrical approach that Chung takes in many passages from the very start. The biggest contrast comes in the portrayal of the heroine. Where Vishnevskaya makes her a ravening fire-eater, with the voice abrasive and aggressive, Maria Ewing's portrait is much more vulnerable, with moods and responses subtly varied, her feminine charms more vividly conveyed in singing far more sensuous, with the beauty of hushed pianissimos most tenderly affecting. Sergei Larin as Katerina's labourer-lover equally gains over his EMI rival, Nicolai Gedda, by sounding more aptly youthful, with his tenor both firm and clear yet Slavonic-sounding. His touch is lighter than Gedda's, with a nice vein of irony. Aage Haugland is magnificent as Boris, Katerina's father-in-law, and Philip Langridge sings sensitively as her husband, Zinovi, while Kurt Moll as the Old Convict provides an extra emotional focus in his important solo at the start of the last Act.

Sibelius, Jean (1865–1957)

Academic march; Finlandia (arr. composer); *Har du mod? Op. 31/2; March of the Finnish Jaeger Battalion, Op. 91/1;* (i) *The origin of fire, Op. 32; Sandels, Op. 28; Song of the Athenians, Op. 31/3.*
** BIS CD 314 [id.]. (i) Sauli Tilikainen, Laulun Ystävät Male Ch., Gothenburg SO, Järvi.

The origin of fire is by far the most important work on this record. Sauli Tilikainen is very impressive indeed, and the playing of the Gothenburg Symphony Orchestra under Neeme Järvi has plenty of feeling and atmosphere. None of the other pieces is essential Sibelius. The singing of the Laulun Ystävät is good rather than outstanding, and the Gothenburg orchestra play with enthusiasm. Fine recording in the best BIS traditions.

Andante festivo; Finlandia, Op. 26; Karelia suite, Op. 11; King Christian II (suite); (i) *Luonnotar, Op. 70. The Oceanides, Op. 73.*
(N) *** DG Dig. 447 760-2 [id.]. (i) Soile Isokoski; Gothenburg SO, Neeme Järvi.

This magnificent, impeccably recorded Sibelius anthology brings one of the best accounts of *The Oceanides* we have had since the celebrated Beecham version, made at the composer's own request, and a first-class *Luonnotar* – again, one of the best ever made. The remaining pieces are hardly less satisfying. The engineering is by the usual Gothenburg team that serviced this orchestra's BIS recordings.

Autrefois (Scène pastorale), Op. 96b; The Bard, Op. 64; Presto in D for strings; Spring song, Op. 16; Suite caractéristique, Op. 100; Suite champêtre, Op. 98b; Suite mignonne, Op. 98a; Valse chevaleresque, Op. 96c; Valse lyrique, Op. 96a.
*** BIS Dig. CD 384 [id.]. Gothenburg SO, Järvi.

A mixed bag. *The Bard* is Sibelius at his greatest and most powerful, and it finds Järvi at his best. The remaining pieces are all light: some of the movements of the *Suite mignonne* and *Suite champêtre* could come straight out of a Tchaikovsky ballet, and Järvi does them with great charm. The last thing that the *Suite*, Op. 100, can be called is *caractéristique*, while the three pieces, Op. 96, find Sibelius in Viennese waltz mood. The rarity is *Autrefois*, which has a beguiling charm and is by far the most haunting of these pastiches. Sibelius introduces two sopranos and their *vocalise* is altogether captivating. The *Presto in D major for strings* is a transcription – and a highly effective one – of the third movement of the *B flat Quartet*, Op. 4. Excellent recording, as one has come to expect from BIS.

(i) *The Bard, Op. 64; En Saga, Op. 9;* (ii) *Finlandia, Op. 26; Kuolema: Valse triste, Op. 44;* (i) *4 Legends, Op. 22;* (ii) *Tapiola, Op. 112.*
(N) (B) *** DG Double 447 358-2 (2) [id.]. (i) Helsinki R. O, Kamu; (ii) BPO, Karajan – GRIEG: *Peer Gynt suites* etc. ***

Okku Kamu offer an exceptionally fine account of *The Bard*, and *En Saga* is hardly less admirable. His set of the four *Legends* is very good indeed. He handles pictorial detail most imaginatively, and the

Helsinki Radio Orchestra responds with enthusiasm and good ensemble to his lively direction. Although his account of *Lemminkäinen and the Maidens of Saari* is a trifle brisk it is certainly exciting, and the famous *Swan* glides in sombrely. The engineers produce a well-balanced and truthful sound-picture and the CD transfer is firm and clear. Karajan's performances come from the mid-1960s. *Finlandia* and *Tapiola* are still among the finest accounts available, and the rather slow *Valse triste* is certainly seductive. Good transfers.

Belshazzar's Feast (suite), Op. 54; Dance intermezzo, Op. 45/2; The Dryad, Op. 45/1; Pan and Echo, Op. 53; Swanwhite, Op. 54.
*** BIS Dig. CD 359 [id.]. Gothenburg SO, Neeme Järvi.

Belshazzar's Feast, a beautifully atmospheric piece of orientalism, and the incidental music for Strindberg's *Swanwhite* may not be Sibelius at his most powerful but both include many characteristic touches and some haunting moments. Neeme Järvi's collection with the Gothenburg orchestra is first class in every way.

Cassazione, Op. 6; Preludio; The Tempest: Prelude & suites 1–2, Op. 109; Tiera.
*** BIS Dig. CD 448 [id.]. Gothenburg SO, Järvi.

Järvi's recording of Sibelius's incidental music to *The Tempest* is the finest and most atmospheric since Beecham and, though it does not surpass the latter in pieces like *The Oak-tree* or the *Chorus of the winds*, it is still impressive and offers first-class modern recording. Järvi also includes the *Prelude*, omitted on Beecham's disc. The *Cassazione* in character resembles the *King Christian II* music, but it is well worth having on disc. Neither *Tiera* nor the *Preludio*, both from the 1890s, is of great interest or particularly characteristic.

Violin concerto in D min. (1903–4 version); *Violin concerto in D min., Op. 47* (1905; published version).
*** BIS Dig. CD 500 [id.]. Leonidas Kavakos, Lahti SO, Osmo Vänskä.

The first performance of the *Violin concerto* left Sibelius dissatisfied and he immediately withdrew it for revision. This CD presents Sibelius's initial thoughts so that for the first time we can see the familiar final version struggling to emerge from the chrysalis. Comparison of the two concertos makes a fascinating study: the middle movement is the least affected by change, but the outer movements are both longer in the original score, and the whole piece takes almost 40 minutes. The Greek violinist, Leonidis Kavakos, proves more than capable of handling the hair-raising difficulties of the 1904 version and is an idiomatic exponent of the definitive concerto. The Lahti orchestra under Osmo Vänskä give excellent support and the balance is natural and realistic. An issue of exceptional interest and value.

Violin concerto in D min., Op. 47.
⊛ *** Sony Dig. SK 44548 [id.]. Cho-Liang Lin, Philh. O, Salonen – NIELSEN: *Violin concerto.* *** ⊛
(Y/B) (M) *** Decca 425 080-2 [id.]. Kyung-Wha Chung, LSO, Previn – TCHAIKOVSKY: *Violin concerto.* ***
(M) *** RCA 09026 61744-2 [id.]. Heifetz, Chicago SO, Hendl – GLAZUNOV: *Concerto;* PROKOFIEV: *Concerto No. 2.* ***
(N) (M) *** Sony Stern Edition I SMK 66829 [id.]. Stern, Phd. O, Ormandy – TCHAIKOVSKY: *Violin concerto.* ***
(M) *** Ph. 420 895-2. Accardo, LSO, C. Davis – DVORAK: *Violin concerto.* ***
(M) *** EMI Dig. CD-EMX 2203; *TC-EMX 2203* [id.]. Little, RLPO, Handley – BRAHMS: *Violin concerto.* ***
*** EMI CDC7 47167-2 [id.]. Perlman, Pittsburgh SO, Previn – SINDING: *Suite.* ***
*** EMI Dig. CDC7 54127-2 [id.]; *EL 7754127-4*. Nigel Kennedy, CBSO, Rattle – TCHAIKOVSKY: *Concerto.* **(*)
(N) *** Erato/Warner Dig. 4509-98537-2 [id.]. Vadim Repin, LSO, Emmanuel Krivine – TCHAIKOVSKY: *Violin concerto.* ***
(M) (***) EMI mono CDH7 61011-2. Ginette Neveu, Philh. O, Susskind – BRAHMS: *Concerto.* (***)
(M) **(*) Sony SMK 47540 [id.]. Francescatti, NYPO, Bernstein – BRAHMS: *Concerto.* **(*)
(BB) *** Naxos Dig. 8.550329; *4550329* [id.]. Dong-Suk Kang, Slovak (Bratislava) RSO, Adrian Leaper – HALVORSEN: *Air Norvégien etc.;* SINDING: *Légende;* SVENDSEN: *Romance.* ***
(N) *** Ph. Dig. 446 131-2 [id.]. Leila Josefovicz, ASMF, Marriner – TCHAIKOVSKY: *Violin concerto.* **(*)
(M) (**) EMI mono CDH7 64030-2 [id.]. Heifetz, LPO, Beecham – GLAZUNOV: *Violin concerto* (***) ⊛; TCHAIKOVSKY: *Violin concerto.* (***)

(i; ii) *Violin concerto;* (ii) *En Saga, Op. 9;* (iii) *Finlandia, Op. 26; Kuolema: Valse triste, Op. 44/1;* (ii) *Legend: The swan of Tuonela, Op. 22/2.*

(N) (M) Sony **(*) SMK 64578 [id.]. (i) Cho-Liang Lin, (ii) Philh. O; (iii) Swedish RSO; Salonen.

(i) *Violin concerto. Karelia suite; Belshazzar's feast (suite), Op. 54.*

(N) **(*) Ondine Dig. ODE 8782 [id.]. (i) Pekka Suusisto; Helsinki PO, Leif Segerstam.

Violin concerto; 2 Serenades, Op. 69; Humoresque No. 1 in D min., Op. 87/1.

(N) *** DG Dig. 447 895-2 [id.]. Anne-Sophie Mutter, Dresden State O, André Previn.

(i) *Violin concerto; Serenade No. 2 in G min., Op. 69. En Saga, Op. 9.*

*** Sony Classical SK 53272 [id.]. (i) Julian Rachlin; Pittsburgh SO, Lorin Maazel.

Cho-Liang Lin's playing is distinguished not only by flawless intonation and an apparently effortless virtuosity but also by great artistry. He produces a glorious sonority at the opening, which must have been exactly what Sibelius wanted, wonderfully clean and silvery, and the slow movement has tenderness, warmth and yet restraint with not a hint of over-heated emotions. Lin encompasses the extrovert brilliance of the finale and the bravura of the cadenza with real mastery. The Philharmonia Orchestra rise to the occasion under Esa-Pekka Salonen, and the recording is first class. Lin's estimable account of the *Violin concerto* is also available at mid-price, coupled with four favourite orchestra pieces. The snag is that *Finlandia* is seriously underpowered and *En Saga* generates real excitement only towards the end, and then it sounds slick. *The Swan of Tuonela* is a fine performance, gentle and poetic. Salonen's rather similar approach to *Valse triste*, if without the panache of Karajan, is quite effective. No complaints about the recording.

Kyung Wha Chung has inimitable style and an astonishing technique, and her feeling for the Sibelius *Concerto* is second to none. André Previn's accompanying cannot be praised too highly: it is poetic when required, restrained, full of controlled vitality and well-defined detail. The 1970 Kingsway Hall recording is superbly balanced and produces an unforced, truthful sound. This is a most beautiful account, poetic, brilliant and thoroughly idiomatic, and must be numbered among the finest versions of the work available; the coupling with Tchaikovsky is very appropriate for reissue in Decca's Classic Sound series.

Heifetz's stereo performance of the Sibelius *Concerto* with the Chicago Symphony Orchestra under Walter Hendl set the standard by which all other versions have come to be judged. It is also one of his finest recordings; in remastered form the sound is vivid, with the Chicago ambience making an apt setting for the finely focused violin line.

Julian Rachlin's account of the Sibelius *Concerto* is pretty stunning; indeed it has a purity of tone and intonation which is remarkable and a silvery, aristocratic quality that is entirely in harmony with Sibelius's conception. There are one or two idiosyncratic touches in the first cadenza, and the music almost comes to a standstill at one point but, given his other qualities, who cares? His slow movement is strikingly fine and without any *zigeuner*-like sentiment. He understands the poignancy of the beautiful *G minor Serenade*, and it is a pity that he did not find room for its companion. Maazel gives excellent support throughout, and his *En Saga* is atmospheric but a bit brisk. The Sony engineers strike an excellent balance between soloist and orchestra, and the recording has great warmth, even if the upper strings could have greater transparency.

Where most violinists treat the opening as a deep meditation, Mutter makes it tougher than usual, less beautiful, using momentarily a vibratoless tone, slightly steely, establishing this more clearly as an *Allegro moderato* first movement rather than a lyrical slow movement. Even if one misses some of the raptness of Mullova or Chung, it is a very valid view, and the sustained power of the reading is reinforced by the relatively close balance of the solo instrument. Like Perlman (among others), she relates this to the Tchaikovsky concerto, giving a performance of extremes, launching into the cadenza for example with rare fierceness. Not that her reading lacks inner qualities for, despite the close balance, the opening of the slow movement finds Mutter playing in rapt meditation on a half-tone. In the finale, taken fast, power is again the keynote. Previn proves a consistently sympathetic partner, drawing a committed performance from an orchestra not noted for playing Sibelius. The all-Sibelius coupling is apt if (at 49 minutes) hardly generous. In the two *Serenades*, Mutter at her most inspired beautifully captures the wayward, improvisatory quality, bringing out the quirky element too in the rather later *Humoresque* with its unpredictable resolution into a sort of wild waltz leading to a final cut-off ending.

Stern's 1969 recording has in the past been rather upstaged by the superb Heifetz version. Yet his performance can match that master in technical assurance. He plays with real passion yet, as the very opening demonstrates, there is no lack of feeling for the work's special atmosphere, and poetry is never in short supply, especially towards the close of the first movement. Ormandy provides a splendid accompaniment and the Philadelphia Orchestra matches Stern's virtuosity and warmth. The violin is forwardly placed, but the balance is much more satisfactory than some recordings from this source, while the remastering has greatly improved the sound: it has plenty of body and resonance.

Of the mid-price versions, Salvatore Accardo and Sir Colin Davis would be a first choice alongside Chung. There is no playing to the gallery, and no schmaltz – and in the slow movement there is a sense of repose and nobility. The finale is exhilarating, and there is an aristocratic feeling to the whole which is just right.

The raptness of Tasmin Little's playing is even more striking in the Sibelius than in the Brahms with which it is generously coupled. Her hushed and mysterious account of the opening theme leads to a performance that is both poised and purposeful, magnetic in her combination of power and poetry. Kyung Wha Chung's reading with André Previn may be more overtly passionate, but Little's is just as deeply felt, with an even wider tonal range, and her virtuosity culminates in an account of the finale in which, as in the Brahms, she finds an element of wit in the pointing of insistent dance rhythms. Throughout she is splendidly matched by the colourful playing of the R LPO under Vernon Handley.

Itzhak Perlman plays the work as a full-blooded virtuoso showpiece and the Pittsburgh orchestra under André Previn support him to the last man and woman. He makes light of all the fiendish difficulties in which the solo part abounds and takes a conventional view of the slow movement, underlining its passion, and he gives us an exhilarating finale. The sound is marvellously alive and thrilling, though the forward balance is very apparent.

Throughout, Nigel Kennedy's intonation is true and he takes the considerable technical hurdles of this concerto in his stride. There is a touch of the *zigeuner* throb in the slow movement, but on the whole he plays with real spirit and panache. This can be confidently recommended if the coupling with the Tchaikovsky, a rather more indulgent performance, is suitable. The playing of the Birmingham orchestra is excellent throughout as, indeed, is the E MI recording.

The purity and refinement of Vadim Repin's performance of the Sibelius are what strike one first. The withdrawn darkness at the very start quickly opens out thrillingly to reveal his total command, the tautness of his control, with tone sharply focused. Here is a young artist who, for all the brilliance of his virtuosity, regularly keeps a degree of emotion in reserve, his very restraint adding to the intensity. The speed in the finale is thrillingly fast, yet Repin with light attack brings out the scherzando element as well as the passion.

The magnetism of Neveu in this, her first concerto recording, is inescapable from her opening phrase onwards, warmly expressive and dedicated, yet with no hint of mannerism. The finale is taken at a speed which is comfortable rather than exciting, but the extra spring of the thrumming dance-rhythms, superbly lifted, is ample compensation, providing a splendid culmination.

Francescatti's account is stunning in its immediacy and impact. With Bernstein fully matching the intensity of his soloist this is a performance impossible to forget. Francescatti's richness of tone is immediately evident in the opening theme and dominates the impassioned reading of the slow movement. The snag is the brightly lit recording, made in the Avery Fisher Hall in 1963, which the remastering serves only to emphasize, with the solo violin artificially balanced well out in front, in a spotlight.

Dong-Suk Kang chooses some popular Scandinavian repertoire pieces, such as the charming Svendsen *Romance in G*, as makeweights. Although this version of the concerto is very fine, he is perhaps a little wanting – albeit only a little – in tenderness as opposed to passion in the slow movement, but there is splendid virtuosity in the outer movements. The orchestral playing is decent rather than distinguished. In the bargain basement, this enjoys a strong competitive advantage, but even if it were at full price it would feature quite high in the current lists.

Helped by a close balance and a full, rich and immediate recording, the Finnish violinist, Pekka Suusisto, barely twenty, gives a strong and passionate reading, very outward-going, lacking some of the meditative, inner qualities that others find but compensating in his volatile imagination. His speeds are on the broad side, but the urgency and concentration are never in doubt. With a Finnish conductor and orchestra too, the result is both magnetic and idiomatic. The playing is equally positive in the two Sibelius suites which come as coupling, with the popular outer movements of *Karelia* bouncy and swaggering and the central *Ballade*, longer than either, equally atmospheric. The exotic colours of *Belshazzar's feast* are then vividly caught.

Still in her teens when she recorded this well-tried coupling, Leila Josefowicz gives strong, positive readings of both works, with far fewer of the feminine nuances which make the rival discs of Chung and Mullova so affecting. If in the Sibelius there is less poetry and mystery, the composer's markings can be taken to suggest a fully lit world, not one of half-lights. She is fast and mercurial in outer movements, but – more controversially – broader than most others in the slow movement, using heavy vibrato. Sir Neville Marriner and the Academy, superbly recorded, provide ideally crisp and clear orchestral support, adding to the impact of the performance.

Although many first recordings have something special that stands out, the Heifetz/Beecham Sibelius

Violin concerto, marvellous though it is, excites admiration rather than affection. And despite Sir Thomas's direction, Heifetz gave the more powerful account of it in his later, Chicago recording with Walter Hendl in the early days of stereo. (The reverse was the case with the Glazunov.) A good transfer nevertheless, and well worth having.

(i; ii) *Violin concerto in D min., Op. 47;* (iii) *En saga, Op. 9;* (ii) *Finlandia, Op. 26; Karelia suite, Op. 11;* (iii) *Symphonies Nos. 1 in E min, Op. 39; 5 in E flat, Op. 82.*

(N) (BB) ** CfP Silver Double CDCFPSD 4763 (2). (i) Sarbu; (ii) Hallé O, Schmidt; (iii) SNO, Gibson.

Eugene Sarbu is a Romanian and was in his early thirties when he recorded the Sibelius *Concerto* in 1980. His vibrato is a little wide and intonation is not always impeccable, though he has plenty of dash and power. He makes the most of every expressive point and underlines romantic fervour rather than spirituality. His is a *zigeuner*-like approach without the purity and refinement of tone which are ideal – and which emerge in such performers as Cho-Liang Lin and Kyung-Wha Chung. There is a nobility in this music that Sarbu does not always convey. But he is well supported by the Hallé, who give Ole Schmidt sensitive and responsive playing, and they are heard to excellent effect in the *Karelia* and *Finlandia* encores. The recording too is excellent. The companion disc includes Sir Alexander Gibson's recordings with the Scottish National Orchestra of the *First* and *Fifth Symphonies*, recorded in 1973–4. As always, he shows a natural feeling for the Sibelian sound world, and these performances are both straightforward and refreshingly unmannered. Both interpretations are sound; neither is inspired, although both (and especially No. 1) make enjoyable listening when the recording is agreeably spacious.

(i) *Violin concerto in D min.; Symphony No. 2 in D, Op. 43.*
(Y/B) (BB) **(*) RCA Navigator Dig./Analogue 74321 17904-2. (i) Dylana Jenson; Phd. O, Ormandy.

Dylana Jenson is a young American violinist, born in 1961, who has the full measure of this concerto. She hardly puts a foot wrong anywhere and her account has all the sense of space, nobility and warmth that one could want. The virtuosity she commands seems quite effortless and is completely at the service of the music. Her tone is fine-spun and vibrant, and she communicates the sense of atmosphere and mystery in the opening to splendid effect. The violin is forwardly placed but naturally caught and the result is most satisfying. In Ormandy's 1972 account of the *Second Symphony* the sound is undoubtedly spacious, although the violin timbre lacks something in refinement because of the close microphones. But they play marvellously and the superbly disciplined response of the whole orchestra cannot fail to hold the listener. Although Ormandy's reading rarely sheds new light on this wonderful score, there is no doubt that the rich sweep of the Philadelphia strings in the big tune of the finale – underpinned by the power and sonority of the brass – is compulsive in its intensity.

(i) *Violin concerto in D min., Op. 47;* (ii) *Symphony No. 7 in C, Op. 105; Tapiola, Op. 112.*
(***) Ondine mono ODE 809-2 [id.]. (i) David Oistrakh, Finnish RSO, Nils-Eric Fougstedt; (ii) Helsinki PO, Beecham.

David Oistrakh's account of the *Violin concerto* has a marvellous strength and nobility, as well as an effortless virtuosity that carries all before it. His artistry inspires a warm response from the Finnish Radio Orchestra under Nils-Eric Fougstedt, who give magnificent support. There was always a special sense of occasion, too, at any Beecham concert and the opening of the *Seventh Symphony* is more dramatically intense and highly charged than his EMI commercial recording with the RPO. *Tapiola* also has great intensity, though the orchestral playing does not have the finesse, magic and tonal subtlety of the RPO recording. Subfusc recording, but a coupling well worth investigating all the same.

(i) *En Saga; Finlandia, Op. 26; Karelia suite; Legend: The Swan of Tuonela, Op. 22/3; Pohjohla's daughter, Op. 49;* (ii) *Symphonies Nos. 2 in D, Op. 43; 5 in E flat, Op. 22.*
(N) (BB) **(*) EMI Seraphim CES5 669134-2 (2) [CDEB 69134]. (i) VPO or BBC SO, Sir Malcolm Sargent; (ii) Sinfonia of L., Tauno Hannikainen.

Sargent's collection of short orchestral works is highly successful and a fine reminder of his affinity with this repertoire. Each performance has conviction and character, and the five pieces complement one another, making a thoroughly enjoyable CD programme. The Vienna Philharmonic bring a distinctive freshness to their playing of music which must have been unfamiliar to them and Sir Malcolm Sargent imparts his usual confidence. The brass is especially full-blooded in *En Saga*, a performance full of adrenalin (as is *Pohjola's daughter*, the one item featuring the BBC Symphony Orchestra). *Finlandia* sounds unhackneyed and, with brisk tempi, *Karelia* has fine impetus and flair. The recordings, made in the Musikverein in 1961 and Kingsway Hall in 1958, are remarkably full and vivid; one would never suspect their age from these vibrant CD transfers, of EMI's best vintage.

The second disc of this inexpensive Seraphim Double offers performances of two symphonies from

Tauno Hainnikainen (originally issued in the UK by the World Record Club), which made a strong impression when they first appeared. The *Second Symphony* is undoubtedly the finer of the two performances. The opening movement is extremely well knit, but it is the slow movement, with its sombre atmosphere and strength of linear feeling, that confirms Hanikainen's empathy for the Sibelian idiom, while the apotheosis of the finale is undoubtedly gripping. The interpretation of the *Fifth* is less telling. There is again a starkness of colour and atmosphere at the opening which is compelling, but the tension is not sustained evenly throughout and the very spacious finale is disappointing. Good, if slightly dry recording. An interesting reissue, especially at this modest price.

(i) *En Saga, Op. 9; Finlandia, Op. 26;* (ii) *Karelia suite, Op. 11;* (i) *Legend: The Swan of Tuonela, Op. 22/2; Tapiola, Op. 112.*
(M) **(*) EMI Analogue/Dig. EMI CDM7 64331-2 [id.]. BPO, Karajan.
(N) (BB) *** Belart 450 018-2 (without *Tapiola*). (i) SRO, Horst Stein; (ii) VPO, Maazel – GRIEG: *Peer Gynt.* ***

Karajan's *En Saga* is more concerned with narrative than with atmosphere at the beginning; but the climax is very exciting and the *lento assai* section and the coda are quite magical. *Tapiola* is broader and more expansive than the first DG version; at the storm section, the more spacious tempo is vindicated and again the climax is electrifying. *The Swan of Tuonela* is most persuasively done. These recordings date from 1977. The later, digital recording of *Karelia* has been added for the current reissue. Here, in the outer movements, which Karajan paces deliberately, the rather weighty bass detracts somewhat from the freshness of the presentation.

Horst Stein shows a gift for the special atmosphere of Sibelius, and these distinguished, exciting and poetic performances offer some of the finest playing we have had from the Suisse Romande Orchestra during the last three decades. Moreover Decca's 1972 recording approaches the demonstration class, especially in *En Saga*. Maazel's *Karelia* is also first rate.

En Saga, Op. 9; Finlandia, Op. 26; Karelia suite, Op. 11; (i) *Luonnotar, Op. 70; Tapiola, Op. 112.*
(M) *** Decca Dig. 430 757-2 [id.]. Philh. O, Ashkenazy, (i) with Elisabeth Söderström.

These are all digital recordings of the first order: Decca sound at its very best. The performances are among the finest available, especially *En Saga*, which is thrillingly atmospheric, while the *Karelia suite* is freshly appealing in its directness. The climax of *Tapiola* is almost frenzied in its impetus – some may feel that Ashkenazy goes over the top here; but this is the only real criticism of a distinguished collection and a very real bargain. *Finlandia* is made fresh again in a performance of passion and precision, and Elisabeth Söderström is on top form in *Luonnotar*, a symphonic poem with a voice (although some ears may find her wide vibrato and hard-edged tone not entirely sympathetic).

En saga, Op. 9; Karelia: Overture, Op. 10; suite, Op. 11; King Christian II suite, Op. 27; Legend: The Swan of Tuonela, Op. 22/2.
(N) (B) **(*) Carlton IMP Dig. PCD 2026 [id.]. New Finnish SO, Jan Engstrom.

Although there are finer individual performances available of all these pieces on record, none are more idiomatic, and the programme here makes for an enjoyable and generous 76-minute concert. The highlight is perhaps the *King Christian II suite*, with some particularly expressive string-playing, but *The Swan of Tuonela* glides in evocatively and both *En Saga* and *Karelia* have their share of colour and excitement. Vivid sound, only just short of the front rank.

En Saga, Op. 9; Scènes historiques, Opp. 25, 66.
*** BIS Dig. CD 295 [id.]. Gothenburg SO, Järvi.

Järvi has the advantage of modern digital sound and the Gothenburg orchestra is fully inside the idiom of this music and plays very well indeed. Järvi's *En Saga* is exciting and well paced.

Finlandia; Karelia suite, Op. 11. Kuolema: Valse triste. Legends: Lemminkäinen's return, Op. 22/4; Pohjola's daughter, Op. 49.
(M) **(*) EMI CDM7 69205-2 [id.]. Hallé O, Barbirolli.

Pohjola's daughter is extremely impressive, spacious but no less exciting for all the slower tempi. *Lemminkäinen's return* is also a thrilling performance. Overall, a desirable introduction to Sibelius's smaller orchestral pieces, with admirable stereo definition.

Finlandia, Op. 26; Karelia suite, Op. 11; Kuolema: Valse triste, Op. 44/1. Legends: The Swan of Tuonela, Op. 22/2. Scènes historiques: Festivo, Op. 25/3. Tapiola, Op. 112.
(N) (M) (***) DG mono 447 453-2 [id.]. BPO, Rosbaud.

Karajan was not the only champion of Sibelius's music in post-war Germany: Hans Rosbaud, the high priest of the Second Viennese School and the 1950s avant-garde, also included it in his repertory and indeed insisted on conducting the *Fourth Symphony* when he came to the BBC Symphony Orchestra, some months before his death in 1962. These recordings come from the mid-1950s and, although some allowance must be made for the mono sound, the performances themselves have the ring of conviction. The *Tapiola* is something special, among the most terrifying evocations of that dark Nordic forest, and worthy to keep company with those of Beecham, Koussevitzky and Karajan. *The Swan of Tuonela* is a little brisk, but it is not wanting in atmosphere. The *Alla marcia* of the *Karelia suite* is a bit sedate, heavy-footed even, but Sibelians will want this disc for Rosbaud's intensely cold *Tapiola*.

Finlandia, Op. 26; Karelia suite, Op. 11; Scènes historiques: Festivo, Op. 25/3; The Chase; Love song; At the drawbridge, Op. 66/1–3; The Tempest (incidental music): *suites Nos. 1–2, Op. 109.*
ⓒ (M) (***) EMI mono CDM7 63397-2 [id.]. RPO, Beecham.

Beecham's mono performance of the incidental music for *The Tempest* is magical – no one has captured its spirit with such insight. A pity that he omits the *Prelude*, which he had done so evocatively on 78s, though the last number of the second suite covers much of the same ground. The four *Scènes historiques* are beautifully done, with the most vivid orchestral colouring: *The Chase* is particularly delectable. No apologies whatsoever need be made about the sound here, though in the *Intermezzo* from *Karelia* (which has a 78-r.p.m. source) the quality is curiously crumbly at the opening and close: surely a better original could have been found. The *Alla marcia* is better, although no one would buy this record for *Finlandia*.

Finlandia, Op. 26; Kuolema: Valse triste, Op. 44; Legend: The Swan of Tuonela, Op. 22/2.
*** DG Gold Dig. 439 010-2 [id.]. BPO, Karajan – GRIEG: *Holberg suite* etc. ***

Coupled with Grieg, this is Karajan at his very finest in the early 1980s, and the remastered digital recording is impressively real and present, particularly in the languorous *Valse triste* and in *The Swan*, Karajan's third and final account on record, powerful in its brooding atmosphere. There is a touch of brashness in the brass in *Finlandia*, but generally this Berlin/Karajan partnership has never been surpassed.

Finlandia, Op. 26; Legends: The Swan of Tuonela, Op. 22/2; The Oceanides, Op. 73; Pohjola's daughter, Op. 49; Tapiola, Op. 112.
(M) **(*) Chandos CHAN 6508 [id.]. SNO, Gibson.

The Oceanides is particularly successful and, if Karajan finds even greater intensity in *Tapiola*, Gibson's account certainly captures the icy desolation of the northern forests. He is at his most persuasive in an elusive piece like *The Dryad*, although *En Saga* is also evocative, showing an impressive overall grasp. The SNO are at the peak of their form throughout these performances.

(i) 6 Humoresques, Opp. 87 & 89; 2 Serenades, Op. 69; 2 Serious melodies, Op. 79; Ballet scene (1891); Overture in E (1891).
*** BIS Dig. CD 472 (i) Dong-Suk Kang, Gothenburg SO, Neeme Järvi.

The *Humoresques* are among Sibelius's most inspired smaller pieces. They are poignant as well as virtuosic and have a lightness of touch, a freshness and a sparkle. The two *Serenades* have great poetic feeling and a keen Nordic melancholy. They are wonderfully played by this distinguished Korean artist, who is beautifully accompanied. The two orchestral works are juvenilia which predate the *Kullervo Symphony*. There are some characteristic touches, but Sibelius himself did not think well enough of them to permit their publication. All the violin pieces, however, are to be treasured, and the recording is top class.

King Christian II (suite), Op. 27; Kuolema (incidental music) *(Canzonetta; Valse romantique, Op. 62a/b; Valse triste; Scene with cranes, Op. 44/1–2); Scaramouche, Op. 71; Scènes historiques: suites Nos. 1, Op. 25; 2, Op. 66. Swanwhite (suite), Op. 54; The Tempest* (incidental music): *suites Nos. 1 & 2, Op. 109/1 & 2.*
(N) (B) ** Decca Double 448 267-2 (2) [id.]. Hungarian State SO, Jussi Jalas.

This is an attractive and inexpensive programme of lesser-known Sibelius, and it includes one real novelty in the ballet-pantomime, *Scaramouche*, composed during the First World War. As Sibelius's son-in-law, Jussi Jalas brings a special authority to this repertoire, but his Hungarian orchestra is not of the front rank. In *King Christian II* and *Swanwhite* the orchestral playing does not rise much above the routine (although in the former the *Elegy* is quite touching). The lacklustre recording does not help: the strings are a little wanting in body and richness of tone, and the wind playing is not distinguished. Jalas takes some of the *Scènes historiques* rather faster than did Barbirolli or Beecham; it must be assumed that this reflects the composer's wishes, but other versions are more convincing. The *Canzonetta* and *Valse romantique*, Op. 62, are two additional pieces that Sibelius wrote for a later production of

Kuolema. The *Scene with cranes* from the same play (Sibelius had an almost mystical feeling for cranes) lacks the final degree of poetic intensity. Jalas's performance of the incidental music from *The Tempest* is certainly idiomatic, yet again the last ounce of poetry and mystery eludes him. The recording is acceptable, but little more; the acoustic could be more open and the string-tone have more blossom.

King Christian II (suite), *Op. 27; Pelléas et Mélisande* (suite), *Op. 46; Swanwhite* (suite: excerpts), *Op. 54.*
*** Chandos Dig. CHAN 9158 [id.]. Iceland SO, Petri Sakari.

The *King Christian II* music is a winner, by far the best on record, and full of the most musical touches. It also includes the *Fool's song*, excellently sung by Sauli Tiilikainen, and a previously unrecorded *Minuet*. Although the *Pelléas et Mélisande* suite does not displace either Beecham or Karajan, it makes a useful alternative to either – and that is praise indeed. It has plenty of atmosphere and, though tempi are on the slow side, there is always plenty of inner life. The *Swanwhite* (five movements only) is attentive to refinements of phrasing and dynamics and at the same time free from the slightest trace of narcissism. Beautifully natural recording, warm and well balanced.

4 Legends, Op. 22 (Lemminkäinen and the maidens of Saari; The Swan of Tuonela; Lemminkäinen in Tuonela; Lemminkäinen's return).
*** BIS Dig. CD 294 [id.]. Gothenburg SO, Järvi.

4 Legends, Op. 22; The Bard, Op. 64; (i) *Luonnotar, Op. 70.*
(M) *** Chandos CHAN 6586 [id.]. SNO, Gibson, (i) with Phyllis Bryn-Johnson.

4 Legends, Op. 22; Tapiola, Op. 112.
(N) *** Ondine ODE 852-2 [id.]. Helsinki PO, Leif Segerstam.

Although Segerstam perversely ignores Sibelius's instructions about the order of the *Legends* (so, for that matter, did Salonen) this is of little moment, given the fact that collectors can easily re-programme the disc. The performances of both the *Legends* and *Tapiola* are first class and are infinitely preferable to the symphony cycle Segerstam recorded in Copenhagen for Chandos. This is now a first recommendation for the *Legends*, while *Tapiola* is the best since Karajan.

Järvi has the advantage of fine, modern digital sound and a wonderfully truthful balance. Järvi gives a passionate and atmospheric reading of the first *Legend* and his account of *The Swan of Tuonela* is altogether magical, one of the best in the catalogue. He takes a broader view of *Lemminkäinen in Tuonela* than many of his rivals and builds up an appropriately black and powerful atmosphere. The slight disappointment is *Lemminkäinen's homeward journey* which, though exciting, hasn't the possessed, manic quality of Beecham's very first record, which sounded as if a thousand demons were in pursuit.

Gibson, however, is at mid-price; he also offers sensitive performances of *The Bard*, which has fine atmosphere and delicate textures, and *Luonnotar*, where the soprano voice is made to seem like another orchestral instrument. The Scottish orchestra play freshly and with much commitment. *The Swan of Tuonela* has a darkly brooding primeval quality, and there is an electric degree of tension in the third piece, *Lemminkäinen in Tuonela*. The two outer *Legends* have ardent rhythmic feeling, and altogether this is highly successful. The recorded sound is excellent.

Rakastava (suite), *Op. 14; Scènes historiques, Opp. 25, 66; Valse lyrique, Op. 96/1.*
(M) *** Chandos CHAN 6591 [id.]. RSNO, Gibson.

Written for a patriotic pageant, the *Scènes historiques* are vintage Sibelius. In the *Love song* Gibson strikes the right blend of depth and reticence, while elsewhere he conveys a fine sense of controlled power. Convincing and eloquent performances that have a natural feeling for the music. Gibson's *Rakastava* is beautifully unforced and natural, save for the last movement which is a shade too slow. The *Valse lyrique* is not good Sibelius, but everything else certainly is. Gibson plays this repertoire with real commitment, and the recorded sound is excellent, with the orchestral layout, slightly distanced, most believable. At mid-price this is a specially desirable collection.

Scaramouche, Op. 71; The Language of the birds: Wedding march.
*** BIS Dig. CD 502 [id.]. Gothenburg SO, Neeme Järvi.

Scaramouche is scored for relatively small forces, including piano (not unlike Strauss's music for *Le bourgeois gentilhomme* of which one is perhaps reminded); at its best it reminds one of the luminous colourings of the *Humoresques* of five years later. A wistful, gentle and haunting score, slightly let down by its uneventful second Act. Sibelius did not think highly enough of the *Wedding march* to Adolf Paul's play, *The Language of the birds*, to give it an opus number but it is in fact quite an attractive miniature. The playing of the Gothenburg orchestra under Neeme Järvi is altogether excellent and so, too, is the BIS recording.

SYMPHONIES

Symphonies Nos. 1–7.
(M) *** Decca Dig. 421 069-2 (4). Philh. O, Ashkenazy.
(B) **(*) Decca 430 778-2 (3). VPO, Maazel.
(M) **(*) Chandos Dig. CHAN 6559 (3). SNO, Sir Alexander Gibson.

(i) *Symphonies Nos. 1–7;* (ii) *Night ride and sunrise;* (i) *The Oceanides; Scene with cranes.*
(M) **(*) EMI CMS7 64118-2 (4) [Ang. CDMD 64118]. (i) CBSO, (ii) Philh. O, Simon Rattle.

Symphonies Nos. 1–7; (i) *Luonnotar. Pohjola's daughter.*
(N) (M) **(*) Sony SX4K 64207 (4) [id.]. NYPO, Leonard Bernstein; (i) with Phyllis Curtin.

Ashkenazy's Sibelius series makes a rich and strong, consistently enjoyable cycle. Ashkenazy by temperament brings out the expressive warmth, colour and drama of the composer rather than his Scandinavian chill, reflecting perhaps his Slavonic background. The recordings are full and rich as well as brilliant, most of them of demonstration quality, even though they date from the early digital period. On four CDs at mid-price, the set makes a most attractive first recommendation.

Simon Rattle's performances with the City of Birmingham Symphony Orchestra are available both as a four-CD boxed set and as individual discs. The best advice is probably to opt for the individual disc for the *Fourth* and *Sixth*, coupled together. They are both impressive, as is his *Seventh*, coupled with the *Fifth* and the highly atmospheric *Scene with cranes*. As a set the box is worth considering, but it would not be first choice.

By far the best of Maazel's performances are the *First* and *Fourth Symphonies*. The *Seventh Symphony*, too, is another landmark in the Sibelius discography and has great majesty and breadth. The *Second* is also successful, but the *Fifth* and, more particularly, the *Sixth* do not come off as well. He sounds uninvolved in both works: the *Third* has a very good first movement but a faster-than-ideal second. The Decca analogue sound is excellent and is vividly transferred, and readers need not hesitate on that score.

Sir Alexander Gibson's Sibelius cycle is impressive, both musically and from an engineering point of view; there are no weak spots anywhere. (Indeed, one respected critic chose Gibson's version of No. 1 as his first choice on a BBC 'Record Review' some years ago.) At the same time it must be conceded that the peaks do not dwarf, say, the Maazel *Fourth* or *Seventh*. The performances are eminently sane, sound and reliable, and no one investing in the set is likely to be at all disappointed. Taken individually, none would be an absolute first choice.

Bernstein recorded his New York cycle between 1961 and 1967 and, whatever their failings, they are performances of stature. His *Second Symphony* is marvellously full-blooded and has even been compared with that of his mentor, Koussevitzky. The *First* is also impassioned and powerful. The *Third* is well paced (far superior to Maazel's, also made in the mid-1960s) and his *Pohjola's daughter* one of the very best accounts of this masterpiece. The only let-down is *Luonnotar*, which is very fast and needs just a little more sense of mystery. Phyllis Curtin is not perhaps the most alluring soloist either. His *Fifth* is marvellously paced and has a sense of exhilaration and majesty, and his *Seventh* is also powerful. In his masterly survey of the symphonies on record, Guy Thomas speaks of them as being worthy of Koussevitzky, on whose Sibelius Bernstein would have been brought up. His *Fourth* has much to commend it too, though he uses some bizarre-sounding tubular bells in the finale. Bernstein aspired to a 'juicy, fat' tone (his own words) in Sibelius, which is perhaps less suited to the *Sixth*. None of these performances is negligible: Nos. 5 and 7 are marvellous, and the Sony engineers have done wonders in improving the sound. All the recordings show a great improvement over their LP originals in terms of spaciousness and tonal warmth.

Symphonies Nos. 1 in E min., Op. 39; 2 in D, Op. 43; 4 in A min., Op. 63; 5 in E flat, Op. 82.
(Y/B) (B) *** Ph. Duo 446 157-2 (2) [id.]. Boston SO, Sir Colin Davis.

Symphonies Nos. 3 in C, Op. 52; 6 in D min., Op. 104; 7 in C, Op. 105; (i) *Violin concerto in D min., Op. 47. Finlandia, Op. 26; Legends: The swan of Tuonela, Op. 22/2; Tapiola, Op. 112.*
(Y/B) (B) *** Ph. Duo 446 160-2 (2) [id.]. (i) Salvatore Accardo; Boston SO, Sir Colin Davis.

Sir Colin Davis's set of the symphonies, recorded during the second half of the 1970s, is undoubtedly among the finest of the collected editions, and now it is not only the least expensive (offered for the cost of two premium-price CDs) but three tone-poems and an estimable account of the *Violin concerto* are thrown in for good measure. Indeed Accardo's performance of the latter is very high on the recommended list. *Tapiola*, too, is atmospheric and superbly played. In terms of sheer mystery and power it stands among the best. Davis's feeling for Sibelius is usually matched by the orchestral response. Nos. 1, 2, 5 and 7 were the first to be recorded, in 1975/6. The idiomatic playing Davis secures from the Boston orchestra is immediately apparent. Tempi are well judged and there is a genuine sense of commitment and power. The recording is not quite as fine as Ashkenazy's on Decca. However, the remastering has undoubtedly improved the overall depth of acoustic. Davis's accounts of the *Third, Fourth* and *Sixth Symphonies* are among the finest on disc and they are excellently recorded. In the *Third* Davis judges the tempi in all three movements to perfection; no conductor has captured the elusive spirit of the slow movement or the power of the finale more effectively. The *Fourth* is arguably the finest of the cycle; there is a powerful sense of mystery, and the slow movement in particular conveys the feeling of communication with nature that lies at the heart of its inspiration. The *Fifth* is a little lacking in atmosphere; it is no match for Karajan. Here Davis is idiomatic and unfussy, as in the *Seventh.* Moreover the recording of these two works is again slightly two-dimensional, although this is less noticeable now than it was on LP. The *Sixth* is altogether more impressive and much more vivid as sound.

Symphonies Nos. 1–4.
(N) (B) *** EMI forte Dig. CZS5 68643-2 (2). Helsinki PO, Berglund.

This is a very impressive set and first-class value as an EMI forte double. Berglund's rugged, sober but powerful readings bring a good feeling for the architecture of the music and no want of atmosphere. Both the playing and the interpretation of the *First* are involving in their breadth and concentration (even if in the first movement the climactic timpani echo of the main theme does not come through). In the *Second*, Berglund is scrupulously faithful to the letter of the score as well as to its spirit, and the build-up to the climax just before the restatement is magnificently handled. The slow movement also comes off well and its contrasting moods are effectively characterized. The Scherzo and finale are of a lower voltage than the finest versions. The Helsinki Philharmonic respond with no mean virtuosity and panache, but the last degree of intensity eludes them. In the *Third*, Berglund adopts sensible tempi throughout and shapes all three movements well; he evokes a haunting feeling of tranquillity in the withdrawn middle section of the slow movement, a passage where Sibelius seems to be listening to quiet voices from another planet. This was Berglund's third account of the *Fourth* and it is a performance of considerable stature: it has a stark grandeur that resonates in the mind, while the slow movement combines brooding power with poetic feeling. There are one or two other things worth noting: the first movement possesses a mystery in its development that eludes him, but the opening is marvellous in Berglund's hands. There is not a great deal of *vivace* in the second movement (Ashkenazy gets the tempo of this movement absolutely right) but Berglund's finale is superb, even if some may find the closing bars not sufficiently cold and bleak. The digital recording throughout the set is excellent.

Symphonies Nos. 1–3; 5; Belshazzar's Feast (incidental music), Op. 51; Karelia suite; Pohjola's daughter, Op. 49; Tapiola, Op. 112.
(N) (M) (***) Finlandia/Warner mono 4509 95882-2 (3). LSO, Robert Kajanus.

When the Finnish government sponsored recordings of the first two symphonies in 1930, Sibelius insisted on having Kajanus as the most authentic interpreter. These performances were all made in 1930 and 1932 and sound amazingly good for the period. The celebrated storm in *Tapiola*, taken at a much slower and more effective tempo than is now usual, still has the power to terrify despite the inevitable sonic limitations, and no conductor has ever given a more spell-binding and atmospheric account of the suite from *Belshazzar's Feast*. The broader, more leisurely view Kajanus takes of the *Third Symphony* comes as a refreshing corrective to the later, more hurried accounts by Anthony Collins and Lorin Maazel. No performer, save Beecham in the *Fourth* and *Sixth* symphonies, came closer to Sibelius's intentions. Essential listening for all Sibelians.

Symphony No. 1 in E min., Op. 39.
**(*) DG Dig. 435 351-2 [id.]. VPO, Bernstein.

Symphony No. 1 in E min.; Finlandia, Op. 26; Karelia suite, Op. 11.
⊛ *** EMI Dig. CDC7 542732 [id.]. Oslo PO, Mariss Jansons.

Symphony No. 1 in E min.; The Oceanides.
(M) **(*) EMI Dig. CDM7 64119-2 [id.]. CBSO, Simon Rattle.

Mariss Jansons's account of the *First Symphony* is the finest to have appeared since Maazel's in the 1960s. The Oslo Philharmonic is on peak form, playing with thrilling virtuosity both in the *Symphony* and *Finlandia* and in the *Karelia suite*. Tempi are well judged, the players are responsive to every dynamic nuance, phrasing is beautifully shaped and the overall architecture of the piece is splendidly realized. A very exciting performance, which has you on the edge of your seat, and very vividly recorded too.

If the whole symphony was as fine as the first movement in Rattle's hands, this would be a clear first recommendation. He has a powerful grasp of both its structure and character. The slow movement is for the most part superb, but he makes too much of the commas at the end of the movement, which are so exaggerated as to be disruptive. The Scherzo has splendid character but is a good deal slower than the marking. *The Oceanides* has an atmosphere that is altogether ethereal. Simon Rattle has its measure and conveys all its mystery and poetry.

Leonard Bernstein gets some electrifying playing from the Vienna Philharmonic and he is superbly recorded at live concerts in the Grosser Saal of the Musikverein in February 1990. Of course there is some expressive self-indulgence, but this is by far the best of Bernstein's recent Sibelius cycle with the Vienna orchestra. However, uncoupled and at full price with only 40 minutes of playing time, it is uncompetitive.

Symphonies Nos. 1 in E min.; 3 in C, Op. 52.
(Y/B) (***) Testament mono SBT 1049 [id.]. Philh. O, Kletzki.

Kletzki's account of the *First Symphony* has never been reissued since it was issued on mono LP in 1954, while his *Third Symphony* has never appeared before in the UK. It is very different in approach from the Anthony Collins LP, which takes a somewhat racy view of both the first and second movements. Kletzki is tauter than the traditional Kajanus school yet far less headlong (or headstrong) than Collins. In both scores he and the Philharmonia Orchestra strike the right balance between the romantic legacy of the nineteenth century and the more severe climate of the twentieth. The recordings are beautifully balanced and have great warmth, and they come up splendidly in these transfers. A valuable addition to the Sibelius compact discography and strongly recommended.

Symphonies Nos. 1 in E min.; 5 in E flat, Op. 82.
(N) (BB) ** RCA Navigator 74321 24216-2. Phd. O, Eugene Ormandy.

The sweep of the Philadelphia Orchestra is always commanding in Sibelius, but Ormandy's readings are flawed. He generates considerable intensity in the *E minor Symphony*, especially in the slow movement, but then spoils the finale by pulling right back at the reintroduction of the big string theme which forms the climax. Similarly in No. 5, while the opening movement is impressive, the concentration falters in the *Andante mosso*, and the work's closing pages bring an exaggerated broadening which, despite the body of tone commanded by his fine orchestra, fails to convince. The recordings (from 1978 and 1975 respectively) are resonantly spectacular, painting the orchestral textures with broad strokes of the brush.

Symphonies Nos. 1 in E min.; 7 in C, Op. 105.
(M) *** Decca Dig. 436 473-2 [id.]. Philh. O, Ashkenazy.
(N) *** Decca Dig. 444 541-2 [id.]. San Francisco SO, Blomstedt.
⊛ (***) Beulah mono IPD 8 [id.]. LSO, Anthony Collins.

Ashkenazy's digital coupling of the *First* and *Seventh Symphonies*, recorded in 1982 and 1984 respectively, is outstandingly successful; at mid-price, it will become a ready first choice for most collectors. The performance of the *First* is held together well and is finely shaped. Throughout, the sheer physical excitement that this score engenders is tempered by admirable control. Only at the end of the slow movement does one feel that Ashkenazy could perhaps have afforded greater emotional restraint, but the big tune of the finale is superbly handled. The recording has splendid detail and clarity of texture, and there is all the presence and body one could ask for, with the bass-drum rolls particularly realistic. The *Seventh Symphony* is also very fine. Ashkenazy does not build up this work quite as powerfully as some others do, but he has the measure of its nobility and there is much to admire – indeed, much that is thrilling in his interpretation. As in the *First Symphony*, the playing of the Philharmonia Orchestra, like the recording, is of the very first order.

To adapt a cocktail metaphor, Herbert Blomstedt and the San Francisco Symphony Orchestra give us Sibelius absolutely ice-cold and straight-up. Blomstedt is faithful to the spirit (and, mostly, the letter) of these scores, and the results that he and his players achieve are remarkably imposing. The *First Symphony* is one of the best we have had in recent years: it can be recommended alongside the Ashkenazy (Philharmonia) version. The *Seventh Symphony* has great strength – it is carefully built up, spacious and dignified; and in both symphonies there is no playing to the gallery. Good recorded sound.

There are those who (justly) count Anthony Collins's magnificent account of the *First Symphony* of 1952, with its haunting, other-worldly opening clarinet solo, as the finest ever put on disc, for the tension throughout the performance is held at the highest level. The electrifying climax of the first movement with the timpani thundering out the main theme is matched by the linear power of the apotheosis of the heart-warming tune of the finale. In between, the powerfully atmospheric *Andante* and the gripping Scherzo are perfectly placed in the overall scheme. The closely integrated *Seventh* is also well understood by Collins, and once again the closing moments of the symphony are drawn together very impressively. The Decca recording remains remarkably vivid and, if the fortissimos are more one-dimensional than we expect today and the massed violins could ideally be fuller, the brass certainly makes a fine impact. There is no lack of underlying fullness, and a little paring of the upper range works wonders. The comparatively rare *Karelia overture*, which was recorded later (1955), makes a brief bonus.

Symphony No. 2 in D, Op. 43.
(N) (M) *** EMI Dig. CDM7 69243-2 [id.]. BPO, Karajan.
**(*) Chesky/New Note CD-3 [id.]. RPO, Barbirolli.
(M) ** Mercury 434 317-2 [id.]. Detroit SO, Paray – DVORAK: *Symphony No. 9 (From the New World)*.
***

Symphony No. 2 in D; Andante festivo; Kuolema: Valse triste, Op. 44/1; Legend: The Swan of Tuonela, Op. 22/2.
*** EMI Dig. CDC7 54804-2 [id.]. Oslo PO, Jansons.

Symphony No. 2 in D; Finlandia, Op. 26; Karelia suite, Op. 11.
(M) *** Decca Dig. 430 737-2 [id.]. Philh. O, Ashkenazy.

Symphony No. 2 in D; Finlandia, Op. 26; Kuolema: Valse triste, Op. 44/1; Romance in C, Op. 42.
*** Decca Dig. 436 566-2 [id.]. Boston SO, Ashkenazy.

Symphony No. 2 in D; Finlandia, Op. 26; Pohjola's daughter, Op. 49; The Swan of Tuonela, Op. 22/2.
(M) (**(*)) RCA mono GD 60294 [09026 60294]. NBC SO, Toscanini.

(i) *Symphony No. 2 in D;* (ii) *Karelia suite, Op. 11.*
(N) (B) **(*) DG Classikon 439 499-2 [id.]. (i) BPO; (ii) Helsinki RSO; Okko Kamu.

Symphony No. 2 in D; Romance for strings in C, Op. 42.
*** BIS Dig. CD 252 [id.]. Gothenburg SO, Järvi.

A very well shaped performance from Ashkenazy in Boston. There is an impressive sense of line throughout and yet no feeling that Sibelius's muse is held on too taut a rein. On the contrary, the first and second movements succeed in conveying a real sense of relaxation as well as excitement. Ashkenazy's approach to the first movement is more measured than earlier maestros (Kajanus, Beecham – and, in more recent times, Järvi). However, many paths lead to the truth and Ashkenazy's performance is even finer than his earlier account for Decca. It is musically very satisfying – and recorded in a very natural concert-hall perspective. The Boston strings respond very ardently but with aristocratic poise in the *Romance in C* and in the remaining works in the programme. Strongly recommended.

Even in a highly competitive field the Oslo Philharmonic account of the *Second Symphony* under Mariss Jansons is a force to be reckoned with. If it lacks something of the high voltage that charged his reading of the *First Symphony*, it has no lack of excitement; it is superbly controlled and tautly held together, with no playing to the gallery in the finale. There is an aristocratic feel to it, and this extends to *The Swan* and the *Andante festivo*, which is distinguished by string playing of great intensity. Jansons whips *Valse triste* into something of a frenzy towards the climax, but elsewhere these performances are totally free from exaggeration. Excellent recording.

Järvi is very brisk in the opening *Allegretto*: this Gothenburg version has more sinew and fire than its rivals, and the orchestral playing is more responsive and disciplined than that of the SNO on Chandos (see below). Throughout, Järvi has an unerring sense of purpose and direction and the momentum never slackens. Of course, there is not the same opulence as with the Boston Symphony under Ashkenazy on EMI, but the BIS performance is concentrated in feeling and thoroughly convincing. The *Romance for strings* is attractively done.

Karajan's 1981 digital version with the Berlin Philharmonic is more spacious than his earlier reading with the Philharmonia. Tempi in all four movements are fractionally broader; nevertheless the first movement is still a genuine *Allegretto* – basically in the brisker tradition of Kajanus, whose pioneering (1930) records were probably closer to Sibelius's intentions than most others. Throughout all four movements there is splendour and nobility here – and some glorious sounds from the Berlin brass. The oboe theme in the trio section of the Scherzo is moulded most expressively, but not all listeners will warm to the grand and measured approach to the finale, though there is no loss of lyrical fervour. It is not as beautifully recorded as the Ashkenazy, but it is undoubtedly a performance of stature. However, without a filler this record is very short measure, even at mid-price.

On Decca, Ashkenazy's control of tension and atmosphere makes for the illusion of live performance in the building of each climax, and the rich digital sound adds powerfully to that impression. Ashkenazy's performances of *Finlandia* and the *Karelia suite* are as fine as any and, like the symphony, are afforded first-class Decca sound.

Barbirolli's version with the RPO is a performance of stature and is by far the finest of the four versions he committed to disc. There is a thrilling sense of live music-making here and a powerful sense of momentum. A high-voltage account, then, and very well recorded, though the upper strings are slightly drier than they were in the LP version on RCA. It retails at full price, which reduces its competitiveness, particularly as it comes without a fill-up.

The Berlin Philharmonic give Kamu excellent support and rich sonority in his 1970 account of the *Second Symphony*, recorded not long after he won the Karajan conducting competition. One or two minor exaggerations apart, he gives a straightforward and dedicated account of the work. However, Karajan's EMI version, recorded with the same orchestra a decade later, is finer in every respect and is to be preferred in spite of the addition to the DG reissue of a fill-up in the form of the *Karelia suite*, expertly played though it is by the Helsinki Radio Orchestra. Nevertheless at bargain price Kamu's disc is undoubtedly value for money.

Three recordings of the *Second Symphony* survive from Toscanini's baton: one from his BBC season in 1938, a second from 1939 and the present issue from 1940. All offer some superb playing but are a shade hard-driven. The account of *Pohjola's daughter* is arguably the most powerful and exciting ever committed to disc and in its elemental power even surpasses Kajanus and Koussevitzky.

Paray's account has plenty of tension – indeed one is immediately gripped by the excitement of the opening movement. The *Andante*, however, does not bring enough contrast and its histrionics seem episodic. The Scherzo has great energy and the finale develops a full head of steam, but overall, in spite of excellent early (1959) Mercury stereo, this reading with its impulsiveness fails to create the feeling of an organic whole.

Symphonies Nos. 2 in D; 3 in C, Op. 52.
(M) *** EMI CDM7 64120-2 [id.]. CBSO, Simon Rattle.

In No. 2 the CBSO play with fervour and enthusiasm except, perhaps, in the first movement where the voltage is lower – particularly in the development, which is not easy to bring off; however, the transition to the finale is magnificent and Rattle finds the *tempo giusto* in this movement. The Birmingham strings produce a splendidly fervent unison both here and elsewhere. Rattle's account of the *Third* is vastly superior to his *First* and *Second*. The slow movement is particularly fine; few have penetrated its landscape more completely, and the movement throughout is magical. The way in which he gradually builds up the finale is masterly and sure of instinct. The recording, made in the Warwick Arts Centre, sounds very well balanced, natural in perspective and finely detailed.

Symphonies Nos. 2 in D; 5 in E flat, Op. 82.
(M) *** Chandos Dig. CHAN 6556 [id.]. SNO, Sir Alexander Gibson.

The *Second* is among the best of Gibson's cycle and scores highly, thanks to the impressive clarity, fullness and impact of the 1982 digital recording. Gibson's reading is honest and straightforward, free of bombast in the finale. Tempos are well judged: the first movement is neither too taut nor too relaxed: it is well shaped and feels right. Overall this is most satisfying, as is the *Fifth*, which has similar virtues: at no time is there any attempt to interpose the personality of the interpreter, and the finale has genuine weight and power.

Symphonies Nos. 2 in D; 6 in D min., Op. 104.
(N) *** RCA Dig. 09026 68218-2 [id.]. LSO, Sir Colin Davis.
(***) Beulah mono 2PD 8 [id.]. LSO, Anthony Collins.
(N) *(*) Sony Dig. SK 53268 [id.]. Pittsburgh SO, Maazel.

The *Sixth* is a work for which Colin Davis has always shown a special affinity and understanding. Its purity of utterance and harmony of spirit give it a special place in the canon. Sir Colin's earlier recording with the Boston orchestra (see above) was one of the best in that magisterial cycle, and this newcomer is if anything even finer. There is 'nothing of the circus' (to quote the composer's own words *à propos* the *Fourth Symphony*) in his reading of the *Second*, and no playing to the gallery. There is a grandeur and a natural distinction about the playing. If this cycle continues as it has begun, it promises to be a first recommendation.

The Decca sound in Collins's 1953 recording of the *Second Symphony* is fuller than in the *First Symphony*. The performance is superb, held together with a tension that carries the listener through from the first bar to the last. The closing pages of the finale, with the timpani again making a telling contribution, are particularly satisfying. The *Sixth* was recorded in 1955, and again the ear notices a further improvement in the sound, particularly at the radiant pastoral opening. The LSO play with much sensitivity, and woodwind and string detail is ever luminous; the conductor's special feeling for Sibelian colour and atmosphere is especially apparent in this work, with the beautiful final coda sustained with moving simplicity. Altogether a lovely performance.

Lorin Maazel comes into direct competition with the Davis/LSO coupling, and comparison is not to his advantage. The *Second Symphony* is overblown and inflated in the manner of his earlier Pittsburgh recordings of Nos. 1 and 7. In the slow movement he adds two minutes to his earlier timing with the Vienna Philharmonic, made for Decca in the 1960s, and nearly as much to the first movement. Not that statistics count for anything – one just longs for a sense of real momentum. The *Sixth Symphony* fares much better. It was the least admired of his earlier cycle. This is very much closer to the spirit of the score and there is relatively little point-making. The tempi are well judged and the wind players of the Pittsburgh orchestra distinguish themselves. All the same, this by no means a first choice.

Symphonies Nos. 2 in D; 7 in C, Op. 105.
(B) *** Sony SBK 53509; *SBT 53509* [id.]. Phd. O, Ormandy.

Ormandy was not so much underrated as taken for granted in an age which had the good fortune to have so many great conductors. The 1957 sound is far better than you might expect and the strings (and practically every other department) are much more sumptuous and responsive than they seem to be in Philadelphia nowadays. The *Second* gets a powerful (and, in the finale, rousing) performance, and the architecture is held together well throughout. The *Seventh*, recorded in 1960, is very impressive indeed: marvellously paced, intense and felt.

Symphony No. 3 in C; King Kristian II (suite), Op. 27.
*** BIS Dig. CD 228 [id.]. Gothenburg SO, Järvi.

With the *Third Symphony* there is a sense of the epic in Järvi's hands and it can hold its own with any in the catalogue. In Gothenburg, the slow movement is first class and the leisurely tempo adopted here by the Estonian conductor is just right. Järvi's coupling is the incidental music to *King Christian II*. This is very beautifully played and recorded.

Symphony No. 3 in C; Nightride and sunrise, Op. 55; Pelléas et Mélisande: suite, Op. 46; Pohjola's daughter, Op. 49.
(***) Beulah mono 3PD8 [id.]. LSO, Anthony Collins.

More outstanding performances from Anthony Collins: only *Nightride and sunrise*, although dramatically effective, is slightly less memorable than the other works here. The other reservation concerns the chosen tempo for the second movement, *Andantino con moto, quasi allegretto*, of the *Third Symphony*. Some listeners find it rather too fast, but the playing has much delicacy of feeling and texture; Collins's approach matches the whole reading, which has a strong momentum overall, and the build-up of tension to the work's climax is satisfyingly controlled. The account of *Pohjola's daughter* is among the most imaginative and colourful available, and the excerpts from the incidental music to *Pelléas et Mélisande* are beautifully played. All the recordings, except *Nightride* (1955), were made in the Kingsway Hall in 1954 and absolutely no apologies need be made for the mono sound, which in this admirable CD transfer is remarkable for its vivid immediacy and fullness.

Symphonies Nos. 3 in C, Op. 52; 5 in E flat, Op. 82.
(Y/B) *** RCA Dig. 09026 61963-2 [id.]. LSO, Sir Colin Davis.
(N) *** EMI Dig. CDC5 55533-2 [id.]. Oslo PO, Jansons.

Sir Colin Davis's account of the *Third Symphony* has a majesty and power that have few rivals. His *Fifth*, too, has tremendous grandeur as well as a feeling for the natural symphonic current that flows in these wonderful works. The recording has a splendour worthy of the music and the players. Both performances (and especially the *Fifth*) offer a marked advance on Davis's earlier, Boston versions – see above.

Mariss Jansons and the Oslo Philharmonic challenge Colin Davis and the LSO on exactly the same ground. It is a logical couping in that both symphonies include some of Sibelius's most innovative formal experiments, the finale of the *Third* and the first movement of the *Fifth*. The Oslo orchestra can certainly hold its own with the LSO in terms of beauty and weight of sonority. Their *Third* is wonderfully lithe and virile, though Sir Colin's broader tempo is perhaps better judged. But everything is marvellously alive and youthful. The *Fifth* is impressive, too, though the transition into the scherzo section of the first movement may strike some listeners used to Karajan, Sargent and Rattle's Philharmonia version as a shade precipitate. Strongly recommended – alongside but not in preference to Sir Colin's classic RCA version.

Symphonies Nos. 3 in C; 6 in D min., Op. 104.
(M) *** Decca Dig. 436 478-2 [id.]. Philh. O, Ashkenazy.

Vladimir Ashkenazy and the Philharmonia Orchestra give a first-class account of both the *Third* and *Sixth Symphonies*. In the first movement of the *Third*, Ashkenazy is a shade faster than the metronome marking, so there is no want of forward momentum and thrust, either here or in the finale. The tempi and spirit of the *Andantino* are well judged, though the withdrawn passage in the slow movement (at fig. 6) could perhaps have more inwardness of feeling; however, Ashkenazy is not helped by the balance, closer than ideal, which casts too bright a light on a landscape that should be shrouded in mystery. It is clear that Ashkenazy has great feeling for the *Sixth* and its architecture. There is no lack of that sense of communion with nature which lies at the heart of the slow movement or the sense of its power which emerges in the finale. Indeed this is possibly the most successful and technically impressive in the current Decca cycle, with the *Seventh* as a close runner-up.

Symphonies Nos. 3 in C; 6 in D min.; 7 in C, Op. 105.
(M) *** Chandos CHAN 6557 [id.]. SNO, Sir Alexander Gibson.

With three symphonies offered, some 74 minutes overall, this is a fine bargain and an excellent way to experience Gibson's special feeling for this composer. The SNO is in very good form. The first movement of the *Third* has real momentum. The *Andantino* is fast, faster than the composer's marking. Such a tempo, while it gives the music-making fine thrust, means that Gibson, like Collins before him, loses some of the fantasy of this enigmatic movement. But there is more here to admire than to cavil at. The *Sixth* is impressive too, with plenty of atmosphere and some radiant playing from the Scottish violin section; the *Seventh* has a rather relaxed feeling throughout, but it does not lack warmth and, as in No. 1, Gibson draws the threads together at the close with satisfying breadth.

Symphonies Nos. 4 in A min.; 5 in E flat, Op. 82.
*** Decca Dig. 425 858-2 [id.]. San Francisco SO, Herbert Blomstedt.
(M) *** Decca Dig. 430 749-2; *430 749-4* [id.]. Philh. O, Ashkenazy.
(***) Beulah mono 4PD 8 [id.]. LSO, Anthony Collins.
(N) ** DG Dig. 445 865-2 [id.]. BPO, Levine.

Blomstedt allows the music to unfold naturally and conveys a real sense of space. The *Fourth Symphony* has the intimacy of chamber music and yet communicates a strong feeling of the Nordic landscape. Blomstedt is particularly attentive to dynamic shading and gets playing of great tonal refinement from the San Francisco orchestra; no one makes the closing bars of the finale sound more affecting. The *Fifth Symphony* is also wonderfully spacious. Some may find the accelerando between the two sections of the first movement a shade steep, but there is a powerful sense of mystery in the development section.

Ashkenazy achieves great concentration of feeling in the *Fourth*. The brightness of the Philharmonia violins and the cleanness of attack add to the impact of this baldest of the Sibelius symphonies, and Ashkenazy's terracing of dynamic contrasts is superbly caught here. Like his other Sibelius readings, this one has something of a dark Russian passion in it, but freshness always dominates over mere sensuousness. The *Fifth*, too, offers Decca's finest Kingsway Hall recording, spacious and well detailed. The reading is a thoroughly idiomatic one and disappoints only in terms of the balance of tempi between the two sections of the first movement.

Collins's opening to the *Fourth Symphony* with its desolate, Nordic atmosphere is remarkably restrained, yet the work as a whole has extraordinary underlying intensity. With Collins, every phrase breathes naturally and the lightening of mood in the Scherzo, with wind and string playing of great delicacy, is merely an interlude, before the powerfully sombre feeling of the *Il tempo largo* gives birth to a climax of compulsive power. In the finale the flux of mood and feeling that comes with its surge of animation is handled with great subtlety. The performance of the *Fifth Symphony* carries all before it, with the reading moving forward in a single sweep. In both symphonies the LSO is marvellously responsive. The 1954/5 Kingsway Hall mono recordings were among the finest in terms of balance and truthfulness that Decca made throughout the mono LP era, and this CD reproduces superbly.

The severe, dark *Fourth Symphony* is rather beautified in Levine's hands, and he lingers all too lovingly over the first and last movements. The slow movement, too, evokes an exotic world that seems nearer Indonesia than Finland. The playing of the Berlin Philharmonic is superlative throughout. The *Fifth Symphony* is less overheated. Levine obviously has considerable feeling for this music, but he is not the ideal Sibelian.

Symphonies Nos. 4 in A min.; 6 in D min.
(M) *** EMI CDM7 64121-2 [id.]. CBSO, Simon Rattle.

Simon Rattle's account of the *Fourth* invokes a powerful atmosphere in its opening pages: one is completely transported to its dark landscape with its seemingly limitless horizons. The string-tone is splendidly lean without being undernourished and achieves a sinisterly whispering pianissimo in the development. The slow movement is magical and the finale is hardly less masterly. Rattle's account of the *Sixth* is almost equally fine. It is still a *Sixth* to reckon with and its closing bars are memorably eloquent.

Symphonies Nos. (i) *4 in A min.;* (ii) *6 in D min., Op. 104;* (i) *The Bard, Op. 64; Lemminkäinen's return, Op. 22/4; The Tempest: Prelude.*
⊛ (M) (***) EMI mono CDM7 64027-2 [id.]. (i) LPO, (ii) RPO, Sir Thomas Beecham.

In its colour Beecham's account of the *Fourth Symphony* reflects his feeling that, far from being an austere work, as is often claimed, it is ripely romantic. No performance brings one closer to the music, while the recording, made over fifty years ago, sounds astonishingly fresh and bleak in this excellent transfer, and there is a concentration, darkness and poetry that few rivalled. Beecham's 1947 account of the *Sixth Symphony* was said to be Sibelius's favourite recording of all his symphonies. Its eloquence is no less impressive. In the three shorter works on the disc Beecham's rhythmic sharpness and feeling for colour vividly convey the high voltage of Sibelius's strikingly original writing. *Lemminkäinen's homeward journey* is positively electrifying, while the *Prelude* to *The Tempest* is every bit as awesome an evocation of a storm as we had remembered. All these performances except the *Sixth Symphony* come from the late 1930s, but few allowances need be made, for they spring vividly to life in these remarkable transfers. Indispensable for all Sibelians.

Symphonies Nos. 4 in A min.; 7 in C; Kuolema: Valse triste.
⊛ (M) *** DG 439 527-2 [id.]. BPO, Karajan.

Karajan's celebrated 1965 account of the *Fourth Symphony* wears well. For many it remains the finest version of the *Fourth* on record, and it certainly ranks along with the Beecham as among the most insightful. The plush sonority of the Berlin Philharmonic at first deceives one into thinking that Karajan has beautified the symphony's landscape, but he comes closer to the spirit of the score than most others. (The symphony meant a great deal to him: he insisted on playing it alongside Beethoven in 1960 at his inaugural concert as the life-conductor of the orchestra at a time when Sibelius was held in the lowest esteem in Germany.) It is a performance of great concentration, deep thought and feeling. Although the new DG transfer of the recording does not have quite the body of violin-tone of the finest digital recordings, the acoustics of the Jesus-Christus-Kirche give weight and depth and a fine resonance to the bass. The performance is undoubtedly a great one. The *Seventh Symphony* is perhaps less successful though it comes off better than in Karajan's Philharmonia version, and the *Valse triste* is seductive. An indispensable record.

Symphony No. 5 (1915 version); *En Saga* (1892 version).
(N) *** BIS Dig. CD 800 [id.]. Lahti SO, Vänskä.

Not long after Sibelius's death, the orchestral material for the first version of the *Fifth Symphony* was discovered in the attic at Ainola. To reconstruct the actual score was a simple matter (RL was shown the score in the mid-1960s). However, Sibelius's heirs opposed it entering the public domain in the conviction that it would have been against the composer's wishes. The next generation have now reconsidered the position and have allowed BIS to proceed with a recording. It offers an invaluable insight into the workings of the creative process and is testimony to Sibelius's refusal to rest content until he had fully realized his vision. The work is in four (not three) movements, the opening horn-call is yet to be discovered; and there are no final hammer-blow chords. But there is much else that is different, and to study these differences offers an endless source of fascination. The *En Saga* we know comes from 1901, when it was extensively revised for Busoni to conduct in Berlin. There are some Brucknerian touches in one or two places, as there were in *Kullervo*, composed earlier the same year, and the orchestration is less expert. Totally dedicated performances which the orchestra committed to tape before the family had actually given permission to release (as opposed to record) them. An essential disc for all Sibelians, and magnificently recorded into the bargain.

Symphony No. 5 in E flat, Op. 82.
(M) *** EMI CDM7 64737-2 [id.]. Philh. O, Rattle – NIELSEN: *Symphony No. 4* etc. ***

Symphony No. 5; Finlandia; Kuolema: Valse triste. Tapiola, Op. 112.
(B) *** DG Classikon 439 418-2 [id.]. BPO, Karajan.

Such is the excellence of the classic Karajan DG *Fifth* that few listeners would guess its age. It is a great performance, and this 1964 version is indisputably the finest of the four he made. The fillers are familiar performances, also from the mid-1960s. *Tapiola* is a performance of great intensity and offers superlative playing; *Finlandia* is also one of the finest accounts available, but *Valse triste* is played very slowly and in a somewhat mannered fashion.

Simon Rattle's account of the *Fifth Symphony* with the Philharmonia was to the 1980s what Karajan's Berlin account was to the 1960s. It collected numerous prizes, even the *Deutscheschallplattenpreis* – and rightly! Everything about it feels right: the control of pace and texture and the balance of energy and repose. The development of the first movement has a compelling sense of mystery and the transition to the Scherzo section is beautifully judged. The Philharmonia Orchestra play splendidly and the EMI recording is very good indeed.

Symphonies Nos. 5 in E flat, Op. 82; 6 in D min., Op. 104; Legend: The Swan of Tuonela, Op. 22/3.
(Y/B) (M) *** DG 439 982-2 [id.]. BPO, Karajan.

Karajan's 1964 *Fifth* is already available on DG's Classikon bargain label, coupled with short orchestral pieces. The new mid-priced reissue is obviously even more attractive, coupled with his glorious 1967 account of the *Sixth*, which remains almost unsurpassed by more recent accounts. The brooding *Swan of Tuonela* is placed between the two symphonies and is played just as admirably by the Berlin Philharmonic on their finest form. The CD transfers are miraculously managed so that the recordings show little sign of their age.

Symphonies Nos. 5 in E flat; 7 in C; Kuolema: Scene with cranes. Night ride and sunrise.
(M) *** EMI CDM7 64122-2 [id.]. CBSO, Simon Rattle.

In the *Fifth Symphony* Rattle is scrupulous in observing every dynamic nuance to the letter and, one might add, spirit. What is particularly impressive is the control of the transition between the first section and the Scherzo element of the first movement. There is a splendid sense of atmosphere in the development and a power unmatched in recent versions, save for the Karajan. The playing is superb, with recording to match. The *Seventh* is hardly less powerful and impressive: its opening is slow to unfold and has real vision. With the addition of an imaginative and poetic account of the *Scene with cranes* from the incidental music to *Kuolema*, this is the finest single disc in Rattle's Birmingham cycle.

Symphony No. 7 in C, Op. 105; Canzonetta, Op. 62a; Kuolema: Valse triste; Scene with cranes, Op. 44; Night ride and sunrise, Op. 55; Valse romantique, Op. 62b.
*** BIS Dig. CD 311 [id.]. Gothenburg SO, Järvi.

Neeme Järvi and the Gothenburg orchestra bring great energy and concentration to the *Seventh Symphony*. The only disappointment is the final climax, which is perhaps less intense than the best versions. However, it is a fine performance, and the music to *Kuolema* is splendidly atmospheric; *Night ride* is strongly characterized. The recording exhibits the usual characteristics of the Gothenburg Concert Hall and has plenty of body and presence.

(i) Symphony No. 7 in C, Op. 105; Pelléas et Mélisande (suite): Mélisande; (ii) A Spring in the Park, Entr'acte, Death of Mélisande. The Tempest: Prelude; suites 1 & 2 (excerpts); Scènes historiques: Festivo, Op. 25/4; In memoriam, Op. 59; Legend: Lemminkäinen's Homeward Journey, Op. 22/4.
(Y/B) (M) (***) Dutton Lab. mono CDAX 8013 [id.]. (i) NYPO (ii) LPO; Sir Thomas Beecham.

Beecham's 1942 performance of the *Seventh Symphony* with the New York Philharmonic has greater power and tautness and its fires burn more intensely than either of his two other performances on CD. Beecham was not satisfied with it (probably the acoustic of the Liederkranz Hall in New York displeased him), and he sued Columbia for issuing it on 78-r.p.m. records without his clearance – and lost! In any event, it makes its first appearance on this side of the Atlantic. It is magisterial and splendid, and sounds magnificent in this transfer. The *Prelude* to *The Tempest* (also available on EMI) has never been surpassed in atmosphere and menace; nor have the *Oak-tree* and the *Intrada and Berceuse* been realized with greater poetry. *Festivo*, too, is a performance of great elegance and style. Whether Beecham's account of *In memoriam* has been equalled is a moot point, but what is incontrovertible is that his *Lemminkäinen's Homeward Journey* has not only never been surpassed but never equalled in its hell-for-leather abandon. These transfers succeed in making them sound more vivid and alive than they have ever done before.

Symphony No. 7 in C, Op. 105; Pelléas et Mélisande: Mélisande. Op. 46/2.
(Y/B) (**) Sir Thomas Beecham Trust mono BEECHAM 6 [id.]. NYPO, Beecham. – MENDELSSOHN:
    Symphony No. 4; TCHAIKOVSKY: *Capriccio italien.* (**)

This is the same recording as that included on the Dutton Laboratory reissue listed above. Sibelians will want to give priority to the former, as it contains material that has not been available since the days of 78-r.p.m. records. It is moreover by far the better transfer. The other two performances, of the *Italian Symphony* and the *Capriccio italien*, are both from 1942 and are of considerable but not necessarily compelling interest. The Tchaikovsky is certainly worth hearing. The recording is opaque but perfectly acceptable for its period.

Tapiola, Op. 112.
(Y/B) (M) *** DG Dig. 445 518-2 [id.]. BPO, Karajan – NIELSEN: *Symphony No. 4.* ***

This is Karajan's fourth and undoubtedly greatest account of *Tapiola*, for he has the full measure of its vision and power. Never has it sounded more mysterious or its dreams more savage; nor has the build-up to the storm ever struck such a chilling note of terror: an awesomely impressive musical landscape; while the wood-sprites, weaving their magic secrets, come vividly to life.

The Tempest (incidental music), *Op. 109* (complete).
*** BIS Dig. CD 581 [id.]. Tiihonen, Passikivi, Hirvonen, Kerola, Heinonen, Lahti Opera Ch. & SO, Osmo Vänskä.
**(*) Ondine Dig. ODE 813-2 [id.]. Groop, Viljakainen, Hynninen, Silvasti, Tiilikainen, Op. Festival Ch., Finnish RSO, Saraste.

The familiar two suites from *The Tempest* plus the *Prelude* have been recorded many times (most notably and magically by Sir Thomas Beecham) but Sibelius's original score for the 1926 Copenhagen production of Shakespeare's play is extensive: it runs to some 34 numbers in all for soloists, mixed chorus, harmonium and orchestra, and takes about 65 minutes. There are some unfamiliar effects here: the muted strings with which we are familiar in the *Berceuse* were an afterthought. In the original, their music is allotted to the harmonium; and although this is at first startling, the effect is other-worldly in a completely unexpected way. There are other master-strokes that are missing (the insinuating bass clarinet in *The Oak-tree*) but much else that will be new. The *Chorus of the winds* with a real chorus is also quite magical – in fact the vocal writing is often highly imaginative – and the singers on the BIS CD are all good. The atmosphere is very strong and puts one completely under its spell. The BIS recording, though good, needs to be reproduced at a higher than usual level setting: some may find it too recessed and there is at the bottom end of the spectrum a certain want of transparency.

If clarity and definition are a first priority, the Ondine version under Saraste is the one to go for. There is good singing here, too, from Monica Groop, Jorma Hynninen and the rest of the cast. The performance is given in Danish (as it would have been in the 1926 version, rather than the Finnish text used by BIS). However, Saraste is nowhere near as sensitive as Vänskä and does not have his sense of mystery or atmosphere. His *Prospero* is too fast, almost routine by comparison with Vänskä, who draws the listener more completely into Sibelius's and Shakespeare's world. Both accounts are recommendable and either is to be acquired rather than none. But the BIS makes a clear first choice.

The Wood nymph (tone-poem), *Op. 15;* (i) *The Wood Nymph* (melodrama) (1895); *A lonely ski-trail; Swanwhite, Op. 54*.
(N) *** BIS Dig. CD 815 [id.]. (i) Lasse Pöysti; Lahti SO, Vänskä.

Sibelius composed *The Wood nymph* in 1894–5 when the four *Lemminkäinen Legends* were taking shape in his mind. It is a re-working of the melodrama written for two horns, piano and strings to accompany the recitation of verses by the mainland Swedish poet, Viktor Rydberg. It is a substantial piece, as long as *En Saga* or the *Seventh Symphony*, though not of comparable quality. Sibelius thought well enough of it to programme it alongside the *First Symphony* at its première in 1899, but he never revised it. It is stirring stuff and begins with echoes of the *Karelia* music and in places comes close to both the first of the *Legends* and *Lemminkäinen's homeward journey*. It improves with every hearing: its main ideas haunt the listener and are difficult to dislodge from the brain! *A lonely ski-trail* is slight, but *The Wood nymph* melodrama is imaginative and highly unusual. The original music to *Swanwhite* has some poetic ideas that did not find their way into the suite, though for the most part there is not a great deal that is unfamiliar. Superb playing from the Lahti orchestra under Osmo Vänskä, and spacious, impeccably balanced recording.

CHAMBER MUSIC

(i) *Piano quartet in C min.* (for piano, two violins and cello); (ii) *String trio in G min.; Suite in A for string trio;* (iii) *Violin sonata in F*.
(Y/B) *** Ondine Dig. ODE 826-2 [id.]. (i) Novikov, Quarta, Miori, Rousi; (ii) Söderblom, Angervo, Gustafsson; (iii) Kovacic, Lagerspetz.

These are all early and uncharacteristic works. The *Violin sonata in F major* (1889) shows Sibelius still under the spell of Grieg. Only three movements of the *Suite in A major* for string trio (1888) survive (these artists give us what remains of the fourth movement, a *Gigue*); and its companion, the *String trio in G minor*, is also unfinished. Only the *Lento* survives intact, though the disc also gives a realization of what remains of the sketches of two other movements. The *Quartet in C minor* for piano, two violins and cello is a set of variations from the composer's Vienna year, 1891. All this is largely uncharacteristic and, save for the opening of the *A major Suite*, offers few glimpses of the mature Sibelius. The performances are dedicated and beautifully recorded.

(i) *Piano quintet in G min.; Piano trio in C (Lovisa); String quartet in E flat.*
*** Finlandia FACD 375 [id.]. Sibelius Ac. Qt, (i) with Tawaststjerna.

(i) *Piano quintet in G min.; String quartet in D min. (Voces intimae), Op. 56.*
*** Chandos Dig. CHAN 8742; *ABTD 1381* [id.]. (i) Anthony Goldstone; Gabrieli Qt.

The *Piano quintet* is a long and far from characteristic piece in five movements. Anthony Goldstone and the Gabrielis reverse the order of the second and third movements so as to maximize contrast. The first movement is probably the finest and Anthony Goldstone, an impressive player by any standards, makes the most of Sibelius's piano writing to produce a very committed performance. The *Voces intimae Quartet* is given a reflective, intelligent reading, perhaps at times wanting in momentum but finely shaped. Good recording.

The early *Quartet in E flat* is Haydnesque and insignificant, and the *Lovisa trio*, so called because it was written in that small town in the summer of 1888, offers only sporadic glimpses of things to come. The *Piano quintet* is given a fine performance on Finlandia, and there is little to choose between it and the more expansive Goldstone/Gabrieli account on Chandos.

String quartets: in E flat (1885); *A min.* (1889); *B flat, Op. 4* (1890); *D min. (Voces intimae), Op. 56.*
(M) *** Finlandia/Warner Dig./Analogue 4509 95851-2 (2). Sibelius Ac. Qt.

The *A minor Quartet* proves a delightful surprise with something of the freshness of Dvořák and Schubert. Sibelius obviously had ambivalent feelings towards the *B flat Quartet* and discouraged its performance. Its second movement bears a slight resemblance to a theme from *Rakastava.* Both are well worth resurrecting even if they do not, of course, match the mature *Voces intimae quartet* in artistry. The playing of the Sibelius Academy Quartet is exemplary and the recordings good: three are digital; *Voces intimae* dates from 1980 and is analogue.

String quartet in D min. (Voces intimae), Op. 56.
(Y/B) (***) Biddulph mono LAB 098 [id.]. Budapest Qt – GRIEG: *Quartet;* WOLF: *Italian serenade.* (***)

A welcome transfer – the first on CD – of the 1933 pioneering *Voces intimae*, still unbeaten. It briefly appeared on LP (on the World Record label) and is newly (and well) transferred here by Ward Marston. Sibelians will need no reminders of its excellence – and the same goes for the couplings.

Music for violin and piano

5 Danses champêtres, Op. 106; Novellette, Op. 102; 5 Pieces, Op. 81; 4 Pieces, Op. 115; 3 Pieces, Op. 116.
(Y/B) *** BIS Dig. CD 625 [id.]. Nils-Erik Sparf, Bengt Forsberg.

Many of the items here, such as the delightful *Rondino* from Op. 81, are little more than salon music, but some of the others are rewarding pieces. Indeed the first of the *Danses champêtres* almost suggests the music to *The Tempest*, written at much the same time. Both the Opp. 115 and 116 pieces contain music of quality. As in the companion disc, Nils-Erik Sparf and Bengt Forsberg prove as imaginative as they are accomplished, and the only marginal criticism concerns the balance, which tends to favour the piano, whose tone sounds a little thick at the bass end of the aural spectrum.

2 Pieces, Op. 2 (2 versions); *Scaramouche: Scène d'amour. 2 Serious melodies, Op. 77; 4 Pieces, Op. 78; 6 Pieces, Op. 79; Sonatina in E, Op. 80.*
(Y/B) *** BIS Dig. CD 525 [id.]. Nils-Erik Sparf, Bengt Forsberg.

This CD offers the first recording of the 1888 versions of the *Grave* and the *Perpetuum mobile*, the two pieces which Sibelius assigned to Opus 2, together with the 1911 versions, in which the former was revised as *Romance in B minor* and the latter overhauled as *Epilogue*. The former bears a certain affinity to the slow movement of the *Violin concerto* and the prevalence of the tritone in the latter acts as a reminder that it was reworked in the wake of the *Fourth Symphony*. Exemplary performances of the later pieces, including *Laetare anima mea* and the 1915 *Sonatina, Op. 80.*

PIANO MUSIC

Autrefois, Op. 96b; 5 Esquisses, Op. 114; Finlandia, Op. 26; 8 Pieces, Op. 99; 5 Pieces, Op. 101; 5 Pieces, Op. 103; Valse chevaleresque, Op. 96c; Valse lyrique, Op. 96a.
(Y/B) *** Continuum CCD 1071 [id.]. Annette Servadei.

6 Bagatelles, Op. 97; Melody for the Bells of Berghäll Church, Op. 65b; 5 Pieces, Op. 75; 13 Pieces, Op. 76; 5 Pieces, Op. 85; 6 Pieces, Op. 94.
(Y/B) *** Continuum Dig. CCD 1070 [id.]. Annette Servadei.

10 Bagatelles, Op. 34; 6 Impromptus, Op. 5; 10 Pieces, Op. 24.
*** Continuum Dig. CCD 1058 [id.]. Annette Servadei.

6 Finnish folksongs; Kavaljeren; Mandolinato; Morceau romantique; Pensées lyriques, Op. 40; 10 Pieces, Op. 58; Spagnuolo; Till trånaden; Valse triste, Op. 44/1.
*** Continuum Dig. CCD 1059 [id.]. Annette Servadei.

Kyllikki, Op. 41; 4 Lyric Pieces, Op. 74; 2 Rondinos, Op. 68; Sonata in F, Op. 12; Sonatinas Nos. 1 in F sharp min., 2 in E; 3 in B flat min., Op. 67/1–3.
*** Continuum Dig. CCD 1060 [id.]. Annette Servadei.

By the exalted standards he set elsewhere, Sibelius's contribution to the keyboard seems limited in inventive resource. The *Melody* he wrote for the bells of Berghäll Church is slight but charming. There are some echoes of the *First Sonatina* in *Aquileja*, and pieces like *När rönnen blommar* ('When the rowan blossoms'), from the Op. 75 set, and *Berger et bergerette* have a certain charm. *Finlandia*, the *Valse lyrique*, *Autrefois* and *Valse chevaleresque* are all transcriptions of orchestral pieces. These were, of course, made when the piano arrangement served to give this music wider currency, a function long overtaken by the gramophone. No pianist, however imaginative and sensitive, could possibly convey the charm of *Autrefois*. The sonatinas attracted the admiration both of Kempff, who never recorded them, and of Glenn Gould, who did. Annette Servadei is a sympathetic and sensitive guide to this repertoire, and on the whole she is well recorded. She produces a wide range of keyboard colour and a good dynamic range. At times she is rather too closely observed by the microphone with a result that *forte* or *fortissimo* passages are insufficiently transparent. But on the whole the Continuum set makes a clear first choice in this repertoire.

Bagatelles, Op. 34; Barcarola, Op. 24/10; Esquisses, Op. 114; Kylliki, Op. 41; 5 Pieces, Op. 75; Piano transcriptions: *Finlandia, Op. 34; Valse triste, Op. 44.*
(N) (***) Ondine Dig. ODE 847-2 [id.]. Ralf Gothoni.

This is how Sibelius's piano music should be played – with the highest musical intelligence and imagination. Gothoni makes the most of every expressive gesture and every gradation of keyboard colour, without indulging in any exaggeration. This makes out a stronger case for Sibelius's piano music than almost any other. Unfortunately it is badly let down by the recording, which is reverberant and clangorous; the piano itself hardly sounds in ideal shape. The repertoire differs from Marita Viitasalo (see below) but, where they overlap, comparison is to Gothoni's advantage. A pity about the sound.

Kylliki, Op. 41; 2 Rondinos, Op. 68; 3 Sonatinas, Op. 67; Sonata in F min., Op. 12; Piano transcription: *Finlandia.*
(N) **(*) Finlandia Dig. 4509-98984-2 [id.]. Marita Viitasalo.

Good performances of *Kyllikki* and the Op. 67 *Sonatinas*, by general consent the finest of Sibelius's piano compositions. Marita Viitasalo is an idiomatic interpreter of this repertoire, though the rival survey by Servedai is marginally better recorded. But there is not much to choose between them, and readers can invest in the Finlandia anthology with reasonable confidence. Why do pianists insist on playing the transcription of *Finlandia*, which was made at the beginning of the century before the gramophone and radio had made it so readily accessible in its original form?

VOCAL MUSIC

(i) *Belshazzar's Feast* (complete score), *Op. 51; The Countess's Portrait (Grefvinnans konterfej);* (ii) *Jedermann (Everyman)* (incidental music), *Op. 83.*
(N) *** BIS Dig. CD 737 [id.]. (i) Passikivi; Lahti SO, Vänskä; (ii) with Lehto, Tiilikainen, Pietiläinen, Lahti Chamber Ch.

BIS is coming up with repertoire which is completely unknown even to keen Sibelians. All three works on this disc are new to the catalogue. The incidental music to Hugo von Hofmannsthal's morality play, *Everyman*, comes from the autumn of 1916, when Sibelius was also working on the second version of his *Fifth Symphony*. The score runs to 16 numbers and takes 40 minutes. Although it was written at the height of the First World War, the theatre was able to muster considerable forces, mezzo-soprano, tenor and baritone, mixed chorus, two flutes and clarinets, oboe, bassoon, two horns and trumpets, timpani, organ and piano, the latter designed to produce bell-sounds, supplemented in this recording by tubular bells. A lot of the music is fragmentary, wisps of sound; all of it is atmospheric and the best of it (the *Largo* section from track 12 onwards) finds Sibelius at his most inspired. The complete score for Hjalmar Procopé's *Belshazzar's Feast* brings us some seven minutes of extra music. The scoring is different from and less effective than the concert suite. There is, for example, no oboe in the original; the seductive descending oboe theme in *Khadra's dance* is assigned to the clarinet. *Grefvinnans konterfej* (*The Countess's Portrait*) is a short, wistful piece for strings which comes from 1906 and was originally designed to accompany a recitation of *Porträtterna*, a poem by the mainland Swedish poet, Anna-Maria Lenngren. Dedicated, sensitive performances from the Lahti Symphony Orchestra and excellent recording. An indispensable disc for admirers of the Finnish master.

Finlandia (version for orchestra and mixed chorus), *Op. 26; Homeland (Oma maa), Op. 92; Impromptu, Op. 19;* (i) *Snöfrid, Op. 29. Song to the earth (Maan virsi), Op. 95; Song to Lemminkäinen, Op. 31; Väinö's song, Op. 110.*
** Ondine Dig. ODE 754-2 [id.]. (i) Stina Rautelin (reciter), Finnish Nat. Op. Ch. & O, Eri Klas.

While most of Sibelius's songs are to Swedish texts, the choral music is predominantly Finnish. *Oma maa* ('Homeland') is a dignified and euphonious work and includes a magical evocation of the wintry nights with Aurora borealis and the white nights of midsummer. *Väinö's song* is an appealing piece which bears an opus number between *The Tempest* and *Tapiola* – though it is not really fit to keep them company. The performances and the recording are decent rather than distinguished.

Kullervo Symphony, Op. 7.
*** Sony Dig. SK 52563 [id.]. Marianna Rørholm, Jorma Hynninen, Helsinki University Ch., LAPO, Salonen.
(N) **(*) Chandos Dig. CHAN 9393 [id.] Isokosi, Laukka, Danish Nat. RSO, Segerstam.

Esa-Pekka Salonen's account of Sibelius's early *Kullervo Symphony* is gripping and held together tautly. The symphony put the composer firmly on the map in his native Finland and is an astonishing achievement, given the musically isolated world in which Sibelius grew up. It is amazing to think that it preceded the *Resurrection Symphony* of Mahler. Sibelius never allowed the work to be heard again after its first performances in 1892, but fortunately it escaped the fate of the *Eighth Symphony* and the score survives. Salonen's is its fourth commercial recording and the fourth in which Jorma Hynninen appears. It is arguably the best so far; it has a sweep and momentum that eluded Salonen's less-than-overwhelming Nielsen cycle. The Los Angeles orchestra, to whom this score must have been new, play with the enthusiasm of fresh discovery and Marianna Rørholm proves a worthy companion to the ubiquitous Hynninen. The first movement is taut, brisk and dramatic – very much as Sibelius's son-in-law took it at its first performance in recent times; the fifth is very imaginatively done, and only the fourth is perhaps a bit too fast, almost headlong.

Segerstam completes his Sibelius cycle with Sibelius's early symphony-cum-symphonic-poem, *Kullervo*, and gives what is for him an uncharacteristically straightforward account of this remarkable work. There are none of the idiosyncrasies that have proved so disruptive elsewhere. His soloists are good and both the playing of the Danish Radio Orchestra and the skill of their engineers are admirable. But this is not a first choice.

(i) *Luonnotar, Op. 70. Night ride and sunrise, Op. 55; The Oceanides, Op. 73.*
(M) **(*) EMI CDM5 65182 [id.]. (i) Gwyneth Jones; LSO, Dorati – NIELSEN: *Symphony No. 5.* **(*)

Gwyneth Jones's version of *Luonnotar* is powerful, though in no respect superior to the somewhat later Valjakka–Berglund. Dorati gives respectable, well-prepared accounts of all three scores, though neither his *Night ride* nor his *Oceanides* is a patch on Rattle's (or, in the case of the latter, Beecham's). All the same, the 1969 recording sounds very good; the coupling, Kubelik's version of Nielsen's *Fifth*, is a performance of some stature.

Songs

7 Songs, Op. 13; 6 Songs, Op. 50; 6 Songs, Op. 90; Resemblance (Likhet); A Song (En visa); Serenade (1888); Skogsrået (Wood-nymph) (1889); The Jewish girl's song (Den judiska flickans sång); (i) *The thought (Tanken) (1915).*
(N) *** BIS Dig. CD757 [id.]. Anne Sofie von Otter, Bengt Forsberg, (i) with Monica Groop.

We welcomed Anne Sofie von Otter's first recital (BIS CD 457), and this is hardly less successful. The Opp. 13 and 90 songs are all settings of Runeberg, Sibelius's favourite poet, but there are rarities such as *Skogsrået* ('The Wood-Nymph') – totally unrelated, by the way, to the melodrama and tone-poem of the same name which he wrote in the early 1890s – and never before recorded. Also new are the duet, *Tanken* ('The thought'), *Resemblance* and *A Song*. Von Otter and her partner characterize each song with the consummate artistry one expects from them, and the only possible reservation concerns the balance, which in some of the early songs favours the piano.

Songs: *Arioso; Autumn evening (Höstkväll); Black roses (Svarta rosor); But my bird is nowhere to be seen (Men min fågel märks dock icke); Come away, death (Komm nu hit, död!); The diamond in the March snow (Diamanten på Marssnön); Did I dream? (Var det en dröm); The first kiss (Den första kyssne); The girl returned from meeting her lover (Flickan kom ifrån sin älsklings möte); On a veranda by the sea (På verandan vit havet); Sigh, rushes, sigh (Säv, säv, susa); Since then I have stopped asking (Se'n har jag ej frågat mera); Spring fleets fast (Våren flyktar hastigt); To the night (Til kvällen).*

(Y/B) (M) *** Decca 440 492-2 [id.]. Kirsten Flagstad, LSO, Oiven Fjeldstad – GRIEG: *Songs* (with: Arne EGGEN: *Praise to the eternal spring of life (Aere det evige forår i livet); Eyvind ALNAES: *About love (Nu brister alle de kløfter); A February morning at the Gulf (Februarmorgen ved Golfen); A hundred violins (De hundrede fioliner); Yearnings of spring (Vålængsler); Harald LIE: *The key (Nykelen); The letter (Skinnvengbrev)* ***).

Some of the Sibelius songs here were orchestrated by the composer, but seven of them remained in their original form (voice and piano) until transformed, usually with great skill, by such arrangers as Jalas, Pingoud, Fougsted and Hellman. This recording, made in the early days of stereo, still sounds astonishingly good, and Sibelius-singing does not come like this any more! These classic performances, now reissued in Decca's Kirsten Flagstad Edition, give a magnificent impression of Sibelius's not inconsiderable range as a song-composer, and the addition of the songs by Grieg and other Norwegian composers will perhaps tempt the listener to explore further in this repertoire. The CD transfers are first class.

Songs with orchestra: *Arioso; Autumn evening (Höstkväll); Come away, Death! (Kom nu hit, död!); The diamond on the March snow (Diamanten på marssnön); The fool's song of the spider (Sången om korsspindeln); Luonnotar, Op. 70; On a balcony by the sea (På verandan vid havet); The Rapids-rider's brides (Koskenlaskian morsiammet); Serenade; Since then I have questioned no further (Se'n har jag ej frågat mera); Spring flies hastily (Våren flyktar hastigt); Sunrise (Soluppgång).*

*** BIS CD 270 [id.]. Jorma Hynninen, Mari Anne Häggander, Gothenburg SO, Panula.

Jorma Hynninen is a fine interpreter of this repertoire: his singing can only be called glorious. Mari-Anne Häggander manages the demanding tessitura of *Arioso* and *Luonnotar* with much artistry, and her *Luonnotar* is certainly to be preferred to Söderström's. Jorma Panula proves a sensitive accompanist and secures fine playing from the Gothenburg orchestra. In any event, this is indispensable.

Arioso; Black roses (Svarta rosor); But my bird is long in homing (Men min fågel märks dock icke); The diamond on the March snow (Diamanten på marssnön); Did I dream? (Var det en dröm?); A dragon-fly (En slända); Driftwood (Lastu lainehilla); The echo-nymph (Kaitar); Enticement (Fågellek); The first kiss (Det första kyssen); 6 Flower songs, Op. 88; Idle wish (Fåfäng önskan); Jubal; The Maiden's Tryst (Flickan kom ifrån sin älsklings möte); May (Maj); The North (Norden); Spring is flying (Våren flyktar hastigt); Swim, duck, swim (Souda, souda, sinisorsa); To evening (Illalle).

(N) ** Ondine Dig. ODE 856-2 [id.] Karita Mattila, Ilmo Ranta.

Although the Sibelius songs are at last gaining ground in the catalogue – though not, alas, in the concert hall – we are still lacking a comprehensive survey. The Finnish soprano, Karita Mattila, who won the very first Cardiff 'Singer of the World' competition in 1983, would on the face of it seem a good choice for this repertoire, but it has to be said that her vocal excellence – a trace of hardness apart – is not always matched by her powers of characterization. Comparisons, where they can be made, with such current rivals as von Otter and Groop, are rarely to her advantage. A qualified success, though; there are, of course, many songs – *Jubal* is one – that come off very well.

Arioso, Op. 3; Narcissus; Pelléas et Mélisande: The three blind sisters. 7 Songs, Op. 17; 6 Songs, Op. 36; 5 Songs, Op. 37; 6 Songs, Op. 88. Souda, souda, sinisorsa.

*** BIS Dig. CD 457 [id.]. Anne Sofie von Otter, Bengt Forsberg.

This lovely recital by Anne Sofie von Otter marks the start of a BIS project to record all the songs; if the remaining issues are as good as this, the set will be a distinguished addition to the Sibelius discography. Miss von Otter always makes a beautiful sound, but she has a highly developed sense of line and brings great interpretative insight to such songs as *My bird is long in homing* and *Tennis at Trianon*, which has even greater finesse than Söderström's. And what a good accompanist Bengt Forsberg is. The recording is good if a bit reverberant.

Diamanten på Marssnön (The diamond in the March snow), Op. 36/6; Drömmen (The dream), Op. 13/5; Flickan kom ifrån sin älsklings möte (The tryst), Op. 37/5; Höstkväll (Autumn evening), Op. 38/1; Kyssens hopp (The kiss's hope), Op. 13/2; Längtan heter min arvedel (Longing is my heritage), Op. 86/2; Lastu lainehilla (Driftwood), Op. 17/7; Näcken (The water-sprite), Op. 57/8; Narciss (Narcissus); Norden (The north), Op. 90/1; På verandan vid havet (On a balcony by the sea), Op. 38/2; Sången om korspindeln (Song of the spider), Op. 27/4; Souda, souda, sinisorsa (Paddle, paddle, little duckling);

Svarta rosor (Black roses), Op. 36/1; Teodora (Theodora), Op. 35/2; Var det en dröm (Was it a dream); Våren flyktar hastigt (Spring flies), Op. 13/4; Vilse (Astray), Op. 17/4.
(Y/B) ** Finlandia Dig. 4509-96871-2 [id.]. Tom Krause, Gustav Djupsjöbacka.

Tom Krause recorded two Sibelius song-recitals in his prime and, together with Elisabeth Söderström, included them all on five LPs in the late 1970s. The present CD, which contains two dozen songs, should not be confused with them. Krause was almost sixty when he made this disc and though, as one would expect from so intelligent an artist, his voice is in generally good shape, it does not have the freshness or the tonal bloom which distinguished his earlier recordings, and his vibrato is now wider at climaxes. He understands this repertoire as few others do, and his insights are as deep – as in the remarkably expressionistic *Teodora*. He is well supported by Gustav Djupsjöbacka, and the recording is truthfully balanced. It is to be hoped that Decca will restore their complete set within the lifetime of this book.

OPERA

The Maiden in the tower (opera). *Karelia suite, Op. 11.*
*** BIS Dig. CD 250 [id.]. Häggander, Hynninen, Hagegård, Kruse, Gothenburg Ch. and SO, Järvi.

The Maiden in the tower falls into eight short scenes. The orchestral interlude between the first two scenes brings us the real Sibelius, and the second scene is undoubtedly impressive; there are echoes of Wagner, such as we find in some of the great orchestral songs of the following decade. All the same, it lacks something we find in all his most characteristic music: quite simply, a sense of mastery. Yet there are telling performances here from Mari-Anne Häggander and Jorma Hynninen and the Gothenburg orchestra. Neeme Järvi's account of the *Karelia suite* is certainly original, with its *Intermezzo* too broad to make an effective contrast with the ensuing *Ballade*.

Simpson, Robert (born 1921)

Energy; Introduction & allegro on a theme by Max Reger; The Four Temperaments; Volcano; Vortex.
*** Hyperion Dig. CDA 66449 [id.]. Desford Colliery Caterpillar Band, James Watson.

The Four Temperaments is a four-movement, 22-minute symphony of great imaginative power, and ingeniously laid out for the band. Simpson played in brass bands as a boy and this is doubtless where he acquired some of his expertise in writing for them. *Energy* came in response to a commission from the World Brass Band Championships. The *Introduction and allegro on a theme by Max Reger* is awesome and impressive. Together with *Volcano* and his most recent piece, *Vortex*, this makes up his entire output in this medium. The Desford Colliery Caterpillar Band under James Watson play with all the expertise and virtuosity one expects, and the recording has admirable clarity and body, though the acoustic is on the dry side.

Symphonies Nos. 2; 4.
*** Hyperion Dig. CDA 66505 [id.]. Bournemouth SO, Vernon Handley.

Robert Simpson's symphonies are at last coming into their own. The *Second*, composed in 1956 for Anthony Bernard's London Chamber Orchestra, is one of the very best; its opening is one of Simpson's most mysterious and inspired ideas, lean and sinuous but full of poetic vision. The variation slow movement is one of the most virtuosic and remarkable exercises in the palindrome, yet such is the quality of Simpson's artistry in concealing his ingenuity that no one coming to it innocently would be aware of this. The *Second* is a work of enduring quality, music that is both accessible yet of substance. The *Fourth Symphony* is the more extended piece. Powerful and inspiriting music in totally dedicated performances by Vernon Handley, and excellent recording quality. Those coming to explore Simpson's symphonic world should start here, for both pieces show him at his most fully characteristic best.

Symphonies Nos. 3 (1961); 5 (1971).
(Y/B) *** Hyperion Dig. CDA 66728 [id.]. RPO, Handley.

Vernon Handley's new disc brings us the première recording of the *Fifth Symphony*, a work of striking power and range. It is combative and intense and enjoys at times an almost unbridled ferocity that enhances the admittedly few moments of repose. No admirer of the composer – and no one who cares about twentieth-century music in general – should pass these performances by, for it is music of a vital and forceful eloquence. Fine playing by the RPO under Handley, and exemplary recording.

Symphonies Nos. 6; 7.
*** Hyperion Dig. CDA 66280 [id.]. R LPO, Handley.

The *Sixth* is inspired by the idea of growth: the development of a musical structure from initial melodic cells in much the same way as life emerges from a single fertilized cell in nature. The *Seventh*, scored for chamber orchestral forces, is hardly less powerful in its imaginative vision and sense of purpose. Both scores are bracingly Nordic in their inner landscape and exhilarating in aural experience. The playing of the Liverpool orchestra under Vernon Handley could hardly be bettered; the recording is first class.

Symphony No. 9.
❊ *** Hyperion Dig. CDA 66299 [id.]. Bournemouth SO, Vernon Handley (with talk by the composer).

What can one say about the *Ninth* of Robert Simpson, except that its gestures are confident, its control of pace and its material are masterly? It is a one-movement work, but at no time in its 45 minutes does it falter – nor does the attention of the listener. The CD also includes a spoken introduction to the piece that many listeners will probably find helpful. It is played superbly by the Bournemouth Symphony Orchestra under Vernon Handley, and is no less superbly recorded.

Horn quartet (for horn, violin, cello & piano); Horn trio (for horn, violin & piano).
(Y/B) *** Hyperion Dig. CDA 66695 [id.]. Richard Watkins, Pauline Lowbury, Christopher Green Armytage, Caroline Dearnley.

The *Quartet for horn, violin, cello and piano* of 1976 is of unfailing quality and imagination, and its development magnificently sustained. The composer's command of large-scale musical thinking is much in evidence – but so, too, is his feeling for sonority. He draws some extraordinary sounds from these four instruments. In some ways this is one of his most deeply original and compelling works. The later *Horn trio*, written for Anthony Halstead, Frank Lloyd and Carol Slater, immediately pre-dates the *Ninth Symphony*. These are most impressive pieces, and the performances are completely dedicated and highly imaginative. Excellent recording too.

String quartets Nos. 1; 4.
*** Hyperion Dig. CDA 66419 [id.]. Delmé Qt.

The *First Quartet* opens in as innocent a fashion as the Haydn *Lark Quartet* or Nielsen's *E flat*, but the better one comes to know it the more it is obvious that Simpson is already his own man. The second movement is a palindrome (most modern composers do not know how to write forwards, let alone backwards as well) but its ingenuity is worn lightly. The *Fourth* is part of the trilogy which Simpson conceived as a kind of commentary on Beethoven's *Rasumovsky quartets*. Yet they live very much in their own right. Excellent performances from the Delmé, and fine recording too.

String quartets Nos. 3 and 6; String trio (Prelude, Adagio & fugue).
*** Hyperion Dig. CDA 66376 [id.]. Delmé Qt.

The *Third Quartet* is a two-movement piece. Its finale is a veritable power-house with its unrelenting sense of onward movement which almost strains the medium. Its first movement is a deeply felt piece that has a powerful and haunting eloquence. The *Sixth* is further evidence of Simpson's remarkable musical mind. The *String trio* is a marvellously stimulating and thoughtful piece. Dedicated performances and excellent recording.

String quartets Nos. 7 and 8.
*** Hyperion Dig. CDA 66117 [id.]. Delmé Qt.

The *Seventh Quartet* has a real sense of vision and something of the stillness of the remote worlds it evokes, 'quiet and mysterious yet pulsating with energy'. The *Eighth* turns from the vastness of space to the microcosmic world of insect-life, but, as with so much of Simpson's music, there is a concern for musical continuity rather than beauty of incident. Excellent playing from the Delmé Quartet, and very good recorded sound too.

String quartet No. 9 (32 Variations & fugue on a theme of Haydn).
*** Hyperion Dig. CDA 66127 [id.]. Delmé Qt.

The *Ninth Quartet* is a set of thirty-two variations and a fugue on the minuet of Haydn's *Symphony No. 47*. Like the minuet itself, all the variations are in the form of a palindrome. It is a mighty and serious work, argued with all the resource and ingenuity one expects from this composer. A formidable achievement in any age, and a rarity in ours. The Delmé Quartet cope with its difficulties splendidly, and the performance carries the imprimatur of the composer. The recording sounds very good in its CD format.

String quartets Nos. 10 (For Peace); 11.
*** Hyperion Dig. CDA 66225 [id.]. Coull Qt.

The subtitle, *For Peace*, of No. 10 refers to 'its generally pacific character' and aspires to define 'the condition of peace which excludes aggression but not strong feeling'. Listening to this *Quartet* is like hearing a quiet, cool voice of sanity that refreshes the troubled spirit after a long period in an alien, hostile world. The one-movement *Eleventh* draws on some of the inspiration of its predecessor. It is a work of enormous power and momentum. Excellent performances and recording.

String quartet No. 12 (1987); (i) String quintet (1987).
*** Hyperion Dig. CDA 66503. Coull Qt, (i) with Roger Bigley.

Robert Simpson's *Twelfth Quartet* is a masterly and absorbing score. His *String quintet* is another work of sustained inventive power. We are unlikely to get another recording, so this is self-recommending; but it must be noted that the heroic demands this score makes on the players keep them fully stretched. The intonation and tone of the leader is not always impeccable, but the playing has commitment and intelligence.

Piano sonata; Michael Tippett, his mystery; Variations and finale on a theme by Beethoven; Variations and finale on a theme by Haydn.
(N) *** Hyperion Dig. CDA 66827 [id.]. Raymond Clarke.

Although he is not a keyboard player himself, Simpson's piano writing is highly individual and he never writes against the grain of the instrument. The *Piano sonata* (1946) was composed before he encountered Nielsen's music and is a concentrated, craggy, powerfully argued piece, not obviously pianistic but bristling with challenges and difficulties. The *Variations and finale on a theme of Haydn* (1948) evince Simpson's lifelong interest in the palindrome (music that sounds the same when played backwards or forwards). The slow movement of Simpson's *Second Symphony* is a palindrome, and the theme he uses here (that of the minuet of Haydn's *Symphony No. 47*) also forms the basis of the mighty variations which comprise the *Ninth String quartet*. The short piece written for Tippett was a contribution to a birthday tribute. The *Variations and finale on a theme of Beethoven* are based on a little-known *Bagatelle*, WoO 61a, and were written by Simpson for Charles Burney's granddaughter, and with the present pianist in mind. The performances are authoritative and, apart from a certain over-resonance, the recording satisfactory.

Sinding, Christian (1856–1941)

Légende, Op. 46.
(BB) *** Naxos Dig. 8.550329 [id.]. Dong-Suk Kang, Slovak (Bratislava) RSO, Adrian Leaper – HAL-VORSEN: *Air Norvégien* etc.; SIBELIUS: *Violin concerto;* SVENDSEN: *Romance*. ***

Dong-Suk Kang plays Sinding's *Légende* with great conviction and an effortless, songful virtuosity. It is by no means as appealing as the Halvorsen and Svendsen pieces but makes a good makeweight for an excellent collection in the lowest price range.

Suite, Op. 10.
*** EMI CDC7 47167-2 [id.]. Perlman, Pittsburgh SO, Previn – SIBELIUS: *Concerto*. ***

Heifetz recorded this dazzling piece in the 1950s, and it need only be said that Perlman's version is not inferior. Such is the velocity of Perlman's first movement that one wonders whether the disc is playing at the right speed.

Sirmen, Maddalena Lombardini (1745–1818)

String quartets Nos. 1 in E flat; 2 in B flat; 3 in G min.; 4 in B flat; 5 in F min.; 6 in E.
(Y/B) *** Cala Dig. CACD 1019 [id.]. Allegri Qt.

Maddalena Lombardini was born in Venice and (with the aid of a scholarship) became a student at one of the *Mendicanti ospedale* (orphanages), the Italian ancestors of our present academies of music. She proved so talented that the governors sent her to continue her studies with Tartini and it was primarily as a violinist, in his view 'absolutely without equal', that she first made her reputation, although she also trained as a singer. Madame Sirman travelled through Europe as a successful virtuoso, and by 1771 she was in London playing at the concerts organized by Abel and J. C. Bach. When her style of fiddling became outmoded (as speed came to be considered more desirable than polish and elegance), she turned to singing and secured a well-paid five-year appointment at the Dresden Opera, then moving on to St Petersburg. Finally Madame Sirmen returned home to Italy, where she spent the last 30 years of her life as teacher rather than performer.

Her *String quartets* (plus a similar batch of string trios and six violin concertos) date from her years at the orphanage and were published in Paris in 1769 by another enterprising woman, Madame Berault. The string quartet medium was at that time in its infancy (the present contribution is approximately contemporary with Haydn's Opus 9 set) and thus her easy skill in handling the medium is the more remarkable. There are two movements to each quartet, but the structure often subdivides into sections using different tempi and, most striking of all, *No. 5 in E minor* introduces a touching *Larghetto* which (within a span of eight minutes) returns after the central allegro. The collection here opens with No. 4 which in its extended first movement (marked *Cantabile*, though it is not slow) uses a typical, simple sonata-form format, with two basic musical ideas. But *No. 1 in E flat* is thematically and structurally a more interesting work, and it has a particularly striking second-movement *Allegretto* which is worthy of the young Mozart. The vivacious finale of the *Second Quartet*, which is used to end the disc, is comparable with Haydn.

The Allegri Quartet obviously lived with this music for some time before this record was made, and they play it with much style and conviction, conveying their own pleasure in part-writing which is obviously enjoyable to play. The leader, Peter Carter, contributes a brief appreciation of the quality of the music as a part of very comprehensive notes. With excellent recording, admirably present but naturally balanced, this is very much worth exploring.

Skroup, František (1801–62)

The Tinker overture.

(N) (**) Sup. mono SU 1914 011. Czech PO, Karel Sejna – DVORAK: *The Cunning peasant overture* (**); SMETANA: *Festive Symphony* etc. (***)

Neither František nor his brother, Jan Nepomuk Skroup, has more than a peripheral hold on the current record catalogue. The author of the sleeve-note speaks of 'the stunning melodic spontaneity' of Skroup's *Overture The Tinker*, which is no small claim. It is not a bad piece, but its melodic invention, while pleasant, is far from stunning. Sejna's performance is marvellously spirited, but the recording was made in 1951 and is rather thin on top!

Smetana, Bedřich (1824–84)

Festive Symphony in E, Op. 6; Festive Overture, Op. 4.

(N) (***) Sup. stereo/mono SU 1914 011. Czech PO, Karel Sejna – DVORAK: *The Cunning peasant overture;* SKROUP: *The Tinker.* (**)

Smetana's *Festive* or *Triumphal Symphony* from 1853 is best known for its effervescent Scherzo, which is often performed on its own. It is also by far the best of the four movements. Karel Sejna's account was recorded in 1966, though the orchestral texture is so well balanced that it can hold its own with more modern recordings. The *Festive overture*, Op. 4, recorded in 1955, is amazingly good for its period.

Håkon Jarl, Op. 16; Prague carnival; Richard III, Op. 11; Wallenstein's Camp, Op. 14 (symphonic poems).

(M) *** DG 437 254-2 [id.]. Bav. RSO, Kubelik – JANACEK: *Sinfonietta.* ***

The jolly *Carnival in Prague*, the composer's last work, was written in 1883; the others are more melodramatic, dating from around 1860. The music has a flavour of Dvořák, if without that master's melodic and imaginative flair. The most spectacular is *Wallenstein's Camp* with its opportunities for offstage brass fanfares – very like Liszt's *Mazeppa* – well managed here. This is very enjoyable in its ingenuous way; but perhaps the most distinguished piece here is *Håkon Jarl*, which has a strong vein of full-blooded romanticism. The playing is first class throughout, the conductor's approach is fresh and committed, and the recording has good body and atmosphere, even if the CD transfer underlines a slight dryness in the bass, characteristic of this source.

Má Vlast (complete).

*** Sup. Dig. 11 1208-2 [id.]. Czech PO, Kubelik.

(Y/B) (BB) *** Naxos Dig. 8.550931 [id.]. Polish Nat. RSO (Katowice), Antoni Wit.

*** Telarc CD 80265 [id.]. Milwaukee SO, Macal.

(Y/B) *** Chandos Dig. CHAN 9366 [id.]. Detroit SO, Neeme Järvi.

(Y/B) (M) *** Ph. Dig. 442 641-2 [id.]. Concg. O, Antal Dorati.

(N) (B) *** EMI forte CZS5 68649-2 (2). Dresden State O, Berglund – DVORAK: *Scherzo capriccioso* etc.; GRIEG: *Old Norwegian romance* etc. ***

(Y/B) (M) *** Virgin/EMI Dig. CUV5 61223-2 [id.]. RLPO, Pešek.

*** DG Dig. 431 652-2 [id.]. VPO, Levine.

(Y/B) ** Sony Dig. SK 58944 [id.]. Israel PO, Mehta.

In 1990 Rafael Kubelik returned to his homeland after an enforced absence of 41 years to open the Prague Spring Festival with this vibrant performance of *Má Vlast*. He had recorded the work twice before in stereo, but this Czech version is special, imbued with passionate national feeling, yet never letting the emotions boil over. At the bold opening of *Vyšehrad*, with the harp strongly profiled, the intensity of the music-making is immediately projected, and the trickling streams which are the source of *Vltava* have a delicacy almost of fantasy but, after the relaxation for the moonlit sequence, one realizes that the return of the chorale as the river flows past Vyšehrad is a key point in Kubelik's reading. *Šárka*, with its bloodthirsty tale of revenge and slaughter, is immensely dramatic, contrasting with the pastoral evocations of the following piece; the Slavonic lilt of the music's lighter moments brings the necessary contrast and release. The recording is vivid and full but not sumptuous, yet this suits the powerful impulse of Kubelik's overall view, with the build-up to the exultant close of *Blaník* producing a dénouement of great majesty.

Antoni Wit and his excellent Polish National Radio Orchestra give us a superbly played and consistently imaginative account of Smetana's *Má Vlast*, a work whose patriotic aspirations can so readily turn into rhetoric. Not here, however. The spacious opening of *Vyšehrad*, marginally slower than usual, glows with romantic evocation; equally the flutes, trickling down from the sources of the *Vltava*, captivate the ear and the famous string-tune is unusually gracious and relaxed. The wedding scene on the river becomes delightfully folksy rather than forcefully rhythmic, then the moonlight glitters on the waters of the lake with a phosphorescent radiance. This idyll is dramatically interrupted by the appearance of the St John's rapids, and there is a superb climax, with thundering (but not exaggerated) timpani, and the main theme gathers pace for the triumphant climax. The opening of *Šárka* brings tingling melodrama, with the neurosis then subsiding naturally for the jaunty theme which follows. *From Bohemia's woods and fields* opens with opulent expansiveness, and later the ethereal high string entry is exquisitely made. The opening horn-call of *Tábor* emerges atmospherically from the mists of the past and the music develops great weight and gravitas. *Blaník* follows on naturally, with the charming pastoral sequence offering more lovely playing from the Polish wind (and horn) soloists. Both the two final symphonic poems are full of incident, and Wit and his players are clearly involved in every bar. Each episode of the narrative is resourcefully presented, not least the charming (almost Tchaikovskian) 'marche miniature' which achieves magnificent grandiloquence, being finally joined – in a satisfyingly broad climax – by the great *Vyšehrad* theme, and the piece closes to joyous fanfares. The warm resonance of the Concert Hall of Polish Radio in Katowice seems right for this very individual reading, full of fantasy, which goes automatically to the top of the list alongside Kubelik's distinguished, and justly renowned, 1990 Czech Philharmonic version on Supraphon, which is rather special.

Macal's new Telarc version offers the finest recording of all; indeed it approaches the demonstration bracket. As with his version of Dvořák's *New World Symphony*, he provides a highly spontaneous and enjoyable performance, imaginatively conceived and convincingly paced. The very opening of *Vyšehrad*, with its relatively gentle harp roulades, sets the atmospheric mood of the reading; other accounts, notably Kubelik's, have greater Slavic fire and find a more red-bloodedly patriotic feeling, but the excellent orchestral playing is responsive to his less histrionic view. *Šárka* has a folksy flavour, the melodrama good-humoured, while in *From Bohemia's woods and fields*, after the radiant high string passage, the horns steal in magically with their chorale. Throughout the brass are full and sonorous, mitigating any rhetorical bombast in the last two symphonic poems; and Macal's Czech nationality ensures that the performance has idiomatic feeling.

Järvi's, too, is an enjoyably vivid performance, and he has the double advantage of first-class playing from the highly committed Detroit orchestra and the splendid acoustics of Symphony Hall. The romantic *Vyšehrad* is fresh and immediate, and the mountain streams of *Vltava* gleam brightly in the sunlight before the string-tune arrives and moves on with plenty of lyrical impetus. The jaunty village wedding is followed by an evocation of lovely, ethereal moonlight (matched by the high strings in *From Bohemia's woods and fields*) and the rapids bring high drama. *Šárka* is very dramatic indeed, with great melodramatic gusto and a heartfelt response from the strings. The opening of *Tábor* is tellingly ominous, and the weight of the Detroit brass makes a powerful contribution to both of the final two sections of the score; the zest of the Detroit music-making is always compelling, and the culminating climax is thrilling rather than expansively grandiloquent.

Dorati's is an extremely fine account of Smetana's cycle, avoiding most of the pitfalls with a reading which brings both vivid drama and orchestral playing of the finest quality. The music-making has a high adrenalin level throughout, yet points of detail are not missed. The accents of *Vyšehrad* may seem too highly stressed to ears used to a more mellow approach to this highly romantic opening piece, and *Vltava* similarly moves forward strongly. In the closing *Blaník*, Dorati finds dignity rather than bombast and the pastoral episode is delightfully relaxed, with a fine rhythmic bounce to the march theme which then leads to the final peroration. The Philips sound is splendid, with a wide amplitude and a thrilling concert-hall presence, and this reissue on the Philips Solo label makes an obvious recommendation in the mid-price range.

Whereas many recorded performances in the past have done well by *Vltava* and *From Bohemia's woods and fields* and then fallen short on the other four pieces, it is in these less well-known works that Berglund is most impressive. Indeed, if there is a criticism of this set it is that *Vltava*, although splendidly played, seems slightly undercharacterized alongside other sections of the score. The opening *Vyšehrad* is most beautifully played, full of lyrical evocation and atmosphere, as is *From Bohemia's woods and fields*, while *Sárka* is arrestingly dramatic. *Tábor* and *Blaník* are played together, and so often in previous accounts they have become engulfed in rhetoric, but not here where the national feeling that is the basis of their inspiration sounds surgingly jubilant. The closing pages of *Tábor* are beautifully managed, and the pastoral interlude in *Blaník* is engagingly lightweight so that when the closing chorale appears it has a lilting step and conjures up memories of *The Bartered Bride* rather than bombastic militarism. The end of the work has a joyous release. Berglund does not shirk the melodrama, but he never lets it get the better of him. The Dresden orchestra plays magnificently and the 1978 recording, made in the Lukaskirche, is full-blooded, with the brilliance never degenerating into fierceness. The Dvořák and Grieg couplings are also very successful, so this forte set is very competitive, if the programme is attractive.

Pešek's reading does not miss the music's epic patriotic feeling, yet never becomes bombastic. There is plenty of evocation, from the richly romantic opening of *Vyšehrad* to the more mysterious scene-setting in *Tábor*, while the climax of *Sárka*, with its potent anticipatory horn-call, is a gripping piece of melodrama. The two main sections of the work, *Vltava* and *From Bohemia's woods and fields*, are especially enjoyable for their vivid characterization, while at the very end of *Blaník* Pešek draws together the two key themes – the *Vyšehrad* motif and the Hussite chorale – very satisfyingly.

Levine is upstaged by Dorati on Philips, who has a considerable price advantage plus the glorious acoustic of the Concertgebouw. Levine's performance is full of momentum and thrust, with much imaginative detail and most beautifully played. In *Tábor* and *Blaník* the VPO play with great vigour and commitment, and these patriotic pieces have both fervour and plenty of colour. The sound is full-bodied, with a wide amplitude and range, but it is less sumptuous and slightly less atmospheric than the Philips version.

After all this excellence it would be easy to undervalue Mehta's Israel performance, but he clearly enjoys the music and so do the Israeli players; the recording, though much less warmly expansive than Wit's or Dorati's – and certainly not in the Chandos bracket – is fuller and somewhat more atmospheric than we often experience in Tel Aviv, although it is at times unrefined and string detail is husky. Mehta's tempi are close to Järvi's in the first three symphonic poems, rather more expansive in the second triptych. *Vyšehrad* comes off quite effectively. But after an attractively delicate opening, the great string-tune of *Vltava* fails really to take off, and the climax needs a more expansive acoustic. The opening of *Tábor* isn't very arresting either, and both here and in *Blaník*, although the adrenalin runs freely, there is an element of bombast (the comparatively dry acoustic does not help) and Mehta seldom displays the imaginative flair of his competitors.

(i) *Má Vlast;* (ii) *Håkon Jarl, Op. 16;* (iii) *The Bartered Bride: Overture; Polka; Furiant.*
(N) (B) ** Decca Double 443 015-2 (2) [id.]. (i) Israel PO, cond. Weller or (iii) Kertész; (ii) Detroit SO, Dorati – DVORAK: *Czech suite* etc. ***

Walter Weller's 1978 recording of *Má Vlast* is of Decca's vintage analogue quality, but the opening of *Vyšehrad* is curiously unevocative and, while Weller provides excellent detail in *Vltava*, the Israel Philharmonic's strings fail to captivate the ear in the glorious theme which spaciously represents the river. Weller is at his best in the later, more melodramatic pieces, and he secures generally good orchestral playing. There are no complaints about *Håkon Jarl* and under Kertész the pieces from *The Bartered Bride* are exceptionally vivid with the separate entries in the overture clearly positioned by the stereo.

Má Vlast: Vltava.
(M) *** Sony SBK 48264; *SBT 48264* [id.]. Cleveland O, Szell – BIZET: *Symphony;* MENDELSSOHN: *Midsummer Night's Dream.* ***
**(*) DG Gold Dig. 439 009-2 [id.]. VPO, Karajan – DVORAK: *Symphony No. 9 (New World).* **(*)
(M) (**) RCA GD 60279 [60279-2-RG]. NBC SO, Toscanini – DVORAK: *Symphony No. 9;* KODALY: *Háry János suite.* (***)
(Y/B) (M) (**) Sony mono SMK 64467 [id.]. NYPO, Bruno Walter – BRAHMS: *Hungarian dances Nos. 1, 3, 10 & 17;* J. STRAUSS: *Overtures; Waltzes.* (***)

The Clevelanders play *Vltava* superbly, from the opening trickle, through the village wedding and the moonlight sequence, to the climax at St John's rapids. The effect is both vivid and dramatic and the dynamic range not too restricted to spoil the element of contrast.

Karajan's VPO performance is characteristically well structured, and the recorded sound sounds quite expansive in this remastered format, even if the balance is not quite natural.

Recorded several years earlier than the other two items on Toscanini's disc, *Vltava* has painfully dry and close sound; but the intensity of Toscanini's performance still makes it a valuable document.

Although the opening has fine delicacy and the moonlight sequence is highly atmospheric, the restricted dynamic range and studio-ish sound prevent Walter's 1941 mono recording from expanding at climaxes.

Má Vlast: Vltava. The Bartered bride: Overture; Polka; Furiant; Dance of the Comedians. The Kiss: Overture. Libuse: Overture. The Two Widows: Overture & Polka.
(N) **(*) Decca Dig. 444 867-2 [id.]. Cleveland O, Dohnányi.

A good Smetana anthology from the Cleveland Orchestra under Christoph von Dohnányi in excellent Decca sound. It is years since *The Bartered bride* – or, for that matter, any other Smetana opera – was given at Covent Garden, though we are at least better served on CD. Charm may not be Dohnányi's strong suit, but this music induces enchantment all by itself. The Cleveland Orchestra play with great brio and virtuosity and, even though there is not too much in the way of spontaneous joy, this anthology will still give pleasure. At 57 minutes and premium price, it is perhaps short measure these days.

Má Vlast: Vltava; Vyšehrad.
*** Chandos Dig. CHAN 9230 [id.]. Detroit SO, Neeme Järvi – FIBICH: *Symphony No. 1.* ***

Järvi's are excellent performances of both pieces, vivid in pictorialism and colour, and they are very well played and recorded. But it is for the Fibich *Symphony* that this Chandos issue is most valuable.

(i) *Má Vlast: Vltava; Vyšehrad; From Bohemia's woods and fields;* (ii) *The Bartered Bride: 3 Dances.*
(Y/B) (B) ** DG 439 451-2 [id.]. (i) Boston SO, Kubelik; (ii) BPO, Karajan.

These excerpts, which offer what many would regard as the three finest of the six tone-poems making up *Má Vlast*, come from Kubelik's second (1970) stereo recording with the Boston Symphony Orchestra which, though perceptive and very well played, suffered from close microphones, thus robbing the orchestra of a good deal of the natural sumptuousness afforded by the acoustics of Symphony Hall, Boston, and in the great string-theme of *Vltava* the massed violins could ideally be richer. However, the ear adjusts and these are otherwise excellent performances. The *Polka, Furiant* and *Entry of the Comedians* from *The Bartered Bride* offer no such problems and are played with much panache by the Berlin Philharmonic under Karajan. But this Classikon bargain disc is not very full at 54 minutes: there would have been room for the overture, too.

Piano trio in G min., Op. 15.
*** Chandos Dig. CHAN 8445; *ABTD 1157* [id.]. Borodin Trio – DVORAK: *Dumky trio.* ***
(N) *** Ara. Dig. Z6661 [id.]. Golub–Kaplan–Carr Trio – TCHAIKOVSKY: *Piano trio.* ***

Writing the *Trio* was a cathartic act, following the death of the composer's four-year-old daughter, so it is not surprising that it is a powerfully emotional work. The writing gives fine expressive opportunities for both the violin and cello, which are taken up eloquently by Rostislav Dubinsky and Yuli Turovsky, and the pianist, Luba Edlina, is also wonderfully sympathetic. In short, a superb account, given a most realistic recording balance. Highly recommended.

Although the balance may place the listener a bit too close to the players for some tastes, the Arabesque CD offers a perfectly pleasing sound and the performance is eminently musical and unaffected. This is the kind of chamber-music playing to inspire confidence in the future: nothing overdriven, mechanized or attention-seeking. While it does not necessarily displace the Borodin Trio, it can be ranked among the best and is the only recording to offer so substantial a partner as the Tchaikovsky Trio – completely uncut, too.

String quartet No. 1 in E min. (From my life).
*** Sony Dig. SK 53282 [id.]. Artis Qt – DVORAK: *String quartet No. 14.* ***
(N) *** Decca Dig. 452 239-2 [id.]. Takács Qt – BORODIN: *Quartet No. 2.* ***
*** EMI Dig. CDC7 54215-2 [id.]. Alban Berg Qt – DVORAK: *String quartet No. 12.* ***
(N) (***) Testament mono SBT 1072 [id.]. Hollywood Qt – DVORAK; KODALY: *Quartets.* (***)
(M) **(*) DG 437 251-2 [id.]. Amadeus Qt – DVORAK: *String quartet No. 12.* **(*)

The Artis Quartet give one of the finest accounts of the *First Quartet* for many years: imaginative, dramatic, ardent and sensitive. It is what one might call a narrative performance in that it holds one completely throughout without ever indulging in expressive overstatement. The Sony recording is in every way first class.

The Takács Quartet play Smetana's autobiographical work with great ardour; indeed it is impossible not to become caught up in the vibrant feeling of this playing. This makes a distinguished alternative to the Artis coupling on Sony for those preferring the (first-class) Borodin coupling. The Decca recording gives the players a very striking presence. However, one can't help reflecting that there was room for more music here.

By the side of the Artis account, the Alban Berg Quartet sound just a shade polished and professional. There is not quite enough spontaneity by comparison with the Artis, who carry one onwards with greater freshness and impulsiveness. All the same, there is much more to admire in the Alban Berg's reading than to cavil at: the first movement comes off well, and the EMI recording is very truthful and present. There is no cause to withhold a third star, particularly as their Dvořák is very successful.

This Hollywood Quartet recording was never issued in the UK in the 1950s when it was made. It is a performance of tremendous fire and passion, with an exhilarating rhythmic drive and a powerful sense of momentum. Yet everything sounds perfectly natural and not overdriven. Great quartet playing – and perfectly acceptable sound, given the mid-1950s date.

A strongly felt and purposeful account of Smetana's autobiographical *Quartet* from the Amadeus on top form: their ensemble, matching of timbre and unanimous of attack, is peerless. At times one feels that Norbert Brainin's lyrical vibrato is not entirely suitable for this very personal utterance: he wears his heart too openly on his sleeve; but there is no doubt that the performance overall is gripping, and the 1977 recording is vividly realistic.

String quartet No. 1 (From my life) – orchestral version by George Szell. *The Bartered Bride: Overture and dances.*
*** Chandos Dig. CHAN 8412 [id.]. LSO, Geoffrey Simon.

The Czech feeling of Szell's scoring is especially noticeable in the *Polka*, but overall there is no doubt that the fuller textures add a dimension to the music, though inevitably there are losses as well as gains. The powerful advocacy of Simon and the excellent LSO playing, both here and in the sparkling excerpts from *The Bartered Bride*, provide a most rewarding coupling. The recording is well up to the usual high Chandos standards.

String quartets Nos. 1 in E min. (From my life); 2 in D min.
*** ASV Dig. CDDCA 777 [id.]. Lindsay Qt (with DVORAK: *Romance; Waltzes Nos. 1–2* ***).
*** Collins Dig. 1323-2 [id.]. Talich Qt (with SUK: *Meditations on the St Wenceslas chorale* ***).

(i) *String quartets Nos. 1 in E min. (From my life); 2 in D min.* (ii) *From the homeland.*
(BB) ** Naxos Dig. 8.550379 [id.]. (i) Moyzes Qt; (ii) Takako Nishizaki, Tatiana Fránova.

The Lindsay Quartet bring dramatic intensity to the *E minor Quartet* and play with great fire and vitality. Their (perhaps slightly forward) recording is very good indeed, and readers wanting both the Smetana *Quartets* together need look no further than them or the Talich Quartet on Collins.

The Talich Quartet have no want of drama or fire either. This is cultured playing, and moreover they are better served by their recording engineers than they were in their earlier, Calliope version. There is not a great deal to choose between the Talich and the Lindsays, and readers can invest in either with confidence. In each case there are attractive bonuses.

The Moyzes Quartet, composed of members of the Slovak Philharmonic, turn in very respectable accounts of both *Quartets*. The recording has less warmth and ambience than its top-price rivals. All the same this is to be preferred to some of the high-powered, jet-set ensembles, and is value for money.

Czech dances I & II; 8 Bagatelles and impromptus.
** Unicorn Dig. DKPCD 9139 [id.]. Radoslav Kvapil.

Radoslav Kvapil is a highly sensitive exponent of this repertoire. The recording is wanting in distinction; it lacks brightness and perspective. It is adequate, while the playing is much more than that.

OPERA

The Bartered Bride: overture.
(Y/B) (M) *** RCA 09026 62587-2 [id.]. Chicago SO, Fritz Reiner – DVORAK: *Symphony No. 9* etc.;
WEINBERGER: *Schwanda: polka and fugue.* ***

The easy, bustling virtuosity of the Chicago strings makes this vivacious performance of Smetana's
famous overture hard to beat when the recording, too, is full yet has clear inner detail.

The Bartered Bride (complete, in Czech).
*** Sup. Dig. 10 3511-2 (3) [id.]. Beňačková, Dvorský, Novák, Kopp, Jonášová, Czech Philharmonic
Ch. and O, Košler.

The digital Supraphon set under Košler admirably supplies the need for a first-rate Czech version of this
delightful comic opera. The performance sparkles from beginning to end, with folk rhythms crisply
enunciated in an infectiously idiomatic way. The cast is strong, headed by the characterful Gabriela
Beňačková as Mařenka and one of the finest of today's Czech tenors, Peter Dvorský, as Jeník. Miroslav
Kopp in the role of the ineffective Vašek sings powerfully too. As Kecal the marriage-broker, Richard
Novák is not always steady, but his swaggering characterization is most persuasive. The CDs offer some
of the best sound we have yet had from Supraphon, fresh and lively. The discs are fairly generously
banded, but this could now be fitted on a pair of CDs, so the set is unnecessarily expensive. The libretto,
however, has been improved and is clear and easy to use.

The Bartered Bride: highlights.
(Y/B) (M) **(*) Sup. 112251-2 [id.] (from above recording, with Beňačková, Dvorský; cond. Košler).

A well-made if not strikingly generous set of highlights from Košler's sparkling complete set. But the
documentation includes only a list of excerpts unrelated to any synopsis, and there is no translation.

The Brandenburgers in Bohemia (complete).
(Y/B) **(*) Sup. 11 1804-2 (2) [id.]. Zídek, Otava, Subrtová, Kalaš, Joran, Vich, Prague Nat. Theatre
soloists, Ch. & O, Jan Hus Tichý.

Smetana was forty before he wrote this, his first opera, understandably a mixture of strong, confident
musical gestures and dramatic ineffectiveness. Though much of the drama centres on the fate of the
heroine, Liduše, abducted by a Prague burgher with the mercenary Germanic name of Tausendmark,
the love interest which must sustain any romantic opera is sketched in only cursorily. The main duet
between Liduše and her beloved, Junoš, is charming and jolly rather than heartfelt, an opportunity
missed. Nevertheless there is much to enjoy in a performance as lively as this, with stirring patriotic
choruses sung with a will, even if their melodic invention is hardly distinguished. The recording was
made as long ago as 1963, but it sounds well in the CD transfer, with the three Acts squeezed on to two
very well-filled discs. Milada Subrtová sings with appealingly sweet, firm tone as Liduše, and the young
Ivo Zídek makes a fresh-voiced hero, strained only a little on top. Tausendmark is sung by a stalwart
veteran, Zdeněk Otava, making up in bite what he lacks in vocal quality. A collector's item.

Dalibor (complete).
(Y/B) *** Sup. 11 2185-2 (2) [id.]. Přibyl, Kniplová, Jindrák, Svorc, Horáček, Prague Nat. Theatre Ch.
& O, Jaroslav Krombholc.

Smetana was at the peak of his creative powers when he wrote *Dalibor*, conceiving it while he was still
writing *The Bartered Bride*. The contrast of mood and subject is extreme between that peasant comedy
and this Gothic historical tragedy. Yet in the development of the plot, when the imprisoned hero's lover
is disguised as the gaoler's assistant, *Dalibor* readily evokes associations with *Fidelio* and the subject
prompted Smetana to write some of his most inspired music. Where in his first opera, *The
Brandenburgers in Bohemia*, the patriotic choruses are conventional, here the opening chorus brings a
stirring and measured number in triple time and a minor key. The confrontations between hero and
heroine also inspire Smetana to some glorious writing, richly lyrical, most notably the love duet in the
prison scene of Act II. This vintage set of 1967, sounding more vivid and fuller-blooded than many
more recent recordings, features in those roles two of the most distinguished Czech singers of their time,
both in their prime, the tenor Vílém Přibyl and the dramatic soprano, Nadezda Kniplová. The other
principals are not so consistent, but Krombholc proves a most persuasive advocate, consistently bringing out the red-blooded fervour of the writing. Highly recommended to anyone who wants to investigate
beyond *The Bartered Bride*. A full translation is provided.

Libuše.
**(*) Sup. Dig. 11 1276-2 633 (3) [id.]. Beňačková, Zítek, Svorc, Vodička, Děpoltová, Prague Nat. Theatre Ch. & O, Košler.

Recorded live at the Prague National Theatre in 1983, this performance vividly communicates the fervour of nationalist aspirations, more intense when shared with an audience. The cast here is even stronger than that of the previous recording under Krombholc, with Gabriela Beňačková-Cápová as Libuše memorable in her prophetic aria in Act III, while Václav Zítek as Přemysl, her consort, provides an attractive lyrical interlude in Act II which, with its chorus of harvesters, has affinities with *The Bartered Bride*. In Act I there is some Slavonic wobbling, notably from Eva Děpoltová as Krasava, but generally the singing is as dramatic as the plot-line will allow. Košler directs committedly; with the stage perspectives well caught, an unintrusive audience and no disturbing stage-noises with such a static plot, the recording is very satisfactory. Now reissued on three discs and with a clearly printed new libretto/ translation, this is made more attractive, although the cues still provide poor internal access for an opera playing for not far short of three hours. Twelve extra index points have been added to the 14 bands – not nearly enough for a work of this kind.

The Two Widows (complete).
(Y/B) ** Sup.11 2122-2 (2) [id.]. Sormová, Machotková, Zahradníček, Horáček, Prague Nat. Theatre Ch. & O, Jílek.
(Y/B) ** Praga/Chant du Monde PR 250 022/3 (2) [id.]. Jonášová, Machotková, Svejda, Jedlička, Prague RSO, Krombholc.

Starting with a jolly chorus, *The Two Widows* gives promise of rivalling in brightness Smetana's earlier comic masterpiece, *The Bartered Bride*. But this is a tale of country life in the big house rather than among the peasantry, with the plot centring on two cousins, both widows, and inconsequential confusions over which of them is going to marry the hero, Ladislav. That said, Smetana offers much delightful music and, if one regrets having choral contributions only at the very beginning and at the ends of each of the two Acts, there are some charming numbers in between, not least an aria for the hero, '*When Maytime arrives*', at the beginning of Act II. Jiří Zahradníček is at his best there, singing lustily, though in gentler moments Slavonic unsteadiness develops. Jaroslav Horáček is effective in the *buffo* bass role of Mumlal but, sadly, the casting of the two widows, both sopranos, involves the major role of Karolina going to the shrill and wobbly Naďa Sormová, while Marcela Machotková, who is altogether sweeter and firmer, with a mezzo-ish quality, is consigned to the role of Anežka with far less to sing, even though it is she who gets the hero. Recorded in 1975, this lively performance under Frantisek Jílek is on the whole well transferred to CD, though in a dry-ish acoustic the Prague Theatre violins sound undernourished. The libretto includes a very necessary translation.

Recorded in 1974, only eighteen months earlier than the Supraphon version, the Praga set, as transferred to CD by Chant du Monde, offers a more genial performance, a degree more expansive but in sound that is rougher and edgier, with less sense of presence. In the role of Ladislav, Miroslav Svejda has a more pleasing lyric tenor than his opposite number and is far more headily beautiful in the hero's aria. Jana Jonášová as Karolina is steadier than Sormová but, if anything, even shriller, not so warmly expressive in her Act II monologue. Again Machotková is excellent as Anežka, and Dalibor Jedlička is a first-rate *buffo* bass. Two balancing points against the Praga set are that Act II starts on the first disc, where Supraphon has one disc per Act, and that Praga offers only an English translation with no Czech text.

Smyth, Ethel (1858–1944)

(i) *Concerto for violin, horn & orchestra. Serenade in D.*
(N) *** Chandos Dig. CHAN 9449 [id.]. (i) Sophie Langdon, Richard Watkins; BBC PO, Odaline de la Martinez.

The *Concerto for violin, horn and orchestra* was one of Dame Ethel's last works, written in 1927. It is a highly successful piece in every respect. The first movement begins with an ambitious string melody, then the soloists enter alternately with the endearing secondary idea (one of the composer's very best tunes), which is imaginatively developed in a free fantasia of flowing and dancing melody and varying moods; only at the recapitulation do the soloists share the opening theme. The romantic central *Elegy* brings a touchingly beautiful and nostalgic exchange between the two soloists: here the horn first dominates passionately, then the violin responds with heartfelt eloquence and it is a delicate violin obbligato that has the last word. The finale dances away spiritedly to an infectious main theme, the development unpredictably quixotic. The highly original joint cadenza brings an improvisatory conversation between the two soloists until the horn descends into its lowest register to play a downward scale of 'chords' with the fiddle dancing flamboyantly above, before the pace quickens into a dashing, exultant finale.

The *Serenade in D major*, Smyth's first orchestral work (1890), might well be Brahms's *Third*! Not only does the rich string writing of the first movement have a glorious sweep, but the harmonic thinking and progressions are *echt*-Brahms. Yet Smyth's invention is of high quality, for all its eclectic associations. The lightly etched Scherzo brings an airy playfulness and the flowing clarinet theme which introduces the *Allegretto grazioso* is comparably graceful; the finale has unquenchable energy, but also a comely, lyrical strain. Its musical motivation is strikingly assured and spontaneous, including a surprise entry of a triumphant brass chorale quite early on in the movement. With superb performances (clearly they are all enjoying themselves, including the first-rate soloists in the *Double concerto*) and warm, sumptuous recording, both these colourful and tuneful works will give great pleasure. This is easily the most impressive Smyth offering yet to have appeared on CD, conducted with understanding and commitment by a highly experienced advocate who has already given us a fine account of *The Wreckers*.

(i) *Double concerto* (trio) *in A for violin, horn & piano* (arr. composer); (ii; iii) *4 Songs: Odelette; La danse; Chrysilla; Ode Anacréonique* (for mezzo soprano and chamber ensemble); (ii; iv) *3 Songs: The clown; Possession; On the road* (for mezzo soprano and piano).
(Y/B) ** Trouba Dig. TRO-CD 1405 [id.]. (i) Renate Eggebrecht-Kupsa, Franz Draxinger, Céline Dutilly; (ii) Melinda Paulsen; (iii) Ens. Schmeller; (iv) Angela Gassenhuber.

Dame Ethel herself arranged the concerto listed above as a chamber work, and one can understand why, for the interplay between violin and horn in the slow movement has a chamber-music feel to it. It works well in its more intimate form. Highly inventive and tuneful, it is despatched here with much feeling and some aplomb, with fine horn playing, even if it has a few rough moments elsewhere. Well worth having on disc. The *Four songs* (1907) are French settings. With flute obbligati, Ravelian influences are strong, but all four are very successful, often exotic and always melodically strong. The three English songs also show Dame Ethel's fine feeling for words. The performances are strong, but Melinda Paulsen is too often inclined to let fly on fortissimos for the vocal line to be always entirely comfortable. The pianist, Angela Gassenhuber, is most supportive. Good recording. Translations are provided, but the notes are a bit sparse.

(i; ii) *Cello sonata in A min., Op. 5;* (iii) *String quartet in C min;* (iii; iv) *String quintet in E, Op. 1;* (v; ii) *Violin sonata in A min., Op. 7.*
(Y/B) ** Trouba Dig. TRO-CD 03 (2) [id.]. (i) Friedemann Kupsa; (ii) Céline Dutilly; (iii) Fanny Mendelssohn Qt; (iv) with Johanna Varner; (v) Renate Eggebrecht-Kupsa.

This music is very eclectic indeed but there is no shortage of good tunes here, even if the *Cello sonata* and, particularly, the *Violin sonata* (both early works dating from 1887) sound as if Brahms had written them. In the *String quintet* (1883) the influences are distinctly Slavonic, with a strong flavour of Dvořák. The *Adagio* is heart-warming; the Scherzo and the ingenuously folksy finale are very lively in their ready flow of ideas. All three performances here, if not immaculate, are warmly persuasive and they project the music admirably. The *String quartet*, written between 1902 and 1912, is a different matter, a much more complex work, by no means backward-looking, with a remarkable slow movement which has something of the searching spirit of Schubert. The *Quartet* is obviously very difficult, for the playing here, though very committed, is rough and ready, with moments of insecure intonation. It is a pity that the discs are not available separately, for the coupling of the *Violin sonata* and *String quintet* is very recommendable. The recording is fully acceptable if not refined.

COMPLETE PIANO MUSIC

Piano sonatas Nos. 1 in C; 2 in F sharp min.; 3 in D; 2 Canons; Aus der Jugendzeit! (To Youth!); 4 Four-part dances; Invention in D; Piece in E; Preludes and fugues: in F sharp; in C. Suite in E; Variations in D flat on an original theme.
(N) ** CPO Dig. 999 327-2 (2) [id.]. Liana Serbescu.

Almost all this music dates from between 1877 and 1890, and the *C major Sonata* was Dame Ethel's first composition when she arrived to study in Leipzig in July 1877. It is a promising work, opening agreeably and with a gentle funeral march for its *Adagio* slow movement, which Liana Serbescu plays touchingly. The *Second Sonata* also has a pleasing but less distinctive *Andante*, and the *Third* is notable for its lively closing Scherzo. However, it cannot be said that any of these works are very distinctive, although the neo-classical *Suite* is jolly, with an engagingly soft-centred Minuet. The extended *Variations*, 'of an exceedingly dismal nature' according to the composer, are indeed rather heavy-going, although the theme itself is agreeable enough. There are immediate reminders of Brahms in the third and fourth of the *Four-part dances* which open the collection, and the two very successful *Preludes and fugues* which close the second CD successfully evoke the world of Mendelssohn. All this music is played sympathetically and is well recorded, but none of it is likely to re-enter the repertoire.

The Wreckers: Overture.
(B) *** CfP CD-CFP 4635; *TC-CFP 4635.* RSNO, Gibson – GERMAN: *Welsh rhapsody;* HARTY: *With the wild geese;* MACCUNN: *Land of the Mountain and Flood.* ***

Ethel Smyth's *Overture* for her opera, *The Wreckers* (first performed in England in 1909), is a strong, meaty piece which shows the calibre of this remarkable woman's personality for, while the material itself is not memorable, it is put together most compellingly and orchestrated with real flair. The recording is full and the CD has refined detail. This CD makes a genuine bargain.

The Wreckers (opera): complete.
(Y/B) **(*) Conifer Dig. 75605 51250-2 (2) [id.]. Sidhom, Owens, Lavender, Wilson-Johnson, Bannatyne-Scott, Roden, Sand, Huddersfield Ch. Soc., BBC PO, Odaline de la Martinez.

Recorded live at the 1994 Proms in a concert performance at the Royal Albert Hall, the Conifer set of *The Wreckers* fills an important gap in the catalogue. The colourful overture has remained reasonably well known, but in melodic invention the rest of the opera hardly lives up to that opening. The plot is strong and sharply conceived, set in Cornwall and culminating in the drowning of the hero and heroine, trapped in a cave by vengeful villagers. That close, which brings some of the most powerful writing in the opera, has been described fairly enough as 'Aida-on-sea', but the close of that death scene is triumphant rather than suffocated. Nevertheless, with Odaline de la Martinez directing a committed performance, this high-romantic melodrama makes an enjoyable piece, for all the lack of hummable tunes. One problem of the casting is that the role of the heroine is given to a mezzo soprano, and Anne-Marie Owens copes valiantly with the extreme range required. Justin Lavender makes a clear-toned hero, ostensibly too light for the role but sounding well on record. The others are stronger – David Wilson-Johnson characterful as the lighthouse keeper, Judith Howarth sweet-toned as the hero's jilted girlfriend and Peter Sidhom most powerful of all as the minister, suggesting that voices of Wagnerian strength might make a difference. Sadly, here the chorus is too backwardly balanced.

Soler, Antonio (1729–83)
KEYBOARD WORKS

Keyboard works: *Sonatas Nos. 1 in A; 3 in B flat; 24–5 in D min.; 28–9 in C; 30–31 in G; 96 in E flat; 118 in A min. Prelude No. 1 in D min.*
** Astrée Dig. E 8768 [id.]. Bob van Asperen (harpsichord).

Sonatas Nos. 2 in E flat; 65 in A min.; 105 in E flat; 111 in D; 117 in D min.; 124 in C; 125 in C; 126a and 126b in C min.; 127 in D; 128 in E min.; 130 in G min.; 131 in A.
** Astrée Dig. E 8779 [id.]. Bob van Asperen (harpsichord).

Sonatas Nos. 4 in G; 5 in F; 6 in F; 49 in D min.; 55 in F; 69 in F; 72 in F min.; 99 in C; 101 in F; 110 in D flat; 114 in D min.; 115 in D min.; 120 in D min.; Prelude No. 4 in F min.
** Astree Dig. E 8777 [id.]. Bob van Asperen (harpsichord).

Sonatas Nos. 7–9 in C; 20–21 in C sharp min.; 95 in A. Prelude No. 3 in C.
** Astrée Dig. E 8769 [id.]. Bob van Asperen (harpsichord).

Sonatas Nos. 8 in C; 35 in G; 38 in C; 70; 71 in A min.; 77 in F sharp min.; 78 in F sharp min.; 79 in F sharp min.; 82 in G; 83 in F; 113 in E min.; 116 in G; Prelude No. 8 in F.
** Astrée Dig. E 8776 [id.]. Bob van Asperen (harpsichord).

Sonatas Nos. 10 in B min.; 11 in B; 12–14 in G; 52 in E min.; 73–4 in D; 92 in D (Sonata des clarines); 106 in E min.; Allegro pastoril; Prelude No. 6 in G.
** Astrée Dig. E 8770 [id.]. Bob van Asperen (harpsichord).

Sonatas Nos. 15 in D min.; 22 in D flat; 23 in D flat; 54 in D min.; 61 in C; 75 in F; 76 in F; 80 in G min.; 81 in G min.; 84 in D; 86 in D.
*(*) Astrée Dig. E 8772 [id.]. Bob van Asperen (harpsichord).

Sonatas Nos. 16 in E flat; 17 in E flat; 32 in G min.; 33 in G; 39 in D min.; 41 in F; 53 in A; 57 in G min.; 60a in C min.; 60b in C min.; 89 in F; Prelude No. 7 in C min.
** Astrée Dig. E 8775 [id.]. Bob van Asperen (harpsichord).

Sonatas Nos. 18 in C min.; 19 in C min.; 26 in E min.; 27 in E min.; 36 in C min.; 85 in F sharp min.; 90 in F sharp min.; 91 in D; 94 in G.
** Astrée Dig. E 8773 [id.]. Bob van Asperen (harpsichord).

Sonatas Nos. 35 in G; 38 in C; 70 in A min.; 71 in A min.; 77 in F sharp min.; 78 in F sharp min.; 79a & 79b in F sharp min.; 82 in G; 83 in F; 113 in E min.; 116 in G; Prelude No. 8 in F.
** Astrée Dig. E 8776 [id.]. Bob van Asperen (harpsichord).

Sonatas Nos. 37 in D; 46 in D; 56 in F; 98 in B flat min.; 100 in C min.; 103 in C min.; 108 in C; 109 in F; 112 in D; Fandango No. 146; Prelude No. 5 in D.
** Astrée Dig. E 8771 [id.]. Bob van Asperen (harpsichord).

Sonatas Nos. 42 in G min.; 43 in G; 47 in C min; 48 in C min.; 50 in C; 58 in G; 59 in F; 62 in E flat; 87 in G min.; 102 in D min.; 104 in D min.; 107 in F; 149 in F; Prelude No. 2 in G min.
** Astrée Dig. E 8778 [id.]. Bob van Asperen (harpsichord).

Sonatas Nos. 45 in C (por la Princesa de Asturias); 51 in C; 88 in D sharp; 93 in F; 97 in A; 119 in B flat; 132 in B flat; 154 in D sharp.
** Astrée Dig. E 8774 [id.]. Bob van Asperen (harpsichord).

An ambitious venture to record the complete keyboard output of Antonio Soler with Bob van Asperen is let down by insensitive engineering. He plays with plenty of vitality but the value of the enterprise is diminished by the oppressively close balance of the recording. Throughout, he uses either a copy of a 1764 Taskin (made by Michael Johnson two centuries later) or a copy of a 1745 Dülcken, made by Rainer Schülze in Heidelberg in 1969. However ingenious and varied in colour the registration of the distinguished Dutch harpsichordist, the effect is reduced to an unrelieved and uniform dynamic level which produces aural fatigue. The music is so characterful and the playing so fresh that these discs must be recommended, but readers will want to listen at low level and to only one or two pieces at a time. Moreover the documentation is too generalized for such an important project, with essays about the composer, the performer, the project research, and a cursory discussion of the music, repeated with each CD. Information is not given about individual works and no attempt is made to differentiate between the single-movement sonatas and the occasional more ambitious three-and four-movement combinations, like Nos. 92 and 98, in which Soler created composite works from movements of the same tonality but diverse character. The spectacular thirteen-minute *Fandango* which opens the fourth disc is presented without comment. Some of these works have no indication of tempo, but Bob van Asperen's judgement in this matter seems impeccable. In spite of the recording balance, overall this is a remarkable achievement.

Keyboard sonatas, S.R. 15, 21, 42, 84–7, 89.
(M) *** Decca 433 920-2 (2) [id.]. Alicia de Larrocha – ALBENIZ: *Sonata* ***; GRANADOS: *Goyescas* etc. *** 🏵

Vital performances of eight sonatas. Like Scarlatti's music, with an advocate of this calibre these works are quite as pleasing heard on the piano rather than the harpsichord. Excellent, truthful 1981 recording.

Keyboard sonatas Nos. 18 in C min.; 19 in C min.; 41 in E flat; 72 in F min.; 78 in F sharp min.; 84 in D; 85 in F sharp min.; 86 in D; 87 in G min.; 88 in D flat; 90 in F sharp; Fandango.
(N) (M) *** Virgin Veritas/EMI VER5 61220-2 [id.]. Maggie Cole (harpsichord or fortepiano).

Maggie Cole plays a dozen Soler pieces, eleven *Sonatas* and the celebrated *Fandango*, half of them on the harpsichord and the remainder on the fortepiano; she gives altogether dashing performances on both. Good pieces to sample are *No. 87 in G minor* (track 5) and, on the harpsichord, *No. 86 in D major* (track 9) or the *Fandango* itself. The playing is all very exhilarating and inspiriting. Played at a normal level-setting, both instruments sound a bit thunderous, but played at a lower level the results are very satisfactory.

Sor, Fernando (1778–1839)

Fantasia, Op. 30; Fantasia, Op. 7; Variations on a theme of Mozart, Op. 9.
(M) **(*) RCA Dig. 09026 61607-2. Julian Bream (guitar) – AGUADO: Collection. **(*)

Both Sor *Fantasias* are ambitious and each has a central set of variations. Bream's approach is spacious and his deliberation – for all the variety and skill of the colouring – means that the listener is conscious of the music's length, although it is all agreeable enough. The more concise Mozartian *Variations* remain Sor's most famous piece, and the variety and flair of the playing demonstrate why. The studio recording, made in New York, is eminently truthful.

'Classic guitar': Grand solo (Introduction and allegro), Op. 14. Sonata in C, Op. 25.
(M) **(*) RCA 09026 61593-2. Julian Bream (guitar) – GIULIANI: *Grand overture, Op. 61* etc.; DIA-
BELLI: *Sonata in A.* **(*)

Sor's *Grand solo* is quite an attractive piece, with an *Andante largo* introduction instead of a slow movement, and it includes the theme and variations seemingly obligatory to this composer. The *Sonata in C*, however, is extremely inconsequential and easily forgettable. But all the music is beautifully played and immaculately recorded.

Sousa, John Philip (1854–1932)

Marches: The Ancient and Honorable Artillery Company; The Black Horse Troop; Bullets and bayonets; The Gallant Seventh; Golden jubilee; The Glory of the Yankee Navy; The Gridiron Club; High school cadets; The Invincible eagle; The Kansas Wildcats; The Liberty Bell; Manhattan Beach; The National game; New Mexico; Nobles of the mystic shrine; Our flirtation; The Piccadore; The Pride of the Wolverines; Riders for the flag; The Rifle Regiment; Sabre and spurs; Sesqui-centennial exposition; Solid men to the front; Sound off.
(M) *** Mercury 434 300-2 [id.]. Eastman Wind Ens., Frederick Fennell.

Fennell's collection of 24 Sousa marches (73 minutes) derives from vintage Mercury recordings of the early 1960s. The performances have characteristic American pep and natural exuberance; the zest of the playing always carries the day. One of the more striking items is *The Ancient and Honorable Artillery Company*, which incorporates *Auld lang syne* as its middle section. The sound, is, of course, first class.

Spohr, Ludwig (1784–1859)

Clarinet concertos Nos. 1 in C min., Op. 26; 4 in E min.
**(*) Orfeo C 088101A [id.]. Leister, Stuttgart RSO, Frühbeck de Burgos.

Clarinet concertos Nos. 2 in E flat, Op. 57; 3 in F min.
**(*) Orfeo C 088201A [id.]. Leister, Stuttgart RSO, Frühbeck de Burgos.

The four *Clarinet concertos* of Spohr – the *Fourth* much grander than the other three – make up an attractive pair of discs, particularly when they are as beautifully played as by the long-time principal of the Berlin Philharmonic, Karl Leister. His smooth tone, the ease and agility with which he tackles virtuoso passage-work and his ability to bring out the smiling quality of much of the inspiration make for delightful performances. The radio recording has relatively little stereo spread, but is undistractingly natural.

Clarinet concerto No. 1 in C min., Op. 26.
(M) *** Decca 433 727-2 [id.]. Gervase de Peyer, LSO, C. Davis – MOZART; WEBER: *Concertos.* ***

Clearly modelled on Mozart's masterpiece, Spohr's *C minor Concerto* primarily exploits the lyrical side of the clarinet. The main theme of the first movement is perfectly conceived for the instrument, and the *Adagio* – very much Mozart-patterned – is charming too. The finale is a captivating Spanish rondo. Gervase de Peyer is just the man for these suave melodic lines and he receives excellent support from Davis. The recording is faithful and sounds hardly dated.

Clarinet concertos Nos. 1 in C min., Op. 26; 3 in F min.; Potpourri for clarinet and orchestra in F on Peter von Winter's opera 'Das unterbrochene Opferfest', Op. 80.
(N) (BB) *(*) Naxos Dig. 8.550688 [id.]. Ernst Ottensamer, Slovak State PO (Košice) or RSO
(Bratislava), Johannes Wildner.

Ottensamer's mellow, nicely turned performances of urbane music that can easily sound bland have not nearly enough flair and sparkle. He is best in the finales which, though low-key, are elegantly jocular; but all his chortling cannot bring the *Potpourri* back to life, for want of really indelible tunes. Warm, full recording.

Symphonies Nos. 1 in E flat, Op. 20; 5 in C min., Op. 102.
**(*) Marco Polo Dig. 8.223363 [id.]. Slovak State PO (Košice), Alfred Walter.

Spohr wrote ten symphonies in all: the *First* when he was in his mid-twenties and still in thrall to Mozart; the *Fifth* comes from the late 1830s and was much admired by Schumann. The latter is certainly a better piece, but there is always a certain blandness about Spohr's invention even when he is at his best. His melodic inspiration is not quite strong enough even in the slow movement, by far the finest and most thoughtful. Although he is no great symphonist, Spohr is an eminently civilized composer, and the case for him is well put by Alfred Walter and the Košice orchestra, who are decently served by the engineers.

Symphonies Nos. 3 in C min., Op. 78; 6 in G, Op. 116.
** Marco Polo Dig. 8.223439 [id.]. Slovak State PO (Košice), Alfred Walter.

The *Third Symphony* makes as good an entry-point as any into the Ten, and is arguably the best of them. Mendelssohn was one of its early champions, but if the symphony suggests his neo-classical romanticism, its invention falls short of either Mendelssohn or Schumann in freshness and character. All the same, the *Third* is well crafted and thoroughly enjoyable, and is far more rewarding than its companion, the *Historical Symphony*, which parodies the styles of various masters to make an unconvincing whole. Alfred Walter draws very good playing from his Slovak forces, who do their best to persuade us as to this music's merits.

Nonet in F, Op. 31; Octet in E, Op. 32.
*** Hyperion Dig. CDA 66699 [id.]. Gaudier Ens.
*** CRD CRD 3354; *CRDC 4054* [id.]. Nash Ens.

Spohr's *Octet* is a work of great charm; the variations on Handel's *Harmonious blacksmith* which form the third movement offer that kind of naïveté which, when played stylishly, makes for delicious listening. Here the Gaudier Ensemble give us a performance as imaginative as it is spontaneous, and the work's finale with its lolloping main theme is joyously spirited. The *Nonet* is also very attractive. Spohr's invention is again at its freshest and his propensity for chromaticism is held reasonably in check. Here there is another vivacious finale, but perhaps one remembers most the *Adagio*, where the expressive mood of the Gaudier performance has a gentle gravitas. The Hyperion recording is fresh and warm, clearly detailed against a resonant acoustic, although this means that the first violin is given a fractional hint of wiriness by the fairly close microphones.

The sound on the competing CRD disc is that bit more mellifluous, yet it remains natural and lifelike; some may prefer the greater suavity of the analogue tonal blend in this urbane music. The Nash Ensemble play both works with much elegance and style, and these performances are very civilized and hardly less spontaneous. They are well worth considering alongside their Hyperion competitors.

Piano trios Nos. 1 in E min., Op. 119; 2 in F, Op. 123; 3 in A min., Op. 124; 4 in B flat, Op. 133; 5 in G min., Op. 142.
(N) *** Orfeo Dig. C 352 952H (2) [id.]. New Munich Piano Trio.
(N) *** CPO Dig. CPO 999 246-2 (3) [id.]. Ravensburg Beethoven Trio.

Piano trios Nos. 2 in F, Op. 123; 4 in B flat, Op. 133.
(N) (BB) ** Naxos Dig. 8.553205 [id.]. Hartley Piano Trio.

Piano trios Nos. 3 in A min., Op. 124; 4 in B flat, Op. 133.
(N) **(*) Chandos Dig. CHAN 9372 [id.]. Borodin Trio.

Spohr's five *Piano trios* are among his freshest, most appealing chamber works, full of attractive ideas and fine craftsmanship. They are late works, the first three composed in 1841–2 and the remaining pair in 1846 and 1849 respectively. The New Munich Piano Trio have their full measure. They also have a fine pianist in Hermann Kechler (one is reminded at times of Menahem Pressler) and the piano is often to the fore. The playing has warmth, a nice degree of elegance and proper touches of wit. In the *First Trio*, with a striking opening movement, after the eloquent *Larghetto* comes a charming Scherzo where, in the trio, the piano decorates the string-tune nimbly with deliciously articulated downward scales. The *Second Trio* brings another fine slow movement, and the *Adagio* of the *Fourth* is even finer, while the bouncing finale brings a buoyant lift. Throughout, the playing combines polish with spontaneity, and the fresh, clear recording is very well balanced. Most enjoyable.

The Ravensburg Trio also give fine performances, mellower, with slightly more gravitas and slightly less sparkle, although they too have an excellent pianist in Inge-Susann Römchild, whose touch is often pleasingly light. The CPO recording is warmer and fuller to suit the playing. In their different way these readings are almost equally enjoyable; indeed some listeners may prefer their more serious mood. But with a greater degree of relaxation the five *Trios* are just too long to fit on a pair of CDs, and the third plays for only 31 minutes.

Of the two individual discs, the Borodin Trio offers plenty of life and the Chandos recording is pleasingly open and vivid. But Luba Edlina's vibrant temperament and timbre do not so readily match Spohr's relatively suave writing, and this coupling is less enjoyable than either of the complete sets.

The Naxos accounts are well played and serviceable, the *Second Trio* rather pleasing, although the Hartley Trio does not exude a very strong collective personality. The other snag is the resonant ecclesiastical acoustic, which means that the microphones have to be fairly close and in consequence the recording is less flattering and not always so cleanly focused.

Piano and wind quintet in C min., Op. 52; Septet in A min. for flute, clarinet, horn, bassoon, violin, cello and piano, Op. 147.
*** CRD CRD 3399; *CRDC 4099* [id.]. Ian Brown, Nash Ens.

These two pieces are among Spohr's most delightful, both the sparkling *Quintet* and the more substantial but still charmingly lighthearted *Septet*. Ian Brown at the piano leads the ensemble with flair and vigour, and the recording quality is outstandingly vivid.

Septet in A min., Op. 147.
(N) *** Decca Dig. 443 892-2 [id.]. Chantal Juillet, Christoph van Kempen, Pascal Rogé, London Winds – BEETHOVEN: *Piano and wind quintet.* ***

The Spohr *Septet* comes from 1853 and was his last chamber work with piano. Scored for violin, flute, clarinet, bassoon, horn, piano and double-bass, it is a model of urbanity. In the hands of Pascal Rogé and his colleagues it radiates a refreshing, invigorating charm that is quite captivating. The Decca recording is in the best traditions of the house. Strongly recommended.

String quartets Nos. 3 in D min., Op. 11; 4 in E flat, Op. 15/1; 6 in G min., Op. 27.
** Marco Polo Dig. 8.223254 [id.]. New Budapest Qt.

The *D minor* is a 'Quatuor brillant' with the focus permanently on the first violin, and the other three players taking very subsidiary roles. The *E flat Quartet*, although still requiring a great deal of virtuosity from the leader, especially in the first movement, is written very much in the spirit of Haydn. *Quartet No. 6 in G minor* is the most ambitious work here and its long first movement (12 minutes 37 seconds) has a very characteristic main theme. It needs rather more grip than these players achieve, and greater polish too. Good recording.

String quartets Nos. 7 in E flat; 8 in C, Op. 29/1–2.
**(*) Marco Polo Dig. 8.22355 [id.]. New Budapest Qt.

The Op. 29 *Quartets* are associated with Johann Tost (dedicatee of Haydn's Opp. 54/5 and 65). Both are written in Spohr's friendly, accomplished style; the first ingeniously bases its opening movement on a two-note motto theme and has an outstanding set of variations for its slow movement, surely worthy of Haydn. The tender *Adagio* of the *C major* is even finer, daring in its expressive chromaticism. Both performances are spontaneous and the players seem inside the music. If the very last ounce of finesse is missing, this is still vibrant, felt quartet-playing, without artifice, and the recording is lively and present.

String quartets Nos. 27 in D min.; 28 in A flat, Op. 84/1–2.
**(*) Marco Polo Dig. 8.223251 [id.]. New Budapest Qt.

These two works, written in 1831–2, exemplify Spohr's smooth, finely integrated quartet-writing at its most characteristic. The slow movement, sustaining a mood of serene simplicity, is the most memorable in each case, although the lyrical finale of the *A flat major Quartet* is also rather appealing. Good performances, lively enough, but capturing the suaveness of the idiom. The recording is truthful.

String quartets Nos. 29 in B min., Op. 84/3; 30 (Quatuor brillant) in A, Op. 93.
**(*) Marco Polo Dig. 8.223252 [id.]. New Budapest Qt.

In many ways *No. 29 in B minor* is the finest of the Op. 84 set, with its touch of melancholy in the first movement, a lively minuet and a pensive slow movement. Op. 93, written in 1835, is more extrovert in atmosphere in the first movement (after a sombre introduction), but it offers another thoughtfully intense slow movement and a very jolly finale. It brings out the best in these players – and there is plenty of bravura for the first violin – and, again, good tonal matching plus a smooth, warm recording combine effectively for this slightly suave music.

String quintet in A min., Op. 91; String sextet in C, Op. 140; Pot-pourri on themes of Mozart, Op. 22.
(N) **(*) Chandos Dig. CHAN 9424 [id.]. ASMF Chamber Ens.

String octet (Double quartet) in D min., Op. 65; String quintet in G, Op. 33/2; String sextet in C, Op. 140.
(N) *** Sony Dig. SK 53370 [id.]. L'Archibudelli & Smithsonian Chamber Players.

To be candid, the *A minor String quintet*, although as always with this composer well crafted, is rather bland, a characteristic the well-rehearsed ASMF performance does very little to counteract. The Mozartian potpourri is much more entertaining: using a theme like *Là ci darem la mano* you can't really go wrong, and here Kenneth Sillito takes the solo violin role like a prima donna. Then comes the fine *String sextet in C major*, one of the composer's last chamber works, from 1848. It has a particularly endearing Brahmsian main theme in the first movement, a hymn-like slow movement and a brilliant finale. The ASMF Chamber Ensemble give a fine, polished account of it, well recorded.

However, the period-instrument performance from L'Archibudelli combined with the Smithsonian Chamber Players is even finer: here is authenticity with much character, giving the *Larghetto* a grave nobility and finding a ready sparkle in the light-textured finale. There is an even more vivacious finale in the *Octet* (marked *Allegro molto*) to which these players respond with virtuosity and the lightest touch, while the preceding slow movement matches that of the *Sextet* in concentration. The *G major String quintet* (using two violas) is hardly less striking in its variety of invention, especially the *Andante* (with very florid variations) and the unusual last movement with its ambivalent atmosphere and strain of nostalgia. (The composer – rightly – thought highly of this work.) There are few recordings on period instruments in which the ear is as consistently beguiled by the transparency of texture and the combination of bravura and warm tonal blending. Highly recommended.

VOCAL MUSIC

Lieder: *An Mignon; 6 German Lieder, Op. 103; 6 Lieder, Op. 154; Lied beim Runetanz; Schlaflied; Scottische Lied; Vanitas!; Zigeuner Lied.*
*** Orfeo Dig. C 103841A [id.]. Julia Varady, Dietrich Fischer-Dieskau, Sitkovetsky, Schoneberger, Hartmut Holl.

The amiable inspiration of Spohr in his songs is delightfully presented in this collection from Dietrich Fischer-Dieskau and Julia Varady. It is characteristic of the composer that, even in his setting of *Erlkönig*, he jogs along rather than gallops, and fails to use the violin dramatically, just giving it an ordinary obbligato. The most attractive songs are the set sung by Varady with clarinet obbligato, but those sung by Fischer-Dieskau are also all highly enjoyable, as long as you do not compare them with the finest of the genre. Excellent recording.

Spontini, Gasparo (1774–1851)

Olympie (opera): complete.
**(*) Orfeo Dig. C 137862H (3) [id.]. Varady, Toczyska, Tagliavini, Fischer-Dieskau, Fortune, Berlin RIAS Chamber Ch., German Op. Male Ch., Berlin RSO, Albrecht.

In Spontini's *Olympie*, based on an historical play by Voltaire about the daughter of Alexander the Great, the writing is lively and committed and, despite flawed singing, so is this performance. Julia Varady is outstanding in the name-part, giving an almost ideal account of the role of heroine, but Stefania Toczyska is disappointingly unsteady as Statire and Franco Tagliavini is totally out of style as Cassandre. Even Dietrich Fischer-Dieskau is less consistent than usual, but his melodramatic presentation is nevertheless most effective. The text is slightly cut.

Stainer, John (1840–1901)

The Crucifixion.
(B) *** CD-CFP 4519; *TC-CFP 4519*. David Hughes, John Lawrenson, Guildford Cathedral Ch., Barry Rose; Gavin Williams.
(BB) ** ASV CDQS 6100. James Griffet, Michael George, Peterborough Cathedral Ch., Stanley Vann; Andrew Newberry.

(i) *The Crucifixion. Come thou long-expected Jesus* (hymn); *I saw the Lord* (anthem).
(B) *** Decca 436 146-2; *436 146-4* [id.]. (i) Richard Lewis, Owen Brannigan, St John's College, Cambridge, Ch., Guest.

All five hymns in which the congregation is invited to join are included on the Decca (originally Argo) record. Owen Brannigan is splendidly dramatic and his voice makes a good foil for Richard Lewis in the duets. The choral singing is first class and the 1961 recording is of Argo's best vintage, even finer than its CfP competitor. Moreover the Decca disc includes two bonuses: a hymn set to the words of Charles Wesley and a fine eight-part anthem, *I saw the Lord*, both of which are equally well sung.

The Classics for Pleasure version (from the late 1960s) is of high quality and, although one of the congregational hymns is omitted, in every other respect this can be recommended. John Lawrenson makes a movingly eloquent solo contribution and the choral singing is excellent. The remastered recording sounds first class, but the Decca version is finer still.

A super-bargain version is welcome, and the ASV performance is sincere and eloquent in a modestly restrained way, although at times there is a lack of vitality. The two soloists make a stronger contribution, and the tenor, James Griffet, is pleasingly lyrical. However, the style of presentation does not wholly avoid hints of the sentimentality that hovers dangerously near all performances of this work. The recording is atmospheric.

Stalder, Joseph Franz Xaver (1725–65)

(i) *Flute concerto in B flat; Symphony No. 5 in G.*
*** Novalis Dig. 150 031-2 [id.]. (i) William Bennett; ECO, Griffiths – REINDL: *Sinfonia concertante in D.* ***

Though Joseph Stalder is not quite as interesting a composer as his younger compatriot, Reindl, both the short *G major Symphony* and the *Flute concerto* have freshness and charm and well repay investigation, particularly in such excellent performances and recording.

Stamitz, Carl (1745–1801)

Sinfonias concertantes: (i) *in C for 2 violins and orchestra;* (ii) *in D for violin, viola and orchestra.*
(Y/B) (BB) **(*) ASV Dig. CDQS 6140 [id.]. Richard Friedman, L. Festival O, Ross Pople; with (i) Steven Smith; (ii) Roger Best – HAYDN: *Sinfonia concertante.* **(*)

Stamitz may not match Mozart but he is a personality in his own right and such a work as the *Sinfonia concertante in C for two violins*, here projected with fine spontaneity, brings a slow movement where one of the two soloists, playing alone, presents a 'singing' cantilena almost worthy of his greater contemporary. This *Andante* is also felicitously scored, with effective writing for the horns. The first movement has some good ideas too, and it is only the *Minuet* finale that lapses into conventionality; even so, like the first movement, the writing for the two soloists is inventively conceived. The companion *Sinfonia concertante for violin and viola*, if not quite so interesting in its material, has a historic link with Mozart's work for the same combination; as such, it makes fascinating listening. However, although the two soloists here play freshly and stylishly, they lack individuality of profile and, while Ross Pople directs the orchestra strongly, with tender feeling in the central *Romance*, the earlier CBS/Sony account of this work by Stern and Zukerman (with the ECO under Barenboim) has far more personality.

Sinfonia concertante in D for violin, viola and orchestra.
(N) (M) *** Sony Stern Edition I SM2K 66472 (2) [id.]. Stern, Zukerman, ECO, Barenboim – VIVALDI: *Concertos.* **(*)

This Stern/Zukerman performance was originally recorded (in 1971) quadraphonically at the EMI Abbey Road No. 1 Studio and was more appropriately coupled with Mozart's much greater *Sinfonia concertante*, featuring the same solo instruments. Stamitz's work is relatively lightweight, but again it gives these vital artists a chance to strike sparks off each other. The recording has plenty of atmosphere but the soloists are balanced unnaturally forward.

Stamitz, Johann (1717–57)

Trumpet concerto in D (arr. Boustead).
*** Ph. Dig. 420 203-2 [id.]. Hardenberger, ASMF, Marriner – HAYDN; HUMMEL: *Concertos* *** ⚘; HERTEL: *Concerto.* ***

This concerto was written either by Stamitz or by a composer called J. G. Holzbogen. The writing lies consistently up in the instrument's stratosphere and includes some awkward leaps. It is quite inventive, however, notably the finale, which is exhilarating on the lips of Håkan Hardenberger. There is no lack of panache here and Marriner accompanies expertly. Good if reverberant recording, with the trumpet given great presence.

Stanford, Charles (1852–1924)

(i) *Concert piece for organ and orchestra;* (ii) *Clarinet concerto in A min., Op. 80; Irish rhapsodies Nos. 1 in D min., Op. 78; 2 in F min. (Lament for the Son of Ossian), Op. 84;* (iii) *3 for cello and orchestra, Op. 137; 4 in A min. (The fisherman of Loch Neagh and what he saw); 5 in G min., Op. 147;* (iv) *6 for violin and orchestra, Op. 191; Oedipus Rex prelude, Op. 29.*
(Y/B) *** Chandos Dig. CHAN 7002/3 [id.]. (i) Gillian Weir; (ii) Janet Hilton; (iii) Raphael Wallfisch; (iv) Lydia Mordkovitch; Ulster O, Vernon Handley.

Stanford's set of *Irish rhapsodies* (two of them concertante pieces with highly responsive soloists) are the more impressive when heard as a set. They originally appeared coupled with the symphonies but sometimes seemed stronger and more concentrated than these more ambitious works. They are splendidly played and recorded. Gillian Weir makes a first-class soloist in the *Concert piece for organ and orchestra* and Janet Hilton is hardly less appealing in the work for clarinet. An essential supplement for those who have already invested in the four-CD box of the symphonies.

Clarinet concerto in A min., Op. 80.
*** Hyperion CDA 66001 [id.]. King, Philh. O, Francis – FINZI: *Concerto.* ***

(i) *Clarinet concerto in A min.* (for clarinet and strings) *Op. 80;* (ii) *3 Intermezzi* (for clarinet and piano).
*** ASV Dig. CDDCA 787 [id.]. Emma Johnson; (i) RPO, Groves; (ii) Martineau – FINZI: *Clarinet concerto etc.* ***

The Stanford *Clarinet concerto* finds Emma Johnson inspired, even freer and more fluent than Thea King on the rival Hyperion disc. It is a delight how Johnson can edge into a theme with extreme gentleness. So her first entry in the slow movement, taxingly high, seems to emerge ethereally from nowhere, while Thea King's firmer, sharper attack is less poetic. In the finale too King is strong and forthright, but Johnson is warmer and more personal with her cheekily witty treatment of the first solo. Sir Charles Groves and the RPO are warmly sympathetic accompanists, very well recorded, though the solo instrument is rather too close.

Piano concerto No. 1 in G, Op. 59.
(N) *** Hyperion Dig. CDA 66820 [id.]. Piers Lane, BBC Scottish SO, Martyn Brabbins – PARRY: *Piano concerto.* ***

Written in 1894, the first of Stanford's two piano concertos brings even clearer Brahmsian echoes than usual, but the finesse of the writing and the ravishing beauty of the slow movement make it almost as enjoyable as the second and better-known concerto, particularly in a performance by turns as brilliant and poetic as Piers Lane's. Full, warm sound.

(i) *Piano concerto No. 2 in C min., Op. 126;* (ii) *Becket, Op. 48: The Martyrdom (Funeral march);* (iii) *The Fisherman of Lough Neagh and what he saw (Irish rhapsody No. 4), Op. 141.*
*** Lyrita SRCD 219 [id.]. (i) Malcolm Binns, LSO; (ii–iii) LPO; (i; iii) Nicholas Braithwaite; (ii) Sir Adrian Boult.

Stanford's *Second Piano concerto*, although in three rather than four movements, is a work on the largest scale, recalling the Brahms *B flat Concerto*. Yet Stanford asserts his own melodic individuality and provides a really memorable secondary theme for the first movement. The piece is enjoyable and uninflated, especially when played with such spontaneous freshness. The recording is surely a demonstration of just how a piano concerto should be balanced. The *Funeral march* comes from incidental music commissioned at the request of Tennyson for Irving's production of his tragedy, *Becket*. It has an arresting opening but otherwise is a fairly straightforward piece, strongly melodic in a Stanfordian manner. Like the more familiar *Irish rhapsody*, it is splendidly played and recorded.

Symphonies Nos. 1–7.
*** Chandos Dig. CHAN 9279/82 (4) [id.]. Ulster O, Handley.

Now available in a box of four CDs, with the fill-ups which accompanied the original CDs now put aside for separate reissue, this is obviously the most attractive way to approach this generally impressive if uneven British symphonic canon. Handley and his Ulster Orchestra are completely at home in this repertoire, and the Chandos recording is consistently of this company's best quality.

Symphonies Nos. 1 in B flat., Op. 78; Irish rhapsody No. 2: The Lament for the Son of Ossian, Op. 84.
*** Chandos Dig. CHAN 9049 [id.]. Ulster O, Handley.

Stanford's mature musical studies had been in Berlin and Hamburg, and he came back to England profoundly influenced by the German symphonic style (the Scherzo of the *First Symphony* (1876) even has the character of a Laendler). His work was duly performed and then, like the *Second*, put in a cupboard. Now we can discover for ourselves that, although he could assemble a convincing structure, his melodic invention was not yet strong enough to achieve real memorability. Handley and the Ulster Orchestra do their persuasive best for a piece which is certainly not a silk purse. The *Irish rhapsody* has distinctly more melodramatic flair. Excellent recording.

Symphony No. 2 in D min. (Elegiac); (i) Clarinet concerto in A min., Op. 80.
*** Chandos Dig. CHAN 8991 [id.]. Ulster O, Handley; (i) with Janet Hilton.

The penultimate issue in Handley's fine series, the *Second Symphony* has until now lain neglected for over a century. The influences of German masters are strong but the work still has its own individuality, for the most part in the scoring. The delightful *Clarinet concerto* makes a splendid coupling, with Janet Hilton at her most seductive, both in timbre and in warmth, and articulating with nimble expertise. A delightful performance.

Symphony No. 3 in F min. (Irish), Op. 28.
(m) *** EMI CDM5 65129-2 [id.]. Bournemouth Sinf., Norman Del Mar – ELGAR: *Scenes from the Bavarian highlands.* ***

Symphony No. 3 in F min. (Irish), Op. 28; Irish rhapsody No. 5, Op. 147.
*** Chandos Dig. CHAN 8545 [id.]. Ulster O, Handley.

This *Third* and most celebrated of the seven symphonies of Stanford is a rich and attractive work, none the worse for its obvious debts to Brahms. The ideas are best when directly echoing Irish folk music, as in the middle two movements, a skippity jig of a Scherzo and a glowing slow movement framed by harp cadenzas. The *Irish rhapsody No. 5* dates from 1917, reflecting perhaps in its martial vigour that wartime date. Even more characteristic are the warmly lyrical passages, performed passionately by Handley and his Ulster Orchestra, matching the thrust and commitment they bring also to the *Symphony*.

  Norman Del Mar directs an equally ripe performance, noting that the finale gives an attractive forward glance to Stanford's pupils, Holst and Vaughan Williams. The EMI recording is warm and well defined.

Symphony No. 4 in F, Op. 31; Irish rhapsody No. 6 for violin and orchestra, Op. 191; Oedipus Rex Prelude, Op. 29.
*** Chandos Dig. CHAN 8884 [id.]. Ulster O, Vernon, (i) with Lydia Mordkovitch.

The *Fourth Symphony*, like the *Third*, is a highly confident piece and an effective symphony, even if it runs out of steam before the close of the finale despite attractive invention. The *Irish* concertante *rhapsody* is a much later work, its nostalgia nicely caught by the soloist here, Lydia Mordkovitch, who is obviously involved. Handley, as ever, takes the helm throughout with ardent commitment and makes the most of the many nice touches of orchestral colour. Excellent recording.

Symphony No. 5 in D (L'Allegro ed il Penseroso), Op. 56; Irish rhapsody No. 4 in A min. (The Fisherman of Lough Neagh and what he saw), Op. 141.
*** Chandos Dig. CHAN 8581 [id.]. Ulster O, Handley.

Stanford's *Fifth Symphony* is colourfully orchestrated and full of easy tunes, illustrating passages from Milton's *L'Allegro* and *Il Penseroso*. The last two movements readily live up to Stanford's reputation as a Brahmsian, representing the *Penseroso* half of the work, and the slow epilogue brings reminders of Brahms's *Third*. The *Irish rhapsody* is more distinctive of the composer, bringing together sharply contrasted, colourful and atmospheric Irish ideas under the title *The Fisherman of Lough Neagh and what he saw*. Excellent recording of the finest Chandos quality.

Symphony No. 6 in E flat (In memoriam G. F. Watts), Op. 94; Irish rhapsody No. 1 in D min., Op. 78.
*** Chandos Dig. CHAN 8627 [id.]. Ulster O, Vernon Handley.

Stanford's *Sixth Symphony* is not the strongest of the set, but it has a rather lovely slow movement, with a pervading air of gentle melancholy. The first movement has some good ideas but the finale is too long, in the way finales of Glazunov symphonies tend to overuse their material. Nevertheless Vernon Handley makes quite a persuasive case for the work and an even better one for the enjoyable *Irish rhapsody No. 1*, which features and makes rather effective use of one of the loveliest of all Irish tunes, the *Londonderry air*. Excellent sound.

Symphony No. 7 in D min., Op. 124; (i) *Concert piece for organ and orchestra, Op. 181;* (ii) *Irish rhapsody No. 3 for cello and orchestra, Op. 137.*
*** Chandos Dig. CHAN 8861 [id.]. Ulster O, Handley; with (i) Gillian Weir; (ii) Raphael Wallfisch.

The *Seventh Symphony* sums up its composer as a symphonist – structurally sound, yet not now so heavily indebted to Germany, and with the orchestration often ear-catching. It is not a masterpiece, but it could surely not be presented with more conviction than here by Handley and his excellent orchestra. The *Irish rhapsody* is very Irish indeed and makes the use of several good tunes. It is most sensitively played by Wallfisch, and Gillian Weir makes a strong impression in the *Organ 'concertino',* where the composer uses only brass, strings and percussion in the accompaniment. The music has a touch of the epic about it.

Serenade (Nonet) in F, Op. 95.
*** Hyperion CDA 66291 [id.]. Capricorn – PARRY: *Nonet.* ***

Like the Parry *Nonet,* with which it is coupled, the *Serenade* is an inventive and delightful piece, its discourse civilized and the Scherzo full of charm. Capricorn play this piece with evident pleasure and convey this to the listener. The recording is very natural and truthfully balanced.

PIANO MUSIC

24 Preludes, Set 1, Op. 163; 6 Characteristic pieces, Op. 132.
(N) *** Priory Dig. PRCD 449 [id.]. Peter Jacobs.

This collection comes as a pleasant surprise: one does not think of Stanford as a composer for the piano, and indeed his 24 *Preludes* are not bravura works like those of Chopin and Rachmaninov. Written in 1918, their chromatic key-sequence would suggest that they are more readily associated with Bach's *Well-tempered Clavier,* and the composer's following set in 1920 (to make a total of 48) seems to emphasize that parallel. But although the very first *C major* piece opens seriously and serenely, by the gently poignant *Second in C minor* we have moved well into the nineteenth century, and this is confirmed by the ardour of *No. 3 in D flat.* Although the writing is eclectic, there is no sense of carbon-copying in its style. There are gentle miniatures that charm, like No. 8, the daintily skipping No. 10, and the occasional lollipop like No. 13 (subtitled *'In the Woodland'*) and the catchy No. 15, while the more solemn *No. 16 in G minor* is entitled *Fantasy.* The poignant funeral march of *No. 22 in B flat* was written in memory of Maurice Gray, the son of the organist at Trinity College, who was tragically killed in 1918, just before the Armistice was signed. He is well remembered. The mood then lightens in the neo-classical *Rondeau* which follows. The variety of Stanford's invention brings a continuing freshness throughout the set, which can be enjoyed as a progression as well as by selecting individual items. The *Charcteristic pieces* were written six years earlier and are also of high quality, with the engaging *Rondel* (No. 4) dedicated to the Schumann of *Kinderszenen.* Peter Jacobs almost never disappoints and his perform-ances here are accomplished, stylish, spontaneous and thoroughly sympathetic, while the recording is first class.

VOCAL MUSIC

Magnificat in B flat, Op. 164; 3 Motets, Op. 38; Motet: Eternal Father, Op. 135.
*** Conifer Dig. 75605 51155-2 [id.]. Trinity College, Cambridge, Ch., Marlow – PARRY: *Songs of farewell.* ***

The *Three Motets,* early works, are settings of Latin hymns; *Eternal Father* is an elaborate setting of Robert Bridges; while the big-scale unaccompanied *Magnificat* for double choir makes a magnificent culmination. Immaculate performances and beautifully balanced, atmospheric recording.

Stanley, John (1712–86)

6 Organ concertos, Op. 10.
*** CRD CRD 3365; *CRDC 4065* [id.]. Gifford, N. Sinfonia.

These bouncing, vigorous performances, well recorded as they are on the splendid organ of Hexham Abbey, present these *Concertos* most persuasively. No. 4, with its darkly energetic C minor, is particu-larly fine. The recording is natural in timbre and very well balanced.

Steffan, Joseph Anton (Štěpán) (1726–97)

Fortepiano concerto in B flat.
(Y/B) *** Teldec/Warner Dig. 4509 94569-2 [id.]. Andreas Staier, Concerto Köln – SALIERI: *Fortepiano concerto*. ***

The Bohemian-born Štěpán was forced by the invading Prussian armies to leave home and make for Vienna, where as a pupil of Georg Wagenseil (who is he, you may well ask!) he became Steffan, before taking over court duties; alas, he began to go blind in the 1770s, although he continued composing; and this work dates from a decade later. It is a fluent and inventive, if slightly overlong piece, with a rather fine slow movement; the concerto also opens with an extended and quite touching *Adagio* in D minor. Staier's performance is highly persuasive and he is given alert and sympathetic support by the excellent Concerto Köln.

Steffani, Agostino (1654–1728)

Stabat Mater.
(N) *** DHM Dig. 05472 77344-2 [id.]. Almajano, Van der Sluis, Elwes, Padmore, Huijts, Van der Kamp, Netherlands Bach Festival Ch. & O, Leonhardt – BIBER: *Requiem à 15 in A*. ***

Agostino Steffani was diplomat and priest as well as a composer, but his music has a strongly individual character. His serene, melancholy *Stabat Mater* has moving and expressive content and much imaginative word-setting, while the *Cujus animam* and *Pro peccatis* are glorious in their expressively rich harmonies. The solo writing is imaginative and the layering of parts in the closing *Quando corpus*, which gathers pace as it proceeds, is very telling. The performance could hardly be bettered, with soloists and chorus equally dedicated. First-rate recording.

Stenhammar, Wilhelm (1871–1927)

(i) *Piano concerto No. 1 in B flat min., Op. 1. Symphony No. 3* (fragment).
*** Chandos Dig. CHAN 9074 [id.]. (i) Widlund; Royal Stockholm PO, Rozhdestvensky.

(i) *Piano concerto No. 1 in B flat min., Op. 1;* (ii) *Florez och Blanzeflor, Op. 3;* (iii) *Two Sentimental Romances, Op. 28.*
*** BIS Dig. CD 550 [id.]. (i) Love Derwinger; (ii) Peter Mattei; (iii) Ulf Wallin, Malmö SO, Paavo Järvi.

Stenhammar's *First Piano concerto* is full of beautiful ideas and the invention is fresh. Love Derwinger proves an impressive and sympathetic intepreter and gets good support from Järvi *fils*. Stenhammar's ballad, *Florez och Blanzeflor* ('Flower and Whiteflower'), Op. 3, is a beautiful piece despite its somewhat Wagnerian overtones, and is sensitively sung by the young Swedish baritone Peter Mattei, of whom we shall surely hear more.

Chandos offer the less substantial coupling, a three-minute fragment from the *Third Symphony*, on which Stenhammar embarked in 1918–19. In itself it is too insignificant a makeweight to affect choice. But in the *Concerto* Mats Widlund proves the more imaginative soloist and brings just that little bit more finesse to the solo part. Rozhdestvensky gives excellent support and the Stockholm orchestra (and in particular their strings) have greater richness of sonority. The Chandos recording also has the edge on its BIS competitor in terms of depth and warmth.

(i; ii) *Piano concerto No. 2 in D min., Op. 23.* (iii) *Serenade for orchestra, Op. 31.* (iii; iv) *Florez och Blanzeflor* (ballad).
(M) *** EMI CDM5 65081-2. (i) Janos Solyom; (ii) Munich PO; (iii) Swedish RSO, Stig Westerberg; (iv) with Ingvar Wixell.

This generously filled mid-price disc could serve as an admirable introduction to this fine Swedish composer. The *Serenade for orchestra* here comes in its finished form, as opposed to Neeme Järvi's Gothenburg recording, which adds the *Reverenza* movement that Stenhammar had excised but which brings no fill-up. Westerberg's 1974 performance is glorious and very well recorded, though the Swedish Radio Orchestra's strings do not have quite the same freshness and bloom as the Järvi set. However, this remains the most recommendable account of the work to date and is to be preferred to the old Kubelik set. Similarly Janos Solyom's dazzling account of the *Second Piano concerto* remains unsurpassed and, like the *Serenade*, still sounds very good indeed. There is a Saint-Saëns-like exuberance and effervescence about this work, and the improvisatory character of the piece is beautifully captured. The early

Florez och Blanzeflor ('Flower and Whiteflower'), a ballad by Oscar Levertin, brings a certain Wagnerian flavour but has a charm that is conveyed well by Ingvar Wixell and Westerberg.

(i) *Symphonies Nos. 1 in F; 2 in G min., Op. 34; Serenade for orchestra, Op. 31* (with *Reverenza* movement); *Excelsior Overture, Op. 13; The Song (Sången): Interlude, Op. 44; Lodolezzi sings (Lodolezzi sjunger): suite;* (ii) *Piano concertos Nos. 1 in B flat min., Op. 1;* (iii) *2 in D min., Op. 23;* (iv) *Ballad: Florez och Blanzeflor;* (v) *2 Sentimental Romances;* (vi) *Midwinter, Op. 24; Snöfrid, Op. 5.*

(Y/B) (M) *** BIS Dig. BIS CD 714/716 [id.]. (i) Gothenburg SO, Neeme Järvi; (ii) Love Derwinger; (iii) Cristina Ortiz; (iv) Peter Matthei; (v) Ulf Wallin; (vi) Gothenburg Ch.; (ii–v) Malmö SO, Paavo Järvi.

Järvi's performances are now repackaged at a distinctly advantageous price. Special points to note are: first, that this is the only version of the *Serenade for orchestra* to include the *Reverenza* movement which Stenhammar subsequently withdrew; secondly, that the *First Piano concerto* makes use of Atterberg's original orchestration, which came to light only recently in America; and, thirdly, this is the most comprehensive compilation of Stenhammar's orchestral music now on the market. All the performances and recordings are of high quality, and the only serious criticism to make affects the first movement of the *Second Symphony*, which Järvi takes rather too briskly. The dazzling performance of the *Second Piano concerto* by Janos Solyom has a slight edge over the Ortiz, but hers is a good account, full of sparkle. All the recordings are digital save for that of the *First Symphony*, which comes from a 1982 concert performance and has great warmth and transparency. Apart from the DG, that is its only recording, and many other works (*Midwinter, Lodolezzi sings* and the *Excelsior overture*) are not otherwise available. Recommended with enthusiasm.

Symphonies Nos. 1 in F (1902–3); 2 in G min., Op. 34; Serenade in F for orchestra, Op. 31; Overture, Excelsior!

(Y/B) *** DG Dig. 445 857-2 (2) [id.]. Gothenburg SO, Neeme Järvi.

As a glance at the above will show, the two-disc DG set is less comprehensive but it contains Stenhammar's orchestral masterpieces, the *Serenade* and the *Second Symphony*, the former without the *Reverenza* movement which the composer excised when he revised the work and transposed the outer movement from E major to F. Neeme Järvi and the Gothenburg Symphony Orchestra record them with the same team and in the same venue as they did for BIS. The *Second Symphony* is a distinct improvement on the earlier recording – the first movement is more measured and dignified, and the steadier tempo allows detail to register more effectively. Only in the fugal section of the finale does Järvi rush things a bit. There is very little to choose between the two versions of the *First Symphony*; perhaps the earlier, analogue recording has the greater warmth and spontaneity. The Gothenburg orchestra plays with real enthusiasm both here and in the *Excelsior! overture*. The *Serenade* comes off well, except for the glorious *Notturno*, which is faster and less atmospheric than before. Despite these provisos, the set is thoroughly recommendable and should do much for Stenhammar's cause in those areas where BIS records are not strongly stocked.

Symphony No. 1 in F.
*** BIS Dig. CD 219 [id.]. Gothenburg SO, Järvi.

The *First Symphony* displays sympathies with such composers as Brahms, Bruckner, Berwald and, in the slow movement, even an affinity with Elgar. Nevertheless there is plenty of originality in it. The recording has complete naturalness, and on CD there is additional presence and range, particularly at the bottom end of the register.

Symphony No. 2 in G min., Op. 34.
*** Cap. CAP 21151 [id.]. Stockholm PO, Westerberg.

Symphony No. 2; Overture, Excelsior!, Op. 13.
*** BIS CD 251 [id.]. Gothenburg SO, Järvi.

This is a marvellous symphony. It is direct in utterance; the melodic invention is fresh and abundant, and the generosity of spirit it radiates is heart-warming. The Stockholm Philharmonic under Stig Westerberg play with conviction and eloquence; the strings have warmth and body, and the wind are very fine too. The recording is vivid and full-bodied even by the digital standards of today: as sound, this record is absolutely first class.

Neeme Järvi takes an altogether brisker view of the first movement than Westerberg, but the playing is spirited and the recording very good indeed, though not quite as distinguished as on the Caprice rival. The special attraction of this issue, however, is the *Overture, Excelsior!* It is an opulent but inventive score in the spirit of Strauss and Elgar and is played with enormous zest.

Piano sonatas Nos. 1 in C; 2 in C min.; 3 in A flat; 4 in G min.; Fantasie in A min.
(N) **(*) BIS Dig. CD634 [id.]. Lucia Negro.

The *Fantasie in A minor* and the *First Sonata* were written when Stenhammar was nine and were followed a year later by another sonata. The *A flat Sonata* comes from 1883 when he was twelve (not two years later as stated on the sleeve-note). They are anonymous though accomplished, as one would expect from so gifted a young musician. All these juvenilia are in the style of Mozart, Weber and Mendelssohn – and it is puzzling why they should be thought worth recording. The *Sonata No. 4 in G minor* is another matter, and in it one recognizes the profile of the real Stenhammar. It comes from 1890, when he was nineteen, and has the breadth and scale of the mature composer. The ideas are long-breathed and the piano writing far more virtuosic and big-boned. It is confident music and well worth hearing. The performances could not be more beguiling. Lucia Negro brings great charm and intelligence to the smaller pieces, which have a certain touching innocence, and she gives the *G minor Sonata* with total conviction. Good recording too. One is hardly likely to play the juvenilia more than once – hence the limitation on the fullest recommendation – despite the excellence of both the playing and recording.

String quartets Nos. 1 in C, Op. 2; 2 in C min., Op. 14; 3 in F, Op. 18; 4 in A min., Op. 25; 5 in C (Serenade), Op. 29; 6 in D min., Op. 35.
*** Cap. CAP 21337/9 [id.]. Fresk Qt; Copenhagen Qt; Gotland Qt.

The *First Quartet* shows Stenhammar steeped in the chamber music of Beethoven and Brahms, though there is a brief reminder of the shadow of Grieg; the *Second* is far more individual. By the *Third* and *Fourth*, arguably the greatest of the six, the influence of Brahms and Dvořák is fully assimilated and the *Fourth* reflects that gentle melancholy which lies at the heart of Stenhammar's sensibility. The *Fifth* is the shortest; the *Sixth* comes from the war years when the composer was feeling worn out and depressed, though there is little evidence of this in the music. The Copenhagen Quartet play this marvellously. Performances are generally excellent, as indeed is the recording.

Allegro con moto ed appassionato; 3 Fantasies, Op. 11; Impromptu; Impromptu-Waltz; Late summer nights, Op. 33; 3 Small piano pieces.
*** BIS Dig. CD-554 [id.]. Lucia Negro.

It is strange that as fine a pianist as Stenhammar left so little music for his own instrument. Brahms is a dominant influence in the early *Allegro con moto ed appassionato* and in the Op. 11 *Fantasies*, but there is a strong individual personality at work too, and the *Sensommarnätter* ('Late summer nights'), which come from the period when Stenhammar was working on the *Serenade for orchestra*, are wonderfully thoughtful and atmospheric pieces that inhabit a wholly personal world. Lucia Negro is thoroughly at home in this repertoire and plays with an effortless assurance and elegance that is very persuasive, and the BIS recording is altogether first rate.

Lodolezzi sings: suite, Op. 39; (i) *Midwinter, Op. 24;* (ii) *Snöfrid, Op. 5; The Song* (interlude).
*** BIS Dig. CD 438 [id.]. (i; ii) Gothenburg Concert Hall Ch., (ii) with Ahlén, Nilsson, Zackrisson, Enoksson; Gothenburg SO, Järvi.

Snöfrid is an early cantata. The young composer was completely under the spell of Wagner at this time and it offers only occasional glimpses of the mature Stenhammar. *Midwinter* is a kind of folk-music fantasy or pot-pourri on the lines of Alfvén's *Midsummer vigil*, though not quite so appealing. *Lodolezzi sings* has much innocent charm. None of this is great Stenhammar but it is well worth hearing; the performances under Neeme Järvi are very sympathetic, and the recording is natural and present.

(i) *The Song (Sången), Op. 44;* (ii) *Two sentimental romances, Op. 28;* (iii) *Ithaca, Op. 21.*
*** Cap. CAP 21358 [id.]. (i) Sörenson, von Otter, Dahlberg, Wahlgren, State Ac. Ch., Adolf Fredrik Music School Children's Ch., (ii) Arve Tellefsen, (iii) Håkan Hagegård, Swedish RSO; (i) Blomstedt; (ii) Westerberg; (iii) Ingelbretsen.

The first half of *The Song* has been described as 'a great fantasy' and is Stenhammar at his best and most individual: the choral writing is imaginatively laid out and the contrapuntal ingenuity is always at the service of poetic ends. The second half is less individual, masterly in its way, a lively choral allegro in the style of Handel. The solo and choral singing is superb and the whole performance has the total commitment one might expect from these forces. The superbly engineered recording does them full justice. The *Two sentimental romances* have great charm and are very well played, and Hagegård is in fine voice in another rarity, *Ithaca*.

7 Songs from Thoughts of Solitude, Op. 7; 5 Songs to texts of Runeberg, Op. 8; 5 Swedish songs, Op. 16; 5 Songs of Bo Bergman, Op. 20; Songs and Moods, Op. 26; Late Harvest.
(Y/B) **(*) BIS Dig. CD 654 [id.]. Mattei, Lundin.

Only two of the three-dozen Stenhammar songs on this disc last longer than four minutes: *Jungfru Blond och Jungfru Brunett* ('Miss Blonde and Miss Brunette') and *Prins Aladin av Lampan* ('Prince Aladdin of the Lamp'), both of which are to be found on the set of 30 songs recorded by Anne Sofie von Otter and Håkan Hagegård – see below. As a song composer Stenhammar was often inspired and never routine in his responses to his poets (he shared Sibelius's taste for Fröding and Runeberg), his crafts-manship is always fastidious and in the posthumously published *Efterskörd* ('Late Harvest') and the *Thoughts of Solitude*, Op. 7, brings to light some songs of great eloquence and beauty that are not readily available outside Sweden. Peter Mattei is an intelligent singer, well endowed vocally; the voice is beautiful, but he has a tendency to colour the voice on the flat side of the note, and on occasion (in *Prins Aladin*, for example) is flat. Bengt-Ake Lundin deserves special mention for the sensitivity and responsiveness of his accompanying, and the recording is excellent.

30 Songs.
*** Caprice MSCD 623. Von Otter, Hagegård, Forsberg, Schuback.

These songs cover the whole of Stenhammar's career: the earliest, *In the forest*, was composed when he was sixteen, while the last, *Minnesang*, was written three years before his death. The songs are unpreten-tious and charming, fresh and idyllic, and nearly all are strophic. Hagegård sings the majority of them with his usual intelligence and artistry, though there is an occasional hardening of timbre. Anne Sofie von Otter is in wonderful voice and sings with great sensitivity and charm. Bengt Forsberg and Thomas Schuback accompany with great taste, and the recording is of the highest quality.

Sterndale Bennett, William (1816–75)

Piano concertos Nos. 1 in D min., Op. 1; 3 in C min., Op. 9.
✪ *** Lyrita Dig. SRCD 204 [id.]. Malcolm Binns, LPO, Nicholas Braithwaite.

Perhaps it was hearing Mendelssohn play his *G minor Concerto* in 1832 that prompted the sixteen-year-old Sterndale Bennett to write his Opus 1, a concerto in D minor and a work of extraordinary fluency and accomplishment. David Byers, who has edited the concertos, speaks of Bennett's 'gentle lyricism, the strength and energy of the orchestral tuttis'; and they are in ample evidence, both here and in the *Third Piano concerto*, composed when he was eighteen. No praise can be too high for the playing of Malcolm Binns whose fleetness of finger and poetic sensibility are a constant source of delight, and for the admirable support he receives from Nicholas Braithwaite and the LPO. The engineers produce sound of the highest quality. A most enjoyable disc.

Piano concertos Nos. 2 in E flat, Op. 4; 5 in F min.; Adagio.
*** Lyrita Dig. SRCD 205 [id.]. Malcolm Binns, Philh. O, Nicholas Braithwaite.

The *Second concerto* proves to be another work of great facility and charm. It takes as its model the concertos of Mozart and Mendelssohn, and the brilliance and delicacy of the keyboard writing make one understand why the composer was so highly regarded by his contemporaries. The *F minor concerto* of 1836 is eminently civilized music with lots of charm; the *Adagio*, which completes the disc, is thought to be an alternative slow movement for Bennett's *Third Concerto* (1837). Whether or not this is the case, it is certainly a lovely piece. Malcolm Binns plays with great artistry, and the accompaniment by the Philharmonia Orchestra and Nicholas Braithwaite is equally sensitive. First-class recording.

(i) *Piano concerto No. 4 in F min.; Symphony in G. min.;* (i) *Fantasia in A, Op. 16.*
(M) *** Unicorn Dig. UKCD 2032. (i) Binns; Milton Keynes CO, Hilary Wetton.

William Sterndale Bennett's eclectic *Fourth Piano concerto* reflects Chopin rather more than Mendelssohn and is agreeable and well structured. Its lollipop slow movement is a winner, an engaging *Barcarolle*. The *Symphony* is amiable, not unlike the Mendelssohn string symphonies. Overall it is very slight, but enjoyable enough. Both performances are uncommonly good ones. Malcolm Binns is a persuasive advocate of the *Concerto*, while Hilary Wetton paces both works admirably and clearly has much sympathy for them. The solo *Fantasia* has been added for the CD issue, which offers excellent sound and a good balance.

Stevens, Bernard (1916–83)

(i) *Cello concerto; Symphony of liberation.*
*** Mer. CDE 84124. (i) Baillie, BBC PO, Downes.

Bernard Stevens came to wider notice at the end of the war when his *Symphony of liberation* won a *Daily Express* competition. What a fine work it proves to be, though the somewhat later *Cello concerto* is even stronger. Dedicated performances from Alexander Baillie and the BBC Philharmonic. Good recording.

(i) *Violin concerto; Symphony No. 2.*
*** Mer. CDE 84174 [id.]. (i) Ernst Kovacic; BBC PO, Downes.

The *Violin concerto* is a good piece and well worth investigating. Stevens is a composer of real substance, and the *Second Symphony* (1964) is impressive in its sustained power and resource. Ernst Kovacic is persuasive in the *Concerto* and Downes and the BBC Philharmonic play well. Good (but not spectacular) recording.

Still, William Grant (1895–1978)

Symphony No. 2 (Song of a new race) in G min.
*** Chandos Dig. CHAN 9226 [id.]. Detroit SO, Neeme Järvi – DAWSON: *Negro Folk Symphony;*
ELLINGTON: *Harlem.* ***

Stokowski conducted the première of this attractive piece in 1937, seven years after the composer's *First Symphony* had been the first work by an African-American composer to be played by a major orchestra (the NYPO). Still worked as an arranger, so he knew how to score (the opening has a particularly fresh colouring) and he had a fund of tunes: the slow movement is haunting, the high-spirited Scherzo whistles along like someone out walking on a spring morning. The idiom is totally American and, if the score is more a suite than a symphony, it remains very personable and rather more coherently structured than the Dawson coupling, although the finale is not its strongest movement. It is played most persuasively here and is given a richly expansive recording.

Stockhausen, Karlheinz (born 1928)

(i) *Mikrophonie 1; Mikrophonie 2;* (ii) *Klavierstücke 1–11.*
(M) *** Sony S2K 53346 (2). (i) Members of W. German R. Ch. & Studio Ch. for New Music, Cologne, Kontarsky, Alings, Fritsch, Bojé, cond. Herbert Schernus; supervised by composer; (ii) Aloys Kontarsky (piano).

This reissue combines two important Stockhausen recordings from the mid-1960s. *Mikrophonie 1* is electronic music proper; *Mikrophonie 2* attempts a synthesis of electronic music and choral sounds, and it is the vocal work that is the more immediately intriguing. It may be in dispute just how valid performances like these are when the composer's score allows many variables, but at least it is the composer himself who is supervising the production. Outstanding recording-quality for its time – as of course it should be with so many musician-engineers around in the Cologne studios.

The *Klavierstücke* provide a stimulating coupling. Aloys Kontarsky plays these eleven pieces – arguably the purest expression yet of Stockhausen's musical imagination – with a dedication that can readily convince even the unconverted listener. Seven of the pieces are very brief epigrammatic utterances, each sharply defined. The sixth and tenth pieces (the latter placed separately on the second disc) are more extended, each taking over 20 minutes. The effect at the begining of the ninth piece provides a clear indication of Stockhausen's aural imagination. The pianist repeats the same, not very interesting discord no fewer than 228 times, and one might dismiss that as merely pointless. What emerges from sympathetic listening is that the repetitions go nagging on so that the sound of the discord seems to vary, like a visual image shimmering in heat-haze. The other pieces, too, bring similar extensions of musical experience, and all this music is certainly communicative. Excellent if forward recording and extensive back-up notes. A good set on which to sharpen avant-garde teeth.

Stimmung (1968).
*** Hyperion CDA 66115 [id.]. Singcircle, Gregory Rose.

Gregory Rose with his talented vocal group directs an intensely beautiful account of Stockhausen's 70-minute minimalist meditation on six notes. Though the unsympathetic listener might still find the result boring, this explains admirably how Stockhausen's musical personality can magnetize, with his variety of effect and response, even with the simplest of formulae. Excellent recording.

Stradella, Alessandro (1644–82)

San Giovanni Battista (oratorio).

⊛ *** Erato/Warner Dig. 2292 45739-2 [id.]. Bott, Batty, Lesne, Edgar-Wilson, Huttenlocher, Musiciens du Louvre, Minkowski.

Stradella's oratorio on the Biblical subject of John the Baptist and Salome is an amazing masterpiece and offers unashamedly sensuous treatment of the story. Insinuatingly chromatic melodic lines for Salome (here described simply as Herodias' daughter) are set against plainer, more forthright writing for the castrato role of the saint, showing the composer as a seventeenth-century equivalent of Richard Strauss. There is one amazing phrase for Salome, gloriously sung here by Catherine Bott, which starts well above the stave and ends after much twisting nearly two octaves below with a glorious chest-note, a hair-raising moment. Herod's anger arias bring reminders of both Purcell and Handel, and at the end Stradella ingeniously superimposes Salome's gloating music and Herod's expressions of regret, finally cutting off the duet in mid-air as Charles Ives might have done, bringing the whole work to an indeterminate close. Quite apart from Catherine Bott's magnificent performance, at once pure and sensuous in tone and astonishingly agile, the other singers are most impressive, with Gerard Lesne a firm-toned counter-tenor in the title-role and Philippe Huttenlocher a clear if sometimes gruff Herod. Marc Minkowski reinforces his claims as an outstanding exponent of period performance, drawing electrifying playing from Les Musiciens du Louvre, heightening the drama. Excellent sound. Not to be missed!

The Strauss family
Strauss, Johann Snr (1804–49) Strauss, Johann Jnr (1825–99)
Strauss, Josef (1827–70) Strauss, Eduard (1835–1916)

(all music listed is by Johann Strauss Jnr unless otherwise stated)

Johann Strauss Jnr: The Complete Edition

Volume 1: Mazurka: *Veilchen, Mazur nach russischen motiven.* Polkas: *Fledermaus; Herzenslust; Zehner.* Quadrilles: *Debut; Nocturne.* Waltzes: *Bei uns z'Haus; Freuet euch des Lebens; Gunstwerber; Klangfiguren; Maskenzug française; Phönix-Schwingen.*
**(*) Marco Polo Dig. 8.223201-2. CSSR State PO (Košice), Alfred Walter.

Volume 2: *Kaiser Franz Josef 1, Rettungs-Jubel-Marsch.* Polkas: *Czechen; Neue Pizzicato; Satanella; Tik-Tak.* Polka-Mazurka: *Fantasieblümchen.* Quadrilles: *Cytheren; Indra.* Waltzes: *Die jungen Wiener; Solonsprüche; Vermälungs-Toaste; Wo die Zitronen blüh'n.*
** Marco Polo Dig. 8.223202-2. CSSR State PO (Košice), Alfred Walter.

Volume 3: Polkas: *Aesculap; Amazonen; Freuden-Gruss; Jux; Vergnügungszug.* Quadrilles: *Dämonen; Satanella.* Waltzes: *Berglieder; Liebeslieder; Lind-gesänge; Die Osterreicher; Wiener Punsch-lieder.*
**(*) Marco Polo Dig. 8.223203-2. CSSR State PO (Košice), Alfred Walter.

Volume 4: Polkas: *Bürger-Ball; Hopser; Im Krapfenwald'l (polka française); Knall-Kügerin; Veilchen.* Marches: *Austria; Verbruederungs.* Quadrille: *Motor.* Waltzes: *Dividenden; O schoener Mai!; Serail-taenze.*
**(*) Marco Polo Dig. 8.223204-2. CSSR State PO (Košice), Richard Edlinger.

Volume 5: *Russischer Marsch Fantasie.* Polkas: *Elisen (polka française); Heiligenstadt rendezvous; Hesperus; Musen; Pariser.* Quadrille: *Sur des airs français.* Waltzes: *Italienischer; Kennst du mich?; Nachtfalter; Wiener Chronik.*
*** Marco Polo Dig. 8.223205-2. CSSR State PO (Košice), Oliver Dohnányi.

Volume 6: *Caroussel Marsch.* Polkas: *Bluette (polka française); Camelien; Warschauer.* Quadrilles: *Nach themen französischer Romanzen; Nordstern.* Waltzes: *Concurrenzen; Kuss; Myrthen-Kränze; Wellen und wogen.*
** Marco Polo Dig. 8.223206-2. CSSR State PO (Košice), Oliver Dohnányi.

Volume 7: *Deutscher krieger Marsch; Kron marsch.* Polkas: *Bacchus; Furioso; Neuhauser.* Polka-Mazurka: *Kriegers liebchen.* Quadrille: *Odeon.* Waltzes: *Ballg'schichten; Colonnen; Nordseebilder; Schnee-Glöckchen; Zeitgeister.*
**(*) Marco Polo Dig. 8.223207-2. Polish State PO, Oliver Dohnányi.

Volume 8: *Banditen-Galopp; Erzherzog Wilhelm genesungs marsch.* Polkas: *Leichtes blut; Wiedersehen; Pepita.* Quadrilles: *Nach motiven aus Verdi's 'Un ballo in maschera'; Saison.* Waltzes: *Cagliostro; Carnevals-Botschafter, Lagunen; Die Sanguiniker; Schallwellen.*
**(*) Marco Polo Dig. 8.223208-2. Polish State PO, Oliver Dohnányi.

This extraordinary Marco Polo enterprise – to record the entire output of the Strauss family – began in 1988, although the first issues did not arrive in the UK until the beginning of 1990. All these initial volumes centre on the music of Johann Junior. Johann and his orchestra were constantly on the move and, wherever they travelled to play, he was expected to come up with some new pieces. While obvious 'hits' and favourites stayed in the repertoire, often the novelties were treated as ephemeral and in many instances only the short piano-score has survived. It was necessary – for the purpose of the recording – to hire professional arrangers to make suitable orchestrations; from these, new orchestral parts could be copied. Such is the perversity of human experience that quite regularly the original orchestral parts would suddenly appear for some of the pieces – after the recording had been made! It is therefore planned to have an appendix and to re-record those items later, from the autographs. So far the recordings have been made in Eastern Europe. Apart from cutting the costs, the Slovak Bohemian tradition provides a relaxed ambience, highly suitable for this repertoire. Much of the music is here being put on disc for the first time and indeed the excellent back-up documentation tells us that three items on the first CD were part of the young Johann's first concert programme: the *Gunstwerber* ('Wooer of favour') *Waltz, Herzenslust* ('Heart's desire') polka and, even more appropriately, the *Debut-Quadrille*, so that makes Volume 1 of the series something of a collector's item, while Volume 3 also seems to have above-average interest in the selection of its programme.

Evaluation of these recordings has not been easy. The first three CDs were made by the Slovak State Philharmonic under Alfred Walter. The mood is amiable and the playing quite polished. With the arrival of Richard Edlinger and Oliver Dohnányi on the scene, the tension seems to increase, and there is much to relish. Of this second batch we would pick out Volumes 5, 7 and 8, all representing the nice touch of Oliver Dohnányi, with Volume 5 perhaps a primary choice, although there are many good things included in Volume 8.

Volume 9: *Habsburg Hoch! Marsch; Indigo marsch.* Polkas: *Albion; Anen; Lucifer.* Polka-Mazurka: *Nachtveilchen.* Quadrille: *Festival quadrille nach englischen motiven.* Waltzes: *Carnevalsbilder, Gedanken auf den Alpen; Kaiser.*
** Marco Polo Dig. 8.223209-2. Polish State PO, Johannes Wildner.

Volume 10: *Pesther csárdás.* Polkas: *Bauern; Blumenfest; Diabolin; Juriston Ball.* Quadrille: *Nach beliebten motiven.* Waltzes: *Feuilleton; Morgenblätter, Myrthenblüthen; Panacea-klänge.*
** Marco Polo Dig. 8.223210-2. Polish State PO (Katowice), Johannes Wildner.

Volume 11: *Revolutions Marsch.* Polkas: *Frisch heran!; Haute-volée; Herrmann; Patrioten.* Polka-Mazurka: *Waldine.* Quadrilles: *Die Afrikanerin; Handels-élite.* Waltzes: *Aus den bergen; Donauweibchen; Glossen; Klänge aus der Walachei.*
**(*) Marco Polo Dig. 8.223211-2. CSSR State PO (Košice), Alfred Walter.

Volume 12: *Krönungs Marsch.* Polkas: *Aurora; Ella; Harmonie; Neues leben (polka française); Souvenir; Stürmisch in lieb' und tanz.* Quadrille: *Fest.* Waltzes: *Die Gemüthlichen; Hofballtänze; Man lebt nur einmal!; Wiener frauen.*
** Marco Polo Dig. 8.223212-2. CSSR State PO (Košice), Alfred Walter.

Volume 13: *Egyptischer Marsch; Patrioten marsch.* Polkas: *Demolirer, Fidelen; Nur fort!; Tanzi-bäri; Was sich liebt, neckt sich (polka française).* Quadrilles: *Nach motiven aus der oper 'Die Belagerung von Rochelle'; Neue melodien.* Waltzes: *Sirenen; Thermen; Die Zillerthaler.*
**(*) Marco Polo Dig. 8.223213-2. CSSR State PO (Košice), Alfred Walter.

Volume 14: *Romance No. 1 for cello and orchestra.* Polkas: *Champagne; Geisselhiebe; Kinderspiele (polka française); Vöslauer.* Quadrilles: *Bal champêtre; St Petersburg (quadrille nach russischen motiven).* Waltzes: *Du and du; Ernte-tänze; Frohsinns-spenden; Grillenbanner, Phänomene.*
**(*) Marco Polo Dig. 8.223214-2. CSSR State PO (Košice), Alfred Walter.

Volume 15: *Jubelfest-Marsch.* Polkas: *Bijoux; Scherz.* Polka-Mazurkas: *Lob der frauen; La Viennoise.* Quadrilles: *Alexander, Bijouterie.* Waltzes: *Die Jovialen; Kaiser-Jubiläum; Libellen; Wahlstimmen.*
** Marco Polo Dig. 8.223215-2. CSR SO (Bratislava), Johannes Wildner.

Volume 16: *Fürst Bariatinsky-Marsch.* Polkas: *Brautschau* (on themes from *Zigeunerbaron*); *Eljen a Magyar!; Ligourianer Seufzer, Schnellpost; Studenten. La berceuse quadrille; Zigeuner-Quadrille* (on themes from Balfe's *Bohemian Girl*). Waltzes: *Bürgerweisen; Freuden-Salven; Motoren; Sangerfährten.*
**(*) Marco Polo Dig. 8.223216 [id.]. CSSR State PO (Košice), Alfred Walter.

With Volume 9, we move to Poland and a new name, Johannes Wildner. He has his moments, but his approach seems fairly conventional. He does not make a great deal of the famous *Emperor Waltz* which closes Volume 9, although he does better with *Gedanken auf den Alpen*, another unknown but charming waltz. Alfred Walter – who began it all – then returns for Volumes 11–14. Of this batch, Volume 11 might be singled out, opening with the jolly *Herrmann-Polka*, while the *Klänge aus der Walachei, Aus den Bergen* ('From the Mountains') and *Donauweibchen* ('Nymph of the Danube') are three more winning waltzes; but the standard seems pretty reliable here, and these are all enjoyable discs. Volume 16 has another attractive batch of waltzes, at least two winning polkas and a quadrille vivaciously drawing on Balfe's *Bohemian Girl.* It also includes the extraordinary *Ligourian Seufzer polka,* in which the orchestra vocally mocks the Ligourians, a despised Jesuitical order led by Alfonso Maria di Ligouri. Another good disc.

Volume 17: *Kaiser Franz Joseph Marsch.* Polkas: *Armen-ball;* '*S gibt nur a Kaiserstadt!* '*S gibt nur a Wien; Violetta (polka française).* Quadrille: *Melodien.* Waltzes: *Adelen; Bürgersinn; Freiheits-lieder; Windsor-klänge.*
*** Marco Polo Dig. 8.223217-2. CSR SO (Bratislava), Alfred Eschwé.

Volume 18: *Alliance-Marsche; Studenten-Marsch.* Polkas: *Edtweder-oder!; Invitation à la polka mazur; Leopoldstädter, Stadt und Land; Cagliostro-Quadrille.* Waltzes: *Grossfürstin Alexandra; Lava-Ströme; Patronessen; Die Pulizisten; Rathausball-Tänz.*
**(*) Marco Polo Dig. 8.223218-2. CSSR State PO, Alfred Walter.

Volume 19: *Hoch Osterreich! Marsch.* Polkas: *Burschenwanderung (polka française), Electro-magnetische; Episode (polka française).* Quadrilles: *Le premier jour de bonheur, Opéra de Auber; Seladon.* Waltzes: *Dorfgeschichten (im Ländlerstyle); Novellen; Rosen aus dem Süden; Seid umschlungen, Millionen; Studentenlust.*
**(*) Marco Polo Dig. 8-223219-2. Czecho-Slovak State PO (Košice), Alfred Walter.

Volume 20: *Dinorah-quadrille nach motiven der oper, 'Die Wallfahrt' nach Meyerbeer. Kaiser-Jäger Marsch. Slovianka-quadrille, nach russischen melodien.* Polkas: *Auf zum tänze; Herzel.* Polka-Mazurkas: *Ein herz, ein sinn; Fata Morgana.* Waltzes: *Aurora-ball-tänze; Erhöhte pulse; Flugschriften; Märchen aus dem Orient; Schwärmereien* (concert waltz).
** Marco Polo Dig. 8.223220-2. Czecho-Slovak State PO (Košice), Alfred Walter.

Volume 21: *Ottinger Reiter Marsch.* Polkas: *Figaro (polka française); Patronessen (polka française); Sans-souci.* Polka-Mazurka: *Tändelei.* Quadrilles: *Orpheus; Rotunde.* Waltzes: *Cycloiden; G'schichten aus dem Wienerwald; Johannis-Käferin.*
** Marco Polo Dig. 8.223221-2. Czecho-Slovak State PO (Košice), Johannes Wildner.

Volume 22: *Klipp-Klapp Galopp. Persischer Marsch.* Polkas: *L'Inconnue (polka française); Nachtigall.* Polka-Mazurka: *Aus der Heimat.* Quadrilles: *Carnevals-spektakel; Der lustige Krieg.* Waltzes: *Controversen; Immer heiterer (im Ländlerstyle); Maxing-tänze; Ninetta.*
** Marco Polo Dig. 8.223222-2. Czecho-Slovak State PO (Košice), Johannes Wildner.

Volume 23: *Deutschmeister-Jubiläumsmarsch.* Polkas: *Maria Taglioni; Die Pariserin (polka française); Rasch in der tat!.* Polka-Mazurka: *Glücklich ist, wer vergisst.* Quadrilles: *Le beau monde; Indigo.* Waltzes: *Gross-Wien; Rhadamantus-klänge; Telegramme; Vibrationen; Wien, mein Sinn!*
** Marco Polo Dig. 8.223223-2. Czecho-Slovak State PO (Košice), Johannes Wildner.

Volume 24: *Gavotte der Königin. Viribus unitis, Marsch.* Polkas: *Demi-fortune (polka française); Heski-Holki; Rokonhangok (sympathieklänge); So ängstlich sind wir nicht!.* Polka-Mazurka: *Licht und Schatten.* Quadrille: *Streina-terrassen.* Waltzes: *Idyllen; Jux-brüder, Lockvögel; Sinnen und Minnen.*
** Marco Polo Dig. 8.223224-2. Czecho-Slovak State PO (Košice), Alfred Walter.

Volume 17 introduces another new name, Alfred Eschwé, and a particularly good collection, one of the highlights of the set, and it is beautifully played. Volume 18 brings back Alfred Walter and another very good mix of waltzes and polkas. Johannes Wildner then directs Volumes 21–23, and it must be said that the middle volume shows him in better light than the other two, and with a well-chosen programme.

Volume 25: *Grossfürsten Marsch*. Polkas: *Bonbon (polka française); Explosions; Lustger Rath (polka française); Mutig voran!* Polka-Mazurka: *Le Papillon*. Quadrilles: *Künstler; Promenade*. Waltzes: *Frauen-Käferin; Krönungslieder; Spiralen; Ins Zentrum!*
** Marco Polo Dig. 8.223225-2. Czecho-Slovak State PO (Košice), Johannes Wildner.

Volume 26: *Es war so wunderschön Marsch*. Polkas: *Elektrophor; L'Enfantillage (polka française); Gut bürgerlich (polka française); Louischen (polka française); Pásmán*. Quadrilles: *Industrie; Sofien*. Waltzes: *Juristen-ball-tänze; Künstlerleben; Pasman; Sinngedichte*.
*** Marco Polo Dig. 8.223226-2. Austrian RSO, Vienna, Guth.

Volume 27: *Spanischer Marsch*. Polkas: *Drollerie; Durch's telephon; Express; Gruss an Wien (polka française)*. Polka-Mazurka. *Annina*. Quadrilles: *Künstler; Sans-souci*. Waltzes: *Aeolstöne; Souvenir de Nizza; Wein, Weib und Gesang; Frühlingsstimmen*.
✹ *** Marco Polo Dig 8.223227-2. Austrian RSO, Vienna, Guth.

Volume 28: *Freiwillige vor! Marsch (1887). Frisch in's feld! Marsch*. Polkas: *Unter Donner und Blitz; Pappacoda (polka française)*. Polka-Mazurkas: *Concordia; Spleen*. Quadrille: *Tête-à-tête*. Waltzes: *Einheitsklänge: Illustrationen; Lebenswecker; Telegraphische depeschen*.
** Marco Polo Dig. 8.223228-2. Czecho-Slovak State PO (Košice), Johannes Wildner.

Volume 29: *Brünner-Nationalgarde-Marsch. Der lustige Krieg, Marsch*. Polkas: *Die Bajadere; Hellenen; Secunden (polka française)*. Polka-Mazurka: *Une Bagatelle*. Quadrille: *Waldmeister*. Waltzes: *Deutsche; Orakel-Sprüche; Schatz; Tausend und eine Nacht; Volkssänger*.
** Marco Polo Dig. 8.223229-2. Czecho-Slovak State PO (Košice), Alfred Walter.

Volume 30: *Fest-Marsch. Perpetuum mobile*. Polkas: *Alexandrinen; Kammerball; Kriegsabenteuer; Par force!* Quadrille: *Attaque*. Waltzes: *Erinnerung an Covent Garden; Kluh Gretelein; Luisen-sympathie-Klänge; Paroxysmen; Reiseabenteuer*.
** Marco Polo Dig. 8.223230-2. Czecho-Slovak State PO (Košice), Alfred Walter.

Volume 31: *Napoleon-Marsch*. Polkas: *Husaren; Taubenpost (polka française); Vom Donaustrande*. Polka-Mazurka: *Nord und Süd*. Quadrilles: *Bonvivant; Nocturne*. Waltzes: *Gambrinus-tänze; Die ersten Curen; Hochzeitsreigen; Die Unzertrennlichen; Wiener bonbons*.
** Marco Polo Dig. 8.223231-2. Czecho-Slovak State PO (Košice), Alfred Walter.

Volume 32: *Wiener Jubel-Gruss-Marsch*. Polkas: *Auf der Jagd; Olge; Tritsch-tratsch*. Polka-Mazurka: *An der Wolga*. Quadrilles: *Methusalem; Hofball*. Waltzes: *Fantasiebilder; Ich bin dir gut!; Promotionen; Wiener Blut*.
** Marco Polo Dig. 8.223232-2. Czecho-Slovak State PO (Košice), Johannes Wildner.

Volume 26 brings another fresh name, and fresh is the right word to describe this attractive programme. From the bright-eyed opening *Elektrophor Polka schnell* this is winningly vivacious music-making and the waltz that follows, *Sinngedichte*, makes one realizes that there is something special about Viennese string-playing, for this is the Orchestra of Austrian Radio. Volume 27 features the same orchestra and conductor and opens with the delectable *Künster-Quadrille*. After the aptly named *Drollerie* polka comes the *Aeolstöne* waltz with its portentous introduction, and the waltz itself is heart-warming. The *Souvenir de Nizza* waltz is hardly less beguiling and *Wine, women and song* and, to end the disc, *Frühlingsstimmen* – two top favourites – simply could not be better played. These two Peter Guth CDs are the finest of the series so far, and we award a token Rosette to the second of the two, although it could equally apply to its companion. After those two marvellous collections it is an anticlimax to return to the following volumes. There is much interesting music here, but the performances often have an element of routine.

Volume 33: *Saschen-Kürassier-Marsch*. Polkas: *Etwas kleines (polka française); Freikugeln*. Polka-Mazurka: *Champêtre*. Quadrilles: *Bouquet; Opern-Maskenball*. Waltzes: *Abschieds-Rufe; Sträusschen; An der schönen blauen Donau; Trau, schau, wem!*.
** Marco Polo Dig. 8.223233-2. Czecho-Slovak State PO (Košice), Wildner.

Volume 34: (i) *Dolci pianti* (Romance for cello and orchestra). *Im russischen Dorfe, Fantasie* (orch. Max Schönherr). *Russischer Marsch. Slaven-potpourri*. Polkas: *La Favorite (polka française); Niko*. Polka-Mazurka: *Der Kobold*. Quadrille: *Nikolai*. Waltzes: *Abschied von St Petersburg; Fünf paragraphen*.
*** Marco Polo Dig. 8.223234-2. Slovak RSO (Bratislava), Dittrich, (i) with Jozef Sikora.

Volume 35: *Zivio! Marsch*. Polkas: *Jäger (polka française); Im Sturmschritt!; Die Zeitlose (polka française)*. Polka-Mazurka: *Die Wahrsagerin*. Quadrilles: *Der blits; Der liebesbrunnen*. Waltzes: *Accelerationen; Architecten-ball-tänze; Heut' ist heut' Königslieder*.

** Marco Polo Dig. 8.223235-2. Slovak State PO (Košice), Wildner.

Volume 36: *Matador-Marsch*. Polkas: *Bitte schön! (polka française); Diplomaten; Kreuzfidel (polka française); Process*. Polka-Mazurka: *Der Klügere gibt nach*. Quadrilles: *Elfen; Fledermaus*. Waltzes: *D'Woaldbuama (im Ländlerstil)* (orch. Ludwig Babinski); *Extravaganten; Mephistos Höllenrufe; Neu-Wien*.
** Marco Polo Dig. 8.223236-2. Slovak State PO (Košice), Alfred Walter.

Among the following batch, the CD that stands out features another new name, Michael Dittrich; working with the Slovak Radio Symphony Orchestra, he produces a splendid collection to make up Volume 34. The flexible handling of the *Slav Potpourri* shows his persuasive sympathy for Strauss, while the *Fünf Paragraphen* waltz has an equally delectable lilt. There is great charm in the elegant *La Favorite* polka and the *Abschied von St Petersburg* waltz has a nicely beguiling opening theme.

Volume 37: *Triumph-Marsch* (orch. Fischer). Polkas: *Das Comitat geht in die Höh!; Sonnnenblume; Tanz mit dem Besenstiel!* (all arr. Pollack); (i) *Romance No. 2 in G min. for cello and orchestra, Op. 35* (arr.Schönherr); Quadrilles: *Die Königin von Leon* (arr. Pollack); *Spitzentuch. Neue Steierische Tänze* (orch. Pollack); *Traumbild II;* Waltzes: *Jugend-Träume* (orch. Pollack); *Schwungräder*.
(Y/B) *** Marco Polo Dig. 8.223237 [id.]. Slovak State PO (Košice), Christian Pollack; (i) with Regina Jauslin.

Volume 37 is among the most interesting and worthwhile issues so far. It includes the waltz with which the nineteen-year-old Johann Junior created his first sensation at Zum Sperlbauer in Vienna. He had taken over the orchestra's direction in February 1845, and during a summer's night festival in August of that same year *Jugend-Träume* was introduced. It received five encores! The waltz is entirely character-istic, opening with a lilting theme on the strings and moving from one idea to another with the easy facility that distinguishes his more famous waltzes. Christian Pollack is a Strauss scholar, and in almost every case here he has worked from piano scores or incomplete scoring. Particularly delectable is the set of *New Styrian dances*, seductively written in the Ländler style of Lanner's *Steyrische Tänze*. Here an almost complete piano version was available, while the orchestral parts end with the third dance; Pollack has therefore scored the fourth dance (very convincingly) in the style of the other three. While the *Romance for cello and orchestra* is agreeably slight, the other striking novelty here is *Traumbild II*, a late domestic work in two sections, the first of which is a gentle and charming 'dream-picture' of Strauss's wife, Adèle; the second shows the other side of her nature – more volatile and capricious. Both are in waltz time. Christian Pollack is not just a scholar but an excellent performing musician, and the playing here is polished, relaxed and spontaneous in an agreeably authentic way.

Volume 38: *Wiener Garnison-Marsch* (orch. Babinsky); *Ninetta-Galopp;* Polkas: *Damenspende; Lagerlust; Maskenzug* (2nd version); *Nimm sie hinn!; Zehner* (2nd version); Quadrilles: *Eine Nacht in Venedig; Serben* (orch. Babinski); Waltzes: *An der Elbe; Faschings-Lieder* (orch. Kulling); *Leitartikel*.
(Y/B) **(*) Marco Polo Dig. 8.223238 [id.]. Slovak State PO (Košice), Alfred Walter.

An der Elbe is a real find among the waltzes, a charming melodic sequence with a striking introduction. But the *Ninetta-Galopp* with its perky main theme and swirling woodwind answer has the potential to become a Strauss lollipop, while the more sedate *Maskenzug-Polka française* closes the programme engagingly. This is one of Alfred Walter's better programmes, nicely played and well recorded.

Volume 39: *Ninetta-Marsch*. Polkas: *I Tipferl; Sylphen; Unparteiische Kritiken;* Quadrilles: *Jabuka; Slaven-Ball* (both orch. Pollack); Quodlibet: *Klänge aus der Raimundzeit;* Waltzes: *Abschied; Irenen* (orch. Babinski); *Hell und voll*.
(Y/B) **(*) Marco Polo Dig. 8.223239 [id.]. Slovak State PO (Košice), Christian Pollack.

The two most interesting items here both date from Johann's last years, the *Abschieds* (Farewell) *waltz* and the *Klänge aus der Raimundzeit* (1898), an affectionate *pot-pourri* including tunes by Johann Senior and Lanner. Johann originally called this good-humoured quodlibet 'Reminiscenz. Aus der guter alten Zeit' ('From the good old days'). The score of the waltz is written in the composer's own handwriting; his widow, Adèle, offered it to be performed posthumously in 1900. The *I Tipferl-Polka française* is based on a popular comic song from Strauss's *Prinz Methusalem*, and the couplet: 'The man forgot – the little dot, the dot upon the i!' is wittily pointed in the music. Christian Pollack directs excellent perform-ances of all the music here which, although of varying quality, is never dull.

Volume 40: *Hochzeits-Praeludium;* Polkas: *Herzenskönigin; Liebe und Ehe; Wildfeuer;* Quadrilles: *Ninetta; Wilhelminen* (orch. Babinski); Waltzes: *Heimats-Kinder* (orch. Babinski); *The Herald* (orch. Schönherr); *Irrlichter; Jubilee* (orch. Cohen).
(Y/B) *(*) Marco Polo Dig. 8.223240 [id.]. Slovak RSO (Bratislava), Bauer-Theussl.

Volume 41: March: *Wo uns're Fahne weht;* Polkas: *Newa; Shawl;* Quadrilles: *Martha; Vivat!;* Waltzes: *Burschen-Lieder, Gedankenflug; Lagunen. Traumbild* (symphonic poem). *Aschenbrödel (Cinderella): Prelude to Act III.*
(Y/B) ** Marco Polo Dig. 8.223241 [id.]. Slovak RSO (Bratislava), Michael Dittrich.

Volume 42: *Hommage au public russe;* March: *Piccolo;* Polkas: *An der Moldau; Auroraball; Grüss aus Osterreich; Sängerlust; Soldatespiel;* Waltzes: *Gartenlaube; Hirtenspiele; Sentenzen.*
(Y/B) **(*) Marco Polo Dig. 8.223242 [id.]. Slovak State PO (Košice), Christian Pollack.

For volumes 40 to 42 Christian Pollack returns, but we also meet a new conductor, Franz Bauer-Theussl. As it turns out, the music-making in Volume 40 under Bauer-Theussl immediately proves heavy-handed in the opening waltz, and the feeling throughout is that he is conducting for the commercial ballroom rather than the concert hall. As Pollack demonstrates in Volume 42, much more can be made of relatively strict tempo versions than Bauer-Theussl does with the *Irrlichter* and *Herald waltzes.* The *Jubilee Waltz* was written for the Strausses' American visit in 1872, when in Boston he conducted its première, played by a 'Grand Orchestra' of 809 players, including 200 first violins! With this kind of spectacle it is not surprising that he chose to end a not particularly memorable piece by including a few bars of the American national anthem in the coda.

Without being exactly a live wire, Michael Dittrich makes a good deal more of Volume 41. He is able to relax and at the same time coax the orchestra into phrasing with less of a feeling of routine, as in the *Shawl-Polka,* which lilts rather nicely, and the comparatively sprightly *Vivat!* Dittrich fails to make a great deal of the one relatively well-known waltz here, *Lagunen,* but he manages the *Aschenbrödel Prelude* colourfully and does very well indeed by the *Traumbild I* ('Dream picture No. 1'), a warmly relaxed and lyrical evocation, quite beautifully scored. It was written towards the end of the composer's life, for his own pleasure.

But when we come to Volume 42, so striking is the added vivacity that it is difficult to believe that this is the same orchestra playing. The opening *Piccolo-Marsch* and the *Auroraball polka française* are rhythmically light-hearted, as are all the other polkas in the programme, and if the *Hirtenspiele* (or 'Pastoral play') *waltz* is not a masterpiece, it is still freshly enjoyable in Pollack's hands, despite the demands of a ballroom tempo. The *Gartenlaube-Walzer* is a real find; it has a charming introduction with a neat little flute solo, then the opening tune, lightly scored, is very engaging indeed. It is a great pity that Marco Polo did not hire the services of Christian Pollack much earlier in the series. Even the recording sounds better-focused here.

Volume 43: *Auf dem Tanzboden* (arr. Pollack); *Reitermarsch.* Polkas: *Herrjemineh; Postillon d'amour; Die Tauben von San Marco.* Quadrilles: *Simplicius; Des Teufels Antheil* (arr. Pollack); Waltzes: *Trifolien; Walzer-Bouquet No. 1; Wilde Rosen* (arr. Babinski & Kulling).
(N) **(*) Marco Polo Dig. 8.223243 [id.]. Slovak State PO (Košice), Christian Pollack.

Volume 44: Polkas: *Auf freiem Fusse; Nur nicht mucken* (arr. Peak); *Von der Börse.* Quadrilles: *Hinter den Coulissen; Monstre* (with Josef STRAUSS). *Maskenfest; Schützen* (with Josef and Eduard STRAUSS). Waltzes: *Altdeutscher* (arr. Pollack); *Aschenbrödel (Cinderella); Strauss' Autograph Waltzes* (arr. Cohen).
(N) ** Marco Polo Dig. 8.223244 [id.]. Slovak State PO (Košice), Christian Pollack.

Volume 45: Ballet music from *Der Carneval in Rom* (arr. Schönherr); *Ritter Pásmán. Fest-Marsch. Pásmán-Quadrille* (arr. Pollack); *Potpourri-Quadrille; Zigeunerbaron-Quadrille.* Waltzes: *Eva; Ischler.*
(N) **(*) Marco Polo Dig. 8.223245 [id.]. Slovak State PO (Košice), Alfred Walter.

With Christian Pollack directing with his usual light touch, Volume 43 is one of the best of the more recent Marco Polo issues, even if the *Walzer-Bouquet* is less winningly tuneful than its title suggests. *Wilde Rosen* is rather better, though not really memorable like *An dem Tanzboden* ('On the dance floor'), which was inspired by a painting. It is a real lollipop with a charming introduction (with clarinet solo) and matching postlude. The main waltz-tune is captivating and Pollack plays it exquisitely. Strauss originally intended to feature a zither in his scoring, but later indicated a pair of flutes instead, which sound delightful here. This is a prime candidate for a New Year concert. The polkas and *Simply delicious quadrille* are amiably diverting too, but the *Trifolien waltz,* though lively enough, is a run-of-the-mill piece.

Volume 44 includes the brief (three-minute) but pleasant *Altdeutscher Waltz,* arranged by the conductor, and the relatively familiar *Aschenbrödel,* which is attractive but not one of Strauss's vintage waltzes. As usual with Pollack, the various quadrilles and polkas are agreeably relaxed but never dull, and the recording is up to standard.

Alfred Walter returns to conduct Volume 45, and he is at his finest in the lively and tuneful waltz which is the central movement of the *Ritter Pásmán ballet*. The other ballet music, from *Der Carneval in Rom*, is scored by Schönherr – and very vividly too. The *Eva waltz* is brief but delightfully graceful; *Ischler*, however, is more conventional. The quadrilles are nicely managed and the sound is very good.

New Year's Day concert in Vienna (1979): Polkas: *Auf der Jagd* (with encore); *Bitte schön! Leichtes Blut; Pizzicato* (with Josef); *Tik-Tak*. Waltzes: *An der schönen blauen Donau; Bei uns zu Haus; Loreley-Rheine-Klänge; Wein, Weib und Gesang*. Josef STRAUSS: *Moulinet polka; Die Emanzipierte polka-mazurka; Rudolfsheimer-Polka; Sphärenklänge waltz*. Johann STRAUSS, Snr: *Radetzky march*. Eduard STRAUSS: *Ohne Bremse polka* (with ZIEHRER: *Herreinspaziert! waltz;* SUPPE: *Die schöne Galathée overture*).
(N) (B) *** Decca 448 572-2 (2). VPO, Willi Boskovsky.

Decca chose to record Boskovsky's 1979 New Year's Day concert in Vienna for their very first digital issue on LP. The clarity, immediacy and natural separation of detail are very striking throughout, and the strings of the Vienna Philharmonic are brightly lit. There is some loss of bloom and not quite the degree of sweetness one would expect now on a record made today in the Musikvereinsaal, but the ear soon adjusts. The music-making itself is another matter. It gains much from the spontaneity of the occasion, and the electricity is very apparent; it reaches its peak when the side-drum thunders out the introduction to the closing *Radetzky March*, a frisson-creating moment which, with the audience participation, is quite electrifying. The whole programe is included here (it was the 25th anniversary of the New Year Concerts and a suitable memento of Boskovsky's long Decca recording period in this repertoire with the VPO). The two discs are reissued most appropriately in Decca's 'Classic Sound' series at the cost of one premium-priced CD.

'1987 New Year Concert in Vienna': Overture: *Die Fledermaus*. Polkas: *Annen; Pizzicato* (with Josef); *Unter Donner und Blitz; Vergnügungszug*. Waltzes: *An der schönen blauen Donau;* (i) *Frühlingsstimmen*. J. STRAUSS Snr: *Beliebte Annen* (polka); *Radetzky march*. Josef STRAUSS: *Ohne Sorgen polka;* Waltzes: *Delirien; Sphärenklänge*.
⊛ *** DG Dig. 419 616-2 [id.]. VPO, Karajan; (i) with Kathleen Battle.

In preparation for this outstanding concert, which was both recorded and televised, Karajan re-studied the scores of his favourite Strauss pieces; the result, he said afterwards, was to bring an overall renewal to his musical life beyond the scope of this particular repertoire. The concert itself produced music-making of the utmost magic; familiar pieces sounded almost as if they were being played for the first time. Kathleen Battle's contribution to *Voices of spring* brought wonderfully easy, smiling coloratura and much charm. *The Blue Danube* was, of course, an encore, and what an encore! Never before has it been played so seductively on record. In the closing *Radetzky march*, wonderfully crisp yet relaxed, Karajan kept the audience contribution completely in control merely by the slightest glance over his shoulder. This indispensable collection makes an easy first choice among any Strauss compilations ever issued.

'New Year in Vienna': *Banditen galop* (from *Prinz Methusalem*); *Perpetuum mobile*. Polkas: *Auf der Jagd; Freut euch des Lebens; Neue pizzicato Polka; Stürmische in Lieb' und Tanz*. Waltzes: *An der schönen blauen Donau; Kaiser; Seid umschlungen, Millionen; Wo die Zitronen blüh'n*. Josef STRAUSS: Polkas: *Auf Ferienreisen; Brennende Liebe; Im Fluge; Die tanzende Muse*. Johann STRAUSS Snr: *Radetzky march*.
*** DG Dig. 437 687-2 [id.]. VPO, Claudio Abbado.

These recordings are taken from Abbado's 1988, 1991 and 1993 New Year VPO concerts, recorded live. Apart from Boskovsky (and Karajan's magical 1987 Concert – see above), the VPO took to Abbado's coaxing direction more naturally than they did to other conductors like Carlos Kleiber and Zubin Mehta, and the result is wholly sympathetic. There is much that is agreeably unfamiliar here, but the two great waltzes sound gloriously fresh. The close of the *Emperor* is wonderfully subtle, and the *Blue Danube* is pretty marvellous too. Elsewhere the playing is as sophisticated in detail as it is joyous in execution, and the audience participation is not intrusive – except, understandably, in *Radetzky*, where Abbado keeps everything well in hand. With 78 minutes of music, this is one of the very finest of modern Strauss anthologies.

'1989 New Year Concert in Vienna': Overture: *Die Fledermaus*. Csárdás: *Ritter Pásmán*. Polkas: *Bauern; Eljen a Magyar!; Im Krapfenwald'l; Pizzicato* (with Josef). Waltzes: *Accelerationen; An der schönen blauen Donau; Frühlingsstimmen; Künstlerleben*. Josef STRAUSS: Polkas: *Jockey; Die Libelle; Moulinet; Plappermäulchen*. Johann STRAUSS, Snr: *Radetzky march*.
**(*) Sony/CBS CD 45938 [id.]. VPO, Carlos Kleiber.

Kleiber's pursuit of knife-edged precision prevents the results from sounding quite relaxed enough, with the Viennese lilt in the waltzes analysed to the last micro-second instead of just being played as a dance. In the delicious polka, *Im Krapfenwald'l*, the cheeky cuckoo-calls which comically punctuate the main theme are made to sound beautiful rather than rustic, and fun is muted elsewhere too. But in one or two numbers Kleiber really lets rip, as in the Hungarian polka, *Eljen a Magyar!* ('Hail to Hungary!'), and in the *Ritter Pásmán Csárdás*. This concert now reappears on a single full-price disc, playing for 76 minutes and omitting just one waltz, *Bei uns zu Haus*. Not everyone responds positively to Kleiber's rather precise style with Viennese rhythms, but this is still an enjoyably spontaneous concert, made the more attractive by the warm, full recording, with the presence of the audience nicely implied without getting in the way.

'*1990 New Year Concert*': Einzugsmarsch (from *Der Zigeunerbaron*). Polkas: *Explosionen; Im Sturmschritt; Tritsch-tratsch*. Waltzes: *An der schönen blauen Donau; Donauweibchen; G'schichten aus dem Wienerwald; Wiener Blut*. Josef STRAUSS: Polkas: *Eingesendet; Die Emancipitre; Sport; Sympathie*. Johann STRAUSS Snr: *Indianer galop. Radetzky march*.
*** Sony Dig. SK 45808. [id.]. VPO, Zubin Mehta.

A worthy successor to Karajan's wonderful 1987 concert, not *quite* its equal but offering a programme of mainly novelties. This was Mehta's finest record for years; he conjures a magical response from the VPO and is just as persuasive in the famous waltzes. In the *Blue Danube* he hardly needs forgiveness for indulging himself (as Karajan sometimes did, only slightly more so) with a gentle, rather mannered reprise of one of the subsidiary melodies. But elsewhere his easy warmth and relaxed rhythmic style are beyond criticism. The recording is superb.

'*1992 New Year Concert*': Overture: *Der Zigeunerbaron*. Polkas: *Neue pizzicato; Stadt und Land; Tritsch-Tratsch; Unter Donner und Blitz; Vergnügungszug*. Waltzes: *An der schönen blauen Donau; Tausend und eine Nacht. Persischer march*. J. STRAUSS Snr: *Radetsky march*. JOSEPH STRAUSS: Waltzes: *Dorfschwalben aus Osterreich; Sphärenklänge* (with NICOLAI: Overture: *The Merry Wives of Windsor*).
**(*) Sony Dig. SK 48376 [id.]. VPO, Carlos Kleiber.

As with his earlier (1989) concert, Kleiber is very precise, and occasionally one wishes for a degree more relaxation. He opens his programme with a beautifully played account of Nicolai's *Merry Wives of Windsor overture*, and the introductions for *1001 Nights* and Josef's so-called '*Village swallows*' and '*Music of the spheres*' are nicely managed and attractively atmospheric. There is plenty of dash in the polkas; but at times elsewhere rubato seems just a trifle calculated, especially so in the *Blue Danube*. The playing and recording are well up to standard, and admirers of the Kleiber Strauss style, which certainly does not lack vitality, will be well pleased. All Straussians will find much to enjoy here.

'*1994 New Year's Day Concert*': Caroussel-Marsch; Lieder-Quadrille, nach beliebten Motiven. Polkas: *Ein Herr und ein Sinn; Enfantillage; Luzifer*. Waltzes: *Accelerationen; An der schönen blauen Donau; G'schichten aus dem Wienerwald; Die Fledermaus: Csárdás*. Johann STRAUSS Snr: *Radetzky march*. Josef STRAUSS: Polkas: *Aus der Ferne; Feuerfest!; Ohne Sorgen*. Eduard STRAUSS: *Mit Chic polka*. with LANNER: *Die Schönbrunner* (waltz).
*** Sony Dig. SK 46694 [id.]. VPO, Lorin Maazel.

Lorin Maazel makes the 1994 New Year concert one of the most effervescent ever, relaxing in a jovial way that one would hardly have expected. His triumph is crowned when in *Tales from the Vienna Woods* he takes up the violin and with Werner Hink from the orchestra plays the slinky duet sections at the beginning and end in an *echt*-Viennese manner. Curiously, the disc fails to mention Maazel's other extra contribution: in the quick polka by Josef Strauss, *Ohne Sorgen* ('Without a care'), Maazel – using an instrument at his elbow, as the television relay revealed – provides decorations on the glockenspiel. Aptly the recording highlights the glockenspiel notes. That polka is just one of the sparkling rarities in the collection – ten of them out of a total of 15 items. The *Schönbrunner waltz* of Joseph Lanner is a first-ever recording, light and charming if not specially characterful, but other rare delights include the French polka *Feuerfest* by Josef Strauss with its clanging hammers and anvils, the *Lucifer polka* with bangs on the drum, and the galumphing *Caroussel march*, both by Johann Strauss Junior. Applause has been tactfully edited, but some may find there is still too much.

'*1995 New Year's Day concert*': An der schönen blauen Donau; Mephistos Höllenrufe; Morgenblätter; Perpetuum mobile; Process; Reitermarsch; Russische Marsche-Phantasie; Schützen; Josef STRAUSS: *Arm in Arm; Auf Ferienreisen; Mein Lebenslauf ist Lieb' und Lust; Thalia*. Eduard STRAUSS: *Electrisch polka;* Johann STRAUSS Snr: *Alice polka; Radetzky march*.
(Y/B) *** Sony SK 66860 [id.]. VPO, Zubin Mehta (with LANNER: *Favorit-Polka*).

Even more than usual, the 1995 New Year Concert reflected the personality of its conductor, Zubin Mehta, a bluff and jolly master of ceremonies. In the programme there is a high proportion of rarities, including two total novelties, buried for a century in some archive in Coburg. The slinky and lyrical Mazurka polka, *Thalia*, by Josef Strauss is particularly delightful, and Eduard Strauss's *Electrisch polka* is as breezily energetic as one would expect. Other rare charmers include the *Alice polka* with Czech overtones, by Johann Strauss the elder, dedicated to Princess Alice, daughter of Queen Victoria, and the *Russian March-fantasy* by Johann Strauss the younger, even more Slavonic in flavour. Lanner's *Favorit polka* includes an authentic Rossini crescendo, and even in this context the swinging waltz, *Mephistos Höllenrufe* (*Mephisto's calls from Hell*), might win a prize for oddity of title. *Morgenblätter* (*Morning Papers*) remains well known, but it is odd, when its main tune is so haunting, that Josef Strauss's waltz, *Mein Lebenslauf ist Lieb' und Lust*, is not played much more. If Mehta's traditional rounding off for the *Perpetuum mobile* polka comes in a little too quickly, and the audience starts clapping in the *Radetzky march* too soon (remember the way Karajan controlled them!), that plainly reflects the exuberance of the occasion, well caught on a very well-filled disc.

'*1996 New Year Concert*': *Fest-Marsch;* Overtures: *Göttin der Vernunft; Waldmeister*. Polkas: *Blumenfest; Furioso Secunden*. Waltzes: *An der schönen blauen Donau; Kaiser; Lagunen; Phönix-Schwingen*. Johann STRAUSS Sr: *Radetzky march*. Eduard STRAUSS: *Mit Vergnügen* (polka). Josef STRAUSS: Polkas: *Jokey; Die Nasswalderin; Die tanzende Muse*.
(N) *** RCA Dig. 09026 68421-2 [id.]. VPO, Maazel (with ZIEHRER: *Wiener Burger*).

Very vividly recorded, for the first time by RCA, the 1996 New Year concert is exceptional for the number of novelties included in the programme. It is amazing how this annual event changes Lorin Maazel from a scowling figure to that of a cosy Viennese: he is pictured on the sleeve, violin in hand, grinning with delight; and the performances, relaxed and idiomatic, consistently reflect his ease. He plays the violin solo in Strauss's little-known *Goddess of Reason Overture*, one of half a dozen delightful rarities that he has unearthed, never before heard at the New Year concerts. Others include the jaunty *Blumenfest polka* and the *Wings of the phoenix waltz*, with one theme like 'Chopsticks' transformed. A free supplementary CD has the encores, the *Furioso polka* and, of course, the *Radetzky march*.

Napoleon-Marsch. Polkas: *Annen; Explosionen; Tritsch-Tratsch*. Waltzes: *An der schönen blauen Donau; Morgenblätter; 1001 Nights; Wein, Weib und Gesang; Wiener Bonbons*. Josef STRAUSS: *Dorfschwalben aus Osterreich*. Johann STRAUSS Snr: *Radetzky march*.
(B) *** Decca 433 609-2; *433 609-4*. VPO, Willi Boskovsky.

A particularly enjoyable concert of Boskovsky repertoire, chosen and ordered with skill, opening with the *Blue Danube* and closing with the rousing *Radetzky march*. The VPO are on their toes throughout. The recording dates range from 1958 to 1976; some are spikier than others in the upper range, but the warm Sofiensaal ambience is always flattering.

(i) Overture: *Die Fledermaus*. Waltzes: (ii) *An der schönen blauen Donau; Carnavals-Botschafter; Donauweibchen; Du and du; Feuilleton; Flugschriften;* (i) *Geschichten au dem Wienerwald; Kaiser;* (ii) *Die Leitartikel; Morgenblätter;* (i) *1001 Nacht;* (ii) *Wein, Weib und Gesang; Wiener Frauen*. Polkas: (i) *Im Krapfenwald'l; Leichtes Blut*. Josef STRAUSS: Waltzes: *Dynamiden; Sphärenklänge*. Johann STRAUSS Sr: *Radetzky march*.
(N) (BB) *** EMI Seraphim Dig./Analogue CES 68535-2 (2) [CDEB 68535]. (i) VPO, Rudolf Kempe;
 (ii) J. Strauss O of V., Willi Boskovsky.

A fascinating juxtaposition of two quite different styles of Johann Strauss performance. From the very opening of the *Blue Danube*, the playing of Boskovsky's Johann Strauss Orchestra balances an evocative Viennese warmth with vigour and sparkle; he is at his very best exploring the novelties – *Donauweibchen* and *Wiener Frauen* are particularly winning – with a few familiar numbers like the vivacious *Morgenblätter*, *Du and du* and *Wein, Weib und Gesang* thrown in. The latter, incidentally, has an abbreviated introduction. The digital recording from the early 1980s is excellent. Kempe opens the second disc with a vivaciously volatile account of the *Die Fledermaus overture*, but in the waltzes he is unashamedly indulgent, especially in the introductions of the two Josef Strauss items, and *1001 Nacht*. With quite gorgeous playing from the VPO strings this is almost decadently voluptuous, moving to a sumptuous climax. Both polkas are infectious and *Im Krapfenwald'l*, with its cuckoo calls, brings an affectionate smile. The recordings, from 1958 and 1961, sound amazingly good. With a playing time of nearly 143 minutes, this is outstanding value.

(i) Overtures: *Die Fledermaus;* (ii) *Waldmeister*. (iii) *Perpetuum mobile*. Polkas: (iv) *Annen;* (v) *Auf der Jagd;* (vi) *Leichtes Blut;* (iv) *Pizzicato* (with Josef); (vii) *Tritsch-Tratsch;* (iv) *Vergnügungszug*. (viii) *Quadrille on themes from Verdi's 'Un ballo in maschera'*. Waltzes: (ix) *Accelerationen;* (x) *An der schönen blauen Donau;* (xi) *Du und Du;* (iv) *Frühlingsstimmen;* (vi) *G'schichten aus dem Wienerwald;* (xii) & (xiii) & (v) *Kaiser;* (iii) *Rosen aus dem Süden;* (ii) *Wein, Weib und Gesang*. Josef STRAUSS: (iv) *Dorfschwalben aus Osterreich;* (v) *Sphärenklänge*. (iv) Johann STRAUSS, Snr: *Radetzky march*.
(M) *** DG mono/stereo 435 335-2 (2). VPO, (i) Maazel; (ii) Boskovsky; (iii) Boehm; (iv) Clemens

Krauss; (v) Karajan; (vi) Knappertsbusch; (vii) Mehta; (viii) Abbado; (ix) Josef Krips; (x) Szell; (xi) Erich Kleiber; (xii) Bruno Walter; (xiii) Furtwängler.

This delectable compilation for the 150th anniversary of the Vienna Philharmonic brings recordings of Strauss made between 1929 and 1990, notably from EMI, whose recordings of Erich Kleiber, Clemens Krauss and George Szell (made in the late 1920s and early 1930s) are particularly atmospheric, very well transferred. Other Clemens Krauss performances, plus more by Boskovsky and Knappertsbusch, come from the Decca label, justly famous in this repertoire. It is fascinating to compare Bruno Walter (1937), Wilhelm Furtwängler (1950) and Karajan (1987), all playing the *Emperor waltz*, and the many well-known favourites are well spiced with a few charming rarities.

Overtures: *Die Fledermaus; Der Zigeunerbaron*. Waltzes: *An der schönen blauen Donau; Geschichten aus dem Wiener Wald; Kaiser; Wiener Blut*.
(Y/B) (M) (***) Bruno Walter Edition: Sony mono SMK 64467 [id.]. Columbia SO, Bruno Walter –
BRAHMS: *Hungarian dances Nos. 1, 3, 10 & 17* (***); SMETANA: *Vltava*. (**)

It is good to have a reminder of Bruno Walter's way with Johann Strauss, full of vivacity, and with *Wiener Blut* obviously the conductor's favourite among the waltzes here, as he coaxes the opening beguilingly and then draws some ravishing playing from the violins. The two overtures are bright and volatile. No apologies whatsoever about the 1956 mono recording, which is warm and spacious and sounds almost like early stereo.

Overture: *Die Fledermaus*. Polkas: *Annen; Auf der Jagd; Explosionen*. Waltzes: *Frühlingsstimmen; Rosen aus dem Süden; Wein, Weib und Gesang; Windsor echoes*. Josef STRAUSS: *Feuerfest polka* (with ZIEHRER: *Kissing polka*).
(M) *** Carlton IMP Classics PCD 902 [id.]. LSO, Georgiadis.

Entitled '*An Evening in Vienna*', the performances have nevertheless a British flavour – which is not to say that there is any lack of lilt or beguiling warmth in the waltzes; they are beautifully done, while the polkas all go with an infectious swing. This is very enjoyable and is John Georgiadis's best record to date.

Pappacoda polka; Der lustige Kreig (quadrille); *Klug Gretelein* (waltz). Josef STRAUSS: *Defilir marsch;* Polkas: *Farewell; For ever*. Eduard STRAUSS: *Weyprecht-Payer marsch;* Polkas: *Mädchenlaune; Saat und Ernte;* Waltzes: *Die Abonnenten; Blüthenkranz Johann Strauss'scher*. J. STRAUSS III (son of Eduard): *Schlau-Schlau polka*.
*** Chandos Dig. CHAN 8527. Johann Strauss O of V., Rothstein, with M. Hill-Smith.

This programme is admirably chosen to include unfamiliar music which deserves recording; indeed, both the *Klug Gretelein waltz*, which opens with some delectable scoring for woodwind and harp and has an idiomatic vocal contribution from Marilyn Hill-Smith, and *Die Abonnenten* (by Eduard) are very attractive waltzes. *Blüthenkranz Johann Strauss'scher*, as its title suggests, makes a pot-pourri of some of Johann's most famous melodies. The polkas are a consistent delight, played wonderfully infectiously; indeed, above all this is a cheerful concert, designed to raise the spirits; the CD sound sparkles.

Perpetuum mobile. Polkas: *Annen; Auf der Jagd; Pizzicato* (with Josef); *Tritsch-Tratsch; Unter Donner und Blitz*. Waltzes: *An der schönen blauen Donau; G'schichten aus dem Wienerwald; Kaiser; Wiener Blut*. Josef STRAUSS: *Delirien waltz*.
(M) **(*) DG 437 255-2 [id.]. BPO, Karajan.

Here is a selection taken from two analogue LPs which Karajan made in 1966 and 1969 respectively. The performances have characteristic flair and the playing of the Berlin Philharmonic has much ardour as well as subtlety, with the four great waltzes of Johann II all finely done (the *Emperor* has a particularly engaging closing section) and the polkas wonderfully vivacious. The current remastering is satisfactory, brightly lit, but with the Jesus-Christus Kirche providing ambient fullness.

Polkas: *Fledermaus* (from *Die Fledermaus*); *Kreigsabenteur* (from *Der Zigeunerbaron*); *Pizzicato* (with Josef); *Unter Donner und Blitz*. Waltzes: *Accelerationen; Rosen aus dem Süden; 1001 Nacht; Wo die Zitronen blüh'n*. Eduard STRAUSS: Polka: *Bahn frei*. Waltz: *Doktrinen*. Josef STRAUSS: Waltzes: *Dynamiden; Sphärenklänge*.
(N) ❀ (M) *** RCA 09026 61688-2 [id.]. Boston Pops O, Arthur Fiedler.

Arthur Fiedler, the doyen of the Boston Pops, never made a better record than this. He shapes the introductions to these famous walzes with captivating charm; his dancing rubato brings an authentic Viennese feel and gives the impression of total spontaneity. Obviously the waltzes by Josef and Eduard especially command his affection, and all polkas go with a swing. Eduard's *Bahn frei* sizzles with energy – an exhilarating showstopper. Strauss records don't come any better than this, and the warm Boston acoustics, superbly caught in the early days of stereo (1956–9), add a special allure to all this music-making.

Polka: *Unter Donner und Blitz;* Waltzes: *An der schönen blauen Donau; Kaiser; Morgenblätter; Rosen aus dem Süden; Schatz; Wiener Blut.* Josef STRAUSS: Waltz: *Dorfschwalben aus Osterreich.*
(N) (M) **(*) RCA 09026 68160-2 [id.]. Chicago SO, Fritz Reiner (with: Richard STRAUSS: *Der Rosenkavalier: Waltzes;* WEBER/BERLIOZ: *Invitation to the dance* ***).

Reiner's collection was recorded in 1957 and 1960, and some of the voluptuousness of the Chicago ambience has disappeared in this fresh remastering. Although the *Thunder and lightning polka* has an unforgettable explosive exuberance, these performances are memorable for their Viennese lilt, especially the *Emperor waltz* (affectionate rather than seeking nobility of outline) and Josef's *Village swallows.* Reiner is especially persuasive in the introductory interchanges of Weber's *Invitation to the waltz* which, like the Richard Strauss *Rosenkavalier* sequence, has been added for the present reissue. The latter shows Reiner at his finest, and here the string-sound has added opulence.

Waltzes: *Accelerationen; An der schönen blauen Donau (Blue Danube); Du und Du; Frühlingstimmen (Voices of spring); Geschichten aus dem Wiener Wald (Tales from the Vienna Woods); Kaiser (Emperor); Künsterleben (Artist's life); Liebeslieder; Morgenblätter (Morning papers); Rosen aus dem Süden (Roses from the South); 1001 Nacht; Wein, Weib und Gesang (Wine, women and song); Wiener Blut (Vienna blood); Wiener Bonbons; Wo die Zitronen blühn (Where the lemon trees bloom).* Josef STRAUSS: *Dorfschwalben aus Osterreich; Sphären-klange (Music of the spheres).*
(Y/B) (B) *** Decca Double 443 473-2 (2) [id.]. VPO, Willi Boskovsky.

These recordings span Willi Boskovsky's long recording career with the VPO for Decca, stretching over two decades, when his records dominated the LP discography in the Strauss family repertoire. The first group to be recorded (*Liebeslieder,* ending disc 1, *Wiener Blut, Wiener Bonbons* and *Artist's life,* which open disc 2) are particularly 'live' and fresh, dating from 1958; and the last, a charmingly lilting performance of Josef Strauss's *Village swallows,* comes from 1976. One might think that such a succession of Strauss waltzes spread over two discs might produce a degree of listening fatigue, but that is never the case here, such is Johann's resource in the matter of melody and freshness of orchestration. The playing is reliably idiomatic in a coaxing, Viennese way and has striking spontaneity and life. Indeed there are some splendid performances and, if the opening item on disc 1, the *Blue Danube* (a little mannered), and the *Emperor* (lacking regality but with a beautiful coda) have been recorded elsewhere with greater memorability, *Tales from the Vienna Woods* is splendid, with a deliciously authentic zither solo; and both *Roses from the South* and *1001 Nights* are superb. *Wo die Zitronen blühn* with unashamed rubato comes off most winningly, and *Wine, women and song* with its four-and-a-half-minute introduction is another success; Josef's *Music of the spheres* is hardly less beguiling. The earliest recordings show their age a bit in the violin tone, but Decca set high technical standards from the beginning, and from the 1960s onwards the strings are tonally more expansive, while the glorious Viennese ambient glow is consistent throughout. Indeed on CD it is remarkable just how well these vintage recordings sound. With 145 minutes of music offered on a Double Decca reissue (two discs for the price of one), this is excellent value.

Waltzes: *An der schönen blauen Donau; Geschichten aus dem Wienerwald; Kaiser; Künstlerleben; Morgenblätter; Schatz; Wiener blut; Wo die Zitronen blüh'n.*
(N) (BB) ** RCA Navigator 74321 24205-2. Phd. O, Eugene Ormandy.

Vividly recorded between 1968 and 1971, these performances have plenty of zest and panache, with the Philadelphia string section making the very most of the sumptuous melodies. Ormandy is clearly enjoying himself and, although there are a few eccentricities of pulse and phrasing and these are obviously not Viennese performances, they are enjoyable for their ready vitality, and this Navigator selection is very modestly priced.

VOCAL MUSIC
Vocal waltzes

(i) *Auf's Korn! Bundesschützen-Marsch.* (ii) *Hoch Osterreich! Marsch.* Polkas: (i) *Burschenwanderung (polka française); 's gibt nur a Kaiserstadt! 's gibt nur ein Wien!;* (ii) *Sängerslust.* Waltzes: *An der schönen blauen Donau;* (i) *Bei uns z'Haus;* (ii) *Gross-Wien;* (i) *Myrthenblüthen;* (ii) *Neu-Wien; Wein, weib und gesang!*
**(*) Marco Polo Dig. 8.223250-2. Wiener Männergesangverein, Czecho-Slovak RSO (Bratislava), (i) Gerhard Track; (ii) Johannes Wildner.

A most enjoyable collection. Wildner is occasionally a bit strong with the beat, but the *Blue Danube* with chorus is much more enjoyable than his performance with orchestra alone. The singers are Viennese, so they have a natural lilt, and the recording has an ideal ambience.

OPERA

Die Fledermaus (complete).
*** Ph. Dig. 432 157-2 (2) [id.]. Kiri Te Kanawa, Gruberová, Leech, Wolfgang Brendel, Bär, Fassbaender, Göttling, Krause, Wendler, Schenk, V. State Op. Ch., VPO, Previn.
(N) (BB) *** CfP Silver Double CDCFPSD 4793 (2). Scheyrer, Lipp, Dermota, Berry, Ludwig, Terkal, Waechter, Kunz, Philh. Ch & O, Otto Ackermann.
(Y/B) (M) *** EMI CMS 7 69354-2 (2). Rothenberger, Holm, Gedda, Dallapozza, Fischer-Dieskau, Fassbaender, Berry, V. State Op. Ch., VSO, Boskovsky.
(M) (***) EMI mono CHS7 69531-2 (2) [Ang. CDHB 69531]. Schwarzkopf, Streich, Gedda, Krebs, Kunz, Christ, Philh. Ch. & O, Karajan.
(N) ** Teldec/Warner Dig. 0630 10024-2 (2) [id.]. Gruberová, Bonney, Hollweg, Protschka, Kmentt, Lipovšek, Netherlands Op. Ch., Concg. O, Harnoncourt.
(N) (B) *(*) Naxos Dig. 8.66017/8 [id.]. Fontana, Hopferwieser, Dickie, Karwautz, Yachmi-Caucig, Martin, Werner, Krämmer, Bratislava City Ch., Slovak RSO (Bratislava), Wildner.

André Previn here produces an enjoyably idiomatic account of Strauss's masterpiece, one which consistently conveys the work's exuberant high spirits. Dame Kiri Te Kanawa's portrait of Rosalinde brings not only gloriously firm, golden sound but also vocal acting with star quality. Brigitte Fassbaender is the most dominant Prince Orlofsky on disc. Singing with a tangy richness and firmness, she emerges as the genuine focus of the party scene. Edita Gruberová is a sparkling, characterful and full-voiced Adèle; Wolfgang Brendel as Eisenstein and Olaf Bär as Dr Falke both sing very well indeed, though their voices sound too alike. Richard Leech as Alfred provides heady tone and a hint of parody. Tom Krause makes a splendid Frank, the more characterful for no longer sounding young. Anton Wendler as Dr Blind and Otto Schenk as Frosch the jailer give vintage Viennese performances, with Frosch's cavortings well tailored and not too extended. This now goes to the top of the list of latterday *Fledermaus* recordings, though with one serious reservation. The Philips production in Act II adds a layer of crowd noise as background throughout the Party scene, even during Orlofsky's solos. Strauss's gentler moments are then seriously undermined by the sludge of distant chatter and laughter, as in the lovely chorus *Bruderlein und Schwesterlein*, yearningly done. Otherwise the recorded sound is superb, with brilliance and bite alongside warmth and bloom, both immediate and well balanced. Like Kleiber on DG, Previn opts for the *Thunder and lightning polka* instead of the ballet.

On a CfP Silver Double, with a synopsis rather than a libretto, comes a vintage *Fledermaus* from 1960. It makes a superb bargain, for the singing is consistently vivacious. Gerda Scheyrer's Rosalinde brings the only relative disappointment, for the voice is not ideally steady; but Wilma Lipp is a delicious Adèle and Christa Ludwig's Orlofsky is a real surprise, second only to Brigitte Fassbaender's assumption of a breeches role that is too often disappointing. Karl Terkal's Eisenstein and Anton Dermota's Alfred give much pleasure, and Erich Kunz's inebriated Frosch in the finale comes off even without a translation. Ackermann's direction has not the subtlety of Karajan, but the final result is lively and polished, with a real Viennese flavour. The sound has come up remarkably vividly – there is a nice combination of atmosphere and clarity.

For those wanting a fairly modern, mid-priced version, EMI have just restored the mid-priced Boskovsky set to the catalogue. Though he sometimes fails to lean into the seductive rhythms as much as he might, his is a refreshing account of a magic score. Rothenberger is a sweet, domestic-sounding Rosalinde, relaxed and sparkling if edgy at times, while, among an excellent supporting cast, the Orlovsky of Brigitte Fassbaender must again be singled out as the finest on record, tough and firm. The entertainment has been excellently produced for records, with German dialogue inserted, though the ripe recording sometimes makes the voices jump between singing and speaking. The remastering is admirably vivid.

The mono recording of Karajan's 1955 version has great freshness and clarity, along with the polish which for many will make it a first favourite. Schwarzkopf makes an enchanting Rosalinde, not just in the imagination and sparkle of her singing but also in the snatches of spoken dialogue (never too long) which leaven the entertainment. As Adèle, Rita Streich produces her most dazzling coloratura; Gedda and Krebs are beautifully contrasted in their tenor tone, and Erich Kunz gives a vintage performance as Falke. The original recording, crisply focused, has been given a brighter edge but otherwise left unmolested.

Harnoncourt, with characteristic concern for scholarship in his version with the Concertgebouw

Orchestra, presents the first recording to use a really full, authentic text, as published in the new editions, including the complete ballet in Act II. The singing cast is very strong, with consistently fresh, clean voices, very well recorded in crisply focused sound. Harnoncourt's direction is unfailingly pointed too, with textures exceptionally clear, and the bright, incisive manner allows the necessary lightness. What nevertheless tends to be missing is the Viennese fizz and vivacity. Some of the aura of a scholarly approach seems to reduce the high spirits, though individual singers give deliciously characterized performances, notably Barbara Bonney as Adèle and Marjana Lipovšek as Orlofsky. Edita Gruberová, similarly characterful, reveals a different side to both her voice and her personality from what we have come to expect, weightier, more dramatic, but unfortunately with a beat beginning to develop in the lower and middle registers. Curiously, instead of spoken dialogue, separate bands are provided containing comment and narration, but non-German speakers can easily programme them out. There is a mid-price highlights disc (72 minutes) which might be considered (Teldec 0630 13816-9).

A bargain version of Johann Strauss's scintillating operetta, well recorded in digital sound, complete with substantial dialogue, clearly has a place, but the singing lets this Naxos set down. After a promising account of the overture, crisp and bright if too rigid, the entry of Alfred signals the worst: lumpish, with coarse Germanic tone. When Adèle arrives, her combination of flutter in the voice and shrillness is equally impossible. Even Gabriele Fontana, who sings Rosalinde, is deeply disappointing, for the voice has plainly deteriorated since she sang the Countess in *Figaro* and Fiordiligi at Glyndebourne. Johannes Wildner is an efficient but inflexible director. The CfP Silver Double set under Ackermann costs about the same as this and is far, far preferable.

Die Fledermaus: highlights.
*** Ph. Dig. 438 503-2 [id.] (from above recording, with Te Kanawa, Gruberová; cond. Previn).
(Y/B) (M) *** EMI CDM7 69598-2 [id.] (from above recording, with Rothenberger, Holm, Gedda; cond. Boskovsky).
(Y/B) (M) **(*) Decca 421 898-2 [id.]. Janowitz, Holm, Kmentt, Kunz, Waechter, Windgassen, V. State Op. Ch., VPO, Karl Boehm.

The 62-minute selection from the exuberantly idiomatic Previn is a fair choice for those wanting a highlights disc, even if it is considerably less generous than some highlights discs; but most should be happy with the excerpts from the mid-priced Boskovsky set.

It is also good to have a generous (76 minutes) set of highlights from Karl Boehm's 1971 recording of *Fledermaus*, which has not yet been issued on CD. Boehm conducts with great warmth and affection, and the recording was made without dialogue, which many will prefer. The stars of the performance are undoubtedly Gundula Janowitz, in rich voice as Rosalinde, and Renate Holm as Adèle. The male principals are rather less impressive and the use of a male Orlovsky has less dramatic point on record than it would on stage. Windgassen, who assumes this role, is vocally here much inferior to, say, Brigitte Fassbaender. But (with fairly good documentation, though with no translation) there is much to enjoy, and the vintage Decca recording was made in the Sofiensaal.

A Night in Venice (Eine Nacht in Venedig): complete.
(Y/B) (M) (***) EMI mono CDH7 69530-2 [id.]. Schwarzkopf, Gedda, Kunz, Klein, Loose, Dönch, Philh. Ch. & O, Ackermann.

A Night in Venice, in Erich Korngold's revision, is a superb example of Walter Legge's Philharmonia productions, honeyed and atmospheric. As a sampler, try the jaunty little waltz duet in Act I between Schwarzkopf as the heroine, Annina, and the baritone Erich Kunz as Caramello, normally a tenor role. Nicolai Gedda as the Duke then appropriates the most famous waltz song of all, the *Gondola song* but, with such a frothy production, purism would be out of place. The digital remastering preserves the balance of the mono original admirably.

Wiener Blut (complete).
(Y/B) (M) (***) EMI mono CDH7 69529-2 [id.]. Schwarzkopf, Gedda, Köth, Kunz, Loose, Dönch, Philh. Ch. & O, Ackermann.

To have Schwarzkopf at her most ravishing, singing a waltz song based on the tune of *Morning Papers*, is enough enticement for this Philharmonia version of the mid-1950s, showing Walter Legge's flair as a producer at its most compelling. Schwarzkopf was matched by the regular team of Gedda and Kunz and with Emmy Loose and Erika Köth in the secondary soprano roles. The original mono recording was beautifully balanced, and the facelift given here is achieved most tactfully.

Der Zigeunerbaron (The Gipsy Baron): complete.
(M) (***) EMI mono CDH7 69526-2 (2). Schwarzkopf, Gedda, Prey, Kunz, Köth, Sinclair, Philh. Ch. & O, Ackermann.

This superb Philharmonia version of *The Gipsy Baron* from the mid-1950s, now restored to the catalogue, has never been matched in its rich stylishness and polish. Schwarzkopf as the gipsy princess sings radiantly, not least in the heavenly Bullfinch duet (to the melody made famous by MGM as *One day when we were young*). Gedda, still youthful, produces heady tone, and Erich Kunz as the rough pig-breeder gives a vintage *echt*-Viennese performance of the irresistible *Ja, das schreiben und das lesen*. The CD transcription from excellent mono originals gives fresh and truthful sound, particularly in the voices.

Der Zigeunerbaron (arr. Harnoncourt; Linke: complete).
(Y/B) *(**) Teldec/Warner Dig. 4509 94555-2 (2) [id.]. Coburn, Lippert, Schasching, Hamari, Holzmair, Oelze, Von Magnus, Lazar, Arnold Schoenberg Ch., VSO, Harnoncourt.

When *Zigeunerbaron*, second only to *Fledermaus* among Strauss operettas, has been so neglected on disc, this new Teldec set, offering a more expanded text than ever before, fills an important gap. Harnoncourt, as a Viennese and with a Viennese orchestra, ensures that the Strauss lilt is winningly and authentically observed from the *pot-pourri* overture onwards, and Harnoncourt's concern (as a period specialist) for clarity of texture gives the whole performance a sparkling freshness. Sadly, the casting is seriously flawed, when the central character of the gypsy princess, Saffi, is taken by a soprano, Pamela Coburn, who, as recorded, sounds strained and unsteady. She projects little of the glamour needed, the quality that Elisabeth Schwarzkopf so radiantly displays on the classic EMI mono set of 1954. The others are better, with Rudolf Schasching catching the fun behind the comic role of the pig-breeder, Zsupán, authentically but without exaggeration, and the light tenor, Herbert Lippert, is charming as the hero, Barinkay. Among the rest, the mezzo, Elisabeth von Magnus, sings in cabaret style in the supporting role of Mirabella, given a major point-number here, often omitted. Christiane Oelze as Arsena, the girl who does not get the hero, sings far more sweetly than Coburn, and Julia Hamari as Saffi's foster-mother, Czipra, sounds younger than her daughter. The recording is full and vivid, but many will feel that there is too much German dialogue – largely accounting for the extended length of two and a half hours.

Strauss, Josef (1827–70)

Josef Strauss: The Complete Edition
Volume 1: Polkas: *Angelica; Bauern; Eislauf; Etiquette; Moulinet; Thalia*. March: *Galenz. Kakadu-quadrille*. Waltzes: *Fantasiebilder; Marien-Klänge; Wiegenlieder*.
(Y/B) ** Marco Polo Dig. 8.223561 [id.]. Budapest Strauss SO, Alfred Walter.

Volume 2: *Amazonen-Quadrille*. Polkas: *Arabella; Diana; Genien; Stiefmütterchen; Sturmlauf; Sympathie. Schottischer Tanz*. Waltzes: *Petitionen; Tranz-Prioriräten*: Arr. of SCHUMANN: *Träumerei*.
(N) ** Marco Polo Dig. 8.223562 [id.]. Slovak State PO (Košice), Alfred Walter.

Volume 3: *Avantgarde march*. Polkas: *Gnomen; Die Lachtaube; Die Naïve; Ohne Sorgen; Sport*. Quadrilles: *Caprice; Flick-flock*. Waltzes: *Assoziationen; Ernst und Humor; Mai-Rosen*.
(N) ** Marco Polo Dig. 8.223563 [id.]. Slovak State PO (Košice), Alfred Walter.

It is good to see Marco Polo now exploring the output of Josef Strauss, of which we know remarkably little. Indeed almost all the items in this first volume are completely unfamiliar. Alfred Walter's easy-going style permeates the whole programme, and most of the polkas are left badly needing a more vital pacing. The waltzes are lilting in a lazy way: Walter shapes the evocative opening of *Fantasiebilder* rather beautifully, helped by polished and sympathetic playing from a group of Hungarian players. *Wiegenlieder* (*Cradle songs*) is another waltz which opens very enticingly and ought to be better known: it has a charming main theme and is nicely scored. The closing *Eislauf polka*, so very like the writing of Johann Junior, ends the concert spiritedly, and this well-recorded disc has great documentary interest, while the back-up notes are equally praiseworthy.

In Volume 2, Walter introduces two more waltzes which are fully worthy of Johann Jnr; *Petitionen* is particularly inventive. The polkas are amiable, with *Diana* aptly introduced by the horns. They are, as usual, played in a relaxed dance tempo: the most successful is the charming, Ländler-like *Stiefmütterchen*. The Schumann arrangement is very straightforward and adds little or nothing to the original piano piece: Walter presents it without any attempt at romantic subtlety.

Volume 3 opens with a sprightly march (not too heavily articulated), but the highlights are the *Assoziationen* and *Ernst und Humor* waltzes and the *Sport polka*, played here with with great spirit. Of the two waltzes the latter ('In a serious and light-hearted manner') has some interesting changes of mood, with modulations to match. It ought to be at least as well known as the closing (and justly renowned) *Ohne Sorgen polka*, which the Slovak players present with much enthusiasm, including the vocal interpolations. Excellent recording.

Strauss, Richard (1864–1949)

Symphonic poems: *An Alpine Symphony, Op. 64; Death and transfiguration, Op. 24; Don Juan, Op. 20; Ein Heldenleben, Op. 40.*
(N) (M) *** Chandos Dig. CHAN 7009/10 [id.]. Royal SNO, Neeme Järvi.

Symphonic poems: *Also sprach Zarathustra, Op. 30;* (i) *Don Quixote, Op. 35. Macbeth, Op. 23; Symphonia domestica, Op. 53; Till Eulenspiegel, Op. 38.*
(N) (M) *** Chandos Dig. CHAN 7011/12 [id.]. Royal SNO, Järvi; (i) with Raphael Wallfisch.

Järvi's generally distinguished survey of the Strauss symphonic poems was recorded in the sumptuous acoustics of the Caird Hall, Dundee, between 1986 and 1989. If occasionally the resonance prevents the sharpest internal clarity, the skilled Chandos engineering ensures that the orchestral layout is very believable, heard within a natural perspective. The account of *An Alpine Symphony* is ripely enjoyable, with the reverberant acoustic here very helpful. Järvi seeks to present a general scenic view within a performance that is not as electrically taut or crisp of ensemble as, say, Karajan's but which is very effective in giving a genial description of the changing landscapes. *Death and transfiguration* shows the orchestra at its finest and here detail is revealed well, within a reading which has impressive control. *Don Juan* is portrayed as a bluff philanderer and the reading seeks sentience and amplitude rather than searing brilliance. *Ein Heldenleben* is strongly characterized and warmly sympathetic from first to last, marked by powerful, thrustful playing, lacking only the last degree of refinement in ensemble.

Järvi's second box opens with the *Symphonia domestica*, a particularly successful performance, with the composer's domestic circumstances and moments of marital ardour indulged good-humouredly; it is followed by a comparably joyful portrait of *Till*. *Macbeth*, less than a masterpiece, is also presented very persuasively; few if any recorded performances make a better case for it. *Don Quixote* then takes a rather leisurely journey, although an amiable one. Raphael Wallfisch, the solo cellist, plays splendidly but, like the excellent violist, John Harrington, is very forwardly balanced, while inner orchestral detail is less than ideally clear. *Also sprach Zarathustra*, which closes the programme, is the least successful of the series, with the reverberant acoustic rather muddying the sound, without bringing compensating richness; moreover the organ pedal at the opening is much too dominant. But overall these two sets represent a considerable achievement, and at mid-price they are undoubtedly competitive, particularly for those collectors who enjoy Chandos's rich tapestries of sound.

An Alpine Symphony, Op. 64.
*** DG Gold Dig. 439 017-2 [id.]. BPO, Karajan.
*** Ph. Dig. 416 156-2 [id.]. Concg. O, Haitink.

An Alpine Symphony; Don Juan, Op. 20.
*** Decca Dig. 421 815-2. San Francisco SO, Blomstedt.

An Alpine Symphony; Don Juan; Salome: Salome's dance of the 7 veils.
(N) (B) **(*) Decca Eclipse Dig. 448 714-2; *448 714-4* [id.]. Cleveland O, Ashkenazy.

An Alpine Symphony; Till Eulenspiegel.
(N) (M) (**) DG mono 447 454-2 [id.]. Dresden State O, Karl Boehm.

Blomstedt's *Alpine Symphony* is superbly shaped and has that rare quality of relating part to whole in a way that totally convinces. He gets scrupulously attentive playing from the San Francisco orchestra and a rich, well-detailed Decca recording.

This DG reissue in the Karajan Gold series is one of the most remarkable in its improvement of the sound over the original CD issue. The acoustic boundaries of the sound seem to have expanded. Detail is not analytically clear, but the sumptuous body of tone created by the orchestra is glorious, with the violins glowing and soaring as they enter the forest. Undoubtedly this performance is very distinguished, wonderfully spacious and beautifully shaped – the closing *Night* sequence is very touching – and played with the utmost virtuosity.

Haitink's account on Philips is a splendid affair, a very natural-sounding recording and strongly characterized throughout. The perspective is excellent, and there is plenty of atmosphere, particularly in the episode of the calm before the storm. Above all, the architecture of the work as a whole is impressively laid out and the orchestral playing is magnificent. This can hold its own with the best.

The Cleveland Orchestra commands as rich a sonority and as much virtuosity as any of its illustrious rivals. Ashkenazy gives a generally well-controlled and intelligently shaped reading of the *Alpine symphony* that has much to recommend it. However, it is not quite as strong in personality as the very finest versions. That applies also to *Don Juan*, which brings comparable virtuosity from the Clevelanders. However, with recording of Decca's top quality, this is good value at bargain price.

Strauss's *Alpine Symphony* is a work that depends a great deal on its panoply of orchestral sound to make its full effect and, while Karl Boehm's 1957 mono recording is marvellously played and dramatically evocative, the recording, though clear, lacks the necessary opulence. His extremely lively portrait of *Till* comes off much better, but he recorded this again in stereo. However, the later, BPO characterization has more of the peasant about him, less of the irrepressible rogue.

(i) *An Alpine Symphony, Op. 64;* (ii) *Der Rosenkavalier* (orchestral suite for silent film).
(***) EMI mono CDC7 54610-2 [id.]. (i) Bav. State O; (ii) augmented L. Tivoli O; composer.

Strauss's 1941 account of the *Alpine Symphony* has been available in various LP formats, but it has never sounded better than it does in this excellent transfer. For all its sonic limitations, the performance still conveys lots of atmosphere, and although one needs the benefit of modern stereo sound to do this sumptuous score full justice Strauss's own reading still has special claims.

An Alpine Symphony, Op. 64; Aus Italien, Op. 16; Dance suite from pieces by François Couperin; (i) *Don Quixote, Op. 35. Macbeth, Op. 23; Metamorphosen for 23 solo strings.*
(M) *** CMS7 64350-2 (3). (i) Paul Tortelier; Dresden State O, Kempe.

This is the third of the three boxes of Richard Strauss's orchestral and concertante music, recorded during the first half of the 1970s. The Dresden orchestra is a magnificent body and the strings produce gloriously sumptuous tone, which is strikingly in evidence in *Metamorphosen*. Rudolf Kempe had recorded the *Alpine Symphony* before with the RPO, and there is little to choose between the two so far as interpretation is concerned: he brings a glowing warmth to this score. His *Aus Italien* is more convincing than any previous version: the sound with its finely judged perspective is again a decisive factor here. He gives a most musical account of the delightful *Dance suite* based on Couperin keyboard pieces, although here some might wish for more transparent textures. Perhaps one could also quarrel with the balance in *Don Quixote*, which gives Tortelier exaggerated prominence and obscures some detail. The performance, however, is another matter and must rank with the best available. *Macbeth* also is convincing, and well paced.

(i) *An Alpine Symphony, Op. 64;* (ii) *Also sprach Zarathustra, Op. 30; Don Juan, Op. 20;* (iii) *Ein Heldenleben, Op. 40;* (ii) *Till Eulenspiegel, Op. 28.*
(B) *** Double Decca 440 618-2 (2) [id.]. (i) Bav. RSO; (ii) Chicago SO; (iii) VPO; Solti.

The Bavarian Radio Orchestra recorded in the Herculessal in Munich could hardly sound more opulent in the *Alpine Symphony* and the superb quality of the 1979 analogue recording tends to counterbalance Solti's generally fast tempi. The performances of *Also sprach Zarathustra, Don Juan* and *Till Eulenspiegel* come from analogue originals, made in Chicago a few years earlier. Solti is ripely expansive in *Zarathustra*, and throughout all three symphonic poems there is the most glorious playing from the Chicago orchestra in peak form. For *Ein Heldenleben* Solti went (in 1977–8) to Vienna, and this is another fast-moving performance, tense to the point of fierceness in the opening tutti and elsewhere. It underlines the urgency rather than the opulence of the writing and, though many Straussians will prefer a warmer, more relaxed view, Solti finds justification in a superb account of the final coda after the fulfilment theme, where in touching simplicity he finds complete relaxation at last, helped by the exquisite playing of the Vienna Philharmonic concertmaster, Rainer Küchl. The Decca recording is formidably wide-ranging to match this high-powered performance and, as with the rest of the programme, the transfers to CD are full-bodied and vividly detailed.

Also sprach Zarathustra, Op. 30; Le bourgeois gentilhomme (suite of incidental music for Molière's play), *Op. 60;* (i) *Violin concerto in D min., Op. 8. Death and transfiguration, Op. 24; Josephslegende, Op. 63; Schlagobers* (waltz), *Op. 70; Symphonia domestica, Op. 53; Der Rosenkavalier: Waltz sequence; Salome: Dance of the 7 veils.*
(M) *** EMI CMS7 64346-2 (3). (i) Ulf Hoelscher; Dresden State O, Kempe.

Ulf Hoelscher's eloquent account of this attractive early *Violin concerto* is more than welcome, as is the *Sinfonia domestica*. Kempe's version of this work is no less desirable than Karajan's, a little more relaxed without being in any way less masterly. His *Also sprach Zarathustra* is completely free of the sensationalism that marks so many newer performances. *Josephslegende*, however, will call for tolerance even in this committed version; Strauss's inspiration is thin here and his craftsmanship runs away with him. The rest of the programme is well worth having, particularly *Le bourgeoise gentilhomme*. Recording and CD transfers are well up to standard.

Also sprach Zarathustra, Op. 30; Le bourgeois gentilhomme: Suite, Op. 60. Der Rosenkavalier: Waltzes.
(M) *** RCA 09026 60930-2 [60930-2]. Chicago SO, Reiner.

Reiner's 1954 account of *Also sprach Zarathustra* with its impressive feeling of space is a wonderful performance that ranks alongside the very best ever committed to disc. The same goes for the suite from *Le bourgeois gentilhomme* – possibly the finest ever, and sounding marvellously fresh considering its date (1956). Incandescent music-making, transferred to CD with stunning success.

(i) *Also sprach Zarathustra, Op. 30;* (ii) *Aus Italien: excerpt: On the shores of Sorrento;* (iii) *Death and transfiguration;* (iv) *Don Quixote;* (v) *Ein Heldenleben.*
(M) (***) RCA mono 09026 60929-2 (2) [60929-2]. (i) Boston SO, Koussevitzky; (ii) Chicago SO, Stock; (iii) Phd. O, Stokowski; (iv) Wallenstein, NYPO, Beecham; (v) NYPO, Mengelberg.

To have *Ein Heldenleben* conducted by its dedicatee seems almost miraculous, recorded in 1928 – only 30 years after its composition – in what was exceptionally good quality for the period. And what a performance it is, and what playing the New York Orchestra could produce in those days! Koussevitzky's superb (1935) Boston account of *Also sprach Zarathustra* was for long the only version in the catalogue. Beecham's New York account of *Don Quixote* with Alfred Wallenstein as soloist, made in 1932 (the year before Strauss's own with Mainardi), is another reading of enormous character (though the transfer has a slightly more strident top than we remember from the LP reissue). Stokowski's *Death and transfiguration* shows the Philadelphia Orchestra with similar opulence of tone and virtuosity.

Also sprach Zarathustra, Op. 30; Death and transfiguration, Op. 24; Don Juan, Op. 20; Ein Heldenleben, Op. 40; Till Eulenspiegel; Der Rosenkavalier: Waltz sequence. Salome: Salome's dance of the seven veils.
(Y/B) (B) *** EMI CZS5 68110-2 (2) [id.]. Dresden State O, Rudolf Kempe.

Kempe's 1974 *Also sprach Zarathustra*, powerful in its emotional thrust, is admirably paced and, while the Dresden orchestra may yield in virtuosity – though not much – to the Berlin Philharmonic under Karajan, whose version was made in the same year, the EMI digital remastering retains the opulence of the Dresden acoustic and the orchestral sound has both body and bloom. Kempe's *Death and transfiguration* and *Till Eulenspiegel* are also marvellously characterized, and the Dresden Staatskapelle is hardly less refined an instrument than the Berlin Philharmonic. The rather mellow portrayal of *Till* is particularly attractive. *Don Juan* is also comparable with Karajan's reading and certainly does not come off second best. *Ein Heldenleben* glows with life under one of the most distinguished Straussians of our time and the closing pages have a special kind of rapt intensity. The richness of string-tone in *Salome's dance*, a sinuously sensuous performance, and in the *Rosenkavalier Waltz sequence* has been superbly caught in the excellent CD transfer. With two discs offered for the price of one, this is a top bargain in the Strauss discography.

Also sprach Zarathustra; Death and transfiguration, Op. 24; Don Juan, Op. 20.
*** DG Gold Dig. 439 016-2 [id.]. BPO, Karajan.
*** Telarc Dig. CD 80167 [id.]. VPO, Previn.

Also sprach Zarathustra; Don Juan.
*** Denon Dig. CO 2259 [id.]. Dresden State O, Blomstedt.

As a performance the 1983 Karajan *Also sprach Zarathustra* (coupled with an exciting account of *Don Juan*) will be hard to beat and could very well be first choice. And the newly remastered CD in the Karajan Gold series has great dynamic range and presence, particularly at the extreme bass and treble, and the massed violins produce wonderfully radiant textures, as in the section marked *Von der grossen Sehnsucht* ('of the great longing'). The soaring main theme of *Don Juan* is hardly less sumptuous and the playing is electrifying in its energy. In Strauss, Karajan has no peer and this is one of his finest records from the early 1980s.

As a recording, the Denon CD could hardly be more impressive. The sound is rich, the acoustic is resonant but never clouds detail, and the range and presence are really quite stunning. The performance has all the sense of architecture and authority we have come to expect from Blomstedt, whose Strauss is always distinctive. The Denon disc also contains a very good *Don Juan*.

Previn draws magnificent playing from the Vienna Philharmonic in powerful, red-blooded readings of the symphonic poems, and the recording is among Telarc's finest. Strongly recommended for anyone wanting this particular coupling, and enjoying spectacularly voluptuous sound-quality.

(i) *Also sprach Zarathustra; Death and transfiguration; Don Juan; Ein Heldenleben; Till Eulenspiegel;* (ii) *Der Rosenkavalier: Waltz sequence.*
(B) *** Ph. Duo Dig./Analogue 442 281-2 (2) [id.]. Concg. O, (i) Haitink; (ii) Jochum.

Haitink's performances are undoubtedly distinguished, superbly played, persuasively and subtly characterized. He finds added nobility in *Death and transfiguration*, while there is no lack of swagger in the accounts of both the *Don* and *Till*. The easy brilliance of the orchestral playing is complemented by the natural spontaneity of Haitink's readings, seamless in the transition between narrative events, without loss of the music's picaresque or robust qualities. Haitink's (1974) *Also sprach Zarathustra* was often spoken of in the same breath as Karajan's analogue alternative, issued in the same year. There is no lack of ardour from the Concertgebouw players and the reading has breadth and nobility. The (1970) *Ein Heldenleben* is also one of Haitink's finest records. He gives just the sort of performance, brilliant and swaggering but utterly without bombast, which will delight those who normally resist this rich and expansive work. In the culminating fulfilment theme, a gently lyrical 6/8, Haitink finds a raptness in restraint, a hint of agony within joy, that links the passage directly to the great Trio from *Der Rosenkavalier*. The Philips sound here is admirably faithful and skilfully remastered. For good measure Jochum's *Waltz sequence* from that very opera has been added, though here the recording, though good for its age (the early 1960s), has not quite the opulence of the Haitink recordings. An indispensable set nevertheless, and one of the finest of all the Duo bargains.

Also sprach Zarathustra; Death and transfiguration; Till Eulenspiegel.
(N) (B) *** Decca Eclipse Dig. 448 224-2; *448 224-4* [id.]. Cleveland O, Ashkenazy.

Glorious Decca Cleveland sound in this triptych and marvellously reponsive playing from the orchestra. As sound, this is in the demonstration bracket; but other readings, notably those of Karajan, are just that bit more characterful.

Also sprach Zarathustra; Don Juan; Till Eulenspiegel.
(B) *(**) DG 439 419-2 [id.]. BPO, Karl Boehm.

Also sprach Zarathustra; Don Juan; Till Eulenspiegel; Salome: Dance of the 7 veils.
(N) (M) *** Decca 448 582-2 [id.]. VPO, Karajan.

Karajan's Decca version of *Also sprach Zarathustra* was a famous early stereo demonstration disc in its day (1959), with its wide dynamic range and thrilling orchestral virtuosity; all its tonal opulence is restored in the CD transfer. The other works were recorded a year later and sound freshly minted, amazingly full and sharply detailed. *Till* is irrepressibly cheeky and full of wit, and *Salome's dance* is decadently sensuous. *Don Juan* brings a similar, richly voluptuous response from the Vienna strings. Again the playing is superb, as beguiling in the love music as it is exhilarating in the chase. An admirable candidate for Decca's 'Classic Sound' series.

Boehm was a fine Straussian, but *Also sprach Zarathustra* is very early stereo (1958) and, for all the ardour of the Berlin Philharmonic, the violins are made to sound thin above the stave, although the Jesus-Christus-Kirche provides plenty of ambient warmth. Boehm's *Don Juan* and *Till* were recorded five years later; the sound is fuller and the orchestral playing is marvellous. *Don Juan* brings glorious leaping strings and rich thrusting horns, and Boehm provides an attractive German-peasant-based characterization of *Till*.

Also sprach Zarathustra, Op. 30; (i) *Don Quixote, Op. 35.*
(M) **(*) Sony SBK 47656; *SBT 47656* [id.]. Phd. O, Ormandy; (i) with Lorne Munroe.

Ormandy's 1963 Sony *Also sprach Zarathustra*, if not as overwhelming as his later, EMI version, has much virtuoso orchestral playing to commend it and many felicities of characterization. His (1961) *Don Quixote* will also give considerable pleasure. There is some marvellous orchestral playing and the two soloists play splendidly with plenty of character but without the 'star soloist' approach favoured by so many record companies. A very competitive coupling.

Also sprach Zarathustra, Op. 30; Ein Heldenleben.
(❀) (M) *** RCA 09026 61494-2 [id.]. Chicago SO, Fritz Reiner.

These were the first stereo sessions the RCA engineers arranged with Fritz Reiner, after the company had taken over the Chicago orchestra's recording contract from Mercury. It must be said – to their enormous credit – that the RCA recording team 'got it right' from the very beginning, and the series of records they made with Reiner and his players in Orchestra Hall remain a technical peak in the history of stereo recording and the impressive feeling of space it conveyed. Later reissues have improved on its definition but none has done so with the stunning success of the present transfer. A wonderful performance that ranks alongside the very best ever committed to disc. *Ein Heldenleben* shows Reiner in equally splendid form. There have been more incisive, more spectacular and more romantic performances, but Reiner achieves an admirable balance and whatever he does is convincing. If anything, the recording sounds even better than *Also sprach* and the warm acoustics of Orchestra Hall help convey Reiner's humanity in the closing pages of the work.

Also sprach Zarathustra, Op. 30; Don Juan, Op. 20; Till Eulenspiegel, Op. 28; Salome: Salome's dance.
(N) (M) *** DG 447 441-2 [id.]. BPO, Karajan.

Karajan's 1974 DG analogue version of *Also sprach Zarathustra* is coupled with his vividly characterized performance of *Till Eulenspiegel* and a thrillingly ebullient *Don Juan*, plus his powerfully voluptuous account of *Salome's dance*. The Berlin Philharmonic plays with great fervour (the timpani strokes at
the very opening are quite riveting) and creates characteristic body of tone in the strings, although the
digital remastering has thrown a much brighter light on the violins.

Also sprach Zarathustra, Op. 30; Symphonia domestica, Op. 53.
(N) (M) **(*) DG Dig. 445 560-2 [id.]. VPO, Maazel.

In a finely played *Also sprach Zarathustra*, Maazel secures some glorious playing from the Vienna
Philharmonic Orchestra. The *Symphonia domestica*, a tone-poem rather than a symphony, is a very
good performance, too. The recordings, dating from 1983 and reissued now in DG's Masters series, are
admirable. A good mid-priced coupling, but there are finer individual versions of both works.

Aus Italien, Op. 16; Die Liebe der Danae (symphonic fragment); *Der Rosenkavalier: waltz sequence No. 2.*
(BB) *** Naxos Dig. 8.550342 [id.]. Slovak PO, Zdeněk Košler.

On Naxos, a very well-recorded and vividly detailed account of *Aus Italien* with an excellent sense of
presence. The orchestra plays very well for Zdeněk Košler both here and in the ten-minute symphonic
fragment Clemens Krauss made from *Die Liebe der Danae* and in the *Rosenkavalier* waltz sequence. The
Slovak Philharmonic is a highly responsive body, with cultured strings and wind departments and, given
the quality of the recorded sound, this represents a real bargain.

Le bourgeois gentilhomme (incidental music); *Divertimento* (after Couperin), *Op. 86.*
*** DG Dig. 435 871-2 [id.]. Orpheus CO.

The Orpheus Chamber Orchestra continue to add to their laurels and enhance their already high
reputation in these superbly vital and sensitive accounts. Straussians will have (or want) the Clemens
Krauss, Beecham and Reiner old records of *Le bourgeois gentilhomme*, but of modern accounts this
version is arguably unsurpassed – and all without the ministrations of a maestro. The performance of
the *Divertimento* after Couperin delights, and the recordings do full justice to them.

(i) *Burleske in D min. for piano and orchestra.* (ii) *Duet-concertino for clarinet, bassoon and strings.* (iii)
Horn concertos Nos. 1–2. (iv) *Oboe concerto in D. Don Juan, Op. 20; Ein Heldenleben, Op. 40.* (v)
*Panathenäenzug for piano (left hand) and orchestra; Parergon to Symphonia domestica for piano (left
hand) and orchestra. Till Eulenspiegel, Op. 28.*
(M) *** EMI CMS7 64342-2 (3). (i) Malcolm Frager; (ii) Manfred Weise, Wolfgang Liebscher; (iii)
    Peter Damm; (iv) Manfred Clement; (v) Peter Rösel; Dresden State O, Kempe.

Volume 1 of the Kempe/EMI Strauss series includes all the major concertante works except the *Violin
concerto*. Most collectors will already have a *Don Juan*, which is perhaps the least electrifying of
Kempe's symphonic poems, and the same surely applies to *Till Eulenspiegel*, although it is an excellent
performance. The *Burleske* is well worth having (it is beautifully recorded) and there are no satisfactory
alternative versions of the *Parergon* to the *Sinfonia domestica* or the *Panathenäenzug*, both written for
the one-armed pianist, Paul Wittgenstein, and played impressively here. Peter Damm's performances of
the *Horn concertos* are first class. Similarly, while Manfred Clement's *Oboe concerto* is a sensitive
reading, his creamily full timbre may not appeal to those brought up on Goossens. There can be no
reservations whatsoever about the *Duet concertino*, where the sounds from bassoon and clarinet are
beguilingly succulent, while the intertwining of both wind soloists with the dancing orchestral violins of
the finale has an irresistible, genial finesse. Throughout, the superb playing of the Dresden orchestra
under Kempe adds an extra dimension to the music-making.

Burleske for piano and orchestra.
(Y/B) (BB) **(*) RCA Navigator 74321 21286-2. Byron Janis, Chicago SO, Reiner – MAHLER:
    Symphony No. 4. **(*)
(B) *(**) Sony SBK 53262; *SBT 53262* [id.]. Rudolf Serkin, Phd. O, Ormandy – BRAHMS: *Piano
    concerto No. 2.* **(*)

(i) *Burleske;* (ii) *Don Quixote, Op. 35.*
(M) *** RCA 09026 61796-2 [id.]. (i) Byron Janis; (ii) Janigro; Chicago SO, Fritz Reiner.

Burleske; Parergon, Op. 73; Stimmungsbilder, Op. 9.
**(*) Ara. Dig. Z 6567 [id.]. Ian Hobson, Philh. O, Del Mar.

(i) *Burleske; Symphonia domestica, Op. 53.*
*** Sony M K 42322 [id.]. (i) Barenboim; BPO, Mehta.

The *Burleske* for piano and orchestra is given with great brilliance and panache by Daniel Barenboim in a beautifully balanced recording, while Mehta's version of the *Symphonia domestica* is humane and relaxed and has great warmth; he certainly gets pretty sumptuous playing from the Berlin Philharmonic and has the advantage of very good sound. A highly recommendable disc.

The brilliance of the *Burleske* is also brought out well by Byron Janis, who does not miss the music's witty or lyrical side. Even at full price, Reiner's *Don Quixote* was a top recommendation. Reiner was a masterly Straussian and this 1959 version was one of the very finest of RCA's Chicago Hall recordings. Antonio Janigro plays stylishly and with assurance; if he brings less intensity than Fournier to the ecstatic solo cadenza in Variation V, his contribution to the close of the work is distinguished. The recording of *Burleske* is somewhat shallower than that of the tone-poem (though a considerable improvement on the original LP), but this helps to ensure that Strauss's youthful writing does not sound too sweet. On the bargain-price Navigator alternative, the recording gives a brilliantly sparkling, some-what dry piano-image, and the orchestra too is brought forward by the comparatively close microphones (although there is no lack of ambience).

Ian Hobson's account of the *D minor Burleske*, on its own terms, is eminently satisfactory, and he is well supported by Norman Del Mar and the Philharmonia, and is well recorded. The *Parergon* for left hand is again very well played. The *Stimmungsbilder* are early, rather Schumannesque pieces, written in 1884: Hobson gives a rather touching account of *Träumerei*, and though one can imagine a performance of the *Intermezzo* with greater charm, there is still much to admire here. Decent recording.

The Sony alternative is a generally excellent performance of what is still a comparative rarity on disc. Serkin plays with great brilliance, and the music's lyrical side – uncharacteristic but winning – is well understood. The current remastering is an improvement on the original, but the piano timbre is bright and somewhat clattery and the orchestral textures are made somewhat two-dimensional by the close microphones. Nevertheless this is an arresting performance.

Horn concerto No. 1 in E flat, Op. 11.
(M) *** EMI Dig. CDM7 64851-2 [id.]. Radovan Vlatkovič, ECO, Tate – MOZART: *Horn concertos Nos. 1–4* etc. ***

Radovan Vlatkovič gives a superb account of the *First Concerto* which, although ripely romantic, has so much in common with the spirit of the Mozart concertos with which it is coupled. He is particularly good in the bold central episode of the *Andante* and caps his performance with an exhilaratingly nimble account of the finale. Tate accompanies admirably and the rich, natural, Abbey Road recording could hardly be better balanced.

Horn concertos Nos. 1 in E flat, Op. 11; 2 in E flat.
(N) ❀ (***) EMI mono CDC7 47834-2 [id.]. Dennis Brain, Philh. O, Sawallisch – HINDEMITH: *Horn concerto*. (***)

Dennis Brain's performances are incomparable and almost certainly will never be surpassed. Sawallisch gives him admirable support, and fortunately the latest EMI CD transfer captures the full quality of the 1956 mono recording. The orchestra is a bit backward, but Brain's glorious melodic line soars aloft ravishingly.

(i) *Horn concertos Nos 1 in E flat, Op. 11; 2 in E flat;* (ii) *Oboe concerto in D;* (iii) *Duet concertino for clarinet, bassoon, strings and harp.*
(M) *** EMI CDM7 69661-2. (i) Peter Damm; (ii) Manfred Clement; (iii) Manfred Weise, Wolfgang Liebscher; Dresden State O, Kempe.

After those of Dennis Brain, Peter Damm's performances of the *Horn concertos* are second to none and, although his use of a (judicious) degree of vibrato may be a drawback for some ears, his tone is gloriously rich. The big striding theme at the centre of the *Andante* of No. 1 is superbly expansive, and the articulation in the finales of both concertos is joyously deft and nimble. Similarly, while Manfred Clement's *Oboe concerto* is a sensitive reading, his creamily full timbre may not appeal to those brought up on Goossens. There can be no reservations whatsoever about the *Duet concertino*, in which the sounds from bassoon and clarinet are beguilingly succulent, while the intertwining of both wind soloists with the dancing orchestral violins of the finale has an irresistible, genial finesse. Throughout, the superb playing of the Dresden orchestra adds an extra dimension to the music-making. Kempe's benign control of the music's ebb and flow shows him always a warmly understanding Straussian. The remastered recording, made in the Dresden Lukaskirche, retains an agreeable ambient glow which pleases the ear greatly.

(i) *Horn concertos Nos. 1 in E flat, Op. 11; 2 in E flat;* (ii) *Duet concertino for clarinet and bassoon. Wind serenade in E flat, Op. 11.*

(Y/B) (M) *** EMI Dig. CD-EMX 2238 [id.]. (i) David Pyatt; (ii) Joy Farrall, Julie Andrews; Britten Sinfonia, Nicholas Cleobury.

David Pyatt gives a ripely exuberant performance of the first of Strauss's two *Horn concertos,* which is very much in the spontaneous style of the Mozart concertos. The more elusive first movement of the *Second Concerto* is shaped – often quite subtly – in an attractively rhapsodical style; the ecstatic solo line of the *Andante,* gently introduced by the oboe, is beautifully played while the finale brings heady, lightly tongued bravura. The outer movements of the gently rapturous *Duet concertino* (a late masterpiece, written the year before the *Vier letzte Lieder*) are presented with enticing delicacy of texture, and the slow movement again brings a most touchingly doleful opening solo, this time from the bassoonist, Julie Andrews. Cleobury and the Britten Sinfonia give sensitive support throughout, and the early *Serenade* is also made the more attractive by the lightness of touch of the wind blending, its sonorities always fresh, never congealing, helped by the naturally balanced recording, made in the Henry Wood Hall, Southwark. For those who want a change from the Dennis Brain Philharmonia accounts of the *Horn concertos* from the 1950s, this would be a distinct contender.

Oboe concerto.

*** Nimbus Dig. NI 5330 [id.]. John Anderson, Philh. O, Simon Wright – FRANCAIX: *L'horloge de flore;* MARTINU: *Concerto.* ***

(M) *** RCA Dig. GD 87989 [7989-2-RG]. John de Lancie, CO, Max Wilcox – FRANCAIX: *L'horloge de flore* *** ✸; IBERT: *Symphonie concertante.* ***

*** ASV Dig. CDCOE 808 [id.]. Douglas Boyd, COE, Berglund – MOZART: *Oboe concerto.* ***

In the summer of 1945 a young American musician/GI (who before the war had been an oboist with the Pittsburgh Symphony Orchestra) suggested to Strauss that he write an oboe concerto, and only months later the eighty-one-year-old composer produced his famous work. That same oboist, John de Lancie, recorded it in 1987, playing persuasively and with much finesse. The chamber accompaniment could ideally sound riper, but the balance is realistic and the sound real.

John Anderson, principal oboe of the Philharmonia, gives a ravishing acount of Strauss's delectable concerto, his timbre slightly riper than that of the concerto's dedicatee, and the Nimbus digital record-ing that bit more modern. But John de Lancie's account is very enjoyable too, so choice can rest with the coupling.

Douglas Boyd winningly brings out the happy glow of Strauss's inspiration of old age, and his warm oboe tone, less reedy than some, brings out the *Rosenkavalier* element in this lovely concerto. With warm, well-balanced recording, the gentle contrast of romantic and classical in this work is conveyed delectably.

Oboe concerto (with alternative endings).

(M) **(*) Carlton Classics 30366 00212-2 [id.]. Robin Canter, LSO, James Judd – VAUGHAN WIL-LIAMS: *Concerto* etc. ***

The great interest of Robin Canter's Pickwick recording is that it offers the finale with alternative endings. If the disc is played straightforwardly, it produces the familiar (revised) close to the work, but the listener can choose instead to programme the CD player to offer Strauss's first thoughts which were very slightly more succinct. The performance itself is enjoyable, although the very opening phrase is almost thrown away: a little more poise here would have been welcome. Otherwise both soloist and accompanists acquit themselves impressively, and the recording is bright and clear.

(i) *Oboe concerto in D.* (ii) *Serenade for wind, Op. 7; Sonatine No. 1 in F for wind (From an invalid's workshop); Suite in B flat for 13 wind instruments, Op. 4; Symphony for wind (The happy workshop).*

(B) *** Ph. Duo 438 733-2 (2) [id.]. (i) Heinz Holliger, New Philh. O; (ii) Netherlands Wind Ens.; Edo de Waart.

The *Serenade* is beautifully played, warm and mellifluous, and so is the *Sonatina,* a late work, written while Strauss was recovering from an illness and appropriately subtitled. It is a richly scored piece, as thoroughly effective as one would expect from this master of wind writing. Both this and the *B flat Suite,* delightful pieces, are given beautifully characterized accounts here, while the performance of the *Symphony for wind instruments* is crisp and alert. Throughout this music-making, the ear is struck by the Netherlanders' beautifully homogeneous tone, and their phrasing is splendidly alive. The recordings (made between 1970 and 1972) are full, well-detailed and truthful. As if this were not bounty enough, Holliger's earlier (1970) version of the *Oboe concerto* is thrown in for good measure. The playing is masterly, an assured, styish account, and Edo de Waart accompanies persuasively. Again very good recording.

(i) *Oboe concerto;* (ii) *4 Last songs;* (iii) Lieder: *Befreit; Cäcile; Frühlingsfeier; Die Heiligen Drei Könige; Muttertändelei.*

(N) (M) *** BBC Radio Classics 15656 91382 [id.]. (i) John Anderson, BBC SO; (ii) Heather Harper, RPO; (iii) Elizabeth Harwood, New Philh.O; all cond. Norman Del Mar.

This ripely enjoyable disc of Strauss in the BBC Radio Collection fills an important gap. Norman Del Mar was not just the author of a definitive study of Strauss's music, he was second to none as a warmly persuasive Strauss conductor. John Anderson, then principal oboe of the BBC orchestra, gives a yearningly beautiful, tenderly elegiac reading of the late *Oboe concerto,* taken from a 1981 performance given on tour in South Korea. Heather Harper is even more radiant in this Prom performance than in her studio recording of the *Four Last songs,* while – filling another gap in the catalogue – the lovely soprano tones of the late Elizabeth Harwood have never been caught more ravishingly than in this 1968 recording of orchestral arrangements of five Strauss songs, including *Cäcilie, Muttertändelei* and the Christmas narrative, *Die Heiligen drei Könige.*

Violin concerto in D min., Op. 8.
*** ASV Dig. CDDCA 780 [id.]. Xue Wei, LPO, Glover – HEADINGTON: *Violin concerto.* *** ✹

With Jane Glover and the LPO warmly sympathetic accompanists, Xue Wei makes a very persuasive case for this very early work of Strauss, with its echoes of Mendelssohn and Bruch.

Death and transfiguration, Op. 24.
(M) (***) RCA mono GD 60312. Phd. O, Toscanini – TCHAIKOVSKY: *Symphony No. 6.* (***)

Toscanini's characteristically taut control of tension goes with what was for him a more warmly expressive style than usual, thanks to the influence of the Philadelphia Orchestra. With the transfer giving good body to the limited sound, it is comparable with his equally intense reading of Tchaikovsky's *Pathétique* from the same period.

Death and transfiguration, Op. 24; Don Juan, Op. 20.
(Y/B) (M) (**(*)) Bruno Walter Edition: Sony mono SMK 64466 [id.]. NYPO, Bruno Walter (with DVORAK: *Slavonic dance, Op. 46/1*) – BARBER: *Symphony No. 1.* (**)

Death and transfiguration, Op. 24; Don Juan, Op. 20; Till Eulenspiegel, Op. 28.
(Y/B) (M) (***) EMI mono CDH5 65197-2 [id.]. VPO, Furtwängler (with SMETANA: *Má Vlast: Vltava* ***).

Furtwängler's are wonderfully rich and humane performances, with that glowing sound the great conductor made so much his own. All these recordings are mono and were produced by Walter Legge or Laurance Collingwood, with Anthony Griffith and Robert Beckett as engineers. They wear their years very lightly indeed. The performances themselves have a tremendous fall-out and resonate in the mind long after they are over. Strongly recommended.

   Walter recorded these tone-poems in the studio in 1952; the sound, though not well balanced, is reasonably expansive for its period, a bit empty-studio-ish but much better than the coupled Barber *Symphony.* The performances are both warmly romantic and high in adrenalin; indeed the playing of the NYPO is at times quite wild in *Don Juan.* Precision of string ensemble is less impressive, but Walter finds a very special atmosphere for the opening and closing pages of *Death and transfiguration.*

Death and transfiguration, Op. 24; Don Quixote, Op. 35.
(M) (**(*)) RCA mono GD 60295 [60295-2-RG]. NBC SO, Toscanini.

By the side of Munch (see below), Toscanini's account of *Don Quixote,* also from 1953 and equally electrifying and masterly, with a superb soloist in Frank Miller, sounds a shade overdriven. It does not have quite the humanity or expressive flexibility of the Piatigorsky–Munch reading. However, his 1952 *Tod und Verklärung* is quite simply stunning.

(i) *Death and transfiguration, Op. 24;* (ii) *Ein Heldenleben, Op. 40.*
(N) (B) ** BBC Radio Classics BBCRD 9122 [id.] (i) BBC SO, Sir John Pritchard; (ii) BBC PO, Günther Herbig.

Taken in isolation, these are both perfectly good performances and the engineers have managed to make a very good job of improving the Maida Vale acoustic for the Pritchard *Tod und Verklärung.* But good broadcasts have to compete with really outstanding commercial recordings by great international orchestras and, put alongside Kempe and Karajan, also available at competitive prices, choice will inevitably fall elsewhere. This is not to say that these performances from the 1970s will not give considerable pleasure.

Death and transfiguration; Metamorphosen for 23 solo strings.
✪ *** DG Dig. 410 892-2 [id.]. BPO, Karajan.

Death and transfiguration; Metamorphosen for 23 solo strings; Till Eulenspiegel.
*** Denon Dig. CO 73801 [id.]. Dresden State O, Blomstedt.

Death and transfiguration; Metamorphosen for 23 solo strings; (i) Drei Hymnen, Op. 71.
*** Chandos Dig. CHAN 8734 [id.]. SNO, Järvi; (i) with Felicity Lott.

Death and transfiguration; Metamorphosen for 23 solo strings; (i) Vier letzte Lieder (4 Last songs).
(Y/B) (M) **(*) DG 447 422-2 [id.]. BPO, Karajan, (i) with Gundula Janowitz.

(i) Death and transfiguration; (ii; iii) Vier letzte Lieder; (ii; iv) Capriccio: closing scene.
(Y/B) (B) ** DG 439 467-2 [id.]. (i) Dresden State O, Boehm; (ii) Gundula Janowitz; (iii) BPO, Karajan; (iv) Bav. RSO, Boehm.

Karajan's digital account of *Metamorphosen* has even greater emotional urgency than the 1971 record he made with the Berlin Philharmonic and there is a marginally quicker pulse. The sound is fractionally more forward and cleaner but still sounds sumptuous, and the account of *Death and transfiguration* is quite electrifying. It would be difficult to improve on this coupling by the greatest Strauss conductor of his day.

The cultured richness of the Dresden string-playing and Blomstedt's spaciously noble interpretation combine to place his performance of the *Metamorphosen* alongside Karajan's in distinction. *Death and transfiguration* is hardly less impressive; perhaps Karajan has the edge in sheer tension, but Blomstedt and his players give the work a special dignified ardour. *Till* is as captivatingly witty as you like, and the Denon sound is first class, gloriously full.

Karajan surpassed his analogue recordings of both *Death and transfiguration* and the *Metamorphosen* when he re-recorded them digitally, but the earlier versions offered here are still powerful and convincing In the *Four last songs*, Janowitz produces a beautiful flow of creamy tone while leaving the music's deeper and subtler emotions under-exposed. The transfers are very impressive, and *Death and transfiguration* can still be regarded as a showpiece among Karajan's earlier Berlin recordings.

Järvi's coupling is also splendidly played and the body of Scottish orchestral tone and ensemble stands up remarkably well in comparison with its Berlin and Dresden competitors. Järvi brings a vibrant feeling to the *Metamorphosen*, and the Chandos recording without lacking sumptuousness allows slightly more detail to emerge than in Dresden. The special attraction here is the inclusion of Felicity Lott's radiant account of the *Drei Hymnen* with their rapturous operatic feeling and, appropriately, including a reference to *Death and transfiguration*. However, this performance is also now available in a separate collection of Strauss orchestral songs (see below).

Boehm's *Death and transfiguration* was recorded live (there is a cough near the opening to prove it) at the 1972 Salzburg Festival. It is a performance of great excitement and strong tensions, but the recording is slightly overweighted at the top. The same Janowitz coupling of the *Vier letzte Lieder* was a curious choice (as Karajan provided the accompaniment), but Boehm returns for the final scene of *Capriccio*, where Janowitz is at her best (though, as in the songs, no match for Schwarzkopf).

(i) Death and transfiguration; Symphonia domestica, Op. 53; (ii) Salome's dance of the seven veils.
✪ (B) *** Sony SBK 53511; *SBT 53511* [id.]. (i) Cleveland O, Szell; (ii) Phd. O, Ormandy.

Szell's *Death and transfiguration* dates from 1957 and it is still unsurpassed. The opening has the most compelling atmosphere and the triumphant closing pages are the more effective for Szell's complete lack of indulgence. The recording has been vastly improved in the present transfer, with Cleveland's Masonic Temple providing a richly expansive ambience. The *Symphonia domestica*, recorded in 1964, is less naturally balanced: the engineers seem more concerned with making every detail tell, but the performance brings such powerful orchestral playing, with glorious strings especially in the passionate *Adagio*, that criticism is disarmed: there is certainly no lack of body here. The programme ends with an extraordinarily voluptuous Philadelphia performance of *Salome's dance*, which conjures up a whole frieze of naked female torsos. Ormandy directs with licentious abandon, and the orchestra responds with tremendous virtuosity and ardour, unashamedly going over the top at the climax. Here the sound is a bit glossy but, with playing like this, one can certainly adjust.

Don Juan, Op. 20.
(N) *** Decca Dig. 444 458-2 [id.]. Carnegie Hall Project O, Solti – BRAHMS: *Variations on a theme of Haydn* **(*); SHOSTAKOVICH: *Symphony No. 9* (with Concert **(*)).

This was recorded at the end of a special workshop in which gifted instrumentalists were assembled in Carnegie Hall and given the opportunity to work with Sir Georg Solti. His *Don Juan* is the best thing on the disc. The playing is very good indeed and Sir Georg gets highly exhilarating results. Both the Brahms and the Shostakovich may seem a little too highly charged for some tastes, but there is no doubt about the electricity Solti engenders.

(i) *Don Juan, Op. 20;* (ii) *Don Quixote, Op. 35;* (iii) *Symphonic fragment from 'Das Liebe der Danae'* (arr. Clemens Krauss).
(N) (M) *** Sony Dig. SMK 66938 [id.]. (i) Cleveland O, Maazel; (ii) Yo-Yo Ma, Boston SO, Ozawa;
    (iii) Toronto SO, Andrew Davis.

This is one of the most thrilling accounts of *Don Juan* on record. With superbly committed bravura support from his Cleveland players, Maazel is totally sympathetic and is clearly relishing every moment. In the love scene the oboe solo is glowingly sensuous yet tenderly feminine, and the final climax is ecstatic, the tempo broadened when the strings take up the great horn tune. The 1979 sound is richly glowing to match, but does not lack clarity, and the brass has telling bite and sonority.

Yo-Yo Ma's portrait of the Don is masterly and, as always, he plays with impeccable taste and refined tone, though at times pianissimos are exaggerated and affectation comes dangerously close. Ozawa is a shade cautious in matters of characterization, as if he is determined not to be thought brash. Karajan's performance has more panache, and the opening theme is a shade more idiomatic in his hands. Although Ozawa pays scrupulous attention to detail (the encounter with the sheep is marvellously done), the very last ounce of Straussian braggadocio is wanting. The CBS recording has a lot going for it: tonally it is very natural and the balance between cello and orchestra is true to life. The orchestral texture is transparent and detail is excellent, though there is a trace of hardness evident when reproduced at a high level setting.

As a unique bonus we are offered Clemens Krauss's sympathetic arrangement of music drawn almost entirely from the closing scene of Strauss's penultimate opera, *Das Liebe der Danae*, ingeniously shaped into an eleven-minute symphonic fragment; its passion and the valedictory feeling at the close are both sensitively caught here by Andrew Davis and his Toronto players.

(i) *Don Juan, Op. 20;* (ii) *Ein Heldenleben, Op. 40;* (i) *Till Eulenspiegel, Op. 28.*
(M) *** Sony SBK 48272; *SBT 48272* [id.]. (i) Cleveland O, Szell; (ii) Phd. O, Ormandy.

Szell's *Don Juan,* sounding really impetuous yet never rushed, delights ear and senses by its forward surge of passionate lyricism, the whole interpretation founded on a bedrock of virtuosity from the remarkable Cleveland players. *Till* is irrepressibly cheeky (the characterization again created from the most polished orchestral response) and here the recording acoustic is almost perfect, with a warm glow on the tone of the players and every detail – and Szell makes sure one can hear every detail – crystal clear, without any loss of momentum or drama.

Ormandy's *Ein Heldenleben* is a really big conception. It is an engulfing performance, and the composite richness of tone and the fervour of the playing, from the Battle section onwards, bring the highest possible level of orchestral tension, finally relaxing most touchingly for the fulfilment sequence and closing with a sonorous brass cadence that is made to sound inevitable. The 1960 recording is more two-dimensional, less full, than the Cleveland recordings (which, surprisingly, were made as early as 1957) but is still appropriately spacious.

Don Juan; Till Eulenspiegel; Salome: Dance of the seven veils.
(Y/B) *** Everest EVC 9004 [id.]. NY Stadium SO, Stokowski – CANNING: *Fantasy on a hymn tune.*
    ***

A justly famous Stokowski triptych from the late 1950s, with the spacious recording now cleaned up and sounding very well indeed. Not surprisingly with the old magician in charge, Salome is made to languish more voluptuously than ever before, and even *Till* in his posthumous epilogue has a languishing mood on him. *Don Juan* indulges himself with rich sensuality, yet leaps off into the fray with undiminished vitality, while the great unison horn-call is held back with a compellingly broadened thrust. As ever, Stokowski is nothing if not convincing, and those looking for really ripe versions of these pieces need not hesitate. The Canning coupling is also worth having.

Don Quixote.
(N) ❀ *** EMI CDC5 55528-2 [id.]. Jacqueline du Pré, New Philh. O, Boult – LALO: *Cello concerto in D min.* ***
(M) (***) RCA mono 09026 61485-2 [id.]. Piatigorsky, de Pasquale, Boston SO, Munch – BRAHMS: *Double concerto.* (***)

(i) *Don Quixote. Till Eulenspiegel.*
(N) (B) *** EMI CZS5 68736-2 (2) [id.]. (i) Tortelier; BPO, Kempe – Concert. ***
(N) **(*) DG Dig. Gold 439 027-2 [id.]. (i) Meneses; BPO, Karajan.

Kempe's recording of *Don Quixote* with Tortelier, unbelievably recorded as early as 1958, is one of the great classics of the gramophone. The recording has ambient warmth yet reveals every smallest detail of Strauss's magical score. The solo cello is admirably balanced, yet Tortelier's splendid contribution is still able to take a leading role in the performance. Kempe's reading is essentially traditional, yet the wit is pointed with delicious lightness of touch, which suggests complete rapport with every member of the orchestra. There is the most refreshing spontaneity throughout, and the Dulcinea passages have a sweetness and lyrical beauty that do not sound out of keeping with the humour of the work. *Till Eulenspiegel* also conveys the sparkle of the work in playing that is brilliant but never forced. Both these picaresque symphonic poems, with their frequent changes of tempo, require the right degree of flexibility, and this Kempe achieves supremely well.

Over 20 years after her playing career was cut short so tragically, Jacqueline du Pré's recorded repertory is thrillingly expanded in previously unpublished recordings of Strauss and Lalo. *Don Quixote* comes in a studio recording, dating from 1968, which has been lovingly pieced together from long-buried tapes. The recording producer, Andrew Keener, discovered in the EMI archive not only session-tapes of *Don Quixote* with Klemperer and the New Philharmonia, but a complete take (except for the first bar) of the whole work, recorded two days later with Boult taking over after Klemperer withdrew. From the Klemperer session Keener was able to restore that first bar and to insert other tiny patches, so putting together a complete performance. One wants to echo Boult's instant cry of 'Bravo!' at the end. No doubt Jacqueline du Pré with more time would have sharpened up some of the bravura passages, but in its tenderness and poignancy this reading is unsurpassed. The lyrical dialogue between Sancho Panza and Quixote in the third variation has a heartfelt warmth, with Herbert Downes a fine partner on the viola. Above all, the final death scene is more yearningly tender than on any rival recording, a magical example of her art. Excellent background notes are provided by Tully Potter as well as by Andrew Keener.

Recorded in 1953 with a Boston Symphony Orchestra which still produced the sound it made for Koussevitzky, Piatigorsky's account of *Don Quixote* is something special even now after the passage of over 40 years. Apart from Piatigorsky's beauty of tone, still discernible for all the sonic limitations, there is Munch's masterly support and excellent contribution from his Sancho Panza, Joseph de Pasquale (who made so signally successful a contribution to Ormandy's *Harold in Italy* a decade or so later). The sound is pretty good for its age and any deficiencies are soon forgotten. This is a great performance.

Karajan's digital recording with Antonio Meneses and Wolfram Christ has been given the 'original image bit re-processing' treatment and there is some improvement in the sound. But the perspective remains far from natural and neither the performance nor the recording is a patch on his earlier versions with Rostropovich (EMI) or the late Pierre Fournier, which latter version remains available at midprice.

(i) *Don Quixote, Op. 35; Death and transfiguration.*
(M) *** DG 429 184-2 [id.]. (i) Fournier; BPO, Karajan.

Fournier's partnership with Karajan is outstanding. He brings great subtlety and (when required) repose to the part. The finale and Don Quixote's death are very moving, while Karajan's handling of orchestral detail is quite splendid. The 1966 recording is of DG's very finest quality and (given its price) this can be strongly recommended, more particularly since the disc includes Karajan's superlative 1973 analogue version of *Death and transfiguration*.

Ein Heldenleben, Op. 40.
*** Denon Dig. C37 7561 [id.]. Dresden State O, Blomstedt.
(N) (M) *** DG 449 725-2 [id.]. BPO, Karajan – WAGNER: *Siegfried idyll.* ***
(N) (B) *** EMI forte CZS5 69349-2 (2) [id.]. LSO, Barbirolli – MAHLER: *Symphony No. 6.* **(*)

Ein Heldenleben; Death and transfiguration, Op. 24.
(N) **(*) DG Dig. Gold 439 039-2 [id.]. BPO, Karajan.

Ein Heldenleben; Till Eulenspiegel.
*** Sony Dig. MK 44817 [id.]. LSO, Tilson Thomas.

Blomstedt shapes his performance with both authority and poetry. There is a genuine heroic stride and a sense of dramatic excitement here, while the Dresden orchestra creates glorious Straussian textures and the whole edifice is held together in a way that commands admiration. In these respects, Blomstedt's account is the most completely satisfying CD.

Although Karajan's 1959 *Heldenleben* cannot quite match Blomstedt's digital Dresden version in sumptuousness, it still sounds remarkably impressive. Its selection for reissue in DG's series of 'Originals' seems particularly apt, since this was not only the first post-war recording Karajan made for DG but also his very first in stereo. It is a superb performance. Playing of great power and distinction emanates from the Berlin Philharmonic and, in the closing section, an altogether becoming sensuousness and warmth. The remastering makes the most of the ambient atmosphere and, while not losing body and warmth, firms up the orchestral detail. The new coupling of Wagner's *Siegfried idyll*, in which Karajan was unsurpassed, could not be be more appropriate.

Michael Tilson Thomas's account is also a performance of genuine authority and no less well laid out than other outstanding versions. His interpretation has an epic breadth and humanity that are impressive. If it does not displace its rivals, it can be recommended with complete confidence alongside them, and moreover it has the additional attraction of *Till Eulenspiegel*.

Barbirolli recorded *Ein Heldenleben* at Abbey Road in 1969, not long before his death. By a strange coincidence, Beecham similarly devoted some of his last recording sessions to this 'hero's life'. The vigour, nobility and richness of the Beecham version seemed to sum up his achievement over the years, and here Barbirolli sets the seal on his Indian summer in the recording studio. With its ripe magic it shows the conductor at his most romantically compelling. All the tempi are slow, even by his latter-day standards. He luxuriates in every moment of this opulent score (his occasional groans of pleasure sometimes punctuating the texture) and the LSO, in superb form, follows him with warmth and ardour through every expressive rallentando. Even the battle scene is not as fast as usual. But never for a moment does the tension slip, nor is the seamless forward movement interrupted. The result is inevitably controversial but, with full-bodied Abbey Road recording and the inescapable electricity of a great occasion, this is a performance which many will relish. The CD transfer has lost some of the original opulence, but there was enough and to spare, and the sound now has greater focus and detail.

Karajan's digital *Heldenleben* has tremendous sweep and all the authority and mastery we have come to expect – and indeed to take for granted. Nor is the orchestral playing anything other than glorious – indeed, in terms of sheer virtuosity, the Berlin players have never surpassed this. There is also a dramatic fire and virtuosity that are quite electrifying. However, in spite of the 'original-image bit re-processing' the early (1983) digital recording falls short of the highest present-day standards. Since Karajan's superb *Death and transfiguration* (recorded only three years later) has been added to it, the ear is drawn to notice that *Ein Heldenleben*, although firmly focused, has less warmth and the strings by comparison lack bloom, while the violins have a certain glassiness in the high treble, characteristic of the early digital era.

Intermezzo: Symphonic interludes.
(N) *** Chandos Dig. CHAN 9357 [id.]. Detroit SO, Neeme Järvi – SCHMIDT: *Symphony No. 1.* ***

Neeme Järvi is an underrated Straussian and here he proves equal to the very best. He and his Detroit musicians give a thoroughly persuasive account of the interludes Strauss extracted from *Intermezzo*, and this comes as a generous fill-up to Schmidt's derivative but delightful *First Symphony*. Strongly recommended.

Josephslegende (ballet): *suite, Op. 63; Symphonia domestica, Op. 53.*
**(*) Delos Dig. DE 3082 [id.]. Seattle SO, Gerard Schwarz.

Strauss composed the *Josephslegende* for Diaghilev on the grandest scale for a large orchestra. There are many felicities, the *Dance of the Turkish Boxers* being a good example, while there are delicious touches in the fourth scene, *Joseph's dance*. Gerard Schwarz gives us the suite from the ballet in addition to a very idiomatic account of the *Symphonia domestica*. There is very good playing from the Seattle orchestra: cultured, thoroughly idiomatic and with splendid sweep; the recording, too, is splendidly detailed, if perhaps just a bit too brightly lit to be ideal.

Metamorphosen for 23 solo strings.
*** Denon Dig. CO 79442 [id.]. Sinfonia Varsovia, Emmanuel Krivine – SCHOENBERG: *Verklaerte Nacht;* WAGNER: *Siegfried idyll.* ***
*** Delos Dig. DE 3121 [id.]. Seattle SO, Gerard Schwarz – HONEGGER: *Symphony No. 2;* WEBERN arr. Schwarz: *Langsamer satz.* ***
(Y/B) (B) **(*) EMI CZS7 67816-2 (2) [id.]. New Philh. O, Barbirolli – MAHLER: *Symphony No. 6.* **(*)

Emmanuel Krivine and the Sinfonia Varsovia give as eloquent an account of Strauss's elegiac masterpiece as any in the catalogue which can be mentioned in the same breath as the celebrated Karajan accounts from the early 1980s. The Polish ensemble produce a sonority of great beauty and flexibility, and they have great expressive and dynamic range; they bring great feeling to this performance, and Krivine characterizes the work with masterly confidence. In addition, the digital sound is very natural and atmospheric.

Gerard Schwarz's account of Strauss's elegiac threnody is sumptuously recorded (it is even more successful in terms of realism than the Honegger with which it is coupled). The performance itself takes 7 minutes longer than Kempe's and 5–6 longer than Karajan – though, to be fair, at no point does it feel too slow. Indeed this *Metamorphosen* is as deeply felt and dignified as it is unhurried, and it should be heard. The listener is completely drawn into its world and, although it does not supersede the Kempe or any of the the Karajan accounts except perhaps in terms of recorded realism, it deserves to be recommended alongside them. At 32 minutes it may be the slowest *Metamorphosen* on disc, but it is certainly one of the best.

Barbirolli's version of the *Metamorphosen* is a fine one, with a warm glow and an intense, valedictory feeling, and the playing of the NPO strings is most eloquent. The 1967 Abbey Road recording still sounds well; however, although it still has weight, the present CD transfer has lost some of its original bloom and opulence.

Schlagobers (ballet), *Op. 70:* complete.
** Denon Dig. CO 73414 [id.]. Tokyo Met. SO, Wakasugi.

Schlagobers comes from the early 1920s, but it is held in low esteem by most Strauss scholars. There are some delights, such as the *March and military exercises of marzipan, Plum soldiers and honey cakes* and the *Dance of the tea cakes* in Act I; but elsewhere his inspiration lapses into routine, as in the *Whipped cream waltz*. Hiroshi Wakasugi gets good results from the Tokyo Metropolitan Orchestra and the recording is more than acceptable, though insufficiently transparent in climaxes.

Symphonia domestica, Op. 53.
(Y/B) (M) *** EMI CDM7 69571-2 [id.]. BPO, Karajan.

Symphonia domestica; (i) *Death and transfiguration.*
(M) **(*) RCA stereo/mono GD 60388 [60388-2-RG]. Chicago SO; (i) (mono) RCA Victor O; Fritz Reiner.

Symphonia domestica, Op. 53; Festliches Praeludium; Till Eulenspiegel, Op. 28.
(Y/B) *** EMI Dig. CDC5 55185-2 [id.]. Phd. O, Sawallisch.

Strauss's much-maligned *Symphonia domestica* is quite admirably served by this mid-priced CD of Karajan's 1973 recording. The playing is stunningly good and the Berlin strings produce tone of great magnificence. The remastered recording demonstrates the wide range of the original; detail is better focused and the ambient atmosphere remains.

Wolfgang Sawallisch's *Symphonia domestica* is *echt*-Strauss, unexaggerated and civilized. He draws excellent playing from the Philadelphia Orchestra and gives a performance that reveals this score for what it is: one of the finest of Strauss's works. This is easily the best *Symphonia domestica* since the Karajan version of the 1970s, and it is accorded refined and well-detailed sound.

Reiner's account of the *Symphonia domestica* comes from 1956, the earliest days of stereo, and is a wonderful performance, a reading of stature, worthy to rank alongside the best. *Death and transfiguration* is a 1950 mono recording, and it was perverse of RCA not to include his marvellous 1957 Vienna Philharmonic version (in surprisingly good stereo even now).

Symphony in F min., Op. 12; (i) *6 Lieder, Op. 68.*
**(*) Chandos Dig. CHAN 9166 [id.]. (i) Eileen Hulse, SNO, Järvi.

The *F minor* is neither a good symphony nor good Strauss, though Järvi makes out a better case for it than any previous recording. The work is cunningly crafted and the young master puts his ideas through their paces with skill and proficiency. But the ideas themselves are not really very distinguished – or indeed characteristic. Järvi paces the score with real mastery and gets very good playing from the Royal Scottish National Orchestra. The glorious Brentano *Lieder*, Op. 68, date from 1918 and Strauss transcribed them for orchestra in 1941. Eileen Hulse produces some beautiful tone and is sensitively supported throughout. Not core repertory this, but a disc for Straussians.

Till Eulenspiegel.
(N) (M) **(*) Decca 448 568-2 [id.]. VPO, Fritz Reiner – BRAHMS: *Hungarian dances;* DVORAK: *Slavonic dances.* **(*)

Reiner's vintage *Till* dates from 1956. The performance is first class, with the orchestra responding to this great Straussian to the manner born. However, the early Sofiensaal stereo does show its age, and this would have been better reissued on a bargain label rather than in Decca's more expensive 'Classic Sound' series.

CHAMBER MUSIC

Capriccio, Op. 85: String sextet.
(Y/B) *** Hyperion Dig. CDA 66704 [id.]. Raphael Ens. – BRUCKNER: *String quintet.* ***
*** Chandos Dig. CHAN 9131 [id.]. ASMF Chamber Ens. – ENESCU: *Octet in C;* SHOSTAKOVICH: *2 Pieces for string octet.* ***

The opening sextet from Strauss's last opera, *Capriccio*, makes an excellent fill-up to the Bruckner *String quintet.* Obviously readers are unlikely to buy the Bruckner for the sake of such a short work, even though it is of great beauty, but those who do will be rewarded by some fine music-making and recording.

The autumnal preface to *Capriccio* is also the expertly played fill-up to Enescu's remarkable *Octet;* very well recorded it is, too.

Cello sonata in F, Op. 6.
**(*) Sony Dig. MK 44980 [id.]. Yo-Yo Ma, Emanuel Ax – BRITTEN: *Sonata.* **(*)

Yo-Yo Ma and Emanuel Ax give a generally fine account of the *Cello sonata*, although there are moments when Ax's fortissimos overpower the cellist and Ma is not wholly free from self-consciousness. The recording is reasonably truthful, though the constraints of the CBS acoustic produce a very slightly synthetic character.

String quartet in A, Op. 2.
**(*) Hyperion Dig. CDA 66317 [id.]. Delmé Qt – VERDI: *Quartet.* **(*)

The Strauss *Quartet* is early and derivative, as one might expect from a sixteen-year-old, but it is amazingly assured and fluent. The Delmé version is well played; however, although the basic acoustic is pleasing, the sound-balance remains a little on the dry side.

Violin sonata in E flat, Op. 18.
*** DG Dig. 427 617-2 [id.]. Kyung Wha Chung, Krystian Zimerman – RESPIGHI: *Sonata.* ***

Among modern versions Kyung Wha Chung is *primus inter pares*, and her version of the Strauss scores over rivals also in the power and sensitivity of Krystian Zimerman's contribution and the excellence of the DG recording. There is, however, a cut of 42 bars in the coda of the first movement (Universal Edition) which appears to be sanctioned, as Heifetz also observed it in his recording.

VOCAL MUSIC

Choral music: (i) *An den Baum Daphne;* (ii) *Der Abend; Hymne, Op. 34/1–2;* (iii) *Deutsche Motette, Op. 62;* (iv) *Die Göttin im Putzzimer.*
*** Chandos Dig. CHAN 9223 [id.]. (i) Marianne Lund, Christian Lisdorf, Copenhagen Boys' Ch.; (iii) Tina Kiberg, Randi Stene, Gert Henning-Jensen, Ulrik Cold; (i–iv) Danish Nat. R. Ch., Stefan Parkman.

Although Stefan Parkman's account of the *Deutsche Motette* does not eclipse memories of the magical singing of the Swedish Radio Choir under Eric Ericson, this disc brings very good performances of some very beautiful and curiously little-known music. The engineers produce a realistic sound too.

8 Lieder, Op. 10; 5 Lieder, Op. 15; 6 Lieder, Op. 17; 6 Lieder, Op. 19; Schlichte Weisen, Op. 21; Mädchenblumen, Op. 22; 2 Lieder, Op. 26; 4 Lieder, Op. 27; Lieder, Op. 29/1 & 3; 3 Lieder, Op. 31; Stiller Gang, Op. 31/4; 5 Lieder, Op. 32; 5 Lieder, Op. 36/1–4; Lieder, Op. 37/1–3 & 5–6; 5 Lieder, Op. 39; Lieder, Op. 41/2–5; Gesänge älterer deutscher Dichter, Op. 43/1 & 3; 5 Gedichte, Op. 46; 5 Lieder, Op. 47; 5 Lieder, Op. 48; Lieder, Op. 49/1 & 2; 4–6; 6 Lieder, Op. 56; Krämerspiegel, Op. 66; Lieder, Op. 67/4–6; Lieder, Op. 68/1 & 4; 5 kleine Lieder, Op. 69; Gesänge des Orients, Op. 77; Lieder, Op. 88/1–2; Lieder ohne Opuszahl.
(M) *** EMI CMS7 63995-2 (6). Dietrich Fischer-Dieskau, Gerald Moore.

Fischer-Dieskau and Moore made these recordings of the 134 Strauss songs suitable for a man's voice between 1967 and 1970, tackling them in roughly chronological order. With both artists at their very peak, the results are endlessly imaginative, and the transfers are full and immediate, giving fine presence to the voice.

Lieder: *Ach, weh mir unglückhaftem Mann; All meine Gedanken; Breit' über mein Haupt; Freundliche Vision; Heimliche Aufforderung; Ich liebe dich; Mein Auge; Morgen; Die Nacht; Nachtgang; Nichts; Ruhe, meine Seele; Ständchen; Traume durch die Dämmerung; Wie solten wir geheim sie halten; Wozu noch, Mädchen; Zueignung.*
(Y/B) (M) *** Ph. 442 744-2 (2) [id.]. Gérard Souzay, Dalton Baldwin – WOLF: *Italienisches Liederbuch.* ***

In subtlety of phrasing and beauty of line Souzay is here at his finest, and songs like *Ich liebe dich* or the delightful *Serenade* sound freshly minted. There is also a superb lightness of touch when called for. The accompaniments are characteristically sensitive and perceptive, and the recording is well balanced. But why did this have to come in harness with the *Italian Lieder Book* (as part of the Philips Early Years series), rather than be available separately?

Lieder: *Allerseelen; Ach Lieb ich muss nun Scheiden; Befreit; Du meines Herzens Krönelein; Einerlei; Heimliche Aufforderung; Ich trage meine Minne; Kling!; Lob des Leidens; Malven; Mit deinen blauen Augen; Die Nacht; Schlechtes Wetter; Seitdem dein Aug; Ständchen; Stiller Gang; Traume durch die Dämmerung; Wie sollten wir geheim; Wir beide wollen springen; Zeltlose.*
*** Ph. Dig. 416 298-2 [id.]. Jessye Norman, Geoffrey Parsons.

Jessye Norman's recital of Strauss brings heartfelt, deeply committed performances, at times larger than life, which satisfyingly exploit the unique glory of the voice. The magnetism of the singer generally silences any reservations, and Geoffrey Parsons is the most understanding of accompanists, brilliant too. Good, natural recording.

Lieder: *Befreit; Hat gesagt, bleibt's nicht dabei; Ich trage meine Minne; Meinem Kinde; Der Rosenband; Die sieben Siegel; Wie sollten wir geheim sie halten.*
*** DG 437 515-2 [id.]. Anne Sofie von Otter, Bengt Forsberg – BERG: *Early Lieder.* KORNGOLD: *Lieder.* ***

Anne Sofie von Otter and Bengt Forsberg follow up their prize-winning disc of Grieg songs with another inspired set of performances. Though they are even more illuminating in Berg and Korngold, the imaginative selection of seven Strauss songs brings warm, intense singing and sensitive accompaniments.

Four Last songs; Orchestral Lieder: *An die Nacht; Der Arbeitsmann; Mein Auge; Das Bächlein; Befreit; Des Dichters Abendgang; Die heil'gen drei Könige aus Morgenland; Ich liebe dich; Morgen!; Das Rosenband; Traum durch die Dämmerung; Zueignung.*
(B) **(*) EMI CDM7 64323-2. Heather Harper, LSO, Hickox.

Heather Harper gives sensitive, sharply characterized readings of the *Four Last songs*, marked by much beautiful singing, but the closeness of the recording exposes the fact that her gorgeous soprano is a degree less pure than it once was. These are performances very much in the light of day, lacking mystery even in *Beim Schlafengehen*. Hickox directs a relatively plain, unmoulded reading of the orchestral accompaniment, fresh and sympathetic but lacking the evocative overtones of the finest versions, again not helped by the closeness of recording. The majority of the twelve songs with orchestral accompaniment work better, when Harper's consistently perceptive characterization distinguishes each one so sharply. It is good to have included *Der Arbeitsmann*, which has never been recorded in orchestral form before; at mid-price, this recital is worth investigating, for there is much to enjoy here.

Four Last songs; Lieder: *Das Bächlein; Befreit; Cäcilie; Freundliche Vision; Die heiligen drei Könige aus Morgenland; Mein Auge; Meinem Kinde; Morgen; Muttertändelei; Ruhe, meine Seele!; Waldseligkeit; Wiegenlied.*
**(*) Chandos Dig. CHAN 9054 [id.]. Felicity Lott, SNO, Järvi.

Drei Hymnen, Op. 71. Orchestral songs: *Des Dichters Abendgang; Frühlingsfeier; Gesang der Apollopriesterin; Liebeshymnus; Das Rosenband; Verführung; Winterliebe; Winterweihe; Zueignung.*
*** Chandos Dig. CHAN 9159 [id.]. Felicity Lott, SNO, Järvi.

Felicity Lott's two discs bring together a whole series of recordings of Strauss songs in their orchestral versions which originally appeared as couplings for Järvi's discs of the Strauss symphonic poems. She sings them beautifully, though the voice is not always caught at its most golden, notably in the *Four Last songs* which yet are movingly done. The second CD includes the first recording of *Drei Hymnen*, Holderlin settings composed in 1921, pantheistic poems about love of nature which are full of ardour and are provided with the most opulent accompaniments. Lott's voice, for the most part well focused, rides over the rich orchestral textures impressively, and throughout both discs there is agreeably warm, full, orchestral sound.

Four Last songs; Lieder: *Befreit; Morgen; Muttertändelei; Ruhe, meine Seele; Wiegenlied; Zueignung.*
(N) (M) **(*) Sony SMK 76794 [id.]. Kiri Te Kanawa, LSO, Andrew Davis.

Four Last songs; Lieder: *Cäcilie; Meinem Kinde; Morgen; Ruhe, meine Seele; Wiegenlied; Zueignung.*
⊛ *** Ph. Dig. 411 052-2 [id.]. Jessye Norman, Leipzig GO, Masur.

(i) *Four Last songs.* (ii) *Arabella* (opera): excerpts. (i) *Capriccio* (opera): Closing scene.
(M) (***) EMI mono CDH7 61001-2 [id.]. Elisabeth Schwarzkopf, (i) Philh. O, Ackermann; (ii) Metternich, Gedda, Philh. O, Von Matačić.

Strauss's publisher Ernest Roth says in the score of the *Four Last songs* that this was a farewell of 'serene confidence', which is exactly the mood Jessye Norman conveys. The start of the second stanza of the third song, *Beim Schlafengehen,* brings one of the most thrilling vocal crescendos on record, expanding from a half-tone to a gloriously rich and rounded forte. In concern for word-detail Norman is outshone only by Schwarzkopf, but both in the *Four Last songs* and in the orchestral songs the stylistic as well as the vocal command is irresistible, with *Cäcilie* given operatic strength. The radiance of the recording matches the interpretations.

Schwarzkopf's 1953 version of the *Four Last songs* comes with both its original coupling, the closing scene from *Capriccio,* also recorded in 1953, and the four major excerpts from *Arabella* which she recorded two years later. The *Four Last songs* are here less reflective, less sensuous, than in Schwarzkopf's later version with Szell, but the more flowing speeds and the extra tautness and freshness of voice bring equally illuminating performances. Fascinatingly, this separate account of the *Capriccio* scene is even more ravishing than the one in the complete set, and the sound is even fuller, astonishing for its period.

Dame Kiri Te Kanawa gives an open-hearted, warmly expressive reading of the *Four Last songs.* If she misses the sort of detail that Schwarzkopf uniquely brought, her commitment is never in doubt. Her tone is consistently beautiful, but might have seemed even more so if the voice had not been placed rather too close in relation to the orchestra. The orchestral arrangements of other songs make an excellent coupling and Andrew Davis directs most sympathetically. A splendid mid-price recommendation.

OPERA

Die Aegyptische Helena (complete).
(M) **(*) Decca 430 381-2 (2) [id.]. Dame Gwyneth Jones, Hendricks, Kastu, Detroit SO, Dorati.

Dorati, using the original Dresden version of the score, draws magnificent sounds from the Detroit orchestra, richly and forwardly recorded. The vocal sounds are less consistently pleasing. Gwyneth Jones has her squally moments as Helen, though it is a commanding performance. Matti Kastu manages as well as any Heldentenor today in the role of Menelaus, strained at times but with a pleasing and distinctive timbre.

Vienna State Opera: Volume V (1933–43): (i) *Die Aegyptische Helena:* excerpts; (ii) *Daphne:* excerpts; (iii) *Die Frau ohne Schatten:* excerpts.
(Y/B) (M) (***) Koch Schwann mono 3-1455-2 (2) [id.]. V. State Op. O, with (i) Viorica Ursuleac, Franz Völker, Margit Bokor, Alfred Jerger, Helge Roswaenge, cond. Clemens Krauss; (ii) Maria Reining, Alf Rauch, Anton Dermota, cond. Rudolf Moralt; (iii) Torsten Ralf, Hilde Konetzni, Elisabeth Höngen, Josef Herrmann, Else Schulz, Herbert Alsen, Emmy Loose, Wenko Wenkoff, cond. Karl Boehm.

These excerpts from *Die Aegyptische Helena* from 1933 are conducted by Clemens Krauss, with Franz Volker superb but with Viorica Ursuleac rather raw in the title-role. The *Daphne* excerpts under Rudolf Moralt date from 1942, with Maria Reining below her best but with two excellent tenors, Alf Rauch as Apollo and the lyrical Anton Dermota as Leukippos. Central to this volume is the selection from *Die Frau ohne Schatten* under Karl Boehm, almost an hour and a half of excerpts with Torsten Ralf as the Emperor and Hilde Konetzni as the Empress, though Boehm went on to make two complete recordings of this opera with infinitely better sound. A fascinating pair of discs, just the same, in spite of the very primitive sound.

Arabella (complete).
*** Orfeo Dig. C 169882H (2). Varady, Fischer-Dieskau, Donath, Dallapozza, Schmidt, Berry, Bav. State Op. Ch. & O, Sawallisch.
*** Decca Dig. 417 623-2 (3) [id.]. Te Kanawa, Fontana, Grundheber, Seiffert, Dernesch, Guttstein, ROHCG Ch. & O, Tate.

(M) **(*) Decca 430 387-2 (2) [id.]. Della Casa, Gueden, London, Edelmann, Dermota, V. State Op. Ch., VPO, Solti.

(Y/B) (M) (***) DG mono 445 342-2 (3) [id.]. Reining, Hotter, Della Casa, Taubmann, VPO, Boehm.

This Orfeo set of *Arabella* has an immediate advantage over the Decca version with Kiri Te Kanawa in being a digital recording on two CDs against the three for the Decca. Moreover the recording is splendid in every way, not just in sound but in the warmth and understanding of Sawallisch, the characterful tenderness of Julia Varady as the heroine, and Fischer-Dieskau's fine-detailed characterization of the gruff Mandryka, *der Richtige* (Mr Right) according to the heroine's romantic view. Helen Donath too is charming as the younger sister, Zdenka, though the voice might be more sharply contrasted. Highly recommended.

Dame Kiri Te Kanawa, in the name-part, gives one of her very finest opera performances on record. It is a radiant portrait, languorously beautiful, and it is a pity that so unsuited a soprano as Gabriele Fontana should have been chosen as Zdenka next to her, sounding all the more shrill by contrast. Franz Grundheber makes a firm, virile Mandryka, Peter Seiffert a first-rate Matteo, while Helga Dernesch is outstandingly characterful as Arabella's mother. Tate's conducting is richly sympathetic and the Decca recording is first class.

Della Casa soars above the stave with the creamiest, most beautiful sounds and constantly charms one with her swiftly alternating moods of seriousness and gaiety. Perhaps Solti does not linger as he might over the waltz rhythms, and it may be Solti too who prevents Edelmann from making his first scene with Mandryka as genuinely humorous as it can be. Edelmann otherwise is superb, as fine a Count as he was an Ochs in the Karajan *Rosenkavalier*. Gueden, too, is ideally cast as Zdenka and, if anything, in Act I manages to steal our sympathies from Arabella, as a good Zdenka can. George London is on the ungainly side, but then Mandryka is a boorish fellow anyway. Dermota is a fine Matteo, and Mimi Coertse makes as much sense as anyone could of the ridiculously difficult part of Fiakermilli, the female yodeller. The sound is brilliant.

Recorded live in August 1947 at the Salzburg Festival, the Boehm recording was issued in 1994 to celebrate the centenary of his birth, a radiant account with an outstanding cast. Maria Reining is here in firm, true voice, conveying not just the dignity of the heroine but the depth of feeling behind her often imperious manner. Hans Hotter too in his early maturity is in splendid voice, a superb Mandryka, characterful and well focused. Lisa della Casa, destined to make the role of Arabella a speciality, is here a charming Zdenka, fresh and girlish; and the rest of the cast includes many Viennese stalwarts of the period. Despite the limitations of the orchestral sound and some very rough playing, it is a most cherishable set.

'Vienna State Opera Live': Volume 15: (i) *Arabella*: excerpts; (ii) *Friedenstag:* complete; (iii) *Ariadne auf Naxos:* excerpts

(Y/B) (M) (**) Koch Schwann mono 3-1465-2 (2) [id.]. (i) Viorica Ursuleac, Margit Bokor, Alfred Jerger, Adele Kern, Gertrude Rünger, Richard Mayr; (ii) Hans Hotter, Ursuleac, Herbert Alsen, Josef Wit, Hermann Wiederman, Mela Bugarinovic; V. State Op. O; both cond. Clemens Krauss; (iii) Anny Konetzni, Sev Svanholm, Kern, Else Schulz, Jerger, Alexander Pichler, Alfred Muzzarelli; V. State Op. O, Rudolf Moralt.

Strauss's one-Act opera, *Friedenstag*, was first heard in 1938, barely a year before the outbreak of the Second World War. It ends in a triumphalist final ensemble which plainly roused the audience, and could well do the same in a modern performance. This is one of only two complete operas in the May Archive of Vienna State Opera recordings, and in one brief patch of 30 seconds the sound is totally submerged beneath the background noise, which remains heavy throughout. Happily, the voices generally come over well. Clemens Krauss, to whom the opera was dedicated, is a warmly responsive interpreter, drawing out the rich lyricism of this score, not least when his wife, the principal soprano, Viorica Ursuleac, is singing. Her monologues, as well as the duets with the heroine's husband, the Commandant of a besieged fortress, are the high points of the score.

It is also fascinating on the first disc to have also four extracts from the first Vienna production of *Arabella*, given only four months after the Dresden première, with the same principals and conductor, Krauss again. In 1933 Ursuleac is even warmer and firmer than in 1939, though the sound is even more seriously obscured by background noise. The *Ariadne* excerpts, recorded in 1941, are also valuable but even more frustrating, with the extracts fading in and out of big numbers at awkward moments. The casting too is flawed, with Anny Konetzni a fruity and none too steady Ariadne, Else Schulz shrill on top as the Composer, while the brilliant contribution of the Zerbinetta, Adele Kern, is undermined by suddenly distant recording.

Ariadne auf Naxos (complete).

❀ (M) (***) EMI mono CMS7 69296-2 (2) [Ang. CDMB 69296]. Schwarzkopf, Schock, Rita Streich, Dönch, Seefried, Cuénod, Philh. O, Karajan.

*** Ph. Dig. 422 084-2 (2) [id.]. Jessye Norman, Varady, Gruberová, Asmus, Bär, Leipzig GO, Masur.

(M) **(*) Decca 430 384-2 (2) [id.]. Leontyne Price, Troyanos, Gruberová, Kollo, Berry, Kunz, LPO, Solti.

(M) **(*) EMI CMS7 64159-2 (2) [Ang. CDMB 61459]. Janowitz, Geszty, Zylis-Gara, King, Schreier, Prey, Dresden State Op. O, Kempe.

(Y/B) (M) (*(**)) DG 445 332-2 (2) [id.]. Della Casa, Gueden, Seefried, Schock, Schöffler, VPO, Boehm.

Elisabeth Schwarzkopf makes a radiant, deeply moving Ariadne, giving as bonus a delicious little portrait of the Prima Donna in the Prologue. Rita Streich was at her most dazzling in the coloratura of Zerbinetta's aria and, in partnership with the harlequinade characters, sparkles engagingly. But it is Irmgard Seefried who gives perhaps the supreme performance of all as the Composer, exceptionally beautiful of tone, conveying a depth and intensity rarely if ever matched. Rudolf Schock is a fine Bacchus, strained less than most, and the team of theatrical characters includes such stars as Hugues Cuénod as the Dancing Master. The fine pacing and delectably pointed ensemble add to the impact of a uniquely perceptive Karajan interpretation. Though in mono and with the orchestral sound a little dry, the voices come out superbly.

Jessye Norman's is a commanding, noble, deeply felt performance, ranging extraordinarily wide; she provides the perfect focus for a cast as near ideal as anyone could assemble today. Julia Varady as the Composer brings out the vulnerability of the character, as well as the ardour, in radiant singing. The Zerbinetta of Edita Gruberová is a thrilling performance and, even if the voice is not always ideally sweet, the range of emotions Gruberová conveys, as in her duet with the Composer, is enchanting. Paul Frey is the sweetest-sounding Bacchus on record yet, while Olaf Bär as Harlekin and Dietrich Fischer-Dieskau in the vignette role of the Music-Master are typical of the fine team of artists here in the smaller character parts. Masur proves a masterly Straussian and he is helped by the typically warm Leipzig recording.

Brilliance is the keynote of Solti's set of *Ariadne*. What the performance is short of is charm and warmth. Everything is so brightly lit that much of the delicacy and tenderness of the writing tends to disappear. Nevertheless the concentration of Solti in Strauss is never in doubt, and Leontyne Price makes a strong central figure, memorably characterful. Tatiana Troyanos is affecting as the composer, and Edita Gruberová establishes herself as the unrivalled Zerbinetta of her generation, though here she is less delicate than on stage. René Kollo similarly is an impressive Bacchus. The Decca CD transfer is characteristically vivid.

Kempe's relaxed, languishing performance of this most atmospheric of Strauss operas is matched by opulent recording, warmly transferred to CD. Gundula Janowitz sings with heavenly tone-colour (marred only when hard-pressed at the climax of the Lament), and Teresa Zylis-Gara makes an ardent and understanding Composer. Sylvia Geszty's voice is a little heavy for the fantastic coloratura of Zerbinetta's part, but she sings with charm and assurance. James King presents the part of Bacchus with forthright tone and more taste than do most tenors. Compared with Karajan's mono set with Schwarzkopf, this is less than ideal, but that has rather dry mono sound and here there is warmth and atmosphere in plenty, and there is a price advantage over the Philips digital stero set with Jesseye Norman.

Boehm's affection for this elegant, touching score glows through the whole performance. Lisa della Casa is a poised, tender Ariadne, totally rapt in the final duet with Bacchus. Even though her later studio recordings of the *Lament* are more assured than this, the passion of the climax of that key solo is most involving. As in Karajan's studio recording, Irmgard Seefried as the Composer and Rudolf Schock as Bacchus have few equals; but what crowns the whole performance is the charming Zerbinetta of Hilde Gueden, not just warmly characterful but fuller-toned than almost any. The snag is the recording, fizzy in the orchestral sound, with even the voices rather thinly recorded.

'Vienna State Opera live': Volume 23: *Ariadne auf Naxos* (complete).

(Y/B) (M) (***) Koch 3-1473-2 (2). Reining, Seefried, Noni, Lorenz, Schoeffler, Vienna State Op. O, Boehm – WAGNER: *Meistersinger:* excerpts. (**)

Recorded live in June 1944, *Ariadne* is here presented in sound that is astonishingly full-bodied for the period. The sense of presence on the voices is most compelling, and it is fascinating to hear Seefried in the first of her three magnificent recorded performances, singing with, if anything, even more passion than later, in full, firm sound. Maria Reining makes a warm, touching Ariadne, and Max Lorenz as Bacchus has rarely been matched in subsequent recordings, sweeter and less strenuous than most

Heldentenoren. Alda Noni makes a bright, mercurial Zerbinetta, not always note-perfect in her coloratura but with plenty of sparkle, and Paul Schoeffler is warm and wise as the Music-master. With 40 minutes of *Meistersinger* excerpts as filler, it is a historic set for non-specialists to consider.

(i) *Ariadne auf Naxos* (excerpts). Lieder: (ii) *Befreit; Einerlei; Hat gesagt; Morgen!; Schlechtes Wetter; Seit dem dein Aug'; Waldseligkeit.*
*** Testament SBT 1036 [id.]. Lisa della Casa, with (i) Rudolf Schock, BPO, Erede; (ii) Sebastian Peschko.

The 1959 stereo recording is full and immediate, bringing out the glories of Della Casa's creamy soprano but failing to convey the full, atmospheric beauty of the music, notably in the echo chorus of Naiads. Della Casa had earlier recorded *Ariadne's Lament* for Decca, but this is even more powerful. The first excerpt is of the opening of the entertainment from the overture through to Ariadne's first solo. There follow her second solo, *Ein Schönes war*, and the *Lament*, while the last extended excerpt has the whole of the final scene from the entry of Bacchus. Rudolf Schock, as in the Karajan version, sings nobly, and Erede brings out the lyrical warmth of the writing. Della Casa is less imaginative in the Strauss Lieder but still sings very beautifully and persuasively. The faithful and full Testament transfers bring out the wide range of the recording, tending to emphasize sibilants in the singing.

Capriccio (complete).
(***) EMI mono CDS7 49014-8 (2) [Ang. CDCB 49014]. Schwarzkopf, Waechter, Gedda, Fischer-Dieskau, Hotter, Ludwig, Moffo, Philh. O, Sawallisch.
(Y/B) (M) **(*) DG 445 347-2 (2) [id.]. Janowitz, Troyanos, Schreier, Fischer-Dieskau, Prey, Ridderbusch, Bav. RSO, Karl Boehm.
(N) ** Decca Dig. 444 405-2 (2) [id.]. Te Kanawa, Hagegård, Heilmann, Bär, Von Halem, Fassbaender, Hollweg, Hotter, VPO, Ulf Schirmer.

In the role of the Countess in Strauss's last opera, Elisabeth Schwarzkopf has had no equals. This recording, made in 1957 and 1958, brings a peerless performance from her, full of magical detail both in the pointing of words and in the presentation of the character in all its variety. Not only are the other singers ideal choices in each instance, they form a wonderfully co-ordinated team, beautifully held together by Sawallisch's sensitive conducting. As a performance this is never likely to be superseded. The mono sound presents the voices with fine bloom and presence, but the digital transfer makes the orchestra a little dry and relatively backward by comparison.

In this elusive opera it is impossible to avoid comparison with Sawallisch's classic mono version with Schwarzkopf and Fischer-Dieskau. Gundula Janowitz is not as characterful and pointful a Countess as one really needs (and no match for Schwarzkopf), but Boehm lovingly directs a most beautiful performance of a radiant score, very consistently cast, beautifully sung and very well recorded for its period (1971). There is full documentation, including translation.

When Strauss's last opera has had great success in many stage productions, it is surprising that it has been recorded so little. That is partly a tribute to the quality of the first two – Schwarzkopf with Sawallisch conducting (EMI mono) and Gundula Janowitz with Karl Boehm. This first digital recording, with a cast as impressive as any that could be devised today, was badly needed but proves a disappointment in two unexpected ways. The recording is refined but, in keeping with Schirmer's relaxed reading, exaggerates the chamber qualities of the piece, so that even the Vienna Philharmonic strings sound thin. The other disappointment is Dame Kiri Te Kanawa, whose soprano as recorded too often lacks the creamily even quality on which she has built her reputation. The climax of the closing scene has the voice sounding even strained, and in that key passage she cannot compare with either Schwarzkopf or Janowitz, both more beautiful as well as more searching with words. The others make a strongly characterized team, notably Brigitte Fassbaender as the actress, Clairon, but that is not enough to offset the disappointments.

Elektra (complete).
*** Decca 417 345-2 (2) [id.]. Nilsson, Collier, Resnik, Stolze, Krause, V. State Op. Ch., VPO, Solti.
(Y/B) (M) ** DG 445 329-2 (2) [id.]. Borkh, Schech, Madeira, Fischer-Dieskau, Dresden State O, Karl Boehm.

Nilsson is almost incomparable in the name-part, with the hard side of Elektra's character brutally dominant. Only when – as in the Recognition scene with Orestes – she tries to soften the naturally bright tone does she let out a suspect flat note or two. As a rule she is searingly accurate in approaching even the most formidable exposed top notes. One might draw a parallel with Solti's direction – sharply focused and brilliant in the savage music which predominates, but lacking the languorous warmth one really needs in the Recognition scene, if only for contrast. The brilliance of the 1967 Decca recording is brought out the more in the digital transfer on CD, aptly so in this work. The fullness and clarity are amazing for the period.

Inge Borkh is tough in the title-role with an apt touch of rawness, while Jean Madeira as Klytemnestra is firm and positive and Dietrich Fischer-Dieskau is incomparable as Orestes; their contributions are very vivid. The clarity of CD with its full body of sound brings an improvement on the original 1960 LPs, but Karl Boehm's masterly timing in this opera deserves to have a more substantial showing. The only weakness to note in the cast is the Chrysothemis of Marianna Schech, thin and unsteady and with touches of shrillness.

(i) *Elektra: Soliloquy; Recognition scene; Finale. Salome: Dance of the seven veils; Finale.*
(M) *** RCA GD 60874 [60874-2-RG]. Inge Borkh, Chicago SO, Fritz Reiner; (i) with Schoeffler, Yeend, Chicago Lyric Theatre Ch.

With Borkh singing superbly in the title-role alongside Paul Schoeffler and Francis Yeend, this is a real collectors' piece. Reiner provides a superbly telling accompaniment; the performance of the Recognition scene and final duet are as ripely passionate as Beecham's old 78-r.p.m. excerpts and outstrip the complete versions. The orchestral sound is thrillingly rich, the brass superbly expansive. For the reissue, Reiner's full-blooded account of *Salome's dance* has been added, and Borkh is comparably memorable in the finale scene. No Straussian should miss this disc.

Die Frau ohne Schatten (complete).
✶ *** Decca Dig. 436 243-2 (3) [id.]. Behrens, Varady, Domingo, Van Dam, Runkel, Jo, VPO, Solti.

In the Heldentenor role of the Emperor, Plácido Domingo, the superstar tenor, gives a performance that is not only beautiful to the ear beyond previous recordings but which has an extra feeling for expressive detail, deeper than that which was previously recorded. Hildegard Behrens as the Dyer's wife is also a huge success. Her very feminine vulnerability is here a positive strength, and the voice has rarely sounded so beautiful on record. Julia Varady as the Empress is equally imaginative, with a beautiful voice, and José van Dam with his clean, dark voice brings a warmth and depth of expression to the role of Barak, the Dyer, which goes with a satisfyingly firm focus. Reinhild Runkel in the key role of the Nurse is well in character, with her mature, fruity sound. Eva Lind is shrill in the tiny role of the Guardian of the Threshold, but there is compensation in having Sumi Jo as the Voice of the Falcon. With the Vienna Philharmonic surpassing themselves, and the big choral ensembles both well disciplined and warmly expressive, this superb recording is unlikely to be matched, let alone surpassed, for many years. Solti himself is inspired throughout.

Intermezzo (complete).
*** EMI CDS7 49337-2 (2) [Ang. CDCB 49337]. Popp, Brammer, Fischer-Dieskau, Bav. RSO, Sawallisch.

The central role of *Intermezzo* was originally designed for the dominant and enchanting Lotte Lehmann; but it is doubtful whether even she can have outshone the radiant Lucia Popp, who brings out the charm of a character who, for all his incidental trials, must have consistently captivated Strauss and provoked this strange piece of self-revelation. The piece inevitably is very wordy, but with this scintillating and emotionally powerful performance under Sawallisch, with fine recording and an excellent supporting cast, this set is as near ideal as could be, a superb achievement. The CD transfer is well managed but – unforgivably in this of all Strauss operas – no translation is given with the libretto, a very serious omission.

Der Liebe der Danae (complete).
(***) Orfeo mono C 292923 A (3) [id.]. Kupper, Felbermeyer, Schoeffler, Gostic, VPO, Krauss.

This belated first recording of *Der Liebe der Danae* ('The love of Danaë') was not made in the spectacular stereo which this sumptuous score cries out for, but in limited mono sound in an Austrian Radio recording from the very first Salzburg Festival performance in August 1952. Despite the limitations and the intrusive stage noises, the opera, under Clemens Krauss, establishes itself as one of Strauss's richest scores. Like *Ariadne auf Naxos, Daphne* and *Die Aegyptische Helena, Der Liebe der Danae* presents Greek myth in light-hearted post-romantic guise. It is not just lyrical in Strauss's *Daphne* manner but a genuinely tuneful score, in places harking back to the diatonic Wagner of *Meistersinger*, and bringing ensembles that were directly influenced by Strauss's favourite Mozart opera, *Così fan tutte*. In the last of the three Acts Strauss lets himself go expansively in a sequence of duets, first between Danaë and Midas, and finally between Danaë and Jupiter, who, rather like Hans Sachs in *Meistersinger* (or the Marschallin in *Rosenkavalier*), nobly cedes any rights in the young lover, a situation that plainly touched the aged Strauss. With the Vienna Philharmonic already restored after the war, Krauss's affectionate reading is backed by some splendid singing, notably from Paul Schoeffler, Sachs-like as Jupiter, and the full-toned heroic tenor, Josef Gostic, as Midas. Annelies Kupper in the title-role has a few raw moments, but she produces pure, creamy tone for the many passages of ravishing cantilena above the stave. With important sequences for Danaë's servant, Xanthe (the resonant Anny Felbermeyer), and four mythical queens, Semele, Europa, Alkmene and Leda, the writing for women's voices brings grateful echoes of the *Rosenkavalier* Trio. Sadly, the three full-price discs come without a libretto, merely providing a note by Strauss's biographer, Willi Schuh, plus a synopsis in fractured English.

Der Rosenkavalier (complete).

❀ *** EMI CDS7 49354-8 (3) [Ang. CDCC 49354]. Schwarzkopf, Ludwig, Stich-Randall, Edelmann, Waechter, Philh. Ch. & O, Karajan.
*** EMI Dig. CDS7 54259-2 (3) [Ang. CDCC 54259]. Kiri Te Kanawa, Anne Sofie von Otter, Rydl, Grundheber, Hendricks, Dresden Op. Ch., Dresden Boys' Ch., Dresden State O, Haitink.
**(*) DG Dig. 423 850-2 (3) [id.]. Tomowa-Sintow, Baltsa, Moll, Perry, Hornik, VPO Ch. & O, Karajan.
(M) (**(*)) Decca mono 425 950-2 (3) [id.]. Reining, Weber, Jurinac, Gueden, V. State Op. Ch., VPO, Erich Kleiber.
(Y/B) (M) **(*) Ph. 442 086-2 (3) [id.]. Lear, Von Stade, Welting, Bastin, Hammond Stroud, Netherlands Op. Ch., Rotterdam PO, Edo de Waart.
(Y/B) (M) ** DG 445 338-2 (3) [id.]. Ludwig, Troyanos, Mathis, Adam, Wiener, VPO, Boehm.

The glory of Karajan's 1956 version, one of the greatest of all opera recordings, shines out the more delectably on CD. Though the transfer in its very clarity exposes some flaws in the original sound, the sense of presence and the overall bloom are if anything more compelling than ever. As to the performance, it is in a class of its own, with the patrician refinement of Karajan's spacious reading combining with an emotional intensity that he has rarely equalled, even in Strauss, of whose music he remains a supreme interpreter. Matching that achievement is the incomparable portrait of the Marschallin from Schwarzkopf, bringing out detail as no one else can, yet equally presenting the breadth and richness of the character, a woman still young and attractive. Christa Ludwig with her firm, clear mezzo tone makes an ideal, ardent Octavian and Teresa Stich-Randall a radiant Sophie, with Otto Edelmann a winningly characterful Ochs, who yet sings every note clearly.

Vocally the biggest triumph of Haitink's beautifully paced reading is the Octavian of Anne Sofie von Otter, not only beautifully sung but acted with a boyish animation to make most rivals sound very feminine by comparison. If the first great – and predictable – glory of Dame Kiri's assumption of the role of the Marschallin is the sheer beauty of the sound, the portrait she paints is an intense and individual one, totally convincing. The portrait of Sophie from Barbara Hendricks is a warm and moving one, but less completely satisfying, if only because her voice is not quite so pure as one needs for this young, innocent girl. Kurt Rydl with his warm and resonant bass makes a splendid Baron Ochs, not always ideally steady, but giving the character a magnificent scale and breadth. Whatever the detailed reservations over the singing, it is mainly due to Bernard Haitink, and his long experience conducting this opera at Covent Garden and elsewhere, that this is the most totally convincing and heartwarming recording of *Rosenkavalier* since Karajan's 1956 set. This recording, unlike the Karajan, opens out the small stage cuts sanctioned by the composer.

Karajan's digital set brings few positive advantages, not even in recorded sound: for all the extra range of the modern recording, the focus is surprisingly vague, with the orchestra balanced too far behind the soloists. For the principal role Karajan chose Anna Tomowa-Sintow; the refinement and detail in her performance present an intimate view of the Marschallin, often very beautiful indeed, but both the darker and more sensuous sides of the character are muted. The Baron Ochs of Kurt Moll, firm, dark and incisive, is outstanding, and Agnes Baltsa as Octavian makes the lad tough and determined, if not always sympathetic. Janet Perry's Sophie, charming and pretty on stage, is too white and twittery of tone to give much pleasure.

Decca's set with Erich Kleiber was the first ever complete recording of *Rosenkavalier*, and it has long enjoyed cult status. Sena Jurinac is a charming Octavian, strong and sympathetic, and Hilde Gueden a sweetly characterful Sophie, not just a wilting innocent. Ludwig Weber characterizes deliciously in a very Viennese way as Ochs; but the disappointment is the Marschallin of Maria Reining, very plain and lacking intensity. She is not helped by Kleiber's refusal to linger; with the singers recorded close, the effect of age on what was once a fine voice is very clear, even in the opening solo of the culminating trio. And ensemble is not good, with even the prelude to Act I a muddle. On the prelude more than anywhere, the CD transfer brings out a shrillness and lack of body in the orchestral sound, though voices are well caught.

The glory of the 1976 set conducted by Edo de Waart is the singing of Frederica von Stade as Octavian, a fresh, youthful performance, full of imagination. Next to her the others are generally pleasing but rarely a match for the finest performances on other sets, though it is good to have Derek Hammond Stroud's Faninal. Evelyn Lear produces her creamiest, most beautiful tone but spreads uncomfortably in the Act III Trio. Jules Bastin gives a virile performance as Ochs; the disappointment is the Sophie of Ruth Welting, often shallow of tone. The Rotterdam orchestra plays very well for its principal conductor of the 1970s and is beautifully recorded.

Boehm's DG set, recorded live at the 1969 Salzburg Festival, is a flawed document, not just because of loud stage-noises but because the stereo recording is thin. Nevertheless it is good to hear Christa Ludwig as the Marschallin, bringing echoes of Schwarzkopf, the Marschallin with whom she sang Octavian. Tatiana Troyanos makes a warm, animated Octavian and Edith Mathis a bright, characterful Sophie, just occasionally forced into shrillness. The snag is the gritty Ochs of Theo Adam, not at all jovial even when he blusters in sing-speech. Boehm is above all a genial interpreter, relishing the waltz-rhythms, but the emotions of a live event lead him at climaxes to draw out the music exaggeratedly in a way uncharacteristic of him.

(i) *Der Rosenkavalier* (abridged version); Lieder: (ii) *All' mein Gedanken; Freundliche Vision; Die Heiligen drei Könige; Heimkehr; Ich schwebe; Des Knaben Wunderhorn: Hat gesagt . . .; Morgen; Muttertändelei; Schlechtes Wetter; Ständchen* (2 versions); *Traum durch die Dämmerung;* (iii) *Mit deinen blauen Augen; Morgen; Ständchen; Traum durch die Dämmerung.*
(M) (***) EMI mono CHS7 64487-2 (2) [Ang. CDHB 64487]. (i) Lehmann, Schumann, Mayr, Olszewska, Madin, V. State Op. Ch., VPO, Robert Heger; (ii) Elisabeth Schumann; (iii) Lotte Lehmann (with var. accompanists).

It is good to have a fresh CD transfer, immaculate in quality, of this classic, abridged, early recording of *Der Rosenkavalier*, containing some 100 minutes of music, made in 1933 in Vienna. Lotte Lehmann as the Marschallin and Elisabeth Schumann as Sophie remain uniquely characterful and, though 78-r.p.m. side-lengths brought some hastening from Heger, notably in the great trio of Act III, the passion of the performance still conveys a sense of new discovery, a rare Straussian magic. There is no libretto, but a synopsis is cued with each excerpt. As a bonus we are offered a glorious Lieder recital, featuring both the principal sopranos, and demonstrating Lehmann's darker timbre, the richness immediately noticeable at her first song, the lovely *Mit deinen blauen Augen*. Versions of *Traume durch die Dämmerung* and the soaring *Ständchen are* sung by both artists, and two different Schumann performances are included of the latter: one (from 1927) fresh and lilting, the other (from 1930) faster and with much clearer sound. *Heimkehr* (1938) is ravishing, and *Die Heiligen drei Könige*, from ten years earlier, with a remarkably well-recorded orchestral accompaniment, is also memorable. No song translations are included, but again the CD transfers are well managed.

Der Rosenkavalier: highlights.
(N) (BB) ** CfP Silver Double CDCFPSD 4739 (2). Dernesch, Howells, Cahill, Michael Langdon, SNO, Gibson – MOZART: *Don Giovanni.* **

The idea of putting on a bargain label highlights of this most warming of twentieth-century operas is an excellent one. The CfP Silver Double presents a coupling with Mozart and, like that selection, this is based on a Scottish Opera production. Though the singing is flawed and the recording is less atmospheric than it might be, it makes a fair enough sampler. In particular it is good to have examples of Helga Dernesch as the Marschallin and Michael Langdon as Baron Ochs. But neither the Presentation of the silver rose nor the final scene of all has quite the magic one expects of a complete performance.

Salome (complete).
*** DG. Dig. 431 810-2 (2) [id.]. Studer, Rysanek, Terfel, Hiestermann, German Opera, Berlin, Ch. & O, Sinopoli.
*** Decca 414 414-2 (2) [id.]. Nilsson, Hoffman, Stolze, Kmentt, Waechter, VPO, Solti.
*** EMI CDS7 49358-8 (2) [Ang. CDCB 49358]. Behrens, Bohme, Baltsa, Van Dam, VPO, Karajan.
(Y/B) *** Decca Dig. 444 178-2 (2) [id.]. Malfitano, Terfel, Riegel, Schwarz, Begley, VPO, Christoph von Dohnányi.
(M) *** RCA GD 86644 (2) [6644-2-RG]. Caballé, Richard Lewis, Resnik, Milnes, LSO, Leinsdorf.
(Y/B) (M) **(*) DG 445 319-2 (2) [id.]. Gwyneth Jones, Fischer-Dieskau, Dunn, Cassilly, Hamburg State Op. O, Boehm.
(Y/B) ** Ph. Dig. 432 153-2 (2) [id.]. Norman, Morris, Raffeiner, Witt, Leech, Dresden State O, Seiji Ozawa.

The glory of Sinopoli's DG version is the singing of Cheryl Studer as Salome, producing glorious sounds throughout. Her voice is both rich and finely controlled, with delicately spun pianissimos that chill you the more for their beauty, not least in Salome's attempted seduction of John the Baptist. Sinopoli's reading is often unconventional in its speeds, but it is always positive, thrusting and full of passion, the most opulent account on disc, matched by full, forward recording. As Jokanaan, Bryn Terfel makes a compelling recording début, strong and noble, though the prophet's voice as heard from the cistern sounds far too distant. Among modern sets this makes a clear first choice, though Solti's vintage Decca recording remains the most firmly focused, with the keenest sense of presence.

Birgit Nilsson is splendid throughout; she is hard-edged as usual but, on that account, more convincingly wicked: the determination and depravity are latent in the girl's character from the start. Of this score Solti is a master. He has rarely sounded so abandoned in a recorded performance. Waechter makes a clear, young-sounding Jokanaan. Gerhardt Stolze portrays the unbalance of Herod with frightening conviction, and Grace Hoffman does all she can in the comparatively ungrateful part of Herodias. The vivid CD projection makes the final scene, where Salome kisses the head of John the Baptist in delighted horror (*I have kissed thy mouth, Jokanaan!*), all the more spine-tingling, with a close-up effect of the voice whispering almost in one's ear.

Hildegard Behrens is also a triumphantly successful Salome. The sensuous beauty of tone is conveyed ravishingly, but the recording is not always fair to her fine projection of sound, occasionally masking the voice. All the same, the feeling of a live performance has been captured well, and the rest of the cast is of the finest Salzburg standard. In particular José van Dam makes a gloriously noble Jokanaan, and in the early scenes his offstage voice from the cistern at once commands attention. Karajan – as so often in Strauss – is at his most commanding and sympathetic, with the orchestra, more forward than some will like, playing rapturously. This is a performance which, so far from making one recoil from perverted horrors, has one revelling in sensuousness.

Dohnányi's is a clear, sharply focused reading, in full-ranging sound more refined than any. With the orchestra set further behind the voices than usual in Decca opera recordings, the violence is to a degree underplayed and the chamber quality of the score (intended by Strauss) enhanced. Catherine Malfitano brings out the girlish element in Salome, while also bringing out her malevolence. The beat in her voice can be distracting, occasionally turning into a wobble, but she rises superbly to the final scene, with full power and precision, a thrilling climax. As Jokanaan, Bryn Terfel is even finer than he was for Sinopoli, rich and firm, with the voice of the prophet from the cistern clearly focused. Kenneth Riegel as a neurotic Herod, Hanna Schwarz as a powerful, sharply dramatic Herodias and Kim Begley as a ringing Narraboth are all outstanding.

Montserrat Caballé's formidable account of the role of Salome was recorded in 1968, utterly different from that of Birgit Nilsson on Decca and much closer to the personification of Behrens on the Karajan set on EMI (both at full price). For some listeners Caballé might seem too gentle, but in fact the range of her emotions is even wider than that of Nilsson. There are even one or two moments of fantasy, where for an instant one has the girlish skittishness of Salome revealed like an evil inverted picture of Sophie. As for the vocalization, it is superb, with glorious golden tone up to the highest register and never the slightest hesitation in attack. Lewis, Resnik and Milnes make a supporting team that matches the achievement of the Decca rivals, while Leinsdorf is inspired to some of his warmest and most sympathetic conducting on record.

In this violent opera Boehm conducts a powerful, purposeful performance which in its rhythmic drive and spontaneity is most compelling, not least in *Salome's dance*, which seems a necessary component rather than an inserted showpiece. Gwyneth Jones, though squally at times, is here at her most incisive, and her account of the final scene is chilling, above all when she drains her voice for the moment of pianissimo triumph, having kissed the dead lips of Jokanaan. Fischer-Dieskau characteristically gives a searchingly detailed, totally authoritative performance as John the Baptist: one believes in him as a prophet possessed. With Richard Cassilly as a powerful Herod, the rest of the cast is strong, making this a fair contender among live recordings.

Jessye Norman has made some outstanding Strauss recordings, but she is miscast as Salome. Though her word-pointing is as detailed and as sensitive as ever, with her massive, rich voice she conveys little that is girlish about the character, let alone anything sinister or depraved. This is a noble Salome, with the evil underplayed. That impression is intensified by Ozawa's smooth, even bland conducting. The playing of the orchestra is beautiful, with many superb woodwind solos, but even Salome's dance lacks the bite and violence that must accompany its sensuousness. The Jokanaan of James Morris is gruff, and only the Narraboth of Richard Leech shines out distinctively.

Die schweigsame Frau (complete).

(Y/B) (M) (***) DG mono 445 335-2 (2) [id.]. Gueden, Wunderlich, Prey, Hotter, VPO, Boehm.

With a cast that could hardly be bettered, Boehm masterfully relishes the high spirits as well as the classical elegance of this late Strauss opera and, though the acoustic is dry and stage noises are often fearsomely intrusive, the sense of presence on the voices makes it consistently involving. Based on Ben Jonson's *Epicene* but updated to 1780 by the librettist, Stefan Zweig, this comic opera about an old bachelor who hates noise is above all centred on lively, sharply pointed ensembles, and the starry cast is here splendidly drilled to bring out the humour. Hans Hotter in his prime makes a wonderfully bluff curmudgeon, pointing every word characterfully. Hilde Gueden – greeted with wild applause on her first entry along with Fritz Wunderlich – is a deliciously minx-ish heroine, using her distinctive golden tone, while the young Wunderlich gives a glorious performance. As the barber who aids the conspiratorial young couple against the old man, Hermann Prey has rarely sounded stronger or more beautiful on disc. With this issue available, the continuing absence of the EMI stereo version under Marek Janowski is far less serious.

Arias from: *Die Aegyptische Helena; Ariadne auf Naxos; Die Frau ohne Schatten; Guntram; Der Rosenkavalier; Salome.*

(M) *** RCA GD 60398 [60398-2-RG]. Leontyne Price, Boston SO or New Philh. O, Leinsdorf; LSO, Cleva.

Leontyne Price gives generous performances of an unusually rich collection of Strauss scenes and solos, strongly accompanied by Leinsdorf (or Cleva in *Ariadne*), always at his finest in Strauss. Recorded between 1965 and 1973, Price was still at her peak, even if occasionally the voice grows raw under stress in Strauss's heavier passages. It is particularly good to have rarities as well as such regular favourites as the Empress's awakening from *Die Frau ohne Schatten*, one of the finest of all the performances here.

Stravinsky, Igor (1882–1971)

The Stravinsky Edition: Volume 1, Ballets, etc.: (i) *The Firebird;* (i) *Fireworks;* (iii) *Histoire du soldat;* (i) *Petrushka;* (iv, iii) *Renard the fox;* (i) *The Rite of spring;* (i) *Scherzo à la russe;* (ii) *Scherzo fantastique;* (v) *The Wedding (Les Noces)* (SM3K 46291) (3) [id.].

Volume 2, Ballets etc.: (vi) *Agon;* (i) *Apollo;* (i) *Le baiser de la fée;* (i) *Bluebird (pas de deux);* (vii) *Jeu de cartes;* (viii) *Orphée;* (ix, i) *Pulcinella;* (ii) *Scènes de ballet* (SM3K 46292) (3) [id.].

Volume 3, Ballet suites: (i) *Firebird; Pétrouchka; Pulcinella* (SMK 45293) [id.].

Volume 4, Symphonies: (i) *Symphony in E;* (ii) *Symphony in C;* (i) *Symphony in 3 movements;* (x, ii) *Symphony of Psalms;* (i) Stravinsky in rehearsal: *Apollo; Piano concerto; Pulcinella; Sleeping beauty; Symphony in C; 3 Souvenirs* (SM2K 46294) [id.].

Volume 5, Concertos: (xi, i) *Capriccio for piano and orchestra* (with Robert Craft); *Concerto for piano and wind;* (xii, i) *Movements for piano and orchestra;* (xiii, i) *Violin concerto in D* (SMK 46295) [id.].

Volume 6, Miniatures: (i) *Circus polka; Concerto in D for string orchestra; Concerto for chamber orchestra, 'Dumbarton Oaks';* (ii) *4 Etudes for orchestra;* (i) *Greeting prelude;* (ii) *8 Instrumental miniatures; 4 Norwegian moods; Suites Nos. 1–2 for small orchestra* (SMK 46296) [id.].

Volume 7, Chamber music and historical recordings: (iii) *Concertino for 12 instruments;* (xiv, xv) *Concerto for 2 solo pianos;* (xv, xvi) *Duo concertante for violin and piano;* (xvii, xviii) *Ebony Concerto (for clarinet and big band);* (iii) *Octet for wind;* (xix, iii) *Pastorale for violin and wind quartet;* (xv) *Piano rag music;* (xviii) *Preludium;* (xx, iii) *Ragtime* (for 11 instruments); (xv) *Serenade in A;* (iii) *Septet;* (xii) *Sonata for piano;* (xxi) *Sonata for 2 pianos;* (xviii) *Tango;* (xxii) *Wind symphonies* (SM2K 46297) [id.].

Volume 8, Operas and songs: (xxiii, iii) *Cat's cradle songs;* (xxiii, xxiv) *Elegy for J. F. K.;* (xxv, ii) *Faun and shepherdess;* (xxvi,iii) *In memoriam Dylan Thomas;* (xxvii, iii) *3 Japanese Lyrics* (with Robert Craft); (xxvii, xxix) *The owl and the pussycat;* (xxvii, iii) *2 poems by K. Bal'mont;* (xxx, i) *2 poems of Paul Verlaine;* (xxiii,i) *Pribaoutki (peasant songs);* (xxiii, i) *Recollections of my childhood;* (xxviii, xxxi) *4 Russian songs;* (xxxvii) *4 Russian peasant songs;* (xxiii, iii) *3 songs from William Shakespeare;* (xxvii, i) *Tilim-Bom (3 stories for children);* (xxxii) *Mavra;* (xxxiii) *The Nightingale* (SM2K 46298) [id.].

Volume 9: (xxxiv) *The Rake's progress* (SM2K 46299) [id.].

Volume 10, Oratorio and melodrama: (xxxv, i) *The Flood* (with Robert Craft); (i) *Monumentum pro Gesualdo di Venosa (3 madrigals recomposed for instruments);* (vii) *Ode;* (xxxvi) *Oedipus Rex;* (xxxvii, xxxviii, i) *Perséphone* (SM2K 46300) [id.].

Volume 11, Sacred works: (x) *Anthem (the dove descending breaks the air);* (x) *Ave Maria;* (xxxix, x, i) *Babel;* (xxviii, xxvi, x, iii) *Cantata;* (xl) *Canticum sacrum;* (x, ii) *Credo;* (x, iii) *Introitus (T. S. Eliot in Memoriam);* (xli) *Mass;* (x, i) *Pater noster;* (xlii, i) *A Sermon, a narrative & a prayer;* (xliii, i) *Threni;* (x, i) *Chorale: Variations on: Vom Himmel hoch, da komm ich her* (arr.); *Zvezdoliki* (SM2K 46301) [id.].

Volume 12, Robert Craft conducts: (xliv, i) *Abraham and Isaac;* (iii) *Danses concertantes;* (xlv) *Double canon: Raoul Dufy in memoriam;* (xlvi) *Epitaphium;* (i) *Le chant du rossignol* (symphonic poem); (i) *Orchestral variations: Aldous Huxley in memoriam;* (xlvii) *Requiem canticles;* (i) *Song of the nightingale* (symphonic poem) (SM2K 46302) [id.].
Complete Stravinsky Edition.
(B) *** Sony SX22K 46290 (22) [id.]. (i) Columbia SO; (ii) CBC SO; (iii) Columbia CO; (iv) Shirley, Driscoll, Gramm, Koves; (v) Allen, Sarfaty, Driscoll, Samuel Barber, Aaron Copland, Lukas Foss, Roger Sessions, American Chamber Ch., Hills, Columbia Percussion Ens.; (vi) Los Angeles Festival SO; (vii) Cleveland O; (viii) Chicago SO; (ix) Jordan, Shirley, Gramm; (x) Festival Singers of Toronto, Iseler; (xi) Philippe Entremont; (xii) Charles Rosen; (xiii) Isaac Stern; (xiv) Soulima Stravinsky; (xv) Igor Stravinsky; (xvi) Szigeti; (xvii) Benny Goodman; (xviii) Columbia Jazz Ens.; (xix) Israel Baker; (xx) Tony Koves; (xxi) Arthur Gold, Robert Fizdale; (xxii) N. W. German RSO; (xxiii) Cathy Berberian; (xxiv) Howland, Kreiselman, Russo; (xxv) Mary Simmons; (xxvi) Alexander Young; (xxvii) Evelyn Lear; (xxviii) Adrienne Albert; (xxix) Robert Craft; (xxx) Donald Gramm; (xxxi) Di Tullio, Remsen, Almeida; (xxxii) Belinck, Simmons, Rideout, Kolk; (xxxiii) Driscoll, Grist, Picassi, Smith, Beattie, Gramm, Kolk, Murphy, Kaiser, Bonazzi, Washington, D. C., Op. Society Ch. & O; (xxxiv) Young, Raskin, Reardon, Sarfaty, Miller, Manning, Garrard, Tracey, Colin Tilney, Sadler's Wells Op. Ch., John Baker, RPO; (xxxv) Laurence Harvey, Sebastian Cabot, Elsa Lanchester, John Reardon, Robert Oliver, Paul Tripp, Richard Robinson, Columbia SO Ch., Gregg Smith; (xxxvi) Westbrook (nar.), Shirley, Verrett, Gramm, Reardon, Driscoll, Chester Watson Ch., Washington, D. C., Op. Society O; (xxxvii) Gregg Smith Singers, Gregg Smith; (xxxviii) Zorina, Molese, Ithaca College Concert Ch., Fort Worth Texas Boys' Ch.; (xxxix) John Calicos (nar.); (xl) Robinson, Chitjian, Los Angeles Festival Ch. & SO; (xli) Baxter, Albert, Gregg Smith Singers, Columbia Symphony Winds & Brass; (xlii) Verrett, Driscoll, Hornton (nar.); (xliii) Beardslee, Krebs, Lewis, Wainner, Morgan, Oliver, Schola Cantorum, Ross; all cond. composer. (xliv) Richard Frisch; (xlv) Baker, Igleman, Schonbach, Neikrug; (xlvi) Anderson, Bonazzi, Bressler, Gramm, Ithaca College Concert Ch., Gregg Smith; cond. Robert Craft.

On these 22 bargain-price discs (each volume also available separately at mid-price) you have the unique archive of recordings which Stravinsky left of his own music. Presented in a sturdy plastic display box that enhances the desirability of the set, almost all the performances are conducted by the composer, with a few at the very end of his career – like the magnificent *Requiem canticles* – left to Robert Craft to conduct, with the composer supervising. In addition there is a handful of recordings of works otherwise not covered, mainly chamber pieces. With some recordings of Stravinsky talking and in rehearsal (included in the box devoted to the symphonies) it makes a vivid portrait.

Stravinsky may not have been a brilliant conductor, but in the recording studio he knew how to draw out alert, vigorous performances of his own music, and every one of these items illuminates facets of his inspiration which other interpreters often fail to notice. There are few if any rival versions of the *Rite of spring* – nowadays, astonishingly, his most frequently recorded work – to match his own recording of 1960 in its compelling intensity and inexorable sense of line.

Of the major ballets, *Petrushka* and *The Firebird* are valuable, but *The Rite* is required listening: it has real savagery and astonishing electricity. The link between *Jeu de cartes* from the mid-1930s and Stravinsky's post-war opera, *The Rake's Progress,* is striking and Stravinsky's sharp-edged conducting style underlines it, while the curiously anonymous-sounding *Scènes de ballet* certainly have their attractive moments. *Orpheus* has a powerful atmosphere, although one of Stravinsky's most classically restrained works. A good performance, with the composer's own authority lending it special interest. However, its invention is less memorable and distinguished than *Apollo,* one of Stravinsky's most gravely beautiful scores. *Agon* is one of the most stimulating of Stravinsky's later works. The orchestra respond with tremendous alertness and enthusiasm to Stravinsky's direction. The recording of *Le baiser de la fée* is a typical CBS balance with forward woodwind. However, if the recorded quality does not inspire too much enthusiasm, the performance certainly does. Stravinsky's recording of *Pulcinella* includes the vocal numbers, which, when well sung, add to the variety and sparkle of the piece, while in the orchestra the clowning of the trombone and the humour generally is strikingly vivid and never too broad. Similarly with the chamber scoring of the suite from *The Soldier's tale,* the crisp, clear reading brings out the underlying emotion of the music with the nagging, insistent little themes given an intensity that is almost tear-laden. There is a ruthlessness in the composer's own reading of *Les Noces* which exactly matches the primitive robustness in this last flowering of Russian nationalism in Stravinsky. The earlier parts are perhaps too rigid, but as the performance goes on so one senses the added alertness and enthusiasm of the performers. *Renard* is a curious work, a sophisticated fable which here receives too unrelenting a performance. The voices are very forward and tend to drown the instrumentalists.

In the early *Symphony in E flat*, Op. 1, the young Stravinsky's material may be comparatively conventional and the treatment much too bound to the academic procedures taught him by his master, Rimsky-Korsakov, but at least in this performance the music springs to life. Each movement has its special delights to outweigh any shortcomings. The performance is obviously as near definitive as it could be. The composer's account of the *Symphony in three movements* is an object lesson for every conductor who has tried to perform this work. Stravinsky shows how, by vigorous, forthright treatment of the notes, the emotion implicit is made all the more compelling. The Columbia Symphony plays superbly and the recording is full and brilliant. Stravinsky never quite equalled the intensity of the pre-war 78-r.p.m. performance of the *Symphony of Psalms*. That had many more technical faults than his later, stereo version, and it is only fair to say that this new account is still impressive. It is just that, with so vivid a work, it is a shade disappointing to find Stravinsky as interpreter at less than maximum voltage. Even so, the closing section of the work is very beautiful and compelling. The CD transfers of the American recordings are somewhat monochrome by modern standards but fully acceptable.

The iron-fingered touch of Philippe Entremont has something to be said for it in the *Capriccio for piano and wind*, but this performance conveys too little of the music's charm. The *Movements for piano and orchestra* with the composer conducting could hardly be more compelling. Stern's account of the *Violin concerto in D* adds a romantic perspective to the framework, and at one time, no doubt, Stravinsky would have objected. But an expressive approach to Stravinsky is permissible in a soloist, when the composer is there to provide the bedrock under the expressive cantilena. Plainly this has the forthright spontaneity of a live performance.

The *Dumbarton Oaks concerto* with its obvious echoes of Bach's *Brandenburgs* is one of the most warmly attractive of Stravinsky's neo-classical works, all beautifully played and acceptably recorded. The *Octet for wind* of 1924 comes out with surprising freshness and, throughout, the unexpected combination of neo-Bach and neo-Pop is most refreshing. The *Ragtime* could be more lighthearted, but Stravinsky gives the impression of knowing what he wants. The *Ebony concerto*, in this version conducted by the composer, may have little of 'swung' rhythm, but it is completely faithful to Stravinsky's deadpan approach to jazz.

In *Le rossignol* the singing is not always on a par with the conducting, but it is always perfectly adequate and the recording is brilliant and immediate. *Mavra* is sung in Russian and, as usual, the soloists – who are good – are too closely balanced, but the performance has punch and authority and on the whole the CD quality is fully acceptable. The songs represent a fascinating collection of trifles, chips from the master's workbench dating from the earliest years. There are many incidental delights, not least those in which the magnetic Cathy Berberian is featured.

The Rake's Progress is one of the highlights of the set and has never since been surpassed. Alexander Young's assumption of the title-role is a marvellous achievement, sweet-toned, accurate and well characterized. In the choice of other principals, too, it is noticeable what store Stravinsky set by vocal precision. Judith Raskin makes an appealing Anne Trulove, sweetly sung if not particularly well projected dramatically. John Reardon too is remarkable more for vocal accuracy than for striking characterization, but Regina Sarfaty's Baba is marvellous on both counts. The Sadler's Wells Chorus sings with even greater drive under the composer than in the theatre, and the Royal Philharmonic play with warmth and a fittingly Mozartian sense of style to match Stravinsky's surprisingly lyrical approach to his score. The CDs offer excellent sound.

The *Cantata* of 1952 is a transitional piece between Stravinsky's tonal and serial periods. However, of the two soloists, Alexander Young is much more impressive than Adrienne Albert, for her voice is entirely unsuitable, with an unformed choirboy sound somehow married to wide vibrato. For the sake of Stravinsky one endures her. The *Canticum sacrum* includes music that some listeners might find tough (the strictly serial choral section). But the performance is a fine one and the tenor solo from Richard Robinson is very moving. The Bach *Chorale variations* has a synthetic modernity that recalls the espresso bar, though one which still reveals underlying mastery. The *Epitaphium* and the *Double canon* are miniatures, dating from the composer's serial period, but the *Canon* is deliberately euphonious.

The *Mass* is a work of the greatest concentration, a quality that comes out strongly if one plays this performance immediately after *The Flood*, with its inevitably slack passages. As directed in the score, trebles are used here, and it is a pity that the engineers have not brought them further forward: their sweet, clear tone is sometimes lost among the lower strands. In *The Flood*, originally written for television, it is difficult to take the bald narrations seriously, particularly when Laurence Harvey sanctimoniously keeps talking of the will of 'Gud'. The performance of *Oedipus Rex*, too, is not one of the highlights of the set. *Perséphone*, however, is full of that cool lyricism that marks much of Stravinsky's music inspired by classical myths. As with many of these vocal recordings, the balance is too close, and various orchestral solos are highlighted.

Of the items recorded by Robert Craft, the *Requiem canticles* stands out, the one incontrovertible masterpiece among the composer's very last serial works and one of the most deeply moving works ever written in the serial idiom. Even more strikingly than in the *Mass* of 1948, Stravinsky conveys his religious feelings with a searing intensity. The *Aldous Huxley variations* are more difficult to comprehend but have similar intensity. Valuable, too, is the ballad *Abraham and Isaac*.

Agon; Jeu de cartes; Orpheus.
(Y/B) **(*) Decca Dig. 443 772-2 [id.]. Deutsches SO, Berlin, Vladimir Ashkenazy.

An intelligently planned disc comprising three of Stravinsky's most exhilarating ballets. Ashkenazy and the Deutsches Symphonie Orkester give us very well-played accounts of all three, and they are accorded more than decent Decca recording. There are slight reservations about the third star because there are rivals which have even greater zest and character.

Apollo (Apollon musagète; complete ballet); (i) *Capriccio for piano and orchestra. Pulcinella* (ballet): *suite.*
(Y/B) (M) *** Decca 443 577-2 [id.]. (i) John Ogdon; ASMF, Marriner.

This newly remastered recording in Decca's Classic Sound series remains a demonstration disc of its period (the two ballets recorded in the Kingsway Hall in 1967), particularly in the *Pulcinella* suite, where the sharp separation of instruments (for example, double-basses against trombones in the *Vivo*) makes for wonderful stereo, with the precision of the playing outshining that of almost all rival versions. The ethereal string-tones of *Apollo* make an ideal coupling, with the elegantly polished response of the Academy players comparing impressively with the outstanding Karajan version. Again, thanks both to the fine recording, made at The Maltings in 1970, and to the pointed playing of the Academy, the neo-classical quality of the *Capriccio*, a charming work, is beautifully underlined, while the soloist, John Ogdon, provides the contrasting element of sinewy toughness. An outstanding disc in every way.

(i) *Apollo (Apollon musagète)* (ballet): complete; *Circus polka;* (ii) *Petrushka* (ballet: 1911 score): complete.
(Y/B) (B) *** DG 439 463-2 [id.]. (i) BPO, Karajan; LSO, Dutoit.

Apollo is a work in which Karajan's moulding of phrase and care for richness of string texture make for wonderful results, especially in the glorious *Pas de deux*. The recording, made in the Jesus-Christus Kirche in 1972, is of DG's highest quality and in no way sounds its age. The *Circus polka* is played with comparable panache. The coupling is Charles Dutoit's first recorded *Petrushka*, made for DG in the Henry Wood Hall in 1975/6. The result is triumphantly spontaneous in its own right, with rhythms that are incisive yet beautifully buoyant, and a degree of expressiveness in the orchestral playing that subtly underlines the dramatic atmosphere. The remastered recording is atmospheric and vivid, though not as smooth on top as the Karajan couplings. Both ballets are generously cued, and altogether this bargain Classikon coupling is very good value.

(i) *Apollo (Apollon musagète); Circus polka; 4 Norwegian moods; Suites Nos. 1–2;* (ii) *The Soldier's tale (L'histoire du soldat);* (iii) *Symphony of Psalms.*
(Y/B) (M) *** Ph. 438 973-2 (2) [id.]. (i) LSO; (ii) Cocteau, Ustinov, Fertey, Tonietti, Parikian & Instrumental Ens.; (iii) Russian State Ac. Ch. & O; Markevitch.

Igor Markevitch's 1963 *Apollon musagète* with the LSO is a beautifully lucid and idiomatic perform-ance with great balletic feeling. The shorter pieces, the *Norwegian moods* and the two *Suites for small orchestra*, are done with great personality. His account of *L'histoire du soldat* was mounted in 1962 to mark his fiftieth birthday, for which he persuaded a less than youthful Jean Cocteau to appear as the narrator and Peter Ustinov as the Devil. The *Symphony of Psalms* was recorded on his visit to the USSR in the same year, and has wonderfully characterful (but not always dead-in-tune) singing. *L'histoire du soldat* is a drier recording than either its London or Moscow companions, but it says much for the skills of the engineers of the 1960s that the sound is so beautifully transparent and the string-tone silky. An altogether admirable and rewarding set.

Apollo (Apollon musagète) (ballet; complete); *Concerto in D for strings; Concerto for chamber orchestra, 'Dumbarton Oaks'; Danses concertantes.*
(Y/B) *** Decca Dig. 440 327-2 [id.]. Montreal Sinf., Charles Dutoit.

Dutoit firmly keeps *Apollo* in its original chamber scale, for the orchestra is not the Montreal Symphony but the Sinfonietta. If inevitably in *Apollo* one lacks the ripe opulence of Karajan and the Berlin Philharmonic, there is a clarity of focus and immediacy that the composer would have approved of, set in glowing sound. Dutoit is adept in bringing out the Stravinskian wit and point that in many numbers is set against the smooth string-lines of this lovely work. The other three works are very well matched and given strongly characterized performances. Though Dutoit could give more lightness to the *Brandenburg*-like textures of the *Dumbarton Oaks concerto*, it would be hard to imagine a more genial version of the *Concerto in D*, full of light and shade, or a more exuberant one of the *Danses concertantes* of 1944.

(i) *Apollo;* (ii) *The Firebird; Petrushka* (1911 score); *The Rite of spring* (complete ballets).
✧ (B) *** Ph. Duo 438 350-2 [id.]. (i) LSO, Markevitch; (ii) LPO, Haitink.

Markevitch gives a gravely beautiful reading of *Apollon musagète*, and the slightly distanced balance is surely ideal, for the focus is excellent. No more refined account of *The Firebird* has ever been put on record than Haitink's. The sheer savagery of *Kashchei's dance* may be a little muted, but the sharpness of attack and clarity of detail make for a thrilling result, while the magic and poetry of the whole score are given a hypnotic beauty, with the LPO at its very finest. The 1973 recording has been remastered with great success, as it has in the other two Haitink ballets, made at the same time. In *Petrushka* the rhythmic feeling is strong, especially in the Second Tableau and the finale, where the fairground bustle is vivid. The LPO wind playing is especially fine; the recording's firm definition and the well-proportioned and truthful aural perspective make it a joy to listen to. The natural, unforced quality of Haitink's *Rite* also brings real compulsion. Other versions may hammer the listener more powerfully, thrust him or her along more forcefully; but the bite and precision of the playing here are most impressive. Outstanding value.

Apollo; Orpheus (ballets).
*** ASV CDDCA 618 [id.]. O of St John's, Lubbock.

The ASV issue offers an ideal coupling, with refined performances and excellent recording. The delicacy of the rhythmic pointing in *Apollo* gives special pleasure, and there is a first-rate solo violin contribution from Richard Deakin. This is one of Stravinsky's most appealing later scores, as readily accessible as the more famous ballets of his early years.

Le baiser de la fée (ballet; complete). TCHAIKOVSKY, arr. STRAVINSKY: *Sleeping Beauty: Bluebird pas de deux*.
*** Chandos CHAN 8360 [id.]. SNO, Järvi.
(N) *** Sony Dig. SK 58949. [id.]. La Scala, Milan, PO, Muti – BARTOK: *2 Pictures*. ***

Le baiser de la fée (ballet; complete); TCHAIKOVSKY, arr. STRAVINSKY: *Sleeping Beauty: Variation d'Aurore; Entr'acte symphonique; Bluebird pas de deux*.
(N) (M) **(*) Virgin/EMI Dig. VM5 61281-2 [id.]. Hong Kong PO, David Atherton.

The scoring here is a constant delight, much of it on a chamber-music scale; and its delicacy, wit and occasional pungency are fully appreciated by Järvi, who secures a wholly admirable response from his Scottish orchestra. The ambience seems exactly right, bringing out wind and brass colours vividly. The condensation of the scoring of the *Sleeping Beauty Pas de deux*, made for a wartime performance when only limited forces were available, also shows Stravinsky's orchestral individuality – he even introduces a piano.

An all-Stravinsky coupling might have made better sense and drawn more collectors to it. However, having said that, Muti gives the *Baiser de la fée* a performance of great elegance and finesse that is as good as any of its rivals. The recording is admirably detailed and the perspective well judged. If the Bartók coupling is suitable, this could be first choice.

David Atherton has been Music Director in Hong Kong since 1989 (though he frequently returns to conduct in Europe and America). He must have regarded the Hong Kong Philharmonic as a challenge. The players are drawn from thirteen different countries and, on the evidence of this record, are a formidable ensemble. They play with considerable sophistication and finesse: the strings still do not possess quite the weight of sonority of the finest European orchestras, but they blend well together; the horns are notably good, while wind and brass rise to the occasion in producing vivid colouring for a ballet that depends so much on the orchestral palette. The performance is enjoyable too for its spontaneous feeling and, indeed, for the conductor's conveyed affection for the simple Tchaikovskian ideas which Stravinsky so cleverly welded into a convincing whole. It is good to have as encores Stravinsky's scoring of the excerpts from Tchaikovsky's *Sleeping Beauty*, not only the well-known *Bluebird pas de deux* of 1941 but also the two earlier movements, arranged for Diaghilev's 1921 London season, notably the concertante *Entr'acte symphonique* in which the orchestra's concertmaster, Mayumi Seiler, plays the violin solo. The recording is excellent and the warm acoustics of Hong Kong Town Hall add plenty of atmosphere.

Le baiser de la fée (Divertimento); The Soldier's tale: suite; Suites for orchestra Nos. 1–2; Octet.
(M) *** Decca Dig. 433 079-2 [id.]. L. Sinf., Chailly.

Chailly's version of the *Le baiser de la fée* divertimento, admirably fresh, is superbly played and Decca's recording is in the finest traditions of the house. The pointing of the lighter rhythmic patterns is especially effective – and the espressivo playing is at once responsive and slightly cool, a most engaging combination. The two *Orchestral suites*, vivid orchestrations of *'Easy' pieces* for piano, provide a kaleidoscopic series of colourful vignettes. The 1922 *Octet* is a considerable piece for flute, clarinet, two bassoons, two trumpets, trombone and bass trombone. It is given a performance of infectious virtuosity, with individual bravura matched by polished ensemble and fine tonal blending. The surprisingly little-recorded concert suite from *The Soldier's tale*, added for this reissue, makes an impressive finale. The performance has great flair and finds sardonic humour in the combination of *Tango, Waltz* and *Ragtime* in the sparkling sixth movement. Throughout the programme, the CD is very much in the demonstration class.

(i) *Capriccio for piano and orchestra;* (ii) *Le chant du rossignol: Marche chinoise;* (iii) *Concerto for 2 solo pianos;* (ii) *Duo concertante; The Firebird: Berceuse; Scherzo. Petrushka: Danse russe;* (ii; iv) *Pastorale;* (ii) *Suite italienne: Serenata II; Scherzino. Piano-rag-music.* (v) *Ragtime. Serenade in A;* (vi) *Octet for wind;* (vii) *Les Noces;* (viii) *Symphony of Psalms.*
(***) EMI mono CDS7 54607-2 (2) [Ang. ZCDB 54607]. Composer (piano or conductor), with (i) Walther Straram Concerts O, Ansermet; (ii) Samuel Dushkin; (iii) Soulima Stravinsky; (iv) Gromer, Durand, Vacellier, Grandmaison; (v) Lavaillotte, Godeau, Devemy, Foveau, Tudesq, Charmy, Volant, Ginot, Juste, Racz, Morel; (vi) Moyse, Godeau, Dhérin, Piard, Foveau, Vignal, Lafosse, Delbos; (vii) Mason, Heward, Lush, Benbow (pianos), Winter, Seymour, Parry Jones, Henderson, BBC Ch.; (viii) Vlassov Ch., Walther Straram Concerts O.

These performances provide the most revealing of all Stravinsky's own recordings of his music. He recorded the *Symphony of Psalms* in 1931, within a year of its première in Boston; the performance, though flawed, has a warmth and energy missing from his later LP recording, made with Canadian forces in 1963. Similarly in 1930 he had recorded another of his newer works of the time, the *Capriccio for piano and orchestra*, taking the solo part himself, with Ernest Ansermet conducting. He was not the greatest pianist, but there is a rhythmic point in the playing which allows a winning flexibility in the jazzy syncopations, while slily bringing out the echoes of Bach. In the last movement of the *Octet* too, which Stravinsky recorded with splendid French wind-players in 1932, the Cuban rhythms have a wit that is missing in his stricter, less expressive American recordings. In London in 1934 he also recorded the ballet, *Les Noces* (The Wedding), using an English translation and excellent British singers, led by the wonderfully firm and true soprano, Kate Winter, with the professional BBC Chorus already beginning to establish a new British choral tradition. The result in what was then a difficult, avant-garde work is still electrifying, despite the limitations of the sound. Much of the second of the two discs is taken up with violin and piano works and transcriptions, in which Stravinsky is joined by Samuel Dushkin; but even more enjoyable are the two jazz inspirations, *Ragtime for eleven instruments* and *Piano-rag-music.*

Capriccio for piano and orchestra; Concerto for piano and wind instruments; Movements for piano and orchestra; Symphonies of wind instruments.
(Y/B) *** Sony Dig. SK 45797 [id.]. Paul Crossley, L. Sinf., Salonen.

This is the sort of repertoire in which Esa-Pekka Salonen excels and in which Paul Crossley is also expert. All three performances can hold their own with the best, as indeed can the *Symphonies of wind instruments*. It is good to make the acquaintance of this CD, which can be confidently recommended to all lovers of the composer. Excellent digital recording too.

Le chant du rossignol (symphonic poem).
*** Erato/Warner 2292 45382-2 [id.]. Fr. Nat. O, Boulez – *Pulcinella.* **(*)

The symphonic poem that Stravinsky made from the material of his opera, *Le Rossignol*, with its extraordinarily rich fantasy and vividness of colouring, deserves a more established place in the concert repertoire. The Boulez performance is masterly; the French National Orchestra on Erato capture detail vividly and have the advantage of a first-class 1982 recording.

(i) *Le chant du rossignol; 4 Etudes for orchestra;* (ii; iii) *L'Histoire du soldat;* (iii; iv) *Pulcinella* (ballet): complete; (v) *3 Pieces for string quartet;* (vi) *Madrid* (étude for pianola); (vii) *4 Russian peasant songs;* (viii) *Le rossignol* (opera; complete).
(Y/B) (M) **(*) Erato/Warner Analogue/Dig. 4509 98955-2 (3) [id.]. (i) O Nat. de France; (ii) Roger Planchon, Patrice Chéreau, Antoine Vitez; (iii) Ens. InterContemporain; (iv) with Murray, Rolfe

Johnson, Estes; (v) InterContemporain Qt; (vi) Rex Lawson (pianola); (vii) Cantin, Melleret, Gantiez, R. France Ch.; (viii) Bryn-Julson, Caley, Laurence, Palmer, George, Howlett, Tomlinson, BBC Singers, BBC SO; Boulez.

An interesting collection which includes a first-class performance of Stravinsky's early opera, *Le rossignol*, as evocative as it is dramatic. It is sung in Russian and is provided with an excellent translation in the fairly well-cued libretto. Phyllis Bryn-Julson is impressively accurate in the Nightingale's complex upper tessitura and sings affectingly in her exchanges with Death, where Elizabeth Laurence's dark mezzo is well contrasted. Ian Caley makes an appealing Fisherman (who introduces and closes the opera). The recording is a bit close but does not lack ambience. However, *L'Histoire du soldat* is presented in French, with the narrator sounding rather verbose in a lengthy text which will not attract most English-speaking listeners as there is no accompanying translation. The performance, too, could be more atmospherically colourful. In both *Le Chant du rossignol* and *Pulcinella*, detail is captured vividly and the playing is often masterly. Boulez's singers in the latter work are splendid in every way; here the pacing is more extreme than Marriner's account (see above), with contrasts between movements almost overcharacterized. Of the shorter pieces, the four succinct *Russian peasant songs* are given an almost medieval character by their bare harmonies, while the three terse, sparc pieces for string quartet are all superbly played and sharply etched. Stravinsky wrote *Madrid* as a result of a commission from the Aeolian pianola manufacturing company and produced a concentrated 'tribute' to Spanish dance music heard through a distorting lens. We hear this piece again as the orchestrated fourth *Etude*, while the *Petrushka*-like second *Etude* was dubbed *Eccentric* by the composer; it evokes a memory of the stage performance of Little Tich, a great London clown whom Stravinsky saw perform in 1914, just before he wrote the string quartet pieces from which the first three *Etudes* are transcribed. Generally recommended, but it would be ideal to have the second disc, with the opera and the shorter works, available separately.

Concerto for chamber orchestra, 'Dumbarton Oaks'; 8 Instrumental miniatures; (i) *Ebony concerto*.
(Y/B) (M) *** DG 447 405-2 [id.]. (i) Michel Arrignon; Ens. InterContemporain, Pierre Boulez – BERG: *Chamber concerto*. ***

A highly suitable coupling for the Berg in DG's 'Originals' series. The close sound almost reminds one of the effect of some early Columbia records which Stravinsky himself made before the war: the dry, spiky, black-and-white images of the early cinema. Yet the effect on DG is never two-dimensional and lacking in ambient colour. The playing of the Ensemble InterContemporain is very brilliant indeed. There is much to enjoy in these performances, which are spiced with the right kind of wit and keenness of edge, and even those who do not normally respond to Boulez's conducting will be pleasantly surprised with the results he obtains here.

Concerto for chamber orchestra, 'Dumbarton Oaks'; Pulcinella (suite).
(Y/B) (M) *** DG Dig. 445 541 [id.]. Orpheus CO – BARTOK: *Divertimento for strings* etc. **(*)

Remarkably fine playing from this conductorless group. Their ensemble in the *Pulcinella suite* is better than that of most conducted orchestras, and the overall impression they convey is one of freshness and spontaneity. Much the same must be said of *Dumbarton Oaks*, which has great zest and brilliance. The DG recording is clean and lifelike and the perspective very natural. While this disc does not eclipse memories of all rivals, it can more than hold its own with most competition, past and present.

Concerto for strings in D.
(N) (M) *** DG 447 435-2 [id.]. BPO, Karajan – HONEGGER: *Symphonies Nos. 2 & 3* *** ⊛

Karajan's version of the *Concerto in D for strings* – written within a few months of the Honegger *Symphonie Liturgique*, with which it is coupled – may strike some listeners as not quite acerbic or biting enough, but the finesse and lightness of touch of the Berlin strings and their rhythmic legerdemain are a delight. The recording is first class.

Ebony concerto.
*** RCA Dig. 09026 61360-2 [id.]. Stoltzman, Woody Herman's Thundering Herd – BERNSTEIN: *Prelude, fugue and riffs;* COPLAND; CORIGLIANO: *Concertos*. ***
*** Sony MK 42227 [id.]. Benny Goodman, Columbia Jazz Ens., composer – COPLAND: *Concerto;* BARTOK: *Contrasts;* BERNSTEIN: *Prelude, fugue and riffs;* GOULD: *Derivations*. (***)

Richard Stoltzman follows Benny Goodman before him in offering a suitably cool, yet lively and entirely idiomatic account of Stravinsky's *Ebony concerto*, coupled with Bernstein's *Prelude, fugue and riffs* and Copland's *Concerto*. Stolzman has the advantage of modern digital sound, and he also includes a fine account of John Corigliano's *Concerto*.

The *Ebony concerto* also sounds strikingly vivid in an apt compilation centred on Benny Goodman's other comparable recordings.

(i; ii) *Ebony Concerto;* (iii) *Violin concerto;* (iv) *Symphony in C; Symphony in three movements;* (ii) *Symphonies for wind instruments;* (v) *Symphony of Psalms.*
(Y/B) (B) **(*) Ph. Duo 442 583-2 (2) [id.]. (i) Pieterson; (ii) Netherlands Wind Ens., Edo de Waart; (iii) Grumiaux, Concg. O, Bour; (iv) LSO, C. Davis; (v) Russian State Ac. Ch. & SO, Markevitch.

A lithe, refined account of the *Violin concerto* from Grumiaux and the Concertgebouw Orchestra. It is enormously vital, but its energy is controlled and the tone never becomes unduly aggressive. The 1967 recording is just a little dated but preserves a good balance between soloist and orchestra. George Pieterson's version of the *Ebony concerto* with the Netherlands Wind Ensemble is not as overtly jazzy as some but it does not lack rhythmic bite, and its dry, sardonic wit and the dark sonorities of the finale make it individual. The *Symphonies for wind instruments* also show the controlled blend of colour for which this Dutch wind group are famous. Sir Colin Davis's account of the *Symphony in C* is splendidly alert, well played and stimulating. The performance of the *Symphony in three movements* is also lively, but compared with Stravinsky's own it is over-tense. Markevitch's 1964 Russian performance of the *Symphony of Psalms* is as vibrantly Slavonic as one could wish, yet the closing 'Alleluias' still bring a frisson in their raptly gentle expressive feeling. The sound is brightly vivid but not harsh.

Violin concerto in D.
(N) (M) (***) Sony mono SMK 64505 [id.]. Stern, Columbia SO, composer – ROCHBERG: *Violin concerto.* *(**)
(M) *** Decca 425 003-2 [id.]. Kyung Wha Chung, LSO, Previn – PROKOFIEV: *Concertos 1–2.* ***
(Y/B) *** Sony Dig. SK 53969 [id.]. Cho-Liang Lin, LAPO, Esa-Pekka Salonen – PROKOFIEV: *Violin concertos Nos. 1 & 2.* *** ❀
(N) (M) *** DG 447 445-2 [id.]. Itzhak Perlman, Boston SO, Ozawa – BERG: *Concerto;* RAVEL: *Tzigane.* ***

Stern's 1951 mono recording with the composer has never been surpased and seldom approached. The outer movements have an exhilarating combination of rhythmic bite and wit, and the two central arias bring a very special subtlety of colour and feeling. The sound is of the highest quality: no apologies whatsoever need be made for it. Listening to the record lifts the spirits, and we would have given it a Rosette were it not for the Rochberg coupling, which (as music) is very much of the second grade, even if Stern's performance is not.

Kyung Wha Chung is at her most incisive in the spikily swaggering outer movements, which with Previn's help are presented here in all their distinctiveness, tough and witty at the same time. In the two movements labelled *Aria,* Chung brings fantasy as well as lyricism, less overtly expressive than Perlman (at full price) but conveying instead an inner, brooding quality. Brilliant Decca recording, the soloist diamond-bright in presence, but with plenty of orchestral atmosphere.

As in the two Prokofiev concertos, so in the Stravinsky Lin plays with power and warmth, while Salonen terraces the accompaniment dramatically, with woodwind and brass bold and full. In this same coupling Chung on mid-priced Decca offers equally compelling readings in excellent analogue sound, with more wit brought out in this Stravinsky work. But in the Prokofiev the balance of advantage goes marginally to Lin.

Perlman's precision, remarkable in both concertos on this disc, underlines the neo-classical element in the outer movements of the Stravinsky. The two *Aria* movements are more deeply felt and expressive, presenting the work as a major twentieth-century concerto. The balance favours the soloist, but no one will miss the commitment of the Boston orchestra's playing, vividly recorded. A fair candidate for DG's 'Originals' series, with the Ravel *Tzigane* now added for good measure.

Complete ballets: *The Firebird;* (i) *Les Noces; Petrushka* (original 1911 score); *The Rite of spring.*
(Y/B) (B) ** Decca 443 467-2 (2) [id.]. SRO, Ansermet; (i) with Retchitzka, Devallier, Cuénod, Rehfuss, Homeffer, Peter, Rossiaud, Aubert, Geneva Motet Ch.

In their day these were much-admired performances and recordings of the three major early ballets. *The Firebird* is very early stereo indeed (1955); *Petrushka* and *The Rite* come from 1957, and *Les Noces* is later (and sounds it: 1961). At this distance of time the shortcomings of the SRO, which in the late 1950s was not the fine body it had been in the immediate post-war period, are evident, and the transfers tend to exaggerate the weakness of timbre in the upper strings by making it seem thin, ill-focused and shrill. *Petrushka* suffers most, and one feels that Ansermet's lively reading could be made to sound better than this. *The Firebird* is much smoother and has plenty of ambience. Detail is exceptionally clear, filled in like vivid embroidery on fine gauze. But the massed strings still sound emaciated. On balance one is prepared to put up with the defects in the orchestra for the sake of Ansermet's view of the *Rite of spring*, which has integrity, besides generating considerable rhythmic excitement and often striking melancholy of atmosphere. Here the sound is better too. *Les Noces* is altogether disappointing. Ansermet fails to capture the essential bite of Stravinsky's sharply etched portrayal of a peasant wedding. The hammering rhythms must sound ruthless, and here they are merely tame.

The Firebird (ballet): complete (with rehearsal).
(Y/B) (M) *** Decca 443 572-2 [id.]. New Philh. O, Ernest Ansermet.

The Firebird (complete); *Le chant du rossignol; Fireworks; Scherzo à la russe*.
✹ (M) *** Mercury 432 012-2 [id.]. LSO, Dorati.

The CD transfer of Dorati's electrifying, 1960 Mercury version of *The Firebird* with the LSO makes the recording sound as fresh and vivid as the day it was made; the brilliantly transparent detail and enormous impact suggest a modern digital source rather than an analogue master made over 30 years ago. The performance sounds completely spontaneous and the LSO wind playing is especially sensitive. Only the sound of the massed upper strings reveals the age of the original master, although this does not spoil the ravishing final climax; the bite of the brass and the transient edge of the percussion are thrilling. The recording of Stravinsky's glittering symphonic poem, *The song of the nightingale*, is hardly less compelling. Dorati's reading is urgent and finely pointed, yet is strong, too, on atmosphere. The other, shorter pieces also come up vividly.

Ansermet came to London in November 1968 to re-record the complete *Firebird* in the Kingsway Hall, only a few months before he died. This London version, though not immaculate in ensemble in *Kaschei's dance*, has more polished playing than that which Ansermet recorded earlier with his own Suisse Romande Orchestra, but generally the interpretations are amazingly consistent. The recording was a demonstration disc in its day and is reissued in Decca's Classic Sound series, well documented by current CD standards. The first-class transfer readily demonstrates the atmosphere and vividly dramatic detail for which this conductor's records were justly famous.

The Firebird; Rite of spring (complete ballets).
(N) (B) *** Decca Eclipse Dig. 448 226-2; *448 226-4* [id.]. Detroit SO, Antal Dorati.

Dorati's Detroit version of *The Firebird* has the benefit of spectacular digital recording. The clarity and definition of dark, hushed passages are amazing, with the contra-bassoon finely focused, never sounding woolly or obscure, while string tremolos down to the merest whisper are uncannily precise. There is plenty of space round woodwind solos, and only the concertmaster's violin is spotlit. The performance is very precise, too; though Dorati's reading has changed little from his previous versions with London orchestras, there is just a little more caution. Individual solos are not so characterful and *Kaschei's dance* lacks just a degree in excitement; but overall this is a strong and beautiful reading, even if the Mercury LP account, an electrifying example of 1960s' analogue engineering, is not entirely superseded.

Similarly, in terms of recorded sound, Dorati's *Rite* with the Detroit orchestra scores over almost all its rivals. This has stunning clarity and presence, exceptionally lifelike and vivid sound, and the denser textures emerge more cleanly than ever before. It is a very good performance too, almost but not quite in the same league as those of Karajan and Muti, generating plenty of excitement. The only let-down is the final *Sacrificial dance*, which needs greater abandon and higher voltage. Nor are the Detroit strings as sumptuous as those of the Berlin orchestra, sounding distinctly undernourished in places. Yet too much should not be made of this. Although Dorati does not match the atmosphere of his finest rivals, the performance is so vivid that it belongs among the very best.

The Firebird: suite (1919 version).
(Y/B) (M) *** DG 447 414-2 [id.]. (i) Grace Bumbry; Berlin RSO, Maazel – FALLA: *El amor brujo* etc.
       **

*** DG Dig. 437 818-2 [id.]. O de l'Opéra Bastille, Chung – RIMSKY-KORSAKOV: *Scheherazade*. ***
(*) Sony SK 45935 [id.]. Concg. O, Giulini – MUSSORGSKY: *Pictures*. *

There has never been a finer recorded account of the 1919 version of the *Firebird suite* than Maazel's. It was recorded in 1958 and the stereo is magically atmospheric. The orchestral playing has great éclat: its colours are wonderfully subtle. In the gentler music the effect is exquisite, with the oboe soloist in the *Dance of the Princesses* and the bassoon in the *Berceuse* playing with the utmost delicacy. The ferocity of the *Infernal dance* breaks the spell momentarily, and Maazel omits the few bars included by Stravinsky to bridge the violent change of mood. But then comes the luminous climax of the finale, with the Berlin violins quite luscious in thirds, even though here the actual sound slightly betrays the age of the recording. This is truly a Legendary Performance, fully worthy of inclusion in DG's set of

'Originals'; but it is a great pity that the equally memorable original coupling of *Le chant du rossignol* was abandoned in favour of the Falla, which by comparison is second rate.

Myung-Whun Chung gets very musical results from his players and there are many imaginative touches. The sound has great warmth and richness (perhaps too much for some tastes) but the perspective is absolutely right and benefits from the technical expertise of Wolfgang Mitelehner and Lennart Dehn, who was Chung's Gothenburg producer.

The Concertgebouw acoustic – as anyone who has experienced live music-making there will know – is less than ideal for fast-moving, sharply dissonant twentieth-century music. Its wide reverberation tends to blur the transients, as here in *Kashchei's dance* which, however, does not lack malignancy. It also brings a voluptuous weight to the richly scored finale, perhaps unmatched on record. Giulini secures wonderfully refined playing in the gentler music, but the lack of rhythmic bite minimizes the balletic feeling and makes the suite seem more symphonic than usual.

Firebird suite; Pastorale.

(N) (M) **(*) Decca Phase 4 443 898-2 [id.]. Czech PO, Stokowski – MUSSORGSKY: *Pictures at an exhibition* **; SCRIABIN: *Poème de l'extase.* **(*)

Tremendously sumptuous sound from Stokowski, while some of the relatively quiet music (the dynamic range is limited by the forward balance) shows the wonderful luminosity he could uniquely command from the orchestra. Rich-textured violins dominate the beginning of the final climax, which is power-fully inflated. *The Pastorale*, a 'song without words' written in 1908, makes a pleasant and unusual bonus. It is warmly played and, again, sumptuously recorded.

Jeu de cartes.

(Y/B) (M) **(*) Sony SMK 57660 [id.]. Novosibirsk PO, Arnold Kaz – RACHMANINOV: *Symphonic dances.* ***

Arnold Kaz is not a celebrated conductor though he produces more musical results than many who are, and the Novosibirsk orchestra is not a virtuoso ensemble, but it is a very good one. There are more brilliant and harder-etched accounts of this score around, but this is very enjoyable indeed – very fresh, far better than routine without quite being touched by real distinction. It comes with a Rachmaninov *Symphonic dances* that is very well worth having. The same goes for the Stravinsky: it is a far more enjoyable performance than some we have from better-known orchestras and glossier maestros, and the recording is eminently satisfactory. Good value for money.

Petrushka (1911 version; complete). *The Firebird: suite* (1919). *Fireworks; Pastoral* (arr. Stokowski).

⊛ (***) Dutton Lab. mono CDAX 8002 [id.]. Phd. O, Stokowski (with: SHOSTAKOVICH: *Prelude in E flat min., Op. 34/14,* arr. Stokowski (***)).

Stokowski's 1937 version of *Petrushka* is very special indeed, the sound tremendously present and amazingly detailed for its period – high fidelity even by today's standards – and the performance is marvellously characterized and full of atmosphere: indeed it is difficult to think of a portrayal of Petrushka himself that is more poignant, keenly felt or brilliantly coloured. (Perhaps Bernstein's CBS account from the 1960s comes closest.) The playing of the Philadelphia Orchestra is quite stunning, and the Dutton transfer gets far more detail on to CD than the RCA rival (see below); it is also smoother on top. The 1935 *Firebird suite* (its ending cut, to fit on a 78-r.p.m. side) takes wing too – equally strongly characterized and full of atmosphere. The shorter pieces are rarities: the Shostakovich *Prelude*, a brand-new piece at this time, was the fill-up to *Firebird*, and the *Pastoral* and *Fireworks* were issued only in the USA. A marvellous collection – indeed, a desert island disc.

(i) *Petrushka* (complete 1911 score); (ii) *The Rite of spring*.

(Y/B) (M) **(*) Sony SMK 64109 [id.]. (i) NYPO; (ii) Cleveland O; Pierre Boulez.

(Y/B) (M) ** Decca 440 064-2 [id.]. (i) Julius Katchen; Paris Conservatoire O, Pierre Monteux.

(M) (***) RCA mono 09026 61394-2. Phd. O, Stokowski.

There is a controlled intensity about Boulez's 1971 New York performance of *Petrushka* which in the original version of the score puts the ballet closer than usual to the barbaric work which followed and it is a pity that the 1971 recording, made in the Avery Fisher Hall, becomes fierce at higher dynamic levels. Similarly in *The Rite of spring*, recorded two years earlier in Severance Hall, Cleveland, tempi are generally measured. Boulez is less lyrical than the composer but compensates with relentless rhythmic urgency. After Stravinsky's own version, which is not only uniquely authoritative but also uniquely compelling, Boulez's is among the most completely recommendable accounts. The massive vividness of sound matches the monolithic quality of the interpretation.

Leopold Stokowski's pioneering recordings of *Petrushka* and *The Rite of spring* make an ideal CD coupling in RCA's Legendary Performers series at mid-price. It is an astonishing tribute to the standards that Stokowski was achieving, that the Philadelphia Orchestra in 1929 was able to play *The Rite* with such flair, and *Petrushka* similarly in 1937. The transfers are bright and vivid but rather shallow, with *Petrushka* no match for the Dutton issue above, and the *Rite* less full-bodied than in the Pearl issue of works that Stokowski included in the Disney film *Fantasia* (GEMM CD 9488).

Monteux's recordings date from the early days of stereo, *The Rite* from 1956 and *Petrushka*, with Julius Katchen recruited to play the solo piano role, a year later. As Monteux conducted the first performance of the former ballet, it is valuable to have his account return to the catalogue. But in neither work is the French orchestral playing anything to write home about. The woodwind in *Petrushka* is at times less than pleasing and the overall ensemble in *The Rite* is not ideally assured. The sound is atmospheric but thin in the upper range.

(i) *Petrushka* (1947 score); *The Rite of spring;* (ii) *4 Etudes for orchestra.*
(M) **(*) Mercury 434 331-2 [id.]. (i) Minneapolis SO; (ii) LSO; Dorati.

Dorati's famous (1959) Mercury recording of *Petrushka* is exceptionally clean and vivid, with the semi-clinical Minneapolis recording bringing stereoscopic detail in the two central tableaux. There is plenty of drama too, and the final scene is touchingly done. Inevitably the sound is dated, with the bright upper range as caught by the Telefunken microphones not quite natural, but this adds a sharp cutting edge and impact to Dorati's extremely violent performance of *The Rite of spring*. His speeds are fast – sometimes considerably faster than is indicated in the score – but the LSO players carry complete conviction, the tautness of the work the more clearly revealed. The orchestral *Etudes* were recorded later (1964) in Watford, and have a fuller ambience.

Petrushka (1947 version); *Symphony in 3 movements.*
*** EMI Dig. CDC7 49053-2 [id.]. CBSO, Sir Simon Rattle.

Using the revised, 1947 scoring, Rattle gives a reading which brings out powerfully the sturdy jollity of the ballet, contrasting it with the poignancy of the puppet's own feelings. The full and brilliant recording is beefy in the middle and bass, but Rattle and his players benefit in clarity from the 1947 scoring, finely detailed to bring out many points that are normally obscured. The *Symphony in three movements*, done with comparable power, colour and robustness, makes an unusual but attractive coupling. With his jazz training, Rattle brings out the syncopations and pop references with great panache.

Petrushka: suite.
(Y/B) (M) ** EMI CDM5 65423-2 [id.]. BPO, Stokowski – HOLST: *The Planets;* RAVEL: *Alborada.*
**(*)

The Berlin Philharmonic seems not completely happy in the *Petrushka* suite, a 16-minute selection from the complete ballet that starts with the *Russian dance*. The Berlin strings sound too saturated in tone for this music, brilliant as the wind playing is, and the 1957 recording is not particularly distinguished.

Pulcinella (ballet) complete.
(M) *** EMI CDM7 64739-2 [id.]. Jennifer Smith, John Fryatt, Malcolm King, N. Sinfonia, Rattle –
    WEILL: *Die sieben Todsünden.* ***
**(*) Erato/Warner 2292 45382-2 [id.]. Murray, Rolfe Johnson, Estes, Ens. InterContemporain, Boulez
    – *Le Chant du rossignol.* ***

(i) *Pulcinella* (complete); *Renard. Ragtime; Octet.*
*** Sony Dig. SK 45965 [id.]. (i) Kenny, Aler, Tomlinson, Robson, Wilson-Johnson; L. Sinf., Esa-Pekka
    Salonen.

Simon Rattle, within a somewhat dry recording acoustic, conveys far more than usual the links between this score and the much later neo-classical opera, *The Rake's Progress*. With lively and colourful playing from the Northern Sinfonia (the solos strong and positive) and with first-rate contributions from the three soloists, the high spirits of this score come over superbly. The current CD transfer adds vividness and presence without loss of bloom, and the new coupling is very generous indeed.

Salonen may be less objective than some rivals, but not only is the fun behind much of this music delightfully brought out, he moulds it sufficiently to suggest a warmth behind neo-classical forms and, frequently, a debt to jazz. That is so not just in *Ragtime* but also in such a work as the delightful *Octet* of 1922–3. When *Pulcinella* is here given with voices, it is good to have another early example of music-theatre in *Renard*, necessarily a rarity in concert, with the Russian folk-tale presented with bluff good humour. Warm recording to match.

Boulez secures superb playing from the Ensemble InterContemporain, and his singers are first class in every way. His is a fine performance, but his pacing is more extreme than some versions, with contrasts between movements almost overcharacterized. However, some may like the periodic added edge, and the Erato recording has been excellently transferred to CD.

(i) *Pulcinella* (ballet; complete); *The Rite of spring.*
(B) *** DG 439 433-2 [id.]. (i) Berganza, Ryland Davies, Shirley-Quirk; LSO, Abbado.

Abbado gives a vividly high-powered reading of the neo-classical score of *Pulcinella*, with rhythms sharply incisive. Not just the playing but the singers too are outstandingly fine and Abbado's feeling for atmosphere and colour is everywhere in evidence, heard against an excellently judged perspective. There is a degree of detachment in *The Rite of spring*; but on points of detail it is meticulous. There is a hypnotically atmospheric feeling at the opening of Part Two, emphasizing the contrast with the brutal music which follows. The drama is heightened by the wide dynamic range of the recording, and the effect is forceful without ever becoming ugly. An excellent Classikon bargain coupling.

The Rite of spring (complete ballet) (see also above, under *Petrushka*).
(M) *** EMI Dig. CDM7 64516-2 [id.]. Phd. O, Muti – MUSSORGSKY: *Pictures.* ***
(M) **(*) Telarc Dig. CD 82001 [id.]. Cleveland O, Maazel – SHOSTAKOVICH: *Symphony No. 5.* ***
(Y/B) **(*) Everest EVC 9002 [id.]. LSO, Sir Eugene Goossens – RACHMANINOV: *Symphonic dances.* ***

The Rite of spring (complete); *4 Etudes for orchestra; Scherzo à la russe.*
(M) **(*) Teldec/Warner Dig. 4509 91449-2 [id.]. Philh. O, Inbal.

Muti's *Rite of spring* offers a performance which is aggressively brutal yet presents the violence with red-blooded conviction. Muti generally favours speeds a shade faster than usual, and arguably the opening bassoon solo is not quite flexible enough, for metrical precision is a key element all through. The recording, not always as analytically clear as some rivals, is strikingly bold and dramatic, with brass and percussion caught exceptionally vividly. At mid-price, coupled with an equally outstanding version of Mussorgsky's *Pictures*, this is very competitive indeed.

The sound on the Cleveland Orchestra version conducted by Lorin Maazel is also pretty spectacular. However, there are a number of sensation-seeking effects, such as excessive ritardandi in the *Rondes printanières* so as to exaggerate the trombone glissandi, which are vulgar. Compare, too, the opening of Part Two in this version with that of Karajan, and one is in a totally different world.

Sir Eugene Goossens seems an unexpected conductor in Stravinsky, yet he gave the first performance of *The Rite of spring* in England. His approach is circumspect and the performance moves forward with a remorseless steadiness, notably so in Part 1, while there is a total absence of romanticism in the long lyrical section which opens Part 2. The playing of the LSO is well disciplined and the recording is very spectacular, a reverberant acoustic (Walthamstow) not clouding the detail but certainly adding sonic excitement, notably in Goossens' bold, dramatic strokes, like the big horn tune towards the end.

Inbal's version was placed among the top three of all available recordings of Stravinsky's ballet in a survey by Michael Stewart in *Gramophone* magazine in September 1992. He admired its 'earthiness', violence and sense of mystery. We find Inbal rather metrical, making the music sound too safe, though the effect is clean and pungent. The couplings are ungenerous but very well played, especially the *Scherzo à la russe* with its flavour of *Petrushka*. The recording is full, smooth and vivid.

The Rite of spring (orchestral & pianola versions).
(M) *** Carlton Classics Dig. MCD 25. Boston PO, Zander.

Benjamin Zander's live recording with the Boston Philharmonic brings a hard-hitting, colourful performance, directly related to the pianola version with which it is coupled. Stravinsky himself in the 1920s supervised the original Pleyela piano roll recording, which Rex Lawson 'plays' very effectively on a resonant Bösendorfer Imperial. The speeds at which everything is presented remain predetermined and unalterable; and here the most striking point on speed is the very fast tempo for the opening of the final *Sacrificial dance*, markedly faster even than Stravinsky's own on the last – and finest – of his three recordings. Zander suggests (and he offers additional documentary evidence) that Stravinsky intended a faster pacing for the ballet's finale and that he modified the tempo only when he discovered that orchestras could not cope with the music at his intended speed. There is no doubt that, played up to this faster tempo, the *Danse sacrale* is electrifying.

The Soldier's tale (complete).
*** Nimbus Dig. NI 5063 [id.]. Christopher Lee, SCO, Lionel Friend.

With the actor Christopher Lee both narrating and taking the individual parts, the Nimbus issue brings an attractively strong and robust reading, lacking the last degree of refinement but with some superb solo playing – from the violinist, for example. The recording is vivid and full of presence, with the speaking voice related to instruments far better than is usual. For a version in English, it makes an excellent investment.

The Soldier's tale (suite).
(M) *** Van. 08.8013.71 [OVC 8013]. Instrumental Ens., Leopold Stokowski – THOMSON: *Film scores.* ***

Stokowski works his magic upon this surprisingly neglected score, making the most of its lyrical warmth as well as the more abrasive Devil's music, which has plenty of rhythmic bite. The septet of expert instrumentalists is naturally recorded in a studio acoustic, but one which has plenty of ambience.

Symphony in E flat; (i) *Violin concerto in D.*
*** Chandos Dig. CHAN 9236 [id.]. (i) Mordkovitch; SRO, Neeme Järvi.

A highly recommendable account of the early *Symphony in E flat* from Neeme Järvi, coupled with a very characterful reading of the *Violin concerto.* This is gutsy and very Russian with a few rough edges (including an out-of-tune first entry). It has bags of character and is highly enjoyable. The Chandos recording is well balanced and finely detailed.

Symphony in C; Symphony in 3 movements.
(M) *** Chandos Dig. CHAN 6577 [id.]. Royal Scottish O, Sir Alexander Gibson.

Even when compared with the composer's own versions, these performances by the Royal Scottish Orchestra – in excellent form – stand up well. The vivid naturalness of the splendid 1982 digital recording compensates for any slight lack of bite, and the inner movements of both works are beautifully played. The cool, almost whimsical beauty of the *Andante* of the *Symphony in three movements* is most subtly conveyed, and altogether this is very enjoyable.

(i) *Symphony in C; Symphony in 3 movements;* (ii) *Symphonies of wind instruments; Scherzo fantastique, Op. 3.*
(M) *** Decca Dig. 436 474-2 [id.]. (i) SRO; (ii) Montreal SO; Dutoit.

The brilliant Decca recording and the alert direction of Charles Dutoit make this a very winning coupling. The *Symphony in C* and *Symphony in three movements* are both exhilarating pieces and Dutoit punches home their virile high spirits and clean-limbed athleticism. The *Symphonies of wind instruments*, the work Stravinsky composed in 1920 in memory of Debussy, is given a very effective and crisp performance, and the sparkling *Scherzo fantastique* also demonstrates the greater polish of the Montreal players.

CHAMBER AND INSTRUMENTAL MUSIC

Concerto for two solo pianos; Scherzo à la russe (arr. Stravinsky); *Sonata for two pianos; Le sacre du printemps* (arr. Stravinsky).
*** Decca Dig. 433 829-2 [id.]. Vladimir Ashkenazy, Andrei Gavrilov.

These two distinguished pianists give a breath-taking exhibition of unanimity, rhythmic projection and keyboard colour. Their account of Stravinsky's own arrangement of *Le sacre du printemps* can only be described as dazzling, and the *Scherzo à la russe*, a rarity in this transcription, is a delight. The *Concerto for two solo pianos*, Stravinsky at his most neo-classical, and the 1943 *Sonata* are given marvellously exhilarating performances by Ashkenazy and Gavrilov, whose virtuosity is matched by a sense of spontaneity and delight in their music-making.

Elégie, for solo viola.
*** EMI CDC7 54394-2 [id.]. Tabea Zimmermann – BRITTEN: *Lachrymae;* SHOSTAKOVICH: *Viola sonata.* ***

Stravinsky's solo *Elégie* is finely played and recorded here and comes with moving accounts of the Britten *Lachrymae* and Shostakovich's deeply felt *Sonata.*

3 Pieces for string quartet.
(N) *** ASV Dig. CDDCA 930 [id.]. Lindsay Qt – DEBUSSY; RAVEL: *Quartets.* **(*)

A vital, finely etched performance of these delightful pieces from the Lindsays. A good fill-up to thoughtful and vigorous account of the Debussy and Ravel *Quartets.* Good recordings.

Suite italienne.
*** BIS Dig. CD 336 [id.]. Torleif Thedéen, Roland Pöntinen – SCHNITTKE: *Sonata;* SHOSTAKOVICH: *Sonata.* ***

Stravinsky made several transcriptions of movements from *Pulcinella*, including the *Suite italienne* for violin and piano. The performances by Torleif Thedéen and Roland Pöntinen, Swedish artists both in their mid-twenties, are felicitous and spontaneous, and they are afforded strikingly natural recording.

PIANO MUSIC

Circus polka; 4 Etudes, Op. 7; Piano-rag-music; Scherzo; Serenade in A; Sonata in F sharp min.; Sonata (1924); Tango.
*** Collins Dig. 1374-2 [id.]. Victor Sangiorgio.

Victor Sangiorgo plays with great character and virtuosity, and in some pieces is more successful and more thoughtful than his previous rivals. He also benefits from vivid and present recording. Thoroughly recommendable.

Circus polka; Piano-rag-music; Serenade in A; Sonata; 4 Studies; Tango.
(M) **(*) Saga EC 3391-2 [id.]. Thomas Rajna.

Some may feel that in Thomas Rajna's hands Stravinsky's piano music is made to sound too soft-centred and without enough rhythmic toughness – even the *Tango* and *Circus polka* have charm. But the *Sonata* is taken seriously and there is an imaginative variety of colour in the *Serenade*: its unexpectedly tranquil closing *Cadenza finala* is played with lucid imperturbability. This is always intelligent as well as sympathetic playing, and many may respond to it who would reject a more percussive approach. The recording is natural but is projected not very forwardly.

3 movements from Petrushka.
(Y/B) (M) *** DG 447 431-2 [id.]. Maurizio Pollini – *Recital.* ***

Staggering, electrifying playing from Pollini, creating the highest degree of excitement. This is part of an outstandingly generous recital of twentieth-century piano music.

Piano sonata; Piano-rag music; Serenade in A.
(Y/B) *** Chandos Dig. CHAN 8962 [id.]. Boris Berman – SCHNITTKE: *Sonata.* ***

Boris Berman is an artist of powerful intelligence who gives vivid and alertly characterized accounts of all these pieces. Excellent piano sound, too, from the Chandos engineers. Strongly recommended.

VOCAL MUSIC

4 Cat's cradle songs; 4 Chants; Elegy for JFK; In memoriam Dylan Thomas; 3 Japanese lyrics; Pastorale; 2 Poems by Konstantin Bal'mont; 2 Poems by Paul Verlaine; Pribaoutki (4 songs); Recollections of childhood (3 songs); 2 Sacred songs (from WOLF: *Spanish Lieder Book); 3 Shakespeare songs; 4 Songs; Tilim-bom; Mavra: Parasha's aria.*
(M) *** DG 431 751-2 [id.]. Bryn-Julson, Murray, Tear, Shirley-Quirk, Ens. InterContemporain, Boulez.

Anyone who thinks a Stravinsky song could not be utterly charming should try the first item of this recital, the *Pastorale*, a song without words for voice and four wind instruments: Phyllis Bryn-Julson's performance is captivating. Practically all of Stravinsky's songs are accommodated on this useful CD. All the singing here is very persuasive and well characterized. The Verlaine songs are, oddly enough, given in Russian (Stravinsky originally set them in French), but Shirley-Quirk makes them sound very appealing nevertheless. The record also includes a 1968 transcription of two of Wolf's Spanish songs, his very last opus. The CD transfer is immaculate, with natural, well-focused sound, and translations are provided where necessary.

(i) *Mass;* (ii) *Les Noces.*
(M) *** DG 423 251-2 [id.]. (i) Trinity Boys' Ch., E. Bach Festival O; (i, ii) E. Bach Festival Ch.; (ii) Mory, Parker, Mitchinson, Hudson; Argerich, Zimerman, Katsaris, Francesch (pianos), percussion; cond. Bernstein.

In the *Mass* the style is overtly expressive, with the boys of Trinity Choir responding freshly, but it is in *Les Noces* that Bernstein conveys an electricity and a dramatic urgency which give the work its rightful stature as one of Stravinsky's supreme masterpieces, totally original and – even today – unexpected, not least in its black-and-white instrumentation for four pianos and percussion. The star pianists here make a superb, imaginative team.

(i) *Perséphone. The Rite of spring.*
(N) (M) *** Virgin/EMI Dig. VMD5 61249-2 (2) [id.]. (i) Anne Fournet, Rolfe Johnson, Tiffin Boys' School Ch., LPO Ch.; LPO, Kent Nagano.

Where Stravinsky himself – at speeds consistently more measured than Nagano's – takes a rugged, square-cut view of *Perséphone*, Nagano, much lighter as well as more fleet, makes the work a far more atmospheric evocation of spring. The playing and singing are consistently more refined, and the modern digital recording gives a warm bloom, while the sung French sounds far more idiomatic from everyone. The narration of Anne Fournet brings out all the beauty of Gide's words, with Anthony Rolfe Johnson free-toned in the taxing tenor solos. Nagano's reading of *The Rite of spring* has similar qualities. If it is less weightily barbaric than many, the springing of rhythm and the clarity and refinement of instrumental textures make it very compelling, with only the final *Danse sacrale* lacking something in dramatic bite. The two separate discs are offered in a box at the cost of a single, premium-price CD.

OPERA

Oedipus Rex (opera-oratorio).
*** Sony Dig. SK 48057 [id.]. Cole, Von Otter, Estes, Sotin, Gedda, Chéreau, Eric Ericson Chamber Ch., Swedish RSO & Ch., Salonen.
*** EMI Dig. CDC7 54445-2 [id.]. Rolfe Johnson, Lipovšek, Tomlinson, Miles, LPO Ch., LPO, Welser-Möst.
** Ph. Dig. 438 865-2 [id.]. Schreier, Norman, Terfel, Peters, Wilson, Shinyukai Male Ch., Saito Kinen O, Ozawa.

Salonen with his Swedish forces and an outstanding cast, more consistent than any previous one, conducts the strongest performance yet on disc of this landmark of modern opera. He offers an ideal combination of rugged power and warmth, delivered expressively but without sentimentality. The pinpoint precision of ensemble of the choruses, substantial but not so big as to impair sharpness of focus, does more than anything else to punch home the impact of this so-called opera-oratorio, with its powerful commentary, Greek-style. The singing of the two principals, Vinson Cole as Oedipus and Anne Sofie von Otter as Jocasta, then conveys the full depth of emotion behind the piece. Simon Estes as Creon and Hans Sotin as Tiresias are both firm and resonant, with Nicolai Gedda still strong as the Shepherd. With recorded sound both dramatically immediate and warm, and with splendid narration in French from Patrice Chéreau, this displaces all rivals, even the composer's own American version.

Franz Welser-Möst and the London Philharmonic take an expressive rather than a severe, neo-classical view. The singing of the men of the London Philharmonic Choir is less incisive than that of the principal rivals but is satisfyingly weighty, and the soloists are on balance the most involvingly characterful of any, led by Anthony Rolfe Johnson, magnificent as Oedipus. Esa-Pekka Salonen's Swedish performance for Sony had an exceptionally light and lyrical Oedipus in Vinson Cole, where Rolfe Johnson is not only weightily heroic but inflects words more meaningfully than any. Marjana Lipovšek brings mature warmth and weight to the role of Jocasta, easily to rival Anne Sofie von Otter on Sony, while John Tomlinson as Creon and John Mark Ainsley as the Shepherd are outstanding too. Only the brisk, prosaic French narration of Lambert Wilson sells the listener short.

Where the prize-winning stage production of *Oedipus Rex* from Japan (available on video) has Philip Langridge in the title-role, the CD offers a very similar cast but with Peter Schreier as Oedipus. Ozawa's conducting is just as warmly dramatic and powerful, and Jessye Norman's Jocasta has a commanding intensity never surpassed, with a relatively short role assuming key importance. Yet Schreier sounds too old and strained to be convincing, robbing the rest of the impact it should have. Only in his final hushed *Lux facta est* does Schreier convey full intensity, but that is hardly enough.

Stravinsky Edition, Volume 9: *The Rake's progress* (complete).
(M) *** Sony SM2K 46299 (2) [id.]. Young, Raskin, Reardon, Sarfaty, Miller, Manning, Sadler's Wells Op. Ch., RPO, composer.

The Rake's progress (complete).
**(*) Decca Dig. 411 644-2 (2) [id.]. Langridge, Pope, Walker, Ramey, Dean, Dobson, L. Sinf. Ch. & O, Chailly.

It was a splendid idea to get Stravinsky to come to London to record *The Rake's progress* in what has many elements of the original Sadler's Wells production – which incidentally the composer attended some time earlier. The casting is uniformly excellent with the Rake of Alexander Young dominating but Judith Raskin an attractive heroine. Regina Sarfaty's Baba is superbly characterized and her anger at being spurned just before the 'squelching' makes a riveting moment. The composer conducts with warmth as well as precision, both chorus and orchestra respond persuasively, and the CD transfer is excellent. A clear first choice.

Riccardo Chailly draws from the London Sinfonietta playing of a clarity and brightness to set the piece aptly on a chamber scale without reducing the power of this elaborately neo-classical work. Philip Langridge is excellent as the Rake himself, very moving when Tom is afflicted with madness. Samuel Ramey as Nick, Stafford Dean as Trulove and Sarah Walker as Baba the Turk are all first rate, but Cathryn Pope's soprano as recorded is too soft-grained for Anne. Charming as the idea is of getting the veteran Astrid Varnay to sing Mother Goose, the result is out of style. The recording is exceptionally full and vivid but the balances are sometimes odd: the orchestra recedes behind the singers and the chorus sounds congested, with little air round the sound.

Strozzi, Barbara (c. 1619–64)

Sacri musicali affetti, Libro I, *Op. 5* (extracts): *Erat Petrus; Hodie oritur; Mater Anna; Nascente Maria; O, Maria; Parasti cor meum; Salve Regina; Salve sancta caro.*

(N) ❀ *** HM Dig. ED 13048 [id.]. Maria Cristina Kiehr, Concerto Soave (with: GIANONCELLI: *Tastegiatas 1–2;* BIAGIO MARINI: *Sonate da chiesa e da camera; Sinfonia secondo tuono;* TARQUINIO MERULA: *Capriccio cromatico; Canzon***).

On the evidence of Maria Kiehr's gloriously sung recital, the Venetian Barbara Strozzi is yet another extraordinarily gifted female composer to emerge from the mists of the past, one whose music's lyrical beauty surely compares with that of Hildegard of Bingen in its soaring allure. Born in about 1619, Strozzi was the adopted daughter of the poet Giulio Strozzi, librettist for Monteverdi and Cavalli, and she became a highly regarded pupil of the latter composer. She initially made her name both as a singer and as a woman of great beauty, and her writing combines purity of feeling and line with a sensuous spiritual ecstasy that is uniquely feminine. Indeed her many Marian celebrations, with their ripely expressive chromaticism, portray the Madonna as a warm, feeling creature with whom any normal woman could identify, rather than a chaste icon. The opening *Salve Regina* with its sighing phrases and melancholy descending scale is wonderfully tender, yet the music has a life-celebrating vitality too. The motet *Erat Petrus* (the Gospel story of Peter set free from prison) is virtually an operatic scena; it matches both Cavalli and Monteverdi in its dramatic confidence, set with great rhythmic variety and using a dialogue device between 'two' voices with aplomb. The melodic line of *Mater Anna* is simple but quite lovely, and here it is a rising scale which brings a ravishing frisson. *Nascente Maria* soars richly, fluently and floridly, and then leads to rapt echoing phrases. Perhaps most remarkable of all is the ravishing F minor *Parasti cor meum*, bringing sliding chromatic glissandi – surely a perfect illustration of the Italian word, *affetti*. Maria Kiehr's singing here is unforgettable, as is her bravura decorative flair; indeed her ornamentation is a model of expressive understanding throughout. She is beautifully accompanied by the appropriately named Concerto Soave. To make the programme even more enjoyable, the vocal items are interspersed with admirably chosen intrumental pieces by Strozzi's contemporaries, featuring – as do the accompaniments – chamber organ as well as harpsichord and the usual continuo instrumentation of the time. The recording is admirably balanced and very natural. This is a treasurable collection and a musical revelation.

Suk, Josef (1874–1935)

Asrael Symphony, Op. 27.

❀ *** Chandos Dig. CHAN 9042 [id.]. Czech PO, Bělohlávek.

*** Virgin/EMI VC7 59638-2 [id.]. RLPO, Pešek.

(***) Sup. mono 11 1902-2 (2) [id.]. Czech PO, Talich (with DVORAK: *Stabat mater* (*)).

*** Panton 81 1101-2 [id.]. Bav. RSO, Kubelik.

Jiří Bělohlávek, the principal conductor of the Czech Philharmonic, draws powerfully expressive playing from the orchestra in a work which in its five large-scale movements is predominantly slow. Next to Pešek's fine Liverpool performance, the speeds flow a degree faster and more persuasively, and the ensemble, notably of the woodwind, is even crisper, phenomenally so. It helps too that the sound is warmer, closer and more involving than the refined but more distant Virgin recording.

Pešek's Liverpool version has altogether greater sensitivity and imagination than the earlier Supraphon account from Vaclav Neumann, and the sympathy of the Liverpool players is very apparent, but there is no doubt that Bělohlávek's gutsier Czech performance has a greater sense of thrust and power, and for those coming new to this fine work it will be a revelation.

Vaclav Talich's pioneering mono account from the early 1950s has great intensity of utterance and poignancy and provides a link with the composer himself. Talich knew him well and conducted many

Suk premières. The sound is very acceptable for the period, and it is a pity that it comes harnessed to a less successful *Stabat Mater*.

Kubelik's performance has all the fervour and pain of the Talich version but has much better sound, emanating from a 1981 studio recording with the Bavarian Radio Symphony Orchestra. It has great expressive refinement and a subtlety of colouring that are quite special. It is as powerful as any *Asrael* on or off record.

A Fairy-tale, Op. 16; Praga (symphonic poem), Op. 26.
*** Sup. Dig. 10 3389-2 [id.]. Czech PO, Libor Pešek.

Suk's *A Fairy-tale* is full of charm and originality, and it is persuasively played here. On this compact disc it is coupled with *Praga*, a patriotic tone-poem reflecting a more public, out-going figure than *Asrael*, which was to follow it. Libor Pešek secures an excellent response from the Czech Philharmonic; the recordings, which date from 1981–2, are reverberant but good.

A Fairy-tale, Op. 16; Serenade for strings in E flat, Op. 6.
*** Chandos Dig. CHAN 9063 [id.]. Czech PO, Jiří Bělohlávek.

This new Chandos account of the unfailingly fresh *Serenade for strings* is probably the most captivating since the days of Talich, and the Czech Philharmonic strings play with their customary warmth and eloquence. *A Fairy tale* (*Pohádka*), a somewhat earlier piece which has a lot of Strauss and Mahler in its pedigree, is beautifully played and certainly better recorded than in the earlier version Bělohlávek made with the Prague Symphony for Supraphon.

Fantasy in G min. (for violin and orchestra), Op. 24.
(N) (M) *** Sup. SU 1928-2 011 [id.]. Josef Suk, Czech PO, Karel Ančerl – DVORAK: *Violin concerto* etc. ***

Suk's *Fantasy* is a brilliant piece which relates to the traditional essays in violin wizardry as well as to the Czech nationalist tradition. The work has music of characteristic fantasy, though the rhetorical brilliance is equally strong. Suk's playing is refreshing and the orchestral accompaniment under Ančerl is no less impressive. Good remastered 1960s sound.

Fantastic Scherzo, Op. 25.
*** Chandos Dig. CHAN 8897 [id.]. Czech PO, Bělohlávek – MARTINU: *Symphony No. 6;* JANACEK: *Sinfonietta.* ***

This captivating piece brings playing from the Czech Philharmonic under Bělohlávek which is even finer than any of the earlier performances and it cannot be too strongly recommended, particularly in view of the excellence of the coupling.

Praga, Op. 28; (i) Ripening, Op. 34 (symphonic poems).
*** Virgin/EMI Dig. VC7 59318-2 [id.]. (i) RLPO Ch.; RLPO, Pešek.

Ripening came after the *Asrael Symphony* and *A Summer tale* and there is no doubt as to its imaginative resource and richness of invention. Libor Pešek and his Liverpool forces give as dedicated an account of this as one could possibly wish. *Prague*, an earlier piece from 1904, is not quite in the same league but it is still an admirable makeweight and is played with exemplary commitment. Very good recorded sound too.

Serenade for strings in E flat, Op. 6.
(BB) *** ASV CDQS 6094. Polish R. CO, Duczmal – TCHAIKOVSKY: *Serenade* ***; GRIEG: *Holberg suite.* **(*)
(BB) *** Naxos 8.550419 [id.]. Capella Istropolitana, Kr(e)chek – DVORAK: *String serenade.* **(*)
(Y/B) (M) **(*) Virgin/EMI Dig. CUV5 61144-2 [id.]. LCO, Christopher Warren-Green – DVORAK: *Serenade.* **(*)

Serenade for strings in E flat, Op. 6; Meditation on an old Czech hymn (St Wenceslas), Op. 35a.
(Y/B) (B) **(*) Discover Dig. DICD 920234 [id.]. Virtuosi di Praga, Oldřich Vlček – JANACEK: *Suite.* ***

Suk's *Serenade* is a gorgeous work and it receives a lovely performance from the Polish Radio Chamber Orchestra under Agnieszka Duczmal. The opening is immediately winning, light and gracious, yet the orchestra can produce a rich body of timbre when needed. The *Adagio* is very beautifully played indeed; it follows Suk's unusual *Allegro ma non troppo e grazioso*, which is nearly a waltz but not quite. The orchestra's sparkling articulation and subtle rhythmic feeling here are most distinctive. This is altogether first rate, and the recording is full-textured and well balanced, bringing out Duczmal's many fine shadings of colour.

On Naxos another entirely delightful account of Suk's *Serenade*, which ought to be far better known. The innocent delicacy of the opening is perfectly caught and the charm of the dance movement which follows is just as winning. The *Adagio* is played most beautifully and then, with a burst of high spirits (and excellent ensemble), the finale bustles to its conclusion with exhilarating zest. The recording is first class, fresh yet full-textured, naturally balanced and transparent.

Warren-Green and his LCO also give a wonderfully persuasive account of Suk's *Serenade*, making obvious that its inspiration is every bit as vivid as in the comparable work of Dvořák. The recording, made in All Saints', Petersham, is fresh, full and natural without blurring from the ecclesiastical acoustic. However, the original CD also included the Tchaikovsky *Serenade*, which is now missing, so even at mid-price this is not such a bargain as it looks, with only 52 minutes' playing time.

Judging by the photo-insert, the Prague Virtuosi have been somewhat expanded from the eleven soloists who made up the original group, to sixteen plus the leader/conductor, Oldřich Vlček. Certainly they create a richly full-bodied sonority here and play this music idiomatically and with ardent, expressive feeling. Some might feel that the *Serenade* benefits from a slightly more subtle and less extrovert approach, but the passionately gripping account of the *Wenceslas meditation* brings an entirely appropriate emotional intensity. Splendidly vivid recording,

PIANO MUSIC

About Mother, Op. 28; Lullabies, Op. 33; 4 Piano pieces, Op. 7; Spring, Op. 22a; Summer, Op. 22b; Things lived and dreamed, Op. 30.
*** Chandos Dig. CHAN 9026/7 [id.]. Margaret Fingerhut.

It is striking how the earliest works here have a carefree, sweetly lyrical character, gentler than Dvořák but typically Czech. Then, after the death in 1904 and 1905 of his mentor, Dvořák, and his wife (Dvořák's daughter), even these fragmentary inspirations, like the massive *Asrael Symphony*, become sharp, sometimes even abrasive. The second disc brings the finest and most ambitious of the suites in which Suk generally collected his genre pieces, *Things lived and dreamed*. Margaret Fingerhut proves a devoted advocate, playing with point and concentration, helped by full-ranging Chandos sound.

Sullivan, Arthur (1842–1900)

The Merchant of Venice (suite); *The Tempest* (incidental music).
(M) *** EMI CMS7 64412-2 (2). CBSO, Sir Vivian Dunn – *Ruddigore*. ***

The longer orchestral work, the suite of incidental music for *The Tempest*, dates from 1861, when the student composer was only nineteen. Not surprisingly it made him an overnight reputation, for it displays an astonishing flair and orchestral confidence. The shorter *Merchant of Venice* suite was composed five years later, and almost immediately the writing begins to anticipate the lively style which was so soon to find a happy marriage with Gilbert's words. The performance here is highly infectious, and the sound is first class.

(i) *Overtures: Cox and Box; Princess Ida; The Sorcerer;* (ii) *Overture in C (In Memoriam).*
(M) **(*) EMI CMS7 764409-2 (2) [Ang. CDMB 64409]. (i) Pro Arte O, Sargent; (ii) RLPO, Groves – *The Pirates of Penzance*. ***

This collects together the overtures from the operas not recorded by Sargent in his EMI series. The performances are characteristically bright and polished. *In Memoriam* is a somewhat inflated religious piece written for the 1866 Norwich Festival.

Overture Di Ballo.
(M) ** EMI CMS7 64400-2 (2). BBC SO, Sargent – *Iolanthe*. ***

Sullivan's gay, Italianate overture, felicitously scored, makes a good bonus for Sargent's *Iolanthe*. However, we are indebted to a reader for pointing out that EMI have mistakenly used Sargent's recording (which is truncated) instead of the much superior Groves/RLPO version.

Overtures: *Di Ballo; The Gondoliers; HMS Pinafore; Iolanthe; Patience; The Pirates of Penzance; Princess Ida; Ruddigore; The Sorcerer; The Yeomen of the Guard* (all arr. Geoffrey Toye).
*** Nimbus Dig. NI 5066 [id.]. SCO, Alexander Faris.

A well-played and well-recorded collection of Sullivan overtures. Mostly they are little more than potpourris, but *The Yeomen of the Guard* is an exception, and the gay *Di Ballo* is vivacious and tuneful and shows Sullivan's scoring at its most felicitous.

Pineapple Poll (ballet; arr. Mackerras).
(M) *** Decca Dig. 436 810-2 (2). Philh. O, Mackerras – *Princess Ida*. ***
(B) *** CfP CD-CFP 4618. LPO, Mackerras – VERDI: *Lady and the fool*. ***

(i) *Pineapple Poll: ballet music* (arr. Mackerras); (ii) *Savoy dances* (arr. Robinson); (i) *Overtures: Iolanthe; Mikado*.
(M) **(*) EMI CDM7 63961-2. Pro Arte O, (i) John Hollingsworth; (ii) Stanford Robinson.

On Decca Mackerras conducts with warmth as well as vivacity, and the elegantly polished playing of the Philharmonia Orchestra gives much pleasure. The record was made in the Kingsway Hall with its glowing ambience, and the CD transfer, though brightly vivid, has a pleasing bloom. Indeed the quality is in the demonstration bracket, with particularly natural string textures.

Mackerras has recorded his vivacious Sullivan arrangement several times, but this LPO version of the suite on CfP, made in the London Henry Wood Hall in 1977, is striking for its brio and warmth. With an apt Verdi coupling, this is excellent value, very well transferred to CD.

Hollingsworth offers a lively reading of *Pineapple Poll*, supported by good orchestral playing, and the slightly brash recorded quality quite suits the ebullience of the score. The upper register is over-bright but can be smoothed out. With its tuneful bonuses more smoothly done, this is enjoyable and quite good value for money. However, Mackerras's own recording of *Pineapple Poll* is even finer.

Symphony in E (Irish).
(M) *** EMI CMS7 64406-2 (2) [Ang. CDMB 64406]. RLPO, Groves – *Patience*. ***

Sullivan's *Irish Symphony* is a pleasing work, lyrical, with echoes of Schumann as much as the more predictable Mendelssohn and Schubert. The jaunty *Allegretto* of the third movement with its 'Irish' tune on the oboe is nothing less than haunting. Groves and the Royal Liverpool Philharmonic give a fresh and affectionate performance, and the CD transfer of the 1968 recording is generally well managed.

Symphony in E (Irish); Imperial march; Overture in C (In Memoriam); Victoria and Merrie England suite.
(Y/B) ** CPO Dig. CPO 999171-2 [id.]. BBC Concert O, Owain Arwel Hughes.

A well-planned and acceptably recorded but, in the last resort, disappointing collection. The first movement of the *Symphony* obstinately refuses to take off and, as Hughes observes the exposition repeat, its 16 minutes' length seems like a lifetime. The other movements are rather more successful, but in almost every way this performance is upstaged by the excellent EMI/Groves version with the Royal Liverpool Philharmonic Orchestra; if you want the symphony, that's the place to go for it. The other items here pass muster, with the ballet suite easily the most enjoyable item, especially the finale, *May Day festivities*, which might well have been an undiscovered interlude from *The Yeomen of the Guard*.

OPERAS
The major Decca and EMI sets

(i) *Cox and Box* (libretto by F. C. Burnand) complete; (ii) *Ruddigore* (complete; without dialogue).
(M) *** Decca 417 355-2 (2). (i) Styler, Riordan, Adams; New SO of L.; (ii) Reed, Round, Sandford, Riley, Adams, Hindmarsh, Knight, Sansom, Allister, D'Oyly Carte Op. Ch., ROHCG O, Godfrey.

The Gondoliers (complete; with dialogue).
(M) *** Decca 425 177-2 (2). Reed, Skitch, Sandford, Round, Styler, Knight, Toye, Sansom, Wright, D'Oyly Carte Op. Ch., New SO of L., Godfrey.

The Gondoliers (complete; without dialogue).
(M) **(*) EMI CMS7 64394-2 (2) [Ang. CDMB 64394]. Evans, Young, Brannigan, Lewis, Cameron, Milligan, Monica Sinclair, Graham, Morison, Thomas, Watts, Glyndebourne Festival Ch., Pro Arte O, Sargent.

(i; ii) *The Grand Duke*. (ii) *Henry VIII: March & Graceful dance*. (iii) *Overture Di Ballo*.
*** Decca 436 813-2 (2) [id.]. (i) John Reed, Meston Reid, Sandford, Rayner, Ayldon, Ellison, Conroy-Ward, Lilley, Holland, Goss, Metcalfe, D'Oyly Carte Op. Ch.; (ii) RPO, Nash; (iii) Philh. O, Mackerras.

HMS Pinafore (complete; with dialogue).
❀ (M) *** Decca 414 283-2. Reed, Skitch, Round, Adams, Hindmarsh, Wright, Knight, D'Oyly Carte Op. Ch., New SO of L., Godfrey.

HMS Pinafore (complete; without dialogue); *Trial by Jury*.

(M) *** EMI CMS7 64397-2 (2) [Ang. CDMB 64397]. George Baker, Cameron, Lewis, Brannigan, Milligan, Morison, Thomas, M. Sinclair, Glyndebourne Festival Ch., Pro Arte O, Sargent.

HMS Pinafore: highlights.

(B) *** Decca 436 145-2; *436 145-4* (from above D'Oyly Carte Opera recording; cond. Godfrey).

Iolanthe (complete; with dialogue).

(M) *** Decca 414 145-2; *414 145-4* (2). Sansom, Reed, Adams, Round, Sandford, Styler, Knight, Newman, D'Oyly Carte Op. Ch., Grenadier Guards Band, New SO, Godfrey.

Iolanthe (complete; without dialogue).

(M) *** EMI CMS7 64400-2 (2). George Baker, Wallace, Young, Brannigan, Cameron, M. Sinclair, Thomas, Cantelo, Harper, Morison, Glyndebourne Festival Ch., Pro Arte O, Sargent – *Di Ballo overture*. **

The Mikado (complete; without dialogue).

(M) *** Decca 425 190-2 (2). Ayldon, Wright, Reed, Sandford, Masterson, Holland, D'Oyly Carte Op. Ch., RPO, Nash.

(M) **(*) EMI CMS7 644403-2 (2) [Ang. CDMB 64403]. Brannigan, Lewis, Evans, Wallace, Cameron, Morison, Thomas, J. Sinclair, M. Sinclair, Glyndebourne Festival Ch., Pro Arte O, Sargent.

Patience (complete; with dialogue).

(M) *** Decca 425 193-2 (2). Sansom, Adams, Cartier, Potter, Reed, Sandford, Newman, Lloyd-Jones, Toye, Knight, D'Oyly Carte Op. Ch. & O, Godfrey.

Patience (complete; without dialogue).

(M) *** EMI CMS7 64406-2 (2) [Ang. CDMB 64406]. Morison, Young, George Baker, Cameron, Thomas, M. Sinclair, Harper, Harwood, Glyndebourne Festival Ch., Pro Arte O, Sargent – *Symphony*. ***

The Pirates of Penzance (complete; with dialogue).

(M) *** Decca 425 196-2; *414 286-4*. Reed, Adams, Potter, Masterson, Palmer, Brannigan, D'Oyly Carte Op. Ch., RPO, Godfrey.

The Pirates of Penzance: highlights.

(B) *** Decca 436 148-2; *436 148-4* [id.]. Reed, Adams, Brannigan, Masterson, Potter, Palmer, D'Oyly Carte Op. Co. Ch., RPO, Godfrey.

The Pirates of Penzance (complete; without dialogue).

(M) *** EMI CMS7 64409-2 (2) [Ang. CDMB 64409]. George Baker, Milligan, Cameron, Lewis, Brannigan, Morison, Harper, Thomas, Sinclair, Glyndebourne Festival Ch., Pro Arte O, Sargent – *Overtures*. **(*)

(i) *Princess Ida* (complete; without dialogue); (ii) *Pineapple Poll* (ballet; arr. Mackerras)

(M) *** Decca 436 810-2 (2) [id.]. (i) Sandford, Potter, Palmer, Skitch, Reed, Adams, Raffell, Cook, Harwood, Palmer, Hood, Masterson, D'Oyly Carte Op. Ch., RPO, Sargent; (ii) Philh. O, Mackerras.

Ruddigore (complete; without dialogue).

(M) *** EMI CMS7 64412-2 (2). Lewis, George Baker, Brannigan, Blackburn, Morison, Bowden, M. Sinclair, Harwood, Rouleau, Glyndebourne Festival Ch., Pro Arte O, Sargent – *Merchant of Venice; Tempest:* incidental music. ***

(i) *The Sorcerer* (complete, without dialogue); (ii) *The Zoo* (libretto by Bolton Rowe).

*** Decca 436 807-2 (2) [id.]. (i) Adams, David Palmer, Styler, Reed, Christene Palmer, Masterson; (ii) Reid, Sandford, Ayldon, Goss, Metcalfe; nar. Geoffrey Shovelton; (i; ii) D'Oyly Carte Op. Ch., RPO; (i) Godfrey; (ii) Nash.

(i) *Utopia Ltd* (complete). Overtures: *Macbeth; Marmion. Victoria and Merrie England*.

**(*) Decca 436 816-2 (2) [id.]. (i) Sandford, Reed, Ayldon, Ellison, Buchan, Conroy-Ward, Reid, Broad, Rayner, Wright, Porter, Field, Goss, Merri, Holland, Griffiths, D'Oyly Carte Op. Ch.; RPO, Nash.

The Yeomen of the Guard (complete; without dialogue).

(M) *** EMI CMS7 64415-2 (2) [Ang. CDMB 64415]. Dowling, Lewis, Evans, Brannigan, Morison, M. Sinclair, Glyndebourne Festival Ch., Pro Arte O, Sargent.

(i) *The Yeomen of the Guard* (complete; without dialogue); (ii) *Trial by Jury*.
(M) *** Decca 417 358-2; *417 358-4*. Hood, J. Reed, Sandford, Adams, Raffell; (i) Harwood, Knight; (ii) Round; D'Oyly Carte Op. Ch.; (i) RPO, Sargent; (ii) ROHCG O, Godfrey.

As can be seen, the two basic sets of recordings of the major Savoy Operas, nearly all from Godfrey (on Decca) and Sargent (on EMI), are now back in the catalogue at mid-price. The Decca series usually has the advantage (or disadvantage, according to taste) of including the dialogue. Certain of the operas are available only in D'Oyly Carte versions, and of these the most fascinating is *Cox and Box*. This pre-Gilbertian one-Acter is based on a play (called *Box and Cox*) with the story of two men sharing the same rooms – one is a hatter, the other works on a newspaper at night – without knowing it, so that Bouncer, the unscrupulous landlord, can collect a double rent. It was written in 1867 and thus pre-dates the first G&S success, *Trial by Jury*, by eight years. One must notice the captivating *Bacon 'Lullaby'*, so ravishingly sung by Joseph Riordan. Later on, in Box's recitative telling how he 'committed suicide', Sullivan makes one of his first and most impressive parodies of grand opera, which succeeds also in being effective in its own right. The D'Oyly Carte performance is splendid in every way. It is given a recording which, without sacrificing clarity, conveys with perfect balance the stage atmosphere.

The Grand Duke, on the other hand, was the fourteenth and last of the Savoy operas. In spite of a spectacular production and a brilliant first night on 7 March 1896, the work played for only 123 performances then lapsed into relative oblivion, although it has been revived by amateur societies. The present recording, the only complete version, came after a successful concert presentation in 1975, and the recorded performance has both polish and vigour, although the chorus does not display the crispness of articulation of ready familiarity. The recording is characteristically brilliant. The bonuses are well worth having, with Mackerras's account of the *Overture Di Ballo* showing more delicacy of approach than usual, though certainly not lacking sparkle.

Turning now to the major G&S successes, it seems sensible to consider the Decca and EMI alternatives together. EMI usually offer some orchestral bonuses and, in the case of *HMS Pinafore*, add *Trial by Jury* as well (as was the practice in the theatre in the heyday of the D'Oyly Carte Opera Company). Godfrey's Decca *Trial by Jury* is saved for inclusion with their outstanding *Yeomen of the Guard*. The Sargent version of *Trial by Jury* (with George Baker as the Judge) is by general consent the best there is, if only by a small margin, and the EMI version of *Pinafore* is wonderfully fresh too, beautifully sung throughout, while the whole of the final scene is musically quite ravishing.

But the 1960 Godfrey set of this opera is very special indeed, and *HMS Pinafore* is in our view the finest of all the D'Oyly Carte stereo recordings. While Owen Brannigan, on EMI, without the benefit of dialogue conveys the force of Dick Deadeye's personality remarkably strongly, Donald Adams's assumption of the role on Decca (which does have the dialogue) is little short of inspired, and his larger-than-life characterization underpins the whole piece. The rest of the cast make a splendid team: Jean Hindmarsh is a totally convincing Josephine – she sings with great charm – and John Reed's Sir Joseph Porter is a delight.

The D'Oyly Carte set of *The Gondoliers* has now been remastered and the quality brought up to Decca's usual high standard. The solo singing throughout is consistently good, the ensembles have plenty of spirit and the dialogue is for the most part well spoken. As a performance this is on the whole preferable to the Sargent account, if only because of the curiously slow tempo Sargent chooses for the *Cachucha*. However, on EMI there is still much to captivate the ear, and Owen Brannigan, a perfectly cast Don Alhambra, sings a masterly *No possible doubt whatever*. The age of the 1957 recording shows in the orchestra but the voices sound fresh and there is a pleasing overall bloom.

With *Iolanthe*, choice between the two alternatives is a case of swings and roundabouts. The 1960 Decca set was given added panache by the introduction of the Grenadier Guards Band into the *March of the Peers*. Mary Sansom is quite a convincing Phyllis, and if her singing has not the sense of style that Elsie Morison brings to the part, she is completely at home with the dialogue. Also Alan Styler makes a vivid and charming personal identification with the role of Strephon, an Arcadian shepherd, whereas John Cameron's dark timbre on EMI seems much less suitable for this role, even though he sings handsomely. However, on EMI the climax of Act I, the scene in which the Queen of the Fairies lays a curse on members of both Houses of Parliament, shows most excitingly what can be achieved with the 'full operatic treatment': this is a dramatic moment indeed. George Baker, too, is very good as the Lord Chancellor: the voice is fuller, more baritonal than John Reed's dryly whimsical delivery, yet he provides an equally individual characterization. Godfrey's conducting is lighter and more infectious than Sargent's in the Act I finale, but both performances offer much to delight the ear in the famous Trio of Act II with the Lord Chancellor and the two Earls.

The 1973 stereo remake of *The Mikado* by the D'Oyly Carte Company directed by Royston Nash is a complete success in every way and shows the Savoy tradition at its most attractive. It is a pity no dialogue is included, but the choral singing is first rate, and the glees are refreshingly done, polished and refined, yet with plenty of vitality. John Reed is a splendid Ko-Ko, Kenneth Sandford a vintage Pooh-Bah and Valerie Masterson a charming Yum-Yum. John Ayldon as the Mikado provides a laugh of terrifying bravura, and Lyndsie Holland is a formidable and commanding Katisha. The Sargent set, with its grand operatic style, brings some fine moments, especially in the finales to both Acts. Owen Brannigan is an inimitable Mikado and Richard Lewis sings most engagingly throughout as Nanki-Poo, while Elsie Morison is freshly persuasive as his young bride-to-be. All in all, there is much to enjoy here, but this remains very much a second choice.

Owen Brannigan was surely born to play the Sergeant of Police in *The Pirates of Penzance*, and he does so unforgettably in both the Decca and EMI sets. On Decca there is a considerable advantage in the inclusion of the dialogue, and here theatrical spontaneity is well maintained. Donald Adams is a splendid Pirate King. John Reed's portrayal of the Major General is one of his strongest roles, while Valerie Masterson is an excellent Mabel. Godfrey's conducting is as affectionate as ever, and one can hear him revelling in the many added touches of colour that are made possible when he has the RPO to play for him. Sargent's version is great fun, too. Its star is George Baker, giving a new and individual portrayal of the Major General. The opera takes a little while to warm up, but there is much to enjoy here. On balance, the Decca set is to be preferred, for Brannigan is especially vivid, and the dialogue undoubtedly adds an extra sense of the theatre.

A 62-minute selection from the vintage 1968 Decca set is self-recommending. The CD transfer is bright and lively, to the point of a degree of sibilance on the solo voices, but there is plenty of theatrical atmosphere.

Patience and *Ruddigore* were the two greatest successes of the Sargent series. Although there is no dialogue in *Patience*, there is more business than is usual in these EMI productions and a convincing theatrical atmosphere. Elsie Morison's Patience, George Baker's Bunthorne and John Cameron's Grosvenor are all admirably characterized, and the many concerted numbers beguile the ear. The extra card in the D'Oyly Carte hand is the dialogue, so important in this opera above all, with its spoken poetry; if Mary Sansom does not quite match her EMI counterpart, both Bunthorne and Grosvenor are well played, while the military numbers, led by Donald Adams in glorious voice, have an unforgettable vigour and presence. The EMI *Ruddigore* is musically superior. The whole performance is beautifully sung and Sargent's essentially lyrical approach emphasizes the associations of this delightful score with the music of Schubert. Pamela Bowden is a first-class Mad Margaret and her duet – after she has reformed – with Owen Brannigan has an irresistible gentility. The drama of the score is well managed too, and the CD transfer is first class. There is even an interesting bonus in Sullivan's Shakespearean incidental music. But here there is competition from the That's Entertainment set, which includes the original finale – see below.

The D'Oyly Carte *Ruddigore*, too, comes up surprisingly freshly, in fact better than we had remembered it, though it is a pity the dialogue was omitted. The performance includes *The battle's roar is over*, which is (for whatever reason) traditionally omitted. There is much to enjoy here (especially Gillian Knight and Donald Adams, whose *Ghosts' high noon* song is a marvellous highlight). Isidore Godfrey is his inimitable sprightly self and the chorus and orchestra are excellent. A fine traditional D'Oyly Carte set, then, brightly recorded, even if in this instance the Sargent version is generally even finer.

Princess Ida is fake feminism with a vengeance, but it makes for a very entertaining opera. Sir Malcolm Sargent is completely at home here, and his broadly lyrical approach has much to offer in this 'grandest' of the Savoy operas. Elizabeth Harwood in the name-part sings splendidly, and John Reed's irritably gruff portrayal of the irascible King Gama is memorable; he certainly is a properly 'disagreeable man'. The rest of the cast is no less strong and, with excellent teamwork from the company as a whole and a splendid recording, spacious and immediate, this has much to offer, even if Sullivan's invention is somewhat variable in quality. The CD transfer is outstanding and the 1965 recording has splendid depth and presence. As a bonus we are offered Mackerras's 1982 digital recording of his scintillating ballet score, *Pineapple Poll*. Mackerras conducts with warmth as well as vivacity, and the elegantly polished playing of the Philharmonia Orchestra gives much pleasure.

The Sorcerer is the Gilbert and Sullivan equivalent of *L'elisir d'amore*, only here a whole English village is affected, with hilarious results. John Reed's portrayal of the sorcerer himself is one of the finest of all his characterizations. The plot drew from Sullivan a great deal of music in his fey, pastoral vein. By 1966, when the set was made, Decca had stretched the recording budget to embrace the RPO, and the orchestral playing is especially fine, as is the singing of the D'Oyly Carte chorus, at their peak. John Reed gives a truly virtuoso performance of his famous introductory song, while the spell-casting scene is equally compelling. The final sequence in Act II is also memorable. The sound is well up to Decca's usual high standard and the CD transfer is first rate, full, atmospheric and with a natural presence for the voices.

Both recordings of *The Yeomen of the Guard*, Decca's and EMI's, are conducted by Sir Malcolm Sargent. Each has many merits. On EMI all the solo singing is very persuasive indeed, and the presence of Owen Brannigan as Wilfred is very much a plus point, while Monica Sinclair is a memorable Dame Carruthers. In both versions the trios and quartets with which this score abounds are most beautifully warm and polished. But the later Decca account has marginally the finer recording and Sir Malcolm's breadth of approach is immediately apparent in the *Overture*. Both chorus and orchestra (the RPO) are superbly expansive and there is again consistently fine singing from all the principals (and especially from Elizabeth Harwood as Elsie). This Decca *Yeomen* is unreservedly a success, with its brilliant and atmospheric recording. In any case, the trump card is the inclusion of Godfrey's immaculately stylish and affectionate *Trial by Jury* with John Reed as the Judge.

Utopia Ltd was first performed in 1893, ran for 245 performances and then remained unheard (except for amateur productions) until it was revived for the D'Oyly Carte centenary London season in 1974, which led to this recording. Its complete neglect is unaccountable; Gilbert's libretto shows him at his most wittily ingenious, and the idea of a utopian society *inevitably* modelled on British constitutional practice suggests Victorian self-confidence at its most engaging. Also the score offers a certain nostalgic quality in recalling earlier successes. Royston Nash shows plenty of skill in the matter of musical characterization, and the solo singing is consistently assured. When Meston Reid as Captain FitzBattleaxe sings 'You see I can't do myself justice' in *Oh, Zara*, he is far from speaking the truth – this is a performance of considerable bravura. The ensembles are not always as immaculately disciplined as one is used to from the D'Oyly Carte, and *Eagle high* is disappointingly focused: the intonation here is less than secure. However, the sparkle and spontaneity of the performance as a whole are irresistible. The CD transfer shows the 1975 recording as being of Decca's best vintage quality. Of the fillers, the *Macbeth overture* is dramatic and brightly coloured but not inspired, and the *Marmion Overture*, too, is not really memorable. The short ballet, *Victoria and Merry England*, includes some pleasing ideas but again is not top-drawer Sullivan. All are vividly played and brightly recorded.

The Zoo (with a libretto by Bolton Rowe, a pseudonym of B. C. Stevenson) dates from June 1875, only three months after the success of *Trial by Jury* – which it obviously seeks to imitate, as the music more than once reminds us. Although the libretto lacks the finesse and whimsicality of Gilbert, it is not without humour, and many of the situations presented by the plot (and indeed the actual combinations of words and music) are typical of the later Savoy Operas. As the piece has no spoken dialogue it is provided here with a stylized narration, well enough presented by Geoffrey Shovelton. The performance is first class, splendidly sung, fresh as paint and admirably recorded, and it fits very well alongside *The Sorcerer*. The CD transfer is more brightly lit than its companion, and the opera has animal noises to set the scene and close the opera.

Other complete recordings

The Gondoliers (complete; without dialogue); *Overture Di Ballo*.
*** That's Entertainment CD-TER2 1187; *ZCTED 1187* (2) [id.]. Suart, Rath, Fieldsend, Oke, Ross, Hanley, Woollett, Pert, Creasy, D'Oyly Carte Op. Ch. & O, John Pryce-Jones.

This new set of *The Gondoliers* represents a new generation of D'Oyly Carte recordings. It was recorded at Abbey Road studios in 1991, offers very good sound and speaks very well indeed for the standards of the resuscitated D'Oyly Carte company. The men are very good indeed: Marco's *Take a pair of sparkling eyes* (David Fieldsend) is fresh and stylish; Richard Suart's Duke of Plaza-Toro is as dry as you could wish, while the voice itself is resonant, and his duet in Act II with the equally excellent Duchess (Jill Pert), in which they dispense honours to the undeserving, is in the best Gilbertian tradition. Perhaps Gianetta (Lesley Echo Ross) and Casilda (Elizabeth Woollett) are less individually distinctive and slightly less vocally secure than their counterparts on the Godfrey and Sargent versions, but they always sing with charm. The chorus is first class – the men are especially virile at the opening of Act II. The orchestral playing is polished, and the ensembles are good, too; John Pryce-Jones conducts with vigour and an impressive sense of theatrical pacing. The finale brings an exhilarating closing *Cachucha* to round the opera off nicely. The acoustic of the recording has both warmth and atmosphere, the vocal balance is not too forward, yet words are remarkably clear. It is a great pity that the dialogue is not included. However, this particular opera stands up well without it.

HMS Pinafore.
(Y/B) ⊛ *** Telarc Dig. CD 80374 [id.]. Suart, Allen, Evans, Schade, Palmer, Adams, Ch. & O of Welsh Opera, Mackerras.

Sir Charles Mackerras here gives an exuberant reading of the first operetta of the cycle. The lyricism and transparency of Sullivan's inspiration shine out with winning freshness. The casting is not just starry but inspired. So in such a number as Captain Corcoran's *Fair moon to thee I sing* one relishes the pure beauty of the melody as sung by Thomas Allen, sharpened by innocent send-up in Gilbert's verses. Even such a jaunty number as the 'encore' trio, *Never mind the why and wherefore*, gains in point when so well sung and played as here, with Allen joined by Rebecca Evans as an appealing Josephine and Richard Suart as a dry Sir Joseph Porter. Michael Schade is heady-toned as the hero, Ralph Rackstraw, while among character roles Felicity Palmer is a marvellously fruity Little Buttercup, with Richard van Allan as Bill Bobstay and the veteran, Donald Adams, a lugubrious Dick Deadeye. As with the previous CDs of *Mikado* and *Pirates of Penzance*, Telarc squeezes the whole score on to a single CD, vividly recorded.

Iolanthe (complete; without dialogue). *Thespis* (orchestral suite).
**(*) That's Entertainment Dig. CD-TER2 1188; *ZCTED2 1188* (2) [id.]. Suart, Woollett, Blake Jones, Richard, Creasy, Pert, Rath, Hanley, D'Oyly Carte Opera Ch. & O, Pryce-Jones.

After the success of the new D'Oyly Carte *Gondoliers*, this fresh look at *Iolanthe* is something of a disappointment. John Pryce-Jones obviously sees it as a very dramatic opera indeed, and he ensures that the big scenes have plenty of impact (the *March of the Peers*, resplendent with brass, quite upstages the Decca version incorporating a Guards band). But his strong forward pressure means that the music feels almost always fast-paced, and the humour is completely upstaged by the drama, especially in the long Act I Finale, which is certainly zestful. The Lord Chancellor's two patter songs in Act I, *The law is the true embodiment* and *When I went to the bar*, are very brisk in feeling, and Richard Suart, an excellent Lord Chancellor, is robbed of the necessary relaxed delivery so that the words can be relished for themselves. Jill Pert is certainly a formidable Queen of the Fairies, but elsewhere the lack of charm is a distinct drawback.

(i) *Iolanthe:* highlights; (ii) *The Mikado* (complete, without dialogue).
(B) *** CfP CD-CDPD 4730; *TC-CFPD 4730* (2). (i) Shilling, Harwood, Moyle, Dowling, Begg, Bevan, Greene, Kern; (ii) Holmes, Revill, Wakefield, Studholme, Dowling, Allister, John Heddle Nash; Sadler's Wells Op. Ch. & O, Alexander Faris.

It is a shame that only highlights are available from the 1962 Sadler's Wells *Iolanthe*, making a rather piecemeal selection; but this means they will fit handily on to a pair of CDs together with the excellent complete *Mikado* from the same year. The Sadler's Wells *Iolanthe* is stylistically superior to Sargent's earlier EMI recording and is often musically superior to the Decca/D'Oyly Carte versions. Alexander Faris often chooses untraditional tempi. *When I went to the bar* is very much faster than usual, with less dignity but with a compensating lightness of touch. Eric Shilling is excellent here, as he is also in the *Nightmare song*, which is really *sung*, much being made of the ham operatic recitative at the beginning. The lovers, Elizabeth Harwood as Phyllis and Julian Moyle as Strephon, make a charming duo, and the Peers are splendid. Their entry chorus is thrilling and their reaction to the Fairy Queen's curse is delightfully, emphatically horrified, while the whole Act I finale (the finest in any of the operas) goes with infectious stylishness. All the solo singing is of a high standard and Leon Greene sings the Sentry song well. But one has to single out special praise for Patricia Kern's really lovely singing of Iolanthe's aria at the end of the opera. The recording has splendid presence and realism.

The Sadler's Wells *Mikado* is traditional in the best sense, bringing a humorous sparkle to the proceedings, which gives great delight. Clive Revill is a splendid Ko-Ko; his performance of *Tit willow* and his verse of *The flowers that bloom in the spring* (aided by a momentary touch of stereo gimmickry) have a charming individuality. John Heddle Nash is an outstanding Pish-Tush, and it is partly because of him that the *Chippy chopper* trio is so effective. Denis Dowling is a superb Pooh-Bah, and Marion Studholme a charming Yum-Yum. Jean Allister's Katisha is first rate in every way. The part is taken very seriously and she is often very dramatic; listen to the venom she puts into the word '*bravado*' in the Act I finale. Even the chorus scores a new point by their stylized singing of *Mi-ya-sa-ma*, which sounds engagingly mock-Japanese. The one disappointment is John Holmes in the name-part. He sings well but conveys little of the mock-satanic quality. But this is a small point in an otherwise magnificent set, which has a vivacious new overture arranged by Charles Mackerras.

The Mikado (complete, but without Overture).
⊛ *** Telarc Dig. CD 80284 [id.]. Donald Adams, Rolfe Johnson, Suart, McLaughlin, Palmer, Van Allan, Folwell, Welsh Nat. Op. Ch. and O, Mackerras.

With the overture omitted (not Sullivan's work) and one of the stanzas in Ko-Ko's 'little list' song (with words unpalatable today), the whole fizzing Mackerras performance is fitted on to a single, very well-filled disc. The full and immediate sound is a credit to Telarc's American engineers. The cast, with no weak link, is as starry as those in EMI's 'Glyndebourne' series of G&S recordings of thirty years ago, yet, far more than Sir Malcolm Sargent on those earlier recordings, Mackerras is electrically sharp at brisk speeds, sounding totally idiomatic and giving this most popular of the G&S operettas an irresistible freshness at high voltage. The tingling vigour of Sullivan's invention is constantly brought out, with performances from the WNO Chorus and Orchestra at once powerful and refined. With that sharpness of focus Sullivan's parodies of grand opera become more than just witty imitations. So Katisha's aria at the end of Act II, with Felicity Palmer the delectable soloist, has a Verdian depth of feeling. It is good too to hear the veteran Savoyard, Donald Adams, as firm and resonant as he was in his D'Oyly Carte recording made no less than 33 years earlier.

Ruddigore (complete recording of original score; without dialogue).
*** That's Entertainment CDTER2 1128; *ZCTED 1128* [MCA MCAD2 11010]. Hill Smith, Sandison, Davies, Ayldon, Hillman, Innocent, Hann, Ormiston, Lawlor, New Sadler's Wells Op. Ch. & O, Simon Phipps.

What is exciting about the New Sadler's Wells production of *Ruddigore* is that it includes the original finale, created by the logic of Gilbert's plot which brought *all* the ghosts back to life, rather than just the key figure. The opera is strongly cast, with Marilyn Hill Smith and David Hillman in the principal roles and Joan Davies a splendid Dame Hannah, while Harold Innocent as Sir Despard and Linda Ormiston as Mad Margaret almost steal the show. Simon Phipps conducts brightly and keeps everything moving forward, even if his pacing is not always as assured as in the classic Sargent version. The recording is first class, with fine theatrical atmosphere.

The Yeomen of the Guard (complete; with dialogue).
(N) **(*) Ph. 438 138-2 (2) [id.]. Thomas Allen, Streit, Dean, Terfel, Mackie, McNair, Collins, Rigby, ASMF and Ch., Marriner.

(i) *The Yeomen of the Guard;* (ii) *Trial by Jury* (both complete; without dialogue).
(N) *** Telarc 2CD 809404 (2) [id.]. (i) Mellor, Archer, Palmer (i; ii) Suart, Adams, Maxwell; (ii) Evans, Banks, Savidge; Welsh Nat. Op. Ch. and O, Mackerras.

Less starrily cast than Sir Neville Marriner's Philips set of *The Yeomen of the Guard*, this fourth Telarc issue of G&S is yet far more involving as a performance, conveying more exuberantly the sparkle as well as the emotional weight of this most serious of the canon. That is clearly due to the fact that all these performers, including the brilliant chorus, were involved in the Welsh National Opera's production which was brought most successfully to Covent Garden in London, the first Gilbert and Sullivan opera ever staged there. Alwyn Mellor makes a far more appealing heroine than Sylvia McNair on Philips, who was well below her best. Among the others, Felicity Palmer makes a delectably fire-snorting Dame Carruthers, and the veteran, Donald Adams, an incomparable Sergeant Meryll. (His cries of 'Ghastly, ghastly' when cornered by the Dame are wonderful.) Richard Suart as Jack Point may be far less effective vocally than Thomas Allen, but he characterizes vividly in authentic style, and the only weak link is the Fairfax of Neil Archer, who too often sounds strained. Even so, the final bringing-together of Fairfax and Elsie could not be more touching. The absence of spoken dialogue allows *Trial by Jury* to be included as a fill-up, with Suart even more aptly cast and Adams again incomparable as the Usher, while the WNO Chorus again sings with ideal clarity. Otherwise it involves different singers, with Rebecca Evans golden-toned as the Plaintiff and Barry Banks firm if light as the Defendant.

Sir Neville Marriner conducts an immaculate performance of the most serious of the G&S canon. It is cast from strength but fails to capture the exuberance and fun in the writing that Mackerras's WNO performance does. It is good to have Thomas Allen as Jack Point, singing beautifully and giving emotional weight to the rejected clown in love with the heroine. The excellent Mozart tenor, Kurt Streit, makes an impressive hero, and even the smallest roles are taken by singers of the calibre of Bryn Terfel, Neil Mackie and Judith Howarth. The big disappointment is the way Sylvia McNair's usually sweet soprano is caught in the role of Elsie: often sour with suspect intonation. Spoken dialogue is included, which for some will be a deciding factor.

'Gilbert and Sullivan classics': Arias, duets and trios from: *The Gondoliers; The Grand Duke; Haddon Hall; HMS Pinafore; Iolanthe; The Mikado; Patience; The Pirates of Penzance; Ruddigore; The Sorcerer; The Yeomen of the Guard.*
(M) *** EMI CDM7 64393-2 [id.]. Valerie Masterson, Sheila Armstrong, Robert Tear, Benjamin Luxon, Bournemouth Sinf., Alwyn; or N. Sinfonia, Hickox.

This collection combines the best part of two recitals of G&S, the first made by Valerie Masterson and Robert Tear with Kenneth Alwyn in 1982 and recorded at the Guildhall, Southampton, and the second, in which the balance is even more realistic, in EMI's No. 1 Studio at Abbey Road, with Sheila Armstrong, Tear and Benjamin Luxon under the direction of Richard Hickox in 1984. Quite apart from the excellence of the singing and the sparkling accompaniments, the programme is notable for the clever choice of material, with items from different operas engagingly juxtaposed instead of being just gathered together in sequence. The singing from the first group is particularly fine. Valerie Masterson's upper range is ravishingly fresh and free and she sings Yum-Yum's famous song from *The Mikado, The sun, whose rays*, with a captivating, ingenuous charm. Robert Tear too is in excellent form and his *A wandering minstrel* is wonderfully stylish, while *A magnet hung in a hardware shop* has fine sparkle. The *Prithee, pretty maiden* duet (also from *Patience*) is hardly less endearing. In the second recital it is the ensemble items that score, notably the duets from *Ruddigore, The Gondoliers* and the vivacious *Hereupon we're both agreed* from *The Yeomen of the Guard*; the star here is Benjamin Luxon. He is left to end the concert superbly with a bravura account of *My name is John Wellington Wells* from *The Sorcerer* and a splendidly timed, beguilingly relaxed account of *When you find you're a broken-down critter* from *The Grand Duke*. The current CD transfer seems at times to add a bit of edge to the voices but this is not too serious.

Highlights from: *The Gondoliers; H M S Pinafore; Iolanthe; The Mikado; The Pirates of Penzance; The Yeomen of the Guard.*
(B) **(*) CfP CD-CFP 4238; *TC-CFP 40238* [id.]. Soloists, Glyndebourne Festival Ch., Pro Arte O, Sargent.

Another attractive selection of highlights offering samples of six of Sargent's vintage EMI recordings. There is some distinguished solo singing and, if the atmosphere is sometimes a little cosy, there is a great deal to enjoy. The recordings have transferred well.

'*The world of Gilbert and Sullivan*': excerpts from: (i) *The Gondoliers; H M S Pinafore; Iolanthe;* (ii) *The Mikado;* (i) *The Pirates of Penzance;* (iii) *The Yeomen of the Guard.*
(M) *** Decca 430 095-2; *430 095-4.* Soloists, D'Oyly Carte Op. Co., New SO or RPO, (i) Godfrey; (ii) Nash; (iii) Sargent.

A quite admirable selection from the vintage series of Decca D'Oyly Carte recordings, with John Reed shining brightly as Koko and Sir Joseph Porter, KCB, in *Pinafore*. Owen Brannigan's unforgettable portrayal of the Sergeant of Police is demonstrated in the excerpts from *The Pirates of Penzance* (as is Valerie Masterson's charming Mabel), and two of the most delectable items are the Second Act trios from *Pinafore* and *Iolanthe*, both liltingly infectious.

'*The world of Gilbert and Sullivan*' Vol. 2: excerpts from: (i) *The Gondoliers; H M S Pinafore; Iolanthe;* (ii) *The Mikado;* (i) *Patience; The Pirates of Penzance;* (iii) *Princess Ida;* (i) *Ruddigore; The Sorcerer;* (iii) *The Yeomen of the Guard.*
(M) *** Decca 433 868-2; *433 868-4* [id.]. Soloists, D'Oyly Carte Op. Co. Ch., New SO, RPO or ROHCG O, (i) Godfrey; (ii) Nash; (iii) Sargent.

Volume 2 covers the ten most popular operas and includes ensembles as well as solo items. As ever, John Reed's contribution is outstanding in *Patience, Ruddigore* (where his role is more lyrical) and especially in *The Sorcerer* (a virtuoso *My name is John Wellington Wells*) and the delicious *If you give me your attention* from *Princess Ida*. But there is plenty to enjoy here, and Donald Adams's *Ghosts' high noon* song from *Ruddigore* is unforgettable. Lively recording with plenty of theatrical atmosphere.

Highlights from: (i; ii) *H M S Pinafore;* (iii; iv) *The Mikado;* (ii; iv; v) *The Pirates of Penzance;* (ii; vi) *Trial by Jury;* (vii) *The Yeomen of the Guard.*
(N) *** Telarc Dig. CD 80431 [id.]. Richard Suart, with (i) Thomas Allen, Felicity Palmer; (ii) Rebecca Evans; (iii) Anthony Rolfe Johnson, Marie McLaughlin, Anne Howells, Janice Watson; (iv) Richard van Allan, Nicholas Folwell; (v) John Mark Ainsley, Julia Gossage; (vi) Barry Banks, Eric Garrett, Peter Savidge, Gareth Rhys Davies; (vii) Neil Archer, Alwyn Mellor, Pamela Helen Stephen; Welsh Nat. Op. Ch. & O, Mackerras.

Even with 76 minutes' playing time, this can be no more than a sampler of Mackerras's effervescent G&S series for Telarc, dominated by the dry-timbred Richard Suart in the key patrician roles. As can be seen, most of the other soloists change with each opera, but the standard remains extraordinarily high. The choice of excerpts is inevitably arbitrary with about half-a-dozen items from each of the two-Act operas and three from *Trial by Jury*. If you buy this, you will inevitably be tempted to go on to one or other of the complete sets. Nevertheless it is a splendid collection in its own right. Characteristically first-class Telarc sound.

Suppé, Franz von (1819–95)

Complete overtures

Volume 1: Overtures: *Carnival; Die Frau Meisterin; Irrfahrt um's Glück (Fortune's Labyrinth); The Jolly Robbers (Banditenstreiche); Pique Dame; Poet and Peasant; Des Wanderers Ziel (The Goal of the Wanderers). Boccaccio: Minuet & Tarantella. Donna Juanita: Juanita march.*
(Y/B) ** Marco Polo Dig. 8.223647 [id.]. Slovak State PO (Košice), Alfred Walter.

Volume 2: Overtures: *Beautiful Galatea (Die schöne Galatea); Boccaccio; Donna Juanita; Isabella; Der Krämer und sein Kommis (The Shopkeeper and his Assistant); Das Modell (The Model); Paragraph 3; Tantalusqualen. Fatinitza march.*
(Y/B) ** Marco Polo Dig. 8.223648 [id.]. Slovak State PO (Košice), Alfred Walter.

Volume 3: Overtures: *Fatinitza; Franz Schubert; Die Heimkehr von der Hochzeit (Homecoming from the wedding); Light Cavalry; Trioche and Cacolet; Triumph. Boccaccio: March. Herzenseintracht polka; Humorous variations on 'Was kommt dort von der Höh'; Titania waltz.*
(Y/B) ** Marco Polo Dig. 8.223683 [id.]. Slovak State PO (Košice), Alfred Walter.

Alfred Walter and Marco Polo, already well on the way towards completing their Johann Strauss Edition, now turn their attention to another composer who made a successful career in Vienna. Yet, in spite of his very German name, Franz von Suppé had a Belgian father and grandfather – though his mother was Viennese-born. In 1840 he made his début as an 'honorary' conductor in the Josefstadt Theatre; his first successful stage work dates from a year later. But it was not until 1860 that he began writing his inconsequential Viennese operettas, and most of his famous overtures (all that have survived of this output outside Vienna) date from the 1860s. *Poet and Peasant* (of which countless arrangements were made) predates the others and was written well before 1846, when the comedy with songs, to which it was finally appended, first appeared.

Walter's performances here are unsubtle, but they have a rumbustious vigour that is endearing and, with enthusiastic playing from the Slovak Orchestra who are obviously enjoying themselves, the effect is never less than spirited. Many of the finest of the lesser-known pieces are already available in more imaginative versions from Marriner – see below. But Walter has uncovered some attractive novelties, as well as some pleasing if inconsequential interludes and dances. On Volume I, *Carnival* (nothing like Dvořák's piece), opens rather solemnly, then introduces a string of ideas, including a polka, a waltz and a galop. *Die Frau Meisterin* also produces an engaging little waltz. *Des Wanderers Ziel* begins very energetically and, after brief harp roulades, produces a rather solemn cello solo and brass choir; later there is an attractive lyrical melody, but there are plenty of histrionics too, and the dancing ending brings distinctly Rossinian influences.

In Volume II *Isabella* is introduced as a sprightly Spanish lady, but Viennese influences still keep popping up, while *Paragraph 3* summons the listener with a brief horn-call and then has another striking lyrical theme, before gaiety takes over. *Das Krämer und sein Kommis* proves to be an early version (the ear notices a slight difference at the dramatic opening) of an old friend, *Morning, noon and night in Vienna*. *Donna Juanita* brings a violin solo of some temperament; then, after some agreeably chattering woodwind, comes a grand march.

On the third CD, *Tricoche and Cacolet* immediately introduces a skipping tune of great charm and, after another of Suppé's appealing lyrical themes, ends with much rhythmic vigour. The biographical operetta about *Schubert* opens with an atmospheric, half-sinister reference to the *Erlkönig* and follows with further quotations, prettily scored; however, the writing coarsens somewhat vulgarly at the end. But the prize item here is a set of extremely ingenuous variations on a local folksong, which translates as *What comes there from on high?*. It seems like a cross between '*A hunting we will go*' and '*The Grand old Duke of York*'.

Overtures: *Beautiful Galathea; Boccaccio; Light cavalry; Morning, noon and night in Vienna; Pique dame; Poet and peasant.*
(M) *** Mercury 434 309-2 [id.]. Detroit SO, Paul Paray – AUBER: *Overtures.* *** ✿

Listening to Paray, one discovers a verve and exhilaration that are wholly Gallic in spirit. His chimerical approach to *Beautiful Galathea* (with a wonderfully luminous passage from the Detroit strings near the very opening) is captivating, and the bravura violin playing in *Light Cavalry* is remarkably deft. With its splendid Auber coupling this is one of Mercury's most desirable reissues.

Overtures: *Beautiful Galathea; Fatinitza; Flotte Bursche; Jolly robbers; Light Cavalry; Morning, noon and night in Vienna; Pique dame; Poet and peasant. March: O du mein Osterreich.*
(BB) **(*) LaserLight Dig. 15 611 [id.]. Hungarian State Op. O, János Sándor.

Sándor's LaserLight collection is very generous and the Hungarian State Opera Orchestra know just how to play this repertoire: the *zigeuner* section in the middle of *Light Cavalry* is most winning, while the cello solo in *Morning, noon and night* has an attractive, romantic simplicity. Sándor offers two extra novelties in *Flotte Bursche* (which brings an amiable quotation of *Gaudeamus igitur*) and a vivid Viennese-style march. The digital recording is basically full-bodied but has brilliance too, and this is a real bargain.

Overtures: *Beautiful Galathea; Fatinitza; Jolly robbers; Light cavalry; Morning, noon and night in Vienna; Pique dame; Poet and peasant.*
*** Decca Dig. 414 408-2 [id.]. Montreal SO, Dutoit.

Dutoit's pacing is splendid, combining warmth and geniality with brilliance and wit, as in the closing *galop* of *Fatinitza*. The orchestral playing is admirably polished, the violins sounding comfortable even in the virtuoso passages of *Light cavalry*, one of the most infectious of the performances here. It is difficult to imagine these being bettered, while the Decca sound is superb, well up to the usual Montreal standards.

Overtures: *Beautiful Galathea; Jolly robbers; Light cavalry; Morning, noon and night in Vienna; Pique dame; Poet and peasant.*
*** BMG/Eurodisc RD 69037. RPO, Gustav Kuhn.

Kuhn takes this music very seriously indeed, lavishing care over every detail. Tempi are spacious, consistently slower than normal, but the effect is not to rob the music of vitality, merely to add to its stature. In the lyrical sections he conjures the most beautiful, expansive playing from the RPO, yet he can be racy in the *galops*, while not rushing the music off its feet. The richly upholstered recording, made in St Barnabas' Church, London, seems exactly right for the music-making.

Overtures: *Die Frau Meisterin; Die Irrfahrt um's Glück; Light cavalry; Morning, noon and night in Vienna; Pique Dame; Poet and Peasant; Tantalusqualen; Wiener-Jubel (Viennese Jubilee).*
⊛ *** EMI Dig. CDC7 54056-2 [id.]. ASMF, Marriner.

Marriner's collection of Suppé *Overtures* goes straight to the top of the list. It is expansively recorded in EMI's No. 1 Studio and, played up to concert volume on big speakers, it produces the most spectacular demonstration quality. The sound has bloom, a wide amplitude, plenty of sparkle and a natural presence. The performances have tremendous exuberance and style: this is one of Marriner's very best records. The novelties are delightful. *Die Irrfahrt um's Glück* – concerned with magical goings-on – has a massively portentous opening, superbly realized here; *Die Frau Meisterin* produces a deliciously jiggy waltz tune, and *Wiener-Jubel*, after opening with resplendent fanfares, is as racy as you could wish. Not to be missed.

Svendsen, Johan Severin (1840–1911)

Romance in G, Op. 26.
(BB) *** Naxos Dig. 8.550329 [id.]. Dong-Suk Kang, Slovak (Bratislava) RSO, Adrian Leaper – HAL-
VORSEN: *Air Norvégien* etc.; SIBELIUS: *Violin concerto;* SINDING: *Légende.* ***

Dong-Suk Kang plays Svendsen's once-popular *Romance in G* without sentimentality but with full-hearted lyricism. The balance places him a little too forward, but the recording is very satisfactory.

Symphonies Nos. 1–2; 2 Swedish folk-melodies, Op. 27.
*** BIS Dig. CD 347 [id.]. Gothenburg SO, Neeme Järvi.

Svendsen excelled (where Grieg did not) in the larger forms and, as befits a conductor, was a master of the orchestra. The *D major Symphony* is a student work of astonishing assurance and freshness, in some ways even more remarkable than the *B flat*. Neeme Järvi is a splendid guide to this terrain; these are first-class performances, sensitive and vital, and the excellent recordings earn them a strong recommendation.

Symphony No. 2 in B flat, Op. 15; Carnival in Paris, Op. 9; Norwegian Artists Carnival, Op. 14; Norwegian Rhapsody No. 2, Op. 19; (i) *Romance in G, for violin and orchestra, Op. 26.*
**(*) Chatsworth Dig. FCM1002 [id.]. (i) Marianne Thorsen; Stavanger SO, Grant Llewellyn.

This Stavanger account of the *Second Symphony* and other popular Svendsen pieces under the Welsh conductor, Grant Llewelyn, is certainly worth considering. The orchestra plays with all the freshness and enthusiasm this captivating music calls for and, though the strings do not have the depth of sonority of their Gothenburg rivals, they produce a very decent sound. The 21-year-old Marianne Thorsen, a pupil of György Pauk, plays with an unaffected simplicity and purity that is most appealing. The recording has the advantage of clean, well-balanced sound with good perspective and presence.

Octet in A, Op. 3; (i) *Romance in G for violin and strings, Op. 26.*
*** Chandos Dig. CHAN 9258 [id.]. (i) Sillito; ASMF Ens. – NIELSEN: *String quintet in G.* ***

Svendsen's youthful *Octet*, Op. 3, a product of his student years at Leipzig, has a strong personality of its own and is full of lively and attractive invention. The Scherzo is particularly delightful. It is beautifully played by the Academy of St Martin-in-the-Fields Chamber Ensemble, whose leader, Kenneth Sillito, is the soloist in the *G major Romance*, composed not long before Svendsen abandoned composition to become what nowadays we would call a 'star' conductor. Three-star performances and recording.

Sweelinck, Jan (1562–1621)

Ballo del Granduca; Echo fantasia; Engelsche Fortuyn; Puer nobis nascitur.
*** Chandos Dig. CHAN 0514 [id.]. Piet Klee (organ of St Laurens Church, Alkmaar) – BUXTEHUDE: *Collection.* ***

Sweelinck lived during the Dutch Golden Age and was a contemporary of Rembrandt. His music is colourful and appealing, and it could hardly be better represented than in this engaging 'suite' of four contrasted pieces, three of which are based on melodies by others. Piet Klee is a very sympathetic advocate and he is given a recording of demonstration standard.

Szymanowski, Karol (1882–1937)

(i) *Violin concerto No. 2, Op. 62;* (ii) *Symphonies Nos. 2, Op. 19;* (iii) *3 (Song of the night), Op. 7.*
(N) (B) **(*) Decca Double Dig. 448 258-2 (2) [id.]. (i) Juillet, Montreal SO, Dutoit; (ii) Detroit SO, Dorati; (iii) with Karczykowski, Jewell Ch. – LUTOSLAWSKI: *Concerto for orchestra* etc. **(*)

Chantal Juillet is a selfless and dedicated interpreter of the *Second Violin concerto* and she is truthfully balanced. Indeed the engineers might have helped her a little, for her small tone does not always sing through Szymanowski's opulently coloured textures. But the orchestral detail emerges with great fidelity and Dutoit's conducting is unfailingly sympathetic. So is Dorati in the two symphonies, and the Decca recording is better detailed than the competing EMI version, with the richness of Szymanowski's textures fully revealed and the chorus clear and well balanced in No. 3. If the Polish performances are in some ways more penetrating, there is no doubting the superiority of the Decca sound.

Symphonies Nos. 1 in F min., Op. 15; 2 in B flat, Op. 19.
** Marco Polo Dig. 8.223248 [id.]. Polish State PO, Stryja.

Neither of Szymanowski's early symphonies is characteristic. The incomplete *First* is undoubtedly a congested and derivative score – as, for that matter, is the more familiar *Symphony No. 2*, which leaves no doubt as to the composer's interest in Strauss and Reger. The withdrawn Dorati recording (Decca) did greater justice to the complex textures of this score, but nevertheless this is well balanced and well played.

Symphonies Nos. (i) *2;* (ii) *3;* (i) *Concert overture in E, Op. 12.*
(M) *** EMI CDM7 65082-2 [id.]. Polish R. Nat. SO; (i) cond. Jacek Kasprzyk; (ii) Wieslaw Ochman, Polish R. Ch. of Krakow, cond. Jerzy Semkow.

The *Second* is not as rewarding a score as the *Third*, but it is unusual in form: there are only two movements, the second being a set of variations culminating in a fugue. The influences of Strauss and Scriabin are clearly audible and not altogether assimilated. *The Song of the night* is one of the composer's most beautiful scores with its heady, intoxicated – and intoxicating – atmosphere. The Polish Radio recordings on EMI date from 1982 and the performances are the most atmospheric and sensitive currently available. The recording is expansive and has impressive atmosphere. The EMI disc also includes a gripping account of the ambitious *Concert overture*, for all the world like an undiscovered symphonic poem by Richard Strauss.

Symphonies Nos. (i) *3 (Song of the Night), Op. 27;* (ii) *4 (Symphonie concertante), Op. 60.*
(N) (M) **(*) BBC Radio Classics BBCRD 9124 [id.]. BBC SO, with (i) Philip Langridge, BBC Singers & Symphony Ch., Del Mar; (ii) Piotr Paleczny, Elder – PANUFNIK: *Symphony No. 8.* **(*)

(i) *Symphony No. 3 (Song of the Night)*; (ii) *Symphony No. 4 (Sinfonia concertante)*; *Concert overture.*
**(*) Marco Polo Dig. 8.223290 [id.]. (i) Ochman, Polish State Philharmonic Ch.; (ii) Taduesz Zmudzinski, Katowice Polish State PO, Karol Stryja.

Both BBC performances come from 1983, the year after the centenary celebrations when the BBC surveyed almost the whole of Szymanowski's output in the course of 22 programmes. The *Third Symphony* or *Song of the Night* comes from the last night of the Proms season, and the *Symphonie concertante* for piano and orchestra was given earlier in the same year at the Royal Festival Hall. Piotr Paleczny is a sensitive and masterly exponent of the concertante part, having recorded it commercially for the EMI/Polish Radio & TV set of the previous year (see below). The acoustic is naturally drier but the results are artistically as convincing, and those wanting these fascinating and rewarding scores need not hesitate.

The Marco Polo version of the *Third Symphony* (but not the *Fourth*) has the advantage of good, well-detailed sound in a resonant hall and Karol Stryja succeeds in getting plenty of atmosphere in No. 3. He uses a tenor rather than a soprano, but his choir is not first class. The *Sinfonia concertante* is not ideally balanced, but the pianist, Taduesz Zmudzinski, plays with refinement and sensitivity, as witness the opening of the *Andante*, which is quite magical. The Straussian *Concert overture* makes a useful make-weight, though the recording is over-resonant and the balance synthetic.

(i) *Symphony No. 3 (Song of the night)*, *Op. 27*; (ii) *Litania do Marii Pany, Op. 59*; (iii) *Stabat Mater, Op. 53*.
(Y/B) *** EMI Dig. CDC5 55121-2 [id.]. (i) Jon Garrison; (ii–iii) Elzbieta Szmytka; (iii) Florence Quivar, John Connell; CBSO Ch., CBSO, Rattle.

Given his sympathetic feeling for Janáček and Nielsen, it was only a matter of time before Simon Rattle turned to another composer with a keen feeling for nature and for the earth. Szymanowski also has that fastidious ear for texture and heightened sense of vision that distinguish mystics, and nowhere is atmosphere more potent than in the *Third Symphony*, the *Song of the night*. Sir Simon is equally committed and persuasive in the *Stabat Mater*, these days a standard coupling, and one of the unequivocally great choral works of the century. These are very good performances and the sumptuous and finely detailed recording is absolutely state-of-the-art.

(i) *Symphony No. 4 (Symphonie concertante)*, *Op. 60*; (ii) *Harnasie* (ballet pantomime), *Op. 55*.
(Y/B) (M) **(*) EMI CDM5 65307-2 [id.]. (i) Piotr Paleczny, Polish Nat. RSO, Jerzy Semkow; (ii) Bachleda, Kwasny, Krakow Polish R. Ch. & SO, Antoni Wit.

Piotr Paleczny is no mean artist and he has all the finesse and imagination as well as the requisite command of colour that the *Symphonie concertante* calls for; Wit provides him with admirable support. On the whole this makes an even stronger impression than the alternative performance on Marco Polo, which anyway is differently coupled. *Harnasie* is also very successful: it reflects Szymanowski's discovery of the folk music of the Tatras. It calls for large forces, including a solo violinist as well as a tenor and full chorus, and poses obvious practical production problems. As always with this composer, there is the sense of rapture, the soaring, ecstatic lines and the intoxicating exoticism that distinguish the mature Szymanowski, and it comes across most tellingly here. The only snag is that the sound, though spaciously wide-ranging, is made a bit fierce on top by the CD remastering.

String quartets Nos. 1 in C, Op. 37; 2, Op. 56.
❀ *** Denon Dig. CO 79462 [id.]. Carmina Qt – WEBERN: *Slow movement for string quartet.* *** ❀
*** Olympia OCD 328 [id.]. Varsovia Qt – LUTOSLAWSKI: *Quartet;* PENDERECKI: *Quartet No. 2.* ***

The Carmina Quartet provides outstanding music-making and is recorded with the utmost realism and fidelity. The opening of the *Second* has always seemed like being in a magical moonlit landscape listening to the Ravel quartet in the distance, and the Carmina succeed in evoking this whispered dreamlike quality to perfection.

The Varsovia Quartet have impeccable intonation and splendid sonority. Theirs are subtle and deeply felt performances. There are glorious things in both works, and the Varsovia play marvellously throughout.

Mythes, Op. 30; Kurpian folk song; King Roger: Roxana's aria (both arr. Kochanski).
❀ (M) *** DG 431 469-2. Kaja Danczowska, Krystian Zimerman – FRANCK: *Violin sonata.* ***

Kaja Danczowska brings vision and poetry to the ecstatic, soaring lines of the opening movement of *Mythes, The Fountains of Arethusa.* Her intonation is impeccable, and she has the measure of these other-worldly, intoxicating scores. There is a sense of rapture here that is totally persuasive, and Krystian Zimerman plays with a virtuosity and imagination that silence criticism. An indispensable issue.

Violin sonata in D min., Op. 9; Mythes, Op. 30; Nocturne and tarantella, Op. 28.
*** Chandos Dig. CHAN 8747 [id.]. Lydia Mordkovitch, Marina Gusk-Grin.

The *Violin sonata in D minor* is an early work, very much in the received tradition; but with the *Mythes* and the *Nocturne and tarantella* the influence of Brahms and Franck has completely gone and we are in a totally different and wholly individual sound-world. Lydia Mordkovitch is ideally attuned to this sensibility and plays both the *Sonata* and the later works beautifully, and she is sensitively partnered by Marina Gusk-Grin. This can be recommended, though this account of the *Mythes* does not displace Danczowska and Zimerman.

PIANO MUSIC

4 Etudes, Op. 4; 12 Etudes, Op. 33; 2 Mazurkas, Op. 62; Shéhérezade (Masques), Op. 34; Variations on a Polish theme, Op. 10.
(M) ** Channel Classics Dig. CDG 9110 [id.]. Arielle Vernède.

In the repertoire that overlaps Dennis Lee's masterly Hyperion anthology, Arielle Vernède offers little real challenge, though her playing is far from wanting in distinction and character. His recital does not include the Op. 10 *Variations* or the demanding but (it must be admitted) unrewarding Op. 33 *Etudes*, and this mid-price CD can be thought of as a useful supplement but not an alternative to the Hyperion CD.

4 Etudes, Op. 4; Fantasy, Op. 14; Masques, Op. 34; Métopes, Op. 29.
*** Hyperion Dig. CDA 66409 [id.]. Dennis Lee.

Dennis Lee not only encompasses the technical hurdles of *Masques* and *Métopes* with dazzling virtuosity but also provides the keenest artistic insights. His Hyperion CD is quite simply the finest record of Szymanowski's piano music to have appeared to date; he conveys the exoticism and hothouse atmosphere of these pieces; moreover he handles the early Chopinesque *Etudes* and the *Fantasy* with much the same feeling for characterization and artistry. The Hyperion sound is very good indeed.

VOCAL MUSIC

(i) *Demeter, Op. 37b; Litany to the Virgin Mary, Op. 59;* (ii) *Penthesilea, Op. 18;* (iii) *Stabat Mater;* (iv) *Veni Creator, Op. 57.*
*** Marco Polo Dig. 8.223293 [id.]. (i) Roma Owsinska; (ii) Anna Malewicz-Madej; (iii) Jadwiga Gadulanka, Krystyna Szostek-Radkova, Andrzej Hiolski; (iv) Barbara Zagórzanka; Polish State PO & Ch., Katowice, Karol Stryja.

Szymanowski's *Stabat Mater* is not only one of his greatest achievements but one of the greatest choral works of the present century. This welcome account has the advantage of highly sensitive conducting and an excellent response from the orchestra, but some of the solo singing is less distinguished, and Jadwiga Gadulanka's intonation is less than perfect. The *Litany to the Virgin Mary* is another late work of great poignancy; but *Demeter*, composed not long after the *Violin concerto* and the *Third Symphony*, has the same exotic, almost hallucinatory textures that distinguish these works. It is all heady and intoxicating stuff, and not to be missed by those with a taste for this wonderful composer.

(i) *3 Fragments of the poems by Jan Kasprowicz, Op. 5;* (ii) *Love songs of Hafiz, Op. 24;* (iii) *Songs of the fairy-tale princess, Op. 31;* (iv) *Songs of the infatuated muezzin, Op. 42.*
*** Schwann Dig. CD 314 001 [id.]. (i) Krystyna Szostek-Radkova; (ii) Krystyna Rorbach; (iii) Izabella Klosińska; (iv) Barbara Zagórzanka, Polish Nat. Op. O, Satanowski.

In the *Songs of the fairy-tale princess*, one feels that Szymanowski must have known Stravinsky's *Le Rossignol* – Izabella Klosińska certainly sings like one. All the singing is very good, but Barbara Zagórzanka in the imaginative *Songs of the infatuated muezzin* deserves special mention. Satanowski achieves marvellously exotic and heady atmosphere throughout, and the recording is excellent.

(i) *3 Fragments of the poems by Jan Kasprowicz, Op. 5;* (ii) *Love songs of Hafiz, Op. 24;* (iii) *Songs of the fairy-tale princess, Op. 31;* (iv) *Songs of the infatuated muezzin, Op. 42;* (v) *King Roger: Roxana's Song.*
**(*) Marco Polo Dig. 8.223294. (i) Anna Malewicz-Madej; (ii & iv) Ryszard Minkiewicz; (iii) Jadwiga Gadulanka; (v) Barbara Zagórzanka; Katowice Polish State PO, Karol Stryja.

On Marco Polo, both the *Songs of the infatuated muezzin* and the *Love songs of Hafiz* are sung by a tenor (Ryszard Minkiewicz) with impressive insight, but the 1989 recording is more resonant and does not flatter him. Jadwiga Gadulanka is hardly less impressive than Klosińska in the extraordinary *Songs of the fairy-tale princess* and Barbara Zagórzanka sings the famous *Chant de Roxane* beautifully, and both she and Anna Malewicz-Madej in the Kasprowicz songs are very well balanced.

STAGE WORKS

(i) *Harnasie, Op. 55;* (ii) *Mandragora, Op. 43.*
*** Schwann Musica Mundi/Koch Dig. 311064. (i) Jozef Stépień; (ii) Paulus Raptus; (i) Polish Nat. Op. Ch.; Polish Nat. Op. O, Robert Satanowski.

Robert Satanowski's version of Szymanowski's choral ballet, *Harnasie*, is the best so far. It is an opulent score and, like the Op. 50 *Mazurkas*, is the product of the composer's encounter with the folk music of the Gorá mountains. It is richly coloured and luxuriant in texture and has a powerfully heady atmosphere. Full justice is done to its opulence and character in this excellent performance. *Mandragora* is a harlequinade for chamber forces, and the performance is persuasive. Both works are very well served by the engineers. A most valuable addition to the catalogue.

(i) *King Roger* (opera; complete); (ii) *Prince Potemkin: incidental music to Act V.*
(Y/B) *(*) Marco Polo Dig. 8.223339/40 [id.]. Hiolski, Ochman, Zagórzanka, Grychnik, Mróz, Malewicz-Madey, Cracow Philh. Boys' Ch., Polish State Philh. Ch. & O (Katowice), Karol Stryja; (ii) Polish Nat. RSO (Katowice), Antoni Wit.

King Roger has one of the most inspired and awe-inspiring openings in all twentieth-century opera and in Roxana's aria one of the most captivating and haunting of musical ideas. Its first Act, still composed in the exotic, heavily scented and heady atmosphere of the *First Violin concerto* and the *Song of the night*, is at variance with the sparer textures of his later folk-inflected idiom, which surfaces in the last part of the opera. There is some good singing from the Roxana of Barbara Zagórzanka and the Shepherd of Wieslaw Ochman, though it must be conceded that Andrzej Hiolski in the title-role is no longer as fresh-timbred or well-focused vocally as he was in Muza's pioneering LP version from the 1960s. But all this is academic, since the *sine qua non* of any *King Roger* is atmosphere – and this Marco Polo alternative has all too little.

Taffanel, Paul (1844–1908)

Wind quintet in G min.
*** Sony Dig. CD 45996. Ens. Wien-Berlin – NIELSEN: *Wind quintet.* ***

This quintet is an urbane, expertly fashioned piece by a musician of obvious culture who knows how to pace the flow of his ideas. The Ensemble Wien-Berlin play it with the utmost persuasion and charm, but this is a very lightweight companion to the Nielsen masterpiece.

Takemitsu, Toru (1930–96)

To the edge of dream.
*** EMI Dig. CDC7 54661-2 [id.]. Julian Bream, CBSO, Rattle – RODRIGO: *Concierto de Aranjuez;* ARNOLD: *Guitar concerto.* ***

A highly sympathetic account of Takemitsu's hypnotically evocative concertante work, using a large orchestra with great economy so as never to overwhelm the soloist. The music is very atmospheric, texturally beautiful but essentially static. It could hardly be better recorded.

A Way A Lone.
*** RCA Dig. 09026 61387-2 [id.]. Tokyo Qt – BARBER: *Quartet;* BRITTEN: *Quartet No. 2.* ***

Takemitsu's *Quartet* was written in response to a commission from the Tokyo Quartet to mark its tenth anniversary in 1981. *A Way A Lone*, as it is subtitled, is rather Bergian but, like so much of Takemitsu's music, shows a refined ear for sonority. Marvellous playing and recording.

Tallis, Thomas (c. 1505–85)

Absterge Domine; Candidi facti sunt; Nazareri; Derelinquat impius; Dum transisset sabbatum; Gaude gloriosa Dei Mater; Magnificat and Nunc dimittis; Salvator mundi.
*** CRD CRD 3429; *CRDC 4129* [id.]. New College, Oxford, Ch., Higginbottom.

The performances by the Choir of New College, Oxford – recorded in the splendid acoustic of the

College Chapel – are eminently well prepared, with good internal balance, excellent intonation, ensemble and phrasing. The *Gaude gloriosa* is one of Tallis's most powerful and eloquent works.

Audivi vocem de celo a 4; Candidi facti sunt Nazarei eius a 5; Dum transisset sabbatum a 5; Hodie nobis celorum rex a 4; Homo quidam fecit cenam magnam a 6; Honor, virtus et potestas a 5; In pace in idipsum a 4; Loquebantur variis linguis a 7; Spem in alium a 40; Videte miraculum a 6.
*** EMI Dig. CDC7 49555-2 [id.]. Taverner Ch. and Cons., Andrew Parrott.

Gaude gloriosa Dei Mater a 6; In jejunio et fletu a 5; Lamentations of Jeremiah I and II a 5; Miserere nostri a 7; O nata lux de lumine a 5; O sacrum convivium a 5; Salvator mundi I and II a 5; Suscipe, quaeso Domine a 7; Te lucis ante terminum (Procol recedant somnia) I a 5.
*** EMI Dig. CDC7 49563-2 [id.]. Taverner Ch. and Cons., Andrew Parrott.

The Taverner style is brighter and more abrasive than we are used to in this often ethereal music, but, quite apart from the scholarly justification, the polyphonic cohesion of the writing comes out the more tellingly. The first of the two discs is the obvious one to investigate initially, containing as it does the 40-part motet, *Spem in alium*, as well as *Videte miraculum* and *Dum transisset sabbatum* – almost as extended in argument. The second of the two discs has the two magnificent *Lamentations of Jeremiah*, as well as an even more expansive motet which Tallis wrote early in his career, *Gaude gloriosa Dei Mater*.

Anthems: *Blessed are those that be undefiled; Christ, rising again; Hear the voice and prayer; If ye love me; A new commandment; O Lord, in Thee is all my trust; O Lord, give thy holy spirit; Out from the deep; Purge me; Remember not, O Lord God; Verily, verily I say: 9 Psalm Tunes for Archbishop Parker's Psalter.*
*** Gimell Dig. CDGIM 007; *1585T-07* [id.]. Tallis Scholars, Phillips.

This disc collects the complete English anthems of Tallis and is thus a valuable complement to the discs listed above. Here, of course, women's voices are used instead of boys', but the purity of the sound they produce is not in question, and the performances could hardly be more committed or more totally inside this repertoire. Strongly recommended.

Derelinquat impius; Ecce tempus idoneum; In jejunio et fletu; In manus tuas; O nata lux; Salvator mundi; (ii) *Sancte Deus;* (i) *Spem in alium* (40-part motet); *Te lucis ante terminum I & II; Veni Redemptor gentium;* (ii) *Videte miraculum; Organ lesson.*
(M) **(*) Decca 433 676-2 [id.]. King's College, Cambridge, Ch., Willcocks; (i) with Cambridge University Musical Society; Langdon; (ii) Andrew Davis.

The highlight of the programme is the magnificent forty-part motet, *Spem in alium*, in which the Cambridge University Musical Society joins forces with King's. But the simpler hymn settings are no less impressive. The two other motets, *Sanctus Deus* and *Videte miraculum*, like *Spem in alium*, organ accompanied, are less well balanced, giving over-prominence to the trebles, but the young Andrew Davis provides an excellent performance of the *Lesson* for organ.

Motets: *Ecce tempus idoneum; Gaude gloriosa Dei Mater; Loquebantur variis linguis; O nata lux de lumine; Spem in alium.*
(B) **(*) CfP CD-CFP 4638; *TC-CFP 4638* [id.]. Clerkes of Oxenford, David Wulstan – SHEPPARD: *Motets.* **(*)

A useful issue, since it not only juxtaposes motets by Tallis against those of his great (but less familiar) contemporary, John Sheppard, but also gives us a strongly sung bargain version of the famous forty-part motet, *Spem in alium*. Here the resonance of Merton College Chapel means that definition could be more refined, and throughout the programme David Wulstan's tempi are somewhat brisk, while at times there is also some sense of strain among the women. (Interestingly, Wulstan's timing for *Loquebantur variis linguis* is almost identical with that of Jeremy Summerly on Naxos, which yet feels slightly less tense.) Reservations notwithstanding, there are fine things on this inexpensive CD, and it can be recommended.

Gaude gloriosa; Loquebantur variis linguis; Miserere nostri; Salvator mundi, salva nos, I and II; Sancte Deus; Spem in alium (40-part motet).
✪ *** Gimell CDGIM 006; *1585T-06* [id.]. Tallis Scholars, Phillips.

Within the admirably suitable acoustics of Merton College Chapel, Oxford, the Tallis Scholars give a thrilling account of the famous 40-part motet, *Spem in alium*, in which the astonishingly complex polyphony is spaciously separated over a number of point sources, yet blending as a satisfying whole to reach a massive climax. The *Gaude gloriosa* is another much recorded piece, while the soaring *Sancte Deus* and the two very contrasted settings of the *Salvator mundi* are hardly less beautiful. The vocal line is beautifully shaped throughout, the singing combines ardour with serenity, and the breadth and depth of the sound are spectacular.

Lamentations of Jeremiah. Motets: *Absterge domine; Derelinquat impius; In jejunio et fletu; In manus tuas; Mihi autem nimis; O sacrum convivium; O nata lux de lumine; O salutaris hostia; Salve intemerata virgo.*
*** Gimell Dig. CDGIM 025; *1385T-25* [id.]. Tallis Scholars, Peter Phillips.

This, the third of the Tallis Scholars' discs devoted to their eponymous composer, is centred on the two great settings of the *Lamentations*. They have often been recorded before, but never more beautifully than here, performances that give total security. As well as the eight fine motets, the collection also has a rare Marian antiphon, *Salve intemerata*, that is among Tallis's most sustained inspirations. Clear, atmospheric recording of striking tangibility.

Alfred Deller Edition: *Lamentations of Jeremiah the Prophet*. 5 hymns: *Deus tuorum militum; Jam Christus astra ascenderat; Jesu Salvator Saeculi; O nata lux de lumine; Salvator mundi Domine.*
(Y/B) (M) ** Van. 08.5062 71 [id.]. Deller Consort (with Wilfred Brown, Gerald English, Eileen McLoughlin (in hymns)), Maurice Bevan, Deller.

Alfred Deller pioneered so much repertoire on LP, and even today Tallis's settings of the *Lamentations of Jeremiah* are not generously represented on disc. They are here given poised, expressive performances and the motets are presented with their alternating plainsong. However, there is comparatively little difference in dynamic range between the plainsong and the hymns, and the closely balanced recording robs the *Lamentations* of much of their atmosphere, while no real pianissimos are possible. The sound itself is full and truthful.

Mass for four voices; Motets: *Audivi vocem; In manus tuas Domine; Loquebantur variis linguis; O sacrum convivium; Salvator mundi; Sancte Deus; Te lucis ante terminum; Videte miraculum.*
(B) *** Naxos Dig. 8.550576 [id.]. Oxford Camerata, Jeremy Summerly.

The Oxford Camerata with their beautifully blended timbre have their own way with Tallis. Lines are firm, the singing has serenity but also a firm pulse. In the *Mass* (and particularly in the *Sanctus*) the expressive strength is quite strongly communicated, while the *Benedictus* moves on spontaneously at the close. The motets respond particularly well to Jeremy Summerly's degree of intensity. The opening *Loquebantur variis linguis* has much passionate feeling, and this (together with the *Audivi vocem*, and especially the lovely *Sante Deus*) shows this choir of a dozen singers at their most eloquent. The recording, made in the Chapel of Wellington College, is very fine indeed, and there is a brief musical note provided by the conductor. Excellent value.

Mass: Puer natus est nobis (for seven voices).
(N) (M) *** EMI Dig. CDM5 65211-2 [id.]. King's College, Cambridge, Ch., Ledger – BYRD: *Mass for 5 voices;* TYE: *Mass: Euge Bone.* ***

The magnificent seven-part writing in the *Mass* (a work assembled in recent years from a variety of sources – see below) contrasts well with the Byrd and Tye *Masses*, both masterpieces, with which it is coupled. The choir, at its finest, is beautifully recorded (digitally, in 1981, whereas the two couplings are analogue) against the ample acoustic of the King's Chapel.

Mass Puer natus est; Motets: *Salvatore mundi; Suscipe quaeso Dominus.*
(N) ✲ (M) *** Cal. CAL 6623 [id.]. Clerkes of Oxenford, David Wulstan – WHITE: *Motets.* ***

A quite outstanding reissue, made the more desirable by the inclusion of the four very beautiful motets by the neglected Elizabethan contemporary of Tallis, Robert White. The Tallis *Mass* was reconstructed by David Wulstan and Sally Dunkley, prompted by the researches and speculations of Joseph Kerman and Jeremy Noble. The details are too complex to be outlined here, and the *Credo* exists only as a fragment, but the results are so beautiful that readers should on no account miss this record. The *Mass* is among the finest Tallis – and, for that matter, the finest music of the period – and it is performed with dedication and authority by these singers. There is no need to hesitate here: this is one of the most important recent reissues of early English choral music, and it is also one of the most successful artistically and technically, for the analogue recording could hardly be bettered.

Missa Salve intemerata Virgo.
(B) *** CfP Dig. CD-CFP 4654; *TC-CFP 4654* [id.]. St John's College, Cambridge, Ch., George Guest – TAVERNER: *Western Wynde mass & song.* ***

Taverner's Mass, *The Western wynde*, with which this is coupled, is based on the celebrated popular tune of the day, while the Tallis derives from an earlier motet of the same name. But the *Missa Salve intemerata Virgo* does in fact rework more of the original than is customary in parody Masses; only about a quarter is completely new. The Choir of St John's College, Cambridge, under George Guest is very well recorded and give a very spirited account of themselves, very different from the small, chamber-like performances which are prevalent nowadays, but musically no less satisfying. At this price, a splendid bargain.

Taneyev, Sergei (1856–1915)

Suite de concert (for violin and orchestra), *Op. 28.*
(Y/B) (M) *** EMI CDM5 65419-2 [id.]. David Oistrakh, Philh. O, Malko – MIASKOVSKY: *Cello concerto.* *** ❀

David Oistrakh's superb account of Taneyev's attractively diverse *Suite*, ranging from rhapsodic ardour in the first (of five movements) to sparkling virtuosity in the *Tarantella* finale, has been available only rarely, even on LP. The early (1956) stereo is of high quality and few would guess the age of the recording from the present CD transfer, which is full-bodied and admirable.

Symphony Nos. (i) *2 in B flat* (ed. Blok); (ii) *4 in C min., Op. 12.*
** Russian Disc RD CD11008. (i) USSR R. & TV Large SO, Fedoseyev; (ii) Novosibirisk PO, Katz.

In the *Fourth Symphony* Arnold Katz gets very good results from the Novosibirsk orchestra; his is a spirited reading and in terms of character and imagination his performance can hold its own against Neeme Järvi's excellent account on Chandos without necessarily displacing it as a first recommendation. The recording, though not quite in the three-star bracket, is more than acceptable. This recording of the *Second Symphony in B flat* would seem to be identical with Fedoseyev's 1969 LP; climaxes are a bit raw and raucous. The performance itself is satisfactory, and there is at present no alternative. The *C minor Symphony* deserves 2½ stars and the B flat 1½, hence the compromise rating.

Symphony No. 4 in C min., Op. 12; Overture The Oresteia, Op. 6.
*** Chandos Dig. CHAN 8953 [id.]. Philh. O, Järvi.

The *Fourth Symphony*, sometimes known as the *First* as it was the first to be published in Taneyev's lifetime, is a long piece of 42 minutes; some of its gestures are predictable, to say the least! Its best movement is the delightful scherzo which betrays his keenness of wit. Elsewhere neither his ideas nor their working out are quite as fresh or as individual as in such pieces as, say, the *Piano quintet.* Neeme Järvi gets very good playing from the Philharmonia and his performance supersedes earlier versions.

Piano quartet in E, Op. 20.
**(*) Pro Arte Dig. CDD 301 [id.]. Cantilena Chamber Players.

The *Piano quartet* is a finely wrought and often subtle work. With a superbly sensitive contribution from Frank Glazer, the performance is altogether first rate, though the acoustic in which it is recorded is not quite big enough.

Piano quintet in G min., Op. 30.
*** Ara. Dig. Z 6539 [id.]. Jerome Lowenthal, Rosenthal, Kamei, Thompson, Kates.

Not only is the *Piano quintet* well structured and its motivic organization subtle, its melodic ideas are strong and individual. It is arguably the greatest Russian chamber work between Tchaikovsky and Shostakovich. The recording is not in the demonstration bracket, but it is very good; and the playing, particularly of the pianist Jerome Lowenthal, is excellent. Strongly recommended.

Piano trio in D, Op. 22.
*** Chandos Dig. CHAN 8592 [id.]. Borodin Trio.

This *Trio* is a big, four-movement work. The invention is attractive – and so, too, is the excellent performance and recording. Strongly recommended.

Tansman, Alexandre (1897–1986)

Symphony No. 5 in D min.; 4 Movements for orchestra; Stèle in memoriam d'Igor Stravinsky.
**(*) Marco Polo Dig. 8.223379 [id.]. Slovak PO (Kosice), Meir Minsky.

The Polish-born Alexandre Tansman was a prolific composer, well-known for his music for guitar which Segovia popularized. Readers will recognize a certain affinity with his countryman Szymanowski; his craftsmanship is fastidious and his command of the orchestra impressive. His music is highly atmospheric, with shimmering textures enhanced by celeste, piano and vibraphones and sensitively spaced pianissimo string chords, plus poignant wind writing. The *Quatre mouvements pour orchestre* is impressive and resourceful. The *Fifth Symphony*, which dates from his Hollywood years, is less successful, though it is well laid out for the orchestra and many of the ideas are pleasing without being as memorable or as individual as the two companion works. The performances are eminently serviceable and the recordings are decent, though there is an ugly edit at the first-time repeat bar in the second movement of *Stèle*. Let us hope that this will lead to more recordings of Tansman's music.

Tarp, Svend Eric (born 1908)

(i) *Piano concerto in C, Op. 39;* (ii) *Symphony No. 7 in C min, Op. 81;* (iii) *The Battle of Jericho, Op. 51;* (iv) *Te Deum, Op. 33.*

**(*) Marco Polo Dacapo Dig. DCCD 9005 [id.]. Danish Nat. RSO, with (i) Per Solo; (i; iii) Schønwandt; (ii) Schmidt; (iv) Danish Nat. R. Ch., Nelson.

The only familiar work here is the neo-classical, Françaix-like *Piano concerto*, a light, attractive piece whose acquaintance is well worth making. There is a distinctively Danish feel to the *Te Deum*, though the piece is eclectic and owes a lot to Stravinsky and may even at times remind English listeners of Walton. The *Seventh Symphony* is neo-classical in feeling, very intelligent music, and only occasionally bombastic; though not the equal of Bentzon or Holmboe in terms of imagination or depth, it is certainly worth hearing. The performances, which come from 1986–90, are enthusiastic and committed, and the recordings are serviceable without being top-drawer.

Tartini, Giuseppe (1692–1770)

Cello concerto in A.

(B) *** DG Double 437 952-2 (2) [id.]. Rostropovich, Zurich Coll. Mus., Sacher – BERNSTEIN: *3 Meditations;* BOCCHERINI: *Cello concerto No. 2;* GLAZUNOV: *Chant du Ménestrel;* SHOSTAKO-VICH: *Cello concerto No. 2;* TCHAIKOVSKY: *Andante cantabile* etc.; VIVALDI: *Cello concertos.* ***

As with the other works in this fine 1978 collection, Rostropovich's view of Tartini's *A major Concerto* is larger than life; but the eloquence of the playing disarms criticism, even when the cellist plays cadenzas of his own that are not exactly in period. This is part of a first-class Double DG anthology which can be recommended almost without reservation.

Violin concertos in C, D.2; F, D.67; A, D.96; A min., D.115; B min, D.125.

(N) (M) ** Erato/Warner 0630 12988-2 [id.]. Piero Toso, Sol. Ven., Claudio Scimone.

These are all attractive concertos. Toso plays them elegantly and is given smooth, warm and polished accompaniments. This is pleasing enough, but the end effect is a bit bland.

Violin concertos: in E min., D.56; in A, D.96; in A min., D.113.

(M) *** Erato/Warner 4509 92188-2 [id.]. Uto Ughi, Sol. Ven.

Tartini is a composer of unfailing originality, and the three violin concertos on this record are all very rewarding. The *Concerto in A major*, which comes last on the disc, has an additional (probably) alternative slow movement, a *Largo Andante* which is particularly beautiful. Uto Ughi's performances are distinguished by excellent taste and refinement of tone, and I Solisti Veneti are hardly less polished. The harpsichord continuo is somewhat reticent, but otherwise the recording is exemplary. Highly recommended.

Tavener, John (born 1944)

Eternal memory.

*** RCA Single 09026 61966-2 [id.]. Steven Isserlis, Moscow Virtuosi, Spivakov – BLOCH: *From Jewish life.* ***

Those who have responded to Tavener's *Protecting veil* (from which the composer actually quotes in this shorter, more succinct evocation) will readily be drawn to this mystical, three-part structure which, unexpectedly, begins with a chant-like whiff of the opening of Tchaikovsky's *1812*, moves on to a motoric central section, then ends in mysticism, a suggestion of the end of mortal existence. Isserlis reaffirms his total identification with Tavener's muse, here bringing an alternation of life's disquieting alarms and its final serenity. The recording is suitably atmospheric and the documentation excellent. The choice of presentation – a CD single – and an apt coupling should also make this a good sampler for those collectors who have not yet ventured beneath *The Protecting veil*.

(i) *The Protecting veil* (for cello and orchestra); *Thrinos*.
*** Virgin/EMI Dig. VC7 59052-2 [id.]. Steven Isserlis, (i) LSO, Rozhdestvensky – BRITTEN: *Cello suite No. 3*. ***

In the inspired performance of Steven Isserlis, dedicatedly accompanied by Rozhdestvensky and the LSO, *The Protecting veil* has an instant magnetism, at once gentle and compelling. Tavener's simplicity of idiom has you escaping at once into a spiritual world, sharing his visions. The 'protecting veil' of the title refers to the Orthodox Church's celebration of a tenth-century vision, when in Constantinople the Virgin Mary appeared and cast her protecting veil over the Christians who were being attacked by the Saracen armies. Tavener, himself a Russian Orthodox convert, echoes the cadences of Orthodox chant, ending each section with passages of heightened lyricism for the soloist. Each time that guides the ear persuasively on into the next section, leading at the end to the work's one sharply dramatic moment, when a sudden surge represents Christ's Resurrection. Much is owed to the performance, with Isserlis a commanding soloist. He is just as compelling in the other two works on the disc, not just the Britten but also the simple lyrical lament, *Thrinos*, which Tavener wrote especially for him. Excellent recording.

The Repentant thief.
*** Collins Dig. Single 2005-2. Andrew Marriner, LSO, Tilson Thomas.

In this memorable work for clarinet and orchestra (Andrew Marriner the keenly responsive soloist) Tavener creates a sharply defined structure, contrasting visionary intensity with rhythmic urgency in alternating *Dances*, *Laments* and *Refrains*.

String quartets: *The Hidden Treasure*; (i) *The Last sleep of the Virgin*.
*** Virgin/EMI Dig. VC5 45023-2 [id.]. Chilingirian Qt, (i) with Iain Simcock (handbells) – PART: *Fratres; Summa*. ***

'Quiet and intensely fragile' is Tavener's guide to performances of *The Last sleep of the Virgin*, a work which might be described as an ethereal suggestion, using the simplest means (string quartet and tolling bell) to convey both the reality and the implications of the death and burial of 'the Mother of God'. *The Hidden Treasure* in its seeking for Paradise offers more violent contrasts (a brief cello cadenza-soliloquy a key factor) with cries of anguish interrupting the flow of the spiritual journey. Tavener's world is all his own and the artists have to create the music's logic with a hypnotic concentration which is certainly achieved here, using a suitable resonance of acoustic. The mystical close of *The Hidden Treasure* brings a shimmering *pianissimo-diminuendo* of remarkable intensity.

VOCAL MUSIC

The Akathist of Thanksgiving.
✹ *** Sony Dig. SK 64446 [id.]. Bowman, Wilson, Westminster Abbey Ch., BBC SO & Singers, Martin Neary.

Even among Tavener's many works inspired by his Russian Orthodox faith, *The Akathist of Thanksgiving* stands out for its concentrated intensity. The composer's personal response to the text by a monk in the Stalin era inspires striking atmospheric contrasts of motif and texture, with the main choir set against a phalanx of 16 soloists, mainly counter-tenors and basses, led by James Bowman and Timothy Wilson. The recording was taken live from the performance given in January 1994 at Westminster Abbey. The result on disc is both warmly atmospheric and well defined, with high dynamic contrasts involving not just choral forces but strings, heavy brass and percussion. Martin Neary proves an inspiring conductor, drawing incandescent tone from the choirs, thrillingly reinforced by the underlying weight of instrumental sound.

Angels; Annunciation; God is with us; Hymns of Paradise; Lament of the Mother of God; Thunder entered her.
*** Virgin/EMI Dig. VC5 45035-2 [id.]. Kringelborn, Kendall, Sweeney, Winchester Cathedral Ch., Hill; Dunnett (organ).

'*Thunder entered her*' is the sobriquet given to a choral collection named after the longest and most striking piece of the six recorded here, which, with distant choirs set against the main body and weighty organ accompaniment, relates closely to the *Akathist*. David Hill conducts the Winchester Cathedral Choir with David Dunnett at the organ, all very atmospherically recorded. Though some of the longer and more meditative pieces rather outstay their welcome, with Tavener resorting too readily to formulae like scalic ostinati and oriental augmented intervals, each one presents a sharply distinctive vision, culminating in a magnificent Christmas proclamation, *God is with us.*

Annunciation; 2 Hymns to the Mother of God; (i) *Innocence; The Lamb;* (ii) *Little Requiem for Father Malachy Lynch; Song for Athene; The Tyger.*
(N) *** Sony Dig. SK 66613 [id.]. Westminster Abbey Ch., Martin Neary; with (i) Patricia Rozario, Graham Titus, Leigh Nixon, Alice Neary (cello), Martin Baker (organ); (ii) ECO.

There is no finer disc than this to represent John Tavener as choral composer. With Martin Neary drawing incandescent singing from the Westminster Abbey Choir, it offers a sequence of Tavener's best-known short works – such as the Blake settings, *The Lamb* and *The Tyger,* and the *Hymns to the Mother of God* – as well as longer pieces in which he movingly exploits spatial effects. *Innocence,* specially written for Westminster Abbey, encapsulates in its 25-minute ritual what many of his more expansive pieces have told us, with multi-layered elements atmospherically contrasted, near and far, starting with apocalyptic organ-sounds and ending with a surging climax parallel to that in Britten's *War Requiem.* The elegiac *Song for Athene* of two years ago is also among Tavener's most beautiful and touching inspirations, a ritual inspired by Orthodox chant over a drone bass. The Sony recording vividly captures the Abbey acoustic, with extreme dynamics used impressively to convey space and distance.

Funeral Ikos; (i) *Ikon of Light. Carol: The Lamb.*
*** Gimell CDGIM 005; *1585T-05* [id.]. Tallis Scholars, (i) Chilingirian Qt (members), Phillips.

Ikon of Light is a setting of Greek mystical texts, with chant-like phrases repeated hypnotically. The string trio provides the necessary textural variety. More concentrated is *Funeral Ikos,* an English setting of the Greek funeral sentences, often yearningly beautiful. Both in these and in the brief setting of Blake's *The Lamb,* the Tallis Scholars give immaculate performances, atmospherically recorded in the chapel of Merton College, Oxford.

We shall see Him as He is.
*** Chandos Dig. CHAN 9128 [id.]. Rosario, Ainsley, Murgatroyd, Britten Singers, Chester Festival Ch., Hickox.

We shall see Him as He is is a sequence of what Tavener describes as musical ikons, setting brief, poetic texts based on the Epistle of St John, each inspired by a salient event in the life of Christ: His baptism, the Wedding Feast at Cana, the cleansing of the Temple, and on to the Last Supper, the Crucifixion and the Resurrection. Each ikon is punctuated by a choral Refrain, setting the words of the work's title in Greek. Though at first the inspiration may seem painfully thin, the simple ritual becomes magnetic, with its structured, highly atmospheric use of large-scale choral forces progressing towards rapt contemplation of the Resurrection, the ultimate ikon. The recording, with Richard Hickox conducting the BBC Welsh Symphony Orchestra, the Britten Singers and Chester Festival Chorus, was made live at the Prom performance, with the dedication totally cancelling out any detailed flaw. The tenor, John Mark Ainsley, in the central solo role of St John sings immaculately with deep feeling, while Patricia Rozario makes her brief, wide-ranging solo a soaring climax.

The Whale.
**(*) Apple/EMI CDP7 98947-2; *SAPCOR 15* [id.]. Anna Reynolds, Raimund Herincx, Alvar Lidell, London Sinf. and Ch., David Atherton; composer (organ & Hammond organ).

The Whale was written well before Tavener turned to the Russian Orthodox Church for inspiration but, with its roots in the biblical story of Jonah, the anticipations of Tavener's later devotional manner are plain, despite the surreal reading from the Encyclopedia Britannica (by Alvar Lidell) with which it starts. Thanks to its dramatic timing as well as Tavener's ear for striking effect, it wears well, though at 31 minutes it makes very short measure for a full-price CD. The new disc is a reissue of the original recording in spectacular sound, made for the Beatles' Apple label by the original performers.

Mary of Egypt (complete).
*** Collins Dig. 7023-2 (2) [id.]. Rozario, Varcoe, Goodchild, Ely Cathedral Ch., Britten-Pears Chamber Ch., Aldeburgh Festival Ens., Lionel Friend.

Mary of Egypt was recorded live at the Aldeburgh Festival first performances in June 1992 and, characteristically, Tavener compels you to accept his slow pacing and paring down of texture. In many ways the disc works better than the live staging, when with the help of the libretto the developments in the bald, stylized plot can be more readily followed. The musical landmarks are sharply defined in clear-cut, memorable motifs, with moments of violence set sharply against the predominant mood of meditation. What is disconcerting is Tavener's use as a frame for each Act of a disembodied voice to represent the

Mother of God. It sounds like a very raw baritone, but in fact is the voice of Chloe Goodchild, using weird oriental techniques. Under Lionel Friend the performance has a natural concentration, with Patricia Rozario as Mary and the baritone, Stephen Varcoe, as Zossima both outstanding. Their confrontation in Act III brings a radiant duet that acts as a climactic centrepiece to the whole work. After that Act IV – a voiceless pageant on Mary's life up to her death – and the equally brief Act V – her burial by Zossima – come almost as epilogue, with the 100 minutes treated as a single span. A synopsis and libretto are provided, but instead of notes there is a 15-minute interview with the composer, informative but disconcertingly overamplified.

Taverner, John (c. 1495–1545)

Missa gloria tibi Trinitas; Audivi vocem (responsory); ANON.: *Gloria tibi Trinitas*.
*** Hyperion CDA 66134 [id.]. The Sixteen, Harry Christophers.

Missa gloria tibi Trinitas; Dum transisset sabbatum; Kyrie a 4 (Leroy).
*** Gimell Dig. CDGIM 004; *1585T-04* [id.]. Tallis Scholars, Phillips.

This six-voice setting of the Mass is richly varied in its invention (not least in rhythm) and expressive in a deeply personal way very rare for its period. Harry Christophers and The Sixteen underline the beauty with an exceptionally pure and clear account, superbly recorded and made the more brilliant by having the pitch a minor third higher than modern concert pitch.

Peter Phillips and the Tallis Scholars give an intensely involving performance of this glorious example of Tudor music. The recording may not be as clear as on the rival Hyperion version, but Phillips rejects all idea of reserve or cautiousness of expression; the result reflects the emotional basis of the inspiration the more compellingly. The motet, *Dum transisset sabbatum*, is then presented more reflectively, another rich inspiration.

Missa Mater Christi; Motets: *Mater Christi; O Wilhelme, pastor bone*.
*** Nimbus Dig. NI 5218 [id.]. Christ Church Cathedral Ch., Stephen Darlington.

This is a liturgical reconstruction by Andrew Carwood for the Feast of the Annunciation of Our Lady, at Eastertide, which intersperses Taverner's *Missa Mater Christi* with the appropriate chant. The disc also includes the Motet *Mater Christi*, on which the Mass itself is built, and the antiphon, *O Wilhelme, pastor bone*. The singing under Stephen Darlington is first class, and the recording made, not at Christ Church, but at Dorchester Abbey, Oxfordshire, is difficult to fault: it is well focused and excellently balanced with a firm image.

Mass, O Michael; Dum transisset sabbatum; Kyrie a 4 (Leroy).
*** Hyperion Dig. CDA 66315 [id.]. The Sixteen, Harry Christophers.

The *Missa O Michael* is an ambitious six-part Mass lasting nearly 40 minutes which derives its name from the respond, *Archangeli Michaelis interventione*, which prefaces the performance. The chant on which the Mass is built appears no fewer than seven times during its course. The so-called Leroy *Kyrie* (the name thought to be a reference to *le roi* Henry) fittingly precedes it: the *Missa O Michael* has no Kyrie. The Easter motet, *Dum transisset sabbatum*, completes an impressive disc.

Missa Sancti Wilhelmi; Dum transisset Sabbatum; Ex eius tumba; O Wilhelme, pastor bone.
*** Hyperion Dig. CDA 66427 [id.]. The Sixteen, Harry Christophers.

The *Missa Sancti Wilhelmi* (known as 'Small Devotion' in two sources and possibly a corruption of *S. Will devotio*) is prefaced by the antiphon, *O Wilhelme, pastor bone*, written in a largely syllabic, note-against-note texture, and the second of his two five-part settings of the Easter respond, *Dum transisset Sabbatum*, and washed down, as it were, by the Matin responds for the Feast of St Nicholas, *Ex eius tumba*, believed to be the only sixteenth-century setting of this text. The singing of The Sixteen under Harry Christophers is expressive and ethereal, and the recording impressively truthful. Recommended with confidence.

Mass: The Western wynde; Song: The Western wynde.
(B) *** CfP Dig. CD-CFP 4654; *TC-CFP 4654* [id.]. St John's Coll., Cambridge, Ch., George Guest –
    TALLIS: *Missa Salve intemerata Virgo*. ***

This St John's performance of John Taverner's mass, *The Western wynde*, is prefaced by the song on which both it and the motet of the same name are based. It also attracted both Tye and Sheppard. The Mass is basically a sequence of 36 variations of much subtlety and ingenuity on the theme and is one of the key works of the period. This spirited and robust performance by the Choir of St John's College,

Cambridge, under George Guest is very well recorded; it is very different in style from the small, chamber-like, vibrato-free performances to which we are becoming accustomed (and by which we are becoming beguiled), but is every bit as valid. An admirable and, at this price, very economical introduction to the composer.

Tchaikovsky, André (1935–82)

String quartet No. 2, Op. 5.
*** ASV Dig. CDDCA 825 [id.]. Lindsay Qt – BARBER: *String quartet;* WIREN: *String quartet No. 3;* WOOD: *String quartet No. 3.* ***

André Tchaikovsky's *Second Quartet* was composed for the Lindsays and recorded at its first performance in 1978. It is a highly concentrated and substantial piece in three interlinked movements, including a central passacaglia. Its musical language is complex and chromatic, of indeterminate tonality rather than twelve-note. It is not 'listener-friendly' but leaves one with the feeling that it is worth taking trouble over.

Tchaikovsky, Peter (1840–93)

Andante cantabile for cello and orchestra, Op. posth; (i) *Variations on a rococo theme, Op. 33.*
(B) *** DG Double 437 952-2 (2) [id.]. Rostropovich, BPO; (i) cond. Karajan – BERNSTEIN: *3 Meditations;* BOCCHERINI: *Cello concerto No. 2;* GLAZUNOV: *Chant du Ménestrel;* SHOSTAKO-VICH: *Cello concerto No. 2;* TARTINI: *Cello concerto;* VIVALDI: *Cello concertos.* ***

Rostropovich indulges himself affectionately in the composer's arrangement of the *Andante cantabile*, and the balance – all cello with a discreet orchestral backing – reflects his approach. Rostropovich's famous and much-praised account of the *Rococo variations* with Karajan (see below) has been added as part of a highly desirable anthology – a real bargain in DG's Double-CD series with two discs offered for the price of one.

(i) *Andante cantabile* (from *String quartet No. 1*, arr. Marriner); (ii; iii) *Capriccio italien;* (iv) *Piano concerto No. 1 in B flat min.;* (v) *Violin concerto in D;* (vi) *1812 Overture;* (vii; viii) *Marche slave; Nutcracker* (extended suite); (ii; ix) *Romeo and Juliet* (fantasy overture); (vii; x) *Serenade for strings;* (vii; viii) *Sleeping Beauty; Swan Lake* (extended suites); (ii; ix) *Symphonies Nos. 4–6 (Pathétique);* (xi) *Waltz* from *Eugene Onegin;* (xii) (Song): *None but the lonely heart* (sung in Russian).
(M) *** EMI Analogue/Dig. CZS 767700-2 (5) [id.]. (i) ASMF, Marriner; (ii) Philh. O; (iii) Ozawa; (iv) Gavrilov, BPO, Ashkenazy; (v) Perlman, Phd. O, Ormandy; (vi) Oslo PO, Jansons; (vii) LSO; (viii) Previn; (ix) Muti; (x) Barbirolli; (xi) RPO, Beecham; (xii) Boris Christoff, Labinsky.

Among all the back-catalogue collections designed to commemorate the centenary of Tchaikovsky's death, this five-CD 'Tchaikovsky Box' from EMI readily takes first place. It includes much of the composer's most inspired music in consistently distinguished performances and vintage recordings, almost all admirably transferred to CD. The only possible technical reservation concerns the CD remastering of the *String serenade*. Barbirolli's account has characteristic vigour and ardour, especially in the *Elegy*, and it is a pity that, although the recording had plenty of body and warmth, the violins playing full out above the stave are made to sound slightly fierce and unrefined. This is the more noticeable as the *Serenade* directly follows Marriner's lovely performance of the *Andante cantabile* (on the first disc), where the Academy strings, digitally recorded, sound warm and natural. However, adjusting the controls works wonders, and this is a small blemish when Muti's accounts of the three greatest *Symphonies*, strong, direct and spontaneous, are as fine as almost any in the catalogue. The two *Concertos* are both highly successful in most respects (although Perlman is too closely balanced), and the shorter pieces are all very enjoyable. Muti (not Jansons as originally indicated in the documentation) directs an exciting and imaginative *Romeo and Juliet*, and Previn is in his element in the *Marche slave* and the three splendid ballet selections. It was good, too, that room was found for Beecham's *Eugene Onegin Waltz* and Boris Christoff's performance of Tchaikovsky's most famous song. The documentation, including some interesting photographs, is first class.

Andante cantabile, Op. 11; Chant d'automne, Op. 37/10; Nocturne, Op. 19/4 (all arr. for cello & orchestra); *Pezzo capriccioso, for cello & orchestra, Op. 62; Sérénade mélancolique, Op. 26; Valse sentimentale, Op. 51/6* (both arr. for cello & orchestra); *Variations on a rococo theme for cello & orchestra, Op. 33; Eugene Onegin: Lensky's aria* (arr. for cello & orchestra).
**(*) RCA Dig. RD 60758 [09026 60758-2]. Ofra Harnoy, LPO, Mackerras.

Ofra Harnoy plays with much lightness and grace in this Tchaikovsky programme, managing to embrace almost every conceivable item which might be transcribed for cello and orchestra. As it so happens, the most successful performance here is *Lenski's aria* from *Eugene Onegin*, which Harnoy plays with gentle lamenting ardour, with the orchestral wind soloists decorating the vocal line with affectionate sensibility. The famous *Variations on a rococo theme* are presented in a similar way – using the published score – and though at times Harnoy fines the melodic line down seductively to just a thread of tone, at others one craves a slightly more robust effect. But in the rest of the programme this delicacy and refinement work well enough. Mackerras accompanies very sensitively and the LPO playing is quite lovely, while the recording balance is ideal, within a pleasingly warm ambience.

Andante cantabile, Op. 11; Nocturne, Op. 19/4; Pezzo capriccioso, Op. 62 (1887 version); *2 Songs: Legend; Was I not a little blade of grass; Variations on a rococo theme, Op. 33* (1876 version).
*** Chandos Dig. CHAN 8347 [id.]. Wallfisch, ECO, Simon.

Andante cantabile, Op. 11; Nocturne, Op. 19/4 (both arr. for cello & orchestra); *Pezzo capriccioso, Op. 62; Variations on a rococo theme, Op. 33* (original versions).
(Y/B) (M) **(*) Virgin/EMI Dig. CUV5 61225-2 [id.]. Isserlis, COE, Gardiner (with GLAZUNOV: *2 Pieces, Op. 20; Chant du ménestrel, Op. 71;* RIMSKY-KORSAKOV: *Serenade, Op. 37;* CUI: *2 Morceaux, Op. 36* ***).

This delightful Chandos record gathers together all of Tchaikovsky's music for cello and orchestra – including his arrangements of such items as the famous *Andante cantabile* and two songs. The major item is the original version of the *Rococo variations* with an extra variation and the earlier variations put in a more effective order, as Tchaikovsky wanted. Geoffrey Simon draws lively and sympathetic playing from the ECO, with Wallfisch a vital if not quite flawless soloist. Excellent recording, with the CD providing fine presence and an excellent perspective.

Isserlis's playing has slight reserve but also an elegant delicacy which is appealing, although it suits Glazunov and Cui rather better than it does Tchaikovsky's *Andante cantabile*. John Eliot Gardiner provides gracefully lightweight accompaniments and the Virgin recording is faithfully balanced, fresh in texture and warm in ambience.

Capriccio italien, Op. 45.
(B) *** CfP CD-CFP 4341; *TC-CFP 4341* [id.]. Philh. O, Kletzki – RIMSKY-KORSAKOV: *Scheherazade.* ***
(Y/B) (**) Sir Thomas Beecham Trust mono BEECHAM 6 [id.]. NYPO, Beecham – MENDELSSOHN: *Symphony No. 4;* SIBELIUS: *Symphony No. 7* etc. (**)

Kletzki's performance is very enjoyable. It offers superb Philharmonia playing (the opening bugle call is most arresting) and is very well recorded indeed for its period (late 1950s).

Sir Thomas recorded the *Capriccio italien* only twice and on both occasions with American orchestras. This account with the New York Philharmonic comes from 1942, the same year as his now celebrated Sibelius *Seventh*, which is also on this disc. It is a thrilling account which finds the New York orchestra and their British guest on excellent musical terms. The recording is somewhat opaque but perfectly acceptable for its period.

Capriccio italien, Op. 45; 1812 Overture, Op. 49; Fatum, Op. 77; Festive overture on the Danish National Anthem, Op. 15; Francesca da Rimini, Op. 32; Hamlet (fantasy overture), *Op. 67a; Romeo and Juliet* (fantasy overture); *The Tempest* (symphonic fantasy), *Op. 18.*
*** Olympia Dig. OCD 512 A/B [id.]. SO of Russia, Dudarova.

This exciting Tchaikovsky compilation includes one of the finest performances of *The Tempest* ever recorded, structurally convincing, full of atmosphere and with the great leaping love-theme for Ferdinand and Miranda wonderfully ecstatic. Veronika Dudarova cannot do quite so much for *Fatum*, which remains an obstinately clumsy structure. *Romeo and Juliet* has passion, excitement and a certain Slavonic reserve at the presentation of the love theme, which make for a very satisfying whole; and a certain spacious gravitas informs *1812*, although it does not lack impetus, with the climax (using drums rather than cannon) bringing a gloriously expansive treatment of the Russian hymn. *Capriccio italien* is very Russian too, especially the nostalgic treatment of the broad string melody, but there is plenty of energy and spectacle, and the end is almost alcoholically rumbustious, with a not quite convincing sudden accelerando at the coda. *Francesca da Rimini* and *Hamlet* here can almost be spoken of in the same breath as the famous Stokowski versions. The former is not as uninhibited at the climax representing the lovers' passion as with Stokowski, but it has some glorious playing in the middle section, full of rich woodwind colouring, and a ferociously demonic portrayal of the inferno and the lovers' final, cataclysmic punishment; the latter has a uniquely touching portrayal of Ophelia's onset of madness (a poignant oboe solo) and a passionately sombre close. The Symphony Orchestra of Russia is apparently a permanent pick-up group, formed from members of other Russian orchestras, who play with great ardour and virtuosity. The 1992 digital recording is red-bloodedly spectacular to suit the music-making, yet not blatant; and Studio No. 5 of Moscow Radio and TV clearly has the proper spacious acoustics to bring out the resonant weight of Tchaikovsky's most brilliant fortissimos.

(i) *Capriccio italien, Op. 45;* (i) *1812 Overture; Marche slave, Op. 31;* (i) *Romeo and Juliet (fantasy overture);* (ii) *Serenade for strings in C, Op. 48;* (ii) *Suite No. 4 in G, Op. 61 (Mozartiana);* Symphonies Nos. (i) *5 in E min., Op. 64;* (i) *6 in B min. (Pathétique).*
(N) (M) (***) Ph. mono 438 311/3-2 (3). (i) Concg. O; (ii) LOP; Paul van Kempen.

Like his Beethoven symphonies, released in this same 'Early Years' series, these performances have not been available since their first appearance on mono LP in the 1950s. Paul van Kempen made several LP recordings before his relatively early death, including a set of Beethoven concertos with Kempff and – unusually for a Dutch conductor – Sibelius's *Seventh Symphony.* The vast majority of these with the Concertgebouw Orchestra come from 1951; those in Paris with the Lamoureux Orchestra come from 1955, the year of his death. For younger collectors he will barely be a name, but these discs leave no doubt that he could generate great excitement and vitality. These are most musical performances and it is good that Philips have made them available again.

(i) *Capriccio italien, Op. 45;* (ii) *Francesca da Rimini, Op. 32;* (i) *Nutcracker suite, Op. 71a;* (ii) *Serenade for strings;* (i) *Eugene Onegin: Polonaise and Waltz.*
(N) (M) **(*) Ph. 442 735-2 (2) [id.]. (i) LPO; (ii) LSO; Leopold Stokowski.

Curiously entitled '*The Early Years*' this Philips box instead includes some of Stokowski's last recordings, made in 1973 (when he was 91) and 1974; he died three years later in September 1977. The performances certainly show his charisma and there are moments of magic, but there is wilful egotism too. *Capriccio italien* brings genuine panache, and the infectiously vigorous *Eugene Onegin* dances have characteristic flair. But in the *Nutcracker suite* (which he played so beautifully for Disney in *Fantasia*), the *Marche* is presented at such a hard-driven pace that the middle section sounds gabbled; then, after introducing the *Sugar Plum Fairy* with a string tremolando, his phrasing is so mannered (with repeated tenutos on the falling clarinet phrase) that few will find this comfortable to live with, even if later the *Waltz of the flowers* is exhilarating. The 1974 account of *Francesca da Rimini*, although not as well controlled as his classic early stereo version with the New York Stadium Orchestra, is very exciting; indeed there is no doubt about the temperament of the reading: the music races off (not entirely convincingly) almost as soon as the performance begins. But the middle section is beautifully played and Stokowski generates a tremendous emotional thrust at the climax. There is no possible doubt about the moment when the lovers are slain, and the ferocious return to Dante's inferno leads to a cataclysmic close, with the cymbals echoing into silence. The *String serenade* is characteristically bold and romantic, with sumptuous tone from the the LSO strings – a real 'Stokowski sound' – and, after the characteristically luscious Waltz, the *Elégie* is ardent and the finale full of energy. The recordings, although resonant, have been splendidly remastered; on LP the quality was never as full-bodied as it is now.

Capriccio italien, Op. 45; 1812 Overture; Marche slave, Op. 31; Romeo and Juliet (fantasy overture).
(BB) *** Naxos Dig. 8.550500; *4550500* [id.]. RPO, Adrian Leaper.

Like Sian Edwards, Adrian Leaper is a natural Tchaikovskian; whether in the colourful extravagance of the composer's memento of his Italian holiday, the romantic ardour and passionate conflict of *Romeo and Juliet*, the sombre expansiveness of *Marche slave* with its surge of adrenalin at the close, or in the extrovert celebration of *1812*, he produces playing from the RPO that is spontaneously committed and exciting. The brilliantly spectacular recording, with plenty of weight for the brass, was made in Watford Town Hall, with realistic cannon and an impressively resonant imported carillon to add to the very exciting climax of *1812*. A splendid disc that would still be recommendable if it cost far more.

Capriccio italien, Op. 45; 1812 Overture, Op. 49; Marche slave, Op. 31; Swan Lake (ballet): *suite.*
**(*) Teldec/Warner Dig. 4509 90201-2 [id.]. Israel PO, Mehta.

This is a quite generously conceived popular Tchaikovsky collection, very well played and given full-bodied, resonant sound, much more flattering than we are used to from the Mann Auditorium in Tel Aviv. With the Israel brass sonorously robust, the concert opens with a lively and warmly conceived *Capriccio italien*, a Slavonically solemn yet exciting *Marche slave* and an exuberant *1812* with a properly spectacular fusillade at the end. The highlight is the suite from *Swan Lake*, played with style and affection and with good solo contributions from woodwind and violin and cello soloists and producing a thrilling *scène finale*. Overall this is an enjoyable concert; if these performances in the last resort are not the finest available, they stand up quite well against the competition if you want this particular programme.

(i) *Capriccio italien; 1812 overture; Romeo and Juliet* (fantasy overture); (ii) Song: *None but the lonely heart; Eugene Onegin: Onegin's aria.*
**(*) Dig. EMI CDC5 55018-2 [id.]. (i) Philh. O, Domingo; (ii) Domingo, Philh. O, Behr.

Here we have Domingo in his newest role as conductor giving heartfelt, somewhat idiosyncratic and quite individual readings of three popular orchestral favourites, with plenty of drama and the passion worn on the sleeve. *1812* is ceremonially measured, with the organ adding breadth and spectacle at the close. The recording is appropriately spacious and resonant. Any lack of sharp co-ordination of ensemble is surely compensated for by the impact throughout. The vocal items show that Domingo can still tug at the emotions in his more familiar role. The recording, made in All Saints', Tooting, provides an expansively resonant panoply of Tchaikovskian hyperbole.

(i) *Capriccio italien, Op. 45; 1812, Op. 49;* (ii) *Fatum, Op. 77; Francesca da Rimini, Op. 32 ; Hamlet, Op. 67;* (i) *Marche slave;* (ii) *Romeo and Juliet* (fantasy overture); *The Tempest, Op. 18; The Voyevoda, Op. 78.*
(B) **(*) Decca Double 443 003-2 (2) [id.]. (i) National SO of Washington, DC; (ii) Detroit SO; Antal Dorati.

Dorati made his recordings of the symphonic poems in Washington in the early 1970s, while the triptych of *Capriccio italien, 1812* and *Marche slave* marked the return of the Detroit orchestra to the recording scene at the beginning of 1979. The recording has the benefit of the splendid Detroit acoustics, although *1812*, rather endearingly, has a spectacular laminated eruption of American Civil War cannon and bells – including Philadelphia's Liberty Bell! – at the end. The result is unbelievable but certainly spectacular, and clearly was aimed at the hi-fi demonstration market of the time. The performance of the *Capriccio* is not without elegance, but *Marche slave* seems almost excessively sombre until the change of mood at the coda, which is taken briskly. The symphonic poems are vividly done, if without the degree of ardour one finds in the competing Russian performances (see above/below). *Fatum* is quite successful, but Dorati's accounts of *Francesca da Rimini* and *Hamlet* are rather underpowered compared with Stokowski, but they are spacious readings, not without individuality, and the central section of *Francesca* is sensitively done. *Romeo and Juliet* takes a while to warm up. When it does, Dorati gives the love theme a distinctive sweep, and the closing pages are very convincing. *The Tempest* obviously excited the conductor's imagination and is vividly done, while the rapturous love theme is played with tingling ardour. *The Voyevoda* is hardly one of the composer's more inspired pieces, although its scoring is sophisticated. Dorati makes the most of its melancholy and dark wind colouring which matches the sombre lower strings.

Capriccio italien, Op. 45; Nutcracker suite, Op. 71a; Sleeping Beauty (ballet): *suite, Op. 66a.*
(M) *** DG 431 610-2 [id.]. BPO, Rostropovich.

We have given the highest praise (and a Rosette) to the Rostropovich triptych combining the three Tchaikovsky ballet suites, which added *Swan Lake* to the two listed here (see below), and that still seems the most appropriate coupling; but anyone whose collection has room for *Capriccio italien* rather than *Swan Lake* will find the present reissue hardly less rewarding. These were among the finest recordings the DG engineers made in the Philharmonie in the late 1970s.

(i) *Concert fantasy, Op. 56; Piano concertos Nos. 1–3;* (ii) *Violin concerto in D;* (iii) *Variations on a rococo theme for cello and orchestra, Op. 33.*
(M) **(*) EMI Dig./Analogue CMS7 64887-2 [id.]. (i) Peter Donohoe, Bournemouth SO, Rudolph Barshai; (ii) Nigel Kennedy, LPO, Okko Kamu; (iii) Paul Tortelier, N. Sinfonia, Yan Pascal Tortelier.

Peter Donohoe's account of the *B flat minor Concerto*, although thoroughly sympathetic and spaciously conceived, lacks the thrust and indeed the electricity of the finest versions. The *Third Piano concerto* is altogether more successful, dramatic and lyrically persuasive, and held together well by Barshai; this is now available at full price, sensibly coupled with the *Second*, and is a better buy than the present box. The *Concert fantasia* is even more in need of interpretative cohesion. A little more poise would have been welcome but there is no denying the spontaneous combustion of the music-making here, and the recording – but for a little too much resonance for the solo cadenza in the opening movement – is effectively spectacular.

Nigel Kennedy gives one of the most expansive readings of the first movement ever put on disc. Though the sound is ample, his idiosyncrasies will not please everyone. For all his many *tenutos* and *rallentandos*, however, Kennedy is not sentimental. The collection is completed by the Torteliers' enjoyably polished account of the *Rococo variations*, not a first choice, perhaps, but a recommendable one and given excellent analogue sound.

Piano concertos Nos. 1–3.
(N) (B) ** EMI forte CZS5 68637-2 (2) [id.]. Gilels, New Philh. O, Maazel – BARTOK: *Piano concerto No. 2;* PROKOFIEV: *Piano concerto No. 5.* *(*)

It is a pity that Gilels elects to play the truncated Siloti edition of the *Second Piano concerto*, for it effectively diminishes the claim that this inexpensive forte set has on the collector's allegiance. His playing is of the highest order of mastery and has the virtue of presenting the works with the freshness of new discovery. The (1972) Abbey Road recording is very good and the New Philharmonia under Maazel provide admirable support. However, this conductor formed a much less fruitful partnership with Richter and the couplings are disappointing.

Piano concertos Nos. 1–3; Concert fantasia.
(M) *** RCA 09026 61631-2 (3). Barry Douglas, LSO or Philh. O, Leonard Slatkin.

A first-class set in every way from Barry Douglas, giving a splendid survey of Tchaikovsky's major concertante works for piano. The *First Concerto* was recorded in 1986, before the others. Barry Douglas – outright winner of the Moscow Tchaikovsky competition that same year – proved an admirable soloist, his bravura always at the service of the music, and he provided many imaginative touches, especially in the first-movement cadenzas and the *Andante*, beautifully done. If Slatkin and the LSO made a more routine response, with a rather heavy reprise of the big tune in the finale, this still proved an impressive and enjoyable account. The other works in this box were all recorded together in June 1992. The *Second Concerto* immediately proves a great success, a performance to rank alongside the Donohoe version in its vigour and romantic sweep, with plenty of sparkle in the finale. The slow movement is beautifully played, with Douglas creating a warmly intimate relationship with the orchestral string soloists. The remaining two works were recorded at EMI's No. 1 Studio at Abbey Road, so yet again a resonant, concert-hall balance creates an expansive effect. Some might feel that in the *Concert fantasy* a more intimate acoustic would be preferable, but soloist and conductor both find plenty of delicacy for the composer's very winning balletic orchestral effects which provide the contrast for the more rhetorical pages. The *Third Concerto* is splendidly done, and here Slatkin's broadly passionate treatment of the main theme immediately reminds us that this work was originally planned as a symphony. The vigorous articulation of the jiggy Allegro is most infectious, and a highlight of the performance is Slatkin's handling of the recapitulation and especially the reprise of Tchaikovsky's lyrical secondary material.

Piano concerto No. 1 in B flat min., Op. 23.
⊛ (M) (***) RCA mono GD 60321. Horowitz, NBC SO, Toscanini – MUSSORGSKY: *Pictures.* (***)
(M) *** RCA 09026 61961-2. Van Cliburn, RCA SO, Kondrashin – BEETHOVEN: *Piano concerto No. 5.* ***
(N) *** Ph. 446 673-2 [id.]. Martha Argerich, Bavarian RSO, Kondrashin – RACHMANINOV: *Piano concerto No. 3.* ***
*** Chesky CD-13 [id.]. Earl Wild, RPO, Fistoulari – DOHNANYI: *Variations on a nursery tune* etc. ***
(M) *** Decca 417 750-2 [id.]. Ashkenazy, LSO, Maazel – CHOPIN: *Concerto No. 2.* ***
(M) *** RCA 09026 61262-2 [id.]. Artur Rubinstein, Boston SO, Leinsdorf – GRIEG: *Concerto.* **(*)
(M) **(*) Mercury 432 011-2 [id.]. Byron Janis, LSO, Menges – SCHUMANN: *Concerto.* ***
(M) (***) RCA mono GD 60449 [60449-2-RG]. Horowitz, NBC SO, Toscanini – MUSSORGSKY: *Pictures* etc. (***)
(Y/B) (M) ** Cziffra Edition, Volume 3: EMI CDM5 65252-2 [id.]. György Cziffra, Philh. O, André Vandernoot – LISZT: *Piano concertos Nos. 1 & 2.* **(*)
(Y/B) (M) (**) DG 447 420-2 [id.]. Sviatoslav Richter, VSO, Karajan – RACHMANINOV: *Piano concerto No. 2.* ***
(N) (B) *(*) Decca Eclipse Dig. 448 221-2; *448 221-4* [id.]. Victoria Postnikova, VSO, Rozhdestvensky – RACHMANINOV: *Piano concerto No. 2.* ***

(i) *Piano concerto No. 1. The Seasons, Op. 37: January; February; April; May; August; October; November; December.*
(Y/B) (B) *** Tring. Dig. TRP 023 [id.]. Ronan O'Hora, (i) with RPO, James Judd.

(i) *Piano concerto No. 1. Theme and variations, Op. 19/6.*
(M) *** EMI CDM7 64329-2 [id.]. Gavrilov, (i) Philh. O, Muti – BALAKIREV: *Islamey;* PROKOFIEV: *Concerto No. 1.* ***

Horowitz's famous record of the *B flat minor Concerto*, recorded at a concert in Carnegie Hall in 1943 with his father-in-law conducting, has achieved legendary status and has dwarfed almost every record of the work made since. The sheer power of the playing means that within seconds the ear makes allowances for the sonic limitations. This performance has now been reissued as part of the Toscanini Edition with a more attractive coupling than in its last incarnation. A record not to be missed on any account. (Readers should note that this live concert version of the Tchaikovsky *Concerto* is still also available coupled with Horowitz's 1952 recording, conducted by Reiner, of Beethoven's *Emperor Piano concerto*, on RCA GD 87992.)

Van Cliburn and the Soviet conductor Kondrashin give an inspired performance with as much warmth as glitter. The 1958 recording is forward and could do with more atmosphere, but the digital remastering has brought a firmer orchestral image, and the piano timbre is also improved. Coupled with an outstanding version of the *Emperor concerto*, this is a very distinguished reissue indeed, even if the piano timbre here is shallower than in the coupling.

Argerich's Philips issue comes from a live performance given in October 1980, full of animal excitement, with astonishingly fast speeds in the outer movements. The impetuous virtuosity is breathtaking, even if passage-work is not always as cleanly articulated as in her superb studio performance for DG. That earlier version also brings more variety of tone; but you will find few more satisfying performances on record than either of these. The CD version clarifies and intensifies the already vivid sound, which is fuller than her DG version of nine years earlier (see below), and the new coupling with her even more sensational account of Rachmaninov's *Third Concerto* makes this a very desirable reissue – even at full price.

Having already given us an outstanding version of the Grieg *Concerto*, Ronan O'Hora and James Judd repeat their success with a memorably fresh, new look at Tchaikovsky's *B flat minor Concerto*. The very opening is gloriously arresting, and then O'Hora sets off with a crisp, sparkling duplet rhythm for the main theme of the allegro, pulling back naturally and poetically for his gentle introduction of the lovely secondary group. The *Andante semplice* brings contrasting delicacy, and in the central section O'Hora's chimerical lightness is like a will-o'-the-wisp. Then the finale makes a fitting culmination, with the joyful spirit of Russian dance paramount, rather than any barnstorming; but the exciting final reprise of the big tune is capped with a stormy bravura flourish from the soloist. The whole performance has the spontaneous feel of a live occasion, and the recording balance is just about ideal, with a bold, natural piano-image set against a richly spacious orchestral tapestry. As with his Grieg record, the pianist chooses a coupling of solo pieces, in this case eight out of the twelve 'months' which make up *The Seasons*. They are presented with an agreeable, impulsive charm and plenty of colour. *May night*, the November *Troika* and the warmly lyrical October *Autumn song* are particularly successful.

Even in the shadow of Horowitz, the spectacular reissue by Earl Wild with the RPO under Fistoulari stands as one of the finest accounts ever of this much-recorded work and needs no apology for its sound, which is vintage quality of the early 1960s, although the violins have become a little drier with the digital remastering for CD. From the first sweep of the opening the reading is distinguished by its feeling of directness and power, yet the lyrical side of the music (the first movement's second subject, the outer sections of the *Andantino*) brings a comparable sensitivity. In the first movement there are some wholly spontaneous bursts of bravura from the soloist which are quite electrifying; the finale too, taken with crackling bravura, again recalls the famous Horowitz/Toscanini live Carnegie Hall recording and Fistoulari makes a superb final climax.

Ashkenazy refuses to be stampeded by Tchaikovsky's rhetoric, and the biggest climaxes of the first movement are made to grow naturally out of the music. In the *Andantino* too, Ashkenazy refuses to play flashily. The finale is very fast and brilliant, yet the big tune is broadened at the end in the most convincing way. The remastering is highly successful: the piano sounds splendidly bold and clear while the orchestral balance is realistic.

Rubinstein re-recorded the work for RCA in stereo in 1963 and is hardly less dashing than Horowitz. Yet, as before, there is a mercurial quality here, not only in the central section of the slow movement but also in the finale. The result, if perhaps not as overwhelming as with Horowitz, is hardly less magnetic, with fine bravura in the outer movements and a poetic *Andante*. Leinsdorf is obviously caught up in the music-making and the Boston Symphony opens the work splendidly and provides plenty of excitement throughout. The sound is remarkably good in its new CD incarnation.

Byron Janis's account is in many ways as dazzling as his Rachmaninov recordings. Menges is not as strong an accompanist as Dorati, most noticeably so in the finale. But this remains a memorable performance, with much dash and power from the soloist in the outer movements and the *Andantino* agreeably delicate. The Mercury sound is excellent, full and resonant, with a big piano image up front.

Horowitz's earlier version, coupled with the Mussorgsky, was made in Carnegie Hall, in 1941, under studio conditions. The recording is altogether better balanced than the live performance by the same artists, and the orchestral sound is much fuller; indeed the quality brooks no real criticism. But throughout one feels that Toscanini – with his soloist responding readily – is forcing the pace, creating enormous urgency. This is an exhilarating listening experience; but the sense of occasion of the live performance created a really great performance which is undoubtedly more satisfying despite its sonic limitations.

Gavrilov is stunning in the finale of the *Concerto*; however, the final statement of the big tune is broadened so positively that one is not entirely convinced. Similarly in the first movement, contrasts of dynamic and tempo are extreme, and the element of self-consciousness is apparent. The *Andante* is full of tenderness and the *prestissimo* middle section goes like quicksilver, displaying the vein of spontaneous imagination that we recognize in Gavrilov's other records. The recording is full and sumptuous. In the *Variations*, Op. 19, Tchaikovsky's invention has great felicity. Gavrilov's playing is stylishly sympathetic here, and the Balakirev and Prokofiev couplings are dazzling.

Cziffra, as always, displays a prodigious technique but the symbiosis he found with Vandernoot and the Philharmonia in Liszt is not sustained here. After a crude opening, during the first movement conductor and soloist seem not wholly agreed on the degree of forward thrust the music needs; sometimes one presses on, sometimes the other. The *Andante* offers nothing special, and the finale is very much a Russian dance and lacks the barnstorming one would expect; the reprise of the big tune is pulled right back very spaciously indeed, almost losing the music's impetus, and only the pianist's final burst of energy saves the day. Despite the use of the Kingsway Hall, the 1958 recording, with its bright primary colours and tendency to harshness of lighting, is comparatively two-dimensional and the strings tend to shrillness.

The element of struggle for which this work is famous is all too clear in the Richter/Karajan performance; not surprisingly, these two musical giants do not always agree: each chooses a different tempo for the second subject of the finale and maintains it, despite the other. However, in both the dramatic opening and the closing pages of the work they are agreed in a hugely mannered, bland stylization which is not easy to enjoy. Clearly two major artists are at work, but it is difficult to praise the end-product as a convincing reading. The recording is full-blooded, with a firm piano image.

The collaboration of wife and husband in the Postnikova/Rozhdestvensky performance makes for a very personal reading, marked by spacious speeds. The very introduction is disconcertingly slow and so is the basic tempo for the central *Andante*, while in other places Postnikova's expressive fluctuations sound studied, even if the clarity of articulation is remarkable.

(i) *Piano concerto No. 1 in B flat min., Op. 23;* (ii) *Violin concerto in D, Op. 35;* (iii) *Hamlet (fantasy overture);* (iv) *Overture, The Storm, Op. 76;* (v) *Romeo and Juliet (fantasy overture);* (vi) *Serenade for strings in C, Op. 48: Waltz and finale. Symphonies Nos. 4 in F min., Op. 36;* (vii) *5 in E min., Op. 64;* (viii) *6 in B min. (Pathétique), Op. 74;* (ix) *Variations on a rococo theme, Op. 33;* (x) *Eugene Onegin:* Act I: *Tatiana's letter scene;* (iii) Act II: *Waltz;* Act III: *Polonaise.*

(N) ✹ (M) (***) EMI mono CHS7 64855-2 (4) [id.]. (i) Solomon, Philh. O, Issay Dobrowen; (ii) Bronislaw Huberman, Staatskapelle Berlin, William Steinberg; (iii) Philh. O, Dobrowen; (iv) Philh. O, Lovro von Matačić; (v) VPO, Karajan; (vi) VPO, Furtwängler; (vii) La Scala, Milan, O, Cantelli; (viii) BPO, Furtwängler; (ix) Tortelier, Philh. O, Menges; (x) Ljuba Welitsch, Philh. O, Walter Susskind.

This is *the* indispensable Tchaikovsky box. It collects great performances, mainly from the late 1940s, including the aristocratic (1949) Solomon account of the *B flat minor concerto* which, in terms of poetry, finesse and virtuosity, can hold its own with any in the catalogue. The two great pre-war records are the wonderfully pure Huberman (1928) account of the *Violin concerto* with the youthful William Steinberg conducting and the electrifying (1938) *Pathétique* from Furtwängler and the Berlin Philharmonic. Collectors will not need reminding of the dramatic intensity of Ljuba Welitsch's Letter scene from *Eugene Onegin*, recorded in 1948, or of Karajan's superb 1946 *Romeo and Juliet* with the Vienna Philharmonic (possibly never surpassed in his later recordings). Re-hearing the Cantelli La Scala performance of the *Fifth Symphony*, recorded at the EMI Abbey Road studios immediately after their appearance at the 1950 Edinburgh Festival, makes one realize why it has become legendary. It is absolutely straight, classical in its proportions, restrained yet totally authentic in feeling, and played marvellously. Furtwängler's account of the *Fourth* with the Vienna Philharmonic is the only performance that could possibly excite controversy, for it does not have the intensity of his *Pathétique*. Tortelier made his first version of the *Rococo variations* with Beecham in 1947. As this is available separately, coupled with Strauss's *Don Quixote*, the choice here was of his later (1955) version with Menges and the Philharmonia. Apart from their excellence artistically, the *Hamlet* and *The Storm* Overture which the Philharmonia recorded with Lovro von Matačić in 1956 pay testimony to the splendid ears of the production team, Lawrance Collingwood and Douglas Larter. Excellent transfers too.

Piano concerto No. 1 in B flat min., Op. 23; Concert fantasy, Op. 56.
*** Virgin/EMI Dig. VC7 59612-2 [id.]. Pletnev, Philh. O, Fedoseyev.

Mikhail Pletnev's masterful account of the *First Concerto* has all the qualities we associate with his remarkable pianism. This high-voltage account, together with that of the *Concert fantasy*, is among the very finest modern recordings in the catalogue. Vladimir Fedoseyev and the Philharmonia Orchestra give excellent support and the production by Andrew Keener is exemplary.

(i) *Piano concerto No. 1;* (ii) *Violin concerto in D, Op. 35.*
(B) *** DG 439 420-2 [id.]. (i) Martha Argerich, RPO, Dutoit; (ii) Milstein, VPO, Abbado.
(Y/B) (BB) *** RCA Navigator 74321 17900-2 [id.]. (i) John Browning; (ii) Erick Friedman; LSO, Ozawa.
(M) **(*) Sony Dig. MDK 44643 [id.]. (i) Gilels, NYPO; (ii) Zukerman, Israel PO; Mehta.
(N) (M) *(*) Ph. 446 203-2 [id.]. (i) Rafael Orozco, Rotterdam PO, Edo de Waart; (ii) Henryk Szeryng, Concg. O, Haitink.

Argerich's 1971 version of the *First Piano concerto* with Dutoit has long been among the top recommendations. The sound is firm, with excellent presence, and its ambience is more attractive than the later version. The weight of the opening immediately sets the mood for a big, broad performance, with the kind of music-making in which the personalities of both artists are complementary. Argerich's conception encompasses the widest range of tonal shading. In the finale she often produces a scherzando-like effect; then the orchestra thunders in with the Russian dance-theme to create a real contrast. The tempo of the first movement is comparatively measured, but satisfyingly so; the slow movement is strikingly atmospheric, yet delicate, its romanticism light-hearted. Milstein's 1973 performance of the *Violin concerto* is equally impressive, undoubtedly one of the finest available, while Abbado secures playing of genuine sensitivity and scale from the Vienna Philharmonic, with a recording that is also well balanced.

Browning's mid-1960s interpretation of the solo role in the *Piano concerto* is remarkable, not only for power and bravura but for wit and point in the many *scherzando* passages, and in the finale he adopts a fast and furious tempo to compare with Horowitz. Erick Friedman, Heifetz's pupil, is a thoughtful violinist who gives a keenly intelligent performance of the companion work, imbued with a glowing lyricism and with a particularly poetic and beautiful account of the slow movement. There is plenty of dash and fire in the finale, and Ozawa gives first-rate support to both soloists. The recording is excellent. Two performances to match those of almost any rival; moreover this disc is in the lowest price-range.

On CBS there are more reservations about the Gilels performance than the Zukerman. The former offers less than first-class orchestral playing and not very distinguished sound, but Gilels's own playing is masterly. In Israel, the sound is much better, and Mehta secures generally good results from the Israel orchestra. The soloist is balanced closely and is made very tangible; Zukerman's warmth is most attractive, and the performance overall has both excitement and spontaneity.

The Philips alternative is uncompetitive. Orozco's version of the *First Piano concerto* is flamboyant enough but, despite the bravura and good (mid-1970s) recording, it fails to be memorable. The *prestissimo* central section of the slow movement is certainly intended by the composer as an opportunity for the soloist to show his mettle, but the lack of refinement here is unattractive. Szeryng is sweetly lyrical in the *Violin concerto*, but he is not helped by Haitink, who provides a rather slack accompaniment. The relaxed manner of the performance of the first movement fails to generate enough impulse and the finale too, although spirited, fails to ignite. This cannot match Szeryng's early stereo version of the work with the Boston Symphony and Munch.

Piano concerto No. 2 in G (complete); Piano sonata No. 1 in G (Grande sonate), Op. 37.
*** Teldec/Warner Dig. 9031 72296-2 [id.]. Elisabeth Leonskaja; (i) Leipzig GO, Kurt Masur.

A splendid new version of Tchaikovsky's *G minor Piano concerto*, weightier and more expansive (more German!) than the famous Donohoe version and certainly compelling. The red-blooded orchestral tuttis are matched by Leonskaja's (forwardly balanced) bold pianism, and if the slow movement misses some of the delicacy of feeling that Donohoe finds, and the extended solos for violin and cello have rather less individuality than with Kennedy and Isserlis, there is much lyrical ardour. The finale, too, is not chimerical but forceful in its exuberance, powerful and exciting, and the rich Leipzig recording matches the style of the performance. The coupling of Tchaikovsky's *Grand Sonata* in the same key is surely an ideal one. Leonskaja has the full measure of its rhetoric and she plays the *Andante* with an appealing spontaneity and freshness.

Piano concertos Nos. 2 in G, Op. 44; 3 in E flat, Op. 75.
✹ *** EMI Dig. CDC7 49940-2 [id.]. Donohoe, Bournemouth SO, Barshai.
*** Ara. Dig. Z 6583 [id.]. Jerome Lowenthal, LSO, Comissiona.

Donohoe's much-praised recording of Tchaikovsky's *Second Piano concerto* is coupled with his excellent account of the *Third*. This superb recording of the full, original score of the *Second* in every way justifies the work's length and the unusual format of the slow movement, with its extended solos for violin and cello; these are played with beguiling warmth by Nigel Kennedy and Steven Isserlis. Barshai's pacing is perfectly calculated. The first movement goes with a splendid impetus, and the performance of the slow movement is a delight from beginning to end. Peter Donohoe plays marvellously and in the finale he is inspired to bravura which recalls Horowitz in the *B flat minor Concerto*. The main theme, shooting off with the velocity of the ball in a pinball machine, is exhilarating, and the orchestral response has a matching excitement. The recording has a fine, spacious ambience and is admirably realistic and very well balanced.

In an obviously attractive coupling of two unjustly neglected works, the energy and flair of Lowenthal and Comissiona combine to give highly spontaneous performances, well balanced and recorded. If the *G major Concerto* has not quite the distinction of the EMI version, it is still satisfyingly alive; the soloist brings an individual, poetic response as well as bravura. With very good sound, this is well worth investigating, as the account of the *Third Concerto* is comparably spontaneous.

Piano concerto No. 3.
(*) Chandos Dig. CHAN 9130 [id.]. Geoffrey Tozer, LPO, Järvi – *Symphony No. 7.* *

It was a very good idea to record the *Third Piano concerto* alongside the *Seventh Symphony*, on whose first movement it is based (see below). Geoffrey Tozer is an excellent soloist and, as in his Medtner performances for Chandos, plays with sympathy as well as powerful bravura. The playing of the London Philharmonic is not so consistent, with violin tone as recorded often thin, not opulent enough for big Tchaikovsky melodies.

(i) *Piano concertos Nos. 1–3;* (ii) *Violin concerto.*
(N) (B) *(*) Decca Double Dig. (2) [id.]. (i) Victoria Postnikova, VSO, Rozhdestvensky; (ii) Kyung-Wha Chung, Montreal SO, Dutoit.

The Postnikova/Rozhdestvensky performance of the *First Concerto* is unconvincing with its very measured tempos (see above). These artists choose the complete original score of the *Second Concerto*, but again, with slow speeds, the performance hangs fire. The long single movement of the *Third Concerto* also needs more consistently persuasive treatment, though the dactylic dance-theme is delectably pointed. Close balance for the piano in a firm, clear recording, enhanced on CD – but the performances remain unenticing. Even at Decca Double price this set cannot be recommended, not even with the inclusion of Chung's splendid account of the *Violin concerto*, which is in a wholly different and higher league.

Violin concerto in D, Op. 35.
(N) *** Teldec/Warner Dig. 4509 90881-2 [id.]. Vengerov, BPO, Abbado – GLAZUNOV: *Violin concerto.* ***

(N) *** Erato/Warner Dig. 4509 98537-2 [id.]. Vadim Repin, LSO, Emmanuel Krivine – SIBELIUS: *Violin concerto.* ***

(Y/B) *** Sony Dig. SK 66567 [id.]. Julian Rachlin, Moscow RSO, Vladimir Fedoseyev – PROKOFIEV: *Violin concerto No. 1.* ***

(Y/B) (M) *** Decca 425 080-2 [id.]. Kyung-Wha Chung, LSO, Previn – SIBELIUS: *Violin concerto.* ***
*** EMI Dig. CDC7 54753-2 [id.]. Sarah Chang, LSO, Sir Colin Davis – BRAHMS: *Hungarian dances.* ***

(BB) *** Naxos Dig. 8.550153; *4550153* [id.]. Takako Nishizaki, Slovak PO, Kenneth Jean – MENDELSSOHN: *Concerto.* ***

(M) *** DG 419 067-2 [id.]. Milstein, VPO, Abbado – MENDELSSOHN: *Concerto.* ***
*** Decca Dig. 421 716-2 [id.]. Joshua Bell, Cleveland O, Ashkenazy – WIENIAWSKI: *Violin concerto No. 2.* ***

(N) (M) *** Sony Stern Edition I SMK 66829 [id.]. Stern, Phd. O, Ormandy – SIBELIUS: *Violin concerto.* ***

(***) Testament mono SBT 1038 [id.]. Ida Haendel, RPO, Goossens – BRAHMS: *Violin concerto.* (***)

(M) (***) EMI mono CDH7 64030-2 [id.]. Heifetz, LPO, Barbirolli – GLAZUNOV: *Violin concerto* (***) ✪; SIBELIUS: *Violin concerto.* (**)

(M) *** RCA 09026 61495-2. Heifetz, Chicago SO, Reiner – BRAHMS: *Concerto.* ***

(N) **(*) Ph. Dig. 446 131-2 [id.]. Josefovicz, ASMF, Marriner – SIBELIUS: *Violin concerto.* **

Violin concerto in D; Sérénade mélancolique, Op. 26; Souvenir d'un lieu cher, Op. 42/3: Mélodie. Valse-scherzo, Op. 34.
*** ASV Dig. CDDCA 713 [id.]. Xue-Wei, Philh. O, Accardo.

Violin concerto in D; Sérénade mélancolique, Op. 26; Valse-scherzo, Op. 34.
(M) *** Erato/Warner 2292 45971-2 [id.]. Pierre Amoyal, Philh. O, Dutoit.

The two most popular romantic Russian violin concertos make an excellent and surprisingly rare coupling, and Vengerov gives inspired performances of both, with magic inspiration breathing new life into music that is well known. This Tchaikovsky reading immediately establishes itself as a big performance, both in the daring manner and in the range of dynamic of the playing. For all his power and his youthfully eager love of brilliance, Vengerov is never reluctant to play really softly. The central *Canzonetta* is full of Russian temperament, free in his natural expressiveness. The finale is sparklingly light, with articulation breathtakingly clean to match the transparency of the orchestral textures. The close brings an eruption of excitement, as in a live performance.

Repin's withdrawn tone in moments of meditation and his fondness for the gentlest pianissimos are as remarkable as his purity and sharpness of focus in bravura. Many interpretative details like sudden pianissimos are remarkably similar to those in the Teldec version by his close colleague, Maxim Vengerov, but this is a tauter reading, with tone less fat, more finely focused. It brings many moments of magic, such as the gentle lead-in to the second subject and the whispered statement of the main theme in the central *Canzonetta*, enhanced by the natural balance of the soloist in refined and well-detailed Erato recording, making this a highly recommendable alternative to Chung and Mullova in this favourite coupling.

As in the Prokofiev, Julian Rachlin gives an exceptionally characterful and distinctive reading, not conventionally high-powered but thoughtful and hushed in intensity, rare qualities in this concerto. He is helped by a natural balance for the solo instrument in these live recordings, made in the Moscow Conservatoire in February 1994. Some may feel that Rachlin's determination to observe every pianissimo marking detracts from the power of his reading, but with magnetic concentration he makes such bravura passages as the big cadenza sound like spontaneous expression, volatile and mercurial, not just a display vehicle. Rachlin uses echo effects – not always marked in the score – in the lyrical episodes of both the central *Canzonetta* and the finale, where he not only plays with yearning beauty but also gives sparkle to the main theme rather than thrusting on with sheer power. The volatile quality of this live recording sets problems for the orchestra, which is not always crisp in its ensemble, but the soloist's performance is what matters.

Chung's earlier recording of the Tchaikovsky *Concerto* with Previn conducting has remained one of the strongest recommendations for a much-recorded work ever since it was made, right at the beginning of her career. Although she recorded it later with Dutoit, anyone should be well satisfied with Chung's 1970 version with its Sibelius coupling. Her technique is impeccable and her musicianship of the highest order, and Previn's accompanying is highly sympathetic and responsive. This has warmth, spontaneity and discipline, every detail is beautifully shaped and turned without a trace of sentimentality. The recording is well balanced and detail is clean, though the acoustic is warm. This is a very distinguished record, very suitable for reissue in Decca's Classic Sound series.

Sarah Chang is a very young artist who, from her first note onwards, compels attention with her poetic and imaginative treatment of each phrase, always sounding spontaneous. Not only does Chang play with exceptionally pure tone, avoiding heavy coloration, her individual artistry does not demand the wayward pulling-about often found in this work. In that she is enormously helped by the fresh, bright and dramatic accompaniment provided by the LSO under Sir Colin Davis, always a sensitive and helpful concerto conductor, and here encouraging generally steady speeds. Even Chang's relatively slow tempo for the central Canzonetta is acceptable, when the tone is so true and sweet and the shading so refined. In the outer movements Chang conveys wit along with the power and poetry, and the intonation is immaculate. She observes the tiny cuts in the passage-work, which until recently were always traditional in the finale. The snag is the ungenerous coupling, but Chang's performances of the four Brahms *Hungarian dances* are delectable.

Xue-Wei gives a warmly expressive reading of this lovely concerto, lacking some of the fantasy and mystery, but, with rich, full tone, he brings out the sensuousness of the work, while displaying commanding virtuosity. The central *Canzonetta* is turned into a simple song without words, not over-romanticized. The coupling will be ideal for many, consisting of violin concertante pieces by Tchaikovsky, not just the *Sérénade mélancolique*, but the *Valse-scherzo* in a dazzling performance, and *Mélodie*, the third of the three pieces that Tchaikovsky grouped as *Souvenir d'un lieu cher*, freely and expressively done. The orchestral playing under another great violin virtuoso is warmly sympathetic but could be crisper, not helped for detail in tuttis by the lively acoustic of St Barnabas Church, Mitcham. However, this makes a very enjoyable collection.

Like Xue-Wei, Pierre Amoyal offers Tchaikovsky's other music for violin and orchestra as coupling, although (unlike the ASV disc) the *Souvenir d'un lieu cher* is not included. However, the Erato collection has a considerable price advantage and the remastered 1981 analogue recording is very beautiful. Even in a strongly competitive field the Amoyal performance of the *Concerto* is strongly recommendable. His is a warmly lyrical performance, yet there is no lack of passionate commitment, and the slow movement is particularly affecting when the sound is so lovely, warm and natural, and much better balanced than with Heifetz. While Dutoit does not press the first movement on as fierily as Reiner, he still gets exciting results from the Philharmonia, and the two shorter pieces, equally sympathetic, make a perfect foil for the major work.

Takako Nishizaki gives a warm and colourful reading, tender but purposeful and full of temperament. As in the Mendelssohn with which this is coupled, the central slow movement is on the measured side but flows sweetly, while the finale has all the necessary bravura, even at a speed that avoids breathlessness. Unlike many, Nishizaki opens out the little cuts which had become traditional. With excellent playing and recording, this makes a first-rate recommendation in the super-bargain bracket.

Milstein's fine 1973 version with Abbado is here coupled with the Mendelssohn *Concerto* and remains one of the best mid-price reissues.

Bell may not have quite the fantasy of a version like Chung's Decca performance, but it is an outstanding account nevertheless, very recommendable if you fancy the unusual coupling of Wieniawski. In the finale of the Tchaikovsky, Bell does not open out the tiny cuts in the passage-work that until recently have been traditional. Full, brilliant recording, with the soloist well balanced.

Stern was on peak form when he made his first stereo recording with Ormandy, and it is a powerfully lyrical reading, rich in timbre and technically immaculate. The playing has undoubted poetry, but it is not helped by the very close balance of the soloist, so that *pianissimos* consistently become *mezzo fortes*. The orchestral sound is vivid but lacks amplitude.

Recorded in mono in 1953, Ida Haendel's red-bloodedly romantic account is such a distinctive, positive and powerful reading, one is grateful to Testament for bringing back so unjustly neglected a recording, and in such a vivid transfer. With speeds on the broad side in the first two movements, and generally kept steady, Haendel's warmly expressive style is the more compelling, leading to a fast and muscular account of the finale. It is generously and ideally coupled with Haendel's masterly reading of the Brahms, similarly neglected.

Heifetz's first (mono) recording of the Tchaikovsky *Violin concerto*, made in 1937, has tremendous virtuosity and warmth. The sound is opaque by modern standards but the ear quickly adjusts, and the performance is special even by Heifetz's own standards. The transfer, too, is very good and, coming as it does with a classic account of the Glazunov and a fascinating Sibelius, this is a real bargain.

There can be no real reservations about the sound of the present remastering of Heifetz's 1957 recording, with the Chicago acoustics ensuring a full ambience to support the brilliance of the orchestra. Heifetz is closely balanced, but the magic of his playing can be fully enjoyed. There is some gorgeous lyrical phrasing, and the slow movement marries deep feeling and tenderness in an ideal performance. The finale is dazzling but is never driven too hard. Reiner always accompanies understandingly, producing fierily positive tuttis. The Brahms coupling is equally desirable and much more generous than the offerings with the older, full-priced CD.

As in the Sibelius, so in the Tchaikovsky, Leila Josefovicz gives a strong, purposeful reading, belying her tender years. If it lacks something in poetry, the warmth makes amends, as well as the excitement of the outer movements, taken very fast. The slow movement is broader than usual, with Josefovicz underlining the *Canzonetta*'s main theme rather heavily. In her thrilling account of the finale she observes the traditional cuts that many nowadays open out.

(i) *Violin concerto;* (ii) *Variations on a Rococo theme, Op. 33.*
**(*) EMI Dig. CDC7 54890-2 [id.]. (i) Nigel Kennedy, LPO, Kamu; (ii) Paul Tortelier, N. Sinfonia, Yan-Pascal Tortelier.

Nigel Kennedy gives a warmly romantic and very measured reading of the *Concerto* (see above), full of temperament. For all his many *tenutos* and *rallentandos*, however, Kennedy is not sentimental, and his range of tone is exceptionally rich and wide, so that the big moments are powerfully sensual. Okku Kamu and the LPO do not always match their soloist; the accompaniment sometimes sounds a little stiff in tuttis, though the final coda is thrilling. This performance is available coupled to an outstanding version of the Sibelius *Concerto* with Simon Rattle (EMI CDC7 54 127-2; *EL 754 127-4*) or in the above pairing with Tortelier's finely wrought account of the *Rococo variations*, which is very enjoyable if of less generous measure. Here the recording is analogue and of excellent quality.

(i) *1812 Overture; Capriccio italien.*

(N) ✿ (M) *** Mercury 434 360-2 [id.]. (i) Bronze French cannon, bells of Laura Spelman Rockefeller Memorial Carillon, Riverside Church, New York City; Minneapolis SO, Dorati (with separate descriptive commentary by Deems Taylor) – BEETHOVEN: *Wellington's victory.* *** ✿

Just as in our listing of this famous Mercury record we have placed *1812* first, so in the credits the cannon and the glorious sounds of the Laura Spelman Carillon take precedence, for in the riveting climax of Tchaikovsky's most famous work the effects completely upstage the orchestra. This is not to suggest that Dorati's performance is in any way lacking. Indeed he makes a great deal of the character and colour of the Russian folk material on which the composer draws so tellingly. But at the end, when the carillon floods into the listener's room and the cannon open fire, the effect is quite overwhelming – far more so than it ever was in its original, LP format, when the narrow grooves could not contain the full amplitude of the sound without some degree of congestion. On this remastered CD the balance is managed spectacularly and the timing of the 'shots' nicely arranged by Wilma Cozart Fine's skilful editing, while the Minneapolis orchestra, who are clearly enjoying themselves both in *1812* and in the brilliant account of *Capriccio italien*, give of their best – even if the (early 1958) stereo is not entirely flattering to the violins. Deems Taylor provides an avuncular commentary on the technical background to the original recording. But heed the cautionary warning on the CD packaging, for before he begins to speak the cannon reopen fire!

(i) *1812 overture;* (ii) *Marche slave.*

(N) (M) **(*) Decca Phase 4 443 896-2 [id.]. (i) Welsh Nat. Op. Ch., Band of Grenadier Guards, RPO Ch., RPO; (ii) LSO; Stokowski – MUSSORGSKY: *Night on the bare mountain* etc. **; BORODIN: *Prince Igor: Polovtsian dances.* **

Stokowski's very eccentric *1812* certainly does not lack spectacle, although it is coarsely recorded. The pyrotechnic effects in the closing pages are accompanied by an overwhelming carillon, then suddenly the chorus appears out of nowhere to sing the Russian hymn. Similarly in *Marche slave* there are gross manipulations of balance to bring out certain instruments (the heavy brass especially) and effects. But it is a powerful performance with a whimsical beginning to the coda.

1812 Overture; Francesca da Rimini; Marche slave; Romeo and Juliet (fantasy overture).
(M) *** EMI Dig. CD-EMX 2152; *TC-EMX 2152.* RLPO, Sian Edwards.

1812 Overture; Hamlet (fantasy overture), *Op. 67; The Tempest, Op. 18.*
*** Delos Dig. D/CD 3081 [id.]. Oregon SO, James DePreist.

The control of the emotional ebb and flow of *Francesca da Rimini* shows Sian Edwards as an instinctive Tchaikovskian. Francesca's clarinet entry is melting and the work's middle section has a Beechamesque sense of colour. The passionate climax, representing the discovery of the lovers, falls only just short of the vehement force of the Stokowski version, while the spectacular recording gives great impact to the closing whirlwind sequence and the despair-laden final chords, where the tam-tam makes its presence felt very pungently. *1812* is also very enjoyable indeed, full of vigour and flair, a majestic final sequence with superbly resounding cannon. In *Romeo and Juliet*, the love-theme is ushered in very naturally and blossoms with the fullest ardour, while the feud music combined with the Friar Lawrence theme reaches a very dramatic climax. *Marche slave*, resplendently high-spirited and exhilarating, makes a perfect foil. The full-bodied recording is well balanced and thrilling in the proper Tchaikovskian way.

The Oregon orchestra show their paces in this vividly colourful triptych, and James DePreist is a highly sympathetic Tchaikovskian. In *1812*, the cannon are perfectly placed and their spectacular entry is as precise as it is commanding. The performance overall is highly enjoyable, energetic but with the pacing unforced, though the ritenuto before the final peroration is not quite convincing. The performances of both *Hamlet* and *The Tempest* are passionately dramatic, the latter generating comparable intensity to (but more melodrama than) Dorati's Decca version, the former approaching yet not quite equalling Stokowski's account in imaginative vividness. But overall this is an impressive CD début.

(i) *1812 Overture;* (ii) *Romeo and Juliet* (fantasy overture); (iii) *Serenade for strings in C, Op. 48.*
(Y/B) (M) **(*) DG Dig. 439 468-2 [id.]. (i) Gothenburg SO, Järvi; (ii) Philh. O, Sinopoli; (iii) Orpheus CO.

Järvi's *1812* is exciting – and not just for the added Gothenburg brass and artillery or for the fervour of the orchestra at the opening. Järvi clearly knows how to structure the piece, and he obviously enjoys the histrionics, and so do we. Sinopoli's reading of *Romeo and Juliet*, however, is not so spontaneous-sounding, with a hint of self-consciousness at the first entry of the big love theme; however, there is plenty of uninhibited passion on the later repeats. In the *Serenade for strings* no one could accuse the Orpheus Chamber Orchestra of lack of energy in the outer movements. Overall it is an impressive performance, even if the problems of rubato without a conductor are not always easily solved. The sound is first class, with the acoustics of the Performing Arts Center at New York State University providing plenty of warmth as well as clarity and a full, firm bass-line, very important in this work.

(i) *Fatum* (symphonic poem), *Op. 77;* (ii; iii) *Francesca da Rimini* (fantasy after Dante), *Op. 32;* (ii; iii) *Hamlet* (fantasy overture), *Op 67a;* (iv; v) *Romeo and Juliet* (fantasy overture); (i) *The Storm, Op. 76; The Tempest, Op. 18; The Voyevoda, Op. 78* (symphonic poems);(iv; iii) *Overture 1812, Op. 49.*

(Y/B) (B) **(*) Ph. Duo 442 586-2 (2) [id.]. (i) Frankfurt RSO, Eliahu Inbal; (ii) New Philh. O; (iii) Igor Markevitch; (iv) Concg. O; (v) Bernard Haitink.

On this two-for-the-price-of-one Duo set come finely committed performances of four of Tchaikovsky's little-known symphonic poems in excellent recordings from the mid-1970s with the right kind of sonority and ambience. The most remarkable piece (which is superbly performed by Inbal and the Frankfurt orchestra) is *The Storm,* a surprisingly coherent structure in sonata form which suddenly appeared in 1864 as Tchaikovsky's first fully fledged orchestral composition (after various student efforts). It has all the fingerprints of the later masterpieces: individual and attractive melodic and harmonic content and an astonishing orchestral flair. Yet the composer never published it. In his splendid biography of the composer, David Brown comments: 'Much of *The Storm* has the familiar and individual sound of Tchaikovsky's own mature orchestration. Already he is showing that natural facility of conceiving his ideas directly in terms of orchestral textures and colour.' *The Voyevoda* is a very late work which is unconnected with the opera of the same name (they are based on different subjects). If not entirely successful, it has some good ideas and characteristic orchestration. But it so dissatisfied its composer – though not the press and public – at its first performance that he tore up the score in anger and despair. Fortunately the orchestral parts survived. *Fatum,* written four years after *The Storm,* is a much less successful and less assured piece and rests completely in the shade of the composer's first great masterpiece, *Romeo and Juliet,* which followed in 1869 (although it was revised twice, in 1870 and 1880). *The Tempest* is notable for its memorably passionate love theme and the atmospheric opening and close depicting Prospero's island and the sea. Here the performance is very ardent, but the reverberant acoustic makes Tchaikovsky's climaxes a bit noisy. Markevitch's accounts of *Francesca da Rimini* and *Hamlet* have characteristic intensity and drive, but are weaker in dealing with the lyrical passages, although there are no complaints about the orchestral playing. Haitink's *Romeo and Juliet* is full of atmosphere and is spaciously conceived, although it builds up a full head of passion rather slowly. *1812* makes a lively bonus, rather individual in its pacing, but not unconvincingly so. But it is for the four novelties that this set is worthwhile.

Festival coronation march in D; (i) *Romeo and Juliet:* duet (orch. Taneyev).
*** Chandos Dig. CHAN 8476 [id.]. (i) Murphy, Lewis, Wilson-Johnson; SNO, Järvi – RACHMANI-NOV: *The Bells* etc. **(*)

Tchaikovsky's *Festival coronation march* is suitably grandiloquent but has a rather engaging trio, plus a whiff of the Tsarist hymn we recognize from *1812.* It is very well played here and superbly recorded. The vocalization of *Romeo and Juliet,* with the music drawn from the famous fantasy overture, was left in the form of posthumous sketches, which Taneyev completed and scored. The effect is more like a symphonic poem with vocal obbligatos, rather than operatic. It is well sung here but is mainly of curiosity value.

Festival overture on the Danish national anthem, Op. 15; (i) *Hamlet: Overture and incidental music, Op. 67 bis. Mazeppa: Battle of Poltava and Cossack dance; Romeo and Juliet* (fantasy overture; 1869 version); *Serenade for Nikolai Rubinstein's saint's day.*
*** Chandos Dig. CHAN 8310/11 [id.]. LSO, Simon, (i) with Janis Kelly, Hammond-Stroud.

Tchaikovsky himself thought his *Danish Festival overture* superior to *1812,* and though one cannot agree with his judgement it is well worth hearing. The *Hamlet* incidental music, however, shows the composer's inspiration at its most memorable. The music from *Mazeppa* and the tribute to Rubinstein make engaging bonuses, but the highlight of the set is the 1869 version of *Romeo and Juliet.* It is fascinating to hear the composer's early thoughts before he finalized a piece which was to become one of the most successful of all his works. The performances here under Geoffrey Simon are excitingly committed and spontaneous; the orchestral playing is nearly always first rate, and the digital recording has spectacular resonance and depth to balance its brilliance. Edward Johnson, who provided the initial impetus for the recordings, writes the excellent notes and a translation of the vocal music.

Francesca da Rimini; Hamlet (fantasy overture), *Op. 67a.*
❀ *** Dell'Arte CDDA 9006 [id.]. NY Stadium O, Stokowski.

Stokowski's famous Everest coupling – one of his greatest records – is here remastered for CD with great success, with the sound cleaner and clearer, yet remarkably expansive in the bass in *Hamlet*. Stokowski's inspired performance is quite sensational: he plays the central lyrical tune so convincingly that, if it has not quite the romantic panache of *Romeo and Juliet*, it has instead the proper sombre passion apt for the altogether different atmosphere of Shakespeare's *Hamlet*. Fascinatingly, Stokowski shows us how intensely Russian the music is; the funeral march at the end is extremely moving. *Francesca* is hardly less exciting: the opening whirlwinds have seldom roared at such tornado speeds before, the central section is played with beguiling care for detail and balance and, when the great polyphonic climax comes and the themes for the lovers' passion intertwine with music to suggest they are discovered, the tension is tremendous. The New York Stadium Orchestra drew on the New York Philharmonic for its players and the tremendous commitment of their response more than makes up for any slight imperfections of ensemble. The recording throughout is astonishingly vivid, and this is an outstanding reissue in every way. An indispensable record for all Tchaikovskians.

Francesca da Rimini; Suite No. 3 in G, Op. 55.
(N) **(*) Chandos Dig. CHAN 9419 [id.]. Detroit SO, Järvi.

This is an unexpected but nicely judged pairing of the most ambitious and most memorable of the *Orchestral Suites* with the much-better-known *Fantasia* after Dante, *Francesca da Rimini*. The perform-ances may not be the most refined we have had but, with Järvi characteristically drawing warmly expressive performances from his Detroit players, the disc can be recommended to anyone who fancies the coupling. For all the warmth and understanding, Järvi's treatment of the *Suite* is a little heavy-handed. The performance is well characterized – not least in the colourfully varied *Variations* which make up the last and longest movement – but lacks something in charm and polish. Järvi is most successful in the thrust of his conducting as he builds up to powerful climaxes. The acoustic of the Detroit Symphony Orchestra Hall is not as helpful as it might be to high fortissimo violins, which need more air round them. The performance of *Francesca da Rimini*, though neither as bitingly dramatic nor as polished as some, gains from the weight of the Chandos sound, with Järvi again a warmly sympa-thetic interpreter, even if the climax of the love-music teeters on the edge of vulgarity, something even Stokowski manages to avoid.

(i) *Hamlet: Overture and incidental music, Op. 67 bis. Romeo and Juliet* (fantasy overture: original (1869) version).
⊛ *** Chandos Dig. CHAN 9191 [id.]. (i) Janis Kelly, Hammond-Stroud; LSO, Simon.

An admirable recoupling. The (1869) original version of *Romeo and Juliet* is very different from the 1880 revision we all know so well: it has a completely different opening section and, after a less well-organized development of the feud and love music, ends sombrely but rather less tellingly than Tchaikovsky's final masterpiece. The composer's second thoughts were undoubtedly superior but, even so, the earlier ver-sion is a most enjoyable work in its own right with at least two unfamiliar tunes, and it remains a very Russian response to Shakespeare's tragedy. Geoffrey Simon is a committed advocate and the perform-ances here are exciting and spontaneous. The *Hamlet incidental music* is hardly less valuable. The overture is a shortened version of the *Hamlet fantasy overture*, but much of the rest of the incidental music is unknown, and the engaging *Funeral march* and the two poignant string elegies show the composer at his finest. *Ophelia's mad scene* is partly sung and partly spoken, and Janis Kelly's perform-ance is most sympathetic, while Derek Hammond-Stroud is suitably robust in the *Gravedigger's song*. A translation of the vocal music is provided. It is sung here in French (as in the original production of *Hamlet*, performed in St Petersburg), using a translation of the play. The digital recording has spectacu-lar resonance and depth to balance its brilliance, and there are excellent new notes by Noël Goodwin, though why Edward Johnson's commentary (which accompanied the original issue) has been replaced is difficult to understand, particularly as he provided the initial impetus for these recordings.

Manfred Symphony, Op. 58.
⊛ *** Chandos Dig. CHAN 8535 [id.]. Oslo PO, Jansons.
*** Virgin/EMI Dig. VC7 59230-2 [id.]. Bournemouth SO, Litton.
(M) *** EMI Dig. CDM7 64872-2 [id.]. Philh. O, Muti.
(N) (***) Testament mono SBT 1048 [id.]. Philh. O, Paul Kletzki – BORODIN: *Symphony No. 2.* (***)
**(*) Teldec/Warner Dig. 9031 73130-2 [id.]. Leipzig GO, Kurt Masur.

Manfred Symphony; Hamlet (fantasy overture).
(M) **(*) Decca 425 051-2 [id.]. VPO, Maazel.

Manfred Symphony; The Tempest, Op. 18.
(N) *** DG Dig. 439 891-2 [id.]. Russian Nat. O, Pletnev.

Since the coming of stereo there has never been a shortage of good recordings of *Manfred*, but Pletnev's tends to trump what has gone before. The actual sounds of the Russian orchestra, the wind as well as the ardent strings, add a touch of plangent colouring to Tchaikovsky's inspired scoring, but Pletnev identifies with the ongoing sweep of the work, yet he can relax glowingly in the pastoral evocation of the slow movement. In *The Tempest*, which is uneven in inspiration, Pletnev again carries the piece through on a wave of passionate romantic feeling. The recording is first class and this is one of the finest new Tchaikovsky records for some time.

Except in a relatively relaxed view of the *vivace* second movement, Jansons favours speeds flowing faster than usual, bringing out the drama but subtly varying the tensions to press each climax home to the full and always showing his mastery of Tchaikovskian rubato: his warmly expressive phrasing never sounds self-conscious when it is regularly given the freshness of folksong. The performance culminates in a thrilling account of the finale, leading up to the entry of the organ, gloriously resonant and supported by luxuriant string sound. The Chandos recording is among the finest in the Oslo series, atmospheric but with fine inner detail.

Litton and the Bournemouth orchestra are particularly successful in the delicate, poetic moments of *Manfred*. The Astarte theme in the first movement has rarely been moulded so affectionately, and Litton, after a relatively lightweight start, controls tension to bring out the narrative sequence of this programme work, the dramatic cohesion. Litton points the chattering semiquavers of the 'Alpine Fairy' Scherzo with engaging wit and fantasy, and his broad speed for the third-movement *Andante* allows the oboist to play his opening solo with a tender expressiveness to make most others seem prosaic. The sound is clean-cut and well balanced, with the organ entry at the end of the finale among the most dramatic of all.

Muti's reading is forceful and boldly dramatic throughout. His Scherzo has a quality of exhilarating bravura, rather than concentrating on delicacy; the lovely central melody is given a sense of joyous vigour. The *Andante*, after a refined opening, soon develops a passionate forward sweep; in the finale the amplitude and brilliant detail of the recording, combined with magnificent playing from the Philharmonia Orchestra, brings a massively compulsive projection of Tchaikovsky's bacchanale and a richly satisfying dénouement. The CD adds to the weight and definition of the recording and, if the effect is slightly less sumptuous than Jansons's Chandos version, the Kingsway Hall ambience adds plenty of warmth and colour.

Like the Borodin with which it is coupled, *Manfred* is given a vintage Philharmonia performance from the mid-1950s. Though, in the manner of the time, Kletzki makes cuts and one or two amendments of orchestration, this is a reading which, far more than usual, carries you warmly and thrustfully through music which can seem unduly episodic. So the electricity which Kletzki generates in the central *Allegro con fuoco* section of the finale is remarkable, with the playing throughout marked by superfine clarity of articulation and subtlety of response to rubato. As to the recording and transfer, the brass and wind have thrilling immediacy, and the dynamic range is astonishing for the time.

Maazel recorded *Manfred* in 1971. It is a keenly alert, fresh performance, direct and often exciting. The slow movement has plenty of ardour to balance its pastoralism, and the Sofiensaal recording is of vintage Decca quality. If other versions are more individual, the generous *Hamlet* coupling may well tempt some collectors. It does not match Stokowski's famous account but is both excitingly dramatic and strong on atmosphere, with the opening and closing pages given a sombre colouring to catch the essence of Shakespeare's tragedy. Again the CD transfer brings a vividly believable orchestral balance.

Masur is less concerned with illustrating the Byronic programme than with building symphonic strength into the music. With a structure that can seem loosely held together, his approach here generally works better than with the numbered symphonies in his Tchaikovsky series for Teldec. In the outbursts of the first movement of *Manfred* there may be little passion but plenty of power. The Leipzig orchestra plays brilliantly, and the very forward recorded sound makes the results bitingly dramatic to the point of fierceness. The second-movement Scherzo is brilliant but lacking in charm, and there is too little affection or tenderness in the third-movement *Andante*. Warm Leipzig sound.

Manfred Symphony; Symphonies Nos. 5–6 (Pathétique); Romeo and Juliet (fantasy overture); *The Tempest* (symphonic fantasy).

(M) *** Virgin/EMI Dig. VMT7 59701-2 (3) [id.]. Bournemouth SO, Andrew Litton.

With Litton's accounts of *Manfred* and the *Pathétique* both among the finest available and the performances of Tchaikovsky's two greatest Shakespearean fantasies equally recommendable, this makes a very attractive mid-priced package. Litton's account of the *Fifth* is also rewarding, although the first movement lacks the high voltage so striking in those other works. The other three movements are first rate. Atmospherically recorded, with slightly distanced sound, this performance certainly has many attractions despite that squarely symphonic view of the first movement.

The Nutcracker (ballet), *Op. 71* (complete).
*** Decca Dig. 433 000-2 (2) [id.]. Finchley Children's Music Group. RPO, Ashkenazy – GLAZUNOV:
   Seasons.
*** Telarc Dig. CD 8137 (2) [id.]. London Symphony Ch., LSO, Mackerras.
(M) *** CfP CD-CFPD 4706; *TC-CFPD 4706* (2) [Ang.CDCB 47267]. Amb. S., LSO, Previn.
(N) (B) *** Decca Double 444 821-2 (2) [id.]. Nat. PO, Bonynge – OFFENBACH: *Le Papillon*. ***
**(*) RCA 09026 61704-2 (2). St Louis Ch. & SO, Leonard Slatkin.
**(*) EMI Dig. CDS7 54600-2 (2) [Ang. CDQB 54649-2]. New L. Children's Ch., LPO, Jansons.

(i) *The Nutcracker* (complete); (ii) *Serenade for strings in C, Op. 48*.
(M) **(*) Mercury 432 750-2 (2). (i) LSO; (ii) Philharmonia Hungarica, Antal Dorati.

(i) *The Nutcracker* (ballet): complete; (ii) *Sleeping Beauty* (ballet): highlights.
(Y/B) (B) *** Ph. Duo 444 562-2 (2) [id.]. (i) Concg. O, with boys' Ch., Dorati; (ii) LSO, Fistoulari.

The Nutcracker (complete); *The Sleeping Beauty: Aurora's Wedding*.
*** Decca Dig. 440 477-2 (2) [id.]. Face School Children's Ch., Montreal SO, Charles Dutoit.

The Nutcracker (complete); *Eugene Onegin: Introduction; Waltz; Polonaise*.
*** Ph. Dig. 420 237-2 (2) [id.]. BPO, Bychkov.

Ashkenazy's digital *Nutcracker* now takes its place fairly easily at the top of the list. It is ideally coupled with Glazunov's *Seasons*, a no less enticing performance, and has the benefit of Walthamstow acoustics and state-of-the-art Decca digital sound, glowingly warm, with much colour and bloom for the wood-wind. The *Snowflakes* choral *waltz* has warmth as well as charm and the famous characteristic dances of the Act II Divertissement match elegance and character with a multi-hued palette of colour. Ideally the recording could be more generously cued in the accompanying documentation, and the narrative needs to be better related to the music in the notes, but for the music-making and recording there can only be the highest praise.

Dutoit's newest Decca recording obviously comes into immediate competition with the Ashkenazy set. It is beautifully played, with much sophisticated detail, and the Montreal acoustic provides brilliance, vivid colouring and striking transparency of detail. The party scene has great zest and character and the famous characteristic dances of the Act II *Divertissement* are made to sound wonderfully fresh, as is the *Waltz of the Snowflakes*, with its charming chorus of children. The sound is less sumptuous than with Ashkenazy (noticeable in the Pine forest journey), but both recordings are of Decca's finest quality and each of the two sets has its own felicities. For a coupling Dutoit offers *Aurora's Wedding*, a truncated version of *The Sleeping Beauty* which swiftly encapsulates the storyline, then moves on to the last-Act *Divertissement*. It makes an agreeable set of highlights, especially when played so spiritedly and elegantly as it is here, and the Decca recording is particularly successful. But Ashkenazy's coupling of Glazunov's *Seasons* is even more enticing.

The Telarc set was recorded in Watford Town Hall, which adds a little glamour to the violins and a glowing warmth in the middle and lower range. When the magic spell begins, the spectacularly wide dynamic range and the extra amplitude make for a physical frisson in the climaxes, while the glorious climbing melody, as Clara and the Prince travel through the pine forest, sounds richly expansive. Before that, the battle has some real cannon-shots interpolated but is done good-humouredly, for this is a toy battle. The great *Pas de deux* brings the most sumptuous climax, with superb sonority from the brass on the Telarc version. The Telarc presentation, too, with a detailed synopsis, is superior to the Decca documentation.

Semyon Bychkov has the services of the Berlin Philharmonic (an orchestra that always identifies readily with Tchaikovsky) and they offer superlative playing, of striking flair and character. Although a concert-hall ambience is favoured, the strings seem more forward, inner detail is very clear and the cymbals have a thrilling metallic clash. There is some superbly stylish playing in the *Divertissement*, and there are many moments when the extra vividness of the Berlin recording is especially compelling; and, of course, Bychkov offers a modest bonus, and the *Eugene Onegin* excerpts are brilliantly done. The Philips notes are extensive but not so conveniently matched to the CD cues.

Dorati's 1975 complete *Nutcracker* with the Concertgebouw Orchestra now makes a clear first choice in the bargain category, more particularly as it is coupled with Fistoulari's equally outstanding 1962 set of highlights from the *Sleeping Beauty*. In the former the playing of the Concertgebouw Orchestra is immensely refined yet often very dramatic. Dorati's conception is both vivid and strong. Its vitality is noticeable from the *Miniature overture* onwards with an engaging rhythmic spring and no forcing of accents. The Pine forest journey has seldom sounded more ardent and is built to a tremendous climax. Then the *Waltz of the Snowflakes* produces the most delightfully fresh choral quality from the Boys'

Choir of St Bravo Cathedral, Haarlem. Dorati's attention to detail is affectionate, and in the dances which make up Act II his characterization is sure, although the *Waltz of the Flowers* could ideally have more lilt. The CD transfer brings less sumptuous sound than on the old LPs, but the Concertgebouw ambience ensures body as well as vividness. Fistoulari's greatness as a ballet conductor is well celebrated by the *Sleeping Beauty* selection, which was extremely well recorded in its day and has transferred to CD with striking amplitude and brilliance. He conducted Tchaikovsky without hysteria yet generated great excitement, as the breadth and power of the *Rose adagio* immediately demonstrates, while the delightful *Panorama* is admirably relaxed and glowing. The selection is well made and satisfying, with plenty of charm and sparkling colours from the LSO wind players.

With Dorati's LSO *Nutcracker* the Mercury engineering is sophisticated, with a natural balance; the hall ambience provides warmth and bloom, yet detail is characteristically refined. Dorati relishes every detail, his characterization is strong, and the playing is full of life and elegance. The *Journey through the pine forest* expands magnificently while the choral delicacy of the *Waltz of the snowflakes* is full of charm. In Act II the characteristic dances have much colour and vitality. Altogether a great success. However, the *Serenade for strings* is less compelling. The slightly dry effect does not capture quite enough of the hall ambience and turns a close scrutiny on ensemble from the Philharmonia Hungarica, who could at times be more polished. It is an affectionate performance, but not an especially vital one.

Previn's earlier (1972) analogue set with the LSO has been freshly remastered. As in his later, digital version (only available combined with the other two ballets), the famous dances in Act II are played with much sophistication, and indeed the orchestral playing throughout is of very high quality. With Act I sounding brighter and more dramatic than in its original LP format, this CfP reissue makes a fine bargain alternative to Dorati's mid-priced Mercury set with the LSO.

Bonynge's set is made the more attractive by its rare and substantial Offenbach coupling. His approach is sympathetic and the orchestral playing is polished, even if in the opening scene he misses some of the atmosphere. With the beginning of the magic, as the Christmas tree expands, the performance becomes more dramatically involving and Bonynge is at his best in the latter part of the ballet, with fine passion in the Act II *Pas de deux* and plenty of colour in the characteristic dances. The Decca Kingsway Hall recording is brilliant on top, yet has a glowing ambient warmth.

Slatkin's 1985 recording has been reissued, sumptuously packaged in a gift box which happily recalls the more lavish days of LP presentation. It is obviously aimed at the younger generation. There are cardboard press-outs of the main characters and robust, free-standing card backgrounds of the principal sets. The quality of the artwork is high and these bonus artefacts will surely delight any young fan of the ballet, the more so as the beautifully illustrated accompanying booklet offers an excellent, user-friendly narrative and in addition relates the story to the music, track by track, describing the orchestration with silhouettes of the orchestral instruments. Charming coloured drawings of Clara, the heroine, and the Nutcracker himself are also beautifully printed on the silver discs. Slatkin's brightly paced reading always keeps the action moving in Act I, and the orchestral playing has plenty of character throughout. Other versions have more charm but are not more vivid. The lively St Louis recording, though spacious, is a little lacking in sumptuousness and richness of woodwind colour, but its vitality is a plus point, especially for younger listeners at whom the set is clearly aimed. With such high production values, it would certainly make a good present.

Jansons's new EMI version is highly dramatic, the histrionic effect emphasized by spectacular recording, especially of the brass which sounds almost Wagnerian at times in its amplitude. This is certainly lively and exciting, and it is stylishly played, but it has less warmth and magic than the Decca Ashkenazy digital recording. Moreover there is no coupling.

The Nutcracker (ballet): excerpts, *Op. 71*.
*** Telarc Dig. CD 80140 [id.]. Tiffin School Boys' Ch., LSO, Mackerras.
(M) *** Sony Dig. MDK 44656 [id.]. Amb. S., Philh. O, Tilson Thomas.

On the face of it, the Tilson Thomas CD would seem to be the strongest recommendation: it offers considerably more music (70 minutes) than the Telarc disc; the bright-eyed Philharmonia playing is always alive and zestful; and the CBS recording is brilliant and well balanced. Moreover the selection is offered at mid-price.

But when one turns to the Telarc disc, which plays for some 55 minutes only, one enters a different, more expansive Tchaikovskian sound-world: the flair of the Battle sequence between the Nutcracker and the Mouse King immediately captures the imagination. Mackerras misses out much of Act I, but not the famous *Marche* nor the sequence called *The Magic Spell begins*, which is superbly expansive. Similarly, the *Scene in the pine forest* with Tchaikovsky's great climbing, scaling melody has a frisson-creating tension, and the *Waltz of the snowflakes* sets the mood for the famous characteristic dances of Act II, all splendidly done, and recorded in Telarc's most spectacular manner. Nevertheless the Sony disc is undoubtedly a bargain in its own way.

Nutcracker suite, Op. 71a.
(M) **(*) Sony SBK 46550; *SBT 46550* [id.]. Phd. O, Ormandy – CHOPIN: *Les Sylphides;* DELIBES: *Coppélia; Sylvia: Suites.* ***

The Philadelphia Orchestra made this wonderful music universally famous in Walt Disney's *Fantasia* and they know how to play it just as well under Ormandy in 1963 as they did under Stokowski. Perhaps there is less individuality in the characteristic dances, but the music-making has suitable moments of reticence (as in the neat *Ouverture miniature*) as well as plenty of flair. In the *Waltz of the flowers* Ormandy blots his copybook by taking the soaring violin tune an octave up on its second appearance.

Nutcracker suite, Op. 71a; Romeo and Juliet (fantasy overture).
(N) **(*) DG Dig. Gold 439 021-2 [id.]. BPO, Karajan.

Originally designed to accompany a picture biography of Karajan, this not very generous Tchaikovsky coupling brings superbly played performances. The suite is delicate and detailed, yet perhaps lacks a little in charm, notably the *Arab dance* which, taken fairly briskly, loses something of its gentle sentience. The performance of *Romeo and Juliet* is both polished and dramatic, but Karajan draws out the climax of the love theme with spacious moulding, and there is marginally less spontaneity here than in his earlier recordings. Nevertheless there is no doubt about the excitement generated at the expansive climax; the sound, characteristic of Berlin, is very well balanced, and this a a case where 'original-image bit re-processing' has transformed the overall (1983) sound-picture, which now has more ambient bloom on the violins, while the wind (especially in the *Nutcracker suite*) and brass solos have striking definition and a natural presence. Our reservation is not about the quality of this music-making, nor its sound, but the short measure: 44 minutes 6 seconds; and this remains at full price.

(i) *The Nutcracker; Sleeping Beauty; Swan Lake:* excerpts.
(B) **(*) EMI CZS7 62816-2 (2) [id.]. LSO, André Previn, (i) with Amb. S.

By the use of two CDs, offering some 148 minutes of music, this EMI box (issued in the 'two for the price of one' series) covers a substantial proportion of the key numbers from all three ballets. *The Nutcracker* selection is particularly generous in including, besides virtually all the most famous characteristic dances, the 13-minute episode in Act I starting with the Battle sequence, continuing with the magical Pine forest journey and finishing with the delightful choral *Waltz of the snowflakes*. Previn and the LSO provide vivacious, charismatic playing and the recording is full, bright and vivid. The remastering, however, loses some of the smoothness and refinement of focus of the original, analogue recordings in the interest of a lively upper range. But this remains very enjoyable and excellent value.

Nutcracker suite; Sleeping Beauty: excerpts; Swan Lake: suite.
(Y/B) *** Decca Dig. 443 555-2 [id.]. Montreal SO, Dutoit.

Dutoit's complete Decca recordings of *The Nutcracker* and *Swan Lake* are highly recommended, and the two suites derived from these sets are elegantly and vividly played, and recorded in Decca's best manner. Readers will note that this means that in the *Nutcracker suite* the *Dance of the Sugar Plum Fairy* has the extended ballet ending, rather than the concert coda. The *Sleeping Beauty* excerpts are taken from Dutoit's recording of *Aurora's Wedding* (a bonus with *The Nutcracker*). Thus the present 22-minute set of excerpts taken from that source misses out some key items, notably the *Panorama*, which is perhaps the composer's finest inspiration in the whole score.

Nutcracker suite; Sleeping Beauty: suite; Swan Lake: suite.
✹ (M) *** DG 449 726-2 [id.]. BPO, Rostropovich.
(M) *** EMI CDM7 64332-2. LSO, Previn.

Rostropovich's triptych of Tchaikovsky ballet suites is very special. His account of the *Nutcracker suite* is enchanting: the *Sugar plum fairy* is introduced with ethereal gentleness, the *Russian dance* has marvellous zest and the *Waltz of the flowers* combines warmth and elegance with an exhilarating vigour. The *Sleeping Beauty* and *Swan Lake* selections are hardly less distinguished, and in the former the *Panorama* is gloriously played. The CD remastering (for inclusion in DG's 'Legendary Recordings' series), which was always outstanding, now approaches demonstration standard, combining bloom with enhanced detail. 69 minutes of sheer joy, and at mid-price too.

The digital remastering has been very successful on the EMI disc, freshening the sound of the excellent recordings, taken from Previn's analogue complete sets (which means that the *Dance of the sugar plum fairy* in *The Nutcracker* has the longer coda rather than the ending Tchaikovsky devised for the *Suite*). The performances are at once vivid and elegant, warm and exciting. Previn's *Panorama* from *Sleeping*

Beauty is hardly less beguiling than Rostropovich's and the recording has comparable warmth. There is nearly 73 minutes of music here, and this version can be strongly recommended alongside the DG disc; it is a most enjoyable record.

Ballet highlights (with narrative) from: *The Nutcracker; Sleeping Beauty; Swan Lake.*
(N) (M) * Conifer Dig. 75605 55018 (*Nutcracker*); 75605 55019 (*Sleeping Beauty*); 75605 55017 (*Swan Lake*). Tony Scotland, ROHCG O, Mark Ermler.

This is a misguided enterprise, and it is difficult to discover at which age-group Tony Scotland's narratives – which he has written himself – are aimed. His manner seems too avuncular for really young children, and older listeners will find there is far, far too much text. Moreover it doesn't bear repetition. In *The Nutcracker*, the background to the events of Petipa's scenario concerning the enigmatic Herr Drosselmeyer is of some interest, but in *Sleeping Beauty*, because the story is so simple and the action limited, every number is described to no advantage at all. Tchaikovsky's music says it all, and that is very well played and recorded here. The three CDs are available separately.

Serenade for strings in C, Op. 48.
(BB) *** ASV CDQS 6094 [id.]. Polish R. CO, Duczmal – SUK: *Serenade* ***; GRIEG: *Holberg suite* etc. **(*)
(M) **(*) RCA 09026 61424-2 [id.]. Boston SO, Munch – BARBER: *Adagio* etc. ***; ELGAR: *Introduction and allegro.* **

The Polish Radio Chamber Orchestra is a first-class body of players, and they give a highly individual reading, full of subtlety and grace. The conductor's imaginative nuancing of dynamic shading is most winning, and this account often finds a rare quality of tenderness alongside its vigour and expansiveness. The Waltz is relaxed and gentle; later there is a wistful delicacy in the *Elégie* as Tchaikovsky's lovely cantilena is floated over gentle pizzicatos. The finale is exquisitely prepared, then the allegro is off with the wind, very fast, light and balletic, again with engagingly crisp articulation. Altogether this is the kind of performance that makes one appreciate this as one of the composer's greatest works, with its Mozartian elegance and perfection of form. The recording is excellent, full, transparent, yet with a fine overall bloom.

A strong, full-blooded reading from Munch, lacking in charm, but with an elegant *Waltz*, an *Elegy* which climaxes with great ardour and a well-prepared finale which generates comparable vigour. The playing of the Boston strings displays considerable bravura and virtuosity, and the 1957 recording sounds remarkably well, robust, well-detailed and with plenty of ambient atmosphere.

Serenade for strings; Souvenir de Florence, Op. 70.
(BB) **(*) Naxos Dig. 8.550404 [id.]. Vienna CO, Philippe Entremont.

Entremont's performances of Tchaikovsky's two major string works communicate above all a feeling of passionate thrust and energy. The *Waltz*, with its neatly managed tenutos, has a nice touch of romantic feeling and, after the ardour of the *Elégie*, the finale steals in persuasively, again producing an unflagging impetus, with dance-rhythms bracing and strong. The unaccountably neglected *Souvenir de Florence* has comparable momentum and eagerness. The dashing main theme of the first movement swings along infectiously, while the wistful secondary idea also takes wing. Entremont brings out the charm and responds easily to the variety of mood, both here and in the *Allegretto*, permeated with a flavour of Russian folksong. Throughout, the commitment and ensemble of the VCO bring the most persuasive advocacy and make one wonder why the *Souvenir* does not have a more central place in the string repertoire.

The Sleeping Beauty (ballet), *Op. 66* (complete).
(BB) *** Naxos Dig. 8.550490/2 [id.]. Slovak State PO (Košice), Andrew Mogrelia.
*** RCA Dig. 09026 61682-2 (2) [id.]. St Louis SO, Leonard Slatkin.
**(*) Ph. Dig. 434 922-2 (3). Kirov O (St Petersburg), Gergiev.
(M) **(*) Decca 425 468-2 (3). Nat. PO, Richard Bonynge – MEYERBEER: *Les Patineurs.* ***

Andrew Mongrelia conducts Tchaikovsky's score with an ideal combination of warmth, grace and vitality. Moreover the Slovak State Philharmonic prove to be an excellent orchestra for this repertoire, with fine wind-players and equally impressive string principals for the important violin and cello solos. Mogrelia relishes the orchestral detail – and there is much inspired Tchaikovskian scoring here – and he moves the music on with a natural sense of pacing and generates plenty of excitement in the big set-pieces: the climaxes which come at the ends of Acts I and II are splendidly expansive. The Naxos digital recording is full and brilliant without being overlit, and the acoustics of the House of Arts in Košice bring a spacious ambience so that the spectacular moments have sufficient room to expand, and the orchestral colours are vivid. A clear first choice among all available recordings, irrespective of cost.

Slatkin's version, like the complete *Nutcracker* above, is impressively packaged with an eye on the younger balletomane. There are cardboard push-out pictures of the Prince and Princess and the Lilac Fairy which are charmingly conceived in a gracious traditional style, while the wicked fairy (Carabosse) looks appropriately like a witch, although she also is given wings. The cardboard set backdrops are handsome and, as with the companion *Nutcracker* set, there is a pleasing and detailed plot summary, plus a cued narrative linked to silhouettes of the orchestral instruments featured in each track. The performance has consistent vitality and plenty of drama and colour, and the Act III *Divertissement* brings both sparkle and grace. The recording is somewhat fuller than the earlier *Nutcracker*, with the hall ambience well conveyed, yet detail is clear and the strings have a realistic sheen. There is not the degree of glowing warmth or expansiveness in the bass one would expect from, say, a Decca recording made at St Eustache, but the sound is very well balanced.

The Kirov recording of Tchaikovsky's complete ballet is in every way satisfying. The playing – from an orchestra completely inside the music – is warmly sympathetic and vital, with no suggestion that familiarity has bred any sense of routine. The woodwind solos, too, are elegant and bring out the full colour of Tchaikovsky's glowing orchestral palette. Gergiev can often be subtle, and his performance of the beautiful *Panorama* floats gently and radiantly over its rocking base. The Act III *Pas de quatre* for all four fairies is a highlight of the sparkling Act III *Divertissement*, while *Puss-in-Boots and the White Cat* are tangible in their feline altercation. The Philips recording is sumptuous without being cloudy and it expands magnificently for Tchaikovksy's rhetorically exciting climaxes without assaulting the ears. All in all, this is first class; however, although as a performance it takes precedence over the Naxos set by a small margin, it costs about 2½ times as much, and the use of three CDs makes it uncompetitive alongside Slatkin, whose presentation is so much more elaborate.

Bonynge secures brilliant and often elegant playing from the National Philharmonic Orchestra and his rhythmic pointing is always characteful. As recorded, however, the upper strings lack sumptuousness; otherwise, the sound is excellent and there is much to give pleasure, notably the drama of the awakening scene and the Act III *Divertissement*. The Decca sound has a fine sparkle here, and the solo violin (Mincho Minchev) and cello (Francisco Gabarro) provide most appealing solo contributions.

Sleeping Beauty (ballet): highlights.
**(*) ROH Dig. ROH 003 [id.]. ROHCG O, Ermler.
(M) ** Sony SBK 46340; *SBT 46340* [id.]. Phd. O, Ormandy – ROSSINI: *Boutique fantasque.* **(*)

Those wishing to sample the Ermler set will find this disc contains 72 minutes of well-chosen key items. One can certainly appreciate the polish and grace of the orchestral playing here, when the recording – made in St Jude-on-the-Hill, Hampstead – is so flattering.

Ormandy provides a sumptuously glossy selection, with nearly an hour's music (the CD plays for 76 minutes overall). Superbly polished and often exciting playing but, with a forward balance, the effect is somewhat overwhelming. The sound is opulently brilliant rather than refined.

Sleeping Beauty (ballet): suite.
(B) **(*) DG Double 437 404-2 (2) [id.]. BPO, Karajan – CHOPIN: *Les Sylphides* *** ⊛; DELIBES: *Coppélia: suite* ***; GOUNOD: *Faust* etc. **(*); OFFENBACH: *Gaîté parisienne:* excerpts; RAVEL: *Boléro.* ***
(BB) ** Naxos Dig. 8.550079; *4550079* [id.]. Czech RSO (Bratislava), Ondrej Lenárd – GLAZUNOV: *The Seasons.* **(*)

Karajan's *Sleeping Beauty* suite generates an equal measure of elegance, warmth and adrenalin and is very well played indeed. But the recording, though quite full-bodied, is very brightly lit in the CD transfer and may need a degree of cutting back on top. It comes as part of a distinctive collection of ballet music, almost all showing the conductor and his orchestra on top form.

The Czech Radio Orchestra under Ondrej Lenárd play Tchaikovsky's ballet suite with spirit and colour, and the recording has plenty of weight and ambience and no lack of brilliance but the *Panorama* is disappointing, taken fast and with a lack of subtlety in the rocking bass rhythm.

(i) *Souvenir d'un lieu cher (Méditation), Op. 42/1;* (ii) *Sérénade mélancolique for violin and orchestra, Op. 26.*
(N) (M) *** Sony Stern Edition I SMK 66830 [id.]. Isaac Stern, with (i) Nat. SO, Rostropovich; (ii) Columbia SO, Brieff – BRUCH: *Violin concerto No. 1;* WIENIAWSKI: *Violin concerto No. 2.* **(*)

Glorious playing from Stern. He is recorded too closely (as is the Columbia Symphony in the *Sérénade*) but his warm timbre is caught lusciously and he knows just how to catch the composer's nostalgic feeling. Both accompaniments are sympathetic.

Suites Nos. 1 in D min., Op. 43; 2 in C (Caractéristique) Op. 53.
(M) *** Melodiya/BMG Dig. 74321 17099-2 [id.]. USSR SO, Svetlanov.
(BB) *** Naxos Dig. 8.550644. [id.]. Nat. SO of Ireland, Stefan Sanderling.

Tchaikovsky's *Orchestral suites* are directly descended from the dance suites of the Baroque era; Svetlanov brings to them an appropriately light touch. The highlight of the *First Suite* is the deliciously orchestrated *Marche miniature* which tends to dwarf everything else in sheer memorability – except perhaps the *Introduction*, where Tchaikovsky's innate melancholy at the opening is effectively dispersed by the following fugato. But the other movements are also immediately attractive, especially the closing *Gavotte*. Svetlanov's inspirational reading of the *Second Suite* is doubly distinctive for making the listener realize that this is a far more substantial and attractive work than was previously thought. The *Scherzo burlesque* has a part for accordions in its central section, but here they are mixed in with folksy woodwind sounds and the effect is highly piquant. In the final *Danse baroque* the Russian energy of the performance bubbles right over. With such sympathetic playing and first-class digital recording this is a prime recommendation at mid-price.

Stefan Sanderling (son of Kurt) also shows how well he understands the music's baroque ancestry in nicely turned performances of works which are neglected on record and almost never heard in the concert hall. The playing of the excellent National Symphony Orchestra of Ireland – another Naxos discovery – is polished and sympathetic to the Tchaikovskian ardour that wells up every now and then. Each of the movements (six in No. 1; five in No. 2) is neatly characterized, and there is much charm and colour. In the *Scherzo burlesque* of No. 2 the four interpolated accordions come through well in the middle section, and the suite's closing *Danse baroque* is very spirited indeed. The recording, made in Dublin's National Concert Hall, is spacious yet allows the intimate detail of the orchestration to emerge vividly. A fine, super-bargain alternative to Svetlanov.

(i) *Suites Nos. 2 in C, Op. 53; 4 in G (Mozartiana), Op. 61;* (ii) *Sérénade mélancolique, Op. 26; Mélodie, Op. 42/3.*
(M) **(*) Sony/CBS Dig. MDK 46503 [id.]. (i) Philh. O, Tilson Thomas; (ii) Zukerman, Israel PO, Mehta.

Michael Tilson Thomas makes a very good case for Tchaikovsky's *Mozartiana suite*. The Philharmonia's response is first class, and the *Second Suite* is also played with great vitality. The bright, slightly dry, early digital recording (made in EMI's No. 1 Studio at Abbey Road), which suits *Mozartiana* rather well, makes the more extrovert, fully scored first movement of the *Second, Jeu de sons*, seem a little aggressive in its brilliance, although the sharp focus is just right for the *Scherzo burlesque*, bustling with its accordions. The fill-ups, if brief, are scarcely apt but are tenderly played and very appealing.

Suites Nos. 3 in G, Op. 55; 4 in G (Mozartiana), Op. 61.
(M) *** Melodiya/BMG Dig. 74321 17100-2 [id.]. USSR SO, Svetlanov.
(BB) **(*) Naxos Dig. 8.550728 [id.]. Nat. SO of Ireland, Stefan Sanderling.

Svetlanov treats Tchaikovsky's finest suite, the *Third*, very freely, supported by the most eloquent response from one of the premier Soviet orchestras. In the *Theme and variations*, some of Svetlanov's tempi are unexpected, and the finale *Polacca* is less overwhelming than in some previous versions, Svetlanov emphasizing its dance rhythms rather than seeking to be grandiose. Svetlanov is hardly less successful in the *Fourth Suite* (*Mozartiana*), where Tchaikovsky's neat scoring is always respectful of the original music. Even so, the *Preghiera*, based on Mozart's *Ave verum*, can sometimes sound too opulent, but not here. The closing *Variations* (where Mozart used Gluck's '*Unser dummer Pöbel meint*' suite) are a delight. With excellent digital recording in both works and an attractive concert-hall ambience this is very recommendable, particularly at mid-price.

Sanderling shows much delicacy of feeling both in the opening *Gigue* of *Mozartiana* and in the *Elégie*, the first movement of the *Third suite*, where he is warm without being carried away; in No. 4, the *Preghiera* is touching without the climax becoming too lavish. The orchestral playing is of the highest quality in terms of sensitivity and polish, and it is a pity that one has reservations about the performances of the sets of variations which Tchaikovsky uses for each finale. In *Mozartiana* Sanderling is very romantic and, although orchestral detail is nicely observed, his affectionate rubato affects the directness of manner with which Mozart's original piano variations would have been presented. The masterly *Theme and variations* which end the *Third suite* are superbly done until the finale, when Sanderling is just that bit too grandiloquent and measured. With such richly expansive recording it cannot fail to make its effect but, with a little more pace and a touch more rhythmic lift, it could have been the overwhelming culmination the composer intended.

Swan Lake (ballet), *Op. 20* (complete).
*** Decca Dig. 436 212-2 (2) Montreal SO, Dutoit.
*** ROH Dig. 301/2 [id.]. ROHCG O, Mark Ermler.
(B) *** CfP Dig. CD-CFPD 4727; *TC-CFPD 4727* (2). Philh. O, John Lanchbery.
(Y/B) **(*) EMI Dig. CDS5 55277-2 (2). Phd. O, Sawallisch.
(M) **(*) Melodiya/BMG 74321 17082-2 (3) [id.]. Russian State SO, Svetlanov.

Dutoit offers the original score virtually complete, as Tchaikovsky conceived it. Into it he poured some of his finest melodic inspiration and colouristic orchestral skill, to provide just over two and a half hours of consistently appealing music in which there is not a single dull bar. The Montreal orchestra play it beautifully, rising to the plot's histrionic moments and (with the help of St Eustache acoustics and the Decca engineers) the final apotheosis, when the great Swan melody achieves its transformation into an exultant B major climax, is gloriously expansive. Dutoit's reading, without lack of drama, emphasizes the warmth and grace of the music, its infinite variety. The Montreal solo violinist, Chantal Juillet, is not a sumptuous-timbred player but plays the *Danse russe* interpolation in Act III with exquisite charm. With wind solos of much character, and warm, nicely turned string phrasing and pacing which alternates bursts of liveliness within a romantically mellow basic conception, Dutoit's reading is easy to enjoy. Lanchbery's digital EMI set (not absolutely complete, but marvellous value on Classics for Pleasure) has a more exhilarating theatrical vitality, but the EMI sound is less glamorously full than the Decca recording.

Released from the Covent Garden pit to record in the warm acoustic of All Saints', Tooting, the players have responded to Ermler's deeply sympathetic direction with both refinement and red-blooded commitment, and one is constantly aware of the idiomatic feeling born of long acquaintance. The sound is exceptionally full and open, with the brass in particular giving satisfying weight to the ensemble without hazing over the detail. The set has now been reissued on a pair of CDs with the break coming in Act II after the *Dance of the little swans*. Ermler's broad speeds consistently convey, more than most rivals', the feeling of an accompaniment for dancing, as in the great andante of the Act I *Pas de deux*. This is a set to have you sitting back in new enjoyment of a gorgeous score.

Lanchbery's 1982 *Swan Lake* makes a superb bargain. The CfP reissue on a pair of CDs, which play for 79 minutes and 75 minutes respectively, accommodates Acts I and II on the first disc and Acts III and IV on the second. Though two numbers are cut, the set includes the extra music (a *Pas de deux*) which Tchaikovsky wrote to follow the *Pas de six* in Act III, when Siegfried dances with Odile, mistakenly believing her to be Odette. The EMI recording, made at Abbey Road, is very fine indeed: spacious, vividly coloured and full, with natural perspective and a wide (but not uncomfortably wide) dynamic range. The orchestral playing is first class, with polished, elegant string phrasing matched by felicitous wind solos. Lanchbery's rhythmic spring is a constant pleasure; everything is alert and there is plenty of excitement at climaxes.

Sawallisch approaches Tchaikovsky's greatest ballet score with appealing freshness as if it had been written yesterday, and the Philadelphia Orchestra play superbly. But, as so often, they are let down by the choice of venue for the recording: in this instance, the Memorial Hall, Fairmount Park, whose apparently intractable acoustics have brought unnaturally close microphone placing. There is no lack of atmosphere, as the very opening demonstrates, yet fortissimos are unrefined, with fierce cymbals, grainy violins, even an element of harshness. But there is also much to enjoy, and splendid vigour, as in the *Allegro giusto* which immediately follows. The first and most famous *Waltz* (gorgeously played) lilts attractively, as again does the later example (track 11 – very affectionate), and how engaging are the cygnets, tripping in very precisely and with irresistible style, while in the famous *pas de deux* of Odette and the Prince the violin and cello duet brings ravishingly serene yet voluptuous solo playing, while in the interpolated *Danse russe* the concert master, Norman Carol, brings a passionate *zigeuner* verve to his violin solo. Above all, Sawallisch's direction combines a flowing spontaneity with an overall feeling for Tchaikovsky's structure. The thrilling final climax (with gorgeously full horn-tone at the restatement of the famous *idée fixe*) makes an overwhelming apotheosis, even if the shrillness added to the violins, who are playing with enormous fervour and weight of sonority, is not a plus factor.

Swan Lake is easily the most successful of Svetlanov's recordings of the three great Tchaikovsky ballets and, were it on two discs instead of three, it would be very competitive. Svetlanov is often exhilarating in his lively pacing, very Slavonic in impetus. Yet all the famous numbers relax glowingly and emerge with flying colours. The opening of Act II with its famous oboe swan theme is ideally paced and the climax is unspoiled by brass blatancy, though they certainly are given their head. Later, the *Danses des cygnes* are very persuasive (with excellent violin and cello soloists) and the Act III *Divertissement* brings vivid solo wind playing. At the end, the spectacular finale has great excitement and passion. The digital recording is admirably full-blooded and the strings have plenty of amplitude.

Swan Lake (ballet), *Op. 20* (slightly abridged recording of the European score).
(Y/B) (B) **(*) Decca Double 440 630-2 (2) [id.]. SRO, Ansermet – PROKOFIEV: *Romeo and Juliet.* **

Returning to Ansermet's 1959 recording of *Swan Lake*, one is amazed by the vigour of the playing and the excellence of the recording. The Drigo version of the score, which Ansermet uses, dates from 1895; Drigo added orchestrations of his own, taken from Tchaikovsky's piano music (Op. 72), yet he left out some 1,600 bars of the original score. Ansermet offers the Act I introduction and Nos. 1–2, 4, 7 and 8; Act II, Nos. 10–13; Act III, Nos. 15, 17–18 and 20–23, with No. 5 (the *Pas de deux*) then interpolated before Nos. 28 and 29 from Act IV. Despite the obvious gaps, most of the familiar favourites are included here, and the music-making has such zest and colour that one cannot but revel in every bar. The solo wind playing is not always as sweet-timbred as in some other versions, but the violin and cello solos are well done, and there is not a dull moment throughout. The transfer is well managed, full-blooded and bright, and there is not too much wrong with the timbre of the upper strings. It was a happy idea to couple this on its Double Decca reissue with a selection of 15 items from the two suites from Prokofiev's *Romeo and Juliet* ballet, even if here the orchestral playing is less impressive.

Swan Lake (ballet), *Op. 20:* highlights.
(B) *** CfP CD-CFP 4296 [Ang. CDB 62713]. Sir Yehudi Menuhin, Philh. O, Efrem Kurtz.

A fine bargain selection on CfP with Menuhin present for the violin solos. He finds a surprising amount to play here. The 1960 recording matches the exuberance which Kurtz brings to the music's climaxes with an expansive dynamic range, and it has atmosphere as well as brilliance. The Philharmonia are on top form and the woodwind acquit themselves with plenty of style, while the string playing is characteristically elegant.

SYMPHONIES

Symphonies Nos. 1–6.
(M) *** DG 429 675-2 (4) [id.]. BPO, Karajan.

Symphonies Nos. 1–6; Andante cantabile; Capriccio italien; Fatum; Francesca da Rimini, Op. 22; Romeo and Juliet (fantasy overture); *Serenade for strings, Op. 48; The Tempest; Voyevoda.*
(B) **(*) BMG/Melodiya 74321 17101-2 (6) [id.]. USSR SO, Svetlanov.

Symphonies Nos. 1–6; Capriccio italien; Manfred Symphony.
❀ (M) *** Chandos Dig. CHAN 8672/8 [id.]. Oslo PO, Jansons.

Symphonies Nos. 1–6; Manfred Symphony; Francesca da Rimini; Romeo and Juliet (fantasy overture).
(N) (M) *** EMI CMS5 65709-2 [CDME 65709] (5) [id.]. LPO, Mstislav Rostropovich.

Symphonies Nos. 1–6; Romeo and Juliet (fantasy overture).
(B) *** Decca 430 787-2 (4) [id.]. VPO, Lorin Maazel.

Jansons' Tchaikovsky series, which includes *Manfred*, is self-recommending. The full romantic power of the music is consistently conveyed and, above all, the music-making is urgently spontaneous throughout, with the Oslo Philharmonic Orchestra always committed and fresh, helped by the richly atmospheric Chandos sound. The seven separate CDs offered here are packaged in a box priced as for five premium discs.

Rostropovich recorded the Tchaikovsky symphonies in the Kingsway Hall in 1977 concurrently with live performances at the Royal Festival Hall; though at certain points (as in some of the *fugato* development sections) the ensemble could be a shade crisper, this is a minor point when the performances have not only passion and electricity but also great charm and refinement. The first three symphonies are done superbly in every way – Rostropovich manages to choose his tempi most persuasively and his rhythmic pointing is consistently delectable – outshining here most of the opposition. Symphonies Nos. 4 to 6 are all characterized by relatively slow but well-pointed accounts of the first movements, and only in No. 5 is there any suspicion of the argument dragging. Otherwise these are sensitive, deeply felt readings which should be easy to live with. The recording is outstandingly warm and full-bodied. The pianissimo string-tone is particularly beautiful. *Manfred* too is most persuasive, with a Scherzo of Berliozian refinement. *Francesca da Rimini* and *Romeo and Juliet* were recorded the following year at Abbey Road. The readings are intensely individual and full of poetic feeling, with the love-theme in *Romeo and Juliet* introduced with the greatest tenderness. Yet although Rostropovich's pacing is as free as his moulding of the melodic lines, the listener is carried along by the expressive vitality of the orchestral playing. *Francesca da Rimini* has an epic scale, with a breathtaking finale, yet again there is touching delicacy in the work's central section, with radiant sounds from the LPO woodwind. The sound remains resonant and spacious, with great body and impact, and the CD remastering loses nothing of the richness, in fact adding to its dramatic profile. To fit the music on to five CDs, the third and sixth symphonies have had to be split across discs, which is a less than ideal arrangement; but in all other respects this set can be recommended with the utmost enthusiasm.

Karajan offers the six symphonies fitted on to four mid-priced CDs, the only drawback being that Nos. 2 and 5 are split between discs. From both a performance and a technical point of view, the accounts of the last three symphonies are in every way preferable to his later, VPO digital versions; all offer peerless playing from the Berlin Philharmonic which the Oslo Philharmonic cannot always quite match, for all their excellence.

Maazel's performances from the mid-1960s have been remastered and reissued on four CDs, necessitating a break only at the centre of No. 4. The recordings come from a vintage Decca period and are remarkably full and vivid. In the early symphonies the hint of edge in the digital remastering (and it is very minimal) increases the bite and sense of urgency at the expense of charm (this is not a strong feature of Nos. 2 and 3 anyway). But in Nos. 4–6 (and especially in No. 4) the performances, always grippingly spontaneous, sound newly minted, helped by the freshness of the VPO playing. Perhaps No. 5 lacks the fullest expansive qualities, but there are few more effective accounts of the March/Scherzo from the *Pathétique*. *Romeo and Juliet* is exciting too, with plenty of romantic flair.

Evgeny Svetlanov's Tchaikovsky cycle of the symphonies comes from 1967; most of the additional orchestral items date from 1970. *Voyevoda*, the *Andante cantabile* and the *Capriccio italien* are later: the late 1980s. The merits of these performances are well known: full-blooded, intense and thoroughly idiomatic, without being in the aristocratic, Mravinsky class. However, they are well worth considering at this price. The boxed package of six CDs is offered at bargain price.

(i) *Symphonies Nos. 1 in G min. (Winter daydreams); 2 in C min. (Little Russian); 3 in D (Polish);* (ii) *Francesca da Rimini.*
(Y/B) (B) *** Ph. Duo 446 148-2 (2) [id.]. (i) LSO; (ii) New Philh. O; Markevitch.

Markevitch is a genuine Tchaikovskian and his readings have fine momentum and plenty of ardour. In the *First Symphony* he finds the Mendelssohnian lightness in his fast pacing of the opening movement, while there is real evocation in the *Adagio* and a sense of desolation at the reprise of the *Andante lugubre*, before the final rousing peroration. In the *Little Russian Symphony* the opening horn solo is full of character and the allegro tautly rhythmic. The *marziale* marking of the *Andantino* is taken literally, but its precise rhythmic beat is well lifted. The finale is striking for its bustling energy rather than its charm. The *Polish Symphony* has a comparably dynamic first movement, but the central movements are expansively warm, the ballet-music associations not missed. The finale is strongly full-blooded. *Francesca da Rimini* is very exciting too, and there is some lovely wind playing from the New Philharmonia in the central section. Excellent sound, warmly resonant and full-bodied.

Symphonies Nos. 1–4.
(M) *** Virgin/EMI VMT7 59699-2 (3) [id.]. Bournemouth SO, Litton.

Litton's box containing Nos. 1–4 is highly recommendable, with only No. 4 marginally less successful than the other three. First-class, modern, digital sound.

Symphony No. 1 in G min. (Winter daydreams), Op. 13.
*** Chandos Dig. CHAN 8402 [id.]. Oslo PO, Jansons.

Symphony No. 1 (Winter Daydreams); Hamlet (fantasy overture), *Op. 67.*
(BB) *** Naxos Dig. 8.550517 [id.]. Polish Nat. RSO, Adrian Leaper.

Refreshingly direct in style, Jansons with his brilliant orchestra gives an electrically compelling performance of this earliest of the symphonies. Structurally strong, the result tingles with excitement, most of all in the finale, faster than usual, with the challenge of the complex fugato passages taken superbly. The recording is highly successful.

Leaper conducts a taut and sympathetic reading of *Winter Daydreams*, with excellent playing from the Polish orchestra enhanced by vivid recording, fresh and clear, with plenty of body and with refined pianissimo playing from the strings in the slow movement. This is among the finest Tchaikovsky recordings on the Naxos list, with all four movements sharply characterized. The overture too comes in a tautly dramatic reading. An outstanding bargain.

Symphonies Nos. 1 (Winter Daydreams); 2 (Little Russian).
*** Virgin/EMI Dig. VC7 59588-2 [id.]. Bournemouth SO, Andrew Litton.

In their Tchaikovsky series for Virgin, Litton and the Bournemouth orchestra here come up with a clear winner, giving urgently spontaneous performances which in every way rival any in the catalogue. With warm and full recording, less distanced than many on this label, the disc earns the strongest recommendation. Litton reveals himself as a volatile Tchaikovskian, free with accelerandos and slowings, yet never sounding self-conscious or too free. The hushed pianissimos of the Bournemouth strings in the slow movement of No. 1 are ravishing, and the *Second Symphony* too brings a beautifully sprung reading which allows plenty of rhythmic elbow-room in the jaunty account of the syncopated second subject in the finale.

Symphony No. 2 in C min. (Little Russian), Op. 17 (original (1872) score); *Festive overture on the Danish national anthem, Op. 15; Serenade for Nikolai Rubinstein's saint's day; Mazeppa: Battle of Poltava; Cossack dance.*
*** Chandos Dig. CHAN 9190 [id.]. LSO, Geoffrey Simon.

This is the first recording of Tchaikovsky's original score of the *Little Russian symphony* and probably the first performance outside Russia. In 1879 Tchaikovsky retrieved the score and rewrote the first movement. He left the *Andante* virtually unaltered, touched up the scoring of the Scherzo, made minor excisions and added repeats, and made a huge cut of 150 bars (some two minutes of music) in the finale. He then destroyed the original. (The present performance has been possible because of the surviving orchestral parts.) There can be no question that he was right. The reworked first movement is immensely superior to the first attempt, and the finale – delightful though it is – seems quite long enough, shorn of the extra bars. However, to hear the composer's first thoughts (as with the original version of *Romeo and Juliet*) is fascinating, and this is an indispensable recording for all Tchaikovskians. Geoffrey Simon secures a committed response from the LSO, and the recording is striking in its inner orchestral detail and freshness, although the lower range is without the resonant richness of some CDs. For the reissue other music has been added. The music from *Mazeppa*, the *Danish Festival overture* and the tribute to Rubinstein make engaging bonuses.

Symphony No. 2 in C min. (Little Russian), Op. 17.
(M) *** Telarc Dig. CD 82011 [id.]. Pittsburgh SO, Lorin Maazel – RIMSKY-KORSAKOV: *Symphony No. 2 (Antar).* ***

Symphony No. 2 (Little Russian); Capriccio italien, Op. 45.
*** Chandos Dig. CHAN 8460 [id.]. Oslo PO, Jansons.

Like other conductors who learned their craft in the Soviet Union, Jansons prefers a fastish speed for the *Andantino* second movement, but what above all distinguishes this version is the joyful exuberance both of the bouncy Scherzo – fresh and folk-like in the Trio – and of the finale, and the final coda brings a surge of excitement, making most others seem stiff. The coupling is a fizzing performance of the *Capriccio italien*, bringing a gloriously uninhibited account of the coda with its deliberately vulgar reprise of the Neapolitan tune. With some edge on violin tone, this is not the finest of the Chandos Oslo recordings, but is still fresh and atmospheric.

Maazel's slow introduction is weightier and much more measured than with his competitors. From then on, he believes in treating Tchaikovsky directly and without sentimentality, incisive of attack, refined of texture. The undistracting freshness of his view – never too tense – is enhanced by excellent, well-balanced recording. If the fine *Antar* coupling is suitable, this is thoroughly worthwhile.

Symphonies Nos. (i) 2 (Little Russian), Op. 17; (ii) 4 in F min.
❋ (B) *** DG 429 527-2. (i) New Philh. O; (ii) VPO, Claudio Abbado.

Abbado's coupling of Tchaikovsky's *Second* and *Fourth Symphonies* is one of the supreme bargains of the current catalogue. His account of the *Little Russian Symphony* is very enjoyable, although the first movement concentrates on refinement of detail. The *Andantino* is very nicely done and the Scherzo is admirably crisp and sparkling. The finale is superb, with fine colour and thrust and a memorably spectacular stroke on the tam-tam before the exhilarating coda. The 1967 recording still sounds excellent. But this is merely a bonus for an unforgettable account of the *Fourth Symphony*, unsurpassed on record. Abbado's control of the structure of the first movement is masterly. The *Andantino*, with its gentle oboe solo, really takes wing in its central section, followed by a wittily crisp Scherzo, while the finale has sparkle as well as power, epitomizing the Russian dance spirit which was Tchaikovsky's inspiration. It was recorded in 1975 in the Musikverein and still sounds very good indeed.

Symphony No. 3 in D (Polish), Op. 29.
*** Chandos Dig. CHAN 8463 [id.]. Oslo PO, Jansons.

Symphony No. 3 (Polish); Hamlet overture; Romeo and Juliet (fantasy overture).
(M) (**) Biddulph mono WHL 014 [id.]. LSO, Albert Coates.

Symphony No. 3 (Polish); The Tempest, Op. 18.
(BB) **(*) Naxos Dig. 8.550518 [id.]. Polish Nat. RSO, Antoni Wit.

Tchaikovsky's *Third* is given a clear, refreshingly direct reading by Jansons, but it is the irresistible sweep of urgency with which Jansons builds the development section of the first movement that sets his performance apart, with the basic tempo varied less than usual. The second movement is beautifully relaxed, the *Andante elegiaco* heartwarmingly expressive, tender and refined, and the Scherzo has a Mendelssohnian elfin quality; but it is the swaggering reading of the finale, always in danger of sounding bombastic, which sets the seal on the whole performance. Though the recording does not convey a genuinely hushed pianissimo for the strings, it brings full, rich and brilliant sound.

Though Wit cannot match Leaper with the same orchestra in the *Symphony No. 1*, with playing a degree less alert and the recording not so full and forward, his *Little Russian Symphony* is still an attractive reading. The first and last movements both have a fine swagger, and if the ensemble could be crisper in the middle movements, Wit characterizes them well. *The Tempest*, an extended fantasia based on Shakespeare, not to be confused with *The Storm*, makes an attractive and unusual coupling and is again given a fine if not distinctive performance.

Made in 1932 and sadly cut, Albert Coates's recording of the *Polish Symphony* was the first ever issued. It compensates for the cuts in a performance that is both urgent and persuasive, with rhythms beautifully sprung. Coates's account of the *Romeo and Juliet overture* is characteristically wilful, but the fire and urgency in his conducting are hard to resist in any of these items.

Symphonies Nos. 4–6.
(Y/B) (M) (***) DG mono 447 423-2 (2) [id.]. Leningrad PO, Evgeny Mravinsky.
(M) *** RCA stereo/mono 09026 61901-2 (2) [id.]. Boston SO, Monteux.
(B) **(*) Ph. Duo 438 335-2 (2) [id.]. LSO, Markevitch.

Symphony No. 4 in F min., Op. 36; Romeo and Juliet (fantasy overture).
(N) (BB) *(*) RCA Navigator 74321 29252-2. Phd. O, Eugene Ormandy.

Symphony No. 5 in E min., Op.64; 1812 overture; Marche slave.
(N) (BB) ** RCA Navigator 74321 21291-2 [(d.) 09026 61853-2]. Phd. O, Eugene Ormandy.

(i) *Symphony No. 6 in B min. (Pathétique)*; (ii) *Serenade for strings in C, Op. 48.*
(N) (BB) **(*) RCA Navigator 74321 24210-2 [(d.) 09026 60908–2]. (i) Phd. O, Ormandy; (ii) Moscow Soloists, Yuri Bashmet.

Symphonies Nos. 4–6; The Nutcracker; Sleeping Beauty; Swan Lake: ballet suites.
(M) (***) EMI mono/stereo CMS7 63460-2 (3) [Ang. CDMC 63460]. Philh. O, Karajan.

Mravinsky re-recorded the three last symphonies of Tchaikovsky with his Leningrad orchestra for DG in stereo, but these legendary earlier, mono performances from the mid-1950s were even more satisfying and they sound marvellously vivid. The earlier readings, without loss of concentration, were less exaggeratedly histrionic, and Mravinsky's speeds for the finale of the *Fourth Symphony* particularly, but also for the *Fifth*, were not as frenetic as in the stereo versions. The opening of the *Fifth* again brings an added dimension of Russian melancholy, and Mravinsky sustains a lyrical intensity throughout the symphony characteristic of all his Tchaikovsky readings. The composer's marking for the slow movement 'con alcuna licenza' is taken very literally: this is a performance of great dramatic extremes, the only drawback for Western ears being the solo horn with his undeniable wobble. The finale has great zest, with blazing perorations from the brass. The emotional power of Mravinsky's *Pathétique* has been equalled elsewhere but never surpassed. The climax of the first movement has tremendous passion, the Scherzo/march is brilliantly pointed yet has plenty of weight, and the finale is deeply eloquent, genuinely touching rather than hysterical. The special rasp of the Russian trombones, which the composer would have recognized, is very telling here, as elsewhere.

Monteux's Boston recordings, part of RCA's Monteux Edition, were made between 1955 and 1958 and are among the finest versions of these works ever committed to disc. Monteux draws a clear distinction between Nos. 4–5 and No. 6. The former are played with a passionate forward romantic sweep and, although there are some interpretative eccentricities in No. 5, notably the finale, the panache of the music-making carries the listener readily through them. The *Pathétique* has rather more reserve and dignity (curiously, the 5/4 movement is pressed on very hard indeed). But although there is no lack of electricity in the first movement, and the Scherzo/march is indeed both a Scherzo and a march, with a broadening at the climax, the finale brings both nobility and great depth of feeling, with the restrained epilogue of the coda especially moving. This is a mono recording, but the full, spacious Boston sound all but covers this up. In Nos. 4 and 5 the recording – unbelievably improved over previous LP incarnations

– is satisfyingly full-blooded and with hardly a hint of the harshness that used to disfigure the equivalent LPs.

The Philharmonia in the early 1950s was an extraordinary body, and these early records are worth having even if you already possess Karajan's later accounts with the Berlin Philharmonic. Nos. 4 and 5 are mono, but the 1959 *Pathétique* is stereo. Exhilarating performances that still sound amazing for their period.

There are many collectors who count Markevitch's Philips recordings from the 1960s as having a similar distinction. Certainly Markevitch's *Fourth* is as exciting as almost any available. It has a superb thrusting first-movement Allegro and, while throughout Markevitch allows himself a degree of rubato in the rocking crescendo passage, as with Monteux it is the forward momentum of the performance that captures the listener. After a less evocative opening than Monteux, Markevitch applies to the first movement of the *Fifth* the forthright, highly charged approach which was so effective in the *Fourth*. He makes no concessions to the second-subject group, which is presented with no let-up on the fast pace at which he takes the main *Allegro*. Tchaikovsky's romanticism is turned into energy and the intended contrast is lost, and in the vigorous finale the final statement of the big tune is slow and rather stolid. In the *Pathétique* Markevitch provides great intensity in his account of the first movement; some might feel that he is too aggressive, even though the performance is always under emotional control. The second movement has both warmth and elegance – more so than with Monteux – and the march is treated broadly, providing suitable contrast before a deeply felt performance of the finale, where the second subject is introduced with great tenderness. With three symphonies offered for the cost of one premium-priced CD, this is certainly worth considering, for all the reservations about the *Fifth*.

Ormandy made his recordings of the *Fourth* and *Fifth Symphonies* in 1973–4, towards the end of his long tenure at Philadelphia and when he himself was in his seventies. The orchestra is still in glorious form, but the readings bring an element of routine, of going through the motions, and the electricity flickers only fitfully. In the first movement of the *Fourth* there are a few individual touches to suggest Ormandy's involvement and, after a somewhat lukewarm *Andantino*, its finale cannot help but make an effect with such magnificent playing; but the *Fifth* brings moments of blandness throughout and here the finale loses its impetus soon after it begins. *Romeo and Juliet* similarly brings relatively subdued passions. This is the coupling for both the *Fourth* and *Fifth Symphonies*, offered at mid-price, in the USA, which is a pity, for Ormandy's *1812* is presented with panache, with a resonant chorus to sing the Russian hymn, as well as some impressive cannon and a carillon at the close. *Marche slave* is very slow and pontifical.

When one turns to the *Pathétique*, recorded some six years earlier in 1968, the transformation is remarkable. This is a vintage Ormandy performance of a work with which he obviously identified closely, and it has even greater individuality and passion than his earlier (1960) account for Sony (see below). The introduction of the beautiful second subject of the first movement is wonderfully tender and, after the riveting development section, its return brings the fullest possible sense of apotheosis. The 5/4 movement winningly combines both warmth and a touch of melancholy, and the March/Scherzo is powerfully arresting. The finale is ardent yet also has dignity, and at the very end Ormandy conveys a touching resignation – all passion spent. The orchestra is on its toes throughout, and the only snag is the very brightly lit sound, much shallower than the later recordings; but this is not enough to detract seriously from the involvement of the performance. Moreover RCA have found a highly appropriate coupling for this Navigator reissue. Yuri Bashmet's account of the *String serenade* with the Moscow Soloists has matching energy and fire, and great finesse in the matter of light and shade. The *Waltz* is light and airy, the tenutos observed without voluptuous emphasis. The *Elégie* opens gently and delicately but develops a volatile ardour at its climax, and the finale is highly animated, its dance-rhythms bursting with energy. The virtuosity of the playing is emphasized by another brightly lit (digital) recording, made two decades later, which has plenty of ambience and a very wide dynamic range. A thoroughly collectable disc, especially at the inexpensive asking price.

Symphony No. 4 in F min., Op. 36.
*** Chandos Dig. CHAN 8361 [id.]. Oslo PO, Jansons.
**(*) DG Gold Dig. 439 018-2 [id.]. VPO, Karajan.

Symphony No. 4; Capriccio italien.
(M) *** DG 419 872-2 [id.]. BPO, Karajan.

Symphony No. 4; Capriccio italien; Romeo and Juliet (fantasy overture).
(N) *** Lodia Dig. LO-CD 791 [id.]. Moscow New Russian O, Carlos Païta.

Symphony No. 4; Francesca da Rimini.
*** DG Dig. 429 778-2 [id.]. NYPO, Bernstein.

(i) *Symphony No. 4;* (ii) *Romeo and Juliet* (fantasy overture).
(M) *** Telarc Dig. CD 82002 [id.]. Cleveland O, Lorin Maazel.

Jansons conducts a dazzling performance of the *Fourth*, unusually fresh and natural in its expressiveness, yet with countless subtleties of expression, as in the balletic account of the second-subject group of the first movement. The *Andantino* flows lightly and persuasively, the Scherzo is very fast and lightly sprung, while the finale reinforces the impact of the whole performance: fast and exciting, but with no synthetic whipping-up of tempo. That is so until the very end of the coda, which finds Jansons pressing ahead just fractionally as he would in a concert, a thrilling conclusion made the more so by the wide-ranging, brilliant and realistic recording.

Karajan's 1977 analogue version is undoubtedly more compelling than his previous recordings and is in most respects preferable to the newer, digital, Vienna version too. It is the vitality and drive of the performance as a whole that one remembers, although the beauty of the wind playing at the opening and close of the slow movement can give nothing but pleasure. The CD transfer is extremely vivid. The ubiquitous *Capriccio italien* is offered as a filler.

Bernstein's is not a performance to compare with any other: it is one that came from an interpreter of genius at a particular moment, white-hot and compellingly recorded, yet the sound is aptly big and fruity. The pizzicato scherzo is not ideally precise of ensemble but it is infectiously sprung and, in Bernstein's big, bold account of the finale, his slowing for the second subject (the *Birch tree* theme) is extreme but persuasive. The close is predictably exciting, with an unashamed accelerando in the closing bars, though without applause and obviously recorded at an editing session. The fill-up, *Francesca da Rimini*, brings a comparably spacious and big-scale performance.

In the early days of CD we gave much praise to Carlos Païta's inspirational version of Dvořák's *Seventh Symphony* (LOD–CD 782) which we hope may be reissued with a worthwhile coupling. Now Païta comes up with a highly compelling, if at times interpretatively eccentric, Tchaikovsky collection, played with great ardour and conviction, if with not always precise ensemble by the Moscow New Russian Orchestra. The recording, made in the Great Hall of the Moscow Conservatoire in 1994, has all the necessary richness and amplitude, and plenty of brilliance; although orchestral textures are at times a little thick, the overall effect is full-bloodedly spectacular. The reading of the symphony is essentially direct and powerful, although there are moments of wildness from the Russian players, notably some skittish woodwind decoration for the second subject of the first movement. Païta is free with *accelerandos*, particularly at the close of movements, and he produces a very Slavonic *decelerando* before the reprise in the *Andantino*, which is then played very beautifully. The Scherzo goes with the wind: it is very fast indeed and produces a bravura piccolo solo in the central section; the finale is exciting without being overdriven until a thrilling, spontaneous burst of bravura in the coda, which reminds one of Szell's famous Decca version. *Romeo and Juliet*, which opens the concert, begins rather sombrely, but there is a riveting climax at the trumpet entry with the Friar Laurence theme and no lack of passion. Païta's *Capriccio italien* makes a superb encore after the symphony. It is exhilaratingly uninhibited, the riveting opening fanfare matched by a sensational climax which almost defeats the engineers by its amplitude.

Maazel's 1979 Telarc Cleveland recording is very similar to his very successful 1965 Decca record, and only in the finale does the new version differ markedly from the old, by seeking amplitude and breadth in preference to uninhibited, extrovert excitement. Maazel's approach generates a strong forward momentum in the first movement and is consistently involving in its directness. Yet he lightens the tension effectively (like Jansons) by his balletic approach to the second-subject group. The slow movement, with a plaintive oboe solo, is distinctly appealing, and at the *Più mosso* Maazel makes a swift, bold tempo change. In the finale the Cleveland Orchestra produces a thrillingly rich body of timbre in the upper strings and the fullest resonance from the lower strings and brass. *Romeo and Juliet*, recorded two years later, is given a spaciously romantic performance, reaching a climax of considerable passion.

The *Fourth* is the most successful of the last three Tchaikovsky symphony recordings which Karajan made in 1985 in connection with the Telemodial video project. Although the playing of the Vienna orchestra does not match that of the Berlin Philharmonic in earlier versions, the performance itself has greater flexibility and more spontaneity. The freer control of tempo in the first movement brings a more relaxed second-subject group, while in the *Andantino* the Vienna oboist is fresher (though the timbre is edgier) than his Berlin counterpart, the phrasing less calculated. The Scherzo is attractively bright, if less precise, and the finale has splendid urgency and excitement. The warmly resonant acoustic is attractive; even if detail is not absolutely clear, there is no lack of fullness, and Karajan admirers should not be disappointed.

(i) *Symphonies Nos. 4 in F, Op. 36;* (ii) *5 in E min., Op. 64; Serenade for strings in C, Op. 48; Suite No. 3 in G, Op. 55: Theme and variations.*
(N) (BB) ** CfP Silver Double CDCFPSD 4784 (2). (i) SNO, Sir Alexander Gibson; (ii) LPO, Norman del Mar.

The generous and attractive-looking package from Classics for Pleasure is inexpensive but uneven in quality. Gibson's is a good honest performance of the *Fourth*, well enough recorded (in 1978). The first movement lacks a little in resilience, while the *Andante* could have more lift; but overall this is effective enough. However, Norman Del Mar's *Fifth*, although undoubtedly exciting and well played (Nicholas Busch's horn solo in the slow movement beautifully done), is exasperatingly wilful. In all the movements but the *Waltz* (which is graciously straightforward) there are eccentric tempo changes. At bar 108 of the first movement there is an inexplicable pulling back; later the preparation for the second subject is spoiled, and the exaggerated rubato in the presentation of the theme itself is equally difficult to take. Throughout there are unmarked accelerandos – and pauses, too – which fail to convince. In the finale Del Mar does not establish his basic tempo at the beginning of the *Allegro vivace* but suddenly quickens as the secondary material arrives. Curiously, the *Serenade for strings* offers no such idiosyncrasies, and the masterly set of variations from the *Third suite* is also very straightforward, though it has its zesful moments, and again the orchestral playing is sensitive (notably the cor anglais in Variation 8, while David Nolan's solo violin in Variation 9 has plenty of flair). In the *Serenade* Del Mar uses the full LPO string section, which provides alert playing with plenty of intensity in the outer movements and nice pointing of the second subject of the first. The *Waltz* is warmly romantic and only slightly indulged. The 1975 recording is brightly lit but quite full.

Symphony No. 5 in E min., Op. 64.
*** Chandos Dig. CHAN 8351 [id.]. Oslo PO, Jansons.
(M) *** Telarc Dig. CD 82015 [id.]. RPO, Previn – RIMSKY-KORSAKOV: *Tsar Saltan: March.* ***
*** Olympia OCD 221 [id.]. Leningrad PO, Mravinsky (with LIADOV: *Baba Yaga, Op. 56.* MUS-SORGSKY: *Khovanshchina: Prelude.* WAGNER: *Tristan: Prelude and Liebstod* ***).
(Y/B) *** RCA Dig. 09026 68032-2 [id.]. N. German RSO, Wand – MOZART: *Symphony No. 40.* ***
**(*) DG Gold Dig. 439 019-2 [id.]. VPO, Karajan.

Symphony No. 5; Francesca da Rimini.
**(*) EMI Dig. CDC7 54338-2 [id.]. Phd. O, Muti

Symphony No. 5; Marche slave.
(M) *** DG 419 066-2 [id.]. BPO, Karajan.

(i) *Symphony No. 5 in E min., Op. 64;* (ii) *Nutcracker suite, Op. 71a.*
(B) *** DG 439 434-2 [id.]. (i) Leningrad PO, Mravinsky; (ii) BPO, Karajan.

Symphony No. 5; (i) Eugene Onegin: Tatiana's letter scene.
⚛ (M) *** EMI Dig. CD-EMX 2187. LPO, Sian Edwards; (i) with Eilene Hannan.

Sian Edwards conducts an electrifying and warm-hearted reading of Tchaikovsky's *Fifth*, which matches any version in the catalogue, particularly when it comes with an unusual and exceptionally attractive fill-up, Tchaikovsky's greatest inspiration for soprano, *Tatiana's letter scene*. That is freshly and dramatically sung, in a convincingly girlish impersonation, by the Australian, Eilene Hannan. Sian Edwards's control of rubato is exceptionally persuasive, notably so in moulding the different sections of the first movement of the symphony, while the great horn solo of the slow movement is played with exquisite delicacy by Richard Bissell. The Waltz third movement is most tenderly done, while the finale brings a very fast and exciting allegro, challenging the orchestra to brilliant, incisive playing.

In the first movement, Jansons's refusal to linger never sounds anything but warmly idiomatic, lacking only a little in charm. The slow movement again brings a steady tempo, with climaxes built strongly and patiently but with enormous power, the final culmination topping everything. In the finale, taken very fast, Jansons tightens the screw of the excitement without ever making it a scramble, following Tchaikovsky's notated slowings rather than allowing extra rallentandos. The sound is excellent, specific and well focused within a warmly reverberant acoustic, with digital recording on CD reinforcing any lightness of bass.

Previn's fine concern for detail is well illustrated by the way that the great horn melody in the slow movement (superbly played by Jeff Bryant) contains the implication of a quaver rest before each three-quarter group, where normally it sounds like a straight triplet. In the first movement, rhythms are light and well sprung, and the third movement is sweet and lyrical yet with no hint of mannerism, for Previn adopts a naturally expressive style within speeds generally kept steady, even in the great climax of the slow movement which then subsides into a coda of breathtaking delicacy. The finale, taken very fast indeed, crowns an outstandingly satisfying reading. The Telarc recording is full and wide-ranging, not as detailed as some, but very naturally balanced.

Mravinsky's Olympia recording of Tchaikovsky's *Fifth* was recorded in Leningrad in 1973; the remaining pieces come from a concert at the Moscow Conservatoire. If anything, the *Symphony* is even more electrifying than either of the earlier DG versions. Climaxes are still somewhat rough on this version – but this is easily overlooked, given the excitement of the playing. Another factor prompting a strong recommendation is the other material on the disc. Liadov's *Baba Yaga* is given a virtuoso performance and is also well recorded; the Mussorgsky is predictably atmospheric, and the Wagner leaves no doubt that Mravinsky must have been a great interpreter of this composer.

However, Mravinsky's earlier stereo version of the *Fifth* with the Leningrad Philharmonic on DG would occupy a distinguished place in any collection. The performance is full of Slavonic vitality and the reading is romantic as well as red-blooded (the second subject of the first movement is both warm and graceful). The solo horn has a faint wobble in the famous solo in the slow movement, and the trumpets in the final peroration of an exhilaratingly fast finale also have a vibrato, but these details are unimportant when the reading has such fire and individuality. The recording, made in Watford Town Hall in 1960, is resonant and full, if not always absolutely clean in focus. By comparison Karajan's 1966 *Nutcracker suite* sounds a little cool, but it is marvellously polished and vivid, and the *Waltz of the flowers* has the most agreeable elegance.

Unexpectedly and generously coupled with Mozart's *G minor Symphony*, Wand's live recording brings a unique reading of Tchaikovsky's *Fifth*, one which might be described as the vision of a great Brucknerian, not in any way dull or boring but rapt, refreshing and intense. His own delight shines out as each fresh idea appears. The rapt account of the slow movement starts with a most beautiful, hushed account of the opening horn solo, and continues from there in an almost devotional manner. The degree of restraint, with pianissimos of breath-catching delicacy, makes the results the more moving, while the climaxes brought by the purified second theme glow even more intensely than usual, with only the second intrusion of the motto theme at all menacing. The waltz lilts easily and delicately, and then the finale brings at last a sense of release, brilliant and exciting, with the slow march of the coda flowing more easily than usual. In all this Wand owes much to the players of the North German Radio Orchestra, helped by the engineers, so that many details which are normally obscured are brought out with distinctive timbres – notably of the horns – set against a glowing acoustic.

Karajan's 1976 recording stands out from his other recordings of the *Fifth*. The first movement is unerringly paced and has great romantic flair; in Karajan's hands the climax of the slow movement is grippingly intense, though with a touchingly elegiac preparation for the horn solo at the opening. The Waltz has character and charm too – the Berlin Philharmonic string playing is peerless – and in the finale Karajan drives hard, creating a riveting forward thrust. The remastered recording brings a remarkable improvement.

Karajan's last VPO version of the *Fifth* brings a characteristically strong and expressive performance; however, neither in the playing of the Vienna Philharmonic nor even in the recorded sound can it quite match his earlier, Berlin Philharmonic version for DG. Though the long takes have brought extra spontaneity, the recording of the strings in the Musikvereinsaal is inconsistent, with front-desk players sharply focused but not the whole body of strings behind them, and with woodwind set at a distance. The slack ensemble and control of rhythm in the waltz movement are specially disappointing. The finale, however, goes especially well, with the Vienna brass biting superbly in the first reprise of the movement's main theme.

The oddity of Muti's Philadelphia version is that, though the first two movements have the disappointingly over-relaxed manners that marked his *Pathétique* earlier, often with surprisingly slack ensemble, the last two movements are played with the high voltage one expects of this conductor and orchestra at their finest. Maybe the change of tension reflects the atmosphere of two separate sessions, the second much sharper than the first. The fill-up too is played at white heat, a powerful performance. It makes a rare and generous coupling. The sound, not as clear as it might be, has warmth and weight beyond most new Philadelphia issues.

Symphony No. 6 in B min. (Pathétique), Op. 74.
*** Chandos Dig. CHAN 8446 [id.]. Oslo PO, Jansons.
(M) (***) RCA mono GD 60312 [60312-2-RG]. Phd. O, Toscanini – R. STRAUSS: *Death and transfiguration.* (***)
**(*) DG Gold Dig. 429 020 [id.]. VPO, Karajan.
**(*) Sony Dig. SK 45836 [id.]. Nat. SO of Washington, Rostropovich (with J. STRAUSS Jnr: *Vergnügungszug polka;* GRIEG: *Peer Gynt: Death of Aase;* PAGANINI: *Moto perpetuo;* PROKOFIEV: *Romeo & Juliet: Death of Tybalt;* GERSHWIN: *Walking the dog;* SOUSA: *Stars & Stripes forever*).

Symphony No. 6 (Pathétique); Capriccio italien; Eugene Onegin: Waltz & Polonaise.
(B) **(*) Sony SBK 47657; *SBT 47657* [id.]. Phd O, Ormandy.

Symphony No. 6 (Pathétique); 1812 Overture.
(N) (M) **(*) RCA 09026 61246-2 [id.]. Chicago SO, Reiner – LISZT: *Mephisto waltz.* ***

Symphony No. 6 (Pathétique); Marche slave, Op. 31.
⊛ *** Virgin/EMI VC7 59661-2 [id.]. Russian Nat. O, Mikhail Pletnev.
(Y/B) (BB) ** Tring Dig. TRP 011 [id.]. RPO, Sir Yehudi Menuhin.

Symphony No. 6 (Pathétique); Nutcracker suite, Op. 71a.
(M) (**) RCA mono GD 60297. NBC SO, Toscanini.

Symphony No. 6 (Pathétique); Romeo and Juliet (fantasy overture).
(M) *** Virgin/EMI Dig. CUV5 61267-2 [id.]. Bournemouth SO, Andrew Litton.
(N) (M) **(*) Mercury 434 352-2 [id.]. LSO, Antal Dorati.
(M) (***) RCA mono GD 60920 [09026 60920-2]. Boston SO, Koussevitzky.

(i) *Symphony No. 6 (Pathétique);* (ii) *Swan Lake* (ballet): *suite.*
(Y/B) (B) *** DG 439 456-2 [id.]. (i) Leningrad PO, Mravinsky; (ii) BPO, Karajan.
(BB) **(*) ASV Dig. CDQS 6091 [id.]. (i) LPO; (ii) RPO, Bátiz.

The *Pathétique* was Mikhail Pletnev's début on record as a conductor with the Russian National Orchestra that has been formed for him. There is no doubt that this is among the most vividly dramatic accounts of this symphony to have appeared for some years. The way in which Pletnev launches us into the development of the first movement still takes one aback, even when one knows what to expect. His hand-picked orchestra is as virtuosic as Pletnev himself can be on the keyboard. The Scherzo may seem too fast for some people but it is marked *Allegro molto vivace* and Koussevitzky (see below) is not much slower. There is a stirring account of *Marche slave* too, and a very fine recording, perfectly balanced, although the effect is a little recessed.

Litton's is an outstanding performance, full of temperament, not just fiery but tender too, arguably the finest of the whole Litton cycle. The Bournemouth playing has never been neater, with the sound bringing out the fine clarity of articulation. The only idiosyncrasy is that in the big second-subject melodies of the outer movements Litton prefers speeds broader than usual, but with no hint of self-indulgence in the finely moulded phrasing. With an account of *Romeo and Juliet* that builds up power-fully from a restrained start, the disc makes a splendid culmination, a match even for the earlier, Virgin version with Pletnev, and more fully and cleanly recorded. It also gains in practical terms even over the Pletnev issue when the coupling is so much more generous.

Mariss Jansons and the Oslo Philharmonic crown their magnetically compelling Tchaikovsky series with a superbly concentrated account of the last and greatest of the symphonies. It is characteristic of Jansons that the great second-subject melody is at once warm and passionate yet totally unsentimental, with rubato barely noticeable. The very fast speed for the third-movement *March* stretches the players to the very limit, but the exhilaration is infectious, leading to the simple dedication of the slow finale, unexaggerated but deeply felt. Fine, warm recording as in the rest of the series.

Mravinsky's very Russian (stereo) account of the *Pathétique* is justly renowned. It is deeply passionate, yet the second subject of the first movement is introduced with much tenderness. The last two move-ments are very fine indeed; the Scherzo/march is brilliantly pointed, yet has plenty of weight, and the finale is very moving without ever letting the control slip. The present transfer of the 1960 recording (made in Wembley Town Hall) maintains the agreeable ambience, even if at times the Russian brass comes over raucously at climaxes. Karajan's *Swan Lake suite* has characteristic charisma and excite-ment, with polished BPO playing seemingly aiming for brilliance, and the recording, made a decade after the symphony, has somewhat less allure in the matter of string sonority. But no one could com-plain of lack of vividness.

Ormandy's fine 1960 performance is a reading of impressive breadth, dignity and power, with no suggestion of routine in a single bar. The orchestra makes much of the first-movement climax and plays with considerable passion and impressive body of tone in both outer movements; yet there is an element of restraint in the finale which prevents any feeling of hysteria. In short, this is most satisfying, a performance to live with; the CD transfer, while brightly lit, avoids glare in the upper range. Ormandy's panache and gusto give the *Capriccio italien* plenty of life without driving too hard, and the dances are rhythmically infectious.

Reiner is given full-blooded 1957 sound but his *Pathétique* – although it has some bursts of excitement in the first movement, and the Chicago ambience adds much to the lively Scherzo/march – as a whole does not completely convince. The last movement is tender rather than producing the intensity and anguish inherent in a Russian performance. *1812* is without cannon but is very enjoyable nevertheless. What makes this reissue distinctive is Reiner's superb account of Liszt's *Mephisto waltz*, perhaps the finest on record.

Dorati's 1960 recording of the *Pathétique* is much better focused on CD than it seemed to be in its rather indifferent Philips LP pressing. Now there is much brilliance, underpinned by the weight and resonance of Watford Town Hall. The reading has plenty of dynamism in the first movement and the 5/4 movement, unusually brisk, is exhilarating, if hardly a conventional reading. There are some minor eccentricities of tempi in the Scherzo/march but the climax is thrilling, and the finale, as so often with this symphony, is finely done, volatile, but grippingly so. *Romeo and Juliet* opens with dignity, is tender in the love music and brings plenty of excitement at the climax. Not a first choice, but there is nothing routine about this music-making.

Rostropovich's reading is intense and passionate. Speeds are on the fast side, and in the great broad melodies of the first and last movements Rostropovich's approach is urgent, with *espressivo* interpreted as a cue for pressing ahead, not drawing back. The string ensemble throughout is excellent, with exceptionally clean articulation, and the principal reservation must be over the recorded sound, very good considering the problems of recording live in Moscow, but with a vagueness of focus in the bass. Among the encores, the Strauss *Excursion train polka* comes not in its usual form but in an extraordinary orchestration by Shostakovich, with witty commentary from percussion and brass. The Grieg then brings ravishing pianissimos from the Washington strings, and Rostropovich reinforces his achievement with the players when the violins *en masse* then play the Paganini showpiece with amazingly precise ensemble.

Koussevitzky's account of the *Pathétique* comes from 1930 but though the sound may lack the vivid colouring of present-day recording, the performance certainly doesn't. This is another version of outsize personality that will have you on the edge of your chair for it is tremendously high voltage. Not that it is free from the odd mannerism: he italicizes the passage immediately after the explosive fortissimo that opens the development in the first movement. The 1936 *Romeo and Juliet* was issued in an RCA Boston Symphony compilation in the 1970s, and ranks as one of the most impassioned accounts of the piece made in that era. The RCA engineers have done their best with the sound which, in spite of some discoloration in climaxes, is more than acceptable.

Toscanini's Philadelphia version of the *Pathétique* glows with the special magic that developed between him and the orchestra over the winter season of 1941–2. Though far more disciplined than most readings, it is altogether warmer than his NBC recording, with the great second-subject melody of the first movement tender in its emotions, not rigid in its easy rubato. He even eases the tempo sympathetically for the fortissimo entries of the march in the third movement. Alongside a magnificent account of the Strauss – an apt link, with death the theme – it makes a superb historical document.

Recorded, like the VPO *Fourth* and *Fifth*, with video as part of the project, Karajan's last digital recording of the *Pathétique* has many characteristic strong points, and the reading has both intensity and spontaneity. If it lacks the supreme grip of the earlier, Berlin Philharmonic recordings, it is still an exciting performance, even if the Vienna ensemble is noticeably slacker than that of the Berliners and the finale in consequence is less powerful. The 5/4 movement is slower than before and rather heavy in style; though the speed of the march movement remains as fast as previously, the result is less tense than before. Even so, the close has plenty of free-flowing adrenalin. The sound is greatly improved in this remastering for the Karajan Gold series.

Bátiz's (1982) reading of the *Pathétique* is distinctly enjoyable, attractively fresh and direct, with the great second-subject melody the more telling for being understated and with transitions just a little perfunctory. The Scherzo/march comes off especially well. The brass are set rather forward, but this makes for a very exciting climax. Otherwise the balance is good and the sound is generally excellent. It is even better in the *Swan Lake suite*, recorded five years later. The RPO playing is very good indeed, polished, warm and alert. Barry Griffiths and Françoise Rive are sensitive string soloists in the *Danse des cygnes*. The suite ends with the great tune near the end of the ballet where the violins are echoed powerfully by the four horns in unison. An excellent super-bargain coupling.

Menuhin's performance has its moments of excitement but in the last resort does not leave a very deep impression. The central movements go best, the third more Scherzo than march. Throughout, ensemble could be crisper and, although the very end of the finale is moving, with an eloquent contribution from the RPO brass, the movement's earlier climax is slightly mannered. There is a proper pause before *Marche slave* and this sparklingly alive and spontaneous performance, despite somewhat over-brilliant sound, demonstrates what is missing in the symphony. Recording good, but artificially balanced and rather two-dimensional.

The 1947 NBC recording for Toscanini, dry and unhelpful, also has high 78 surface hiss, which detracts from a characteristically powerful and intense performance. Speeds are all on the fast side, but only in the first movement do the results ever sound perfunctory, and the middle movements are delectably pointed in rhythm, while the slow finale at a flowing speed is both noble and passionate. The sound for the *Nutcracker* is far clearer, a crisp, bright interpretation, even if the Sugar-Plum Fairy is heavy-footed.

(i) *Symphony No. 6 (Pathétique); Romeo and Juliet (fantasy overture);* (ii) *The Nutcracker; Sleeping Beauty; Swan Lake:* excerpts.

(Y/B) (BB) *** EMI Seraphim CES5 68537-2 (2) [CDEB 68537]. Philh. O, with (i) Carlo Maria Giulini; (ii) Erfrem Kurtz; with Y. Menuhin.

Giulini's EMI performance of the *Pathétique* was recorded with the Philharmonia on top form in 1959, and this reissue still sounds excellent in the CD transfer. Giulini takes a spacious view of the symphony. There is a degree of restraint in the way he interprets the big melodies of the first and last movements, which are given an almost Elgarian nobility. Yet passionate intensity is conveyed by the purity and concentration of the playing, which equally builds up electric tension and excitement without hysteria. It now comes coupled with his equally fine performance of *Romeo and Juliet*, recorded two years later, a not dissimilar reading and equally superbly played. The work's climax is dramatically very powerful. The second of the two CDs in this inexpensive package also shows the Philharmonia Orchestra at its absolute peak. The early (late 1950s) stereo sounds astonishingly full, and the performances combine elegance and finesse with sparkle and colour. Here all of the *Nutcracker suite* is included except the *Chinese dance*, an inexplicable omission that would have nicely fitted on, as the programme plays for 77 minutes 39 seconds. A splendid super-bargain compilation.

Symphony No. 7 (arr. Bogatyrev).
*** Chandos Dig. CHAN 9130 [id.]. LPO, Neeme Järvi – *Piano concerto No. 3.* **(*)

Symphony No. 7 in E flat (reconstructed Bogatyrev); (i) *Variations on a rococo theme for cello and orchestra, Op. 33.*
(M) ** Sony MPK 46453 [id.]. Phd. O, Ormandy; (i) with Leonard Rose.

Just over 30 years after Eugene Ormandy and the Philadelphia Orchestra first recorded Bogatyrev's completion of Tchaikovsky's *Symphony No. 7*, Neeme Järvi provided this valuable alternative, helpfully coupled with the one-movement *Piano concerto No. 3* which Tchaikovsky drew from the symphony's first movement. This reconstructed symphony, abandoned not long before Tchaikovsky wrote his culminating masterpiece in the *Pathétique Symphony*, may be no match for the regular canon, but it brings many Tchaikovskian delights. Having symphony and concerto side by side makes it very easy to compare Bogatyrev's reconstruction of the original version, in structure identical except for the central solo cadenza which Tchaikovsky inserted in the concerto. In the *Symphony* Järvi, with speeds a degree more expansive than Ormandy in all four movements, finds more poetry, more fantasy, and the modern digital recording allows far more light and shade over a much wider dynamic range. With Järvi, the Scherzo, drawn from the tenth of Tchaikovsky's Opus 72 piano pieces, is lighter and more resilient and, though in the finale the opening is less exciting, the march theme of the second subject, which with Ormandy is square and banal, is made to sound delightfully jaunty. Apart from the thinness on the upper strings, the recorded sound is satisfyingly full and warm. Geoffrey Tozer – see above – gives a fine performance of the *Concerto* but there are more reservations here, notably about the orchestral string timbre.

On the Sony CD, Leonard Rose's warm and elegant account of the *Rococo variations* comes like balm to the ears after the noisy finale of the symphony.

Variations on a rococo theme for cello and orchestra (original version).
*** Ph. Dig. 434 106-2 [id.]. Julian Lloyd Webber, LSO, Maxim Shostakovich – MIASKOVSKY: *Cello concerto.* ***

At last the composer's own version of the *Variations on a rococo theme* is coming into its own. A scholarly edition appeared as long ago as 1941, but the corrupt edition retained its hold on the repertory. Lloyd Webber's approach is leisurely and, aided no doubt by the exemplary Philips recording, he produces a pleasingly cultured sound. Not as virtuosic in outlook or as strongly profiled as Rostropovich's version of the corrupt score, but very musical and refreshingly enjoyable.

Variations on a rococo theme for cello and orchestra, Op. 33.
(Y/B) ⊛ (M) *** DG 447 413-2 [id.]. Rostropovich, BPO, Karajan – DVORAK: *Cello concerto.* *** ⊛
(N) (BB) *** CfP Silver Double CDCFPSD 4775 (2). Robert Cohen, LPO, Macal – BEETHOVEN: *Triple concerto;* DVORAK: *Cello concerto;* ELGAR: *Cello concerto.* ***
(Y/B) *** EMI Seraphim CES5 68521-2 (2) [CEDB 68521]. (i) Paul Tortelier, N. Sinfonia, Yan Pascal Tortelier – DVORAK: *Cello concerto* etc. ***
(M) *** Decca 425 020-2 [id.]. Harrell, Cleveland O, Maazel – BRUCH: *Kol Nidrei* ***; DVORAK: *Cello concerto.* ***

*** RCA Dig. RD 71003. Ofra Harnoy, Victoria SO, Freeman – OFFENBACH: *Concerto;* SAINT-SAENS: *Concerto No. 1.* ***

(B) *** Sony SBK 48278; *SBT 48278* [id.]. Leonard Rose, Phd. O, Ormandy – BLOCH: *Schelomo* ***; FAURs: *Élégie* ***; LALO: *Concerto.* **(*)

**(*) Virgin/EMI Dig. VC7 59325-2 [id.]. Truls Mørk, Oslo PO, Jansons – DVORₐK: *Cello concerto.* **(*)

Rostropovich uses the published score rather than the original version which more accurately reflects the composer's intentions. But this account, with Karajan's glowing support, is so superbly structured in its control of emotional light and shade that one is readily convinced that this is the work Tchaikovsky conceived. The recording (made in the Jesus-Christus Kirche) is beautifully balanced and is surely one of the most perfect examples of DG's analogue techniques. It sounds remarkably real and present in this superb remastering and well deserves its place at the head of DG's 'Legendary Recordings series'.

As in the Dvořák concerto, with which his performance of the *Rococo variations* is coupled, Robert Cohen tends to avoid pronounced rubato, yet the result is warmly expressive as well as strong. The 1978 recording is first rate, and anyone fancying the other three works included on this Classics for Pleasure Silver Double will find Cohen's artistry is consistently rewarding.

A finely wrought account from Tortelier *père*, accompanied by the Northern Sinfonia under Tortelier *fils*. This is very enjoyable, if perhaps not quite so distinguished as Rostropovich on DG. Well worth considering when the Dvořák couplings are so generous.

An assured, vividly characterized set of *Variations* from Lynn Harrell, with plenty of matching colour from the Cleveland woodwind. The analogue recording is bright and colourful.

Ofra Harnoy's scale is smaller, the style essentially elegant, not missing the colour or ardour but never forgetting the word 'rococo' in the title. It is a considerable performance, stylish yet emotionally responsive, and Paul Freeman's accompaniment is first class, too.

Leonard Rose's warm and elegant – yet at times quite ardent – account of these splendid variations is balm to the senses, and Ormandy provides admirable support. The recording is forwardly balanced but the dynamic range remains reasonably wide, and the cello is firmly and realistically focused.

A fine performance from Truls Mørk, with plenty of energy and finesse, and the *Andante* of Variation 11 played with an appealingly Slavonic, plaintive feeling. Very good recording too, but in sheer elegance and panache this is no match for Rostropovich.

CHAMBER AND INSTRUMENTAL MUSIC

Album for the young, Op. 39: (i) original piano version; (ii) trans. for string quartet by Dubinsky.
*** Chandos CHAN 8365 [id.]. (i) Luba Edlina; (ii) augmented Borodin Trio.

These 24 pieces are all miniatures, but they have great charm; their invention is often memorable, with quotations from Russian folksongs and one French, plus a brief reminder of *Swan Lake*. Here they are presented twice, in their original piano versions, sympathetically played by Luba Edlina, and in effective string quartet transcriptions arranged by her husband, Rostislav Dubinsky. The Borodin group play them with both affection and finesse. The CD has plenty of presence.

Piano trio in A min., Op. 50.
*** EMI Dig. CDC7 49865-2 [id.] Chung Trio – SHOSTAKOVICH: *Piano trio No. 1.* ***
(N) *** Ara. Dig. Z6661 [id.]. Golub–Kaplan–Carr Trio – SMETANA: *Piano trio.* ***
**(*) EMI CDC7 47988-2 [id.]. Ashkenazy, Perlman, Harrell.
(Y/B) **(*) Sony Dig. SK 53269 [id.]. Yefim Bronfman, Cho-Liang Lin, Gary Hoffman – ARENSKY: *Piano trio No. 1.* **(*)
** Mezhdunarodnaya Kniga Dig. MK 417001 [id.]. Timofeyeva, Fedotov, Rodin.

An ardent and committed performance comes from the Chung Trio. Myung-Whun is very much the dominant partner (at times his virtuosity would seem more at home in a concerto) but he plays with great delicacy and charm. Some of the variations (Nos. 2 and 8) are played better here than in any of the rival versions, and the recording is splendidly truthful and realistic. Moreover they give us the whole work uncut (as did Perlman, Ashkenazy and Harrell). The only snag is the somewhat reticent playing of Myung-Wha Chung: she is a refined cellist, but her sound is not as big or her personality as strong as either her brother or sister. All the same, this is so likeable a performance that it must go to the top of the list, the more particularly since it has such a worthwhile coupling.

What we say about the Golub/Kaplan/Carr account of the Smetana *G minor Piano trio*, with which this is coupled, applies equally to the Tchaikovsky, which has the merit of being completely uncut. Perhaps the balance places the listener a bit too close to the players, but the sound is perfectly pleasing and the performance is eminently musical and refreshingly unaffected. Nothing is overdriven, mechanized or attention-seeking. While it does not necessarily displace the Chung Trio or Ashkenazy, Perlman and Harrell, it can be ranked alongside them.

The dominating keyboard role of the first movement of Tchaikovsky's *Piano trio* can so easily sound rhetorical, as well as gripping and commanding – and that element is not entirely avoided by Ashkenazy, Perlman and Harrell. But the *Variations* which form the second part of the work are very successful, with engaging characterization and a great deal of electricity in the closing pages. Indeed, generally this group carry all before them, with their sense of artistic purpose and through their warmth and ardour. The sound is on the dry side, with the digital remastering increasing the sharpness of focus, where a little more ambience would have been a more attractive addition; moreover this is still at full price and comes without a coupling.

The new Sony account from Yefim Bronfman, Cho-Liang Lin and Gary Hoffman is a keenly lyrical and expressive performance of this work, which suffers from a less than ideally balanced recording. Yefim Bronfman is allowed to swamp the texture when the dynamic level rises, even though, as in the Arensky with which it is coupled, it is obvious that he is playing with delicacy. Both Cho-Liang Lin and Gary Hoffman are marvellous players whose refinement and purity give unfailing delight. If you can make allowances for the bias towards the piano, this could be your preferred choice.

Lyubov Timofeyeva, Maxim Fedotov and Kirill Rodin have impressive credentials as prize-winners and their account of the *Trio* brings the sort of playing one might have encountered in a highly cultured Russian home at the turn of the century, communicating a sensitivity and reticence that make a refreshing change in these days of glamourized, packaged sentiment. But having said this, the fact remains that the tempo in the first movement is expansive, almost sluggish, minimizing any contrast between the two movements. Many of the variations are beautifully done but, despite their refined musicianship, one ends up feeling the need for just a bit more projection. Decent recording, but short measure in that there is no coupling.

Souvenir de Florence, Op. 70.
(N) *** Chandos Dig. CHAN 9878 [id.] ASMF Chamber Ens. – GLAZUNOV: *String quintet.* ***
** Mer. Dig. CDE 84211 [id.]. Arienski Ens. – ARENSKY: *String quartet No. 2* ***; BORODIN: *Sextet movements.* **

On Chandos, a very musical and well-recorded account of *Souvenir de Florence* which, though not necessarily superior to the Borodin performance, certainly deserves a warm recommendation. Its coupling, which brings a Glazunov rarity, strengthens its claims on the collector.

A very good rather than a distinguished performance of Tchaikovsky's eloquent *Souvenir de Florence* on Meridian, very decently recorded. The strength of the issue lies in the interest of its coupling, an Arensky rarity, the *A minor Quartet*, from which the well-known *Variations on a theme of Tchaikovsky* derive, and two Mendelssohnian movements from the Borodin *Sextet*.

String quartets Nos. 1 in D, Op. 11; 2 in F, Op. 22; 3 in E flat, Op. 30; (i) *Souvenir de Florence* (string sextet), *Op. 70.*
*** EMI Dig. CDS7 49775-2 (2). Borodin Qt, (i) with Y. Bashmet, N. Gutman.

String quartet in B flat; String quartets Nos. 1–3; (i) *Souvenir de Florence.*
(M) *** BMG/Melodiya 74321 18290-2 (2) [id.]. Borodin Qt, (i) with Rostropovich, Talalyan.
*** Teldec/Warner Dig. 4509 90422-2 (2) [id.]. Borodin Qt, (i) with Yurov, Milman.

String quartets Nos. 1 in D, Op. 11; 3 in E flat, Op. 30.
**(*) Nimbus Dig. NI 5380 [id.]. Franz Schubert Qt.

String quartet No. 2 in F, Op. 22; (i) *Souvenir de Florence.*
**(*) Nimbus Dig. NI 5399 [id.]. Franz Schubert Qt, (i) with Flieder, Schultz.

The EMI set with the three *Quartets*, dating from 1978–9 plus the *Souvenir de Florence* with Bashmet and Natalia Gutman of 1980, was reissued and repackaged in 1993 as part of the centenary celebrations. Given performances of this distinction and music of this quality of inspiration, the set is self-recommending. The digital recording is very nearly as outstanding as the performances, and there is no reason to qualify the strength and warmth of our recommendation. The mid-priced BMG/Melodiya set is of earlier provenance in the case of the *Souvenir de Florence* with Rostropovich and Talalyan; it comes from 1965, whereas the three *Quartets* plus the student *Quartet movement* that Tchaikovsky wrote in 1865 were all recorded at roughly the same time (1979–80). The Teldec set, made in 1993 in the Berlin Teldec studios, is digital and the sound is a shade drier: it also includes the early (and, to be frank, not wildly interesting) *B flat movement*. All the same, all three are superb and are without peer, and either the EMI/Melodiya or BMG/Melodiya are unassailable recommendations; the Teldec is hardly less impressive. One need look no further.

The two Nimbus discs have the same advantage as the Shostakovich on Olympia (see below) of being available separately. The two couplings, of *No. 1 in D major* and *No. 3 in E flat*, and the *F major quartet* and the *Souvenir de Florence*, offer good playing and the sound-balance offers one of the best chamber-music recordings Nimbus have given us. The Franz Schubert Quartet possess smooth, beautifully produced sound and good ensemble. All the same, as a performance the playing is not in the same league as the Borodins.

String quartets Nos. 1 in D, Op. 11; 2 in F, Op. 22; 5 early pieces for string quartet.
** Olympia OCD 521 [id.]. Shostakovich Qt.

String quartet No. 3 in E flat, Op. 30; (i) *Adagio molto in E flat for string quartet & harp.*
**(*) Olympia OCD 522 [id.]. (i) Moskvitina; Shostakovich Qt – GRECHANINOV: *String quartet.* **(*)

The versions by the Shostakovich Quartet are also masterly but not in the Borodins' league. The performances emanate from Moscow Radio broadcasts from 1976 (*No. 1*) and 1978 (*No. 2*) and 1973 in the case of the early pieces dating from the composer's student years at the St Petersburg Conservatoire (not masterpieces, though they are of interest, as is almost anything that the master penned, to Tchaikovsky lovers). Coming to them immediately after any of the Borodins, they sound just a shade strident at the upper end of the spectrum, though this is easily tamed. Indeed in the *Third Quartet*, recorded in 1976, this is barely noticeable; the sound has warmth and presence. The *Adagio* for string quartet and harp is one of the few Tchaikovksy rarities that are not of real interest. The coupling is unusual – a pleasing if unmemorable quartet by Grechaninov, better known for his vocal and choral music.

String quartet No. 1 in D, Op. 11.
(N) (M) *** Cal. CAL 6202 [id.]. Talich Qt – BORODIN: *Quartet No. 2.* **(*)
(Y/B) (***) Testament mono SBT 1061 [id.]. Hollywood Qt – GLAZUNOV: *5 Novelettes;* BORODIN: *String quartet No. 2 in D.* (***)
(M) **(*) Decca 425 541-2 [id.]. Gabrieli Qt – BORODIN; SHOSTAKOVICH: *Quartets.* **(*)
(N) **(*) Collins Dig. 1450-2 [id.]. Duke Qt – SCHNITTKE: *String quartet No. 2;* SHOSTAKOVICH: *String quartet No. 8.* **(*)

A glorious account of Tchaikovsky's best-loved quartet from the Talich group. They play the opening movement with an unassertive, lyrical feeling that is quite disarming, while the famous *Andante canta-bile* has never sounded more beautiful on record, shaped with a combination of delicacy of feeling and warmth that is wholly persuasive. The Scherzo has plenty of verve, and the finale winningly balances the music's joyful vigour and its underlying hint of melancholy with the same lightness of touch that makes the first movement so enjoyable. The 1987 digital recording is beautifully balanced, not too brightly lit but well integrated, with a natural presence. Very highly recommended.

The Hollywood Quartet's LP first appeared in 1953 and this account is a performance of real fervour that has a persuasive eloquence which still puts one under its spell. The sound has been improved, and the addition of the Glazunov, which is new to the catalogue, enhances its value. The disc runs to one second short of 80 minutes, and the sleeve warns that some CD players may have difficulty in tracking it. We have not found this to be the case, but some caution may be necessary on the part of readers with older players.

The Gabrielis give a finely conceived performance, producing well-blended tone-quality, and the 1977 recording is clean and alive; but ideally the upper range could be less forcefully projected.

An intelligent and expressive account of the *D major Quartet* from the Duke Quartet on Collins. If it is not a first choice, it is because of an upfront balance which does not enhance the quartet's beauty of tone. Readers with high-grade equipment will find this more worrying than others. The playing is of considerable artistry.

PIANO MUSIC
Piano duet

Capriccio italien, Op. 45 (arr. composer). *Swan Lake: 3 Dances* (arr. Debussy). *Sleeping Beauty: suite* (arr. Rachmaninov/Siloti). *Marche slave* (arr. Batalin).
(N) **(*) Ph. Dig. 442 778-2 [id.]. Katia & Marielle Labèque (with SCRIABIN: *Fantasy in A min.* **(*)).

The composer's own arrangement (of *Capriccio italien*) is the least effective here, with the opening 'brass fanfare' sounding bare and uncompelling. But the Labèques obviously enjoy the 'echo' theme and they produce plenty of brilliance later for the *Tarantella* (as Tchaikovsky intended); elsewhere, and especially in the dazzling closing *Marche slave*, they make one almost forget the orchestra. The *Swan Lake* arrangement is by the young Debussy, made while he was staying with Madame von Meck; and the

Sleeping Beauty suite was the work of another young composer, Rachmaninov, even though – in view of Tchaikovsky's dissatisfaction – his cousin, the pianist-conductor Siloti, reworked it. There is much that is charismatic and the one complete disappointment is the *Panorama* from *Sleeping Beauty*, where the rocking bass is quite prosaic and the lovely floating melody has no magic. The Scriabin *Fantasy* is an early work (1889) and was written for two pianos: it is played sympathetically but is not especially memorable. Excellent, very present recording.

Solo piano music

Album for the young, Op. 39; Aveu passioné in E min.; Capriccio in G flat, Op. 8; Dumka, Op. 59; Impromptu in A flat; Impromptu-caprice in G; Military march in B flat; Momento Lyrico in A flat; 6 Morceaux composés sur un seul thème, Op. 21; 2 Morceaux, Op. 10; 3 Morceaux, Op. 9; 6 Morceaux, Op. 19; 6 Morceaux, Op. 51; 12 Morceaux, Op. 40; 18 Morceaux, Op. 72; 2 Pieces, Op. 1; Potpourri on themes from the opera 'Voyevoda'; Romance in F min., Op. 5; 3 Romances; (i) arr: 50 Russian folksongs. The Seasons, Op. 37b; Sonata No. 1 in C sharp min., Op. 80; (Grand) Sonata (No. 2 in G), Op. 37a; 3 Souvenirs de Hapsal, Op. 2; Theme and variations in A min.; Valse caprice in D, Op. 4; Valse-scherzo in A; Valse-scherzo in A, Op. 7.
**(*) Erato/Warner Dig. 2292 45969-2 (7) [id.]. Viktoria Postnikova, (i) Gennady Rozdestvensky.

Piano sonata No. 1 in C sharp min.; The Seasons, Op. 37b.
**(*) Erato/Warner Dig. 2292 45512-2 [id.] (from above). Viktoria Postnikova.

It is no secret that Tchaikovsky was a remarkable melodist and almost every one of these pieces is attractive in this respect; each is also well crafted and needs care, polish and real style in presentation. Viktoria Postnikova has obviously lived with this music and her imagination is patently caught by even the simplest inspirations. In her hands nothing sounds trivial. The *Grand sonata* has a comparable rhetoric to the first movements of the *Second Piano concerto* and the *Piano trio*, yet the result here is never hectoring and the slow movement is most sensitively played. The two most famous sets of genre pieces, *The Seasons* and the Op. 39 collection for young people, are affectionately and perceptively characterized. Rozdestvensky joins her for Tchaikovsky's four-handed arrangements of the 50 Russian folk-songs. Many of them are very brief, but one can see how they became part of the composer's musical consciousness, for the sixth is instantly familiar from its use in the second movement of the *Little Russian Symphony*. Similarly, the Scherzo of the *C sharp minor Sonata* which (in spite of its high opus number) is a student work, brings a reminder of the *Winter Daydreams Symphony*. This somewhat Schumannesque sonata is available separately, coupled to *The Seasons*. The *Theme and variations in A minor* is an engaging piece and the *Pot-pourri on themes from The Voyevoda* offers a fascinating sampler of ideas from a virtually unknown opera. In short, everything here is well worth having, and the last item on the very first disc of early pieces brings a *Humoresque* (Op. 10/2) which Stravinsky appropriated and scored for horns to produce one of the most memorable themes in his *Baiser de la fée* pastiche ballet score. Postnikova in her notes makes the point that it was apt for some of these recordings to be made in France, where the composer's piano music was recognized and performed during his own lifetime. The only snag is that the recording quality, while live and present, is sometimes a bit hard on top.

Capriccioso in B flat, Op. 19/5; Chanson triste, Op. 40/2; L'espiègle, Op. 72/12; Humoresque in G, Op. 10/ 2; Méditation, Op. 72/5; Menuetto-scherzoso, Op. 51/3; Nocturne in F, Op. 10/1; Rêverie du soir, Op. 19/1; Romances: in F min., Op. 5; in F, Op. 51/5; The Seasons: May (White nights), June (Barcarolle), November (Troika); January (By the fireplace). Un poco di Chopin, Op. 72/15; Valse de salon, Op. 51/2; Waltz in A flat, Op. 40/8; Waltz-scherzo in A min., Op. 7.
*** Olympia Dig. OCD 334 [id.]. Sviatoslav Richter.

It is good to hear Richter (recorded in 1993 by Ariola-Eurodisc) given first-class, modern, digital sound and on top technical form, showing that he has lost none of his flair. These miniatures are invested with enormous character in playing of consistent poetry; there is never a whiff of the salon. The opening *Nocturne in F major*, the charming neo-pastiche called *Un poco di Chopin* and the haunting *Rêverie du soir* readily demonstrate Richter's imaginative thoughtfulness, while the apparently simple *Capriccioso in B flat* produces a thrilling burst of bravura at its centrepiece. They are all captivating, and the bolder *Menuetto-scherzoso* also shows Tchaikovsky at his most attractively inventive, as of course does the *Humoresque* which Stravinsky used so indelibly (scored for horns) in his *Baiser de la fée* ballet music. In Richter's hands the famous *Barcarolle* (*June*) from *The Seasons* is full of charming nostalgia, while the more quirky *Troika* (*November*) is hardly less winning. With its very truthful sound-picture, this is a first recommendation for anyone wanting a single CD of Tchaikovsky's piano music.

The Seasons, Op. 37a.
**(*) Chandos Dig. CHAN 8349 [id.]. Lydia Artymiw.

The Seasons, Op. 37b; Dumka, Op. 59; Romance in F min., Op. 5; Valse-scherzo in A, Op. 7.
(M) **(*) Carlton IMP Classics Dig. PCD 976. James Lisney.

The Seasons, Op. 37b; 6 Pieces, Op. 21.
(Y/B) *** Virgin/EMI Dig. VC5 45042-2 [id.]. Mikhail Pletnev.

Tchaikovsky's twelve *Seasons* (they would better have been called 'months') were written to a regular deadline for publication in the St Petersburg music magazine, *Nuvellist*. They are lightweight but attractively varied in character and style. Mikhail Pletnev has exceptional feeling for Tchaikovsky and finds more in this music than any other pianist. His insights reveal depths that are hidden to most interpreters and he grips one here from first note to last, not only in *The Seasons* but also in the charming and touching *Six morceaux*, Op. 21. This is the best account of both to have reached the gramophone, given fresh and natural recorded sound.

James Lisney provides a fine, stylish set of these pieces. His playing is not very Slavonic in its expressive feeling. Yet if there is a touch of Mendelssohn's *Songs without words*, they are warmly presented, along with the other genre pieces, and are well recorded.

It is the gentler, lyrical pieces that are most effective in the hands of Lydia Artymiw, and she plays them thoughtfully and poetically. Elsewhere, she sometimes has a tendency marginally to over-characterize the music. The digital recording is truthful.

Sleeping Beauty (excerpts) arr. Pletnev.
✹ *** Virgin/EMI Dig. VC7 59611-2 [id.]. Mikhail Pletnev – MUSSORGSKY: *Pictures at an exhibition.*
*** ✹

In the present transcription Pletnev gives us about 30 minutes of *The Sleeping Beauty* in a dazzling performance. In sheer clarity of articulation and virtuosity this is pretty remarkable – also in poetry and depth of feeling. An altogether outstanding issue and in every way a *tour de force.*

Piano sonata in G, Op. 37; 6 Morceaux, Op. 51.
(N) (BB) * Naxos Dig. 8.553063 [id.]. Oxana Yablonskaya.

Tchaikovsky's piano music is much patronized and underrated. Played by a Richter or a Pletnev, the *G major Sonata* can sound masterly. Oxana Yablonskaya is not the most subtle of artists, given to grand gestures and over-free use of rubato. The price is competitive but it is better to spend more and buy this often endearing music in a performance of greater stature. Postnikova's Erato version will do well enough, although it is coupled with *The Seasons*, and for that one must turn to Pletnev.

VOCAL MUSIC

Liturgy of St John Chrysostum, Op. 41; Liturgical hymns: *Blessed are they who Thou hast chosen; The hymn of the Cherubim; It is meet; Now the angels are with us; Our Father; To Thee we sing.*
(N) (B) *** EMI forte CZS5 68661-2 (2) [id.]. Grigorov-Teres, Spasov, Manolov, Nikolov, Svetoslav, Obretenov, Bulgarian A Capella Ch., Georgi Robev.

One does not think of Tchaikovsky as a composer of religious music. Yet, listening to these ardent and moving performances by this splendid Bulgarian choir – not only of the *Liturgy* but also the simple hymns – one realizes that, like most Russians, he found a religious dimension within himself and was clearly moved by the words he was setting. Much of the music here is simple and traditionally homophonic (for that was essential if it was to achieve church performance) but Tchaikovsky's ready melodic gift brought its own individuality, as in the beauty of the simple downward scale at the opening of the *Cherubic hymn*; as in the comparable Rachmaninov work, this is a lyrical highlight. Elsewhere he tries a little imitative polyphony all his own with his 'Alleluias', as in *Praise ye the Lord.* There are moments of high drama too in the postlude for the Creed (and elsewhere), while the closing section of *Thine own of Thine own* is gloriously serene. Tchaikovsky was again obviously deeply touched by the words beginning 'Especially for our most holy', and his music for the Lord's Prayer is directly appealing. The Bulgarian singing has great intensity of feeling and, aided by the cathedral acoustic, the effect is wonderfully spacious. Indeed, all this music could hardly be performed more convincingly, and the recording is superb.

The Snow Maiden (Snegourotchka): complete incidental music.
(Y/B) *** Chandos Dig. CHAN 9324 [id.]. Irina Mishura-Lekhtman, Vladimir Grishko, Michigan University Musical Soc., Detroit SO, Järvi.

Alexander Ostrovsky's play, *The Snow Maiden*, based on a Russian folk-tale, is best known in the West through Rimsky-Korsakov's opera, but Tchaikovsky, well before his colleague, wrote this incidental music for a stage production of the play at the Bolshoi in 1873, using and adapting folk themes. It remained a favourite work of his and, until Rimsky stole a march on him, he intended to turn it into an opera. The consistent freshness and charm of invention comes out in Järvi's reading of the 19 numbers, lasting just under 80 minutes. It makes a delightful, undemanding cantata, very well played and sung, and vividly recorded. It is instructive of Tchaikovsky's mastery to compare the alternative versions of a single song for the shepherd, Lel, equally effective but one lighter than the other. This now replaces the earlier Chant du Monde version (LDC 278904).

Songs

Ah, if only you could for one moment; Amid the din of the ball; I bless you, forests; I should like in a single word; It happened in the early spring; The love of a dead man; My protector, my angel, my friend; On the golden cornfield; Not a word, O Beloved; We sat together; Whether the day reigns.
(Y/B) ** Ph. Dig. 442 536-2 [id.]. Dmitri Hvorostovsky, Mikhail Arkadiev – RIMSKY-KORSAKOV; RACHMANINOV: *Songs.* **

The eleven songs recorded here with Mikhail Arkadiev are not generously enough represented in the catalogue for us to look askance at 'My restless soul', which is what Philips call this CD. Hvorostovsky makes a glorious sound but, while he looks after the sounds, the sense does not always take care of itself. The lack of characterization of which some have complained is well to the fore here. After a while one song sounds all too much like the next. Very good recording.

Songs: *Amid the noise of the ball; As over burning ashes; The cuckoo; Cradle song; Deception; Do not believe it, my friend; Evening; The fearful minute; If I'd only known; It was in the early spring; Les larmes; Last night; Mezza notte; My guiding spirit, my angel, my friend; The nightingale; None but the lonely heart; O do sing that song; Poème d'octobre; Serenade (Aurore); Simple words; Spring; The sun has never set; Take my heart away; To forget so soon; Whether day reigns; Why?; Why did I dream of you?; Zemfira's song.*
(M) *** Decca Analogue/Dig. 436 204-2 [id.]. Elisabeth Söderström, Vladimir Ashkenazy.

This song collection brings many delights, including *Zemfira's song* – in which a young girl repulses the attentions of an old man – and the spoken exchanges briefly present Ashkenazy as an actor. This and *Amid the noise of the ball* (which surely has an affinity with Tatiana in *Eugene Onegin*), plus the famous *None but the lonely heart*, are among Tchaikovsky's finest inspirations, but even the lighter numbers are enchanting as sung by this artist, with Ashkenazy an ever-imaginative partner. Fine Decca recording from 1982/3, with the artists given a natural presence. (Generous measure, too: 74 minutes.)

Songs: *Amid the noise of the ball; Behind the window; The canary; Cradle song; The cuckoo; Does the day reign?; Do not believe; The fearful minute; If only I had known; It was in the early spring; Last night; Lullaby in a storm; The nightingale; None but the lonely heart; Not a word, O my friend; Serenade; Spring; To forget so soon; Was I not a little blade of grass?; Why?; Why did I dream of you?*
*** Hyperion Dig. CDA 66617 [id.]. Joan Rodgers, Roger Vignoles.

The warmly distinctive timbre of Joan Rodgers' lovely soprano has been heard mainly in opera but she is equally compelling in this glowing first solo disc of songs. Her fluency with Russian texts as well as the golden colourings of her voice make this wide-ranging collection a delight from first to last. Though the voice is not quite at its richest in the most celebrated song of all, *None but the lonely heart*, the singer's subtle varying of mood and tone completely refutes the idea that Tchaikovsky as a song-composer was limited. One of the finest discs issued to mark the Tchaikovsky centenary in 1993.

OPERA

Eugene Onegin (complete).
*** Decca 417 413-2 (2) [id.]. Kubiak, Weikl, Burrows, Reynolds, Ghiaurov, Hamari, Sénéchal, Alldis Ch., ROHCG O, Solti.
**(*) DG Dig. 423 959-2 (2) [id.]. Freni, Allen, Von Otter, Schicoff, Burchuladze, Sénéchal, Leipzig R. Ch., Dresden State O, Levine.
**(*) Ph. Dig. 438 235-2 (2) [id.]. Hvorostovsky, Focile, Shicoff, Borodina, Anisimov, St Petersburg Chamber Ch., O de Paris, Bychkov.
(M) (**) BMG/Melodiya mono 74321 17090-2 (2) [id.]. Belov, Vishnevskaya, Lemeshev, Avdeyeva, Bolshoi Theatre Ch. & O, Khaikin.

Solti, characteristically crisp in attack, has plainly warmed to the score of Tchaikovsky's colourful opera, allowing his singers full rein in rallentando and rubato to a degree one might not have expected of him. The Tatiana of Teresa Kubiak is most moving – rather mature-sounding for the *ingénue* of Act I, but with her golden, vibrant voice rising most impressively to the final confrontation of Act III. The Onegin of Bernd Weikl may have too little variety of tone, but again this is firm singing that yet has authentic Slavonic tinges. Onegin becomes something like a first-person story-teller. The rest of the cast is excellent, with Stuart Burrows as Lensky giving one of his finest performances on record yet. Here, for the first time, the full range of musical expression in this most atmospheric of operas is superbly caught, with the Decca CDs capturing every subtlety – including the wonderful off-stage effects.

The DG version brings a magnificent Onegin in Thomas Allen, the most satisfying account of the title-role yet recorded. It is matched by the Tatiana of Mirella Freni, even at a late stage in her career readily conveying girlish freshness in her voice. The other parts are also strongly taken. The tautened-nerves quality in the character of Lensky comes out vividly in the portrayal by Neil Shicoff, and Anne Sofie von Otter with her firm, clear mezzo believably makes Olga a younger sister, not the usual over-ripe character. Paata Burchuladze is a satisfyingly resonant Gremin and Michel Sénéchal, as on the Solti set, is an incomparable Monsieur Triquet. What welds all these fine components into a rich and exciting whole is the conducting of James Levine with the Dresden Staatskapelle: passionate, at times even wild in Slavonic excitement, yet giving full expressive rein to Tchaikovskian melody, allowing the singers to breathe. The Leipzig Radio Choir sings superbly as well. The snag is that the DG recording is unevocative and studio-bound, with sound close and congested enough to undermine the bloom on both voices and instruments. In every way the more spacious acoustic in the Solti set is preferable.

Dmitri Hvorostovsky makes a strong, heroic Onegin in the Philips set, though Bychkov's conducting does not always encourage him to be as animated as one wants, and the voice at times comes near to straining. Nuccia Focile also emerges at her most convincing only in the final scene of confrontation with Onegin. Earlier, her voice is too fluttery to convey the full pathos of the young Tatiana in the *Letter scene*, edgy at the top. The digital recording may well exaggerate unevenness of production, for Neil Shicoff as Lensky also suffers, though he sings with passionate commitment, conveying the neurotic element in the poet's character. As Gremin, Alexander Anisimov also has a grainy voice. Olga Borodina sings impressively as Olga, but on balance the other characters are better cast in Solti's earlier, Decca set, which is clearly to be preferred.

The BMG transfer of the 1955 Bolshoi recording clarifies the sound, with voices focused well forward, even though big ensembles bring serious distortion. With Boris Khaikin a deeply sympathetic conductor, this is a powerfully idiomatic performance which captures the authentic Russian tradition more persuasively than most recordings from the Soviet period, with the genre numbers crisply sprung and with some first-rate playing from some of the Bolshoi instrumentalists, even if the horn adopts a typical howling tone. Though the mono sound is limited, the voices are not constricted, and the off-stage choruses, so important in this work, are well balanced to make them as atmospheric as possible. As Onegin, Evgeni Belov is clear and forthright, while Galina Vishnevskaya, near the beginning of her Bolshoi career, is firm and bright, if rarely able to convey subtler half-tones, partly thanks to the close-up recording. Also very Russian-sounding, but clear and not whining, is the Lensky of Sergei Lemeshev. A historic set, worth investigating. Only brief notes are provided, with no libretto or translation.

Eugene Onegin: highlights.
(Y/B) (M) **(*) DG Dig. 445 467-2 [id.] (from above set, with Allen, Freni, Von Otter, Shicoff, Burchuladze; cond. Levine).

Even though the Levine set is not our first choice for the complete opera, this 75-minute selection brings out the superb qualities of the singing. It includes the Letter scene (with Freni a freshly charming Tatiana), the Waltz and Polonaise scenes (with the excellent Leipzig Radio Chorus), also the Act II Duel scene and other key arias, all strongly characterized, and the entire closing scene (11 minutes). The recording, made in the Dresden Lukaskirche, is too closely balanced and unatmospheric; but as a sampler this is clearly valuable.

Mazeppa (complete).
(Y/B) *** DG Dig. 439 906-2 (3) [id.]. Leiferkus, Gorchakova, Larin, Kotscherga, Dyadkova, Stockholm Royal Op. Ch., Gothenburg SO, Neeme Järvi.

Full of magnificent music, *Mazeppa* – dating from 1884, five years after *Eugene Onegin* – has been sadly neglected on disc. Apart from a Russian set, briefly available, this is the first complete recording of the opera, and it satisfyingly fills an important gap with a performance thrillingly sung and vividly conducted. Sergei Leiferkus sings the title-role superbly, with his very Russian-sounding tone a little grainy and tight in the throat, and entirely apt for the character. There is no flaw either among the other principals. Sergei Larin, in what might seem the token tenor part of Andrey, sings with such rich, heroic tone and keen intensity that the character springs to life. Equally, the magnificent, firm-toned bass, Anatoly Kotscherga, father of the heroine, Maria, confirms the high impressions he created in his Boris recording with Abbado. As Maria, Galina Gorchakova also emerges as one of the latter-day stars among Russian singers, with her rich mezzo gloriously caught, even if the final lullaby for her dead lover, Andrei, could be more poignant. Järvi draws electric playing from the Gothenburg orchestra, not least in the fierce battle music which opens Act III. The only disappointment is that the opportunity was not taken of also recording the conventional finale to the opera which Tchaikovsky originally wrote.

The Queen of Spades (Pique Dame) (complete).
*** Ph. Dig. 438 141-2 (3) [id.]. Grigorian, Putilin, Chernov, Solodovnikov, Arkhipova, Gulegina, Borodina, Kirov Op. Ch. & O, Gergiev.
**(*) Sony Dig. S3K 45720 (3) [id.]. Dilova, Evstatieva, Toczyska, Konsulov, Ochman, Masurok, Bulgarian Nat. Ch., Sofia Festival O, Tchakarov.
** RCA Dig. 09060 60992-2 (3) [id.]. Freni, Atlantov, Hvorostovsky, Forrester, Leiferkus, Katherine Ciesinski, Tanglewood Festival Ch., Boston SO, Seiji Ozawa.
(Y/B) (M) ** BMG/Melodia 74321 17091-2 (3) [id.]. Atlantov, Milashkina, Levko, Fedosseiev, Borisova, Valaitis, Bolshoi Theatre Soloists, Ch. & O, Mark Ermler.

When each new recording of this opera for many years has been flawed, it is good that Gergiev and his talented team from the Kirov Opera in St Petersburg have produced a winner. The very opening, refined and purposeful, sets the pattern, with Gergiev controlling this episodic work with fine concern for atmosphere and dramatic impact, unafraid of extreme speeds and telling pauses. Though the engineers fail to give a supernatural aura to the voice of the Countess when she returns as a ghost, the recorded sound is consistently warm and clear. It is good to have the veteran Irina Arkhipova singing powerfully and bitingly in that key role, while the other international star, Olga Borodina, is unforgettable as Pauline, singing gloriously with keen temperament. Otherwise Gergiev's chosen team offers characterful Slavonic voices that are yet well focused and unstrained, specially important with the tenor hero, Herman, here dashingly sung by Gegam Grigorian. As the heroine, Lisa, Maria Gulegina sings with warm tone and well-controlled vibrato, slightly edgy under pressure.

Tchakarov in his Sony series of Russian operas conducts a fresh, expressive and alert account of *Queen of Spades*, very well recorded. Wieslaw Ochman makes an impressive Herman, amply powerful and only occasionally rough. Yuri Masurok is a superb Yeletsky, and the duet of Lisa and her companion, Pauline, is beautifully done by Stefka Evstatieva and Stefania Toczyska, one of Tchaikovsky's most magical inspirations. As the old Countess, Penka Dilova has a characteristically fruity Slavonic mezzo, very much in character, if with a heavy vibrato. The Countess's famous solo is taken very slowly indeed but is superbly sustained. Ensembles and chorus work are excellent, timed with theatrical point.

The RCA version conducted by Ozawa is a live recording spliced together from performances in Boston and New York, the acoustic unhelpfully dry, allowing little bloom on the voices, and with the orchestra consigned to the background. The rich contralto of Maureen Forrester fares best in the role of the Countess. Ozawa moulds the music most persuasively and draws keenly polished playing from the orchestra, but this is not as volatile or naturally dramatic a performance as that on the Sony set from Bulgaria. The chorus sing with knife-edged precision but sound far less idiomatic than their Bulgarian counterparts. Vocally what is disappointing in the set is the contributions of the two principals, Vladimir Atlantov and Mirella Freni, who are no longer young enough to be fully convincing in the roles of Herman and Lisa. The advantage of having star names in the rest of the cast, notably Dmitri Hvorostovsky and Sergei Leiferkus, need not weigh too heavily when their roles are so incidental.

This Bolshoi version was recorded in 1974 and now passes from the Philips label to RCA. The sense of presence and atmosphere makes up for shortcomings in the singing, with Vladimir Atlantov as Herman too taut and strained, singing consistently loudly, and with Tamara Milashkina producing curdled tone at the top, not at all girlish. Both those singers, for all their faults, are archetypally Russian, and so – in a much more controlled way – is Valentina Levko, a magnificent Countess, firm and sinister.

Yolanta (complete).
(M) **(*) Erato/Warner Dig. 2292 45973-2 (2) [id.]. Vishnevskaya, Nicolai Gedda, Groenroos, Petkov, Krause, Cortez, Tania Gedda, Anderson, Dumont, Groupe Vocale de France, O de Paris, Rostropovich.

Tchaikovsky's imagination was obviously touched by the fairy-tale story of a blind princess in medieval Provence who is finally cured by the arrival of the knight who falls in love with her. The libretto may be flawed but the lyrical invention is a delight. The performance offered here was recorded at a live concert performance in the Salle Pleyel in December 1984, with excellent, spacious sound. Rostropovich's performance has a natural expressive warmth to make one tolerant of vocal shortcomings. Though Vishnevskaya's voice is not naturally suited to the role of a sweet young princess, she does wonders in softening her hardness of tone, bringing fine detail of characterization. Gedda equally by nature sounds too old for his role, but again the artistry is compelling and ugly sounds are few. More questionable is the casting of Dimiter Petkov as the King, far too wobbly as recorded. However, now reissued on a pair of mid-priced CDs, this is well worth exploring.

Arias from: *The Enchantress; Eugene Onegin; Iolantha; Mazeppa; The Queen of Spades.*
*** Ph. Dig. 426 740-2 [id.]. Dmitri Hvorostovsky, Rotterdam PO, Gergiev – VERDI: *Arias.* ***

Hvorostovsky presents an eager, volatile Onegin, a passionate Yeletski in *Queen of Spades* and an exuberant Robert in *Iolantha*. One can only hope that he will be guided well, to develop such a glorious instrument naturally, without strain.

Tcherepnin, Alexander (1899–1977)

Le Pavillon d'Armide (ballet; complete).
(N) **(*) Marco Polo Dig. 8.223779 [id.]. Moscow SO, Henry Shek.

Le Pavillon d'Armide was the ballet with which Diaghilev opened his first *Ballets russes* season introducing Nijinsky. Its invention is fluent, owing much to Tcherepnin's teacher, Rimsky-Korsakov, and to Tchaikovsky. It is not as atmospheric or as interesting as *Le Royaume enchanté*, which Pletnev has recorded with the Russian National Orchestra, nor is it as well played. It runs to well over an hour and its inspiration is of uneven distinction. At its best, though, it has real charm, and the scoring is always full of colour. It is very well recorded.

La Princesse lointaine; Le royaume enchanté.
(N) *** DG Dig. 447 084-2 [id.]. Russian Nat. O, Mikhail Pletnev – LIADOV: *Baba-Yaga* etc; RIMSKY-
KORSAKOV: *Suite: Le Coq d'or.* ***

Like Liadov, Nikolai Tcherepnin was a pupil of Rimsky-Korsakov, whose opera, *Le Coq d'or*, he introduced to Parisian audiences. He was Diaghilev's conductor for the latter's very first Paris season, and he taught conducting for a time and numbered Prokofiev among his pupils. His best-known work is the *Pavillon d'Armide*, but the two pieces recorded here are full of interest. Both inhabit the same world as Rimsky, and *Le royaume enchanté* ('The enchanted kingdom'), which gives its name to the whole record, blends his master's voice with that of French impressionism. It is based on the same fairy-tale as *Firebird*, and is prefaced by the words: 'A spell-bound calm binds the kingdom of Kashchei.' It is quite magical in its way, highly atmospheric and well worth resurrecting. It enjoys the most persuasive advocacy from Pletnev and the Russian National Orchestra, and good recording.

Symphony No. 4, Op. 91; Romantic overture, Op. 67; Russian dances, Op. 50; Suite for orchestra, Op. 87.
*** Marco Polo Dig. 8.223380 [id.]. Czech-Slovak State PO (Košice), Wing-Sie Yip.

The *Fourth Symphony* is probably Tcherepnin's best work. Written in the mid-1950s, it is colourful and tautly compact, neo-classical in idiom, very well organized and full of lively and imaginative musical invention. The *Suite*, Op. 67, is less individual and in places recalls the Stravinsky of *Petrushka* and *Le chant du rossignol*. Like the much earlier *Russian dances*, it is uneven in quality but far from unattractive. The *Romantic overture* was composed in wartime Paris when taxis and private cars were forbidden and there was a return to horse-drawn traffic, which reminded Tcherepnin of his childhood in St Petersburg. Generally good performances, decently recorded too under the young Chinese conductor, Wing-Sie Yip, who draws a lively response from her players.

Telemann, Georg Philipp (1681–1767)

Concertos: for 2 chalumeaux in D min.; for flute in D; for 3 oboes, 3 violins in B flat; for recorder & flute in E min.; for trumpet in D; for trumpet & violin in D.
*** DG Dig. 419 633-2 [id.]. Soloists, Col. Mus. Ant., Goebel.

As Reinhard Goebel points out, Telemann 'displayed immense audacity in the imaginative and ingenious mixing of the colours from the palette of the baroque orchestra', and these are heard to excellent effect here. Those who know the vital *B flat Concerto* – or, rather, A major, for that is how it actually sounds – for three oboes and violins, from earlier versions, will find the allegro very fast indeed and the slow movement quite thought-provoking. The chalumeau is the precursor of the clarinet, and the concerto for two chalumeaux recorded here is full of unexpected delights. Marvellously alive and accomplished playing, even if one occasionally tires of the bulges and nudges on the first beats of bars.

Concerto for flute, oboe d'amore and viola d'amore in E; Concerto polonois; Double concerto for recorder and flute in E min.; Triple trumpet concerto in D; Quadro in B flat.
*** O-L Dig. 411 949-2 [id.]. AAM with soloists, Hogwood.

'An attentive observer could gather from these folk musicians enough ideas in eight days to last a lifetime,' wrote Telemann after spending a summer in Pless in Upper Silesia. Polish ideas are to be found in three of the concertos recorded here – indeed, one of the pieces is called *Concerto polonois*. As always, Telemann has a refined ear for sonority, and the musical discourse with which he diverts us is unfailingly intelligent and delightful. The performances are excellent and readers will not find cause for disappointment in either the recording or presentation.

(i) *Concerto for 2 flutes, 2 oboes and strings in B flat;* (ii) *Triple concerto for flute, oboe d'amore, violin and strings in E; Oboe d'amore concerto in D; Trumpet concerto in D;* (iii) *Concerto for trumpet, 2 oboes in D;* (ii) *Double viola concerto in G;* (i) *Concerto for 3 trumpets, 2 oboes, timpani and strings in D;* (iv) *Double concerto for violin, trumpet and strings in D;* (i) *Suite in G (La Putain); Tafelmusik, Part I: Conclusion in E min. for 2 flutes and strings.*
(M) *** Van. 08.9138.72 (2) [id.]. (i) Soloists, Esterhazy O, David Blum; (ii) Soloists, I Solisti di Zagreb, Antonio Janigro; (iii) Peter Masseurs, Amsterdam Bach Soloists; (iv) Mincho Minchev, Nikolai Chochev, Sofia Soloists, Vasil Kazandiev.

The sheer interest of the repertoire here outweighs any minor reservations about the recording, which comes from the 1960s. However, the sound, particularly in the Esterhazy recordings, is warm and full and the performances are expert. The diversity of Telemann's inexhaustible invention is well demonstrated. In the *Concerto for two violas* the soloists interweave inseparably from the orchestral texture, a device borrowed from Vivaldi who named it 'violette all'inglese'. The solo *Oboe d'amore concerto* and *Trumpet concerto* are both fine, four-movement works, but it is the collective concertos that offer the greatest interest. The *Concerto for two flutes, two oboes and strings* begins elegantly with richly mellifluous blending; then, after a busy *Presto*, the two oboes open the *Cantabile* unaccompanied in a gravely Handelian melody. The *Triple concerto for flute, oboe d'amore and violin in E major* opens with an imposingly spacious *Andante*, very like an introduction to an aria or a chorus from an oratorio; then, after a lively allegro, comes a particularly fine *Siciliano*. The *Concerto for three trumpets, two oboes and timpani* brings a sprightly Handelian fugue, including trumpets and oboes within the part-writing. The oboes gently dominate the gravely expressive *Largo* arietta, and the piece ends with more rollicking interplay between all concerned. The result is an irresistible masterpiece. The suite, *La Putain* ('The Prostitute'), contains an invitation by way of a folksong (*Ich bin so lang nicht bei dir g'west*) to 'Come up and see me sometime'. The suite of strongly characterized dances which follow reminds one not a little of the incidental music of Lully and Rameau in its feeling for colour. The *Concerto for trumpet and two oboes in D* is added on to the end of the first CD, and the performance by the Amsterdam Bach Soloists (with Peter Masseurs a splendid soloist) appears to use original instruments. The second CD closes the programme with a brief contribution from Sofia, the *Concerto for violin, trumpet and strings in D*, vividly played but rather thinly recorded. But overall this highly stimulating set must receive the warmest possible welcome.

Horn concerto in D; Double horn concerto in D; Triple horn concerto in D; Suite in F for 2 horns and strings; Tafelmusik, Book 3: *Double horn concerto in E flat.*
*** Ph. Dig. 412 226-2 [id.]. Baumann, Timothy Brown, Hill, ASMF, Iona Brown.

The *E flat Concerto* comes from the third set of *Tafelmusik* (1733) and is the best-known of the four recorded here. The playing here and in the other concertos is pretty dazzling, not only from Hermann Baumann but also from his colleagues, Timothy Brown and Nicholas Hill. Mention should also be made of the concertante contributions from the two violinists. Telemann's invention rarely fails to hold the listener, and the recording has warm ambience and excellent clarity.

Oboe concertos: in C min.; D (Concerto gratioso); E; E flat; F; Oboe d'amore concerto in G.
*** Unicorn Dig. DKPCD 9128 [id.]. Sarah Francis, L. Harpsichord Ens.

Oboe concertos in C min.; D min.; F min.; Oboe d'amore concertos in E; E min.; (i) *Triple concerto for oboe d'amore, flute and viola d'amore.*
*** Unicorn Dig. DKPCD 9131 [id.]. Sarah Francis; (i) Graham Mayer, Elizabeth Watson; L. Harpsichord Ens.

Sarah Francis is making a survey of Telemann's *Oboe* and *Oboe d'amore concertos* for Unicorn and, though these are modern-instrument performances, they are a model of style. The *G major Oboe d'amore concerto* on the first disc is particularly gracious (the first movement marked *soave* and the colouring dark-timbred like a cor anglais). The *Concerto gratioso*, too, is aptly named, although that sobriquet is centred on the first movement. The *C minor Oboe concerto* begins with a *Grave*, then the main Allegro brings a witty dialogue between soloist and violins, with the theme tossed backwards and forwards like a shuttlecock. But it is the works for oboe d'amore that are again so striking. Most imaginative of all is the *Triple concerto* with its sustained opening *Andante* (a bit like a Handel aria) and *Siciliano* third movement with the melody alternating between oboe d'amore and viola d'amore, and nicely decorated by flute triplets. The performances are full of joy and sparkle and are equally impressive for their nicely judged expressive feeling. They are beautifully recorded and make a very good case for playing this repertoire on modern instruments.

Oboe concertos: in C min.; D; D min.; E min.; F min.
*** Ph. Dig. 412 879-2 [id.]. Holliger, ASMF, Iona Brown.

The *C minor Concerto* with its astringent opening dissonance is the most familiar of the concertos on Holliger's record. Telemann was himself proficient on the oboe and wrote with particular imagination and poignancy for this instrument. The performances are all vital and sensitively shaped and a valuable addition to the Telemann discography. Well worth investigation.

Oboe concertos: in D min.; E min.; F min.
(Y/B) (M) *** Virgin Veritas/EMI Dig. VER5 61152-2 [id.]. Hans de Vries, Alma Musica Amsterdam, Bob van Asperen – ALBINONI: *Concertos from Op. 9.* ***

Hans de Vries is a very fine player and he produces an attractively full yet refined timbre from his baroque oboe (which dates from 1735). Apart from the stylishness of his phrasing, there are absolutely no intonation problems and the bravura articulation in the *moto perpetuo Allegro molto* second movement of the *E minor Concerto* is astonishingly clean. The authentic accompaniments are alert and stylish and not in the least vinegary. The solo balance seems excessively forward, but that may be partly the result of the acoustic, and the accompanying strings remain well in the picture.

Frans Brüggen Edition, Volume 10: *Recorder concerto in C; Concerto à 6 in F; Suite (Overture) in A min., TWV 55:a2*
(Y/B) (M) *** Teldec/Warner 4509 97472-2 [id.]. Frans Brüggen, VCM, Harnoncourt.

The *Suite in A minor* is Telemann's equivalent of Bach's *Orchestral Suite No. 2 in B minor*. It is one of his finest works, with some movements given enticing sobriquets: *Les Plaisirs*, *Air à l'Italien* and *Rejouissance*. The couplings here also show the composer on top form. The *Concerto a flauto dolce* (recorder) *in C* has an opening *Allegretto* melody worthy of Handel, then produces a most effective pizzicato accompaniment. The central movements are hardly less inventive, then the finale is a fast minuet in which Brüggen has chance for nimble bravura. The bassoonist, Otto Fleischmann, is very much the co-star of the ambitious four-movement *Concerto à 6* (for recorder, bassoon and string quartet). This also opens graciously, with a solemn bassoon contribution, and it is the bassoon which leads the dialogue of the following *Vivace*. The part-writing in the finale is particularly felicitous. With superb solo playing and lively but not too abrasive accompaniments from Harnoncourt's VCM, this can be cordially recommended. Excellent 1960s recording, admirably transferred.

Recorder concertos in C; in F; Suite in A min; (i) *Sinfonia in F.*
**(*) Hyperion Dig. CDA 66413 [id.]. Peter Holtslag, Parley of Instruments, Peter Holman or (i) Roy Goodman.

The three solo concertos here are a delight. Peter Holtslag's piping treble recorder is truthfully balanced, in proper scale with the authentic accompaniments, which are neat, polished, sympathetic and animated. The *Sinfonia* is curiously scored, for recorder, oboe, solo bass viol, strings, cornett, three trombones and an organ, with doubling of wind and string parts. Even with Roy Goodman balancing everything expertly the effect is slightly bizarre, if stimulating. About the great *Suite in A minor* we have some reservations: it is played with much nimble bravura and sympathy on the part of the soloist, but the orchestral texture brings a degree of anorexia; after hearing how grand this piece can sound on a modern string group, the results here are faintly dispiriting.

Recorder concerto in C; (i) *Double concerto for recorder and bassoon.*
*** BIS Dig. CD 271 [id.]. Pehrsson, (i) McGraw; Drottningholm Bar. Ens. – VIVALDI: *Concertos.* ***

Clas Pehrsson and Michael McGraw are most expert players, as indeed are their colleagues of the Drottningholm Baroque Ensemble; the recordings are well balanced and fresh.

Recorder concerto in G min.; Double concerto in A min. for recorder, viola da gamba and strings; Double concerto in A for 2 violins in scordatura; Concertos for 4 violins: in C and D.
(b) **(*) DG 439 444-2 [id.]. Soloists, Col. Mus. Ant., Goebel.

These are chamber concertos rather than solo concertos such as we associate with Vivaldi. They are diverting and inventive, without at any point reaching any great depths: like so much of Telemann, they are pleasing without being memorable. Nevertheless they are eminently well served by these artists and well recorded. There is an edge on the sound of the string ripieno which not all ears will enjoy, but any reservations are almost forgotten when one looks at the price of this CD.

Double concerto in F, for recorder, bassoon & strings; Double concerto in E min., for recorder, flute & strings; Suite in A min., for recorder & strings.
*** Ph. Dig. 410 041-2 [id.]. Petri, Bennett, Thunemann, ASMF, Iona Brown.

The *E minor Concerto* for recorder, flute and strings is a delightful piece and is beautifully managed, even though period-instrument addicts will doubtless find William Bennett's tone a little fruity. The playing throughout is highly accomplished and the *Suite in A minor*, Telemann's only suite for treble recorder, comes off beautifully. The orchestral focus is not absolutely clean, though quite agreeable.

(i–iii) Double concerto in E min. for recorder and transverse flute; (iv) Viola concerto in G; (i; v) Suite in A min. for flute and strings; (iii) Overture des Nations anciens et modernes in G.
✹ (m) *** Teldec/Warner 9031 77620-2 [id.]. (i) Frans Brüggen, (ii) Franz Vester, (iii) Amsterdam CO, André Rieu; (iv) Paul Doctor, Concerto Amsterdam, Brüggen; (v) SW German CO, Friedrich.

All these works show Telemann as an original and often inspired craftsman. His use of contrasting timbres in the *Double concerto* has considerable charm; the *Overture des Nations anciens et modernes* is slighter but is consistently and agreeably inventive, and the *Suite in A minor*, one of his best-known works, is worthy of Handel or Bach. Frans Brüggen and Franz Vester are expert soloists and Brüggen shows himself equally impressive on the conductor's podium accompanying Paul Doctor, the rich-timbred soloist in the engaging *Viola concerto*. The sound, splendidly remastered, is unbelievably good, with fine body and presence: it is difficult to believe that these recordings are now three decades old.

Trumpet concerto in D; (i) Double trumpet concerto in E flat; (ii) 2 Concertos in D for trumpet, 2 oboes & strings; (i; iii) Concerto in D for 3 trumpets & strings.
*** Ph. Dig. 420 954-2 [id.]. Hardenberger, with (i) Laird; (ii) Nicklin, Miller; (iii) Houghton; ASMF, Iona Brown.

The effortless higher tessitura of Hardenberger and his admirable sense of style dominate a concert where all the soloists are expert and well blended by the engineers. The concertos with oboes offer considerable variety of timbre and have fine slow movements; there is for instance an engaging *Poco andante* where the oboes are given an *Aria* to sing over a simple but effective continuo, given here to the bassoon (Graham Sheen). That same work is structured unusually in five movements, with two short *Grave* sections to provide pivots of repose. Telemann is always inventive and, with such excellent playing and recording, this can be recommended to anyone who enjoys regal trumpet timbre.

Concerto in D for 3 trumpets, 2 oboes and strings; Suite in G min. for 3 oboes, bassoon and strings; Tafelmusik, Production II: Suite (Overture) in D.
*** DG Dig. 439 893-2 [id.]. E. Concert, Pinnock.

As usual, Pinnock lifts rhythms engagingly and keeps everything fresh and vital. The *Suite in G minor*, using regal trumpets but never upstaging the oboes, is a particularly felicitous example of the composer's own special semi-*concerto grosso* style, with the soloists and ripieno in a colourful interplay; yet in some ways the *G minor Suite*, using three oboes, is even more ear-tickling. Here two of the inner movements have sobriquets: *Les Irresoluts* and *Les Capricieuses*, while there is also a French *Loure* and a robust *Gasconnade* for good measure. The closing excerpt from the *Tafelmusik* has a single trumpet to brighten the texture and the invention is remarkably consistent. Excellent recording and splendid music.

(i) Viola concerto in G; (ii) Suite in A min. for recorder and strings; Tafelmusik, Part 2: (iii) Triple violin concerto in F; Part 3: (iv) Double horn concerto in E flat.
✹ (bb) *** Naxos Dig. 8.550156; *4550156* [id.]. (i) Kyselak; (ii) Stivín; (iii) Hoelblingova, Hoelbling, Jablokov; (iv) Z. & B. Tylšar, Capella Istropolitana, Richard Edlinger.

Our Rosette is awarded for enterprise and good planning – to say nothing of good music-making. It is difficult to conceive of a better Telemann programme for anyone encountering this versatile composer for the first time and coming fresh to this repertoire, having bought the inexpensive Naxos CD on impulse. Ladislav Kyselak is a fine violist and is thoroughly at home in Telemann's splendid four-movement concerto; Jiři Stivín is an equally personable recorder soloist in the masterly *Suite in A minor*;

his decoration is a special joy. The *Triple violin concerto* with its memorable *Vivace* finale and the *Double horn concerto* also show the finesse which these musicians readily display. Richard Edlinger provides polished and alert accompaniments throughout. The digital sound is first class.

Darmstadt overtures (suites), TWV 55/C6 (complete).
(M) *** Teldec/Warner 4509 93772-2 (2) [id.]. VCM, Harnoncourt.

What strikes one with renewed force while listening to these once again is the sheer fertility and quality of invention that these works exhibit. This is music of unfailing intelligence and wit and, although Telemann rarely touches the depths of Bach, there is no lack of expressive eloquence either. The performances are light in touch and can be recommended with real enthusiasm. This would make an excellent start to any Telemann collection.

Suites: in B flat, TW 55/B 10; in C, TWV 55/C6; in D, TWV 55/D 19.
*** DG Dig. 437 558-2 [id.]. E. Concert, Trevor Pinnock.

There is some marvellous music here, and each suite has its own lollipops, the *Hornpipe* and charming *Plainte* in the *B flat major Suite*, the sensuous *Someille* in the C major work (although one can imagine this would sound even creamier on modern wind instruments) while the D major work has a most fetching *Bourrée*, fully worthy of Handel. It brings a feather-light *moto perpetuo* for strings at its centre, and the *Ecossaise* with its witty Scottish snap has a similar contrast, bringing the neatest possible articulation from the English Concert players. There is lots of vitality here and crisp, clean rhythms. Just occasionally one feels the need for more of a smile and greater textural warmth – the rasping, integrated hunting horns don't add a great deal to the *D major Suite* – but this is still a very worthwhile and generous collection (76 minutes), realistically recorded.

Tafelmusik (Productions 1–3) complete.
(Y/B) (M) *** Teldec/Warner 4509 95519-2 (4) [id.]. Concerto Amsterdam, Frans Brüggen.
*** DG Dig. 427 619-2 (4) [id.]. Col. Mus. Ant., Reinhard Goebel.

Brüggen's Teldec set was made in the mid-1960s. The playing is very good indeed, and the recorded quality, like so many of these Das Alte Werk reissues, is first rate, with the usual proviso that the balance is forward, reducing the range of dynamic. The solo playing is expert (Hermann Baumann and Adriaan van Woudenberg are the impressive horn players in the *Double concerto* in the Third Book). The performances have vitality throughout, the sound is full yet has a spicing of astringency, and this mid-priced reissue compares very favourably with the premium-priced sets.

    The playing of the Musiqua Antiqua is distinguished by the highest order of virtuosity and unanimity of ensemble and musical thinking. They also have the advantage of very vivid and fresh recording quality; the balance is close and present without being too forward and there is a pleasing acoustic ambience.

Tafelmusik: Production 1: *Quartet in G for flute, oboe, violin & continuo; Trio in E flat for 2 violins & continuo;* Production 2: *Quartet in D min. for 2 flutes, cello & harpsichord; Trio in E min. for flute, oboe & continuo;* Production 3: *Quartet in E min. for flute, violin, cello & continuo; Trio in D for 2 flutes & continuo.*
(N) (M) *** DG Dig. 447 296-2 [id.]. Col. Mus. Ant., Goebel.

Only in the *String trio* from Production 1 could there be any reservation about Reinhard Goebel's meagre period-violin timbre, and that relatively minor; the wind quartets and trios here are sheer delight and are played with the lightest touch. The recording is closely balanced but the ambience is warm, making this an excellent entertainment (nearly 70 minutes) to accompany a dinner party.

Tafelmusik, Production 3: *Overture in B flat; Quartet in E min.;* Production 2: *Concerto in F; Trio sonata in E flat; Solo (Violin) sonata in A; Conclusion in B flat.*
*** DG Dig. 429 774-2 [id.] (from above set, directed Goebel).

For those not wanting a complete set, this arbitrary but well-chosen 75-minute selection may prove useful. The recording is faithful, though the edginess of Goebel's violin timbre will not suit all tastes.

Water Music (Hamburg Ebb and Flow); Concertos in A min.; B flat; F.
**(*) DG Dig. 413 788-2 [id.]. Col. Mus. Ant., Goebel.

Telemann's *Water Music* is one of his best-known works and, save for the opening *overture*, is given a very lively performance, with sprightly rhythms and vital articulation. The eccentric opening is less than half the speed of Marriner's (deleted) version on Argo or Wenzinger's famous old Archiv account. Of particular interest are the three *Concertos* which form the coupling, two of which (in F major and A minor) are new to records. The invention is of unfailing interest, as is the diversity of instrumental colouring. The balance is admirably judged and the recording excellent.

CHAMBER MUSIC

Essercizii musicale: Trio sonata in C min. for recorder, oboe and continuo, TWV 42:c2. Der getreue Musik-Meister: Sonata for recorder and violino piccolo, TWV 40:111. Quartets: in A min. for recorder, oboe, violin and continuo, TWV 43:a3; in G for recorder, oboe, violin and continuo, TWV 43:g6; in G min. for recorder, two violins and continuo, TWV 43:g3; in G min. for recorder, violin, viola and continuo, TWV 43:g4; Trio Sonatas: in A min. for recorder, violin and continuo, TWV 42:a1; in A min. for recorder, violin and continuo, TWV 42:a4; in A min. for recorder, oboe and continuo, TWV 42:a6; in C for recorder, pardessus de viole and continuo, TWV 42:c2; in C min. for recorder, oboe and continuo, TWV 42:c7; in D min. for recorder, pardessus de viole and continuo, TWV 42:d7; in D min. for recorder, violin and continuo, TWV 42:d10; in E min. for recorder, oboe and continuo, TWV 42:e6; in F for recorder, pardessus de viole and continuo, TGWV 42:f6; in F for recorder, violin and continuo, TWV 42:f8; in F for recorder, oboe & continuo, TWV 42:f9; in F for recorder, oboe and continuo, TWV 42:f15; in F min. for recorder, violin and continuo, TWV 42:f2; in G min. for recorder, pardessus de viole and continuo, TWV 42:g9.

(Y/B) (M) *** Teldec/Warner 4509 97455-2 (3) [id.]. Kees Boeke, Walter van Hauwe, Hans de Vries, Alice Harnoncourt, Anita Mitterer, Woulter Möller, Bob van Asperen.

There is a great deal of music here, lasting for nearly three hours, but Telemann admirers will find nearly all of it aurally fascinating. The works are cunningly selected from a great range of works of a similar nature, often showing the composer at his most inventive. As can be seen, there is considerable variety of texture, and within there is a fair variety of style. Performances are expressive and lively and there is much unostentatious virtuosity; in this case, scholarship and authenticity do not intimidate the music-making and it communicates readily. As with most Das Alte Werk reissues from the 1970s, the sound is closely balanced, which reduces the range of dynamic, although the playing itself is expert and has plenty of light and shade. This is not music to be played all at once: the listener must make his own choice. But on the second disc, for instance, there is an intriguing *Sonata for recorder and violino piccolo* (from *Der getreue Musik-Meister*) and the *Trio sonata* (for recorder, oboe and continuo) and two *Quartets* which follow all show the composer on top form.

Frans Brüggen Edition, Volume 1: *Essercizii musici: Sonata in C, TWV 41:c5; in D min., TWV 41:d4. Fantasias: in C, TWV 40:2; in D min., TWV 40:4; in F, TWV 40:8; in G min., TWV 40:9; in A min., TWV 40:11; in B flat, TWV 40:12. Der getreue Music-Meister: Canonic sonata in B flat, TWV 41:b3; Sonatas in C, TWV 41:c2; in F, TWV 41:F2; in F min., TWV 41:f1.*

(Y/B) (M) *** 4509 93688-2 [id.]. Frans Brüggen, Anner Bylsma, Gustav Leonhardt.

In this single-disc anthology of Telemann's chamber music Brüggen plays with his usual mastery and, as one would expect from Gustav Leonhardt's ensemble, the performances have polish and authority, and they are excellently recorded. The music itself is highly inventive and entertaining.

12 Fantasias for unaccompanied violin (complete).
(N) (M) *** Maya Dig. MCD 9302 [id.]. Maya Homburger.

Telemann's *12 Fantasias* for solo violin are a decade later than Bach's *Partitas* and *Sonatas,* and they are less ambitious and demanding. Each is in either three or four movements, usually opening with a *Largo* or *Grave,* alternating with *Allegros.* Their invention is of high quality and they make very enjoyable listening, especially when played with such life and style. Maya Homburger uses a baroque violin and has joined in recordings with the Academy of Ancient Music, English Baroque Soloists and the English Concert, so she has thoroughly absorbed and mastered period-instrument techniques. This is cheerful music and it would be difficult to imagine these works being played more freshly or with a more sensitive espressivo. Homburger is recorded most naturally against a warm but not too resonant acoustic, and there is not a trace of vinegar in her timbre.

Der getreue Music-Meister (complete).
(N) ✳ (B) *** DG 447 722-2 (4) [id.]. Mathis, Töpper, Haefliger, Unger, McDaniel, Würzburg Bach Ch., Instrumental soloists, including Linde, Tarr, Melkus, Schäffer, Elza van der Ven, Ulsamer.

We award a Rosette for sheer enterprise to DG's Archiv division in recording (in 1966–7) a 'complete' version of Telemann's *Der getreue Music-Meister* ('The constant Music Master') which has been called the first musical periodical. Telemann published 25 issues or 'lessons' in all, resourcefully serializing works so that, in order to collect a multi-movement sonata, subscribers would have to wait over three or four issues until publication was complete. (Needless to say, each work is performed here with the movements gathered together.) Other composers were invited to contribute, although Telemann stipulated that they should pay their own postage in sending manuscripts to him for inclusion! Thus the present box includes a lute piece by Weiss, a *Gigue sans basse* by Pisandel and an ingenious choral canon by Zelenka. There is also a great deal of refreshing instrumental music of Telemann with the widest variety of instrumentation, with various combinations of recorder, flute, oboe, chalumeau, bassoon, trumpet and various stringed instruments, including a *Burlesque suite* for 2 violins ingeniously depicting scenes from *Gulliver's Travels*. The operatic arias from *Eginhard*, *Belsazar* and *Sacio* are of considerable interest, while the comic fable from *Aesopus* concerns 'The she-goat's wooing of the lion'. Among the other vocal items there is an aria about 'The woman who is going out of tune'. Sixty-two pieces are recorded here, spread over four CDs (originally five LPs). Performances are almost invariably of excellent quality, and Edith Mathis and Ernst Haefliger stand out among the vocal soloists. Excellent documentation includes full vocal texts. The recording sounds delightfully fresh and natural.

Der getreue Music-Meister: Nos. 4, 7, 13, 20, 28, 31, 35, 50, 53, 59, 62.
*** Denon Dig. C37 7052 [id.]. Holliger, Thunemann, Jaccottet.

This CD offers three of the most important works from *Der getreue Music-Meister* for oboe and continuo, two *Sonatas* and a *Suite*, as well as the *F minor Sonata*, designated for recorder or bassoon and played here by Klaus Thunemann. They are interspersed with various miniatures, all well played and recorded. Holliger's playing is unusually expressive and his eloquence alone makes this selection worth having.

(i) *6 Paris quartets (Nouveaux quatuors en six suites)* (1738): *Nos. 1 in D min.; 2 in A min.; 3 in G; 4 in B min.; 5 in A; 6 in E min.;* (ii) (Orchestral) *Suites: in E flat (La Lyra) for strings;* (iii) *in F for solo violin, 2 flutes, 2 oboes, 2 horns, strings & timpani.*
(Y/B) ✪ (M) *** Teldec/Warner 4509 92177-2 (2) [id.]. (i) Quadro Amsterdam (Frans Brüggen, Jaap Schröder, Anner Bylsma, Gustav Leonhardt); (ii) Concerto Amsterdam, Frans Brüggen; (iii) with Schröder.

In 1730 Telemann published a set of six quartets for violin, flauto traverso, viola da gamba and bass continuo, and these were sufficiently popular to be pirated by the French publishing house, Le Clerk, and reprinted in 1736 – without the composer's permission. Telemann learned by this experience. During a long and fruitful visit to Paris in 1737/8, by virtue of a *Privilège du Roi*, he was able himself to publish a new and even finer set. When these records first appeared, we commented: 'The performances are of such a high order of virtuosity that they silence criticism, and Frans Brüggen in particular dazzles the listener.' Moreover the recording is of the very first class, beautifully balanced and tremendously alive (like the performances themselves), and the CD transfer, as is invariably the case with these Das Alte Werk reissues, is immaculate. To fill out the space on the second CD, we are offered a pair of orchestral suites. The *Suite in F* is the more ambitious and probably dates from the beginning of the 1730s; the autograph score was found in Dresden, and this was almost certainly one of the works '*per molti strumenti*' written (and not only by Telemann), for the local orchestra, so famous at the time. The *La Lyra Suite in E flat major* is much earlier, but its invention is hardly less resourceful and in the third movement, *La Vielle*, Telemann gives a more than passable imitation of a hurdy-gurdy.

Paris quartets Nos. 1 in D; 5 in A; Hamburg quartets (1730): *Sonata No. 2 in G min.; Suite No. 2 in B min.*
(Y/B) (M) *** Virgin/EMI VC5 45045-2 [id.]. Wilbert Hazelzet, Trio Sonnerie.

Hazelzet and the Trio Sommerie, in what is clearly going to be an ongoing series, offer us two of the most attractive *Paris quartets*, plus a pair of the slightly less ambitious earlier quartets, which turn out to be of a higher quality than their reputation led one to expect. The performances are of a high calibre and are representative of modern practice, using original instruments, bringing lighter textures and greater delicacy of style. Thus they have a different kind of charm. Tempi with the Trio Sonnerie are almost always brisker, with both losses and gains; for instance, the *Tendrement* second movement of the *Paris Quartet No. 1* is just that bit more seductive in Amsterdam, while in the *Gai* second movement of *No. 5 in A* Hazelzet probably wins on points. The Trio Sonnerie are led by the expert Monica Huggett, and their timbre is cleaner, more transparent than Brüggen's group; but who can say which is the more authentic? Certainly the results on Virgin Veritas are refreshingly different, while the sound is truthful and again very well balanced.

Sonatas for two recorders Nos. 1–6.
*** RCA Dig. RD 87903. Michala Petri and Elisabeth Selin.

Sonatas for two recorders Nos. 1–6; Duetto in B flat.
*** BIS Dig. CD 334 [id.]. Clas Pehrsson, Dan Laurin.

Canon sonatas Nos. 1–6; Duettos Nos. 1–6.
*** BIS Dig. CD 335 [id.]. Clas Pehrsson, Dan Laurin.

All the *Duet sonatas* are in four movements, the second being a fugue; the *Canon sonatas* are for two flutes, violins or bass viols. Needless to say, listening to two recorders for longer than one piece at a time imposes a strain on one's powers of endurance, however expert the playing – and expert it certainly is.

The RCA and BIS versions can be recommended alongside each other, although the BIS disc does contain one extra work. The playing of Michala Petri and Elisabeth Selin is particularly felicitous and the recording first class. However, although it is good to have the two treble recorders blending so well together, a clearer degree of separation would have been advantageous in the imitative writing.

Sonatas for 2 flutes, TW 40: 130–35.
(N) **(*) Lyrichord Dig. LEMS 8019 [id.]. Kimberley Reighley, Tom Moore.

Telemann wrote four sets of sonatas for two flutes, all designed for amateurs to play and enjoy, for they do not make too many bravura demands. However, this fourth series (which remained unpublished but which probably dates from the end of the 1730s or the beginning of the 1740s) uses keys which were more difficult for the one-keyed flute of that time, so these works were clearly aimed at players with fair performance skills. They are each in four movements, and the slow movement is usually marked *Dolce* or *Amoroso*, which gives some indication of their somewhat ingenuous character. They are well presented here on period instruments although, amiable as it is, this is music to take in small doses.

Sonata Metodiche Nos. 1–6 (1728); *7–12* (1732).
(N) *** Accent Dig. ACC 94104/5D (2) [id.]. Barthold and Wieland Kuijken, Roberts Kohnen.

Telemann's *Methodical sonatas* were written in two sets of six, the first designated 'for violin or flute', the second 'for flute or violin', which is a curious alternation of emphases, the more so as the second set sometimes uses keys which are less comfortable for the baroque flute. Not that this is apparent in these expert performances, lively and expressive by turns. All the sonatas of the first set are in four movements; four out of the second six add a fifth, and there is plenty of variety in the music itself. One of the purposes of these sonatas was to instruct amateurs in the art of ornamentation, so Telemann wrote out ornaments in the French style for each first movement, while mixing French and Italian styles in the writing itself. The ornamentation used here is not confined to the composer's original suggestions but is thoroughly convincing. A worthwhile addition to the catalogue, very well recorded, though these are not works to be heard all at one go!

VOCAL MUSIC

Pimpinone (opera; complete).
(N) (M) *** Teldec/Warner 0630 12323-2 [id.]. Spreckelsen, Nimsgern, Ens. Florilegium Musicum, Hans Hirsch (with TESSARINI: *Violin concerto, Op. 1/8*. VIVALDI: *Violin concerto in C, Op. 7/2* (Franz-Josef Maier); ALBINONI: *Oboe concerto Op. 9/8* (Albert Sous) ***).

This charming chamber opera anticipates *La serva padrona* and offers music of great tunefulness and vivacity. The opera has only two characters, no chorus whatsoever and a small orchestra. Yet its music is as witty as its libretto, and from the very opening one can sense that Telemann is enjoying every minute of this absurd comedy about a serving maid (Vespetta) who battens on to a wealthy gentleman (Pimpinone), eventually persuading him not only to marry her but also to give her the freedom of his purse and at the same time do her bidding. Uta Spreckelsen is a charmingly vivacious Vespetta and Nimsgern a wonderful buffoon of a Pimpinone. With excellent direction from Hans Ludwig Hirsch the overall impression is one of freshness and the music is so delightful that it deserves the widest currency. The recording, too, is both lively and atmospheric. The opera divides into three Acts or Intermezzi, and appropriate baroque concertos have been placed between them, with the first acting as an opening 'sinfonia concertante'. However, without them it is possible that the opera might just have fitted on to a single CD. The excellent documentation includes a full translation.

Teixeira, Antonio (1707–*c.* 1759)

Te Deum.
(N) *** Collins Dig. 1359-2 [id.]. The Sixteen Ch. & O, Christophers.

Here is another remarkable Portuguese composer who, courtesy of his king (João V), like his contemporary, Almeida – see above – was sent to study in Rome for a decade (although he was only ten years old when he arrived!). He returned in due course and in 1734 produced this spectacular work for diverse soloists, five choirs and a large orchestra. Quite how The Sixteen spread themselves for such an occasion suggests some sort of miracle comparable with the biblical tale of the loaves and fishes; but they do, and no one could complain of any lack of choral spectacle. For the most part Teixeira's invention matches his ambitious canvas, and the stylistic result, like Handel's oratorios, lies somewhere between opera and oratorio. The soloists are tested, too, and here are not found wanting; the result is nothing less than an aural feast, filling a single CD almost to the point of overflowing. The recording is suitably spacious and wide-ranging.

Thomas, Ambroise (1811–96)

Overtures: *Mignon; Raymond.*
(M) *** Mercury 434 321-2 [id.]. Detroit SO, Paray – BIZET: *L'Arlésienne; Carmen: suites.* **(*)

These justly famous overtures are almost never heard in the concert hall nowadays. *Mignon*, opening with a delightful series of lyrical ideas on flute, clarinet and then horn, is matched by the ebullience of *Raymond*, perhaps more of a bandstand piece. The Detroit orchestra play both with wonderful finesse and Gallic spirit: this is repertoire which Paray directs as to the manner born, like his Auber overtures on the same label. The excellent (1960) recording was made in the Cass Technical High School Auditorium.

Hamlet (complete).
*** EMI Dig. CDS7 54820-2 (3) [Ang. CDCC 54820]. Hampson, Anderson, Ramey, Graves, Kunde, Garino, Le Roux, Trempont, Amb. S., LPO, Antonio de Almeida.
(M) *** Decca Dig. 433 857-2 (3) [id.]. Milnes, Sutherland, Morris, Winbergh, Conrad, Tomlinson, WNO Ch. & O, Bonynge.

Thomas's *Hamlet* may be an unashamed travesty of Shakespeare, complete with happy ending (in its original form), but it remains a strong and enjoyable example of French opera of its period. So much was evident from Richard Bonynge's 1983 Decca set. If the EMI set is even more strikingly successful, it is not just that it provides an unusually full text – with the tragic, so-called Covent Garden ending and the ballet music in an appendix – but that Thomas Hampson gives such a commanding performance in the title-role. Hampson's superb, finely shaded singing goes with truly Shakespearean power in the acting, and the character emerges as a young hero, ardent but vulnerable, endlessly self-questioning. One no longer finds the aria, *Etre ou ne pas être*, sounding conventional or trivial, and consistently Hampson magnetizes the attention the moment he begins to sing. June Anderson is not so happily cast as Ophelia. The voice is inclined to sound too edgy, and she is hardly more successful at sounding girlish than Sutherland at the end of her career, hardly matching her older rival in the Act III ballad, but the singing is felt and expressive. The rest of the cast may not be as starry as that in the Decca version, but there is no serious weakness. Almeida is understanding, and the presentation of the full text, conveniently, with trivia consigned to the appendix, and with a recently discovered duet for Claudius and Gertrude a valuable extra, makes it a highly enjoyable set.

On the Decca set, Ophélie has priority vocally in brilliant and beautiful numbers, with Sutherland taking all the challenges commandingly. Ophelia's famous Mad scene was one of the finest of her early recordings, and here, 24 years later, she still gives a triumphant display, tender and gentle as well as brilliant in coloratura. The heroine's primacy is reinforced when the role of Hamlet is for baritone, here taken strongly if with some roughness by Sherrill Milnes. Outstanding among the others is Gösta Winbergh as Laërte (in French without the final 's'), heady and clear in the only major tenor role. John Tomlinson as Le Spectre sings the necessary monotones resonantly, James Morris is a gruff Claudius and Barbara Conrad a fruity Gertrude. The compelling success of the whole performance of a long, complex opera is sealed by Bonynge's vigorous and sympathetic conducting of first-rate Welsh National Opera forces, brilliantly and atmospherically recorded. The layout, with Act I on the first CD and the other four Acts, two apiece, on the other two, is surely ideal, and the documentation is good.

Thomson, Virgil (1896–1989)

Film scores: *The Plow that broke the Plains; The River* (suites).
(M) *** Van. 08.8013.71 [OVC 8013]. Symphony of the Air, Leopold Stokowski – STRAVINSKY: *Soldier's Tale.* ***

Virgil Thomson's orchestral music may be sub-Copland (he too uses cowboy tunes like *Old paint*), but in Stokowski's charismatic hands these two film scores emerge with colours glowing and their rhythmic, folksy geniality readily communicating. The recording is resonantly atmospheric, but vivid too. Most enjoyable, and with a worthwhile coupling. This is at upper mid-price in the USA.

Lord Byron (complete).
** Koch Dig. 3-7124-2Y6 (2) [id.]. Lord, Zeller, Johnson, Mercer, Woodman, Owen, Ommerlé, Fortunato, Csengery, Jonason, Vanderlinde, Dry, Monadnock Music, Bolle.

Lord Byron is a weird piece, set mainly in Poet's Corner in Westminster Abbey after Byron's death, with his heirs and friends in dispute and his ghost periodically commenting. The settings of Byron's own words are fluent but do not avoid blandness, and the lyrical if shortwinded invention takes you effectively through the offbeat plot. The main trouble is that under James Bolle the playing of the Monadnock Festival Orchestra is limp. Soloists are efficient enough. Only periodically does Thomson let you know what he could have done as an opera-composer when, Puccini-like, he tellingly points the opening of a big number, as with Byron's solo at the end of Act I or in a splendid duet for Byron and his sister in Act II.

Ticheli, Frank (born 1958)

Postcard; Radiant voices.
(Y/B) *** Koch Dig. 3-7250-2 [id.]. Pacific SO, Carl St Clair -CORIGLIANO: *Piano concerto.* ***

Frank Ticheli, composer-in-residence to this Pacific orchestra largely made up of musicians from film studios, here offers two warm, unproblematic works, ingeniously and wittily argued, full of engaging echoes of composers from Bartók and Copland to John Adams, with a flavouring of Walton in the jazz rhythms. First-rate performances and sound. An attractive coupling for the ambitious, similarly communicative *Piano concerto* of John Corigliano.

Tiomkin, Dimitri (1894–1979)

Film music: *The Fall of the Roman Empire: Overture; Pax Romana. The Guns of Navarone: Prologue-Prelude; Epilogue. A President's country. Rhapsody of steel. Wild is the wind.*
(N) (M) **(*) Unicorn UKCD 2079 [id.]. Royal College of Music O, Willcocks; D. King (organ).

Dimitri Tiomkin contributed scores to some of the most famous movies of all time, for Hitchcock and Frank Capra among others. But it was Carl Foreman's *High noon* that produced his most memorable idea, and he quotes its famous theme, among others, in *A President's country*, a well-crafted medley used as background music for a documentary about President Johnson's Texas. *Wild is the wind* is another familiar melody; Christopher Palmer's arrangement makes a tastefully scored showcase. The latter has arranged and orchestrated all the music here except *Rhapsody of steel*, a complex pseudo-symphonic score written for another documentary, which lasts some 22 minutes. The music of *Pax Romana* has the robust character of a typical Hollywood epic costume spectacular, featuring a bold contribution from the organ. All the music is played with obvious enjoyment by the Orchestra of the Royal College of Music; no apologies need be made for their technique, which is fully professional. Sir David Willcocks conducts with understanding of the idiom and great personal conviction. The recording is very impressive too, though the balance gives brass and percussion rather too much prominence.

Tippett, Michael (born 1905)

Concerto for orchestra; (i) Triple concerto.
(N) *** Chandos Dig. CHAN 9384-2 [id.]. (i) Levon Chilingirian, Simon Rowland-Jones, Philip de Groote; Bournemouth SO, Hickox.

Hickox's coupling of these two major orchestral works is a fine supplement to his set of the four Tippett symphonies, also with the Bournemouth orchestra, warmly recorded in well-focused sound. Levon Chilingirian makes a powerful leader for the trio of soloists, heightening the sharp contrasts of the elliptical argument in Tippett's late return to lyricism. The *Concerto for orchestra*, written in very much the same vein as the opera, *King Priam*, is presented with similar concentration and concern for lyrical warmth.

Concerto for double string orchestra.
(N) (BB) *** CfP Silver Double CDCFPSD 4754 (2). LPO, Handley – BRITTEN: *Violin concerto in D min.* etc. ***; VAUGHAN WILLIAMS: *Tallis fantasia* etc. ***; WALTON: *Belshazzar's feast.* **(*)

Perhaps Barshai's account has a slight edge over Vernon Handley's as a performance, but this CfP Silver Double is a first-rate bargain compilation, including the Vaughan Williams *Tallis fantasia* as well as the

Tippett, two of the warmest and most memorable string works of the present century in strong, committed performances. No one could miss the passion behind the sharp, rhythmic inspirations of the outer movements here or the glorious lyricism of the slow movement. The spacious (1974) recording was made in the Fairfield Hall, Croydon.

(i) *Concerto for double string orchestra; Divertimento on 'Sellinger's round' (for chamber orchestra); Little music for string orchestra;* (ii) *Sonata for 4 horns.*
(N) *** EMI Dig. CDC5 55452-2 [id.]. (i) ASMF, Marriner; (ii) Michael Thompson Horn Qt.

Marriner conducts the Academy in immaculate performances of these fine chamber works which yet have plenty of energy and bounce. Consistently they bring out the joyful exuberance of Tippett's inspiration in his first full maturity. Full and well-balanced sound. This performance of the *Concerto* now supersedes Barshai's version, although hopefully the composer's own version on Virgin Classics will return to the catalogue during the lifetime of this book.

Concerto for double string orchestra; Divertimento on 'Sellinger's round'; Little music for strings; (i) *The Heart's assurance* (orch. Meirion Bowen).
(N) **(*) Chandos Dig. CHAN 9409 [id.]. City of L. Sinf., Richard Hickox, (i) with John Mark Ainsley.

Hickox draws warm and energetic performances from his chamber orchestra, opulently recorded with fine definition. The first movement of the *Concerto* may lack a little in bite, but the slow movement is ravishing and the finale fizzes with energy. The playing may not always be quite as polished as that of the Academy on the rival, EMI disc, but the big bonus is the first recording of the song-cycle, *The Heart's assurance*, in the orchestration prepared by Meirion Bowen with the composer's express approval. What with piano accompaniment can seem a gritty, uncompromising piece here emerges with warmth and beauty, thanks also to the fine singing of John Mark Ainsley.

(i) *Concerto for double string orchestra;* (ii) *Fantasia concertante on a theme of Corelli;* (iii; iv) *Piano concerto;* (v) *String quartet No. 1;* (iii) *Piano sonatas Nos. 1–2.*
(M) *(**) EMI CMS7 63522-2 (2). (i) Moscow CO & Bath Festival O, Barshai; (ii) Y. Menuhin, Masters, Simpson, Bath Festival O, composer; (iii) John Ogdon; (iv) Philh. O, Sir Colin Davis; (v) Edinburgh Qt.

Tippett's eloquent *Concerto for double string orchestra* is well served by Barshai's performance, which has both warmth and vitality. The recording is lively but a shade dry in the upper range. The string textures are clear but not ideally expansive. The *Fantasia concertante* is not as immediately striking as its predecessor but, with the composer in charge and Menuhin as principal soloist, its inventiveness and expressive feeling are never in doubt. Again, the sound is clear and vivid but could be more sumptuous. The *Piano concerto* also represents Tippett's complex-textured and starkly conceived earlier style. Ogdon gives it a fine performance, although he does not rescue it from waywardness, while the recording, if not ideal, now sounds clearer than originally. The *First String quartet* is played rather slackly here; the sound is on the thin side. Ogdon plays the two *Piano sonatas* well and is especially convincing in the *First*. The work has a vitality of invention that it is easy to admire, even if as piano writing it is not as effective in the traditional sense as Tippett's later essay in this form. This is much more compressed in its argument, and though a more uninhibited approach can bring out the point of Tippett's scheme better, Ogdon displays his usual integrity, as well as virtuosity. The recording is faithful but a shade hard.

(i) *Piano concerto;* (ii) *Triple concerto.*
(N) *** Nimbus Dig. NI 5301 [id.]. (i) Tirimo; (ii) Kovacic, Caussé, Baillie; BBC PO, composer.

Though written over 20 years apart, the *Piano concerto* and the *Triple concerto* have many stylistic similarities in their easy lyricism and genially wayward argument. Tippett in his eighties is a mellow interpreter of his own music. That he chooses speeds consistently broader than usual means that these readings are not as taut as those of rivals, but they have a glowing dedication – helped in the *Piano concerto* by Tirimo's thoughtful intensity – which makes them equally magnetic, helping to explain the emotional thrust behind the music. Recorded with the help of the BBC in Manchester, the sound is very good, though slightly distanced.

Little music for string orchestra.
(M) **(*) Chandos Dig. CHAN 6576 [id.]. Soloists of Australia, Ronald Thomas – BLISS: *Checkmate*; RUBBRA: *Symphony No. 5.* ***

Tippett's *Little music* was written in 1946 for the Jacques Orchestra. Its contrapuntal style is stimulating but the music is more inconsequential than the *Concerto for double string orchestra*. It receives a good if not distinctive performance here, truthfully recorded.

Praeludium for brass, bells & percussion; Suite for the birthday of Prince Charles; The Midsummer marriage: (i) *Ritual dances;* (ii) *Sosostris's aria.*
**(*) Nimbus Dig. NI 5217 [id.]. (i; ii) Alfreda Hodgson, (i) Ch. of Opera North; E. N. Philh. O, Tippett.

Tippett draws a committed performance, not the most brilliant account but, quite apart from the composer's insight, it brings an obvious advantage in including the vocal parts in the fourth dance. *Sosostris's aria* makes another good concert item, but the soloist, Alfreda Hodgson, like the chorus, is balanced much too far behind the orchestra. The *Praeludium* is a sustained ceremonial piece, marked by sharp contrasts of dynamic and texture, wayward and distinctive. The *Prince Charles suite* offers another example of Tippett's occasional music, idiosyncratically bringing together echoes of Elgar, Vaughan Williams and Holst in a very Tippett-like way. With warm, atmospheric recording this is more than just an invaluable document.

Symphony No. 1; (i) *Piano concerto.*
(Y/B) *** Chandos Dig. CHAN 9333 [id.]. (i) Howard Shelley; Bournemouth SO, Richard Hickox.

Those who thought that Sir Colin Davis's pioneering recordings of the first three Tippett symphonies (which are currently withdrawn) were definitive will find fresh revelation in Richard Hickox's readings, not least in the *First Symphony*. Hickox may be less biting, but he gives an extra spring to the chattering motor rhythms at the start, and from then on the Bournemouth performance is regularly warmer and more expressive, as in the distinctive trumpet melody in the slow movement. In the last two movements too, Hickox finds more fun and jollity in Tippett's wild inspirations. The *Piano concerto*, with Howard Shelley a superb soloist, brings another revelatory performance, warm and affectionate but purposeful too, rebutting any idea that with their fluttering piano figurations these are meandering arguments. Warm, full, atmospheric sound, with the piano balanced within the orchestra instead of in front of it. This must now be a first recommendation.

Symphony No. 2; New Year (opera): *suite.*
(Y/B) *** Chandos Dig. CHAN 9299 [id.]. Bournemouth SO, Richard Hickox.

As in the *First Symphony*, Hickox with extra lift in the rhythms brings out the joy behind Tippett's inspirations without ever losing a sense of purpose. This may be a less biting performance than Sir Colin Davis's was on Decca, but it is consistently warmer, with extra fun and wit in the third-movement Scherzo. The coupling is also valuable, when Tippett's own suite from his last opera, *New Year*, brings out the colour and wild energy of this inspiration of his mid-eighties. If anything, the music seems the more telling for being shorn of the composer's own problematic libretto. The obbligato instruments – saxophones, electric guitars and kit drums – are most evocatively balanced in the warm, atmospheric recording.

(i) *Symphony No. 3. Praeludium for brass, bells and percussion.*
(Y/B) *** Chandos Dig. CHAN 9276 [id.]. Bournemouth SO, Richard Hickox; (i) with Faye Robinson.

In two long movements, each lasting nearly half an hour, the *Third Symphony* is not easy to hold together and, though Richard Hickox and the Bournemouth orchestra cannot match the original performers, Sir Colin Davis and the LSO, in sheer power, they find more light and shade over the long span. Hickox gives wit to the Stravinskian syncopations in the first section and then dedicatedly carries concentration through the pauses of the slow second half of the movement. Hickox brings fun to the galumphing introduction to the second movement – 'Like a juggler with five different objects in the air at once,' said Tippett – leading to the sequence of blues sections with soprano soloist. Though Faye Robinson's voice is not as warm or firm as Heather Harper's was, she is more closely in tune with the blues idiom, helping to build the sequence to a purposeful conclusion in the long final scena. The recording is full and warm to match. The *Praeludium for brass, bells and percussion* was written in 1962 for the 40th anniversary of the BBC, a gruff, angular piece hardly suggesting celebration, but none the less welcome in a well-played performance.

Symphony No. 4; (i) *Byzantium.*
*** Decca Dig. 433 668-2 [id.]. (i) Faye Robinson; Chicago SO, Solti.

Symphony No. 4; Fantasia concertante on a theme of Corelli; (i) *Fantasia on a theme of Handel* (for piano and orchestra).
(Y/B) *** Chandos Dig. CHAN 9233 [id.]. (i) Howard Shelley; Bournemouth SO, Hickox.

Byzantium, written to celebrate Sir Georg Solti's 30-year association with the Chicago orchestra, is an extended setting for soprano of the Yeats poem of that name. This is Tippett at his most exotic, responding vividly to the words; and the live recording (made in Carnegie Hall, New York, at one of the first performances) can hardly be faulted. Faye Robinson, taking over from Jessye Norman at the last minute, gives a radiant performance, triumphantly breasting the problems of the often stratospheric and angular vocal-line; equally, Solti draws brilliant, responsive playing from the orchestra. It is apt to have Tippett's *Symphony No. 4* as coupling, another work written for, and played by, Solti and the Chicago orchestra, though most Tippett devotees will already have this 1981 recording.

In the *Fourth Symphony* Richard Hickox and the Bournemouth Symphony are less weighty than the work's originators, but they are generally warmer and more atmospheric. In place of Solti's fiery brilliance, Hickox brings an element of wildness to the fast sections and he also finds a vein of tenderness in the meditative sections. The well-known *Corelli Variations* have never sounded quite as sumptuous and resonant as here, and the disc is generously rounded off with a welcome rarity: the early *Handel Fantasia for piano and orchestra*. Howard Shelley is most convincing in the weighty piano-writing, like his accompanists giving the music warmth. Full-blooded sound to match.

String quartets Nos. 1–5.
(N) *** ASV Analogue/Dig. CDDCS 231 (2) [id.]. Lindsay Qt.

String quartet No. 4.
*** ASV Dig. CDDCA 608 [id.]. Lindsay Qt – BRITTEN: *Quartet No. 3.* ***

String quartet No. 5.
*** ASV Dig. CDDCA 879 [id.]. Lindsay Qt (with BROWN: *Fanfare to welcome Sir Michael Tippett;* MORRIS: *Canzoni ricertati;* PURCELL: *3 Fantasias;* WOOD: *String quartet ***).

This neatly brings together the première recordings of Tippett's last two quartets, each written for the Lindsays, with the recordings the same players made in the 1970s for L'Oiseau-Lyre of the first three quartets in the series, long unavailable. Neatly fitted into a slim double jewel-case, this issue completely upstages the Collins set of the first four quartets. The notes include the composer's own commentary on the first three quartets, written for the original issue. He explains that he regards these works, written between 1935 and 1946, as a sequence, each developing out of the other. One of the most beautiful movements is the *Lento cantabile* of No. 1, written as a replacement for the original two central movements. No. 2 is the most classically balanced in four movements, while the five movements of No. 3, the longest and weightiest of these early works, reflect Tippett's experience of hearing the Bartók *Quartets*, not in idiom but in broad approach. There followed a long gap before hearing the Lindsays play led Tippett to write No. 4 in 1977–8, developing the birth-to-death theme he adopted in the *Symphony No. 4*. He followed that with No. 5 in 1990–91, using late Beethoven as a conscious model. The Lindsays give performances as near definitive as could be, making one realize why they inspired the composer so positively. The analogue sound for Nos. 1–3, as transferred, is brighter with less body than the digital recordings for Nos. 4 and 5.

As can be seen, the *Fourth* and *Fifth Quartets* are also available separately, the *Fourth* well coupled with Britten's *Third*. The other varied items which come on CDDCA 879 with No. 5 are designed as a pendant to the Tippett, music by composers with whom he is associated, from Purcell, always a strong influence, to Christopher Brown from a young generation, paying tribute in a vigorous fanfare. R. O. Morris and Charles Wood were Tippett's teachers, both represented in beautifully crafted quartet pieces, the one a pair of contrasted fugal movements, the other a crisp, four-movement work with echoes of Irish folksong and dance-rhythms, a most attractive piece.

Piano sonatas Nos. 1 (Fantasy sonata); 2–4.
*** CRD Dig. CRD 34301; *CRD C 4130/1* (2) [id.]. Paul Crossley.

Paul Crossley has been strongly identified with the Tippett sonatas; he recorded the first three for Philips in the mid-1970s: indeed, No. 3 was written for him. The *Fourth* and most recent (1983–4) started life as a set of five bagatelles. Crossley contributes an informative and illuminating note on the sonata and its relationship with, among other things, Ravel's *Miroirs*; his performance has all the lucidity and subtlety one would expect from him. These masterly accounts are matched by truthful and immediate sound-quality on CD, with chrome cassettes of high quality.

VOCAL MUSIC

A Child of our time (oratorio).
*** Collins Dig. 1339-2. Robinson, Walker, Garrison, Cheek, CBSO Ch. & SO, composer.
(N) (M) *** BBC Radio Classics BBCRD 9130 [id.]. Gomez, Watts, Woollam, Shirley-Quirk, BBC SO Ch. & O, Rozhdestvensky.
*** Chandos Dig. CHAN 9123 [id.]. Haymon, Clarey, Evans, White, L. Symphony Ch., LSO, Hickox.

Sir Michael Tippett in his mid-eighties may not secure the best-disciplined performance on record of this earliest of his oratorios, but it is generally the most moving. The spirituals which punctuate the story like chorales in a Bach Passion have a heart-easing expressiveness, warmly idiomatic, while the lightness and resilience of *Nobody knows* allows the syncopations to be pointed with winning jazziness. Next to Sir Colin Davis's taut, tough reading on Philips this may be relatively slack, taking a full five minutes longer overall, but the Collins sound is fuller and warmer than that of rival versions. The soloists are placed well forward, an outstandingly characterful team of singers specially associated with Tippett's music. On the whole this must be counted first choice.

Rozhdestvensky's is the most passionate account of the work on disc, a radio recording of a 1980 performance in the Royal Festival Hall which is incandescent from first to last, with bright, forward choral sound adding to the impact. As in Vaughan Williams's *Fifth Symphony*, Rozhdestvensky here shows how naturally he responds to the English idiom, moulding phrases with love yet with no sentimentality, not least in the spirituals, and justifying speeds faster than usual by the extra urgency and sense of purpose. Jill Gomez outshines all rivals in the soprano solos, a ravishing performance, and the other soloists make a characterful team – Helen Watts and John Shirley-Quirk both bringing out word-meaning incisively, and with Kenneth Woollam a strong partner, despite a slight unevenness in his tenor. The composer's own version remains special and it is better recorded, but this BBC version is a disc to recommend not just to devotees but to anyone who has yet to find Tippett.

Hickox's version of Tippett's oratorio, *A Child of our time*, establishes its place against severe competition largely through the exceptionally rich recording and its distinctive choice of soloists, a quartet of black singers. Not only do Cynthia Haymon, Cynthia Clarey, Damon Evans and Willard White make the transitions into the spirituals (used in the way Bach used chorales) seem all the more natural, their timbres all have a very sensuous quality. The London Symphony Chorus, though not at its most incisive, sings well, responding to Hickox's warmly expressive style, often even more expansive than the composer himself on his recent recording.

(i) *A Child of our time* (oratorio); (ii) *The Knot Garden* (opera; complete).
(Y/B) *** Ph. 446 331-2 (2) [id.]. (i) Norman, J. Baker, Cassily, Shirley-Quirk, BBC Singers, BBC Ch. Soc. & SO; (ii) Herinx, Minton, Gomez, Barstow, Carey, Tear, Hemsley, ROHCG O; C. Davis.

We have had to wait a long time for Sir Colin Davis's superb recorded performance of *The Knot Garden* to appear on CD; but now it arrives, aptly coupled with Davis's 1975 recording of the oratorio, *A Child of our time*, on a pair of well-filled CDs, but at full price. As Tippett has grown older, so his music has grown wilder, and those accustomed to the ripe qualities of *The Midsummer marriage* may be disconcerted by the relative astringency of the later opera, a garden conversation-piece to a libretto by the composer, very much in the style of a T. S. Eliot play. The brief central Act, called *Labyrinth*, has characters thrown together two at a time in a revolving maze, a stylized effect which contributes effectively to Tippett's process of psychiatric nerve-prodding. But the whole thing projects splendidly here when recorded so vividly, even if the sound itself is a little dry. The recording of *A Child of our time* is also cleanly defined, here suiting Davis's performance, more sharply focused than most. Speeds are on the fast side, both in the spirituals, which here take the place that Bach gave to chorales, and in the other numbers. Consistently Davis allows himself far less expressive freedom than the composer in his outstanding Collins version and he misses the tenderness which can make the setting of *Steal away* at the end of Part 1 so moving. He has a superb quartet of soloists; and their fine contribution, together with that of the chorus, matches this approach. The result makes a refreshing alternative to the composer's own account.

The Ice-break.
*** Virgin/EMI Dig. VC7 59048-2 [id.]. Sylvan, Harper, Wilson-Johnson, Page, Tear, Clarey, Randle, L. Sinf., Atherton.

The Ice-break is presented here more as a modern dramatic oratorio than as an opera. The music has the physical impact characteristic of later Tippett, but with less of the wildness that developed in his works of the 1980s. Centrally in Act II comes a lament for one of the principal black characters, the nurse Hannah (beautifully sung by Cynthia Clarey). In its bald simplicity that solo provides a vital, touching moment of repose, warmly emotional, to contrast with the tensions of a plot that centres on the Cold War period, with violence, racial conflict and student demonstrations part of the scheme. David Atherton directs an electrically tense performance, with the American baritone, Sanford Sylvan, singing superbly in the central role of Yuri, a second-generation immigrant, set against Heather Harper as his mother, Nadia, full-voiced and characterful, and David Wilson-Johnson as Lev, the father who in the first scene arrives after 20 years of prison and exile. The single disc comes boxed with libretto and excellent notes by Meirion Bowen.

The Mask of Time.
(M) *** EMI Dig. CMS7 64711-2 (2) [id.]. Robinson, Walker, Tear, Cheek, BBC Singers, BBC Ch., BBC SO, Andrew Davis.

There is richness, generosity and overwhelming vigour in this 'Seven Days of Creation for a Nuclear Age', astounding in a composer who was nearing eighty when he wrote it. With his BBC forces, Andrew Davis brilliantly clarifies and sharpens the ever-busy score, and the fine discipline brings out a creative, purposeful control behind the wildness, while the poetry of the piece emerges the more intensely, culminating in the lovely setting for soprano and humming chorus of lines by Anna Akhmatova in *Hiroshima, mon amour*. The final wordless chorus then projects the role of music into eternity, under the title, *The singing will never be done*. Davis draws incandescent singing from the BBC Symphony Chorus and attendant professionals. The quartet of soloists is also outstanding, three of them in the original Boston performance. No finer recording has ever been made in the difficult acoustics of the Royal Festival Hall. This is most welcome, back in the catalogue at mid-price.

The Midsummer marriage (complete).
(N) ✪ *** Lyrita SRCD 2217 (2) [id.]. Remedios, Carlyle, Burrows, Herinx, Harwood, Watts, Ch. & O of ROHCG, Sir Colin Davis.

At long last this outstanding (originally Philips) 1970 recording of Tippett's masterpiece appears on CD in anticipation of a brand-new production. It is a work that should be in the standard repertoire, alongside Britten's *Peter Grimes*, for the music consistently has that inspired melodic flow which distinguishes all great operas. That Tippett's visionary conception, created over a long period of self-searching, succeeds so triumphantly on record – if anything with greater intensity than in the opera house – is a tribute above all to the exuberance of the composer's glowing inspiration, his determination to translate the beauty of his vision into musical and dramatic terms. Any one minute from this 154-minute score should be enough to demonstrate the unquenchable energy of his writing, his love of rich sounds. There are few operas of any period which use the chorus to such glorious effect, often in haunting offstage passages, and, with Sir Colin Davis a burningly committed advocate and with a cast that was inspired by live performances in the opera house, this is a set hard to resist, even for those not normally fond of modern opera. The so-called 'difficulties' of the libretto, with its mystical philosophical references, fade when the sounds are so honeyed in texture and so consistently lyrical, while the story – for all its complications – preserves a clear sense of emotional involvement throughout. The singing is glorious, the playing magnificent and the recording outstandingly atmospheric, and the new Lyrita transfer brings an extraordinay sense of realism, the feeling of sitting in the stalls inside an opera house with quite perfect acoustics – even though the recording was made in Wembley Town Hall.

King Priam (complete).
(N) *** Chandos Dig. CHAN 9406/7 [id.]. Bailey, Harper, Allen, Palmer, Langridge, Minton, Tear, Roberts, L. Symphony. Ch., LSO, Atherton.

'The future of any twentieth-century opera depends quite a lot on recording,' Sir Michael Tippett said on the appearance of this superb set, and it is no exaggeration that it set the seal on the acceptance of a masterly work which yet seemed disconcerting when it first appeared in 1962. The dry fragmentation of texture and choppy compression of the drama then seemed at odds with an epic subject, particularly after the lyrical, expansive warmth of Tippett's preceding opera, *The Midsummer marriage*. With an outstanding cast of the finest British singers of the time, Atherton in this 1980 recording brings out the sharp cogency of the writing, the composer's single-mindedness in pursuing his own individual line. The Wagnerian, Norman Bailey, sounds agedly noble in the title-role, with Robert Tear a shiningly heroic Achilles and Thomas Allen a commanding Hector, illuminating every word. The digital recording, originally made by Decca, comes out brilliantly on CD, with each Act fitted conveniently on a single disc.

Tishchenko, Boris (born 1939)

Symphony No. 5.
*** Olympia OCD 213 [id.]. USSR MoC SO, Rozhdestvensky.

Boris Tishchenko's *Fifth Symphony* was composed in 1976, the year of Shostakovich's death; and it pays tribute to Shostakovich not only in the various quotations but at a deeper level; throughout these strong resonances Tishchenko still speaks his own language. A powerful document, this is played with enormous conviction by the Ministry of Culture Symphony Orchestra under Gennady Rozhdestvensky, and is vividly recorded.

Toch, Ernst (1887-1964)

Symphony No. 3.
(N) (M) *** EMI CDM5 65868-2. Pittsburgh SO, Steinberg – HINDEMITH: *Mathis der Maler* **(*);
MARTIN: *Petite symphonie concertante.* ***

Until 1950, when he was sixty-three, Ernst Toch, the expatriate German composer who settled in America, had not written a symphony; then, in a sudden burst of creative energy, he produced three in quick succession. This one, first performed in 1955, was commissioned by the American Jewish Tercentenary Committee of Chicago, and the composer himself attaches to it a quotation from Goethe – 'Certainly I am but a wanderer on the earth, a pilgrim – are you anything more?' Toch linked this in his mind with the idea of the Wandering Jew and, though there is no specific programme for the symphony, this was the idea which lay beneath his thoughts during the writing of it. It is an impressive work, thoughtful and exciting by turns, with the central *Andante tranquillo-Allegro* (slow movement and Scherzo combined) especially appealing. Toch adopts no conventional form and links the whole work together with a striking motto theme. But, while the symphony is essentially rhapsodic in feeling, it is the sense of continuity, of musical arguments following naturally after one another in what seems a spontaneous flow, which marks it out. In Steinberg's superb performance it makes a powerful impression as a work which is deeply sincere and serious, but readily approachable. The early stereo (1957) is remarkably atmospheric and clear; only a degree of thinness on top dates the sound. Toch's exotic orchestration – steam valve and all – is beautifully caught, and one is even reconciled to the idea of a Hammond organ in the score, when it is made to sound so effective. A highly recommendable reissue, with intelligent couplings.

5 Pieces for wind and percussion.
(N) *** Virgin/EMI Dig. VC5 45056-2 [id.]. Deutsche Kammerphilharmonie Wind – HINDEMITH:
Septet for Wind; WEILL: *Violin concerto.* ***

The Viennese-born Ernst Toch is better known as a teacher than as a composer (incidentally, his pupils in Berlin included Vagn Holmboe) and, of course, for his inventive, spoken *Geographical Fugue* for chorus. While he was an influential figure in Germany in the 1920s and early '30s, he never really recovered the ground lost when he was forced out of Germany by the Nazis. Hardly any of the seven symphonies he composed between 1950 and his death in 1964 have made their way into the repertoire, though the *Third* has now appeared on CD. If any of the others have such beguiling and delightful invention as these *Five Pieces for wind and percussion* of 1959, they should be recorded as a matter of urgency. These are absolutely charming pieces, lyrical and full of imagination – as well as (in the third, *Night Music*) humour (as in the second *Caprice*) and a gentle melancholy, as in the *Roundelay*. Beautiful playing and superbly life-like, well-balanced recording. Recommended with enthusiasm.

Tomkins, Thomas (1572–1656)

The Great service (No. 3); Anthems: *Know you not; Oh, that the salvation; O Lord, let me know mine end; Organ voluntaries: in A; in C; in G.*
*** CRD Dig. CRD 3467; *CRDC 4167* [id.]. New College, Oxford, Ch., Edward Higginbottom;
David Burchell.

The Great service (No. 3); When David heard; Then David mourned; Almighty God, the fountain of all wisdom; Woe is me; Be strong and of a good courage; O sing unto the Lord a new song; O God, the proud are then risen against me.
*** Gimell Dig. CDGIM 024; *1585T-24* [id.]. Tallis Scholars, Phillips.

Tomkins is a madrigalist and fluent contrapuntist in the Elizabethan manner who found his highest fulfilment in church music like the magnificent examples contained on this Gimell disc. The *Great Service*, in no fewer than ten parts, sets the four canticles – *Te Deum, Jubilate, Magnificat* and *Nunc dimittis* – with a grandeur rarely matched, using the most complex polyphony. The following motets bring comparable examples of his mastery. These complex pieces bring the flawless matching and even tone for which the Tallis Scholars are celebrated, and with recording to match, yet *O sing unto the Lord a new song* should surely bring some clearer expression of joy.

Many will prefer the more direct and throatier style of the Choir of New College, Oxford; even if the choral sound (recorded in the chapel of New College) is less sharply defined, the effect is very satisfying and real. The service is given added variety by the inclusion of three organ voluntaries, well if not strikingly played by David Burchall. What makes this record especially attractive is the inclusion of three of Tomkins' most beautiful anthems. The treble solos in *Know you not* and *Oh, that the salvation* are ravishingly done, and the alto soloist in *O Lord, let me know mine end* is hardly less impressive.

Tomlinson, Ernest (born 1924)

Aladdin: 3 dances (Birdcage dance; Cushion dance; Belly dance); Comedy overture; Cumberland Square; English folk-dance suite No. 1; Light music suite; Passepied; (i) Rhapsody and rondo for horn and orchestra; Rigadoon; Shenandoah (arrangement).
(Y/B) *** Marco Polo Dig. 8.223513 [id.]. (i) Richard Watkins; Slovak RSO (Bratislava), composer.

This second collection of the light music of Ernest Tomlinson is every bit as enjoyable as the first. The opening *Comedy overture* is racily vivacious, and there are many charming vignettes here, delectably tuneful and neatly scored, and the pastiche dance movements are nicely elegant. The *Pizzicato humoresque* (from the *Light music suite*) is every bit as winning as other, more famous pizzicato movements, and in the *Rhapsody and rondo* for horn Tomlinson quotes wittily from both Mozart and Britten. The composer finally lets his hair down in the rather vulgar *Belly dance*, but the concert returns to grace for the charming closing *Georgian miniature*. As before, the playing is elegant and polished, its scale perfectly judged, and the recording is first class.

An English overture; 3 Gaelic sketches: Gaelic lullaby. Kielder Water; Little serenade; Lyrical suite: Nocturne. Nautical interlude; 3 Pastoral dances: Hornpipe. Silverthorne suite; 2nd Suite of English folk dances; Sweet and dainty. arr. of Coates: The fairy coach; Cinderella waltz.
*** Marco Polo Dig. 8.223413 [id.]. Slovak RSO (Bratislava), the composer.

Ernest Tomlinson's orchestral pieces charm by the very lightness of their being, with scoring as frothy as lace. The delicately winning *Little serenade*, which opens the disc, is the most famous, but the gentle, evocative *Kielder Water*, the captivating *Canzonet* from the *Silverthorne suite* and the *Nocturne* are hardly less appealing. *Love-in-a-mist* is as intangible as it sounds, with the most fragile of oboe solos, and it is not surprising that *Sweet and dainty* has been used for a TV commercial. Of course there is robust writing too, in the *Folk song suite* – but not too robust, although the jolly *English Overture* begins with *Here's a health unto His Majesty* and certainly does not lack vitality. The music is played with much grace and the lightest possible touch by the remarkably versatile Slovak Radio Orchestra under the composer, and the vivid recording has delightfully transparent textures, so vital in this repertoire.

Tosti, Francesco (1846–1916)

Songs: L'alba separa della luce l'ombra; Aprile; 'A vucchella; Chanson de L'adieu; Goodbye; Ideale; Malia; Marechiare; Non t'amo; Segreto; La serenata; Sogno; L'ultima canzone; Vorrei morire.
(M) *** Ph. 426 372-2. José Carreras, ECO, Muller.

Tosti (knighted by Queen Victoria for his services to music) had a gently charming lyric gift in songs like these, and it is good to have a tenor with such musical intelligence – not to mention such a fine, pure voice – tackling once-popular trifles like *Marechiare* and *Goodbye*. The arrangements are sweetly done, and the recording is excellent.

Truscott, Harold (1914–92)

Symphony in E; Elegy for string orchestra; Suite in G.
(Y/B) *** Marco Polo 8.223674 [id.]. Nat. SO of Ireland, Gary Brain.

Here is another British symphonic name to conjure with. Harold Truscott broadcast as a pianist for the BBC, specializing in Schubert. Two of his own piano sonatas were heard on the radio in 1969, played by John Ogdon. But in general his music was a casualty (like the work of so many other 'traditional' composers) of the William Glock regime in the 1960s. This record suggests that his writing, for all its eclectic influences, has genuine individuality and power. The moving *Elegy* for strings, elliptical in structure, is little short of a masterpiece, and the three-movement *Symphony* (premièred as a complete work on this record), which dates from the end of the 1940s, is a powerfully argued piece. The *Suite in G* shows Truscott's vivid orchestral sense. Its *Molto Andante* confirms the intensity of feeling the composer could create with string textures. Gary Brain seems to have an instinctive feel for all these works and holds together the turbulent moods of the first movement of the *Symphony* coherently, while the Dublin orchestra rise to the occasion and play with much conviction throughout. The recording is full-bodied, with the resonance at the service of the music but without clouding textures. Well worth exploring.

Tubin, Eduard (1905–82)

(i) *Balalaika concerto; Music for strings; Symphony No. 1.*
*** BIS Dig. CD 351 [id.]. (i) Sheynkman; Swedish RSO, Järvi.

The opening of the *First Symphony* almost puts one in mind of Bax, and there is a Sibelian breadth; but for the most part it is a symphony apart from its fellows. The quality of the musical substance is high; its presentation is astonishingly assured for a young man still in his twenties; indeed, the scoring is quite masterly. Emanuil Sheynkman's account of the *Balalaika concerto* with Neeme Järvi is first class, both taut and concentrated. Excellent recording.

(i) *Ballade for violin and orchestra;* (ii) *Double-bass concerto;* (i) *Violin concerto No. 2; Estonian dance suite; Valse triste.*
*** BIS Dig. CD 337 [id.]. (i) Garcia; (ii) Ehren; Gothenburg SO, Järvi.

Tubin's highly imaginative *Double-bass concerto* has an unflagging sense of momentum and is ideally proportioned; the ideas never outstay their welcome and one's attention is always held. The *Second Violin concerto* has an appealing lyricism, is well proportioned and has a strong sense of forward movement. The *Ballade* is a work of gravity and eloquence. *Valse triste* is a short and rather charming piece, while the *Dance suite* is the Estonian equivalent of the *Dances of Galánta*. Splendid performances from both soloists in the *Concertos* and from the orchestra under Järvi throughout, and excellent recording.

Symphonies Nos. 2 (The Legendary); 6.
*** BIS CD 304 [id.]. Swedish RSO, Järvi.

The opening of the *Second Symphony* is quite magical: there are soft, luminous string chords that evoke a strong atmosphere of wide vistas and white summer nights, but the music soon gathers power and reveals a genuine feeling for proportion and of organic growth. If there is a Sibelian strength in the *Second Symphony*, the *Sixth*, written after Tubin had settled in Sweden, has obvious resonances of Prokofiev – even down to instrumentation – and yet Tubin's rhythmic vitality and melodic invention are quietly distinctive. The Swedish Radio Symphony Orchestra play with great commitment under Neeme Järvi, and the engineers have done a magnificent job.

Symphonies Nos. 3; 8.
*** BIS Dig. CD 342 [id.]. Swedish RSO, Järvi.

The first two movements of the wartime *Third Symphony* are vintage Tubin, but the heroic finale approaches bombast. The *Eighth* is his masterpiece; its opening movement has a sense of vision and mystery, and the atmosphere stays with you. This is the darkest of the symphonies and the most intense in feeling, music of real substance and importance. Järvi and the Swedish orchestra play it marvellously and the recording is in the demonstration bracket.

Symphonies Nos. (i) *4 (Sinfonia lirica);* (ii) *9 (Sinfonia semplice); Toccata.*
✪ *** BIS Dig. CD 227 [id.]. (i) Bergen SO, (ii) Gothenburg SO, Järvi.

The *Fourth* is a highly attractive piece, immediately accessible, the music well argued and expertly crafted. The opening has a Sibelian feel to it but, the closer one comes to it, the more individual it seems. The recording comes from a concert performance and has an exceptionally well-behaved audience. The *Ninth Symphony* is in two movements: its mood is elegiac and a restrained melancholy permeates the slower sections. Its musical language is direct, tonal and, once one gets to grips with it, quite personal. If its spiritual world is clearly Nordic, the textures are transparent and luminous, and its argument unfolds naturally and cogently. The playing of the Gothenburgers under Järvi is totally committed in all sections of the orchestra. The performances are authoritative and the recording altogether excellent.

Symphony No. 5 in B min.; Kratt (ballet suite).
*** BIS Dig. CD 306 [id.]. Bamberg SO, Järvi.

The *Fifth* makes as good a starting point as any to investigate the Tubin canon. Written after he had settled in Sweden, it finds him at his most neo-classical; the music is finely paced and full of energy and invention. The ballet suite is a work of much character, tinged with folk-inspired ideas and some echoes of Prokofiev.

Symphony No. 7; (i) *Concertino for piano and orchestra; Sinfonietta on Estonian motifs.*
*** BIS Dig. CD 401 [id.]. (i) Roland Pöntinen; Gothenburg SO, Järvi.

The *Seventh* is a marvellous work and it receives a concentrated and impressive reading. As always with Tubin, you are never in doubt that this is a real symphony which sets out purposefully and reaches its goal. The ideas could not be by anyone else and the music unfolds with a powerful logic and inevitability. Neeme Järvi inspires the Gothenburg orchestra with his own evident enthusiasm. The *Concertino for piano and orchestra* has some of the neo-classicism of the *Fifth Symphony*. Roland Pöntinen gives a dashing account of the solo part. The *Sinfonietta* is a fresh and resourceful piece, a Baltic equivalent of, say, Prokofiev's *Sinfonietta*, with much the same lightness of touch and inventive resource. Superb recording – a quite indispensable disc.

Symphony No. 10; (i) *Requiem for fallen soldiers.*
*** BIS Dig. CD 297 [id.]. Gothenburg SO, Järvi; (i) with Lundin, Rydell, Hardenberger, Lund Students' Ch., Järvi.

Tubin's *Requiem*, austere in character, is for two soloists (a contralto and baritone) and male chorus. The instrumental forces are merely an organ, piano, drums, timpani and trumpet. The simplicity and directness of the language are affecting and the sense of melancholy is finely controlled. The final movement is prefaced by a long trumpet solo, played here with stunning control and a masterly sense of line by the young Håkan Hardenberger. It is an impressive and dignified work, even if the quality of the choral singing is less than first rate. The *Tenth Symphony* is a one-movement piece that begins with a sombre string idea, which is soon interrupted by a periodically recurring horn call – and which resonates in the mind long afterwards. The recordings are absolutely first class and in the best traditions of the house.

(i; iii) *Ballade; Capricci Nos. 1 & 2; The Cock's dance; Meditation; 3 Pieces; Prelude.* (i) *Sonata for unaccompanied violin.* (i; iii) *Violin sonatas Nos. 1 & 2; Suite of Estonian dance tunes; Suite on Estonian dances.* (ii; iii) *Viola sonata; Viola sonata* (arr. of *Alto saxophone sonata*).
*** BIS Dig. CD 541/542 (2) [id.]. (i) Leibur; (ii) Vahle; (iii) Rumessen.

Although the smaller pieces are finely wrought, Tubin seems to come into his own on a larger canvas. Particularly impressive are the *Second Violin sonata* (*In the Phrygian mode*), the visionary *Second Piano sonata*, and the two sonatas for viola, one a transcription of the alto-saxophone sonata with its foretaste of the *Sixth Symphony* (1954) in which that instrument plays a prominent, almost soloistic role, and the later *Viola sonata* (1965). As so often with Tubin's non-symphonic music, there is much of interest to reward the listener. Highly accomplished and cultured performances from Arvo Leibur and Petra Vahle, and exceptionally thorough documentation from the pianist Vardo Rumessen, with over 40 music-type examples. The recording is truthful, but the acoustic lends a shade too much resonance to the piano, which is often bottom-heavy.

Complete piano music: *Album leaf; Ballad on a theme by Maat Saar; 3 Estonian folk-dances; 4 Folksongs from my country; A little march for Rana; Lullaby; 3 Pieces for children; Prelude No. 1; 7 Preludes; Sonatas Nos. 1–2; Sonatina in D min.; Suite on Estonian shepherd melodies; Variations on an Estonian folk-tune.*
*** BIS Dig. CD 414/6 [id.]. Vardo Rumessen.

Tubin's first works for piano inhabit a world in which Scriabin, Ravel and Eller were clearly dominant influences but in which an individual sensibility is also to be discerned. The resourceful *Variations on an Estonian folk-tune* is a lovely work that deserves a place in the repertoire, as does the *Sonatina in D minor*, where the ideas and sense of momentum are on a larger scale than one would expect in a sonatina. The *Second Sonata* is a key work in Tubin's development. It opens with a shimmering figure in free rhythm, inspired by the play of the aurora borealis, and is much more concentrated than his earlier piano works. Vardo Rumessen makes an excellent case for it and it is impressive stuff. The performances are consistently fine, full of understanding and flair, and the recording is very natural.

OPERA

Barbara von Tisenhusen.
*** Ondine Dig. ODE776-2 (2). Raamat, Sild, Kuusk, Puurabar, Ants Kollo, Estonian Op. Company & O, Peeter Lilje.

Tubin's opera with its theme of illicit passion is not long, consisting of three Acts of roughly 30 minutes each. It has pace and variety of dramatic incident and musical textures, and the main roles in the action are vividly characterized. The musical substance of the opera is largely based on a chaconne-like figure of nine notes heard at the very outset, yet the theme changes subtly and skilfully to meet the constantly shifting dramatic environment so that the casual listener will probably not be consciously aware of the musical means Tubin is employing. All the singers are dedicated and serve the composer well and, though the orchestra is not first class, it too plays with spirit and enthusiasm under Peeter Lilje. The recording produces a sound comparable to that of a broadcast relay rather than the opulent sound one can expect from a commercial studio recording. A strong recommendation.

The Parson of Reigi; (i) *Requiem for fallen soldiers.*
*** Ondine Dig. ODE783-2 (2). Maiste, Eensalu, Tônuri, Kuusk, Estonian Op. Company & O, Paul Mägi; (i) Urve Tauts; Talevaldis Deksnis, Urmas Leiten; Rein Tiido, Rein Roos, Estonian Nat. Male Ch., Eri Klas.

After the success of *Barbara von Tisenhusen,* the Estonian Opera immediately commissioned Tubin to compose *The Parson of Reigi,* and it, too, concerns an illicit relationship. Tubin's music powerfully evokes the claustrophobic milieu of a small, closely knit fishing community and is particularly successful in conveying atmosphere. The dawn scene where the parson, Lampelius, blesses the departing fishermen is particularly imaginative, as is the evocation of the white summer nights in the Garden scene, where the heroine confesses her illicit passion. As in the case of *Barbara von Tisenhusen,* Tubin's powers of characterization of both the major and supporting roles are striking, and there is a compelling sense of dramatic narrative as well as variety of pace. The performance of the three principal singers is very good – especially the parson, splendidly sung by the baritone, Teo Maiste – and the only let-down is in the quality of the orchestral playing, which is little more than passable.

The coupled *Requiem for Fallen Soldiers* is generally to be preferred to the rival account on BIS coupled with the *Tenth Symphony* (see above). The Estonian singers produce better focused and darker tone than their Swedish colleagues, though the BIS recording has some amazingly lyrical playing by Håkan Hardenberger. The Estonian player, Urmas Leiten, is very eloquent too. Strongly recommended.

Turina, Joaquin (1882–1949)

Danzas fantásticas, Op. 22; La procesión del Rocio, Op. 9; Ritmos, Op. 43; Sinfonia sevillana, Op. 23.
*** RCA Dig. RD 60895 [09026 60895-2]. Bamberg SO, Antonio de Almeida.

La procesión del Rocio (1913) was Turina's first great success in picaresque Spanish tone-painting, corruscating with *seguidilla* and *garrotín* dance-rhythms. We are more than familiar with the three equally exotic *Danzas fantásticas* (1918), with the opening shaft of bright sunlight of *Exaltación* leading to chimerical mood-changes, and evening bells in *Ensueño.* The closing *Orgía,* for all its flamenco vigour, later also brings dreamlike imagery of floral perfumes drifting on the night air. The three-movement *Sinfonia sevillana* is no less descriptive, beginning with a *Panorama,* then suggesting the river which runs through the centre of Seville and ending with an exuberant *Fiesta.* *Ritmos* (1928), subtitled '*Fantasía coreográfica*', is a series of sharply characterful vignettes, ear-tickling in their tunefulness and the diversity of their orchestral palette. The Bambergers clearly relish the southern sunshine, balmy nocturnal breezes and glittering flamenco dances and, with Almeida directing persuasively, they respond with distinction to this evocative repertoire. The recording too is spacious, with the necessary resonance hardly clouding the more garish tuttis and bringing lustrously translucent strings and glowing wind.

La Oración del Torero (version for string orchestra).
*** Chandos Dig. CHAN 9288 [id.]. I Musici di Montréal, Yuli Turovsky – SHCHEDRIN: *Carmen ballet suite* etc. ***

The composer's string-orchestral version of the haunting *Oración del Torero* is warmly and sensitively played and very well recorded here, and if the quartet version is even more subtle (see below) this makes an enjoyable foil for Shchedrin's brilliant arrangement of music from Bizet's *Carmen.*

Rapsodia sinfónica (arr. Halffter).
(N) (B) *** Decca Eclipse Dig. 448 243-2; *448 243-4* [id.]. Alicia de Larrocha, LPO, Frühbeck de Burgos – ALBENIZ: *Rapsodia española;* RODRIGO: *Concierto de Aranjuez* etc. ***

Turina's *Rapsodia sinfónica* has been recorded by others, but in the hands of Alicia de Larrocha it is played with such éclat that it becomes almost memorable and thoroughly entertaining. Excellent, vivid sound.

CHAMBER MUSIC

La Oración del Torero.
*** Collins Dig. 1267-2 [id.]. Britten Qt – CHERUBINI; VERDI: *Quartets.* ***
(Y/B) (***) Testament mono SBT 1053 [id.]. Hollywood Qt – CRESTON: *Quartet;* DEBUSSY: *Danses sacrées;* RAVEL: *Intro and allegro;* VILLA-LOBOS: *Quartet No. 6.* (***)

Turina's seductively gentle evocation was conceived with lutes in mind, but quartet playing of this calibre makes the string medium seem exactly right for the music, and brings a refined ravishing of the senses. The performance is full of lush Andalusian atmosphere, yet has an element of restraint and never becomes over-ripe, helped by superb recording and a most sympathetic acoustic. The *'delicadisimo'* close is quite magical.

It is difficult to imagine Turina's famous piece being played with greater expressive eloquence or more perfect ensemble than by the incomparable Hollywood Quartet and it comes as part of a valuable and beautifully transferred anthology.

Turnage, Mark-Anthony (born 1960)

Greek (opera; complete).
*** Argo Dig. 440 368-2. Quentin Hayes, Richard Suart, Fiona Kimm, Helen Charnock, Greek Ens., Bernas.

Turnage's opera, *Greek*, is out to shock at all costs, beginning with a spoken introduction from the central character, Eddy, rich in vulgarities. This is the Oedipus myth freely adapted to the East End of London ('Eddy-pus' you might deduce). The colour and energy of Turnage's writing, violently dissonant with copious percussion, is brilliantly caught. The unprepared listener may resist at first, but Turnage with his echoes of popular music and his element of lyricism is a powerful communicator. What comes out less well than on stage is the humour, which seems heavy-handed, though the parody of a music-hall duet for Mum and Dad at the end of Act I has plenty of wit. Quentin Hayes has all the impact needed as the central rough diamond, with Richard Suart as Dad, Fiona Kimm as Wife and Helen Charnock as Mum all singing with bite and conviction, tackling not just those roles but incidentals too. On a single disc with libretto and notes, it can be strongly recommended to the adventurous.

Tye, Christopher (c. 1505–c. 1572)

Mass: Euge bone; Peccavimus patribus nostris.
*** Proudsound Dig. PROUCD 126; *PROU 126* [id.]. Clerkes of Oxenford, David Wulstan – SHEPPARD: *Collection.* ***

Christopher Tye was a clerk at King's College, Cambridge, before moving on to Ely Cathedral in the 1540s. Mass settings of the period were often based on a setting of a votive antiphon, using the opening to provide a motto for each Mass section. Tye's *Euge bone* belongs to this genre. It is a work of great beauty; it is sung here with characteristic tonal sophistication by the Clerkes of Oxenford under David Wulstan, and splendidly recorded in a spacious but not over-reverberant acoustic.

Mass: Euge bone (in 6 parts).
(N) (M) *** EMI CDM5 65211-2 [id.]. King's College, Cambridge, Ch., Ledger – BYRD: *Mass for 5 voices;* TALLIS: *Mass: Puer natus est nobis.* ***

Christopher Tye's *Mass for six voices* is one of the glories of early Tudor music, amazingly rich and complex. This fine (1980) recording – attractively coupled with Byrd's masterpiece and the wonderfully reconstructed Tallis work – is well balanced between clarity and atmosphere, and the quality of the singing is a fine tribute to Ledger's work with this unique choir.

Ullmann, Viktor (1898–c. 1944)

(i) *Der Kaiser von Atlantis* (opera; complete); (ii) *Hölderlin Lieder: Abendphantasie; Der Frühling; Wo bist du?*
(Y/B) *** Decca Dig. 440 854-2 [id.].(i) Kraus, Berry, Vermillion, Lippert, Mazura, Leipzig GO, Lothar Zagrosek; (ii) Vermillion, Alder.

In Decca's *Entartete Musik* series, *Der Kaiser von Atlantis* ('The Emperor of Atlantis') stands out as a work actually written in a Nazi concentration camp. Sharp, Weill-like writing, with the chance availability of such instruments as organ and banjo heightening the flavour, is tempered by echoes of Zemlinsky and Berg. The result is a strongly drawn sequence involving not just the central character, Kaiser Overall, a caricature of Hitler, but the key figure of Death, Harlequin, a Drummer-girl and two soldiers, one of them, Bubikopf, sung by a soprano. The death theme from Suk's *Asrael Symphony* is the centre of a complex web of references intended for the Terezin audience, a cultural élite. The mixture of satire with an element of poignancy is undoubtedly moving, not least in the use of Luther's hymn, *Ein feste Burg*, in the finale. Zagrosek conducts an outstanding performance with a characterful, well-cast team of soloists, led superbly by the baritone, Michael Kraus, as Overall. The three settings of Hölderlin, written in the same year, are mellower in style, with Ullmann's admiration of Berg flowering in warmly romantic, tonal writing. They are beautifully sung by Iris Vermillion, accompanied at the piano by Jonathan Alder. Excellent recording. The single CD comes in a box with libretto, text and translations, plus copious notes.

Vainberg, Moishei (born 1919)

The Golden Key (ballet), *Op. 55: suites Nos. 1–3; suite 4:* excerpts.
(Y/B) *** Olympia OCD 473 [id.]. Bolshoi Theatre O, Mark Ermler.

The Golden Key is a full-length ballet dating from 1955, based on a story by Alexis Tolstoy. The scenario concerns a troupe of puppets with a Petrushka or Pierrot-like figure at the centre. This generous selection (not far short of 80 minutes) gives a good idea of the quality of Vainberg's invention and his skill in making telling character-studies. One does not necessarily want to play all 26 of the movements at one go, without the benefit of stage action, but there is some arresting music here and it is well performed by Bolshoi forces under Mark Ermler, and decently recorded.

Symphonies Nos. (i) *6 in A min.;* (ii) *10 in A min.*
(Y/B) ** Olympia mono/stereo OCD 471 [id.]. (i) Moscow Ch. School Boys' Ch., Moscow PO, Kondrashin; (ii) Moscow CO, Barshai.

Moishei (since 1985 Mieczyslaw) Vainberg is enormously prolific and has some 22 symphonies to his credit. The *Sixth Symphony* is a dark and powerful work, ultimately more satisfying than the *Tenth* for strings, whose invention does not fully sustain its length. Both works are nevertheless worth exploring and, though the recordings are analogue (and, in the case of the *Sixth*, only in mono), they are, if not three-star, more than acceptable. The performances under Kirill Kondrashin and Rudolf Barshai are persuasive and authoritative.

Symphonies Nos. (i) *7, Op. 81;* (ii) *12, Op. 114 (In memory of Dmitri Shostakovich).*
(N) **(*) Olympia OCD 472 [id.]. (i) Moscow CO, Barshai; (ii) USSR TV & R. SO, Maxim Shostakovich.

Moishei Vainberg is enjoying greater exposure on disc, thanks to the enterprise of the Olympia label. The present issue couples the *Seventh Symphony*, written for the unusual combination of strings and harpsichord and which comes from the early 1960s, and the *Twelfth*, which takes 52 minutes and was written in 1976 after Shostakovich's death. As Per Skans's exceptionally informative and interesting notes remind us, Vainberg was the dedicatee of Shostakovich's *Tenth Symphony*. David Fanning speaks in *Guide to the Symphony* of 'a steady flow of expressive, inventive and expertly controlled music, much indebted to, but never wholly overshadowed by, Shostakovich' – and thus it is in these impressive works. Both the recordings are analogue and come from 1967 and 1979 respectively, but they reproduce decently. An interesting issue.

Vaňhal, Jan (1739–1813)

(i) *Double bassoon concerto in F; Sinfonias: in A min.; F.*
**(*) BIS CD 288 [id.]. (i) Wallin, Nilsson; Umeå Sinf., Saraste.

The best thing here is the *Concerto*, which is an arresting and inventive piece. The slow movement has real distinction, touching a deeper vein of feeling than anything else on this record. It is not too fanciful to detect in some of the harmonic suspensions the influence of Gluck, with whose music Vaňhal came into contact in the late 1760s. The two *Sinfonias* are less musically developed but far from uninteresting: the minuet of the *F major* has a distinctly 'Sturm und Drang' feel to it: Vaňhal's symphonies may well have paved the way for Haydn at this period; they were certainly given by Haydn while Kapellmeister at the Esterhazy palace. The recording is good, as one has come to expect from this source, even if the acoustic is on the dry side. The playing of the Umeå ensemble is eminently respectable.

Violin concerto in B.
(N) (B) *** Discover Dig. DICD 920265 [id.]. Ivan Zenaty, Virtuosi di Praga, Oldrich Vlček –
   MYSLIVECEK: *Violin concerto*. ***

Like his Bohemian contemporary, Mysliveček, Vaňhal was born in Bohemia almost a generation before
Mozart; he similarly wrote inventive, lively music, of which this violin concerto is an appealing example,
with the central slow movement a nostalgic intermezzo. On this well-recorded bargain issue Ivan Zenaty
with his clean, full tone again proves an outstanding advocate, with the Virtuosi di Praga providing
lively support on modern instruments. Excellent recording.

Varèse, Edgar (1883–1965)

Amériques; Arcana; Density 21.5; Intégrales; Ionisation; Octandre; Offrandes.
(M) *** Sony Analogue/Dig. SK 45844 [id.]. Yakar, NYPO, Ens. InterContemporain, Boulez.

In the inter-war period Varèse was regarded as a wild man of the avant-garde in writing a work like
Ionisation for percussion alone and abandoning conventional argument in favour of presenting blocks
of sound. Yet performances like these show what a genius he had – not for assaulting but for tickling the
ear with novelty. Boulez brings out the purposefulness of his writing, not least in the two big works for
full orchestra, the early *Amériques* and *Arcana*, written for an enormous orchestra in the late 1920s.
Those two works are here played by the New York Philharmonic and are not digitally recorded. The
selection recorded more recently in digital sound covers his smaller but just as striking works for
chamber ensembles of various kinds, with Rachel Yakar the excellent soprano soloist in *Offrandes*.

Amériques; (i; ii) Ecuatorial; (ii) Nocturnal (ed. & completed Chou Wen-Chung).
(M) **(*) Van. 08 4031-71 [OVC 4031]. (i) Ariel Bybee; (ii) University Civic Choral Bass Ens.; Utah SO,
   Abravanel (with HONEGGER: *Pacific 231* **).

Amériques was written when the composer was still under the spell of his first impressions of New York.
Its rhythms are unpredictable and its cross-currents and dissonant colourings suggest the organized
chaos of the metropolitan civilization of the twentieth century. The *Nocturnal* was commissioned by the
Koussevitzky Foundation, and the composer began it in 1961. But Varèse did not live to finish his music,
and it was first performed in an incomplete state. However, the composer also left notes about intended
changes, although these are sometimes ambiguous. Chou Wen-Chung has bravely edited the completed
portion of the piece and added closing material from the composer's sketches. The result is surprisingly
convincing and, although we know where Chou Wen-Chung's section begins, the ear does not detect any
sudden drop in intensity or quality. Like the account of *Amériques*, the performance is not lacking in
exuberance and even humour (even if perhaps this is not all intentional). *Ecuatorial* is a stronger and
more directly emotional work, mystical, and based on a high-flown but poetic text by Miguel Asturias.
The music in some ways recalls Milhaud's *L'homme et son désir* in creating a background atmosphere
suggestive of a tropical jungle. The voices are used with great colouristic imagination. All these performances are most convincing, with the orchestra plainly enjoying themselves, and the characteristically atmospheric Utah acoustic seems ideal for these scores; even if Honegger's picture of a railway
engine, which is added as a fill-up, is less well-focused, the sound is never ugly. An important reissue,
with texts included.

Arcana; Intégrales; Ionisation.
(N) **(*) Decca 448 580-2 [id.]. LAPO, Mehta – KRAFT: *Concerto for 4 percussion soloists and orchestra*
   etc. **(*)

Decca's 1971 vintage stereo recording of these three key works with their unusual timbres and textures
remains highly recommendable. The performances under Mehta have the easy expressiveness that comes
from close and warm acquaintance by the players. However, the coupled music by William Kraft wears
less well.

Vaughan Williams, Ralph (1872–1958)

(i) *Concerto accademico in D min. Fantasia on a theme of Thomas Tallis.*
(M) (***) Dutton mono CDAX 8007 [id.]. (i) Frederick Grinke; Boyd Neel O, Neel – BRITTEN: *Simple
   Symphony* etc. (***)

The Boyd Neel String Orchestra was formed in the early 1930s and soon established itself as the premier ensemble of its kind in England. In 1936 they made what were the first recordings of the *Tallis fantasia* (in the presence of the composer) and, three years later, the *Concerto accademico* with Frederick Grinke as soloist. Sir Adrian Boult's version with the BBC Symphony Orchestra rather stole its thunder at the time and was better recorded. The *Concerto accademico* has hardly been surpassed and is splendidly fresh and down-to-earth. The *Variations on a theme of Frank Bridge*, with which these works are coupled, is also indispensable. There is nearly always something very special about pioneering recordings in terms of imaginative freshness and communicative intensity. Michael Dutton has done a splendid job in restoring these discs, and those who are acquainted with or possess the originals will be astonished at his results. The same applies to the *Simple Symphony*, which they recorded some months later; but it is the hauntingly atmospheric *Tallis fantasia* that resonates in the memory.

Concerto grosso for strings; (i) *Concerto accademico for violin;* (ii) *Oboe concerto;* (iii) *Piano concerto in C;* (iv) *Tuba concerto. Two Hymn-tune Preludes;* (v) *The Lark ascending. Partita for double string orchestra;* (vi) *Towards the unknown region.*
*** Chandos Dig. CHAN 9262/3 [id.]. (i) Sillito; (ii) Theodore; (iii) Shelley; (iv) Patrick Harrild; (v) Michael Davis; (vi) LSO Ch.; LSO, Bryden Thomson.

Chandos offer here as a separate compendium the series of mostly concertante works that were used as fillers for Bryden Thomson's set of the *Symphonies*, and with generous measure and characteristically fine recording this pair of CDs is very attractive. With immaculate LSO string ensemble, the *Concerto grosso* under Thomson's persuasive direction shows how in glowing sound its easy, unforced inspiration can transcend its utilitarian background and bring it close to the world of the *Tallis fantasia*. While many performances of the *Concerto accademico* make the composer's neo-classical manner sound like Stravinsky with an English accent, Thomson and Sillito find a rustic jollity in the outer movements that is very characteristic of Vaughan Williams and a gentle, withdrawn quality in the slow movement. David Theodore's plangent tones in the *Oboe concerto* effectively bring out the equivocal character of this highly original work, making it far more than just another pastoral piece, sharply emphasizing the contrasts of mood and manner. Howard Shelley addresses the neglected *Piano concerto* with flair and brilliance, making light of the disconcerting cragginess of the piano writing and consistently bringing out both the wit and the underlying emotional power. The bluff good humour of the *Tuba concerto* is beautifully caught in Patrick Harrild's rumbustious account and this outstanding tuba soloist plays with wit and panache, even if the instrument as recorded sounds rather muffled by the resonance. Michael Davis makes a rich-toned soloist in *The Lark ascending*, presenting it as more than a pastoral evocation.The *Hymn-tune Preludes* are unashamedly pastoral in tone; then the *Partita* finds the composer in more abrasive mood, less easily sympathetic. This curiously angular work sounds more convincing in a more purposeful performance than this, but in the *Fantasia* finale – a replacement movement that Vaughan Williams wrote after the rest – Thomson effectively brings out the foretastes of the dark first movement of the *Sixth Symphony*, helped by string timbre with more edge on it than is usual with Chandos. *Towards the unknown region* is the only relative disappointment – a setting of Whitman that antedates the *Sea Symphony*. The choral sound is beautiful, but this early work really needs tauter treatment than Thomson provides.

Concerto grosso; (i) *Oboe concerto. English folksongs suite; Fantasia on Greensleeves; Fantasia on a theme by Thomas Tallis;* (ii) *Romance for harmonica and strings.*
(M) **(*) Decca 440 320-2 [id.]. (i) Celia Nicklin; (ii) Tommy Reilly; ASMF, Marriner.

With the addition of the *Tallis fantasia* to the original collection, this fairly lightweight programme is given added ballast. Celia Nicklin gives a most persuasive account of the elusive *Oboe concerto*, while the *Concerto grosso* is lively and polished. The atmospheric *Romance* is not one of the composer's most inspired works but is still worth having, and the *Folksongs* could hardly be presented more breezily. The *Tallis fantasia* is given a performance at once vital and refined. Here the sound might ideally have had an even greater resonance in the acoustic (though it is by no means studio-ish), but the performance has considerable intensity.

Oboe concerto in A min.; 6 Studies in English folk songs (arr. Canter, for oboe d'amore and strings).
(M) *** Carlton IMP Classics Dig. 30366 0021-2 [id.]. Robin Canter, LSO, Judd – R. STRAUSS: *Concerto.* **(*)

Robin Canter gives a first-rate account of Vaughan Williams's elusive *Oboe concerto*, holding its florid cantilena together most convincingly. He has arranged the *Folk songs* (originally scored for cello and piano) most persuasively for this new combination, and the performance is equally winning. These settings are most appealing. Excellent recording.

(i) *Oboe concerto. Fantasia on Greensleeves;* (ii) *The Lark ascending.*
(M) *** DG 439 529-2 [id.]. (i) Neil Black; (ii) Zukerman, ECO, Barenboim – DELIUS: *Aquarelles* etc.;
WALTON: *Henry V.* ***

Neil Black's creamy tone is particularly suited to Vaughan Williams's *Oboe concerto* and he gives a
wholly persuasive performance. Zukerman's account of *The Lark ascending* is full of pastoral rapture –
even if perhaps not totally idiomatic, the effect is ravishing. The recordings from the late 1970s have not
lost their allure or atmospheric warmth in the digital remastering.

(i) *Oboe concerto. Fantasia on Greensleeves; Fantasia on a theme of Thomas Tallis; Five variants of Dives
and Lazarus; The Lark ascending; The Wasps: Overture.*
(M) *** Nimbus Dig. NI 7013 [id.]. (i) Maurice Bourgue; English String O or SO, William Boughton.

Opening with an exuberant account of *The Wasps overture*, this is a very attractive and generous 70-
minute collection of favourite Vaughan Williams orchestral pieces, most sympathetically played under
William Boughton and presented amply and atmospherically. The spacious acoustic of the Great Hall
of Birmingham University ensures that the lyrical string-tune in the overture is properly expansive
without robbing the piece of bite, and that both the deeply felt *Tallis fantasia*, with its passionate climax,
and *Dives and Lazarus* have a rich amplitude of string-sound. Michael Bochmann, the sympathetic
soloist in *The Lark ascending*, playing simply yet with persuasive lyrical freedom is nicely integrated with
the warm orchestral backing. More questionable is the *Oboe concerto*, with the superb French soloist,
Maurice Bourgue, balanced too close. Nevertheless Bourgue's playing, sharply rhythmical and with a
rich, pastoral timbre, makes a good case for a comparatively neglected piece.

Piano concerto in C.
*** Lyrita SRCD 211 [id.]. Howard Shelley, RPO, Handley – FOULDS: *Dynamic triptych.* ***
(N) (M) *** EMI Dig. CD-EMX 2239 [id.]. Piers Lane, RLPO, Handley – DELIUS: *Piano concerto;*
FINZI: *Eclogue.* ***

This was the first recording of the *Concerto* in solo form, not quite as originally written, because the
definitive score, published not too long before this Lyrita record was made and giving the alternatives of
one or two pianos, opts for ending with a serene coda instead of the original brief dispatching coda of
ten bars. That is certainly an improvement, and the wonder is that, though the solo piano writing is
hardly pianistic, the very challenge to as fine an exponent as Shelley brings out an extra intensity to a
highly individual work. Despite the thick textures, there is lightheartedness in much of the writing,
whether the urgently chattering *Toccata* or the *Alla tedesca* which emerges out of the toughly chromatic
fugue of the finale. Since this record was made, Shelley has re-recorded the piece digitally for Chandos
(see below), but that is coupled with the *Ninth Symphony*, and many may find the stimulating
Foulds coupling on Lyrita even more enticing. The 1984 recording is very impressive in its remastered
form.

   Piers Lane defies the old idea of this as a grittily unpianistic work, giving it a powerful, refreshing
reading, helped by fine playing from the RLPO under Handley, always a sympathetic Vaughan
Williams interpreter. Though this hardly outshines Howard Shelley's Lyrita version with its more
involving, less distant recording, the apt and unusual coupling can be warmly recommended.

(i) *Piano concerto; Symphony No. 9 in E min.*
*** Chandos Dig. CHAN 8941 [id.]. (i) Howard Shelley, LPO, Bryden Thomson.

Perhaps the most strikingly original of the three movements of the *Piano concerto* is the imaginative and
inward-looking *Romanza*, which has some of the angularity of line one finds in *Flos campi*, while the
finale presages the *Fourth Symphony*. The piece abounds in difficulties of the most demanding nature,
which Howard Shelley addresses with flair and brilliance. He makes light of the disconcerting cragginess
of the piano writing and consistently brings out both the wit and the underlying emotional power.
Bryden Thomson conducts a powerful performance of the last of Vaughan Williams's symphonies.
Though the playing may not be as crisply incisive as that on Previn's 1971 version with the LSO, it
brings out an extra warmth of expression. Both performances are greatly helped by the richness and
weight of the Chandos sound, warmly atmospheric but with ample detail and a fine sense of presence.

English folksongs suite; Fantasia on Greensleeves; In the Fen Country; (i) *The Lark ascending; Norfolk
rhapsody No. 1;* (ii) *Serenade to music.*
(M) *** EMI CDM7 64022-2 [id.]. LPO, LSO or New Philh. O, Sir Adrian Boult; (i) with Hugh Bean;
   (ii) 16 soloists.

All the music here is beautifully performed and recorded. Hugh Bean understands the spirit of *The Lark
ascending* perfectly and his performance is wonderfully serene. The transfers are fresh and pleasing; in

the lovely *Serenade* (which Boult does in the original version for 16 soloists) the voices are given greater presence.

English folksongs suite; Fantasia on a theme by Thomas Tallis; Fantasia on Greensleeves; (i) *The Lark ascending. The Wasps: Overture; Entr'acte No. 1; March of Kitchen Utensils.*
(Y/B) (BB) ** Tring Dig. TRP 031 [id.]. (i) Jonathan Carney; RPO, Christopher Seaman.

The highlight here is a rapt account of the idyllic *Lark ascending*, with Jonathan Carney the highly sensitive soloist often sustaining a haunting pianissimo solo line. The *Tallis fantasia* is also a fine performance, both ethereal and passionate; but this, like the whole programme, is affected by too close microphones in a reverberant acoustic. The dynamic range of the recording is realistically wide, but fortissimos inevitably bring fierceness, even though the basic ambience is spacious.

English folksongs suite; Toccata marziale.
(BB) *** ASV CDQS 6021. London Wind O, Denis Wick – HOLST: *Military band suites* etc. ***

As in the Holst suites, the pace of these performances of the original scores is attractively zestful, and if the slow movement of the *English folksongs suite* could have been played more reflectively, the bounce of *Seventeen come Sunday* is irresistible.

English folksongs suite; Sea songs (march).
(M) *** EMI Dig. CDM5 65122-2. Central Band of the RAF, Wing Commander Eric Banks – HOLST: *Suites;* GRAINGER: *Lincolnshire posy* etc.

Both these works were written for military band – and how well they sound here! The solo playing in the darkly atmospheric central movement of the suite, *Intermezzo* (*My bonny boy*), is specially sensitive. This movement is quite haunting in its original scoring, conjuring up an impression of mist drifting over the lowland Fen country. The marches have great spirit and ebullience, and the recording is first class in every way.

Fantasia on Greensleeves; (i) *Fantasia on a theme of Thomas Tallis.*
(N) ✸ EMI CDC7 47537-2 [id.]. Sinfonia of L., (i) with Allegri Qt; Barbirolli – ELGAR: *Introduction and allegro* etc. *** ✸
(Y/B) (BB) *** RCA Navigator 74321 17905-2. Phd. Ch. & O, Ormandy – HOLST: *The Planets.* (***)
(M) **(*) Carlton IMP Classics Dig. PCD 930 [id.]. LSO, Frühbeck de Burgos – ELGAR: *Cello concerto.* ***
(N) (M) * DG Dig. 445 561-2 [id.]. Orpheus CO (with BRITTEN: *Simple symphony* ***) – ELGAR: *Elegy* etc. *(*)

The rich projection of the Tallis theme on which Vaughan Williams based his *Fantasia* when it first appears in full, after the pizzicato introduction, sets the seal on Barbirolli's quite outstanding perform-ance of the *Tallis fantasia*, one of the great masterpieces of all music. The wonderfully ethereal and magically quiet playing of the second orchestra is another very moving feature of this remarkable performance. The remastered CD retains all the warmth, amplitude and ambient bloom of the superb (1963) recording; it is beautifully focused, so that the gently radiant closing section is particularly moving. The delightful *Greensleeves fantasia* makes an irresistible bonus, presented with pleasing freshness.

Gloriously ripe performances of both works from Ormandy and the Philadelphia strings, recorded in 1970 and 1972 respectively. Subtlety is not the strong point and the second orchestra in the *Tallis fantasia* is made to seem too close; but the warm intensity of the playing confounds such criticism and there is a gravity in the way Ormandy presents the famous *Greensleeves* melody that is very endearing. There are few recordings that in their resonant opulence show the body of tone the Philadelphia strings could command at that time.

Though Frühbeck is rather heavy-handed in his treatment of these Vaughan Williams favourites, the playing of the LSO is refined and the recording first rate.

Even more than in the coupled Elgar, the Orpheus performance of the *Tallis fantasia* suggests a lack of the kind of familiarity and innate understanding of the music which comes with frequent performance. Though there are moments of passion, they are short-lived and the overall pacing is unconvincing. The bright, vividly clear recording confirms the need for a greater weight and body of tone to help the work to expand emotionally.

Fantasia on Greensleeves; Fantasia on a theme by Thomas Tallis; Five variants on 'Dives and Lazarus'; In the Fen Country; (i) *The Lark ascending. Norfolk rhapsody No. 1.*
**(*) Argo Dig. 440 116-2 [id.]. New Queen's Hall O, Barry Wordsworth; (i) with Hagai Shaham.

The re-formed New Queen's Hall Orchestra concentrate on late-nineteenth-century and early-twentieth-century repertoire, playing instruments in use at the turn of the century. The stringed instruments use gut rather than steel strings, brass instruments have a narrow bore, reedy French bassoons are favoured rather than the mellower, fatter-timbred German instrument, and wooden flutes are preferred to metal ones. The horns are genuine French (or Viennese) and not the more elaborate (and more reliable) German double horns. *Portamento* is featured in the string style but here it is applied very judiciously, and for the most part the ear notices the fuller, warmer sonority of the violins, the treble less brilliant in attack. In works like the *Tallis fantasia* and *Dives and Lazarus* one can readily wallow in the richly refined textures, but Wordsworth's performance of *Tallis* misses the final degree of intensity at the climax, and the opening of *Dives and Lazarus* is also rather relaxed, even indulgent, in relishing the sheer breadth of sonority achieved, though the closing pages are ethereally lovely. For *The Lark ascending*, Hagai Shaham is placed within the orchestra and she plays very gently, displaying a rather recessive personality. Although the effect has a simple, serene beauty, the rapt intensity of the closing solo passage is here rather subdued. The performers are at their finest in the evocative opening of the *Norfolk rhapsody*, while *In the Fen Country* has a fine idyllic ardour, with some very sensitive playing from wind and brass in the coda. The Argo recording, made in the Walthamstow Assembly Hall, is splendidly expansive and natural, and we await other CDs from this source with great interest.

Fantasia on Greensleeves; Fantasia on a theme by Thomas Tallis; (i) *The Lark ascending.*
(M) *** Virgin/EMI Dig. CUV5 61126-2 [id.]. (i) Christopher Warren-Green; LCO, Warren-Green –
    ELGAR: *Introduction and allegro* etc. ***

Fantasia on Greensleeves; Fantasia on a theme of Thomas Tallis; Five variants of Dives and Lazarus; (i)
Flos Campi.
(M) *** Van. 08.4053.71 [OVC 4071]. (i) Sally Peck, Utah University Ch.; Utah SO, Maurice
    Abravanel.

Christopher Warren-Green and his London Chamber Orchestra give a radiant account of *The Lark ascending*, in which Warren-Green makes a charismatic solo contribution, very free and soaring in its flight and with beautifully sustained true pianissimo playing at the opening and close. For the *Tallis fantasia*, the second orchestra (2.2.2.2.1) contrasts with the main group (5.4.2.2.1) and here, though the effect is beautifully serene, Warren-Green does not quite match the ethereal, other-worldly pianissimo that made Barbirolli's reading unforgettable. But that is a minor quibble; the performance overall has great ardour and breadth, almost to match the coupled *Introduction and allegro* of Elgar in its intensity. The recording, made at All Saints' Church, Petersham, is quite ideal in its resonant warmth and atmosphere, yet has good definition. This is an altogether superb disc.

On Vanguard *Greensleeves* is slow and gracious, and there are more passionate versions of the *Tallis fantasia* available; but the noteworthy point is the way Abravanel catches the inner feeling of the music. Both here and in *Dives and Lazarus* the full strings create a gloriously rich sonority. Sally Peck, the violist, is placed with her colleagues rather than as a soloist in *Flos Campi* (following the composer's expressed intention), yet her personality still emerges well. Abravanel, always a warm, energetic conductor, displays real understanding, allowing the music to relax as it should in this evocation of the Song of Solomon, but never letting it drag either. The CD transfer is excellent, retaining the naturalness of the original recording.

Fantasia on Greensleeves; (i) *The Lark ascending.*
(Y/B) (B) *** DG 439 464-2 [id.]. (i) Zukerman; ECO, Barenboim – BRITTEN: *Serenade*; DELIUS: *On
    hearing the first cuckoo in spring* etc. ***

This DG Classikon bargain CD makes a most attractive anthology. Zukerman's account of *The Lark ascending* has a uniquely rapturous pastoralism and it is beautifully played and recorded.

Fantasia on a theme of Thomas Tallis.
(Y/B) (M) **(*) BBC Radio Classics BBCRD 9107 [id.]. New Philh. O, Stokowski (with Concert) –
    BRAHMS: *Symphony No. 4;* RAVEL: *Rapsodie espagnole.* **(*)
(Y/B) (BB) ** BBC Radio Classics BBCRD 9119 [id.]. New Philh. O, Sir Adrian Boult (with Concert)
    – LEIGH: *Harpsichord concertino;* FINZI: *Clarinet concerto* etc. **(*)

The Stokowski performance comes from an Albert Hall concert in May 1974 and is scrupulously prepared. Stokowski recorded the piece commercially in 1952, and this later reading is marginally more expansive. There is a characteristic sophistication of texture and a strong sense of atmosphere, while dynamic shadings and nuances are meticulous. But the BBC sound, though warm, is not transparent; the close microphones restrict full dynamic expansion of climaxes. All the same, this is a relatively inexpensive disc, well worth investigating, not least for the sake of the Brahms *Symphony*.

Sir Adrian's performance with the New Philharmonia comes from a Cheltenham Festival concert of

1972. Strong, atmospheric and firmly focused, rather bottom-heavy recording. Not superior to any of Boult's commercial recordings either artistically or technically, but again this is part of an enjoyable bargain concert which includes fine concertante works by Finzi and Walter Leigh.

Fantasia on a theme of Thomas Tallis; Five variants of Dives and Lazarus; In the Fen Country; Norfolk rhapsody.
*** Chandos Dig. CHAN 8502 [id.]. LPO, Bryden Thomson.

Boult recorded *In the Fen Country* and the *Norfolk rhapsody* successfully, but neither is otherwise available in modern digital sound. Bryden Thomson is a thoroughly persuasive guide in all this repertoire, and in the other two pieces more than holds his own with most of the opposition.

Fantasia on a theme by Thomas Tallis; Five variants of Dives and Lazarus; In the Fen country; Norfolk Rhapsody No. 1 in E min.; Variations for orchestra (orch. Jacob); *The Wasps: Overture.*
(Y/B) **(*) Ph. Dig. 442 427-2 [id.]. ASMF, Marriner.

Opening with a bright and brisk account of *The Wasps overture*, this collection is valuable in including the rare *Variations*, written as a brass band test-piece in 1957 and skilfully orchestrated by Gordon Jacob. Not a masterpiece, but worth having on disc. The other works are very well played; but *Tallis*, though beautiful, lacks the last degree of ethereal intensity. Marriner makes up with the climax of *Dives and Lazarus* which is richly expansive, and he and the ASMF are at their finest in the gentle, evocative opening and closing sections of the *First Norfolk rhapsody. In the Fen country* brings more fine playing; and overall this is an enjoyable programme, if not showing these artists at their very finest. The recording too, though spacious, is good rather than outstanding.

(i) *Fantasia on a theme by Thomas Tallis; Five variants of Dives and Lazarus; Norfolk rhapsody No. 1;* (ii) *In Windsor Forest;* (i; iii) *Toward the Unknown Region.*
(M) *** EMI CDM5 65131-2 [id.]. (i) CBSO; (ii) Bournemouth Symphony Ch. & Sinf.; (iii) with CBSO Ch.; Norman Del Mar.

Norman Del Mar's strong and deeply felt account of the *Tallis fantasia* is given a splendid digital recording, with the second orchestral group creating radiant textures. The direct approach, however, lacks something in mystery, and not all of the ethereal resonance of this haunting work is conveyed. The early (1907) cantata, *Toward the Unknown Region,* set to words of Walt Whitman, and *In Windsor Forest,* which the composer adapted from his Falstaff opera, *Sir John in love,* make a perfect coupling. The movements are not always exact transcriptions from the opera, for the composer rethought and amplified certain passages. Norman Del Mar directs warmly sympathetic performances, given excellent sound.

Fantasia on a theme of Thomas Tallis; Prelude and fugue in D min.
(N) (BB) *** CfP Silver Double CDCFPSD 4754 (2). LPO, Handley – BRITTEN: *Violin concerto in D min.* etc. ***; TIPPETT: *Concerto for double string orchestra* ***; WALTON: *Belshazzar's feast.* **(*)

Vernon Handley proves a passionately persuasive interpreter of the masterly *Tallis fantasia,* and the recording is appropriately full-bodied yet clear. The *Prelude and fugue* is an orchestral arrangement of an organ piece (made by the composer) for the Three Choirs Festival, Hereford, in 1930; this was its first recording.

Fantasia on Sussex folk tunes for cello and orchestra.
*** RCA Dig. RD 70800. Lloyd Webber, Philh. O, Handley – DELIUS: *Cello concerto;* HOLST: *Invocation.* ***

The *Fantasia on Sussex folk tunes* has lain neglected since its first performance by Casals, and it proves something of a discovery. This is a highly appealing work, most persuasively performed too. The recording is first class.

Five variants of Dives and Lazarus; (i) *The Lark ascending.*
(M) *** Decca 440 325-2 [id.]. (i) Iona Brown, ASMF, Marriner – BUTTERWORTH: *Banks of green willow* etc.; WARLOCK: *Capriol suite* etc. ***

Iona Brown is second to none in her beautiful (1972) account of *The Lark ascending,* and the account of *Dives and Lazarus* has comparable intensity and refinement. With excellent transfers, this generous collection in Decca's 'British Classics' series readily reflects the excellence of the (originally Argo) recordings.

Five variants of Dives and Lazarus; (i) *The Lark ascending; The Wasps: Overture and suite.*
(M) *** EMI Dig. CD-EMX 9508; *TC-EMX 2082.* (i) David Nolan; LPO, Handley.

The immediacy of the recording allows no mistiness in *The Lark ascending*, but it is still a warm, understanding performance. The overture is spaciously conceived and it leads to charming, colourful accounts of the other, less well-known pieces in the suite, tuneful and lively. The *Five Variants of Dives and Lazarus* is superbly played and recorded. The sound is fresh and clear, if rather brightly lit.

Job (A masque for dancing); Variations for orchestra (orch. Jacob).
*** EMI Dig. CDC7 54421-2 [id.]. Bournemouth SO, Richard Hickox.

Job (A masque for dancing); The Wasps overture.
(N) (BB) (***) Belart mono 461 122-2 [id.]. LPO, Boult.
(Y/B) *(**) Everest EVC 9006 [id.]. LPO, Boult (with ARNOLD: *4 Scottish dances*: cond. composer **(*)).

Richard Hickox conducts a strong and spacious account of Vaughan Williams's biblical ballet-score, warmly recorded. In its fine pacing it brings out the spiritual intensity of the music, while presenting dramatic contrasts at full power. The coupling is a welcome rarity. The composer scored it for brass band, but here it is given in the fine orchestral arrangement by Gordon Jacob, a fresh and colourful little work, sharply structured.

Boult made four LP recordings of *Job*, and this Belart/Decca mono version has a special kind of warmth and freshness. No apologies need be made for the mono recording, which sounds fuller and more atmospheric than some early digital stereo discs; and the same comment might apply to the delightful incidental music for *The Wasps*, with the lovely string-tune in the *Overture* as spacious as one could ask and the delicious *March past of the kitchen utensils* comparably piquant.

The Everest performance of *Job* under the work's dedicatee was Boult's second LP of Vaughan Williams's ballet. The Everest version is sensitive and spontaneous but, unusually for this label, the recording, although basically spacious, is made aggressive at climaxes because of the close microphoning of the brass, which sound strident, while the massed strings are somewhat tight. The venue was the Royal Albert Hall, and obviously the engineers could not cope with the hall's notorious resonance. *The Wasps overture* was done at Walthamstow and sounds full and unconfined. What an outstanding performance, too, with plenty of sparkle but with a very broad tempo for the beautiful secondary theme. Malcolm Arnold conducts his own *Scottish dances* with élan and is especially persuasive in the third with its glorious picture of the Highland scenery, which produced one of the loveliest tunes the composer ever wrote. This is properly expansive; otherwise the brightly vivid sound is not quite as smooth as the best Everest reissues.

The Lark ascending.
*** RCA 09026 61700-2 [id.]. Anne Akiko Meyers, Philh. O, Andrew Litton – MENDELSSOHN: *Violin concerto.* ***

Meyers' opening brings a pianissimo of breathtaking intensity, for the raptness of Miss Meyers' playing is magnetic, and Andrew Litton – who from the start of his career has shown what sympathy he has for British music – makes the most understanding accompanist. The atmospheric intensity of the performance is enhanced by the refinement of sound, with the violin set naturally rather than spotlit.

(i) *Suite for viola and orchestra;* (ii) *Flos campi;* (iii) *Hymn-tune preludes Nos. 1 & 2; Overture: The poisoned kiss; The running set.*
(M) **(*) Chandos CHAN 6545 [id.]. Bournemouth Sinf., (i) with Riddle, cond. Del Mar, (ii) with Ch.; (iii) cond. Hurst.

The *Suite* is lightweight but engaging, unpretentious music to be enjoyed, with its charming *Carol* and quirky *Polka mélancolique*. Frederick Riddle is an eloquent soloist, even if the playing is not always technically immaculate, and Norman Del Mar directs sympathetically. The overture to the opera *The poisoned kiss* is merely a pot-pourri, but it is presented most persuasively here. *The running set* is an exhilarating fantasy on jig rhythms. Fine performances under George Hurst.

SYMPHONIES

Symphonies Nos. 1–9.
**(*) Chandos Dig. CHAN 9087/91 [id.]. LSO, Thomson (with Yvonne Kenny, Brian Rayner Cook in *No. 1*; Kenny in *No. 3*; Catherine Bott in *No. 7*; London Symphony Ch. in *Nos. 1 & 7*).

Symphonies Nos. 1–9 (complete); *Fantasia on Greensleeves; Fantasia on a theme of Tallis; Norfolk rhapsody No. 1; 5 Variants of Dives and Lazarus.*
(M) **(*) RCA 09026 61460-2 (6) [id.]. Philh. O, Slatkin.

Symphonies Nos. 1–9; (i) *Flos campi; Serenade to music.*
(Y/B) (M) *** EMI Dig./Analogue CD-BOXVW 1 (6) [id.]. Soloists, Liverpool Philharmonic Ch., RLPO, Vernon Handley; (i) with Christopher Balmer.

Handley's set consists of the six individual CDs in a handsome blue slipcase, and it will especially suit those needing both economy and modern, digital sound; only the *Sinfonia Antartica* is analogue – and that is still a fine modern recording, offering also the orchestral version of the *Serenade to music* as a fill-up. In all his Vaughan Williams recordings Handley shows a natural feeling for expressive rubato and is totally sympathetic. Many of his performances are first or near-first choices and No. 5 is outstanding in every way. This disc also includes a very successful account of *Flos campi.*

Leonard Slatkin, following in the footsteps of André Previn in the earlier VW cycle for RCA, shows consistent sympathy for the idiom. Like the composer himself in his surviving recordings, Slatkin prefers speeds faster than usual, and that makes the central symphonies of the cycle less warmly expressive and less atmospheric than some rivals, but the earliest and, notably, the last symphonies find Slatkin at his finest. His achievement in this cycle is above all to demonstrate that the last three symphonies make a worthy conclusion, unconventionally but tellingly symphonic. Fine playing and generally full, atmospheric recording. The six CDs are offered for the price of four.

By omitting the various fillers, Chandos have fitted the nine Vaughan Williams symphonies on to five CDs; each work is offered without a break. However, Bryden Thomson's achievement is somewhat uneven through the cycle. In the *Sea Symphony* the chorus lacks the sharpest focus and the microphone is not kind to Brian Rayner Cook, the baritone soloist. In the *Pastoral Symphony* the orchestral sound is almost too tangible, losing some of the more gentle atmospheric feeling, and this applies also to the *Sinfonia Antartica.* Generally there is no lack of power, and the readings certainly have both individuality and warmth and, of course, the advantage of modern, digital recording. But in the last resort both Previn and Boult have more to say and greater insights to express in this music.

A Sea Symphony (No. 1).
(M) **(*) EMI Dig. CD-EMX 2142. Rodgers, Shimell, Liverpool PO Ch., RLPO, Handley.
(N) (M) *** BBC Radio Classics 15656 91502 [id.]. Blighton, Cameron, New Zealand Christchurch Harmonic Ch., BBC Ch., BBC Choral Soc., BBC SO, Sargent.
(BB) (***) Belart mono 450 144-2. Baillie, Cameron, LPO Ch. & O, Boult.
*** EMI Dig. CDC7 49911-2 [id.]. Lott, Summers, LPO Ch., LPO, Haitink.
(M) *** RCA GD 90500 [60580-2-RG]. Harper, Shirley-Quirk, London Symphony Ch., LSO, Previn.
(M) *** EMI CDM7 64016-2 [id.]. Armstrong, Carol Case, LPO Ch., LPO, Boult.
*** RCA Dig. 09026 61197-2 [id.]. Benita Valente, Thomas Allen, Philh. Ch. & O, Leonard Slatkin.
(N) ** Teldec/Warner Dig. 4509 94550-2 [id.]. Roocroft, Hampson, BBC SO and Ch., Andrew Davis.

Vernon Handley conducts a warmly idiomatic performance, which sustains relatively slow speeds masterfully. The reading is crowned by Handley's rapt account of the slow movement, *On the beach at night alone,* as well as by the long duet in the finale, leading on through the exciting final ensemble, *Sail forth,* to a deeply satisfying culmination in *O my brave Soul!* Joan Rodgers makes an outstandingly beautiful soprano soloist, with William Shimell drier-toned but expressive. The recording, full and warm, presents problems in its extreme dynamic range, while placing the two soloists rather distantly. Yet to have such a performance in modern digital sound on a mid-price issue is self-recommending.

The *Sea Symphony* is just the work to bring out the best in Sargent, and though the radio sound (recorded in the Royal Festival Hall) is not as open as regular recordings, the electricity and passionate thrust of the performance make it compelling from first to last, with the sound of the massed choirs well caught. Speeds are more urgent than in most rival recordings, notably in the extended finale, which builds up rivetingly over its contrasted sections. Elaine Blighton and John Cameron are clear, sympathetic soloists.

As a performance, Boult's (early 1952) Decca mono recording with outstanding soloists and incisive and sympathetic singing from the LPO Choir has never been surpassed. However diffuse the argument may be, conveyed here is the kind of urgency one normally gets only at a live performance. The realistic presence of the dramatic opening has not lost its power to astonish. Boult was at his most inspired. This newly transferred Belart CD makes the very most of the master tape, and only the lack of body of the massed upper strings betrays the age of the original. The choral sound is full and well focused and the Kingsway Hall acoustic spacious and warm; the closing section, *Away O soul,* is particularly beautiful.

As in the rest of his Vaughan Williams series, Bernard Haitink takes what to traditional English ears may seem a very literal view, not at all idiomatic but strong and forthright. Speeds are almost all unusually spacious, making this (at well over 70 minutes) the slowest version on record; but Haitink sustains that expansive manner superbly. It is the nobility of the writing, rather than its emotional warmth, that is paramount. The recording is the fullest and weightiest yet given to this work, with the orchestra well defined in front of the chorus. Felicity Lott and Jonathan Summers are both excellent.

Previn does not always relax, even where, as in the slow movement, he takes a rather measured tempo. The finale similarly is built up over a longer span, with less deliberate expressiveness. The *Epilogue* may not be so deliberately expressive, but it is purer in its tenderness and exact control of dynamics. Previn has clear advantages in his baritone soloist and his choir. The rich ambience remains, with the performers set slightly back.

Boult's stereo version demonstrates his affectionate style, drawing consistently expressive but never sentimental phrasing from his singers and players. John Carol Case's baritone does not sound well on disc with his rather plaintive tone-colour, but his style is right, and Sheila Armstrong sings most beautifully. The set has been remastered with outstanding success.

With Slatkin drawing passionate playing and singing from his Philharmonia performers and with Thomas Allen outstanding among the baritones who have tackled this role, the RCA version is a strong contender. Slatkin's ability to lift the folk-like rhythms of the early Vaughan Williams makes for idiomatically expressive results, though he cannot match Handley, for example, in conveying the mystery behind some of these Whitman settings. The bright, clear tones of the soprano soloist, Benita Valente, are marred by an intrusive vibrato, robbing the sound of purity. The recording of the chorus is full and bright, with soloists balanced relatively close.

Helped by clear, finely focused sound, Andrew Davis conducts a performance that can hardly be faulted on any detail whatever but which fails quite to add up to the sum of its parts: it is a degree too literal. So you have two of the finest international soloists available who yet convey too little of the mystery behind these settings of Walt Whitman, and even with bright, clean choral sound one is less involved than with the finest rival versions.

A London Symphony (*No. 2;* original score).
(***) Biddulph mono WHL 016 [id.]. Cincinnati SO, Eugene Goossens – WALTON: *Violin concerto*
(***) (with Concert (***)).

This is the only recording ever made of the 1920 version of Vaughan Williams's *London Symphony*. That involves three minutes of intensely poetic music, later excised in RVW's definitive 1936 edition. The sessions immediately followed the first recording of the Walton *Violin concerto* with Heifetz in 1941 in which Goossens and the Cincinnati orchestra provided the accompaniment. The coupling (together with other British music) is among the most valuable of all the reissues in the Biddulph catalogue, for the CD transfers are of high quality.

A London Symphony (*No. 2*).
(M) **(*) EMI CDM5 65109-2 [id.]. Hallé O, Barbirolli – IRELAND: *London overture.* ***
(N) (BB) ** ASV Dig. CDQS 6162 [id.]. Philh. O, Arwel Hughes – ELGAR: *Cockaigne.* **

A London Symphony; (i) *Concerto accademico; The Wasps: Overture.*
(M) *** RCA GD 90501 [60581-2-RG]. LSO, Previn; (i) with James Buswell.

A London Symphony; Fantasia on a theme of Thomas Tallis.
(M) *** EMI CDM7 64017-2. LPO, Boult.
*** EMI CDC7 49394-2 [id.]. LPO, Haitink.

A London Symphony; (i) *The Lark ascending.*
*** Telarc Dig. CD 80158 [id.]. RPO, Previn; (i) with Barry Griffiths.

A London Symphony; Partita for double string orchestra.
(Y/B) (BB) *** Belart mono/stereo 461 008-2 [id.]. LPO, Sir Adrian Boult.

A London symphony; The Wasps: Overture.
(BB) *** Naxos Dig. 8.550734. Bournemouth SO, Kees Bakels.

Previn's Telarc version brings an exceptionally spacious reading, marked by a vivid and refined sound-balance, and the slow movement in particular brings a radiant, deeply poetic performance, caressing the ear. The faster movements consistently bring out the conductor's natural idiomatic feeling for this music, with rhythms nicely sprung – not least the sharp syncopations – and with melodies warmly moulded, though without sentimentality. Barry Griffiths' account of *The Lark ascending* is a welcome bonus, but it is not as instinctively rapturous a performance as those by Iona Brown or Warren-Green.

On RCA, though the actual sonorities are subtly and beautifully realized by Previn, the architecture is presented equally convincingly, with the great climaxes of the first and last movements powerful and incisive. Most remarkable of all are the pianissimos which here have great intensity, a quality of frisson as in a live performance. The LSO play superbly and the digitally remastered recording, made in

Kingsway Hall, still sounds well with its wide range of dynamic. The fill-ups are welcome, especially James Buswell's fine account of the *Concerto*.

The sound remains spacious on Boult's splendid 1970 version and the orchestral playing is outstandingly fine. The orchestra produces lovely sounds, the playing deeply committed; and criticism is disarmed. With Boult's noble, gravely intense account of the *Tallis fantasia* offered as a coupling, this remains an attractive alternative to Previn. The new CD transfer is remarkably successful.

In jaunty themes Haitink's straight manner at times brings an unexpected Stravinskian quality, and the expansively serene handling of the lovely melodies of the slow movement brings elegiac nobility rather than romantic warmth. In the *Tallis fantasia* the straight rhythmic manners make the result sound somewhat unidiomatic too, but very powerful in its monumental directness. The recording has spectacular range, though it is not quite as transparent or as atmospheric as Previn on Telarc.

The Naxos version of Vaughan Williams's *London Symphony*, coupled with the *Wasps Overture*, is powerful and dedicated. Kees Bakels draws ravishing sounds from the Bournemouth Symphony Orchestra, notably the strings, with the slow movement both warm-hearted and refined, and with pianissimos that have you catching the breath. The problem is the extraordinary range of dynamic in the recording. If you adjust the volume-level for the pianissimo at the start, you are quickly blasted out of your seat by the first fortissimo. A thrilling experience none the less, and throughout this is a performance to stimulate the ear, not least the Scherzo, which is full of atmosphere with VW's clever scoring very nicely realized.

In his 1968 EMI recording of the *London Symphony*, Barbirolli did not quite achieve the intensity of his earlier, Pye version (see below), choosing a more relaxed and spacious approach. In many places this brings a feeling of added authority, as at the end of the first movement where the threads are drawn together with striking breadth. The slow movement gains from the fuller recording but has less passion, while the Scherzo, taken relatively slowly, is more controversial. The powerful finale and finely graduated pages of the Epilogue make considerable amends, and this remains an impressive account.

Boult's 1952 recording of the *London Symphony* has great atmosphere and intensity. His later, EMI performance is warmer, but the voltage of this first LP version is very compelling, bringing the feeling of a live performance. The mono sound is spacious and basically full, but the violins sound very thin above the stave, and the remastering has not improved matters, especially in the glorious slow movement. But such is the magnetism of the music-making that the ear readily adjusts. The *Partita* was recorded in the earliest days of stereo in 1956. It is not one of the composer's most remarkable works (it was originally a double string trio) and it does not inspire Boult as does the symphony; but it is well played and the string sound here is more agreeable, if not outstanding.

Owain Arwel Hughes's version comes as the main component in a musical celebration of London, coupled with Elgar's *Cockaigne*. The orchestral sound is admirably refined but, with consistently slow speeds and rhythms often rather heavy, it cannot compare with the finest available. Recommendable to those who fancy the package.

(i) *A London Symphony (No. 2); Fantasia on Greensleeves; The Wasps Overture;* (ii) *Serenade to music.*
(M) (***) Dutton Laboratories mono CDAX 8004 [id.]. (i) Queen's Hall O; (ii) Isobel Baillie, Stiles Allen, Elsie Suddaby, Eva Turner, Margaret Balfour, Astra Desmond, Muriel Brunskill, Mary Jarred, Heddle Nash, Walter Widdop, Parry Jones, Frank Titterton, Roy Henderson, Robert Easton, Harold Williams, Norman Allin, BBC SO; Sir Henry Wood.

The historic Decca recording of Vaughan Williams's *London Symphony*, with the specially assembled group of musicians designated as the 'Queen's Hall Orchestra', conducted by Sir Henry Wood, brings a most striking discrepancy of pace with modern performances. The first movement alone takes over three minutes less than in most latter-day recordings. The not-so-slow introduction may lack mystery but there has never been a more passionate account of the work than this on record, and even with limited dynamic range – no true pianissimo is caught – the hushed intensity of the slow movement is tellingly conveyed in a way that only Barbirolli has since matched in his early stereo recording for Pye. The *Symphony* comes coupled with shorter Vaughan Williams works, *The Wasps Overture*, *Greensleeves* and, best of all, the original (1938) Columbia recording of the *Serenade to music*, with the 16 soloists specified in the score, a stellar group of quite remarkable distinction. The gently soaring phrase 'of sweet harmony' has never sounded so sweetly angelic as when sung here by Isobel Baillie. The Dutton Laboratory transfers are outstandingly true to the originals.

A London Symphony (No. 2); Fantasia on a theme of Thomas Tallis; Norfolk rhapsody.
**(*) RCA Dig. 09026 61193-2 [id.]. Philh. O, Slatkin.

Characteristically, Slatkin takes a brisk view of many of the themes of the *London Symphony*, opting for a direct rather than a warmly expressive style. The result is less atmospheric than with many rivals but, more than most, he keeps the work tautly symphonic. The sound is refined but not as immediate as it might be, except with the opulent Philharmonia brass. The coupling is unusual and generous, offering a refined rather than weighty account of the *Tallis Fantasia*, as well as the rare and attractive *Norfolk rhapsody*.

A London Symphony (No. 2); Symphony No. 8 in G min.
✸ (M) *** EMI CDM7 64197-2 [id.]. Hallé O, Sir John Barbirolli.
(M) *** EMI Dig. CD-EMX 2209; *TC-EMX 2209*. RLPO, Handley.
(Y/B) *(*) Teldec/Warner 4509 90858 [id.]. BBC SO, Andrew Davis.

Barbirolli's 1957 recording of the *London Symphony* was an inspirational performance, entirely throwing off the fetters of the studio. The reading gathers power as it proceeds and the slow movement has great intensity and eloquence, with the Hallé strings surpassing themselves; its climax sounds surprisingly full. Indeed the recording, besides having a wide dynamic range, has plenty of atmosphere and warmth. The digital remastering is wholly successful, with the background subdued. The new coupling of the *Eighth Symphony* makes the CD doubly attractive. 'Glorious John' (the composer's appreciative description of the work's dedicatee) gave its première, and this record was made (by Mercury engineers) just a month afterwards. It is a robust performance rather than a subtle one, but full of character and feeling, matched by most vivid sound. For many, this will be regarded as a first choice for both these works.

Vernon Handley gives a beautifully paced and well-sprung reading of the *London Symphony*, not as crisp in ensemble as some and with the sound diffused rather than sharply focused. The result is warmly sympathetic and can be strongly recommended, if the generous coupling of the *Eighth Symphony*, an underestimated work, is preferred.

The Teldec recording has magnificent presence and definition. This would be a front runner if the performances had been of equal quality. Of course there are good things – in particular the Scherzo of the *London Symphony*. There is impressive atmosphere at the very beginning of the symphony, but as a whole this is no match in terms of grip or concentration for the best rivals – and certainly not for Barbirolli's remarkable EMI (originally Pye) version.

(i) *A Pastoral Symphony (No. 3); Symphony No. 4 in F min.*
(M) *** RCA GD 90503 [60583-2-RG]. (i) Heather Harper; LSO, Previn.
(M) *** EMI Dig. CD-EMX 2192. (i) Barlow; RLPO, Vernon Handley.

(i) *A Pastoral Symphony (No. 3); Symphony No. 4 in F min.; Fantasia on Greensleeves.*
**(*) RCA Dig. 09026 61194-2 [id.]. (i) Linda Hohenfield; Philh. O, Slatkin.

Previn draws an outstandingly beautiful and refined performance from the LSO, the bare textures sounding austere but never thin, the few climaxes emerging at full force with purity undiminished. In the *F minor Symphony* only the somewhat ponderous tempo Previn adopts for the first movement lets it down. But on the whole this is a powerful reading, and it is vividly recorded.

Although Vernon Handley's speeds are relatively fast – as those of his mentor, Boult, tended to be – he has the benefit of refined modern digital recording to help bring out the element of mystery in the *Pastoral Symphony*. The extra bite and warmth of expressiveness in Previn's view brings even greater dividends in the *Fourth Symphony*, when he sustains generally slower speeds. Handley's approach is lighter and less violent. But in a symphony that is less brutal than was originally thought, there is a case for this sympathetic alternative approach.

Taking his cue from the composer's own recording of the *Fourth Symphony*, Slatkin's speeds not just for that violent work but for the elusive *Pastoral Symphony* are consistently on the fast side. In the *Pastoral* it tends to mean – as it did even with Boult – that mystery is lacking and, though the *Fourth* gains in power and urgency, the rhythms are sprung less infectiously. The recording is atmospheric but clearly focused, which helps the *Fourth* more than its predecessor. In this coupling the older, RCA version from Previn and the LSO offers even more powerful, dramatic and evocative performances, with 1960s sound still giving a vivid illusion of presence.

(i) *A Pastoral Symphony (No. 3); (ii) Symphony No. 5 in D.*
(M) *** EMI CDM7 64018-2. (i) Margaret Price, New Philh. O; (ii) LPO, Sir Adrian Boult.
(N) (BB) (***) Belart mono 461 118-2. (i) Margaret Ritchie; LPO, Boult.

On EMI, in the *Pastoral Symphony* Boult is not entirely successful in controlling the tension of the short but elusive first movement, although it is beautifully played. The opening of the *Lento moderato*, however, is very fine, and its close is sustained with a perfect blend of restraint and intensity. Boult gives a loving and gentle performance of No. 5, easier and more flowing than most rivals', and some may prefer it for that reason, but the emotional involvement is a degree less intense, particularly in the slow movement. Both recordings have been very successfully remastered.

It is good to have the earlier, Kingsway Hall recordings back in the catalogue. They were made in 1952/3 with the composer present; although some allowances have to be made for the lack of amplitude in the upper string climaxes, the present transfer is impressively full and the recording is basically full and luminous. The translucent textures Boult creates in the *Pastoral Symphony* (the opening is hauntingly ethereal) and his essential delicacy of approach are balanced by his intensity in the *Fifth*, where the climax of the first movement has wonderful breadth and passion. The LPO play with great sympathy and warmth in music that was still new, the *Fifth* only a decade old, at the time this record was made.

A Pastoral Symphony (No. 3); Symphony No. 6 in E min.
(Y/B) (BB) **(*) Naxos Dig. 8.550733 [id.]. Bournemouth SO, Kees Bakels.

Kees Bakels' serenely expressive account of the *Pastoral* has moments of drama to heighten its quiet intensity of atmosphere. There is much lovely orchestral playing, with the soloists in the Bournemouth Symphony Orchestra very sympathetic to the music's subtle, lyrical resonance. The account of the *Sixth* does not catch the degree of underlying menace in the *Lento* second movement that seemed so prophetic at the symphony's broadcast première (under Boult) but the performance overall has plenty of life and vigour, and Bakels sustains the epilogue with an ethereal, glowing pianissimo. First-rate Naxos recording in both works.

Symphony No. 4 in F min.; Fantasia on Greensleeves; Fantasia on a theme of Thomas Tallis; (i) Serenade to music.
(Y/B) (M) *** Sony SMK 47638 [id.]. NYPO, Bernstein; (i) with Addison, Amara, Farrell, Chookasian, Tourel, Verrett-Carter, Bressler, Tucker, Vickers, London, Flagello, Bell.

This is one of the most rewarding of the reissues in the Bernstein Edition. The account of the *Fourth Symphony* is strangely impressive. Bernstein's first movement is slower than usual but powerful and very well controlled; he captures the flavour and intensity of the score as well as the brooding intensity of the slow movement. The New York orchestra play very well indeed, particularly in the extremely characterful Scherzo. This is a thoroughly competitive reading, freshly thought out and with a compelling integrity to commend it. The 1965 Avery Fisher recording, though not first class, is very well transferred. The *Tallis fantasia*, spacious and essentially serene, is just short of being romantic but retains its elegiac atmosphere. Here the venue is the more resonant Manhattan Center, and the 1976 sound is full and rich-textured. The *Greensleeves fantasia*, also taken expansively, uses a solo violin in its central section. The performance of the *Serenade* features a star-studded cast and, though they are rather forwardly balanced, the ambience has agreeable warmth and the performance catches the work's radiance, with Adele Addison singing Portia's closing solo (*Soft stillness and the night*) quite beautifully.

Symphonies Nos. (i) 4 in F min.; (ii) 5 in D.
(Y/B) (M) (***) Dutton Lab. mono CDAX 8011 [id.]. (i) BBC SO, composer; (ii) Hallé O, Barbirolli.
(Y/B) ** Teldec/Warner Dig. 4509 90844-2 [id.]. BBC SO, Andrew Davis.

In 1937 Vaughan Williams recorded his violent *Fourth Symphony* with the BBC Symphony Orchestra, then at its pre-war peak, and he proved a bitingly urgent inspirer. This historic recording has been transferred to CD by Michael Dutton in astonishingly full-bodied sound, bringing out the high voltage of the playing, never quite matched since on record. Aiming to shock, RVW said he wasn't sure he liked the piece, but it was what he meant. After that, the *Fifth Symphony*, inspired by Bunyan, held no shocks; but, more than anyone, Sir John Barbirolli in this première recording of 1944, made in the year following its first performance, brings out a rare passion behind the seamless pastoral idiom. The great climaxes in the first and third movements are more red-blooded than in any recordings since. Though the string-playing of the wartime Hallé may not be as immaculate as one would expect today, this inspired performance, vividly transferred, has one consistently magnetized.

Though Andrew Davis draws beautiful, refined playing from the BBC orchestra in both symphonies, there is a lack of dramatic tension, which – particularly in the violent No. 4 – prevents the performance from catching fire. One can pick out many passages which, with the help of superb recorded sound, are as beautiful as any ever recorded, but the parts do not add up to a satisfying whole.

Symphonies Nos. 4 in F min.; 6 in E min.
(M) **(*) EMI CDM7 64019-2 [id.]. New Philh. O, Sir Adrian Boult.
(N) (BB) (**(*)) Belart mono 461 117-2 [id.]. LPO, Boult (with speech by the composer).

Symphony Nos. (i) *4 in F min.;* (ii) *6 in E min.;* (i) *Fantasia on a theme by Thomas Tallis.*
(B) (***) Sony mono SBK 62754; *SBT 62754* [id.]. NYPO, (i) Mitropoulos; (ii) Stokowski.

The recordings of Vaughan Williams's two apocalyptic symphonies made by the New York Philharmonic – No. 4 conducted in 1956 by Dmitri Mitropoulos (in a reading approved by the composer himself) and No. 6 in 1949 by Stokowski (directing with unsentimental thrust) – make a fascinating coupling. As transferred to CD they sound far better than they ever did on LP. Both demonstrate what idiomatic power and brilliance American players could bring to the composer's two most abrasive symphonies. Stokowski's reading is the more controversial, disconcertingly fast in the slow movement and unpointed in the slow, visionary finale. Mitropoulos in a generous fill-up shows equal understanding of the rarefied *Tallis Fantasia.* Not to be missed – truly an 'Essential Classic'.

In the *Fourth Symphony* Sir Adrian procures orchestral playing of the highest quality from the New Philharmonia, and the slow movement is particularly successful. The recording, too, is first class, and this increases the sense of attack in the first movement of the powerful *Sixth Symphony.* Here, the strange finale is played beautifully, and the atmosphere is not without a sense of mystery, but a greater degree of underlying tension is needed.

On Belart, Boult, as ever, shows himself to be a master interpreter of Vaughan Williams, but in the tearingly dramatic *Fourth Symphony* the age of the recording and its relative lack of amplitude blunt the fullness of the work's impact, powerful as it still is. The performance of the *Sixth* is another matter: it drew from Boult and the LPO some of the very finest and most committed playing in the whole cycle; certainly Boult never matched it in his later recording for EMI. After the ebullience of the first movement comes the frightening warning of the slow movement, with its slow triplet rhythm built into a climax of the utmost menace. Following the brash and popular Scherzo the work closes in a mood of almost complete desolation which is wonderfully sustained here and brings a spoken eulogy of praise from the composer, who was present at the sessions. Here the Decca mono recording is very impressive indeed.

Symphonies Nos. (i) *4 in F min;* (ii) *8 in D min.*
(N) (M) **(*) BBC Radio Classics 15656 91312 [id.]. BBC SO; (i) Sargent; (ii) Stokowski.

These Prom performances, recorded respectively in 1963 and 1964, have a warmth and fiery thrust that are instantly compelling, amply compensating for incidental shortcomings such as imprecise ensemble and audience noise. Sargent is here far more electrifying than he generally was in the recording studio, bringing out the biting urgency of the inspiration in this darkest of the VW symphonies. Stokowski is even more magnetic, shaping each phrase magically, terracing the big contrasts to give cogency to the free structure and consistently challenging his players, as in the hectic speed for the woodwind Scherzo.

Symphony No. 5 in D; The England of Elizabeth: 3 Portraits (arr. Mathieson).
(M) *** RCA GD 90506 [60586-2-RG]. LSO, Previn.

Symphony No. 5 in D; (i) *Flos campi* (suite).
❀ (M) *** EMI Dig. CD-EMX 9512; TC-EMX 2112 [Ang. CDM 62029]. RLPO, Handley; (i) with Christopher Balmer & Liverpool Philharmonic Ch.

Symphony No. 5 in D; (i) *The Lark ascending. Norfolk rhapsody.*
(N) *** EMI Dig. CDC5 55487-2 [id.]. LPO, Haitink, (i) with Sarah Chang.

Vernon Handley's disc is outstanding in every way, a spacious yet concentrated reading, superbly played and recorded, which masterfully holds the broad structure of this symphony together, building to massive climaxes. The warmth and poetry of the work are also beautifully caught. The rare and evocative *Flos campi*, inspired by the Song of Solomon, makes a generous and attractive coupling, equally well played, though the viola solo is rather closely balanced. The sound is outstandingly full, giving fine clarity of texture.

Previn refuses to be lured into pastoral byways. His tempi may be consistently on the slow side, but the purity of tone he draws from the LSO, the precise shading of dynamic and phrasing, and the sustaining of tension through the longest, most hushed passages produce an outstanding performance, very well transferred to CD. Previn's later, Telarc version with the RPO does not match this in raptness and emotional thrust. The *England of Elizabeth suite* is a film score of no great musical interest but is undoubtedly pleasant to listen to.

Haitink's measured, dedicated view of VW, broad and steady in tempo, goes with beautiful playing from the LPO, notably in extreme pianissimos from the refined string section. This may not be as passionate as some other versions in climaxes, but it compensates in monumental strength. After the measured speeds in earlier movements, the finale brings extra purposefulness in a flowing tempo. Haitink draws out comparable qualities in the rare *Norfolk rhapsody*, while Sarah Chang proves an intensely poetic soloist in *The Lark ascending*, volatile at the start in the bird-like fluttering motif and magnetically concentrated throughout. Full, atmospheric recording to match.

Symphony No. 5 in D; (i) *Sancta civitas.*
(N) (M) **(*) BBC Radio Classics BBCRD 9125 [id.]. BBC SO, Rozhdestvensky, (i) with Gareth Roberts, Brian Rayner Cook, BBC Singers, BBC SO Ch.

Rozhdestvensky, a passionate interpreter of English music as he is of Russian, here gives a rich, thrusting account of the *Fifth* in which he resolves the big climaxes in the first and third movements with a heartfelt warmth to remind one of Barbirolli, who made the first ever recording. Only in the finale does the performance momentarily lack focus, before the conductor's passion thrusts forward again. Though the radio recording could be more open, string-tone is most refined. *Sancta civitas* makes a generous and apt coupling, with visionary intensity reinforced by red-blooded passion, with dramatic contrasts underlined.

Symphonies Nos. 5 in D; 6 in E min.
**(*) RCA Dig. RD 60556 [60556-2-RD]. Philh. O, Leonard Slatkin.

Except in the third movement *Romanza* of No. 5 and the pianissimo finale of No. 6 Slatkin opts for speeds on the fast side, yet with his preference for keeping a very steady beat, he remains a restrained interpreter of RVW. The big climaxes of the *Preludio* in No. 5 and of the *Romanza* lack the emotional weight they can have, and the second movement of No. 6 with its insistent anapaestic interruptions lacks menace. Yet there is still much to enjoy in these performances, with refined and intensely beautiful string playing from the Philharmonia.

Symphony No. 6 in E min.; Fantasia on a theme of Thomas Tallis; (i) *The Lark ascending.*
*** Teldec/Warner Dig. 9031 73127-2 [id.]. (i) Tasmin Little; BBC SO, Andrew Davis.

Andrew Davis's reading of the *Sixth* is taut and urgent, with emotions kept under firm control. The two shorter works which come as supplement are given more warmly expressive, exceptionally beautiful performances, with Tasmin Little an immaculate soloist in *The Lark ascending*. Teldec's wide-ranging sound, setting the orchestra at a slight distance, slightly blunts the impact of the symphony in the first three movements, but then works beautifully in the chill of the hushed pianissimo meditation of the finale, as it does too in the fill-ups.

Symphonies Nos. 6 in E min.; 9 in E min.
(M) *** RCA GD 90508 [60588-2-RG]. LSO, Previn.
(N) (M) *** EMI Dig. CD-EMX 2230; *TC-EMX 2230* [id.]. RLPO, Vernon Handley.

In the first three movements Previn's performance is superbly dramatic, clear-headed and direct, with natural understanding. His account of the mystical final movement with its endless pianissimo is not, however, on the same level, for the playing is not quite hushed enough, and the tempo is a little too fast. The *Ninth* stimulates Previn to show a freshness and sense of poetry which prove particularly thought-provoking and rewarding. The RCA recording is highly successful.

Handley, with rich, full recording, gives warm-hearted readings of Nos. 6 and 9, two works that in their layout – both ending on measured, visionary slow movements – can be seen as related, quite apart from sharing the same key. Next to Previn in the same coupling, Handley lacks some of the darker, sharper qualities implied. Though his speeds are consistently faster, he is more comfortable, and the recording adds to that impression. Handley's approach is a valid one, when the slow pianissimo finale, here presented as mysterious rather than desolate, was inspired not by a world laid waste by nuclear war, but by Prospero's 'cloud-capp'd towers' in Shakespeare's *The Tempest*.

Sinfonia Antartica (No. 7).
*** EMI Dig. CDC7 47516-2 [id.]. Sheila Armstrong, LPO Ch., LPO, Haitink.

(i) *Sinfonia Antartica (No. 7); Five Variations of Dives and Lazarus; Sea songs* (Quick march).
**(*) RCA Dig. 09026 61195-2 [id.]. (i) Linda Hohenfield; Women of Philh. Ch.; Philh. O, Slatkin.

(i) *Sinfonia Antartica (No. 7); Serenade to music.*
(M) *** EMI Dig. CD-EMX 2173. (i) Alison Hargan; RLPO and Ch., Vernon Handley.

(i) *Sinfonia Antartica (No. 7); The Wasps* (incidental music): *Overture and suite.*
(M) **(*) EMI CDM7 64020-2 [id.]. (i) Sheila Armstrong; LPO, Sir Adrian Boult.

With stunningly full and realistic recording, Haitink directs a revelatory performance of what has long been thought of as merely a programmatic symphony. Based on material from VW's film music for *Scott of the Antarctic*, the symphony is in fact a work which, as Haitink demonstrates, stands powerfully as an original inspiration in absolute terms. Only in the second movement does the 'penguin' music seem heavier than it should be, but even that acquires new and positive qualities, thanks to Haitink.

As in his other Vaughan Williams recordings, Handley shows a natural feeling for expressive rubato and draws refined playing from the Liverpool orchestra. At the end of the epilogue Alison Hargan makes a notable first appearance on disc, a soprano with an exceptionally sweet and pure voice. In well-balanced digital sound it makes an outstanding bargain, particularly when it offers an excellent fill-up, the *Serenade to music*, though in this lovely score a chorus never sounds as characterful as a group of well-chosen soloists. This can be recommended alongside Haitink but costs much less.

Sir Adrian gives a stirring account and is well served by the E M I engineers. The inclusion of Vaughan Williams's Aristophanic suite, *The Wasps*, with its endearing participation of the kitchen utensils plus its indelibly tuneful *Overture*, is a bonus, although in the *Overture* the upper strings sound a bit thin.

The Slatkin version offers an exceptionally strong and dramatic account of the *Sinfonia Antartica* which, thanks to speeds brisker than usual, notably in the first movement, is presented as a symphonic structure rather than a programme work, just a series of atmospheric sound-pictures. The slow movement may not convey the same chill as other versions, with the cleanly focused recording dispelling mistiness, but the originality of instrumentation adds to a feeling of tautness in the argument, not usually conveyed in this work. The soprano soloist could also sound more mysterious, but she sings with bright, clear tone. The couplings, idiomatically done, are unusual and attractive.

Sinfonia Antartica (No. 7).
(N) (BB) *** RCA Navigator 74321 29248-2. Heather Harper, Ralph Richardson, London Symphony Ch., LSO, André Previn – WALTON: *Cello concerto*. ***

(i) *Sinfonia Antartica (No. 7); Symphony No. 8 in D min.*
(M) *** RCA GD 90510 [60590-2-RG]. (i) Harper, Richardson, London Symphony Ch.; LSO, Previn.

In the *Sinfonia Antartica* Previn's interpretation concentrates on atmosphere rather than drama in a performance that is sensitive and literal. Because of the recessed effect of the sound, the portrayal of the ice-fall (represented by the sudden entry of the organ) has a good deal less impact than on Vernon Handley's version. Before each movement Sir Ralph Richardson speaks the superscription written by the composer on his score. Previn's account of the *Eighth* brings no reservations, with finely pointed playing, the most precise control of dynamic shading, and a delightfully Stravinskian account of the bouncing Scherzo for woodwind alone. Excellent recording, which has been opened up by the digital remastering and made to sound more expansive. As can be seen, Previn's *Sinfonia Antartica* is also available coupled with Walton's *Cello concerto* – a real bargain on RCA's super-budget Navigator label.

Symphonies Nos. 8 in D min.; 9 in E min.
(M) *** EMI CDM7 64021-2 [id.]. LPO, Sir Adrian Boult.

Symphonies Nos. 8 in D min.; 9 in E min.; Flourish for Glorious John.
*** RCA Dig. 09026 61196 [id.]. Philh. O, Slatkin.

The concluding disc brings a deeply satisfying culmination to Slatkin's Vaughan Williams cycle, arguably the finest of all, brilliantly played and recorded. The *Flourish*, never previously recorded, is a 90-second work that says much more than its brevity might suggest, a tribute to Sir John Barbirolli that seems almost to present the composer's work in microcosm. Both the last two symphonies are seriously underestimated, and Slatkin's bitingly intense performances, adopting speeds faster than usual, give them a tautness that has rarely been appreciated. So the finales of both symphonies prove exceptionally satisfying, not just the bell-like ostinatos of No. 8 but the elusive string-writing of No. 9, which here emerges as a close relation to the visionary slow finale of No. 6. Bright, immediate recording, with more presence than in most of the series, and splendid playing.

Boult's account of the *Eighth* may not be as sharply pointed as Slatkin's version, but some will prefer the extra warmth of the Boult interpretation with its rather more lyrical approach. The *Ninth* contains much noble and arresting invention, and Boult's performance is fully worthy of it. He draws most committed playing from the LPO, and the recording is splendidly firm in tone. The digital remastering is well up to the high standard EMI have set with these reissues of Boult's recordings.

Symphony No. 9 in E min.
(Y/B) **(*) Everest EVC 9001 [id.]. LPO, Boult – ARNOLD: *Symphony No. 3*. **(*)

Boult's first stereo record of the *Ninth* on Everest is prefaced on CD by a brief speech from the conductor, regretting the composer's death seven months before the recording was undertaken. The sound was very good for its day with a wide dynamic range, and it sounds even better now, although the actual tonal quality has not the warmth and lustre of more recent versions of the work. Boult's interpretation changed very little over the years; this early version seems tauter than the later remake for EMI, but this may be partly the effect of the less expansive sound.

CHAMBER MUSIC

(i) *Phantasy quintet* (for 2 violins, 2 violas & cello); *String quartet No. 2 in A min. (For Jean on her birthday);* (ii; iii) *6 Studies in English folk-song for cello and piano;* (iii; iv) *Violin sonata in A.*
(M) *** EMI CDM5 65100-2 [id.]. (i) Music Group of London; (ii) Eileen Croxford; (iii) David Parkhouse; (iv) Hugh Bean.

This collection of relatively little-known chamber works, very well performed and recorded at Abbey Road in 1972/3, can be recommended strongly – and not only to devotees of Vaughan Williams. The *Phantasy quintet* dates from the composer's full maturity in 1912. It is conceived in a compressed one-movement form but falls into four distinct sections: these to be played (attacca) without a break, as advocated by W. W. Cobbett. The ethereal opening is Vaughan Williams at his most ecstatically pastoral in feeling, and the *Alla Sarabanda* third section is also very beautiful. The *Six studies in English folk-song* are highly characteristic, while the *Violin sonata* (1954) is a relatively gawky work but one which, like much later Vaughan Williams, has a tangily distinctive flavour, especially in a performance as fine as this. The *Second quartet*, written between the *Fifth* and *Sixth Symphonies*, was offered as a birthday present to a viola player friend of the composer, Jean Stewart. It contains some strikingly original ideas, notably in the purposefully sombre but bleakly haunting *Largo* with its harmonium-like textures and, in the plangent Scherzo, with its *tremolandos* and *sul ponticello* devices. The performances by the Music Group of London bring out the deeper qualities of both this and the richly scored *Quintet*.

6 Studies in English folksong for clarinet and piano.
*** Chandos Dig. CHAN 8683 [id.]. Hilton, Swallow – BAX: *Sonata* **(*); BLISS: *Quintet*. ***

These *Folksong studies*, which Vaughan Williams published in arrangements for the viola and cello, come from the mid-1920s and are really very beautiful; they are played with the utmost sensitivity by Janet Hilton and Keith Swallow.

VOCAL MUSIC

(i) *10 Blake songs* (for voice and oboe); (ii) *Songs of travel.* Songs: *Linden Lea; Orpheus with his lute; The water mill; Silent noon.*
(M) *** Decca 430 368-2. Robert Tear; (i) Neil Black; (ii) Philip Ledger – BUTTERWORTH: *Shropshire lad.* ***

Robert Tear, recorded in 1972, cannot match Ian Partridge in his wonderfully sensitive account (currently withdrawn) of the *Blake songs*, but his rougher-grained voice brings out a different kind of expressiveness, helped by Neil Black's fine oboe playing. The *Songs of travel*, here presented complete with the five extra songs published later, are also most welcome, as are the other four songs, notably *Silent noon*, added for this reissue. Ledger is a most perceptive accompanist.

(i) *3 Choral hymns (Easter hymn; Christmas hymn; Whitsunday hymn);* (ii) *Communion service in G min.:* Sanctus. (i) *Come down, O love divine.* (ii) *Festival Te deum.* (i) *For all the Saints; O taste and see; Prayer to the Father; Te deum in G; Valiant for truth; We've been awhile a-wandering; Wither's Rocking hymn.*
(M) ** Chandos CHAN 6550 [id.]. (i) Worcester Cathedral Ch., Christopher Robinson; H. Bramma; (ii) Westminster Abbey Ch., Douglas Guest.

A useful if not distinctive collection of Vaughan Williams's shorter choral works. Besides the short *Te Deum* and the *Festival Te Deum*, among the more striking settings is *Valiant for truth*, a much subtler piece than its Salvation Army-like title would suggest. The three *Choral hymns* are spaciously conceived but would have benefited from a recording with more bite. As it is, the sound is atmospheric but not very clear in detail. The performances generally are of a good standard. The documentation provides all the words but no comments about the settings.

Dona nobis pacem; 4 Hymns; Lord, Thou hast been our refuge (Psalm 90); O clap your hands (Psalm 47); Toward the unknown region.
(N) *** Hyperion Dig. CDA 66655 [id.]. Judith Howarth, John Mark Ainsley, Thomas Allen, Corydon Singers & O, Matthew Best.

Using a relatively small choir and orchestra, Best takes an intimate view of *Dona nobis pacem* but one which as a result is even sharper in focus, capturing the dramatic contrasts as a big performance would, with words unusually clear. The sweet-toned Judith Howarth and the warmly expressive Thomas Allen are ideal soloists. *Toward the unknown region* was VW's first big choral work, not as distinctive as his later music but with many typical fingerprints. Best brings out the beauty of the choral writing, as he does in the even rarer *Four Hymns* for tenor, viola and strings, which the composer intended as a counterpart to the *Five Mystical songs*. Ainsley is the clear tenor soloist, though strained just a little at the top. The setting of *Psalm 90* is the more effective here for having, instead of a semi-chorus, the optional baritone soloist, with Allen again singing with deep dedication. Another welcome issue in Best's excellent Vaughan Williams series for Hyperion.

Dona nobis pacem; 5 Mystical songs.
*** Chandos Dig. CHAN 8590 [id.]. Wiens, Rayner-Cook, LPO Ch., LPO, Bryden Thomson.

The *Dona nobis pacem* is well performed on this Chandos disc by Edith Wiens and Bryan Rayner-Cook. The latter gives an eloquent account of the much earlier *Five Mystical songs*. Bryden Thomson gets playing of total commitment from the London Philharmonic Orchestra. The recording is made in an appropriately resonant acoustic and the orchestral detail registers well.

(i; ii) *Dona nobis pacem;* (ii; iii) *Sancta civitas.*
(N) *** EMI CDC7 544788-2 [id.]. (i) Yvonne Kenny; (ii) Bryn Terfel; (iii) Philip Langridge, St Paul's Cathedral Choristers; L. Symphony Ch., LSO, Hickox.

These two visionary masterpieces, both seriously neglected, both with Latin titles and both dating from the interwar period, make an ideal and generous coupling. Drawing passionate performances from his choir and soloists (notably from Bryn Terfel in both works), Hickox brings out not only the visionary intensity and atmospheric beauty – as in the offstage trumpets and '*Alleluias*' near the start of *Sancta civitas* – but also the dramatic power. Both these works may be predominantly meditative, but they have moments of violence which relate directly to the dark side of VW, as expressed in the *Fourth Symphony*, such as the chorus, '*Beat! beat! drums!*', the second section of *Sancta civitas*. In that same work it is fascinating to have the words '*Babylon the great is fallen*' set as a hushed lament instead of as a shout of triumph, as in Walton's *Belshazzar's Feast*. Hickox is a degree broader in his speeds than previous interpreters on disc, but is all the warmer for it.

(i) *Epithalamion;* (ii) *Merciless Beauty.*
(M) *** EMI Dig./Analogue CDM7 64730-2 [id.]. (i) Roberts, Shelley, Bach Ch., LPO, Willcocks; (ii) Langridge, Endellion Qt – *Riders to the sea.* ***

Vaughan Williams's setting of *Epithalamion* began life as a masque in the late 1930s and, only a year before he died, he expanded it into the coolly lyrical cantata recorded here. Scored for baritone and small orchestra with piano (Howard Shelley quite superb) and solo parts for flute and viola, it is an eloquent and thoroughly characteristic piece. Stephen Roberts gives a beautiful account of it, and Philip Langridge is hardly less impressive in *Merciless beauty*, three much earlier settings for voice and string trio. *Riders to the sea* is also indispensable – see below. This reissue makes a most valuable addition to the Vaughan Williams discography. The first two works were recorded digitally; *Riders to the sea* is analogue (1970) but sounds equally vivid and well focused. Splendid performances throughout.

(i) *Fantasia on Christmas carols;* (ii) *Flos Campi;* (i) *5 Mystical songs;* (iii) *Serenade to music.*
*** Hyperion Dig. CDA 66420 [id.]. (i) Thomas Allen, (ii) Imai & Corydon Singers; (iii) 16 soloists; ECO, Best.

This radiant record centres round the *Serenade to music* and, as in the original performance, sixteen star soloists are here lined up; though the team of women does not quite match the stars of 1938, the men are generally fresher and clearer. Above all, thanks largely to fuller, modern recording, the result is much more sensuous than the original, with ensemble better matched and with Matthew Best drawing glowing sounds from the English Chamber Orchestra. The other items are superbly done too, with Nobuko Imai a powerful viola soloist in the mystical cantata, *Flos campi*, another Vaughan Williams masterpiece. Thomas Allen is the characterful soloist in the five *Mystical songs*. Warmly atmospheric sound to match the performances.

Fantasia on Christmas carols; Hodie.
**(*) EMI Dig. CDC7 54128-2 [id.]. Gale, Tear, Roberts, London Symphony Ch., LSO, Hickox.

Though the three soloists cannot match the original trio in Sir David Willcocks's pioneering version (on EMI, now withdrawn), Hickox directs a more urgent and more freely expressive reading of the big Christmas cantata, *Hodie*, helped by more refined and incisive choral singing. As on the earlier disc, the *Christmas carol fantasia* proves an ideal coupling, also warmly done.

(i) *Flos campi. Household music (3 Preludes on Welsh hymn tunes).*
(N) *** Chandos Dig. CHAN 9392 [id.]. (i) Philip Dukes, N. Sinfonia, Richard Hickox – *Riders to the sea.* ***

Philip Dukes proves a rich and eloquent viola soloist in *Flos campi*, in which the Northern Sinfonia Chorus is balanced more forwardly and powerfully than usual, and this is a remarkably successful performance on all counts. The *Household music*, never recorded before, offers three delightful miniatures, written in 1941 as a wartime exercise, intended for amateur musicians as well as professionals.

Alfred Deller Edition: Arrangements of folksongs (with Deller Consort, Desmond Dupré, lute): *An acre of land; Bushes and briars; Ca' the yowes; The cuckoo and the nightingale; The dark-eyed sailor; Down by the riverside; A farmer's son so sweet; Greensleeves; John Dory; Just as the tide was flowing; The jolly ploughboy; Loch Lomond; The lover's ghost; My boy Billy; The painful plough; The spring time of the year; The turtle dove; Ward the pirate; Wassail song.*
(Y/B) (M) ** Van. 08.5073.71 [id.].

These highly artistic folksong settings can be effectively performed either by choir or by soloists. Although basically Deller allocates one voice to each part, there are some doublings where – for example – the two voices do not blend well. The spirit in which these settings are performed is, however, admirable. Deller himself sings *Down by the riverside* as a solo, with lute accompaniment, and this is effectively followed by the gentle choral version of *Bushes and briars*. Similarly, Deller's *My boy Billy* is followed by the atmospheric *The spring time of the year*, and the solo *The cuckoo and the nightingale* by the choral *Loch Lomond*, one of the most enjoyable arrangements here. The recording is a little dry, but the stereo adds to the sense of atmosphere.

Folksong arrangements: *An acre of land; Bushes and briars* (2 versions); *Ca' the yowes; Early in the spring; 5 English folksongs (The dark-eyed sailor; The spring time of the year; Just as the tide was flowing; The lover's ghost; Wassail song* (2 versions)); *Greensleeves; John Dory; Loch Lomond; The seeds of love; The turtle dove; The unquiet grave; Ward the pirate.*
(N) (M) *** EMI CMS5 65123-2 (2) [id.]. London Madrigal Singers, Bishop – HOLST: *Choral songs;* ELGAR: *Part-songs* etc. ***

As recording manager, Christopher Bishop has supervised many fine records of Vaughan Williams's music (as well as much else); here, with a choir of hand-picked singers, he shows that he is a first-rate interpreter of the composer in his own right. This is a delightful collection of part-songs, far more varied than one might expect. There is nothing at all pretentious about the settings and each one shows subtly the distinction of RVW's mind, never falling into mere routine. The singing of the London Madrigal Singers is admirably lithe and sensitive, and this is altogether a lovely recital, beautifully engineered. Additional performances of *Bushes and briars* and the *Wassail song* in their versions for men's voices (the latter arranged by Herbert Pierce) come as part of the second half of this collection. This includes music by Elgar, Howells, Bax, Delius, Britten and Warlock, sung no less impressively by the Baccholian Singers of London. An invaluable reissue.

Lord Thou hast been our refuge; Prayer to the Father of Heaven; A vision of aeroplanes.
*** Chandos Dig. CHAN 9019 [id.]. Finzi Singers, Spicer – HOWELLS: *Requiem* etc. ***

These three choral pieces make an apt coupling for the Howells choral works on the Finzi Singers' disc. *A vision of aeroplanes* improbably but most imaginatively uses a text from Ezekiel.

Mass in G min.; Te Deum in C.
*** Hyperion CDA 66076 [id.]. Corydon Singers, Best – HOWELLS: *Requiem.* ***

Matthew Best and the Corydon Singers give as committed an account of the *Mass* as King's College Choir and, despite the spacious acoustic, there is admirable clarity of texture.

5 Mystical songs; O clap your hands.
(N) (M) *** EMI CDM5 65588-2 [id.]. John Shirley-Quirk, King's College, Cambridge, Ch., ECO, Willcocks – FINZI: *Dies natalis;* HOLST: *Choral fantasia; Psalm 86.* ***

In the *Five Mystical songs* to words by George Herbert, John Shirley-Quirk sings admirably, and the motet, *O clap your hands*, makes a fine bonus for a recommendable triptych of English vocal works.

(i) *On Wenlock Edge;* (ii) *Songs of travel* (song-cycles).
(M) *** EMI Dig. CDM7 64731-2 [id.]. (i) Robert Tear; (ii) Thomas Allen, CBSO, Rattle – BUTTERWORTH; ELGAR: *Songs.* ***

Vaughan Williams's own orchestration of his famous song-cycle, made in the early 1920s, has been curiously neglected. It lacks something of the apt, ghostly quality of the version for piano and string quartet, but some will prefer the bigger scale. The orchestral version brings home the aptness of treating the nine songs as a cycle, particularly when the soloist is as characterful and understanding a singer as Thomas Allen. The Housman settings in the other cycle are far better-known, and Robert Tear – who earlier recorded this same orchestral version with Vernon Handley and the Birmingham orchestra – again proves a deeply perceptive soloist, with his sense of atmosphere, feeling for detailed word-meaning and flawless breath control. Warm, understanding conducting and playing, and excellent sound.

On Wenlock Edge (song-cycle from A. E. Housman's *A Shropshire Lad*); (i) *10 Blake songs for voice and oboe. 4 Hymns: (Lord, come away!; Who is this fair one?; Come love, come Lord; Evening hymn); Songs: Merciless beauty;* (ii) *The new ghost; The water mill.*
(N) (M) *** EMI CDM5 65589-2 [id.]. Ian Partridge, (i) Janet Craxton, Music Group of London; (ii) Jennifer Partridge.

The EMI mid-priced CD is an outstandingly beautiful record, with Ian Partridge's intense artistry and lovely individual tone-colour used with compelling success in Vaughan Williams songs both early and late. The Housman cycle has an accompaniment for piano and string quartet which can sound ungainly but which here, with playing from the Music Group of London, matches the soloist's sensitivity; the result is atmospheric and moving. The *Ten Blake songs* come from just before the composer's death: bald, direct settings that with the artistry of Partridge and Craxton are darkly moving. The tenor's sister accompanies with fine understanding in two favourite songs as a welcome extra. The other (much rarer) items make an attractive bonus, with the *Four Hymns* distinctively accompanied by viola and piano.

The Shepherds of the Delectable Mountains; 3 Choral hymns; Magnificat; A Song of thanksgiving; Psalm 100.
*** Hyperion Dig. CDA 66569 [id.]. Gielgud, Dawson, Kitchen, Wyn-Rogers, Ainsley, Bowen, Thompson, Opie, Terfel, Best, Corydon Singers, L. Oratory Junior Ch., City of L. Sinfonia, Best.

With Sir John Gielgud as narrator and Lynne Dawson as the sweet-toned soprano soloist, Best gives *A Song of thanksgiving* a tautness and sense of drama, bringing out the originality of the writing, simple and stirring in its grandeur, not for a moment pompous. The *Magnificat* brings more buried treasure, a massive setting designed not for liturgical but for concert use. With its haunting ostinatos it is closer to Holst's choral music than most Vaughan Williams. The *Three Hymns* and the setting of *Psalm 100* are comparably distinctive in their contrasted ways, and it is good to have a recording of the Bunyan setting, *The Shepherds of the Delectable Mountains.* Most of the solo singing is excellent, and the chorus is superb, helped by warmly atmospheric recording.

Songs of travel; The House of Life (6 sonnets); *4 Poems by Fredegond Shove; 4 Last songs: No. 2, Tired; Songs: In the spring; Linden Lea.*
**(*) Chandos Dig. CHAN 8475 [id.]. Benjamin Luxon, David Williams.

Though Benjamin Luxon's vibrato is distractingly wide, the warmth and clarity of the recording help to make his well-chosen collection of Vaughan Williams songs very attractive, including as it does not only the well-known Stevenson travel cycle but the Rossetti cycle, *The House of Life* (including *The Water mill*), as well as the most famous song of all, *Linden Lea.*

The Pilgrim's progress (incidental music, ed. Palmer).
*** Hyperion CDA 66511; *KA 66511* [id.]. Sir John Gielgud, Richard Pasco, Ursula Howells, Corydon Singers, City of L. Sinfonia, Best.

Vaughan Williams had a lifelong devotion to Bunyan's great allegory, which fired his inspiration to write incidental music for a BBC radio adaptation of the complete *Pilgrim's Progress.* Much of the material, but not all, then found a place in the opera. Christopher Palmer has here devised a sequence of twelve movements, which – overlapping with the opera and the *Fifth Symphony* – throws up long-buried treasure. Matthew Best draws warmly sympathetic performances from his singers and players, in support of the masterly contributions of Sir John Gielgud, taking the role of Pilgrim as he did on radio in 1942, and Richard Pasco as the Evangelist.

(i) *5 Tudor Portraits;* (ii) *Benedicite;* (iii) *5 variants of Dives and Lazarus.*
(M) *** EMI CDM7 64722-2 [id.]. (i) Bainbridge, Carol Case, Bach Ch., New Philh. O; (ii) Harper, Bach Ch., LSO; (iii) Jacques O; Willcocks.

Ursula Vaughan Williams reports in her biography of the composer that the first performance of the *Five Tudor portraits* – in Norwich in 1936 – was remarkable for shocking many of the audience. The composer deliberately chose bawdy words by the early Tudor poet, John Skelton, and set them in his most rumbustious style. This is a good, strong performance, but the soloists are not earthy enough for such music. It is a pity that the humour was not underlined more strongly, but the musical invention is still more than enough to sustain compelling interest, and the digital remastering has brought splendid bite and projection to the chorus without losing too much of the original ambience. The *Benedicite* is another strong work, compressed in its intensity, too brief to be accepted easily into the choral repertory, but a fine addition to the RVW discography. The *Five variants of Dives and Lazarus* is beautifully played and warmly recorded and adds a touch of serenity and balm after the vigour of the vocal works.

OPERA

Hugh the Drover (complete).
*** Hyperion Dig. CDSA 66901/2 [id.]. Bonaventura Bottone, Rebecca Evans, Sarah Walker, Richard Van Allan, Alan Opie, Corydon Singers & O, Matthew Best.

Described as a ballad opera, *Hugh the Drover* uses folk-themes with full-throated Puccinian warmth. The Hyperion version in atmospheric digital sound offers a fresh, light view, resilient and urgent in the first Act, hauntingly tender in the second. Rebecca Evans is superb as the heroine, Mary, with Bonaventura Bottone an amiable Hugh, only occasionally strained, well supported by a cast of generally fresh young singers.

The Pilgrim's Progress.
(M) *** EMI CMS7 64212-2 (2). Noble, Burrowes, Armstrong, Herincx, Carol Case, Shirley-Quirk, Keyte, LPO Ch., LPO, Boult.
(M) **(*) RNCM PP1/2 (2) [id.]. Richard Whitehouse, Wyn Griffiths & soloists, Ch. & O of Royal N. Coll. of Music, Igor Kennaway.

The Pilgrim's Progress is crammed full of delectable ideas. John Noble gives a dedicated performance in the central role of Pilgrim, and the large supporting cast is consistently strong. Vanity Fair may not sound evil here, but Vaughan Williams's own recoil is vividly expressed, and the jaunty passage of Mr and Mrs By-Ends brings the most delightful light relief. Boult underlines the virility of his performance with a fascinating and revealing half-hour collection of rehearsal excerpts, placed at the end of the second CD. The outstanding recording quality is confirmed by the CD transfer, which shows few signs of the passing of two decades.

Enterprisingly, in 1992 the Royal Northern College of Music in Manchester presented a staging which effectively brought out the operatic qualities of a work too often dismissed as an oratorio. Obviously student voices cannot match those of the front-rank singers of the 1970s who appear on the earlier recording, but the vitality is what matters. Richard Whitehouse as the Pilgrim boldly shoulders the weightiest individual burden, but this is an opera in which good teamwork is more important than individual performances, and under Igor Kennaway the young singers and players perform with a dedication that could hardly be more compelling. The two CDs can be obtained direct from the College and are in the mid-price range.

Riders to the sea (opera) complete.
(N) *** Chandos Dig. CHAN 9392 [id.]. Finnie, Daymond, Dawson, Attrot, Stephen, N. Sinfonia, Richard Hickox – *Flos campi* etc. ***
(M) *** EMI CDM7 64730-2 [id.]. Burrowes, M. Price, Watts, Luxon, Amb. S., L. O Nova, Meredith Davies – *Epithalamion; Merciless Beauty*. ***

The one-Act opera, *Riders to the sea*, is among Vaughan Williams's supreme masterpieces, a word-by-word setting of J. M. Synge's one-Act play which heightens an already darkly intense drama. As in other Vaughan Williams works, Hickox takes a broad, warmly idiomatic view, less urgent than the previous, EMI recording, more timeless and mysterious, helped by opulently atmospheric recording. He is helped too by an excellent cast. Even if Linda Finnie as the old woman, Maurya, who loses all her sons to the sea, cannot quite match Helen Watts on the original recording, her final monologue of lament and resignation provides a moving, deeply expressive culmination. Among the others, Karl Daymond as Bartley, the last son to drown, is a newcomer to note, as impressive here as he was in Hickox's recording of Purcell's *Dido*. The generous coupling adds to the disc's attractions.

The earlier, EMI recording is also beautifully recorded, though there is too much wind machine. The analogue recording, clear yet wonderfully atmospheric, approaches the demonstration bracket in its CD format and, with its equally rare couplings, this can be strongly recommended alongside the Chandos version. All who care about this composer should investigate one or other of these records.

Veracini, Francesco Maria (1690–1768)

Overtures (Suites) Nos. 1 in B flat; 2 in F; 3 in B flat; 4 in F; 6 in B flat.
(Y/B) *** DG Dig. 439 937-2 [id.]. Col. Mus. Ant., Goebel.

The flamboyant and eccentric Florentine composer, who spent almost the entire middle period of his life working away from home, successfully penetrated and then established himself at the Dresden court (something Vivaldi never managed to do). Dresden represented the peak of his career, and these concertos were composed for the Dresden court orchestra, probably around 1716. Their character brings a curious amalgam of Italian volatility and German weight, and they have something in common with the orchestral suites of Telemann. Yet Telemann loved instrumental light and shade, whereas Veracini favoured tutti scoring and, although oboes and bassoons are included, they are used to reinforce and colour the texture rather than provide solo instrumental contrast. There is of course the interplay of counterpoint, but Veracini seemed to relish the favourite Dresden device of the time, a unison minuet, with the fullness of orchestral sonority paramount. The music is strong in personality and there is no shortage of ideas, but energy is more important than expressive lyricism, with usually a single brief sarabande to provide contrast as the centrepiece of up to half-a-dozen dance movements. Musica Antiqua of Cologne, with their pungent tuttis, seem custom-made for this repertoire, playing with consistent vitality and obviously enjoying the music's Germanic flavour. The recording is first class, within a spacious acoustic.

12 Sonate accademiche, Op. 2.
(Y/B) *** Hyperion Dig. CDA 66871/3 (3). Locatelli Trio.

Alongside his fame as a composer, Veracini was renowned as a master of the violin, and he knew it, boasting that there 'was but one God and one Veracini', so that even Tartini was initimidated by his prowess. The twelve *Sonate accademiche* date from 1744. They are much more Italianate than the overtures, though German influence remains strong. The writing has a rhapsodic exuberance and drive, in common with the orchestral works, and, like the overtures, the format is heavily laced with dance movements. But there are touching lyrical interludes and some really lovely slow movements. The last *Sonata* is quite masterly, opening with a descending minor scalic theme, which is first used for a *Passacaglia*, then for a *Capriccio cromatico*, and finally provides the basis for an ambitious closing *Ciaccona*. In short, these are fascinatingly inventive works, showing their little-known composer as a great deal more than a historical figure. The Locatelli Trio, led by Elizabeth Wallfisch, are a first-class group and their authentic style, strongly etched, is full of joy in the music's vitality, while the composer's lyrical side is most persuasively revealed. Paul Nicholson's continuo is very much a part of the picture, especially in the works using an organ – which is very pleasingly balanced. The recording is vividly real and immediate.

Verdi, Giuseppe (1813–1901)

(i) *Ballet music from: Aida (including Triumphal march); Macbeth; Otello.* (ii) Overtures: *Aroldo; La forza del destino; Giovanna d'Arco; Luisa Miller; Nabucco; Oberto, conte di San Bonifacio; I vespri siciliani.*
(N) (B) *** Decca Eclipse Dig. 448 238-2; *448 238-4* [id.]. (i) Bologna Teatro Comunale O; (ii) Nat. PO; Chailly.

Chailly's version enjoys brilliant Decca recording. Besides the ballet music, which is presented with gusto and style, he offers the four most obviously desirable overtures plus three rarities, including the overture to Verdi's very first opera, *Oberto*, and the most substantial of the early ones, *Aroldo*. Crisp and incisive, Chailly draws vigorous and polished playing from the excellent National Philharmonic.

The Lady and the fool (ballet suite; arr. Mackerras).
(B) *** CfP CD-CFP 4618. LPO, Mackerras – SULLIVAN: *Pineapple Poll.* ***

Mackerras's arrangement of Verdi has not caught the public fancy in quite the way of the coupled *Pineapple Poll*, but the scoring is witty and the music vivacious, and it is very well played and recorded here.

Overtures and Preludes: *Aida: Prelude. Alzira: Sinfonia. Aroldo: Sinfonia. Attila: Prelude. Un ballo in maschera: Prelude. Il Corsaro: Prelude. Luisa Miller: Sinfonia. Oberto, Conte di San Bonifacio: Sinfonia. La Traviata: Preludes to Acts I & III. I vespri siciliani: Sinfonia.*
(N) (BB) **(*) Naxos Dig. 8.553018 [id.]. Hung. State Op. O, Pier Giorgio Morandi.

Overtures and Preludes: *La battaglia di Legnano: Sinfonia. Don Carlo: Prelude to Act III. I due Foscari: Prelude. Ernani: Prelude. La forza del destino: Sinfonia. Un giorno di regno: Sinfonia. Giovanna d'Arco: Sinfonia. Macbeth: Sinfonia. I Masnadieri: Prelude. Nabucco: Overture. Rigoletto: Prelude.*
(N) (BB) **(*) Naxos Dig. 8.553089 [id.]. Hung. State Op. O, Pier Giorgio Morandi.

Morandi has served his time conducting at La Scala and he gives ripely robust accounts of these colourful overtures and sinfonias, with excellent playing from his Hungarian musicians, notably from the strings in the *Traviata* and *Aida Preludes* and from the brass in *Nabucco. La forza del destino* ends the second disc strongly. Full-bloodedly resonant sound (with the second collection at times marginally sharper in definition) means that this pair of bargain discs is worth anyone's money, even if the readings are not as dramatically individual as those of Chailly and Karajan.

Overtures and Preludes: *Aida* (Prelude); *Alzira; Aroldo* (Overtures); *Attila; Un ballo in maschera* (Preludes); *La battaglia di Legnano; Il Corsaro* (Sinfonias); *Ernani* (Prelude); *La forza del destino; Un giorno di regno; Giovanna d'Arco* (Sinfonias); *Luisa Miller* (Overture); *Macbeth; I Masnadieri* (Preludes); *Nabucco* (Overture); *Oberto, Conte di San Bonifacio* (Sinfonia); *Rigoletto; La Traviata* (Preludes); *I vespri siciliani* (Overture).
(Y/B) (M) *** DG 439 972-2 (2) [id.]. BPO, Karajan.

It is good to have Karajan's complete set of Overtures and Preludes back in the catalogue. The 1975 recording was one of the very best made in the Philharmonie: the sound combines vividness with a natural balance and an attractive ambience. As we have commented before, the performances have an electricity, refinement and authority that sweep all before them. The little-known overtures, *Alzira, Aroldo* and *La battaglia de Legnano*, are all given with tremendous panache and virtuosity. Every bar of this music is alive and, with all the exuberance, Karajan skirts any suggestion of vulgarity. Try the splendid *Nabucco*, or the surprisingly extended (8-minute) *Giovanna d'Arco* to discover the colour and spirit of this music-making, with every bar spontaneously alive, while there is not the faintest suggestion of routine in the more familiar items.

Le quattro stagioni (*The four seasons:* ballet from *I vespri siciliani*).
(M) *** Decca 425 052-2 [id.]. Cleveland O, Maazel – RESPIGHI: *Feste romane* etc. ***

Verdi's *Seasons* ballet is not great Verdi but is tuneful and nicely scored. Maazel, who obviously enjoys the music, succeeds in securing first-class playing from the Cleveland Orchestra, and he is given admirable recorded quality which, though bright, is not clinical and combines detail with atmosphere. A good bonus for some outstanding Respighi performances.

String quartet in E min.
*** Collins Dig. 1267-2 [id.]. Britten Qt – CHERUBINI: *Quartet No. 1;* TURINA: *La Oración del Torero.* ***

*** CRD CRD 3366; *CRDC 4066* [id.]. Alberni Qt – DONIZETTI: *Quartet No. 13;* PUCCINI: *Crisantemi.* ***

**(*) Hyperion Dig. CDA 66317 [id.]. Delmé Qt – R. STRAUSS: *Quartet.* **(*)

A quite outstanding performance of Verdi's only *String quartet* from the Britten group. They match polished energy in the outer movements with much warmth and elegance in the inner ones, particularly the charming Neapolitan serenade theme at the centre of the miniature scherzo. With full, immediate, yet transparent sound this is very impressive indeed.

The Alberni Quartet's performance is also strong and compelling, and it is most imaginatively and attractively coupled with the Puccini and Donizetti pieces.

The Delmé are not a 'high-powered', jet-setting ensemble and they give a very natural performance of the Verdi which will give much pleasure: there is the sense of music-making in the home among intimate friends, and it is refreshingly unforced, even if the sound is just a shade on the dry side.

Requiem Mass.
(N) (B) *** EMI forte CZS5 68613-2 (2) [id.]. Scotto, Baltsa, Luchetti, Nesterenko, Amb. Ch., Philh. O, Muti – CHERUBINI: *Requiem in C min.* ***
(Y/B) ❀ (B) (***) DG Double mono 439 684-2 (2) [id.]. Stader, Dominguez, Carelli, Sardi, St Hedwig's Cathedral Ch., Berlin RIAS SO, Fricsay – ROSSINI: *Stabat Mater.* (***)
(M) (***) DG mono 447 442-2 [id.]. Stader, Radev, Krebs, Borg, St Hedwig's Cathedral Ch., Berlin RIAS O, Fricsay.
(N) (M) (**(*)) EMI mono CMS5 65506-2 (2). Schwarzkopf, Dominguez, Di Stefano, Siepi, La Scala, Milan, Ch. & O, De Sabata (with: VERDI: *La Traviata: Preludes to Acts I & III. I vespri siciliani: overture.* WOLF-FERRARI: *Susanna's secret: Overture and Intermezzo.* RESPIGHI: *The Fountains of Rome.* ROSSINI: *William Tell overture* **(*)).

(Y/B) (M) (***) Dutton Lab. mono CDLX 7010 [id.]. Caniglia, Gigli, Stignani, Pinza, Rome Opera Ch. & O, Serafin.

**(*) Decca 411 944-2 (2) [id.]. Sutherland, Horne, Pavarotti, Talvela, V. State Op. Ch., VPO, Solti.

(M) **(*) RCA 09026 61403-2 (2) [id.]. L. Price, J. Baker, V. Luchetti, Van Dam, Chicago Symphony Ch. & SO, Solti.

(B) **(*) DG Double 437 473-2 (2) [id.]. Freni, Ludwig, Cossutta, Ghiaurov, V. Singverein, VPO, Karajan.

(N) **(*) DG Dig. Gold 439 033-2 (2) [id.]. Tomowa-Sintow, Baltsa, Carreras, Van Dam, V. State Op. Konzertvereingung, VPO, Karajan.

(M) **(*) Sony SM2K 47639 (2) [id.]. Arroyo, Veasey, Domingo, Raimondi, L. Symphony Ch., LSO, Bernstein.

(N) (B) ** Sony SB2K 53252 (2) [id.]. Amara, Forrester, Tucker, London, Westminster Ch., Phd. O, Ormandy – ROSSINI: *Stabat Mater*. **

(i) *Requiem Mass;* (ii) *4 Sacred pieces.*
(Y/B) *** Ph. Dig. 442 142-2 (2) [id.]. (i) Orgonasova, Von Otter, Canonici, Miles; (ii) Donna Brown; Monteverdi Ch., ORR, Gardiner.

*** DG Dig. 435 884-2 (2) [id.]. Studer, Lipovšek, Carreras, Raimondi, V. State Op. Ch., VPO, Abbado.

**(*) EMI CDS7 47257-8 (2) [Ang. CDCB 47257]. (i) Schwarzkopf, Ludwig, Gedda, Ghiaurov; (ii) J. Baker; Philh. Ch. & O, Giulini.

(N) (B) **(*) Decca Double 444 833-2 (2) [id.]. (i) L. Price, Elias, Bjoerling, Tozzi, V. Musikverein, VPO, Reiner; (ii) Minton, Los Angeles Master Ch., LAPO, Mehta.

(i) *Requiem Mass.* Choruses from: *Aida; Don Carlo; Macbeth; Nabucco; Otello.*
*** Telarc Dig. CD 80152 (2) [id.]. (i) Dunn, Curry, Hadley, Plishka; Atlanta Ch. & SO, Shaw.

Gardiner, using period forces, is searingly dramatic and superbly recorded, with fine detail, necessary weight and atmospheric bloom. It can be recommended as a first choice among modern digital recordings even to collectors not drawn to period performance, notably in the *Dies irae*, where the bite and clarity of the textures, both choral and orchestral, intensify Gardiner's thrusting sense of drama. With a choir of 70, all of them keenly disciplined professionals, Gardiner has the best of both worlds: as recorded, there is ample weight and power as well as a rare refinement in the singing. The soloists make a characterful quartet, with the vibrant Orgonasova set against the rock-steady von Otter, and with Canonici bringing welcome Italianate colourings to the tenor role. Alistair Miles is a strong bass, not quite ideally dark but untroubled by the tessitura. The *Four Sacred pieces* are equally revealing. The longest and most complex, the final *Te Deum*, is the most successful of all, marked by thrillingly dramatic contrasts, as in the fortissimo cries of '*Sanctus*'.

Fricsay's second recording, which DG have now reissued on a bargain Double coupled with Rossini, is of a live performance given in 1960, the very last he conducted before his untimely death. In biting drama it has never been surpassed, and even though speeds are often measured when compared with his fine studio recording (which DG have also currently reissued on a single disc as an 'Original'), such is the voltage of this later performance that it doesn't sound slower. Moreover it is underpinned by a commanding gravity that plainly reflects the conductor's own emotions during his last illness. Like him, the two male soloists are Hungarian, and both are first rate, with the tenor, Gabor Carelli, pleasingly Italianate of tone (his *Ingemisco* is ravishing). Maria Stader, the soprano soloist, is common to both performances; here she sings with clear, pure tone, if very occasionally suffering intonation problems, which did not trouble her in the earlier version. Oralia Dominguez is the rich mezzo. The chorus is superbly disciplined, yet ardent: the *Dies irae* is electrifying, the *Sanctus* is wonderfully light and joyful and the closing *Lux aeterna* raptly beautiful, for Fricsay's concentration never falters. The CD transfer enhances the bite of the choral projection without losing the atmospheric warmth of a recording which, even today, can startle by its immediacy of sound.

Fricsay's superb mono studio recording of Verdi's *Requiem* caused a sensation when it first appeared on LP in 1954. Its tingling drama anticipated the later version, and though tempi are generally faster than in that live account there is marginal extra precision and polish. This makes a worthy reissue in DG's 'Legendary Recordings' series, with the full, spacious mono recording already showing that the DG engineers, using mono techniques, could achieve a combination of clarity and atmosphere – especially in recording the big choral climaxes – to anticipate their later stereo records. The solo team is first class with the contribution of Kim Borg standing out, although in the latter part of the work the solo ensembles are at times even more eloquent in the live performance. But this earlier version makes an equally astonishing impact.

Claudio Abbado's DG live recording was taken from performances at the Vienna Musikverein with the Vienna Philharmonic and Vienna choirs, as well as Cheryl Studer, Marjana Lipovšek, José Carreras and Ruggero Raimondi, all in superb voice and finely matched, even if Carreras has to husband his resources. In detail Abbado's reading is little different from his earlier, La Scala version, but the sense of presence, of the tension of a live occasion, makes the later account far more magnetic from the hushed murmurings of the opening onwards. The Vienna forces are not only more expressive but more polished too, and this now must count as the finest of digital versions using modern instruments, generously coupled with the *Four Sacred Pieces*, also superbly done in another live recording.

Robert Shaw, in the finest of his Atlanta recordings, may not have quite the same searing electricity as Toscanini's rough old NBC recording, but it regularly echoes it in power and the well-calculated pacing. In the *Dies irae*, for example, like Toscanini he gains in thrust and power from a speed marginally slower than usual. With sound of spectacular quality, beautifully balanced and clear, the many felicities of the performance, not least the electricity of the choral singing and the consistency of the solo singing, add up to an exceptionally satisfying reading, more recommendable than those of even the most eminent conductors. The fill-up of five Verdi opera choruses is more colourful, and again brings superb choral singing. An outstanding issue.

With spectacular analogue sound – not always perfectly balanced, but vividly wide in its tonal spectrum – Muti's 1979 Kingsway Hall performance makes a tremendous impact and is in almost all respects preferable to his later version, recorded live eight years later at La Scala. Characteristically he prefers fast speeds, and in the *Dies irae* he rushes the singers dangerously, making the music breathless in its excitement rather than grandly dramatic in its portrayal of the Day of Wrath. It is not surprising that Muti opted for a professional choir, and the engineers are able to give it fine impact. Unashamedly, from first to last this is an operatic performance, with a passionately committed quartet of soloists, under-pinned by Nesterenko in glorious voice, giving priestly authority to the *Confutatis*. Scotto is not always sweet on top, but Baltsa is superb, and Luchetti sings freshly. Now offered very inexpensively, and aptly coupled with a splendid (digital) account of Cherubini's *C minor Requiem*, so admired by Berlioz, this readily goes to the top of the list of bargain recommendations.

What Giulini proves is that refinement added to power can provide an even more intense experience than the traditional Italian approach. In this concept a fine English chorus and orchestra prove exactly right. The array of soloists could hardly be bettered. Schwarzkopf caresses each phrase, and the exactness of her voice matches the firm mezzo of Christa Ludwig in their difficult octave passages. Gedda is at his most reliable, and Ghiaurov with his really dark bass actually manages to sing the almost impossible *Mors stupebit* in tune without a suspicion of wobble. Giulini's set also finds space to include the *Four Sacred pieces* and there is no doubt that in a performance as polished and dramatic as this the element of greatness in these somewhat uneven works is magnified. The CD is successful enough in the *Sacred pieces*; but it tends to emphasize the occasional roughness of the heavy climaxes in the *Requiem*, even though generally the quality is fully acceptable.

Victor de Sabata's legendary 1954 recording unashamedly adopts the most spacious speeds and a deeply devotional manner, helped by a starry quartet of soloists. When it came out, it was not well received by many, who found the slow speeds self-indulgent, the very opposite of those adopted by Tullio Serafin, whose early recording made an obvious comparison, lasting a full 22 minutes less. Also this de Sabata version, master-minded by Walter Legge, was due to be superseded ten years later by Giulini's stereo version, ensuring that it never reappeared on LP, making this CD transfer very welcome, limited in sound but with fine dynamic contrasts. Unlike the Fricsay version, the electrical urgency – well illus-trated in some of the orchestral fill-ups on the set – flashes out only occasionally in sudden dynamic bursts, as in the *Dies irae*. Otherwise dedication is the keynote. Far more than the later Giulini set, de Sabata's is a performance of extremes, totally concentrated but very personal in its new look, often with underlining that draws attention to itself, as in *Te decet hymnus*. Where de Sabata rides triumphant is in his spine-tingling authority, however controversial he may be, and the four superb soloists respond with total commitment, Schwarzkopf most of all, in radiant voice. Oralia Dominguez excels herself, as cleanly focused as Schwarzkopf, with her rapid flicker-vibrato adding character to the firm mezzo timbre. Giuseppe di Stefano sings with headily fresh tone and de Sabata even woos the occasional *mezza voce* from him, while Siepi, not quite as rock-like or imaginative as Pinza for Serafin, is splendid too. The chorus sing lustily but with characteristic Italian reluctance to match in an ensemble. The fill-ups com-plete the picture of de Sabata: the *Traviata Preludes*, rapt and finely shaded, the Respighi sensuously atmospheric, the *William Tell overture* given surprising refinement. Best of all are the two little Wolf-Ferrari items, in their point and sparkle deliciously witty in a way one might not have expected from de Sabata. For all one's reservations, this remains a revelatory set.

Reiner's opening of the *Requiem* is very slow and atmospheric. He takes the music at something like half the speed of Toscanini and shapes everything very carefully. Yet as the work proceeds the performance quickly sparks into life, and there is some superb and memorable singing from a distinguished team of soloists. The recording has a spectacularly wide dynamic range, enhanced by the CD format, and, with the chorus singing fervently, the *Dies irae* is almost overwhelming. Mehta's performance of the *Sacred pieces* has much more brilliant, sharply focused recording than Giulini's, but in every other way Giulini's performance of Verdi's last work (or group of works) provides a deeper, more searching experience. However, that is at full price.

The Dutton Sound transfer of Serafin's historic recording of 1939 relates the work to the Verdian operatic tradition more closely than most latter-day versions. The beefy, Italianate sound of the chorus is what Verdi himself no doubt had in mind, and the team of soloists is characterfully representative of the finest Italian singing at that period. The recording was built round Beniamino Gigli, singing with his most golden tone. Though his tendency to aspirate the vocal line and to bring his half-tone down to a gentle croon may upset the purists, few performances are as winning as his, and both Ebe Stignani and Ezio Pinza are at their supreme best, rarely matched since. The soprano, Maria Caniglia, is more variable but, always dramatic, she rises splendidly to the challenge of the final *Libera me*. Whether because of co-ordination problems between such distinguished soloists, a brief *a cappella* passage of 11 bars for mezzo, tenor and bass soloists is omitted towards the end of the *Lux aeterna*.

There is little or nothing reflective about Solti's Decca account, and those who criticize the work for being too operatic will find plenty of ammunition here. The team of soloists is a very strong one, though the matching of voices is not always ideal. It is a pity that the chorus is not nearly as incisive as the Philharmonia on the EMI set – a performance which conveys far more of the work's profundity than this. But if you want an extrovert performance, the firmness of focus and precise placing of forces in the Decca engineering of 1967 make for exceptionally vivid results on CD.

On RCA, with an unusually sensitive and pure-toned quartet of soloists – Luchetti perhaps not as characterful as the others, Leontyne Price occasionally showing strain – and with superb choral singing and orchestral playing, Solti's 1977 Chicago version has all the ingredients for success. The set is well worth having for Janet Baker's deeply sensitive singing, but the remastered recording – less than ideally balanced – tends to be fierce on climaxes and in sound; and in other ways too, Solti's earlier, Decca/Vienna set is preferable.

Karajan's earlier recording of the *Requiem* has been greatly enhanced in its CD transfer, with the whole effect given greater presence and immediacy. He has a fine team of soloists, too. However, Karajan's reading still smooths over the lines of Verdi's masterpiece. The result is often beautiful, but, apart from the obvious climaxes, such as the *Dies irae*, there is a lack of dramatic bite. However, with two discs offered for the price of one, many collectors may be tempted to try this.

Though Karajan's smooth style altered relatively little since he recorded this work before, the overall impression in the DG 'Gold' version is notably fresher, and it would be more so if the recording were more consistent. The current 'original image bit reprocessing' has improved the focus and impact, but this is still not among the finest recordings of Verdi's spectacular work and the *Dies irae* remains less sharply dramatic than in Fricsay's version, for instance. Soloists are good, naturally and warmly expressive. Though Tomowa-Sintow's un-Italian soprano sometimes brings a hint of flutter, she sings most beautifully in the final rapt account of *Libera me*. But at premium price this is by no means a first choice.

Bernstein's 1970 *Requiem* was recorded in the Royal Albert Hall. By rights, the daring of that decision should have paid off; but with close balancing of microphones the result is not as full and free as one would have expected. Bernstein's interpretation remains marvellously persuasive in its drama, exaggerated at times, maybe, but red-blooded in a way that is hard to resist. The quartet of soloists is particularly strong.

Ormandy's is a sincere, warm-blooded performance, with ardent choral singing and plenty of drama. The snag lies with the soloists, who all fall far short of their rivals on other bargain sets (notably Fricsay's). One has only to sample their contribution to the *Kyrie* to hear that this is not really distinguished singing.

(i; ii) *Requiem Mass;* (iii; iv) *Inno delle nazione;* (ii) *Te Deum;* (iii) *Luisa Miller: Quando le sere al placido.* (iv) *Nabucco: Va pensiero.*

(M) (***) RCA mono GD 60299; *GK 60299* (2) [60299-RG-2; *60299–RG-4*]. (i) Nelli, Barbieri, Di Stefano, Siepi; (ii) Robert Shaw Ch.; (iii) Jan Peerce; (iv) Westminster Ch.; NBC SO, Toscanini.

Toscanini's account of the *Requiem* brings a supreme performance, searingly intense. The opening of the *Dies irae* has never sounded more hair-raising, with the bass-drum thrillingly caught, despite the limitation of dry mono recording. And rarely has the chorus shone so brightly in this work on record, while the soloists are near-ideal, a vintage team. The other works make fascinating listening, too. The *Te Deum* was one of Toscanini's very last recordings, a performance more intense than usual with this work, and it is good to have the extraordinary wartime recording of the potboiling *Hymn of the Nations*.

The *Internationale* is added to Verdi's original catalogue of national anthems, to represent the ally, the USSR.

OPERA

Aida (complete).

(Y/B) (M) *** EMI CMS7 69300-2 (3) [Ang. CDMC 69300]. Freni, Carreras, Baltsa, Cappuccilli, Raimondi, Van Dam, V. State Op. Ch., VPO, Karajan.

*** Decca 417 416-2 (3) [id.]. Leontyne Price, Gorr, Vickers, Merrill, Tozzi, Rome Op. Ch. & O, Solti.

(M) *** Decca 414 087-2 (3) [id.]. Tebaldi, Simionato, Bergonzi, MacNeil, Van Mill, Corena, V. Singverein, VPO, Karajan.

(M) (***) RCA mono GD 86652 (3) [6652-2-RG]. Milanov, Bjoerling, Barbieri, Warren, Christoff, Rome Op. Ch. & O, Perlea.

(**) EMI mono CDS7 49030-8 (3) [Ang. CDCC 49030]. Callas, Tucker, Barbieri, Gobbi, La Scala, Milan, Ch. & O, Serafin.

(M) (**) RCA mono GD 60300 (3) [60300-RG-2]. Nelli, Gustavson, Tucker, Valdengo, Robert Shaw Ch., NBC SO, Toscanini.

On EMI, Karajan's is a performance of *Aida* that carries splendour and pageantry to the point of exaltation. Yet Karajan's fundamental approach is lyrical. On record at least, there can be little question of Freni lacking power in a role normally given to a larger voice, and there is ample gain in the tender beauty of her singing. Carreras makes a fresh, sensitive Radames, Raimondi a darkly intense Ramphis and Van Dam a cleanly focused King, his relative lightness no drawback. Cappuccilli here gives a more detailed performance than he did for Muti on EMI, while Baltsa as Amneris crowns the whole performance with her fine, incisive singing. Despite some over-brightness on cymbals and trumpet, the Berlin sound for Karajan, as transferred to CD, is richly and involvingly atmospheric, both in the intimate scenes and, most strikingly, in the scenes of pageant, which have rarely been presented on record in greater splendour. The set has been attractively re-packaged and remains first choice for the opera, irrespective of price.

Leontyne Price is an outstandingly assured Aida on Decca, rich, accurate and imaginative, while Solti's direction is superbly dramatic, notably in the Nile Scene. Merrill is a richly secure Amonasro, Rita Gorr a characterful Amneris, and Jon Vickers is splendidly heroic as Radames. Though the digital transfer betrays the age of the recording (1962), making the result fierce at times to match the reading, Solti's version otherwise brings full, spacious sound, finer, more open and with greater sense of presence than most versions since.

On Decca, as on EMI, Karajan was helped by having a Viennese orchestra and chorus; but most important of all is the musicianship and musical teamwork of his soloists. Bergonzi in particular emerges here as a model among tenors, with a rare feeling for the shaping of phrases and attention to detail. Cornell MacNeil too is splendid. Tebaldi's creamy tone-colour rides beautifully over the phrases and she too acquires a new depth of imagination. Among the other soloists Arnold van Mill and Fernando Corena are both superb, and Simionato provides one of the very finest portrayals of Amneris we have ever had in a complete *Aida*. The recording has long been famous for its technical bravura and flair. CD enhances the overall projection, but the brightness on top at times strikes the ear rather too forcibly. Nevertheless this remains a remarkable technical achievement.

All four principals on the historic RCA set are at their very finest, notably Milanov, whose poise and control in *O patria mia* are a marvel. Barbieri as Amneris is even finer here than in the Callas set, and it is good to hear the young Christoff resonant as Ramphis. Perlea conducts with great panache.

The Nile Scene has never been performed more powerfully and characterfully on record than in this vintage La Scala set. Though Callas is hardly as sweet-toned as some will think essential for an Aida, her detailed imagination is irresistible, and she is matched by Tito Gobbi at the very height of his powers. Tucker gives one of his very finest performances on record, and Barbieri is a commanding Amneris. The mono sound is more than acceptable, but this remains at full price.

Toscanini's 1949 performance of *Aida* is the least satisfying of his New York opera recordings. Richard Tucker sings well but makes a relatively colourless Radames, and Herva Nelli lacks weight as Aida, neatly though she sings and with some touching moments. Nancy Gustavson's Amneris lacks all menace, and Valdengo as Amonasro is the only fully satisfying principal. Yet Toscanini is so electrifying from first to last that his admirers will accept the limited, painfully dry recording.

Aida: highlights (scenes & arias).

(M) *** Decca 417 763-2 [id.] (from above set, with Tebaldi, Bergonzi, cond. Karajan).

Aida: highlights.
(M) (***) RCA mono GD 60201 [60201-2-RG] (from above recording with Milanov, Bjoerling; cond. Perlea).
(M) *** Decca 433 444-2 [id.] (from above recording, with Leontyne Price, Gorr, Vickers, Merrill, Tozzi; cond. Solti).
(Y/B) (B) **(*) DG Dig. 439 482-2 [id.] (from complete recording, with Ricciarelli, Obraztsova, Domingo, Nucci, Ghiaurov; cond. Abbado).

The selection from the Solti recording is generous (71 minutes) and would seem an obvious first choice for those wanting a highlights CD from this opera. Nevertheless the alternative Decca compilation called 'Scenes and arias' from John Culshaw's Karajan recording, made during the early stereo era, remains particularly enticing. The RCA highlights disc is valuable above all for providing a sample of one of Milanov's most compelling performances on record, poised and commanding.

In Abbado's 1981 La Scala *Aida*, it was the men who stood out, Domingo a superb Radames, Ghiaurov as Ramphis, Nucci a dramatic Amonasro, and Raimondi as the King. Ricciarelli is an appealing Aida, but her legato line is at times impure above the stave, and Elena Obraztsova produces too much curdled tone as Amneris. The recording is bright and fresh, but not ideally expansive in the ceremonial scenes. As is usual with DG's bargain Classikon series, the documentation is good, though without translations. The selection offers 64 minutes of music.

Alzira (complete).
*** Orfeo CO 57832 (2) [id.]. Cotrubas, Araiza, Bruson, George, Bonilla, Bav. R. Ch., Munich R. O, Gardelli.

Alzira is the shortest of the Verdi operas, but its concision is on balance an advantage on record. In musical inspiration it is indistinguishable from other typical early operas, with Verdian melodies less distinctive than they became later, but consistently pleasing. Gardelli is a master with early Verdi, and the cast is strong, helped by warm and well-balanced recording supervised by Munich Radio engineers.

Aroldo (complete).
** Sony CD 79328 [M2K 39506] (2). Caballé, Cecchele, Lebherz, Pons, NY Oratorio Soc., Westminster Ch. Soc., NY Op. O, Queler.

Aroldo is Verdi's radical revision of his earlier unsuccessful opera, *Stiffelio*: he translated the story of a Protestant pastor with an unfaithful wife into this tale of a crusader returning from the Holy Land. Less compact than the original, it contains some splendid new material such as the superb aria for the heroine, beautifully sung by Caballé. The final scene too is quite new, for the dénouement is totally different. The storm chorus (with echoes of *Rigoletto*) is most memorable – but so are the rum-ti-tum choruses common to both versions. This recording of a concert performance in New York is lively, though the tenor is depressingly coarse.

Attila (complete).
(M) *** Ph. 426 115-2 (2). Raimondi, Deutekom, Bergonzi, Milnes, Amb. S., Finchley Children's Music Group, RPO, Gardelli.

With its dramatic anticipations of *Macbeth*, the musical anticipations of *Rigoletto* and the compression which (on record if not on the stage) becomes a positive merit – all these qualities, helped by a fine performance under Gardelli, make this Philips version of *Attila* an intensely enjoyable set. Deutekom, not the most sweet-toned of sopranos, has never sung better on record, and the rest of the cast is outstandingly good. The 1973 recording is well balanced and atmospheric.

Un ballo in maschera (complete).
*** Decca Dig. 410 210-2 (2) [id.]. Margaret Price, Pavarotti, Bruson, Ludwig, Battle, L. Op. Ch., Royal College of Music Junior Dept Ch., Nat. PO, Solti.
*** DG Dig. 427 635-2 (2) [id.]. Domingo, Barstow, Nucci, Quivar, Sumi Jo, V. State Op. Konzertvereinigung, VPO, Karajan.
*** DG 415 685-2 (2) [id.]. Ricciarelli, Domingo, Bruson, Obraztsova, Gruberová, Raimondi, La Scala, Milan, Ch. & O, Abbado.
(M) *** RCA GD 86645 (2) [6645-2-RG]. L. Price, Bergonzi, Merrill, Grist, Verrett, Flagello, RCA Italiana Op. Ch. & O, Leinsdorf.
(M) *** EMI CMS7 69576-2 (2) [Ang. CDMB 69576]. Arroyo, Domingo, Cappuccilli, Grist, Cossotto, Howell, ROHCG Ch., New Philh. O, Muti.
(M) **(*) Decca 440 042-2 (2). Tebaldi, Pavarotti, Milnes, Donath, Regina Resnik, Santa Cecilia Academy, Rome, Ch. & O, Bartoletti.

(M) (***) RCA mono GD 60301 (2) [60301-2-RG]. Herva Nelli, Jan Peerce, Robert Merrill, Virginia Haskins, Claramae Turner, Nicola Moscona, NBC Ch. & SO, Toscanini.

(N) ** Teldec/Warner Dig. 4509 98408-2 (2) [id.]. Leech, Chernov, Criser, Zaremba, Bayo, WNO Ch. and O, Rizzi.

Shining out from the cast of Solti's set of *Ballo* is the gloriously sung Amelia of Margaret Price in one of her richest and most commanding performances on record, ravishingly beautiful, flawlessly controlled and full of unforced emotion. The role of Riccardo, pushy and truculent, is well suited to the extrovert Pavarotti, who swaggers through the part, characteristically clear of diction, challenged periodically by Price to produce some of his subtlest tone-colours. Bruson makes a noble Renato, Christa Ludwig an unexpected but intense and perceptive Ulrica, while Kathleen Battle is an Oscar whose coloratura is not just brilliant but sweet too. Solti is far more relaxed than he often is on record, presenting a warm and understanding view of the score. The recording is extremely vivid within a reverberant acoustic.

Recorded in Vienna early in 1989, *Un ballo in maschera* was Karajan's last opera recording and it makes a fitting memorial, characteristically rich and spacious, with a cast – if not ideal – which still makes a fine team, responding to the conductor's single-minded vision. Standing out vocally is the Gustavo of Plácido Domingo, strong and imaginative, dominating the whole cast. He may not have the sparkle of Pavarotti in this role, but the singing is richer, more refined and more thoughtful. Amelia is Josephine Barstow's finest achievement on record, and dramatically she is most compelling. Leo Nucci, though not as rough in tone as in some of his other recent recordings, is over-emphatic, with poor legato in his great solo, *Eri tu*. Sumi Jo, a Karajan discovery, gives a delicious performance as Oscar, the page, coping splendidly with Karajan's slow speed for her Act I solo. Florence Quivar produces satisfyingly rich tone as Ulrica. Though the sound is not as cleanly focused as in the Decca recording for Solti, it is warm and full.

Abbado's powerful reading, admirably paced and with a splendid feeling for the sparkle of the comedy, remains highly recommendable. The cast is very strong, with Ricciarelli at her very finest and Domingo sweeter of tone and more deft of characterization than on the Muti set of five years earlier. Bruson as the wronged husband Renato (a role he also takes for Solti) sings magnificently, and only Obraztsova as Ulrica and Gruberová as Oscar are less consistently convincing. The analogue recording clearly separates the voices and instruments in different acoustics, which on CD is distracting only initially and after that brings the drama closer.

The reissued RCA set makes a fine bargain. Leontyne Price is a natural for the part of Amelia, spontaneous-sounding and full of dramatic temperament. Only in the two big arias does Price for a moment grow self-conscious. Robert Merrill here seems to have acquired all sorts of dramatic, Gobbi-like overtones to add to the flow of firm, satisfying tone. Bergonzi is a model of sensitivity, while Reri Grist makes a light, bright Oscar, and the Ulrica of Shirley Verrett has a range of power, richness and delicacy coupled with unparalleled firmness that makes this one of her most memorable recorded performances. Excellent recording, hardly showing its age, with the voices rather forward.

On EMI the quintet of principals is also unusually strong, but it is the conductor who takes first honours in a warmly dramatic reading. Muti's rhythmic resilience and consideration for the singers go with keen concentration, holding each Act together in a way he did not quite achieve in his earlier recording for EMI of *Aida*. Arroyo, rich of voice, is not always imaginative in her big solos, and Domingo rarely produces a half-tone, though the recording balance may be partly to blame. The sound is vivid, but no translation is provided for this mid-price reissue.

The main interest in the earlier Decca set rests in the pairing of Tebaldi and Pavarotti. The latter was in young, vibrant voice, but Tebaldi made her recording in the full maturity of her career. Much of her singing is very fine indeed, but there is no mistaking that her voice here is nowhere near as even as it once was. For the command of her performance this is a version well worth hearing and the supporting cast is strong, not only Milnes as Renato and Donath as Oscar, but Resnik a dark-voiced Ulrica. Bartoletti directs the proceedings dramatically, and the (1970) Decca recording remains strikingly vivid and atmospheric.

Un ballo was the very last of the complete operas that Toscanini conducted in New York in concert performance. It was given in Carnegie Hall in January 1954, just three months before the maestro finally retired. Though the performance cannot match in exhilaration his unique reading of *Falstaff*, it stands as one of the most cherishable mementoes of his conducting of Verdi. Speeds are often fast and the control characteristically taut, but it is wrong to think of the performance as rigid, when rubato is often so freely expressive. Peerce misses some of the lightness of the role, clear in diction but not very characterful, yet Herva Nelli here gives one of her finest performances, with a beautiful, finely moulded line in her big numbers, including the two arias. Robert Merrill is superb as Renato, singing magnificently in *Eri tu*, while Claramae Turner is firm as a rock as Ulrica. The sound is typically dry, not at all atmospheric, but clean and well detailed.

There is a good case to be made for a recording of this opera which takes a lightweight view, with its sparkling party and ball scenes, and Carlo Rizzi is an excellent choice of conductor for such an approach. He draws crisp, amiably relaxed performances from his Welsh National Opera forces, yet the result is in many ways disappointing. Too many of the cast have voices which do not take easily to recording, with wobbles and vibrato exaggerated by the microphone. That is specially true of the soprano, Michele Criser, who sings Amelia, sounding too gusty in her big arias. The Russian baritone, Vladimir Chernov, as Renato uses a distinctively Slavonic timbre, not always steady, if very characterful, and it is the same with his compatriot, the Russian mezzo, Elena Zaremba, as Ulrica. Richard Leech as Riccardo adds to the feeling of a lightweight reading with his tenor, as recorded, sounding lighter and more lyrical than usual, stylish but not as commanding as the big guns, Plácido Domingo (Karajan) and Luciano Pavarotti (Solti). Most successful among the soloists is the bright, clear Spanish coloratura, Maria Bayo, as Oscar. For all these shortcomings, the warmth and the point of the writing, particularly in the many important ensembles, come over well, thanks largely to Rizzi. Clear recording, a little backward.

Un ballo in maschera: highlights.
(Y/B) (M) *** DG Dig. 445 468-2 [id.] (from above set, with Ricciarelli, Domingo, Bruson, Gruberová, Raimondi; cond. Abbado).
(N) (BB) *** CfP Silver Double CDCFPSD 4742 (2). Deutekom, Craig, Hay, Derksen, McCue, Van den Berg, Scottish Op. Ch., SNO, Gibson – LEHAR: *The Merry Widow*. **(*)

The 68-minute selection from the Abbado version, which includes the *Prelude* and opens brightly with *S'avanza il conte*, makes a good mid-priced choice, with a cued synopsis of the narrative for the listener to follow the action. The excerpts are well chosen to represent Domingo, but Ricciarelli's splendid contribution is not neglected. The CD transfer faithfully reflects the qualities of the complete set.

The Classics for Pleasure hour-long set of highlights from the 1975 Scottish Opera production of *Un ballo in maschera* is something of a collector's item. Everyone is on top form, and Christina Deutekom's vibrant assumption of the role of Amelia matches her fine contribution to the complete recording of *Attila*. She is extremely well partnered by Charles Craig (heard too rarely in Verdi on record) and their Love duet which climaxes Act II (*Teco io sto . . . O qual soave brivido*) is memorable. In Act III it is the strong, dark-voiced Anckarstroem of Jan Derksen who stands out. But none of the other principals lets the side down, and Gibson directs with fine vigour and spontaneity, so that one has the feeling of a live performance. The recording is excellent, vivid and atmospheric. Only the briefest synopsis is provided, but this very enjoyable if unlikely Silver Double coupling with Lehár is well worth trying.

La Battaglia di Legnano (complete).
(M) *** Ph. 422 435-2 (2). Ricciarelli, Carreras, Manuguerra, Ghiuselev, Austrian R. Ch. & O, Gardelli.

La Battaglia di Legnano is a compact, sharply conceived piece, made the more intense by the subject's obvious relationship with the situation in Verdi's own time. One weakness is that the villainy is not effectively personalized, but the juxtaposition of the individual drama of supposed infidelity against a patriotic theme brings most effective musical contrasts. Gardelli directs a fine performance, helped by a strong cast of principals, with Carreras, Ricciarelli and Manuguerra all at their finest. Excellent recording, with the depth of perspective enhanced on CD.

Il Corsaro (complete).
(M) *** Ph. 426 118-2 (2). Norman, Caballé, Carreras, Grant, Mastromei, Noble, Amb. S., New Philh. O, Gardelli.

In *Il Corsaro*, though the characterization is rudimentary, the contrast between the two heroines is effective, with Gulnara, the Pasha's slave, carrying conviction in the *coup de foudre* which has her promptly worshipping the Corsair, an early example of the Rudolph Valentino figure. The rival heroines are taken splendidly here, with Jessye Norman as the faithful wife, Medora, actually upstaging Montserrat Caballé as Gulnara. Gardelli directs a vivid performance, with fine singing from the hero, portrayed by José Carreras. Gian-Piero Mastromei, not rich in tone, still rises to the challenge of the Pasha's music. Excellent, firmly focused and well-balanced Philips sound.

Don Carlos (complete).
(Y/B) (M) *** EMI CMS7 69304-2 (3) [Ang. CDMC 69304]. Carreras, Freni, Ghiaurov, Baltsa, Cappuccilli, Raimondi, German Op. Ch., Berlin, BPO, Karajan.
*** EMI CDS7 47701-8 (3) [Ang. CDCC 47701]. Domingo, Caballé, Raimondi, Verrett, Milnes, Amb. Op. Ch., ROHCG O, Giulini.

**(*) Sony Dig. S3K 52500 (3) [id.]. Furlanetto, Millo, Zajick, Sylvester, Chernov, Ramey, Battle, NY Met. Ch. & O, James Levine.

**(*) DG Dig. 415 316-2 (4) [id.]. Ricciarelli, Domingo, Valentini Terrani, Nucci, Raimondi, Ghiaurov, La Scala, Milan, Ch. & O, Abbado.

(M) (**(*)) EMI mono CMS7 64642-2 [CDMC 64642] (3). Christoff, Stella, Nicolai, Mario Filippeschi, Gobbi, Neri, Rome Op. Ch. & O, Santini.

(M) **(*) DG 437 730-2 (3) [id.]. Christoff, Stella, Cossotto, Labò, Bastianini, La Scala, Milan, Ch. & O, Santini.

Karajan opts firmly for the later, four-Act version of the opera, merely opening out the cuts he adopted on stage. The *Auto da fé* scene is here superb, while Karajan's characteristic choice of singers for refinement of voice rather than sheer size consistently pays off. Both Carreras and Freni are most moving, even if *Tu che le vanità* has its raw moments. Baltsa is a superlative Eboli and Cappuccilli an affecting Rodrigo, though neither Carreras nor Cappuccilli is at his finest in the famous oath duet. Raimondi and Ghiaurov as the Grand Inquisitor and Philip II provide the most powerful confrontation. The sound is both rich and atmospheric and is made to seem even firmer and more vivid in its current remastering, giving great power to Karajan's uniquely taut account of the four-Act version. The set's presentation has also been attractively redesigned, and this set remains at the top of the recommended list.

There is extra joy in the *Auto da fé* scene as it is pointed by Giulini, who uses the full, five-Act text. Generally the cast is strong; the only major vocal disappointment among the principals lies in Caballé's account of the big aria *Tu che le vanità* in the final Act. The CD transfer of the 1971 analogue recording brings astonishing vividness and realism, a tribute to the original engineering of Christopher Parker. Even in the big ensembles the focus is very precise, yet atmospheric too, not just analytic.

The heavy-handedness of Levine as a Verdian is exaggerated by the full, forward sound. With Levine the *Auto da fé* ensemble may lack refinement, taken fast, but it is certainly dramatic, and the whole performance has a thrust and bite that reflect opera-house experience. The cast is very acceptable, if not ideally distinguished. In the title-role the American tenor, Michael Sylvester, produces fine, clear, heroic tone and, unlike most rivals, he is not afraid to shade his voice down to a pianissimo. Aprile Millo's ripe soprano is very apt for the role of Elisabetta and, though her vibrato tends to become obtrusive, she controls her line well, not least in the perilous phrases of her big Act V aria, *Tu che le vanità*. As Eboli, Dolora Zajic's fruity mezzo is not well caught by the close-up recording, again with unevenness exaggerated, but this is a rich characterization. As King Philip, Ferruccio Furlanetto is not as firm as he usually is, while Vladimir Chernev as Rodrigo is not flattered either, with fluttery timbre exaggerated. He makes little of the character, the key to the whole opera, leaving a disappointing blank where one wants the keenest intensity. But this remains the best digital recommendation for the full, five-Act score.

Abbado's set was the first recording to use the language which Verdi originally set, French, in the full five-Act text, and, by rights, this should be the definitive recording of the opera. The first disappointment lies in the variable quality of the sound, with odd balances, so that although the Fontainebleau opening, with its echoing horns, is arrestingly atmospheric, the *Auto da fé* scene lacks bite, brilliance and clarity. In addition, large-scale flair and urgency are missing; once that is said, however, the cast of singers is a strong one. Domingo easily outshines his earlier recording with Giulini (in Italian), while Katia Ricciarelli as the Queen gives a tenderly moving performance, if not quite commanding enough in the Act V aria. Ruggero Raimondi is a finely focused Philip II, nicely contrasted with Nicolai Ghiaurov as the Grand Inquisitor in the other black-toned bass role. Lucia Valentini Terrani as Eboli is warm-toned if not very characterful, and Leo Nucci makes a noble Posa.

The vintage EMI mono recording offers a seriously cut version of the four-Act score, indifferently conducted by Gabriele Santini, but it is still an indispensable set, with performances from Tito Gobbi as Rodrigo and Boris Christoff as Philip which have never been remotely matched. Gobbi's singing in the Death scene is arguably the finest recorded performance that even this glorious artist ever made, with a wonderful range of tone and feeling for words. The bitingly dark tone of Christoff as the King also goes with intense feeling for the dramatic situation, making his big monologue one of the peaks of the performance. Antonietta Stella, never a very distinctive artist, gives one of her finest recorded performances as Elisabetta, only occasionally squally. As Eboli, Elena Nicolai controls her fruity mezzo well, even if the vibrato becomes obtrusive; and the most serious blot is the singing of the tenor, Mario Filippeschi, and even that is not as coarse or strained as we have often had latterly.

Two of the principal soloists on the analogue DG set – Christoff and Stella – as well as the conductor are the same as in the old HMV mono recording, but this newer set has the advantage of including the Fontainebleau forest scene. Christoff is again superb. No other bass in the world today comes anywhere near him in this part in vocal strength, musicianship or power of characterization. The tragic dilemma of the ageing King Philip II has an intense nobility when in Act IV he faces the grim demands of the Inquisitor. Antonietta Stella is no more successful here than she was on EMI: she still has poor discipline, and in her big aria, *Tu che le vanità*, this makes for some squally sounds. Fiorenza Cossotto proves a warm-voiced Eboli who copes strongly with the difficulties of *O don fatale*. Labò is a surprisingly good Don Carlos. Unlike Filippeschi on the old mono set, he sings expressively and intelligently. The real loss, of course, is the replacement of Tito Gobbi by Bastianini. Firm and rich as Bastianini unfailingly is, he does not begin to plumb the character in that way. The DG recording-balance favours the voices, while the orchestra is comparatively distant; but the lively CD transfer makes everything sound more vivid, even if the orchestra is masked in the moments of spectacle. But this is such a wonderful opera that even these flaws cannot prevent this recording from proving a most moving experience.

Don Carlos: highlights.
(M) *** EMI CDM7 63089-2 (from above recording, with Domingo, Caballé; cond. Giulini).
(Y/B) (M) **(*) Sony Dig. SMK 53507 [id.] (from above recording, with Furlanetto, Millo, Zajick, Sylvester, Chernov; cond. Levine).

Giulini's disc of highlights can be highly recommended. In selecting from such a long opera, serious omissions are inevitable; nothing is included here from Act III, to make room for the *Auto da fé* scene from Act IV – some 37 minutes of the disc is given to this Act. With vivid sound this is most stimulating; the only reservation concerns Caballé's *Tu che le vanità*, which ends the selection disappointingly.

Although, like Levine's *Aida*, his Met. *Don Carlos* highlights was recorded in the Mahattan Center, the sound is comparatively full and vivid. Michael Sylvester (as Don Carlos) and Aprile Millo (as Elisabetta) are both well cast and, if the rest of the team are more uneven and Ferruccio Furlanetto is a less than ideal King Philip, this 74-minute selection makes a more than acceptable mid-priced sampler.

I due Foscari (complete).
(M) *** Ph. 422 426-2 (2). Ricciarelli, Carreras, Cappuccilli, Ramey, Austrian R. Ch. & SO, Gardelli.

I due Foscari brings Verdian high spirits in plenty, erupting in swinging cabalettas and much writing that anticipates operas as late as *Simon Boccanegra* and *La forza del destino*. The cast here is first rate, with Ricciarelli giving one of her finest performances in the recording studio to date and with Carreras singing tastefully as well as powerfully. The crispness of discipline among the Austrian Radio forces is admirable, but there is less sense of atmosphere here than in the earlier, London-made recordings in the series.

Ernani (complete).
(M) *** RCA GD 86503 (2) [6503-2-RG]. Leontyne Price, Bergonzi, Sereni, Flagello, RCA Italiana Op. Ch. & O, Schippers.
**(*) EMI Dig. CDS7 47083-2 (3) [Ang. CDC 47082]. Domingo, Freni, Bruson, Ghiaurov, La Scala, Milan, Ch. & O, Muti.
(N) (M) **(*) Ph. Dig. 446 669 [id.]. Lamberti, Sass, Kovats, Miller, Takacs, Hungarian State Op. Ch. & O, Gardelli.

At mid-price, Schippers' set, recorded in Rome in 1967, is an outstanding bargain. Leontyne Price may take the most celebrated aria, *Ernani involami*, rather cautiously, but the voice is gloriously firm and rich, and Bergonzi is comparatively strong and vivid, though Mario Sereni, vocally reliable, is dull, and Ezio Flagello gritty-toned. Nevertheless, with Schippers drawing the team powerfully together, it is a highly enjoyable set, with the digital transfer making voices and orchestra sound full and vivid.

The great merit of Muti's set, recorded live at a series of performances at La Scala, is that the ensembles have an electricity rarely achieved in the studio, even if the results may not always be so precise and stage noises are often obtrusive. The singing, generally strong and characterful, is yet flawed. The strain of the role of Elvira for Mirella Freni is plain from the big opening aria, *Ernani involami*, onwards. Even in that aria there are cautious moments. Bruson is a superb Carlo and Ghiaurov a characterful Silva, but his voice now betrays signs of wear. As Ernani himself, Plácido Domingo gives a commandingly heroic performance, but under pressure there are hints of tight tone such as he rarely produces in the studio. The CD version gives greater immediacy and presence, but also brings out the inevitable flaws of live recording the more clearly.

Originally issued on Hungaraton, this early digital set now returns to the catalogue on Philips at mid-price with full libretto and translation. Gardelli's conducting is most sympathetic and idiomatic in the Hungarian version and, like Muti's, it is strong on ensembles. Sylvia Sass is a sharply characterful Elvira, Callas-like in places, and Lamberti a bold Ernani, but their vocal flaws prevent this from being a first choice. Capable rather than inspired or idiomatic singing from the rest. The digital recording is bright and well balanced, although the CD transfer brings out the fact that the recording acoustics are very resonant. An enjoyable set all the same.

Falstaff (complete).

*** DG Dig. 410 503-2 (2) [id.]. Bruson, Ricciarelli, Nucci, Hendricks, Egerton, Valentini Terrani, Boozer, LA Master Ch., LAPO, Giulini.

*(**) EMI CDS7 49668-2 (2) [Ang. CDCB 49668]. Gobbi, Schwarzkopf, Zaccaria, Moffo, Panerai, Philh. Ch. & O, Karajan.

(M) (***) RCA mono GD 60251 (2) [60251-RG-2]. Valdengo, Nelli, Merriman, Elmo, Guarrera, Stich-Randall, Robert Shaw Ch., NBC SO, Toscanini.

Giulini's *Falstaff* brings a care for musical values which at times undermines the knockabout comic element. On record that is all to the good, for the clarity and beauty of the playing are caught superbly on CD. Bruson, hardly a comic actor, is impressive on record for his fine incisive singing, giving tragic implications to the monologue at the start of Act III after Falstaff's dunking. The Ford of Leo Nucci, impressive in the theatre, is thinly caught, where the heavyweight quality of Ricciarelli as Alice comes over well, though in places one would wish for a purer sound. Barbara Hendricks is a charmer as Nannetta, but she hardly sounds fairy-like in her Act III aria. But the conviction of the whole performance puts it among the most desirable of modern readings.

This earlier (1956) Karajan recording presents not only the most pointed account orchestrally of Verdi's comic masterpiece (the Philharmonia Orchestra at its very peak) but the most sharply characterful cast ever gathered for a recording. If you relish the idea of Tito Gobbi as Falstaff (his many-coloured voice, not quite fat-sounding in humour, presents a sharper character than usual), then this is clearly the best choice, for the rest of the cast is a delight, with Schwarzkopf a tinglingly masterful Mistress Ford, Anna Moffo sweet as Nannetta and Rolando Panerai a formidable Ford. Unfortunately the digital remastering has been mismanaged. While the precision and placing of voices on the stereo stage, a model even today, comes out the more clearly on CD, the transfer itself, at a low level and with high hiss, has lost the bloom and warmth of the original analogue master which was outstanding for its time.

Toscanini's fizzing account of Verdi's last masterpiece has never been matched on record, the most high-spirited performance ever, beautifully paced for comedy. Even without stereo, and recorded with typical dryness, the clarity and sense of presence in this live concert performance set the story in relief. The cast is excellent, led by the ripe, firm baritone, Giuseppe Valdengo. Such singers as Nan Merriman as Mistress Page, Cloe Elmo as a wonderfully fruity Mistress Quickly and Frank Guarrera as Ford match or outshine any more recent interpreters. Toscanini's favourite soprano in his last years, Herva Nelli, is less characterful as Mistress Ford, rather over-parted but still fresh and reliable.

La forza del destino (complete).

*** RCA RD 81864 (3) [RCD3-1864]. Leontyne Price, Domingo, Milnes, Cossotto, Giaiotti, Bacquier, Alldis Ch., LSO, Levine.

*** DG Dig. 419 203-2 (3) [id.]. Plowright, Carreras, Bruson, Burchuladze, Baltsa, Amb. Op. Ch., Philh. O, Sinopoli.

(M) *** RCA GD 87971 (3) [4515-2-RG]. Leontyne Price, Tucker, Merrill, Tozzi, Verrett, Flagello, Foiani, RCA Italiana Op. Ch. & O, Schippers.

(N) (M) * Decca 443 678-2 (3) [id.]. Milanov, Di Stefano, Warren, Elias, Tozzi, Santa Cecilia, Rome, Ch. and O, Previtali.

James Levine directs a superb performance. The results are electrifying. Leontyne Price recorded the role of Leonora in an earlier RCA version made in Rome in 1956, but the years have hardly touched her voice, and details of the reading have been refined. The roles of Don Alvaro and Don Carlo are ideally suited to the regular team of Plácido Domingo and Sherrill Milnes so that their confrontations are the cornerstones of the dramatic structure. Fiorenza Cossotto makes a formidable rather than a jolly Preziosilla, while on the male side the line-up of Bonaldo Giaiotti, Gabriel Bacquier, Kurt Moll and Michel Sénéchal is far stronger than on rival sets. In a good, vivid transfer of the mid-1970s sound, this is a strong, well-paced version with an exceptionally good and consistent cast.

Sinopoli draws out phrases lovingly, sustaining pauses to the limit, putting extra strain on the singers. Happily, the whole cast seems to thrive on the challenge, and the spaciousness of the recording acoustic not only makes the dramatic interchanges the more realistic, it brings out the bloom on all the voices, above all the creamy soprano of Rosalind Plowright. Though José Carreras is sometimes too conventionally histrionic, even strained, it is a strong, involved performance. Renato Bruson is a thoughtful Carlo, while some of the finest singing of all comes from Agnes Baltsa as Preziosilla and Paata Burchuladze as the Padre Guardiano, uniquely resonant.

On RCA, Leontyne Price's voice (in 1964) was fresher and more open; on balance this is a more tender and delicate performance than the weightier one she recorded with Levine. Richard Tucker as Alvaro is here far less lachrymose and more stylish than he was earlier in the Callas set, producing ample, heroic tone, if not with the finesse of a Domingo. Robert Merrill as Carlo also sings with heroic strength, consistently firm and dark of tone; while Shirley Verrett, Giorgio Tozzi and Ezio Flagello stand up well against any rivalry. The sound is remarkably full and vivid.

Decca must be scraping the bottom of the barrel to bring out Previtali's early stero set (originally issued on RCA) which, even when it first appeared, was compared adversely to its main competitor, dominated by Tebaldi and conducted by Molinari-Pradelli – which itself has long been outclassed by subsequent recordings. In Rome, Milanov as Leonora was beginning to show her age, with occasional gusty swoops, her performance hardly comparable with Tebaldi's exquiste *mezza voce*; and Di Stefano, a relatively pale Alvaro, still was not entirely free of crudeness. Rosalind Elias as Preziosilla sounds fruity and bosomy. Perhaps the set may be regarded as a memorial to Leonard Warren, a fine Don Carlo; but with uninspired conducting from Previtali this reissue has little to recommend it.

La forza del destino (slightly abridged).
(***) EMI mono CDS7 47581-8 (3) [Ang. CDCC 47581]. Callas, Tucker, Tagliabue, Clabassi, Nicolai, Rossi-Lemeni, Capecchi, La Scala, Milan, Ch. & O, Serafin.

Though there are classic examples of Callas's raw tone on top notes, they are insignificant next to the wealth of phrasing which sets a totally new and individual stamp on even the most familiar passages. Apart from his tendency to disturb his phrasing with sobs, Richard Tucker sings superbly; but not even he – and certainly none of the others (including the baritone Carlo Tagliabue, well past his prime) – begin to rival the dominance of Callas. Serafin's direction is crisp, dramatic and well paced, again drawing the threads together. The 1955 mono sound is less aggressive than many La Scala recordings of this vintage and has been freshened on CD.

La forza del destino: highlights.
** EMI Dig. CDC7 54326-2 [id.]. Freni, Domingo, Zancanaro, Zajic, Pliskhka, La Scala, Milan, Ch. & O, Muti.

Few are likely to choose Muti's complete set of *La forza del destino*, because of its indifferent digital sound, but those wanting to sample Domingo's arresting Don Alvaro might consider this highlights disc. He is included in two excerpts from Act III and three from Act IV. The CD includes 67 minutes of music and is well documented, but it comes at full price.

Un giorno di regno (complete).
(M) *** Ph. 422 429-2 (2). Cossotto, Norman, Carreras, Wixell, Sardinero, Ganzarolli, Amb. S., RPO, Gardelli.

Un giorno di regno may not be the greatest comic opera of the period, but this scintillating performance under Gardelli clearly reveals the young Verdi as more than an imitator of Rossini and Donizetti, and there are striking passages which clearly give a foretaste of such numbers as the duet *Si vendetta* from *Rigoletto*. Despite the absurd plot, this is as light and frothy an entertainment as anyone could want. Excellent singing from a fine team, with Jessye Norman and José Carreras outstanding. The recorded sound is vivid.

I Lombardi (complete).
(M) *** Ph. 422 420-2 (2). Deutekom, Domingo, Raimondi, Amb. S., RPO, Gardelli.

I Lombardi reaches its apotheosis in the famous *Trio*, well known from the days of 78-r.p.m. recordings. By those standards, Cristina Deutekom is not an ideal Verdi singer: her tone is sometimes hard and her voice is not always perfectly under control, yet there are also some glorious moments and the phrasing is often impressive. Domingo as Oronte is in superb voice, and the villain Pagano is well characterized by Raimondi. Among the supporting cast Stafford Dean and Clifford Grant must be mentioned. Gardelli conducts dramatically and the action projects vividly.

(i) *I Lombardi, Act III: Trio.* (ii) *Rigoletto, Act IV* (complete).
(M) (**) RCA mono GD 60276 (2); [60276-2-RG]. (i) Della Chiesa, Peerce, Moscona; (ii) Warren, Milanov, Peerce, Moscona, Merriman, All City Highschool Ch. & Glee Clubs, NBC SO, Toscanini – BOITO: *Mefistofele: Prologue.* (***)

It is interesting to find a little-known singer, Vivian della Chiesa, emerging strongly alongside Jan Peerce and Nicola Moscona. The last Act of *Rigoletto* was given in a wartime fund-raising concert in Madison Square Garden and, though the brittleness of sound is at times almost comic and the tautness of Toscanini's control was unrelenting, the performances of the principals are formidable, with Zinka

Milanov at her most radiant. With Toscanini's searing account of the *Mefistofele Prologue*, this makes a generous compilation.

Luisa Miller (complete).
*** Sony Dig. S2K 48073 (2) [id.]. Domingo, Millo, Chernov, Rootering, Quivar, Plishka, Met. Op. O and Ch., Levine.
*** Decca 417 420-2 (2) [id.]. Caballé, Pavarotti, Milnes, Reynolds, L. Op. Ch., Nat. PO, Maag.
*** DG 423 144-2 (2) [id.]. Ricciarelli, Obraztsova, Domingo, Bruson, ROHCG Ch. & O, Maazel.
(M) *** RCA GD 86646 (2) [6646-2-RG]. Moffo, Bergonzi, Verrett, MacNeil, Tozzi, Flagello, RCA Italiana Op. Ch. & O, Cleva.

Levine conducts his forces from the Met. in a red-blooded, exceptionally high-powered reading of this elusive opera. In the role of Miller, the heroine's father, Chernov is even more characterful and musically more individual than any of his main rivals on the other sets, with the power of his singing brought home by the close balance of the voice. Though the sound tends to make Levine's direction seem less subtle than it is, less elegant than Maag on Decca, less refined in texture than Maazel on DG, the impact of the score is brought home formidably. It is significant how Plácido Domingo, who takes the role of the hero Rodolfo for both Maazel and Levine, sings with much greater animation in the New York recording. Among the others Jan-Henrik Rootering, Florence Quivar and Paul Plishka all sing powerfully, even if all three suffer from occasional unsteadiness. The snag is the variable quality of Aprile Millo's singing in the title-role. She has the right Verdian timbre, more girlish-sounding than her rivals, but in Act I the coloratura taxes her severely; however, by the final Act she produces some lovely singing with some beautifully floated high pianissimos. It is in that final Act that the extra dramatic bite of Levine's reading tells most in its impact.

On Decca, Caballé, though not as flawless vocally as one would expect, gives a splendidly dramatic portrait of the heroine and Pavarotti's performance is full of creative, detailed imagination. As Federica, Anna Reynolds is distinctly preferable to Obraztsova, and Maag's sympathetic reading, by underlining the light and shade, consistently brings out the atmospheric qualities of Verdi's conception. Vividly transferred, this Decca recording has the balance of advantage over the DG set.

Though taut in his control, Maazel uses his stage experience of working with these soloists to draw them out to their finest, most sympathetic form. Ricciarelli gives one of her tenderest and most beautiful performances on record, Domingo is in glorious voice and Bruson as Luisa's father sings with velvet tone. Gwynne Howell is impressive as the Conte di Walter and Wladimiro Ganzarolli's vocal roughness is apt for the character of Wurm. The snag is the abrasive Countess Federica of Elena Obraztsova.

In many ways the Cleva RCA set provides a performance to compete with the full-price versions and is just as stylish, with Moffo at her very peak, singing superbly, Carlo Bergonzi unfailingly intelligent and stylish, and Verrett nothing less than magnificent in her role as a quasi-Amneris. MacNeil and Tozzi are also satisfyingly resonant, and Fausto Cleva tellingly reveals his experience directing the opera at the Met. Good recording.

Luisa Miller: highlights.
(Y/B) (M) *** Sony Dig. SMK 53508 [id.] (from above recording, with Domingo, Millo, Chernov; cond. Levine).

This is easily the finest of the current Sony series of Verdi highlights recorded at the Met. under James Levine. The 75-minute selection is well chosen and, with Chernov (as Miller) and Domingo (as Rodolfo) both on top form, this can be strongly recommended.

Macbeth (complete).
*** Ph. Dig. 412 133-2 (3) [id.]. Bruson, Zampieri, Shicoff, Lloyd, German Op. Ch. & O, Berlin, Sinopoli.
(N) (M) *** DG 449 732-2 (2) [id.]. Cappuccilli, Verrett, Ghiaurov, Domingo, La Scala, Milan, Ch. & O, Abbado.
(M) *** EMI CMS7 64339-2 (2) [Ang. CDMB 64339]. Milnes, Cossotto, Raimondi, Carreras, Amb. Op. Ch., New Philh. O, Muti.
(M) **(*) Decca 440 048-2 (2) [id.]. Fischer-Dieskau, Suliotis, Ghiaurov, Pavarotti, Amb. Op. Ch., LPO, Gardelli.
(M) **(*) RCA GD 84516 (2) [4516-2-RG]. Warren, Rysanek, Bergonzi, Hines, Met. Op. Ch. & O, Leinsdorf.
(N) (M) (*(**)) EMI mono CMS7 64944-2 (2) [CDMB 64944]. Callas, Mascherini, Tajo, Penno, Della Pergola, La Scala, Milan, Ch. & O, Victor de Sabata.

Even more than his finest rivals, Sinopoli presents this opera as a searing Shakespearean inspiration, scarcely more uneven than much of the work of the Bard himself. In the Banqueting scene, for example, Sinopoli creates extra dramatic intensity by his concern for detail and his preference for extreme dynamics, and Renato Bruson and Mara Zampieri respond vividly. Zampieri's voice may be biting rather than beautiful, occasionally threatening to come off the rails, but, with musical precision an asset, she matches exactly Verdi's request for the voice of a she-devil. Neil Shicoff as Macduff and Robert Lloyd as Banquo make up the excellent quartet of principals, while the high voltage of the whole performance clearly reflects Sinopoli's experience with the same chorus and orchestra at the Deutsche Oper in Berlin. CD adds vividly to the realism of a recording that is well balanced and focused but atmospheric.

At times Abbado's tempi are unconventional, but with slow speeds he springs the rhythm so infectiously that the results are the more compelling. The whole performance gains from superb teamwork, for each of the principals – far more than is common – is meticulous about observing Verdi's detailed markings, above all those for *pianissimo* and *sotto voce*. Verrett, hardly powerful above the stave, yet makes a virtue out of necessity in floating glorious half-tones, and with so firm and characterful a voice she makes a highly individual, not at all conventional Lady Macbeth. As for Cappuccilli, he has never sung with such fine range of tone and imagination on record as here, and Plácido Domingo makes a real, sensitive character out of the small role of Macduff. Excellent recording, splendidly remastered as one of the first operas to be included in DG's 'Legendary Recordings' series, and now at mid-price and on two discs.

Muti's 1976 version of *Macbeth*, made at Abbey Road, appeared within weeks of Abbado's, confirming that, in this opera, new standards were being set on record. Though Muti and his team do not quite match the supreme distinction of Abbado and, later, Sinopoli, they provide a valid alternative. Both Milnes and Cossotto sing warmly and are richly convincing in their relatively conventional views of their roles, while the comfortable reverberation and warmth of the EMI recording conceal any slight shortcomings of ensemble. The reissue therefore provides a firm mid-priced recommendation for this opera, and it fits neatly on to a pair of CDs.

Fischer-Dieskau does not give a traditional performance in this great tragic role, for characteristically he points the words in full Lieder-style. Nor is he in his freshest voice, growing gritty in some climaxes; but it is still a marvellous, compelling performance which stands repeated hearing. Suliotis is – to put it kindly – a variable Lady Macbeth. In the first aria there are moments when her voice runs completely out of control, but she still has imagination, and her 'voice of a she-devil' (Verdi's words) is arguably the precise sound needed. Certainly she settles down into giving a striking and individual performance, while Ghiaurov as Banquo and Pavarotti as MacDuff sing with admirable poise. Gardelli and the LPO are treated to specially vivid recording which has transferred vibrantly to CD.

Leinsdorf's version brings a large-scale performance featuring three favourite principals from the Met. Leonie Rysanek here gives one of her finest performances on record, producing her firmest, creamiest sound for the Sleepwalking scene, even though the coloratura taxes her severely. Leonard Warren, much admired in this part before his untimely death (on stage, singing Don Carlo in *La forza del destino*), gives a strong, thoughtful reading, marred by the way the microphone exaggerates his vibrato. Carlo Bergonzi is a stylish, clear-toned Macduff. Good sound for its period.

The role of Lady Macbeth could hardly have been more perfectly suited to Maria Callas, and though there are serious flaws in this live recording of 1952 – evidently taken off a radio relay – the commanding presence, the magnetic musical imagination and the actual vocal quality abrasive enough to qualify as the 'she-wolf' Verdi wanted, make this a unique experience. In 1952 the vocal flaws that beset Callas were largely in the future, with thrilling sound in every register. Also Victor de Sabata, despite some odd misjudgements like his brisk tempo for the Sleepwalking scene, is comparably incisive as a conductor. Sadly, nothing else in the performance matches such mastery, with Enzo Mascherini a dull, uncharacterful Macbeth and only the resonant Italo Tajo as Banquo otherwise commanding attention. Scrubby, limited sound which most ears will still accommodate for the sake of such a performance.

I Masnadieri (complete).
(M) *** Ph. 422 423-2 (2). Caballé, Bergonzi, Raimondi, Cappuccilli, Amb. S., New Philh. O, Gardelli.
(M) **(*) Decca Dig. 433 854-2 (2) [id.]. Sutherland, Bonisolli, Manuguerra, Ramey, WNO Ch. & O, Bonynge.

Few will seriously identify with the hero-turned-brigand of *I Masnadieri* who stabs his beloved rather than lead her into a life of shame; but, on record, flaws of motivation are of far less moment than on stage. The melodies may only fitfully be of Verdi's more memorable quality, but the musical structure and argument often look forward to a much later period with hints of *Forza*, *Don Carlo* and even *Otello*. With Gardelli as ever an urgently sympathetic Verdian, and a team of four excellent principals, splendidly recorded, the set can be warmly welcomed.

Sutherland's is a weightier view than Caballé took in the earlier, Philips recording, conveying more light and shade. The cabaletta for her great Act II aria brings a coloratura display, with Sutherland still at her very peak. Though Bonisolli sings with less refinement than Bergonzi on the rival set, he has great flair, as in his extra flourishes in the final ensemble of Act II. Manuguerra sings strongly too. He may not be as refined as his rival, Cappuccilli, but he sounds more darkly villainous. Ramey as Massimiliano sings with fine clarity, but the voice does not sound old enough for a father. The Welsh National Opera Chorus projects with the lustiness of stage experience, even if the Kingsway Hall acoustic clouds some choral detail slightly. Even so, the digital sound is very impressive in its fullness and depth, and at mid-price this is certainly worth considering, especially by Sutherland fans.

Nabucco (complete).
*** DG Dig. 410 512-2 (2) [id.]. Cappuccilli, Dimitrova, Nesterenko, Domingo, Ch. & O of German Op., Berlin, Sinopoli.
*** Decca 417 407-2 (2) [id.]. Gobbi, Suliotis, Cava, Previdi, V. State Op. Ch. & O, Gardelli.

With Sinopoli one keeps hearing details normally obscured. Even the thrill of the great chorus *Va, pensiero* is the greater when the melody first emerges at a hushed pianissimo, as marked, sound almost offstage. Dimitrova is superb in Abigaille's big Act II aria, noble in her evil, as is Cappuccilli as Nabucco, less intense than Gobbi was on Gardelli's classic set for Decca, but stylistically pure. The rest of the cast is strong too, including Domingo in a relatively small role and Nesterenko superb as the High Priest, Zaccaria. Bright and forward digital sound, less atmospheric than the 1965 Decca set with Gobbi and Suliotis, conducted by Gardelli.

On Decca, the Viennese choral contribution was less committed than one would ideally like in a work which contains a chorus unique in Verdi's output, *Va, pensiero*; but in every other way this is a masterly performance, with dramatically intense and deeply imaginative contributions from Tito Gobbi as Nabucco and Elena Suliotis as the evil Abigaille. Suliotis made this the one totally satisfying performance of an all-too-brief recording career, wild in places but no more than is dramatically necessary. Though Carlo Cava as Zaccaria is not ideally rich of tone, it is a strong performance, and Gardelli, as in his later Verdi recordings for both Decca and Philips, showed what a master he is at pointing Verdian inspiration, whether in the individual phrase or over a whole scene, simply and naturally, without ever forcing. Vividly real and atmospheric 1965 Decca recording.

Nabucco: highlights.
(M) *** Decca 421 867-2 (from above recording with Gobbi; cond. Gardelli).

Suliotis's impressive contribution is well represented on the Decca highlights disc, and there are fine contributions too from Gobbi. Needless to say, the chorus *Va, pensiero* is given its place of honour and the selection runs for 58 minutes.

Oberto (complete).
*** Orfeo C 105843 F (3) [id.]. Dimitrova, Bergonzi, Panerai, Baldani, Bav. R. Ch., Munich R. O, Gardelli.

In every way this issue matches the success of Gardelli's earlier, Philips recordings, despite the change of venue to Munich. Gardelli successfully papers over the less convincing moments, helped by fine playing from the orchestra, an outstanding chorus and first-rate principals. Ghena Dimitrova makes a very positive heroine, powerful in attack in her moment of fury in the Act I finale, but also gently expressive when necessary. Only in cabalettas is she sometimes ungainly. The veterans, Carlo Bergonzi and Rolando Panerai, more than make up in stylishness and technical finesse for any unevenness of voice, and Ruza Baldani is a warm-toned Cuniza, the mezzo role. First-rate recording.

Otello (complete).
(Y/B) *** DG Dig. 439 805-2 (2) [id.]. Domingo, Studer, Leiferkus, Ch. & O of Bastille Opera, Myung-Whun Chung.
*** Decca Dig. 433 669-2 (2) [id.]. Pavarotti, Te Kanawa, Nucci, Rolfe Johnson, Chicago SO & Ch., Solti.
*** RCA RD 82951 (2) [RCD2-2951]. Domingo, Scotto, Milnes, Amb. Op. Ch., Nat. PO, Levine.
(M) *** RCA GD 81969 (2) [1969-2-RG]. Vickers, Rysanek, Gobbi, Rome Op. Ch. & O, Serafin.
(M) *** EMI CMS7 69308-2 (2) [Ang. CDMB 69308]. Vickers, Freni, Glossop, Ch. of German Op., Berlin, BPO, Karajan.
(N) (M) (***) EMI mono CHS5 65751-2 (2) [CDHB 65751]. Vinay, Martinis, Schoefler, Dermota, V. State Op. Ch., VPO, Furtwängler.
(M) **(*) Decca 440 045-2 (2) [id.]. Cossutta, M. Price, Bacquier, V. Boys' Ch., V. State Op. Ch., VPO, Solti.
(M) (**(*)) RCA mono GD 60302 (2) [60302-2-RG]. Vinay, Valdengo, Nelli, Merriman, Assandri, NBC Ch. & SO, Toscanini.

Plácido Domingo's third recording of *Otello* proves to be his finest yet, more freely expressive, even more involved than his previous ones. In the earliest, with James Levine conducting (RCA), the voice may be more ringingly heroic, but the baritonal quality of his tenor now brings new darkness, with the final solo, *Niun mi tema*, poignantly tender. Cheryl Studer gives one of her finest performances as Desdemona, the tone both full and pure, while Sergei Leiferkus makes a chillingly evil Iago, the more so when his voice is the opposite of Italianate, verging on the gritty, which not everyone will like. With plenty of light and shade, Myung-Whun Chung is an urgent Verdian, adopting free-flowing speeds yet allowing Domingo full expansiveness in the death scene. The Chorus and Orchestra of the Bastille Opera excel themselves, setting new standards for an opera recording from Paris, and the sound is first rate, though transferred at a slightly low level. This now makes a pretty clear first choice for this much-recorded opera.

In the Decca Chicago set the key element is the singing of Pavarotti, new to his role of Otello, as was Nucci as Iago. Following the pattern of the whole performance, Pavarotti often adopts faster speeds than usual. Whatever the detailed reservations, this is a memorable reading, heightened by Pavarotti's acutely observed feeling for the words and consistently golden tone. With a close microphone-balance, like the others he is prevented from achieving genuine pianissimos; but above all he offers a vital, animated Otello, no mere replacement for Domingo but a magnificent alternative. Dame Kiri Te Kanawa produces consistently sumptuous tone; the *Willow song* is glorious. The impact of the whole is greatly enhanced by the splendid singing of the Chicago Symphony Chorus, helped by digital sound that is fuller and more vivid than on any rival set.

On RCA, Domingo as Otello combines glorious heroic tone with lyrical tenderness. Scotto is not always sweet-toned in the upper register, and the big ensemble at the end of Act III brings obvious strain; nevertheless, it is a deeply felt performance which culminates in a most beautiful account of the all-important Act IV solos, the *Willow song* and *Ave Maria*, most affecting. Milnes too is challenged by his role: this Iago is a handsome, virile creature beset by the biggest of chips on the shoulder. In the transfer of the 1977 analogue original the voices are caught vividly and immediately, and the orchestral sound too is fuller and cleaner than in many more recent versions. But this should now be reissued at mid-price.

No conductor is more understanding of Verdian pacing than Serafin and, with sound that hardly begins to show its age (1960), this presents two of the finest solo performances on any *Otello* recording of whatever period: the Iago of Tito Gobbi has never been surpassed for vividness of characterization and tonal subtlety; while the young Jon Vickers, with a voice naturally suited to this role, was in his prime as the Moor. Leonie Rysanek is a warm and sympathetic Desdemona, not always ideally pure-toned but tender and touching in one of her very finest recorded performances. The sense of presence in the open, well-balanced recording is the more vivid on CD, thanks to a first-rate transfer.

Karajan directs a big, bold and brilliant account, for the most part splendidly sung and with all the dramatic contrasts strongly underlined. There are several tiny, but irritating, statutory cuts, but otherwise on two mid-price CDs this is well worth considering. Freni's Desdemona is delightful, delicate and beautiful, while Vickers and Glossop are both positive and characterful, only occasionally forcing their tone and losing focus. The recording is clarified on CD.

Furtwängler, dedicated to the German repertory, at the 1951 Salzburg Festival broke with tradition by presenting Verdi's masterpiece, no doubt intending to rival the pre-war Toscanini. The result is incandescent, a performance of extremes. Set against rapt concentration and tender expressiveness in such passages as the Act I love duet and Desdemona's final scene, the fierily dramatic attack of the main drama is heightened all the more. So the oath duet of Otello and Iago in Act II is thrilling, and the clarity of both Ramon Vinay in the title-role and of Paul Schoeffler as a clean-cut, rather Germanic Iago adds to the bite. Vinay, who recorded the role with Toscanini four years earlier, has a focus and power ideally suited to the role, even if the voice is rarely beautiful. It matters surprisingly little that the Austrian Radio recording of the stage production often balances him distantly. Dragica Martinis, whose career was sadly short, is here revealed as a tender and charming Desdemona, every bit a match for her more celebrated colleagues. The orchestral sound is limited and dim, with intrusive stage-noises, but the electricity and atmosphere still come over well.

The warmth and tenderness of Solti's Vienna reading of *Otello* as well as its incisive sense of drama take one freshly by surprise. The recording is bright and atmospheric to match, which leaves the vocal contributions as a third and more debatable deciding point. Of the very finest quality is the singing of Margaret Price as Desdemona, a ravishing performance, with the most beautiful and varied tonal quality allied to deep imagination. Carlo Cossutta as Otello is not so characterful a singer but, more than most rivals, he sings with clear, incisive tone and obvious concern for musical qualities. Gabriel Bacquier gives a thoughtful, highly intelligent performance as Iago, but his relative weakness in the upper register brings obvious disappointment. The Decca recording, however, has a sense of spectacle (notably in the opening scene) and perspective which is particularly appealing.

Toscanini's historic 1947 reading suffers more than usual from dry, limited sound but in magnetic intensity it is irresistible, bringing home the biting power of Verdi's score as few other recorded performances ever have. Ramon Vinay makes a commanding Otello, baritonal in vocal colouring but firm and clear, with a fine feeling for words. Giuseppe Valdengo had few rivals among baritones of the time in this role, strong, animated and clean in attack, though the vocal differentiation between hero and villain is less marked than usual. Herva Nelli is sweet and pure if a little colourless as Desdemona. The recording prevents her from achieving a really gentle pianissimo, and Toscanini, for all his flowing lines, fails to allow the full repose needed.

Otello: highlights.
(N) *** DG Dig. 445 876-2 [id.] (from above complete set, with Domingo, Studer, Leiferkus; cond. Chung).
(Y/B) **(*) Decca Dig. 440 843-2 [id.] (from above set, with Pavarotti, Te Kanawa, Nucci; cond. Solti).

This DG disc offers some 75 minutes from our current primary recommendation for this opera, with all the key numbers, including the spectacular opening and of course the opera's tragic close. It seems a pity that, at full price, texts and translations are not included, but there is a good cued synopsis.

Those preferring a complete set with Domingo as Otello may be glad to try the Pavarotti/Te Kanawa/ Nucci alternative in highlights form, even if the selection is not very generous for a full-priced CD (59 minutes). Dame Kiri's *Willow song* is glorious and Pavarotti's contribution is also memorable. Solti conducts vividly, while the contribution from the Chicago Chorus adds much to the impact of a set where the digital sound is well up to Decca's usual Vienna standard.

Otello (complete; in English).
(Y/B) (B) **(*) CfP CFPD 4736 (2) [id.]. Craig, Plowright, Howlett, Bottone, ENO Ch. & O, Mark Elder.

Recorded live at the Coliseum in London, the ENO version of *Otello* is inevitably flawed in the sound; but those who seek records of opera in English need not hesitate, for almost every word of Andrew Porter's translation is audible, despite the very variable balances inevitable in recording a live stage production. Less acceptable is the level of stage noise, with the thud and blunder of wandering feet all the more noticeable on CD. The performance itself is most enjoyable, with dramatic tension building up compellingly. Charles Craig's Otello is most moving, the character's inner pain brought out vividly, though top notes are fallible. Neil Howlett as Iago may not have the most distinctive baritone, but finely controlled vocal colouring adds to a deeply perceptive performance. Rosalind Plowright makes a superb Desdemona, singing with rich, dramatic weight but also with poise and purity. The Death scene reveals her at her finest, radiant of tone, with flawless attack.

Rigoletto (complete).
*** Ph. Dig. 412 592-2; *412 592-4* (2) [id.]. Bruson, Gruberová, Shicoff, Fassbaender, Lloyd, St Cecilia Ac., Rome, Ch. & O, Sinopoli.
*** Decca 414 269-2 (2) [id.]. Milnes, Sutherland, Pavarotti, Talvela, Tourangeau, Amb. Op. Ch., LSO, Bonynge.
(***) EMI mono CDS7 47469-8 (2) [Ang. CDCB 47469]. Gobbi, Callas, Di Stefano, Zaccaria, La Scala, Milan, Ch. & O, Serafin.
(M) **(*) RCA GD 86506 (2) [6506-2-RG]. Merrill, Moffo, Kraus, Elias, Flagello, RCA Italiana Op. Ch. & O, Solti.
(Y/B) (B) ** Decca Double 443 853-2 (2) [id.]. MacNeil, Sutherland, Cioni, Siepi, Malagu, Academy of Santa Cecilia, Rome, Ch. & O, Sanzogno.

Edita Gruberová might have been considered an unexpected choice for Gilda, remarkable for her brilliant coloratura rather than for deeper expression, yet here she makes the heroine a tender, feeling creature, emotionally vulnerable yet vocally immaculate. Similarly, Renato Bruson as Rigoletto does far more than produce a stream of velvety tone, detailed and intense, responding to the conductor and combining beauty with dramatic bite. Even more remarkable is the brilliant success of Neil Shicoff as the Duke, more than a match for his most distinguished rivals. Here the *Quartet* becomes a genuine climax. Brigitte Fassbaender as Maddalena is sharply unconventional but vocally most satisfying. Sinopoli's speeds, too, are unconventional at times, but the fresh look he provides makes this one of the most exciting Verdi operas on disc, helped by full and vivid recording, consistently well balanced.

Just over ten years after her first recording of this opera, Sutherland appeared in it again, this time with

Pavarotti who is an intensely characterful Duke: an unmistakable rogue but an unmistakable charmer, too. Thanks to him and to Bonynge above all, the *Quartet*, as on the Sinopoli set, becomes a genuine musical climax. Sutherland's voice has acquired a hint of a beat, but there is little of the mooning manner which disfigured her earlier assumption, and the result is glowingly beautiful as well as being technically supremely assured. Milnes makes a strong Rigoletto, vocally masterful and with good if hardly searching presentation of character. The digital transfer is exceptionally vivid and atmospheric.

There has never been a more compelling performance of the title-role in *Rigoletto* than that of Gobbi on his classic Scala set of the 1950s. At every point, in almost every single phrase, Gobbi finds extra meaning in Verdi's vocal lines, with the widest range of tone-colour employed for expressive effect. Callas, though not naturally suited to the role of the wilting Gilda, is compellingly imaginative through-out, and Di Stefano gives one of his finer performances. The transfer of the original mono recording is astonishingly vivid in capturing the voices, but this remains at full price.

Anna Moffo makes a charming Gilda in the Solti set of 1963. Solti at times presses too hard, but this is a strong and dramatic reading, with Robert Merrill producing a glorious flow of dark, firm tone in the name-part. Alfredo Kraus is as stylish as ever as the Duke, and this rare example of his voice at its freshest should not be missed. A good bargain, though there are statutory cuts in the text.

The earlier Sutherland recording came a decade before her triumphant partnership with Pavarotti. Cornell MacNeil was a resonant but uncharacteful Rigoletto, although Cioni, if conventional, sings well enough as the Duke of Mantova. Sutherland's own performance epitomizes her soft-grained style at its most extreme. The result is often intensely beautiful, particularly in *Caro nome*, but as a dramatic experience it cannot compare with the later Decca set. Nino Sanzogno jogs through everything very neatly, but it is the fine technical quality of the recording and the reliability of the singing that engage the attention, rather than the drama.

Simon Boccanegra (complete).
⊛ *** DG 415 692-2 (2) [id.]. Cappuccilli, Freni, Ghiaurov, Van Dam, Carreras, La Scala, Milan, Ch. & O, Abbado.
(M) (***) EMI mono CMS7 63513-2 (2) [Ang. CDMB 63513]. Gobbi, Christoff, De los Angeles, Campora, Monachesi, Dari, Rome Op. Chor & O, Santini.
(Y/B) (B) **(*) Discover Dig. DICD 920225/6 [id.]. Tumagian, Gauci, Aragall, Mikulas, Sardinero, BRTN Philharmonic Ch. and O, Alexander Rahbari.

Abbado's 1977 recording of *Simon Boccanegra* is one of the most beautiful Verdi sets ever made. Under Abbado the playing of the orchestra is brilliantly incisive as well as refined, so that the drama is underlined by extra sharpness of focus. The cursing of Paolo after the great Council Chamber scene makes the scalp prickle, with the chorus muttering in horror and the bass clarinet adding a sinister comment, here beautifully moulded. Cappuccilli, always intelligent, gives a far more intense and illuminating performance than the one he recorded for RCA earlier in his career. He may not match Gobbi in range of colour and detail, but he too gives focus to the performance; and Ghiaurov as Fiesco sings beautifully too. Freni as Maria Boccanegra sings with freshness and clarity, while Van Dam is an impressive Paolo. With electrically intense choral singing as well, this is a set to outshine even Abbado's superb *Macbeth* with the same company, superbly transferred to CD.

Tito Gobbi's portrait of the tragic Doge of Genoa is one of his greatest on record, and it emerges all the more impressively when it is set against equally memorable performances by Boris Christoff as Fiesco and Victoria de los Angeles as Amelia. The Recognition scene between father and daughter has never been done more movingly on record; nor has the great ensemble, which crowns the Council Chamber scene, been so powerfully and movingly presented, and that without the help of stereo recording. The transfer is full and immediate, giving a vivid sense of presence to the voices, though tape-hiss is on the high side.

On the Discover bargain label Rahbari's well-paced reading is newly recorded in good digital sound with strong casting. Excellent East European principals are joined by the long-established Spanish tenor, Giacomo Aragall, and the baritone, Vincente Sardinero. Miriam Gauci is a vibrant, sympathetic Amelia, and though Eduard Tumagian is not the most characterful Boccanegra and Peter Mikulas could be darker-toned in the bass role of Fiesco, their voices are clear and well-focused, despite backward balance. Libretto in Italian only. Good value.

Stiffelio (complete).
(M) *** Ph. 422 432-2 (2). Carreras, Sass, Manuguerra, Ganzarolli, Austrian R. Ch. & SO, Gardelli.

Coming just before the great trio of masterpieces, *Rigoletto, Il Trovatore* and *La Traviata, Stiffelio* is still a sharply telling work, largely because of the originality of the relationships and the superb final scene in which Stiffelio reads from the pulpit the parable of the woman taken in adultery. Gardelli directs a fresh performance, at times less lively than Queler's of *Aroldo* but with more consistent singing, notably from Carreras and Manuguerra. First-rate recording from Philips, typical of this fine series.

La Traviata (complete).

(Y/B) 🌀 *** Decca Dig. 448 119-2 (2) [id.]. Gheorghiu, Lopardo, Nucci, ROHCG Ch. & O, Solti.

*** Decca Dig. 430 491-2 (2) [id.]. Sutherland, Pavarotti, Manuguerra, L. Op. Ch., Nat. PO, Bonynge.

(M) **(*) EMI Dig. CDS7 47538-8 (2) [Ang. CDC 47538]. Scotto, Kraus, Bruson, Amb. Op. Ch., Philh. O, Muti.

*** Teldec/Warner Dig. 9031 76348-2 (2) [id.]. Gruberová, Shicoff, Zancanaro, Amb. S., LSO, Rizzi.

(B) **(*) CfP CD-CFPD 4450 (2) [Ang. CDB7 67576]. De los Angeles, Del Monte, Sereni, Rome Op. Ch. & O, Serafin.

(B) **(*) Double Decca 443 002-2 (2) [id.]. Lorengar, Aragall, Fischer-Dieskau, Ch. & O of German Op., Berlin, Maazel.

(M) **(*) Decca 411 877-2 (2) [id.]. Sutherland, Bergonzi, Merrill, Ch. & O of Maggio Musicale Fiorentino, Pritchard.

**(*) Ph. Dig. 438 238-2 (2) [id.]. Te Kanawa, Kraus, Hvorostovsky, Maggio Musicale (Florence) Ch. & O, Mehta.

(M) (*(**)) EMI mono CMS7 63628-2 (2) [Ang. CDMB 63628]. Callas, Di Stefano, Bastianini, La Scala Ch. & O, Giulini.

** DG Dig. 435 797-2 (2) [id.]. Studer, Pavarotti, Pons, Met. Op. Ch. & O, Levine.

(M) (**) RCA mono GD 60303 (2) [id.]. Albanese, Peerce, Merrill, NBC Ch. & SO, Toscanini.

Defying the problems of recording opera live at Covent Garden, the Decca engineers here offer one of the most vivid and involving versions ever of *La Traviata*, full and immediate in sound. In a magnetic reading Solti treats the piece, not with his old fierceness, but with refinement and tenderness as well as emotional weight from the ravishingly hushed opening of the Prelude onwards. The intensity of a live occasion comes over consistently, with little or no intrusion from stage or audience noises, merely an enhancement of the event. As on stage, Gheorghiu brings heartfelt revelations, using her rich and vibrant, finely shaded soprano with consistent subtlety. Youthfully vivacious in the first Act, dazzling in her coloratura, she already reveals the depths of feeling which compel her later self-sacrifice. In Act II she finds ample power for the great outburst of '*Amami, Alfredo*', and in Act III almost uniquely uses the second stanza of *Addio del passato* (often omitted) to heighten the intensity of the heroine's emotions. Frank Lopardo emerges as a fresh, lyrical Alfredo with a distinctive timbre, passionate and youthful-sounding too. Leo Nucci, a favourite baritone with Solti, provides a sharp contrast as a stolid but convincing Germont. This is now a leading contender among all the many rival sets and for many it will be a first choice. A video version – taken from a single performance, not (like the CDs) an edited compendium of a series – is also offered (VHS 071 431-3; Laserdisc 071 428-1), letting one appreciate how Gheorghiu's physical beauty matches her voice, and how elegant and atmospheric Richard Eyre's Covent Garden production is, with sets by Bob Crowley.

Sutherland's second recording of the role of Violetta has a breadth and exuberance beyond her achievement in the earlier version of 1963, conducted by John Pritchard, and the richness and command of the singing put this among the very finest of her later recordings. Pavarotti too, though he over-emphasizes *Di miei bollenti spiriti*, sings with splendid panache as Alfredo. Manuguerra as Germont lacks something in authority, but the firmness and clarity are splendid. Bonynge's conducting is finely sprung, the style direct, the speeds often spacious in lyrical music, generally undistracting. The digital recording is outstandingly vivid and beautifully balanced but the CD booklet is not ideal.

Muti has no concern for tradition; at the start of the Act I party music, he is even faster than Toscanini, but the result is dazzling; and when he needs to give sympathetic support to his soloists, above all in the great Act II duet between Violetta and Germont, there is no lack of tenderness. Overall, it is an intensely compelling account, using the complete text (like Bonynge), and it gains from having three Italy-based principals. Scotto and Kraus have long been among the most sensitive and perceptive interpreters of these roles, and so they are here; with bright digital recording, however, it is obvious that these voices are no longer young, with Scotto's soprano spreading above the stave and Kraus's tenor often sounding thin. Scotto gives a view of Violetta which even amid the gaiety of Act I points forward to tragedy. Bruson makes a fine, forthright Germont, though it does not add to dramatic conviction that his is the youngest voice. Small parts are well taken, and the stage picture is projected clearly on CD, with the pleasant reverberation clarified.

Carlo Rizzi in his first major opera recording draws subtle, refined playing from the LSO, which in turn brings refined singing from a well-matched cast. Giorgio Zancanaro is a characterful Germont, giving depth of feeling to the first scene of Act II up to *Di Provenza il mar*. Though Edita Gruberová's bright soprano acquires an unevenness under pressure, she is freshly expressive and increasingly through the opera, up to the great challenge of the death scene, produces the most delicate pianissimos, with phrasing and tone exquisitely shaded. She may not match the finest Violettas of the past, and the tenor, Neil Shicoff, sings with markedly less finesse than the other principals, but this stands high in the list of modern, digital versions of this opera.

Even when Victoria de los Angeles made this EMI recording in the late 1950s, the role of Violetta lay rather high for her voice. Nevertheless it drew from her much beautiful singing, not least in the coloratura display at the end of Act I which, though it may lack easily ringing top notes, has delightful sparkle and flexibility. As to the characterization, De los Angeles was a far more sympathetically tender heroine than is common; though neither the tenor nor the baritone begins to match her in artistry, their performances are both sympathetic and feeling, thanks in part to the masterly conducting of Serafin. All the traditional cuts are made, not just the second stanzas. The CD transfer is vivid and clear and at bargain price this is worth any collector's money, though only a synopsis is provided.

The 1968 Maazel set was more complete in its text than some earlier three-disc versions. As to the performance, much will depend on the listener's reaction to Lorengar's voice. Her interpretation is most affecting, deeply felt and expressively presented, but the vibrato is often intrusive to the point where the tone-colour is seriously marred. That will not worry all ears – and in any case with Fischer-Dieskau a searchingly intense Germont (if hardly an elderly-sounding one) and Aragall making impressive trumpet-sounds as Alfredo, this is a strong cast. Maazel's conducting is characteristically forceful. The recording quality is excellent and, as usual with Decca, the CD transfer belies its age.

In Sutherland's 1963 recording of *La Traviata*, it is true that her diction is poor, but it is also true that she has rarely sung on record with such deep feeling as in the final scene. The *Addio del passato* (both stanzas included and sung with an unexpected lilt) merely provides a beginning, for the duet with Bergonzi is most winning, and the final death scene, *Se una pudica vergine*, is overwhelmingly beautiful. This is not a sparkling Violetta, true, but it is vocally closer to perfection than almost any other in a complete set. Bergonzi is an attractive Alfredo and Merrill an efficient Germont.

Though both Alfredo Kraus as Alfredo and Dmitri Hvorostovsky as Germont sing well on Philips, they offer an unconvincing partnership. Kraus's musical imagination is masked by dry tone and strain on top, with a very gusty entry for example in the duet *Parigi o cara*. Equally the rich-toned Hvorostovsky hardly sounds fatherly, though he does his best in a firm, spacious account of the aria, *Di Provenza*. Dame Kiri Te Kanawa is tenderly beautiful as Violetta, finely poised in *Ah fors'è lui* and the Farewell, as well as in a hushed, intense account of the Act II duet with Germont.

Callas's version with Giulini was recorded in 1955, three years before the Ghione Lisbon set, when the voice was fresher. There is no more vividly dramatic a performance on record than this, unmatchable in conveying Violetta's agony; sadly, the sound, always limited, grows crumbly towards the end. It is sad too that Bastianini sings so lumpishly as Germont *père*, even in the great duet of Act II, while di Stefano also fails to match his partner in the supreme test of the final scene. The transfer is fair.

DG, relying on a superstar, Luciano Pavarotti, offers a set recorded in New York, with James Levine conducting a cast based on the Metropolitan Opera production, with Cheryl Studer as Violetta and Juan Pons as Germont. There is much to be said for the beefy energy of Levine in this score, but the recorded sound is relatively coarse, and Pavarotti, for all his detailed feeling for words, does not match his previous recording for Decca opposite Joan Sutherland. Studer too is more exaggerated in expression than she usually is, and Pons is ill-cast as Germont, singing with none of the paternal weight needed.

Toscanini's live recording, made in December 1946, was one of the first he made of complete operas in his final years in New York, following after *La Bohème* in the previous February. Here, even more than in the Puccini and certainly more than in his later Verdi recordings, his speeds are not just fast but relentless. Even so, the high tension of the drama is hair-raising, and both Licia Albanese and Jan Peerce respond impressively, not letting the strict discipline mar their vocal production. The sound, as always with Toscanini recordings of this period, is painfully dry but very clear and forward.

La Traviata: highlights.
(M) *** EMI CDM7 63088-2 (from above complete set, with Scotto, Kraus, Bruson; cond. Muti).
(B) **(*) DG 439 421-2 [id.]. Cotrubas, Domingo, Milnes, Bav. State Op. Ch. & State O, Carlos Kleiber.

Muti's complete set is at full price and it isn't a first choice, so many will be glad to have this fairly generous (61 minutes) mid-price disc of highlights, including both the Act I and Act III *Preludes* and a well-balanced selection from each of the three Acts, with most of the key numbers included.

For many, Cotrubas makes an ideal star in *Traviata*, but unfortunately the microphone-placing in Carlos Kleiber's complete set (DG 415 132-2) exaggerates technical flaws and the vibrato becomes too obvious at times. Such is her magic that some will forgive the faults, for her characterization combines strength with vulnerability, but Kleiber's direction is equally controversial with more than a hint of

Toscanini-like rigidity in the party music and an occasionally uncomfortable insistence on discipline. However, the strong contributions of Domingo and Milnes make this bargain-priced Classikon highlights CD very worthwhile, as it contains 71 minutes of music, including the two *Preludes*. The documentation is well thought out, except that it omits a track-by-track synopsis of the narrative.

La Traviata (complete, in English).

(N) (BB) **(*) CfP Silver Double CDCFPSD 4799 (2). Masterson, Brecknock, Du Plessis, E. Nat. Op. Ch. & O, Mackerras. /

Mackerras directs a vigorous, colourful reading which brings out the drama, and Valerie Masterson is at last given the chance on record she has so long deserved. The voice is caught beautifully, if not always very characterfully, and John Brecknock makes a fine Alfredo, most effective in the final scene. Christian Du Plessis' baritone is less suitable for recording. The conviction of the whole enterprise is infectious – but be warned, Verdi in English has a way of sounding on record rather like Gilbert and Sullivan.

Il Trovatore (complete).

⊛ *** RCA RD 86194 (2) [6194-2-RC]. Leontyne Price, Domingo, Milnes, Cossotto, Amb. Op. Ch., New Philh. O, Mehta.

*** DG Dig. 423 858-2 (2) [id.]. Plowright, Domingo, Fassbaender, Zancanaro, Nesterenko, Ch. & O of St Cecilia Academy, Rome, Giulini.

*** Sony Dig. S2K 48070 (2) [id.]. Millo, Domingo, Chernov, Zajick, Morris, Kelly, Met. Op. Ch. & O, Levine.

(***) EMI CDS7 49347-2 (2) [Ang. CDCB 49347]. Callas, Barbieri, Di Stefano, Panerai, La Scala, Milan, Ch. & O, Karajan.

(M) (***) RCA mono GD 86643 (2) [6643-2-RG]. Milanov, Bjoerling, Warren, Barbieri, Robert Shaw Ch., RCA Victor O, Cellini.

(Y/B) (M) **(*) EMI CMS7 69311-2 (2) [CDMB 69311].Price, Bonisolli, Cappucilli, Obraztsova, Raimondi, German Op. Ch., Berlin Ch., BPO, Karajan.

(N) (B) **(*) DG Double 445 451-2 (2) [id.]. Stella, Bergonzi, Cossotto, Bastianini, La Scala, Milan, Ch. & O, Serafin.

(Y/B) ** Decca Dig. 430 694-2 (2) [id.]. Pavarotti, Banaudi, Verrett, Nucci, Maggio Musicale Fiorentino Ch. & O, Mehta.

The soaring curve of Leontyne Price's rich vocal line (almost too ample for some ears) is immediately thrilling in her famous Act I aria, and it sets the style of the RCA performance, full-bodied and with the tension consistently held at the highest levels. The choral contribution is superb; the famous *Soldiers'* and *Anvil choruses* are marvellously fresh and dramatic. When *Di quella pira* comes, the orchestra opens with tremendous gusto and Domingo sings with a ringing, heroic quality worthy of Caruso himself. There are many dramatic felicities, and Sherrill Milnes is in fine voice throughout; but perhaps the highlight of the set is the opening section of Act III, when Azucena finds her way to Conte di Luna's camp. The ensuing scene with Fiorenza Cossotto is vocally and dramatically quite electrifying. The CDs are transferred vibrantly to make one of the most thrilling of all early Verdi operas on record.

Giulini flouts convention at every point. The opera's white-hot inspiration comes out in the intensity of the playing and singing, but the often slow tempi and refined textures present the whole work in new and deeper detail. Rosalind Plowright, sensuous yet ethereal in *Tacea la notte*, masterfully brings together the seemingly incompatible qualities demanded, not just sweetness and purity but brilliant coloratura, flexibility and richly dramatic bite and power. Plácido Domingo sings Manrico as powerfully as he did in the richly satisfying Mehta set on RCA, but the voice is even more heroic in an Otello-like way, only very occasionally showing strain. Giorgio Zancanaro proves a gloriously firm and rounded Count di Luna and Evgeny Nesterenko a dark, powerful Ferrando, while Brigitte Fassbaender, singing her first Azucena, finds great intensity and detail, matching Giulini's freshness. The recording is warm and atmospheric with a pleasant bloom on the voices, naturally balanced and not spotlit.

James Levine conducts his Met. cast in a performance that with full, forward sound brings out the blood-and-thunder of the piece, not least in ensembles. Plácido Domingo as Manrico shows few if any signs of wear in the voice, even in relation to his singing on two of the very finest earlier sets – with both Mehta on RCA and Giulini on DG. Aprile Millo as Leonora has never been more impressive on record, disciplining a voice that can often sound unruly. Vladimir Chernov is a magnificent Count di Luna, with James Morris formidably cast as Ferrando. Dolora Zajick is aptly fruity-toned as Azucena, but heavy vibrato in the voice disturbs her legato singing. Strong as the performance is, it yields before both the vintage Mehta with Leontyne Price at her finest and the inspired Giulini, in which Rosalind Plowright sings far more beautifully and movingly than Millo.

The combination of Karajan and Callas is formidably impressive. There is toughness and dramatic determination in Callas's singing, whether in the coloratura or in the dramatic passages, and this gives the heroine an unsuspected depth of character which culminates in Callas's fine singing of an aria which used often to be cut entirely – *Tu vedrai che amore in terra*, here with its first stanza alone included. Barbieri is a magnificent Azucena, Panerai a strong, incisive Count, and Di Stefano at his finest as Manrico. On CD the 1957 mono sound, though dry and unatmospheric, is one of the more vivid from La Scala at that period.

Though dating from 1952, using a cut text as in the Met. production, the Cellini version brings a vivid reminder of that great opera house at a key period. Milanov, though at times a little raw in Leonora's coloratura, gives a glorious, commanding performance, never surpassed on record, with the voice at its fullest. Bjoerling and Warren too are in ringing voice, and Barbieri is a superb Azucena, with Cellini – rarely heard on record – proving an outstanding Verdian.

The later Karajan set with Leontyne Price promised much but proved disappointing, largely because of the thickness and strange balances of the recording, the product of multi-channel techniques exploited over-enthusiastically. So the introduction to Manrico's aria, *Di quella pira*, provides full-blooded orchestral sound, but then the orchestra fades down for the entry of the tenor, who in any case is in coarse voice. In other places he sings more sensitively, but at no point does this version match that of Mehta on RCA. CD clarifies the sound but makes the flaws in the original recording all the more evident.

There is room in the catalogue for a really recommendable bargain set of *Il Trovatore*, and Serafin's DG Double La Scala set fills the bill nicely. The documentation is inadequate, but that matters less in such a popular opera where the narrative is easy enough to follow from the very basic synopsis. The performance itself is immensely enjoyable, with the contributions of Cossotto as Azucena and Carlo Bergonzi, splendid as Manrico, as satisfying in those roles as almost any on record. Stella and Bastianini give flawed performances, but they have many impressive moments; as Leonora's opening aria readily demonstrates, Stella is in full voice and identifies strongly with the heroine. The conducting of Serafin is crisp and stylish, and the 1963 recording is transferred to CD with fine vividness, yet has plenty of atmosphere. Excellent value. Playing time: 126 minutes.

Recorded in 1990, Pavarotti responds with a bravura performance, with crystal-clear words delivered as characterfully as ever. Yet the performance is marred by mannerisms that on disc more than in live performance grow irritating, notably a throaty roaring in moments of climax and the ending of phrases on little effortful grunts. Mehta's speeds are consistently fast so that, for all its exhilaration, the speed of *Di quella pira* at the end of Act III makes it sound a little perfunctory. Pavarotti devotees will hardly worry, and the other three principals make a strong, reliable team. Antonella Banaudi sings cleanly and firmly, with a mezzo-ish tinge in the tone, fine flexibility and a precise trill. Yet, next to Pavarotti, her reading seems undercharacterized. Shirley Verrett makes as firm an Azucena as ever and Leo Nucci is strong and reliable as the Count but not very imaginative. Mehta is vital as well as brisk in an opera which brings out the best in him, but this cannot match his classic reading for RCA with Leontyne Price and the young Domingo.

I vespri siciliani (complete).
**(*) RCA RD 80370 (3) [0370-2-RC]. Arroyo, Domingo, Milnes, Raimondi, Ewing, Alldis Ch., New Philh. O, Levine.
**(*) EMI CDS7 54043-2 (3) [Ang. CDCC 54043]; *EX 754043-4*. Merritt, Studer, Zancanaro, Furlanetto, Ch. & O of La Scala, Milan, Muti.

This opera has been sadly neglected on record; Levine's 1974 RCA set, made in London, remains a first choice, dominated by the partnership of Plácido Domingo and Sherrill Milnes. Their Act II duet, using a melody well known from the *Overture*, is nothing short of magnificent, with both singers at their very peak. Though Martina Arroyo is less responsive than Studer on Muti's EMI alternative version, Domingo, Milnes and the young Ruggero Raimondi are all preferable to the La Scala singers, and the sharpness of focus in both performance and recording exposes the relative fuzziness of Muti's live account. The rest of the singing in the RCA cast is good if rarely inspired, and James Levine's direction is colourful and urgent. Good recording, vividly remastered.

The EMI set is the most successful yet of the live recordings made by Muti at La Scala, Milan, plagued by a difficult acoustic which is dispiritingly dry for the engineers. The atmosphere is well caught and, though Muti can be too tautly urgent a Verdian, his pacing here is well geared to bring out the high drama. Outstanding in the cast is Cheryl Studer as the heroine, Elena, singing radiantly; while the tenor Chris Merritt as Arrigo sounds less coarse and strained than he has in the past. Giorgio Zancanaro also responds to the role of Monforte – the governor of Sicily, discovered to be Arrigo's father – with new sensitivity, and though Ferruccio Furlanetto as Procida lacks the full weight to bring out the beauty of line in the great aria, *O tu Palermo*, his is a warm performance too.

COLLECTIONS

Arias & excerpts (recorded 1906–16, with Gadski, Hempel, Scotti, Alda, Ruffo, Tetrazzini, Jacoby, Amato, Gluck, Schumann-Heink) from: *Requiem; Aida; Un ballo in maschera; Don Carlo; La forza del destino; I Lombardi; Macbeth; Otello; Rigoletto; La Traviata; Il Trovatore.*
(M) (***) RCA mono 09026 61242-2 [id.].

Like the miscellaneous Caruso collections transferred at the same time, these recordings were restored by Thomas Stockham using the Soundstream digital process which removes unwanted horn resonances; the improvement in sound is phenomenal. The voice often sounds pristine, and only the heavily scored accompaniments serve to remind the listener of the early recording dates. There are many famous recordings here and it is good that other singers are featured too, Gadski in *La fatal pietra* from *Aida*, Hemel in *La rivedrà nell'estasi* from *Un ballo in maschera*, Scotti in the excerpts from Act I of *Don Carlo* and Act III of *La forza del destino*, and so on. The version of the *Quartet* from *Rigoletto* (*Bella figlia*) includes Tetrazzini, Josephine Jacoby and Amato. The programme is well chosen and the sound revelatory. Sample the superbly stylish *Questa o quella* or *La donna è mobile* (from *Rigoletto*), or the soaring *Ah sì, ben mio* (*Il Trovatore*), all recorded in 1908, which sound amazingly free from the mechanical problems of the early recording process. Surface noise is reduced, but still present; yet the ear soon programmes it out.

Arias: *Aida: Ritorna vincitor. Un ballo in maschera: Ecco l'orrido campo. Don Carlos: Tu che le vanità. Ernani: Ernani involami. I Lombardi: O Madre dal cielo. Macbeth: Nel dì della vittoria; La luce langue una macchia. Nabucco: Anch'io dischiuso un giorno. I vespri siciliani: Arrigo! Oh parli.*
*** EMI CDC7 47730-2 [id.]. Maria Callas, Philh. O, Rescigno.

In this first of two Verdi recital records issued to commemorate the tenth anniversary of Callas's death, the great soprano is at her most commanding, not flawless but thrilling, both in her creative musicianship and in her characterizations. Generally good transfers and clean sound.

Arias: *Don Carlo: Son io, mio Carlo . . . Per me giunto . . . O Carlo, ascolta. Luisa Miller: Sacra la scelta. Macbeth: Perfidi! All'anglo contra me v'unite . . . Pietà, rispetto, amore. La Traviata: Di Provenza il mar. Il Trovatore: Tutto è deserto . . . Il balen.*
*** Ph. Dig. 426 740-2 [id.]. Dmitri Hvorostovsky, Rotterdam PO, Gergiev – TCHAIKOVSKY: *Arias.* ***

With a glorious voice, dark and characterful, and with natural musical imagination, Dmitri Hvorostovsky on this disc made his recording début in the West not just in Tchaikovsky arias, but here in Verdi, stylishly sung. With a voice of such youthful virility, he hardly sounds like the father-figure of the *Traviata* and *Luisa Miller* items, but the legato in Macbeth's Act IV aria is most beautiful. He also brings the keenest intensity to Posa's death-scene aria from *Don Carlo*.

Arias: *Don Carlos: Tu che le vanità. La Traviata: Ah fors'è lui. Il Trovatore: Timor di me.*
*** Sony Dig. MK 37298 [id.]. Kiri Te Kanwa, LPO, Pritchard – PUCCINI: *Arias.* ***

The Verdi part of Kiri Te Kanawa's Verdi–Puccini recital brings three substantial items, less obviously apt for the singer, but in each the singing is felt as well as beautiful. The coloratura of the *Traviata* and *Trovatore* items is admirably clean, and it is a special joy to hear Elisabetta's big aria from *Don Carlos* sung with such truth and precision. Good recording, enhanced on CD.

Arias & duets: *Un ballo in maschera: Teco io sto. Il Corsaro: Egli non riede ancora! Don Carlos: Non pianger, mia compagna. Giovanna d'Arco: Qui! Qui! Dove più s'apre libero il cielo; O fatidica foresta. Jérusalem: Ave Maria. I Masnadieri: Dall'infame banchetto io m'involai; Tu del mio; Carlo vive. Otello: Già nella notte densa; Ave Maria. Il Trovatore: Timor di me; D'amor sull'ali rosee; Tu vedrai che amor in terr. I vespri siciliani: Arrigo! Ah, parli a un cor.*
(M) *** RCA GD 86534 [6534-2-RG]. Katia Ricciarelli, Plácido Domingo, Rome PO or St Cecilia Ac. O, Gavazzeni.

At mid-price this collection of Verdi arias and duets from two star singers, both in fresh voice, makes a good bargain. The inclusion of rarities adds to the attractions, and though the sound is not the most modern, it is more than acceptable in the bright digital transfer.

Choruses from: *Aida; Un ballo in maschera; Don Carlo; I Lombardi; Macbeth; I Masnadieri; Nabucco; Otello; Rigoletto; La Traviata; Il Trovatore. Requiem Mass: Sanctus.*
*** Decca Dig. 430 226-2 [id.]. Chicago Symphony Ch. & SO, Solti.

The Solti collection is not drawn from the maestro's previous complete opera sets but is a first-class studio production, recorded in Orchestra Hall, Chicago, with Decca's most resplendent digital sound. The choral balance is forward, but there is also plenty of depth and a wide dynamic range. Solti is on top form. Besides the many exciting histrionic moments there are many refined touches too, notably in the stylish *La Traviata* excerpt, with soloists from the chorus, and the flashing fantasy of *Fuoco di gioia* from *Otello*. Full translations are included.

Choruses from: *Aida; La Battaglia di Legnano; Don Carlo; Ernani; La forza del destino; Macbeth; Nabucco; Otello; La Traviata; Il Trovatore.*
(BB) *** Naxos Dig. 8.550241; *4.550241* [id.]. Slovak Philharmonic Ch. & RSO, Oliver Dohnányi.

The super-bargain Naxos collection by the excellent Slovak Philharmonic Choir brings very realistic sound and the slightly recessed choral balance in the Bratislava Radio Concert Hall is very natural: it certainly does not lack impact and, in the *Fire chorus* from *Otello*, detail registers admirably. Under Oliver Dohnányi's lively direction the chorus sings with admirable fervour. The collection ends resplendently with the Triumphal scene from *Aida*, omitting the ballet but with the fanfare trumpets blazing out on either side most tellingly. With a playing time of 56 minutes this is excellent value in every respect.

'*The world of Verdi*': (i) *Aida: Celeste Aida;* (ii) *Grand march and ballet.* (iii) *La forza del destino: Pace, pace mio Dio.* (iv) *Luisa Miller: O! Fede negar potessi ... Quando le sere al placido.* (v) *Nabucco: Va pensiero.* (vi) *Otello: Credo. Rigoletto:* (vii) *Caro nome;* (viii) *La donna è mobile;* (vii; viii; ix) Quartet: *Belle figlia dell'amore.* (x) *La Traviata: Prelude, Act I;* (vii; xi) *Brindisi: Libiamo ne'lieti calici. Il Trovatore:* (xii) *Anvil chorus;* (xiii) *Strida la vampa;* (viii) *Di quella pira. I vespri siciliani:* (xiv) *Mercè, diletti amiche.*
(M) *** Decca 433 221-1; *433 221-4.* (i) Vickers; (ii) Rome Op. Ch. & O, Solti; (iii) G. Jones; (iv) Bergonzi; (v) Amb. S., LSO, Abbado; (vi) Evans; (vii) Sutherland; (viii) Pavarotti; (ix) Tourangeau, Milnes; (x) Maggio Musicale O, Fiorentino, Pritchard; (xi) Bergonzi; (xii) L. Op. Ch., Bonynge; (xiii) Horne; (xiv) Chiara.

Opening with the *Chorus of the Hebrew Slaves* from *Nabucco* and closing with Pavarotti's *Di quella pira* from *Il Trovatore*, this quite outstandingly red-blooded Verdi compilation should surely tempt any novice to explore further into Verdi's world, yet at the same time it provides a superbly arranged 74-minute concert in its own right. The choice of items and performances demonstrates a shrewd knowledge of both popular Verdi and the Decca catalogue, for not a single performance disappoints. Joan Sutherland's melting 1971 *Caro nome* with its exquisite trills is the first of three splendid excerpts from *Rigoletto*, ending with the famous Quartet, and other highlights include Dame Gwyneth Jones's glorious *Pace, pace, mio Dio*, introduced of course by the sinisterly scurrying *Forza del destino* motif, Sir Geraint Evans's superb account of Iago's evil *Credo* from *Otello* – here the Decca sound adds to the riveting impact – and Marilyn Horne's dark-timbred *Strida la vampa* from *Trovatore*. Solti, too, is at his most electric in the great March scene from *Aida*. The stereo throughout is splendidly vivid, and this mid-priced collection is worth every penny of its modest cost.

Victoria, Tomás Luis de (c. 1548–1611)

Ascendens Christus (motet); *Missa Ascendis Christus in altum; O Magnum mysterium* (motet); *Missa O Magnum mysterium.*
*** Hyperion Dig. CDA 66190 [id.]. Westminster Cathedral Ch., David Hill.

Missa Ave maris stella; O quam gloriosum est regnum (motet); *Missa O quam gloriosum.*
⊛ *** Hyperion CDA 66114 [id.]. Westminster Cathedral Ch., David Hill.

The Latin fervour of the singing is very involving; some listeners may initially be surprised at the volatile way David Hill moves the music on, with the trebles eloquently soaring aloft on the line of the music. The spontaneous ebb and flow of the pacing is at the heart of David Hill's understanding of this superb music. The recording balance is perfectly judged, with the Westminster acoustic adding resonance (in both senses of the word) to singing of the highest calibre, combining a sense of timelessness and mystery with real expressive power.

Ave Maria; Ave Maris stella (hymn). *Missa Vidi speciosam. Ne timeas, Maria; Sancta Maria, succurre miseris; Vidi speciosam* (motets).
*** Hyperion Dig. CDA 66129 [id.]. Westminster Cathedral Ch., David Hill.

An outstanding collection of some of Victoria's most beautiful music celebrating the Virgin Mary. The four-part *Ave Maria* may not be authentic, but the composer would surely not be reluctant to own it. The Westminster Choir again show their flexibly volatile response to this music with that special amalgam of fervour and serenity that Victoria's writing demands. The acoustics of Westminster Cathedral add the right degree of resonance to the sound without clouding.

Officium defunctorum.
*** Gimell Dig. CDGIM 012; *1585T-12* [id.]. Tallis Scholars, Phillips (with LOBO: Motet: *Versa est in luctum* ***).
*** Hyperion Dig. CDA 66250 [id.]. Westminster Cathedral Ch., David Hill.

The *Officium defunctorum* was Victoria's swan-song – he died only six years later. It is a work of great serenity and beauty. Honours are fairly evenly divided between the Westminster Cathedral Choir on Hyperion and the Tallis Scholars under Peter Phillips. The Westminster Choir has the advantage of boys' voices and larger forces; they are recorded in a warmer, more spacious acoustic. By comparison with the Gimell recording, the sound seems a little less well focused, but on its own terms it is thoroughly convincing. They permit themselves greater expressiveness, too. Moreover the *Requiem* is set in the wider liturgical context by the use of some chants. The Tallis Scholars achieve great clarity of texture; they are twelve in number and, as a result, the polyphony is clearer, and so too are their words. They offer also a short and deeply felt motet by Alonso Lobo (*c.* 1555–1617). The recording has a warm, glowing sound which almost persuades you that you are in the imperial chapel.

Missa Surge propera; Stabat Mater.
(M) *** Carlton IMP Classics Dig. PCD 970 [id.]. Mixolydian, Piers Schmidt – PADILLA: *Missa Ego flos campi* etc. ***

The *Missa Surge propera* is a five-voiced parody Mass, published in 1583, the only one of Victoria's works to be based on Palestrina. It is a beautiful work and, like the *Stabat Mater*, is very well sung by Mixolydian under Piers Schmidt and is recorded with exemplary skill.

Responsories for Tenebrae.
*** Hyperion Dig. CDA 66304 [id.]. Westminster Cathedral Ch., David Hill.
** Gimell Dig CDGIM 022; *1385T-22* [id.]. Tallis Scholars, Peter Phillips.

The *Tenebrae responsories* are so called because of the tradition of performing them in the evening in increasing darkness as the candles were extinguished one by one. The Tallis Scholars sound absolutely perfect in both blend and intonation but are curiously uninvolving. They are beautifully recorded and technically immaculate but convey little real intensity of feeling. The Westminster Cathedral Choir under David Hill on Hyperion find far more atmosphere in this music and bring a sense of spontaneous feeling to their performance. Of recent versions, this can be welcomed without reservation.

(i) *Responsories for Tenebrae;* (ii) *Litaniae de Beata Virgine. Motets: Ascendens Christus in altum; Ave Maria; Gaudent in coelis; O magnum mysterium.*
(M) *** Decca 425 078-2 [id.]. (i) Westminster Cathedral Ch., George Malcolm; (ii) St John's College, Cambridge, Ch., George Guest.

The music here offers Victoria's settings for Maundy Thursday, Good Friday and Holy Saturday. The three sections between them tell the story of the Crucifixion from Judas's betrayal through to the burial of Jesus. This (originally Argo) recording dates from 1959, a period when the Westminster Cathedral Choir under George Malcolm was at its peak. The performance has great vigour and eloquence, and the recording is very fine. The coupled motets from the St John's Choir must be numbered among the finest Victoria gave us. The performances are admirably done and, if one accepts the fact that English choirs lack the harsh lines drawn by the firmer-toned Spanish bodies, there is little at which one can cavil. Indeed this record would be a useful starting-point for any library. The transfers are clear and well focused.

Vierne, Louis (1870–1937)

Suite No. 3, Op. 54: Carillon de Westminster.
*** DG Dig. 413 438-2 [id.]. Simon Preston (organ of Westminster Abbey) – WIDOR: *Symphony No. 5.*
***

The Vierne *Carillon de Westminster* is splendidly played by Simon Preston and sounds appropriately atmospheric in this spacious acoustic and well-judged recording. It makes an attractive makeweight to the Widor *Fifth Symphony*.

Symphonies Nos. 1 in D min., Op. 14; 2 in E min., Op. 20.
*** Mer. CDE 84192 [id.]. David Sanger (organ of La Chiesa Italiana di San Pietro, London).

Symphonies Nos. 3 in F sharp min., Op. 28; 4 in G min., Op. 32.
*** Mer. CDE 84176 [id.]. David Sanger (organ of La Chiesa Italiana di San Pietro, London).

Symphonies Nos. 5 in A min., Op. 47; 6 in B min., Op. 59.
*** Mer. CDE 84171 [id.]. David Sanger (organ of La Chiesa Italiana di San Pietro, London).

David Sanger's recordings of the Vierne *Organ symphonies* are highly rewarding and can be strongly recommended, especially as Marie-Claire Alain's set on Erato has been withdrawn. Indeed some listeners are likely to prefer the very appealing patina of the San Pietro organ. There is no cause to complain of the sound quality, which maintains the high standards Meridian have set themselves: the resonance of the pedals is very telling without muddying the overall sound-picture.

Symphonies Nos. 1 in D min., Op. 14; 3 in F sharp min., Op. 28.
**(*) Telarc Dig. CD 80329 [id.]. Michael Murray (organ of St Ouen Abbey, Rouen).

Strong, direct performances from Michael Murray, attractively registered. The Telarc engineers also create a spectacularly full-blooded sound-picture of the Cavaillé-Coll organ at Rouen. But in the last resort Murray seems less naturally at home in this repertoire than his competitors.

Vieuxtemps, Henri (1820–81)

Violin concerto No. 5 in A min., Op. 37.
(N) *** EMI Dig. CDC5 55292-2 [id.]. Sarah Chang, Philh. O, Dutoit – LALO: *Symphonie espagnole.* ***
(Y/B) (M) *** Sony Dig. SMK 64250 [id.]. Cho-Liang Lin, Minnesota O, Marriner – BRUCH; MENDELSSOHN: *Concertos.* ***
*** DG Dig. 427 676-2 [id.]. Mintz, Israel PO, Mehta – LALO: *Symphonie espagnole;* SAINT-SAENS: *Intro & Rondo capriccioso.* ***
(Y/B) *** Denon Dig. CO 78913 [id.]. Chee-Yun, LPO, Lopez-Cóboz – MENDELSSOHN: *Concerto.* ***
(M) **(*) Sony SBK 48274 [id.]. Zukerman, LSO, Mackerras – BRUCH: *Concerto No. 1;* LALO: *Symphonie espagnole.* **(*)

Sarah Chang's newest recording, coupling a scintillating account of the Lalo *Symphonie espagnole*, goes readily to the top of the list. It is beautifully recorded, with a well-nigh perfect balance, in an agreeably warm acoustic. Chang's vitality is matched by Dutoit and her playing has a magically gentle tenderness in presenting the engaging lyrical themes of the first movement and the *Adagio*. The brief finale has splendid élan.

Cho-Liang Lin plays with flair and zest and is well supported by Sir Neville Marriner and the Minnesota Orchestra. The recording is first class, and the couplings of the more famous concertos of Bruch and Mendelssohn could not be more appropriate.

Mintz's performance has enormous dash, and real lyrical magic too. Mehta, obviously caught up in the inspiration of the solo playing, provides an excellent accompaniment; this is another example of a memorable live performance recorded 'on the wing', and if the acoustic is not especially flattering the sound is obviously truthful and well balanced.

The young South Korean violinist, Chee-Yun, made her début with the Vieuxtemps No. 5 at the tender age of thirteen in the 1980s, with the NYPO; and her performance shows how well she understands the piece in its attractive combination of affection and maturity. The plaintive *Andante* is touching and the brief finale given with comparable dash and sparkle. She is well recorded, but this Denon record is short measure by comparison with Lin's Sony CD, which also has a price advantage.

Zukerman provides here an enjoyable bonus to his dazzling accounts of the Bruch and Lalo works. There is comparable dash for Vieuxtemps, yet he coaxes the *Adagio* tenderly. Again a very forward balance, but the ear adjusts.

Villa-Lobos, Heitor (1887–1959)

Amazonas; Dawn in a tropical forest; Erosão; Gênesis.
*** Marco Polo Dig. 8.223357 [id.]. Czecho-Slovak RSO (Bratislava), Roberto Duarte.

These are imaginative scores with lots of tropical colouring and exotic textures, all sounding rather similar in their luxuriance – but who cares! *Amazonas* is the earliest and most astonishing score, dating from the First World War, and in its vivid sonorities affirms Villa-Lobos's contention that his first harmony book was the map of Brazil. The Bratislava strings could perhaps be more opulent, but the performances under a Brazilian conductor are really very good indeed and so is the recording.

Bachianas brasileiras Nos. 1–9; Chôros Nos. 2 (for flute & orchestra); *5* (for piano, Alma Brasileira); *10* (for chorus & orchestra); (i) *11* (for piano & orchestra). *2 Chôros (bis)* (for violin & cello); (i) *Piano concerto No. 5; Descobrimento do Brasil; Invocação em defesa da Patria;* (i) *Momoprecoce* (fantasy for piano & orchestra); *Symphony No. 4. Qu'est-ce qu'un Chôros?* (Villa-Lobos speaking).

(M) (**(*)) EMI mono CZS7 67229-2 (6). De los Angeles, Kareska, Basrentzen, Braune, Tagliaferro, Du Frene, Plessier, Cliquennois, Bronschwak, Neilz, Benedetti; (i) Blumental; Chorale des Jeunesses Musicales de France, Fr. Nat. R. & TV Ch. & O, cond. composer.

This six-CD box is a colourful, warm-hearted collection, not helped by dull mono recordings and ill-disciplined performances, but full of a passionately surging intensity that plainly reflects the personality of a composer of obvious charisma, if of limited ability as a conductor. Endearingly, there is a 10-minute track spoken in French by Villa-Lobos himself. All nine of the *Bachianas brasileiras* are recorded here, including the celebrated No. 5 for soprano and eight cellos, with Victoria de los Angeles a radiant soloist. That recording is already well known, but most of the others have had very limited circulation. They make an enjoyable collection for, despite the dull sound, the warmth of the writing never fails to come over.

Bachianas Brasileiras Nos. (iii) *1;* (i; iii) *5;* (i; ii) *Suite for voice and violin.* (iii) arr. of BACH: *The Well-tempered clavier: Prelude in D min., BWV 583; Fugue in B flat, BWV 846; Prelude in G min., BWV 867; Fugue in D, BWV 874.*

*** Hyperion Dig. CDA 66257 [id.]. (i) Jill Gomez, (ii) Peter Manning, (iii) Pleeth Cello Octet.

Jill Gomez is outstanding in the popular *Fifth Bachianas Brasileiras* and with the violinist, Peter Manning, in the *Suite* (1923). Villa-Lobos' favourite 'orchestra of cellos' produce sumptuous sounds in both the *Bachianas Brasileiras*, and an added point of interest is the effective transcriptions for cellos of unrelated Bach preludes and fugues. An eminently attractive introduction to this most colourful of composers.

Bachianas Brasileiras No. 2: The little train of the Caipira.

(Y/B) **(*) Everest EVC 9007 [id.]. LSO, Sir Eugene Goossens – ANTILL: *Corroboree* **(*); GINAS-TERA: *Estancia; Panambi.* ***

It is good to have a recommendable mid-priced version of Villa-Lobos's engaging tone-picture of a little country train in São Paulo, Brazil, which the composer experienced in 1931. The composer uses Brazilian percussion instruments to suggest train noises over which there is a soaring theme in the strings. The performance is excellent and the recording vivid. It is slightly over-resonant, which implies close microphones, and there is a slight edge to the violins. But the resulting sound-picture is strongly projected.

Bachianas Brasileiras Nos. 2 (The little train of the Caipira); 4; (i) *5 for soprano and 8 cellos;* (ii) *Chorus No. 10: Rasga o Coraçâo;* (iii) *Miniaturas Nos. 2 (Viola); 3, Cantilena;* (iv) *Momoprecoce* (Fantasy for piano and orchestra).

(Y/B) (***) EMI stereo/mono CDC5 55224-2 [id.]. (i) French Nat. RO, composer; (i) with Victoria de los Angeles; (ii) Ch. des Jeunesses Musicales de France; (iii) Fredrick Fuller; (iv) Magda Tagliaferro.

No one has been more persuasive than the composer in *The little train of the Caipira*, and the recording certainly has plenty of local colour with its exotic percussive effects. Victoria de los Angeles' golden voice sounds ravishing in the famous *Bachianas Brasileiras No. 5*, even if the recording is not entirely flattering; and the other, rarer works, notably the *Fantasy for piano and orchestra*, are welcome in this reissue in EMI's Composer in Person series, which now takes the two most familiar items into the premium-price bracket.

Guitar concerto.

(BB) *** Naxos Dig. 8.550729 [id.]. Norbert Kraft, Northern CO, Nicholas Ward – CASTELNUOVO-TEDESCO: *Concerto* ***; RODRIGO: *Concierto de Aranjuez.* ***

An excellent account from Norbert Kraft, spontaneous and catching well the music's colour and atmosphere. If it is not quite as individual as Bream's version, it has the advantage of vivid, well-balanced, modern, digital recording and excellent couplings. Another genuine Naxos bargain.

(i) *Guitar concerto. 12 Etudes; 5 Preludes.*

(M) *** RCA 09026 61604-2. Julian Bream, (i) LSO, André Previn.

A highly distinguished account of the *Guitar concerto* from Bream, magnetic and full of atmosphere in the slow movement and finale. Previn accompanies sympathetically and with spirit. The rest of the programme also shows Bream in inspirational form. He engages the listener's attention from the opening of the first study and holds it to the last. The recording has a nice intimacy in the concerto and the solo items have fine presence against an attractive ambience.

Piano concertos Nos. 1–5.
*** Decca Dig. 430 628-2 (2) [id.]. Cristina Ortiz, RPO, Gómes-Martínez.

What emerges from the series of concertos, as played by Cristina Ortiz here, is that the first two are the most immediately identifiable as Brazilian in their warm colouring and sense of atmosphere, even though the eclectic borrowings are often more unashamed than later, with many passages suggesting Rachmaninov with a Brazilian accent. No. 3, the work Villa-Lobos found it hard to complete, tends to sound bitty in its changes of direction. No. 4, more crisply conceived, has one or two splendid tunes, but it is in No. 5 that Villa-Lobos becomes most warmly convincing again, returning unashamedly to more echoes of Rachmaninov. With Ortiz articulating crisply, there is much to enjoy from such colourful, undemanding music, brilliantly recorded and sympathetically performed.

Discovery of Brazil: suites Nos. 1–3; (i) 4.
**(*) Marco Polo Dig. 8.223551 [id.]. Slovak RSO (Bratislava), Roberto Duarte; (i) with Adam Blazo, Slovak Philharmonic Ch.

The *Discovery of Brazil* derives from an ambitious film project and Villa-Lobos fashioned three orchestral suites from it, plus a fourth which employs a soloist and choir. To be frank, although there are good things in this music and some exotic orchestral effects, the colours are not quite as vivid and dazzling as one would have expected from this prolific Brazilian master. Not three-star music exactly, but the performances are really rather good, and so is the recording.

CHAMBER MUSIC

Berceuse, Op. 50; Divigação; O canto do capadócio; O canto do cisne negro; O canto do nossa terra; Sonhar, Op. 14.
** Marco Polo Dig. 8.223298 [id.]. Rebecca Rust, David Apter – ENESCU: *Cello sonata.* **

These pieces are all new to the catalogue and are well played and recorded, but they are a bonus for the Enescu *First Cello sonata*, some 37 minutes long, which may not hold the attention of all listeners to the last bar!

String quartets Nos. 4 (1917); 6 (Quarteto Brasileiro) (1938); 14 (1953).
*** Marco Polo Dig. 8.223391 [id.]. Danubius Qt.

The three quartets recorded here are all well crafted and their ideas are of quality. The *Fourth* is perhaps the most Gallic; the *Sixth* (*Quarteto Brasileiro*) is one of the most individual and rewarding. It makes intelligent use of Brazilian folk-material. The *Fourteenth*, like so much of Villa-Lobos, is not entirely free from note-spinning. The Danubius Quartet are an accomplished ensemble and play with evident commitment. The recording places them rather forward in the aural picture.

String quartet No. 6 (Quarteto Brasileiro).
(Y/B) (***) Testament mono SBT 1053 [id.]. Hollywood Qt – CRESTON: *Quartet;* DEBUSSY: *Danses sacrées;* RAVEL: *Intro and allegro;* TURINA: *La Oración.* (***)

The *Sixth Quartet* is a slight but amiable score, ultimately facile but pleasing and well crafted. It would be hard to imagine a finer performance than this.

Suite populaire brésilienne; Etudes Nos. 5 in C; 7 in E.
(M) *** RCA 09026 61596-2. Julian Bream – Recital: *'Twentieth-century guitar II'.* ***

The *Suite populaire brésilienne* is deservedly among Villa-Lobos's most popular music. The composer disclaims the idea that these four chôros (pieces in the style of Brazilian street-bands) were intended as a suite, but they fit together remarkably well. Bream plays them with his usual flair and brings out all their vivid colouring. The two contrasted *Etudes* are also fine pieces. Excellent late-1970s recording.

PIANO MUSIC

Alma brasileira, Bachiana brasileira No. 4; Ciclo brasileiro; Chôros No. 5; Valsa da dor (Waltz of sorrows).
*** ASV Dig. CDDCA 607 [id.]. Alma Petchersky.

Alma Petchersky's style is romantic, and some might find her thoughtful deliberation in the *Preludio* of the *Bachianas Brasileira No. 4* overdone. Her very free rubato is immediately apparent in the *Valsa da dor* which opens the recital. Yet she clearly feels all this music deeply, and the playing is strong in personality and her timbre is often richly coloured. She is at her finest in the *Brazilian cycle*. The recording is first class.

VOCAL MUSIC

Bachianas Brasileiras No. 5 for soprano and cellos.
(N) (B) *** Decca Double Dig. 444 995-2 (2) [id.]; *444 995-4*. Kiri Te Kanawa, Lynn Harrell and instrumental ens. – CANTELOUBE: *Songs of the Auvergne*. ***
(M) *** RCA GD 87831 [7831-2-RG]. Anna Moffo, American SO, Stokowski – CANTELOUBE: *Chants d'Auvergne;* RACHMANINOV: *Vocalise*. ***

The Villa-Lobos piece makes an apt fill-up for the Canteloube songs, completing Kiri Te Kanawa's recording of all five books. It is, if anything, even more sensuously done, well sustained at a speed far slower than one would normally expect. Rich recording to match.

Anna Moffo gives a seductive performance of the most famous of the *Bachianas Brasileiras*, adopting a highly romantic style (matching the conductor) and warm tone-colour.

Magdalena.
*** Sony Dig. SK 44945 [id.]. Kaye, Rose, Esham, Gray, Hadley, O, Evans Haile.

Magdalena is a colourful, vigorous piece, alas lacking the big tunes you really need in a musical, but full of delightful ideas. It tells the sort of story that Lehár might have chosen, only translated to South America. Sadly, in spite of an enthusiastic response from everyone, it closed on Broadway in 1948 after only eleven weeks. The present recording was prompted by a concert performance to celebrate the Villa-Lobos centenary, a splendid, well-sung account of what is aptly described as 'a musical adventure'.

Viotti, Giovanni Battista (1755–1824)

Violin concerto No. 13 in A.
*** Hyperion Dig. CDA 66210 [id.]. Oprean, European Community CO, Faerber – FIORILLO: *Violin concerto No. 1*. ***

Viotti wrote a great many violin concertos in much the same mould, but this is one of his best. Adelina Oprean's quicksilver style and light lyrical touch give much pleasure – she has the exact measure of this repertoire and she is splendidly accompanied and well recorded. The measure, though, is short.

Vivaldi, Antonio (1675–1741)

L'Estro armonico (12 Concertos), Op. 3.
*** DG Dig. 423 094-2 (2) [id.]. Standage & soloists, E. Concert, Trevor Pinnock.
*** O-L 414 554-2 (2) [id.]. Holloway, Huggett, Mackintosh, Wilcock, AAM, Hogwood.
(Y/B) (B) **(*) Ph. Duo 446 169-2 (2) [id.]. Garatti, Altobelli, Colandrea, Cotogni, Gallozzi, Michelucci, Vicari, I Musici.

L'estro armonico, Op. 3; (i) *Bassoon concerto in A min., RV 498;* (ii) *Flute concerto in C min., RV 441;* (iii) *Oboe concerto in F, RV 456;* (i; iii; iv) *Concerto in F for 2 oboes, bassoon, 2 horns and violin, RV 574.*
(Y/B) (B) *** Decca Double 443 476-2 (2) [id.]. ASMF, Marriner; with (i) Martin Gatt; (ii) William Bennett; (iii) Neil Black; (iv) Celia Nicklin, Timothy Brown, Robin Davis, Iona Brown.

Vivaldi's *L'Estro armonico* includes some of his finest music and had great influence. This new chamber version from Pinnock (with one instrument to a part) seems instinctively to summarize and amalgamate the best features from past versions: there is as much sparkle and liveliness as with Hogwood, for rhythms are consistently resilient, ensemble crisp and vigorous. Yet in slow movements there is that expressive radiance and sense of enjoyment of beauty without unstylish indulgence that one expects from the ASMF. The recording was made in EMI's Abbey Road studios and the balance and ambient effect are judged perfectly.

Those who have not been won over to the more abrasive sound of original instruments will find Marriner's set no less stylish. As so often, he directs the Academy in radiant and imaginative perform-ances of baroque music and yet observes scholarly good manners. The delightful use of continuo – lute and organ as well as harpsichord – the sharing of solo honours and the consistently resilient string playing of the ensemble make for compelling listening. The 1972 recording, made in St John's, Smith Square, is immaculately transferred, and as a bonus we are offered four of Vivaldi's most inventive concertos which occupied a whole LP to themselves when first issued in 1977. Each work has its own individuality and its own special effects. The *A minor Bassoon concerto* has a delightful sense of humour and in RV 441 the flute chortles like a bird. The work for oboes and horns is agreeably robust but has an imaginatively scored slow movement. The recording is a model of clarity and definition and has plenty of warmth and atmosphere.

There is no question about the sparkle of Christopher Hogwood's performance with the Academy of Ancient Music. The captivating lightness of the solo playing and the crispness of articulation of the accompanying group bring music-making that combines joyful vitality with the authority of scholarship. Hogwood's continuo is first class, varying between harpsichord and organ, the latter used to add colour as well as substance. The balance is excellent, and the whole effect is exhilarating.

The Philips Duo offers fresh and lovely performances; melodies are finely drawn and there is little hint of the routine which occasionally surfaces in I Musici – and, for that matter, in Vivaldi himself. However, in making comparisons this group often yields to St Martin-in-the-Fields, who have crisper textures and convey greater enthusiasm. Even so, I Musici are a good choice and are certainly recommendable. However, whereas the Decca Marriner set (at the same cost) offers extra works as a bonus, this Philips reissue, with its overall playing time of just two hours, offers none.

La Stravaganza (12 concertos), *Op. 4* (complete).
(N) ❀ (B) *** Decca Double 444 821-2 (2). Soloists, ASMF, Marriner.

Marriner's performances make the music irresistible. The solo playing of Carmel Kaine and Alan Loveday is superb and, when the Academy's rhythms have such splendid buoyancy and lift, it is easy enough to accept Marriner's preference for a relatively sweet style in the often heavenly slow movements. As usual, the contribution of an imaginatively varied continuo (which includes cello and bassoon, in addition to harpsichord, theorbo and organ) adds much to the colour of Vivaldi's score. The recording, made in St John's, Smith Square, in 1973/4, is of the very highest quality and the CD transfers are in the demonstration class.

The Trial between harmony and invention (12 Concertos), Op. 8.
(B) **(*) Ph. Duo 438 344-2 (2). Felix Ayo, I Musici.

Felix Ayo recorded the first four concertos (*The Four Seasons*) in 1959 and his was one of the finest of the early versions, although the recording was rather resonant. The remaining concertos in the set – full of typically Vivaldian touches which stamp these works as among the best of their time – date from 1961/2 and the recording, though still full-bodied, is less reverberant. The solo playing is very good and an undoubted freshness pervades the music-making here, although Maria Teresa Garatti's continuo fails to come through adequately. Good value.

The Four Seasons, Op. 8/1–4.
(M) *** Virgin/EMI CUV5 61145-2. Christopher Warren-Green with LCO – ALBINONI: *Adagio;* PACHELBEL: *Canon.* ***
(Y/B) *** DG Dig. 439 933-2 [id.]. Gil Shaham, Orpheus CO – KREISLER: *Violin concerto in the style of Vivaldi.* ***
**(*) Argo 414 486-2 [id.]. Alan Loveday, ASMF, Marriner.
**(*) DG Dig. 400 045-2 [id.]. Simon Standage, E. Concert, Pinnock.
**(*) BIS Dig. CD 275 [id.]. Nils-Erik Sparf, Drottningholm Bar. Ens.
(Y/B) (M) **(*) Carlton Classics Dig. PCD 2000 [id.]. Jaime Laredo, SCO.
**(*) EMI Dig. CDC7 49557-2 [id.]. Nigel Kennedy, ECO.
(B) *** DG 427 221-2. Schneiderhan, Lucerne Festival Strings, Baumgartner (with ALBINONI: *Adagio;* PACHELBEL: *Canon & Gigue;* PURCELL: *Chacony;* BACH: *Suite No. 3, BWV 1068: Air* ***).

The Four Seasons, Op. 8/1–4 (with sonnets in Italian and English).
*** Helios/Hyperion CDH 88012; *KH 88012* [id.]. Bruni, Edwards (readers), Adelina Oprean, European Community CO, Faeber.

The Four Seasons, Op. 8/1–4; Violin concertos: in E flat (La tempesta di mare), RV 253; in C (Il piacere), RV 108, Op. 8/5–6.
*** Teldec/Warner Dig. 4509 91683-2 [id.]. Marieke Blankestijn, COE.
(M) **(*) Teldec/Warner 4509 91851-2 [id.]. Alice Harnoncourt, VCM, Harnoncourt.

The Four Seasons, Op. 8/1–4; Violin concertos: in E flat (La tempesta di mare), RV 253; in C (Il Piacare), RV 108; in B flat (La Caccia), RV 362; in D, RV 210, Op. 8/5–6, 10–11.

(Y/B) (M) *** Virgin Veritas/EMI Dig. VER5 61172-2 [id.]. Monica Huggett, Raglan Bar. Players, Nicholas Kraemer.

(i; ii) The Four Seasons, Op. 8/1–4; (i; iii) Violin concerto in E flat (La tempesta di mare), Op. 8/5, RV 253; (iv) Triple concerto in F for flute, oboe and bassoon, RV 570; Double concerto in G min. for flute and bassoon (La Notte), RV 104.

(Y/B) (BB) *** ASV Dig. CDQS 6148 [id.]. (i) José-Luis Garcia; (ii) ECO; (iii) Fort Worth CO, Giordano; (iv) William Bennett, Neil Black, Robin O'Neill, ECO, Malcolm.

(i) The Four Seasons, Op. 8/1–4; (ii) Violin concertos: L'Estro armonico: in A min., Op. 3/6. La Stravaganza: in A, Op. 4/5. Concerto in C min. (Il sospetto), RV 199.

(M) *** EMI CDM7 64333-2. Perlman, (i) LPO; (ii) Israel PO.

The Four Seasons; (i) L'Estro armonico: Quadruple violin concerto in B min., RV 580, Op. 3/10.

(B) *** Discover Dig. DICD 920202 [id.]. Oldřich Vlček; (i) with Hessová, Kaudersová, Nováková; Virtuosi di Praga.

The Four Seasons; (i) L'Estro armonico: Quadruple violin concerto in B min., RV 580, Op. 3/10. Sinfonia in B min. (Al Santo Sepolcro), RV 169.

✺ *** Sony Dig. SK 48251 [id.]. Jeanne Lamon, Tafelmusik.

The Four Seasons, Op. 8/1–4; La Stravaganza: Concerto in A min., Op. 4/4; Concerto in E min., RV 278.

*** RCA Dig. RD 60369 [60369-2-RC; 60369-4-RC]. Vladimir Spivakov, Moscow Virtuosi.

(i) The Four Seasons; Concerto for strings in G (Alla rustica), RV 151; (ii) Violin concerto in E (L'amoroso), RV 271; Sinfonia in B min. (Al Santo Sepolcro), RV 169.

(B) *** DG 439 422-2 [id.]. (i) Michel Schwalbé; (ii) Thomas Brandis; BPO, Karajan.

(i) The Four Seasons, Op. 8/1–4; Quadruple violin concerto in B flat, RV 553. Concerto for strings in G (alla rustica), RV 151; Sinfonia in G, RV 146.

(Y/B) (M) *** Virgin/EMI VC5 45117-2 [id.]. (i) Chiara Banchini, Alison Bury, John Holloway, Elizabeth Wallfisch; Taverner Players, Andrew Parrott.

(i) The Four Seasons. Concerto funèbre; Concerto per l'orchestra di Dresda; Concerto per la Solennità di San Lorenzo.

(N) (B) **(*) Decca Eclipse Dig. 448 225-2; 448 225-4 [id.]. (i) Franco Gulli; I Filarmonici de Teatro Comunale di Bologna, Chailly.

(i) The Four Seasons, Op. 8/1–4; (ii) Mandolin concerto in C, RV 425; (iii) Double mandolin concerto in G, RV 532; (iv) Double trumpet concerto in C, RV 537.

(N) (M) *** Ph. Dig/Analogue 442 393-2 [id.]. (i) Salvatore Accardo, I Solisti delle Settimane Internazionali di Napoli; (ii) Parisi; (iii) Del Vescovo, Ruta; (iv) Adelbrecht, Mathez; (ii-iv) I Musici.

Tafelmusik offer a superbly imaginative version of Vivaldi's *Four Seasons* on original instruments, which is for the 1990s what Marriner's famous ASMF version was for the '70s. The playing is at once full of fantasy and yet has a robust gusto that is irresistible. The opening of *Spring*, with its chirruping bird calls, sets the scene and the second movement brings a lovely cantilena from Jeanne Lamon, while the barking dog is as musical as he is gruff. The performances throughout are full of dramatic contrasts. The same shimmering delicacy in *Summer* alternates with invigoratingly robust tutti from the lower strings in the finale. The sleepy *Adagio* of *Autumn* brings a gentle, musing commentary from the archlute, followed by the gutsy hunting music over which the soloist soars with dazzling bravura. The weird frozen landscape of *Winter* is introduced in a half-light, but the solo entry is soon dramatically dominant. After *Winter*'s roisterous finale comes the hauntingly austere texture of the opening of the highly original *Sinfonia al Sepulcro*; and the famous *Concerto for four violins* makes a fitting finale. The Sony recording is first class, absolutely clean in focus, with plenty of body and the most refined detail.

For those still preferring the fuller texture of modern instruments, the Teldec version provides the perfect alternative. The chimerical solo playing of Marieke Blankestijn is a delight and her clean style shows that she has learned from authentic manners. There is more imaginative delicacy here, particularly in the improvisatory central movement of *Summer* and the gentle haze of *Autumn*, where the gutsy finale has splendid bite and energy; and the opening of *Winter* mirrors the impressionism of the Tafelmusik version. However, the cheerful COE approach to the *Largo* central movement is even more attractive than with Tafelmusik, to make the finale the more distinctive. With two extra concertos from

Opus 8 also included, this is now also a strong primary recommendation. The Teldec recording is superb.

Monica Huggett's stimulating Virgin Veritas CD makes a fine mid-priced alternative to the premium version by Jean Lamon and Tafelmusik, even if Huggett does not quite match it in sheer exuberance of pictorialism. The shepherd's dog on Virgin is in a mellower mood, but the light texture and dancing tempo of the finale of *Spring* is matched by the sense of fantasy in the central movement of *Summer*, while the sheer rumbustious energy of the latter's last movement is gloriously invigorating. The *Adagio* of *Autumn* has a delicate, sensuous somnambulance, and only the opening of *Winter* is relatively conventional, although certainly not lacking character. Four other concertos from Op. 8 are also included, all played in fine style; the supple solo line is a constant pleasure, as is Monica Huggett's easy, exhilarating bravura, well matched by Raglan's zestful accompaniments.

Salvatore Accardo's version is of particular interest in that he uses a different Stradivarius for each of the four concertos – period instruments with a difference! Thanks to this aristocrat of violinists, the sounds are of exceptional beauty. The performances are much enhanced, too, by the imaginative continuo playing of Bruno Canino, who is not given a credit in the booklet provided with this reissue. The notes also neglect to say that these were live performances, recorded digitally at the Cremona Festival in 1987. They have all the virtues of live music-making but none of the drawbacks. The other concertos are excellently played, and the analogue recording is first class.

Christopher Warren-Green makes a brilliantly charismatic soloist, with the London Chamber Orchestra providing delectably pointed bird-imitations in *Spring* and *Summer*. Tempi of allegros are very brisk, but the effect is tinglingly exhilarating when the soloist's bravura is so readily matched by the accompanying ensemble. Slow movements offer the widest contrast, with delicate textures and subtle use of the continuo, as in *Winter* where Leslie Pearson makes a delightful surprise contribution to the finale, having already embroidered the opening allegro and prevented it from being too chilly. The recording, made in All Saints' Church, Wallington, has plenty of ambient fullness but remains bright and fresh. With its equally attractive couplings, this can be recommended to those who like their Vivaldi to be dashing and vital, and yet imaginatively pictorial at the same time.

The Taverner Players offer yet another authentic version which stimulates the ear without acerbity. They are not the first group to use a different soloist for each of Vivaldi's *Four Seasons*, and this works well, with plenty of tingling vitality overall and a good deal of imaginative freedom from each in turn, with Chiara Banchini setting the style in her duets with the leader in her volatile account of *Spring*. In the *Adagio* of *Summer*, Alison Bury's timbre is pure with a minimum of vibrato, yet the playing is appealingly expressive. There is no lack of sensuous lustre in the hazy evocation of the slow movement of *Autumn* (the brooding harpsichord continuo particularly effective) and Elizabeth Wallfisch's contribution to the outer movements gleams with bravura. John Holloway's upper tessitura in *Winter* is suitably mercurial. The four players join together for the *Concerto for four violins in B flat*, offered as the principal bonus; it is an interesting work, if not quite as memorable as its more familiar companion in B minor, but it demands and receives much virtuosity from its soloists. The *Sinfonia* and *Concerto alla rustica* bring much energy and tonal bite from the orchestral strings, and the recording is suitably vivid throughout.

The ASV version of *The Four Seasons*, with José-Luis Garcia as soloist and musical director, is particularly pleasing, with the violins of the accompanying group sweetly fresh and the soloist nicely balanced. The overall pacing is beautifully judged, and each movement takes its place naturally and spontaneously in relation to its companions. The effects are well made, but there are no histrionics and, although the continuo does not always come through strongly, the unnamed player makes a useful contribution to a performance that is very easy to live with. The one drawback to this issue is that there is only one track for each of the *Four Seasons*. The new couplings add two versions of *La tempesta del mare*, both the one with solo violin (from Op. 8) and the even more engaging triple concerto arrangement for flute, oboe and bassoon. The equally attractive flute/bassoon version of *La Notte* completes the listener's pleasure. The wind soloists are illustrious and George Malcolm's accompaniments are a model of baroque style.

Gil Shaham and the excellent, conductorless Orpheus Chamber Orchestra combine to present a strongly characterized, eminently musical set of *Seasons* which, orchestrally at least, seeks in some ways to emulate period-instrument performances with bright, bracingly athletic string-textures – sample the opening movement of *Autumn* – and gutsy virility when called for, as in the summer storms (tracks 5–6). Gil Shaham plays beautifully and with freshness, but in the last resort this performance has nothing really new to say about this much-recorded work. It is given first-rate sound with plenty of presence.

Perlman's imagination holds the sequence together superbly, and there are many passages of pure magic, as in the central *Adagio* of *Summer*. The digital remastering of the 1976 recording is managed admirably, the sound firm, clear and well balanced, with plenty of detail. Now this record has been made much more competitive by the addition of three extra violin concertos, all fine works. Although the acoustic is somewhat dryish, this does not prevent these extra works from sounding very good.

Schneiderhan's 1959 version of *The Four Seasons* re-emerges, as fresh as paint, now well buttressed by Pachelbel's *Canon*, Purcell's *Chacony* and the famous Bach *Air* all sounding serenely spacious, while the Albinoni/Giazotto *Adagio* also has a certain refined dignity. Schneiderhan's timbre, pure and sweetly classical, suits Vivaldi very well indeed. The aptly chamber-scaled performance, with brisk tempi and alert orchestral playing, is full of life, with the pictorial detail emerging naturally but without being overcharacterized.

There are innumerable recordings of Vivaldi's *Four Seasons* and it seems to us that those versions offered without fill-ups in a crowded marketplace have become uncompetitive. However, Marriner's 1970 Academy of St Martin-in-the-Fields version with Alan Loveday is an exception and still remains near the top of the list of recommended CDs. The performance is as satisfying as any and will surely delight all but those who are ruled by the creed of authenticity. It has an element of fantasy that makes the music sound utterly new; it is full of imaginative touches, with Simon Preston subtly varying the continuo between harpsichord and organ. The opulence of string tone may have a romantic connotation, but there is no self-indulgence in the interpretation, no sentimentality, for the contrasts are made sharper and fresher, not smoothed over. But without any coupling this now calls for reissue on a lower-priced label.

Karajan's 1972 recording of *The Four Seasons* was an undoubted success and remains very enjoyable. Its tonal beauty is not achieved at the expense of vitality and, although the harpsichord hardly ever comes through, the overall scale is acceptable. Michel Schwalbé is a memorable soloist; his playing is neat, precise and very musical, with a touch of Italian sunshine in the tone. The current remastering for DG's bargain label, Classikon, has restored the body and breadth of the original, and in the additional works (recorded in the St Moritz Französische Kirche in Switzerland two years earlier) the string-sound is glorious. The sheer charisma of the BPO playing, notably in the *Sinfonia al Santa Sepolcro*, where the first movement is presented with great expressive depth, is difficult to resist, and the *Concerto alla rustica* sounds wonderfully sumptuous. Vivaldi would surely have been amazed!

An excellent bargain version from the Virtuosi di Praga, fresh, bright and clean, with a strong, highly responsive soloist in Oldřich Vlček. *Spring* is immediately vivacious and the viola produces a nice little rasp for the shepherd's dog. *Autumn* is delicately somnambulant, and the opening of *Winter* is well below zero and is decorated with a clink from the continuo. The *Concerto for four violins* makes for a popular encore. Excellent sound and very good value.

The Archiv version by Simon Standage with the English Concert, directed from the harpsichord by Trevor Pinnock, creates a relatively intimate sound, though their approach is certainly not without drama, while the solo contribution has impressive flair and bravura. The overall effect is essentially refined, treating the pictorial imagery with subtlety. The result finds a natural balance between vivid projection and atmospheric feeling. The digital recording is first class. Authenticists should be well satisfied.

The BIS recording by Nils-Erik Sparf and the Drottningholm Baroque Ensemble has astonishing clarity and presence; and as playing, it is hardly less remarkable in its imaginative vitality. These Swedish players make the most of all the pictorial characterization without ever overdoing anything: they achieve the feat of making one hear this eminently familiar repertoire as if for the very first time.

Vladimir Spivakov's highly enjoyable account of Vivaldi's *Four seasons* is made the more attractive by opening with two more of Vivaldi's most imaginative violin concertos. Both are very well played indeed by soloist and orchestra alike, as is the more famous main work, given an essentially chamber-style account, yet one not lacking its robust moments. Characterization is strong. There is plenty of vigour for the summer storms and *Spring* is tinglingly fresh, with its central movement played with contrasting gentle delicacy. Altogether this is highly successful, with the vivid, well-balanced recording achieving excellent presence against the background ambience of L'Eglise du Liban, Paris.

The novelty of the Helios issue is the inclusion of the sonnets which Vivaldi placed on his score to give his listeners a guide to the illustrative detail suggested by the music. Before each of the four concertos, the appropriate poem is read, first in a romantically effusive Italian manner and then in BBC English (the contrast quite striking). On CD, of course, one can programme out these introductions; one would hardly want to hear them as often as the concertos. The performances are first class. Adelina Oprean is an excellent soloist, her reading full of youthful energy and expressive freshness; her timbre is clean and pure, her technique assured. Faeber matches her vitality, and the score's pictorial effects are boldly characterized in a vividly projected sound-picture.

Jaime Laredo's performance has great spontaneity and vitality, emphasized by the forward balance which is nevertheless admirably truthful. The bright upper range is balanced by a firm, resonant bass. Laredo plays with bravura and directs polished, strongly characterized accompaniments. Pacing tends to be on the fast side; although the reading is extrovert and the lyrical music – played responsively – is made to offer a series of interludes to the vigour of the allegros, the effect is exhilarating rather than aggressive. However, there is no extra music.

Kennedy's account is certainly among the more spectacular in conveying its picaresque imagery; only *Autumn* brings a degree of real controversy, however, with weird special effects, including glissando harmonics in the slow movement and percussive applications of the wooden part of the bow to add rhythmic pungency to the hunting finale. There is plenty of vivid detail elsewhere. The ECO's playing is always responsive, to match the often very exciting bravura of its soloist, and allegros have an agreeable vitality. However, at 41 minutes, with no fillers, this is not generous and it would not be our first choice for repeated listening.

There is an element of eccentricity in Harnoncourt's approach to Vivaldi's Op. 8, and his control of dynamics and tempi, with allegros often aggressively fast and chimerical changes of mood, will not convince all listeners. Alice Harnoncourt's timbre is leonine and her tone-production somewhat astringent in the 'authentic' baroque manner. The dramatic style of her solo playing is certainly at one with the vivid pictorialism of Vivaldi's imagery, even if it is somewhat overcharacterized. The interpretative approach throughout emphasizes such strong contrasts: the languorous opening of *Summer* makes a splendid foil for the storm and buzzing insects, yet the zephyr breezes are wistfully gentle. The continuo uses a chamber organ to great effect, and picaresque touches of colour are added to the string texture. The CD includes two other colourful works from the set and the sound is extremely lively to match the playing.

The digital Decca Eclipse version from Chailly, with an assured and highly musical soloist in Franco Gulli, has the advantage of top-drawer sound and brings performances that are warmly animated and well characterized (without exaggeration), using modern instruments to pleasing effect. The Bologna Philharmonic accompanies spiritedly, if without the very last degree of polish. *The Four Seasons* starts at band 8 of the CD, and the programme opens with the three other works, as imaginative as anything in the vast Vivaldi repertory. They are very well played too. Enjoyable though this is, it cannot rise to the very top of a crowded list.

(i) *The Four Seasons, Op. 8/1–4;* (ii) *L'Estro armonico: Double violin concerto in A min., Op. 3/8* (arr. Franko); *Double violin concertos, RV 509, 512, 514, 517;* (iii) *Double concertos for flute and violin, RV 516, 524* (arr. Rampal); (iv) *Triple violin concerto in F, RV 551.*

(N) (M) **(*) Sony Stern Edition I Analogue/Dig. SM2K 66472 (2) [id.]. Isaac Stern, with (i) Jerusalem Music Centre CO; (ii) David Oistrakh, Phd. O, Ormandy; (iii) Jean-Pierre Rampal, Franz Liszt CO, Rolla; (iv) Zukerman, Perlman, NYPO, Mehta – CARL STAMITZ: *Sinfonia concertante.* ***

Stern's *Four Seasons*, recorded in Jerusalem in 1977, is bright and extrovert, with impressive bravura playing and strong characterization in outer movements. There is plenty of orchestral bustle to support the solo line, with the summer winds blowing furiously and a positively icy opening for *Winter*. Stern's articulation is impressively brilliant and he offers a serene contrast in slow movements, providing a novelty in the *Largo* of *Spring* by decorating the reprise of the solo line. The *Double concerto* from *L'Estro armonico* is the earliest recording here (1955) and Sam Franko's arrangement turns it into a concerto for strings with concertante violin parts; this is emphasized by the full Philadelphia string-textures. The other four *Double concertos* with David Oistrakh were recorded in 1959. These performances are the highlight of the present compilation. It certainly makes a difference when soloists of this calibre combine in such a series. The performances are so spontaneous and musical that one's attention is closely held throughout, especially in the often glorious slow movements. In spite of Ormandy's apparant reluctance to control the final ritardando of quick movements, there is also much to admire in the orchestral playing. Taken individually, Oistrakh and Stern have distinct and easily identifiable tonal characteristics. When playing along in thirds, however, the effect is almost like that of two Oistrakhs or two Sterns. There is a satisfying variety of key here and useful though unexaggerated separation for the two soloists, who are at their peak in the slow movement of the *G minor*, RV 517, and the first Allegro of the *D major*, RV 512. Excellent, full sound so that one forgets that no one plays Vivaldi like this any more! Rampal's arrangements of RV 516 and RV 524 are also of works intended for a pair of violins. The playing is very fast and brilliant and will surely give any signed-up member of the early-music lobby a seizure. The *Triple violin concerto* comes from Stern's sixtieth-birthday concert in the autumn of 1980, and the enjoyment of the participants on this occasion is well conveyed.

(i) *The Four seasons, Op. 8/1–4;* (ii) *Cello concerto in E min., RV 40;* (iii) *Guitar concerto in D, RV 93;* (iv; v) *Double mandolin concerto in G, RV 532;* (vi) *Piccolo concerto in C, RV 443;* (vii) *Double trumpet concerto in C, RV 537;* (viii; v) *Double concerto for viola d'amore & guitar;* (ix; x) *Flute concerto in G (La Notte), Op. 10/2, RV 239;* (x) *Concertos for strings: in D min. (Madrigalesco), RV 129; in G (alla rustica), RV 151;* (xi; x) *Violin concertos: in D (L'inquietudine), RV 234; in E (L'Amoroso), RV 271. Sinfonia in B min. (Al Santo Sepolcro), RV 169.*

(N) (B) *** DG Double 447 346-2 (2) [id.]. (i) Schneiderhan; (ii) Fournier; both with Lucerne Festival Strings, Baumgartner; (iii) Behrend, I Musici; (iv) Takashi & Silvia Ochi; (v) CO, Paul Kuentz; (vi) Linde, Seiler CO, Hofmann; (vii) Scherbaum, Haubold, with Hamburg Bar. Ens.; (viii) Monique Frasca-Columbier, Yepes; (x) BPO, Karajan; with (ix) Blau; (xi) Brandis.

Scheiderhan's admirably stylish account of *The Four seasons* (see above) here comes as part of a DG Double offering an attractive mélange of favourite concertos from a variety of sources but all expertly played and well recorded. The second CD centres on Karajan's highly individual Berlin Philharmonic collection from the beginning of the 1970s, which shows the maestro affectionately indulging himself in repertoire for which he may not have the proper stylistic credentials but which he obviously loves. The sheer charisma of the playing and the rich body of tone the orchestra creates within a resonant acoustic, notably in the extraordinary *Sinfonia al Santo Sepolcro*, are difficult to resist. The orchestra dominates even the solo concertos and the fine soloists, notably Thomas Brandis (violin), seem to float, concertante style, within the glowing ambience. The refinement of execution is remarkable and all the music comes to life, if in an inflated way. This is a Vivaldi collection like no other.

'The world of Vivaldi': (i) *The Four Seasons, Op. 8/1–4;* (ii) *Guitar concerto in D, RV 43;* (iii) *Piccolo concerto in C, RV 443;* (iv) *Concerto for strings in G (alla rustica), RV 151;* (v) *Double trumpet concerto in C, RV 537.*

(M) **(*) Decca 433 866-2; *433 866-4.* (i) Kulka, Stuttgart CO, Münchinger; (ii) Fernández, ECO, Malcolm; (iii) Bennett, ASMF, Marriner; (iv) Lucerne Festival Strings, Baumgartner; (v) Wilbraham, Jones, ASMF, Marriner.

Konstanty Kulka's performance of *The Four Seasons* from the early 1970s has stood the test of time. The solo playing is first class and Münchinger's accompaniment is stylish and lively. It was Münchinger who, with a different soloist, put this famous concertante work on the map with his first mono LP recording in the 1950s (the first in the UK – though Scherchen pioneered the work in the USA in the late 1940s) and so it is good to have the present reminder of his Vivaldi sympathies. The sound is a little astringent on top but does not lack body, and its brightness adds to the freshness. The quartet of concertos now offered as ballast certainly give a good cross-section of Vivaldi's world, all played with expertise and well recorded. The *Concerto for guitar* is digital; the *Double trumpet concerto* sounds a shade over-bright.

The Four Seasons, Op. 8/1–4 (arr. for flute and strings).
(M) *** RCA GD 60748 [60748-2-RG]. James Galway, Zagreb Soloists.

James Galway's transcription is thoroughly musical and so convincing that at times one is tempted to believe that the work was conceived in this form. The playing itself is marvellous, full of detail and imagination, and the recording is excellent, even if the flute is given a forward balance, the more striking on CD.

La Cetra (12 Violin concertos), Op. 9.
(N) (M) *** Virgin Veritas/EMI Dig. VED5 61246-2 (2) [id.]. Monica Huggettt, Raglan Bar. Players, Kraemer.
*** O-L Dig. 421 366-2 (2) [id.]. Standage, AAM, Hogwood.

(i) *La Cetra;* (ii) *Double oboe concerto in D min., RV 535;* (iii) *Piccolo concerto in C, RV 443.*
(N) ❀ (B) *** Decca Double 448 110-2 (2) [id.]. (i) Iona Brown, ASMF; (ii) Neil Black; (iii) Celia Nicklin; both with ASMF, Marriner.

La Cetra (The Lyre) was the last set of violin concertos Vivaldi published. Iona Brown, for some years the leader of St Martin's Academy, here acts as director in the place of Sir Neville Marriner. So resilient and imaginative are the results that one hardly detects any difference from the immaculate and stylish Vivaldi playing in earlier Academy Vivaldi sets. There is some wonderful music here; the later concertos are every bit the equal of anything in *The Trial between harmony and invention*, and they are played gloriously. The recording too is outstandingly rich and vivid, even by earlier Argo standards with this group, and the Decca transfer to CD retains the demonstration excellence of the original analogue LPs, with a yet greater sense of body and presence. For the Double Decca reissue, two of Vivaldi's most engaging wind concertos have been added, winningly played by two estimable Academy soloists and made the more attractive in slow movements by the imaginative continuo from Kenneth Heath (cello), Christopher Hogwood (harpsichord) and Colin Tilney (organ). The sound is every bit as good as in the concertos for violin.

Monica Huggett and the Raglan Baroque Players offer performances so accomplished and in such good style that they are unlikely to be surpassed in authentic-instrument versions of *La Cetra*. She is in excellent form and her virtuosity always appears effortless. The Raglan Baroque Players are of the same size as the Academy of Ancient Music and some players are common to both groups. First-class recording.

On Oiseau-Lyre, Simon Standage gives an attractive and fluent account of the set, and the recording is excellent, slightly dry but very clean.

6 Flute concertos, Op. 10.
*** DG Dig. 437 839-2 [id.]. Patrick Gallois, Orpheus CO.
*** DG Dig. 423 702-2 [id.]. Liza Beznosiuk, E. Concert, Pinnock.
(Y/B) (M) *** O-L 444 163-2 [id.]. Stephen Preston, AAM, Hogwood.
(M) *** Carlton Classics Dig. PCD 961 [id.]. Judith Hall, Divertimenti of L., Paul Barritt.
(M) **(*) RCA 09026 61351-2. James Galway, New Irish CO.

These works are extremely well served on CD, and it is almost impossible to suggest a clear first choice. However, among recent issues this Gallois/Orpheus set is arguably the lightest and most spirited of any, be they on period instruments or not. Collectors who recall Gallois' dazzling account of the Nielsen *Concerto* will know what to expect: effortless virtuosity, refined musicianship, intelligence and taste. He has an excellent rapport with the splendid Orpheus Chamber Orchestra and is very well served too by the engineers. A most distinguished issue.

There is some expressive as well as brilliant playing on the DG Archiv CD, which should delight listeners. Try track 8 (the *Largo* movement of *Concerto No. 2 in G minor, La Notte*) for an example of the beautifully refined and cool pianissimo tone that Liza Beznosiuk can produce – and almost any of the fast movements for an example of her virtuosity. Trevor Pinnock and the English Concert provide unfailingly vital and, above all, imaginative support. The DG recording is exemplary in its clarity. Recommended with enthusiasm.

Stephen Preston plays a period instrument, a Schuchart, and the Academy of Ancient Music likewise play old instruments. Their playing is eminently stylish, but also spirited and expressive, and they are admirably recorded, with the analogue sound enhanced further in the CD format. This makes a clear first choice among period performances at medium price .

Judith Hall's record of the Op. 10 *Flute concertos* is fresh and brightly recorded. She plays with considerable virtuosity and a great deal of taste. The Divertimenti of London is a modern-instrument group and the players are both sensitive and alive.

James Galway directs the New Irish Chamber Orchestra from the flute – and to generally good effect. The playing is predictably brilliant and the goldfinch imitations in *Il Gardellino* (which comes first on the disc) are enticing. Slow movements demonstrate Galway's beauty of timbre and sense of line to consistently good effect, although some may find the sweet vibrato a bit too much for baroque repertoire. No complaints about the recording quality.

6 Violin concertos, Op. 11.
*** O-L Dig. 436 172-2 [id.]. Stanley Ritchie, Frank de Bruine, AAM, Hogwood.

The Vivaldi repertoire convincingly using original instruments continues to expand. The last of the Op. 11 set is given an accomplished performance by Frank de Bruine (oboe), and Stanley Ritchie is a vital and suitably expressive soloist in the others (which include the familiar *Il Favorito*). Accompaniments are fresh and bracing in the way of the Academy of Ancient Music, and Hogwood's continuo uses organ as well as harpsichord, besides featuring the theorbo.

Complete bassoon concertos

Bassoon concertos.
(M) *** ASV Dig. CDDCX 625 (6). Daniel Smith, ECO, Ledger; Zagreb Solists, Ninić.

Bassoon concertos: in C, RV 466; in C, RV 467; in F, RV 486; in F, RV 491; in A min., RV 499; in A min., RV 500.
**(*) ASV Dig. CDDCA 565 [id.]. Daniel Smith, ECO, Ledger.

Bassoon concertos in C, RV 469; in C, RV 470; in C, RV 474; in C, RV 476; in F, RV 487; in G, RV 494.
**(*) ASV Dig. CDDCA 571 [id.]. Daniel Smith, ECO, Ledger.

Bassoon concertos: in C, RV 472; in C, RV 477; in C, RV 479; in D min., RV 481; in F, RV 488; in B flat (La notte), RV 501.
**(*) ASV Dig. CDDCA 662 [id.]. Daniel Smith, ECO, Ledger.

The bassoon seems to have uncovered a particularly generous fund of inspiration in Vivaldi, for few of his 37 concertos for that instrument are in any way routine. Daniel Smith's achievement in recording them all is considerable, for he plays with constant freshness and enthusiasm. His woody tone is very attractive and he is very well caught by the engineers. This set can be welcomed almost without reservation and, dipped into, the various recordings will always give pleasure. We have listened to every one of these concertos and have come up smiling. Daniel Smith is a genial and personable player and he has considerable facility; even if some of the more complicated roulades are not executed with exact precision, his playing has undoubted flair. He is balanced well forward, but the orchestral accompaniment has plenty of personality and registers well enough.

Bassoon concertos: in C, RV 471; in C, RV 475; in F, RV 490; in G, RV 492; in G min., RV 495; in G min., RV 496.
*** ASV CDDCA 734 [id.]. Daniel Smith, Zagreb Soloists, Tonko Ninić.

Bassoon concertos: in C, RV 473; in C, RV 478; in E flat, RV 483; in F, RV 485; in A min., RV 497; in A min., RV 498; in B flat, RV 502.
**(*) ASV CDDCA 752 [id.]. Daniel Smith, Zagreb Soloists, Tonko Ninić.

For the last three CDs of the series the Zagreb Soloists take over the accompaniments and offer alert, vivacious playing that adds to the pleasure of the performances. Daniel Smith too, responds with more vigour and polish and overall there is plenty of affectionate warmth.

Bassoon concertos: in C min., RV 480; in E min., RV 484; in F, RV 489; in G, RV 493; in B flat, RV 503; in B flat, RV 504.
*** ASV Dig. CDDCA 751 [id.]. Daniel Smith, Zagreb Soloists, Tonko Ninić.

This is the record to begin with if you intend sampling this enterprising ASV series. Almost all the works here show Vivaldi at his most inventively spontaneous. Smith and the Zagreb group rise to the occasion and the recording is pleasingly vivid.

Bassoon concerto in F, RV 485; (i) *Double concerto in G min., for recorder and bassoon (La Notte), RV 104.*
*** BIS Dig. CD 271 [id.]. McGraw, (i) Pehrsson, Drottningholm Bar. Ens. – TELEMANN: *Concertos.*
***

The concerto subtitled *La Notte* exists in three versions: one for flute (the most familiar), RV 439; another for bassoon, RV 501; and the present version, RV 104. Clas Pehrsson, Michael McGraw and the Drottningholm Baroque Ensemble give a thoroughly splendid account of it, and the *Bassoon concerto in F major* also fares well. Excellent recording.

Complete cello concertos

Volume 1: *Cello concertos: in C, RV 398; in C, RV 399; in D, RV 404; in D min., RV 406; in F, RV 410; in F, RV 412; in A min., RV 419.*
(Y/B) (BB) *** Naxos Dig. 8.550907 [id.]. Raphael Wallfisch, City of L. Sinfonia, Nicholas Kraemer.

Volume 2: *Cello concertos: in C, RV 400; in C min., RV 401; in E flat, RV 408; in G, RV 413; in A min., RV 422;* (i) *Double cello concerto in G min., RV 531.*
(Y/B) (BB) *** Naxos Dig. 8.550908 [id.]. Raphael Wallfisch, (i) with Keith Harvey; City of L. Sinfonia, Nicholas Kraemer.

Volume 3: *Cello concertos: in C min., RV 402; in D, RV 403; in D min., RV 407;* (i) *in E min., RV 409; in A min., RV 418; in B flat, RV 423; in B min., RV 424.*
(Y/B) ✿ (BB) *** Naxos Dig. 8.550909 [id.]. Raphael Wallfisch, (i) with Johanna Graham; City of L. Sinfonia, Nicholas Kraemer.

Volume 4: *Cello concertos: in D min., RV 405; in F, RV 411; in G, RV 414; in G min., RV 416 & RV 417; in A min., RV 420 & RV 421.*
(Y/B) (BB) *** Naxos Dig. 8. 550910 [id.]. Raphael Wallfisch, City of L. Sinfonia, Nicholas Kraemer.

Vivaldi liked to write for instruments playing in the middle to lower register, and he left 27 solo concertos for the cello, all of which are here. This Naxos series is part of an overall survey, with plans eventually to record every one of the Vivaldi concertos! Certainly the company has begun admirably and the choice of Raphael Wallfisch as soloist could hardly have been bettered. He forms an admirable partnership with the City of London Sinfonia, directed from the harpsichord or chamber organ by Nicholas Kraemer. The first concerto of Volume 1, the fine *F major*, RV 412, sets off with great energy and produces a characteristically atmospheric central *Larghetto*. Wallfisch plays with restrained use of vibrato and a nicely judged expressive feeling. In the *A minor* work which follows (RV 419), Kraemer effectively uses an organ continuo to enliven the opening tutti and underpin the singing cello line in the *Andante*. The alert, resilient orchestral string-playing in the allegros is a pleasure in itself.

Besides several very striking solo works, Volume 2 of the Naxos series includes Vivaldi's only *Double cello concerto*, with much bustling interchange in the outer movements and the soloists answering each other eloquently in the *Largo*. In the *G major* solo *Concerto*, RV 413, there is a brilliantly articulated *moto perpetuo* semiquaver theme which alternates between soloist and orchestra; then follows a thoughtful slow movement, somewhat improvisatory in feeling, in which Wallfisch is in his element, suspended over Kraemer's gentle organ continuo. Bravura passage-work returns in the finale. Throughout these performances one admires the soloist's subtle use of light and shade and his partnership with the accompanying group and Nicholas Kraemer's continuo.

Volume 3 is a particularly fine collection and as good a place to start as any. The soloist's bravura staccato playing at the opening on the *B flat major*, RV 423, commands the listener's attention at the very beginning of the disc, and this work has a matching good-humoured finale. The *Concerto in D minor*, RV 407, is one of Vivaldi's very best, and its central *Largo e sempre piano* again brings a touching solo response. Vivaldi is never predictable, and perhaps the most striking work of all here is the *E minor Concerto*, RV 409, where the cello is joined by a subservient and somewhat doleful solo bassoon. In the *Adagio–Allegro molto* opening movement, the two soloists wind their way through a melancholy recitativo, regularly interrupted by modest bursts of energy from the string tutti, reminding one of *The Four Seasons*; then in the much briefer *Allegro–Adagio* slow movement the procedure is reversed: the orchestral strings are gently sustained and the soloists busy. The finale is more conventional in manner, but the presence of the bassoon ensures that the effect is still aurally intriguing.

Volume 4 brings a further batch of concertos notable for their vitality and the vigorous bravura demanded from the soloist. Throughout these four discs there is never a hint of routine. Wallfisch's playing has extraordinary precision, and both he and the accompanying group continually communicate their enthusiasm for this endlessly inventive music. The recording is vividly realistic and the balance seems very well judged indeed within the warm but never clouding ambience of All Saints' Church or Conway Hall, London. A remarkable achievement, standing very high indeed in the Vivaldi discography. We award a token Rosette to Volume 3, but the final volume is hardly less stimulating, and our accolade could surely apply to either of the other two.

Cello concertos: in C, RV 398; in G, RV 413.
(B) *** DG Double 437 952-2 (2) [id.]. Rostropovich, Zurich Coll. Mus., Sacher – BERNSTEIN: *3 Meditations;* BOCCHERINI: *Cello concerto No. 2;* GLAZUNOV: *Chant du Ménestrel;* SHOSTAKOVICH: *Cello concerto No. 2;* TARTINI: *Cello concerto;* TCHAIKOVSKY: *Andante cantabile* etc. ***

Performances of great vigour and projection from Rostropovich; every bar comes fully to life. Spendidly lively accompaniments and excellent CD transfers, bright and clean with no lack of depth. Rostropovich's performances come as part of a very generous Double DG compilation, with the two discs offered for the price of one.

Cello concertos: in C, RV 399; in C min., RV 401; in D min., RV 405; in B flat, RV 423; in F, RV 538; Largo. (i) *Concerto in E min. for cello and bassoon, RV 409.*
*** RCA Dig. RD 87774 [7774-2-RC]. Harnoy, (i) McKay, Toronto CO, Robinson.

Cello concertos: in C min., RV 402; in D, RV 403; in D min., RV 406; in F, RV 412; in G, RV 414; in A min., RV 422; in B min., RV 424.
*** RCA Dig. RD 60155 [60155-2-RC]. Ofra Harnoy, Toronto CO, Paul Robinson.

Cello concertos: in D, RV 404; D min., RV 407; F, RV 411; G min., RV 417; A min., RV 420; (i) *Double concerto for violin, cello and strings in F (Il Proteo o sia il mondo), RV 544.*
*** RCA Dig. 09026 61578-2 [id.]. Ofra Harnoy, (i) with Igor Oistrakh; Toronto CO, Paul Robinson.

Ofra Harnoy's are traditional performances with modern instruments; she plays with style, impeccable technique and eloquence. In short, she is a first-class artist with a good lyrical sense. Her strength lies not so much in her tone, which is not big, but in her selfless approach to this repertoire. She does not regard this music as a vehicle for her own personality but plays it with an agreeable dedication and a delight in its considerable felicities. The *Double concerto* brings an excellent partnership with Igor Oistrakh, and here the *Adagio* is particularly touching. She is given good support from the Toronto Chamber Orchestra under Paul Robinson, and is very well recorded.

Cello concertos: in G, RV 413; in G min., RV 417.
(M) **(*) EMI CDM7 64326-2 [id.]. Lynn Harrell, ECO, Zukerman – HAYDN: *Concertos.* **(*)

Though Lynn Harrell is hardly a classical stylist among cellists (as he shows in the Haydn coupling), he gives lively, imaginative performances of two fine Vivaldi concertos (the *G major* particularly attractive) and is well accompanied by Zukerman. The sound is lively and full, if not as smooth as on the Haydn concertos, which are interspersed with Vivaldi on the generous (74-minute) CD.

Frans Brüggen Edition, Volume 8: *Chamber concertos in C, RV 87; in D, RV 92 & RV 94; in G min., RV 105; in A min., RV 108; in C min., RV 441; in F, RV 442.*

(Y/B) (M) *** Teldec/Warner 4509 97470-2 [id.]. Frans Brüggen, Jürg Schaeflein, Otto Fleischmann, Alice Harnoncourt, Walter Pfeiffer, Nikolaus Harnoncourt, Gustav Leonhardt; VCM, Harnoncourt; Concerto Amsterdam, Schröder.

Vivaldi's *Chamber concertos* are among his most aurally stimulating with period instrumental combinations of recorder, oboe, violin and bassoon. The *G minor Concerto*, RV 105, offers all four, with the most piquant interplay. However, the opening *Concerto in D*, RV 94, catches the ear since for its *Largo* Vivaldi borrows a movement from *The Four Seasons*. All the small-scale works here use soloists from Harnoncourt's group, with Alice's violin notable for its abrasive edge, while in the *C minor Concerto*, RV 441, the Vienna Concentus Musicus bring characteristically bright, thin string-timbre. But its clean profile sets off Bruggen's virtuosity, and he provides some astonishing roulades in the closing *Presto*. The Concerto Amsterdam provide the backing for the final work on the disc, the strings (still period instruments, although muted) much warmer and sweeter. This is one of Vivaldi's most imaginative concertos. In the first movement there is some delicious interplay between the recorder and the solo violin (Jaap Schröder), then, after a lovely central *Siciliano*, the recorder and violin have more lively imitative dialogue. No complaints about the excellent Das Alte Werk sound, vividly transferred.

Flute concertos: in A min., RV 108; in F, RV 434; Double flute concerto in C, RV 533; Sopranino recorder concertos: in C, RV 443 & RV 444; in A min., RV 445.

(BB) *** Naxos Dig. 8.550385; 4550385 [id.]. Jálek, Novotny, Stivin, Capella Istropolitana, Oliver Dohnányi.

The Capella Istropolitana, who are drawn from the excellent Slovak Philharmonic, play with vitality and sensitivity for Oliver Dohnányi and the soloists show appropriate virtuosity and flair. As always, there are rewards and surprises in this music, revealed by Jiří Stivin's undoubted artistry. The sound is very good indeed, and so is the balance.

Flute concertos in D, RV 427; in D (Il gardellino), RV 428; in D, RV 429; in G, RV 436; in G, RV 438; in A min., RV 440; (i) in C, for 2 flutes, RV 533.

*** HM Dig. HMC 905193 [id.]. Janet See, (i) S. Schultz; Philh. Bar. O, McGegan.

Janet See is not only a first-class player but also a real artist whose phrasing is alive and imaginative. Moreover the Philharmonia Baroque Orchestra, a West Coast American group, give her excellent support. Vivaldi deserves some of the credit for all this, too. The diversity and range of these pieces is astonishing. Highly enjoyable.

Guitar concertos in C, RV 82; in D, RV 93.

(Y/B) (M) *** DG 439 984-2 [id.]. Siegfried Behrend, I Musici – CARULLI: *Concerto in A;* GIULIANI: *Concerto in A, Op. 30.* ***

Both these concertos are transcriptions of chamber works intended for the lute. They work well enough on guitar and are most elegantly played here. Although – as the opening of the *D major* shows – there is no lack of life in the performances, their predominating characteristic is of smooth elegance, and a more robust and sinewy effect can be more telling in this repertoire.

Guitar concerto in D, RV 93.

(N) (B) *** Sony SBK 58168; SBT 58168 [id.]. John Williams, ECO – GIULIANI: *Concerto, Op. 30;* RODRIGO: *Concierto de Aranjuez* etc. ***

This is a familiar work but none the less delightful for that. It is played with predictable liveliness and artistry and, although the balance (as so often with this solo instrument) places the soloist too forward, the orchestra is well in the picture and the ambience is pleasing.

Guitar concertos in D, RV 93; in B flat, RV 524; in G min., RV 531; in G, RV 532. Trios: in C, RV 82; in G min., RV 85.

*** DG Dig. 415 487-2 [id.]. Söllscher, Bern Camerata, Füri.

Göran Söllscher further enhances his reputation both as a master-guitarist and as an artist on this excellently recorded issue, in which he has first-class support from the Camerata Bern under Thomas Füri. In RV 532, Söllscher resorts to technology and plays both parts. The DG balance is admirably judged.

(i) *Lute concerto in F, RV 93; Double concerto in G, RV 532;* (ii) *Sonatas for lute and harpsichord: in C; in G, RV 82 & 85* (arr. from *Trio sonatas*).

(M) **(*) RCA 09026 61588-2 [id.]. Julian Bream, Monteverdi O, Gardiner – HANDEL; KOHAUT: *Concertos.* **(*)

The *Lute concerto* receives a first-class performance from Bream, and he is well accompanied. The slow movement with its delicate embroidery over sustained strings is particularly fine. In the arrangement of the *Double mandolin concerto* Bream is able by electronic means to assume both solo roles. This too is a highly effective performance, though the forward balance makes the solo instruments sound larger than life and negates much of the dynamic contrast with Gardiner's excellent accompanying group. The two chamber works were originally *Trio sonatas for lute, violin and continuo*, but as the violin part doubles much of what the lute has to contribute it can be omitted without problems arising. The music is pleasingly lightweight and the performances are fresh and imaginative. Once again, however, the balance is unnaturally forward.

Mandolin concerto in C, RV 425; Double mandolin concerto in G, RV 532; (Soprano) Lute concerto in D, RV 93; Double concerto in D min. for viola d'amore and lute, RV 540. Trios: in C, RV 82; in G min., RV 85.
*** Hyperion CDA 66160 [id.]. Jeffrey, O'Dette, Parley of Instruments, Goodman and Holman.

These are chamber performances, with one instrument to each part, and this obviously provides an ideal balance for the *Mandolin concertos*. There are other innovations, too. An organ continuo replaces the usual harpsichord, and very effective it is; in the *Trios* and the *Lute concerto* (but not in the *Double concerto*, RV 540) Paul O'Dette uses a gut-strung soprano lute. The delightful sounds here, with all players using original instruments or copies, are very convincing. The recording is realistically balanced within an attractively spacious acoustic.

Oboe concertos: in C, Op. 8/12, RV 64; in C, RV 447 & RV 452; in D, RV 453; in D min., RV 454; in F, RV 456; in A min., RV 461; in B flat, RV 464.
(B) *** Erato/Warner 2292 45944-2 [id.]. Pierre Pierlot, Sol. Ven., Scimone.

As in his companion collection of Albinoni *Concertos* on the same Erato Bonsai label, Pierre Pierlot proves an ideal soloist, his small, sweet timbre expressive without being overly romantic, and there is pleasingly nimble articulation in allegros. Scimone accompanies sympathetically and the playing of I Solisti Veneti is alert and stylish. Excellent sound, too, from the late 1960s. These eight performances have the right kind of charm, and the disc makes a generous (70 minutes) bargain. Alas, no information is provided about the music itself.

Oboe concertos: in C, RV 447 & RV 451; in F, RV 455 & RV 457; in A min., RV 461 & RV 463.
(BB) *** Naxos Dig. 8.550860 [id.]. Stefan Schilli, Budapest Failoni CO, Béla Nagy.

Oboe concertos: in C, RV 450 & RV 452; in D, RV 453; in D min., RV 454; (i) *Double oboe concertos: in C, RV 534; D min., RV 535; A min., RV 536.*
(BB) *** Naxos Dig. 8.550859 [id.]. Stefan Schilli; (i) with Diethelm Jonas; Budapest Failoni CO, Béla Nagy.

Excellent playing from these Budapest musicians, who seem set to provide us with a survey of Vivaldi's concertante works for oboe. The second of these two discs offers the three *Double concertos*, and the two CDs between them include half the solo works. They are often surprisingly florid, requiring considerable bravura from the soloist. A good example is the Minuet finale of RV 447, which is a cross between a Rondo and a theme and variations. Vivaldi is never entirely predictable, except that his invention never seems to flag, and many of the simple *Grave, Larghetto* and *Largo* slow movements are very pleasing indeed.

(i) *Oboe concertos: in C, RV 540; in D min., RV 454; in F, RV 457;* (i–ii) *Double oboe concerto in D min., RV 535;* (i; iii) *Double concerto for oboe, bassoon and orchestra in G, RV 545;* (i–iii) *Concerto for 2 oboes, 2 violins, bassoon and orchestra, RV 557;* (i) *Recorder concerto in F, RV 442.*
(Y/B) (B) *** HM Dig. HMA 1903018 [id.]. (i) Marie Wolf (oboe or recorder); (ii) Márton Brandisz; (iii) Paul Tognon; Capella Savaria, Pál Németh.

While two of the solo oboe concertos here were conceived for bassoon, Marie Wolf with her warm phrasing and clean tonguing makes them all sound custom-made for her principal instrument. Indeed she creates robust yet creamy tone on her baroque oboe, especially in the *Largo* of RV 454, while the chromatic 'slides' in the work's first movement are most seductively managed. In the double concertos the other wind soloists produce equally characterful timbres: the two oboes blend well together, yet have individuality, while the combination of oboe and the chortling, woody bassoon must surely make the listener smile at the genial exchanges. Then Marie Wolf turns to her recorder and charms us yet again. The delightful slow movement of RV 442 is made the more fragile by the use of muted strings in the orchestra and the accompaniments have finesse and transparency. Indeed there are few more appealing bargain collections of Vivaldi wind concertos played on original instruments than this. The recording is beautifully balanced and truthful.

Concertos for strings and continuo: in C, RV 114; in C min., RV 118; in C min., RV 120; in D min., RV 128; in E min., RV 133; in F min., RV 143; in G (Alla rustica), RV 151; in G min., RV 152; in G min., RV 157; in A, RV 158; in B flat (Conca), RV 163; in B flat, RV 167. Sinfonias for strings and continuo: in C, RV 116; in E, RV 132; in E min., RV 134; in F, RV 137; in F, RV 140; in G, RV 146; in B min., RV 168.
(Y/B) (M) *** Erato/Warner Analogue/Dig. 4509 96382-2 (2) [id.]. Sol. Ven., Claudio Scimone.

For Vivaldi the terms sinfonia and concerto for strings seem to be interchangeable; indeed RV 134, which has a fugal opening movement, was first called a concerto, and the composer added the description 'sinfonia' later to the manuscript. The finales of RV 120 and RV 152, both called concertos, are also contrapuntal and these fugues show an attractive, extrovert vitality. But Vivaldi is never predictable, and many of the individual movements here show his imagination at full stretch. The *Sinfonia in G*, RV 146, opens the first disc with typically arresting flourishes, followed by a wistful *Andante*, with the melody floating over gentle pizzicatos like a song with mandolin, while the *Concerto in C*, RV 114, has a highly inventive *Chaconne* for the finale. It is a fast movement and so within its 3 minutes 25 seconds a great deal happens. We all know the *Alla rustica Concerto*, but RV 163 (curiously subtitled *Conca*) is another short but masterly piece, its three movements all springing from the opening phrase. The central *Andante* is for all the world like an operatic aria without the vocal line. Indeed many of the slow movements here are very touching, not least the restless *Andante molto* of RV 152, the lyrical A minor cantilena of RV 158, the solemn *Largo* of RV 120 and, perhaps most strikingly of all, the *Sinfonia in F*, RV 137, where the 'singing' *Andante*, with its touch of chromatic melancholy, contrasts so well with the very positive outer movements. This makes a fine close to a fascinating programme, revealing a little-known side of a great composer. The performances (using modern instruments) are vital and expressively penetrating, and the recording, whether analogue or digital (as with RV 116, 118, 137 and 143), is fresh and naturally balanced.

Viola d'amore concertos: in D, RV 392; in D min., RV 393, 394 & 395; in A, RV 396 & 397.
(M) **(*) Erato/Warner 4509 92190-2 [id.]. Nane Calabrese, Sol. Ven., Scimone.

Nane Calabrese is an excellent player with a full timbre and excellent intonation. If the viola d'amore does have its limitations, the quality of Vivaldi's invention is surprisingly high; although the orchestra, using modern instruments, makes an ample sound, the balance is cleverly contrived so that the continuo detail comes through well. Well worth exploring.

Violin concertos, Op. 8, Nos. 5 in E flat (La Tempesta di mare), RV 253; 6 in C (Il Piacere), RV 180; 10 in B flat (La Caccia), RV 362; 11 in D, RV 210; in C min. (Il Sospetto), RV 199.
(B) *** CfP Dig. CD-CFP 4522. Sir Yehudi Menuhin, Polish CO, Jerzy Maksymiuk.

Menuhin's collection of five concertos – four of them with nicknames and particularly delightful – brings some of his freshest, most intense playing in recent years. Particularly in slow movements – notably that of *Il Piacere* ('Pleasure') – he shows afresh his unique insight in shaping a phrase. Fresh, alert accompaniment and full digital recording.

Violin concertos: in C (Per la Sanctissima Assunzione di Maria Vergine), RV 581; in C min. (Il sospetto), RV 199; in D (L'inquietudine), RV 234; in E (Il riposo), RV 270; in E min. ('Il favorito'), RV 277.
(N) *** Ph. Dig. 442 145-2 [id.]. Mariana Sirbu, I Musici.

A programme of well-known Vivaldi violin concertos played with exemplary aplomb and flair by Mariana Sirbu and I Musici. For those who have had enough of period-instrument performances, these will come as an enormous relief. Sirbu and I Musici offer great expressive range and make a glorious sound. They are beautifully recorded.

MISCELLANEOUS CONCERTO COLLECTIONS

Concerti 'con molti instromenti': Bassoon concerto in E min., RV 484; Flute concerto in G min. (La notte), Op. 10/2, RV 439; Double mandolin concerto in G, RV 532; Concerto con multi instromenti in C, RV 558; Double concerto for oboe and violin in B flat, RV 548; Concerto for strings (alla rustica), RV 151; Concerto for 2 violins and two cellos in G, RV 575; L'estro armonico: Concerto for 4 violins in D, Op. 3/1, RV 549.

(N) (M) *** DG Dig. 447 301-2 [id.]. Soloists, E. Concert, Pinnock.

This extremely generous 72-minute collection of very varied works is very enticing at mid-price, showing Pinnock and the English Concert at their liveliest and most refreshing, although not always so strong on charm. (The account of the *Bassoon concerto* is perhaps an unintentional exception, for the solo timbre has a certain bovine character.) The *Concerto for four violins* is very lithe, and throughout the concert the solo playing is predictably expert. The orchestral concerto, RV 558, involves an astonishing array of instruments.

Bassoon concertos: in A min., RV 497; in B flat (La Notte), RV 501; Double mandolin concerto in G, RV 532; Piccolo concerto in C, RV 443; Viola d'amore concerto in D min., RV 394; Double violin concerto for violin and violin per eco lontano in A, RV 552.
(N) (M) *** Pierre Vernay Dig. PV 730052 [id.]. Soloists, Paul Kuentz CO, Kuentz.

Although described as 'six rare concertos', this most enjoyable, 71-minute collection is made up entirely of favourites, all played with much character. The two mandolinists, Takashi and Sylvia Ochi, are as personable as the sprightly bassoonist, Fernand Corbillon, with his woody French timbre, while the *Echo violin concerto* (the echoes feature in the ripieno as well as the solo writing) comes off to great effect. Fine accompaniments from Kuentz and first-rate digital sound, naturally balanced.

Double cello concerto in G min., RV 531; Flute concerto in C min., RV 441; Concerto in G min., for flute and bassoon (La notte), RV 104; Concerto in F for flute, oboe and bassoon (La tempesta di mare), RV 570; Guitar concerto in D, RV 93; Concerto in F for 2 horns, RV 539; Concerto in B flat for violin and cello, RV 547.
*** ASV Dig. CDDCA 645 [id.]. Soloists, ECO, Malcolm.

With George Malcolm in charge it is not surprising that this 65-minute collection of seven diverse concertos is as entertaining as any in the catalogue. Perhaps most striking of all is the *Double cello concerto*, vigorously energetic in outer movements, but with a short, serene central *Largo*, with overlapping phrases at the beginning, to remind one of the slow movement of Bach's *Double violin concerto*. The concert ends with the duet version of *La notte*, which has much to charm the ear. Accompaniments are sympathetic and stylish, and the whole programme beams with vitality and conveyed enjoyment. The digital sound is vivid and realistic.

Double concertos: for 2 cellos in G min., RV 531; 2 flutes in C, RV 533; 2 oboes in D min., RV 535; 2 mandolins in G, RV 532; 2 trumpets in C, RV 537; 2 violins, RV 523.
(M) *** Ph. 426 086-2. I Musici.

This makes an attractively diverse collection. Most of these concertos are admirably inventive and the performances show I Musici at their very best, on sparkling form. The sound is good too.

Double cello concerto in G min., RV 531; Lute (Guitar) concerto in D, RV 93; Oboe concerto in F, F.VII, No. 2 (R.455); Double concerto for oboe and violin; Trumpet concerto in D (trans. Jean Thilde); Violin concerto in G min., Op. 12/1; RV 317.
(BB) *** Naxos Dig. 8.550384; 4550384 [id.]. Capella Istropolitana, Jaroslav Kr(e)chek.

This is a recommendable disc from which to set out to explore the Vivaldi concertos, especially if you are beginning a collection. Gabriela Krcková makes a sensitive contribution to the delightful *Oboe concerto in F major*, F.VII, No. 2 (R.455), and the other soloists are pretty good too. Should this programme meet your particular needs, there is no need for hesitation.

Double concertos: for 2 cellos in G min., RV 531; 2 flutes in C, RV 533; 2 trumpets in C, RV 537; Concerto for Flautino (sopranino recorder) in C, RV 443; Concertos for strings: in D min. (Madrigalesco), RV 129; in G (Alla rustica), RV 151; in G min., RV 153; Quadruple concerto for 2 violins & 2 cellos in D, RV 564; L'Estro armonico: Quadruple violin concerto in B min., Op. 3/10, RV 580.
(Y/B) (M) *** O-L 443 198-2 [id.]. Soloists, AAM, Hogwood.

Not everything in this issue is of equal substance: the invention in the *Double trumpet concerto*, for example, is not particularly strong; but for the most part it is a rewarding and varied programme. It is especially appealing in that authenticity is allied to musical spontaneity. The *Concerto for two flutes* has great charm and is dispatched with vigour and aplomb. Performances and recording alike are first rate. For the reissue, three extra works have been added (giving an overall playing time of 70 minutes), most notably the famous *Quadruple violin concerto* from *L'Estro armonico*, taken from the Academy's splendid complete set, with John Holloway, Monica Huggett, Catherine Mackintosh and Elizabeth Wilcock the excellent soloists.

Double cello concerto in G min., RV 531; Double concerto for violin & cello in F, RV 544; Triple concerto for violin & two cellos in C, RV 561; Quadruple concerto for 2 violins & 2 cellos in D, RV 564; Double violin concerto for violin & violin per eco lontano in A, RV 552; Triple violin concerto in F, RV 551.
(Y/B) **(*) Teldec/Warner Dig. 4509 94552-2 [id.]. Christophe Coin, Il Giardino Armonico, Milan, Giovanni Antonini.

Easily the most striking of the six concertos here, all performed on original instruments, is the *Concerto in A*, RV 552, for violin and 'violino per eco lontano', where the echo effects are most engagingly managed. Christophe Coin is the only soloist listed on the frontispiece – and that is perhaps appropriate, as the *Double cello concerto* is a memorably fine performance, especially the melancholy interplay of the *Largo* and the bustling bravura of the finale. Coin's excellent partner is Paolo Beschi. The other concertos are all lively enough, but the overall effect is a little anonymous. The tuttis have plenty of life, helped by the bright, slightly astringent upper range. The recording itself is agreeably spacious, but there are more attractive groupings of Vivaldi concertos which cost less than this.

L'Estro armonico: Quadruple violin concerto in B min., Op. 3/10; La Stravaganza: Violin concerto in B flat, Op. 4/1; Cello concerto in C min., RV 401; Double horn concerto in F, RV 539; Concerto in F for 2 oboes, bassoon, 2 horns and violin, RV 569; Double trumpet concerto in C, RV 537.
(M) *** Decca 425 721-2. ASMF, Marriner.

An excellent collection from the considerable array of Vivaldi concertos recorded by Marriner and his ASMF (on modern instruments) between 1965 and 1977. The soloists are all distinguished, offering playing that is constantly alert, finely articulated and full of life and imagination.

(i) *Flute concertos: in D, RV 429; in G, RV 435, Op. 10/4; Recorder concerto in F, RV 434, Op. 10/5;* (ii) *Concertos for strings: in D, RV 121; in G min., RV 156;* (iii) *Double concerto for viola d'amore, lute and strings in D min., RV 540; Concerto for lute, 2 violins and continuo in D, RV 93;* (ii) *Sonata in E flat (Al Santo Sepolcro), RV 130.*
(B) *** CfP CD-CFP 4655; *TC-CFP 4655.* (i) Hans-Martin Linde, Prague CO; (ii) ECO, Leppard; (iii) Win Ten Have, Anthony Bailes, Danske Strings (members).

By combining first-rate analogue recordings from three separate sources, Classics for Pleasure have assembled a representative and first-rate collection to show almost every aspect of Vivaldi's unique contribution to the baroque concerto. The German flautist, Hans-Martin Linde, has an attractively fresh tone on both flute and recorder and is splendidly accompanied by the excellent strings of the Prague Chamber Orchestra. Leppard's string concertos are equally attractive, with the playing polished and committed. The standard of invention is high and, although *Al Santo Sepolcro* has only two brief movements, they are strongly contrasted. These performances all use modern instruments, but now we are offered a stimulating contrast as the concerto pairing viola d'amore and lute is heard on original instruments. To create a fragile effect, Vivaldi has all the instruments muted. The companion work for lute is equally delicate, a chamber concerto with the accompaniment scored for two violins and continuo. This stimulating group of concertos should find a useful niche in any collection.

Double concertos: for 2 flutes in C, RV 533; for 2 horns in F, RV 538 & RV 539; for 2 trumpets in C, RV 537; for oboe and bassoon in G, RV 545; Concerto (Sinfonia in D) for strings, RV 122; Quadruple concerto for 2 oboes and 2 clarinets, RV 560.
(Y/B) (BB) *** Naxos Dig. 8.553204 [id.]. Soloists, City of L. Sinfonia, Nicholas Kraemer.

An enjoyably lively clutch of concertos, very well recorded in All Saints' Church, East Finchley. The opening double concertos for two horns, RV 539, two flutes, RV 533, and two trumpets, RV 537, all go well enough and offer expert solo contributions, but then at the arrival of the *Quadruple concerto for two oboes and two clarinets* the playing suddenly sparks into extra exuberance, and one senses the musicians' enjoyment of one of Vivaldi's most imaginatively scored multiple works. The *Concerto for two horns* which follows (RV 538) has a similar (bold) ebullience, and the concert is rounded off by a captivating account of RV 545, where both the oboe and bassoon clearly relish every bar of their engaging dialogue. Throughout, Kraemer's accompaniments are polished and spirited.

Double flute concerto in C, RV 533; Double horn concerto in F, RV 539; Double mandolin concerto in G, RV 536; Double oboe concerto in A min., RV 536; Concerto for oboe and bassoon in G, RV 545; Double trumpet concerto in D, RV 563.
*** Ph. Dig. 412 892-2 [id.]. Soloists, ASMF, Marriner.

Apart from the work for two horns, where the focus of the soloists lacks a degree of sharpness, the recording often reaches demonstration standard. On CD, the concerto featuring a pair of mandolins is particularly tangible, with the balance near perfect, the solo instruments in proper scale yet registering admirable detail. The concertos for flutes and oboes are played with engaging finesse, conveying a sense of joy in the felicity of the writing. Once again Marriner makes a very good case for the use of modern wind instruments in this repertoire.

Concertos for strings: in D min. (Concerto madrigalesco), RV 129; in G (Alla rustica), RV 151; in G min., RV 157. (i) Motet: In turbato mare irato, RV 627; Cantata: Lungi dal vago volto, RV 680. Magnificat, RV 610.
*** Hyperion Dig. CDA 66247 [id.]. (i) Kirkby, Leblanc, Forget, Cunningham, Ingram, Tafelmusik Ch. & Bar. O, Lamon.

Mingling vocal and instrumental items, and works both well-known and unfamiliar, Jean Lamon provides a delightful collection, with Emma Kirkby a sparkling, pure-toned soloist in two items never recorded before: the motet, *In turbato mare irato*, and the chamber cantata, *Lungi dal vago volto*. The performance is lively, with fresh choral sound. The Tafelmusik performers come from Canada, and though the use of period instruments has some roughness, their vigour and alertness amply make up for that. Good, clear recorded sound.

CHAMBER MUSIC

Cello sonatas Nos. 1–9, RV 39/47.
*** CRD Dig. CRD 3440; *CRDC 4140* [id.] (*Nos. 1–4*); CRD 3441; *CRDC 4141* [id.] (*Nos. 5–9*). L'Ecole d'Orphée.

All nine *Sonatas* are given highly musical performances on CRD; they do not set out to impress by grand gestures but succeed in doing so by their dedication and sensitivity. Susan Sheppard is a thoughtful player and is well supported by her continuo team, Lucy Carolan and Jane Coe. The CRD recording is well focused and very present.

VOCAL MUSIC

Beatus vir, RV 597; Credo, RV 592; Magnificat, RV 610.
(M) *** Ph. 420 651-2. Soloists, Alldis Ch., ECO, Negri.

Beatus vir, RV 598; Dixit Dominus in D, RV 594; Introduzione al Dixit: Canta in prato in G, RV 636 (ed. Geigling); Magnificat in G min., RV 611 (ed. Negri).
(M) *** Ph. 420 649-2. Lott, Burgess, Murray, Daniels, Finnie, Collins, Rolfe Johnson, Holl, Alldis Ch., ECO, Negri.

Crediti propter quod, RV 105; Credo, RV 591; Introduction to Gloria, RV 639; Gloria, RV 588; Kyrie, RV 587; Laetatus sum, RV 607.
(M) *** Ph. 420 650-2. M. Marshall, Lott, Finnie, Rolfe Johnson, Alldis Ch., ECO, Negri.

Dixit dominus, RV 595; In exitu Israel, RV 604; Sacrum, RV 586.
(M) *** Ph. 420 652-2. Alldis Ch., ECO, Negri.

Introduction to Gloria, RV 642; Gloria in D, RV 589; Lauda Jerusalem in E min., RV 609; Laudate Dominum in D min., RV 606; Laudati pueri Dominum in A, RV 602.
(M) *** Ph. 420 648-2. Marshall, Lott, Collins, Finnilä, Alldis Ch., ECO, Negri.

These Philips recordings come from the late 1970s. Vittorio Negri does not make use of period instruments, but he penetrates as deeply into the spirit of this music as many who do, and they come up splendidly in their new format, digitally refurbished. Any lover of Vivaldi is likely to be astonished that not only the well-known works but the rarities show him writing with the keenest originality and intensity. There is nothing routine about any of this music, nor any of the performances either.

Beatus vir, RV 597; Dixit Dominus, RV 595; Gloria, RV 588; Magnificat, RV 610; Nisi Dominus, RV 608; Stabat Mater, RV 621.
(B) **(*) Erato/Warner 4509 91936-2 (2) [id.]. Soloists; Lausanne Vocal Ens. & CO; Lisbon Gulbenkian Foundation Ch. & O; E. Bach Festival Ch. & Baroque O; Corboz.

The recordings on Corboz's Duo-Bonsai issue derive from three different sources. Those from the English Bach Festival, which include the *Gloria*, RV 588 (shorn of its three-movement *Introduction* on a non-liturgical text), and *Nisi Dominus* (beautifully sung by Helen Watts), offer baroque orchestral playing on authentic instruments. The *Beatus vir, Dixit Dominus*, RV 595, and *Magnificat* come from Lausanne, and modern instruments are used to produce a warm, well-focused sound; the acoustic is spacious and the performances vital and musical. The professional singers of the Lausanne Choir are generally admirable and the soloists are sweet-toned. The *Magnificat* is given in its simpler first version on a relatively small scale, with the chorus singing the alto solo, *Fecit potentiam*. The *Stabat Mater* (a most affecting piece, thought to have been composed at great speed) was recorded in Lisbon, and here the performance is pleasingly old-fashioned with robust tone and modern instruments. There is much to enjoy on this pair of CDs and this is a recommendably inexpensive way to get to know some of Vivaldi's finest choral music.

Motets: *Canto in prato, RV 623; In furore giustissimae irae, RV 626; Longa mala umbrae tertores, RV 640; Vos aurae per montes (per la solennita di S. Antonio), RV 634.*
(Y/B) (M) *** Erato/Warner Dig. 4509 96966-2 [id.]. Cecilia Gasdia, Sol. Ven., Scimone.

Though the booklet for this collection of Vivaldi rarities fails to provide texts for these four solo motets, they make a delightful collection, also displaying the formidable talent of a rising star among Italian sopranos, Cecilia Gasdia. Vivaldi's solo motets might be described structurally as concertos for voice, but generally with a recitative between first movement and slow movement. *Canto in prato* is the exception, with three jolly, rustic allegros in succession. Lively performances and well-balanced recording.

(i) *Gloria in D, RV 588; Gloria in D, RV 589;* (ii) *Concerto for guitar and viola d'amore, RV 540.*
(N) (B) *** Decca Eclipse Dig. 448 223-2; *448 223-4* [id.]. (i) Russell, Kwella, Wilkens, St John's College, Cambridge, Ch., Wren O, Guest; (ii) Fernández, Blume, ECO, Malcolm.

(i) *Gloria in D, RV 588; Gloria in D, RV 589;* (ii; iii) *Beatus vir in C, RV 597; Dixit dominus in D, RV 594;* (iv; iii) *Magnificat in G min., RV 610.*
(Y/B) (B) *** Decca Double Dig./Analogue 443 455-2 (2) [id.]. (i) Russell, Kwella, Wilkens, Bowen, St John's College, Cambridge, Ch., Wren O, Guest; (ii) Jennifer Smith, Buchanan, Watts, Partridge, Shirley-Quirk, ECO, Cleobury; (iii) King's College, Cambridge, Ch.; (iv) Castle, Cockerham, King, ASMF, Ledger.

The two settings of the *Gloria* make an apt and illuminating pairing. Both in D major, they have many points in common, presenting fascinating comparisons, when RV 588 is as inspired as its better-known companion. Guest directs strong and well-paced readings, with RV 588 the more lively. Good, warm recording to match the performances. *Dixit dominus* cannot fail to attract those who have enjoyed the better-known *Gloria*. Both works are powerfully inspired and are here given vigorous and sparkling performances with King's College Choir in excellent form under its latest choirmaster. The soloists are a fine team, fresh, stylish and nimble, nicely projected in the CD format. But what caps this outstanding Vivaldi compilation is the earlier King's account of the inspired *Magnificat in G minor*. Ledger uses the small-scale setting and opts for boys' voices in the solos such as the beautiful duet (*Esurientes*) which is most winning. The performance overall is very compelling and moving, and the singing has all the accustomed beauty of the King's records. The transfer of an outstanding (1976) analogue recording to CD is admirable, even richer than its digital companions.

As can be seen, those seeking an inexpensive disc of the two *Glorias* will find the Eclipse CD a satisfactory alternative, and the *Concerto for guitar and viola d'amore* makes an attractively lightweight interlude between the two choral works.

Gloria in D, RV 589.
(M) *** Decca 421 146-2. Vaughan, J. Baker, King's College, Cambridge, Ch., ASMF, Willcocks – HAYDN: *Nelson Mass*. ***
*** EMI Dig. CDC7 54283-2 [id.]. Hendricks, Murray, Rigby, Heilmann, Hynninen, ASMF Ch. & O, Marriner – BACH: *Magnificat*. ***
(M) *** O-L 443 178-2 [id.]. Nelson, Kirkby, Watkinson, Ch. of Christ Church Cathedral, Oxford, AAM, Simon Preston – HANDEL: *Utrecht Te Deum and Jubilate*. ***
*** DG Dig. 423 386-2 [id.]. Argenta, Attrot, Denley, Ch. & E. Concert, Pinnock – A. SCARLATTI: *Dixit Dominus*. ***

Gloria, RV 589; Ostro picta, armata spina, RV 642.
*** Chandos Dig. CHAN 0518 [id.]. Kirkby, Bonner, Chance, Coll. Mus. 90, Hickox – BACH: *Magnificat*. ***

The CD remastering of the stylish 1962 Willcocks recording of Vivaldi's *Gloria* is strikingly vivid and, with excellent choral and solo singing, this makes a fine and generous bonus for the Haydn *Nelson Mass*.

Both Richard Hickox and Neville Marriner couple the more popular of the two D major *Glorias* with the Bach *Magnificat* and offer a pretty clear choice between period and modern instruments. Honours are fairly evenly divided between them: Hickox directs a strong musical account and has the benefit of a fine team of soloists and good Chandos recording; Marriner's performance with the Academy on modern instruments is well paced, as is the Bach *Magnificat*. His soloists are also very fine, and the recording has warmth and immediacy. Both can be recommended with confidence.

The freshness and point of the Christ Church performance of the *Gloria* are irresistible; anyone who normally doubts the attractiveness of authentic string technique should sample this, for the absence of vibrato adds a tang exactly in keeping with the performance. The soloists too keep vibrato to the minimum, adding to the freshness, yet Carolyn Watkinson rivals even Dame Janet Baker in the dark intensity of the Bach-like central aria for contralto, *Domine Deus, Agnus Dei*. The choristers of Christ Church Cathedral excel themselves, and the recording is outstandingly fine. This now comes generously coupled with Handel, making a total playing time of 74 minutes.

Trevor Pinnock directs a bright, refreshing account of the grander and better known of Vivaldi's *Gloria* settings, with excellent playing and singing from the members of the English Concert. Unusually but attractively coupled with the rare Scarlatti setting of *Dixit Dominus*, and very well recorded, it makes a first-rate alternative recommendation.

Gloria in D, RV 589; Kyrie in G min., RV 587.
(M) *** DG 427 142-2. Regensburg Cathedral Ch., V. Capella Academica, Schneidt – BACH: *Motets.* ***

In the superb setting of the *Kyrie*, and the well-known *Gloria*, Schneidt with his fresh-toned Regensburg Choir (the celebrated Domspatzen, 'cathedral sparrows') brings out what may seem a surprising weight for an 'authentic' performance. The use of semi-chorus for solo numbers is questionable, but no one hearing these performances is likely to dismiss the music as trivial.

Laudate pueri dominum, RV 601; Nisi Dominus, RV 608.
*** Mer. Dig. CDE 84129 [id.]. Lynne Dawson, Christopher Robson, King's Consort, Robert King.

The present setting of Psalm 113, RV 601, is a strong work whose inspiration runs at a consistently high level; Lynne Dawson sings with an excellent sense of style and is given splendid support. The coupling, the *Nisi Dominus*, a setting of Psalm 127, is much better known but makes an attractive makeweight. It is also given an excellent performance by Christopher Robson. Good recording.

(i) *Nisi dominus (Psalm 127), RV 608;* (ii) *Nulla in mundo pax sincera, RV 630.*
(Y/B) (M) *** O-L 443 199-2 [id.]. (i) James Bowman; (ii) Emma Kirkby; AAM, Preston – BACH: *Magnificat;* KUHNAU: *Der Gerechte kommt um.* ***

The solo motet, *Nulla in mundo pax sincera*, has Emma Kirkby as soloist coping splendidly with the bravura writing for soprano. James Bowman is also a persuasive soloist in the more extended, operatic-styled setting of Psalm 127. But since Vivaldi probably wrote *Nisi Dominus* for the Pietà, a Venetian orphanage for girls, readers might prefer a soprano voice.

OPERA

Opera overtures: Armida al campo d'Egitto; Arsilda, Regina di Ponto (Orlando Furioso); Bajazet (Tamerlano); Dorilla in Tempe; Farnace; Giustino; Griselda; L'Incoronazione di Dario; L'Olimpiade; Ottone in Villa; La verità in cimento.
(Y/B) (M) *** Erato/Warner 4509 96381-2 [id.]. Sol. Ven., Scimone.

Although the concerto grosso element with its bold dynamic contrasts remains strong, the inclusion of a courtly minuet section in nearly all of these overtures adds to their appeal. The first piece here, *Dorilla in Tempe*, brings a familiar Vivaldi tune, drawing on *Spring* from *The Four Seasons*, ready for the opera's opening chorus, which has the same theme. *Ottone in Villa* reverts unashamedly to concerto grosso style by featuring a concertino of two violins and two oboes. *Griselda* is rhythmically a very characterful piece but it too includes a stately central dance, and in *La verità in cimento* the rather beautiful flowing central tune is heard against a pizzicato accompaniment, a device repeated in *Arsilda, Regina di Ponto. Bajazet*, unexpectedly, includes horns to fill out the sonority in the outer sections. The performances here are full of life and colour, and the excellent 1978 analogue recording projects the music vividly. Not a CD to be played all at one go, but offering plenty of colourful ideas.

Catone in Utica (partially complete).
(N) (M) *(*) Erato/Warner Dig. 0630 11232-2 (2) [id.]. Gasdia, Palacio, Schmiege, Zimmermann, Lendi, Rigacci, Sol. Ven., Scimone.

When so few Vivaldi operas have been recorded, it is disappointing that this set can be given only a limited recommendation. It is a curious choice, seeing that the first Act is missing and the other two Acts are not as musically rich as other Vivaldi operas. Cecilia Gasdia sings impressively, and Scimone conducts a fair, middle-of-the-road interpretation; but more is needed if the cause of the music is to be argued effectively. Good sound.

Orlando Furioso (complete).
*** Erato/Warner 2292 45147-2 (3) [id.]. Horne, De los Angeles, Valentini Terrani, Gonzales, Kozma, Bruscantini, Zaccaria, Sol. Ven., Scimone.

Outstanding in a surprisingly star-studded cast is Marilyn Horne in the title-role, rich and firm of tone, articulating superbly in divisions, notably in the hero's two fiery arias. In the role of Angelica, Victoria de los Angeles has many sweetly lyrical moments, and though Lucia Valentini Terrani is less strong as Alcina, she gives an aptly clean, precise performance. The remastering has somewhat freshened a recording which was not outstanding in its analogue LP form.

Tito Manlio (complete).
(N) (M) **(*) Ph. 446 332-2 (4) [id.]. Luccardi, Wagemann, Hamari, Finnnilä, Marshall, Trimarchi, Lerer, Ahnsjö, Berlin R. Ch. & CO, Negri.

Vivaldi claimed that he wrote this massive score in a mere five days – which sounds improbable, even for him. The inspiration of the set numbers, most of them short, simple arias, is generally lively, and they are attractively spiced with obbligato solos. The overture sets the classical scene well, with its pomposo, trumpet-full style; the main snag for the modern listener is the sheer length, which achieves Wagnerian proportions. First issued on LP in the tercentenary year, the opera is given here uncut except for some snipping of *secco* recitatives, which still make up a very substantial proportion of the whole. The performance, using modern instruments, is crisp and stylish, sympathetically directed by Negri and with generally excellent solo singing, though (with women taking three male parts) it is hard to follow the story, since the timbres are not as distinct as they might be. The recording quality has an attractive bloom on it which has not been lost in the CD transfer, and for the dedicated Vivaldian this will undoubtedly give pleasure.

Vives, Amadeo (1871–1932)

Doña Francisquita.
(Y/B) **(*) Sony Dig. S2K 66563 (2) [id.]. Domingo, Arteta, Mirabal, Del Portal, Cordoba Theatre Ch., Sevilla SO, Roa.

Even among the hundred and more zarzuelas written by this composer, *Doña Francisquita*, a light-hearted love story, is by far the most popular: no fewer than 5,000 performances were given in Spain over the twenty years after its first performance in 1923. It is full of charming ideas, skilfully presented. This version stands out from previous complete recordings through the strength of Plácido Domingo in the role of the hero, Fernando. Domingo's love of the genre shines out in every note he sings, with his diction immaculately clear. Even if vocally he is hardly matched by Ainhoa Arteta in the title-role, her light, bright, agile soprano is well suited to the part of an ingénue. Linda Mirabel, a warm-toned mezzo, sings Aurora, the actress, though the second tenor, Enrique del Portal, as the hero's friend, Cardona, is very thin-toned. At least there is no confusion with Domingo. Enrique Roa, who earlier conducted an electrifying account of Penella's *El gato montes* for DG, also with Domingo as the hero, understands the idiom perfectly, but here with an indifferent orchestra and the sound a little backward the impact of the performance is less, for all the brightness and energy.

Voříšek, Jan Vaclav (1791–1825)

Symphony in D, Op. 24.
(N) *** Hyperion Dig. CDA 66800 [id.]. SCO, Sir Charles Mackerras – ARRIAGA: *Symphony in D min.* etc. ***

Voříšek is as close as the Czechs got to producing a Beethoven, and this remarkably powerful work has fingerprints of the German master everywhere while managing to retain a certain individuality. The slow movement is impressive and, after an attractive Scherzo, the finale has something in common with that of Beethoven's *Fourth*. Mackerras offers the finest account this work has received on record so far. The Hyperion recording is warmly reverberant, but this serves to increase the feeling of Beethovenian weightiness, and the Scherzo is particularly imposing. Moreover the Arriaga coupling is indispensable.

Fantasia, Op. 12; Impromptus Nos. 1–6, Op. 7; Sonata in B flat min., Op. 19; Variations in B flat, Op. 19.
*** Unicorn Dig. DKPCD 9145 [id.]. Radoslav Kvapil.

Voříšek's *Sonata in B flat minor* (1920), like his *D major Symphony*, is one of his most representative and well-argued works and is the centrepiece of this beautifully played recital. Radoslav Kvapil is a highly sensitive and imaginative artist, deeply committed to this repertoire. The slightly later *B flat variations* will be a welcome discovery for those who do not know them, and Kvapil's accounts of the *Impromptus* are as good as, if not better than, any predecessor's. The recording, though not outstanding, serves him well, certainly more faithfully than in Fibich's diary pieces in the same series.

Impromptus Nos. 1–6, Op. 7.
(Y/B) (M) ** Carlton IMP Classics Dig. 30367 00902 [id.]. Dirk Joeres – SCHUBERT: *Impromptus* etc. ******

It was an intelligent idea to couple these *Impromptus*, which inspired the whole genre, with Schubert's better-known and more searching pieces. The German pianist, Dirk Joeres, is a sensitive and imaginative player, and his playing will give pleasure, though his recording is just a shade bass-heavy.

Wagenseil, George (1715–77)

Harp concerto in G.
(B) ***** DG 427 206-2. Zabaleta, Paul Kuentz CO –** HANDEL: *Harp concerto;* MOZART: *Flute and harp concerto.* *******

Wagenseil's *Harp concerto* is a pleasant example of the *galant* style; the felicity of the writing in the first two movements is capped by a very jolly finale. Both performance and recording here can be commended and the remastering is fresh and clear.

Wagner, Richard (1813–83)

Der Ring des Nibelungen: an introduction to *The Ring* by Deryck Coooke, with 193 music examples.
(Y/B) (M) *** Decca 443 581-2 (2) [id.]. VPO, Solti.

The reissue in Decca's Classic Sound series of Deryck Cooke's fascinating and scholarly lecture is most welcome. Even though the CD reissue omits the printed text, the principal musical motives are all printed out in the accompanying booklet and they demonstrate just how the many leading ideas in *The Ring* develop from one another, springing from an original germ. The discourse is riveting, though even dedicated Wagnerians may not want to hear it many times over. The music examples, many of them specially prepared, are not always inserted with the skill one is accustomed to on BBC Radio 3, but this is still a thoroughly worthwhile acquisition for those who already have recordings of the operas.

Siegfried idyll.
(N) (M) ***** DG 449 725-2 [id.]. BPO, Karajan –** R. STRAUSS: *Ein Heldenleben.* *******
(Y/B) (M) ***** DG 439 969-2 (2) [id.]. BPO, Karajan –** BRUCKNER: *Symphony No. 8.* *******
*** Denon Dig. CO 79442 [id.]. Sinfonia Varsovia, Krivine – SCHOENBERG: *Verklärte Nacht;* R. STRAUSS: *Metamorphosen.* *******
(N) (M) ***** Carlton IMP Classics Dig. 30367 0029-2. SCO, Jaime Laredo –** DVORAK: *String serenade* etc. *******
(M) ****(*) EMI CMS7 63277-2 (2) [Ang. CDMB 63277]. Philh. O, Klemperer –** MAHLER: *Symphony No. 9.* *******

Karajan's account of Wagner's wonderful birthday present to Cosima is unsurpassed; it has never sounded better than in this new transfer for DG's series of 'Legendary Recordings', aptly coupled with Strauss's *Ein Heldenleben*, Karajan's very first stereo recording for DG.

Emmanuel Krivine gives a strongly characterized and obviously well-thought-out view of the piece and gets a very sensitive and totally committed response from his Warsaw orchestra. Both the wind and the strings give us playing of the utmost warmth, and they are beautifully recorded. In such oft-recorded repertoire one cannot speak of first choices, but this disc comes very high on the list.

A beautiful performance from Jaime Laredo and the Scottish Chamber Orchestra, warm and poised and ending serenely, yet moving to a strong central climax. The recording, made in Glasgow City Hall, has a pleasingly expansive ambience, yet textures are clear.

Klemperer favours the original chamber-orchestra scoring and the Philharmonia players are very persuasive, especially in the score's gentler moments. However, the balance is forward and, although the sound is warm, the ear craves a greater breadth of string tone at the climax.

(i; ii) *Siegfried idyll*. (iii; iv) *Overture: Der fliegende Holländer*. (i; v) *Götterdämmerung: Siegfried's Rhine journey. Lohengrin:* (i; ii) *Prelude to Act I;* (vi; iv) *Prelude to Act III. Die Meistersinger:* (vi; iv) *Overture;* (vii; viii) *Prelude to Act III.* (ix; viii) *Parsifal: Prelude & Good Friday music. Overtures:* (vi; iv) *Rienzi;* (vii; x) *Tannhäuser. Tristan:* (iii; iv) *Preludes to Acts I & III;* (vi; iv) *Death of Isolde.* (i; v) *Die Walküre: Ride of the Valkyries.*

(B) *** DG Double 439 687-2 (2) [id.]. (i) BPO; (ii) Kubelik; (iii) Bayreuth Festival O; (iv) Karl Boehm; (v) Karajan; (vi) VPO; (vii) Deutsche Op., Berlin, O; (viii) Jochum; (ix) Bav. RSO; (x) Otto Gerdes.

The *Siegfried idyll* is beautifully shaped by Kubelik and equally beautifully played by the Berlin Philharmonic. He also conducts an impressive *Lohengrin Act I Prelude*, again with the BPO, who have played it under everyone who matters, including, of course, Furtwängler. Boehm not only provides a richly sustained opening for *Rienzi* but is pretty exciting in *Der fliegende Holländer* and at his finest in the *Tristan Preludes* – taken from his 1966 Bayreuth complete set – which glow with intensity. Surprisingly, Karajan contributes only two items, but both bring plenty of adrenalin. But the highlight of the set comes last, Jochum's electrifying and Rosette-worthy performance of the *Prelude and Good Friday* music from *Parsifal*. Recorded in the Munich Herculessaal, it is not only a demonstration record from the earliest days of stereo, but the playing has a spiritual intensity that has never been surpassed. Elsewhere the recordings, dating from the late 1950s to the early 1980s, have all been transferred vividly, with some sounding fuller and more refined than others. The documentation, as with the rest of this series, is totally inadequate.

Siegfried idyll. Die fliegende Holländer: Overture. Lohengrin: Prelude to Act III. Rienzi: Overture. Tannhäuser: Overture.
(BB) *** Tring Dig. TRP 008 [id.]. RPO, Vernon Handley.

The *Siegfried idyll* is beautifully played and radiantly recorded, but the highlight is Handley's excitingly rumbustious account of the *Rienzi overture* with thrilling brass and an exuberant contribution from the side-drum, snares a-rattling. This is a demonstration item. The heavy brass also makes a splendidly weighty contribution to the famous *Lohengrin Act III Prelude* and is hardly less effective at the climax of the *Ride of the Valkyries*. Handley uses the concert ending in both these pieces, and his spacious treatment of the reprise of the Pilgrim's chorale at the close of the *Tannhäuser overture* makes a satisfying close to a programme which is played as well as it is recorded (in the suitable resonance of St Augustine's Church, Kilburn).

Siegfried idyll (with rehearsal); *Der fliegende Holländer: Overture; Die Meistersinger: Prelude to Act I; Lohengrin: Prelude to Act I; Parsifal: Prelude to Act I and Good Friday music; Tannhäuser:* (i) *Overture and Venusberg music.*
(N) (M) *** Sony SMK 64456 (2) [id.]. (i) Occidental College Ch.; Columbia SO, Bruno Walter.

Walter's is above all a gentle performance of the *Siegfried idyll*; the opening is quite lovely. The 1963 recording seems fuller than before, with more ambient warmth, especially at the climax – which has no lack of ardour – while the rapt quality of the closing ritenuto is magical. Before the performance, we hear an extended rehearsal sequence lasting three-quarters of an hour, which most listeners will find fascinating. The rest of the programme was recorded in 1959. Highlights include the glowing *Parsifal Prelude* and *Good Friday music*, matching Jochum in its simple intensity, and the superb account of the *Tannhäuser Overture* and *Venusberg music* with its thrillingly sensuous climax, and the closing pages – the Occidental College Choir distantly balanced – bringing a radiant hush. The years have not diminished its impact, and again one notices that both here and in the *Flying Dutchman* and *Meistersinger overtures* the orchestra has more body and weight, while the *Lohengrin Prelude*, relaxed but beautifully controlled, sounds radiant.

Siegfried idyll; Lohengrin: Prelude to Act III. Die Meistersinger von Nürnberg: Prelude. Parsifal: Prelude. Rienzi: Overture. Tristan und Isolde: Prelude; (i) *Liebestod.*
(N) **(*) EMI Dig. CDC5 55479-2 [id.]. (i) Jane Eaglen; L. Classical Players, Norrington.

By traditional standards of Wagnerian interpretation, Norrington's tempi here are eccentric and the *Meistersinger Prelude*, swinging off joyfully, two-in-a-bar, has the imprimatur of the composer's own treatise, 'On Conducting'. Wagner tells us that his own tempo for this piece was 'a few seconds over eight minutes'; Norrington's timing is 8 minutes 28 seconds. On the other hand, the performance here of the *Rienzi overture* is, above all else, grandly spacious and this certainly brings more gravitas, with the bandstand flavour all but banished. Anyone used to Bruno Walter's gentle treatment of the *Siegfried idyll* will surely be disconcerted by the way Norrington presses forward, beautifully though it is played. And in the *Parsifal Prelude* he is very different from Jochum. Certainly the ardent thrust works well in *Tristan*, and Jane Eaglen rises to the occasion in the *Liebestod*. So these performances are all refresh-

ingly different; the orchestral response is impressive, committed and spontaneous, while detail is sophisticated. The Abbey Road recording is superb.

*Siegfried idyll. Lohengrin: Preludes to Acts I & III. Die Meistersinger: Prelude to Act I. Parsifal: Prelude
to Act I. Tristan und Isolde: Prelude and Liebestod.*
(M) *** Ph. 420 886-2. Concg. O, Haitink.

The addition of Haitink's simple, unaffected reading of the *Siegfried idyll* to his 1975 collection of
Preludes enhances the appeal of a particularly attractive concert. The rich acoustics of the
Concertgebouw are surely ideal for *Die Meistersinger*, given a memorably spacious performance, and
Haitink's restraint adds to the noble dignity of *Parsifal*. The *Lohengrin* excerpts are splendidly played.
The digital remastering is almost entirely beneficial.

*Siegfried idyll. Lohengrin: Prelude to Acts I & III. Die Meistersinger: Overture. Die Walküre: Ride of the
Valkyries;* (i) *Wotan's farewell and Magic fire music.*
*** ASV Dig. CDDCA 666 [id.]. Philh. O, Francesco d'Avalos, (i) with John Tomlinson.

The opening *Siegfried idyll* has all the requisite serenity and atmosphere; here, as elsewhere, the
Philharmonia play most beautifully. The boldly sumptuous recording brings a thrilling resonance and
amplitude to the brass, especially trombones and tuba, and in the expansive *Meistersinger overture*, and
again in *Wotan's farewell* the brass entries bring a physical frisson. John Tomlinson's noble assumption
of the role of Wotan, as he bids a loving farewell to his errant daughter, is very moving here, and the
response of the Philharmonia strings matches the depth of feeling he conveys. With the Valkyries also
given a splendid sense of spectacle, this collection should have a wide appeal.

Siegfried idyll. Tannhäuser: overture. (i) *Tristan: Prelude and Liebestod.*
*** DG Dig. 423 613-2 [id.]. (i) Jessye Norman; VPO, Karajan.

This superb Wagner record was taken live from a unique concert conducted by Karajan at the Salzburg
Festival in August 1987. The *Tannhäuser overture* has never sounded so noble, and the *Siegfried idyll* has
rarely seemed so intense and dedicated behind its sweet lyricism; while the *Prelude and Liebestod*, with
Jessye Norman as soloist, bring the richest culmination, sensuous and passionate, but remarkable as
much for the hushed, inward moments as for the ineluctable building of climaxes.

ORCHESTRAL EXCERPTS FROM THE OPERAS

(i) *Der fliegende Höllander: Overture.* (ii) *Lohengrin: Prelude to Act I. Die Meistersinger: Overture.* (iii)
Parsifal: Prelude and Good Friday music. (iv) *Tannhäuser: Overture.*
(Y/B) (B) **(*) DG 439 445-2 [id.]. (i) Bayreuth (1971) Festival O, Boehm; (ii) BPO, Kubelik; (iii) Bav.
RSO, Jochum; (iv) German Op. O, Berlin, Otto Gerdes.

Most of these performances are duplicated in a particularly attractive DG Double set of Wagner's
orchestral excerpts mentioned above, but this shorter, Classikon bargain collection includes Jochum's
superb account of the *Parsifal* excerpts and is quite worthwhile in its own right.

Der fliegende Holländer: Overture. Lohengrin: Prelude to Act I. Die Meistersinger: Overture. (i)
Tannhäuser: Overture and Venusberg music. Tristan: Prelude and Liebestod.
(M) *** EMI CDM7 64334-2 [id.]. BPO, Karajan; (i) with German Op. Ch.

All the music here is played excellently, but the *Overture and Venusberg music* from *Tannhäuser* (Paris
version, using chorus) and the *Prelude and Liebestod* from *Tristan* are superb. In the *Liebestod* the
climactic culmination is overwhelming in its sentient power, while *Tannhäuser* has comparable spaciousness and grip. There is an urgency and edge to the *Flying Dutchman overture*, and *Die Meistersinger* has
weight and dignity, but the last degree of tension is missing.

*Götterdämmerung: Dawn and Siegfried's Rhine journey. Lohengrin: Preludes to Acts I & III. Die
Meistersinger: Prelude to Act I. Das Rheingold: Entry of the Gods into Valhalla. Rienzi: Overture.
Siegfried: Forest murmurs. Tannhäuser: Overture. Die Walküre: Ride of the Valkyries; Wotan's farewell
and Magic fire music.*
(N) (B) *** EMI forte Dig. CZS5 68616-2 (2). BPO, Tennstedt.

This EMI forte double combines two highly successful collections from the early days of the digital era.
The recordings were made in the Philharmonie between 1981 and 1983; they could ideally be more
opulent in the middle and bass, but the brilliance is demonstrable, and there is weight, too, and fine
detail, especially in the atmospheric *Forest murmurs*. Moreover the orchestral playing is superb and the
sense of spectacle is in no doubt. Tennstedt amalgamates something from the combined Furtwängler
and Klemperer traditions with his broad, spacious readings, yet the voltage is consistently high. The

opening and closing sections of the *Tannhäuser overture* are given a restrained nobility of feeling without any loss of power or impact. Similarly the gorgeous string melody at the opening of *Rienzi* is elegiacally moulded, and later when the brass enter in the allegro there is no suggestion of the bandstand. In the Act I *Lohengrin Prelude*, Tennstedt lingers in the pianissimo sections, creating radiant detail, then presses on just before the climax. The Berlin Philharmonic are on top form throughout.

(i) *Götterdämmerung: Siegfried's Rhine journey and Funeral music.* (ii) *Lohengrin: Prelude to Act III.* (i) *Die Meistersinger: Overture; Prelude to Act III; Dance of the apprentices; Procession of the Masters.* (ii) *Tannhäuser: Grand march.*
(M) ** RCA (i) stereo / (ii) mono 09026 61792-2 [id.]. (i) Chicago SO; (ii) RCA Victor O; Fritz Reiner.

It is rare that one has to complain about the stereo sound achieved by the RCA engineers in Chicago's Orchestral Hall in the late 1950s, but in the stereo Wagner sessions included here the sound is too sumptuously inflated: all amplitude, with no sparkle in the treble. It makes Reiner's spacious account of the *Die Meistersinger overture* seem too weighty and overblown, although the close of the *Procession of the Masters* is more effective. However, there is some glorious playing from the horns in the great *Prelude to Act III* from the same opera, and the opening of *Siegfried's Rhine journey* has plenty of tension and atmosphere. The other three items use an East Coast pick-up orchestra and were recorded in mono in New York's Manhattan Center in 1950.

Götterdämmerung: Dawn and Siegfried's Rhine journey; Siegfried's funeral march. Lohengrin: Prelude to Act III. Die Meistersinger: Prelude. Tannhäuser: Overture & Bacchanale. Die Walküre: Ride of the Valkyries.
(N) **(*) Decca Dig. 448 155-2 [id.]. Concg. O, Chailly.

Anyone wanting a good Wagnerian wallow and plenty of excitement will enjoy this superbly recorded collection. It sounds as if Chailly is nodding in Norrington's direction, for his exhilarating account of the *Die Meistersinger overture* is only 27 seconds longer than the EMI performance, although it dossn't have quite the thrust Norrington generates. The Third Act *Lohengrin Prelude*, too, is only four seconds longer than Norrington's. The *Valkyries* ride out with comparable gusto, and Siegfried sets off on his *Rhine journey* as if there were no tomorrow. The Concertgebouw acoustic seems ideal for this programme and the playing is first class, with plenty of adrenalin running. But a little more subtlety would have been welcome at times.

Götterdämmerung: Dawn and Siegfried's Rhine journey; Funeral march. Lohengrin: Preludes to Acts I & III. Die Meistersinger: Overture; Dance of the apprentices. Die Walküre: Ride of the Valkyries.
(B) *** CfP Dig. CD-CFP 9008 [CDB7 62007-2]. LPO, Rickenbacher.

Karl Anton Rickenbacher secures first-class playing from the LPO with the strings at their peak in the radiant opening of the *Lohengrin Prelude*. Some might feel that his pacing of the *Die' Meistersinger overture* is fractionally fast. The CD sound is firm and full; indeed the *Prelude to Act III* of *Lohengrin* makes a splendid demonstration recording; an exciting performance, particularly vividly projected.

Götterdämmerung: Dawn and Siegfried's Rhine journey; Siegfried's death and funeral march. Lohengrin: Prelude to Act I. Tannhäuser: Overture and Venusberg music. Tristan und Isolde: Liebestod. Die Walküre: Ride of the Valkyries.
(M) (***) RCA mono GD 60306 [09026 60306-2]. NBC SO, Toscanini.

Götterdämmerung: Dawn; (i; ii) Zu neuen Taten; Willst du mir Minne schenken; O heilige Götter; Siegfried's Rhine journey; Brünnhilde's immolation: (i) Starke Scheite schichtet mir dort; Wie Sonne lauter strahlt mir sein Licht; Mein Erbe nun nehm'ich zu eigen; Fliegt heim ihr Raben!; Grane, Mein Ross, sei mir gegrüsst. Siegfried: Forest murmurs.
(M) (***) RCA mono GD 60304 [09026 60304-2]. (i) Helen Traubel; (ii) Lauritz Melchior; NBC SO, Toscanini.

Toscanini's special brand of electricity comes over vividly in these characteristic Wagner performances. The *Lohengrin Prelude* and the soaring *Tristan Liebestod* have typical intensity and, although the dynamic range is compressed, the sound is surprisingly good, as it is in the tenderly sensuous *Venusberg* sequence in *Tannhäuser*. One is offered a choice here of the *Götterdämmerung Dawn* sequence with or without the vocal contribution in which both Helen Traubel and Melchior are strong enough musical personalities to stand up against Toscanini. The recordings date from the 1940s and 1950s and, as transferred, are surprisingly full, with something of a concert-hall effect in the Carnegie Hall *Immolation* sequence of 1941. Traubel rides over the orchestra with considerable dominance.

Götterdämmerung: Dawn and Siegfried's Rhine journey; Siegfried's death and funeral march; (i)
Brünnhilde's immolation. Siegfried: Forest murmurs. Die Walküre: Ride of the Valkyries.
*** Erato/Warner Dig. 2292 45786-2 [id.]. (i) Deborah Polaski; Chicago SO, Barenboim.

Here Barenboim dons his Furtwänglerian mantle to splendidly spacious effect. Even with tempi measured, he secures playing of great concentration and excitement from the Chicago orchestra, and the
recording is one of the finest made in Chicago's Orchestra Hall for many years. Deborah Polaski makes
a bold, passionate Brünnhilde, and if her voice is not flattered by the microphones, and under pressure
her vibrato widens and there is a loss of focus at the climax of the *Immolation scene*, this is still
histrionically thrilling, and Barenboim and the orchestra provide an overwhelming final apotheosis.

*Götterdämmerung: Dawn and Siegfried's Rhine journey; Siegfried's death and funeral music. Die
Meistersinger: Prelude. Das Rheingold: Entry of the Gods into Valhalla. Siegfried: Forest murmurs.
Tristan und Isolde: Prelude & Liebestod. Die Walküre: Wotan's farewell and Magic fire music.*
⊛ (M) *** SBK 48175; *SBT 48175* [id.]. Cleveland O, Szell.

The orchestral playing here is in a very special class. Its virtuosity is breathtaking. Szell generates the
greatest tension, particularly in the two scenes from *Götterdämmerung*, while the *Liebestod* from *Tristan*
has never been played on record with more passion and fire. The *Tristan* and *Meistersinger* excerpts
(from 1962) have been added to the contents of the original LP, which contained the *Ring* sequences
made later (in 1968), and the improvement in quality with the latest remastering for CD is little short of
miraculous. Like the similarly remastered Dvořák *Slavonic dances*, this is reasonably worthy of Szell's
extraordinary achievement in Cleveland in the 1960s, even if the forward balance of the recording places
a limit on the dynamic range.

*Götterdämmerung: Siegfried's Rhine journey & Funeral music. Parsifal: Prelude to Act I. Siegfried: Forest
murmurs. Tristan und Isolde: Prelude & Liebestod. Die Walküre: Ride of the Valkyries.*
*** Collins Dig. 1207-2 [id.]. Philh. O, Yuri Simonov.

If you want a spectacular, modern, digital recording of Wagnerian orchestral excerpts, this one is hard
to beat. The magnificent account of *Siegfried's Rhine journey* (with a splendid horn solo) is followed by
a performance of the *Funeral music* which has blazing drama and enormously expansive sound, with the
brass biting venomously at Siegfried's betrayal. The *Prelude and Liebestod* from *Tristan* brings playing
of great ardour from the Philharmonia strings, while – at a very spacious tempo – they find considerable
intensity in the *Parsifal Prelude*. The *Valkyries* come in at a fine canter, nostrils flaring yet not driven too
hard.

Lohengrin: Preludes to Acts I & III. Parsifal: Preludes to Acts I & III.
(N) (BB) *** EMI Seraphim CES5 69092 (2) [CDEB 69092]. BPO, Karajan – BRUCKNER: *Symphony
No. 8.* ***

Karajan's Act I *Lohengrin Prelude* is graduated superbly; the *Parsifal* excerpts, too, are nobly shaped, yet
here the tension is held at a marginally lower level. The *Parsifal* excerpts bring rapt serenity. This is
magnificent playing, and the 1975 recording has an attractively wide amplitude.

*Die Meistersinger: Prelude to Act III. Tannhäuser: Overture and Venusberg music. Tristan und Isolde:
Prelude and Liebestod.*
(N) **(*) DG Dig. Gold 439 022-2 [id.]. BPO, Karajan.

In Karajan's digital concert the orchestral playing is altogether superlative; artistically there need be no
reservations here. But, in spite of the reprocessing, the upper strings lack an ideal amount of space in
which to open out, and climaxes are not altogether free. The overall effect is slightly clinical in its detail,
instead of offering a resonant panoply of sound. But Brangäne's potion still remains heady, and the
playing is eloquent and powerful. As can be seen, the measure is not particularly generous for a reissued
premium-price CD.

VOCAL MUSIC

Das Liebesmal der Apostel (cantata).
(M) **(*) Carlton Classics PCD 1042 [id.]. Ambrosian Male Voice Ch., L. Symphonica, Wyn Morris –
BRUCKNER: *Helgoland.* ***

Wagner's strange Pentecostal cantata was written originally for massed choirs in Dresden at a time when
he was composing *Tannhäuser* (so very obvious from the music). Some 1,200 singers from all over
Saxony gathered for the première in 1843 – even so, the composer was disappointed with the lack of
impact! There is no lack of impact here, and the balance with the large orchestra is expertly managed
when it finally appears – two-thirds of the way through the piece. But its spectacular framework tends to

underline the relative smallness of the choral group. Yet the Ambrosians sing incisively and with much fervour, and the thrills remain when the direction is so strong. If the climax is not as monumental as the composer undoubtedly envisaged, it is still most compelling.

Lieder: *Les deux Grenadiers; Lied des Mephistopheles (Es war einmal ein König; Was machst du mir); Mignonne; Der Tannenbaum; Tout n'est qu'images fugitives.*
⊛ *** EMI Dig. CDC5 55047-2 [id.]. Thomas Hampson, Geoffrey Parsons – BERLIOZ: *Irlande;* LISZT: *Lieder.* *** ⊛

Starting with a charming French salon piece, *Mignonne*, to words by Ronsard, the Hampson collection presents a virtually unknown side of the composer. As well as another French love-song, there is a setting in French of the Goethe poem about the two grenadiers, not as subtle as Schumann's version but building to a tremendous climax with a reference to the *Marseillaise*. Two of Mephistopheles' songs from *Faust* (in German) date from earlier, including a jaunty setting of the *Song of the flea*. With Hampson in magnificent voice, powerfully accompanied by Geoffrey Parsons, this makes up a winning disc, very well recorded.

Wesendonk Lieder.
(Y/B) (M) *** Decca 440 491-2 [id.]. Kirsten Flagstad, VPO, Boult – MAHLER: *Kindertotenlieder* etc. **(*)

Now, like the operatic reissues below, part of Decca's Kirsten Flagstad Edition, this performance remains treasurable. Flagstad's glorious voice is perfectly suited to the rich inspiration of the *Wesendonk Lieder. Im Treibhaus* is particularly beautiful. Fine accompaniment, with the 1956 recording sounding remarkable for its vintage, and skilfully remastered.

Wesendonk Lieder: Der Engel; Stehe still; Im Treibhaus; Schmerzen; Träume. Götterdämmerung: Starke Scheite schichet mir dort. Siegfried: Ewig war ich. Tristan: Doch nun von Tristan?; Mild und leise.
(M) (***) EMI mono CDH7 63030-2 [id.]. Kirsten Flagstad, Philh. O, Furtwängler, Dobrowen.

Recorded in the late 1940s and early '50s, a year or so before Flagstad did *Tristan* complete with Furtwängler, these performances show her at her very peak, with the voice magnificent in power as well as beautiful and distinctive in every register. The *Liebestod* (with rather heavy surface noise) may be less rapt and intense in this version with Dobrowen than with Furtwängler but is just as expansive. For the *Wesendonk Lieder* she shades the voice down very beautifully, but this is still monumental and noble rather than intimate Lieder-singing.

OPERA

Die Feen (complete).
*** Orfeo Dig. C062833 (3) [id.]. Gray, Lovaas, Laki, Studer, Alexander, Hermann, Moll, Rootering, Bracht, Bav. R. Ch. & SO, Sawallisch.

Wagner was barely twenty when he wrote *Die Feen*, yet even when he has a *buffo* duet between the second pair of principals, the result is distinctive and fresh, delightfully sung here by Cheryl Studer and Jan-Hendrik Rootering. Sawallisch gives a strong and dramatic performance, finely paced; central to the total success is the singing of Linda Esther Gray as Ada, the fairy-heroine, powerful and firmly controlled. John Alexander as the tenor hero, King Arindal, sings cleanly and capably; the impressive cast-list boasts such excellent singers as Kurt Moll, Kari Lovaas and Krisztina Laki in small but vital roles. Ensembles and choruses – with the Bavarian Radio Chorus finely disciplined – are particularly impressive, and the recording is generally first rate.

Der fliegende Holländer (complete).
(M) *** Ph. Dig. 434 599-2 (2) [id.]. Estes, Balslev, Salminen, Schunk, Bayreuth Festival (1985) Ch. & O, Nelsson.
(B) *** Naxos Dig. 8.660025/6 [id.]. Muff, Haubold, Knodt, Seiffert, Budapest R. Ch., Vienna ORF SO, Steinberg.
(M) **(*) EMI Dig. CMS7 64650-2 (2) [Ang. CDMB 64650]. Van Dam, Vejzovic, Moll, Hofmann, Moser, Borris, V. State Op. Ch., BPO, Karajan.
**(*) Decca 414 551-2 (3) [id.]. Bailey, Martin, Talvela, Kollo, Krenn, Isola Jones, Chicago SO Ch. & O, Solti.
(M) **(*) Decca 417 319-2 (2) [id.]. London, Rysanek, Tozzi, ROHCG Ch. & O, Dorati.
** Decca Dig. 436 418-2 (2). Hale, Behrens, Rydl, Protschka, Vermillion, Heilmann, V State Op. Konzertvereinigung VPO, Dohnányi.

(Y/B) ** EMI CDS5 55179-2 (3). Adam, Silja, Talvela, Kozub, Burmeister, Unger, BBC Ch., New Philh. O, Klemperer.

Woldemar Nelsson, with the team he had worked with intensively through the season, conducts a performance even more glowing and responsively paced than those of his starrier rivals. The cast is more consistent than any, with Lisbeth Balslev as Senta firmer, sweeter and more secure than any current rival, raw only occasionally, and Simon Estes a strong, ringing Dutchman, clear and noble of tone. Matti Salminen is a dark and equally secure Daland and Robert Schunk an ardent, idiomatic Erik. The veteran, Anny Schlemm, as Mary, though vocally overstressed, adds pointful character, and the chorus is superb, wonderfully drilled and passionate with it. Though inevitably stage noises are obtrusive at times, the recording is exceptionally vivid and atmospheric. On two mid-priced discs only, it makes an admirable first choice.

Pinchas Steinberg, who has been outstandingly successful as music director of the O R F Orchestra and who was responsible for RCA's brilliant recording of Massenet's *Cherubin*, here proves a warmly sympathetic Wagnerian. More than most rivals, he brings out the light and shade of this earliest of the regular Wagner canon, helped by the refined, well-balanced recording, and by brilliant, sharply dramatic playing from the orchestra. His speeds are more urgent than most, with rhythms well sprung and melodic lines understandingly moulded. The chorus too sings with a bite and precision to match any rival. The cast of soloists may not be in that league, but they sing clearly and on the whole freshly, avoiding most of the cardinal faults of Wagner singers today. Alfred Muff as the Dutchman attacks the notes cleanly, with vibrato only occasionally intrusive. The vibrato of Ingrid Haubold is more of a problem but, except under pressure, it is well controlled, and she begins *Senta's Ballad* with a meditative pianissimo, a rare achievement. Both tenors are excellent, Peter Seiffert as Erik and Joerg Hering as the Steersman, and though Erich Knodt with rather a gritty baritone is an uncharacterful Daland, his Act II aria is light and refreshing, thanks to Steinberg's fine rhythmic pointing. The recording is both atmospheric and clear, and the set comes with libretto, translation, notes and very detailed synopsis, an outstanding bargain.

The extreme range of dynamics in EMI's recording for Karajan, not ideally clear but rich, matches the larger-than-life quality of the conductor's reading. He firmly and convincingly relates this early work to later Wagner, *Tristan* above all. His choice of José van Dam as the Dutchman, thoughtful, finely detailed and lyrical, strong but not at all blustering, goes well with this. Van Dam is superbly matched and contrasted with the finest Daland on record, Kurt Moll, gloriously biting and dark in tone, yet detailed in his characterization. Neither the Erik of Peter Hofmann, nor – more seriously – the Senta of Dunja Vejzovic matches this standard; nevertheless, for all her variability, Vejzovic is wonderfully intense in *Senta's Ballad* and she matches even Van Dam's fine legato in the Act II duet. The CD transfer underlines the heavyweight quality of the recording, with the *Sailors' chorus* for example made massive, but effectively so, when Karajan conducts it with such fine spring.

What will disappoint some who admire Solti's earlier Wagner sets is that this most atmospheric of the Wagner operas is presented with no Culshaw-style production whatever. Characters halloo to one another when evidently standing elbow to elbow, and even the Dutchman's ghostly chorus sounds very close and earthbound. But with Norman Bailey a deeply impressive Dutchman, Janis Martin a generally sweet-toned Senta, Martti Talvela a splendid Daland, and Kollo, for all his occasional coarseness, an illuminating Erik, it remains well worth hearing.

Dorati, with rhythms well sprung, draws strong and alert playing and singing from his Covent Garden forces in a consistently purposeful performance, helped by Culshaw-style sound-effects. The well-spread recording is full and atmospheric and, like the Philips set, the reissue is offered on two mid-price CDs. George London's Dutchman brings one of his most powerful performances on disc, occasionally rough-toned but positive. Leonie Rysanek may sound too mature for Senta, but as a great Wagnerian she brings a commanding presence and the most persuasive sense of line. There is no weak link in the rest of the cast, well set up at the start by the characterful Richard Lewis as the Steersman.

Issued around the same time as the Naxos version, Dohnányi's Decca set, also made in Vienna but with starrier forces, is disappointing. The sound is rich and full, if not as clear on detail as the Naxos, but Dohnányi's relatively sluggish speeds go with rhythms too often square and unsprung. In all he takes over 10 minutes longer than Nelsson in his Bayreuth set on Philips – on balance still the finest – and almost as many more than Steinberg. Nor does his cast fulfil expectations. Robert Hale is a powerful, intense Dutchman but, as recorded, the voice is ill-focused, lacking necessary firmness. Hildegard Behrens too has trouble with vibrato, which is intrusive except when her voice opens out richly at the top, and even Kurt Rydl's ripely characterful Daland is not as steady as it might be.

Predictably, Klemperer's reading is spacious in its tempi – involving a third disc in its CD reissue – and the drama hardly grips you by the throat. But the underlying intensity is irresistible. This could hardly be recommended as a first choice, but any committed admirer of the conductor should try to hear it. It is a pity that Anja Silja was chosen as Senta, even though she is not as squally in tone here as she can be. Otherwise a strong vocal cast, much beautiful playing (particularly from the wind soloists) and a lively if not particularly atmospheric recording, made to sound drier still in its CD format.

Der fliegender Holländer: highlights.
(N) (M) **(*) Ph. Dig. 446 618-2 [id.] (from above complete (1985) Bayreuth set, with Estes, Balslev, Salminen, Schunk; cond. Nelsson).

A generous (76 minutes) and well-chosen selection from this outstanding set is let down by the absence of any documentation, save a list of the 12 excerpts.

Götterdämmerung (complete).
*** Decca 414 115-2 (4) [id.]. Nilsson, Windgassen, Fischer-Dieskau, Frick, Neidlinger, Watson, Ludwig, V. State Op. Ch., VPO, Solti.
*** DG 415 155-2 (4) [id.]. Dernesch, Janowitz, Brilioth, Stewart, Kelemen, Ludwig, Ridderbusch, German Op. Ch., BPO, Karajan.
*** Ph. 412 488-2 (4) [id.]. Nilsson, Windgassen, Greindl, Mödl, Stewart, Neidlinger, Dvořáková, Bayreuth Festival (1967) Ch. & O, Boehm.
(Y/B) *** Teldec/Warner Dig. 4509 94194-2 (4) [id.]. Jerusalem, Anne Evans, Kang, Von Kannen, Bundschuh, Meier, Turner, Bayreuth (1991) Festival Ch. & O, Barenboim.
*** EMI Dig. CD7 54485-2 (4) [Ang. CDCD 54485]. Marton, Jerusalem, Tomlinson, Adam, Hampson, Bundschuh, Lipovšek, Bav. R. Ch., RSO, Haitink.
(M) *** Ph. 434 424-2 (4) [id.]. G. Jones, Jung, Hübner, Becht, Mazura, Altmeyer, Killebrew, (1979) Bayreuth Festival Ch. & O, Boulez.
(Y/B) *** DG Dig. 439 385-2 (4) [id.]. Goldberg, Behrens, Salminen, Wlaschiha, Studer, Weikl, Schwarz, NY Met. Op. Ch. & O, Levine.

Solti's *Götterdämmerung* represented the peak of his achievement in recording the *Ring* cycle. His reading had matured before the recording was made. He presses on still, but no longer is there any feeling of over-driving, and even the *Funeral march* is made into a natural, not a forced, climax. There is not a single weak link in the cast. Nilsson surpasses herself in the magnificence of her singing: even Flagstad in her prime would not have been more masterful as Brünnhilde. As in *Siegfried*, Windgassen is in superb voice; Frick is a vivid Hagen, and Fischer-Dieskau achieves the near impossible in making Gunther an interesting and even sympathetic character. As for the recording quality, it surpasses even Decca's earlier achievement, and the CDs bring added weight to balance the brilliant upper range.

Karajan's singing cast is marginally even finer than Solti's, and his performance conveys the steady flow of recording sessions prepared in relation to live performances. But ultimately he falls short of Solti's achievement in the orgasmic quality of the music. Karajan is a degree less committed, beautifully as the players respond, and warm as his overall approach is. Dernesch's Brünnhilde is warmer than Nilsson's, with a glorious range of tone. Brilioth as Siegfried is fresh and young-sounding, while the Gutrune of Gundula Janowitz is far preferable to that of Claire Watson on Decca. The matching is otherwise very even.

Boehm's urgently involving reading of *Götterdämmerung*, very well cast, is crowned by an incandescent performance of the final Immolation scene from Birgit Nilsson as Brünnhilde. It is an astonishing achievement that she could sing with such biting power and accuracy in a live performance, coming to it at the very end of a long evening. The excitement of that is matched by much else in the performance, so that incidental stage noises and the occasional inaccuracy, almost inevitable in live music-making, matter hardly at all. Josef Greindl is rather unpleasantly nasal in tone as Hagen, and Martha Mödl as Waltraute is unsteady; but both are dramatically involving. Thomas Stewart is a gruff but convincing Gunther and Dvořáková, as Gutrune, strong if not ideally pure-toned. Neidlinger as ever is a superb Alberich.

Recorded at the 1991 Bayreuth Festival, a year earlier than *Siegfried*, Barenboim's live recording is not quite the culmination one had hoped for in his cycle for Teldec. There is also the problem in this opera, more than the rest of the *Ring*, of stage noises, particularly at the end of the Immolation scene, rather undermining its rapt intensity, when the fulfilment motif enters at last. Anne Evans sweetly and purely rises to the challenge of that radiant close of the tetralogy, compensating for any lack of power in the clarity of focus and expressive intensity of her singing, making Brünnhilde a very human figure to excite the deepest sympathy. Whatever reservations have to be made about the recording, it is satisfyingly weighty and has more presence than its direct digital rivals, recorded in the studio under Haitink (EMI) and Levine (DG). On balance, it stands as the most recommendable of latterday versions of this final opera, thanks not only to the beauty as well as the imagination of Evans's singing, more satisfying than that of her squally rivals, but also to the superb singing of Siegfried Jerusalem who outshines his already outstanding achievement in the same role in the Haitink version, even if the stresses of a long evening begin to show by the end. Eva-Maria Bundschuh makes a fresh, bright Gutrune and Waltraud Meier a powerful Waltraute, giving an animated account of her Act I narration. Bodo Brinkmann is an old-sounding, rather uneven Gunther, Philip Kang a powerful but gritty Hagen and Gunter von Kannen an unsinister Alberich. Any disappointment there is small compared to the keen tension and excitement of this live recording under Barenboim, consistently gripping in a way studio recordings tend to be. As a performance it may not outshine either Solti's pioneering version or Karl Boehm's live account from Bayreuth – both of which still sound splendid – but it satisfyingly completes the finest of modern *Ring* cycles on disc.

Haitink's reading is magnificent. In its strength, nobility and thrustfulness it crowns all his previous Wagner, culminating in a forceful and warmly expressive account of the final Immolation scene. Siegfried Jerusalem clearly establishes himself as the finest latterday Siegfried, both heroic and sweet of tone. Thomas Hampson is a sensitive and virile Gunther, John Tomlinson a sinister but human Hagen, Marjana Lipovšek a warmly intense Waltraute and Eva-Maria Bundschuh a rich, rather fruity Gutrune. The obvious reservation to make is with the singing of Eva Marton as Brünnhilde, when the unevenness of the vocal production is exaggerated by the microphone in a way that at times comes close to pitchless yelping. However, that drawback is clearly outweighed by the set's positive qualities, and the scale of her singing is in no doubt, an archetypal Brünnhilde voice in timbre if not in firmness.

Boulez's 1979 analogue recording is warm and urgent. The passion of the performance is established in the Dawn music before the second scene of the Prologue and, with a strong if not ideal cast, it has a clear place as a first-rate mid-price recommendation. Manfred Jung as Siegfried gives a fresh, clean-cut performance. Jeannine Altmeyer sings Gutrune, sweet but not always ideally clean of attack; Fritz Hübner is a weighty Hagen, Franz Mazura a powerful Gunther and Gwendoline Killebrew a rich, firm Waltraute. Dame Gwyneth Jones as Brünnhilde, always very variable, has some splendid moments, notably at the close of the Immolation scene. The sound is aptly atmospheric but lacks something in weight in the brass, though there is no lack of excitement at the end of Act II.

Levine's hardly less compelling reading of *Götterdämmerung* stands out from the other three operas in his *Ring* cycle, with the sound rather more ample than in the earlier operas. The cast is a powerful one, with even the Norns cast from strength. Cheryl Studer as Gutrune, Matti Salminen as Hagen and Ekkehard Wlaschiha as Alberich have few equals, even if the contributions of both Hildegard Behrens as Brünnhilde and Rainer Goldberg as Siegfried are flawed, the one too edgy to convey beauty of line, whatever her power, the other growing gritty under pressure even in this, one of his finest recordings. For those wanting to sample the Levine *Ring*, this is the opera to go for.

Götterdämmerung: scenes (sung in German): *Dawn; Brünnhilde and Siegfried's entrance; Siegfried's Rhine journey; Siegfried's funeral march; Brünnhilde's immolation.*
(Y/B) (M) *** CfP CD-CFP 4670; *TC-CFP 4670* [id.]. Rita Hunter, Alberto Remedios, LPO, Mackerras.

This Classics for Pleasure disc of highlights was made in 1972, six years before the classic complete set in English by the same artists. Vocally what stands out in Hunter's performance is the pinging precision of even the most formidable exposed notes. Here she revealed herself to be a natural competitor in the international league, and her simple, fresh manner in the most intense moment of the *Immolation*, the hushed farewell of *Ruhe, du Gott*, is caught most affectingly. Remedios is also in splendid form, and Mackerras draws dedicated and dramatic playing from the LPO. The recording still sounds very impressive indeed, full-blooded and present, with the closing scene magnificently vivid. An outstanding bargain.

Götterdämmerung: highlights.
(N) (M) *** Teldec/Warner Dig. 0630 13823-9 [id.] (from above complete (1991) Bayreuth set, with Jerusalem, Evans; cond. Barenboim).
(N) (M) **(*) Ph. 446 616-2 [id.] (from above complete (1979) Bayreuth set, with Jones, Jung; cond. Boulez).

The 73 minutes of highlights are satisfactorily chosen from the Barenboim set and a synopsis is provided though not keyed directly to the 18 excerpts.

Many collectors will want to sample the Boulez set, and this CD offering 78 minutes of highlights should serve admirably, except for the lack of either translation or synopsis – or, indeed, any kind of documentation at all except for detailing the 16 excerpts. They include *Siegfried's Rhine journey* and *Funeral march* and the final Immolation scene, so telling here.

The Twilight of the Gods (*Götterdämmerung:* complete; in English).
(M) *** EMI CMS7 64244-2 (5) [id.]. Hunter, Remedios, Welsby, Haugland, Hammond-Stroud, Curphey, Pring, E. Nat. Op. Ch. & O, Goodall.

Goodall's account heightens the epic scale. The few slight imprecisions and the occasional rawness of wind tone actually seem to enhance the earthiness of Goodall's view. Both Rita Hunter and Alberto Remedios give performances which are magnificent in every way. In particular the golden beauty of Remedios's tenor is consistently superb, with no Heldentenor barking at all, while Aage Haugland's Hagen is giant-sounding to focus the evil, with Gunther and Gutrune mere pawns. The voices on stage are in a different, drier acoustic from that for the orchestra, but considering the problems the sound is impressive. As for Goodall, with his consistently expansive tempi he carries total concentration – except, curiously, in the scene with the Rhinemaidens, whose music (as in Goodall's *Rhinegold* too) lumbers along heavily.

The Twilight of the Gods (Götterdämmerung): Act III: excerpts (in English).
(M) *** Chandos CHAN 6593 [id.]. Rita Hunter, Alberto Remedios, Norman Bailey, Clifford Grant, Margaret Curphey, Sadler's Wells Opera Ch. & O, Goodall.

Originally recorded by Unicorn in the early 1970s, even before the Sadler's Wells company had changed its name to the English National Opera, this single Chandos CD brings an invaluable reminder of Reginald Goodall's performance of the *Ring* cycle when it was in its first flush of success. The two-LP set is here transferred on to a single CD, lasting 66 minutes and covering the closing two scenes. In many ways it possesses an advantage over even the complete live recording of the opera, made at the Coliseum five years later, when Rita Hunter and Alberto Remedios are here obviously fresher and less stressed than at the end of a full evening's performance. It is good too to have this sample, however brief, of Clifford Grant's Hagen and Norman Bailey's Gunther, fine performances both. Fresh, clear recording, not as full as it might be. But at mid-price this CD is well worth investigating.

Lohengrin (complete).
(Y/B) *** DG Dig. 437 808-2 (3) [id.]. Jerusalem, Studer, Meier, Welker, Moll, Schmidt, V. State Op. Ch., VPO, Claudio Abbado.
⊛ *** Decca Dig. 421 053-2 (4) [id.]. Domingo, Norman, Nimsgern, Randová, Sotin, Fischer-Dieskau, V. State Op. Concert Ch., VPO, Solti.
*** EMI CDS7 49017-2 (3) [Ang. CDCC 49017]. Jess Thomas, Grümmer, Fischer-Dieskau, Ludwig, Frick, Wiener, V. State Op. Ch., VPO, Kempe.
(N) (M) **(*) Ph. 446 337-2 (3) [id.]. Jess Thomas, Silja, Vinay, Varnay, Crass, Krause, Bayreuth Festival Ch. & O, Sawallisch.
(N) **(*) RCA Dig. 09026 62646-2 (3) [id.]. Heppner, Sweet, Leiferkus, Rootering, Marton, Terfel, Bav. State Op. Ch., Bav. R. Ch. & O, Sir Colin Davis.

Lohengrin has been a lucky opera on disc, and Claudio Abbado adds another magnificent reading to set alongside such classic performances as Kempe's and Solti's. But where Solti takes a very measured view, Abbado keeps Wagner's square rhythms flowing more freely, allowing himself a greater measure of rubato. That in turn reflects his experience with these same performers at the Vienna State Opera, and throughout the set one registers that, though this has all the benefits of a studio performance in precision, it consistently reflects stage experience, never more so than in the final dénouement and Lohengrin's departure. That Abbado's speeds are generally faster than Solti's (with the Act III *Prelude* a notable exception, where Abbado's compound time is more springy) means that the complete opera is squeezed on to three instead of four discs, giving it the clearest advantage. For the general collector this will now be first choice. As Elsa, matching her earlier, Bayreuth performance on Philips, Cheryl Studer is at her sweetest and purest, bringing out the heroine's naïvety more touchingly than Jessye Norman, whose weighty, mezzo-ish tone is thrillingly rich but is more suited to portraying other Wagner heroines than this. Though there are signs that Siegfried Jerusalem's voice is not as fresh as it once was, he sings commandingly, conveying both beauty and a true Heldentenor quality. Where Plácido Domingo, producing even more beautiful tone, tends to use a full voice for such intimate solos as *In fernem Land* and *Mein lieber Schwann*, Jerusalem sings there with tender restraint and gentler tone. Among the others, Waltraud Meier as Ortrud and Kurt Moll as King Heinrich are both superb, as fine as any predecessor, and though in the role of Telramund Hartmut Welker's baritone is not ideally steady, that tends to underline the weakness of the character next to the positive Ortrud.

It is Plácido Domingo's achievement singing Lohengrin that the lyrical element blossoms so consistently, with no hint of Heldentenor barking; at whatever dynamic level, Domingo's voice is firm and unstrained. Jessye Norman, not naturally suited to the role of Elsa, yet gives a warm, commanding performance, always intense, full of detailed insights into words and character. Eva Randová's grainy mezzo does not take so readily to recording, but as Ortrud she provides a pointful contrast, even if she never matches the firm, biting malevolence of Christa Ludwig on the Kempe set. Siegmund Nimsgern, Telramund for Solti, equally falls short of Fischer-Dieskau, his rival on the Kempe set; but it is still a strong, cleanly focused performance. Fischer-Dieskau here sings the small but vital role of the Herald, while Hans Sotin makes a comparably distinctive King Henry. Radiant playing from the Vienna Philharmonic, and committed chorus work too. This is one of the crowning glories of Solti's long recording career.

Kempe's is a rapt account of *Lohengrin* which has been surpassed on record only by Solti's Decca set and which remains one of his finest monuments in sound. The singers seem uplifted, Jess Thomas singing more clearly and richly than usual, Elisabeth Grümmer unrivalled as Elsa in her delicacy and sweetness, Gottlob Frick gloriously resonant as the king. But it is the partnership of Christa Ludwig and Fischer-Dieskau as Ortrud and Telramund that sets the seal on this superb performance, giving the darkest intensity to their machinations in Act II, their evil heightening the beauty and serenity of so much in this opera. Though the digital transfer on CD reveals roughness (even occasional distortion) in the original recording, the glow and intensity of Kempe's reading come out all the more involvingly in the new format. The set is also very economically contained on three CDs instead of the four for all rivals, though inevitably breaks between discs come in the middle of Acts.

The Sawallisch recording was of a live performance at Bayreuth in 1962 and has a propulsive thrust over Wagner's expansive paragraphs through the presence of an audience. For this dramatic tension one naturally has to pay in stage-noises, occasional slips and odd balances, but the recording captures the unique flavour of the Festspielhaus splendidly. What above all will dictate a listener's response is his reaction to the voices of Anja Silja as Elsa and of Astrid Varnay as Ortrud. Though Silja has been far less steady on record in other sets, this is often not a pretty sound, and Varnay was firmer in her earlier Bayreuth recording for Decca in mono. Jess Thomas is here not as reliable as he has been in other performances; but Sawallisch's direction is superb, fresh and direct, never intrusive. Considering the problems of recording, on CD the sound is marvellously refined as well as atmospheric. The opera fits neatly on three discs, with each Act complete and unbroken.

Among Wagner operas *Lohengrin* has been lucky on disc, and the RCA version from Munich, conducted by Sir Colin Davis, stands out both for the refinement and spaciousness of the reading and for the unstrained singing of the Canadian Heldentenor, Ben Heppner, in the title-role. Though he hardly outshines such direct rivals as Plácido Domingo for Solti on Decca or Siegfried Jerusalem for Abbado on DG, he provides a ringingly fresh, strong alternative. The other male singers make a formidable team. With grit in the voice, Sergei Leiferkus makes Telramund more of a villain than usual, less of a dupe, with Jan-Henrik Rootering as the King and Bryn Terfel as the Herald both full and firm. Sharon Sweet as Elisabeth scales her voice down well for the lyrical moments, but the vibrato grows obtrusive under pressure, while the set's big snag is the gusty and wobbly Ortrud of Eva Marton.

Lohengrin: highlights.
(N) *** DG Dig. 445 869-2 [id.] (from above complete set, with Jerusalem, Studer, Meier, Welker; cond. Abbado).
(N) (M) **(*) Ph. Dig. 446 619-2 [id.]. Frey, Studer, Schnaut, Wlaschiha, Schenk, (1990) Bayreuth Festival Ch. and O, Peter Schneider.

Cheryl Studer's Elsa – the role which won her international fame – is common to both sets, and in the earlier, Bayreuth recording she tangibly brings out the equivocal development of the character. Paul Frey proves a strong and noble Lohengrin, though with a slow vibrato occasionally obtruding on the sweetness of his tone. Wlaschiha is a dark, sinister Telramund; but this generous 77-minute disc of highlights is let down – like the rest of the current Philips series of Wagnerian excerpts – by the total absence of documentation except for a brief list of its 15 items. Most collectors will therefore turn to the alternative, Abbado CD – preferable as a performance, with Studer at her very best – since it is equally generous and includes a full synopsis.

Die Meistersinger von Nürnberg (complete).
*** DG 415 278-2 (4) [id.]. Fischer-Dieskau, Ligendza, Lagger, Hermann, Domingo, Laubenthal, Ludwig, German Op. Ch. & O, Berlin, Jochum.
(Y/B) *** EMI CDS5 55142-2 (4) [id.]. Weikl, Heppner, Studer, Moll, Lorenz, Van der Walt, Kallisch, Bav. State Op. Ch., Bav. State O, Sawallisch.
**(*) Decca 417 497-2 (4) [id.]. Bailey, Bode, Moll, Weikl, Kollo, Dallapozza, Hamari, Gumpoldskirchner Spatzen, V. State Op. Ch., VPO, Solti.
(Y/B) (M) (*(**)) Decca mono 440 057-2 (4) [id.]. Schoeffler, Gueden, Treptow, Edelmann, Dönch, Poell, Dermota, Schürhoff, V. State Op. Ch., VPO, Knappertsbusch.

Jochum's is a performance which, more than any, captures the light and shade of Wagner's most warmly approachable score, its humour and tenderness as well as its strength. Above all, Jochum is unerring in building long Wagnerian climaxes and resolving them – more so than his recorded rivals. The cast is the most consistent yet assembled on record. Though Caterina Ligendza's big soprano is a little ungainly for Eva, it is an appealing performance, and the choice of Domingo for Walther is inspired. The key to the set is of course the searching and highly individual Sachs of Fischer-Dieskau, and Horst Laubenthal's finely tuned David matches this Sachs in applying Lieder style. The recording balance favours the voices, but on CD they are made to sound slightly ahead of the orchestra. There is a lovely bloom on the whole sound and, with a recording which is basically wide-ranging and refined, the ambience brings an attractively natural projection of the singers.

Sawallisch's fine set was the first studio recording of *Meistersinger* to be made in digital sound, and Wagner's great ensembles have never been heard on disc with such glorious warmth and fullness. Sawallisch also paces the work in reflection of his long experience of performing it in the opera house with the same musicians. Add to that the most radiant and free-toned Walther on disc, the Canadian, Ben Heppner, and you have a superb set, one that for many will be a clear first choice. In sheer beauty Heppner even outshines Plácido Domingo on Jochum's DG set, as he does in variety of expression and feeling. Cheryl Studer's contribution is hardly less remarkable than Heppner's, at once powerful and girlishly tender, with the voice kept pure. If she is less affecting than she might be in the poignant duet with Sachs in Act II and in the great *Quintet* of Act III, that has something to do with a limitation in Sawallisch's reading, fine as it is. It rarely brings a gulp to the throat, rarely finds the poetic magic that this of all Wagner's operas can convey, and Act II, with the opening prelude too soft-grained for this buoyant music, rather lacks freshness. Bernd Weikl makes a splendid Sachs, firm and true of voice, but something of the nobility of the master-shoemaker is missing. Deon van der Walt is a strong David, clear-cut and fresh, with Cornelia Kallisch making a traditionally fruity yet firm Magdalene. Siegfried Lorenz is a well-focused Beckmesser who refuses to caricature the much-mocked Town Clerk, and Kurt Moll is a magnificent Pogner. The chorus (balanced a little backwardly) and orchestra play with the warmth and radiance associated with recordings made in the Herkulessaal in Munich.

The great glory of Solti's set is the mature and involving portrayal of Sachs by Norman Bailey. Kurt Moll as Pogner, Bernd Weikl as Beckmesser and Julia Hamari as Magdalene are all excellent, but the shortcomings are comparably serious. Both Hannelore Bode and René Kollo fall short of their far-from-perfect contributions to earlier sets, and Solti for all his energy gives a surprisingly square reading of this most appealing of Wagner scores, pointing his expressive lines too heavily and failing to convey real spontaneity. It remains an impressive achievement for Bailey's marvellous Sachs, and the Decca sound comes up very vividly on CD.

Knappertsbusch takes a characteristically spacious view, but one which brings out the comedy as well as the poignancy of the piece. Maybe in reflection of the order of recording, Act II stands out as one of the most moving on disc, matched since but not surpassed. Paul Schoeffler with his dark, slightly metallic tone makes a searching Hans Sachs, wise and benevolent but unsentimental. Hilde Gueden is an enchanting Eva, with her unmistakable golden tone making the heroine provocative, even minxish. Her duet with Sachs is a high point, touching rare depths of emotion when Sachs remembers the wife and family who died, while then selflessly refusing to push himself forward as Eva's partner. The rest of the cast, though not so characterful, is still very strong, notably Anton Dermota as David and Karl Dönch as Beckmesser, with Günther Treptow not too strenuous as Walther. Sadly, the Decca transfer is edgy, with string-tone far more acid-sounding than on the original LP, even if voices come over well.

'Vienna State Opera live': Volume 23: *Die Meistersinger*: excerpts: *Fliedermonolog* and Sachs–Eva duet; Sachs–Beckmesser duet; Act III: Quintet, Sachs's final monologue.
(Y/B) (M) (**) Koch-Schwann mono 3-1473-2 (2) [id.]. Herrmann, Kunz, Lorenz, Reining, Klein, Vienna State Op. O, Boehm – R. STRAUSS: *Ariadne auf Naxos*. (***)

This 40-minute selection of excerpts from a Vienna State Opera performance of *Meistersinger* in 1943, conducted by Karl Boehm (Vol. 23 of the Vienna State Opera series), comes as a supplement to Boehm's historic recording of Strauss's *Ariadne auf Naxos*. The funereally slow account of Sachs's *Fliedermonolog* from Josef Herrmann leads on to charming performances of the duets with Eva and with Beckmesser. The sound is dim, and the recordings of Walther's *Prize song*, superbly sung by Max Lorenz, and of Sachs's final monologue are unceremoniously cut off; but the sense of occasion is most compelling, making this a valuable document.

Die Meistersinger: highlights.
(Y/B) (M) *** DG 445 470-2 [id.] (from above set, with Fischer-Dieskau, Domingo, Ligendza; cond. Jochum).

(Y/B) (M) (***) EMI mono CD-EMX 2228 [id.]. Frantz, Schock, Grümmer, Frick, Kusche, Unger, Höffgen, St Hedwig's Cathedral Ch., German Op., Berlin, Ch., Berlin State Op. Ch., BPO, Kempe.

(N) (M) ** Ph. 446 621-2 [id.]. Ridderbusch, Bode, Sotin, Hirte, Cox, Stricker, (1974) Bayreuth Festival Ch. & O, Varviso.

Jochum's DG excerpts are especially valuable for giving fair samples of the two most individual performances: Fischer-Dieskau as a sharply incisive Sachs, his every nuance of mood clearly interpreted, and Domingo a golden-toned if hardly idiomatic Walther. Needless to say, the 76-minute selection, opening with the *Overture*, includes the Act III Quintet, also the opera's closing scene. The recording, made in March 1976 in the Berlin Jesus-Christus Kirche with the voices placed rather closely, matches the fine quality of the complete set.

The 72-minute selection from Kempe's classic EMI mono set is not dissimilar, this time demonstrating Ferdinand Frantz's comparatively weighty, dark-toned Sachs, while Rudolph Schock, with his distinctive timbre between lyrical and heroic, is ideally suited to the role of Walther. Elisabeth Grümmer is a meltingly beautiful Eva, particularly so in the great Act III Quintet. Again voices are closely balanced and there is striking clarity of focus so that, although the orchestra sounds relatively thin, one soon adjusts when the singing is so fine and there is good ambience.

The 1974 Bayreuth performance is flawed (and the big crowd scenes bring obtrusive stage-noises), but the Swiss conductor, Silvio Varviso, is a persuasive Wagnerian, one who inspires the authentic ebb and flow of tension. With the exception of Hannelore Bode's disappointing Eva, much of the singing here is very enjoyable, with Karl Ridderbusch a firmly resonant Hans Sachs and the other Masters really singing their parts. But this set of highlights (nearly 78 minutes) is let down, like the others in this Philips series, by the absence of a synopsis to relate the excerpts to the narrative.

Parsifal (complete).

⊛ *** DG Dig. 413 347-2 (4) [id.]. Hofmann, Vejzovic, Moll, Van Dam, Nimsgern, Von Halem, German Op. Ch., BPO, Karajan.

(N) *** Teldec Dig. 9031 74448-2 (4) [id.]. Jerusalem, Van Dam, Hölle, Meier, Von Kannen, Tomlinson, Berlin State Op. Ch., BPO, Barenboim.

*** Decca 417 143-2 (4) [id.]. Kollo, Ludwig, Fischer-Dieskau, Hotter, Kelemen, Frick, V. Boys' Ch., V. State Op. Ch., VPO, Solti.

(N) **(*) Koch-Schwann 3-1348-2 (4) [id.]. Kollo, Adam, Cold, Schröter, Bunger, Teschler, Leipzig and Berlin R. Choirs, Thomanenchor Leipzig, Leipzig RSO, Kegel.

(Y/B) **(*) DG Dig. 437 501-2 (4) [id.]. Domingo, Norman, Moll, Morris, Wlaschiha, Rootering, Met. Op. Ch. & O, James Levine.

**(*) DG 435 718-2 (3) [id.]. James King, Gwyneth Jones, Stewart, Ridderbusch, McIntyre, Crass, (1970) Bayreuth Festival Ch. & O, Boulez.

**(*) Ph. 416 390-2 (4) [id.]. Jess Thomas, Dalis, London, Talvela, Neidlinger, Hotter, (1962) Bayreuth Festival Ch. & O, Knappertsbusch.

(N) (M) **(*) EMI CMS5 65665-2 (4) [CDMD 65665]. Ellsworth, Joll, McIntyre, Meier, Gwynne, Folwell, Welsh Nat. O Ch. & O, Goodall.

Communion, musical and spiritual, is what this intensely beautiful Karajan set provides. The playing of the Berlin orchestra is consistently beautiful; but the clarity and refinement of sound prevent this from emerging as a lengthy serving of Karajan soup. Kurt Moll as Gurnemanz is the singer who, more than any other, anchors the work vocally, projecting his voice with firmness and subtlety. José van Dam as Amfortas is also splendid. The Klingsor of Siegmund Nimsgern could be more sinister, but the singing is admirable. Dunja Vejzovic makes a vibrant, sensuous Kundry who rises superbly to the moment in Act II when she bemoans her laughter in the face of Christ. Only Peter Hofmann as Parsifal leaves any disappointment; at times he develops a gritty edge on the voice, but his natural tone is admirably suited to the part and he is never less than dramatically effective. He is not helped by the relative closeness of the solo voices, but otherwise the recording is near the atmospheric ideal, a superb achievement. The four CDs are still among DG's finest so far.

With Siegfried Jerusalem a superb Parsifal, one of the finest ever, both characterful and mellifluous, Daniel Barenboim's is a dedicated version with an excellent cast. Like Karajan, Barenboim draws glorious sounds from the Berlin Philharmonic, even if he cannot quite match his predecessor in concentrated intensity, well sustained as his control of long paragraphs is. Waltraud Meier as in rival versions is an outstanding, darkly intense Kundry, unsurpassed today, and José van Dam is superb as Amfortas, clean of attack, as he was for Karajan. John Tomlinson is a resonant, if young-sounding Titurel, and Gunther von Kannen a clear and direct, if unvillainous, even noble Klingsor. The relatively weak link is the Gurnemanz of Matthias Hölle, warm-toned but slightly unsteady, not quite in character. The four-disc format is more convenient than most, with Acts II and III each complete on a single disc.

Solti's singing cast could hardly be stronger, every one of them pointing words with fine, illuminating care for detail; and the complex balances of sound, not least in the *Good Friday music*, are beautifully caught; throughout, Solti shows his sustained intensity in Wagner. There remains just one doubt, but that rather serious: the lack of a rapt, spiritual quality. The remastering for CD, as with Solti's other Wagner recordings, opens up the sound, and the choral climaxes are superb.

Recorded live at a concert performance in East Berlin in 1975, the Kegel version presents a refreshing alternative to most latterday interpretations, brisk and electric, bringing out the dramatic thrust of the piece far more than usual at speeds that flow fluently and easily. Kegel, best known as the creator of the Leipzig Radio Choir, is a more passionate Wagnerian than Pierre Boulez, similarly brisk in this opera. Kegel draws incandescent singing from his massed choirs, with the spacious recording capturing the bloom on the vocal sound atmospherically, with choral antiphonies most beautiful. René Kollo as Parsifal and Theo Adam as Amfortas were then still in their prime and sing magnetically. The others, less celebrated, still comprise a generally fresh-sounding team, clean of attack, notably Ulric Cold as Gurnemanz. Gisela Schröter, lighter of tone than usual for Kundry with a tight vibrato, also sings beautifully. Reid Bunger is a youngish-sounding Klingsor with a villainous snarl. The layout on four discs is not only inconvenient (with breaks in each Act) but extravagant, when it could easily have been accommodated on three.

James Levine's speeds outstrip almost anyone in slowness; indeed at times the New York studio performance seems to hang fire -as in the Transformation scene of Act I. Many will find it a small price to pay for a performance, vividly recorded, involving a cast as starry as any that could be assembled. Jessye Norman as Kundry and Plácido Domingo in the title-role give performances that in every way live up to their reputations, not just exploiting beauty of sound but backing it with keen characterization and concern for word-meaning. Kurt Moll as Gurnemanz and Ekkehard Wlaschiha as Klingsor are both magnificent, firm and characterful, while James Morris as Amfortas gives a powerful performance, with slightly gritty tone adding to the character's sense of pain. Jan-Henrik Rootering's bass as Titurel is atmospherically enhanced by an echo-chamber, pointing the relative lack of reverberation in the main, firmly focused recording, one of the most vivid yet made in the Manhattan Center. If Levine's slow speeds will prevent this from being a first choice with most Wagnerians, this version brings many compensations.

Boulez's speeds are so consistently fast that in the age of CD it has brought an obvious benefit in being fitted – easily – on three discs instead of four, yet Boulez's approach, with the line beautifully controlled, conveys a dramatic urgency rarely found in this opera, and never sounds breathless, with textures clarified in a way characteristic of Boulez. Even the flower-maidens sing like young apprentices in *Meistersinger* rather than seductive beauties. James King is a firm, strong, rather baritonal hero, Thomas Stewart a fine tense Amfortas, and Gwyneth Jones as Kundry is in strong voice, only occasionally shrill, though Franz Crass is disappointingly unsteady as Gurnemanz. The live Bayreuth recording is most impressively transferred to CD.

Knappertsbusch's expansive and dedicated 1962 reading is caught superbly in the Philips set, arguably the finest live recording ever made in the Festspielhaus at Bayreuth, with outstanding singing from Jess Thomas as Parsifal and Hans Hotter as Gurnemanz. Though Knappertsbusch chooses consistently slow tempi, there is no sense of excessive squareness or length, so intense is the concentration of the performance, its spiritual quality; and the sound has undoubtedly been further enhanced in the remastering for CD. The snag is that the stage noises and coughs are also emphasized, with the bronchial afflictions particularly disturbing in the *Prelude*.

EMI have reissued the Goodall version at mid-price and on four CDs instead of the original five, which brings considerable savings on the original cost. There are no complaints about the sound, which is admirably full and vivid. Goodall in his plain, unvarnished, patiently expansive reading characteristically finds deep intensity in a strong, rough-hewn way. He may lack the ethereal beauties of Karajan, for here *Parsifal* is brought down to earth, thanks not just to Goodall but to the cast which with one exception stands up well to international competition. It was plainly a help that these same singers had appeared together under Goodall on stage in the Welsh National Opera production. Donald McIntyre gives one of his very finest performances as Gurnemanz, with more bloom than usual. Waltraud Meier's powerful, penetrating voice suits the role of Kundry well, while the American, Warren Ellsworth, has power and precision, if little beauty, as Parsifal. Only the ill-focused Amfortas of Phillip Joll is disappointing, too gritty of tone, though he too makes the drama compelling.

Parsifal: highlights.

(N) *** Teldec/Warner Dig. 4509 97910-2 [id.] (from complete recording, with Jerusalem, Van Dam, Hölle, Von Kannen, Meier; cond. Barenboim).

(N) **(*) DG Dig. 445 868-2 [id.] (from above set, with Domingo, Norman, Moll; cond. Levine).

(N) (M) ** Ph. Dig. 446 622-2 [id.]. Hofmann, Meier, Estes, Salminen, Sotin, (1985) Bayreuth Festival
    Ch. & O, Levine.

Both the Teldec and DG highlights are generous (77 and 78 minutes respectively) but the choice of
items is different, with the Teldec selection using some 19 minutes for the Preludes to Acts I and III and
concentrating on key interchanges between Siegfried Jerusalem's Parsifal and Waltraude Meier's
Kundry. The synopsis is not keyed directly to the excerpts, as is the better-produced DG booklet. The
DG selection, understandably, centres very much on Domingo's Parsifal, although it also has the key
choral scenes and Jessye Norman's *Ich sah das Kind*.

The (75 minutes) Philips selection from Levine's earlier Bayreuth recording includes the Act I Prelude
only. The singing of Peter Hofmann as Parsifal is flawed, although Waltraud Meier is an outstanding
Kundry. Perhaps surprisingly, the contribution of Hans Sotin as Gurnemanz is strongly featured when
he is vocally less reliable than usual. In any case, these highlights are hardly enticing when the meagre
back-up documentation fails to relate the excerpts to a plot synopsis.

Das Rheingold (complete).
*** Decca 414 101-2 (3). London, Flagstad, Svanholm, Neidlinger, VPO, Solti.
*** Teldec/Warner Dig. 4509 91185-2 (2) [id.]. Tomlinson, Brinkmann, Schreibmayer, Clark, Finnie,
    Johansson, Svendén, Von Kannen, Pampuch, Hölle, Kang, Liedland, Küttenbaum, Turner, (1991)
    Bayreuth Festival O, Barenboim.
(M) *** Ph. 434 421-2 (2) [id.]. McIntyre, Schwarz, Zednik, Pampuch, Becht, (1980) Bayreuth Festival O,
    Boulez.
**(*) DG 415 141-2 (3) [id.]. Fischer-Dieskau, Veasey, Stolze, Kelemen, BPO, Karajan.
**(*) Ph. 412 475-2 (2) [id.]. Adam, Nienstedt, Windgassen, Neidlinger, Talvela, Böhme, Silja,
    Soukupová, (1967) Bayreuth Festival Ch. & O, Boehm.
(Y/B) ** DG Dig. 445 295-2 (2) [id.]. Morris, Wlaschiha, Ludwig, Häggander, Svendén, Jerusalem,
    Lorenz, Mark Baker, Zednik, Moll, Rootering, Hong, Kesling, Parsons, Met. Op. O, James Levine.
(N) *(*) Decca Dig. 443 690-2 (2) [id.]. Hale, Schwarz, Gustafson, Schulte, Sunnegardh, Begley,
    Schreier, Zaremba, Kapellmann, Cleveland O, Dohnányi.

The first of Solti's cycle, recorded in 1958, *Rheingold* remains in terms of engineering the most spectacular on CD. The immediacy and precise placing are thrilling, while the sound-effects of the final scenes,
including Donner's hammer-blow and the Rainbow bridge, have never been matched since. Solti gives a
magnificent reading of the score, crisp, dramatic and direct. Vocally, the set is held together by the
unforgettable singing of Neidlinger as Alberich. He vocalizes with wonderful precision and makes the
character of the dwarf develop from the comic creature of the opening scene to the demented monster
of the last. Flagstad learned the part of Fricka specially for this recording, and her singing makes one
regret that she never took the role on the stage. George London is sometimes a little rough, but this is a
dramatic portrayal of the young Wotan. Svanholm could be more characterful as Loge, but again it is a
relief to hear the part really sung. An outstanding achievement.

Barenboim's recording of the *Ring* cycle for Teldec, made during the 1991 Bayreuth Festival, may not
outshine the finest of previous versions but is most welcome as easily the most involving of modern
versions. When Barenboim as Wagnerian has at times seemed lethargic, what is particularly surprising is
the dramatic tension of the performance. Even with slow speeds, the sense of flow carries the ear on,
where neither of the two most recent rival recordings, Haitink's for EMI and Levine's for DG, ever
quite lets you forget the atmosphere of the studio. Even with often-thunderous stage noises, the
Barenboim performances magnetize you much more consistently, with the atmosphere of the
Festspielhaus well caught by the engineers. It is very satisfying too to have on disc John Tomlinson's
magnificent performance as Wotan, Graham Clark as an electrifying, dominant Loge and Linda Finnie
a thoughtful, intense Fricka.

Like the Boehm set, also recorded live by Philips at Bayreuth, the Boulez version, taken from the 1980
Festival, comes on only two discs and has the advantage of a more modest medium price. The early
digital sound has plenty of air round it, giving a fine impression of a performance in the Festspielhaus
with all its excitement, though voices are not caught as immediately as on the Boehm set. Sir Donald
McIntyre here gives a memorable and noble performance, far firmer than his rival for Boehm, Theo
Adam. Heinz Zednik is splendid as Loge and Hanna Schwarz is a powerful Fricka, while Siegfried
Jerusalem brings beauty of tone as well as distinction to the small role of Froh. Hermann Becht is a
weighty rather than incisive Alberich, and the only weak link is Martin Egel's unsteady Donner. Though
not as bitingly intense as Boehm, Boulez, with speeds almost as fast, shatters the old idea of him as a
chilly conductor.

Karajan's very reflectiveness has its less welcome side, for the tension rarely varies. One finds such
incidents as Alberich's stealing of the gold or Donner's hammer-blow passing by without one's pulse

quickening as it should. On the credit side, however, the singing cast has hardly any flaw at all, and Fischer-Dieskau's Wotan is a brilliant and memorable creation, virile and expressive. Among the others, Veasey is excellent, though obviously she cannot efface memories of Flagstad; Gerhard Stolze with his flickering, almost *Sprechstimme* as Loge gives an intensely vivid if, for some, controversial interpretation. The 1968 sound has been clarified in the digital transfer, but generally the lack of bass brings some thinness.

Boehm's preference for fast speeds here brings the benefit that the whole of the *Vorabend* is contained on two CDs. The pity is that the performance is marred by the casting of Theo Adam as Wotan, keenly intelligent but rarely agreeable on the ear, at times here far too wobbly. On the other hand, Gustav Neidlinger as Alberich is superb, even more involving here than he is for Solti, with the curse made spine-chilling. It is also good to have Wolfgang Windgassen as Loge; among the others, Anja Silja makes an attractively urgent Freia.

Originally issued on three CDs, Levine's version has sensibly been re-transferred on to two, making it more competitive with other latterday versions. The casting is strong, based on the live production at the Met. in New York, but, with little sense of presence in the recording, the voices lose some of their bloom. James Morris here sounds rougher than for Haitink on his EMI set, but Ekkehard Wlaschiha is a magnificent Alberich, with Heinz Zednik a well-focused Mime, Siegfried Jerusalem a powerful if undercharacterized Loge and Christa Ludwig a characterful Fricka. Yet neither in sound nor in pacing does the performance capture the sense of a live occasion very vividly, and this set will appeal mainly to those who have had experience of the opera-house performances.

Some 35 years after Sir Georg Solti made his pioneering recording of *Rheingold* and subsequently a complete *Ring* cycle for Decca, the same company sought to follow up that success with another cycle. The ingredients may be promising but, disappointingly, Dohnányi's version of *Rheingold*, very vividly recorded, lacks the dramatic fire which made its predecessor so compelling. This feels like a comfortable, well-played concert performance in which the climactic moments fail to convey the tension of a stage event, and Robert Hale's bland, undercharacterized performance as Wotan, not to mention Franz-Josef Kapellmann's mild Alberich, intensifies that impression. Without a believable central figure and with the conductor concentrating on beauty of sound, the others can do little to bring the performance to life, though Hanna Schwarz as Fricka gets nearest and Kim Begley sings impressively as Loge. Compare the new Dohnányi with the old Solti in the moment, towards the end of the piece, when Donner wields his hammer, and even the glory of very full-ranging, modern, digital sound seems to fade.

Das Rheingold: highlights.
(N) (M) (***) Teldec/Warner Dig. 0630 13820-9 [id.] (from above set, with Tomlinson, Finnie; cond. Barenboim).
(N) (M) *(**) Ph. 446 613-2 [id.] (from above set, with McIntyre, Schwarz; cond. Boulez).

It is difficult to recommend a set of highlights which contains barely 51 minutes of music, with John Tomlinson's magnificent Wotan not as well represented as he might be; although the Barenboim Teldec recording is highly recommendable, collectors would do better to go for the complete set.

The Philips collection is much more generous (78 minutes) and, with Sir Donald McIntyre another superb Wotan splendidly partnered by Hanna Schwarz's powerful Fricka and Heinz Zednik's Loge, this would be much more recommendable had Philips troubled to provide adequate documentation and a proper synopsis.

The Rheingold (complete, in English).
(M) **(*) EMI CMS7 64110-2 (3). Bailey, Hammond-Stroud, Pring, Belcourt, Attfield, Collins, McDonnall, Lloyd, Grant, English Nat. Op. O, Goodall.

Goodall's slow tempi in *Rheingold* bring an opening section where the temperature is low, reflecting hardly at all the tensions of a live performance, even though this was taken from a series of Coliseum presentations. Nevertheless the momentum of Wagner gradually builds up so that, by the final scenes, both the overall teamwork and the individual contributions of such singers as Norman Bailey, Derek Hammond-Stroud and Clifford Grant come together impressively. Hammond-Stroud's powerful representation of Alberich culminates in a superb account of the curse. The spectacular orchestral effects (with the horns sounding glorious) are vividly caught by the engineers and impressively transferred to CD, even if balances (inevitably) are sometimes less than ideal.

Rienzi (complete).
(M) ** EMI CMS7 63980-2 (3) [Ang. CDMB 63980]. Kollo, Wennberg, Martin, Adam, Hillebrand, Vogel, Schreier, Leipzig R. Ch., Dresden State Op. Ch., Dresden State O, Hollreiser.

It is sad that the flaws in this ambitious opera prevent the unwieldy piece from having its full dramatic impact. This recording is not quite complete, but the cuts are unimportant and most of the set numbers make plain the youthful, uncritical exuberance of the ambitious composer. Except in the recitative, Heinrich Hollreiser's direction is strong and purposeful, but much of the singing is disappointing. René Kollo at least sounds heroic, but the two women principals are poor. Janis Martin in the breeches role of Adriano produces tone that does not record very sweetly, while Siv Wennberg as the heroine, Rienzi's sister, slides most unpleasantly between notes in the florid passages. Despite good recording, this can only be regarded as a stop-gap.

Der Ring des Nibelungen (complete).

✧ (M) *** Decca 414 100-2 (15) [id.]. Nilsson, Windgassen, Flagstad, Fischer-Dieskau, Hotter, London, Ludwig, Neidlinger, Frick, Svanholm, Stoltze, Böhme, Hoffgen, Sutherland, Crespin, King, Watson, Ch. & VPO, Solti.

(Y/B) (B) *** Ph. 446 057-2 (14) [id.]. Nilsson, Windgassen, Neidlinger, Adam, Rysanek, King, Nienstedt, Esser, Talvela, Böhme, Silja, Dernesch, Stewart, Hoeffgen, (1967) Bayreuth Festival Ch. & O, Boehm.

(M) *** DG 435 211-2 (15) [id.]. Veasey, Fischer-Dieskau, Stolze, Kelemen, Dernesch, Dominguez, Jess Thomas, Stewart, Crespin, Janowitz, Vickers, Talvela, Brilioth, Ludwig, Ridderbusch, BPO, Karajan.

(M) (***) EMI mono CZS7 67123-2 (13) [Ang. CDZM 67123]. Suthaus, Mödl, Frantz, Patzak, Neidlinger, Windgassen, Konetzni, Streich, Jurinac, Frick, RAI Ch. & Rome SO, Furtwängler.

(Y/B) (M) ** DG Dig. 445 354-2 (14) [id.]. Behrens, Goldberg, Morris, Norman, Ludwig, Moll, Met. Op. O, Levine.

Solti's was the first recorded *Ring* cycle to be issued. Whether in performance or in vividness of sound, Solti's remains the most electrifying account of the tetralogy on disc, sharply focused if not always as warmly expressive as some. Solti himself developed in the process of making the recording, and *Götterdämmerung* represents a peak of achievement for him, commanding and magnificent. Though CD occasionally reveals bumps and bangs inaudible on the original LPs, this is a historic set that remains as central today as when it first appeared.

Anyone who prefers the idea of a live recording of the *Ring* cycle can be warmly recommended to Boehm's fine set, more immediately involving than any. Recorded at the 1967 Bayreuth Festival, it captures the unique atmosphere and acoustic of the Festspielhaus very vividly. Birgit Nilsson as Brünnhilde and Wolfgang Windgassen as Siegfried are both a degree more volatile and passionate than they were in the Solti cycle. Gustav Neidlinger as Alberich is also superb, as he was too in the Solti set; and the only major reservation concerns the Wotan of Theo Adam, in a performance searchingly intense and finely detailed but often unsteady of tone even at that period. The sound, only occasionally constricted, has been vividly transferred. Philips are currently offering this version of the *Ring* in a 14-disc limited edition (which means in effect for a limited time) at bargain price. Waverers should snap this up while it is still around and before it returns to mid-price under its earlier catalogue number (420 325-2).

Karajan's recording of *The Ring* followed close on the heels of Solti's for Decca, providing a good alternative studio version which equally stands the test of time. The manner is smoother, the speeds generally broader, yet the tension and concentration of the performances are maintained more consistently than in most modern studio recordings. Casting is not quite consistent between the operas, with Régine Crespin as Brünnhilde in *Walküre*, but Helga Dernesch at her very peak in the last two operas. The casting of Siegfried is changed between *Siegfried* and *Götterdämmerung*, from Jess Thomas to Helge Brilioth, just as strong but sweeter of tone. The original CD transfers are used without change for this mid-price compilation.

When in 1972 EMI first transferred the Italian Radio tapes of Furtwängler's studio performances of 1953, the sound was disagreeably harsh, making sustained listening unpleasant. In this digital transfer, the boxiness of the studio sound and the closeness of the voices still take away some of the unique Furtwängler glow in Wagner, but the sound is acceptable and actually benefits in some ways from extra clarity. Furtwängler gives each opera a commanding sense of unity, musically and dramatically, with hand-picked casts including Martha Mödl as a formidable Brünnhilde, Ferdinand Frantz a firm-voiced Wotan and Ludwig Suthaus (Tristan in Furtwängler's recording) a reliable Siegfried. In smaller roles you have stars like Wolfgang Windgassen, Julius Patzak, Rita Streich, Sena Jurinac and Gottlob Frick.

DG have sensibly repackaged Levine's New York *Ring* cycle on 14 discs at a special mid-price, and some listeners will welcome so strongly cast a recording in up-front studio sound, even though aggressively digital and not always kind to voices. The glory of the cycle is the conclusion, Levine's powerful reading of *Götterdämmerung*, with the sound rather fuller than in the earlier operas. Yet overall this is a set with too many flaws and disappointments, best recommended to those who have enjoyed Levine's spacious reading at the Met. or relayed on television.

'The best of The Ring': excerpts from *Das Rheingold; Die Walküre; Siegfried; Götterdämmerung.*
(N) (B) *** Ph. Duo 454 020-2 (2) (from (1967) Bayreuth Festival recordings; cond. Karl Boehm).

Although the Solti and Kajan single-disc selections have their own appeal – and, of course, there are more extended highlights available from each opera – as potted 'Rings' go, this is probably the best buy. The only snag is that Bernard Jacobson's very brief synopsis of the narrative fails to relate each track to the story. However, since not too much happens in each of the four operas, and what does isn't too complicated, this Philips Duo set, taken from Boehm's outstanding complete recording, can certainly be enjoyed as a summary of Wagner's intentions, and virtually all the key scenes are included.

The Ring 'Great scenes': *Das Rheingold: Entry of the Gods into Valhalla. Die Walküre: Ride of the Valkyries; Magic fire music. Siegfried: Forging scene; Forest murmurs. Götterdämmerung: Siegfried's funeral march; Brünnhilde's immolation scene.*
(M) *** Decca 421 313-2. Nilsson, Windgassen, Hotter, Stolzel, VPO, Solti.

These excerpts are often quite extended – the *Entry of the Gods into Valhalla* offers some 10 minutes of music, and the *Forest murmurs* from *Siegfried* starts well before the orchestral interlude. Only *Siegfried's funeral march* is in any sense a 'bleeding chunk' which has to be faded at the end; and the disc closes with 20 minutes of Brünnhilde's Immolation scene.

The Ring: highlights: *Das Rheingold: Lugt, Schwestern! Die Wenken lacht in den Grund; Zur Burg führt die Brücke. Die Walküre: Der Männer Sippe sass hier im Saal; Ride of the Valkyries; Wotan's farewell and Magic fire music. Siegfried: Forest murmurs; Aber, wie sah meine Mutter wohl aus?; Nun sing! Ich lausche dem Gesang; Heil dir, Sonne! Heil dir, Licht!. Götterdämmerung: Funeral music; Fliegt heim, ihr Raben!.*
(B) *** DG 439 423-2 [id.] (from above complete recording; cond. Karajan).

The task of selecting highlights to fit on a single disc, taken from the whole of the *Ring* cycle, is daunting. But the DG producer of this Classikon super-bargain issue has extended the previous selection to 77 minutes and managed to assemble many key items, either very well tailored or ending satisfactorily. The whole of Wotan's great *Farewell* scene with the *Magic Fire music* is included, and much else besides. Moreover the *Funeral music* from *Götterdämmerung* (where the previous CD ended) is now followed by *Brünnhilde's Immolation* and continues to the end of the opera. The transfers are extremely brilliant (the *Ride of the Valkyries* is given an edge of excitement) and this makes a magnificent bargain reissue. It seems carping to complain that the notes do not find space to detail what happens in each excerpt. But sonically this should surely tempt any novice in this repertoire to want to go on and explore Wagner's masterly cycle still further.

Siegfried (complete).
*** Decca 414 110-2 (4). Windgassen, Nilsson, Hotter, Stolze, Neidlinger, Böhme, Hoffgen, Sutherland, VPO, Solti.
(Y/B) *** Teldec/Warner Dig. 4509 94193-2 (4) [id.]. Jerusalem, Anne Evans, Tomlinson, Clark, Von Kannen, Philip King, Svendén, Leidland, (1992) Bayreuth Festival Ch. & O, Barenboim.
*** Ph. 412 483-2 (4) [id.]. Windgassen, Nilsson, Adam, Neidlinger, Soukupová, Köth, Böhme, (1967) Bayreuth Festival Ch. & O, Boehm.
(M) *** Ph. Dig. 434 423-2 (3). Jung, G. Jones, McIntyre, Zednik, Becht, Wenkel, Hübner, Sharp, (1980) Bayreuth Festival O, Boulez.
** DG 415 150-2 (4) [id.]. Dernesch, Dominguez, Jess Thomas, Stolze, Stewart, Kelemen, BPO, Karajan.
** DG Dig. 429 407-2 (4) [id.]. Goldberg, Behrens, Morris, Zednik, Wlaschiha, Moll, Battle, N Y Met. O, Levine.

Siegfried has too long been thought of as the grimmest of the *Ring* cycle, but a performance as buoyant as Solti's reveals that, more than in most Wagner, the message is one of optimism. Each of the three Acts ends with a scene of triumphant optimism. Solti's array of singers could hardly be bettered. Windgassen is at the very peak of his form, lyrical as well as heroic. Hotter has never been more impressive on record, his Wotan at last captured adequately. Stolze, Neidlinger and Böhme are all exemplary, and predictably Joan Sutherland makes the most seductive of woodbirds. With singing finer than any opera house could normally provide, with masterly playing from the Vienna Philharmonic and with Decca's most vivid recording, this is a set likely to stand comparison with anything the rest of the century may provide.

Barenboim's live recording of *Siegfried*, made at the Bayreuth Festival in 1992, is the finest of latterday digitally recorded versions. There is no finer interpreter of the role of Mime today than Graham Clark.

On disc the characterization may sometimes sound extreme, but here is a powerful, clean-cut tenor voice that makes the dwarf into an intensely compelling character. In the title-role Siegfried Jerusalem completely outshines his already fine performance on Haitink's studio recording for EMI. His voice has grown fuller and more powerful without losing any beauty, and the recording helps to give it more weight. Few Siegfrieds since Wolfgang Windgassen begin to match him, and John Tomlinson is the firmest, most darkly projected Wanderer among current rivals. You may argue that the older Wotan should not sound so virile, but Tomlinson's superb singing goes with keen musical imagination and concern for word-meaning. As for Anne Evans as Brünnhilde, she too brings out the beauty of Wagner's lines, focusing cleanly and purely, with some thrilling top notes and not a suspicion of a wobble. The fifth principal is the splendid Erda of Brigitta Svendén, with other roles cast well, if not outstandingly. But what confirms this, recorded last in the series, as the high point in Barenboim's Bayreuth cycle is the incandescence of his conducting, given extra impact by the vivid sound and consistently reflecting his experience of working with these musicians.

The natural-sounding quality of Boehm's live recording from Bayreuth, coupled with his determination not to let the music lag, makes his account of *Siegfried* as satisfying as the rest of his cycle, vividly capturing the atmosphere of the Festspielhaus, with voices well ahead of the orchestra. Windgassen is at his peak here, if anything more poetic in Acts II and III than he is in Solti's studio recording, and vocally just as fine. Nilsson, as in *Götterdämmerung*, gains over her studio recording from the extra flow of adrenalin in a live performance; and Gustav Neidlinger is unmatchable as Alberich. Erika Köth is disappointing as the woodbird, not sweet enough, and Soukupová is a positive, characterful Erda. Theo Adam is at his finest as the Wanderer, less wobbly than usual, clean and incisive.

Like the first two music-dramas in his Bayreuth *Ring* cycle, Boulez's version takes a disc less than usual and comes at mid-price in the Philips Bayreuth series. Here the advantage is even greater when each Act is complete on a single disc. It was recorded in 1980. If anything, Boulez is even more warmly expressive than in *Rheingold* or *Walküre*, directing a most poetic account of the *Forest murmurs* episode and leading in each Act to thrillingly intense conclusions. Manfred Jung is an underrated Siegfried, forthright and, by latterday standards, unusually clean-focused, and Heinz Zednik is a characterful Mime. As in the rest of the cycle, Sir Donald McIntyre is a noble Wotan, though Hermann Becht's weighty Alberich is not as strongly contrasted as it might be. Norma Sharp as the Woodbird enunciates her words with exceptional clarity and, though Gwyneth Jones as Brünnhilde has a few squally moments, she sings with honeyed beauty when the Idyll theme emerges, towards the end of the love duet. The digital sound is full and atmospheric, though it is a pity that the brass is not caught as weightily as it might be.

When Siegfried is outsung by Mime, it is time to complain, and though the DG set has many fine qualities – not least the Brünnhilde of Helga Dernesch – it hardly rivals the Solti or Boehm versions. Windgassen on Decca gave a classic performance, and any comparison highlights the serious shortcomings of Jess Thomas. Even when voices are balanced forward, the digital transfer helps little to make Thomas's singing as Siegfried any more acceptable. Otherwise, the vocal cast is strong, and Karajan provides the seamless playing which characterizes his cycle. Recommended only to those irrevocably committed to the Karajan cycle.

Levine is markedly less successful than any of his competitors in conveying the feeling of a live, dramatic performance. Behrens sings steadily but is over-stressed as Brünnhilde, and Reiner Goldberg's Siegfried is seriously flawed. James Morris is impressive as the Wanderer.

Siegfried: highlights.
(N) (M) (***) Teldec/Warner Dig. 0630 13822-9 [id.] (from above set, with Jerusalem, Clark, Tomlinson; cond. Barenboim).
(N) (M) *(**) Ph. Dig. 446 615-2 [id.] (from above set, with Jung, Zednik, Gwyneth Jones; cond. Boulez).

The Teldec selection from *Siegfried* (46 minutes 30 seconds) is even less generous than the companion highlights CD from *Das Rheingold*, but it does at least include the Act I dialogue between John Tomlinson's memorable Wanderer and Graham Clark's unforgettable portrayal of Mime. Sir Donald McIntyre's noble contribution is omitted altogether from the Philips selection, which concentrates on the Mime/Siegfried duologues in Act I, then on Siegfried entirely in Act II (apart from the Woodbird), and on the Siegfried/Brünnhilde interchanges in Act III. As usual in this Philips series, the snag is that neither a translation nor a cued synopsis is provided, only a list of excerpts and participants.

Siegfried (complete, in English).
(M) *** EMI CMS7 63595-2 (4). Remedios, Hunter, Bailey, Dempsey, Hammond-Stroud, Grant, Collins, London, Sadler's Wells Op. O, Goodall.

More tellingly than in almost any other Wagner opera recording, Goodall's spacious direction here conveys the genuine dramatic crunch that gives the experience of hearing Wagner in the opera house its unique power, its overwhelming force; this is unmistakably a great interpretation caught on the wing. Remedios, more than any rival on record, conveys not only heroic strength but clear-ringing youthfulness, caressing the ear as well as exciting it. Norman Bailey makes a magnificently noble Wanderer, steady of tone, and Gregory Dempsey is a characterful Mime, even if his deliberate whining tone is not well caught on record. The sound is superbly realistic, even making no allowances for the conditions. Lovers of opera in English should grasp the opportunity of hearing this unique set.

Tannhäuser (Paris version; complete).
*** DG. Dig. 427 625-2 (3) [id.]. Domingo, Studer, Baltsa, Salminen, Schmidt, Ch. & Philh. O, Sinopoli.
*** Decca 414 581-2 (3) [id.]. Kollo, Dernesch, Ludwig, Sotin, Braun, Hollweg, V. State Op. Ch., VPO, Solti.

Plácido Domingo here makes another Wagnerian sortie, bringing balm to ears wounded by the general run of German heroic tenors, producing sounds of much power as well as beauty. Giuseppe Sinopoli here makes his most passionately committed opera recording yet, warmer and more flexible than Solti's Decca version, always individual, with fine detail brought out, always persuasively, and never wilful. Agnes Baltsa is not ideally opulent of tone as Venus, but she is the complete seductress. Cheryl Studer – who sang the role of Elisabeth for Sinopoli at Bayreuth – gives a most sensitive performance, not always ideally even of tone but creating a movingly intense portrait of the heroine, vulnerable and very feminine. Matti Salminen in one of his last recordings makes a superb Landgrave and Andreas Schmidt a noble Wolfram, even though the legato could be smoother in *O star of Eve*.

Solti gives one of his very finest Wagner performances to date, helped by superb playing from the Vienna Philharmonic and an outstanding cast, superlatively recorded. Dernesch as Elisabeth and Ludwig as Venus outshine all rivals; and Kollo, though not ideal, makes as fine a Heldentenor as we are currently likely to hear. The compact disc transfer reinforces the brilliance and richness of the performance. The sound is outstanding for its period (1971), and Ray Minshull's production adds to the atmospheric quality.

Tannhäuser (Dresden version; complete).
**(*) Ph. 420 122-2 (3) [id.]. Windgassen, Waechter, Silja, Stolze, Bumbry, (1962) Bayreuth Festival Ch. & O, Sawallisch.

Though CD brings out all the more clearly the thuds, creaks and audience noises of a live performance (most distracting at the very start), the dedication of Sawallisch's version is very persuasive, notably in the Venusberg scene where Grace Bumbry is a superb, sensuous Venus and Windgassen – not quite in his sweetest voice, often balanced rather close – is a fine, heroic Tannhäuser. Anja Silja controls the abrasiveness of her soprano well, to make this her finest performance on record, not ideally sweet but very sympathetic. Voices are set well forward of the orchestra, in which strings have far more bloom than brass; but the atmosphere of the Festspielhaus is vivid and compelling throughout.

Tannhäuser (Dresden version): highlights.
(N) (M) *(**) Ph. 446 620-2 [id.] (from above set, with Windgassen, Silja; cond. Sawallisch).

With a generally good cast, and with Bumbry's sensuous Venus getting the opera off to an impressive start, many collectors will be glad to have these extensive (78 minutes) excerpts from Sawallisch's dedicated performance of the Dresden version of *Tannhäuser*; once again, the considerable drawback is the lack of a cued synopsis.

Tristan und Isolde (complete).
(Y/B) (M) *** EMI CMS7 69319-2 (4) [Ang. CDMD 69319]. Vickers, Dernesch, Ludwig, Berry, Ridderbusch, German Op. Ch., Berlin, BPO, Karajan.
(Y/B) *** Teldec/Warner Dig. 4509 94568-2 (4) [id.]. Meier, Jerusalem, Lipovšek, Salminen, Struckmann, Berlin State Op. Ch., BPO, Barenboim.
*** Ph. 434 425-2 (3) [id.]. Windgassen, Nilsson, Ludwig, Talvela, Waechter, (1966) Bayreuth Festival Ch. & O, Boehm.
(M) *** Decca 430 234-2 (4) [id.]. Uhl, Nilsson, Resnik, Van Mill, Krause, VPO, Solti.
(***) EMI mono CDS7 47322-8 (4) [Ang. CDC47321]. Suthaus, Flagstad, Thebom, Greindl, Fischer-Dieskau, ROHCG Ch., Philh. O, Furtwängler.
(Y/B) (M) *** Decca 443 682-2 (4) [id.]. Mitchinson, Gray, Howell, Joll, Wilkens, Folwell, Welsh Nat. Op. Ch. & O, Goodall.

Karajan's is a sensual performance of Wagner's masterpiece, caressingly beautiful and with superbly refined playing from the Berlin Philharmonic. Dernesch as Isolde is seductively feminine, not as noble as

Flagstad, not as tough and unflinching as Nilsson; but the human quality makes this account if anything more moving still, helped by glorious tone-colour through every range. Jon Vickers matches her in what is arguably his finest performance on record, allowing himself true pianissimo shading. The rest of the cast is excellent too. The recording has been remastered again for the present reissue and the 1972 sound has plenty of body, making this an excellent first choice, with inspired conducting and the most satisfactory cast of all. The set has also been attractively repackaged with cleanly printed documentation.

Daniel Barenboim follows up his live recording of the *Ring* cycle, made at Bayreuth, with this glowing account of *Tristan*, recorded in opulent sound under studio conditions in the Philharmonie. As a Furtwängler devotee, Barenboim has learnt much from that master's classic recording, and Act I is comparably spacious. After that the urgency of the drama prompts speeds that move forward more readily than Furtwängler's. The cast is an exceptionally strong one, with Waltraud Meier as Isolde graduating from mezzo soprano to full soprano, breasting the top Cs easily, showing no sign of strain, and bringing a weight and intensity to the role that reflect her earlier experience. The vibrato sometimes grows obtrusive, and even in the final *Liebestod* there is a touch of rawness under pressure; but the feeling for line is masterly, always with words vividly expressed. Siegfried Jerusalem, with a more beautiful voice than most latterday Heldentenoren, makes a predictably fine Tristan, not quite as smooth of tone as he once was and conveying the poignancy of the hero's plight in Act III rather than his suffering. Marjana Lipovšek is among the most characterful of Brangänes, strong and vehement, while Matti Salminen is a resonant, moving King Mark. Only the gritty tones of Falk Struckmann as Kurwenal fall short, a particular blemish in Act III. With weighty, full-ranging and well-balanced sound, this is a first-rate recommendation for a modern digital set.

The benefit is enormous with Boehm's Bayreuth performance in presenting one of the big Wagner operas for the first time on disc without any breaks at all, with each Act uninterrupted. Boehm is on the urgent side in this opera and the orchestral ensemble is not always immaculate; but the performance glows with intensity from beginning to end, carried through in the longest spans. Birgit Nilsson sings the *Liebestod* at the end of the long evening as though she was starting out afresh, radiant and with not a hint of tiredness, rising to an orgasmic climax and bringing a heavenly pianissimo on the final rising octave to F sharp. Opposite Nilsson is Wolfgang Windgassen, the most mellifluous of Heldentenoren; though the microphone balance sometimes puts him at a disadvantage to his Isolde, the realism and sense of presence of the whole set have you bathing in the authentic atmosphere of Bayreuth. Making up an almost unmatchable cast are Christa Ludwig as Brangäne, Eberhard Waechter as Kurwenal and Martii Talvela as King Mark, with the young Peter Schreier as the Young Sailor.

Solti's performance is less flexible and sensuous than Karajan's, but he shows himself ready to relax in Wagner's more expansive periods. On the other hand the end of Act I and the opening of the Love duet have a knife-edged dramatic tension. Nilsson is masterly in her conviction and – it cannot be emphasized too strongly – she never attacks below the note as Flagstad did, so that miraculously, at the end of the Love duet the impossibly difficult top Cs come out and hit the listener crisply and cleanly, dead on the note; and the *Liebestod* is all the more moving for having no soupy swerves at the climax. Fritz Uhl is a really musical Heldentenor. Dramatically he leaves the centre of the stage to Isolde, but his long solo passages in Act III are superb and make that sometimes tedious Act into something genuinely gripping. The Kurwenal of Tom Krause and the King Mark of Arnold van Mill are both excellent and it is only Regina Resnik as Brangäne who gives any disappointment. The production has the usual Decca/ Culshaw imaginative touch, and the recording matches brilliance and clarity with satisfying co-ordination and richness.

Wilhelm Furtwängler's concept is spacious from the opening *Prelude* onwards, but equally the bite and colour of the drama are vividly conveyed, matching the nobility of Flagstad's portrait of Isolde. The richly commanding power of her singing and her always distinctive timbre make it a uniquely compelling performance. Suthaus is not of the same calibre as Heldentenor, but he avoids ugliness and strain, which is rare in Tristan. Among the others, the only remarkable performance comes from the young Fischer-Dieskau as Kurwenal, not ideally cast but keenly imaginative. One endearing oddity is that – on Flagstad's insistence – the top Cs at the opening of the Love duet were sung by Elisabeth Schwarzkopf. The Kingsway Hall recording was admirably balanced, catching the beauty of the Philharmonia Orchestra at its peak. The CDs have opened up the original mono sound and it is remarkable how little constriction there is in the biggest climaxes, mostly shown in the *fortissimo* violins above the stave.

Based on the much-praised production of the Welsh National Opera company, Goodall's recording of *Tristan* was made in 1980/81, not on stage but at Brangwyn Hall, Swansea, just when the cast was steamed up for stage performances. Typically from Goodall, it is measured and steady, but the speeds are not all exceptionally slow and, with rhythms sharply defined and textures made transparent, he keeps the momentum going. The WNO orchestra is not sumptuous, but the playing is well-tuned and responsive. Neither Linda Esther Gray nor John Mitchinson is as sweet on the ear as the finest rivals, for the microphone exaggerates vibrato in both. But Mitchinson never barks, Heldentenor-style, and Gray provides a formidable combination of qualities: feminine vulnerability alongside commanding power. Gwynne Howell is arguably the finest King Mark on record, making his monologue at the end of Act II, so often an anti-climax, into one of the noblest passages of all. This may not have the smoothness of the best international sets but, with its vivid digital sound, it is certainly compelling, and a libretto in three languages is an additional bonus.

Tristan und Isolde (slightly abridged).
(M) (***) EMI mono CHS7 64037-2 (3) [Ang. CDHC 64037]. Melchior, Flagstad, Herbert Janssen, Margarete Klose/Sabine Kalter, Sven Nilsson/Emanuel List, ROHCG Ch., LPO, Beecham/Reiner.

In both recordings used here, Melchior and Flagstad take the title-roles, with Herbert Janssen as Kurwenal, three legendary singers in those roles, but the parts of King Mark and Brangäne were sung by different singers – and, above all, Fritz Reiner was the conductor in the 1936 recordings. It is astonishing to find that the warmly expansive account of Act I is the work of Reiner, while it is Beecham who is responsible for the urgent view of Act II with its great love duet – part of it cut following the manner of the day. Act III is divided between Beecham in the first part, Reiner in the second. Whatever the inconsistencies, the result is a thrilling experience, with Flagstad fresher and even more incisive than in her studio recording with Furtwängler of 15 years later, and with Melchior a passionate vocal actor, not just the possessor of the most freely ringing of all Heldentenor voices.

Tristan und Isolde: highlights.
(N) (M) *** Ph. 446 617-2 [id.] (from above (1966) Bayreuth Festival recording, with Windgassen, Nilsson, Talvela; cond. Boehm).

Tristan with its seamless flow is less suitable than most of Wagner's operas for selecting excerpts from an ongoing performance but, with 77 minutes included, these highlights from the 1966 Boehm Bayreuth set, including the Act I Prelude, are excellent value save for the absence of a proper documented synopsis.

Die Walküre (complete).
*** Ph. 412 478-2 (4) [id.]. King, Rysanek, Nienstedt, Nilsson, Adam, Burmeister, (1967) Bayreuth Festival Ch. & O, Boehm.
*** Decca 414 105-2 (4) [id.]. Nilsson, Crespin, Ludwig, King, Hotter, Frick, VPO, Solti.
*** Teldec/Warner Dig. 4509 91186-2 (4) [id.]. Elming, Hölle, Tomlinson, Secunde, A. Evans, Finnie, Johansson, Floeren, Close, (1992) Bayreuth Festival O, Barenboim.
(M) (***) EMI mono CHS7 63045-2 (3) [Ang. CHS 63045]. Mödl, Rysanek, Frantz, Suthaus, Klose, Frick, VPO, Furtwängler.
**(*) EMI Dig. CDS7 49534-2 (4) [Ang. CDCD 49534]. Marton, Studer, Morris, Goldberg, Salminen, Meier, Bav. RSO, Haitink.
(M) **(*) Ph. 434 422-2 (3) [id.]. Hofmann, Altmeyer, G. Jones, McIntyre, Schwarz, Salminen, (1980) Bayreuth Festival O, Boulez.
**(*) DG 415 145-2 (4) [id.]. Crespin, Janowitz, Veasey, Vickers, Stewart, Talvela, BPO, Karajan.

Rarely if ever does Boehm's preference for fast speeds undermine the music; on the contrary, it adds to the involvement of the performance, which never loses its concentration. Theo Adam is in firmer voice here as Wotan than he is in *Rheingold*, hardly sweet of tone but always singing with keen intelligence. As ever, Nilsson is in superb voice as Brünnhilde. Though the inevitable noises of a live performance occasionally intrude, this presents a more involving experience than any rival complete recording. The CD transfer transforms what on LP seemed a rough recording, even if passages of heavy orchestration still bring some constriction of sound.

Solti sees Act II as the kernel of the work, perhaps even of the whole cycle, with the conflict of wills between Wotan and Fricka making for one of Wagner's most deeply searching scenes. That is the more apparent when the greatest of latterday Wotans, Hans Hotter, takes the role, and Christa Ludwig sings with searing dramatic sense as his wife. Before that, Act I seems a little underplayed. This is partly because of Solti's deliberate lyricism – apt enough when love and spring greetings are in the air – but also (on the debit side) because James King fails both to project the character of Siegmund and to delve into the word-meanings as all the other members of the cast consistently do. Crespin has never sung more beautifully on record, but even that cannot cancel out the shortcoming. As for Nilsson's Brünnhilde, it has grown mellower, the emotions are clearer, and under-the-note attack is almost eliminated.

Barenboim's reading of *Die Walküre* is by a fair margin the most involving of modern versions, with orchestra and soloists after four years of the same production totally in sympathy. Barenboim's control of dramatic tension is masterly. Even with characteristically slow speeds, the results are magnetic. Consistently there is a natural sense of flow so that, despite intrusive stage noises, Barenboim compels attention from first to last. It could not be more welcome to have on disc John Tomlinson's magnificent performance as Wotan, even more demanding in *Walküre* than in *Rheingold*. The other British singer who stands out in this opera is Anne Evans, at last showing her paces on disc as a radiant Brünnhilde. Maybe she is not as powerful as such rival loud ladies, Eva Marton and Hildegard Behrens, but she is far truer and clearer in focusing notes, singing with more expressive variety. With Barenboim conveying the full emotional thrust, the final duet between Brünnhilde and Wotan has rarely been so moving on disc. Also outstanding is the Danish tenor, Poul Elming, as Siegmund. Again the Bayreuth atmosphere is very well caught.

Furtwängler, an excellent cast and the Vienna Philharmonic in radiant form match any of their successors. Ludwig Suthaus proves a satisfyingly clear-toned Heldentenor, never strained, with the lyricism of *Wintersturme* superbly sustained. Neither Léonie Rysanek as Sieglinde nor Martha Mödl as Brünnhilde is ideally steady, but the intensity and involvement of each is irresistible, classic performances both. Similarly, the mezzo of Margarete Klose may not be very beautiful, but the projection of words and the fire-eating character match the conductor's intensity. Gottlob Frick is as near an ideal Hunding as one will find, sinister but with the right streak of arrogant sexuality; while the Wotan of Ferdinand Frantz may not be as deeply perceptive as some, but to hear the sweep of Wagner's melodic lines so gloriously sung is a rare joy. The 1954 sound is amazingly full and vivid, with voices cleanly balanced against the inspired orchestra. The only snag of the set is that, to fit the whole piece on to only three CDs, breaks between discs come in mid-Act.

Haitink's is a broad view, strong and thoughtful yet conveying monumental power. That goes with searching concentration and a consistent feeling for the detailed beauty of Wagner's writing, glowingly brought out in the warm and spacious recording, made in the Herkulessaal in Munich. The outstanding contribution comes from Cheryl Studer as Sieglinde, very convincingly cast, giving a tenderly affecting performance to bring out the character's vulnerability in a very human way. At *Du bist der Lenz* her radiant singing brings an eagerly personal revelation, the response of a lover. Despite some strained moments, Rainer Goldberg makes a heroic Siegmund, far finer than most today; and Eva Marton is a noble, powerful Brünnhilde, less uneven of production than she has often been on record. Waltraud Meier makes a convincingly waspish and biting Fricka and Matti Salminen a resonant Hunding. James Morris is a fine, perceptive Wotan, and the voice, not an easy one to record, is well focused here.

The major advantage of the Boulez Bayreuth version of 1980 is that it comes at mid-price on only three discs, with atmospheric digital sound and a strong, if flawed, cast. Jeannine Altmeyer is a generally reliable Sieglinde, but Peter Hofmann's tenor had already grown rather gritty for Siegmund and in Act I is not as mellifluous as he should be. Donald McIntyre makes a commanding Wotan, Hanna Schwarz a firm, biting Fricka and Gwyneth Jones is at her least abrasive, producing beautiful, gentle tone in lyrical passages. Boulez's fervour will surprise many, even if he does not match Boehm's passionate urgency in this second instalment of the tetralogy.

The great merits of Karajan's version are the refinement of the orchestral playing and the heroic strength of Jon Vickers as Siegmund. With that underlined, one cannot help but note that the vocal shortcomings here are generally more marked, and the total result does not add up to quite so compelling a dramatic experience: one is less involved. Thomas Stewart may have a younger, firmer voice than Hotter, but the character of Wotan emerges only partially; it is not just that he misses some of the word-meaning, but that on occasion – as in the kissing away of Brünnhilde's godhead – he underlines too crudely. Josephine Veasey as Fricka conveys the biting intensity of the part. Gundula Janowitz's Sieglinde has its beautiful moments, but the singing is ultimately a little static. Crespin's Brünnhilde is impressive, but nothing like as satisfying as her study of Sieglinde on the Decca set. The DG recording is good, but not quite in the same class as the Decca and the bass is relatively light.

Die Walküre: Act I (complete).
(Y/B) (M) *** Ph. 442 640-2 [id.]. Leonie Rysanek, James King, Gerd Nienstedt, (1967) Bayreuth Festival O, Boehm.
(M) (***) EMI mono CDH7 61020-2 [id.]. Lehmann, Melchior, List, VPO, Bruno Walter.

It seems not unusual to have Act I of *Die Walküre* offered alone on disc, and indeed the sequence of events between Siegmund, Sieglinde and Hunding make a miniature opera in their own right, so collectors who have the Solti *Ring* will welcome this well-transferred CD as a sampler of a highly involving performance from 1967.

One is consistently gripped by the continuity and sustained lines of Walter's reading, and by the intensity and beauty of the playing of the Vienna Philharmonic. Lotte Lehmann's portrait of Sieglinde, arguably her finest role, has a depth and beauty never surpassed since, and Lauritz Melchior's heroic Siegmund brings singing of a scale and variety – not to mention beauty – that no Heldentenor today begins to match. Emanuel List as Hunding is satisfactory enough, but his achievement at least has latterly been surpassed.

Die Walküre: Act III (complete).
(N) (M) *** Decca 448 575-2 [id.]. Flagstad, Edelmann, Schech, VPO, Solti.
(N) (M) (***) EMI mono CDH7 64704-2 [id.]. Varnay, Rysanek, Bjoerling, (1951) Bayreuth Festival O,
   Karajan.

The Solti recording was made in 1957. Flagstad came out of retirement to make it, and Decca put us eternally in their debt for urging her to do so. She sings radiantly. The meticulousness needed in the recording studio obviously brought out all her finest qualities, and there is no more than a touch of hardness on some of the top notes to show that the voice was no longer as young as it had been. Edelmann is not the ideal Wotan, but he has a particularly well-focused voice and when he sings straight, without sliding up or sitting under the note, the result is superb, and he is never wobbly. But it is Solti's conducting that prevents any slight blemishes from mattering. Not surprisingly, the recording too is remarkably vivid, anticipating the excellence of the great *Ring* project which was to follow, and so makes an obvious choice for reissue in Decca's 'Classic Sound' series.

Recorded in 1951, the first season after the war, Karajan's Bayreuth version of Act III shows the still-young conductor working at white heat. Speeds are far faster than in his DG studio recording, and very close to those in his live recording made at the Met. in 1969 (Nuova Era). Ensemble inevitably is not as taut as it was in the studio performance, but the electricity is far keener, and his cast is a characterful one. Astrid Varnay is an abrasive Brünnhilde, presenting the Valkyrie as a forceful figure, even in penitence prepared to stand up against her father. Leonie Rysanek is a warm Sieglinde, powerful rather than pure, with a rather obtrusive vibrato even at that date. Sigurd Bjoerling by contrast, the least-known of the principals, proves a magnificently virile Wotan, steady as a rock in the *Farewell*, but colouring the voice with a near-shout at the command, '*Loge, hier!*' The mono sound is transferred with bright immediacy, with some harshness on top but plenty of weight in the bass. This makes a splendid supplement to Karajan's superb Bayreuth *Meistersinger*, also recorded live in 1951.

Die Walküre: highlights.
(N) (M) *** Teldec/Warner Dig. 0630 13821-9 [id.] (from above set, with Elming, Hölle, Tomlinson;
   cond. Barenboim).
*** EMI Dig. CDC7 54328-2 [id.] (from above set, with Goldberg, Marton, Studer, Morris; cond.
   Haitink).
(N) (M) *** Ph. 446 614-2 [id.] (from above (1980) Bayreuth Festival recording, with Hofmann,
   Altmeyer, G. Jones; cond. Boulez).

With *Die Walküre*, Teldec are back on form in offering a well-planned 75-minutes selection following the opera's narrative line admirably (though, as usual, the synopsis is not cued).

Those who have chosen another complete set will surely want a reminder of Haitink's glowingly spacious EMI set. The selection here is generous (76 minutes), and it includes Cheryl Studer's *Du bist der Lenz* within the 21 minutes from Act I, while the excerpts from Act III include the *Ride of the Valkyries* and end with the *Magic fire music* sequence at the end of the opera. Splendidly rich recording.

As with the others in this otherwise excellent Philips series of Wagnerian highlights, the documentation is totally inadequate, with the excerpts listed baldly and with no synopsis provided to relate each to the narrative. But as this is by no means a first choice among recordings of this opera, many collectors will be interested in such a generous sampler (78 minutes) rather than the complete recording.

The Valkyrie (complete; in English).
(M) *** EMI CMS7 63918-2 (4). Hunter, Remedios, Curphey, Bailey, Grant, Howard, E. Nat. Op. Ch.
   & O, Goodall.

The glory of the ENO performance lies not just in Goodall's spacious direction but in the magnificent Wotan of Norman Bailey, noble in the broadest span but very human in his illumination of detail. Rita Hunter sings nobly too, and though she is not as commanding as Nilsson in the Solti cycle she is often more lyrically tender. Alberto Remedios as Siegmund is more taxed than he was as Siegfried in the later opera (lower tessituras are not quite so comfortable for him) but his sweetly ringing top register is superb. If others, such as Ann Howard as Fricka, are not always treated kindly by the microphone, the total dramatic compulsion is irresistible. The CD transfer increases the sense of presence and at the same time confirms the relative lack of sumptuousness.

VOCAL COLLECTIONS

'*Wagner singing on record*': Excerpts from: (i) *Der fliegende Holländer;* (ii) *Götterdämmerung;* (iii) *Lohengrin;* (iv) *Die Meistersinger von Nürnberg;* (v) *Parsifal;* (vi) *Das Rheingold;* (vii) *Siegfried;* (viii) *Tannhäuser;* (ix) *Tristan und Isolde;* (x) *Die Walküre.*

(M) (***) EMI mono/stereo CMS7 640082 (4) [id.]. (i) Hermann, Nissen, Endrèze, Fuchs, Beckmann, Rethberg, Nilsson, Hotter; (ii) Austral, Widdop, List, Weber, Janssen, Lawrence; (iii) Rethberg, Pertil, Singher, Lawrence, Spani, Lehmann, Lemnitz, Klose, Wittrisch, Rosavaenge; (iv) Schorr, Thill, Martinelli, Bockelmann, Parr, Williams, Ralf, Lemnitz; (v) Leider, Kipnitz, Wolff; (vi) Schorr; (vii) Nissen, Olszewska, Schipper, Leider, Laubenthal, Lubin; (viii) Müller, Lorenz, Janssen, Hüsch, Flagstad; (ix) Leider, Marherr, Larsen-Todsen, Helm, Melchior, Seinemeyer, Lorenz; (x) Lawrence, Journet, Bockelmann.

This collection, compiled in Paris as '*Les Introuvables du Chant Wagnerien*', contains an amazing array of recordings made in the later years of 78-r.p.m. recording, mostly between 1927 and 1940. In 49 items, many of them substantial, the collection consistently demonstrates the reliability of the Wagner singing at that period, the ability of singers in every register to produce firm, well-focused tone of a kind too rare today. Some of the most interesting items are those in translation from French sources, with Germaine Lubin as Isolde and Brünnhilde and with Marcel Journet as Wotan, both lyrical and clean-cut. The ill-starred Marjorie Lawrence, a great favourite in France, is also represented by recordings in French, including Brünnhilde's Immolation scene from *Götterdämmerung*. Not only are such celebrated Wagnerians as Lauritz Melchior, Friedrich Schorr, Frida Leider, Lotte Lehmann and Max Lorenz very well represented, but also singers one might not expect, including the Lieder specialist, Gerhard Husch, as Wolfram in *Tannhäuser* and Aureliano Pertile singing in Italian as *Lohengrin*. Significantly, Meta Seinemeyer, an enchanting soprano who died tragically young, here gives lyric sweetness to the dramatic roles of Brünnhilde and Isolde; and among the baritones and basses there is none of the roughness or ill-focus that marks so much latter-day Wagner singing. It is a pity that British-based singers are poorly represented, but the Prologue duet from *Götterdämmerung* brings one of the most impressive items, sung by Florence Austral and Walter Widdop. First-rate transfers and good documentation.

(i) *Götterdämmerung: Starke Scheite (Immolation scene);* (ii) *Lohengrin: Einsam in trüben Tagen. Parsifal: Ich sah das Kind. Die Walküre,* Act I: *Der Männer Sippe; Du bist der Lenz;* (iii) Act II: *Siegmund! Sieh' auf mich! (Todesverkündigung).*

(Y/B) (M) **(*) Decca stereo/mono 440 495-2 [id.]. Kirsten Flagstad; (i) Oslo PO or Norwegian State R. O, Fjeldstad; (ii) VPO, Knappertsbusch; (iii) VPO, Solti.

Kirsten Flagstad's 1956 Wagner recordings with Knappertsbusch were uneven. Sieglinde's solo (*Der Männer Sippe*) is magnificent, but the scale of the voice makes *Elsa's dream* from *Lohengrin* seem a little unwieldy; and, fine as it is vocally, Kundry's *Herzeleide* (*Parsifal*) sounds rather staid for a seductress. However, to redress the balance Decca have added the 1957 *Death announcement scene* from the partial recording of Act II of *Die Walküre*, with Set Svanholm as Siegmund. He sings intelligently, if not always with grateful tone-colour, but it is Solti's conducting that prevents any slight blemishes from mattering here. The recording, too, is remarkably vivid. The collection ends with Flagstad's mono recording of the *Immolation scene* from *Götterdämmerung*, with Fjeldstad providing passionate support. She was over sixty when this was made, in the studio of Norwegian Radio in 1956, but the result is vocally thrilling and, despite the degree of hardness of the mono recording and the two-dimensional orchestra, it is the highlight of the disc.

Arias: *Götterdämmerung:* (i) *Zu neuen Taten; Starke Scheite schichtet mir dort. Lohengrin: Euch Lüften mein Klagen. Parsifal:* (i) *Ich sah' das King. Tristan: Mild und leise. Die Walküre: Du bist der Lenz; Ho-jo-ho!.*

(M) (***) RCA mono GD 87915 [87915-2-RG]. Flagstad, (i) with Melchior, San Francisco Op. O, or Victor SO (both cond. Edwin McArthur); Phd. O, Ormandy.

Recorded for RCA in America between 1935 and 1940, this first generation of Wagner recordings by Flagstad reveals the voice at its noblest and freshest, the more exposed in consistently close balance on the 78s of the period. It is a pity that only two of the shortest items – from *Lohengrin* and *Walküre* – have Ormandy conducting. Most of the rest are conducted by Flagstad's protégé, Edwin McArthur, including the two longest, the big duet for Parsifal and Kundry and Brünnhilde's Immolation scene. Yet the grandeur of Flagstad's singing is never in doubt, the commanding sureness, and, though the orchestral sound is unflatteringly dry, the voice is gloriously caught in clean transfers.

Choruses from: *Der fliegende Holländer; Lohengrin; Die Meistersinger; Parsifal; Tannhäuser*.
(M) *** Decca 421 865-2 (from complete sets, cond. Solti).

Solti's choral collection is superb, with an added sophistication in both performance and recording. The collection opens with a blazing account of the *Lohengrin* Act III *Prelude*, since of course the *Bridal chorus* grows naturally out of it. But the *Pilgrims' chorus*, which comes next, creates an electrifying pianissimo and expands gloriously, while the excerpts from *Die Meistersinger* and *Parsifal* show Solti's characteristic intensity at its most potent.

Waldteufel, Emile (1837–1915)

Polkas: *Les Bohémiens; Retour des champs; Tout ou rien*. Waltzes: *Ange d'amour; Dans des nuages; España; Fontaine lumineuse; Je t'aime; Tout-Paris*.
** Marco Polo Dig. 8.223438 [id.]. Slovak State PO (Košler), Alfred Walter.

Polkas: *Camarade; Dans les bois; Jeu d'esprit*. Waltzes: *Bien aimés; Chantilly; Dans tes yeux; Estudiantina; Hommage aux dames; Les Patineurs*.
** Marco Polo Dig. 8.223433 [id.]. Slovak State PO (Košice), Walter.

Polkas: *L'esprit français; Par-ci, par-là; Zig-zag*. Waltzes: *Hébé; Les Fleurs; Fleurs et baisers; Solitude; Toujours ou jamais; Toujours fidèle*.
**(*) Marco Polo Dig. 8.223450 [id.]. Slovak State PO (Košice), Walter.

Invitation à la gavotte; Polkas: *Joyeux Paris; Ma Voisine*. Waltzes: *Pluie de diamants; Les Sirènes; Les Sourires; Soirée d'été; Très jolie; Tout en rose*.
** Marco Polo Dig. 8.223441 [id.]. Slovak State PO (Košice), Alfred Walter.

Béobile pizzicato. Polka-mazurka: *Bella*. Polka: *Château en Espagne*. Waltzes: *Acclamations; La barcarolle; Brune ou blonde; Flots de joie; Gaîté; Tout à vous*.
(N) **(*) Marco Polo Dig. 8.223684 [id.]. Slovak State PO (Košice), Alfred Walter.

Grand vitesse galop. Mazurka: *Souveraine*. Polka: *Les folies*. Waltzes: *Amour et printemps; Dolorès; Mello; Mon rêve; Pomone; Sous la voûte étoilée*.
(N) ** Marco Polo Dig. 8.223451 [id.]. Slovak State PO (Košice), Alfred Walter.

Waldteufel's music, if not matching that of the Strauss family in range and expressive depth, has grace and charm and is prettily scored in the way of French ballet music. Moreover its lilt is undeniably infectious. The most famous waltz, *Les Patineurs*, is mirrored in style here by many of the others (*Dans les nuages*, for instance), and there are plenty of good tunes. *Plus de diamants*, with lots of vitality, is among the more familiar items, as is the sparkling *Très jolie*, but many of the unknown pieces are equally engaging. Like Strauss, Waldteufel usually introduces his waltzes with a section not in waltz-time, and he is ever resourceful in his ideas and in his orchestration. The polkas are robust, but the scoring has plenty of character. The third disc listed (Volume 3 in the overall Marco Polo series) is a good starting point for the collector wanting to explore. It begins with *Zig-zag*, a lively polka featuring a solo cornet; then the horns open *Les Fleurs*, which produces yet another of the composer's best singing melodies. Both *Solitude* and *Fleurs et baisers* have much charm. Yet another cornet solo appears in *Toujours fidèle*, but the strings join him when the main waltz begins. *L'Esprit français*, a very gay French polka with a whiff of Offenbach, then makes a good foil for the two final waltzes, *Toujours ou jamais* and *Hébé*, which is Straussian in its melodic contour and worthy of the Viennese master. The performances are direct and have fresh, unmannered rubato. They are played with warmth and a good deal of finesse and, if Alfred Walter emerges as a sympathetic rather than an individual exponent, better this than exaggerated presentation, pulling the rhythms out of shape. The French style is understood as being more *galant*, less languorously indulgent, than the Viennese manner.

Volume 5 (8.223451) includes two favourites, *Pomone* (with its enticing opening nicely judged) and *Mon rêve*, but everything else is unfamiliar. The *Souveraine* mazurka has a pleasingly *galant* style and the polka, *Les folies* (delicated to M. Prevet, a soloist of the Garde de Paris), is a sprightly concertante interchange for cornet and orchestra. Walter ends his programme galloping with élan and *Grand vitesse*.

Flots de joie which opens Volume 6 (8.223684) brings a regal polonaise introduction which Walter handles with pleasing rhythmic lightness, and he is no less enticing in the following *Château en Espagne* polka and *Bella*, an equally engaging polka mazurka. The waltzes *Gaîté* and *Brune ou blonde* open with notable delicacy from the violins, and in the closing *Béobile* the playing sparkles so that this brief novelty rivals Johann Strauss's *Pizzicato polka* in sparkle when played as vivaciously as it is here. This is one of the best CDs in the series so far and it is very well recorded.

Grand vitesse galop. Polkas: *Les folies.* Mazurka: *Souveraine.* Waltzes: *Amour et printemps; Dolorès; Mello; Mon rêve; Pomone; Sous la voûte étoilée.*
(N) ** Marco Polo Dig. 8.223451 [id.]. Slovak State PO (Košice), Alfred Walter.

Polkas: *Bella; Château en Espagne. Béobile* (pizzicato). Waltzes: *Acclamations; La barcarolle; Brune ou blonde; Flots de joie; Gaîté; Tout à vous.*
(N) **(*) Marco Polo Dig. 8.223684 [id.]. Slovak State PO (Košice), Alfred Walter.

Galop: *Prestissimo.* Polkas: *Bella bocca; Nuée d'oiseaux.* Waltzes: *Au revoir; Coquetterie; Jeunesse dorée; Un premier bouquet; Rêverie; Trésor d'amour.*
**(*) Marco Polo Dig. 8. 223685 [id.]. Slovak State PO (Košice), Alfred Walter.

Waldteufel's waltzes are fairly straightforward in their layout, theme and key sequences, but every so often (though not nearly as often as with Johann Strauss) he does something less predictable and the introductions often bring a greater degree of imagination. The quality of the tunes varies and it is not surprising that *Pomone*, which opens the first of these three latest collections, is a favourite, while *Mon rêve* is enticing from its very opening bars. The rest of the concert is more ordinary, although *Sous la voûte étoilée*, once it gets under way, produces another characteristically smooth yet catchy main theme. The *Grand vitesse galop* ends the concert vigorously and makes one reflect that these discs would be more enjoyable if they had a greater proportion of non-waltz material.

Volume 6 brings an expansive polacca introduction for *Flots de joie*, and *Gaîté* is not mis-titled. Although the programme is all unfamiliar repertory, it shows the composer in fairly consistent good form: the dancing strings which open *Brune ou blonde* lead to another pleasing main tune, and *La barcarolle* (though nothing like Offenbach) lilts nicely. However, the highlight here is a superbly ebullient pizzicato, *Béobile*, which ends the concert fizzingly.

Volume 7 brings a comparably lively opening with the *Prestissimo galop*; *Rêverie*, after a nicely pointed introduction, is a waltz that fits its name. Yet another sleek tune provides *Un premier bouquet*; the flutes set the mood nicely for the charming *Trésor d'amour*, while the closing *Au revoir* is suitably nostalgic. The recording is excellent and Walter's performances are well up to standard throughout, sometimes really rather good, although his lazy rubato at the opening of *Pomone*, seductive as it is, would better suit a Viennese waltz.

Walton, William (1902–83)

'*Walton edition*': (i; ii) *Viola concerto;* (i; iii) *Violin concerto;* (iv) *Coronation marches: Crown imperial; Orb and sceptre; Façade (suites Nos. 1–2); Hamlet: Funeral march. Henry V* (scenes from the film with Sir Laurence Olivier & chorus; suite, arr. Mathieson); *Johannesburg festival overture; Partita for orchestra; Portsmouth Point overture; Richard III: Prelude & suite. Spitfire prelude and fugue; Symphony No. 1 in B flat min.;* (v) *The Wise Virgins (ballet suite)* & (iv) *Sheep may safely graze;* (iv; vi) *Belshazzar's Feast.*
(Y/B) (M) *** EMI stereo/mono CHS5 65003-2 (4) [CDHD 65003]. (i) Sir Yehudi Menuhin; (ii) New
  Philh. O; (iii) LSO; (iv) Philh. O; (v) Sadler's Wells O; (vi) with Donald Bell, Philh. Ch.; all cond.
  composer.

EMI follows up its revelatory Elgar Edition with this handsome Walton Edition, bringing together the composer's own EMI recordings not previously available on CD, with some of the most important dating from the mono interregnum before stereo arrived. The big revelation is Walton's own recording of the *First Symphony*, made in mono in October 1951, and here presented with far more bite and body than ever it had on the long-deleted LP. It emerges as among the most exciting versions ever, consistently displaying the Walton characteristic – faithfully observed later by such devotees as Previn – of treating the persistent syncopated rhythms with a jazzy freedom. The passion behind the performance is intense, most of all in the slow movement, which gains from superb woodwind playing from the Philharmonia soloists. Comparing Walton's 1959 stereo version of *Belshazzar's Feast* here with his earlier one of 1943 is fascinating, with speeds consistently more spacious, but with tensions just as keen and ensemble consistently crisper, though with less mystery conveyed. The one snag is the soloist, Donald Bell, clean of attack but uncharacterful.

Belshazzar and the *Symphony* make up the first disc, very generous measure, and all four discs are very well filled indeed. The second disc, entirely stereo, couples Menuhin's recordings of the *Violin* and *Viola concertos* with his version of the *Partita*, made in 1959. The new transfer of that last, fuller than before, reveals what extra fun Walton himself finds, bouncing the rhythms. Though Menuhin's account of the *Viola concerto* is a little effortful, not always flowing as it should, his viola sound is gloriously rich and true, and when it comes to the *Violin concerto*, recorded in July 1969, this is a vintage Menuhin performance, marked by his very distinctive tone and poignantly tender phrasing.

The third disc, mono except for Walton's scintillating account of the *Johannesburg Festival overture* and the *Hamlet Funeral march*, brings together the shorter pieces. This 1955 account of the *Façade suites* lacks the tautness of Walton's consistently brisker pre-war versions, not helped by less immediate recording. The *Coronation marches* and *Portsmouth Point*, recorded in 1953 to celebrate the Queen's coronation, have a beefy strength, with Walton as conductor bringing out not just the swagger but also the full-throated emotion behind the marches. The 1953 sessions also produced a new version of the Bach arrangement, *Sheep may safely graze*, warmer and more refined than the one in the original (1940) recording of *The Wise Virgins*. That was made with the Sadler's Wells Orchestra in July 1940, bright and vigorous, even if the ensemble is not of the crispest.

The final disc contains the film music – the *Spitfire Prelude and fugue*, the *Richard III Prelude* and *Suite* and the *Henry V Suite*, all made in 1963 as a package. Most important is the belated restoration of the complete Henry V sequence with Laurence Olivier, recorded in 1946 on four 78-r.p.m. records, but reissued on LP by RCA with seven minutes of cuts from the opening and closing scenes. The transfer is again first rate, with the atmospheric quality of the writing vividly caught, even if the mono sound lacks a little in body. The sound of arrows at the climax of the Agincourt charge has never been matched on subsequent recordings. What consistently comes out throughout the set is that in his seemingly reticent way Walton was just as inspired a conductor of his own music as Elgar was of his.

Anniversary fanfare; Crown imperial; March for the history of the English-speaking peoples; Orb and sceptre; A Queen's fanfare; (i) *Antiphon; 4 Christmas carols: All this time; King Herod and his cock; Make we now this feast; What cheer?. In honour of the City of London; Jubilate Deo; Where does the uttered music go?.*
*** Chandos Dig. CHAN 8998 [id.]. (i) Bach Ch.; Philh. O, Willcocks.

Sir David Willcocks conducts performances of the two *Coronation marches* full of panache, with the brass superbly articulated and inner detail well caught. Also the *March for the history of the English-speaking peoples*. The *a cappella* choral items are very well done too, if less intimately than on the Conifer disc of Walton choral music from Trinity College Choir. With the original organ parts orchestrated, the *Jubilate* and *Antiphon* gain greatly from having full instrumental accompaniment. The brief fanfares, never previously recorded, are a welcome makeweight, with the *Anniversary fanfare*, designed to lead directly into *Orb and sceptre*, which is what it does here.

Capriccio burlesco; The First shoot (orch. Palmer); *Granada* (Prelude for orchestra); *Johannesburg festival overture; Music for children. Galop finale* (orch. Palmer); *Portsmouth Point: overture; Prologo e fantasia; Scapino.*
*** Chandos Dig. CHAN 8968 [id.]. LPO, Bryden Thomson.

The *Capriccio burlesco* is ravishingly orchestrated, with some apt echoes of Gershwin, and the *Prologo e fantasia* completes an American group. The *Granada* Prelude, written for the television company, taps Walton's patriotic march vein in a jaunty way. *The First shoot* comes in Christopher Palmer's brilliant orchestration of the brass band suite. The opening *Giocoso* is a re-run of *Old Sir Faulk*, and the other movements bring more echoes of *Façade*. As for the other novelty, the ten brief movements of *Music for children* are here supplemented by a *Galop final*. Palmer has here orchestrated the piano score. Though the opulent Chandos recording tends to take some of the bite away from Walton's jazzily accented writing, the richness of the orchestral sound is consistently satisfying.

(i) *Capriccio burlesco*; (ii) *Music for children; Portsmouth Point overture*; (i) *The Quest* (ballet suite); *Scapino overture*; (ii) *Siesta*; (i; iii) *Sinfonia concertante.*
*** Lyrita SRCD 224 [id.]. (i) LSO or (ii) LPO, composer; (iii) with Peter Katin.

When Walton made these recordings, he was in his late sixties, and his speeds had grown a degree slower and safer. *Portsmouth Point* loses some of its fizz at so moderate a speed. By contrast *Scapino* suffers hardly at all from the slower speed, rather the opposite, with the opening if anything even jauntier and the big cello melody drawn out more expressively. *Siesta* too brings out the piece's romantically lyrical side, rather than making it a relatively cool intermezzo. The *Capriccio burlesco* and the ten little pieces of the *Music for children* are delightful too, with the subtleties of the instrumentation beautifully brought out. Much the biggest work here is the *Sinfonia concertante*, and in the outer movements the performance lacks the thrust that Walton himself gave it in his very first wartime recording, in which Phyllis Sellick was a scintillating soloist. Yet Peter Katin is a very responsive soloist too, and the central slow movement is much warmer and more passionate than on Conifer, with orchestral detail rather clearer. It is good too to have the first stereo recording of the suite from Walton's wartime ballet based on Spenser's 'Faerie Queene', *The Quest*, only a fraction of the whole but bright and colourful.

Cello concerto.
(M) *** Sony Dig. SMK 53333 [id.]. Yo-Yo Ma, LSO, Previn – ELGAR: *Cello concerto.* ***
(N) (BB) *** RCA Navigator 74321 29248-2. Piatigorsky, Boston SO, Munch – VAUGHAN WILLIAMS:
    Sinfonia Antartica. ***
(M) *** RCA 09026 61498-2. Piatigorsky, Boston SO, Munch – DVORAK: *Concerto.* **(*)

Yo-Yo Ma and Previn give a sensuously beautiful performance. With speeds markedly slower than usual
in the outer movements, the meditation is intensified to bring a mood of ecstasy, quite distinct from
other Walton, with the central allegro becoming the symphonic kernel of the work, far more than just a
scherzo. In the excellent CBS recording, the soloist is less forwardly and more faithfully balanced than
is common.

The *Cello concerto* was written for Piatigorsky and he plays it with a gripping combination of full-
blooded eloquence and subtlety of feeling, readily capturing the bitter-sweet melancholy of its flowing
lyrical lines. The closing pages of the final variations are particularly haunting. Munch provides a totally
understanding accompaniment, with the strings of the Boston Symphony finding that special quality of
lyrical ecstasy which is such a distinctive part of this concerto. The 1957 recording is a bit close, but the
improvement of the CD over the old LP is enormous, and the ambience of Symphony Hall is much
more apparent than before. As can be seen, this performance is also available coupled to Previn's fine
account of Vaughan Williams's *Sinfonia Antartica* on RCA's bargain-basement Navigator label.

(i; ii) *Cello concerto;* (ii) *Improvisations on an impromptu of Benjamin Britten; Partita for orchestra;* (i)
Passacaglia for solo cello.
*** Chandos Dig. CHAN 8959 [id.]. (i) Rafael Wallfisch; (ii) LPO, Bryden Thomson.

With his rich, even tone, Wallfisch is just as warm and purposeful in the solo *Passacaglia* as in the
Concerto, while Thomson relishes the vivid orchestral colours in both the *Improvisations*, here wider-
ranging in expression than usual, and the brilliant *Partita*. Excellent Chandos sound.

(i) *Cello concerto. Symphony No. 1 in B flat min.*
(N) *** Decca Dig. 443 450-2 [id.]. (i) Robert Cohen; Bournemouth SO, Litton.
*** EMI Dig. CDC7 54572-2 [id.]. (i) Lyn Harrell; Birmingham SO, Rattle.

Like the other two Decca Walton discs issued simultaneously, Andrew Litton's coupling of the
Symphony No. 1 and the *Cello concerto* crowns his formidable achievement as principal conductor of the
Bournemouth Symphony Orchestra. It even outshines Sir Simon Rattle's similar coupling for EMI.
Not since André Previn's vintage recordings of Walton has a conductor on disc so thrillingly conveyed
the element of wildness in Walton's finest inspirations, notably in the *First Symphony*. Litton's success
lies not just in his ability to screw up tension to breaking point but also in his treatment of the jazzy
syncopations which are a vital element in this music. Like Previn – and, for that matter, Walton himself
– Litton treats the jazz rhythms with a degree of idiomatic freedom, consistently making the music
crackle with electric energy. The exceptionally full and vivid recording brings out the opulence as well as
the sensuousness of Walton's orchestration, not least in the bitingly dramatic contrasts of brass and
percussion, with the Bournemouth orchestra unsurpassed by any rival. In the symphony, Litton more
than anyone makes the finale into a fitting culmination, bold and brazen, resolving into the concluding
climax triumphantly on a shattering outburst of timpani. In the *Cello concerto* Harrell on the Rattle disc
remains unrivalled in power and tonal resonance, where Robert Cohen for Litton is the more mercurial
as well as the more tender, following a deeper, more hushed, meditative approach. The way that Cohen
makes the opening note of the slow finale seem to emerge from afar is magical.

Harrell is both noble and deeply reflective, and in the second-movement *Allegro appassionato* he is at
once mercurial while establishing the movement's symphonic power. With Harrell more than his rivals
there is no feeling of the slow music in this largely lyrical work overbalancing the fast, and his most
remarkable achievement comes in the variation finale. The solo instrument is placed well forward, but
not aggressively so. Coupled with an equally compelling account of the *Symphony*, this is highly
recommendable.

Simon Rattle's disc with the CBSO is outstanding, not just because of the electrifying account of the
First Symphony, but because it has as the most generous coupling the most powerful version of the *Cello
concerto* yet. Where Rattle scores very strongly in the *Symphony* is that, like Previn in his classic 1966
version (RCA), he combines idiomatic rhythmic freedom in jazzy syncopations with keen precision of
ensemble. Though the EMI sound could have more beef in it, it has an exceptionally wide dynamic
range and Rattle exploits it powerfully to intensify the drama, and his control of tension is unerring in
its contrasts of light and shade. After pressing home the marking *con malizia* in the Scherzo, Rattle finds
a poignancy as well as power in the slow movement, with the recording again heightening the contrasts
of light and shade. In the finale he touchingly brings out the Last Post overtones in the hushed trumpet-

theme of the epilogue, again finding natural poignancy. With its brilliant, wide-ranging digital sound it will be a clear first choice for many, particularly when the coupling proves so commanding (see above). In every way an outstanding issue.

Viola concerto; Violin concerto.
*** EMI Dig. CDC7 49628-2 [id.]. Nigel Kennedy, RPO, Previn.

Kennedy's achievement in giving equally rich and expressive performances of both works makes for an ideal coupling, helped by the unique insight of André Previn as Waltonian. Kennedy on the viola produces tone as rich and firm as on his usual violin. The Scherzo has never been recorded with more panache than here, and the finale brings a magic moment in the return of the main theme from the opening, hushed and intense. In the *Violin concerto* too, Kennedy gives a warmly relaxed reading, in which he dashes off the bravura passages with great flair. He may miss some of the more searchingly introspective manner of Chung in her 1971 version, but there are few Walton records as richly rewarding as this, helped by warm, atmospheric sound.

(i) *Viola concerto. Johannesburg festival overture; Symphony No. 2.*
(N) (BB) *** Naxos Dig. 8.553402 [id.]. (i) Tomter; E. N. Philh. O, Paul Daniel.

With Paul Daniel drawing brilliantly pointed, keenly idiomatic playing from the English Northern Philharmonia, this first of the Naxos Walton series could not be more promising, helped by warm, clear and well-balanced recording. Pride of place goes to the thoughtful, deeply felt reading of the *Viola concerto* with the Norwegian viola-player, Lars Anders Tomter. Though Tomter's tight vibrato is at times obtrusive, he brings out the tender poetry of this most elusive of Walton's string concertos, with its mixture of melancholy and wit. More than others, Tomter observes pianissimo markings, and rightly he adopts a flowing speed for the first movement while refusing to be rushed in the Scherzo and finale, which with delectable pointing acquire extra scherzando sparkle. The overture is given the most exuberant performance, rivalling the composer's own, with the orchestra's soloists playing brilliantly. In the *Symphony No. 2* Daniel gives extra transparency to the often heavy orchestration, making the work less weighty than usual but just as warmly expressive. A superb bargain.

(i) *Viola concerto; Sonata for string orchestra; Variations on a theme of Hindemith.*
*** Chandos Dig. CHAN 9106 [id.]. (i) Nobuko Imai; LPO, Jan Latham-Koenig.

Imai is satisfyingly firm and true in all her playing, keenly confident in the virtuoso passages, with the central Scherzo not at all breathless-sounding. Imai uses a very broad *Andante* to bring out the full lyrical warmth, but it means that the following bravura section enters with a jolt rather than developing naturally. The movement is not helped either by the forward balance of the soloist. Though the recording also obscures some orchestral detail, not just a question of balance, Jan Latham-Koenig secures crisply rhythmic playing from the orchestra in all three movements. The main theme of the finale is even jauntier than usual, again at a speed fractionally slower than normal.

The warmth of the LPO string-tone comes over impressively in the *Sonata for strings*. Though the extra weight and tonal warmth are often very satisfying, as in the opening of the slow movement, the contrast between the passages for solo string quartet (echoing the original quartet version) and the full string ensemble is too extreme. Latham-Koenig is also warmly expressive in the *Hindemith variations*, which is not as lightly pointed or cleanly detailed as it might be, partly a question of the recording, but with extra weight and thrust to make it richly satisfying. Any reservations are peripheral when the three works on the disc not only make an exceptionally generous triptych, but one which reflects Walton's mastery over the full range of his career.

(i) *Viola concerto;* (ii) *Symphony No. 1;* (iii) *3 Songs from Façade.*
🏵 (M) (***) Dutton Laboratories mono CDAX 8003 [id.]. (i) Riddle, LSO, composer; (ii) LSO, Harty; (iii) Dora Stevens, Foss.

This first ever recording of the *Viola concerto*, made for Decca in December 1937 with Walton conducting the LSO and with Frederick Riddle as soloist, puts a totally different complexion on the piece from usual. Riddle's performance has never been surpassed by even the starriest viola-players since for, unlike almost every rival today, he takes the first movement, *Andante comodo*, at a flowing speed that avoids over-romanticizing the yearning melody at the start. Yet Riddle finds a poignant tenderness in the concerto. In the central Scherzo he is more relaxed, with wittily sprung rhythms, while after a fast, spiky account of the finale the epilogue is wistful rather than tragic. Amazingly, this historic recording was never transferred to LP, making the superb transfer from Dutton Laboratories doubly welcome. It is coupled ideally with the very first recording of Walton's *First Symphony*, made in 1935 by the LSO under Sir Hamilton Harty. Though the playing is not always as polished as in modern versions, the emotional thrust under Harty has never been surpassed. Again the sound is beefy and full, amazingly so when you think that Decca's improvised studio was in a warehouse building near Cannon Street station. The songs, with Dora Stevens accompanied by her husband, Hubert Foss, Walton's publisher from OUP, are a charming makeweight.

Violin concerto.
(M) *** Decca 440 324-2 [id.]. Kyung Wha Chung, LSO, Previn – *Belshazzar's Feast* etc. ***
(M) *** EMI CDM7 64202-2 [id.]. Ida Haendel, Bournemouth SO, Berglund – BRITTEN: *Violin concerto.* ***
(***) Biddulph mono WHL 016 [id.]. Heifetz, Cincinnati SO, Goossens – VAUGHAN WILLIAMS: *A London Symphony (No. 2)* (***) (with Concert (***)).

In the brooding intensity of the opening evocation, Kyung Wha Chung presents the first melody with a depth of expression, tender and hushed, that has never been matched on record, not even by Heifetz. With Previn as guide and with the composer himself a sympathetic observer at the recording sessions, Chung then builds up a performance which must remain a classic, showing the *Concerto* as one of the greatest of the century in this genre. Outstandingly fine recording, sounding the more vivid in its CD format. This now comes, coupled with Solti's *Belshazzar's Feast* and the *Coronation anthem*, at 78 minutes a generous CD if ever there was one.

A sunny, glowing, Mediterranean-like view of the concerto from Ida Haendel, with brilliant playing from the soloist and eloquent orchestral support from the Bournemouth orchestra under Paavo Berglund. The CD transfer of the fine (1977) recording, made in the Guildhall, Southampton, brings a brilliant orchestral tapestry to provide the necessary contrast and, given the quality of the playing (as well as the interest of the equally successful Britten coupling), this is an eminently desirable reissue.

Jascha Heifetz made the very first recording in 1941 with Eugene Goossens and the Cincinnati orchestra, and it has never quite been matched since for its passionate urgency as well as its brilliance. Speeds are much faster than has latterly become the norm, but the romantic warmth of the work has never been more richly conveyed. Here in an excellent CD transfer it is coupled with the only existing recording of the original score of Vaughan Williams's *London Symphony*, plus other British music.

(i) *Violin concerto;* (ii; iii) *Capriccio burlesco;* (iv; iii) *Façade suite No. 1; Johannesburg festival overture.*
(M) *** Sony SMK 58931 [id.]. (i) Francescatti, Phd. O, Ormandy; (ii) orchestra; (iii) André Kostelanetz; (iv) NYPO.

Zino Francescatti's 1959 recording of the Walton *Violin concerto* with Eugene Ormandy and the Philadelphia Orchestra comes close to matching the power and thrust of both the Heifetz versions that preceded it. In a first-rate transfer to CD in Sony's British Heritage series, it is very well coupled with the Walton recordings made in New York by André Kostelanetz, far more than a light-music specialist. These include the characteristically bustling showpiece that Walton dedicated to him, the *Capriccio burlesco*, given a performance of tremendous brio, the ever-delectable *Façade* pieces as well as the most lovable and exuberant of Walton's three witty overtures, the *Johannesburg Festival*, stunningly done. Forward, larger-than-life recording.

(i) *Violin concerto. Capriccio burlesco; Henry V: Suite; Spitfire prelude & fugue.*
**(*) HM Dig. HMU 907070 [id.]. (i) Aaron Rosand; Florida PO, Judd.

Judd draws warmly idiomatic playing from the Florida Philharmonic Orchestra in the colourful pieces based on wartime film music, for *The First of the Few* and *Henry V*, with the oboe solo in the *Bailero* theme after the Agincourt music achingly beautiful, and with the brass consistently ripe and resonant. The *Capriccio burlesco* is aptly witty and spiky. It is good to have Aaron Rosand returning to the recording studio, and in this formidable concerto he shows that his virtuosity is as impressive as ever. Against the latterday trend, Rosand comes near to matching the formidable drive and agility of Heifetz himself in the work, without sounding over-stressed. The snag is that the recording balances the soloist so close that orchestral detail is dim, and tuttis lack the bite and thrust they need. Despite the dryness of sound in the concerto and a lightness in bass, the bite and thrust of Rosand's performance are most refreshing, while the *Henry V* and *Spitfire music* are treated with great warmth.

Violin concerto; 2 Pieces for violin and orchestra; Sonata for violin and orchestra (both orch. Palmer).
*** Chandos Dig. CHAN 9073 [id.]. Mordkovitch, LPO, Jan Latham-Koenig.

Lydia Mordkovitch gives the most expansive account of the Walton *Violin concerto* on disc, sustaining spacious speeds warmly and persuasively. Latham-Koenig may not have quite the spark that Previn brings to the orchestral writing in both the Chung and Kennedy versions but he is keenly idiomatic, both in his feeling for sharply syncopated rhythms and in flexible rubato for Walton's romantic melodies. The characteristically warm Chandos recording is also a help, allowing plenty of detail to be heard, but helping to give extra cohesion to such a passage as the final march coda. Christopher Palmer's scoring of the *Sonata* offers a sensuousness of sound comparable with that in the opera *Troilus and Cressida*. Though his use of the harp or pizzicato strings for arpeggio accompaniments is not always comfortable, Palmer is right in seeing much of the piano part as already implying orchestration. With Mordkovitch just as powerful and rich-toned as in the regular concerto, the work makes a far bigger impact than in its original chamber form, a valuable addition to the Walton repertory. The two shorter pieces make an agreeable supplement, with Palmer's lush orchestration removing them even further from their medieval source-material.

(i) *Violin concerto. Symphony No. 2; Scapino overture.*
(N) *** Decca Dig. 444 114-2. (i) Tasmin Little; Bournemouth SO, Litton.

On the second of Litton's three Walton discs, the *Symphony No. 2* is given an even sharper focus than in Ashkenazy's earlier Decca version with the RPO. On the disc it follows – as in a concert – the *Scapino Overture* and the *Violin concerto*. Tasmin Little as soloist gives the most tenderly beautiful performance, matching Litton in her control of Waltonian contrasts between tender lyricism and sparkling wit. Like Litton, she is able to hold full tension through pauses, often daringly extending them as in a live performance, so that the cadenzas in the first and last movements have a rare intensity. This is a work which has inspired many outstanding performances, not least from women violinists, and Little in spontaneity and tenderness is unsurpassed.

Coronation marches: Crown imperial; Orb and Sceptre; Façade suites Nos. 1 & 2; (i; ii) *Gloria;* (ii) *Te Deum.*
(M) *** EMI CDM7 64201-2 [id.]. (i) Robothom, Rolfe Johnson, Rayner Cook, CBSO Ch.; (ii) Choristers of Worcester Cathedral; CBSO, Frémaux.

The three Walton works inspired by coronations are here splendidly coupled with the grand setting of the *Gloria*. Frémaux directs a highly enjoyable performance but it rather pales before the Coronation *Te Deum*, which may use some of the same formulas but has Walton electrically inspired, exploiting every tonal and atmospheric effect imaginable between double choirs and semi-choruses. The two splendid marches are marvellously done too. The rich, resonant recording is apt for the music, spacious and with excellent perspectives, and it has transferred splendidly to CD, with the brass both sonorous and biting and the choral sound fresh as well as with plenty of weight. The *Façade suites* have been added for the CD and here the remastering is even more telling, adding point to playing which is already affectionately witty. Frémaux's rhythmic control gives a fresh, new look to familiar music: his jaunty jazz inflexions in *Old Sir Faulk* are deliciously whimsical.

Crown Imperial (concert band version).
⍟ (M) *** Mercury 432 009-2 [id.]. Eastman Wind Ens., Fennell – BENNETT: *Symphonic songs;* HOLST: *Hammersmith;* JACOB: *William Byrd suite.* ***

Paced with dignity, yet with joyously crisp articulation, Fennell's splendidly spacious performance is part of a highly recommendable collection of music for concert band; the entry of the organ at the climax brings a frisson-creating dynamic expansion which is unforgettably exciting. The coda, too, is quite superb. The Mercury sound, from the late 1950s, remains in the demonstration bracket.

Façade (original version; complete).
(Y/B) (BB) ** Belart 450 136-2 [id.]. Dame Peggy Ashcroft, Paul Schofield, L. Sinf., composer.

Façade (complete, including *Façade 2*).
**(*) ASV Dig. CDDCA 679 [id.]. Prunella Scales, Timothy West, L. Mozart Players (members), Jane Glover.
**(*) Chandos Dig. CHAN 8869 [id.]. Lady Susana Walton, Richard Baker, City of L. Sinfonia (members), Richard Hickox.

Façade (absolutely complete).
(Y/B) (B) *** Discover Dig. DICD 920125 [id.]. Hunter, Melologos Ens., Van den Broeck.

Enterprisingly the Discover International label at bargain price offers the most complete version of Walton's Entertainment yet, using a group of Belgian instrumentalists, the Melologos Ensemble, under Silveer van den Broeck. When the reciter, Pamela Hunter, has made a speciality of reciting these Edith Sitwell poems, not exactly imitating Dame Edith herself but observing the strictly stylized, rhythmically crisp manner originally laid down, it makes a welcome and delightful disc. Five items appear here for the first time, adding to those resurrected by Walton himself in *Façade 2*. What one registers here, even more than with *Façade 2* alone, is that the early settings are more experimental and less sharply parodistic than the later, well-known ones, though in the accompaniment to one of them, *Aubade* ('Jane, Jane, tall as a crane'), there is a clear tongue-in-cheek reference to Stravinsky's *Rite of spring*. The recording is cleanly focused, balanced with the voice in front of the players yet obviously in the same acoustic, not superimposed; and the clarity and point of the solo playing, notably from the flute and clarinet, are splendid. Pamela Hunter is excellent too, happily characterizing with a minimum of 'funny voices'. At the price, a disc to recommend to all.

Scales and West as a husband-and-wife team are inventive in their shared roles, and generally it works well. *Scotch rhapsody* is hilariously done as a duet, with West intervening at appropriate moments, and with sharply precise Scots accents. Regional accents may defy Edith Sitwell's original prescription – and her own example – but here, with one exception, they add an appropriate flavour. The exception is *Popular song*, where Prunella Scales's cockney accent clashes horribly with the allusive words, with their 'cupolas, gables in the lakes, Georgian stables'. For fill-up the reciters have recorded more Sitwell poems, but unaccompanied.

Susana Walton, widow of the composer, makes a bitingly characterful reciter, matching with her distinctive accent – she was born in Argentina – the exoticry of many numbers. Richard Baker, phenomenally precise and agile in enunciating the Sitwell poems, makes the perfect foil, and Hickox secures colourful and lively playing from members of the City of London Sinfonia, who relish in particular the jazzy inflexions. *Façade 2* consists of a number of poems, beyond the definitive series of 21. All of them are fun and make an apt if not very generous coupling for the regular sequence. Warm sound, rather too reverberant for so intimate a work.

Walton's own stereo version from the early 1970s makes a fascinating supplement. Peggy Ashcroft is aptly characterful. She often lags behind the beat, but this adds to the sense of magnetic idiosyncrasy, and she is recorded so close that her breath is constantly in one's ear. Paul Schofield is the slowest and least rhythmic of reciters, but the composer keeps the music going as a subtle, quiet commentary in the background, and the effect is unique. The stereo is both atmospheric and immediate, and you can hear every word. Not a first choice, but an interesting bargain supplement to the essential Discover version.

(i) *Façade;* (ii) *Belshazzar's Feast.*
(N) (M) ** Sony mono/stereo SMK 46685 [id.]. (i) Edith Sitwell, David Horner, CO, Frederick Prausnitz; (ii) Walter Cassel, Rutgers University Ch., Phd. O, Ormandy.

Dame Edith Sitwell made this flawed New York recording of the *Façade* entertainment in January 1949, and though as ever her ripely characterful voice is magnetic, it was not agile enough to cope with the rhythmic complexities or even to get the words right. In one number, *Tango-Pasodoble*, she is helped out by David Horner. A fascinating supplement to the classic recording with Peter Pears as well as Dame Edith, but no replacement. Ormandy directs a strong and purposeful, if not always idiomatic account of *Belshazzar's Feast*, recorded in upfront stereo sound, making a generous coupling.

Façade: suites Nos. 1–3; Overture Portsmouth Point (arr. Lambert); *Siesta;* (i) *Sinfonia concertante.*
WALTON/ARNOLD: *Popular birthday.*
*** Chandos Dig. CHAN 9148 [id.]. (i) Eric Parkin; LPO, Latham-Koenig or Thomson.

Adapted from a ballet score written for Diaghilev (but then rejected), the *Sinfonia concertante*, with its sharply memorable ideas in each movement and characteristically high voltage, has never had the attention it deserves. Like the Conifer issue with Kathryn Stott as soloist, the Chandos recording restores the original version, though the differences are hardly noticeable without close study of the score. Eric Parkin as soloist is perfectly attuned to the idiom, warmly melodic as well as jazzily syncopated, making this the most sympathetic account on disc since the original version of 1945 with Phyllis Sellick as soloist and Walton himself conducting, even if the *Maestoso* introduction is hardly grand enough. The recording sets the piano a little more backwardly, no doubt to reflect the idea that this is not a full concerto. Jan Latham-Koenig gives the witty *Façade* movements just the degree of jazzy freedom they need. The third suite, devised and arranged by Christopher Palmer, draws on three apt movements from the *Façade* entertainment, ending riotously with the rag-music of *Something lies beyond the scene*. That is a first recording, and so is Constant Lambert's arrangement for small orchestra of the *Overture Portsmouth Point*, clearer than the original. *Siesta* is given an aptly cool performance under Bryden Thomson, and the *Popular birthday* is Malcolm Arnold's fragmentary linking of 'Happy birthday to you' with the *Popular song* from *Façade*, originally written for Walton's seventieth birthday.

Façade: suites 1 & 2.
*** Hyperion Dig. CDA 66436 [id.]. E. N. Philh. O, Lloyd-Jones – BLISS: *Checkmate* ***; LAMBERT: *Horoscope.* *** ⊛

Brilliantly witty and humorous performances of the two orchestral suites which Walton himself fashioned from his 'Entertainment'. This is music which, with its outrageous quotations, can make one chuckle out loud. Moreover it offers, to quote Constant Lambert, 'one good tune after another', all scored with wonderful felicity. The playing here could hardly be bettered, and the recording is in the demonstration bracket with its natural presence and bloom.

Film scores

As you like it: suite. The Battle of Britain: suite. Henry V: suite. History of the English speaking peoples: March. Troilus and Cressida (opera): *Interlude.*
(Y/B) (M) *** EMI Dig. CDM5 65585-2 [id.]. LPO Ch. & O, Carl Davis.

The Battle of Britain suite presents the music that (for trumpery reasons) was rejected for the original film, including a Wagnerian send-up and a splendid final march. Another vintage Walton march here was written for a television series based on Churchill's history, but again was never used. It is a pity that the *Henry V* suite does not include the Agincourt charge, but it is good to have the choral contributions to the opening and closing sequences. Best of all, perhaps, is the long-buried music for the 1926 Paul Czinner film of *As You Like It*. If only he had allowed himself to throw off music like this rather more often, we would all have gained by it. Warm, opulent recording.

As you like it; Hamlet.
*** Chandos Dig. CHAN 8842 [id.]. Catherine Bott, Sir John Gielgud, ASMF, Marriner.

Walton's score for *Hamlet*, thanks to the diligence of Christopher Palmer, offers some 40 minutes of music, a rich and colourful suite, superbly played and recorded, and much enhanced by the contribution of Sir John Gielgud in two of Hamlet's soliloquies, 'O that this too, too solid flesh' and 'To be or not to be'. The selection of music from the pre-war film of *As you like it* makes a valuable fill-up. It adds the splendid setting of *Under the greenwood tree* in a radiant performance by Catherine Bott. Marriner and the Academy draw out all the romantic warmth of both scores, and the sound is richly atmospheric to match.

The Battle of Britain (suite); Escape me never (suite); The First of the Few: Spitfire prelude and fugue; Three Sisters; A Wartime sketchbook.
*** Chandos Dig. CHAN 8870 [id.]. ASMF, Marriner.

The Spitfire prelude and fugue, from *The First of the Few,* was immediately turned into a highly success-ful concert-piece, but we owe it to Christopher Palmer that there is the 'Wartime Sketchbook', drawing material from three of the wartime films, plus scraps that Colin Matthews did not use in the suite from the much later *Battle of Britain* film music and not least in the stirring theme from the credits of the film, *Went the day well*. The brief suite from the music for Olivier's film of Chekhov's *The Three Sisters,* from much later, brings more than one setting of the *Tsar's Hymn* and a charming imitation of *Swan Lake.* Earliest on the disc is *Escape me never,* the first of Walton's film-scores, written in !935 in a more popular idiom; but the war-inspired music is what this delightful disc is really about. Marriner and the Academy give richly idiomatic performances, full of panache. Aptly opulent recording.

Henry V: A Shakespeare scenario (arr. Christopher Palmer).
*** Chandos Dig. CHAN 8892 [id.]. Christopher Plummer (nar.), Westminster Cathedral Ch.,
    ASMF, Marriner.

Few film-scores can match Walton's for the Olivier film of *Henry V* in its range and imagination, the whole lasting just over an hour. The most controversial change is to 'borrow' the first section of the march which Walton wrote much later for a projected television series on Churchill's *History of the English-speaking Peoples*; otherwise, the chorus's call to arms, *Now all the youth of England is on fire,* would have had no music to introduce it. As an appendix, three short pieces are included which Walton quoted in his score. Sir Neville Marriner caps even his previous recordings in this series, with the Academy and Westminster Choir producing heartfelt playing and singing in sumptuous sound. As narrator, Christopher Plummer makes an excellent substitute for Olivier, unselfconsciously adopting a comparably grand style.

Henry V: Passacaglia; The Death of Falstaff; Touch her soft lips and part.
(M) *** DG 439 529-2 [id.]. ECO, Barenboim – DELIUS: *Aquarelles* etc.; VAUGHAN WILLIAMS: *Oboe concerto* etc. ***

These two fine Walton string pieces make an admirable complement to a sensuously beautiful collection of English music, with Barenboim at his most affectionately inspirational and the ECO very responsive, and with the 1975 recording retaining its warmth and bloom.

Macbeth: Fanfare & march. Major Barbara (suite); Richard III (Shakespeare scenario).
*** Chandos Dig. CHAN 8841 [id.]. Sir John Gielgud (nar.), ASMF, Marriner.

Disappointingly, Sir John Gielgud underplays Richard III's great 'Now is the winter of our discontent' speech, but working to the underlying music – much of it eliminated in the film – may have cramped his style. The performance generally has all the panache one could wish for, leading up to the return of the grand Henry Tudor theme at the end. The six-minute piece, based on Walton's music for Gielgud's wartime production of *Macbeth*, is much rarer and very valuable too, anticipating in its Elizabethan dance-music the *Henry V* film-score. *Major Barbara* also brings vintage Walton material. Marriner and the Academy give performances just as ripely committed as in their previous discs in the series, helped by sonorous Chandos sound.

The Quest (ballet): complete; *The Wise Virgins* (ballet): suite.
*** Chandos Dig. CHAN 8871 [id.]. LPO, Bryden Thomson.

Walton's two wartime ballet-scores make an attractive coupling. Walton, even in a hurry, could not help creating memorable ideas and, with the help of Constant Lambert – not to mention Christopher Palmer, who has expanded the instrumentation in line with the suite – the orchestral writing is often dazzling. Quite apart from the dramatic power of the performance, the recording is superb, among the fullest and clearest from Chandos. The sound for *The Wise Virgins* is more reverberant and the perform-ance has less electricity, though Walton's distinctive arrangements of Bach cantata movements – includ-ing *Sheep may safely graze* – remain as fresh as ever.

Sinfonia concertante for piano & orchestra (original version).
*** Conifer Dig. 74321 15007-2 [id.]. Kathryn Stott, RPO, Handley – BRIDGE: *Phantasm;* IRELAND: *Piano concerto.* ***

Kathryn Stott, warmly and strongly accompanied by Vernon Handley and the RPO, gives an outstand-ing reading of the work's original version, and the result seems to strengthen what is a consistently memorable work, built from vintage Walton material. First-rate recorded sound, and a coupling both generous and apt.

Symphonies Nos. 1–2.
(M) *** EMI Dig. CD-EMX 2206. (i) LPO; (ii) LSO; Sir Charles Mackerras.

Where too often No. 2 has been dismissed as Walton imitating himself, saying nothing new, Mackerras firmly establishes the work's distinction, above all in its control of argument and its brilliant use of a very large orchestra. The thematic material may not be as striking as in the high-voltage *First Symphony*, with its eruption of youthful inspiration, but there is consistent lyrical warmth. Mackerras's reading of No. 1, using the LPO, adopts broader speeds than usual. It may not be as bitingly dramatic as the very finest versions, but the richness and strength of the symphony, one of the key British works of its period, come over powerfully. Warm, full recording in both symphonies. An outstanding bargain.

Symphony No. 1 in B flat min. (see also above, under *Cello concerto; Viola concerto*).
(M) *** RCA GD 87830 [7830-2-RG]. LSO, Previn (with VAUGHAN WILLIAMS: *Wasps overture* ***).

Symphony No. 1; Coronation marches: Crown Imperial; Orb and Sceptre.
(Y/B) (M) **(*) Telarc Dig. CD 82016 [id.]. RPO, André Previn.

Symphony No. 1; Portsmouth Point overture.
(Y/B) (M) **(*) Virgin/EMI Dig. CUV5 61146-2 [id.]. LPO, Slatkin.

Symphony No. 1; Varii Capricci.
*** Chandos Dig. CHAN 8862 [id.]. LPO, Bryden Thomson.

On RCA Previn gives a marvellously biting account of the magnificent *First Symphony*. His fast tempi may initially make one feel that he is pressing too hard, but his ability to screw the dramatic tension tighter and tighter until the final resolution is most assured. '*Presto con malizia*' says the score for the Scherzo, and malice is exactly what Previn conveys, with the hints of vulgarity and humour securely placed. In the slow movement Previn finds real warmth, giving some of the melodies an Elgarian richness; and the finale's electricity here helps to overcome any feeling that it is too facile, too easily happy a conclusion. The bright recording – made by Decca engineers in the vintage 1960s – has splendid focus in its CD remastering, yet does not lack body.

Thomson's is a warmly committed, understandingly idiomatic account of the work, weighty and rhythmically persuasive, which brings out the full emotional thrust. In the slow movement his tender expressiveness goes with a flowing speed, well judged to avoid exaggeration. If the Scherzo is a degree less demonic than it might be, at a speed fractionally slower than usual, it is infectiously sprung. The

Chandos coupling is not as generous as some but is very welcome when it brings the first recording of *Varii capricci*, the orchestral suite in five compact movements which Walton developed from his set of guitar *Bagatelles*, written for Julian Bream. With a brilliant performance and sumptuous sound, it makes a fine supplement.

Previn's view of Walton's electrifying *First Symphony* has grown broader and less biting with the years. The sumptuous Telarc recording also makes for warmth rather than incisiveness. Those who know Previn's incomparable earlier reading for RCA may well be disappointed; however, with fine playing from the RPO and with the slow movement more richly luxuriant than before, this is still a most enjoyable reading. The two *Coronation marches* make a colourful and welcome fill-up. *Crown Imperial* sounds especially expansive, with full-bodied Telarc sound, and altogether this is well worth acquiring as a more mature alternative to the indispensable RCA version of the symphony.

The brilliance, bite and clarity of sound in Slatkin's version of the *First Symphony* reinforce the tautness of the performance, nagging the mind with repetitive rhythms and tension piled on tension. Slatkin does not have quite the rhythmic mastery in giving a jazzy lift to syncopations or in moulding Waltonian melody that you find in both Previn's versions, and the Scherzo is almost breathlessly fast. But the finale is magnificent, bringing thrust and power, and culminating superbly in the uninhibited triple timpani passage near the end. Slatkin takes an equally electric view of the *Overture*, again played brilliantly by the LPO.

Symphony No. 2 (see also above, under *Viola concerto; Violin concerto*).
*** (M) Carlton RPO Dig. CDRPO 8023 [id.]. RPO, Ashkenazy – BRITTEN: *Serenade;* KNUSSEN: *Symphony No. 3*. ***

Symphony No. 2; Partita for orchestra; Variations on a theme by Hindemith.
❀ (M) *** Sony MPK 46732 [id.]. Cleveland O, Szell.

In a letter to the conductor, Walton expressed himself greatly pleased with Szell's performance of the *Second Symphony*: 'It is a quite fantastic and stupendous performance from every point of view. Firstly it is absolutely right musically speaking, and the virtuosity is quite staggering, especially the Fugato; but everything is phrased and balanced in an unbelievable way.' Listening to the splendidly remastered CD of this 1961 recording, one cannot but join the composer in responding to the wonderfully luminous detail in the orchestra. Szell's performance of the *Hindemith variations* is no less praiseworthy. Finally comes the *Partita*, which was commissioned by the Cleveland Orchestra and given its première a year before the recording was made. The recordings are bright, in the CBS manner, but the ambience of Severance Hall brings a backing warmth and depth, and these are technically among the finest of Szell's recordings in this venue.

In this live recording, ensemble is inevitably less crisp than in most studio performances – as in the fugato of the finale – but the power and passion of Ashkenazy's reading amply compensate. He is somewhat brisker and more urgent than either Previn or Mackerras in the outer movements, bringing out the scherzando element in the finale even more effectively. He then most tellingly draws out the lyrical warmth of the central slow movement at a marginally slower speed. It could hardly be more sensuous, helped by sound that is amazingly good, considering the problems of live recording, atmospheric with plenty of detail and, on the whole, a natural balance.

CHAMBER MUSIC

(i) *5 Bagatelles for solo guitar;* (ii; iii) *Duets for children;* (iv; ii) *2 Pieces for violin and piano; Toccata for violin and piano;* (ii) (Piano) *Façade: Valse;* (v; i) *Anon in love* (for tenor & guitar); (v; ii) *2 Songs for tenor: The Winds, The Tritons.*
(Y/B) *** Chandos Dig. CHAN 9292 [id.]. (i) Carlos Bonell; (ii) Hamish Milne; (iii) Gretel Dowdeswell; (iv) Kenneth Sillito; (v) John Mark Ainsley.

The *Toccata for violin and piano* is a curious mixture of cadenza and rhapsody of 15 minutes in a disconcertingly un-Waltonian style. Two songs for tenor are fascinating too, with a rushing accompaniment for *The Winds*, while *The Tritons* is chaconne-like, with a melody quite untypical of Walton. Milne and Dowdeswell bring out what charming, sharply focused ideas are contained in the ten *Duets for children*. The piano arrangement of the *Valse* from *Façade* is so thorny that even Hamish Milne has to go cautiously. The two violin pieces – using French troubadour songs – are spin-offs from the *Henry V* incidental music and, in the second, *Scherzetto*, reflect what their composer had learnt, writing for Heifetz. The two works with guitar are well known in Julian Bream's performances and recordings. Bonell is lighter and more delicate than Bream (see under Concerts, below), both in the *Bagatelles* and in *Anon in Love*, but is no less persuasive. Similarly, John Mark Ainsley lacks some of the punch of Peter Pears, for whom the cycle was written, but in a gentler way taps the wit and point of these Elizabethan conceits. A delightful collection, full of revealing insights into the composer's complex character.

Passacaglia for solo cello.
*** Chandos Dig. CHAN 8499 [id.]. Raphael Wallfisch – BAX: *Rhapsodic ballad;* BRIDGE: *Cello sonata;* DELIUS: *Cello sonata.* ***

William Walton's *Passacaglia* for solo cello was composed in the last year of his life. It has restraint and eloquence, and Raphael Wallfisch gives a thoroughly sympathetic account of it. Excellent recording.

(i) *Piano quartet; String quartet in A min.*
**(*) Mer. Dig. CDE 84139 [id.]. John McCabe, English Qt.

The *Piano quartet* is a work of Walton's immaturity, though there are many indications of what is to come. It is coupled with the mature *String quartet*; this is a substantial piece with stronger claims on the repertoire. McCabe and the English Quartet give a convincing enough account of the early piece, but the latter's account of the *String quartet* does not present a strong challenge to the finest rival versions. If you want this particular coupling rather than the Elgar, however, this is certainly worth investigating.

Piano quartet; Violin sonata.
*** Chandos Dig. CHAN 8999 [id.]. Sillito, Smissen, Orton, Milne.

This performance of the *Piano quartet* with Hamish Milne as pianist makes one marvel that such music could have been the inspiration of a 16-year-old. Admittedly Walton revised the piece, but here is music which instantly grabs the ear, with striking ideas attractively and dramatically presented in each movement. This is a more sharply focused reading than the rival Meridian one, both in the performance and in the recorded sound, with speeds generally flowing more freely and strongly and the string sound more satisfyingly resonant. The two principal performers from the quartet make a warmly sympathetic rather than high-powered duo for the *Violin sonata* of 1949. Yet the combination of Sillito's ripely persuasive style and Milne's incisive power, clarifying textures and giving magic to the phrasing, keeps tensions sharp. The satisfyingly full sound helps too.

String quartet No. 1 (ed. Christopher Palmer); *String quartet in A min.*
*** Chandos Dig. CHAN 8944 [id.]. Gabrieli Qt.

Coupled ideally with the mature *String quartet in A minor*, completed in 1946, is the atonal quartet, long thought to be lost, which Walton wrote when an undergraduate at Oxford. The result is hardly recognizable as Walton at all but is full of fire and imagination. The first movement is 'pastoral-atonal', lyrical in its counterpoint, but the Scherzo, built on vigorously rhythmic motifs and jagged ostinatos, has much more of Bartók in it than of Schoenberg, while the fugue of the finale seeks to emulate Beethoven's *Grosse Fuge* in its complexity and massive scale, alone lasting almost 16 minutes. The Gabrieli performance brings out all the latent power and lyrical warmth, often implying an underlying anger. It provides a fascinating contrast with the highly civilized *A minor* work of 25 years later. That comes in a red-blooded Gabrieli recording of 1986, earlier available in coupling with the Elgar *Quartet*. Both recordings were made in the warm, rich acoustic of The Maltings, Snape, with little discrepancy between them.

String quartet in A min.
(Y/B) *** Hyperion Dig. CDA 66718 [id.]. Coull Qt – BRIDGE: *3 Idylls;* *** ELGAR: *Quartet.* **(*)
*** Collins Dig. 1280-2 [id.]. Britten Qt – ELGAR: *Quartet.* ***
*** Virgin/EMI Dig. VC7 59026-2 [id.]. Endellion Qt – BRIDGE: *String quartet No. 3.* ***
(Y/B) ✹ *** Testament mono SBT 1052 [id.]. Hollywood Qt – HINDEMITH: *Quartet No. 3;* PROKOFIEV: *Quartet No. 2.* (***) ✹

The Elgar and Walton *Quartets* make an apt and attractive coupling, and here the Coulls, unlike their direct rivals, offer as bonus a fine example of Frank Bridge's quartet-writing. In the Walton, the reading captures movingly the spirit of Waltonian melancholy, bringing out the elegiac intensity of the extended *Lento* slow movement, taken at a very measured pace. The Coulls are splendid too in capturing the element of fun in Walton's scherzando ideas. The Brittens on Collins, also offering the Elgar, find less fantasy.

The Britten Quartet, bitingly powerful, bring out the emotional intensity, playing with refinement and sharp focus, finding a repose and poise in the slow movement that brings it close to late Beethoven. The contrasts of wistful lyricism and scherzando bite in the first movement make most other versions seem clumsy by comparison, and the incisiveness of Walton's jaggedly rhythmic writing is a delight.

The contrast between haunting melancholy and spiky wit also suits the Endellion players. The warmth of their understanding culminates in an outstanding performance of the *Lento* slow movement, superbly sustained at a very measured speed. The marked difference of style and mood here between this work and the other fine quartet on the disc is beautifully brought out, the Walton resigned, the

Bridge angry in a way that Walton had rather left behind in his pre-war work. Excellent, warm sound.

In many ways the pioneering account by the Hollywood Quartet, made in 1950, has still not been surpassed. It first appeared on a Capitol LP in harness with the Villa-Lobos *Sixth Quartet*. The sound comes up very well, though it is not, of course, state of the art. Moreover it comes with equally strong couplings and cannot be too strongly recommended.

CHORAL MUSIC

All this time; Antiphon; Chichester service: Magnificat; Nunc dimittis. Jubilate Deo; King Herod and the cock; A Litany (Drop drop slow tears); Make we now joy in this fest; Missa brevis; Set me as a seal upon thine heart; The Twelve; What cheer?; Where does the uttered music go?.
**(*) Nimbus Dig. NI 5364 [id.]. Christ Church Cathedral Ch., Oxford, Stephen Darlington.

There are special reasons for welcoming performances from Christ Church Cathedral Choir. It was this choir which Walton joined as a boy of ten, and he was still a member when at the age of fifteen he wrote the beautiful *a cappella* setting of Phineas Fletcher's *A Litany*, the first item on this disc. Later he wrote both the powerful setting of the *Jubilate* and the longest piece here, *The Twelve*, setting words specially written by another Christ Church man, W. H. Auden. The clear distinction between the Christ Church performances and those of the two other choirs, giving a strikingly different timbre as well as a different scale, is that you have boy trebles singing instead of sopranos. The trebles on their own even manage the tricky opening of the *Kyrie* of the *Missa brevis* with confidence at a flowing speed, and in the *Missa brevis* Christ Church observes the revised order of the Mass in the Church of England, with the *Gloria* after the *Kyrie*. Unfortunately, that reordering makes nonsense of Walton's intended musical scheme, which is that after the three *a cappella* sections the organ should enter dramatically for the *Gloria*. What works superbly is the Christ Church performance of *Where does the uttered music go?*, the setting of John Masefield written as a memorial tribute to Sir Henry Wood. At a much faster speed than usual, it has new freshness and a winning flexibility, bringing out the word-meaning. The snag about the Nimbus version is that it omits a major item included by both rivals, the *Cantico del sole* of 1974, setting words of St Francis of Assisi in the original Italian.

All this time; Cantico del sole; Jubilate Deo; King Herod and the cock; A Litany; Magnificat and Nunc dimittis; Make we joy now in this feast; Missa brevis; Set me as a seal (antiphon); The Twelve; What cheer?; Where does the uttered music go?.
*** Conifer Dig. 75605 51164-2 [id.]. Trinity College Ch., Richard Marlow.

On Conifer, sung by the choir of Trinity College, the *Missa brevis* for Coventry Cathedral in its spareness strikes a darker, deeper note. The *Cantico del sole*, idiomatically setting Italian words of St Francis, is warmly distinctive, and the longest piece, *The Twelve*, to words specially written by W. H. Auden, is far more than an occasional piece. Marlow draws phenomenally responsive singing from his talented choir, with matching and ensemble that approach the ideal. The recording is just as alive and immaculate.

Anon in love (song-cycle).
(M) *** RCA 09026 61601-2. Peter Pears, Julian Bream (guitar) – BRITTEN: *Songs from the Chinese* etc; SEIBER: *Four French folk songs*. ***

Walton wrote his cycle, *Anon in love*, for Pears and Bream, and the melisma of the opening song, *Fain would I change that note*, soars aloft in a way that Pears made his own. The other songs progress from nostalgia and romantic feeling to jolly revelry (*I gave her cakes and ale*) and consummation (*To couple is a custom*), with the closing number in the form of a brilliantly earthy scherzando. With attractive couplings this (Volume 18) is one of the most attractive and valuable reissues in the Julian Bream Edition, providing an entire programme played and sung by the artists who inspired the music.

Antiphon; Cantico del sole; 4 Christmas carols; Coronation Te Deum; Jubilate Deo; A Litany; Magnificat & Nunc dimittis; Missa brevis; Set me as a seal upon thine heart; The Twelve; Where does the uttered music go?.
**(*) Chandos Dig. CHAN 9222 [id.]. Finzi Singers, Paul Spicer; Andrew Lumsden.

The significant advantage of the Chandos collection of shorter choral works over the Conifer version from Trinity College Choir is that it offers an additional item, the setting of the *Te Deum* which Walton wrote for the coronation of Queen Elizabeth II in 1953. That comes in the version with organ, suitable for use on rather less grand occasions. The loss of weight makes it less stirring, but the clarity of Walton's structure, a simplified sonata-form, and the ingenuity with which he fits it to the long and complex text of the *Te Deum* comes over all the more clearly. What matters is that the Finzi Singers' freshness and liveliness is equally winning in bringing out the rich variety of Walton's inspiration in this field.

Belshazzar's Feast.
(N) (BB) **(*) CfP Silver Double CDCFPSD 4754 (2). Rippon, Hallé Ch. and O, Loughran – BRIT-
TEN: *Violin concerto in D min.* etc; TIPPETT: *Concerto for double string orchestra;* VAUGHAN WIL-
LIAMS: *Tallis fantasia* etc. ***

(i) *Belshazzar's Feast. Coronation march: Crown Imperial; Henry V* (film incidental music): *suite.*
(N) *** Decca Dig. 448 134-2. (i) Bryn Terfel, Bournemouth Symphony Ch., Waynflete Singers,
L'Inviti; Bournemouth SO, Litton.

(i) *Belshazzar's Feast. Henry V* (film score): *suite.*
(M) *** Carlton Dig. CDRPO 8001 [id.]. (i) Luxon, Brighton Festival Ch., L. Coll. Mus., RPO, Previn.

(i) *Belshazzar's Feast. Henry V: 2 Pieces for strings. Partita for orchestra.*
(M) **(*) RCA Dig. RD 60813 [60813-2-RC]. (i) Allen, LPO Ch.; LPO, Slatkin.

(i) *Belshazzar's Feast. Improvisations on an impromptu of Benjamin Britten; Overtures: Portsmouth Point;
Scapino.*
(M) *** EMI CDM7 64723-2 [id.]. LSO, Previn, (i) with John Shirley-Quirk, L. Symphony Ch.

(i) *Belshazzar's Feast. In honour of the City of London.*
(M) *** EMI Dig. CD-EMX 2225; *TC-EMX 2225* [id.]. (i) David Wilson-Johnson; L. Symphony Ch.,
LSO, Hickox.

(i) *Belshazzar's Feast;* (ii) *Coronation Te Deum.*
(M) *** Decca 440 324-2 [id.]. (i) Benjamin Luxon, LPO Ch.; (ii) Choirs of Salisbury, Winchester &
Chichester Cathedrals; LPO, Solti – *Violin concerto.* ***

Belshazzar's Feast; Coronation Te Deum; Gloria.
**(*) Chandos Dig. CHAN 8760 [id.]. Howell, Gunson, Mackie, Roberts, Bach Ch., Philh. O,
Willcocks.

Richard Hickox not only conducts one of the most sharply dramatic accounts of *Belshazzar's Feast*
currently available, even crisper and keener (if less jazzy) than Previn's superb (1971) EMI version; but
he couples it with the one major work of Walton left unrecorded: his cantata, *In honour of the City of
London.* With forces almost as lavish as those in the oratorio, its vitality and atmospheric colour come
over on this record to a degree generally impossible in live performance. As for *Belshazzar* under
Hickox, its voltage has never seemed higher on record, thanks not just to the LSO and Chorus – in far
sharper form than for Previn, 17 years earlier – but also to the full and brilliant digital recording. The
dramatic soloist is David Wilson-Johnson, colouring his voice with chilling menace in the writing-on-
the-wall sequence. Now reissued on EMI's mid-priced Eminence label, this makes a very strong
recommendation.

Where the first two of Litton's Walton discs were recorded in the helpful acoustic of the Southampton
Guildhall, *Belshazzar's Feast* was put into the grander setting of Winchester Cathedral. The reverberation time is formidably long, yet, thanks to brilliant balancing, there is ample detail and fine focus in
exceptionally incisive choral and orchestral sound. The great benefit is that this emerges as a performance on a bigger scale than its rivals, with the contrasts between full chorus and semi-chorus the more
sharply established. The vividly dramatic soloist is Bryn Terfel, pointing the words as no one else ever
has. He was magnetic enough in his 1994 Last Night of the Proms performance with Andrew Davis
(issued on Teldec), but his expressive colourings are even more individual here, both in the 'shopping-
list' – 'Babylon was a great city' – and in his spine-chilling narration describing the writing on the wall.
The other items, the *Henry V suite* and *Crown Imperial*, were recorded, like *Belshazzar*, in Winchester
Cathedral, but sadly the opportunity was not taken for using a chorus in *Henry V.* The fanfares have
never been more evocative, and the build-up of the Agincourt charge is thrilling. Despite the reverberation, *Crown Imperial* is also given a stirring performance.

Previn's EMI version of *Belshazzar's Feast* remains among the most spectacular yet recorded. The
digital remastering has not lost the body and atmosphere of the sound but has increased its impact. This
fine performance was recorded with Walton present on his seventieth birthday and, though Previn's
tempi are occasionally slower than those set by Walton himself in his two recordings, the authenticity is
clear, with consistently sharp attack and with dynamic markings meticulously observed down to the
tiniest hairpin markings. Chorus and orchestra are challenged to their finest standards, and John
Shirley-Quirk proves a searching and imaginative soloist. The *Improvisations*, given a first recording,
make a generous fill-up alongside the two overtures in which Previn, the shrewdest and most perceptive
of Waltonians, finds more light and shade than usual. Again the remastered sound is excellent.

Sir Georg Solti directs a sharply incisive performance which brings out the symphonic basis rather than the atmospheric story. Fresh, scintillating and spiky, it is a performance that gives off electric sparks, not always quite idiomatic, but very invigorating. Solti observes Walton's syncopations very literally, with little or none of the flexibility that the jazz overtones suggest. But with generally excellent singing from the chorus and a sympathetic contribution from Luxon (marred only slightly by vibrato) this is a big-scale reading which overall is most convincing. Moreover from the very opening with its dramatic trombone solo, one is aware that this is to be a Decca spectacular, with superbly incisive and clear choral sound, slightly sparer in texture in *Belshazzar's Feast* than in the *Te Deum*. And for this reissue in the 'British Classics' series, Decca have added Chung's classic account of the *Violin concerto*.

André Previn's RPO digital version of Walton's oratorio brings a performance in some ways even sharper and more urgent than his fine earlier version for EMI with the LSO. The chorus, singing with biting intensity, is set realistically behind the orchestra, and though that gives the impression of a smaller group than is ideal, clarity and definition are enhanced. Benjamin Luxon – who earlier sang in Solti's Decca version – is a characterful soloist, but his heavy vibrato is exaggerated by too close a balance. The five-movement suite from Walton's film-music for *Henry V* makes an attractive coupling. Previn was the first conductor on record since Walton himself to capture the full dramatic bite and colour of this music, with the cavalry charge at Agincourt particularly vivid.

Willcocks scores over some rivals in his pacing which, far more than is common, follows the example set by the composer himself in his two recordings. Speeds tend to be a degree faster, as in *By the waters of Babylon* which flows evenly yet without haste. The soloist, Gwynne Howell, firm and dark of tone, is among the finest of all exponents but, with the Bach Choir placed rather more distantly than in most versions, this is not as incisive as its finest rivals. The *Coronation Te Deum* receives a richly idiomatic performance, and Willcocks also gives weight and thrust to the *Gloria*, with the tenor, Neil Mackie, outstanding among the soloists. The microphone unfortunately catches an unevenness in Ameral Gunson's mezzo. The recording is warmly reverberant, not ideally clear on choral detail but easy to listen to.

Loughran's version is forthright and dramatic, helped by brilliant (1973) recording. The orchestra is particularly well caught, and so is the excellent soloist, firm and clear in attack. The snag is the work of the chorus, relatively small and placed rather close to the microphones so that details of imperfect ensemble and intonation tend to be exaggerated. The result is still a fine, convincing account of a gripping masterpiece; all the couplings offered on this Silver Double set are highly recommendable, making it outstanding value at the modest price asked.

Leonard Slatkin conducts the briskest of all modern versions of *Belshazzar*. In the final chorus, *Then sing, sing aloud*, Slatkin is even fractionally faster than Walton, but the syncopated jollity of the music is then diminished. Despite some questionable intonation, the choral ensemble is first rate, and the singing of the baritone soloist, Thomas Allen, is superb, covering the broadest tonal and expressive range. Sadly, the recording places him, like the chorus, rather at a distance, with too little feeling of presence. It lacks the biting impact the work needs. The distancing of sound affects the *Partita*, even if this account hardly replaces the original Szell version. In the two little string-pieces from the *Henry V* music Slatkin sustains very slow speeds well.

(i) *Christopher Columbus (suite of incidental music);* (ii) *Anon in love;* (iii) *4 Songs after Edith Sitwell: Daphne; Through gilded trellises; Long steel grass; Old Sir Faulk. A Song for the Lord Mayor's table; The Twelve (an anthem for the Feast of any Apostle).*
*** Chandos Dig. CHAN 8824 [id.]. (i) Linda Finnie, Arthur Davies; (ii) Martyn Hill; (iii) Jill Gomez; Westminster Singers, City of L. Sinfonia, Hickox.

The composer's own orchestral versions of his song-cycles *Anon in love* (for tenor) and *A Song for the Lord Mayor's table* (for soprano) are so beautifully judged that they transcend the originals, and the strength and beauty of these strongly characterized songs is enormously enhanced, particularly in performances as positive as these by Martyn Hill and Jill Gomez. The anthem, *The Twelve*, also emerges far more powerfully with orchestral instead of organ accompaniment. The four Sitwell songs were orchestrated by Christopher Palmer, who also devised the suite from Walton's incidental music to Louis MacNeice's wartime radio play, *Christopher Columbus*, buried for half a century. It is a rich score which brings more happy anticipations of the *Henry V* film-music in the choral writing, and even of the opera *Troilus and Cressida*, as well as overtones of *Belshazzar's Feast*. Warmly committed performances, opulently recorded.

OPERA

The Bear (complete).
*** Chandos Dig. CHAN 9245 [id.]. Della Jones, Opie, Shirley-Quirk, Northern Sinfonia, Hickox.

In its way the one-Acter *The Bear*, based on Chekhov, matches in its point and flair any of Britten's own chamber operas written for Aldeburgh, with Walton producing textures that are sumptuous rather than spare. It is a masterly score, with the farcical element reflected in dozens of parodies and tongue-in-cheek musical references, starting cheekily with echoes of Britten's own *Midsummer Night's Dream*. Richard Hickox paces with members of the Northern Sinfonia paces the music superbly, flexibly heightening the moments of mock-melodrama that punctuate this tale of a mourning widow who faces the demands of one of her dead husband's creditors. The casting of the three characters is ideal, with Della Jones commanding as the affronted widow, with words clear, Alan Opie clean-cut and incisive as the creditor or 'Bear' of the title, and with John Shirley-Quirk as the old retainer. In many ways this is a piece – with its climactic duel scene leading to an amorous *coup-de-foudre* – which comes off even better on disc than on stage.

Troilus and Cressida (complete).
(Y/B) ✸ *** Chandos Dig. CHAN 9370/1 (2) [id.]. Arthur Davies, Howarth, Howard, Robson, Opie, Bayley, Thornton, Owen-Lewis, Opera North Ch., English N. Philh. O, Richard Hickox.
(Y/B) (M) **(*) EMI CMS5 65550-2 (2) [id.]. Cassilly, J. Baker, Bainbridge, English, Luxon, Van Allan, Rivers, Lloyd, ROHCG Ch. and O, Lawrence Foster.

Few operas since Puccini have such a rich store of memorable tunes as *Troilus and Cressida*. As Chandos's magnificent recording shows, based on Opera North's 1995 production – using Walton's tautened score of 1976 but with the original soprano register restored for Cressida – this red-bloodedly romantic opera on a big classical subject deserves to enter the regular repertory. Judith Howarth portrays the heroine as girlishly vulnerable, rising superbly to the big challenges of the love duets and final death scene. Arthur Davies is an aptly Italianate Troilus, an ardent lover, and there is not a weak link in the rest of the characterful cast, with Nigel Robson a finely pointed Pandarus, comic but not camp, avoiding any echoes of Peter Pears, the originator. As Evadne, Cressida's maid, Yvonne Howard produces firm, rich mezzo tone, and the role of Calkas, Cressida's father, is magnificently sung by Clive Bayley. The role of Diomede, Cressida's Greek suitor, can seem one-dimensional but Alan Opie, in one of his finest performances on record, sharpens the focus, making him a genuine threat, a noble enemy. Richard Hickox draws magnetic performances from chorus and orchestra alike, bringing out the many parallels with the early Walton of *Belshazzar's Feast* and the *Symphony No. 1*. As for the recorded sound, the bloom of the Leeds Town Hall acoustic allows the fullest detail from the orchestra, enhancing the Mediterranean warmth of the score, helped by the wide dynamic range. The many atmospheric effects, often offstage, are clearly and precisely focused, and the placing of voices on the stereo stage is also unusually precise.

The great glory of EMI's live recording, made at Covent Garden during the 1976 revival, is the singing of Dame Janet Baker in the role of Cressida. Though the dry acoustic takes some of the bloom away from the voice, the glorious variety of her tonal colourings still gives a superb idea of Dame Janet's masterly singing in opera at the very peak of her career: the weight, beauty and heartfelt expressiveness are wonderfully telling, giving a distinctive slant to the whole opera. It is good to have this historic document on CD, even if in face of the magnificent Chandos recording, based on the Opera North production, it inevitably remains second best, not helped by intrusive audience noises. The one compensation of the very dry Covent Garden sound is that the dramatic bite is often enhanced. Otherwise the beauty of Walton's writing, for voices and orchestra alike, is minimized and the voices are never flattered. Richard Cassilly as Troilus uses his powerful Heldentenor tone intelligently, but the lower register is often gritty. The bite and purposefulness of Lawrence Foster's conducting – with speeds regularly faster than Hickox's – comes over well, even if he fails to match Hickox in expressive warmth or natural feeling for the Walton idiom.

Troilus and Cressida: Scenes: (i) Act I: *Is Cressida a slave?; Slowly it all comes back;* Act II: *How can I sleep if one last doubt remain;* (ii) *Is anyone there?;* (i) *If one last doubt; Now close your arms; Interlude; From isle to isle chill waters;* Act III: *All's well!; Diomede! Father!.*
(M) *** EMI (i) mono; (ii) stereo CDM7 64199-2. (i) Lewis, Schwarzkopf, M. Sinclair, Philh. O; (ii) Collier, Pears, ROHCG O; composer.

Walton wrote this superbly lyrical and atmospheric opera with Schwarzkopf in mind to play the heroine. She never sang the part on stage, but these highlights are more than enough to show what we missed. The melodies may not be as immediately striking as Puccini's but they grow more haunting on repetition, and it would be hard to find a more directly appealing modern romantic opera. The selections are well chosen, and for the reissue a reminder of Sir Peter Pears's Pandarus is now included. As a Decca artist he was not included in the original EMI recording, but now his brief duet with Maria Collier (the

Cressida of the 1963 Covent Garden revival) can happily be included. It was recorded in stereo in 1968, again using the Kingsway Hall, the venue for the original sessions 13 years earlier. With Walter Legge then producing, it is not surprising that the mono quality is almost as impressive as the later stereo, particularly the scene in Act III (*All's well*) with Cressida, Evadne and the Watchman which has a magical sense of perspective. A most valuable and rewarding reissue.

Ward, John (1571–1638)

Madrigals: *Come sable night; Cruel unkind; Die not, fond man; Hope of my heart; If heaven's just wrath; If the deep sighs; I have retreated; My breast I'll set; Oft have I tender'd; Out from the vale; Retire, my troubled soul; Sweet Philomel.*
*** Hyperion Dig. CDA 66256 [id.]. Consort of Musicke, Anthony Rooley.

Ward's music speaks with a distinctive voice, free from the self-conscious melancholy that afflicts some of his contemporaries. He chooses poetry of high quality and his music is always finely proportioned and organic in conception. These settings represent the madrigal tradition at its finest; such is the quality of this music and the accomplishment with which it is presented that collectors who respond to this repertoire should not hesitate.

Cor mio, deh non languire; Cruel unkind; Down in a dale; Fantasias a 6: Nos. 1 in A min.; 2 in F; 3 in A min.; 4 in G min.; 7 in C min. If Heaven's just wrath; In nomine a 6: No. 2 in C min. My breast I'll set upon a silver stream; No object dearer, Well-sounding pipes.
(Y/B) *** Musica Oscura Dig. 070981 [id.]. Consort of Musicke, Anthony Rooley.

Down caitive wretch/Prayer is an endless chain; Have mercy upon me; How long wilt thou forget me; I will praise the Lord; Let God arise; O let me tread in the right path; O Lord consider my great moans; Praise the Lord, O my soul (2 versions); *This is a joyful, happy, holy day.*
(Y/B) *** Musica Oscura Dig. 070982 [id.]. Consort of Musicke, Anthony Rooley.

As Anthony Rooley and the Consort of Musicke have shown, John Ward was one of the greatest madrigalists of the Jacobean period. On this showing his church music was just as inspired in its dark intensity, a model for Purcell's finest. All but one of these ten Psalm-settings and anthems are in the minor mode, with grinding suspensions regularly bringing astonishingly adventurous chromatic harmonies in complex polyphony. Emma Kirkby leads the team of soloists, sensitively accompanied by the viols of Rooley's Consort.

Warlock, Peter (1894–1930)

Capriol suite.
(Y/B) (BB) ** BBC Radio Classics BBCRD 9104 [id.]. Hirsch Chamber Players, Leonard Hirsch (with Concert) – FINZI: *Clarinet concerto* etc.; LEIGH: *Harpsichord concertino;* VAUGHAN WILLIAMS: *Tallis fantasia.* **(*)

Capriol suite (for strings); *Serenade for strings (for the sixtieth birthday of Delius).*
(M) *** Decca 440 325-2 [id.]. ASMF, Marriner – BUTTERWORTH: *Banks of green willow* etc.; VAUGHAN WILLIAMS: *Lark ascending* etc. ***

Warlock's gentle *Serenade*, written for Delius, is beautifully played and recorded here by Marriner, an unjustly neglected work receiving its due. The *Capriol suite*, based on Elizabethan dances, is given a comparably lively, polished and stylish account which readily reveals the freshness of Warlock's invention. The recording is first rate.

A very decent, lively and well-articulated performance of the *Capriol suite* from Hirsch that dates from 1965. Although it is well played, it is not very special – and the *Capriol suite* is not a rarity. The sound is very good for its date, better in fact than some of the other material in this BBC series.

Capriol suite (orchestral version); *Serenade for strings (for the sixtieth birthday of Delius).*
*** Chandos Dig. CHAN 8808 [id.]. Ulster O, Vernon Handley – MOERAN: *Serenade* etc. ***

The *Capriol suite* exists in piano-duet form, the very familiar version for strings (both from 1926), and the present full orchestral score, which followed in 1928. The effect is to rob the music of some of its astringency. A dryish wine is replaced with one with the fullest bouquet, for the wind instruments make the textures more rococo in feeling as well as increasing the colour. There are losses as well as gains, but it is good to have Handley's fine performance, made to sound opulent by the acoustics of Ulster Hall, Belfast. The lovely *Serenade*, for strings alone, is also played and recorded very beautifully.

'*Centenary collection':* (i) *Capriol suite;* (ii) *Serenade to Frederick Delius on his 60th birthday.* Songs: (iii) *Adam lay ybounden;* (iv) *Autumn twilight;* (v) *Balulalow;* (vi) *Bethlehem Down;* (vii) *Captain Stratton's fancy;* (viii) *The Curlew* (song-cycle); (ix) *I saw a fair maiden;* (x) *The Lady's birthday* (arrangement); (v) *Pretty ring time;* (x) *The shrouding of the Duchess of Malfi;* (xi) *Where riches is everlasting;* (xii) *Yarmouth Fair.*
(M) *** EMI CDM5 65101-2 [id.]. (i) E. Sinf., Neville Dilkes; (ii) Bournemouth Sinf., Norman Del Mar; (iii) Robert Hammersley, Gavin Williams; (iv) Frederick Harvey, Gerald Moore; (v) Janet Baker, Philip Ledger; (vi) Guildford Cathedral Ch., Barry Rose; (vii) Robert Lloyd, Nina Walker; (viii) Ian Partridge, Music Group of London; (ix) Westminster Abbey Ch., Douglas Guest; (x) Baccholian Singers, Jennifer Partridge; (xi) King's College, Cambridge, Ch., Willcocks; (xii) Owen Brannigan, Ernest Lush.

A splendid anthology of Warlock – less well-known as the music critic, Peter Heseltine. Opening with one of our favourite versions of the *Capriol suite* from the English Sinfonia under Neville Dilkes, brightly coloured and full of vigour, followed by Warlock's touchingly tender tribute to Delius, the selection ranges over a well-chosen selection of favourite songs, solo and choral. The other key item is *The Curlew*, Warlock's most striking and ambitious work, a continuous setting of a sequence of poems by Yeats which reflect the darker side of his complex personality. Ian Partridge, with the subtlest shading of tone-colour and the most sensitive response to word-meanings, gives an intensely poetic performance, beautifully recorded. Among other performances those of Dame Janet Baker stand out, but many of the songs here are persuasively beautiful. At the very close of the recital Owen Brannigan restores our high spirits with his characteristically ebullient delivery of *Yarmouth Fair*. The transfers are consistently well managed.

(i) *Capriol suite;* (ii) *The Curlew* (song-cycle); *5 Nursery jingles. The Birds; Chopcherry; Fairest May; Mourn no moe; My gostly fader; Sleep; The water lilly.*
(Y/B) (BB) **(*) ASV CDQS 6143 [id.]. (i) RPO, Barlow; (ii) James Griffett, Haffner Qt; Mary Murdoch, Mary Ryan.

Though Griffett's performance of *The Curlew* is not so beautiful or so imaginative as Ian Partridge's, it is good to have a bargain record of songs by a composer with a strikingly distinctive feeling for English verse. Each one of these songs is a miniature of fine sensitivity, and James Griffett sings them with keen insight, pointing the words admirably. The instrumental playing is most sensitive, and the recording, made in Christ Church, Chelsea, is warmly atmospheric yet clear. The performance of the *Capriol suite* is also a very good one, and the digital recording is first rate. This CD is well worth its modest cost.

Songs: *As ever I saw; Autumn twilight; The bachelor; The bayly berith the bell away; Captain Stratton's fancy; First mercy; The fox; Hey, trolly, loly lo; Ha'nacker Mill; I held love's head; The jolly shepherd; Late summer; Lullaby; Milkmaids; Mourne no more; Mr Belloc's fancy; My gostly fader; My own country; The night; Passing by; Piggesnie; Play-acting; Rest, sweet nymphs; Sleep; Sweet content; Take, o take those lips away; There is a lady sweet and fair; Thou gav'st me leave to kiss; Walking the woods; When as the rye; The wind from the west; Yarmouth Fair.*
*** Chandos Dig. CHAN 8643 [id.]. Benjamin Luxon, David Willison.

Songs like *Autumn twilight*, the powerfully expressive *Late summer* and *Captain Stratton's fancy* are appealing in utterly different ways, and there is not a single number in this programme that does not show the composer either in full imaginative flow or simply enjoying himself, as in *Yarmouth Fair*. Luxon's performances are first class and David Willison provides sensitive and sparkling accompaniments. The recording is first class.

Wassenaer, Unico Wilhelm (1692–1766)

Concerti armonici Nos. 1–6.
*** Hyperion Dig. CDA 66670 [id.]. Brandenburg Cons., Goodman.

These splendid concertos have long been attributed to Pergolesi, but finally (in 1979) their true source was discovered, one Unico Wilhelm, Graf von Wassenaer, a Dutch part-time composer of remarkable accomplishment. Their invention, vigorous and expressive, is sustained by a remarkably harmonic individuality: in short they are first-class works, almost on a par with the *concerti grossi* of Handel.

These fine new performances restore them to the catalogue in the most presentable manner and Hyperion's recording is very good indeed, to eclipse previous issues of this rewarding repertoire.

Waxman, Franz (1906–67)

Film scores: *Bride of Frankenstein: Creation of the female monster; Old Aquaintance: Elegy for strings. Philadelphia Story: Fanfare; Main title; True love. A Place in the Sun: suite. Prince Valiant: suite. Rebecca: suite. Sunset Boulevard: suite. Taras Bulba: suite.*

✹ (M) *** RCA GD 80708; *GK 80708* [0708-2-RG; *0708-4-RG*]. Nat. PO, Charles Gerhardt.

Of the many European musicians who crossed the Atlantic to make careers in Hollywood, Franz Waxman was among the most distinguished. His first important score was for James Whale's *Bride of Frankenstein*, a horror movie to which many film buffs give classic status. His marvellously evocative music for *The creation of the female monster* was restored by the conductor, mainly from listening to the film sound-track, as the orchestral parts are lost. Waxman stayed on to write for 188 films over 32 years. The opening of the first item on this CD and tape, the *Suite* from *Prince Valiant*, immediately shows the vigour of Waxman's invention and the brilliance of his Richard Straussian orchestration, and this score includes one of those sweeping string tunes which are the very epitome of Hollywood film music. Perhaps the finest of these comes in *A Place in the Sun*, and in the *Suite* it is used to preface an imaginative rhapsodical movement for solo alto sax (brilliantly played here by Ronnie Chamberlain). The collection ends with *The ride to Dubno* from *Taras Bulba* (Waxman's last film-score), which has thrilling impetus and energy and is scored with great flair. The orchestral playing throughout is marvellously eloquent, and the conductor's dedication is obvious. The recording is rich and full, with no lack of brilliance in this very successful transfer to compact disc.

Weber, Carl Maria von (1786–1826)

Bassoon concerto in F, Op. 75.
*** Denon Dig. CO 79281 [id.]. Werba, V. String Soloists, Honeck – HUMMEL; MOZART: *Concertos.* ***

Michael Werba's performance of the Weber concerto completes an attractive triptych. Both he and the accompanying group under Rainer Honeck capture the grand operatic flourishes of the first movement and the geniality of the finale. The recording is well balanced and vivid.

Clarinet concertino in E flat, Op. 26.
*** ASV Dig. CDDCA 559 [id.]. Emma Johnson, ECO, Groves – CRUSELL: *Concerto No. 2* *** ✹;
    BAERMANN: *Adagio ***; ROSSINI: Introduction, theme and variations. ***

Emma Johnson is in her element in Weber's delightful *Concertino*. Her phrasing is wonderfully beguiling and her use of light and shade agreeably subtle, while she finds a superb lilt in the final section, pacing the music to bring out its charm rather than achieve breathless bravura. Sir Charles Groves provides an admirable accompaniment, and the recording is eminently realistic and naturally balanced.

Clarinet concertos Nos. 1 in F min., Op. 73; 2 in E flat, Op. 74; Clarinet concertino in E flat, Op. 26.
✹ *** Denon Dig. CO 79551 [id.]. Paul Meyer, RPO, Günther Herbig.
*** Virgin/EMI Dig. VC7 59002-2 [id.]. Antony Pay, O of Age of Enlightenment.
(BB) *** Naxos Dig. 8.550378 [id.]. Ernst Ottensamer, Slovak State PO (Košice), Johannes Wildner.

The brilliant twenty-year-old Paul Meyer shows his prowess here in scintillating accounts of these three Weberian showpieces. He takes every risk in the book, using the widest possible dynamic range, at one moment using a robust cutting edge to his tone, at another fining it down to a magical *sotto voce*. In the slow movement of the *F minor Concerto* he blends delicately with the horn chorale and then, after a beautifully controlled diminuendo, dashes off, chortling through the finale with great glee. He is fortunate in having an excellent accompanist in Günther Herbig, and the RPO provides admirable support: the opening tutti of the *E flat Concerto* is particularly impressive. The *Concertino* is sheer delight from beginning to end. With fine recording this record is in a class of its own.

   Antony Pay and the Orchestra of the Age of Enlightenment offer period-instrument performances. Pay uses a copy of a seven-keyed clarinet by Sinriot of Lyons from 1800. The sonority is cleaner and less bland than can be the case in modern performances, and the solo playing is both expert and sensitive. A further gesture to authenticity is the absence of a conductor; however, the ensemble might have been even better and the texture more finely judged and balanced had there been one. The recording is vivid and truthful.

Ernst Ottensamer is a highly sensitive clarinettist, who has played with the major Viennese orchestras and is a member of the Vienna Wind Ensemble. His account of the two *Clarinet concertos* can hold its own against nearly all the competition in the current catalogue in any price category. The Košice orchestra also responds well to Johannes Wildner's direction, and the recorded sound is very natural and well balanced. A real bargain.

Clarinet concerto No. 2 in E flat, Op. 74.
(M) *** Decca 433 727-2 [id.]. Gervase de Peyer, LSO, C. Davis – MOZART; SPOHR: *Concertos.* ***

This first appeared in 1961, coupled with Spohr. For the reissue, the Mozart has been added to make an entertaining triptych, well recorded. With its operatic *Andante* and witty finale, the work invites and receives masterly playing from Gervase de Peyer – he is quite captivating in the closing *Rondo*, with some hair-raising roulades towards the end. The studio recording is a little dryish, but not excessively so. Excellent value.

Horn concertino in E min., Op. 45.
*** Ph. Dig. 412 237-2 [id.]. Baumann, Leipzig GO, Masur – R. STRAUSS: *Horn concertos.* **(*)

Baumann plays Weber's opening lyrical melody so graciously that the listener is led to believe that this is a more substantial work than it is. At the end of the *Andante* Baumann produces an undulating series of chords (by gently singing the top note as he plays) and the effect is spine-tingling, while the easy virtuosity of the closing *Polacca* is hardly less breathtaking. Masur's accompaniment has matching warmth, while the Leipzig Hall adds its usual flattering ambience.

Piano concertos Nos. 1 in C, Op. 18; 2 in E flat, Op. 32; Konzertstück, Op. 79.
(N) (B) **(*) Discovery Dig. DICD 920222 [id.]. Dana Protopopescu, Belgian R. & TV O, Rahbari.

Piano concertos Nos. 1–2; Konzertstück, Op. 79; Polacca brillante (L'hilarité), Op. 72 (orch. Liszt).
(N) (BB) *** Naxos Dig. 8.550959 [id.]. Benjamin Frith, Dublin R. & TV Sinf., Prionnsias O'Duinn.

The young Hungarian pianist, Dana Protopopescu, plays all three works with striking freshness and an almost Chopinesque feeling in the lyrical music. Her sparkling passage-work and the chimerical changes of tempo and character of the *Konzertstück* are deftly managed. She is persuasively partnered by Alexander Rahbari, who enters fully into the spirit of her romantic style, convincing the listener that these works gain much from the added colour of a modern piano. Excellent recording.

However, Benjamin Frith's accounts are even finer and he receives splendid support from O'Duinn and the excellent Dublin Sinfonietta. In consequence, these performances all have more depth (the *Konzertstück* is particularly fine). Both slow movements in the concertos bring rapt concentration; Frith's playing has plenty of dash, yet its impetuosity is never inclined to run away with itself (as from time to time it almost does with Dana Protopopescu). The Naxos CD is not only better recorded and less expensive, it also includes the appropriately named *L'hilarité Polacca brillante*, which Frith plays with attractive panache.

Konzertstück in F min., Op. 79.
*** Ph. 412 251-2 [id.]. Brendel, LSO, Abbado – SCHUMANN: *Piano concerto.* ***

This Philips version of Weber's programmatic *Konzertstück* is very brilliant indeed, and finds the distinguished soloist in his very best form: Brendel is wonderfully light and invariably imaginative. In every respect, including the recording quality, this is unlikely to be surpassed for a long time.

Overtures: *Der Freischütz; Oberon.*
(M) *** DG 415 840-2 [id.]. Bav. RSO, Kubelik – MENDELSSOHN: *Midsummer Night's Dream.* ***

Kubelik offers Weber's two greatest overtures as a fine bonus for his extended selection from Mendelssohn's *Midsummer Night's Dream* incidental music. The playing is first class and compares favourably with the Karajan versions.

Symphonies Nos. 1 in C; 2 in C.
**(*) ASV Dig. CDDCA 515 [id.]. ASMF, Marriner.

Symphonies Nos. 1 in C; 2 in C, J.50/51. Die Drei Pintos: Entr'acte. Silvana: Dance of the young nobles; Torch dance. Turandot: Overture; Act II: *March;* Act V: *Funeral march.*
(Y/B) 🏵 (BB) *** Naxos Dig. 8.550928 [id.]. Queensland PO, John Georgiadis.

Symphonies Nos. 1 in C; 2 in C; (i) *Konzertstück, Op. 79.*
(Y/B) *** EMI Dig. CDC5 55348-2 [id.]. L. Classical Players, Roger Norrington; (i) with Melvyn Tan.

Weber wrote his two symphonies in the same year (1807) and, though both are in C major, each has its own individuality. The witty orchestration and operatic character of the writing are splendidly caught in these sparkling Queensland performances, while in the slow movements the orchestral soloists (notably the languishing viola in the *Adagio* of No. 2) relish their solos, for all the world like vocal cantilenas. Weber's scoring is often adventurous and he finds plentiful opportunities for the horns to shine, especially in the playful main theme of the *Presto* finale of No. 1. Weber's writing is often unpredictable, not least in the surprising closing bars of No. 2; and Georgiadis and his players present both works with striking freshness and spontaneity. The Naxos recording is in the demonstration class, and the disc is made the more attractive for the inclusion of orchestral excerpts from two little-known operas and incidental music from *Turandot*. The *Entr'acte* from the incomplete *Die Drei Pintos* was put together by Mahler from Weber's sketches.

If you want period performances, Roger Norrington's with the London Classical Players meet the bill admirably and the symphonies come up with striking freshness. Compared with the sound of modern instruments, the effect is undoubtedly gruffer, but there is also rather more gravitas and the drama is heightened, with the spirit of Beethoven not far away, although neither of the symphonies is a weighty work in a Beethovenian sense. Norrington favours relatively relaxed allegros, yet rhythms are so well sprung that there is no hint of sluggishness. The quirkiness of some of the writing is reinforced; the bite is greater with period instruments, with contrasts of light and shade emphasized, with the braying of the hand horns adding to the character. However, though the textures are refined, the recording sometimes clouds big tuttis in a way one does not expect with simulated authenticity. Particularly beautiful are the oboe solos from Anthony Robson and the long cello solo in the *Adagio* of No. 2, here gloriously played by Jennifer Ward-Clarke: one is reminded of a slow movement of Haydn. As his bonus, Norrington offers the *Konzertstück*, with Melvyn Tan playing a Derek Adlam copy of an appropriate Streich instrument of 1815. He makes an impressive case for using an authentic fortepiano with its rather dry treble response, although the piece is made to seem more lightweight than usual. Personal taste will decide whether this relatively romantic work sounds better on a modern concert grand, as played, say, by Alfred Brendel. Here it remains a display piece, not because of conventional keyboard bravura but through the diamond clarity of the rapid figuration as delivered by Tan, even if the result is to suggest an occasional banality of argument.

Sir Neville Marriner also has the full measure of Weber's two symphonies; these performances combine vigour and high spirits with the right degree of gravitas (not too much) in the slow movements. The recording is clear and full in the bass, but the bright upper range brings a touch of digital edge to the upper strings.

CHAMBER AND INSTRUMENTAL MUSIC

Clarinet quintet in B flat, Op. 34.
(Y/B) (M) *** O-L 444 167-2 [id.]. Alan Hacker, The Music Party – HUMMEL: *Clarinet quartet.* ***
*** O-L Dig. 433 044-2 [id.]. Antony Pay, AAM Chamber Ens. – BEETHOVEN: *Septet.* **(*)

(i) *Clarinet quintet; Introduction, theme and variations for clarinet and string quartet, Op. posth.;* (ii) *Grand duo concertante in E flat, Op. 48; 7 Variations on a theme from Silvana in B flat, Op. 33* (both for clarinet and piano).
(N) (BB) *** Naxos Dig. 8.553122 [id.]. Kálmán Berkes, with (i) Auer Qt; (ii) Jenö Jandó.

Clarinet quintet; Flute trio in G min., Op. 63 (for flute, cello and piano).
*** CRD CRD 3398; *CRDC 4098* [id.]. Nash Ens.

(i) *Clarinet quintet;* (ii) *Grand duo concertante, Op. 48; 7 Variations on a theme from Silvana, Op. 33.*
**(*) Chandos Dig. CHAN 8366 [id.]. Hilton, (i) Lindsay Qt; (ii) Keith Swallow.

If you want to hear how Weber's *Clarinet quintet* must have sounded during his lifetime, Alan Hacker and the Music Party will probably be your first choice. The Gerock clarinet Hacker uses is from 1804, eleven years before the first complete performance of the *Quintet*. Hacker plays with his customary artistry and sensitivity, and with lots of bite and sparkle in the bravura passages. The recording is clear and vivid. Hacker has a price advantage and an ideal coupling.

On the CRD version, Antony Pay (playing a modern instrument) makes the very most of the work's bravura, catching the exuberance of the *Capriccio* third movement and the breezy gaiety of the finale. The Nash players provide an admirable partnership and then adapt themselves readily to the different mood of the *Trio*, another highly engaging work with a picturesque slow movement, described as a *Shepherd's lament*. The recording is first class, vivid yet well balanced.

For his second Oiseau-Lyre recording, Antony Pay uses a reconstruction of an 1810 clarinet and he has completely tamed it. This is another fresh and pleasing performance, with a finely sensitive *Adagio*, a brilliant third movement and some splendid giocoso roulades in the bravura finale. Those wanting an authentic account will find this hard to beat.

Naxos conveniently gather together expert and winning performances of Weber's major chamber works featuring the clarinet. If the *Introduction, theme and variations* is now considered spurious, it is still an agreeably amiable piece. The *Quintet* is particularly successful. Berkes leads a lusciously appealing account af the *Adagio* and then sets off, chortling with great zest, in the *Capriccio presto* Minuet; the finale is no less infectious in its sparkling virtuosity. With Jandó an admirable partner, the *Grand duo concertante* is hardly less successful, and the two sets of variations are presented with both elegance and panache. The recording, made in the Scottish Church, Budapest, is realistic if too resonant, but the charisma and spontaneity of this Hungarian music-making carry the day in spite of this.

Janet Hilton plays with considerable authority and spirit though she is not always as mellifluous as her rivals. However, her account of the *Grand duo concertante* is a model of fine ensemble, as are the *Variations on a theme from Silvana* of 1811, in both of which Keith Swallow is an equally expert partner. At times the acoustic seems almost too reverberant in the two pieces for clarinet and piano, but the sound in the *Quintet* is eminently satisfactory.

7 Variations on a theme from Silvana in B flat, Op. 33.
*** Chandos Dig. CHAN 8506 [id.]. Gervase de Peyer, Gwenneth Pryor – SCHUBERT: *Arpeggione sonata;* SCHUMANN: *Fantasiestücke* etc. ***

These engaging Weber *Variations* act as a kind of encore to Schubert's *Arpeggione sonata* and with their innocent charm they follow on naturally. They are most winningly played by Gervase de Peyer; Gwenneth Pryor accompanies admirably. The recording is first class.

PIANO MUSIC

Piano sonata No. 1 in C, Op. 24 (J.138); Invitation to the dance, Op. 65 (J.260); 6 Variations on an original theme, Op. 40 (J.7); 9 Variations on a Russian theme: 'Schöne Minka', Op. 40 (J.179).
(Y/B) (BB) ** Naxos Dig. 8.550988 [id.]. Alexander Paley.

Piano sonata No. 2 in A flat, Op. 39 (J.199); Grande Polonaise, Op. 21 (J.59); 6 Variations on Naga's aria: 'Woher mag dies wohl kommen?' from Vogler's opera, Samori, Op. 6 (J.43); 7 Variations on a gypsy song, Op. 55 (J.219).
(Y/B) (BB) ** Naxos Dig. 8.550989 [id.]. Alexander Paley.

Piano sonata No. 3 in D min., Op. 49 (J.206); Momento capriccioso, Op. 12 (J.56); 7 Variations on an original theme, Op. 9 (J.55); 7 Variations on Binchi's air: 'Vien quà, Dorina bella', Op. 7 (J.53); 8 Variations on the Air de ballet from Castore e Polluce by Abbé Vogler, Op. 5 (J.40).
(Y/B) (BB) ** Naxos Dig. 550990 [id.]. Alexander Paley.

Piano sonata No. 4 in E min., Op. 70 (J.287); Les Adieux, Op. 81 posth.; Polacca brillante (L'hilarité), Op. 72 (J.268); Rondo brillante (La gaîté), Op. 62 (J.252); 7 Variations on a theme from Méhul's opera, Joseph, Op. 28 (J.141).
(Y/B) (BB) **(*) Naxos Dig. 8.553006 [id.]. Alexander Paley.

Alexander Paley's survey of Weber's piano output is certainly comprehensive. His playing has finesse and polish and is often thoughtful, but it tends to reveal relatively little below the surface of the music. The result is generally pleasing, although at times Paley's rubato in Weber's secondary lyrical ideas is a little fussy and in the sets of variations, after announcing each theme characterfully, the playing seems to slip back into routine as if Paley were not really involved with Weber's invention. What does fire him is the bravura writing, and the Mendelssohnian *Momento capriccioso* on the third disc is vivaciously done. For some reason, the *Fourth E minor Sonata* also excites a strong response and this is easily the most compelling performance of the four. Then the closing *Rondo* and *Polacca* are thrown off infectiously. So disc four is the place to start if you are tempted by these inexpensive discs, which are all well recorded. But the sonata performances by Hamish Milne and Martin Jones are well worth their extra cost.

Piano sonatas Nos. 1 in C, Op. 24; 2 in A flat, Op. 39.
(M) *** Pianissimo Dig. PP 20792 [id.]. Martin Jones.

Piano sonatas Nos. 1–2; Rondo brillante in E flat (La Gaîté), Op. 52; Invitation to the dance, Op. 65.
*** CRD Dig. CRD 3485; *CRDC 4185* [id.]. Hamish Milne.

These two Weber *Sonatas* are not easy to bring off, with their classical heritage and operatic freedom of line. Martin Jones is clearly at home in both works, pacing the music so that it never sounds brittle, revealing an unexpected depth where some pianists would find only opportunities for surface display. He is particularly impressive in the *A flat major* work, concluding the Rondo finale with a fine balance between virtuosity and grazioso feeling. The recording, made in the resonant but not too-resonant acoustic of the Concert Hall of Cardiff University, is admirable and seems just right for his relatively grand manner.

Hamish Milne's style is less overtly expansive, more chimerical, his performances have a lightness of touch that is most appealing, without ever being superficial, and his playing in the slow movements has attractive lyrical feeling. If you want added gravitas, turn to Jones, but Milne's readings are equally truthful to the composer's intentions. Moreover he also provides a sparkling account of the *Rondo brillante* and, as a final encore, a totally captivating account of the charming *Invitation to the dance*, making it sound every bit as appealing on the piano as in Berlioz's orchestration. He is realistically recorded in the BBC Studios at Pebble Mill in Birmingham.

Piano sonata No. 2 in A flat, Op. 39.
*** Ph. Dig. 426 439-2 [id.]. Alfred Brendel – BRAHMS: *4 Ballades*. ***

Masterly playing from Alfred Brendel, who makes out a strong case for the Weber *Sonata* which in his hands has seriousness and strength as well as charm. Everything is thoroughly thought out, and one feels that the slightest hesitation is carefully calculated. If there is a certain want of spontaneity, there is no want of mastery. Brendel is recorded in sound of marvellous presence and clarity.

Piano sonata Nos. 3 in D min., Op. 49; 4 in E min., Op. 70; Polacca brillante in E (L'Hilarité) (with LISZT: *Introduzione (Adagio)*).
*** CRD Dig. CRD 3486; *CRDC 4186* [id.]. Hamish Milne.

Hamish Milne here completes his admirable survey of the Weber *Piano sonatas* with a sterner approach to the opening *Allegro feroce* of *No. 3 in D minor*, cast in an almost Beethovenian mould. But Weber was always himself, and operatic feeling inevitably creeps into the lyrical material as well as the passage-work. The last sonata is more introspective in its colouring and feeling, and the work concludes with a ruthless Tarantella, driven on by its own restless energy. The *Polacca brillante* returns to the world of dazzling articulation and sparkling display. It is heard here with a slow introduction which Liszt arranged from the *Grande Polonaise* of 1808. Hamish Milne's playing is thoroughly inside Weber's world and technically equal to the composer's prodigious demands. He is very well recorded.

OPERA

Die drei Pintos (complete; adapted Mahler).
(N) (M) *** RCA 74321 32246-2 (2) [id.]. Popp, Hollweg, Prey, Scovotti, Moll, Munich PO, Bertini.

A valuable addition to the catalogue, even though the assurance on the box, 'libretto enclosed', is misleading for there is only the German text. *Die drei Pintos* was left unfinished by Weber; he started work on it in 1820 but managed to sketch only seven numbers. Mahler completed it in the 1880s, adding 15 more, 11 of which were rearrangements of other Weber. The performance here is recorded complete with the spoken dialogue separately cued so that one can bypass it if necessary. The soloists are excellent and the whole production is lively and dramatic, while the orchestral support under Gary Bertini is first rate. So is the chorus, and you will need to sample only the engaging opening *Auf Wiedersehn* ensemble, with Werner Hollweg a fresh-voiced Gaston, to be won over immediately. The sound is excellent, warmly atmospheric and with cleaner detail than on the original LPs.

Der Freischütz (complete).
(M) *** EMI CMS7 69342-2 (2). Grümmer, Otto, Schock, Prey, Wiemann, Kohn, Frick, German Op. Ch., Berlin, BPO, Keilberth.
*** DG 415 432-2 (2) [id.]. Janowitz, Mathis, Schreier, Adam, Vogel, Crass, Leipzig R. Ch., Dresden State O, Carlos Kleiber.
(Y/B) **(*) RCA Dig. 09026 62538-2 (2) [id.]. Sweet, Ziesak, Seiffert, Rydl, Scharinger, Berlin R. Ch., German Opera, Berlin, O, Janowski.
(B) ** DG Double 439 717-2 (2) [id.]. Seefried, Holm, Streich, Böhme, Waechter, Bav. R. Ch. & O, Jochum.
** Ph. Dig. 426 319-2 (2) [id.]. Karita Mattila, Francisco Araiza, Eva Lind, Ekkehard Wlaschiha, Kurt Moll, Dresden Op. Ch. & State O, Sir Colin Davis.
(Y/B) (M) ** Decca 443 672-2 (2) [id.]. Behrens, Donath, Meven, Kollo, Moll, Brendel, Grumbach, Bav. R. Ch. & SO, Kubelik.

Keilberth's is a warm, exciting account of Weber's masterpiece which makes all the dated conventions of the work seem fresh and new. In particular the Wolf's glen scene on CD acquires something of the genuine terror that must have struck the earliest audiences and which is far more impressive than any mere scene-setting with wood and cardboard in the opera house. The casting of the magic bullets with each one numbered in turn, at first in eerie quiet and then in crescendo amid the howling of demons, is superbly conveyed. The bite of the orchestra and the proper balance of the voices in relation to it, with the effect of space and distance, helps also to create the illusion. Elisabeth Grümmer sings more sweetly and sensitively than one ever remembers before, with Agathe's prayer exquisitely done. Lisa Otto is really in character, with genuine coquettishness. Schock is not an ideal tenor, but he sings ably enough. The Kaspar of Karl Kohn is generally well focused, and the playing of the Berlin Philharmonic has plenty of polish. The overall effect is immensely atmospheric and enjoyable.

The DG set marked Carlos Kleiber's first major recording venture and this fine, incisive account of Weber's atmospheric and adventurous score fulfilled all expectations. With the help of an outstanding cast, excellent work by the recording producer, and transparently clear recording, this is a most compelling version of an opera which transfers well to the gramophone. Only occasionally does Kleiber betray a fractional lack of warmth, but the full drama of the work is splendidly projected in the enhanced CD format.

In full-bodied, if not always refined, sound, with voices well forward, Marek Janowski conducts a strong, generally enjoyable performance that does not replace earlier versions such as Carlos Kleiber's or indeed Keilberth's. Outstanding in the cast are Ruth Ziesak as Aennchen, light and sparkling, and Peter Seiffert who, as Max, produces unstrained, heroic tone. As Kaspar, Kurt Rydl suffers from the closeness of the recording, which exaggerates an unevenness of production, though the characterization is strong. The key figure is that of the heroine, Agathe, with Sharon Sweet generally controlling her weighty soprano well in the lovely legato lines of her two big arias, but sounding too lusty, rarely producing a true pianissimo. This hardly matches the finest performances in this difficult role. As for the big dramatic moments, the forward sound adds to their power, atmospheric subtlety is lacking, even in the Wolf's Glen scene.

On the face of it, Jochum's cast is as impressive as that on the EMI version, but there are too many disappointments here for the DG set to measure up. To begin with, Seefried is decidedly off-colour. There is nothing 'inner'; it is all too matter-of-fact, with the usual creamy tone sounding beautiful but hardly ever moving or in character. Streich sings her charming coquettish song, *Kommt ein schlanker Bursch gegangen*, with delicious lightness, but again the characterization is not very well conveyed and what dialogue remains here is not done as dramatically as on the HMV set. The recording weighs heavily in favour of the voices at the expense of the orchestra, and in the Wolf's Glen scene this detracts from the sense of excitement. Overall the performance is lively enough and the CD transfer of a set first published on LP in 1960 is remarkably vivid, but the reservations remain while the inadequate documentation offers only a very brief synopsis.

Sir Colin Davis paces this magic score very well indeed, and the Dresden forces respond with some fine playing and singing. To add to the drama there are plenty of production sounds, even including the barking of hounds, with shots that have you jumping out of your seat. Even so, this is a set that fails to convey the full power of the Wolf's Glen scene, where the casting of the magic bullets sounds tame, not frightening at all. The singing is flawed too. Karita Mattila's warm, vibrant soprano is apt enough for Agathe, and she controls the soaring lines of her two big arias very beautifully, but *Und ob die Wolke* brings under-the-note coloration which may distress some ears. As Max, Francisco Araiza is seriously stressed, with the basically beautiful voice sounding throaty, and Eva Lind is unpleasantly fluttery and shallow as Aennchen. Ekkehard Wlaschiha, best known as Alberich in the *Ring*, is darkly sinister as Kaspar, and it is good too to have Kurt Moll as the Hermit.

Kubelik takes a direct view of Weber's high romanticism. The result has freshness but lacks something in dramatic bite and atmosphere. There is far less tension than in the finest earlier versions, not least in the Wolf's Glen scene, which in spite of full-ranging, brilliant recording seems rather tame. The singing is generally good – René Kollo as Max giving one of his best performances on record – but Hildegard Behrens, superbly dramatic in later German operas, here as Agathe seems clumsy in music that often requires a pure lyrical line. The sound has been successfully remastered; but this cannot compare with Keilberth's early EMI set.

Der Freischütz: highlights.
(Y/B) (B) *** DG 439 440-2 [id.] (from above recording, with Janowitz, Mathis; cond. Carlos Kleiber).

Anyone looking for a set of highlights from *Der Freischütz* cannot better this bargain Classikon disc, taken from a compelling performance which is consistently well sung and dramatically conducted by

Carlos Kleiber. The 73-minute selection includes the full Wolf's Glen scene at the end of Act II, and the 1973 recording still sounds very well indeed.

Oberon (complete).

(M) *** DG 419 038-2 (2) [id.] Grobe, Nilsson, Domingo, Prcy, Hamari, Schiml, Bav. R. Ch. & SO, Kubelik.

Weber's delicately conceived score is a sequence of illogical arias, scenas and ensembles strung together by an absurd pantomime plot. Although, even on record, the result is slacker because of that loose construction, one can appreciate the contribution of Weber, in a performance as stylish and refined as on DG. The original issue included dialogue and a narrative spoken by one of Oberon's fairy characters. In the reissue this is omitted, cutting the number of discs from three to two, yet leaving the music untouched. With Birgit Nilsson commanding in *Ocean, thou mighty monster*, and excellent singing from the other principals, helped by Kubelik's ethereally light handling of the orchestra, the set can be recommended without reservation, for the recording remains of excellent quality.

Webern, Anton (1883–1945)

(i) *Concerto for nine instruments, Op. 24; 5 Movements for string quartet* (orchestral version), *Op. 5; Passacaglia, Op. 1; 6 Pieces for large orchestra, Op. 6; 5 Pieces for orchestra, Op. 10; Symphony, Op. 21; Variations for orchestra, Op. 30.* Arrangements of: BACH: *Musical offering: Fugue* (1935). (ii) SCHUBERT: *German dances* (for small orchestra), *Op. posth.* Chamber music: (iii) *6 Bagatelles for string quartet, Op. 9; 5 Movements for string quartet, Op. 5;* (iv; v) *4 Pieces for violin and piano, Op. 7;* (v; vi) *3 Small pieces for cello and piano, Op. 11;* (v; vii) *Quartet, Op. 22* (for piano, violin, clarinet & saxophone); (iii) *String quartet, Op. 28; String trio, Op. 20;* (v) *Variations for piano, Op. 27.* (Vocal) (viii; i) *Das Augenlicht, Op. 26;* (ix; x) *5 Canons on Latin texts, Op. 16;* (viii; ix; i) *Cantata No. 1, Op. 29;* (viii; ix; xi; i) *Cantata No. 2, Op. 31;* (viii) *Entflieht auf leichten Kähnen, Op. 2;* (ix; x) *5 Sacred songs, Op. 15;* (xii; v) *5 Songs, Op. 3; 5 Songs, Op. 4;* (xii; x) *2 Songs, Op. 8;* (xii; v) *4 Songs, Op. 12;* (xii; x) *4 Songs, Op. 13; 6 Songs, Op. 14;* (ix; x; xiii) *3 Songs, Op. 18;* (viii; i) *2 Songs, Op. 19;* (xii; v) *3 Songs, Op. 23;* (ix; v) *3 Songs, Op. 25;* (ix; x) *3 Traditional rhymes, Op. 17.*

(M) *** Sony SM3K 45845 (3) [id.]. (i) LSO (or members), Pierre Boulez; (ii) Frankfurt R. O, composer (recorded December 1932); (iii) Juilliard Qt (or members); (iv) Stern; (v) Rosen; (vi) Piatigorsky; (vii) Majeske, Marcellus, Weinstein; (viii) John Alldis Ch.; (ix) Lukomska; (x) with Ens., Boulez; (xi) McDaniel; (xii) Harper; (xiii) with John Williams. Overall musical direction: Boulez.

These three CDs contain all Webern's works with opus numbers, as well as the string orchestra arrangements of Op. 5 and the orchestration of the *Fugue* from Bach's *Musical offering*. A rare recording of Webern himself conducting his arrangement of Schubert dances is also included. What Pierre Boulez above all demonstrates in the orchestral works (including those with chorus) is that, for all his seeming asceticism, Webern was working on human emotions. The Juilliard Quartet and the John Alldis Choir convey comparable commitment; though neither Heather Harper nor Halina Lukomska is ideally cast in the solo vocal music, Boulez brings out the best in both of them in the works with orchestra. Rarely can a major composer's whole *oeuvre* be appreciated in so compact a span. There are excellent notes, every item is cued, and perhaps it is carping to regret that the *Passacaglia* and *Variations for orchestra* were not indexed.

Concerto for 9 instruments, Op. 24.

(M) *** Chandos CHAN 6534 [id.]. Nash Ens., Simon Rattle – SCHOENBERG: *Pierrot Lunaire*. ***

This late Webern piece, tough, spare and uncompromising, makes a valuable fill-up for Jane Manning's outstanding version of Schoenberg's *Pierrot Lunaire*, a 1977 recording originally made for the Open University. First-rate sound and a beautifully clean CD transfer.

Langsamer satz (arr. Schwarz).

*** Delos Dig. DE 3121 [id.]. Seattle SO, Gerard Schwarz – HONEGGER: *Symphony No. 2;* R. STRAUSS: *Metamorphosen.* ***

The slow movement Webern composed in 1905 for string quartet sounds even more Mahlerian in Gerard Schwarz's transcription for full strings, which is eloquently played and sumptuously recorded.

5 Movements, Op. 5; Passacaglia, Op. 1; 6 Pieces for orchestra, Op. 6; Symphony, Op. 21.

(M) *** DG 427 424-2 (3) [id.]. BPO, Karajan – BERG: *Lyric suite; 3 Pieces;* SCHOENBERG: *Pelleas und Melisande; Variations; Verklaerte Nacht.* ***

(M) *** DG 423 254-2 [id.]. BPO, Karajan.

Available either separately or within Karajan's three-CD compilation, this collection, devoted to four compact and chiselled Webern works, is in many ways the most remarkable of all. Karajan's expressive refinement reveals the emotional undertones behind this seemingly austere music, and the results are riveting. Karajan secures a highly sensitive response from the Berlin Philharmonic, who produce sonorities as seductive as Debussy. Incidentally, he plays the 1928 version of Op. 6. A strong recommendation, with excellent sound.

Passacaglia for orchestra.
(N) (BB) *** RCA Navigator 74321 29243-2. Cologne RSO, Wakasugi – BERG: *Violin concerto;* SCHOENBERG: *Verklärte Nacht.* ***

The Cologne Radio Symphony Orchestra understand what this music is about and under Hiroshi Wakasugi give a powerfully committed and very well-played account of Webern's most spectacular orchestral work. The 1977 recording is full and atmospheric, and the couplings on this inexpensive CD of key twentieth-century works are equally recommendable, despite inadequate documentation.

5 Pieces for orchestra, Op. 10.
(M) *** Mercury 432 006-2 [id.]. LSO, Dorati – BERG: *3 Pieces* etc; SCHOENBERG: *5 Pieces.* ***

Webern's *Five pieces*, Op. 10, written between 1911 and 1913, mark a radical point in his early development. Their compression is extreme. The couplings could hardly be more fitting, and the whole record can be strongly recommended to anyone wanting to explore the early work of Schoenberg and his followers before they formalized their ideas in twelve-note technique. Bright, clear, 1962 recording to match the precision of the writing.

6 Pieces for orchestra, Op. 6.
*** EMI Dig. CDC7 49857-2 [id.]. CBSO, Rattle – SCHOENBERG: *5 Pieces;* BERG: *Lulu: suite.* ***
*** DG Dig. 419 781-2 [id.]. BPO, Levine – BERG: *3 Pieces;* SCHOENBERG: *5 Pieces.* ***

Rattle and the CBSO bring out the microcosmic strength of the six Webern *Pieces*, giving them weight and intensity without inflation. Warmth is rightly implied here, but no Mahlerian underlining. A superb performance, given sound of demonstration quality.

Levine brings out the expressive warmth of Webern's writing, with no chill in the spare fragmentation of argument and with much tender poetry. With the longest of the six tiny movements, the *Funeral march*, particularly powerful, it complements the other works on the disc perfectly. Ripe recording, with some spotlighting of individual lines.

Slow movement for string quartet (1905).
✲ *** Denon Dig. CO 79462 [id.]. Carmina Qt – SZYMANOWSKI: *String quartets Nos. 1 & 2.* *** ✲
*** DG Dig. 437 836-2. Hagen Qt – DEBUSSY; RAVEL: *Quartets.* ***

The single-movement Webern *Quartet* was composed in Carinthia in the summer of 1905 and was first heard in the 1960s. It has an intense and chromatic study, and is played with great refinement by the Hagen Quartet and beautifully recorded. An excellent *bonne bouche*, if that term is appropriate, for a superb Debussy and Ravel coupling.

On Denon, Webern's early quartet movement is equally beautifully played and comes as a pendant to an altogether outstanding performance and recording of the two Szymanowski quartets.

Weill, Kurt (1900–1950)

Violin concerto.
(N) *** Virgin/EMI Dig. VC5 45056-2 [id.]. Christian Tetzlaff, Deutsche Kammerphilharmonie Wind – HINDEMITH: *Septet;* TOCH: *5 Pieces for wind and percussion.* ***

Weill's *Concerto for violin and winds* dates from 1924, just after the twenty-four-year-old had completed his studies with Busoni. It has a seriousness of purpose and an originality that are persuasive, no doubt much helped by the highly sensitive and imaginative performance given by Christian Tetzlaff and the winds of the Deutsche Kammerphilharmonie. There are rival versions on the market; however, this is a marvellous performance and recording in every way; it is coupled with most interesting repertoire. It will surely convert any doubters about the quality of this work as it has us.

Symphonies Nos. 1–2.
(N) (M) ** EMI CDM7 65869-2 [id.]. BBC SO, Gary Bertini – BUSONI: *Berceuse élégiaque* ***; SCHOENBERG: *Chamber Symphony No. 2.* **(*)

Kurt Weill's unpredictable symphonies are fascinating, the first a student piece written in Berlin in 1921 when Weill was still a Busoni pupil. However, the influences were mainly from Mahler and Schoenberg, and the youthful urgency and imagination of the argument in a complex interlinked form carries the work off most successfully. No. 2 (1933–4) is obviously a more mature work, with three colourful and effective movements that are nearer to the idiom of Shostakovich and Kabalevsky. Behind the characteristic ostinatos and near-vulgar melodies there is a lurking seriousness. The performances are committed but could be better disciplined. No complaints about the late-1960s recording.

The Ballad of Magna Carta; Der Lindberghflug.
*** Capriccio Dig. 60012-l [id.]. Henschel, Tyl, Calaminus, Clemens, Cologne Pro Musica Ch. & RSO, Latham-König; Wirl, Schmidt, Feckler, Minth, Scheeben, Berlin R. Ch. & O, Scherchen.

Der Lindberghflug ('The Lindbergh Flight') is a curiosity, a radio entertainment on the subject which was then (in 1927) hitting the headlines: the first solo flight across the Atlantic by Charles Lindbergh. Brecht wrote the text, and Weill started on the music, but for the Baden-Baden Festival it was diplomatic to ask Hindemith to set some of the numbers, and that is how it first appeared. Only later did Weill set the complete work, and that is how it is given in this excellent Cologne recording. As a curiosity, a historic 1930 performance of the original Weill–Hindemith version, conducted by Hermann Scherchen, is given as an appendix, recorded with a heavy background roar but with astonishingly vivid voices. One can understand why Weill was so enthusiastic about the fine, very German tenor who sang Lindbergh in 1930, Erik Wirl. The tenor in the new recording is not nearly so sweet-toned, and the German narrator delivers his commentary in a casual, matter-of-fact way. Otherwise the performance under Jan Latham-König fully maintains the high standards of Capriccio's Weill series; and the other, shorter item, *The Ballad of Magna Carta*, another radio feature, written in America in 1940 to fanciful doggerel by Maxwell Anderson, is most enjoyable too, a piece never recorded before. Clear, if rather dry, recording with voices vivid and immediate.

Die Dreigroschenoper (The Threepenny Opera): complete.
*** Decca Dig. 430 075-2 [id.]. Kollo, Lemper, Milva, Adorf, Dernesch, Berlin RIAS Chamber Ch. & Sinf., Mauceri.
*** Sony MK 42637 [id.]. Lenya, Neuss, Trenk-Trebisch, Hesterberg, Schellow, Koczian, Grunert, Ch. & Dance O of Radio Free Berlin, Brückner-Rüggeberg.

Decca's all-star production is fitted on to a single, generously filled CD. There are obvious discrepancies between the opera-singers, René Kollo and Helga Dernesch, and those in the cabaret tradition, notably the vibrant and provocative Ute Lemper (Polly Peachum) and the gloriously dark-voiced and characterful Milva (Jenny). That entails downward modulation in various numbers, as it did with Lotte Lenya, but the changes from the original are far less extreme. Kollo is good, but Dernesch is even more compelling. The co-ordination of music and presentation makes for a vividly enjoyable experience, even if committed Weill enthusiasts will inevitably disagree with some of the controversial textual and interpretative decisions.

The CBS alternative offers a vividly authentic abridged recording, darkly incisive and atmospheric, with Lotte Lenya giving an incomparable performance as Jenny. All the wrong associations, built up round the music from indifferent performances, melt away in the face of a reading as sharp and intense as this. Bright, immediate, real stereo recording, made the more vivid on CD.

Happy End (play by Brecht with songs); *Die sieben Todsünden (The Seven deadly sins)*.
(M) *** Sony mono/stereo MPK 45886 [id.]. Lotte Lenya, male quartet & O, Ch. & O, Brückner-Rüggeberg.

The Sony/CBS performance of *The Seven deadly sins*, with the composer's widow as principal singer, underlines the status of this distinctive mixture of ballet and song-cycle as one of Weill's most concentrated inspirations. The rhythmic verve is irresistible and, though Lenya had to have the music transposed down, her understanding of the idiom is unique. The recording is forward and slightly harsh, though Lenya's voice is not hardened, and the effect is undoubtedly vivid. *Happy end* was made in Hamburg-Harburg in 1960. Lenya turned the songs into a kind of cycle (following a hint from her husband), again transposing where necessary, and her renderings in her individual brand of vocalizing are so compelling they make the scalp tingle.

The Rise and fall of Mahagonny (complete).
**(*) Sony MK 77341 (2) [M2K 37874]. Lenya, Litz, Gunter, Mund, Gollnitz, Markworth, Saverbaum, Roth, Murch (speaker), NW German R. Ch. and O, Brückner-Rüggeberg.

Though Lotte Lenya, with her metallic rasping voice, was more a characterful *diseuse* than a singer, and this bitterly inspired score had to be adapted to suit her limited range, it remains a most memorable performance. The recording lacks atmosphere, with voices (Lenya's in particular) close balanced. Yet even now one can understand how this cynical piece caused public outrage when it was first performed in Leipzig in 1930.

Der Silbersee (complete).
*** Capriccio Dig. 60011-2 (2) [id.]. Heichele, Tamassy, Holdorf, Schmidt, Mayer, Korte, Thomas, Cologne Pro Musica Ch., Cologne RSO, Latham-König.

This restoration of the original score of *Der Silbersee*, written just before Weill left Nazi Germany, aims to cope with the basic problem presented by having his music as adjunct, not to a regular music-theatre piece, but to a full-length play by Georg Kaiser. Between Weill's numbers a smattering of the original dialogue is here included to provide a dramatic thread and the speed of delivery adds to the effectiveness. Led by Hildegard Heichele, bright and full-toned as the central character, Fennimore, the cast is an outstanding one, with each voice satisfyingly clean-focused, while the 1989 recording is rather better-balanced and kinder to the instrumental accompaniment than some from this source, with the voices exceptionally vivid.

Die sieben Todsünden (The seven deadly sins) complete.
(M) *** EMI Dig. CDM7 64739-2 [id.]. Ross, Rolfe Johnson, Caley, Rippon, Tomlinson, CBSO, Rattle – STRAVINSKY: *Pulcinella*. ***

(i) *Die sieben Todsünden (The seven deadly sins); Kleine Dreigroschenmusik.*
(Y/B) (M) *** Sony Dig. SMK 44529 [id.]. (i) Migenes, Tear, Kale, Opie, Kennedy; LSO, Tilson Thomas.

(i) *Die sieben Todsünden (The seven deadly sins);* (ii) *Mahagonny Singspiel.*
*** Decca Dig. 430 168-2 [id.]. Lemper, Wildhaber, Haage, Mohr, Jungwirth, Berlin RIAS Chamber Ens., Mauceri, (ii) with J. Cohen.

(i; ii) *Die sieben Todsünden (The seven deadly sins);* (i) *Songs: Berlin im Licht; Complainte de la Seine; Es regnet; Youkali; Nannas Lied (Meine Herren, mit Siebzehn); Wie lange noch?.*
**(*) HM Dig. HMC 90 1420 [id.]. (i) Fassbaender; (ii) Brandt, Sojer, Komatsu, Urbas; Hanover R. PO, Garben.

Rattle's moving account of this Brecht–Weill collaboration gives it a tender but refreshing new look. The key point is the casting of Elsie Ross as the two Annas, the one idealistic, the other practical, who in this sharply drawn sequence visit various American cities and their respective deadly sins. It was the first version to use the original soprano pitch (as does the newer account with Fassbaender on Harmonia Mundi). The higher pitch makes it easier for Elsie to contrast the singing of Anna I with the speaking of Anna II. The final epilogue brings them back to where they started, beside the Mississippi in Louisiana; and the agony of disillusion is presented with total heartache, thanks to Miss Ross's acting. Her singing is sweet and tender, rather than a more abrasive cabaret style: she is far less aggressive than Lotte Lenya's version (see above, under *Happy end*), and though Rattle's direction is sharp and analytical the spring in the rhythm and nicely judged expressiveness of phrase give a warmth which is very attractive and also brings out the work's often Mahlerian intensity. Rattle's speeds – nearer to Tilson Thomas's fast ones than to Mauceri's slow – have the dramatic bite of the one and the poignancy of the other, and the vocal quartet has the best voices of all, but loses some impact from being balanced (like the soprano) relatively distantly. But with such a generous coupling and at mid-price, it must be our primary recommendation. The digital recording has plenty of theatrical atmosphere.

Using the lower-pitch version of *The Seven deadly sins* originally designed for Lotte Lenya, but with Weill's original instrumentation, the Decca issue presents Ute Lemper in one of her finest performances on record. Her sensuous, tough voice, in the tradition of Lenya but very distinct from her in its characterfulness, exactly suits the role of the first Anna, who does all the singing. Mauceri's speeds, consistently slower than those of Rattle or Tilson Thomas, also enhance the sensuous element while bringing out the strange poignancy of the Prologue and Epilogue. The chattering ensemble of four male singers – closely balanced in a slightly different acoustic from the orchestra – is well cast with voices apt for German cabaret style, and John Mauceri equally brings out the tang of the instrumental writing. He is rather less successful in the Singspiel, perhaps reflecting the fact that Lemper's role – mainly in duet with a singer of similar timbre – is less distinctive. Yet with similar forces required, it makes the ideal coupling. Full, bright sound to bring out the bite of the music.

In Tilson Thomas's performance with the LSO, Julia Migenes also uses the lower version of the score, colouring the voice even more boldly than Ute Lemper, echoing, even imitating, Lenya closely. With voices and instruments forwardly focused in the same consistent acoustic, the bite of the writing and its tangy beauty are put over powerfully, with Tilson Thomas's relatively brisk speeds adding to the power rather than to the poignancy. This makes a formidable mid-priced alternative to the Rattle and Mauceri versions, in some ways more forceful than either, but with a coupling, apt as it is, rather less generous.

The Harmonia Mundi version stars Brigitte Fassbaender who, using the original pitch, brings a Lieder-singer's feeling for word-detail and a comparable sense of style. Her account is obviously less street-wise than Lemper's but there is a plangent feeling that is highly appropriate. The songs are equally impressive, mostly connected in some way or another with the main piece. The vocal quartet make an impressive team but, especially alongside Rattle, the conductor, Cord Garben, at times seems on the leisurely side in his choice of tempi. Excellent, vivid recording.

Street scene (opera): complete.
*** TER Dig. CDTER2 1185 (2) [id.]. Kristine Ciesinski, Janis Kelly, Bottone, Van Allan, ENO Ch. and O, Carl Davis.

Street scene was Kurt Weill's attempt, late in his Broadway career, to write an American opera as distinct from a musical. The TER set was made with the cast of the ENO production at the Coliseum, and the idiomatic feeling and sense of flow consistently reflect that. Some of the solo singing in the large cast is flawed, but never seriously, and the principals are all very well cast – Kristine Ciesinski as the much-put-upon Anna Maurrant, Richard van Allan as her sorehead husband, Janis Kelly sweet and tender as the vulnerable daughter, and Bonaventura Bottone as the diffident young Jewish neighbour who loves her. Those are only a few of the sharply drawn characters, and the performance on the discs, with dialogue briskly paced, reflects the speed of the original ENO production. Warm, slightly distanced sound.

Der Zar lässt sich Photographieren (complete).
**(*) Capriccio Dig. 60 007-1 [id.]. McDaniel, Pohl, Napier, Cologne R. O, Latham-König.

This curious one-act *opera buffa* is a wry little parable about assassins planning to kill the Tsar when he has his photograph taken. Angèle, the photographer, is replaced by the False Angèle, but the Tsar proves to be a young man who simply wants friendship, and the would-be assassin, instead of killing him, plays a tango on the gramophone, before the Tsar's official duties summon him again. Jan Latham-König in this 1984 recording directs a strong performance, though the dryly recorded orchestra is consigned to the background. The voices fare better, though Barry McDaniel is not ideally steady as the Tsar.

Weinberger, Jaromír (1896–1967)

Schwanda the Bagpiper: Polka and fugue.
(Y/B) (M) *** RCA 09026 62587-2 [id.]. Chicago SO, Fritz Reiner – DVORAK: *Symphony No. 9* etc.; SMETANA: *Bartered Bride: overture.* ***

This infectious orchestral display-piece was better known in the days of 78s. Reiner and his fine orchestra give a bravura performance, building to a huge climax. The Chicago recording is excellent and this CD overall is most attractive.

Weiner, Léo (1885–1960)

Hungarian folkdance suite, Op. 18.
(N) *** Chandos Dig. CHAN 9029 [id.]. Philh. O, Järvi – BARTOK: *Miraculous Mandarin.* **(*)

Though he was born in Budapest just four years after Bartók, Weiner remained orientated towards the German and French schools until after the First World War. This charming suite, completed in 1931, represents a Hungarian folk style far milder than Bartók's; but, with purposeful direction from Järvi, fine dramatic playing from the orchestra and ripely resonant recording, the full range of colour is brought out in these four movements lasting almost half an hour. They make an attractive and well-contrasted coupling for the violent Bartók ballet.

Weir, Judith (born 1954)

OPERA

Blond Eckbert (complete).
(Y/B) *** Collins Dig. 1461-2 [id.]. Nerys Jones, Owens, Ventris, Folwell, ENO Ch. & O, Sian Edwards.

Not everyone will respond to the bald style of the libretto, with characters on entry tending to sing monologues about their life-stories rather than joining in conversation. Yet the bright clarity and fresh invention of Weir's writing follows on the style she has adopted with such success in previous operas and mini-operas. The original English National Opera staging was over-elaborate for so basically simple a piece, which makes this disc welcome in letting one appreciate the musical qualities without distraction. The singing is clean-cut and generally fresh, with Christopher Ventris excellent in multiple tenor roles, but with Nicholas Folwell gruff-sounding in the title-role. Excellent sound.

(i) *The Consolations of scholarship;* (ii) *Missa del Cid;* (iii) *King Harald's Saga.*
(Y/B) *** United Dig. 88040 CD [id.]. (i) Linda Hirst, Lontano, Odaline de la Martinez; (ii) Herrett, Combattimento, Mason; (iii) Jane Manning.

King Harald's Saga is a 13-minute sequence in three Acts, based on the Norwegian invasion of Britain under Harald Hardradi in 1066. With Jane Manning the magnetic soloist, it has the singer unaccompanied in a virtuoso performance. In the other two operas on this disc, Weir again uses spoken dialogue freely, with the solitary singer in each freely ringing the changes, but the chamber accompaniments expand the range of expression. *The Consolations of scholarship* has a libretto reflecting the style of Yuan drama, the oldest form of Chinese play. The mixture of speech, declamation and aria was suggested by the original text, involving a surprisingly elaborate story about a boy thwarting a wicked general's plot against the Emperor. The *Missa del Cid* of 1988, also lasting 20 minutes, is simpler in outline though again involving an elaborate story, with the exploits of El Cid told by an Evangelist in a sequence built on the six sections of the Latin Mass. The idiom in each opera is distinctive and new, but not hard to take in, with the story element more clearly established than in many far longer operas. Performances and recording are excellent, with Linda Hirst joined by Odaline de la Martinez in *Consolations* and Nick Herrett with Combattimento under David Mason in the *Missa.*

Weiss, Silvius (1686–1750)

Overture in B flat; Suite in D min.; Suite No. 17 in F min.
(M) *** RCA GD 77217 [77217-2-RG]. Konrad Junghänel (lute).

The Silesian composer Silvius Leopold Weiss was an almost exact contemporary of J. S. Bach and was regarded in his day as the greatest lutenist of the Baroque. Konrad Junghänel plays a Baroque 13-string lute by Nico van der Waals with splendid authority and musicianship, though, as so often with recordings of soft-spoken instruments like the lute or the clavichord, the level is too high and best results are obtained by playing this at a lower volume setting.

Wert, Giaches de (1535–96)

Il settimo libro de madrigali.
(Y/B) (M) *** Virgin Veritas/EMI Dig. VER5 61177-2 [id.]. Consort of Musicke, Anthony Rooley.

Giaches de Wert was Monteverdi's predecessor in Mantua at the court of Count Alfonso Gonzaga. He was fairly prolific: this is the seventh of twelve books of madrigals, published in 1581 to celebrate the nuptials of the Duke's son, Vincenzo, and the final dialogue madrigal, *In qual parte sì ratto* ('Where are his swift pinions'), cleverly embroiders the elements of the bridegroom's family (an eagle) and those of his bride (the hyacinth: 'A flawless white pearl'). The opening madrigal is celebratory: *Sorgi e rischiara* ('Arise, light up the sky with thy approach, Holy Mother of love, lead in the day'), but many of the other varied settings are concerned with the trials and disappointments of love. De Wert certainly emerges here as a composer of expressive depth and personality and with a fine feeling for words. He is not another Monteverdi but his art is well worth knowing, and the singing here is persuasive, expressively responsive and beautifully blended, even if it does not always make the music project irresistibly. The recording is well up to the high standard of this stimulating Veritas series.

Westlake, Nigel (born 1958)

Antartica (suite for guitar and orchestra).
(Y/B) *** Sony Dig. SK 53361 [id.]. John Williams, LSO, Paul Daniel – SCULTHORPE: *Nourlangie* etc.

Nigel Westlake was born in Perth, Australia, and his music makes a fine coupling for the works by his older contemporary, Peter Sculthorpe. *Antartica* is a film-score written to accompany an Imax large-screen documentary about the frozen continent. Westlake's music is highly imaginative and inventive and stands up memorably on its own. The guitar is used both with the orchestra and to play haunting, improvisatory-styled interludes. The suite is consistently compelling, and the scoring and writing for the solo instrument are very resourceful indeed. John Williams clearly relishes the considerable demands of the solo part, and Paul Daniel shapes the music spontaneously and skilfully. The recording is in the demonstration bracket, though the solo guitar is very forwardly balanced. Well worth exploring: there is no barbed wire here.

Weyse, Christoph Ernst Friedrich (1774–1842)

Symphonies Nos. 1 in G min., DF117; 2 in C, DF118; 3 in D, DF119.
(Y/B) ** Marco Polo/Da Capo 8.224012 [id.]. Royal Danish O, Schønwandt.

Weyse's seven symphonies all date from the early part of his career (1795–9) and the three recorded here were all composed in 1795, when he was twenty-one. The example of Haydn affected Weyse strongly, and the minor-key symphonies in particular are reminiscent of Haydn's *Sturm und Drang* symphonies. Michael Schønwandt gives vital yet sensitive accounts of all three symphonies and is well served by the engineers. This lively music is worth investigating.

White, Robert (c. 1538–74)

Motets: *Christe qui lux es; Domine quis habitavit; Portio mea Domine; Regina coeli.*
(N) ✪ (M) *** Cal. CAL 6623 [id.]. Clerkes of Oxenford, David Wulstan – TALLIS: *Mass Puer natus est etc.* *** ✪

Robert White, another neglected master of Elizabethan polyphony, married the daughter of Christopher Tye while based at Ely Cathedral; he then moved on to Chester, ending his days as choir-master of St Peter's Cathedral in Westminster. His style of writing has a basic restraint and often shows a gentle, Dowland-like melancholy, so striking at the opening of *Domine quis habitavit*. But this is often offset by the soaring trebles, especially in the ravishing *Portio mea Domine*, while *Christe qui lux es*, the last motet on this record, is very touching indeed. Glorious performances by Wulstan and the Clerkes of Oxenford, who have the full measure of this repertoire. The analogue recording could hardly be bettered. Not to be missed.

Widor, Charles-Marie (1844–1937)

Organ symphony No. 5 in F min., Op. 42/1.
*** DG Dig. 413 438-2 [id.]. Simon Preston (organ of Westminster Abbey) – VIERNE: *Carillon de Westminster.* ***
*** Chandos Dig. CHAN 9271 [id.]. Ian Tracey (organ of Liverpool Cathedral), BBC PO, Yan Pascal Tortelier – GUILMANT: *Symphony No. 1 for organ and orchestra* ***; POULENC: *Concerto.* **(*)

Organ symphonies Nos. 5 in F min., Op. 42/1 (complete); 6 in B, Op. 42/2: 1st movt; 8 in B, Op. 42/4: 4th movt (Prelude).
(Y/B) (M) *** Saga EC 3361-2 [id.]. David Sanger (organ of St Peter's Church, Clerkenwell, London).

David Sanger's account of the Widor *Symphony No. 5* is first class in every respect and is recorded with fine bloom and clarity. His restraint in registering the central movements prevents Widor's cosy melodic inspiration from sounding sentimental, and the finale is exciting without being overblown. The other symphonic movements are well done but serve to confirm the conclusion that the famous *Toccata* from No. 5 was Widor's masterpiece. The Clerkenwell organ has a pleasingly wide palette of colour, perhaps surprisingly well suited to this repertoire.

Simon Preston also gives a masterly account of the Widor *Fifth Symphony*, with a fine sense of pace and command of colour; there is a marvellous sense of space in this DG recording.

The long reverberation-period of Liverpool Cathedral gives a special character to Widor's *Fifth Symphony*, especially the mellow central movements. Ian Tracey makes the most of the colouristic possibilities of his fine instrument and also uses the widest possible range of dynamics, with the tone at times shaded down to a distant whisper. Yet the famous *Toccata* expands gloriously if without the plangent bite of a French instrument.

Symphonies Nos. 5, Op. 42/1: Adagio & Toccata; 6, Op. 42/2: 1st movt: Allegro; 8, Op. 42/4: Moderato cantabile; Allegro; 9 (Symphonie gothique), Op. 70 (complete); 3 Nouvelles pièces, Op. 87.
*** Argo Dig. 433 152-2 [id.]. Thomas Trotter (Cavaillé-Coll organ of Saint-François-de-Sales, Lyon).

The inner movements of the *Symphonie gothique* are attractive and the finale undoubtedly inventive – it is essentially in variation form with an extended coda. The excerpts from the *Eighth Symphony* are also very agreeable. Thomas Trotter is an impressive advocate and he is splendidly recorded on an organ highly suited to this repertoire.

Wieniawski, Henryk (1835–80)

Violin concertos Nos. 1 in F sharp min., Op. 14; 2 in D min., Op. 22; Légende, Op. 17.
*** DG Dig. 431 815-2 [id.]. Gil Shaham, LSO, Lawrence Foster – SARASATE: *Zigeunerweisen.* ***

Listening to Gil Shaham's DG record, it becomes even more mystifying that Wieniawski's *First Violin concerto* should always be upstaged by the *Second*, which is so often recorded. The Paganinian pyrotechnics in the first movement can be made to dazzle, as Shaham readily demonstrates and Lawrence Foster makes a good deal of the orchestral part. Both soloist and orchestra are equally dashing and lyrically persuasive in the better known *D minor Concerto*, and make an engaging encore out of the delightful *Légende*. With first-class DG recording this record is very recommendable.

Violin concerto No. 2 in D min., Op. 22.
*** Decca Dig. 421 716-2 [id.]. Joshua Bell, Cleveland O, Ashkenazy – TCHAIKOVSKY: *Violin concerto.* ***

(N) (M) **(*) Sony Stern Edition I SMK 66830 [id.]. Stern, Phd. O, Ormandy – BRUCH: *Violin concerto No. 1* **(*); TCHAIKOVSKY: *Méditation; Sérénade mélancolique.* ***

Joshua Bell gives a masterly performance, full of flair, even if he does not find quite the same individual poetry in the big second-subject melody or in the central *Romance* as Shaham. Excellent recording, brilliant and full.

Stern's recording comes from 1957, and the very close balance is not flattering to his upper range (although of course this playing can stand any kind of scrutiny). The songful slow movement is played simply and beautifully, and the finale is very *energico* indeed. Stern's virtuosity is both thrilling and astonishing in its clean articulation. Ormandy, as usual, provides fine support and the orchestra, though also balanced artificially, plays against a warm ambience.

Capriccio-waltz, Op. 7; Gigue in E min., Op. 27; Kujawiak in A min.; Légende, Op. 17; Mazurka in G min., Op. 12/2; 2 Mazurkas, Op. 19; Polonaise No. 1 in D, Op. 4; Russian carnival, Op. 11; Saltarello (arr. Lenehan); Scherzo-tarantelle in G min., Op. 16; Souvenir de Moscou, Op. 6; Variations on an original theme, Op. 15.
(Y/B) (BB) **(*) Naxos Dig. 8.550744 [id.]. Marat Bisengaliev, John Lenehan.

All the dazzling violin fireworks are ready to bow here, from left-hand pizzicatos in the *Russian carnival* to multiple stopping (and some lovely, warm lyricism) in the *Variations on an original theme*, plus all the dash you could ask for in the closing *Scherzo-tarantelle*. The four *Mazurkas* have plenty of animated folk feeling and local colour, while the beautiful *Légende* (which Wieniawski dedicated to his wife as a nuptial gift) is both touchingly gentle and passionately brilliant. Marat Bisengaliev is without the larger-than-life personality of a Perlman, but he is a remarkably fine player and a stylist, as well as being able to produce a sparkling moto perpetuo at will, as in the Neapolitan *Saltarello*, arranged by the pianist, John Lenehan, who provides his partner with admirable support throughout. The snag is the very reverberant acoustic of the Rosslyn Hill Chapel, Hampstead – so obviously empty. One adjusts to this (with some reluctance); otherwise the sound and balance are natural enough.

Wikmanson, Johan (1753–1800)

String quartet No. 2 in E min., Op. 1/2.
*** CRD CRD 3361; CRDC 4061 [id.]. Chilingirian Qt – BERWALD: *Quartet.* ***
*** CRD CRD 33123 (2) [id.]. Chilingirian Qt – ARRIAGA: *String quartets Nos. 1–3.* ***

Wikmanson was a cultured musician, but little of his music survives and two of his five *Quartets* are lost. The overriding influence here is that of Haydn and the finale of the present quartet even makes a direct allusion to Haydn's *E flat Quartet*, Op. 33, No. 2. The Chilingirian make out a persuasive case for this piece and are very well recorded. As can be seen, this work is available coupled with either Arriaga or Berwald.

Wirén, Dag (1905-86)

(i) *Violin concerto, Op. 23;* (ii) *String quartet No. 5, Op. 41;* (iii) *Triptych, Op. 33;* (iv) *Wind quintet, Op. 42.*

** Cap. Dig./Analogue CAP 21326. (i) Nils-Erik Sparf, Stockholm PO, Comissiona; (ii) Saulesco Qt; (iii) Stockholm Sinf., Wedin; (iv) Stockholm Wind Quintet.

Wirén is a 'one-work composer', and little of his music is widely known or shares the celebrity of the *Serenade for strings.* The best piece here is probably the post-war *Violin concerto* whose first two movements are often imaginative and inventive; it is very well played by Nils-Erik Sparf and the Stockholm Philharmonic under Sergiu Comissiona. Only the finale is a let-down. The other three pieces, the *Triptych,* the *Fifth String quartet* and the *Wind quintet,* are all disappointingly thin and scrappy. Excellent performances and recordings all the same.

Serenade for strings in G, Op. 11.
(Y/B) *** RCA Dig. R D 60439 [60439-2-RC] [id.]. Guildhall String Ens., Robert Salter – *Concert.* ***
(Y/B) (BB) *** Naxos Dig. 8.553106 [id.]. Bournemouth Sinf., Richard Studt – Concert: *Scandinavian string music.* ***

The engaging *String serenade* is Dag Wirén's one claim to international fame, and it is superbly played by the Guildhall String Ensemble under Robert Salter within a first-class collection of comparable pieces, given state-of-the-art sound.

It is good also to welcome an outstanding super-bargain version of Dag Wirén's deservedly popular *Serenade.* The natural impetus and lyrical charm of the first movement is most winning and the Scherzo brings fizzing bravura, while the colour and mood of the *Andante* is aptly caught. The finale certainly earns its hit status, full of spontaneous, lilting energy. First-rate recording within an entirely recommendable concert of Scandinavian string music, not all of it familiar.

String quartet No. 3 in D min.
*** ASV Dig. CDDCA 825 [id.]. Lindsay Qt – BARBER: *String quartet;* A. TCHAIKOVSKY: *String quartet No. 2;* WOOD: *String quartet No. 3.* ***

Dag Wirén's is a small-scale talent, even if he speaks with a distinctive voice. His was one of the most natural and instinctive of musical gifts, and the *Sinfonietta* for orchestra, the *Cello Concerto* and the neglected *Divertimento* for orchestra all betray a vein of poetic feeling that is quite haunting. The *Third* of his five quartets speaks with his familiar and engaging accents, but the thematic substance is short-breathed and deficient in contrast. A very good live performance and recording from the (1987) BBC's Lunchtime Concerts at St John's, Smith Square.

Wolf, Hugo (1860-1903)

Italian serenade.
(Y/B) (***) Biddulph mono L A B 098 [id.]. Budapest Qt – GRIEG; SIBELIUS: *Quartets.* ***

A welcome transfer – the first on CD – of the 1933 pioneering *Italian serenade.* It has a spring in its step and a lightness of touch that are almost unique, and it is well transferred here by Ward Marston. The couplings also show how special this ensemble was in the 1930s.

String quartet in D min.
(M) ** DG 437 128-2 (2) LaSalle Qt – (with BRAHMS: *Quartets Nos. 1–2 *(*)).

The *String quartet* was written when Wolf was only twenty. The finale was added later. It is an ambitious work (41 minutes long), original in its metric flow, and the music has all the direct passion of youth. It suits the LaSalle Quartet better than the Brahms couplings (which are much less recommendable). Though they press hard at times, the long slow movement is eloquent and often beautifully played and the finale has plenty of impetus. Bright, immediate, 1967 sound. We hope this may be reissued, differently coupled.

Lieder: Frage nicht; Frühling übers Jahr; Gesang Weylas; Kennst du das Land? (Mignon); Heiss mich nicht reden (Mignon I); Nur wer die Sehnsucht kennt (Mignon II); So lasst mich scheinen (Mignon III); Der Schäfer; Die Spröde.

*** DG Dig. 423 666-2 [id.]. Anne Sofie von Otter, Rolf Gothoni – MAHLER: *Das Knaben Wunderhorn* etc. ***

It is astonishing that so young a singer can tackle even the most formidable of Wolf's *Mignon* songs, *Kennst du das Land?*, a culminating peak of Lieder for women, with such firm, persuasive lines. The gravity of such a song is then delightfully contrasted against the delicacy of *Frühling übers Jahr* or *Die Spröde*. The sensitivity and imagination of Rolf Gothoni's accompaniment add enormously to the performances in a genuine two-way partnership. Well-balanced recording.

6 Lieder für eine Frauenstimme. Goethe-Lieder: Die Bekehrte; Ganymed; Kennst du das Land?; Mignon I, II & III; Philine; Die Spröde. Lieder: *An eine Aeolsharfe; Auf einer Wanderung; Begegnung; Denk es, o Seele; Elfenlied; Im Frühling; Sonne der Schlummerlosen; Wenn du zu den Blumen gehst; Wie glänzt der helle Mond; Die Zigeunerin.*
(M) **(*) EMI CDM7 63653-2. Elisabeth Schwarzkopf, Gerald Moore or Geoffrey Parsons.

This is a superb collection, representing the peak of Schwarzkopf's achievement as a Lieder singer. It is disgraceful that no texts or translations are provided as this will seriously reduce its appeal for some collectors; but the selection of items could hardly be better, including many songs inseparably associated with Schwarzkopf's voice, like *Mausfallen spruchlein* and, above all, *Kennst du das Land?*.

Italienisches Liederbuch (complete).
(Y/B) *** Hyperion Dig. CDA 66760 [id.]. Felicity Lott, Peter Schreier, Graham Johnson.
(Y/B) (M) *** EMI CDM7 63732-2 [id.]. Elisabeth Schwarzkopf, Dietrich Fischer-Dieskau, Gerald Moore.
(Y/B) (M) *** Ph. 442 744-2 (2) [id.]. Elly Ameling, Gérard Souzay, Dalton Baldwin – R. STRAUSS: *Lieder.* ***
(Y/B) **(*) Teldec/Warner Dig. 9031 72301 [id.]. Barbara Bonney, Håkan Hagegård, Geoffrey Parsons.

No accompanist, not even Gerald Moore himself, has revealed quite so profound an understanding of this cycle as Graham Johnson, and with two of his favourite Lieder-singers on Hyperion he conjures up a performance full of magic, compelling from first to last. Yet, so far from being intrusive in his playing, he consistently heightens the experience, drawing out from Felicity Lott one of her most intense and detailed performances on record, totally individual, with few echoes of the inevitable model, Schwarzkopf. Peter Schreier, one of the supreme masters of Lieder today, responds to his characterful accompanist, eager to accept the challenge and to intensify his expression of word-meaning, his shading of tone-colours. If, under pressure, his voice shows signs of wear, it is a small price to pay, and having a tenor instead of the usual baritone brings many benefits in this sharply pointed sequence. The triumph of this issue is crowned by the substantial booklet provided in the package, containing Johnson's uniquely perceptive commentary on each song – alone worth the price of the disc. Excellent sound.

All 46 songs of Wolf's *Italienisches Liederbuch* are here, sung by Schwarzkopf and Fischer-Dieskau on an EMI CD playing for two seconds over 79 minutes, generous measure indeed at mid-price! These songs show the composer at his most captivatingly individual. Many of them are very brief fragments of fantasy, which call for the most intense artistry if their point is to be fully made. No one today can match the searching perception of these two great singers in this music, with Fischer-Dieskau using his sweetest tones and Schwarzkopf ranging through all the many emotions inspired by love. Note particularly the little vignette, *Wer rief dich denn?*, which Schwarzkopf interprets more vividly than anyone else: scorn mingling with hidden heartbreak. Gerald Moore is at his finest, and Walter Legge's translations will help bring the magic of these unique songs even to the newcomer. The well-balanced 1969 recording has been admirably transferred, giving the artists a fine presence.

Elly Ameling, delicately sweet and precise, contrasts well with Souzay, with his fine-drawn sense of line. The charm and point of these brief but intensely imaginative songs are well presented, with perceptive accompaniment from Dalton Baldwin. The coupled Richard Strauss recital also shows Souzay at his most perceptive. However, the unforgettable 1969 version with Schwarzkopf and Fischer-Dieskau has the advantage of being offered uncoupled, on a single, mid-priced CD.

Recorded in Berlin, the Teldec CD presents a fresh, direct and intensely satisfying reading of this characterful sequence of 46 songs. Barbara Bonney uses her bright, clear soprano with keen imagination, often with echoes of Schwarzkopf, but with many individual insights. Håkan Hagegård is less individual but still gives a strong, firm reading, even if his baritone has often sounded more beautiful on disc. Geoffrey Parsons is the keenly responsive accompanist, sharply reflecting his singers' approach to each poem. First-rate sound.

(i; ii) *Italienisches Liederbuch* (complete). (ii) Eichendorf Lieder: *Erwartung; Der Freund; Der Glücksritter; Heimweh; Lieber Alles; Liebesglück; Der Musikant; Die Nacht; Nachtzauber; Der Schreckenberger; Der Scholar; Seemanns Abschied; Der Soldat I & II; Das Ständchen; Unfall; Verschwiegene Liebe; Der verzweifelte Liebhaber. In der Fremde I, II & IV; Nachruf; Rückkehr.* Michelangelo Lieder: *Alles endet, was entstehet; Fühlt meine Seele das ersehnte Licht; Wohl denk'ich oft an mein vergangnes Leben.*

(Y/B) (M) *** DG 439 975-2 (2) (i) Christa Ludwig; (ii) Dietrich Fischer-Dieskau; Daniel Barenboim.

Fischer-Dieskau is superb in these varied items from the *Italian Song Book*, always underlining the word-meanings with the inflexion of a born actor, helped by the understanding accompaniment of Barenboim. In the women's songs, Christa Ludwig is less uninhibited and, after Schwarzkopf's accounts of such jewels as *Wer rief dich denn*, these may seem undercharacterized, with the voice not always perfectly steady; but Ludwig too has natural compulsion in her singing and responds splendidly to the pointed playing of Barenboim. The *Eichendorf* and *Michelangelo Lieder* make a splendid supplement for the CD issue, and the mid-1970s recording gives an entirely natural effect.

Mörike Lieder: An den Schlaf; Auf ein altes Bild; Auf einer Wanderung; Begegnung; Bei einer Trauung; Denk'es, o Seele!; Der Feuerreiter; Fussreise; Der Gärtner; Gebet; Gesang Weylas; Im Frühling; In der Frühe; Jägerlied; Der Knabe und das Immlein; Lebe wohl; Nimmersatte Liebe; Peregrina 1 & 2; Schlafendes Jesuskind; Selbstgeständnis; Storchenbotschaft; Das verlassene Mägdlein; Verborgenheit; Zum neuen Jahr.

*** Decca Dig. 440 208-2 [id.]. Brigitte Fassbaender, Thibaudet.

Here is a dangerous, even violent singer who, with light in the eye, heightens the character of each song, bringing out the good humour in such a song as *Fussreise*, rambling, drawing out the beauty of line in *Verborgenheit*, but often positively taking an individual approach. So there is passionate intensity as much as rapt concentration behind *Schlafendes Jesuskind*, and the loss of a lover in *Das verlassene Mägdlein* is treated not as tragedy but as something to be shrugged off by the servant-girl. Characteristically, Fassbaender concludes with a shattering account of the most violent of Wolf songs, normally reserved for men, *Der Feuerreiter* ('The fire-rider').

Spanisches Liederbuch (complete).

(M) *** DG 423 934-2 (2) [id.]. Schwarzkopf, Fischer-Dieskau, Moore.

(Y/B) *** EMI CDS5 55325-2 (2) [id.]. Anne Sofie von Otter, Olaf Bär, Geoffrey Parsons.

In this superb CD reissue the sacred songs provide a dark, intense prelude, with Fischer-Dieskau at his very finest, sustaining slow tempi impeccably. Schwarzkopf's dedication comes out in the three songs suitable for a woman's voice; but it is in the secular songs, particularly those which contain laughter in the music, where she is at her most memorable. Gerald Moore is balanced rather too backwardly – something the transfer cannot correct – but gives superb support. In all other respects the 1968 recording sounds first rate, the voices beautifully caught. A classic set.

Completed barely six months before Geoffrey Parsons' untimely death, the EMI set of the *Spanish Songbook* makes a superb memorial to that great accompanist, here working with two of the most searching and stylish Lieder singers of the present generation. After experience of performing the complete cycle in concert, they opt for an order of the songs quite different from the original published order, seeking to find 'a dramatic shape that worked in the atmosphere of a concert'. Quite apart from Parsons' superb contribution, rapt and dark in the sacred songs, volatile and sparklingly articulated in the secular, the performances of both soloists vie with those on the classic DG set with Schwarzkopf and Fischer-Dieskau. Generally in the new set the manner is more intimate, often more subdued, with speeds generally broader, making a seven-minute difference overall. For the lighter songs von Otter uses a much brighter tonal range than elsewhere, though in such a song as *In dem Schatten meiner Locken* she remains more intimate than Schwarzkopf, pointing the words and phrases with comparable character. Generally the pointing of words is even more vivid in the earlier set but, helped by the extra sparkle of Parsons' playing, this provides a superb alternative, very well recorded.

Wolf-Ferrari, Ermanno (1876–1948)

L'amore medico: Overture; (i) *Intermezzo. Il Campiello: Intermezzo; Ritornello. La Dama Bomba: Overture. I gioielli della Madonna (suite). I 4 rusteghi: Prelude & Intermezzo. Il segreto di Susanna: Overture & Intermezzo.*

*** EMI CDC7 54585-2 [id.]. ASMF, Marriner, (i) with Stephen Orton.

*** ASV Dig. CDDCA 861 [id.] (without *Il segreto* & *L'amore medico Intermezzi*). RPO, José Serebrier.

In spite of the considerable attractions of his opera, *Susanna's secret*, Wolf-Ferrari holds a permanent place in the catalogue only with recordings of his operatic *intermezzi* – not surprising, perhaps, when they are so readily tuneful and charmingly scored. Marriner and the Academy are only marginally short of their finest form here, and this concert makes a delightful entertainment, with everything elegantly played and warmly (if a little resonantly) recorded at Abbey Road.

Serebrier's performances are by no means upstaged. He conjured at times exquisite playing from the RPO (especially the strings) and, even though he takes Susanna's sparkling overture slightly slower than Marriner, it is hardly less successful. What is specially memorable is his delicate treatment of the gossamer string-pieces from *I quattro rusteghi* and the *Ritornello* from *Il Campiello* which almost have a Beecham touch. The ASV recording, made in the Henry Wood Hall, is slightly more open and indeed marginally more transparent and fresh. But the snag is that the ASV collection omits three of the more delectable pieces included by Marriner (and even the latter gives us only 54 minutes), including the concertante *Intermezzo* from *L'amore medico* in which Stephen Orton takes the solo cello role most winningly.

Piano trios Nos. 1 in D, Op. 5; 2 in F sharp, Op. 7.
(N) *** ASV Dig. CDDCA 935 [id.]. Raphael Trio.

Best known for his light-hearted, tuneful operas, Ermanno Wolf-Ferrari, half-German, half-Italian, wrote these two ambitious *Piano trios* at the very beginning of his career. They may not be masterpieces, but the large-scale first movements show how well he had learnt his academic lessons. More importantly, his themes already show the gift of easy memorability which marks his operas. So the slow movement of No. 1 is like a Mascagni lament, and the chattering finale might be a sketch for an operatic interlude. No. 2 is even odder in its layout, with the first movement twice as long as the other two put together, but with well-disciplined performances from the Raphael Trio – an American group – the colour and charm of the writing is persuasively brought out.

Wood, Haydn (1882–1959)

Apollo overture; A Brown bird singing (paraphrase for orchestra); *London cameos:* suite (*Miniature overture: The City; St James's Park in the spring; A State ball at Buckingham Palace); Mannin Veen* (Manx tone-poem); *Moods* (suite): *Joyousness* (concert waltz). *Mylecharane* (rhapsody); *The Seafarer (A nautical rhapsody); Serenade to youth; Sketch of a Dandy.*
*** Marco Polo Dig. 8.22340-2. Slovak RSO (Bratislava), Adrian Leaper.

Haydn Wood was an almost exact contemporary of Eric Coates and nearly as talented. Wood spent his childhood on the Isle of Man, and much of his best music is permeated with Manx folk-themes (original or simulated), which often bring a Celtic flavour to his invention. Now most of his output is all but forgotten, although military bands in the parks stay faithful to him and *Mannin Veen* ('Dear Isle of Man') is a splendid piece, based on four Manx folksongs. The companion rhapsody, *Mylecharane*, also uses folk material if less memorably, and *The Seafarer* is a wittily scored selection of famous shanties, neatly stitched together. The only failure here is *Apollo*, which uses less interesting material and is over-ambitious and inflated. But the English waltzes are enchanting confections. This generous collection (69 minutes) opens with a most engaging miniature, *Sketch of a Dandy*, endearingly dated but deliciously frothy and elegant, and played here with an ideal lightness of touch. Adrian Leaper is obviously much in sympathy with this repertoire and knows just how to pace it; his Czech players obviously relish the easy tunefulness and the sheer craft of the writing (as do all orchestral musicians, anywhere). With excellent recording in what is surely an ideal acoustic, this is very highly recommendable.

Wood, Hugh (born 1932)

Piano concerto, Op. 31.
*** Collins Single Dig. 2007-2 [id.]. Joanna MacGregor, BBC SO, Andrew Davis.

Hugh Wood's *Piano concerto*, written for Joanna MacGregor, who studied with him at Cambridge, is one of his most important new works – a three-movement piece whose central movement is a haunting set of variations on *Sweet Lorraine*, the song popularized in the 1950s by Nat King Cole. Expert playing from both the soloist and the BBC Symphony Orchestra under Andrew Davis, and first-class recorded sound.

String quartet No. 3, Op. 20.
*** ASV Dig. CDDCA 825 [id.]. Lindsay Qt – BARBER: *String quartet;* A. TCHAIKOVSKY: *String quartet No. 2;* WIREN: *String quartet No. 3.* ***

Wood has a highly sophisticated feeling for sonority and texture, and his *Third Quartet* (1978) is the product of skilled musicianship and a well-stocked imagination. His music shows that the example of Schoenberg and the Second Viennese School need not be inhibiting if it is intelligently absorbed. His *Third Quartet* is a one-movement work, musically dense and varied; not one to yield up its secrets on a casual hearing but worth perseverance and study. The Lindsay performance, recorded at St John's, Smith Square, in 1980 is admirably prepared and dedicated, and the BBC recording eminently well balanced.

Wordsworth, William (1908–88)

Symphonies Nos. 2 in D, Op. 34; 3 in C, Op. 48.
*** Lyrita Dig. SRCD 207 [id.]. LPO, Nicholas Braithwaite.

William Wordsworth was a direct descendant of the poet's brother, Christopher; on the evidence of this disc, he was a real symphonist. The *Second*, dedicated to Tovey, has a real sense of space; it is distinctly Nordic in atmosphere and there is an unhurried sense of growth. It is serious, thoughtful music, both well crafted and well laid out for the orchestra. At times it almost suggests Sibelius or Walter Piston in the way it moves, though not in its accents, and the writing is both powerful and imaginative. The *Third* is less concentrated and less personal in utterance, but all the same this is music of integrity, and readers who enjoy, say, the symphonies of Edmund Rubbra should sample the *Second Symphony*. Nicholas Braithwaite gives a carefully prepared and dedicated account of it, and the recording is up to the usual high standard one expects from this label.

Ysaÿe, Eugène (1858–1931)

6 Sonatas for solo violin, Op. 27.
*** Chandos Dig. CHAN 8599 [id.]. Lydia Mordkovich.

Lydia Mordkovich plays with great character and variety of colour and she characterizes No. 4 (the one dedicated to Kreisler, with its references to Bach and the *Dies Irae*) superbly. These *Sonatas* can seem like mere exercises, but in her hands they sound really interesting. Natural, warm recorded sound. Recommended.

Zandonai, Riccardo (1883–1944)

Francesca da Rimini: excerpts from Acts II, III & IV.
(M) **(*) Decca 433 033-2 (2) [id.]. Olivero, Del Monaco, Monte Carlo Op. O, Rescigno – GIORDANO: *Fedora.* **(*)

Magda Olivero is a fine artist who has not been represented nearly enough on record, and this rare Zandonai selection, like the coupled set of Giordano's *Fedora*, does her some belated justice. Decca opted to have three substantial scenes recorded rather than snippets, and though Mario del Monaco as Paolo is predictably coarse in style, his tone is rich and strong and he does not detract from the achievement, unfailingly perceptive and musicianly, of Olivero as Francesca herself. Excellent, vintage 1969, Decca sound.

Zelenka, Jan (1679–1745)

Lamentationes Jeremiae Prophetae (Lamentations for Holy Week).
(M) *** HM/BMG GD 77112 [77112-2-RG]. Jacobs, De Mey, Widmer, Instrumentalists of the Schola Cantorum Basiliensis, Jacobs.

These solo settings of the six *Lamentations* for the days leading up to Easter reinforce Zelenka's claims as one of the most original composers of his time. The spacious melodic lines and chromatic twists in the harmonic progressions are often very Bachian, but the free-flowing alternation of arioso and recitative is totally distinctive. This mid-price issue of René Jacobs's 1983 recording for Deutsche Harmonia Mundi follows close on a very recommendable full-price version on the Hyperion label with the

Chandos Baroque Players. Here, too, all three soloists are excellent, with the least-known, the baritone Kurt Widmer, easily matching the other two in his exceptionally sweet and fresh singing. But, quite apart from price, this BMG disc has the advantage of focusing the voices more cleanly and offering a rather less abrasive instrumental accompaniment, with speeds generally more flowing.

Missa dei Filii; Litaniae Laurentanae.
*** HM/BMG Dig. RD 77922 [7922-2-RC]. Argenta, Chance, Prégardien, Gordon Jones, Stuttgart Chamber Ch., Tafelmusik, Bernius.

This fine set offers not only one of Zelenka's late Masses, but also a splendid *Litany* too, confirming him – for all the obscurity he suffered in his lifetime – as one of the most inspired composers of his generation. The *Missa dei Filii* (Mass for the Son of God), is a 'short' mass, consisting of *Kyrie* and *Gloria* only. It seems that Zelenka never heard that Mass, but his *Litany*, another refreshing piece, was specifically written when the Electress of Saxony was ill. Zelenka, like Bach, happily mixes fugal writing with newer-fangled concertato movements. Bernius provides well-sprung support with his period-instrument group, Tafelmusik, and his excellent soloists and choir.

(i) *Requiem in D min., ZWV 48;* (ii) *Miserere (Psalm 50) in C min., ZWV 57.*
(N) ** Sup. Dig. SU 0052-2 231 [id.]. (i) Pellarová, Kozená, Ladislav Richter, Pospísil; (ii) Anna Hlavenková; Czech Chamber Ch., Bar. Ens. 1994, Roman Válek.

The Dresden *Requiem in D minor* is a recent rediscovery (in Prague, with individual parts surviving in Modra, Slovakia). It is quite a compelling work; if not quite as individual as its C minor companion it is notable for including no fewer than seven fugues, of which the most striking is in the *Benedictus*. It is a grave, solemn setting but gives plenty of opportunities to the chorus, who respond with vigour, and the soloists, who are uneven and whose unreliable intonation is unsettling. A robust period-instrument group accompanies with spirit. The much shorter *Miserere* shows the composer returning to his imaginative harmonic and melodic form, and here the soprano soloist, Anna Hlavenková, is both secure and pleasingly eloquent. Excellent recording, but poor presentation, with no texts.

Zemlinsky, Alexander von (1871–1942)

Piano trio in D min., Op. 3.
(Y/B) *** Ph. Dig. 434 072-2. Beaux Arts Trio – KORNGOLD: *Piano trio.* ***

This is a transcription of the *Trio for clarinet, piano and cello* which Zemlinsky himself made, and which in some ways is to be preferred to the original. The textures are better balanced and more transparent. The Beaux Arts play this early work with great spirit and just the right blend of vitality and sensitivity. The recording is exemplary.

String quartets Nos. 1, Op. 4; 2, Op. 15; 3, Op. 19; 4, Op. 25.
(M) *** DG Dig. 427 421-2 (2). LaSalle Qt.

None of the four Zemlinsky *Quartets* is in the least atonal: the textures are full of contrapuntal interest and the musical argument always proceeds with lucidity. There is diversity of mood and a fastidious craftsmanship, and the listener is always held. The musical language is steeped in Mahler and, to a lesser extent, Reger, but the music is undoubtedly the product of a very fine musical mind and one of considerable individuality. Collectors will find this a rewarding set: the LaSalle play with polish and unanimity, and the recording is first class, as is the admirable documentation.

VOCAL MUSIC

Gesänge Op. 5, Books 1–2; Gesänge (Waltz songs on Tuscan folk-lyrics), Op. 6; Gesänge, Opp. 7–8, 10 & 13; Lieder, Op. 2, Books 1–2; Op. 22 & Op. 27.
*** DG Dig. 427 348-2 (2) [id.]. Barbara Bonney, Anne Sofie von Otter, Hans Peter Blochwitz, Andreas Schmidt, Cord Garben.

Thanks to recordings, the art of Alexander von Zemlinsky is coming to be ever more widely appreciated, and this two-disc DG collection of songs can be warmly recommended for the fresh tunefulness of dozens of miniatures. With Cord Garben accompanying four excellent soloists, the charm of these chips from the workbench comes over consistently. Best of all is Von Otter, more sharply imaginative than the others, making the one consistent cycle that Zemlinsky ever wrote, the six Maeterlinck Songs, Opus 13, the high-point of the set.

6 Maeterlinck Lieder, Op. 13.
(Y/B) (B) *** Decca Double 444 871-2 (2) [id.]. Concg. O, Chailly – MAHLER: *Symphony No. 6.* ***

Beautifully sung by Jard van Nes in her finest recording to date, these ripely romantic settings of Maeterlinck make an unusual but valuable fill-up for Chailly's rugged and purposeful reading of the Mahler *Symphony*. This is very much the world of medieval chivalry which inspired *Pelléas et Mélisande*, and Zemlinsky responds wholeheartedly. The rich, vivid recording captures van Nes's full-throated singing with new firmness.

Eine florentinische Tragödie (opera; complete).
*** Schwann Dig. CD 11625 [id.]. Soffel, Riegel, Sarabia, Berlin RSO, Albrecht.

A Florentine Tragedy presents a simple love triangle: a Florentine merchant returns home to find his sluttish wife with the local prince. Zemlinsky in 1917 may have been seeking to repeat the shock tactics of Richard Strauss in *Salome* (another Oscar Wilde story) a decade earlier; but the musical syrup which flows over all the characters makes them far more repulsive, with motives only dimly defined. The score itself is most accomplished; it is compellingly performed here, more effective on disc than it is in the opera house. First-rate sound.

Der Gerburtstag der Infantin (opera; complete).
*** Schwann Dig. CD 11626 [id]. Nielsen, Riegel, Haldas, Weller, Berlin RSO, Albrecht.

The Birthday of the Infanta, like its companion one-Acter, was inspired by a story of Oscar Wilde, telling of a hideous dwarf caught in the forest and given to the Infanta as a birthday present. Even after recognizing his own hideousness, he declares his love to the princess and is casually rejected. He dies of a broken heart, with the Infanta untroubled: 'Oh dear, my present already broken.' Zemlinsky, dwarfish himself, gave his heart to the piece, reproducing his own rejection at the hands of Alma Mahler. In this performance, based on a much-praised stage production, Kenneth Riegel gives a heartrendingly passionate performance as the dwarf declaring his love. His genuine passion is intensified by being set against lightweight, courtly music to represent the Infanta and her attendants. With the conductor and others in the cast also experienced in the stage production, the result is a deeply involving performance, beautifully recorded.

Collections

Because of space limitations this is a very selective list. We hope to include many more collections in our next volume. The Julian Bream Edition CDs not included in the Composer section, above, will also be found therein, together with comprehensive coverage of the BMG/Melodiya Mravinsky Edition.

Concerts of Orchestral and Concertante Music

Art of conducting

'The Art of conducting': Video: 'Great conductors of the past' (Barbirolli, Beecham, Bernstein, Busch, Furtwängler, Karajan, Klemperer, Koussevitzky, Nikisch, Stokowski, Richard Strauss, Szell, Toscanini, Walter, Weingartner): BRUCKNER: Symphony No. 7: Rehearsal (Hallé O, Barbirolli). GOUNOD: Faust: ballet music (with rehearsal) (RPO, Beecham). Silent film (BPO, Nikisch). Richard STRAUSS: Till Eulenspiegel (VPO, Richard Strauss). WEBER: Der Freischütz overture (Paris SO, Felix Weingarner). WAGNER: Tannhäuser overture (Dresden State O, Fritz Busch). MOZART: Symphony No. 40 (BPO, Bruno Walter). BRAHMS: Symphony No. 2 (rehearsal) (Vancouver Festival O, Bruno Walter). BEETHOVEN: Egmont overture; Symphony No. 9 (Philh. O, Klemperer). WAGNER: Die Meistersinger overture. SCHUBERT: Symphony No. 8 (Unfinished). BRAHMS: Symphony No. 4 (both rehearsals) (BPO, Furtwängler). VERDI: La forza del destino overture; La Traviata: Coro di zingarelle. RESPIGHI: The Pines of Rome (NBC SO, Toscanini). PURCELL (arr. Stokowski): Dido and Aeneas: Dido's lament. RESPIGHI: The Pines of Rome (BBC SO). TCHAIKOVSKY: Symphony No. 5 (NYPO) (both cond. Stokowski). BEETHOVEN: Egmont overture (Boston SO, Koussevitzky). TCHAIKOVSKY: Violin concerto (Heifetz, NYPO, Reiner). BEETHOVEN: Symphony No. 7 (Chicago SO, Reiner). BRAHMS: Academic festival overture. BEETHOVEN: Symphony No. 5 (Cleveland O, Szell). BEETHOVEN: Symphony No. 5. DEBUSSY: La Mer (BPO, Karajan). SHOSTAKOVICH: Symphony No. 5 (rehearsal and performance) (LSO). MAHLER: Symphony No. 4 (VPO; both cond. Bernstein). BEETHOVEN: Symphony No. 9 (Philh. O, Klemperer). (Commentary by John Eliot Gardiner; Isaac Stern, Jack Brymer, Beecham, Menuhin, Oliver Knussen, Suvi Raj Grubb, Szell, Walter, Klemperer, Hugh Bean, Werner Thäruchen, Richard Mohr, Stokowski, Julius Baker, Karajan).
(N) ✪ *** Teldec/Warner VHS 4509 95038-3 [id.].

This extraordinary video offers a series of electrifying performances by the great conductors of our century, all seen and heard at their very finest. Enormous care has been taken over the sound, even in the earliest recordings, for it is remarkably full-bodied and believable. But most of all it is to watch conductors weaving their magic spell over the orchestra which is so fascinating. And sometimes they do it imperceptibly, like Richard Strauss conducting Till Eulenspiegel with apparent nonchalance, yet making music with the utmost aural vividness; Fritz Busch creating great tension in Wagner; Bruno Walter wonderfully mellow in Brahms; Klemperer in Beethoven hardly moving his baton and yet completely in control; Furtwängler rehearsing the finale of Brahms's Fourth Symphony with a tremendous flow of adrenalin; Toscanini the martinet in Verdi; Stokowski moulding gloriously beautiful sound with flowing movements of his hands and arms; and, most riveting of all, Bernstein creating enormous passion with the LSO in Shostakovich's Fifth Symphony. Of the many commentaries from other artists and various musicians, the experience of Werner Thäringen stands out. He was participating in a Berlin performance when he suddenly realized that the sound around him had changed: it had become uncannily more beautiful. Not understanding why, he looked to the back of the hall . . . and saw that Furtwängler had just walked in. The great Nikisch is seen conducting (on silent film) but not heard – and no one knows what the music was!

'The Art of conducting: Great conductors of the past' (Barbirolli; Beecham; Bernstein; Busch; Furtwängler; Karajan; Klemperer; Koussevitzky; Nikisch; Reiner; Stokowski; Richard Strauss; Szell; Toscanini; Walter; Weingartner): WEBER: Der Freischütz overture (LSO, Arthur Nikisch). BRAHMS: Symphony No. 4 (LSO, Felix Weingartner). Richard STRAUSS: Der Rosenkavalier: suite of film music (Augmented L. Tivoli Theatre O, Richard Strauss). BRAHMS: Tragic overture. WAGNER: Parsifal: Prelude and Good Friday music (BBC SO, Arturo Toscanini). BEETHOVEN: Fidelio overture. SCHUBERT: Symphony No. 8 in B min. (Unfinished) (both VPO). WAGNER: Tristan und Isolde: Prelude, Act III (Philh. O; all conducted Wilhelm Furtwängler). MOZART: Così fan tutte overture (Glyndebourne Festival O, Fritz Busch). MOZART: Serenade: Eine kleine Nachtmusik. WAGNER: Siegfried idyll. MAHLER: Symphony No. 5: Adagietto (VPO, Bruno Walter). WAGNER: Tristan und Isolde: Prelude, Act I

(LPO, Fritz Reiner). SIBELIUS: *Symphony No. 7* (BBC SO, Serge Koussevitzky). CHABRIER: *Joyeuse marche*. DELIUS: *Irmelin Prelude*. SIBELIUS: *Tapiola* (RPO, Sir Thomas Beecham). ELGAR: *Introduction and allegro for strings* (L. Sinfonia, Sir John Barbirolli). DVORAK: *Symphony No. 8 in G* (Cleveland O, George Szell). BEETHOVEN: *Symphony No. 7* (Philh. O, Otto Klemperer). *Symphony No. 8*. SMETANA: *Má Vlast: Vltava* (BPO, Herbert von Karajan). BACH/STOKOWSKI: *Toccata and fugue in D min.* RESPIGHI: *The Pines of Rome* (Symphony O or Symphony of the Air, Leopold Stokowski). BERLIOZ: *Harold in Italy* (O Nat. de France, Leonard Bernstein, with Donald McInnes, viola). Comparisons: BEETHOVEN: *Symphony No. 5:* first movt (BPO, Nikisch; VPO, Furtwängler; Philh. O, Karajan; Philh. O, Klemperer). Rehearsal sequences (excerpts): BEETHOVEN: *Symphony No. 5*. MOZART: *Die Entführung aus dem Serail* (with Gottlob Frick). HAYDN: *Symphony No. 100 (Military)* (all RPO, Beecham). BEETHOVEN: *Overture Leonora No. 3* (Stockholm PO, Furtwängler). TCHAIKO-VSKY: *Symphony No. 4:* Finale (Hallé O, Barbirolli).
(N) (M)(***) EMI CMS5 65915-2 (7) [CDMG 65915].

Opportunely EMI have issued this carefully prepared seven-disc set to offer further examples of the art of the musicians in the video. There is much here that is treasurable. Now we can hear as well as see Nikisch – in Weber. Felix Weingartner conducts a glowingly lyrical account of Brahms's *Fourth Symphony* which shows his natural mastery of Brahmsian phrasing and line; Koussevitzky is heard in Sibelius, Furtwängler in Beethoven, Wagner and Schubert, Beecham in Delius and Chabrier, and Barbirolli is uniquely warm-blooded in Elgar. We have both Klemperer and Karajan in complete performances of Beethoven symphonies and, after various rehearsal sequences, we are given the chance to compare Nikisch, Furtwängler, Karajan, Klemperer and Beecham in the first movement of the Beethoven *Fifth Symphony*.

Australian Chamber Orchestra, Richard Tognetti

JANACEK: *Kreutzer Sonata for strings* (arr. Tognetti from *String quartet No. 1*). BARBER: *Adagio for strings, Op. 11a*. WALTON: *Sonata*.
(N) *** Australia Sony Dig. SK 48252 [id.].

The third disc from this excellent chamber orchestra won an award in Australia – and understandably so. The arrangement for strings of Janáček's *String quartet* is very successful and the performance has a chimerical spontaneity and freedom, as well as great expressive feeling. Similarly the climax of the Barber *Adagio* has tingling intensity, and one's only cavil is that there is an unnecessary brief final surge of fervour in the coda, interrupting the diminuendo, which may be telling but is not what the composer intended. The Walton *Sonata* is, of course, another string quartet adaptation (by the composer) and it caps this collection with its vigour and wit. The recording approaches the demonstration bracket: it is very vivid and tangible.

BBC Philharmonic Orchestra, Matthias Bamert

Stokowski Encores: HANDEL: *Overture in D min.* GABRIELI: *Sonata piano e forte*. CLARKE: *Trumpet Prelude*. MATTHESON: *Air*. MOZART: *Rondo alla turca*. BEETHOVEN: *Adagio* from *Moonlight sonata*. SCHUBERT: *Serenade*. FRANCK: *Panis Angelicus*. CHOPIN: *Funeral march*. DEBUSSY: *The Girl with the flaxen hair*. IPPOLITOV-IVANOV: *In the manger*. SHOSTAKOVICH: *United Nations march*. TCHAIKO-VSKY: *Andante cantabile*. ALBENIZ: *Festival in Seville*. SOUSA: *The Stars and Stripes for ever*. (all arr. Leopold Stokowski).
(Y/B) *** Chandos Dig. CHAN 9349 [id.].

However outrageous it may seem to take a tiny harpsichord piece by a contemporary of Bach and Handel, Johann Mattheson, and inflate it on full strings, the result caresses the ear, and the Chandos engineers come up with recording to match. Amazingly, Mozart's *Rondo Alla Turca* becomes a sparkling moto perpetuo, Paganini-like, with Stokowski following Mozart himself in using 'Turkish' percussion, *Entführung*-style. The opening *Adagio* of Beethoven's *Moonlight sonata* with lush orchestration then echoes Rachmaninov's *Isle of the Dead*, with menace in the music. Stokowski's arrangement of the Handel *Overture in D minor* (taken from the *Chandos anthem No. 2*) is quite different from Elgar's transcription of the same piece, opulent in a different way, with timbres antiphonally contrasted. If Bamert cannot match the panache of Stokowski in the final Sousa march, *The Stars and Stripes for ever*, that is in part due to the recording balance, which fails to bring out the percussion, including xylophone. The least attractive item is Schubert's *Serenade*, given full Hollywood treatment not just with soupy strings but with quadruple woodwind trilling above. Hollywood treatment of a different kind comes in the *United Nations march* of Shostakovich, in 1942 used as the victory finale of an MGM wartime musical, *Thousands Cheer*. Stokowski promptly cashed in with his own non-vocal arrangement. A disc for anyone who likes to wallow in opulent sound.

Bell, Joshua (violin), RPO, Litton

SAINT-SAENS: *Introduction and rondo capriccioso, Op. 28.* MASSENET: *Thaïs: Méditation.* SARASATE: *Zigeunerweisen, Op. 20.* CHAUSSON: *Poème.* YSAYE: *Caprice d'après l'étude en forme de valse de Saint-Saëns.* RAVEL: *Tzigane.*
(Y/B) *** Decca Dig. 433 519-2 [id.].

A splendid showcase for a first-rate American virtuoso and musician of the younger generation who has not yet established his personality as an artist in Britain as firmly as on the other side of the Atlantic. Whether in Sarasate, Saint-Saëns or Ysaÿe the easy, sparkling brilliance of bow on string (with dashes of pizzicato) is balanced with a warm melodic line that can be sultry or chimerical by turns. He plays with style and an impressive range of colour. While the Chausson *Poème* has much delicacy of feeling, the Ravel *Tzigane* brings a gutsy, almost malevolent, incandescent energy. Litton accompanies with characteristic polish and feeling for detail, and Decca produce vividly realistic projection for their soloist.

(i) Berlin Philharmonic Orchestra; (ii) Berlin RIAS Symphony Orchestra; (iii) Berlin Radio Symphony Orchestra; (iv) Vienna Philharmonic Orchestra; (v) South German Radio Symphony Orchestra, Ferenc Fricsay

'Ferenc Fricsay Portrait': (i) BEETHOVEN: *Symphony No. 9* (with Irmgard Seefried, Maureen Forrester, Ernst Haefliger, Dietrich Fischer-Dieskau, St Hedwig's Cathedral Ch.) (stereo; 445 401-2).
BARTOK: *Violin concerto No. 2* (with Tibor Varga); (ii) *Dance suite; Cantata profana* (with Helmut Krebs, Dietrich Fischer-Dieskau, RIAS Chamber Ch., St Hedwig's Cathedral Ch.) (mono; 445 402-2).
(ii) R. STRAUSS: *Don Juan, Op. 20; Duet-Concertino for clarinet, bassoon, strings and harp* (with Heinrich Geuser, Willi Fugmann); *Burleske, Op. 11* (with Margrit Weber); (i) *Till Eulenspiegel, Op. 28* (mono; 445 403-2).
(ii) LIEBERMANN: *Furioso.* BLACHER: *Paganini variations, Op. 26.* EGK: *French suite.* (iii) VON EINEM: *Piano concerto, Op. 20* (with Gerty Herzog); *Ballade for orchestra, Op. 23* (mono/stereo; 445 404-2).
STRAVINSKY: (ii) *The Rite of spring; Petrushka* (1947 version); (iii) *Movements for piano and orchestra* (with Margrit Weber) (mono/stereo; 445 405-2).
(ii) ROSSINI: *Overtures: Il barbiere di Siviglia; Tancredi; Il Signor Bruschino; La gazza ladra; Semiramide.*
VERDI: *Overtures: Nabucco; La traviata* (Preludes to Acts I & III); *La forza del destino; Aida; I vespri siciliani* (mono; 445 406-2).
BRAHMS: (iv) *Symphony No. 2 in D, Op. 73;* (iii) *Variations on a theme of Haydn, Op. 56a; Alto rhapsody, Op. 53* (with Maureen Forrester, RIAS Chamber Ch.) (mono; 445 407-2).
MOZART: (ii) *Requiem Mass No. 19 in D min., K.626* (with Elisabeth Grümmer, Gertrude Pitzinger, Helmut Krebs, Hans Hotter, RIAS Chamber Ch., St Hedwig's Cathedral Ch.); (iii) *Adagio and fugue in C min., K.546* (mono/stereo; 445 408-2).
TCHAIKOVSKY: (i) *Symphony No. 6 (Pathétique);* (ii) *Violin concerto in D, Op. 35* (with Yehudi Menuhin) (mono; 445 409-2).
KODALY: (ii) *Dances of Marosszék;* (iii) *Symphony; Psalmus hungaricus, Op. 13* (with Ernst Haefliger, St Hedwig's Cathedral Ch.) (mono/stereo 445 410-2).
Bonus CD: (v) SMETANA: *Má Vlast* (extracts): *Vltava* (rehearsal and concert performance) (mono; 445 411-2).
(Y/B) ✪ (M) *** DG mono/stereo 445 400-2 (10) [id.] (records available separately).

Although many younger collectors know their Furtwängler, Beecham and Monteux, the Hungarian conductor, Ferenc Fricsay, never enjoyed cult status. The appearance of this ten-CD box offers an excellent opportunity to evaluate him, and DG deserve congratulations on its planning and presentation – and on making each disc separately available as well, thus bringing it within the grasp of any serious collector. To many, we are sure, it will come as something of a revelation: indeed, although we admired and respected Fricsay in the 1950s and '60s, coming back to these performances (or, in some cases, hearing them for the first time) serves afresh to reaffirm his stature.

One striking feature of the collection is the sheer quality of the sound produced by the DG engineers of the 1950s. One thing is quite self-evident: that the original mono pressings did scant justice to their achievement. The original LPs did not reproduce such vivid detail, such presence or body. Among the riches that are assembled here, one of the surprises is *The Rite of spring* (445 405-2), far removed from any vestige of the current view of the work as some kind of sanitized orchestral showpiece. This brings this score alive with a freshness and ferocity that remind one of the first encounter with this extraordinary score. *The Rite* is far more savage and powerful than Markevitch's celebrated account with the Philharmonia that came out at the same time. This is a must.

Naturally the contemporary music with which Fricsay was specially associated must have first claim. The DG Dokumente version of the Bartók *Divertimento* and *Music for strings, percussion and celeste* (see our main volume) does not prepare you for the excellence of the Bartók disc here (445 402-2). His *Dance suite* is one of the best ever committed to disc, wonderfully idiomatic, vital and yet relaxed; the *Cantata profana* too is excellent, though Tibor Varga's account of the *Violin concerto* does not displace Menuhin. Of particular value is the disc coupling Rolf Liebermann's *Furioso*, Werner Egk's *French suite*, two von Einem works, and Boris Blacher's *Paganini variations* (445 404-2). The Blacher was almost a popular warhorse in the 1950s, so frequently did it appear; it is a resourceful and diverting piece which, like his engaging *Concertante musik*, should be a popular repertory piece. Apart from these and the Kodály (445 410-2), which are effortlessly idiomatic and thrillingly alive, Fricsay is no less impressive in the mainstream repertoire.

In Richard Strauss he is hardly less persuasive, and the disc devoted to that master is to be particularly recommended for a delightful performance of the *Duet-Concertino for clarinet, bassoon, strings and harp*. We remember what an enormous impact his splendid Tchaikovsky *Pathétique* made on collectors when it first appeared: it remains one of the most vital and intense of all recorded performances and still carries an enthusiastic recommendation. The Brahms *Second Symphony*, one of his later recordings (1961), which has not appeared before in Britain, has a rich, lyrical warmth and a sense of forward movement worthy of Bruno Walter. Needless to say, the box is not comprehensive: there are Mozart symphonies and operas, now in currency separately, and the three Bartók *Piano concertos* with Géza Anda reappear among DG's 'Originals'. Those buying the ten CDs as a package get a bonus disc, which includes a 1960 performance of Smetana's *Vltava*, made with the orchestra of Süddeutsches Rundfunk, with an hour-long rehearsal in their Stuttgart studios. It is easy to follow but there is a précis of his remarks in both English and French. We do not normally give rosettes for this kind of compilation, but this should certainly have one in recognition of the care lavished on it, and the artistic and technical excellence of these performances.

Berlin Philharmonic Orchestra, Paris Conservatoire Orchestra or Belgian Radio & TV Orchestra, André Cluytens

'Artist profile': BEETHOVEN: *Symphony No. 6 in F (Pastoral), Op. 68.* BERLIOZ: *L'enfance du Christ: La fuite en Egypte: Overture; Shepherds' farewell* (with René Duclos Ch.). DEBUSSY: *Jeux.* FRANCK: *Le chasseur maudit.* PIERNE: *Concertstück, Op. 39, for harp and orchestra* (with Annie Challan). ROUSSEL: *Bacchus et Ariane, Op. 43: suite No. 2; Sinfonietta, Op. 52; Le festin de l'araignée (fragments symphoniques), Op. 17.*
(Y/B) ✲ (B) *** EMI CZS5 68220-2 (2) [id.].

There is something special about this compilation. André Cluytens was a much-underrated conductor and, though his account of the *Pastoral Symphony* with the Berlin Philharmonic was highly acclaimed on its first appearance, he was generally taken for granted during his lifetime. His 1957 recording of the *Pastoral* with the same orchestra was in mono, and some would say it was even more inspired. In any event it made a sufficient impression to encourage EMI to re-record it in 1960 and then to go on to do a complete cycle. The stereo version (offered here) is radiant and glowing – as good as any made during the 1960s, and better than many that followed. His account of *Jeux* with the Orchestre de la Société des Concerts du Conservatoire was vastly more atmospheric than the Boulez account with the Philharmonia (CBS) which came out at much the same period, though some of the subtlety, delicacy and the slight haze of the old LPs have been lost in the transfer. (The original opens out and has much greater range, but the present disc is still very good and reproduces smoothly on most machines.) The Pierné rarity is also beautifully done and makes a welcome addition to the catalogue. The second *Bacchus et Ariane* suite is both exhilarating and atmospheric, and never has Roussel's spider feasted so sumptuously and in such an exotic ambience as it does here. Let us hope that EMI will restore Cluytens' account of Debussy's *Images* and the Roussel *Third* and *Fourth Symphonies*. At full price these two discs would be well worth having, but for so modest an outlay they represent an altogether outstanding bargain. One of the most rewarding issues of the year.

(i) **Berlin Philharmonic**, (ii) **Royal Philharmonic**, (iii) **Vienna Philharmonic** or (iv) **Philharmonia Orchestra, Rudolf Kempe**

R. STRAUSS: (i) *Till Eulenspiegels lustige Streiche; Don Quixote* (with Paul Tortelier). (ii) SMETANA: *The Bartered Bride: Overture and suite*. HUMPERDINCK: *Hänsel und Gretel: Overture and suite*. (iii) LEHAR: *Gold and Silver waltz*. Josef STRAUSS: *Sphärenklänge waltz*. WEBER: *Oberon overture*. (iv) HAYDN: *Symphony No. 104 in D (London)*.
(N) (B) *** EMI CZS5 68736-2 (2) [id.].

Kempe's recording of *Don Quixote* with Tortelier, recorded as early as 1958 but sounding remarkably full and fresh, is one of the great classics of the gramophone. *Till Eulenspiegel*, more than almost any other recorded performance, conveys the wit and sparkle of the music in playing that is brilliant but never forced. And the rest of the programme here is hardly less treasurable, the *Bartered Bride* music played with plenty of Slavonic sparkle balanced by Kempe's characteristic warmth, which latter quality also suits the rare Humperdinck suite so readily. The two *Waltzes* are affectionately mannered but still most enjoyable, and Weber's *Oberon overture*, with its romantic opening horn solo, comes from another area of repertoire in which Kempe is thoroughly at home. The Haydn symphony is a heavyweight account by today's standards but the orchestral playing is first class: outer movements are rhythmically buoyant and the lovely slow movement is attractively mellow. Excellent sound throughout.

Boston Symphony Orchestra, Serge Koussevitzky

COPLAND: *El Salón México*. FOOTE: *Suite in E min., Op. 63*. HARRIS: *Symphony (1933); Symphony No. 3*. MCDONALD: *San Juan Capistrano – Two Evening Pictures*.
(M) (***) Pearl mono GEMM CD 9492.

Koussevitzky's performance of the Roy Harris *Third Symphony* has never been equalled in intensity and fire – even by Toscanini or Bernstein – and Copland himself never produced as exhilarating an *El Salón México*. The Arthur Foote *Suite* is unpretentious and has great charm. Sonic limitations are soon forgotten, for these performances have exceptional power and should not be missed.

Boston Symphony Orchestra, Chicago Symphony Orchestra or San Francisco Symphony Orchestra, Pierre Monteux

'*Pierre Monteux Edition*': BEETHOVEN: *Symphonies Nos. 4, Op. 60; 8, Op. 93; Overture: The Ruins of Athens*. BACH: *Passacaglia & fugue in C min*. (09026 61892-2). BERLIOZ: *Symphonie fantastique; Benevenuto Cellini overture; Les Troyens: Act II Prelude. La damnation de Faust: Rákóczy march* (09026 61894-2). BRAHMS: *Symphony No. 2, Op. 73; Schicksalslied, Op. 54*. MAHLER: *Kindertotenlieder* (with Gladys Swarthout) (09026 61891-2). CHAUSSON: *Symphony, Op. 20; Poème de l'amour et de la mer*. CHABRIER: *Le roi malgré lui: Fête-polonaise* (09026 61899-2). DEBUSSY: *Images; Sarabande; Nocturnes* (09026 61900-2). LISZT: *Les Préludes*. SCRIABIN: *Poème de l'extase, Op. 54*. SAINT-SAENS: *Havanaise, Op. 83*. DEBUSSY: *La mer* (09026 61890-2). DELIBES: *Coppélia: suite; Sylvia: suite*. GOUNOD: *Faust: ballet music* (09026 61975-2). FRANCK: *Symphony in D min; Pièce héroïque*. D'INDY: *Istar* (symphonic variations), *Op. 42* (09026 61967-2). D'INDY: *Symphony on a French mountain air (cévenole), Op. 25; Fervaal, Op. 40; Symphony No. 2, Op. 57* (09026 61888-2). RIMSKY-KORSAKOV: *Scheherazade* (symphonic suite), *Op. 35; Sadko, Op. 5; Symphony No. 2 (Antar), Op. 9* (09026 61897-2). R. STRAUSS: *Ein Heldenleben, Op. 40; Death and transfiguration, Op. 24* (09026 61889-2). STRAVINSKY: *Petrushka; The Rite of spring* (09026 61898–2). TCHAIKOVSKY: *Symphonies Nos. 4, 5 & 6 (Pathétique)* (09026 61901-2).
(M) (***) RCA 09026 61893-2 (15) [id.].

Monteux was born in 1875, thirteen years after Debussy and seven before Stravinsky, and the great French conductor's career was to co-exist and readily adapt to the enormous changes that came in music in the first half of the twentieth century. He made recordings from the 1920s onwards and, while he obviously brought special insights to French music, there is universal agreement that his repertoire had no geographical limitations and his interpretative versatility was extraordinary: everything was made to sound fresh. He loved the German repertoire and hated to be type-cast as a French specialist. His insights were as compelling in a Beethoven or Brahms symphony as in Stravinsky's *Rite of spring*, of which he conducted the 1913 world première in the city of his birth. (Noting the dismayed fury of the public at the *Rite of Spring*'s début, he confessed with great candour that 'At that time I did not understand one note!') Later, of course, he came to know every note and worked with the composer on the score before it entered his concert repertoire. He also directed the opening performances of *Petrushka*, *Daphnis et Chloé* and *Jeux* for Diaghilev's Ballets Russes.

For Americans, his name will always be associated with the San Francisco Symphony, whose musical director he became in 1936 and where he stayed for 16 years, until 1952. From 1951, he also conducted regularly at Boston, where he recorded both French and Russian repertory. In the mid-1950s he also came regularly to London, where he made some of his finest later recordings with the LSO for Decca. Yet his San Francisco coupling of the Beethoven *Fourth* and *Eighth Symphonies* has all the exuberant freshness one associates with his Beethoven.

In his 1945 *Symphonie fantastique*, one of the finest ever recorded, the volatile manipulation of tempo in the first movement grows naturally out of the music and, with the sparkling waltz providing a pleasingly elegant interlude, the slow movement combines Byronic romanticism with intensity. The last two movements generate great excitement and the clipped rhythms of the *March to the scaffold* are full of Gallic character. The close balance of the mono recording also means that not only are the strings given plenty of body in their slow-movement cantilena but remarkable detail also registers in the finale.

Monteux had a very special place in his heart for Brahms and he recorded the *Second Symphony* four times. In many ways his later, VPO version is the finest and it includes the first-movement exposition repeat. But the present San Franciso performance is unerringly paced and has great warmth and energy. The Chausson *Symphony* is warm, fresh and subtly coloured in the first movement, the *très lent*, darker, more intense without neurosis, while the finale is certainly exuberantly *animé*. A refreshing reading, remarkably well recorded. In Debussy's *Images*, the *Gigues* has every bit as strong an atmosphere as one remembered; so, too, has the middle movement of *Ibéria* (*Parfums dans la nuit*), which never appeared in the UK (according to W.E.R.M., the complete set appeared on LP in France). The *Sarabande* (orchestrated by Ravel), recorded in 1946, is masterly and elegant. The 1955 *Nuages* is a great improvement in sound and is marvellously paced, with sumptuous string sonority – one of the best *Nuages* ever! It has the advantage of the ambience of Boston's Symphony Hall. So has *La Mer*, another performance showing Monteux's ear for detail and atmosphere, the *Dialogue du vent et de la mer* exciting without going over the top.

The performance of Liszt's *Les Préludes* has tremendous panache and gusto. Scriabin's *Poème de l'extase* has refined, translucent detail and a passionate climax, achieved in spite of the comparatively limited dynamic range of the recording. These performances were made in Carnegie Hall and are close-miked, but for Saint-Saëns's *Havanaise* we return to Boston and join Leonid Kogan, who gives a sparkling and deliciously sultry account (with the advantage of stereo). This piece, like many of the other orchestral works, has individual sections banded, so one can isolate the coda and enjoy Kogan's wonderfully chimerical closing bars.

Monteux's ballet experience was not confined to twentieth-century scores and he knew just how to bring a sparkle to the eyes and a bloom to the cheeks of *Coppélia* and *Sylvia*. The Boston acoustics add bloom and this 1953 recording sounds almost like stereo; Gounod's ballet suite from *Faust* was recorded in San Francisco six years earlier, and the Opera House acoustics are also pleasing.

The stereo César Franck *Symphony*, dating from 1961, is masterly – perhaps Monteux's very finest recording. The addition of Charles O'Donnell's orchestration of the *Pièce héroïque* is a distinct bonus. Its chromatic links with the *Symphony* are the more obvious in its orchestral format: it sounds rather like a symphonic poem with a brassy dénouement. The 1941 mono recording (like the *Faust* ballet music) shows the excellence of the acoustics of San Francisco's War Memorial Opera House. Vincent d'Indy's *Istar* (from 1945) completes Volume 8. It is a colourful and increasingly energetic piece. Although the sound is boxier, the strings have plenty of middle sonority and the performance is unlikely to be bettered, since Monteux was a friend of the composer and took special care with recordings of his music (as did Beecham with Delius).

Volume 9, devoted entirely to the music of d'Indy, is an especially valuable disc, since the *Second Symphony* held a special place in Monteux's affections. This was its first commercial recording and it remained the only one for the best part of 40 years. The 1941 recording of the *Symphonie sur un chant montagnard français* is splendidly paced and comes up sounding very fresh, even though there is some distortion in the lower end of the range and the piano tone calls for some tolerance. The Russian-born pianist, Maxim Schapiro, relatively little known nowadays, is very good indeed. The *Second Symphony* is a marvellous performance, though this transfer is a bit flat. Checked against the LP (RCA LCT 1125) and a tuning fork, we made it over half a semitone down!

Monteux made his complete recording of *Daphnis et Chloé* for Decca, but the *First suite* (initially described as 'symphonic fragments') has remarkable allure, even if the sound is not quite secure at the opening. It includes not only a chorus but also a wind-machine. The other Ravel pieces are distinctive (some of the *Valses nobles* have captivating delicacy), but Lalo's melodramatic overture and Ibert's translucent *Escales* suffer from the restricted mono sound. No such complaints about the 1942 *Scheherazade*, where once more the resonance of the San Francisco Opera House provides mono sound of unexpected warmth and allure. With the orchestra's concertmaster, Naoum Blinder (very well balanced), taking the role of the heroine with panache this is a tremendously compelling performance. The orchestra produces sumptuous tone and in the finale the playing is so riveting that the ear hardly notices that there is any dynamic restriction: the final climax is truly magnificent. In many ways this is even finer than Monteux's later, stereo, Decca record. *Sadko* is hardly less intoxicating and *Antar* has plenty of exotic colour and impetus, but here the sound is two-dimensional.

As a recording, the 1947 *Ein Heldenleben* must be counted a virtual failure. In spite of the use of the San Francisco Opera House, the engineers obviously sought brilliance above all and the violins are made to sound paper-thin and shrill. However, Monteux's glorious 1960 *Death and transfiguration*, recorded in California Hall, ranks with the very finest, as gripping as – and even more sumptuous than – Szell's Cleveland version. Like his Brahms, it shows just how well this extraordinarily versatile conductor could handle main-line German repertoire, with the San Francisco brass sounding like Reiner's Chicago players and the transformation scene at the end both radiant and thrillingly voluptuous.

The Stravinsky coupling offers the finer of Monteux's two stereo *Petrushkas*, coupled with a remarkably fine mono *Rite of spring* from 1951. *Petrushka* is much better played here than the later, Decca version with the Paris Conservatoire Orchestra: vivid throughout, with the tension especially high in the final scene, and all the bustle of the Shrovetide Carnival brilliantly conveyed. *The Rite* is marvellously played and, because of the Boston ambience, sounds remarkably like stereo. There is plenty of rhythmic vehemence and the closing *Danse de la terre* of Part 1 brings thrillingly menacing articulation. Although the balance is close, the *Cercles mystérieux des adolescentes* is hauntingly evocative and the final *Sacrificial dance* with its snarling brass brings a powerful climax and a quickening of tension in the very last bars.

The three great Tchaikovsky *Symphonies* were recorded in Boston between 1955 and 1959 and are among Monteux's finest records. The *Fourth* is a most compulsive reading which sweeps through the score with its momentum sustained from first to last. The *Fifth* (1958) is direct, full-blooded and exciting, still among the finest versions available. The remastered recording is a revelation: strings and brass sound wonderfully rich and this is one of the best of all the RCA recordings made in Boston in the early stereo era. There are a few minor eccentricities of tempo, and in the finale Monteux makes a few agogic distortions, but the performance has such panache that he convinces the listener in all he does.

The *Pathétique* is a mono recording, but the ear would hardly guess when the Boston sound has such amplitude and depth. The reading is essentially dignified, except in the *Allegro con grazia*, which has a curious feeling of urgency, even of hurry. The finale, the apex of the reading, is heartfelt and spontaneously passionate without ever gushing. The orchestra responds nobly, especially in the restrained, dignified coda.

Bournemouth Sinfonietta, Richard Studt

Scandinavian string music: GRIEG: *Holberg suite.* Dag WIRÉN: *Serenade, Op. 11.* SVENDSEN: *2 Icelandic melodies; Norwegian folksong; 2 Swedish folksongs, Op. 27.* NIELSEN: *Little suite in A min., Op. 1.*
(Y/B) (BB) *** Naxos Dig. 8.553106 [id.].

The liltingly spontaneous account of the Dag Wirén *Serenade* ensures a welcome for this enjoyable collection of Scandinavian music. The performance of Grieg's perennially fresh *Holberg suite* is hardly less successful in its combination of energy and polish, folksy charm and touching serenity in the famous *Air*. Nielsen's *Little suite* also has plenty of style and impetus, the changing moods of the finale neatly encompassed. The Svendsen folksong arrangements belong to the 1870s. The two *Icelandic melodies* are melodically robust but the *Norwegian folksong* is gentler and quite lovely. Yet it is the second of the two *Swedish folksongs* that most reminds the listener of Grieg. All are played with a natural expressive feeling, and the recording, made in the Winter Gardens, Bournemouth, has a fine, full sonority to balance its natural brilliance.

Brendel, Alfred (piano)

'The Art of Alfred Brendel' (complete)
(N) (B) *** Ph. Analogue/Dig. 446 920-2 (25) [id.] (includes bonus CD).

'The Art of Alfred Brendel' Volume 1: HAYDN: *Andante con variazione in F min., Hob. XVII/6; Piano sonatas in E flat, Hob. XVI/49; in C, Hob. XVI/50; Sonata in E flat, Hob. XVI/52.* MOZART: *Piano concertos Nos. 14 in E flat, K.449; 15 in B flat, K.450; 19 in F, K.459; 21 in C, K.467; 26 in D (Coronation), K.537; 27 in B flat, K.595; Double piano concerto in E flat, K.365* (with ASMF, Marriner; K.365 with Imogen Cooper). *Adagio in B min., K.540; Piano sonatas Nos. 8 in A min., K.310; 11 in A, K.331; 13 in B flat, K.333; 14 in C min., K.457; Fantasia in C min., K.475; Rondo in A min., K.511.*
(N) (M) *** Ph. Analogue/Dig. 446 921-2 (5) [id.].

Volume 2: BEETHOVEN: *Piano concertos Nos. 4 in G, Op. 58; 5 in E flat (Emperor), Op. 73* (with Chicago SO, Levine). *Andante in F (Andante favori), WoO 57; Bagatelle in A min. (Für Elise), WoO 59; 6 Bagatelles, Op. 126; 6 Ecossaises, WoO 83; Piano sonatas Nos. 3 in C, Op. 2/3; 11 in B flat, Op. 22; 18 in E flat, Op. 31/3; 23 in F min. (Appassionata), Op. 57; 24 in F sharp, Op. 78; 29 in B flat (Hammerklavier), Op. 106; 30 in E, Op. 109; 5 Variations on 'Rule Britannia', WoO 79; 6 Variations in F, Op. 34; 15 Variations and fugue on a theme of Prometheus (Eroica), Op. 35; 33 Variations on a waltz by Diabelli, Op. 120.*
(N) (M) **(*) Ph. Dig./Analogue 446 922-2 (5) [id.].

Volume 3: SCHUBERT: *Sonatas Nos. 4 in A min., D.537; 13 in A, D.664; 14 in A min., D.784; 15 in C, D.840; 16 in A min. (Relique), D.845; 19 in C min., D.958; 20 in A, D.959; 21 in B flat, D.960; Allegretto in C min., D.915; 11 Ecossaises, D.781; Fantasy in C (Wanderer), D.760; 12 German dances, D.790; 16 German dances, D.783; Hungarian melody in B min., D.817; 6 Moments musicaux, D.780.*
(N) (M) *** Ph. Analogue/Dig. 446 923-2 (5) [id.].

Volume 4: LISZT: *Piano concertos Nos. 1–2; Totentanz* (paraphrase on the *Dies irae*) (with LPO, Haitink); *Années de Pèlerinage: Book 1: 1st year: Italy; Book 2: 2nd & 3rd years: Italy; Sonata in B min.* Concert paraphrase: WAGNER: *Tristan: Isoldes Liebestod; Csárdás macabre; En rêve (Nocturne); Harmonies poétiques et religieuses: Invocations; Bénédiction de Dieu dans la solitude; Pensée des morts; Funérailles. Klavierstück in F sharp; Légendes; La lugubre gondola Nos. 1–2; Mosonyis Grabgeleit; RW (Venezia); Schlaflos! Frage und Antwort; Trübe Wolken (Nuages gris); Unstern: Sinistre; Valse oubliée No. 1; Vexilla regis Prodeunt; Weinachtsbaum (Christmas tree/Arbre de Noël) suite* (excerpts); *Weinen, Klagen, Sorgen Zagen.*
(N) (M) *** Ph. Analogue/Dig. 446 924-2 (5) [id.].

Volume 5: BRAHMS: *Piano concertos Nos. 1–2* (with BPO, Abbado). *4 Ballades, Op. 10; Theme and variations in D min.* (from *String sextet, Op. 18*). SCHUMANN: (i) *Piano concerto in A min., Op. 54* (with LSO, Abbado). (ii) *Abendlied, Op. 85/12; Adagio and Allegro in A flat, Op. 70; Fantasiestücke, Op. 73; 3 Romances, Op. 94; 5 Stücke im Volkston, Op. 102* (with Heinz Holliger). *Etudes symphoniques, Op. 13. Fantasia in C, Op. 17; Fantasiestücke, Op. 12; Kinderszenen, Op. 15; Kreisleriana, Op. 16.*
(N) (M) *** Ph. Analogue/Dig. 446 925-2 (5) [id.].

Weihnachtsbaum (A Christmas tree) (suite).
(N) (***) Ph. mono 454 140-2 [id.] (bonus disc).

'The Art of Alfred Brendel' subdivides into five boxes, each of five CDs, and we have surveyed them in some depth under their composer entries. Brendel aficionados will have to decide whether to invest in the complete set (with the five individual boxes in a slip-case), which offers some saving in cost, or to pick and choose. Brendel's overall achievement in a wide breadth of repertoire is quite remarkable, as indeed is the consistency of the Philips engineering: few (if any) artists have enjoyed such reliably truthful recording. However, while the Haydn/Mozart, the Liszt and the Schubert boxes can be recommended almost without serious reservation, the Beethoven collection is slightly marred by the inclusion of Brendel's digital recordings of the *Fourth* and *Emperor Piano concertos*, which are considerably inferior on almost all counts to his earlier, analogue versions. Perversely, the problem with the Brahms collection is the inclusion of Brendel's recent digital versions of both concertos, which are outstandingly fine and thus will probably have already found their way into the collections of most of his admirers! The choice for Volume 4 of his most recent 1991 recording of the Liszt *Sonata* is also difficult to fathom when, by general consensus, both his earlier versions are superior in almost all respects. But the rest of the Liszt package is very impressive indeed, as is the Schubert box, which offers many of his analogue recordings not otherwise available.

With the complete set comes a bonus disc of Liszt's *Christmas tree suite*, a mono recording from 1951–2.

While it is unique, its appeal is limited by its poor technical quality: a blurred focus at higher dynamic levels, and moments of distortion. The music itself, written by Liszt for his granddaughter to play, is of relatively limited interest.

(i) British Symphony Orchestra, (ii) London Symphony Orchestra, (iii) Symphony Orchestra, (iv) Queen's Hall Orchestra, (v) London Philharmonic Orchestra; Sir Henry Wood

'*Proms favourites*': (iv) COATES: *London suite; London Bridge march*. GRAINGER: (i) *Molly on the shore; Mock Morris*. (iv) *Handel in the Strand*. (iv) WAGNER: *The Ride of the Valkyries*. (v) BERLIOZ: *Roman carnival overture*. (v) GOUNOD: *Funeral march of a marionette*. ELGAR: (v) *Pomp and circumstance marches Nos. 1 in D (Land of hope and glory); 4 in G*. (ii) *Fantasia on British sea songs* (arr. Wood). (iii) JARNEFELT: *Praeludium*.

(M) (**(*)) Dutton Laboratories mono CDAX 8008 [id.].

In the early days, the Proms were the exact opposite of what they have become under the BBC's current programming policy, and this collection of 'pops' is representative of the kind of music Wood introduced, especially on Saturday evenings, to draw in the widest audience. It includes the famous *Sea-songs* which became a staple of the 'Last night' celebrations, put together in 1905 to celebrate the centenary of the Battle of Trafalgar. It sounds incredibly vivid here, especially the famous *Sailor's hornpipe*, where one is immediately tempted to clap and which works up into such a zestful frenzy at the end that the listener is left breathless. Wood conducts everything with aplomb. The programme is slight and, for all the skill of the transfer engineers, one needs modern stereo for the shorter lollipops to sound their best; even so, the *Carnaval romain overture* (from 1940) has a strikingly convincing ambience. The early Decca recordings included here sound rather dry and studio-ish, especially the unexpansive *Ride of the Valkyries* (not Wood's fault). But the lollipop which leaps off the original shellac is track 7, Wood's own re-orchestration of Grainger's *Handel in the Strand*, and this is surely the demonstration item. This record and its companion set above are issued to coincide with Arthur Jacobs' splendid new biography, *Henry J. Wood, Maker of the Proms*.

(i) Chicago Symphony Orchestra, Frederick Stock; (ii) Cincinnati SO, Eugene Goossens; (iii) with Jascha Heifetz (violin)

English music: (i) BENJAMIN: *Overture to an Italian comedy*. ELGAR: *Pomp and circumstance march No. 1*. (ii) VAUGHAN WILLIAMS: *A London Symphony (No. 2;* original version); (ii; iii) WALTON: *Violin concerto*.

(***) Biddulph mono WHL 016 [id.].

This superbly transferred Biddulph issue celebrates the fact that some of the very finest recordings of British music have come from America. Heifetz's historic first recording of the Walton *Violin concerto* is imaginatively coupled with the only recording ever made (also by Goossens and the Cincinnati Orchestra immediately following the Walton sessions in 1941) of the 1920 version of Vaughan Williams's *London Symphony*. As welcome fill-ups come Elgar's *Pomp and Circumstance No. 1* and Arthur Benjamin's *Overture to an Italian comedy*, brilliantly played by the Chicago orchestra under Frederick Stock.

Cincinnati Pops Orchestra, Erich Kunzel

'*The Fantastic Leopold Stokowski*' (transcriptions for orchestra): BACH: *Toccata & fugue in D min., BWV 565; Little fugue in G min., BWV 578*. BOCCHERINI: *Quintet in E flat: Minuet*. BEETHOVEN: *Moonlight sonata: adagio sostenuto*. BRAHMS: *Hungarian dance No. 6*. DEBUSSY: *Suite bergamasque: Clair de lune; La cathédrale engloutie*. ALBENIZ: *Fête-Dieu à Seville*. RACHMANINOV: *Prelude in C sharp min., Op. 3/2*. MUSSORGSKY: *Night on the bare mountain; Pictures at an exhibition: The Great gate of Kiev*.

(❀) *** Telarc Dig. CD 80338 [id.].

Stokowski began his conducting career in Cincinnati in 1909, moving on to Philadelphia three years later; so a collection of his orchestral transcriptions from his first orchestra is appropriate, particularly when the playing is so committed and polished and the recording so sumptuous. Indeed, none of Stokowski's own recordings can match this Telarc disc in sheer glamour of sound. The arrangement of *La cathédrale engloutie* is very free and melodramatically telling. Most interesting is *Night on the bare mountain*, which has a grandiloquent brass chorale added as a coda. Any admirer of Stokowski should regard this superbly engineered CD as an essential purchase. It is now reissued with two extra items added, the Brahms *Hungarian dance No. 6* and Stokowski's extraordinary transcription of *The Great Gate of Kiev* from Mussorgsky's *Pictures at an exhibition*. Kunzel has the advantage of Telarc's bass-drum recording, and at the very close there is a highly imaginative added touch as the old magician introduces an evocation of Moscow cathedral bells.

Columbia Symphony Orchestra or New York Philharmonic Orchestra, Bruno Walter

Bruno Walter Edition Volume 1 (complete)
(N) (M) **(*) Sony stereo/mono SX10K 66246 (10) [id.].

MAHLER: *Symphonies Nos.* (i) *1 (Titan)* (with Columbia SO); (ii) *2 (Resurrection)* (with Emilia Cundari, Maureen Forrester, Westminster Ch., NYPO); (iii) *Lieder eines fahrenden Gesellen* (with Mildred Miller, Columbia SO) (SMK 64447) (2) [id.].
MAHLER: *Symphony No. 4* (with Desi Halban, NYPO); (ii) *Lieder und Gesänge: Frühlingsmorgen; Erinnerung; Hans und Grethe; Ich ging mit Lust durch einen grünen Wald; Starke Einbildungskraft; Ablösung im Sommer; Scheiden und Meiden; Nicht wiedersehen* (Halban & Walter, piano) (mono SMK 64450) [id.].
MAHLER: (i) *Symphony No. 5* (with NYPO) (mono SMK 64451) [id.].
MAHLER: *Symphony No. 9* (with rehearsal & conversation between Bruno Walter and Arnold Michaelis) (with Columbia SO) (SMK 64452) (2) [id.].
MAHLER : *Das Lied von der Erde* (with Mildred Miller, Ernst Haefliger, NYPO) (SMK 64455) [id.].
WAGNER: *Siegfried idyll* (with rehearsal); *Der fliegende Holländer: Overture; Die Meistersinger: Prelude to Act I; Lohengrin: Prelude to Act I; Parsifal: Prelude to Act I; Tannhäuser: Overture and Venusberg music* (with Columbia SO) (SMK 64456) (2) [id.].
BEETHOVEN: *Violin concerto* (with Joseph Szigeti, NYPO). MENDELSSOHN: *Violin concerto* (with Nathan Milstein, NYPO) (Sony mono SMK 64459) [id.].

The first volume of Sony's Bruno Walter Edition understandably concentrates on Mahler, with the recordings of the *First*, *Second* and *Ninth Symphonies* and, to a lesser extent, *Das Lied von der Erde*, an indispensable part of the catalogue. Nos. 4 and 5 are mono, but Walter aficionados will want these too although, for all the conductor's magnetism, the orchestral playing in New York is less refined. In the first movement of the *Fifth*, Walter's seamless and seemingly spontaneous control of the Funeral march is memorable, as of course is the glowing *Adagietto*. The Lieder recital, which is a makeweight to the glorious mono version of the *Fourth Symphony*, is made special by his piano accompaniments for Desi Halban, reticent as it is. Walter's Wagner orchestral recordings also show him at his finest, and here the ear notices the greater amplitude and weight with which the Sony engineers have enhanced the sound. Szigeti's account of Beethoven's *Violin concerto* comes from New York in 1947. His classical purity of line is still evident, but the loss of bloom on his timbre and the moments of disturbing vibrato which troubled the great violinist in the last decade of his career had already begun to surface. Milstein's patrician account of the Mendelssohn *Concerto* was recorded two years earlier and is undoubtedly distinguished, although he re-recorded the work in stereo with Abbado for DG with equal success. All these recordings are available separately, and the stereo CDs are discussed in greater detail under the appropriate composer listing. The rehearsal recordings add to the value and interest of these important reissues.

Columbia Symphony Orchestra, Bruno Walter

Bruno Walter Edition, Volume 2 (complete)
(Y/B) (M) **(*) Sony stereo/mono SX10K 66247 (10) [id.].

BEETHOVEN: *Symphonies Nos. 1 in C, Op. 21; 2 in D, Op. 36; Coriolan Overture* (SMK 64460).

BEETHOVEN: *Symphonies Nos. 3 in E flat (Eroica), Op. 55; 8 in F* (SMK 64461).
BEETHOVEN: *Symphonies Nos. 4 in B flat, Op. 60; 6 in F (Pastoral), Op. 68* (SMK 64462).
BEETHOVEN: *Symphonies Nos. 5 in C min., Op. 67; 7 in A, Op. 92* (SMK 64463).
BEETHOVEN: *Symphony No. 9 in D min., Op. 125* (with Cundari, Rankin, Da Costa, Wilderman, Westminster Ch. (SMK 64464)).
BEETHOVEN: *Symphonies Nos. 4, 5, 7 & 9* (rehearsals) (SMK 64465).
BARBER: *Symphony No. 1, Op. 9.* Richard STRAUSS: *Don Juan; Death and transfiguration.* DVORAK: *Slavonic Dance, Op. 46/1* ((mono) SMK 64466).
Johann STRAUSS Jnr: Waltzes: *An der schönen blauen Donau; Geschichten aus dem Wiener Wald; Kaiser Weiner Blut;* Overtures: *Die Fledermaus; Der Zigeunerbaron.* BRAHMS: *Hungarian dances Nos. 1, 3, 10 & 17.* SMETANA: *Vltava* (both with NYPO) ((mono) SMK 64467).
MOZART: (i) *Violin concertos Nos. 3 in G, K.216; 4 in D, K.218; Serenade No. 13 (Eine kleine Nachtmusik), K.525* ((i) with Zino Francescatti (SMK 64468)).
BRAHMS: (i) *German Requiem;* (ii) *Alto rhapsody, Op. 53* (with (i) Seefried, London, Westminster Ch., NYPO; (ii) Mildred Miller, Occidental College Concert Ch., Columbia SO ((mono/stereo) SMK 64469).

Although he enjoyed a position of pre-eminence in the 1930s, Bruno Walter was never invited to record a Beethoven cycle. Duplication was less frequent then than it is now, and Weingartner and Toscanini dominated the field. (Walter's glorious pre-war records of the *Pastoral Symphony* with the Vienna Philharmonic give some idea of how good it might have been.) After he settled in the United States he recorded all nine symphonies with the New York Philharmonic and Philadelphia orchestras, but the set offered here is with the Columbia Symphony, made in California in 1958/9, not long before he died, and by general consent the finer of the two by a considerable margin. These performances embody the humane, songful approach which characterized his finest work, their warmth standing out in contrast against the gaunt, often matter-of-fact approach of Klemperer. Tempi are not exaggerated and, although Walter may not have had the electricity and fiery qualities that distinguish Toscanini's NBC Beethoven, there is no lack of either rhythmic vitality or lyrical intensity. There is also a rehearsal disc (available as part of the set) which shows his courteous, gentle, yet firm approach to music-making in the slow movement of the *Fourth*, the first movements of the *Fifth* and *Seventh* and the Scherzo of the *Ninth*. All these recordings are discussed more fully under their individual entries, as they are all available separately. Of particular interest in the present set is the 1945 version of Barber's *First Symphony*, which makes its first appearance since the two blue-label 78-r.p.m. discs were withdrawn in the early 1950s. Not only is this the only *American* symphony, it is the only *contemporary* symphony Walter recorded: his repertoire never embraced much modern music (though he did conduct Wellesz's *Prospero's spell*). Like the two Strauss tone-poems with which it is coupled, it is a mono disc and, though the resulting transfer produces cleaner and better-focused sound than the originals, it still calls for some tolerance. Walter's Mozart was particularly notable for its humane qualities, and he gives admirable support to Francescatti, his soloist in the two best-known violin concertos, who is at times over-tense – what the French would call *nerveux*. The Brahms *Requiem* with the youthful Irmgard Seefried and George London comes from 1954 and is also in mono. Its companion, the *Alto Rhapsody*, with Mildred Miller comes from 1962, the year of his death, and is less successful. However, this is a collection which serious collectors will want to have.

Columbia Symphony Orchestra or New York Philharmonic Orchestra, Bruno Walter

Bruno Walter Edition, Volume 3 (complete)
(Y/B) (M) **(*) Sony stereo/mono SX10K 66248 (10) [id.].

BRAHMS: *Symphony No. 1 in C min., Op. 68; Variations on a theme of Haydn, Op. 56a; Academic festival overture.*
(N) (M) *** Sony SMK 64470 [id.]. Columbia SO, Walter.

BRAHMS: *Symphonies Nos. 2 in D, Op. 73; 3 in F, Op. 90.*
(N) (M) *** Sony SMK 64471 [id.]. Columbia SO, Walter.

BRAHMS: *Symphony No. 4 in E min., Tragic overture;* (i) *Song of Destiny (Schicksalslied), Op. 54.*
(N) (M) *** Sony SMK 64472 [id.]. Columbia SO, Walter; (i) with Occidental College Concert Ch.

MOZART: (i) *Symphonies Nos. 25 in G min., K.183; 28 in C, K.200; 29 in A, K.201;* (ii) *35 in D (Haffner), K.385.*
(N) (M) (***) Sony mono SMK 64473 [id.]. (i) Columbia SO; (ii) NYPO, Walter.

MOZART: *'The birth of a performance':* (recorded rehearsals of *Symphony No. 36*); (i) *Symphonies Nos. 36 in C (Linz), K.425;* (ii) *38 in D (Prague), K.504.*
(N) (M) *** Sony mono SM2K 64474 (2) [id.]. (i) Columbia SO; (ii) NYPO, Walter.

MOZART: *Symphonies Nos. 39 in E flat, K. 543; 40 in G min., K.550; 41 in C (Jupiter), K.551.*
(N) (M) (**) Sony mono SMK 64477 [id.]. NYPO, Walter.

SCHUBERT: *Symphony No. 9 in C (Great); Rosamunde: Overture; Ballet music; Entr'acte No. 3.*
(N) (M) **(*) Sony SMK 64478 [id.]. Columbia SO, Walter.

BEETHOVEN: (i) *Triple concerto for piano, violin and cello in C, Op. 56.* (ii) BRAHMS: *Double concerto for violin, cello and orchestra in C, Op. 102.*
(N) (M) *(**) Sony mono/stereo SMK 64479 [id.]. (i) Walter Hendl, John Corigliano, Leonard Rose, NYPO; (ii) Francescatti, Fournier, Columbia SO, Walter.

(i) BRUCKNER: *Te Deum.* (ii) MOZART: *Requiem mass in D min., K.626.*
(N) (M) ** Sony mono 64480 [id.]. (i) Yeend, Lipton, Lloyd, Harrel; (ii) Seefried, Tourel, Simoneau, Warfield; Westminster Ch., NYPO, Walter.

Walter's set of the Brahms symphonies is self-recommending, still standing high on the list of recommendations. The present remastering has improved detail, with a very slight loss of bloom on the violins. His Schubert *Ninth* is also endearing, and the mono Mozart recordings from the 1950s also bring much refreshment – although, surprisingly, the last three symphonies are less successful than the earlier ones. The rehearsal sequence for the *Linz Symphony* remains as fascinating as ever. All these recordings are discussed fully under their composer entries. The relative disappointments are the Beethoven *Triple concerto*, which is unattractively balanced, and the two choral works. Both are spaciously dramatic performances (and the Mozart *Requiem* has a splendid solo team), but the choral singing, although ardent, is not as polished as we would expect today.

Bruno Walter Edition Volume 4 (complete).
(N) (B) **(*) Sony stereo/mono SX9K 66249 (9) [id.].

BRUCKNER: *Symphony No. 4 in E flat (Romantic)* (SMK 64481) [id.].
BRUCKNER: *Symphony No. 7 in E* (SMK 64481) [id.].
BRUCKNER: *Symphony No. 9 in D min.* (❀ SMK 64483) [id.].
DVORAK: *Symphonies Nos. 8 in G; 9 in E min. (New World)* (SMK 64484) [id.].
(all above with Columbia SO)
HAYDN: *Symphonies Nos. 88 in G; 100 in G (Military)* (with Columbia SO); *102 in B flat* (with NYPO) (stereo/mono SMK 64485) [id.].
HAYDN: *Symphony No. 96 in D (Miracle)* (with NYPO). MOZART: *3 German dances, K.605/1–3; Masonic funeral music, K.477; Minuets, K.568 & 599; Overtures: Così fan tutte; The Impresario; Le nozze di Figaro; Die Zauberflöte* (with Columbia SO) (mono/stereo SMK 64486) [id.].
SCHUBERT: *Symphonies Nos. 5 in B flat, D.485; 8 in B min. (Unfinished).* BEETHOVEN: *Overture: Leonora No. 3* (with Columbia SO or NYPO) (stereo/mono SMK 64487) [id.].
SCHUMANN: *Symphony No. 3 in E flat (Rhenish)* (with NYPO). BEETHOVEN: *Overtures: Egmont; Leonora No. 2* (with Columbia SO) (mono/stereo SMK 64488) [id.].
BEETHOVEN: *Piano concerto No. 5 (Emperor)* (with Serkin, NYPO). SCHUMANN: *Piano concerto in A min.* (with Eugene Istomin, Columbia SO) (mono/stereo SMK 64489) [id.].

The highlights of this set are Bruckner's *Fourth* and (especially) the *Ninth Symphony*; by their side the *Seventh* is comparatively disappointing. The coupling of Dvořák's *Eighth* and *New World Symphonies* is also very special, and Walter's way with Schubert has an endearing grace and warmth. The Haydn symphonies are of more mixed appeal. Only Nos. 88 and 100 are stereo (made in 1961) and the glorious slow movement of the former drags, while similarly slow tempi in the *Military Symphony* also bring heaviness. The finales of both works are the most successful movements; overall, the effect is more of a rehearsal than live performances. The Mozart programme is much more characteristic. Walter's tempi in the overtures are unerringly apt, but readers should note that these are not Walter's more recent, stereo recordings but his earlier, mono versions made in 1954. The account of the *Masonic funeral music* is particularly fine. Good sound, too. The performance of Schumann's *Rhenish Symphony* is impressive, although this is mono; of the Beethoven overtures, *Leonora No. 2* is really outstanding. This is stereo; the other two are mono. However, neither of the concertos could be placed among the more remarkable versions of these works in the current catalogue, although Serkin's mono *Emperor* is more memorable than Istomin's Schumann (which is early stereo).

Concerts Straram Orchestra, Walther Straram

'The Premier Parisian Orchestra between the wars': (i) RAVEL: *Alborada del gracioso; Daphnis and Chloé: suite No. 2.* DEBUSSY: *Prélude à l'après-midi d'un faune.* ROUSSEL: *Le festin de l'araignée.* IBERT: *Escales.*
(i) Philippe Gaubert; (ii) Walther Straram.
(N) (**) VAI mono VAIA 1074-2 [id.].

As older collectors will recall, such repertoire as Roussel's *Le festin de l'araignée* was available only on the light-blue French Columbia label from the Straram Orchestra, whose discography also included Stravinsky's *Capriccio.* Roussel's own recording of *Le festin,* though very good, is nowhere near as atmospheric as the Straram. There is some distinguished playing here which older collectors will welcome the chance of re-hearing. Acceptable, rather than distinguished, transfers.

Du Pré, Jacqueline (cello)

'The Art of Jaqueline Du Pré': (with (i) LSO, Sir John Barbirolli; (ii) RPO, Sir Malcolm Sargent; (iii) New Philh. O; (iv) Chicago SO; (v) ECO; (vi) Daniel Barenboim; (vii) Valda Aveling; (viii) Gerald Moore; (ix) Ernest Lush; (x) Steven Bishop). (i) ELGAR: *Cello concerto in E min., Op. 85.* (ii) DELIUS: *Cello concerto.* (iii; vi) SAINT-SAENS: *Cello concerto No. 1 in A min., Op. 33.* (iv; vi) DVORAK: *Cello concerto in B min., Op. 104; Waldesruhe, Op. 68.* (iii; vi) SCHUMANN: *Cello concerto in A min., Op. 129.* (i; vii) MONN: *Cello concerto in G min.* HAYDN: *Cello concertos in* (i) *C and* (v; vi) *D, Hob VIIb/1–2.* (vi) CHOPIN: *Cello sonata in G min., Op. 65.* (vi) FRANCK: *Cello sonata in A.* (viii) FAURE: *Élégie in C min., Op. 24.* (viii) BRUCH: *Kol nidrei, Op. 47.* BACH: *(Unaccompanied) Cello suites Nos. 1–2, BWV 1007/8.* (ix) HANDEL: *Cello sonata in G min.* BEETHOVEN: (vi) *Variations in G min, WoO 45; on Judas Maccabeus: See the conqu'ring hero comes;* (x) *Cello sonatas Nos. 3, in A, Op. 69; 5 in D, Op. 102/2.* (vi) *Variations on themes from 'The Magic Flute': 7 variations in D, WoO 46 (Bei Männern, welche Liebe fühlen); 12 variations in F, WoO 66 (Ein Mädchen oder Weibchen).*
(B) *** EMI CZS5 68132-2 (6) [id.].

Admirers of this remarkably gifted artist, whose career ended so tragically, will welcome this survey of her major recordings, made over the incredibly brief period of a single decade. Her first recordings (1961) have a BBC source and her last (the Chopin and Franck *Sonatas*) were made at Abbey Road in 1971. But of course she made her real breakthrough in 1965 with the justly famous Kingsway Hall recording of the Elgar *Concerto* with Barbirolli. Some items included here are not otherwise currently available (including the *Concerto* by Matthias Georg Monn) and, with excellent transfers, this set is an admirable and economical way of exploring her art. There are good if brief notes and some heart-rending photographs showing this young prodigy playing with characteristic concentration and joyously in conversation with her equally young husband, Daniel Barenboim.

English music

English music ((i) LPO; (ii) New Philh. O; (iii) Sir Adrian Boult; (iv) ASMF, Marriner; (v) Hirsch Chamber Players, Leonard Hirsch; (vi) BBC Northern SO, Bryden Thomson): BUTTERWORTH: (i; iii) *The Banks of green willow.* VAUGHAN WILLIAMS: (ii; iii) *Fantasia on a theme of Thomas Tallis.* (iv) LEIGH: *Harpsichord concertino* (with George Malcolm). (v) WARLOCK: *Capriol suite.* FINZI: (vi) *Clarinet concerto* (with Janet Hilton); (i; iii) *Introit for violin and orchestra* (with Gerald Jarvis).
(Y/B) (B) **(*) BBC Radio Classics BBCRD 9119 [id.].

This mixed bag of BBC recordings from various sources offers a delightful collection. The charming Walter Leigh *Concertino* in three compact movements – including a heavenly central *Andante* – has never been recorded so ravishingly as by George Malcolm. It is also good to have a Finzi novelty in the beautiful *Introit* (with another memorable main theme), though the soloist, Gerald Jarvis, could be sweeter. Janet Hilton is an agile soloist in the Finzi *Clarinet concerto,* though the transfer gives her instrument a flutter in the finale. Boult as ever is most persuasive in all he conducts, and it is good to have a vintage artist like Leonard Hirsch conducting his own orchestra in the Warlock, even if the performance itself is a little bland. The sound is good throughout and this 77-minute concert is well worth its modest cost.

Gould, Glenn (piano)

Glenn Gould Edition

BACH: *Harpsichord concertos Nos. 1–5; 7, BWV 1052/6 & BWV 1058* (with Columbia SO, Bernstein (No. 1) or Golschmann).
(Y/B) (M) (**) Sony mono (No. 1)/stereo SM2K 52591 (2) [id.].

BACH: *Fugues, BWV 953 & BWV 961; Fughettas, BWV 961 & BWV 902; 6 Little Preludes, BWV 933/ 938; 6 Partitas, BWV 825/830; Preludes, BWV 902 & 902/1a; Prelude and fugue, BWV 895; 2 Preludes & fughettas, BWV 899/900.*
(Y/B) (M) (**) Sony SM2K 52597 (2) [id.].

BACH: *Goldberg variations, BWV 988; Three-part Inventions, BWV 788/801.*
(Y/B) (M) (**) Sony SMK 52685 [id.] (live recordings from Salzburg and Moscow).

BACH: *Goldberg variations, BWV 988; Well-tempered Clavier: Fugues in E, BWV 878; F sharp min., BWV 883.*
(Y/B) (M) (**(*)) Sony mono SMK 52594 [id.] (1955 recording).
(Y/B) (M) (**) Sony Dig. SMK 52619 [id.] (*Variations* only).

BACH: *15 Two-part Inventions; 15 Three-part Inventions, BWV 772/801.*
(Y/B) (M) (**) Sony SMK 52596 [id.].

BACH: *Well-tempered Clavier, Book I, Preludes and fugues Nos. 1–24, BWV 858/869.*
(Y/B) (M) (**) Sony SM2K 52600 (2) [id.].

BACH: *Well-tempered Clavier, Book II, Preludes and Fugues Nos. 25–48, BWV 882/893.*
(Y/B) (M) (**) Sony SM2K 52603 (2) [id.].

BACH: *Well-tempered Clavier: Preludes and fugues: in E, BWV 878; in F sharp min., BWV 883.* HANDEL: *Harpsichord suites Nos. 1–4, HWV 426/9.*
(Y/B) (M) (**) Sony mono/stereo SMK 52590 [id.].

BACH: *Sonata for violin and harpsichord No. 4 in C min. BWV 1017.* BEETHOVEN: *Violin sonata No. 10 in G, Op. 96.* SCHOENBERG: *Phantasy for violin and piano, Op. 47* (all with Yehudi Menuhin).
(Y/B) (M) (**) Sony mono SMK 52688 [id.].

BEETHOVEN: *Piano concertos Nos. 1–5* (with Columbia SO, Golschmann (No.1); Columbia SO, Bernstein (Nos. 2–3); NYPO, Bernstein (No. 4); America SO, Stokowski (No. 5)).
(Y/B) (M) (***) Sony SM3K 52632 (3) [id.].

BEETHOVEN: *7 Bagatelles, Op. 33; 6 Bagatelles, Op. 126; 6 Variations in F, Op. 34; 15 Variations with fugue in E flat (Eroica), Op. 35; 32 Variations on an original theme in C min., WoO 80.*
(Y/B) (M) (**) Sony SM2K 52646 (2) [id.].

BEETHOVEN: *Piano sonatas Nos. 24 in F sharp, Op. 78; 29 in B flat (Hammerklavier).*
(Y/B) (M) (**) Sony SMK 52645 [id.].

BIZET: *Nocturne No. 1 in F; Variations chromatiques.* GRIEG: *Piano sonata in E min., Op. 7.* SIBELIUS: *Kyllikki (3 Lyric pieces), Op. 41; Sonatines Nos. 1–3, Op. 67/1–3.*
(Y/B) (M) (**(*)) Sony SM2K 52654 (2) [id.].

BRAHMS: (i) *Piano quintet in F min., Op. 34.* SCHUMANN: (i) *Piano quartet in E flat, Op. 47* (with (i) Montreal Qt; (ii) Juilliard Qt (members)).
(Y/B) (M) (**) Sony SMK 52684 [id.].

BRAHMS: *4 Ballades, Op. 10; Intermezzi, Op. 76/6–7; Op. 116/4; Op. 117/1–3; Op. 118/1, 2 & 6; Op. 119/1; 2 Rhapsodies, Op. 79.*
(Y/B) (M) (**) Sony Analogue/Dig. SM2K 52651 (2) [id.].

HAYDN: *Piano sonata in E flat, Hob XVI:49.* MOZART: *Piano concerto No. 24 in C min., K.491* (with CBC SO, Walter Süsskind); *Fantasia (Prelude) and fugue in C, K.394; Sonata in C, K.330.*
(Y/B) (M) (**) Sony SMK 52626 [id.].

HINDEMITH: (i) *Alto horn sonata in E flat;* (ii) *Bass tuba sonata;* (i) *Horn sonata;* (iii) *Trombone sonata;* (iv) *Trumpet sonata* (with: (i) Mason Jones; (ii) Abe Torchinsky; (iii) Henry Charles Smith; (iv) Gilbert Johnson).
(Y/B) (M) (**) Sony SM2K 52671 (2) [id.].

HINDEMITH: *Piano sonatas Nos. 1–3.*
(Y/B) (M) (**(*)) Sony SMK 52670 [id.].

LISZT: *Concert paraphrases* of Beethoven's *Symphonies Nos. 5 in C min.; 6 in F (Pastoral): 1st movt.*
(Y/B) (M) (**) Sony SMK 52636 [id.].

LISZT: *Concert paraphrase* of Beethoven's *Symphony No. 6 in F (Pastoral).*
(Y/B) (M) (*) Sony SMK 52637 [id.].

Richard STRAUSS: *Piano sonata in B min., Op. 5; Enoch Arden, Op. 38; 5 Pieces, Op. 3;* (i) *Ophelia Lieder, Op. 67* (with Elisabeth Schwarzkopf).
(Y/B) (M) (**(*)) Sony Dig./Analogue SM2K 52657 (2) [id.].

Contemporary music: MORAWETZ: *Fantasy in D min.* ANHALT: *Fantasia.* HETU: *Variations, Op. 8.*
PENTLAND: *Ombres.* VALEN: *Piano sonata No. 2.*
(Y/B) (M) (**) Sony SMK 52677 [id.].

Consort music: BYRD: *1st Pavane & Galliard.* GIBBONS: *Fantasy in C min.; Allemande; Lord Salisbury's pavane & galliard.* BYRD: *Hugh Ashton's ground; 6th Pavane & galliard; A Voluntary; Selliger's round.*
SWEELINCK: *Fantasia in D (Fantasia cromatica).*
(Y/B) (M) (**) Sony stereo/mono SMK 52589 [id.].

GOULD: *Lieberson madrigal; So you want to write a fugue* (McFadden, Keller, Fouchécourt, Van Kamp, Naoumoff, Ens., Rivvenq); *String quartet No. 1* (Monsaingeon, Apap, Caussé, Meunier); *2 Pieces for piano; Piano sonata* (unfinished) (Naoumoff); *Sonata for bassoon and piano* (Marchese, Naoumoff).
(Y/B) (M) (**) Sony Dig. SMK 47814 [id.].

Glenn Gould is an artist who excites such strong passions that guidance is almost superfluous. For his host of admirers these discs are self-recommending; those who do not respond to his pianism will not be greatly interested in this edition. For long he enjoyed cult status, enhanced rather than diminished by his absence from the concert hall. There is too much that is wilful and eccentric in these performances for any of them to rank as a sole first recommendation. Yet if for his devotees virtually all his recordings are indispensable, for the unconverted a judicious approach is called for.

Generally speaking, his earlier recordings are to be recommended to those who are sceptical as to his gifts. There is nothing eccentric about the early recordings. His 1957 performances of the Beethoven *Second Piano concerto* with Ladislav Slovák in Leningrad and Bernstein in New York are first rate in every respect. He leaves everything to his fingers rather than his head, and his performance is eminently sensitive. We have commented on these individually and on the set of Beethoven concertos, made with Golschmann, Bernstein and Stokowski. (The *C major Concerto,* with Vladimir Golschmann, is particularly exhilarating, and both this and the *C minor* with Bernstein command admiration.) There is no questioning Gould's keyboard wizardry or his miraculous control of part-writing in Bach, for which he had much intuitive feeling. The majority of his Bach discs evince strong personality and commitment throughout, even though the tiresome vocalise (which became an increasing source of frustration, particularly later in his recording career) is a strain. The famous 1955 38-minute repeatless mono recording of the *Goldberg* sounds more of a curiosity nowadays, but it is nothing if not a remarkable feat of digital prestidigitation.

Gould possessed a fine and inquiring mind and both a sharp and an original intellect, as readers of the strongly recommended collection of his writings on music, *The Glenn Gould Reader,* will know. (Judging from the sampler Sony CD, widely available also on videocassette and laserdisc and containing *So you want to write a fugue* and some of his CBC television appearances, his sense of humour was less sophisticated, in fact pretty cringe-making.) His enterprise and intellectual curiosity, however, inspire respect. Everything he does is the result of artistic conviction, whether it is championing Bizet's *Nocturne* and *Variations chromatiques* ('a giddy mix of Chopin and Chabrier') or Schoenberg. He had great feeling for Hindemith and championed this composer at a time when he had become comparatively unfashionable, and likewise *Kyllikki* and the three *Sonatinas* of Sibelius. In fact his tastes are always unpredictable: Strauss's *Enoch Arden,* Grieg's early *Sonata,* and the *Second Piano sonata* of the Norwegian 12-note master, Fartein Valen. And who, nowadays, would dare to play Byrd and Gibbons on the piano?

Sony deserve congratulations on this formidable enterprise, and collectors will note that the sound-quality of the originals has in the main been much improved – as indeed it needed to be. However, the sound generally has insufficient freshness and bloom, and the eccentricity (some might say ego-centricity) of some of Gould's readings and the accompanying vocalise are often quite insupportable.

Grumiaux, Arthur (violin)

'*Favourite violin concertos*' (with (i) Concg. O; (ii) New Philh. O; (iii) Sir Colin Davis; (iv) Bernard Haitink; (v) Jan Krenz): BEETHOVEN: (i; iii) *Concerto in D;* (i; iv) *Romance No. 2 in F.* BRAHMS: (ii; iii) *Concerto in D.* (ii; v) MENDELSSOHN: *Concerto in E min.* TCHAIKOVSKY: *Concerto in D.*
🏵 (B) *** Ph. Duo 442 287-2 (2) [id.].

Another extraordinary Duo bargain set from Philips, containing some of the great Belgian violinist's very finest performances. He recorded the Beethoven twice for Philips, and this is the later account from the mid-1970s with Sir Colin Davis. Grumiaux imbues this glorious concerto with a spirit of classical serenity and receives outstanding support from Davis. If we remember correctly, the earlier account with Galliera had slightly more of a sense of repose and spontaneous magic in the slow movement, but the balance of advantage between the two versions is very difficult to resolve as the Concertgebouw recording is fuller and richer and (even if there is not absolute orchestral clarity) there is less background noise. The performance of the Brahms, it goes without saying, is full of insight and lyrical eloquence, and again Sir Colin Davis lends his soloist the most sympathetic support. The (1973) account of the Mendelssohn is characteristically polished and refined, and Grumiaux, even if he does not wear his heart on his sleeve, plays very beautifully throughout: the pure poetry of the playing not only lights up the *Andante* but is heard at its most magical in the key moment of the downward arpeggio which introduces the second subject of the first movement. In the Tchaikovsky his playing similarly – if less overtly emotional than some – has the usual aristocratic refinement and purity of tone to recommend it. His reading is beautifully paced and has a particularly fine slow movement; both here and in the brilliant finale he shows superb aplomb and taste. With excellent accompaniments in both works from Krenz, this adds to the attractions of the set, for the 1970s recording has a wide range and is firmly focused in its CD format.

Hallé Orchestra, Sir John Barbirolli

French music: DEBUSSY: *Prélude à l'après-midi d'un faune.* FAURE: *Pelléas et Mélisande – suite.* IBERT: *Divertissement.* SAINT-SAENS: *Carnival of the animals* (with Rawicz & Landauer). BIZET: *L'Arlésienne*: excerpts: *Prélude; Adagietto; Farandole.*
(Y/B) (M) (***) Dutton Lab. mono CDSJB 1002 [id.].

Dating from between 1950 and 1954, these heart-warming recordings not only show off Barbirolli's Hallé at a vintage period, but consistently demonstrate what natural sympathy he had for this French repertory. Regularly he brings out the red-blooded qualities of French music, alongside the subtle evocation of atmosphere. Equally his sense of humour and fun bubbles over in the riotous 'Italian Straw Hat' music of Ibert's *Divertissement*. Thanks to the Barbirolli Society, these recordings come in transfers by Dutton Sound, using CEDAR-based techniques on more recent material than that company had tackled previously. The absence of surface hiss is particularly welcome in such a piece as the Debussy, an easily flowing reading presented with a vivid sense of presence and weight of sound. For the Saint-Saëns *Carnival of the animals* EMI brought in the most popular piano duo of the day, Rawicz and Landauer, offering energy and brilliance to match Barbirolli's own. Again the fun of the piece is brought out, though it is a pity that *The Swan* is given to the full cellos, hardly a match for a cello section today.

Heifetz, Jascha (violin)

'*The Acoustic Recordings 1917–1924*' (with André Benoist; Samuel Chotzinoff; O, Pasternak): SCHUBERT: *Ave Maria.* DRIGO: *Valse bluette.* ELGAR: *La Capricieuse, Op. 17.* SARASATE: *Malagueña, Habanera, Op. 21/1 & 2; Introduction and tarantelle, Op. 43; Zapateado, Op. 23/2; Zigeunerweisen, Op. 20/1; Carmen fantasy, Op. 25.* BAZZINI: *La ronde des lutins.* BEETHOVEN: *Ruins of Athens: Chorus of Dervishes; Turkish march.* WIENIAWSKI: *Scherzo-Tarantelle, Op. 16; Concerto No. 2, Op. 22: Romance.* ACHRON: *Hebrew melody, Op. 33; Hebrew lullaby, Hebrew dance, Op. 35; Stimmung, Op. 32.* PAGANINI: *Moto perpetuo; Caprices, Nos. 13 & 20.* KREISLER: *Minuet; Sicilienne et Rigaudon.* GLAZUNOV: *Meditation; Valse.* MOSZKOWSKI: *Guitarre, Op. 45/2.* CHOPIN: *Nocturnes, Op. 9/2; Op. 27/2.* TCHAIKOVSKY: *Souvenir d'un lieu cher: Scherzo, Op. 42/2. Serenade: Valse, Op. 48/2. Concerto, Op. 35: Canzonetta. Sérénade mélancolique, Op. 26.* MENDELSSOHN: *On wings of song, Op. 34/2; Concerto in E min.: finale.* DVORAK: *Slavonic dances, Op. 46/2; Op. 72/2 & 8.* SCHUMANN: *Myrthen: Widmung, Op. 25/1.* LALO: *Symphonie espagnole, Op. 21: Andante.* MOZART: *Divertimento No. 17, K.334: Minuet. Haffner Serenade, K.250: Rondo.* D'AMBROSIO: *Serenade, Op. 4.* JUON: *Berceuse, Op. 28/3.* GOLDMARK: *Concerto*

in A min., Op. 28: Andante. GODOWSKY: *Waltz in D.* BRAHMS: *Hungarian dance No. 1 in G min.* HAYDN: *Quartet (Lark), Op. 64/5: Vivace.* GRANADOS: *Danzas españolas, Op. 37/5; Andaluza.* BOULANGER: *Nocturne in F; Cortège.* SCOTT: *The gentle maiden.* SAINT-SAENS: *Havanaise, Op. 83.*
(M) (***) RCA mono 09026 61732-2 [61732-2-RG] (3).

These recordings serve as a salutary reminder of Heifetz's extraordinary powers. The earliest records come from the year of the Russian Revolution, when Heifetz was still sixteen and only five years after he had made his début in St Petersburg. As always with Heifetz, even the highest expectations are surpassed: his effortless technical mastery is dazzling, the golden tone strong and pure, the accuracy of his intonation almost beyond belief and his taste impeccable. The collector will also be agreeably surprised by the quality of sound; the earliest was made only two weeks after his Carnegie Hall début, when the art of recording was still relatively primitive, and the original 78–r.p.m. disc was single-sided. Seventy or more years later, his brilliance remains undimmed. The recordings are arranged in chronological order, though the differences during the period are relatively small. This set is a mandatory purchase for all who care about the art of violin playing.

Hofmann, Josef (piano)

'*The Complete Josef Hofmann*', Vol. 2 (with Curtis Institute Student O, cond. Reiner or Hilsberg): BRAHMS: *Academic festival overture.* RUBINSTEIN: *Piano concerto No. 4 in D min.* CHOPIN: *Ballade No. 1 in G min., Op. 23; Nocturne in E flat, Op. 9/2; Waltz in A flat, Op. 42; Andante spianato e Grande Polonaise brillante in E flat, Op. 22* (2 versions); *Nocturne in F sharp, Op. 15/2; Waltz in D flat, Op. 64/1; Etude in G flat, Op. 25/9; Berceuse in B flat, Op. 57; Nocturne in C min., Op. 48/1; Mazurka in C, Op. 33/ 3; Waltz in A flat, Op. 34/1.* HOFMANN: *Chromaticon for piano & orchestra* (2 versions). MENDELSSOHN: *Spinning song in C, Op. 67/4.* RACHMANINOV: *Prelude in G min., Op. 23/5.* BEETHOVEN–RUBINSTEIN: *Turkish march.* MOSZKOWSKI: *Caprice espagnole, Op. 37.*
(Y/B) ✸ (***) Vai Audio mono VAIA/IPA 1020 (2) [id.].

Josef Hofmann's amazing 1937 performance of Rubinstein's *Fourth Piano concerto* has long been a much-sought-after item in its LP format, and those who possess it have treasured it. The performance was attended by practically every pianist around, including Rachmaninov and Godowsky. (It was the latter who once said to a youngster who had mentioned a fingerslip in one of Hofmann's recitals, 'Why look for the spots on the sun!') In no other pianist's hands has this music made such sense: Hofmann plays his master's best-known concerto with a delicacy and poetic imagination that are altogether peerless. Olin Downes spoke of his 'power and delicacy, lightning virtuosity and the capacity to make the keyboard sing, the richness of tone colouring and incorruptible taste'. The 1937 concert included the Brahms overture, a speech by Walter Damrosch, the incomparable performance of the Rubinstein concerto and, after the interval, a Chopin group. One is tempted to say that the *G minor Ballade* has never been surpassed. The second CD includes four later items, recorded in 1945. Once again – and it can't be said too often – the Rubinstein is phenomenal.

Horowitz, Vladimir (piano)

The '*Horowitz Editions*'
Obviously these expensive compilations are designed for libraries and ambitious private collectors. The RCA set includes concertos, so is listed here under Orchestral Collections. The smaller Sony (CBS) set consists entirely of solo piano music and is listed below in our Recitals section. In one sense, both sets are highly desirable and to choose between them is almost impossible.

'*The Vladimir Horowitz Edition*': (complete RCA recordings with var. orchestras & conductors): BEETHOVEN: *Sonatas Nos. 14 (Moonlight); 21 (Waldstein); 23 (Appassionata)* (GD 60375). CHOPIN: *Sonata No. 2; Nocturnes, Op. 9/2; 55/1; Impromptu No. 1, Op. 29; Etudes, Op. 10/3–4; Ballade No. 1, Op. 23; Mazurka, Op. 30/4; Scherzo No. 1, Op. 20* (GD 60376). PROKOFIEV: *Sonata No. 7, Op. 83; Toccata, Op. 11.* BARBER: *Sonata, Op. 26.* KABALEVSKY: *Sonata No. 3, Op. 46.* FAURE: *Nocturne No. 13.* POULENC: *Presto in B flat* (GD 60377). MUSSORGSKY: *Pictures at an exhibition; By the water.* TCHAIKOVSKY: *Concerto No. 1* (with NBC SO, Toscanini) (GD 60449). CZERNY: *La Ricordanza (Variations on a theme by Rode), Op. 33.* MOZART: *Sonata, K.332.* MENDELSSOHN: *Variations sérieuses, Op. 54.* SCHUBERT: *Sonata, D.960* (GD 60451). SCARLATTI: *Sonata, Kk.380.* BACH (arr. Busoni): *Nun komm' der Heiden Heiland (Come Redeemer).* HAYDN: *Sonata, Hob XVI/52.* BEETHOVEN: *Sonata No. 14 (Moonlight).* BRAHMS: *Violin sonata No. 3* (with Nathan Milstein). SCHUMANN: *Träumerei* (GD

60461). SCHUMANN: *Kinderszenen; Clara Wieck variations.* LISZT: *Valse oublié No. 1; Hungarian rhap-sody No. 6.* DEBUSSY: *Sérénade à la poupée.* FAURE: *Impromptu No. 5.* MENDELSSOHN: *Songs without words: May breezes.* BRAHMS: *Waltz in A flat.* CHOPIN: *Barcarolle; Nocturne, Op. 15/2; Mazurkas Opp. 24/4; 30/4; Scherzo No. 3.* LISZT/BUSONI: *Etude No. 2* (GD 60463). BRAHMS: *Concerto No. 2, Op. 83* (with NBC SO, Toscanini); *Intermezzo, Op. 117/2.* SCHUBERT: *Impromptu, D.899.* LISZT: *Au bord d'une source; Sonetto No. 4 del Petrarca; Hungarian rhapsody No. 2* (GD 60523). MUSSORGSKY: *Pictures at an exhibition.* SCRIABIN: *Etude, Op. 2/1; Preludes Nos. 11/5; 22/1; Sonata No. 9.* HOROWITZ: *Danse excen-trique.* TCHAIKOVSKY: *Dumka.* BIZET/HOROWITZ: *Carmen variations.* PROKOFIEV: *Sonata No. 7: III.* RACHMANINOV: *Humoresque; Barcarolle.* DEBUSSY: *Sérénade à la poupée.* SOUSA/HOROWITZ: *The Stars and stripes forever* (GD 60526). SCRIABIN: *Sonatas Nos. 3, Op. 23; 5, Op. 53; Preludes, Op. 11/1, 3, 9–10, 13–14, 16; 13/6; 15/2; 16/1, 4; 27/1; 48/3; 51/2; 59/2; 67/1; Etudes, Op. 8/7, 12; 42/5* (GD 86215). SCHUMANN: *Sonata No. 3 (Concerto without orchestra); Humoresque, Op. 20; Fantasiestücke, Op. 111; Nachtstücke, Op. 23* (GD 86680). CHOPIN: *Polonaise-Fantaisie, Op. 61; Ballades Nos. 1, Op. 23; 4, Op. 52; Barcarolle, Op. 60; Etudes, Opp. 10/5; 25/7; Waltz, Op. 69/1; Andante spinato & grande polonaise, Op. 22* (GD 87752). CLEMENTI: *Sonatas, Opp. 14/3; 26/2; 33/3 (Sonata quasi concerto); 34/2; 47/2 (rondo)* (GD 87753). RACHMANINOV: *Sonata No. 2, Op. 36; Moment musical, Op. 16/2; Prelude, Op. 32/5; Polka V. R.; Concerto No. 3* (with RCA Victor SO, Fritz Reiner) (GD 87754). BIZET/HOROWITZ: *Carmen variations.* SAINT-SAENS/LISZT/HOROWITZ: *Danse macabre.* MOZART: *Rondo alla turka.* MENDELSSOHN/LISZT/HOROWITZ: *Wedding march & variations.* MENDELSSOHN: *Songs without words: Elégie; Spring song; The Shepherd's complaint.* DEBUSSY: *Sérénade à la poupée.* MOSZKOWSKI: *Etudes in A flat; in F; Etincelles.* CHOPIN: *Polonaise, Op. 53.* SCHUMANN: *Träumerei.* MENDELSSOHN: *Scherzo a capriccio.* LISZT/HOROWITZ: *Rakóczy march.* RACHMANINOV: *Prelude in G min.* SOUSA/HOROWITZ: *The Stars and stripes forever* (GD 87755). TCHAIKOVSKY: *Concerto No. 1* (with NBC SO, Toscanini). BEETHOVEN: *Concerto No. 5 (Emperor)* (with RCA Victor SO, Fritz Reiner) (GD 87992). SCARLATTI: *Sonatas, Kk.46; 87; 322; 380; 455; 531.* SCARLATTI/TAUSIG: *Capriccio (Sonata, K.20/L.375).* BEETHOVEN: *Sonata No. 7.* CHOPIN: *Mazurka, Op. 30/3; Nocturnes, Opp. 27/1; 72/1; Waltzes, Opp. 34/ 2; 64/2; Ballade No. 3, Op. 47.* VON DOHNANYI: *Concert étude, Op. 28/6 (Capriccio)* (09026 60986-2). CHOPIN: *Scherzos Nos. 1–2; Mazurkas, Opp. 7/3; 41/1; 50/3; 59/3; 63/2–3* (09026 60987-2). *God save the queen.* CHOPIN: *Polonaise-fantaisie, Op. 61; Ballade No. 1.* SCHUMANN: *Kinderszenen, Op. 15.* SCRI-ABIN: *Etude, Op. 8/12* (09026 61414-2). LISZT: *Sonata in B min.; Ballade No. 2; Consolation No. 3; Funerailles; Mephisto waltz No. 1* (09026 61415-2). SCARLATTI: *Sonatas, L.33; 118; 186; 189; 224; 494.* CHOPIN: *Ballade No. 4; Waltz (L'adieu), Op. 69/1.* LISZT: *Ballade No. 2.* RACHMANINOV: *Prelude, Op. 23/5* (09026 61416-2). RACHMANINOV: *Concerto No. 3* (with NYPO, Ormandy) (09026 61564-2).

(M) (***) RCA Dig./analogue mono/stereo 09026 61655-2 (22) [id.].

The RCA set comprises 22 CDs, ranging from the 1940s through to the 1980s before he was lured to DG – and omitting the period when he was out of the public eye or with the CBS label. Included in the survey are the two accounts of the Rachmaninov *Third Piano concerto*, the 1951 account with Reiner (which is to be preferred) and the 1978 account with Ormandy. There are two versions of the *Pictures at an exhibition*, one from 1947 and the other from a Carnegie Hall recital in 1951. Not to be missed in the RCA set are the epoch-making Barber *Sonata* and Prokofiev *Seventh*, his Clementi sonata disc and his Scriabin *Third* and *Fifth sonatas*, as well as the electrifying Tchaikovsky *B flat minor Concerto* with Toscanini. His 1951 *Emperor concerto* with Reiner has been consistently underrated and has a splendid authority; his Brahms *Second* with Toscanini is less compelling and lacks spontaneity and, in the slow movement, warmth. His Liszt *Sonata* is magnificent but not as breathtaking as the 1933 version, included in the EMI set. The recordings vary greatly: many are an improvement on the originals – though in many cases they needed to be. As suggested below, advice for those considering the boxes in juxtaposition would be to buy the Sony set complete and choose liberally from among the CDs singled out for special mention in the RCA set, most of which are discussed individually in our composer section.

Koussevitzky, Serge (double-bass and conductor)

Collections (with (i) Pierre Luboshutz; (ii) Boston SO; (iii) Bernhard Zighera, Pierre Luboshutz): BEETHOVEN: (i) *Minuet in G* (arr. Koussevitzky): (ii) *Symphony No. 6 in F (Pastoral).* (iii) ECCLES: *Largo.* (i) LASKA: *Wiegenlied.* KOUSSEVITZKY: *Concerto, Op. 3: Andante; Valse miniature.* (ii) Johann STRAUSS Sr: *Wiener Blut; Frühlingstimmen.*

(M) (***) Biddulph mono WHL 019 [id.].

In his youth and before he was established as a conductor of international celebrity, Koussevitzky was regarded as the greatest double-bass virtuoso of the age. In 1928–9, in his mid-fifties, he was enticed into the New York Studios to record the above with the pianist, Bernard Zighera, but he then re-recorded everything with Pierre Luboshutz the following year. These performances confirm that he brought to the double-bass the same lyrical intensity and feeling for line and sonority that distinguished his conducting. Judging from the two concerto movements included here, he was no great composer, but the 1928 recording of the *Pastoral Symphony* with the Boston Symphony Orchestra is little short of a revelation. As an interpretation it feels just right; generally speaking, it is brisk but totally unhurried, each phrase wonderfully shaped. Given the fact that he never lingers, the paradox is that this performance seems strangely spacious. One young and knowledgeable collector to whom we played this thought it quite simply 'among the best *Pastorals* ever'; moreover the recorded sound is remarkable for its age and comes up very freshly.

Liverpool Philharmonic Orchestra, Sir Malcolm Sargent

English and Irish music (with (i) Webster Booth; (ii) Huddersfield Choral Soc.; (iii) David Wise): IRE-LAND: *A London overture.* HARTY: *A John Field suite.* COLERIDGE TAYLOR: (i) *Hiawatha's Wedding feast: On away awake beloved.* BALFOUR GARDINER: *Shepherd Fennell's dance.* VAUGHAN WILLIAMS: (iii) *The Lark ascending.* HOLST: (ii) *The Hymn of Jesus.*
(Y/B) (M) (***) Dutton mono CDAX 8012 [id.].

This centenary tribute to Sir Malcolm Sargent concentrates on his remarkable wartime work with the Liverpool Philharmonic, an orchestra which had him as chief conductor from the time in 1942 when it became a permanent body. Sargent quickly put the orchestra on the map, not least as a recording band. As the recordings here confirm (all but *The Lark ascending* dating from wartime, 1943–4), the woodwind team was outstanding, with the *Nocturne* in Harty's *John Field suite* offering a magical clarinet solo from Reginald Kell. Far rougher was the string ensemble, and the Harty in particular, involving only a small body of players, sounds seedy, for all the rhythmic verve. Consistently Sargent's rhythmic control, from the vivid account of the Ireland overture onwards, amply compensates for string shortcomings. CD transfers are first rate, with the satisfyingly full-bodied sound one expects from the Dutton use of the CEDAR process. The Coleridge Taylor – with Webster Booth producing shiningly clear tenor tone – has a higher surface hiss, and the Holst is a degree mistier than the rest – apt enough for such evocative choral writing. The performance has a thrust and dramatic intensity unsurpassed since. *The Lark ascending* dates from 1977, offering marginally clearer sound, with David Wise a tenderly responsive, totally unmannered soloist. A heartwarming centenary tribute, representing Sargent at his finest.

London Philharmonic Orchestra, Sir Thomas Beecham

'Vintage Beecham': HANDEL: *Solomon: Arrival of the Queen of Sheba.* DVORAK: *Legend, Op. 59/3.* BIZET: *Carmen suite.* DELIUS (arr. Fenby): *Koanga: La Calinda.* MENDELSSOHN: *A Midsummer Night's Dream: Incidental music, Op. 61.* J. STRAUSS Jnr: *Waltz: Voices of spring.* BORODIN: *Prince Igor* (excerpts).
❀ (M) (***) Dutton Laboratories mono CDLX 7003 [id.].

The quality of Michael Dutton's transfers here is even more remarkable than on the companion disc, above. All the repertoire comes from the 1930s, yet for most of the time the ear has to make few concessions to enjoy this music-making, almost as if it had been put on disc yesterday. The opening *Arrival of the Queen of Sheba* has remarkable tangibility and profile, and no one ever 'magicked' the *Barcarolle* from the *Tales of Hoffmann* as did Beecham. But it is the *Carmen* excerpts which help to make this collection indispensable, played with such glowing, lyrical feeling and colour – the cultivated way Beecham builds up the climax of the *Danse bohème* is an object lesson in combining orchestral finish with a steadily increasing spontaneous surge of energy. The Borodin *Polovtsian dances* (a famous recording from the 1934 Leeds Festival) is a tribute to Walter Legge's skill with location recording – something much less easy to manage then than now – and the result is breathtaking. Even Beecham's later stereo version does not quite achieve the sheer abandon at the end, yet the Leeds performance was not recorded 'live'. Detail is less than perfect, but the full-bodied choral sound, topped by the percussion, yet with plenty of weight in the bass, makes a glorious impact, and the final accelerando is breathtaking. The the 73-minute concert concludes with a bitingly Russian *Polovtsian march.*

London Symphony Orchestra, Bruno Walter

'The Classic 1938 HMV recordings': BEETHOVEN: *Overture Coriolan, Op. 62.* HAYDN: *Symphony No. 86 in D.* SCHUMANN: *Symphony No. 4 in D min., Op. 120.* SMETANA: *The Bartered Bride overture.* CORELLI: *Concerto grosso in G min. (Christmas), Op. 6/8.*

✿ (M) (***) Dutton Laboratories mono CDLX 7008 [id.].

How remarkably Beethoven encapsulated the spirit of *Coriolan* in his seven-minute overture, and how well Bruno Walter balances its lyrical and dramatic elements. The Haydn *D major Paris Symphony* bursts with energy, although there is an unashamed rallentando for the second subject. The Minuet and trio is most fetching. The Schumann *Fourth* has great lyrical warmth, the transition to the finale not as remarkable as with Furtwängler, but the close of the finale is very spirited indeed. The *Bartered Bride overture* isn't rushed but still has energy and the Corelli *Concerto grosso* shows that, even with a relatively large body of strings and a close balance Walter knew just how to preserve the element of contrast between solo group and ripieno. The performances all have total spontaneity, and it is impossible to believe that they were put on wax four minutes at a time! Dutton Labs have worked their usual magic with the transfers, and the sound itself is so full and believable that one forgets the 78–r.p.m. source within a minute or so of the music commencing.

New Philharmonia Orchestra, Leopold Stokowski

BRAHMS: *Symphony No. 4 in E min., Op. 98.* KLEMPERER: *Merry waltz.* RAVEL: *Rapsodie espagnole.* VAUGHAN WILLIAMS: *Fantasia on theme of Thomas Tallis.*

(Y/B) (B) **(*) BBC Radio Classics BBCRD 9107 [id.].

This BBC recording of May 1974 makes a fascinating document, allowing us to witness one of the very last live concerts that Leopold Stokowski conducted. The pity is that in the reverberant acoustic of the Royal Albert Hall the sound takes away from the bite which marked Stokowski's last appearances, and the close microphones are unflattering to the violins. The expansive account of the Vaughan Williams works best, warm and atmospheric rather than intense, although the dynamic range is reduced; and the Ravel too gains from atmospheric sound, even if the excitement of the final *Feria* is dampened a little – the performance itself short of electrifying. Klemperer's *Merry waltz* is a charming tribute from one veteran conductor to another who had died the previous July. The Brahms suffers most from the recording and cannot compare with some of the superb studio recordings Stokowski made in the months and years after this concert. Speeds are on the brisk side, especially in the outer movements, and Stokowski's control of tension is masterly; though ensemble is slacker than would have been accepted in the studio, this remains highly compelling music-making, and the CD is well worth its modest cost.

New York Philharmonic Orchestra, Sir John Barbirolli

Barbirolli in America (1938–9): DEBUSSY: *Images: Ibéria.* TCHAIKOVSKY: *Francesca da Rimini.* SCHUBERT: *Symphony No. 4 in C min. (Tragic).*

(N) (B) (***) Dutton Laboratories mono CDEA 5000 [id.].

Along with Beecham in Mozart, Walter in Haydn and Schubert, and Casals and Szell in Dvořák, this is one of four vividly transferred historic issues from Dutton Laboratories being offered at bargain price. Barbirolli's brilliant recordings of 1938–9, made with the New York Philharmonic Symphony, here totally refute the myth that Barbirolli as successor to Toscanini was a failure. All three of these works were rarities on disc at the time – even the Schubert, which comes in a forceful, high-powered reading which yet has a Schubertian smile. The crisp attack in the Tchaikovsky is thrillingly caught too, though sadly some cuts are made – common practice at the time. The Debussy brings a white-hot performance and the most vivid sound of all, weighty and full, with castanets and brass leaping out from the speakers. Not to be missed by fans of this remarkably volatile and inspirational conductor.

Philadelphia Orchestra, Leopold Stokowski

'Fantasia': BACH, orch. Stokowski: *Toccata and Fugue in D min.* DUKAS: *L'apprenti sorcier.* MUSSORGSKY, arr. Stokowski: *A Night on the Bare Mountain.* STRAVINSKY: *The Rite of spring.* TCHAIKOVSKY: *Nutcracker Suite.*

(M) (***) Pearl mono GEMMCD 4988.

A self-recommending disc. *The Rite of spring* comes from 1929–30 and the *Nutcracker* from as early as 1926, though one would never believe it. Everything Stokowski did at this period was full of character, and the engineers obviously performed miracles. The latest recording is Stokowski's amazing arrangement of *A Night on the Bare Mountain*, which dates from 1940. Such is the colour and richness of sonority Stokowski evokes from the fabulous Philadelphians that surface noise and other limitations are completely forgotten. The transfers are very good.

Philadelphia Orchestra, Wolfgang Sawallisch

Stokowski orchestral transcriptions: BACH: Chorales from cantatas: *Sheep may safely graze; Wachet auf; Ein feste Burg is unser Gott. Toccata and fugue in D min., BWV 565.* BOCCHERINI: *Minuet, Op. 13/ 5.* BEETHOVEN: *Piano sonata No. 14 (Moonlight): 1st movt.* CHOPIN: *Prelude in E min., Op. 28/4.* FRANCK: *Panis angelicus.* TCHAIKOVSKY: *Andante cantabile, Op. 11; At the ball* (with Marjana Lipovšek). DEBUSSY: *Suite bergamasque: Clair de lune. Prélude: La cathédrale engloutie.* RACHMANI-NOV: *Prelude in C sharp min., Op. 3/2.*
(N) **(*) EMI Dig. CDC5 55592-2 [id.].

Though Stokowski's own recordings, even those he made in extreme old age, generally have a degree more flair and dramatic bite than any of these from the latterday Philadelphia Orchestra, this makes a fine tribute from the great orchestra he created. The selection of items is an attractive one, not least the Tchaikovsky song orchestration, with Marjana Lipovšek an aptly Slavonic-sounding soloist, though balanced too close. Sawallisch brings out the evocative magic of Stokowski's impressionistic view of the *Moonlight sonata* movement, and *Clair de lune* is similarly free in its expressiveness. With warm, resonant sound, firmer in bass than usual from this source, this makes a sumptuous collection, even if some will prefer the brighter, sharper focus of rival Stokowski collections such as Kunzel's on Telarc or Bamert's on Chandos. It is worth noting that Bamert's even more generous selection of 15 encore pieces overlaps in only three items, and it includes more fun pieces.

Philharmonia Orchestra or NBC Symphony Orchestra, Guido Cantelli

'Artist profile': MOZART: *A musical joke, K.522; Symphony No. 29 in A, K.201.* BEETHOVEN: *Symphony No. 7 in A, Op. 92.* SCHUBERT: *Symphony No. 8 in B min. (Unfinished).* FRANCK: *Symphony in D min.*
(Y/B) (B) *** EMI CZS5 68217-2 (2) [id.].

Not only do Cantelli's classic accounts have the authority of a master-conductor, they also have a perfect sense of proportion, phrasing that is alive and supple, and a natural elegance. The Mozart *A major Symphony*, K.201, blends style and an expressive freedom which seems totally spontaneous yet which is beautifully shaped and controlled. This is music-making of an order of which period-instrument groups should be envious. The Beethoven *Seventh Symphony* is well held together without being in the least overdriven, and the Schubert *Unfinished* is also a selfless reading, free of idiosyncrasy and all the more full of character for being so. The Franck *Symphony*, recorded with the NBC Symphony for which he was being groomed after Toscanini, is also a performance of some stature. The recordings wear their years lightly: they are now 40 years old and are still going strong.

(i) Philharmonia Orchestra, (ii) Royal Philharmonic Orchestra, Paul Kletzki

'Paul Kletzki profile': (i) GLINKA: *Jota aragonesa.* RIMSKY-KORSAKOV: *Tsar Saltan* (suite). TCHAIKO-VSKY: *Andante cantabile.* SIBELIUS: *Symphony No. 2.* SCHUBERT: (ii) *Rosamunde overture.* MAHLER: (i) *Symphonies Nos. 4 in G; 5: Adagietto* (only).
(B) *** EMI CZS7 67726-2 (2) [id.].

Kletzki was the most sympathetic of Mahler conductors, evoking the underlying emotions with great sensitivity and showing them, not as neurotic self-searchings, but as full-blooded and warm. In the first movement of the *Fourth Symphony* his affectionately relaxed approach, full of warmly individual touches, means that the structure is loosely held. But there is little else to criticize in the reading; Kletzki's simplicity of style in the finale, with Emmy Loose singing very beautifully, makes for a perfect conclusion. The Kingsway Hall recording was considered outstanding in its day for its lovely bloom, and so it is on CD. The *Adagietto* from the *Fifth Symphony* is slow and languorous but has a sudden surge of adrenalin at the climax. The Sibelius *Second Symphony* is finely conceived as a whole and generates considerable tension in the opening movement, even if the closing pages are not as overwhelming as they might be. However, the spacious stereo adds to the impact of a performance which was certainly among the finest of the early stereo era. The Glinka and Rimsky-Korsakov pieces are also vividly played and brilliantly recorded and make the strongest impression.

Philharmonia Orchestra or Royal Philharmonic Orchestra, Efrem Kurtz

'Artist profile': RIMSKY-KORSAKOV: *The snow maiden: suite. Le Coq d'or: suite; Dubinushka, Op. 62.* LIADOV: *Kikimora, Op. 63; Baba-Yaga, Op. 56; The enchanted lake, Op. 62; A musical snuffbox, Op. 32.* SHOSTAKOVICH: *Symphony No. 1 in F, Op. 10.* KHACHATURIAN: *Masquerade: Waltz; Galop.* GLINKA: *A life for the Tsar* (ballet music). KABALEVSKY: *The Comedians: suite, Op. 26.* PROKOFIEV: *Symphony No. 1 in D (Classical), Op. 25.*
(Y/B) (B) *** EMI CZS7 67729-2 (2) [id.].

These Kurtz recordings were made between 1957 and 1963, but the sound has dated hardly at all and on CD sounds both colourful and lustrous. The playing of the Philharmonia in the Prokofiev and Shostakovich symphonies is superbly polished and responsive and the performances combine wit and high spirits with much character; the Rimsky-Korsakov suites and Liadov tone-poems (with the RPO playing in the latter) bring comparable finesse and plenty of atmosphere. The effect in *Le Coq d'or* is vividly refined rather than sultry, but *The snow maiden* sparkles, and the Kabalevsky *Comedians suite* has ebullience without vulgarity. Glinka's attractive dances from *A life for the Tsar* show why he was regarded as the 'father' of Russian orchestral music. It is good to have Kurtz's distinguished contribution to the early EMI stereo catalogue properly represented in what is one of the very best of EMI's 'Artist profile' series: this is well worth its modest cost.

Philharmonia Orchestra, Carlo Maria Giulini

'Carlo Maria Giulini Profile': RAVEL: *Aborado del gracioso; Daphnis et Chloé: suite No. 2.* BRITTEN: *Peter Grimes: 4 Sea interludes; The Young person's guide to the orchestra.* TCHAIKOVSKY: *Symphony No. 2 (Little Russian).* SCHUMANN: *Manfred* (overture). FRANCK: *Psyché et Eros.*
(B) *** EMI CZS7 67723-2 (2) [id.].

Giulini's Ravel offers most refined Philharmonia playing and *Daphnis et Chloé* has genuine ecstasy. The performance of the Britten works again brings outstandingly good playing and the performances are scrupulously attentive to the composer's demands, but there is a curiously detached quality about the readings, even though they remain compelling for their lucidity. Tchaikovsky's *Little Russian Symphony* is full of energy, if rather less strong on charm, although the *Andantino marziale* brings the most refined orchestral response. Giulini sets a brisk pace in the finale, and the crisp articulation adds to the feeling of vitality. The first movement of the Franck *Symphony*, though not unspontaneous, takes a while to get properly underway, and this is one of those readings where the conductor never really establishes a firm tempo in the first movement. The slow movement is most beautifully done and the finale, too, is a success – although Giulini's temptation to linger is again felt when the earlier themes are recalled. Nevertheless, with good sound, this is certainly not dull or predictable, and the Love scene from *Psyché* is also beautifully played, if rather lacking in eroticism.

Rostropovich, Mstislav (cello)

'The Rostropovich Edition': Cello concertos: DVORAK: *Concerto in B min., Op. 104* (with LPO, Giulini). BRAHMS: *Double concerto for violin and cello in A min., Op. 102* (with David Oistrakh, Cleveland O, Szell). HAYDN: *Cello concertos in C & D, Hob VIIb/1–2* (with ASMF, Marriner). BLOCH: *Schelomo* (with O Nat. de France, Bernstein). Richard STRAUSS: *Don Quixote, Op. 35* (with BPO, Karajan). MIASKOVSKY: *Cello concerto in C min., Op. 66* (with Philh. O, Sargent).
(N) (M) **(*) EMI CMS5 65701-2 (3) [CDMC 65701].

Rostropovich recorded the Dvořák *Concerto* three times before this version (with Talich, Boult and Karajan), and this 1977 EMI performance is his least successful on record. He makes heavy weather of most of the concerto, and his unrelieved emotional intensity is matched by Giulini, who focuses attention on beauty of detail rather than structural cohesion. Even so, there are many incidental beauties that compel admiration, and the engineering is impressive. The Brahms *Double concerto* (recorded eight years earlier in Cleveland with David Oistrakh and Szell) is a different matter altogether and can be counted among the most powerful and eloquent performances on record (in the same league as Heifetz/Feuermann and Thibaud/Casals). In Bloch's *Hebrew rhapsody* the collaboration of Rostropovich and Bernstein is a triumph. The ripe expressiveness of both artists blends superbly, so that the rhapsodic flow conveys total concentration from the deeply meditative opening phrases (*con somma espressione*) onwards. The recording is ripe to match, but spotlights the soloist. The two solo Haydn *Concertos*, which date from 1975, are more controversial. Rostropovich's earlier recording of the *C major Concerto* with Britten was brilliant enough but, at even faster speeds in the outer movements, his virtuosity in the EMI performance is astonishing. However, apart from the extra haste (which brings its moments of breathless phrasing) both here and in the more familiar *D major Concerto*, there is a degree of self-indulgence in the warmth of expressiveness. However, the Karajan/Rostropovich *Don Quixote*, which came a year later, rights the balance. It is predictably fine and its only failing is a tendency for Rostropovich to dominate the aural picture. He dominates artistically too. His Don is superbly characterized and the expressiveness and richness of tone he commands are a joy in themselves. There are moments when one wonders whether the intensity of his response does not lead to over-emphatic tone, but in general both the cello and viola soloists and the Berlin orchestra under Karajan silence criticism. In many ways the Miaskovsky *Concerto*, the earliest recording here (1956), is the most valuable item of all, and Rostropovich's recording with Sir Malcolm Sargent remains unsurpassed. Fortunately it is also available separately – see under its composer listing.

'*Masterpieces for cello*' (with various orchestras and conductors): BERNSTEIN: *3 Meditations for cello and orchestra* (from *Mass*). BOCCHERINI: *Cello concerto No. 2*. GLAZUNOV: *Chant du Ménestrel*. SHOSTAKOVICH: *Cello concerto No. 2*. TARTINI: *Cello concerto*. TCHAIKOVSKY: *Andante cantabile; Variations on a rococo theme*. VIVALDI: *Cello concertos, RV 398 and RV 413*.
(Y/B) (B) *** DG Double 437 952-2 (2) [id.].

A self-recommending set, with two CDs for the price of one. Each of the works included is discussed under its composer entry. The only drawback is the inadequate documentation.

Royal Philharmonic Orchestra, Sir Thomas Beecham

French music: BIZET: *Carmen suite No. 1*. FAURE: *Pavane, Op. 60; Dolly suite, Op. 56*. DEBUSSY: *Prélude à l'après-midi d'un faune*. SAINT-SAENS: *Le rouet d'Omphale*. DELIBES: *Le Roi s'amuse* (ballet suite).
❀ (M) *** EMI CDM7 63379-2 [id.].

No one conducts the *Carmen Prelude* with quite the flair of Sir Thomas, while the last movement of the *Dolly suite*, *Le pas espagnole* (in Rabaud's orchestration) has the kind of dash we associate with Beecham's Chabrier. But for the most part the ear is beguiled by the consistently imaginative and poetic phrasing that distinguished his very best performances. Delibes' pastiche ballet-score, *Le Roi s'amuse*, is given the special elegance that Sir Thomas reserved for music from the past unashamedly rescored to please the ear of later generations. The remastering is marvellously managed.

Royal Philharmonic Orchestra, Sir Charles Groves

'*An English celebration*': ELGAR: *Serenade for strings, Op. 20*. BRITTEN: *Variations on a theme of Frank Bridge, Op. 10*. VAUGHAN WILLIAMS: *Fantasia on a theme by Thomas Tallis*. TIPPETT: *Fantasia concertante on a theme of Corelli*.
❀ (B) *** Carlton IMP Classics Dig. 30367 0068-2 [id.].

With gloriously full and real recording, providing the most beautiful string textures, this is one of Sir Charles Groves's very finest records and it makes a worthy memorial to the achievement of the closing decade of his long career. The RPO players give deeply felt, vibrant accounts of four great masterpieces of English string music.

(i) **Royal Philharmonic Orchestra;** (ii) **Vienna Philharmonic Orchestra, Rafael Kubelik**

'*Artist profile*': (i) BRAHMS: *Hungarian dances Nos. 17–21.* (ii) BORODIN: *Symphony No. 2 in B min.* TCHAIKOVSKY: *Symphony No. 4 in F min., Op. 36.* MARTINU: *Les fresques de Piero della Francesca.* JANACEK: *Taras Bulba.* BARTOK: *Concerto for orchestra.*
(Y/B) (B) *** EMI CZS5 68223-2 (2) [id.].

Kubelik's concert opens well. In the Brahms *Hungarian dances* he sounds as if he is enjoying himself, and the RPO responds with good-humoured virtuosity, while in the 1960 Borodin *Second* there is an agreeable warmth. The finale bursts with colour and makes a satisfying culmination. Kubelik's Tchaikovsky *Fourth* is a fine and often brilliant reading. If not electrifying, it has very real qualities of understanding and sympathy for the composer's intentions, plus a remarkable freedom from idio-syncrasies, notably in the first movement which offers both drama and excitement in a way that makes it a fine performance to live with. The finale is splendid, not rushed but with plenty of adrenalin, the well-prepared coda among the most exciting on record, helped by a 1960 recording of substantial weight as well as brilliance.

The Bartók *Concerto for orchestra* (1958) offers first-rate playing and apt tempi, and the vigour of the intepretation reflects the music's inherent virtuosity, especially in the outer movements, without going over the top. One could say the same for *Taras Bulba*, recorded at the same time. Indeed it is difficult to credit the recording date, so vivid and full-blooded is the quality. No less persuasive is the pioneering stereo account of the *Frescoes of Piero della Francesca*, inspired by the fifteenth-century frescoes by the Umbrian painter of that name in the church of San Francesco at Arezzo in Italy, depicting 'The History of the True Cross'. Kubelik conducted its première only two years before making this recording, which is vivid and full of intensity.

Sargent, Sir Malcolm

'*Sir Malcolm Sargent conducts British music*' (with (i) LPO; (ii) LSO; (iii) Mary Lewis; Tudor Davies & O; (iv) Royal Choral Soc.; (v) New SO): (i) HOLST: *Perfect fool: suite.* (ii) BRITTEN: *Young person's guide to the orchestra.* (iii) VAUGHAN WILLIAMS: *Hugh the Drover: Love duet.* ELGAR: (iv) *I sing the birth;* (ii) *Pomp & Circumstance Marches Nos. 1 & 4.* (v) COLERIDGE-TAYLOR: *Othello: suite.* (ii) BAX: *Coronation march.*
(Y/B) (***) Beulah mono 1PD13 [id.].

Sargent was at his finest in this repertory, and it is very welcome to have his personal electricity so vividly conveyed throughout the disc, and most of all in the recording, taken from the sound-track of the original COI film, of Britten's *Young person's guide*. The optical transfer by Martin Sawyer produces far more vivid and satisfyingly weighty results than one would ever expect. The *Love duet* from *Hugh the Drover* was recorded in 1924 in limited pre-electric sound, but the Elgar part-song, recorded live at the Royal Albert Hall in 1928, also soon after the first performance, is vividly atmospheric. The *Othello suite* of Coleridge-Taylor, another première recording, is a sequence of brief genre pieces, with recording more than lively and colourful enough to make one forget the high surface-hiss. The three marches at the end were recorded for the Queen's coronation in 1953, with Sargent taking an uninhibitedly broad view of the great tunes in both the Elgar favourites, and with Bax doing a fair imitation of Walton.

Solomon (piano), **Philharmonia Orchestra, Herbert Menges**

'*Solomon Profile*': BEETHOVEN: *Concertos Nos. 1 in C, Op. 15; 3 in C min., Op. 37; Sonata No. 27 in E min., Op. 90.* GRIEG: *Concerto in A min., Op. 16.* SCHUMANN: *Concerto in A min., Op. 54.*
(B) *** EMI CZS7 67735-2 (2) [id.].

Solomon is at his most inspired throughout. The Beethoven *Concertos* are particularly fresh and spon-taneous, and his Grieg/Schumann coupling has been highly praised by us since the earliest days of stereo. The Op. 90 *Sonata* is unsurpassed in wisdom. The (1956) Abbey Road recordings have never sounded better, and Solomon's wide range of colour is faithfully caught.

Stern, Isaac (violin)

'*A Life in Music*' (Boxes I–III)
'*A Life in music*': Box I
(N) (M) *** Sony Analogue/Dig. SX11K 67193 (11) [id.].

Volume 1: VIVALDI: *The Four Seasons, Op. 8/1–4* (with Jerusalem Music Centre CO); *Concertos for 2 violins, RV 516, 524* (arr. Rampal) (with Jean-Pierre Rampal (flute), Franz Liszt CO); *Concerto for 3 violins, RV 551* (with Pinchas Zukerman, Itzhak Perlman, NY PO, Mehta); *L'estro armonico: Double concerto in A min., Op. 3/8* (arr. Franko); *Concertos for 2 violins, RV 514, 517, 509, 512* (with David Oistrakh, Phd. O, Ormandy). Carl STAMITZ: *Sinfonia concertante in D* (with Pinchas Zukerman (viola), ECO, Barenboim) (SM2K 66472 (2)) [id.].

Volume 2: BACH: *Violin concertos 1–2, BWV 1041–2* (with ECO, Schneider); *Concerto for 2 violins, BWV 1043* (with Itzhak Perlman, NYPO, Mehta); *Concerto for oboe & violin in C min., BWV 1060* (with Harold Gomberg, NYPO, Bernstein) (SMK 66471) [id.].

Volume 3: MOZART: (i) *Violin concertos No. 1, K.207;* (ii) *No. 2, K.211;* (iii) *No. 3, K.216;* (ii) *No. 4, K.218;* (i) *No. 5, K.219;* (ii) *Adagio in E, K.261; Rondo in C, K.373.* (iv) *Concertone for 2 violins in C, K.190;* (v) *Sinfonia concertante for violin & viola, K.364.* (i) Columbia SO, Szell; (ii) ECO, Schneider; (iii) Cleveland O (members), Szell; (iv; v) Pinchas Zukerman, ECO; (iv) Schneider; (v) Barenboim (SM3K 66475 (3)) [id.].

Volume 4: BEETHOVEN: *Violin concerto in D, Op. 61* (with NYPO, Barenboim); (i) *Triple concerto in C, Op. 56* (with Eugene Istomin (piano)); BRAHMS: *Double concerto in A min., Op. 102* (i) (with Leonard Rose (cello), Phd. O, Ormandy); *Violin concerto in D, Op. 77* (with NYPO, Mehta) (SM2K 66941 (2)) [id.].

Volume 5: MENDELSSOHN: *Violin concerto in E min., Op. 64.* DVORAK: *Violin concerto in A min., Op. 53; Romance in F min., Op. 11* (with Phd. O, Ormandy) (SMK 66827) [id.].

Volume 6: TCHAIKOVSKY: *Violin concerto in D, Op. 35.* SIBELIUS: *Violin concerto in D min., Op. 47* (with Phd. O, Ormandy) (SMK 66829) [id.].

Volume 7: WIENIAWSKI: *Violin concerto No. 2 in D min., Op. 22.* BRUCH: *Violin concerto No. 1 in G min., Op. 26* (with Phd. O, Ormandy). TCHAIKOVSKY: *Méditation, Op. 42/1* (orch. Glazunov) (with Nat. SO, Rostropovich); *Sérénade mélancolique, Op. 26* (with Columbia SO, Brieff) (SMK 66830) [id.].

There is a feast of superb playing here. It is a pity that the choice of the Beethoven and Brahms *Concertos* features Stern's recent versions instead of his more inspired, earlier accounts (with Bernstein and Ormandy respectively) and the Dvořák *Concerto*, too, is something of a disappointment. But the Bruch, Mendelssohn, Sibelius and Tchaikovsky are glorious, and both the Bach *Double concerto* and Mozart *Sinfonia concertante* bring comparably inspirational music-making. The solo Mozart *Concertos* also give much pleasure, while in the Vivaldi collection, where Stern's partner is David Oistrakh, there are some more marvellous performances of baroque double concertos, and the results are very compelling indeed. Although too often recordings are balanced very forwardly, the remastered sound is a very great and consistent improvement on the old LPs.

'*A Life in music*': Box II
(N) (M) **(*) Sony SX9K 67194 (9) [id.].

Volume 8: LALO: *Symphonie espagnole.* SAINT-SAENS: *Introduction & Rondo capriccioso.* RAVEL: *Tzigane* (with Phd. O, Ormandy). SAINT-SAENS: *Violin concerto No. 3* (with O de Paris, Barenboim). SARASATE: *Zigeunerweisen.* WAXMAN: *Carmen-Fantasie* (with O, Waxman). FAURE: *Berceuse, Op. 16.* CHAUSSON: *Poème, Op. 25* (with O de Paris, Barenboim). DEBUSSY: (i) *La fille aux cheveux de lin;* (ii) *Clair de lune* (with Columbia SO, (i) Brieff (ii) Katims) (SM2K 64501 (2)) [id.].

Volume 9: BARTOK: *Violin concertos Nos.* (i) *1;* (ii) *2* ((i) with Phd. O, Ormandy; (ii) with NYPO, Bernstein) (SMK 64502) [id.].

Volume 10: PROKOFIEV: *Violin concertos Nos. 1–2* (with NYPO, Mehta). BARTOK: *2 Rhapsodies for violin and orchestra* (with NYPO, Bernstein) (SMK 64503) [id.].

Volume 11: BERG: *Violin concerto* (with NYPO, Bernstein); *Chamber concerto for piano, violin & 13 wind* (with Peter Serkin, LSO (members), Abbado) (SMK 64504) [id.].

Volume 12: STRAVINSKY: *Violin concerto in D* (with Columbia SO, cond. composer). ROCHBERG: *Violin concerto* (with Pittsburgh SO, Previn) (SMK 64505) [id.].

Volume 13: BARBER: *Violin concerto, Op. 14* (with NYPO, Bernstein). MAXWELL DAVIES: *Violin concerto* (with RPO, Previn) (SMK 64506) [id.].

Volume 14: HINDEMITH: *Violin concerto* (with NYPO, Bernstein). PENDERECKI: *Violin concerto* (with Minnesota O, Skrowaczewski) (SMK 64507) [id.].

Volume 15: BERNSTEIN: *Serenade for violin, strings, harp and percussion, after Plato's Symposium* (with Symphony of the Air, cond. composer). DUTILLEUX: *Violin concerto 'L'Arbre des songes'* (with O Nat. de France, Maazel) (SMK 64508) [id.].

Although there are a few more reservations here than with Box I, there are some unforgettable performances too. The Barber *Concerto* remains unsurpassed and unsurpassable, as does the Stravinsky, recorded in mono with the composer, while the Dutilleux and Hindemith works are almost as fine. In the Stravinsky, no apology need be made for the sound and the performance is electrifying. The two-disc set which includes music of Lalo, Saint-Saëns, Chausson and others is particularly enticing and makes a good sample of the sheer calibre and remarkable charisma of Stern's playing.

'A Life in music': Box III
(N) (M) **(*) Sony Analogue/Dig. SX12K 67195 (12) [id.].

Volume 16: (i) BACH: *Trio sonatas in G, BWV 1038; in C min., BWV 1079.* W. F. BACH: *Trio sonata in A min.* (ii) J. C. BACH: *Trio sonata in C.* (iii) *Sonata in C.* (ii) TELEMANN: *Quartet (Trio sonata) in E min.* (with (i; ii; iii) Jean-Pierre Rampal (flute); (i) Leslie Parnas (cello); (ii) Mstislav Rostropovich (cello); (i; iii) John Steele Ritter ((i) harpsichord; (iii) fortepiano); (ii) Matthias Spaeter (lute)) Sony Dig. SMK 64509 [id.].

Volume 17: BEETHOVEN: *Piano trios Nos. 1–3, Op. 1/1–3; 8, WoO 38; 10 (Variations in E flat), Op. 44;* (with Leonard Rose (cello), Eugene Istomin (piano)) Sony SM2K 64510 [id.].

Volume 18: BEETHOVEN: *Piano trios Nos. 4 in B flat, Op. 11; 5 in D (Ghost), Op. 70/1; 6 in E flat, Op. 70/ 2; 7 in B flat (Archduke), Op. 97; 9 in B flat, WoO 39; 11 (Variations on 'Ich bin der Schneider Kakadu'), Op. 121a* (with Leonard Rose (cello), Eugene Istomin (piano)) Sony SM2K 64513 [id.].

Volume 19: (i) SCHUBERT: *Piano trios Nos. 1–2, Op. 99, 100.* (ii) MOZART: *Piano quartet No. 2 in E flat, K.493.* (i) HAYDN: *Piano trio in E flat, Hob XV/10* ((i) with Leonard Rose (cello); (ii) with Milton Katims (viola), Mischa Schneider (cello); (i; ii) with Eugene Istomin (piano)) Sony SM2K 64516 (2) [id.].

Volume 20: MENDELSSOHN: *Piano trios Nos. 1 in D min., Op. 49; 2 in C min., Op. 66* (with Leonard Rose (cello), Eugene Istomin (piano)) Sony SMK 64519 [id.].

Volume 21: BRAHMS: *Piano trios Nos. 1 in B, Op. 8; 2 in C, Op. 87; 3 in C min., Op. 101* (with Leonard Rose (cello), Eugene Istomin (piano)); *Piano quartets Nos. 1 in G min., Op. 25; 2 in A, Op. 26; 3 in C min., Op. 60* (with Jaime Laredo (viola), Yo-Yo Ma (cello), Emanuel Ax (piano)) Sony SM3K 64520 (3) [id.].

Volume 22: (i) ANON.: *Greensleeves.* FOSTER: *I dream of Jeannie with the light brown hair.* KREISLER: *Liebesleid.* SCHUBERT: *Ave Maria.* (ii) MENDELSSOHN: *On wings of song.* (i) BRAHMS: *Hungarian Dance No. 5.* DVORAK: *Humoresque.* RIMSKY-KORSAKOV: *Flight of the bumblebee.* (ii) RACHMANINOV: *Vocalise.* (i) TCHAIKOVSKY: *None but the lonely heart.* (ii) BORODIN: *Nocturne.* (i) BENJAMIN: *Jamaican Rumba.* (ii) SATIE: *Gymnopédie No. 3.* (i) GERSHWIN: *Bess, you is my woman now.* COPLAND: *Hoedown* (with (i, ii) Columbia SO; (i) Milton Katims; (ii) Frank Brieff) Sony SMK 64537 [id.].

With Box III it is perhaps better to pick and choose rather than to go for the complete box. The *Trio sonatas* by Bach and his sons plus an attractive work of Telemann offer some very distinguished playing (especially in the performances featuring Rostropovich) and one can adjust to the up-front balance. The Beethoven and Brahms *Piano trios* and *Quartets* are indispensable, but the Schubert and Mendelssohn are not. Many will enjoy the final selection of lollipops, sumptuously recorded, although the effect is a bit schmaltzy and they are best taken in small doses. Superb playing, of course, as throughout all three Boxes. All the records (or smaller compilations) are available separately and most are discussed in detail under their composer entries. Overall this is a remarkable achievement.

Vienna Philharmonic Orchestra, Claudio Abbado

'New Year Concert 1988' (with Vienna Boys' Ch.): REZNICEK: *Donna Diana: overture.* Josef STRAUSS: *Brennende Liebe; Auf Ferienreisen; Im Fluge* (polkas). Johann STRAUSS, Jnr: *Die Fledermaus overture; Neue pizzicato polka; Freut euch des Lebens* (waltz); *Chit-chat polka; Un Ballo in maschera: Quadrille on themes from Verdi's opera. Liechtes Blut polka; Seid unschlungen Millionen* (waltz); *Perpetuum mobile; Banditen-Galopp; An der schönen blauen Donau.* Johann STRAUSS, Snr: *Radetzky march.*
*** DG Dig. 423 662-2; 423 662-4.

If this record, which also includes the Vienna Boys' Choir, does not quite match Karajan's, it still has a real sense of occasion and offers some delectable performances. Obvious favourites like *The Blue Danube, Die Fledermaus overture* and, of course, the *Radetzky march* are duplicated, but most of the programme is new. With Rezniček's *Donna Diana* opening the proceedings vivaciously, the mixture is nicely varied to include the familiar and the unfamiliar, and both playing and recording are excellent.

Vienna Philharmonic Orchestra, Herbert von Karajan

(N) *'The great Decca recordings':* BRAHMS: *Symphonies Nos. 1 in C min., Op. 68; 3 in F, Op. 90; Tragic overture, Op. 81.* HAYDN: *Symphonies Nos. 103 in E flat (Drumroll); 104 in D (London).* MOZART: *Symphonies Nos. 40 in G min., K.550; 41 in C (Jupiter), K.551.* TCHAIKOVSKY: *Romeo and Juliet* (fantasy overture); *Nutcracker suite; Swan Lake* (ballet): *suite; Sleeping Beauty* (ballet) *suite.* ADAM: *Giselle* (ballet; abridged). BEETHOVEN: *Symphony No. 7 in A, Op. 92.* DVORAK: *Symphony No. 8 in G, Op. 88.* GRIEG: *Peer Gynt* (incidental music): *suite No. 1; suite No. 2: Ingrid's lament; Solveig's song.* HOLST: *The Planets* (suite), *Op. 31.* Johann STRAUSS Jnr: *Die Fledermaus: Overture and ballet music. Der Zigeunerbaron: Overture.* Polkas: *Annen; Auf der Jagd.* Waltz: *Geschichten aus dem Wiener Wald.* Josef STRAUSS: *Delirien waltz.* Richard STRAUSS: *Till Eulenspiegel; Salome: Dance of the 7 veils. Don Juan, Op. 20; Also sprach Zarathustra, Op. 30.*
(N) (B) **(*) Decca 448 042 (9) [id.].

Following directly on after his EMI Philharmonia recordings with Walter Legge, Karajan's five-year Decca period with the Vienna Philharmonic – master-minded by producers John Culshaw and Erik Smith – lasted from 1959 until 1964. Though the epithet 'great' can be applied to only a handful of the recordings in this box, almost all of them have far more character and musical appeal than many of the more anonymous records flooding the present-day CD market. Certainly Karajan's 1960 *Romeo and Juliet* stands the test of time, not only for its passion but also for its delicacy of feeling in the 'moonlight' music, and his virtually complete (1961) recording of Adam's *Giselle* (with sumptuous sound still approaching demonstration standard) shows what a fine ballet conductor he was, the playing combining affectionate warmth, elegance and drama. The suites from the three Tchaikovsky ballets have comparable panache and generate considerable excitement; apart from the rather plangent timbre of the VPO's principal oboe, they have plenty of glowing colour, with the *Panorama* from *Sleeping Beauty* endearingly suave and the final climax from *Swan Lake* riveting in its histrionic power. The *Nutcracker suite* has more vivid characterization than the later, Berlin Philharmonic account, with the *Waltz of the flowers* lilting agreeably. The remastering scores over the analogue DG versions in its greater ambient depth.

The excerpts from *Peer Gynt* bring the freshest reponse from the VPO, with gutsy Trolls galloping into the *Hall of the Mountain King*, and *Solveig's song* radiantly beautiful. Again, the 1961 Decca recording stands up well alongside the later DG analogue version (which we count as marginally the most alluring of his three stereo accounts) and in many ways is superior in body and naturalness. As for *The Planets*, dating from that same vintage year, this is certainly a great performance, with *Mars* among the most thrilling ever put on disc. With whining Wagnerian tubas it makes a terrifying impact; then *Venus* follows, transmuted into sensuous balm – the *Venus* of gentle ardour rather than mysticism. *Jupiter* is bucolic and breezy, the Vienna strings bringing their own characteristic tone-colour to the big central tune. *Saturn* with its slow, sad march and *Uranus* with superb VPO brass are no less outstanding, and the wordless chorus at the end of *Neptune* is more atmospheric than in almost any other version. The analogue recording is so stunningly vivid that it could have been made yesterday.

Karajan never surpassed his 1960 VPO collection of overtures, polkas and waltzes by Johann and Josef Strauss until he came to make his wonderful (DG) 1987 New Year concert with the same orchestra. His later, BPO records sound glossy by comparison, yet here his rhythmic touch is unerring in the two overtures, while the polkas have all the flair you could ask for. However, the highlight is the highly seductive account of *Tales from the Vienna woods*, played most beautifully, an account which may have been equalled, but has never been surpassed.

The superlative performances of Richard Strauss tone-poems are hardly less remarkable, and they sound wonderfully fresh. In this repertoire no one can quite match Karajan in the panache and point of his conducting. This programme is available separately in Decca's 'Classic Sound' series and is discussed above under its composer entry.

In the symphonic repertoire the results are less even. Of the two Haydn symphonies, No. 103 is more urbane than No. 104, though both offer enjoyably polished VPO playing: there is plenty of robust vigour in the latter and both slow movements are beautifully shaped. The same comments might apply to Mozart's *Fortieth* and *Jupiter Symphonies*. In the *G minor* every detail remains beautifully in place, each phrase nicely contoured and in perspective. Beautifully articulate, this performance has genuine dramatic power, even though one feels that it all moves within carefully regulated limits. The reading of the *Jupiter* is strong and direct and has breadth as well as warmth. Exposition repeats are observed in the first movements of each symphony, but not in the finale of the *Jupiter*. Of the two Brahms symphonies, No. 3 is more successful than No. 1, which gives the impression of being over-rehearsed. Its pacing does not always seem spontaneous, with an overall lack of tension; though towards the end of the finale Karajan cannot help creating genuine excitement, this is dissipated in a very slow chorale reference in the coda. The *Third* is much more successful. Here is another case in which the Vienna performance rivals the quality of the later, DG Berlin version. In both, Karajan takes the opening expansively; in both, he omits the exposition repeat. The third movement, too, is very slow, but the overall reading has plenty of grip and tension, and the Decca recording has a fuller and more resonant bass than the DG, and this well suits Brahms. The recording of Beethoven's *Seventh* is also full-bodied, though not as fine as that for the Dvořák *Eighth*. 1961 was certainly a vintage year for the Decca engineers. The Beethoven performance is massive rather than incandescent and refuses to catch fire or grip the listener emotionally. The Dvořák is another matter, a most winning performance with superb orchestral playing. There are moments of slight self-indulgence in the Trio of the Scherzo, but the result is delectable when the Vienna strings are at their creamiest; overall, this account blends polish and spontaneity in almost equal measure. The orchestra sound as if they are enjoying themselves and so do we.

Vienna Philharmonic Orchestra, Carlos Kleiber

'1992 New Year Concert': J. STRAUSS Jnr: Overture: *Der Zigeunerbaron*. Polkas: *Neue pizzicato; Stadt und Land; Tritch-Tratch; Unter Donner und Blitz; Vergnügungszug*. Waltzes: *An der schönen, blauen Donau; Tausend und eine Nacht. Persischer march*. J. STRAUSS Snr: *Radetsky march*. Joseph STRAUSS: Waltzes: *Dorfschwalben aus Osterreich; Sphärenklänge*. NICOLAI: Overture: *The Merry wives of Windsor*.
*** Sony Dig. SK 48376 [id.].

When Carlos Kleiber conducted the 1989 event, he seemed at times a little stiff. But here he manages precision alongside lilt, discipline as well as verve. There is plenty of elegance and warmth too, in a programme entirely without novelties but where the waltzes nearly always go as spontaneously as the polkas, though the *Blue Danube* is no match for Karajan's version two years earlier. The recording is well up to standard, vivid yet spacious and full.

Vienna Philharmonic Orchestra, Riccardo Muti

'1993 New Year Concert': J. STRAUSS Snr: *Sperl-Galop; Radetzsky march*. J. STRAUSS Jnr: *Klipp Klapp galop; Egyptischer Marsch; Overture Indigo und die Vierzig Rauber; Perpetuum mobile;* Polkas: *Auf der Jagd; Diplomaten; Pizzicato polka; Veilchen;* Waltzes: *Die Publicisten; An der schönen blauen Donau*. Josef STRAUSS: *Transaktionen*. LANNER: *Steyrische-Tänz; Hans-Jörgel*.
*** Ph. Dig. 438 493-2; *438 493-4 [id.]*.

Riccardo Muti seems an unlikely candidate for sweet-toothed Vienna *bon-bons*, but the atmosphere of this celebrated occasion has its usual effect and he clearly lets his hair down after a while. Once again there are novelties and they sparkle readily when Muti can produce such unselfconscious Straussian manners. Lanner's *Steyrische-Tänz* provides the surprise of the CD by unexpectedly turning out to be the source of the barrel-organ waltz in Stravinsky's *Petrushka*. The tension is not quite consistent throughout the concert, with the second half (beginning with the overture) setting an even more compelling atmosphere; but overall this is such a happy occasion that one cannot but enjoy the experience. Applause is nicely edited and is not too much of a problem. The documentation reveals the history of the event, fascinating in itself. Excellent recording.

Instrumental Recitals

Beaux Arts Trio

'*A Celebration (1955–1995)*': RAVEL: *Piano trio in A min.* HAYDN: *Piano trio in G, Hob XV/25.* FAURE: *Piano trio in D min., Op. 120.* BEETHOVEN: *Piano trio No. 7 (Archduke).* SCHUMANN: *Piano trio No. 2 in F, Op. 80.* MENDELSSOHN: *Piano trio No. 1 in D min., Op. 49.* HAYDN: *Piano trio in F sharp min., Hob XV/26.* SCHUBERT: *Piano quintet in A (Trout), D.667* (with Samuel Rhodes & Georg Hörtnagel); *Piano trio No. 1 in B flat, D.898.* BRAHMS: *Piano trio No. 1 in B, Op. 8.* TCHAIKOVSKY: *Piano trio in A min., Op. 50.* ROREM: *Spring music.*
(Y/B) (M) *** Ph. Analogue/Dig. 446 360-2 (4 + 1) [id.].

As can be seen, the present set celebrates the fiftieth anniversary of the Beaux Arts Trio, and even if over the years there have been changes in personnel the character of their playing (with its immaculate ensemble and spontaneity of feeling) has been stimulated and masterminded throughout by the unostentatious dominance of the pianist, Menahem Pressler, always sharply imaginative, who remains as influential as ever. The earliest recordings here (the Ravel, Haydn *G major Trio*, Hob XV/25, and the Fauré) are offered on a separate bonus disc which comes in a separate cardboard sleeve, inside the slipcase. Daniel Guilet's violin is somewhat meagre in timbre, especially in the Ravel and Fauré, but the cello and piano are naturally focused. Some recording dates for the other works are not stated at all and so we have listed the works in approximate order of recording. Rightly, the earlier (1965) account of the *Archduke Trio* is included; it has more spontaneity than the later version, and the overall feeling is of lightness and grace. The Scherzo is a delight, and elsewhere there is an attractive pervading lyricism, so typical of the Beaux Arts style. Some of the other works have been re-recorded digitally with even greater success, notably the Ravel (where originally we noted a lack of charm on the part of Daniel Guilet). But the earlier versions remain thoroughly worthwhile. The playing in the Mendelssohn *D minor Trio* is thoroughly alive and musical, and the Schubert *Trout* is delightfully fresh. Every phrase is splendidly alive, there is no want of vitality and sensitivity; the *B flat Piano trio*, however, is the later, digital version from the mid-1980s, and the performance, though enjoyable, is not quite as spontaneous as the earlier, analogue version. The Brahms, also digital, shows the later group (including Cohen) at its finest, the playing always vital and sensitive, as does the Tchaikovsky *Trio*. This is a another case where the later version is distinctly superior to the earlier, analogue account. The fugue (originally omitted) is now restored, although there is still a sizeable cut in the final coda. But this remains a fine reading, and the recording is very vivid and present.

Hamelin, Marc-André (piano)

'*Live at Wigmore Hall*': BEETHOVEN (arr. Alkan): *Piano concerto No. 3:* first movt. CHOPIN (arr. Balakirev): *Piano concerto No. 1: Romanza.* ALKAN: *Trois grandes études.* BUSONI: *Sonatina No. 6 (Chamber Fantasy on Carmen).* MEDTNER: *Danza festiva, Op. 38, No. 3.*
(Y/B) ⊛ *** Hyperion Dig. CDA 66765.

This is among the most spectacular piano issues of the decade. It captures live one of the programmes given in June 1994 at Wigmore Hall by the French-Canadian pianist, Marc-André Hamelin, in a series called 'Virtuoso Romantics'. Bizarre as the mixture is, it works magnificently, thanks not only to Hamelin's breathtaking virtuosity, finger-perfect, but to his magnetism. As well as the *Three Grandes Etudes* of Alkan, he plays Alkan's arrangement of the first movement of Beethoven's *Third Piano concerto*. Thanks to his sharp clarity, one marvels afresh at the purposefulness of the writing, and he revels in Alkan's manic six-minute cadenza, which in dotty inspiration even quotes the finale of Beethoven's *Fifth Symphony*. Balakirev's arrangement of the *Romanza* from Chopin's *First Piano concerto* then offers yearning poetry, with two flamboyant display-pieces as encores: Busoni's *Carmen fantasy* and Medtner's *Danza festiva*.

Headington, Christopher (piano)

British piano music of the twentieth century: BRITTEN: *Holiday Diary.* DELIUS: *3 Preludes.* ELGAR: *Adieu; In Smyrna; Serenade.* HEADINGTON: *Ballade-image; Cinquanta.* IRELAND: *The island spell.* MOERAN: *Summer valley.* PATTERSON: *A Tunnel of time, Op. 66.*
*** Kingdom Dig. KCLD 2017; *CKCL 2017* [id.].

The novelties here are fascinating. The Delius *Preludes* (1923) have much of the luminous atmosphere of the orchestral music, while Britten's *Holiday Diary* (what a happy idea for a suite!), written when he was just twenty, is most winning. The Elgar pieces are well worth having, and Headington again reveals himself as an appealing composer. Both his pieces were written for fiftieth-birthday celebrations and the *Ballad-image* expressly seeks to conjure up an atmosphere combining the influences of Chopin and Debussy. It is most engaging. John Ireland's *Island spell* is beautifully played. A 69-minute recital which is skilfully planned to be listened to in sequence. Good, if not outstanding, recording.

Horowitz, Vladimir (piano)

'*The Horowitz Edition*': CHOPIN: *Sonata No. 2; Etudes, Opp. 10/12; 25/7; Scherzo No. 1.* RACHMANI-NOV: *Etudes-tableaux, Opp. 33/2; 39/5.* SCHUMANN: *Arabesque, Op. 18; Kinderszenen, Op. 15; Toccata, Op. 7.* LISZT: *Hungarian rhapsody No. 19* (trans. Horowitz). D. SCARLATTI: *Sonatas, Kk. 322, 455, 531.* BEETHOVEN: *Sonata No. 8.* SCHUBERT: *Impromptu No. 3.* DEBUSSY: *3 Préludes, Book II.* SCRIABIN: *Poème, Op. 32/1; Etudes, Opp. 2/1; 8/12* (S2K 53457). SCARLATTI: *Sonatas, Kk. 25, 33, 39, 52, 54, 96, 146, 162, 197, 198, 201, 303, 466, 474, 481, 491, 525, 547* (SK 53460). BACH/BUSONI: *Toccata, Adagio & Fugue, BWV 564.* SCHUMANN: *Fantaisie, Op. 17; Träumerei, Op. 15/7; Blumenstück, Op. 19.* SCRIABIN: *Sonatas Nos. 9–10; Poème, Op. 32/1; Etude in C sharp min., Op. 2/1.* CHOPIN: *Mazurkas, Opp. 30/4; 33/4; Etude, Op. 10/8; Ballade No. 1; Polonaise-fantaisie, Op. 61; Nocturne, Op. 72/1.* DEBUSSY: *Serenade for the doll; L'Isle joyeuse.* MOSZKOWSKI: *Etude in A flat, Op. 72/11.* MOZART: *Sonata No. 11, K.331.* HAYDN: *Sonata, Hob XVI/23.* LISZT: *Vallée d'Obermann.* CHOPIN: *Ballade No. 1; Nocturne, Op. 55/1; Polonaise, Op. 44.* D. SCARLATTI: *Sonatas, Kk. 55; 380.* SCHUMANN: *Arabeske, Op. 18; Traümerei.* SCRIABIN: *Etude, Op. 8/12.* HOROWITZ: *Variations on a theme from Carmen.* (SK 53465). CLEMENTI: Excerpts from: *Sonatas, Opp. 12/2; 25/3; 50/1. Adagio sostenuto in F, from Gradis ad Parnassum, Book I/14.* J. S. BACH: *Chorale prelude: 'Ich ruf zu dir, Herr Jesu Christ'.* D. SCARLATTI: *Sonatas, Kk. 260; 319.* HAYDN: *Sonata, Hob XVI/48.* BEETHOVEN: *Sonata No. 28, Op. 101.* (SK 53466). BEETHOVEN: *Sonatas Nos. 14, Op. 27/2 (Moonlight); 21, Op. 53 (Waldstein); 23, Op. 57 (Appassionata).* (SK 53467). CHOPIN: *Mazurkas, Opp. 7/3; 17/4; 30/3; 33/2; 41/2; 50/3; 59/3; Etudes, Op. 10/3–6, 12; 3 Nouvelles études, No. 2; Introduction & rondo, Op. 16; Waltzes, Op. 34/2; 64/2; Polonaises, Opp. 40/1; 53; Prélude, Op. 28/6, 15.* SCHUMANN: *Variations on a theme by Clara Wieck; Kreisleriana, Op. 16.* (S2K 53468). SCHUBERT: *Impromptus, D.899/2, 4; D.935/1–2.* LISZT: *Consolation No. 2; Scherzo & Marsch.* DEBUSSY: *Pour les arpèges composées; La terrasse des audiences du clair de lune.* MENDELSSOHN: *Etude, Op. 104b/3.* (SK 53471). SCRIABIN: *Feuillets d'album Opp. 45/1; 58; Etudes, Opp. 8/2, 8, 10–11; 42, 3–5; 65/3; 2 Poèmes, Op. 69; Vers la flamme.* MEDTNER: *Fairy tale, Op. 51/ 3.* RACHMANINOV: *Sonata No. 2; Prélude, Op. 32/12; Moment musical, Op. 16/3; Etudes-tableaux, Opp. 33/2, 5; 39/9.*

(M) (***) Sony mono SX13K 53456 (13) [id.].

The strength of the Sony box which runs to 13 CDs and includes all Horowitz's recordings from 1962–73 resides in the fact that nearly all these discs are essential repertory for Horowitz collectors but in any case are not now obtainable separately in the UK. Hardly any of these performances can be passed over, whether it be the Scarlatti sonatas or the stunning accounts of Scriabin's *Ninth* and *Tenth*. There is almost nothing that does not show him in top form – and the sound, though not ideal, is greatly improved. Advice for those considering the boxes rather than individual releases would be to buy the Sony and choose liberally from among the CDs singled out for special mention in the RCA set.

'*In London*': *God save the Queen* (arr. Horowitz). CHOPIN: *Ballade No. 1 in G min., Op. 23; Polonaise No. 7 in A flat (Polonaise-Fantaisie), Op. 61.* SCHUMANN: *Kinderszenen, Op. 15.* SCRIABIN: *Étude in D sharp min., Op. 8/12.*

(M) *** RCA 09026 61414-2 [id.].

Horowitz's London and New York recitals were both recorded live by RCA and now reappear at mid-price. The highlights from the memorable 1982 London recital omit the elegant Scarlatti sonatas he played on that occasion, doubtless because it would duplicate '*Horowitz at the Met*.' – see below. However, room could surely have been found for the Rachmaninov *Sonata* or for his encores, as the CD is not generously filled. As those who attended this electrifying recital will know, there were idiosyncratic touches, particularly in the *Kinderszenen* (and also in the Chopin *Ballade*), but this is remarkable testimony to his wide dynamic range and his refined *pianopianissimo*. There are many fascinating points of detail in both works (but notably in the Chopin) which give one the feeling of hearing the music for the first time.

'At the Met.': D. SCARLATTI: *Sonatas: in A flat, Kk. 127; in F min., Kk. 184 & 466; in A, Kk. 101; in B min., Kk. 87; in E, Kk. 135.* CHOPIN: *Ballade No. 4 in F min., Op. 52; Waltz No. 9 in A flat, Op. 69/1.* LISZT: *Ballade No. 2 in B min., G. 171.* RACHMANINOV: *Prelude No. 6 in G min., Op. 23/5.*
(M) *** RCA 09026 61416-2 [id.].

The playing is in a class of its own, and all one needs to know is that this recording reproduces the highly distinctive tone-quality Horowitz commanded. This recital, given at the Metropolitan Opera House and issued here at the time of his London Festival Hall appearance in 1982, comes closer to the real thing than anything else on record, except his DG recitals. The quality of the playing is quite extraordinary.

Recital: BACH/BUSONI: *Chorale prelude: Nun komm der Heiden Heiland.* MOZART: *Piano sonata No. 10 in C, K. 330.* CHOPIN: *Mazurka in A min., Op. 17/4; Scherzo No. 1 in B min., Op. 20; Polonaise No. 6 in A flat, Op. 53.* LISZT: *Consolation No. 3 in D flat.* SCHUBERT: *Impromptu in A flat, D. 899/4.* SCHUMANN: *Novellette in F, Op. 21/1.* RACHMANINOV: *Prelude in G sharp min., Op. 32/12.* SCRIABIN: *Etude in C sharp min., Op. 2/1.* MOSZKOWSKI: *Etude in F, Op. 72/6* (recording of performances featured in the film *Vladimir Horowitz – The Last Romantic*).
*** DG Dig. 419 045-2 [id.].

Recorded when he was over eighty, this playing betrays remarkably little sign of frailty. The Mozart is beautifully elegant and the Chopin *A minor Mazurka,* Op. 17, No. 4, could hardly be more delicate. The only sign of age comes in the *B minor Scherzo,* which does not have the leonine fire and tremendous body of his famous 1950 recording. However, it is pretty astonishing for all that.

'The studio recordings': SCHUMANN: *Kreisleriana, Op. 16.* D. SCARLATTI: *Sonatas: in B min., Kk. 87; in E, Kk. 135.* LISZT: *Impromptu (Nocturne) in F sharp; Valse oubliée No. 1.* SCRIABIN: *Etude in D sharp min., Op. 8/2.* SCHUBERT: *Impromptu in B flat, D. 935/3.* SCHUBERT/TAUSIG: *Marche militaire, D. 733/ 1.*
❀ *** DG 419 217-2 [id.].

The subtle range of colour and articulation in the Schumann is matched in his Schubert *Impromptu,* and the Liszt *Valse oubliée* offers the most delicious, twinkling rubato. Hearing Scarlatti's *E major Sonata* played with such crispness, delicacy and grace must surely convert even the most dedicated authenticist to the view that this repertoire can be totally valid in terms of the modern instrument. The Schubert– Tausig *Marche militaire* makes a superb encore, played with the kind of panache that would be remark- able in a pianist half Horowitz's age. With the passionate Scriabin *Etude* as the central romantic pivot, this recital is uncommonly well balanced to show Horowitz's special range of sympathies.

'In Moscow': D. SCARLATTI: *Sonata in E, Kk. 380.* MOZART: *Sonata No. 10 in C, K. 330.* RACHMANI- NOV: *Preludes: in G, Op. 32/5; in G sharp min. Op. 32/12.* SCRIABIN: *Etudes: in C sharp min., Op. 2/1; in D sharp min., Op. 8/12.* LISZT/SCHUBERT: *Soirées de Vienne; Petrarch Sonnet 104.* CHOPIN: *Mazurkas, Op. 30/4; Op. 7/3.* SCHUMANN: *Kinderszenen: Träumerei.*
*** DG Dig. 419 499-2 [id.].

This is familiar Horowitz repertoire, played with characteristic musical discernment and spontaneity. Technically the pianism may not quite match his finest records of the analogue era, but it is still both melting and dazzling. The sound too is really excellent, much better than he ever received from his American engineers in earlier days.

'The Private Collection': BACH: *Toccata and fugue in C min., BWV 911.* CHOPIN: *Fantaisie in F min., Op. 49; Polonaise in C sharp min., Op. 26/1; Mazurka in B min., Op. 30/2.* CLEMENTI: *Sonatas: Op. 36/1; Op. 24/2: Allegro con brio; Op. 34/1: Un poco andante.* MENDELSSOHN: *Song without words in B flat, Op. 67/3.* LISZT: *Consolations Nos. 4 & 5.* RACHMANINOV: *Etude-tableau in C min., Op. 39/7.*
(Y/B) (***) RCA mono 09026 62643-2 [id.].

This is the first of two discs that emanate from Carnegie Hall concerts Horowitz gave during 1945–50 and which were recorded for his own use and stored in his New York home. Not long before his death he gave the collection to Yale University Library. His friend and producer, Thomas Frost, discovered among them some two hours of repertoire that Horowitz had never committed to disc, and they make their appearance now. The playing is in every way quite remarkable, whether it is the energy generated in the Clementi or the feather-like delicacy the great pianist can harness when he so desires. The Rachmaninov is tremendously intense and imbued with a hypnotic atmosphere that is quite individual. Never mind the surface imperfections inevitable in acetates, this playing makes one realize why people still speak of these concerts with awe.

'Discovered Treasures (1962–1972)': BACH/BUSONI: *Chorale prelude: Ich ruf zu dir, Herr Jesus Christ.* CHOPIN: *Nouvelle étude No. 1 in A flat; Etude in E flat min., Op. 10/6; Prelude in D flat (Raindrop) Op. 28/15.* CLEMENTI: *Piano sonata in E flat, Op. 12/2: Rondo. Gradus ad Parnassum, Book 1, No. 14: Adagio sostenuto in F; Piano sonata in B flat, Op. 25/3: Rondo. Piano sonata in A, Op. 50/1: Adagio.* LISZT: *Consolation in E.* MEDTNER: *Fairy tale in A, Op. 51/3.* SCARLATTI: *Sonatas in G, Kk 547; B min., Kk 197; F sharp min., Kk 25; D min., Kk 52; G, Kk 201; C min., Kk 303.* SCRIABIN: *Feuille d'album, Op. 58; Etude, Op. 65/3.*
(N) *** Sony SK 48093-2 [id.].

The earliest of these recordings, the Liszt *Consolation*, comes from 1962, and the last, the Scriabin *Feuille d'album* and the *Etude*, Op. 65, No. 3, from 1972. All were made in the studio and were approved by Horowitz himself but were never included on records, purely for planning reasons. Horowitz was fastidious in seeing that each of the LPs he released made a logical programme, and hence there was quite a lot of studio material unused in the Archives.

'The private collection' (live performances recorded in Carnegie Hall, 1945–9): DEBUSSY: *Etudes, Book 1/1, 4 & 6.* PROKOFIEV: *Cinderella: Intermezzo & Valse lente.* POULENC: *Intermezzo No. 2; Novellette No. 1.* KABALEVSKY: *Preludes, Op. 38/1, 3, 8, 10, 16–17, 22 & 24; Sonata No. 2, Op. 45.* BARBER: *Excursions, Op. 20/1, 2 & 4.*
(N) (***) RCA mono 09026 61644-2 [id.].

During the late 1940s, Horowitz gave 13 recitals at Carnegie Hall. None of these was recorded commercially, but the great pianist did have them recorded for his own private use. These were donated some time before his death to the Yale University Library, and this is the first of two CDs devoted to repertoire that Horowitz never otherwise recorded. Thomas Frost, who heard all the recordings, calls them 'a series of stunning recitals by Horowitz at the height of his middle period' – and stunning is the word. The actual recorded sound is better than one fears, though some of the audiences are more bronchial than one might expect. The colours Horowitz produces in the Debussy and the imagination he shows in the Prokofiev transcriptions would be amazing were it not for the fact that one never ceases to wonder at Horowitz's playing. Self-recommending.

Hough, Stephen (piano)

'The Piano Album': MACDOWELL: *Hexentanz, Op. 12.* CHOPIN: *Chant polonaise No. 1.* QUILTER: *The crimson petal; The fuchsia tree.* DOHNANYI: *Capriccio in F min., Op. 28/8.* PADEREWSKI: *Minuet in G, Op. 14/1. Nocturne in B flat, Op. 16/4.* SCHLOZER: *Etude in A flat, Op. 1/2.* GABRILOWITSCH: *Mélodie in E; Caprice-burlesque.* RODGERS: *My favourite things.* WOODFORDE-FINDEN: *Kashmiri song.* FRIEDMAN: *Music box.* SAINT-SAENS: *Carnival: The Swan.* ROSENTHAL: *Papillons.* GODOWSKI: *The gardens of Buitenzorg.* LEVITZKI: *Waltz in A, Op. 2.* PALMGREN: *En route, Op. 9.* MOSZKOWSKI: *Siciliano, Op. 42/2; Caprice espagnole, Op. 3.*
❀ *** Virgin Dig. VC7 59509-2 [id.].

There are few young pianists who can match Stephen Hough in communicating on record. This Virgin Classics collection captures more nearly than almost any other recent record the charm, sparkle and flair of legendary piano virtuosos from the golden age of Rosenthal, Godowski and Lhévinne. MacDowell's *Hexentanz* (*Witches' dance*) launches the listener into pure pianistic magic, with playing totally uninhibited and with articulation and timing that are the musical equivalent of being tickled up and down the spine. Hough's own arrangements of Roger Quilter and Amy Woodforde-Finden, in their tender expressiveness, are most affecting. In the grand tradition, Hough does a Valse-caprice arrangement he himself has made of *My favourite things* from *The Sound of Music*, as well as firework pieces by Rosenthal and Moszkowski, among others, along with old-fashioned favourites like Paderewski's *Minuet in G* and Godowski's arrangement of the Saint-Saëns *Swan*. It is a feast for piano-lovers, very well recorded in venues in both London and New York.

Hurford, Peter (organ of Ratzeburg Catherdral)

'Organ masterpieces, Volume I': WIDOR: *Symphony No. 5: Toccata. Symphony No. 6: Allegro* (1st movt). VIERNE: *Pièce en style libre: Berceuse. Symphony No. 1, Op. 14: Finale.* KARG-ELERT: *Marche triomphale: Nun danket alle Gott.* ALAIN: *3 Pièces: Litanies.* LISZT: *Prelude and fugue on B-A-C-H.* REGER: *Benedictus, Op. 59/9; Introduction and Passacaglia in D min.* LANGLAIS: *Paraphrase grégorienne: Hymne d'action de grâce, Te Deum, Op. 5/3.* BOELLMANN: *Suite gothique, Op. 25* (complete).

(N) ❀ (M) *** Decca Dig. 444 567-2 [id.].

There are not many records of Romantic organ music to match this in colour, breadth of repertory and brilliance of performance, superbly recorded – to say nothing of generosity of content (76 minutes). The ever-popular Widor item leads to pieces just as effective at bringing out Hurford's imaginative variety of organ registration, such as the imposing Karg-Elert or the jaunty Alain. These are performances which defy all thought of Victorian heaviness, and the splendid Ratzeburg organ produces sounds which are both piquant and beautiful and, when required, gloriously expansive too. For the other volumes in Decca's outstanding 'Organ masterpieces' series, see above under the composers: Franck (Volume II), J. S. Bach (Volume III) and Brahms and Mendelssohn (Volume IV).

Lloyd Webber, Julian (cello)

'British cello music' (with (i) John McCabe, piano): (i) RAWSTHORNE: Sonata for cello and piano. ARNOLD: Fantasy for cello. (i) IRELAND: The Holy Boy. WALTON: Passacaglia. BRITTEN: Teme (Sacher); Cello suite No. 3.
*** ASV Dig. CDDCA 592 [id.].

A splendid recital and a most valuable one. Julian Lloyd Webber has championed such rarities as the Bridge Oration at a time when it was unrecorded and now devotes this present issue to English music that needs strong advocacy; there is no alternative version of the Rawsthorne Sonata, in which he is most ably partnered by John McCabe. He gives this piece – and, for that matter, the remainder of the programme – with full-blooded commitment. Good recording.

British cello music, Vol. 2 (with John McCabe (piano)):
STANFORD: Sonata No. 2, Op. 39. BRIDGE: Elegy; Scherzetto. IRELAND: Sonata in G min.
❀ *** ASV CDDCA 807 [id.].

The Stanford Second Cello sonata (1893 – written between the Fourth and Fifth Symphonies) is revealed here as an inspired work whose opening theme flowers into great lyrical warmth on Lloyd Webber's ardent bow. The focus of the recording is a little diffuse, but that serves to add to the atmosphere. Ireland's Sonata, too, is among his most richly inspired works, a broad-spanning piece in which ambitious, darkly intense, outer movements frame a most beautiful Poco largamente. Again Lloyd Webber, who has long been a passionate advocate of the work, conveys his full expressive power. The Bridge Elegy (written as early as 1911) is another darkly poignant evocation which points forward to the sparer, more austere style of the later Bridge and the Scherzetto (even earlier, 1902) and makes a winning encore: it should ideally have been placed at the end of the recital. John McCabe is a sympathetic partner – in spite of the balance – but this collection offers what are perhaps Lloyd Webber's finest performances on disc.

Malcolm, George (harpsichord)

'The world of the harpsichord': BACH: Italian concerto, BWV 971; Chromatic fantasia and fugue in D min., BWV 903; French suite No. 5 in G, BWV 816; Toccata in D, BWV 912. PARADIES: Toccata. DAQUIN: The cuckoo. RIMSKY-KORSAKOV: Flight of the bumble-bee (arr. Malcolm). RAMEAU: Pièces de clavecin: La Poule; Le rappel des oiseaux; Tambourin. François COUPERIN: Pièces de clavecin: Le rossignol-en-amour; Le carillon de Cithère. TEMPLETON: Bach goes to town. MALCOLM: Bach before the mast.
(N) ❀ (M) *** Decca 444 390-2 [id.].

This is a delectable collection, a CD of harpsichord music that should be in even the smallest collection, spanning as it does the gamut of the late George Malcolm's wide repertory. His Bach performances are very considerable indeed; the Chromatic fantasia has an appropriate improvisatory element, the Italian concerto is full of vitality, and the best known of the French suites has a genial, lyrical intimacy to offset the buoyant Toccata in D. The comparative gravitas of Bach goes well with the charm of Rameau and Couperin, with their descriptive pieces realized with flair, notably Le rappel des oiseaux and Le carillon de Cithère. The two witty Bach imitations make a tempting hors d'oeuvre and the Rimsky-Korsakov is similarly a fun piece, played with great bravura; but no one should dismiss the mixture, for there is plenty of real substance here and playing of great distinction. The 1960s recording of the harpsichord (unnamed, but almost certainly a modern copy of a fine baroque instrument) is in the demonstration class, beautifully balanced – not too close – and natural within an airy but not over-resonant acoustic.

Peyer, Gervase de (clarinet), Gwenneth Pryor (piano)

French music for clarinet and piano: SAINT-SAENS: *Sonata, Op. 167.* DEBUSSY: *Première rhapsodie; Arabesque Nó. 2; Prélude: La fille aux cheveux de lin.* POULENC: *Sonata.* SCHMIDT: *Andantino, Op. 30/1.* RAVEL: *Pièce en forme de habanera.* PIERNE: *Canzonetta, Op. 19.*
⊛ *** Chandos Dig. CHAN 8526.

A gorgeous record. The Saint-Saëns *Sonata* is an attractively crafted piece, full of engaging invention. Poulenc's *Sonata* is characteristically witty, with contrast in its lovely central *Romanza* (*très calme*); and the other short pieces wind down the closing mood of the recital, with De Peyer's luscious timbre drawing a charming portrait of *The girl with the flaxen hair* before the nimbly tripping closing encore of Pierné. This is a quite perfect record of its kind, the programme like that of a live recital and played with comparable spontaneity. The recording is absolutely realistic; the balance could hardly be improved on.

Richter, Sviatoslav (piano)

BEETHOVEN: *Piano sonatas Nos. 3 in C, Op. 2/3; 4 in E flat, Op. 7; 27 in E min., Op. 90.*
(Y/B) **(*) Olympia OCD 336 [id.].

SCHUBERT: *Piano sonatas Nos. 19 in C min., D.958; 21 in B flat, D.960.*
(Y/B) **(*) Olympia Dig. OCD 335 [id.].

RACHMANINOV: *Etudes-tableaux, Opp. 33 & 39; 6 Preludes, Op. 23/1–2, 4–5, 7–8; 7 Preludes, Op. 32/1– 2, 6–7, 9–10, 12.*
(Y/B) **(*) Olympia Dig./Analogue OCD 337 [id.].

Sonically these recordings leave a good deal to be desired: in most instances the balance is fairly close and the acoustic on the dry side, without being unacceptably so. They call for tolerance, but this is well worth extending for the sake of this music-making. The early Beethoven sonatas are from 1975 and the *E minor*, Op. 90, comes from 1971. The *C major Sonat*a, Op. 2, No. 3, is far more powerful than one is used to encountering, particularly in the intensity of the slow movement; Richter's view of the *E flat*, Op. 7, familiar from an earlier recording Philips issued in the 1960s, is further deepened. There is a marvellously inward feeling and a sense of profound euphony in the *E minor*, Op. 90.

The Schubert sonatas were recorded in the early 1970s; the *C minor Sonata*, D.958, in 1973, the *B flat*, D.960, in the previous year; neither has been in currency in the UK. Richter's way with Schubert is well known. Some listeners have difficulty in coming to terms with the sheer scale of his first movement: it seems almost timeless, just as the almost static inwardness of the slow movement is not for those in a hurry.

Some of the Rachmaninov *Etudes-tableaux* have been available before, but again most are new to this country. The majority of the pieces were recorded in 1971 but others are later. The playing is of a rare order of mastery and leaves strong and powerful resonances. Richter's conception goes far beyond the abundant virtuosity this music calls for, and the characterization of this music is strong and searching. If you invest in no other of these Olympia CDs, this is the one that is unique – which makes the poor sound-quality particularly regrettable.

'The Philips Richter Authorised Edition'

(Y/B) **(*) Ph. 438 612-2 (21) (includes book: Sviatoslav Richter Portraits).

BACH: *Concerto in the Italian style, BWV 971; 4 Duets, BWV 802–5; English suites Nos. 3 in G min., BWV 808; 4 in F, BWV 809; 6 in D min., BWV 811; Fantasy in C min., BWV 906; French suites Nos. 2 in C min., BWV 813; 4 in E flat, BWV 815a; 6 in E, BWV 817; Overture (Partita) in the French style, BWV 831; Toccatas: in D min., BWV 913; in G, BWV 916.*
(Y/B) **(*) Ph. 438 613-2 (3) [id.].

BEETHOVEN: *Piano sonatas Nos. 19 in G min.; 20 in G, Op. 49/1–2; 22 in F, Op. 54; 23 in F min. (Appasssionata), Op. 57; 30 in E, Op. 109; 31 in A flat, Op. 110; 32 in C min., Op. 111.*
(Y/B) **(*) Ph. Dig. 438 486-2 (2) [id.].

BEETHOVEN (with (i) Moraguès Qt; (ii) members of the Borodin Qt): (i) *Piano quintet in E flat, Op. 16;* (ii) *Piano trio in B flat, Op. 97. Rondos: in C; in G, Op. 51/1–2; Piano sonatas Nos. 18 in E flat, Op. 31/3; 28 in A, Op. 101.*
(Y/B) **(*) Ph. Dig. 438 624-2 (2) [id.].

BRAHMS: *Ballade in G min., Op. 118/3; Capriccio in C, Op. 76/8; Intermezzo in E min., Op. 116/5; Rhapsody in E flat, Op. 119/4; Piano sonatas Nos. 1 in C, Op. 1; 2 in F sharp min., Op. 2; Variations on a theme by Paganini, Op. 35.* SCHUMANN: *Blumenstück, Op. 19; 3 Concert Etudes on Caprices by Paganini, Op. 10/4–6; Fantasy in C, Op. 17; March in G min., Op. 76/2; 4 Nachtstücke, Op. 23; Novelette in F, Op. 21/1.*
(Y/B) **(*) Ph. Dig. 438 477-2 (3) [id.].

HAYDN: *Piano sonatas Nos. 39 in D, Hob XVI/24; 62 in E flat, Hob XVI/52.* WEBER: *Piano sonata No. 3 in D min., Op. 49.* BEETHOVEN: *Piano sonatas Nos. 9 in E, Op. 14/1; 11 in B flat, Op. 22; 12 in A flat, Op. 26; 27 in E min., Op. 90.*
(Y/B) **(*) Ph. Analogue/Dig. 438 617-2 (2) [id.].

MOZART: *Piano sonatas Nos. 2 in F, K.280; 5 in G, K.283; 13 in B flat, K.333; 14 in C min., K.457; Sonata in F: Andante and allegro, K.533; Rondo, K.494; Fantasia in C min., K.475.*
(Y/B) **(*) Ph. Dig. 438 480-2 (2) [id.].

SCHUBERT: *Piano sonatas Nos. 9 in B, D.575; 15 in C (Relique), D.840; 18 in G, D.894.*
(Y/B) *** Ph. 438 483-2 (2) [id.].

CHOPIN: *Barcarolle in F sharp, Op. 60; Etudes, Op. 10/1–5, 10–12; Etudes, Op. 25/5–8, 11–12; Nocturne in F, Op. 15/1; Polonaises: in C sharp min., Op. 26/1; in C min., Op. 40/2; Polonaise-Fantaisie in A flat, Op. 61; Preludes, Op. 28/6–11, 17, 19, 23–24.* LISZT: *Consolation No. 6; Etudes d'exécution transcendante, Nos. 1–3, 5, 7–8, 10–11; Etudes de concert: 'Un sospiro'; 'Gnomenreigen'; Hungarian rhapsody No. 17; Klavierstück in F sharp; Mephisto-Polka; Polonaise No. 2 in E; Piano sonata in B min.; Scherzo in G min.; Trübe Wolken.*
(Y/B) **(*) Ph. Dig. 438 620-2 (3) [id.].

SCRIABIN: *2 Dances: 'Guirlandes'; 'Flammes sombres', Op. 73; Fantasie in B min., Op. 28; Poème-Nocturne; Vers la flamme, Op. 72.* PROKOFIEV: *Cinderella: excerpts, Op. 87; Danza and waltz, Op. 32/1 & 4; Légende, Op. 26/6; Piano sonatas: Nos. 4 in C min., Op. 29; 6 in A, Op. 82; Visions fugitives, Op. 22/3–6, 8–9, 11, 14–15; 18.* SHOSTAKOVICH: *Preludes and fugues, Op. 87/4, 12, 14–15, 17, 23.*
(Y/B) *** Ph. 438 627-2 (2) [id.].

Unusually for Philips, the documentation concerning the date and provenance of these records is meagre or non-existent. So, although many of the recordings appear to be digital, the quality of the sound is extremely variable. But, generally speaking, these are self-recommending performances which admirers of this pianist will want to have anyway. In Beethoven, Richter's voice is uniquely authoritative, in Schubert his profoundly spacious readings, recorded live, have extraordinary concentration. The indispensable compilation of Prokofiev, Scriabin and Shostakovich is a combination of studio recordings and live recitals; the Mozart collection brings dryness of timbre to match a very positive, classical style. The Liszt playing is little short of inspired, especially the *Sonata*, but the recordings are again confined. The Schumann performances, too, inhabit an area of repertoire in which Richter has something very special to say, and the playing triumphs over any sonic limitations; the Brahms sonatas, on the other hand, are made to sound hard at higher dynamic levels. All the Bach performances, aristocratic and masterly, were recorded live, and these superbly controlled interpretations, unashamedly pianistic, are often surprisingly generous with repeats.

CHOPIN: *Préludes, Op. 28/2; 4–11; 13; 19; 21 & 23.* TCHAIKOVSKY: *Nocturne in F, Op. 10/1; Valse-scherzo in A, Op. 7.* RACHMANINOV: *Etudes-tableaux, Op. 33/3, 5 & 6; Op. 39 1–4; 7 & 9.*
*** Olympia OCD 112 [id.].

Some marvellous playing here from Richter. He plays an odd assortment of Chopin *Preludes*, Nos. 4 through to 10 in the published sequence, then 23, 19, 11, 13, 23 and 21! These obviously derive from a public concert, as there is applause. He is distinctly ruminative and wayward at times. The two Tchaikovsky pieces are done with extraordinary finesse and the Rachmaninov is masterly. The recordings are not top drawer and the disc gives no details of their provenance; but the sound is perfectly acceptable.

DEBUSSY: *Estampes; Préludes, Book I: Voiles; Le vent dans la plaine; Les collines d'Anacapri.* PROKOFIEV: *Visions fugitives, Op. 22, Nos. 3, 6 & 9; Sonata No. 8 in B flat, Op. 84.* SCRIABIN: *Sonata No. 5 in F sharp, Op. 53.*
✹ (M) *** DG 423 573-2.

The Debussy *Préludes* and the Prokofiev *Sonata* were recorded at concerts during an Italian tour in 1962, while the remainder were made the previous year in Wembley Town Hall. The former sound more open than the rather confined studio acoustic – but what playing! The Scriabin is demonic and the Debussy could not be more atmospheric. The performance of the Prokofiev *Sonata* is, like the legendary Gilels account, a classic of the gramophone.

Recital: BACH: *Well-tempered Klavier: Preludes and fugues Nos. 1–6, BWV 846–53.* HAYDN: *Piano sonata in G min.* SCHUBERT: *Allegretto in C min., D.915; Ländler in A, D.366.* CHOPIN: *Polonaise-fantaisie, Op. 61; Etudes: in C; C min. (Revolutionary), Op. 10/7 & 12.* SCHUMANN: *Abegg variations, Op. 1.* DEBUSSY: *Estampes; Préludes: Voiles; Le vent dans la plaine; Les collines d'Anacapri.* SCRIABIN: *Sonata No. 5 in F sharp min., Op. 53.* RACHMANINOV: *Prelude in G sharp min., Op. 32/12.* PROKOFIEV: *Visions fugitives, Op. 22/3, 6 & 9; Sonata No. 8 in B flat, Op. 84.*
(N) (B) *** DG Double 447 355-2 [id.].

This remarkable Richter treasury collects the stereo recordings he made for DG (or which were licensed to DG) between 1962 and 1965. They are all of good quality and often the sound is excellent, if a little dry. The recordings, taken from live recitals during his Italian tour, bring a cough or two. The opening Bach *Preludes and fugues* immediately bring rapt concentration. The Chopin selection opens with a wonderfully poetic account of the *Polonaise-fantaisie*, and the *Revolutionary study* is almost overwhelming in its excitement. The audience noises may be found intrusive both here and in the superb Debussy performances, yet *Jardins sous la pluie* is quite magical, as is the gentle exoticism of *Pagodes* (both from *Estampes*). Richter's Schumann is no less special, and in the delicious account of the Schubert *Ländler* one can sense the smile in his eyes. Both in the Scriabin and Prokofiev *Sonatas* it is the powerful dynamism of Richter's technique that projects the music so vividly, but of course there is much poetic feeling too. As an inexpensive cross-section of his art, this could hardly be bettered.

Melodiya Richter Edition (complete)
(N) (M) (*(**)) RCA mono 74321 19460-2 (10) [id.].

Volume 1: BACH: *English suite No. 3 in G min., BWV 808. Piano concerto in D min., BWV 1052* (with USSR SO, Kurt Sanderling). *Double piano concerto in C, BWV 1061* (with Anatoly Vedernikov, Moscow CO, Barshai).
(N) (M) (**) RCA mono 74321 19461-2 [id.].

Volume 2: BEETHOVEN: *Piano sonatas Nos. 8 in C min. (Pathétique); 23 in F min. (Appassionata), Op. 57; Bagatelles, Op. 33/3 & 5; Op. 119/ 2, 7 & 9; Op. 126/1, 4 & 6.*
(N) (M) (**(*)) RCA mono 74321 29462-2 [id.].

Volume 3: SCHUBERT: *Piano sonatas Nos. 16 in A min., D.845; 17 in D, D.850.*
(N) (M) (***) RCA mono 74321 29463-2 [id.].

Volume 4: SCHUMANN: *Fantasiestücke, Op. 12; Humoreske in B flat, Op. 20; Novelleten, Op. 21.*
(N) (M) (***) RCA mono 74321 29464-2 [id.].

Volume 5: SCHUBERT: *Moments musicaux, D.780/1, 3 & 6.* CHOPIN: *Etudes: in E, Op. 10/3; in E min., Op. 25/5. Polonaise No. 1 in C sharp min., Op. 26/1.* FRANCK: *Prélude, choral et fugue.* BARTOK: *15 Hungarian peasant songs.*
(N) (M) (**(*)) RCA mono 74321 29465-2 [id.].

Volume 6: CHOPIN: *Piano concerto No. 2 in F min., Op. 21* (with USSR SO, Svetlanov). SAINT-SAENS: *Piano concerto No. 5 in F, Op. 103.* FRANCK: *Les Djinns* (both with Moscow Youth O, Kondrashin).
(N) (M) (*(**)) RCA mono 74321 29466-2 [id.].

Volume 7: RACHMANINOV: *Piano concertos Nos. 1 in F sharp min., Op. 1; 2 in C min., Op. 18* (with USSR R. & TV Large SO or Leningrad PO, both cond. Kurt Sanderling).
(N) (M) (***) RCA mono 74321 29467-2 [id.].

Volume 8: RIMSKY-KORSAKOV: *Piano concerto in C sharp min., Op. 30.* GLAZUNOV: *Piano concerto No. 1 in F min., Op. 92.* PROKOFIEV: *Piano concerto No. 1 in D flat, Op. 10* (with Moscow Youth O, Kondrashin).
(N) (M) ((***)) RCA mono 74321 29468-2 [id.].

Volume 9: TCHAIKOVSKY: *Piano sonata in G, Op. 37.* MUSSORGSKY: *Pictures at an exhibition.*
(N) (M) (**(*)) RCA mono 74321 29469-2 [id.].

Volume 10: SCRIABIN: *12 Etudes: Op. 2/1; Op. 8/5 & 11; Op. 42/2–6 & 8; Op. 65/1–3; Piano sonata No. 6, Op. 62.* MIASKOVSKY: *Piano sonata No. 3 in C min., Op. 19.* PROKOFIEV: *Piano sonata No. 7 in B flat, Op. 83.*
(N) (M) ((***)) RCA mono 74321 29470-2 [id.].

All these discs which Richter made for the Melodiya label are available separately; the only gain in acquiring them all is a sturdy slipcase. Each disc is annotated separately, and the annotations are all authoritative and full of interest. Most of these recordings will be familiar to collectors of the older generation, but not all of them were issued on Western labels. The oldest of the recordings is of the *G minor English Suite*, which comes from 1948 when Richter would have been in his early thirties and, for all its sonic limitations, it is wonderfully alive. The *Bach D minor Concerto*, made in 1955 with Kurt Sanderling, originally appeared in the UK in a Parlophone series called 'Music from the USSR' not long after Richter's breakthrough Schumann recital on DG. At that time it was coupled with his Rachmaninov *First* from the same year – a dazzling performance, which here appears more logically coupled in the seventh volume of the set with the *Second*, made in 1959 (not as well recorded as his DG set with Stanislaw Wislocki and the Warsaw Philharmonic the following year); but some feel the 1959 version to be a stronger performance, and certainly the orchestral support is impressive.

The Beethoven performances are of early provenance and call for some tolerance as far as the actual sound is concerned, though they are a great improvement on such original Melodiya LPs as we have. The *Pathétique* and the *Bagatelles* come from 1948 and 1955, and the recordings are shallow and a bit clangorous at climaxes. The *Appassionata* was recorded at a public concert in 1960 and was Richter's own preferred version. (He was not satisfied with the studio performance he made with RCA in America.) These are all performances of stature. The *Choral Fantasy*, sung in Russian, comes from 1952 and, although the sound calls for some tolerance, the performance is tremendously compelling.

The Schubert *Sonata in A minor*, D.845, had a disc to itself (with an *Impromptu* as fill-up) when it appeared on blue-label Melodiya LPs, complete with wow, swish and fairly heavy background noise, and it is good to renew its acquaintance in more acceptable sound. (These LPs were never officially issued here but were obtainable in an austere, sleeveless presentation for a derisory sum.) Although Richter made later Schubert recordings for EMI, this *A minor* is in a class of its own for sheer depth of feeling. The two Schubert sonatas were recorded in mono in 1957–8.

Like Perahia, Richter has a special feeling for Schumann. The *Humoreske* in this set is the 1956 account mentioned above, and the *Fantasiestücke* come from roughly the same period as the famous DG LP, which was also recorded in 1956 while Richter was in Prague. If you have the DG disc, there is no need to add the present issue to your library except for the sake of the magisterial *Humoreske*.

The Schubert and Chopin on the next disc are of early provenance (1952), and again the recording is wanting in freshness and bloom – but not the playing! The Franck was made four years later and the Bartók comes from 1972. Like so much in this collection, it is self-recommending.

The Chopin *Concerto No. 2 in F minor* and the Saint-Saëns *Fifth Concerto*, the so-called *Egyptian*, are much less well-known and the dated sound-quality of the Saint-Saëns and Franck couplings, which come from 1952–3, may perhaps have limited their wider dissemination, though the RCA engineers have freshened them up considerably – and many will tolerate the shallowness and distortion of the climaxes for the sake of the performance. The *F minor Concerto* is of much later provenance (1966) and, though the sound is hardly the 'highest of fi', it is serviceable.

The Russian concertos on Volume 6 have all been available at one time or another in the 1950s and '60s though the recordings sounded execrable. The Glazunov, recorded way back in 1952, has never been better played, and the same probably holds for the Rimsky-Korsakov, which Richter made with Kondrashin in 1950. The Prokofiev from 1952 is simply dazzling and is perhaps even more remarkable than the later (and better-recorded) version he made in Prague with Karel Ančerl. However, while the RCA engineers have improved the sound, there are limits to what even they can do with the shrill, hollow orchestral climaxes which suffer from distortion.

The famous 1956 account of the Tchaikovsky *Sonata in G major* shared a Parlophone disc with the Schumann *Humoreske* and is one (if not *the*) classic account of the piece on disc. The 1958 *Pictures at an exhibition* is not to be confused with the live performance Richter gave in Sofia, which was released on Philips. The Melodiya recording might at best be described as 'so-so'. (The notes remind us that Richter is an accomplished painter himself.)

The Scriabin *Etudes* come from 1952, and the *Sixth Sonata* was recorded three years later; he penetrates this music as few artists do. The Miaskovsky *Third Sonata*, recorded in 1953, is an interesting work and it is difficult to envisage more sympathetic advocacy. Much the same must be said of the stunning, demonic account Richter gives of the *Seventh Sonata* which makes most other pianists sound quite tame. Richter had given the first Moscow performance of this sonata in 1943 and this 1958 account finds him at the height of his powers. This extraordinary performance comes over in spite of all the distortion.

To sum up: despite the skill and dedication of those concerned with this project, considerable allowances have to be made for shallow sound-quality, and sometimes distortion too, while the occasional cough can disturb the listener in the live performances. However, allowances are worth making, as most of these performances find Richter in his youthful prime. For those who do not want the whole box, prime recommendations lie with the Schubert sonatas (Volume 3), the Rachmaninov concertos (7), the Tchaikovsky *G major Sonata* and the *Pictures* (9), and the stunning Prokofiev *Seventh Sonata* (10).

Russian Piano School

Russian Piano School: '*The great pianists*' Volumes 1–10.

RCA/Melodiya are currently offering eleven CDs that survey the Russian piano tradition from the generation of Goldenweiser and Neuheus, whose pianistic pedigree goes back to the nineteenth-century masters, through to such younger virtuosi as Pletnev and Kissin. All of them have been digitally remastered with great care with 20-bit technology and NoNoise processing and, though the results are inevitably variable (particularly in the earlier recordings), the series affords an invaluable opportunity to steep oneself in the Russian pianistic tradition. Although the set is available in a slipcase, with a small saving in cost (74321 25172-2), the discs are also available separately at mid-price.

Goldenweiser, Alexander Borisovich

Volume 1: ARENSKY: *Forgotten rhythms: Sari, Op. 28/4.* BORODIN: *Petite suite: Mazurka.* GOLDEN-WEISER: *Song and dance.* MEDTNER: *Novella in C min., Op. 17/2.* RACHMANINOV: *Morceaux de salon: Barcarolle in G min., Op. 10/3. Suite No. 2, Op. 17* (with Grigori Ginsburg). TCHAIKOVSKY: *Dialogue in B, Op. 72/8; Meditation, Op. 72/5; Romance in F, Op. 51/5; Valse sentimentale in F min., Op 51/6.*
(Y/B) (M) (***) RCA mono 74321 25173-2 [id.].

Alexander Goldenweiser (1875–1961) was a pupil of Siloti, Rachmaninov's cousin and himself a pupil of Liszt, and his class-mates at the Moscow Conservatoire included Scriabin, Rachmaninov and Medtner. His composition studies were with Arensky, Ippolitov-Ivanov and Taneyev, all pupils of Tchaikovsky. He lived to be eighty-six and recorded these pieces between 1946 and 1955, when he would have been in his seventies. His own pupils included Tatiana Nikolayeva, Lazar Berman, Dmitri Bashkirov and the composer Kabalevsky. Of particular interest is his powerful 1948 recording of the Rachmaninov *Second Suite* (with Grigori Ginsburg as the second pianist), since the composer dedicated the piece to him. He wears his virtuosity lightly and, like all the greatest pianists, his lightness of touch leaves one unaware of hammers. The Tchaikovsky pieces of Op. 72 have a particularly touching quality. The recordings come up surprisingly well, given their age.

Neuhaus, Heinrich

Volume 2: MOZART: *Rondo in A min., K.511; Sonata in D for two pianos, K.448* (with Stanislav Neuhaus). DEBUSSY: *Préludes, Books I & II: Danseuses de Delphes; La sérénade interrompue; La puerta del vino; Des pas sur la neige; Les sons et les parfums tournent dans l'air du soir; Les collines d'Anacapri; Bruyères; Minstrels.* PROKOFIEV: *Visions fugitives, Op. 22.*
(Y/B) (M) (***) RCA mono 74321 25174-2 [id.].

Heinrich Neuheus (1888–1964) is one of the most legendary figures among Russian pianists, the teacher of Richter and Gilels among others, a cousin of Szymanowski, much spoken of but scarcely glimpsed on a record label. He studied with Tausig and Godowsky before going on to become an influential teacher, as was his son, Stanislav (1927–80), with whom he recorded the Mozart *Sonata in D major*, K.488, in 1950. The eight Debussy *Préludes*, recorded in 1946 and 1948, have a powerful atmosphere and a refined sense of colour. Acceptable sound, though with not a great deal of top. It is difficult to imagine the *Visions fugitives*, recorded in 1956 when Neuheus was in his late sixties, being played with greater character.

Feinberg, Samuil

Volume 3: BACH, trans. Feinberg: *Sonata No. 5 in C, BWV 529: Largo. Chorale preludes: Allein Gott in der Höh sei Ehr, BWV 711; Allein Gott in der Höh sei Ehr, BWV 662* (two versions); *Wer nur den lieben Gott lässt walten, BWV 647; Allein Gott in der Höh sei Ehr, BWV 663.* MOZART: *Piano sonatas Nos. 4 in E flat, K.282; 18 in D, K.576; Fantasia and fugue in C, K.394; 12 Variations on an allegretto in B flat, K.500.*
(Y/B) (M) (***) RCA mono/stereo 74321 25175-2 [id.].

Samuil Yevgenyevich Feinberg (1890–1972) was a pupil of Goldenweiser and will be one of the discoveries of this collection for many non-specialist collectors. So wide a range of colour and sonority does he command that one is at times tempted to believe that there is more than one pianist playing. His style has a melting lyricism, a limpid tone-quality and a miraculous *pianissimo*; his sonority is of exceptional richness and finesse. He is the opposite of the modern jet-setting virtuoso, and both the transcriptions of Bach organ works and the Mozart are of altogether exceptional beauty. The recordings date from 1951–3, with the exception of four of his Bach transcriptions, which date from 1962. The recordings are very acceptable indeed: playing of this artistry deserves the widest dissemination.

Yudina, Maria

Volume 4: BARTOK: *Mikrokosmos, Books 5 & 6:* excerpts. BERG: *Sonata, Op. 1.* HINDEMITH: *Sonata No. 3.* KRENEK: *Sonata No. 2, Op. 59.* STRAVINSKY: *Serenade in A.*
(Y/B) (M) (***) RCA mono/stereo 74321 25176-2 [id.].

Maria Yudina (1899–1970) studied at first with the legendary Essipova, herself a Leschetizky pupil, and, after her death, was a fellow-student at Leningrad with Sofronitsky; Glazunov appointed her to a teaching post on the spot during her graduation recital. Her openness to modern developments in the West is well illustrated by the recordings assembled here. She carried on a long correspondence with Stravinsky, with whom she is pictured (in the sleeve-note) on his visit to Russia in 1962. These are impressive records: she makes Hindemith's *Sonata No. 3* sound more compelling than almost any other artist who has recorded it, and she succeeds in making Krenek's *Second Sonata* sound like music – no mean achievement! The recordings date from 1960–64 and are of eminently acceptable quality.

Sofronitsky, Vladimir

Volume 5: CHOPIN: *Nocturnes in F & F sharp, Op. 15/1–2; Scherzo No. 1 in B min., Op. 20.* MOZART: *Fantasia in C min., K.475.* PROKOFIEV: *Grandmother's Tales, Op. 31; Pieces for piano, Op. 12/2, 3 & 6–9; Sarcasm, Op. 17/3; Vision fugitive, Op. 22/7.* RACHMANINOV: *Moments musicaux, Op. 16/2 & 5.* SCHUBERT: *Impromptus, D.899/3 & 4.* SCHUMANN: *Sonata No. 1 in F sharp min., Op. 11.* SCRIABIN: *Sonata No. 4 in F sharp, Op. 30; Poème tragique, Op. 34; Valse in A flat, Op. 38; Etude in B flat min., Op. 8/11.*
(Y/B) (M) (**(*)) RCA mono 74321 25177-2 (2) [id.].

Vladimir Sofronitsky (1901–61) is best remembered as a Scriabin interpreter (he married the composer's daughter and was hailed by Tatiana Schloezer, Scriabin's widow, as the finest interpreter of her husband's music). He studied in Warsaw and had attracted the attention of Glazunov, who sent him to study with Alexander Michalowski. In the late 1920s he spent some time in Warsaw and Paris, where he earned the admiration of Prokofiev, whose friendship he enjoyed after his return to the Soviet Union. Sofronitsky was never cultivated by the Soviet regime and rarely appeared in the West, eventually succumbing to drink and drugs. All except the Prokofiev pieces come from a recital at the Small Hall of the Tchaikovsky Conservatoire in the year before his death. The Prokofiev Op. 31 comes from 1946 and the remainder of the group from 1953, recorded in the Scriabin Museum. In the fullness of time RCA will doubtless get round to reissuing all his Scriabin. In the meantime the *Fourth Sonata* gives a good idea why he is so much admired in this composer.

Richter, Sviatoslav

Volume 6: BACH: *Concerto in F in the Italian style, BWV 971.* BEETHOVEN: *Sonata No. 12 in A flat, Op. 26.* CHOPIN: *Ballades Nos. 1 in G min., Op. 23; 2 in F, Op. 38.* HAYDN: *Sonata No. 50 in C, Hob. XVI:50.*
(Y/B) (M) (*(*)) RCA mono 74321 25178-2 [id.].

The Bach *Italian concerto* was recorded in 1948, though it is difficult to credit it, given the excellence of its sound and the relative indifference (to put it mildly) of the later recordings offered here. It is much superior to the 1960 Haydn or Beethoven. Like most of the repertoire on this disc, it is given a performance of much distinction. The Haydn, Beethoven and Chopin items were recorded at recitals in 1960–63, but if the sound is shallow and poor in quality the playing is not. Richter recorded these pieces in the West, and older readers will doubtless recall the various CBS, RCA and EMI LP issues. Perhaps the first movement of the Haydn is too fast for comfort – but still, what playing! The Beethoven sounds very papery in tone and, though the playing is magisterial, the unpleasing sound makes its claims less pressing than many of the other discs in this collection.

Gilels, Emil

Volume 7: BACH: *Prelude and fugue in D, BWV 532.* BEETHOVEN: *32 Variations on an original theme, WoO 80.* LISZT: *Rapsodie espagnole.* PROKOFIEV: *Visions fugitives, Op. 22/1, 3, 5 & 11.* WEBER: *Sonata No. 2 in A flat, Op. 39.*

(Y/B) (M) (**(*)) RCA mono 74321 25179-2 [id.].

Gilels is represented by a recital given in the Grand Hall of the Philharmonic in Leningrad in January 1968. Such is the quality of his pianism that the (very much less than state-of-the-art) recording does not make this anything other than a highly recommendable issue. There are some smudges (as was often the case with Gilels in the concert hall) but they are of little account, given the musical insights and the beauty of sound he produced. The Liszt *Rapsodie espagnole* is pretty breathtaking and the Weber *Sonata No. 2 in A flat* is played with elegance and finesse. Despite the fact that it was January in Leningrad, the audience is very quiet, warmed no doubt by the white-hot, risk-taking pianism which confronted them.

Berman, Lazar

Volume 8: LISZT: *Etudes d'exécution transcendante; Hungarian Rhapsody No. 9 in E flat.*
(Y/B) (M) (**(*)) RCA mono 74321 25180-2 [id.].

The recordings of the *Etudes d'exécution transcendante* were made in the early part of 1959 and the *Hungarian rhapsody* (*Pesther Carneval*) two years later – and they leave something to be desired in terms of presence. However, the sound is vastly superior to the Richter CD reviewed above. As with the latter, no quarrels with the playing, which is absolutely stunning. Effortlessly virtuosic and brilliant, yet poetic and tender when required, and obviously with an immense dynamic range, only partly captured by the engineers. Pianistically this is without question a three-star recommendation.

Pletnev, Mikhail

Volume 9: MOZART: *Sonata No. 16 in B flat, K.570.* PROKOFIEV: *Sonata No. 7 in B flat, Op. 83.* SHCHEDRIN, arr. Pletnev: *Prologue and Horse-racing from Anna Karenina.* TCHAIKOVSKY, arr. Pletnev: *Nutcracker suite.*
(Y/B) 🏵 (M) *** RCA Analogue/Dig. 74321 25181-2 [id.].

We have long been urging the reissue of Mikhail Pletnev's astonishing transcription of the *Nutcracker suite* which he recorded when he was twenty-one. (EMI originally issued this, but they never promoted it with vigour and, as a result, it disappeared within a couple of years.) Pletnev produces a wider range of colour from the keyboard than most orchestras command, and in the Shchedrin *Anna Karenina* an extraordinarily wide dynamic range. Small wonder that he has become so effective a conductor. Like the Prokofiev *Seventh Sonata*, these were all recorded after he won the Tchaikovsky Competition in 1978. The Mozart is later (1984) and completes a recital which is pre-eminent even in this remarkable series.

Kissin, Yevgeni

Volume 10: PROKOFIEV: *Visions fugitives, Op. 22/10, 11, 16 & 17; Dance in F sharp min., Op. 32/1.* RACHMANINOV: *Etudes-Tableaux, Op. 39/1–6, 9; Preludes: in G flat, Op. 23/10; A min., Op. 32/8. Lilacs, Op. 21/5* (trans. Kissin). SCRIABIN: *Preludes, Opp. 27/1–2; 37/1–4; Etude in C sharp min., Op. 42/5; 4 Pieces, Op. 51.* KISSIN: *2 Inventions.*
(Y/B) (M) *** RCA 74321 25182-2 [id.].

These recordings were made at recitals given at the Grand Hall of Moscow Conservatoire in 1984 and 1986 when Kissin was twelve and fourteen respectively. (He had, after all, played both the Chopin *Concertos* when he was thirteen!) What is there left to say about this remarkable youngster, save that the playing has extraordinary assurance, dazzling technical address and splendid taste. This listener was left spellbound by the sheer passion and brilliance of the playing. The acoustic is a bit reverberant but, given this youth's poetic insight and artistry, technical reservations are of minimal importance.

Vocal Recitals and Choral Collections

Many operatic recitals are not included here; they can be found in our companion volume, *The Penguin Guide to Opera on Compact Disc*

Baillie, Dame Isobel (soprano)

'The unforgettable Isobel Baillie': HANDEL: *Samson: Let the bright Seraphim. Rodelinda: Art thou troubled. Messiah: I know that my Redeemer liveth; If God be with us. Theodora: Angels ever bright and fair. Joshua: Oh! Had I Jubal's lyre.* BACH: *Cantata No. 68: My heart ever faithful; Cantata No. 201: Ah yes, just so* (arr. Mottl). MOZART: *La finta giardiniera: A maiden's is an evil plight. The marriage of Figaro: O come, do not delay.* HAYDN: *The Creation: With verdure clad.* MENDELSSOHN: *Elijah: Hear ye, Israel.* OFFENBACH: *Tales of Hoffmann: Doll's song.* SCHUBERT: *The shepherd on the rock* (with Charles Draper, clarinet); *To music.* ARNE: *Where the bee sucks.*
(Y/B) ✸ (M) *** Dutton Lab. mono CDLX 7013 [id.].

It must be unique for a soprano's recording career to span over half a century, yet over all that time Isobel Baillie rarely if ever let down her maxim which provided the title of her autobiography: 'Never sing louder than lovely'. Handel's *I know that my Redeemer liveth* was certainly her most popular record during the war years. Alan Blyth describes this famous 1941 performance in the accompanying insert leaflet: 'Notes are hit fully and truly in the middle, and they are joined together in a seamless line. At the same time Baillie was able to swell and diminish her tone with total ease.' Like the rest of the pro- gramme, it is flawlessly transferred by the miraculous Dutton/CEDAR process, and one can enjoy Leslie Heward's warm Hallé accompaniment alongside the voice. In her duet with the trumpet (Arthur Lockwood) which opens the disc, *Let the bright Seraphim*, her bright, gleaming tone wins out every time, and elsewhere there are dazzling displays of agility (as in the 1930 *Doll's song* and the delightful Arne *Where the bee sucks* from 1943) as well as purity and loveliness (as in the 1941 *Art thou troubled* or Susanna's aria from *The marriage of Figaro*, recorded in 1927). Her simplicity of style was just right for Schubert, and her account of *The Shepherd on the rock*, recorded a year later, shows the bright, fresh timbre, which was uniquely hers, under perfect control. The timbre of Charles Draper, the distinguished clarinettist who plays the obbligato, by comparison seems dry and lustreless. A record to treasure on all counts.

Baker, Dame Janet (mezzo-soprano)

Lieder (with Martin Isepp, piano): SCHUMANN: *Frauenliebe und Leben* (song-cycle), *Op. 42* *** ✸. SCHUBERT: *Heimliches Lieben; Minnelied; Die Abgeblühte Linde. Der Musensohn.* BRAHMS: *Die Mainacht; Das Mädchen spricht; Nachtigall; Von ewiger Liebe.*
(Y/B) (M)*** Saga EC 3361-2 [id.].

Janet Baker's inspirational account of *Frauenliebe und Leben*, part of this early Lieder recital for Saga, has never been surpassed. The Schubert songs are not quite on this level (*Der Musensohn* a little jerky), but the Brahms are beyond praise. This is singing of a quality that you find only once or twice in a generation and – whatever the price – this CD is a collector's piece. The stereo on the original LP was curiously balanced, with voice and piano unnaturally separated, but the CD transfer transforms the sound, with oddities ironed out. Set in a dryish acoustic, the quality is now full-bodied, with a vivid sense of presence to make the transcendental performances even more involving.

'Grandi voci': RAVEL: *3 Poèmes de Stéphane Mallarmé; Chansons madécasses.* CHAUSSON: *Chanson perpétuelle, Op. 37.* DELAGE: *4 Poèmes hindous* (with the Melos Ensemble). Arias from: PURCELL: *Dido and Aeneas.* RAMEAU: *Hippolyte et Aricie* (with ECO, Lewis). BACH: *Cantata, BWV 170* (with ASMF, Marriner). CAVALLI: *La Calisto* (with LPO, Leppard).
(Y/B) ✸ (M) *** Decca 440 413-2 [id.].

The performances of French mélodies included on this record are very beautiful indeed. Chausson's extended cantilena about a deserted lover has a direct communication which Dame Janet contrasts with the subtler beauties of the Ravel songs. She shows great depth of feeling for the poetry here and an equally evocative sensitivity to the songs about India, written in 1912 by Ravel's pupil, Maurice Delage, which are by no means inferior to the songs by his more famous contemporaries. With superb, atmos- pheric playing by the Melos group and an outstanding 1966 (originally Oiseau-Lyre) recording, this ravishing collection must be placed among Dame Janet's most outstanding recordings. For the current reissue, more remarkable examples of her art have been generously added, not least the lovely Bach aria, *Vergnügte Ruh'*, the dramatic excerpt from Cavalli's *La Calisto* in Raymond Leppard's imaginative realization, and, of course, her heartrending account of Dido's lament, *When I am laid in earth*.

RAVEL: *Shéhérazade* (with New Philh. O, Barbirolli). CHAUSSON: *Poème de l'amour et de la mer*. DUPARC: *Phidylé; La vie antérieure; Le manoir de Rosamonde; Au pays où se fait la guerre; L'invitation au voyage* (with LSO, Previn). SCHUMANN: *Frauenliebe und Leben* (with Barenboim). BRAHMS: *Vier ernste Gesänge, Op. 121; 2 Lieder, with viola, Op. 91* (with Aronowitz, Previn); *4 Duets, Op. 28* (with Fischer-Dieskau, Barenboim).

(N) (B) *** EMI forte CZS5 68667-2 (2).

Dame Janet Baker was always at her finest in French music, and with her 1967 performance of *Shéhérazade* she inspired Barbirolli to one of his most glowing performances in this atmospherically scored music; her range of tone and her natural sympathy for the French language make for heartwarming singing which has a natural intensity. The account of Chausson's *Poème de l'amour et de la mer* is comparably glorious and heart-felt, both radiant and searching, so that this picture of love in two aspects, first emergent, then past, has a sharpness of focus often denied it; in this she is superbly supported by Previn and the LSO. Their partnership is hardly less persuasive in the five Duparc mélodies which the composer orchestrated himself – each a jewelled miniature of breathtaking beauty, with the extra richness and colour of the orchestral accompaniment adding to the depth and intensity of the exceptionally sensitive word-settings, especially in the greatest of them all, *Phidylé*. It was Schumann's *Frauenliebe und Leben* that helped to establish Baker's early reputation, and she returned to this favourite cycle in early maturity with renewed freshness in the light of deeper experience. Where on her Saga record (see Composer index) she transposed most of the earlier songs down a full tone, the later version keeps them in the original keys. Then by contrast it is the later songs which she transposes, reserving her warmer tones for those expressions of motherhood. The wonder, the inwardness, are even more intense, while the final song in some ways brings the most remarkable performance of all ('*Now you have hurt me*'), not at all a conventional expression of mourning. With Barenboim an endlessly imaginative – if sometimes reticent – accompanist, this is another classic example of Baker's art. The Brahms Lieder were the last to be recorded, in 1977, and the gravity and nobility of her singing in the *Four Serious Songs* underlines the weight of the biblical words while presenting them with a far wider and more beautiful range of tone-colour than is common. André Previn's piano is placed rather backwardly, but his rhythmic control provides fine support, and in the two viola songs, which are ravishingly sung and played, these artists are partnered by the late Cecil Aronowitz, making his last appearance on record. To cap the recital come the four varied duets of Op. 28, in which Baker is joined by Dietrich Fischer-Dieskau, recorded at a live recital at London's Queen Elizabeth Hall in 1969. The vivacious closing *Der Jäger und sein Liebchen* makes a spiritedly vivacious coda to a collection which could hardly be bettered. Even if the presentation here omits texts and translations, this set still makes an amazing bargain.

Bartoli, Cecilia (soprano)

'*A Portrait*': Arias from: MOZART: *La clemenza di Tito; Così fan tutte; Le nozze di Figaro; Don Giovanni*. Concert aria: *Ch'io mi scordi di te?* ROSSINI: *Semiramide; Maometto II; La Cenerentola*. Song: *Bella crudèle*. PARISOTTI: *Se tu m'ami*. GIORDANO: *Caro mio ben*. CACCINI: *Amarilli*. SCHUBERT: *La pastorella; Metastasio: Vedi quanto adoro ancora ingrato!*.

(N) *** Decca Dig. 448 300-2 [id.].

Cecilia Bartoli's portrait, covering a recording period from 1991 to 1995, could hardly be more enticing. Every lyrical aria displays her truly lovely voice with astonishing consistency. The very opening *Parto, parto, ma tu ben mio* from *La clemenza di Tito* could hardly be more inviting, with its engaging basset clarinet obbligato from Lesley Schatzberger, and *Come scoglio* shows her dramatic and vocal range to powerful and moving effect. There is a delicious combination of charm and sparkle in Despina's *In uomini, in soldate* (wonderfully crisp trills echoing the orchestral violins), while Cherubino's *Voi che sapete* brings delightful innocence, and Susanna's *Deh vieni* the sunny joy of loving anticipation which ravishes the ear, especially at the leisurely close. The simpler classical songs bring contrast, with the silken line of *Caro mio ben* followed by the very touching and gloriously sung *Amarilli* of Caccini. Finally Rossini, where Bartoli is unsurpassed among the present generation of mezzos (and measures up impressively to famous names from the past). After the beautifully spun line of the aria from *Maometto II* (with choral support) she captivates with a fizzing, crisply articulated and joyfully humorous *Non più mesta*. Top-class Decca recording throughout ensures the listener's pleasure and this hugely enjoyable

collection would have earned a Rosette but for the totally inadequate documentation, with no translations – unacceptable in a premium-priced record.

Callas, Maria (soprano)

Operatic recital: CILEA: *Adriana Lecouvreur: Ecco, respiro appena . . . Io son l'umile; Poveri fiori.*
GIORDANO: *Andrea Chénier: La mamma morta.* CATALANI: *La Wally: Ebben? Ne andro lontana.* BOITO:
Mefistofele: L'altra notte. ROSSINI: *Il barbiere di Siviglia: Una voce poco fa.* MEYERBEER: *Dinorah:
Shadow song.* DELIBES: *Lakmé: Bell song.* VERDI: *I vespri siciliani: Boléro.* CHERUBINI: *Medea: Dei tuoi
figli.* SPONTINI: *La Vestale: Tu che invoco; O Nume tutelar, Caro oggetto.*
⊛ (***) EMI mono CDC7 47282-2 [id.].

This fine recital disc is a conflation of two of Callas's most successful earlier LPs. The *Medea* and
Vestale items were originally coupled with extracts from complete opera sets and might otherwise have
been left in limbo. These are recordings from the 1950s, when the voice was still in fine condition and the
artistry at its most magnetic. Callas's portrait of Rosina in *Una voce* was never more sparklingly viperish
than here, and she never surpassed the heart-felt intensity of such numbers as *La mamma morta* and
Poveri fiori. Some items may reveal strain – the *Bell song* from *Lakmé,* for example – but this has many
claims to be the finest single Callas recital on CD, very well transferred.

Cambridge Singers, John Rutter

'*There is sweet music*' (English choral songs): STANFORD: *The blue bird.* DELIUS: *To be sung of a summer
night on the water I & II.* ELGAR: *There is sweet music; My love dwelt in a Northern land.* VAUGHAN
WILLIAMS: *3 Shakespearean songs: Full fathom five; The cloud-capp'd towers; Over hill, over dale.*
BRITTEN: *5 Flower songs, Op. 47.* Folksongs: arr. MOERAN: *The sailor and young Nancy.* Arr.
GRAINGER: *Brigg Fair; Londonderry air.* Arr. CHAPMAN: *Three ravens.* Arr. HOLST: *My sweetheart's
like Venus.* Arr. BAIRSTOW: *The oak and the ash.* Arr. STANFORD: *Quick! We have but a second.*
⊛ *** Coll. Dig. COLCD 104 [id.].

Opening with an enchanting performance of Stanford's *The blue bird* and followed by equally expressive
accounts of Delius's two wordless summer evocations, this most attractive recital ranges from Elgar and
Vaughan Williams, both offering splendid performances, to various arrangements of folksongs, less
fashionable today than they once were, but giving much pleasure here. The recording, made in the Great
Hall of University College, London, has an almost ideal ambience: words are clear, yet the vocal timbre
is full and natural. A highly recommendable anthology, and if you enjoy this you will enjoy other fine
compilations from this group: English madrigals on '*Flora gave me fairest flowers*' (COLCD 105) and
English church music on '*Faire is the Heaven*' (COLCD 107) and '*Hail gladdening light*' (COLCD
113).

Clare College, Cambridge, Choir and Orchestra, John Rutter

'*The Holly and the ivy*' (Carols): RUTTER: *Donkey carol; Mary's lullaby.* TRAD., arr. RUTTER: *King Jesus
hath a garden; Wexford carol;* (Flemish) *Cradle song; Child in a manger, In dulci jubilo; I saw three ships;
The holly and the ivy.* TRAD., arr. WOODWARD: *Up! Good Christian folk.* TRAD., arr. WILLCOCKS:
Gabriel's message; Ding! dong! merrily on high; Quelle est cette odeur agréable. TRAD., arr. PETTMAN: *I
saw a maiden.* DARKE: *In the bleak mid-winter.* PRAETORIUS: *The noble stem of Jesse; Omnis mundus
jocundetur.* TCHAIKOVSKY: *The crown of roses.* POSTON: *Jesus Christ the apple tree.* TRAD., arr.
VAUGHAN WILLIAMS: *Wassail song.*
⊛ (M) *** Decca 425 500-2.

This outstanding collection, recorded by Argo in the Lady Chapel at Ely Cathedral in 1979, is a model
of its kind. Rutter's admirers, among whom we can be counted, will surely want this disc for the
Christmas season. The opening arrangement of *King Jesus hath a garden,* using a traditional Dutch
melody, immediately sets the mood with its pretty flute decorations. Moreover Rutter's own gentle
syncopated *Donkey carol,* which comes fourth, is indispensable to any Christmas celebration. The whole
programme is a delight – not always especially ecclesiastical in feeling, but permeated throughout by the
spirit of Christmas joy.

Domingo, Plácido (tenor)

'Domingo favourites'; Arias from: DONIZETTI: L'elisir d'amore. VERDI: Ernani; Il trovatore; Aida; Nabucco; Don Carlos. HALEVY: La Juive. MEYERBEER: L'Africaine. BIZET: Les Pêcheurs de perles; Carmen. PUCCINI: Tosca; Manon Lescaut.
(Y/B) (M) *** DG Dig. 445 525-2 [id.].

The greater part of this collection is taken from a 1980 digital recital, recorded in connection with yet another gala in San Francisco. The result is as noble and resplendent a tenor recital as you will find. Domingo improves in detail even on the fine versions of some of these arias he had recorded earlier, and the finesse of the whole gains greatly from the sensitive direction of Giulini. Though the orchestra is a little backward, the honeyed beauty of the voice is given the greatest immediacy. The other items are taken from Domingo's complete sets of Don Carlos (with Abbado), Nabucco, Manon Lescaut and Tosca (with Sinopoli), and are well up to the high standards this great tenor consistently sets for himself.

Ferrier, Kathleen (contralto)

'The world of Kathleen Ferrier': TRAD.: Blow the wind southerly; The Keel Row; Ma bonny lad; Kitty my love. arr. BRITTEN: Come you not from Newcastle. HANDEL: Rodelinda: Art thou troubled? Serse: Ombra mai fu. GLUCK: Orfeo: What is life? MENDELSSOHN: Elijah: Woe unto them; O rest in the Lord. BACH: St Matthew Passion: Have mercy, Lord, on me. SCHUBERT: An die Musik; Gretchen am Spinnrade; Die junge Nonne; Der Musensohn. BRAHMS: Sapphische Ode; Botschaft. MAHLER: Rückert Lieder: Um Mitternacht.
❀ (B) (***) Decca mono 430 096-2; 430 096-4.

This selection, revised and expanded from the original LP issue, admirably displays Kathleen Ferrier's range, from the delightfully fresh folksongs to Mahler's Um Mitternacht in her celebrated recording with Bruno Walter and the VPO. The noble account of O rest in the Lord is one of the essential items now added, together with an expansion of the Schubert items (Die junge Nonne and An die Musik are especially moving). The CD transfers are remarkably trouble-free and the opening unaccompanied Blow the wind southerly has uncanny presence. The recital plays for 65 minutes and fortunately there are few if any technical reservations to be made here about the sound quality.

'The world of Kathleen Ferrier' Volume 2: TRAD.: Ye banks and braes; Drink to me only (both arr. QUILTER); I have a bonnet trimmmed with blue; Down by the Sally Gardens; The stuttering lovers (all arr. Hughes). PURCELL: The Fairy Queen: Hark! the echoing air. HANDEL: Atalanta: Like the love-lorn turtle. GLUCK: Orfeo: Che puro ciel. MAHLER: Rückert Lieder: Ich bin der Welt abhanden gekommen. SCHUMANN: Frauenliebe und Leben: Er, der Herrlichste von allen. BRAHMS: Geistliches Wiegenlied; Von ewiger Liebe. SCHUBERT: Du bist die Ruh; Rosamunde: Romance. BACH: Mass in B min.: Agnus Dei. HANDEL: Messiah: He was despised.
(N) (M) *** Decca mono 448 055-2; 448 055-4 [id.].

Volume II offers a comparable mixture, opening with more delightful folksongs, notably the charming 'stuttering lovers', although it is Ye banks and braes and Drink to me only that show the full richness of this glorious voice. Che puro ciel stands out among the opera arias for its simple eloquence, and the Brahms Geistliches Wiegenlied, with its somewhat wan viola obbligato, is gently ravishing. The passionate Du bist die Ruh, the Rosamunde Romance and Von ewiger Liebe come from a BBC acetate disc of her 1949 Edinburgh Festival recital with Bruno Walter at the piano, and here there is some uneven background noise and the quality deteriorates in the Brahms song. But the CD closes with one of her very last recordings, her unforgettably poignant He was despised, with those words given an uncanny presence.

Fischer-Dieskau, Dietrich (baritone)

'Fischer Dieskau Lieder Edition' (complete).
(Y/B) ❀ (BB) *** DG 447 500-2 (44) [id.].

To celebrate the seventieth birthday of the great German baritone, DG published a justifiably extravagant Lieder Edition, summing up the astonishing achievement of the greatest male Lieder singer of our time – although, in making such a claim, one must not forget Gérard Souzay's inestimable contribution in the area of French art-song. The set is offered at budget price, with two discs thrown in for good measure (44 CDs for the price of 42).

Each individual composer grouping is also available separately, still very competitively priced. With consistent artistry from all concerned and with first-class transfers, these CDs are self-recommending. We have discussed the Schubert in previous volumes, and much else, too, in individual issues. Fischer-Dieskau's mastery never ceases to amaze. Sample this set at almost any point and the same virtues emerge: characteristic beauty of vocal tone and an extraordinarily vivid power of characterization and vocal colouring. No less remarkable are his accompanists, including the incomparable Gerald Moore and Daniel Barenboim, whose sensitivity and command of keyboard colour make for consistently memorable results. The Liszt collection is especially valuable. As in a number of other fields, Liszt has been severely under-appreciated as a song composer. This collection of 43 songs plus an accompanied declamation should do much to right the balance. The sheer originality of thought and the ease of the lyricism are a regular delight. Fischer-Dieskau's concentration and inspiration never seem to falter, especially in the most famous of the songs, the *Petrarch Sonnets*, and Barenboim's accompaniments could hardly be more understanding.

SCHUBERT: Lieder (with Gerald Moore, piano): Volume 1 (1811–17); Volume 2 (1817–28). Song-cycles: *Die schöne Müllerin; Schwanengesang; Die Winterreise.*
(Y/B) (M) *** DG 437 214-2 (21) [id.].

Lieder, Volume I (1811–17): *Ein Leichenfantasie; Der Vatermörder* (1811); *Der Jüngling am Bache* (1812); *Totengräberlied; Die Schatten; Sehnsucht; Verklärung; Pensa, che questo istante* (1813); *Der Taucher* (1813–15); *Andenken; Geisternähe; Erinnerung; Trost, An Elisa; Die Betende; Lied aus der Ferne; Der Abend; Lied der Liebe; Erinnerungen; Adelaide; An Emma; Romanze: Ein Fräulein klagt' im finstern Turm; An Laura, als sie Klopstocks Auferstehungslied sang; Der Geistertanz; Das Mädchen aus der Fremde; Nachtgesang; Trost in Tränen; Schäfers Klagelied; Sehnsucht; Am See* (1814); *Auf einen Kirchhof; Als ich sie erröten sah; Das Bild; Der Mondabend* (1815); *Lodas Gespenst* (1816); *Der Sänger* (1815); *Die Erwartung* (1816); *Am Flusse; An Mignon; Nähe des Geliebten; Sängers Morgenlied; Amphiaraos; Das war ich; Die Sterne; Vergebliche Liebe; Liebesrausch; Sehnsucht der Liebe; Die erste Liebe; Trinklied; Stimme der Liebe; Naturgenuss; An die Freude; Der Jüngling am Bache; An den Mond; Die Mainacht; An die Nachtigall; An die Apfelbäume; Seufzer; Liebeständelei; Der Liebende; Der Traum; Die Laube; Meeres Stille; Grablied; Das Finden; Wandrers Nachtlied; Der Fischer; Erster Verlust; Die Erscheinung; Die Täuschung; Der Abend; Geist der Liebe; Tischlied; Der Liedler; Ballade; Abends unter der Linde; Die Mondnacht; Huldigung; Alles um Liebe; Das Geheimnis; An den Frühling; Die Bürgschaft; Der Rattenfänger; Der Schatzgräber; Heidenröslein; Bundeslied; An den Mond; Wonne der Wehmut; Wer kauft Liebesgötter?* (1815); *Der Goldschmiedsgesell* (1817); *Der Morgenkuss; Abendständchen: An Lina; Morgenlied: Willkommen, rotes Morgenlicht; Der Weiberfreund; An die Sonne; Tischlerlied; Totenkranz für ein Kind; Abendlied; Die Fröhlichkeit; Lob des Tokayers; Furcht der Geliebten; Das Rosenband; An Sie; Die Sommernacht; Die frühen Gräber; Dem Unendlichen; Ossians Lied nach dem Falle Nathos; Das Mädchen von Inistore; Labetrank der Liebe; An die Geliebte; Mein Gruss an den Mai; Skolie – Lasst im Morgenstrahl des Mai'n; Die Sternenwelten; Die Macht der Liebe; Das gestörte Glück; Die Sterne; Nachtgesang; An Rosa I: Warum bist du nicht hier?; An Rosa II: Rosa, denkst du an mich?; Schwanengesang; Der Zufriedene; Liane; Augenlied; Geistes-Gruss; Hoffnung; An den Mond; Rastlose Liebe; Erlkönig* (1815); *Der Schmetterling; Die Berge* (1819); *Genügsamkeit; An die Natur* (1815); *Klage; Morgenlied; Abendlied; Der Flüchtling; Laura am Klavier; Entzückung an Laura; Die vier Weltalter; Pflügerlied; Die Einsiedelei; An die Harmonie; Die Herbstnacht; Lied: Ins stille Land; Der Herbstabend; Der Entfernten; Fischerlied; Sprache der Liebe; Abschied von der Harfe; Stimme der Liebe; Entzückung; Geist der Liebe; Klage: Der Sonne steigt; Julius an Theone; Klage: Dein Silber schien durch Eichengrün; Frühlingslied; Auf den Tod einer Nachtigall; Die Knabenzeit; Winterlied; Minnelied; Die frühe Liebe; Blumenlied; Der Leidende; Seligkeit; Erntelied; Das grosse Halleluja; Die Gestirne; Die Liebesgötter; An den Schlaf; Gott im Frühling; Der gute Hirt; Die Nacht; Fragment aus dem Aeschylus* (1816); *An die untergehende Sonne* (1816/17); *An mein Klavier; Freude der Kinderjahre; Das Heimweh; An den Mond; An Chloen; Hochzeitlied; In der Mitternacht; Trauer der Liebe; Die Perle; Liedesend; Orpheus; Abschied; Rückweg; Alte Liebe rostet nie; Gesänge des Harfners aus Goethes Wilhelm Meister: Harfenspieler I: Wer sich der Einsamkeit ergibt; Harfenspieler II: An die Türen will ich schleichen; Harfenspieler III: Wer nie sein Brot mit Tränen ass. Der König in Thule; Jägers Abendlied; An Schwager Kronos; Der Sänger am Felsen; Lied: Ferne von der grossen Stadt; Der Wanderer; Der Hirt; Lied eines Schiffers an die Dioskuren; Geheimnis; Zum Punsche; Am Bach im Frühling* (1816); *An eine Quelle* (1817); *Bei dem Grabe, meines Vaters; Am Grabe Anselmos; Abendlied; Zufriedenheit; Herbstlied; Skolie: Mädchen entsiegelten; Lebenslied; Lieden der Trennung* (1816); *Alinde; An die Laute* (1827); *Frohsinn; Die Liebe; Trost; Der Schäfer und der Reiter* (1817); *Lob der Tränen* (1821); *Der Alpenjäger; Wie Ulfru fischt; Fahrt zum Hades; Schlaflied; Die Blumensprache; Die abgeblühte Linde; Der Flug der Zeit; Der Tod und das Mädchen; Das Lied vom Reifen; Täglich zu singen; Am Strome; Philoktet; Memnon; Auf dem See; Ganymed; Der Jüngling und der Tod; Trost im Liede* (1817).

(Y/B) (B) *** DG 437 215-2 (9) [id.].

Lieder, Volume II (1817–28): *An die Musik; Pax vobiscum; Hänflings Liebeswerbung; Auf der Donau; Der Schiffer; Nach einem Gewitter; Fischerlied; Das Grab; Der Strom; An den Tod; Abschied; Die Forelle; Gruppe aus dem Tartarus; Elysium; Atys; Erlafsee; Der Alpenjäger; Der Kampf; Der Knabe in der Wiege* (1817); *Auf der Riesenkoppe; An den Mond in einer Herbstnacht; Grablied für die Mutter; Einsamkeit; Der Blumenbrief; Das Marienbild* (1818); *Litanei auf das Fest Allerseelen* (1816); *Blondel zu Marien; Das Abendrot; Sonett I: Apollo, lebet noch dein Hold verlangen; Sonett II: Allein, nachdenken wie gelähmt vom Krampfe; Sonett III: Nunmehr, da Himmel, Erde schweigt; Vom Mitleiden Mariä* (1818) ; *Die Gebüsche; Der Wanderer; Abendbilder; Himmelsfunken; An die Freunde; Sehnsucht; Hoffnung; Der Jüngling am Bache; Hymne I: Wenige wissen das Geheimnis der Liebe; Hymne II: Wenn ich ihn nur hab; Hymne III: Wenn alle untreu werden; Hymne IV: Ich sag es jedem; Marie; Beim Winde; Die Sternennächte; Trost; Nachtstück; Prometheus; Strophe aus Die Götter Griechenlands* (1819); *Nachthymne; Die Vögel; Der Knabe; Der Fluss; Abendröte; Der Schiffer; Die Sterne; Morgenlied* (1820); *Frühlingsglaube* (1822); *Des Fräuleins Liebeslauschen* (1820); *Orest auf Tauris* (1817); *Der entsühnte Orest; Freiwilliges Versinken; Der Jüngling auf dem Hügel* (1820); *Sehnsucht* (1817); *Der zürnenden Diana; Im Walde* (1820); *Die gefangenen Sänger; Der Unglückliche; Versunken; Geheimes; Grenzen der Menschheit* (1821); *Der Jüngling an der Quelle* (1815); *Der Blumen Schmerz* (1821); *Sei mir gegrüsst; Herr Josef Spaun, Assessor in Linz; Der Wachtelschlag Ihr Grab; Nachtviolen; Heliopolis I: Im kalten, rauhen Norden; Heliopolis II: Fels auf Felsen hingewälzet; Selige Welt; Schwanengesang: Wie klage'ich's aus; Du liebst mich nicht; Die Liebe hat gelogen; Todesmusik; Schatzgräbers Begehr; An die Leier; Im Haine; Der Musensohn; An die Entfernte; Am Flusse; Willkommen und Abschied* (1822); *Wandrers Nachtlied: Ein Gleiches; Der zürnende Barde* (1823); *Am See* (1822/3); *Viola; Drang in die Ferne; Der Zwerg; Wehmut; Lied: Die Mutter Erde; Auf dem Wasser zu singen; Pilgerweise; Das Geheimnis; Der Pilgrim; Dass sie hier gewesen; Du bist die Ruh; Lachen und Weinen; Greisengesang* (1823); *Dithyrambe; Der Sieg; Abendstern; Auflösung; Gondelfahrer* (1824); *Glaube, Hoffnung und Liebe* (1828); *Im Abendrot; Der Einsame* (1824); *Des Sängers Habe; Totengräbers Heimwehe; Der blinde Knabe; Nacht und Träume; Normans Gesang; Lied des gefangenen Jägers; Im Walde; Auf der Bruck; Das Heimweh; Die Allmacht; Fülle der Liebe; Wiedersehn; Abendlied für die Entfernte; Szene I aus dem Schauspiel Lacrimas; Am mein Herz; Der liebliche Stern* (1825); *Im Jänner 1817 (Tiefes Leid); Am Fenster; Sehnsucht; Im Freien; Fischerweise; Totengräberweise; Im Frühling; Lebensmut; Um Mitternacht; Über Wildemann* (1826); *Romanze des Richard Löwenherz* (1827); *Trinklied; Ständchen; Hippolits Lied; Gesang (An Silvia); Der Wanderer an den Mond; Das Zügenglöcklein; Bei dir allein; Irdisches Glück; Wiegenlied* (1826); *Der Vater mit dem Kind; Jägers Liebeslied; Schiffers Scheidelied; L'incanto degli occhi; Il traditor deluso; Il modo di prender moglie; Das Lied im Grünen; Das Weinen; Vor meiner Wiege; Der Wallensteiner Lanzknecht beim Trunk; Der Kreuzzug; Das Fischers Liebesglück* (1827); *Der Winterabend; Die Sterne; Herbst; Widerschein* (1828); *Abschied von der Erde* (1825/6).

(Y/B) (B) *** DG 437 225-2 (9) [id.].

Lieder, Volume III: Song-cycles: *Die Schöne Müllerin; Schwanengesang; Die Winterreise.*

(Y/B) (M) *** DG 437 235-2 (3) [id.].

SCHUMANN: Lieder (with Christoph Eschenbach, piano): *Myrten, Op. 25/1–3; 5–8; 13; 15–19; 21–2; 25–6. Lieder und Gesänge, Op. 27/1–5; Op. 51/4; Op. 77/1 & 5; Op. 96/1–3; Op. 98/2, 4, 6 & 8; Op. 127/2–3. Gedichte, Op. 30/1–3; Op. 119/2. Gesänge, Op. 31/1 & 3; Op. 83/1 & 3; Op. 89/1–5; Op. 95/2; Op. 107/3 & 6; Op. 142/1, 2 & 4; Schön Hedwig, Op. 106. 6 Gedichte aus dem Liederbuch eines Malers, Op. 36. 12 Gedichte aus Rückerts Liebesfrühling, Op. 37. Liederkreis, Op. 39. 5 Lieder, Op. 40. Romanzen und Balladen, Op. 45/1–3; Op. 49/1–2; Op. 53/1–3; Op. 64/3; Belsatzar, Op. 57. Liederkreis, Op. 24. 12 Gedichte, Op. 35. Dichterliebe, Op. 48. Spanisches Liederspiel, Op. 74/6, 7 & 10. Liederalbum für die Jugend, Op. 79; Der Handschuh, Op. 87. 6 Gedichte von Nikolaus Lenau und Requiem (Anhang, No. 7), Op. 90. Minnnespiel, Op. 101. 4 Husarenlieder, Op. 117. Heitere Gesänge, Op. 125/1–3. Spanische Liebeslieder, Op. 138/2, 3, 5 & 7. Balladen, Op. 122/1–2. Sechs frühe Lieder, Op. posth. (WoO 21).*

(Y/B) (B) *** DG 445 660-2 (6) [id.].

BRAHMS: Lieder (with Daniel Barenboim, piano): *Gesänge, Op. 3/2–6; Op. 6/2–6; Mondnacht, Op. 7/1–4 & 6; Op. 43/1–4; Op. 46/1–4; Op. 70/1–4; Op. 71/1–5; Op. 72/2–5. Lieder und Romanzen, Op. 14/1–8; Gedichte, Op. 19/1–3, 3 & 5; Lieder und Gesänge, Op. 32/1–9; Op. 57/2–8; Op. 58/1–8; Op. 59/1–4, 6–7; Op. 63/1–9; Romanzen, Op. 33/1–15; Lieder, Op. 47/1–4; Op. 48/1, 2, 5–7; Op. 49/1–5; Op. 85/1–2, 4–6; Op. 86/2–5; Op. 94/1–3 & 5; Op. 95/2, 3 & 7; Op. 96/1–4; Op. 97/1–3, 5–6; Op. 105/4–5; Op. 106/1–5; Op. 107/1–2 & 4. Neuen Gesänge, Op. 69/3, 5 & 7. Vier ernste Gesänge, Op. 121.*

(Y/B) (B) *** DG 447 501-2 (6) [id.].

LISZT: Lieder (with Daniel Barenboim, piano): *Der Alpenjäger; Anfangs wollt' ich fast verzagen; Angiolin dal biondo crin; Blume und Duft; Comment, disaient-ils; Die drei Zigeuner; Du bist wie eine Blume; Der du von dem Himmel bist; Enfant, si j'étais roi; Eine Fichtenbaum steht einsam; Es muss ein Wunderbares sein; Es rauschen die Winde; Der Fischerknabe; Gastibelza; Gestorben war ich; Der Hirt; Hohe Liebe; Ich möchte hingehn; Ihr Glocken von Marling; Im Rhein, im schönen Strome; In Liebeslust; J'ai perdu ma force et ma vie; Klinge leise, mein Lied; Lässt mich ruhen; Die Lorelei; Morgens steh' ich auf und frage; Oh! quand je dors; O Lieb, so lang du lieben kannst; Petrarch sonnets Nos. 1–3; Schwebe, schwebe blaues Auge; S'il est un charmant gazon; Die stille Wasserrose; Des Tages laute Stimmen schweigen; La tombe et la rose; Der traurige Mönch; Uber allen Gipfeln ist Ruh; Die Vätergruft; Vergiftet sind meine Lieder; Le vieux vagabond; Wer nie sein Brot mit Tränen ass; Wieder möcht' ich dir Begegnen; Wie singt die Lerche schön.*
(Y/B) (M) *** DG 447 508-2 (3) [id.].

Richard STRAUSS: Lieder (with Wolfgang Sawallisch, piano): *5 kleine Lieder, Op. 69; Lieder, Op. 10/2–7; Op. 15/2 & 5; Op. 17/2; Op. 19/1–6; Op. 26/1–2; Op. 27/1, 3 & 4; Op. 29/1 & 3; Op. 31/4; Op. 32/1–5; Op. 36/1 & 4; Op. 37/1–2, 5–6; Op. 49/6; Op. 56/1 & 3; Op. 67/6. Schlichte Weisen, Op. 21; Vier Gesang, Op. 87.*
(Y/B) (M) *** DG 447 512-2 (2) [id.].

WOLF: Lieder (with Daniel Barenboim, piano): *23 Eichendorf Lieder; 42 Goethe Lieder; 7 Heine Lieder; 4 Lenau Lieder; 3 Gedichte von Michelangelo; Mörike Lieder* (complete); *6 Reinick Lieder; 4 Gedichte von Robert Reinick. 3 Gedichte nach Shakespeare und Lord Byron.* Miscellaneous Lieder by Peitl; Von Matthisson; Körner; Herlossohn; Hebbel; Von Fallersleben; Sturm; Von Scheffel.
(Y/B) (B) *** DG 447 515-2 (6) [id.].

Flagstad, Kirsten (soprano)

Kirsten Flagstad Edition

Kirsten Flagstad Edition (complete).
(Y/B) (M) **(*) Decca stereo/mono 440 490-2 (5) [id.].

MAHLER: *Kindertotenlieder; Lieder eines fahrenden Gesellen* (with VPO, Boult). WAGNER: *Wesendonck Lieder* (with VPO, Knappertsbusch) (440 491-2).
SIBELIUS: Songs: *Arioso; Autumn evening (Höstkväll); Black roses (Svata rosor); But my bird is nowhere to be seen (Men min fågel märks dock icke); Come away, death (Komm nu hit, död!); The diamond on the March snow (Diamanten på Marssnön); Did I dream? (Var det en dröm); The first kiss (Den första kyssne); The girl returned from meeting her lover (Flickan kom ifrån sin älsklings möte); On a veranda by the sea (På verandan vit havet); Sigh, rushes, sigh (Säv, säv, susa); Since then I have stopped asking (Se'n har jag ej frågat mera); Spring fleets fast (Våren flyktar hastigt); To the night (Til kvällen).* GRIEG: *Autumn storms (Efteråsstormen); I give my song to the spring (Jeg giver mit digt til våren); I would like a waistcoat of silk (Og jeg vil ha mig en silkevest); To you (Til én) I & II.* Arne EGGEN: *Praise to the eternal spring of life (Aere det evige forår i livet).* Eyvind ALNAES: *About love (Nu brister alle de kløfter); A February morning at the Gulf (Februarmorgen ved Golfen); A hundred violins (De hundrede fioliner); Yearnings of spring (Vårlængsler).* Harald LIE: *The key (Nykelen); The letter (Skinnvengbrev)* (with LSO, Oivin Fjeldstad) (440 492-2).
GRIEG: *Haugtussa (The Mountain maid; song-cycle), Op. 67;* Songs: *Ambition (Der ærgjerrige); Among roses (Millom rosor); At Gjaetle Brook (Ved Gjætle-Bekken); Blueberry slope (Blåbær-Li); Children's dance (A hipp og hoppe); A dream (En drøm); The encounter (Møte); Enticement (Det syng); Eros; The first meeting (Det første møte); Fra Monte Pincio (from Monte Pincio); High up in the leafy hills (I liden højt der oppe); I give my song to the spring (Jeg giver mit digt til våren); I love you (Jeg elsker Dig); In the boat (Der gynger en Båd på Bølge); The little hut (Hytten); Little Kirsten (Liten Kirsten); The little maiden (Veslemøy); Love (Elsk); Sorrowful day (Vond Dag); The water-lily (Med en vanlilje); With a primrose (Med en primulaveris)* (with Edwin McArthur) (mono 440 493-2).
BRAHMS: *Vier ernste Gesänge (4 Serious songs);* Lieder: *Alte Liebe; Am dem Kirchhofe; Am Sonntag Morgen; Bei dir sind meine Gedanken; Dein blaues Auge; Treue Liebe; Wie Melodien zieht es mir; Wir waldelten.* SCHUBERT: *Am Grabe Anselmos; An Der Erlkönig; Ave Maria; Das Mädchens Klage; Dem Unendlichen* (with Edwin McArthur) (mono 440 494-2).
WAGNER: (with (i) Oslo PO or Norwegian State RO, Fjeldstad; (ii) VPO, Knappertsbusch; (iii) VPO, Solti): (i) *Götterdämmerung: Starke Scheite schichtet mir dort (Immolation scene);* (ii) *Lohengrin: Einsam in trüben Tagen. Parsifal: Ich sah das Kind. Die Walküre, Act I: Der Männer Sippe; Du bist der*

Lenz; (iii) Act II: *Siegmund! Sieh' auf mich! (Todesverkündigung)* (stereo/mono 440 495-2).

The Decca producer John Culshaw was (understandably) a great admirer of the art of Kirsten Flagstad and it was he who persuaded her to come out of retirement in the mid-1950s. Not only did she contribute to Solti's great *Ring* cycle, singing the part of Fricka (for the first time) in *Das Rheingold*, but other recordings were planned, and most of them are here. She had recorded some of this repertoire earlier for EMI when she was in her prime in the mid-1940s, notably the Grieg and Norwegian songs. Yet the later, Decca recordings, which have more faithful sound, demonstrate again her masterly sense of pacing and of vocal colour and her command of evocation. These and the equally fine Sibelius songs are discussed more fully under their composer entries.

In Lieder, Flagstad may not have the evenness of line or bring the perception of word-meanings of the greatest German Lieder singers, but her voice is admirably suited to the *Four Serious songs* of Brahms, of which the third, *O Tod, O Tod, wie bitter bist du,* is most deeply felt, while among the other Brahms songs *Am Sonntag Morgen* brings wonderfully radiant tone and *Dein blaues Auge* is very touching. In Schubert, although the voice at times seems less than wieldy, the operatic drama of *Der Erlkönig* is as memorable as the gently ravishing cantilena of *Am Grabe Anselmos* and the hardly less sympathetic *Alte Liebe*. Here, as elsewhere, Edwin McArthur's accompaniments are a model of support for the great voice and make a sensitive and imaginative impression in their own right. The mono recordings, made at Decca's West Hampstead studios in the spring and late autumn of 1956, are naturally atmospheric, and the ear would hardly guess the sound was not early stereo. The stereo Wagner recordings with Knappertsbusch are uneven, although Flagstad was a superb Sieglinde, and her glorious voice is perfectly suited to the rich inspiration of the *Wesendonk Lieder*. Moreover the excerpt from Solti's partial recording of Act II of *Die Walküre* and the earlier (mono) Immolation scene from Fjeldstad's 1956 *Götterdämmerung* provide an outstanding reminder of one of the finest Brünnhildes of our time. Throughout this set (which presents the five individual CDs in a slipcase) the transfers are consistently vivid, and the documentation is good, with translations provided throughout.

'The Flagstad Legacy': Volume 1: Opera arias from: BEETHOVEN: *Fidelio.* WAGNER: *Götterdämmerung; Lohengrin; Parsifal; Tannhäuser; Tristan und Isolde; Die Walküre.* WEBER: *Oberon.* Songs and arias by ALNAES; BEETHOVEN; BISHOP; BRAHMS; BULL; FRANZ; GRIEG; GRONDAHL; HURUM; LIE; NOR-DRAAK; PALENZ; ROSENFELDT; SCHUBERT; SINDING; R. STRAUSS; THOMMESEN; THRANE. (N) (***) Simax mono PSC 1821 (3).

These three Simax CDs make up the first of five sets, running to 13 CDs in all, which promise the most comprehensive overview of this great singer's legacy on records. It comes with a substantial article by Arne Dørumsgaard, himself a composer and translator. The contents range from the period of the First World War through to 1941, though the 1940 *Haugtussa* is not included. There is a thrilling *Dich, teure Halle* from *Tannhäuser*, recorded in New York in 1935 (hardly surprising that Flagstad took America by storm) and a *Liebestod* from the same year, as well as the 1936 Copenhagen recordings of Grieg and other Norwegian songs. There are some Philadelphia and San Francisco Opera recordings under Ormandy with Melchior, and many feature her lifelong accompanist, Edwin McArthur. In Norwegian song, Grieg is not the whole story even if he is most of it. Flagstad included a number of her other and less familiar countrymen in her discography. These include Ole Bull, the violinist-composer who encouraged Grieg's family to send the boy to Leipzig, and whose *Sæterjentens Søndag* ('The Herd Girl's Sunday') would have been mandatory at the time. Eyvind Alnæs's song, *Lykkan mellem To Mennseskor* ('Happiness between two people') was also a favourite of hers. Dørumsgaard tells of the 'disarming simplicity' of her 1929 version, the finest of her early electrics, released 'before fame struck'. It is indeed quite amazing and fresher than the 1936 record, which also suffers from the rather dry acoustic of the Copenhagen studio. The Simax will be indispensable to the serious collector, both for its comprehensiveness and for the generally high standard of its transfers.

Fretwork

'The English Viol' (with Catherine Bott, soprano, Jeremy Budd, treble, Michael Chance, counter-tenor and (i) Red Byrd): ANON.: *The dark is my delight; Allemande and Galliard* (from *Lumley Books*); *In paradise.* FERRABOSCO I: *In Nomine a 5.* HOLBORNE: *Pavan and Galliard.* BYRD: *Christe redemptor a 4; In nomine a 5 No. 4; Ah silly soul.* DOWLAND: *Lachrimae gementes; Semper Dowland, semper dolens; M. Bucton his Galiard.* FERRABOSCO II: *Pavan and Alman.* GIBBONS: *Fantasia a 6 No. 2; Fantasia a 3 for the 'Great dooble bass'; The silver swan; Fantasia a 2. The cry of London, Part II.* LAWES: *Fantazy a 5 on the playnesong in G min.; Gather ye rosebuds; Aire a 6 in G min.* LOCKE: *Consort of 4 parts in F.* PURCELL: *Fantasia a 4 in B flat No. 5; In nomine a 6.*

(Y/B) ❀ (M) *** Virgin Veritas/EMI Dig. VER5 61173-2 [id.].

Fretwork was one of the really outstanding groups of artists which Virgin Records promoted from their inception and they offer viol playing which is in a class of its own. This superb 77–minute anthology draws on recordings made between 1988 and 1994: the excellence is unvarying: these players catch perfectly the spirit of the later-Tudor and early-Stuart periods. The playing itself has immaculate ensemble and intonation, restrained feeling and great freshness. Much of the music is relatively austere but the effect on the listener is hypnotic. The special character of Elizabethan romantic melancholy is well caught by Dowland (especially in his autobiographical *Semper Dowland, semper dolens*), but there is lively part-writing too, notably from Lawes and Locke. Lawes's *Fantasy a 5 'on the playnesong'* is touchingly expressive, the music's sonority coloured subtly by an (uncredited) chamber organ continuo, while the two pieces by Purcell are also quietly moving. The instrumental music is sprinkled with brief, cheerful, vocal items, delightfully sung, and the selection includes an excerpt from *The Cry of London*, where the vocal group, Red Byrd, offer every conceivable commodity for sale, from a pair of oars and a good sausage to bread and meat 'for the prisoners of the Marshalsea'. Altogether an ideal introduction to a period in English history which was musically very productive. The recording could hardly be bettered.

Gheorghiu, Angela (soprano)

Arias (with Ch. & O of Teatro Regio, Turin, John Mauceri) from: VERDI: *Falstaff*. MASSENET: *Hérodiade; Chérubin*. CATALANI: *La Wally*. BELLINI: *I Capuleti e i Montecchi*. PUCCINI: *La Bohème*. BOITO: *Mefistofele*. GOUNOD: *Faust*. DONIZETTI: *Don Pasquale*. GRIGORIU: *Valurile Dunarii*. (N) **(*) Decca Dig. 452 417-2 [id.].

The new star of Decca's *La Traviata* here makes her solo début in a recital which offers much lovely singing – the very opening excerpt from Verdi's *Falstaff* brings a ravishing line (and some fine orchestral playing, too) and the Massenet aria is quite melting and full of charm. But there is too little difference of characterization between the different heroines, not enough fiery passion or, indeed, displays of temperament, which means that the *Jewel song* from *Faust* fails to sparkle as it should. Nevertheless the sample of Mimì in *La Bohème* promises well. The back-up here, from John Mauceri and the Turin chorus and orchestra, is impressive, and so is the glowing Decca recording.

Gheorghiu, Angela (soprano), Roberto Alagna (tenor)

Opera arias and duets from: MASCAGNI: *L'amico Fritz*. MASSENET: *Manon*. DONIZETTI: *Anna Bolena; Don Pasquale*. OFFENBACH: *La belle Hélène*. BERNSTEIN: *West Side story*. GOUNOD: *Faust*. G. CHARPENTIER: *Louise*. BERLIOZ: *Les Troyens*. PUCCINI: *La Bohème*. (N) *** EMI Dig. CDC5 56117-2 [id.].

If Angela Gheorghiu's solo début is a little disappointing, this record of duets with her husband, Roberto Alagna, is not. Clearly they are a natural couple as artists as well as human beings. There is much here to delight, not least the opening *Cherry duet* from *L'amico Fritz*, in which the voices blend delightfully. *Manon* brings a comparable symbiosis, and the Donizetti items are as winning as the unexpected excerpt from *Les Troyens*. Solo arias also come off well here, notably Gheorghiu's aria from *Anna Bolena*, which suits her exactly; Alagna turns in a stylishly heady account of the delicious Waltz song from *La belle Hélène*. The excerpt from *West Side story* is tenderly touching but, as nearly always, the voices sound too mature for these star-crossed young lovers. Again the promise of that future complete *Bohème* comes in the closing all-too-short *O soave fanciulla*. First-rate accompaniments under Richard Armstrong and superb sound contribute to the great success of this immensely pleasurable operatic hour.

Jo, Sumi (soprano)

Virtuoso arias (with Monte Carlo PO, Olmi) from: ROSSINI: *Il barbiere di Siviglia*. BELLINI: *La sonnambula*. DONIZETTI: *Lucia di Lammermoor*. DELIBES: *Lakmé*. R. STRAUSS: *Ariadne auf Naxos*. VERDI: *Rigoletto*. MEYERBEER: *Dinorah*. BERNSTEIN: *Candide*. MOZART: *Die Zauberflöte* (with O de Paris Ens., Jordan). YOUNG-HA HOON: Song: *Boribat*. (Y/B) *** Erato/Warner Dig. 4509 97239-2 [id.].

This is among the most brilliant and commanding recitals of coloratura arias made in the 1990s.

Though the recording brings out a slight flutter in Sumi Jo's lovely voice, the sweetness and tenderness of her singing, so different from the hardness of many coloratura sopranos, is formidably established over the widest range of arias. Sumi Jo's clarity, with no hint of stridency, coupled with a dreamy quality in the delivery, reminds one of the remark of an opera critic many years ago, that Galli-Curci sounded like 'a nightingale half-asleep'. Not that there is anything sleepy in Sumi Jo's singing, which is beautifully controlled. That is so both in firework arias like Rosina's *Una voce poco fa* from Rossini's *Barber* and over the sustained spans of the big aria in Bellini's *La sonnambula* (full recitative leading to *Ah non credea mirarti* and *Ah! non giunge*) and the Mad scene from Donizetti's *Lucia di Lammermoor*. Though *Glitter and be gay* from Bernstein's *Candide* lacks a little in fun, Delibes' *Bell song* from *Lakmé* is aptly sensuous and Zerbinetta's aria from *Ariadne auf Naxos* aptly extrovert, while the reading of the Queen of the Night's second aria from Mozart's *Zauberflöte* is lighter and even faster than with Solti in his Decca set. With tenderness and poise a regular ingredient alongside brilliance, not least in the honeyed sounds of the final Korean song, all ten arias are to be cherished. The voice is well caught, though the orchestral accompaniment has less presence.

'Carnaval!' (with ECO, Richard Bonynge): French coloratura arias from: OFFENBACH: *Un mari à la porte*. MASSENET: *Don César de Bazan*. Félicien DAVID: *La Perle du Brésil*. GRETRY: *L'Amant jaloux*. BALFE: *Le puits d'amour*. MESSAGER: *Madame Chrysanthème*. THOMAS: *Le songe d'une nuit d'été*. ADAM: *Les pantins de Violette*; *Si j'étais roi*. HEROLD: *Le pré aux clercs*. DELIBES: *Le roi l'a dit*. BOIELDIEU: *La fête du village voisin*. MASSE: *La Reine Topaze: Carnaval de Venise*.
(Y/B) ✹ *** Decca Dig. 440 679-2 [id.].

If anything, this singing is even more astonishing than Sumi Jo's Erato recital, above. The music may be more frivolous, but what delectable freshness and vocal sparkle there is in every number, and this repertoire is far rarer. After the frothy Offenbach introduction, the nightingale lightness and precision in Massenet's *Sevillana* from *Don César de Bazan* is matched by the vocal poise in the *Couplets du Mysoli* from David's *La Perle du Brésil*, with William Bennett playing the flute solo. Equally, Jo trills along seductively in Adam's *Chanson du canari*, in which the song's pensive quality is also nicely caught. This is Galli-Curci territory, and Sumi Jo doesn't come second best; moreover her voice is fuller and warmer. The softness and delicious ease of her pianissimo top notes also recall Rita Streich at her finest, in both Adam and Thomas, and in the Grétry *Je romps la chaîne qui m'engage*. Her ravishingly easy legato in Balfe's *Rêves d'amour* is a joy, while Hérold's *Jours de mon enfance* brings a duet with a solo violin (the excellent Anthony Marwood), and here one is reminded of the young Sutherland. Delibes' *Waltz song* from *Le roi l'a dit* is bewitching, and the recital ends with a sparkling *Boléro* of Boieldieu and an unforgettable interpolation of the *Carnival of Venice* into an aria by Victor Massé, with astonishingly free divisions. Throughout, Bonynge provides stylish and beautifully pointed accompaniments, as he has done for Sutherland in the past, and the Decca recording could hardly be bettered.

New College, Oxford, Choir, Higginbottom

'O Sing unto the Lord' (with Instrumental Ens. led by Roy Goodman): VAUGHAN WILLIAMS: *O Clap your hands* (motet). STANFORD: *Magnificat and Nunc dimittis in G*. TAVERNER: *Mater Christi* (motet). PURCELL: *O Sing unto the Lord* (Verse anthem). BAINTON: *And I saw a new heaven*. BRITTEN: *Missa brevis*. MONTEVERDI: *Beatus vir*. HARVEY: *I love the Lord*.
✹ *** Proudsound PROUCD 114 02; *PROU 114* [id.].

It is difficult to conceive of a better or more rewarding collection of (mainly British) church music than this, marvellously sung by this fine choir of 16 trebles and 12 men. The recording, made in New College Chapel, is ideally balanced, very real indeed, and offers the most beautiful choral textures, used over the widest range of dynamic. The programme opens quite spectacularly with Vaughan Williams's brief but ambitious setting of Psalm 47 for double chorus, brass, percussion and organ (a demonstration item if ever there was one) and continues with Stanford's inspired *Magnificat and Nunc dimittis in G*. Then the programme ranges from Taverner's fine motet, *Mater Christi*, written some 400 years earlier, to Harvey's rich modern setting of Psalm 16, with its satisfyingly pungent dissonances.

Oberlin, Russell (counter-tenor), Seymour Barab (piano)

Troubadour and trouvère songs, Volume 1: BRULE: *Cil qui d'amor me conseille*. DE BORNEIL: *Reis glorios, verais lums e clartatz*. DANIEL: *Chanson do – Ih mot son plan e prim*. D'EPINAL: *Commensmens de dolce saison bele*. RIQUIER: *Ples de tristor, marritz e doloires*; DE VENTADOUR: *Can vei la lauzeta mover*.

(Y/B) *** Lyrichord LEMS 8001 [id.].

It is good to see the legendary Russell Oberlin return to the catalogue. Older readers will recall his Covent Garden appearance as Oberon in Britten's *Midsummer Night's Dream*. Unfortunately his concert career was cut short and he has since pursued a distinguished career as a scholar. This 1958 recital of *Troubadour and trouvère songs* first appeared on the Experiences Anonymes label and, like so many of his all-too-few recordings (including an incredible Handel aria disc), has long been sought after. This voice was quite unique, a *real* counter-tenor of exquisite quality and, above all, artistry. The disc is expertly annotated and is of quite exceptional interest. LEMS stands for Lyrichord Early Music Series, and the discs we have so far heard (and on which we will report in the next edition) are artistically impressive.

Oxford Camerata, Jeremy Summerly

'*Lamentations*': WHITE: *Lamentations*. TALLIS: *Lamentations, Sets I & II*. PALESTRINA: *Lesson I for Maundy Thursday*. LASSUS: *Lessons I & III for Maundy Thursday*. Estâvão DE BRITO: *Lesson I for Good Friday*.

❀ (BB) *** Naxos Dig. 8.550572 [id.].

On the bargain Naxos label come nearly 70 minutes of sublime polyphony, beautifully sung by the fresh-toned Oxford Camerata under Jeremy Summerly. All these *Lamentations* (*Lessons* simply means collection of verses) are settings from the Old Testament book, *The Lamentations of Jeremiah*. They were intended for nocturnal use and are usually darkly intense in feeling. The English and Italian *Lamentations* have their own individuality, but the most striking of all is the *Good Friday Lesson* by the Portuguese composer, Estâvão de Brito. This is very direct and strong in feeling for, as the anonymous insert-note writer points out, Portugal was under Spanish subjugation at the time and de Brito effectively uses dissonance at the words *non est lex* ('there is no law') to assert his nationalistic defiance. The recorded sound is vividly beautiful within an ideal ambience.

Oxford Pro Musica Singers, Michael Smedley

20th-century sacred choral music: TAVENER: *Annunciation; Ikon of the Nativity; The Lamb; A Nativity; Today the Virgin; The Lord's prayer; Many years; Wedding prayer; He that hath entered Heaven; The acclamation.* PART: *Magnificat; Summa.* GORECKI: *Euntes Ibant; Totus tuus; Amen.*

❀ *** Proudsound Dig. PROUCD 136 [id.].

The ten pieces by John Tavener – although written at different times over the last decade and a half – make a remarkably cohesive whole when heard in the sequence presented here. They are framed by the *Annunciation* which opens gently and ethereally with a quartet of solo voices placed in the distance and answered immediately and powerfully by the full choir, and the *Acclamation* which reaches a climax of great splendour. The haunting carol, *The Lamb*, is the most familiar of these works, but the most ambitious setting of all, *He that hath entered Heaven*, brings within its stillness and beauty the tinkling sounds of a set of suspended handbells, used very discreetly, until the treble line, released, soars rapturously. Arvo Pärt's *Magnificat* is more mellifluously static but undoubtedly eloquent, and it makes a positive statement of faith, as does the *Summa* (a setting of the Creed) with its lines flowing like the waves of the ocean. Górecki's *Euntes Ibant et Flebant* is a 12-part Psalm setting with phrases mystically repeated over a sustained pedal note, bringing some scrumptious dissonance. *Totus tuus* is a characteristic affirmation. Finally comes a similarly elliptical *Amen* that has much in common with Barber's *Adagio for strings*. The whole programme is gloriously sung, and this well-rehearsed group of 32 singers sustains tension as movingly at pianissimo level as they do in the great arching climaxes. The dynamic range is wide and the very generous resonance of St Barnabas' Church, Oxford, adds atmosphere and beauty to the sound without clouding the focus.

Luciano Pavarotti (tenor)

'*Tutto Pavarotti*': VERDI: *Aida: Celeste Aida. Luisa Miller: Quando le sere al placido. La Traviata: De' miei bollenti spiriti. Il Trovatore: Ah si ben mio; Di quella pira. Rigoletto: La donna è mobile. Un ballo in maschera: La rivedrà nell'estasi.* DONIZETTI: *L'elisir d'amore: Una furtiva lagrima. Don Pasquale: Com'è gentil.* PONCHIELLI: *La Gioconda: Cielo e mar.* FLOTOW: *Martha: M'appari.* BIZET: *Carmen: Flower song.* MASSENET: *Werther: Pourquoi me réveiller.* MEYERBEER: *L'Africana: O paradiso.* BOITO:

Mefistofele: Dai campi dai prati. LEONCAVALLO: *Pagliacci: Vesti la giubba.* MASCAGNI: *Cavalleria Rusticana: Addio alla madre.* GIORDANO: *Fedora: Amor ti vieta.* PUCCINI: *La Fanciulla del West: Ch'ella mi creda. Tosca: E lucevan le stelle. Manon Lescaut: Donna non vidi mai. La Bohème: Che gelida manina. Turandot: Nessun dorma.* ROSSINI: *Stabat Mater: Cuius animam.* BIZET: *Agnus Dei.* ADAM: *O holy night.* DI PAPUA: *O sole mio.* TOSTI: *A vucchella.* CARDILLO: *Core 'ngrato.* TAGLIAFERRI: *Passione.* CHERUBINI: *Mamma.* DALLA: *Caruso.*
(M) *** Decca 425 681-2; 425 681-4 (2) [id.].

Opening with Dalla's *Caruso*, a popular song in the Neapolitan tradition, certainly effective, and no more vulgar than many earlier examples of the genre, this selection goes on through favourites like *O sole mio* and *Core 'ngrato* and one or two religious items, notably Adam's *Cantique de Noël*, to the hard core of operatic repertoire. Beginning with *Celeste Aida*, recorded in 1972, the selection of some 22 arias from complete sets covers Pavarotti's distinguished recording career with Decca from 1969 (*Cielo e mar* and the *Il Trovatore* excerpts) to 1985, although the opening song was, of course, recorded digitally in 1988. The rest is a mixture of brilliantly transferred analogue originals and a smaller number of digital masters, all or nearly all showing the great tenor in sparkling form. The records and equivalent tapes are at mid-price, but there are no translations or musical notes.

Schwarzkopf, Dame Elisabeth (soprano)

'Elisabeth Schwarzkopf sings operetta' (with Philh. Ch. and O, Ackermann): HEUBERGER: *Der Opernball: Im chambre séparée.* ZELLER: *Der Vogelhändler: Ich bin die Christel; Schenkt man sich Rosen. Der Obersteiger, Sei nicht bös.* LEHAR: *Der Zarewitsch: Einer wird kommen. Der Graf von Luxembourg: Hoch Evoë, Heut noch werd ich Ehefrau. Giuditta: Meine Lippen.* J. STRAUSS Jr: *Casanova: Nuns' chorus; Laura's song.* MILLOCKER: *Die Dubarry: Ich schenk mein Herz; Was ich im Leben beginne.* SUPPE: *Boccaccio: Hab ich nur deine Liebe.* SIECZYNSKY: *Wien, du Stadt meiner Träume (Vienna, city of my dreams;* song).
✵ *** EMI CDC7 47284-2 [id.].

This is one of the most delectable recordings of operetta arias ever made, and it is here presented with excellent sound. Schwarzkopf's 'whooping' manner (as Philip Hope-Wallace called it) is irresistible, authentically catching the Viennese style, languor and sparkle combined. Try for sample the exquisite *Im chambre séparée* or *Sei nicht bös*; but the whole programme is performed with supreme artistic command and ravishing tonal beauty. This outstanding example of the art of Elisabeth Schwarzkopf at its most enchanting is a disc which ought to be in every collection. The compact disc transfer enhances the superbly balanced recording even further, manages to cut out nearly all the background, give the voice a natural presence, and retain the orchestral bloom.

'Diva': Arias from: MOZART: *Nozze di Figaro; Don Giovanni; Così fan tutte.* BEETHOVEN: *Fidelio.* WEBER: *Der Freischütz.* WAGNER: *Lohengrin.* SMETANA: *The Bartered Bride.* R. STRAUSS: *Der Rosenkavalier; Ariadne auf Naxos; Arabella.* HEUBERGER: *Der Opernball.* Johann STRAUSS Jr: *Die Fledermaus.*
(N) (M) *** EMI stereo/mono CDM5 65577-2 [id.].

This single CD in EMI's 'Diva' series offers an excellent and shrewdly selected survey of Schwarzkopf's opera and operetta recordings. Mozart is very well represented, with Schwarzkopf as both Susanna and the Countess in *Figaro*, as Donna Elvira in *Don Giovanni* (from the masterly Giulini recording) and as Fiordiligi in *Così fan tutte* (commanding in *Come scoglio* under Boehm). From Richard Strauss there is not only the Marschallin's monologue (from the Karajan recording of *Rosenkavalier*) but also Ariadne's lament and Arabella's final solo, another of her most compelling Strauss performances. Immaculate accounts of Weber (Agathe's *Leise, leise* from *Freischütz*) and of Wagner (Elsa's Dream from *Lohengrin*) have been drawn from one of the finest of all her discs, with Heuberger's *Im chambre séparée* as an enchanting operetta tailpiece. Excellent transfers.

'Schwarzkopf Songbook' (with Gerald Moore, Geoffrey Parsons, Nicolas Medtner, Cyril Skalkiewicz (piano)): MOZART: *Warnung; Der Zauberer, Das Veilchen; Der Zauberer.* SCHUBERT: *Ungeduld; Liebe schwärmt.* MENDELSSOHN: *Auf Flügeln des Gesanges.* SCHUMANN: *6 Lieder from Liederkreis, Op. 39; Aufträge; Widmung.* LISZT: *Die drei Zigeuner.* BRAHMS: *Vergebliches Ständchen; Immer leiser, Wie Melodien; Der Jäger, Liebestreu; Ständchen.* JENSEN: *Murmelndes Lüftchen.* MAHLER: *Lob des hohen Verstandes.* R. STRAUSS: *Ach, was Kummer, Wer lieben will; 3 Ophelia Lieder.* WOLF: *25 Lieder from the Italienisches Liederbuch; 8 Goethe Lieder, 4 Mörike Lieder, Keine gleicht von allen Schönen; Wienlied (Im Sommer); Mausfallensprüchlein; In dem Schatten meiner Locken.* GRIEG: *Farmyard song; Ich liebe dich;*

Mit einer Wasserlilie; Letzter Frühling; Erstes Begegnen; Zu Rosenzeit; Mit einer Primula veris; Lauf der Welt. DVORAK: *Songs my mother taught me.* TCHAIKOVSKY: *Nur wer die Sehnsucht kennt.* MUS-SORGSKY: *In den Pilzen.* MEDTNER: *The muse; The rose; The waltz; When roses fade; 7 Goethe Lieder; Praeludium; Winternacht; Die Quelle.* SIBELIUS: *Die Echo-Nymph; Der Norden; Hundert Wege; Schiff, Schiff, säusle; Der Kuss; Der erste Kuss; War es ein Traum?; Schwarze Rosen.*
(N) (M) *** EMI mono/stereo CHS5 65860-2 (3) [CDHC 65860].

Issued to celebrate Schwarzkopf's eightieth birthday in December 1995, these three discs offer many rarities selected from many different periods in her career. So the second of the three, devoted entirely to Wolf, has 25 songs from the *Italian Songbook* in the mono recordings she made in 1959, four more than she contributed to the joint recording of that cycle, much better known, which she made with Fischer-Dieskau ten years later. These earlier examples are more intimate and often more intense. The Mozart song recordings range from a girlish account of *Warnung*, recorded in 1947, and of *Der Zauberer*, recorded in 1951, to a 1970 recording of that second song, warmer, more positive and with more detail. Similarly in the Schumann selection, a 1951 recording of *Aufträge* is set against six songs from the Opus 39 *Liederkreis*, recorded as late as 1974. Brahms is generously represented, mainly from 1970 sessions, with an alternative version of *Vergebliches Ständchen* from 1954, lighter and fresher if less dramatic. Liszt's *Three gypsies* prompt aptly throaty tone, while a song by Adolf Jensen brings one of the loveliest performances of all. The first disc is rounded off with a Strauss group, including a previously unpublished radio recording of the Ophelia songs, compellingly characterized. The third disc is devoted to songs outside the German repertory, mainly done in German, as for example the eight Grieg songs. Medtner is the accompanist in 11 of his own tenderly lyrical songs, while the greatest treasure of all is the final group of eight Sibelius songs, recorded live in 1955 by Finnish Radio in inspired performances, never previously published.

Seefried, Irmgard (soprano)

Lieder (with Erik Werba, piano): MOZART: *Das Veilchen; Die Verschweigung; Das Lied der Trennung; Das Kinderspiel; Die kleine Spinnerin; Als Luise die Briefe ihres ungetreuen Liebhabers verbrannte; Einsam ging ich jüngst im Haine; An Chloe; Abendempfindung; Sehnsucht nach dem Frühling.* SCHU-BERT: *Auf dem Wasser zu singen; Lachen und Weinen.* BRAHMS: *Dein blaues Auge hält so still; Ständchen.* MUSSORGSKY: *The Nursery* (cycle). BARTOK: *Village scenes* (cycle). WOLF: *An eine Äolsharfe; Das verlassene Mägdlein; Begegnung.* R. STRAUSS: *Ständchen.* SCHUMANN: *Die Lotosblume; Mit Myrten und Rosen; Du bist wie eine Blume; Frauenliebe und Leben* (cycle). SCHUBERT: *Der König in Thule; Das Lied im Grünen; Die junge Nonne; Fischerweise; Seligkeit; Die Forelle; An die Musik.* R. STRAUSS: *Traum durch die Dämmerung; Meinem Kinde; Allerseelen; Morgen.*
(❀) (M) *** DG mono/stereo 437 348-2 (2).

This tribute to a much-loved singer of German Lieder in the 1950s and early '60s has been lovingly assembled to make a superb continuous recital which, taken in two sections, gives some two hours and fifteen minutes of sheer delight. After the Mozart group, which she sings with appealing freshness (the last two songs, *Abendempfindung* and *Sehnsucht nach dem Frühling*, are given a Schubertian lilt), comes an enchanting series of live recordings made in 1953, including the sparkling Bartók *Village scenes* and the hardly less engaging Mussorgsky group, ending with a rapturous account of Strauss's *Ständchen*. The songs in the second half are hardly less captivating. Schumann's *Die Lotosblume* and *Du bist wie eine Blume* are ravishing, and Seefried brings her own experience to the great *Frauenliebe und -leben* cycle. The last song may not have quite the passionate intensity of Dame Janet Baker's famous version, but the colourless tone and withdrawn emotion create a strong impression after the earlier songs have revelled in the young bride's happier experiences, with the song about the wedding ring (*Du Ring an meinem Finger*) particularly poignant. Erik Werba accompanies with complete understanding and the vivid sound is equally realistic throughout; the ear can hardly tell that only the closing Schubert and Strauss songs, recorded mainly in 1958, are in stereo. Full documentation makes this a very desirable set indeed.

Souzay, Gérard (baritone)

Mélodies (with Jacqueline Bonneau): FAURE: *Tristesse; Au bord de l'eau; Après un rêve; Clair de lune; Arpège; En sourdine; L'Horizon chimérique; Spleen; C'est l'extase; Prison; Mandoline.* CHAUSSON: *Nanny; Le charme; Sérénade italienne; Le Colibri; Cantique à l'épouse; Les papillons; Le temps de lilas.* Airs: BOESSET: *Me veux-tu voir mourir?.* ANON.: *Tambourin.* BATAILLE: *Cachez, beaux yeux; Ma ber-gère non légère.* CANTELOUBE: *Brezairola; Malurous qu'o uno fenno.*

⊛ (M) (***) Decca mono 425 975-2.

The great French baritone made these recordings for Decca when he was at the very peak of his form. The Fauré were recorded in 1950 and the glorious Chausson songs in 1953. Souzay was endowed with the intelligence of Bernac as well as his powers of characterization, the vocal purity of Panzera and a wonderful feeling for line. The Decca transfer does complete justice to the original sound, and it is good to have these performances without the surface distractions of LP. Full texts and translations are provided. A marvellous record worth as many rosettes as stars!

Souzay, Gérard (baritone), Dalton Baldwin (piano)

Mélodies françaises: FAURE: *Chanson du pêcheur; Poème d'un jour, Op. 21; Les berceaux; Le secret; Aurore; Fleur jetée; La rose; Madrigal; 5 Mélodies de Venise, Op. 58; La bonne chanson, Op. 61; Le parfum impérissable; Arpège; Prison; Soir; Dans la forêt de septembre; La fleur qui va sur l'eau; Le don silencieux; La chanson d'Eve, Op. 95,* excerpts *(Eau vivante; O mort, poussière d'étoiles). Le jardin clos, Op. 106,* excerpts *(Exaucement; Je me poserai sur ton cœur). Mirages, Op. 113; L'horizon chimérique, Op. 118.* POULENC: *Chansons villageoises; Calligrammes; Le travail du peintre; La fraîcheur et le feu; Airs chantés: Air vif. La grenouillère; Métamorphoses: Reine des mouettes. Priez pour paix.* RAVEL: *5 Mélodies populaires grecques; Epigrammes de Clément Marot; Histoires naturelles; Chansons mad-écasses; 2 Mélodies hébraïques; Don Quichotte à Dulcinée; Les grands vents venus d'outre-mer; Sainte; Sur l'herbe.* LEGUERNEY: *20 Poèmes de la Pléiade,* excerpts *(Ma douce jouvence est passée; A son page).* HAHN: *L'heure exquise.* DUPARC: *L'invitation au voyage; Sérénade florentine; La vague et la cloche; Extase; Le manoir de Rosemonde; Lamento; La vie antérieure; Testament; Phidylé; Chanson triste; Elégie; Soupir.* GOUNOD: *L'absent; Sérénade.* CHABRIER: *Les cigales; Chanson pour Jeanne.* BIZET: *Chanson d'avril.* FRANCK: *Nocturne.* ROUSSEL: *Le jardin mouillé; Le bachelier de Salamanque.*
(Y/B) ⊛ (M) *** Ph. 438 964-2 (4) [id.].

Now here is something to make the pulse quicken: Gérard Souzay, recorded while still in his prime and in repertoire in which he was unmatched in his day. Only Bernac had as refined an interpretative intelligence and, of an older generation, only Panzera commanded an equal authority and tonal beauty. Souzay's 1963 recording of Fauré's *La bonne chanson* is one of the classics of the gramophone and has been extensively discussed in the *Stereo Record Guide* over the years. It was chosen by RL as one of his 'desert-island' discs in 'The Great Records' ('rich in artistry, imagination and insight'). The recording of the *Deux mélodies hébraïques* is captivating, though Souzay made an even more haunting version for French EMI in the late 1950s; and one is hard pressed to choose between his *Don Quichotte à Dulcinée* and those of Panzera and Bernac. After Souzay's Philips disc with *La bonne chanson* came further recordings of Fauré, an anthology of other French *mélodies* and an LP of the Duparc songs, in every way superior to his later, EMI re-make in the early 1970s. This is treasure-trove which no lover of the French repertoire should be without. It is as essential an acquisition for Souzay admirers as the Schumann *Dichterliebe* – see above, under the composer). Not everyone can afford four CDs all at one go, even at mid-price, and Philips would be wise to re-package the Fauré songs as part of their bargain Duo series, and issue the Duparc separately as well.

Sutherland, Dame Joan (soprano)

'Grandi voci': BELLINI: *Norma: Sediziose voci . . . Casta diva . . . Ah! bello a me ritorna. I Puritani: Qui la voce sua soave . . . Vien, diletto* (with ROHCG O, Molinari-Pradelli). VERDI: *Atilla: Santo di patria . . . Allor che i forti corrono . . . Da te questo or m'è concesso* (with LSO, Bonynge). DONIZETTI: *Lucia di Lammermoor: Ancor non giunse! . . . Regnava nel silenzio; Il dolce suono mi colpi di sua voce! . . . Ardon gl'incensi* (Mad scene). *Linda di Chamounix: Ah! tardai troppo . . . O luce di quest'anima.* VERDI: *Ernani: Surta è la notte . . . Ernani! Ernani, involami. I vespri siciliani: Mercè, dilettte amiche (Boléro).*
(Y/B) ⊛ (M) *** Decca 440 404-2 [id.].

Sutherland's 'Grandi voci' disc is one of the most cherishable of all operatic recital records, bringing together the glorious, exuberant items from her very first recital disc, made within weeks of her first Covent Garden success in 1959, and – as a valuable supplement – the poised accounts of *Casta diva* and *Vien, diletto* she recorded the following year as part of the 'Art of the Prima Donna'. It was this 1959 recital which at once put Sutherland firmly on the map among the great recording artists of all time. Even she has never surpassed the freshness of these versions of the two big arias from *Lucia di Lammermoor*, sparkling in immaculate coloratura, while the lightness and point of the jaunty *Linda di*

Chamounix aria and the *Boléro* from *I vespri siciliani* are just as winning. The aria from *Attila* comes from 'The age of bel canto' (1963). The sound is exceptionally vivid and immediate, though the accompaniments under Nello Santi are sometimes rough in ensemble.

Terfel, Bryn (bass-baritone), Malcolm Martineau (piano)

'The Vagabond and other English songs': VAUGHAN WILLIAMS: *Songs of travel (The vagabond; Let beauty awake; The roadside fire; Youth and love; In dreams; The infinite shining heavens; Whither must I wander; Bright in the ring of words; I have trod the upward and the downward slope).* BUTTERWORTH: *Bredon hill (Bredon hill; Oh fair enough; When the lad for longing sighs; On the idle hill of summer; With rue my heart is laden); The Shropshire lad* (6 songs): *Loveliest of trees; When I was one-and-twenty; Look not in my eyes; Think no more, lad; The lads in their hundreds; Is my team ploughing?* FINZI: *Let us garlands bring (Come away, death; Who is Silvia?; Fear no more the heat of the sun; O mistress mine; It was a lover and his lass).* IRELAND: *Sea fever; The vagabond; The bells of San Marie.*
(Y/B) ✹ *** DG Dig. 445 946-2 [id.].

No other collection of English songs has ever quite matched this one in its depth, intensity and sheer beauty. Terfel, the great Welsh singer of his generation, here shows his deep affinity with the English repertory, demonstrating triumphantly in each of the 28 songs that this neglected genre deserves to be treated in terms similar to those of the German *Lied* and the French *mélodie*. The Vaughan Williams songs are perhaps the best known, nine sharply characterized settings of Robert Louis Stevenson which, thanks to Terfel's searching expressiveness and matched by Martineau's inspired accompaniments, reveal depths of emotion hardly suspected.

The five Shakespeare settings by Finzi are just as memorable in their contrasted ways, five of the best-known lyrics from the plays that have been set countless times but which here are given new perspectives, thanks both to the composer and to the singer. The eleven Butterworth settings of Housman are among the finest inspirations of this short-lived composer, and it is good to have three sterling Ireland settings of Masefield, including the ever-popular *Sea fever*, which with Terfel emerges fresh and new. The singer's extreme range of tone and dynamic, down to the most delicate, firmly supported half-tones, is astonishing, adding intensity to one of the most felicitous song-recital records in years. The warm acoustic of Henry Wood Hall gives a glow both to the voice and to the piano.

'Impressions' (with (i) E. Bar. Soloists, Gardiner; (ii) Malcolm Martineau, piano; (iii) Philh. O, Sinopoli; (iv) BPO, Abbado): (i) MOZART: *Le nozze di Figaro: Se vuol ballare; Non più andrai; Aprite un po' quegli occhi.* (ii) SCHUBERT: *Litanei auf das Fest Allerseelen. Die Forelle; An die Musik; Erlkönig.* (iii) MAHLER: *Kindertotenlieder.* (ii) VAUGHAN WILLIAMS: *The vagabond; The roadside fire.* (iv) WAGNER: *Die Meistersinger: Wie duftet doch der Flieder. Tannhäuser: O! du mein holder Abendstern.*
(N) *** DG Dig. 449 190-2 [id.].

Ranging over the recordings made for DG up to his English song disc, this sampler gives a formidable idea of this brilliant young singer's powers, very well chosen not just from his solo discs but from complete opera sets and discs with orchestra.

Operatic arias (with Metropolitan Op. O, James Levine) from: MOZART: *Le nozze di Figaro; Così fan tutte; Don Giovanni; Die Zauberflöte.* WAGNER: *Tannhäuser; Der fliegende Holländer.* OFFENBACH: *Contes d'Hoffmann.* GOUNOD: *Faust.* BORODIN: *Prince Igor.* DONIZETTI: *Don Pasquale.* ROSSINI: *La Cenerentola.* VERDI: *Macbeth; Falstaff.*
(N) ✹ *** DG Dig. 455 866-2 [id.].

Not many operatic recital discs match this formidable, keenly enjoyable one offering, in Terfel's own words, 'a future diary of my opera plans' and demonstrating not just the warmth and musical imagination of this brilliant young singer but his range and power too. This account of *Non più andrai* is weightier, marginally broader and even more characterful than the one he recorded as part of John Eliot Gardiner's complete set, and that is typical of his development. Though Mozart remains central to his repertory, it is striking that the most thrilling items of all are those which test him most severely, such as Igor's aria from Borodin's *Prince Igor* and the Dutchman's monologue. The Falstaff monologue from Act I of Verdi's comic masterpiece similarly finds him presenting a larger-than-life portrait with no holds barred over the widest dynamic range. This is singing that is not just strong, varied and imaginative but consistently beautiful too.

Von Otter, Anne Sofie (soprano)

'*Wings in the night*' (Swedish songs; with Bengt Forsberg, piano): PETERSON-BERGER: *Aspåkers-polska (Aspåker's polka); Återkomst (Return); Böljeby-vals (Böljeby waltz); Like the stars in the sky (Som stjärnorna på himmeln); Marits visor (3 songs, Op. 12); Nothing is like the time of waiting (Intet är som väntanstider); When I walk by myself (När jag går för mig själv)*. SJOGREN: *6 Songs from Julius Wolff's Tannhäuser.* Sigurd von KOCH: *In the month of Tjaitra (I månaden Tjaitra); Of lotus scent and moon-shine (Af Lotusdoft och månens sken); The wild swans (De vilda svanarna) (3 songs)*. STENHAMMAR: *Miss Blond and Miss Brunette (Jungfru blond och jungfru brunett); In the maple's shade (I lönnnens skymning); Jutta comes to the Volkungs (Jutta kommer till Folkungarna); A seaside song (En strand-visa); A ship is sailing (Det far ett skepp); The wanderer (Vandraren).* RANGSTROM: *The farewell (Afskedet); Old Swedish (Gammalsvenskt); Melodi; Pan; Supplication to night (Bön till natten); Wings in the night (Vingar i natten).* ALFVEN: *The forest is asleep (Skogen sover); I kiss your white hand (Jag kysser din vita hand)*.

(N) 🏵 *** DG Dig. 449 189-2 [id.].

So often Swedish singers, once they have made a name for themselves in the world, neglect their native repertoire in favour of Schumann, Brahms, Strauss and Wolf. Anne Sofie von Otter is an exception and, fresh from her recent successes in Scandinavian repertoire, above all her Grieg *Haugtussa* and her Sibelius recitals on BIS, she gives us a splendid anthology of Swedish songs. The disc takes its name from one of Ture Rangström's most haunting songs, *Vingar i natten* (*Wings in the night*), and, indeed, his are some of the loveliest songs in the Swedish *romans* repertoire. (*Romans* is the Nordic equivalent of *lied*.) *Bön till natten* (*Prayer to the night*) is arguably the most beautiful of all Swedish songs and has the innocence and freshness of Grieg combined with a melancholy and purity that are totally individual. Von Otter also includes songs by the composer-critic, Wilhelm Peterson-Berger, whose criticism was much admired in his native Sweden and who was compared with Bernard Shaw (he is in fact an opinionated windbag) but whose songs have a certain wistful charm. The Stenhammar songs are among his finest, and she adds some familiar Alfvén and less familiar repertoire by Emil Sjögren and Sigurd (not to be confused with Erland) von Koch. A disc to be treasured.

Walker, Sarah (mezzo-soprano), Thomas Allen (baritone)

'*The Sea*' (with Roger Vignoles, piano): IRELAND: *Sea fever.* HAYDN: *Mermaid's song; Sailor's song.* DIBDIN: *Tom Bowling.* WALTON: *Song for the Lord Mayor's table; Wapping Old Stairs.* WOLF: *Seemanns Abschied.* FAURE: *Les Berceaux; Au cimetière; L'horizon chimerique.* SCHUBERT: *Lied eines Schiffers an die Dioskuren.* BORODIN: *The Sea; The Sea Princess.* DEBUSSY: *Proses lyriques: De grêve.* IVES: *Swimmers.* SCHUMANN: *Die Meersee.* BERLIOZ: *Nuits d'été: L'ile inconnue.* MENDELSSOHN: *Wasserfahrt.* BRAHMS: *Die Meere.* TRAD.: *The Mermaid.* Arr. BRITTEN: *Sail on, sail on.*

🏵 *** Hyperion CDA 66165 [id.].

With Roger Vignoles as master of ceremonies in a brilliantly devised programme, ranging wide, this twin-headed recital celebrating 'The Sea' is a delight from beginning to end. Two outstandingly charac-terful singers are mutually challenged to their very finest form, whether in solo songs or duets. As sample, try the setting of the sea-song, *The Mermaid*, brilliantly arranged by Vignoles, with hilarious key-switches on the comic quotations from *Rule Britannia*. Excellent recording.